R. N. Champlin, Ph.D.
ENCICLOPÉDIA de BÍBLIA, TEOLOGIA & FILOSOFIA

VOLUME 1 | A/C

hagnos

©1991 por Russel N. Champlin

1ª edição: 1991
14ª reimpressão: abril de 2021

REVISÃO
Equipe Hagnos

CAPA
Maquinaria Studio

DIAGRAMAÇÃO
Imprensa da Fé

EDITOR
Aldo Menezes

COORDENADOR DE PRODUÇÃO
Mauro Terrengui

IMPRESSÃO E ACABAMENTO
Imprensa da Fé

As opiniões, as interpretações e os conceitos emitidos nesta obra são de responsabilidade do autor e não refletem necessariamente o ponto de vista da Hagnos.

Todos os direitos desta edição reservados à
EDITORA HAGNOS LTDA.
Av. Jacinto Júlio, 27
04815-160 — São Paulo, SP
Tel.: (11) 5668-5668

E-mail: hagnos@hagnos.com.br
Home page: www.hagnos.com.br

Dados Internacionais de Catalogação na Publicação (CIP)
Angélica Ilacqua CRB-8/7057

Champli, Russel Norman, 1933-2018.

Enciclopédia de Bíblia, Teologia & Filosofia. Vol. 1: A-C. / Russel Norman Champlin — São Paulo: Hagnos, 1991. 6 vols.

ISBN 978-85-88234-33-8

1. Bíblia – Enciclopédias 2. Teologia – Enciclopédias 3. Filosofia – Enciclopédias I. Título

21-0891   CDD 220.3

Índices para catálogo sistemático:
1. Bíblia – Enciclopédias 220.3

Editora associada à:

DEDICAÇÃO

Dedico esta *Enciclopédia* às quatro pessoas que mais me ajudaram na minha carreira de escritor:

••• •••

Vera Lúcia de Oliveira
Que persistia no trabalho de tal maneira que se tornou o próprio modelo de dedicação.

Irene Champlin
Que desde a produção das minhas teses de pós-graduação esteve sempre pronta e entusiasmada para começar – mais um projeto.

João Marques Bentes
O maior tradutor de literatura bíblica portuguesa de todos os tempos.

In Memoriam
Mrs. Margaret Hutzel
Que contribuiu com grandes somas de dinheiro para a publicação dos meus projetos – e sempre me encorajou a continuar lutando.
"...as suas obras a sigam". (Apo. 14:13)

HOMENAGENS

••• •••

ao *Professor Leonidas Hegenberg,*
o maior filósofo brasileiro
de todos os tempos.

ao *missionário Bill Barkley*, um
homem de dedicação e convicção
que ele combina com tolerância
e generosidade.

(Ver as homenagens mais completas: ao Prof. Leonidas, ao fim do artigo sobre *Filosofia*; ao Rev. Barkley, ao fim do artigo sobre *Comentários sobre a Bíblia*).

AGRADECIMENTOS

Agradeço à

Zondervan Publishing House cuja obra, The *Zondervan Pictorial Encyclopedia of the Bible*, muito nos ajudou em compilar os artigos bíblicos da presente Enciclopédia. Talvez 5 % da presente obra tenha sido emprestada diretamente daquela enciclopédia, com pouca modificação.

Marlene Gomes de Oliveira que dedicou diligentemente muitas horas tediosas na correção gráfica do texto.

Maria de Jesus Ferreira Aires, perita em língua portuguesa, que zelosamente revisou esta Enciclopédia, de capa a capa, garantindo uma expressão decente.

Darrell Steven Champlin, meu filho, pela compilação do *Índice* desta Enciclopédia, e pela contribuição de um número considerável de trabalhos artísticos que embelezam a obra.

Autor da Enciclopédia

Russell Norman Champlin

Russell Norman Champlin nasceu no dia 22 de Dezembro de 1933 em Salt Lake City, Utah, EUA. Fez o grau B.A. em Literatura Bíblica no Immanuel College; os graus M.A. e Ph.D. em Línguas Clássicas na University of Utah; escreveu suas teses na área dos manuscritos gregos antigos do Novo Testamento; fez estudos de especialização (no nível de pós-graduação) no Novo Testamento na University of Chicago. Na sua carreira como professor universitário e escritor, publicou mais de 45.000 páginas de literatura. Sua *magnum opus* foi *O Novo Testamento Interpretado*. Publicou mais sete livros e colaborou na publicação de diversos outros; escreveu um número significativo de artigos sobre a filosofia que foram publicados em revistas especializadas no Brasil. A estas realizações, acrescenta, agora, a *Enciclopédia de Bíblia, Teologia* e Filosofia que contém 13.000 artigos.

••• •••

AOS LEITORES
Ler para considerar não para condenar.

•••

É útil lembrar que a busca da verdade continua e que a verdade não morre com a morte de alguém. Também, é impossível estagná-la dentro de um sistema qualquer que tolamente acha ter toda a verdade e ter resolvido todos os problemas. *Erasmo* certamente tinha razão quando insistia em que a linguagem humana não pode aprisionar o *infinito*. Ele certamente tinha razão quando defendeu, com vigor, a *liberdade da investigação.*

Da covardia que teme novas verdades,
Da preguiça que aceita meias-verdades,
Da arrogância que pensa saber toda a verdade,
Ó Senhor, livra-nos. (Arthur Ford)

A grande maioria dos artigos desta *Enciclopédia* são simplesmente informativos e serão proveitosos para pessoas de todos os credos e denominações. *Alguns* dos artigos incluídos são *controvertidos* e criarão discussões animadas. Debates não devem ser conduzidos no *Ódio Teológico.* (Ver o artigo sob esse título). O debate expande o escopo do nosso conhecimento e aprimora a investigação, portanto, não deve ser receado nem evitado. Mas o amor é a própria essência e a *prova* da espiritualidade (I João 4:7,8,12,16) e deve governar todas as nossas atividades. O conhecimento e o amor são as duas grandes colunas da espiritualidade, mas «se eu conhecesse todos os mistérios e toda a ciência... e não tivesse amor, nada seria». (I Cor 13:2)

Combinamos nesta *Enciclopédia* as três áreas, Bíblia, Teologia e Filosofia, as três sendo intrinsecamente inter-relacionadas. A Teologia é a irmã da Bíblia e a Filosofia nos ajuda tanto a entender como a expressar nossa teologia.

••• •••

É nossa esperança que esta *Enciclopédia* seja útil para aumentar os conhecimentos dos leitores sobre os três campos tratados. Emprestamos liberalmente dos trabalhos dos outros (como a *Bibliografia* mostra) porque ninguém escreve uma enciclopédia deste volume só de conta própria. Informações estão sendo acumuladas ao longo dos séculos, e nós transmitimos estes dados aos leitores, essencialmente, através de compilação. Esperamos, todavia, ter acrescentado algumas coisas novas — a nossa pequena contribuição pessoal.

••• •••

A Editora Hagnos publicou a *Enciclopédia de Bíblia, Teologia e Filosofia* por ela ser um grande tesouro de informações sobre as três áreas tratadas. Porém, não concordamos com a inclusão de alguns artigos nem com todas as crenças do autor, Russel Normal Champlin, e não nos responsabilizamos pelas mesmas.

... ...

VITÓRIA ESPIRITUAL

Conquista de Terreno Espiritual

Estágios da Inquirição

1. *Materialismo*

    A alma é imersa no bem-estar físico; dominada pelo egoísmo; afligida pelo agnosticismo e ateísmo.

2. *Superstição*

    As evidências de poderes super-humanos são suficientes para convencer a alguns de que a abordagem materialista não pode explicar todos os fenômenos. Mas bem pouco é reconhecido acerca de tais forças.

3. *Fundamentalismo Rígido, Farisaico*

    Livros Sagrados tornam-se objetos de adoração. Credos rígidos dominam o pensamento. Porções dos Livros Sagrados são distorcidas ou omitidas na tentativa de criar um credo sem conflitos ou problemas.

4. *A Mente Inquiridora, Iluminada*

    Os homens começam a pensar; as convicções espirituais são mantidas, mas há menos dependência ao mero dogma. O intelecto é posto por detrás da inquirição espiritual.

5. *Perseguição e Perseverança*

    A alma do indivíduo é afligida por profundos anelos espirituais. Há tensão interior, ou mesmo angústia espiritual. O amor de Deus passa a ser enfatizado acima de tudo.

6. *A Vereda Mística*

    A alma esforça-se por desvencilhar-se dos muitos dogmas e sistemas parciais. A alma procura a Presença de Deus. A iluminação é procurada com todo o coração.

7. *Estágio Final*

    Transformação à imagem do *Logos* na Visão Beatífica.

Artigos para Consultar

    Vitória Espiritual

    Transformação Segundo a Imagem de Cristo

    Desenvolvimento Espiritual, Meios de

    Visão Beatífica

...

O oposto de injustiça não é justiça — é *amor.*

BIBLIOGRAFIA

••• ••• •••

Ver uma lista alfabética completa dos autores e
editores incorporados nesta lista de abreviações, ao
fim da mesma.

A

A   *Greek-English Lexicon of the New Testament and Other Early Christian Literature*, Arndt, William F. e Gingrich, F.Wilbur, 1963.

AAA   *Annals of Archaeology and Anthropology*.

AASOR *Annual of the American School of Anthropology*.

AB   Abetti, Giorgio, *The History of Astronomy*, 1952.

ABB   *A Bibliography of Bible Study*, Princeton, 1960.

ABE   Abernathy, George L. e Thomas, A. Langford, *Philosophy of Religions*, 1962.

ABR   Abrahamson, I., *Studies in Pharisaism and the Gospels*, 1917.

ACM   McGiffert, A.C., *Protestant Thought Before Kant*, 1911.

AD   Adolph, R, *Missions Health Manual*, 1964.

ADA   Adams, A.M.C., *The Evolution of Urban Society*, 1966.

ADM   Adams, J.M., *Biblical Backgrounds*, 1965.

AG   *A Guide to Christian Reading*.

AH   Aharoni, Y., *The Land and The Bible*, 1967; «The Problem of Canaanite Arad», in *Israel Exploration Journal*, 1964; *The Land of the Bible, a Historical Geography*, 1967; *The Archaeological Survey of Massada*, (1956); *The Stratification of Israelite Megiddo* (1982).

AJ   Nichols, James, *The Works of Jacobus Arminius*, 1875.

AJA   *American Journal of Archaeology*.

AJP   *American Journal of Philology*.

AJSL   *American Journal of Semitic Languages and Literature*.

AJT   *American Journal of Theology*.

AL   Alford, Henry, *The Greek Testament*, 1871.

ALA   Aland, K. *The Problem of the New Testament Canon*, 1962.

ALB   Albright, W.F., *Archaeology and the Religion of Israel*, 1956.
(1935) «Egypt and the Early History of the Negeb», JPOS, XV, 1935.
(1936) «The Song of Deborah in the Light of Archaeology», BASOR, 62, 1936.
(1957) «The High Place in Ancient Palestine», 1957.
The Bible and the Ancient Near East, «The Roll of the Canaanites in the History of Civilization», 1961.

ALL   Allen, A.B., *The Romance of the Alphabet*, 1937.

ALLE   Allegro, John M., *The Dead Sea Scrolls*, 1964.

ALS   Alston, William, *Religious Belief and Philosophical Thought*, 1963.

ALT   Altizer, T.J.J., *The Gospel and Christian Atheism*, 1967.

AM   *Encyclopedia Americana*, 1970.

AMI   Amiran, R., *Ancient Pottery of the Holy Land*, 1970.

AN   Anderson, Alan R., *Minds and Machines*, 1964.

AND   Anderson, B.W., *The Old Testament and Christian Faith*, 1964.

AND(2) Anderson, G.H., *The Theology of the Christian Mission*, 1961.

ANEA   *Ancient Near Eastern Archaeology*.

ANEP   Pritchard: *Ancient Near East in Pictures*, 1954.

ANET   Pritchard: *Ancient Near Eastern Texts*, 1956.

ANF   Roberts and Donalson: *The Ante-Nicene Fathers*.

ANS   Anson, P.F., *The Call of the Cloister*, 1964.

ANT   James, M.R., *The Apocryphal New Testament*, 1924.

AO   Allis, O.T., *God Spoke by Moses*, 1951.

AOTS   Thomas, D.R., *Archaeology and Old Testament Study*, 1982.

AP   Thomas, D.R., *A Primer of Old Testament Textual Criticism*, 1965.

APEF   *Annual of the Palestine Exploration Fund*.

APOT   Charles, R.H., *Apocrypha and Pseudepigrapha of the Old Testament*, 1914.

AR   Richardson, Alan, *Religion in Contemporary Debate*, 1966.

ARAB   Luckenbill: *Ancient Records of Assyria and Babylonia*.

ARB   Arbesmann, Rudolph, *Fasting and Prophecy in Pagan and Christian Antiquity*, 1949.

ARC   Archer, G., *A Survey of Old Testament Introduction*, 1964.

ARE   Breasted, J.H., *Ancient Records of Egypt*, 1975.

ARN   Arnason, H.H., *The History of the Chalice of Antioch*, 1941.

ARNO   Arnold, P., *Birds of the Bible*, 1962.

AS   Abbott-Smith, *Manual Greek Lexicon of the Testament*, 1978.

ASH   Ashby, Robert H., *The Guidebook for the Study of Psychical Research*, 1972.

AT   Altizer, Thomas, e Hamilton, Wm., *Radical Theology and the Death of God*, 1966.

ATHR   *Anglican Theological Review*.

ATT   Attwater, D., *A Dictionary of Mary*, 1956.

AU   *Novo Dicionário Aurélio*, 1980.

AUG   Augustine, *Confessions of St. Augustine*, Warner, Rex (ed.), 1963.

AUL   Aulon, G., *The Faith of the Christian Church*, 1961.

AV   Ave Jonah, Michael, *Jerusalem*, 1962.

AY   Ayer, A.J., *Language, Truth and Logic*, 1936

B

B   *Baker's Dictionary of Christian Theology*, Harrison, E.F. (ed.), 1960.

BA   Altaner, B., *Patrology*, 1960.

BA   (revista) *Biblical Archaeology*.

BAD   Badawy, A., *Architecture in Ancient Egypt and the Near East*, 1966.

BAG   Baggot, J., *A New Approach to Colossians*, 1961.

BAI   Bailey, A., *Daily Life in Bible Times*, 1943.

BAIL   Bailey, D.D., *The Mystery of Love and Marriage*, 1955.

BIBLIOGRAFIA

BAL   Baly, D., *The Geography of the Bible*, 1967.

BALL   Ballow, R.O., *The Bible of the World*, 1939.

BAR   Barton, G.A., *Archaeology and the Bible*, 1937.

BARC   Barclay, W., *The Mind of Jesus*, 1960.

BARK   Barkley, W.P., *Twelve Who Were Chosen*, 1959.

BART   Barth, Karl, *Church Dogmatics*, 1936-1962; *The Epistle to the Romans*, 1933; *The Knowledge of God and the Service of God*, 1938.

BARTS   Bartsch, W., *Jesus Christ and Mythology*, 1960.

BASOR   *Bulletin of the Evangelical Theological Society*.

BAU   Baur, Ferdinand Christian, *The Christ Party in the Christian Church*, 1831; *Paul, the Apostle of Jesus Christ*, 1845; *Compendium of Christian Doctrine*, 1847; *Christianity and the Christian Church of the First Three Centuries*, 1853; *History of the Christian Church*, 1863.

BAY   Bayless, Raymond, *Apparitions and Survival of Death*, 1973.

BDB   Brown, Driver e Beges, *Hebrew-English Lexicon of the Old Testament*, 1980.

BE   Bentley, John C., *Philosophy, An Outline History*, 1962.

BEA   Bea, Augustine, *The Unity of Christians*, 1963.

BEC   Beccaria, G., *Crime and Punishment*, 1964.

BEL   Bell, Sir Charles Alfred, *The Religions of Tibet*, 1931.

BEN   Bentzen, A., *An Introduction to the Old Testament*, 1952.

BENS   Benson, Clarence H., *A Popular History of Christian Education*, 1946.

BES   Besnier, M., *Les Catacombes de Rome*, 1900.

BEV   Bevan, E.R., *The House of Seleucus*, 1902; (1927), *A History of Egypt Under the Ptolemaic Dynasty*.

BI   Bickerman, E., *Chronology of the Ancient World*, 1968.

BIR   Birley, E., *Roman Britain and the Roman Army*, 1953.

BJ   Burnet, J., *Early Greek Philosophy*, 1930.

BJR   Roberts, B.J., *The Old Testament Manuscripts, Text and Versions*, 1969.

BK   Blackman, E., *The Epistle of James*, 1957.

BL   Blair, E.P., «Soundings of Anata», *Bulletin of the American Schools of Oriental Research*, 62, 1936.

BLA   Blackwood, A.W., *Leading in Public Prayer*, 1958.

BLAC   Black, Matthew, *An Aramaic Approach to the Four Gospels and Acts*, 1953.

BLAS   *A Greek Grammar of the New Testament and Other Early Christian Literature*, 1961. Blass, F. e Debrunner, A., 1961.

BLAU   Blau, C., Bath Kol, *JE*, II, 1909.

BLM   Blackman, G.E., *The New Testament in the Apostolic Fathers*, 1905.

BLR   Blackmore, Susan J., *Experiências Fora do Corpo*, 1990.

BM   Beasley, Murray, R., *Baptism Today and Tomorrow*, 1966.

BMU   Burn-Murdoch, *The Development of the Papacy*, 1954.

BN   Bowman, R.A., «Arameans, Aramaic and the Bible», *Journal of Near Eastern Studies*, 1948.

BO   Box, H.S., *The Assumption of the Blessed Virgin Mary*, 1963.

BOD   Bodheimer, F.S., *Animals and Man in Bible Lands*, 1960.

BOE   Boettner, E., *Immortality*, 1956.

BOH   Bohl, F.M., *King Hammurabi of Babylon in the Setting of his Time*, 1946.

BOK   Bert, J. e Priscilla, F., *The Milky Way*, 1957.

BON   Bonhoeffer, Dietrich, *Ethics*, 1955.

BOR   Borger, R., *Die Inscripten Asarhaddons Konigs von Assyrian*, 1956.

BOT   Botsford, G.W.. e Robinson, C.A., *Hellenic History*, 1956.

BOU   Bouyer, K.E., *The Meaning of the Monastic Life*, 1955.

BOW   Bowman, G.W., *The Dynamics of Confession*, 1969.

BOX   Box, C.H., *The Ascension of Isaiah*, 1919.

BOY   Boyle, Isaac, *Ecclesiastical History*, 1966.

BR   *Encyclopedia Britannica*, 1982.

BRA   Brav, S.R., *Marriage and the Jewish Tradition*, 1951.

BRE   Breasted, J.H., *The History of Egypt*, sem data.

BRI   Bright, J., *A History of Israel*, 1959.

BRIG   Bright, J., *The Kingdom of God in Bible and Church*, 1955; *Jeremiah*, 1966.

BRIG(2)   Brightman, E.S., *A Philosophy of Religion*, 1942.

BRIN   Brinker, R., *The Influence of Sanctuaries in Early Israel*, 1946.

BRO   Bromiley, G.W., *The Baptism of Infants*, 1955.

BROA   Broad, C.D., *The Mind and Its Place in Nature*, 1925.

BROC   Brockington, L.H., *A Critical Introduction to the Apocrypha*, 1961.

BRON   Bronstein, Daniel J., e Schulweis, Harold M., *Approaches to the Philosophy of Religion*, 1954.

BRU   Bruce, F.F., *The Book of Acts*; 1954; «Israel and the Nations», ANET, 176-281.

BRUN   Brunner, E., *The Christian Doctrine of God*, 1949; *Eternal Hope*, 1954.

BS   *Biblioteca Sacra*.

BU   Burr, Harold S., *Blueprint for Immortality; The Electrical Patterns of Life*, 1972.

BUB   Buber, Martin, *I and Thou*, 1958.

BUC   Buchan, J., «Augustus Caesar», *Cambridge Ancient History*, X, 1930.

BUD   Budge, A.W., *A History of Ethiopia, Nubia and Abyssinea*, 1928.

BUH   Buhl, F., «Muhammed», *Encyclopedia of Islam*, 1892-95.

BULL   *Bulletin of the Theological Students' Fellowship*, 1970.

BULT   Bultman, R., *Die Geschichte der Synoptischen Tradition*, 1931; *Form Criticism*, 1932; *Theology of the New Testament*, 1955; *Jesus Christ and Mythology*, 1960.

BUR   Burkitt, F.C., *Jewish and Christian Apocalypses*, 1914.

BUS   Bush, F.O., *The Five Herods*, 1958.

BW   Brownlee, William H., *The Meaning of the Qumran Scrolls for the Bible*, 1964.

C

C   *A Dictionary of Christian Theology*, Richardson, Alan (ed.), 1969.

BIBLIOGRAFIA

CA   De Camp, L.S., *The Ancient Engineers*, 1963.

CAD   Cadbury, Henry J., *The Making of Luke-Acts*, 1927; *The Book of Acts in History*, 1955.

CAL   Callaway, J.E., *Burials in Ancient Palestine*, BA, XXVI, 1963.

CALM   *Calmet's Dictionary*, 1732.

CALV   Calvin, John, *Calvin's Commentaries*, 1949.

CAM   Cook, A.S., *Cambridge History of English Literature*, 1909-1961.

CAR   Carey, K.M. (ed.), *The Historic Episcopate*, 1954.

CARN   Carnell, John E., *The Philosophy of the Christian Religion*, 1952.

CARR   Carrington, P., *The Primitive Christian Catechism*, 1946.

CAS   Cassell's, *Latin-English, English-Latin Dictionary*, 1957.

CB   Enslin, Morton Scott, *Christian Beginnings*, 1956.

CBQ   *Catholic Biblical Quarterly*.

CC   Curran, Charles (ed.), «Absolute Norms in Moral Theology», *Norm and Concept in Christian Ethics*, 1968.

CD   *Catholic Dictionary of Theology*, Davis, Mon. H. (ed.), 1962.

CDC   *Cairo Genezan Document of the Damascus Covenanters*.

CE   *Catholic Encyclopedia*, Hebermann, Charles G. (ed.), 1954.

CEM   Montefiore, C.G., *Lectures on the Origin and Growth of Religion*, 1892.

CEN   *Collier's Encyclopedia*, 1964.

CER   Cerny, B.J., *Ancient Egyptian Religion*, 1952

CG   Gordon, C., *Recent Discoveries and the Patriarchal Age*, 1940.

CGG   Cameron, George Glen, *History of Early Iran*, 1936.

CGT   *Cambridge Greek Testament*.

CH   Charles, R.H., *Apocrypha and Pseudepigrapha of the Old Testament*, 1913, *The Ascension of Isaiah*, 1900.

CHA   Chafer, Lewis S., *Systematic Theology*, 1947.

CHAV   Chavasse, C., *The Bride of Christ*, 1939.

CHE   Chetwynd, Tom, *How to Interpret Your Own Dreams*, 1980.

CHI   Chainey, George, *Jerusalem, The Holy City*, 1933.

CHI(2)   Chisholm, Roderick, M., *Theory of Knowledge*, 1966.

CIL   *Corpus Inscriptionum Lationorum*.

CKB   Barrett, C.K., *The Fourth Gospel in Recent Criticism and Interpretation*, 1955.

CL   Clay, A., *The Empire of the Amorites*, 1919.

CLA   Clark, Gordon H., *Hellenistic Philosophy*, 1940; *A Christian Vision of Man and Things*, 1952.

CLAP   Clapp, F.G., «The Site of Sodom and Gomorrah», AJA, 1936.

CLAR   Clarke, Adam, *Clarke's Commentary*, sd.

CM   Cary, Max, *A History of the Greek World*, 1963.

CN   Cameron, G.C., *History of Early Iran*, 1936; *Persepolis Treasury Tablets*, 1948.

CO   Copleston, Frederick, *A History of Philosophy*, 1962.

COB   Cobb, J.B., *A Christian Natural Theology*, 1968.

COB(2)   Cobern, C., *The New Archaeological Discoveries*, 1917.

COH   Cohen, H., «Day of Atonement», I, *Judaism*, 1968 (summer); e II, III, *Judaism*, 1969 (winter, spring).

COH(2)   Cohen, S.S., *What We Jews Believe*, 1931.

COM   *Comprehensive Commentary on the Holy Bible*, 1887.

COP   Cope, G., *Ecclesiology Then and Now*, 1964.

COPL   Ver CO.

COR   Corbishley, Thomas, *Roman Catholicism*, 1950.

COT   Cottrell, L., *The Last Pharoahs*, 1950; *Life Under the Pharoahs*, 1960.

COW   Cowley, A., *Aramaic Papyri of the 5th Century*, 1923.

CR   Carr, Harvey, *The Interpretation of Animal Mind in Psychological Research*, 1917.

CRI   Cripps, R.S., *Critical and Exegetical Commentary on Prophecy in Amos*, 1958.

CRIP   Crippa, Adolpho, (ed.), *As Idéias Filosóficas no Brasil*, 1978.

CS   Chiera, E.; Speiser, E.A., «A New Factor in the History of the Ancient Near East», AASOR, VI, 1926.

CSEG   *Corpus Scriptorum Ecclesiasticorum Graecorum*.

CSEL   *Corpus Scriptorum Ecclesiasticorum Latinorum*.

CUM   Cumont, F., *Oriental Religions in Roman Paganism*, 1911.

CW   Williams, Colin, *John Wesley's Theology Today*, 1960.

CY   Richardson, Cyril Charles, *Library of Christian Classics*, «Early Church Fathers», 1933.

D

D   Denzinger, H., *Enchiridion Symbolorum Definitionum et Declarationum de Rebus Fidei et Morum*, 1957.

DA   Connolly, R.H., *Didascalia Apostolorum*, 1929.

DAL   Dalman, G., *Sacred Sites and Ways*, 1935.

DALB   Dalby, J., *Christian Mysticism and the Natural World*, 1950.

DAN   Dancy, J.C., *A Commentary on I Maccabees*, 1954.

DANA   Dana, E.S., *A Textbook on Minerology*, 1954.

DANR   Daniel-Ropes, H., *Daily Life in Palestine at the Time of Christ*, 1962.

DAR   Darling, James, *Encyclopedia Bibliographica* 1854-1859.

DAV   Davies, J.G., *Introduction to Pharisaism*, 1954; *Members One of Another; Aspects of Koinonia*, 1958.

DAVI   Davidson, A.B., *The Theology of the New Testament*, 1925.

DB   Baille, D.M., *God was in Christ*, 1948.

DBF   Japiassu, Hilton, e Marcondes, Danilo, *Dicionário Básico de Filosofia*, 1990.

DCJ   Ducasse, C.J., *Belief in Life After Death*, 1948.

DD   Davbe, D., *Studies in Biblical Law*, 1947.

DE   *Dicionário-Enciclopédia*, Den Born (ed.), 1969.

DEIS   Deismann, A., *Light From the Ancient East*, 1927; Paul, *A Study in Social and Religious History*, 1926.

DEL   Delitzsch, F., *Biblical Commentary on the Prophecies of Isaiah*, 1866.

BIBLIOGRAFIA

DEN   Dennis, James Shepherd, *Christian Missions and Social Progress*, 1906.

DF   *Dicionário de Filosofia*, Brugger, Walter, 1962.

DH   Dhorme, M., *A Commentary on the Book of Job*, 1926.

DI   Dixon, Jeane, *My Life and Prophecies*, 1969.

DIR   Diringer, David, *The Alphabet a Key to the History of Mankind*, 1948; *The Story of the Alpha-Beth*, 1960; *Writing*, 1962.

DK   Diels, H., Franz, W., *Die Fragments der Vorsokratiker*, 1951.

DL   *Enciclopédia Delta Larouse*, 1980.

DLI   *Diretório Litúrgico da Igreja no Brasil*, 1986.

DM   Driver, G.R., e Miles, J., *The Babylonian Laws*, 1952.

DO   Doresse, J., *The Secret Book of the Egyptian Gnostics*, 1960.

DOD   Dodd, C.H., *The Parables of the Kingdom*, 1935; *The Bible and the Greeks*, 1960.

DOL   Dolan, John P., *History of the Reformation*, 1965.

DOT   Dothan, T., *The Philistines and Their Natural Culture*, 1967.

DOTT   Drumm: *Documents from Old Testament Times*.

DOU   Dougherty, R.P., *Nabonidus and Belshazzar*, 1929.

DOW   Downey, E., *A History of Antioch in Syria from Seleucus to the Arab Conquest*, 1961.

DP   Rouse, W.H.D. (tradutor), *Great Dialogues of Plato*, 1956.

DR(1)   Daniel-Ropes, H., *Daily Life in Palestine at the Time of Christ*, 1962

DR(2)   Ross, Sir David e Smith, J.A., *The Basic Works of Aristotle*, 1956.

DRE   Champlin, Russell N., *Como Descobrir o Significado de seus Sonhos*, 1983.

DRI(1)   Driver, G.R., *Birds in the Old Testament*, 1955.

DRI(2)   Driver, S.R., *Notes on the Hebrew Texts of the Book of Samuel*, 1913.

DRIV   Driver, G.R., *Aramaic Documents of the 5th Century*, 1954.

DRO   Drower, M.S., *Water Supply, Irrigation and Agriculture; A History of Technology*, 1954.

DS   Denzinger, H., e Schonmetzer, A., *Enchiridion Symbolorum Definitionum et Declarationum de Rebus Fidei et Morum*, 1965.

DT   Doughty, C.M., *Travels in Arabia Deserta*, 1953.

DU   Ducasse, C.W. (ed.), *The Interpretation of the Bible*, 1964.

DUB   Dubberstein, W.H., «The Chronology of Cyrus and Cambyses», em AJSL, 416-419, 1938.

DUC   Duchesne, L., *Christian Worship, Its Origin and Evolution*, 1923.

DUN   Dunlap, Jane, *Explosive Inner Space*, 1961.

DV(1)   Davidson, A.B., *An Introductory Hebrew Grammar*, 1962.

DV(2)   Dvornik, Francis, *The Ecumenical Councils*, 1961.

E

E   *Encyclopedia of Religion*, Ferm, Vergilius (ed.), 1964.

EA   Eaton, J.H., *Obadiah, Nahum, Habbukkuk and Zephaniah*, 1961.

EAU   Bourke, Vernon, *The Essential Augustine*, 1964.

EB   Brunner, E., *Revelation and Reason*, 1947.

EBI   *Encyclopedia Biblica*.

EC   Champlin, Russell N., *Evidências Científicas Demonstram que Você Vive Depois da Morte* 1981.

ED   Edersheim, Alfred, The Temple, Its Ministry and Services, 1874; *Life and Times of Jesus the Messiah*, 1883; *Sketches of Jewish Social Life*, 1927; *Bible History*, 1956.

EDD   Eddy, R., *History of Universalism*, 1955.

EDE   Ver ED.

EDER   Ver ED.

EDI   Edidin, B.M., *Jewish Holidays and Festivals*, 1940, in K.

EDM   Edmunds, C. Gordon, *Medical Ethics*, 1966.

EF   *Enciclopedia Filosófica*, Firenze: G.C. Sansoni, 1967.

EGT   *Expositor's Greek Testament*, Nicoll, W. Robertson (ed.), 1956.

EI   Eisen, G.A., *The Great Chalice of Antioch*, 1953.

EIS   Eissfeldt, *The Old Testament, An Introduction*, 1965.

EL   Eliot, H.W., *Excavations in Mesopotamia and Western Iran*, 1950.

ELE   Elert, W., *The Structure of Lutheranism*, 1962.

ELL   Ellison, H.L., Ezekiel, *The Man and His Message*, 1951.

ELLI   Ellicott, Charles John, *Ellicott's Commentary on the Whole Bible*, 1954.

EN   Enslin, Morton Scott, *Literature of the Christian Movement*, 1956.

ENI   *Encyclopedia of Islam*, 1965.

EP   *Encyclopedia of Philosophy*, Edwards, Paul (ed.), 1967.

ERR   *Encyclopedia of Religion and Religions*, Pike, Royston E. (ed.), 1959.

ES   Rader, Melvin (ed.), *A Modern Book of Esthetics*, 1967.

ET   Melden, A., I. (ed.), *Ethical Theories*, 1955.

EU   Eusebius, *Historia Ecceles*.

EUG   Eugene, Maly, *The World of David and Solomon*, 1961.

EW   *The Concise Encyclopedia of Western Philosophy and Philosophers*, Urmson, J.O. (ed.), 1960.

EW(2)   Ewing, W., *Bethsaida*, in ISBE, I., 1929; *ibid, Galilee*, 1929.

EX   *Expositor's Bible*, Nicoll, Robertson, (ed.), 1956.

EXPT   *The Expository Times*.

EXT   Spanos, William V., *A Casebook on Existentialism*, 1966.

F

F   *Dictionary of Philosophy*, Flew, Antony, 1968.

FA(1)   *Bible Encyclopedia and Dictionary*, Fausset, A.R., *sd*.

FA(2)   Fairbairn, M., *The Place of Christ in Modern Theology*, 1898.

FAI   Fairbridge, R.W., *The Encyclopedia of Geomorphology*, 1968.

FAL   Falkner, E., *Games, Ancient and Oriental*, 1892.

FAR   Farrar, F.W., *The Message of the Book*, sd.

FARQ   Farquhar, John, *A Primer of Hinduism*, 1912.

BIBLIOGRAFIA

FE   Shaffer, Jerome A., *Filosofia do Espírito*, 1968.

FI   Filson, F.V., *Origins of the Gospels*, 1939; *Jesus Christ, The Risen Lord*, 1956.

FIN   Finegan, J., *Light From the Ancient Past*, 1946, *Handbook of Biblical Chronology*, 1964.

FK   Kenyon, Frederick, *The Bible and Archaeology*, 1940.

FL   Flemington, W.F., *The New Testament Doctrine of Baptism*, 1948.

FO   *Classical Greek Dictionary*, Foilett, 1960.

FOE   Foerster, W., *From the Exile to Christ*, 1964.

FOR   Forbes, R.J., *Studies in Ancient Technology*, 1981.

FP   Bornheim, Gerd A., *Os Filósofos Pré-Socráticos*, 1977.

FR   Frazer, J.G., *Adonis, Attis and Osiris; Studies in the History of Oriental Religion*, 1906.

FRA   Frankfort, H.H., *The Art and Architecture of the Ancient Orient*, 1954.

FRAN   Frankfort, H., *Kingship and the Gods*, 1948.

FRE   Free, J.P., *Archaeology and Bible History*, 1956; (1953-1960): Artigos diversos sobre descobertas arqueológicas: American Schools of Oriental Research, and BASOR.

FREE   Freeman, H.E., *An Introduction to the Old Testament Prophets*, 1963.

FREE(2)   Freeman, David Hugh, *A Philosophical Study of Religion*, 1976.

FREU   Freud, Sigmund, *The Interpretation of Dreams*, 1900; *Wit and Its Relationship to The Unconscious*, 1916.

FRI   Friedrich, J., *Strabo*, XII; *Monumenta Asiae Minores Antiqua; Anatolean Studies*, REK, XX, pp. 781-891.

FRO   Frost, H.W., *The Great Commission*, 1934.

FW   Farmer, W.R., *Maccabeus, Zealots and Josephus*, 1956.

G

G   *Dr. Gill's Commentary on the Whole Bible*, sd.

GA   Gaebelein, Frank E., *Christian Education in a Democracy*, 1951.

GAD   Gadd, Cyril John, *The Assyrian Sculptures*, 1934; *The Stones of Assyria*, 1936.

GAS   Gaster, M., *Jewish Magic*, HA, VIII, 3000-3005.

GB   *Great Books of the Western World*, Hutchins, R. (ed.), 1952.

GC   Clark, Gordon, *Hellenistic Philosophy*, 1940.

GCH   Gordon, G.H., «Biblical Customs and the Nuzi Tablets», BA iii (1940), 1—12.

GD   Goodspeed, E.J., *The Formation of the New Testament*, 1926; *Strange New Gospels*, 1931; *The Meaning of Ephesians*, 1933; *The Story of the Apocrypha*, 1939; *Early Christian Literature*, 1942; «Modern Apocrypha», *The Princeton Seminary BULLETIN*, 1957.

GE   Gilson, Étienne, *History of Christian Philosophy in the Middle Ages*, 1955; *God and Philosophy*, 1961.

GEI   Geikie, C., *Old Testament Characters*, 1888.

GEO(1)   Geoffrey, Parmiter, *King David*, 1961.

GEO(2)   George, P.R., *Communion with God in the New Testament*, 1953.

GES   Gesenius, W., *Hebrew Grammar*, 1910.

GEY   Geyser, A.S., *The Youth of John the Baptist: New Testament*, 1956.

GG   Blass, F. e Debrunner, A., *Greek Grammar of the New Testament and Other Early Christian Literature*, 1961.

GH   Ghirshman, R., *Iran*, 1954.

GI   Ginzberg, H.L., *The Apocalypse of Abraham*, 1906.

GL   Glueck, N., *The Other Side of Jordan*, 1940; *Some Ancient Towns in the Plains of Moab*, 1943; *The River Jordan*, 1946; *Rivers in the Desert*, 1960.

GLO   Glover, R.H., *The Biblical Basis of Missions*, 1946.

GLU   Ver GL (1943).

GN   Green, W.H., *Higher Criticism: and the Pentateuch*, 1895.

GO   Ver GD (1933 e 1942).

GOL   Goldschmidt, Victor, *A Religião de Platão*, 1963.

GOOD   Goodman, Jeffrey, *We Are the Earthquake Generation*, 1981.

GOR   Gordon, C.H., «The Story of Jacob and Laban in the Light of the Nuzi Tablets», BASOR, 66, 1937; «Biblical Customs and the Nuzi Tablets», BA, 3, 1940; *Old Testament Times*, 1953; *Ugaritic Textbook*, 1965.

GORD   Ver GOR (1953).

GOT   Gottwald, N.K., *Studies in the Book of Lamentations*, 1954; *A Light to the Nations*, 1959.

GP   Grimal, Pierre, *Hellenism and the Rise of Rome*, 1968.

GR   Grant, R.M., *The Apostolic Fathers*, 1964.

GRA   Grant, E., «Beth Shemash», 1928, AASOR, IX, 1-15.

GRAD   Gradenwitz, P., *The Music of Israel*, 1949.

GRAN   Grant, F.C., *Form Criticism*, 1939.

GRE   Greenberg, M., «The Biblical Concept of Asylum», *Journal of Biblical Literature*, 78.

GREE   Greenslade, S.L. (ed.), *The Cambridge History of the Bible from the Reformation to the Present*, 1963.

GRI   Griffith, G.T., *Alexander the Great: The Main Problems*, 1956.

GREN   Grenfell, B.P., e Hunt, A.S., *The Oxyrhynchus Papyri*, 1888-1889.

GRO   Groves, C.P., *The Planting of Christianity in Africa*, 1948.

GROL   Grollenberg, L.H., *Atlas of the Bible*, 1957.

GS   Ver GD (1939).

GSM   Smith, G. (ed.), *The Teaching of the Catholic Church*, 1948.

GT   *The Greek New Testament*, United Bible Societies, 1975.

GU   Guthrie, D., *New Testament Introduction*, 1965.

GUI   Guillamont, A., *La Designation des Couleurs en Hebreu et en Araméan, en Meyerson*, ed., *Problems de la Couluer*, 1957.

GUN   Gunday, R.H., *A Survey of the New Testament*, 1970.

GY   Gray, J., *The Canaanites*, 1964.

H

H   *Baker's Dictionary of Christian Ethics*, Henry, Carl F.H. (ed.), 1978.

HA   *Encyclopedia of Religion and Ethics*, Hastings, James (ed.), 1940.

BIBLIOGRAFIA

HAZ Barnes, Hazel E., *An Existentialist Ethics*, 1967.

HDB *Harper's Bible Dictionary*, 1978.

HEA Healy, Edwin, F., *Medical Ethics*, 1956.

HEI Heidel, Alexander, *The Gilgamesh Epic and the Old Testament Parallels*, 1949.

HEN Hennecke, Edgar, *The New Testament Apocrypha*, 1963.

HER(1) Herodotus, *History*.

HER(2) Herford, R.Y., *Sayings of the Fathers*, 1962.

HF *História da Filosofia*, Hirschberger, Johannes, 1969.

HI Hick, John, *Philosophy of Religion*, 1963.

HIC Ver HI.

HIE Hiers, R.H., *The Kingdom of God in the Synoptic Tradition*, 1970.

HIR Hirsch, F.E., «Punishment», ISBE, IV, 1955.

HIT Hitti, P.K., *The History of the Arabs*, 1970.

HJ Jonas, H., *The Gnostic Religions*, 1963.

HO(1) Hodge, C., *Systematic Theology*, 1874.

HO(2) Howard, Clingbell, *Understanding and Counselling the Alcoholic*, 1968.

HOD(1) Hodgson, Leonard, *The Ecumenical Movement*, 1951.

HOD(2) Hodgson, P.C., *The Formation of Historical Theology, a Study of Ferdenand Christian Bauer*, 1966.

HOR Horowitz, E., *How the Hebrew Alphabet Grew*, 1961.

HOS Hoskins, H., *The Religion of Ancient Israel*, 1967.

HOU Houston, M.G., «Ancient Egyptian and Persian Costume and Decoration», ANEP, 1954.

HOW Howlet, D., *The Essenes and Christianity*, 1957.

HP Clark, Gordon H., *Hellenistic Philosophy*, 1940.

HR Harrison, A.W., *Arminianism*, 1937.

HAD Hadas, M., *Aristeas to Philocrates*, 1951.

HAH Hahn, H.F., *The Old Testament and Modern Research*, 1954.

HAL Holmgard and Hall, *History of Technology*, 1954.

HALD Haldar, A., *Studies in the Book of Nahum*, 1947.

HALL Halley, Henry, H., *Pocket Bible Handbook*, 1948.

HAN Hanson, R.P.C., *Allegory and Event*, 1959.

HANS Hanson, S., *The Unity of the Church in the New Testament*, 1946.

HAR Harding, G.L., *The Antiquities of Jordan*, 1959.

HARN Harnack, Adolf von, *The Acts of the Apostles*, 1909, *The History of Dogma*, 1958.

HARR Harrison, R.K., *The Dead Sea Scrolls*, 1961; *Archaeology of the New Testament*, 1964, *Introduction to the Old Testament*, 1969.

HART Hartfelder, Karl, *Melanchthon als Praetor Sermaniae*, 1889.

HAT Hatch, Edwin, *The Influence of Greek Ideas on Christianity*, 1957.

HAU Haupart, Raymond, «Lachish, Frontier Fortress of Judah», BA, 1938.

HAY Hayes, W.C., *The Scepter of Egypt*, 1959.

HRL Harris, H.L., *Inspiration and Canonicity of the Bible*, 1957.

HRM Hare, R.M., *The Language of Morals*, 1952.

HRR Harrison, P.N., «Onesimus and Philemon», *Anglican Theological Review*, xxxii, 1950.

HS Schoeps, Hans, *The Jewish Christian Argument*, 1963.

HTR *Harvard Theological Review*.

HU Hughes, Philip, *A History of the Church*, 1947.

HUCA *Hebrew Union College Annual*.

HUN Hunt, I., *The World of the Patriarchs*, 1966.

HUS Smith, Huston, *The Religions of Man*, 1958.

HY Hughes, T. Hawel, *The Philosophical Basis of Mysticism*, 1937.

I

I *International Critical Commentary*, Driver, Samuel R., Plummer. Alfred e Briggs, Charles, A. (eds.), 1961.

IB *Interpreter's Bible*, Buttrick, George, (ed.), 1946.

ID *Interpreter's Dictionary of the Bible*, 1962.

IOT Young, E.J., *Introduction to the Old Testament*, 1941.

IR Iranaeus, *Against Heresies*.

IRA Ira, Progoff, *Jung's Psychology and its Social Meaning*, 1953.

ISBE *International Standard Bible Encyclopedia*, 1975.

J

J Charlesworth, James H., *The Old Testament Pseudepigrapha, Apocalyptic Literature and Testaments*, 1983.

JA *The New Schaff-Herzog Encyclopedia of Religious Knowledge*, Jackson, Samuel (ed.), 1950.

JAL Jalland, Tig, *The Church and the Papacy*, 1944.

JAM James, M.R., *The Apocryphal New Testament*, 1924.

JAME James, E.D., *Creation and Cosmology*, 1969.

JAOS *Journal of American Oriental Society*.

JAR Jarrett, James L. e McMurrin, Sterling M., *Contemporary Philosophy*, 1954.

JAS Jastrow, M., «Did the Babylonian Temples Have Libraries?» JAOS, 27:147-182, 1906.

JB Baille, J., *Our Knowledge of God*, 1939.

JBL *Journal of Biblical Literature*.

JD Daniélou, J., *Shadows to Reality*, 1960.

JE *The Universal Jewish Encyclopedia*, 1943.

JEL Jellicoe, S., *The Septuagint in Modern Study*, 1969.

JF Fabricus, J.F., *Codex Apocryphus Novi Testamenti, sd.*

JFB *Critical and Experimental Commentary*, Jamison, Fausset e Brown, 1948.

JG Goodman, Jeffrey, *We Are the Earthquake Generation*, 1974; *Psychic Archaeology; Time Machine to the Past*, 1979.

JL Lewis, John, «Marxism and Ethics», *Marxism and the Open Mind*, 1957.

JM Montgomery, J., *Kings*, 1951.

JNES *Journal of Near Eastern Studies*.

JO Josephus, *Antiquities and Wars*.

JOH Johler, K., *Jewish Theology*, 1918.

JOHN Johnson, A.R., *Sacral Kingship in Ancient Israel*, 1955.

JON Jones, A.H.M., *The Cities of the Roman Provinces*, 1937.

JP Pederson, J., *Israel*, 1959.

JPOS *Journal of the Palestine Oriental Society*.

JQ Quaston, J., *Patrology*, 1950.

JR *Journal of Religion and Psychic Research*.

JSS *Journal of Semitic Studies*.

BIBLIOGRAFIA

JTS   *Journal of Theological Studies.*

JU   Jung, Carl, *Modern Man in Search of a Soul,* 1933; *The Psychology of Religion,* 1938; *Memories, Dreams and Reflexions,* 1963.

JUD   Judge, E.A., *The Social Patterns of the Christian Groups of the First Century,* 1960.

JUN   June, Leo, *The Jewish Library,* 1934.

K

K   *Theological Dictionary of the New Testament,* Kittle, Gerhard (ed.), 1964.

KA   Kassis, H., «Gath and the Structure of Philistine Society», BL, 84, 1965.

KAH   Kahler, Martin, *The So-Called Historical Jesus and the Historical Biblical Christ,* 1964.

KAP   Kapelrud, Arvid S., *Joel's Prophecies,* 1948.

KD   *Commentary on the Old Testament,* Keil e Delitzsch.

KE   Kenyon, Sir Fredric, *Our Bible and the Ancient Manuscripts,* 1962; *Archaeology in the Holy Land,* 1970.

KEI   Keil, C.F., *Books of Ezra, Nehemiah and Esther,* 1950; *Jeremiah,* 1960; *Chronicles,* 1966.

KEL   Kelson, J., com Albright, W., *Excavations of Bethel,* AASOR, vol. 39, 1968.

KELL   Kelly, J.N.D., *The Pastoral Epistles,* 1963.

KELS   Kelso, J.L., «Excavations at Jericho», AASOR, vols. 29-30, 1955; «Excavations at Jerusalem», BA, XXVII, 1964.

KEN   Kent, R.G., *Old Persia,* 1950.

KENN   Kennedy, R., «Crimes and Punishment», HA, 1963.

KENY   Kenyon, K., *Digging up Jericho; Excavations at Jericho,* 1960.

KI   Kidner, D., *Proverbs,* 1964.

KIN   Kinsey, Alfred C., *Sexual Behavior in the Human Male,* 1948; *Sexual Behavior in the Human Female,* 1953.

KK   Kitchen, K.A., *Ancient Orient and the Old Testament,* 1966.

KL   Lake, Kirsopp, *The Apostolic Fathers,* 1913.

KLA   Klausner, J., *The Messianic Ideal in Israel,* 1956.

KLI   Kline, M.G., *Structure of Biblical Authority,* 1972.

KLIN   Klink, A., *Home Life in Biblical Times,* 1959.

KM   Hiltner, Seward e Menninger, Karl, *The Constructive Aspects of Anxiety,* 1967.

KN   Knight, G.A.F., *A Christian Theology of the Old Testament,* 1959.

KNE   Kneller, George, *Introdução à Filosofia da Educação,* 1964.

KO   Kopp, C., *The Holy Places in the Gospels,* 1963.

KOH   Gordis, Robert, *Koheleth, The Man and His World,* 1951.

KR(1)   Kraeling, C.H., *John the Baptist,* 1951.

KR(2)   Kraft, C.F., *Judges, Book of.*

KR(3)   Kraft, R.A., *Barnabas and the Didache,* 1961.

KRA   Kramer, S.N., *History Begins at Sumer,* 1956.

KRAU   Kraus, H.J., *Worship in Israel,* 1966.

KU   Kurtz, Prof., *Church History, sd.*

KY   Kyle, M.G., *Moses and the Monuments,* 1920, «The Story of Ancient Sodom in the Light of Modern Science», BS, LXXI, July, 1924.

L

L   *Twentieth Century Encyclopedia of Religious Knowledge,* Letcher, Letterts, A (ed.), 1955.

LA   Lampe, G.W.N., e Woolcombe, K., *The Doctrine of Justification by Faith,* 1954.

LA(2)   Lang, C.H.. *Pictures and Parables,* 1955.

LAB   Labby, Daniel H., *Life or Death; Ethics and Option,* 1968.

LAE   Laetsch, A., *Jonah, The Minor Prophets,* 1956.

LAK   Foakes, Jackson e Lake, K., *The Beginnings of Christianity,* 1920-33.

LAM   Lamon, R.S., *Megiddo,* 1931.

LAN   *Lange's Commentary,* Lange, P., sd.

LANG   Langton, E., *Essentials of Demonology,* 1949.

LAS   La Sor, W., «The Messianic Idea in Qumran», *Studies and Essays in Honor of Abraham Neuman,* 1962.

LAT   Latourette, K.S., *A History of the Expansion of Christianity,* 1945.

LE   Leuick, B., *Roman Colonies in Southern Asia Minor,* 1967.

LEA   Lea, H.C., *History of Sacred Celibacy in the Christian Church,* 1956.

LEO   Leon-Dufour, *Vocabulário de Teologia Bíblica,* 1984.

LEU   Leupolo, H.C., *Exposition of Genesis,* 1942; (1967) *Christian Reflections.*

LEW   Lewis, C.S., *Miracles,* 1947.

LEX   *Analytical Greek Lexicon,* Bagster S., 1958.

LI   Little, F.H., *The Anabaptist Doctrine of the Church,* 1952.

LIG   Lightfoot, J.B., *Clement of Rome,* 1890; *Apostolic Fathers,* 1890; *Dissertation on the Apostalic Age,* 1892.

LIL   Lillie, W., *Studies in New Testament Ethics,* 1961.

LIN   Linstrom, Harold, *Wesley and Santification,* 1946.

LINN   Linnemann, E., *Parables of Jesus,* 1966.

LL   Lloyd, R., *The Chruch of England in the 20th Century,* 1960.

LLO   Lloyd, S., *The Art of the Ancient Near East,* 1961.

LO   *Loeb Classical Library,* Lake, K., 1912.

LOT   Lotz, Johannes Baptist, *How the Reformation Came,* 1965.

LOU   Loud, G., *The Megiddo Ivories,* 1939.

LOW   Lowther, Clarke (ed.), *Liturgy and Worship,* 1943.

LU   *Luther's Works,* Philadelphia, Fortress (ed.), *sd.*

LUT   Lutz, H.F., *Textiles and Costumes Among the Peoples of the Near East,* 1923.

LUTH   Luther, Martin, *A Commentary on St. Paul's Epistle to the Galatians,* 1535.

LY   Lyttleton, Raymond A., *The Modern Universe,* 1957.

LW   Lambert, W.G., *Babylonian Wisdom Literature,* 1960.

M

M   Mansel, H.L., *The Limits of Religious Thought, 1957.*

MA   Macgregor, C.H.C., «The Concept of the Wrath of God in the New Testament», *N.T. Studies,* 1961.

MAC   Macintosh, H.R., *Types of Modern Theology,* 1963.

BIBLIOGRAFIA

MACA Macalister, R.A.S., *The Excavations of Gezer*, 1912; *The Philistines, Their History and Civilization*, 1913.

MAG Maggs, J.T.L., *The Spiritual Experience of Paul*, 1901.

MAL Mallowan, M.E.L., *Twenty-Five Years of Mesopotamian Discoveries, and Nimrod and its Remains*, 1962.

MAN Manley, *The Book of the Law*, 1957.

MAR Marmor, Judd, (ed.), *Sexual Inversion; The Multiple Roots of Homosexuality*, 1965.

MARI Marias, Julian, *Introdução à Filosofia*, 1966.

MAY May, H.C., *Material Remains of the Megiddo Cult*, 1935.

MC *Dicionário Bíblico*, McKenzie, John L., (ed.), 1978.

MCC McCown, C.C., «Hebrew High Places and Cult Remains», JBL LXIX, 1950.

MCG McGiffert, A.C., *A History of Christianity in the Apostalic Age*, 1920.

MCN McNeill, J.T., *The History and Character of Calvinism*, 1954.

ME Metzger, Bruce, *An Introduction to the Apocrypha*, 1957; *The Text of the New Testament*, 1964.

MEL Melden, A.I., (ed.), *Human Rights*, 1970.

MER Mercer, S.A.B., *The Religion of Ancient Egypt*, 1949.

MET Taylor, Richard, *Metaphysics*, 1965.

MEY Meyer, M.A., *History of the City of Gaza*, 1907.

MEYE Meyer, Heinrich August Wilhelm, *Meyer's Commentary on the New Testament*, 1884.

MG Goguel, M. *The Primitive Church*, 1964.

MH Mornschuh, M., *Studien Zur Epistula Apostolorum*, 1965.

MI *Encyclopedia Mirador Internacional*, 1976.

MIC Micklem, N., «Leviticus» em IB, 1953.

MICH Nichols, R., *The New Testament Speaks*, 1969.

MIL Miller, J.L., *Encyclopedia of Bible Life*, 1949

MILL Millard, A.R., *Archaeology and the Life of Jacob*, 1963.

MIT Mitton, C., *The Epistle of James*, 1966.

MK McKnight, W.J., *The Apocalypse of Jesus Christ; John to the Seven Churches*, 1927.

MM McMurrin, S., e Fuller, B.A.G., *History of Philosophy*, 1955.

MO Moffatt, J., *The Historical New Testament*, 1901; *Moffatt New Testament Commentary*, 1938.

MOF Ver MO.

MOO Moody, Raymond, A., *Life After Life*, 1977; *Reflections on Life after Life*, 1978.

MON Montgomery, J.A., *Arabia and the Bible*, 1934.

MONT Montgomery, J.A., «Aesthetics in Hebrew Religion», JBL, LVI, 1937.

MONTE Montefiore, *The Epistle to the Hebrews*, 1964.

MOR Moore, G.F., *Judaism*, 1927.

MORN Morgan, G. Campbell, *Commentary on the Four Gospels*, 1977.

MOU Moule, C.F.D., *An Idiom Book of the New Testament*, 1960.

MOUR Mourant, John A., *Readings in the Philosophy of Religion*, 1954.

MR Moore, G.E., *Principia Ethica*, 1903.

MST *Cyclopedia of Biblical, Theological and Ecclesiastical Literature*, Moulton and Milligan, 1975.

MU Murray, H.J.C., *A History of Board Games other than Chess*, 1952.

MUR Murray, Gilbert, *Five Stages of Greek Religion*, 1951.

MW Weber, M., *Ancient Judaism*, 1952.

MY Myers, F.W.H., *Human Personality and its Survival of Bodily Death*, 1903.

N

N Nelson, Leonard, *Systems of Ethics*, 1956.

NA Navarra, Fernand, *The Forbidden Mountain*, 1958.

NAI Nairne, A., *The Faith of the New Testament*, 1920.

NAP Napier, B.P., *Exodus*, 1963.

NAS Nash, Arnold S., (ed.), *Protestant Thought in the Twentieth Century*, 1951.

NB Newberry, Thomas, *The Newberry Study Bible*, 1959.

NBC *New Bible Commentary*, Davidson, F., (ed.), 1953 (português).

NCE *The New Catholic Encyclopedia*.

ND *Novo Dicionário da Bíblia*, 1968.

NE(1) Newell, William R., *Hebrews Vs. by Vs.*, 1947; *Romans Vs. by Vs.*, 1952.

NE(2) Neve, Juergen, L., *History of Christian Thought*, 1946.

NI Nida, Eugene, *Customs and Cultures*, 1970.

NIC *New International Commentary*.

NIE Niebuhr, H., Richard, *Christ and Culture*, 1952.

NIL Nilson, P., *Primitive Time Reckoning*, 1920.

NTI Champlin, Russell Norman, *O Novo Testamento Interpretado*, 1979.

NO Noth, M., *The Old Testament World*, 1966.

NOK Nock, A.D., Festugiere, A.J., *Corpus Hermeticum* (4 vols), 1960.

NOT Noth, M., *Geshichte und Altes Testament*, «Mare und Israel», 1953, pp. 127-152; *Exodus*, 1962.

O

O Piper, O., *The Biblical View of Sex*, 1960.

OA Oates, W.J., *The Basic Works of St. Augustine*, 1948.

OC O'Callaghan, R.T., *Aram Naharaim*, 1948.

OD Odeberg, Hugo, *III Enoch or the Hebrew Book of Enoch*, 1928.

OE(1) Oesterley, W.O.E., *The Sacred Dance*, 1923; (1937) *Fresh Approach to the Psalms*, 1937.

OE(2) Oehler, G.F., *Theology of the Old Testament*, 1882.

OES Oesthorn, *Torah in the Old Testament*, 1945; *Yahweh and Baal: Studies in the Book of Hosea*, 1956.

OG(1) Ogden, Schubert M., *The Reality of God*, 1962.

OG(2) Ogg, G., *The Chronology of the Public Ministry of Jesus*, 1940.

OIC *Oriental Institute Communications*.

OLM Olmstead, A.T., *History of the Persian Empire*, 1948; *History of Assyria*, 1960.

OLMS Ver OLM. 1960.

OP Oppenheim, A.L., *Ancient Mesopotamia*, 1964; *Letters from Mesopotamia*, 1967.

OR Orni, E., e Efrat, E., *Geography of Israel*, 1966.

ORE Orr, J., *Revelation and Inspiration*, 1910.

ORR Orr, James, *The Problem of the Old Testament*, 1966.

BIBLIOGRAFIA

OS Seyffert, Oskar, *Dictionary of Classical Antiquities*, 1964.

OSI Osis, K., *Deathbed Observations by Physicians and Nurses*, 1961.

OX *Oxford Dictionary of the Christian Church*, Cross, F.L., 1957.

P

P *Dictionary of Philosophy and Religion*, Reese, W.L., 1983.

PA Patterson, S., *The Concept of God in the Philosophy of Aquinas*, 1933.

PAD Padovani, Humberto e Castagnola, Luis, *História da Filosofia*, 1964.

PAL Pallis, E.H., *Mandean Studies*, 1926.

PAR Parrot, A., *Ninevah and the Old Testament*, 1955; *The Flood and Noah's Ark*; 1956, *Babylon and the Old Testament*, 1958.

PAS Pastor, Ludwig von, Baron, *History of the Popes*, (trans. Kerr, R.F.,), 1925.

PAT Paterson, J., *The Wisdom of Job; Job and Proverbs*, 1961.

PAU Pauck, Wilhelm, *Nature of Protestantism*, 1937; *The Heritage of the Reformation*, 1950.

PAY(1) Payne, J.B., *The Theology of the Older Testament*, 1962.

PAY(2) Payne, Barton, *An Outline of Hebrew History*, 1954.

PE Peeters, Evangeles, *Apocryphes*, II, 1914.

PEA Peak, A.S., *The Bible, Its Origin, Its Significance and Its Abiding Worth*, 1913; *Elijah and Jezebel*, 1927.

PEAK Ver PEA.

PED Pederson, J., *Israel, Its Life and Culture*, 1926.

PEL Pelikan, J., *From Luther to Kierkegaard, A Study of the History of Theology*, 1963.

PEQ *Palestine Exploration Quarterly*.

PER Perowne, S., *Life and Times of Herod the Great*, 1958; *The Later Herods*, 1958.

PET Petrie, F., «Ancient Gaza», I-IV, *The Egyptian Research Account, and the British School of Archaeology in Egypt*, LVI-LVIII, 1931-34.

PETA Petavel, E., *The Struggle for Eternal Life*, 1875.

PETR Petrie, W.F., *Tools and Weapons*, 1917.

PF Pfeiffer, Robert H., *The Books of the Old Testament*, 1962.

PFE Pfeiffer, C.F., *The Patriarchal Age*, 1961.

PH Price, H.A., «Appearing and Appearances», *American Philosophical Quarterly*, 1932.

PHI Philo, *Legattio and Gaium*.

PHIL Philipson, D., *The Reform Movement in Judaism*, 1931.

PM Montet, P., *Everyday Life in Egypt*, 1958.

PO Pommerenke, C.H., «Artificial Insemination, Genetic and Legal Implications», *Obstetrics and Gynecology*, 9:189, 1957.

POE Poebel, Arno, «The Assyrian King List From Khorsalead», JNES, Vols. 1,2; 1942-43.

PPH Freeman, Kathleen, *Ancilla to the Pre-Socratic Philosophers*, 1956.

POR Porter, Frank E., *The Mind of Christ in Paul*, 1939.

PR Prat, F., *Jesus Christ, His Life, His Teaching and His Work*, 1960.

PRI Pritchard, J.B., *Ancient Near Eastern Tests*, 1955; *Studies in Ancient Technology*, 1956; *Gibeon Where the Sun Stood Still*, 1962.

PRIT Ver PRI

PS Smith, T.V., (ed.), *Philosophers Speak for Themselves*, 1956.

PSBA *Proceedings of the Society of Biblical Archaeology*.

PT Peters, P.W., *The Hebrew Attitude to Education in the Hellenistic Era*, 1967.

PTR *Princeton Theological Review*.

PU Pusey, E.B., *The Minor Prophets*, 1957.

Q

QDAP *Quarterly of the Department of Antiquities of Palestine*.

QS Quell, Gottfried; Schrenk, G. (trans. Coats, J.R.), *Righteousness*, 1951.

R

R *Encyclopedia of Theology*, Rahner, Karl (ed.), 1975.

RA Von Rad, Gerhard, *Old Testament Theology*, 1962.

RAM Ramsay, M., *A Historical Commentary on St. Paul's Epistle to the Galations*, 1900; *Letters to the Seven Churches*, 1904; *St. Paul the Traveller and the Roman Citizen*, 1909; *The Cities of St. Paul*, 1949.

RAMM Ramm, B., *The Christian View of Science and Scripture*, 1954.

RAN Randall, John L., *Parapsychology and the Nature of Life*, 1977.

RAND Randall, John Herman e Buchler, Justus, *Philosophy, An Introduction*, 1942.

RE Reed, W.L., *The Asherah of the Old Testament*, 1949.

REA Read, H.H., *Rutley's Elements of Minerology*, 1970.

REG Regush, Nicholas M., Frontiers of Healing, 1977.

REI Reider, J., *An Index to Aquila*, 1966.

REIF Reifenberg, A., *Ancient Hebrew Arts*, 1950.

REIN *Reincarnation, An East-West Anthology*, Head, Joseph, e Cranston, S.L., 1981.

REIS Reis, J.K.S., *The Biblical Doctrine of the Ministry*, 1955.

REN Rentz, G., *The Encyclopedia of Islam*, 1960.

REU Reu, M., *Catechetics and Theory and Practice of Religious Education*, 1927.

RG Grant, R.M., *Reader in Gnosticism*, 1961.

RH Rhine, J.B., *The Reach of the Mind*, 1947.

RI Richardson, A., *Historical Theology and Biblical Theology*, 1955.

RIC Richardson, E.C., *Biblical Libraries*, 1915.

RID Ridderbos, H., *Paul and Jesus*, 1958.

RIN Ring, Kenneth, *Life at Death: A Scientific Investigation of the Near Death Experience*, 1983.

RO Robertson, A.T., *John the Loyal*, 1912; *Word Pictures in the New Testament*, 1930; *A Grammar of the Greek New Testament in the Light of Historical Research*, 1931; *The Body*, 1952.

ROB Robertson, H.W., *The Christian Doctrine of Man*, 1926.

ROB(2) Robinson, T., *The Poetry of the Old Testament*, 1947.

ROBIN Robinson, S., *Biblical Researches*, 1841.

ROBINS Robinson, J., *A New Quest of the Historical Jesus*, 1959.

BIBLIOGRAFIA

ROS   Rose, Herbert J., *A Handbook of Greek Literature*, 1951; *A Handbook of Latin Literature*, 1960.

ROT   Roth, C., *Jewish Art*, 1961.

ROU   Rouse, Ruth, *A History of the Ecumenical Movement*, 1948.

ROUT   Routley, Eric, *Hymns, Today and Tomorrow*, 1964.

ROW   Rowley, H.H., *From Joseph to Joshua*, 1950; *The Old Testament and Modern Study*, 1951; *Men of God*, 1963.

ROWE   Rowe, L.A., *Topography and the History of Beth-Shan*, 1930.

RP   Sahakian, William e Lewis, Mabel, *Realms of Philosophy*, 1965.

RU   Russell, D.S., *The Jews from Alexander to Herod*, vols. 5 e 6, *The New Carendom Bible*, 1967; *The Method and Message of Jewish Apocaliptic Literature*, 1964.

RUN   Runes, Dagobert D., *Twentieth Century Philosophy*, 1943.

RUS   Russell, Bertrand, *Principia Mathematica*, 1912.

RV   Devaux, R., *Ancient Israel*, 1962.

RW   Wilson, R. Mcl. *Gnostic Problems*, 1958; *Gnosis and the New Testament*, 1968.

RY   Rynne, Xavier, *Vatican II*, 1967.

RYR   Ryrie, C., *Biblical Theology and the New Testament*, 1959.

S

S   *Bible Encyclopedia and Scriptural Dictionary*, Howard-Severance (ed.), 1904.

SA   Sabom, Michael, *Recollections of Death*, 1982.

SAC   Sachs, *A History of Musical Instruments*, 1940.

SAG   Saggs, H.W.F., *The Greatness That Was Babylon*, 1962.

SAL   Salmond, S.D.F., *The Christian Doctrine of Immortality*, 1901.

SAM   Samuel, H.E., *Ptolemaic Chronology*, 1962.

SAU   Sauer, E., *From Eternity to Eternity*, 1954.

SB   Muller, A., *The Sacred Books of the East*, 1910.

SC   Scurti, S.J., *Short History of Philosophy*, 1950.

SCH   Schaff, Philip, *History of the Christian Church*, 1892.

SCHO   Schonfield, Hugh J., *Reader's A to Z Bible Companion*, 1967.

SCHW   Schweitzer, Albert, *The Quest of the Historical Jesus*, 1910.

SCO   Scofield, C.I., *The Scofield Reference Bible*.

SE   Seiss, Joseph, *Letters to the Seven Churches*, 1956.

SEG   Segal, J.B., *The Hebrew Passover*, 1963.

SET   Seters, J. Van, *The Hyksos, a New Investigation*, 1966.

SH   Schurer, E., *A History of the Jewish People*, 1891.

SHE   Sherman, Harold, *Know the Powers of Your Own Mind*, 1960.

SHER   *The New Schaff-Herzog Encyclopedia of Religious Knowledge*.

SHO   Short, Rendel, *The Bible and Modern Medicine*, 1953.

SHS   Singer, Charles, *A Short History of Scientific Ideas*, 1959.

SHU(1)   Shultz, S.J., *The Prophets Speak*, 1968.

SHU(2)   Shut, R.J.H., *Studies in Josephus*, 1961.

SI   Simons, J., *The Geographical and Topographical Text of the Old Testament*, 1959.

SIM   Simpson, E.K., *The Pastoral Epistles*, 1954.

SIN   Singer, C., (ed.), *A History of Technology*, 1958.

SK   Kierkegaard, Soren, *The Concept of Dread*, 1946.

SKE   Skeat, T.C., *The Reign of the Ptolemies*, 1954.

SL   Ostrander, Sheila e Shroeder, Lynn, *A Handbook of Psychic Discoveries*, 1968.

SM   Smith, J.B., *Greek-English Concordance*, 1955.

SMI   Smith, J.A., *The Historical Geography of the Holy Land*, 1896.

SMID   Smid, T., *Protevangelium Jacobi, a Commentary*, 1965.

SMIT   Smith, W.R., *The Religion of the Semites*, 1927.

SN   Snaith, H.H., *Mercy and Sacrifice*, 1953.

SO   Souter, A., *The Text and Canon of the New Testament*, 1954.

SOC   Mondolfo, R., *Sócrates*, 1967.

SP   Spitzer, Walter, e Saylork, Carlyle, I., (eds.), *Birth Control and the Christian; A Protestant Symposium on the Control of Human Reproduction*, 1961.

ST   Strong, Augustus, *Systematic Theology*, 1907.

STA   Stanley, Arthur Penrhyn, *The Jewish Church*, 1886.

STAI   Stainer, J., *The Music of the Bible*, 1914.

STAN   Stanley, David, M., *The Apostolic Church in the New Testament*, 1965.

STE   Stendall, K., (ed.), *Immortality and Resurrection*, 1964.

STI   Stibbs, A.M., *The Meaning of the Word Blood in Scripture*, 1947; *God's Church*, 1959.

STO   Stokes, W.L., *Essentials of Earth History; An Introduction to Historical Geography*, 1963.

STOI   Hadas, Moses (ed.), *Essential Works of Stoicism*, 1961.

STON   Stonehouse, Paul, *Before the Aeropagus*, 1956.

STONE   Stonehouse, N.B., *Origins of the Synoptic Gospels*, 1964.

STOR   Storr, C., *Ancient Ships*, 1895.

STR   Striwe, Otto, *The Universe*, 1962.

STRA   Strawson, W., *Jesus and the Future Life*, 1959.

STRAC   Strack, H.L., *Introduction of the Talmud and Midrash*, 1931.

STRE   Streeter, B.H., *The Four Gospels*, 1930.

STRO   Strong, James, *Exhaustive Concordance of the Bible*, 1951.

SU   Suetonius, *Gaius Caligula Dio*.

SW   Swete, H.B., *Essays on the Early History of the Church and the Ministry*, 1921.

T

T   *Baker's Dictionary of Practical Theology*, Turnball, Ralph (ed.), 1982.

TA   Taylor, V., *The Gospels*, 1960.

TAR   Tarn, William W., e Griffith, Guy T., *Hellenistic Civilization*, 1961.

BIBLIOGRAFIA

TAY Taylor, C., *Sayings of the Jewish Fathers*, 1900.

TC Tcherikover, V., *Hellenistic Civilization and the Jews*, 1959.

TCE *The Twentieth Century Encyclopedia of Religious Knowledge*, Loetscher, 1979.

TCH Chan, Thomas, *The Adam and Eve Story*, 1963.

TE Tenny, M.C., *The New Testament, A Historic and Analytical Survey*, 1953; *Galatians: The Charter of Christian Liberty*, 1954.

TEC Techenie, *Euprat und Tigris*, 1934.

TEN Ver TE.

TH Thomas, D., Winston, *Archaeology and Old Testament Study*, 1967.

THA Thackeray, H., *Josephus the Man and the Histories*, 1929.

THI Thiel, A., *The Mysterious Numbers of the Hebrew Kings*, 1965.

THO Thomas, D.W., *Documents from Old Testament Times*, 1958.

THOM Thompson, R.C., *The Epic of Gilgameh*, 1930.

THU Thomas, C., e Hutchinson, R.W., *A Century of Exploration of Nineveh*, 1929.

TI Titus, Eric Lane, *Essentials of New Testament Study*, 1958.

TIL Tillich, Paul, *The Dynamics of Faith*, 1957.

TIS Tischendorf, Constantinus, *Novum Testamentum Graece*, 1869.

TJ Jallard, Trevor, *Church and Papacy*, 1944.

TL Thorndike, Lynn, *A History of Magic and Experimental Science*, 1938.

TO Torbet, R.G., *A History of the Baptists*, 1950.

TON Tonybee, J., *The Shrine of St. Peter and the Vatican Excavation*, 1956; *The History of Civilization*, 1959.

TOR Torrey, C.C., *Ezra Studies*, 1910; *Pseudo-Ezekiel and the Original Prophecy*, 1930.

TOR(2) Torrey, R.A., (ed.), *The Topical Textbook*, sd.

TR Tristan, H.B., *Eastern Customs in Bible Lands*, 1984.

TRA Trawick, Buckner B., *The New Testament as Literature*, 1964.

TT *The New Topical Textbook*, Fleming and Revel, sd.

TVS Smith, T.V., *Philosophers Speak for Themselves*, 1956.

TYN *Tyndale New Testament Commentary*, 1958.

U

U Uhlhorn, G., *Christian Character in the Ancient Church*, 1883.

UL Ullendorff, E., «The Moabite Stone», *Documents from OT Times*, 1958; *Ethiopia and the Bible*, 1968.

UL(2) Ver UL (1958).

UN Unger, Merrill F., *Unger's Bible Dictionary*, 1966. Ver tambem UNA.

UN(1952) Unger, Merrill, F., *Biblical Demonology*, 1952.

UN(1957) Unger, Merrill, F., *Israel and the Aramaeans of Damascus*, 1957.

UNA Unger, Merrill, *Archaeology and the New Testament*, 1960; *Archaeology and the Old Testament*, 1962.

UNN Van Unnick, W.C., *Newly Discovered Gnostic Writings*, 1960.

UT *Ugaritic Textbook*.

V

V Vriezen, S., *An Outline of Old Testament Theology*, 1962.

VA Vaux, R., *Ancient Israel*, 1961.

VAS Vasilieve, *History of the Byzantine Empire*, 1929.

VE Velikovsky, R.B.Y., *Worlds in Collision*, 1950.

VI Vincent, A., *La Religion des Judeo-Arameens D'Eléphantine*, 1957.

VIN Vincent, Marvin R., *Word Studies in the New Testament*, 1946.

VO Vos, E., *The Teaching of the Epistle to the Hebrews*, 1956.

VR Vriezen, Th.C., *An Outline of Old Testament Theology*, 1963.

VT *Vocabulário de Teologia Bíblica*, Xavier-Leon-Dufour, SJ (ed.), 1984.

W

W Richardson, Alan, *A Theological Word Book*, 1962.

WA *Funk and Wagnalls Standard Dictionary*, 1968.

WA(2) Wallace, R.S., *Many Things in Parables*, 1955.

WAL Walker, W., *All the Plants of the Bible*, 1958

WALK Walker, G.P., *Mammals of the World*, 1964.

WALL Wallace, R.S., *Elijah and Elisha*, 1957.

WAT Watson, Thomas, *The Ten Commandments*, 1965.

WAX Waxman, Meyer, *The History of Jewish Literature*, 1960.

WBC *Wycliffe Bible Commentary*, 1962.

WC Westerman, C., *Essays of Old Testament Interpretation*, 1958.

WE Eichrodt, W., *Theology of the Old Testament*, 1961.

WEA Weatherhead, L.D., *Psychology, Religion and Healing*, 1951.

WEB Webre, A.L., e Liss, P.H., *The Age of Cataclysm*, 1974.

WEH Howard, F.H., *Christianity According to St. John*, 1946.

WEI Weiser, A., *The Psalms*, 1905.

WEI(2) Weigall, A., *The Life and Times of Cleopatra*, 1925.

WES *Westminster Commentaries*.

WEST Westermach, E., *A Short History of Marriage*.

WG Wright, George E., *The Book of Isaiah*, 1964; *The Old Testament and Theology*, 1969.

WH Whale, J.S., *Christian Doctrine*, 1941.

WHB Brownlee, H.H., *The Text of Habakkuk in the Ancient Commentary from Qumran*, 1959.

WHE Whesluright, Philip, *A Critical Introduction to Ethics*, 1959.

WHG Green, W.H., «Primeval Chronology», *Bibliotheca Sacra*, 1890.

WHI White, H.G.I., *The Sayings of Jesus from Oxyrhnchus*, 1920.

WHI(2) White, John, *Pole Shift*, 1982.

BIBLIOGRAFIA

WHIS Whiston, W., *The Life and Works of Josephus*, 1906.

WHIT Whitcomb, J.C. Jr., *Darius the Mede: A Study in Historical Identification*, 1963.

WI Wilson, R., *The Gnostic Problem*, 1958.

WI(2) Wright, F., Ver WRIG.

WIE Wiegard, T., *Baalbek*, 1921-25.

WIK Wilkenhauser, A., *New Testament Introduction*, 1958; *Pauline Mysticism*, 1960.

WIL Eastman e Wilson, *Drama in the Church*, 1942.

WILS Wilson, J.A., *The Culture of Ancient Egypt*, 1956.

WIR Wirgman, A.T., *The Blessed Virgin and All the Company of Heaven*, 1905.

WIS Wiseman, J., *Chronicles of Chaldean Kings in the British Museum*, 1956.

WOD Wood, J.A., *Bible Animals*, 1869.

WOO Wooley, C.L., *Charchemish*, I-III, 1914-52, 1962.

WOR Worrell, W., «Israel and the Dance», D.D. Runes (ed.), *The Hebrew Impact on Western Civilization*, 1951.

WORD Wordsworth, Charles, *The Greek Testament*, 1875.

WOU Woudstra, M.H., *The Ark of the Covenant from Conquest to Kingship*, 1965.

WRI Wright, G., *Biblical Archaeology*, 1957.

WRIG Wright, F., *Manners and Customs of Bible Lands*, 1954.

WT Whitehead, A.N., *Process and Reality*, 1929.

WTJ *Westminster Theological Journal*.

WW(1) Comay, Joan E Brownrigg, Robert, *Who's Who in the Bible*, 1980.

WW(2) Walker, Willinston, *History of the Christian Church*, 1959.

WY Wycherley, Richard C., *How the Greeks Built Cities*, 1962.

X

XJ Jacques, X., *Orientalia*, 1969.

Y

Y Young, E.J., *The Prophecy of Daniel*, 1949.

YA Yahudu, A.S., *The Accuracy of the Bible*, 1934.

YAD Yadin, Y., *The Art of Warfare in Biblical Lands*, 1963; *The Ben-Sira Scroll from Mosada*, 1965; *Masada, Herod's Fortress and the Zealots Last Stand*, 1966.

YAT Yates, Kyle, *Studies in the Psalms*, 1953.

YE Yeivin, S., «The Palestino-Sinaitic Inscriptions», PEQ, 1937.

YO Young, E.J., *Studies in Isaiah*, 1954; Introduction to the Old Testament, 1958; *History of the Literary Criticism of the Pentateuch*, 1970.

Z

Z *The Zondervan Pictorial Encyclopedia of the Bible*, Tenney, Merril C., (ed.), 1977.

ZAE Zaehner, R.C., *The Dawn and Twilight of Zorastrianism*, 1961.

ZE Zeitlin, S., *A Historical Study on the Canonization of the Old Testament*, 1950.

ZEL Zeller, Eduard, *Outlines of the History of Greek Philosophy*, 1950.

ZEU Zeuner, F.E., *A History of Domesticated Animals*, 1963.

ZY Zyl, A.H., Van, *The Moabites*, 1960.

••• ••• •••

AUTORES E EDITORES
EM ORDEM ALFABÉTICA

Abbott-Smith, Ver AS.
Abernathy, George L., Ver ABE.
Abetti, Giorgio, Ver AB.
Abrahamson, I., Ver ABR.
Adams, A.M.C., Ver ADA.
Adams, J.M., Ver ADM.
Adolph, R., Ver AD.
Aharoni, Y., Ver AH.
Aland, K., Ver ALA.
Albright, W.F., Ver ALB e KEL.
Alford, Henry, Ver AL.
Allegro, John M., Ver ALLE.
Allen, A.B., Ver ALL.
Allis, O.T., Ver AO.
Alston, William, Ver ALS.
Altaner, B., Ver BA.
Altizer, T.J.J., Ver ALT.
Amiran, R., Ver AMI.
Anderson, Alan R., Ver AN.
Anderson, B.W., Ver AND.
Anderson, G.H., Ver AND(2).
Anson, P.F., Ver ANS.
Arbesmann, Rudolph, Ver ARB.
Archer, G., Ver ARC.
Arnason, H.H., Ver ARN.
Arndt, William F., Ver A.

Arnold, P., ARNO.
Ashby, Robert H., Ver ASH.
Attwater, D., Ver ATT.
Augustine, Ver AUG.
Aulon, G., Ver AUL.
Ave Jonah, Michael, Ver AV.
Ayer, A.J., Ver AY.
Badawy, A., Ver BAD.
Baggot, J., Ver BAG.
Bagster, S., Ver LEX.
Bailey, A., Ver BAI.
Bailey, D.D., Ver BAIL.
Baille, D.M., Ver DB.
Baille, J., Ver JB.
Baly, D., Ver BAL.
Ballow, R.O., Ver BALL.
Barclay, W., Ver BARC.
Barkley, W.P., Ver BARK.
Barnes, Hazel E., Ver HAZ.
Barrett, C.K., Ver CKB.
Barth, Karl, Ver BART.
Barton, G.A., Ver BAR.
Bartsch, W., Ver BARTS.
Baur, Ferdinand Christian, Ver BAU.
Bayless, Raymond, Ver BAY.

Bea, Augustine, Ver BEA.
Beasley, Murray R., Ver BM.
Beccaria, G., Ver BEC.
Bell, Sir Charles Alfred, Ver BEL.
Benson, Clarence H., Ver BENS.
Bentley, John C., Ver BE.
Bentzen, A., Ver BEN.
Bert, J., Ver BOK.
Besnier, M., Ver BES.
Bevan, E.R., Ver BEV.
Bickerman, E., Ver BI.
Birley, E., Ver BIR.
Black, Matthew, Ver BLAC.
Blackman, E., Ver BK.
Blackman, G.E., Ver BLM.
Blackmore, Susan J., Ver BLR.
Blackwood, A.W., Ver BLA.
Blair, E.P., Ver BL.
Blass, F., Ver BLAS.
Blau, C., Ver BLAU.
Bodheimer, F.S., Ver BOD.
Boettner, E., Ver BOE.
Bohl, F.M., Ver BOH.
Bonhoeffer, Dietrich, Ver BON.
Borger, R., Ver BOR.
Bornheim, Gerd A., Ver FP.

BIBLIOGRAFIA

Botsford, G.W., Ver BOT.
Bourke, Vernon, Ver EAU.
Bouyer, K.E., Ver BOU.
Bowman, G.W., Ver BOW.
Bowman, R.A., Ver BN.
Box, C.H., Ver BOX.
Box, H.S., Ver BO.
Boyle, Isaac, Ver BOY.
Brav, S.R., Ver BRA.
Breasted, J.H., Ver ARE e BRE.
Briggs, Charles A., Ver I.
Bright, J., Ver BRI e BRIG.
Brightman, E.S., Ver BRIG(2).
Brinker, R., Ver BRIN.
Broad, C.D., Ver BROA.
Brockington, L.H., Ver BROC.
Bromiley, G.W., Ver BRO.
Bronstein, Daniel J., Ver BRON.
Brown, David, Ver JFB.
Brown, Driver e Beges, Ver BDB.
Brownlee, H.H., Ver WHB.
Brownlee, William H., Ver BW.
Brownrigg, Robert, Ver WW(1).
Bruce, F.F., Ver BRU.
Brugger, Walter, Ver DF.
Brunner, E., Ver BRUN e EB.
Buber, Martin, Ver BUB.
Buchan, J., Ver BUC.
Buchler, Justus, Ver RAND.
Budge, A.W., Ver BUD.
Buhl, F., Ver BUH.
Bultman, R., Ver BULT.
Burkitt, F.C., Ver BUR.
Burnet, J., Ver BJ.
Burr, Harold S., Ver BU.
Bush, F.O., Ver BUS.
Buttrick, George Arthur, Ver IB.
Cadbury, Henry, J., Ver CAD.
Callaway, J.E., Ver CAL.
Calvin, John, Ver CALV.
Cameron, G.C., Ver CN.
Cameron, George Glen, Ver CGG.
Carey, K.M., Ver CAR.
Carnell, John E., Ver CARN.
Carr, Harvey, Ver CR.   CR.
Carrington, P., Ver CARR.
Cary, Max, Ver CM.
Cassell, Ver CAS.
Castagnola, Luis, Ver PAD.
Cerny, B.J., Ver CER.
Chafer, Lewis S., Ver CHA.
Chainey, George, Ver CHI.
Champlin, Russell N. Ver DRE,
  EC e NTI.
Chan, Thomas, Ver TCH.
Charles, R.H., Ver APOT e CH.
Charlesworth, James H., Ver J.
Chavasse, C., Ver CHAV.
Chetwynd, Tom, Ver CHE.
Chiera, E., Ver CS.
Chisholm, Roderick M., Ver
  CHI(2).
Clapp, F.G., Ver CLAP.
Clark, Gordon H., Ver CLA, GE e
  HP.
Clarke, Adam, Ver CLAR.
Clay, A., Ver CL.
Cobb, J.B., Ver COB.
Cobern, C., Ver COB(2).
Cohen, H., Ver COH.
Cohen, S.S., Ver COG(2).
Comay, Joan, Ver WW(1).
Connolly, R.H., Ver DA.
Cope, G., Ver COP.

Copleston, Frederich, Ver CO.
Cook, A.S., Ver CAM.
Corbishley, Thomas, Ver COR.
Cottrell, L., Ver COT.
Cowley, A., Ver COW.
Cranston, S.L., Ver REIN.
Crippa, Adolpho, Ver CRIP.
Cripps, R.S., Ver CRI.
Cross, F.L., Ver OX.
Cumont, F., Ver CUM.
Curran, Charles, Ver CC.
Dalby, J.C., Ver DALB.
Dalman, J.C., Ver DAL.
Dana, E.S., Ver DANA.
Dancy, J.C., Ver DAN.
Daniélou, J., Ver JD.
Daniel-Ropes, H., Ver DANR.
Darling, James, Ver DAR.
Davbe, D., Ver DD.
Davidson, A.B., Ver DAVI e DV(2)
Davidson, F., Ver NBC.
Davies, J.G., Ver DAV.
Davis, Mon. H., Ver CD.
Debrunner, A., Ver BLAS.
De Camp, L.S., Ver CA.
Deismann, A., Ver DEIS.
Delitzsch, F., Ver DEL e KD.
Den Born, Ver DE.
Dennis, James Shepherd, Ver DEN.
Denzinger, H., Ver D e DS.
Devaux, R., Ver RV.
Dhorme, M., Ver DH.
Diels, H., Ver DK.
Diringer, David, Ver DIR.
Dixon, Jeane, Ver DI.
Dodd, C.H., Ver DOD.
Dolah, John, P., Ver DOL.
Doresse, J., Ver DO.
Dothan, T., Ver DOT.
Dougherty, R.P., Ver DOU.
Doughty, C.M., Ver DT.
Downey, E., Ver DOW.
Driver, G.R., Ver DM, DRI(1) e
  DRIV.
Driver, S.R., Ver DRI(2) e I.
Drower, M.S., Ver DRO.
Dubberstein, W.H., Ver DUB.
Ducasse, C.J., Ver DCJ.
Ducasse, C.W., Ver DU.
Duchesne, L., Ver DUC.
Dunlap, Jane, Ver DUN.
Dvornik, Francis, Ver DV(2).
Eastman e Wilson, Ver WIL.
Eaton, J.H., Ver EA.
Eddy, R., Ver EDD.
Edersheim, Alfred, Ver ED, EDE e
  EDER.
Edidin, B.M., Ver EDI.
Edmunds, C. Gordon, Ver EDM.
Edwards, Paul, Ver EP.
Eichrodt, W., Ver WE.
Eisen, G.A., Ver EI.
Elert, W., Ver ELE.
Eliot, W., Ver EL.
Ellicott, Charles John, Ver ELLI.
Ellison, H.L., Ver ELL.
Enslin, Morton Scott, Ver CB e EN.
Eugene, Maly, Ver EUG.
Eusebius, Ver EU.
Ewing, W., Ver EW(2).
Fabricus, J.F., Ver JK.
Fairbairn, M., Ver FA(2).
Fairbridge, R.W., Ver FAI.
Falkner, E., Ver FAL.

Farmer, W.R., Ver FW.
Farquhar, John, Ver FARQ.
Farrar, F.W., Ver FAR.
Fausset, A.R., Ver FA(1) e JFB.
Ferm, Vergilius, Ver E.
Ferreira, Aurélio Buarque de Ho-
  landa, Ver AU.
Filson, F.V., Ver FI.
Finegan, J., Ver FIN.
Firenze, Ver EF.
Flemington, W.F., Ver FL.
Flew, Antony, Ver F.
Foakes, Jackson, Ver LAK.
Foerster, W., Ver FOE.
Foilett, Ver FO.
Forbes, R.J., Ver FOR.
Frankfort, H., Ver FRAN.
Frankfort, H.H., Ver FRA.
Franz, W., Ver DK.
Frazer, J.G., Ver FR.
Free, J.P., Ver FRE.
Freeman, David Hugh, Ver
  FREE(2).
Freeman, H.E., Ver FREE.
Freeman, Kathleen, Ver PPH.
Freud, Sigmund, Ver FREU.
Friedrich, J., Ver FRI.
Frost, H.W., Ver FRO.
Gadd, Cyril John, Ver GAD.
Gaebelein, Frank E., Ver GA.
Gaster, M., Ver GAS.
Geikie, C., Ver GEI.
Geoffrey, Parmiter, Ver GEO(1).
George, P.R., Ver GEO(2).
Gesenius, W., Ver GES.
Geyser, A. S., Ver GEY.
Ghirshman, R., Ver GH.
Gill, John, Ver G.
Gilson, Étienne, Ver GE.
Gingrich, F. Wilbur, Ver A.
Ginzberg, H.L., Ver GI.
Glover, R.H., Ver GLO.
Glueck, N., Ver GL.
Goguel, M., Ver MG.
Goldschmidt, Victor, Ver GOL.
Goodman, Jeffrey, Ver GOOD e JG.
Goodspeed, E.J., Ver GD.
Gordis, Robert, Ver KOH.
Gordon, C.H., Ver CG, GCH e
  GOR.
Gottwald, N.K., Ver GOT.
Gradenwitz, P., Ver GRAD.
Grant, E., Ver GRA.
Grant, F.C., Ver GRAN.
Grant, R.M., Ver GR. e RG.
Gray, J. Ver GY.
Green, W.H., Ver GN e WHG.
Greenberg, M., Ver GRE.
Greenslade, S.L., Ver GREE.
Grenfell, B.P., Ver GREN.
Griffith, Guy, Ver TAR.
Griffith, G.T., Ver GRI.
Grimel, Pierre, Ver GP.
Grollenberg, L.H., Ver GROL.
Groves, C.P., Ver GRO.
Guillamont, A., Ver GUI.
Gunday, R.H., Ver GUN.
Guthrie, D., Ver GU.
Hadas, M., Ver HAD e STOI.
Hahn, H.F., Ver HAH.
Haldar, A., Ver HALD.
Hall, (e Holmgard), Ver HAL.
Halley, Henry, H., Ver HALL.
Hanson, R.P.C., Ver HAN.

BIBLIOGRAFIA

Hanson, S., Ver HANS.
Harding, G.L., Ver HAR.
Hare, R.M., Ver HRM.
Harnack, Adolf von, Ver HARN.
Harnack, G.L., Ver HAR.
Harris, H.L., Ver HRL.
Harrison, A.W., Ver HR.
Harrison, E.F., Ver B.
Harrison, P.N., Ver HRR.
Harrison, R.K., Ver HARR.
Hartfelder, Karl, Ver HART.
Hastings, James, Ver HA.
Hatch, Edwin, Ver HAT.
Haupart, Raymond, Ver HAU.
Hayes, W.C., Ver HAY.
Head, Joseph, Ver REIN.
Healy, Edwin, Ver HEA.
Heberman, Charles E., Ver CE.
Heidel, Alexander, Ver HEI.
Hennecke, Edgar, Ver HEN.
Henry, Carl F.H., Ver H.
Henry, Matthew, Ver COM.
Herford, R.Y., Ver HER(2).
Herodotus, Ver HER(1).
Hick, John, Ver HI.
Hiers, R.H., Ver HIE.
Hiltner, Seward, Ver KM.
Hirsch, F.E., Ver HIR.
Hirschberger, Johannes, Ver HF.
Hitti, P.K., Ver HIT.
Hodge, C., Ver HO(1).
Hodgson, Leonard, Ver HOD(1).
Hodgson, P.C., Ver HOD(2).
Holmgard e Hall, Ver HAL.
Horowitz, E., Ver HOR.
Hoskins, H., Ver HOS.
Houston, M.G., Ver HOU.
Howard, Clingbell, Ver HO(2).
Howard, F.H., Ver WEH.
Howard-Severance, Ver S.
Howlet, D., Ver HOW.
Hughes, Philip, Ver HU.
Hughes, T. Hawel, Ver HY.
Hunt, I., Ver HUN.
Hutchins, B., Ver GB.
Ira, Progoff, Ver IRA.
Iranaeus, Ver IR.
Jackson, Samuel, Ver JA.
Jacques, X., Ver XJ.
Jalland, Tig, Ver JAL.
Jallard, Trevor, Ver TJ.
James, E.D., Ver JAME.
James, M.R., Ver ANT e JAM.
Jamieson, Robert, Ver JFB.
Japiassu, Hilton, Ver DBF.
Jarrett, James L., Ver JAR.
Jastrow, M., Ver JAS.
Jellicoe, S., Ver JEL.
Johler, K., Ver JOH.
Johnson, A.R., Ver JOHN.
Jonas, H., Ver HJ.
Jones, A.H.M., Ver JON.
Josephus, Ver JO.
Judge, E.A., Ver JUD.
June, Leo, Ver JUN.
Jung, Carl, Ver JU.
Kahler, Martin, Ver KAH.
Kapelrud, Arvid S., Ver KAP.
Kassis, H., Ver KA.
Keil, C.F., Ver KD e KEI.
Kelly, J.N.D., Ver KELL.
Kelso, J.L., Ver KELS.
Kelscn, J., Ver KEL.
Kennedy, K., Ver KENY.

Kent, R.G., Ver KEN.
Kenyon, Frederick, Ver FK. e KE.
Kenyon, K., Ver KENY.
Kidner, D., Ver KI.
Kierkegaard, Soren, Ver SK.
Kinsey, Alfred C., Ver KIN.
Kitchen, K.A., Ver KK.
Kittle, Gerhard, Ver K.
Klausner, J., Ver KLA.
Kline, M.G., Ver KLI.
Klink, A., Ver KLIN.
Kneller, George, Ver KNE.
Knight, G.A.F., Ver KN.
Kopp, C., Ver KO.
Kraeling, C.H., Ver KR(1).
Kraft, C.F., Ver KR(2).
Kraft, R.A., Ver KR(3).
Kramer, S.N., Ver KRA.
Kraus, H.J., Ver KRAU.
Kurtz, Prof., Ver KU.
Kyle, M.G., Ver KY.
Labby, Daniel H., Ver LAB.
Laetsch, A., Ver LAE.
Lake, Kirsopp, Ver KL e LAK e LO.
Lambert, W.G., Ver LW.
Lamon, R.S., Ver LAM.
Lampe, G.W.N., Ver LA.
Lang, C.H., Ver LA(2).
Lange, P., Ver LAN.
Langford, A., Ver ABE.
Langton, E., Ver LANG.
La Sor, W., Ver LAS
Latourette, K.S., Ver LAT.
Lea, H.C., Ver LEA.
Letcher, Lefferts A., Ver L.
Leon-Dufour, Ver LEO.
Leuick, B., Ver LE.
Leupolo, H.C., Ver LEU.
Lewis, C.S., Ver LEW.
Lewis, John, Ver JL.
Lewis, Mabel, Ver RP.
Lightfoot, J.B., Ver LIG.
Lillie, W., Ver LIL.
Linnemann, E., Ver LINN.
Linstrom, Harold, Ver LIN.
Liss, P.H., Ver WEB.
Little, F.H., Ver LI.
Lloyd, R., Ver LL.
Lloyd, S., Ver LLO.
Loetscher, Ver TCE.
Lotz, Johannes Baptist, Ver LOT.
Loud, G., Ver LOU.
Lowther, Clarke, Ver LOW.
Luckenbill, Ver ARAB.
Luther, Martin, Ver LU e LUTH.
Lutz, H.F., Ver LUT.
Lyttleton, Raymond A., Ver LY.
Macalister, R.A.S., Ver MACA.
Macgregor, C.H.C., Ver MA.
Macintosh, H.R., Ver MAC.
Maggs, T.J.L., Ver MAG.
Mallowan, M.E.L., Ver MAL.
Manley, Ver MAN.
Mansel, H.L., Ver M.
Marcondes, Danilo, Ver DBF.
Marias, Julian, Ver MARI.
Marmor, Judd, Ver MAR.
May, H.C., Ver MAY.
McCown, C.C., Ver MCC.
McGiffert, A.C., Ver ACM e MCG.
McKenzie, John L., Ver MC.
McKnight, W.J., Ver MK.
McMurrin, Sterling M., Ver JAR e MM.

McNeile, A.H., Ver I.
McNeill, J.T., Ver MCN.
Melden, A.I., Ver ET e MEL.
Menninger, Karl, Ver KM.
Mercer, S.A.B., Ver MER.
Metzger, Bruce, Ver ME.
Meyer, Heinrich August Wilhelm, Ver MEYE.
Meyer, M.A., Ver MEY.
Michols, R., Ver MICH.
Micklem, N., Ver MIC.
Millard, A.R., Ver MILL.
Miller, J.L., Ver MIL.
Mitton, C., Ver MIT.
Moffatt, J., Ver MO.
Mondolfo, R., Ver SOC.
Montefiore, C.G., Ver CEM.
Montefiore, Ver MONTE.
Montet, P., Ver PM.
Montgomery, J., Ver JM.
Montgomery, J.A., Ver MON e MONT.
Moody, Raymond, A., Ver MOO.
Moore, G.E., Ver MR.
Moore, G.F., Ver MOR.
Morgan, G., Campbell, Ver MORN.
Mornschuh, M., Ver MH.
Moule, C.F.D., Ver MOU.
Moulton e Milligan, Ver MST.
Mourant, John A., Ver MOUR.
Muller, R., Ver SB.
Murray, Gilbert, MUR.
Murray, H.J.C., Ver MU.
Myers, F.W.H., Ver MY.
Nairne, A., Ver NAI.
Napier, B.P., Ver NAP.
Nash, Arnold S., Ver NAS.
Navarra, Fernand, Ver NA.
Nelson, Leonard, Ver N.
Neve, Juergen L., Ver NE(2).
Newberry, Thomas, Ver NB.
Newell, William R., Ver NE(1).
Nichols, James, Ver AJ.
Nicoll, W. Robertson, Ver EGT e EX.
Nida, Eugene, Ver NI.
Niebuhr, H. Richard, Ver NIE.
Nilson, P., Ver NIL.
Nock, A.D., NOK.
Noth, M., NO.
Oates, W.J., Ver OA.
O'Callaghan, R.T., Ver OC.
Odeberg, Hugo, Ver OD.
Oehler, G.F., OE(2).
Oestborn, Ver OES.
Oesterley, W.O.E., Ver OE(1).
Ogden, Schubert M., Ver OG(1).
Ogg, G., OG(2).
Olmstead, A.T., Ver OLM e OLMS.
Oppenheim, A.L., Ver OP.
Orni, E., Ver OR.
Orr, J., Ver ORE.
Orr, James, Ver ORR.
Osis, K., Ver OSI.
Ostrander, Sheila, Ver SL.
Padovani, Humberto, Ver PAD.
Pallis, E.H., Ver PAL.
Parrot, A., Ver PAR.
Pastor, Ludwig von, Baron, Ver PAS.
Paterson, J., Ver PAT.
Pauck, Wilhelm, Ver PAU.

BIBLIOGRAFIA

Payne, Barton, Ver PAY(2).
Payne, J.B., Ver PAY(1).
Pederson, J., Ver JP e PED.
Peak, A.S., Ver PEA.
Peeters, Evangeles, Ver PE.
Pelikan, J., Ver PEL.
Perowne, S., Ver PER.
Petavel, E., Ver PETA.
Peters, P.W., Ver PT.
Petrie, F., Ver PET.
Petrie, W.F., Ver PETR.
Pfeiffer, C.F., Ver PFE.
Pfeiffer, Robert H., Ver PF.
Pike, Royston, Ver ERR.
Piper, O., Ver O.
Philipson, D., Ver PHIL.
Philo, Ver PHI.
Plummer, Alfred, Ver I.
Poebl, Arno, Ver POE.
Pommerenke, C.H., Ver PO.
Porter, Frank E., Ver POR.
Prat, F., Ver PR.
Pritchard, J.B., Ver ANEP, ANET e PRI.
Pusey, E.F., Ver PU.
Quaston, J., Ver JQ.
Quell, Gottfried, Ver QS.
Rader, Melvin, Ver ES.
Rahner, Karl, Ver R.
Ramsay, M., Ver RAM.
Ramm, B., Ver RAMM.
Randall, John Herman, Ver RAND.
Randall, John L., Ver RAN.
Read, H.H., Ver REA.
Reed, W.L., Ver RE.
Reese, W.L., Ver P.
Regush, Nicholas M., Ver REG.
Reider, J., Ver REI.
Reifenberg, A., Ver REIF.
Reis, J.K.S., Ver REIS.
Rentz, G., Ver REN.
Reu, M., Ver REU.
Rhine, J.B., Ver RH.
Richardson, Alan, Ver AR, C, RI e W.
Richardson, Cyril Charles, Ver CY.
Richardson, E.C., Ver RIC.
Ridderbos, H., Ver RID.
Ring, Kenneth, Ver RIN.
Roberts, B.J., Ver BJR.
Roberts, Donalson, Ver ANF.
Robertson, A.T., Ver RO.
Robertson, H.W., Ver ROB.
Robinson, C.A., Ver BOT.
Robinson, J., Ver ROBINS.
Robinson, S., Ver ROBIN.
Robinson, T., Ver ROB(2).
Rose, Herbert, J., Ver ROS.
Ross, Sr. David, Ver DR(2).
Roth, C., Ver ROT.
Rouse, Ruth, Ver ROU.
Rouse, W.H.D., Ver DP.
Routley, Eric, Ver ROUT.
Rowe, L.A., Ver ROWE.
Rowley, H.H., Ver ROW.
Runes, Dagobert, D., Ver RUN.
Russell, Bertrand, Ver RUS.
Russell, D.S., Ver RU.
Rynne, Xavier, Ver RY.
Ryrie, C., Ver RYR.
Sabom, Michael, SA.
Sachs, K., Ver SAC.
Saggs, H.W.F., Ver SAG.
Sahakian, William, Ver RP.
Salmond, S.D.F., Ver SAL.

Samuel, H.E., Ver SAM
Sansoni, G.C., Ver GC.
Sauer, E., Ver SAU.
Saylork, Carlyle, Ver SP.
Schaff, Philip, Ver SCH.
Schoepes, Hans, Ver HS.
Schonfield, Hugh, Ver SCHO.
Schonmetzer, A., Ver DS.
Schulweis, Harold M., Ver BRON.
Schurer, E., Ver SH.
Schweitzer, Albert, Ver SCHW.
Scofield, C.I., Ver SCO.
Scurti, S.J., Ver SC.
Segal, J.B., Ver SEG.
Seiss, Joseph, Ver SE.
Seters, J., Ver SET.
Seyffert, Oskar, Ver OS.
Shaffer, Jerome A., Ver FE.
Sherman, Harold, Ver SHE.
Short, Rendel, Ver SHO.
Shrenk, G., Ver QS.
Shroeder, Lynn, Ver SL.
Shultz, S.J., Ver SHU(1).
Shut, R.J.H., Ver SHU(2).
Simons, J., Ver SI.
Simpson, E.K., Ver SIM.
Singer, C., Ver SIN.
Singer, Charles, Ver SHS.
Skeat, T.C., Ver SKE.
Smid, T., Ver SMID.
Smith, G., Ver GSM.
Smith, Huston, Ver HUS.
Smith, J.A., Ver DR(2) e SMI.
Smith, J.B., Ver SM.
Smith, T.V., Ver PS e TVS.
Smith, W.R., Ver SMIT.
Snaith, H.H., Ver SN.
Souter, A., Ver SO.
Speiser, G.A., Ver CS.
Spitzer, Walter, Ver SP.
Spanos, William V., Ver EXT.
Stainer, J., Ver STAI.
Stanley, Arthur Penrhyn, Ver STA.
Stanley, David M., Ver STAN.
Stendall, K., Ver STE.
Stibbs, A.M., Ver STI.
Stokes, W.L., Ver STO.
Stonehouse, N.B., Ver STONE.
Stonehouse, Paul, Ver STON.
Storr, C., Ver STOR.
Strack, H.L., Ver STRAC.
Strawson, W., Ver STRA.
Streeter, B.H., Ver STRE.
Striwe, Otto, Ver STR.
Strong, Augustus, Ver ST.
Strong, James, Ver STRO.
Suetonius, Ver SU.
Swete, H.B., Ver SW.
Tarn, William W., Ver TAR.
Taylor, C., Ver TAY.
Taylor, Richard, Ver MET.
Taylor, V., Ver TA.
Tcherikover, V., Ver TC.
Techenie, Ver TEC.
Tenny, M.C., Ver TE e Z.
Thackeray, H., Ver THA.
Thiel, A., Ver THI.
Thomas, C., Ver THU.
Thomas, D.R., Ver AOTS e AP.
Thomas, D.W., Ver THO.
Thompson, R.C., Ver THOM.
Thorndike, Lynn, Ver TL.
Tillich, Paul, Ver TIL.
Tischendorf, Constantinus, Ver TIS.

Titus, Eric Lane, Ver TI.
Tonybee, J., Ver TON.
Torbet, R.G., Ver TO.
Torrey, C.C., Ver TOR.
Torrey, R.A., Ver TOR(2).
Trawick, Buckner B., Ver TRA.
Tristan, H.B., Ver TR.
Turnball, Ralph G., Ver T.
Uhlhorn, G., Ver U.
Ullendorff, E., Ver UL.
Unger, Ver UN, UN(1952), UN(1957) e UNA.
Urmsoh, J.O., Ver EW.
Van Unnick, W.C., Ver UNN.
Vasilieve, Ver VAS.
Vaux, R., Ver VA.
Velikovsky, R.B.Y., Ver VE.
Vincent, A., Ver VI.
Vincent, Marvin R., Ver VIN.
Von Rad, Gerhard, Ver RA.
Vos, E., Ver VO.
Vriezen, S., Ver V.
Vriezen, Th.C., Ver VR.

Walker, G.P., Ver WALK.
Walker, W., Ver WAL.
Walker, Willinston, Ver WW(2).
Wallace, R.S., Ver WA(2) e WALL.
Warner, Rex, Ver AUG.
Watson, Thomas, Ver WAT.
Waxman, Meyer, WAX.
Weatherhead, L.D., Ver WEA.
Weber, M., Ver MW.
Webre, A.L., Ver WEB.
Weigall, A., Ver WEI(2).
Weiser, A., Ver WEI.
Westermach, E., Ver WEST.
Westerman, C., Ver WC.
Whale, J.S., Ver WH.
Whesluright, Philip, Ver WHE.
Whiston, W., Ver WHIS.
Whitcomb, J.C., Ver WHIT.
White, H.G.I., Ver WHI.
White, John, Ver WHI(2).
Whitehead, A.N., Ver WT.
Wiegard T., Ver WIE.
Wilkenhauser, A., Ver WIK.
Wilson, Colin, Ver CW.
Wilson, J.A., Ver WILS.
Wilson, R., Ver WI.
Wilson, R. Mcl., Ver RW.
Wirgman, A.T., Ver WIR.
Wiseman, J., Ver WIS.
Wood, J.A., Ver WOD.
Woolcombe, K., Ver LA.
Wooley, C.L., Ver WOO.
Wordsworth, Charles, Ver WORD.
Worrell, W., Ver WOR.
Woudstra, M.H., Ver WOU.
Wright, F., Ver WRIG.
Wright, G., Ver WRI.
Wright, George E., Ver WG.
Wycherley, Richard C., Ver WY.

Xavier-Leon-Dufour, Ver VT.
Yadin, Y., Ver YAD.
Yahudu, A.D., Ver YA.
Yates, Kyle, Ver YAT.
Yeivin, S., Ver YE.
Young, E.J., Ver IOT, Y e YO.

Zaehner, R.C., Ver ZAE.
Zeitlin, S., Ver ZE.
Zeller, Eduard, Ver ZEL.
Zeuner, F.E., Ver ZEU.
Zyl, A.H., Van, Ver ZY.

1. Formas Antigas

fenício (semítico), 1000 A.C.   grego ocidental, 800 A.C.   latino, 50 D.C.

2. Nos Manuscritos Gregos do Novo Testamento

a λ α

3. Formas Modernas

A A a a   AA a a   *A a*   **AA a a**

4. História

A é a primeira letra do alfabeto português. Originalmente, essa letra era consoante, nos alfabetos semíticos. No hebraico o seu nome era '*aleph*, «boi». V representava o boi, com os chifres apontando para cima. Mas, finalmente, a letra passou a ser desenhada com as pontas para baixo, o que explica a aparência do «A» moderno. Os eruditos pensam que essa letra foi tomada por empréstimo dos hieróglifos egípcios, do símbolo que representava o boi. O idioma grego não tinha uso para um *A* consonantal, tendo transformado essa letra em uma vogal. Como é óbvio, não havia similaridade de som entre o '*aleph* semítico e o *alpha* grego, o nome que os gregos deram a essa letra. Do alfabeto grego, o emblema passou para o latim, e daí para o português.

5. Usos e Símbolos

A é o nome da sexta nota musical, também chamada *lá*, na escala de Dó. Representa também o primeiro de uma série; algo de primeira qualidade. Pode indicar o começo de qualquer coisa. Nos sistemas de gradação, representa *excelente*. Cristo é o alfa e o ômega, o começo e o fim, o originador e o alvo final. Ver o artigo *Alfa e Ômega*. No português, apenas duas palavras consistem em um simples «a», a saber: o artigo definido feminino, *a*; e a preposição simples, *a* (também temos a preposição craseada, *à*, cuja forma masculina é ao). *A* é usado como símbolo do *Codex Alexandrinus*, que é descrito em um artigo separado sob *A*.

Caligrafia de Darrell Steven Champlin

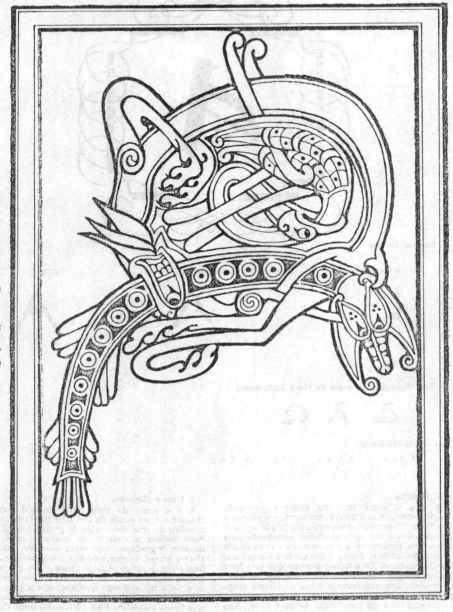

Letra A decorativa, Evangelho de Lucas, Livro de Kells

A

A

A primeira letra de quase todos os alfabetos. No hebraico chama-se *Alef* que significa *boi*. Essa letra é usada para designar o antiqüíssimo manuscrito *Codex Sinaiticus*. Ver o artigo sobre os *Manuscritos* da Bíblia. No antigo alfabeto fenício, essa letra era desenhada mais ou menos como a cabeça de um boi, daí o seu nome. (Plutarco, *Quest. Sympos.* ix:2; Genessi *Thesaur.* Heb. p. 1).

No alfabeto grego, a letra é chamada *Alfa*. Tem sido usada simbolicamente para indicar o Senhor, como o *Primeiro*, em combinação com *Ômega*, a última letra do alfabeto grego, para aludir à sua eternidade e divindade, Apoc. 1:11, 21:6, 22:13. Is. 44:6 usa-a para indicar a eternidade de Deus. Ver o artigo sobre o *Alfa e o Ômega*.

A letra *A* é usada para designar o antigo manuscrito *Codex Alexandrinus*. (A AL I ME)

AALAR

Em I Esdras 5:36, um lugar de onde vieram alguns judeus que se diziam sacerdotes, embora não pudessem provar sua linhagem, em razão do que também não podiam oficiar. Alguns têm identificado esse lugar com a Imer de Esd. 2:59 e Nee. 7:61.

AARÁ

No hebraico, *após o irmão*. Um filho de Benjamim (ver I Crô. 8:1). Em outros trechos bíblicos é chamado Eï (Gên. 46:21), Airã (Núm. 26:38) e Aer (I Crô. 7:12). (UN Z)

AARÃO

1. *Significado do nome*. Não há certeza quanto ao que esse nome quer dizer. Pelo menos desde os dias de Jerônimo, pensava-se que vem de um vocábulo hebraico que significa *monte de força*. Outros, porém, têm conjecturado *montanhista* ou *iluminador*. Visto que a própria Bíblia não nos dá explicação sobre o sentido desse nome, nenhum sentido especial tem sido vinculado ao mesmo. Somente Aarão, irmão de Moisés, tem esse nome na Bíblia inteira.

2. *Família*. Aarão foi o filho mais velho do levita Anrão e de Joquebede (Êxo. 6:20; Núm. 26:59). Era irmão de Moisés e Miriã, sendo três anos mais velho do que o legislador (Êxo. 7:7). Conjecturas situam seu nascimento em torno do ano 1725 A.C., que foi o ano anterior ao decreto de Faraó acerca da eliminação dos meninos hebreus. Os trechos de Êxo. 6:16-20 e I Crôn. 6:1-3 indicam que Aarão estava na terceira geração depois de Levi, pelo que teríamos Levi, Coate, Anrão, Aarão, embora as genealogias com freqüência fossem apenas representativas, e não completas. Seja como for, Aarão era levita por parte de seu pai e de sua mãe (Núm. 26:29). A esposa de Aarão foi Eliseba, irmã de Naassom, aparentemente o príncipe de Judá, que foi ancestral de Davi (Êxo. 6:23; Rute 4:20; I Crô. 2:10; Mat. 1:4). Aarão e Eliseba tiveram quatro filhos: Nadabe, Abiú, Eleazar e Itamar. Os dois mais velhos foram mortos pelo fogo caído do céu, por motivo de um ato de sacrilégio (Lev. 10:1 ss.). A classe dos sumos sacerdotes deriva-se dos outros dois filhos, em Israel (I Crô. 24:1 ss).

3. *Nomeação divina*. Moisés foi nomeado por Deus para tirar o povo de Israel do Egito. Deus também nomeou Aarão para ser assistente e porta-voz de Moisés, por ser mais eloqüente do que este (Êxo. 4:14-16; 7:1). O hebraico aqui é pitoresco. De Moisés é dito que ele era «pesado de boca e pesado de língua».

E sobre Aarão declara-se: «Certamente ele pode falar».

Moisés foi instruído a deixar Midiã (onde estivera durante quarenta anos, aproximadamente de 1688 a 1648 A.C., preparando-se no deserto para a sua missão), a fim de retornar ao Egito. Encontrou-se com Aarão no monte Horebe, que para ali fora mandado por divina orientação (Êxo. 4:29-31). No dia seguinte, apresentaram-se a Faraó, e o grande drama teve início.

4. *Resistência de Faraó*. Faraó não deu crédito à mensagem, nem se deixou assustar por Moisés e Aarão, como embaixadores divinos. A princípio, expulsu-os de sua presença com opróbrio; intensificou os labores dos israelitas, para não serem infectados pelo desejo de liberdade. Então os dois irmãos enfrentaram a oposição do próprio povo de Israel, porquanto aumentara muito o peso das cargas e da opressão contra eles. Porém, os dois irmãos mantiveram-se firmes, reiterando o propósito divino, encorajando o povo a suportar a servidão e a buscar a liberdade (Êxo. 5).

Novos encontros com Faraó tiveram lugar, envolvendo espantosos milagres. Em todas essas entrevistas, Aarão usou sua eloqüência em favor dos escravizados hebreus (Êxo. 6-9). Mas Faraó, pensando no trabalho escravo sobre o qual se alicerçava a economia egípcia, não tinha intenção de dar atenção à mensagem dos «fanáticos» irmãos.

Ouvimos em seguida sobre Aarão quando o êxodo já era um sucesso. A narrativa de Êxo. 17:8 ss descreve o ataque dos amalequitas contra Israel. Ele e Hur seguraram as mãos de Moisés, a fim de que Israel prevalecesse em batalha.

Aarão, seus filhos sobreviventes e os setenta anciãos tiveram permissão de ver a glória do Senhor de longe, enquanto só Moisés pôde contemplá-la de perto (Êxo. 24:1,9,10). Isso, naturalmente, juntamente com o incidente do bezerro de ouro, demonstra a inferioridade da espiritualidade e da missão de Aarão, em contraste com Moisés.

5. *O sacerdócio*. Moisés recebeu as tábuas da lei no monte Sinai. Foi nessa ocasião que Aarão e os anciãos de Israel viram de longe a glória do Senhor (Êxo. 24:1-11). Foi então que o sacerdócio foi estabelecido. Aarão e seus filhos receberam esse ofício, e, subseqüentemente, a tribo inteira à qual pertencia Aarão, a tribo de Levi, tornou-se uma casta sacerdotal e erudita (Lev. 8). O trecho de Sal. 133:2 traz o nome de Aarão como o primeiro sacerdote a ser designado.

6. *A impaciência produziu um lapso*. Moisés demorou-se por quarenta dias no monte. O povo se impacientou e exigiu que Aarão fabricasse deuses para eles adorarem, porque haviam desistido de Moisés (Êxo. 33:1 ss). Foram dissolvidos todos os tipos de objetos de ouro. Usando o material, Aarão fabricou um infame bezerro de ouro. O bezerro provavelmente representava o deus-boi, Ápis, de Mênfis, cuja adoração era comum no Egito inteiro. Tão pusilânime quanto o povo, Aarão proclamou o absurdo que aquele era o deus que tirara Israel do Egito. O incidente inteiro exibe a natureza primitiva da fé hebréia nesse estágio da história. Moisés foi informado acerca do lapso do povo (Êxo. 32:7). Imediatamente Moisés desceu o monte, trazendo consigo as tábuas da lei. Ao aproximar-se do acampamento, ele jogou as tábuas no solo, quebrando-as. Moisés exigiu arrependimento, e foi atendido.

7. *Arrependimento e consagração*. A princípio,

AARÃO — AARÃO, A VARA DE

Aarão buscou justificar-se de seu lapso, mas então reconheceu a necessidade de arrependimento. Como sempre, Deus usou homens imperfeitos, pecaminosos, mas perdoados, a fim de ajudarem na realização de Sua obra. O tabernáculo foi erigido e as instituições foram estabelecidas. Aarão e seus filhos foram consagrados com óleo santo, e foram investidos com as vestes sagradas (Êxo. 40; Lev. 8). Porém, nem bem as cerimônias foram instituídas quando os dois filhos mais velhos de Aarão ousaram queimar incenso no tabernáculo com fogo estranho (Lev. 10:1-11). Por causa do sacrilégio, foram mortos pelo fogo divino. Assim Aarão perdeu seus dois filhos mais velhos. Mas sofreu a perda com magnanimidade.

8. *Longa fidelidade*. Aarão aplicou-se aos seus deveres por quase quarenta anos. Sim, teve problemas de ciúmes com Moisés, seu superior. Ele e sua irmã, Miriã, apoiando-se no fato de que Moisés casara-se em segundas núpcias com uma mulher cuxita, puseram em dúvida a autoridade do legislador. O provável problema de Miriã é que ela temia a perda de seu lugar de honra, agora que outra mulher fora trazida para o acampamento, que provavelmente estaria mais próxima de Moisés do que ela. Miriã foi castigada com lepra temporária, o que devolveu o bom senso a Aarão. Ele buscou e obteve o perdão para ambos (Núm. 12).

9. *Moisés e Aarão sob ataque*. O trecho de Núm. 16 mostra como Moisés e Aarão foram os alvos da rebelião encabeçada por Coré, Datã e Abirão. A praga enviada por Deus demonstrou o desprazer divino ante o incidente. A revolta envolvia a autoridade sacerdotal exercida por Aarão e seus filhos, e também a autoridade civil investida em Moisés. Coré, da tribo de Levi, e Datã e Abirão, da tribo de Rúben, queriam modificações radicais que resultariam na exaltação deles, quando poderiam exercer autoridade. A resultante luta pelo poder terminou mediante a praga, que Aarão (por ordens de Moisés) fez cessar, quando encheu um incensário com fogo tirado do altar, correu e «pôs-se em pé entre os mortos e os vivos» (Núm. 16:48). O incidente inteiro demonstrou ao povo que a autoridade constituída permaneceria. Foi dado um sinal adicional. Entre as varas dos diferentes filhos de Israel, somente a de Aarão floresceu (Núm. 17:8). Essa vara foi guardada na arca como testemunho contra qualquer rebelião futura. (Núm. 17:10).

10. *Fracasso*. Aarão não recebeu permissão para entrar na Terra Prometida em face de sua incredulidade (compartilhada por Moisés), manifestada quando a rocha foi ferida, em Meribá (Núm. 20:8-13).

11. *Morte*. Pouco depois desse fracasso, Aarão morreu, com 123 anos (Núm. 33:32). Por ordem de Deus, Aarão, seu filho Eleazar e Moisés subiram ao topo do monte Hor, à vista de todo o povo. Ali as vestes pontificiais foram transferidas para Eleazar, e, pouco depois, Aarão morreu (Núm. 20:23-29). Seu filho e seu irmão sepultaram-no em uma caverna da montanha. (Ver as notas sobre *Hor, Monte*). Houve lamentação por trinta dias por Aarão. Até hoje, no monte Abe, os judeus organizam uma cerimônia, comemorando a morte de Aarão. Os árabes apontam para o local tradicional de seu sepulcro, que seria em Petra. Naturalmente, a localização exata é desconhecida.

12. *Descendentes*. O trecho de Jos. 21:4,10,13 chama-os de «os filhos de Aarão». Eles formavam o sacerdócio em geral. Seus descendentes diretos foram os sumos sacerdotes, ofício limitado ao primogênito na sucessão. Nos dias de Davi, seus descendentes

formavam um grupo muito numeroso (I Crô. 12:27).

13. *Caráter e lições espirituais de Aarão*. Ele foi um homem eloqüente, espiritualmente forte a longo prazo, mas com alguns lapsos sérios. Sua devoção era séria, embora ocasionalmente fosse vitimado por alguma súbita tentação.

14. *Símbolo*. Seu sumo sacerdócio foi designado para ser «sombra das realidades celestes», para conduzir a comunidade religiosa para coisas «melhores», quando um outro Sacerdote, da ordem de Melquisedeque, houvesse de aparecer, suplantando todos os sacerdócios anteriores. Esse Sacerdote foi Jesus Cristo (Heb. 6:20 e 7).

Como tipo de Cristo. 1. Como sumo sacerdote, oferecendo holocaustos, Heb. 8:1 ss. 2. Como o sacerdote que oferecia expiação ao entrar no Santo dos Santos, Heb. cap. 9; Jo. 17:3. 3. Ao ser ungido, passou a atuar como intercessor. Sua unção prefigurou o poder do Espírito Santo na vida de Cristo, e subseqüentemente, na vida de Seus irmãos, Rom. 8:14. 4. Ele transportava todos os nomes das tribos de Israel em seu peito e em seus ombros, assim representando a todos eles. Cristo é o Salvador universal (Efé. 1:10,23; João 3:16; 12:32). 5. Ele foi o mediador das mensagens divinas, utilizando-se dos místicos Urim e Tumim. Cristo é o nosso Mediador (Heb. 8:6 ss ; 9:15; I Tim. 2:5). (FA S Z)

AARÃO, A VARA DE

A vara de Aarão floresceu para vindicar a autoridade que recebera de Deus para ser o sumo sacerdote (Núm. 17:8). Um dos eventos mais importantes dos quarenta anos de peregrinação de Israel pelo deserto (Núm. 15:19), foi quando Coré e seus companheiros desafiaram a autoridade civil de Moisés e a posição sumo sacerdotal de Aarão (Núm. 16 e 17). Moisés requereu que as varas dos príncipes das tribos fossem postas «perante o Senhor na tenda do testemunho» (Núm. 17:7). No dia seguinte, a vara de Aarão havia florescido, mas as demais varas continuavam comuns. Esse era todo o testemunho necessário quanto à autoridade de Aarão. Então a vara foi posta diante da arca, no Santo dos Santos, para servir de contínua afirmação da instituição ordenada por Deus, em contradistinção às pretensões espirituais espúrias. Nos dias de Salomão, esse costume continuava sendo observado. Somente as tábuas da lei estavam dentro da arca (I Reis 8:9). É possível que posteriormente a própria vara tenha sido posta dentro da arca, conforme Heb. 9:4 talvez indique.

É provável que a vara em discussão fosse uma vara de pastor, que Moisés tivera, por ocasião de sua comissão (Êxo. 4:2), que se transformou em serpente. Isso serviu de sinal da autoridade de Moisés ao próprio Moisés, a Aarão, ao povo de Israel e a Faraó.

Referências e Idéias:

a. A vara era *de Deus* (Êxo. 4:20; 17:9). b. A vara era de Moisés (Êxo. 4:17). c. A vara era de Aarão (Êxo. 7:14-20). d. A vara era usada, sendo estendida (Êxo. 8:5; 9:22,23). e. Tornou-se vara de provocação quando Moisés, que meramente deveria «falar à rocha» (Núm. 20:8), a fim de obter água, feriu a rocha por duas vezes (Núm. 20:11). Esse ato de presunção, que envolveu Moisés e Aarão, foi severamente punido, sendo essa uma das razões por que nenhum deles teve a permissão de entrar na Terra Prometida (Núm. 20:12). f. Com o nome de «vara de Deus», representava a autoridade divina investida em homens. Todo verdadeiro homem de Deus possui sua própria vara especial de ação. Algo é investido nele que pode transmitir o poder do Senhor aos homens,

AAREL — ABÃ

para benefício deles. (FA S UN Z)

AAREL

No hebraico significa *irmão de Raquel*. A LXX diz «irmão de Recabe». Era filho de Harum, da tribo de Judá (ver I Crô. 4:8). (S)

AARONITAS

Eram os levitas da família de Aarão; os sacerdotes que serviam no santuário(Núm. 4:5 ss). Em Israel, o sacerdócio estava limitado aos filhos de Aarão (Êxo. 28:1; Lev. 1:3). Os dois filhos mais velhos de Aarão foram eliminados por pecado de sacrilégio (Lev. 10), pelo que todos os sacerdotes legítimos descendiam dos dois irmãos mais novos, Eleazar e Itamar. Nos dias de Davi, a tribo era muito numerosa, e ele a dividiu em vinte e quatro turnos (I Crô. 24:1-6), dezesseis da linhagem de Eleazar e oito da linhagem de Itamar. Após o exílio babilônico, cerca de quatro mil sacerdotes retornaram em companhia de Zorobabel, cerca de um décimo do total original. As reivindicações de outros ao sacerdócio foram repelidas (Esd. 2:62 ss), demonstrando que deviam conservar cuidadosos registros genealógicos, para garantir a pureza. Um sacerdote não podia ter qualquer defeito físico, pelo que nem todos os descendentes de Aarão estavam qualificados para ocupar o ofício sacerdotal. (ND S Z)

AASBAI

No hebraico, *florescência*, embora outros interpretem como *refugiei-me em Yahweh*. Era um maacatita, pai de Elifelete, um dos homens poderosos de Davi (ver II Sam. 23 e 24). Em I Crô. 11:35,36, em vez de Aasbai, lemos «Ur, Héfer». Parece ter havido uma corrupção textual em um desses dois lugares. (S)

AAVA

No hebraico, *água*, nome de um rio ou canal onde os exilados judeus reuniram sua segunda caravana, sob a liderança de Esdras, quando voltavam a Jerusalém. (Ver Esd. 8:21,31). Com base em Esd. 8:15, parece que recebeu o nome devido a uma cidade com o mesmo apelativo: «Ajuntei-os perto do rio que corre para Aava...» Porém, nenhuma cidade desse nome tem sido encontrada pelos arqueólogos. Os eruditos têm conjeturado que o rio Aava, ou Pelegue-Ava, é o Palacopas, um ribeiro que corre para o sul da Babilônia. Outros identificam-no com o rio Is de Herd. i:179, um rio que atravessava ao meio de uma aldeia do mesmo nome, atualmente chamada Hit. Porém, nada se sabe sobre essas questões com qualquer grau de certeza. (S Z)

AB

Vem de uma forma hebraica *Tisha b'Ab*. Um dia festivo dos judeus em comemoração à queda de Jerusalém e à destruição do templo pelos romanos em 70 D.C. Além do jejum, havia a abstenção de todas as atividades recreacionais e as observâncias religiosas nas sinagogas assumiam um aspecto austero, com a remoção de todos os ornamentos. Eram lidas as Lamentações. Ver o artigo sobre as *Festas* dos judeus. (E)

AB

Significa «pai». Usado em nomes hebraicos compostos, como Abner, «pai da luz», Abiézer, «pai da ajuda». Algumas vezes era usado em nomes femininos, como Abigail, «pai da alegria» (I Sam. 25:14). Nesse caso, a idéia de «pai» tem o sentido de autor, causa ou fonte originária. (E Z)

ABA

Essa palavra aparece por três vezes no N.T.: 1. Marcos 14:36, na oração de Jesus no Getsêmani; 2. Romanos 8:15, o nome de Deus no coração do crente; e 3. similarmente, em Gálatas 4:6. Sempre aparece na tradução grega, *ho pater*, «o pai». O termo em questão vem do aramaico, *abba*, e alguns eruditos pensam que tem a força de «meu pai». Parece que o vocábulo começou a ser usado em fórmulas litúrgicas desde bem cedo. A doutrina de que Deus é «pai» figura entre os mais elevados conceitos da fé religiosa. Dá a entender a eventual participação na natureza divina, por parte dos filhos de Deus, conforme se lê em II Ped. 1:4, e isso mediante a ligação com o Filho e a transformação em Sua imagem. Quanto a notas detalhadas sobre esses conceitos, ver «Aba, Pai», em Rom. 8:15, no NTI. Ver as notas sobre a salvação como filiação, em Rom. 8:29; 2 Cor. 3:18, no NTI (B NTI).

Forma Enfática e Definitiva

Forma aramaica da palavra hebraica que significa «papai». Tal palavra não ocorre no Antigo Testamento. Encontra-se no Novo Testamento no texto de três orações: Mar. 14:36; Rom. 8:15 e Gál. 4:6, sempre acompanhada por seu equivalente grego, *«pater»*. Os dialetos aramaicos não têm o artigo definido na forma que se encontra no hebraico. Compensam isso adicionando uma sílaba ao fim do substantivo comum, asssim produzindo uma forma distintiva, chamada pelos gramáticos de *enfática* ou *definitiva*. Essa forma também podia ser usada como um vocativo, o que se dá com todas as ocorrências de «aba» no Novo Testamento. Em algumas das igrejas orientais (siríaca, cóptica e etíope), «aba» tornou-se o título dos bispos. O vocábulo era usado na antiguidade pelos filhos para se dirigirem a seus pais naturais, mas o título não podia ser usado por escravos ou servos da casa, quando se dirigiam àqueles homens. Ver Isa. 8:4: «Porque antes que o menino saiba dizer meu pai ou minha mãe...» No original, «pai» e «mãe» são traduções de *Abi* e *Immi*.

Usos neotestamentários: 1. Em Marcos, Jesus usou a palavra para dirigir-se ao Pai, em Sua agonia no Getsêmani. Embora a palavra não apareça em outros trechos dos evangelhos, é possível que ela esteja por detrás de «pater», em Mat. 11:26; 26:39,42. 2. O uso que Paulo faz da palavra, nas duas outras referências, provavelmente reflete um uso litúrgico da Igreja primitiva. No sentido supremo, Deus é o «aba». Esse termo veio a expressar a consciência dos homens sobre esse relacionamento especial. Filiação é óbvio, é um sinônimo virtual de «salvação», pois nosso destino é sermos transformados segundo a imagem do *Filho* (Rom. 8:29), tornando-nos assim filhos que estão sendo conduzidos «à glória» (Heb. 2:10). O silêncio quase total do Antigo Testamento acerca de Deus como *pai* tem feito os intérpretes perceberem um avanço na teologia do Novo Testamento, sobre esse particular, dentro do significado da salvação. (FA IB MTI S)

ABÃ

No hebraico quer dizer *irmão de um inteligente*.

ABADESSA — ABATER

Era filho de Abisur, da tribo de Judá (I Crô. 2:29). Foi o primeiro dos dois filhos de Abisur e Abiail a ser chamado por nome. O outro era Molide. Viveu em cerca de 1471 A.C. Nada mais se sabe acerca dele. (S)

ABADESSA

Superiora de um convento de doze freiras ou mais. Embora não goze da jurisdição própria dos abades, ela usa o crucifixo como símbolo de sua posição e um anel. O título aparece entre as beneditinas, as clarissas, e outras.

ABADIA

Um mosteiro independente e canonicamente erigido, que abriga pelo menos doze membros. O complexo de edifícios inclui um templo, um claustro, uma hospedaria, uma enfermaria, um refeitório, etc. Quando ocupada por monges, é dirigida por um abade, termo que vem do aramaico *abba*, pai. Aparentemente o primeiro a usar o termo nesse contexto foi Benedito, que aplicou o nome ao superior de um mosteiro. O ofício é eletivo, através de voto secreto dos membros da abadia. A autoridade da abadia geralmente se estende aos seus próprios membros, mas exerce influência sobre o clero e os leigos que vivem no território em redor da abadia. Após sua eleição, o abade recebe do bispo a bênção, a mitra, o crucifixo, o anel, a cruz peitoral e outros emblemas de ofício. (E)

ABADON

Nome dado a um anjo satânico em Apo. 9:11. Ele aparece como o rei de uma horda de gafanhotos-monstros sobrenaturais, enviados como uma praga contra a humanidade. O grego traduz o termo hebraico como *o destruidor*. A palavra hebraica aparece no A.T. indicando o sheol ou hades, e literalmente significa «destruição». Ver Sal. 88:12; Pro. 15:11; 27:20; Jó 26:6; 31:12. Ver nota no *Novo Testamento Interpretado*, de Russell N. Champlin, em Apo. 9:11, quanto a maiores detalhes. As interpretações variam desde a tentativa de identificar algum anjo específico até postular alguma significação simbólica. Alguns dizem simplesmente que Satanás está em pauta, mas a maioria dos intérpretes vê aqui um elevado poder diabólico que agirá sob o controle de Satanás. Mas outros vêem nessa passagem o anticristo ou algum outro vulto da história, como algum notável herege cristão, ou alguma poderosa força anticristã. (B NTI)

ABAGTA

Um dos sete eunucos da corte persa de Assuero (Est. 1:10), acerca de quem nada se sabe além do que está implícito nesse versículo. (UN)

ABANA

Nome de um dos rios aludidos por Naamã (II Reis 5:12), no qual poderia ter sido imerso em seu próprio país, e não em Israel, a fim de ficar curado de sua lepra. Uma variante no texto hebraico diz *Amana*. Esse é o nome da serra de onde desce o rio, e pode ter sido o nome original do rio, ou pode ser uma variante do nome, visto que o «b» e o «m» com freqüência são intercambiáveis nos idiomas orientais. A Septuaginta diz «Abana».

Há várias conjeturas sobre a identidade do atual rio que na antiguidade era chamado *Abana*. A mais

comum é o *Barada*. Nasce nos montes de Antilíbano, e cruza a moderna cidade de Damasco. Oitenta quilômetros abaixo de Damasco, o rio desemboca em um lago raso. Podemos justificar Naamã por sua preferência, devido ao fato de que o Barado é constante e abundante em seu fluxo (a palavra Amana significa «perene»), ajudando a tornar as cercanias de Damasco uma das mais belas do mundo. Em comparação, os rios de Israel são pequenos, —e muitas vezes secam. Os gregos chamavam aquele rio de «correnteza dourada», porquanto transformava em verdadeiro oásis uma Damasco que de outro modo seria árida. (F A UM Z)

ABANDONO

1. Uma das idéias mais básicas do existencialismo ateu (segundo expresso por Sartre) é que, visto que Deus não existe, não pode haver objetividade alguma na vida, e nem valores finais que envolvam o homem ou a humanidade. Visto inexistirem tais valores, o homem se acha «abandonado». Portanto, ele deve tomar suas próprias decisões, aprendendo a distinguir entre o certo e o errado de um ponto de vista prático e experimental. O homem não dispõe de qualquer mão orientadora da qual possa depender, e deve assumir pessoalmente toda a responsabilidade. Ver *Existencialismo*. Contrastar com o conteúdo dos artigos sobre a *Redenção*, a *Imortalidade* e *Deus*.

2. No campo da ética, o termo tem sido usado para aludir à prática do infanticídio, mediante abandono e exposição às intempéries, ou à negligência quanto aos aleijados e à expulsão dos idosos e enfermos da vida comunitária.

3. O termo também pode referir-se ao próprio senso de abandono, derivado da ausência de fé, do temor da morte e do senso de impotência, em um Universo que aparentemente está fora de controle e é fútil. Esse conceito é o que mais se aproxima da primeira significação.

4. Positivamente, a palavra pode referir-se à abnegação ou *sacrifício* pelo próximo. O supremo exemplo é a dedicação de Cristo à Sua missão, sob a vontade do Pai. Ver as notas no NTI em Fil. 2:5-8, que expandem em muito esse tema. (H NTI)

ABARIM

Forma plural do termo hebraico que significa «do outro lado» ou «além». Refere-se à cadeia montanhosa a suleste do mar Morto. Pisga, o pico mais alto do monte Nebo, faz parte dessa cadeia (Deu. 3:27; 32:49). Houve tempo em que Israel acampou no local (Núm. 33:47,48). A cadeia do Abraim dá frente para o Mar Morto, mil e duzentos metros abaixo. Foi do monte Pisga que Moisés contemplou a Terra Prometida, imediatamente antes de sua morte. Nos tempos antigos, a cadeia se localizava no que se chamava Moabe, defronte de Jericó. Comparar Núm. 27:12; 33:47,48; Deut. 3:27. (ID UN Z)

ABATER

Verbo que no hebraico significa «fugir», «diminuir». Usado em Deu. 34:7 acerca das energias físicas de Moisés, as quais, apesar de seus 120 anos de idade, não se tinham «abatido». O mesmo termo é usado em relação ao rebaixamento das águas do dilúvio (Gên. 8:8), e em relação à ira dos efraimitas contra Gideão (Juí. 8:3).

4

ABATTACHIM — ABE

ABATTACHIM

Termo hebraico que figura apenas em Núm. 11:5, onde os israelitas murmuradores disseram: «Lembramo-nos dos peixes que no Egito comíamos de graça; dos pepinos, dos melões...» Essa última palavra é que no hebraico é *abattachim*. No árabe, a palavra que significa «melão» é similar ao termo hebraico. Portanto, parece quase certo que a tradução tradicional dessa palavra é correta. (IB S)

ABDA

Vem de um termo hebraico que significa «servo», «escravo» ou «adorador» de Deus.

1. Pai de Adonirão, que foi um oficial que recolhia tributos, sob Salomão, I Reis 4:6.

2. Filho de Samua (Nee. 11:17), chamado Obadias em I Crô. 9:16 (444 A.C.).

A palavra pode ser uma forma abreviada de Obadias, a fim de eliminar a pronunciação do nome divino *Yah*. (FA UN)

ABDEEL

No hebraico, *disciplinado por Deus* ou *anelante por Deus*. Vem do árabe, *milagre de Deus* (?), mencionado nas genealogias de Abraão (ver Gên. 25:13; I Crô. 1:29) como o terceiro dos doze filhos de Ismael, neto de Abraão e Hagar, a egípcia. Nos registros assírios de Tiglate-Pileser, os descendentes de Abdeel são chamados Idibi ilu, uma tribo de beduínos arameus. (S Z)

ABDI

Vem de uma palavra hebraica que significa *meu servo*, como nome de três pessoas no Antigo Testamento:

1. Um levita ou merarita que viveu nos dias de Davi, ancestral de Etã, o cantor (I Cor. 6:44).

2. Pai de Quis, um merarita, durante o reinado de Ezequias (II Crô. 29:12).

3. Um dos filhos de Elão, que divorciou-se de sua esposa estrangeira, após o retorno do exílio babilônico (Esd. 10:26), em 459 A.C.

ABDIAS

Forma latina de Obadias, em algumas versões, em II Esd. 1:39.

ABDIAS, HISTÓRIA APOSTÓLICA DE

Coletânea de lendas latinas acerca dos doze apóstolos, incluindo Paulo. As fontes dessa obra são o Novo Testamento, a literatura pseudoclementina e um antigo Atos apócrifo. Parece datar do fim do século VI D.C. O prefácio afirma que Abdias, bispo da Babilônia, companheiro dos apóstolos Simão e Judas, escreveu a obra, e que ele mesmo fora testemunha ocular de Jesus e de suas realizações. Tudo isso não passa de fabricação, conforme é o mais provável. A obra está dividida em dez livros, cada um dos quais teria sido escrito por algum apóstolo. A obra tem valor por citar obras antigas, algumas das quais pereceram. Ver o artigo sobre os *Livros Apócrifos do Novo Testamento*, que ilustra e descreve esse tipo de atividade literária. (JF HEN Z)

ABDIEL

Vem de um vocábulo hebraico que significa **servo**

de Deus (El). Era filho de Gemi e pai de Aí, um dos principais residentes gaditas em Gileade (I Crô. 5:15), entre 1093-782 A.C. Seu filho, Selemias, foi um dos nomeados para deterem Jeremias e Baruque, o escriba (Jer. 36:26), antes de 606 A.C. (FA S UN)

ABDON

Vem de uma palavra hebraica que significa «servo». Vários indivíduos e um lugar são assim designados.

1. Um filho de Hilel, da tribo de Efraim, o décimo segundo juiz de Israel. Sucedeu a Elom e governou Israel por oito anos (1233-1225 A.C.). Sua administração foi pacífica. Tudo quanto sabemos sobre ele é que tinha catorze filhos e trinta sobrinhos, montados em jumentinhos, um sinal da importância deles (Juí. 12:13-15). Morreu em 1225 A.C. Provavelmente é o Bedam de I Sam. 12:11, mas que em nossa versão portuguesa diz-se «Baraque».

Josefo escreveu sobre ele: «Está registrado que ele foi feliz com seus filhos; pois os negócios públicos eram tão seguros e pacíficos, que ele não teve oportunidade de realizar atos gloriosos» (*Ant.* v. 7,15). Pratim, onde ele vivia, tem sido identificada com a moderna Ferata, a dez quilômetros a oeste de Siquém de Nablus.

2. Primogênito de Jeiel e Maaca, da tribo de Benjamim, residente de Jerusalém (II Crô. 8:30 e 9:36), onde temos a genealogia de Saul.

3. Filho de Mica, contemporâneo de Josias (II Crô. 34:20), 628 A.C. Em II Reis 22:12 ele é chamado Acbor.

4. Filho de Sasaque e chefe benjamita de Jerusalém (I Crô. 8:23), 624 A.C.

5. Uma importante cidade da tribo de Aser, dada aos levitas da família de Gérson (Jos. 21:30; I Crô. 6:74). Em alguns manuscritos, o mesmo lugar é mencionado em Jos. 19:29, talvez idêntico a Hebrom. Talvez ocupasse o sítio da moderna Khirbet Abdah, a vinte e quatro quilômetros ao sul de Tiro. (FA S).

ABDUÇÃO

Vem do latim *ab* (para longe) e *ducere* (levar).

1. Para Aristóteles, abdução é um silogismo no qual a premissa maior é veraz, mas a premissa menor é apenas provável.

2. Para C.S. Peirce, o termo é usado para indicar a formulação criativa de novas hipóteses estatísticas que explicam um dado conjunto de fatos.

3. Como termo legal, a palavra é usada para indicar o ato de levar ilegalmente uma pessoa, geralmente à força ou por fraude. Na ética, o termo significa a violação do direito de autodeterminação e de liberdade pessoal que Deus deu a outrem. O exemplo mais óbvio desse fato é a escravidão - a qual pode assumir muitas formas, como a prática de muitos empregadores que forçam seus empregados a trabalharem por um baixo salário. Também são culpados desse erro, pelo menos em algum grau, aqueles que não são generosos ou que se mostram desonestos em seus negócios.

ABE

Esse era o nome do quinto mês eclesiástico e do décimo primeiro mês civil do povo hebreu. A própria palavra não aparece nas Escrituras, sendo substituída pelo termo «quinto» mês (Núm. 33:38). O termo é de origem caldaica, tendo sido introduzida no vocabulá-

ABECEDARIANOS — ABEL

rio hebreu após o cativeiro babilônico. Começava com a lua nova e corresponde mais ou menos aos nossos meses de julho e agosto. Quanto a detalhes, ver *Calendário*. (E S)

ABECEDARIANOS

Uma seita extrema da Reforma que rejeitava todo estudo e erudição, negando-se mesmo a aprender a ler e a escrever. Diziam que o Espírito Santo é tudo que se faz necessário. Seu nome vem do abecedário que rejeitavam. (B)

ABEDE-NEGO

Vem de um nome caldaico que provavelmente significa «servo de Nego (Nebo)», com quem alguns eruditos identificam Mercúrio, intérprete ou mensageiro dos deuses. Outros sugerem que o nome vem de Arad-Ishtar, que significa «servo de Istar» (segundo diz o ISBE). Esse foi o nome dado por um oficial do rei da Babilônia a Azarias, um dos três companheiros de Daniel. Juntamente com seus dois amigos, Sadraque e Mesaque, foi miraculosamente livrado da fornalha, onde foram lançados por terem se recusado a adorar a estátua de ouro que Nabucodonosor mandara erigir na planície de Dura (Dan. 3). A identificação desse homem com Esdras é improvável, visto que este último era sacerdote da tribo de Levi (Esd. 7:5), ao passo que Azarias era de sangue real, e portanto, da tribo de Judá (Dan. 1:3-6). Viveu em cerca de 600 A.C. Antes de sua grande provação, foi oficial de uma província babilônica. Foi deposto por haver-se recusado a participar da idolatria, e depois passou por seu grande teste. (S UN Z)

ABEGARO (ABAGARO)

Abegaro e as Epístolas de Cristo datam de algum tempo antes de 260 D.C. Rei de Edessa e do distrito de Osroene; o décimo sétimo dos vinte monarcas desse nome e contemporâneo de Cristo. O nome não ocorre na Bíblia, embora seja celebrado na história eclesiástica por causa da suposta correspondência trocada entre ele e Cristo. A lenda diz que Abegaro escreveu a Jesus, solicitando dEle que viesse curá-lo da lepra. Jesus teria respondido que Ele mesmo não poderia fazer a viagem, mas que enviaria um de Seus apóstolos. E teria enviado Tadeu, ainda segundo a mesma fonte. O relato envolve duas cartas, que ocupam lugar dentro da literatura apócrifa do Novo Testamento. Eusébio, *Hist*. I.13 (onde estão contidas essas cartas), afirma tê-las traduzido de documentos sórios, localizados nos arquivos de Edessa. Eusébio (segundo Quasten) igualmente teria conhecimento dos Atos de Tadeu, em grego (Lipsius, *Acta apos apocry*. I.273 ss), mas a verdade da questão parece ser que ele somente escreveu a narrativa.

A lenda espalhou-se sob várias formas e em diversos idiomas. Encontra-se no *Doctrine Addaei* siríaco, em Agostinho (*Contra Faustum* 28:4) e em Jerônimo (em Ezech. 44:29). Abegaro V de Edessa foi um personagem histórico contemporâneo de Jesus, mas a lenda era desconhecida antes da época de Eusébio, sendo uma evidente fabricação. (JQ)

ABEL

Vem de um termo hebraico que significa *respiração*. Mas a etimologia é incerta, e outros sentidos têm sido sugeridos, como «vapor», «fragilidade» e «filho». É possível que esse nome esteja associado ao termo acadiano *aplu*, «filho», ou ao sumeriano *ibila*, «filho».

1. *História da família*. Era o segundo filho de Adão e Eva, talvez gêmeo de Caim (Gên. 4:1,2). Foi instruído na adoração ao Criador e trabalhava como pastor. Seu irmão, Caim, era agricultor. Devido a essas circunstâncias, Abel ofereceu em sacrifício um animal, ao passo que Caim trouxe os frutos da terra (Gên. 4:3-5). O trecho de Heb. 11:4 mostra que Deus agradou-se do sacrifício de Abel, mas não do de Caim. Despertou-se-lhe a inveja, e segundo diz o texto samaritano, ele *convidou* Abel para o campo, onde o matou. O texto hebraico disponível silencia sobre o convite, embora registre o homicídio. Seja como for, é certo que o ato foi premeditado.

2. *Tradição judaica*. Segundo esta, Abel foi morto na planície de Damasco, e seu túmulo é ali mostrado aos turistas, perto da vila de Sinie ou Sineiah, acerca de dezenove quilômetros a noroeste de Damasco, na estrada para Baalbeque, embora tudo isso não passe de fantasia.

3. Interpretações simbólicas baseadas no nome «Abel». a. Se seu sentido é «filho», então o nome simplesmente assinala o fato de seu nascimento. Visto que Caim significa «possessão», esse foi o nome do primogênito, porque ele foi uma possessão significativa para seus pais. b. Se seu sentido é «fraqueza», «vaidade» ou «lamentação», seu nome predizia seu fim súbito e triste, tendo nele o primeiro quadro de um justo sob perseguição, fisicamente impotente perante um poder físico superior.

4. *Um nome de fé*. O trecho de Heb. 11:4 elogia Abel por sua fé, do que resultou um sacrifício superior. Seu nome figura no início da grande lista dos fiéis, tendo sido ele elogiado pelo próprio Senhor Jesus (Mat. 23:35). Presume-se que ele obedeceu a alguma ordem específica, acerca do sacrifício, que Caim ignorou, embora isso não seja declarado no Antigo Testamento.

5. *Simbolismo*. Abel tornou-se um tipo de Cristo porquanto ofereceu um sacrifício cruento, superior (Heb. 9:26; 10:12). Ele tipifica Cristo como o Messias e Servo sofredor, o Cordeiro de Deus (João 1:29; Isa. 53:7). Ele testifica sobre a necessidade de um sacrifício de sangue (Heb. 9:22; 11:4).

6. *Nos escritos dos pais da Igreja*. Crisóstomo chamou-o de tipo do Cordeiro de Deus, gravemente injustiçado, em vista de sua inocência (*Ad Stagir* ii.5). Agostinho chamou-o de «peregrino», porquanto foi morto antes de poder residir em qualquer cidade terrena, pelo que aguardava uma cidade celeste, onde pudesse habitar em justiça (*De Civitate Dei*, xv.1). Caim, por sua vez, fundou uma cidade terrena e ali habitou em meio à iniqüidade. Irineu observou sobre como Abel mostrou que os justos sofrem nas mãos dos ímpios, e como as virtudes dos justos são assim magnificadas. (*Contra Haeres*. iii.23)

7. Jesus referiu-se a Abel como o primeiro mártir (Mat. 23:35), conceito esse que teve prosseguimento na Igreja primitiva. Evidentemente, Jesus o considerava um personagem histórico. O sangue de Abel é contrastado com o sangue de Cristo, em Heb. 12:24 (IB ND S Z)

ABEL

Vem de um termo hebraico que significa *prado* ou *lugar de relva*. É usado como prefixo nos nomes de vários lugares, por exemplo Abel-Sitim (prado das acácias), em Núm. 23:49; e o trecho de I Sm. 6:18 tem «o grande prado» (que em nossa versão portuguesa se traduz por «a grande pedra», seguindo a Septuaginta). Esse prado ou essa pedra estava localizada perto

ABELARDO DE BATH — ABEL-MIZRAIM

de Bete-Semes, onde os filisteus puseram a arca, quando a devolveram a Israel. (S Z)

ABELARDO DE BATH

Escritor inglês do século XII sobre assuntos filosóficos, que transmitiu a erudição científica dos árabes ao ocidente. Sua obra principal foi *De Eoden et Diverso* (Sobre a Identidade e a Diferença). Ele argumentava que espécie e gênero não são afetados pelas características individualizantes. Um objeto do entendimento pode ser considerado como um individual ou como um universal, segundo sua doutrina da «indiferença». Não obstante, ele supunha que a perspectiva platônica era superior. Outros livros seus foram: *Sobre as Coisas da Natureza* e *Sobre as Questões da Natureza.* (AM F P)

ABELARDO, PEDRO

Teólogo e filósofo francês (1079-1142), conhecido na literatura romântica por causa de seu romance com Heloísa. Foi um dos maiores intelectuais da Idade Média. Ele nasceu em Palais ou Le Pallet, na Bretanha. Estudou com Roscelin e Guilherme de Champeaux, e sob famosos mestres da Escola de Chartres. Abriu várias escolas de filosofia e teologia, sobretudo em Paris, onde começou, em 1113, seu célebre mas infeliz relacionamento com Heloísa. Abelardo anelava assumir uma abordagem mais racionalista dos problemas teológicos. Sua primeira obra, sobre a *Divina Unidade e Trindade*, foi condenada como herética em Soissons, e foi queimada. Foi abade de São Gildas, em 1125, e conferenciou em Santa Genoveva, em Paris, de 1136 a 1139. Bernardo acusou-o de herege e ele foi condenado pelo concílio de Sens, em 1141. Finalmente, o papa Inocente II proibiu-o de continuar ensinando. Retirou-se para Cluny, onde permaneceu até à morte. Porém, sua paixão pela aplicação da razão à teologia atraiu muita atenção e ajudou a dar forma a um novo clima intelectual.

Idéias:

Abelardo desempenhou importante papel na controvérsia sobre os *universais* (ver o artigo). Assumiu posição anti-realista, especialmente censurando o realismo radical que supunha que só há dez objetos, a saber, as dez categorias aristotélicas (ver o artigo). Segundo essa posição, qualquer diferença, como entre uma rocha e um cavalo, por exemplo, seria apenas variações dentro de um único objeto. Abelardo salientou o absurdo da idéia asseverando que, nesse caso, *a mesma coisa* tinha, simultaneamente, qualidades contrárias. Também opunha-se à teoria da coleção, do realismo, segundo a qual o universal seria o conjunto de todos os objetos em questão. Assim, o homem universal é simplesmente *todos os homens.* Também combatia o *nominalismo* radical (ver o artigo). Roscelin cria que o universal é mero vocábulo, ou *flatus vocis.* A posição de Abelardo era o *conceitualismo* (ver o artigo): os universais são reais apenas como *conceitos* da mente humana.

Seu livro, *Sic et Non* (Sim e Não), foi uma coletânea de opiniões contraditórias dos padres, sob as principais questões da teologia e da filosofia, onde são abordadas cento e cinqüenta questões. Seu propósito era demonstrar que o indivíduo tem o direito de fazer suas próprias investigações e de meditar. Ele parecia promover o primado da razão sobre a fé, nesse seu método investigativo.

Em seu *Scito Te Ipsum* (Conhece-te a Ti Mesmo), procurou mostrar que o pecado implica tanto em conhecimento como em intuito de fazer o mal, pelo que reside na vontade. Sua abordagem forçou ajustes na doutrina do pecado original.

ABEL-BETE-MAACÁ

Vem do hebraico e significa «prado da casa da opressão» (ver II Sam. 20:14,15; I Reis 15:20; II Reis 15:29). Era uma localidade ao norte da Palestina, que modernamente se identifica com Abi-el-Qamh. Nos tempos antigos deve ter sido um lugar importante, próspero e fortificado, porquanto foi chamado de «uma mãe em Israel» (II Sam. 20:19). Foi assediado por Joabe, Ben-Hadade e Tiglate-Pileser (II Sam. 20:14; I Reis 15:20; II Reis 15:29). Seba estabeleceu-se ali, quando se revoltou contra Davi. Oitenta anos mais tarde, Ben-Hadade invadiu o lugar, e após duzentos anos, Tiglate-Pileser o conquistou, e enviou seus habitantes como cativos para a Assíria. (II Reis 15:29).

Descobertas arqueológicas têm aumentado nossos conhecimentos sobre o local. Uma coleção de textos de maldições, chamados Textos de Execração, pertencente ao século IX A.C., compostos no Egito, incluem uma alusão a esse lugar, juntamente com Ijom, Lais e Hazor. Figura na lista composta por Tutmés III sobre cento e dezenove aldeias cananéias, como a de número 92, soletrada *i-b-r.* Um texto fragmentar no tablete de Ninrode (deixado por Tiglate-Pileser) dá um relato sobre sua invasão nesse lugar, paralelo à narrativa de II Reis 15:29. Tal destruição foi apenas uma dentre uma longa série de conquistas. *Abi* foi declarada como cidade da fronteira entre Bete-Omri (Israel) e Bete-Hazel (Aram, Damasco). (Ver evidências das inscrições na obra do Dr. J. Wiseman, Iraq, xvii, 1956, 117 ss). (N D S Z)

ABEL-MEOLÃ

Vem do hebraico e tem o sentido de «prado da dança», supostamente uma aldeia próxima do rio Jordão, —cerca de dezesseis quilômetros (no dizer de Eusébio) ao sul de Bete-Seã ou Citópolis (I Reis 4:12). Alguns conjeturam que provavelmente não distava muito de onde desemboca o Wady el-Maleh, no vale do Jordão ou Aulon, onde está localizado o moderno Tell Abu Sifri, a oeste do Jordão, a meio-caminho entre o mar da Galiléia e o mar Morto. Um outro sítio possível é o Tell el-Mazlub, no Wadi el-Jabis (no dizer de AASOR xxv-xxviii, 1951, pág. 216). — É melhor conhecida devido à sua conexão com a vitória de Gideão sobre os midianitas (Juí. 7:22), e também como o local onde nasceu Eliseu (I Reis 19:16). Durante o reinado de Salomão, Abel-Meolá é mencionada como pertencente à área de Baaná (I Reis 4:12), um dos doze oficiais administradores dos distritos governamentais de Salomão.

ABEL-MIZRAIM

No hebraico significa «prado do Egito». Localização desconhecida. Esse era o nome da eira onde parou o cortejo de Jacó a caminho de Hebrom. Ali foram levados a efeito sete dias de lamentação (Gên. 50:10,11). A palavra hebraica «ebel» significa «luto», pelo que o nome poderia ser chamado de «prado do luto». O texto de Gênesis, acima mencionado, nos leva a entender que assim deveríamos interpretar o nome, embora haja um óbvio jogo de palavras aqui devido à similaridade dos vocábulos «abel» (prado) e

ABEL-NAIM — ABENÇOAR

«ebel» (luto). O sentido real era «prado», mas o jogo de palavras faz o sentido ser «luto», devido às circunstâncias históricas envolvidas. O local era chamado de eira de Atade, antes dos cananeus darem-lhe o nome acima discutido. Ficava «além do Jordão», o que podia significar «na região de». Portanto, podia ficar no lado oriental ou ocidental do rio Jordão (S Z)

ABEL-NAIM

Nome alternativo de Abel-Bete-Maacá, encontrado em II Crô. 16:4, em relação às conquistas militares de Bene-Hadade. (FA)

ABEL-QUERAMIM

Vem de uma expressão hebraica que significa «prados» ou «vinhedos». Alguns eruditos pensam que seria uma aldeia amonita, cerca de dez quilômetros de Filadélfia ou Rabvate Amom, de acordo com Eusébio. Na época, o lugar ainda tinha vinhedos. Ver *Onomasticon* 32:15,16. Jefté perseguiu os amonitas até essa aldeia. Portanto, foi uma das vinte cidades amonitas que Jefté conquistou. Não se sabe o seu local exato. Ver Juí. 11:33.

ABEL-SITIM

No hebraico temos as palavras que significam «prado» e «acácias». Era o nome de uma aldeia nas planícies de Moabe, no lado oriental do Jordão onde entre essa e Bete-Jesimote houve o último acampamento dos israelitas naquela margem do rio Jordão (Núm. 33:49), antes de terem-no cruzado para entrar em Canaã. Os espias foram enviados daquele lugar (Jos. 2:1). Mais comumente era denominada apenas Sitim (Núm. 25:1; Jos. 2:11; Miq. 6:5). Eusébio afirma que ficava próxima ao monte Peor. No tempo de Josefo era conhecida como Abila, a sessenta estádios do Jordão (*Ant.* iv.81; v.1,1). O local é lembrado como o sítio onde Israel foi severamente punido, por ter sido seduzido a adorar Baal-Peor, quando se associaram aos moabitas e amonitas. Provavelmente é o moderno Tell Kefrein, a leste de Jericó, doze a catorze quilômetros a leste do rio Jordão (Buhl, *Geography*, pág. 116, 265). Até hoje as acácias ladeiam os terraços verdes do Jordão. Também têm sido aventadas outras localizações possíveis, como Tell el-Hammam e Wadi es-Sant (J.A. Bewer, *Joel*, ICC, 1912, pág. 142).

O trecho de Joel 3:18 fala sobre as águas vivificadoras que a região receberá no dia do Senhor. Essa é uma predição sobre as bênçãos e a prosperidade da era do reino, após a grande restauração de Israel. (FA ND S)

ABELHA

A palavra hebraica para abelha significa *ordeira*, podendo ser achada em Deu. 1:44; Juí. 14:8; Sal. 118:12 e Isa. 7:18. De acordo com a lei, era um inseto imundo (ver Lev. 11:23). O nome científico da família é *apidae*, e a abelha melífera é a *apis mellifica*. Todas as espécies são aladas, alimentando-se quase exclusivamente de néctar e de pólen das flores, em cuja atividade elas transportam o pólen fertilizador. A maioria das espécies compõe-se de indivíduos solitários, mas a abelha melífera forma uma sociedade altamente organizada. A abelha era a origem do elemento açucarador até o século XVIII, continuando a sê-lo até hoje, em muitos lugares. As

passagens bíblicas sobre as abelhas sugerem o seguinte: 1. Em Juízes 14:8, se lê que as abelhas ocuparam a carcaça de um leão que Sansão havia matado, o que deu origem à idéia equivocada de que as abelhas eram geradas dos corpos mortos dos animais. Porém, tudo quanto está envolvido no episódio é o fato de que as abelhas usaram parte da estrutura óssea do leão morto, como o crânio, como lugar para construírem uma colméia. 2. Usualmente, porém, as abelhas buscam localizações naturais, como fendas nas rochas ou cavidades nos troncos das árvores. (Ver Deu. 32:13; Sal. 81:16). 3. As abelhas abundam no deserto da Judéia (ver Mat. 3:4). 4. Elas representam grande fúria, como se fosse o ataque de um numeroso inimigo (ver Deu. 1:44 e Sal. 118:12). 5. O mel de abelhas era muito procurado como alimento (ver Pro. 24:13; 25:16,17). 6. A vida das abelhas, e o mel por elas produzido, provêem várias lições morais: a. A mensagem espiritual pode ser doce, mas também pode tornar-se amarga, quando rejeitada (ver Eze. 3:1-3). b. As leis do Senhor são grandemente desejáveis, tão doces quanto o mel. c. As palavras agradáveis são como um favo de mel, uma doçura para a alma, e para a saúde da mesma (ver Pro. 16:24). d. Assoviando, o Senhor convoca as abelhas para julgar, um símbolo de inimigos invasores (ver Isa. 7:18). É corrente que alguns habitantes da Palestina podiam chamar as abelhas pelo assobio e é provável que isso esteja por detrás dessa idéia do versículo. e. As abelhas simbolizam a indústria e a frutificação, o que explica o nome feminino *Débora*, que significa abelha, quando as mulheres tinham tais qualidades (ver Gên. 35:8; Juí. 4). (FA HA UN Z)

ABENÇOAR

Vem do termo grego *eulogeo*, cujo sentido básico é de prosperidade e bondade, envolvendo a adoração a Deus como um ser bom, recebendo dEle favores e benfeitorias; salienta as idéias de *falar bem*, de *louvar*, de *exaltar*, em face dos benefícios recebidos.

1. Quando o homem bendiz: a. Ele louva ou exalta a Deus (ver Sal. 104:1); b. agradece pelas misericórdias recebidas (ver Sal. 16:7); c. deseja e invoca a felicidade para outras pessoas (ver Gên. 49); d. ora para que a bondade de Deus seja conferida a outras pessoas (ver Núm. 6:23,24); e. dá valor aos benefícios espirituais recebidos (ver Isa. 65:16; Jer. 4:2); f. expressa isso em uma saudação, desejando a outras pessoas paz e prosperidade (ver Sal. 129:8); g. ora em favor e fala favoravelmente acerca de outras pessoas (ver Luc. 6:28); h. mas tudo isso pode ser pervertido, pois um homem pode imaginar-se espiritualmente abençoado ao prosperar materialmente, ainda que possa ser espiritualmente pobre e materialmente rico (ver Deu. 29:19).

2. Quando Deus abençoa: a. Os que são abençoados recebem o favor divino (ver Gên. 24:48); b. Deus anuncia Seu favor e o confere (ver Gên. 27-29), através de líderes religiosos, como o chefe de uma família, ou os líderes do povo (ver Núm. 6:22-27), ou através de um rei (ver II Sam. 6:18), ou através de pactos firmados (ver Deu. 28:3-6).

3. Esse conceito era expresso através do vocábulo grego *makarios*. Esse indicava a *felicidade* dos deuses, dentro da literatura pagã, bem como a felicidade daqueles que haviam sido beneficiados mediante dons e avanços espirituais. Ver o artigo sobre as *bem-aventuranças*, quanto a maiores detalhes.

4. Responsabilidade de quem é abençoado. As bem-aventuranças, no Novo Testamento, antecedem a

ABES — ABIAS

chamada à obediência, a qual é desenvolvida nas muitas injunções do Sermão do Monte (Mat. 5 e 6). Paulo iniciava suas epístolas com uma bênção, a qual armava o palco para instruções sobre as responsabilidades espirituais e morais. (Ver Efé. 1:3-14).

ABES

No hebraico é um metal, «estanho», que alternativamente pode ser soletrado *ebez*. O nome designava uma aldeia de Issacar, supostamente perto da fronteira mencionada entre Quisiom e Remete (Jos. 19:20). O território de Issacar ocupava a maior parte da fértil planície de Esdrelom. Desconhece-se a localização exata de Ebes. (S)

ABGAR (ABGARUS) e as Epístolas de Cristo.

Ver o artigo sobre *Doctrina Addaei*.

ABHIDHARMAKOSA

Ver a Terminologia Budista.

ABHINIVESHA

Termo sânscrito que indica o amor à vida e o temor da morte, uma das cinco espécies de ilusões com as quais os homens se envolvem.

ABI

No hebraico, «pai de», que forma a primeira parte de diversos nomes próprios hebreus. O termo é usado exclusivamente para denotar o pai natural de alguém. Pode funcionar como sujeito, com alguma indicação explanatória, como «pai da abundância» (Abiatar), ou «Jah é pai» (Abias).

Abi era a mãe do rei Ezequias (II Reis 18:2), mas ela também é chamada de Abia (II Crô. 19:1). O nome do pai dela era Zacarias, talvez aquele que Isaías tomou como testemunha (Isa. 8:2). (S Z)

ABIAIL

No hebraico, «pai da luz» ou «esplendor». Há aqui uma variante que envolve uma letra, fazendo a palavra significar «pai da força». A diferença é entre Abiail e Abicail. Talvez Abiail envolva um erro pré-massorético, visto que uma nota naquele texto confirma a variante.

1. Mãe de Maalate, esposa de Reobão, rei de Judá. Ela é chamada filha de Jerimote, filho de Davi (II Crô. 11:18), 972 A.C. Porém, visto que Davi já reinava há mais de oitenta anos antes do casamento dela, sem dúvida devemos entender que ela era apenas *descendente* de Eliabe. Uma ambiguidade no texto de II Crô. 11:18 tem levado alguns eruditos a verem essa mulher como a segunda esposa de Reobão. O vs. 19, entretanto, parece indicar que ele só teve uma esposa.

2. Abiail, filho de Huri, um dos chefes de família da tribo de Gade, que se estabeleceu em Basã (I Crô. 5:14), entre 1093-782 A.C.

3. Pai de Zuriel, que foi o pai da tribo levítica de Merari (Núm. 3:25).

4. Pai da rainha Ester e irmão de Mordecai (Est. 2:15), 538 A.C.

5. Esposa de Abisur e mãe de Abã e Molide (I Crô. 2:29), consideravelmente antes de 1612 A.C.

ABI-ALBOM

No hebraico quer dizer «valente», «pai da força».

Um dos heróis de Davi (II Sam. 23:31). Em uma passagem paralela ele é chamado Abiel (I Crô. 11:32). Provavelmente era natural de Bete-Arabá, uma aldeia fronteiriça entre Judá e Benjamim (Jos. 15:6,61; 18:22). (FA S)

ABIAS

No hebraico significa «de quem Deus é pai». Há versões que registram diversas variantes de seu nome, embora nossa versão portuguesa sempre registre o nome nessa forma. Essas variantes são: Abijam, I Reis 15:1 e Nee. 10:7. Abiah, em I Sam. 8:2. Abia em I Crô. 3:10; Mat. 1:7; Luc. 1:5.

1. Filho de Bequer, um dos filhos de Benjamim (I Crô. 7:8), após 1856 A.C.

2. Filha de Maquir e esposa de Hezrom (I Crô. 7:8), cerca de 1612 A.C.

3. Segundo filho de Samuel (I Sam. 8:2; I Crô. 6:28), cerca de 1093 A.C.

4. Filho de Jeroboão, primeiro rei de Israel. Foi afetado por perigosa enfermidade. Sua mãe disfarçou-se e visitou o profeta Aías, para saber se ele se recuperaria ou não. Aías disse que ele morreria, e que seria a única pessoa da família que teria um sepultamento honroso, sendo lamentado em Israel (I Reis 14:1-18). A razão do disfarce é que Deus havia rejeitado abertamente a Jeroboão. Seja como for, o disfarce foi inútil, porque o profeta soube da visita antes que a mesma ocorresse, por advertência divina. Em toda a casa de Jeroboão, somente Abias tinha alguma coisa que o Senhor Deus de Israel aprovou (I Reis 14:13). Cerca de 930 A.C.

5. Descendente de Eleazar, filho de Aarão. Foi cabeça do oitavo turno dos vinte e quatro turnos sacerdotais (I Crô. 24:10; Luc. 1:5). Cerca de 1014 A.C.

6. Em nossa versão portuguesa, esse personagem é chamado de «Abião», em I Reis 14:31, mas «Abias» em I Reis 15:1. A primeira dessas formas significa «pai do mar» ou «pai do ocidente», ou ainda «marinheiro». Era filho de Reobão e neto de Salomão, e foi o segundo rei de Judá (I Crô. 3:10). Sucedeu a seu pai antes de 918 A.C. e reinou apenas por três anos de acordo com alguns eruditos entre 913 e 911 A.C. Lemos que ele andou em todos os pecados de seu pai (I Reis 15:3), e que fez guerra contra Jeroboão, rei de Israel. Porém, em II Crô. 13, ele é apresentado como alguém que zelava pela honra de Deus e pelo sacerdócio levítico. Os dois relatos parecem contraditórios. Talvez isso se deva às observações e opiniões de diferentes autores. Ou então o seu reinado foi marcado, de modo geral, por várias formas de iniquidade, embora também assinalado por alguns breves períodos de piedade. Seu melhor momento foi quando da derrota de Jeroboão. Ele condenou o norte por sua apostasia e declarou que o próprio Deus defendera a causa de Judá, como seu grande «Capitão». A despeito da vantagem de dois para um, favorável ao norte, Abias saiu-se vitorioso e capturou Betel, Jesana e Efrom (II Crô. 13:19). Ele considerava a separação entre o norte e o sul como um ato de rebelião, e no seu conflito com o norte teve o propósito de reunificar os dois reinos.

Dificuldade vinculada à maternidade. Há uma dificuldade relativa à mãe de Abias. Em I Reis 15:2, lemos «sua mãe Maacá, filha de Abisalão». Mas em II Crô. 13:2, lemos: «Era o nome de sua mãe Micaías, filha de Uriel de Gibeá». Maacá e Micaías eram variações do mesmo nome; e Abisalão provavelmente é o mesmo Absalão, filho de Davi. A palavra hebraica

ABIASATE — ABIEL

ban, traduzida por «filha», é aplicada na Bíblia não somente à filha de um homem, mas também a uma sobrinha, neta ou bisneta. Portanto, é provável que Uriel de Gibeá tenha se casado com Tamar, a linda filha de Absalão (II Sam. 14:27), da qual teve como filha Maacá, que era assim filha de Uriel e neta de Absalão.

Abias acumulou um total de catorze esposas, que lhe deram um total de vinte e dois filhos e dezesseis filhas (II Crô. 13:21).

7. Filha de Zacarias, esposa de Acaz e mãe de Ezequias, rei de Judá (II Crô. 29:1). Também era chamada Abi (sobre quem ver as notas), segundo lemos em II Reis 18:2.

8. Um dos sacerdotes que provavelmente assinou o pacto feito com Neemias (Nee. 10:7), em 410 A.C. Provavelmente retornou com Zorobabel da Babilônia, embora na época já fosse muito idoso (Nee. 12:4), em 536 A.C. Tinha um filho chamado Zicri (Nee. 12:17).

9. Alguns eruditos propõem um outro Abias, diferente do anterior, e que retornou da Babilônia com Zorobabel (Nee. 12:4). Na lista cronológica dos sacerdotes, que aparece em Nee. 12:10-21, Zicri é alistado como o descendente seguinte a governar a casa de Abias (12:17).

ABIASATE

No hebraico significa «pai da colheita», o mais jovem dos três filhos do levita Coré (Êxo. 6:24), após 1740 A.C. O termo pode aplicar-se a uma divisão dos levitas, descendentes de Coré. Em I Crônicas, Abiasafe é alistado entre os porteiros, embora seja incerta a identificação dos dois. Entre os descendentes notáveis figurava o profeta Samuel, filho de Elcana (I Sam. 1:1), e o cantor Haman. (ND Z)

ABIATAR

No hebraico, «pai da abundância». O homem desse nome foi o décimo terceiro sumo sacerdote dos judeus, e o quarto descendente de Eli. Quando o sumo sacerdote Abimeleque, pai de Abiatar, foi morto com os sacerdotes, em Nobe, por suspeita de parcialidade para com o fugitivo Davi, Abiatar escapou ao massacre, levando consigo a porção mais essencial das vestes sacerdotais.

1. *Como sumo sacerdote*. Davi o acolheu bem e o nomeou sacerdote de seu grupo, durante o seu período de exílio. Com freqüência era o mediador das mensagens divinas a Davi. Ao tornar-se rei de Judá, Davi nomeou Abiatar sumo sacerdote. Saul havia nomeado Zadoque como sumo sacerdote. A nomeação de Abiatar foi feita em harmonia com a divina sentença de deposição, decretada através de Samuel, sobre a casa de Eli (I Sam. 2:30-36). Quando Davi tornou-se rei de todo o povo de Israel, ele não tinha base para desmerecer a Zadoque. Por essa razão, permitiu que ambos, Abiatar e Zadoque, funcionassem como sumo sacerdotes (I Reis 4:4). Não somos informados como os deveres sumo sacerdotais foram divididos entre os dois.

2. *Deposição*. Abiatar tentou impedir Salomão de ficar com o trono de Davi, preferindo apoiar Adonias. Se não fossem os favores prestados a Davi, Abiatar poderia ter sido executado. Salomão meramente removeu-o do ofício sumo sacerdotal, banindo-o para Anatote (I Reis 2:26,27). Assim, a sucessão sumo sacerdotal foi confinada a Zadoque, da linhagem do filho mais velho de Aarão. Desse modo chegou ao fim o domínio da casa de Eli, sendo assim cumprida a profecia de I Sam. 2:31-35.

3. *Aparente discrepância*. Em Marcos 2:26 são descritas circunstâncias que teriam ocorrido nos dias de Abiatar, sumo sacerdote, mas que com base em I Sam. 21:1, teriam realmente ocorrido quando seu pai, Abimeleque, era o sumo sacerdote. Numerosas soluções têm sido oferecidas para essa dificuldade. Alguns sugerem: «...nos dias de Abiatar, que *depois* foi o sumo sacerdote». Mas isso abre uma outra dificuldade, originada da precisa referência oposta (II Sam. 8:17; I Crô. 18:16; 24:3,6,31): «...Abimeleque, *filho* de Abiatar...», como a pessoa que era sumo sacerdote, juntamente com Zadoque, e que foi deposta por Salomão; ao passo que a história descreve essa personagem como Abiatar, filho de Abimeleque. Uma sugestão que poderia remover *todas* essas dificuldades — embora dificilmente possa ser considerada plenamente satisfatória.— é que tanto o pai quanto o filho tinham os dois nomes, Abimeleque e Abiatar, podendo ser chamados por um ou por outro desses nomes. Embora não fosse incomum que os judeus tivessem dois nomes, também *não* era incomum que um pai e seu filho tivessem um mesmo nome. Frente a tais dificuldades, alguns intérpretes têm pensado ser melhor deixar de lado a passagem de Mar. 2:26, conforme foi explicado acima, concluindo que as outras discrepâncias surgiram devido a alguma fácil e óbvia transposição de palavras, por parte dos copistas, perpetrada posteriormente. Os intérpretes que supõem que nenhum equívoco de cópia desse tipo poderia ter ocorrido, tentam promover a harmonia a qualquer preço, embora sacrificando a verdade da questão. A espiritualidade e a fé não são promovidas por esquemas dessa ordem. (ND S Z)

ABIDA

No hebraico, «pai do julgamento», ou «juiz». Era filho de Gideoni, príncipe de Benjamim (Núm. 1:11; 2:22; 10:25), 1210 A.C. Por ocasião da ereção do templo, sua contribuição caiu no nono dia (Núm. 7:60-65). Representou sua tribo como recenseador.

ABIDE

No hebraico significa «espiga». Esse era o mês da colheita do grão, ou o mês quando o cereal amadurecia. Correspondia mais ou menos aos nossos meses de março e abril, durante o tempo em que se observava a páscoa. Aparentemente, a palavra vem do termo cananeu mais antigo para o mês de nisã (Êxo. 13:4; 23:15; Deu. 16:1). Era costumeiro dar nomes aos meses do ano, através da observação das funções da natureza. Vários nomes cananeus aparecem entre as inscrições fenícias, embora o nome *abibe* até agora não tenha sido encontrado. Ver o artigo sobre o *calendário* (FA ND)

ABIEL

No hebraico significa «pai da força» ou «aquele cujo pai é Deus».

1. Pai de Quis, cujo filho Saul foi o primeiro rei de Israel, e de Ner (I Crô. 8:33; 9:39), cujo filho, Abner, foi capitão do exército de seu primo, Saul (I Sam. 9:1; 14:51), 1093 A.C. Alguns supõem que Jeiel, em I Crô. 8:29; 9:35, pai de Ner, seja o mesmo Abiel. Nesse caso, Abiel foi avô de Quis, e bisavô de Saul. Um elo na genealogia pode estar faltando, o que era ocorrência comum.

2. Abiel, um arbatita, um dos trinta mais distintos elementos da guarda pessoal de Davi (I Crô. 11:32), cerca de 1000 A.C. Também era chamado Abi Albom (II Sam. 23:31), nome que tem o mesmo sentido. (S Z)

ABIÉZER — ABILENE

ABIÉZER

No hebraico significa «pai da ajuda», *ajudador*.

1. O segundo dos três filhos de Hamolequete, irmão de Gileade, neto de Manassés (Núm. 26:30; I Crô. 7:18), 1170 A.C. Tornou-se o fundador do clã ao qual pertencia Gideão, que era conhecido por seu nome, os abiezritas (Juí. 6:34; 8:2; Jos. 17:2). Nos dias de Gideão, o clã tinha por sede, Ofra, a oeste do rio Jordão (Juí. 6:11,24). O nome Jezer (Núm. 26:30) é uma contração. Foi em Ofra que o anjo do Senhor apareceu a Gideão, e desse distrito ele convocou seus primeiros soldados, a fim de combater contra os midianitas (Juí. 6:34). Esse ato provocou a inveja de Efraim. Gideão, porém, abrandou-os, proferindo um provérbio: «Não são porventura os rabiscos de Efraim melhores do que a vindima de Abiézer?» (Juí. 8:2). O clã de Gideão aparentemente era um dos mais pobres de Manassés (Juí. 6:15).

2. Um nativo de Anatote, um dos trinta principais heróis de Davi (II Sam. 23:27; I Crô. 11:28). Anatote ficava a três quilômetros e pouco, ao norte de Jerusalém. Abiézer comandava o exército de Davi no nono mês (I Crô. 27:12). Certo número de comandantes se intercambiavam na liderança, em base mensal. (MD S)

ABIEZRITAS

No hebraico significa «pai dos ezritas», uma designação antiga dos descendentes de Abiézer (Juí. 6:2,4; 8:32). (S)

ABIGAIL

No hebraico quer dizer «pai da alegria» ou «exultação».

1. Esposa de um próspero criador de ovelhas, Nabal, que habitava em Maom, no distrito de Carmelo, a oeste do mar Morto (I Sam. 25:3; 27:3), 1000 A.C. Era conhecida por sua beleza física. Mostrou-se pronta e discreta nas medidas que tomou para afastar a indignação de Davi, violentamente excitado pelo tratamento insultante que seus mensageiros receberam da parte de Nabal, quando buscavam provisões. Apressadamente ela preparou um suprimento liberal de provisões, de que as tropas de Davi muito necessitavam, e saiu ao encontro dele com uns poucos servos à sua frente. Davi estava a caminho para exterminar Nabal e tudo quanto ele tinha. A ação de Abigail abrandou a ira de Davi, ao ponto dele ver que estava exagerando, e que poderia ter cometido grande injustiça. A beleza e a prudência de Abigail impressionaram de tal modo a Davi que, não muito tempo depois, quando Nabal falecera, ele mandou buscá-la para ser sua esposa (I Sam. 25:14-42). Dali por diante ela tornou-se sua companheira inseparável em todas as coisas, boas e más (I Sam. 27:3; 30:5; II Sam. 2:2). Acredita-se que eles tiveram dois filhos, Quileabe e Daniel, mas alguns estudiosos crêem que o Quileabe de II Sam. 3:2 é o mesmo Daniel de I Crô. 3:1.

2. Filha de Naás (Jessé) (filha de Naás, II Sam. 17:25, ou de Jessé, I Crô. 2:13-16), irmã de Davi, esposa de Jeter ou Itra, um ismaelita, e mãe de Amasa, 1008 A.C. Provavelmente era meia-irmã de Davi. Se Naás não é o mesmo Jessé, é possível que Jessé tenha se casado com a viúva de Naás. A maioria dos críticos modernos acredita que «Naás» é um erro escribal em lugar de Jessé. Pelo menos é certo que essa Abigail e Davi tiveram a mesma mãe (se não o mesmo pai). O filho de Abigail, Amasa, por algum tempo foi o comandante do exército de Davi (II Sam. 20:4). (UM Z)

ABI-JONAS

Em Eclesiástico 12:5, ele figura como personagem cujo nome significa «desejo». Ou então é alusão à «abionote», pequena fruta silvestre, da família do morango. Presumivelmente consumida como condimento e estimulante, ou seja, como afrodisíaco.

ABILA

Capital da Abilene de Lisânias (Luc. 3:1), e que deve ser distinguida de outros lugares com o mesmo nome, como Abila de Lisânias e Abila do Líbano. O sentido básico do apelativo parece ser «lugar de relva», ou «prado», derivado do hebraico *abel*. Também não é o mesmo local que Abel-Bete-Maacá, pois esta era cidade de Naftali, ao passo que Abila não o era.

1. *Tradição*. Uma antiga tradição faz de Abila o lugar onde Caim matou Abel, concordando com a suposição que Damasco fica no local do antigo jardim do Éden. Mui provavelmente, a tradição surgiu devido à similaridade dos nomes Abila e Abel. Um monumento, no cume de uma elevada colina, perto do manancial do rio Barrada, presumivelmente assinala o túmulo de Abel. Mas tudo não passa de fantasia. A lenda é tão fantástica que se diz que o comprimento do túmulo é de trinta metros, e que essa teria sido a altura de Abel.

2. *Localização*. Acha-se na estrada de Heliópolis (Baalbeque) a Damasco, entre as quais cidades -trinta e duas milhas romanas da primeira e dezoito da segunda — fica situada Abila, no itinerário de Antônio. Suas ruínas ainda são visíveis ao redor da aldeia de Es-Suk, a trinta e dois quilômetros de Damasco.

3. *Provas arqueológicas*. Mais ou menos à mesma distância a noroeste de Damasco, fica localizada Souk Wady Barrada, onde há inscrições que identificam o local com a Abila de Lisânias. Há algumas inscrições desse lugar. Uma delas, no verso, estampa um grande cacho de uvas, sugerindo a abundância de vinhedos na região. Uma outra traz uma meia-figura do rio Barrada, com a inscrição: «Chrysoroas Claudianus». No reverso há o nome «Leucadion», nome grego da cidade. Visto que Abila adicionou o nome de Cláudio aos seus outros apelativos (o que parece ser óbvio na moeda), podemos supor que a cidade revestia-se de alguma importância e magnitude. (FA S Z)

ABILENE

Ver Luc. 3:1. Era um pequeno distrito do território que derivava seu nome da cidade principal, Abila, acima descrita. Não se sabe quais os seus limites exatos, embora saiba-se que, para o norte, devia ultrapassar o Barrada Superior, a fim de incluir Abila, sendo possível que sua fronteira sul chegasse ao sopé do monte Hermom. Parece ter incluído as vertentes orientais do Antilíbano. Seja como for, era conhecida como linda e fértil região, bem arborizada e regada, com excelentes e amplas pastagens. Portanto, fazia contraste com as estéreis vertentes ocidentais das montanhas do Antilíbano.

Embora pequena, a região de Abilene obviamente tinha certa importância, o que é indicado na nota acima, sobre sua capital, Abila. Uma inscrição ali existente menciona a dedicação do templo ao «Senhor dos Senhores», provavelmente título aplicado a Tibério, 14-37 D.C. A dedicação foi feita por

ABIMAEL — ABINOÃO

«Lisânia, o tetrarca». Josefo alude a ele como tetrarca de Abilene, ao registrar que o imperador Gaio (Calígula), ao subir ao trono, em 37 D.C., concedeu a tetrarquia de Lisânia a Agripa (Josefo, *Ant.* xix,v.1; xx.vii.1). Esses detalhes mostram que Abilene tinha alguma importância para Roma.

Sua menção no Novo Testamento (Luc. 3:1), deve-se ao desejo de Lucas em «datar» o começo do ministério de João Batista, aludindo a certo número de governantes da época.

Aparente discrepância. Lucas atribui o governo de Abilene a Lisânias, na mesma época em que Josefo o dá a Filipe. Tem sido demonstrado que o território fora dividido e que, na realidade, tanto Lisânias quanto Filipe governaram Abilene, cada qual em sua porção. (S UN Z)

ABIMAEL

No hebraico quer dizer «o pai é Deus», ou então «pai de Mael». Foi um dos filhos de Joctã, na Arábia (Gên. 10:28; I Crô. 1:22), algum tempo depois de 2414 A.C. Foi o nono descendente de Joctã, descendente de Sem, ao qual se atribui a fundação de uma tribo árabe. (S Z)

ABIMELEQUE

No hebraico, «pai do rei», ou, talvez, «pai real» (Maleque é pai). Nome usado para indicar várias pessoas na Bíblia.

1. Nome do rei filisteu de Gerar, nos dias de Abraão (cerca de 2200 A.C.), referido em Gên. 21:1 ss. Porém, talvez se tratasse de um título distintivo para os governantes filisteus, como Faraó, no Egito, e não um nome pessoal. Esse homem, apaixonando-se pela esposa de Abraão (pois este dissera que Sara era sua irmã), resolveu tomá-la como esposa. Essa circunstância mostra-nos o grande poder dos antigos reis, que podiam fazer o que quisessem e com quem quisessem, incluindo as mulheres locais e as mulheres que porventura passassem pelo seu território. Ver esse costume implicado nos trechos de Gên. 12:15 e Est. 2:3. Mas Deus advertiu Abimeleque, e fez o que Abraão deveria ter feito, mostrando que, algumas vezes, a proteção divina é dada quando não a merecemos. Por qual motivo Sara não disse alguma coisa? A resposta é «por temor». O rei local podia fazer o que lhe agradasse com as mulheres de seu reino, mesmo que alguma mulher estivesse ali como estrangeira, casada ou solteira. Provavelmente Abraão apelou para uma mentira a fim de preservar a própria vida, dispondo-se a permitir que Sara fosse tomada pelo rei, se isso fosse necessário. Deus, revelando que Abraão era um Seu profeta, exigiu respeito da parte de Abimeleque; e este, além de devolvê-la ao marido, enviou-lhe presentes. Contudo, aproveitou o ensejo para repreender a Abraão com observações sarcásticas (Gên. 20:14,16). Por duas vezes Sara escapou de fazer parte de haréns reais. Alguns anos depois, os servos dos dois homens discordaram por causa de alguns poços, tendo sido firmado um pacto à beira do poço chamado Beerseba (fonte de sete ou do juramento), a fim de pôr fim ao conflito. (Ver Gên. 21:22-24).

2. Incidente similar ocorreu cerca de um século mais tarde, entre Isaque e um outro Abimeleque, de Gerar (Gên. 26:1-11). Isaque disse que Rebeca era sua irmã, e a história se repetiu, incluindo até mesmo a intervenção divina. Novamente houve uma disputa por causa de poços, cujo resultado foi um acordo (ver Gên. 26:17-32). Nesse relato, bem como naquele relativo a Abraão, aparece o nome Picol (Gên. 21:22 e 26:26). Por causa dessas similaridades, alguns eruditos têm pensado que as duas narrativas na realidade são duas versões do mesmo incidente, aplicadas a dois personagens diferentes. Não há uma maneira *clara* de resolver o problema. Abimeleque, apesar de ser inimigo natural de Isaque, procurou cultivar a sua amizade, por ver como Deus o fazia prosperar. (Ver Gên. 26:8-31).

3. Rei de Siquém, filho de Gideão por meio de uma concubina (ver Juí. 8:31). Isso envolveu um casamento matrilinear, segundo o qual a esposa vive na casa de seus pais, e os filhos ficam pertencendo ao clã materno. Após o falecimento de Gideão, esse homem procurou tornar-se rei, primeiro através dos chefes de seu clã, e mais tarde por aclamação popular. A fim de consolidar a sua autoridade, matou os setenta filhos de seu pai. Jotão, único sobrevivente do massacre, postou-se no monte Gerizim, com seus seguidores armados, e pronunciou sua famosa fábula de *rei-espinheiro*, que não tinha capacidade de governar. A fábula também predizia a destruição mútua de Abimeleque e de seus súbitos. (Ver Juí. 9:7-11).

Após três anos, houve uma revolta contra o cruel Abimeleque, tendo sido preparada uma emboscada para matá-lo, quando retornasse a Siquém. Mas o rei descobriu o conluio, e foi capaz de frustrar os sequemitas, destruindo a cidade de Siquém.

Em um ataque contra Tebes, cidade que distava cerca de vinte e um quilômetros de Siquém, para o nordeste, uma mulher, do alto da torre, deixou cair a pedra superior de um moinho em sua cabeça, deixando-o moribundo. A fim de que sua morte não fosse atribuída a uma mulher, ele rogou a seu armeiro que o matasse à espada, o que foi feito. (Ver Juí. 9:54).

4. Um sumo sacerdote dos dias de Davi (I Crô. 18:16), embora tenhamos ali um erro escribal em lugar de Aimeleque, filho de Abiatar, conforme se vê em II Sam. 8:17; I Crô. 24:6, a Septuaginta e doze manuscritos de I Crô. 18.16 (ND UN VT Z).

ABINADABE

No hebraico, «pai da generosidade», nome dado a diversas figuras bíblicas.

1. Um dos oito filhos de Jessé, e um dos três que seguiram a Saul, na guerra contra os filisteus (I Sam. 17:13). O incidente do desafio de Golias contra as tropas de Israel envolve o seu nome.

2. Um dos filhos de Saul que foi morto quando da batalha de Gilboa (I Sam. 31:2), em 1001 A.C. (Ver também I Sam. 31:2; I Crô. 8:33; 9:39; 10:2).

3. Um levita de Quiriate-Jearim, em cuja casa, localizada em uma colina, foi depositada a arca da aliança, depois que os filisteus a devolveram. Foi entregue aos cuidados de seu filho, Eleazar, tendo ficado ali por setenta anos, até que foi removida por Davi, em cerca de 1030 A.C. (I Sam. 7:1,2; II Sam. 6:3,4; I Crô. 13:7).

4. Pai de um dos doze oficiais nomeados por Salomão para proverem mantimentos, alternadamente, para o rei e sua corte (I Reis 5:1,2), em cerca de 1170 A.C. (DE S)

ABINOÃO

No hebraico, «pai da agradabilidade» ou «pai da graça», genitor de Baraque, o juiz (Juí. 4:6, 12; 5:1,

ABIRÃO — ABISMO

12), após 1170 A.C. Ele é mencionado na narrativa referente à vitória de Baraque sobre os cananeus, sob Jabim e Sísera, bem como no cântico de Débora e Baraque. (S Z)

ABIQUEILA Ver *Queila (Abiqueila)*

ABIRÃO

No hebraico, «pai da altura», ou «exaltado». Dois homens recebem esse nome, nas páginas da Bíblia:

1. Um dos chefes da família da tribo de Rúbem, o qual, juntamente com Natã e Om, pertencentes à mesma tribo, uniram-se a Coré, da tribo de Levi, em conspiração contra Aarão e Moisés (Núm. 16:1-7; 26:9; Deu. 11:6; Sal. 106:17), em cerca de 1620 A.C. A terra os engoliu vivos.

2. Filho mais velho de Hiel, de Betel (I Reis 16:34). Hiel reconstruiu Jericó durante o reinado de Acabe. A obra incluiu o lançamento dos alicerces, o que, em vários lugares da Palestina, era realizado em meio ao holocausto de crianças, embora não haja evidências absolutas do que sucedeu no caso relacionado a Hiel e Abirão. O trecho de I Reis 16:34 atribui a morte dos filhos de Hiel ao cumprimento da maldição de Josué, embora alguns interpretem que, na ocasião, Hiel sacrificou Abirão. O ponto continua em disputa.

ABISAGUE

Uma bela e jovem mulher sunamita, da tribo de Issacar, que foi escolhida pelos assessores de Davi para fazer parte do harém real a fim de ministrar pessoalmente a ele, em sua idade avançada. Parece que poderia ser encontrada outra solução de manter o idoso monarca aquecido, em vez de submeter a jovem àquela absurda situação. Mas, na época, as mulheres não tinham direitos reconhecidos, e coisas assim ridículas continuamente aconteciam com elas. (I Reis. 1:3,15). Após a morte de Davi, Adonias, filho mais velho dele, tentou obter permissão para casar-se com a mulher, mas Salomão mandou-o executar, supondo que a tentativa fazia parte de um plano para Adonias apossar-se do trono (ver I Reis 1:1-4; 2:13-25). Além disso, havia a questão da propriedade do possível casamento, porquanto a mulher fora esposa de seu pai, embora o matrimônio nunca se tivesse consumado. (DE FA S UN Z)

ABISAÍ

No hebraico quer dizer «pai dos presentes» ou, como alguns preferem, «pai de Jessé», embora o sentido do nome seja incerto. Era o filho mais velho de Zeruia, irmã de Davi, e irmão de Joabe e Asael (I Crô. 2:16). Foi um daqueles que se devotaram fielmente a Davi, durante sua peregrinação, quando era perseguido por Saul, antes de tornar-se rei. Abisai apresentou-se voluntariamente para ir com Davi ao centro do exército de Saul, que dormia. Poderia ter matado a Saul, se não tivesse sido restringido por Davi. Foi uma das duas pessoas que se atreveu a tanto (ver I Sam. 26:5-9). Quando Davi fugia de Absalão, para o outro lado do Jordão, novamente Abisai acompanhou o rei, tendo-lhe sido confiado o comando de uma das três divisões do exército que esmagou com êxito os rebeldes (ver I Sam. 18:2). Posteriormente, foi enviado pelo rei contra Seba, filho de Bicri (II Sam. 20:6-10), em cerca de 1049 A.C.

Quando Davi envelheceu, Abisai o salvou de morrer na batalha contra os filisteus, ao enfrentar o gigante Isbi-Benobe, que foi morto por Abisai. Ficou célebre devido a outros feitos de heroísmo, como quando

enfrentou trezentos homens e os matou com sua lança. Sua história envolve violência e matança, e os homens louvam aos homens por causa desses feitos.

Sua posição exata, entre os heróis de Davi, não é clara. Aparentemente, ele não fazia parte dos três maiores (ver II Sam. 23:8,9,11), mas parece ter sido um dos mais proeminentes entre os demais heróis de Davi. As variantes textuais em II Sam. 23:18,19 e I Crô. 11:20,21 obscurecem o problema, o qual, para começar, não se reveste de grande importância. Também são desconhecidas as circunstâncias de sua morte, antes da luta entre Adonias e Salomão, visto que ele não é mencionado como partidário de um ou de outro. (FA S UN Z)

ABISALÃO

Avô de Maacá, esposa de Reoboão. A palavra «filha», em I Reis 15:2, provavelmente significa «neta», e a palavra «mãe» (ali e em I Reis 15:10), significa «avó». (Z)

ABISMO

No grego, *ábussos*, «sem fundo». Termo que figura por nove vezes: Luc. 8:31; Rom. 10:7; Apo. 9:1,2,11; 11:7; 17:8; 20:1,3. Segundo os antigos imaginavam, o abismo era uma fenda existente no interior do mundo, como parte do submundo ou hades (que vide), cujo fundo não podia ser sondado. Na LXX, o vocábulo grego aparece como tradução da palavra hebraica *tehom*, «abismo» (ver Sal. 135:6).

O termo grego assim traduzido é *abyss*. Também traduzido por «abismo sem fundo». No grego clássico, a palavra é um adjetivo que significa «sem fundo» ou «sem limites». Na Septuaginta, a palavra é usada por cerca de trinta e cinco vezes, referindo-se ao fundo do mar, ou à habitação dos mortos (Eze. 31:15). No N.T., a palavra é usada para indicar a habitação dos demônios (Luc. 8:31), bem como o lugar de tormento (Apoc. 9:1), aparentemente como sinônimo de *hades*. Romanos 10:7 inclui o termo para indicar a habitação dos mortos. No Apocalipse, esse lugar tem um rei chamado «Destruidor». Em Apoc. 17:8, o anticristo surge de dentro do abismo, confirmando a antiga idéia judaica que o hades não é um lugar de residência permanente, de onde alguém pode sair. É interessante observarmos que o autor pensa que é possível alguém sair do hades, reencarnar-se e efetuar outra missão maligna. Ver os comentários em Apoc. 17:8, 10,11, no NTI, relativos a completas descrições sobre essas questões. Ver o artigo sobre *Hades*.

Antigas idéias cosmológicas. Alguns dos antigos, como os hebreus, os gregos, os romanos e vários povos orientais, supunham que a Terra flutuasse sobre águas sem fundo, estando sobre o *abismo*. A Terra estaria alicerçada sobre um abismo (Sal. 24:2; 136:6). Sob essas águas, ou no abismo propriamente dito, os espíritos maus dos mortos teriam sua residência final. Essa idéia foi modificada de tal modo que o *abismo* passou a ser concebido como se estivesse no interior do próprio globo terrestre, em uma espécie de caverna subterrânea, a grande cúpula do hades. Por essa razão fala-se no «submundo» como lugar dos espíritos perdidos, humanos ou demoníacos. Alguns cristãos até hoje concebem isso de forma bem literal. Mas, por certo o hades é um mundo espiritual, e os mundos espirituais, os lugares de habitação dos demônios, nada têm a ver com a geologia. O hades é uma dimensão espiritual, e não um local geológico.

De acordo com a cosmogonia semítica, a terra

ABISSÍNIA — ABIÚDE

flutuaria sobre um vasto lençol de água, que seria o manancial de todas as fontes e rios (Gên. 1:2; Sal. 24:2; 136:6). Esse oceano subterrâneo algumas vezes é descrito como «águas debaixo da terra» (Êxo. 20:4). Segundo o trecho de Jó. 41:32, o *tehom* é o habitat do leviatã. Interessante é observar que a LXX nunca usa o termo grego *ábussos* para traduzir *sheol*, o qual equivale ao *hades* do Novo Testamento (ver os artigos sobre o *sheol* e o *hades*). E isso quer dizer que o *tehom* nunca indica o «lugar dos mortos», que é o sentido ordinário de *sheol*. Portanto, não se deve confundir o abismo com o hades. O salmista usa a palavra *tehom* de maneira figurada, em Sal. 71:20, para indicar as dificuldades por ele experimentadas (cf. Jon. 2:5).

Quando chegamos ao Novo Testamento, a palavra grega *ábussos* indica o «lugar dos demônios». Segundo alguns estudiosos, pelo menos em Rom. 10:7, a palavra equivale ao *hades*. Todavia, Rom. 10:7 é citação de Deu. 30:13; e, nesta passagem, figura a palavra *yam*, «mar», e não a palavra *tehom*. Por conseguinte, permanece de pé a contenção que *tehom* não equivale ao *hades*.

O Novo Testamento distingue entre o *hades* e a *geena* (ver Apo. 20:14, onde se lê: «Então a morte e o *inferno* foram lançados para dentro do lago do fogo...», onde «inferno» corresponde ao original grego, «hades»), o que também nos permite concluir que o abismo não é a mesma coisa que *geena* ou lago do fogo. Antes, o abismo parece corresponder ao «Tártaro», referido em II Ped. 2:4, e que a nossa versão portuguesa, com muita dose de razão, traduz por «abismos de trevas». Em confirmação disso, vemos que os demônios, expulsos do endemoninhado geraseno, não queriam ir para o «abismo», seu lugar de castigo, segundo se lê em Lucas 8:31. Sumariando: *tehom* = abismo ou Tártaro; *sheol* = *hades*. A *geena*, um conceito tipicamente neotestamentário, corresponde a grosso modo ao «inferno», embora não exatamente, pois o inferno pertence às idéias latinas, e não hebréias ou gregas.

A cosmogonia bíblica é difícil de ser acompanhada, sobretudo em face do caráter evolutivo da revelação, que vai acrescentando, — à medida que avançamos na Bíblia. E o quadro complica-se mais ainda quando lemos as Escrituras sob a forma de traduções, que não são homogêneas e precisas. Ver os artigos sobre *Inferno, Hades, Geena* e *Lago do Fogo*.(B NTI S Z)

ABISSÍNIA

Ver Etiópia.

ABISUA

No hebraico, significa «pai da segurança», nome de dois personagens bíblicos:

1. Filho de Finéias e quarto sumo sacerdote dos judeus (I Crô. 6:4,5,50). Não se sabe exatamente quando ele começou a oficiar, mas isso evidentemente incluiu o período de servidão a Eglom, de Moabe. Alguns sugerem 1352-1302 A.C. como suas datas, mas outros falam em 1513-1463 A.C. Foi bisneto de Aarão. Foi chamado Abiézer por Josefo, *Ant.* v.12,5.

2. Um dos filhos de Bela, primogênito de Benjamim (I Crô. 8:4), após 1856 A.C. Alguns o identificam com Jeremote, em I Crô. 7:7. (DE FA S UN)

ABISUM

No livro apócrifo de I Esdras 1:2, figura como forma variante de Abisua, filho de Finces e pai de Bocas. (S Z)

ABISUR

No hebraico, «meu pai é um muro», um dos dois filhos de Samai, na lista genealógica de Jeremeel, da tribo de Judá. Sua esposa era Abiail. I Crô. 2:28,29. (FA S Z)

ABITAL

No hebraico, significa «pai do orvalho», isto é, *frescor*. Foi a quinta esposa de Davi (ver II Sam. 3:4; I Crô. 3:3), 1052 A.C. Era a mãe de Sefatias.

ABITUBE

No hebraico, «pai da bondade». Foi um benjamita, um dos dois filhos de Saaraim, de sua primeira esposa, Husim, uma moabita. Ele é incluído na genealogia de Benjamim (I Crô. 8:11).

ABIÚ

No hebraico, «de quem Deus é pai». Foi o segundo dos filhos de Aarão e Eliseba (Êxo. 6:23; Núm. 3:2; 26:60; I Crô. 6:3; 24:1). Juntamente com seus irmãos Nadabe, Eleazar e Itamar, Abiú foi separado e consagrado para o sacerdócio (Êxo. 28:1).

1. *Estabelecimento da adoração cerimonial.* Quando do estabelecimento da adoração cerimonial, as vítimas colocadas sobre o grande altar de bronze eram consumidas por fogo descido do céu. Foram dadas ordens para que esse fogo fosse mantido aceso, e que o incenso diariamente oferecido fosse queimado em incensários cheios de brasas tiradas do grande altar.

2. *Negligência fatal.* Certo dia, Nadabe e Abiú olvidaram dessa regra e ofereceram incenso em incensários cheios de fogo «estranho», isto é, fogo comum, e não daquele que fora mantido no fogo divino. Por causa disso foram instantaneamente mortos pelo fogo (relâmpago?) e assim foram violentamente tirados do ofício sacerdotal. Então foram retirados e sepultados com as vestes que traziam no momento, fora do acampamento (Lev. 10:1-11). Ver também Núm. 3:4; 26:61; I Crô. 24:2. Sem dúvida, esse foi um aviso severo para mostrar que a adoração instituída deveria ser cumprida exatamente conforme as instruções baixadas, incluindo os menores detalhes.

3. *O vinho proibido.* Pouco depois do incidente acima descrito, houve a proibição do uso de vinho pelos sacerdotes que tivessem de entrar no tabernáculo. Com base nessa circunstância, podemos depreender que Nadabe e Abiú estavam embriagados quando ofereceram o fogo «estranho». Não estavam impelidos pela presença do Espírito, mas pela força do vinho. Um dos símbolos do Espírito é o vinho.

4. *A linhagem sacerdotal continua através dos outros irmãos.* Nem Nadabe e nem Abiú tinham filhos (Núm. 3:4; I Crô. 24:2), pelo que a sucessão sacerdotal continuou através de seus irmãos mais novos.

5. *Simbolismo envolvido.* O ofício e o sacrifício único é indispensável a Cristo (cf. Heb. 7:22 ss ; 8:6; 9:28). (ID ND S)

ABIÚDE

No hebraico, «pai de renome» ou «pai da majestade».

ABLUÇÃO — ABOBOREIRA

1. Um dos dois filhos de Bela, filho de Benjamim (I Crô. 8:3), talvez também conhecido como Aiúde (I Crô. 8:7), depois de 1856 A.C.

2. Trineto de Zorobabel e pai de Eliaquim, na linhagem paterna de Jesus, em Mat. 1:13. Provavelmente deve ser identificado com Jodá, filho de Joanã e pai de José, na linhagem materna de Jesus (Luc. 3:26, se é que podemos fazer distinção entre a linhagem paterna e a linha materna de Jesus). Ele também pode ser identificado com Obadias, filho de Arnã e pai de Secanias mencionados em I Crô. 3:21, antes de 410 A.C. (ND S Z)

ABLUÇÃO

Na religião judaica havia quatro tipos de lavagem cerimonial. 1. A lavagem das mãos, não explicitamente requerida no A.T., embora inferida com base em Lev. 15:11. Nos dias do N.T., a prática torna-se generalizada e séria (Mar. 7:3; Mat. 15:2). A lavagem dos pés era uma prática similar. Há notas completas no NTI, sobre a lavagem das mãos em Mat. 15:2 e sobre a lavagem dos pés em João 13:5. 2. A segunda era a lavagem dos pés e das mãos, em preparação para o serviço sacerdotal (Êxo. 30:19; 40:31). O tabernáculo e o templo tinham uma bacia para esse fim. 3. A terceira é a imersão do corpo inteiro, que simboliza a purificação do homem inteiro, a fim de poder participar plenamente da adoração ao Senhor. Notemos os casos do sumo sacerdote, no dia da expiação (Lev. 16:24), de Aarão e seus filhos (Lev. 8:6) e dos leprosos ou daqueles que se tivessem maculado por causa de contatos proibidos (Lev. 14:8; 15:5-10; Núm. 19:19). Os prosélitos tinham que passar por essa ablução. Provavelmente, ela participa do pano de fundo do batismo cristão. 4. Também havia a lavagem de vasos, casas, vestes e outros itens usados para propósitos religiosos. Ver notas completas em Mar. 7:4, no NTI. Ver Lev. 14:52; 15:6-8; Êxo. 19:14.

Simbolismo. A preocupação com a pureza apropriada (santidade), de modo a estar isento de poluções do mundo, e assim poder aproximar-se do Deus Santo. No cristianismo, tudo isso é substituído por um coração limpo. Sem a santificação, ninguém verá a Deus. (Heb. 12:14). Como é óbvio, abusava-se das abluções na prática antiga, — quando os homens substituíam a substância da fé religiosa por alguma forma de sinal ou ato externo. Alguns queixavam-se que muitos rabinos tinham trocado o santuário pela cozinha, tão intenso era o espírito de lavagens e tantas eram as coisas que precisavam ser lavadas. (B IB NTI)

ABNER

No hebraico, «pai da luz» ou «iluminador». Filho de Ner, irmão de Quis, pai de Saul, e portanto, primo deste último. Tornou-se o comandante-em-chefe do exército de Saul (I Sam. 17:55; 20:25; I Crô. 26:28), em cerca de 1030 A.C.

1. *Associação com Saul.* Foi o comandante militar durante o reinado deste. Após a morte de Saul, defendeu a causa periclitante da casa de Saul. Tirou vantagem dos sentimentos contra Judá e contra Davi como rei, para promover seu próprio nome.

2. Não se candidatou ao trono, mas tomou Isbosete, filho sobrevivente de Saul, de pouca capacidade mental, para sentá-lo ao trono. Todas as tribos (excetuando apenas Judá) reconheceram-no como rei. Essa circunstância prosseguiu por algum tempo. Abner encontrou-se e lutou contra Joabe, general de Davi, em Gibeão, em uma das diversas batalhas em que os partidos contendores se mediram.

3. Em Gibeão, Abner foi derrotado e fugiu. Mas foi perseguido por Asael, irmão de Joabe; e foi morto por Abner (II Sam. 2:8-32). Isso deixou Abner como o único membro da casa de Saul que tinha capacidade de liderança. Uma discussão com Isbosete deixou-o indignado, e ele se dispôs a bandear-se para a causa de Davi.

4. Davi recebeu-o respeitosamente, e resolveu torná-lo chefe de seu exército. Mas Joabe, indignado diante da ameaça ao seu poder, vingou a morte de seu irmão, Asael. Então convidou Abner a um encontro amigável, mas matou-o à espada. Davi ordenou grande lamentação por Abner, o qual recebeu honras fúnebres (II Sam. 4:12). Todavia, Joabe, o vingador do sangue, escapou à punição (II Sam. 3:6-39).

5. O lamento de Davi, registrado em II Sam. 3:33, é significativo:

Teria de morrer Abner como se fora um perverso?
As tuas mãos não estavam atadas,
Nem os teus pés carregados de grilhões;
Caíste como os que caem diante dos filhos da maldade.

Abner foi sepultado em Hebrom, com a reputação de um herói e homem de caráter, tendo sido lamentado pelos poderosos. Os matadores são os heróis dos homens. (UN S Z)

ABÓBADA CELESTE

No hebraico temos uma palavra que significa faixa ou cúpula, mas que também pode indicar as algemas dos prisioneiros (ver Isa. 58:6), um bando de homens (II Sam. 2:25) ou a cúpula dos céus. Em Amós 9:6 indica os aposentos celestes — em português, «suas (de Deus) câmaras no céu».

ABOBOREIRA

Ver o artigo geral sobre o *reino vegetal.* No hebraico, a palavra em foco é *qiqayon* (ver Jon. 4:6-10), uma planta de crescimento muito rápido. Na Septuaginta é usada a *abóbora*, curcubita pepo, que faz parte da família dos colocíntidas. A planta era nativa da área do mar Cáspio. Foi introduzida na Assíria em alguma data desconhecida, mas antes da época de Jonas. Alguns pensam que a espécie vegetal em foco, no caso de Jonas seria a greco-egípcia *kiki*, nome hebraico similar ao daquele que é usado em Jonas. Essa seria a mamona, chamada também de palma christi. Seu nome científico é *Ricinus communis.* Essa também é uma planta de desenvolvimento rápido, capaz de atingir a altura de três metros. No relato de Jonas, porém, nenhuma explicação natural pode explicar a rapidez do crescimento daquela planta, pelo que preferimos pensar em um sinal divino.

As colocíntidas, no hebraico, *paqquah* («que abre-se pelo meio») (ver II Reis 4:39), foi a planta ingerida pelos filhos dos profetas. Essa planta produz um fruto que se assemeiha à laranja, quanto ao tamanho e ao formato, embora tenha casca dura e uma polpa amarela, com manchas verdes e brancas. Assemelha-se ao melão, e pertence à mesma família. Tal planta era comum na Palestina. Também produzia uma substância usada como medicamento e catártico. Trata-se de uma erva ereta, com caule e ramos quebradiços.

Lição espiritual da planta de Jonas. Sua presença alegrou Jonas, devido à sombra projetada pela

ABOMINAÇÃO — ABORTO

mesma. Mas seu desaparecimento deixou-o irritado, visto que sua preciosa sombra lhe fora tirada. O contexto também sugere que Jonas teve dó da planta, por causa de sua breve vida e súbita morte. Seja como for, a planta era muito importante para ele, embora fosse apenas uma planta. No entanto, entristeceu-se porque Deus poupara Nínive e sua multidão de habitantes, dos quais *Deus* se condoera. Essa é uma excelente lição. Deus tem mais misericórdia dos homens do que os homens têm dos seus semelhantes. Podemos esperar mais da misericórdia de Deus do que a maioria dos homens espera. Essa é uma porção que nunca se ausenta da mensagem do evangelho, posto que é quase totalmente ignorada. Ver o artigo sobre a *restauração*. (ID ND S)

ABOMINAÇÃO

Quatro vocábulos hebraicos são assim traduzidos, e no N.T. grego, *bdeluma* é o veículo desse conceito.

Usos populares, não-religiosos. Os israelitas tinham aversão a certas pessoas e as excluíam de sua comunidade. Por sua vez, os egípcios tinham os israelitas como abomináveis. (Deu. 23:7). Uma pessoa podia ser rejeitada por causa de alguma enfermidade (Sal. 88:8) ou aflição (Jó 19:19). Certos animais ou alimentos em potencial eram evitados (Eze. 8:10; Isa. 66:17). Acima de tudo, era repelida a idolatria pagã. Assim, os termos hebraicos envolvidos refletiam tais usos, como *shegez* (carnes de animais proibidos); *shigguz* (ódio à idolatria); *piggul* (repugnância à carne sacrificial estragada). A mais comum dessas palavras, *to'ebah*, era usada para indicar qualquer tipo de abominação.

A abominação da idolatria. A idolatria repele a ordem própria das coisas e perverte a idéia da divindade, substituindo-a por uma variedade qualquer das simulações humanas, deixando de lado a adoração ao Deus único. Ver Deu. 17:4-5; II Reis 23:13; Dan. 9:27; 11:31; 12:11. A idolatria não apenas perverte a idéia de divindade, mas também é uma irresponsabilidade moral, porque, através dela, o homem é iludido acerca de quem ele tem responsabilidade. Outrossim, a prática da idolatria tem produzido muitas práticas desumanas, violentas e corruptas. A queixa de Jeremias (7:1-15) leva em conta as implicações morais da idolatria. Ezequiel lamentou a corrupção da vida nacional por causa das práticas idólatras, (7:3 ss ; 20:4 ss). As coisas especificamente mencionadas, nessa conexão, são o homossexualismo, o orgulho, a mentira, a violência contra os inocentes, o testemunho falso, a discórdia, etc., coisas essas que só deviam ser esperadas da parte dos pagãos, mas que também apareciam nas vidas dos chamados justos. (Ver Lev. 18:23). Os trechos de Deuteronômio 12:31 condena o sacrifício de crianças; 3:28-32, a desonestidade nos negócios; 6:16-19, a altivez, a mentira, o falso testemunho, a perturbação da ordem; 15:26, os pensamentos malignos; 17:15, a inversão da justiça. Em suma, todas as práticas estranhas à boa ética são abomináveis. (B WZ)

ABOMINÁVEL DA DESOLAÇÃO

Essa expressão se acha em Mat. 24:15 e Mar. 13:14. Sua origem está em Dan. 11:31 e 12:11. Poderia ser traduzida por «abominação que desola». Essas palavras foram aplicadas a Antíoco Epifânio, que erigiu um altar a Zeus, no altar de Yahweh. O relato encontra-se em I Mac. 1:54-64, e também em *Antiguidades* xii 5:4, de Josefo. Em cerca de 170 A.C., esse monarca selêucida perpetrou o que se considerou atrocidades contra os judeus e sua religião, mediante a poluição do templo de Jerusalém. Porém ele serviu apenas de tipo simbólico do grande anticristo que virá e que é um dos temas do N.T. (II Tess. 2:3. Ver a nota detalhada sobre o anticristo). O futuro anticristo aparecerá e assumirá o controle do templo, proclamar-se-á Deus, realizará muitas maravilhas falsas, controlará o mundo inteiro, afinal, por breve período. Ele será tão intensamente iníquo que só se poderá comparar ao próprio Satanás. Alguns acreditam que houve personagens de menor envergadura e que serviram de material para o conceito da *abominação da desolação*. Alguns acreditam que Marcos liga isso às circunstâncias da guerra dos judeus contra Roma. É verdade que ao tempo da destruição de Jerusalém, os romanos ofereceram sacrifícios às suas insígnias, postas diante da porta oriental do templo. Mas isso serviu de mero símbolo da blasfêmia maior que ainda jaz no futuro. Israel, afinal, lhe fará oposição e muito sofrerá por causa disso. Entretanto, o anticristo assumirá o controle do templo e obrigará o povo a adorá-lo ali, como se fosse Deus. Essa ação é justamente o «abominável da desolação». Fala de grande apostasia, a idolatria máxima.

Satanás será adorado em um homem, porque o anticristo será o filho do diabo, fazendo parte da trindade maligna (Satanás, o anticristo e o falso profeta). Essa será a idolatria máxima que Deus abominará. A tradição profética assegura-nos que chegará tempo quando o mal predominará violentamente sobre o mundo, quando o Espírito Santo se ausentará, exceto dos corações de um pequeno remanescente. O anticristo encabeçará essa revolta. Ver o artigo «Tradição Profética e a Nossa Época». (AI B NTI RO Z)

ABORDAGEM CIENTÍFICA À CRENÇA NA ALMA E EM SUA SOBREVIVÊNCIA ANTE A MORTE FÍSICA

Ver o artigo com este título entre os artigos apresentados sobre a *Imortalidade da Alma*.

ABORTO

O assunto é complexo e não admite qualquer solução simples, no terreno médico, social ou ético-religioso. Quanto a essa questão, os argumentos são numerosos e complexos, tanto favoráveis quanto contrários. Porém, apesar de não haver qualquer solução fácil, a teologia ética por certo pode sugerir-nos algumas diretrizes.

1. *A vida é dom de Deus*, e um *feto tem vida*. Os teólogos não têm podido chegar a um acordo sobre quando o espírito vem fazer-se presente em um feto. Alguns dizem que isso se sucede no momento da concepção. Se isso é verdade, então o aborto desfaz uma verdadeira personalidade humana, e, com a única exceção da necessidade de se salvar a vida da mãe, é uma forma de homicídio. Porém, outros insistem que a porção imaterial do homem não entra no corpo senão por ocasião do nascimento, ou pouco antes ou depois do nascimento. Com freqüência, essas idéias estão ligadas ao conceito da pré-existência da alma. Quanto a notas completas sobre a alma, sua natureza, origem e destino, ver o artigo sobre a alma. Se a alma ainda não está presente por ocasião do aborto, então o ato não destrói uma personalidade humana. Nesse caso, dificilmente poderíamos falar em assassinato de uma vida humana, através do aborto.

ABORTO OCULTO — ABRAÃO

2. *Questão do sofrimento*. Mesmo que o aborto não envolva homicídio, envolve o sofrimento físico, pois estamos informados de que o feto pode sentir, e muito deve sofrer ante os métodos de aborto que são utilizados. Não há como duvidar que é errado provocar sofrimento, mesmo que isso não redunde em homicídio. Os indivíduos e as civilizações mais avançadas interessam-se pelo bem-estar não apenas das pessoas, mas também dos animais, e declaram-se contrários à provocação de sofrimento desnecessário.

3. *A santidade da vida*. O feto, mesmo que não seja humano enquanto a alma não lhe é dada, é uma forma de vida, e merece o nosso respeito, já que é o futuro veículo da alma humana. Certamente deveria ser respeitado, pelo menos tanto quanto uma vida animal, que as pessoas boas e espirituais honram, procurando poupar dos sofrimentos.

4. *Considerações bíblicas e teológicas*. a. Trechos como Êxodo 21:22-24 e Jeremias 1:5 indicam que a vida no ventre materno deve ser respeitada como uma vida humana. Lucas 1:41 diz que o bebê saltou no ventre de Isabel por motivo de alegria, o que indica algo mais que uma vida animal. b. Apesar do corpo não ser a pessoa essencial, deve ser respeitado como um maravilhoso instrumento, produto de desígnio, e, conseqüentemente, algo que não deve ser destruído caprichosamente. c. Dificilmente se pode justificar uma mulher que mata o filho de suas entranhas por querer evitar o escândalo ou a carga financeira extra. Sua culpa, todavia, variaria dependendo da presença da alma ou não, a partir do momento da concepção. d. O mandamento bíblico que diz «Não matarás», e que proíbe especificamente o homicídio, mas que envolve o ódio e a malícia, usualmente de forma preconcebida (ver Mat. 5:21-22), apesar de não haver sido baixado tendo em mira o aborto, *até certo ponto* pode ter aplicação ao caso, mesmo que a alma não se faça presente senão por ocasião do nascimento.

5. *Exceções*. Os argumentos favoráveis ao aborto, nos casos de incesto ou estupro, ou quando a mãe do feto corre perigo de vida, parecem dar licença ao aborto, mesmo que a alma se faça presente no feto desde o instante da concepção. Resolver provocar um aborto, com base em uma dessas razões, envolve um grande problema pessoal, que cada mulher deve resolver individualmente. Penso que não podemos ter certeza sobre o que é correto em tais casos, e que devemos ser moderados no julgamento.

6. *Perdão dos pecados*. Todos os pecados podem ser perdoados. O arrependimento e a fé são suficientes para tanto. Mas há castigo (a colheita) para os erros praticados, inteiramente à parte do perdão. Isso é algo que o indivíduo deve estar disposto a enfrentar, ao mesmo tempo que prossegue em sua mudança de atitude, assim evitando futuros atos pecaminosos. Não somente é possível, mas também é nosso dever prosseguir para uma maior espiritualidade, após praticarmos algum ato maligno. Todas as pessoas envolvidas em casos de aborto, a mulher e algum homem que a tenha encorajado a isso, deveriam buscar uma mais elevada realização espiritual, a fim de contrabalançar o passado, além de evitarem a conduta similar no futuro.

7. *Estados psicológicos*. Somos informados de que o aborto origina sérias tensões psicológicas, nesmo em mulheres que não antecipavam qualquer reação negativa. Sem importar a razão, isso deveria servir de aviso de que o aborto, tal como muitos outros pecados, envolve pelo menos parte de sua própria punição.

ABORTO OCULTO

No hebraico temos uma palavra que vem do verbo «cair», e que significa «aborto»; no grego temos uma palavra, *éktroma*, «aborto».

A palavra hebraica ocorre por três vezes, em Jó 3:16; em Sal. 58:8 e em Ecl. 6:3, referindo-se ao feto que sai sem vida do útero materno. O mesmo pensamento reaparece em Núm. 12:12, onde o hebraico tem outro termo, embora a nossa versão portuguesa também a traduza por «aborto», e onde a LXX também a traduz por *éktroma*. O apelo de Aarão em favor de sua irmã Miriã, era que ela não ficasse com a aparência de um aborto, por causa da lepra, isto é, como se ela tivesse saído do ventre de sua mãe com parte de suas carnes consumidas.

A *referência figurada* a um aborto, com a qual Paulo diminuiu a sua própria importância como apóstolo, aparece em I Coríntios 15:8, como o último dos apóstolos a quem o Senhor ressurrecto aparecera; aponta para o atraso com que ele foi chamado ao apostolado, de modo súbito e inesperado. Era como se seu apostolado se devesse a um «nascimento monstruoso». Outros estudiosos preferem esquecer o atraso de sua chamada, em relação aos outros apóstolos, salientando mais o fato de que Paulo assim se considerava devido à sua indignidade ao ofício, em face de ter perseguido à Igreja de Deus. Paulo sentia que o elevadíssimo privilégio de ver o Cristo ressurrecto tornava-o mais indigno ainda. E assim, tudo quanto ele era e realizava, foi por ele atribuído não a si mesmo, mas à graça divina (ver I Cor. 15:10).

ABRAÃO

No hebraico significa «pai de uma multidão», o fundador da nação hebréia. Até Gên. 17:4,5, ele é chamado de Abrão, «pai da elevação», ou «pai exaltado», embora o sentido desse nome seja incerto. O nome mais longo evidentemente foi adotado por causa da promessa de sua numerosa posteridade.

1. *Fontes informativas*. A narrativa veterotestamentária, em Gên. 11:26-25:18, é primária e importantíssima. Mas muitas descobertas arqueológicas têm aumentado nosso conhecimento sobre a época e o mundo de Abraão.

2. *História primitiva*. Era nativo da Caldéia. Por meio de Eber, estava na nona geração depois de Sem, filho de Noé. Seu pai foi Terá que teve dois outros filhos, Naor e Harã. Harã morreu cedo, deixando seu filho Ló, que se apegou a seu tio Abraão. Harã também deixou duas filhas, uma das quais, Sara, tornou-se esposa de Abraão. Lemos, em Gên. 20:12, que Abraão chamou Sara de «irmã», filha de seu pai, mas não de sua mãe. Mas alguns eruditos compreendem que o hebraico diz que Harã era meio-irmão de Abraão e, nesse caso, Sara era sobrinha de Abraão. De acordo com um hebraico elementar, isso poderia ser indicado chamando-a «irmã» de Abraão. Mas o ponto é disputado.

Abrão nasceu em cerca de 2333, em Ur dos caldeus (Gên. 11:28), mas todas essas datas antigas são questionáveis e incertas. Nada sabemos sobre a sua vida senão quando ele já tinha setenta anos de idade. Há tradições que procuram preencher os claros, mas mui provavelmente sem base nos fatos. Terá é apresentado como um idólatra e fabricante de ídolos.

3. *Ur dos caldeus* (ver o artigo a respeito). A arqueologia moderna usualmente identifica essa cidade com a atual Tell el-Muquyyar, a 15 quilômetros a oeste de Nasireyeh, à beira do Eufrates, no sul do Iraque. Terá viajou por cerca de mil quilômetros de Ur até Harã, localizada à beira do rio Balique,

ABRAÃO

tributário do Eufrates, onde se estabeleceu (Gên. 11:26-32). Há lendas que dizem que Abraão, desgostoso com a idolatria de seu povo, foi perseguido por Ninrode e foi lançado em uma fornalha acesa, embora tivesse sido livrado da morte por um milagre. Alguns acreditavam que Abraão trouxera a astronomia (astrologia) da Caldéia para o ocidente, tendo ensinado essa ciência aos egípcios (Josefo, *Ant.* i.8), mas nada se sabe quanto à exatidão desses relatos, e o próprio Josefo duvidava da maioria deles.

4. *Chamada de Abraão*. Abraão tinha sessenta anos de idade quando sua família deixou Ur e foi para Harã. Não sabemos com o motivo da imigração, embora Josefo (*Ant.* i.6,5) tenha dito que a razão foi a tristeza de Terá ante a morte de seu filho Harã. Mas o trecho de Judite 5:6-8 afirma que o motivo foi a revolta contra a idolatria. Outros supõem que a mudança de lugar teve razões econômicas, a fim de buscar algum lugar mais próspero.

Com a idade de setenta e cinco anos, Abraão, sua esposa Sara e seu sobrinho Ló, com suas possessões, em resposta à chamada divina, partiram para a terra de Canaã, cerca de seiscentos e cinqüenta quilômetros de Harã. Durante a jornada, pernoitaram em Siquém e Betel. (Ver Gên. 12:1 quanto à chamada de Abraão por parte do Senhor). A princípio ele se estabeleceu no Neguebe, mas, devido a um período de escassez, continuou viagem até o Egito. Devido à sua beleza física, Sara atraiu a atenção do Faraó. Mas a providência divina interveio mediante pragas, impedindo qualquer consternação. Após a crise, Abraão retornou a Neguebe (ver Gên. 12:1-20). Posteriormente, mudaram-se para as vizinhanças de Betel. E a prosperidade ditou que Abraão e Ló deveriam dividir suas possessões, tornando-se independentes um do outro. Abraão permitiu que Ló escolhesse seu território, e este escolheu o vale do Jordão e a cidade de Sodoma. Abraão estabeleceu-se na área de Hebrom. Invasores vindos do norte arrebataram cativos a Ló e aos reis do vale do Jordão. Abraão combateu-os, havendo grande matança; e dos despojos, deu dízimos a Melquisedeque, sacerdote do Deus Altíssimo e rei de Salém (Gên. 14:1-24).

5. *O herdeiro*. Não tendo filhos, Abraão nomeou Eliézer, de Damasco, como seu herdeiro. Mas Deus lhe prometeu, mediante pacto, um filho e a posse da terra (Gên. 15:1-21). Passaram-se dez anos, sem o nascimento de um filho. Então Sara deu Hagar como concubina a Abraão. E assim nasceu Ismael. Porém, com o tempo, mãe e filho foram rejeitados e enviados ao deserto. Abrão tornou-se Abraão (pai das multidões), como sinal da certeza do nascimento de um filho e herdeiro. A circuncisão foi instituída como sinal do pacto (ver Gên. 17:10-14). Entrementes, Ló caiu em dificuldades e em pecado, e o anjo advertiu-o de que Sodoma e Gomorra seriam destruídas, o que não demorou a cumprir-se. Na fuga, a mulher de Ló foi castigada por sua teimosia, e foi transformada em estátua de sal. Mediante incesto com seu pai (inconsciente este do que estava sucedendo), suas filhas engravidaram. E nasceram Moabe e Amom, cujos descendentes tornaram-se os moabitas e os amonitas. (Ver Gên. 19:24-38).

Várias vicissitudes, incluindo o incidente em que Abimeleque quisera tomar Sara como sua mulher (ver Gên. 20:1 ss.), não puderam impedir o cumprimento da promessa. E assim, através da intervenção divina, Isaque nasceu, quando Sara estava com cem anos de idade (Gên. 20:1-18). Nesse ínterim, divinamente preservado, Ismael migrou-se para o deserto de Parã, onde haveria de tornar-se pai de uma grande nação, de acordo com uma promessa divina.

O incidente que envolveu a tentativa de Abimeleque tomar Sara como sua esposa é muito revelador quanto aos costumes da época. Um rei local tinha autoridade para dispor das vidas a seu talante, incluindo as mulheres casadas ou solteiras, e até mesmo aquelas que meramente passassem pelos seus domínios. Provavelmente, Abraão disse que Sara era sua irmã, por ter temido que poderia ser morto se o rei soubesse que ela era sua mulher, e quisesse tê-la. Portanto, Abraão arriscou-se a deixar Sara terminar no harém do rei, a fim de continuar vivo. A intervenção divina deu solução à crise. Algumas vezes, é disso que precisamos.

6. *A prova da fé*. Deus (segundo Abraão tinha a certeza) requereu a imolação de Isaque quando este estava com cerca de vinte anos de idade. Sem dúvida, ainda havia sacrifícios humanos na época, ou Abraão não teria dado ouvidos ao *impulso interior para* realizar tal sacrifício. O fato de que Isaque era herdeiro único tornou extremamente difícil a decisão. A fé de Abraão mostrou ser profunda (ver Heb. 11:17-19), confiando denodadamente na provisão divina (ver Gên. 22:7,8). Isaque foi poupado da morte por intervenção divina. Os eruditos e críticos da Bíblia têm discutido desde há muito sobre essa narrativa. Orígenes e outros dos primeiros pais da Igreja viam no relato sentidos místicos e alegóricos importantes, embora defendendo a idéia de que Deus jamais ordenaria, realmente, um sacrifício humano, embora se tratasse apenas de uma prova da fé. Sem dúvida, eles estavam com razão em sua contenção. O patriarca agiu de boa-fé, crendo que o sacrifício humano estava sendo requerido da parte dele. Porém, cumpre-nos supor que ele deve ter chegado a algum mal-entendido sobre a questão. Seu pano de fundo cultural e religioso deve ter confundido sua mente de algum modo. Nosso conceito de Deus avançou além do de Abraão, por essa altura de sua vida.

7. Sara faleceu em Quiriate-Arba, com 126 anos de idade, e foi sepultada na caverna do campo de Macpela (ver Gên. 23:1 ss.). O local, na área de Hebrom, tornou-se o local de sepultamento da família.

8. Com quarenta anos de idade, Isaque obteve noiva em Mesopotâmia, por intermédio do servo Eliézer, que conseguiu Rebeca, filha de Naor, para ser esposa do filho de Abraão.

9. Abraão faleceu com a idade de 175 anos, tendo sido sepultado por seus filhos Isaque e Ismael, na caverna de Macpela (ver Gên. 24:1 - 25:18).

10. *Caráter de Abraão*. A despeito de suas falhas e de alguns deslizes notáveis, Abraão tem sido reconhecido como um dos maiores líderes espirituais da humanidade, como homem de fé inabalável, por muitas religiões subseqüentes, como a judaica, a cristã e a islâmica. Ele desfrutava de íntima comunhão mística com Deus (Gên. 18:33; 24:40), sendo esse um dos segredos de sua grandeza. Sua fé era exemplificada na sua decidida obediência a Deus. Para onde quer que Deus o chamasse, ele ia: a. O incidente de Ur (Gên. 11:31; 15:7). b. A partida de Harã (Gên. 12:1,4). c. Aceitou uma vida seminomádica mesmo na terra de Canaã (Gên. 13:15; 15:18). d. Sacrifício de Isaque e confiança na sua ressurreição (Gên. 22:12,18; Heb. 11:9). Os cuidados de Abraão por sua família eram notáveis (Gên. 17:19). E ele era generoso e hospitaleiro (Gên. 18:2-8; 21:8; 13:8; 14:23).

11. *Abraão como tipo*. a. Tornou-se pai da raça espiritual, representando um aspecto da missão de Cristo como Cabeça da raça e Restaurador de todas as coisas (ver Efé. 1:10). b. Sua vida de peregrinações

Abraão

O Sacrifício de Isaque

Araão e Ló fazem um pacto (Gên. 13:10)

ABRAÃO — ABRAÃO, APOCALIPSE DE

simboliza o tipo de vida que a inquirição espiritual requer de nossa parte. c. Sua incontável posteridade simboliza as famílias que pertencem a Cristo. d. O incidente com Isaque é retrato da ressurreição, da vida dentre a morte. e. A expulsão de Hagar representa a rejeição divina dos não-herdeiros, aqueles que estão *sob a lei* e não entram no estado da *graça*, por meio de Cristo (Gál. 4:24,25). f. Seu pacto é tipo do pacto entre Deus e os homens, por intermédio de Cristo. g. Ele representa os *verdadeiros* crentes, que abandonam a idolatria e seguem a Deus, quando *chamados*.

12. *A arqueologia e Abraão*. As descobertas arqueológicas têm mostrado que a vida e os tempos de Abraão, segundo o registro do livro de Gênesis, concordam com o conhecimento recentemente adquirido sobre o segundo milênio A.C., principalmente o século XIX A.C. Têm sido encontrados muitos nomes de pessoas e de coisas que correspondem ao registro do livro de Gênesis. As informações de que dispomos sobre as leis e os costumes de então confirmam e nos fazem entender melhor os relatos de Gênesis. Essas descobertas desencorajam o ponto de vista de que Abraão personifica alguma tribo ou antiga deidade tribal, ou é apenas uma personagem mística de alguma antiga saga tribal.

Descobertas arqueológicas específicas:

a. Escavações feitas em Nuzu, à margem do rio Tigre, revelaram informações sobre leis de herança e outros costumes da época de Abraão, justificando assim a preocupação de Abraão com a questão. Um homem podia adotar um servo ou escravo, ou qualquer outra pessoa, para ser seu herdeiro, cumprindo assim todos os deveres relativos à família e à tribo. E isso explica o caso de Eliézer (Gên. 15:2-4).

b. Um herdeiro podia ser obtido através de uma concubina ou esposa-escrava, o que explica o caso de Hagar e Ismael (Gên. 16).

c. A *circuncisão* (ver o artigo) era uma prática comum da época, e Abraão tornou-a como sinal do pacto, provavelmente devido à sua associação com a *geração*.

d. A concubina não podia tomar o lugar da esposa na casa; mas a esposa também não podia expulsá-la. Isso explica a relutância de Abraão em expulsar Hagar. Só uma ordem divina foi capaz de demovê-la (ver Gên. 21:12-21).

e. O código legal hitita (descoberto na antiga capital hitita de Bogascoi, na Ásia Menor) lança luz sobre a compra do campo para sepultamento, feita por Abraão. Segundo essas leis, certas obrigações feudais estavam incluídas quando era vendido um terreno inteiro, o que não sucedia quando somente uma parte do terreno trocava de dono. Embora Abraão quisesse comprar somente a caverna, as estipulações de Efrom foram a venda da propriedade inteira, e assim, é provável que ele tivesse transferido para Abraão certas responsabilidades feudais. As árvores da propriedade eram indicadas no documento de venda, conforme usualmente se fazia nos documentos hititas. (Ver Gên. 23:17 ss).

f. *Canaã*. Após a morte de Terá, Abraão partiu de Harã e foi para a terra de Canaã (ver Gên. 12:4,5). A região montanhosa era pouco ocupada por uma população rarefeita, na Idade Média do Bronze (2000-1500 A.C.), pelo que as descrições de Gênesis, que fazem os patriarcas percorrerem as colinas da Palestina central e as terras secas do sul (havendo muito espaço e pouca gente para opor-se a eles), são corretas. As cidades que são mencionadas como lugares habitados nos tempos dos patriarcas, como Mispa, Gibeá, Siquém, Betel, Dotã, Gerar, Jerusalém (Salém), Beerseba, etc., foram todas encontradas mediante as escavações, e suas antigas histórias têm sido confirmadas.

g. O local de Nuzu, perto da moderna Quircuque, foi escavado entre 1925 e 1941. Data do século XV A.C. Milhares de tabletes têm sido desenterrados, ilustrando leis do matrimônio (ver Gên. 16:1-16), da primogenitura (ver Gên. 25:27-34), dos terafins (ver Gên. 31:34), e muitas outras práticas, costumes e leis. Descobertas similares têm sido feitas em Mari, um local próximo da moderna Abou Kemal, no médio Eufrates. Foi encontrado o nome *Abraão*, embora não especificamente relacionado ao personagem da Bíblia.

13. *Abraão e o Antigo Testamento*. Além das narrativas de Gênesis, há alusões a Abraão em vários trechos do resto do Antigo Testamento: No pacto mencionado por Moisés (Deu. 1:8; 6:10; 9:5), Canaã era a terra dada a Israel dentro do pacto firmado com Abraão (Deu. 34:4); o povo de Israel, — descendia de Abraão, o amigo de Deus (II Crô. 20:7); o Deus de Israel era o Deus de Abraão (I Reis 18:36); a proteção e a misericórdia divinas derivavam-se do pacto com Abraão (II Reis 13:23); os salmos mencionam Abraão em várias conexões (Sal. 47:9; 105:6,9,42); Abraão também é mencionado em trechos como Isaías 29:22; 41:8; 51:2; 63:16. Abraão é mencionado como pai da nação de Israel em Jer. 33:26; Eze. 33:24; Miq. 7:20.

Os livros apócrifos do Antigo Testamento (ver o artigo a respeito) dão prosseguimento a esse uso, enfatizando o fato de que Abraão foi grande profeta e também o homem do pacto com Deus. Ver Eclesiástico 44:19-21. Outro tanto diz a literatura rabínica, como Bereshith Rabba, Pirque Aboth 5:4, e também Josefo, em *Ant.* 1:7-8. Várias lendas figuram no livro de Judite e nas obras de Josefo, apresentando-o como astrônomo de primeira grandeza (um astrólogo?), que teria compartilhado de sua sabedoria com reis do Oriente e do Ocidente.

14. *Abraão e o Novo Testamento*. Jesus aparece como filho de Abraão, em Mat. 1:1; e ser alguém descendente de Abraão é reconhecido como fator significativo, embora isso não envolva direitos religiosos automáticos, sem a correspondente espiritualidade (Mat. 1:2,17; 3:9; 8:11; 22:32; Mar. 12:26; João 8:33-58). Abraão figura com proeminência na pregação dos apóstolos (Atos 3:13,25; 7:2-32; 13:26). Nos escritos de Paulo, Abraão ilustra o modo da justificação (Rom. 4:1-16). Na epístola aos Gálatas, a descendência espiritual de Abraão é a Igreja. Na epístola aos Hebreus, Abraão é o grande herói da fé (11:8 ss), bem como o ancestral do sacerdócio levítico (7:5). (AM CG KK UN S Z)

ABRAÃO, APOCALIPSE DE

Uma obra extracanônica, existente em uma versão no eslavônico antigo, baseada em uma tradução grega de um original hebraico ou aramaico. Os nomes semitas existentes na obra parecem mostrar uma origem semítica.

Oito capítulos introduzem a obra, falando sobre a juventude de Abraão. Essa parte provavelmente foi escrita antes do ano 50 D.C. O Apocalipse propriamente dito ocupa o restante do livro. Essa seção parece ser posterior, talvez do ano 100 D.C. ou mais tarde.

A narrativa é essencialmente um tipo de comentário de Gênesis 15, narrando como o anjo Jaoel escoltou Abraão ao sétimo céu, onde foi testemunha de eventos

ABRAÃO BEN SAMUEL ABULIAFA — ABSALÃO

passados, como a queda de Adão e Eva (ali atribuída a um pecado sexual, ocasionado pela sedução de Azazel, ou Satanás). As revelações incluídas falam sobre profecias, o advento do Messias, a destruição do templo, a restauração de Israel e o julgamento dos ímpios.

São discutidos alguns problemas teológicos, como o problema do mal - incluindo por que Azazel (Satanás) é tolerado. A resposta é a comum, que o livre-arbítrio é necessário, resultando disso, naturalmente, o mal.

Azazel é ali idêntico ao Belial do Testamento dos Doze Patriarcas. É identificado com a serpente de Gênesis 3.

Essa obra usa a elaborada angelologia da religião hebréia posterior, ilustrada no anjo Jaoel, que se afirma possuidor dos poderes do nome inefável. Em outras obras apócrifas, isso é atribuído a outros anjos, como Miguel e Metraton (Sanh. 38b). Ver os artigos sobre os livros apócrifos e pseudepígrafos do Antigo e do Novo Testamentos. (J NTI Z)

ABRAÃO BEN SAMUEL ABULIAFA

Cabalista judeu. Ver o artigo sobre a *Cabala*.

ABRAÃO, SEIO DE

Essa figura de linguagem aparece na discussão de Jesus sobre Lázaro e o rico, em Lucas 16:22-23. Três expressões eram comumente usadas entre os judeus, para expressar o futuro estado da bem-aventurança: 1. O jardim do Éden, ou paraíso; 2. o trono da glória; e 3. o seio de Abraão. É justamente esta que figura na história de Jesus, em Lucas 16. De conformidade com a teologia judaica, esse paraíso ou seio de Abraão fazia parte do hades, que abrigava os bem-aventurados ou justos. A idéia do seio de Abraão tem por detrás o pensamento de comunhão e filiação. O homem justo, com toda a razão, era considerado filho de Abraão. Na passagem de João 18:23, vemos que jazer no seio era o lugar dos convivas mais favorecidos. Essa referência, naturalmente, não deve ser entendida literalmente, mas sim, da posição mais próxima ao mestre, no arranjo dos móveis. Na qualidade de hóspede favorecido no céu, ou paraíso, Lázaro descansava no seio de Abraão, pai da família espiritual. Sua alma sobrevivia à morte teológica, e isso sem interrupção alguma da própria consciência. Ver o artigo sobre a «imortalidade».

O seio de Abraão é usado para fazer forte contraste com a outra porção do hades, onde impera o castigo. Na história de Lucas, um grande abismo foi fixado, não podendo haver comunicação entre os lados bom e mau do hades. Isso sugere destinos fixos. Mas a narrativa da descida de Cristo ao hades, em I Pedro 3:18 - 4:6, mostra-nos que a missão de Cristo anulou qualquer estagnação nos destinos, pelo menos até o juízo final, após o milênio. Quanto a notas completas sobre esse conceito, ver o artigo sobre a descida de Cristo ao hades. (B G IB NTI Z) Ver o artigo sobre *O Julgamento*.

ABRAÃO, TESTAMENTO DE

Essa obra é um antigo livro apócrifo judaico, onde há um relato lendário sobre as experiências de Abraão por ocasião da morte, com sua subseqüente ascensão ao céu. Provavelmente foi escrito no século II D.C., por um judeu, ou, talvez, por um judeu cristão. Mais provavelmente ainda, é obra judaica com posteriores interpolações cristãs.

Abraão viveu até idade avançada. Miguel revela-lhe sua morte para breve. Abraão reluta, não querendo entregar seu corpo, pelo que o anjo o arrebata, em uma carruagem. Chegando ao firmamento, Abraão olha para baixo e vê a grande iniqüidade dos homens, e invoca contra eles o juízo. Então Abraão contempla a estrada larga que leva à perdição, e a estrada estreita, que conduz à vida. Ele vê a pesagem das almas, no juízo. Contudo, ainda não quer dar seu espírito; mas a morte o arrebata e o conduz honrosamente ao paraíso.

Essa obra é similar ao Testamento de Jó e ao Apocalipse de Abraão, extraindo subsídios de muitos dos mesmos conceitos da sociedade judaica. Miguel aparece como o anjo supremo que conduz na jornada, como é comum nos escritos judaicos. Há também o anjo da morte, igualmente um elemento comum das obras apócrifas e pseudepígrafas.

Essa obra expõe três julgamentos: 1. Um juízo dirigido por Abel; 2. um juízo das doze tribos de Israel; 3. o juízo divino, no último dia. O Messias não participa de qualquer desses juízos, no Testamento de Abraão. (E J Z) Ver os artigos sobre os livros apócrifos e pseudepígrafos dos judeus.

ABRÃO

No hebraico significa «pai das alturas», ou «pai elevado», o nome original de Abraão (ver Gên. 17:5).

ABRON

Rio mencionado no livro apócrifo de Judite, — o qual alguns identificam com o Habor de II Reis 17:6 e 18:11, ou com o Abdom de Jos. 21:30 e I Crô. 6:74. Porém, a palavra pode ser uma corruptela para a palavra hebraica que significa «além do rio», lida como se fora um nome próprio.

ABSALÃO

No hebraico quer dizer «o pai é da paz», terceiro filho de Davi e seu único filho com Maacá, filha de Talmai, rei de Gesur (II Sam. 3:3), nascido em 1000 A.C. Era admirado por sua beleza sem defeito, distinguido por sua longa e vasta cabeleira. O peso inconveniente da mesma compelia-o a cortá-la a cada ano, orçando em cerca de 2 kg. Os registros a respeito variam. A Septuaginta fala em cerca de 1,1 kg.

A poligamia produziu seus frutos fatais, engendrando o ciúme entre as famílias das várias esposas, cada qual com seu próprio lar (II Sam. 13:8; 14:24). A lassidão sexual fomentou a paixão de Davi, que terminou em adultério e homicídio, além de muitos vexames sofridos. Absalão foi apenas uma dimensão dessa história.

1. *A narrativa de Tamar*. Com Maacá, Davi teve uma filha, Tamar, que se tornou uma bela mulher. Foi estuprada pelo filho mais velho de Davi, Amom (II Sam. 13:1,20), em cerca de 1050 A.C. Absalão, seu irmão, conservou-a reclusa em sua casa e planejou vingar-se. Esperou por dois anos inteiros, e então convidou todos os filhos de Davi para a festa da tosquia das ovelhas, em Baal-Hazor, perto de Efraim. Davi também foi convidado, mas não aceitou o convite, embora os demais convidados tivessem atendido. Houve comidas e bebidas, e os servos de Absalão, segundo orientações prévias, no momento em que menos se esperava, assassinaram Amom. Os restantes fugiram para Jerusalém e contaram o ocorrido a Davi, para sua grande consternação. Então Absalão foi para

ABSALÃO — ABSOLUTO

Gesur e ali, permaneceu por três anos com seu avô, o rei Talmai (Ver II Sam. 13:30-38).

2. *A volta a Jerusalém*. Absalão continuava muito amado por seu pai, e desejava poder voltar. Através da mediação de Joabe, Davi o chamou de volta. Porém, durante mais dois anos, não foi admitido à presença do rei. Finalmente, a reconciliação foi completa (ver II Sam. 14:21-33), em 1036 A.C.

3. *Ambições de Absalão*. Ele começou a traçar planos mais ousados. Amom, o irmão mais velho, estava morto. Restava ainda Quileabe; mas somente Absalão era de nobre nascimento, por meio de sua mãe, filha de um rei. Parece que seu irmão mais velho morreu cedo, pois após II Sam. 3:3 não há mais menção a seu respeito. Portanto, ali estava Absalão, o filho restante mais velho, e o pai ficando cada vez mais idoso. Todavia, se assim quisesse fazê-lo, o rei poderia rejeitar Absalão e escolher um dos filhos mais jovens. Tal direito foi eventualmente exercido por Davi, e Salomão veio a tornar-se rei, embora não fosse ele o herdeiro presuntivo, por questão de idade. O trecho de II Sam. 7:12 havia predito que o rei seria sucedido por um filho que na época da profecia, ainda não havia nascido. Muitos sabiam disso, talvez incluindo o próprio Absalão. Ele agiu astutamente, furtando a lealdade de muitos para a sua causa (ver II Sam. 15:6), insinuando que dispensaria a justiça melhor do que o seu pai estava fazendo (ver II Sam. 15:2-4).

4. *A revolta*. A campanha de Absalão foi ganhando vulto. Quatro anos depois de seu retorno de Gesur a Jerusalém, ele estava preparado para dar seu golpe. Retirou-se para uma antiga capital de Davi, Hebrom, e ali declarou-se rei. Contava com maciço apoio popular, pelo que Davi deixou Jerusalém e foi para Maanaim, do outro lado do Jordão (II Sam. 15:7-18), para proteger-se e para planejar a resistência.

5. *Triunfo de Davi em Jerusalém*. Absalão, ouvindo que Davi abandonara Jerusalém, para ali se dirigiu e apossou-se do poder sem qualquer oposição. Aitofel, ex-conselheiro de Davi, ajudava Absalão. A sabedoria desse homem era tão grande que suas opiniões eram tidas como oráculos, em Jerusalém (ver II Sam. 15:30,31). Isso fortaleceu ainda mais a causa de Absalão. Davi enviou Husai, para tentar fazer virar a maré. Aitofel aconselhou Absalão a perseguir imediatamente a Davi, antes que este tivesse tempo de recuperar-se do golpe recebido (ver II Sam. 17:1,2); mas Husai, procurando ganhar tempo, persuadiu Absalão a não arriscar uma possível derrota, mas a reunir forças de todo Israel tão superiores que garantíssem a vitória. Fatalmente para Absalão, ele ouviu esse conselho. Entrementes, Davi reuniu suas forças. Davi conseguiu reunir uma força poderosa, três divisões comandadas por Joabe, Abisai e Itai (ver II Sam. 18:2).

6. *A batalha*. Joabe era o comandante-em-chefe. Sua tática foi de atrair o adversário para os bosques, para então cercá-lo. Isso foi feito, e os homens de Absalão foram destruídos facilmente, — 20.000 deles, enquanto que os demais fugiram. Isso teve lugar na floresta de Efraim (II Sam. 18:3-6).

7. *Morte de Absalão*. Este montou em uma mula ligeira, mas enquanto fugia, os galhos de uma árvore enroscaram-se em seus longos cabelos e ele ficou suspenso no ar. Davi havia ordenado que não o matassem, mas Joabe apressou-se ao lugar e o transpassou com três dardos. Seu corpo foi arriado e lançado em uma cova, com um montão de pedras por cima (II Sam. 18:7-17) em cerca de 967 A.C.

8. *A tristeza de Davi*. O amor do rei por seu filho

Absalão não se abatera, e a notícia da morte de Absalão causou amarga tristeza a Davi (II Sam. 18:24-33). Seu lamento era: «Meu filho Absalão, meu filho, meu filho Absalão! Quem me dera que eu morrera por ti. Absalão, meu filho, meu filho!» Essas palavras têm sido aproveitadas na composição de um breve mas lindo hino. Davi parece ter sido um pai amoroso, mas fraco, com seus favoritos, o que talvez tivesse sido um fator no desvio de Absalão. (FA S UN Z)

ABSALÃO, O Embaixador

Um embaixador no exército de Jônatas Macabeu, pai de Matatias e de Jônatas (I Mac. 11:9,70; 13:11; II Mac. 11:17). Alguns não identificam como uma só as duas pessoas desse nome, em I e II Macabeus. (Z)

ABSINTO

No hebraico temos essa palavra, e também no grego. A palavra hebraica é usada por oito vezes (ver Deu. 29:18; Pro. 5:4; Jer. 9:15; 23:15; Lam. 3:15,19; Amós 5:7 e 6:12). E a palavra grega, *ápsinthos* de onde se deriva nossa palavra portuguesa, «não-bebí-vel», é usada por duas vezes, em Apo. 8:11. Apesar do sentido da palavra grega, o absinto tornou-se um dos mais populares aperitivos na França, embora de gosto realmente intragável para os iniciantes! Esse aperitivo é feito com base na planta *Artemesia absinthium* que é uma espécie de vegetal perene, tipo herbáceo. Produz pequenas flores amarelas, em grande quanti-dade. A bebida alcoólica é atualmente manufaturada na Jordânia.

É provável que essa bebida fosse conhecida desde os dias do Antigo Testamento, pois Jeremias queixou-se: «Fartou-me de amarguras, saciou-me de absinto» (Lam. 3:15). Por outro lado, por mais de uma vez as Escrituras aludem ao gosto amargo e desagradável do absinto: «...mas o fim dela é amargoso como o absinto...» (Prov. 5:4); e também: «...não haja entre vós raiz que produza erva venenosa e amarga» (Deu. 29:18), onde o original hebraico diz «absinto», e nossa versão portuguesa diz «amarga».

Como se vê, o absinto tornou-se símbolo para descrever os sentimentos negativos de tristeza, calamidade e mesmo crueldade.

Na Palestina há duas outras espécies de vegetais similares, a *Artemesia herba-alba*, que tem um odor de cânfora e é extremamente amarga ao paladar, e a *Artemesia judaica*. Esta última espécie era e continua sendo usada, em alguns lugares, para repelir traças e as larvas de moscas de peças feitas de lã. As plantas, uma vez secas, são colocadas entre as peças de lã.

É interessante observar que a LXX traduz a palavra hebraica em foco de várias maneiras, mas nunca por seu equivalente grego. E também que há espécies da planta que são usadas para a manufatura de anti-helmínticos.

No Novo Testamento e na Septuaginta, palavra grega que indica uma planta de gosto proverbialmen-te amarga, a fim de denotar aflição ou amargura moral (Deu. 29:18; Pro. 4:5; Jer. 9:15). O nome é dado à estrela fatal de Apo. 8:10,11. O nome do gênero vegetal é artemísia, havendo certa variedade da espécie. (S)

ABSOLUTO

Vem do latim, *absolutus*, que significa *perfeito* ou

ABSOLUTOS MORAIS — ABSOLVIÇÃO

completo. O termo é usado em oposição ao que é *relativo*, e com freqüência indica a negação do que é relativo. As idéias contidas no termo são independência, completa e sem qualificações. A palavra é usada em aplicação a Deus, à natureza, à verdade, ao tempo, ao espaço e à virtude. Devido à larga gama de usos, não é possível qualquer definição fácil ou completa, pelo que se segue uma descrição:

Descartes. Ele usava o termo para princípios auto-evidentes, para proposições demonstradas das quais podemos derivar outros conceitos.

Fichte. Ele aplicava o termo ao *ego*, como o poder originador do conhecimento e da realidade.

Nicolau de Cusa. Usava-o para indicar Deus, que para ele era tanto o absoluto máximo quanto o absoluto mínimo. Muitos teólogos passaram então a aplicar o termo a Deus.

Hegel. Falava sobre o Espírito absoluto com suas dimensões de verdade e beleza absolutas, um tipo de Deus panteísta, impessoal, do qual todas as outras coisas se derivam, e para o qual se movem. A realidade é espiritual, mas não no sentido ordinário, antropomórfico e teísta. Outros idealistas alemães compartilhavam desse ponto de vista.

Soloviev. Esse filósofo russo empregou o termo para indicar a totalidade da realidade, que ele considerava uma espécie de organismo vivo.

Bradley. A totalidade das coisas, dentro do que se reconcilia ou harmoniza tudo quanto é contraditório e incoerente no mundo das meras aparências.

Sir Aurobindo. Teólogo e filósofo hindu, que usava a palavra para indicar Bramá, o Deus absoluto.

Spinoza falava da realidade como uma única substância espiritual, *Deus sive Natura*; Deus ou a Natureza, enquanto que o termo «absoluto» era usado para indicar a totalidade das coisas:

Na filosofia e na teologia, o vocábulo é usado para indicar aquilo que é necessário, em contraste com o contingente, aquilo que é independente, em contraste com o que é derivado, aquilo que é eterno, em contraste com o temporal. (C E F P)

ABSOLUTOS MORAIS

A ética pode ser dividida em três categorias bem gerais: 1. A ética absoluta; 2. a ética relativa; e 3. a ética de valores. Na ética *absoluta*, os valores usualmente são concebidos como externos ao homem, impostos ao homem por uma força superior ou pessoa, como Deus. O homem não é o criador da ética, mas está sob uma lei ética instituída por poderes externos e superiores a ele. A maioria dos sistemas religiosos assume essa posição. Os valores morais são absolutos, isto é, fixos, eternos e perfeitos. O homem aprende no que consistem esses valores, e procura segui-los. Não é ele o inventor dos valores.

Na *ética relativa*, o homem é o criador dos valores. Isso ele faria através da experiência humana. Visto que as experiências variam, variam também os valores, pelo que nenhum valor poderia ser considerado fixo, perfeito ou eterno. Ademais, meus valores não são necessariamente aceitáveis para outrem, e vice-versa.

Na *ética de valores*, os valores morais são considerados *constantes*, mas não fixos. Esse é um conceito intermediário entre os outros dois. Não podemos alterar os valores de um dia para o outro, e nem de uma pessoa para outra, embora os valores realmente se alterem após longos períodos de tempo, pelo menos no caso de muitos deles. Em conseqüên-

cia, o homem deriva valores do meio externo e do seu interior. Valores lhe são impostos, mas ele também cria valores.

No cristianismo, Deus é o criador e sustentador dos valores morais, pelo que são sempre obrigatórios, sem importar situações ou pessoas. Os valores são revelados ou são conhecidos pela razão, e não produzidos através das experiências e vicissitudes dos homens. Os livros sagrados são originadores do conhecimento dos juízos morais. Deus tem falado por meio dos profetas. Os profetas registraram seus discernimentos. Os livros sagrados se desenvolveram em torno dos escritos dos profetas. As organizações eclesiásticas existem a fim de proteger a revelação. Conseqüentemente, podemos dizer que a ética é um ramo da revelação. As ciências sociais não aceitam sem protesto esse arranjo, e pregam uma ética dependente das situações.

Argumentos contra a ética absoluta:

1. O sistema inteiro depende da validade da revelação, ou da exatidão inerente à razão. Ambas as coisas são largamente questionadas.

2. Os homens regularmente criam Deus à sua própria imagem, razão pela qual os supostos valores divinos variam de culutra para cultura.

3. É impossível que uma mente finita fale em termos de absolutos, que se tornam inalcançáveis quanto mais são rebuscados.

4. Finalmente, há um conflito de absolutos, ao passarmos de um sistema para outro, ou mesmo dentro de um único sistema, quando se trata de determinar quais supostos absolutos se aplicam a todos os homens. Nossas escolhas morais nem sempre são feitas entre o bem e o mal. Algumas vezes, são feitas entre o mal e o pior, como quando um jovem é convocado para ir à guerra e matar. Deve ele ir, ou não? Ou deve abortar uma mulher que engravidou por ato de estupro?

Respostas a esses argumentos:

1. Os absolutos existem, mas nem sempre são perfeitamente conhecidos por nós. Nossa busca é pela luz, para conhecermos e agirmos melhor.

2. Os conflitos culturais apenas mostram que uma cultura qualquer tem um entendimento imperfeito acerca da vontade de Deus, e não que Deus não tenha uma vontade absoluta.

3. Onde houver conflito - um jovem deve ir à guerra? - essa é uma questão altamente pessoal, que não pode ser respondida por alguma declaração simplista. Novamente, faz-se necessária a iluminação. O mesmo sucede no caso da mulher que é estuprada e engravida, quando então vem à tona a questão do aborto.

4. A existência de valores absolutos não envolve o perfeito conhecimento desses valores. Se assim fosse, não haveria inquirição moral. Mas, se os princípios morais são fixos e certos, então pelo menos dispomos de diretrizes dignas de confiança acerca de muitas questões, e podemos escapar do subjetivismo profundo que assinala a ética relativa.

ABSOLVIÇÃO

Vem do latim **absolvo**, «libero». Na teologia, o termo denota a remissão de pecados mediante o ato remidor de Jesus Cristo. Na teologia católica-romana, envolve o ensino que deu autoridade aos apóstolos e seus sucessores para perdoar pecados, através do sacramento da penitência. A palavra é usada para indicar o perdão real de pecados, efetuado por esse sacramento. O trecho de João 20:23 é usado como

ABSTINÊNCIA — ABUNDÂNCIA

texto de prova bíblica dessa doutrina. Esse versículo é altamente controvertido, e recomendo que o leitor examine minha exposição da questão no NTI, naquela referência. Os trechos de Mat. 16:19 e 18:18, que descrevem o uso das *chaves*, são outros textos do N.T., usados em apoio àquela doutrina. Esses versículos são abundantemente iluminados no NTI, *in loc*.

Os intérpretes protestantes naturalmente contradizem frontalmente a idéia de que esses versículos possam ser interpretados corretamente desse modo, dando o direito de perdoar a Deus e ao Filho de Deus, com exclusividade, e aludindo aos apóstolos e a outros ministros apenas como veículos da mensagem, e não como quem foi autorizado a perdoar diretamente.

Descobrimos na história que o rito da absolvição foi sujeitado a um amplo desenvolvimento, integrando-se no sistema sacramental na época do escolasticismo. Tomás de Aquino (1227-1274) evidentemente foi o primeiro a defender formalmente o tipo de absolvição que se tornou comum na Igreja Católica Romana atual, e que envolve a confissão auricular e a declaração formal de absolvição, por meio das penitências e do ofício mediatório do padre. Como é óbvio, em sua substância, o rito já existia muito antes da defesa formal feita por Tomás de Aquino.

O termo tem continuado a ser usado em algumas comunidades protestantes, embora aplicado à declaração que Deus perdoa gratuitamente o pecado de quem se arrepende, mas por meio de Cristo, de Sua missão e ofício, sem o concurso de qualquer mediador humano. Porém, encoraja-se ali a confissão de pecados, mas «uns aos outros», devido aos seus favoráveis efeitos psicológicos.

Como em todas as controvérsias, é pecado mais grave exibir hostilidade para com outrem do que errar no tocante a dogmas. Além disso, o debate é bom, se não for efetuado em meio ao ódio. O amor é a prova da espiritualidade do indivíduo, e deveria manifestar-se em todos os casos de controvérsia. (B E H P)

ABSTINÊNCIA

Ver também **proibição e temperança**. A abstinência é a renúncia voluntária de certos alimentos, bebidas alcoólicas, prazeres carnais, atos egoístas, e atos duvidosos que podem ofender ao próximo.

Israel. Essa nação cultivava a abstinência, cujas leis incluíam várias proibições acerca de alimentos. Ver Levítico 11-15. Com o desenvolvimento do judaísmo, a lista chegou a aproximar-se do ascetismo. Certos grupos, como os essênios, adicionaram mais itens, tornando-se francamente ascéticos.

A vida de Jesus foi um testemunho contra o ascetismo, pois Ele não se retirou do mundo e da vida social, aceitou a hospitalidade oferecida por pecadores e transformou a água em vinho (João 2). E os Seus inimigos chamaram-nO de beberrão e glutão (Mat. 11:19).

O Novo Testamento. Os crentes abstêm-se das concupiscências carnais (I Ped. 2:11), da impureza e imoralidade— (Col. 3:5), da cobiça (Col. 3:5). Para agradar os judeus, mas não com base em algum princípio moral absoluto, os primitivos cristãos se abstinham de animais sufocados, bem como da carne com sangue (Atos 15:2-29). Os princípios morais requerem a abstinência de bebidas alcoólicas (Gál. 5:21), bem como de todas as formas conhecidas de mal (Sal. 119:101). Esse princípio envolve ações duvidosas que possam ofender ao próximo, ainda que não sejam ofensivas à própria pessoa (I Cor. 7:5). O

jejum é um bom exercício espiritual, se não for levado ao exagero (Mat. 6:16-18).

O *ascetismo* é condenado (Col. 2:20-23; I Tim. 4:1-3), conforme essas referências o demonstram. O ascetismo, e não apenas o vício, pode originar-se da influência demoníaca. Ver completas explicações sobre esses versículos, no NTI. (H NTI S)

ABSTRAÇÃO

Vem do latim **abstractus**, particípio passado de *abstrahere*, «extrair».

1. Em Aristóteles e Tomás de Aquino, esse é o processo por meio do qual as idéias universais podem ser apropriadas pela mente. Tal processo é possível por causa da natureza *hilomórfica* da substância, isto é, a substância compõe-se de matéria e forma. A mente detecta informes sensoriais, extraindo daí a forma, contanto que ela seja universal.

2. Para Locke, a abstração é o ato de extrair aquilo que é *comum* a um grupo de coisas individuais, mediante comparação de similaridades e diferenças. Todas as classificações devem envolver o processo da abstração, a fim de se chegar ao que é comum. Isso envolve a «eliminação» de elementos não-comuns. Se abstrairmos a cor amarela em um grupo de objetos que tenham essa cor, teremos de deixar de lado outras considerações, a fim de chegarmos a um fator comum.

3. Na lógica e na matemática contemporâneas, a abstração é o nome dado àquela operação sobre uma variável, que produz uma função. (F P)

ABUBO

Pai de Ptolomeu, governador militar de Jericó, que assassinou seu sogro, Simão, o hasmoneano, e seus dois filhos, em Jericó (I Mac. 16:15), em 135 A.C. (Z)

ABU HANIFA

Faleceu em 767. Foi islamita persa, fundador de uma das quatro escolas ortodoxas de jurisprudência; seus seguidores supunham-no intérprete infalível do Alcorão e do Suna (ver os artigos a respeito). Era considerado homem dotado de juízo supremo, que dependia mais do juízo pessoal independente do que das tradições, em casos não tratados pela lei e pelo Alcorão. A fim de garantir a justiça, quando necessário, ele rejeitava até mesmo as claras indicações do Alcorão. (E)

ABUNDÂNCIA

Em Gên. 49:26, «bênçãos»; em I Reis 10:13 e Est. 1:7, «generosidade»; em Sal. 116:12, «benefícios». O salmista louvou a Deus pela generosidade do Senhor, pela abundância das coisas que Ele dá, material e espiritualmente falando (ver Sal. 13:6; 65:11; 116:7,12). A generosidade divina inspira-nos confiança (ver Sal. 142:7), e o salmista orou a respeito disso (ver Sal. 119:17). Lemos em Gên. 49:26: «As bênçãos de teu pai excederão as bênçãos de meus pais até o cimo dos montes eternos...» Aos crentes, Deus dará uma abundância maior e eterna.

O Novo Testamento ensina que, no campo espiritual, aqueles que semearem com abundância colherão com abundância (ver II Cor. 9:6). Mas também há a promessa de um abundante suprimento de bens materiais, a fim de podermos labutar espiritualmente, sem o empecilho da pobreza e suas restrições (ver II Cor. 9:8). Oxalá seja essa a nossa

ABUNDÂNCIA, GENEROSIDADE — ACABE

sorte! A abundância é prova do amor que Deus nos tem. E quando compartilhamos de nossa abundância com outras pessoas, estamos apenas cumprindo a lei do amor, prova da espiritualidade (ver I João 4:7).

ABUNDÂNCIA, GENEROSIDADE

A palavra hebraica que mais corresponde à idéia por detrás dessas palavras portuguesas é *shoa*, «magnânimo», que figura somente em Isa. 32:5 e Jó 34:19. Palavras afins são *chesed*, «generosidade» e *tob* ou *tub*, «bondade». *Chesed* figura por noventa e quatro vezes (por exemplo: Êxo. 34:6; Sal. 33:5). *Tob* figura por mais de quinhentas e sessenta vezes (por exemplo: Êxo. 18:9; Sal. 16:2; Jer. 2:7; 33:9; Zac. 9:17, etc.).

Conceitos Básicos. 1. Generosidade, sobretudo da parte de Deus, porquanto toda a abundância começa com o Senhor (Sal. 13:6; 65:11; 116:7,12; 142:7).

2. Os homens deveriam orar para que a abundância divina lhes seja conferida (Sal. 119:17).

3. A abundância de bênçãos é prometida àqueles que se mostram generosos com os pobres (Pro. 22:9).

4. A bênção divina é eterna e abundante, conforme se vê na vida de José, dentro da bênção proferida por Jacó: «As bênçãos de teu pai excederão às bênçãos de meus pais até o cimo dos montes eternos; estejam elas sobre a cabeça de José, e sobre o alto da cabeça do que foi distinguido entre seus irmãos» (Gên. 49:26).

5. O rei Salomão, o mais rico de todos os monarcas hebreus, deixou a rainha de Sabá admirada com sua generosidade e abundância (I Reis 10:13), e ele obteve suas riquezas buscando, em primeiro lugar, a sabedoria, para que o primeiro lugar fosse dado às coisas mais importantes. Com isso concorda o princípio exarado em Mat. 6:33: «...buscai, pois, em primeiro lugar, o seu reino e a sua justiça, e todas estas cousas vos serão acrescentadas».

6. Paulo levantou uma abundante oferta para os pobres de Jerusalém, enviada pelas igrejas gentílicas, como sinal de fraternidade e comunicação com suas necessidades (II Cor. 9:11).

7. A generosidade é um princípio geral espiritual de que aqueles que semeiam pouco também colhem pouco, e que aqueles que semeiam abundantemente também colhem com abundância (II Cor. 9:6), e isso aplica-se tanto às questões financeiras como a tudo em que pomos a mão. (HA ID NTI Z)

ABUTRE

Essa ave aparece em quinto lugar entre as aves declaradas imundas (ver Deu. 14:13). No entanto, algumas traduções (como nossa versão portuguesa), preferem traduzir o termo hebraico envolvido por «falcão». O pássaro em questão é dotado de grandes asas, capaz de voar bem alto, sendo espécie tanto residente na Palestina como migratória. O falcão é ave com boa variedade de cores, desde escuras até pálidas, passando pela cor de mel. Qualquer ave de rapina, mui naturalmente, era proibida pela lei mosaica como alimento humano. As aves de rapina são transmissoras de enfermidades, devido a seus hábitos alimentares. (ID Z)

ACÃ

No hebraico, «perturbador» (Jos. 7:1). Era filho de Carmi, da tribo de Judá. Recebe o nome de Acar, em I Crô. 2:7, onde é apodado de «o perturbador de Israel».

1. *O pecado de Acã*. Por causa de um único ato impensado, ele obteve uma lamentável notoriedade. Jericó e tudo quanto nela estava, excetuando Raabe e seus familiares, foram destinados à total destruição. Tudo teve de ser queimado, e todo o metal foi dedicado a Deus (ver Deu. 7:16,23-26 e Jos. 6:17-19). Após a queda de Jericó (em cerca de 1400 A.C.), essa maldição foi rigidamente cumprida, excetuando o ato de Acã. Ele preservou para si mesmo uma boa capa babilônica, duzentos siclos de prata e uma barra de ouro do peso de cinqüenta siclos. (Ver Jos. 7:21).

2. *Castigo contra o pecado*. Ai havia sido visitada por espias que disseram que esta poderia ser facilmente conquistada. Mas três mil homens não foram capazes do feito. Josué indagou do Senhor a razão da derrota, e foi-lhe revelado que alguém havia pecado. Foram lançadas sortes para descobrir o ofensor, e Acã foi detectado. Os intérpretes sentem dificuldades em explicar o uso de um aparente jogo de azar, pelo qual Acã foi descoberto. Mas outros têm afirmado que não houve envolvimento de qualquer *chance*, pois o Senhor estava interessado pela questão. Ainda outros salientam o baixo nível de espiritualidade requerido por tal, embora, observem que o primeiro capítulo de Atos também envolve esquema idêntico, se é que isso nos ajuda em alguma coisa. Ver o artigo sobre a *adivinhação*. Seja como for, Acã, seus familiares e suas possessões foram levados ao vale de Acor (tribulação), onde as pessoas foram apedrejadas e queimadas (ver Jos. 7:25). Dessa circunstância surge o outro problema principal, a saber, se tal castigo foi próprio. Alguns intérpretes supõem que a família de Acã tinha consciência de seu pecado e o promoveu, pelo que mereceram o que receberam. Outros apenas frisam que se tratava de uma era brutal, e que aqueles que queimaram e destruíram tudo em Jericó, não hesitaram em matar alguns parentes de Acã, mesmo que eles, como indivíduos, talvez fossem inocentes. Outros afirmam que, de modo geral, a iniqüidade de Canaã estava agora tão cheia que o juízo lhes sobreveio de modo *geral* (ver Gên. 15:16). Ainda outros pensam que é ridículo tentar justificar cada ato de violência, só porque está narrado na Bíblia, lançando a culpa sobre Deus. É inútil apontar para Deu. 24:16, que proíbe que os filhos sejam mortos por causa dos pecados de seus pais, porquanto isso seria considerado um caso de «culpa por convivência», um justo castigo contra o próprio Acã. De qualquer modo, a vida humana era e continua sendo barata. Intérpretes como Orígenes, que encontrava problemas morais com narrativas assim, simplesmente as alegorizava para descobrir sentidos espirituais; e não reputava instrutivo o evento literal, e nem característico das coisas boas que Deus faz. Ver o artigo sobre *Interpretação Alegórica*. (S UN Z)

ACÃ

No hebraico, **torcido**. Um dos filhos de Eser, filho de Seir, descendente de Esaú (ver Gên. 36:27). Em I Crô. 1:42 ele é chamado Jaacã. (S Z)

ACABE

No hebraico, **irmão do pai**. 1. Filho de Onri e sexto rei de Israel. Reinou por vinte e um anos, entre 918 e 897 A.C., aproximadamente. Foi um dos reis mais fracos e corruptos de Israel. Parece ter tido bons sentimentos e disposições, mas facilmente desviava-se para o mal. Sua história aparece principalmente em I Reis 16 - 22. A narrativa mostra que a debilidade, por

ACABE — ACÁCIA

parte de alguma alta autoridade, pode produzir tanto o mal quanto a impiedade direta. Foi influenciado por sua associação com os fenícios, e vários erros por ele cometidos podem ser atribuídos a esse fato.

a. *Influência fenícia.* Havia laços comerciais, provenientes do tempo de Davi e Salomão. Tais associações, após a divisão de Israel em dois reinos, tiveram fim em Judá, mas permaneceram fortes no norte, em Israel.

b. Jezabel, sua esposa, era filha de Etbal, rei de Tiro. Era mulher enérgica, mas ímpia e pagã, e conseguiu dominar completamente a Acabe. Por meio da influência dela, pois, foi estabelecido o culto aos deuses fenícios, sobretudo o deus-sol, Baal, no reino do norte.

c. Antes disso houvera incidências de idolatria em Israel, mas agora caíram por terra todas as restrições. O rei erigiu um templo em Samaria, levantou uma imagem e consagrou um trecho arborizado a Baal. Muitos sacerdotes de Baal eram mantidos, ao ponto da idolatria tornar-se a religião predominante em Israel. Tão poderoso foi o movimento que parecia que a antiga fé dos judeus se perderia para sempre.

d. *Elias* (ver o artigo) era o homem certo para enfrentar a emergência. Ele se opôs vigorosamente à idolatria e à autoridade real que lhe dava o apoio. Foi autor de predições e milagres que visavam a fazer o povo voltar-se de novo para o Senhor.

e. *O caso de Nabote.* Perto do palácio de Acabe, em Jezreel, havia um cidadão chamado Nabote, cuja vinha Acabe desejava. Acabe tentou convencer Nabote a vendê-la, mas este recusou-se devido a direitos de herança de sua família (por lei divina). Jezabel tomou a questão nas mãos, quando viu o desapontamento de Acabe, pressionando os anciãos da cidade e subornando falsas testemunhas contra Nabote. Foi assassinado por alegadas blasfêmia e traição. Acabe tomou posse da vinha, mas, em sua volta para casa, Elias saiu ao encontro dele e predisse que cães lamberiam o seu sangue no lugar onde havia sido lambido o sangue de Nabote; que Jezabel seria comida por cães, perto das muralhas de Jezreel, e que o resto da família teria seus cadáveres devorados pelos cães da cidade, ou pelas feras e aves. Acabe ficou aterrorizado e arrependeu-se, e a execução plena da profecia foi adiada até depois de sua morte, no reinado de Jeorão, seu filho (ver I Reis 21).

f. *Morte de Acabe.* Ele morreu de ferimentos recebidos em batalha contra os sírios, algo que fora predito por Micaías, embora o rei não tivesse crido na predição. Militarmente, ele fora bem-sucedido, mantendo seu governo e autoridade, o que é indicado pela Pedra Moabita, linhas sétima e oitava, onde somos informados que Onri e seu filho, Acabe, governaram a terra de Medeba (conquistada por Onri), durante quarenta anos. Porém, quando Acabe envolveu-se em guerra contra os sírios, Moabe se rebelou.

g. *Cumprimento da profecia de Elias.* Acabe foi morto por um homem que atirou sua flecha ao acaso. Conseguiu manter-se de pé em seu carro de guerra, e morreu à tardinha, e seu exército dispersou-se. (Ver I Reis 22). Ao ser trazido para ser sepultado em Samaria, os cães lamberam o seu sangue, enquanto um servo lavava o seu carro de guerra.

h. *Acabe e a arqueologia.* O nome dele aparece com preeminência nos monumentos assírios do grande conquistador Salmaneser III (859-824 A.C.). A inscrição Monolítica, atualmente no Museu Britânico, narra o choque entre o exército assírio, em 853 A.C. com uma colisão de reis sírios em Carcar, ao

norte de Hamate, uma fortaleza que guardava os acessos para toda a baixa Síria. Essa inscrição mostra que Acabe conseguiu sustar com sucesso o avanço assírio. Acabe lançou dois mil homens nessa batalha, mais que qualquer outro. Ultrapassado somente pelo estado damasceno, ele mostrou ser a força militar mais poderosa na Síria central e inferior, nos meados do século IX A.C.

i. O aspecto mais triste da história de Acabe é o seu fracasso espiritual, tendo-se oposto abertamente a Elias, por influência de sua esposa. O pecado dele afetou negativamente gerações sucessivas, o que foi condenado por Osé. 1:4 e Miq. 6:16.

j. Surpreendentemente, nosso Senhor descendia de Acabe e Jezabel! Ver Mat. 1:8,9. O Uzias ali mencionado é o mesmo Uzias ou Amazias, filho de Joás, neto de Atália e bisneto de Acabe e Jezabel.

2. *Acabe, filho de Colias.* Esse homem foi um falso profeta, autonomeado, que falava em nome de Deus entre os exilados na Babilônia, pouco depois que Jeconias (Jeoiachim) foi levado para o exílio, no fim do reinado de Judá (598/597 A.C.), cerca de onze anos mais tarde. Ele é mencionado em Jer. 29:21-23. Ele e um certo Zedequias foram culpados de grosseira imoralidade. Foi predito que ele seria morto na presença daquele a quem enganara, e que, no futuro, tornar-se-ia um dito popular: «...o Senhor te faça como a Zedequias e como a Acabe, os quais o rei de Babilônia assou no fogo» (Jer. 29:21,22). Tal dito popular tornou-se uma maldição comum. O código de Hamurabi, um antigo monarca babilônio, prescrevia a pena de morte contra o adultério. Portanto, isso foi parte do julgamento decretado contra Acabe. Acabe e Zedequias são identificados como os dois anciãos malignos da narrativa apócrifa de Susana. (ND S UN Z)

ACÁCIA

No hebraico temos uma palavra cujas letras transliteradas para as letras latinas dariam *sitâ*. Da árvore desse nome é que se tirava a madeira de acácia, mencionada por vinte e seis vezes no Antigo Testamento, principalmente no livro de Êxodo. Entretanto, o trecho de Isaías 41:19 menciona a árvore propriamente dita. A forma plural da palavra hebraica daria algo como *sitim*. Foi o nome de uma localidade com esse nome que Josué enviou os espias, pois sem dúvida ali havia uma floresta de acácias (ver Jos. 2:1).

Há duas espécies dessa árvore, a *Acacia seyal* e a *Acacia tortilis*. São as únicas árvores que se desenvolvem bem nas regiões áridas. A *tortilis* é maior e também mais comum do que a outra. Sua madeira de cor marrom tem grão fino, sendo muito usada no fabrico de móveis. Essa madeira foi própria para a fabricação da arca da aliança, do altar e das mesas do tabernáculo. Os egípcios, que foram os primeiros a chamar a espécie de tal nome, usavam a sua madeira no fabrico de navios, móveis e imagens de escultura, pois, apesar de leve, tal madeira é dura e incorruptível. A abundância da espécie no vale do Jordão explica topônimos como Sitim (Jos. 2:1; 3:1, etc.), Bete-Sita (Juí. 7:22) e Abel-Sitim (Núm. 33:49).

Outras Variedades

Um arbusto do qual há certa variedade de espécies. 1. A *acácia nilótica*, que pode ser vista em abundância ao redor do mar Vermelho, onde é chamada de espinheiro. É referida no livro de Êxodo como *sarça*. 2. Nos trechos de Êxo. 25:5,10; 13:23; 26:15; 16:26; Deu. 10:3; Jos. 2:1; 3:1,18; Isa. 41:19 e Miq. 6:5, temos a *acácia torilis*, chamada *sitim*. Trata-se de

ACÁCIO DE CESARÉIA — ACAIA

uma madeira dura, de cor amarronzada, usada para o fabrico de móveis até os tempos modernos. Nos tempos antigos, tal como hoje, a planta era abundante. 3. A *acácia arábica*, que talvez seja a espécie referida em Êxodo 3, e que produz a goma-arábica. Essa árvore não era nativa no norte da Palestina, e nem é especificamente mencionada na Bíblia. 4. A *acácia catechu*, de onde talvez fosse extraída a *hena*, referida em Cantares de Salomão 1:14 e 4:13. Era misturada à cânfora, formando uma pasta. (ID UN Z)

ACÁCIO DE CESARÉIA

Faleceu em cerca de 366. Foi discípulo, sucessor e biógrafo (340) de Eusébio de Nicomédio, que também (como ele) foi líder do partido ariano. Ver sobre Ário e o arianismo. Foi amargo opositor de Cirilo de Jerusalém. (E)

ACADE

No hebraico significa **fortaleza**, antiquíssimo centro do poder imperial camita, fundado por Ninrode (Gên. 10:10). Essa cidade deve ser identificada com Agrade, que Sargão I trouxe à fama como capital de seu império semita, e que dominou o mundo mesopotâmico em cerca de 2360 - 2180 A.C. Ficava à beira do rio Eufrates, a pouca distância da moderna Bagdá. A *região* derivou o nome de sua capital, incluindo a planície aluvial sem pedras do sul da Babilônia e do norte da Suméria. A expressão «terra de Sinear», onde se desenvolveu o primeiro poder imperial do mundo, incluía as cidades de Babel, Ereque (Uruque), Acade e Calné. Os habitantes originais da região provavelmente foram sumerianos não-semitas, mas de origem camita (ver Gên. 10:8-10), inventores da escrita cuneiforme, precursores culturais dos posteriores conquistadores semitas da Babilônia. Esse império perdurou por dois séculos, considerado pelos babilônios como um império ideal, representante de uma espécie de idade áurea. O termo Acade veio a ser aplicado a todo o norte da Babilônia, a fim de contrastar com a Suméria, o sul da Babilônia. *Acadiano* é atualmente usado como termo para referir-se à mais antiga língua escrita, utilizada durante o reinado de Sargão de Acade, chamado «acadiano antigo». Essa palavra também designa os idiomas semíticos assírio e babilônio. (ND S UN Z)

ACADEMIA DE PLATÃO

Está em pauta a escola ou universidade de grande duração, fundada por Platão, em Atenas (385 A.C. até 529 D.C.). Recebeu o nome de «academia» devido ao lugar onde estava localizada, um lugar público dedicado ao herói grego Academus. Especializava-se essa escola na matemática, na música, na astronomia, na dialética, e, naturalmente, nos vários ramos da filosofia.

Divisões Históricas:

1. A primeira academia, que refletia influências pitagoreanas e sua preocupação com os números. As principais figuras desse período foram Speusipo, Xenócrates, Hérclides do Ponto, Pólemon, Crates, Crantor e Platão. A epistemologia era um dos grandes interesses da academia.

2. A segunda academia deu continuação a ênfase sobre a epistemologia, mas, já sem contar com Platão, a escola voltou-se para um ceticismo moderado, que não teria agradado ao fundador. Arcésilas (ver o

artigo a seu respeito) foi a grande figura desse período.

3. A terceira academia, ainda de tendências céticas mais fortes, desenvolveu interesse pela teoria das probabilidades. As principais figuras desse período foram Carnéades e Clitômaco (ver os artigos a respeito deles).

4. A quarta academia caracterizava-se pelos interesses ecléticos e pelo neoplatonismo. Seus principais membros foram Filo de Larissa, Antico de Ascalom, Gaio, Eudoro de Alexandria, Plutarco de Alexandria, Teom de Esmirna, Albino, Nicóstrato, Ático, Celso, Máximo de Tiro e Severo. Ver artigos separados sobre cada uma dessas personagens. (EP P)

ACADEMIA FLORENTINA

Foi uma tentativa feita em Florença, na Itália, no século XV, para produzir um centro de erudição para a renascença, no espírito da academia de Platão. As igrejas grega e latina trouxeram a Florença o neoplatonista Gemistos Pleton (ver o artigo a respeito), o qual fez conferências acerca de Platão e dos místicos de Alexandria. A sociedade florentina correspondeu com entusiasmo e a idéia se desenvolveu, resultando em uma espécie de reavivamento da academia de Platão. Marsílio Ficino (ver o artigo a respeito) era o nome que encabeçava a lista de interessados, além de vários membros da família dos Médicis e outros mestres famosos, como Ângelo Poliziano, Cristóforo Lantino, e outros, que foram convidados a participar. Obras gregas e alexandrinas foram traduzidas e explicadas. Mediante tais atividades, o neoplatonismo recebeu um novo impulso, tendo exercido poderosa influência sobre a literatura européia do século XVI. (AM P)

AÇAFRÃO

O termo aparece somente em Cantares 4:14, como uma das especiarias ali exaltadas. Talvez fosse o crocus da Índia, de cuja planta se fabricava um pó aromático, usado para dar certo gosto aos alimentos. Esse pó era extraído do Crocus sativus. Eram necessárias mais de quatro mil flores da planta para produzir cerca de um quarto de quilo desse pó.

As flores eram colhidas quando elas começavam a abrir-se, e então os pistilos das mesmas eram cuidadosamente removidos. Então os mesmos eram ressecados em um forno portátil, a fim de que se evaporasse a umidade.

Nos países de clima quente, os estigmas podiam ser ressecados ao sol. E o pó daí resultante era usado para dar sabor a bolos, assados e molhos. Era planta nativa da Palestina, pelo que era conhecida por Salomão, que escreveu o único livro da Bíblia onde ela é mencionada. (ID Z)

ACAIA

Uma região da Grécia que, no sentido restrito, ocupava a porção noroeste do Peloponeso, incluindo Corinto e seu istmo (Estrabão, viii. págs. 438 ss). O uso poético permitia que o termo designasse a Grécia inteira, de tal modo que os acaianos eram os gregos. Sob os romanos, a Grécia foi dividida em duas províncias, Macedonia e Acaia. A primeira incluía a Macedônia propriamente dita e o Ilírico, o Épiro e a Tessália; e a segunda toda a porção ao sul da mesma. É nesse sentido que o termo é empregado no Novo Testamento (Atos 17:12-16; 19:21; Rom. 15:26; I Cor. 16:15; II Cor. 1:1; 9:2; 11:10; I Tess. 1:7,8). A

ACAMPAMENTO — ACAZ

princípio, a Acaia foi uma província senatorial, governada por procônsules (Dion, Cass. liii. par. 704). Tibério transformou ambas essas regiões em províncias imperiais, sob procuradores (Tácito, *Annal*. 1:76). Mas Cláudio restaurou-as ao senado bem como à forma proconsular de governo. (Suet. *Claud*. 25). Nisso se vê a exata e minuciosa propriedade com que Lucas se expressou, ao dar a Gálio o título de procônsul, o qual foi nomeado para governar a província no tempo de Cláudio. Ver Atos 18:12. (ID ND S)

Era natural da Acaia e se tornou discípulo de Paulo. Juntamente com Estéfanas e Fortunato, Acaico foi portador da primeira epístola aos Coríntios, onde é elogiado por Paulo diante dos coríntios, como merecedor de seu respeito especial (ver I Cor. 16:7). Eles haviam servido bem a Paulo, e agora o apóstolo pedia que lhes fosse dado esse tratamento pelos coríntios. (S Z)

ACAMPAMENTO

Ver o artigo sobre **Exército**. 1. O livro de Números descreve os acampamentos dos israelitas, durante o êxodo. O povo se punha em ordem ao redor do tabernáculo, em seus quatro lados (ver Núm. 2:2). O tabernáculo, pois, ficava cercado pelas doze tribos, que formavam os lados externos de um retângulo. No oriente ficavam Judá, Issacar e Zebulom. Ao sul ficavam Rúben, Simeão e Gade. Ao norte ficavam Dã, Aser e Naftali. No ocidente ficavam Efraim, Manassés e Benjamim. Dentro dessa formação, e ao redor do tabernáculo, ficavam os levitas e os transportadores de bagagens, bem como os currais de animais domésticos. 2. *Uso militar*. Não era seguida pelos militares qualquer formação única. Proteções naturais como colinas, vales e rios podiam ser utilizados como proteções, determinando a formação. Linhas de defesa eram estabelecidas (ver I Sam. 17:20; 26:5). Sentinelas eram estacionados (ver Juí. 7:19). Quando arrebentava alguma batalha, alguns ficavam para trás, para guardar o acampamento. 3. *No Novo Testamento*. Os romanos tinham barracas e quartéis (ver Atos 21:34,37; 22:24; 23:10,16,32). Arraiais específicos eram usados (ver Heb. 11:34. Ver também Heb. 13:11,13 e Apo. 20:9). 4. Espiritualmente falando, há um acampamento espiritual dos soldados espirituais, os quais acampam em um território hostil, e cuja segurança e sucesso depende da estrita obediência ao comandante-em-chefe.

Essa expressão refere-se ao acampamento que Israel tinha na noite antes da destruição do exército egípcio no mar Vermelho, localizado entre Migdol e o mar, de acordo com Êxo. 14:2. Isso sucedeu na vizinhança de Baal-Zefom e Pi-Hairote, ambas as localidades são descritas em artigos separados nesta obra. A localização exata depende da interpretação sobre a rota exata do *êxodo* (ver o artigo a respeito). Se os hebreus seguiram uma rota para o norte, o acampamento então ficava às margens do lago Sirbonis; se seguiram uma rota para o sul, então ficava às margens do atual mar Vermelho; e se seguiram uma rota central, então o acampamento ficava entre esse lago e o mar Vermelho.

ACAR

Variante do nome **Acã**, que lhe é dada em I Crônicas 2:7.

ACAZ

No hebraico significa **possuidor**. É forma abreviada

de Jeoacaz, *possuído por Yahweh*. Trata-se do mesmo Acazias, com mera transposição de letras. Sua história aparece em II Reis 16:1-20 e II Crô. 27:9. Ele envolveu-se em desastrosas aventuras religiosas, militares e diplomáticas. Foi o décimo terceiro monarca judeu da linhagem de Davi. Reinou por dezesseis anos (735-719 A.C.).

1. *Família*. Casou-se com Abia, filha de Zacarias, a qual foi mãe de Ezequias, um dos melhores reis de Judá. Seu avô e seu bisavô também foram monarcas dignos.

2. *Reinado*. Acaz tornou-se rei aos vinte anos de idade. Há um problema acerca das datas de seu reinado. Em II Crô. 28:1 e II Reis 16:2, aparentemente ele faleceu com trinta e seis anos. Mas, em II Crô. 29:1, seu filho Ezequias subiu ao trono com vinte e seis anos, quando da morte de Acaz, fazendo com que Acaz tivesse apenas onze anos quando do nascimento de seu filho, Ezequias. Na Septuaginta, a idade de Acaz seria de vinte anos em II Reis 16:2; mas, em II Crô. 29:1, sua idade aparece como vinte e cinco anos. Os manuscritos variam e confundem mais ainda o quadro. É verdade que, nos países orientais, casavam-se adolescentes ainda bem jovens, e geravam filhos. Porém, parece mais provável que alguma corrupção textual tenha entrado na história, e não que Acaz tornara-se pai aos onze anos de idade.

3. *Idolatria*. Acaz entregou-se à mais abominável idolatria. Um de seus filhos foi sacrificado ao ídolo Moloque. Ele mesmo ordenou ativamente sacrifícios e observâncias pagãs em lugares altos, colinas e bosques. Sacrificava aos ídolos da Síria, que ele supunha serem a causa de suas calamidades. Quebrou os vasos sagrados do templo e erigiu ídolos em toda a terra. Foi um dos mais corruptos reis da história de Judá, acerca de ritos pagãos, ao mesmo tempo em que desrespeitava o antigo culto de Israel. Finalmente, fechou o templo de Jerusalém.

4. *Guerras*. Como de costume, houve então muitas guerras. No mundo temos a história do homem, o selvagem, o caçador implacável, o destruidor. Os comentadores procuram desculpar muito dessa selvageria, diminuindo o efeito dos atos bárbaros, ou mesmo lançando toda a culpa sobre Deus, como se Ele fosse o grande Chefe da horta de assassinos. Mas, a mente espiritual sente-se repelida ante a idéia que Deus é o líder de tribos selvagens.

Perto do fim do reinado do pai de Acaz, os sírios, sob Rezim, e os israelitas, sob Peca, começaram a assediar Judá. Pensavam que Acaz era um rei fraco, e resolveram derrubá-lo do trono, fazendo de Tabeel o seu testa-de-ferro em Judá. A invasão veio, o povo ficou aterrorizado, mas o profeta Isaías garantiu a Acaz que Judá reteria sua independência. A invasão foi derrotada, embora as tribulações de Acaz tivessem continuado. Rezim atacou novamente, e Peca matou cento e vinte mil homens do exército de Acaz em um único dia, levando duzentos mil prisioneiros, incluindo seu filho, Maasséias. Mas o profeta Oded interveio, e vários líderes persuadiram as tropas a soltar os prisioneiros. Soltos, estes voltaram a Judá. Mas então os idumeus do sul atacaram o país e levaram a muitos como escravos. No oeste, os filisteus invadiram e tomaram Bete-Semes, Aijalom, Gederote, Socó, Timnate e Ginzo, povoando essas localidades com sua própria gente.

5. *Acaz torna-se um rei vassalo*. Desesperado, Acaz voltou-se para impiedade ainda maior, profanou a adoração tradicional, substituindo-a pela idolatria, e transformou tudo em um verdadeiro caos. Tornou-se vassalo de Tiglate-Pileser, rei da Assíria, ao implorar

ACAZ — ACEITAÇÃO

o seu socorro contra os seus inimigos. Tiglate-Pileser derrotou os sírios, mas impôs pesado tributo a Acaz, deixando-o desesperado em outro sentido. Foi a Damasco congratular-se com o rei assírio, e ali observou um altar pagão, do qual gostou. Ordenou que fosse feita uma réplica do mesmo, e o pôs no templo, no lugar do altar de bronze. Esse altar pagão, pois, tornou-se o centro da adoração. Esse culto envolvia a adoração às estrelas e aos planetas, o sacrifício infantil e a feitiçaria (ver II Crô. 28:22-25; Isa. 8:19). O nome de Acaz, portanto, ficou ligado à adoração ao sol, e as abominações pagãs prosseguiram até um século mais tarde (ver II Reis 23:11).

6. *Sua morte*. Acaz morreu no décimo sexto ano de seu reinado, e sepultaram-no em Jerusalém, embora não nos túmulos reais (ver I Reis 15:36; 16:2; II Crô. 28 e Isa. 7).

7. *Arqueologia*. O nome de Acaz ocorre em uma inscrição do famoso imperador assírio, Tiglate-Pileser III (744-727 A.C.), chamado *Pul* (Pulu). Acaz é mencionado como quem pagava tributos à Assíria sob a forma de ouro, prata, chumbo, ferro, estanho, peças de lã colorida, linho e toda espécie de objetos valiosos, produtos do mar e da terra, cavalos reais, mulas e tesouros. (DE FA ND S UN Z)

ACAZ

Bisneto de Jônatas, filho do rei Saul, um dos quatro filhos de Mica. Foi pai de Jeoada ou Jaerá (ver I Crô. 8:35,36 e 9:42), acerca de quem nada se sabe. (S)

ACAZIAS

No hebraico, **a quem Yahweh sustenta** (I Reis 22:40,41 tem uma forma mais longa do nome; e II Reis 1:2, uma forma mais breve). Foi filho e sucessor de Acabe, como rei de Israel. Foi o oitavo rei de Israel. Reinou apenas por dois anos (cerca de 853-852 A.C.). Jezabel exerceu sua péssima influência sobre ele, tal como influenciara seu pai, tendo seguido toda espécie de coisas malignas.

1. *Revolta*. Por ocasião da morte de Acabe, os moabitas revoltaram-se e recusaram-se a pagar tributo a Israel, o qual consistia de cem mil ovelhas e de um igual número de carneiros (ver II Reis 1:1 e 3:4,5).

2. *Acazias e Josafé*, rei de Judá. Esses dois monarcas tentaram reavivar o tráfico marítimo por via do mar Vermelho, mas o projeto terminou em nada (ver II Crô. 20:35,37).

3. *Acazias e o oráculo*. Acazias caiu pelas grades de um quarto elevado em seu palácio, e quis saber se teria chances de recuperação. Então enviou alguém para consultar o oráculo de Baal-Zebube, deus de Ecrom. Mas Elias saiu ao encontro do grupo, enviando-os de volta, a fim de informarem ao rei que ele não mais recuperaria a saúde (ver II Reis 1:4). Assim sucedeu, e Acazias foi substituído no trono por seu irmão, Jeorão (ver II Reis 1:17; II Crô. 20:35). (S UN)

ACAZIAS

Foi sobrinho do Acazias anterior. Foi o oitavo rei da linhagem de Davi, tendo reinado em Judá por menos de um ano, em 842 A.C. Em II Crô. 21:17 e 25:23, ele é chamado de Jeoacaz. Continuou refletindo a péssima influência da ímpia Jezabel, voltando-se para todas as formas de mal, no breve período de seu reinado. Era filho de Jeorão e Atália, sendo esta filha

de Acabe e Jezabel (ver II Reis 8:24-27). A família inteira era corrupta, e sua mãe influenciou-o a participar da idolatria. «Ele também andou no caminho da casa de Acabe porque sua mãe foi quem o aconselhou a proceder iniquamente» (II Crô. 22:3). Uniu-se a seu tio, Jeorão, de Israel, em uma expedição contra Hazael, rei da Síria, na tentativa de recuperar Ramote-Gileade (ver II Reis 8:27,28). Esse Jeorão era filho de Josafé, rei de Judá (872-849 A.C.). Casou-se com Atália, filha de Acabe e Jezabel. Portanto, houve o envolvimento de dois homens com o nome de Jeorão, pai e tio de Acazias (ver o artigo sobre Jeorão). Foram bem-sucedidos na campanha, mas Jeorão foi mortalmente ferido e retirou-se para Jezreel (cidade ao sul do lago Quinerete, dentro do território israelita), a fim de recuperar-se. Depois disso, Acazias foi visitar Jeorão. Os dois reis saíram em seus carros de guerra ao encontro de Jeú. Jeorão recebeu uma flechada que lhe atravessou o coração, e Acazias, ao tentar escapar, foi alcançado e gravemente ferido. Atingiu Medigo, onde faleceu. Seu corpo foi levado a Jerusalém, para ser sepultado. O Senhor escolheu Jeú para destruir a casa de Acabe. (Ver II Reis 8:26,27). O julgamento divino, pois, estava sendo imposto. Jeú havia sido ungido rei antes disso, pelo que seu ato fez parte da consolidação de seu reino. (DE ND S UN Z)

ACBOR

No hebraico, **rato, roedor**, designado no Antigo Testamento. 1. O pai de Baal-Hanã, rei dos idumeus (Gên. 36:38,39; I Crô. 1:49). 2. Um oficial de Josias (II Reis 22:12,14; Jer. 26:22; chamado Abdom, em II Crô. 34:20 (cerca de 624 A.C.). Era filho de Micaías (II Reis 22:12), e pai de Elnatã (Jer. 26:22). Josias ordenou que ele fosse com outros consultar a profetisa Hulda, acerca do recém-descoberto livro da lei. (S)

ACEITAÇÃO

Termo que significa que uma pessoa ou ato é aprovado ou bem recebido por outrem. A palavra também é usada para indicar a aceitação de um conceito ou verdade por meio da fé. Nesse contexto, a teologia medieval distinguia três facetas na fé: 1. *Notitia*, entendimento; 2. *assensus*, assentimento; e 3. *fiducia*, confiança. As duas primeiras indicam o assentimento da pessoa à verdade revelada, e a terceira indica seu ato final de fé, na qual ela aceita o que a Igreja ensina, por haver crido que o revelador é o próprio Deus. Tal fato significa que há um ato de submissão à autoridade da Igreja, e à plena aceitação da revelação.

No que tange a Cristo, a pessoa aceita-O como Salvador e Senhor com base em seu assentimento, que termina no ato de outorga. Muitos objetam ao ato cego de submissão à Igreja, insistindo que se trata antes de um relacionamento direto com Cristo. Essa era a posição de Lutero. O fundamentalismo com freqüência tem ressaltado a necessidade da «doutrina correta» ao ponto em que o assentimento às proposições doutrinárias corretas, evidenciado por meio de uma confissão pública, com freqüência substitui qualquer outorga real à pessoa de Cristo.

A aceitação de Deus. Sob o antigo pacto, isso era simbolicamente representado na realização das exigências rituais e cerimoniais (Lev. 22:20), bem como nas qualidades morais e éticas, como a guarda da lei (Prov. 21:3), que é salientado nos escritos dos profetas (Isa. 1:12-15; Jer. 6:20; Miq. 5:21-24).

Acéldama — O Campo de Sangue, Vale de Hinom
Cortesia, Matson Photo Service

O CAMPO DOS PASTORES, COM BELEM A DISTANCIA — Cortesia Matson Photo Service

ACÉLDAMA — ACIDENTE

No Novo Testamento, a aceitação alicerça-se sobre a obra remidora de Cristo (Efé. 1:6; I Ped. 2:5), que se dá segundo a graça de Deus (Efé. 2:8-9), mas também é algo que deve ser operante na vida, ou será em vão (Fil. 2:12-13). A verdadeira aceitação por Deus manifesta-se mediante uma vida dedicada, que envolve renúncia e sacrifício (Rom. 12:1-2). A verdadeira aceitação imita a do Filho pelo Pai (Mat. 3:17). Aquele que é aceito faz coisas aceitáveis, especialmente cumprindo a lei do amor (Fil. 4:18; Heb. 13:15,16; Gál. 5:22). Aquele que é recebido por Deus também aceita a outros, embora estes se mostrem deficientes em sua fé e em sua prática religiosa (Efé. 4:32; 5:2; Rom. 14:1-2; 15:7).

Paul Tillich e os teólogos-filósofos existencialistas usam o termo *aceitação* para indicar «nós» aceitamos, a saber, as idéias essenciais do credo, a liberdade humana, a busca pelo fugidio absoluto, que nunca pode ser apreendido, embora continuamente buscado. Buscamos corajosamente, e essa coragem vence o estado natural do homem, caracterizado por desesperança e dúvida, embora não de forma total. Porém, mesmo na dúvida somos aceitos pela graça de Deus. Mediante a coragem, vencemos a alienação. (B C E Z. Ver o NTI em Efé. 1:6. Ver o artigo sobre o *Existencialismo*).

Na filosofia, a *aceitação* indica que uma pessoa aceitou uma idéia ou teoria. Na filosofia da ciência, essa aceitação é sempre provisória, porque nunca se obtém toda a evidência. Cria-se um conflito com as certezas diárias que se repetem continuamente em nosso mundo, e também com as tecnologias que parecem atingir elevado grau de exatidão. Na filosofia, a aceitação pode ser tida como completa se os meios de conhecimento não são empíricos, por serem intuitivos, racionais ou místicos. Todavia, muitos negam a validade ou a absoluta validade desses meios de conhecimento. Ver os artigos sobre o *Empirismo*, o *Racionalismo*, a *Intuição* e o *Misticismo*. (E F)

ACÉLDAMA

A palavra Acéldama (Atos 1:19), é uma transliteração grega do termo aramaico *akeldamach*. Alguns estudiosos pensam que essa palavra significa «campo de sono» ou «cemitério», mas o sentido, «Campo de Sangue» é preferível e apropriado, por causa do suicídio de Judas, descrito nessa passagem em termos cruentos.

«O campo pertencia originalmente a um oleiro, e provavelmente era um terreno que já havia dado toda a argila possível para servir aos seus propósitos, tendo-se tornado, por conseguinte, inútil. Jerônimo relata que continuava existindo, no lado sul do monte Sião, em cujas circunvizinhanças, até os dias presentes há um leito de argila branca». (Alford, em Atos 1:19). (Ver o trecho de Mat. 27:10 no NTI quanto a outros significados ligados à questão do *oleiro*. Ver também Mat. 27:7).

Esse campo, conforme alguns têm asseverado, foi cercado por quatro muros, à maneira de uma torre, no pináculo da qual havia sete portas distintas, como janelas, por onde os corpos dos mortos eram descidos. Essa muralha cercava um terreno com cerca de vinte e dois metros de comprimento por quinze metros de largura, não ficando longe do vale de Hinon, na vertente sul do monte Sião. Essa construção foi feita por ordem da imperatriz Helena, mãe de Constantino (300 D.C.), a qual procurou assinalar esse e muitos outros locais associados à vida terrena do Senhor Jesus. Jerônimo afirma que em seus tempos («De

Locis Hebraicis», fol. 89, C e 95 H; *de nominibus Hebraicis*, fol. 105 H) ainda se podia ver tal construção. Másio fala sobre uma altíssima montanha, próxima de Jerusalém, chamada de Acéldama, que teria obtido seu nome de um campo adjacente, e que se pensava ser o mesmo lugar mencionado em Atos. (Comentário em *Josuam*, par. 283). Atualmente, entretanto, parece não haver qualquer evidência da existência desse antigo campo, exceto que nas cercanias existem várias camadas de argila.

ACEPÇÃO DE PESSOAS

Ver **Respeito (Acepção) de Pessoas.**

ACESSO

O termo grego assim traduzido é **prosagoge**, figurando em três lugares do N.T. (Rom. 5:2; Efé. 2:18 e 3:12). A forma verbal significa «trazer à frente», «aproximar» (prosago), podendo ser encontrada em seis lugares (Mat. 18:24; Luc. 9:41; Atos 12:6; 16:20; 27:27 e I Ped. 3:18). Só Pedro usa o termo (verbalmente) com significado teológico, e o conceito neotestamentário reside no substantivo. A noção geral, na literatura sagrada e profana, onde se encontra esse vocábulo, é que alguém é introduzido à presença de alguma autoridade ou poder superior. Mediante a sua identificação com Cristo, os filhos de Deus têm acesso ao Pai.

Os monarcas orientais ou os altos oficiais contavam com alguém cuja função consistia em trazer pessoas à sua presença, se tinham direitos ou negócios legítimos para obterem tal acesso. Também nos aproximamos da Presença real e obtemos esse direito, por meio da missão de Cristo, e por termos nos tornado filhos, tal como Ele é o Filho. Deus é o rei da criação inteira (Sal. 29:10; 47:7; 96:10), não sendo coisa de somenos ter o direito de acesso a Ele. Não há tal acesso sem a santificação (Heb. 12:14). A própria salvação é o processo e a substância desse acesso. Quanto a notas mais completas, ver *acesso* em Rom. 5:2, no NTI, e ver *salvação*, em Heb. 2:3. Ver também o artigo nesta obra, sobre a *salvação*. O ofício mediatário de Cristo provê acesso diário, enquanto aguardamos sua fruição futura (Rom. 8:26-27). As operações do Espírito preparam a alma humana para aproximar-se de Deus, tanto agora como no futuro (Efé. 2:18). Esse acesso é obtido conforme vamos sendo transformados à imagem do Filho (II Cor. 3:18), sendo esse um processo eterno. Portanto, o acesso não consiste meramente em nos aproximarmos do Senhor, onde Ele se encontra, em alguma bem-aventurança futura, mas consiste em nos transformarmos em filhos, participantes da natureza divina (II Ped. 1:4). Destarte somos membros da família divina, pelo que temos acesso ao Pai.

Natureza desse acesso. 1. É um dom de Deus (Sal. 65:11); 2. através de Cristo (João 10:7-8); 3. através do Espírito Santo (Efé. 2:18); 4. condicionado à reconciliação (Col. 1:21-22); 5. garante todas as bênçãos espirituais (Heb. 4:16); 6. tem aspectos presentes e futuros (Heb. 10:17); 7. mediado através da filiação (João 1:12; Rom. 8:15-17); 8. resulta na filiação a Deus (João 6:25-26; II Cor. 3:18; II Ped. 1:4). (B NTI S W Z)

ACIDENTE

Vem do latim, **accidens**, particípio presente de *accidere*, «acontecer». Na filosofia aristotélica e na teologia escolástica, era termo usado para indicar algo que adere ou acompanha uma entidade ou substância, embora sem fazer parte necessária da mesma, como a cor vermelha de uma maçã. Pode haver uma

ACIFA — AÇÕES DE GRAÇA

maçã que não seja vermelha; uma menina pode não ser loura, embora possa ser um acidente próprio de algumas meninas. Um *acidente* não tem existência independente e não é auto-suficiente. É uma qualidade não-essencial. Tal conceito tem certa importância nas tentativas de explicações de alguns teólogos, quando falam sobre a doutrina da transubstanciação (ver o artigo a respeito). O pão e o vinho transmutam-se no corpo e no sangue de Cristo, isto é, a substância deles torna-se a substância do corpo e do sangue de Cristo. Mas os acidentes, como peso, extensão e espaço, qualidades químicas, etc., não se alteram, pois todas as considerações materiais são apenas acidentais. Ver o artigo sobre *substância*.

O termo *acidente* é usado na ética para denotar coisas que sucedem, totalmente sem causa, ou sem qualquer causa conhecida. São as coisas que nos parecem surpreendentes, deixando-nos perplexos, pois nenhuma delas é danificadora, exceto devido a motivos fortuitos. O trecho de Rom. 8:20, ao falar sobre a «vaidade» ou inutilidade a que o mundo foi sujeitado, provavelmente inclui a idéia de acidentes prejudiciais. Notemos, porém, que até mesmo nesse caso, Deus permite catástrofes para ensinar ao homem a atitude de dependência, para que eventualmente apele para Deus como seu refúgio. Naturalmente, estamos tratando com o *problema do mal*, amplamente comentado em Rom. 3:8, no NTI. Ver também sobre esse assunto, na presente obra. (C F H NTI)

ACIFA
Uma forma de **Hacufa**.

ACMETA
Ver **Ecbatana**.

ACO
Uma cidade da costa mediterrânea, a 49 km ao sul de Tiro, e a 16 km do monte Carmelo (Juí. 1:31). Os antigos gregos e romanos conheciam-na pelo nome de Ptolemaida, por causa de Ptolomeu, rei do Egito, que a reconstruiu em 100 A.C. Na Idade Média tornou-se conhecida como Acra, e então Santa Joana d'Acra. Paulo visitou o local (ver Atos 21:7).

O porto ali existente é o melhor de toda a costa marítima da Palestina, circundado por montanhas. Esta cidade era um importante centro populacional dos tempos do Antigo Testamento, por ser o único porto natural em toda a costa sul da Fenícia. Diversas rotas vinculavam-na ao território da Galiléia, ao lago da Galiléia, ao vale do rio Jordão e a outros pontos geográficos mais além. A localidade foi distribuída entre a tribo de Aser, ainda que nunca tenha sido conquistada, tendo permanecido uma localidade fenícia durante todo o período do Antigo Testamento.

O trecho de Juízes 1:31 é a única referência a essa cidade no Antigo Testamento, embora fosse freqüentemente mencionada na literatura extrabíblica e figure nas listas topográficas dos séculos XV a XIII A.C., bem como nos famosos tabletes de Amarna.

Nos dias de *hegemonia assíria*, Senaqueribe, rei da Assíria, mencionou essa cidade como parte integrante do reino de Tiro e Sidom. Passou sucessivamente pelo domínio dos ptolomeus, assírios, babilônios, persas e romanos (Estrabão xvi.2:25). Nos tempos da dominação romana, a cidade foi feita uma colônia e o imperador Cláudio estabeleceu ali uma divisão de seu exército. Ao tempo da revolta e da guerra dos judeus

contra os romanos, no ano de 70 D.C., cerca de dois mil judeus foram mortos ali. Após o período romano, seu antigo nome foi restaurado. Já nos tempos das cruzadas, ficou famosa sob o nome Santa Joana d'Arc. Nos tempos modernos, essa cidade perdeu muito de sua antiga proeminência, tendo sido sobrepujada por Haifa, situada diretamente do outro lado da baía. (ND S UN Z)

AÇÕES DE GRAÇA

I. Referências e Idéias
1. Cristo deixou-nos o grande exemplo de ações de graças (ver Mat. 11:25; 26:27; João 6:11 e 11:41). 2. Até mesmo seres celestiais ocupam-se desse ato de devoção (ver Apo. 4:9; 7:11, 12 e 11:16,17). 3. Trata-se de um ato de devoção ordenado por Deus (ver Sal. 50:25; Fil. 4:6 e I Tes. 5:18). 4. Trata-se de coisa boa, sendo benéfica para quem se mostra grato ao Senhor (ver Sal. 92:1). 5. Deve ser expressa a gratidão a Deus (ver Sal. 50:14), a Cristo (ver I Tim. 1:12), em nome de Cristo (ver Efé. 5:20), na adoração pública (ver Sal. 35:18), na adoração individual (ver Dan. 6:10), em tudo (ver I Tes. 5:18), por todas as coisas (ver Efé. 5:20). 6. Devem ser expressas contínuas ações de graças (ver Efé. 1:16; 5:20 e I Tes. 1:2). 7. Devem ser expressas ações de graças pela bondade e pela misericórdia de Deus (ver Sal. 106:1; 107:1; 136:1-3). 8. Devem ser dadas ações de graças ante o sucesso em qualquer empreendimento (ver Nee. 12:31,40). 9. Também pelo suprimento das necessidades físicas, e antes das refeições (ver João 6:11 e Atos 27:35). 10. Por causa do grande dom de Cristo (ver II Cor. 9:15).

II. Em tudo Dai Graças
Assim fala I Tess. 5:18. Efé. 5:20 fala ainda mais forte: *por tudo*.

Na vontade de Deus a nosso respeito muitas coisas estão inclusas. Entre elas figura o nosso senso de gratidão. Essa atitude faz-nos lembrar nossa posição de dependência a ele; faz-nos recordar de sua bondade para conosco, o que leva nossos espíritos a entrarem em harmonia com ele, reconhecendo que ele é o grande Benfeitor da humanidade, aquele a quem devemos toda a vida e o sustento. Nesse reconhecimento, porém, devemos envolver-nos com *vidas agradecidas*, e não meramente com externas «ações de graças». Nossas próprias vidas diárias, pois, deveriam ser uma forma de agradecimento. Em face de toda a bondade e de todos os benefícios divinos, deveríamos dedicar nossas vidas a nosso Pai. «Se eu tivesse mil vidas, todas elas seriam tuas», deveria ser a autêntica expressão dos nossos corações. Com base nisso pode-se ver que um autêntico espírito de gratidão resulta do desenvolvimento espiritual, em razão do que nos tornamos espiritualmente úteis a outros. Somente então encontraremos muitas razões para dar graças ao Senhor. Pois quando cumprimos a vontade de Deus, descobrimos muitos motivos para lhe sermos gratos.

III. Em Cristo
É na pessoa de Cristo que nos são conferidas todas as bênçãos espirituais (ver Efé. 1:3); pelo que ele mesmo é a razão, a fonte e a inspiração de toda a nossa gratidão. A vontade de Deus opera dentro da esfera de Cristo, isto é, quando estamos associados a ele, mediante a comunhão mística, como servos seus. Então é que a vontade de Deus atua poderosamente em nós, especialmente no que concerne a fazer a vontade de Deus; e isso nos fornece abundantes motivos para sermos gratos a Ele. A vontade de Deus,

Aco, fortificações —
Cortesia, Levant Photo Service

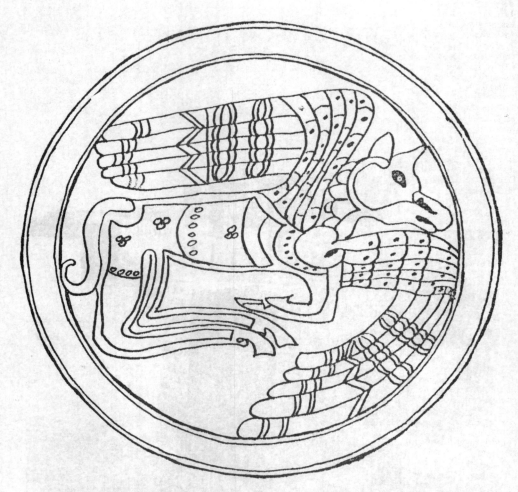

Arte céltica — o boi, símbolo do evangelho de Lucas, Livro de Kells

Reprodução Artística de
Darrell Steven Champlin

AÇÕES DE GRAÇA — AÇOITE

pois, envolve essa «exigência» divina de sermos gratos.

«A gratidão é possível, porque Deus determinou que assim fosse, no dom do Senhor Jesus. Esses conceitos, como alegria, constância na oração e ação de graças também aparecem nos trechos de Rom. 12:12; Col. 4:2,3 e Efé. 6:18, e pertencem essencialmente à vida cristã, conforme Paulo vivia e ensinava» (Bailey, em I Tess. 5:18).

A conduta cristã, quando está de acordo com a vontade de Deus, segundo ela nos é esclarecida em Cristo, deve incluir as ações de graça como parte de nossa devoção, tal como a oração faz parte da mesma, pois tal devoção não é algo sem fundamento e sem motivos.

Esses mandamentos todos assumem maior significação quando consideramos as pessoas para quem foram dados. Os crentes tessalonicenses estavam sendo perseguidos, e muitos eram afligidos. Reconhecendo a bondade de Deus, e tendo a certeza do triunfo final em Cristo, até mesmo sobre a morte e a sepultura, somos impelidos a dar ações de graças. Deus deseja que cheguemos a esse ponto de devoção e dedicação em nossas vidas espirituais, ou que cheguemos a esse estágio do desenvolvimento espiritual para que seja possível esse tipo de gratidão. Sim, a expressão de ações de graças é um meio de reavivarmos nossa alegria, nossa confiança e nossa esperança; portanto, é uma prática muito útil, além de ser um meio de glorificar a Deus pela sua bondade. Em Cristo Jesus, tudo é nosso (ver I Cor. 3:21); e as ações de graças nos trazem tudo isso à memória. Por causa de seus muitos usos e benefícios, Deus ordena o uso das ações de graças. Posto que estamos associados a Deus, participando de seus muitos benefícios, temos muitas razões para sermos gratos; e a vontade de Deus é que assim façamos, para que possamos reconhecer claramente o que ele tem feito por nós, vivendo em gratidão, esperançosos e na luz de um reconhecimento grato.

IV. Observações

1. As introduções de quase todas as epístolas paulinas trazem uma seção que contém ações de graças. (Ver I Cor. 1:4-9 e Col. 1:13-14).

2. Somente a epístola aos Gálatas não tem de forma alguma essa característica, talvez porque Paulo não se sentia muito grato ao escrever para aqueles crentes, considerando como o legalismo havia invadido a comunidade.

3. Apesar de que todas as igrejas tinham problemas, e que todas as epístolas de Paulo têm o propósito de corrigir tais problemas, ele sempre encontrava algum motivo para sentir-se grato, e algo para louvar a seus leitores.

«É o começo que vale, conforme nos lembra aquele provérbio que diz: 'Uma coisa bem começada já foi feita pela metade'. Invariavelmente Paulo iniciava suas epístolas com uma afirmação forte e confiante de agradecimento. Nisso há mais do que mera idiossincrasia de composição. Pelo contrário, tal atitude se origina da firme convicção do apóstolo dos gentios de que a gratidão, que tem por fruto o louvor, é um dos elementos primários e necessários da atitude cristã. Trata-se de uma psicologia elementar sã; e, quando é transferida para o campo religioso, explica o preponderante papel desempenhado pelas ações de graças no livro de Salmos. Aqueles que têm sido ensinados, por um livramento real, acerca daquilo que Deus tem feito por eles, não podem guardar silêncio». (John Knox, em Rom. 1:8).

«Sete das epístolas de Paulo têm início com tais ações de graças, as quais tanto transmitem os elogios que o amor regozija em dar, sempre que possível, como também atribuem todas as virtudes espirituais diretamente à sua Fonte, o Senhor. E em Rom. 1:8, essas virtudes são atribuídas não somente ao 'Senhor', mas também ao 'meu Deus', uma frase usada, em todo o N.T., exclusivamente pelo apóstolo Paulo, excetuando a exclamação de Cristo moribundo: 'Eli, Eli...'» (Moule, em Rom. 1:8).

«*mediante Jesus Cristo*», Rom. 1:8. O Verbo eterno sempre foi e sempre será o mediador de todos os privilégios e graças do cristianismo, até mesmo no caso das expressões de ação de graças. Jesus é a base de nossa aceitação por parte de Deus Pai. (Ver Efé. 1:5,6). A passagem de Efé. 5:20 recomenda que sejamos gratos por tudo, em nome do Senhor Jesus Cristo. Ele é o mediador de todos quantos se achegam a Deus, conforme lemos em Efé. 2:18.

(FA I LAN NTI)

AÇOITE

O objeto e a ação de açoitar envolvem três termos hebraicos e cinco termos gregos. Açoitar era uma forma comum de castigo entre os povos antigos, embora quase todas as menções ao ato de açoitar, no Antigo Testamento, sejam metafóricas. Assim, a figura é usada acerca da língua (Jó 5:21) que ataca subitamente (ver Jó 9:23, onde nossa versão portuguesa diz «flagelo»), acerca do juízo divino (Isa. 28:15,18). Lê-se em Isaías 10:26 que nosso Deus tem um açoite, e também que as nações cananéias poderiam tornar-se um flagelo nas ilhargas de Israel (Jos. 23:13).

As únicas referências ao açoite como um instrumento de castigo são I Reis 12:11,14 e II Crônicas 10:11,14, trecho quase idêntico ao outro. Mas não é claro se a palavra «escorpiões», que ocorre nessas passagens como um sinônimo de «açoite», é apenas um símbolo vívido do mesmo objeto, ou um açoite munido com pontas de metal, correspondente ao *scorpio* dos romanos. A lei mosaica permitia que, em tribunal, uma pessoa considerada culpada fosse castigada com açoites. A sentença era executada na presença do juiz, com a pessoa prostrada. O número de golpes sem dúvida era proporcional à gravidade da ofensa, embora não pudesse exceder a quarenta (ver Deu. 25:1-3). Posteriormente, os judeus passaram a usar um açoite com três línguas, mas nunca ultrapassaram o limite, sempre cessando em trinta e nove, para compensar qualquer erro possível na contagem (2 Cor. 11:24). As autoridades locais das sinagogas e os membros do Sinédrio administravam o castigo de açoites por motivo de ofensas contra a lei (ver Mat. 10:17). Parece que, com base em Deuteronômio 22:18 e Josefo (ver *Anti*. IV.viii.23), a difamação era uma das ofensas castigadas dessa forma, mas não há registro de outros crimes pelos quais uma pessoa pudesse ser assim punida. A *Mishnah Mokkah* 11:12 descreve o método empregado. Após ter averiguado que o réu estava em boas condições físicas, suas mãos eram atadas a um poste, enquanto que suas costas e seu peito eram desnudados. Treze golpes eram aplicados no peito, e treze sobre cada ombro. Se a vítima morresse, nenhuma acusação era feita aos que tinham aplicado o castigo. A lei romana porciana proibia o castigo de açoites contra qualquer cidadão romano (ver Atos 22:25), mas os escravos e os que não eram cidadãos romanos podiam ser interrogados com o uso desse método de castigo (ver Atos 22:24).

Os romanos habitualmente usavam um tipo de açoite munido de pedacinhos de metal ou de osso nas

ACOMODAÇÃO — ACOR

pontas; mas a palavra grega *rabdizein* (ver Atos 16:22 e II Cor. 11:25) indica que as varas dos lictores foram usadas nas ocasiões mencionadas. Usualmente, os crucificados eram então castigados com açoites, de acordo com o que diz Lívio 33,36, mas aparentemente tal castigo foi aplicado a Jesus de modo inverso, isto é, antes de ser Ele crucificado. Isso assim sucedeu porque Pilatos julgava que o castigo de açoites satisfaria aos judeus, e que Jesus não teria de ser crucificado (ver Luc. 23:16,22; João 19:1).

Resta ser dito que alguns estudiosos pensam que entre os judeus não havia o castigo com açoites, mas tão-somente com varas, sobretudo com base no que se lê em Provérbios 10:13, e que os romanos foram os introdutores do castigo com açoites, pelo menos nas páginas sagradas. (ND UN)

ACOMODAÇÃO

1. **Descrição de Deus e das entidades espirituais** São usados termos antropomórficos, mas isso exige interpretação. Deus não é semelhante ao homem, mas certas características humanas podem dizer-nos algo sobre a pessoa de Deus. Quanto mais primitiva for a teologia, mais antropomórfica ela será. Acomodamos nossa linguagem para descrever Deus.

2. **Descrições da natureza.** Dizemos que o sol se levanta e se põe, embora saibamos que os movimentos do globo terrestre é que dão essa impressão. Acomodamos nossa linguagem às aparências.

3. Usamos acomodação de linguagem quando não sentimos estar justificada a interpretação literal da Bíblia ou de outros livros, como se dá com os símbolos apocalípticos. Também podemos falar sobre o grande exemplo deixado pelo sacrifício de Abraão, quando ele ofereceu Isaque, sem aprovar o sacrifício de crianças. Podemos negar que Deus ordenaria tal coisa, acomodando a verdade à narrativa, negando que a mesma deva ser literalmente compreendida. Alegorias e parábolas são meios de acomodar a linguagem literal a fim de explicar alguma verdade.

4. **Significações duplas.** Se trechos proféticos têm um duplo significado, então o texto é acomodado (alterado) para ensinar tal coisa.

5. A Bíblia usa termos e idéias pagãs dando-lhes um colorido judaico ou cristão, como na doutrina do Logos (João 1:1) e as antigas cosmologias (Gên. 1, quanto à história da criação). Pelo menos em parte, a angelologia é uma acomodação às religiões orientais, que exerceram influência sobre o pensamento hebreu. Aquilo que é acomodado não é necessariamente falso, e então recebe foros de verdade mediante a acomodação. A idéia tomada por empréstimo talvez já contenha a sua verdade, embora obscura e parcial. A acomodação, pois, pode aclarar a verdade.

6. **O uso de textos do A.T. e do N.T. com freqüência exibe acomodação,** por que os versículos podem ser usados com sentidos diferentes ou modificados, não inerentes aos trechos citados do A.T. Alguns vêem acomodação em Mat. 2:17-18, citando Jer. 31:15-17.

7. Em sentido geral, a revelação por si mesma é uma acomodação, porque o grande Deus transmite Suas mensagens ao minúsculo homem. Ninguém pode entender Deus e os Seus mistérios (Rom. 11:33 ss). Em conseqüência, o conhecimento transmitido ao homem deve vir mediante veículos e símbolos apropriados ao seu estágio intelectual e ao seu estado espiritual. Isso não quer dizer que não possuímos a verdade, mas significa que vemos a verdade através de um espelho fosco, que distorce e obscurece, conforme Paulo assevera em I Cor. 13:12. Isso visa a eliminar o orgulho humano no tocante ao conhecimento e à verdade. Todos estamos nos estágios iniciais da inquirição pela verdade, sem importar onde nos encontramos em relação uns aos outros.

8. **Na filosofia.** Aprendemos que toda a verdade é emblemática, porque nada conhecemos de modo completo e preciso. Os meios de conhecimento das coisas, como o empirismo, o racionalismo, a intuição e o misticismo são todos meios parabólicos de busca pela verdade. Em outras palavras, fornecem-nos uma visão simbólica da verdade, e jamais algo como descrições completas.

9. Para ilustrar o sexto ponto, textos neotestamentários usam referências ao Antigo Testamento, com acomodações. Compare estes textos (apenas alguns, dentre muitos outros possíveis):

Gên. 15:5, em Rom. 4:18; Gên. 15:6, em Rom. 4:3; Gál. 3:6 e Tia. 2:23; Gên. 18:10, em Rom. 9:9; Êxo. 9:16, em Rom. 9:17; Lev. 11:45, em I Ped. 1:16; Jos. 1:5, em Heb. 13:5; I Sam. 21:6, em Mat. 12:3,4; Mar. 2:25,26 e Luc. 7:3,4; I Reis 14:14,18, em Rom. 11:3,4; Sal. 19:4, em Rom. 10:18; Sal. 34:12-16, em I Ped. 3:10-12; Sal. 78:3, em Mat. 13:35; Pro. 10:12, em I Ped. 4:8; Isa. 52:7 e Naum 1:15, em Rom. 10:15; Isa. 52:11,12, em II Cor. 6:17; Jer. 31:15, em Mat. 2:17,18; Hab. 2:4, em Rom. 1:17; Joel 2:32, em Rom. 10:13; Mal. 1:2,3, em Rom. 9:13

Naturalmente, alguns intérpretes procuram eliminar a teoria da acomodação, no tocante a muitas dessas referências, especialmente quando estão envolvidos elementos proféticos.(B S Z)

ACONSELHAMENTO PASTORAL

Ver o artigo sobre **Conselheiro (Aconselhamento)**.

ACONTECIMENTO PIVOTAL

Dentro da filosofia de Whitehead (ver o artigo a respeito), essa expressão indica o limite ideal de um acontecimento, com suas dimensões uniformemente restringidas.

ACOR

No hebraico significa tribulação. Era um vale entre Jericó e Ai, que recebeu esse nome por causa da derrota dos israelitas ante o pecado de Acã (ver Jos. 7:24). Ver sobre *Acã.* O local é atualmente identificado com o Wadi Daber e com o Wadi Mulelik. O nome do vale tornou-se proverbial (ver Osé. 2:15), e Oséias acrescenta «E lhe darei... o vale de Açor por porta de esperança» (Osé. 2:15, indicando que a disciplina e o juízo podem resultar em esperança. (S UN Z)

AÇOR

Ver Deu. 14:13; Isa. 34:15 e Lev. 11:14. A ave em foco é um gavião ou um falcão. Duas espécies de falcão existem na Palestina, o vermelho e o negro, o qual é levemente menor que o primeiro. O falcão pode ser distinguido de outras aves de rapina por sua longa cauda em tesoura. Alimentam-se os falcões de grande variedade de animais, desde insetos, peixes, ratos, pequenas aves, ou carniça. Há gravuras desse pássaro na escrita hieroglífica.

A ave em questão provavelmente pertence à classe dos falcões (ver Lev. 11:14). Em nossa versão portuguesa, essa ave não aparece na lista de Levítico 11, mas figura na lista de Deuteronômio 14 (ver vs. 13). Nessa última referência talvez haja, no hebraico,

AÇOR — ACRÓPOLE

um erro textual, em lugar de «ave de rapina». A raiz da palavra hebraica significa «voar rapidamente» ou «dardejar no ar». O açor era uma ave imunda, ou seja, não era própria para consumo humano. (ID S)

ACOSMISMO

Vem do grego a (não) e kosmos (mundo), palavra cunhada por Hegel a fim de referir-se à idéia de que o mundo físico, na realidade, é ilusório e irreal, visto que, em um sentido verdadeiro, só Deus existe. A idéia é comum nas religiões orientais. Shankara e F.H. Bradley diziam que coisa alguma é real, exceto o inefável e o supercósmico Um. Tudo quanto existe no espaço, no tempo, e todas as coisas finitas, são apenas maya, isto é, mera «aparência». O termo cabe dentro do conceito idealista da realidade, onde, em um sentido verdadeiro, somente o que é espiritual é real, ao passo que o que é material é apenas um epifenômeno do espírito. Ver o artigo sobre Idealismo. (E P)

ACRA

No grego, cidadela, termo usado para indicar o lugar elevado ao norte do templo, onde foi construída uma cidadela por Antíoco Epifânio, para dominar o lugar santo. Tornou-se a acrópole de Jerusalém. Josefo descreveu o lugar como semicircular, dizendo que quando Simão Macabeu conseguiu expulsar dali a guarnição síria, não somente demoliu a cidadela, mas nivelou até mesmo a colina, para que nenhum local dali por diante fosse mais alto ou tão alto quanto o local onde estava o templo. O povo havia sofrido tanto por causa daquela guarnição que voluntariamente trabalhou, dia e noite, durante três anos, nessa grande obra de remoção (ver Josefo, Ant. xiii:6,6; Bel. Jud. v.4,1). Posteriormente, o palácio de Helene foi construído no local, que reteve seu antigo nome.

ACRABATENA

1. Um distrito da toparquia da Judéia, que ia desde Siquém (não Nablua) a Jericó, inclinando-se para o leste. Tinha cerca de dezenove quilômetros de comprimento. Não é mencionado no Antigo Testamento, mas ocorre em Josefo (Bell. Jud. ii.12,4; iii.3-5). Distava nove milhas romanas a leste de Neápolis, na estrada para Jericó.

2. Um distrito da Judéia que jazia próximo à extremidade sul do mar Morto, ocupado pelos idumeus durante o cativeiro, e mais tarde conhecido como Iduméia. É mencionado em I Mac. 5:3; Josefo, Ant. xii.8.1. Supõe-se que seu nome derivava do Maalh Akrabbim ou Barranco dos Escorpiões, mencionado em Núm. 34:4 e Jos. 15:3, como extremidade sul do território de Judá. (S)

ACRABATENE

Ver Acrabim.

ACRABIM

No hebraico, escorpiões (Jos. 15:3; 34:4). Um passo entre as montanhas no lado sul do mar Morto (Núm. 34:4; Jos. 15:3 e Juí. 1:36), identificado com o moderno Nqb es-Safa, embora outros o identifiquem com Umm el-'Aqarab, no lado ocidental do mesmo. Nesse lugar, Judas Macabeu derrotou os idumeus (ver I Mac. 5:3). O lugar ficava na fronteira entre a Judéia e a Iduméia. Josefo parece referir-se ao lugar, situando-o a suleste de Siquém (ver Guerras, II.xii.4;

IV.ix.9). Mas talvez ele tenha aludido a um lugar diferente. A cadeia montanhosa veio a ser conhecida como montanhas de Edom. (S Z)

ACRE

No hebraico, jugo, a área de terra que uma junta de bois podia arar em um dia, pelo que é uma medida de superfície dos hebreus (ver I Sam. 14:14; Isa. 5:10). Ver pesos e medidas. (UN)

ACRISOLAR, REFINAR

No hebraico há duas palavras com inflexão como verbos finitos e particípios. E há muitas palavras gregas diferentes na LXX, com o sentido de testar, refinar, acrisolar, purificar, etc. No N.T. temos o verbo puróo, usado apenas em Apo. 1:15 e 3:18. Indica o processo de eliminação de impurezas, especialmente no caso de metais.

Normalmente, uma dessas palavras hebraicas é usada em alusão a metais, mas em Jó 36:27, ela é usada em alusão à chuva («destilar», em nossa Bíblia portuguesa), e, em Isa. 25:6, é usada em alusão ao vinho («clarificar», em nossa Bíblia portuguesa). Visto que o sentido básico desse verbo é destilar, compreende-se seu uso em relação a líquidos. A outra palavra hebraica é usada exclusivamente acerca de metais, exceto quando usada em sentido figurado.

O processo de refinação era bastante simples. Aquecia-se o minério ao ponto de dissolver-se, e então extraía-se o metal. Este era refinado ou por aquecimento até o estado líquido, quando então era retirada a impureza da superfície, ou mediante assopro. Naturalmente, o ouro ou a prata refinados eram mais preciosos e caros. O altar do incenso era feito de ouro refinado (I Crô. 28:18), e a igreja de Laodicéia foi aconselhada a comprar desse tipo de ouro (Apo. 3:18). A Bíblia nos dá algumas indicações sobre o processo. Sal. 12:6 menciona a fornalha de refino. Isa. 1:25 refere-se à potassa química, e Jer. 6:29 fala sobre o fole, usado no processo.

O processo de refinação ilustra a maneira de Deus tratar Seu povo. Ele é o refinador, e eles são o metal. Isaías disse, figuradamente: «Eis que te acrisolei, mas disso não resultou prata; provei-te na fornalha da aflição» (48:10; cf. 1:25). Malaquias usa ambas as palavras hebraicas: «Assentar-se-á como derretedor e purificador de prata; purificará os filhos de Levi, e os refinará como ouro e como prata...» O salmista orou para que nele fosse efetuado esse processo, quando disse: «...sonda-me o coração e os pensamentos» (Sal. 26:2).

ACRÓPOLE

No grego, um lugar elevado em uma cidade, usualmente colinas fortificadas de onde se avistavam cidades greco-romanas. A acrópole de Atenas elevava-se a quase 154 m de altura. Era adornada por templos esplêndidos quando Paulo visitou a cidade (ver o artigo sobre Atenas). O escultor Fídias (falecido em 432 A.C.) fez uma gigantesca estátua de Atena, posta na acrópole. O magnificente Partenom foi ali edificado para abrigar uma grande estátua de ouro e marfim de Atena, feita por Fídias. Mais tarde, completou-se a majestosa entrada, a Propiléia, tendo sido construídos o templo do Erecteu e o santuário de Atena Nique, deusa da vitória. As ruínas hoje existentes são belíssimas. A cultura antiga culminou em Atenas, cidade famosa e exaltada em sua acrópole. Em sua segunda viagem missionária, Paulo

ACRÓSTICO — ADA

visitou outras cidades com acrópoles fortificadas, como Filipos e Corinto, mas em Atenas foi onde seu espírito mais se agitou, diante da exibição de idolatria pagã, culminando na acrópole da cidade. Ver Atos 17:16. (UN)

ACRÓSTICO

Vem do grego **akron**, «extremidade» e **stixos**, «verso», uma composição escrita, geralmente versificada, em que a primeira e a última das letras das linhas, em suas estâncias, uma em cada linha, formam um nome ou sentença. Por exemplo, no Salmo 119, as linhas ou versos começam com as letras do alfabeto hebraico. Cada estrofe tem oito linhas, cada uma delas começando com a mesma letra, as primeiras oito linhas começando com alefe, as próximas oito linhas com bete, etc. As Lamentações de Jeremias compõem-se quase inteiramente de acrósticos, e o último capítulo de Provérbios no hebraico tem as letras iniciais de seus últimos vinte e dois versos, em ordem alfabética. Ao todo, o Antigo Testamento contém catorze poemas acrósticos, onde as vinte e duas letras do alfabeto hebraico aparecem, com leves variações, como em: a. cada linha (Lamentações 3); b. cada linha ou cada metade de versos de duas linhas (Sal. 111 e 112); c. cada verso, cada segunda linha de versos de duas linhas (Sal. 25, 35; 119, 145; Pro. 31:10-31; Lam. 4); d. cada segunda linha ou cada metade de versos de quatro linhas (Naum 1:2-10); e. cada verso, cada terceira linha de versos de três linhas (Lam. 1 e 2); f. cada quarta linha, ou cada dois versos de versos de duas linhas (Sal. 9, 10 e 37). Outros arranjos podem ser vistos em outros lugares.

Além de servir de decoração poética, os acrósticos ajudavam na memorização. Algumas reconstruções textuais têm sido possíveis por causa da presença desses artifícios literários.

O Novo Testamento não tem acrósticos. Mas, como uma espécie de código, os antigos cristãos usavam a palavra *peixe* (em grego), para indicar as suas crenças principais.

IXTHYS — I (Ihsous — Jesus); X (Xristós — Cristo); TH (Theou — de Deus); Y (Yios — Filho); S(Sothr — Salvador). Portanto: Jesus Cristo, (o) Filho de Deus, Salvador.

ACSA

No hebraico, **amuleto**, filha de Calebe, oferecida em casamento a qualquer um que liderasse o ataque à cidade de Debir e a tomasse. O prêmio foi ganho por seu sobrinho, Otniel. Quando a noiva era conduzida com as cerimônias usuais ao seu futuro lar, ela desmontou do jumento e implorou a seu pai doar-lhe fontes de água nas terras que seriam suas. Um pedido, naquele instante seria difícil de repelir, e ela obteve o que queria. Recebeu várias fontes situadas perto de Debir (ver Jos. 15:16-19; Juí. 1:9-15). (S UN Z)

ACSAFE

No hebraico, **feitiçaria** ou **encantamento**. Cidade real dos cananeus (ver Jos. 11:1) a qual muitos supõem ser a mesma Aczibe, ambas no território da tribo de Aser. Porém, a consideração cuidadosa de Jos. 19:25 e 29 parece indicar que eram lugares diferentes. A arqueologia a tem identificado com Tell Kisan, cerca de dez quilômetros a suleste de Aco. É mencionada nos Textos de Execração do Egito, dos séculos XIX e XVIII A.C., na lista de lugares conquistados por Tutmés III (1490 - 1436 A.C.), em Karnak, bem como nas cartas de Tell el-Amarna, do século XIV A.C., e em uma carta egípcia do século XIII A.C., o papiro Anastasi. (FA S UN Z)

ACTUS PURUS

Expressão latina que significa «ato puro» ou «realidade pura». Nome comum para Deus na filosofia escolástica. Sendo puramente real, Deus é a única coisa destituída de potencialidade, sendo assim o Ser mais elevado e o Único verdadeiramente completo. (P)

ACUA

Forma alternativa de **Acube**.

ACUBE

Forma variante de **Babuebuque**, em manuscritos gregos.

ACUBE

No hebraico, **insidioso**. Uma forma abreviada de Jacó.

1. Filho de Elioenai, da família de Davi (I Crô. 3:24).

2. Um porteiro do templo de Salomão (I Crô. 9:17).

3. Uma família de servos que servia no templo (Esd. 2:45; I Esd. 5:28).

4. Um sacerdote empregado por Esdras para ajudar o povo a compreender a lei (Mee. 8:7). (ND S)

AÇUDE DE HASSELÁ Ver **Poço do Aqueduto**.

ACZIBE

Devemos considerar uma palavra hebraica grafada de várias maneiras, que tem o sentido de «enganador», «desapontador».

a. Uma aldeia de Aser, na costa do mar Mediterrâneo, a 32 km de Acre. Nos dias do Novo Testamento chamava-se Ecdipa. Modernamente chama-se ez-Zib.(Ver Jos. 19:29 e Juí. 1:31).

b. Uma aldeia nas terras baixas de Judá, a sudoeste de Adulão, identificada com a moderna Tell el-Beida. Em Gên. 39:5, nossa versão grafa Quezibe; em Jos. 15:44 e Miq. 1:14, Aczibe. As traduções variam na forma da palavra.

c. Homens de Cozeba, que pertenciam aos descendentes de Selá, filho de Judá (ver I Crô. 4:22).

d. Em I Esdras 5:31, Caseba, uma família de serviçais do templo, que retornaram da Babilônia após o exílio. (Z)

ADA

No hebraico, **adorno** ou **beleza**. Há duas delas no Antigo Testamento: 1. A primeira esposa de Lameque, mãe de Jabel e Jubal (ver Gên. 4:19-21), diante de quem Lameque recitou seu poema de auto-exaltação. 2. Uma das esposas de Esaú, filha de Elom, o heteu (ver Gên. 36:4), chamada Basemate, em Gên. 26:34. Ela é a primeira esposa de Esaú mencionada por nome, embora fosse sua terceira esposa. Mas alguns supõem que havia duas esposas com o mesmo nome, talvez ambas filhas de Elom. Porém, isso é apenas conjectura. Nenhuma solução da aparente discrepância tem sido encontrada, e nem a questão é importante. O casamento de Esaú e Ada

ADADA — ADÃO

introduziu sangue cananeu, e chegou a influenciar a vida dos israelitas. Essa mulher foi antepassada de seis tribos iduméias (ver Gên. 36:2-4,15,16). (FA S UN Z)

ADADA

Seu sentido no hebraico é incerto, talvez **festividade** ou *fronteira*, uma cidade de Judá na fronteira suleste, perto de Edom (ver Jos. 15:22). A localização é desconhecida, embora tenha sido sugerida Khirbet 'Ar 'arah, cerca de dezesseis quilômetros a suleste de Berseba. Outros identificam-na com Aroer, em Judá. A ordem das palavras, no livro de Josué, sugere que esse lugar ficaria na região de Arade e Aroer. (Z)

ADAGA

Essa palavra indica qualquer instrumento agudo, mas, especialmente, uma arma de guerra (ver Juí. 3:16,21,22). Ver o artigo geral sobre *Armas, Armadura*.

ADAÍAS

No hebraico, **Yahweh adornou** ou **agradável a** *Yahweh*, nome de várias pessoas no Antigo Testamento:

1. Avô materno do rei Josias (ver II Reis 22:1).
2. Um levita da família de Gérson, talvez o mesmo que Ido, que nasceu em cerca de 632 A.C. (ver I Crô. 6:20,21,41).
3. Filho de Bani, um israelita que se divorciou de sua esposa gentia, depois do cativeiro (ver Esd. 10:29).
4. Outro descendente de Bani, culpado da mesma ofensa (ver Esd. 10:39).
5. Um dos benjamitas, residente em Jerusalém antes do cativeiro (ver I Crô. 8:21), em cerca de 586 A.C.
6. Pai de Maaséias, um dos capitães de cem, que apoiou Jeoiada (ver II Crô. 23:1).
7. Filho de Joiaribe, pai de Hazaías, da tribo de Judá (ver Nee. 11:5), de cuja posteridade alguns vieram a residir em Jerusalém, após o cativeiro (cerca de 445 A.C.).
8. Um sacerdote, filho de Jeroão, o qual, após o retorno da Babilônia, foi empregado na obra do santuário (ver I Crô. 9:12 e Nee. 11:12). (FA S UN)

ADÁLIA

Termo hebraico, mas de origem persa, de sentido desconhecido, um dos dez filhos de Hamã, o inimigo dos judeus. Foi executado pelos judeus sob o edito real em Susã (ver Est. 9:8), em cerca de 447 A.C. (S)

ADAM

Variante de **Adom**.

ADAMÁ

No hebraico, **terra**, cidade fortificada de Naftali (ver Jos. 19:36). Era uma das dezenove cidades fortificadas. Não se conhece com certeza a sua localização, mas parece que ficava ao norte do mar da Galiléia. Não são muito prováveis as identificações com Adami-Neguebe, e com o local onde se encontram os rios Jaboque e Jordão. (S UN Z)

ADAMATA

No hebraico, **terreno(?), escuro**, um dos sete príncipes da Pérsia e da Média, «que se avistavam pessoalmente com o rei, e se assentavam como principais no reino» (Est. 1:14). A rainha Vasti foi banida por Assuero, devido ao conselho que ele deu, em cerca de 519 A.C. (S Z)

ADAMI-NEGUEBE

No hebraico, **terras vermelhas do passo**, ou *fortaleza do passo*, ou mesmo *terreno do passo* (ver Jos. 19:33). Era um lugar perto da fronteira de Naftali, provavelmente identificável com Khirbet Damiyeh, uma localidade da Idade do Bronze, a oito quilômetros a sudoeste de Tiberíades, no lado ocidental do mar da Galiléia. Ficava na rota de caravanas da área leste da Galiléia para a planície de Aco. (UN Z)

ADÃO

Biblicamente falando, é o primeiro homem e pai da raça humana. O termo deriva-se do hebraico *adamah*, «terra», a substância da qual foi formado o corpo físico de Adão. Adão representa, na teologia judaica, a fonte primária de toda a vida humana. Simbolicamente, ele é tratado nessa teologia como a unidade básica e a igualdade de toda a humanidade. Ele representa a propensão humana para a fraqueza e o pecado, embora originalmente o homem tivesse sido dotado de virtude. Ver os artigos sobre a *queda do homem* e o *pecado original*. O termo «adão» aparece por 560 vezes no A.T., para indicar homem ou humanidade; mas no começo do livro de Gênesis indica o primeiro homem, e é um nome próprio.

Várias interpretações acerca de Adão:

1. *Bíblico-literal*. Adão foi um homem real, de fato, o primeiro homem, não somente da atual raça humana, mas em sentido absoluto. Ele veio à existência por um ato especial da criação, e não mediante algum processo evolutivo. A mulher foi literalmente formada de uma costela extraída do homem. A queda no pecado sucedeu tal como é historiado, mediante a tentação de uma serpente capaz de falar, acerca de um fruto proibido. Em suma, tudo quanto é dito no começo do livro de Gênesis deve ser compreendido literalmente, e não como parabólico ou simbólico em qualquer sentido. Mediante cálculos derivados de Gênesis, por meio das genealogias, a Terra deve ser vista como tendo menos de 7000 anos de idade, e todas as descobertas geológicas, embora pareçam antiqüíssimas, de alguma maneira devem ser encaixadas dentro desse espaço de tempo. Embora não seja um livro científico, a Bíblia não incorre em erros científicos.

O Novo Testamento obviamente aceita que Adão foi uma personagem histórica, não devendo ser entendido como um símbolo da humanidade. Ver Luc. 3:38, onde a genealogia de Jesus retrocede até Adão. Falando sobre a queda, o trecho de I Tim. 2:13-14 não mostra indícios de que se tencionava uma alegoria. Judas 14 faz Enoque ser o sétimo depois de Adão, sem qualquer tentativa de afirmar qualquer coisa que não seja evidente fato histórico. Paulo estabelece o contraste entre o primeiro e o último Adão (Rom. 5:12-21; I Cor. 15:22-45, vinculando a origem do pecado ao primeiro Adão, e da redenção, ao último Adão). O último Adão é uma pessoa histórica indiscutível, ficando implícito que isso se dá também com o primeiro.

2. *Bíblico-literário modificado*. Adão foi um

35

ADÃO

personagem histórico, literal, mas as genealogias dos hebreus com freqüência são incompletas, tornando-se símbolos de descendência, e não de declarações exatas. Biblicamente, não há como reconstituir a cronologia. Outrossim, tendo sido Adão o primeiro homem da presente raça (homo sapiens), pode ter havido raças pré-adâmicas de criaturas similares ao homem. As descobertas científicas podem estar desenterrando tais raças, e longas eras podem ter-se escoado antes da criação, conforme as conhecemos atualmente. Ademais, há um grande hiato de tempo entre Gên. 1:1 e Gên. 1:2. Houve uma criação original que entrou em caos. E então houve uma recriação, quando apareceu a atual raça humana. Essa linhagem humana começou com a figura literal de Adão, pelo que ele é o primeiro homem da narrativa bíblica; mas pode ter havido numerosas outras eras e raças sobre as quais nada sabemos, por não serem espiritualmente importantes para nós. O hiato entre Gên. 1:1 e Gên. 1:2 abre espaço para todas as descobertas geológicas e paleontológicas que não possam ser racionalmente encaixadas dentro de menos de sete mil anos.

3. *Líbero-radical*. As narrativas bíblicas sobre Adão, a criação, a queda, etc., não têm qualquer valor histórico, sendo frontalmente contraditas por tudo quanto a ciência tem sido capaz de produzir. Essas narrativas são meros mitos, e bastante crus. Para começar, o homem foi apenas uma estátua de argila, e a mulher foi formada de uma costela, mostrando quão destituído de imaginação foi o autor do livro de Gênesis, que expôs descrições das origens realmente cruas. Outrossim, temos em Gên. 1 a teoria astronômica da *cúpula invertida*. Segundo a teologia hebraica, o «firmamento» era uma tampa firme, sólida e semi-esférica, que tampava a Terra em seu interior. Em outras palavras, era uma espécie de cúpula que encobria a Terra. As estrelas não seriam corpos luminosos separados, mas apenas perfurações que permitiam que a luz celeste chegasse à Terra. Quem investigar a cosmologia dos hebreus descobrirá que eles não formavam idéias aceitáveis para a astronomia moderna. A serpente que andava e falava é outro elemento cru e sem imaginação da narrativa do autor. Precisamos lembrar que a teologia hebréia original não representava essa serpente como Satanás. Isso foi uma associação posterior. Além disso, é um toque estranho, dentro dessa narrativa, fazer com que algo tão crítico como a queda e o destino humano dependam do ato de comer certo fruto no jardim do Éden. Por certo, o caos da degradação humana deve ter tido uma origem bem diferente disso, que não passa de uma invenção simplista e sem sofisticação.

Finalmente, devemos lembrar que as declarações de que a Bíblia não contém erro alicerçam-se sobre o dogma humano e levaram séculos para se desenvolver. A própria Bíblia não reivindica isso para si mesma. Em conseqüência, ao negarmos elementos fantásticos da Bíblia, estamos meramente repelindo os dogmas humanos, e não o que a Bíblia diz por si mesma. O livro de Gênesis, pelo menos em suas porções iniciais, onde encontramos questões sobre origens remotas, foi composto para responder indagações que intrigavam mentes primitivas, e vários mitos foram compilados para dar essas respostas. O homem primitivo perguntava: «Por que o homem é tão pecaminoso? Por que ele sofre? Por que a mulher sofre dores durante o parto? Por que crescem as ervas daninhas? De onde vem tanto caos?» O primeiro capítulo de Gênesis sonda esses mistérios, embora de forma bastante primitiva e mal-informada.

4. *Abordagem líbero-neo-ortodoxa*. Se não pode-mos afirmar que Gên. 1 seja um verdadeiro registro histórico dos primórdios humanos, podemos afirmar que é importante a teologia contida em seus *símbolos*. Não precisamos da história para formarmos teologia. A ciência demole as narrativas antigas do ponto de vista histórico. Apesar de que algumas coisas na história são importantes para o cristianismo, como a vida de Jesus, a Sua morte e ressurreição (coisas que podem ser aceitas como históricas e literais), outras coisas, como as que dizem respeito a origens absolutas, não são expostas em termos históricos literais nos documentos sagrados. De fato, simples-mente desconhecemos como as coisas começaram e como o homem caiu, ou como a mulher veio à existência, se seu começo diferiu do começo do homem. E nem é moral e espiritualmente importante que saibamos dessas coisas. Cremos que tudo teve origem em Deus, e que Ele efetuou um ato especial de criação para trazer o homem à existência; mas poderia ter instituído um processo evolutivo que envolvesse esse propósito. O que sabemos é que o homem está aqui, e é um ser decaído. Mediante a narrativa de Gênesis, podemos obter discernimentos quanto à condição espiritual do homem.

Os trechos neotestamentários que dão apoio ao Adão histórico fazem-no porque era nisso que os autores sagrados acreditavam. Mas, supor que eles tivessem de estar certos em tudo não passaria de dogmas humanos que precisavam de séculos para se desenvolver. Os próprios autores não reivindicaram inerrância; e mesmo que o tivessem feito, não poderiam comprová-la. Aquele que precisa apelar para o mito da inerrância é um infante espiritual que precisa de mamadeira adredemente preparada. A espiritualidade não se parece com isso. De fato, a espiritualidade (em seu aspecto de conhecimento) é uma aventura, uma inquirição. Existem grandes verdades subjacentes como Deus, a existência e a sobrevivência da alma, e muitos detalhes dotados de base histórica. Porém, é vão tentar encaixar historicamente e sem erros tudo quanto encontramos na Bíblia:

Consideremos também este pequeno exemplar da teologia hebréia. O autor de Gên. 1 e 2 não tencionava descrever o começo da alma humana. O «sopro divino» no barro, que animou o homem, de acordo com o pensamento hebreu, não tinha a intenção de colocá-lo em um elemento imaterial e eterno. Embora o Pentateuco fale sobre Deus e os anjos, ali não há qualquer explicação sobre a alma humana. Assim, a narrativa de Gênesis não pretende dizer-nos de onde veio a *alma*; e a alma é o homem real, e o seu corpo é apenas um veículo temporário. Portanto, desse ângulo, não temos qualquer relato sobre como começou o *homem real*. Somente no tempo dos Salmos e dos Profetas é que a teologia hebréia incluiu a alma. Ela já fazia parte de outras antigas religiões e filosofias, por longo tempo, antes de entrar no pensamento dos hebreus. Em razão disso, devemos ser cautelosos quanto aos relatos antigos, porque, espiritualmente falando, há muita coisa a ser dita sobre o homem que não foi incluído ali, sem importar se consideramos essas narrativas historicamente verazes ou não.

Não obstante, a teologia é um negócio sério, e a representação simbólica em Gênesis faz parte disso.

Acima das controvérsias: — Ignorando por ora as controvérsias que cercam a história de Adão, devemos observar importantes ensinos contidos nessa narrativa:

1. Originalmente o homem era um ser elevado, de

Adão e Eva e a Rebelião

REBELIÃO CONTRA DEUS

••• •••

Proibida (Núm. 14:9; Jos. 22:19)
Provoca a Deus (Núm. 16:30; Nee. 9:26)
Provoca a Cristo (comp. Êxo. 23:20 com I Cor.

10:9)
Vexa ao Espírito Santo (Isa. 63:10)

Exibida:
  Na incredulidade (Deu. 9:23)
  Na rejeição do governo divino (I Sam. 8:7)
  Na revolta contra Deus (Isa. 1:5)
  No desprezo de sua lei (Nee. 9:36)
  No desprezo aos seus conselhos (Sal. 107:11)
  Na desconfiança quanto ao seu poder (Eze.
  17:15)
  Na murmuração contra Deus (Núm. 20:3,10)
  Na recusa de dar-lhe ouvidos (Deu. 9:23)
  No afastar-se de Deus (Isa. 59:13)

A Culpa devido à Rebeldia:
  É agravada pelos cuidados paternais de
  Deus (Isa. 1:2)
  É agravada pelos incessantes convites de
  Deus, para que o rebelde retorne a ele
  (Isa. 65:2)
  Deve ser lamentada (Jos. 22:29)
  Deve ser confessada (Lam. 1:18,20)

Perdão:
  Só Deus pode perdoá-la (Nee. 9:17)
  É perdoada em face do arrependimento
  (Nee. 9:26,27)

Os Ministros:
  São advertidos contra ela (Eze. 2:8)
  São enviados aos rebeldes (Mar. 12:4-8)
  Devem advertir contra a mesma (Núm. 14:9)
  Devem testificar contra a mesma (Isa.
  30:8,9)
  Devem relembrar o passado a seus
  líderes (Deu. 9:7; 31:27)

••• •••

ADÃO — ADÃO, O ÚLTIMO (SEGUNDO)

grande inteligência e de notáveis qualidades espirituais. A origem do homem, o verdadeiro homem, o espírito, não se encontra no reino animal. Ele traz a «imagem de Deus». Inferiores são outros pontos de vista do homem, como o humanismo e o marxismo. O homem não é um produto natural, e nem apenas economicamente formado. Em sua origem há o toque divino.

2. Por ter a imagem de Deus, o homem, finalmente, através da redenção, terá a semelhança divina, a Sua natureza essencial, embora em escala finita (II Ped. 1:4).

3. Isso resulta da missão do *último Adão* (ver o artigo seguinte), que se identifica com toda a humanidade. (Rom. 5:12 ss ; I Cor. 15:45-47).

4. O que é físico serviu de veículo, mas o homem realmente não pertence ao terreno físico. Os pais alexandrinos, seguindo idéias platônicas, supunham que o verdadeiro homem pertencia a uma criação espiritual anterior e antiqüíssima, e que a sua união eventual com o corpo físico, e sua história subseqüente representam estágios da história humana, mas não a sua substância. Com ou sem esses ensinos, precisamos reconhecer que o homem é um ser espiritual cujo destino não está (finalmente) relacionado à esfera terrestre. Sua porção espiritual é transcendental. Quanto à origem da alma, ver o artigo sobre *a alma*.

5. A intervenção divina na história humana, ou *teísmo*, em contraste com o *deísmo*. O teísmo (ver o artigo) ensina que Deus se interessa pelo homem e intervém em sua história, recompensando ou punindo, guiando e cuidando. Neste mundo operam propósito e desígnio. O deísmo (ver o artigo) apesar de admitir alguma força criadora, pessoal ou impessoal, acredita que a mesma esteja divorciada da criação, deixando que as leis naturais a governassem. Portanto, essa força não faria qualquer intervenção, nem se importaria e nem castigaria ou puniria o homem. A narrativa bíblica põe-se inteiramente ao lado do teísmo.

6. Contra um Universo mecânico e materialista, Deus e o espírito estavam presentes desde o começo. Ver o artigo sobre *o materialismo*.

7. O conhecimento espiritual é oferecido ao homem, conforme é simbolicamente representado pela árvore do conhecimento. Deus transmite, e o homem pode aprender. Ver o artigo sobre *o misticismo*.

8. Pecaminosidade. O homem e a mulher viram que estavam nus, quando pecaram. Na humanidade há delito e desgraça, e isso requer redenção. Ver o artigo sobre esse assunto e sobre *a salvação*.

9. Há a vida eterna. Isso é representado pela árvore da vida. Ver o artigo sobre *a vida eterna*.

10. A confusão causada pelo pecado. Quanto caos foi provocado pelo pecado! Ver o artigo sobre *o pecado*.

11. O princípio maligno. O mal também é pessoal, e não apenas circunstancial. Existem seres malignos que impedem e destroem. Ver os artigos sobre *Satanás* e *os demônios*. A serpente (ver o artigo) representa essas forças negativas.

12. A penalidade. Adão e Eva foram expulsos por causa do pecado. Ver o artigo sobre *o julgamento*. (B EB JB NTI S V W WH Z)

ADÃO, CIDADE DE

Cidade a alguma distância a leste do rio Jordão, diante ou abaixo da qual cessou o fluxo das águas daquele rio, permitindo a passagem dos israelitas por seu canal. Ficava localizada onde deságua no Jordão o segundo maior rio da Transjordânia, o Jaboque. Ver Jos. 3:9-17. Esse nome também se encontra na inscrição de Faraó Sisaque, onde ele descreve suas invasões na Palestina, no quinto ano de Reoboão, filho de Salomão. Essa inscrição foi preservada no templo de Amom, em Carnaque. O nome moderno do lugar é Tell ed-Damiyeh. O nome dessa antiga cidade, Adão (vermelho), provavelmente derivava-se da cor da argila da região. (S Z)

ADÃO, LIVROS DE

Esse é um título geral que alude a várias obras não-canônicas e que abordam diversos eventos fantasiosos nas vidas da primeira família. Há uma versão em grego, no *Apocalipse de Moisés*. Há uma outra versão na obra latina *Vida de Adão e Eva*. A primeira dessas obras parece ser a mais antiga, embora ambas possam ter uma origem comum. Devido à ausência de quaisquer elementos cristãos, o original (em hebraico ou aramaico) provavelmente foi escrito por um judeu (de Alexandria?) algum tempo após 60 D.C., mas talvez até ao século IV D.C.

Versões menores existem em outras línguas, como o armênio, e eslavônico, o etíope, o siríaco e o árabe. A versão armênia é a que mais se aproxima do manuscrito do *Apocalipse de Moisés*, e a versão eslavônica é a mais parecida com a versão grega em geral.

A estória. Expulsão do jardim do Éden; Eva prevê o assassinato de Abel em um sonho; Adão sofre enfermidade e dor, em resultado da queda; Sete e Eva procuram obter azeite da árvore da vida, para curar Adão, mas uma fera os ataca para impedir isso. Miguel, o arcanjo, declara que a doença de Adão é incurável. Adão morre e vai para o terceiro céu. Anjos sepultam o corpo de Adão. Eva ordena que sejam registrados em pedra alguns relatos. Eva morre uma semana depois de Adão. Miguel restringe o período de lamentação a seis dias.

A versão latina acrescenta os elementos seguintes: Após a expulsão, Eva pede que Adão a mate, por causa de seu pecado e da calamidade resultante. Adão sugere um período de arrependimento. Ele fica no Jordão por quarenta dias, e ela no Tigre, por trinta e sete dias. Ali ela sofre uma segunda tentação por parte de Satanás, no décimo oitavo dia. Adão diz a Eva que deixe o rio, por haver sido perdoada. Adão desmascara o engodo. Satanás explica que ele agiu por motivo de inveja, porque a todos os anjos de Deus fora ordenado que adorassem a Adão (Sal. 8:2). (CH GI J S Z)

ADÃO, O ÚLTIMO (SEGUNDO)

Um título aplicado por Paulo a Cristo, tendo o apóstolo desenvolvido o paralelismo e o contraste entre Adão e Cristo. Cristo é o último Adão (I Cor. 15:45), e também o segundo Adão (I Cor. 15:47). Em Rom. 5:14, Adão é apresentado como o tipo contrastante de Cristo. Paulo enfatiza a solidariedade da raça humana inteira, primeiramente com Adão, quanto à origem física, e então com Cristo, por ser Ele a fonte da vida espiritual. O primeiro trouxe a morte por meio do pecado, e o segundo trouxe a vida, mediante Sua missão salvatícia (Rom. 5:12). O pecado de Adão é visto como algo que afetou a humanidade inteira, talvez por meio da hereditariedade, ou então mediante a afinidade espiritual. Talvez o autor sagrado visse todos os homens

ADAR — ADIÁFORA

biologicamente presentes em Adão, pelo que fariam parte de sua personalidade. Em consequência, todos participam daquilo que ele foi. O «velho homem» está em todos nós, pois participamos da queda de Adão (Rom. 6:6; Efé. 4:22; Col. 3:9). A experiência parece comprovar que os homens não se tornam pecadores meramente devido ao fator ambiental. Até crianças conforme Freud demonstrou, têm todas as formas de horrendos répteis ocultos na mente. Portanto, não é que meramente morremos; merecemos morrer. Porém, nossa salvação é assegurada mediante a identidade com o Cabeça da raça espiritual, a saber, Jesus Cristo, o último Adão, que faz reverter o caos criado pelo primeiro Adão.

Somos incorporados na *nova humanidade* que é uma raça espiritual, e cujo alvo é a participação na natureza divina (II Ped. 1:4). Tal como Cristo participou de nossa natureza humana, assim também, finalmente, participaremos da natureza divina, compartilhando da imagem de Cristo (Rom. 8:29; II Cor. 3:18). Uma *nova criação* está sendo trazida à existência (II Cor. 5:17). A imagem desfigurada do Criador está sendo renovada no homem.

Provisão universal. Por meio do pecado de Adão, o juízo sobreveio a *todos os homens.* Mas, mediante a retidão do último Adão, o dom gratuito da salvação e da vida 'eterna é oferecido a *todos os homens* (Rom. 5:18). Diversas interpretações têm surgido no tocante a isso, conforme damos abaixo:

1. Cristo anulou o pecado original, com o resultado que agora os seres humanos nascem sem pecado e tornam-se pecadores devido à influência do meio ambiente e por escolha pessoal, com base no livre-arbítrio. A experiência não parece apoiar tal idéia. Ninguém precisa ensinar as crianças como se peca. Pecar faz parte da substância de seus seres.

2. A provisão de Cristo é absolutamente universal e foi franqueada a todos os que quiseram. Em outras palavras, todos podem ser salvos. Isso concorda com trechos bíblicos como I Tim. 2:4. Ver as notas no NTI sobre o *livre-arbítrio,* bem como o artigo nesta obra, sobre o mesmo assunto. As Escrituras também ensinam o *determinismo.* Ver o NTI em Efé. 1:4, bem como o artigo nesta obra.

3. Os universalistas vêm nesse texto uma prova de sua doutrina, de que todos os homens, eventualmente serão salvos, embora talvez isso ocupe muito tempo. Quanto a notas sobre a plena extensão da missão de Cristo, ver o NTI, em Efé. 1:10. Ver o artigo sobre *a restauração.* É impossível que viesse a falhar a missão de Cristo, não atingindo a todos os homens, de todos os lugares, afinal de contas. Mas, como ela alcança aos mesmos pode ser diversificadamente definido, e as notas aludidas abordam a questão. Ver o artigo sobre *o universalismo.* (EB NTI V W Z)

ADAR

No acadiano, **escuro ou nebuloso,** um nome posterior do décimo segundo mês do ano judaico, tomado por empréstimo dos judeus, quando exilados na Babilônia. Esse mês ia da lua nova de fevereiro à lua nova de março. Quando necessário, por causa do ano lunar, era usado um segundo mês de Adar, intercalado. (Ver Eze. 6:15; 3:7,13; 8:12; 9:1,15-21). As importantes comemorações desse mês eram as seguintes: a. A morte de Moisés, no sétimo dia, que era relembrada com um jejum (ver Deu. 34:5,6), embora as autoridades discordem quanto a essa data. Josefo, *Ant.,* diz-se que essa comemoração ocorria no primeiro dia desse mês. As referências talmúdicas dão apoio ao sétimo dia. b. Hilel e Shammai, uma

comemoração no nono dia, relembrava a separação dessas duas escolas teológicas dos judeus, o que ocorreu poucos anos antes do nascimento de Cristo. c. O jejum de Ester, no décimo terceiro dia, por três dias (ver Est. 4:16), e que incluía a preparação para a festividade seguinte, a festa de Purim. d. Uma festividade em memória da derrota e morte de Nicanor (ver II Mac. 15:36). e. A festa de *Purim* (ver o artigo a respeito), nos dias 14 e 15 desse mês. Ver sobre *Calendário.*

ADAR

No hebraico, **eira, lugar espaçoso.** 1. Filho de Bela e neto de Benjamim (ver I Crô. 8:3). Também foi chamado Arde em Gên. 46:21 e Núm. 26:40. 2. Cidade fortificada na fronteira sul de Judá, perto de Cades-Barnéia, que talvez possa ser identificada com Khirbet el-qudeirat, a oito quilômetros a noroeste de Cades-Barnéia. (FA Z)

ADASA

Cidade que não é mencionada no Antigo Testamento, embora aludida em I Mac. 7:40,45 e em Josefo, *Ant.* xii.10:5, localizada entre Bete-Horom e Jerusalém, provavelmente a moderna Khirbet 'Addaseh, a onze quilômetros de Bete-Horom. Ali, Judas Macabeu, com três mil homens, derrotou o exército sírio comandado por Nicanor, o que é comemorado no décimo terceiro dia do mês de Adar (ver I Mac. 7:49).

ADEGA Ver **Depósito.**

AD HOC

Latim, **para isto.** Na lógica, uma hipótese **ad hoc** é formada a fim de explicar um dado fenômeno, embora diferindo de hipóteses poderosas, por não 'derivar-se de outros fenômenos ou por não resultar em outras consequências comprováveis. O valor dessas hipóteses, que se aplica somente a certos fenômenos específicos, é que lança dúvida não estribada em evidências comprobatórias. Geralmente, o termo significa apenas «no tocante a esta coisa particular».

ADI

No grego, **ornamento** (ver Luc. 3:28). Era filho de Cosã e pai de Melqui, o terceiro acima de Salatiel, na genealogia de Jesus Cristo. O termo pode ser uma forma variante de Adna (ver o artigo a respeito). (S Z)

ADIABENE

Nome grego da principal das seis províncias em que foi dividida a Assíria. Plínio (*Hist. Nat.* v:12) e Amiano (xxiii:6, sec. 20), referiam-se à Assíria inteira por esse termo. A região não é mencionada na Bíblia. Mas Josefo (*Ant.* x:2,4; *Bel. Jud.* ii:16,19; v:4,6,11) diz que a rainha Helena e seu filho Izates, de Adiabene, tornaram-se israelitas.

ADIÁFORA

Essa é uma palavra grega que significa «coisas indiferentes», referindo-se a questões que não são consideradas essenciais à fé, que podem ser toleradas em si mesmas, mas que com frequência devem ser evitadas, a fim de que outras pessoas não nos critiquem.

Exemplos bíblicos. Jesus e Paulo, apesar de denunciarem o alcoolismo (Luc. 21:23; I Cor. 5:11), não condenaram a ingestão moderada de bebidas

ADIÁFORA — ADITUM

alcoólicas (João 2:1-12; Mat. 11:19; I Tim. 5:23). Era questão indiferente para eles. Mas a ciência tem demonstrado que o álcool no sangue mata células cerebrais, pelo que a ingestão de bebidas alcoólicas em qualquer dose não pode ser correta, segundo o princípio declarado em I Cor. 6:19-20. Para Paulo, a circuncisão e a ingestão de certos alimentos eram questões livres para o crente (I Tim. 4:3-5; Gál. 2:3; 5:6). Ele acreditava que existiam muitas coisas dessa natureza. «Todas as cousas me são lícitas, mas nem todas me convêm» (I Cor. 6:12). Esse vocábulo, «todas», é aqui limitado pelo contexto, indicando aquelas coisas sem conteúdo moral, isto é, que não são realmente nem certas e nem erradas. Uma pessoa pode comer todo tipo de carne (I Cor. 6:13; I Tim. 4:4) porque, ingerir carne, em si mesmo, não é ato pecaminoso. Porém, uma vez que se aprenda pela ciência que certas carnes contêm muito colesterol, por motivos de saúde, devemos ingerir menos dessas carnes e procurar ter uma dieta equilibrada, de acordo com as pesquisas modernas. Não há como negar que o avanço da ciência pode aprimorar-nos na moralidade, acima dos antigos preceitos, que eram puramente teológicos.

Na história eclesiástica. Além das coisas que a Bíblia considera moralmente indiferentes, aparecem outras na história da Igreja, como o celibato. Algumas seitas dos primeiros séculos cristãos insistiam que o celibato era necessário à santidade, como os gnósticos ascéticos. A Igreja assumiu posição moderada e deixou que o celibato dependesse da escolha pessoal (Crisóstomo, Hom. 15:2, em Heb., comentário sobre Gál. 2:11 ss.).

Uma vez formadas as denominações protestantes, vários grupos passaram a discutir se seria certo ou errado reter certas práticas católicas. Melancton declarou que a confirmação, a veneração aos santos, a confissão auricular, a extrema-unção, os ritos, o cerimonial, os dias santos, etc., podiam ser praticados, por serem espiritualmente indiferentes. Mas muitos luteranos negavam o acerto de tais práticas, por serem uma transigência sincretista. Eles também insistiam que as coisas indiferentes (res mediae), quando *impostas* pelas autoridades, tornavam-se erradas por violarem a liberdade cristã. Alguns (incluindo os puritanos posteriores) tomaram a posição extrema de dizer que coisas *não explicitamente permitidas* nas Escrituras são condenáveis. Mas isso reflete ascetismo e legalismo. Os anglicanos têm considerado como adiáforas muitas coisas permitidas, mas não obrigatórias, como são certas práticas religiosas tradicionais, embora não apoiadas por textos bíblicos de prova.

As diversões, por toda a história da Igreja, têm sido motivo de debates, se seriam ou não adiáforas; ou quais delas são permissíveis e quais não a são. Essa é uma questão complexa, porque uma diversão, embora inofensiva em si mesma, pode tornar-se prejudicial se conduzida em um lugar moralmente degradante. Essas são questões debatíveis, devendo ser esclarecidas, para que os crentes ajam segundo a consciência individual ou coletiva. A liberalidade quase sempre desliza para o pecado, mas o ascetismo estrangula, pelo que é difícil encontrar o ponto de equilíbrio. Em tempos modernos, a música própria de clubes noturnos foi introduzida nas igrejas a fim de entreter e de atrair ouvintes. Visto que a música exerce uma influência moral, tal música na igreja dificilmente pode ser tida como questão indiferente. Deve ser rejeitada a qualquer custo. (H NTI)

ADIÇÕES A ESTER

Ver **Ester, Adições a.**

ADIDA

Forma grega que na Vulgata é Addus. Uma cidade fortificada da tribo de Judá. Em 1 Mac. 12:38 ficamos sabendo que Simão Macabeu fortificou o lugar. Eusébio diz que o nome que se dava nesse tempo ao território aberto perto de Eleuterópolis era Sefelá. Adida, em Sefelá, provavelmente é o mesmo local mencionado em I Mac. 13:13. A cidade estava situada em uma colina, acima das planícies da Judéia, em uma estrada que levava a Jerusalém. Talvez seja a Hadida do Antigo Testamento. Simão Macabeu usou o local em sua luta contra Tripom (ver I Mac. 13:13), e foi ali que Aretas, rei da Arábia, derrotou Alexandre Janeu em batalha (ver Josefo, *Ant.* xiii.15,2). (S)

ADIEL

No hebraico significa **ornamento de Deus**. 1. Um dos chefes da tribo ue Simeão, que aparentemente conquistou a terra de Gedor (ver I Crô. 4:36). 2. Um sacerdote, filho de Jazera e pai de Maasai. Seu filho ajudou na reconstrução do templo, após o cativeiro (ver I Crô. 9:12), em cerca de 536 A.C. 3. Pai de Azmavete, tesoureiro de Davi (ver I Crô. 27:25). (UN S)

ADIM

No hebraico, **efeminado**. 1. Cabeça de uma das famílias israelitas, cujos descendentes retornaram com Zorobabel da Babilônia a Jerusalém, em cerca de 536 A.C. O número deles era de 454, de acordo com Esd. 2:15, mas Nee. 7:20 fala em 655 descendentes. Ocorreu aqui algum erro de transcrição. A diferença de 54 e 55 pode ser explicada pelo próprio autor, no segundo caso. 2. Um homem que assinou o pacto feito por Neemias com o povo, após terem retornado a Jerusalém (ver Nee. 10:16), em cerca de 445 A.C. (S)

ADINA

No hebraico, **magro, delicado**. Era filho de Siza, um rubenita, capitão de trinta de seus companheiros de tribo, um dos guerreiros de Davi (ver I Crô. 11:42), cerca de 1000 A.C. (S Z)

ADINU

Forma alternativa de **Adim**.

ADINUS

Forma alternativá de **Jamim**.

ADITAIM

Seu sentido no hebraico é incerto. Uma cidade de Judá (ver Jos. 15:36), de localização desconhecida. Posteriormente, o nome parece haver sido mudado para Hadide (*Cadide*) e para Adida. (S)

ADITUM

No grego vem de a, «não», e dein, «entrar». Indicava algum santuário secreto, em certos lugares de adoração, na antiguidade. Apontava para algum lugar inacessível ou impenetrável, como era o caso do

ADIVINHAÇÃO

Santo dos Santos do templo de Jerusalém. Metaforicamente, a palavra tem sido usada para indicar o coração ou a consciência do ser humano, ou, algumas vezes, o significado profundo e espiritual da Palavra de Deus. (S)

ADIVINHAÇÃO

I. A Prática Da Adivinhação Nas Escrituras

O A.T. condena todas essas práticas entre os povos pagãos (Lev. 19:26; Deu. 18:9-14; II Reis, 17:17 e 21:6). Porém, é fato fácil de ser demonstrado que o próprio povo de Israel muito se envolveu com tais práticas, e que freqüentemente o fez sem qualquer censura.

Abaixo oferecemos um sumário sobre a questão, mostrando os oito métodos geralmente empregados nas páginas das Escrituras ou na cultura judaica:

1. *Rabdomancia* (ver Eze. 21:21). Varetas ou flexas eram atiradas para o ar, e os presságios eram deduzidos das posições em que esses objetos caíam. Talvez a passagem de Osé. 4:12 seja uma referência a isso.

2. *Hepatoscopia* (ver Eze. 21:21). Esse método de adivinhação consistia no exame do fígado ou outras entranhas dos animais sacrificados. Sentidos prováveis eram atribuídos aos diversos sinais desses órgãos, mais ou menos semelhantes ao que fazem as quiromantes, ao examinarem as marcas das palmas das mãos de seus fregueses.

3. *Terafins*. Eram imagens de antepassados mortos. (Ver I Sam. 15:23; Eze. 21:21 e Zac. 10:2). Alguns estudiosos acreditam que esse método representava alguma forma remota de espiritismo.

4. *Necromancia*. Era a consulta aos mortos, isto é, aos espíritos desencarnados de tais indivíduos. (Ver Deut. 18:11; I Sam. 28:7; II Reis 21:6; Isa. 8:19,20). Essa prática era estritamente condenada pela lei mosaica. (Ver Lev. 18:31 e 20:6). Supunha-se que o chamado *médium* ou intermediário possuía um espírito familiar, ou, usando termos modernos, um *controle*. O vocábulo «necromante» é utilizado em Deut. 18:11, e significa, literalmente, «aquele que interroga os mortos». Não há razão alguma em supormos que o A.T. queria dar a entender que essa prática é impossível; e as pesquisas modernas parecem indicar que, pelo menos em alguns casos, se obtém contatos genuínos, e que mensagens genuínas são transmitidas assim. Porém, de mistura com essa prática sem dúvida alguma surgem formas freqüentes de demonismo, quando alguns espíritos malignos fingem ser seres humanos já falecidos. Outrossim, a maioria dos espíritos de mortos que podem entrar em contato com os vivos são os de natureza *maligna e inferior*.

Regressam Os Espíritos dos Mortos?

a. A doutrina judaica condenava o contato com os espíritos dos mortos, mas não considerava isso algo impossível.

b. A doutrina judaica comumente associava os demônios aos espíritos humanos desencarnados depravados e aviltados. Essa idéia foi seguida por muitos dos primeiros pais da igreja. O mais provável é que entre os demônios havia tanto anjos decaídos como espíritos humanos desencarnados aviltados, além de outros tipos de seres espirituais, sobre os quais não temos nenhum conhecimento maior.

c. Não há razão para dúvidas de que, em tempos modernos, os chamados «médiuns» sejam capazes de entrar em contato com certa variedade de espíritos, incluindo espíritos humanos que se acham no mundo intermediário, a saber, o mundo espiritual onde os destinos ainda não estão bem definidos. (Ver notas em I Ped. 4:6 no NTI sobre como os «destinos eternos» não serão determinados enquanto não houver a segunda vinda de Cristo). Apesar de poder haver tais contatos — em meio a muita fraude — isso não é desejável, a menos que Deus, por alguma razão específica, envie um desses espíritos em missão, para dar alguma mensagem. Consideramos que esses casos são raríssimos, e que não devem ser buscados abertamente pelos vivos.

d. Ver no NTI as notas completas sobre os «demônios», em Mar. 5:2; sobre a «possessão demoníaca», em Mat. 8:28; sobre «Satanás», em Luc. 10:18.

5. *Astrologia*. Tal prática tira as suas conclusões mediante as posições dos astros celestes, como o sol, a lua, os planetas e as constelações em relação ao zodíaco (que é o cinturão imaginário, no firmamento que se estende por oito graus, de ambos os lados da vereda aparentemente seguida pelo sol incluindo tanto a lua como os principais planetas; tal campo está dividido em doze partes iguais, também chamadas *signos*, cada uma das quais recebeu o nome de alguma constelação) e em relação uns aos outros desses corpos celestes. A Bíblia, a despeito de não condenar abertamente tais especulações, despreza-as entretanto, conforme vemos em Isa. 47:13 e Jer. 10:2.

A história sobre os *magos* ou *astrólogos* que vieram do Oriente, a fim de apresentarem os seus presentes ao menino Jesus, era geralmente interpretada pelos pais da igreja como uma admissão de que havia tais estudos em tempos antigos e que Cristo foi a perfeita revelação de Deus que eliminou tais ciências, porquanto tais homens prostraram-se ante a face de Cristo. (Ver Mat. 2:1-12 quanto a essa narrativa e sua devida interpretação).

Três Variedades De Astrologia

a. Há quem pense que os planetas e as estrelas, ao emanarem energia, produzem efeitos, negativos ou positivos, sobre os homens, os quais, afinal de contas, são campos de energia eletromagnética. Naturalmente, o sol e a lua produzem tais efeitos, mas é difícil crer que a débil energia dos planetas também os produzam.

b. Outros crêem numa forma de astrologia que operaria segundo o princípio da «coincidência cheia de significado». Isso daria a entender que Deus, em um desígnio total fantástico, teria equiparado as experiências de cada ser humano com os movimentos dos planetas, da lua e do sol. Essa teoria nega, essencialmente, que os corpos celestes realmente influenciem os homens por meio de emanações de energia. Contudo, pensa-se que as posições e os movimentos de tais corpos coincidem com os eventos das vidas humanas, e isso por um desígnio divino. A vida de um ser humano, por conseguinte, poderia ser lida nas estrelas, pois ali ela seria lida por aqueles que possuem o conhecimento apropriado.

c. Também existe uma astrologia cristã. Alguns têm afirmado serem capazes de encontrar, em vários aspectos do zodíaco, várias afirmações e ilustrações acerca da glória de Cristo. Em outras palavras, cada sinal desvendaria algo dis 1into a respeito dele. As vidas dos homens envolvidas nele como estão, naturalmente também seriam exibidas através daqueles signos.

6. *Hidromancia*. Esse método de adivinhação pode assumir diversas formas. Uma delas consiste em encher uma taça ou copo com água, procurando produzir com tal objeto um transe passageiro. Nesse estado mental podem-se obter informações, ou da

ADIVINHAÇÃO

parte de algum ser superior, que então poderia penetrar na mente e influenciá-la, ou da parte da porção subconsciente da mente do próprio adivinho, naqueles casos em que as pessoas possuem poderes telepáticos e de clarividência que ordinariamente não dispõem os homens, embora o conhecimento assim obtido possa ser transmitido a um indivíduo em estado de sonho. Trata-se, realmente, de uma forma de adivinhação com *bola de cristal*, que é apenas a sua forma moderna, embora alguns desses adivinhos prefiram usar a água. Alguns indivíduos podem até mesmo produzir tais efeitos contemplando alguma superfície plana e polida, como a superfície de uma mesa ou de outro objeto polido. A única referência bíblica insofismável a respeito desse método aparece no trecho de Gên. 44:5, onde se lê que José afirmou que usava o seu cálice de prata com tal propósito. Os intérpretes têm feito muitas contorções para negar que José realmente usava tal método de adivinhações; mas tal esforço é desnecessário, pois os servos de José, meramente repetiram o que ele ordenou que se dissesse. No entanto, isso é tentar fazer as culturas antigas e suas práticas se adaptarem *ao ideal cristão*, conforme esse ideal é contemplado pela igreja cristã moderna. Sabemos que José era possuidor de dons psíquicos, conforme os seus sonhos, interpretações de sonhos e predições indicam claramente; e como há razão real alguma para duvidarmos que ele usasse um ou mais de outros métodos antigos para provocar seu discernimento sobre tais questões. Além disso, o mal consiste na *fonte informativa* espiritual com a qual ele entraria em contato, e não no próprio método usado. Se porventura ele entrava em contato meramente com o nível subconsciente de sua própria mente, dificilmente poder-se-ia dizer que ele entrava em contato com alguma fonte maligna; porém, se ele se deixava arrastar por transes profundos (o que não é usual no método da «bola de cristal»), então sua mente subconsciente poderia ficar aberta ante os poderes malignos; e isso é que seria perigoso.

Por essa mesma razão, não é sábio que indivíduo algum, exceto sob a observação e as recomendações médicas mais estritas possíveis, submeta-se *ao hipnotismo*, porquanto isso franqueia a mente subconsciente para alguém de fora, sendo exercidas possíveis influências malignas, além de ficar debilitado o poder da vontade do indivíduo. Essa prática também cria a dependência psicológica, por parte do hipnotizado, ao hipnotizador; o que é um grande mal. Casos de possessão demoníaca se têm verificado em resultado direto do hipnotismo, porquanto a mente do indivíduo hipnotizado é enfraquecida pela influência externa.

Deveríamos ainda *advertir* neste ponto, que muito daquilo que passa por manifestações espirituais, no seio da igreja evangélica, como o falar em línguas, os pronunciamentos proféticos, as visões, etc., podem nada ser além do produto da mente subconsciente de alguns indivíduos, da influência telepática exercida por terceiros ou por alguma entidade espiritual, quer um espírito humano terreno, quer um espírito humano desencarnado, quer da parte de algum *outro ser* espiritual qualquer. E tudo isso mediante a entrada do indivíduo em uma forma de transe hipnótico, superficial ou profundo. Tais manifestações podem ser induzidas pelo próprio indivíduo ou por outros, os quais, sincera mas ignorantemente, buscam os dons espirituais ou o contato especial com o Espírito Santo. Esse contato espiritual, necessário é que se diga, pode ser real, mas não com o Espírito Santo. Esses são os casos de mistificação. Isso não significa, entretanto, que não existam manifestações genuínas do Espírito Santo.

No que diz respeito à adivinhação por bola de cristal, alguns estudiosos acreditam que *Balaão* pode ter-se utilizado de suas capacidades de clarividência através desse método. (Ver Núm. 24:1).

7. Sonhos. Muitas são as instâncias de sonhos reveladores, tanto no Antigo como no Novo Testamentos, que foram dados por Deus como meios para guiar os homens. O caso de José é uma ilustração que nos vem dos tempos anteriores à lei mosaica; o caso de Daniel é um exemplo do tempo dos profetas. (Ver Gên. 35:40,41 e Dan. 2:4,7). No N.T. diversos exemplos de sonhos místicos são historiados. (Ver Mat. 1:20; 2:12,13,19,22 e Atos 2:17, onde os sonhos são definidamente declarados como meios de comunicação entre Deus e os homens, como cumprimento de parte de uma profecia que aparece em Joel 2:28). O trecho de Zac. 10:2 mostra-nos que os falsos profetas geralmente dependem muito de sonhos falsos e mentirosos.

Os estudos modernos sobre o fenômeno dos sonhos têm mostrado que os sonhos comuns geralmente *combinam* o passado, o presente e o futuro dos indivíduos, essencialmente com o propósito de *resolver problemas*. É óbvio, pois, que a mente subconsciente tem a capacidade de atuar como um computador, recolhendo dados das experiências passadas e presentes, e até mesmo dos acontecimentos futuros, que se sabem fazer parte da experiência necessária do indivíduo, fazendo juízos com base em tais informes; e então, mediante um sonho, fornece orientação à pessoa. Através desses estudos se tem verificado positivamente que todas as mentes humanas têm consciência, em nível profundo, de acontecimentos futuros, sobretudo no que tange ao próprio indivíduo, sendo uma das funções da *psique* humana.

Não existe experiência psíquica mais comum que a do sonho de conhecimento prévio. Tal sonho é uma função da personalidade humana, que fornece orientação ao indivíduo, ou que tem por finalidade prepará-lo psicologicamente para alguma ocorrência acerca da qual a mente subconsciente foi adredemente avisada. A maioria dos sonhos não é lembrada, após o despertar, e somente os mais vívidos é que são relembrados. Alguns estudos têm indicado que *todos* os principais acontecimentos, e talvez até mesmo todos os acontecimentos, são primeiramente sonhados. Dessa forma, pois, parece que a função inteira dos sonhos é de servir de dom de Deus aos homens, ajudando-os em suas existências terrenas de maneira mais ordeira.

Com base em tudo aquilo que já sabemos ou que estamos aprendendo concernente aos sonhos, não nos devemos surpreender que Deus use de tais recursos para comunicar-se com os homens. Afinal de contas, o homem é um ser espiritual, — apesar de temporariamente viver preso a um corpo físico, porém, possui faculdades espirituais inegáveis. Se porventura encontrássemos algum meio de fazer as nossas horas de sono se voltarem para Deus, como também nossas horas despertas, sem dúvida muito proveito espiritual tiraríamos disso.

8. Sortes. (Quanto a informações sobre esse método de adivinhação, ver as notas expositivas sob ponto II).

O único uso que se faz no N.T. do termo *adivinhação*, aparece no trecho de Atos 16:16, onde é contada a história de uma jovem que era possuída por um espírito adivinhador. Tal caso possivelmente pode ser classificado sob o ponto número (4), que aparece acima. O famoso délfico ficava no distrito de Pito (na Grécia central). De Pito é que nos veio o termo

41

ADIVINHAÇÃO

pitonisa, termo esse que indica as mulheres que adivinham as coisas. Tal termo era evidentemente utilizado de forma irrestrita, para indicar qualquer pessoa sobrenaturalmente inspirada, como sucedia às sacerdotisas de Delfos.

II. Como ilustrada em Atos 1:26

Então deitaram sortes a respeito deles e caiu a sorte sobre Matias, e por voto comum foi ele contado com os onze apóstolos.

Esta história nos faz lembrar das práticas do A.T. Por enquanto a igreja primitiva ainda não usava da imposição de mãos, mas uma espécie de cerimônia que provavelmente vinha desde os tempos de Moisés. O método de «lançar sortes» consistia em colocar pedras ou tabuinhas, com nomes escritos, em um vaso, o qual era sacudido até que uma delas caísse. Aquele cujo nome estivesse nessa pedra ou tabuinha, era considerado como a pessoa escolhida por Deus, porquanto pensava-se que de algum modo o Senhor Deus é quem causara aquela ação particular. Não obstante, alguns estudiosos têm pensado que tudo quanto se fazia em tais casos era «tomar um voto», o que seria uma antiga expressão idiomática acerca do lançamento de sortes. No entanto, a maioria dos intérpretes tem-se manifestado contrariamente a essa noção, a qual, mui provavelmente, apareceu como tentativa de «limpar» o texto sagrado, posto que muitos cristãos modernos pensam que esse tipo de ação é muito estranha, posto ser uma forma antiga de adivinhação.

«Interpretada à luz da oração que se fez, Atos 1:24, bem como pela palavra «caiu», que aqui aparece, parece não restar dúvidas de que a passagem fala sobre lançamento de 'sortes', e não sobre 'votos'.» (E.H. Plumptre, *in loc.*).

A literatura antiga revela-nos que essas práticas eram extremamente comuns em outras culturas da época, como, por exemplo, entre os gregos. A bem conhecida história do estratagema de Cresponto, na divisão do território, após a invasão dos dóricos (Sófocles, *Aias*, 1285), é um exemplo disso. A passagem de Pro. 16:33 reflete tanto essa prática como também a confiança que Deus se utilizava desses meios para revelar a sua vontade: «A sorte se lança do vaso, mas do Senhor procede toda a sua disposição». Isso pode refletir um tipo de diferente modo de proceder, em que se punham várias sortes dentro de um vaso; quando estas eram retiradas, as primeiras a saírem eram as favorecidas, sem importar quais decisões estavam sendo tomadas.

No tocante a essa passagem, John Gill diz o seguinte (in loc.): «...lançadas em seu colo, nas vestes de um homem, no seu seio, em seu chapéu, capa, urna ou o que quer que tivesse no colo, de onde eram retiradas. Essa prática era usada na escolha de líderes, tanto civis como eclesiásticos, nas divisões de heranças e na determinação de casos duvidosos; também no estabelecimento de contendas e para pôr fim aos conflitos e desentendimentos, o que, de outro modo, não se poderia conseguir...o juízo que se deveria fazer mediante essa prática, acerca de pessoas ou de coisas...era assim dirigido por Deus, de tal modo que (a sorte) caía sobre a pessoa certa, ou então ficava conhecido aqui o que era o motivo da dúvida...Isso deveríamos atribuir não ao acaso cego ou à sorte, ou à influência das estrelas, ou a qualquer ser criado invisível, anjo ou demônio, e, sim, somente ao próprio Senhor. Pois não existe aquilo que se convencionou chamar de *sorte* , e nem acontecimentos fortuitos; tais ocorrências, ainda aquelas que parecem mais fortuitas ou contingentes, são todas dispostas,

ordenadas e governadas pela vontade soberana de Deus». (Isso dizia John Gill referindo-se ao trecho de Pro. 16:31. Ver também o uso dessa prática por parte de Aarão, em Lev. 16:8. Ver também Núm. 34:13; I Crô. 24:6; João 1:17 e Luc. 1:9, referências bíblicas essas que mostram que a ordem particular do serviço prestado pelos sacerdotes, isto é, quando e como haveriam de servir, em suas várias capacidades no templo, era determinada por alguma forma de *sorte*, quando se empregavam diversos sistemas possíveis, conforme fica subentendido nas notas expositivas acima).

Outras alusões antigas a essa prática, fora da cultura hebraica, são as seguintes: *Lívio* xxiii.3; Sófocles, *Aias*, 1285. Josefo menciona igualmente tal prática, no trecho de *Antiq.* vi. 5, havendo referências à mesma nos antiqüíssimos escritos de Homero.

Recair sobre Matias. Sem importar qual método de lançamento de sortes foi usado, o resultado é que Matias foi considerado *apóstolo* por escolha divina, porquanto se aceitou o fato de que Deus havia dirigido o salto da sorte para fora do vaso ou urna; ou que, no caso da mesma haver sido retirada com a mão, de algum recipiente, que Deus orientara a mão para que retirasse o nome escolhido pelo Senhor. Desse modo Matias tomou lugar, junto com os outros onze apóstolos, no ofício apostólico.

Com base nessa circunstância, ficamos sabendo da grande fé dos apóstolos na providência divina, e que eles não criam que as coisas acontecem por acaso.

Ver o artigo separado sobre a *astrologia*. Ver também o artigo sobre os *sonhos*.

III. Comentários, críticas e observações. — 1. O fato de que os sonhos regularmente prevêem o futuro, mostra-nos que o homem comum recebeu de Deus a capacidade de prever o futuro. Portanto, é absurda a idéia de alguns, de que há algo de errado ou mesmo demoníaco nos sonhos. Como no caso de tudo o mais, essa capacidade, ou a tentativa de desenvolvê-la abusivamente, pode tornar-se prejudicial, quando a utilizamos com finalidades erradas.

2. As capacidades psíquicas, por si mesmas, não são boas e nem más. Os estudos feitos em laboratórios têm demonstrado que todas as pessoas são psíquicas. De fato, mui provavelmente é essa capacidade, posta em uso diariamente, que permite a manipulação de nossos corpos. Em outras palavras, o controle da mente sobre a matéria é a essência mesma da interação entre o corpo e o espírito. A força psíquica é usada como um instrumento pelo espírito, a fim de controlar o seu veículo físico, o corpo. Porém, quando as habilidades psíquicas são usadas abusivamente, no interesse próprio, ou para influenciar outras pessoas para o mal, ou para prover meios para algum espírito estranho, ou para forçar sobre nós influências diversas, então tais capacidades tornam-se um instrumento maligno. Mas somente em tais casos.

3. A Bíblia pronuncia-se contrária à adivinhação (ver Deu. 18:10-12), quando esta é abusiva. Pois há provas óbvias de que os hebreus usavam formas de adivinhação, como também o fizeram os apóstolos, em Atos 1:26. Uma questão tão séria como a questão de substituir Judas Iscariotes no apostolado foi resolvida mediante o lançamento de sortes. Pode-se presumir que os pagãos regularmente abusam da adivinhação, pelo que buscar a ajuda psíquica de pessoas incrédulas, devido a essa circunstância, não é apenas uma medida inútil, mas até mesmo pode ser prejudicial. Além disso, os poderes demoníacos, que atuam sobre os incrédulos, são reais, e precisam ser evitados pelo crente.

ADLAI — ADOÇÃO

4. O simples ato de tentar obter discernimento psíquico acerca dos problemas, sem importar se isso envolve ou não conhecimento quanto ao futuro, dificilmente pode ser algo errado, porque isso é o que os. nossos sonhos fazem regularmente. Os estudos mostram que quase tudo quanto fazemos, dotado de qualquer importância, além de muitas coisas totalmente triviais, são previstas pelos nossos sonhos. O truque consiste em lembrar os sonhos, pois apesar de podermos ter mais de vinte sonhos a *cada noite*, talvez possamos relembrar apenas quatro ou cinco deles por semana. Não há que duvidar que os sonhos fazem parte de uma herança dada por Deus, para nossa orientação. Os sonhos de cunho moral castigam-nos e nos fornecem instruções espirituais. Os sonhos espirituais revelam-nos mistérios. Os sonhos psicossomáticos advertem-nos de coisas que adoecem o corpo. Os estudos feitos no campo dos sonhos mostram que há um intercâmbio telepático regular entre as pessoas que se tornam íntimas, e muitos sonhos são compartilhados de forma literal ou simbólica. Isso simplesmente faz parte dos sonhos. Portanto, dificilmente pode ser errado enviar e receber impulsos psíquicos ou telepáticos. Isso sucede conosco o tempo todo, se estivermos despertos ou dormindo. Não obstante, a negra mão do mal intromete-se em tudo, até mesmo em nosso comer e beber, quando nos tornamos gulosos ou bebemos coisas prejudiciais à saúde.

5. O crente espiritual, conduzido pelo Espírito, recebe orientação de alguma fonte mais elevada do que aquela que serve à adivinhação comum. Essa fonte mais elevada é a que os crentes deveriam desenvolver. Os demais fenômenos, mesmo quando não forem malignos em si mesmos, serão apenas uma curiosidade para nós, mais do que qualquer coisa. E, quando tais fenômenos forem decididamente perversos, devem ser evitados por nós, para que os espíritos malignos não tenham oportunidade para atacar-nos. Já temos problemas suficientes, em nós mesmos, não havendo necessidade alguma de convidar poderes estranhos para nos afetarem a vida.

6. *Os extremos usualmente são absurdos*. Afirmar que toda e qualquer adivinhação, excetuando aquela praticada por Israel e pela Igreja primitiva, é demoníaca, ou má em si mesma, de forma automática, é uma posição extremada, manifestamente absurda. Dizer que a adivinhação não passa de um jogo, também é um absurdo. Supor que não pode haver a intervenção da malignidade de poderes sinistros nessa prática, é outro absurdo. De fato, a adivinhação pode ser tudo isso: demoníaca, má por si mesma, indiferente (isto é, nem boa e nem má), dotada apenas de discernimento psíquico, ou então boa, ou mesmo apenas um jogo que diverte as pessoas. (IB ID NTI SH)

Ver informações sobre assuntos relacionados no artigo sobre a *Parapsicologia*.

ADLAI

No hebraico, **Yahweh é justo**. Era pai de Safate, e cuidava dos rebanhos reais ao tempo de Davi (ver I Crô. 27:29), depois de 1000 A.C. (UN)

ADMÁ

No hebraico, **terra vermelha**, uma das cidades do vale de Sidim (ver Gên. 10:19), que tinha seu próprio rei, Sinabe (ver Gên. 14:2). A cidade foi destruída juntamente com Sodoma e Gomorra (ver Gên. 19:24; Deu. 29:23; Osé. 11:8). Alguns identificam esse lugar com a Adão, em Josué, 3:16. (UN)

ADMINISTRAR, ADMINISTRAÇÃO

No grego, **diakonia**, «gerenciar», «distribuir» como mordomo (ver II Cor. 8:19). O termo «administração» aponta para o ofício público e para a execução desse ofício (ver I Cor. 12:5). Tem o sentido de «aliviar», «ministrar», em II Cor. 9:12. A raiz da palavra é a idéia de *prestar serviço*, espiritual ou materialmente falando.

ADMIRAÇÃO

Vários vocábulos gregos são usados para expressar essa emoção, a saber: *thambein*, Mar. 1:27; *existanai*, Mar. 2:12; *ekplessesthai*, Mar. 1:22; *thaumazein*, Mar. 1:22; *fobeisthai*, Mar. 5:20. Estão envolvidas idéias como espanto, admiração e temor.

Essas palavras adquirem importância ao serem aplicadas a Jesus. Por duas vezes é dito que Jesus se «admirou», ou ficou muito surpreso (Mat. 8:10; Mar. 6:6). Nesse caso, a palavra é *thaumazein*, enfatizando a reação de Jesus a situações consternadoras. Em Mar. 14:33, a reação de Jesus, no Getsêmani, é descrita com o termo *ekthambeisthai*, que é usado para indicar um grande alarme, aflição ou temor. Na Septuaginta, a palavra enfatiza temor ou medo (ver I Sam. 14:15; II Sam. 22:5). As origens da emoção de Jesus, nesse caso, eram as horrendas implicações da cruz. Aqueles que concebem um Cristo docético, que seria humano apenas na aparência, ficam perplexos quando lêem que Jesus foi capaz de ter temor. Porém, do ponto de vista da humanidade de Cristo, isso não nos deveria surpreender. Ver o artigo sobre *a Humanidade de Jesus Cristo*. Ver o artigo a *Divindade de Cristo*. (A B)

ADMOESTAÇÃO

O termo grego **nouthesia** aparece por três vezes no Novo Testamento, em I Cor. 10:11; Efé. 6:14 e Tito 3:10, denotando a idéia de «meter na mente». O cognato verbal aparece por quatro vezes: Rom. 15:14; Col. 3:16; I Tes. 5:12 e II Tes. 3:15. A transmissão da mensagem divina requer que ela seja injetada nas mentes alheias, por meio do ensino e da exortação.

Idéias. 1. A aplicação de exemplo santo. 2. A transmissão de ensino espiritual, de modo geral. 3. A repreensão aos hereges. 4. O ministério dos líderes que deve ser respeitado. 5. A repriıenda a um irmão em erro. Quanto à questão da repreensão, no âmbito da disciplina eclesiástica, ver as notas no NTI, em Mat. 18:15-17.

ADNA

No hebraico, **prazer**. No Antigo Testamento há quatro homens com esse nome: 1. Um israelita descendente da família de Paate-Moabe, que se divorciou de sua mulher gentia, após o cativeiro (ver Esd. 10:30). 2. Um sumo sacerdote, filho de Harim, contemporâneo de Joiaquim (ver Nee. 12:15), em cerca de 536 A.C. 3. Um dos principais homens da tribo de Manassés, que aliou-se a Davi em Ziclague (ver I Crô. 12:20), antes de 1000 A.C. 4. Um guerreiro da tribo de Judá e capitão sob Josafá (ver I Crô. 17:14), em cerca de 836 A.C. (UN S Z)

ADOÇÃO

Ver o artigo sobre o **adopcionismo**, a alegada doutrina de Cristo como Filho adotivo de Deus. Ver abaixo, neste artigo, sob o quinto ponto, sobre a «adoção» em relação ao Filho, Cristo, onde o trecho de

ADOÇÃO

Rom. 1:4 é cuidadosamente considerado.

Adoção traduz um termo grego que significa «colocar como filho». A palavra portuguesa tem o termo latino *adopter*, «selecionar», como sua base. Trata-se do ato legal mediante o qual uma pessoa faz de outra pessoa, com a qual não tem relação de parentesco, ou, pelo menos, que não é seu filho natural, seu filho aos olhos da lei. O Antigo Testamento não contém qualquer vocábulo equivalente ao termo grego traduzido por «adoção», embora ocorram alguns poucos exemplos da prática. No Novo Testamento, o termo grego *uiothesia*, «filiação», pode ser encontrado em Rom. 8:15,23; 9:4; Gál. 4:5; Efé. 1:5, num total de cinco vezes. O costume da adoção é aludido, embora não haja o relato de qualquer ato de adoção em todo o Novo Testamento.

1. *Origem da prática*. A origem da mesma foi o desejo de ter um descendente do sexo masculino, para que a herança continuasse na família, quando não havia nenhum filho natural do sexo masculino.

2. *No Antigo Testamento*. O caso de Moisés no Egito (ver Êxo. 2:10), provavelmente envolveu um caso de adoção. Outros exemplos são a adoção de Eliezer, por Abraão (ver Gên. 15:2,3), e a de Ester, por Mordecai (ver Est. 2:15). No passado, até mesmo um escravo algumas vezes era adotado como filho. Uma forma de adoção estava envolvida naqueles casos em que uma esposa dava uma serva a seu marido, mediante a qual ela geraria filhos, se o casal não pudesse gerá-los, como o filho que nasceu de Abraão e Hagar. Jacó adotou como seus os dois filhos de José, Efraim e Manassés, com os mesmos direitos de Rúben e Simeão, seus dois filhos mais velhos. (Ver Gên. 48:5). Destarte, Jacó pôde dar a José, seu filho favorito, uma partilha maior da herança. Desse modo, as tribos tornaram-se treze, embora Levi não viesse a receber terras na partilha; ou então Efraim e Manassés foram considerados como metades, compondo uma única tribo. Em I Crônicas 2, Maquir deu sua filha a Hezrom de Judá, e ela deu à luz a Segube, pai de Jair. Ele herdou vinte e três cidades de Gileade, por meio de sua avó. Embora pertencente a Judá, por meio de seu avô, em Números 23:41 ele foi contado como pertencente a Manassés, por causa da herança que recebeu por meio de sua avó.

3. *Gregos e romanos*. As alusões existentes no Novo Testamento refletem costumes entre esses dois povos. No Oriente, a prática sempre foi comum, mormente entre os povos semitas. A prática confinava-se a filhos, e a narrativa bíblica não menciona a adoção somente de uma filha (Ester, por parte de Mordecai), se é que ali temos uma verdadeira adoção. Isso se devia, em primeiro lugar, à questão inteira da herança e da perpetuação da família, bem como ao sentimento geral que era melhor ter filhos do que ter filhas. Isso concorda com um provérbio chinês, que diz: «É mais feliz com filhas aquele que só tem filhos» (*Mem. sur les Chinois*, t, x:149). A prática era mais comum entre os romanos do que entre os gregos. Isso provê uma bela ilustração da função do evangelho, pois não é pequena a vantagem de alguém passar da posição de um escravo, pertencente a um senhor, para a posição de um filho, que agora tem um pai. Na adoção, pois, o filho adotado tornava-se legalmente *morto* para todas as anteriores obrigações e ligações, e assumia posição de um filho dentro de uma nova família, juntamente com os direitos e obrigações nisso envolvidos. Há uma outra excelente ilustração da realização do evangelho, que faz com que homens que antes pertenciam à pecaminosa família adâmica, agora se tornem membros da família de Deus (ver Rom. 8:15 ss).

Segundo a lei romana de adoção, que requeria um documento legal, o filho adotivo tinha direito ao nome, às possessões e à posição do pai adotivo na sociedade e nas questões religiosas. Era o herdeiro de seu pai adotivo como se fora um filho natural. O pai também tinha direito à propriedade do filho adotivo, tornando-se seu proprietário absoluto. Os judeus não tinham precisamente esses costumes, mas a literatura judaica mostra que eles estavam familiarizados com as determinações das leis romanas.

4. *Idéias neotestamentárias associadas à adoção*. a. Transformar um escravo em filho, segundo foi comentado acima (ver Rom. 8:15 e Gál. 4:5). b. A adoção é efetuada por meio do Irmão mais velho, Jesus Cristo (ver Efé. 1:5). Ali faz-se presente a idéia do *amor* da família divina. c. Em Rom. 8:15 ss. temos uma introdução ao elevado destino dos filhos adotados, a saber, a transformação segundo a imagem do Irmão mais velho, sendo eles os herdeiros de tudo quanto Ele herdar. Assim os homens participarão da natureza divina, por se tornarem membros reais da família divina. (Ver II Ped. 1:4; Col. 2:10; II Cor. 3:18). d. A adoção inclui a redenção futura do corpo, a participação na glorificação, a mudança de natureza, da humana para a divina, no mesmo sentido em que o Filho participa dessa natureza, embora em grau finito. (Ver Rom. 8:23). e. Todo esse processo é um ato voluntário de Deus, originado em Sua vontade soberana (ver Efé. 1:4-6). f. Mediante a influência do Espírito Santo, os homens recebem a certeza de seu novo relacionamento com Deus, pelo que clamam «Aba, Pai». (Ver Mar. 14:36; Rom. 8:15,16). Isso é o contrário exato da anterior escravidão ao pecado. g. Filiação é sinônimo de salvação, pois tudo quanto está envolvido na *salvação* (ver o artigo a respeito), também está envolvido em nossa posição de filhos (ver Rom. 8:29 ss). h. A criação inteira participa nos resultados da adoção dos filhos, o que é claramente ensinado em Rom. 8:22 ss. Isso significa que haverá um benefício universal, resultante da missão de Cristo, e que a adoção de filhos é uma garantia dessa universalidade, embora só os eleitos participem desse benefício em sentido primário. Os demais receberão benefícios secundários. Ver o artigo sobre a *restauração*. A missão de Cristo não pode falhar no tocante a qualquer coisa viva ou inanimada. i. Isso garante a solução final para o *problema do mal* (ver o artigo a respeito).

5. *Adoção em relação ao Filho, Cristo*. Isso leva em conta o que lemos em Romanos 1:4. Ver também o artigo sobre o *adopcionismo*, quanto a detalhes sobre essa doutrina. «Com poder foi declarado Filho de Deus segundo o espírito de santidade, pela ressurreição dentre os mortos, Jesus Cristo, nosso Senhor».

6. *Luz da arqueologia* sobre a adoção pré-abraâmica. A descoberta dos arquivos de Nuzi (ver sobre *Nuzi*, no artigo referente à *arqueologia*) nos fornece alguma compreensão sobre a adoção entre os povos semitas. Em Nuzi era costume que um casal sem filhos adotasse um filho, que primeiramente servia os seus pais adotivos, enquanto eles vivessem, e então cuidava do sepultamento deles, de acordo com os costumes vigentes. Em recompensa, ele ficava com a herança. Se, após o ato de adoção, o casal gerasse filhos, os filhos naturais ficavam com a porção maior da herança, mas o filho adotivo ainda assim participava da mesma. Algum modo de proceder como esse provavelmente esteve envolvido na adoção de Eliezer por Abraão (ver Gên. 15:2 ss).

7. *Como um termo ético*. Deus está interessado na solidariedade da família e nos órfãos (ver Tia. 1:27). Portanto, é a qualidade do amor que inspira as

ADOÇÃO EM RELAÇÃO AO FILHO

pessoas a adotarem crianças que não lhes pertencem, conferindo às mesmas todos os privilégios de filhos naturais. O amor é a raiz e o solo onde medram todas as virtudes (Gál. 5:22). O amor também é a prova da espiritualidade (ver I João 4:7 ss.). A adoção, pois, expressa, de certa maneira, esse amor. (A DE HA ND S UN Z)

ADOÇÃO EM RELAÇÃO AO FILHO, Considerando Rom. 1:4.

Ver o artigo sobre *Adopcionismo*.

com poder foi declarado Filho de Deus segundo o espírito de santidade, pela ressurreição dentre os mortos—Jesus Cristo nosso Senhor...

Grande número de diferentes interpretações tem surgido em torno deste vers., no que diz respeito à natureza da filiação de Jesus Cristo. O vocábulo grego aqui traduzido por *demonstrado* pode ter outros significados, e são justamente esses outros sentidos possíveis que modificam a interpretação do versículo. Por exemplo, algumas traduções dizem que Cristo foi «nomeado» Filho de Deus; mas outras preferem dizer que Cristo foi «instalado» como Filho de Deus, sugestão esta que dá a impressão de que Jesus não era realmente o Filho de Deus enquanto não atingiu a ressurreição. As interpretações centrais a esse respeito são as seguintes:

1. A cristologia da adoção pura. — Alguns dos primitivos cristãos acreditavam que, em algum tempo da vida de Jesus, ele «tornou-se» Filho de Deus, e não que eternamente o tivesse sido, ou que tivesse nascido já com esse elevado ofício. Assim sendo, Cristo teria sido «adotado» como Filho porque veio merecer tal adoção, através de sua vida de santidade. A maioria dos que defendiam essa teoria afirmava que no **batismo é que Cristo** chegara ao ponto, dentro do tempo, de receber sua divindade, quando foi batizado pelo Espírito Santo. Nessa oportunidade é que ele teria recebido sua natureza especial elevada e seus poderes extraordinários. Outros estudiosos, seguindo a suposta indicação dada por este versículo, crêem que a plena adoção não ocorreu enquanto Jesus Cristo não ressuscitou. O termo aqui empregado, «Filho de Deus», pode subentender divindade; mas, de conformidade com essa teoria, Cristo se tornou divino por uma dádiva de Deus, tendo sido elevado a essa categoria, e não porque o fosse eternamente, ainda que, olhando-se para o futuro, ele o seja eternamente.

2. O ponto de vista da teoria da adoção radical. Alguns dos antigos gnósticos ensinavam que o Verbo eterno se apossou do corpo humano de Jesus, quando de seu batismo, mas que não podem ser identificadas essas duas personalidades, por não serem iguais. Isso significaria que o homem Jesus jamais foi divino, mas que o ser divino se apossou de seu corpo quando do batismo no rio Jordão. Ainda de acordo com essa teoria, o Verbo eterno teria abandonado o corpo de Jesus quando de sua morte na cruz. Essa idéia, naturalmente, não se adapta bem dentro da cristologia ordinária do N.T., e nem mesmo a este presente versículo, que faz da ressurreição de Cristo um acontecimento especial. É evidente que para fazer este versículo ensinar tal teoria, seria mister supormos um «retorno» do Verbo eterno para reavivar o corpo morto de Jesus, e novamente produzir a *adoção*. No entanto, esse retorno, incoerentemente, não faz parte da teoria dos «adopcionistas», isto é, daqueles que ensinam essa teoria.

3. Em contraste com a teoria da adoção, acima descrita, encontramos o ensino verdadeiro sobre a

encarnação, conforme ela é tão enfática e claramente ensinada no primeiro capítulo do evangelho de João. O Verbo eterno não é nenhuma personagem separada do homem Jesus; mas antes, assumiu sobre si mesmo a natureza humana, ao mesmo tempo que jamais deixou de ser divino. Para sermos francos, não sabemos dizer como é que tal coisa pôde suceder; mas, apesar disso, podemos continuar afirmando, com base nas Escrituras, a dualidade da personalidade de Cristo. Assim sendo, Jesus Cristo não foi «adotado» por Deus para ser divino, porquanto já pertencia à divindade, e desde a eternidade, já que a preexistência eterna do Senhor Jesus é também claramente ensinada na Bíblia. Assim sendo, não podemos aceitar traduções que digam que Jesus foi «instalado» como Filho de Deus, ou «feito», ou «nomeado», — todos esses termos podem ser tradução de um termo grego um tanto ambíguo; mas antes, devemos traduzi-lo por *demonstrado*, «designado» ou «declarado» Filho de Deus. A filiação de Jesus Cristo foi declarada, foi demonstrada pela sua ressurreição, não tendo sido criada naquele momento. Jesus sempre foi o Filho de Deus; mas a ressurreição dentre os mortos se tornou a demonstração poderosa dessa filiação divina, uma prova empírica da mesma.

Essa é a interpretação ordinária sobre a passagem em pauta, ainda que alguns intérpretes acreditem que este versículo reflita o ponto de vista da «adoção», e que alguns dos crentes de Roma, ou talvez até mesmo aquela comunidade inteira, defendiam essa teoria, e que o apóstolo Paulo, propositalmente, usou um vocábulo de sentido ambíguo a fim de não ofender aqueles para quem escrevia. Não temos meio algum para julgar as crenças doutrinárias dos crentes de Roma a esse respeito; mas sabemos, com base no segundo capítulo da epístola aos Colossenses, que uma teoria de «adoção» pura e radical é contrária à teologia paulina.

4. Adoção modificada. Uma verdade da teoria da adoção. — Considerado apenas como **homem**, inteiramente à parte de sua identidade com o Logos, por ser o Pioneiro de nossa fé (ver Heb. 2:10), por haver aprendido coisas por meio daquilo que sofreu (ver Heb. 5:8,9), e por ter sido aperfeiçoado através desse sofrimento, Jesus tornou-se divino naquele sentido em que o *homem-Jesus* não era divino. Ele se tornou o primeiro *Deus-homem*.

a. Jesus, nesta capacidade, é o *arquétipo* da redenção humana.

b. Essa forma de filiação divina ele dá a todos quantos nele confiam (ver II Cor. 3:18).

c. Ele compartilha de sua plenitude com os homens (isto é, sua natureza divina e os atributos acompanhantes), e assim os homens, em Cristo, são adotados na filiação divina (ver Col. 2:10).

d. Um novo tipo de ser divino veio à existência quando Jesus saiu imortalizado do túmulo, através de sua ressurreição. (Ver I Cor. 5:20 quanto ao significado da «ressurreição»). A ressurreição de Jesus produziu uma nova forma de vida, da qual os homens podem participar, pois Deus está duplicando o Filho nos filhos.

Não é provável, entretanto, que o apóstolo tenha propositalmente usado uma palavra grega ambígua para agradar aos romanos que não compartilhavam de seus pontos de vista cristológicos. Historicamente, entretanto, sabemos que alguns dos primitivos cristãos aferravam-se à teoria da «adoção». Foi preciso um longo tempo para que as verdades cristológicas

ADOM — ADONI-ZEDEQUE

ficassem esclarecidas na igreja cristã, e alguns pontos de vista distintos vieram a ser aceitos de modo geral. Naturalmente durante toda a história eclesiástica têm persistido grandes divergências em torno dessa questão.

Sem importar a interpretação que aceitarmos, é óbvio que a ressurreição é encarada nas Escrituras como um acontecimento literal, revestindo-se de capital importância, tanto para Jesus Cristo, em sua posição cosmológica, como para todos quantos nele confiam. (G I IB NTI RO)

ADOCIANISMO Ver Adopcianismo.

ADOM

No hebraico, **poderoso**. Lugar mencionado em Nee. 7:71, de onde vieram certos israelitas da Babilônia, que não puderam provar, pelas genealogias, que eram israelitas e pertenciam à classe sacerdotal. (S)

ADONAI

No hebraico, **Senhor, mestre**. Antiga forma plural do substantivo *adon*, usada como o *pluralis excellentiae* (para dignificar um singular), como nome de Deus. Uma forma similar é usada sobre homens, como no caso de José, em Gên. 42:30,33. Por motivo de respeito, os judeus evitavam pronunciar o nome divino, Yahweh. Assim, misturavam as consoantes desse nome com as vogais de Adonai, produzindo o nome Jeová. Portanto, dizer *Jeová* era evitar a pronunciação do nome de Deus. O nome de Deus era por demais sagrado para ser proferido. Contrastemos isso com certos cristãos modernos que dizem «o Senhor, o Senhor» a cada três linhas, em seus diálogos, atribuindo a Ele tudo quanto crêem, pensam ou fazem. Certamente isso exibe falta de respeito, ainda que tal hábito vise mostrar piedade. A linguagem frívola pode tentar ocultar a superficialidade. (PAY S)

ADONIAS

No hebraico, **Yahweh é meu Senhor**. Nome de várias pessoas no Antigo Testamento.

1. Quarto filho de Davi, por meio de Hagite. Adonias nasceu depois que seu pai se tornara rei, embora ainda estivesse reinando somente sobre Judá (ver II Sam. 3:4). Depois da morte de seus irmãos, Amom e Absalão, ele poderia ter-se tornado rei. Mas foi preterido em favor de Salomão, que nasceu quando Davi era rei de todo o Israel. Não se deixando abalar pelo trágico exemplo de revolta de Absalão, ele resolveu que seria o rei. Assumiu a posição de herdeiro presuntivo, e em vista da avançada idade de Davi, em breve poderia ser o rei. Não se revoltou abertamente contra seu pai, mas esperou até que Davi aparentemente chegasse ao fim. Então convocou vários homens influentes, que lhe apoiavam a causa, e proclamou-se rei. Deram-lhe apoio homens como Joabe, chefe do exército de Davi, e Abiatar, sumo sacerdote, ambos os quais sempre estiveram ao lado de Davi, sem se importar com o que lhe sucedesse. Isso mostra a força do princípio de hereditariedade entre os antigos hebreus. O conluio foi frustrado por Davi, que prontamente proclamou que Salomão fosse o rei, guindando-o ao exercício da autoridade. Quando Adonias percebeu que havia fracassado, buscou abrigo diante do altar, de onde recusou-se a sair, até receber a promessa de perdão por parte do rei Salomão. Esse lhe foi concedido, mas com o aviso de que ele não mais entrasse em conluios.

Então veio o seu segundo grande erro. Procurou obter permissão para casar-se com a virgem e jovem última esposa de Davi, Abisague (ver o artigo acerca dela). Mas isso foi interpretado como outra tentativa para tentar subir ao trono. Salomão ordenou imediatamente a sua execução (ver I Reis 2:23-25), em cerca de 960 A.C. (FA S Z)

2. Um dos levitas enviados por Josafá para ensinar a lei ao povo, nas cidades de Judá (ver II Crô. 17:8).

3. Um daqueles que assinaram o pacto, no tempo de Esdras. (Ver Nee. 10:16). Tem sido identificado com o Adonicão de Esd. 2:13. (FA S Z)

ADONI-BEZEQUE

No hebraico, **senhor de Bezeque**. Bezeque era uma aldeia cananéia. Eusébio situou-a a 27 quilômetros a leste de Neápolis, em Siquém. A pequena extensão dos reinos na Palestina e ao derredor, ao tempo da invasão dos hebreus, é demonstrada pelo fato de que o rei de Bezeque, Adoni-Bezeque, havia subjugado setenta desses reinos, embora ele mesmo tivesse um reino minúsculo. A crueldade das lutas entre as tribos é demonstrada por seu costume de decepar os polegares das mãos e os dedões dos pés de todos os prisioneiros, obrigando-os a viver juntando o alimento sob as mesas de seus captores. Esse costume provavelmente era seguido por outros chefes da época. Essas conquistas faziam de Adoni-Bezeque um peixe grande entre as piabas. Como cabeça dos cananeus e perizeus, ele lutou contra as tribos invasoras de Israel. Seu exército foi derrotado e ele foi aprisionado. Então foram decepados os seus polegares e os dedos grandes dos pés, uma aplicação da *lei de talião*. Portanto, os israelitas não eram menos bárbaros que seus contemporâneos. Basta-nos ler os registros. Adoni-Bezeque foi levado a Jerusalém, onde morreu dos ferimentos recebidos. (Ver Juí. 1:5-7). (FA S)

ADONI-ZEDEQUE

No hebraico, **senhor da justiça, rei de Zedeque** ou *senhor justo*. Foi um rei cananeu de Jerusalém, no tempo em que os israelitas invadiram a Palestina. A similaridade do nome dele ao de Melquisedeque (um rei ainda mais antigo de Jerusalém, sugere que *Zedeque* talvez fosse um antigo nome de Jerusalém), Seja como for, Adoni-Zedeque foi o primeiro dos príncipes nativos a oferecer considerável resistência à invasão israelita, sob as ordens de Josué (ver Jos. 10:1,3). Ao ouvir sobre a queda de Ai e a liga entre os gibeonitas e Israel, ele entrou em colisão com outros quatro reis amorreus, ao sul e a oeste de Jerusalém, com o propósito específico de punir os habitantes de Gibeom. Seus aliados eram os reis de Hebrom, Jarmute, Laquis e Eglom. —Não combateram os israelitas invasores diretamente, mas assediaram os gibeonitas, a fim de desencorajar outros a entrarem em aliança com Israel, mostrando o que sucederia aos tais. Josué ouviu falar sobre a batalha e marchou a noite inteira desde Gilgal, caindo inesperadamente sobre o inimigo e pondo-o imediatamente em fuga.

A perseguição ao inimigo. A caçada foi longa, assinalada pela famosa ordem de Josué para que o sol parasse, e também pela tremenda saraiva que atingiu os fugitivos. Os cinco reis refugiaram-se em uma caverna, em Maquedá, mas foram descobertos. Os chefes hebreus puseram então os pés sobre os pescoços dos reis prostrados, um antigo sinal de triunfo, acerca do que há muita evidência arqueológica. Então os reis foram executados, e seus corpos

ADONICÃO — ADOPCIONISMO

foram pendurados em árvores até à noite, pois a lei proibia exposição mais longa dos mortos (ver Deu. 21:23). Seus corpos foram arriados e lançados na caverna, e a boca da caverna foi entulhada com grandes pedras, as quais ali permaneceram por muito tempo (ver Jos. 10:1-27). Aquela era uma guerra de extermínio, e os judeus nem eram melhores e nem piores que as selvagens tribos da época. (DE HA ND UN)

ADONICÃO

No hebraico significa **estabelecido pelo Senhor**, ou então *meu Senhor ergueu-se*. Era nome de uma das famílias que retornaram do exílio (ver Esd. 2:13 e Nee. 7:18). Adonicão tinha 666 descendentes, embora o livro de Neemias fale em 667 descendentes. Nessas duas listas, que envolvem 153 dados numéricos cada, há diferença em vinte e nove desses dados, dos quais treze casos envolvem diferença de um número apenas. Alguns dizem que o próprio Adonicão foi adicionado à lista em Neemias, perfazendo a diferença; mas isso é apenas uma entre as várias conjecturas que explicam discrepâncias, as quais não se revestem de grande importância, mesmo que sejam reais. Mais tarde, três de seus descendentes imediatos, com sessenta seguidores do sexo masculino, vieram com Esdras (ver Esd. 8:13), em cerca de 458 A.C. Parece que ele é o mesmo Adonias de Nee. 10:16. (UN Z)

ADONIRÃO (Hadorão, Adorão)

No hebraico, **senhor da altura** ou **senhor exaltado**. É nome de pelo menos duas personagens da Bíblia. Os comentadores não concordam acerca da questão. O nome é exibido em forma contraída, Adorão, em II Sam. 20:24 e I Reis 12:18, ou Hadorão, em II Crô. 10:18. Se se tratava da mesma pessoa, viveu em cerca de 930 A.C.

1. Adonirão ou Hadorão, filho de Toi, rei de Hamate, que foi enviado por seu pai para congratular-se com Davi por sua vitória sobre o inimigo comum, Hadarezer, rei da Síria (ver I Crô. 18:10). É chamado Jorão, em II Sam. 8:10.

2. Uma pessoa, ou pessoas com esse nome, aparece no departamento de trabalhos forçados de Salomão. A prolongada duração do serviço pode significar que mais de uma pessoa ocupou o ofício, ambas com o mesmo nome. Contudo, o ponto é disputado. Ele é identificado como o oficial que, no final do reinado de Davi e no começo do reinado de Reoboão, ocupava esse ofício, e tinha uma forma contraída desse nome, Adorão (ver II Sam. 20:24 e I Reis 12:18). Ele é chamado filho de Abda e superintendente de trinta mil homens de Israel, servindo em três turnos de dez mil homens cada, que iam ao Líbano atrás de cedro e cipreste (ver I Reis 5:8,13,14). Talvez Davi tivesse estabelecido o sistema como meio de recolher impostos ou dívidas, ou o próprio trabalho forçado fosse uma forma de taxação. O sistema cananeu da época incluía a prática, conforme testificam os textos administrativos ugaríticos (Ras Shamra). É possível que Davi tenha copiado a idéia de seus vizinhos pagãos. Muitos faziam objeção ao sistema, e quando Reoboão recusou-se a descontinuá-lo, as tribos do norte separaram-se de Judá e Benjamim (ver I Reis 12:1-16; II Crô. 10:1-11). Insensatamente, procurando preservar o sistema, Reoboão enviou o grande símbolo do sistema, Adorão, para impor a cobrança de tributo; mas Adorão foi prontamente morto por apedrejamento (ver I Reis 12:18 e II Crô. 10:18). (FA S UN Z)

ADÔNIS

No grego, **senhor**. Uma divindade síria da vegetação, que se ressecava sob os cálidos raios de sol do verão. Em acadiano, ele era chamado *duzu* ou *tamuzu*. Mas, na Síria e na Fenícia, ele era chamado por um nome grego, *adoni*. Seu culto era muito generalizado, envolvendo grande parte do Oriente Próximo, do Egito e da Grécia. Uma festa o celebrava em junho/julho. A lenda dizia que quando a vegetação começava a ressecar-se, ele descia ao mundo inferior. Sua esposa, a deusa Istar, descia a fim de reavivá-lo, para que chegasse a primavera. Ambas essas divindades estavam envolvidas com a questão da fertilidade. O trecho de Eze. 8:14 registra a história de mulheres que choravam em um dos portões do templo, por causa da morte de Tamuz (*tamuzu*). É possível que o trecho de Isa. 17:10, que fala sobre «plantações formosas», indique os jardins dedicados a Adônis, visto que em sua honra eram plantadas ervas. (FO FR WE)

ADOPCIANISMO

Um dos grandes problemas do cristianismo consiste em explicar como, em uma só pessoa, podem residir o humano e o divino. Uma dessas tentativas de explicação é o **adopcianismo**. Essa é a doutrina de que Cristo, que nasceu como um ser humano mortal, *tornou-se* Filho de Deus por adoção. Jesus, embora homem, foi adotado pelo Verbo e incorporado na deidade. O Cristo humano, através do brilhante cumprimento de Sua missão, foi considerado digno de lhe serem conferidos os atributos divinos, com a alteração de Sua natureza, da humana para a divina. Essa doutrina apareceu, sob várias formas, nos primeiros três séculos da era cristã. Historicamente, culminou na **controvérsia adopcianista** do século VIII, na Espanha, tendo sido condenada por sínodos patrocinados por Carlos Magno, nos anos de 792, 794 e 799.

Exponentes desse ponto de vista. Teodoto de Bizâncio, excomungado pelo papa Vítor (190-198), os ebionitas (185), Paulo de Samosata, bispo de Antioquia (260-272), Teodoro de Mopsuéstia (350-428), colega de estudos de João Crisóstomo e presbítero de Antioquia. Mais tarde, ele tornou-se bispo de Mopsuéstia, na Cilícia. A posição adopcianista era forte na escola de Antioquia. Nos tempos modernos, muitos teólogos protestantes liberais têm adotado esse ponto de vista, vendo nele uma salvaguarda da humanidade de Cristo.

Extremo oposto. Muitos evangélicos modernos, ansiosos por salvaguardar o ensino da divindade de Cristo, têm virtualmente eliminado qualquer doutrina autêntica de Sua humanidade, tendo assim caído no erro do docetismo (ver o artigo). Essa doutrina ensina que a humanidade de Cristo era apenas *aparente*. Enquanto esses evangélicos crêem na realidade do corpo humano de Jesus, outros atribuem à Sua divindade a tudo quanto Ele fez. Assim, Seu conhecimento especial, Seus milagres, Suas elevadas qualidades morais e espirituais são vistos como atributos de Sua divindade. Alguns têm chegado ao extremo de negar que Jesus tinha alma humana, afirmando que Cristo meramente se utilizou de um corpo humano como veículo. Mas, o ensino neotestamentário é que Jesus foi homem em todos os sentidos, embora não tenha caído no pecado. Naturalmente, ali também é ensinada a divindade real de Cristo. Como podem habitar duas naturezas em uma só pessoa é um grande mistério, e nem o

ADOR (ADORA) — ADORAÇÃO

adopcianismo e nem o docetismo o esclarecem. Quanto a notas completas sobre essas idéias, ver os artigos sobre a **Humanidade de Cristo**; a **Divindade de Cristo**; e **Docetismo**.

Forma correta de adopcianismo. Esse termo pode ser usado para descrever uma realidade metafísica acerca de Jesus. O *Verbo* é o princípio do Filho, dentro da trindade (ver artigo). O Verbo é divino e eterno, e em sentido algum foi adotado, embora possa ser chamado de ı«gerado». Porém, quando esse termo é usado a respeito dEle, Sua eterna geração é ressaltada, isto é, o fato de que Ele sempre foi o Filho. Através do termo «gerado» expressamos a idéia de «Filiação», não dando a entender qualquer começo de tempo. Nesse contexto, trata-se de um termo de relacionamento, nada tendo a ver com alguma ordem cronológica. Mas Jesus, como homem, tornou-se divino. Isto é, Sua *humanidade* foi incorporada ao Verbo, que é o *Filho eterno*. Portanto, há aquela forma de divindade que incorpora a humanidade. O princípio divino-humano, pois, torna-se o alvo de todos os filhos de Deus, que tornar-se-ão divinos, participantes da natureza divina (II Ped. 1:4), embora em sentido secundário, sem participação na trindade. O homem Jesus foi o pioneiro no caminho da salvação (pois a filiação divina é a salvação). Ele conduzirá muitos filhos à glória, para compartilharem de Sua natureza divina, da mesma maneira que Ele, em Sua missão messiânica, compartilhou da natureza humana. Ver Heb. 2:10; Rom. 8:29; II Cor. 3:18 e Col. 2:9-10, bem como a exposição desses versículos no NTI. Essa afirmação visa indicar que em Jesus veio à existência uma forma de divindade que não existia antes, embora o Verbo-filho sempre tivesse sido Deus. A divindade incorporou a humanidade, transmutando-a em uma forma real de divindade. Portanto, há uma família divina, da qual participam muitos filhos, e não somente o Filho.

Há *uma* só pessoa no Verbo-Filho-Jesus-Homem, porque Jesus, como homem, foi apanhado no drama divino, havendo uma completa fusão de naturezas, resultando em uma única pessoa. Esse é um grande mistério, não havendo explanações adequadas para o mesmo. Porém, a questão inteira serve de alicerce da nossa salvação, porque Jesus é o pioneiro desse caminho, no que tange às aspirações dos outros filhos de Deus. Se meus raciocínios, nos dois parágrafos acima, não têm valor, então cumpre-nos resolver o que fazer com a humanidade de Jesus nos céus. Jesus continua existindo como *homem* imortal nos céus? Em caso contrário, alguma transformação deve ter tido lugar em Sua natureza *humana*. Opino que houve uma imensa transformação em Sua humanidade por ocasião de Sua *glorificação*, e da qual participamos. Conseqüentemente, Ele não levou para o céu qualquer forma de humanidade que nós conhecemos. A humanidade glorificada *tornou-se* parte da natureza divina. Mas o Verbo *sempre foi* o Filho de Deus. (B D DB E NTI)

ADOR (ADORA)

Cidade da Iduméia capturada por Hircano (Josefo, *Ant*. xiii.9,1). Também é mencionada em I Mac. 13:20. (Z)

ADORAÇÃO
Observações
A Palavra

Palavra latina composta, de *ad*, «à» e *os*, *oris*,

«boca». Literalmente, pois, adorar é «aplicar a mão à boca», ou seja, «beijar a mão». Ou então é a combinação de *ad* e *orare*, «falar», «adorar», embora a palavra-raiz seja «boca».

1. Envolve a reação religiosa, a oração, o rogo, a adoração, a homenagem prestada a Deus ou a algum ser ou pessoa superior. Em sentido estrito, somente Deus é objeto de nossa adoração. Mas, em sentido secundário, um profundo afeto por outro ser humano pode ser chamado de adoração, sem que isso infrinja contra o nosso amor a Deus. Amar a outrem é amar a Deus, pois todo amor origina-se em Deus.

2. A reação da adoração é uma estrada com direção dupla: é inspirada por Deus, mas o homem corresponde. Alguma coisa existe no próprio homem que busca uma Idéia Suprema que possa exigir seu amor e adoração, porquanto a queda no pecado não obliterou esse algo, embora o tenha debilitado. Quando Deus fala por meio de Cristo, esse sentimento interior é levado à sua plena fruição. Quando os homens buscam a Beleza Suprema, encontram em outras pessoas e objetos algo da beleza de Deus, a ser buscada e cultivada. Devemos buscar ao Senhor enquanto Ele puder ser achado, mas Deus também buscou ao homem por meio de Cristo.

Atos e Objetos

Atos físicos que exibem adoração. Inclinar a cabeça (Êxo. 34:8), ajoelhar-se (I Reis 8:54), prostrar-se (Gên. 17:3; Apo. 1:17). Esses atos mostram o estado da alma, diante do poder de Deus.

Deus é o objeto da adoração. Os Salmos 94, 95-100 ilustram esse princípio com muitas referências. Deus é adorado em vista de Sua majestade, poder, santidade, bondade, retidão e providência em favor dos homens. O termo latino *adorare* contém as idéias de orar, de rogar, de venerar, de homenagear. Esses são os atos envolvidos na adoração. Em sentido amplo, pode-se expressar uma queda de admiração no tocante a algo, incluindo outra pessoa, sendo essa uma forma legítima de veneração, mas que ainda não envolve adoração. Nesse último sentido, alguns sentiram que os santos podiam ser venerados; mas logo envolveu abusos, e os homens passaram a adorar os santos. É muito difícil ver como imagens e relíquias podem ser veneradas em qualquer sentido, sem que ocorra a idolatria. A adoração a objetos materiais é severamente proibida na Bíblia (Êxo. 20:1-6; Isa. 44:12-20).

O Novo Testamento atesta sobre a justiça da adoração a Cristo, em primeiro lugar como o Messias de Deus, e então como o Filho de Deus. Jesus foi adorado quando de Seu nascimento (Mat. 2:11), durante Seu ministério (Mat. 8:2; 9:18), após a Sua ressurreição (Mat. 28:8,17). Homens (João 9:38), anjos (Heb. 1:6) e mesmo demônios (Mar. 5:6) ocuparam-se nessa adoração. Essa atitude emocional é também uma atitude da alma. Os homens correspondem à graça divina, e suas almas são transformadas nessa reação favorável. (B E Z)

Elementos Necessários

Há vários elementos necessários à verdadeira adoração:

1. Um despertamento íntimo, no indivíduo e na coletividade, que crie o desejo de buscar e adorar a Deus.

2. A convicção de que a própria vida requer adoração a Deus, sendo produzida profunda insatisfação pelo tipo de vida que a omite.

3. Associação com outras pessoas de iguais atitudes

ADORAÇÃO

mentais, para que possa existir uma comunidade que adora.

4. Confissão e arrependimento de pecados.

5. Reiterada outorga a Deus, para que sejam renovados o espírito e a essência da adoração.

6. A disposição para enfrentar os aspectos negativos do próprio indivíduo e da coletividade, no esforço de tentar obter reformas, visando o bem geral.

7. A tentativa de buscar uma condição ideal, para o indivíduo e para a coletividade, em que cada pessoa procura aprimorar a si mesma e a sua função.

8. Os elementos de oração, louvor, ação de graças, meditação e adoração devem fazer-se todos presentes. Desse modo, o caminho é largamente aberto até a presença de Deus, podendo ser exercido controle sobre cada indivíduo e sobre a comunidade adoradora inteira.

Adorar e Venerar

A Igreja Católica Romana faz muita questão de distinguir entre «adorar» e «venerar», afirmando que os seus adeptos não adoram, mas somente veneram as imagens de escultura. Mas isso é fugir da questão, pois as Escrituras não nos ordenam que veneremos as imagens de escultura. Na realidade, para todos os efeitos práticos, «adorar» e «venerar» são sinônimos perfeitos. Quem adora, venera; e quem venera, adora.

Na linguagem religiosa, o termo é usado para indicar a devoção, o serviço e a honra que prestamos a Deus, em público ou individualmente. Os templos evangélicos são lugares de adoração, e as formas de culto divino, seguidas pelas diversas denominações cristãs, são formas de adoração. O verbo «adorar» pode ser usado tanto transitivamente, «adorar a Deus», como intransitivamente, «participar da adoração».

Visto que a adoração inclui todos os seus elementos constitutivos, por exemplo, louvor, oração e pregação, e visto que também envolve várias questões associadas, como templos, música, hinos, o número de vocábulos hebraicos e gregos envolvidos nesta ato é muito elevado e diversificado. Nosso estudo estará alicerçado sobre o exame de cinco termos gregos básicos, embora devamos mencionar ao menos o sentido de certas palavras hebraicas mais importantes, como «prostrar-se», «fazer um ídolo», «servir», «inclinar-se». No hebraico, a primeira dessas palavras é usada por cerca de cento e setenta e duas vezes nos vários livros do Antigo Testamento. Abaixo damos o esboço do artigo:

ESBOÇO

I. *Termos gregos importantes*
    A. Gónu
    B. Proskuneîn
    C. Latreía
    D. Leitourgía
    E. Omología

II. *Adoração no Antigo Testamento*
    A. Princípios básicos
    B. Adoração doméstica
        1. Introdução
        2. Louvor e oração
        3. Sacrifícios
        4. Instrução
    C. Adoração pública
        1. O tabernáculo
        2. O templo de Jerusalém
        3. A sinagoga

    D. Adoração individual
    E. Idolatria
        1. Introdução
        2. Cultos cananeus
        3. Influências estrangeiras
    F. O testemunho dos profetas
        1. O lugar dos profetas
        2. Idolatria
        3. Formalismo
        4. Adoração verdadeira

III. *Adoração no Novo Testamento*
    A. Formas de adoração
        1. Nos evangelhos
        2. No livro de Atos e nas epístolas
    B. Elementos componentes da adoração
        1. Oração
        2. Louvor
        3. Confissão de pecado
        4. Confissão de fé (batismo)
        5. Leitura da Bíblia
        6. Pregação
        7. Ceia do Senhor
        8. Coletas?
        9. Cultos ocasionais?
    C. A essência da adoração
        1. Cristo
        2. O Espírito Santo

I. Termos Gregos Importantes

A. Gónu e gonupetéo são palavras usadas na Bíblia para denotar o ato de ajoelhar-se. No grego, joelho é *gónu*. Mas também indica o ato de prostrar-se. Essas palavras são importantes porque descrevem um gesto de adoração que também simboliza a atitude interna.

No mundo greco-romano, esses termos poderiam também ter uma referência secular, pois os escravos ajoelhavam-se diante de seus senhores. O culto oficial pagão não incluía o ato de ajoelhar-se, embora tivesse papel na adoração das divindades sujeitas à influência oriental.

A genuflexão era ato comum no Antigo Testamento. Algumas vezes era praticado diante de homens, como, por exemplo, diante de homens de Deus (ver II Reis 1:13), ou diante dos reis (ver I Crô. 29:20). Por outro lado, embora o ato de pôr-se de pé fosse a atitude normal, por ocasião da oração (ver Gên. 18:22; I Sam. 1:26), era costume ajoelhar-se diante de Deus (ver I Reis 8:54; Dan. 6:10). Ajoelhar-se era sinal de humildade, de auto-aviltamento e de homenagem (ver Isa. 45:23). Posteriormente, os rabinos fizeram distinção entre a genuflexão parcial e o prostrar-se inteiramente, com as mãos e os pés estendidos. Os padres da Igreja Católica Romana, no decurso da missa, também reconhecem mais de uma forma de genuflexão.

No Novo Testamento, há alusão quase que exclusiva ao ato de ajoelhar-se. O ato era empregado principalmente em conexão com a oração a Deus (ver Luc. 22:41), com petições feitas ao Senhor (ver Mat. 17:14), com saudações ao mestre (ver Mar. 10:17), e com homenagens prestadas ao rei (cf. Mat. 27:29), a Baal (ver Rom. 11:4), ao Juiz divino (ver Rom. 14:10,11) ou a Jesus, em suas manifestações públicas como Senhor (ver Fil. 2:10). Tal gesto era expressão de humildade, necessidade, respeito, submissão e adoração. Na Igreja primitiva era usado na oração individual e na oração pública.

B. Prokuneîn. Essa palavra está intimamente ligada a **gónu** e **gonupetéo**, sendo o termo de sentido

ADORAÇÃO

mais amplo, e em muitos sentidos é a palavra que mais rresponde à palavra portuguesa «adorar». Toda.ıa. são obscuras a etimologia e a história primitiva do vocábulo *proskuneín*, embora os estudiosos favoreçam a vinculação etimológica com a palavra «beijo». Conjectura-se que na Grécia antiga o ato de beijar o chão era praticado como meio de honrar às divindades terrestres. Por sua vez, isso envolvia um gesto de inclinação ou prostração, que originalmente era estranho aos gregos, em outras atividades. Portanto, esse verbo passou a significar «prostrar-se como sinal de reverência», «prestar homenagem». E visto que desde o princípio a adoração parecia implícita, nesse gesto, foi apenas natural que a palavra também viesse a indicar a atitude interna de adoração.

Visto que o ato de submissão já era um gesto comum na adoração veterotestamentária, não é de surpreender que *proskuneín* ocorra com freqüência na LXX. Até hoje pode envolver a idéia de beijar (cf. o paralelo em Êxo. 18:7), embora o sentido predominante seja o de inclinar-se (até o solo), em atitude de submissão ou obediência, isto é, de prestar reverência, homenagem, adoração. O ato podia ser prestado a homens, como a um profeta ou a um rei. Também podia ser um gesto próprio da corte (cf. Abraão, em Gên. 23:7,12); mas, em outros casos, só era prestado ao indivíduo que fosse representante de Deus (cf. I Sam. 20:41). Mordecai recusou-se a prestar tal submissão a Hamã (ver Est. 3:2). Os anjos, como mensageiros de Deus, poderiam ser tidos como objetos de adoração. Entretanto, a palavra grega, mesmo na LXX, é reservada para a adoração de alguma divindade, sem importar se fosse um ídolo (ver Êxo. 20:5, para exemplificar) ou o verdadeiro Deus (ver Gên. 22:5, para exemplificar). Isso posto, a palavra grega tem o mesmo sentido que a palavra portuguesa «adorar», mormente no caso de adoração a Deus, ainda que não nos devamos olvidar do sentido secundário. A principal diferença é que a palavra grega, em sua origem, está mais intimamente ligada com o gesto de prostrar-se ou de prestar homenagem.

No Novo Testamento, o uso de *proskuneín* limita-se quase que exclusivamente aos evangelhos, ao livro de Atos e ao Apocalipse, onde aparece por cinqüenta e quatro vezes. À parte de duas citações do Antigo Testamento, na epístola aos Hebreus, a única instância dessa palavra nas epístolas é em I Coríntios 12:45. E mesmo nesse caso, a palavra é usada acerca de um homem que age como incrédulo. No livro de Atos, o termo nunca é usado para indicar a adoração cristã, exceto aquela ligada à primitiva adoração no templo. Mesmo quando os membros da Igreja primitiva se ajoelhavam em oração, era usada alguma frase juntamente com *gónu*, e não o verbo *proskuneín*. Parece que *proskuneín* era deliberadamente evitado como termo para indicar a primitiva adoração cristã, talvez devido à sua reconhecida associação com a adoração visível de alguma divindade do paganismo.

Nos evangelhos sinópticos, esse verbo grego é reservado para indicar a obediência e adoração a Deus e a Jesus. A aparente exceção (ver Mat. 18:26) é controlada pelo fato de que, como é óbvio, Deus está por detrás do senhor que aparece na parábola. Talvez a característica mais interessante em Mateus e Marcos seja a homenagem prestada a Jesus, principalmente em Mateus. Cf. o leproso (8:2), Jairo (9:18), etc. À luz da adoração dos magos (Mat. 2:2,11) e da recusa do Senhor Jesus em adorar ao diabo (Mat. 4:9,10), pouca dúvida pode haver quanto ao fato de que Mateus não usava o termo meramente para denotar um gesto convencional de respeito a Jesus. Consciente ou inconscientemente, aqueles que adoravam e adoram a Jesus estão reconhecendo a Sua deidade. Essa é a ironia por detrás da homenagem zombeteira dos soldados, em Marcos 15:19. Os discípulos de Jesus só começaram a adorá-Lo quando perceberam que Ele era o Filho de Deus (ver Mat. 14:33), ou quando estavam na presença do Senhor ressurrecto (ver Mat. 28:9,17). No livro de Atos, lemos que Pedro não permitiu que Cornélio o adorasse (ver Atos 10:25,26), e o anjo baixou proibição similar (ver Apo. 19:10).

No evangelho de João, há um importante uso de *proskuneín*, em 4:20-24. Em contraste com a adoração localizada, que aparece na pergunta feita pela mulher, Jesus refere-se ali à adoração em Espírito e em verdade. Deixou então de vigorar o preceito atinente à adoração em um único lugar. Mas o uso de *proskuneín* mostra que a adoração propriamente dita não era concebida apenas como uma questão externa. A verdadeira adoração, sem dúvida alguma é um ato de espírito. A homenagem externa não é um pré-requisito e nem uma garantia da verdadeira adoração. No entanto, aparece a mesma ambivalência na mensagem profética, pois a adoração interna não é, de modo algum, incompatível com a expressão externa, podendo até mesmo exigir essa expressão. O máximo que podemos dizer, pois, é que Jesus desvinculou a verdadeira adoração de qualquer gesto externo, em qualquer lugar determinado. E o testemunho das epístolas sem dúvida confirma isso, pois ali *proskuneín* não é mais essencial à adoração. Na prática, a Igreja primitiva aparentemente não sentiu ser possível guardar a idéia da adoração interna paralelamente à palavra que indicava um gesto externo; e, por essa razão, abandonou o uso da palavra.

No livro de Apocalipse, porém, **proskuneín** volta a ser uma palavra importante. Ali é feita a distinção entre a adoração à besta e a adoração a Deus, no Seu santuário celeste. O ato está obviamente em foco, embora certamente tenha significação simbólica nas grandiosas cenas retratadas nos capítulos quatro e cinco do Apocalipse. O ponto alto é que por detrás de *proskuneín* jaz o reconhecimento final de reivindicações totais em conflito. No fim, entretanto, as nações do mundo adorarão a Deus (ver Apo. 15:4).

O fato de que o verbo *proskuneín* é novamente usado quando da homenagem final, por ocasião da *parousia* ou segunda vinda de Cristo, confirma a tese de alguns de que esse verbo, quando usado no Novo Testamento, requer um ato visível ou um gesto concreto de submissão a uma deidade visível. Isso foi possível durante a encarnação e os quarenta dias entre a páscoa e a ascensão do Senhor; daí o seu uso nos evangelhos sinópticos. Isto será possível, novamente, por ocasião da segunda vinda do Senhor, o que justifica o seu uso em Apo. 15:4. No período. intermediário, porém, esse verbo grego não era o termo apropriado para indicar a adoração cristã, o que explica por que o mesmo é evitado no livro de Atos (à parte da adoração no templo de Jerusalém) e nas epístolas (excetuando o caso da adoração prestada pelos incrédulos, em I Cor. 14). Não obstante, se não confinar-se a algum lugar ou gesto específicos, a Igreja pode ocupar-se em adoração verdadeira, não apenas espiritualmente, mas no Espírito, por meio de Quem o Cristo se faz continuamente presente ao Seu povo.

C. Latreía. Tanto esse substantivo quanto a sua forma verbal, **latreúo**, levam-nos a uma **esfera** inteiramente diferente daquela visada por *gonupetéo* e *proskuneín*. O sentido básico desse novo vocábulo

ADORAÇÃO

grego é o de salário, ou de um serviço mais geral prestado a alguém, embora sem a idéia conseqüente de recompensa, no entanto, abarcando um conceito muito mais amplo do que o de escravidão. Devemos pensar em algum serviço fisicamente prestado, como, por exemplo, o ofício de um copeiro. Mas essa palavra também pode ser usada para indicar os cuidados pelo corpo físico. Não se tratava de um termo religioso por exclusividade, apesar de podermos encontrar instâncias de uso dessa palavra em conexão com o culto prestado aos ídolos. Parece, então, estar em foco a preparação associada ao culto.

Na tradução da LXX, esse verbo grego ocorre principalmente nos livros de Êxodo, Deuteronômio, Josué e Juízes, onde tem o sentido de serviço religioso, como ocorre por todo o Antigo Testamento, porém, tendo sempre em vista o ato de sacrifício cultual. Também foi palavra livremente usada para indicar o serviço prestado a deuses falsos (ver Êxo. 20:5, para exemplificar), ainda que a todo tempo as Escrituras insistam que Israel deveria servir ao único Deus vivo e verdadeiro. Isso empresta um elemento mais profundo ao ato de culto. Servir ao Senhor por meio de oferendas alicerça-se sobre uma decisão ou dedicação do coração. Isso é bem destacado em Deu. 10:12 ss, que alude ao amor e ao serviço a Deus com todo o seu coração e com toda a sua alma. Esse serviço requer um aspecto ético e um aspecto cúltico, pois o homem que ama e serve a Deus desse modo observa os mandamentos e estatutos de Deus. O convite de Josué para que o povo de Israel escolhesse entre servir ao Senhor ou servir a outros deuses (ver Jos. 24:14 ss, especialmente o vs. 19), tem essa mesma ênfase.

O substantivo *latreía* é muito menos comumente usado do que o verbo. É empregado quase que exclusivamente para apontar à adoração cúltica, de modo geral ou específico, por exemplo, a páscoa, em Êxo. 12:25,26. Uma característica notável, em contraste com o uso geral do termo grego, que se deu seu uso não-religioso foi quase virtualmente abandonado. Todavia, *latreía* não é um termo muito geral, por um lado (o serviço prestado a Deus), e nem muito específico, por outro lado (o ministério sacerdotal). Simplesmente denota a adoração cúltica a Deus. Conforme se deduz do seu verbo cognato, em última análise repousa sobre uma profunda autodedicação a Deus, com o impulso do amor e do santo temor.

Tal como sucede na LXX, como também no Novo Testamento, o verbo é mais comum do que o substantivo. *Latreúo* ocorre mais freqüentemente em Lucas e Atos, e também na epístola aos Hebreus. Sob influência do Antigo Testamento, esse verbo sempre tem um sentido religioso. E o serviço envolvido é o serviço prestado a Deus (ou aos deuses). Na epístola aos Hebreus, está em pauta o ministério de sacrifícios levíticos (em distinção ao serviço prestado aos deuses falsos). Uma importante diferença, em relação ao uso que se vê no Antigo Testamento, é que em Hebreus 8:5 e 13:10, o autor sagrado parece haver rompido com a rígida distinção, feita pela LXX, entre *latreúo*, para indicar o serviço cúltico, e *leitourgéo*, para indicar o ministério específico dos sacerdotes levitas; cf. também Heb. 9:9. Apesar disso, o impulso geral do Novo Testamento é ampliar, e não estreitar o alcance do sentido religioso. À parte de seu uso, em Mat. 4:10, onde *latreúo* denota a adoração que alguém deve oferecer a Deus, em contraste com a submissão exigida pelo diabo, essa ampliação envolve as três áreas básicas da oração, das obras e da vida diária.

a. O uso dessa palavra, para indicar o ministério da oração, ocorre nos escritos de Lucas. Ver o caso de Ana (Luc. 2:37), onde suas orações e jejuns faziam parte integrante de sua adoração, e não meros adjuntos. E há uma referência similar em Atos 26:7. Isso contrasta com o uso veterotestamentário, onde a oração não fazia parte integrante do culto.

b. Mais significante é o uso de *latreúo* na obra do ministério neotestamentário. Essa é a contribuição específica de Paulo, em Rom. 1:9. Se ele tivesse dito apenas «com meu espírito», poderíamos pensar tratar-se da adoração em espírito e em verdade. Mas a expressão «no evangelho», indica a pregação do evangelho, conforme se vê em II Cor. 8:18. O que Paulo fazia era descrever o ministério da Palavra em termos de culto (cf. o uso que ele faz da palavra «sacrifício»). Tal ministério não é apenas serviço, é culto ou adoração. Isso posto, todo o seu empenho em favor do evangelho é um serviço prestado a Deus, nesse sentido.

c. A vida inteira do crente também pode formar o conteúdo de *latreúo*. Isso pode ser visto até no Benedictus, onde o serviço a Deus deve ser prestado em santidade e retidão (ver Luc. 1:74). Uso similar acha-se em Atos 24:14, onde Paulo insiste que, com seus pais, servia fielmente à lei, embora de maneira que os judeus considerariam herética (cf. vs. 16 e também as palavras «com consciência pura», em II Tim. 1:3). Hebreus 12:28 encerra a mesma linha de pensamento, onde se lê no serviço prestado a Deus com reverência e piedade, e onde a alusão certamente é à conduta diária (cf. cap. 13). E é possível que em Filipenses 3:3 a referência seja ainda mais ampla, onde a verdadeira circuncisão, que é o culto espiritual, é contrastado com a circuncisão física. Naturalmente, é possível que ali a idéia seja de que a adoração espiritual é comparada com a adoração segundo os ritos, embora o contexto favoreça mais o contraste entre duas maneiras de viver totalmente diversas, a saber, o caminho jubiloso do Espírito e o penoso caminho da inculpabilidade legal.

A palavra *latreía* ocorre apenas por cinco vezes em todo o Novo Testamento, e em três instâncias alude ao culto sacrificial do Antigo Testamento (ver Rom. 9:4; Heb. 9:1,6). Em João 16:2 talvez haja um indício de pano de fundo sacrificial também, quando Jesus diz que alguns matariam os discípulos como se estivessem prestando um serviço a Deus. Por igual modo, a *logike latreía* de Rom. 12:1 aparece dentro do contexto da apresentação do corpo como um sacrifício vivo oferecido a Deus. Nesse caso, porém, esse sacrifício consiste na autoconsagração que abarca a renovação e a transformação da vida. Esse serviço também é *«lógico»* no sentido de que é a coisa razoável a ser feita, mas também que segue um padrão lógico, que tem sua base última no Logos. Assim, a *latreía* irrompe os limites do que é cúltico e adquire uma referência total interna e externa. Apesar disso, preserva a associação cúltica, pois o âmago mesmo da *latréia* é o auto-oferecimento a Deus, com base no fato de que Deus ofereceu a Si mesmo a nós. Assim, o verdadeiro serviço cristão só ocorre quando, em sua essência, consiste em uma adoração que se expressa de forma legítima em atos de oração e louvor.

D. Leitourgia. Esse substantivo e o verbo **leitourgéo** relacionam-se, etimologicamente, ao serviço prestado em favor de um povo ou nação, isto é, o corpo político. Desde seus mais antigos exemplos, essas palavras têm um certo sentido técnico no mundo grego. Aludem aos serviços específicos que os ricos, de modo voluntário ou compulsório, prestavam à cidade ou comunidade, de seu próprio bolso. No período imperial, essa palavra assumiu um sentido ainda mais amplo, envolvendo todo o serviço oficial compulsório

ADORAÇÃO

prestado ao estado ou à comunidade. Posteriormente, o vocábulo adquiriu um sentido muito amplo e frouxo, desaparecendo do mesmo o elemento oficial. Assim, os escravos prestavam serviço (leitourgía) a seus senhores, as mães a seus bebês, os amigos a seus amigos, etc. Nas religiões misteriosas, a palavra adquiriu ainda um novo sentido técnico. E os que serviam nos templos, segundo se dizia, prestavam uma liturgia aos deuses.

O uso cúltico predomina na LXX. Dentre cerca de cem usos desse verbo, na LXX, apenas alguns poucos casos são não-religiosos, o que também se dá com cerca dos quarenta exemplos do substantivo. Ali não restam traços do sentido clássico original da palavra, e mesmo o sentido geral da mesma mais ou menos desapareceu. O objeto da liturgia era Deus ou o Seu tabernáculo. Assim, as funções sacerdotais tornam-se liturgias, quase sempre no sentido literal da palavra. Somente nos livros apócrifos de Eclesiástico e Sabedoria de Salomão vê-se a tendência de espiritualizar o conceito. Incidentalmente, é altamente improvável que os tradutores da LXX tenham usado *leitourgéo* e *leitourgía* porque já eram termos usados nas religiões misteriosas. Fazendo contraste com *latreía* e *diakonía*, a palavra *leitourgía* envolve a dignidade associada ao serviço público, sendo esse, mui provavelmente, o fator decisivo no seu significado.

É interessante observar que as palavras *leitourgéo* e *leitourgía* não se revestem da mesma importância no Novo Testamento que têm na LXX. De fato, no Novo Testamento, o verbo ocorre apenas por três vezes, e o substantivo por seis vezes (ver Atos 13:2; Rom. 15:27; Heb. 10:11; Luc. 1:23; II Cor. 9:12; Fil. 2:17,30; Heb. 8:6; 9:21). Apesar da importância que esse grupo de palavras adquiriu na cristandade medieval e moderna, dificilmente podemos considerá-las palavras de importância capital no Novo Testamento.

Na epístola aos Hebreus, como também em Lucas 1:23 o uso assemelha-se ao do Antigo Testamento. Assim, Zacarias estaria cumprindo os deveres de sua liturgia. Mais interessante ainda é a transferência do termo para o próprio Cristo, o qual ofereceu uma melhor liturgia quando se entregou sobre a cruz (ver Heb. 8:6). A alusão sacrificial do termo justifica seu uso em relação ao ministério sumo sacerdotal de nosso Senhor.

Até este ponto poderia parecer que *leitourgía* seria um termo grego impróprio para indicar a adoração cristã. Suas associações com os sacrifícios certamente nos indicam uma extensão de idéias sacerdotais quanto aos serviços dos cristãos. Entretanto, em Atos 13:2 a liturgia dos profetas e mestres sugere-nos a oração e o jejum, juntamente com a espiritualização desse vocábulo, dentro do período intertestamental (cf. Filo). Paulo vai ainda mais adiante, aplicando a palavra tanto à coleta que organizara para a igreja em Jerusalém (ver II Cor. 9:12), como também à oferta que os filipenses lhe fizeram (ver Fil. 2:30; cf. Rom. 15:27). Seja como for, descobre-se uma certa aproximação do desenvolvimento que já se pôde observar no tocante à palavra *latreía*. Certamente, *leitourgía* não é palavra usada para indicar as funções oficiais efetuadas pelos apóstolos, profetas, evangelistas, pastores e mestres da Igreja primitiva. Por conseguinte, se tal palavra foi usada em relação à Igreja, deve-se evitar pensar que a mesma tenha implicações sacerdotais como, por exemplo, alguma aplicação especial à Ceia do Senhor.

Leitourgós é termo usado para indicar o próprio Cristo em Hebreus 8:2 «...como **ministro** do

santuário e do verdadeiro tabernáculo...» O trecho de Heb. 1:7 (cf. *Leitourgikós*, em Heb. 1:14) denota os anjos como instrumentos da vontade de Deus. Parece ser esse também o sentido em Rom. 13:6, onde os governantes são chamados *leitourgoí* de Deus. Epafrodito aparece como um *leitourgós*, ao trazer a dádiva dos crentes de Filipos (ver Fil. 2:25), pois era o agente que prestava serviço, o executor de uma benfeitoria pública, ou o servo de um ato cúltico (ver Fil. 2:30). Finalmente, em um trecho com tons um tanto mais sacerdotalistas, o próprio Paulo aparece como um *leitourgós* de Jesus Cristo no tocante aos gentios (ver Rom. 15:16). Esse ministério é explicitamente vinculado à pregação do evangelho, e também ao oferecimento da fé dos gentios (cf. Fil. 2:17). Parece, portanto, que Paulo estava novamente usando uma metáfora sacrificial para indicar o ministério do evangelho. Ao assim fazer, estava caracterizando esse ministério como a adoração suprema que, com base na própria liturgia prestada por Cristo, o crente pode oferecer a Deus.

E. Homologia e sua forma verbal, **homologeîn**, têm o sentido básico de dizer a mesma coisa, de concordar em uma declaração (*homo* = o que é comum; *logos* = palavra). Isso a levou a um variegado uso dentro do vocabulário das leis e do comércio, como, por exemplo, admitir o que disse, confessar uma acusação, confirmar uma importância recebida, aceitar uma proposta ou promessa, etc. O substantivo *homologia* pode dar a entender um acordo em uma discussão, a concordância da prática com a teoria, ou mesmo um acordo ou pacto. O conceito de viver-se harmoniosamente com a natureza era uma idéia importante para o estoicismo. Em sentido religioso, que é um sentido adquirido, e não original, o conceito denota aceitação de votos, ou mais comumente, a confissão de pecados. Sob a influência oriental, essa confissão podia ser feita a um sacerdote, tendo em vista aplacar a ira de alguma divindade, em período de aflição.

Se a confissão de pecados é uma noção básica no Antigo Testamento, parece estar aqui associada a um tipo bem diferente de confissão, a saber, a confissão de louvor a Deus, devido a Seus atos poderosos. Salmos como 22,30, etc., exibem essa conexão. Ao reconhecer o seu pecado, o salmista encontrou a salvação, e seu arrependimento tornou-se louvor e ação de graças. Destarte, a confissão muda de caráter. A admissão de pecado transforma-se em reconhecimento da graça e do poder de Deus. A confissão dos atos errados praticados transmuta-se em confissão a Deus, não tanto no sentido de uma confissão de fé, mas antes, no sentido de uma confissão de louvor, de magnificência a Deus.

Para exprimir essa confissão, tanto de pecado como de louvor, a LXX prefere usar formas compostas, em lugar das simples palavras *homologéo* e *homologia*, embora, fora da Bíblia, uma palavra como *eksomologeîsthai* não seja usada no sentido de *enaltecer*. A palavra hebraica por detrás da mesma, que tem a força tanto de louvor quanto de confissão de pecados, controla a tradução da LXX nesse ponto (cf. I Reis 8:33,34 e Nee. 9:3). O que fica pressuposto, tanto no hebraico quanto no grego, é que a confissão e o louvor têm lugar publicamente, diante da congregação. Isso significa que o louvor envolve também um elemento de proclamação. Assim, confessar as obras graciosas de Deus consiste em declará-las (ver Sal. 118:17 ss). E o elemento de oração também não deve ser esquecido, porquanto confessar o nome do Senhor pode ser um ato de oração que corresponde à invocação do nome do

ADORAÇÃO

Senhor. Desse modo, a simples palavra «homologuia» ou confissão pode unir, de forma ímpar, os elementos que constituem, fundamentalmente, a verdadeira adoração, a saber, a confissão de pecados, o louvor a Deus, a declaração de atos e a oração a Ele dirigida. Tudo isso pressupõe, naturalmente, a confissão de fé, como é claro.

No Novo Testamento, o primeiro sentido de chamar à atenção é dado a uma declaração solene. Essa declaração pode ter um caráter bem geral (cf. a promessa de Herodes, em Mat. 14:7). Mas também pode envolver o ato bíblico mais específico de confessar pecados. Assim, em Hebreus 11:13, os indivíduos que confessaram-se estrangeiros e peregrinos, não estavam meramente confirmando ou admitindo o fato, mas estavam fazendo uma declaração de fé. Com base nisso, foi fácil galgar-se para o sentido de prestar testemunho, que tem raízes óbvias no uso legal clássico, mas que assume um caráter distintivo nas páginas do Novo Testamento. Assim, testificar é predominantemente testificar acerca de Jesus Cristo. Confessar ou não confessar a Cristo tem significações escatológicas (ver Mat. 10:32), porquanto quando alguém confessa a Cristo, Ele, por sua vez, o confessa como Seu. A própria negação pode assumir a forma de uma confissão de ignorância (ver Mat. 7:23). Confessar a Jesus como o Messias podia envolver a idéia de que o tal seria expulso da sinagoga (ver João 9:22).

Confessar a Jesus também envolvia a confissão de fé (ver Rom. 10:9,10). Paulo vinculava a fé ao coração, que Deus ressuscitou a Jesus dentre os mortos, e também a confissão dos lábios, a saber, que Jesus é o Senhor. Essa combinação assegura a certeza de salvação. A doutrina específica da ressurreição é o tema da confissão (ver Atos 23:8; os fariseus). João emprega o termo *homologeîn* para indicar a confissão cristológica, que ele procurava proteger contra os falsos mestres (cf. I João 4:2,3; II João 7). Os verdadeiros mestres cristãos, pois, podem ser distinguidos dos falsos mediante a confissão que fazem.

O próprio Cristo fez sua boa confissão na presença de Pilatos. Ao fazê-lo assim, Jesus deu o bom exemplo para ser seguido por todos os cristãos (ver I Tim. 6:13). O batismo em água provê uma excelente oportunidade para se fazer a confissão básica de fé, a qual pode assumir a forma de uma interrogação (cf. Mat. 16:13 ss.; João 1:19 ss.; Atos 8:37). Se todos os crentes devem confessar, então aqueles chamados à obra ministerial têm uma tarefa específica de confissão. A ênfase recai aqui não tanto sobre o testemunho acerca da fé, mas sobre a proclamação, o testemunho, o evangelismo ou mesmo o ensino pessoal. Confessar é fazer a confissão de Jesus, o que envolve aquilo que Deus tem feito através Dele. Essa confissão apostólica faz pesar sobre os ouvintes a obrigação de confessarem seus pecados, aliando-se na confissão de Jesus como Salvador e Senhor. Visto que o tema da confissão é a reconciliação graciosa que Deus operou por meio de Cristo, a confissão redunda na honra e na glória de Deus, prestando-se admiravelmente ao louvor e à ação de graças.

O substantivo *homología* raramente é usado no Novo Testamento. Reveste-se de certa fluidez de sentido que demonstra quão rico é esse conceito. O autor sagrado denota a fixa confissão de fé, da qual a Igreja não podia desviar-se, confissão essa que talvez tivesse a forma de um hino. A confissão de Timóteo (ver I Tim. 6:12,13) também poderia referir-se a um conjunto fixo de doutrinas, recitadas por ocasião do batismo ou da ordenação ao ministério; mas a ênfase parece recair mais sobre o elemento de compromisso público assumido. Paulo usa de modo bastante livre essa palavra, em II Coríntios 9:13. A coleta evidenciava a reação e a obediência dos crentes de Corinto, o que servia para redundar na glória de Deus. Indícios da declaração do evangelho e da confissão de fé jazem por detrás do vocábulo, nesse exemplo. O fato de que a confissão e a obediência avançam de mãos dadas mostra que não há qualquer discrepância fundamental entre Paulo e Tiago, o qual afirma que meras palavras, sem o acompanhamento de obras, são ocas e destituídas de valor (ver Tia. 2:14 ss.).

No que concerne à forma grega composta, *eksomologeísthai*, esta é a mais importante. Usada como «pecados», no acusativo, denota confissão pública (ver Rom. 14:11; Atos 19:18; Tia. 5:16). Mais comumente, porém, trata-se de um termo que expressa louvor. Paulo empregou o termo nesse sentido, em Rom. 15:7 ss. Cristo é confessado como o Senhor, para glória de Deus Pai (ver Fil. 2:11). Essa confissão final da criação já é antecipada à adoração efetuada pela Igreja Cristã. Os magníficos cânticos existentes no livro de Apocalipse podem ser descritos como homológicos quanto à forma e ao conteúdo, embora a própria palavra grega não apareça.

A palavra «homologia» não é um equivalente direto de adoração. Não obstante, de todos os termos gregos que a Bíblia usa para indicar a adoração a Deus, esse é o mais abrangente e significativo. Isso porque, com nenhum outro termo, esse é capaz de combinar as características mais importantes da genuína adoração cristã. A nova ênfase neotestamentária sobre a declaração e confirmação de Cristo e da obra salvatícia de Deus em Cristo, adiciona substância e profundidade àquilo que aparece no uso da LXX. A confissão de pecados continua ali a desempenhar um papel indispensável na adoração. A confissão ou louvor a Deus, em oração, também retém o seu papel. Todavia, a confissão de fé emerge como o ato central de adoração. E isso tem um duplo conteúdo: é a confissão acerca de Jesus, e também é a confissão dos fatos e doutrinas relacionadas a Ele. Também reveste-se de uma dupla forma: é a pública profissão na congregação e também é a declaração do evangelho no testemunho apostólico e no evangelismo. A pregação, longe de ser uma alternativa da adoração, é um de seus aspectos intrínsecos. A confissão acerca de Jesus Cristo, na congregação ou para o mundo, visa o louvor da glória de Deus. Tal como na «homologia» do Antigo Testamento, é o louvor a Deus que culmina nas antenas celestiais e no reconhecimento de Jesus Cristo, como Senhor, por parte da criação. A compreensão sobre a «homologia» bíblica talvez seja a grande chave para a compreensão da adoração expressa na Bíblia.

II. Adoração No Antigo Testamento

A. Princípios básicos. O estudo das palavras gregas associadas à adoração mostra-nos que, se certos conceitos, como ajoelhar-se ou prestar submissão, envolvem o aspecto humano, as raízes da adoração bíblica devem ser procuradas não nas emoções humanas, mas no relacionamento divinamente estabelecido entre Deus e o homem.

Isso é importante porque significa que a base da adoração é teológica, e não antropológica. A comum indagação que pergunta se a origem da adoração deve-se encontrar em emoções como o temor, o respeito e a veneração aos antepassados, torna-se indagação fora de lugar, do ponto de vista bíblico. Tal indagação pressupõe que a adoração é algo subjetivo,

ADORAÇÃO

que se origina do íntimo do próprio indivíduo, que é uma realidade intrínseca para o homem, e que mesmo como uma reação adquire substância no interior da pessoa que reage, não havendo necessidade alguma de qualquer objeto externo que corresponda às emoções internas.

Que emoções e reações humanas estão envolvidas no ato de adoração é algo inegável, naturalmente. Admiração, temor, gratidão e amor podem ser emoções experimentadas na adoração. O que se deve ressaltar, porém, é que esses não são fatores controladores. Não constituem a verdadeira essência da adoração. Na Bíblia, o começo jaz no objeto da adoração, e não no sujeito. E tal objeto também não é indefinido. Não é o mistério por detrás do universo. Nem é o próprio universo. Não é algum fator desconhecido. Não é a potencialidade do próprio ser humano. O objeto da adoração é, ao mesmo tempo, o ponto inicial e o fator controlador, e não uma projeção do ser humano. Esse objeto é Deus.

Deus declara sobre Si mesmo, na Bíblia, como o Deus vivo que existe de eternidade a eternidade, o qual criou o mundo, criou o homem segundo a Sua imagem, e se pôs em posição de relacionamento com o homem. Em todo o relacionamento entre Deus e o homem, a iniciativa fica com Deus. Ele é o sujeito, bem como o objeto. Deus diz ao homem o que ele pode fazer e o que ele não pode. Deus controla o destino do homem. Deus julga as falhas humanas e salva o homem de seus pecados. Esse Deus é o Deus cuja pessoa e cujos atos formam o tema e o princípio formativo da adoração genuína. Se a adoração envolve admiração, essa admiração é a admiração a Deus; se há amor, é o amor a Deus; se há louvor, é o louvor a Deus; se a adoração é a reação humana, trata-se da reação do homem ao Deus vivo, que se fez conhecido do homem, através de Suas obras e de Suas palavras.

A reação da adoração não é uma reação qualquer. A adoração é controlada pelo seu objeto, que também é o sujeito. Portanto, devemos pensar em uma adoração sob formas específicas. Em primeiro lugar, há a forma de louvor confessional a Deus, a declaração de Sua graça e de Seus atos poderosos. Essa confissão combina a recitação do que Deus tem feito e o louvor a Deus por esses Seus atos. Na prática, por um lado, esses elementos podem ser separados na leitura e na proclamação, e, por outro lado, no cântico de salmos e hinos. Não obstante, quando a adoração é genuinamente bíblica, há uma indissolúvel relação entre esses dois elementos. A proclamação genuína consiste em louvor, e o louvor genuíno também consiste em proclamação.

Em segundo lugar, há a forma de serviço, capaz de larga expansão, mas que também tem seu aspecto mais estreito, a saber, a prestação de serviços a Deus, mediante a realização de atos de culto. Quanto a isso a Bíblia preserva um admirável equilíbrio. Os exercícios religiosos não podem servir de substitutos de um serviço total da vida. Por outro lado, o serviço total da vida não deveria excluir os serviços específicos prestados a Deus, expressos sob a forma de exercícios religiosos. Dentro desse serviço a Deus, o ministério sacrificial desempenha um importante papel no Antigo Testamento. E tal ministério também não é eliminado no Novo Testamento; antes é consumado em, e através do ministério sumo sacerdotal de Jesus Cristo. Porém, mesmo no Antigo Testamento, traz à luz um aspecto decisivo da adoração. A relação entre Deus e o homem é tal que o homem degenerou-se mediante a sua revolta e pecado. A expiação torna-se necessária, para que haja a restauração dessa relação.

O ministério sacerdotal do Antigo Testamento prefigura o mais elevado de todos os atos libertadores de Deus, a saber, o ato mediante o qual, encarnado em Seu Filho, Ele levou sobre Si, graciosamente, a pena do pecado, e assim proveu para sua remissão e para a restauração do homem à comunhão Consigo mesmo. O ministério sacerdotal não foi algum acidente errático dentro da estrutura total da adoração. Em sua forma cumprida no Novo Testamento, tanto é um tema supremo de adoração como também é aquilo que capacita o homem a oferecer serviço e louvor aceitáveis. Em sua forma veterotestamentária, faz parte do serviço prestado a Deus, um convite ao arrependimento e à dedicação da vida, bem como a prefiguração da obra divina que é o âmago e a substância da confissão do louvor. Sem isso, não haveria adoração autêntica, mas apenas uma idolatria mal-orientada e uma temível expectação de juízo.

Finalmente, há a forma de oração. Em si mesmo, esse é um outro aspecto da adoração a Deus, por dois motivos: inclui a confissão de pecados e é a confissão do nome de Deus, uma confiante invocação do Deus que intervém em favor do homem, inclinando-se graciosamente em favor do solicitador, e tendo em vista à satisfação de suas necessidades. O próprio fato de que Deus toma a iniciativa indica que a oração, tanto quanto o louvor, faz parte da própria essência da adoração, pois a oração também envolve proclamação e louvor. As orações oferecidas a Deus rememoram as grandes coisas realizadas por Deus. Deus é magnificado por causa dessas coisas. Longe de ser um grito desesperado nas trevas, é uma solicitação confiante ao Deus que a Si mesmo se revela, com base naquilo que Ele tem revelado sobre Si mesmo. A própria urgência da crise ou queixa não pode ocultar essa confiança subjacente, a qual é sustentada não pela justiça própria, mas pela verdade e pela fidelidade divinas.

Um ponto adicional é que a adoração bíblica não é deixada sujeita ao capricho humano. A adoração bíblica não é controlada por desejos arbitrários ou por necessidades contingentes. Não indaga que coisas serão mais úteis, ou que melhor expressam o impulso para adorar, do ponto de vista do homem. Aprende como adorar da parte de Deus que é o objeto da adoração. Isso é especialmente claro no Antigo Testamento, onde Deus diz a Moisés, com detalhes minuciosos, como o povo que Ele redimiu do Egito, haveria agora de adorá-Lo e servi-Lo, tanto no deserto, como, mais tarde, na Terra Prometida. Mas o povo de Israel não tinha nem o desejo e nem o instinto de obedecer a muitas daquelas coisas. Eles sentiam-se muito mais simpáticos aos ritos dos deuses estrangeiros. Assim sendo, a lição bíblica certamente é clara. Na adoração, como em tudo o mais, o crente não deve confiar em seus próprios instintos. Ele não sabe o que lhe é mais útil e melhor. Antes, precisa aprender a adorar a Deus. E isso conforme as instruções baixadas pelo próprio Deus. Esse rígido detalhamento, naturalmente, não mais se vê nas páginas do Novo Testamento. Mas o mesmo princípio continua a ter aplicação ali, embora de maneira diferente. Toda ação cristã está sujeita à supervisão do Espírito e às normas determinadas pela Palavra. Se não há mais regulamentos detalhados, o fato é que os elementos constitutivos básicos da adoração fazem-se claramente presentes tanto no Antigo quanto no Novo Testamentos. As formas de adoração usadas pelos cristãos, embora sejam muito variadas quanto aos detalhes, devem ser moldadas de tal modo que expressem e incluam esses elementos essenciais

ADORAÇÃO

em sua devida proporção, pureza e poder.

B. Adoração doméstica.

1. Introdução. A mais antiga forma de adoração, no Antigo Testamento, é a adoração doméstica. Antes mesmo de Israel tornar-se uma nação, já existia uma família que adorava, a família de Abraão, Isaque e Jacó. Após o êxodo, quando os filhos de Israel tornaram-se uma nação, e foram estabelecidas formas nacionais de adoração, a família continuou a desempenhar um importante papel na adoração. O surgimento da sinagoga, posteriormente, possibilitou uma forma mais contínua de vida congregacional, oferecendo novas oportunidades de instrução. Mas nem mesmo isso excluiu a família como unidade de adoração.

2. Louvor e oração. Uma das dificuldades existentes na era patriarcal consistia em distinguir entre a oração doméstica e a oração pessoal. Apesar disso, parece que quando Abraão invocou o nome do Senhor em vários lugares (por exemplo, Gên. 12), toda a sua casa participou na adoração. Não é dada a substância dessa invocação, mas pouca dúvida há no sentido de que ali estão contidos os elementos fundamentais da oração e da ação de graças. Isso é expresso na oração do servo de Abraão (ver Gên. 24). Essa oração deixa transparecer claramente a natureza doméstica da adoração, pois o servo, no décimo segundo versículo, invocou o Senhor Deus de Abraão. Nos dias de adoração nacional, o papel central dos holocaustos, no santuário, removeu dos lares uma das grandes ocasiões para oração e louvor, embora não haja razões para supormos que, em conseqüência disso, tenha perecido a oração doméstica. Dar graças por ocasião das refeições torna-se um hábito fixo, no final do período do Antigo Testamento, ou mesmo muito antes disso. Quando e com qual extensão os salmos foram usados no lar é algo difícil de ser determinado. O hino entoado por ocasião da última Ceia serviu de indicação de que, pelo tempo de Jesus, o saltério era usado nos lares. O cântico do Hilel, por ocasião da Páscoa, é confirmado por meio de outras fontes informativas, embora a informação seja escassa quanto ao uso mais amplo do saltério e, embora, sem dúvida alguma, a prática variasse consideravelmente de família para família.

3. Sacrifícios. Os sacrifícios oferecidos pelos patriarcas hebreus tinham natureza doméstica ou pessoal. Assim, Abraão foi erigindo altares nos lugares onde invocava a Deus. Em Betel, Jacó erigiu uma coluna e derramou azeite sobre a mesma, para ungi-la. Incidentalmente, esse uso não significa que os patriarcas copiavam sua religião dos povos em derredor; eles simplesmente usavam formas comuns de adoração ao verdadeiro Deus. A páscoa também era uma instituição doméstica, pois cada família a observava com a doação de um cordeiro. Entretanto, quando a instituição da tenda ou do templo central de Jerusalém pôs fim às oferendas oferecidas pelas famílias, essa regra continuou sendo observada, embora as ofertas tivessem de ser feitas em um lugar central. Porém, a centralização de maneira alguma destruiu esse aspecto doméstico, pois as famílias continuaram jornadeando a Jerusalém, a fim de apresentarem suas oferendas em grupos (tal como a adoração doméstica pôde ser mantida na adoração da congregação, através de cultos domésticos). Tal como o sinal de livramento, o grande sinal do pacto, a circuncisão, também era uma questão familiar. Esse sinal do pacto foi dado a princípio a Abraão, como ordenança de ser observada por toda a sua casa (ver Gên. 17:9 ss). E mesmo quando a adoração de Israel obteve dimensões nacionais, persistiu o caráter doméstico da circuncisão (cf. Luc. 2:21 ss). Em último recurso, como é natural, a nação como um todo fazia as suas ofertas na qualidade de família de Abraão, Isaque e Jacó.

4. Instrução. Um aspecto da vida religiosa que foi claramente entregue aos cuidados das famílias, nos dias do Antigo Testamento, era o aspecto da instrução tanto na fé de Israel como também no tocante à sua adoração. Nos tempos dos patriarcas, isso pode ser pressuposto por nós. Após o êxodo, foi claramente ordenado ao povo que assim se fizesse, nas exortações constantes no livro de Deuteronômio. O«Ouve, ó Israel» devia ser ensinado diligentemente pelos pais aos seus filhos (ver Deu. 6:4 ss). Aos pais também cabia explicar os mandamentos a seus filhos (ver Deu. 6:20 ss). A explicação sobre os mandamentos envolvia a rememorização dos grandiosos atos de Deus (ver Deu. 6:21 ss). O dever dos israelitas de não ocultarem esses fatos a seus filhos e netos sublinha um dos grandes salmos históricos (ver Sal. 78; cf. vs. 3 e 4). Os trechos de Êxodo 12:26 e 13:14 dizem a mesma coisa, onde se aprende que era mister falar, não somente sobre os ritos da páscoa, mas também sobre o grande ato de livramento divino, que a páscoa comemora. Conforme já se pôde observar, grande parte desse dever de instruir posteriormente foi delegada às sinagogas; mas às famílias cabia o direito de assegurar que essa instrução estava sendo dada. Se não fora isso, tal instrução não teria continuado a ser dada quando veio a dispersão dos judeus.

C. Adoração Pública

1. O tabernáculo. Pode-se dizer que a adoração pública de Israel começou por ocasião da observância da páscoa, no Egito. A isso seguiu-se a instituição de um sistema inteiro de adoração, estabelecido pelo próprio Deus, mediante as revelações dadas através de Moisés. Essa adoração girava em torno do tabernáculo ou da tenda da congregação. Durante as marchas pelo deserto, uma tenda era a única estrutura que podia ser usada de maneira prática pelos israelitas, embora talvez esteja envolvido também um importante princípio, a saber, o fato de que o Deus vivo por assim dizer não está limitado a alguma estrutura permanente (cf. Atos 7).

Os detalhes da adoração prescrita para o tabernáculo são tão variegados que é simplesmente impossível falar sobre todos eles neste artigo, podendo-se apenas chamar a atenção para certos pormenores mais significativos, que são quatro:

a. As festividades religiosas. A adoração a Deus, por parte de Israel, concentrava-se quase toda em torno das grandes festas religiosas da páscoa, do pentecoste e dos tabernáculos. Os israelitas tinham o dever de fazer-se presentes a essas festas, em Jerusalém, para fazerem as ofertas apropriadas. Eram ocasiões de rememorização jubilosa e agradecida, pelo que envolviam o aspecto declaratório e confessional da adoração. A páscoa era a festa da liberação, representando simbolicamente a nossa salvação em Cristo; o pentecoste era a festa da constante provisão de Deus, que se cumpre na experiência cristã com o Espírito de Deus; e a festa do tabernáculo era a festa da orientação divina ao povo que peregrinava pelo deserto, representando a colheita final do povo de Deus, por ocasião da segunda vinda de Cristo.

b. Os sacrifícios. Desde o começo os holocaustos faziam parte da adoração bíblica. Quando da revelação dada no Sinai, eles receberam uma forma organizacional de âmbito nacional. As ofertas foram divididas em Levítico em várias categorias, a saber: os

ADORAÇÃO

holocaustos ou ofertas queimadas; as ofertas de manjares; as ofertas pelo pecado; e as ofertas pela culpa. Cada uma dessas categorias tinha uma finalidade diferente. (Ver Sacrifícios e Ofertas). O que importa entender é que no âmago do sistema de sacrifícios brilha a verdade de que Deus fazia provisão, através dos sacrifícios, para fazer expiação, sem o que nenhuma adoração verdadeira seria possível. Essa verdade é particularmente expressa no grande ritual anual do dia da expiação, quando o santuário, os sacerdotes e o povo eram todos purificados (ver Lev. 16).

c. A arca da aliança. Esta ocupava posição de proeminência no tabernáculo. Servia de memória dos fatos de que Deus não pode ser representado através de imagens de escultura; de que a base da adoração prestada no tabernáculo era o pacto que Deus estabelecera com o Seu povo; e de que a adoração efetuada no santuário não excluía, não substituía, nem debilitava os requisitos de um serviço mais amplo a Deus, em cumprimento dos imperativos éticos da lei. O estabelecimento da arca da aliança dentro da tenda mostrava que qualquer divisão entre o ministério sacerdotal e o ministério profético só surgiria se a adoração básica de Israel não fosse devidamente compreendida. O culto efetuado no santuário não era uma esfera autônoma. A ausência de alguma representação visível de Deus não se devia a alguma falta de objetividade. Antes, Deus não deve jamais ser identificado com as coisas por Ele criadas.

d. O sábado. Uma instituição sui-generis é o sábado. Não era alguma cerimônia, e nem estava centralizada no santuário. Deveria ser classificado sob a adoração doméstica ou individual. No entanto, tinha que ser observado pelo povo inteiro de Israel. Era mais um dia de descanso, do que um dia de adoração, pois caracterizava-se mais pelo que não era feito do que por aquilo que era feito. Por outro lado, o sábado tinha um lado positivo, do ponto de vista da adoração. Era um memorial permanente: a. da criação (ver Êxo. 19:11) e b. do livramento da servidão egípcia (ver Deu. 5:15). Mas a santificação daquele dia também destacava um aspecto fundamental da adoração, a saber, a santificação do nome Deus e de toda a vida e atividade no nome de Deus. Através dos séculos, a observância do sábado tem servido para separar Israel como povo consagrado ao serviço do Deus vivo e verdadeiro; em um estágio posterior da história de Israel, essa observância proveu-lhe do dia natural para a adoração nas sinagogas.

2. O templo. Quando os israelitas entraram na Terra Prometida, houve a localização da adoração, a princípio em Silo (talvez mediante uma estrutura semipermanente), e mais tarde em Jerusalém. A adoração no templo de Jerusalém seguia as diretrizes básicas da adoração na tenda, porém, melhor organizada, especialmente no tocante ao sacerdócio. Se o dia da expiação continuava ocupando posição de proeminência, no templo, há trechos nos Salmos que sugerem que a festa do Ano Novo foi adquirindo importância cada vez maior. As novas festividades, incluídas após o exílio, como a festa de Purim, por exemplo, não se revestiam de importância suficiente para serem aqui comentadas. A grande contribuição da adoração no templo foi o desenvolvimento do lado musical e poético, mormente por organização de Davi (ver II Sam. 6:5 e I Crô. 25). O livro de Salmos tornou-se o grande hinário que é o núcleo de todo o louvor bíblico, e boa parte dos salmos é de autoria davídica. (Ver Salmos).

A presença de Deus no templo era simbolizada pelo seu resplendor que encheu a casa quando a arca foi trazida para seu interior (ver I Reis 8:10,11), mas que Ezequiel viu afastando-se do templo, porque o mesmo havia sido contaminado pela idolatria (ver Eze. 10:18; cf. I Sam. 4:22). Deus era adorado no santuário porque ali Ele estabelecera o Seu nome. Contudo, Ele era e continua sendo o Deus que não pode ser contido pelo céu dos céus (ver I Reis 8:27). No céu, principal lugar das manifestações de Deus, Ele ouviria as orações que Lhe fossem dirigidas, tanto do interior quanto do exterior do templo. Isso indica que a adoração de Israel continuava livre de restrições cúlticas, atitude essa que passa diretamente ao culto prestado a Deus no Novo Testamento. Explicou Jesus à samaritana: «Mulher, podes crer-me, que a hora vem, quando nem neste monte, nem em Jerusalém adorareis o Pai... vem a hora, e já chegou, quando os verdadeiros adoradores adorarão o Pai em espírito e em verdade; porque são estes que o Pai procura para seus adoradores» (João 4:21 e 23).

3. A sinagoga. A destruição do templo de Jerusalém, por ocasião do exílio, criou uma nova situação, o aparecimento das sinagogas. E mesmo quando foi erigido o segundo templo, as sinagogas tiveram prosseguimento em Israel e nas terras da dispersão. Visto que a adoração sob a forma de sacrifícios só podia ter lugar em Jerusalém, foi mister a criação de uma nova forma de adoração, nas sinagogas. Essa palavra, que vem do grego, significa «ajuntamento», «congregação». Na LXX aparece como uma forma alternativa para *ekklesia*, «igreja». A partir do tempo de Esdras, a leitura, a exposição e os ensinamentos da lei ganharam maior importância, os quais iam bem além dos rudimentos ensinos dados nos lares. Isso ajudou os judeus a preservarem a integridade de sua fé, por onde quer que estivessem exilados. Quando o Senhor Jesus esteve neste mundo, encontrou tanto o templo de Jerusalém quanto sinagogas, praticamente em todas as cidades e aldeias de Israel. Paulo também se utilizou das sinagogas para ali anunciar a Cristo (ver Atos 9:20, por exemplo). O culto, nas sinagogas, estilizou-se e distanciou-se mais ainda do primitivo culto de Israel após a queda de Jerusalém, no ano 70 D.C. Nas sinagogas não há sacerdotes, e, sim, rabinos, isto é, «mestres».

D. Adoração individual. Nem a adoração doméstica e nem a adoração pública excluíram a riquíssima prática da religião pessoal em Israel. Os patriarcas foram os primeiros a dar o exemplo disso. Moisés também desfrutou de profunda relação pessoal com Deus. A lei provia muitos atos de piedade individual, até mesmo dentro do contexto da adoração pública. Nos dias dos últimos juízes, Ana serve de notável exemplo de súplica e ação de graças pessoais. Davi, e profetas como Jeremias, também foram grandes figuras dessa forma de piedade, para não falarmos em Neemias e Daniel. Muitos dos salmos foram escritos na primeira pessoa do singular, pois expressam a piedade individual de seus autores, sob a forma de oração, queixa, confissão de pecados, confissão de fé e protestos de esperança e louvor. Além de serem a expressão da piedade de vários grandes santos do Antigo Testamento, proviam inesgotável tesouro de devoção e orientação para a vida diária. A idéia de piedade pessoal é reiterada no Novo Testamento: «Exercita-te pessoalmente na piedade. Pois o exercício físico para pouco é proveitoso, mas a piedade para tudo é proveitosa, porque tem a promessa da vida que agora é e da que há de ser» (I Tim. 4:7,8).

E. Idolatria.

1. Introdução. Idolatria é palavra que vem de

ADORAÇÃO

«ídolo» e «latreia», indicando o serviço a ídolos e a deuses falsos. Toda a adoração que não tem por objeto o verdadeiro Deus é idolatria. A idolatria em Israel surgiu não porque a adoração a Yahweh se desenvolveu com base em cultos pagãos, mediante um processo de evolução religiosa, mas porque o povo de Israel resistia ao conhecimento e à adoração de Deus, inclinando-se por aceitar costumes religiosos dos povos ao redor. A idolatria geralmente origina-se do impulso humano de buscar objetos visíveis de adoração. No Sinai, enquanto Moisés recebia os mandamentos, Israel construía um desses objetos de culto idólatra, o bezerro de ouro. — A história subseqüente de Israel pode ser vista como um conflito entre a adoração prescrita, que nunca foi totalmente abandonada, e os cultos idólatras, que constantemente ameaçavam introduzir-se. Isso produziu períodos de declínio espiritual e períodos de reforma religiosa. Juízes, reis e profetas empenharam-se no combate à tendência idólatra. Os reis maus abandonavam a adoração a Yahweh, aceitando algum culto estrangeiro. Israel perdeu essa tendência à idolatria após o exílio babilônico. Os cristãos foram ensinados pelos apóstolos a fugirem da idolatria (ver I João 5:21). Na Igreja Católica Romana não se adoram diretamente deuses do paganismo antigo, mas os «santos» são venerados, como também os anjos, embora as Escrituras ensinem que só o Criador deve ser adorado, e jamais a criatura. E tais «santos» sempre recebem uma representação visível (quer sob a forma de «ídolos», quer sob a forma de «ícones», na Igreja Católica Grega). Essa representatividade sob forma palpável é o âmago da tendência idólatra.

2. Cultos cananeus. Embora a idolatria de Israel tivesse se manifestado ainda no deserto, foi na terra de Canaã que os israelitas receberam o primeiro forte impulso para seguirem essa corrupção. É que os israelitas ocuparam um lugar que já contava com seus santuários, sacerdotes e práticas religiosas idólatras. Fundamentalmente, esses cultos veneravam a Baal, deus da fertilidade (cf. Juí. 10:6), com centros em lugares como Dã, Gilgal, Siquém e Betel. Os israelitas ou apelavam para o sincretismo do culto a Yahweh com o culto a Baal, ou substituíam aquele por este, com práticas morais degradantes como um inevitável acompanhamento. Assim, a imoralidade dos filhos de Eli, na tenda da congregação (ver I Sam. 2:22), parece ter sido um reflexo da prostituição templária. E o valor quase supersticioso dado à arca (ver I Sam. 4:3) sugere mais o fetichismo e a mágica do que a fé genuína em Deus.

Quando começaram a ser esculpidas imagens, no reino do norte (ver I Reis 12:28), isso representou mais um degrau descendente para o paganismo em Israel. Para tanto, até mesmo razões políticas tinham o seu efeito. Essa tendência idólatra no reino do norte começou com Jeroboão, que além de estabelecer um sacerdócio e um santuário rivais de Jerusalém, levantou também dois bezerros de ouro para serem venerados em Dã e Betel. E no reino do sul, os reis piedosos foram considerados tais por terem combatido a prática de oferecerem sacrifícios e ofertas queimadas nos lugares altos, em desafio à adoração verdadeira a Yahweh (ver II Reis 14:4; 15:4,35; 16:4; 17:10, etc.). Sacrifícios humanos enegreceram ainda mais o quadro (ver II Reis 16:4 e 21:6). A introdução de tais abominações na própria Jerusalém mostra-nos que a pura adoração a Yahweh havia sido praticamente abandonada ou corrompida (ver II Reis 21:7). Como castigo e correção, veio o exílio babilônico.

3. Influências estrangeiras. A adoração a Yahweh sofria ataques internos e externos. Os casamentos políticos de Salomão, com princesas estrangeiras, trouxeram em sua esteira formas estranhas de adoração (ver I Reis 11:1-8). O clímax desse processo foi atingido nos dias de Acabe, dominado que era por sua esposa libanesa de Sidom, Jezabel. Acabe começou o seu reinado já errando, edificando a Baal, em Samaria, um templo e um altar (ver I Reis 16:32). Jezabel foi mais além, perseguiu os verdadeiros adoradores de Yahweh, e tirou a vida de muitos profetas de Deus. Ela ensinou a Israel o típico despotismo oriental, e, mediante alianças feitas por casamento, afetou também o reino do sul (ver II Reis 8:18). Acaz fez uma réplica de um altar que tinha visto em Damasco (II Reis 16:10 ss). Manassés adorava a «todo o exército dos céus» (II Reis 21:3). Josias mal conseguiu fazer virar a maré idólatra iniciada por Salomão (ver II Reis 23:13), pois Ezequiel retratou um quadro negro de vis práticas religiosas, até mesmo na parte mais interior do templo (ver Eze. 8:7 ss). E Jeremias informa-nos que aqueles que escaparam para o Egito, voltaram-se para a veneração à rainha do céu, tal como seus pais, reis e príncipes haviam feito nas cidades de Judá e nas ruas de Jerusalém (ver Jer. 44).

F. O Testemunho dos Profetas.

1. O lugar dos profetas. Os profetas do Antigo Testamento sempre foram os campeões da verdadeira teologia e da ética pura, e, por conseqüência, da adoração genuína a Yahweh. Ao lutarem em prol de uma verdadeira teologia, opunham-se às idéias pagãs; e ao contenderem por uma ética pura, condenavam as práticas religiosas imorais e o divórcio entre a adoração e a retidão pessoal e coletiva. Uma das grandes tarefas dos profetas era conclamar Israel a retornar da adoração falsa à adoração ao verdadeiro Deus.

2. Idolatria. O protesto principal dos profetas era contra a idolatria. Assim, um homem de Deus veio de Judá a Betel protestar contra o altar de Jeroboão (ver I Reis 13:1 ss). O profeta Aías proferiu juízo contra Jeroboão por haver apelado para divindades estrangeiras e para imagens esculpidas (ver I Reis 14:7 ss). Elias obteve tremenda vitória contra os profetas de Baal (ver I Reis 18). Amós clamou contra o santuário real de Betel (ver Amós 4:4; 5). Oséias anunciou que Efraim seria castigado devido a seus muitos altares idólatras (ver Osé. 8:11). Miquéias mostrou ao povo qual seria o fim das imagens de escultura e dos bosques onde os idólatras costumavam reunir-se em sua adoração espúria (ver Miq. 5:13 ss). E assim, cada profeta contribui sua parte nessa luta incessante contra a tendência à idolatria.

3. Formalismo. Os profetas foram cada vez mais se empenhando contra o externalismo, na adoração que salientava mais a forma externa do que a atitude interna. Esse tema foi claramente enunciado por Samuel, em seu famoso: «Eis que o obedecer é melhor do que o sacrificar, e o atender melhor do que a gordura de carneiros» (I Sam. 15:22). Outro tanto ensinou Natã a Davi. Esse formalismo andava de mãos dadas com a injustiça no trato com o próximo. Tal injustiça tornava-se abominável aos olhos do Senhor nas grandes ocasiões religiosas nacionais. O que Deus queria era que o povo fosse reto e justo: «...corra o juízo como as águas, e a justiça como ribeiro perene» (Amós 5:24). Esse é um estribilho dos profetas.

4. Adoração verdadeira. Alguns têm concluído erroneamente que os profetas do Antigo Testamento, devido a esses seus ataques contra o formalismo tornaram-se adversários do sistema levítico, como se

ADORAÇÃO

houvesse uma espécie de rivalidade entre profetas e sacerdotes, uns representantes da verdadeira fé e outros do culto mediante sacrifícios. Mas tal tese cai por terra quando consideramos que alguns dos maiores profetas, como Jeremias e Ezequiel, também eram sacerdotes levitas. A destruição do templo de Jerusalém foi predita pelos profetas como não sendo uma cirurgia que faria o culto falso dar lugar ao culto verdadeiro. Uma das principais funções dos profetas Ageu e Zacarias foi a de encorajar os judeus a reconstruírem o templo, convocando o povo a participar ativamente dessa forma de adoração prescrita pelo Senhor. Portanto, erram muito os que pensam que em Israel havia um conflito entre os sacerdotes e os profetas.

E quando os profetas desencorajavam sacrifícios, jejuns, assembléias solenes e até mesmo orações, faziam-no porque essas coisas eram oferecidas em meio a práticas idólatras, e não por causa das próprias práticas religiosas, ou porque não refletiam a piedade interna, mas apenas uma religiosidade superficial. O que os profetas almejavam realmente era a purificação da adoração. Eles tomaram os princípios fundamentais da lei e dali extraíram os grandes princípios de uma religião ideal — a autêntica piedade para com Deus e a retidão no trato entre homem e homem. Somente quando essas coisas estão presentes é que torna-se possível uma verdadeira adoração. Já vimos que, por sua própria natureza, a adoração consiste em confissão e serviço. Por outro lado, as formas externas prescritas não substituem e nem são substituídas pela atitude íntima aprovada por Deus, uma atitude de fé e obediência. Em outras palavras, ofertas e festividades não têm qualquer valor sem um coração penitente, fiel e obediente. Isso posto, os profetas foram campeões da adoração genuína, em contraste com simulacros indignos.

III. Adoração No Novo Testamento
A. Formas de Adoração.
1. Nos Evangelhos. Os evangelhos pressupõem as formas de adoração nativas ao judaísmo da Palestina, no começo do século I D.C. Isso significa que o templo continuava ocupando um lugar importante na adoração primitiva do Novo Testamento. Zacarias, pai de João Batista, era sacerdote, e a revelação divina lhe foi dada quando ele estava cumprindo o ritual do ministério no templo (ver Luc. 1:5 ss). José e Maria tiveram o cuidado de observar a lei da circuncisão e a lei da purificação (ver Luc. 2:21 ss). Quando Jesus atingiu a idade apropriada, Ele subiu ao templo para observar a festa da páscoa; e é significativo que Seu ministério proléptico, naquela ocasião, teve lugar entre os mestres de Israel, no templo, tendo então dado a Seus pais a resposta que encerra a sugestão de que o templo, a casa de Deus, era o lugar que Lhe competia (ver Luc. 2:42 ss). Uma característica digna de atenção, no evangelho de Lucas, é que os primórdios do evangelho são assim claramente engastados dentro da vida e das práticas de Israel.

O templo manteve sua importância durante todos os dias do ministério de Jesus, e Ele participou das festas religiosas: a páscoa, a festa dos tabernáculos e a festa da dedicação. E tirou proveito dessas festas para salientar certos aspectos de Seu ministério. Ao ensinar no átrio do templo, por ocasião da festa dos Tabernáculos, Ele ensinou qual era a verdadeira água da vida. A páscoa foi aproveitada para estabelecer tanto a instituição da Ceia do Senhor quanto a realização do novo êxodo, mediante Sua auto-oferta na cruz, como o Cordeiro que tira o pecado do mundo. E, mui significativamente, o derramamento do Espírito Santo teve lugar por ocasião da festa de Pentecoste.

Quando Jesus criticava a adoração que se efetuava no templo, fazia-o contra os abusos daqueles que corrompiam e contaminavam essa adoração, e não contra a adoração propriamente dita. Por isso foi que Ele expulsou do templo os cambistas e negociantes (cf. João 2:17), o que despertou a hostilidade somente dos eclesiásticos e aproveitadores. Contudo, Jesus predisse que o templo seria destruído, embora tenha-o feito com a tristeza de um verdadeiro adorador, e não com o zelo enlouquecido de um revolucionário, ainda que muitos O tenham acusado de ser apenas tal coisa.

Os vários templos que foram construídos e que Deus permitiu que fossem destruídos mostram-nos que a verdadeira promessa era a de que Deus edificaria para Si mesmo uma casa, dentre a linhagem de Davi. Essa casa era o próprio Jesus, Aquele por meio de quem Deus armara tenda entre os homens. Por esse motivo, o templo chegara ao fim de sua utilidade e alvo. Jesus era o antítipo do templo, mas não podia e nem queria preservá-lo. Só podia «cumpri-lo» (cf. João 1:14; 2:19 ss.).

Outro tanto aplica-se aos sacrifícios e ao ministério do templo. A vida de Jesus tinha por finalidade oferecer o sacrifício único, que tiraria os pecados para sempre (ver Heb. 10:12), cumprindo assim a páscoa, as ofertas regulares e os ritos especiais do dia da expiação. E quando o templo de Jerusalém foi finalmente destruído, no ano 70 D.C., não houve mais necessidade de restaurá-lo. E, por igual modo, Jesus aceitou o sacerdócio aarônico durante o Seu ministério encarnado. Não obstante, Ele veio para cumprir o ministério do sumo sacerdote eterno, segundo a categoria de Melquisedeque (ver Heb. 7:1 ss). Como já foi dito, o atual sistema judaico das sinagogas não conta com sacerdotes. Sendo Jesus o sumo sacerdote, o altar dos holocaustos, a expiação e todo o sistema levítico foi cessado.

Mas, enquanto o Senhor Jesus não deu por nós a Sua vida, Ele continuou vivendo como um judeu piedoso o faria. Freqüentava a sinagoga nos sábados (ver Luc. 4:16). No primeiro período de Seu ministério Ele percorreu todas as aldeias da Galiléia, pregando em suas sinagogas (ver Mat. 4:23; 9:35). Mas foi também na sinagoga que Ele sofreu violenta oposição (ver Mar. 3:1 ss), tendo avisado a Seus seguidores que eles seriam açoitados nas sinagogas (ver Mat. 10:17). E no período final de Seu ministério, embora as multidões continuassem a segui-Lo (ver Mat. 19:2), Ele já não era mais bem acolhido nas sinagogas, pois até os Seus seguidores eram expulsos das mesmas (ver João 9:22; 12:42). Não obstante, não houve rompimento definitivo com a sinagoga antes da crucificação, e mesmo quando saíram a campo os primeiros missionários cristãos; aparentemente eles continuaram sendo recebidos nas sinagogas da dispersão.

Os evangelhos dão evidência de piedade individual e pública. Ali há alusões a pessoas piedosas como Ana e Simeão. João Batista foi um dedicado profeta do ermo, que levava vida ascética. E o próprio Senhor Jesus, apesar de todo o contraste que Ele mesmo traçou entre Sua pessoa e a de João (ver Mat. 11:16 ss.), jamais se descuidou de dedicar-se à oração. Jesus proibiu Seus seguidores de exibicionismo (ver Mat. 6:1 ss.), mas recomendou que se ocupassem em esmolas secretas, oração e jejum, ensinando-lhes que oração e jejum são práticas necessárias para a realização de certas obras (ver Mat. 17:21). Também insistiu que Seus discípulos vivessem em atitude de vigilância (ver Mat. 24:42). É interessante observar-

ADORAÇÃO

mos a lição objetiva dada por Cristo a Pedro, Tiago e João (ver Mat. 26:38,41). Tendo começado Seu ministério com um período de quarenta dias de jejum e oração, Jesus preparou-se para a crise final retirando-se para o jardim do Getsêmani, para encontrar forças para obedecer às cruéis dores envolvidas no ato de obediência à vontade do Pai. E as orações e súplicas que Jesus expressou até Seu último instante de vida, na cruz, demonstram a Sua profunda piedade pessoal.

Seguindo a verdadeira tradição profética, Jesus não tolerava a perversão da piedade mediante o formalismo oco. Jesus censurou não somente o exibicionismo na oração, mas também a oração que consiste em repetições sem sentido (ver Mat. 6:7). E também condenou severamente a ênfase exagerada das práticas rituais, como substituição da retidão genuína (ver Mar. 7:6 ss). Apesar disso, Jesus não rejeitava nem as formas externas (cf. a oração do Pai Nosso e o novo ritual da Ceia do Senhor) e nem os ritos como tais (ver Mat. 23:23). Mas ensinou que a substância dessas observâncias encontra-se na conduta motivada por uma autêntica consagração e pela busca pela retidão.

2. No livro de Atos e nas epístolas. O testemunho desses livros do Novo Testamento é similar ao testemunho dos evangelhos. A única diferença importante foi que devido à missão entre os gentios e a crescente separação do templo e das sinagogas, as igrejas locais tiveram de desenvolver suas próprias formas de adoração comum. Os próprios judeus cristãos tiveram de sofrer sob a pressão da hostilidade das autoridades religiosas dos judeus, indignados ante o evangelismo persistente dos cristãos.

O templo continuou desempenhando importante papel na adoração da Igreja infante. Após a ascensão de Jesus, os discípulos não arredavam o pé do templo, louvando e bendizendo a Deus (ver Luc. 24:51-53). Parte da comunhão da igreja de Jerusalém era a freqüência diária ao templo (ver Atos 2:46). Pedro e João curaram o coxo quando estavam entrando no templo (ver Atos 3:1 ss). Tal como Jesus o fizera, os apóstolos também ensinavam o povo no templo (ver Atos 5:25). Alguns anos mais tarde, Paulo muito desejou estar em Jerusalém, para a festa do Pentecoste (ver Atos 20:16). Um de seus primeiros atos ao chegar à cidade foi dirigir-se ao templo para fazer os preparativos para o ritual da purificação (ver Atos 21:23 ss). Mas o testemunho de Estêvão mostra-nos que a Igreja primitiva sabia do caráter transitório do templo terreno (ver Atos 7:47 ss). O problema criado pelos judaizantes surgiu porque muitos judeus convertidos ao cristianismo continuavam dando excessiva importância ao templo, e queriam que os gentios se adaptassem à adoração que ali se processava. Mas Estêvão e Paulo perceberam que isso nem era possível e nem correto. A epístola aos Gálatas é um libelo contra as tendências judaizantes. Mas, enquanto perdurou de pé o templo de Jerusalém, este continuou sendo um centro apropriado para a adoração realizada pelos cristãos, que se verifica em meio à fé, à obediência, à sinceridade e à verdade.

A pregação do evangelho entre os judeus dividiu-os em duas facções, os crentes e os incrédulos diante da mensagem cristã. E isso forçou os crentes a organizarem suas próprias reuniões. Na verdade, nem todas as reuniões dos primeiros discípulos, após a ascensão do Senhor, tiveram lugar no templo (ver Atos 1:14; 4:23; 12:12). Isso mostra que desde o começo os cristãos demonstraram a tendência de se organizarem à parte dos judeus incrédulos. Não obstante, durante muito tempo os cristãos não tiveram lugares especiais de reunião, ou templos. Antes, reuniam-se nas casas, talvez nas mais espaçosas dos irmãos na fé (ver File. 2; Rom. 16:5; I Cor. 16:19, etc.). Os apóstolos tomaram providências com o intuito de melhor organizar essas novas assembléias (ver Atos 14:22). Seguindo até certo ponto o padrão da sinagoga, os dois principais ministros das igrejas locais primitivas eram o ancião (também chamado pastor ou bispo = supervisor) e o diácono, embora também leiamos sobre profetas e evangelistas. Os mestres eram os pastores que se dedicavam ao ensino. (Ver I Tim. 5:17).

Que tipo de adoração era levado a efeito nas assembléias cristãs? O Novo Testamento nos fornece bem pouca informação detalhada a respeito. Pelos primeiros capítulos do livro de Atos depreende-se que as orações, e o partir do pão eram básicos. As únicas outras fontes informativas detalhadas são Atos 20 e I Cor. 11 e 14. O trecho de Atos 20:7 registra uma reunião no primeiro dia da semana, quando os discípulos partiram o pão e Paulo pregou; e tal reunião parece ter-se dado no começo da noite. O trecho de I Coríntios 11 também alude a uma refeição, que certamente era a Ceia do Senhor (vs. 23 ss), embora provavelmente em combinação com uma refeição comum. O trecho de I Coríntios 14 menciona uma reunião na qual os membros contribuíam com salmos, doutrinas, línguas, revelações ou interpretação de línguas, mas na qual a ênfase recai sobre dois pontos, edificação e boa ordem. A ordem baixada em I Cor. 16:2 talvez seja um outro indício de que essas assembléias tinham lugar no primeiro dia da semana. Embora possa-se argumentar que, por essa altura dos acontecimentos a adoração cristã ainda não se cristalizara completamente, pelo menos podemos ver nessa epístola de I Coríntios uma estrutura reconhecida, com oração, louvor, exposição e leitura das Escrituras, a celebração da Ceia do Senhor e o exercício de dons espirituais, sem falarmos em certos toques litúrgicos. O conteúdo das orações (conforme se pode depreender de I Tim. 2:1 ss e Atos 4:24) usava frases litúrgicas extraídas do Antigo Testamento. Visto que a Igreja primitiva herdou tão rica tradição do judaísmo e do Antigo Testamento, seria estranho se as coisas não tivessem sido assim. O poder e o espírito dos cristãos jazia na nova compreensão sobre as antigas formas, com adaptações convenientes das mesmas.

A piedade pessoal foi muito bem exemplificada pelos apóstolos. Para exemplificar o ponto, Paulo praticava (ver I Tes. 3:10) e recomendava (ver I Tes. 5:17) a oração incessante. Ele solicitava aos crentes que orassem em favor do seu ministério (ver Efé. 6:18). As orações que aparecem nas epístolas de Paulo são quase sempre intercessórias (ver Fil. 1:4 ss e Col. 1:9 ss), embora nem sempre (ver Fil. 3:8 ss). O trecho de Efé. 3:14 ss nos permite ver melhor ainda o tipo de oração daquele apóstolo, tendo em vista a concretização da vontade do Senhor nas vidas dos crentes, para cumprimento cabal do plano de Deus neles.

Em adição à oração, Paulo recomendava o estudo diligente das Escrituras, mediante leitura ou memorização (cf. II Tim. 3:15 ss e Efé. 6:17). Ele também exorta a uma vida cristã bem disciplinada, incluindo, em alguns casos, o ideal celibatário, se essa fosse a vontade divina (ver I Cor. 7:1 ss.). O que importava, realmente, era que os crentes mantivessem o corpo sob controle, para que os mesmos prestassem um melhor serviço cristão (ver I Cor. 9:24). O jejum

59

ADORAÇÃO

não é negligenciado por ele (ver II Cor. 11:27). A atitude de ação de graças também deveria ser uma constante na vida dos crentes (ver I Tes. 5:9). Uma conduta grave e sóbria era esperada da parte dos pastores e diáconos (ver I Tim. 3). Timóteo, como homem de Deus que era, foi exortado a seguir a piedade pessoal (ver I Tim. 6:11). Apesar da adoração do crente individual mesclar-se com a adoração coletiva, de mistura com a retidão de vida e conduta, o exercício pessoal da religião cristã não é um aspecto de pequena importância na adoração neotestamentária.

B. Elementos Componentes da Adoração

1. Oração. A oração no sentido mais específico de petição, naturalmente era um dos elementos básicos da adoração cristã primitiva. Entre a ascensão do Senhor e o derramamento do Espírito, a Igreja recebeu ordens para dedicar-se à oração cheia de expectação. As perseguições sofridas também levaram os crentes a caírem de joelhos diante do Senhor. E todas as necessidades que foram surgindo também proveram motivo e material para intercessão. Todavia, não há nenhuma descrição de como essas orações eram feitas. Talvez um líder orasse por todos; talvez indivíduos orassem um por vez. O que é surpreendente é que não há qualquer menção da recitação da oração do Pai Nosso, o que parece indicar que os crentes primitivos usavam orações extemporâneas, e não fórmulas fixas. O «amém», devido ao exemplo dado pelo Senhor Jesus, adquiriu um sentido ainda mais profundo do que tinha no Antigo Testamento (cf. II Cor. 1:20). Frases feitas, como *Maranata*! talvez também fossem usadas de vez em quando (ver I Cor. 16:22; cf. Apo. 22:20 e o Didaqué 10:7). Doutro modo, é difícil entender-se por qual motivo essas frases teriam sido preservadas em aramaico. As «bênçãos» também se fizeram presentes desde o começo, segundo se vê em II Cor. 13:14 e Apo. 22:21. E as epístolas testificam sobre o aparecimento de um distinto vocabulário cristão, usado nas orações. O que é importante não esquecer é que essas orações eram consideradas parte integrante da adoração neotestamentária, o que não sucedia no Antigo Testamento.

2. Louvor. O louvor está intimamente ligado à oração. O louvor é a confissão da natureza e das obras de Deus. De fato, oração na forma de ação de graças também é louvor. Quase todas as orações registradas nas páginas do Novo Testamento contêm um elemento doxológico. Essas orações relembram os atos de Deus, e assim soam uma nota de certeza e triunfo. Inteiramente à parte da oração, porém, o louvor a Deus tem seu próprio papel na adoração neotestamentária. Muitos hinos cristãos e cânticos espirituais louvam a Deus. Paulo alude ao cântico de Salmos, durante a adoração, em uma de suas epístolas aos Coríntios, e a hinos e cânticos espirituais em Efé. 5:19. Os estudiosos têm percebido possíveis fragmentos de primitivos hinos cristãos em trechos como Fil. 2:6 ss e I Tim. 3:16. Os hinos constantes no Apocalipse mostram que tanto na adoração terrestre quanto na adoração celeste são entoados hinos de louvor, embora outros pensem que Apocalipse 4 e 5 podem estar baseados na adoração da congregação. É bem possível que o saltério fosse o hinário da Igreja primitiva, embora haja uma referência na carta de Plínio a Trajano (Epp. x.96) a hinos cristológicos o que dá a entender que novos hinos e mais especificamente cristãos foram compostos.

3. Confissão de pecados. A confissão de pecados acha-se no âmago da adoração, pois, quando a dignidade de Deus é exaltada, a indignidade do homem requer ser reconhecida. As orações e os salmos do Antigo Testamento estão repletos do reconhecimento de culpa, paralelamente aos pedidos de perdão e restauração, bem como a louvores e ações de graças pela misericórdia e perdão divinos. Por sua própria natureza, o evangelho é uma palavra divina dirigida a pecadores. O batismo de João aparece logo no início do evangelho com sua conclamação ao arrependimento e à conversão. Jesus deu prosseguimento à mesma conclamação, o que foi seguido pelos Seus apóstolos, segundo se vê no livro de Atos. Pedro, confrontado por Jesus, confessou-se um homem pecador (ver Luc. 5:8). Segundo certo relato de Jesus, a oração que Deus ouviu no templo foi a oração penitente do publicano, e não a oração autocongratulatória do fariseu (ver Luc. 18:9 ss). O ato de batismo em água é a grande oportunidade que o novo convertido tem para confessar-se pecador, ao renunciar sua antiga vida pecaminosa e ao aceitar a nova vida de fé e obediência a Cristo. Com base em I João 1:8 ss , tem-se a nítida impressão de que a confissão de pecados a Deus, individualmente ou em grupos, continuou desempenhando um importante papel na vida dos crentes primitivos. Em suas epístolas, Paulo refere-se, por diversas vezes, que ele mesmo e todos os crentes primitivos viviam na dependência da misericórdia divina. Portanto, mesmo que não haja grandes evidências de orações específicas de confissão de pecados, na adoração neotestamentária, esse elemento precisa ser pressuposto como base de toda oração e louvor da Igreja primitiva. As orações precisavam ser dirigidas ao Pai em nome de Jesus, visto que nada há em cada crente que constitua base sólida para acesso a Deus ou para recebimento da resposta divina (cf. o papel de Jesus como sumo sacerdote e intercessor, no sétimo capítulo da epístola aos Hebreus).

4. Confissão de fé (batismo). No Antigo Testamento, embora a recitação do «Ouve, ó Israel...» fosse um mandamento, também servia de confissão de fé: o Senhor, nosso Deus, é uma unidade. Por essa razão, o *shema* achou caminho até a adoração nas sinagogas. Todavia, tal recitação não encontrou eco na Igreja primitiva. E a razão disso não é que essa confissão básica tivesse sido abandonada, mas antes, é que agora fora adicionada a confissão distintamente cristã: Jesus é o Senhor, ou seja, é Yahweh. A fé da Igreja primitiva era a fé em Jesus como Salvador e Deus. Pedro fez essa afirmação primária em Mat. 16:16. E isso pode ser visto novamente na confissão de Tomé (ver João 20:28). O evangelho de João foi escrito tendo em vista mostrar exatamente esse fato (ver João 20:31). A obra do Espírito Santo faz com que os crentes afirmem e confessem que Jesus é o Senhor (I Cor. 12:3). Finalmente, essa verdade será reconhecida em todas as línguas (ver Fil. 2:11). Sobre essa crença repousa a plena confissão do Deus triúno (ver Mat. 28:19). Essa crença é especificamente confessada por ocasião do batismo em água, o qual pode ser ministrado em nome de Jesus (ver Atos 2:38). O eunuco professou fé no Senhor (ver Atos 8:37). Cornélio foi batizado em nome de Jesus (ver Atos 10:48). O carcereiro filipense foi batizado quando creu no Senhor e foi salvo (ver Atos 16:30 ss). Alguns escritos dos pais da Igreja (ver Justino, Apologia I,61, etc.) testificam sobre a mesma coisa.

5. Leitura da Bíblia. A leitura do Antigo Testamento, nas reuniões da Igreja primitiva, nunca é declarada diretamente, mas apenas indiretamente. Mas as epístolas de Paulo eram lidas publicamente (ver I Tes. 5:27). Os textos tradicionais referentes à Ceia do Senhor também eram freqüentemente

ADORAÇÃO

recitados, (ver I Cor. 11). Mas, se a leitura do Antigo Testamento não é diretamente referida, o extenso uso e citação do Antigo Testamento, no Novo Testamento, o conhecimento que os crentes primitivos demonstravam ter daquelas Escrituras, bem como durante o período pós-apostólico e nos escritos dos pais da Igreja, nos faz crer que o Antigo Testamento era tão lido e estudado quanto o cânon neotestamentário em formação. Os cristãos primitivos pregavam. Nas sinagogas, os sermões consistiam primariamente em exposição. Ora, a pregação dos primeiros cristãos visava, antes de mais nada, mostrar que o Antigo Testamento tinha o seu cumprimento na pessoa e na realização de Jesus Cristo. Além disso, a menção a alguma interpretação parece subentender uma referência no Antigo Testamento. O alto valor conferido pelos primeiros cristãos às Escrituras (ver II Tim. 3:15 ss.), é outro fato que precisa ser considerado. Assim, a leitura do Antigo Testamento, e cada vez mais, do Novo Testamento, certamente era uma porção constitutiva da adoração cristã primitiva.

6. Pregação. Em contraste com a leitura da Bíblia, o ato de pregar é solidamente confirmado no Novo Testamento. Em Corinto, transparece a pregação sob a forma de exortação. Seguindo o exemplo deixado pelo Senhor Jesus; e ante a necessidade de evangelizar, de instruir e de edificar, o ministério da Palavra sem dúvida era incluído em todos os encontros dos cristãos. Os apóstolos foram chamados especificamente para o ministério da Palavra (ver Atos 6). Posteriormente, aprende-se que os pastores deveriam ser aptos para ensinar (ver II Tim. 3:2). Assim, a pregação combinava diversos aspectos da adoração: a declaração das obras de Deus, a confissão de fé, a oração subjacente a todas as atividades dos cristãos, o clímax atingido nos louvores, etc. Embora essa pregação não fosse exclusivamente expositiva, era-o quase totalmente de tal natureza. Entre os crentes gentios, especialmente, muita informação precisava-lhes ser transmitida mediante a pregação. Dos gentios convertidos não era esperado a mesma familiaridade com as Escrituras que tinham os judeus convertidos ou os primeiros «tementes a Deus». Apolo, homem poderoso nas Escrituras, exerceu poderoso ministério nesse campo (ver Atos 18:24 ss). A prédica jamais deixou de ocupar papel saliente nas reuniões dos cristãos evangélicos, através dos séculos. Todo período de reavivamento espiritual é antecedido por intensa e firme prédica.

7. Ceia do Senhor. Não somente o batismo, mas especialmente a Ceia do Senhor, constituíam adendos à adoração nas sinagogas. Tanto os escritos do Novo Testamento como o testemunho patrístico mostram que a Ceia fazia parte integrante da adoração cristã primitiva, semana após semana. Cada reunião dos cristãos incluía não somente oração, louvor, leitura das Escrituras e pregação, mas também uma santa refeição com a celebração da Ceia. A Ceia do Senhor veio substituir não somente a páscoa, mas também as ofertas do templo. Por essa razão é que uma linguagem própria dos sacrifícios veio a ser usada em relação à Ceia (cf. Mal. 1:1). Todavia, não há apenas um elemento de substituição. A Ceia do Senhor tanto rememora o grande e único sacrifício de Cristo pelos pecados, para sempre, como também anuncia a segunda volta de Cristo. (Ver I Cor. 11:26). O fato de que Cristo é o sumo sacerdote para sempre obviou um ministério sacerdotal. E essa é a razão pela qual os ministros da Ceia do Senhor, não importando se apóstolos, profetas, pastores ou diáconos, são todos verdadeiros ministros («servos»), e não sacerdotes. O ponto enfocado na Ceia é a morte e a ressurreição de

Jesus Cristo. Essa é a base da comunhão desfrutada pelos crentes com Deus Pai e uns com os outros. Portanto, em última análise, a Ceia do Senhor é cristológica, e não litúrgica, no sentido veterotestamentário mais estreito. Classificá-la como quinta-essência da liturgia é perder de vista o seu verdadeiro significado. A Ceia serve de memorial perene do fato de que a adoração autêntica só é possível com base na expiação no sangue de Cristo.

8. Coletas. A alusão a uma coleta semanal, em I Cor. 16, a significação litúrgica atribuída às esmolas, em Fil. 4:18, e a menção a ofertas nos escritos patrísticos, têm dado margem para o ponto de vista de que as coletas faziam parte da adoração cristã primitiva. A grande dificuldade no caminho dessa interpretação é que todas as alusões às coletas mostram que elas precisavam ser espontâneas. Por outro lado, alguns destacam que a doação de esmolas tinha uma antiqüíssima história no Antigo Testamento, e que os apóstolos não se descuidavam desse aspecto. (Ver Gál. 2:10, para exemplificar). Alguns estudiosos pensam que o ósculo santo (ver I Cor. 16:20) poderia receber idêntica classificação.

9. Cultos ocasionais? Alguns têm comentado que não há cultos de matrimônio ou cultos fúnebres nas páginas do Novo Testamento. Porém, deveríamos lembrar que tais cultos são apenas uma aplicação dos elementos básicos da adoração, a saber, a oração, o louvor, a leitura expositiva das Escrituras e a Ceia do Senhor, e isso em situações específicas. De fato, o Novo Testamento menciona certas ocasiões, como a confirmação efetuada pelos apóstolos, a ordenação de ministros e talvez a unção dos enfermos com azeite, quando eram usados certos sinais bíblicos (a unção e a imposição de mãos) juntamente com outros elementos litúrgicos. Isso significa que pode haver uma rápida adaptação dos elementos fundamentais da adoração a novas necessidades. A consagração de Paulo e Barnabé ao serviço missionário, em Antioquia, nos provê um instrutivo exemplo quanto a isso (ver Atos 13:2 ss.). Ainda que algum tipo de culto particular não encontre antecedentes nas páginas do Novo Testamento, certamente o novo pacto nos oferece material suficiente para nele basearmos formas de culto legítimas; e a injunção de que tudo seja feito no Senhor significa que a introdução de elementos de adoração jamais deve ser considerada uma intrusão.

C. A Essência da Adoração

1. Cristo. Embora, no Novo Testamento, os elementos da adoração sejam os mesmos que aparecem no Antigo Testamento, há dois novos fatores no coração do Novo Testamento, que dão à adoração neotestamentária uma decisiva reorientação. O primeiro é que a adoração cristã, em sua própria essência, consiste na adoração de Deus Pai através de Deus Filho. Os elementos permanecem; mas a orientação cristológica é uma novidade. Nesta breve conclusão, algumas poucas indicações são suficientes. O adorador, no Novo Testamento mantém-se em uma relação pessoal de filiação a Deus, com base em sua adoção em Cristo. O crente ora no nome do Filho (ver João 16:23). As obras de Deus, através do Filho, formam o tema de Seu louvor (ver Efé. 1:3 ss). Seu apelo por perdão é que Cristo deu a Si mesmo como perfeito sacrifício pelo pecado (ver I João 1:7 ss). Sua confissão é a confissão de Jesus como Senhor (ver I Cor. 12:3). Tanto o Antigo quanto o Novo Testamentos testificam sobre Cristo (ver João 5:39). A pregação consiste na exposição de Cristo, em Sua obra reveladora e reconciliadora (ver II Cor. 5:18). A Ceia do Senhor é a páscoa do atual

61

ADORAÇÃO AO IMPERADOR

e final êxodo, a exibição do único grande sacrifício pelos pecados (ver I Cor. 11:26). A doação de esmolas, por parte dos cristãos, adquire uma nova base, à luz do dom de Deus em Cristo (ver II Cor. 9:15), bem como à luz que todos os dons são dados em Cristo (ver Mat. 25:31 ss). A adoração é aceitável, em vários pontos da vida do crente, porque toda a vida cristã consiste em vida no Senhor (ver Rom. 14:8). O ponto decisivo, pois, não é que novas formas de adoração são instauradas, ou que novos níveis de devoção sejam assegurados, mas que Deus, em Cristo, veio pessoalmente a este mundo, a fim de dar cumprimento à Sua graciosa realização. Destarte, à adoração é conferida uma nova profundidade e conteúdo, que de modo algum podia ter nos dias do Antigo Testamento, de acordo com as expectações judaicas.

2. O Espírito Santo. O segundo dos novos fatores da adoração cristã é que o mesmo consiste em adoração a Deus Pai através do Filho de Deus, bem como em, e através de Deus Espírito Santo. A verdadeira adoração tanto foi em espírito como foi no Espírito; e, conforme Jesus mostrou, Seu próprio ministério resultou em uma vinda específica do Espírito, tornando possível a plenitude da adoração que é em espírito e em verdade. Assim, a oração é feita com a ajuda do Espírito (ver Rom. 8:26 s.). O louvor consiste em regozijo no Espírito (ver Efé. 5:18,19). A confissão do pecado processa-se sob a convicção do Espírito (ver João 16:8). A confissão de fé consiste em confissão ajudada pelo Espírito (ver I Cor. 12:3). As Santas Escrituras, dadas a nós mediante o Espírito, são iluminadas pelo Espírito (ver II Cor. 3:6 ss). A pregação é efetuada em demonstração do Espírito e do poder (ver I Cor. 2:4). A comunhão em torno da Ceia do Senhor é a comunhão do Espírito (cf. Atos 2). A liberalidade cristã flui do amor que é um dos aspectos do fruto do Espírito (ver Gál. 5:22). A vida de oração, louvor e proclamação das boas-novas consiste em andar no Espírito (cf. Rom. 8:1 ss). O que está em foco não é tanto uma adoração espiritual, em distinção a uma adoração litúrgica, mas é o ministério interior do Espírito, com Seu poder regenerador e santificador. O indivíduo que nasceu do Espírito e é dirigido pelo Espírito é o homem que, mesmo em suas expressões externas, oferece a Deus, por meio de Cristo, uma adoração apropriada e aceitável.

ADORAÇÃO AO IMPERADOR (DEIFICAÇÃO)

Pano de fundo. A Bíblia mostra haver um grande e intransponível abismo entre Deus e o homem, para que nenhum homem se sinta tentado a adorar a seu semelhante. Mas o coração humano, que tende à adoração a heróis, tem seus objetos de veneração entre os guerreiros e os artistas. As nações ao redor de Israel tinham certas formas de adoração ao rei. Os mitos gregos, que tão facilmente misturavam seres mortais com imortais, e cujos heróis são semideuses, promoviam a adoração de homens, pelo menos a partir do século V A.C. Naturalmente, Alexandre o Grande foi adorado nas terras orientais por ele conquistadas, e os seus sucessores esperavam receber o mesmo tipo de bajulação. Antíoco IV Epifânio, mostrou-se suficientemente ridículo ao chamar-se de Zeus e de Deus, nas suas moedas. No Egito, era tradicional considerar os monarcas como divindades. E a família dos Ptolomeus, tanto os membros vivos quanto os mortos, recebiam honras absurdas, que os consideravam divinos.

Adoração ao imperador, em Roma. Como estamos vendo, há um amplo pano de fundo que encorajava o desenvolvimento da adoração aos imperadores romanos. A princípio, o culto ao imperador era essencialmente uma medida política, que começou espontaneamente, nas províncias orientais do Império, e que Augusto, Tibério e seus sucessores usaram como uma útil manobra política. Esse culto serviu para consolidar e unificar as forças do império, que lutavam para estabilizar as fronteiras e mesclar os díspares elementos formativos do mesmo. A partir de Júlio César, a deificação tornou-se uma prática cuidadosamente cultivada. A prática era restringida na própria capital do império, mas eram exageradas pelas comunidades ao redor. Augusto promoveu a adoração do *Divus Julius*, embora não tenha promovido com grande empenho o culto à sua própria pessoa. Ele e a maioria dos seus sucessores foram oficialmente deificados após a morte. Em seu leito de morte, Vespasiano teve a ousadia de dizer, em tom jocoso: «Penso que estou me tornando um deus», sabendo que seu período de vida era curto. Governantes romanos psicologicamente desequilibrados, como Calígula, Nero e Domiciano insistiram em receber honras divinas quando ainda vivos, e aparentemente levavam a sério a sua pretensão. Conta-se que um deles, ao ser ferido, espantou-se ao verificar que seu sangue era vermelho, como o de qualquer mortal. Esse culto caiu no ridículo quando parentes, oficiais e amigos especiais dos imperadores tornaram-se uma espécie de família divina, exigindo atenção especial da parte do povo. Era uma idolatria em uma de suas formas mais doentias, embora não muito diferente do louco fanatismo demonstrado pelo povo em relação a atletas, estrelas de cinema e músicos de rock-and-roll. O movimento da deificação dos imperadores atingiu o clímax com Diocleciano e o movimento anticristão dos fins do século III D.C. Constantino, ao tornar-se cristão, pôs fim a essa forma de adoração. Antes disso, porém, vitimou a muitos cristãos, pois se alguém não adorava ao imperador podia ser acusado de traição ao estado, crime esse punido com a morte.

Formas dessa adoração. 1. Os imperadores eram considerados divindades encarnadas. 2. Os imperadores eram tidos como instrumentos de um *gênio*, uma espécie de possessão divina. 3. Os imperadores, segundo se acreditava, tornavam-se deuses, quando morriam. Sem importar a forma envolvida, juramentos de lealdade e submissão eram requeridos de todos os cidadãos e súditos, algo que os cristãos recusavam-se a fazer, e em razão disso foram perseguidos e mortos (ver Plínio a Trajano, *Ep.* 96; *Martírio de Policarpo*). O trecho de Apo. 2:10, 13 refere-se a uma situação assim, na igreja de Pérgamo.

Uma profundíssima verdade bíblica. O evangelho promete aos crentes a participação na imagem do Filho de Deus (ver Rom. 8:29), e portanto, a participação na própria natureza divina (ver II Ped. 1:4). E isso de maneira real, e não meramente poética ou moral. De todas as doutrinas do evangelho, essa é a mais elevada. Haverá uma participação finita na divindade, que nunca porá em perigo o caráter ímpar da Trindade. Porém, nenhum homem pode conquistar tal privilégio por seus próprios esforços. Isso resultará de uma mui longa transformação espiritual, em que o crente irá passando de um estágio de glória para outro. Por ocasião da morte física (embora não apenas porque o crente morre), essa transformação recebe extraordinário impulso (ver II Cor. 3:18). Ver também Col. 2:9,10 e a exposição a respeito no NTI. Ver o artigo, nesta enciclopédia, sobre *Natureza Divina, Participação Humana na Mesma*. (B Z)

ADORAÇÃO AO SOL — ADORAÇÃO

ADORAÇÃO AO SOL

A adoração ao sol é uma antiga prática da humanidade. Evidências desse tipo de adoração podem ser encontradas em muitas culturas, incluindo as da Índia, da Grécia, dos maias e dos incas da América Central e do Sul. Reveste-se de particular importância a prática na Babilônia e no Egito antigos.

Na Babilônia e na Assíria, locais especiais, como Sopara e Larsa, eram dedicados à adoração ao sol. Na Fenícia, o Baal solar chamava-se Baal-Hamom. Além disso, o deus Sames era um deus-do-sol.

No delta do Egito, em On (Heliópolis), estava centralizada a adoração ao sol entre os egípcios. Desde os tempos remotos, — os egípcios adoravam a Rá, nome geral que eles davam ao deus-sol. Mais especificamente, ele era chamado de Atom ou Amom, e os seus sacerdotes controlavam o mundo religioso egípcio. Durante o reinado de Amenotepe IV, foi feita uma tentativa para estabelecer a adoração ao disco solar como o único deus do Egito, com o nome de Aton. Mas tal reforma só perdurou durante o período de vida desse Faraó, o qual chegou ao extremo de edificar a sua própria cidade capital, para servir de centro dessa forma de idolatria.

As Escrituras proíbem claramente tal forma de adoração. A adoração ao sol e a imagens do sol (que até mereceram um vocábulo próprio no hebraico) é proibida pela lei de Deus (ver Deu. 17:3). Deus adverte que Ele destruirá os adoradores e as próprias imagens do sol (ver Deu. 4:19 e Lev. 26:30), e conforme se vê na primeira referência dada neste parágrafo, a pena imposta aos adoradores do sol era a morte por apedrejamento, se para tanto houvesse duas ou três testemunhas.

Nos dias que se seguiram ao reino dividido, essas práticas idólatras foram seguidas por alguns dos reis de Judá e Israel. Manassés, filho de Ezequias, erigiu

ADORAÇÃO AOS ANCESTRAIS

Um fenômeno complexo, existente de uma maneira ou de outra entre muitos povos. Em suas formas rudimentares, nas religiões primitivas, a crença de que os espíritos dos mortos demoram-se em torno dos antigos lugares costumeiros durante a vida física, inspirou os sacrifícios de alimentos e outras oferendas, além das tentativas de comunicação. Essa crença usualmente é acompanhada pela noção de que esses espíritos são ciumentos da atenção que presumivelmente merecem, podendo punir àqueles que os negligenciam mediante o infortúnio, as doenças, etc.

Motivações comuns a essa doutrina. 1. Desejo de servir aos mortos, ou por motivo de medo ou de afeto e respeito. 2. Temor dos danos que as visitas dos fantasmas podem causar, resultando daí o desejo de aplacar. 3. Desejo de ser protegido e abençoado, o que seria conferido por tais espíritos. 4. A idéia de que os mortos avançam para um nível mais alto da existência, e são dignos de respeito, ou mesmo de veneração. Normalmente, é a família que cuida dessa adoração, visto que cada família tem seus próprios espíritos para venerar e aplacar. Algumas vezes, os heróis tribais ou nacionais são venerados em uma comunidade, o que pode levar à deificação. A prática pode tornar-se mais elaborada com ritos e santuários apropriados. Em nosso século, a prática continua comum na China e no Japão. Nesse último país, isso tem sido importante não somente para a vida familiar, mas para a vida nacional, tendo adquirido conseqüências políticas. (AM E)

altares dedicados ao exército do céu e foi culpado dessa forma de idolatria, chegando a instalá-la na própria casa do Senhor (ver II Reis 21:3-5). Alguns dos reis de Judá dedicaram cavalos e carruagens à adoração ao sol, ao qual também queimaram incenso (ver II Reis 23:5,11).

Entre os povos vizinhos a Israel, os árabes do sul e os fenícios consideravam o sol como uma divindade feminina, ao passo que os egípcios, sumérios e acádios como uma divindade masculina. Mas os heteus tanto tinham um deus-sol quanto uma deusa-sol. Para os babilônios o deus-sol, considerado inferior à deusa lunar, Sin, era a luz do mundo, do qual dependiam a vida e a boa ordem do universo. E, como vencedor da noite e da morte, para eles essa divindade era o herói por excelência. E, em face da penetração de sua luz por toda a parte, eles também o consideravam o legislador supremo e o juiz onisciente, o qual aplicaria bênção ou castigo aos homens, conforme suas ações. Na Babilônia, o santuário central do deus-sol ficava em Sipar, onde era adorado juntamente com Aia, a «esposa». Alguns estudiosos pensam que é devido à influência dessas idéias, cultivadas por povos com os quais os israelitas estavam tão ligados, que o autor de Salmos 19 comparou o sol nascente a um esposo que sai de seu aposento e, qual atleta, percorre heroicamente o seu curso (vs. 6 e 7). E nos vs. 8-13 do mesmo Salmo, onde a lei do Senhor é exaltada, o sol é lembrado como símbolo do direito e da lei.

O profeta Jeremias revela-nos que os reis de Judá amavam, serviam e adoravam o sol, (ver Jer. 8:2). Ezequiel nos prove um quadro muito descritivo dos adoradores do sol, na casa do Senhor, de rostos voltados para o oriente, prostrados diante do sol (ver Eze. 8:16).

Como é natural, houve em Israel reações contra essa invasão idólatra. Assim, Asa (ver II Crô. 14:5) e Josias (ver II Crô. 34:4,7) procuraram eliminar tal forma de adoração, derrubando os altares dedicados ao sol nas cidades de todo o Israel. Contudo, por ocasião da queda de Jerusalém, diante dos babilônios, tal prática prosseguia (ver Jer. 19:13; Eze. 6:4,6). (E ID)

ADORAÇÃO DA NATUREZA

Envolve a expressão do sentimento de dependência e/ou de gratidão, para com o meio ambiente natural, naquilo em que esse ambiente nos ajuda, ou devido às óbvias provisões que a natureza nos oferece. Além disso, os homens temem as forças naturais. E isso leva-os a tentar aplacar as forças da natureza mediante sacrifícios, orações, etc. A maioria das divindades das culturas antigas de alguma maneira estava vinculada à natureza. Na natureza, os homens descobrem tanto ajuda quanto ameaça, sendo apenas natural que eles tenham imaginado deuses de acordo com as forças naturais. Os homens sentem-se agradecidos ante as frutas, raízes, castanhas, água, ar, etc., que lhes são dadas gratuitamente. Mas ficam aterrorizados diante das tempestades, dos terremotos, dos relâmpagos e trovões, das enchentes, das erupções vulcânicas, etc. As coisas que escapam ao controle humano adquirem certo senso de respeito. E os homens, em suas primitivas formas religiosas, tentam mostrar-se à altura das mesmas. A adoração às forças da natureza terminou por evoluir sob a forma de adoração a espíritos da natureza, do que resultaram divindades inferiores, supostamente associadas a mananciais, cavernas, montanhas, etc. (E)

Toda e qualquer adoração dessa natureza é um desvio provocado pelo pecado, sendo condenado por

ADORADORES DO DIABO — ÁDRIA

Deus. Diz Paulo: «...eles mudaram a verdade de Deus em mentira, adorando e servindo a criatura, em lugar do Criador, o qual é bendito eternamente. Amém» (Rom. 1:25).

ADORADORES DO DIABO

A comunidade religiosa Yezidi, que conta com cerca de vinte mil pessoas, no Curdistão, a leste de Mosul e perto de Alepo, em Diarbekr e em Bitlis, é intitulada de adoradores do diabo. O termo yezidi vem do persa moderno, *ized*, que significa anjo ou divindade, sendo usado especificamente para aludir aos adoradores do diabo. Eles chamam a si mesmos de Dasin ou Dasni, e quase todos falam o curdo. Isolaram-se do resto da humanidade, supondo que somente eles descendem de Adão. A religião deles mistura elementos do paganismo, do zoroastrismo, do maniqueísmo, do judaísmo, do nestorianismo e do islamismo (há artigos sobre cada uma dessas religiões). Eles têm dois livros sagrados: o Livro da Revelação e o Livro Negro. A divindade superior deles é deísta (ver sobre o deísmo), sendo uma divindade passiva no mundo. Sete elevados anjos realizam a obra dele, e o mais importante desses anjos é o Malak Ta'us, o anjo pavão, o qual teria caído, mas posteriormente ter-se-ia arrependido. O inferno foi extinto devido às suas lágrimas de remorso. Esse anjo é adorado por ser bom e ativo. Seu nome real é *Satanás*, embora nenhum dos seguidores da seita ouse pronunciar tal nome. Ele manifesta-se através de Shaikh 'Adi (falecido em 1161), um profeta que tornou-se divino por meio de transmigração da alma, e que no mundo atual vive em espírito.

Outras aplicações. Em nossos dias, o satanismo está desfrutando de grande reavivamento. Igrejas têm sido formadas em alguns lugares, visando à adoração ao diabo. Algumas formas de bruxaria prestam lealdade confessada a Satanás, embora não o vejam como um ser maligno. O movimento de rock-and-roll tem sido infiltrado por elementos que adoram abertamente ao diabo.

Alguns religiosos têm o péssimo costume de chamar de seguidores do diabo a todos aqueles que não fazem parte de sua agremiação religiosa. Os católicos dizem isso sobre os protestantes, os protestantes sobre os católicos; e ambos sobre os espíritas. Muitos dizem que o satanismo também tem influenciado a certos indivíduos, dentro do movimento carismático. Porém, a não ser em casos inequívocos, em que as pessoas prestam lealdade declarada a Satanás, deveríamos ter o cuidado de não chamar este ou aquele indivíduo de seguidor do diabo.

ADORAIM

No hebraico significa **duas colinas** ou **duas habitações**. Era uma aldeia no sul de Judá, enumerada juntamente com Hebrom e Maressa, como uma das cidades fortificadas por Reoboão (ver II Crô. 11:5-9). Nos livros apócrifos aparece com o nome de *Adora* (ver I Mac. 13:20), como também em outra literatura (Josefo, *Ant.* 8:10, 1, xiii.6,4,15,4; *Bel. Jud.* 1:2,6,8.4). Josefo usualmente ligava o lugar com Maressa, como cidades iduméias. Foi capturada por Hircano e reconstruída por Gabínio (Jos. *Ant.* xiii.9,1; xiv.5,3). Depois de Josefo, nenhuma outra menção foi feita da cidade, embora tenha sido descoberta pela arqueologia, em tempos modernos. Gabínio transformou-a em um de seus distritos administrativos (Jos. *Bel. Jud.* I.xiii.4,5). No Livro dos Jubileus 38:9 ss, lê-se que Esaú foi morto ali, por forças de Jacó, onde o nome dado é Adurã. Segundo esse livro, Esaú foi sepultado ali. (S UN Z)

ADRAMELEQUE

No hebraico, **esplendor do rei**, isto é, **de Moloque**. 1. Um ídolo mencionado em II Reis 17:31, juntamente com Anameleque, como um dos ídolos cuja adoração os habitantes de Sefarvaim estabeleceram em Samaria, quando para ali foram transferidos pelo rei da Assíria, e ao qual adoravam mediante o sacrifício de seus filhos na fogueira. Isso constitui tudo quanto sabemos com certeza sobre esse ídolo. O nome pode significar Hadade é rei, um nome confirmado pela arqueologia em Tell Halaf. A forma variante, Anameleque, pode estar relacionada ao deus sumério-acadiano Anu, conforme diz Albright em *Archaeology and the Religion of Israel*, págs. 162-164. Por detrás do ídolo uma divindade era adorada, mas não há unanimidade de opinião quanto à divindade assim indiretamente adorada. Alguns têm sugerido algum corpo celeste, misturando a questão com a astrologia. 2. Outros identificam esse ídolo como parte da adoração a Moloque, baseados no fato de que a sacrifício de crianças na fogueira e a significação geral do nome são a mesma coisa em ambos os casos. Porém, outros pensam que Saturno, ou o sol, seriam o «deus» adorado através desse ídolo. O elemento *melek*, do nome Adrameleque, pode aludir ao deus Atar-Vênus. Atar tem sido encontrado pelos arqueólogos em Hará e na Síria. Todas essas muitas conjecturas não solucionam o problema, embora saibamos que estamos tratando com algum tipo de divindade pagã, a qual os assírios transplantaram para Samaria após 722 A.C. 3. Um homem tinha esse nome, filho de Senaqueribe, rei da Assíria. O rei estava habitando em Nínive, após sua desastrosa expedição contra Ezequias. Enquanto adorava no templo de Nisroque, seu deus, Senaqueribe foi assassinado por seus dois filhos, Adremeleque e Sareza, em cerca de 681 A.C. Após o homicídio, os dois irmãos fugiram para a Armênia. (Ver II Reis 19:36,37 e Isa. 37:38). (S Z)

ADRAMITINO

Adramítio era o nome de um antigo porto marítimo na província da Mísia, na Ásia Menor, defronte da ilha de Lesbos e de uma colônia ateniense (Estrabão xiii. par. 606; Herod. viii.42). É mencionado na Bíblia portuguesa somente em Atos. 27:2, sob o substantivo coletivo *adramintino*, devido ao fato de que o navio em que Paulo embarcou em Cesaréia, como prisioneiro a caminho da Itália, pertencia a Adramítio. Alguns identificam esse lugar com a Pédaso de Homero, mas outros supõem que a cidade foi fundada por Adramis, irmão de Creoso, em 6 A.C. Provavelmente existia uma colônia ateniense no local, antes disso. O local original é atualmente conhecido como Karatahs. O navio adramitino levou Paulo e seus companheiros de viagem a Mira, na Lícia, e ali tomaram um navio alexandrino, rumo à Itália.

Nos tempos antigos, a cidade contava com um bom porto, e era importante como um centro comercial, incluindo cunhagem de moedas e preparação de ungüentos (Plínio, HN xiii.2:5). Parece que a cidade era um centro da adoração a *Polux e Castor* (ver o artigo a respeito). (DE S UN Z)

ÁDRIA

O termo alude ao mar Adriático, o moderno golfo

ADRIANO — ADULTÉRIO

de Veneza, o *Mare Supernum* dos romanos, em distinção ao *Mare Inferum* ou mar Tirreno. Provavelmente o nome deriva-se de Ádria, cidade da Ístria. O trecho marítimo inteiro fica entre a Itália, ao ocidente, e a Dalmácia, a Macedônia e a Acaia, ao oriente, —estendendo-se até o Mediterrâneo central, incluindo as águas entre Creta e Malta, onde o navio de Paulo foi açoitado pelo tufão na viagem para Roma (ver Atos 27:27). Nos tempos mais antigos, o nome era aplicado somente às águas perto da foz do rio Pó, enquanto que mais ao sul a mesma região marítima era conhecida como mar Jônico. Todavia, esses termos tornaram-se intercambiáveis. Estrabão usava o termo Ádria para indicar toda aquela região marítima (Estrabão ii.123, vii.187). Terminou incluindo toda a região marítima da foz do Pó ao Mediterrâneo central, conforme Ptolomeu, cientista e geógrafo do século II A.C. e Josefo (Vida iii.15), usaram o vocábulo. Foi nesse mar que Paulo experimentou seu dramático naufrágio, descrito em Atos 27.

ADRIANO

Décimo quinto imperador de Roma, não mencionado no Novo Testamento. Mas alguns supõem que ele é aludido no trecho de Apo. 8:10,11, onde alguns pensam que há uma predição acerca de Barcocheba, o famoso impostor judeu, embora não haja boas evidências em favor disso. Tendo criado distúrbios durante o reinado de Trajano, os judeus foram enviados a Jerusalém para formarem uma colônia, com o propósito de serem mantidos em ordem. Adriano também mandou construir dentro da cidade, um templo em honra a Júpiter. Os judeus pegaram as armas (134 D.C.) e Barcocheba, fingindo ser o Messias, animou a rebelião. Após várias batalhas, durante quase três anos, os judeus foram derrotados. A maioria dos sobreviventes foi vendida à servidão, — e Jerusalém ficou sem habitantes judeus. Houve a devastação dos judeus e do judaísmo. Depois disso, Adriano reconstruiu Jerusalém, mudando seu nome para Elia (ver o artigo a respeito). Isso deu início a grande dispersão judaica, que só foi revertida em nossos dias, sobretudo a partir de 1948. (AM S)

ADRIANO IV, Papa (1154-1159)

Único papa nascido na Inglaterra. Seu nome era Nicolau Breakspear. Mostrou-se insubordinado como monge, em São Rufo, na França, e perdeu sua posição de abade. Então, em 1152, foi enviado em delicada e importante missão à Escandinávia como legado papal (ver artigo a respeito). Em Trandjem ele encontrou as relíquias de São Olaf e deu início a reformas, aprimorando as instituições civis e religiosas. Ao tornar-se papa, obteve a reputação de fazer oposição ao domínio da Sicília pelos normandos. Também resistiu às pretensões imperiais de Frederico I (1152-1190) na Alemanha. Adriano envolveu-se em várias controvérsias políticas e religiosas que envolveram os poderes relativos à Igreja e ao estado. As questões chegaram a um clímax em amarga controvérsia quando da dieta de Besancon (1157) e na declaração dos juristas bolonheses, quando da convocação em Roncaglia, em 1158, acerca das prerrogativas imperiais.

Adriano mostrou-se inflexível diante da posição e do poder do papado medieval, visto que os imperadores, segundo o costume da época, brandiam o poder através do poder papal, sendo considerados filhos do pai de toda a cristandade, pai esse que seria o próprio papa. Temporalmente, o imperador também era tido como dependente dos papas, visto que a superioridade do imperador sobre todos os demais príncipes cristãos europeus dependia da bênção e aprovação papal. Essas controvérsias continuaram durante o pontificado de Alexandre III (ver o artigo a respeito), sucessor de Adriano.

ADRIEL

No hebraico significa *rebanho de Deus*, ou *Deus é o meu socorro*. Era o nome do filho de Barzilai, que viveu no vale do Jordão, não longe do sul de Belém, a pessoa a quem Saul deu sua filha Merabe em casamento, embora originalmente ela tivesse sido prometida a Davi (ver I Sam. 18:19). Dessa união nasceram cinco filhos. Esses estavam entre os sete descendentes de Saul que Davi entregou aos gibeonitas (ver II Sam. 21:8), para vingarem-se das crueldades perpetradas por Saul contra eles. Em II Sam. 21:8, o nome *Mical* aparece como a mãe dos filhos de Adriel. Mas sabe-se que ela não teve filhos (ver II Sam. 6:23). O artigo sobre Mical inclui uma tentativa de explicação sobre esse erro aparente. (DE ND UN)

ADULÃO

No hebraico significa **refúgio**. Era uma antiga cidade cananéia. (Ver Gên. 38:1,12,20), na região plana da tribo de Judá (ver Jos. 15:35). Era uma das cidades reais dos cananeus (ver Jos. 12:15). Foi uma das aldeias fortificadas por Reoboão (ver II Crô. 11:7; Miq. 1:15), sendo mencionada após o exílio babilônico (ver Nee. 40:30 e II Mac. 12:38). Eusébio e Jerônimo afirmam que ela ficava a leste de Eleuterópolis, mas eles seguiram a Septuaginta, que a confunde com Eglom. Eram lugares diferentes com reis distintos nos dias de Josué (ver Jos. 12:12,15). Adulão era uma das cidades do vale ou da planície entre a região montanhosa de Judá e o mar Mediterrâneo. A julgar pela lista onde seu nome aparece, talvez ficasse próxima da cidade filistéia de Gate. O local é identificado com o moderno Tell esh-esheikh Madhkur, perto de Khirbet 'ele el-Ma, a meio caminho entre Laquis e Jerusalém.

A caverna de Adulão. Saindo da cidade de Gate (ver I Sam. 22:1), Davi retirou-se para uma caverna, quando fugia de Saul. Mas nenhum trecho bíblico liga essa caverna com a cidade, e nem tem sido encontrada qualquer caverna nas proximidades capaz de ocultar quatrocentos homens. É possível que a caverna de Adulão ficasse no ermo montanhoso a oeste de Judá, na direção do mar Morto, onde existem cavernas. O esconderijo de Davi ficava nessa região. Uma caverna nessa região parece mais certa, em face do fato de que Davi chamou para ali os seus pais e eles viviam em Belém. Mas alguns eruditos defendem a área perto da cidade de Adulão. Têm sido encontradas algumas cavernas a meio caminho entre Socó e Queila, a dezesseis quilômetros a noroeste de Hebrom, que poderiam ter servido como refúgio e fortaleza de Davi. Ao que parece, essa caverna não ficava distante do lugar onde Davi entrou em luta com Golias. Mas, acerca de tudo isso, não temos certeza de nada. Ver I Sam. 22:1; II Sam. 23:13-17; I Crô. 11:16-19. (FA S Z)

ADULTÉRIO

No A. Testamento. Contato sexual de uma mulher casada ou comprometida com alguém que não esteja seu marido ou noivo. Ou de um homem casado com

ADULTÉRIO

uma mulher que não fosse sua esposa. Todavia, o concubinato era extremamente comum no Antigo Testamento, pelo que um homem casado podia ter muitas mulheres, contanto que não fossem casadas, e se houvesse contratos apropriados, sob forma escrita, estipulando as condições segundo as quais o relacionamento deveria ocorrer. Outrossim, a poligamia era uma prática comum. A poliandria (vários maridos para uma só mulher), todavia, nunca foi reconhecida na lei e nos costumes dos judeus. Os versículos que proíbem o adultério incluem Êxo. 20:14; Lev. 18:20; Mat. 19:3-12; Gál. 5:19-21. O sétimo mandamento proíbe o adultério.

Base original da monogamia. O trecho de Mat. 19:4-8 registra as declarações de Jesus em favor da monogamia e contra o divórcio. Ele alicerçou o Seu ensino na narrativa da criação do homem. Podemos supor, pois, que, apesar da permissividade do Antigo Testamento em relação ao concubinato e à poligamia (para os homens somente, como é natural), a monogamia é o ideal espiritual.

Por que o adultério é proibido? A fim de preservar a santidade do lar (Êxo. 20:14; Deu. 5:18). Também está envolvida a questão da herança da família e a preservação da pureza tribal. Finalmente, o próprio ato era considerado um crime sério, um ato de contaminação (Lev. 18:20). Por esse motivo, era imposta a pena de morte, envolvendo a execução de ambos os culpados (Êxo. 20:14; Lev. 20:1 ss). Injunções similares podem ser achadas no código babilônico de Hamurabi (129), e, opcionalmente, na primitiva lei romana (Dion. Hal. *Antiguidades Romanas*). A pena de morte mostra que as sociedades antigas encaravam o adultério não meramente como um ato privado errado, mas que ameaçava o arcabouço do lar e da sociedade. O fato de que o homem e a mulher tornam-se *uma carne* no matrimônio (Gên. 2:24; Efé. 5:31,32) sugere uma comunicação mística de energias vitais físicas e espirituais, e isso deve acontecer somente entre duas pessoas. Quanto a notas sobre esse conceito, ver NTI na referência de Efésios. No adultério, o indivíduo é furtado de sua identidade, e a união mística de seres é perturbada, talvez assemelhando-se ao homicídio, embora certamente com menores conseqüências morais.

Severidade do Novo Testamento. Jesus transferiu a questão do adultério ao campo dos pensamentos e emoções. O homem que deseja uma mulher já se tornou culpado (Mat. 5:28). Portanto, a moralidade estrita envolve as intenções, as palavras e os pensamentos do indivíduo, e não apenas os seus atos. E assim, todos os homens e mulheres caem sob a condenação, no espírito do sétimo mandamento, e ninguém pode jactar-se de sua santidade quanto a esse preceito.

Uso metafórico. A idolatria e a infidelidade a Deus, sob qualquer forma, é adultério espiritual (Jer. 3). Paulo dá a isso um colorido cristão, pois o homem pode cometer adultério contra Cristo (I Cor. 6:9-20). O Espírito residente no crente faz de seu corpo um templo. Assim, qualquer poluição do corpo é uma forma de infidelidade contra o Espírito ali residente, uma execração desse templo. Visto que o Espírito habita no crente, e entre os crentes como uma coietividade, quando um membro peca, todos os demais membros são envolvidos quanto ao resultado disso (I Cor. 5:6; 12:27; Efé. 5:28-31). A união sexual não envolve somente o que o indivíduo faz — afeta a substância daquilo que ele é (I Cor. 6:16). Todos os pecados sexuais são proibidos no Novo Testamento, e não apenas o adultério (I Cor. 6:9; Gál. 5:19).

Em outras sociedades, antigas e modernas. O código babilônico de Hamurabi (128) mostra-nos que pelo menos alguns povos antigos, além dos hebreus, encaravam desaprovadoramente o adultério. Nas sociedades grega e romana o adultério era tratado com severidade, posto que nem sempre de forma coerente. Na sociedade grega, um homem não podia ser divorciado de sua esposa, somente por esse motivo. O sexo antes do casamento era geralmente tolerado, não sendo reputado um erro grave. Nos ritos de fertilidade entre os egípcios, babilônios, gregos e romanos praticamente não havia regras, e parece que se isso fosse feito como parte de crenças e práticas religiosas, muitas coisas que não eram permissíveis na vida diária comum seriam permitidas. Essas práticas, por via de Canaã, penetraram na vida israelita (Amós 2:7 ss ; Miq. 1:7; I Reis 14:24). O homossexualismo com freqüência fazia parte dos cultos antigos.

As religiões de todos os povos consideram que os atos sexuais praticados entre pessoas não casadas são errados, exceto nas sociedades onde a poligamia continua sendo praticada. A maioria dos países europeus, bem como os Estados Unidos da América, permitem o divórcio em razão de adultério. Nesse último país, desde 1955, o adultério não está incluído no código criminal, embora continue sendo motivo comum para o divórcio. Ali ninguém é preso por causa de um romance com uma mulher que não seja sua esposa.

A lei do amor. O adultério pode ser perdoado por meio do arrependimento. Disse Jesus: «Nem eu tão pouco te condeno; vai, e não peques mais» (João 8:11)

Ver os artigos sobre o *divórcio*, a *fornicação*, a *monogamia*, o *matrimônio* e a *inseminação artificial*.

Comentários adicionais, considerando I Cor. 6:18.

Fugi da prostituição. Qualquer outro pecado que o homem comete, é fora do corpo; mas o que se prostitui peca contra o seu próprio corpo.

Não convém que enfrentemos frontalmente esse pecado, oferecendo-lhe resistência através da força da vontade. Nosso plano de batalha, nesse caso, consiste em fugir. E nessa fuga que fujamos para os braços de Cristo, desenvolvendo Nele as virtudes morais positivas (ver Gál. 5:22,23), as quais nos protegerão dessa forma de pecados. A alma remida que permanece em comunhão com Cristo, através de seu Espírito, mediante a meditação, o estudo das Escrituras, a oração, e, idealmente, mediante as experiências místicas reais, perderá seu apetite pelas concupiscências carnais.

Paulo já havia declarado algo similar, com o mesmo sentido básico, na passagem de Rom. 13:14: «...*mas revesti-vos do Senhor Jesus Cristo, e nada disponhais para a carne, no tocante às suas concupiscências*». Assim sendo, não devemos freqüentar aqueles lugares, ler aquelas coisas, ter contato com aquelas pessoas, que formariam provisões para as ações sensuais. Pelo contrário, «revistamo-nos do Senhor Jesus Cristo». Que seja ele o nosso revestimento espiritual. Que ele nos cubra e proteja com o seu sangue.

Com esses pensamentos podemos comparar o ensinamento de Jesus Cristo sobre o *adultério visual* (ver Mat. 5:28). E também podemos confrontar a admoestação e censura de Simão Pedro, que diz: «...tendo olhos cheios de adultério e insaciáveis no pecado, engodando almas inconstantes...» (II Ped. 2:14). Existem homens que vivem em estado permanente de concupiscência, em razão do que vivem procurando sempre alguém com quem adulte-

ADUMIM — ADVENTISTAS

rar. Seus olhos percorrem a terra, procurando quem queira pecar com eles, — e a vitalidade de seus seres é desperdiçada nessa pervertida atividade. Conforme a tradução inglesa de Williams (aqui vertida para o português), os olhos dessas pessoas são «insaciáveis pelo pecado». Jamais ficam satisfeitas, sempre precisando de quem queira compartilhar de sua sensualidade. Tornaram-se escravos completos do sexo. Tais indivíduos, em vez de fugirem dessa forma de pecado, buscam situações favoráveis para o pecado, sempre fazendo coisas que provocam o seu apetite. Tais homens não passam de escravos. e somente a ajuda «vinda do alto» poderá salvá-los.

Sófocles, no diálogo de autoria de Platão, intitulado *República* (329), ao ser interrogado sobre como vinha manuseando as questões do «amor», retrucou: «Mui alegremente tenho 'escapado' do mesmo, e sinto como se tivesse escapado de um senhor louco e furioso». Sim, o sexo pervertido pode ser uma entidade assim, e feliz é aquele que consegue escapar do mesmo.

«Pecar 'contra o corpo' é defraudá-lo da parte que o mesmo tem com Cristo, é cortá-lo de seu destino eterno. Esse é o efeito da fornicação em um grau sem-par... Aquilo que o apóstolo Paulo assevera sobre a fornicação, nega a respeito de qualquer outro pecado». (Robertson e Plummer, *in loc.*).

«...*fora...*», nesse caso, é palavra que significa algo como «sem efeito sobre o destino do corpo» (novamente falando apenas em sentido relativo). Por essa razão é que Alford (*in loc.*) comenta a respeito dessa questão como segue: «A assertiva do apóstolo é estritamente veraz. O alcoolismo e a glutonaria são pecados feitos no corpo e através do corpo, sendo praticados no abuso do mesmo, porém, são coisas *introduzidas de fora*, erradas em seu *efeito*, cujo efeito é dever de cada indivíduo prever e evitar. Mas a fornicação é a 'alienação daquele corpo que pertence ao Senhor, fazendo do mesmo, corpo de uma prostituta'; não é um 'efeito' sobre o corpo deles, com base na participação de coisas vindas de fora, mas antes, é uma 'contradição da verdade' do corpo, proveniente 'de dentro' de si mesmo».

É bem provável que Paulo concordaria com essa opinião de Alford. O que é inegável é que Paulo não subscreveria àquela filosofia que afirma que todos os pecados são igualmente maus, não havendo qualquer gradação de pecado. (AL IB LAN NTI RO)

ADUMIM

No hebraico significa **rochas vermelhas,** ou talvez *lugar sangrento*, um passo acerca de dez quilômetros a sudoeste de Jericó, uma rota comercial desde tempos remotos, desde o vale do Jordão, nas vizinhanças de Jericó, até à região montanhosa, incluindo Jerusalém. Fazia parte da fronteira norte de Judá (ver Jos. 15:7), sendo usada como ponto de referência no estabelecimento da localização de Gelilote, na fronteira sul de Benjamim (ver Jos. 18:17). Era um caminho perigoso por causa dos freqüentes assaltos, de cujo fator (conforme Jerônimo e outros conjecturaram) talvez se derivasse o seu nome. — O caminho era, notoriamente, perigoso, fazendo parte da cena da história do bom samaritano, em Lucas 10:30. Jerônimo informa-nos que um fortim ou guarnição era mantido nas vizinhanças, para proteger os viajantes. Atualmente há uma hospedaria, onde antes estivera o fortim, e cujo nome é Hospedaria do Bom Samaritano. O nome árabe do passo é Talat ed-Damm, que significa «subida de sangue». Mas a alusão mais provável é devido às formações de rocha vermelha, e não ao tratamento sangüinário dado aos viajantes, durante muitos séculos, naquele lugar. (FA S Z)

ADUS

Um homem cujos descendentes retornaram com Zorobabel, da Babilônia (ver I Esd. 5:34). Seu nome é omitido nas listas paralelas de Esdras 3 e Neemias 7.

ADVAITA

Esse termo sânscrito significa «não-dualismo». Era usado para referir-se a uma das idéias centrais da filosofia vedanta, de que o «eu» do homem o *atman*, bem como a alma das coisas, *bramá* (ver os artigos), são idênticos. Ver o artigo sobre a *Vedanta*. A tarefa espiritual da vida humana consiste em dissipar nossas crenças equivocadas, por estarmos separados de Bramá, ficando assim rejeitado o dualismo. Os principais representantes dessa escola são Guadapada e Shankara (ver os artigos). (P)

ADVENTISTAS

Estão em foco algumas seitas religiosas que se originaram com o movimento do advento, resultante dos ensinos de William Miller (1782-1849). Os membros desse movimento enfatizavam c segundo advento pré-milenar de Cristo e a renovação da terra como habitação dos remidos, após a ressurreição física dos mortos. Miller (ver o artigo) levava muito a sério as passagens proféticas e apocalípticas da Bíblia; e através da manipulação dos dados que aparecem no livro de Daniel, ele concluiu que o segundo advento ocorreria entre 1843 e 1844. Passou a fazer muitas conferências, começando em Dresden, NY. Anunciou a condenação iminente e um grande número de pessoas converteu-se. Assim, uma nova seita nasceu. O espírito geral de temor provocou excessos. As pessoas venderam as suas propriedades, e muitas abandonaram as atividades normais da vida diária. Periódicos passaram a ser publicados, alertando o mundo, a saber: *Clamor de Meia-Noite*, *Sinais dos Tempos* e *Trombeta da Alarma*. Quando as predições de Miller falharam, alguns abandonaram o movimento, mas este agora já estava firmemente estabelecido. E assim nasceu uma nova denominação.

Idéias principais. a. Aniquilamento dos ímpios. b. Sono da alma, desde a morte física ao dia do juízo. c. Criação de novos céus e de nova terra, sendo que este seria o lar dos remidos ressuscitados. d. Um milênio entre a primeira e a segunda ressurreição, onde esta última apenas assinalaria um juízo que resultaria no total aniquilamento dos perdidos. e. Não haveria conversão do mundo ao evangelho. f. Satanás continuaria assediando o trabalho dos remidos até o fim. Em outras doutrinas, são essencialmente evangélicos.

Desistência. Vários grupos adventistas desistiram de acompanhar o movimento original. Jonathan Cummings dizia que a imortalidade é um dom de Cristo dado apenas a alguns poucos, que seriam escolhidos quando da ressurreição. E organizou um movimento chamado Igreja Cristã do Advento, em Worchester, Massachusetts, em 1861. Esse grupo continua sendo uma agremiação bastante numerosa, com muitas igrejas. James Bates e James White, em 1844, declararam-se a favor da observância do sétimo dia como sagrado, permitindo que somente a Bíblia fosse usada como regra de fé e prática. Em uma conferência, efetuada em Battle Creek, em Michigan, em 1860, formou-se a denominação: Adventistas do Sétimo Dia. Suas idéias básicas são as seguintes: a. As Escrituras são leis acerca de tudo. b. Adoração e descanso no sétimo dia. c. Expulsão de membros que

ADVENTO — ADVOGADO

usam o tabaco ou qualquer outra forma de intoxicantes. d. Ênfase sobre o segundo advento de Cristo, como um retorno iminente, embora de data desconhecida. Um outro grupo separou-se sob a liderança de Elder Cranmer, em protesto a reivindicação de inspiração divina por parte de um dos membros fundadores da denominação dos Adventistas do Sétimo Dia. Esse grupo, embora menor que o anterior, continua contando com um bom número de igrejas. Seu nome é Igreja de Deus Adventista. Todavia, ainda um outro grupo se formou, chamado União de Vida e Advento, fundado em Nova Iorque, em 1863, sob a liderança de John T. Walsh, que deixou de acreditar na ressurreição dos ímpios, terminado o milênio. Pois se os ímpios serão apenas julgados, para logo serem aniquilados, por que ressuscitariam? Esse grupo tem continuado pequeno até hoje. Finalmente, temos as Igrejas de Deus em Jesus Cristo, que vieram à existência em novembro de 1888. Esse grupo defende todas as doutrinas adventistas originais. Tem sobrevivido até nossos dias com modesto número de igrejas.

ADVENTO

1. O nascimento de Jesus Cristo, a vinda do Filho de Deus a este mundo, em forma humana, na encarnação. Ver os artigos sobre *Jesus* e *Cristo*. Ver a *encarnação* e o *nascimento virginal*.

2. A segunda vinda de Cristo. Quanto a notas completas sobre o assunto ver sob esse título.

3. A observância luterana e católica-romana de quatro domingos anteriores ao Natal, como preparação para a festa da Natividade. Tais celebrações tiveram início em meados do século VI D.C., desde quando o *advento* passou a assinalar o começo do ano eclesiástico.

Essa palavra vem do latim *adventus*, que geralmente corresponde ao termo grego *parousia*, ou «vinda». Justino Mártir, em seu Diálogo contra Trifo, caps. 52 e 121, fala da primeira e da segunda *parousia*, aludindo ao nascimento e à segunda vinda de Cristo. O Novo Testamento também usa o vocábulo *epifaneia* para indicar ambos esses adventos. Quanto ao primeiro, ver II Tim. 1:10; quanto ao segundo, I Tim. 6:14. Ver os artigos sobre a *epifânia* e a *parousia*. (A B E SM Z)

ADVERSÁRIO

De modo geral, um inimigo de qualquer categoria, como em Naum 1:2, que diz: «... o Senhor toma vingança contra os seus adversários...» Especificamente, indica alguém que se opõe injustamente a outrem. Assim, Penina é intitulada adversária de Ana (ver I Sam. 1:6). No Antigo Testamento, algumas vezes, a palavra *adversário* é tradução do vocábulo que basicamente significa «amarrar» ou «esforçar-se». O trecho de Isa. 1:8, traduz a palavra que significa alguém que tem uma *causa judicial* em andamento contra outrem.

•••

Um dos nomes de Satanás (que vide). Ele é o oponente e o *acusador*, o inimigo por excelência daqueles que prestam lealdade a Deus. Ver Jó 1 e Zac. 3. Seu intuito é destruir. Grande é a cooperação que ele recebe daqueles que são destruidores. É como um leão que ruge, querendo devorar (I Ped. 5:8), e nós lhe devemos resistir (vs. 9). O termo grego usado nesse trecho é *antídikos*, usado por cinco vezes no Novo Testamento, para indicar vários tipos de adversários.

A própria palavra envolve a idéia de adversário, acusador, inimigo, oponente. O acusador é o contrário do advogado, que é Cristo. Em sentido moral, a história do homem é a história de como ele tem prestado lealdade a Deus ou ao diabo, para seu benefício ou para sua perdição. Essa oposição é variegadamente pintada no Novo Testamento. Satanás primeiramente testou a Jesus (Mat. 4:10). Ele é o líder da oposição ao reino do Senhor (Mat. 12:26), e é o responsável pela queda e pelo pecado (Mat. 16:23; Atos 5:3), podendo causar enfermidades (Luc. 13:16), a fim de assediar àqueles a quem se opõe. E é o responsável pela tentação e pelas possessões demoníacas (Mat. 7:22; 12:24). A personalidade humana está sujeita às suas invasões (Juí. 6:34). A libertação vem através da resistência e da lealdade a Deus (I Ped. 5:9). (A SM W)

ADVOGADO

No grego é **parakletos**, alguém que pleiteia a causa de outrem. O vocábulo também é usado para indicar alguém que exorta, defende ou ora em favor de outrem. O título é conferido ao Espírito Santo (ver João 14:16; 15:26; 16:7) e a Cristo (ver I João 2:1). Ver também Rom. 8:34 e Heb. 7:25.

1. Essa palavra pode significar um advogado legal, que pleiteia o caso de outrem. Em Sua missão, Cristo assume essa função, e nós somos aceitos no Amado (Efé. 1:6), transformados à Sua imagem, de modo a sermos dignos dessa aceitação (Rom. 8:29. Ver o NTI e a nota geral sobre esse assunto, nessa referência). Portanto, a obra de nosso Advogado é eficaz.

2. O vocábulo também pode significar «intercessor». Ver I João 2:1 no tocante a isso e à obra do Espírito, cumprindo a mesma função. (Rom. 8:26).

3. Um ajudador. Com base em Sua morte propiciatória e em Seu poder transformador, Cristo ajuda àqueles que nEle confiam (Rom. 8:35 ss).

Etimologicamente, a palavra empregada significa «chamado para o lado de outrem», como em um tribunal, para defender uma causa, para interceder ou ajudar. Ver João 14:16,26; 15:26; 16:7, quanto a usos da palavra, no tocante ao Espírito. Ver *Paracleto*.

Uso secular. Na sociedade judaica era desconhecida a função do advogado, que defende ou pleiteia pelas causas alheias, pelo menos em sentido formal. Os romanos desenvolveram-na ao mais alto nível, embora a função já existisse entre os gregos. A lei romana regulamentava a prática e o ofício dos advogados. Nos tempos do Novo Testamento podiam ser encontrados advogados em todas as províncias romanas. Também manuseavam com negócios legais, e não apenas com julgamentos em tribunal. Os judeus empregaram um advogado para defender a causa deles contra Paulo, perante Félix, um certo Tertulo (Atos 24:1). Ali é usado o termo grego *retor*, um «orador», mas a idéia de advocacia também se faz presente no termo.

No grego, *nomikós*, «especialista na lei». O termo é usado para designar os homens eruditos na lei mosaica oral e escrita, ou nas leis civis, conforme se vê em Tito 3:3. Um sinônimo grego é *nomodidáskalos*, «mestre da lei», conforme se vê mediante a comparação das passagens de Mat. 22:35; Mar. 12:28; Luc. 5:17,21; 10:25 e 11:44-46. Cada detalhe da vida do povo de Israel era regulamentado por lei, e isso exigia que especialistas interpretassem e pusessem em vigor a lei mosaica.

Deveres dos advogados. Eles deviam estudar,

AEDIAS — AFECA

interpretar, expor e ensinar a lei, na vida privada, nas escolas e nas sinagogas. Também atuavam como juízes. Vários sinédrios ou tribunais foram formados com esse propósito, embora um único indivíduo pudesse ser convocado para atuar como juiz.

Freqüência da palavra. O termo grego aparece por dez vezes, em Mat. 22:35; Luc. 7:30; 10:25; 11:45,46,52,53; 14:3; Tito 3:9,13.

Os advogados e Jesus. Os «intérpretes da lei», conforme eles são chamados em nossa versão portuguesa, participaram ativamente na oposição a Jesus, em liga com os fariseus (ver Luc. 7:30). Jesus denunciou-os por causa dos abusos que cometiam (ver Luc. 11:45-52). Eles se opuseram às curas efetuadas por Jesus em dia de sábado (ver Luc. 14:3). Um deles tentou embaraçar Jesus com perguntas difíceis, durante a semana da paixão (ver Mat. 22:35). A resposta de Jesus exprime um magnífico sumário da doutrina cristã, em nossos deveres relativos a Deus e ao próximo: «Destes dois mandamentos dependem toda a lei e os profetas» (Mat. 22:40). (ID S UN Z)

AEDIAS

Em I Esdras 9:27, uma forma alternativa para Elias.

AENESIDEMUS

Filósofo grego do primeiro século A.C., nascido em Creta. Ensinou em Alexandria. Reviveu o *pirronismo* (ver o artigo), sistematizando os seus argumentos. Foi um cético extremista, que se opunha ao estoicismo e ao ceticismo moderado. Seus escritos, perdidos exceto em referências, foram *Discursos Pirronianos* e *Esboço do Pirronismo*.

Juntamente com Pirro (ver o artigo), ele suspendia o juízo sobre todas as coisas e promovia a *ataraxia* (tranqüilidade), como o alvo moral ideal. Desenvolveu dez modos ou *tropos*, que explicam porque os juízos devem ser suspensos. Os tropos são: ·a. a percepção manifesta-se de vários modos; b. diferentes classes de homens manifestam diferenças individuais; c. os informes dos sentidos diferem uns dos outros; d. um organismo tem diferentes percepções em diferentes estados; e. a variedade de posições de um objeto afeta a percepção, como também a distância; f. o meio através do qual a percepção se faz a afeta; g. diferenças nos estados de um objeto percebido afeta a percepção; h. a impossibilidade de eliminar contradições e discriminações entre a multiplicidade de fatores envolvidos no juizo; i. a freqüência ou raridade da ocorrência de qualquer dado faz uma coisa tornar-se corriqueira ou maravilhosa em nosso juízo, distorcendo a avaliação; j. diferenças de julgamento, devido a costumes, crenças e estágios de desenvolvimento das pessoas afetam o juízo. Em adição, ele argumentava contra o conceito de causalidade, afirmando que é impossível determinar o momento exato da causa-efeito, o que obscurece o conceito inteiro de causa. O resultado disso é que não temos conhecimento seguro sobre qualquer coisa, o que equivale ao *ceticismo* (ver o artigo). (AM F P)

AEON

Esse é o termo grego que significa **era**, cujo sentido indica a duração de uma vida humana ou a própria vida (Homero), ou então um período interminável, a perpetuidade do tempo, a eternidade.

Declaração geral. 1. No plural, *as eras*, a idéia é a de divisões de tempo, passados e futuros (ver Efé. 2:7 e 3:9). Por esse motivo, Deus é chamado de «Rei dos séculos» (I Tim. 1:17). 2. Dentro do uso escatológico, a era presente em contraste com a era vindoura, com as idéias enfáticas da natureza temporal do presente e da natureza eterna da era vindoura. O mal impera no mundo atual, mas Deus imperará na era vindoura. (Ver Mar. 10:30). 3. Ou então a palavra pode indicar um período indefinido de tempo, no passado ou no futuro. (Ver Luc. 1:70). A tradução «para sempre», em Lucas 1:33, transmite essa idéia. Somente o contexto pode ajudar-nos a mostrar se essa qualidade está ali em foco.

Fórmulas que expressam a idéia de eternidade, no Novo Testamento:

1. Por todas as gerações, para todo o sempre (Efé. 3:21). A eternidade é encarada como um ciclo interminável de eras, e as eras são compostas de gerações. Os homens pensam em *eras* compostas por anos, mas, neste texto, a eternidade é concebida como composta de eras — eras das eras (*aionon*).

2. *Pelas eras* (*aeon*, de novo), ou *para sempre* (ver Rom. 1:25; 9:5; II Cor. 9:9).

3. *Pelas eras das eras*, usualmente traduzida como *para todo o sempre*. (Ver Gál. 1:5; Fil. 4:10; I Tim. 1:17; II Tim. 4:18; Apo. 1:16; 4:9; 5:13; 7:12 e 10:6, etc.).

4. *Pela era das eras* (em III Esdras 4:38 e Dan. 7:18). (A AL FA NTI UN Z)

AER

No hebraico, **outro**, ou **depois**. Era descendente de Benjamim (I Crô. 7:12). É identificado com Ará (ver I Crô. 8:1) ou Airã (ver Núm. 26:38).

AESORA (ESORA)

Uma aldeia nas fronteiras da Samaria, alistada juntamente com Bete-Horom, Jericó, e outras. Não se conhece a sua localização, mas alguns a identificam com Hazor (ver Jos. 11:1,10; Juí. 4:2,17 e Nee. 11:33). (Z)

AFARSAQUITAS

O vocábulo aparece em Esd. 4:9; 5:6 e 6:6. Trata-se do nome do povo ao qual pertenciam alguns dos colonos que os assírios enviaram para a Samaria. Têm sido identificados com os paratacenes da Média, referidos pelos geógrafos gregos (ver Estrabão 11.522, xv. 732; Plínio xvi.29). A época do estabelecimento deles em Samaria foi entre 669 e 626 A.C. (FA ID S)

AFARSITAS

Aparecem em Esd. 4:9, provavelmente um povo persa, uma tribo transferida para a Samaria pelos assírios, em cerca de 464-424 A.C. (KEI)

AFECA

No hebraico, **fortaleza**. Uma cidade na região montanhosa da Jùdéia, perto de Bete-Tapua (Jos. 15:53). Tem sido identificada com a moderna Khirbet ed-darrame, ou Khirbet Kanaan, mas que outros estudiosos preferem considerar de localização desconhecida. (ND Z)

••• ••• •••

AFEQUE — AFINIDADE

AFEQUE

No hebraico, **força**. Designa uma cidadela ou cidade fortificada. Quatro cidades do Antigo Testamento são assim chamadas:

1. Uma cidade no território de Aser (ver Jos. 12:18; 13:4; 19:30). Em Juí. 1:31 aparece como uma das cidades cujos habitantes, os membros da tribo de Aser, não conseguiram desapossar, pelo que esses povos habitaram entre os aseritas. Comumente é identificada com Tell Kurdaneh, acerca de dez quilômetros a suleste de Aco, ao norte de Beirute.

2. Um lugar localizado na fronteira norte do território cananeu, com os amorreus (ver Jos. 13:4). Ver o artigo sobre os *amorreus*. As referências bíblicas dizem respeito às terras que não foram ocupadas, ao norte. Com freqüência tem sido identificada com Afqa, antiga Afaca, acerca de 37 km ao norte de Beirute. Nos tempos antigos, foi o centro do culto de Astarte-Adonis.

3. Uma importante cidade, uma das diversas que havia na planície de Sarom. Seu rei foi morto por Josué, durante a conquista de Canaã (ver Jos. 12:18). Foi o lugar de onde partiram as forças filisteias que capturaram a arca e destruíram Silo, em cerca de 1050 A.C. (ver I Sam. 4:1). Foi ali, igualmente, que os filisteus reuniram suas forças, quando estavam em campanha contra Saul, o que resultou na morte dele (ver I Sam. 29:1). O lugar foi capturado na segunda campanha de Amenhotepe II, do Egito, contra as planícies de Sarom e Jezreel (em cerca de 1440 A.C.). Fez parte da província de Samaria durante o reinado de Esar-hadom (681-669 A.C.).

Posteriormente, o local foi ocupado pela cidade de *Antípatris* (ver o artigo a respeito). Tem sido identificada com a moderna Ras el-'Ain, nas cabeceiras do Nahr el-'Auga, acerca de 18 km a nordeste de Jopa.

4. Uma cidade ao norte da Transjordânia, distrito de Basã, na estrada de Damasco a Bete-Sean, atravessando o vale de Jezreel. Ficava localizada cerca de seis quilômetros a leste do mar da Galiléia. Era uma cidade forte de Bete-Sean. Foi perto dali que Ben-Hadade, o rei sírio, foi derrotado por Acabe, de Israel. Ben-Hadade fugiu para a própria cidade e pediu clemência da parte de Acabe (ver I Reis 20:26-34). Joás derrotou Ben-Hadade, filho de Hazarel, da Síria, nesse lugar, conforme predissera o moribundo Eliseu (ver II Reis 13:14-25). Tem sido identificada com Fiq ou Afiq, na cabeceira do Wadi Fiq, a leste do mar da Galiléia.(AH ID ND WRI)

AFEREMA

Um dos três distritos tirados de Samaria e adicionados à Judéia pelo rei da Síria, Demétrio Nicator (ver Josefo, *Anti.* xiii.iv.9; I Macabeus 10:38). Ficava perto de Betel, representando a forma aramaica de um lugar chamado Efraim. Nos tempos modernos, o local é identificado com et-Taiyibeh. (Z)

AFERRA

Chefe de uma família de servos de Salomão que retornou do cativeiro com Zorobabel (ver I Esdras 5:34). O nome não aparece nos paralelos de Esd. 2:57 e Nee. 7:59. (Z)

AFETOS

Tradução do termo grego **splagchnon**, «intestinos, órgãos vitais» (II Cor. 7:15; Col. 3:12), de *froneo* (pensar, mentalizar, II Cor. 7:15), e de *pathos* (sentimento, paixão, Col. 3:5; Rom. 1:26). Esses conceitos podem ter sinônimo em afetos. Os afetos podem ser distinguidos das paixões por serem menos intensos, naturais e espirituais. Nesse sentido, podem resultar da operação da lei do amor na vida, a principal de todas as virtudes (Gál. 5:22). Esses sentimentos fazem parte fundamental da consciência, juntamente com a tomada de consciência. Podem operar à parte da vontade, originando-se do instinto interior daquilo que é certo. São os mananciais da ação e fazem parte essencial da vida espiritual (Mar. 12:30,31). (A B K P SM ST)

Em sua forma nominal, «afeto» é o termo usado na psicologia racional de Spinoza para dar nome a certa variedade de sentimentos, propósitos e impulsos que nos motivam. Visto que os afetos são internos, sua influência sobre nós parece permitir um tipo de autodeterminação. Ver sobre o *livre-arbítrio*.

AFIA

No hebraico, **soprado**, isto é, **refrescado**. Um benjamita que foi um dos antepassados de Saul (ver I Sam. 9:1). (S)

ÁFIA

No grego, o sentido do nome é desconhecido. Era nome de uma mulher (ver Filemom 2), que aparece com os nomes de Arquipo e Filemom, e que provavelmente era esposa deste último (64 D.C.). Nada se sabe acerca dela, exceto aquilo que é dito nesse versículo. Mas a tradição diz que ela foi apedrejada até à morte nos dias de Nero, juntamente com Filemom e Arquipo. O dia 22 de novembro foi consagrado à sua memória, pela Igreja Grega.

O nome era comum na Ásia Menor, sendo bem possível que ela fosse nativa da Frígia, região onde estavam localizadas as cidades de Laodicéia, Hierápolis e Colossos. O evangelho chegara àquelas áreas quando Paulo estava em Éfeso. (ID NTI)

AFINIDADE (relativa ao matrimônio)

Uma afinidade é um relacionamento criado por casamento, e não por *consangüinidade* (que vide).

1. Nos tempos antigos, como no livro de Gênesis, encontramos casamentos de um homem com sua irmã ou meia-irmã, como os casos de Caim e Abel, e Abraão. A prática era comum no Egito, e a literatura antiga nos revela que era generalizada em muitas sociedades antigas.

2. *Graus de afinidade e regulamentação* (ver Lev. 18:7 ss quanto às leis judaicas sobre a questão, em um período posterior). a. Um homem não podia casar-se com a viúva de seu pai (nem com sua madrasta). b. Nem podia casar-se com a filha da esposa de seu pai, por outro marido. c. Nem com a viúva de seu tio paterno. d. Nem com a viúva de seu irmão, se este tivesse tido filhos com ela. Em caso contrário, um homem solteiro deveria casar-se com a viúva de seu irmão, a fim de gerar filhos que continuassem a família. Era a chamada lei do levirato.

3. *Em relação aos casamentos polígamos*. a. Um homem não podia casar-se com uma mulher e com sua filha, ao mesmo tempo. b. Nem podia casar-se com duas irmãs ao mesmo tempo, a fim de evitar a inevitável competição e ciúmes. Porém, o casamento com a irmã de uma esposa falecida era aceitável. (S)

AFIRMAÇÕES DE JESUS — ÁGABO

AFIRMAÇÕES DE JESUS DE OXYRYNCHUS
Ver **Oxyrynchus, Afirmações de Jesus de**.

AFIRMATIVAS

Entre os judeus, a fórmula de assentimento ou afirmação era: «Você o disse»; ou então: «Você disse com razão». Tais fórmulas continuam prevalentes em alguns países orientais. Isso explica por que Jesus (ver Mat. 26:25), quando interrogado se era ou não o Cristo, o Filho de Deus, replicou: «Tu o disseste». Isso equivalia a uma afirmação em português: «Eu o sou». Não equivalia a uma negativa, como se Ele tivesse dito: «Você é que está dizendo isso; eu não estou dizendo», conforme alguns têm pensado. No Talmude encontramos muitos exemplos disso. Assim, alguém indagou: «O rabino morreu?» E a resposta foi: «Você o disse» (o que equivalia a um «sim»). (T. *Hieros*. *Kilaim*, xxxii.2). Essa maneira de afirmar era comum entre os gregos e os romanos, pelo que a resposta de Jesus certamente foi bem entendida. (NTI S)

AFLIÇÃO
Ver sobre **Sofrimento**.

AFO

Epíteto aplicado a Jônatas, quinto filho de Matatias (ver I Macabeus 2:5). O sentido do apelido é desconhecido, embora alguns suponham que signifique *desmantelador*, que poderia ter sido obtido pelo fato que Jônatas enganou a tribo de Jambri, que havia assassinado seu irmão, João (ver I Macabeus 9.37-41). (Z)

A FORTIORI

Expressão latina que significa «do mais forte», com o sentido de «mais ainda» ou «ainda mais certo». É um tipo de argumento em que dois casos são comparados, um menor e um maior. O argumento vai do menor ao maior. Por exemplo: Se um dono de casa dá um pão, e não uma pedra, a um estranho que bate à sua porta, *a fortiori* dará um pão a seu filho. O argumento também é usado do maior para o menor, por alguns. Por exemplo: Todos os homens são mortais, *a fortiori* Sócrates também deve ser mortal.

ÁFRICA

Um dos sete continentes. O nome não aparece na Bíblia, embora esta aluda a certas áreas que pertencem à moderna África.

1. *Antigas designações*. Os gregos chamavam esse continente de *Libya*, mas não sabemos o quanto eles conheciam da verdadeira extensão desse continente. Heródoto, no século V a.C., pensava que o mesmo estava cercado de água (*Hist*. iv.42).

2. *Antigo Testamento*. Israel preocupava-se muito com o Egito, e este fazia parte da África (ver o artigo sobre o *Egito*). Israel passou ali por muitas tribulações, mas permaneceu um terno sentimento pelo Egito, após o êxodo, pois, apesar de todas as desvantagens, o Egito fora a sua pátria. Há profecias que dizem que o Egito compartilhará com Israel do conhecimento e da adoração do Senhor (ver Isa. 19). Diversos outros povos africanos são mencionados no Antigo Testamento, como Lubim, Pute, Cuxe (Etiópia), cujas designações apontam para terras além do Egito. Há ali comentários sobre a pigmentação da pele e o tipo físico daqueles habitantes (ver Jer. 13:23; Isa. 45:14; e talvez Isa. 18:2,7). Esperava-se que os juízos divinos cairiam sobre tais povos, — e que Israel obtivesse eventualmente a supremacia sobre eles (ver Isa. 43:4; Eze. 30:4 ss ; Isa. 45:14). E também foi antecipado que tais povos terminariam recebendo os benefícios de Deus (Ver Sal. 87:4; 68:31). Alguns intérpretes pensam que a maldição de Cão (ver Gên. 9:25) foi o que fez os africanos tornarem-se negros, sujeitos à servidão a outros povos. Mas muitos eruditos modernos objetam a esse tipo de interpretação, que dá sanção bíblica aos preconceitos e aos abusos raciais.

3. *No Novo Testamento*. Jesus foi hospitaleiramente recebido na África (ver Mat. 2:13 ss.). Simão, que ajudou a transportar a cruz, era de Cirenaica, e seus filhos aparentemente eram discípulos cristãos bem conhecidos (Mar. 15:21). Judeus, egípcios e cirênios participaram do Pentecoste (ver Atos 2:10). O eloqüente Apolo era um judeu alexandrino (ver Atos. 18:24). Alguns dos obreiros no começo da missão entre os gentios eram convertidos cirênios (ver Atos 9:20 ss). A tradição afirma que Marcos foi missionário pioneiro em Alexandria (Eusébio, *HE*, ii.16). O evangelho entrou na África mediante o eunuco (ver Atos 8:26 ss). Algumas das mais fortes igrejas cristãs encontravam-se na África do Norte e no Egito, no fim do século II D.C. (GRO NE Z)

ÁGABA

Variante de Hagaba (I Esdras 5:30), uma fortaleza perto de Jerusalém que Galesto, seu governador, devolveu a Aristóbulo, filho de Alexandre Janeu. (Josefo *Ant*. xii.24). (S)

ÁGABO

O termo grego tem sentido incerto, embora possa significar *gafanhoto* ou *amor*. Foi um profeta do Novo Testamento, o qual, segundo uma tradição posterior, era um dos setenta discípulos (ver Luc. 10:1), e veio a ser um dos mártires cristãos. Juntamente com outros, ele veio da Judéia para Antioquia, estando Paulo e Barnabé ali. Ágabo anunciou uma fome que se aproximava, e que ocorreu no ano seguinte (44 D.C.). Tácito *Anais* xii.43; Suetônio *Cláudio* 18, Josefo, *Ant*. XX.ii.5, v.2. Essa predição fez a igreja de Antioquia reunir uma oferta de alívio para a igreja judaica (ver Atos 11:27,28). O «mundo inteiro» da profecia, naturalmente, significa o mundo daquela área, talvez confinada à Judéia. No templo de Cláudio houve quatro severas fomes locais, sendo possível que aquela sob consideração tenha ocorrido no seu quarto ano de governo, espraiando-se pela Palestina. A rainha de Adiabene comprou trigo do Egito, para aliviar a fome (ver Josefo, *Ant*. xx.2,6). Para alívio dos cristãos, foram feitas contribuições pela igreja de Antioquia. Paulo e Barnabé foram os portadores da oferta. Muitos anos depois, esse mesmo Ágabo encontrou Paulo em Cesaréia, e avisou-o sobre os sofrimentos que o esperavam, se ele continuasse viagem a Jerusalém (ver Atos 21:11-14). Isso efetivamente ocorreu, e Paulo começou sua viagem para Roma como prisioneiro. Esse acontecimento marcou o fim da terceira viagem missionária de Paulo.

Conhecimento prévio. Estudos têm demonstrado que todas as pessoas têm essa capacidade, em maior ou menor grau. Os sonhos incluem constantemente previsões sobre o futuro. Não precisa ser um sinal nem do Espírito Santo e nem do diabo, embora possa ser de um ou de outro. Um profeta religioso, entretanto,

AGAGITA — AGAPAO

essencialmente é um mestre dotado de forte mensagem, que ocasionalmente pode ter uma experiência pré-cognitiva para o bem da comunidade, ou, então, para seu próprio bem, embora não seja tal experiência que faça dele um profeta. Ver os artigos sobre *profeta* e *parapsicologia*. (ND S Z)

AGAGITA

Um termo usado em Ester 3:1 e 9:24 para descrever Hamã. Talvez se tratasse de um termo geral para indicar um inimigo, ou uma figura de linguagem: o que Agague (ver o artigo) fora para Saul, Hamã foi para Mordecai, isto é, um inimigo mortal. Josefo (*Ant*. xi.6,5) explica que era um sinônimo de Amaleque (ver também Esth. iii.1,10; viii.3,5). (S)

AGAGUE

No hebraico significa **chama**, embora outros prefiram o sentido de *alto* ou *guerreiro*. Nome de dois reis dos amalequitas (embora pudesse ser um título, como era o caso dos Faraós do Egito). Ver Núm. 24:7; I Sam. 15:8,9,20,32. Agague viveu em torno de 1020 A.C. 1. A primeira das referências dá a entender que o rei dos amalequitas era um grande monarca, e que o seu povo era mais importante do que comumente se supõe. Ver o artigo sobre os *amalequitas*. 2. As últimas referências dizem respeito ao rei amalequita cuja vida foi poupada por Saulo, contrariamente ao solene voto de total destruição, por causa de sua firme resistência à entrada de Israel na região (ver Êxo. 17:10; Núm. 14:45). Samuel, ouvindo que Agague fora poupado, ordenou que ele fosse trazido e o despedaçou. Isso foi um ato de vingança, porquanto fora dito: «Assim como a tua espada desfilhou mulheres, assim desfilhada ficará tua mãe entre as mulheres» (I Sam. 15:33). Aparentemente Agague adquirira uma notoriedade infame, em seu tratamento aos prisioneiros, incluindo aqueles de Israel. (N D S)

AGAPAO, relação com phileo

Ver João 21:15-17.

Sim, Senhor, tu sabes que te amo. É comum, entre os intérpretes, observarem aqui que dois vocábulos diferentes, no original grego, são usados para traduzir a palavra «amar». O Senhor usou o termo grego «agapao», nas duas primeiras indagações, e o vocábulo grego «fileo» na terceira inquirição. Pedro usou sempre o termo grego «fileo», em suas três respostas. Muito se tem explorado sobre essas diferenças verbais, segundo as seguintes citações nos indicam:

«No grego é *'agapas'*, amor profundo; usado com respeito ao amor divino (João 14:21), bem como sobre aquele amor exigido pela lei. No grego, o verbo 'fileo' significa 'ter simpatia'. Trata-se de um grau inferior de amor que *agapas*». (C.I. Scofield, Scofield Reference Bible, *in loc*.).

«Ele, 'Jesus' usa...a palavra que indica o amor mais elevado, intelectual, enquanto que Pedro replica com a declaração da afeição pessoal». (Ellicott, *in loc*.)

Essas citações bastam-nos para mostrar que tipos de distinção, entre essas duas palavras gregas — *agapao* e *fileo* — têm feito os intérpretes. Entretanto, e certamente de forma correta, outros intérpretes negam que haja a intenção de entendermos aqui qualquer diferença de sentido, porquanto tais palavras são meros sinônimos. Pois qualquer pessoa que se muna de uma concordância do N.T. grego e

acompanhe o uso dos termos *agapao* e *fileo*, logo se convencerá de que são palavras sinônimas, e que as diferenças expostas por alguns intérpretes, são artificiais. Por exemplo, em João 13:23, o amor de Jesus por João (o discípulo a quem o Senhor amava), é expresso pelo termo «agapao». Porém, em expressão quase exata em outro trecho, o amor de Jesus por João é expresso por *fileo* (ver João 20:2). Ver também João 11:3,5,36. Nessas citações, que se referem ao amor de Jesus por Lázaro, Marta e Maria, as duas palavras são usadas alternadamente. Na realidade, na passagem que ora comentamos, essa alternância pode ser também observada, porquanto no versículo décimo sétimo, o Senhor Jesus usou *fileo*, e não *agapao*, como fizera nas duas indagações anteriores. É altamente improvável, pois, que o autor sagrado, ao registrar a presente secção, estivesse pensando em estabelecer qualquer diferença de sentido, ao usar essas duas palavras.

Confirmando a veracidade da interpretação exposta no parágrafo acima, Wilbert F. Howard (*in loc*.), tem o seguinte a dizer: «Não há necessidade alguma em se fazer *distinção* entre as duas palavras que indicam 'amar', nestes versículos, posto que 'agapao' e 'fileo' são usadas alternadamente neste mesmo evangelho, até mesmo em um só contexto...O maneirismo joanino, que alternava sinônimos gregos, em seus escritos, mostra não ser um sábio basearmos quaisquer sutilezas exegéticas sobre palavras diferentes usadas para 'apascenta' (boskein) e 'pastoreia' (poimainein), ou mesmo para 'cordeiros' e 'ovelhas'. Por conseguinte, essa regra também se aplica às duas palavras diferentes usadas para indicar 'amar'».

No que diz respeito ao verbo *fileo*, como se este indicasse um amor de qualidade inferior, segundo alguns intérpretes afirmam, fica provado que essa é uma idéia totalmente *falsa* quando se acompanha o seu uso nas páginas de N.T. Por exemplo, neste mesmo evangelho de João (5:20), *fileo* é empregado para indicar o amor do Pai pelo Filho. Diríamos, pois, que Deus Pai «tem simpatia» pelo Filho? Em João 16:27 a palavra é empregada para indicar o amor do Pai pelos discípulos de Jesus, bem como para indicar o amor dos discípulos por Jesus. No trecho de Tito 3:15, o termo é usado para indicar o amor dos santos pelo apóstolo Paulo. Essa palavra — *fileo* — é usada por vinte e cinco vezes no N.T., não há nessas ocorrências nenhuma evidência em favor da teoria de que ela pode ser distinguida em seu sentido do verbo *agapao*, como se houvesse qualquer inferioridade daquela em relação a esta última.

Agapao é, dentre esses dois vocábulos, o mais usado no N.T., onde figura por nada menos de cento e quarenta e duas vezes em sua forma verbal e por cento e dezesseis vezes, em sua forma substantivada. Seus usos são extremamente diversos, e a própria palavra pode indicar a esfera inteira das afeições humanas, da afeição divina, da afeição dos seres humanos uns pelos outros, da afeição a Deus como ser divino, ou mesmo da afeição por objetos físicos. Em suma, *agapao* era usada no grego *koiné* mais ou menos do modo livre como empregamos modernamente a palavra *amor*, com uma grande multiplicidade de sentidos.

Por conseguinte, o argumento contra as sutilezas exegéticas que pretendem estabelecer distinções na passagem que ora comentamos, por causa de duas palavras diferentes que aqui foram usadas, para indicar *amor*, é conclusivo, podendo ser sumariado como segue:

1. O uso antigo e o desenvolvimento do vocábulo *agapao* (isto é, no grego clássico), não consubstancia a

AGAPAO — AGAPE

idéia de que essa palavra seja diferente, em grau ou em categoria, do termo *fileo*; porquanto, no grego clássico, embora *fileo* ocorresse com maior freqüência, não diferia em sentido da outra palavra. Eram meros sinônimos.

2. Esse uso das duas palavras, como sinônimos, passou de modo completo para as páginas do N.T., apesar de que, no grego helenístico, ou, pelo menos no grego *koiné* utilizado no N.T., *agapao* fosse a palavra mais freqüentemente usada.

3. Ambos esses vocábulos podem expressar *todas as formas* de emoção, desde o «ter simpatia» até ao amor mais intenso.

4. O autor do quarto evangelho tendia a usar *livremente* palavras sinônimas, até mesmo numa única passagem, sem que com isso quisesse dar a entender qualquer diferença de sentido.

5. O propósito inteiro dessa seção, — que é o de demonstrar a restauração de Simão Pedro ao ofício apostólico, e, por conseguinte, a sua autoridade autêntica na igreja cristã, labora *contra* a idéia de que este texto apresenta-o como alguém que, por enquanto, tinha ainda apenas *simpatia* por Jesus, isto é, votava-lhe um afeto que, de alguma maneira, era inferior àquele que o Senhor dele esperava. Pois, nesse caso, bem poderíamos supor que Pedro não fora ainda plenamente restaurado pelo Senhor Jesus. No entanto, o autor sagrado procurava demonstrar justamente o oposto.

6. Se realmente houvesse o intuito de estabelecer uma distinção entre esses dois vocábulos, o autor sagrado dificilmente teria dito que Pedro *entristeceu-se* (ver o vs. 17), quando Jesus persistiu em suas perguntas, o que poderia indicar uma dúvida concernente à qualidade de seu amor pelo Senhor, posto ter Pedro usado uma palavra inferior para indicar *amor*, que de algum modo mostrava que esse afeto era menor que aquele que Jesus esperava de sua parte. Nesse caso, dificilmente Pedro poderia ter-se entristecido ante a pergunta insistente de Jesus. A tristeza de Pedro, bem pelo contrário, mostra que, ante a persistência de Jesus, ele usava o termo que expressava o máximo amor que ele conhecia, que envolvia tudo quanto Pedro pensava que Jesus requeria dele.

7. Finalmente, devemos observar que Jesus e Pedro não conversavam em grego (idioma em que na narrativa do episódio, foram usadas as palavras «agapao» e «fileo»), e, sim, em *aramaico*, onde tal distinção não existia. Portanto, não foram usadas palavras diferentes por Pedro e Jesus, no tocante ao «amor». Mas o autor sagrado, ao narrar o caso em grego, por força de *hábito estilístico*, empregou duas palavras sinônimas, não tencionando dar a entender que o Senhor Jesus exigia uma afeição mais elevada que o amor que Pedro lhe oferecia. (A I IB NTI RO)

AGAPE

Vem do grego **agapao**, amar; ou de **agape**, amor.

1. Usado para designar uma «festa de amor», uma refeição comum para promover a fraternidade cristã, associada à antiga prática, à Ceia do Senhor do protestantismo e à eucaristia do catolicismo romano. Comemora o sacrifício de amor realizado por Cristo e a intensa expectação por Seu retorno.

Há decisivas indicações no Novo Testamento de que o «agape» consistia em uma refeição completa, tomada antes do partir do pão e do beber do vinho. (Ver Atos 2:42-47; 20:6-12; I Cor. 11:17-34). Paulo descreve abusos de glutonaria e excesso de vinho, ou

de negligência quanto aos pobres, enquanto os membros abastados da igreja se empanturravam. Tais abusos levaram à recomendação de que a refeição fosse evitada, com a passagem do tempo; e também que cada pessoa deveria tomar a sua própria refeição em casa. Essa tornou-se a regra na prática da Igreja posterior. Na maioria das denominações, a participação no pão e no vinho, em pequenas doses, passou a representar o holocausto de Cristo e a expectativa por Seu retorno. Pelos fins do século VII D.C., parece haver cessado, quase universalmente, qualquer refeição separada associada à eucaristia.

História. Alguns procuram achar a origem dessa festa nas guildas pagãs, ou nas refeições comuns dos judeus. Mas outros vêem nela um reflexo do incidente no lago de Tiberíades, onde Jesus compartilhou de Seu quebra-jejum com sete de Seus discípulos (João 21). Essa interpretação é favorecida pelo fato de que algumas pinturas, encontradas nas catacumbas, mostram grupos de sete pessoas participando de uma refeição comum. Porém, parece melhor supormos que a refeição estava ligada à páscoa, pois Jesus e Seus discípulos estavam envolvidos, quando da primeira «Ceia do Senhor». Jesus ordenou que nos amássemos mutuamente (*agape*) por ocasião da Ceia, pelo que é próprio que a idéia de comunhão e companheirismo seja vinculada à Ceia do Senhor.

A refeição original era efetuada à noitinha, tencionando promover a fraternidade e beneficiar os pobres. Pelo segundo século de nossa era, foi distinguida da eucaristia, tendo persistido até hoje como evento separado. Aparentemente Judas 12 reflete essa situação. Posteriormente, no que toca ao pão e ao vinho, cada pessoa recebia o pão abençoado das mãos do oficial residente (chamado então eulogia, e não eucaristia), e cada qual tomava e abençoava o cálice de vinho. Esses elementos foram tomados por empréstimo dos costumes judaicos. Após a oficialização do cristianismo por Roma, em 313 D.C., a festa de amor começou a perder seu caráter religioso em muitos lugares, até ser suspensa pela Igreja.

Inácio, *ad Smyrnaeos* viii.2. refere-se ao *agape*, como também o faz o *Didache* x. 1; xi.9, onde é sugerido que a refeição antecedia à eucaristia. Nos dias de Tertuliano (*Apol.* xxxix; *De Jejuniis* xvii; *De Corona Militis* iii), a festa era celebrada distintamente — da eucaristia —. É possível que Plínio tenha aludido a esse arranjo, em *Epp. x.96. Clemente* de Alexandria (Paedagogus ii.1 e *Stromata* iii.2) e Crisóstomo (*Hom.* xxvii sobre I Cor. 11:17), mencionam os dois aspectos como distintos. Crisóstomo descreve a festa de amor como «lindíssimo e benéfico hábito», porquanto favorecia o amor, era um alívio para os pobres e um disciplinamento de humildade. Festas de amor eram efetuadas nas prisões, em tempos de perseguição, — nas festas de casamento e em outros eventos significativos (Gregório Nazianzeno, *Epçp.* i.14).

Porém, a prática caiu sob abusos durante e após o século IV D.C. Agostinho menciona abusos (Confissões vi.2). Os cânones 26 e 27 do concílio de Laodicéia (363) tentaram corrigir os abusos. O terceiro concílio de Cartago (393) e o segundo concílio de Orleãs (541) proibiram banquete na Igreja. Isso se radicalizou de tal modo que o concílio de Trullan, em 692, ameaçou excomungar aqueles que efetuassem festas de amor. Depois disso, o rito desapareceu quase inteiramente, a única exceção aparecendo na Igreja oriental. Ali, persiste até os nossos dias. Tem reaparecido em algumas denominações, aqui ou acolá, no mundo ocidental. Os «quebra-jejuns paroquianos», após a

AGAR — AGEU

participação na eucaristia em algumas igrejas, têm restaurado os elementos essenciais do *agape*.

2. A palavra *Agape* vem de *agapao*. No grego clássico significava acolher, entreter, gostar de, amar, contentar-se com. «Agape» fala de «amor». O termo figura no Novo Testamento grego por 116 vezes, com a idéia de «amor», «caridade», «querido» e «festa de amor». A forma verbal aparece por 142 vezes no Novo Testamento, dando a entender «amar» ou «ser amado».

Fileo é um sinônimo grego. A tentativa de aplicar o *agape* ao amor divino e o *fileo* ao amor humano, fracassa totalmente, quando se acompanha esses vocábulos em uma boa concordância. Por toda parte são usados como sinônimos. Em João 21, onde as duas palavras são usadas, os pregadores têm procurado estabelecer distinção entre elas, por motivos puramente homiléticos, mas a passagem de uma para outra é apenas uma variação estilística da parte do autor sagrado. O amor divino também é descrito por *fileo*.

Eros também significa *amor, desejo*; e o amor religioso também pode ser indicado por essa palavra. Contudo, com freqüência está associada ao amor apaixonado. Eros era o deus do amor. Essa palavra nunca aparece no Novo Testamento.

No *eros*, o homem busca satisfação. No *agape*, Deus busca o homem, e vice-versa. O *agape* ama aos que erram, aos que não merecem amor, aos inimigos. O *eros* busca a auto-satisfação. O *agape* é a virtude suprema, pois o amor é a base de todas as virtudes (Gál. 5:22), a prova da espiritualidade (I João 4:7). Essa é a única qualidade moral que é usada como título do próprio Deus (I João 4:8). (A AM B C E FO K S Z) Ver os artigos *eucaristia* e *amor*.

AGAR — Ver **Hagar**

AGARENES

Em Bar. 3:23, uma forma de **Hagar**.

ÁGATA

No hebraico, o sentido é desconhecido. Na Sept. temos *achates*, na Vulgata Latina, *achates* pedra preciosa e ornamental, usada entre outras no peitoral do sumo sacerdote (ver Exo. 28:19; 29:12). Era uma variedade da calcedônia, similar ao jaspe. Sílica muito refinada (dióxido de sílica), com camadas distintas e alternadas principalmente de branco, azul e marrom claro. A maioria das ágatas ocorrem em cavidades nas lavas antigas, podendo ser encontradas em muitos países. As camadas sucessivas são mais ou menos paralelas às paredes da cavidade, resultantes da reação da gelatina de sílica, coagulada com água, levando sílica em solução, e reagindo com a rocha ferrosa adjacente. A formação pode assumir muitas combinações diversas, dando à pedra uma variedade quase infinita, o que explica sua grande beleza. Os trechos bíblicos onde a pedra é mencionada mostram que ela era usada para gravação. Muitas ágatas antigas gravadas podem ser encontradas em museus e coleções. (Ver Êxo. 28:19; Isa. 54:12; Eze. 26:17). As duas últimas referências envolvem um termo hebraico diferente da primeira. Talvez se trate de uma pedra diferente, possivelmente o rubi. (S UN Z)

AGÉ

No hebraico significa **fugitivo**. Era pai de Samá, um dos homens poderosos de Davi (ver II Sam. 23:11). Era hararita. (Z)

AGEU

Declaração introdutória.

O primeiro livro profético de tempos pós-exílicos foi o de Ageu, que registra quatro discursos dirigidos aos judeus que retornaram do exílio a Jerusalém, entre agosto e dezembro de 520 A.C. A comunidade, com dezoito anos de existência, estava desencorajada devido ao fracasso nas colheitas, à seca e à hostilidade das populações vizinhas, ao ponto que já se dispunha a retornar à Babilônia. Ageu repreendeu-os por terem deixado o templo semidestruído. Após terem iniciado uma pequena estrutura, Ageu falou novamente, convocando o povo para construir um edifício ainda mais glorioso que o de Salomão. Ele também queria restaurar a monarquia, tendo Zorobabel como monarca. Ageu foi diferente dos outros profetas reformadores de antes do exílio, por ser mais sacerdotal em caráter, salientando a adoração no templo e os rituais, como a chave a uma maior prosperidade.

Ageu foi um daqueles chamados de doze profetas menores, e o primeiro dentre os três que profetizaram após o retorno dos judeus do cativeiro babilônico (ver o artigo a respeito). Esses profetas são chamados *menores* não por haverem sido menos importantes do que os profetas *maiores*, mas apenas porque os volumes que escreveram são *menos volumosos*.

Esboço do conteúdo

1. Autor
2. Pano de fundo do livro
3. Data
4. Lugar de origem
5. Destino
6. Propósito
7. Canonicidade
8. Texto
9. Unidade
10. Conteúdo
11. Perspectiva teológica

1. Autor

A palavra **Ageu** parece ter-se derivado do termo hebraico que significa *festividade*, provavelmente porque seu nascimento coincidiu com uma das festas judaicas ou festividades (ver o artigo a respeito). Coisa alguma nos é informada sobre seu passado, família, genealogia, etc. Desconhecemos totalmente o lugar de seu nascimento, a época de seu nascimento, e até mesmo os principais acontecimentos de sua vida. Mas sabemos que ele começou a profetizar no segundo ano de Dario Histaspes (ver Ageu 1:1), e, juntamente com o profeta Zacarias, salientou fortemente a reiniciação da construção do templo, tendo obtido a permissão e a assistência do rei (ver Eze. 5:1 e 6:14). O povo judeu, animado por esses líderes, completou a construção no sexto ano do reinado de Dario I (520 A.C.). Podemos inferir pelas circunstâncias que Ageu era homem dotado de elevados propósitos, que exercia grande influência e era dotado de profunda espiritualidade. Presumivelmente, foi um dos exilados que retornaram a Jerusalém, embora isso não seja dito em parte alguma da Bíblia.

2. Pano de fundo do livro

A declaração introdutória fornece essa informação.

3. Data

É possível determinarmos precisamente a data

AGEU

desse livro, porque as profecias teriam ocorrido durante o reinado de Dario I (522-486 A.C.). A primeira ocorreu no primeiro dia do sexto mês, no começo da atividade profética de Ageu, a saber, em agosto e setembro de 520 A.C. Então, a sua quarta profecia, sucedeu no nono dia do quarto mês, isto é, novembro e dezembro de 520 A.C., imediatamente depois que Zacarias deu início ao seu ministério.

4. Lugar de origem
Os exilados retornaram da Babilônia e estabelece-ram-se na área de Jerusalém. As profecias estão associadas ao lugar do templo arruinado. Isso significa que a própria cidade de Jerusalém, ou algum lugar das proximidades, foi o lugar onde o livro foi escrito.

5. Destino
Está em questão uma área muito restrita. Em primeiro lugar, houve o encorajamento para recons-truir o templo (ver 2:1-9). Os sacerdotes foram incluídos no terceiro discurso. O encorajamento dado a Zorobabel, governador civil da Judéia, no quarto oráculo (2:20-23), alude à mesma localização geral. Todas as referências, pois, apresentam a Judéia e, especificamente, Jerusalém, como os lugares para onde as mensagens foram enviadas.

6. Propósito
O alvo era o de encorajar os desanimados repatriados a reconstruírem o templo, restabelecendo a autoridade civil e religiosa da nação, e reconhecendo a vida comunitária, após o padrão do estado judaico original. Israel não tinha por intuito ser apenas um ajuntamento de pessoas em certo lugar, para então surgir um governante que organizasse as coisas. Antes, Israel deveria ser uma teocracia e uma fraternidade, com propósito e serviço espirituais. Não bastava os israelitas serem libertados do cativeiro. A restauração geral de Israel, em todos os seus aspectos, era algo necessário. Deus os escolhera como um povo, e deles era exigido que correspondessem a essa responsabilidade.

7. Canonicidade
Esse livro foi o primeiro dos três livros proféticos pós-exílicos (Ageu, Zacarias e Malaquias). Todos esses livros tratam da questão da restauração de Israel, após o cativeiro babilônico. Desde o começo, Ageu foi um livro aceito, tendo sido contado entre os doze profetas menores. Esdras atestou a validade e a importância da profecia de Ageu (ver Esd. 5:1 e 6:14), o que sem dúvida aumentou o prestígio do livro entre o povo. Na maioria dos antigos catálogos, Ageu não é mencionado por nome, mas sempre houve a referência aos doze profetas menores, que necessaria-mente incluíam o seu livro. Nos tempos do N.T., temos a citação em Heb. 12:26. (ver Ageu 2:6-8,22). Josefo chamou Ageu e Zacarias (ver *Anti*. xi.4,5, par. 557) de «os profetas». Ver o artigo geral sobre o «Cânon, Antigo Testamento».

8. Texto
De modo geral, o texto do livro está em boa ordem, como se dá com o texto massorético em geral. Ver o artigo sobre a Massora. Entretanto, há algumas corrupções em Ageu 1:7,9,10,12; 2:6,15,17. Há uma possível deslocação de texto, em Ageu 2:15-18. A Septuaginta tem uma adição em Ageu 2:9, que ajuda a reconstituir o texto hebraico.

9. Unidade
Alguns estudiosos têm dividido o livro em duas partes, escritas por dois autores distintos. Em primeiro lugar, há uma porção narrativa, não-proféti-ca; em segundo lugar, há os oráculos. O primeiro escritor poderia ter incorporado as profecias do

segundo em seu livro. O fato de que as profecias foram redigidas na terceira pessoa talvez dê apoio a essa teoria. Por que o profeta não usou o «eu», ao entregar suas próprias profecias? O autor diz «o profeta Ageu», ao referir-se às profecias dadas, como se estivesse designando uma pessoa distinta de si mesma. (Ver Ageu 1:1 e 2:1,10). O autor evidente-mente estava bem familiarizado com os eventos profetizados, mas isso poderia mostrar apenas que ele era um contemporâneo, e não que ele mesmo foi quem recebera as profecias. Portanto, ele pode ter sido o porta-voz da mensagem, embora não o autor da mesma. Outrossim, as profecias são resumos extre-mamente reticentes, e não extensas profecias, o que poderia apontar para o trabalho de um redator ou editor. Não há como solucionar a questão com qualquer grau de certeza; mas ela não se reveste de qualquer importância real. Se um autor qualquer incorporou fielmente os oráculos de um profeta em sua obra, o resultado poderia ser corretamente chamado pelo nome do profeta, e seria uma profecia genuína do mesmo.

10. Conteúdo
A. **Ageu 1:1-11. Sexto mês, primeiro dia. Primeiro** oráculo. É mencionada a negligência do povo. Eles não haviam construído o templo, (ver Esd. 3:4), enquanto concentravam seus esforços em suas próprias residências (ver Ageu 1:4). Os desastres por eles sofridos, a seca e a ausência de colheita eram lembretes de Deus de que eles deveriam pôr em primeiro lugar as coisas principais.

b. **Ageu 2:1-9. Sétimo mês, vigésimo primeiro dia.** O futuro templo seria maior que o de Salomão. Os próprios gentios contribuiriam para torná-lo assim. A profecia talvez inclua o templo de Herodes, que foi maior que o de Salomão; e espiritualmente falando, poderia referir-se ao novo templo formado por judeus e gentios, encarnado na Igreja, na era do evangelho (ver Efé. 2:17-22). Seja como for, o futuro referente ao templo e ao seu sentido espiritual é grande, e isso deveria encorajar-nos a fazer investimentos nessa realização.

c. **Ageu 2:10-19. Nono mês, vigésimo quarto dia.** A lei ritual nos fornece uma lição. Se um homem estivesse transportando a carne dos sacrifícios e se suas roupas tocassem em algo, a coisa tocada nem por isso tornar-se-ia santa. Mas as vestes de um homem que estivesse ritualmente impuro, contaminariam tudo aquilo em que elas tocassem. Portanto, a imundícia contamina. As ruínas do templo eram imundas, e contaminavam a nação judaica. Somente se o novo templo substituísse o antigo, mediante reconstrução, a nação poderia ficar isenta da imundícia que lhes servia de obstáculo e atraía contra eles o juízo divino. Finalmente, o reavivamento resultou no lançamento de um novo alicerce (ver Esd. 3:10), em 536 A.C. E isso foi feito segundo a filosofia do profeta.

d. **Ageu 2:20-23. Nono mês, vigésimo quarto dia.** Aparece uma promessa, feita a Zorobabel, de que ele seria mantido em segurança, a despeito das perturbações que agitavam o império persa.

11. Perspectiva teológica
a. A prosperidade material não serve de sinal seguro de prosperidade espiritual; mas, quando se põem as coisas principais em primeiro lugar (primeiro as coisas espirituais, e só então as materiais), isso resulta em bênçãos de todas as modalidades. Isso se coaduna à mensagem de Jesus em Mateus 6:33 (ver Ageu 1:1-11).

b. Os reveses na vida de um crente podem ser devidos a questões espirituais às quais não atende-

75

AGGIORNAMENTO — AGNOSTICISMO

mos. (Ver Ageu 1:6 ss.).

c. O ritual é importante, se dele participarmos com a correta atitude espiritual. Dentro do contexto judaico, essa é uma questão importante, porque ali o ritual continuava sendo um importante indicador do destaque que se dava às questões religiosas (ver Ageu 2:12 ss.).

d. Em seu terceiro oráculo, o profeta salientou quão penetrante é o mal, ainda mais que o bem. Por esse motivo, deve ser evitado (ver Ageu 2:12 ss.).

e. Se um homem recebe de Deus uma missão, o Senhor cuidará para que ele seja protegido, até cumprir a sua missão, o que não é um pequeno consolo (ver Ageu 2:21 ss). (G I IB ID)

AGGIORNAMENTO

Palavra italiana que significa «adiamento» ou «atualização». As obras teológicas modernas, em suas discussões, usam-na com o sentido de «atualização». O Papa João XXIII usou a palavra ao expressar seu desejo de modernizar a Igreja Católica Romana. Não se deve confundir esse termo com «modernismo» (ver artigo a respeito). (C)

AGNI

Palavra sânscrita que significa «fogo». Um dos deuses mais importantes dos Vedas. Agni era deus do fogo do altar, representado pela trindade terrestre do fogo, do relâmpago e do sol. Era um deus-sacerdote, visto que as oferendas eram feitas aos deuses por meio do fogo. Também tinha funções éticas, como perdoador e castigador de pecados. Ver o artigo sobre *Deuses do fogo*. (E P)

AGNOETAE

Termo grego que significa **não-onisciente**. O nome foi aplicado a uma seita do século IV D.C., que negava a onisciência de Deus, dizendo que Ele não se lembrava do passado sem refletir, e que tinha conhecimento incerto quanto ao futuro. O líder deles foi Teofrônio de Capadócia. Uma outra seita, do século VI D.C., intitulada de monofisitas, asseverava o mesmo no tocante ao espírito humano e a Cristo. Também eram chamados temistianos, por causa do diácono Temisto, que adotou essa posição. Alguns, mesmo em tempos modernos, aceitam esse conceito no tocante a Deus, a fim de preservarem a noção do livre-arbítrio humano. Para alguns, a presciência de Deus anula a liberdade humana. Ver os artigos sobre a *presciência*, o *livre-arbítrio* e o *determinismo*. Se Deus prevê que o homem agirá livremente, então o homem assim o fará. Esse contraconceito remove o problema, do ponto de vista filosófico. (E)

AGNOSTICISMO

Vem do grego **a** (não) e **ginosko** (conhecer). O vocábulo foi cunhado por T.H. Huxley (1869), para exprimir a idéia de «crença suspensa», ou seja, o indivíduo nem crê, nem deixa de crer. Huyley usou a palavra para aplicá-la a qualquer proposição para a qual não há provas suficientes para ser crida. Entretanto, o termo é mais freqüentemente aplicado à crença sobre Deus. Nesse contexto, o agnóstico não nega que existam evidências pró ou contra Deus; porém afirma que as evidências, positivas ou negativas, não são suficientes para provar ou negar a existência de Deus. O *ateísmo* diz que existem provas negativas da existência de Deus, pelo que poderíamos ter certeza de que Ele não existe. O agnosticismo diz que há provas, negativas e positivas, embora inconclusivas. O positivismo lógico declara que não há provas negativas ou positivas, porque a questão toda está acima de nosso conhecimento, o qual só pode envolver coisas detectadas pela percepção dos sentidos, e não possuímos órgãos capazes de detectar Deus. Portanto, o ateísmo e o agnosticismo afirmam que tal conhecimento é possível, mas o positivismo lógico nega a possibilidade de tal conhecimento. Por sua vez, o teísmo afirma que o conhecimento de Deus é possível e que as evidências são positivas. Deus existe.

Raízes filosóficas. O agnosticismo tem raízes nos filósofos céticos pré-socráticos, nos sofistas, que eram oponentes de Sócrates e de Platão (450A.C.), e sobretudo nos filósofos Pirro (300-270 A.C.) e Sexto Empírico (século III D.C.). Esses filósofos levantaram questões que os modernos agnósticos têm utilizado e desenvolvido. Quanto a notas completas sobre as idéias acerca de Deus, ver o artigo *Deus, idéias concernentes a*. Ali também oferecemos as provas filosóficas da existência de Deus, sob o título *Deus, provas de Sua existência*.

O agnosticismo opõe-se tanto ao teísmo como ao ateísmo. Alguns agnósticos supõem que é impossível a obtenção de provas da existência de Deus, e que sempre será assim. Outros supõem que algum dia poderão surgir evidências nesse sentido, que até hoje não dispomos. As razões para a suspensão da fé são as seguintes: 1. O intelecto humano é incapaz de manusear problemas dessa dimensão, ou seja, sofre de uma fraqueza inerente. 2. As evidências poderiam produzir tal crença, e o homem poderia ser capaz da mesma. Mas o homem ainda não dispõe dos meios e do acúmulo de provas necessárias. Kant desenvolveu o conceito da razão limitada, em sua *Crítica da Razão Pura*. Argumentava ele que o conhecimento é limitado à percepção dos sentidos, e, como é óbvio, Deus está fora do alcance de nossa percepção. Assim, Deus pode existir ou não. Nossos sentidos simplesmente são incapazes de detectá-lO. Os agnósticos do século XIX, como J.S. Mill e Leslie Stephen, aceitaram o raciocínio de Kant como válido, mas também supunham que as investigações científicas mostram a natureza precária da teologia em geral, e das provas da existência de Deus, em particular. Se o único conhecimento que podemos adquirir vem por meio dos laboratórios, então é improvável que cheguemos a afirmar a existência de Deus, a qual não está sujeita às pesquisas de laboratório.

O agnosticismo também tem sido favorecido por processos usados no seio da própria Igreja, onde os ensinos bíblicos são aceitos sem qualquer crítica — método sujeitado a ataques. Kant exerceu grande influência em certos grupos protestantes, e os teólogos começaram a basear conceitos religiosos sobre a fé e não sobre a razão ou sobre provas empíricas. O catolicismo ortodoxo continua a crer que a razão natural e as evidências empíricas na natureza podem consubstanciar evidências da existência de Deus, sem ou com a revelação. De fato, isso faz parte do dogma católico tradicional, visto que Tomás de Aquino expôs argumentos cosmológicos, etiológicos, teleológicos e contingentes em favor de provas racionais e empíricas da existência de Deus. Os documentos cristãos partem do pressuposto que Deus pode ser conhecido através da razão (Rom. 1:20), embora, não tentem qualquer prova formal. Ver Sabedoria 13, quanto a uma antiga declaração, bem como DS 2853, 3004, 3026 e 3475, dentro da teologia católica.

AGNUS DEI — AGORÁ

Argumentos contrários:

1. *Filósoficos.* Há muitos argumentos racionais e filosóficos em prol da existência de Deus, não baseados na percepção dos sentidos, válidos inteiramente à parte das investigações científicas. Ver o artigo sobre *Deus, provas de Sua existência*, e as notas em Rom. 1:20, no NTI, quanto ao desenvolvimento dessa tese. Devemos notar que um de nossos melhores argumentos positivos é o argumento moral de Kant, que ele extraiu da razão. Assim, o que Kant derrubou em sua *Crítica da Razão Pura*, restaurou em sua *Crítica da Razão Prática*.

2. *Científicos.* Quanto mais se desenvolve a ciência, mais evidente se torna que há um fantástico desígnio em todos os aspectos da existência. De fato, nada há de mais comum em toda a natureza do que suas evidências de desígnio. Ora, se há desígnio, então há um Planejador. Estamos falando aqui sobre o argumento *teleológico* em prol da existência de Deus, incluído no artigo acima mencionado. Alguns cientistas são teístas, não por motivos religiosos, mas por motivos científicos.

A *parapsicologia* (ver o artigo), uma novel e crescente ciência, serve de impressionante e compelidora evidência da existência da alma. Ora, se alma e espírito existem, não é preciso um grande salto de fé para supormos que há um Criador de espíritos.

A experiência humana da morte, investigada pelos cientistas, tem demonstrado que não há perda da consciência no processo da morte. Essas experiências são chamadas (experiências próximas da morte) EPM, ou «retorno após a morte clínica». Em outras palavras, uma pessoa, segundo todos os testes clinicamente aplicados, está morta; mas, durante esse tempo, antes de seu retorno ao corpo físico, não há perda da consciência, e muitas experiências notáveis têm lugar. Se isso é verdade, e se o homem é um ser espiritual, conforme sempre afirmaram a filosofia e a teologia, então não é necessário nenhum grande salto de fé para postular a existência do Criador das almas.

3. *Místicos.* A base de toda a fé religiosa é o *misticismo* (ver o artigo). Isto é, é possível o contato com um Ser ou seres espirituais, mais elevados do que nós. Qualquer contato dessa ordem, como no ministério do Espírito Santo, os dons do Espírito, as visões, as revelações, os sonhos, etc., são experiências místicas em sua definição mais fundamental. Apesar de haver falsas experiências místicas, como é óbvio, e de que algumas delas são inexatas quanto àquilo que transmitem, ao passo que outras são simples alucinações, há um âmago de experiências místicas sobre o qual se alicerça toda a religião; mediante esse âmago verdadeiro, são continuamente transmitidas certas verdades básicas e universais. Duas dessas comunicações principais são que a alma existe e Deus existe, embora pouco saibamos sobre a natureza de uma ou de outra.

Não se reivindica, em qualquer sentido significativo, que Deus possa ser conhecido em Sua natureza. Quando muito, sabemos coisas acerca de Suas obras. A Bíblia declara que Deus não pode ser conhecido, no tocante à Sua augusta natureza (Rom. 11:33; I Tim. 6:16). Os teólogos católicos romanos, ao defenderem a tese de que Deus pode ser conhecido por meios racionais e empíricos, admitem isso (D 254, 428, 1782). Porém, podemos saber que Ele existe, e podemos saber algo sobre Ele mesmo, itens extremamente importantes de conhecimento para a vida de qualquer pessoa. Tal conhecimento pode ter várias origens, conforme foi sugerido acima. Ver o artigo sobre o *ceticismo*, posição aparentada do agnosticismo. (AM B C D DS E F MM P R SA)

AGNUS DEI

Significa «Cordeiro de Deus», simbolizando Jesus em Sua missão expiatória (João 1:29). Esse trecho tornou-se parte da invocação litúrgica: «Ó Cordeiro de Deus, que tira os pecados do mundo, tem misericórdia de nós», usada por ocasião da missa (ver o artigo), ou durante a Santa Comunhão. (E)

AGONIA

O termo grego **agonia** geralmente denotava uma *luta* ou *competição*, como se via nos jogos atléticos, embora também indicasse qualquer tipo de luta, angústia, agonia. No Novo Testamento, é usado somente para indicar a agonia de Jesus no jardim do Getsêmani (ver Luc. 22:44). As passagens paralelas nos fornecem maiores detalhes, embora não usem a palavra específica. (Ver Mat. 26:36-46; Mar. 14:32,42 e Heb. 5:7,8). Os evangelistas, ao usarem o vocábulo, tencionavam mostrar a intensidade da luta de Jesus. O pedido específico de Jesus foi que o *cálice* de sofrimento fosse removido, qualificando com isso o desejo expresso de que fosse feita a vontade do Pai. Esse cálice tem sido variegadamente interpretado como o sofrimento físico, como o sofrimento mental e espiritual, como a situação de Jesus, como portador de nosso pecado, envolvendo agonia espiritual. Talvez devêssemos pensar na situação como um todo, incluindo todas essas particularidades. Ver o NTI em Mat. 26:36-46, quanto a completos detalhes.

Implicações teológicas. Os teólogos têm visto corretamente na questão uma prova da humanidade de Jesus, um instrumento para combater todas as variedades de *docetismo* (ver o artigo a respeito), as negações da verdadeira humanidade de Jesus. Ver o artigo sobre *a humanidade de Cristo*. É curioso que o evangelho de João, que tão fortemente enfatiza a divindade de Cristo, tenha omitido essa cena, pois o autor sagrado sem dúvida sentia que tal pormenor debilitaria o seu propósito. Em contraste, o autor da epístola aos Hebreus mostra que os sofrimentos de Jesus foram parcialmente responsáveis por seu «aperfeiçoamento», de acordo com o que aprendeu na obediência, tornando-se um homem perfeito. O mistério do Cristo divino-humano é precisamente *isso*, um *mistério*. Porém, não solucionaremos a questão ignorando um dos lados da questão. A teologia não visa explicar todas as coisas. Caso contrário, teríamos uma teologia bem fraca, teríamos uma «explicação de crenças humanas», e não um «estudo do Ser divino». Os sistemas que buscam harmonia a qualquer preço reduzem a teologia a uma mera pesquisa do humano. Exigindo harmonia e conforto mental, podemos desferir um golpe mortal na própria teologia. (Ver NTI em Heb. 5,7,8). (A NTI S W)

AGORÁ

No grego significa **mercado, local de reuniões**, ou a própria *assembléia*. Em Atenas, o *agorá* era o centro da vida da cidade, um mercado; mas também um local de reuniões públicas. Tal como em outras cidades gregas, era o centro da vida comercial, judicial e religiosa. Normalmente era adornada com templos, estátuas, edifícios públicos, jardins; e geralmente tinha a forma de um quadrado. Muitas descobertas arqueológicas têm sido feitas no *agorá* de Atenas, efetuadas pela American School of Classical Studies, entre 1930 e 1964. Têm sido encontrados o *Tholos*, onde eram guardados os pesos e as medidas

AGORAIOS — AGOSTINIANISMO

padrões; o *Metroon*, ou depósito de arquivos; o *Bouleuterion*, ou câmara do conselho; um templo de Apolo; o templo de Hefaísto, deus da metalurgia; urnas micenas do século XIV A.C.; e muita ostraca, vasos e jóias. Paulo conhecia os *agorá* de várias cidades gregas, além daquele de Atenas. No grego era *agorá* e no latim era *forum*. No Novo Testamento, a palavra aparece em Mat. 11:16; 23:7; Mar. 6:56; 7:4; 12:38; Luc. 11:43; 20:46; Atos 16:19 e 17:17. (A FO OS SM UN)

AGORAIOS

No grego, **pertencente ao agorá** (mercado, forum). Em Atos 19:38, é aplicado aos dias onde eram efetuados julgamentos públicos no forum, e em Atos 17:5, denota indivíduos ociosos que perambulavam pelo mercado ou por outros lugares públicos, dotados de vil caráter, que poucò tinham a fazer –além de vaguear sem rumo, procurando algo em que se intrometer.

AGOSTINHO

Era descendente de cartagineses. Sua vida e carreira coincidiram com a desintegração do Império Romano do Ocidente. *Aurélio Agostinho* nasceu a 13 de novembro de 354 D.C., em Tagaste, Norte da África, atualmente Souk-Ahras, na Argélia. Era filho de Patrício, oficial romano, que continuou pagão até pouco antes de sua morte, e de Mônica, uma cristã devota. Tinha um irmão chamado Navígio, e uma irmã, Perpétua, que se tornou freira. Sua educação inicial envolveu gramática e aritmética. Odiava o idioma grego, e nunca adquiriu qualquer conhecimento completo do mesmo. Porém, conhecia profundamente a literatura latina. Sua formação e meio ambiente pagãos influenciaram adversamente a sua formação. Em cerca de 370, a leitura da obra de Cícero, *Hortensius*, causou-lhe profunda impressão e a partir de então voltou-se para a filosofia. Continuou seus estudos em Cartago, onde vivia com uma amante, que lhe deu um filho, Adeodato, em 371. Tornou-se maniqueu (ver o artigo), e foi muito ativo como membro da seita. Em 373-374, ensinou gramática em Tagaste; e então, durante nove anos, dirigiu uma escola de retórica, em Cartago. Mudou-se para Roma, onde estabeleceu uma escola similar. Então abandonou o maniqueísmo e tornou-se um cético. Um ano mais tarde, fundou uma escola em Milão.

Conversão ao cristianismo. A filosofia platônica libertou sua mente do paganismo crasso, dando-lhe razão para ter esperanças em Deus e na alma. Um amigo, Simpliciano, e a sua própria mãe, influenciaram-no profundamente no tocante à fé cristã. Finalmente, recebeu uma experiência mística, na qual lhe foi dito: «Tolle, lege» (Toma, lê), quando ele estava diante de um manuscrito do Novo Testamento, em Rom. 13:13,14. Isso lhe conferiu convicção moral, e a sua conversão foi completa.

Retornando a Tagaste, em 388 ele vendeu seu patrimônio e distribuiu o dinheiro entre os pobres, conservando consigo apenas uma casa, que transformou em uma comunidade monástica. Ele e seus amigos viviam como monges. Entre os primeiros membros do grupo estava Adeodato, seu filho, jovem de brilhante intelecto. Mas o jovem logo faleceu, com dezenove anos. Agostinho não tencionava tornar-se «padre», mas as circunstâncias e a sua própria convicção levaram-no exatamente nessa direção. Assim, em 391, foi ordenado na cidade próxima de

Hipona (moderna Anaba, na Argélia). Em 395-396, foi ordenado bispo auxiliar de Hipona, e pouco depois, já era o bispo da diocese. Mostrou ser um hábil administrador, pregador, polemista, correspondente, e acima de tudo, autor, cujos escritos exerceram vasta influência em sua época, como até hoje o fazem.

Os últimos anos de sua vida foram assinalados por desastres e guerras, quando se esborooou o império romano. Em agosto de 420 (serviu como bispo pelo espaço de quarenta anos), os vândalos, que marchavam para o oeste, após terem-se apossado de Cartago, lançaram cerco a Hipona. Em meio ao assalto, a 28 de agosto de 430, morreu Agostinho, na santidade e na pobreza em que vivera por tantos anos. Os vândalos destruíram quase toda a cidade de Hipona, excetuando a catedral e a biblioteca de Agostinho, que foram deixadas intactas. De acordo com uma tradição, seu corpo repousa em Pávia, na Itália. A data de sua morte é celebrada como sua festa. Ver sobre o *Agostinianismo*.

AGOSTINHO DE CANTERBURY

Foi o apóstolo dos anglo-saxões, enviado à Inglaterra por Gregório I (ver o artigo), à testa de uma missão de quarenta monges beneditinos. Chegou em Kent em 597, converteu o rei Ebelterto e fundou a sé de Canterbury. Tornou-se seu primeiro arcebispo. Sua obra assinalou o reavivamento do interesse da Igreja pela obra missionária. Entre os celtas havia um cristianismo que se arrastara por vários séculos. Agostinho procurou entrar em acordo com os bispos celtas, mas eles recusaram-se a cooperar com a missão romana, ou a desistir de seus costumes acerca do batismo e da data da Páscoa. Por ocasião da morte de Agostinho (609), sua obra ainda não se espraiara muito; mas, após sua morte, o esforço conjunto das igrejas romana e celta converteu a Inglaterra inteira ao cristianismo, em menos de cem anos. O dia da festa de Agostinho é 26 de maio. (AM E)

AGOSTINIANISMO

Nome dado aos ensinos gerais filosófico-religiosos de Agostinho. Os escritos onde se acham essas doutrinas são os seguintes: *Sobre o Livre-Arbítrio*; *Concernente ao Mestre; Confissões; Sobre a Doutrina Cristã; Inquirições da Fé, da Esperança e do Amor; Sobre a Trindade; e A Cidade de Deus*. Em seus escritos e ensinos, Agostinho é o elo de ligação entre o pensamento grego e as especulações dos escolásticos. Foi o maior dos pais latinos da Igreja, não tendo rivais na Igreja Cristã, desde o Apóstolo Paulo, na opinião de alguns. Deu à Igreja oriental suas definições cristológicas, e à Igreja ocidental a sua vida. Nele convergem os ideais católicos e as convicções protestantes posteriores. O Santo Império Romano foi fundado sobre os seus conceitos, contidos na obra *A Cidade de Deus*, que por mil anos dominou os desenvolvimentos políticos da Idade Média.

As combinações de Agostinho. Talvez seja por demais simplista asseverar que Agostinho era um teólogo e filósofo cristão-platônico. Não há que duvidar que estava pesadamente endividado a Platão, e boa parte de sua teologia cristã foi expressa através das idéias e das terminologias platônicas. Naturalmente, ele estava fortemente escudado na Bíblia, mas Platão, corretamente manuseado, não é antibíblico.

Sua inspiração. Seu pensamento era controlado por dois pólos: Deus e a alma. Escreveu ele: «Desejo conhecer Deus e a alma. Nada mais? Nada mais!» E

AGOSTINHO

Santo Agostinho — 354-430

Santo Agostinho, o elo que ligou o pensamento grego e a filosofia escolástica; pensador original e pai da igreja *por excelência;* bispo de Hippo por quarenta anos; a maior figura na Igreja desde o Apóstolo Paulo.

Agostinho deu a Igreja Oriental suas definições da cristologia e a Igreja Ocidental a sua própria vida. Nele os ideais católicos se unem com as convicções protestantes.

•••

AGOSTINHO

Procurando a Vereda Mística
O Toque Místico — A Presença de Deus

Santo Agostinho em êxtase, por B. Gozzoli.

• • •   • • •

AGOSTINIANISMO

também: «Ó Deus, Tu és sempre o mesmo. Oxalá eu conhecesse a mim mesmo e conhecesse a Ti». (*Confissões*)

Elementos do agostinianismo:

1. *A vereda da felicidade e da salvação*. É a senda do autoconhecimento, em que o indivíduo vem a conhecer a alma e suas exigências, divinamente outorgadas, mediante a razão e as Escrituras. Essa vereda caracteriza-se pela formosura, pela verdade e pela bondade. Quando conhecemos a nós mesmos, chegamos a conhecer o criador do nosso «eu» — Deus. Nossos corações não têm descanso enquanto não encontram descanso nEle.

2. *Teísmo*. A única posição intelectualmente válida para o cristão é o *teísmo* (ver o artigo). Usando idéias platônicas, Agostinho definiu como obtemos esse conhecimento. Há uma base racional e filosófica para crermos na existência de entidades imateriais, as *idéias eternas* ou *rationes aeternas*. Essas existem na mente de Deus (ver o artigo sobre o *conceitualismo*). Naturalmente, para tanto, Agostinho também empregava conceitos bíblicos.

3. *Importância da defensibilidade filosófica*. Ele tinha fé, crendo na revelação. — Mas buscava intensa e incansavelmente uma base racional para a fé, tendo-a encontrado em Platão, em contraste com os céticos.

4. *Refutação do ceticismo*. A verdade só floresce onde se acha a fé, e o ceticismo é trevas. O ceticismo é contrário ao autoconhecimento, uma das grandes colunas-mestras de Agostinho. Ele não podia evitar a idéia da verdade. «Se duvido, estou certo da verdade que duvido. Se estou equivocado, então ao menos devo existir, para que possa ter-me equivocado». (*Si fallor, sum*). Isso, naturalmente, antecipou a famosa declaração de Descartes: «Penso. Portanto, existo». Pode ter sido a inspiração da mesma.

5. *Formosura e bondade*. Essas idéias também são inatas ao homem, não podendo ser evitadas, tal como se dá com a verdade, de modo geral. A consciência da verdade, da beleza e da bondade são juízos do homem interior, da alma. Temos consciência natural dessas coisas (ver o artigo sobre a *intuição*). Nos juízos que formamos, estão implícitas certas normas. A tomada de consciência dessas normas nos faz tomar consciência de Deus, pois Deus é o verdadeiro Bem, a verdadeira Beleza, a própria Verdade. Temos aí as *idéias* platônicas, cristianizadas. Ver o artigo sobre *formas*, as idéias platônicas.

6. *A descoberta de Deus*. Há uma vereda interior que conduz a Deus, e os elementos de verdade, beleza e bondade são nossos grandes guias. O décimo capítulo das *Confissões* de Agostinho traça essa vereda, partindo de visões e ruídos, de impressões e percepções, partindo daí para idéias destituídas de imagem. Estão envolvidas a razão e a intuição, mas o Ser que buscamos é «luz inextinguível» e «luz inteligente». Toda outra luz, toda outra inteligência derivam-se dEle. E somente através das experiências místicas, relativas a agora, e absolutas no mundo futuro da luz, realmente chegaremos a conhecer a Deus. A luz do intelecto do indivíduo encontra-se dentro da Luz, não da própria, mas daquela que tem afinidade com a ele. Essa é a vereda que alicerça a Deus. Naturalmente, Agostinho também se alicerçava sobre conceitos bíblicos, e essa vereda passa pela missão de Cristo.

7. *Evidências de Deus*. Há «vestígios» de Deus na natureza. Agostinho usava o argumento teleológico sobre a existência de Deus (ver o artigo sobre esse argumento). A existência de desígnio requer a existência de um Planejador.

8. *O mal*. O mal é a privação do bem, e não uma entidade em si mesma, já que não é positivo. Assim, a cegueira é a privação de luz. O mal também se assemelha às sombras escuras de uma pintura, que não são atrativas, mas que, consideradas como um todo, contribuem para a beleza. Portanto, o mal consiste em: 1. privação; 2. falta de percepção. Essa atitude para com o mal, sem dúvida deficiente, surgiu na tentativa de explicar como o mal pode existir em um mundo governado por um Deus todo-bom e todo-poderoso. Ver o artigo sobre *o problema do mal*.

9. *Fé no cristianismo*. Agostinho reconhecia as doutrinas cristãs, aceitando a autoridade do Novo Testamento. Onde não se podia explicar ou descrever a razão, assim ele se contentava com a simples fé no dogma.

10. *A natureza de Deus*. Agostinho declarava sua crença nos atributos tradicionais de Deus (ver o artigo a respeito), como a perfeição, a eternidade, a infinitude, a simplicidade, a unidade. Deus, em Sua essência, desconhece acidentes, tendo criado o mundo do nada, conhecendo tudo, passado e futuro. Com Sua presciência, Deus vê que o homem agirá livremente, sendo isso uma garantia da liberdade humana, longe de ser um fator predestinador. Deus é a causa inabalável de tudo, o sustentador de todas as coisas. O conceito agostiniano de Deus como um ser infinito foi o padrão durante mais de mil anos, após os seus dias.

11. *Sobre as obras de Deus*. Agostinho repelia a posição de Plotino (ver sobre Plotino), de que o Universo é uma emanação de Deus. Embora Deus houvesse planejado sua criação desde a eternidade (um conceito de Sua mente), Ele o criou dentro do tempo, do nada (*ex nihilo*). As coisas materiais pertenceriam ao nível mais baixo da criação. Dentro delas, porém, Deus plantou as Suas *rationes seminales*, ou sementes da razão. Por causa dessa implantação, novas formas de vida podem continuar a surgir, uma espécie de conceito de «lei natural», que governaria a esfera inferior, sem a intervenção direta da parte de Deus.

12. *Sobre o tempo*. Há uma esfera destituída do fator tempo. A esfera eterna pertence a uma outra qualidade. A abordagem agostiniana do tempo antecipou a teoria da relatividade, embora a ideia já estivesse contida nos *particulares de Platão* (objetos deste mundo) e nas *formas* (realidades espirituais que dão origem aos particulares (ver o artigo a respeito). Seu estudo sobre o tempo é considerado a única filosofia original vazada em língua latina, embora os gregos já tivessem dito coisas semelhantes. Ele confessava a sua ignorância sobre a natureza real do tempo, embora frisasse seus aspectos psicológicos, considerando o tempo como uma distensão da alma.

13. *Sobre o conhecimento*. «Credo ut intelligam» (creio, a fim de compreender). Não há conhecimento sem fé. O ceticismo nos faz mergulhar nas trevas. Há percepção, mas esta envolve apenas verdades triviais, mundanas. Há a razão, que ultrapassa aos sentidos; e há a intuição, inerente ao homem, a qual pode definir muitas verdades. Além disso, há o contato direto com a Inteligência, Deus, por meio das experiências místicas, culminando na visão beatífica (ver o artigo a respeito), que é o ponto culminante do conhecimento. O conhecimento não consiste em mero entendimento teórico sobre algum assunto. Mas é o que sucede à alma em sua busca pelo conhecimento de Deus. Agostinho usava a Bíblia para definir artigos de fé, mas não hesitava em alegorizar trechos, quando

AGOURO — AGRADECIMENTO

pensava que isso era necessário para a obtenção da verdade que ultrapassava a mera letra inadequada. Ver o artigo sobre as *alegorias*. Deus e a alma são os verdadeiros alvos do conhecimento, mas todo conhecimento reflete a mente de Deus, pelo que faz parte da teologia. A ciência conduz a Deus quando corretamente manuseada. Temos nisso a doutrina da *unidade da verdade*, um útil conceito.

14. *Sobre o homem*. O mal moral deve-se ao livre-arbítrio humano. O homem poderia desejar ser feliz, seguindo a vereda necessária para tanto (*eudemonismo*). Mas falta ao homem a visão do mundo eterno, e cada pecado é a rejeição desse mundo. Os problemas morais específicos ventilados por Agostinho foram: veracidade, autopreservação, castidade, paz e guerra. Para que haja uma guerra justa, deve haver: a. uma autoridade legítima; b. uma causa justa; c. uma correta intenção; d. todos os outros meios devem ter sido exauridos. A vontade divina, *por si mesma*, não é oposta à guerra, se essas condições forem satisfeitas. Contudo, a guerra só pode ser justificada após terem falhado todas as tentativas para conservar a paz. Se os bons soldados merecem ser elogiados, muito mais o merecem aqueles que procuram eliminar a guerra.

O homem está tão profundamente inoculado pelo pecado original, transmitido de geração em geração, que não merece ser salvo. Em Sua graça, Deus predestina alguns para a salvação, mas deixa outros receberem o que merecem (artigo sobre a *reprovação passiva*).

A temporalidade humana contrasta com a eternidade divina, e o próprio tempo é aquilatado pela alma do homem; mas Deus está acima do tempo. O homem, união de uma alma eterna com um corpo físico temporal, não tem sentido apenas na esfera terrena, mesmo que a preexistência não lhe possa ser postulada. Ver o artigo sobre a *alma*, que inclui teorias das origens.

A dupla atração. A encruzilhada de todas as questões morais é o amor. O homem tem dois amores: o amor a Deus e o amor ao próprio «eu». Todos os problemas morais têm começo no amor-próprio. Mediante o amor a Deus pode ser atingida a felicidade, porquanto nisso o homem avizinha-se do Deus eterno e chega a participar de Sua natureza, mediante a visão beatífica.

15. *Política*. Em sua obra, *A Cidade de Deus*, Agostinho produziu a primeira e maior filosofia da história. A motivação foi a captura e o saque da cidade de Roma pelos bárbaros, em 410 D.C. Visto que isso poderia provocar acusações contra os cristãos (alguns disseram que o surgimento do cristianismo correspondeu à queda de Roma), a primeira preocupação de Agostinho foi apologética; mas, à medida que escrevia, — ampliava seu tema, transformando-a em uma filosofia da história. Ali ele concebe duas cidades: Jerusalém, a cidade de Deus, que é a Igreja Católica, e Babilônia, a cidade terrena, o estado, aliás, o *estado pagão*. Tal como no homem há dois amores em choque, assim também se dá na sociedade dos homens. As sociedades humanas aproximam-se mais do amor a este mundo, ou do amor a Deus, segundo a vontade das massas. A cidade do homem está sempre sujeita à ruína, estando ali presentes todos os riscos da contingência. Mas a cidade de Deus está acima de tudo, e pode influenciar e aprimorar a cidade do homem. A cidade de Deus é superior à cidade do homem, e deveria exercer autoridade sobre ela. Daí a mescla de Igreja e estado, criando a base filosófica para muitos séculos de conflito. O estado moldado pela cidade de Deus é denominado Roma, e isso apresenta uma terceira alternativa. Visto que a cidade de Deus em seus ideais, é superior à cidade do homem. Conseqüentemente, a voz da Igreja sempre deveria ser ouvida pelas autoridades civis.

Os quatro períodos da história. 1. Paraíso, antes da queda; 2. o mundo após a queda; 3. o período da lei; 4. o período da graça, desde a vinda de Cristo, à época em que vivemos. Algumas vezes, Agostinho preferia uma divisão em sete períodos, para corresponder aos sete dias da semana.

16. *Um filho da Igreja*. O conhecimento e o uso da Bíblia por parte de Agostinho foi crescendo após sua conversão, e ele fez significativas contribuições para a teologia. Foi chamado de «o doutor da graça». Opôs-se à heresia de Pelágio (ver o artigo). A vontade de Deus depende de Deus, e somente por meio da graça divina o homem pode chegar à salvação e à perfeição. Devido ao livre-arbítrio, o homem é responsável por seus atos. Deus oferece Sua graça eficaz, mas o homem pode rejeitá-la. Deus prevê que o homem agirá livremente, pelo que a previsão divina não pode determinar as escolhas humanas. Entre outros assuntos, Agostinho abordou o da encarnação, o da redenção, e o da Igreja como corpo místico de Cristo, fazendo-o com profundeza. Escreveu sobre os sacramentos e demorou-se especialmente sobre a doutrina do amor. Muito fez para mostrar a relação entre a fé e a razão, embora sempre salientando o lugar primacial da fé.

Sua influência. Agostinho tem sido chamado de «o maior doutor da Igreja». Ele influenciou, em termos decisivos, a fé e a teologia da Igreja ocidental. Através da Idade Média, mestres representativos apelavam para a sua autoridade. Pode-se ver sua influência nas obras de Anselmo, Tomás de Aquino, Alberto Magno, Pedro Lombardo, os membros das escolas franciscana e vitorina, e outros. Agostinho é estimado como um dos grandes pensadores da humanidade, dentro ou fora da Igreja. (AM B BE C E EP H OE P)

AGOURO Ver sobre **Presságio**.

AGRADECIMENTO

Tanto o verbo quanto o substantivo aparecem, quase uniformemente, no hebraico, sob a forma de uma única palavra. No grego a situação é idêntica, em cujo caso a palavra original é *euxaristéo* e seus cognatos. Digno de observação, porém, é que se a palavra grega tem o sentido usual de «agradecer», a palavra hebraica adquire força através do contexto, porquanto é mais um sinônimo de «louvar» ou «abençoar» (que vide). Geralmente, a LXX traduz o termo hebraico pelo grego *eksomologeo*, que significa «falar juntamente» ou «louvar». Com isso pode-se comparar o uso dos termos gregos *homologéo*, «confessar», «homologar», que aparece no Novo Testamento por cerca de trinta e duas vezes, como verbo ou substantivo (para exemplificar, Mat. 10:32; João 1:20; Rom. 10:9,10; Rom. 3:5) e *anthomologéomai*, «agradecer», que aparece exclusivamente em Luc. 2:38, na boca da profetisa Ana. Os gregos também usavam a palavra *charis* «graça», com o sentido de «agradecer», conforme se vê em Luc. 6:32-34, ou com o sentido de «favor», conforme se vê em I Ped. 2:19, mas que nossa versão portuguesa traduz, respectivamente, por «recompensa» e «grato».

A palavra grega *eucharistía*, «agradecimento», tornou-se um termo técnico cristão para indicar a Ceia do Senhor. Mas isso, segundo dizem as autoridades da teologia histórica, começou somente nos escritos de Inácio e no Didache. A razão disso

ÁGRAFOS — AGRICULTOR

talvez se encontre nas palavras de Paulo, em I Cor. 11:24, onde ele relata como o Senhor instituiu a Ceia: «...e, tendo dado graças, o partiu e disse: Isto é o meu corpo, que é dado por vós; fazei isto em memória de mim». As palavras, «tendo dado graças», é tradução do verbo grego *euxaristéo*. Jesus deu graças pelo alimento. Porém alguns cristãos antigos começaram a denominar a Ceia com base nessa ação de graças, embora não haja base real para tanto. A Igreja Católica Romana, que transformou a celebração da Ceia em um «sacrifício» (com o reparo feito por seus teólogos de que se trata de um sacrifício incruento, isto é, sem a presença de sangue), insiste, apesar desse reparo, que por ocasião das palavras da consagração, proferidas pelo sacerdote, a hóstia transforma-se no corpo, no sangue, na alma e na divindade de Jesus, fazendo do ato o ponto culminante da missa, que seria o maior mistério cristão, ainda segundo esses mesmos teólogos. Incidentalmente, isso mostra-nos que a história da doutrina deve ser disciplina estudada pelo crente, a qual lhe permite perceber que todo desvio doutrinário começa com alguma pequena distorção, e que, com a passagem do tempo, vai recebendo adendos progressivamente distorcidos, até que a doutrina torna-se inteiramente diferente do que era no cristianismo primitivo. Todas as grandes verdades cristãs têm sido sujeitadas a essa distorção. Devemos tomar conhecimento de que as Escrituras prevêem desde o início, que a verdade revelada por Deus não permaneceria pura no cristianismo. Muitos haveriam até de preferir as fábulas (ver II Tim. 4:4)—em vez da verdade divina. E Paulo ajunta que isso se deve a uma operação satânica planejada, conforme se depreende de suas palavras: «Com efeito, o mistério da iniqüidade já opera...» (II Tes. 2:7). Esse mistério, uma vez devidamente desenvolvido, frutificará na carreira monstruosa do anticristo, o qual será adversário de Cristo e negará tudo quanto Ele representa. (HA ID ND)

ÁGRAFOS

Coisas não-escritas, termo usado para falar sobre as declarações de Jesus que não foram registradas nos evangelhos. Algumas delas se acham em outros trechos do Novo Testamento (Atos 20:35 e I Tes. 4:15), e outras nos evangelhos apócrifos; mas a maioria se encontra nos escritos dos primeiros pais da Igreja. Descobertas recentes têm trazido à luz certo número de declarações até agora desconhecidas de Jesus, sobretudo duas folhas de papiro encontradas em Oxyrhynchus. Tais declarações obviamente faziam parte de um número muito maior delas. Os ágrafos existentes podem ser contados na casa das centenas, mas bem poucos deles, talvez apenas vinte, dão mostras de serem genuínos.

Exemplos:

1. *No Novo Testamento*. O trecho de João 21:25 mostra que houve muitas afirmativas de Jesus que não foram registradas na Bíblia, sendo conhecidas apenas através da tradição oral. Diz Atos 20:35: ...é mister... recordar as palavras do próprio Senhor Jesus: «Mais bem-aventurado é dar do que receber». O trecho de Tia. 1:12 subentende uma declaração de Jesus sobre a coroa da vida que será dada aos justos. No codex Bezae (D), em Luc. 6:4, aparece uma declaração adicional de Jesus: «No mesmo dia, contemplando alguém trabalhando no sábado, disse-lhe: Homem, se sabes o que fazes, é bendito; mas, se não sabes, és maldito e transgressor da lei».

2. *Nos primitivos escritos cristãos*. Esses existem até

o século IV D.C. — Resch coligiu 74 que ele considerava genuínos, e 103 que considerava apócrifos. A maioria desses ágrafos ilustra o ensino de Jesus em um ponto ou outro, sendo difícil ou mesmo impossível julgar sua genuinidade. Jesus teria dito: «Aquele que está perto de mim está perto do fogo; e aquele que está longe de mim está longe do reino». E também: «Aquele que é fraco será salvo por aquele que é forte».

3. A *Logia*, ou Declarações do Senhor, encontradas em manuscritos descobertos em Oxyrhynchus, a 274 km ao sul do Cairo, no Egito, por B.F. Grenfell e Arthur S. Hunt, em 1896. a. Logion 1: «...e então verás claramente para tirar o argueiro que está no olho de teu irmão». b. Logion 2: «Disse Jesus: Se não jejuardes para o mundo, de modo algum encontrareis o reino de Deus, e se não guardardes o sábado, não vereis o Pai». c. Logion 3: «Jesus disse: Estive no mundo e encontrei todos os homens embriagados, e nenhum deles estava com sede. E minha alma se entristece com os filhos dos homens, porque estão cegos em seus corações». d. Logion 4: Indecifrável. e. Logion 5. «Disse Jesus: Onde houver... e há um...somente, e estou com ele. Erguei a pedra, e ali me encontrareis, parti a lenha, e ali estou eu». f. Logion 6. «Jesus disse: «Um profeta não é aceitável em seu próprio país, e nem um médico cura àqueles que o conhecem». g. Logion 7: «Jesus disse: Uma cidade edificada no alto de uma elevada colina fica firme, e não pode cair e nem ser escondida». h. Logion 8: Indecifrável.

AGRAMATOS

No grego significa analfabeto, sem escolaridade. No trecho de Atos 14:13 é aplicado pelos líderes judeus a Pedro e a João; em João 7:15 é aplicado a Jesus. Apesar desse termo poder significar absolutamente analfabeto, nesses dois casos era uma observação descaridosa sobre as realizações acadêmicas desses homens. É provável que os judeus quisessem dizer que aqueles cristãos e o próprio Jesus não tinham educação suficiente para conhecer bem a lei, pelo que não se deveria confiar neles quanto a questões religiosas, pois cer...mente não eram autoridades religiosas que deveriam ser seguidas. (A S)

AGRICULTOR

Vários nomes são dados na Bíblia ao indivíduo que trabalhava no solo, ou que se ocupava das lides próprias do campo: agricultor, viticultor, lavrador, jardineiro, etc. (Ver João 15:1 e Mat. 21:33 ss). O termo hebraico *ikkar* (na LXX, *georgós*) era usado para indicar quem cultivava o solo e colhesse o fruto da terra. (Ver Jer. 14:4). Ele é chamado «lavrador» em Jer. 51:23 e em Amós 5:16. No Novo Testamento, o termo grego *georgós* é usado para indicar a mesma profissão (ver II Tim. 2:6 e Tia. 5:7). Jesus contou uma parábola que envolvia lavradores, em Mat. 21:33 ss e paralelos, pois era atividade bem conhecida, a fim de indicar os que labutam no reino de Deus.

Uso metafórico. Os obreiros do evangelho são co-lavradores, que procuram obter uma respeitável produção no campo espiritual (ver I Cor. 3:6 ss). A propagação e cultivo da mensagem espiritual assemelha-se ao trabalho dos semeadores (Mat. 13:3), conforme se vê nas parábolas relativas à semeadura. O abuso no trabalho espiritual é ilustrado na parábola dos lavradores maus (ver Mat. 21:33 ss ; Mar. 12:1 ss ; Luc. 20:9 ss). O homem que aguarda com paciência a concretização dos propósitos de Deus,

AGRICULTURA

especialmente a vinda de Cristo ou «parousia» (ver o artigo a respeito), assemelha-se ao lavrador que planta e espera pacientemente o tempo da colheita (ver Tia. 5:7,8). O lavrador que trabalha arduamente tem o direito de compartilhar do fruto de seu labor; e outro tanto se dá no caso do obreiro espiritual. Este último não perderá a sua recompensa (ver II Tim. 2:6). Todos os aspectos de nossa vida e bem-estar espirituais resultam de nossa união com a vinha, na qualidade de ramos (João 15). Quanto a detalhes sobre esses assuntos, ver a exposição no NTI. (ID NTI Z)

AGRICULTURA

A arqueologia tem demonstrado que a Palestina foi uma das primeiras áreas agrícolas de que se tem notícia. Desde cerca de 7500 A.C. há evidências de uma agricultura razoavelmente boa ali. O vale do Jordão, com seus tributários e as áreas adjacentes, eram áreas intensamente cultivadas. A agricultura de Israel estava intimamente relacionada aos antigos povos do Médio Oriente. Plantavam-se mais cereais, comuns no crescente fértil. E também havia animais domésticos, leite e lã.

1. *Antes do dilúvio*. A história primitiva de Caim e Abel (ver Gên. 4:2,3), mostra que desde o começo do relato bíblico, a agricultura foi uma atividade básica. Porém, acerca do tempo antes do dilúvio, pouquíssimo se sabe sobre a questão. Há evidências de que Noé e seus filhos ocupavam-se em atividades agrícolas (ver Gên. 9:20), e descobertas feitas em Canaã mostram que até onde nossa história pode recuar, aquela região do mundo já era cultivada.

2. *No Egito*. O Egito era um país agrícola, enquanto que os hebreus eram essencialmente pastores. As primeiras lições de agricultura os hebreus aprenderam dos egípcios.

3. *Ao entrarem na terra prometida*. Israel invadiu uma terra já cultivada, e continuou a prática, após ter-se apossado dela.

4. *Evidências extrabíblicas*. A maioria dos arqueólogos, antropólogos e estudiosos da pré-história acredita que a princípio o homem foi caçador, recolhendo alimentos naturalmente supridos pela terra, sem qualquer cultivo humano. Esses estudiosos **afirmam que há cerca de dez mil anos (8000 A.C.) o homem começou a plantar e a criar, no que se chama de Idade Neolítica. Mas outros eruditos crêem que a** agricultura foi a principal ocupação humana desde o princípio. Outros expõem seus argumentos e escassas descobertas em favor da idéia do homem como caçador, como pastor e então como agricultor. O fato de que não se chega a um acordo sobre a questão, mostra que nenhum dos lados conta com provas conclusivas. Os fatos são muito escassos em relação aos primeiros séculos da história humana. Também é possível que em algumas áreas primeiro tenha havido a agricultura, e que em outras tenha havido primeiro a caça ou a criação de gado. Seja como for, assim que começamos a examinar os registros bíblicos, vemos a agricultura desde o começo. Temos de considerar ainda a questão das civilizações pré-bíblicas, se nossa raça atual é um acontecimento comparativamente recente, ao mesmo tempo o passado remoto esconde de nós muitas e talvez grandes civilizações pré-bíblicas. Há evidências de mais de quatrocentos grandes **cataclismos**, como o dilúvio de Noé, provocados pela mudança de posição dos pólos, com a conseqüente destruição de quase tudo que havia na superfície da terra. O registro referente a Adão, assim sendo, falaria sobre o **penúltimo cataclismo universal**. E a

história do dilúvio aparentemente é um registro da última vez em que um desses **grandes cataclismos**teve lugar. Mas, que dizer sobre os outros quatrocentos episódios? Parece seguro afirmar que nossa história é apenas uma *história moderna*, em comparação com as imensas eras em que criaturas similares ao homem viveram sobre a terra. Portanto, em termos absolutos, é muito dúbio o debate sobre o princípio do homem, se como agricultor, como caçador ou como pastor, e qual era a ordem dessas atividades. No **Oriente (vale do Eufrates)** sob certo tipo de terreno, foi encontrada uma camada de *vidro verde*. Que estranho! Pois o vidro é manufaturado pelo homem, e não um produto natural. Também lembramo-nos que nos desertos da porção ocidental dos Estados Unidos da América, onde foram efetuados os primeiros testes atômicos acima do solo, na área de uma das explosões apareceu uma camada de vidro verde, criado sobre a superfície da areia. E então os homens descobriram outras tais camadas de vidro verde em lugares tão distantes, no tempo e no espaço, da moderna nação norte-americana! Pense sobre isso, irmão! Alguns eruditos bíblicos crêem em raças pré-adâmicas, supondo que todas elas perderam-se entre Gên. 1:1 e Gên. 1:2, e que a nova raça humana, encabeçada por Adão, é uma ocorrência recente, uma autêntica história moderna. Cabe confessarmos que conhecemos muito pouco. Nosso conhecimento é parcial e localizado, e grandes mistérios envolvem nossa existência. Os homens gostam de conhecer superficialmente as coisas, impondo ridículas restrições sobre como e o quê pode ser sabido. Destarte eles se sentem mentalmente tranqüilos, com um falso senso de sabedoria. Porém, os limites que eles estabelecem são apenas os limites de suas próprias mentes, e não os limites da verdade.

5. *As estações do ano*. As estações e as condições de clima são questões fundamentais para a agricultura. Na Palestina, as variações de chuva e de luz solar confinam-se à porção final do outono e ao inverno. No resto do ano o céu fica praticamente sem nuvens, e a chuva é muito rara. As chuvas de outono usualmente começam perto do fim de outubro, no começo de novembro. As chuvas continuam durante os meses de novembro e dezembro. Continuam caindo algumas chuvas até março, mas, depois disso, a chuva é muito rara. O inverno não é rigoroso, pelo que as atividades agrícolas nunca cessam completamente. A neve cai nos lugares mais elevados, ou mesmo em lugares mais baixos, embora não fique muito tempo na superfície. Nas planícies e nos vales o calor do verão é opressivo, mas não nos lugares mais elevados. No outono, os poços estão quase vazios, e o terreno fica estorricado, exceutando áreas artificialmente irrigadas. A colheita da cevada se faz pouco antes da do trigo, que se faz no começo de maio, embora em alguns lugares se faça no fim de maio. A colheita da uva se faz em setembro, embora as primícias das uvas já estejam maduras em julho. Os métodos modernos têm modificado muitas coisas, mas o que dizemos aqui representa condições que prevalecem até hoje.

6. *O solo e seu uso*. Trechos do solo eram marcados, divididos para plantios específicos (ver I Sam. 14:14 e Isa. 28:25), cercados e protegidos dos animais (ver Isa. 5:5 e Núm. 22:24). O solo era fertilizado com estrume (ver II Reis 9:30 e Sal. 83:10). Carcaças e sangue de animais, como também sal para promover a putrefação da escória, eram usados (ver II Reis 9:37; Sal. 83:10; Mat. 5:13; Luc. 14:34,35). O solo podia ser enriquecido com cinzas (ver Isa. 61:3). Eram feitos terraços para conservar espaço e impedir a erosão do solo. Ele era quebrado, por animais, de maneira crua. Atrás vinham

AGRICULTURA

Debulhando os grãos

Mulheres debulhando

Debulhador

AGRICULTURA

Machado egípcio

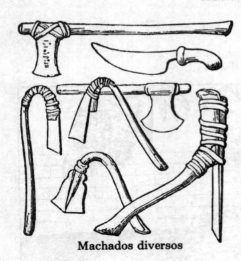
Machados diversos

Machado assírio

Metáforas Agriculturais

Foices

Garfo

Ver o artigo sobre *Agricultura, Metáfora de.*
O fruto do Espírito é amor, gozo, paz, longanimidade, benignidade, bondade, fé, mansidão, temperança. (Gál. 5:22)

...eis que semeio em ti a minha lei, e ela produzirá fruto, e serei glorificado nela para sempre. (IV Esdras)
...a palavra do reino...o que lhes foi semeado no coração. (Mat. 13:19)
Se as primícias são santas, também a massa o é; se a raiz é santa, também os ramos o são. (Rom. 11:16)

AGRICULTURA, METÁFORA DE

homens com enxadas para quebrar ainda mais os torrões (ver Isa. 28:24). Em seguida era plantada a semente.

7. *As espécies*. As principais colheitas eram a do trigo e a do centeio. O milho era *desconhecido* na Palestina. Outras colheitas incluíam a espelta, painço, a lentilha, o linho, o pepino, o melão, o feijão, o cominho e o funcho. Desconhecia-se o feno e a cevada com palha moída era dada como alimento aos animais (ver Gên. 24:25,32; Juí. 19:10 ss). A semeadura começava após a festa dos Tabernáculos (fim de outubro ou começo de novembro), quando as chuvas de outono estavam chegando. Os frutos do verão (painço, feijões, etc.), eram plantados em janeiro e fevereiro. A colheita da cevada dava início à colheita do ano (ver II Sam. 21:9), cerca de duas semanas antes da colheita do trigo. As lentilhas eram colhidas mais ou menos no tempo da cevada. O linho e o algodão (ver I Crô. 4:21) aparentemente eram cultivados. Linho e lã podiam ser encontrados em todas as casas (ver Osé. 2:9 e Pro. 31:13).

8. *Semeadura*. As pinturas egípcias mostram que o semeador acompanhava o arado e lançava a semente. Ele levava uma cesta com a semente. Também havia o método em que a semente era espalhada frouxamente por sobre a superfície da terra (ver Mat. 13:3-8). Sempre que as condições o permitiam, a semeadura era feita sem se passar antes o arado (ver Deu. 11:10).

9. *A colheita*. Conforme já dissemos, a cevada, as lentilhas e então o trigo, eram colhidos desde o começo de maio até o fim de junho. A colheita era assinalada por muita celebração e ação de graças. O cereal era cortado com a foice (ver Deu. 16:9), embora também existisse o método de puxar a planta com suas raízes. Quando cortado, o cereal era arrumado em feixes e colocado em montões (Can. 7:2 e Rute 3:7). Havia eiras para a separação entre o grão e a palha. Usualmente as eiras eram em algum terreno elevado, de chão bem batido. Faziam passar bois por sobre os grãos para quebrar as cascas com seus cascos (ver Osé. 10:1). Pequenos vagões com rodas cilíndricas baixas também eram usados (ver Isa. 28:27; 41:15). O peneiramento era feito com uma pá larga ou com um tridente de madeira, com os dentes curvos. A massa da palha era lançada no ar, o vento soprava a palha e o grão caía no chão.

10. *Leis*. Ver o artigo sobre *lei agrária*. Além das que já foram mencionadas ali, havia também o descanso sabático (ver Lev. 19:3). O solo era deixado sem cultivo durante os anos sabáticos e de jubileu (ver Lev. 25:3 ss e 25:11). Um boi e um jumento não podiam ser postos na mesma canga (ver Deu. 22:10), pois um era considerado animal limpo e o outro era considerado imundo, pela lei cerimonial. Sementes de diferentes espécies também não podiam ser misturadas (ver Lev. 19:19 e Deu. 22:9). Não podia ser usada a semente que tivesse se umedecido com a carcaça de um animal imundo (ver Lev. 11:37,38). As extremidades de um campo semeado não podiam ser colhidas, deixando para os pobres virem respigar (ver Lev. 19:9; Deu. 24:19). Uma pessoa que passasse pelo caminho em meio a um campo plantado podia colher espigas (ver Mat. 12:1 e Luc. 61:1). As primícias de todos os tipos de plantio pertenciam a Deus, doador da produção da terra, para sustento da tribo sacerdotal. O fruto dos pomares não podia ser usado durante os três primeiros anos de produção; o quarto ano era doado a Deus; somente do quinto ano em diante pertencia aos homens (ver Lev. 19:23).

11. *A metáfora agrícola*. (Ver o artigo separado intitulado, — *Agricultura, Metáfora de*). Essa atividade natural prestava-se a diversas aplicações espirituais, como aquelas empregadas nas Escrituras e nos escritos dos filósofos morais. (G I IB S TCH UN WI WRI Z)

AGRICULTURA, METÁFORA DE

I. A Palavra Implantada

O termo «palavra», tal como em Tiago 1:21 indica o *evangelho*. Essa questão pode ser entendida de diversos modos:

1. Deus *enxerta* a sua palavra (a mensagem concernente a Cristo) em nossas almas. Essa planta lança raízes e se propaga rapidamente. Ao espalhar-se, cativa o ser inteiro, de maneira que a alma é transformada em consonância com a natureza do organismo nela enxertado. Isso pode ser confrontado com o trecho de Mat. 13:19, que diz: «...a palavra do reino... o que lhes foi semeado no coração...» A vida está envolvida em tudo isso; de fato uma *modalidade de vida*. Deus nos confere a natureza divina de seu Filho, com todos os atributos pertinentes (ver Col. 2:10), porquanto é a sua vida que se propaga em nós e que, finalmente, nos transforma, em cada célula de nosso ser, em células semelhantes às dele mesmo.

2. Outros supõem que o cultivo de um campo plantado, está em mira na parábola do semeador, no décimo terceiro capítulo de Mateus. Essa é uma idéia menos provável, no que concerne ao texto presente, mas a mensagem por ela exposta não difere em muito daquela.

3. Seja como for, a palavra *implantada* ou a palavra *enxertada*, é indicação de que o evangelho de Cristo se apossa de nosso ser inteiro, formando em nós uma nova modalidade de vida. Por conseguinte, pode ser dito com plena sinceridade: «Porquanto, para mim o viver é Cristo...» (Fil. 1:21); e também que a vida que agora floresce em mim não é minha própria, mas «Cristo vive em mim» (Gál. 2:20). Bem-aventurado é o homem cuja espiritualidade chegou a essa condição!

II. Poderoso para Salvar

Ver Tiago 1:21. A Palavra, como uma expressão do Espírito, em seu poder regenerador, é capaz de levar à perfeição a obra da salvação. (Comparar isso com Heb. 4:12, onde se lê acerca da Palavra como «...viva e eficaz...» Quanto à própria «salvação», ver Heb. 2:3). Essa obra de salvação pode ser realizada porque é feita pelo poder divino, que opera através do evangelho de Cristo, o qual anuncia esse poder aos homens. Assim também, em Rom. 1:16, vê-se que o evangelho é o «poder de Deus para a salvação», embora somente para aqueles que crêem. O próprio Cristo é a Palavra personalizada (ver João 1:1).

Ver o artigo sobre a *Alma*. Ver sobre *Imortalidade*.

O livro de IV *Esdras* diz: «...eis que semeio em ti a minha lei, e ela produzirá fruto, e serei glorificado nela para sempre...» (Ver declaração um tanto similar em IV *Esdras* 8:6; Deut. 30:11-14; Mar. 4:20 e Luc. 8:13). Pensando que o autor sagrado se escudara em tais conceitos do A.T., alguns intérpretes supõem que o termo *Palavra*, usado em Tiago 1:21, é «a lei sob trajos cristãos», ou seja, a «verdade acumulada de Deus», atingida na dispensação cristã. Porém, conforme é esclarecido em Tiago 1:18, o «evangelho» é que está aqui em foco.

III. Gál. 5:22,23. Os frutos ou virtudes espirituais e éticas, são uma cultivação do Espírito Santo. Eles são as características espirituais da pessoa. Ver o artigo sobre *O Fruto do Espírito*. (AL I IB NTI)

AGRIPA — ÁGUA

AGRIPA
Ver Herodes.

AGRIPA
Filósofo grego dos séculos II ou III D.C. Era cético do estilo de Aenesidemus (ver o artigo). Apresentou cinco tropos ou modos, para mostrar por qual motivo não podemos ter qualquer conhecimento seguro (ver sobre o *ceticismo*). Seus tropos são: 1. Não há como determinar quais filósofos (se é que os há) estão certos em sua abordagem do conhecimento, se através dos sentidos, da razão, ou de uma combinação de ambos. 2. Cada prova requer premissas que repousam sobre outras, em um regresso infinito, o que é fatal para o conhecimento certo. 3. Todos os informes são relativos, quer venham dos sentidos, quer venham da razão, pelo que nunca podemos saber algo por si mesmo. 4. A fim de fazer estacar um regresso infinito de premissas, temos de postular uma *hipótese*, a alegada verdade a qual é aceita sem provas. Portanto, a suposta verdade repousa, finalmente, sobre a fé. Se uma hipótese não for provada, então as premissas podem ser levadas a sério? 5. Há um círculo vicioso na tentativa de estabelecer pela razão o que é sensível, visto que a própria razão precisa apoiar-se sobre os sentidos. (P)

AGRIPA VON NETTESHEIM, Henrique Cornélio
Filósofo e cabalista alemão (ver o artigo sobre a *Cabala*), 1486-1535. Estudou em Colônia, serviu a quatro chefes de estado, incluindo Carlos V, e por algum tempo foi o médico da rainha-mãe de Francisco I. Conferenciou em universidades, publicou várias obras controvertidas e promoveu a erudição cabalista. Porém, sua obra principal rebate essa erudição, as ciências e as artes, advogando o retorno ao cristianismo primitivo e à devoção às Escrituras. Escritos: *Sobre a Filosofia Oculta*, 1531; *Sobre a Incerteza e a Vaidade das Ciências e das Artes*, 1530. (P)

ÁGUA
1. Considerações Gerais. Tanto no hebraico como no grego temos a considerar apenas uma palavra. No grego é *údor*, um líquido composto de hidrogênio e oxigênio (H_2O), convertível em vapor d'água quando aquecido convenientemente, ou em gelo, se sua temperatura cair a 0° centígrados ou menos. A maior parte da água existente deriva-se diretamente dos oceanos. Mediante evaporação, condensa-se sob a forma de nuvens e precipita-se como chuva, neve, cerração, etc., caindo sobre a superfície do solo, onde origina rios, lagos ou águas subterrâneas (lençóis freáticos). Essas águas subterrâneas reaparecem na superfície como fontes, ou então retornam ao mar.

Naturalmente, a água potável arrasta consigo várias impurezas, em variegados graus. No processo da evaporação, os sais dissolvidos nas águas oceânicas são deixados para trás, mas a água da chuva adquire traços de sais de amônia e de vários gases do ar. Nas regiões montanhosas, a água dos rios e lagos é relativamente pura, — mas à medida que a água avança ela vai dissolvendo sais e apanhando minerais ou matéria vegetal em pequenas quantidades. Quando uma corrente de água termina em algum lago fechado, como é o caso do mar Morto, a proporção de sais vai aumentando progressivamente, conforme ocorre a evaporação. As águas subterrâneas, por serem filtradas pelas rochas, geralmente são claras e limpas de matéria em suspensão. Por outro lado, em sua passagem pelas camadas rochosas, essas águas podem conter quantidades consideráveis de sais minerais, particularmente nas regiões de pedra calcária, onde se formam soluções próprias de cavernas (vide). — Alguns sais minerais, particularmente os sais de magnésio, tornam a água imprópria para o consumo humano ou dos animais. Na maioria dos casos, tais águas têm um gosto amargo. Mas outras águas subterrâneas contêm bem pouca matéria dissolvida (ver Tia. 3:12).

Visto que a água é essencial para a existência humana, bem como para os animais e as plantas (ver Isa. 1:30; 55:10), as antigas civilizações desenvolviam-se em lugares onde havia chuva suficiente para servir aos animais e às plantas, bem como aos seres humanos; ou onde havia rios como o Eufrates, o Tigre e o Nilo, que eram rios perenes. Quando os homens concentravam-se em áreas distantes dos rios, eles dependiam muito da água subterrânea disponível, em cujo caso as fontes naturais (cf. Deu. 8:7), que davam origem a correntes e riachos, eram importantes (cf. Gên. 26:18) e até mesmo vitais para os criadores de gado. Cidades como Jerusalém e Jericó precisavam de suprimento suficiente de água, como uma das principais considerações, inclusive para efeito de defesa. Jerusalém, que a Bíblia descreve como a mais significativa cidade do mundo (ver Sal. 87:2-5), por ser também a habitação de Deus (I Reis 8:13); a existência da fonte de Giom, nas adjacências do vale do Cedrom (ver II Crô. 32:30; Isa. 7:3), era um fator vital.

O suprimento de água sempre foi o fulcro da contenda, por toda a história do Oriente Próximo, entre os agricultores e os criadores de gado (ver Gên. 4:2). Ante o aumento progressivo da agricultura, os nômades daquela região são forçados a abandonar territórios dotados de bom suprimento de água. Como uma espécie de revide, os nômades geralmente atacam às populações fixas, procurando destruir quaisquer arranjos hidráulicos das mesmas. E os criadores de gado geralmente lutam uns contra os outros, pela posse das fontes e poços (ver Gên. 26:20).

Não é de surpreender que *água e pão* são as grandes necessidades da existência humana (ver I Sam. 25:11; I Reis 18:4). E a doação ou a possessão dessas coisas era considerado algo de magna importância (ver Deu. 23:4; Mat. 10:42). A provisão de água é mesmo considerada uma provisão divina. As bênçãos divinas são aludidas em termos de água (ver Isa. 44:3; João 4:13), e tanto a escassez como o desejo de vida espiritual são descritos em termos de sede de água (ver Amós 8:11; Mat. 5:6). Tanto o costume de transportar água até à residência (ver Mar. 14:13) como a maneira como a água era sorvida (ver Jul. 7:5,6) eram usados como sinais. E o costume de lavar os pés dos visitantes (ver Gên. 43:24), foi usado por Jesus como meio de ensinar certa lição (ver João 13:5-9), ou como um indicador das atitudes das pessoas (ver Luc. 7:37,38,44). O emprego da água nos ritos aparece tanto no Antigo Testamento (por exemplo, Êxo. 29:4; Lev. 15:12) como no Novo Testamento (por exemplo, Mar. 1:5,9).

Na narrativa bíblica, não somente as águas continentais, mas também os mares adjacentes são importantes. Grande parte da chuva que caía na Terra Santa era devida que se evaporava do mar Mediterrâneo, o qual desempenhava importante papel no comércio (por exemplo, dos fenícios) e no transporte (ver Atos 27). Para Israel, o mar Vermelho e o golfo de Áqaba também proviam meios de acesso para o comércio (ver I Reis 9:26), sobretudo com a

ÁGUA

Arábia, com o nordeste e o leste da África, e talvez, até com a Índia. E também lhes provia certos recursos naturais, como as pérolas, a oníquia, etc.

2. Chuva, evaporação e infiltração. Os ventos ocidentais prevalecentes (ver I Reis 18:42-45) sobre o Mediterrâneo oriental transportam a umidade que se precipita quando o ar é forçado a subir para as terras altas da Judéia e da porção oriental do vale do Jordão. A maior parte dessa precipitação ocorre sob a forma de chuvas sobre as terras altas, havendo também algum granizo. Essa precipitação geralmente acontece de outubro a maio, com máximas de dezembro a março. A precipitação média anual é maior que 1000 mm nas terras altas a sudeste de Damasco, e maior que 500 mm sobre o Líbano, certas porções da Síria e Israel, e porções limitadas do Jordão (ver fig. 1). Mas essa média está sujeita a grandes variações. Assim a média anual de chuvas, em Jerusalém, de 1850 a 1960, foi de 620 mm, com um máximo de 1090 mm e com um mínimo de 210 mm. Boa parte do leste do Jordão e do leste da Síria conta com uma precipitação inferior a 200 mm anuais. Para o sul a precipitação anual ainda é inferior a isso, apesar das elevações maiores das terras altas do Jordão, em comparação com a região mais ao norte. Isso resulta do fato de que os ventos sopram principalmente do sul, provenientes do seco continente norte-africano, onde, nas regiões desérticas, a água se deposita apenas como orvalho matinal (ver Êxo. 16:13). A precipitação de chuvas, na porção sul do vale do Jordão e na região adjacente ao mar Morto também é bem baixa.

Uma boa porcentagem da chuva evapora-se, causando uma taxa de umidade, na margem esquerda do Jordão, da ordem de setenta e cinco por cento no inverno, e de trinta e cinco por cento no verão. Em certa região do norte do rio Jordão, onde a precipitação anual é de 415 mm, a taxa de umidade chega a oitenta e um por cento. Mas noventa por cento da água desaparece no sistema de drenagem da superfície, e dez por cento infiltra-se no solo. Em outras regiões, com taxas pluviais comparavelmente moderadas, tão pouco quanto cinco por cento, ou tanto quanto quinze por cento das chuvas se infiltra, aumentando os depósitos vitais de águas subterrâneas (cf. Deu. 11:11). Mas, nas regiões onde o índice pluviométrico é menor que 200 mm, há pouca ou nenhuma infiltração direta, exceto quando há alguma súbita enchente, nos wadis que atravessam os lençóis freáticos.

3. Água subterrânea. O aproveitamento de águas subterrâneas, incluindo a emergência da água como fontes e poços, quase sempre depende inteiramente de fatores geológicos. Esses fatores incluem a porosidade e a permeabilidade das camadas do solo e as formações que transmitem água ou não, a inclinação das camadas e a existência de características estruturais como dobras e falhas. Grande parte da água que se infiltra no solo e nas rochas superficiais aloja-se em alguma zona onde as rochas ficam saturadas de água. A superfície superior dessa zona saturada é chamada de mesa de água, e sua altura, em qualquer lugar, depende do nível em que a água permanece em algum poço dos proximidades.

Há dois grupos principais de águas subterrâneas na Terra Santa, a saber, as águas subterrâneas das seções permeáveis das regiões montanhosas onde há dobras e falhas, e aquelas que se ajuntam nos sedimentos das principais planícies. Nas regiões montanhosas, como as da Judéia, Samaria e Galiléia, as águas subterrâneas geralmente depositam-se em profundidades consideráveis, abaixo da superfície do solo, embora a mesa de água ondule. Onde essa mesa encontra a superfície, nos vales entre terrenos mais elevados, a água emerge na forma de fontes (ver Deu. 8:7). Muitas dessas fontes ocorrem onde há uma junção inclinada de camadas porosas e não porosas à superfície (ver fig. 2), ou onde há uma junção com falha, entre dois tipos de camadas assim. Essas fontes geralmente são perenes, formando por sua vez riachos (ver II Sam. 17:20). Nas vertentes dos vales também há fontes, onde a mesa de água chega até a superfície. Mas as variações pluviométricas, bem como os longos períodos de seca, causam variações no nível da mesa de água, o que faz com que certas fontes deixem de jorrar água, durante certos períodos (ver II Reis 2:19). Outras fontes intermitentes só fluem nas faldas dos vales após uma infiltração anormal, depois de prolongadas chuvas, o que faz com que a mesa de água eleve-se acima do normal, até chegar à superfície (fig. 2). E onde a elevação do terreno não é grande, como nas colinas da Judéia, diminui a profundidade do lençol de água, e esta pode ser aproveitada em fontes relativamente rasas.

Em alguns casos, as águas subterrâneas podem percorrer dezenas de quilômetros antes de aflorarem nas fontes. Esse é o caso de alguns raros e isolados lugares servidos por água abundante no deserto do sul da Judéia, entre o mar Morto e o golfo de Áqaba.

4. Sistema de drenagem do rio Jordão. O rio Jordão, seus tributários, o lago de Tiberíades e o mar Morto constituem os principais elementos do sistema de drenagem superficial da Terra Santa. O rio Jordão tem dois braços originários principais. Um deles fica perto de Banias (Cesaréia de Filipe; ver Mat. 16:13), na base sul da cadeia do monte Hermom, na Síria, onde o riacho Banias sai de uma caverna, e o outro em uma fonte em Tell el-Kadi (no território de Dã). Dois córregos mais longos, embora com menos água, também formam as cabeceiras do rio Jordão, a saber, o Hasbani, que ocupa a continuação norte do vale do Jordão (talvez devido a algum antigo terremoto, que vide), e o Bareighit. Esses quatro riachos juntam-se abaixo do Banias, e fluem para o lago Hulete, atualmente drenado (Merom? de Jos. 11:5), que se formou quando rochas vulcânicas barraram o rio. A partir dali forma-se um rio encachoeirado, abaixo do nível do mar, e nos quinze quilômetros até o lago de Tiberíades, o rio baixa 180 m de nível. Em suas margens oriental e ocidental ficam, respectivamente, as cidades de Betsaida (ver Mar. 6:45) e Cafarnaum (ver João 6:17), na altura de sua entrada no lago.

O lago de Tiberíades, que tem dezenove quilômetros de comprimento e em alguns pontos até onze quilômetros de largura, também deve sua existência ao represamento do rio Jordão por meio de rochas vulcânicas, havendo fontes termais contendo cloretos e sulfetos perto de suas margens. Seu antigo nome veterotestamentário, mar de Quinerete, resulta de seu formato de harpa, quando visto do alto. Nomes que lhe são dados no Novo Testamento são lago de Genezaré (ver Luc. 5:1) e mar de Tiberíades (ver João 6:1). Cerca de três quartas partes da água que chega ao lago vem do rio Jordão, e um quarto vem das fontes, das águas subterrâneas, da chuva e das inundações nos wadis. A água desse lago é morna, variando de 12,5º a 30º centígrados. Entre fevereiro e agosto há plâncton abundante no lago, e também muito peixe. Isso permitia a grande indústria pesqueira que ali se desenvolvia, nos dias do Novo Testamento (ver João 21:3). Ventos fortes e secos, que sopram do leste, afetam o lago durante o inverno, causando tufões de inverno, e também vendavais súbitos durante o verão, em resultado do vento que

ÁGUA AMARGA

sopra do oeste (ver Mar. 4:37).

O rio Jordão, ao sul do lago de Tiberíades, torna-se barrento e serpeia por mais de 290 km, para atravessar apenas 97 km de deserto, ao mesmo tempo em que o fundo de seu leito baixa apenas 275 m. Nos períodos de enchente, o rio transborda por suas várzeas, mas no verão, em alguns lugares, ele atinge menos de 30 m de largura e menos de 90 cm de profundidade. Por mais de uma vez, suas águas já foram represadas por rochas que caem perto de Adão, acerca de trinta e oito quilômetros ao norte de sua entrada no mar Morto. Provavelmente isso se deve aos abalos sísmicos comuns ao longo do vale em que corre o rio Jordão, o que também poderia explicar a passagem em seco dos israelitas, sob o comando de Josué (ver Jos. 3:16). A planície do Jordão foi escolhida por Ló devido à sua abundância de água (ver Gên. 13:10,11). Esse rio desempenhou um importante papel nas vidas de Elias (ver II Reis 2:6) e Eliseu (ver II Reis 6:2). Suas águas barrentas pareceram repugnantes a Naamã, o general sírio leproso, que provinha de um distrito dotado de rios de águas claras (ver II Reis 5:12). Entretanto, devido à sua associação com Jesus, incluindo o Seu batismo, perto de Betabara (ver Mar. 1:9), e o batismo de João (ver Mar. 1:5), o rio Jordão tornou-se símbolo de purificação e pureza.

O mar Morto, que também é chamado de «mar Salgado» (Gên. 14:3; Jos. 3:16), é alimentado principalmente pelas águas do rio Jordão, que lhe fornece cerca de três quartos da água. O mar Morto, que é interior, não tem saída e está situado na porção mais profunda do vale do Jordão. Tem cerca de 71 km de norte a sul, com uma largura média de treze quilômetros. A península de Lisã projeta-se de sua margem oriental, dividindo o lago em uma bacia rasa, ao sul, e em uma bacia funda, ao norte, as quais formam cerca de três quartas partes de sua área total de 142 km (2). Há evidências que sugerem que a última enchente da bacia sul teve lugar a mil e quinhentos anos atrás, e que era local seco nos tempos bíblicos. A temperatura da água varia entre 19-23° centígrados, em dezembro e janeiro, e 34-36° centígrados, em julho e agosto. O recorde da temperatura máxima está registrado em 38°. A gravidade específica de suas águas é de 1,206 g/cm(3), em comparação com 1,0 g/cm(3) de água pura, e sua salinidade média é de 31,5 por cento, a maior do mundo.

5. Uso da água. Havia o uso profano e o uso religioso.

A. *Uso profano.* A água era a bebida mais comum, mas também era tomada misturada com um pouco de vinagre (ver Rute 2:14) ou com um pouco de vinho (ver II Mac. 15:39). A água que manava da fonte era mais apreciada do que a água parada, de poço. Às mulheres cabia a tarefa de buscar água para casa (ver Gên. 24:11,15; I Sam. 9:11; João 4:7). Josué encarregou os gibeonitas de buscarem água para o santuário (ver Jos. 9:21,23,27), de acordo com Deu. 29:10.

B. *Uso religioso.* Lavar o corpo como ato religioso aparece pela primeira vez na história de Jacó (ver Gên. 35:2). Israel recebeu ordem de preparar-se para o encontro com Yahweh, mediante a lavagem (ver Êxo. 19:10). Outro tanto foi ordenado a Aarão e seus filhos, para sua consagração sacerdotal (ver Êxo. 29:4; Lev. 8:6). A lavagem do corpo ou de partes do corpo fazia parte das prescrições legais dos sacerdotes, ao executarem seu ofício (ver Êxo. 30:17-21; 40:31 s. e Núm. 19:7). Também servia para todos que

tivessem contraído alguma impureza cerimonial (ver Lev. 14).

Roupas e outros objetos também eram lavados, devido à impureza cerimonial (ver Lev. 11-15). Às vezes, bastava a aspersão de água para um objeto tornar-se cerimonialmente puro (ver Nú. 19). Além disso, certas porções dos animais sacrificados eram lavadas (ver Lev. 1:9-13; 8:21; 9:14). O derramamento de água diante de Yahweh, em I Sam. 7:6, foi apenas um ato simbólico, pois a água nunca fez parte integrante de qualquer holocausto.

No decurso dos séculos, os judeus acrescentaram muitos detalhes aos rituais de purificação dos preceitos levíticos (ver Mar. 7:3 s.), e os fariseus observavam escrupulosamente essas prescrições. O lava-pés, que até então era um simples sinal de hospitalidade, e que geralmente era efetuado pelos servos, na Última Ceia adquiriu um novo sentido, ensinando a humildade e a igualdade entre os crentes (ver João 13:1-17). Interessante é o uso de água amargosa na prova de infidelidade, no caso de uma mulher suspeita de adultério (ver Núm. 5:12-31).

Após o cativeiro babilônico, a água adquiriu papel de destaque na celebração da festa dos Tabernáculos. Um sacerdote tirava água do poço de Siloé, com um jarro de ouro, de capacidade de cerca de litro e meio. A água era solenemente transportada para o templo e derramada sobre o altar dos holocaustos, juntamente com a libação de vinho. Antes mesmo do ministério de João Batista, já era costumeiro imergir pessoas em água, se quisessem tornar-se prosélitos do judaísmo. O batismo cristão, porém, é administrado por motivos bem diferentes, simbolizando a lavagem da regeneração, que é aplicada pelo Espírito ao coração penitente, bem como a integração do batizando na comunidade cristã.

6. Uso metafórico da água. Esse uso da água é muito freqüente nas Escrituras. O Senhor chama a si mesmo de «manancial de águas vivas» (Jer. 2:13; 17:13). E Jesus classificou-se também como tal (ver João 7:37-39; 4:10-13 ss). A «água», prometida por Jesus, representa a *vida sobrenatural*. Nessas imagens, Jesus dava continuação às do Antigo Testamento, onde as bênçãos divinas (ver Sal. 1:3; 17:8; 23:2, etc.), e mais ainda os bens messiânicos (ver Isa. 11:3-9; 32:2-20; 41:18; 43:19, etc.) são descritos em termos de águas abundantes, ou em termos de águas que transmitem vida e fertilidade. É natural representar o desejo pelas bênçãos divinas como uma sede ou anelo (ver Sal. 63:2; 143:6). Em Provérbios 5:15, «beber água da própria cisterna» significa não ter relações sexuais com mulher alheia. Água corrente é símbolo daquilo que passa e não volta mais (ver Jó 11:16). Idêntico sentido tem a metáfora da água derramada, que não mais pode ser recolhida (ver II Sam. 14:14; Sal. 58:8). Nos períodos chuvosos, os córregos podiam transbordar e ameaçar as propriedades. Por isso, a água às vezes simboliza um inimigo poderoso, que já se aproxima (ver Jer. 47:2; Isa. 8:7,8; 17:12; 28:2-17), ou então algum perigo iminente (ver Sal. 88:17,81; Osé. 5:10). (HA IB LAN NTI)

ÁGUA AMARGA

Essa era uma bebida que continha água santa, pó extraído do soalho do Tabernáculo e tinta de uma maldição escrita. Era preparada por um sacerdote, que a dava de beber a uma mulher suspeita de adultério por seu marido. (Ver Núm. 5:11-31). O propósito era fazer a mulher passar por uma prova ou teste. A arqueologia não tem descoberto evidências do

ÁGUA BENTA — ÁGUA DE IMPUREZA

uso desse rito, exceto entre os hebreus, embora os povos primitivos tenham inventado outros tipos de provas para tais mulheres. A inocência ou culpa da mulher presumivelmente era estabelecida pela reação dela à bebida. Se ela sofresse fortes dores e distorções no baixo abdômen, era considerada culpada; em caso contrário, era declarada inocente.

O rito. O marido que suspeitasse de sua mulher, trazia-a à presença do sacerdote, trazendo também uma oferta de manjares. Ela era posta «diante do Senhor», segurando a oferta. Seus cabelos eram soltos. O sacerdote preparava a mistura. A tinta usada era a mesma que servira para escrever uma maldição. A tinta era dissolvida em água. A mulher era então forçada a beber a poção. Alguns supõem que a reação violenta de algumas mulheres devia-se à mistura da tinta, e não ao adultério. Mas outros vêem em tudo uma intervenção divina. Assim, ela adoecia porque Deus a tornava doente. Mas há aqueles que preferem uma explicação psicológica, uma espécie de sugestão induzida. A mulher, sentindo-se culpada, sofria uma reação intestinal. Nesse caso, no rito encontramos uma espécie de antigo teste de detecção de mentira, que também funciona com base no princípio da mente que produz efeitos sobre o corpo. Prefiro pessoalmente essa última explicação. A ciência tem demonstrado amplamente o poder da mente para afetar o corpo. Por exemplo, alguns prisioneiros eram postos em uma cela, sendo-lhes dito que recentemente morrera ali um homem de varíola, embora isso não fosse verdade. Assim, em pouco tempo, os prisioneiros manifestaram todos os sintomas da enfermidade, embora não estivesse presente qualquer agente bacteriológico. A medicina psicossomática oferece intermináveis ilustrações do fato.

Duração. Há referências literárias que demonstram que esse rito continuou sendo efetuado até o início da era cristã. Josefo menciona o mesmo (ver *Anti.* III.xi.6). A *Mishna* mostra que a prática sofreu algumas modificações, como pôr a mulher na porta Oriental do templo, vestida de negro e com os seios aparecendo (1:5,6). O livro apócrifo, *Proto-evangelho* contém a fantasia de que tanto Maria quanto José foram submetidos ao teste (parte 16), e que, naturalmente, eles foram aprovados. O rabino Johannan ben Zakkai (século I D.C.) declarou que a prática foi abolida finalmente, porque o adultério tornou-se extremamente comum. (I IB ID)

ÁGUA BENTA

Trata-se apenas de água comum, santificada pela bênção sacerdotal. Adiciona-se sal à água a fim de dar a entender que agora ela está preservada da corrupção. Em seguida, a água é usada em várias cerimônias que transmitem alguma bênção. Do ponto de vista *filosófico*, da variedade cética, a água benta não é outra coisa senão água salgada, que foi *declarada* benta. Sua singularidade deriva-se do seu uso e da boa intenção por detrás dela. Porém, a água benta continua sendo apenas água. Do ponto de vista *parapsicológico*, alguns supõem que tal água realmente pode absorver certa energia, positiva ou negativa, quando bento ou maldita, de tal modo que, na realidade, a água benta pode ter um conteúdo de energia diferente do que sucede à água comum. Essa idéia assemelha-se ao uso de peças de roupa nas curas, segundo o registro de Atos 19:12. A roupa dos homens de Deus curava ou expelia demônios. Presumivelmente, o manuseio dessas peças, por parte de Paulo, transmitia alguma forma de energia

espiritual às mesmas, surtindo um efeito; ou então poderíamos dizer que o Espírito Santo honrava o ato; como um símbolo, mas Ele é quem realizava a operação. A explicação *teológico-dogmática* da água benta é que o próprio Espírito de Deus lhe empresta a eficácia.

Experiências em laboratório mostram que as plantas regadas com água benta crescem mais rapidamente e com maior força e saúde do que aquelas aguadas com água comum. Mas isso sucede em alguns casos selecionados. *Algumas* pessoas aparentemente são capazes de transmitir alguma forma de energia à água, o que promove o crescimento e a saúde das plantas. Pessoas conhecidas como taumaturgos têm obtido sucesso nisso, sendo provável que a energia da cura tenha natureza similar ou igual à energia transmitida à água benta. (E NTI)

ÁGUA DE IMPUREZA ou ÁGUA PURIFICADORA

A *água purificadora* (ver Núm. 19:9,13,20,21 e 31:23) era um agente de purificação, usado para pessoas ou coisas que tivessem sido contaminadas mediante o contato com corpos mortos, ou por outras razões.

As cinzas de uma novilha vermelha eram adicionadas à «água corrente», que era então aplicada ao objeto contaminado. O animal usado para tal cerimônia precisava ser uma novilha de cor marrom-avermelhada, sem qualquer defeito físico, que nunca fora atrelada a jugo. A novilha era queimada «fora do acampamento», por inteira, incluindo seu sangue, com a exceção de uma pequena porção do sangue que era usado para aspersão, diante da tenda, uma vez reduzido a cinzas. Isso distinguia tal cerimônia dos sacrifícios rituais levíticos. Um pedaço de madeira de cedro e um molho de hissopo, amarrado com um pano de cor escarlate, eram queimados juntamente com a novilha.

As cinzas eram conservadas «fora do acampamento, em um lugar limpo», até serem misturadas com água de fonte, para uso nas cerimônias específicas de purificação. Essa «água purificadora» era aplicada à pessoa ou objeto contaminados mediante aspersão, com um ramo de hissopo. A cerimônia era efetuada no terceiro e no sétimo dia depois que a pessoa era considerada limpa, tendo-se banhado e lavado as suas vestes, dando-lhe assim o direito de ser restaurada ao convívio comunitário, que antes a excluíra. O episódio relatado em Números 31:13 diz respeito a objetos contaminados, que haviam sido tomados em batalha.

Os judeus, nos dias de Jesus, haviam legislado extensamente sobre essa questão. Basta dizer que quando foi preparada a coleção da Mishnah, o livro maior dedicava-se às leis da purificação, com trinta capítulos do mesmo dedicados somente à descrição da purificação de vasos.

Em João 2:1-11 vemos que os judeus tinham seis grandes jarras de água, usadas para cerimônias de purificação, quando do casamento em Caná. Em João 3:25 lemos sobre uma controvérsia entre os discípulos de Jesus e os judeus. Para todo judeu, a questão revestia-se de imensa importância. Um judeu sentia que precisava manter-se cerimonialmente puro, se tivesse de ser justo e quisesse merecer a aprovação de Deus.

O Senhor Jesus, porém, desprezou todas essas leis relativas à purificação, sobretudo no tocante aos preceitos adicionados ao código levítico, e que formavam a «tradição dos anciãos» (ver Mat. 15:2 e

ÁGUA E SANGUE — ÁGUA, TRANSFORMAÇÃO EM VINHO

Mar. 7:3-13). Jesus ensinava que não havia impureza cerimonial, mas apenas moral e espiritual. Esse ensino foi absorvido pelos Seus apóstolos. Paulo não considerava nada impuro por si mesmo (ver Rom. 14:14-20; Tito 1:15). Apesar disso, é ensino bíblico que ninguém deve violar os escrúpulos de sua própria consciência, ou a consciência de um seu irmão na fé, pondo uma pedra de tropeço em seu caminho. A suprema lei cristã é o amor, e não o cerimonialismo. Ao submeter-se ao voto de purificação, em Jerusalém, Paulo estabeleceu exemplo sobre esse princípio (ver Atos 21:26).

ÁGUA E SANGUE
Ver o artigo sobre **Sangue e Água**.

ÁGUA E SANGUE, CRISTO VEIO POR
Cristo veio por água e sangue; *Testemunho do Espírito* (I Jo. 5:6-12)

Neste texto o autor sagrado apressa-se a voltar à sua polêmica e declara agora o valor da morte de Cristo como expiação. Os gnósticos, (ver o artigo sobre *Gnosticismo*), não criam que o Espírito-Cristo pudesse encarnar-se, porquanto consideravam a matéria como o próprio princípio do pecado, e o corpo humano participaria desse princípio. Se algum «aeon» ou o Cristo (o qual seria apenas um dentre muitos *aeons*) se encarnasse na «matéria», ficaria contaminado. Além disso, parece que não criam na possibilidade metafísica da «encarnação». Pensavam, portanto, que o Espírito-Cristo meramente viera apossar-se do corpo do homem Jesus de Nazaré, quando de seu batismo, tendo-o abandonado quando de sua crucificação. Nunca houve *uma pessoa*, ao mesmo tempo, divina e humana.

Essa *rejeição à encarnação* levava os gnósticos a pensarem que a autoridade de Cristo residia somente em seu *batismo*. Diziam eles: «Cristo veio pela água». Porém, não acreditavam que um *aeon* (como seria Cristo) pudesse morrer. Assim sendo, somente o *homem* Jesus teria morrido. Sua morte teria sido, quando muito, a morte de um mártir que morrera por uma causa boa — não poderia ter qualquer valor como expiação, como se o próprio Cristo não pudesse sofrer ou morrer. Isso significa, além disso, que Cristo não viera «pelo sangue», pois sua missão não poderia ter incluído a morte. Portanto, não haveria qualquer valor expiatório na missão de Cristo. A seção a nossa frente ataca essa suposição errônea. A autor sagrado já havia demonstrado que Cristo realmente se encarnara, pelo que fora possível a «morte de Cristo». Agora, o autor sagrado haverá de mostrar que assim, realmente, sucedera, e que a morte de Cristo fora o motivo da expiação, ficando assim incorporada essa questão em sua missão e autoridade. Cristo viera «pelo sangue», e não somente pela água.

A verdadeira confissão, por conseguinte, reconhece sua encarnação; e a sua morte expiatória também está em foco, e não meramente a autoridade do batismo de Jesus Cristo. Os gnósticos reconheciam somente a autoridade de seu batismo, quando o «aeon» descera supostamente sobre o homem Jesus. Nisso, pois, os gnósticos haviam reduzido consideravelmente a compreensão da missão de Cristo. O Espírito Santo, entretanto, dá testemunho acerca da encarnação e da expiação de Cristo, porquanto o Espírito Santo é da verdade e propaga a verdade. Sobre a terra há três testemunhos: o do Espírito (que é o mediador da missão de Cristo em favor dos homens); a água (o

batismo — o seu e o nosso, ao identificar-se conosco); e o sangue, que é a expiação de Cristo, e a nossa participação na mesma. (LAN NTI RO)

ÁGUA, Milagre do Andar Sobre. Ver **Milagre**.

ÁGUA, TRANSFORMAÇÃO EM VINHO
I. Declaração introdutória
O milagre da transformação da água em vinho serve de fachada para o evangelho de João: Ver João 2:12 ss.

«De certa feita, em um grupo de ministros do evangelho, para minha surpresa descobri que eu era o único, dentre eles, que pregava acerca dos milagres, por que os outros sentiam ser tática adversa e psicologia deficiente escolher por assunto um tema que tende a fazer alguns dos ouvintes tropeçarem, ficando assim fechadas as suas mentes para qualquer coisa edificada sobre o que poderiam considerar como fundamento inseguro. No que diz respeito aos milagres de cura, tal atitude, naturalmente, é inteiramente antiquada. É J.A. Hadfield, com a sua imensa experiência, que nos diz secamente: 'Houve tempo em que as pessoas diziam que *milagres não acontecem*; e a implicação disso era que as narrativas sobre milagres, existentes nos evangelhos, são inverídicas. Atualmente, porém, praticamente todos os *milagres de cura* do Novo Testamento têm sido reproduzidos...por muitas e muitas vezes'. (*Psychology and the Church*, Nova Iorque: The MacMillan Co., 1925, pág. 190). Muitas coisas, próprias dos evangelhos, que anteriormente serviam de motivo de zombaria, por vezes confiantes e zombeteiras, agora são aceitas como *auto-evidentemente verazes*, e, de alguma maneira, a maravilha das realizações de Cristo aparentemente vem sendo reproduzida, em muitos lugares, o que ele antecipou, há dois mil anos. Até a ciência está fazendo descobertas confirmativas».

«É de modo um tanto semelhante que o episódio do casamento em Caná serve de fachada para o Evangelho de João, sumariando numa narrativa gráfica o que viria a seguir: como nosso Senhor solucionava as dificuldades do povo; quão incrivelmente ele sofria por causa de cada dificuldade; e, acima de tudo, como ele enriqueceu as coisas para nós. O que a água era para o vinho, o que a embaraçosa insuficiência era para o alívio que ele concedeu ao anfitrião da festa, assim também se compara qualquer outra vida com a plenitude, com o colorido, com a aventura, com a realização que ele proporciona... Porém, se essa é a lição principal, também muitos outros pensamentos se evidenciam e nos atraem, ao nos aproximarmos dela. Temos aqui o fato de que Cristo se achava presente; que eles mesmos desejavam que ele ali estivesse; que eles não temiam que ele se sentisse fora de seu elemento, ou não conseguisse adaptar-se, ou que deixasse os outros um tanto embaraçados, segundo teria ocorrido no caso de João Batista fazer-se presente, com o seu ascetismo. E podemos estar certos de que não houve qualquer silêncio embaraçoso naquela porção da mesma onde ele estava reclinado. Pois Cristo não se conservava afastado da felicidade inocente dos homens, fato esse que muitos de nós, seus seguidores, temos esquecido, com resultados suficientemente trágicos, transformando a sua religião em algo muito mais austero do que ele jamais tencionou; e por essas caricaturas espantamos muitos daqueles que lhe pertencem por direito natural». (Arthur John Gossip, em Jo. 2:12, IB).

88

ÁGUAS DE MEGIDO — ÁGUAS DE MEROM

II. Diversas interpretações

Interpretações (típicas) dos milagres. Diversas interpretações têm sido oferecidas para explicar, para eliminar mesmo, este milagre; e essas explanações também são comumente aplicadas a outras narrativas sobre milagres, nos evangelhos. Abaixo damos um sumário dessas explicações:

1. *Explicações naturais* (do baixo racionalismo). O que Jesus fez foi tão-somente uma brincadeira própria para uma festa de casamento. Ele trouxera grande quantidade de vinho para a festa, e misturou o vinho com a água das talhas. Outros da mesma escola dizem que se tratou de *um presente* de casamento, para surpreender os noivos.

2. *Explicações místicas*. A narrativa não deveria ser aceita como um acontecimento histórico, mas antes, como uma espécie de *poema religioso*, como lenda inconscientemente (ou conscientemente) produzida, e que foi honestamente acreditada pela igreja cristã primitiva. A base desse milagre se encontraria na narrativa do A.T., que conta como as águas amargosas se tornaram potáveis (ver Êxo. 15:23 e II Reis 2:19). Ou a origem do mesmo poderia ser encontrada na literatura antiga dos gregos e romanos, como o caso da história de Dionísio, o deus grego do vinho e da inspiração. Uma narrativa similar a essa (transformação de água em vinho) se encontra nos escritos de Plínio (*História Natural* II,231; XXXI.16). Essa opinião pode ter sido até mesmo sugerida pela interpretação alegórica do V.T. criada por Filo. Por exemplo, em sua obra, *Interpretações Alegóricas* (III. 26.82), ele apresenta o *Logos* a ordenar a Melquisedeque que dê vinho, em vez de água, e ali o vinho serve de símbolo da «embriaguez divina, mais sóbria que a própria sobriedade».

3. *Interpretações simbólicas*. A narrativa não seria nem fictícia e nem histórica, mas conteria meros símbolos, tal como chegara o tempo para Jesus tirar os seus discípulos da «água» de João Batista para o vinho de seu reino superior; ou então, de modo geral, que o vinho é símbolo da superioridade da nova religião, em comparação com os princípios ensinados por João Batista, ou com as doutrinas do judaísmo do estilo antigo. (Ver João 1:26,33 e Efé. 5:18).

4. *Interpretações históricas*. Existem muitas e variegadas interpretações e modificações. a. Interpretação absoluta: Foi um milagre físico, uma *intervenção divina* na natureza, sem qualquer ajuda por parte de processos naturais. Foi um milagre sem quaisquer condições humanas de qualquer sorte. b. Interpretação *condicional*: Foi uma transformação possibilitada por condições. Olshausen assevera ter havido uma aceleração dos processos naturais, o que, naturalmente, não faz sentido algum. c. Teria sido uma modificação dos acidentes, em que a água, como no caso de algumas águas minerais, assume *sabores diversos*. Este último ponto de vista não permite qualquer transformação real na *substância* da água, mas, tão-somente, em como a percepção dos sentidos humanos a julgava. d. *Modificação substancial*: A própria «substância» da água foi transformada, e' juntamente com isso, os seus «acidentes», ou seja, aquelas qualidades sujeitas à percepção dos sentidos humanos, tais como cor, sabor, peso, aroma, etc. A posição da modificação substancial poderia ser alistada sob «interpretação histórica absoluta» ou sob «interpretação condicional»; neste último caso, o milagre teria ocorrido ajudado por algumas condições. Mas os comentadores não têm jamais apresentado quaisquer condições apropriadas e compreensíveis. As condições mais apropriadas, coerentes com os próprios ensinamentos de Jesus, seriam que ele, como homem, mediante o desenvolvimento dado pelo Espírito Santo, tornou-se um tipo de ser humano que, apesar de continuar sendo mortal, podia realizar essas maravilhas físicas. Essa idéia poderia incluir aquela ainda mais avançada, a saber, que outros homens, crentes em Cristo, mediante o mesmo processo de desenvolvimento espiritual, em seu caminho de transformação segundo a imagem de Cristo, podem realizar milagres similares, como expressão de seus seres espiritualizados em graus diversos.

III. Considere estes fatos.

1. O Senhor possui os recursos para solucionar as dificuldades do povo.

2. Suas soluções abarcam as duas esferas: a física (necessidades terrenas) e a espiritual (necessidades da alma).

3. Jesus fez o que o anfitrião não tinha recursos para fazer. Os homens são limitados, mesmo nas coisas desta vida, e mormente, no tocante a qualquer provisão para a vida no além.

4. Os feitos de Jesus proporcionaram uma solução definitiva e feliz.

5. A própria missão de Cristo tinha por intuito resolver aquilo que os homens, por si mesmos, não poderiam resolver. Considere a mensagem de textos como Rom. 5:1, Efé. 2:8, João 1:12 e Tito 3:5.

IV. Sumário e polêmica

1. O ministério de Jesus foi o do Messias; portanto, de elevadíssima estatura.

2. Portanto, apesar de poderoso, o ministério de João foi secundário e preparatório apenas.

3. O antigo judaísmo estava ultrapassado, e doravante teria de buscar seu cumprimento no ministério do Messias.

4. A encarnação (que vide) do Logos trouxe um novo dia, o dia profético, o cumprimento das esperanças dos profetas.

5. O Messias combinava, em si mesmo, as naturezas divina e humana, e tinha o direito e o poder de revelar Deus aos homens. Ver os artigos sobre a *Humanidade de Cristo*, e sobre sua *divindade*. (AL DE FA I IB NTI)

ÁGUAS DE MEGIDO

No cântico de vitória de Débora, em Juízes 5:19, é empregada essa expressão, provavelmente alusiva ao wadi que drenava a região por detrás de Megido. Entre esse local e as colunas mais ao sul, acampou Tutmés III. Dali ele lançou o ataque contra Megido. A passagem bíblica sugere que em vez de dividirem os despojos, o que teriam feito se estivessem no lado sul do vale de Jezreel, os reis cananeus foram varridos pela torrente de Quisom (ver o artigo a respeito), que ficava no centro da planície. (Z)

ÁGUAS DE MEROM

A palavra hebraica envolvida significa «altura» ou «águas superiores». De acordo com alguns estudiosos, era um massa de água em forma triangular, com cerca de quase sete quilômetros e meio de extensão e 800 m de largura. Fica a 82,5 m abaixo do nível do mar Mediterrâneo. O Jordão atravessa essa massa de água, sendo esse o local onde Josué obteve grande vitória sobre os cananeus (ver Jos. 11:5-7). Fica localizada na porção superior das colinas de Naftali, onde começam as vertentes do Hermom, que alcançam 3.050 m de altura. Trata-se do lago que Josefo

ÁGUIA — AGULHA

chamou de Semeconitis (ver *Ant.* v.5,1; *Guerras* iii.10,7). Na Bíblia esse lago só é mencionado no livro de Josué. Ao que parece, modernamente é o lago de Hulleh. Alguns estudiosos identificam a Mermo dos tempos bíblicos com a atual aldeia de Merom, à base do Jebal Jermak, a oeste de Safede, onde há uma importante fonte.

Tutmés III (cerca de 1480 A.C.), referiu-se a *Mrm*, que talvez fosse a mesma localidade bíblica que estamos considerando. Ainda outros estudiosos pensam que Merom seja a atual Kirbet el-Bijar, perto de Marun er-Ras, onde há muitas fontes. Todas essas propostas identificações envolvem problemas, tanto aquelas feitas na antiguidade como as de nossos dias. Entretanto, a fixação da cidade de Merom, nas vizinhanças do Jebel Marun harmoniza-se muito bem com todas as fontes informativas que mencionam essa cidade, provendo uma razoável explicação topográfica para aquela batalha ganha por Josué. Ficava situada na estrada principal que partia de Aco, via Gate. Era um local apropriado para o encontro de aliados que viessem da planície de Aco e de Hazor. Sua localização fica a curta distância do lago de Quinerete, mais para o noroeste. Seja como for, em resultado da vitória obtida por Josué, os israelitas foram capazes de conquistar as cidades cujos reis caíram em Merom. E nenhuma dessas cidades aparece na lista de aldeias não conquistadas, no primeiro capítulo do livro de Juízes (ver Juí. 1:27-36). Todas essas aldeias, excetuando Merom, figuram entre as aldeias atribuídas às tribos do norte, no livro de Josué. (UN Z)

ÁGUIA

As **palavras hebraica e grega envolvidas são** traduzidas como *águia* e como *abutre*, em diferentes traduções. A águia encabeça a lista de aves consideradas imundas, pela lei levítica (ver Lev. 11:13 ss.), talvez por causa de seu grande tamanho e aspecto impressionante. Por ser uma ave de rapina, a águia era repulsiva aos hebreus, embora vários trechos bíblicos demonstrem admiração, conforme se lê em Êxo. 19:4: «...vos levei sobre asas de águias...», ou como em Jer. 49:22: «Eis que como águia subirá...», ou como Pro. 23:5: «...como a águia que voa pelos céus». Nesse último trecho, o rápido vôo da águia representa como as riquezas podem desaparecer facilmente, não devendo tornar-se o alvo principal na vida de alguém. O trecho de Êxo. 19:4 também encerra uma alusão figurada, falando sobre a proteção de Deus, que se assemelha a uma águia que pode sustentar outros em suas imensas asas.

Há várias espécies desse pássaro na Palestina, distinguidas por seu tamanho, coragem, poderes de vôo e capacidade de ataque. As espécies maiores têm uma envergadura de asas com 2,10 m ou mais, com um comprimento de corpo de cerca de 1,05 m. Todavia, há referências bíblicas que claramente apontam para o abutre, como se vê em Mat. 24:28. Essas aves de rapina atingem grande altura em seu vôo, mantendo-se bem afastadas umas das outras. Quando alguma delas baixa subitamente o vôo, isso serve de sinal de que há algo de interesse para elas no solo, e as demais rapidamente juntam-se, para o banquete. Esse é um hábito observado em várias espécies. O grifo, que é um abutre, talvez esteja em foco em Miq. 1:16. A cabeça dessa ave é coberta por uma pele enrugada clara, que pode ser vista à grande distância. Nesse trecho, lê-se sobre a «calva» da águia.

Outros usos simbólicos, além daqueles sugeridos acima: 1. Reis conquistadores, como os da Assíria,

Babilônia e Egito, que se lançam à matança e ao saque (ver Eze. 17:3,7; Osé. 8:1). 2. Os exércitos dos caldeus, que agiam como se dotados de asas de águias, pois atacavam e matavam com grande rapidez (ver Jer. 4:13; Lam. 4:19; Dan. 7:4). 3. Os exércitos romanos também são comparados com as águias, por motivos similares (ver Mat. 24:28; Luc. 17:37). 4. Os idumeus, que faziam fortificações em rochas inacessíveis em seu país, protegendo-se assim de qualquer possível derrota (ver Jer. 49:16 e Oba. 4). 5. Como sinal de lamentação pela destruição iminente, foi recomendado a Israel que se fizesse calva como a águia (ver Miq. 1:16). Todavia, nesse trecho está em foco uma espécie de abutre. Um antigo provérbio, preservado no Talmude, refere-se à águia como ave que, da Palestina, era capaz de divisar uma carcaça na distante Babilônia, ou vice-versa. (ID S Z)

ÁGUIA MARINHA

É mencionada em Lev. 11:13 e Deu. 14:12. Era uma ave de grande porte, que alguns estudiosos pensam pertencer à espécie do abutre. Mas outros pensam em uma espécie que alimentava-se de peixes. Como o peixe não é abundante na Palestina, essa espécie era um tanto rara. Além disso, tal ave, por ser ictiófaga, deveria pertencer à espécie dos gaviões. Isso explica a versão portuguesa «águia marinha».

AGUILHÕES

Vem de um termo hebraico que significa «aprender» ou «ensinar», bem como de um vocábulo grego que significa «ferrão», um instrumento aguçado e pontudo. O aguilhão era usado para guiar bois. Tinha um longo cabo, usualmente com uma ponta aguçada em uma das extremidades. Além de ser usado para tanger animais de grande porte, era usado como uma arma, conforme se vê em Juízes 3:31, onde lemos que Sangar, filho de Anate, feriu a seiscentos filisteus «com uma aguilhada de bois». Algumas vezes, o aguilhão tinha uma ponta de ferro, que também podia ser usada para limpar arados. Metaforicamente, a palavra fala de encorajamento e repreensão (ver Ecl. 12:11). O único uso da palavra, no Novo Testamento, aparece em Atos 26:14, onde o aguilhão refere-se à divina repreensão e orientação, contra o que Saulo lutava, em sua louca perseguição contra os cristãos. Embora convencido de que estava fazendo a vontade de Deus com grande zelo, na verdade ele estava se comportando como um boi recalcitrante, resistindo aos planos reais de Deus para ele, o que certamente é comum à experiência da maioria das pessoas.

AGULHA

Essa palavra encontra-se na Bíblia somente em um provérbio de Jesus: «E ainda vos digo que é mais fácil um camelo passar pelo fundo de uma agulha, do que entrar um rico no reino de Deus» (Mat. 19:24). Certa variante textual diz «corda», em vez de *camelo*, mas isso, embora pareça interessante, conta com menor apoio textual. Ver a exposição desse versículo, no NTI. O sentido geral é que as riquezas atraem a atenção de seu possuidor de tal maneira que é difícil o tal apreciar as realidades da vida espiritual. Portanto, tal indivíduo está negligenciando as coisas que realmente importam na vida, a saber, o bem-estar espiritual. O quinto capítulo do livro de Tiago desenvolve o tema dos aspectos prejudiciais das riquezas materiais.

AGULHA — AI

Trabalho com agulhas. A arte de costurar e de bordar foi uma das primeiras realizações humanas. O trecho de Gênesis 3:7 fala em costura de folhas, para a confecção de aventais que encobriam a nudez de Adão e Eva. As primeiras agulhas eram feitas de osso, tendo sido encontradas agulhas pertencentes ao sexto milênio A.C. Em Israel, em tempos posteriores, as agulhas passaram a ser fabricadas de bronze, e tinham uma perfuração ou um pequeno gancho para formar o buraco da agulha. Os arqueólogos têm descoberto agulhas feitas de outros materiais, como ferro, marfim, etc., e de variegados tamanhos, desde 12 mm até 13,5 cm. Bordadeiras habilidosas são mencionadas em Êxodo 36:37 e 39:29. Homens envolviam-se nesse tipo de trabalho (ver Êxo. 35:34,35). O apóstolo Paulo era fabricante de tendas, o que envolvia o trabalho de costurar (ver Atos 18:3). Ver os artigos sobre *Buraco da Agulha* e *Bordado.* (NTI Z)

AGULHA, BURACO DA

Ver o artigo sobre **Agulha.** Os evangelhos sinópticos aludem ao buraco da agulha (ver Mat. 19:24; Mar. 10:25 e Luc. 18:25), onde se lê que é mais fácil um camelo passar pelo buraco de uma agulha, do que um rico entrar no reino de Deus. Jesus tinha o costume de usar objetos familiares em Suas parábolas. Havia agulhas em qualquer casa. O buraco de uma agulha, que era uma perfuração ou um pequeno gancho, era uma pequena abertura, por onde era difícil fazer passar um fio, quanto mais um camelo! Alguns manuscritos gregos dizem aqui «corda», em vez de *camelo*, — pois essas duas palavras são similares nesse antigo idioma; mas a variante «corda» tem muito menor apoio textual. É possível que um provérbio original dissesse «elefante», e não «camelo»; mas Jesus falou em camelo, por ser esse o maior animal que havia na Palestina. (Ver no NTI a exposição dessa afirmação de Jesus, e as dificuldades textuais existentes em Mat. 19:25). Outros estudiosos pensam que Jesus falava na pequena abertura existente na muralha de Jerusalém, por onde um camelo só podia passar se se ajoelhasse; mas a maioria dos estudiosos rejeita essa especulação, ainda que haja algum indício de que tal abertura era chamada de «buraco». O que Jesus quis dizer é que é *muito difícil* um rico entrar no reino de Deus, embora também possamos entender Sua declaração como indicação de total impossibilidade, se a entendermos literalmente. Ver também o quinto capítulo de Tiago, que fala sobre os empeceilhos à vida espiritual, representados pelas riquezas materiais. Uma coisa é certa: os ricos deste mundo não são favorecidos quanto às coisas espirituais, conforme o são quanto às coisas terrenas. Contudo, há ricos piedosos, tal como há esmoleiros que vão para o inferno. Ver também o artigo sobre *Bordados.* (ND S Z)

AGUR

No hebraico significa **colhedor** ou **mercenário.** Era filho de Jaque e foi o autor das declarações contidas em Provérbios 30. O título descreve-o como compositor de preceitos entregues por «Agur, filho de Jaque», aos seus amigos «Itiel e Ucal». Além disso, só há conjecturas sobre essas pessoas. Alguns supõem que o verdadeiro autor foi Salomão, embora ninguém explique por qual razão ele teria escrito sob um pseudônimo. A Vulgata Latina, em Pro. 31:1 diz: *Verba Congregantis filii Vomentis,* o que faz de Agur irmão de *Lemuel* (ver o artigo). (Z)

AHIMSA

Termo sânscrito que significa **não-injúria.** Jainos, budistas e outros acreditam que é matar qualquer ser vivo, por humilde que seja. A crença subjacente para essa convicção é que todas as criaturas vivas possuem almas, essencialmente da mesma natureza que a alma humana. Por meio da transmigração a alma de um ser humano temporariamente pode ser cativada em alguma forma inferior de vida. Isso posto, merecem respeito todas as formas de vida. A vida é *sagrada.* Todas as criaturas vivas estariam esforçando-se na direção da salvação. Ver *reencarnação.* (E F)

AHRIMAN

Conhecido também como Angra Mainyu, deus malévolo do zoroastrismo. Ele se opõe à força do bem, especificamente ao deus benevolente, Ahura Mazda. Ver *zoroastrismo.*

AI

No hebraico, **montão** ou **ruína.** Uma cidade dos cananeus, associada a Betel, Jericó e Jerusalém, que estabelece sua localização naquela área (ver Gên. 12:8; 13:3; Jos. 7:2-5; 8:1-29; 10:1,2; 12:9; Esd. 2:28; Nee. 7:32; Jer. 49:3). Ela é mais lembrada por ter sido capturada e destruída por Josué (ver Jos. 7:2-5 e 8:1-29). Mais tarde foi reconstruída, e foi mencionada por Isaías (10:28). No tempo de Eusébio e Jerônimo, suas ruínas aparentemente ainda eram conhecidas. Atualmente, o local é Et Tell Kisa, cerca de três quilômetros de Tell Beitin (Betel). Joseph A. Callaway, arqueólogo, pensa que essa é a única conclusão satisfatória com base em um estudo dos antigos nomes envolvidos, da topografia e do óbvio íntimo relacionamento que tinha com Betel, Jerusalém e Jericó. Seus estudos e escavações têm sido feitos desde 1964. Antes disso houve escavações nessa área, em 1928 (John Garstang), 1933-1935 (Judith Marquet Krause). As escavações mostram que houve uma ocupação pré-urbana de Ai desde 3200 A.C., e que no período de 3000-2500 A.C. houve ali uma próspera população, na chamada Idade do Bronze Primitiva. Evidências arqueológicas mostram que Ai foi atacada por duas vezes em sua história, deixando traços óbvios. Os artefatos encontrados mostram forte influência egípcia, podendo ser identificada com a Palestina egípcia da era das pirâmides. Ainda não foram encontradas evidências arqueológicas sobre a própria Ai, mas sabemos que naquela época havia ali apenas um minúsculo povoado (ver Jos. 7:3). Alguns têm conjecturado que a Ai dos dias de Josué não era exatamente no local antigo, mas nas proximidades, e que o nome foi transferido para esse novo local. Isso explicaria as evidências diretas de Ai no tocante a Josué. A transferência do nome de uma cidade arruinada ou abandonada, para um novo local, era um fenômeno comum na Palestina. (FK ND S UN)

AI

Tradução portuguesa de sete interjeições hebraicas e de uma grega. Algumas delas usadas apenas por uma vez, conforme se vê em Sal. 120:5; Eze. 2:10 e 30:2. Duas das interjeições hebraicas são usadas por vinte e duas e por trinta e seis vezes, respectivamente, a primeira como simples interjeição de tristeza (ver, para exemplificar, Núm. 21:29; I Sam. 4:7,8; Isa. 3:9-11; Jer. 4:13; 48:46; Lam. 5:16; Eze. 16:23; Osé. 7:13), e a segunda como interjeição de tristeza, de advertência ou de exortação (ver, para exemplificar,

AI — AÍAS

Isa. 5:8,11,18,20,21,22; Jer. 22:13; Eze. 13:3; Amós 5:18; Miq. 2:1; Naum 3:1; Hab. 2:6; Sof. 2:5; Zac. 11:17). A palavra grega *ouaí* é usada por vinte e oito vezes, de Mat. 11:21 a Apo. 12:12.

Quando essa interjeição era usada, Deus não estava pronunciando um juízo final, mas descrevendo a miserável condição daqueles que estavam sendo descritos. Viviam em um paraíso de tolos, inconscientes do terrível destino que os esperava. Jesus, em Luc. 6:24-26, mostrou que a miséria de certos homens jaz no fato de que eles são dotados de mente materialista, cegos quanto às suas necessidades espirituais, estando auto-satisfeitos, mas não demonstrando simpatia para com o próximo e vivendo na impenitência, embora desfrutando de certa popularidade. O zelo hipócrita, a falta de proporções quanto aos valores espirituais, o amor à aclamação popular, e a autocomplascência dos fariseus e escribas, também os tornava pessoas dignas de lamentação (ver Mat. 23:13-33; Luc. 11:42-52). No tocante aos habitantes impenitentes de Corazim e Betsaida, os «ais» proferidos por Jesus contra eles deviam-se à indiferença deles para com a pregação e as evidências comprobatórias, na forma de milagres, de Jesus, com a consequente inexorável condenação que os aguardava (ver Mat. 11:21).

Paulo sabia que sua situação espiritual tornar-se-ia digna de lamentação se ele negligenciasse no anúncio do evangelho (ver I Cor. 9:16). Por isso mesmo, empenhava-se em fazer a boa-mensagem ser ouvida onde quer que lhe fosse dada oportunidade. Cumpre-nos aceitar esse cuidado (ver II Tim. 4:1-5).

A queda da Babilônia também é anunciada no Apocalipse em meio a «ais» (ver Apo. 18:10-16). E as várias tremendas pragas e desastres destrutivos que acompanharão o juízo final também são expressos por «ais», emitidos pelo Espírito de Deus (ver Apo. 9:12 e 11:14).

AI

Termo chinês para **amor**, e termo-chave da religião de Mo Tzu e Han Yu. Ali o amor é encarado como o principal meio para alguém atingir o bem e o direito.

AI (DE MOABE)

Uma cidade moabita de localização desconhecida (ver Jer. 49:3). Mas alguns identificam-na com a mesma cidade referida acima.

AÍ

No hebraico, **irmão** ou **meu irmão**. 1. Forma usada em nomes compostos, a fim de significar «irmão» ou «meu irmão», como Joai, «Yahweh é irmão» ou Aimeleque, «irmão do rei». 2. Um certo Aí era *membro da tribo de Gade* (ver I Crô. 5:15). Um outro desse nome era *membro da tribo de Aser* (ver I Crô. 7:34), embora algumas traduções, nessa segunda instância, entendam isso como «seu irmão». (S Z)

AIA

Uma cidade do território da tribo de Efraim (ver I Crô. 7:28). Em algumas versões aparece como Gaza ou Aza. De fato, alguns manuscritos hebraicos dizem ali Gaza. Se a forma está correta, ainda assim não deve ser confundida com a Gaza dos filisteus, bem mais ao sul do que aquela. Alguns estudiosos sugerem sua identificação com a «Aia» de Neemias 11:31, fazendo os dois nomes se referirem a uma só cidade.

Mas, em Neemias a menção é a uma cidade benjamita, e não efraimita. (Z)

AIA

Outra forma alternativa de **Ai** (ver o artigo). Essa forma encontra-se em Nee. 11:31.

AIÁ

No hebraico, **falcão** ou **grito do falcão**. — Há dois homens com esse nome no Antigo Testamento.

1. O filho de Zibeão, filho de Seir, o horita (cerca de 1500 A.C.), antepassado de um clã de Edom (ver Gên. 36:24 e I Crô. 1:40).

2. Pai de Rispa. Rispa era concubina de Saul. Dois incidentes que a envolvem se destacam. Isbosete, filho de Saul, acusou Abner de ter tido um caso amoroso com ela (ver II Sam. 3:7), o que Abner repeliu irada e sarcasticamente. E Isbosete calou-se — porque o temia. Mais tarde, quando houve escassez de alimentos, Davi procurou saber do Senhor a razão para a mesma. A resposta do Senhor foi que o ato de Saul, matando os gibeonitas, precisava ser vingado. Para tanto, sete de seus filhos foram enforcados. Entre os mesmos, havia dois filhos de Rispa, a saber, Armoni e Mefibosete.

AIÁ

No hebraico, **fraternal**. Era membro da tribo de Manassés, filho de Semida (ver I Crô. 7:19), cerca de 1856 A.C. (S)

AIÃO

No hebraico significa **irmão da mãe**. Foi um dos heróis de Davi, um dos trinta mais valentes (ver II Sam. 23:33). Era filho de Sarar (II Sam. 23:33) ou Sacar (I Crô. 11:35). Alguns estudiosos supõem que esse nome é uma variante de Aquiabe, que significa *irmão do pai*. (S UN)

AÍAS

No hebraico, **meu irmão é Yahweh**, ou **irmão de** *Yahweh*. Forma abreviada de Aimeleque. Várias pessoas recebem esse nome no Novo Testamento:

1. Aías, um profeta que residia em Siló nos tempos de Salomão e Jeroboão. Parece que ele registrou algumas das transações do primeiro desses reis: ver II Crô. 9:29. Sua tarefa foi de anunciar a separação dos dez tribos (Israel) da casa de Davi (duas tribos: Judá e Benjamim), bem como a fundação da dinastia de Jeroboão. E, após muitos anos, anunciou a queda de Jeroboão (ver I Reis 11:29-39 e 14:2-18). Protestou contra a idolatria que se tornara parte do reinado de Salomão e dividiu simbolicamente as suas vestes em doze pedaços, dez dos quais deu a Jeroboão (um oficial secundário do governo de Salomão). Predisse que esses dez lhe seriam sujeitos. A fim de escapar da ira de Salomão, fugiu para o Egito. Após a morte de Salomão, tudo isso teve cumprimento. Reoboão provocou a divisão do reino. Jeroboão tornou-se rei de Israel, ocupando o trono de 933 a 901 A.C. Jeroboão, porém, conduziu Israel à idolatria, e foi denunciado por Aías, que predisse a morte de seu filho e a extinção de sua casa, bem como o futuro cativeiro de Israel (ver I Reis 14:6-10). A profecia de Aías, o silonita, foi uma das fontes informativas usadas na

AIATE — AIESER

história de Salomão (ver II Crô. 9:29). O último dos filhos de Jerameel a ser chamado por nome (ver I Crô. 2:25), em cerca de 1600 A.C. Era irmão de Calebe, de Judá. Alguns manuscritos da Septuaginta e da versão siríaca dizem «seu irmão», em vez do nome pessoal, Aías.

2. Filho de Aitube, sumo sacerdote durante o reinado de Saul (ver I Sam. 14:3,18), que alguns pensam ser o mesmo que Aimeleque. Era descendente de Eli por meio da linhagem de Finéias (ver I Sam. 14:3). Seu nome era uma forma abreviada de Aimeleque, o que, por sua vez, tem sido confundido com Abimeleque. Aías (ou Aimeleque), pai de Abiatar, serviu como sacerdote em Nobe, usou a estola sacerdotal e foi encarregado da arca de Deus, tendo consultado os oráculos em favor de Saul (ver I Sam. 14:18ss). Foi ele quem ofereceu a Davi os pães da proposição, quando ele e seus homens tiveram fome enquanto fugiam de Saul (ver I Sam. 21:1-10).

3. Um dos príncipes de Salomão (ver I Reis 4:3), filho de Sisa ou Eliorefe. Ambos os irmãos eram escribas de Salomão.

4. Pai de Baasa, rei de Israel (ver I Reis 15:27,33), em cerca de 953 A.C. Conspirou contra Nadabe, filho de Jeroboão, e governou em seu lugar. Pertencia à tribo de Issacar.

5. Um dos heróis de Davi (ver I Crô. 11:36), em cerca de 1050 A.C. Era pelonita e um dos trinta principais heróis de Davi, a elite militar. Ver Também II Sam. 23:34.

6. Um levita durante o reinado de Davi (ver I Crô. 26:20), em cerca de 1015 A.C. Governava os tesouros da casa de Deus. A Septuaginta e muitos eruditos traduzem essa palavra, nesse trecho, como «irmão deles», em vez de um nome próprio.

7. Um dos líderes de Israel, que se uniu em pacto com Neemias (ver Nee. 10:25), em cerca de 445 A.C.

8. Um descendente de Benjamim (I Crôn. 8:7), um dos filhos de Eúde. O International Critical Commentary supõe que os três nomes: Naamã, Aías e Gera formariam uma ditografia (ver I Crô. 8:4). Os nomes Aías (vs. 7), Aoá (vs. 4) e Eí (Gên. 46:21) são variações escribais de um texto que originalmente dizia Airã (ver Núm. 26:38).

9. Pai de Aitube, antepassado de Esdras (II Esd. 1:1 ss.). (FA UN Z)

AIATE

Forma alternativa de Ai (ver o artigo). Essa forma encontra-se em Isa. 10:28.

AIÇÃO

No hebraico significa **meu irmão levantou-se** ou *irmão do inimigo*. Um dos quatro homens de distinção a quem Josias enviou para consultar a profetisa Hulda, a respeito da lei (ver II Reis 22:12-14). Ele e seus familiares foram poupados pela proteção conferida ao profeta Jeremias (ver Jer. 26:24 e 39:4), o qual, de outro modo, poderia ter morrido. Era pai de Gedálias, a quem Nabucodonosor tornou-se governador da terra, após a destruição de Jerusalém. (FA S Z)

AICAR, LIVRO DE

Aicar era sobrinho de Tobias, filho do irmão deste, Anael (ver Tobias 1:21,22; 2:10; 11:18; 14:10). Tal como Tobias, foi personagem da antiga literatura de sabedoria do Oriente Próximo, sendo usado como o herói do livro de Aicar, do qual fazemos uma breve descrição abaixo.

Trata-se de uma lenda popular, com o intuito de ensinar conceitos éticos. Fala-se de uma época entre 500 e 600 A.C., embora a data do livro seja incerta. Há várias versões da narrativa em aramaico, siríaco, árabe, etíope, armênio, grego, turco e eslavônico. O original provavelmente foi escrito em aramaico, mas os nomes ali contidos quase todos são de origem assíria. O livro tem muitos paralelos literários e elementos tomados por empréstimo, sobretudo do Antigo Testamento, dos livros apócrifos do Antigo Testamento, de Tobias, de Ben Siraque, de Demócrito, de Esopo, do Alcorão e do Novo Testamento. Como é óbvio, a história foi aproveitando adições e modificando-se ao longo do caminho, para poder incorporar tão grande gama de literatura.

Principais elementos da narrativa:

1. Aicar era o vizir (oficial mais alto) de Senaqueribe, rei da Assíria (704 - 681 A.C.). 2. Era conhecido por sua sabedoria. 3. Visto que não tinha filhos, adotou o filho de sua irmã, Nadã, e criou-o para ser o seu sucessor na corte de Senaqueribe. 4. Deu ao menino todas as vantagens, embora este fosse como uma maçã estragada, aparentemente bonita por fora, cujo âmago porém, estava apodrecido. 5. Quando Aicar ameaçou substituir o menino, Nadã escreveu cartas fraudulentas aos soberanos do Egito e da Pérsia, oferecendo-se para trair as tropas assírias. O pior é que disse a Senaqueribe que Aicar era traidor da pátria e então foi condenado à morte. Afortunadamente, o proposto executor de Aicar era um bom amigo seu, que colocou um criminoso em lugar dele, dando tempo assim para que a cólera do monarca se abrandasse. 6. Aicar teve de ocultar-se. Surgiram circunstâncias que levaram o rei a consultar alguém que fosse tão sábio quanto Aicar. O Egito exigiu que a Assíria pagasse pesado tributo e este poderia ser dispensado se alguém pudesse construir um castelo no ar, com cordas tecidas de areia. 7. Aicar é trazido à presença do rei, porém, agora um homem alquebrado, com cabelos longos e unhas como as presas de uma águia. 8. Então ele confrontou seu sobrinho com provérbios de repreensão, como, por exemplo: «Oh, meu rapaz! você foi para comigo como um homem que viu seu companheiro despido no frio do inverno e derramou sobre ele água gelada». Ouvindo essas repreensões, o corpo de Nadã inchou e seu ventre estourou. 9. A fim de resolver o problema egípcio, Aicar usou duas águias para transportar dois meninos para o ar, os quais então pediram aos egípcios que lhes dessem tijolos e cimento, para poderem construir o castelo. Visto que não podiam fazer isso, foi dispensada a obrigação da construção do castelo. Então Aicar foi restaurado ao seu posto original.

Esse livro, sob várias formas e em vários idiomas, foi muito popular na literatura folclórica por muitos séculos. Foi encontrado um fragmento do livro nas ruínas de Elefantina, com data de cerca de 500 A.C. Mas é óbvio que vários elementos da história foram sendo acrescentados com a passagem do tempo. Seu texto mais **autoritário** é um papiro em aramaico. (C Z)

AIESER

No hebraico, **irmão é ajuda.** É o nome de duas pessoas do Antigo Testamento:

1. Filho de Amisadai, o qual, no tempo de Moisés, representava a tribo de Dã, o que fez em certo número de importantes ocasiões (ver Núm. 1:12; 2:25;

AIJALOM — AIMAÁS

7:66,71; 10:25). Saiu do Egito à testa de setenta e dois mil homens.

2. Um homem mencionado em I Crô. 12:3, chefe danita que se aliou a Davi, quando se esondia em Ziclague, para não ser morto por Saul. Era um exímio arqueiro. (UN Z)

AIJALOM

No hebraico, **lugar de veados** ou **carvalhos**. Havia duas cidades com esse mesmo nome:

1. Uma cidade e um vale na tribo de Dã (ver Jos. 19:42), que foi dada aos levitas (ver Jos. 21:24; I Crô. 6:69), não distante de Bete-Semes (ver II Crô. 28:18). Foi um dos lugares fortificados por Reoboão (ver II Crô. 11:10). Estava entre os fortes que os filisteus tomaram de Acaz (ver II Crô. 28:18). O nome aparece pela primeira vez na Bíblia no discurso de Josué, após a derrota dos amorreus: «Sol, detém-te em Gibeom, e tu, lua, no vale de Aijalom» (Jos. 10:12). Veio a tornar-se uma cidade de refúgio (ver Jos. 21:24). Quando da divisão da terra, os danitas não conquistaram a cidade (ver Juí. 1:35), mas Saul e Jônatas obtiveram grandes vitórias nas proximidades da mesma (ver I Sam. 14:31). Mais tarde foi habitada por efraimitas (I Crô. 6:69), e mais tarde ainda, por benjamitas (I Crô. 8:13). Quando Israel e Judá se dividiram, ela ficou com Judá. Então Reoboão tornou-a uma fortaleza (ver II Crô. 11:10). No reinado de Acaz, foi capturada pelos filisteus (ver II Crô. 28:18).

2. Uma cidade no território da tribo de Zebulom (ver Juíz. 12:12). O juiz Elom foi ali sepultado. A localização moderna é desconhecida. (AH ND UN S)

AIJELETE (Hash-shahar)

Ver **instrumentos musicais**. A palavra ocorre no título do Salmo 22, no hebraico. Pode indicar a melodia com que esse Salmo era cantado. Em nossa Bíblia portuguesa, essa melodia aparece com o nome de Corça da Manhã, no título desse salmo.

AILUDE

Desconhece-se seu sentido em hebraico, mas talvez signifique *irmão do nascido*, ou *irmão do Lídio*.

1. Pai de Josafá, cronista e escrivão do reino, nos governos de Davi e Salomão (ver II Sam. 8:16; 20:24; I Reis 4:3).

2. Pai de Baana, um dos oficiais de Salomão (ver I Reis 4:12). Mas alguns estudiosos pensam que «1» e «2» são a mesma pessoa.

AIM

No hebraico, **fonte**. Há duas cidades com esse nome no Antigo Testamento:

1. Uma aldeia na extremidade nordeste de Canaã, assim chamada devido a uma fonte existente no local. O trecho de Núm. 34:11 mostra que ficava perto de Ribla (mas não a Ribla do Orontes). Os textos da Vulgata e dos rabinos dizem *Dafne*, em lugar de Aim, mas aquela ficava próxima do lago Hulé. Josefo (*Guerras* iv.3) estava amiliarizado com o lugar. Este era um marco fronteiriço natural na Palestina oriental. Alguns a têm identificado com a 'Ain el-'Azy, um dos braços formadores do Orontes, que é uma poderosa fonte de água potável.

2. Uma cidade que a princípio foi dada à tribo de Judá (ver Jos. 15:32), e que mais tarde foi dada a Simeão (ver Jos. 19:7 e I Crô. 4:32). Era uma das cidades dos levitas (ver Jos. 21:16). Em I Crô. 6:59, o nome de Aim é mudado para Asã. Ficava localizada a nordeste de Canaã, entre Ribla e o mar da Galiléia.

Em Josué e I Crôn. 4:32, as cidades de Aim e Rimom aparecem como cidades separadas. Alguns estudiosos, porém, preferem entender que havia uma única cidade, com o nome de *Aim-Rimom*.

3. A mesma palavra significa a décima sexta letra do alfabeto hebraico, assim chamada porque seu traçado se parece com um olho. Também figura no alfabeto de Ugarite. Na Septuaginta, foi usada a letra grega *gama* para transliterá-la, conforme se vê nos nomes próprios locativos Gomorra e Gaza, que no hebraico começam com a letra *aim*.

AIMÃ

No hebraico, **irmão de um presente, liberal** ou **meu irmão é fortuna**.

1. Um dos três famosos gigantes anaquins que habitavam em Hebrom, avistados pelos espias e por Calebe (ver Núm. 13:22), em cerca de 1600 A.C. Posteriormente, os gigantes foram exterminados por Josué (ver Jos. 11:21), ou foram mortos pela tribo de Judá (ver Juí. 1:10).

2. Um dos porteiros levitas do templo, após o exílio. (Ver I Crô. 9:17). (FA UN S)

AIMAÁS

No hebraico, **meu irmão é ira**, ou **irascível**. É o nome de várias pessoas no Antigo Testamento:

1. Pai da esposa de Saul, Ainoã (ver I Sam. 14:50).

2. Filho e sucessor de Sadoque, foi sumo sacerdote juntamente com ele durante o reinado de Davi, e talvez tenha sido o único sumo sacerdote nos dias de Salomão. Sua história cabe mais no tempo de Davi, a quem prestou um importante serviço, quando da revolta de Absalão. Na ausência de Davi em Jerusalém, os sumos sacerdotes Sadoque e Abiatar ali ficaram para cuidar dos negócios do reino. Mas seus filhos, Aimaás e Jônatas ocultaram-se fora da cidade, prontos a levar a Davi qualquer informação importante acerca das atividades de Absalão. Foi assim que Husai, tendo transmitido aos sacerdotes o resultado do conselho de guerra, em que seu conselho foi preferido ao de Aitofel, enviou uma menina (para evitar suspeitas) a Aimaás e Jônatas, para que eles levassem a notícia a Davi. Mas isso foi detectado, e os mensageiros foram perseguidos. Refugiaram-se em um poço vazio, e a dona da casa escondeu-os cobrindo o poço e disfarçando-o com grama seca. E disse aos perseguidores que os mensageiros haviam passado por ali com grande pressa. Desse modo, puderam continuar e transmitir a mensagem a Davi (ver II Sam. 15:27-36; 17:17-20). Aimaás tornou-se conhecido por ser um corredor veloz, o que demonstrou ainda em uma outra ocasião, quando convenceu Joabe a permitir-lhe levar notícias a Davi. Um outro homem, Cusi, estava a caminho, embora Aimaás tivesse corrido mais do que ele, chegando primeiro para dar as notícias. A notícia envolvia a vitória do exército de Davi sobre o de Absalão, e a morte deste último. Mas o mensageiro não falou sobre a morte de Absalão, respeitando os sentimentos de Davi. Alguns duvidam que ele tivesse substituído Sadoque como sumo sacerdote, visto que ele não aparece entre os oficiais de Salomão (ver I Reis 4:2), e por parecer que Azarias é que preenchia essa função.

3. Genro de Salomão, que casou-se com a filha

AIMELEQUE — AISAR

deste, Basemate, e foi um dos doze oficiais do rei, encarregados de prover o alimento para a casa real, financiado pelo oitavo distrito, o de Naftali (ver I Reis 4:15). Viveu em cerca de 950 A.C. (FA S UN Z)

AIMELEQUE

No hebraico significa **irmão do rei** ou **amigo do rei**. Nome aplicado a três personagens do Antigo Testamento.

1. Um outro nome para Aías. Ele é a terceira pessoa desse nome que é discutida.

2. Um heteu que seguia Davi enquanto ele estava fugitivo no deserto, escondendo-se de Saul (ver I Sam. 26:6).

3. Um filho de Abiatar também atendia por esse nome (ver II Sam. 8:17; I Crô. 18:16). Era neto do primeiro Aimeleque, acima. Alguns supõem que o pai e o filho de Abiatar não teriam o mesmo nome; mas a verdade é que esse era um fenômeno comum. Outros supõem que o texto deveria dizer «Abiatar, filho de Aimeleque», e não «Aimeleque, filho de Abiatar», tornando assim esse homem idêntico ao primeiro homem. Entretanto, não há necessidade desse esquema. (ALB UN)

AIMOTE

No hebraico quer dizer **meu irmão é morte**, ou *destrutivo*. Era levita, descendente de Coate (ver I Crô. 6:25). Elcana, pai de Samuel, descendia dele. Em I Crô. 6:26 é chamado Naate.

AINADABE

No hebraico, **irmão é nobre** ou **irmão liberal**. Um dos doze oficiais que, nos doze distritos em que o país foi dividido, conseguia suprimentos para a mesa real, em regime mensal. O distrito de Ainadabe era constituído da metade sul da região além do Jordão (ver I Reis 4:14), no sul de Gileade. E sua sede ficava em Maanaim. (S Z)

AIN FESHKA

Um oásis a três quilômetros ao sul de Khirbet Qumran, na costa ocidental do mar Morto. Esse lugar pode ter sido o centro agrícola das seitas de Qumran. Ver sobre *Qumran*. Essa comunidade produzia certa variedade de legumes, e contava com um curtume, que provavelmente incluía a produção de pergaminho. (Z)

AIN KARIM

Uma aldeia cerca de seis quilômetros a oeste de Jerusalém, onde, segundo a tradição, viviam Zacarias e Isabel, pais de João Batista (ver Luc. 1:24,39). Maria, mãe de Jesus, foi ali visitar sua prima. (DAL Z)

AINOÃ

No hebraico, **irmão da graça** ou **irmão é deleite**. Era nome de duas mulheres referidas no Antigo Testamento.

1. Uma mulher de Jezreel, uma das esposas de Davi, mãe de Amom. Ela foi levada cativa pelos amalequitas, quando eles assaltaram Ziclague, mas foi resgatada por Davi (ver I Sam. 25:43; 27:3; II Sam. 2:2 e 3:2). Após a morte de Saul, Ainoã e Abigail subiram a Hebrom com Davi, e ali Ainoã de

à luz ao primeiro filho de Davi, Amom (ver I Sam. 15:43; 27:3; I Crô. 3:1). Abigail foi a mãe de seu segundo filho.

2. Filha de Aimaás, esposa de Saul (ver I Sam. 14:50). (S Z)

AIO Ver sobre **Guia**.

AIO

No hebraico, **fraternal**. Há três pessoas com esse nome no Antigo Testamento:

1. Um dos filhos de Abinadabe, o qual, com seu irmão Uzá, guiaram a carruagem nova em que a arca foi posta, quando da primeira tentativa de Davi de removê-la para Jerusalém. Aio foi na frente, para guiar os bois, enquanto Uzá caminhava ao lado da carruagem (ver II Sam. 6:3,4). Assim a arca foi removida da casa de Abinadabe e voltou a Jerusalém.

2. Um benjamita, filho de Elpaal (ver I Crô. 8:14).

3. Um filho de Jeiel, irmão de Quis, e pai de Saul (ver I Crô. 8:31 e 9:37). (UN)

AIRA

No hebraico significa **irmão do mal**, ou, talvez, **sem** *sorte*. Era chefe da tribo de Naftali, quando os israelitas deixaram o Egito (ver Núm. 1:15 e 2:29). Foi nomeado um dos assessores de Moisés para fazer o recenseamento do povo. Fez sua contribuição para o culto sagrado no décimo segundo dia das ofertas (ver Núm. 7:78,83; 10:27), em cerca de 1440 A.C. (UN Z)

AIRÃ (airamitas)

No hebraico, *irmão exaltado*. 1. O terceiro dos filhos de Benjamim (ver Núm. 26:38). Na lista de I Crô. 8:1, o terceiro nome, Aará, provavelmente é uma forma variante (ou corrupta) de Airão, o que talvez seja o mesmo caso de Aer, em I Crô. 7:12. A genealogia de Benjamim, em Gên. 46:21, diz *Eí*, que pode ser uma forma abreviada de Airã. Nessa lista aparecem 10 filhos, mas alguns desses nomes podem aludir a descendentes mais remotos, em outras listas. 2. Um rei fenício de Gebal (mais tarde, Biblos). Seu magnificante sarcófago foi descoberto, no qual há inscrições que representam um elo no desenvolvimento do alfabeto fenício. Esse sarcófago e as jóias de Airã estão atualmente no Museu Nacional de Beirute. Os eruditos não identificam esse homem com o Hirão de Tiro, aliado de Salomão, embora os nomes sejam evidentemente idênticos. Talvez fossem contemporâneos. (S UN Z)

AIRAMITAS

A família ou os descendentes de Airã (ver Núm. 26:38).

AISAAR

No hebraico, **irmão da alvorada**. Era benjamita, filho de Bilã, neto de Benjamim (ver I Crô. 7:10), em cerca de 1658 A.C. (S)

AISAMAQUE

No hebraico, **irmão de ajuda, socorro**. Pai de Aoliabe, o danita, um dos famosos artífices que construíram e adornaram o tabernáculo. Ver Êxo. 31:6; 35:34. Viveu antes de 1657 A.C.

AISAR

No hebraico, **irmão da canção**. Era o mordomo da

AITOFEL — AJUDAS

casa de Salomão (ver I Reis 4:6).

AITOFEL

No hebraico significa **irmão da insensatez**, ou **tolo**. Foi um homem que, no tempo de Davi, tornou-se conhecido por todo o Israel por causa de sua sabedoria secular. Sua sabedoria era tão grande que seus conselhos eram considerados oráculos (ver II Sam. 16:23). O verdadeiro nome desse homem pode ter sido Aifelete (irmão do livramento), cujas letras foram transpostas para que o seu nome significasse *tolo*. Os escribas poderiam ter feito isso para assinalar a sua insensatez ao ter participado da revolta de Absalão contra Davi.

1. *Sabedoria política*. Ele é mencionado no Antigo Testamento como homem dotado de grande sagacidade política. Fazia parte do grupo de conselheiros de Davi; mas estava em Giló, seu lugar nativo, quando Absalão proclamou sua revolta e convocou-o para vir a Jerusalém.

2. *Defecção*. Supomos que Aitofel pesou as possibilidades do caso, tendo calculado que Absalão seria o vencedor. Portanto, resolveu dar apoio à rebelião (ver II Sam. 15:12). Davi ficou alarmado diante da defecção, e orou para que Deus transformasse o sábio conselho de Aitofel em insensatez. A fim de ajudar nesse propósito, enviou Husai a Absalão, para que ele fingisse estar-se aliando àquele, a fim de enfraquecer a influência de Aitofel. Talvez o trecho de Sal. 55:12-14 contenha um lamento de Davi, diante da traição de Aitofel, sendo ele ali chamado de «meu igual, meu companheiro e meu íntimo amigo», mas agora em liga com o adversário. Aitofel aconselhou Absalão a apossar-se do harém de Davi, e isso pôs fim a toda possibilidade de reconciliação (ver II Sam. 16:20-23). E é provável que a medida tivesse precisamente essa finalidade. Também aconselhou Absalão a perseguir e a eliminar Davi e suas tropas sem a menor demora, antes que tivessem a oportunidade de se reorganizarem. Mas Husai, tendo desempenhado bem o seu papel, convenceu Absalão a esperar e ser cauteloso. Isso deu a Davi o tempo necessário para organizar o contra-ataque.

3. *Suicídio*. Quando Aitofel viu que seu conselho fora rejeitado, desistiu de seguir Absalão, como uma causa perdida, e imediatamente retornou à sua casa, em Giló, pôs em ordem os seus negócios e suicidou-se. Não há como duvidar que, em sua sabedoria, ele viu que Davi sairia vencedor, sendo ele deixado na ridícula posição de haver promovido uma causa errada e perdida. Foi sepultado no sepulcro de seu pai (ver II Sam. 17:23), em cerca de 967 A.C. Esse é o único caso de suicídio registrado no Antigo Testamento, a menos que consideremos como tais os atos de desespero de Sansão e Saul. Ver o artigo sobre o *suicídio*. É curioso que seu filho, Eliã tenha permanecido fiel a Davi; porquanto foi um de seus trinta valentes guerreiros (ver II Sam. 23:34) (FA ND S UN Z)

AITUBE

No hebraico, **irmão da bondade**. É nome de várias pessoas do Antigo Testamento:

1. Filho de Finéias, neto do sumo sacerdote Eli. Seu pai, Finéias, foi morto quando a arca de Deus foi tomada pelos filisteus. Sucedeu a seu avô como sumo sacerdote (em cerca de 1141 A.C.), e por sua vez, foi sucedido por seu filho, Aías (ver I Sam. 14:3), em cerca de 1093 A.C. Ele é chamado de Aimeleque, o

sacerdote, em I Sam. 22:9,11,20.

2. Nome do pai de Sadoque. Sadoque foi feito sumo sacerdote após a morte de Abimeleque (ver II Sam. 8:17 e I Crô. 6:8). Portanto, ocupava esse ofício nos dias de Davi. Em I Crô. 9:11, Aitube é chamado avô de Sadoque. Essas confusões eram provocadas nas listas genealógicas do Antigo Testamento porque os escribas tinham o hábito de deixar de fora, propositalmente, certos nomes, preferindo dar listas representativas, e não listas completas; e também pelo fato de que o termo «pai de» pode referir-se a algum antepassado mais distante, ao mesmo tempo que «filho de» pode ter a força de «descendente». Esses termos eram usados como expressões de ligação, não exprimindo necessariamente relacionamentos exatos. Não há qualquer evidência em prol da conjectura que Aitube tivesse chegado a ser sumo sacerdote.

3. Um outro Aitube era descendente ou filho de Amarias, pai de um outro Sadoque. Estava na sétima geração de Aitube, alista sob o segundo número acima, em I Crô. 6:11; Esd. 8:2; II Esd. 1:1 e Esd. 7:2.

4. Um antepassado de Judite (ver Juí. 8:1). (S UN Z)

AIÚDE

No hebraico quer dizer **irmão é majestade**, ou *irmão de um famoso*. É o nome de dois personagens do Antigo Testamento:

1. Um príncipe da tribo de Aser, o qual, juntamente com outros cabeças de tribos, cooperou com Josué e Eleazar na divisão da terra prometida (ver Núm. 34:27), em cerca de 1172 A.C.

2. Um dos filhos de Eúde, da tribo de Benjamim (ver I Crô. 8:7). O texto não é claro (talvez tenha sido corrompido), e ele poderia ser identificado como filho de Gera ou de Heglã. (UN Z)

AJATIVADA

Termo sânscrito para «não-organização». A única realidade seria o Absoluto, que não tem origem. Usado para indicar Guadapada.

AJOELHAR Ver **Joelho, ajoelhar**.

AJUDADOR

Essa é uma tradução possível do termo grego *paracleto*, um dos nomes dados ao Espírito Santo, a fim de designar o Seu ofício de ajuda, consolo e exortação, visando ao benefício dos crentes. Ver o artigo sobre o *Paracleto*.

AJUDA ECONÔMICA

Ver *Nações Subdesenvolvidas*.

AJUDAS

No grego temos **antilempsis**, «ajudas», «apoios». Ver I Cor. 12:28. O sentido básico da forma verbal é *levar pessoalmente a carga de outrem*, ou seja, levar o fardo alheio.

Usos da palavra. O termo grego é usado nos clássicos para indicar ajuda ou assistência. (Por exemplo, Diod. Sic. i:87). A Septuaginta traduz o termo hebraico correspondente por «socorro», conforme se vê em Sal. 22:19. Outro tanto sucede nos escritos de Josué (ver Guerras iv.5.1) e em II Mac. 11:26.

AKIBA — ALAMOTE

No Novo Testamento. No trecho de I Cor. 12:28, a palavra assume o sentido especial de ser um dos vários dons do Espírito. Os intérpretes muito têm disputado sobre o significado desse dom, exatamente no que consiste, como ele opera, etc.

Idéias. A palavra grega não representa aqui um ofício, como é o caso de apóstolos, pastores, mestres, profetas e evangelistas, os quais, como indivíduos, ocupavam uma posição oficial ou não na Igreja. Refere-se antes a uma função desempenhada por tais homens. Portanto, está em foco o que alguém faz, como atos de misericórdia, doação em dinheiro ou em comestíveis para alívio da pobreza e da necessidade, etc. É nesse campo que os *diáconos* mostram-se ativos, e assim exercem o dom de ajudar ao próximo. A passagem de I Tessalonicenses 5:14 afirma que devemos consolar os desanimados e amparar os fracos. Isso está relacionado à questão. E Paulo também diz que cada qual deve ajudar com seu labor. (Ver Atos 20:35; comparar também Luc. 1:54).

Uma pessoa dotada com esse dom poderia ser um diácono, impulsionado pelo Espírito Santo a preocupar-se com os pobres e necessitados; ou então qualquer indivíduo generoso, que tenha prazer em prestar ajuda e fazer doações voluntárias. A verdade é que há pessoas que se regozijam em dar, não se preocupando muito com aquilo que lhes resta. A generosidade é um dos aspectos do amor, e isso, por si mesmo, é o maior de todos os aspectos do fruto do Espírito (ver Gál. 5:22, bem como as notas do NTI a respeito). Ver também o artigo sobre o *amor.* Aquele que tem esse dom de socorro pode viver de acordo com a lei do amor em sentido material, satisfazendo sua alma ao ver que outras pessoas têm supridas as suas necessidades. Esse dom pode não parecer muito espetacular, como a profecia ou o falar em línguas. Porém, nada existe de tão grande e satisfatório quanto a lei do amor, que é a substância da lei e a prova da espiritualidade (ver I João 4:7,8,20,21). (NTI UN)

AKIBA

Um dos maiores mestres judeus palestinos (50-135 D.C.). Até aos quarenta anos era um pastor analfabeto. Encorajado por sua esposa, Raquel, começou a estudar a lei, e após doze anos, distinguiu-se como mestre. Sistematizou a *Halakah* (prática religiosa, ver o artigo a respeito) e estabeleceu novos métodos de interpretação, incluindo a descoberta de sentidos secretos em cada letra e palavra das Escrituras, um método ilusório que, nos séculos posteriores, haveria de perturbar a vida de muitos. Entretanto, foi um grande erudito que se distinguiu como filósofo e teólogo, expandindo-se o escopo da erudição judaica. Mereceu o título de «pai do judaísmo rabínico». Deu apoio à revolta anti-romana em 132 D.C., encabeçada por Bar Cocheba, a quem Akiba proclamou como o Messias. Ignorou as proibições romanas contra o estudo da lei, e finalmente, foi executado por escoriação (segundo diz o Talmude). (AM E)

ALABASTRO

O antigo alabastro era uma espécie de mármore. Plínio informa-nos que era abundante nas cercanias de Tebas, no Egito, bem como ao redor de Damasco, na Síria. Era usado para manufaturar vasos e jarras de ungüento (ver Mat. 26:7; Mar. 14:3). Muitos vasos eram chamados *alabastro*, embora, na realidade, fossem feitos de várias substâncias, como ouro, prata, vidro, etc. Geralmente o mármore tem veios do chamado ônix-mármore, que consiste em zonas concêntricas de calcita ou aragonita, cujos materiais são carbonato de cálcio. Quando puro, o alabastro é branco ou translúcido. Com impurezas, assume várias cores, creme, amarelo, marrom e vermelho, devido à presença do óxido de ferro. A formação resulta de depósitos de soluções em água fria, em cavernas, particularmente estalactites e estalagmites, em fendas e em torno das saídas de fontes. O alabastro moderno é uma variedade muito fina e compacta de gesso (sulfato de cálcio hidratado), usado em trabalhos de ornamentação interior. No Novo Testamento ver Mat. 26:6,7; Mar. 14:3; Luc. 7:37 e João 12:3. (FA S Z)

ALABE

No hebraico, **gordura, fértil**. Uma cidade de Aser, identificada com a moderna Khirbet el-Mahalib, na Galiléia superior, a pouco mais de seis quilômetros a nordeste de Tiro (ver Juí. 1:31).

ALAI

No hebraico, **oxalá!** 1. Filha de Sesã, a quem ele deu por mulher a seu escravo egípcio, Jará. Ela pertencia à tribo de Judá (ver I Crô. 2:31,34). 2. O pai de Zabade, um dos homens poderosos de Davi (I Crô. 11:41), em cerca de 1046 A.C. (UN Z)

ALAMELEQUE

No hebraico, **carvalho do rei**, uma cidade no território de Aser, identificada com Wady-el-Malek, a dez quilômetros de terra adentro de Haifa, embora não haja certeza quanto à sua localização. (Ver Jos. 19:26). (S Z)

ÁLAMO

Essa árvore é mencionada apenas por duas vezes na Bíblia (ver Gên. 30:37 e Osé. 4:13, embora nesta última referência a nossa versão portuguesa diga «choupos»). Na primeira referência há menção à utilidade de sua madeira; e, na segunda, são mencionadas as ofertas feitas debaixo de suas sombras. Cientificamente, a árvore é chamada *Populus elba*, podendo atingir a uma altura de 18 m. Produz boa sombra, devido à sua densa folhagem. As folhas são de cor cinza brilhante, brancas por baixo, o que explica o termo álamo prateado. Durante a primavera, os botões que produzem as folhas, emitem um odor fragrante. Bosques de álamos eram usados na adoração pagã, e evidentemente essa adoração incluía a queima de incenso debaixo das árvores (ver Isa. 65:3, segundo a tradução de Moffatt). Jacó utilizou-se de varas de álamo para tentar influenciar as ovelhas a produzirem crias de determinado colorido. Naturalmente, nisso há certa dose de superstição; e se algo influenciou tal colorido, além dos fatores genéticos, temos de pensar em Deus, e não em varas de álamo. (ID Z)

ALAMOTE

No hebraico, **virgens**. Nossa versão portuguesa traduz a palavra como «voz de soprano», em Sal. 46 e I Crô. 15:20. Ou era um instrumento musical ou era uma melodia. Ver sobre *instrumentos musicais*.

Ver os artigos sobre *Estética* e *Música*.

••• ••• •••

ALBERTO MAGNO — ÁLCIMO

ALBERTO MAGNO

Filósofo e teólogo escolástico (1193-1280); famoso pela extensão de sua sabedoria. Foi intitulado, com justiça, Doutor Universal. Foi um dominicano alemão, educado em Paris, Pádua e Bolonha, tendo lecionado em Paris e em Colônia. Escreveu comentários sobre Aristóteles e transmitiu à Idade Média o conhecimento grego e islâmico acerca das ciências naturais. Promoveu o método empírico e as ciências naturais, sendo o precursor de Roger Bacon (ver o artigo). Foi o intelecto organizador da Idade Média e teria maior renome, se o seu discípulo, Tomás de Aquino, não tivesse obtido estatura intelectual maior ainda. Trouxe a atenção de muitos eruditos europeus a filosofia e a ciência de Aristóteles, as quais doutra sorte teriam permanecido na ignorância. Foi também expositor das idéias e das obras de Pedro Lombardo (ver o artigo). Suas obras abrangem o conhecimento inteiro de sua época, tendo sido o único erudito medieval a comentar sobre todas as obras de Aristóteles, autênticas e pseudas.

Em 1651, foram impressos 21 volumes de suas obras, cujo editor foi P. Jammy. A obra foi reimpressa em 1890-1899. O Instituto Alberto Magno de Colônia dedicou-se a publicar suas obras. Foram impressos quarenta volumes, os quais não eram disponíveis ao público antes disso. Oh, o poder de uma única vida, embora tenha estado na Terra há setecentos anos!

Escritos: Comentário sobre as Sentenças de Pedro Lombardo, 1240-1249; *Manual Sobre as Criaturas*, 1240-1243; *Comentário sobre o Pseudo-Dionísio*, 1248-1254; *Sobre a Unidade do Intelecto e Manual de Teologia* (incompleto), 1270-1280.

Idéias e realizações: 1. Expôs Aristóteles à mente européia; fundiu o aristotelianismo e o neoplatonismo. 2. Deus é o ser necessário, idêntico em Seu ser e existência. Provas de Deus: com base no movimento e na impossibilidade de um regresso infinito nos princípios. Deus é um ser inteligente, onipotente, vivo, livre e unitário em Sua natureza. 3. Porém, sabemos principalmente o que Deus não é, e não aquilo que Ele é. 4. Deus emana a realidade, tal como o neoplatonismo. 5. Alberto distinguiu claramente a teologia da filosofia, visto que a lógica não podia demonstrar os grandes temas teológicos. Porém, ele sentia que a alma podia ser demonstrada pela filosofia. A filosofia vê Deus como o Primeiro Ser; a teologia vê Deus como um Ser revelado, alvo da fé. A filosofia usa a razão como o seu grande princípio. A teologia depende da revelação, da iluminação e da fé. 6. Alberto estudou as ciências empíricas, principalmente a botânica e a zoologia, respaldando-se sobre o empirismo. 7. Sua maior contribuição foi a exposição das idéias aristotélicas aos europeus, através de traduções latinas, além de ter reconhecido e ressaltado os talentos de Tomás de Aquino à atenção dos eruditos da Europa. (AM BR E EP P)

ALBIGENSES, DOUTRINA DOS

Os albigenses herdaram as idéias distorcidas e dualistas dos bogomilos e dos paulicianos. Seu centro era a cidade de Albi, no suleste da França. Floresceram também no norte da Espanha e no norte da Itália, durante o século XII. Também eram conhecidos por cátaros ou patarinos.

Adotaram a noção gnóstica de que a matéria encerra o princípio do mal, e que os mundos materiais foram criados por uma força maligna. Rejeitavam porções do Antigo Testamento e salientavam o evangelho de João. Formavam uma comunidade anti-sacerdotal, protestando contra os abusos da Igreja medieval.

Estavam divididos em dois grupos, os *perfecti* e os *credenti*. Os discípulos «perfeitos» eram celibatários e praticavam a comunidade de bens. E os «crentes» ou discípulos podiam casar-se, ter propriedades e participar dos sacramentos da Igreja de Roma.

A consolação. Esse era o rito cátaro do batismo *espiritual*, administrado por imposição de mãos e sem água. Presumivelmente isso transmitia o *consolo* do perdão dos pecados, a liberdade do mundo material, a introdução no reino celestial de Deus. O rito só podia ser administrado por quem já o tivesse recebido e usualmente só era aplicado imediatamente antes da morte. Os que o recebiam durante a vida, eram os «perfeitos». Consideravam tal rito necessário à salvação. Uma vez que alguém se tornasse perfeito, tinha que viver no celibato, abstendo-se também de leite, ovos ou carne, visto que esses alimentos despertam a atividade sexual nos animais. Eram pacifistas, não podendo ter propriedades. Criam na reencarnação como um meio de se continuar a busca pela salvação.

Alguns batistas modernos, ansiosos para encontrarem seitas «batistas» antes da Reforma, apelam ignorantemente para os albigenses, como um elo histórico com o passado. Mas nada havia de batista entre os albigenses, exceto que eles também se opunham à Igreja de Roma. (B E)

ALBINO

Filósofo grego do século II D.C., membro da escola de Gaio (ver o artigo), e associado à quarta academia. Ver o artigo sobre a Academia de Platão. Ele sistematizou as doutrinas de Gaio, combinando Platão, Aristóteles e o estoicismo. Defendeu a idéia neoplatônica de que o conhecimento é um meio de se chegar ao discernimento religioso. Há três divisões da realidade: forma pura, idéias e matéria. Deus é o movedor inabalável, com duas *hipóstases* (ver o artigo a respeito).

ALBO, JOSÉ

Suas datas foram 1380-1444. Um seguidor popular e não-original de seu mestre, Crescas, um filósofo judeu-espanhol que extraiu suas idéias, em estilo eclético, de fontes judaicas, islâmicas e cristãs escolásticas, a fim de prover uma justificação racional para o judaísmo. Seus três grandes princípios eram: a existência de Deus; a revelação; a recompensa e a punição após a morte; em conseqüência disso, a imortalidade da alma. Segundo ele encarava as coisas, os sistemas religiosos derivam princípios secundários desses princípios. Seus escritos tornaram-se populares entre os judeus, sendo admirados por alguns teólogos cristãos posteriores, como Grócio e Ricardo Simon. (E F)

ÁLCIMO

Forma grega de Eliaquim e Joachim (nomes com freqüência intercambiados). Foi sumo sacerdote em Jerusalém entre 163 e 161 A.C. É mencionado em I Mac. 7:4-50; 9:1-57; II Mac. 14:1-27 e em Josefo, *Anti.* xii.7. Consideremos alguns pontos a seu respeito:

1. Descendia de Aarão, mas não era da casta sacerdotal. Foi expulso do ofício por judeus de Jerusalém.

2. Fez oposição a Judas Macabeu, e liderou um

Alexandre, o Grande na batalha de Issus
Art Reference Bureau, Ancram

Moeda de prata de Lysimachus, Rei de Trácia
A Cabeça de Alexandre o Grande, deificado, — Cortesia, Museum of Fine Arts, Boston

Tetradracma de Prata, Alexandre o Grande, Século III
Tetradracma de Prata de Heliocles de Báctria
Tetradracma de Prata de Antimachus I de Báctria
Cortesia de Museum of Fine Arts, Boston

ALCMÉON DE CRÓTONA — ALCORÃO

grupo de homens perversos para aliar-se ao rei Demétrio. Acusou falsamente a Judas e seus irmãos de terem assassinado todos os amigos de Demétrio.

3. Demétrio enviou Baquides com Álcimo para vingar-se. Baquides fingiu ser portador de uma missão pacífica, mas Judas percebeu a fraude. Cerca de sessenta homens, envolvidos no ludíbrio, foram mortos.

4. Álcimo tentou ser nomeado sumo sacerdote, e obteve algum apoio; mas, ao fracassar em seu propósito, retornou a Demétrio.

5. Nicanor foi enviado para destruir Israel, e também tentou enganar Judas. Quase conseguiu seu intuito, mas Judas percebeu o logro e houve uma batalha. Nicanor foi morto com cinco mil de seus homens.

6. Então Demétrio enviou Baquides e Álcimo com um poderoso exército. O exército de Judas abandonou-o, e ele foi morto. Seu irmão Jônatas tornou-se seu sucessor.

7. Jônatas e suas forças foram obrigados a deixar Jerusalém, e Álcimo tornou-se o sumo sacerdote. Ordenou que o átrio interior do santuário fosse derrubado e destruiu as obras dos profetas. Ele foi afetado por uma praga, ficou paralítico e morreu entre agonias. Então houve paz na terra.

8. II Macabeus pinta Nicanor como mais amigável a Judas do que se vê em I Macabeus; e Josefo diz que Álcimo morreu antes de Judas ser morto. Portanto, há alguns problemas com a antiga narrativa. Josefo também menciona seguidores de Álcimo, chamando-os de renegados, além de haver atribuído a enfermidade de Álcimo ao juízo divino. (Z)

ALCMÉON DE CRÓTONA

Filósofo grego do século V A.C., discípulo de Pitágoras. Salientou a lei da harmonia universal, que se aplicaria aos mundos natural e social. Interessava-se mormente pela medicina, pensando que a saúde requer um equilíbrio de fatores opostos (ou poderes contrários), no organismo. Acreditava na alma imortal, embora julgasse o cérebro essencial em todos os sentidos. Identificava a alma com o movimento circular perfeito, descobrindo tal movimento no homem e nas estrelas. À tabela pitagoreana dos contrários, alegadamente ele adicionava as qualidades secundárias e relativas do doce-amargo, do branco-negro e do grande-pequeno. Ver o artigo sobre *Pitágoras* e o *pitagorianismo*. (E EP P)

ALCOOLISMO

O alcoolismo é uma condição crônica e patológica, causada pela ingestão excessiva de bebidas alcoólicas. O termo *alcoólatra* é usado para falar daqueles que se tornam dependentes físicos e psicológicos dessa substância. Os alcoólatras manifestam perturbações mentais, mudanças de caráter e de personalidade para pior, deterioração física, destruição maciça de células cerebrais, e, finalmente, por causa dessas circunstâncias, incapacidade de conviver na sociedade.

Sendo um fenômeno quase mundial, o alcoolismo tem-se tornado um dos problemas sociais mais graves. Nos Estados Unidos da América, aparece como a quarta maior causa de enfermidades, após os distúrbios mentais, as doenças do coração e o câncer. Dentre os oitenta milhões de pessoas que ingerem álcool naquele país, seis milhões são consideradas viciadas no álcool, ou alcoólatras. Muitos outros milhões são afetados pela conduta dos alcoólatras, pelo que um número enorme de pessoas são afetadas pelas desgraças produzidas pelo vício do alcoolismo.

Enfermidade ou pecado? Há grande controvérsia sobre essa questão. Alguns pensam que a ingestão excessiva de álcool origina-se da debilidade moral, e vêem a questão como um problema ético, e não como uma questão médica. Outros insistem que certas pessoas são constituídas de tal modo que ingerir álcool para elas é fácil, logo tornando-se excessivo o uso do mesmo. Apontam para desordens da personalidade e outros fatores psicológicos. De fato, é estranho que haja indícios de que hereditariedade esteja envolvida no caso, mesmo quando filhos que não conheceram seus pais, seguem-nos no vício. O fator hereditário parece apontar para alguma causa física, que não pode ser explicada pelo meio ambiente ou pelas pressões sociais. Aqueles que crêem na reencarnação respondem que os alcoólatras trazem consigo as reminiscências de outra vida física, condições morais e espirituais que favorecem outra existência como alcoólatra. Nesse caso, o alcoólatra é responsável pelo que faz, já que ele desenvolveu o vício. Outro tanto pode ser dito inteiramente à parte do qualquer conceito de reencarnação. Os alcoólatras estabelecem um padrão de vida que fomenta o vício. Pavimentam seu caminho por meio da imprudência. Parece ser melhor concluirmos que o alcoolismo tanto é uma debilidade quanto é um pecado, e que nós podemos nos aproximar do problema de ambos os ângulos.

A Bíblia e o alcoolismo. As Escrituras nos aconselham à moderação em todas as coisas, embora não proíbam terminantemente a ingestão de bebidas alcoólicas. João Batista era total abstêmio; e Jesus bebia vinho com moderação. (Ver João 2; I Tim. 3:3 e 5:23). Porém, a ciência moderna tem demonstrado que qualquer partícula de álcool na corrente sangüínea destrói células do cérebro. Com base em I Cor. 6:19-20, a única resposta espiritual, considerando-se o que a ciência tem descoberto, é a abstinência total.

Tratamento. Os Alcoólatras Anônimos, usando princípios espirituais e religiosos, bem como a solidariedade entre as vítimas do álcool, é a organização que se tem mostrado mais eficaz na reabilitação de viciados no álcool. A Igreja evangélica deve desempenhar seu papel, aplicando princípios idênticos e conclamando os homens a se entregarem a Cristo. E, naturalmente, a ciência médica pode aplicar seus conhecimentos e ajudar as vítimas; mas essa raramente é suficiente, se tiver de atuar isoladamente. Ver as notas em I Tim. 5:23, no NTI. (H HO NTI)

ALCORÃO

A palavra vem do árabe Quran, da palavra cognata *qara'a*, que significa «ler». O sentido resultante é *leitura* ou *lição*. Trata-se do Livro Sagrado do islamismo, tido como eterna palavra de Deus, e que o arcanjo Gabriel teria entregue a Maomé (ver o artigo a seu respeito), em 622 D.C. Após haver chegado em Medina, Maomé começou a ditar os seus oráculos a um discípulo, à medida que lhe iam sendo revelados. O termo *Quran* a princípio foi aplicado a cada revelação, ao ser anunciada pelo profeta, mas, eventualmente, o termo foi dado ao livro inteiro compilado após a morte de Maomé, por seu secretário, Zaid Ibn Thabit, por ordem do califa Abu Bekr. Parte do conteúdo do Alcorão deriva-se do período de Meca, antes de 622. O resto veio à

ALCORÃO

existência entre 622 e 632. Quando Maomé faleceu, o livro existia sob forma de fragmentos, o que explica a necessidade de compilação. Porém, antes mesmo disso, muitos islamitas conheciam de memória grandes trechos do mesmo, o que mostra o poder do livro, desde os seus primórdios. Os redatores arranjaram a obra em capítulos, ou *suras*, os mais longos no princípio e os mais breves no fim do livro. Esse arranjo, pois, ignora a lógica e a cronologia. Há 114 *suras*, totalizando cerca de 77.638 palavras. Em páginas batidas à máquina, espaço e meio, daria cerca de 150 páginas, ou seja, um livro de tamanho relativamente pequeno. O estilo do mesmo é métrico. Suas fortes cadências e suas reiterações cumulativas são lidas em voz alta e com eloqüência, o que muito atrai os ouvintes islamitas. O livro foi escrito em árabe clássico, tendo-se tornado modelo de outras variedades literárias, como ciências, filosofia, ética, etc.

Características e mensagens:

1. O orador é Deus, do princípio ao fim, que se comunica com os homens através de um anjo. Da primeira à última página é enfatizado o *monoteísmo*.

2. As primeiras *suras* são apaixonadas, contendo vívidas descrições de casos de ressurreição, de julgamento, do céu, etc.

3. As últimas *suras* são menos vívidas e contêm exortações acerca da fé, das virtudes, do cerimonial, das leis civis e religiosas. Os judeus são atacados violentamente, Deus é exaltado e a idolatria é combatida. É deplorada a deificação dos homens (como no caso de Cristo). Os homens são exortados a defender a fé.

4. O Alcorão contém relatos cujo intuito é ensinar lições morais e espirituais, mormente sobre como Deus recompensa os fiéis e julga os incrédulos. Personagens como Abraão, Moisés, José (do Antigo Testamento), alguns do N.T., bem como aqueles pertencentes à cultura árabe, são usados como veículos dessas narrativas. Aquelas narrativas baseadas na Bíblia são distorcidas.

5. O conteúdo da obra é unificado no fato de que sempre se faz presente o fluxo da comunicação divina, através do anjo, ao profeta. O conteúdo centraliza-se nas exortações à obediência e na busca da salvação através da obediência.

6. *Uma sura notável*. Essa é chamada de *alfatiha* (abertura), também denominada Oração do Senhor dos islamitas. Diz como segue:

«No nome de Deus, o misericordioso compassivo. Louvado seja Deus, o Senhor dos mundos, o misericordioso compassivo, o soberano do dia do julgamento. Adoramos a ti e te imploramos a ajuda. Dirige-nos pelo reto caminho, no caminho daqueles a quem tens agraciado, em quem não há ira, e que não se desviam».

7. Cristo aparece ali como profeta, e importante, mas não como ser divino.

8. *Alvo geral do Alcorão*. «...orientação para os piedosos que crêem nos mistérios da fé, fazem orações e dão esmolas».

9. *Autoridade*. O Alcorão é aceito como isento de erros, é encarado com profunda reverência, é tido como acima de qualquer crítica. Sua influência e autoridade, no mundo islâmico, não pode ser exagerada.

10. *Texto original*. O livro terreno presumivelmente seria apenas uma cópia física do Alcorão que há no céu, que seria eterno e não teria sido criado.

Um protesto:

Com o devido respeito aos sentimentos e à fé religiosa de outras pessoas, sinto-me obrigado a deixar aqui registrada a minha observação de que é lamentável que a maioria das pessoas religiosas, se não mesmo todas, quando são fortemente conservadoras (tanto no islamismo como em vários segmentos do judaísmo e do cristianismo) sinta-se na obrigação de resolver todos os problemas de conhecimento e fé por meio da revelação que resulta em algum livro. Uma vez que tal livro esteja completo, supõe-se que nada naquele livro está errado, e que o *livro* é final. Esse tipo de crença só pode estagnar a busca pela verdade e o desenvolvimento espiritual, por estar alicerçado em um *dogma*, e não nos requisitos do processo de revelação. Isso é o que os *homens* dizem sobre suas revelações e livros sagrados, e não o que a própria revelação sagrada requer. Jamais haverá tempo em que Deus deixará de revelar-se. Jamais chegará o tempo em que o caminho espiritual não continuará sendo aberto à nossa frente, ao passarmos de um estágio de glória para outro (ver II Cor. 3:18), em que nossas almas são transformadas segundo os moldes da natureza de Deus (ver II Ped. 1:4). Também não é possível que um único livro, ou uma coletânea, contenha toda a verdade de Deus. Continua sendo labor do Espírito conduzir-nos a *toda* a verdade. Em conseqüência, devemos respeitar as revelações, mas não podemos pô-las no lugar do próprio Deus Todo-Poderoso, o qual é maior que qualquer uma ou que a soma total de Suas revelações. Além disso, também devemos afirmar que a revelação não é o único meio através do qual obtemos conhecimento, sagrado ou profano. Há outros meios válidos de obtenção de conhecimento, mediante os quais chegamos a conhecer a Deus e às obras. Podemos buscar o conhecimento através do método empírico, conforme nos mostra a ciência. A intuição e a razão são meios frutíferos de obtenção de conhecimento. Tudo isso é criação e dom de Deus, e tudo pode ser útil na investigação dos variegados aspectos da verdade de Deus. O homem é um ser temporal e finito. Portanto, ele busca sofregamente pontos finais e conforto mental. Fica aterrorizado diante de questões não resolvidas e de um eterno futuro misterioso, que se estende ininterruptamente diante dele. Em conseqüência, a sua fé religiosa fá-lo tornar-se um construtor de cercas e de limitações. Porém, essas limitações são autoconfinadoras apenas. Tais cercas, tão cuidadosamente erigidas por meio de dogmas, confinam a maneira dos homens pensarem acerca de Deus e da inquirição espiritual. Porém, não confinam a Deus e nem ao poder que Ele tem de revelar-se. Devemo-nos lembrar que o próprio Deus é o nosso alvo, que Cristo é o nosso caminho, e que o Espírito é quem nos dá energia. Se concentrarmos toda a nossa busca em um livro sagrado, teremos posto um ponto final em nosso raciocínio, mas não na própria busca.

Quão freqüentemente, na história das religiões, encontramos a convicção e a declaração que diz: «O nosso grupo é o único e o melhor. Nosso livro sagrado é a última das revelações de Deus». Isso foi dito pelo judaísmo. Jesus e Paulo foram perseguidos porque pregaram novas idéias, tendo algo mais a declarar além do que já fora dito. Essa (nosso grupo é o único e o melhor) tem sido uma constante declaração que se ouve na Igreja. O islamismo a reitera. Muitos cultos e seitas assim afirmam. Tem sido dito até mesmo por pequenos grupos cismáticos da fé cristã. Tais grupos, derivados do cristianismo central, têm a audácia de dizer: «Somente nós sabemos o que o Mestre quis dizer. Somente nós praticamos o que Ele ordenou».

Os dois grandes absurdos. Em primeiro lugar, a fé

ALCUÍNO — ALEGORIA

religiosa, em qualquer forma em que ela possa expressar-se, será errada e fútil. Assim asseveram o ceticismo e o ateísmo. Em segundo lugar, qualquer grupo que, com seus livros sagrados e suas interpretações particulares, tenta monopolizar a Deus.

As reivindicações de qualquer religião ou seita particular, de que atingiu um ponto de verdade completa ou final, quanto ao método ou quanto às crenças atinentes a Deus, à alma e à inquirição espiritual, são por demais ridículas para lhes darmos um momento sequer de atenção. Porém, o extremo oposto, que afirma que a experiência religiosa inteira é apenas uma gigantesca ilusão, é igualmente ridículo. (AM E P)

ALCUÍNO

Eclesiástico e educador inglês. Estudou na escola da catedral de Iorque, e tornou-se o maior erudito de sua época. Foi convidado para ser membro da corte de Carlos Magno, tendo sido comissionado para fundar escolas. Propagou a cultura latina entre os francos, fundando bibliotecas e academias. Em 790, retornou à Inglaterra, mas por diversas vezes esteve novamente entre os francos, cumprindo tarefas especiais. Nos seus últimos anos de vida cuidou da abadia de São Martin, em Tours. Seus escritos incluem cartas e poemas, manuais de gramática, dialética retórica, comentários sobre a Bíblia e um tratado teológico, intitulado *Sobre a Trindade*. Opunha-se ao *adopcionismo* (ver o artigo). (E P)

ALDRAVA

Três palavras hebraicas são assim traduzidas, referindo-se à *maçaneta do ferrolho* (ver Can. 5:5), à *alça* de um vaso de barro (ver Isa. 45:9), e ao *cabo* de um machado (ver Deu. 19:5). A forma verbal da palavra é traduzida em nossa versão portuguesa por «manejar», em II Crô. 25:5, e por «levar», em Juí. 5:14. (S Z)

ALEFE

1. Primeira letra do alfabeto hebraico, correspondente ao ALFA grego e ao *a* do idioma português e das línguas modernas. Porém, no hebraico, o alefe é uma consoante, sendo transliterada em português pelo apóstrofe ('). Encabeça cada um dos oito primeiros versos do Salmo 119.

2. Esse símbolo é usado para indicar o Codex Sinaiticus, um manuscrito bíblico do século IV D.C., encontrado por Tischendorf, em Sinae, e atualmente no Museu Britânico. Ver o artigo sobre *manuscritos*. (ME Z)

ALEGORIA

1. A palavra aparece em **Gálatas 4:24, sob a forma** «alegóricas», na expressão:«Estas cousas são alegóricas». Indica a explicação ou expressão de alguma coisa por meio do nome ou imagem de outra coisa. Fazer a Hagar e seus filhos corresponderem à atual Jerusalém e aos judeus (que, na realidade, descendiam de Abraão e Sara, e não de uma escrava), parece uma estranha distorção. Mas Paulo apontava para um aspecto da *servidão espiritual*. Aqueles que se tinham deixado escravizar espiritualmente, tinham-se tornado descendentes espirituais de Hagar e seu filho, e não de Sara e seu filho, o qual nasceu livre. Quanto a detalhes sobre isso, ver o NTI em Gál. 4:24.

O termo grego compõe-se de *allos* e *agoreuein*,

«outro» e «falar». Quem alegorizava, falava ou escrevia sobre alguma coisa por intermédio de outra, procurando desvendar sentidos simbólicos ou espirituais ocultos e inesperados. Assim, Jesus disse: «Ide dizer a essa *raposa...*» (Luc. 13:32), ao referir-se a Herodes, pois este demonstrava possuir a natureza ardilosa e má de uma raposa. Se uma narrativa ou ilustração contém vários de tais usos, — chamamo-la de *alegoria*; mas, se apenas um desses artifícios literários é usado, chamamos esse uso de *metáfora* ou *símile*. O termo grego pode ser usado para indicar um uso isolado ou um uso reiterado desse artifício. Consideremos os pontos abaixo:

2. *Distinções*. a. Uma *metáfora* ou *símile* é uma única comparação mediante a qual uma coisa é explicada por meio de outra, segundo se vê na ilustração acima, em que *raposa* toma o lugar de *Herodes*. b. Uma *parábola*, por estrita definição, é uma estória que contém uma ou algumas poucas lições, ilustradas por seu intuito geral. Todavia, a maioria das parábolas (ver o artigo a respeito) do Novo Testamento consiste, realmente, de alegorias. Nas alegorias, muitos itens têm um sentido simbólico, isto é, são usadas muitas símiles ou metáforas. A parábola do semeador, contada por Jesus, envolve um sentido para cada item. E isso, segundo a definição moderna, é uma alegoria, e não uma parábola. c. Uma *analogia* é a comparação de uma coisa com outra, que tenciona instruir quanto à natureza da coisa em questão. Uma analogia também pode envolver muitos itens de comparação, mas é antes uma análise racional, ao passo que uma alegoria usa uma coisa de natureza inteiramente diferente para ilustrar alguma coisa. Uma analogia envolve a *semelhança* entre uma coisa e outra, em um ponto ou mais. A *bondade* de um homem pode ser usada para descrever a bondade divina, porque se assemelha a esta, em algum grau. Todos os atributos de Deus são concebidos por nós por analogia com as melhores qualidades humanas, posto que multiplicadas ao infinito. d. Um *tipo* envolve a circunstância em que uma coisa ou pessoa simboliza outra, ou um aspecto de outra pessoa ou coisa, tal como o sacerdócio de Aarão tipificava o sacerdócio de Cristo quanto a certo aspecto, ou como José, em algumas de suas qualidades pessoais, prefigurava as qualidades de Cristo, servindo assim de tipo do Senhor Jesus. O livro aos Hebreus contém muitos tipos.

3. *Alegorias na Bíblia*. Há alegorias no livro de Ezequiel, nos capítulos primeiro e trigésimo sétimo, neste último a famosa alegoria dos ossos secos. Alguns pensam que o livro Cantares de Salomão é uma alegoria elaborada, retratando o amor de Cristo por Sua Igreja. No Novo Testamento, a maioria das parábolas com múltiplos sentidos consiste em alegorias (ver Mat. 13:18-23; Mar. 4:14-20). Jesus como a porta, o pão e a água, no evangelho de João, pode ser concebido alegoricamente, em consonância com o uso de Gál. 4:24; todavia, é melhor chamar esses usos de símiles ou metáforas, de conformidade com a terminologia moderna. O Apocalipse contém a alegoria da mulher (12:1 ss), do cavalo branco (19:11-16) e muitas símiles e metáforas. Paulo usou uma outra alegoria em I Cor. 9:9 ss , usando a imagem do *boi* a fim de indicar o ministério cristão. Já vimos a alegoria de Gál. 4:24, à qual se assemelha a alegoria de Cristo como a *rocha*, em I Crô. 1:4.

4. *Interpretação alegórica*. Um artigo separado trata do assunto, sob esse título. A interpretação alegórica é anterior a tal tratamento dado na Bíblia. Os escritos homéricos (a antiga Bíblia grega, para todos os propósitos práticos) eram interpretados

101

ALEIJADO — ALEMBERT

alegoricamente em tempos posteriores, a fim de fixar as idéias ali contidas sobre os deuses e a fim de serem descobertos sentidos ocultos. Teógenes de Rédio (c. de 520 A.C.) provavelmente foi o primeiro alegorista homérico. Homero falara sobre os deuses em termos das injustiças, imoralidades e muitas imperfeições, e os gregos posteriores, usando os escritos de Homero como sagrados e inspirados, tiveram de apelar para a alegoria a fim de evitar a aplicação de suas terríveis descrições aos seres divinos.

Em relação à Bíblia, um judeu chamado Aristóbulo, do início do século II A.C., incorporou a interpretação alegórica aos seus ensinos e escritos. Ele tentou encontrar os ensinos de Platão nos escritos de Moisés, mediante interpretações fantasiosas. Nessa atividade ele chegou a incríveis extremos, como quando alegorizou o relato do adultério de Davi, transformando-o em um homem virtuoso, em seu ato! O que falta ser dito sobre a questão da interpretação alegórica, reservo para ser dito no artigo que trata especificamente do assunto.

ALEIJADO

A palavra indica alguém defeituoso nos membros; se nos membros inferiores, um «coxo». A razão do aleijão podia ser congênita, por motivo de enfermidade ou devido a algum acidente. Uma forma comum de aleijão, no Oriente Médio, era a cilose, ou pés atrofiados. Uma outra forma era a atrofia da perna inteira. Grande parte desses aleijões eram conseqüências de acidentes. Sem importar a causa, qualquer aleijão desqualificava um homem para servir como sacerdote, segundo a lei do Antigo Testamento. Mas um homem assim aleijado podia comer as carnes oferecidas em sacrifício, praticando qualquer outra coisa relativa à fé religiosa judaica, sem qualquer impedimento (ver Lev. 21:17-23). Ficamos sabendo, com base em II Samuel 5:6,8, que durante o início da monarquia havia muitos aleijados em Israel.

Jesus, os apóstolos e os aleijados. Durante Seu ministério terreno, Jesus curou a muitos aleijados (ver Mat. 15:30 e 21:14). Pedro e João curaram um coxo, em uma notável ocasião (ver Atos 3:2-8). Ao relatar o ocorrido, Lucas usou os termos *basis*, «pé» e *sfura*, «artelhos». Portanto, o caso envolvia um problema com os pés. Paulo curou em Listra a um «aleijado» (ver Atos 14:8-10).

Implicações metafóricas. Podemos pensar em pessoas espiritualmente aleijadas. A debilidade geral humana também pode ser assim retratada. O fato de que não podia haver sacerdotes levitas aleijados sugere-nos que aquilo que é oferecido em serviço a Deus precisa ser perfeito, não podendo ser deformado em qualquer sentido. A espiritualidade importa em saúde, e coisa alguma que sugerisse o contrário podia estar envolvida no ministério do templo, da mesma forma que, em Cristo, os crentes são considerados hígidos e perfeitos. (ID S Z)

ALELUIA

1. *A palavra.* Vem dos termos hebraicos **halal**, «louvor», e **Yah**, uma forma abreviada de «Yahweh», Senhor. Portanto, significava «louvor ao Senhor». No hebraico, a palavra era hifenizada, de tal modo que os dois elementos sempre apareciam distintos. Em outros idiomas, porém, tornou-se um nome composto, incluindo no grego da Septuaginta. Atualmente, a expressão tornou-se universal. Encontra-se no começo e no fim de vários dos Salmos, tendo-se tornado um convite padrão para se louvar a Deus na adoração do templo.

2. *Seu uso nos Salmos.* Esse uso divide-se em dois grupos: a. Salmos 104 e 115 (no fim); 106 (no começo e no fim). Esse último uso parece parte da doxologia do quarto livro do saltério. b. Salmos 111-118 (no começo); 115 - 117 (no fim). Na Septuaginta, há uma repetição no fim do Salmo 113 e no começo do Salmo 114, que assim completa a série. E, mui provavelmente, isso está correto. c. Salmo 135 (no começo); mas a Septuaginta põe o vocábulo no começo do Salmo 136. d. Salmos 146 - 160 (no começo de cada um). Portanto, a palavra «Aleluia» é usada nos Salmos por um total de quinze vezes.

3. *No Novo Testamento.* Em Apo. 19:1,3,4,6 há uma convocação para louvor e adoração por meio de «Aleluia», agora transformada em uma exclamação cristã, com o uso da mesma fórmula. Portanto, o uso desse vocábulo está limitado aos Salmos e ao livro de Apocalipse. E, neste último, o louvor envolve um coro celestial.

4. *Usos festivos.* Esse termo passou a ser usado como uma expressão de louvor, nas festividades da Páscoa, do Pentecoste e dos Tabernáculos. Os Salmos 105 e 106 eram usados nessas festas. O grupo dos Salmos 113 - 118 passou a ser conhecido como o Hallel Egípcio, devido à sua associação com o livramento de Israel da servidão egípcia. Esses Salmos eram usados por ocasião das três principais festividades, e por ocasião da dedicação do templo. Por ocasião da Páscoa, eram entoados os Salmos 113 e 114, antes da refeição pascal, e os Salmos 115 a 118, após a mesma, conforme foi observado por Jesus e seus discípulos, na última Ceia (ver Mat. 26:30).

5. *Usos modernos do vocábulo.* Além do uso popular dessa expressão, na Igreja cristã, como uma expressão de louvor, a palavra é usada para designar o sábado antes do domingo da ressurreição. Além disso, também é usada por alguns para aludir ao próprio domingo da ressurreição. (AM AU ID NTI)

Ver o artigo sobre o *Hallel*, relacionado a este assunto.

ALEMA

Uma cidade de Gileade, além do Jordão, uma dentre meia dúzia de cidades onde os gentios aprisionaram os judeus (ver I Mar. 5:24-26). Judas Macabeu foi ali, libertou os judeus e executou os cidadãos (I Mac. 5:28-44). O lugar tem sido identificado com Alma, na planície do Haurã, talvez sendo a mesma Helã referida em II Sam. 10:16, embora não haja certeza quanto a esse particular. (S Z)

ALEMBERT, JEAN LE ROND D'

Suas datas são 1717-1783. Filósofo e matemático francês, nascido em Paris. Estudou no Colégio Jansenista de Mazarin, fez contribuições à matemática e à física, e foi editor da grande *Enciclopédia* (juntamente com Diderot). Obras: *Tratado sobre a Dinâmica*, 1743; *Discurso Preliminar da Enciclopédia*, 1791; *Mescla de Literatura, História e Filosofia* (5 volumes), 1752; *Ensaios sobre os Elementos da Filosofia*, 1759; opúsculos matemáticos, 1761-1780.

Idéias:

1. Todo conhecimento tem origem empírica. As percepções cooperam com a memória; a memória com a história; a razão com as ciências e a filosofia; a imaginação com as artes.

ALÉM DO JORDÃO — ALEXANDRE O GRANDE

2. A matemática, por igual modo, é empírica. Ele trabalhou com a teoria das probabilidades, embora estivesse essencialmente equivocado quanto a essa área.

3. A filosofia deveria guiar os estudos científicos, não desperdiçando tempo com temas transcendentais. Ele aproximou-se do ateísmo e do materialismo.

4. Deu apoio aos ideais do Iluminismo e ao papel da educação, no tocante ao mesmo.

ALÉM DO JORDÃO

As palavras hebraicas envolvidas poderiam indicar perto, ou do outro lado do Jordão, ou mesmo nas margens do Jordão ou no cruzamento do Jordão. Porém, o sentido mais comum é *Jordânia*, ou seja, a região do Jordão. A expressão ocorre por cerca de trinta e três vezes no A.T., usualmente referindo-se ao território a leste daquele rio, embora nem sempre. Os trechos de Gên. 50:10,11; Deu. 3:20,25; 11:30; Jos. 9:1 e I Reis 4:21 parecem requerer a idéia da margem ocidental. Portanto, o termo pode aludir a qualquer das duas margens do rio, dependendo da perspectiva do escritor, no momento. Os trechos de Jos. 5:1 e 12:7 referem-se especificamente à margem ocidental do rio. A referência em Mat. 4:15 designa a Peréia, um novo lugar onde Jesus levaria a efeito um ministério evangelístico, e ali está em foco a margem oriental. (HA UN Z)

ALÉM DO RIO

O rio em foco é o Eufrates. Essa expressão ocorre por cerca de vinte vezes no A.T. Pode estar em pauta qualquer das duas margens do rio. Lemos que os sírios estavam localizados *além do rio* (ver II Sam. 10:16; I Crô. 19:16), havendo ali alusão à margem oriental. Outro tanto era dito a respeito dos assírios (ver Isa. 7:20), e Josué faz alusão idêntica, em Jos. 24:3,14,15. Portanto, o reino de Salomão incluía a região deste lado do rio, ou seja, o lado ocidental do Eufrates (ver I Reis 4:21). No período persa, o termo aludia ao lado ocidental, tendo-se tornado uma expressão fixa, designativa daquele território. (Ver Eze. 4:10,11,16,17,20; 5:3,6; 6:8,13; 7:21; Nee. 2:7,9; 3:7). (Z)

ALEMETE

No hebraico, **cobertura, ocultamento**. Nome de duas pessoas e de um lugar no Antigo Testamento.

1. Filho de Jeoada, ou Jará, um benjamita, descendente de Jônatas, filho de Saul (I Crô. 8:36; 9:42).

2. Um benjamita, filho de Bequer. É o último dentre nove filhos nomeados. Fluorit em 1856 A.C.

3. Cidade levítica de Benjamim, I Crô. 6:60. Em Jos. 21:18 é denominada Almom. (FA S UN)

ALEXANDRA

Salomé Alexandra, esposa de Aristóbulo I (104-103 A.C.), e depois do falecimento deste, esposa de seu irmão, Alexandre Janeus, talvez um casamento levirato (103-76 A.C.). Ela foi uma rainha macabéia, a única rainha judia que reinou por direito próprio, se exceturamos a usurpadora Atália. Alexandre, após um reinado muito perturbado, deixou-lhe o trono, aconselhando-a a estabelecer a paz com os fariseus. Foi o que ela fez, e durante o reinado dela, os fariseus obtiveram grande dose de poder (76-67 A.C.),

tornando-se, pela primeira vez, membros do Sinédrio. O reinado de Alexandra foi pacífico e próspero. Simão Ben Shetach, famoso fariseu, aparentemente era irmão dela. (Ver Jos. *Ant*. XIII.xvi.1,5,6). (Z)

ALEXANDRE, Bispo de Alexandria

Suas datas: 273-326 D.C. Foi o superior eclesiástico de Ário (ver o artigo), iniciador da controvérsia ariana (ver o artigo sobre o *arianismo*), do ponto de vista ortodoxo. Sua posição era essencialmente aquela do credo niceno, e a formulação desse credo muito se deveu a ele. Foi patrono e predecessor episcopal de Atanásio (ver o artigo a respeito).

ALEXANDRE DE HALES

Suas datas: 1185-1245. Autor da **Summa Universae Theologicae**, — que qualifica como fundador do escolasticismo, no sentido estrito. Essa obra (inacabada) é um volumoso manual de teologia especulativa, dialeticamente elaborado. Ele expressou idéias de Agostinho, Anselmo e Hugo de São Vítor, mediante a ajuda das categorias aristotélicas. Foi o primeiro mestre a familiarizar-se bem com Aristóteles. Sua *Summa* expõe questões e respostas baseadas na fé e nos pais latinos, bem como na razão, com o apoio da filosofia grega clássica. Dentro do *escolasticismo* (ver o artigo), ele originou a abordagem tríplice dos assuntos em *pró*, *contra* e *solução*, aplicando a dialética ao dogma. Sua visão do conhecimento religioso tornou-se a norma seguida pelos franciscanos.

Pano de fundo:

Hales foi um filósofo e teólogo inglês, nascido em Shrospshire. Estudou e ensinou na Universidade de Paris. Entre os seus notórios alunos estava Boaventura (ver o artigo). Outros escritos: *Comentário sobre as Sentenças de Pedro Lombardo*; *Questões Disputadas*. Seu estilo claro e convincente obteve para ele o título de «Doutor Irrefragável».

Hales tornou-se franciscano em 1237, fazendo parte do movimento agostiniano do século XIII. Sua *Summa* tinha como alvo principal a justificação da tradição agostiniana. (BE CO E EP P)

ALEXANDRE JANEU

Ver **Janeu, Alexandre**, e também **Hasmoneanos**.

ALEXANDRE O GRANDE

No grego significa **defensor de homens**, um nome comum nos tempos helenistas, utilizado de várias maneiras em muitos idiomas.

1. *A família de Alexandre*. Ele nasceu em 356 A.C., filho de Filipe II da Macedônia e Olímpias do Épiro. Foi rei da Macedônia desde o falecimento de seu pai, em 336 A.C., até seu próprio falecimento, em 323 A.C. Aristóteles foi seu mestre (ver o artigo sobre Aristóteles).

2. *Vida pregressa e conquistas*. Antes de Alexandre, durante cerca de duzentos anos as repúblicas gregas tinham permanecido sob a influência persa, cujos reis acaemenidas governavam desde o mar Egeu até o rio Indo, e desde o Afeganistão até o Egito. Houve algumas vitórias isoladas dos gregos, como as de Maratona e de Salamis, que obtiveram alguma independência para eles, nos séculos V e IV A.C. Mas o domínio persa continuava vasto. Filipe II subjugou a península grega, o que o deixou à testa de uma confederação de estados gregos, com os quais formou

ALEXANDRE O GRANDE— ALEXANDRE, SAMUEL

uma frente unida contra a Pérsia. Dois anos após essa conquista, Alexandre herdou o trono. Primeiramente Alexandre consolidou o seu governo sobre os gregos. Ao cruzar o Helesponto com cerca de 40 mil homens, obteve a primeira vitória sobre os gregos, no Granico. Tomou posse dos estados gregos da Ásia menor e então marchou sobre a Síria. Dario tomou conhecimento do fato, e lhe cortou a retirada com poderoso exército. Mas a cavalaria grega deu a vitória a Alexandre, em Isso, em 333 A.C. As mulheres do harém real da Pérsia caíram em suas mãos, e Dario retirou-se para o Oriente. Em vez de perseguir Dario, Alexandre ocupou a Fenícia e o Egito, base do poder marítimo persa, que disputava a hegemonia sobre o mar Egeu. Tiro foi conquistada mediante um brilhante assédio. A mole que Alexandre construiu até hoje une a cidade ao continente. No Egito, Alexandre fundou Alexandria, a mais famosa dentre as várias cidades que receberam o seu nome. Então ele recebeu honras como se fosse um novo Faraó.

Em seguida, Alexandre voltou a atenção para a tarefa principal, a de derrotar Dario e os persas em seu próprio território. Derrotou Dario em Gaugamela, do outro lado do rio Tigre. Uma série de vitórias conferiu-lhe o controle da Babilônia, da metrópole Susa, sede do poder, e de Persépolis, onde havia o tesouro e o mausoléu dos acaemenidas. — Os acaemenidas eram a dinastia dominante do primeiro império persa, razão pela qual se chamava império acaemenida. Sob essa dinastia, o governo persa estendia-se do Nilo ao Danúbio. Esse império foi fundado por Ciro o Grande (559-529 A.C.). A dinastia recebeu esse nome de seu ancestral, *Acaemenes*.

Em Susa e Persépolis, Alexandre apossou-se do tesouro imperial, cerca de cento e oitenta mil talentos em moedas e barras de ouro, além de incontáveis riquezas, que caíam nas mãos do conquistador, por todos os lados.

Dario retrocedeu para o norte e o leste, até que foi assassinado por seu sátrapa de Báctria, em vista do que Alexandre declarou-se sucessor do trono persa. Após dois anos de duras lutas, ele subjugou a Báctria, atualmente os modernos Afeganistão e Casaquistão. Então transportou-se para o vale do rio Indo, em 327 A.C. Ali, ele chegou ao que era considerado o fim do mundo, mas precisava atravessar o rio Ganges. Seus soldados se revoltaram. Para castigá-los, ele fê-los marchar de volta à Babilônia, através do estéril deserto Gedrosiano, no Irã. Sua frota naval investigou as costas próximas, e Alexandre sentiu-se inspirado por novas ambições a fazer explorações navais. Queria saber se o mar Cáspio levava ao oceano, na direção norte, e se a Arábia representava outra Índia, para o sul. Em meio a tais planos de conhecer e avançar interminavelmente, cansado de bebedeiras e orgias, tendo contraído uma febre (malária? ou teria sido envenenado?), Alexandre morreu com a idade de trinta e três anos, em 323 A.C.

3. *Alexandre e a profecia bíblica*. Ele é o leopardo com quatro asas (prodigiosa força e rapidez) de Dan. 7:6. Também é o bode de um chifre só, que corria tão veloz que não tocava na terra, e que atacou e derrotou o carneiro com dois chifres — Média e Pérsia — que representava Dario, o último dos monarcas persas, em Dan. 8:4-7. Na estátua de Nabucodonosor, em Dan. 2:39, Alexandre é o ventre de bronze, ao passo que as pernas de ferro representam os seus sucessores. Presumivelmente, estando ainda na Macedônia, ele teve uma visão do Deus dos judeus, que lhe apareceu vestido como sumo sacerdote judaico, e a figura encorajou-o a marchar sobre a Ásia, prometendo-lhe a conquista da Pérsia. Seja como for, o fato é que

Alexandre tratou os judeus gentilmente, tendo recebido deles considerável apoio, em troca da liberdade de viverem com independência, excetuando tributo a ser pago. Essas condições foram aceitas por ambas as partes. (Ver Josefo, *Anti*. xi.314 ss.). Josefo dá-nos essa informação em conexão com uma visita feita por Alexandre a Jerusalém, quando alguns detalhes do acordo vieram à tona. A maioria dos eruditos modernos, entretanto, duvida da historicidade dessa visita e das histórias a respeito. Várias outras estórias ou lendas foram criadas, envolvendo Israel de alguma maneira.

4. *Alexandre, o universalista*. Alexandre chocou seus companheiros macedônios ao adotar o estilo da corte persa, incluindo a formação de um harém. Casou-se com uma princesa bactriana, Roxana, e encorajou seus homens a lhe seguirem o exemplo. Nobres persas foram retidos como sátrapas para ajudá-lo a governar o império. Aparentemente, Alexandre visava um reino universal, uma confraternização de povos, sem distinções nacionais. Muitos historiadores modernos, no entanto, — duvidam do escopo e da sinceridade de suas tentativas. Seja como for, a influência grega, que já era geral, tornou-se ainda mais ampla por causa de suas conquistas, de tal modo que, com Alexandre o Grande passamos para o *período helenista*, um período em que a cultura grega tornou-se universal, embora misturada com outras culturas.

5. *Universalidade do idioma grego*. Parte do processo de helenização consistiu na propagação do idioma grego a todos os pontos do mundo então conhecido. Sabemos que o grego era falado até mesmo em Jerusalém. Paulo falava o grego como seu idioma nativo, embora não fosse essa a sua única língua. Ver o artigo sobre o idioma grego. O Novo Testamento foi escrito em grego, primeiramente por ser um veículo verdadeiramente universal, e em segundo lugar, porque todos os escritores sabiam o grego ou conseguiram amanuenses que escreveram seus livros. Nem todos falavam ou liam grego como língua nativa. O livro de Apocalipse, por exemplo, foi escrito por um autor que aprendera o grego, mas que nunca conseguira dominar a sintaxe grega e o uso dos casos, escrevendo com mentalidade aramaica, uma língua sem declinações. II Pedro é um livro grego, com alguns sinais de artificialismo. Hebreus foi escrito em excelente grego, quase clássico. Paulo tinha um bom grego *koiné* literário. Ver o artigo sobre a *Língua do Novo Testamento*.

6. *Resultados para as Terras Bíblicas*. A Palestina tornou-se parte do império de Alexandre; mas, por ocasião de sua morte, seus generais dividiram o império. Seleuco, um dos generais de menor importância de Alexandre, ficou com o controle das satrapias do extremo oriente, e a dinastia ali iniciada tomou o nome *selêucida*. A capital ocidental era Antioquia, da qual veio o nome de Antíoco, nome de treze reis da dinastia selêucida. Ver os artigos sobre ambos os termos. Os macabeus finalmente derrotaram essa dinastia, obtendo uma independência temporária para os judeus. Esta terminou devido às conquistas dos romanos. O idioma grego, porém, continuou tendo influência universal, tornando-se o veículo lingüístico do Novo Testamento. (AM BOT GRI S UN Z)

ALEXANDRE, SAMUEL

Suas datas: 1859-1938. Filósofo inglês, nascido em Sidney, Austrália. Estudou em Oxford e foi professor da Universidade de Manchester.

Alexandria, Porto
Cortesia, Matson Photo Service

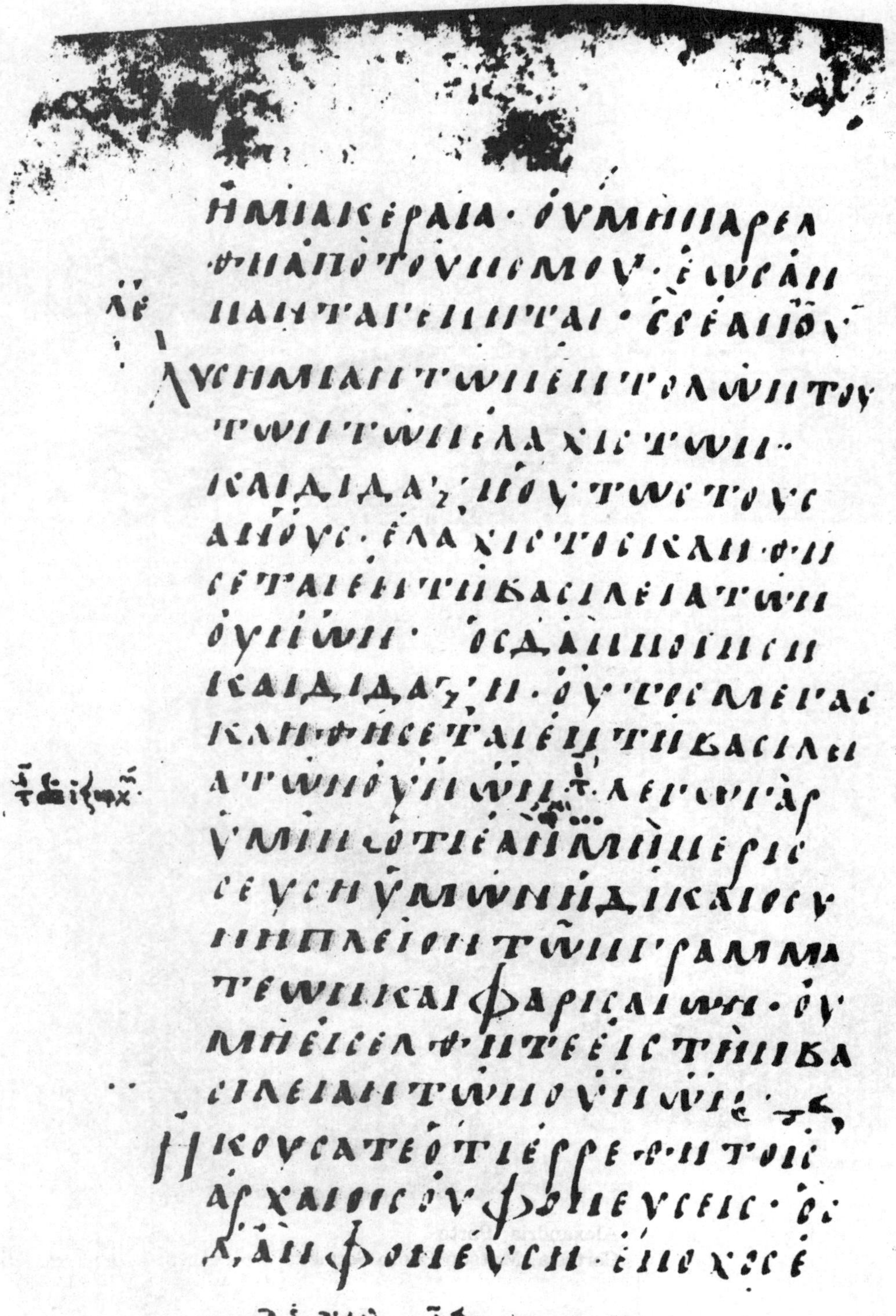
η μια κεραια ου μη παρελ
θη απο του νομου εως αν
παντα γενηται. ος εαν ουν
λυση μιαν των εντολων του
των των ελαχιστων
και διδαξη ουτως τους
ανους ελαχιστος κληθη
σεται εν τη βασιλεια των
ουνων. ος δ αν ποιηση
και διδαξη ουτος μεγας
κληθησεται εν τη βασιλει
α των ουνων. λεγω γαρ
υμιν οτι εαν μη περισ
σευση υμων η δικαιοσυ
νη πλειον των γραμμα
τεων και φαρισαιων ου
μη εισελθητε εις την βα
σιλειαν των ουνων.
Ηκουσατε οτι ερρεθη τοις
αρχαιοις ου φονευσεις. ος
δ αν φονευση ενοχος ε

Codex Pi, 9º séc., Mat. 5:18 *ss*
Cortesia, Public Library, Leningrad

ALEXANDRE III, Papa—ALEXANDRIA

Escritos: *Ordem Moral e Progresso*, 1889; *Locke*, 1908; *Espaço, Tempo e Divindade*, 1920; *Spinoza e o Tempo*, 1921; *Arte e Instinto*, 1927; *Beleza e Outras Formas de Valor*, 1933; *Peças Filosóficas e Literárias*, 1939.

Idéias:

1. Na epistemologia, ele foi um realista. O erro seria criado quando um objeto é deslocado de seu devido lugar, ou mal compreendido, por meio da ilusão. Mas a verdade seria relativa, tornando-se obsoleta, e podendo transformar-se em falsidade.

2. Na metafísica, ele cria em uma evolução emergente, tudo fazendo parte de movimentos complexos. O espaço-tempo, como movimento puro, seria a origem de todos os demais movimentos. A divindade consistiria no fato de que acima de qualquer nível evolutivo, surgiria um novo nível emergente. Mas Deus (mediante contraste) seria o mundo inteiro do espaço-tempo, o *nisus* (o exercício de poder agindo ou tentando agir) que se movimenta na direção do próximo emergente. Ou, com «Deus», entenderíamos a característica da transcendência, que se manifestaria no próximo emergente. Esse emergente é que seria a *divindade*.

3. Os emergentes manifestam-se hierarquicamente: físicos, químicos, fisiológicos, mentais. A evolução, ao usar esses elementos, tem um *nisus* (um esforço) que busca níveis superiores.

4. A alma humana é deidade em relação ao corpo. A evolução produzirá, a partir do homem, uma espécie de super-homem, que será divindade em relação ao homem atual.

5. *Mente-corpo*. O corpo de qualquer coisa é o aspecto externo da natureza, unificado naquela perspectiva particular. A mente é a *idéia* ou qualidade interna distintiva que provê o *nisus* evolutivo.

ALEXANDRE III, Papa (1159-1181)

Membro de famosa família de Siena, Orlando Bardinelli distinguiu-se como canonista (escreveu um comentário sobre o Decretum Gratiani), em Bolonha. Em 1150 foi chamado a Roma pelo papa Eugênio III. Ali ocupou vários ofícios como cardeal diácono, cardeal e camareiro papal. Tornou-se conselheiro de confiança de Adriano IV (ver o artigo). Encabeçou um movimento que visava livrar Roma do poder alemão, aliando a Igreja de Roma aos normandos de Nápoles. Afirmou publicamente, quando da dieta de Besancon (1157), diante de Frederico Barborroxa, que o ofício imperial era possível devido ao *beneficium* papal, e assim atiçou a ira dos príncipes. Escapou por pouco de ser morto no local. Ao candidatar-se ao papado, apesar da oposição do estado, recebeu dezenove dentre vinte e dois votos, e assumiu o papado com o nome de Alexandre III. Um oponente, cardeal Otaviano, embora tivesse recebido apenas três votos, foi coroado como antipapa, com o nome de Víctor IV (1159-1164). Alexandre III respondeu a isso excomungando o imperador, a 11 de fevereiro de 1160, isentando seus súditos de lealdade a ele. Em seguida, aliou-se a Liga Lombarda, e estes edificaram a cidade de Alessandria, em sua honra. O cisma prosseguiu na Igreja, tendo havido três antipapas adicionais que chegaram à sé de Roma, a saber, Pascal III (1164-1168), Calisto III (1168-1179) e Inocente III (1179-1180). Esse movimento perdurou por dezessete anos, e terminou somente depois da batalha de Legnano, em 1175, na qual Barbarroxa, em Veneza, foi forçado a render-se incondicionalmente. Que o papa pôs o pé triunfalmente sobre o pescoço do imperador, não passa de uma lenda infantil.

Alexandre teve de enfrentar outras controvérsias entre a Igreja e o estado. Exilado na França, entre 1162 e 1165, chegou a conhecer Henrique II, da Inglaterra, o qual, no seu tempo, foi o mais poderoso monarca do Ocidente. Subseqüentemente, o papa foi arrastado à controvérsia relativa aos poderes do estado versus os poderes da Igreja, que surgiu entre Henrique II e Thomas Becket, arcebispo de Canterbury. Becket foi finalmente assassinado, por ordem de Henrique. Mas as areias movediças da história correram a favor da Igreja de Roma, e Henrique foi forçado a retratar-se, pedindo perdão diante do túmulo do mártir.

Um dos triunfos de Alexandre foi a regra baixada pelo Terceiro Concílio Luterano (1179), que ordenava que um papa só podia ser eleito com dois terços da maioria dos votos dos cardeais. Essa conferência contou com trezentos bispos, e marcou a história da Igreja de Roma com uma importante decisão, para evitar futuros cismas.

Alexandre III era um erudito canonista, não inferior a Bonifácio VIII ou Inocente III, um estrategista diplomata e um enérgico defensor das liberdades e poderes da Igreja de Roma.

ALEXANDRES (vários)

Ver o artigo anterior, sobre *Alexandre o Grande*.

1. Alexandre, cognominado Balas, devido à sua mãe, Bala. Um personagem que aparece na história dos Macabeus (I Mac. 10) e nos escritos de Josefo. Ele derrubou Demétrio I em 150 A.C., e por sua vez foi substituído pelo filho daquele, Demétrio II, em 145 A.C. Era marido de Cleópatra e filho pretenso do rei selêucida Antíoco IV. As guerras civis das quais ele participou enfraqueceram os poderes dos monarcas selêucidas.

2. Alexandre, filho de Simão, o cireneu (Mar. 15:21), bem - conhecida figura entre os primitivos cristãos. Juntamente com Rufo, aparentemente era bem conhecido pelos leitores originais do evangelho de Marcos.

3. Alexandre, membro da família sumo sacerdotal (ver Atos 4:6). Excetuando aquilo que sobre ele é dito no livro de Atos, trata-se de uma pessoa desconhecida.

4. Um judeu, ou talvez convertido ao cristianismo, a quem a multidão de Éfeso, excitada por Demétrio, o ourives, recusou-se a ouvir (ver Atos 19:33).

5. Um crente efésio, entregue «a Satanás», juntamente com Himeneu (ver I Tim. 1:20). Ver detalhes no NTI, nessa referência.

6. Um latoeiro, provavelmente residente em Éfeso, que muito prejudicou a Paulo (ver II Tim. 4:14). Alguns o identificam com o Alexandre «4» ou com o Alexandre «5». (S UN Z)

ALEXANDRIA

Essa cidade foi fundada no ano de 332 A.C., por Alexandre o Grande, da Macedônia, e dele derivou o seu nome. Era um grande porto marítimo situado na costa noroeste do delta do rio Nilo, no Egito, no estreito istmo existente entre o mar e o lago Mareotis. Evidentemente só o pequeno povoado egípcio denominado Racotis tem assinalado o antigo local, até que foi absorvido pela nova cidade de Alexandria, com a passagem do tempo.

Os engenheiros do exército de Alexandre traçaram os planos da fundação da nova cidade. E, nesse ínterim, Alexandre o Grande visitou o famoso templo

ALEXANDRIA

do antiqüíssimo e mui venerado deus egípcio, *Amom*, localizado no coração do deserto, — atualmente conhecido como oásis de Siwa. Dessa visita, Alexandre voltou com o título de *filho de Zeus-Amom*, que lhe foi aplicado pelo sumo sacerdote daquele culto. Tudo isso fazia parte dos planos que Alexandre tinha de deificar-se, evidentemente como um meio de exaltar o seu próprio orgulho e prestígio de grande conquistador militar.

Depois do falecimento de Alexandre, o Grande, passou a governar o Egito Ptolomeu I Soter (323- 283) A.C.). Foi sucedido no trono egípcio por Ptolomeu II Filadelfo (285-247 A.C.). Este último não poupou esforços por completar a já notável biblioteca de Alexandria, que Ptolomeu I havia fundado, e muitos outros tesouros foram levados para Alexandria. Foi igualmente sob os seus auspícios (conforme a tradição nos revela) que se iniciou a famosa tradução das Escrituras hebraicas para o grego, a qual, uma vez pronta, passou a ser chamada de tradução da Septuaginta, vertendo as Escrituras do A.T. para o mesmo idioma internacional em que o N.T. estava destinado a ser lançado.

Pouquíssimas descobertas arqueológicas se têm podido fazer em Alexandria, devido ao fato de que a cidade antiga foi inapelavelmente sepultada sob a sua moderna sucessora. Por essa razão é que a maior parte do conhecimento de que dispomos acerca da natureza da antiga cidade obrigatoriamente deve ser extraída de referências literárias, muitas das quais não são muito precisas.

Foi sob o governo de *Ptolomeu* II que Alexandria atingiu, pela primeira vez, o seu resplendor arquitetural, que se destaca de tal modo nas referências literárias da antiguidade. Entre a ilha de Faros e a praia continental se estendia um caminho elevado chamado «Heptastaidion», devido ao fato de que se prolongava por «sete estádios», ou seja, cerca de dois quilômetros. Esse caminho elevado vinculava o continente com a ilha, e dividia o ancoradouro em um porto ocidental e em um porto oriental, também denominado *Grande*, cuja entrada era dominada pela torre do farol de Faros. Havia também um chamado porto Real, o qual era ladeado, a leste, pelo palácio real. A cidade de Alexandria ficava ao sul da linha costeira, e se estendia ao longo da mesma, por detrás, até o lago Mareotis.

Os portos de Alexandria, descritos no parágrafo acima, eram próprios tanto para as atividades comerciais como para os movimentos bélicos. Alexandria era um dos principais portos de embarque de cereais do império romano. O navio mencionado no trecho de Atos 27:6, que velejaria de Alexandria para a Itália tinha «carga» (ver Atos 27:10), e provavelmente essa carga era de trigo.

Desde os tempos mais antigos que Alexandria contava com *três elementos* étnicos mais proeminentes em sua população: gregos, egípcios e judeus. Visto que os judeus não sofriam perseguições nessa cidade, mas antes, desfrutavam de iguais privilégios juntamente com quaisquer outros, eles estabeleceram ali uma poderosíssima colônia. E assim, apesar de continuarem os judeus considerando Jerusalém como a sua cidade santa, passaram a possuir a sua própria versão das Escrituras do A.T. em grego (a chamada *Septuaginta*), bem como o seu próprio templo, em Leontópolis. Foi nessa cidade que a revelação hebraica entrou em contato íntimo com a filosofia grega. Filo Judeus (viveu em cerca de 50 D.C.) foi o mais famoso de todos os filósofos judeus, seguindo as tendências neoplatônicas. O seu esforço maior consistiu na tentativa de reconciliar as revelações

dadas aos hebreus com a filosofia grega, para o que ele se utilizou sobretudo das idéias platônicas. Alguns judeus consideravam-no como o Moisés de língua grega; mas outros (talvez mais corretamente), preferiam reputá-lo como um Platão de fala hebraica. Não foi ele o criador, mas foi quem desenvolveu um pouco mais a doutrina do «logos», que finalmente aparece, sob forma cristã, em João 1:1.

Sob os governantes *Ptolomeus*, Alexandria foi feita capital do Egito, não demorando a tornar-se a maior cidade helenista de sua época, tanto no que diz respeito à erudição como no que tange à sua importância política e comercial. Alexandria continuou sendo a capital administrativa do Egito durante o período de Roma imperial e durante o tempo bizantino. Essa cidade era o centro bancário do Egito, bem como a sua principal cidade comercial, e ali se manufaturavam principalmente tecidos, vidro e papiro. Sua população, durante a era cristã primitiva, orçava em mais de um milhão de habitantes.

Por igual modo, Alexandria tornou-se o grande centro intelectual da dispersão judaica. Além da tradução da Septuaginta e dos volumosos escritos do filósofo Filo, há também o livro apócrifo do A.T., intitulado *Sabedoria*, que teve a sua origem nessa cidade. Os remanescentes literários testificam da energia intelectual, da preocupação missionária e da seriedade com que os judeus ali enfrentavam a mensagem de suas Escrituras sagradas, a despeito de alguns desvios importantes do judaísmo ordinário.

No tempo dos monarcas da casa dos Ptolomeus, a biblioteca de Alexandria aumentou até atingir a cifra de mais de meio milhão de rolos de papiro, e diversos eruditos famosos ocuparam a posição de bibliotecário ali.

De Alexandria é que chegou até nós a versão Septuaginta, isto é a tradução do A.T. hebraico para o grego (250 - 150 A.C.). O nome dessa versão se deve ao fato de que, segundo uma tradição, teriam sido setenta os seus tradutores, que trabalharam por orientação sobrenatural, os quais trabalharam somente durante setenta e dois dias até terminar o seu trabalho. Ali vivia também o grande filósofo neoplatônico dos judeus, Filo, que talvez tivesse sido o mestre de Apolo, que foi um dos grandes pregadores cristãos, antes da conversão deste ao cristianismo.

O Talmude menciona uma sinagoga judaica separada, em Jerusalém, para os judeus de Alexandria; e isso pesa em favor da interpretação de alguns eruditos que dizem que, a despeito de traduções aparentemente melhores de que havia apenas duas sinagogas (em que os três primeiros patronímicos formariam uma sinagoga, e os dois últimos formariam outra), Atos 6:9, quer dizer que havia cinco sinagogas separadas de conformidade com a nacionalidade de seus membros. (*Juchasim*, fol. 26,2 e Talmude *Hieros*. *Megilla*, fol. 73:4). Também somos informados de que Alexandria possuía uma população de cerca de cem mil habitantes por essa época, e os judeus que dali haviam retornado a Jerusalém eram suficientemente numerosos para organizarem a sua própria sinagoga, tendo formado ao menos uma delas.

A cidade de Alexandria possuía a terceira maior população judaica de todas as cidades do mundo, só sendo ultrapassada por Roma e Jerusalém. Os judeus tinham o seu próprio distrito, que lhes foi designado por Ptolomeu Filadelfo, e que governavam como uma república independente, por um etnarca judeu (ver Josefo, *Antiq*. xiv.7,2). A passagem de *Antiq*. mostra-nos que os judeus eram reconhecidos como

ALEXANDRIA, BIBLIOTECA DE

cidadãos por seus senhores romanos.

Sabemos que Alexandria se tornou um importante centro de cristianismo, embora não sejam muito abundantes as informações autênticas de que dispomos sobre a igreja cristã ali existente. O que se sabe sobre o movimento cristão ali é que era herdeiro do judaísmo alexandrino. Clemente de Alexandria (212 D.C.) é um dos mais conhecidos pais da igreja provenientes daquela área. A doutrina por ele ensinada exibe influências do neoplatonismo, tal como sucede com os escritos de Filo. Isso também ocorre no tocante aos escritos de *Orígenes*, outro famoso pai da igreja que era natural de Alexandria (250 D.C.)

Atualmente, em Alexandria, existe a famosa Biblioteca do Patriarcado Grego, que entesoura a *segunda* maior coletânea de manuscritos bíblicos do mundo, ocupando posição inferior somente em relação ao mosteiro de Stª Catarina, no Sinai.

Ver o artigo sobre *Alexandria, Biblioteca de*.

Alexandria não é mencionada no Antigo Testamento, e só incidentalmente é mencionada no Novo (ver Atos 2:10; 6:9; 18:24 e 27:6). No entanto, teve imensa importância histórica no tocante a Israel e ao cristianismo primitivo. Ali estudaram e ensinaram vários importantes pais da Igreja. Ver o artigo sobre a *teologia alexandrina*. (AM DE FA HA ND NTI UN Z)

ALEXANDRIA, BIBLIOTECA DE

A biblioteca de Alexandria foi a mais completa e mais famosa do mundo antigo. Foi fundada por Ptolomeu I (c. 300 A.C.), em conjunção com o Museu e a Universidade, com um corpo docente de eruditos sustentados pelo estado. O *Museu* tinha diversas divisões: uma faculdade de aprendizagem semita e grega, um centro de pesquisa internacional e a biblioteca. As instalações incluíram um número de edifícios e jardins semelhantes aos das Universidades de Oxford e Cambridge. Os estudiosos mais brilhantes da época a freqüentavam para ler os manuscritos e para fazer pesquisa. Ptolomeu atraiu alguns dos homens mais brilhantes da época para trabalhar e lecionar em Alexandria, oferecendo-lhes dinheiro e privilégios. Assim foi, que Alexandria substituiu Atenas como o centro cultural da época. Por cerca de um século, Alexandria não tinha rival. Mais tarde a biblioteca de Pérgamo (A. Menor) ganhou uma reputação admirável como um centro de erudição.

O filho de Ptolomeu compartilhava a visão do pai e aumentou imensamente o número dos manuscritos da biblioteca de Alexandria. Seu bibliotecário, Demétrio de Falero, tentou adquirir cópias de todos os livros do mundo. Quando iniciou seu trabalho, a biblioteca tinha 200.000 manuscritos e ele acrescentou mais. Ptolomeu III (247-222 A.C.) estabeleceu uma biblioteca menor no Serápeo, o templo de Júpiter Serápis, no mesmo local. Sêneca nos informa que 400.000 livros foram queimados na biblioteca na campanha de guerra que César fez na cidade. Mas a biblioteca foi reconstruída e Aulo Gélio, no século II D.C. declarou que, no tempo dele, a biblioteca tinha 700.000 livros. Segundo a tradição judaica, foi para esta biblioteca que a tradução do Antigo Testamento foi feita, sendo chamada de Septuaginta, da tradição de 70 eruditos que produziram a obra. Esta informação foi registrada na *Carta de Arísteas*.

Os manuscritos foram adquiridos de todas as partes do mundo conhecido na época, e em muitas linguagens. Eruditos e sacerdotes tinham livros e coleções particulares por séculos, mas foi em Alexandria que a primeira grande biblioteca foi estabelecida. Além disso, a biblioteca tornou-se um centro de traduções, fabricação e duplicação de manuscritos. Lá a filologia tornou-se uma ciência. A teoria gramática do grego clássico foi desenvolvida e melhorada em Alexandria. Interpretações críticas sobre muitas obras foram produzidas pelos eruditos da biblioteca. Entre as muitas obras importantes lá produzidas está o tratado de Hipócrates sobre a medicina (460-377 A.C.). A ciência da cartografia também foi lá desenvolvida em cerca de 300 A.C. Euclides, o pai da geometria científica, trabalhou na cidade em cerca de 300 A.C., escrevendo seu livro «Os Elementos da Geometria». Seus conceitos têm sido ensinados por mais de 2000 anos, e este livro tem sido chamado «o livro texto mais bem-sucedido de todos os tempos». Erastóstenes, um dos bibliotecários da biblioteca, no terceiro século A.C. descreveu a forma globular da terra, e falou de terras além do horizonte. Ele usou sombras lançadas pelo sol para calcular a circunferência da terra, e errou em apenas 1100 milhas. Strabo desenvolveu a ciência da geografia em Alexandria, e publicou seu livro «*Geografia*» em 23 D.C. O grande erudito Ptolomeu de Alexandria (127-151 D.C.), escreveu sobre diversas ciências, geografia, cartografia, matemática, e principalmente sobre astronomia. Seu trabalho sobre a geografia tinha 8000 nomes geográficos e seus livros tratavam sobre a astronomia de todos os planetas e 1022 estrelas. Mas ele cometeu o grande erro de localizar a terra no centro do universo, e só muitos séculos depois este erro foi corrigido.

A leitura de todas as realizações dos eruditos de Alexandria se lê como um livro de «*Quem é Quem*» do mundo antigo, e os nomes e livros citados aqui são somente representativos da grande atividade daquele centro de erudição e literatura. Os judeus nunca tiveram um homem mais erudito que Filo, nem os cristãos, alguém mais erudito que Orígenes, e ambos foram nativos de Alexandria. Nesta cidade se desenvolveu a célebre Escola de Teologia de Alexandria que tinha alguns entendimentos mais sábios do que aqueles da Igreja Ocidental, sobre um número de assuntos que têm influenciado a teologia cristã, especialmente na Igreja Oriental e na Igreja Anglicana.

Destruições irracionais

1. A parte principal da biblioteca foi danificada num incêndio que resultou do ataque de Júlio César contra Alexandria em 47 A.C. Mas a biblioteca foi reconstruída e renovada.

2. Na guerra civil, no tempo do Imperador Aurélio, perto do fim do terceiro século depois de Cristo, a biblioteca foi novamente destruída por fogo e depois restaurada.

3. A coleção do Serápio e o próprio templo que serviu como seu depósito, foram totalmente destruídos em 391 D.C. pelos cristãos, cumprindo a ordem do Imperador Teodósio—uma destruição incrivelmente irracional, inspirada pelo preconceito e ódio religioso.

4. Finalmente, o golpe fatal foi aplicado pelo Caliph Omar, em 641 D.C., que queimou os livros da biblioteca para esquentar os banhos de Alexandria. Tais ações absurdas são repetidas em tempos modernos por terroristas que queimam bibliotecas de países inimigos, por razões políticas. Hoje, em Alexandria, existe a Biblioteca do Patriarcado Grego, que depois do mosteiro do Sinai, tem a maior coleção de manuscritos bíblicos do mundo. (AM E)

ALEXANDRIA, TEOLOGIA DE — ALFABETO (ESCRITA)

ALEXANDRIA, TEOLOGIA DE

Orígenes (186-255) foi o maior teólogo-filósofo e figura do cristianismo da Igreja, antes do concílio de Nicéia. Nasceu em Alexandria e ali ficou até o ano 232. Sua erudição lhe dá uma proeminência na Igreja antiga que só foi ultrapassada por Jerônimo. Era bem versado na filosofia e procurou expressar a fé cristã por meio da filosofia, sobretudo no platonismo; particularizando-se no neoplatonismo. A escola alexandrina (mormente Orígenes e Clemente) desenvolveu uma forma distintiva de cristianismo. Foi Clemente de Alexandria quem declarou que a porção melhor da filosofia grega (como as idéias de Platão) serviu de mestre-escola para conduzir os gregos a Cristo, segundo a lei de Moisés fizera no caso dos judeus.

Características distintivas da teologia alexandrina:

1. A ênfase sobre a missão universal do Logos, que opera através de meios para salvar os homens, meios não confinados à Igreja cristã. Em outras palavras, o Logos (ver o artigo) teria uma missão que vai além dos limites da Igreja cristã, agora e após a morte física. O conhecimento viria lentamente, embora com segurança, para todos os homens (Orígenes), mesmo no caso das multidões que durante toda a sua vida terrena não têm contato com o cristianismo. Essa idéia de forma alguma é anticristã, visto que Cristo é o Logos em uma de Suas missões. Mas o Logos não está restringido a qualquer organização ou cultura.

2. A preexistência da alma, e a queda de todas elas antes da associação com o corpo físico. A vida na Terra é encarada como um campo de provas para almas já caídas no pecado.

3. Os homens penetram nesse campo de provas como seres humanos ou como espíritos angelicais caídos, por não haver diferença substancial entre o alma humana e os anjos (ver o artigo a respeito), exceto quanto à extensão da queda.

4. Orígenes criou o útil conceito da «eterna geração» do Filho, conferindo ao Logos um eterno aspecto de filiação. Essa idéia ajudou na formulação da doutrina da trindade.

5. Interpretações simbólicas ou alegóricas de trechos bíblicos problemáticos, mormente do Antigo Testamento. Por exemplo, o sacrifício de Isaque refletiria uma fé muito primitiva, que ainda contemplava a utilidade e a correção dos sacrifícios humanos. Tal idéia é totalmente inaceitável diante de uma visão iluminada de Deus e daquilo que Ele requer do homem. É difícil imaginar que Deus submeteria alguém a esse tipo de teste, assim sancionando o conceito da correção dos sacrifícios humanos. Portanto, rejeitamos a narrativa em seu aspecto literal, embora possamos extrair dela lições quanto à dedicação suprema. Outras questões difíceis, no terreno histórico ou científico, foram similarmente alegorizadas por Orígenes, como a história da criação. Orígenes postulava três níveis de interpretação: 1. O literal; 2. o simbólico ou alegórico; e 3. o místico. As mais profundas necessidades da alma só podem ser satisfeitas com a interpretação mística.

6. A oportunidade não cessaria por ocasião da morte biológica. A missão do Logos não seria limitada pelo tempo. A morte põe fim à vida do corpo, mas não confina a alma. A missão de Cristo pode atingir os homens bem longe, no corredor da eternidade futura. Orígenes pensava em um *universalismo* absoluto (ver o artigo). Outros membros da mesma escola pensavam em ampla oportunidade para além da morte biológica. Ver o NTI sobre Efé. 1:10 e o relato

sobre a descida de Cristo ao hades, em I Ped. 3:18, onde há uma longa nota expositiva a respeito. Ver o artigo sobre *a restauração*, nesta obra, bem como sobre *a descida de Cristo ao hades*.

7. As chamas purgatoriais do juízo seriam necessárias, porque o homem precisa pagar por seus erros, visto que não há salvação sem santificação, por meio da purificação. Todavia, o julgamento é remedial, e não meramente retributivo, tornando-se um dos meios de levar os homens a Cristo, na pós-vida. (Ver I Ped. 4:6).

Vários dos itens acima satisfazem o anelo do coração humano por um tipo de cristianismo mais otimista e abrangente. Certas dessas características têm sido preservadas na Igreja do Oriente ortodoxa e eslavônica), ou pela Igreja Anglicana, sobretudo no que toca à ampla oportunidade de salvação, que não terminaria no túmulo. Textos bíblicos como Efé 1:10 e I Ped. 3:18-4:6 são utilizados para demonstrar a sabedoria alexandrina quanto a alguns desses pontos. (B C E NTI)

ALEXANDRINOS

São mencionados em Atos 6:9. Judeus de Alexandria estabeleceram-se em Jerusalém, onde tinham uma sinagoga.

ALEXANDRINUS

O Codex Alexandrinus, simbolizado por A, um importante manuscrito bíblico grego. Ver o artigo sobre os *manuscritos*.

Alfa e o Ômega Ver depois de **Alfabeto (Escrita)**.

ALFABETO (ESCRITA)

Deriva-se essa palavra do grego **alfabetos**, passando pelo latim. Esse nome vem das duas primeiras letras do alfabeto grego, *alfa* e *beta*. Têm-se encontrado obras escritas no Oriente Próximo datadas de pelo menos 3.100 A.C. No segundo milênio A.C., várias experiências levaram ao desenvolvimento de um alfabeto. O alfabeto é uma coleção de letras (símbolos) para representar sons ou fonemas, e portanto, palavras. Isso nos fornece a *fala escrita*. As culturas atuais mais avançadas têm esse modo de expressão escrita, embora os símbolos chineses e japoneses não sigam o desenvolvimento comum, pois a escrita deles é mais ideográfica.

Esboço:
1. O termo alfabeto
2. Escrita pré-alfabética
3. Escritas alfabéticas
4. Origem do alfabeto
5. Ilustrações de princípios
6. Principais ramos alfabéticos
7. Alfabeto dos hebreus
8. O ramo aramaico
9. O alfabeto grego
10. A invenção da imprensa

1. *O termo alfabeto*. Esse termo, que vem do latim *alphabetum*, foi pela primeira vez usado pelos eruditos cristãos Tertuliano e Jerônimo. A maioria dos nomes das letras do alfabeto grego tem origem semítica, embora não haja uma exata correspondência de uso.

2. *Escrita pré-alfabética*. Primeiramente apareceram os auxílios mnemônicos ou de memória, como varetas com nós, cordões com nós; em seguida, vieram os símbolos iconográficos, geométricos, com figuras de animais e de objetos naturais, que datam

ALFABETO

SEMITA				GREGO			ETRUSCO		LATIM	
Semita Norte	Fenício	Nome	Valor Fonético	Cedo	Clássico	Nome	Cedo	Clássico	Cedo	Clássico
		ʾALEPH	ʾ			ALPHA				A
		BETH	B			BETA				B
		GIMEL	G			GAMMA				C
		DALETH	D			DELTA				D
		HE	H			ĔPSILON				E
		WAW	W			DIGAMMA				F
										G
		ZAYIN	Z							
		ḤETH	Ḥ			ĒTA				H
		TETH	Ṭ			THETA				
		YOD	Y			IOTA				I
										(J)
		KAPH	K			KAPPA				K
		LAMED	L			LAMBDA				L
		MEM	M			MU				M
		NUN	N			NU				N
		SAMEKH	S							
		ʾAYIN	ʿ			ŎMICRON				O
		PE	P			PI				P
		SADE	Ṣ							
		QOPH	Q							Q
		REŠ	R			RHO				R
		ŠIN	SH — S			SIGMA				S
		TAW	T			TAU				T
						UPSILON				V
										X
						CHI				Y
										Z
						ŌMEGA				

Cortesia, Encyclopedia Americana

ALFABETO

Tabela de Alfabetos

INGLÊS	ÁRABE	HEBRAICO	GREGO	RUSSO	ALEMÃO
A a	Alif *l* — Alif *l*	א Aleph *3*	A α Alpha (ã)	А а (ã)	$\mathfrak{A}$ $\mathfrak{a}$ (ã)
B b	ب Be (b)	ב Beth (b)	B β Beta (b)	Б б (b)	$\mathfrak{A}$ ä (e)
C c	ت Te (t)	בּ Veth (v) *4*	Γ γ Gamma (g)	В в (v)	$\mathfrak{B}$ $\mathfrak{b}$ (b)
D d	ث Se (th)	ג Gimel (g)	Δ δ Delta (d)	Г г (g)	$\mathfrak{C}$ c (k, ts, s)
E e	ج Jim (j) *2*	ד Daleth (d)	E ε Epsilon (e)	Д д (d)	$\mathfrak{Ch}$ $\mathfrak{ch}$ (H, kh)
F f	ح He (h) *2*	ה Heh (h)	Z ζ Zeta (z)	Е е (ye)	$\mathfrak{D}$ $\mathfrak{d}$ (d)
G g	خ Khe (kh) *2*	ו Vav (v)	Η η Eta (ã)	Ж ж (zh)	$\mathfrak{G}$ $\mathfrak{e}$ (e, ã)
H h	د Dal (d)	ז Zayin (z)	Θ θ Theta (th)	З з (z)	$\mathfrak{F}$ $\mathfrak{f}$ (f)
I i	ذ Zal (*th*)	ח Kheth (kh)	I ι Iota (ê)	И и (i, ê)	$\mathfrak{G}$ $\mathfrak{g}$ (g, kh)
J j	ر Re (r)	ט Teth (t)	Κ κ Kappa (k)	Й й (ê) o	$\mathfrak{H}$ $\mathfrak{h}$ (h)
K k	ز Ze (z)	י Yod (y)	Λ λ Lambda (l)	К к (k)	$\mathfrak{I}$ $\mathfrak{i}$ (i, ê)
L l	س Sin (s) *2*	כ ך Kaph (k) *5*	M μ Mu (m)	Л л (l)	$\mathfrak{I}$ $\mathfrak{j}$ (y)
M m	ش Shin (sh) *2*	כ ך Khaph (kh) *4, 5*	N ν Nu (n)	М м (m)	$\mathfrak{R}$ $\mathfrak{t}$ (k)
N n	ص Sad (s) *2*	ל Lamedh (l)	Ξ ξ Xi (ks)	Н н (n)	$\mathfrak{L}$ $\mathfrak{l}$ (l)
O o	ض Dad (*th*) *2*	מ ם Mem (m) *5*	O o Omicron (o)	О о (ô, o)	$\mathfrak{M}$ $\mathfrak{m}$ (m)
P p	ط Ta (t)	נ ן Nun (n) *5*	Π π Pi (p)	П п (p)	$\mathfrak{N}$ $\mathfrak{n}$ (n)
Q q	ظ Za (z)	ס Samekh (s)	P ρ Rho (r)	Р р (r)	$\mathfrak{O}$ $\mathfrak{o}$ (ô, ô)
R r	ع Ain *l, 2*	ע Ayin *3*	Σ σ ς Sigma (s) *5*	С с (s)	$\mathfrak{O}$ ö (ô)
S s	غ Ghain (kh) *2*	פ ף Peh (p) *5*	T τ Tau (t)	Т т (t)	$\mathfrak{P}$ $\mathfrak{p}$ (p)
T t	ف Fe (f) *2*	פ ף Feh (f) *4, 5*	Υ υ Upsilon (u, ôô)	У у (ôô)	$\mathfrak{Q}$ (u) $\mathfrak{q}$ (u) (kv)
U u	ق Qaf (kã) *2*	צ ץ Tsadi (ts) *5*	Φ φ Phi (f)	Ф ф (f)	$\mathfrak{R}$ $\mathfrak{r}$ (r)
V v	ك Kef (k) *2*	ק Koph (k)	X χ Chi (H)	Х х (kh)	$\mathfrak{S}$ $\mathfrak{s}$ (s, z) *5*
W w	ل Lam (l) *2*	ר Resh (r)	Ψ ψ Psi (ps)	Ц ц (ts)	$\mathfrak{Sch}$ $\mathfrak{sch}$ (sh)
X x	م Mim (m) *2*	שׂ Sin (s)	Ω ω Omega (ô)	Ч ч (ch)	$\mathfrak{T}$ $\mathfrak{t}$ (t)
Y y	ن Nun (n) *2*	שׁ Shin (sh) *4*		Ш ш (sh)	$\mathfrak{U}$ $\mathfrak{u}$ (ôô)
Z z	ه He (h)	ת Tav (t)		Щ щ (shch)	$\mathfrak{ü}$ ü (u)
	و Waw (w)	ת Thav (th, s)		Ъ ъ *7*	$\mathfrak{V}$ $\mathfrak{v}$ (f)
	ي Ye (y) *5*			Ы ы (ê)	$\mathfrak{W}$ $\mathfrak{w}$ (v)
				Ь ь *8*	$\mathfrak{X}$ $\mathfrak{x}$ (ks)
				Э э (e)	$\mathfrak{Y}$ $\mathfrak{y}$ (e, u)
				Ю ю (u)	$\mathfrak{Z}$ $\mathfrak{z}$ (ts)
				Я я (yã)	

Marcas Diacríticas

- ◌ֹ (ô, ô)
- ◌ָ (ã)
- ◌ֵ (ã)
- ◌ֶ (e)
- ◌ִ (i, ê)
- ◌ְ (silent)
- ◌ּ (ôô)

ALFABETO (ESCRITA)

de até 20.000 A.C., encontrados nas paredes de muitas cavernas. Esses símbolos comunicavam uma forma de escrita pré-alfabética. Em seguida apareceu uma série de quadros para comunicar uma mensagem, resultando nas escritas cuneiformes, nos hieróglifos egípcios e nas escritas maia e asteca, que já eram parcialmente fonéticas.

Escrita fonética. Um exemplo dessa forma escrita encontra-se na escrita linear minoana B, de cerca de 1.500 A.C. (e, nos idiomas modernos, no japonês e no coreano). Cada elemento corresponde a um fonema ou som específico. Os *sinais* individuais representam sílabas e vogais. os menores elementos das palavras que são capazes de serem isolados e pronunciados.

3. *Escritas alfabéticas.* Esse é o último e mais desenvolvido estágio da escrita, e também o mais eficiente. Cada símbolo individual representa *fonemas* (sons consoantes e vogais), como os tijolos que formam uma parede. A história do alfabeto é muito complexa mas os historiadores da linguagem concordam que todos os alfabetos existentes podem ser explicados por um único (mas contínuo) desenvolvimento histórico, que retrocede ao fim do segundo milênio A.C.

4. *Origem do alfabeto.* Muita discussão envolve esse problema, com sugestões de que as origens podem ser encontradas nos hieróglifos egípcios, na escrita cuneiforme ou nas escritas cretense e fenícia. A maior parte das evidências gira em torno da Terra Santa e regiões circunvizinhas, com datas entre 1.700 e 1.300 A.C. Partindo dali, muitos têm conjecturado como o alfabeto teve seu início. As inscrições paleo-sinaíticas fornecem-nos alguma indicação sobre a possível origem do alfabeto, o que representa um passo intermediário entre os hieróglifos egípcios e o alfabeto norte-semítico. Outros, entretanto, têm pensado que a escrita pseudo-hieroglífica de Biblos seja o protótipo do alfabeto. Essa idéia fundamenta-se sobre inscrições em bronze e em pedra (século XV A.C. ou antes), encontradas em 1929, no local do antigo porto de Biblos. Porém, surgiu uma terceira teoria por causa do descobrimento de milhares de tabletes de argila, desenterradas em Ras Shamra (antiga Ugarite), na Síria, na costa do mar Mediterrâneo. Esses tabletes contêm um alfabeto cuneiforme de trinta letras, em uso entre os séculos XV e XIII A.C. Todavia, alguns objetam a isso, dizendo que essa forma de escrita dependia do alfabeto norte-semítico, que já era usado na região; e novas descobertas e estudos parecem confirmar isso. Portanto, esses tabletes representam um estágio posterior de escrita, por meio de um alfabeto, e não a origem real do alfabeto. A solução do quebra-cabeça pode provir da Palestina, onde, desde 1929, diversas inscrições da idade do bronze média e posterior (conhecidas como canaanita antiga) têm sido descobertas. Podem ser divididas em três grupos, entre os séculos XVII e XIII A.C., correspondentes aos períodos bíblicos dos patriarcas, de Josué e dos Juízes. Parece que a conjectura mais provavelmente correta é que a origem do alfabeto pode ser encontrada no alfabeto norte-semítico ou no seu protótipo. Os hieróglifos egípcios, as escritas cuneiformes e outras exerceram influência sobre esse protótipo. Porém, qualquer das teorias propostas deixa sem solução grandes problemas, especialmente no que tange ao inter-relacionamento entre as antigas formas de linguagem escrita.

5. *Ilustrações de princípios.* Falamos aqui sobre o desenvolvimento das letras. Usando o antigo hebraico como exemplo, temos o *yod* = y, com a figura de uma *mão; mem* = m, com a figura de *água corrente, num* = n, com a figura de um *peixe; alef* = uma consoante glotal suave, com a figura de um *boi; gimel* = g, com a figura de um *bumerangue.* Ver o gráfico adiante quanto aos detalhes dos símbolos.

6. *Principais ramos alfabéticos.* Em cerca de 1000 A.C., já existiam quatro ramos principais do alfabeto semítico original. Havia o sul-semítico, o cananeu, o aramaico e o grego. Cada um desses ramos contava com seus sub-ramos. O hebraico pertencia ao ramo cananeu (fenício).

7. *Alfabeto dos hebreus.* O primitivo alfabeto dos hebreus era um sub-ramo do alfabeto cananeu, tendo florescido no período pré-exílico (1000 a 500 A.C.), embora continuasse em uso até o século III A.C. Moedas judaicas do período dos macabeus têm inscrições que se derivam desse ramo. O alfabeto quadrado hebraico deriva-se do ramo aramaico norte-semítico, o alfabeto que deu origem ao hebraico moderno. Pode ser seguido até o século III A.C. Com algumas modificações, era usado nos rolos bíblicos antes da era cristã, sendo essencialmente preservado na Bíblia impressa. A moderna forma hebraica manuscrita é mais cursiva, tendo muitas variedades locais.

8. *O ramo aramaico.* Os arameus originalmente eram nômades semitas, acerca de quem primeiramente ouvimos na Assíria, no século XII A.C. Esses povos foram derrubados pelos assírios no século IX A.C. A língua aramaica e sua forma escrita tornou-se a *língua franca* do Oriente Próximo, perto do final do século VII A.C. Subseqüentemente, tornou-se um idioma em que foram escritas pequenas porções das Escrituras, originadora do hebraico quadrado, protótipo do hebraico moderno. Tornou-se o protótipo dos alfabetos de idiomas semíticos e não-semíticos, como o árabe, o sírio-nestoriano, e certos idiomas asiáticos na Índia, no Irã, no Iraque e em certas regiões da Rússia, além de muitas outras. O aramaico era a língua falada pelos judeus nos dias de Jesus.

9. *O alfabeto grego.* A escrita hieroglífica *linear B* de Cnossus e Micenas sugere que o grego pode ter sido escrito de maneira diferente do que o foi mais tarde. E, nesse caso, essa forma mais antiga perdeu-se por ocasião da queda desses reinos (cerca de 1150 A.C.). Seja como for, o alfabeto grego (inscrições que datam do século VIII A.C.) teve origem semítica. Isso se comprova pelos nomes das letras que não têm sentido no grego, e sim, nos idiomas semíticos. Ademais, o alfabeto grego original segue a mesma ordem das letras que se vê no norte-semítico, com um sinal adicional no fim. Além disso, o formato das letras é bastante similar tanto no norte-semítico quanto no grego. Uma prova adicional da origem semítica do alfabeto grego é o fato que, originalmente, a escrita se processava da direita para a esquerda, conforme se vê até hoje nas línguas semíticas. Finalmente, a maioria dos sinais gregos equivale em som aos seus equivalentes semíticos. As diferenças existentes envolvem fonemas semíticos que não existem no grego, deixando alguns sinais sem função no grego (a saber, alefe, he, ayin e yod). Por outro lado, algumas vogais gregas têm sons que não são usados nas línguas semíticas.

Do alfabeto grego surgiram os alfabetos de vários idiomas como o cóptico, o etrusco, o latim e o gótico (dezenove ou vinte do grego, e cinco ou seis do latim). O alfabeto cirílico, do qual procedem o russo moderno, o búlgaro e outras línguas eslavas, tem sua base no grego. Desses alfabetos fundamentais desenvolveram-se todos os alfabetos europeus.

ALFA E O ÔMEGA — AL-KINDI

O alfabeto grego ocupa uma posição ímpar na história da escrita. Embora os gregos não tivessem inventado o alfabeto, transformaram a escrita semítica consonantal em um alfabeto moderno, conferindo-lhe simetria e arte. O alfabeto latino desenvolveu-se do grego, por meio do etrusco; e o latim, adotado como língua oficial pela Igreja Católica Romana, tornou-se o idioma comum do mundo intelectual europeu. Várias formas da escrita latina tornaram-se a base dos estilos incorporados nos idiomas ocidentais modernos.

10. *A invenção da imprensa.* No tempo da invenção da impressão, em 1450 D.C., dois estilos principais do alfabeto latino posterior dominavam: as letras negras (também chamadas estilo gótico ou estilo alemão — este último erroneamente assim chamado) e a forma mais arredondada (atualmente chamada tipo romano), a *littera antiqua.* A forma romana era a mais popular e espalhou-se pelo mundo. Essa foi a forma que se tornou mais usada do que qualquer outra.

O alfabeto foi uma das mais úteis invenções humanas, a fonte mais fundamental de toda cultura e ciência. Tornou-se o veículo de todo o conhecimento reduzido à forma escrita, incluindo o conhecimento espiritual. (ALL AM DIR ND Z)

ALFA E O ÔMEGA

1. *Itens do alfabeto.* Essas são a primeira e a última letra do alfabeto grego, equivalentes aos nossos *a* e *z.* Os hebreus usavam sua primeira e sua última letra para indicar «o primeiro e o último», uso esse que foi adotado no Novo Testamento. Os termos também podem significar «do começo ao fim», englobando tudo. A «totalidade de uma coisa» é indicada e significada pela glória Shekinah. A idéia de eternidade também pode estar envolvida.

2. *No Novo Testamento.* Ver Apo. 1:8; 21:6; 22:13. O artigo definido se repete: «o Alfa e o Ômega». Provavelmente os trechos de Isa. 44:6 e 48:12 estavam na mente do autor sagrado: «Eu sou o primeiro, e eu sou o último», asseverando a eternidade e a transcendência de Deus. O mesmo conceito está envolvido, sem essas palavras, em Efé. 1:10 e Rom. 11:26. Naturalmente, a grandeza do Pai, no Antigo Testamento, é transferida para a grandeza do Filho, no Novo Testamento (Apo. 22:13), o que subentende a Sua divindade (ver o artigo *a divindade de Cristo*). No Filho encontramos o começo da criação espiritual e o seu final, ou o alvo da criação, a saber, a participação em Sua imagem (II Cor. 3:18), e em Sua divindade (II Ped. 1:4), no caso dos outros filhos de Deus. Cristo deu início à glória em Sua encarnação, e cumpriu-a em Sua glorificação. Os outros filhos de Deus participam de ambas essas realidades espirituais. Ver o NTI, em Rom. 8:29, quanto a uma completa explicação sobre esse conceito.

Na literatura cristã patrística e posterior, essa expressão aparece com freqüência na idéia de nosso relacionamento com Cristo, tendo-se tornado parte da terminologia cristológica. Ver os artigos sobre *o primeiro e o último* e o *Logos.* (A B MK MTI S SE Z)

AL-FARABI

Famoso filósofo árabe (falecido em 950), que tentou harmonizar a filosofia helenista e o misticismo islâmico. Ele tomou por empréstimo idéias neoplatônicas, em apoio a seu *Sufi* (ver o artigo), ou misticismo. Ele tentou combinar Aristóteles, Platão e sua fé religiosa em uma única filosofia.

Escritos: Sobre os Princípios dos Pontos de vista dos Habitantes do Estado Excelente, ou *A Cidade Ideal; Comentário sobre Aristóteles: Breve Comentário sobre a Análise Posterior de Aristóteles; O Fusul Al-Madani; Aforismos sobre o Estadista de Al-Farabi.*

Idéias:

1. Deus é o Um em quem se identificam a essência e a existência. Da inteligência de Deus procedem a alma do mundo e o cosmos. O mundo é uma eterna emanação de Deus.

2. O alvo da vida humana é a identificação com o Um.

3. *Argumentos em prol da existência de Deus:* a. Necessidade de explicar o movimento e todas as formas de desenvolvimento. Deus é a causa, o Movedor primário. b. O argumento cosmológico (ver o artigo a respeito). Os efeitos devem ter uma causa, e deve haver uma Causa Primária. c. Argumento baseado na necessidade. Todos os objetos têm existência dependente. Não são suas próprias causas. Deve haver um Ser necessário, sua causa, auto-existente. Tomás de Aquino desenvolveu esse argumento como uma de suas *cinco maneiras* de provar a existência de Deus. Ver o artigo sobre *Deus,* primeiro ponto: Provas de Sua Existência.

4. A lógica é um estudo introdutório à filosofia, necessário para nosso desenvolvimento mental, e, portanto, para nosso desenvolvimento religioso, que inclui várias perfeições, incluindo a perfeição mental.

5. A filosofia tem duas divisões principais, a teórica e a prática. A divisão prática é a *ética,* a ciência da conduta ideal entre os homens. (E EP P)

AL-GHAZZALI

O maior dos teólogos do Islã (1050-1111). Foi professor da Academia Nizamita de Bagdá por muitos anos, mas abandonou a carreira para fazer uma peregrinação na qual buscava a certeza. Tinha profundos conhecimentos sobre o islamismo, tendo sido chamado de Agostinho do Islã. Ajudou no estabelecimento da escola mística do *sufismo* (ver o artigo a respeito).

Escritos: Intenções dos Filósofos; Auto-Destruição dos Filósofos; Reavivamento das Ciências Religiosas; Incoerência dos Filósofos; Livramento do Erro; Começo da Orientação; A Incoerência da Incoerência.

Idéias:

1. Ele opunha-se à idéia da eternidade do mundo, ensinada por Al-Farabi e Avicena, seguindo Aristóteles. Defendia a *criação,* e não a emanação. Deus fez a criação, dentro do tempo e ex-nihilo, isto é, do nada.

2. A soberania divina manifestar-se-ia no *motivismo* (ver o artigo). Deus não seria apenas a Causa Primária, mas também a Causa Única.

3. A razão, não apenas os sentidos, seria um dos meios para se adquirir o conhecimento. Também precisamos do misticismo para tanto. A capacidade mística é posta à disposição do indivíduo que pratica os exercícios ascéticos apropriados. O homem precisa utilizar-se da oração, do jejum e evitar a sensualidade, a fim de obter contato com Deus.

4. O Alcorão é um dos meios de busca da verdade, pois contém verdades *reveladas.* (E EP P)

AL-KINDI

Filósofo islâmico (813-873), membro da Escola de Bagdá, viveu em Basra e em Bagdá, onde morreu. Foi o primeiro seguidor árabe influente de Aristóteles.

ALFARROBAS — ALIANÇAS

Traduziu os livros quarto a sexto da Eneadas de Plotino, que equivocadamente foram atribuídos a Aristóteles, e que circularam até o século XIII como a *Teologia de Aristóteles*. Sua obra principal é *A Metafísica*. Também escreveu sobre geometria, astronomia, astrologia, aritmética, música, física, medicina, psicologia, meteorologia e política.

Idéias:

Foi essencialmente um neoplatonista muito endividado a Aristóteles. No campo da *ontologia* ele tratou como reais as categorias aristotélicas, intitulando de substâncias primárias a matéria, a forma, o movimento, o lugar e o tempo. Ensinava que muitas verdades nos chegam mediante a revelação de que a filosofia não dispõe. Também ensinava que Deus criou tudo do nada (criação, e não emanação); mas dizia que a criação, que veio do nada, eventualmente reverterá ao nada. Considerava a astrologia uma ciência genuína.

ALFARROBAS

Alfarrobas é o nome dado à semente da **Ceratonia siliqua**, árvore verde perene das margens do Mediterrâneo. As alfarrobas eram dadas ao gado e aos porcos como alimento, mas os pobres também as consumiam. Na história do filho pródigo, o fato de que ele foi submetido a comer alfarrobas simbolizava o baixo estado de penúria a que fora reduzido por seus desperdícios, ilustrando ainda o que o pecado finalmente nos faz na vida. Anteriores estados de glória não demoram a ser anulados, devido à destruição causada pela obra do mal. (Ver Luc. 15:16). (NTI)

ALFEU

1. **Pai de Levi (Mar. 2:14)**. Levi é identificado com o apóstolo Mateus (ver Mat. 9:9 e 10:3). Essa é a única informação que nos é dada sobre Alfeu.

2. Pai de Tiago, o menor, assim chamado para distingui-lo do Tiago melhor conhecido, irmão de João (ver Mat. 10:3 e Mar. 3:18). Alguns o identificam com o pai de Levi, mas sem provas convincentes. Alguns também o identificam com Cléopas (ver Luc. 24:18) ou com Clopas (João 19:25). A maioria dos eruditos, entretanto, duvida do acerto de todas essas identificações, e supõe que Cléopas e Clopas eram homens diferentes. É verdade que a forma aramaica de Alfeu é *Halphal*, que poderia ser transliterada como Clopas; mas até mesmo com esse fato a identificação não se firma. Outros, fazendo a comparação entre João 19:25 e Luc. 24:10 e Mat. 10:3, chegam à conclusão que Alfeu é a forma grega e que Cléopas é a forma hebraica ou siríaca do mesmo indivíduo. Esse argumento pressupõe que Maria, esposa de Clopas, a qual esteve presente à crucificação, junto com outras mulheres, é a mesma Maria, mãe de Tiago, que também esteve presente à crucificação (ver Mat. 27:56 e Mar. 15:40). Tiago, filho de Maria (ver Mat. 27:56), portanto, seria filho de Clopas e Maria (ver João 19:25). Porém, isso é contrabalançado pela declaração de que Cléopas é nome de origem grega, ao passo que Clopas é derivado do aramaico. Aqueles que afirmam que Alfeu e Clopas são a mesma pessoa também pensam que Alfeu tinha dois nomes, tal como acontecia a muitas pessoas daquela época, como, por exemplo, Saulo e Paulo. Em vista do exposto, concluímos que nada se sabe acerca disso com certeza. (ND PR UN Z)

••• ••• •••

ALFORJE

Tradução portuguesa de um termo grego que aparece por seis vezes no Novo Testamento, *péra* (ver Mat. 10:10; Mar. 6:8; Luc. 9:3; 10:4; 22:35,36). Trata-se de uma sacola de couro, a qual Lucas contrasta com o *ballántion*, «bolsa» (ver Luc. 10:4 e 22:35). Que o alforje era uma sacola usada para o transporte de provisões (de boca) torna-se claro em Judite 13:10, em cujo livro apócrifo é adicionada a expressão «de alimentos». Usualmente era usada pelos antigos pastores, em suas andanças pelos campos, tangendo seus rebanhos. Nos quatro evangelhos também há menção a outros receptáculos. Ver *Vasos*. Alforje é sinônimo de «surrão», que os interioranos brasileiros do nordeste usam em suas cavalgadas pela caatinga.

ALFREDO, O GRANDE

Datas: 849-899. Rei dos saxões ocidentais, guerreiro e erudito cristão. Foi cultural e religiosamente importante, devido às suas traduções das obras de Orósio, Boécio, Bede e Gregório o Grande, e por haver promovido a educação. (AM E)

ALGODÃO

O termo hebraico *karpas*, ocasionalmente traduzido por «verde», indica o algodão. (Ver Est. 1:6). O algodão é cultivado na Judéia desde 490 A.C., e a arqueologia tem demonstrado que algumas múmias eram envoltas nesse material. Os judeus aprenderam como cultivar e utilizar o algodão, estando cativos na Pérsia, na época de Assuero (598-536 A.C.). A planta existente na Palestina e na Índia é a Gossypium herbaceum, que é um arbusto que atinge cerca de 1,80 m de altura. O fruto, quando amadurece, abre-se e produz massas brancas muito tênues. Essa variedade de algodão é um tanto mais amarelada que as variedades que existem noutras regiões do mundo.

ALHOS SILVESTRES

Esses alhos são mencionados em Números 11:5, juntamente com pepinos, melões, cebolas e alhos. Esse tipo de alho é um vegetal bulboso, similar à cebola, cultivado no Egito desde os tempos mais remotos. Eram comidos crus, com pão; ou então eram usados como condimento. Depois que saíram do Egito, os israelitas sentiram a falta desse alimento.

Os alhos silvestres têm sido cultivados pelo mundo todo para servirem como parte da alimentação, e também com finalidades medicinais. Há duas espécies, o *allium porrum* e o *trigonella foenumgra cum*. Ambas as variedades existiam no Egito. Continua sendo um alimento popular, até hoje, entre os egípcios e israelitas. (S Z)

ALIANÇAS — Ver também sobre **Pactos**.

Consideremos os pontos abaixo:

1. *Usos bíblicos*. Em Gên. 14:3, *entrar em liga com*. Em II Crô. 20:36, *combinar, ter afinidade com*, como no caso de um casamento. Em Gên. 15:18 e 21:27, *estabelecer um pacto*.

2. *Natureza das alianças*. Um acordo, usualmente sobre questões políticas e militares; uma aliança envolvia questões pessoais e religiosas. Todavia, não há uma clara distinção entre essas duas modalidades.

3. *Interdito mosaico*. Moisés baixou uma lei que proibia o povo de Israel de entrar em pacto com as nações pagãs, sem dúvida a fim de que os israelitas

ALIANÇAS — ALIENAÇÃO DO HOMEM

não fossem encorajados a adquirir os hábitos idólatras de tais povos, deixando assim de ser um povo especial e separado. (Ver Êxo. 34:15 ss. e Deu. 7:3 ss.).

4. *Alianças na antiguidade*. No Antigo Testamento encontramos as seguintes: De Abraão com três chefes dos amorreus (Gên. 14:12); mais tarde, com Abimeleque, rei de Gerar (Gên. 21:22-34). Isaque entrou em aliança com Abimeleque, o que deu nome ao poço de Beerseba (Gên. 26:26-33). Jacó e Labão entraram em aliança, sendo estabelecida a fronteira de Galeede, entre Israel e a Síria (Gên. 31:44-54). Moisés estabeleceu aliança com os queneus, quando se casou com uma mulher quenita (Êxo. 18; Núm. 10:29 ss e Juí. 1:16 e 4:11). Josué entrou em aliança com seis tribos cananéias (Jos. 9:1 ss) e mais tarde, enganado por um artifício, entrou em aliança com os gibeonitas (Jos. 9). Davi, exilado na Filístia, entrou em aliança com o rei Aquis, mediante a qual a cidade de Ziclague tornou-se sua (I Sam. 27:5-12); mais tarde, Davi entrou em aliança com Abner, em conseqüência da qual todas as tribos submeteram-se a Davi (II Sam. 3:12-21), e finalmente, Davi entrou em aliança com seus vizinhos, Hirão, rei de Tiro, e Toi, rei de Hamate (II Sam. 5:11 e 8:9-12).

5. *Resultados*. De modo geral, a sabedoria da proibição mosaica ficou confirmada, pois muitos danos foram sofridos por Israel, devido às alianças formadas. Além das alianças militares, consideramos as alianças por casamento, formados por Salomão, que tão prejudiciais foram para o espírito religioso de Israel (ver I Reis 11:1-8). Os profetas com freqüência alçaram a voz em protesto contra as alianças (ver I Reis 20:38; II Crô. 16:7; 19:2; 25:7 e Isa. 7:17).

6. *Alianças por casamento*. Usualmente essa espécie de aliança era feita por motivos políticos, a fim de fomentar boas relações com vizinhos potencialmente perigosos. Davi tinha vinte ou mais esposas e concubinas, duas das quais envolviam alianças dessa ordem (ver II Sam. 3:2-5; 5:13-16). Salomão entrou em muitas dessas alianças (ver I Reis 3:1; 9:16 e 11:1). Onri e Etbaal formaram aliança entre Israel e a Fenícia, ratificando-a com o casamento de Acabe com Jezabel (ver I Reis 16:23-31), com os mais desastrosos resultados.

7. *Princípio espiritual envolvido*. Paulo estabelece diretrizes para associações íntimas dos crentes, em II Cor. 6:14, as quais proíbem-nos de estabelecer «jugos desiguais» com os incrédulos. Assim, ele estabeleceu o princípio espiritual como guia para todas as associações íntimas que poderiam comprometer nossas vidas espirituais. (FA RV U UN Z)

ALICERCE Ver diversos artigos sobre **Fundamentos**.

ALIENAÇÃO

1. *Na teologia*. A crença que o homem caiu e assim tornou-se um ser alienado, necessitado de restauração, reconciliação e salvação. A teologia localiza a alienação do homem em sua condição moral, provocada pela revolta espiritual. (Ver Rom. 3:9 ss). O *modernismo*, abandonando a explicação sobrenatural da alienação humana, retrocedeu a um evangelho social, cujo intuito é ajudar o homem a assumir seu lugar em uma sociedade utópica. À medida que guerras, pobreza, ódio e violência generalizada embotam essa visão, a *neo-ortodoxia* postula um abrigo na reação existencial interna do homem à realidade transcendental. Entrementes, o homem não pode entender esse tipo de conceito, e continuou alienado. O *existencialismo* declara que a alienação é uma piada da natureza, por ser a própria substância do não-sistema mundial que o homem perdeu voluntária mas irrecuperavelmente. O cosmos é apenas uma existência caótica e irracional; através da piada da evolução, fomos envolvidos no caos. O homem só pode vencer a alienação forçando seus próprios valores sobre este mundo amoral.

A resposta dada pelo cristianismo é que mesmo o caos é útil a Deus por disciplinar o homem que busca a salvação (Rom. 8:20). Além disso, há a provisão da missão de Cristo, que restaura o homem e capacita-o a participar da família divina (Rom. 8:18 ss).

2. *No campo político e filosófico*. O conceito de Marx da alienação foi descrito em seus manuscritos econômicos e filosóficos, em 1844. Primeiro, o indivíduo é alienado de seu trabalho e de sua produção, porque as riquezas que ele produz não são suas, nem participa ele das decisões que trazem à existência essas riquezas. Aprofundando-se na pobreza, o homem é alienado de seus semelhantes, visto que o sistema econômico na realidade é uma espécie de guerra de competição na qual os homens lutam uns contra os outros. Finalmente, o homem se aliena de si mesmo como um ser humano, quando sua natureza é pervertida pelos abusos econômicos. O grande equívoco de Marx, naturalmente, foi que não percebeu que por detrás de todas essas formas de alienação, alicerçadas sobre os abusos econômicos, há a pior forma de alienação, que é a que provoca todos os tipos de alienação social, ou seja, como um ser decaído, o homem naturalmente explora seus semelhantes e causa os abusos econômicos. Nenhum sistema econômico estará isento de abusos enquanto aqueles que tomam as decisões não se reconciliarem espiritualmente com Deus.

Hegel falava sobre a alienação do espírito de si mesmo, na natureza e na história, e de como essa alienação vem sendo gradualmente diminuída, dentro do processo histórico. Marx obteve em Hegel as suas noções básicas, tendo-as desenvolvido naquele tipo de considerações econômicas que mostramos acima. (H E F)

ALIENAÇÃO DO HOMEM em Col. 1:21

A vós também, que outrora éreis estranhos, e inimigos no entendimento pelas vossas obras más.

Temos aqui um paralelo das condições dos pagãos, descritas em Efé. 2:1-3,5, exceto que ali a descrição é mais envolvida. O décimo segundo versículo daquele capítulo acrescenta os pensamentos de que são «estranhos» à promessa de bem-estar espiritual, de que estão «distantes», mas que agora foram «aproximados» mediante o sangue de Cristo (ver o décimo terceiro versículo). Assim, pois, foi estabelecida a «paz», mediante a «reconciliação» (versículos quinze e dezesseis, respectivamente), porquanto a «inimizade» foi abolida «na sua carne» (em sua cruz, em sua expiação terrena). Tudo isso resultou no fato de que agora temos *acesso* ao próprio Deus Pai.

I. **Estranhos**. Grego «apallotrio», ser **estranho, excluído**, termo derivado da palavra básica «allotrio», *pertencente a outro*, ou seja, «estrangeiro», «alienígena», «hostil». Essa palavra também é usada em Efé. 2:12, em alusão ao estado alienado dos pagãos em relação aos pactos de Israel; ou então de esposas privadas de seus esposos (ver I Clemente 6:3); ou mesmo da alienação de alguém da vida de Deus, em Efé. 4:18. Neste caso, os pagãos é que estão alienados de Deus, por não possuírem sua vida, por se mostrarem hostis à sua influência, afastados do seu evangelho, segundo o mesmo se acha em Cristo. Pertenciam à província do inimigo, e não eram

ALIENAÇÃO DO HOMEM

cidadãos da pátria celeste (ver Fil. 3:20). Antes, eram cidadãos do reino das trevas, e não do reino da luz (ver Col. 1:13). Por assim dizer, estavam «banidos» das realidades espirituais. Estavam em «hostilidade» contra o reino da luz, necessitados do poder reconciliador de Cristo, para que fossem levados à harmonia com ele e seu reino.

II. Inimigos. Sendo inimigos no entendimento, eram também inimigos de Deus, de modo ativo. A palavra pode ser «ativa», ou seja, «inimigo»; ou então «passiva», ou seja, «odioso», conforme se vê em Rom. 11:28. Aqueles eram «hostis» em sua mente, como também eram «inimigos ativos». Provavelmente, isso é o que está em foco aqui. Comparar essa idéia com o que se lê em Rom. 5:10, que mostra que a reconciliação foi feita com quem estava em inimizade com Deus, através da expiação. O ensinamento gnóstico supunha que a mera matéria crassa e a participação do homem na mesma fosse a totalidade de nossos problemas; pois, segundo eles, a matéria seria totalmente incapaz de redenção, ao passo que a morte física libertaria à alma que busca o bem. Paulo nega tal pensamento, pois até mesmo a matéria, bem como todas as coisas, estão sujeitas à reconciliação com Deus, ao mesmo tempo que o espírito pode mostrar-se inimigo de Deus, pervertido; e isso não sucede apenas ao corpo. Por isso é que Paulo diz *inimigos no entendimento*, tradução mais exata que a de certas versões, pois o termo grego «dianoia» significa «entendimento», «inteligência», «mente», o órgão de pensamento e racionalização. Esse vocábulo também pode significar «disposição», ou «pensamento». Seja como for, assinala àqueles que se acham alienados de Deus, sendo inimigos do Senhor em todo o seu intelecto ou processo mental. E isso, como bases neotestamentárias, também aponta para a alma, pois a função intelectual faz parte da alma, e não meramente do cérebro físico. A maldade daquela gente, portanto, maculava-lhes a própria alma, e não apenas o corpo material; e nesta mesma passagem eles são chamados de inimigos de Deus, como característica essencial de seu comportamento espiritual. Isso pode ser confrontado com o trecho de Rom. 1:19 e ss, onde a apostasia pagã se alicerça sobre bases mentais e do conhecimento. Dessa maneira, alienados de Deus, eram levados à perversão, de corpo e alma. Deixavam-se arrastar por «tolas imaginações», julgando-se «sábios» quando, na realidade, não passavam de «tolos». Tinham «concupiscência», a qual partia do «coração», e não queriam reter a Deus em seu «conhecimento». Por isso é que seguiam a terrível apostasia, na qual Deus os «entregara» a todas as formas de perversão. Conforme diz Robertson, *in loc.*: «É sempre uma tragédia ver os homens usarem ativamente suas mentes contra Deus».

> O morcego e a coruja habitam ali:
> A serpente se aninha no altar de pedra:
> Os vasos sagrados mofam perto:
> A imagem de Deus desapareceu!
>
> Naquele duro mundo pagão caíram
> O desgosto e o nojo secreto;
> Profundo cansaço e concupiscência concentrada
> Fizeram da vida humana um inferno.
>
> (Matthew Arnold).

III. Pelas vossas obras malignas. O original grego tem o substantivo «ergon», que normalmente significa «trabalho», «feito», «ação», «realização», e o adjetivo «poneros», que significa «mal-intencionado», «ímpio». Algumas vezes, esse adjetivo é usado em sentido personificado, apontando para Satanás — ele é a personificação do mal, em quem não se pode achar bem nenhum, isto é, nenhum bem que não seja maculado por alguma perversão. Assim também os pagãos eram inteiramente dominados pela maldade, sendo seus praticantes, e se regozijavam na maldade praticada (ver Rom. 1:32). Gloriavam-se em seus atos vergonhosos (ver Fil. 3:19); sua depravação era tão grande que era vergonhoso até mesmo o uso das palavras para descrever à mesma (ver Efé. 5:12). O trecho de Rom. 1:29 tem a grande lista de vícios dos pagãos. Quanto ao uso de listas de vícios, nos ensinamentos morais, o que era uma prática comum na antiguidade, ver as notas sobre I Cor. 5:13, no NTI. O Senhor julga os homens segundo as obras dos mesmos, sejam elas boas ou más. (Ver o NTI em Rom. 2:6 e Apo. 20:12, acerca desse tema). Paulo ensinava que é mister um poder imenso para libertar os homens de suas práticas ímpias; e que esse poder se acha em Cristo, e não em supostos *aeons* remidores ou salvadores.

IV. Outras considerações

Referências e idéias. Ignorar a Deus:

1. Ignorar a Cristo é ignorar a Deus (ver João 8:19).
2. Isso é evidenciado pela falta de amor (ver I João 4:8). 3. Pela desobediência a seus mandamentos (ver I João 2:4). 4. Pela vida no pecado (ver Tito 1:16 e I João 3:6). 5. Ignorar a Deus conduz ao erro (ver Mat. 22:29). 6. À idolatria (ver Isa. 44:19; Atos 17:29,30). 7. Ao alienamento de Deus (ver Efé. 4:18). 8. Às paixões pecaminosas (ver I Tes. 4:5 e I Ped. 1:14). 9. À perseguição contra os santos (ver João 15:21 e 16:3). 10. Ignorar a Deus não é desculpa para o pecado (ver Lev. 4:2 e Luc. 12:48).

V. Causas da alienação

1. *A indiferença*. O homem tem suas tribulações e fracassos, seus desejos, seus anelos, seu senso de futilidade, mas com freqüência não reconhece que o seu próprio problema é essencialmente de ordem espiritual. Deixou Deus inteiramente fora de sua vida, e preferiu enfatizar os valores terrenos, com detrimento dos valores celestes. Por isso mesmo, ficou alienado do Pai celestial.

2. A separação também pode assumir a forma de *ressentimento* contra o Senhor Deus. Essa pode assumir uma forma ativa e consciente, ou então subconsciente. Alguns homens odeiam a Deus, especialmente por causa do problema do mal, o moral e o natural. (Ver o artigo sobre o *problema do mal*). Os homens podem até mesmo aceitar a Deus como bom, dentro de um artigo de fé; mas se ressentem contra Ele quando as coisas não correm bem e a tragédia os atinge. Essa forma de alienação pode ser um ressentimento contra toda e qualquer autoridade, e está identificada com Deus, direta ou indiretamente, por ser ele a autoridade suprema.

3. A alienação também se dá por causa do *egoísmo*, em que o indivíduo busca somente os seus próprios interesses, até mesmo quando a sua consciência reconhece a maldade das próprias ações, ou, pelo menos, quando percebe que Deus não vem apropriadamente servido. O egoísmo aliena o homem do homem, e também de Deus. Já o amor é uma poderosa força que os une.

4. O senso de separação também pode ocorrer através do senso de *culpa*, sobretudo se este for exagerado, mórbido. A psicologia tem revelado quão prevalente é esse senso, destrutivo do bem-estar físico e espiritual do homem.

Em Cristo é obtido o perdão dos pecados e a questão deveria ser deixada nesse ponto, até onde o abandono ao pecado diz respeito. Porém, os homens

ALIMENTOS

se castigam criando auto-acusações mórbidas que estabelecem uma barreira entre eles mesmos e Deus, provocando atribulação em suas vidas mentais e espirituais. E daí resulta uma espécie de alienação entre eles e Deus. Não obstante, o senso de culpa é algo garantido pelo Espírito de Deus, como parte integrante da existência humana. (AL IB NTI)

ALIMENTOS (Ver também, Limpo e Imundo)

São substâncias físicas, vegetais ou animais, que podem ser consumidas pelo homem e pelos animais, sustentando-lhes as energias físicas. Metaforicamente, estão em pauta aqueles elementos espirituais que sustentam a causa e produzem o desenvolvimento espiritual.

1. *Tempos primitivos*. Os alimentos são limitados principalmente por razões geográficas, podendo ser de natureza vegetal ou animal. As culturas mais abastadas dispõem de uma dieta mais rica, mediante a manipulação local e as importações. Nos tempos primitivos, os homens alimentavam-se do que podiam colher, como raízes, legumes, frutas, castanhas, e mediante a caça de animais selvagens. Somente após o dilúvio a Bíblia menciona especificamente o uso da carne de animais na alimentação humana (ver Gên. 9:3), embora isso se deva mais provavelmente à ausência de menção, - e não a um reflexo da realidade das coisas. O trecho de Gên. 7:8, com sua divisão de animais limpos e imundos, por certo sugere que o consumo de carne é de data antiquíssima.

2. *Era patriarcal*. Nesse período, eram consumidas as carnes de animais selvagens e domesticados. A agricultura foi desenvolvendo-se com o cultivo do feijão, das ervilhas, dos cereais, da lentilha, etc. Também havia castanhas, mel e especiarias (ver Gên. 43:11). O pão era, talvez, o alimento mais comum.

3. *Outras culturas*. a. As pinturas murais egípcias mostram que a dieta dos egípcios era variada. O quadragésimo capítulo de Gênesis mostra que a família real era servida por profissionais. Havia copeiros, padeiros e cozinheiros. Os egípcios consumiam aves, peixes, carnes, vinhos, temperos e acepipes importados. Homens e mulheres freqüentavam banquetes, usando vestes suntuosas para a ocasião. As pinturas existentes na cidade de Aquenaton (edificada em cerca de 1387 - 1366 A.C.) exibem o rei e sua princesa, Nefertiti, e três filhas, banqueteando-se em um espaçoso salão, decorado com grinaldas e servido por escravos. Penas de avestruz eram usadas como leques, havia luzes coloridas e cadeiras almofadadas. b. Entre os habitantes da Mesopotâmia era costume consumir-se feijão, lentilha, ervilha, cebolas, pepinos, abóboras, trigo, cevada e outros cereais. Também havia grande variedade de frutas, incluindo as tâmaras. Um selo cilíndrico de lápis-lazúli, atualmente no museu da Universidade da Pennsylvania (de cerca de 3000 A.C.) retrata um banquete da rainha Shubade, com pratos raros por todo o lado, e escravos que ventilavam o ambiente com leques. Também havia música ao vivo.

4. *Israel e a lei mosaica*. No Egito, os filhos de Israel comiam bem, conforme se lê em Êxodo 16:3: «...quando estávamos sentados junto às panelas de carne, e comíamos pão a fartar!» No deserto, os israelitas lembravam com saudade o peixe, os pepinos, os melões, os alhos porros, os alhos, as cebolas e outros acepipes (ver Núm. 11:5). Com a lei mosaica apareceram certas restrições, mas o próprio fato de que tantas coisas puderam ser vedadas, em contraste com a grande variedade de alimentos permitidos, serve para mostrar que a dieta dos antigos era variada.

a. *Proibições*. Os animais foram classificados na lei levítica como limpos e imundos, isto é, próprios e impróprios para o consumo humano. Os quadrúpedes que não ruminam e que não têm os cascos das patas divididos, foram proibidos (ver Lev. 11:4-8; Deu. 14:7,8). Os peixes lisos, isto é, sem escamas, como as enguias, para exemplificar, também foram proibidos (ver Lev. 11:9-12). Toda ave de rapina, bem como aquelas que se alimentam de carniça, foram vedadas (ver Lev. 11:13-19). Outro tanto se dava com serpentes, insetos e algumas variedades de gafanhotos. Todo sangue era absolutamente proibido para o consumo humano (ver Lev. 3:17; 7:26; Deu. 12:16,23). A mesma coisa se pode dizer com relação às porções gordas dos animais sacrificados, e a qualquer coisa consagrada aos ídolos (ver Lev. 3:17; Êxo. 34:15). Além disso, por óbvias razões sanitárias, a carne do gado que morrera por si mesmo, ou que fora despedaçada pelas feras, não podia ser consumida (ver Êxo. 22:31; Lev. 11:39 ss). Também não se podia cozinhar alimentos na água onde tivesse caído o corpo morto de algum inseto (ver Lev. 11:33,34). Alimentos sólidos e líquidos, preservados em receptáculos descobertos, na tenda de algum moribundo ou de algum morto, não podiam ser utilizados. A proibição acerca do cozimento de um cabrito, no leite de sua mãe (ver Êxo. 23:19), surgiu porque os cananeus usavam tal prática em seus ritos sagrados, pelo que era considerada uma abominação pagã. Essa informação foi descoberta nos tabletes de Ras Shamra. A reverência ao ancestral Jacó aparentemente não permitia que seus descendentes usassem na alimentação o nervo do quadril, na articulação da coxa (ver Gên. 32:32).

b. *Alimentos permitidos*. Eram permitidos carnes e legumes, bem como muitos condimentos. Os alimentos de origem animal incluíam carnes de carneiro, de boi, de cabras, de veado, de antílope, de corço, além de grande variedade de aves. Muitas variedades de peixes eram pescadas no lago de Genezaré (ver João 21:11), e também havia peixes trazidos do mar por comerciantes fenícios (ver Nee. 13:16). Gafanhotos eram consumidos pelos pobres (ver Lev. 11:22 e Mat. 3:4).

c. *Preparação dos alimentos*. Muitos povos primitivos ingerem seu alimento com pouca ou nenhuma preparação prévia, até mesmo em nossos dias. O trecho de Mateus 12:1 mostra que as pessoas, nos dias de Jesus, às vezes ingeriam o cereal tirado diretamente da espiga. Desde os tempos pré-históricos, o fogo vem sendo usado para cozinhar, assar e tostar. A invenção do moinho possibilitou o surgimento da farinha de trigo e de outros cereais, pelo que pães e bolos passaram a ser feitos, às vezes com cereais misturados. Ver o artigo sobre o pão. Com base em Gênesis 25:29,34, ficamos sabendo que sopas eram preparadas desde os tempos mais remotos. Legumes, ervas e carnes eram cozidos em panelas (ver II Reis 4:38; Núm. 11:8 e Juí. 6:19). O espeto era usado no preparo de carnes assadas, desde os tempos mais antigos (conforme se vê nos escritos homéricos), e essa prática já existia em Israel, embora a cozedura e o frigir também fossem comuns (ver I Sam. 2:15). Os animais mortos eram cozidos imediatamente, para evitar que a carne se estragasse. O leite era usado como um agente. Os gafanhotos eram tostados, mas não antes de serem extraídos os intestinos, as asas e os pés. Eram tostados ou cozidos, e também preservados em vasos, em uma solução salina. Mulheres e escravos cozinhavam e serviam os

ALIMENTOS — ALMA

alimentos, mas ao chefe da casa cabia abater os animais (ver Gên. 18:2-6; Juí. 6:19). As pessoas de classe elevada contavam com cozinheiros profissionais, e também com padeiros, copeiros, etc. (ver II Sam. 9:23 ss).

d. *Refeições*. Os israelitas contavam com um simples quebra-jejum, além de duas refeições mais substanciais, uma delas ao meio-dia (ver Gên. 18:1 e 43:16), e a outra, que era a refeição principal, às seis ou sete horas da noite (ver Gên. 19:1 ss ; Rute 3:7). As mãos eram bem lavadas, primeiramente por motivo de exigência cerimonial, que fazia parte dos requisitos religiosos, e em segundo lugar, como meio de higiene. Ver sobre *Lavagens*. Eram oferecidas orações de agradecimento às refeições (ver I Sam. 9:13). Nos tempos mais remotos, as pessoas sentavam-se à mesa (ver Gên. 27:19; Juí. 19:6; I Reis 13:19). Os gregos e os romanos introduziram a prática de comer reclinados em divãs ou colchões. O alimento era levado à boca com a mão direita (ver Rute 2:14; Pro. 26:15 e João 13:6).

e. *Preço dos alimentos*. Pouco se sabe exatamente sobre esses preços, embora saibamos que um alqueire de farinha de trigo e dois de cevada eram vendidos por um siclo (ver II Reis 7:1,16). Dois pardais eram vendidos por um asse (ver Mat. 10:29). No livro de Apocalipse — uma medida de trigo valerá um denário (salário de um dia de trabalho), e três medidas de cevada terão o mesmo valor. No trecho de Mat. 20:1-16 aprendemos que um denário era um bom salário por um dia de trabalho, o que nos dá alguma base para julgar o preço dos alimentos. Essa referência no Apocalipse, entretanto, mostra-nos preços em tempos de necessidade e inflação. Tremenda será realmente a inflação, quando um dia inteiro de trabalho puder comprar somente cerca de menos de 900 g de trigo. Ver o artigo sobre *Dinheiro*, para efeito de comparação.

f. *Alimentos oferecidos aos ídolos*. Nos templos pagãos, as carnes dos sacrifícios eram oferecidas aos deuses, e mais tarde essas carnes eram vendidas nos mercados. Surgiu então o problema, se os cristãos podiam ou não adquirir tais carnes. Talvez a questão também envolvesse o caso em que uma festa fosse oferecida no próprio templo, quando as carnes eram oferecidas a alguma divindade. Um crente poderia estar presente a tais festas, contanto que dissesse em seu coração: «Os ídolos nada são, e estou aqui apenas em um evento social»? Seja como for, a ingestão de tais alimentos foi proibida pelo decreto apostólico registrado em Atos 15:29. Mas Paulo, comentando que um ídolo nada significa, e que nenhum alimento nos melhora nos piora espiritualmente, deixou a ingestão de qualquer alimento ao encargo da consciência de cada um, contanto que, no processo, a consciência fraca de algum irmão não fosse ofendida (ver I Cor. 10:25; Rom. 14:13 ss e I Cor. 8:1-13). O trecho de Apocalipse 2:14 mostra que a questão continuava em vigor por muito tempo, e que a atitude mais liberal de Paulo não era considerada por muitos cristãos como a norma a ser seguida. Ali, a ingestão de carnes sacrificadas a ídolos é severamente criticada.

g. *Usos metafóricos*. a. Uma pessoa pode dilapidar seu dinheiro com acepipes que não satisfazem a alma (ver Isa. 55:1 ss.). b. Jesus é o pão da vida, é o nosso sustento espiritual (ver João 6). c. Israel comeu o maná, no deserto, porque a provisão divina para as nossas necessidades espirituais, que é o próprio Jesus, é o maná dos crentes (ver João 6). d. Jesus alimentava-se cumprindo a vontade do Pai e realizando a Sua missão (ver João 4:34), e feliz é o crente que segue o Seu exemplo. e. O crente recém-convertido deve ser como uma criança infante, faminta pelo leite espiritual, o que aponta para a fome da alma acerca das realidades espirituais. f. Não obstante, os crentes que, após algum tempo no caminho da fé, continuam alimentando-se só de leite, podem ser classificados como crentes infantis. O alimento sólido, o avanço nas questões espirituais, deveria ser nosso alvo da vida cristã (ver I Cor. 3:2 e Heb. 5:14). g. Os poderes preservativos do sal representam a capacidade que os discípulos de Cristo têm de influenciar este mundo, mediante o qual eles cumprem a vontade de Deus em suas vidas (ver Mat. 5:13 e Mar. 9:50). h. O poder que o sal tem de transmitir sabor representa o uso próprio da linguagem, no trecho de Colossenses 4:6. i. Também devemos considerar a árvore da vida e seus frutos, bem como suas folhas, que servirão para curar as nações, segundo se vê em Apocalipse 2:7 e 22:2. j. Várias realizações do Espírito Santo, na vida do crente, são chamadas fruto do Espírito (ver Gál. 5:22,23). Devemos pensar, nesse caso, em virtudes morais e espirituais, bem como em realizações espirituais. No NTI, nessas referências, damos notas que muito acrescentam quanto aos detalhes sobre essas questões.

ALJAVA

Palavra que aparece pela primeira vez na Bíblia, em Gên. 27:3. Era um receptáculo para flechas, geralmente feito de couro, pendurado ao ombro do caçador ou soldado. Jó 39:23 e Isa. 22:6 aludem à aljava em conexão com outros equipamentos militares.

As outras quatro ocorrências do termo são metafóricas. Sal. 127:5 fala da família de um homem como sua aljava, e de seus filhos como as flechas. O profeta, uma flecha de Deus, está oculto em sua aljava, de acordo com Isa. 49:2. Visto que um assassino usa as suas flechas, Jeremias equipara a aljava a um túmulo aberto (Jer. 5:16). E, em Lam. 3:13, «as flechas da sua aljava» é tradução do hebraico, que diz, literalmente: «os filhos da sua aljava», referindo-se ao golpe mortal desfechado pelo inimigo.

ALLAH

No árabe, **alilah**, indicando Deus como o Adorado, o nome próprio de Deus no islamismo. Nos tempos antigos, os árabes parecem ter usado essa palavra a fim de indicar o Deus supremo, talvez em contraste com divindades secundárias. Por meio das reformas de Maomé, o termo passou a significar o único Deus. O primeiro artigo do credo islâmico é: «Não há Deus senão Alá». Os cristãos sírios também usam essa palavra para indicar Deus.

ALMA

Ver o artigo sobre a **Imortalidade da Alma** que inclui tratados de outros escritores sobre o assunto. Ver o artigo sobre o *Problema Corpo-Mente*. Os artigos sobre a Imortalidade da Alma incluem um do ponto de vista científico, intitulado, *Abordagem Científica à Crença na Alma e na sua Sobrevivência ante a Morte Física*. Ver o artigo sobre *Experiências Perto da Morte*. Ver o artigo sobre a *Reencarnação*.

Esboço

 I. A Origem da Alma
 II. A Natureza da Alma

ALMA

III. O Destino da Alma
IV. Provas da Existência e Sobrevivência da Alma
V. O Problema Antropológico

Temos bom ânimo, mas desejamos antes estar ausentes deste corpo para estarmos presentes com o Senhor. (II Cor. 5:8)

I. A Origem da alma

1. O criacionismo. A idéia de que Deus cria uma nova alma, quando da concepção de cada corpo físico. É a noção teológica mais comum, e algumas vezes o trecho de Gên. 2:7 é empregado em apoio a essa idéia. Porém, a teologia dos hebreus não contemplava uma entidade separada, imaterial, como a vida da carne. Isso é de desenvolvimento posterior, que mui provavelmente foi tomado por empréstimo de outras culturas. O trecho de Gênesis 2:7 significa somente que havia uma forma animal dotada de animação. Que Deus tenha tido a necessidade de criar uma alma para cada nova concepção, faz dele um ser extremamente ocupado, em uma única tarefa, ainda que não possamos dizer que tal tarefa seja impossível para ele. Porém, pelo menos para este autor, a razão é contrária a esse pensamento, embora seja o ponto de vista mais comum, hoje em dia, no cristianismo.

A teologia também é contra esta teoria. Como podemos reconciliar esta idéia com a doutrina do pecado original? Parece que uma alma criada diretamente por Deus não pode ser inerentemente pecaminosa. Ou podemos supor que Deus cria almas pecaminosas?

2. O traducionismo. Os estóicos, e mais tarde, Agostinho, defendiam essa teoria, a qual supõe que homem e mulher, como seres físico-espirituais que são naturalmente, e sem qualquer intervenção direta e contínua da parte de Deus, produzem seres que são tanto físicos como espirituais — os seus filhos. E isso significa que tanto a «alma» como o espírito seriam produtos da «procriação». Essa idéia é razoável, não se podendo negar que é um grande mistério como o «espírito» pode ser produzido por meios naturais. Porém, também não sabemos ainda como o «corpo físico» pode ser produzido por meios naturais. Tanto uma como a outra coisa são misteriosas. Se os progenitores, que são tanto físicos como espirituais, podem produzir um corpo físico, mediante um processo tão misterioso e estupendo, quem pode negar que também possam produzir o «espírito»?

3. A fulguração. Em uma teoria não muito bem definida, Leibniz supôs que Deus fez o mundo e tudo quanto nele existe, não por «criação» direta, proveniente do nada, e, sim, por «fulguração», ou seja, por fagulhas de seu próprio ser, que teriam se projetado a fim de formar o mundo físico, com a inclusão do «espírito», segundo o mesmo é conhecido por nós, tanto no nível humano como no angelical, isto é, tudo quanto não é o próprio Deus, mas antes, é parte de sua «criação». Haveria um «ponto no tempo» em que tudo isso teria começado, mas não a criação proveniente do nada. Como esta idéia pode evitar o *panteísmo*, Leibniz não esclareceu, mas somente disse que se trata de um «mistério». De alguma maneira, nesse processo de fulguração, aquilo que era projetado do ser divino não retinha a própria natureza do seu ser, pelo que não temos um mundo panteísta, que compartilhe de idêntica natureza do poder emanador. Podemos ousar dizer, porém, que essa idéia é uma ficção filosófica.

4. A eternidade. Platão e outros filósofos antigos e modernos têm especulado que a «substância da alma» — é eterna —, proveniente de Deus e a ele semelhante em sua natureza. Não obstante, a *individualização* dessa substância, para formar um «ser» espiritual, distinto de Deus, teria tido lugar em algum tempo remoto da eternidade passada. Assim sendo, a alma, o homem real, seria preexistente. Na qualidade de um poder espiritual preexistente e muito elevado, o homem caiu no pecado, e essa queda, eventualmente, levou-o a assumir obrigatoriamente uma forma física como veículo, a fim de manifestar-se nesta dimensão terrena inferior. Ora, o que é físico sempre será mortal, pelo que o homem passou a ser classificado como um ser mortal. O ponto todo da vida é o bem dessa alma imortal, do ser espiritual, levando-o a retornar ao mundo celeste de onde decaiu. A união com um corpo físico, portanto, é quase um acidente dentro da filosofia platônica, e certamente degradante para o próprio espírito (ou alma). Para Platão, o corpo é considerado a «prisão» da alma. Pitágoras chamava o corpo de *sepulcro* da alma, expressando idêntica atitude.

5. A preexistência. Para diversos teólogos cristãos, como Justino Mártir, Clemente e Orígenes, a alma seria parte da criação angelical, não tendo substância diversa da dos anjos, quanto à sua natureza básica. Os anjos e os homens caíram no pecado, e, nessa queda, os homens finalmente assumiram corpo físico, o que é sinal evidente da degradação e descendência da alma. Mas, em seu retorno para Deus, o homem se libertará finalmente do corpo físico, e habitará nos mundos da imortalidade. Essa idéia também era a mais comum entre os hebreus, depois que a teologia judaica abandonou a sua errônea doutrina da «inexistência da alma», que é o ponto de vista dominante no Pentateuco, onde somente leves indícios da crença no após-vida podem ser percebidos. A natureza humana de Jesus incluía a alma, segundo quase todos os teólogos afiançam. Porém, a sua alma humana não seria decaída. Através dessa teoria, essa alma humana também foi preexistente, como todas as almas humanas o seriam. Não tendo caído no pecado, a alma humana de Jesus teria retido o seu poder semelhante ao dos anjos, e isso explicaria as obras e as palavras de Jesus, até mesmo em sua encarnação e humilhação. A alma de Jesus fundiu-se ao *Logos eterno*, formando uma única pessoa e isso para todo o sempre. Isso constituiria um profundíssimo mistério, que não admite racionalização humana.

Essa idéia da preexistência da alma tem ocupado grande lugar na história da igreja; e a despeito de atualmente ser defendida por uma exígua minoria, tem ocupado uma grande posição na história da Igreja, como já dissemos, merecendo cuidadosa consideração. Existem boas evidências, fornecidas pela ciência moderna, em favor da inteligência da alma de um indivíduo, de natureza não-comunitária, o que indica que um indivíduo qualquer, agora visto em um corpo físico, é antiquíssimo, tendo conhecido a vida em outros níveis da existência, e, talvez, neste nível de existência.

Os pais alexandrinos acreditaram na preexistência da alma sem reencarnação na vida física da terra, com a exceção de casos especiais. Outros fazem da reencarnação uma doutrina paralela com a idéia da preexistência.

Vários poetas têm louvado o seu valor, conforme esta bela seção do poema de Wordsworth, intitulado «Subentendidos da Imortalidade»:

Nosso nascimento é apenas um sono e esquecimento:
A alma que se eleva conosco, nossa estrela da vida,

ALMA

Tem tido algures o seu lugar,
E vem de longe:
Não totalmente olvidada,
E nem em completa nudez,
Mas arrastando nuvens de glória
é que procedemos
De Deus, que é o nosso lar.

Para o autor deste artigo esta idéia é a mais provável das possibilidades.

6. Emanação desde a eternidade. Trata-se de um ponto de vista panteísta sobre a alma. Temos aqui uma variação da quarta posição, que faz da alma uma simples emanação do espírito universal, divino, ou seja, da mente divina, e não diferente quanto à sua natureza, ainda que tenha adquirido uma forma diferente. Mas, de acordo com esse sistema, tudo quanto existe tem a natureza divina, porque tudo seria Deus, e Deus seria tudo; Deus é o cabeça da existência e o mundo ou a existência seria o corpo de Deus. O *destino*, de conformidade com esse sistema, consiste na reabsorção de tudo pela mente divina, com a perda total da distinção pessoal.

II. A natureza da alma

1. A palavra **alma** é aqui usada como sinônimo de «espírito» como em quase todas as suas ocorrências nesta enciclopédia. Haveria a emanação da mente ou espírito divino. Uma forma especial de *imaterialidade* está em foco, isto é, uma imaterialidade que participa da divindade. Trata-se de uma idéia exaltadíssima, não havendo maneira para descrevermos o que nela está envolvido. Contudo, por enquanto nem ao menos fazemos boa idéia do que significa a materialidade; e quanto menos qualquer forma de imaterialidade. Mas pelo menos podemos dizer que a alma, sob qualquer descrição de imaterialidade, não consiste em partículas «atômicas».

2. *A idéia platônica* sobre a alma afirma que a alma é uma individualização operada por Deus, mas fazendo parte de sua natureza. Assim sendo, a alma participaria das qualidades dos «universais», tais como a imaterialidade, a eternidade, o absoluto, a perfeição, não pertencendo nem ao tempo e nem ao mundo dos universais, o mundo eterno.

3. O ponto de vista *alexandrino* sobre a alma, estipulado pelos pais da igreja Justino Mártir, Clemente e Orígenes, diz que a alma é de natureza equivalente à dos anjos, sem qualquer diferenciação real. Seria «espírito», e, por conseguinte, seria imaterial; e teria elevados poderes, não menores que os dos anjos. Essa «alma» não seria divina, conforme se dá no caso da primeira posição, porquanto seria separada da divindade. Todavia, pertenceria a uma elevadíssima natureza. Essa natureza teria sido prejudicada e degradada quando da queda. Esta é igualmente a posição tomada pelo autor deste artigo.

4. *Alguns estudiosos pensam que a alma seria uma substância semifísica* ou mesmo «física», com modificações de natureza para nós desconhecida. Poderia ser uma «substância mais rarefeita» que a do corpo, embora continuasse sendo física. E podemos supor que isso também significa que se comporia de partículas «atômicas». Os estóicos mantinham esse ponto de vista, como também fazem os «mórmons», entre os cristãos da atualidade. Os estóicos pensavam que se alguém tivesse de ser morto esmagado debaixo de uma pedra, seria melhor que o fosse com uma pedra pequena, porquanto se uma pedra grande caísse sobre uma pessoa, prendendo-a debaixo da mesma, a alma talvez não pudesse escapar dali.

5. O homem seria constituído de corpo, alma e espírito. A alma seria a sede emocional do homem, ou de sua porção intelectual, o que significa que talvez seja sinônimo de «mente». Já o «espírito», designaria o homem essencial em sua inteligência, a porção do homem que sobrevive. Neste ponto usamos a palavra «espírito» conforme o vocábulo «alma» vem sendo empregado por todo este artigo. O termo «espírito», aqui empregado, pode ser definido de qualquer das maneiras descritas acima. (Quanto ao problema «dicotomia-tricotomia», ver as notas expositivas sobre os trechos de Rom. 11:3; Heb. 4:12 e I Tes. 5:23 no NTI).

6. Alguns estudiosos pensam que a «alma» indica tão-somente o corpo animado, não dando a entender qualquer entidade separada. Essa é a antiga posição dos hebreus, a posição refletida pelo Pentateuco, e que foi aceita pelos Adventistas do Sétimo Dia, entre os cristãos modernos.

7. Para outros a alma não seria substancial, mas antes, se assemelharia à idéia dos «fantasmas». Essa é a antiga idéia entre os judeus e gregos, anterior a Platão, e que pode ser percebida facilmente nos escritos de Homero, onde a alma aparece como uma espécie de forma sem substância, fugidia, destituída de memória, representada nos desenhos antigos como uma pequena ave a esvoaçar. Havia na personalidade humana um fantasma, sem memória, não sendo a personalidade essencial, embora podendo ser identificada com a «dupla» personalidade. Seria, assim sendo, uma energia mental, que pelo menos em alguns casos poderia sobreviver ao corpo, embora eventualmente venha a dissipar-se. Evidentemente alguma comunicação com ela seria possível, mas sempre em um baixo nível intelectual; e ninguém aprenderia alguma coisa de grande significado, da parte dessas entidades. Especulamos, portanto, que o homem é uma *trindade*, isto é, se compõe de três complexos distintos de energia: o físico (o corpo), o semifísico (o fantasma, a dupla personalidade, a mente), e o espiritual (o espírito, ou alma).

Apesar de tudo que possamos dizer acerca da «natureza» da alma, na realidade não podemos apresentar qualquer descrição sobre a sua «substância»;e isso porque, no momento, o máximo que podemos asseverar é que ela é «imaterial», não estando sujeita às leis que governam a matéria, conforme as conhecemos no momento.

III. O destino da alma

O que aqui dizemos dependerá de nossas crenças religiosas e filosóficas. Por essa razão, existem quase tantos «destinos» quantos são os pensadores, ainda que as diferenças sejam leves, em alguns casos.

1. A mais antiga idéia entre os hebreus é que não existe alma, e, portanto, também não há destino. O destino humano, entretanto, estaria reservado para quando da ressurreição do corpo. A crença na ressurreição, não nos olvidemos, é um pensamento hebreu posterior, não se alicerçando sobre o Pentateuco. Esse destino variaria desde os prazeres sensuais sem-fim, conforme se vê em certas religiões orientais, até prazeres sensuais moderados, com a ênfase sobre os valores espirituais, conforme se verifica no antigo pensamento dos hebreus.

2. A alma-fantasma. Nos escritos de Homero, como também no pensamento posterior dos hebreus, a alma aparecia como uma forma sem substância, sem memória e sem inteligência essencial, pelo que também não haveria qualquer verdadeiro destino pessoal.

3. Também há aqueles que crêem em transmigração da alma, em reencarnação. Em sua busca pela

ALMA

perfeição, a alma teria de atravessar muitos estados intermediários, em cada um dos quais aprenderia determinadas lições. Mas seria eterna, pelo que também não se desintegraria, embora seja confinada à necessidade de passar por vidas repetidas, em corpos físicos. A «transmigração» é um termo geral, o qual pode significar a habitação em um corpo humano ou em um corpo animal; porém, quando esse termo é contrastado com a idéia da *reencarnação*, então sempre significa a habitação em um corpo «animal», ao passo que a reencarnação usada sem outros qualificativos, significa quase sempre a habitação em um corpo «humano». Uma vez tendo atingido um grau suficiente de perfeição, a alma escaparia à dimensão física e entraria no terreno espiritual. Ali chegando, a alma faria progresso muito mais rápido na direção de Deus. A teologia dos hebreus, uma vez aceita a idéia da existência da alma, quase sempre aceitou a idéia da reencarnação, sendo isso especialmente verdadeiro entre os rabinos cabalistas. As escolas dos fariseus ensinavam tal conceito, como também o faziam pelo menos alguns dentre os essênios.

A crença na reencarnação fala apenas sobre destinos *intermediários*, e não sobre o destino final das almas. O destino final seria determinado pela experiência religiosa do indivíduo, para além da consideração de reencarnação; porquanto, em qualquer sistema, isso é apenas *um meio* para o fim, e não o próprio fim.

4. *Reabsorção*. Essa palavra expressa a tendência, verificada nas religiões orientais, para pensar que a alma encontra o seu destino mais elevado na reabsorção pela mente ou espírito divino. E isso importaria na perda da identidade pessoal. Não é muito claro se alguns admitem que, nessa reabsorção, o «ego» se transmuta no *superego*, o que significaria que a consciência humana passa a assumir a consciência divina. Platão defendia a individualidade temporária da alma, uma vez que ela ascendesse às regiões celestes, com a eventual absorção no espírito divino; mas, uma vez mais, não sabemos se ele entendia que isso significa que o «ego» passa a ser o «superego», com uma correspondente consciência. A filosofia idealista germânica, conforme aparece nos escritos de Hegel e de Fichte, imaginava essa espécie de reabsorção. O destino da alma, segundo esse ponto de vista, é extremamente elevado, embora lhe falte o interesse da individualidade. Eriugena, um filósofo-teólogo da metade da Idade Média, igualmente aceitava essa idéia da reabsorção, embora pareça ter procurado preservar também a idéia de individualidade, de conformidade com o pensamento cristão ordinário. Acreditava ele que todos os homens seriam redimidos a fim de participar na vida do «logos», e que os eleitos seriam elevados à divindade de Deus Pai.

No caso da religião hindu, o retorno da alma individual (atmã) ao Bramá, algumas vezes é referido de tal maneira a dar a idéia da retenção da individualidade e existem trechos nos Upanishads e na Vedante que parecem indicar exatamente essa idéia. Entretanto, a interpretação predominante parece ser que a individualidade, agora mesmo, é apenas uma ilusão, para nada dizermos sobre o tempo em que a alma retornar completamente ao Bramá. Através das experiências místicas, nesta vida terrena, haveria uma união de êxtase com a divindade; mas a verdadeira união teria de esperar até que nos víssemos libertos da carne.

Os místicos cristãos têm falado bastante em tais termos; e mui provavelmente alguns deles tenham esperado uma verdadeira reabsorção, embora isso seja contrário à corrente principal do pensamento cristão. (Assim podemos depreender nos escritos de Royce, Eckhart, Stª Teresa e Jacó Boehme). O pensamento dessa completa união com a divindade tem penetrado em alguns hinos, como naquele de autoria de George Matheson: «Dou-te de volta a vida que possuo, para que em tuas profundezas oceânicas ela flua mais rica, mais plena». Porém, não é muito provável que esses autores tenham tido o intuito de ensinar a perda da individualidade, ao usarem tais expressões.

5. *A imortalidade cristã*. No conceito bíblico e cristão esta é sempre individual, importando em consciência pessoal. Saberei que eu sou eu, o mesmo ser que fui, ainda que então me encontrarei em estado exaltado. A imortalidade, dentro do conceito paulino, é sempre vinculada ao corpo ressurrecto, como veículo da alma remida; mas esse corpo é também chamado de «espiritual», não sendo material e nem formado por partículas atômicas. (Ver no NTI as notas expositivas completas sobre a natureza do «corpo ressurrecto, em I Cor. 15:20, *ss*, e nos versículos 35 e 40). A alma atingirá um elevado estado de glorificação quando receber o seu novo veículo, mediante o qual a completa personalidade humana será restaurada, ainda que em termos totalmente não-corporais. O padrão da natureza desse corpo novo é o próprio Senhor Jesus Cristo, porquanto haveremos de ser transformados conforme a sua imagem (ver Rom. 8:29), e por isso compartilharemos de sua própria divindade (ver II Ped. 1:4). Uma vez que nos tornemos seres elevados acima dos anjos, dotados de maior poder, inteligência e perfeição do que eles, seremos instrumentos capazes de feitos notáveis. Em conexão com a idéia do destino da alma, além das referências que já foram dadas, ver os artigos sobre *vida eterna*, *galardões* e *coroas*.

IV. Provas da existência e sobrevivência da alma

Os artigos existentes na introdução ao NTI, que versam sobre a «imortalidade da alma», fornecem um estudo mais completo sobre o presente tópico. Algumas das provas principais são alistadas aqui, em forma de esboço:

1. *O consensus gentium*, ou seja, a «opinião popular». Todas as culturas humanas incluem a crença na existência da alma e sua sobrevivência. Para não crer nisso, é mister que o indivíduo seja treinado a não crer. Por razão e intuição, o homem reconhece certas verdades básicas, tais como a existência de Deus e da alma, a necessidade de justiça, a necessidade de galardão e castigo, enfim, a garantia de um universo «moral». É verdade que muitas crenças quase universais, como a idéia de uma «terra chata», do «giro do sol em torno da terra», etc., são incorretas. Não obstante, tais tipos de verdades não podem ser reputadas como aquelas que a intuição e a razão (conferidas como dom de Deus) dariam aos homens. Por outro lado, os dons da razão e da intuição, implantados no homem pelo Espírito, poderiam ser instrumentos para o reconhecimento de Deus e da alma humana, sem a necessidade de qualquer revelação divina. O primeiro capítulo da epístola aos Romanos dá apoio a essa forma de idéia, embora não exatamente sob os mesmos termos. Mediante essa forma de raciocínio, a verdade pode ser *a priori*, isto é, anterior a quaisquer experiências empíricas, verificada pela razão pura ou pela intuição.

2. *O desejo universal*. Pode-se supor que o desejo universal de sobreviver à morte física é mais do que

ALMA

um anelo caprichoso; antes, na realidade, resulta da consciência íntima de que a imortalidade é um fato. A maneira de consubstanciar tal crença é essencialmente a mesma que a do primeiro caso.

3. *Os argumentos platônicos* com base na razão pura (argumentos *a priori*). Consideremos os três seguintes subpontos: a. A geração dos opostos. (Argumento acerca dos contrários). O dia segue-se à noite; — a morte segue-se ao nascimento, e é lógico assumir que a vida se siga à morte. Podemos descobrir várias analogias na natureza, que talvez indiquem essa verdade, tal como no caso das estações do ano. b. A alma é o «princípio vivo», sendo «simples», e não complexa; por conseguinte, não estaria sujeita à dissolução, tal como sucede ao corpo, que é extremamente complexo. Uma alma «morta», pois, é uma contradição de termos. O homem participa do «princípio vivo», por meio da alma, que é a sua manifestação terrena, embora a própria alma seja eterna em sua substância, proveniente que é do mundo eterno. c. A preexistência e as reminiscências. A alma, sendo eterna em sua substância, e antiquíssima em sua individualização, é preexistente. Portanto, também é pós-existente, porquanto não depende do corpo quanto à sua origem, e nem dele depende para a sua continuidade. E certos estudos, feitos no terreno da parapsicologia, parecem indicar a verdade da preexistência da alma.

4. *A bondade de Deus*. É ilógico supormos que um Deus bondoso e sábio criaria um ser tão complexo como é o homem, a fim de permitir-lhe tão breve duração de existência, para logo em seguida deixá-lo ser reduzido ao nada, à extinção.

5. *A probabilidade teísta*. Não é provável que Deus criasse um ser vivo como é o homem, para em seguida permitir que ele seja reduzido ao nada, sendo um ser tão complexo, conhecedor do bem e do mal, aspirante às realidades celestiais. A probabilidade simples, inteiramente à parte de Deus, mostra-nos que não é provável que um ser tão complexo como é o homem, com tantos refinamentos em sua natureza, pudesse existir somente por um pouco de tempo. O homem é superior ao tempo, o que significa que sobreviverá ao mesmo.

6. *A evolução*. O processo da evolução, se o admitirmos como verdadeiro, criou, como sua maior realização, uma alma que sobrevive à morte física.

7. *A revelação*. Diversos profetas, de inúmeras religiões no decorrer dos séculos, mediante visões, sonhos ou revelações místicas, conferidas por seres de outros mundos, ou por Deus, afirmam a realidade da imortalidade da alma. Temos confiança nos místicos e naquilo que têm dito, o que é pelo menos parcialmente confirmado pelas provas empíricas das tradições proféticas. Em outras palavras, pode-se mostrar que a profecia é verídica, através de provas empíricas. Os místicos deram-nos a profecia. E eles também afirmam a veracidade da imortalidade de Deus, da justiça final, dos galardões, do castigo final e de outros temas importantíssimos. Inclinamo-nos a crer neles porque têm um registro convincente de veracidade em muitas coisas, se não mesmo acerca de tudo. Para os crentes, existem documentos, tanto no Antigo como no Novo Testamentos que contêm essas revelações. Os *trechos bíblicos* que subentendem ou ensinam claramente a existência da alma e sua sobrevivência ante a morte física, são os seguintes: a. No A.T.: Sal. 86:13; Pro. 15:24; Eze. 26:20; 32:21; Is. 14:9,10; Ecl. 12:7 e Jó 32:8. b. No N.T.: Mat. 10:28; 17:1-4; Marc. 8:36,37; Luc. 16:19-31; 23:43; Atos 7:59; Fil. 1:21-23; II Cor. 5:8; 12:1-4; Heb. 12:23; I Ped. 3:18-20; 4:6; Apo. 6:9,10 e 20:4.

8. *Os efeitos da fé* — O impacto prático da fé sobre a sociedade: uma crença tão bela e tão poderosa na sociedade, sobre o que tantas pessoas alicerçam a sua vida, fazendo com que a vida «visível» se fundamente sobre a «invisível», deve ser verdadeira, porquanto o erro dificilmente poderia produzir benefícios e efeitos de âmbito tão mundial.

9. *O argumento moral de Emanuel Kant*. A imortalidade da alma deve ser uma verdade, porque é evidente que a justiça não se concretiza neste mundo. Assim, pois, deve haver uma esfera de seres vivos, os mesmos seres que um dia viveram à face da terra, onde impera a justiça, onde os galardões e as punições são aplicadas. Se isso não é uma verdade, então este mundo é apenas um caos. Nossa rejeição ao conceito do caos requer, por semelhante modo, a aceitação da fé na imortalidade da alma. Esse argumento moral também prova a existência de Deus, porquanto deve haver um juiz capaz de exercer justiça. E esse juiz só pode ser um ser que esteja conforme o conceito de Deus — nenhum outro ser poderia ter estatura suficiente para ocupar-se com êxito dessa tarefa.

10. *Argumentos empíricos ou científicos*. É facilmente possível que, dentro da nossa própria geração, a ciência chegará a provar a existência da alma e a sua sobrevivência ante a morte física. A imortalidade é outra questão, que está além do campo de investigação da ciência, visto que a imortalidade implica em uma existência «para sempre», aquela forma de vida que não está sujeita à dissolução. Mesmo que a ciência pudesse confirmar continuamente a existência de uma alma, em forma desencorporada, por cem anos, ainda assim se poderia dizer que o período de existência de uma alma é de cem anos e um dia; e, «teoricamente», ninguém poderia negar essa possibilidade, embora pudesse duvidar do cálculo. A sobrevivência da alma ante a morte física poderia vir a ser eventualmente comprovada pela ciência: mas a imortalidade permanecerá para sempre além do escopo da investigação científica, o que requer a renovação contínua de informes e de uma avaliação que leve em conta qualquer novo fator que porventura surja. De um ponto de vista teórico, o corpo pode durar 70 anos, e a alma pode durar dois mil anos. Mas a ciência dificilmente poderá falar em «para sempre», porquanto a «eternidade» não está sujeita à percepção dos sentidos, que serve de base para todas as investigações científicas.

Ver o artigo intitulado, *Abordagem Científica à Crença na Alma e Em sua Sobrevivência Ante A Morte Física*, entre os artigos sobre a *Imortalidade da Alma*.

A ciência está às vésperas de demonstrar a existência e a sobrevivência da alma; e isso é tremendamente importante, tanto para os crentes como para os incrédulos. Se se pudesse demonstrar essa verdade, e viesse ela a ser aceita por toda a comunidade científica em geral, o impacto seria tão grande que levaria o mundo inteiro a reviver o seu interesse pelos princípios religiosos, os quais sempre têm confirmado essa verdade. As grandes inquirições sobre o *destino da alma*, sobre as «regiões espirituais da existência» se tornariam importantíssimas para todos os homens, necessariamente; porquanto assim estaríamos investigando sobre o que acontecerá «conosco».

V. O problema antropológico

O que é o homem? Será ele apenas uma forma de energia, a energia física, e, portanto, sujeita à dissolução final? (Assim pensa o *materialismo*). Será

ALMA DO MUNDO — ALMA DOS ANIMAIS

o homem formado de dois complexos de energia que agem entre si — a alma com o corpo? (Essa é a posição do *interacionismo*). Será ele composto de três formas de energia, uma material, outra semimaterial, e outra ainda espiritual, em que a energia espiritual pertence ao mundo eterno, e não a este mundo, o que significa que o verdadeiro homem é transcendental? (Essa é a posição do *substancialismo*).

Ver sobre *Problema Corpo-Mente* e também, *Imortalidade, Afirmações Teológicas*.

ALMA DO MUNDO

De modo geral, temos aí o conceito do divino, como extensivo ao espaço, incluindo o mundo como seu meio ambiente interno.

1. Em *Platão* (ver o artigo a respeito), a alma do mundo representa a divindade secundária, «tão divina quanto uma coisa mutável pode ser divina», que se auto-impulsiona, sendo o princípio de animação em todas as outras coisas. Esse conceito está relacionado à idéia do *demiurgo* (ver o artigo).

2. Entre os *estóicos*, o mundo era identificado com Deus (*panteísmo*; ver o artigo a respeito), sendo referido em termos de alma. O ser se estenderia pelo universo inteiro, sendo idêntico ao universo. Os estóicos pensavam que esse ser era material, e o fogo seria a força que, mediante modificações, transformar-se-ia em todas as coisas.

3. Entre os *platônicos*, a expressão passou a significar a «deidade última», embora não se misturassem a matéria e o espírito.

4. De acordo com *Plotino*, a alma do mundo seria uma *emanação* de Deus, o qual seria o Um. E essa emanação dar-se-ia por meio da mente (*nous*), ou seja, a força espiritual que atua no mundo físico, e que contém o mundo físico como seu corpo. (Ver o artigo sobre *nous*).

5. O *panteísmo*, de modo geral, fala sobre Deus como a cabeça, e sobre o mundo como o corpo. E a alma do mundo seria Deus, coletivamente falando.

6. No *pampsiquismo*, a alma, na essência imaterial, permearia todas as coisas, incluindo todos os objetos materiais. E essa essência imaterial seria a alma do mundo, ou estofo da mente. (E EP P)

ALMA DOS ANIMAIS

Platão foi um dos primeiros a expressar a crença de que nenhum ser vivo é meramente físico. Toda vida seria *psíquica*, e a parte material, apenas um veículo. Todas as coisas vivas têm sua «forma» ou «idéia», que é a causa sustentadora das mesmas. Essa «forma» é imaterial. Alguns têm afirmado que é impossível explicar o comportamento dos animais em termos meramente físicos. Há neles qualidades de pensamento, razão e emoção que sugerem que os animais têm alma. A observação empírica de aparições de animais, além de tentativas cruas (aparentes) de comunicação com antigos proprietários de animais, por parte de animais de estimação mortos, tem servido para convencer alguns de que os animais têm alma. As religiões orientais têm dado apoio às idéias de desenvolvimento espiritual nas almas dos animais, e até mesmo de intercâmbio entre almas humanas e de animais, em veículos animais, por meio da transmigração (ver o artigo a respeito). Ver o artigo sobre os *animais*, primeiro ponto, sob Argumentos em prol do respeito aos animais, e seus direitos, quanto a outros argumentos em favor da existência de alma nos animais. Ver os artigos sobre *transmigração, reencarnação e idéias*.

Nas religiões orientais, é um dogma que os animais têm alma. Há uma base filosófica para isso em Platão e no platonismo. Porém, as grandes controvérsias sobre a questão não tiveram início na filosofia senão com Descartes, cujo dualismo não deixava espaço de discussão sobre os animais. Ele defendia a idéia de que os animais são puras máquinas e agem instintivamente e não mediante raciocínio. Seus argumentos baseavam-se mais em pressupostos teológicos do que em qualquer outra consideração. A crença na existência de alma nos animais parecia ameaçar as crenças religiosas tradicionais, incluindo a suposta natureza ímpar do homem, dentro da criação. Muitos raciocínios teológicos adquirem peso dentro da questão, como aquele de que os animais são impecáveis, pelo que não podem sofrer punição por erros morais. Presumivelmente, segundo alguns crêem, por não terem alma, os animais não sofrem. E isso também justificaria o homem ao explorar, matar e comer os animais, visto que eles não teriam alma, e portanto, não teriam valor metafísico. A Descartes parecia degradante atribuir alma aos animais, pois isso seria privilégio exclusivo do homem. Além disso, ele aplicava o argumento lingüístico, dizendo que visto que os animais não têm a capacidade de falar, por meio da qual poderiam exprimir pensamentos, obviamente são criaturas destituídas de alma. Para Descartes, ver um chimpanzé comunicando-se através do teclado de um computador seria uma cena extremamente perturbadora. Mas é isso que está se sucedendo atualmente. De fato, quanto mais a ciência aprende sobre os animais, — mais fracos vão ficando tais argumentos.

A teoria mecânica não tem sido bem-sucedida ao explicar os processos biológicos. Quanto mais a ciência descobre mais nos convencemos de que há uma inteligência com propósitos por detrás dos fenômenos biológicos. Muitos e poderosos ataques foram desfechados contra Descartes e seu conceito de animais-máquinas. Os peripatéticos, usando conceitos aristotélicos, postulavam uma substância intermediária entre a matéria e a mente, atribuindo aos animais uma alma sensível (tal como Aristóteles já havia feito). Presumivelmente, a alma de um animal poderia refletir, raciocinar e exercer sua vontade. Mas, a ausência de evidências empíricas debilitava essa tentativa de explicação. Alguns admitiam que os animais têm uma espécie de alma, mas não do tipo capaz de sobreviver. Muitos naturalistas assumem essa posição. Diferentes graus de mentalidade são atribuídos às várias espécies de animais. Aos animais é negada qualquer propriedade que possa conceber a própria verdade, ou que considere coisas como o destino ou as questões metafísicas, o que seria propriedade exclusiva do homem.

A questão inteira chegou ao ponto do absurdo quando o padre Bougeant, um jesuíta, escreveu em 1739 uma convincente crítica da doutrina cartesiana e suas várias alternativas. Surpreendentemente concluiu que as almas dos animais na realidade são demônios ou anjos caídos, os quais, como uma forma de castigo, vêm habitar nos corpos de animais. Assim, os animais teriam toda a inteligência, a volição e o propósito que queiramos imaginar, mas somente porque esses também são atributos do diabo. Desnecessário é dizer que os demais jesuítas reagiram fortemente contra aquele padre, e essa teoria foi merecidamente esquecida.

Locke distinguia entre a sensação (dos animais) e a reflexão (do homem) e achava a fonte de ambos em uma espécie de teoria atômica, que mantinha a discussão inteira dentro do campo naturalista.

ALMAS DEBAIXO DO ALTAR

Somente o homem é capaz da abstração. Outros, como Condillac, atribuíam a órgãos de sentidos inferiores a capacidade mental inferior dos animais. Ainda outros pensavam em funções cerebrais inferiores para os animais, reduzindo assim a mente ao cérebro. Essa abordagem provocou a grande discussão do *Problema Corpo-Mente* (ver o artigo). Muitos filósofos, e grande número de cientistas, simplesmente não podem ver como o cérebro pode explicar as funções da mente. As descobertas da parapsicologia moderna muito têm contribuído para mostrar que a mente é distinta do cérebro. A entrada da teoria da evolução na realidade não alterou em grande coisa o quadro, porque a evolução materialista não tem podido explicar a vontade humana, o raciocínio especulativo e metafísico, as emoções, o senso de desígnio e destino, as sensibilidades espirituais, etc. Tudo quanto o homem tem sido capaz de investigar, no campo da inteligência artificial, não tem eliminado a necessidade de programar uma máquina com uma inteligência inteiramente separada da máquina. Evidências em prol da porção imaterial do homem são dadas no artigo sobre a *alma*. Nesse artigo, foram incluídos estudos científicos.

Alguns, como McTaggart, apesar de crerem na evolução do corpo, têm suposto que a própria evolução tem produzido a mente e a alma como sua mais significativa realização. Isso significa que temos uma alma natural; mas alma, afinal de contas. Porém, há boas provas de que a alma é transcendental, as quais são citadas no artigo sobre a alma.

Skinner e seu behaviorismo metodológico representam um retorno ao mecanismo animal cartesiano, estando sujeitos às mesmas objeções. Quanto mais a ciência descobre, menos provável parece ser a teoria *reducionista* (ver o artigo a respeito), pois vai-se tornando mais e mais evidente de que há realidades e eventos mentais que não podem ser explicados pelas funções cerebrais ou *reduzidos* às mesmas. Os artigos sobre a *alma* e a *parapsicologia* demonstram isso de forma adequada.

As várias abordagens não-espirituais que tencionam explicar a inteligência, a emoção e a vontade, animal ou humana, não têm podido eliminar o princípio da *teleologia* (ver o artigo), isto é, o princípio de desígnio e propósito na natureza. De fato, a própria ciência depende em muito do princípio da constância, da *invariabilidade*. Se ao menos quisermos ter ciência, precisamos ter a confiança de que as experiências podem ser repetidas, e que há algo na natureza que requer e dá apoio a um desígnio que funciona. Em outras palavras, há leis naturais, e, se há leis e invariabilidade, podem elas existir sem a existência da mente e do propósito nas coisas? (AN CR EP F)

ALMAS DEBAIXO DO ALTAR

I. Debaixo do altar as almas, Apo. 6:9.

São aquelas que sofreram o martírio, durante os selos segundo a quarto. — Apesar do autor sagrado ter incluído os mártires de todas as eras, o seu propósito primário foi o de mostrar que aqueles que o império romano havia martirizado, não estavam na inatividade. Suas orações e apelos atrairão os juízos divinos contra os perseguidores da igreja. Isso significa, profeticamente, que durante a Grande Tribulação, os tempos serão terríveis e a igreja se encontrará na tribulação a fim de ser perseguida. Essas almas são de mártires cristãos, e não de Israel, porquanto, por essa altura dos acontecimentos, a

nação de Israel não se terá ainda convertido. Lembremo-nos que o Apocalipse foi escrito a fim de fortalecer a igreja *perseguida* e não a fim de evitar que ela *escapasse* a perseguição. Isso se deu no caso da perseguição «histórica» movida por Domiciano, o «segundo *Nero*», que estava assediando a igreja quando o Apocalipse foi escrito. E assim sucederá profeticamente, quando a besta romana perseguir a igreja, durante a Grande Tribulação.

Por qual razão essas almas estão debaixo do altar? 1. Alguns estudiosos supõem que assim como o sangue escorria para a valeta que havia ao pé do altar, e assim como «a vida está no sangue», assim também aqueles mártires, cujo sangue for derramado, tomarão a posição correspondente ao sangue dos sacrifícios. Os trechos de II Tim. 4:6 e Fil. 2:17 vêem os mártires como sacrifícios oferecidos a Deus. (Ver também Inácio, *Ad Rom*. ii.2, quanto a essa idéia). Portanto, o martírio à face da terra, como se a vida fosse oferecida a Deus em sacrifício celestial, tem esse significado. Deus fica satisfeito com essa elevada dedicação, e a alma humana obtém um acesso especial a Deus, não conferido a outras. 2. Em *Aboth* R.N. xxi é refletida a crença de que as almas justas estão sob o altar, para *proteção* e preservação divinas; e essa idéia parece estar incluída em Apoc. 6:9. (Ver também *Shabb*. 152b, «as almas dos justos são preservadas sob o altar da glória»). Outras citações rabínicas indicam a mesma coisa. Portanto, aquilo que é dito acerca de todos os santos, é aqui particularmente aplicado aos mártires. Simbólica e espiritualmente, aquilo que Paulo requeria de todos os crentes, que sejam «sacrifícios vivos», atinge seu cumprimento «ideal» nos mártires. (Ver Rom. 12:1,2).

II. Aceitação especial dos mártires

A crença judaica ordinária não conferia aos santos a entrada imediata nos céus. Antes, tinham de permanecer na porção boa do hades, no mundo intermediário, até que entrasse o número total dos eleitos. E então o grupo inteiro, em um bloco, ascenderia aos lugares celestiais. (Ver II Baruque 23:4,5, Yebamoth 62a, II Esdras 4:35-37; 2:41 e I Enoque 47:4, quanto a esse tipo de ensinamento). O sétimo capítulo do Apocalipse, com os seus «cento e quarenta e quatro mil», pode ser uma alusão ao número dos mártires, mas o vidente João lhes atribui acesso já obtido aos céus, o que o judaísmo antigo não concebia.

Os privilégios dos mártires podem ser sumariados como segue:

1. Ocorrendo a sua morte, têm acesso imediato ao trono, sendo, por assim dizer, «sacrificados», o que significa que serão capazes de render um elevado serviço a Deus, mediante uma total dedicação, o que não está imediatamente disponível no caso de outros santos.

2. Não precisam ascender através dos vários níveis até os lugares celestiais (sete níveis, segundo a teologia judaica), a fim de chegarem ao trono; chegam ali de imediato.

3. Em contraste com a grande multidão dos santos, eles escapam ao «mundo intermediário», a boa seção do hades.

4. Recebem a vestimenta do novo corpo, antes da ressurreição, as «vestes brancas». (G I IB NTI)

III. A teologia desta cena

Esta cena demonstra que a alma existe e sobrevive a morte biológica. É impossível supor que representa um grupo especial que sobrevive *exclusivamente*.

ALMODÁ — ALTAR

ALMODÁ

No hebraico talvez signifique **agitador**. Foi o filho mais velho de Joctã (Gên. 10:26; I Crô. 1:20). Aparentemente ele vivia no sul da península da Arábia, mas nada se sabe com certeza quanto a isso. A Septuaginta, em Gên. 10:26, diz Elmodá (Deus é amigo). Somos informados de que ele foi o fundador de uma tribo árabe, de localização incerta. (S UN)

ALMOM-DIBLATAIM

No hebraico, **Almom do duplo bolo de figos**. Foi a qüinquagésima primeira estação onde os israelitas estacionaram a caminho entre o monte Hor e as planícies de Moabe (ver Núm. 33:46,47), identificada com Bete-Diblataim (Jer. 48:22), cuja localização exata, porém, é desconhecida. Alguns têm sugerido Deleilat el-Gharbiyeh, uma aldeia que domina três estradas, a seis quilômetros de Libe, como sua moderna localização. (S UN Z)

ALNATAN

No hebraico, **Deus deu**. Foi um dos principais líderes do retorno da Babilônia a Israel (ver I Esdras 8:44). Ele solicitou que fossem enviados sacerdotes que servissem na casa do Senhor. (S Z)

ALOÉS

Trata-se do **lignum aloes** ou do **aloe succotrina**. Uma planta mencionada tanto no Antigo quanto no Novo Testamento. A árvore era altamente valorizada, havendo diversas espécies que cresciam sem cultivo na Índia, na China e na Arábia. O material era usado como incenso ou como perfume. (Ver Núm. 24:6; Sal. 45:8; Pro. 7:17; Can. 4:14 e João 19:39). Da flor nasce um fruto semelhante a uma ervilha grande, branca e vermelha. Um suco é extraído das folhas e guardado em frascos. Na antiguidade esse suco era muito dispendioso, e valia mais do que o ouro quanto ao peso (ver Núm. 24:6). Um perfume era fabricado do óleo, que se concentrava na forma de resina, dentro do tronco. A substância era usada como repelente de insetos e também para perfumar leitos e vestes.

Alguns identificam essa espécie com a *Aquilaria agallochum*. O mais provável é que várias espécies de vegetais estivessem em foco. Os egípcios usavam o material em seus embalsamamentos, misturando-o com mirra, salpicando a mistura entre as tiras de pano. (Ver João 19:39 no NTI quanto a detalhes a esse respeito). Nicodemos usou cerca de 34 kg (cem libras romanas) para embalsamar o corpo de Jesus. O material era importado, o que significa que o ato envolveu grande dispêndio em dinheiro.(FA ND NTI S Z)

ALOGENES SUPREMO

No grego, **allogenes** significa «de outra raça». Esse é o título de uma das obras gnósticas escritas em cóptico, encontrada em Quenobósquiom, em 1946. Talvez se trate do mesmo Apocalipse de Alegenes, citado por Porfírio em sua biografia de Plotino. Contém muitas revelações espúrias atribuídas a Sete e seu sucessor. Data do começo do século III D.C. (DO UN Z)

ALOGI

Nome dado zombeteiramente àqueles que rejeita-

vam a doutrina do Logos, no evangelho de João. Floresceram perto do fim do século II D.C., e seu líder principal era Gaio, contra quem Hipólito escreveu um livro que não mais existe. A palavra «alogos» pode ter dois sentidos. 1. Contrário ao Logos; ou 2. destituído de razão. Ver o artigo sobre o *Logos*. (E GO).

ALOM

Vem do hebraico, e significa **carvalho**. A Vulgata Latina diz *Quercus*.

1. Como designação de um carvalho, ver Gên. 35:8; Jos. 19:32; Isa. 2:13; 6:13, etc. Na Síria os carvalhos não são comuns senão nas colinas. Notemos, porém, a expressão «carvalhos de Basã» (Isa. 2:13; Eze. 27:6; Zac. 11:2), que mostram que eles eram comuns naquela região. Densas florestas de carvalhos existiam nas regiões da Basã e Gileade.

2. Uma cidade na fronteira da Naftali, entre Helefe e Zaanim (ver Jos. 19:33), embora alguns pensem que se tratava apenas de um marco de fronteira, vinculado a algum carvalho, e não uma cidade (que é o parecer de nossa versão portuguesa, onde se lê: «do carvalho em Zaanim»).

3. Filho de Jedaías e pai de Sifi (I Crô. 4:37). Era um chefe simeonita, da família que expulsou os camitas do vale de Gedor. (S UN)

ALOM-BACUTE

No hebraico esse nome significa «carvalho do pranto», a árvore sob a qual foi sepultada Débora, enfermeira de Raquel (ver Gên. 35:8). Aparentemente, Débora, a juíza, não está em vista, embora presumivelmente ela fosse a pessoa que mais apropriadamente seria honrada por um memorial dessa natureza. Mas, a serva de Raquel e Jacó os serviu com dedicação, tendo sido afetuosamente lembrada dessa maneira. (UN Z)

ALTA CRÍTICA

Ver também **Crítica da Bíblia**. A expressão «alta crítica» aponta para o exame crítico da Bíblia, envolvendo qualquer coisa que vá além do próprio texto bíblico, isto é, questões que digam respeito à autoria, à data, à forma de composição, à integridade, à proveniência, às idéias envolvidas, às doutrinas ensinadas, etc. A *baixa crítica* é a crítica do texto. A alta crítica pode ser positiva ou negativa em sua abordagem, ou pode misturar ambos os pontos de vista. Por si mesmo, a expressão «alta crítica» não é negativa. Um crítico pode manifestar-se em favor dos pontos de vista interpretativos tradicionais, e no entanto, ser um crítico que usa da alta crítica.

ALTA IGREJA

Um termo aplicado no tempo da rainha Ana, da Inglaterra, para apoiar os que defendiam a causa da Igreja Anglicana, quanto à política. Posteriormente, esse título foi dado aos anglicanos que tinham em alta conta a igreja e seus sacramentos. Ver sobre os *anglo-católicos*. (E)

ALTAR

Lugar de se entrar em contato com o poder divino ou com os mortos, por meio de um *sacrifício* (ver o artigo) e de *oferendas* (ver o artigo). As religiões primitivas supunham que o altar de uma divindade

ALTAR

seria o lugar onde ela manifestava a sua presença. O altar (do latim, *altus*, estrutura elevada), presumivelmente chamava a atenção do poder invocado. Oferendas eram postas nessas estruturas a fim de aplacar ou solicitar o favor do deus do altar.

I. Altares pagãos. Eram de muitos tipos, formatos e dimensões. Na Idade do Bronze Antiga, alguns altares eram de meras pedras arrumadas. Na Idade do Bronze Moderna, alguns altares eram retangulares, feitos de tijolos ou de pedras, erguidos com cimento de argila. Alguns altares eram estruturas imensas, e outros eram pequenos. Montões de pedras também serviam de altares, entre os povos pagãos.

II. Semitas. Eram similares aos altares acima descritos, em diferentes épocas. Altares foram edificados por Noé (Gên. 8:20), Abraão, em Siquém (Gên. 12:7), Isaque, em Beerseba (Gên. 26:25), Jacó, em Siquém (Gên. 33:20) e em Betel (Gên. 35:7), Moisés, em Refidim (Êxo. 17:15) e Horebe (Êxo. 24:4). Na cultura semita, os altares usualmente eram erigidos com propósitos sacrificiais, mas não exclusivamente. Muitos eram feitos de rocha natural, com canais para que escorresse o sangue; ou eram montes de terra ou rochas escavadas, com valetas ao redor, com o mesmo propósito. Cria-se que o sangue derramado sobre o altar estava carregado com o poder da divindade, sendo assim útil para vários ritos de purificação e busca de poder.

III. Altar do tabernáculo. Na verdade, dois eram os altares do tabernáculo. Um deles, que ficava na metade oriental do átrio, era de «bronze» (influência fenícia, dizem alguns), recoberto de madeira de acácia (Êxo. 27:1-8). As suas dimensões eram 2,5 m x 2,5 m x 1,5 m. Era o altar dos holocaustos. Tinha chifres que se projetavam nas pontas, bem como argolas e varas para ser transportado. Não havia topo, e talvez contasse com uma armação gradeada de metal, cheia de terra, o que explica como era resistente ao fogo ali posto. O segundo desses altares era menor, com 0,5 m x 0,5 x 1,0 m, de madeira de acácia recoberto de ouro (Êxo. 30:1-10). Tinha quatro chifres e uma borda de ouro, com argolas e varas para ser transportado. Era o altar do incenso, símbolo de nossas orações e intercessões (Lev. 16:12).

IV. Dos templos. No átrio exterior (Jer. 36:10) do templo de Salomão, em Jerusalém, estava localizado um vasto altar de bronze, com 4,5 m de altura e 9,0 m de comprimento. Era uma réplica em tamanho grande do altar do tabernáculo, ao qual se obtinha acesso por um lance de escadas. O interior oco do mesmo era cheio de pedras e terra, e o resplendor do mesmo podia ser visto do átrio abaixo (II Crôn. 4:1). Orações eram feitas diante desse altar, e sacrifícios eram ali oferecidos. Existiu por quase três séculos. Acaz (735-717 A.C.) removeu esse altar para o lado norte, pondo um altar seu no local original. O novo altar tornou-se o centro das atividades. Talvez o altar original tenha sido finalmente restaurado ao seu lugar (II Crô. 33:16), como parte das reformas. Todavia, parece que o altar de Salomão, ou suas partes essenciais de metal, foram removidas por Nabucodonosor para a Babilônia (Jer. 52:17-20). O segundo templo tinha seus altares, provavelmente dois, segundo certa tradição. Antíoco Epifânio levou um altar de incenso, todo de ouro, no ano de 169 A.C. (I Mac. 1:21). Dois anos mais tarde ele profanou o altar dos holocaustos (I Mac. 1:54). Posteriormente, os Macabeus restauraram ambos os altares (I Mac. 4:44-49). Não se sabe qual a disposição exata dos altares no templo de Salomão, que substituiu o templo mais antigo. Apenas sabe-se que o altar dos holocaustos era uma pilha de pedras não-lavradas, ao qual se obtinha acesso por meio de uma rampa, e não por meio de degraus.

V. No Novo Testamento. A fé do N.T. eliminou o judaísmo suntuoso e complexo. Templos humildes substituíram o templo de Jerusalém e seus móveis. No início, os templos cristãos eram apenas as residências dos crentes. Tudo quanto fazia parte do judaísmo, passou então a ser considerado típico das realidades espirituais. O batismo reteve certos aspectos da imersão judaica de prosélitos, e de conceitos de purificação inerentes às abluções. A Ceia do Senhor reteve as idéias de sacrifício, expiação e comunhão. Mas agora —o altar— é a alma do crente, onde a adoração a Deus é levada a efeito. Conforme diz um hino: «Meu coração é o altar, e Teu amor é o fogo».

O uso literal que se faz da palavra «altar», no Novo Testamento, alude ao altar do templo de Jerusalém, figurando por oito vezes nos evangelhos: Mat. 5:23,24; 23:18-20; Luc. 11:51. Ou alude a vários altares (Rom. 11:3; I Cor. 9:13; 10:18; Heb. 7:13; Tia. 2:21). O vocábulo é usado em sentido figurado, em Apo. 6:9; 8:3,5; 9:13, etc.

O altar pagão mencionado no sermão feito no Areópago (no grego, *bomós*), é mencionado em Atos 17:22,23. Trazia a inscrição: «Ao Deus Desconhecido». Ver a passagem no NTI, onde há uma completa exposição. Uma outra referência pagã é ao altar de Pérgamo, em Apo. 2:13, o trono de Satanás. Foi um dos mais famosos altares do mundo antigo. Ver o artigo sobre *Pérgamo, altar de*. Foi descoberto em 1871 e levado para a Alemanha, onde foi reconstruído e agora está no Museu de Berlim. Ver também no NTI, o trecho de Apo. 2:13, quanto a notas completas.

1. Simbolismo do altar

Trata-se do lugar onde podemos nos aproximar de Deus, mediante sacrifício e oração; lugar onde Deus vem ao encontro das necessidades humanas, conforme as exigências por ele estabelecidas. O altar fala da «comunicação» entre Deus e os homens; esse é o lugar onde um homem pode encontrar-se com o poder divino. O altar é igualmente o lugar onde o homem pode trazer seus dons a Deus, onde pode prestar serviço e lealdade.

2. Em Heb. 13:10. Um entendimento cristão

Temos um altar, do qual não têm direito de comer os que servem ao tabernáculo.

Um altar. Essa palavra indica tudo quanto Cristo fez em sua vida, em sua expiação e em seu ofício medianeiro. Nada de específico é indicado, como a cruz, a mesa da Ceia do Senhor, ou o próprio Cristo. Antes, o autor sagrado junta todas as idéias de acesso e aproximação a Deus, que fazem parte da expiação, do perdão, da aceitação e da filiação, e se refere a elas sob o símbolo de um «altar»; porquanto esse era o símbolo da aproximação de Deus, por parte de homens pecaminosos. O autor sagrado era dono de uma mentalidade mística, e não sacramentalista; portanto, dificilmente ele podia ter a eucaristia ou Ceia do Senhor em vista, porquanto isso também é apenas símbolo da comunhão com Cristo, e não um meio mágico para a mesma. Se qualquer coisa específica está em foco, na palavra «altar», então só pode ser o «santuário celestial», onde Cristo entrou, a fim de oferecer o seu sangue expiatório, obtendo assim acesso até à presença mesma de Deus Pai. (Ver Heb. 6:20 e 9:12). Torna-se imediatamente evidente que o altar cristão não é de natureza a precisar de

ALTAR ALTO — AL-TASCHITH

refeições sacrificiais, e nem é acompanhado por práticas cerimoniais. Ultrapassou e substituiu a tudo isso.

Esse altar é o mesmo que se encontrava no antigo tabernáculo. O altar não era o ofertante, e muito menos ainda a vítima. Era o lugar onde a vítima era apresentada e morta. Em parte alguma Cristo é chamado de *altar*; e nem a cruz recebe tal nome. De fato, o décimo primeiro versículo, o principal ponto da passagem, não dá apoio a tal idéia.

Do qual não têm direito. Aqueles que repeliam a provisão de acesso em Cristo, retornando aos antigos caminhos, rejeitavam o altar de Deus, pelo que também não tinham mais direito a ele. Ou aqueles que nunca se tinham aproximado de Cristo, mas antes, permaneciam nos antigos caminhos, por se recusarem a reconhecer o novo caminho de acesso a Deus, automaticamente se tinham eliminado de seus benefícios, condenando a si mesmos às futilidades do antigo caminho. As palavras *os que ministram* apontam para os que se apegavam às normas legalistas e cerimoniais, e não meramente para os sacerdotes, que realmente efetuavam os ritos.

VI. Culto verdadeiro. O coração humano se deleita em cerimônias externas e em ritos elaborados. E relativamente fácil levar um cordeiro a um templo, fazer uma peregrinação a Meca ou a Roma, freqüentar um culto na igreja, revestir-se dos paramentos externos da religião. Essas coisas nos confortam com o pensamento agradável que, pelo menos, fizemos coisas que agradam a Deus. Mas o verdadeiro culto é o sacrifício (dedicação) absoluto do próprio ser. (Ver Rom. 12:1-2). (AL I IB LAN NTI)

ALTAR ALTO

Em um templo da Igreja Católica Romana, o altar principal, em distinção aos altares laterais, menores.

ALTAR DE INCENSO

Esse altar era um dos móveis que havia no tabernáculo, no deserto. (Ver Êxo. 30:1-11). Tinha cerca de meio metro de lado e um metro de altura, com pontas em forma de chifres, nos quatro cantos. Era feito de madeira de acácia e recoberto de ouro. (Ver Êxo. 37:25-38). A fim de ser transportado, esse altar contava com argolas por onde eram passadas as varas. O sumo sacerdote queimava incenso sobre o mesmo pela manhã e à tardinha, todos os dias. Como é evidente, esse altar é chamado de «altar de ouro», em Êxo. 39:38, sendo assim distinguido do outro altar, maior e de bronze, que ficava no meio do átrio descoberto. Ver o artigo geral sobre o *altar*. A posição do altar de incenso, dentro do tabernáculo, parece ter sido dentro do santuário, diante da arca da aliança (ver Êxo. 40:5 e Lev. 16:11-14), onde o sumo sacerdote aspergia sangue uma vez por ano (ver Êxo. 30:10). No templo de Salomão, o altar de ouro ficava dentro do Lugar Santo (ver I Reis 6:20,22). Mas, no terceiro templo, parece ter sido posto do lado de fora do véu, embora ainda dentro do santuário (ver Luc. 1:10). O trecho de Hebreus 9:3 parece dizer que esse altar ficava dentro do Santo dos Santos, embora os intérpretes tenham disputado sobre a questão da sua posição exata. (Ver as notas sobre essa questão no NTI, em Heb. 9:3). Como é óbvio, se esse altar ficasse no Santo dos Santos, nenhum sacerdote poderia ter queimado incenso sobre o mesmo a cada manhã e cada fim de tarde, pois ali somente o sumo sacerdote entrava, e isso apenas uma vez por ano, no dia da expiação. Naturalmente, é possível que, com a passagem do tempo, a posição desse altar fosse sendo modificada, como também as suas funções.

Uso metafórico. Esse altar era o lugar das orações, da intercessão, do acesso a Deus por meio da oração, os mesmos sentidos que são atribuídos ao próprio *incenso*. Ver o artigo sobre esse assunto, bem como os trechos de Sal. 141:2; Mal. 1:11; Atos 10:4 e Apo. 4:8; 8:4. (ID NTI Z)

ALTAR DE JOSUÉ

Um antigo altar recentemente descoberto, feito de pedra, com cerca de trinta e quatro séculos de antiguidade, foi desenterrado em Israel, em um monte na margem ocidental do Jordão, onde a Bíblia diz que Josué erigiu um altar, após haver introduzido os filhos de Israel à Terra Prometida. O arqueólogo israelense, Adam Zartal, descreveu o achado à *Associated Press*, afirmando que a estrutura de pedra de 9,15 m × 7 m, foi identificada pela presença de ossos de ovelhas, cinzas e uma substância escura, talvez sangue coagulado. A descoberta foi feita a 21 de outubro de 1983. A Universidade de Haifa confirmou a autenticidade da descoberta. Evidentemente, trata-se de um dos mais antigos altares encontrados em solo israelense, e talvez seja mesmo o altar de Josué. Disse o professor Benjamim Mazar, da Universidade Hebraica, e um dos mais respeitados arqueólogos de Israel: «O Monte Ebal é bem conhecido através de todos os relatos sobre a ocupação do povo israelita na antiga terra de Israel, e ali temos encontrado restos arqueológicos que servem de testemunho da santidade daquele antigo local». Porém, segundo Mazar frisou, maiores pesquisas ainda são necessárias. A cerâmica encontrada no local tem sido datada pelo método do carbono-14, como pertencente ao século XII A.C. (Ver Jos. 8:30,31 e Deu. 27:5).

ALTAR DE PÉRGAMO

Ver **Pérgamo, Altar de**.

ALTAR DO TESTEMUNHO

Está em foco um altar erigido na margem ocidental do rio Jordão pelas tribos de Rúben, Gade e Manassés, que se estabeleceram no lado oriental desse rio. A finalidade do altar foi dar testemunho do fato de que eles, bem como as tribos do lado ocidental do rio «tinham parte no Senhor» (Jos. 22:21-34). Isso causou pequena comoção entre aquelas tribos e as demais tribos de Israel, até que a questão foi devidamente justificada.

ALTAR GRANDE E VISTOSO

No hebraico, *ed*, que significa «testemunho». Tratava-se de um altar erigido pelos rubenitas, gaditas e pela meia-tribo de Manassés, que se estabeleceram no lado leste do rio Jordão. Esse altar prestava testemunho da lealdade daqueles israelitas a Yahweh. (Ver Jos. 22:34).

AL-TASCHITH

No hebraico, **não destruas**, ou **não corrompas**. É título que aparece nos Salmos 52, 59 e 75, embora nossa versão portuguesa não o inclua no título do primeiro desses salmos. Talvez as palavras sejam o começo de um cântico entoado por ocasião da vindima, conforme é sugerido em Isa. 65:8. (S Z)

ALTÍSSIMO—ALTURA, PROFUNDIDADE

ALTÍSSIMO

No hebraico, **Elyon**, o Altíssimo. Acredita-se que esse é um dos mais antigos nomes hebraicos de Deus. Melquisedeque era sacerdote de El Elyon, e não de Yahweh (ver o artigo a respeito). O título «Altíssimo» é usado no livro de Salmos por vinte e uma vezes (para exemplificar, Sal. 7:17; 9:2; 18:13). Aparece por três vezes no livro de Daniel (ver Dan. 7:22,25,27). No Novo Testamento, os demônios chamaram Jesus de Filho do Altíssimo (ver Mat. 5:7 e Luc. 8:28).

ALTRUÍSMO E EGOÍSMO

Altruísmo (do latim, **alter**, outro), é a devoção ao interesse do próximo, ou ação desinteressada, ou seja, ação que não tem alguma razão pessoal, mas que realmente busca os interesses alheios. Como uma teoria ética, surgiu nos fins do século XVII, sendo uma reação ao hedonismo psicológico de Thomas Hobbes (1588-1679), segundo o qual o indivíduo serve a si mesmo, mediante variadas formas de prazer. O altruísmo afirma que existem impulsos no homem para fazer o bem ao próximo, inteiramente à parte de qualquer coisa que ele possa ganhar para si mesmo. Hobbes havia argumentado que todos os impulsos naturais podem ser atribuídos a alguma forma de auto-interesse, embora isso possa ser escondido em certas ocasiões. Por exemplo, quando alguém sente «dó» de outrem, não é porque sinta horror pela calamidade de outrem, mas porque vê a si mesmo como vítima potencial da calamidade, em algum tempo futuro, ou mesmo no presente, por causa do significado que a outra pessoa tem para ele. Isso equivale a dizer que ninguém é capaz de ter um amor desinteressado — ficando assim destruída a própria base da moralidade bíblica, e, de fato, todos os códigos morais e todas as religiões proclamam que a lei do amor é o maior princípio moral de todos, o sol orientador no firmamento ético.

O *egoísmo* distingue entre o auto-interesse crasso e o auto-interesse iluminado. O primeiro é brutalmente egoísta. O segundo é sutilmente egoísta, pois leva em conta os interesses alheios, mas sempre com objetivo de algum interesse próprio. Por exemplo, farei o bem aos meus filhos, mas não exclusivamente a eles, como pessoas distintas de mim mesmo. Antes, o bem que farei em favor deles voltará para mim de diversas maneiras: 1. Eles me devolverão o bem recebido; 2. a sociedade me aprovará por causa de minha bondade; 3. eu me sentirei bem (derivando disso um tipo de prazer), por haver cumprido meu dever; 4. e mesmo do ponto de vista religioso, Deus *me* recompensará. Se eu servir à sociedade, isso a ajudará a ser uma sociedade mais estável e próspera, o que, por sua vez, será um lugar melhor para *eu* viver. Obedeço às leis porque, em última análise, elas *me* beneficiam.

O altruísmo, em contraste, apesar de admitir que as pessoas realmente agem egoisticamente, ao mesmo tempo que se fingem altruístas, afirma que o indivíduo é capaz de ações totalmente altruístas. Se um homem corre para dentro de um edifício em chamas, a fim de salvar seu filho de uma morte horrenda, poderá sacrificar *alegremente* sua própria vida, a fim de cumprir seu propósito. Em tal caso, ele fará isso por seu *filho*, e não por temer o que os outros diriam se ele não fizesse tal esforço. De fato, seu filho talvez seja mais importante para ele, do que ele é para si mesmo. Outrossim, o altruísmo afirma que o interesse por outras pessoas, por causa delas mesmas, é uma condição necessária à verdadeira moralidade,

pois o egoísmo sempre corrompe a boa lei do amor.

Biblicamente falando, a lei do amor sempre ocupa o primeiro lugar na lista das virtudes espirituais (Gál. 5:22), sendo a grande prova da espiritualidade de alguém (I João 4:7-8). Visto que nos é mandado que amemos (João 13:34), fica entendido que somos capazes de amar. O trecho de Gál. 5:22 ss mostra que as virtudes espirituais são fruto ou *cultivo* do Espírito. Através disso aprendemos que o amor é uma qualidade espiritual e divina, em sua mais alta manifestação, fazendo parte de nossa transformação espiritual. O amor aumenta na proporção em que crescemos na espiritualidade. Ver os artigos separados sobre *Amor* e *Altruísmo e Egoísmo*. (EP F H NTI)

ALTURA, PROFUNDIDADE

Rom. 8:29: *Nem a altura, nem a profundidade, nem qualquer outra criatura nos poderá separar do amor de Deus, que está em Cristo Jesus nosso Senhor.*

Esses termos são vagos, e isso significa que os mesmos estão sujeitos a muitas interpretações:

1. Alguns estudiosos pensam que a alusão é a *vastidão do espaço*, pelo que nada existente no espaço é capaz de separar o crente do seu Senhor. Se essa é realmente a interpretação certa sobre essas palavras, então «espaço» é simplesmente uma maneira de expressar o que é misterioso. Diz Sanday (*in loc.*): «Não há nada remoto no espaço». De maneira geral, poderíamos dizer que, segundo essa interpretação, nada existe, na vasta expansão da criação de Deus, que nos possa prejudicar espiritualmente.

2. Estendendo um pouco mais essa idéia, alguns intérpretes têm pensado que esses vocábulos se referem aos *céus* e ao *submundo* ou hades. O apóstolo Paulo foi elevado aos «lugares celestiais», onde ouviu e viu coisas que não podia revelar. (Ver II Cor. 12:2 e s.). Nada existe, naquelas alturas, que possa separar-nos do amor de Cristo, nenhuma surpresa que não possamos antecipar agora, que possa ter esse efeito. O próprio Cristo atravessou todos os céus, e chegou à mão direita de Deus Pai, no Santo dos Santos celeste, para dali fazer intercessão por nós. (Ver Rom. 8:34). Por conseguinte, não precisaríamos temer qualquer força proveniente dessas elevadíssimas regiões, como se alguma delas pudesse arruinar o destino que nos foi prometido em Cristo. De fato, tais poderes são nossos aliados, e os lugares celestiais são nosso lar futuro. (Ver Efé. 2:6 sobre esse tema). Cristo, entretanto, também desceu ao mundo inferior, ao hades, conforme se lê em trechos como Efé. 4:9; Rom. 10:7 e Mat. 12:40 . Mas as portas do inferno não podem prevalecer contra a igreja de Cristo. (Ver Mat. 16:18).— Nem qualquer agente do mundo inferior pode reivindicar qualquer direito sobre o homem que confia em Cristo. Por essa razão é que Jesus disse: «Não temas; eu sou o primeiro e o último, e aquele que vive; estive morto, mas eis que estou vivo pelos séculos dos séculos, e tenho as chaves da morte e do inferno» (Apo. 1:17,18). Por conseguinte, nenhuma «profundidade» pode ser-nos prejudicial.

3. Ainda outros eruditos pensam que essas palavras significam *céu* e *terra*, respectivamente.

4. Ainda outros pensam em «felicidade» e «infelicidade».

5. Existem alguns que opinam em favor de «honra» e «opróbrio».

6. Ainda outros preferem «exaltação» e «humilhação».

7. Há aqueles que pensam em — «espíritos superiores» e «espíritos inferiores».

125

ALUS — ALVO DA VIDA

8. Finalmente, há certos intérpretes que pensam que temos aqui uma expressão de natureza «astrológica», como se a mesma aludisse à mais alta posição atingida por qualquer estrela, ou o lugar mais baixo, o abismo, abaixo do horizonte. As posições das estrelas, nos dias do apóstolo Paulo, eram aceitas por muitos (tal como na moderna astrologia) como algo que exerce influências diversas sobre as vidas humanas, chegando mesmo a controlar-lhes o destino, ou bom ou mau. Se porventura isso faz parte do sentido dessas palavras de Paulo, o que é inconcebível, mesmo assim ele então salientava que sem importar a *suposta* influência das estrelas, elas não têm a capacidade de «separar-nos do amor de Deus em Cristo Jesus, nosso Senhor».

Na astrologia judaica antiga (como entre outras culturas) a idéia foi que as estrelas são seres vivos de imenso poder, ou lugares de habitação de tais seres. Naturalmente, estes seres teriam poder sobre a vida de seres humanos. Não há qualquer evidência de que Paulo compartilhou destas idéias, mas pode ser que ele negou, aqui neste texto, que tais seres (se existissem), teriam poder sobre os homens.

Dentre essas oito possibilidades, contudo, as que contam com maiores probabilidades de estarem conforme o pensamento do apóstolo dos gentios, são a primeira, a segunda e a oitava. Não obstante, criando ainda uma nona interpretação, alguns estudiosos preferem pensar que esses termos são poéticos, não tendo por intuito referir-se a qualquer coisa ou estado de coisas específicos, mas que tão-somente asseguram-nos que nenhuma condição pode existir que seja capaz de separar-nos do amor de Deus, em Cristo Jesus. (AL I IB NTI RO)

Ver o artigo sobre *Segurança Eterna do Crente*.

ALUS

No hebraico talvez signifique **desolação**. Foi um dos lugares onde os israelitas descansaram, a caminho do monte Sinai (ver Núm. 33:13,14). Ficava entre Dofka e Refidim. A cronologia judaica *Seder Olam Rabba*, c. 5, par. 27, afirma que ficava a dezenove quilômetros da primeira dessas estações, e a treze quilômetros da segunda. Como interpretação do trecho de Êxo. 16:1, alguns supõem que o sábado foi pela primeira vez instituído e observado ali. Desconhece-se o local moderno. (S)

ALVÃ

No hebraico, **alto, sublime**. Foi um chefe de Edom, filho de Sobal, um descendente de Seir (ver Gên. 36:23; I Crô. 1:51), c. 1907-1760 A.C. Talvez o nome deva ser identificado com Aliã, em I Crô. 1:40. (Z)

ALVO

Tradução de uma palavra hebraica que aparece uma única vez, em Jó 16:12, onde aquele servo de Deus diz: «Em paz eu vivia, porém ele (Deus) me quebrantou; pegou-me pelo pescoço, e me despedaçou. Pôs-me por seu alvo...»

ALVO DA VIDA

Para quem existimos (I Cor. 8:6).

I. Idéias gerais

1. Nas páginas do N.T., vida jamais é mera existência, e a vida eterna nunca é considerada como existência sem fim. Pelo contrário, a vida eterna é uma «modalidade de vida», a participação no tipo de vida que tem o próprio Deus (ver João 5:25,26), em sua essência e atributos (ver Efé. 3:19). Deus possui a mais elevada forma de vida, e os homens chegarão a participar de sua forma de vida e de sua natureza (ver II Ped. 1:4).

2. Isso é mediado através da participação humana na natureza e essência de Cristo (ver Rom. 8:29), em que os crentes, como filhos, serão levados à glória do Filho (ver as notas em Heb. 2:10 no NTI).

3. Isso significa que os homens compartilham dos atributos do Filho, com base na participação em sua natureza divina, (ver Col. 2:10).

4. A missão de Cristo terá efeitos absolutamente universais. Ver o artigo sobre a *Restauração*. Ver no NTI os comentários sobre Efé. 1:10.

5. A glorificação é um alvo infinito, portanto, terá de ser um processo eterno. E posto que há uma infinitude com a qual seremos cheios, também deve haver um enchimento infinito. Ver em NTI sobre Rom. 8:29.

II. Meios de desenvolvimento espiritual

1. O treinamento do intelecto, através do estudo dos escritos sagrados.

2. A prática da oração (ver o artigo).

3. A meditação em busca de iluminação espiritual (ver Efé. 1:18).

4. A santificação (ver o artigo).

5. A prática da lei do amor, que é comprovação de espiritualidade (ver I João 4:7).

6. O uso dos dons espirituais, que nos ajudam a cumprir nossas respectivas missões individuais.

Para quem existimos. Essas palavras foram ditas a respeito de Deus Pai. Mas as palavras, *e nós também por ele*, se referem ao Senhor Jesus Cristo. Pode-se observar aqui, por igual modo, o emprego enfático do vocábulo «Senhor». Ter alguém a Jesus Cristo como seu «Senhor» significa que esse alguém vive *por ele*, isto é, por intermédio dele. Sim, porque a verdadeira vida não consiste de mera existência. Antes, é uma vida dominada, possuída e absolutamente dirigida pelo Senhor Deus.

O indivíduo irreligioso, sem piedade, é um «louco» no sentido que não possui conceito real da vida. Talvez se trate de um grande cientista, e conheça muitos argumentos acerca de alguns segmentos da criação divina. Mas, quão absurdo é que tal homem não reconheça o Criador de todas as coisas. Tal homem ficou totalmente absorvido pelas coisas criadas, mas falhou, não reconhecendo o Criador. Ocupou sua mente com uma verdade bem diminuta e parcial, mas nada soube a respeito de «a Verdade». Assim também ocorre no caso de todos os demais homens, que não se deixam redimir pelo sangue de Cristo. Atarefam-se com verdades pequeníssimas, mas às vezes até mesmo com verdades religiosas. No entanto, nada representam, se não reconhecem a verdade da pessoa de Deus, a verdade que Jesus Cristo é «o Senhor».

A verdadeira vida é aquela inteiramente envolvida por Cristo, que se orienta na direção dele. Nós, os remidos, estamos sendo transformados segundo a imagem de Cristo, tanto moral como metafisicamente falando. E disso é que consiste realmente a vida eterna, a vida superior que Deus tenciona dar aos homens, partindo da criação deles em diante. Pois, por maior que tivesse sido o homem, em seu esplendor celeste, no princípio (supondo nós que o homem original foi o «espírito» e não o corpo, entre os anjos, e Orígenes fazia a identificação entre o homem original e os anjos, como *espécie*, e que a «queda», em seus diversos níveis para baixo é que estabeleceu a diferença que agora há entre homens e anjos), contudo, em Cristo, aquela glória celeste original é em muito ultrapassada, atingindo os remidos o cume mesmo da mais elevada serra do Espírito. Esta vida terrena, quando está sendo vivida como deve, o que só pode suceder no caso dos remidos, consiste de um processo contínuo em que o crente se vai aproximando do grande alvo. Assim sendo, aquelas experiências a que chamamos de conversão, regeneração e santificação, etc., são tão-somente termos que descrevem o caminho pelo qual chegaremos à glorificação em Cristo. Mas aquele que nada sabe dessas admiráveis experiências místicas na realidade não está «vivendo», conforme os termos de I Cor. 8:6. Antes, estão mortos em seus delitos e transgressões, estão atolados nas trevas da rebelião e da condenação eterna.

A encarnação do Filho de Deus, Jesus Cristo, é que trouxe para os homens esse grande dom de Deus; pois foi como homem que o Filho de Deus, embora em um corpo mortal, mostrou aos homens de que modo se pode retornar a Deus.

José em Belém
Até mesmo um carpinteiro, às vezes, precisa de palavras,
E eu, que sou descendente de Davi,
Que entregou a sua vida, em amor a Ti.
(IB FA NTI)

ALVORADA
Ver Jó 38:12 e Juí. 19:25, para indicar a alvorada literal. Em Isa. 8:19,20, o termo é usado como símbolo de veracidade e discernimento. Em Lucas 1:78, a expressão «o sol nascente» indica a vinda do Messias. Simbolicamente, a alvorada representa o começo de algo novo, de renovação da esperança, que ultrapassa aquilo que é velho. Também pode ser um símbolo imaginário da juventude, diante da qual se desenrola o dia inteiro da experiência da terra. (TO Z)

AMA
A palavra pode indicar uma mulher que amamenta uma criança, embora também possa significar «governanta». A filha de Faraó aceitou a sugestão de Miriã de ser encontrada uma mulher hebréia para amamentar o infante Moisés (ver Êxo. 2:7). Noemi tomou a seus cuidados seu neto infante (ver Rute 4:16).

A ama que substituísse a mãe de uma criança, nesse mister da amamentação, adquiria certo prestígio na família, mesmo depois que a criança não mais precisasse ser amamentada. Esse costume vem desde os tempos mais remotos. Há duas ou três gerações atrás era costumeiro haver a *mãe-preta*, uma escrava africana que ajudava a amamentar um filho do senhor branco e a quem a criança se apegava emocionalmente, para nunca mais esquecê-la. O pai deste tradutor falava de vez em quando na sua «mãe-preta». Rebeca fez-se acompanhar por uma ama. Quando sua ama faleceu, o acontecimento foi considerado suficientemente importante para ficar registrado nas Escrituras. (Ver Gên. 35:8). Além disso, o local onde Débora, ama de Rebeca, faleceu, foi chamado Alom-Bacute, isto é, «carvalho do pranto», porquanto ela foi sepultada ao pé de um carvalho.

Uso metafórico. Diz Isaías 49:23: «Reis serão os teus aios, e rainhas as tuas amas...» Isso alude às bênçãos divinas especiais sobre Israel, de acordo com o discernimento do profeta. Paulo diz que Deus agiu como uma ama para Israel, enquanto esse povo vagueava pelo deserto (ver Atos 13:18). E, em I Tessalonicenses 2:7, Paulo se compara com uma «ama», em relação a seus convertidos, face ao gentil tratamento que lhes dispensava. (NTI S Z)

AMÃ
No hebraico, côvado. Era uma colina próxima de Gia, em Benjamim, no deserto de Gibeom, onde Joabe e Abisai cessaram a perseguição a Abner, depois que suas forças o derrotaram na batalha de Gibeom (ver II Sam. 2:24-32). Seguiu-se um período de trégua, e as duas forças armadas retornaram aos seus lares. O local é desconhecido. (S Z)

AMÃ
No hebraico, **lugar de reunião**. Uma cidade próxima de Sema e Moladá, no território sul da tribo de Judá (ver Jos. 15:26). Talvez ficasse situada no território posteriormente dado à tribo de Simeão (ver Jos. 19:1-9). O local é atualmente desconhecido. (S UN)

Em Tobias 14:2 e em I Esdras 10:7; 12:6; 13:3,12; 14:17 e 16:10,17, esse nome aparece como a forma grega do nome Hamã. (Ver sob *Hamã*).

AMADE
No hebraico, **povo durável**. Era uma aldeia ou território na fronteira de Aser, próximo de Alameleque (ver Jos. 19:26). Alguns identificam-na com Shefa Omar ou Shefa Amar, uma cidade-mercado a leste de Haifa. Mas o local é considerado desconhecido. (S Z)

AMADO
Notamos que no trecho de Rom. 1:7, Paulo usa esse vocábulo em conexão aos *eleitos*, e os santos são os chamados de Deus, os amados. Temos nisso o amor de Deus (ver o artigo sobre o *amor*), que enviou Cristo ao mundo, a fim de salvar aos homens (ver João 3:16). Ver as notas expositivas sobre esse versículo, no NTI, *in loc*. Ver Gál. 5:22 no NTI, que comenta sobre o amor como um dos aspectos do fruto do Espírito. Foi no amor que Deus nos predestinou para a adoção de filhos (ver Efé. 1:5). Israel, no tocante à eleição, é *amado* de Deus (ver Rom. 11:28). Os crentes são designados pelo adjetivo *amados* (ver Rom. 1:7; 12:19; 16:8,9,12; I Cor. 4:14,17; 10:14; 15:58; II Cor. 7:1; 12:19; Efé. 7:21; Fil. 2:12; 4:1; Col. 3:12; 4:7,19; I Tes. 1:4 e II Tes. 2:13). Fomos aceitos *no Amado* (Cristo) (ver Efé. 1:6). Com base na posição que os crentes têm no Amado, Paulo exige que eles possuam as diversas virtudes espirituais. Precisam possuí-las, a fim de ficar comprovada a validade e a realidade de sua posição espiritual. O amor requer amor da parte dos amados, sendo também a fonte de todas as virtudes espirituais (ver Gál. 5:22,23). Paulo usa o termo *amado* por trinta e duas vezes. Aparece por doze vezes nas epístolas de João. Ver o artigo sobre o *discípulo amado*. O livro Cantares de Salomão encerra a maioria das referências à palavra *amado* do Antigo Testamento (vinte e oito dentre as quarenta e quatro referências no A.T.). Ali temos o símbolo do amor de Cristo por Sua Igreja, bem como o amor da Igreja por Cristo, referido simbolicamente dentro da história romântica narrada no livro. O A.T., tal como o Novo, refere-se aos eleitos como *amados* (ver Deu.

AMAL — AMALEQUITAS

33:12; Nee. 13:26; Sal. 60:5; Jer. 11:15; 12:7; Dan. 9:3). (I IB NTI).

AMAL

No hebraico, **labutador**. Um aserita, o último nomeado dos quatro filhos de Helém (ver I Crô. 7:35), cerca de 1658-1600 A.C.

AMALEQUE

No hebraico, **habitante do vale**. Filho de Elifaz e sua concubina, Timna, e neto de Esaú. Sucedeu Gaetã no governo de Edom, ao sul de Judá (ver Gên. 36:12,16 e I Crô. 1:36). Há uma referência aos amalequitas, em Gên. 14:7, onde Quedorlaomer (c. 1900 A.C.) e seus associados subjugaram os amalequitas, entre outros povos. Essa referência pode ser um anacronismo, embora seja possível que algum outro Amaleque (desconhecido) esteja em foco; ou esse termo pode ter sido usado para identificar a terra que mais tarde tornou-se a pátria dos descendentes amalequitas de Esaú. Em Números 24:20, Balaão refere-se a Amaleque como «o primeiro das nações», mas que seria destruído. Isso não é uma alusão a tempos mais primitivos, mas apenas uma declaração de que os amalequitas seriam a primeira entre as nações a atacar Israel, quando do êxodo do Egito (ver Êxo. 17:8; Núm. 14:45). Os edomitas apossaram-se do território dos horeus. Nos tempos de Ezequias, os últimos redutos amalequitas em Edom foram dispersos pelos simeonitas (ver I Crô. 4:42,43). (FA S UN Z)

AMALEQUITAS

No heraico, **habitantes do vale**. Filo interpretava como *povo que lambe*. Nome de um povo que habitava a região ao sul da Palestina, entre a Iduméia e o Egito, bem como a leste do mar Morto e do monte Seir. De acordo com Josefo, os amalequitas habitavam Gobolites e Petra, e eram a nação mais aguerrida daquelas regiões. Ele assevera que ocupavam desde Pelúsio, no Egito, até o mar Vermelho. Ocupavam aquela porção de Israel que coube à tribo de Efraim. A primeira menção aos amalequitas se faz em Gênesis 14:7. Também exerciam influência para o norte, no território dos filisteus e na região de Efraim, conforme se aprende em Juí. 12:15. Os trechos de I Sam. 27:5-7 e 30:1 mostram que eles lançavam ataques contra aldeias da Filístia, como Ziclague, a poucos quilômetros ao norte de Beerseba, e que Áquis dera a Davi.

1. *Os primeiros atacantes*. Depois que Israel iniciou o êxodo, os amalequitas foram os primeiros adversários atacantes (ver Êxo. 17:8-13). Alguns têm sugerido que é improvável que em um período de tempo tão curto os descendentes do neto de Esaú pudessem ser suficientemente numerosos e poderosos ao ponto de formarem um exército capaz de desfechar esse ataque. Porém, mais ou menos no mesmo período, a tribo de Efraim crescera de tal modo que pôde lançar em armas 40.500 homens; e Manassés, 32.200. O ataque foi lançado contra a parte mais fraca das hostes de Israel, quando estavam cansados e desanimados (ver Deu. 25:17,18), porquanto a guerra nunca poupa os fracos e os inocentes. No Pentateuco, os amalequitas são freqüentemente mencionados em conjunto com os moabitas e amonitas. (Ver Juí. 3:13). E também são mencionados junto com os midianitas (Juí. 6:3). Eram tão numerosos como gafanhotos, possuidores de inúmeros camelos, numerosos como a areia do mar. Em I Samuel 15:6 também são mencionados paralelamente aos queneus. Israel venceu a batalha, mas com muitas perdas de vidas. Uma vez instalado em sua terra, o povo de Israel deveria exterminar os amalequitas (ver Deu. 25:19).

2. *Próximo encontro armado*. Os espias enviados para investigar a terra, trouxeram relatório de que o inimigo ao norte de Cades-Barnéia, no deserto de Parã e ao sul de Canaã, que incluía os amalequitas, era por demais forte e numeroso para ser derrotado pelos israelitas. Cabele e Josué protestaram contra esse parecer, mas a palavra deles não prevaleceu. Os israelitas rebelaram-se. Deus retirou deles a Sua bênção. Mais tarde, os israelitas atacaram os amalequitas por sua própria iniciativa, e foram derrotados (ver Núm. 14:39-45; Jos. 12:14 e 15:30). Os amalequitas mereciam o temor que infundiam, porquanto eram assassinos e assaltantes, desde o começo de sua história.

3. *No tempo dos Juízes*. Os amalequitas continuamente atacavam Israel com estocadas. Associavam-se então aos queneus (I Sam. 15:5,6), aos moabitas, amonitas e midianitas, todos eles ocupados em atividades pilhadoras (ver Juí. 3:12-14). Ver também Juízes 5:14, que sugere que havia contínuas batalhas entre os israelitas e os amalequitas. O trecho de Juízes 6:3,4 mostra a extensão desses ataques e suas conseqüências. De algumas vezes, Israel saía-se vencedor; de outras vezes, perdedor. Era uma guerra tribal sem qualquer trégua, desde o começo até o fim da história deles.

4. *Nos dias de Saul*. Saul, disposto a vingar-se, atacou o território dos midianitas com um exército de 210 mil homens, destruindo o inimigo com grande matança, embora o rei deles, Agague, fosse preservado em vida (ver I Sam. 15:1 ss). A vida desse rei foi poupada contrariamente à ordem divina de que os amalequitas fossem totalmente extintos, e ali mesmo Saul foi rejeitado como rei de Israel (ver I Sam. 15:10-23). Agague foi despedaçado pelo próprio profeta Samuel (ver I Sam. 15:24-33).

5. *Nos dias de Davi*. O conflito com os amalequitas prosseguiu. Durante cerca de vinte anos eles foram atacados por Davi (ver I Sam. 27:8), quando ele residia entre os filisteus, deixando para trás um rastro de sangue e destruição. Mas os amalequitas, em represália, não muito depois incendiaram Ziclague (ver I Sam. 30). Porém, exatamente quando celebravam a vitória, banqueteando-se, bebendo e dançando, Davi os apanhou de surpresa. Matou a todos, exceuando quatrocentos homens que conseguiram fugir em lombo de camelo (ver I Sam. 30:17). Portanto, o morticínio prosseguiu, aqui ou acolá, de um ou de outro lado da refrega, sendo surpreendente que alguém tenha sobrevivido às matanças. Essas são as atitudes dos homens que não dão lugar a Deus em suas vidas.

6. *Nos dias de Ezequias, rei de Judá*. Quinhentos homens dentre os descendentes de Simeão foram ao monte Seir e liquidaram o remanescente dos amalequitas, aparentemente o pequeno número que escapara das outras matanças. (Ver I Crô. 4:43). Depois disso, as Escrituras nunca mais mencionam os amalequitas. Talvez tivessem sido totalmente exterminados como nação. Na península do Sinai há maciças construções de pedras, pedras que têm entre 2 m e 2,5 m de comprimento. Alguns acreditam que são restos de construções das tribos amalequitas. (BA S SMI Z)

••• ••• •••

AMANA

No hebraico significa **fixo**, dando a entender um pacto. O cume montanhoso mencionado em Can. 4:8, na cadeia do Antilíbano, perto do rio que também se chamava Amana, como forma variante de Abana (conforme diz a nossa versão portuguesa, em II Reis 5:12). Parece que o nome do cume derivava-se do nome do rio. (S UN)

AMANTE

Palavra que no hebraico significa concubina. Em Ezequiel 23:20, a palavra refere-se a um amante do sexo masculino, mas nos outros trechos alude a uma mulher (ver, por exemplo, Gên. 22:24; Juí. 8:31, etc.). O termo hebraico aparece por trinta e sete vezes no Antigo Testamento. Em Daniel 5:2,3,23, embora nossa versão portuguesa e outras também digam «concubina», temos uma palavra hebraica diferente, que significa «jovem cantora». (Z)

AMARELO

Não há menção na Bíblia a algum corante dessa cor. Na antiguidade, corantes dessa cor eram produzidos provenientes de várias pétalas e ervas, como o açafrão, a romã verde, etc. (Ver também *Cores*). Algumas versões dizem *amarelo* em Salmos 68:13, onde a nossa versão portuguesa diz «brilho flavo do ouro», e onde outras versões dizem «esverdeado». Trata-se de um brilho iridescente, como se vê nas penas do pavão. A glória de Israel, enquanto a nação andava nos caminhos de Deus, é descrita como tal. Uma outra palavra hebraica, que algumas versões (como a nossa versão portuguesa) traduzem por «amarelo», descreve a aparência dos pêlos em meio a alguma infecção leprosa (ver Lev. 13:30). Quando presentes, esses pêlos indicavam a presença de uma enfermidade leprosa. Seu desaparecimento indicava que a doença era curável, e que não era do tipo de lepra que definha o organismo.

Em Apo. 6:8, quando o Senhor Jesus abriu o quarto selo, apareceu a João um cavalo «amarelo», representando a morte. O grego diz *chlorós* «esverdeado», palavra de onde vem nossa palavra moderna «clorofila», que dá a cor verde às folhas das plantas.

O amarelo simboliza as atividades intelectuais, tal como o vermelho simboliza fortes emoções, como a ira, e o azul simboliza as atividades espirituais, concordando com as cores da aura dos seres vivos, que podem ser fotografadas pelo método de Kirlian.

AMARGO

Ver Êxo. 1:14 e Jer. 9:15. A palavra é usada literal e simbolicamente, a fim de indicar aflição e miséria. A amarga servidão de Israel, no Egito, é representada por ervas amargosas. 1. Há o dia de amarguras (ver Amós 8:10). 2. Os caldeus foram chamados de «nação amarga e impetuosa» (Hab. 1:6). A *força* deles importava em miséria amarga para outros povos. 3. Há o fel de amargura, em Atos 8:3, que denota um estado de extrema perversidade, prejudicial ao próximo e ao próprio indivíduo. 4. Em Hebreus 12:15 lemos sobre uma «raiz de amargura», que indica pessoas ímpias que ensinam doutrinas contrárias à verdade, ou então qualquer pecado perigoso, que leve à apostasia. 5. O teste da água amarga tinha por intuito descobrir casos ocultos de adultério, ou era usado para aliviar os ciúmes de um marido cheio de suspeitas (ver Núm. 5:18-27). 6. Condições morais más são como uvas amargas (Deu. 32:32). 7. O julgamento divino é amargo (ver Jer. 4:18; Amós 8:12 e Apo. 8:11). (I IB ID NTI S)

AMARIAS

No hebraico significa **palavra de Yahweh**. É nome de várias pessoas do Antigo Testamento:

1. Um levita da linhagem de Eleazar, filho de Meraiote e avô de Sadoque, o sacerdote (ver I Crô. 6:7,52). Era pai de Aitube, pai de Sadoque, cerca de 1100 A.C.

2. Um levita da linhagem de Coate, nos dias de Davi (ver I Crô. 23:19 e 24:23). — Cerca de 1015 A.C.

3. Um levita da linhagem de Eleazar, filho de Azarias. Ministrou no templo de Salomão (ver I Crô. 6:11; Eze. 7:3 e Esdras 8:2), como sumo sacerdote.

4. Sumo sacerdote durante o reinado de Josafá (ver II Crô. 19:11). Não somos informados sobre o nome de seu pai (cerca de 912-895 A.C.).

5. Filho de Sefatias de Judá, um antepassado de Ataías (ver Nee. 11:4). Descendia de Peres, filho de Judá, e talvez fosse o mesmo Inri, referido em I Crô. 9:4. Cerca de 465 A.C.

6. Um levita que viveu durante o reinado de Ezequias (ver II Crô. 31:15), que ajudou na distribuição das ofertas entre as cidades sacerdotais, em cerca de 430 A.C.

7. Homem da tribo de Judá, filho de Bani, que se casou com uma mulher estrangeira (ver Eze. 10:42), em cerca de 465 A.C.

8. Um sacerdote que regressou a Jerusalém com sua família e assinou o pacto junto com Neemias (ver Nee. 10:3 e 12:2). Foi pai de Joanã, sacerdote do tempo de Joaquim (ver Nee. 12:13). Alguns o identificam com Imer (ver I Crô. 24:14 e Esd. 2:37; 10:20; I Esdras 5:24). Cerca de 430 A.C.

9. Antepassado do profeta Sofonias, filho de Ezequias (talvez o rei). Ver Sof. 1:1. Cerca de 630 A.C. Talvez tivesse sido o avô de Sofonias. (S UN Z)

AMARNA, TELL EL

Ver sobre **Tell el-Amarna**.

AMASA

No hebraico, **carga** ou **carregador de carga**. Nome de duas pessoas no Antigo Testamento:

1. Amasa, capitão do exército israelita, nomeado por Absalão quando tentou destronar Davi. Era filho de Jeter ou Itra e Abigail, irmã de Davi, pelo que era primo de Absalão (ver II Sam. 17:25; I Crô. 2:17 e I Reis 2:5,32). Também era primo de Joabe, cuja mãe, Zeruia, também era irmã de Davi (ver I Crô. 2:16,17). Quando o conflito ocorreu, Amasa foi derrotado por Joabe. Após a eliminação dos partidários de Absalão, Davi, desgostoso com Joabe por ter matado Absalão contra as suas ordens, ofereceu a Amasa o perdão e o comando do exército, em substituição a Joabe, cuja insolência o tornara insuportável (ver II Sam. 19:13). Quando Seba, filho de Bicri, revoltou-se, Davi ordenou a Amasa que reunisse todo o Judá para atacar àquele; mas Amasa procrastinou. Então Davi ordenou que Abisai cumprisse a ordem. Joabe, com seus homens, o acompanhou. Ao atingirem a grande pedra em Gibeom, Amasa veio com suas forças para unir-se a eles. Joabe, incendiado pelo ciúme, tomou Amasa pela barba e disse: «Vais bem, meu irmão?», como se fosse saudá-lo com um ósculo, mas em vez

AMASAI — ÂMBAR

disso, matou-o à espada (ver II Sam. 20:4-14). Não sofreu qualquer castigo por causa disso, e liderou as forças combinadas, levando-as à vitória sobre Seba. Em meio a tantas mortes, o que significava mais uma?

2. Um chefe efraimita que, tal como outros, resistiu com veemência à retenção de prisioneiros que Peca, rei de Israel, levara cativos, em uma bem-sucedida campanha com Acaz, rei de Judá (ver II Crô. 27:12), em cerca de 741 A.C. Era filho de Hadlai (ver II Crô. 28:8-15). Uniu-se ao profeta Odede na advertência contra o ato de conservar escravizados os prisioneiros, e então providenciou para que retornassem a Jericó. (S UN Z)

AMASAI

No hebraico, **carregador de cargas**. Foi nome de várias pessoas no Antigo Testamento:

1. Um coatita, pai de Maate, um antepassado de Samuel (ver I Crô. 6:25,35; II Crô. 19:11), cerca de 1410-1045 A.C.

2. O principal capitão dos homens das tribos de Judá e Benjamim que se aliaram a Davi, em Ziclague (ver I Crô. 12:18), em cerca de 1061 A.C. Um dos trinta homens da elite de Davi, poderosos guerreiros. Alguns o identificam com Amasa, o chefe militar nomeado por Absalão (ver II Sam. 17:25). Mas outros o identificam com Abisai, irmão de Joabe (ver I Crô. 11:20). O problema envolvido nessas identificações permanece porque nenhum desses três nomes (Amasai, Amasa ou Abisai) aparece nas listas dos trinta heróis, conforme se lê em II Sam. 23 e I Crô. 11.

3. Um sacerdote que ajudou no transporte da arca à casa de Obede-Edom (ver I Crô. 15:24), em cerca de 1043 A.C.

4. Um outro coatita, pai de um diferente Maate, no reinado de Ezequias (ver II Crô. 19:12), e talvez da mesma família. Certamente não há qualquer possibilidade de identificação com o primeiro desta lista, a despeito das semelhanças de nomes envolvidos. (FA S Z)

AMASIAS

No hebraico, **Yahweh tem força**. Foi filho de Zicri, da tribo de Judá. Foi chefe do exército de Josafá (ver II Crô. 17:16), em cerca de 440 A.C. (UN)

AMASIS

Supõe-se ter sido o **Faraó** cuja residência em **Taínes** é mencionada em Jer. 43:9, e que reinou entre 569 e 525 A. C. (S)

AMASSAI

Provavelmente um erro textual em lugar de Amasai. Foi filho de Azareel, um valente sacerdote do tempo de Neemias (Nee. 11:13), talvez o mesmo Masai de I Crô. 9:12. Cerca de 445 A.C. (S)

AMAZIAS

No hebraico quer dizer **força de Yahweh**, nome de quatro pessoas no Antigo Testamento:

1. Filho e sucessor de Joás. Foi o nono rei de Judá, tendo subido ao trono com a idade de 25 anos. Reinou por vinte e nove anos (ver II Reis 14:1,2; II Crô. 25:1), cerca de 800-771 A.C. A informação dada em II Reis 14:2 parece ser contradita por II Reis 14:17:

«Amazias...viveu quinze anos depois da morte de Jeoás», o que poderia significar que ele não era a autoridade executiva real de seu reino. Nenhuma solução convincente tem sido encontrada para esse problema; e outros informes sobre outros reis também envolvem problemas. Amazias começou seu reinado executando aqueles que haviam assassinado seu pai, embora tivesse poupado os filhos dos homicidas (ver Deu. 24:16). No décimo segundo ano de seu reinado tentou recuperar Edom, que se revoltara durante o reinado de Jeorão. Organizou um exército de trezentos mil homens e também contratou cem mil mercenários (primeira menção de tal força armada na história de Israel). Porém, despediu os mercenários, em vista da ordem dada por um profeta. Regressando à terra deles, eles saquearam várias cidades de Judá para mostrarem seu descontentamento por haverem sido dispensados. Amazias obteve grande vitória, tendo sido mortos dez mil edomitas, além do que outros dez mil foram despedaçados e lançados abaixo das rochas de Sela. Ele tomou muito despojo, incluindo os ídolos de monte Seir; e então caiu no erro de lhes prestar culto. Por causa disso, os desastres tiveram início. Desafiou o mais poderoso Jeoás, rei de Israel (ver II Reis 14:7-19) e subseqüentemente, perdeu seu reinado e seu povo ficou sujeito a Israel (ver II Reis 14:8-14; II Crô. 15:17-24). Permaneceu no trono, mas durante quinze anos não foi o verdadeiro mandatário da nação. Então ele foi vitimado por uma intriga da corte, foi perseguido até Laquis, e ali foi assassinado. Seu corpo foi transportado de volta a Jerusalém, e foi sepultado nos túmulos reais, fora do monte Sião (ver II Reis 14:3-20 e II Crô. 25:2-28).

2. Pai de Joás. Posteriormente, Joás tornou-se um dos chefes simeonitas que expulsaram os amalequitas do vale de Gedor, no tempo de Ezequias (ver I Crô. 4:34), em cerca de 726 A.C. Acerca do pai de Joás, nada se sabe dizer.

3. Um levita, filho de Merari (I Crô. 6:45). Era cantor e estava a serviço do tabernáculo que havia defronte da área onde mais tarde Salomão edificou o templo, antes de 1000 A.C.

4. Um sacerdote dos bezerros de ouro em Betel, no tempo de Jeroboão II, cerca de 786-746 A.C. Sentiu-se perturbado com as profecias condenatórias de Amós, e exortou-a a ir para o reino de Judá para profetizar ali. Amós o pôs no seu devido lugar, falando sobre a grande degradação que sua família sofreria quando do vindouro cativeiro do reino do norte (ver Amós 7:10-17). Cerca de 770 A.C. (ND UN Z)

ÂMBAR

Uma resina vegetal fóssil, amarela e translúcida que, por meio da perda de substâncias voláteis, oxidação e polimerização, atinge um estado estável. O período de sepultamento necessário para que esse estado seja atingido pode alcançar milhões de anos; e, visto que um *fóssil* implica em uma vida pré-histórica, a resina deve ter sido exudada por alguma árvore pelo menos antes de qualquer história conhecida. O âmbar aparece como módulos irregulares ou sob a forma de gotas, em todos os tons amarelos, com algumas manchas alaranjadas, marrons, e, mais raramente, vermelhas (ver Eze. 1:4, onde algumas traduções preferem dizer «metal brilhante», como nossa versão portuguesa, *bronze* ou *metal amarelo*). Há variedades em coloração, de translúcidas a transparentes. O material é muito valorizado para o fabrico de jóias, e isso desde tempos pré-históricos. Na passagem de Ezequiel referida acima, o termo hebraico *chasmal*, «âmbar», provavelmente indicava um metal (metal polido), e não a resina fóssil. Em Ezequiel 1:4,27 e 8:2, a glória divina e o resplendor estão em pauta. A palavra grega ali usada, *elektron*, pode referir-se à resina ou a uma liga de ouro e prata, que os mineralogistas modernos chamam de *electrum*. Não se sabe com certeza se os hebreus estavam familiarizados com a substância fóssil. A palavra traduzida *âmbar* era usada para designar a cor amarela brilhante (característica do âmbar). Ver também Apo. 1:15 e Eze. 8:27. (FA UN Z)

AMBIÇÃO

Ver o artigo sobre o **orgulho**. O desejo de cumprimento ou realização é bom e significativo em qualquer vida, incluindo a vida motivada pelo conhecimento espiritual. Paulo usa palavras e expressões como «avançar», «esquecer o passado», «a corrida», «o alvo a ser atingido», além de termos concernentes à aprovação de Deus diante de tais ações. O fato de que João Marcos foi rejeitado a princípio por Paulo parece ter-se baseado sobre a maneira fácil em que o primeiro abandonou seu dever (ver Atos 15:38). Sua posterior aceitação por Paulo, como «útil» (II Tim. 4:11), mostra-nos que Marcos corrigiu a sua falta de ambição espiritual, e não que Paulo se tornou mais generoso.

A qualidade de ambição espiritual, porém, pode ser distorcida pelo orgulho e pelo auto-interesse. Os homens podem construir templos a fim de serem elogiados pelos homens, ou para receberem maiores ofertas em dinheiro. Os homens podem pregar sermões eloqüentes e obter vasto acúmulo de conhecimento a fim de se distinguirem, e não a fim de glorificar Aquele que os enviou. Nossa ambição deve ser Cristocêntrica; e então será digna de louvor. Especialmente repelente é a competição no seio da Igreja, as lutas pelo poder, alicerçadas sobre as ambições pessoais. Ver o NTI em I Cor. 3:3 ss. (H NTI)

AMBIENTE

1. *Cosmológico*. Uma parte do argumento em favor de Deus, com base no *cosmos* (argumento cosmológico) é a observação de que seria impossível sustentar a vida sem a localização própria do globo terrestre em um lugar, e sob circunstâncias que permitiriam a vida, como condições atmosféricas e proximidade suficiente do sol para haver luz e calor suficientes, mas não perto demais, para que o calor não fosse excessivo. Quem é teísta vê em tudo isso a mão providencial de Deus. Faz parte de um desígnio, pelo que a questão do meio ambiente constitui um aspecto do argumento teleológico. Ambos os argumentos são descritos em artigos separados. No artigo sobre Deus, sob o subtítulo Provas da Existência de Deus, são oferecidas muitas dessas provas. As causas, portanto, não são meramente lineares, isto é, não acontecem em uma seqüência histórica. Também são presentes e hierárquicas. Em outras palavras, qualquer acontecimento presente é produzido por uma série de causas presentes. Por exemplo: Para que um homem continue a viver, seu coração precisa continuar batendo. Para que seu coração bata, ele precisa das condições físicas apropriadas, em seu próprio organismo. Mas, para tanto, ele precisa das condições externas apropriadas, no meio ambiente. Ele não pode permanecer debaixo da água sem equipamento especial, e nem pode subir alto demais, onde não há oxigênio. Além disso, o globo terrestre, dentro do sistema solar, precisa estar localizado em um local favorável, a fim de que seja possível a sustentação da vida biológica na terra, porque, em caso contrário, seria inútil ter um coração que pudesse funcionar, se não houvesse também o meio ambiente cosmológico apropriado. Portanto, temos uma hierarquia de causas presentes que são necessárias para sustentar a vida, bem como a Causa Primária que deu origem à vida, antes de mais nada.

2. *Meio ambiente natural*. Onde o homem deve viver, como ele está localizado, são questões importantes do ponto de vista prático e ético. Por quai razão transportaríamos água para um deserto, localizando ali milhões de pessoas? Por que não localizar aquelas pessoas perto da água? Por que construir represas apenas para impedir dilúvios? Por que não localizar as pessoas em áreas sem risco de enchentes e dilúvios? É um erro construir casas e convidar pessoas para virem residir nelas, em áreas onde se sabe que há o perigo constante de terremotos, conforme já tem acontecido na já infame fratura de San Andreas, na Califórnia.

3. *Aspecto local e prático*. As cidades e as casas onde os homens vivem afetam a maneira deles pensarem sobre si mesmos. A higiene ou a imundície nas cidades refletem o estado moral interno das pessoas. Escrever bobagens nas paredes e nos edifícios é um desrespeito à propriedade e aos direitos de outros, bem como um reflexo da ausência de senso de beleza, por parte dos que assim fazem. Tem-se mostrado que a decoração das salas de aula, e o uso de tapetes para amortecer os ruídos e emprestar beleza ao ambiente, produzem um melhor comportamento da parte dos alunos. Os projetos de renovação das favelas e pardieiros têm demonstrado duas coisas: Algumas pessoas reagem a um novo e melhor meio ambiente por um senso renovado de valor pessoal, e assim esforçam-se por preservar o que há de melhor. Outras pessoas, entretanto, transformam em um novo pardieiro ou favela um novo distrito residencial no espaço de alguns poucos anos. Ambos os grupos estão demonstrando condições internas. Para que se tire um homem de sua favela, será mister primeiro tirar a favela do coração daquele homem. As questões primárias são sempre espirituais e morais, e esses valores são refletidos nas condições físicas que as pessoas criam ao redor de si mesmas.

4. *Fatores sociológicos*. Uma vez que um homem tenha um lugar para residir, e meios razoáveis de subsistência, ele começará a cercar-se de estruturas sociais, políticas e religiosas que haverão de governar a maneira em que ele viverá, bem como a maneira como ele se relacionará com outras pessoas. As leis de um povo, como elas são cumpridas, dizem-nos muito sobre aquele povo. As ênfases na indústria revelam-nos o que é importante para um povo qualquer. Israel, por exemplo, a despeito de todas as suas falhas e de sua história violenta, era uma nação sã, com forte fervor religioso e moral. E, embora pequena, deixou uma influência permanente sobre o mundo inteiro. Por essa razão foi que Israel foi escolhida para promover grandes alterações históricas, de cunho espiritual, como se deu nos casos da instituição da lei e do primeiro advento de Cristo. E isso sucederá novamente, ao começar a era milenar. Um novo movimento religioso produzirá uma mais elevada espiritualidade para toda a humanidade; e Israel, como nação, tornar-se-á importante por esse motivo. A ameaça de destruição por armas atômicas deriva-se da perversidade interna das pessoas e de toda a humanidade. Os gastos com as indústrias de

AMBIENTE E HERANÇA

armamentos destruidores ultrapassam em muito ao que é gasto com a educação, a saúde e o bem-estar público, mostrando-nos muito da real natureza decaída do homem. O Brasil já é o quinto maior produtor mundial de instrumentos bélicos, e atualmente é um importante fator econômico em nosso país. Muitos encaram a questão com orgulho, visto que o tanque de guerra brasileiro opera com maior eficiência destrutiva que o tanque de guerra francês. Porém, é difícil perceber como as pessoas podem orgulhar-se daquilo que promove a destruição e o ódio. Lemos narrativas sobre o velho oeste norte-americano, tempo em que certos indivíduos produziam e vendiam armas tanto para os criadores de gado quanto para os índios, pouco se importando com a matança daí resultante, contanto que eles vendessem as armas e se enriquecessem. Se uma nação faz a mesma coisa em escala internacional, a moralidade envolvida seria superior à moralidade envolvida naquela venda de armas para «cowboys» e índios? (B E)

AMBIENTE E HERANÇA

Um homem é o que é por causa do ambiente no qual vive, ou aquilo que ele herda determina o tipo de ambiente que ele produzirá? Nessa controvérsia, apresso-me a acrescentar que um grande fator tem sido deixado fora das nossas cogitações. Também há uma hereditariedade espiritual, uma certa qualidade de alma, que os homens trazem consigo. Isso quase sempre é desprezado pelos estudiosos do meio ambiente, e por aqueles que supõem que tudo depende da herança genética.

1. O crime como exemplo. Tem sido provado que pelo menos a metade dos criminosos, nos Estados Unidos da América, não se tornam tais por razões econômicas. De fato, alguns de nossos piores criminosos têm sido aqueles que dispõem de mais dinheiro e vivem no mais alto estilo de vida. A Máfia é um exemplo disso, que não pode ser ignorado. Os estudos têm demonstrado que existe uma *mentalidade criminosa*. Certos indivíduos são diferentes desde os seus mais tenros anos, mentindo, furtando e abusando do próximo, embora pertencentes a boas famílias, e contando com irmãos e irmãs inteiramente normais. Um artigo publicado pela *Reader's Digest*, intitulado «*The Criminal Mind: A Startling New Look*», de junho de 1978, destacou diante da atenção geral fatos dessa natureza. Muitos tipos criminosos crescem, diferenciando-se desde a infância dos demais, e terminam transgredindo em três áreas do crime: a propriedade alheia, o sexo e a integridade física de outras pessoas. Marianne Rasmuson, pesquisadora sueca, professora da Universidade de Umea, no norte da Suécia, tentou provar em tese que o crime é hereditário, e que as tendências criminosas passam de pai para filho, em muitos casos. Os estudos feitos por ela centralizaram-se em torno do exame de mil crianças que vieram a tornar-se criminosas; e a conclusão dela foi que, na maioria dos casos, as condições ambientais pouco tinham a ver com o que sucedeu àquelas pessoas. Porém, levemos um pouco mais adiante essa questão da hereditariedade. Não haverá também uma herança espiritual? Esta última poderia assumir várias formas, a saber: a. *A preexistência da alma*. Os pais alexandrinos da Igreja ensinavam que a alma vem a este mundo depois de já haver passado por uma antiga história, como uma entidade espiritual, trazendo consigo a sua própria bagagem moral e espiritual. Se isso é verdade, então é fácil explicar tanto os criminosos quanto os gigantes espirituais; e nenhum desses casos teria qualquer coisa a ver com as influências ambientais. João Batista foi cheio do Espírito Santo desde antes de seu nascimento, quando ainda era feto. Mas isso foi uma simples e caprichosa escolha divina, ou João Batista já era uma entidade espiritual bem desenvolvida, cujo começo nada teve a ver com a sua associação com o corpo físico, com uma existência terrena tão breve? Cremos na preexistência de Cristo. Ele não foi o que foi, meramente porque desenvolveu-se espiritualmente com espantosa rapidez em Sua vida física. Outro tanto poderia ocorrer com todas as pessoas, as quais, de fato ou potencialmente, são irmãs dEle. Ver o artigo sobre a *alma*, onde se incluem teorias sobre a origem da mesma. b. *A reencarnação*. A herança espiritual que alguém traz consigo poderia envolver mais de uma vida física, além de uma prévia e longa existência da alma. O Novo Testamento mostra que assim se dá, pelo menos em alguns dos casos. Espera-se que Elias cumprirá uma outra missão terrena (ver Mat. 11:10,14; 17:10 ss.). É doutrina judaica padrão que não apenas Elias, mas também vários outros profetas do Antigo Testamento terão mais de uma vida e missão terrenas, o que se reflete em Mat. 16:14. Além disso, acerca do anticristo, é dito que ele já tivera outra existência terrena, descera ao hades, e retornará para a sua missão destruidora final (ver Apo. 17:8,10,11). Portanto, do ponto de vista da Bíblia, podemos dizer que pelo menos algumas pessoas são o que são por causa de vidas anteriores, quer espirituais, quer físicas, ou mesmo ambas as coisas. No tocante a argumentos em prol e contra a *reencarnação*, ver o artigo sobre esse assunto. c. Ademais, é possível que certos aspectos da condição espiritual de alguém tenham sido herdados de atitudes morais e espirituais, mediadas *através do veículo físico*, especificamente as qualidades cerebrais.

Entretanto, a experiência humana demonstra amplamente que os criminosos também são formados por meio de fatores ambientais como a pobreza, o aprendizado com criminosos, devido à associação com eles, a defesa dos direitos e da honra do indivíduo, a fome, a perversão das atitudes, devido a uma comunidade violenta. Parece correto dizer, pois, que os atos anti-sociais, tal como as atividades criminosas e todas as demais atitudes, os vícios e as qualidades de uma pessoa podem todas derivar-se de três origens: 1. O meio ambiente; 2. a hereditariedade genética (herança física) e 3. a herança espiritual, sem importar exatamente como ela opera.

2. O ambiente e a hereditariedade interagem. Uma coisa não pode ser separada da outra. É verdade que as variações na estatura física dependem de diferenças genéticas. Mas também é verdade que a altura média das pessoas aumenta dramaticamente como resultado de uma melhor nutrição. Portanto, o meio ambiente pode alterar o que sucede aos genes, embora isso requeira tempo. A radiação ou certos elementos químicos podem alterar o material genético. Os genes podem influenciar o meio ambiente; quando uma pessoa é o que é devido à herança genética, muda seu meio ambiente. Não somos escravos de nosso meio ambiente. Podemos alterar o meio em que vivemos. Mas alguns estados psicóticos são definidamente herdados. No caso da esquizofrenia, por exemplo, o risco de gêmeos idênticos serem afligidos por essa perturbação é de cinquenta por cento, ao passo que no caso de outros irmãos e irmãs a incidência é de cerca de dez a quinze por cento apenas, o que ainda assim é taxa bem mais alta do que no caso da população em geral. O filho de uma mulher

AMBIENTE, POLUIÇÃO DO — AMBIGÜIDADE

esquizofrênica, embora removido para longe da influência dela, ainda assim retém a mesma porcentagem de risco de vir a tornar-se um esquizofrênico como se tivesse ficado com sua mãe. A habilidade nativa quanto ao quociente de inteligência está bem intimamente ligada à herança genética, embora, como é óbvio, qualquer pessoa pode melhorar muito aquilo que herdou, chegando mesmo a produzir maravilhas com uma mente apenas mediana.

3. Responsabilidade espiritual. a. Devemos usar e desenvolver nossas habilidades naturais ao máximo. b. Devemos ser sensíveis ao meio ambiente, alterando-o para melhor. c. No caso dos cientistas, devem identificar — elementos físico-químicos prejudiciais, removendo-os do meio ambiente. Consideremos os produtos industriais, destacando entre eles a indústria do fumo. Governos e igrejas também têm responsabilidade de manifestar-se quanto a esse particular. d. Devemos estar interessados na herança espiritual, aprendendo mais sobre ela e promovendo-a, pois esse, afinal, é o mais importante de todos os fatores.

AMBIENTE, POLUIÇÃO DO

1. *Causas da poluição*. Excesso de população, acúmulo de riquezas e ganância, bem como o abuso da tecnologia. As soluções técnicas não funcionam bem enquanto não houver mudança de atitude. Do ponto de vista teológico, pode-se dizer que uma maior apreciação pela beleza da natureza, vinculada a uma cobiça menor, poderia ser a base filosófica da inovação.

2. *O problema populacional*. Há excesso populacional quando o país envolvido não tem meios para manter sua população em níveis razoáveis de vida. Um país muito grande, com vasta extensão territorial, pode sofrer de excesso de população se não dispor de agricultura e de tecnologia suficientes para servir aos seus habitantes. O câncer é um crescimento, mas não é saudável. É nesse ponto que entram as questões morais do aborto e do controle de nascimento. Nossas atitudes básicas sobre a vida determinam o que pensamos acerca dessas coisas. Algumas pessoas estão convencidas de que é um crime destruir um feto, ou a destruição do esperma masculino por meios artificiais. Outros, entretanto, dispõem-se a não destruir um feto, mas estão prontos para destruir o esperma masculino, porque há abundância do mesmo. Ainda outros, sem hesitação dispõem-se a destruir tanto uma coisa quanto outra. Ver os artigos sobre *aborto* e *controle de nascimentos*. Cidades superpopulosas produzem condições ambientais poluídas.

3. *O problema das riquezas materiais*. O desejo de possuir mais inspira as indústrias a produzirem mais, por razões puramente econômicas. A ganância sempre está envolvida. Disso resulta a poluição industrial. Além disso, a produção desenfreada de bens de consumo resulta no abuso dos recursos naturais, na dilapidação da terra, na poluição dos rios mediante os resíduos industriais, na poluição do ar devido à fumaça tóxica das chaminés das fábricas. Aqueles que querem juntar mais dinheiro não pretendem reduzir seus lucros fazendo caros investimentos em aparelhos que controlam a poluição, e os governos que querem o dinheiro proveniente dos impostos, favorecem o desenvolvimento industrial descontrolado.

4. *O abuso da tecnologia*. Nos Estados Unidos da América, a poluição multiplicou dez vezes mais rapidamente que o produto nacional bruto. A tecnologia tem sido usada para produzir muitos produtos que não podem ser reciclados, que não se desintegram com a passagem do tempo. Têm sido desenvolvidas fontes de energia que não se incomodam em preservar a natureza.

5. *Ecologia*. A ecologia é o estudo do inter-relacionamento entre os organismos e seus meios ambientes. *Princípios básicos*. a. Todas as coisas estão interligadas umas às outras. b. Tudo deve ir para algum lugar. É impossível simplesmente desfazermo-nos de alguma coisa. Qualquer coisa que joguemos fora terá alguma influência em algum lugar. c. As extrações impensadas da natureza não nos fornecem nenhuma refeição grátis, pois, em algum lugar e em algum tempo teremos de pagar por tais extrações. d. A introdução de substâncias artificiais no meio ambiente pode ser altamente prejudicial. Mesmo nas regiões árticas, onde não há indústrias, os resíduos industriais sujam o gelo e a neve. O conceito de «vizinhança» internacionalizou-se. O homem labora em erro ao pensar que seus avanços tecnológicos libertaram-no de sua dependência à natureza. Se as plantas verdes forem mortas, a vida animal deixará de existir. Se envenenarmos a vegetação, as pessoas ficarão doentes.

6. *Um ponto de vista ético da natureza*. É errado prejudicarmos outras pessoas. E também é errado prejudicarmos o meio ambiente em que as pessoas vivem. São Francisco, o santo patrono dos ecologistas, acreditava na autonomia espiritual de todas as porções da natureza. Não apenas o homem, mas a própria natureza tem direitos. O homem não pode exercer um domínio absoluto sobre as coisas. São Benedito insistia para que os monges aprendessem a cuidar da terra, vivendo dela. O Antigo Testamento tem provisões acerca da natureza e de todas as formas de vida, conforme podemos ver em Salmos 104. O trecho de Êxodo 23:10 impunha o ano sabático, a fim de promover a fertilidade da terra e impedir abusos. O pacto de Deus com Noé incluiu todos os tipos de vida, e não apenas a vida humana (ver Gên. 9). Deus criou a natureza, pelo que a natureza, inteiramente à parte do homem, tem valor. A terra pertence ao Senhor (Sal. 24:1). Deus tanto é o criador quanto é o sustentador, e os homens deveriam cuidar para ajudar nessa sustentação.

7. *O homem como um mordomo*. O homem tanto está na natureza como está sujeito a ela. Também foi-lhe determinada uma função dentro da natureza, do que resulta sua responsabilidade em protegê-la e preservá-la. Foi-lhe determinado que subjugasse e exercesse domínio (ver Gên. 1), mas também foi-lhe ordenado que cultivasse a terra (ver Gên. 2). O homem é mordomo de grande variedade de bênçãos, tanto espirituais quanto materiais. Deve mostrar-se ativo na manutenção de ambas as formas. O homem precisa aprender a exercer domínio, sem tornar-se destruidor. Coisa alguma, na atualidade, é tão horrenda quanto a ameaça de destruição atômica. O avanço tecnológico do homem tem ultrapassado em muito o seu progresso moral e espiritual. O monstro criado pelo homem agora volta-se para despedaçá-lo. O homem tem abusado da natureza, e a natureza talvez tenha de vergastá-lo, a fim de devolver-lhe o bom senso. (E H)

AMBIGÜIDADE

1. *Ambigüidade verbal*. Muitas palavras têm dois sentidos ou mais. O contexto precisa definir o sentido tencionado, ou a comunicação será obscura ou falaz.

2. **Ambigüidade sistemática**. Palavras e expressões que sempre têm o mesmo sentido no contexto de um sistema; mas diferentes sentidos quando são usadas em um sistema ou disciplina diferente. Tanto pessoas quanto lugares podem ser adjetivados de «saudáveis», mas não faz sentido perguntar se uma cidade é mais saudável do que uma pessoa que vive naquela cidade. As duas categorias não podem ser comparadas.

3. **Ambigüidade teológica**. Isso ocorre devido a dois fenômenos principais. Em primeiro lugar, dentro do vocabulário teológico. As palavras que usamos para descrever conceitos grandiosos se esboroam ante a tentativa. Em segundo lugar, os próprios conceitos são conhecidos apenas imperfeitamente. Por exemplo, chamamos Deus de «espírito». Isso faz algum sentido, pois o que não é matéria, é espírito, e negamos qualquer materialidade em Deus. Porém quando tentamos definir *espírito*, topamos com ambigüidade tanto verbal quanto de conceito. Falamos sobre livre-arbítrio e determinismo, e compreendemos apenas imperfeitamente ambas as idéias. E muito menos ainda somos capazes de reconciliar uma com a outra. Ver os artigos sobre ambos esses assuntos. E então com tristeza vemos que os homens separam amigos, igrejas e denominações por causa dessas questões, que permanecem essencialmente misteriosas, e não cedem diante de nossas descrições verbais. (F)

AMBROSIANOS

1. Nome dado a uma ordem monástica fundada sob o patrocínio de Ambrósio, por Alexandre Givelli, Antônio Petrasancta e Alberto Besazzi, perto de Milão. Em 1375, Gregório XII confiou a eles a regra de Agostinho, modificada por certas constituições especiais. A nova ordem adotou então o nome de *Frates Sancti Ambrosii ad Nemus*. Eles seguiram o rito ambrosiano na liturgia, e seus deveres incluíam a pregação e o ensino. Em 1441, Eugênio IV unificou todos os mosteiros ambrosianos, até ali então unidos apenas na idéia e nos costumes. Em 1579, Carlos Borromeu reformou a disciplina da ordem. Em 1589, Xisto V uniu os Irmãos de São Barnabé à Congregação de Santo Ambrósio. Mas, em 1650, a ordem foi dissolvida. (E)

2. Seita anabatista radical, do séc. 16, que afirmava ter comunicação imediata com Deus, por meio do Espírito. Não tinham um ministério formal. Ambrósio, seu líder, dizia ter recebido revelações, as quais, para ele e seus seguidores, tinham maior autoridade do que a das Escrituras.

AMBROSIASTRO

O pseudo-Ambrósio, autor desconhecido de um breve mas importante comentário sobre as epístolas de Paulo, escrito em Roma, entre 366 e 384. Na Idade Média, a obra era comumente atribuída a Ambrósio. Essa obra reveste-se de certa importância no terreno da crítica textual do Novo Testamento, por causa do texto antigo que a mesma preserva, quanto aos escritos paulinos. (E GT KE ME)

AMBRÓSIO DE MILÃO

Suas datas: 340-397. Um dos mais notáveis exegetas, teólogo-filósofos, compositores de hinos e oradores da Igreja Cristã antiga. Foi a ponte intelectual que ligou Cipriano a Agostinho (ver os artigos sobre eles). Foi bispo de Milão, e atarefou-se no ensino e na defesa das doutrinas cristãs, opondo-se à heresia ariana que afirmava que Cristo e Deus não são da mesma substância, pondo em dúvida a divindade de Cristo. Exerceu influência sobre Agostinho, quanto a estas idéias: a. A fé repousa sobre a autoridade da Bíblia; b. a razão é importante na explicação e defesa da verdade; c. a propagação física do pecado adâmico na raça humana; d. justificação somente pela fé; e. ênfase sobre a missão de Cristo contra a religião legalista; f. ensinos sobre o batismo e a Igreja, que correspondem às interpretações de Agostinho, e que talvez as influenciaram; g. de modo geral, a doutrina paulina, especialmente aquela exposta na epístola aos Romanos; h. separação entre Igreja e estado, contra o ensino posterior de Agostinho, de que a Igreja seria mestra do estado, e superior ao mesmo.

Embora fosse erudito na Bíblia e expositor, Ambrósio conhecia os escritos clássicos e foi influenciado pelos mesmos, vendo a importância da filosofia grega e do conhecimento através da razão. Foi o primeiro teólogo cristão a usar a expressão «virtudes cardeais», que encontrou nos escritos de Cícero sobre as classificações morais de Platão. Foi professor eloqüente, que empregou o método alegórico dos alexandrinos.

Ambrósio foi zeloso promotor do monasticismo no Ocidente. Seus sermões exaltavam tão poderosamente a virgindade que muitas famílias proibiam suas filhas a ouvirem-nos.

Obras: *De Mysteriis*, sobre o batismo e a eucaristia; *De fide*, cinco livros; *De Spiritu*, três livros; *De Incarnationis sacramento*, doutrinas fundamentais da fé, em oposição ao arianismo; muitas exposições de livros do Antigo Testamento; *Sermones*, e noventa e duas epístolas. Todos os seus escritos distinguem-se pela nobreza e pela eloqüência.

AMÉM (amém, amém: ver **Em verdade, em verdade**)

Vem de um adjetivo hebraico que significa «verdadeiro, certo, digno de confiança», ou de uma forma adverbial com o sentido de «é digno de confiança ou veraz». O verbo correlato, *aman*, significa «sustentar», «apoiar». O uso do «amém» como uma explicação, significa «certamente», «assim seja», no verdade». Ver Sal. 41:13; 72:19; 89:52; 106; 48; I Crô. 16:36 e Nee. 8:6. O trecho de Isa. 65:16 faz de Yahweh o Deus do Amém, isto é, aquele que fala com verdade, em quem todos podem confiar.

No Novo Testamento, o uso grego emprega o vocábulo para indicar «verdadeiramente», «de fato», «assim seja», «isso mesmo». O termo tornou-se comum nas orações, nas doxologias, nas respostas congregacionais, nas exclamações de aprovação. Nos evang. sinópticos, a palavra é dita por Jesus por 54 vezes. Só o evangelho de João contém 25 repetições do termo, sempre em forma dupla, *amém, amém*, para ênfase especial. Algumas ocorrências do termo aparecem em: João 1:51; 3:3; 5:19,24,25; 12:24; 14:12. Paulo também usou-o, como se vê em Rom. 15:3; 16:27; I Cor. 16:24; Gál. 6:18; Efé. 3:21. Em doxologias, ver Heb. 13:21; I Ped. 4:11; 5:11; II Ped. 3:18; Jud. 25. No Apocalipse, a palavra aparece por nove vezes, e a mais importante delas é quando figura como nome próprio de Cristo, o Amém em Apo. 5:14. Em Cristo culmina a certeza da mensagem espiritual. (A B S W)

AMÉM, Título de Cristo em Apo. 3:14.

Em cada uma das sete cartas do Apocalipse, Cristo recebe um título e descrições diferentes; e, em cada caso, esses elementos se aplicam especialmente à igreja que está sendo endereçada. Assim, no caso da igreja em Éfeso, Cristo é visto a andar entre as igrejas,

AMÉM — AMETISTA

pois sua presença e poder foram especialmente fortes na era apostólica. No caso da igreja dos mártires, Esmirna, Cristo se caracteriza como aquele que morreu, mas está vivo para sempre. No caso da corrupta igreja de Pérgamo, Cristo mostra-se como aquele que tem a espada aguda de dois gumes, com a qual promete julgamento. No caso da igreja de Filadélfia, aquele com uma «porta aberta de serviço», Cristo é visto a brandir as «chaves de Davi», que ele pode usar com toda a autoridade, para qualquer propósito que queira, especialmente para a admissão no reino de Deus. Assim também no caso presente, da igreja apóstata de Laodicéia, Cristo continua sendo o «Amém». Ele continua a ser a sua própria confirmação, a prova de seu próprio ministério e de sua pessoa, embora os membros da igreja laodicense o tivessem abandonado. Cristo continua sendo uma «testemunha fiel e verdadeira», apesar de terem rejeitado o seu testemunho e de se terem mostrado infiéis à sua causa. Cristo continua sendo o «princípio», a «causa primária», tanto da criação física quanto da criação espiritual, a despeito do fato de que os crentes de Laodicéia não reivindicassem à vida eterna, por intermédio dele, não o considerando mais como o Alfa e o Ômega.

Amém. É possível que isso seja um eco do trecho de Isa. 65:16, onde Deus é chamado de *Deus, que dirá amém*. O autor não hesita, em lugar nenhum do Apocalipse, de dar a Cristo toda a honra atribuída, nas páginas do A.T. a Deus Pai. Isso é prova insofismável de sua divindade. Ver o artigo sobre a *Divindade de Cristo*. Ver também sobre sua *Humanidade*. Em todo o Novo Testamento, a única ocorrência da palavra *Amém*, como nome próprio, se verifica aqui. (Ver João 1:51, quanto ao seu uso como confirmação ou imperativo). Essa palavra pode ser uma afirmação: «É assim». Ou pode ser um imperativo: «Assim seja!» Desenvolveu-se na prática litúrgica judaica, e era vocábulo usado nos cultos de adoração como afirmação de fé na validade ou veracidade da mensagem que era lida ou proferida. Em face do que se diz neste parágrafo, consideremos os pontos seguintes:

Ao usar o termo *Amém*, Cristo afirmou:
1. A validade da mensagem cristã, a qual é a Palavra de Deus para os homens. Ele mesmo é o tema central dessa mensagem.
2. Cristo é a afirmação da boa vontade de Deus para com os homens.
3. Cristo é o meio divino que confere aos homens as bênçãos motivadas por essa boa vontade; é o mediador entre Deus e o homem, e quem justifica o homem perante Deus.
4. Cristo é o «Amém», na qualidade de verdade de Deus, como aquele que transmite essa verdade aos homens.
5. O «Amém» é a garantia dada por Deus aos homens de que ele se importa com eles; o «Amém» é a expressão divina de amor.
6. O «Amém» confirma a validade do pacto de Deus, sendo o seu promulgador.
7. O «Amém» de Deus faz contraste com a corrupção contra a verdade, por parte de indivíduos como os laodicenses, que tinham esquecido a Palavra de Deus, passando a ter como seus deuses o dinheiro e o próprio «eu». O testemunho de Cristo é sempre veraz e afirmativo, sem importar os desvios dos homens. (Quanto a outras notas expositivas sobre o «Amém», que ajudam a iluminar o presente conceito, ver I Cor. 14:16 no NTI). (AL G IB NTI RO)

••• ••• •••

AMÊNDOAS

No hebraico, a palavra significa, aparentemente, «despertada», porque florescia bem cedo no ano. (Ver Gên. 43:11; Núm. 17:8; Ecl. 12:5; Jer. 1:11). Trata-se da *Prunus Amygdalus communis*, que é seu nome científico. Uma árvore nativa da Síria e da Palestina. Por causa de sua inflorescência, é altamente ornamental. Talvez tenha sido introduzida no Egito quando José era o governador da terra. Na Palestina, ela floresce já no mês de janeiro. As flores são róseas, e algumas vezes, brancas, o que explica a sua analogia com um ancião encanecido (ver Ecl. 12:5). Sua beleza tem inspirado a decoração em trabalhos de entalhe, onde a amêndoa é retratada. Também parece ter sido a origem de um óleo valioso.

Símbolo espiritual. O trecho de Jer. 1:11,12 menciona a amêndoa em conexão com a idéia de que Deus cumpre prontamente as Suas promessas. (ND S Z)

AMENDOEIRA

Trata-se de um arbusto baixo, abundantemente encontrado ao longo das costas do Mediterrâneo, o qual produz uma flor usada como especiaria desde tempos remotos. As referências clássicas mostram que a florescência (ou a baga que a produz) era usada como afrodisíaco e condimento. Provavelmente, a planta é a *Capparis spinosa*. Ela é mencionada somente em Eclesiástico 12:5, onde está em foco a intensificação do desejo sexual, — declinando à medida que a pessoa avança em idade. O processo de envelhecimento leva, finalmente, ao rompimento do fio de prata (o que produz a morte). Ver o artigo sobre o *fio de prata*, o filamento de energia que liga a alma ao corpo, como se fora uma espécie de cordão umbilical. À medida que a pessoa se aproxima desse momento, suas energias declinam-se, e ela pode tentar reverter alguns aspectos do envelhecimento mediante o uso de medicamentos ou tonificantes, como é o caso do emprego da amendoeira. (G I IB LAN)

AMESHA SPENTAS

Auxiliares de Ormazde (ver o artigo sobre *Ahura Mazda*), importantes deuses do zoroastrismo. Seriam personificações do caráter de Ormazde: bons pensamentos, retidão perfeita, reino desejável, santa harmonia, saúde salvadora, imortalidade. Ver o artigo sobre o *zoroastrismo*. (E)

AMETISTA

Uma variedade de quartzo transparente, violeta ou púrpura (dióxido de sílica), usada como pedra preciosa ou jóia ornamental (ver Apo. 21:20). O colorido é atribuído à presença do manganês, ou talvez ao material orgânico. Os antigos egípcios usavam a ametista como uma jóia. É mencionada no Antigo Testamento como a nona pedra do peitoral do sumo sacerdote (ver Êxo. 28:19 e 39:12), e como o décimo segundo material dos alicerces da Nova Jerusalém (ver Apo. 21:20). A ametista ocorre nos veios minerais associadas ao granito ou como margens da ágata oca, em nódulos. A ametista oriental era rara, muito dura e de grande brilho e beleza. O material era muito usado para o fabrico de anéis e camafeus, em parte porque se prestava bem ao corte, segundo nos informa Plínio (*Hist. Nat.* 37:9). Os antigos acreditavam que a pedra possuía a capacidade de fazer passar a embriaguês alcoólica, por meio do

AMI — AMINADABE

simples toque. Daí deriva-se o nome grego *amethustos*, que significa «não intoxicado». Alguns rabinos pensavam que a pedra, ao ser usada, produziria sonhos e que poderia ser usada por aqueles que desejassem ter sonhos. No hebraico, o nome da pedra significa «pedra de sonho». É bem possível que a pedra fosse usada como ponto de concentração mental, como o cristal, para efeitos de adivinhação; ou a sua presença no peitoral do sumo sacerdote visasse a provocar sonhos ou experiências psíquicas que poderiam ter utilidade para se conhecer a vontade de Deus. No Novo Testamento, a ênfase recai sobre a beleza da pedra, fazendo-nos lembrar a beleza das obras de Deus. (A FO S UN Z)

AMI

No hebraico, **meu povo**. Nome simbólico aplicado a Israel, em contraste com Lo-Ami, *não meu povo*. O povo tornou-se de Deus por meio da reconciliação. Oséias deu esse nome ao seu terceiro filho com Gomer (ver Osé. 2:1 e 1:9,10), dando assim a entender que Deus pode rejeitar um povo que antes era considerado Seu, por motivo do pecado. Todavia, isso foi pronunciado acerca de Israel, tendo em vista uma futura restauração que reverteria a situação. No evangelho, os gentios, que antes não eram povo de Deus, poderiam tornar-se povo de Deus mediante a conversão, segundo vemos em Rom. 9:25,26, onde Paulo cita essa profecia de Oséias. (Ver Também I Ped. 2:10). (ID S UN Z)

AMI (AMOM)

Antepassado de um dos servos de Salomão (ver Esd. 2:57). Chamado Amom em Nee. 7:59, e que algumas traduções dão como Alom.

AMIDIANOS

Uma família que retornou do cativeiro babilônico com Zorobabel (ver I Esdras 5:20). Esse nome não está contido no paralelo do sétimo capítulo do livro de Neemias. (Z)

AMIEL

No hebraico significa **povo de Deus**. Nome dado a várias pessoas no Antigo Testamento.

1. Filho de Gemali, um dos doze espias enviados por Moisés para explorarem a terra de Canaã (ver Núm. 13:12).

2. Pai de Maquir (II Sam. 9:4,5 e 17:27). Foi em sua casa que Mefibosete se escondeu de Davi. Mais tarde, Maquir tornou-se amigo de Davi.

3. Pai de Bate-Seba, esposa de Urias (e depois de Davi). Ver I Crô. 3:5. Em II Sam. 11:3 ele é chamado Eliã.

4. O sexto filho de Gemali, um dos porteiros do templo (ver I Crô. 26:5).

AMIGO, AMIZADE

Amigo é uma pessoa com quem temos associação amigável, nos vários tipos de relacionamento humano: a. Um companheiro fiel ou vizinho ajudador (ver Gên. 38:20; Jer. 6:21; Luc. 11:5-8). b. Um aderente político (ver I Sam. 3:26; 2 Sam. 3:8). c. Uma pessoa amada (ver Deu. 13:6). d. Alguém fiel em seus relacionamentos (ver Sal. 35:14; Pro. 17:17). Também há falsos amigos (ver Pro. 18:14), aqueles que traem a amizade (ver Jó 6:14,27); aqueles que são egoístas (ver Pro. 19:4,6 s.).

A amizade com Cristo. Aqueles que se dedicam à observância dos mandamentos de Cristo são Seus amigos (ver Mat. 12:46-50 e João 15:14). Eles O amam e promovem a honra de Seu nome.

A amizade prejudicial é a amizade com o mundo (ver Tia. 4:4; Mat. 6:24; Luc. 16:13; I João 2:15 ss.).

As amizades especiais, que envolvem um forte sentimento de amor, conforme a amizade de Davi e Jônatas (ver I Sam. 18:1-4 e 19:1-7).

A forma mais elevada de amizade, a amizade com Deus (ver II Crô. 20:7; Isa. 41:8; Tia. 2:23), é exemplificada no caso de Abraão, conforme se vê na referência de Tiago.

O amigo do noivo era João Batista (ver João 3:29). Alguns pensam que isso representa a classe dos remidos (como Israel), que não fazem parte da Igreja cristã. (I ID LAN NTI)

AMIGO DO NOIVO Ver **Matrimônio**.

AMIGOS DE DEUS

Termo que designa um grupo informal de místicos alemães, quase sempre leigos, que existiu no século XIV. Seus principais líderes eram João Tauler e Henrique Suso. Ver os artigos sobre eles. O misticismo busca a comunhão com Deus, um contato direto com Deus, ultrapassando as doutrinas e as proposições intelectuais, sendo apenas natural que uma sociedade de místicos tenha recebido esse título.

AMIGOS, SOCIEDADE DE

(Ver **Sociedade de Amigos**).

AMILENIALISMO

Essa doutrina tem assumido várias formas. Talvez a mais comum seja a idéia de que o milênio ou reino milenial seja o tempo que vai da ressurreição de Cristo à Sua segunda vinda. Portanto, o milênio, em termos literais de mil anos de paz, prosperidade e avanço espiritual, *após* a segunda vinda de Cristo, não existiria. Em conseqüência, temos a definição da palavra, *amilenial,* que significa não-milênio, ou seja, não haveria um milênio. Essa declaração é apenas preliminar. Uma descrição detalhada do amilenismo aparece no artigo sobre o *milênio,* onde são consideradas outras doutrinas relacionadas, como o *pós-milenismo* e o *pré-milenismo,* além de outro número de pontos de vista acerca do próprio milênio, segundo afirmam os milenistas.

AMINADABE

No hebraico, **meu parente é generoso** ou **nobre**. Nome de várias pessoas no Antigo Testamento:

1. Filho de Arão, pai de Naasom (Mat. 1:4). Em Luc. 3:33, encontramos a seguinte ordem de nomes: «Aminadabe, filho de Admim, Admim filho de Arni, Arni, filho de Esrom...» Naasom era príncipe da tribo de Judá por ocasião do primeiro recenseamento de Israel, no segundo ano após o êxodo (ver Núm. 1:7 e 2:3), antes de 1210 A.C. Era pai de Eliseba, esposa de Aarão (ver Êxo. 6:23). Foi ascendente de Davi, da quarta geração de Judá, e antepassado de Jesus Cristo. Pouco se sabe sobre ele; mas o casamento de sua filha com Aarão assinala a mais antiga instância de aliança entre a linhagem real de Davi e a linhagem sacerdotal de Aarão. O nome Nadabe, dado ao filho mais velho de Aarão, provavelmente visava a honrar seu avô, Aminadabe.

2. Um levita que ajudou a transportar a arca de volta a Jerusalém, nos dias de Davi (ver I Crô. 15:10,11). Era um dos filhos de Uziel. Foi um dos cento e doze homens nomeados por Davi para executarem a tarefa.

3. Na Septuaginta, em Ester 2:15 e 9:29, Aminadabe é chamado pai de Ester. Mas o texto judaico tradicional (massorético) diz *Abiail*, que é o texto preferido. Massorético é adjetivo que se deriva de «massoretas», compiladores e comentadores da Bíblia hebraica, que produziram um texto padronizado do Antigo Testamento. Ver o artigo sobre o *texto massorético*.

4. De acordo com I Crô. 6:22, Aminadabe figura como filho de Coré, descendente de Levi; mas isso não pode ser o texto correto, pois Aminadabe aparece como o sogro de Aarão, em Êxo. 6:23. Na lista paralela de I Crô. 6, aparece o nome Jizar (vs. 38 ss) o que concorda com a genealogia dada em Êxo. 6:18,22. Os manuscritos A e L da Septuaginta trazem o texto correto, Jizar, em I Crô. 6:22. (ICC ND UN Z)

AMINADIBE

Forma variante de **Aminadabe**, uma pessoa mencionada em Can. 6:12, cujo carro aparece como veloz — tudo segundo algumas versões. Mas a passagem é obscura, talvez tendo sofrido alguma corrupção, pelo que outras versões preferem a tradução que se vê em nossa versão portuguesa: «no carro do meu nobre povo» ou «no carro ao lado de meu príncipe», deixando de lado a idéia de velocidade. Nesse caso, a palavra hebraica não é lida como um nome próprio. (ND UN Z)

AMIRALDISMO

O termo vem do nome próprio Amiraldo (Moisés Amiraldo, 1596-1664), da escola reformada francesa em Saumur. Ele defendia um «universalismo hipotético», afirmando que Deus deseja que todos os homens sejam salvos, embora o intelecto humano seja incapaz de fazer a vontade acreditar, à parte da operação específica de Deus no coração dos eleitos. Isso posto, no caso dos não-eleitos, Deus retém essa operação, ficando anulada a suposta potencialidade do homem salvar-se. Os calvinistas modernos ainda usam essa noção na tentativa de explicar aqueles versículos bíblicos que aludem ao interesse de Deus por todos os homens. Mas, ao assim fazerem, não lhe conferem qualquer potencialidade verdadeira ou importante. Pequeno é o consolo ao dizer que todos os homens *podem* ser salvos, mas que, de fato, *não podem*, porque não podem crer no evangelho. Isso é uma teologia podre. Ver *Livre-arbítrio* e *determinismo*.

AMISADAI

No hebraico, **Shaddai é meu parente**. Pai de Aieser, um danita, líder durante a jornada pelo deserto (ver Núm. 1:12; 2:25; 7:55,71 e 10:25). (UN Z)

AMITABHA

Salvador da Terra Pura, seita do budismo mahaiana. E também o Patshen Lama reencarnado, do *lamaísmo* (ver o artigo a respeito).

AMITAI

No hebraico significa **fiel**. Era pai do profeta Jonas (ver II Reis 14:25 e Jon. 1:1), o qual era natural de Gate-Hefer, no território de Zebulom. (S)

AMIÚDE

No hebraico, **meu parente é glorioso**. Esse é o nome de várias pessoas no Antigo Testamento:

1. Um efraimita, pai de Elisama. Elisama foi nomeado chefe da tribo na época do êxodo (ver Núm. 1:10; 2:18; 7:48,53; 10:22; I Crô. 7:26). Antes de 1210 A.C.

2. Pai de Samuel, que posteriormente foi o chefe simeonita nomeado para fazer parte da comissão que fez a divisão da Terra Prometida — (ver Núm. 34:20), antes de 1452 A.C.

3. Membro da tribo de Naftali cujo filho, Pedael, príncipe daquela tribo, foi nomeado para ajudar na divisão da terra (ver Núm. 34:28), antes de 1452 A.C.

4. Pai de Talmai, rei de Gesur. Após ter assassinado seu meio-irmão Amom, Absalão fugiu para a companhia de Talmai (ver II Sam. 13:37). Antes de 1030 A.C.

5. Filho de Onri, da tribo de Judá e descendente de Peres. Foi pai de Utai, tendo sido este último um dos primeiros a residir em Jerusalém, após o retorno da Babilônia (ver I Crô. 9:4). Antes de 536 A.C.

AMIZADABE

No hebraico, **o parente concedeu**. Era filho de Benaia, que fazia parte da guarda pessoal de Davi e capitão dos trinta mais valentes guerreiros. Ele servia como líder da divisão no terceiro mês do ano (ver I Crô. 27:6). Cerca de 1000 A.C. (UN Z)

AMNOM

No hebraico significa **fiel**. É o nome de duas pessoas no Antigo Testamento.

1. O filho mais velho de Davi e Ainoã, a jezreelita (ver II Sam. 3:2 e I Crô. 3:1). Ele nasceu em Herom, em cerca de 1056 A.C. Estuprou sua própria meia-irmã Tamar, e dois anos depois foi assassinado por Absalão, irmão de Tamar, por causa desse ato. Ver a narrativa em II Sam. 13.

2. Um filho de Simão (ver I Crô. 4:20), descendente de Judá. (S)

AMOM

No hebraico, **construtor** (ver Jer. 46:25). Mas outros pensam que o vocábulo significa *verdadeiro* ou *fiel*.

1. Nome de uma divindade egípcia, associada por antigos escritores a Zeus ou Júpiter. Sua primitiva sede de adoração parece ter sido Meroe. Dali seu culto mudou-se para Tebas, e então propagou-se para o Oásis de Siwah e Dodona (ver Heródoto ii.54). Em todos esses lugares, os oráculos dessa divindade eram celebrados. Porém, o verdadeiro centro de sua adoração era Tebas. Nos monumentos egípcios, esse deus é apresentado como um homem sentado com cabeça de carneiro, ou então como um carneiro. Parece ter sido, basicamente, uma divindade da fertilidade. Quando Tebas tornou-se a capital do Egito, Amom foi vinculado a Rá, o deus-sol.

2. Governador da cidade de Samaria, no tempo de Acabe (ver I Reis 22:26 e II Crô. 8:25), em cerca de 900 A.C. Nessa passagem, lemos que Acabe ordenou que Micaías, o profeta, fosse levado a Amom para ser encarcerado.

AMOM (AMONITAS) — AMOR

3. Filho de Manassés, e décimo quinto rei de Judá, que começou a reinar em 644 A.C. e que governou por dois anos. Ele restaurou a idolatria e reergueu os ídolos que Manassés havia derrubado. Foi assassinado em uma conspiração na corte, e então os homicidas foram executados pelo povo. Seu filho, Josias, tornou-se rei, quando estava apenas com oito anos de idade (ver II Reis 21:18-26 e II Crô. 33:21-25).

4. Filho de Manassés, e um dos antepassados de Cristo (ver Mat. 1:10). (S UN)

AMOM (AMONITAS)

Descendentes de Amom, filho mais novo de Ló (ver Gên. 19:38) e da sua filha mais jovem. Originalmente, os amonitas ocupavam uma faixa de terras a leste dos amorreus, vivendo separados dos moabitas pelo rio Arnon.

1. *O nome Amom.* — A filha mais jovem de Ló deu à luz um filho de seu próprio pai, chamando-o Ben-Ami, cuja tradução não é certa. Alguns dizem que significa «filho de meu povo»; outros pensam que significa «filho de meu tio paterno» (ou clã paterno). Ainda outros supõem que significa «filho de meu próprio pai», em consonância com o incidente envolvido. O nome isolado não aparece em nenhum outro trecho bíblico, embora apareçam seus compostos, como «Lo-Ami» (*não-meu-povo*, na profecia de Oséias 1:9). Outras formas compostas são Amiel, Amiúde, Amiur, Amizadabe e Aminadabe (ver os artigos respectivos), além de outros.

2. *Localização.* Os amonitas tomaram um território antes ocupado por uma raça de gigantes (ver Deu. 2:20). Aos israelitas, ao atingirem as fronteiras da Terra Prometida, foi ordenado que não molestassem os filhos de Amom, por serem descendentes de Ló. Todavia, os amonitas não demonstraram hospitalidade para com os israelitas, pelo que foram proibidos de entrar na congregação do Senhor, isto é, de serem membros da comunidade civil dos israelitas, até à *décima* geração, o que alguns entendiam como uma proibição perpétua (ver Nee. 13:1).

3. *Hostilidade contra Israel.* Em Juízes 3:13 lemos que esse povo mostrou-se hostil para com Israel. Uniram-se em ataque combinado a Israel com outros adversários do povo de Deus. Cerca de cento e quarenta anos mais tarde, lemos que os israelitas caíram na idolatria, servindo aos deuses de várias nações, incluindo os deuses amonitas. Os amonitas foram hostis a Israel tanto antes (ver I Sam. 11:11) quanto depois do cativeiro (ver Nee. 4:3; Judite 5 - 7 e I Macabeus 7:30-43), o que prosseguiu até que os romanos engoliram todas as facções em litígio, incluindo os judeus. No tempo de Justino Mártir (cerca de 150 D.C.), os amonitas continuavam sendo um povo numeroso; mas, pela época de Orígenes (cerca de 186-254 D.C.), eles já se tinham amalgamado com os árabes. Quanto a atos específicos de hostilidade, ver estas referências: Juí. 3:13; 11:12; I Sam. 11:11; II Sam. 10:4,19; 12:26-31 e II Crô. 20:25.

4. *O cativeiro de Israel.* Quando Israel foi levado cativo, os amonitas tomaram posse das cidades pertencentes à tribo de Gade (ver Jer. 49:1), e rejubilaram-se diante do infortúnio dos israelitas (ver Eze. 25:3,6). Após o cativeiro, a antiga hostilidade prosseguiu (ver Nee. 4:3,7,8).

5. *Outros pontos de interesse.* Os amonitas eram governados por um rei (ver I Sam. 12:12). A divindade nacional era Moloque (ver I Reis 11:7; Chamado Milcom, em I Reis 11:5 e 33). A capital deles era Rabá (Rabate Amom). Posteriormente, essa cidade tomou o nome de Filadélfia, em honra a Ptolomeu Filadelfo. Atualmente chama-se Amam. A língua deles era semítica. Atualmente todas aquelas regiões foram arabizadas, e fala-se o árabe. Salomão casou-se com mulheres amonitas. A mãe de Reoboão era Naama, mulher amonita (ver I Reis 14:31), um mau exemplo seguido por Israel (ver Nee. 13:23). Condenação e destruição estão prometidas aos amonitas, devido à hostilidade deles para com Israel — atualmente os amonitas fazem parte da liga árabe, cujo propósito declarado é expulsar Israel da Palestina — e por causa de sua impiedade (ver Eze. 25:5,10 e Sof. 2:9). Essas predições se têm cumprido parcialmente considerando que a raça amonita desapareceu misturada com outras raças semitas. A arqueologia tem descoberto extensas ruínas, principalmente de origem romana, no local moderno de Amam. (GL HAR S UN Z)

AMOMUM

Palavra latina derivada do grego **amomon**, um *hapax legomena* que aparece em Apo. 18:13, que alguns traduzem como «odores». Mas trata-se do nome de uma planta odorífera usada no preparo de ungüentos dispendiosos, o que justifica a tradução que se vê em nossa versão portuguesa «especiarias». A planta é nativa na Índia, pertencente ao gênero chamado Scitamineoe, que medra nas áreas tropicais do mundo antigo, aparentada do gengibre. Essas plantas são herbáceas, com raízes trepadeiras e folhas grandes. Tanto as sementes quanto as folhas são aromáticas. A espécie mencionada em Apocalipse tinha sementes grandes como uvas, que eram usadas no fabrico de ungüento. Esse produto é alistado entre os muitos itens dispendiosos consumidos pelos ricaços romanos, por meio do comércio e do escambo, e que o profeta condena como um luxo que caracterizará o estágio final da Babilônia. (NTI UN)

AMÔNIO SACCAS

Filósofo helenista (175-242 D.C.). Nasceu cristão mas converteu-se ao helenismo, membro da Escola Alexandrina (ver o artigo). Foi mestre ilustre, e Plotino foi um dos seus alunos por onze anos. Um outro famoso estudante seu foi Orígenes (ver o artigo a seu respeito). Sua filosofia aparentemente tinha caráter neoplatônico, e algumas vezes, ele, e não Plotino, é chamado de fundador desse movimento. A natureza exata de sua filosofia não pode ser determinada com certeza, visto que os seus discípulos juravam manter segredo de suas idéias, mas parece que ele procurava reconciliar as idéias de Platão e Aristóteles. (P)

AMOQUE

No hebraico quer dizer **profundo**. Era ancestral de Héber, um sacerdote do tempo de Joiaquim (ver Nee. 12:20). Amoque foi um dos sacerdotes que retornou do exílio com Zorobabel (ver Nee. 12:7). (Z)

AMOR

Discussão Preliminar

Tradução do termo hebraico *aheb*, palavra de larga conotação. Outros vocábulos também eram usados no Antigo Testamento, com sentidos variegados, associados a amor, desejo, amante, etc. No N.T., temos

Amor

Ainda que eu falasse as línguas dos homens e dos anjos, e não tivesse Caridade, seria como o metal que soa ou como o sino que tine. E ainda que tivesse o DOM de profecia, e conhecesse todos os mistérios e toda a ciência, e ainda tivesse toda a fé, de maneira tal que transportasse os montes, e não tivesse Caridade, NADA seria. E ainda que distribuísse toda minha fortuna para o sustento dos pobres, e ainda que entregasse o meu corpo para ser queimado, e NÃO tivesse Caridade, nada disso ME Aproveitaria.

I aos Coríntios 13 1~3

Caligrafia de Darrell Steven Champlin

AMOR

••• ••• •••

O círculo do amor de Deus não tinha início,
e não terá fim. O amor de Deus inspirou
e *garantiu* a execução da

missão tridimensional

do Logos. Ele ministrou e ministra na terra,
no hades e nos céus para ser tudo para todos,
   — afinal — .

••• ••• •••

O amor de Deus é *real* universalmente,
   — não meramente potencial.
O amor de Deus será absolutamente *efetivo*,
   — afinal —.
Limites de pedra não podem conter o amor.
E o que o amor *pode* fazer, isso o amor
   ousa fazer.
   (William Shakespeare)

O oposto de injustiça não é justiça — é *amor*.

••• ••• •••

AMOR

agape (agapao), comum na Septuaginta, e *phileo*, sinônimo de *agapao*. *Agapao* aparece por 142 vezes no Novo Testamento; *agape*, por 116 vezes, e *phileo* por 25 vezes. *Agapao* tem todo o alcance possível de significado que a nossa palavra *amor* exibe; e mediante o uso dessa palavra, não se pode estabelecer a diferença entre o amor divino e o amor humano, em contraste com *phileo*. A suposta diferença entre essas duas palavras torna-se nula quando simplesmente tomamos um léxico e lemos as referências onde figuram os dois termos. Ver o artigo sobre *agape*, como ilustração desse fato, e quanto a outras informações. A mudança de uma para outra palavra, em João 21, é simples questão estilística, não envolvendo qualquer sentido oculto. *Eros*, com freqüência usada para indicar o amor apaixonado e sexual, não se encontra no Novo Testamento. Também pode ser usado para indicar o amor nobre e espiritual, embora envolvendo, em muitos casos pelo menos, um sentido menos nobre do que aqueles achados no caso de *agapao* e *phileo*. Nas Escrituras, o amor aparece tanto como um atributo de Deus como uma virtude humana moral, pelo que o assunto do amor pertence tanto à *teologia* quanto à *ética*. O amor é fundamental à verdadeira religião e à filosofia moral, e de fato, até na maior parte das filosofias pessimistas, como na de Schopenhauer, onde é encarado favoravelmente sob o título de *simpatia*. O amor é uma parte importante e mesmo dominante da fé judaico-cristã, básica ao evangelho. (Ver João 3:16). É um elemento essencial em todo o relacionamento humano. Portanto, tanto mais atônitos ficamos em face do fato de que quase todos os credos denominacionais evangélicos deixam-no totalmente de lado, ao alistarem seus itens de crença (ver o artigo sobre Credos). Paulo declara que o amor é a maior de todas as graças cristãs (ver I Cor. 13:13, onde aparece a exposição do NTI, quanto a muitos dos atributos e características do amor). Nos escritos de Paulo, também é o solo de onde brotam todas as outras virtudes (ver Gál. 5:22,23). Trata-se da marca distintiva de que alguém é filho de Deus (ver Mat. 5:44 ss.). É um pré-requisito absoluto para que alguém seja uma pessoa espiritual, um bom cidadão, um bom vizinho, um bom marido, esposa ou pai, ou qualquer outra coisa, que envolva boas qualidades divinas ou humanas.

I. Tipos de amor

1. Há o amor de Deus (João 3:16), o qual é a fonte de todo outro amor, até mesmo aquele manifestado pelos incrédulos. O Espírito de Deus, atuando no mundo, impede-o de transformar-se em floresta completa, porquanto propaga ao redor o seu amor, e muitas pessoas fazem o que fazem por motivos puramente altruístas.

2. Há o amor de Cristo pelo homem, o qual é uma extensão do amor de Deus; e, em sua essência, é a mesma coisa. (Ver II Cor. 5:14 e as notas expositivas no NTI sobre esse amor, que nos constrange a atitudes que expressam o cristianismo).

3. Há o amor do indivíduo por si mesmo, num afeto inteiramente egoísta, pois só se preocupa consigo mesmo.

4. Há o amor de um homem por outro ser humano. Quando alguém ama outrem, deseja para o próximo o que deseja para si mesmo, ou transfere o cuidado por si mesmo para outra pessoa, desejando o seu bem-estar, tal como deseja o seu próprio bem-estar. Pode-se imaginar quase qualquer homem a amar um filho ou filha predileta. Por causa de seus cuidados por seu filho, ele fará sacrifícios e procurará protegê-lo. Pensará em como suprir às suas necessidades, e desejará a felicidade de seu filho. Em outras palavras, fará em prol de outra pessoa (sem importar quão mau seja, quanto a outras questões) aquilo que faria por si mesmo. O amor-próprio é fácil; não é muito difícil a transferência desse amor pelo menos a uma outra pessoa. Mas aqueles que amam verdadeiramente são os que descobriram como transferir o amor-próprio para um grande número de pessoas. Aqueles que assim fazem são a isso impelidos pelo Espírito de Deus, sem importar se são ou não discípulos de Cristo, no sentido tradicional.

5. Há o amor dirigido a Cristo, o Filho de Deus, ou então a Deus Pai, o que se verifica quando amamos aos nossos semelhantes. (Ver as notas expositivas sobre esse conceito no NTI em Mat.25:35 e ss).

6. Há o amor do homem a Cristo ou a Deus Pai, diretamente expresso. Essa modalidade de amor requer um senso altamente desenvolvido, e normalmente se expressa por meios místicos, mediante a ascensão da alma, que passa a contemplar a Deus. Certamente essa foi a forma de amor que o escritor sagrado tinha em mente, em João 4:7-21, embora o contexto contemple muitos resultados «diários» e «práticos» da mesma, como o evangelismo dos perdidos, a vida santa, a lealdade a Cristo e as ações de caridade em favor do próximo.

Cristo como uma figura distante. Os crentes de Éfeso(Apo. 2), reduziram Cristo a uma figura distante a despeito de continuarem a fazer prodígios espirituais e apesar de seu poder no Espírito. Quantas pessoas hoje em dia, quando pregam, somente atacam várias formas de males, como o mundanismo, o modernismo, o comunismo, embora suas mensagens reflitam pouquíssimo do amor conquistador de Cristo. Tornaram-se polemistas profissionais, mas pouco ou nada sabem do amor construtivo. Perderam a visão do Cristo, em meio à batalha.

Há um caminho melhor do que esse. É o caminho do amor. O amor à semelhança da morte, transforma a tudo quanto toca. Os homens são atraídos pelo amor. As coisas semelhantes se atraem mutuamente. Os homens amam quando são amados. E odeiam quando são odiados.

*Pois limites de pedra não podem conter ao amor,
E o que o amor pode fazer, isso ousa tentar.*

(«*Romeu e Julieta*», Shakespeare).

II. O Amor de Deus pelo mundo, a base do Evangelho

1. Este mundo não é o mundo dos eleitos — mas sim, de *todos* os indivíduos do mundo, de *todas* as épocas, sem exceção alguma.

2. Deus, sendo um ser inteligente, tem consciência da existência deste mundo e ama a todos os homens que nele habitam. De alguma maneira, posto que indefinida, exceto conforme entendemos as pessoas, Deus possui qualidades emocionais. O seu amor é a mais alta forma de amor, a mais pura, ao ponto de ser chamado de *amor*, conforme lemos no trecho de I João 4:8. Esse princípio de amor, que faz com que Deus tenha o destino perfeito do homem, a sua felicidade e a sua utilidade perfeita e cumprimento da existência, sempre perante os seus olhos, e que é a força central motivadora de todas as suas ações para com os homens, também é compartilhado pelo homem, para ser exercido em direção aos seus semelhantes. A passagem de I João 4:16 expressa essa idéia, como também o faz o Sermão do Monte (Mat. 5:7 e 22:38,39). Esse amor de Deus pelos homens deve ser recíproco — dos homens por Deus, e, em seguida, por todos os homens. O amor, por

AMOR

conseguinte, é a força dinâmica de toda a criação, bem como a origem de toda autêntica bondade, porquanto a lei inteira se alicerça no amor, conforme também nos ensina o trecho de Mat. 22:40, declaração essa confirmada por Paulo, em Rom. 13:9. A grandeza do amor de Deus impeliu o apóstolo Paulo a escrever o seu soneto imortal, o qual lemos no décimo terceiro capítulo de sua primeira epístola aos Coríntios; e nenhuma literatura superior a essa, sobre a questão, foi jamais escrita. E ainda que esse apóstolo nada mais houvesse deixado escrito, isso bastaria para assegurar-lhe o lugar de um dos maiores autores do mundo.

III. O amor de Deus pelo Filho e na Família divina

O amor de Deus Pai por Deus Filho é mencionado e enfatizado em João 10:17, 14:31; 15:9, 17:23,24,26. Fica entendido que esse amor é mútuo. João 14:21 destaca o amor mútuo no seio da família de Deus. Este evangelho apresenta o amor como um autêntico requisito para que a obediência aceitável, além de ser um grande *motivo* para agirmos corretamente, diante de Deus.

IV. Deus é amor (I Jo. 4:8)
Implicações desta grande declaração:

Isso é o que ensinam as Escrituras. Essa é uma das grandes afirmativas das Escrituras, que quase todas as crianças de Escola Dominical conhecem. Certamente é uma das mais bem conhecidas declarações da primeira epístola de João. O amor, naturalmente, é um *atributo* de Deus; mas permeia a todas as coisas, de tal modo que é legítima a declaração que «Deus é amor». Por igual modo se diz que «Deus é luz» (I João 1:5) e «Deus é Espírito» (João 4:24). Com idêntica propriedade poder-se-ia dizer que «Deus é Justiça», «Deus é Bondade» e «Deus é Verdade», ficando assim personificados e elevados os seus atributos infinitos. Platão, ao descrever a realidade última, expressou-se desse modo. Assim sendo, as «idéias» finais (formas espirituais finais, copiadas e imitadas por tudo quanto existe no plano terrestre) seriam a «Bondade», a «Beleza» e a «Justiça». Em última análise, Deus é essas coisas; no nível terrestre, vê-se apenas imitações das «idéias divinas», as quais representam a realidade espiritual final. As Escrituras Sagradas, entretanto, preferem dizer que «Deus é Amor», porquanto todas as demais qualidades são atributos baseados sobre o amor divino. Portanto, a «bondade» de Deus se baseia sobre o seu amor; ele expressa bondade porque ama. E a sua justiça, embora se mostre severa em certas ocasiões, se baseia no amor; pois até mesmo os juízos de Deus são medidas pelas quais ele mostra ao homem o erro de seus distorcidos caminhos, levando-o a pagar dívidas necessárias, levando-o a reconhecer a verdade e a justiça. Além disso, o amor de Deus se expressa através da «beleza». O plano de Deus, relativo à redenção humana, reveste-se de beleza esplendorosa. É a beleza do evangelho que atrai a ele mesmo tantas pessoas, e não a sua lógica, as suas ameaças e as suas promessas.

Deus, como amor, é contrastado com outras noções religiosas, conforme se vê nos pontos abaixo:

1. Os antigos gregos imaginavam deuses tão *imperfeitos* como eles mesmos, e em doses sobre-humanas. Seus deuses eram supremamente invejosos, desprezíveis, destruidores, vingativos e odiosos. Estavam envolvidos em todas as formas de «concupiscências», mas em doses sobre-humanas. Quão impuro e destruidor era Zeus, com sua resmungadora esposa Hera, que sempre procurava levá-lo a fazer algo que ele não queria fazer! Quão *licencioso* era Zeus, embora ninguém pudesse chamá-lo à ordem! Em contraste com esse horrendo quadro de Zeus destaca-se o Deus do N.T. - caracterizado pela pureza, pelo amor, pela bondade, pela justiça.

2. Além disso, Aristóteles fazia de Deus um Impulsionador Inabalável. Para ele a deidade seria pensamento puro, a contemplar-se a si mesmo, porque nada haveria digno de contemplação fora dele. Ele não tinha amor pelo universo, e, na realidade, nem tinha consciência dele, porquanto nem merecia ser conhecido por ele—não amaria ao seu universo, mas moveria todas as coisas, sendo amado. O N.T., entretanto, nega tais conceitos. Antes, ali se ensina que Deus contempla seu universo e é levado a amá-lo; seu amor ativo faz o mundo prosseguir.

3. Os gnósticos pensavam que Deus seria um ser totalmente *transcendental*. Ele tinha contato com seus universos somente através de uma longa linhagem de sombrias emanações angelicais ou mediadores, como eram os «aeons». Deus seria elevado por demais para ter qualquer contato direto com este mundo, ou mesmo para ao menos interessar-se pela sua criação. O «deísmo» deles fazia de Deus um ser intocável, inatingível para qualquer ser mortal.

4. Pontos de vista religiosos modernos, que exageram a vontade divina ou seu senso de vingança, às expensas de seu amor, também contradizem o quadro que o N.T. faz dele. Aqueles que crêem em «reprovação ativa» e em amor limitado; Deus amaria não ao mundo, mas exclusivamente aos «eleitos», na realidade não acreditam que Deus seja amor. Aqueles que vêem apenas retribuição e vingança no julgamento divino, ignorando passagens como o primeiro capítulo da epístola aos Efésios e as passagens de I Ped. 3:18-20 e 4:6, ou então pervertendo-as, na realidade não podem dizer que «Deus é amor». Até mesmo o juízo de Deus é uma medida de seu amor, porque o juízo opera através do amor. Primeiramente mostra ao homem o quanto «custa» o erro de seu caminho; em seguida, mostra ao homem o próprio erro; e em seguida modifica a mente do homem acerca de Cristo, de tal modo que até aqueles «debaixo da terra» (ver Fil. 2:10, que fala sobre o «hades», lugar da prisão e do juízo de almas perdidas) eventualmente virão a inclinar-se diante de «Jesus» (Salvador) e Cristo, que é o Senhor. Deus dá a todos uma vida espiritual (ver I Ped. 4:6), embora não seja o mesmo tipo de vida dos eleitos. Chegam a ter utilidade e propósito em Cristo, porquanto o mistério da vontade de Deus é que, eventualmente, o Cristo seja «tudo para todos», conforme se aprende em Efé. 1:23. Os demais não chegarão a compartilhar da própria natureza de Deus (ver II Ped. 1:4), conforme sucederá aos eleitos, mas acharão em Cristo o propósito e alvo da existência; e o próprio julgamento será um meio para ensinar-lhes essa lição. Assim, pois, o «juízo» serve de aquilatação do amor de Deus, e não algo contrário ao mesmo. O julgamento é um dedo na mão do amor de Deus. Ver o artigo sobre *Julgamento*. Ver o artigo sobre os *atributos* de Deus.

V. O Amor é a Prova da Espiritualidade

1. Sabemos que o amor é a maior de todas as virtudes cristãs, mais importante que a fé ou a esperança (ver I Cor. 13:12).

2. Sabemos que o amor é o solo mesmo onde brotam e se desenvolvem todas as demais virtudes espirituais (ver Gál. 5:22,23).

3. Porém, o que talvez nos surpreenda é que não terá havido o novo nascimento, sob hipótese alguma, sem que o amor haja sido implantado na alma. A

AMOR

alma egoísta não pode ser uma alma regenerada. I João 4:7 declara — ousadamente — que o amor é produto do próprio novo nascimento. Deus é amor, e o amor vem da parte de Deus. Aquele que nasceu de Deus recebeu o implante da natureza altruísta. Tal indivíduo automaticamente amará a seu próximo, embora isso sempre deva ser fortalecido e incrementado, conforme a alma se vai tornando mais espiritual.

4. Portanto, afirmamos que o amor é a prova mesma da espiritualidade de uma pessoa. Trata-se da maior das virtudes espirituais, o solo onde todas as outras virtudes têm de medrar. Assim sendo, realmente é de estranhar que alguns pensem que o conflito e o ódio sejam a prova de sua espiritualidade!

5. Fomos aceitos no «Amado» (ver Efé. 1:6), e assim, no seio da família divina, existe uma comunhão de amor. Essa participação no espírito de amor deve necessariamente caracterizar qualquer verdadeiro filho de Deus. Aquele que odeia pertence ao diabo.

6. *Nossa espiritualidade imita Deus, o Pai.* Deus é amor. Ele é a origem de todo o pensamento e ação altruísta. Os filhos de Deus serão inspirados tanto por seu exemplo como através do cultivo do amor na alma, uma realização do Espírito.

7. A prática da lei do amor é um dos meios de desenvolvimento espiritual. De cada vez que fazemos o bem para alguma outra pessoa, impelidos por motivos puros, o nível da nossa espiritualidade se eleva. Outros meios de crescimento espiritual são o estudo dos livros sagrados, a oração, a meditação, a santificação e o emprego dos dons espirituais, que nos ajudam a cumprir nossas respectivas missões.

VI. O Amor é a Cultivação, o Fruto do Espírito Santo

1. Gál. 5:22, o amor é o primeiro fruto do Espírito na alma e a vida de uma pessoa, e torna-se o solo no qual todos os demais frutos crescem.

2. Como o produto supremo do Espírito, o amor torna-se a força por detrás de todos os *dons espirituais*, sendo maior que qualquer um deles, isoladamente ou em conjunto (ver I Cor. 13). Sem o amor nada somos.

3. Deus nos confere o seu amor, pela operação do Espírito na alma. O amor é uma planta tenra da qual o Espírito cuida. Se o amor estiver ausente, então é que o Espírito não habita em nós.

VII. O Amor como Altruísmo, cumprimento da Lei

1. Capacidade de olvidar-se de si mesmo no serviço ao próximo. Isso é amar a Cristo, Mat. 25:31 e ss.

2. O amor não consiste em mera emoção. É uma qualidade da alma, mediante a qual o indivíduo sente ser natural servir ao próximo, tal como sempre quererá servir a si mesmo. Essa qualidade da alma é produzida pela influência transformadora do Espírito, segundo se vê em Gál. 5:22.

3. — O amor consiste no interesse por nossos semelhantes como aquele que temos naturalmente por nós mesmos. Trata-se de um altruísmo puro, a negação do próprio «eu» visando o bem-estar alheio. Consiste em desejar as vantagens e a prosperidade, física e espiritual, em favor dos outros, como naturalmente anelamos para nós mesmos. Esse amor ao próximo é, ao mesmo tempo, amor a Cristo, conforme aprendemos no vigésimo quinto capítulo do evangelho de Mateus (ver Mat. 25:31 e ss). Poucas almas podem amar diretamente a Deus, e somente quando a alma já ascendeu o suficiente na direção de Deus é que esse amor pode ocorrer, na forma de contemplação. Porém, parte dessa ascensão consiste no amor por aqueles para quem Deus outorgou a vida eterna. Assim sendo, é impossível amar a Deus e odiar a um ser humano. (Ver I João 4:7). Só ama verdadeiramente aquele que nasceu de Deus, porquanto o «amor cristão» é uma qualidade eminentemente espiritual. (Ver I João 4:7). Outrossim, aquele que não ama também não conhece a Deus (ver I João 4:8), porque Deus é a própria essência do amor, sendo altruísmo puro. Por semelhante modo, não amar é andar nas trevas (ver I João 2:11). O amor é o caminho mais rápido de retorno ao Senhor Deus, porquanto é a virtude moral suprema que precisamos possuir a fim de compartilhar da sua imagem moral, permitindo que todas as demais virtudes possam ser bem mais facilmente adquiridas. Somente quando já somos possuidores da natureza moral divina é que podemos possuir a natureza metafísica, que está destinada aos remidos, a saber, a própria natureza de Jesus Cristo, o Filho de Deus. Somente então é que nos tornamos verdadeiros filhos de Deus, juntamente com o Filho de Deus, dentro da família divina, participantes da natureza divina. (Ver II Ped. 1:4).

«...segundo J.R. Seeley expressou o conceito, Cristo adicionou um novo hemisfério ao mundo moral». (*Ecce Homo*, págs. 201 e 202. Ver o capítulo inteiro sobre a 'Moralidade Positiva'). Paralelamente à moralidade negativa, e acima dela, ele estabeleceu a moralidade positiva. Alguém poderia guardar com perfeição os Dez Mandamentos e, no entanto, estar longe de praticar o verdadeiro cristianismo. Para nós não existem dez mandamentos, e, sim onze. O décimo primeiro consiste em: *Amarás*. Nessa pequena palavra, *amor*, no dizer de Cristo, está sumariado o dever inteiro de um homem. Em tudo isso Cristo manifesta muita originalidade do que percebemos. Assim também é que T.R. Glover, na obra 'Influence of Christ in the Ancient World', um excelente estudo acerca do cristianismo e dos rivais mais próximos, declara: 'As filosofias epicúrea e estóica haviam posto grande ênfase na 'imperturbabilidade' e 'liberdade' de toda emoção, o que, em cada caso, é essencialmente um câson muito egoísta da vida'. Esse autor admite que no caso do estoicismo isso era sempre modificado pela memória do descanso do cosmos. Todavia, *Liberdade das emoções*? A palavra grega era e continua sendo, nesse caso *apatia*. 'Não me ponho ao lado', disse o gentil Plutarco, 'daqueles que entoam hinos à selvagem e dura apatia'». (Cambridge, University of Cambridge Press, 1929, págs. 76 e 77). Não era esse o ideal de Cristo. Tal como o seu Mestre, o crente deve expor-se a 'sentir o que os miseráveis sentem'.

Para sermos justos para com os antigos, deveríamos acrescentar neste ponto que, tanto na moral de Sócrates, em sua busca pelas definições universais acerca da questões éticas, fundamentadas em sua confiança de que todo o princípio ético é eterno e imutável, contido na mente universal, como também na moral de Platão, em seus universais e em suas 'realidades últimas', que seriam eternos, perfeitos e imutáveis, que também incluem princípios éticos e que, em seu diálogo sobre as «Leis», são identificados com «Deus», há uma aproximação bem delicada do ideal do amor cristão.

Tennyson escreveu:
Se por acaso amo a algum outro
....
Não devo ter cuidado com tudo quanto penso,

AMOR — AMOREIRAS

Sim, até mesmo daquilo que como e bebo,
....
Se por acaso amo a algum outro?

Nessas linhas transparece a percepção do poeta de que *nenhum indivíduo vive isolado* dos outros, somente para si mesmo, porquanto nenhuma pessoa é uma ilha.

«Amor é uma disposição de caráter que leva a pessoa a considerar seus semelhantes *com estima*, *respeito, justiça* e *compaixão*. Amor cristão é, obviamente, esse sentimento inspirado e exemplificado por Cristo, e praticado pelos seus servos, em seu nome. O amor permeia e rege todo o evangelho. Foi por amor que Deus enviou Jesus ao mundo (João 3:16): o amor é o resumo da lei de Deus (Mat. 22:34-40). O amor é a finalidade dos mandamentos (I Tim. 1:5). O amor se constitui num mandamento específico de Jesus para com seus discípulos, Jo. 15:12. O amor é uma das evidências da regeneração. O amor é, em resumo, a essência do cristianismo. Por isso mesmo é necessário que cada servo de Jesus faça uma reavaliação de seu procedimento, para que verifique o quanto tem obedecido ao Senhor no tocante à prática do amor em sua vida». (Delcyr de Souza Lima, *Pontos Salientes*, 1970, Casa Publicadora Batista, Rio de Janeiro, GB).

A mensagem de I João é: *O amor é a prova da espiritualidade.*

Não há nunca amor perfeito
Sem tortura e sem cuidado.
Amar é ter Deus no peito,
Outra vez crucificado.
  (Augusto Gil, Porto, Portugal, 1873-1929).

«Agora, pois, permanecem a fé, a esperança e o amor, estes três; porém, o maior destes é o amor». (I Cor. 13:13).

VIII. Citações que ilustram a nobreza do Amor

O Matrimônio de Mentes Verazes
Que ao matrimônio de mentes verazes
Não admitia eu empecilhos. Amor não é amor
Se se altera quando encontra alterações,
Ou se se inclina para remover o removedor.
Oh, não! Mas é um alvo sempre fixo,
Que encara tempestades e nunca se abala:
É a estrela de toda barca ao léu,
Cujo valor desconhece, embora sua altura seja tomada.
O amor não é escravo do tempo, embora lábios e faces rosadas
Apareçam dentro da encurvada foice;
O amor não se altera com as horas e as semanas,
Mas resiste até mesmo à beira da condenação:
Se isso labora em erro, e for provado contra mim,
Nunca escrevi, e nenhum homem jamais ensinou.
  (William Shakespeare, 1565 — 1616).

O amor altera e enobrece as coisas:
Deus seja louvado, a pior de suas criaturas
Jacta de dois lados na alma, uma para enfrentar o mundo,
E outra para mostrar a uma mulher, quando a ama.
  (Robert Browning)

Ai! o amor das mulheres! sabe-se
Que é coisa amável e temível.
  (Lord Byron)

«Os estóicos definem o amor como a tentativa de formar uma amizade inspirada pela beleza». (Cícero, *Turculanae Disputationes*).

«Todos nós nascemos para amar...Esse é o princípio da existência e sua única finalidade». (Benjamim Disraeli, *Sybil*).

O amor concede em um momento
O que o trabalho não poderia obter em uma era.
  (Goethe, «Torquato Tasso»).

«Se queres ser amado, ama». (Hecato, *fragmentos*, 550 A.C.).

O amor é a prova da *espiritualidade*:
Amados, amemo-nos uns aos outros, porque o amor é de Deus; e todo o que ama é nascido de Deus e conhece a Deus. (I Jo. 4:7)
Deus é amor. (I Jo. 4:8)

«O amor é o símbolo da eternidade. Apaga todo o senso de tempo, destruindo toda a memória de um começo e todo o temor de um fim». (Madame de Stael, *Corinne*).

Amor é felicidade trêmula.
......
O amor apaixonado é uma sede insaciável.
......
O amor, como a morte, muda tudo.

«O químico que pode extrair de seu próprio coração os elementos de compaixão, de respeito, de anelo, de paciência, de lamento, de surpresa e de perdão, compondo-os em um só, pode criar aquele átomo que se chama Amor».
  (*The Spiritual Sayings of Kahlil Gibran*)

«Ninguém tem maior amor do que este: de dar alguém a própria vida em favor dos seus amigos» (João 15:13).

«No amor não existe medo; antes, o perfeito amor lança fora o medo» (I João 4:18).

«...aonde quer que fores, irei eu, e onde quer que pousares, ali pousarei eu; o teu povo é o meu povo, o teu Deus é o meu Deus» (Rute 1:16).

«As muitas águas não poderiam apagar o amor, nem os rios afogá-lo...» (Can. 8:7). (B IB NTI RO S UN Z)

AMOREIRA

No grego, **sukáminos**, palavra que pode ser traduzida por «amoreira», e, segundo alguns estudiosos, até mesmo «figueira». Tal palavra aparece somente em Luc. 17:6, nas palavras de Jesus: «Se tivésseis fé como um grão de mostarda, diríeis a esta amoreira...» A amoreira é a *Morus nigra*, que é natural da Palestina e da Grécia, havendo também a *Morus alba*, que é uma variante. Mas a primeira é cultivada por seu fruto, ao passo que a segunda é cultivada por causa de suas folhas, que são o principal alimento do bicho-da-seda. A amoreira pode crescer até cerca de onze metros de altura, com densa folhagem, produzindo uma sombra bastante densa. *Morus nigra* existe na Palestina desde os tempos mais remotos, mas a *Morus alba* só foi introduzida na Palestina há cem anos. A árvore a qual nosso Senhor se referiu, portanto, sem dúvida alguma era a primeira. (Ver *Sicômoro*).

AMOREIRAS

A palavra hebraica aparece em quatro trechos: II Sam. 5:23,24 e I Crô. 14:14,15. Provavelmente está em vista a *Populus euphratica*, uma espécie vegetal abundante no vale do Jordão, e que também pode ser a mesma espécie chamada «salgueiro», em Sal. 137:2, em cujas árvores os judeus penduravam suas harpas, na tristeza decorrente do cativeiro. A árvore pertence à mesma família do algodoeiro. Os bichos-da-seda alimentam-se das folhas de uma espécie de amoreira, a *Morus alba*. E a *Morus nigra*, uma amora preta, produz um fruto comestível. É possível que a amoreira, mencionada por Jesus em Lucas 17:6, seja a amora branca. No hebraico, a palavra *baka* significa «choro», indicando gotas que destilavam, o que leva alguns estudiosos a pensar que não está em foco a moderna amoreira, embora a referência em Lucas seja à amoreira genuína. No livro apócrifo de I Macabeus 6:24 há uma referência a essa árvore. (UN Z)

AMORREUS

1. *Nome*. No acadiano, **amurru**. Traduzia o sumério *mar-tu*, que parece significar «ocidental». Mas, se isso corresponde à realidade, por que esse povo chamava a si mesmo desse modo? Alguns têm sugerido «habitantes dos cumes», que parece mais provável como um nome, embora conte com menos apoio do que a primeira possibilidade. A conclusão é que a origem e o significado desse nome permanece na dúvida.

2. *Lugar*. Os amorreus ocupavam um território bastante pequeno, começando da metade do mar Morto para o norte, para o leste do mar Morto, passando por cima do mesmo, ao longo da margem oriental do rio Jordão. Mas, quando os israelitas entraram na Terra Prometida, os amorreus aparentemente ocupavam ambas as margens do Jordão, acima do mar Morto.

3. *O povo*. Eles eram cananeus, e aparentemente a mais poderosa das tribos cananéias. O trecho de Gên. 14:7 é a primeira referência bíblica a eles, localizando-os no deserto da Judéia, não longe do mar Morto, em um local posteriormente denominado En-Gedi. Seu território posterior, porém, estendia-se até o outro lado do mar Morto. Nas promessas feitas a Abraão (ver Gên. 15:16,21), os amorreus foram especificamente mencionados como um dos povos cujo território seria dado à posteridade de Abraão. Quando Israel ocupou a terra, os territórios a leste do mar Morto, que antes eram dos amorreus, ficaram com as tribos de Rúben, Gade e a meia-tribo de Manassés.

Referências extrabíblicas. Os amorreus eram tão proeminentes entre os cananeus que o nome deles podia ser usado para indicar todos os cananeus (ver Jos. 24:8). Nas cartas de Tel-el-Amarna o nome *Amurri* inclui a Palestina-Fenícia. Os registros mostram que Sargão o Grande, de Acade, enviou pelo menos duas expedições à terra de *Amurru*, e esse vocábulo envolvia o que agora faz parte da Síria. Outras evidências mostram que porções da Mesopotâmia também eram chamadas por esse nome, e o próprio rei Hamurabi da Babilônia (cerca de 1792-1750 A.C.) foi chamado de amorreu. No quinto ano de Ibbi-Sin de Ur (2025 A.C.), os amorreus penetraram profundamente na Suméria, isolando Nipur e Isin, no norte da capital de Ur, que ficava no sul. O poder deles propagou-se por toda aquela região, com a deteriorização do poder de Ur. Em cerca de 1895 A.C., um chefe amorreu de nome Sumabum, começou a reinar sobre a Babilônia. Em cerca de 1814 A.C., um amorreu chamado Shamshi-Adad começou a reinar na Assíria. Veio assim a controlar um reino que se ampliava desde o leste do rio Tigre até bem dentro da Síria, no oeste. Seu filho, Iasmaque-Adade, governou a cidade de Mari por dezessete anos (1796-1780 A.C.), o que foi a idade áurea dos amorreus. Pode-se ver através desses detalhes que os amorreus da Bíblia representavam apenas uma parcela pequena do que fora antes um vasto império.

4. *As conquistas israelitas*. No tempo da invasão israelita da Palestina, os reis amorreus Seom, de Hesbom, e Ogue, rei de Basã, governavam a maior parte da Transjordânia (ver Jos. 12:1-6; Juí. 1:36). A conquista desses dois reinos foi o primeiro estágio da possessão da Terra Prometida. Gade, Rúben e a meia-tribo de Manassés ocuparam a terra deles, que mais tarde foi uma das doze regiões que davam sustento à corte de Salomão (ver I Reis 7:7). Os habitantes de Ai eram chamados amorreus, e houve tempo em que Jerusalém, Hebrom, Jarmute, Laquis e Eglon eram fortalezas dos amorreus que Israel foi forçado a vencer (ver Jos. 10:1-27).

5. *A absorção*. Os amorreus foram reduzidos à servidão e foram sendo gradualmente absorvidos (ver I Reis 9:20). Deixaram de existir como uma nação, mas a sua memória permaneceu na idolatria, a qual era comparada à de Acabe e Manassés que adotaram costumes pagãos (ver I Reis 21:26 e II Reis 21:11).

6. *Idioma*. A maior parte do nosso conhecimento da língua dos amorreus deriva-se dos tabletes de Mari, que chegam a milhares. Mari (Tell Hariri) era uma das capitais dos amorreus. Esses tabletes estão atualmente no Museu de Louvre, em Paris. Escavações começaram nesse antigo local dos amorreus em 1933. Os tabletes, cerca de vinte em número, dão todos os tipos de informação sobre aqueles antigos povos e também iluminam aspectos da vida patriarcal da Palestina. Esses tabletes mostram que a língua dos amorreus pertencia ao ramo ocidental da família semítica de idiomas, aparentada do ugarítico, do cananeu, do hebraico e do árabe. A língua dos amorreus era a mãe da língua aramaica. O Antigo Testamento contém algumas palavras diretamente tomadas por empréstimo da língua que aparece nos textos de Mari.

7. *O deus Amurru*. No século XVIII A.C., Degã era a principal divindade dos amorreus, e o deus Tesube prevalecia no reino de Amurru, da época de Amarna (1400-1200 A.C.). O nome *Amurru* (no sumério, *Mar-tu*) também tem sido encontrado na Assíria e na Babilônia. Amurru-Martu era o filho do deus-firmamento An. Amurru era um típico deus das tempestades, violento, destruidor de cidades, provocador de confusão, uma espécie de Zeus secundário. Naturalmente, a idolatria fazia parte desse culto, não havendo apenas uma divindade. Baal e Astarte eram outros bem conhecidos deuses dos amorreus (ver Jos. 24:15 e Juí. 6:10). Tais divindades exerceram uma influência corruptora sobre os israelitas. (AM CL ND OP UN Z)

AMÓS

Ver sobre *Autoria*, item três do artigo sobre o livro *Amós*.

AMÓS

No hebraico, **forte**. Era o pai do profeta Isaías e irmão de Amazias, rei de Judá (ver II Reis 19:2; 20:1,2; II Crô. 26:22; 27:20,32; Isa. 1:1; 2:1; 13:1; 20:2 e 37:2). Todavia, alguns dos primeiros escritores cristãos confundiram-no com o profeta Amós, como Clemente de Alexandria (*Strom*. 1:21; sec. 111). (S)

••• ••• •••

AMÓS, LIVRO DE

Esboço:
1. Pano de fundo
2. Data
3. Autoria e unidade
4. Lugar de origem e destino
5. Canonicidade e texto
6. Mensagem e conteúdo
7. Amós e o Novo Testamento

Introdução. Amós foi um dos doze profetas menores, sendo nativo de Tecoa, cidade a dez quilômetros ao sul de Belém. Era pastor, mas foi chamado por Deus a fim de profetizar nos dias dos reis Uzias, de Judá, e Jeroboão, de Israel, em cerca de 786-746 A.C. Os *profetas menores* não são aqueles que se revestem de menor importância, como alguns poderiam entender a expressão, e, sim, aqueles que *escreveram menos.* Sua vida tranqüila foi perturbada por uma séria de visões que o levaram à conclusão hesitante de que Israel estava prestes a ser aniquilada como nação, a despeito de afirmar-se sob a perpétua proteção de Deus. Yahweh, que lhe deu a mensagem, é visto como o criador e soberano de toda a natureza, bem como o justo juiz da história, o qual intervém na vida humana. Isso expõe um ponto de vista *teísta*, e não *deísta* de Deus. Ver os artigos sobre esses termos. O teísmo ensina que Deus não somente criou, mas também está interessado e faz intervenções em Sua criação, recompensando ou punindo. Por sua vez, o deísmo ensina que o criador, ou alguma força cósmica que deu origem às coisas, abandonou a sua criação, deixando-a sob o controle das leis naturais.

1. Pano de fundo

Uzias, de Judá, e Jeroboão II, de Israel (ambos reinaram no mesmo período), desfrutaram de paz e prosperidade. Os inimigos militares estavam quietos ou haviam sido esmagados. A Assíria havia derrotado a Síria, permitindo que Jeroboão II ampliasse as suas fronteiras (ver II Reis 14:25). O comércio trouxe novo surto de riquezas. Tanto Judá (ao sul) quanto Israel (ao norte) cresceram, e o reino de Israel combinado com o de Judá chegou a ter quase as mesmas dimensões que tivera na época de Davi e Salomão, a era áurea de Israel. Embora a Assíria estivesse se tornando uma ameaça militar, sob o governo de Tiglate-Pileser III (745-727 A.C.), qualquer ameaça vinda daquela direção parecia remota àqueles que descansavam na prosperidade de Israel.

Sucedeu que a prosperidade material, como é usual, provocou suas corrupções sociais e religiosas. A vida fácil estava debilitando moralmente o povo (ver Amós 2:6-8; 5:11,12). Amós sentiu ser necessário denunciar a vida de luxo, a idolatria e a depravação moral do povo, advertindo sobre julgamento e cativeiro final. A adoração do Baal dos cananeus foi incorporada no culto de Israel, e a arqueologia tem demonstrado que a religião cananéia contemporânea do profeta era a religião mais corrupta que havia no Oriente Próximo. A prostituição ritual fazia parte desse culto. Alcoolismo, violência, grosseira sensualidade e idolatria eram fatores constantes. Israel participava dessa corrupção (ver Amós 4:4,5 e 5:5), corrompendo totalmente o ideal do *monoteísmo* (ver o artigo a respeito). A degradação geral degenerou para a injustiça judicial, onde os ricos exploravam os pobres, produzindo um virtual estado escravocrata.

A arqueologia tem trazido a lume evidências da extensão da prosperidade do comércio nessa época, em Samaria, riquezas que se espalhavam para outras partes de Israel. As ostraca samaritanas, atribuídas ao reinado de Jeroboão II, alguns sessenta e três casos inscritos à tinta, recuperados em 1910, encontrados pela expedição Harvard à Samaria, em ruínas a oeste do local do palácio real, contêm detalhes sobre o comércio, sobre os impostos e sobre itens luxuosos, sobre o vinho e o azeite. O selo de jaspe de Sema, servo de Jeroboão, descoberto em Megido, em 1904, ilustra as realizações artísticas do povo daquela época. Seus leitos eram decorados com engastes de mármores, com representações de lírios, veados, leões, esfinges e figuras humanas aladas. Foi um período de vida ociosa, riqueza, arte e lassidão moral. Em outras palavras, Israel tornara-se uma nação doente, como sucede à maioria das sociedades abastadas. A opressão contra os pobres era intensa (ver Amós 2:6 ss), os faminitos eram deixados faminitos (ver Amós 6:3-6), a justiça se vendia a quem subornasse mais (ver Amós 2:6 e 8:6), os agiotas exploravam suas vítimas (ver Amós 5:11 ss ; 8:4-6). A religião não era negligenciada, mas havia sido pervertida (ver Amós 3:4; 4:4 e 7:9). O julgamento divino era iminente.

2. Data

Corria o segundo quartel do século VIII A.C., durante os reinados de Uzias, rei de Judá (779-740 A.C.) e Jeroboão, rei de Israel (Samaria) (783-743 A.C.). Esses dois reis reinaram ao mesmo tempo pelo espaço de trinta anos, de 779 a 743 A.C. Durante parte desse tempo, Amós profetizou e escreveu o seu livro. Foi-lhe ordenado que retornasse à sua terra nativa de Judá, após ter pregado em Israel durante algum tempo (ver Amós 7:10-13), e isso pôs fim à sua carreira como profeta de Yahweh. Não há como determinar a data exata da escrita de seu livro, embora o período geral seja óbvio.

3. Autoria e unidade

a. *O homem Amós.* Nasceu em Tecoa, aldeia a dez quilômetros ao sul de Belém. Era pastor, sem treinamento teológico, acerca de quem nada sabemos até o momento de sua chamada. Também trabalhava como cultivador de sicômoros (ver Amós 7:14). Migrava em certo período do ano para o território mais fértil de Efraim, onde trabalhava com os sicômoros. Portanto, era um *leigo* humilde e seminômade, e não um membro da classe profética (ver I Reis 22:6 ss), tendo-se recusado a ser chamado de profeta, embora admitindo ter sido forçado a entrar no ministério profético, por comissão divina. Em uma série de visões, provavelmente no fim da primavera ou no verão de 751 ou 750 A.C., (ver Amós 7:1-9 e 8:1-3) ele recebeu sua espantosa mensagem concernente à iminente destruição e deportação do povo de Israel. Foi acusado de conspiração contra Jeroboão e foi ameaçado por Amazias, sumo sacerdote de Betel. Após ter cumprido sua missão, Amós retornou a Judá. Permanecem desconhecidos o tempo e a maneira de sua morte, bem como quaisquer detalhes subseqüentes de sua vida.

b. *A escrita.* Como é óbvio, a mensagem de Amós foi genuinamente preservada no livro intitulado por seu nome. Mas o texto hebraico não indica que o próprio Amós tenha escrito o seu livro. Alguns supõem que as profecias de Amós existiam a princípio como tradição oral, posteriormente reduzida à forma escrita por uma pessoa ou mais. Contra isso, argumenta-se que a notável higidez do texto hebraico do livro, além de sua evidente unidade, sugere, se não mesmo prova que Amós ou um amanuense de sua escolha escreveu o livro. Naturalmente, não há como provar coisa alguma no tocante a isso. O evangelho de Marcos poderia ser intitulado evangelho de Pedro, visto que preserva, essencialmente, suas memórias

AMÓS, LIVRO DE

(embora, como é óbvio, tenha havido outras fontes informativas). Isso é verdade, apesar do fato de que o próprio Pedro não escreveu o evangelho de Marcos. Por igual modo, o livro de Amós pode com razão ser chamado «livro de Amós», porquanto preserva a mensagem desse profeta, mesmo que o livro não tenha sido produção literária de sua pena.

c. *Unidade*. O vocábulo *unidade* é usado para destacar que a matéria do livro em pauta vem de um mesmo período, por um único autor, ou se representa uma compilação e obra de um editor (ou editores, em diferentes períodos). Alguns problemas sugeridos: 1. Alguns estudiosos sugerem que as visões (ver Amós 7:1-9; 8:1-3 e 9:1-4) pertencem a um período anterior à missão de Amós a Israel, e que já existiam como um documento separado antes do terremoto (ver Amós 1:1), o que serviu para salientar a mensagem condenatória dessas visões. A isso, presumivelmente foi adicionado o trecho de Amós 8:4-14 algum tempo mais tarde. 2. Em seguida, os capítulos primeiro a sexto são encarados como uma unidade separada, coligida no final do ministério de Amós a Israel. Então, presumivelmente esses dois documentos foram unidos nos dias do exílio ou após o exílio. 3. A essa combinação, foram acrescentados alguns comentários editoriais. Dois documentos separados seriam sugeridos na terminologia de Amós 1:1, «Palavras que, em visão, vieram a Amós...» e em Amós 7:1: «Isto me fez ver o Senhor...», onde a palavra «visão» não é diretamente usada. 4. Outros estudiosos aceitam o livro como essencialmente uno, embora supondo que houve pequenas adições, sugerindo como tais os trechos de Amós 1:9,10,11,12 e 2:4,5, além das três doxologias, em 4:13; 5:8 e 9:5,6, e a passagem messiânico-milenial de 9:11-15. Outros retrucam que essas supostas adições são fragmentos de imaginações dos eruditos, que entendem mal a história do desenvolvimento da religião de Israel. Conceitos posteriores, segundo alguns, poderiam ter existido em uma época anterior à que geralmente se supõe. Contra a dupla divisão do livro, alguns argumentam que um exame cuidadoso do livro revela que não há diferença real entre essas duas porções, quanto ao conteúdo ou à natureza teológica, e que dividir o livro em «palavras» (primeira seção) e «visões» (segunda seção) é um artificialismo que não resiste à investigação séria. A conclusão disso tudo é que o livro é essencialmente uma unidade homogênea, com algumas possíveis adições editoriais, feitas ou pelo escriba original, ou por algum editor posterior. E contrariando o argumento de que houve adições teológicas pertencentes a uma data posterior (o que teria ocorrido em Amós 4:13; 5:8 e 9:5,6), alguns salientam que as supostas idéias posteriores, ali contidas, já se encontram firmemente arraigadas na lei mosaica. (Idéias envolvidas: Deus como criador, misterioso, desconhecido, majestático; o controlador de toda a natureza, misterioso em Sua atuação, imanente na natureza, causa de tudo quanto acontece. Esses conceitos são expressos em forma poética exaltada, mas todos os conceitos ali encontrados podem ser vistos nas mais antigas Escrituras Sagradas, pelo que não refletem necessariamente uma época posterior à de Amós).

4. Lugar de origem e destino

Conforme já dissemos, Amós era de Tecoa, a dezesseis quilômetros ao sul de Jerusalém, atualmente representada pelas ruínas de um local de cinco acres de área, em Khirbet Taqu'a. Foi para Samaria e profetizou em Betel, de onde foi expulso. Então voltou para sua casa. É impossível dizermos onde escreveu seu livro, ou se escreveu porções do mesmo em diversos lugares (ver Amós 1:1 e 7:12,14,15). Embora tivesse profetizado no reino do norte (Israel), suas profecias foram endereçadas a todo o povo israelita, do norte e do sul, de Israel e Judá (ver Amós 1:1 e 2:4), incluindo uma denúncia contra todas as nações que se recusam a adorar a Deus de maneira certa, mas que têm corrompido o seu caminho (ver Amós 1:3,6,9,11 e 2:1,4,6).

5. Canonicidade e texto

Amós aparece como o terceiro entre os doze profetas menores. Mas, cronologicamente, ele foi um dos primeiros profetas escritores. O livro é amplamente confirmado por autoridades judaicas e cristãs, como Filo, Josefo, o Talmude, e naturalmente, catálogos do cristianismo antigo, desde os primórdios cristãos. Nos dias de Jesus, os fariseus aceitavam os Salmos e os Profetas como livros canônicos, juntamente com o Pentateuco; mas os saduceus aceitavam somente o Pentateuco como canônico. Os judeus da dispersão aceitavam os escritos apócrifos, representados na Septuaginta, tradução da Bíblia hebraica para o grego. (Ver o artigo sobre os *livros apócrifos*). O Novo Testamento cita e faz alusão a esses livros, e podemos supor que os cristãos primitivos (pelo menos muitos deles) defendiam o cânon representado pela Septuaginta. Seja como for, Amós era livro canônico na situação cristão-judaica, com a única exceção dos saduceus. Ver o artigo sobre o *cânon*.

O texto hebraico do livro de Amós acha-se em boas condições, embora alguns eruditos vejam problemas nos trechos de 2:7; 3:13; 5:6,26; 7:2 e 8:1, onde sugerem textos variantes e emendas. A versão da Septuaginta, além de outras versões antigas, parece ter sido traduzida de um texto relacionado ao texto massorético (ver o artigo a respeito). Os fragmentos do livro de Amós, encontrado nas cavernas de Qumran não apresentam quaisquer diferenças importantes do texto tradicional, embora a Septuaginta algumas vezes exponha o texto correto, e não esse texto.

6. Mensagem e conteúdo

a. *O conceito de Deus*. Amós tinha um elevado conceito de Deus. Deus é o criador (4:13), além de ser o sustentador da criação (4:8; 9:6). Deus julga e castiga o pecado sob a forma de fome (ver 4:6-11), ou confere a abundância (9:13). Deus controla os destinos dos povos (1:5). Ele é o Juiz e o determinador das leis morais, considerando os homens responsáveis por seus atos (1:3-2:3).

b. *A lei moral*. Amós deixou claro que nenhuma formalidade, rito, cerimônia, festividade ou qualquer outro fator, pode substituir a moralidade e a piedade básicas. Se os homens não seguirem as implicações dessa verdade, terão de enfrentar o julgamento (ver 5:27). Deus ameaça os ímpios (9:1). Ele denuncia a injustiça social (ver 2:6-8; 4:1 ss. e 6:1 ss.).

c. *Arrependimento*. Esse é o objetivo colimado das profecias condenatórias (ver 5:4,11,15,24).

d. *O julgamento não é a palavra final*. O profeta encerra com uma promessa de dias mais brilhantes (ver 9:11-15), dizendo que essa será a obra divina no futuro. Ver Rom. 11:26. Contudo, a profecia de Amós foi rejeitada. E suas ameaças tiveram cumprimento, cerca de cinquenta anos depois.

Esboço do conteúdo:

I. Juízos proferidos contra várias nações, Damasco, Filístia, Fenícia, Edom, Amom, Moabe (1:1 - 2:3), Israel (2:6-16) e Judá (2:4,5).

II. Acusação de Deus contra a família inteira de Jacó (3:1 - 9:10).

1. Três sermões de denúncia (3:1 - 6:15)
2. Cinco visões simbólicas (7:1 - 9:10)
III. A futura bênção do reino dada a Israel (9:11-15).
1. O reinado do Messias (9:11,12)
2. A prosperidade do milênio (9:13)
3. A nação judaica restaurada (9:14,15)

7. Amós e no Novo Testamento

Estêvão, em seu discurso diante do Sinédrio (ver Atos 7:42,43), citou o trecho de Amós 5:25-27. Tiago, falando diante do concílio de Jerusalém (ver Atos 15:16), citou o trecho de Amós 9:11. Essa circunstância demonstra, naturalmente, que Amós, um livro do V.T., era considerado autoritário, por judeus e cristãos do século I D.C. (AM CRI HAR I ND UN Z)

AMOSIS

Um monarca egípcio, fundador da XVII dinastia, que se tornou rei em cerca de 1585 A.C. O período de sua subida ao trono e a mudança que então teve lugar na família reinante, sugerem que ele foi o novo rei do Egito «que não conhecera a José» (Êxo. 1:8). Se ele fosse da distante província de Tebas, seria natural que os hebreus lhe fossem estranhos, e que ele os olhasse com desconfiança e desprezo. (S)

AMPLIATIVO

Vem do latim, **ampliare**, «ampliar». Os juízos ampliativos são os juízos *sintéticos*, isto é, aqueles cujos predicados não estão implícitos no sentido de seus termos, conforme se vê em uma declaração como: «As órbitas dos planetas são elipses». O termo órbita não requer a descrição «elipse», visto que as órbitas podem ter outras formas, como a circular. Portanto, elipse seria um juízo sintético, visto que acrescenta algo à idéia de órbita, descrevendo-a, conforme se vê em certos casos. O contrário do juízo ampliativo ou sintético é o juízo analítico (ver o artigo), onde o predicado é logicamente subentendido no sujeito. (EP F MM)

AMPLÍATO

Um crente de Roma ou da Ásia Menor, a quem Paulo enviou saudações, em cerca de 60 D.C., chamando-o de «meu dileto amigo no Senhor» (Rom. 16:8). Era um nome comum na época, com o sentido de *honrado* ou *expandido*. Foi encontrado por duas vezes no cemitério de Domitila, em Roma. A mais antiga das duas inscrições data do século I A.C. Alguns eruditos acreditam que o décimo sexto capítulo de Romanos representa um acréscimo feito a essa epístola, sendo o fim de uma carta menor por si mesma, recomendando Febe aos crentes da Ásia Menor, e não de Roma. As evidências em prol dessa conjectura são abordadas na introdução ao décimo sexto capítulo de Romanos, no NTI. Se tal conjectura tem razão, então o homem aqui em foco era crente da Ásia Menor e não de Roma, provavelmente um dos convertidos de Paulo em suas primeiras viagens missionárias. (A NTI)

AMULETO

Provavelmente vem do vocábulo árabe que significa *pendente*, ou *levar* (ver Isa. 3:20). Desde os dias mais remotos, os orientais criam na influência das estrelas, na bruxaria, nos encantamentos, nos poderes sobrenaturais que se ocultam em certos lugares e que podem ser influenciados para ajudar ou prejudicar outras pessoas, curar enfermidades e proteger do mal. Em relação a tais coisas, quase todos os povos antigos usavam *amuletos* (ver Plínio, *hist. Nat.* xxx.15). Com freqüência eram inscritos com sentenças sagradas, orações ou encantamentos, com o propósito de curar enfermidades, proteger contra qualquer dano, físico ou espiritual, etc., conforme sugerimos acima. O trecho de Isaías 3:20, em uma lista de jóias e enfeites condenados, inclui a palavra, usando o termo que literalmente significa *sussurro, encantamento*, e também o silvo de uma serpente, enfim, tudo o que sugere a prática dos encantadores de serpentes. Comparar com Sal. 58:5; Ecl. 10:11 e Jer. 8:17.

Os amuletos tinham muitos formatos e eram feitos dos mais diferentes materiais. A arqueologia tem desenterrado inúmeras espécimes. Eram jóias lapidadas, talhadas e inscritas com fórmulas mágicas; pedras, discos lunares associados à adoração de Astarte ou Istar; conchas furadas, origem dos camafeus; pérolas, dentes, brincos, anéis, etc. Embora a prática fosse condenada, os hebreus não resistiam e usavam amuletos. A multidão reunida diante do Sinai tinha jóias e pendentes suficientes para prover a Aarão o material suficiente para fabricar o bezerro de ouro. Judas Macabeu ficou horrorizado quando encontrou amuletos sob as túnicas dos soldados mortos em batalha, os quais evidentemente não cumpriram o seu papel (ver II Macabeus 12:40). É possível que as filactérias, pequenas caixas contendo citações extraídas da lei (especialmente trechos de Êxo. 13:1-16 e Deu. 6:4-9; 11:18), usadas no antebraço ou na testa, fossem usadas como amuletos, para todos os intuitos e propósitos. A palavra filactéria (no grego, *fulakterion*) (ver Mat. 23:5) significa «salvaguarda», e a conexão com a filosofia dos amuletos é óbvia. Os tufos de tecidos, com cordões vermelhos, que eram usados nos quatro cantos das vestes (ver Núm. 15:37-41 e Mat. 23:5), bem como as sinetas que decoravam as vestes do sumo sacerdote, provavelmente tinham o intuito de funcionar como amuletos.

Muitos crentes do primeiro século cristão usavam amuletos assinalados com a figura de um peixe, um símbolo de Cristo e do cristianismo; ou então um pentângulo, que consistia de três triângulos em intersecção, com as linhas arranjadas de tal modo que apontavam para os lugares onde o Salvador fora ferido. Mais tarde, fitas com sentenças extraídas das Escrituras eram penduradas no pescoço. O concílio de Trulo ordenou que os fabricantes de amuletos fossem excomungados, o que foi uma medida contra tais superstições.

Agostinho falou severamente contra os brincos, usados como amuletos, em seus dias (ver *Epist.* 75, *ad Pos.*). A prática persistiu até os tempos modernos. O reformador Calvino escarneceu dos alegados fragmentos da cruz e de inúmeros cravos que supostamente foram tirados da cruz de Cristo, considerando as relíquias dos santos e mártires, embora não fossem amuletos propriamente ditos, como artigos de superstição. (AM S UN Z)

ANA

No hebraico, **graça**. Nome de várias pessoas na Bíblia.

1. A esposa de Tobias (ver Tobias 1:9).
2. Uma idosa viúva, filha de Fanuel, da tribo de Aser. Ela casara-se cedo, mas, após sete anos de casamento, seu marido falecera. Seguiu-se uma longa

viuvez, na qual ela demonstrou grande piedade, servindo no templo de manhã e à tarde. Embora a sua tribo tivesse sido levada pelo cativeiro assírio, e nunca houvesse retornado oficialmente, genealogias foram preservadas e devolvidas à Terra Prometida, de tal modo que se conhecia a linhagem a que pertencia aquela mulher. Ou Ana tinha 84 anos de idade quando o infante Jesus foi levado ao templo, ou o grego pode querer dizer que ela já vivia como viúva fazia 84 anos. Se esta alternativa é a verdadeira, então ela deveria ter bem mais de cem anos quando viu Jesus. Se ela se casou com 15 anos (comum em Israel), esteve casada por sete anos, — e agora era viúva há 84 anos, isso lhe daria 106 anos de idade, por ocasião da visita do infante Jesus ao templo. Jesus foi trazido ao templo por Sua mãe. Tomando Jesus nos braços, Simeão, impulsionado pelo Espírito de Deus, proferiu sua ação de graças. Então Ana irrompeu em louvores (ver Luc. 2:36-38). O Messias foi reconhecido.

3. Nome da mãe de Maria e avó materna de Jesus, de acordo com o apócrifo *Protevangelium de Tiago*. (Ver o artigo a respeito). As lendas relatam que durante muitos anos Ana foi estéril, mas que ela e seu marido, Joaquim, receberam a promessa de que a situação se reverteria, em resposta às suas orações. Isso sucedeu quando Maria nasceu, tendo sido dedicada ao Senhor por toda a sua vida. Aos três anos de idade, Maria foi levada ao templo por Ana, e ali permaneceu, alimentada pelos anjos, até à idade de 12 anos. Ornatos posteriores fazem Ana tornar-se mãe de duas outras meninas, ambas também chamadas Maria, que se tornaram esposas de Alfeu e Zebedeu.

4. Uma forma variante de Hana (ver I Sam. 1:2). Ana é a forma que aparece ali, em nossa versão portuguesa.

Ver o artigo que segue.

ANA

No hebraico significa **graça, favor**. Era esposa de Elcana, um levita de Efrata, e mãe de Samuel. (Ver I Sam. 1 e 2).

1. *Como esposa sem filhos*. Visto que Ana não tinha filhos, Penina (a outra esposa de Elcana) tornou-se arrogante e insultuosa, multiplicando o opróbrio de Ana entre as mulheres, pois uma esposa sem filhos era considerada uma desgraça em Israel. O fato de que ela era a esposa favorita de Elcana não a ajudava muito, e o favoritismo provavelmente só servia para agravar a atitude de Penina.

2. *Oração para resolver o problema*. Ana orou durante um ano inteiro a respeito da questão, prometendo ao Senhor que se lhe fosse dada uma criança, esta seria dedicada a Deus. A família vivia perto de Ramataim-Zofim, e como era requerido pela lei, eles faziam uma viagem anual a Siló, lugar onde estava o altar de Yahweh. As mulheres não tinham obrigação de fazer-se presentes, mas muitas delas o faziam, por motivo de piedade. Ana também fazia as viagens, embora evitasse as cerimônias. De certa feita, ela foi e ali fez o seu voto. Ela orava em voz baixa (aparentemente os votos eram feitos em voz alta), e o sacerdote Eli pensou que ela estivesse embriagada. Porém, ela explicou o que estava fazendo. Algo lhe segredava que Deus ouvira a sua oração, porque ela retornou de coração alegre.

3. *Nascimento de Samuel*. Antes do fim daquele ano, Ana tornou-se mãe de um menino, destinado a ser o profeta Samuel. Desde seu nascimento, ele foi posto sob os votos do nazireado, aos quais sua mãe o dedicou, cumprindo a sua parte na promessa feita. Isso sucedeu em cerca de 1171 A.C.

4. *Outra viagem a Siló*. Ana não retornou ali enquanto Samuel não atingiu idade suficiente para seguir sozinho na sua vida. Ele foi entregue ao sumo sacerdote, e seu aprendizado teve início. Ela lembrou ao sacerdote de que estava cumprindo o seu voto (ver I Sam. 1:27). Seu regozijo posteriormente produziu um alegre cântico, que tornou-se um notável espécime de antiga poesia lírica (ver I Sam. 3:1-10). Esse cântico foi repetido, em suas formas essenciais, pela virgem Maria, em ocasião similar (ver Luc. 1:46 ss.).

5. *O poder de Deus*. Basta que alguém faça o inesperado para que esse acontecimento inesperado resulte em uma fruição especial na vida desse alguém. Ana não apenas obteve um filho, mas um profeta e sacerdote de grande estatura espiritual.

6. *Depois disso*, Ana continuou a fazer uma viagem anual a Siló, trazendo a Samuel novas vestes, em cada ocasião. A bênção do Senhor continuou sobre ela, e ela teve outros três filhos e duas filhas. (ID S)

ANÁ

No hebraico significa **resposta**. É nome de duas pessoas no Antigo Testamento:

1. Ou um filho ou uma filha de Zibeão, e também pai ou mãe de Oolibama, uma das esposas de Esaú (ver Gên. 36:2,14,18,25; I Crô. 1:40 ss.). O livro de Gênesis diz que tal pessoa era hevéia, que pode significar um heveu. O trecho de Gên. 36:24 diz que ele era o Aná que achou as fontes termais no deserto, e que algumas traduções dizem *mulas*, em vez de fontes termais. As traduções também variam quanto ao gênero dessa pessoa, embora não fosse provável que uma mulher pudesse cumprir as funções descritas no Antigo Testamento acerca de tal pessoa.

2. Filho de Seir, o horeu, e um dos cabeças de uma tribo (ver Gên. 36:29 e I Crô. 1:38). Alguns identificam essa pessoa com a anterior. Outros conjecturam que a diferença quanto ao gênero, nas versões antigas (refletida nas traduções modernas) deve-se ao fato de que duas pessoas diferentes e muito próximas uma de outra eram indicadas pelo mesmo nome. Mas nada se sabe com certeza a esse respeito. (ND S UN Z)

ANÃ

No hebraico, **nuvem**. Há dois homens com esse nome, no Antigo Testamento:

1. Um chefe israelita que assinou o pacto sagrado por ocasião do retorno da Babilônia (ver Nee. 10:26), em cerca de 445-450 A.C.

2. Um homem que retornou do exílio, e que I Esdras 5:30 chama de Hana e também Hanã (ver Eze. 2:46 e Nee. 7:49). (S Z)

ANAARATE

No hebraico, *garganta*. Uma cidade de Issacar (ver Jos. 19:19), provavelmente na porção norte daquele território, localizada no vale de Jezreel (ver Jos. 19:19). Tem sido identificada com a moderna En-Na'urah, a três quilômetros de En-Dor. (S Z)

ANABATISTAS

Esse termo, que significa «rebatizadores», é usado frouxamente para indicar aqueles que questionavam a validade do batismo infantil e requeriam o rebatismo

ANABATISTAS — ANÁFORA

daqueles que quisessem tornar-se membros de seu grupo. Mais especificamente, o termo se aplica àquelas seitas que surgiram em cerca de 1521, em Zurique, pouco antes, durante e após a Reforma Protestante, dependendo do grupo particular em questão. Os anabatistas não formavam uma seita única ou coerente, mas representavam vários graus de ortodoxia. A maior parte dos grupos, porém, afastou-se muito da posição ortodoxa, conforme será delineado no presente artigo. Os grupos variavam de uma relativa ortodoxia, como era a posição evangélica de Conrado Grebel (1485-1528), até à posição mais radical e menos ortodoxa de Baltasar Huebmaier (1485-1528) e de Hans Denk (falecido em 1527). O denominador comum era a insistência deles sobre a necessidade de batizar adultos convertidos apenas, rejeitando terminantemente a validade do batismo infantil. O bastimo de adultos, porém, continuou a ser praticado por aspersão (segundo a maioria dos eruditos), e não por imersão. Entretanto, esse ponto tem sido disputado. Quanta imersão era usada? Católicos e protestantes opunham-se a eles decisivamente, especialmente por causa de suas doutrinas não-ortodoxas, e por serem o centro de revolta e agitação. Primeiramente foram expulsos de Wittenberg, e depois de outras cidades. Muenzer, pregando cada vez mais radicalmente acerca de questões religiosas e políticas, contribuiu para os acontecimentos chamados Guerra dos Aldeões. Opondo-se ao feudalismo, Muenzer promoveu um tipo de comunismo teocrático. O esforço da luta unificou os aldeões alemães contra os abusos políticos e econômicos. Os aldeões foram violentamente suprimidos. Lutero denunciou em termos radicais a revolta e encorajou a repressão.

Suas Doutrinas Distintivas

1. Rejeição do batismo infantil e batismo somente de adultos convertidos. Isso requeria o rebatismo (daí se derivando o nome deles) daqueles que abandonavam outras seitas, e que tinham sido batizados na infância. Esse ponto doutrinário foi radicalizado na forma da convicção de muitos anabatistas de que somente seu grupo era detentor da verdade, e que os membros de outros grupos (incluindo os protestantes) eram pessoas perdidas.

2. Comunidade de bens e de propriedades, como característica constante. Portanto, praticavam uma espécie de comunismo teocrático.

3. A maioria dos anabatistas tinha um conceito não-trinitariano de Deus, e uma noção marcionita (docética) da encarnação. Assim, eles negavam tanto a divindade quanto a humanidade de Jesus Cristo. Ver *Márcion* e o *docetismo*. Cristo, não sendo o vero Deus, de acordo com esse ponto de vista, também não era verdadeiro homem, pois Sua humanidade era apenas aparente. O docetismo é nome derivado do grego *doken*, «parecer». Muitos anabatistas eram antitrinitarianos declarados.

4. Liberdade religiosa e separação entre a Igreja e o estado.

5. Pacifismo, estrita disciplina eclesiástica, prática dos princípios do sermão do monte, reconhecimento e prática da lei do amor.

6. Forte ênfase missionária, pois criam que cada crente tem o dever de ser uma testemunha.

7. Ênfase sobre o dom profético, que algumas vezes era abusado, levando a muitos cismas. Ressaltavam a «palavra interna», e não a «palavra externa», as Escrituras. Isso debilitava entre eles a autoridade da Palavra escrita e permitia um excessivo individualismo.

8. Negação de doutrinas como a total depravação do homem, o pecado original, a eleição e a condenação eterna. Muitos deles eram universalistas. Enfatizavam a capacidade do homem buscar e achar a Deus diretamente, no nível da alma. Portanto, havia um forte elemento místico na fé deles.

Os anabatistas e a história: Os modernos menonitas estão ligados historicamente aos anabatistas, visto que pertencem ao ramo daquela denominação liderado por Meno Simons, após 1536. Ele afastou a seita do radicalismo e a aproximou da ortodoxia evangélica. Outras denominações, como os batistas, os amigos, os irmãos e os hutteritas incorporaram certos aspectos da doutrina anabatista em seus respectivos sistemas. Alguns batistas modernos, ansiosos por encontrarem seitas «batistas» antes da reforma, têm errado ao escolher os anabatistas como um elo com o passado. Mas esse elo não existe nem histórica e nem teologicamente, conforme o demonstram as notas acima. Em suas doutrinas, os anabatistas estavam longe de ser batistas, a despeito da similaridade fortuita dos apelativos desses dois grupos. (AM B C E H LI)

ANABE

No hebraico, **cidade da uva**. Era uma das cidades da região montanhosa de Judá, de onde Josué expulsou os anaquins (ver Jos. 11:21 e 15:13,14). O local ficava a sudoeste de Debir, estando localizada no sítio da moderna Khirbet 'Anab, perto da aldeia de'Anab (antiga Debir), a sudoeste de Hebrom, a vinte e um quilômetros para sudoeste. (S UN Z)

ANACORETA

Vem do grego **anachoreo**, «separar», «retirar-se». O anacoreta era um tipo extremado de asceta cristão, um *recluso*. Certos homens criam que poderiam servir melhor a Deus vivendo uma existência solitária, procurando a vitória sobre os desejos carnais e ocupando-se na meditação e na oração, em busca do desenvolvimento espiritual. Parecia não terem qualquer senso de missão no tocante ao serviço ao próximo. E é precisamente essa deficiência, sem importarem-se com o que de bom tenham feito, que assinalou tal movimento como espiritualmente equivocado.

Antônio, no Egito (250?-356?) foi o primeiro anacoreta cristão, não demorando para que muitos o imitassem. O deserto e as cavernas egípcias do Oriente Médio tornaram-se lugares favoritos para esses retiros. O clima europeu era por demais severo para encorajar ali o movimento. Muitos anacoretas praticavam um ascetismo extremado, com abusos praticados contra o corpo, exposição às intempéries, abrigos e vestes inadequadas, etc. Alguns chegaram ao ponto de passarem anos sentados sobre colunas. Esse tipo de vida satisfazia espiritualmente a um número reduzido, e o *monasticismo* foi iniciado por Pacômio (292?-349), que rejeitou a vida de solidão absoluta. Ver o artigo sobre *o monasticismo*. (AM B E WO)

ANAEL

Irmão de Tobitas e pai de Aicar, que era o tesoureiro, copeiro e guardador do sinete de Senaqueribe, rei da Assíria (ver Tobias 1:21,22). (Z)

ANÁFORA

Vem de um termo grego que significa «oferecer a».

No latim é *oblatio*, a oração eucarística consagratória das liturgias orientais, que corresponde ao Prefácio e ao Cânon da missa romana (ver artigo a respeito). O mais antigo exemplo aparece na *Tradição Apostólica* de Hipólito, cerca de 220 D.C. Essa oração de consagração faz parte essencial do rito eucarístico, que culmina na comunhão. A *anáfora* começa com uma exortação dirigida pelo sacerdote ao povo, para que elevem seus corações, o que recebe a resposta apropriada. Segue-se então uma oração de ação de graças. A oração é interrompida pelo cântico do *Sanctus*, o hino angelical, «Santo, Santo, Santo». O *Sanctus* não fazia parte da mais antiga oração eucarística conhecida por Hipólito, mencionada acima. Mas é seguido por um memorial da obra remidora de Deus em Cristo, bem como um relato da instituição da própria eucaristia, após o que, nas liturgias orientais, segue-se uma *Epiclesis* (ver o artigo a respeito), que ordena que os elementos do pão e do vinho transformem-se no corpo e no sangue de Cristo. Segue-se então a intercessão final para a comunhão e a doxologia. (C E)

ANAÍAS

No hebraico, **Yahweh respondeu**. Nome de duas pessoas no Antigo Testamento:

1. Um levita que se postou à mão direita de Esdras enquanto este lia a lei ao povo, e que provavelmente o ajudou na tarefa (ver Nee. 8:4; I Esdras 9:43).

2. Um dos chefes do povo que se aliou a Neemias em um pacto sagrado (ver Nee. 10:22), em cerca de 445 A.C.

ANALOGIA

Vem do grego **ana**, «conforme», e **logos**, «taxa», «proporção». Dois termos, coisas, situações ou pessoas são positiva ou negativamente comparadas, de onde emergem seus pontos de semelhança ou de contraste.

1. Uma relação de semelhança entre duas coisas ou mais, na busca de conclusões prováveis ou necessárias, dependendo do tipo de relação em pauta. Ao encontrarmos similaridades em alguns pontos, raciocinamos, por analogia, que haverá similaridades em outros pontos. No caso das similaridades não serem suficientes, mediante tal raciocínio concluímos haver ali um caso de *falsa* analogia.

Fracasso da analogia. As analogias podem prover-nos discernimento, embora também possam distorcer (como quando se reduz Deus a um tipo de super-homem, mediante o uso de terminologia da antropologia). Com freqüência são vagas e ilusórias, autocontraditórias ou impróprias. Se tomarmos por empréstimo uma idéia da natureza ou dos relacionamentos humanos, já estaremos manuseando coisas imperfeitas. Aplicá-las então a Deus, deixa-nos com imperfeições ou mesmo erros. Dizemos que Deus está «irado», mas isso dificilmente pode ser entendido em termos das emoções dos seres humanos. Kant mostrou que todos os termos de nossa linguagem envolvem relações de espaço e tempo. Ora, se Deus está além do espaço e do tempo, então nenhuma analogia aplicada a Ele pode ser perfeita, embora comunique importantes conceitos.

2. *Três comuns e importantes analogias*. a. A social: Deus como Pai, e, assim sendo, benévolo e cuidadoso, uma analogia altamente teísta (ver o artigo *teísmo*). b. A analogia mente-corpo: Deus é a alma do universo, tal como a alma do homem é seu ser real. Portanto, a mais elevada Realidade é Deus, que funciona como a Alma de tudo. c. A analogia do artista: Deus produz e amolda criativamente o universo, sendo seu Artista e Artesão. Em tudo há desígnio e beleza, unidade e harmonia. Cada analogia tem seus pontos fortes e fracos, servindo apenas de ilustração, não sendo uma maneira exata para se definir a natureza de Deus.

3. *Outras aplicações*. Guilherme de Ockham negava a validade desse método de se criar proposições teológicas, argumentando que não pode haver analogia do ser, visto que o conceito do ser é unívoco, ou seja, tem apenas um significado apropriado. Ele não achava ser possível o raciocínio ir de um finito conhecido para um infinito desconhecido. Guilherme Paley desenvolveu a linda e ilustrativa analogia baseada no relógio, a fim de demonstrar a existência de Deus por via da necessidade de haver um Planejador para o universo. Karl Barth substituiu a *analogia entis* pela *analogia fidei*, a analogia da fé, visto que a verdade religiosa é dada por Deus.

Tomás de Aquino. Raciocinava ele que, visto que tanto a criatura como o Criador fazem parte da mesma escala metafísica do ser, deveria haver analogias que extraíssem elementos do inferior para ilustrar o superior. Se o homem tem conhecimento, então Deus o tem, em grau eminente. Se o homem tem bondade, então Deus deve ser superbom. Se o homem tem qualidades que buscam a perfeição, então Deus deve ser perfeito. Apesar de Ockham estar com a razão, ao afirmar que é precário raciocinar com base em um finito conhecido para se chegar a um infinito desconhecido, nem por isso a analogia torna-se inútil, porquanto Deus criou o homem à Sua própria imagem, e deve haver alguma coisa nele que seja reflexo do Criador.

4. *A analogia da verdade*. Uma outra analogia útil é aquela que aborda a verdade. Supõe-se que Deus seja a fonte de toda a verdade. Portanto, qualquer verdade descoberta, em qualquer campo do conhecimento, é um reflexo de Deus e Sua inteligência, isto é, o homem pode pensar os pensamentos de Deus, após Ele. Desse modo, todo raciocínio *verdadeiro* é análogo, —e aponta para a Inteligência Superior.

5. *A analogia do ser, ou analogia entis*. Os escolásticos tentaram usar a própria escala do ser para descrever Deus em alguns aspectos. O homem é a imagem de Deus (*imago Dei*, Gên. 1:27), e o resto da criação, fora do homem, é o *vestigium Dei* (Rom. 1), ou seja, vestígios, indícios de Deus. O exame de Sua imagem ou de Seus vestígios presumivelmente produz conhecimento sobre o Criador dessas entidades. O homem inclina-se até certo ponto à perfeição, pelo que presumimos que há um Ser Perfeito. O homem tem alguma inteligência, pelo que deve haver a suprema Inteligência. Pode-se dizer que Deus é como um Pai, uma Luz, um Rei, etc.

6. *Analogias filosóficas*. Aristóteles ficou conhecido por sua declaração: «Como a vista é para o corpo, o entendimento é para a alma...» (*Nicomachean Ethics*, 1096, b.28). Tal fato favorece a idéia da percepção intuitiva da alma, tanto ao usar os dados da percepção dos sentidos, como ao receber «lampejos de entendimento», não necessariamente inerentes aos informes dos sentidos. Aristóteles limitou sua analogia às questões do conhecimento, mas Platão, tal como os escolásticos depois dele, pensava que algo de útil poderia ser dito sobre a Realidade Última, mediante a observação da natureza da realidade inferior. Isso poderia ser feito mediante *negações* (o infinito *não* é como o finito em vários particulares, como temporalidade, finitude, confinamento ao

ANALOGIA FALSA — ANAMNESE

espaço e ao tempo, etc.), mediante *causalidade* (o infinito é a causa do finito), e mediante a analogia da *imagem do homem* (o homem tem muitas qualidades como bondade, beleza, inteligência, etc., que podem ser reflexos do divino). (B C E EP F HA P PA)

ANALOGIA FALSA

Ver o artigo sobre **analogia**. As analogias podem ser úteis para aclarar-nos o entendimento; mas também podem ser abusadas e tornar-se prejudiciais, pervertendo a verdade. Uma analogia teísta é que «Deus é Pai», o que exprime uma profunda verdade. Mas isso pode ser pervertido se introduzirmos as qualidades e defeitos dos pais terrenos, e então dizermos que Deus deve compartilhar dos mesmos. Por exemplo, Deus teria uma esposa ou esposas, daí derivando-se Seus filhos espirituais, que seriam as almas humanas. Assim pensa o islamismo. Uma analogia útil é aquela que diz que Deus é um artista. Sua criação seria Sua obra-prima; e aquilo que aparentemente não se encaixa dentro da analogia, poderia ser comparado com as cores que parecem estar fora de lugar em uma pintura, até que o artista complete a sua obra. E então vemos como todas as coisas ajustam-se aos seus lugares. Porém, podemos levar isso muito longe, conforme têm feito alguns filósofos e teólogos, os quais negam a própria existência do mal, que presumivelmente, não seria uma entidade real, mas apenas a existência de algum bem. William Palley desenvolveu a bela e complexa analogia do relógio, mostrando que a criação pode ser comparada a um relógio, em todo o seu intricado inter-relacionamento, o que requer que creiamos na existência de um projetista desse relógio, pois um instrumento dessa natureza não pode surgir ao acaso. Por igual modo, a misteriosa e majestática criação, que contemplamos com nossos olhos, exige que pensemos em um divino Planejador, o Criador. E isso é exposto no *argumento teleológico*, sobre o qual escrevi um artigo separado. Não obstante, Deus é diferente e muito superior a qualquer fabricante de relógios.

Dentro da lógica, falamos sobre a falácia das falsas analogias. Essa falácia é cometida quando alguém argumenta com base em uma analogia, mas daí conclui aquilo que não se segue necessariamente. Por exemplo: «Ambulâncias e viaturas policiais podem desrespeitar a luz vermelha dos semáforos, se estão com urgência; assim, se eu estou com pressa, posso fazer a mesma coisa». No campo moral, poderíamos dizer que visto que certo espião, durante a guerra, ao ser capturado pelo inimigo negou que era espião, e visto que seus captores não puderam obter evidências comprobatórias, ele escapou à morte; assim também quando eu estiver em alguma dificuldade, poderei mentir a fim de escapar de resultados adversos. Ou então, que em vista de existirem sociedades onde seus velhos são abandonados e deixados ao relento para morrerem, em meu próprio caso posso abandonar meus pais, em circunstâncias adversas, para que sobrevivam segundo puderem ou para morrerem de inanição. Além disso, precisamos considerar a doutrina de Deus, com Seus atributos e propósitos. A maior parte das descrições que fazemos são antropomórficas. Falamos em termos de Deus como um super-homem. Apesar de termos de nos limitar, naturalmente, a tais analogias, a maioria delas continua deixando-nos a indagar: Como é Deus? (EP F NTI)

ANALOGIAS DA EXPERIÊNCIA

Para Kant, os princípios **a priori** que tornam possível a unidade da experiência humana. Os três princípios, derivados da categoria de relação, são: substância, causalidade e reciprocidade. Para Kant, os princípios são derivados dos tipos básicos de proposições, dando a entender a ordenação de substância, causa e comunidade, segundo os quais interpretamos a experiência. (E P)

ANALÓGICA, TIPO DE INTERPRETAÇÃO

Vem do grego **anagogo**, «levar para cima». A palavra refere-se à descoberta de uma verdade espiritual oculta em algum texto literal da Bíblia. Assemelha-se à interpretação alegórica. Ver o artigo sobre *alegoria*. A idéia é que o indivíduo é «elevado» do literal para o simbólico, para as verdades espirituais e místicas. (P E)

ANAMELEQUE

No hebraico, **rocha do rei** (ver II Reis 17:31), mencionado juntamente com Adrameleque, como uma divindade em honra da qual os habitantes de Sefarvaim, que colonizaram a Samaria, queimavam seus filhos em sacrifício. Alguns eruditos preferem soletrar o nome como *Anu-Melque*, porquanto *Anu* era o deus-firmamento da Babilônia. O nome Anu-Melque indica que Anu era adorado com os ritos do deus Moloque.

ANAMIM

No hebraico, **homens das rochas**. Consideremos estes dois pontos:

1. Segundo filho de Mizraim (ver Gên. 10:13), acerca de quem nada se sabe.

2. Uma tribo relacionada aos egípcios, cujos progenitores são mencionados em Gên. 10:13. De acordo com alguns estudiosos, estavam localizados no Alto Egito, no moderno grande oásis de Chargeh. Mas outros localizam-nos na Cirenaica. (UN Z)

ANAMNESIS

Termo grego para indicar «memória», «lembrança».

1. Ao instituir a Ceia do Senhor (I Cor. 11:23 ss), Jesus baixou esta instrução: «...fazei isto em memória de mim» (anamnese). A maioria dos intérpretes protestantes dizem que isso significa: a. O ato de relembrar: «Fazei isto quando vos relembrardes de mim»; ou b. como um memorial: «Este é o meu memorial»; ou seja, a cerimônia tornar-se-ia um memorial. Os católicos romanos vêm nisso um «chamar de volta». «Chamai de volta esse ato original, para que chegue ao momento presente, trazendo consigo sua eficácia original». Em outras palavras, o ato renova a eficácia da participação no corpo e no sangue de Cristo. Essa forçada interpretação, pois, favorece a teoria da transubstanciação. Naturalmente isso é uma interpretação, e não uma simples explicação do trecho e dos termos envolvidos. Ver o artigo sobre *a transubstanciação*.

2. Em Platão, o termo é usado para indicar «memórias» ou «reminiscências» da alma. Sendo preexistente, a alma conhece muitas coisas sem ter que aprender mediante a percepção dos sentidos. Esse conhecimento envolve as realidades divinas, bem como coisas deste mundo, e certamente inclui as idéias morais. No diálogo *Meno*, a palavra aponta para a geometria. Em *Phaedo*, aponta para elevadas verdades espirituais, jamais adequadamente aprendidas neste mundo físico. (C EP F)

ANANIAS — ANAQUE (ANAQUIM)

ANANIAS

No hebraico significa **protegido por Yahweh**. É o nome de muitas pessoas no Antigo Testamento:

Há a forma hebraica do nome, *Ananiah*:

1. Pai de Maaséias e avô de Azarias, que ajudou a reconstruir as muralhas de Jerusalém, após o cativeiro (ver Nee. 3:23), em cerca de 446 A.C.

2. Uma cidade da tribo de Benjamim, localizada entre Nob e Hazor (ver Nee. 11:32), que talvez deva ser identificada com a moderna el 'Aziriyeh (Betânia), quanto à sua localização. (S Z)

Há a forma grega do nome, *Ananias*:

1. Algumas traduções usam essa forma em lugar de Hananias, como nome de um dos três companheiros de Daniel (ver Dan. 1:6).

2. Forma usada em lugar de Anias, em I Esdras 5:16, cabeça de uma família que retornou do cativeiro em companhia de Zorobabel.

3. Forma usada em lugar de Hanani, filho de Imer, em I Esdras 9:21 e Esd. 10:20. Um sacerdote que despediu sua esposa estrangeira, terminado o cativeiro.

4. Forma usada em lugar de Hananiah, filho de Bebai, em I Esdras 9:29 e Ezeq. 10:28. Era levita e estava casado com uma mulher estrangeira.

5. O pai de Azarias (ver Tobias 5:12). Rafael, o anjo, identificou-se como filho de Ananias, parente de Tobias.

6. Um personagem do Novo Testamento, esposo de Safira, membro da igreja apostólica de Jerusalém. Tornou-se culpado por enganar a igreja no tocante à soma mediante a qual vendera uma propriedade sua, com o propósito de dar o dízimo aos pobres, por meio dos apóstolos. (Ver Atos. 5:1-10 quanto à história). Uma vez feita a venda, ele e sua esposa guardaram uma parte do dinheiro, em ato de pura cobiça, ou por temerem sofrer necessidades mais tarde, e apresentaram sua dádiva como correspondente à quantia total, a fim de obter glória e elogios da parte da comunidade cristã. Ver Atos 4:32-37 para notar como a igreja cristã da época estava ocupada nesse tipo de projeto, que visava aliviar os pobres. O pecado não consistiu em reter uma parte (o que tinham plena liberdade de fazer) mas em enganar a igreja quanto aos motivos que tinham. Pedro interrogou-os em separado e apanhou-os na mentira. Primeiramente, Ananias caiu fulminado, e sua esposa, indagada mais tarde, teve igual sorte. A narrativa ilustra o incomum poder dos *apóstolos* (ver o artigo acerca deles) bem como a seriedade de tratarmos com honestidade as questões religiosas. Não há qualquer indício no relato de que Pedro tenha apelado para qualquer ato de violência pessoal. O incidente é apresentado como um juízo divino, conforme freqüentemente se vê nas narrativas do Antigo Testamento. Há algumas instâncias similares na Igreja cristã moderna, onde a intervenção divina põe fim a algum cristão ofensor. Compare essa narrativa com outra parecida, em I Cor. 5:1, onde há a ameaça de morte pelo poder divino, pronunciada contra um ofensor moral.

7. Um crente de Damasco (ver Atos 9:10-17 e 22:12). Sua reputação era grande entre os crentes, e o Senhor apareceu-lhe em uma visão, ordenando-lhe que fosse à rua chamada Direita, procurar por Saulo de Tarso na casa de Judas. Saulo estava orando, após sua conversão, e buscando orientação. Ananias quase não podia crer que a mensagem recebida era autêntica, pois sabia que Saulo muito havia perseguido aos cristãos. Mas, certo de que recebia uma ordem do Senhor, realizou sua tarefa, e foi instrumento usado na recuperação da vista de Saulo. *Paulo*, agora preparado para a sua missão, foi imerso nas águas e começou a pregar que Jesus era o Cristo.

A tradição representa Ananias como um dos setenta discípulos (ver Lucas 10), o primeiro que pregou o evangelho em Damasco, e que posteriormente tornou-se bispo naquele lugar. Os judeus, irados diante de seu sucesso, agarraram-no, açoitaram-no, e finalmente, apedrejaram-no até morrer, no mesmo local onde sua igreja se reunia. Visto que muitas dessas histórias são lendárias, não se sabe o quanto da narrativa é veraz, ou ao menos se o incidente aconteceu.

8. Um sumo sacerdote, filho de Nebedeu, no tempo do procurador Tibério Alexandre. Foi nomeado sumo sacerdote em 48 D.C. por Herodes, rei de Calcis (ver Josefo, *Anti*. XX.v.5). Quadrato, legado da Síria, enviou-o a Roma em 52 D.C., para responder a acusações de crueldade, mas foi inocentado por Cláudio, por influência de Agripa, o Jovem (ver Josefo, *Anti*. XX.x1.2.3). Permaneceu no ofício sumo sacerdotal até 58 D.C. Era um saduceu orgulhoso, rico e inescrupuloso (ver Josefo, *Anti*. XX.ix.2), que cooperava com assassinos para realizar os seus propósitos. Colaborou com os romanos a fim de fomentar seus próprios interesses, e por esse motivo era odiado pelos judeus nacionalistas. Quando rebentou a guerra entre Israel e Roma, em 66 D.C., foi caçado e morto por assassinos (ver Josefo, *Guerras* II.xvii.9). Os historiadores consideram-no o mais indigno de todos os ocupantes da cadeira sumo sacerdotal.

No Novo Testamento, foi perante ele que Paulo foi levado, durante o governo do procurador Félix, depois que o apóstolo foi preso em Jerusalém (ver Atos 22:30 - 23:5). Paulo afirmou que havia vivido diante de Deus com boa consciência, e Ananias, ofendido, ordenou que ele fosse espancado na boca. Então Paulo chamou-o de «parede branqueada» (Atos 23:3), não sabendo que ele era o sumo sacerdote. Posteriormente, Ananias apareceu em pessoa para reforçar as acusações contra Paulo, em Cesaréia. Esse julgamento foi efetuado diante de Félix (ver Atos 24:1). (ND S UN Z)

ANÃO

A única referência bíblica a esse defeito do nanismo aparece em Lev. 21:20, onde vários defeitos físicos são declarados motivos desqualificadores na descendência de Aarão, para alguém servir como sacerdote. A própria palavra, que no hebraico significa basicamente *mirrado*, também é usada para descrever gado ou espigas de trigo (ver Gên. 41:3-7), o maná que era minúsculo (ver Êxo. 16:14), a poeira (ver Isa. 29:5) ou um sussurro (ver I Reis 19:12). A proibição bíblica a respeito do nanismo pode referir-se a pessoas doentias, extenuadas, não estando em foco os anões literais, embora muitas traduções prefiram sempre usar o termo *anão*. A Septuaginta e a Vulgata traduzem o termo por «olho defeituoso», mas quase certamente tal tradução é incorreta. Seja como for, no Oriente Próximo, na antiguidade, pensava-se que os anões eram possuidores de poderes mágicos especiais, e isso seria razão suficiente para desqualificar os anões para o sacerdócio, à parte de qualquer outro problema físico. (ID ND Z)

ANAQUE (ANAQUIM)

No hebraico, **pescoço longo**. Anaque foi o progenitor de uma raça de gigantes chamados *anaquins.* Era um povo nômade que habitava o sul de Canaã, antes da chegada dos israelitas. (Ver Núm. 13:33; Deu. 9:2; Jos. 15:13,14; 21:1; Juí. 1:20). O lugar de origem de Anaque ou era a cidade de Arba (ver Jos. 15:13) ou a cidade de Hebrom (= Quiriate-Arba), mais provavelmente esta última, conforme Núm. 13:22 parece indicar, e onde os cabeças de Herom declaradamente eram descendentes de Anaque. O trecho de Deuteronômio 9:1,2 situa essa raça na Cisjordânia, de modo geral. Calebe expulsou-os dali, e foram habitar em Gaza, Gate e Asdode, na Filístia. Ver Jos. 11:22. Os espias enviados para explorar a terra, desanimaram quando viram esses gigantes (ver Deu. 1:28), mas, finalmente, guerras sangrentas e muitas perdas de vida os forçou a sair da região. Eram tão altos e tão poderosos fisicamente que o nome deles tornou-se proverbial. Os israelitas perguntaram: «Quem poderá resistir aos filhos de Anaque?» (Deu. 9:2). Ver também Deu. 1:28; 2:10,21. Textos de execração dos séculos XIX e XVIII A.C., encontrados no Egito, provavelmente aludem a esses povos, sob o título de Iy-canaq, cujos três príncipes tinham nomes semíticos. (FA ND S UN Z)

ANARQUISMO

Vem do grego **an**, «sem», e **arche**, «governo». Uma teoria social que considera o estado como a origem da maioria dos males sociais e morais. Em primeiro lugar, busca a destruição da antiga ordem, mediante métodos violentos ou outros; em segundo lugar, busca substituir a antiga ordem por uma outra que, presumivelmente, surja espontaneamente, por meio da cooperação de indivíduos livres, organizados em grupos puramente voluntários, territoriais e funcionais, que, segundo se esperava, produziria e distribuiria os bens e serviços necessários à sociedade. Essa teoria pressupõe que a natureza humana básica é boa, e que se for deixada livre para agir, produzirá o bem. Portanto, o homem não precisa de leis coercivas.

Tipos. 1. Individualista, que aceita a propriedade privada isenta de todas as restrições do controle do estado. 2. Comunista, que repudia o coletivismo forçado do marxismo, em favor da possessão comum dos meios de produção, por livre acordo e cooperação entre os elementos da sociedade. 3. Terrorista, que advoga a violência, incluindo o assassinato de figuras chaves a fim de atingir os seus propósitos. 4. Cristã, que presumivelmente deriva os seus princípios dos ensinamentos de Cristo. Os anarquistas cristãos advogaram a isenção de leis humanas, como inerente à liberdade dada por meio de Cristo. Os proponentes dessa variedade de anarquismo puderam ser encontrados entre os *Levelers* e *Diggers* do século XVII, os anabatistas e os doukhobors. William Godwin, um escritor político inglês, pensava que o progresso moral gradual do homem terminaria no anarquismo. Tolstoy defendia a revolução moral, que levaria à abolição do estado.

Em contraste com essa filosofia, Agostinho, Lutero, Calvino e outros argumentavam que o *pecado* requeria o governo civil, o que, naturalmente, refletia a posição da Bíblia (ver Rom. 13:1 ss.).

ANÁS

Forma contraída de Ananias (no hebraico, **protegido por Yahweh**). Foi sumo sacerdote dos judeus (ver Luc. 3:2; João 18:13,24; Atos. 4:6). Em Lucas ele é mencionado como sumo sacerdote juntamente com Caifás, seu genro. No tempo de Cristo, o ofício sumo sacerdotal tornara-se extremamente instável, porquanto eram nomeados e destituídos sumos sacerdotes ao sabor do capricho das autoridades romanas. Assim sucedeu que, embora removido do ofício, Anás reteve grande autoridade, quando seus filhos e seu genro, *Caifás* (ver o artigo a seu respeito), tornaram-se sumos sacerdotes. Anos após haver sido deposto, continuava grande a sua autoridade, pois em Atos 4:6 ele é o primeiro nome a aparecer na lista de líderes sacerdotais. No trecho de João 18:19,22, ele é o sumo sacerdote em questão, embora Caifás esteja em foco nos vs. 13 e 24.

Anás era filho de Sete, nomeado sumo sacerdote por Quirínio, governador da Síria, mas deposto por Valério Gratus. No Antigo Testamento, esse ofício era vitalício, e um novo sumo sacerdote só podia ser nomeado em face da morte do anterior. Porém, a ocupação romana alterou essa norma. Como sumo sacerdote oficial, Anás governou de 6 a 25 D.C.

Ele é referido em conexão com o ministério de João Batista (ver Luc. 3:2). Quando Jesus foi aprisionado, foi levado diante desse homem (ver João 18:13). Foi ele quem interrogou Jesus acerca de Seus discípulos e de Seu ensino, e quem também deu ordem a um dos soldados que batesse em Jesus com a mão (ver João 18:19-22). Após ter sido interrogado, Jesus foi enviado amarrado para Caifás. Semanas mais tarde, esteve presente à reunião do Sinédrio quando Pedro e João defenderam-se acerca da pregação da nova fé (ver Atos 4:6).

O fato de ser ele chamado de sumo sacerdote tem deixado alguns comentadores perplexos, posto que Caifás, seu genro, nos evangelhos, é apresentado como o sumo sacerdote. Com base no trecho de Luc. 3:2, ficamos sabendo que Anás e Caifás eram reputados, ambos, como sumos sacerdotes que atuavam ao mesmo tempo; e este versículo do livro de Atos (4:6), informa-nos que Anás ainda era considerado pelos judeus como o líder inconteste, embora deposto pelos romanos, tendo sido substituído no ofício por seu próprio genro, Caifás. Todavia, os judeus não reconheceram como legítima essa substituição vitalícia, isto é, o cargo era ocupado pelo mesmo indivíduo enquanto vivesse. No ano em que o Senhor Jesus foi crucificado no entanto, José Caifás já era o presidente oficial do sinédrio, bem como o sumo sacerdote legal, por nomeação dos romanos. O historiador judeu, Josefo (*Antiq*. xviii. 2,1) revela-nos como o ofício sumo sacerdotal caíra em desordem. E esse mesmo escritor presta-nos a seguinte informação: Anás foi nomeado como sumo sacerdote com a idade de trinta e sete anos, no ano 7 D.C., por Quirínio, governador da Síria. Tendo sido deposto, foi substituído por Ismael, em 14 D.C. Seguiram-se mais duas modificações antes que seu genro, José Caifás, tivesse subido a essa posição. Caifás permaneceu no ofício até o ano 37 D.C., ao passo que Anás continuou a ser uma espécie de sumo sacerdote *«de jure»* (por direito, segundo a opinião e a lei do povo judeu), embora Caifás fosse o sumo sacerdote «de facto» ainda que, segundo o ponto de vista dos romanos, Caifás fosse o sumo sacerdote «de jure». A verdade, entretanto, é que para todos os efeitos práticos, Anás ainda retinha grande dose de autoridade, e Caifás sempre pareceu relutante em tomar qualquer decisão importante, sem primeiramente consultá-lo. No devido tempo, diversos dos filhos de Anás ocuparam, sucessivamente, o ofício sumo sacerdotal.

O ofício sumo sacerdotal propriamente dito se tornara corrupto, por ter-se transformado em motivo de jogo político, sendo comprado e vendido a dinheiro. Caifás sucedera a Simeão bem Camhith no

ANASIB — ANÁTEMA

ofício, mas sua permanência no posto sumo sacerdotal foi de curta duração. Simeão bem Camhith substituíra Ismael bem Phabi. Todos esses sumos sacerdotes foram nomeados por Valério Grato, governador romano. Josefo (ver *Antiq.* xx.10) mostra-nos que, além de Caifás, houve um total de vinte e oito sacerdotes, em um período de cento e sete anos. (FA ND NTI Z)

ANASIB

Em algumas traduções como Sanasib, progenitor de uma família de sacerdotes que voltou do cativeiro com Zorobabel, I Esd. 5:24, cujo nome não aparece nas listas em Esd. 5:24 e Nee. 7:38.

ANATA

Um termo sânscrito usado pela escola Teravada de budismo, que significa *sem alma.* Essa escola acredita na reencarnação, porém não na reencarnação de uma alma que vai de um corpo para outro, em uma série de vidas físicas, mas sim, na reencarnação da disposição mental, dos desejos, das atitudes de um indivíduo, transferidos para outro ser humano. Assim sendo, continuaria o *karma* (ver o artigo a respeito) e não uma alma, levando tal bagagem a uma nova existência. Ver os artigos sobre o *budismo* e sobre a *terminologia budista*, e também sobre a *reencarnação*. (E EP P)

ANATE

No hebraico significa **resposta**, isto é, à oração.
1. Esse era o nome do pai de Sangar, que foi o terceiro juiz de Israel, após a morte de Josué (ver Juí. 3:31), em cerca de 1250 A.C.
2. Anate era o nome de uma deusa guerreira em Ugarite, considerada irmã ou esposa de Baal. Essa deusa atualmente é bem conhecida devido à literatura épica religiosa, descoberta em Ras Shamra (antiga Ugarite). Era patrocinadora do sexo e da guerra. Deve ser identificada com a *rainha do céu*, à qual os judeus ofereciam incenso nos dias de Jeremias (ver Jer. 44:19). Figurinhas sensuais, representando-a, têm sido encontradas em vários locais da Palestina, em níveis que datam do terceiro e do segundo milênios A.C. As degradadas religiões da Palestina pagã degradaram Israel, despertando a indignação e as denúncias dos profetas do Senhor. (ALB UN)

ANÁTEMA

No grego ático, **anathema** significa algo «posto de lado» ou «suspenso», como uma oferta prometida, separada para um deus. Isso era suspenso em um templo ou outro lugar de adoração. Na Septuaginta, veio a indicar qualquer coisa devotada a Deus, proibida para uso ordinário, ou algo destinado à destruição (Lev. 27:19; Jos. 6:17). No Novo Testamento, tem o sentido de *maldito*, em Rom. 9:3; I Cor. 12:3 e Gál. 1:8,9. A palavra veio a ser associada a exclusão, visto que o excluído tornava-se «maldito». Alguns pensavam que desde o tempo refletido em Esd. 10:8, o termo (por meio do grego), indicava exclusão. Assim foi empregado no Talmude e nos escritos dos pais gregos, com regularidade. Ver o artigo sobre *a exclusão*. As referências do Novo Testamento não envolvem a idéia de exclusão eclesiástica, mas sim, de maldição espiritual. Em I Cor. 16:22, a palavra aparece lado a lado com o termo aramaico *maranatha* (nosso Senhor vem, ou o imperativo, vem, nosso Senhor). A interpretação comum disso é que aquele que não amar nosso Senhor, por ocasião de Sua vinda, ao ter de defrontar-se com Ele, será espiritualmente amaldiçoado. Isso é um lembrete da constante doutrina cristã de que a vinda do Senhor imporá o julgamento, e não somente a bênção. Ver os artigos sobre *o julgamento* e *os galardões*.

História:
1. Antes do Novo Testamento. As ofertas votadas, nas comunidades hebréias e não-hebréias; algo maldito; talvez a exclusão, em alguns casos.
2. No Novo Testamento. As ofertas votadas, Luc. 21:5; algo espiritualmente maldito, ver as referências acima.
3. Na Igreja primitiva. Especialmente entre os pais gregos, a exclusão, bem como um pronunciamento sobre os hereges e suas doutrinas, presumivelmente envolvendo uma maldição espiritual, um uso comum entre os séculos III e VI de nossa era.
4. Após o século VI D.C., com freqüência a palavra era usada com sentido mais forte do que a exclusão, que podia ser a simples interrupção da comunhão com a igreja, um fato que fossem vedados a adoração e os ritos. Esse uso mais forte presumivelmente pronunciava um corte espiritual de Deus e da salvação em Cristo. Os homens têm-se mostrado prontos a perseguir e amaldiçoar àqueles que lhes parecem diferentes. Jesus e Paulo não escaparam a isso. Essa circunstância deveria limitar o orgulho daqueles que amaldiçoam.

A palavra traduzida por *anátema*, originalmente era utilizada para indicar apenas uma oferta qualquer, e tanto nos escritos clássicos como na Septuaginta (tradução do A.T. hebraico para o grego, que já estava completa por volta do século II A.C.), o uso regular da palavra é esse. Essa forma substantivada se deriva do verbo *anatithemi*, que significa «dedicar», «tal como uma oferta votiva». Essa palavra gradualmente foi se revestindo de um sentido negativo, como algo «devotado» ao mal ou à destruição, certamente sugerido pelo fato de que os sacrifícios eram consumidos. Foi daí que a palavra assumiu o seu sentido negativo de maldição, em que o indivíduo é declarado separado de Deus e maldito, ou seja, oficialmente separado da vinculação à igreja ou sinagoga. (Pode-se comparar com isso as passagens de Gál. 1:8,9; I Cor. 12:3 e 16:22, onde esse tipo de uso negativo da palavra «anátema» é usado nas páginas do N.T.).

O Uso em Rom. 9:3.
Pouca dúvida pode haver de que Paulo usava o vocábulo em Rom. 9:3 em sentido negativo; e o desejo hipotético, cuja impossibilidade ele esqueceu momentaneamente, seria que ele desejava ser *separado de Cristo*, sendo assim lançado na destruição fatal da alma. Alguns intérpretes, entretanto, têm procurado suavizar o desejo expresso aqui por Paulo, fazendo com que esse *anátema* seja menos do que o próprio Paulo tencionava que fosse. Como exemplos disso, alguns têm pensado que:
1. Paulo queria dar a entender a morte física, e não a espiritual.
2. O apóstolo queria indicar a exclusão da igreja, e não a condenação da sua alma.
3. Paulo pensava na alienação entre sua pessoa e Deus, embora isso não envolvesse, necessariamente, a condenação de sua alma.

Entre os judeus, a exclusão dos membros das sinagogas era realizada gradualmente: a. Havia a exclusão do templo; b. havia a expulsão da congregação, em que o disciplinado ficava separado dos outros, já com maior severidade na disciplina. Neste segundo caso, ordinariamente se supunha que Deus tomava o mesmo ponto de vista sobre os culpados que as autoridades eclesiásticas; e isso significava que o réu corria o perigo de ser condenado por Deus, no estado eterno. Se porventura Paulo fez alguma alusão a essas idéias judaicas, então o texto deixa plenamente indicado que esse desejo hipotético se estendia até a condenação divina, e que ele desejaria ter ficado maldito por Deus, contanto que isso trouxesse o povo de Israel de volta ao seu Deus. Ora, não há que duvidar que isso é o que Paulo queria dizer, o que significa que não há nenhuma necessidade de suavizarmos nem o tipo de desejo expresso por ele, e nem o sentido da palavra grega «anátema». Pode-se observar que *Moisés* fez uma declaração similar, não menos radical do que a de Paulo, conforme se lê no registro de Êxo. 32:32: «Agora, pois, perdoa-lhe o pecado; — ou, senão, risca-me, peço-te, do livro que escreveste».

Bacon considerava essa atitude de «êxtase de amor e infinito sentimento de comunhão» com outras pessoas. Bengel observou sobre Rom. 9:3: «Não é fácil calcular a medida do amor de um Moisés ou de um Paulo. Porque a nossa razão tão limitada não a apreende, tal como uma criança não pode compreender a coragem dos guerreiros!»

Moule (em Rom. 9:3), aplicando um raciocínio estritamente lógico a essa questão, observa: «Desejar a maldição de Deus é desejar não apenas o sofrimento, mas igualmente a alienação moral longe dele, a retirada da capacidade que a alma tem de amá-lo. Por conseguinte, esse desejo na realidade seria um ato de 'maior amor ao próximo do que a Deus'. Além disso, a alma redimida 'não pertence mais a si própria': desejar que o 'eu' seja amaldiçoado e cindido de Cristo seria desejar a perda daquilo que foi 'comprado e feito de Cristo'. Porém, a razão lógica desse desejo transparece na leitura do oitavo capítulo da epístola aos Romanos, e nisso percebemos quão inteiramente impossível, moralmente falando, era para Paulo realmente desejar a realização desse anelo».

Não há razão alguma para supormos, entretanto, que o apóstolo Paulo, arrebatado em seu fervor momentaneamente, não tivesse levado em conta tais «impossibilidades morais» dos desejos por ele expressos, ainda que mui provavelmente soubesse que tal anelo, de fato, era impossível. (A B IB NTI RO)

ANATEMATA

Essa palavra designa ornamentos separados para a decoração de igrejas. Em Lucas 21:5, a palavra (traduzida por «ornado») é aplicada aos ornamentos usados no templo de Jerusalém. Em sentido mais estrito, o vocábulo era usado para denotar *memoriais* de grandes favores recebidos pelos homens da parte de Deus. Havia um costume nos tempos antigos, que prevalece até hoje, relativo às curas recebidas. Quem fosse curado, a fim de mostrar sua gratidão, mandava fazer uma figura do membro do corpo curado, em ouro ou em prata. Tal figura era chamada ectipoma. Era doada à igreja como sinal de gratidão. (DE S UN)

ANATIKAYA

Uma palavra sânscrita que significa «não-físico», usada no jainismo (ver o artigo a respeito), dentro da frase *anastikaya dravya*, «substância não-física».

ANATOTE

No hebraico, **respostas**, isto é, às orações. Nome usado para pessoas e para designar um lugar, no Antigo Testamento:

1. Um dos líderes de Israel que assinou o pacto estabelecido por Neemias, após o retorno do cativeiro babilônico (ver Nee. 10:19), em cerca de 445 A.C.

2. O oitavo dos nove filhos de Bequer, filho de Benjamim (ver I Crô. 7:8), em cerca de 445 A.C.

3. Uma das cidades pertencentes aos sacerdotes, na tribo de Benjamim, e que era cidade de refúgio (ver o artigo a respeito; ver Jos. 21:18; Jer. 1:1; II Sam. 23:27; Esd. 2:23 e Nee. 7:27). É melhor conhecida como terra natal e residência usual do profeta Jeremias (ver Jer. 1:1; 11:21-23 e 29:27). No tempo de Jerônimo, parece que tinha o nome de Jeremias (ver *Onomast.* sob Anatote). Ele situava a três milhas romanas ao norte de Jerusalém (ver *Comment.* em Jer. 1:1), que corresponde aos vinte estádios de Josefo (ver *Anti.* x.7,3). Nos dias veterotestamentários, o nome talvez fosse uma forma plural de Anate, uma deusa dos cananeus, sugerindo que fora um centro da adoração a essa divindade. Isaías refere-se a Anatote como um dos lugares no caminho trilhado por exércitos invasores. Ocorre em um jogo de palavras em conjunção com a palavra *responder*, que tem som semelhante, em Isa. 10:30. Após o cativeiro babilônico, 128 homens daquele lugar retornaram em um grupo, na companhia de Zorobabel (ver Esd. 2:23). Alguns supõem que a moderna cidade de Anata, a cinco quilômetros ao norte de Jerusalém, seja o mesmo lugar. Mas outros preferem pensar em Ras el-Harrubeh, perto dessa aldeia, como a sua verdadeira localização. Escavações feitas na região têm mostrado que vem sendo habitada desde tempos antigos. Abiézer, um dos guerreiros de Davi (ver II Sam. 23:27), e Jeú, que veio unir-se a Davi em Ziclague (ver I Crô. 12:3), eram anatotitas. Originalmente era uma cidade murada, uma fortaleza; mas atualmente é uma aldeia pobre e minúscula. (BL FA S UN Z)

ANAXÁGORAS de Clazômenas

Discípulo de Anaxímenes (vide). — Nasceu na Jônia, em 499 A.C., mas alcançou fama como um dos homens notáveis do círculo de Péricles. Platão informa-nos que ele tinha discípulos, entre os quais talvez estivessem Arquelau e Eurípedes. Ele requeria que a verdade fosse abordada sob vários ângulos, pois reconhecia que a verdade que havia em cada escola de pensamento era limitada. Seu principal escrito foi *Sobre a Natureza*, que agora existe somente sob a forma de citações feitas por outros autores.

Idéias:

1. Ele afirmava que a lua se compunha de terra e rochas, e que o sol era uma massa incandescente. Mas quase todos os atenienses julgavam que esses astros eram deuses, pelo que a idéia de Anaxágoras pareceu altamente herética. Josefo (Diels, 46 A 19) afirma que por esse motivo ele foi encarcerado e condenado à morte, mas que ele escapou e retornou à Jônia, na Ásia Menor.

2. Dizia: «Há uma porção de tudo em tudo», com o que propunha a teoria de um mundo composto de «partículas», ou «sementes», conforme ele as chamava. A *mistura* dessas partículas produziria os objetos grosseiros que ferem os nossos sentidos.

3. Geração e destruição, como também alteração, ocorrem através do rearranjo espacial dessas partículas. As diferenças nos objetos também dependeriam

do tipo de mistura (*migma*) envolvido.

4. Ele não fez qualquer tentativa de explicar a *origem* das partículas, que a princípio existiriam apenas em um estado caótico, primevo.

5. *Nous*: termo grego que significa «mente», era uma de suas doutrinas distintivas. A «mente» também se comporia de partículas (as menores e mais puras entre elas). Não haveria mistura com outras coisas, provendo o impulso inicial de movimento para a massa caótica. Portanto, as *partículas mentais* ativariam as outras partículas, de onde se derivaria o tipo de mundo que vemos ao nosso redor. A «mente» estaria presente em tudo. Ela seria simples, sem mistura, conheceria tudo, governaria tudo, seria infinita e se autogovernaria.

6. Todos os mundos evoluem partindo de causas naturais, tal como se dá com todas as formas de vida.

7. *Percepção*. Percebemos as coisas através do contraste. Visto que há uma porção de tudo em tudo, só podemos ver algo como distinto quando nossos órgãos dos sentidos detectam qualidades contrastantes.

8. *Vários movimentos na natureza*. A Terra seria chata; Sol e Lua seriam corpos naturais, e não divinos; a Lua refletiria a luz do Sol. Os terremotos, o relâmpago e o trovão teriam causas naturais (embora ele tivesse errado em suas explicações). Os gregos inclinavam-se por ver algo divino em todos esses fenômenos. Os eclipses dever-se-iam à interposição da Terra. A Terra seria chata e flutuaria no espaço. Os corpos celestes se incandesceriam devido a um movimento de revolução. Anaxágoras tentou determinar as dimensões do Sol, e determinou as fases da Lua. Procurou explicar a produção da vida e seu desenvolvimento em forma de muitas espécies.

9. *A «mente» seria a grande qualidade divina*. A filosofia de Anaxágoras fala sobre vários atributos que são característicos da deidade. A «mente» *põe em ordem* tudo quanto era, é, e será, embora não seja a criadora de tudo. Alguns filósofos falam em prol de uma «mente» não-material na filosofia de Anaxágoras, mas outros concebem a «mente» como matéria, posto que de substância mais fina. A questão não está resolvida. Seja como for, sua doutrina estabelece uma distinção radical entre a matéria comum e a mente, distinção essa que se tornou importante na filosofia. Naturalmente, tal noção fazia parte das religiões orientais desde muito tempo antes. (AM E EP MN P)

ANAXIMANDRO

Filósofo grego (610-547 A.C.), nascido em Mileto, membro de uma família nobre. Liderou emigrantes milesianos para formarem uma nova colônia. Alega-se que ele inventou o relógio de sol e o mapeamento geográfico. Tales de Mileto (ver o artigo) deu início à filosofia ocidental com as especulações de Anaximandro sobre a substância primária na natureza. Anaximandro aparentemente foi o segundo filósofo a inquirir sobre essa questão. Tales postulou a água como a substância primária, mas Anaximandro falava sobre o *indeterminado*, uma substância básica que subjaz a tudo, embora desconhecida em si mesma. A *apeiron* (realidade indeterminada) tanto é a origem quanto é a substância à qual todas as coisas finalmente retornarão.

Idéias:

1. A *apeiron*, descrita no fim do parágrafo acima. Uma substância indefinida e *ilimitada*, que proveria explicação tanto para a variedade como para as transformações das coisas. Seria algo eterno, não-criado, mas caracterizado por movimento e agitação constantes e eternas. Em suas manifestações, faz surgir outras substâncias. Na sua obra, *Sobre a Natureza das Coisas*, Anaximandro expõe sua filosofia essencial, onde a *apeiron* é intitulada de *arche*, o ponto de partida de tudo. Termos que usualmente são atribuídos à divindade são conferidos à *arche*, como um poder sem idade, imortal, não-gerado, imperecível, transcendental e eterno. Portanto a *apeiron* dele seria um conceito físico, metafísico e teológico. Lançou a base para o vácuo infinito dos atomistas, a deidade cósmica de Xenófanes, Aristóteles e os estóicos.

2. A desintegração da substância, ou retorno à *apeiron*, é descrita poeticamente como uma forma de justiça cósmica, porquanto todas as coisas de certa maneira são injustas e merecem ser extintas.

3. O espaço, que em alguns pontos pode ser identificado com o *ilimitado*, estende-se indefinidamente para cima, pelo que haveria a possibilidade de muitos mundos.

4. O Sol, a Lua e as Estrelas vieram à existência mediante a fragmentação de uma esfera em chamas, que a princípio envolvia a Terra. Os eclipses eram por ele explicados mediante a suposição de que vemos os corpos celestes através de perfurações ou respiradouros, que algumas vezes são bloqueados. A Terra teria a forma de um cilindro, com comprimento um terço maior que a sua largura. Flutuaria livremente no espaço, e ficaria eqüidistante de todas as coisas que existem no sistema cósmico.

5. *Evolução*. A vida teria tido origem na umidade (do oceano), e todos os animais teriam evoluído de outras espécies. Os antepassados do homem seriam peixes. Ele sentia que os seres humanos jamais sobreviveriam como infantes e que nada poderiam fazer por si mesmos; mas «devem ter nascido de outros seres vivos, visto que os outros animais podem procurar rapidamente o seu próprio alimento, mas somente o homem requer cuidados maternais prolongados». (Diels, H. e Kranz, W). (AM DK EP F. MM)

ANAXÍMENES DE MILETO

Compatriota mais jovem e discípulo de Anaximandro (ver o artigo). Suas datas são 588-524 A.C.

Idéias:

1. *A substância básica de tudo é o ar*, identificada como o sopro da *vida*. Essa terminologia tem levado alguns filósofos à suposição de que a sua idéia era *psíquica*, e não física. Mas a questão tem sido disputada. Alguns deles têm suposto que os filósofos naturalistas, pré-socráticos (Tales, Anaximandro e Anaxímenes) na verdade estavam promovendo o pampsiquismo (ver o artigo), e não várias modalidades de materialismo; isso com base nas diversas descrições que eles davam às suas substâncias, de acordo com as quais pareciam estar falando sobre Deus ou alguma energia espiritual. Todavia, não há certeza quanto a isso. Seja como for, para Anaxímenes o *ar* é que manteria todas as coisas em seu lugar, neste mundo, como uma espécie de princípio divino, a chave de toda origem, combinação, modificação e desintegração.

2. Ocorrem modificações através da condensação e da rarefação. Tal processo envolveria as pedras, a terra, as nuvens, o vento e o fogo, que seriam modificações atenuadas da mesma substância básica, o ar.

3. A terra, o sol, a lua e as estrelas são

ANCIÃO DE DIAS — ANCIÃO

substâncias em ignição, repousando sobre o ar. Os astros estariam girando em torno da Terra. Ele explicava a noite supondo que o Sol se ocultaria por detrás de pontos mais elevados da Terra, como se o Sol se movesse ao redor dos cumes da Terra, como se fora um boné ao redor da cabeça. O arco-íris seria produzido pelos raios do sol incidindo sobre ar condensado, mais espesso. Os terremotos seriam produzidos pela sequidão ou pela umidade da Terra, o que criaria condições caóticas.

4. O ar é a origem de tudo, animado, inanimado, terreno, os deuses e as realidades divinas. O movimento do ar, que é incessante, dá origem a causa e efeito, e a todas as modificações. O ar rarefeito gera o fogo; o ar condensado produz as nuvens; as nuvens condensadas produzem a água; a água condensada produz a terra; a terra condensada produz as rochas, etc. O calor e o frio seriam os fatores modificadores mais importantes utilizados pelo ar.

5. O ar é a causa de tudo, e a teleologia seria a finalidade de tudo. O Ar divino, que envolve a Terra, regula com êxito todas as coisas. Tales, Anaximandro e Anaxímenes formam a escola milesiana da filosofia. (AM BJ DK EP MM)

ANCIÃO DE DIAS

Nome dado a Deus em uma visão de Daniel (7:9,13,22), o único trecho da Bíblia onde se acha essa designação. A palavra tem sua raiz no árabe, no acadiano e no siríaco (aramaico não-bíblico), com o sentido de «avanço», de onde vem a idéia de *dias* que avançam na marcha ininterrupta do tempo. A figura simbólica é a de um homem idoso, cujos dias já avançaram extraordinariamente; mas o Deus eterno é o verdadeiro *ancião de dias*. Por meio de Cristo, compartilhamos da eternidade, mediante a nossa participação em Sua natureza (ver II Ped. 1:4), possuidores que somos da vida eterna (ver João 3:15; Tito 1:2 e I João 2:25), a mais profunda e ampla de todas as doutrinas da Bíblia. No livro de Daniel, o termo enfatiza a eternidade de Deus e do Seu reino, em contraste com os quatro sucessivos reinos temporais (simbolizados pelas quatro feras). Portanto, a eternidade do mundo espiritual é ressaltada em contraste com este mundo temporal e físico. A grandiosidade resplandece no mundo celestial, o desespero caracteriza este mundo terreno, a não ser quando Deus faz o que é temporal redundar na vida eterna. (I Y Z)

ANCIÃO No Antigo e Novo Testamentos

Discussão Preliminar

De modo geral, *ancião* é uma palavra que se refere aos líderes de um grupo ou comunidade, presumindo-se que os mesmos tenham idade avançada e sejam dotados de caráter maduro. No Antigo Testamento, o termo se aplicava a vários ofícios. Era o caso de Eliézer, o «mais antigo servo» de Abraão, em Gên. 24:2; certos oficiais da casa de Faraó, em Gên. 50:7; os principais servos de Davi, em II Sam. 12:17; e os «anciãos de Gebal» (ver Eze. 27:9). No Egito, mui provavelmente os anciãos eram funcionários do estado, pelo que o termo aplicava-se ali aos líderes e chefes políticos. Isso também sucedia entre os israelitas, moabitas e midianitas (ver Núm. 22:7). Não há que duvidar que o direito de primogenitura, bem como a capacidade de chefe da família, influenciaram tal uso, porquanto presumia-se que a idade tinha algo a ver com o amadurecimento e a sabedoria, o que se refletia em boa variedade de costumes. Os líderes das tribos naturalmente vinham dentre os anciãos pertencentes a essas tribos. Moisés e Aarão, ao chegarem no Egito, reuniram os anciãos de Israel e anunciaram ao povo a comissão divina que haviam recebido, para liderarem o povo, tirando-o do Egito (ver Êxo. 3:16,18; 4:29). Os anciãos do povo acompanharam a Moisés na primeira entrevista deste com o Faraó (ver Êxo. 31:9). Moisés também se comunicava com o povo por meio dos anciãos (ver Êxo. 19:7 e Deu. 31:9). Setenta anciãos de Israel acompanharam Moisés até o monte (Êx. 24:1). Esses anciãos também tinham o título de «príncipes». De acordo com a legislação mosaica, esses anciãos tinham seus respectivos deveres e poderes (ver Deu. 19:12 e 21:3). Era responsabilidade deles governarem e cuidarem para que a lei fosse cumprida (ver Jos. 20:4; Juí. 8:16 e Rute 4:2). Nos salmos, os anciãos são aludidos como uma classe distinta de autoridade (ver Sal. 107:32. Ver também Lam. 2:10 e Eze. 14:1). Após o exílio, eles receberam uma autoridade muito significativa.

Em cada sinagoga, havia um grupo governante de anciãos, de número variado, dependendo do número dos membros da congregação. Era dentre esses anciãos, finalmente, que se formava o superior tribunal, o Sinédrio (ver o artigo).

Nos arquivos de Mari, do século XVIII A.C., e até mesmo na correspondência real da dinastia de Sargão, no período VIII A.C., os anciãos aparecem como representantes do povo e defensores dos interesses populares, embora antes disso eles não tivessem quaisquer funções administrativas. No império hitita, entretanto, eles controlavam as questões municipais. Tais costumes eram praticamente universais entre os povos antigos, e os israelitas não eram exceção. Mas, no caso de Israel esse costume era associado às questões religiosas, visto que Israel era uma teocracia.

No Novo Testamento. Dentro do contexto judaico, nos dias neotestamentários, encontramos os anciãos associados aos principais sacerdotes (ver Mat. 21:23) e aos escribas (ver Mat. 16:21), bem como ao concílio (ver Mat. 26:29). Esses anciãos sempre exerciam alguma atividade, provavelmente porque seus membros acabavam tornando-se membros de alguma dessas três categorias. Lucas alude ao grupo inteiro dos anciãos, usando o termo grego coletivo *presbutérion* (ver Luc. 22:66; Atos 22:5), como também Paulo, em I Tim. 4:14, embora o apóstolo, nesse caso, estivesse falando ao grupo de pastores de alguma igreja cristã local. No tocante aos anciãos ou pastores da Igreja cristã, não contamos com qualquer informação específica acerca de sua origem, mas tão-somente que os títulos «ancião», «bispo = supervisor» e «pastor» são intercambiados (ver, para exemplificar, Atos 20:28). A importância dos anciãos cristãos aumentou, quando a Igreja se dispersou. Esses anciãos eram líderes, pastores, mestres, supervisores, enfim, autoridades cristãs (ver Atos 15:22,23; Efé. 4:11; Atos 20:28; Heb. 13:7 e I Tes. 5:12).

No decorrer dos séculos, — alguns anciãos passaram a receber o título de «bispos = supervisores», por exercerem autoridade sobre certas áreas, e não meramente dentro de alguma igreja local. As Ep. Pastorais parecem indicar esta possibilidade. Mas no resto do NT, um homem é um «ancião», devido à sua experiência e maturidade espiritual; era também um «bispo» porque supervisionava alguma congregação local; e era também um «pastor» porque

ANCIÃO

cuidava das ovelhas espirituais do rebanho. Muitas igrejas pentecostais de nossos dias distinguem entre «pastor» e «ancião». Isso também é um erro, porque as mesmas qualificações e deveres são dados na Bíblia a um e a outro. O mais estranho nessas igrejas, porém, é que eles não têm uma classe de oficiais chamados «bispos». Se queriam fazer distinção entre títulos, então deveriam ter três títulos para indicar três funções. Conforme funcionam as igrejas pentecostais, porém, os «anciãos» não encontram funções específicas nas Escrituras, como um ofício separado dos pastores, e isso os deixa muito confusos quanto à utilidade e serviço deles dentro das igrejas.

Origens na Igreja primitiva. Consideremos estes dois pontos: 1. Os anciãos, os ofícios e a autoridade deles no judaísmo, foram transferidos para a comunidade cristã. Esse título procede do judaísmo. 2. Os bispos (título esse que procede de um modelo gentílico) tinham funções análogas às dos anciãos, pois, na verdade, indicavam os mesmos oficiais. No paganismo, os bispos eram os presidentes de fraternidades e agremiações, e seus deveres principais eram o levantamento e a administração de fundos. No grego, o ofício era chamado *epíscopos,* de onde procede nossa palavra portuguesa «bispo».

Na cristandade moderna. 1. A Igreja Católica Romana, a Igreja Anglicana e a Igreja Episcopal Protestante têm os seus «padres». Esse título, que significa «pais» (ver como Jesus proibiu o uso de títulos dessa natureza, entre os Seus seguidores, em Mat. 23:9), enfeixa em suas mãos uma autoridade desconhecida para os primitivos pastores cristãos, como, por exemplo, a de perdoar ou não pecados, o que lhes dá o direito de determinarem o destino eterno das pessoas. Na Igreja Católica Romana há várias ordens eclesiásticas, nenhuma das quais é referida ou sugerida na Bíblia: o papa (que se arroga o título de substituto ou «vicário» de Cristo), os cardeais, os arcebispos (que governam sobre alguma área ou distrito extenso), os bispos (que governam áreas ou distritos), os padres, os diáconos, e um bom número de outros títulos. No anglicanismo, antes que alguém possa tornar-se sacerdote, precisa ser diácono. 2. No metodismo há três ordens: bispos, anciãos e diáconos. Os bispos são escolhidos como *primii inter pares,* para supervisionarem alguma região como superintendentes. 3. Na Igreja Presbiteriana há dois tipos de anciãos: os anciãos mestres (pastores) e os anciãos governantes (leigos). 4. Nos grupos evangélicos com governo congregacional as questões mais importantes são decididas mediante o voto da congregação (governo democrático). Os líderes de cada congregação local são os pastores, dirigentes espirituais usualmente envolvidos no ensino com o direito de decidir sobre as questões mais importantes que afetam a igreja local. Nessas igrejas, os pastores são assessorados pelos diáconos, cuja função principal é a de cuidar das questões materiais da igreja local.

Alguns grupos evangélicos estão procurando renovar o ministério diversificado que aparece nos dias do Novo Testamento (ver Efé. 4:11). Esse é o ministério neotestamentário ideal. A dificuldade consiste em achar apóstolos autênticos, que preencham todos os requisitos bíblicos (por exemplo, ter visto a Jesus, conforme se vê em I Cor. 9:1, onde Paulo indaga: «...não sou apóstolo? não vi a Jesus, nosso Senhor?...»

1. Origem e desenvolvimento do ofício no N.T.
Originalmente, os «anciãos», eram os líderes das igrejas domésticas de Jerusalém, a saber, aquelas congregações que se reuniam em lares particulares, porquanto não havia ainda templos, naqueles primeiros dias da história cristã, que os crentes usassem.

Todavia, devemos observar, em Atos 15:6,23, que os *anciãos* aparecem lado a lado com os apóstolos como uma espécie de concílio eclesiástico; e isso indica que, por essa altura da história, eles já haviam obtido todo o prestígio que era desfrutado pelos anciãos das sinagogas judaicas. É bem provável que, desde o começo do cristianismo os «anciãos» ocupassem a mesma função dos «presidentes» das sinagogas dos judeus, os quais eram os principais elementos daquela estrutura eclesiástica israelita, embora, mui certamente, não fossem esses «presidentes» consagrados para ocuparem suas funções, por meio de qualquer cerimônia específica. No entanto, desde o princípio do cristianismo, a consagração de líderes, como os «anciãos», se tornou costumeira. Essa ordenação ao ofício, não se há de duvidar, era efetuada por meio da imposição de mãos, o que é outra continuação da prática judaica. (Quanto a notas expositivas sobre a história e a significação do rito da «imposição de mãos», ver Atos 6:6 no NTI).

No trecho de Atos 20:17, são usados alternadamente os vocábulos «presbítero» (ou ancião) e *bispo,* o que também se verifica em Tito 1:5,7. Conforme já pudemos esclarecer, mais acima, «ancião» ou «presbítero» se deriva da terminologia judaica, ao passo que «bispo» ou «supervisor» é de origem gentílica. É bem provável que, originalmente, não houvesse distinção alguma entre as palavras «ancião» e *diácono..* Mas, gradualmente, esses termos vieram a indicar ofícios distintos, ainda que as qualificações para ambos os ofícios tenham permanecido essencialmente as mesmas, segundo também nos mostra a leitura do terceiro capítulo da primeira epístola a Timóteo. Os *diáconos,* evidentemente, ocupavam um ofício um tanto inferior, talvez mais ocupado com as questões materiais das congregações locais, tendo ao seu encargo mais a responsabilidade pelas necessidades físicas dos membros das igrejas locais; porém, existem indicações fortes de que os diáconos também eram pregadores, desempenhando um papel ativo nesse ministério, por semelhante modo. Não obstante, os anciãos ou presbíteros eram os principais líderes espirituais das igrejas locais, estando especificamente encarregados do ensino, da pregação e da evangelização.

Ver Tito 1:5-8 e I Tim. 3:1-13, onde aparece que já na era do NT, o bispo tinha autoridade sobre uma *área* e não somente sobre uma igreja local.

2. Qualificações dos anciãos ou supervisores

Ver Tito 1:5-8 e I Tim. 3:1-13 onde aparecem as qualificações e funções dos pastores e dos diáconos.

Notemos que o vocábulo *ancião* é usado em Tito 1:5, ao passo que no sétimo versículo é usada a palavra «bispo», isto é, «supervisor». (No grego, essas palavras são, respectivamente, «presbuteros» e «episkopos»). Essas palavras parecem ser usadas intercambialmente, o que está de conformidade com o uso normal das mesmas, em todo o N.T. E se porventura há alguma diferença de sentido entre elas, então «presbuteros» pode indicar o próprio «indivíduo», em seu título, ao passo que «episkopos» se refere ao seu *ofício.* Essa distinção, popular até recentemente, bem como a identificação dos dois termos, perdeu o apoio dos eruditos modernos. — As epístolas pastorais mostram clara e — definitivamente — que os *bispos* exercem autoridade sobre outros ministros, tal como sucede aos bispos modernos, podendo nomeá-los, exigindo seu discipulado, etc. Portanto, podemos distinguir três ofícios: bispos, anciãos e diáconos,

ANCIÃO

possuidores de autoridade nessa ordem descendente. O bispo podia exercer autoridade sobre uma região; o ancião, sobre uma igreja local, juntamente com outros pastores liderantes, ou anciãos; e o diácono se ocupava de um serviço secundário, mas não de natureza física, exclusivamente, porquanto se ocupava da administração de esmolas, etc.

Normalmente o «bispo» ou «supervisor» se levantava dentre a ordem dos «anciãos». Apesar dessas distinções nem sempre serem estabelecidas com base no sentido dos próprios vocábulos gregos usados, contudo, percebe-se que esses níveis de autoridade eclesiástica vinham surgindo, ao tempo em que foram escritas as «epístolas pastorais». (Ver a seção IV do artigo sobre *Epístolas Pastorais*, sob o título *«Para Quem foram Escritas».*

As principais qualificações dos *supervisores*, conforme as encontramos em Tito 1:5 e no terceiro capítulo da primeira epístola a Timóteo, são as mesmas, a saber:

1. Eles precisam ter bom testemunho dos «de fora» (da comunidade ou sociedade não-cristã), bem como daqueles que fazem parte da igreja cristã.

2. Indivíduos recentemente convertidos devem ser barrados do ministério da Palavra. Deve haver tempo para que obtenham experiência.

3. Devem ser homens casados apenas uma vez.

4. **Devem possuir filhos obedientes, o que demonstra sua capacidade de governar o próprio lar, antes de governarem a família de Deus.**

5. Devem ser pessoas dotadas de piedade geral, livres de qualquer vício tipicamente pagão.

6. Devem ser hospitaleiros.

7. Devem ser possuidores dos dons espirituais, o que fica subentendido no fato de que devem ser *aptos* ou «qualificados» para ensinar, embora isso só seja dito diretamente no trecho de I Tim. 3:2.

8. Tanto a primeira epístola a Timóteo como a Tito estabelecem regras similares para as «diaconisas», embora essas regras só apareçam no segundo capítulo da epístola a Tito. Ali também aprendemos que as diaconisas devem ser «mestras», mas apenas de mulheres (ver Tito 2:4), porquanto é proibido pelo autor sagrado que as mulheres ensinem aos homens (ver I Tim. 2:11-15).

Os anciãos são realmente nomeados por Deus (ver Atos 20:28), devendo ser selecionados entre aqueles que demonstrem suas qualificações espirituais em uma vida diária, caracterizada pela piedade, com o acompanhamento da posse dos dons ministeriais e carismáticos. Não há nenhum caso, em todo o N.T., de um único «ancião» em uma igreja — o ministério de um único indivíduo foi produto de uma época posterior, quando o ministério cristão já se encontrava *profissionalizado*, devido à ausência dos dons espirituais. Alguma ênfase é posta sobre a questão da «consagração» desses anciãos, porquanto esse é o método pelo qual a igreja é resguardada dos falsos mestres, os quais procuram introduzir ensinamentos errôneos. É mister que tenham autoridade apropriada e isso conforme lhes for conferida pelo apóstolo dos gentios ou por aqueles nomeados pela sua «sucessão». (Quanto a idéias adicionais a esse respeito, ver a introdução aos trechos de I Tim. 3:1,8 no NTI).

3. Outros comentários — considerando I Tim. 5:17-25.

O Sustento e a Disciplina dos Ministros

No primeiro versículo deste capítulo é usado o termo «ancião», referindo-se a algum «homem idoso», e ali são dadas regras sobre como um «jovem pastor» deve tratar com o mesmo; havendo em seguida instruções acerca de outros grupos de idade. Mas, neste ponto, o «ancião» é um título eclesiástico, indicando um pastor, um dirigente da congregação local, juntamente com outros «anciãos», embora em posição inferior ao «bispo» ou «supervisor». É correto dizer-se que, no restante, do N.T., os «anciãos» e os «bispos» ou supervisores, são as mesmas pessoas, porquanto «ancião» e «supervisor» são termos sinônimos. Mas, nestas «epístolas pastorais», não se dá exatamente o mesmo.

Neste ponto, damos o comentário extraído do *Word Studies*, de autoria de Vincent, acerca desse assunto:

«A opinião dos críticos modernos tem abandonado quase inteiramente o ponto de vista que o governo cristão original imitava o governo da sinagoga. As autoridades seculares e religiosas das comunidades judaicas, pelo menos em localidades puramente judaicas, eram as mesmas; e bastaria esse fato contra a probabilidade de tal norma ter sido diretamente transferida para a igreja cristã. As prerrogativas dos anciãos do judaísmo nada têm que correspondam ao que sucedia nas comunidades cristãs. Funções que emergem posteriormente, nas comunidades judaico-cristãs da Palestina, não existem na sociedade palestino-cristã inicial. Quando muito, segundo observa Wiezsacker, tudo se resumiu no empréstimo de um título corrente.

Penso que a crítica moderna compele-nos a abandonar a idéia de que os títulos de bispo e ancião são idênticos, idéia essa que tem obtido larga aceitação, especialmente entre os eruditos ingleses, mediante as discussões de Lightfoot e Hatch. O testemunho de Clemente de Roma (Epístola aos Coríntios) mostra que os bispos (*egoúmenoi* ou *proegoúmenoi*) eram distinguidos dos anciãos, e que se os bispos eram aparentemente designados como anciãos, isso se devia ao fato de terem aqueles sido escolhidos dentre os anciãos, tendo retido o mesmo nome, mesmo depois de terem deixado de manter o ofício. Por essa razão, os bispos falecidos eram chamados anciãos. Nos escritos de *Clemente*, os anciãos indicam uma classe ou estado — membros de longa data e de caráter aprovado, e não titulares de ofício, regularmente nomeados. Entre esses é que os bispos devem ser procurados. Os bispos são reputados anciãos, não porque um ancião, como tal, seja um bispo, mas porque um bispo, como tal, seja um ancião. Nas Epístolas pastorais, os bispos e diáconos são associados uns aos outros, sem haver menção aos anciãos (ver I Tim. 3:1-13). Os anciãos são referidos em I Tim. 5:17-19, mas em uma conexão inteiramente diferente. As qualificações dos bispos e diáconos são detalhadas na primeira dessas passagens, e a lista de qualificações termina com a declaração de que assim estava organizada a igreja, como casa de Deus (ver os versículos catorze e quinze). Os ofícios são exauridos na descrição dos bispos e diáconos. Nada é dito acerca dos anciãos até o quinto capítulo desta primeira epístola a Timóteo, onde as relações de Timóteo com membros individuais da igreja são prescritas; e em Tito 2:2 e ss , onde esses membros são descritos como 'homens idosos' (presbútas). Fica implícita certa distinção entre duas classes de bispos — aqueles que governam bem, e aqueles que não o fazem; mas a distinção é obviamente feita entre os membros de igreja antigos e honrados, coletivamente considerados, formando o corpo do presbitério, e certos dentre seu número, que mostram suas qualificações por terem sido nomeados como supervisores. Os anciãos, como tais, não estavam investidos de qualquer ofício.

ANCIÃO — ÂNCORA

Não havia ato formal constitutivo dos anciãos. Os bispos eram contados entre os anciãos, mas estes últimos não formavam um ofício.

Dessa maneira, precisamos explicar as alusões aos anciãos 'nomeados' (em Tito 1:5 e Atos 14:23). Os anciãos devem ser nomeados como supervisores ou bispos, pois os supervisores devem ter as qualificações de anciãos aprovados. A consagração de anciãos consiste da dedicação de anciãos para a posição de supervisores. O presbitério denota um estado honroso e influente, na igreja, com base na idade, na duração como membro de igreja e no caráter aprovado. Somente os bispos eram 'nomeados'. Não havia nomeação para o presbitério. Ao término da epístola de Clemente aos Coríntios, as qualificações de um ancião são indicadas na descrição dos três comissários, enviados pela igreja romana, que eram os portadores da epístola, e aos quais nenhum título oficial foi conferido. Eram antigos membros da igreja romana, onde estavam desde a juventude, sem mácula na vida, crentes e sóbrios.

O falecido dr. Hort, em sua 'Ecclesia', afirmava que 'bispo' não era a designação de um ofício, e, sim, de uma função. Era uma descrição da função dos anciãos. — Diz ele: 'Atualmente, se reconhece bem que não temos aqui (na palavra *episkopos*) um ofício diferente, mantido por alguma pessoa, em contraste com o plural «anciãos». E acrescenta ele: 'É dificilmente menos errôneo compreender (*episkopos*) como mero segundo título, capaz de ser usado intercambiavelmente com «presbúteros», (pág. 190).

Além dessas distinções, feitas por Vincent, deveríamos salientar que os «bispos» ou «supervisores», os quais, portanto, tinham autoridade sobre um território ou distrito, e não meramente sobre alguma igreja local, que era o caso relacionado aos «anciãos». E embora talvez não houvesse supervisores com toda a autoridade e com todos os deveres atribuídos aos «bispos» posteriores, contudo, pelo tempo em que estas epístolas foram escritas, grandes passadas tinham sido dadas na formação de um autêntico bispado. E isso significa que o «bispo» era mais que uma palavra para indicar as *funções* de um ancião. Antes, trata-se de um vocábulo que indica autoridade superior à dos anciãos, ainda que não tivesse o total sentido que veio a adquirir nos meados do segundo século de nossa era, conforme se vê nas epístolas de Inácio. Ver o artigo sobre as Epístolas pastorais, no item intitulado, «A Quem foram Dirigidas».

••• ••• •••

A seção que se segue mostra-nos que apesar de todos os «anciãos» terem autoridade na igreja, fazendo parte do governo eclesiástico, alguns deles se ocupavam da pregação e do ensino. Os anciãos eram, essencialmente, oficiais administrativos, embora alguns tivessem também outras funções. Alguns dos anciãos, ou mesmo todos eles, recebiam algum pagamento da congregação local, por seus serviços, mas os pregadores e mestres deveriam receber um salário mais amplo. (Ver os versículos dezessete e dezoito deste capítulo). É bem possível que muitos deles trabalhassem gratuitamente, conforme faziam os rabinos judeus mais espirituais, ou como faziam Paulo e Barnabé (ver I Cor. 9:6). Contudo, o ofício de ancião era visto como algo que merecia remuneração de alguma sorte. Com base nisso devemos supor que foi imposto um limite ao número dos homens que seriam reputados anciãos, em uma igreja local; e que ainda que houvesse um número excessivo deles, alguns tinham tal ofício como «honra», apenas, sem receber qualquer recompensa financeira por seus labores, embora pudessem compartilhar também do governo. Todavia, o trecho que temos à frente não entra em detalhes sobre essa questão, pelo que também não sabemos como essas questões eram regulamentadas.

Hoje em dia, um dos grandes problemas da igreja é a determinação de quais líderes da igreja devem ser considerados dignos de salário. Na congregação média, esse problema é solucionado mediante o ministério «profissional», que postula o «governo de um homem», o qual é o único que recebe salário da Igreja. Isso, naturalmente, passou a ocorrer quando os dons ministeriais espirituais desapareceram, tornando-se mister o aparecimento de um ministério profissional. Mas isso não representa as verdadeiras condições existentes na igreja cristã primitiva; e se a igreja atual ainda contasse com *anciãos*, segundo o molde primitivo, ainda assim o problema financeiro permaneceria de pé. O texto sagrado é bastante definido sobre um ponto — aqueles que pregam e ensinam deveriam ser os primeiros da lista a receber ajuda financeira, o que lhes permitiria serem melhores mestres, se **prepararem-se melhor**, fim de exercerem suas habilidades sem empecilhos de ordem financeira.

Esta seção também envolve o tópico necessário da disciplina dos líderes da igreja. Infelizmente essa disciplina é necessária, e homens bons, até mesmo homens de Deus, caem em pecados e erros sérios. A igreja deve contar com algum meio de tratar com os tais. A antiga regra judaica, de serem apresentadas duas ou três testemunhas, para que alguma acusação fosse feita contra os anciãos, é aplicada aqui (ver o décimo nono versículo deste capítulo). E o vigésimo versículo parece aplicar a regra democrática da disciplina, embora não haja menção alguma de «voto» que anule o ofício dado a alguém por chamada divina, ou mesmo que o exclua, ainda que tal ação drástica se torne necessária. O trecho de Mat. 18:15 e ss, tal como a passagem de I Cor. 5:4 e ss., dá a entender a necessidade de ação democrática em todos os casos de disciplina. (AM B IB FA ND NTI UN Z)

ÂNCORA

As âncoras mais primitivas eram pedras preparadas de modo a serem seguras por uma corda. Antigas âncoras desse tipo têm sido encontradas no Mediterrâneo. Começaram a existir âncoras similares às atuais por volta do século I A.C., completas com a barra transversal, os dentes e vários tipos de projeções, e também feitas de variegados materiais. As primeiras âncoras desse modelo eram feitas de madeira, com uma barra transversal de chumbo. Em Atos 27:29, lemos que quatro âncoras foram arriadas da popa do navio.

Usos figurativos

Âncora da alma, Heb. 6:19. (Ver I Tim. 1:19 quanto à mesma figura simbólica implícita). O navio precisa de uma âncora, para segurá-lo na tempestade. Mediante essa medida é obtida a segurança. A alma também enfrenta perigos, e deve ser protegida. A esperança de Deus, dada em Cristo é que nos fornece a segurança necessária. O navio ancorado no porto, embora agitado pelo vento e pela tempestade, acha-se em segurança, pois é resguardado de áreas eivadas de perigo. Por isso é que tanto na literatura antiga como no tempo moderno, a âncora é símbolo de esperança e segurança. «A 'esperança' básica em uma falsa suposição é como confiar em uma âncora fraca» (Sócrates). E mais adiante, no mesmo texto (*Stob.*

ÂNCORA — ANDAR

Serm. 109), diz Sócrates: «Um navio não deve confiar em uma âncora, e nem a vida em uma só esperança». Na igreja primitiva, a âncora era símbolo, não menos que a cruz, das realidades cristãs. No Túmulo de Gordon, que muitos crêem ter sido o sepulcro de Cristo (que vide), sobre o lugar onde o corpo esteve, aparece uma âncora, esculpida sobre a parede de pedra. Os túmulos de cristãos antigos e mais recentes com freqüência têm sido decorados com a representação de uma âncora. Trata-se de um símbolo bem apropriado para a esperança, posto que se agarra a algo «invisível», mas bem real. Por isso, o autor sagrado reputa que, em Cristo, a esperança é segura, embora ainda precise concretizar-se e ser desfrutada.

Filo também se utilizou desse símbolo (ver *De somniis* 1:39), e é bem possível que o autor sagrado obteve a idéia da parte dele, posto que neste tratado se pode ver muito da influência de Filo. Eurípedes (ver *Helena*, 277), Aristófanes (ver *Cavaleiros*, 1244) e Pitágoras (ver *Stob. Ecolg.* 3), usaram da âncora como símbolo da segurança. Pitágoras rejeita tais coisas como glória, governos, honrarias, etc., como âncoras fracas, tanto quanto o corpo humano físico. As virtudes, porém, como a prudência, a magnanimidade e a fortaleza seriam âncoras inabaláveis.

«A alma se apega, como que com temor do naufrágio, a uma âncora, e não vê para onde vai o cabo da âncora, e nem onde esta ficou presa: mas sabe que está segura além do véu que oculta a glória futura, e que se ela mesma ao menos segurar-se firmemente na âncora, com o tempo será levada para onde está esta última, isto é, ao Santo dos Santos, pelas mãos do nosso Libertador». (Ebhard, em Heb. 6:19).

«A âncora é firme e constante; é segura em sua própria natureza e é constante quanto ao seu objetivo, visto que está presa à rocha, a Rocha dos séculos; não está presa à areia, mas está segura para além do véu e em Cristo». (Matthew Henry, em Heb. 6:19).

«O homem que não encontra sua segurança para além do véu torna-se vítima de forças mundanas que o tratam como um brinquedo. É desviado de seu curso. Seu frágil batel muda de direção ao elevar-se e baixar-se a qualquer onda. Até mesmo as estrelas morais são apagadas quando não há marcos de terra que meçam o 'avanço'. É patente que o reconhecimento dos perigos que enfrentamos, tanto do lado de fora como do lado de dentro, encontrando nossa 'âncora segura', nossa esperança no Deus que fez a promessa, é salvação para todo homem, para toda a circunstância, para toda geração». (Cotton, em Heb. 6:19).

Tua âncora se manterá firme no temporal da vida
Quando as nuvens desdobram suas asas contenciosas?
Quando as marés se levantam e os cabos ficam tensos,
Tua âncora se desviará ou permanecerá firme?
......
Temos uma âncora que mantém a alma
Segura e firme, enquanto as ondas rolam,
Segura à Rocha que não pode mover-se,
Bem segura e profunda no amor do Salvador.

(Priscilla J. Owens)

Segura e firme, Heb. 6:19. Alguns aplicam isso à *esperança*; e outros à âncora. Alguns aludem à idéia do «refúgio», que transparece no décimo oitavo versículo, mas isso é menos provável. A esperança torna-se a âncora, a âncora da esperança, dentro do simbolismo combinado; portanto a questão da segurança e da firmeza está envolvida em ambos os elementos. O termo *segura* deriva-se do vocábulo gr. «asphale», «firme», como se dá com alicerces «seguros», sendo um derivativo de «spallein», «cambalear»; era termo usado metaforicamente com o sentido de «deixar perplexo» ou «frustrar». «Firme» vem de «bebaios»; «permanente», «bem firmado».

Penetra além do véu, Heb. 6:19. A metáfora é mantida, e agora somos informados sobre onde a âncora se firma, de onde procede a nossa segurança. A âncora se firma *além do véu*, isto é, na presença mesma de Deus, para onde Cristo Jesus já foi. Os cabos da âncora vão de nós para ele, firmando-nos na sua presença.

Além do véu é a realidade invisível e eterna do mundo celeste. Dois símbolos são aqui combinados; a. o mundo como mar; a alma como um navio; o fundo oculto do oceano como a realidade oculta do mundo celestial; b. a vida presente nos átrios externos do templo; a bem-aventurança futura do santuário dentro do véu. A alma como navio tangido pela tempestade, mas que é mantido firme pela âncora. A alma no átrio externo do templo é segura, pela fé, à bendita realidade no interior do templo». (Vincent em Heb. 6:18).

«A âncora está fora de vista, mas ela se mantém firme. Isso é o que importa» (Robertson em Heb. 6:19). O trabalho de Cristo, como nosso Sumo Sacerdote (o tema agora tem prosseguimento, com vinculações com o trecho de Heb. 5:10), é o que garante a chegada segura no porto, o bem-estar eterno da alma. (FA NTI Z)

ANDAR

Esse verbo é tradução de cerca de sete vocábulos hebraicos, no Antigo Testamento, e de cinco palavras gregas, algumas das quais raramente usadas. Naturalmente, há um sentido literal e sentidos figurados da ação. Os sentidos figurados podem ser antropomórficos, como quando se lê que Deus andava pelo jardim do Éden na viração do dia (ver Gên. 3:8), ou metafóricos, quando se lê sobre a maneira de andar do coração (ver Jó 31:7), da língua dos ímpios (ver Sal. 73:9), do trajeto das pestes (ver Sal. 91:6) ou do curso da lua (ver Jó 31:26). O uso metafórico mais comum dessa ação representa a conduta do homem, bem como a atitude de Deus para com essa maneira de andar. Por exemplo, ver Lev. 26:23,24: «Se...porém, andardes contrariamente comigo, eu também serei contrário a vós outros...»

Mais raramente, o termo pode ser usado em um sentido mais limitado, referindo-se às leis e preceitos para observância por parte dos homens (ver Atos 21:21). E no evangelho de João tem o sentido de atividade incansável (ver João 11:9), ou mesmo de aparição em público (ver João 7:1).

Quando Jesus curava alguém da paralisia, restaurando-lhe a capacidade de andar, não o fazia somente para que a pessoa readquirisse sua movimentação, mas para ensinar que há necessidade de uma renovação interna, que capacite o pecador a prosseguir caminho, uma vez arrependido (ver Mar. 2:9: «Qual é mais fácil, dizer ao paralítico: Estão perdoados os teus pecados, ou dizer: Levanta-te, toma o teu leito, e anda?») No caso de Pedro, ao imitar Jesus, que caminhava por sobre as águas, continuar andando ou afundar era questão de fé. Quando a atenção de Pedro desviou-se de Jesus para a força das ondas, e ele começou a afundar e recorreu a Jesus, este perguntou: «Homem de pequena fé, por que

ANDAR, METÁFORA DE

duvidaste?» (Mat. 14:31).

O ato do batismo cristão indica que o crente deixou de andar pelo caminho da auto-suficiência pecaminosa e passou a andar pelo novo «caminho» (ver Rom. 6:4), da mesma maneira que, após Sua ressurreição, Jesus estava andando em uma nova maneira de viver. Assim, o crente é exortado a «andar no Espírito» (Gál. 5:16), e não mais a andar segundo a carne. O «andar dignamente» (ver Rom. 13:13) é melhor compreendido quando contrastado com o andar indigno de quem vive em orgias e bebedices, imoralidades e dissoluções, contendas e ciúmes. A idéia de progressão espiritual também é retratada pelo ato de andar. Promete Jesus, àqueles que não se macularem, não acompanhando o exemplo de outros, os quais abandonavam a integridade cristã: «...andarão de branco junto comigo, pois são dignos». No céu não haverá estagnação, mas a progressão espiritual será perene.

Essas e outras idéias proveitosas estão ligadas metaforicamente ao ato de andar. O estudioso da Bíblia muito aproveitará se meditar sobre as passagens que usam dessa metáfora.

ANDAR, Metáfora de

1. A metáfora do ato de **andar** expressa a natureza geral da vida espiritual. Isso é comum nas páginas do NT. Ver Gál. 5:16,25; 6:16; Rom. 4:12; 6:4; 8:1,4; 13:13; I Cor. 3:3; 7:17; Efé. 2:10; 4:1,17; 5:2,8,15; Fil. 3:16-18; Col. 1:10; 2:6; 4:5; I Tes. 2:12; 4:1,12; II Tes. 3:11. A metáfora se encontra em Paulo 33 vezes, e no resto do NT, 16 vezes. Nos filósofos éticos, também é comum.

2. A orientação do Espírito. Andar no Espírito, na comunhão e sob a influência do Espírito, o Poder Divino que cultiva em nós seus frutos. «Devemos dar os nossos passos pela ajuda e orientação do Espírito». (Robertson, em Gál. 5:25).

Andai na luz!
Assim conhecereis aquela comunhão de amor,
Que somente seu Espírito pode dar,
E que reina na luz superior.

Andai na luz!
E nem mesmo o sepulcro terá sombra temível;
A glória espantará sua tristeza,
Pois Cristo conquistou também ali.

(Bernard Barton)

3. Os mandamentos e o andar

a. Todos os mandamentos éticos do N.T., estão relacionados ao modo de «andar», ou seja, à maneira do crente conduzir-se neste mundo. O ato de andar é uma série de quedas interrompidas. Em nossas imperfeições, caímos com freqüência, e mesmo quando andamos, levamos conosco muitas quedas. Porém, o crente autêntico acaba encontrando a vitória cabal sobre todos os vícios.

b. O andar do crente precisa envolver as seguintes características:

Honestidade (ver I Tes. 2:12).

Ser digno de Deus (ver I Tes. 2:12), ser digno do Senhor (ver Col. 1:10), e ser digno de nossa vocação (ver Efé. 4:1). No Espírito (ver Gál. 5:25), e como filhos da luz (ver Efé. 5:8).

«*digno de Deus*», I Tess. 2:12. No grego encontramos o termo *aksios*, — um advérbio muito bem traduzido aqui, isto é, de maneira tal que o crente possa ser aprovado por ele, cuja vida seja agradável ao Senhor, sendo conduzido ao destino que o Senhor planejou para nós, em Cristo Jesus. (Comparar com Col. 1:10). Essa passagem diz: «...a fim de viverdes de modo digno do Senhor, para o seu inteiro agrado, frutificando em toda boa obra, e crescendo no pleno conhecimento de Deus». É dessa maneira que podemos cultivar uma conduta digna. Também se pode comparar com o trecho de Efé. 4:1: «Rogo-vos, pois, eu, o prisioneiro no Senhor, que andeis de modo digno da vocação a que fostes chamados...» Essa expressão tem sido encontrada em vários papiros e inscrições de tipo diverso do N.T., bem como em antiqüíssimos documentos cristãos, como em I *Clemente* 21:1 e Policarpo 5:2.

4. A maneira digna de andar

Aspectos da conduta ideal:

a. O seu exemplo é Cristo, o qual, como homem em que se tornou, enfrentou as mesmas tentações e problemas com que nos defrontamos, mas triunfou sobre tudo e muito aprendeu disso. (Ver Heb. 5:9). Dessa maneira se tornou o Pioneiro de nossa fé, mostrando-nos a vereda a seguir e como podemos enveredar por esse caminho. (Ver as notas a respeito, em Heb. 2:10, no NTI). Ele dizia: «Vinde após mim?» (Mat. 4:19).

b. A maneira ideal de andar leva-nos a uma missão específica que precisa ser cumprida, pois cada indivíduo é singular e tem uma obra singular a realizar. (Ver notas completas sobre esse conceito em Apo. 2:17 no NTI). Assim como o Pai enviou o Filho em sua missão, assim também somos agora enviados (ver João 17:18).

c. A maneira ideal de andar inclui a nossa comunhão com Deus, através do Espírito, ao ponto mesmo de sermos o templo do Espírito Santo, o lugar onde ele habita. (Ver Efé. 4:3 e Efé. 2:10).

d. A maneira digna de andar requer que o crente ponha em prática *os meios de desenvolvimento espiritual:*

O estudo dos documentos sagrados, bem como de outros livros que sejam espiritualmente úteis.

A oração (ver o artigo)

A meditação (ver o artigo)

A santificação (ver o artigo)

A vida diária segundo a lei do amor, as boas obras (ver no NTI em I João 4:7,8).

A possessão e o uso dos dons espirituais (ver no NTI em Efe. 4:11 e ss).

5. Através desse meios é que nos tornamos «dignos» de Deus, o qual nos chamou como seus filhos.

O Lado Negativo: O Andar nas Trevas

O «curso» geral da vida conduz às pessoas aos vícios do paganismo, à participação na rebeldia maléfica, fazendo-os enveredar por avenidas de degradação do corpo e do espírito. A expressão, «andar nas trevas» é usada somente nas obras joaninas. (Comparar com João 8:12 e 12:35). Para que não andemos nas trevas, precisamos da iluminação sobrenatural, pois o andar espiritual é inspirado e dirigido pelo Espírito de Deus. É impossível tal alvo para o homem natural. Este precisa de iluminação, de transformação, de inspiração e de ajuda da parte de Deus. A experiência mostra isso para nós, porque freqüentemente falhamos em nossas próprias forças; e quando a nossa santidade depende de nossa própria iniciativa, tornamo-nos profanos. Para andarmos santamente precisamos «nascer de novo» (ver I Ped. 1:23); é o poder residente, do Espírito Santo, em nós infundido, que nos confere a natureza moral de Cristo (ver Gál. 5:22,23). (I IB ND NTI)

••• ••• •••

ANDAR SOBRE ÁGUA

ANDAR SOBRE ÁGUA, O milagre de
Ver Mat. 14:22-27, Mar. 6:45,46 e João 6:15-21. As diversidades contidas nos relatos provavelmente indicam que a história foi preservada em mais do que uma fonte na tradição primitiva evangélica, antes da formação dos Evangelhos canônicos.

Tanto em Marcos quanto em João, a história está vinculada na seqüência com a multiplicação miraculosa; e disso obtemos a impressão de que o grande Cristo, que pode multiplicar pães, também pode vencer a força da gravidade, e andar por sobre a água. Não há motivo para duvidarmos disso, pois até hoje, entre os fenômenos psíquicos, tal fenômeno não é de todo desconhecido. O homem Jesus, por ser altamente espiritualizado, devido às operações do Espírito Santo, na realidade prática nem pertencia a este mundo, tão grande era o seu desenvolvimento, que ele demonstrou ocasionalmente. Interpretações céticas também são apresentadas neste ponto, por aqueles que ignoram o que pode ser feito mediante o desenvolvimento espiritual, ou por aqueles que estão cegos para a significação de tal desenvolvimento. Jesus teria andado «através» da água e não «sobre» a água; mas os discípulos se equivocaram sobre o que sucedeu. Tais idéias não merecem nossa consideração, e refletem a ignorância do ceticismo quanto às realidades espirituais. Agostinho dizia que somente na «fé», é que uma mente está em condição de acolher a verdade espiritual, pois o ceticismo resulta do fato de que a verdade espiritual foi amortecida para os céticos. Por isso é que ele dizia: *Creio, para que possa entender.* Sem dúvida temos nisso grande verdade espiritual. A experiência humana demonstra tal coisa. Os místicos que podem ver a aura humana (a qual atualmente pode ser fotografada por um tipo de radiografia) dizem-nos que as auras dos céticos são manchadas com máculas negras e sem cor, ilustrando o fato de que suas faculdades espirituais foram prejudicadas. Quão certo estava Agostinho, mesmo sem qualquer prova científica.

Este Milagre, tal como o da multiplicação dos pães, tem atraído muita atenção, bem como grande número de interpretações. As principais são representadas pelas seguintes idéias:

1. Interpretação às vezes denominada *monofisista*, porque os monofisistas ensinavam que Cristo possuía apenas uma natureza, composta da divina e da humana. Parte da igreja cóptica manteve essa crença. Essa interpretação diz que o Filho de Deus exerce controle sobre os elementos da natureza por ser Deus e homem. Essa doutrina não dá muita importância à natureza humana de Jesus, e pode incluir a idéia de docetismo (palavra que vem do verbo grego que significa «perecer»), que indica que o corpo de Cristo, nessa aparição, era apenas uma miragem, e não um autêntico corpo humano. Mas o texto indica, aqui, que Jesus não somente tinha poder sobre as forças da natureza, mas também sobre o seu próprio corpo. As Escrituras ensinam que Jesus foi homem verdadeiro, dotado de um corpo humano.

2. Alguns interpretam que Jesus realmente não andou sobre a *superfície* do mar, mas que somente dava aos discípulos a impressão de andar sobre o mar, quando a realidade é que andava sobre a terra, à beira-mar, ou então em água muito rasa. Mas o próprio texto impossibilita essa interpretação. O grego diz que ele andou «sobre» o mar, e seria impossível fazer isso significar *sobre* a terra ou em água de pouca profundidade. Por semelhante modo, o incidente da tentativa de Pedro em fazer a mesma coisa, e o fato de que eles conversaram, ilustra a impossibilidade de se crer que essa conversa, e a atitude de Pedro, tivessem lugar enquanto Jesus ficava em terra, ao passo que Pedro estava a «muitos estádios» da terra.

3. Outros pensam que a ocorrência foi modificada pelo autor do evangelho, e que representa um acontecimento comum, onde não houve qualquer milagre, mas que a tradição floreou o incidente. Parece que seria melhor dizer (pelo menos haveria mais razão nisso) que a ocorrência foi *invenção* do autor (ou dos três autores, ou pelo menos que isso foi aceito por três pessoas, Mateus, Marcos e João), pois é difícil entender como é que um acontecimento sem qualquer elemento fora do comum poderia provocar tantas modificações ao ponto de transformar-se em um dos milagres notáveis de Jesus.

4. Um intérprete sugere que Jesus apenas *nadou!* Mas essa interpretação refuta a si mesma.

5. Outros oferecem a interpretação *mitológica*, uma história marinha, como muitas outras, com possíveis reflexos de II Reis 2:14; 6:6 e Jó. 9:8, além de certos mitos estrangeiros.

6. Alguns pensam que Cristo manifestou poderes especiais, inerentes à natureza superior de sua *corporalidade*. Mas as Escrituras nunca indicam que Jesus tivesse um corpo diferente do homem comum, e a sua morte parece deixar isso bem patente.

7. Alguns expositores interpretam a história como se fora uma *alegoria* que apenas anota certas lições espirituais, sem aceitar a narrativa como acontecimento histórico.

8. Sabemos, por incidentes modernos de pessoas chamadas *sonâmbulas* que andam pelas vizinhanças, em estado de sono ou transe, que andar sobre a água não é algo impossível para a natureza humana. Outros, mesmo não estando em estado de transe, têm demonstrado essa habilidade, e isso deve ser incluído nas manifestações psíquicas, sobre as quais até hoje não sabemos muito. Pelo menos parece que essa façanha não é impossível à natureza humana, sob determinadas condições. Alguns expositores não aceitam essa ação como algo possível à natureza humana, mas pensam que tais pessoas devem contar com a ajuda de algum *poder externo*, como o dos demônios, etc. Mas, quando entramos nessas discussões, entramos na esfera das especulações, porque simplesmente não temos conhecimento suficiente sobre a questão para afirmar muitas coisas. Porém, é errôneo atribuir ao diabo tudo quanto não entendemos. Lembremo-nos que os antigos atribuíam o relâmpago e o trovão a deuses bons ou maus. Em geral, os estudos psíquicos ilustram o fato de que a personalidade humana é muito *mais poderosa* do que se tem pensado até hoje e que parecem quase não ter limites as possibilidades da personalidade humana. Isso seria ainda mais evidente não fora o peso e os efeitos do pecado, dos quais Jesus estava isento. E quem pode negar que, na transformação à imagem de Cristo, o homem adquirirá muito maior poder do que a capacidade de caminhar sobre a água? Também precisamos lembrar que o Cristo estava em processo de transformação espiritual, sendo homem, e assim ia adquirindo maior poder, dia-a-dia. Não nos olvidemos, ainda, que os poderes por ele adquiridos tornavam-se expressões *permanentes* de sua personalidade. (Ver Heb. 5:8,9). Por outro lado, a verdade é que esse desenvolvimento era espiritual, mediante a participação no poder do Espírito Santo. Através do conhecimento que temos até o presente, talvez possamos asseverar que o milagre aqui realizado por Jesus foi resultado direto da influência divina sobre

ANDORINHA— ANDRÉ E MATIAS, ATOS DE

ele (talvez o uso *direto* desses poderes de sua própria natureza como Deus), mas é verdade, igualmente, que a transformação do ser humano, pelo poder de Deus, enquanto o homem está no processo do retorno a ele, fará com que o homem se torne mais e mais uma pessoa capaz de fazer tais maravilhas. Ler notas sobre Rom. 8:29 no NTI. Ver comentários sobre a nossa participação na divindade em II Ped. 1:4 no NTI.

Também notamos que dois dos evangelhos sinópticos, Mateus e Marcos, têm a mesma história em conjunto com o evangelho de João. Assim sendo, a suposição de alguns intérpretes, que dizem que somente João exagerou os elementos miraculosos na vida de Jesus, não têm base. Talvez a diferença entre os evangelhos, nesse sentido, não seja tão grande como alguns têm imaginado. (I IB LAN NTI)

ANDORINHA

Ver o artigo geral sobre **Aves** da Bíblia. Nas traduções, há duas palavras hebraicas, *agur* e *sus* (ver Isa. 38:14 e Jer. 8:7) que foram intercambiadas. Esses termos hebraicos indicam, respectivamente, grou e andorinha. Ambas são aves migratórias. Neste artigo, interessa-nos a segunda delas. No hebraico, *sus* significa *rápida*. Há espécies migratórias e espécies residentes de andorinhas. Quando elas eram abundantes na Palestina, os habitantes usavam-nas como alimento. E os hebreus também tiveram permissão de consumi-las em sua dieta. Há traduções que usam somente a palavra «grou» para ambas essas passagens; outras que usam somente a palavra «andorinha», em ambas. Nossa versão portuguesa as distingue.

Temos a considerar duas palavras hebraicas, uma delas usada em Sal. 84:3 e Pro. 26:2, e a outra usada em Isa. 38:14 e Jer. 8:7. Alguns estudiosos opinam que a primeira dessas palavras seria a verdadeira andorinha, ao passo que a outra seria a grou. Driver (PEQ, 1955, pág. 131) vê uma clara distinção entre uma espécie e outra; mas a verdade é que essa diferenciação não é tão simples como pode parecer à primeira vista. Esses pássaros pertencem a espécies totalmente diferentes, embora com hábitos similares. Ambas as espécies buscam o seu alimento no ar, onde passam a maior parte das horas do dia, pois são quase incapazes de tocar no solo, e fazem os seus ninhos em construções feitas pelo homem. A Palestina conta com seis membros da família das andorinhas (Hirundinidae). Dois desses membros são residentes, e os outros são migratórios. Mas o caso é que os escritores antigos dificilmente distinguiram entre essas duas espécies com precisão. No hebraico, a palavra traduzida por «andorinha», em Sal. 84:3 e Pro. 26:2, também significa «liberdade» (em letras latinas, essa palavra hebraica daria algo como *derôr*). Alguns têm sugerido que essa é uma palavra mais geral, que inclui todos os pássaros insetívoros, que se alimentam enquanto voam. Por esse motivo, tanto uma espécie quanto a outra se ajustariam aos contextos de Sal. 84:3 e Pro. 26:2, o que talvez explique por que nossa versão portuguesa traduz duas palavras hebraicas diferentes por uma só, «andorinha». (Z)

ANDRÉ

O nome dele está incluído entre aqueles que esperaram no cenáculo, após a ascensão de Cristo (ver Atos 1:13). Porém, depois disso, seu nome não mais é mencionado no Novo Testamento. A tradição, como usual, adiciona toda a espécie de detalhes. Talvez alguns desses detalhes correspondam à realidade.

Eusébio, *Hist.* III.1, registrou uma tradição que afirma que posteriormente trabalhou na Cítia. Por essa razão, ele foi adotado como santo patrono da Rússia. Porém, outras tradições vinculam-no à Lídia, à Trácia e à Acaia. O evangelho apócrifo chamado *Atos de André* diz que ele evangelizou a Acaia, e que finalmente foi ali martirizado em uma cruz com a forma de «X». Esse tipo de cruz, a *crux decussata*, veio a chamar-se Cruz de Santo André. Por causa dessa tradição, ele tornou-se o santo patrono da Grécia. As tradições se multiplicam, afirmando que então seu corpo foi transferido para Constantinopla, e dali para a Itália, durante as cruzadas da Idade Média. Uma tradição posterior diz que um de seus *braços* foi trazido para a costa oriental da Escócia, por Régulo; e assim André tornou-se também o santo patrono da Escócia.

André não possuía a habilidade nativa e a agressividade de seu irmão Pedro, mas desempenhou — importante papel na evangelização, — que prosseguiu dando apoio às atividades do grupo apostólico. A vontade de Deus dirige as atividades de cada ser humano, embora, como é óbvio, o desenvolvimento espiritual pessoal e a iniciativa do indivíduo tenham um grande peso no tocante ao que acontece a uma pessoa durante esta vida. Seja como for, trata-se de um ensino espiritual, digno de atenção, onde cada um de nós tem uma missão especial a realizar, e não somente neste momento do tempo que chamamos de vida terrena, mas igualmente por toda a eternidade. Isso fica subentendido no trecho de Apo. 2:17, o que é comentado pormenorizadamente no NTI.

ANDRÉ, ATOS DE PEDRO E

Ver *Pedro e André, Atos de*, nos *Livros Apócrifos do Novo Testamento*.

Os Atos Leucianos:

Há um grande número de Atos apócrifos, mas os principais são os de Paulo, Pedro, Tomé (Judas), João e André. Os maniqueus reuniram muitas dessas obras, formando uma coleção. A maioria desses livros tem origem gnóstica. O bibliófilo do século IX D.C., Fótio, encontrou a coleção inteira atribuída a um certo *Leucius Charinus*; mas parece que o nome Leucius era o nome fictício do autor de Atos de João (o livro mais ortodoxo desse grupo). Seja como for, seu nome veio a ser associado a esse grupo de livros.

Atos de André. Quanto à data, esse é o mais recente desses livros (cerca de 260 D.C.), e também o mais fragmentado nos manuscritos existentes. Reveste-se de um caráter fortemente gnóstico, comentado por Eusébio em *Hist*. iii.25. Fala-se ali sobre a suposta pregação de André entre povos canibais e outros, seus vários milagres e suas exortações em favor da virgindade e do celibato.

ANDRÉ E MATIAS (MATEUS), ATOS DE

Essa obra existe em várias versões—latina, **grega** e **siríaca** — sendo uma alegada história romântica apócrifa das maravilhosas obras de André e Mateus. Não faz parte do livro Atos de André. A obra tem por intuito narrar mais os feitos de Matias (ver Atos 1:26), e não do evangelista Mateus; mas, em algumas versões posteriores da obra, Mateus toma o lugar de Matias.

A narrativa. O mundo estaria dividido em vários campos missionários, e os apóstolos encarregaram-se de entrar nesses campos, cada qual com sua área individual. Matias foi enviado a um território de canibais, que tratavam violentamente os estrangeiros, aprisionando-os, — matando-os, e, finalmente, devorando-os. Matias foi apanhado e cego, — mas conseguiu reter a consciência e orou pedindo ajuda. André foi a resposta às suas orações e o socorreu. Uma visita de Jesus foi o meio de transmitir a mensagem. André e alguns companheiros tomaram um barco cujo piloto era Jesus, embora não o tivessem reconhecido. A caminho, André (provocado por Jesus) historiou as poderosas obras de Jesus, incluindo a fantástica estória da visita feita a um templo pagão, onde os sumos sacerdotes judeus foram refutados por uma esfinge falante.

Ao chegarem, André liberta Matias, e ele e seus companheiros são arrebatados em uma nuvem, mas André fica para trás. Opera grandes milagres, mas é aprisionado e torturado. Como protesto, ele quase destrói a cidade, invocando grandes torrentes de água de uma estátua. O povo da cidade arrepende-se e ele restaura a cidade. Então traça planos para a construção de um templo, e o povo é batizado. (HEN JAM Z)

ANDRÉ E PAULO, ATOS DE

Essa história que só existe como fragmentos em cóptico, é um dos Atos apócrifos posteriores. Paulo desejava visitar *Amente* (o submundo), pelo que mergulhou no mar. Deixara uma mensagem endereçada a André, instruindo-o a trazê-lo de volta, chegado o tempo próprio. Ao retornar, Paulo conta como se encontrou com Judas, a única alma deixada em Amente. Embora Judas tivesse sido perdoado por haver traído a Jesus, caiu no erro de adorar a Satanás e movido pelo temor, suicidou-se. Portanto, foi condenado a permanecer no submundo, até o dia do juízo.

Depois Paulo e André visitaram uma cidade (na terra). Mas os judeus não permitiram a sua entrada, pelo que Paulo derrubou os portões com um pedaço de madeira que ele tinha trazido de Amente. Então os judeus rebeldes foram engolidos pela terra. Grande disputa seguiu-se entre os sobreviventes, e dois mil e setecentos judeus se converteram. (XJ Z)

ANDRÉ, HISTÓRIA FRAGMENTADA DE

Um livro apócrifo posterior, existente somente em cóptico, e em forma fragmentada, fala sobre uma mulher que matou sua criancinha dando-a como alimento para um cão. Os apóstolos viram-na e tentaram aproximar-se; porém, ela fugiu. Mas o cão ficou e explicou o sucedido. André orou pedindo um milagre, aludindo a como, uma vez, no monte Gebal, Jesus ordenara que todas as pedras espalhadas e todos os grãos de areia se reunissem em um só lugar, o que aconteceu de fato. A oração de André foi eficaz, e a criança voltou à vida. (Z)

ANDRÔNICO

1. Governador regente de Antíoco Epifânio, o qual por ordem de Menelau, depôs e executou o sumo sacerdote Onias, por causa do qual ele mesmo foi morto, ao regressar a Antíoco (ver II Macabeus 4), em cerca de 169 A.C.

2. Um oficial a quem Antíoco Epifânio, após saquear Jerusalém, deixou no governo, em Gerizim (ver I Macabeus 5:23).

3. Um cristão de Roma, ou de Éfeso (se é verdade que o décimo sexto capítulo da epístola aos Romanos foi uma pequena carta originalmente enviada à Ásia Menor, a fim de apresentar Febe). Ver o problema ser discutido no artigo sobre a epístola aos Romanos, na Seção VIII, *Integridade da Epístola*, quase no final da mesma. Seja como for, Paulo o saúda em Rom. 16:7. Evidentemente ele era crente antigo, já convertido quando Paulo o conheceu. O termo usado por Paulo, «parentes», provavelmente significa apenas que ele era judeu. Ele também é chamado um dos «companheiros de prisão», o que deve ser entendido literalmente. Todavia, não se sabe onde ele compartilhou com Paulo de algum encarceramento. Ver o artigo sobre *prisões*. Visto que o seu nome é associado ao de «Júnias», é possível que fossem marido e mulher. É possível que os dois tivessem se convertido no dia de Pentecoste, ou que fariam deles crentes experientes, antes de conhecerem o apóstolo dos gentios. Eles eram «notáveis entre os apóstolos», indicando que eram pessoas notórias na Igreja cristã. Alguns intérpretes acham que essas palavras indicam que eles mesmos eram alistados entre os apóstolos, no sentido mais amplo ou secundário do termo. Ver o artigo sobre *apóstolos*. Ver também os comentários sobre Atos 14:4 no NTI, quanto a esse uso mais amplo do termo «apóstolos». Ver os trechos de Gál. 1:19; Fil. 2:25; I Tess. 2:6 e I Cor. 4:9, onde fica entendido esse uso mais amplo do termo. Mui provavelmente ele conheceu Paulo em 60 D.C. De conformidade com Hipólito, ele tornou-se bispo da Panônia, mas Doroteu afirma que ele tornou-se bispo na Espanha. (DE MAG NTI RAM)

ANDRÔNICO DE RODES

Um filósofo helenista do século I A.C. Encabeçou um ressurgente movimento aristotélico, que recuperou as idéias de Aristóteles de numerosas vicissitudes sofridas em outras mãos. Por algum tempo, perderam-se os escritos de Aristóteles, mas Andronico os trouxe à tona. Foi ele quem cunhou o termo *metafísica*, usando-o para dar título a um tratado ao qual Aristóteles não dera nome. Também comentou sobre as obras de Teofrasto (ver o artigo), além de fazer suas próprias investigações no campo da lógica. (MM P)

ANEL

Palavra que aparece tanto no Antigo quanto no Novo Testamento. No grego é *daktúlios*, palavra que se origina do termo grego que significa «dedo». Anéis eram usados desde a antiguidade mais remota, conforme os arqueólogos têm descoberto entre os assírios, os babilônios e os egípcios. Provavelmente, os patriarcas do povo de Israel também os usassem. Usualmente os anéis eram confeccionados em ouro ou prata, embora também houvesse anéis de bronze. Os anéis de selar, sua forma mais primitiva, podem ter sido usados a princípio como substitutos do cordão de pôr no pescoço, onde ficava pendurado o selo (ver Gên. 38:18). Os egípcios que usavam muitos anéis, usavam-nos nos dedos. Posteriormente, os israelitas usavam o anel de selar em algum dedo da mão direita (ver Jer. 22:24). Os selos, esculpidos em uma chapa no anel, representavam certa variedade de emblemas, como um leão, um touro, um escaravelho, um crocodilo, além de vários emblemas reais. O anel de selar era usado para selar (equivalente à moderna assinatura) vários acordos, especialmente no caso de contratos matrimoniais. Era um objeto especialmente importante para a realeza, a nobreza e para

ANÉM — ANGLO-CATOLICISMO

indivíduos de alta posição social (ver Tia. 2:2). Faraó deu um desses anéis de selar a José, como símbolo de autoridade (ver Gên. 41:42). Por semelhante modo, Assuero deu a Hamã o seu anel de selar, para que este confirmasse com o mesmo o decreto real (ver Est. 3:10,12). O filho pródigo, da parábola de Jesus, recebeu um anel de seu pai, como símbolo de dignidade (Luc. 15:22).

Além de anéis, mulheres e crianças também usavam brincos que eram pendurados nas orelhas (ver Gên. 35:4; Êxo. 32:2), conforme se tem descoberto em Gezer, Megido e Taanaque. Argolas para o nariz também eram bastante populares entre os adornos femininos (ver Gên. 24:22,47; Isa. 3:21). Os anéis são mencionados por mais de quarenta vezes, dentre os objetos de uso religioso, em Êxo. 25:39. — E lemos que Moisés baixou instruções quanto ao uso dos mesmos na arca, nas cortinas do tabernáculo, no peitoral e na estola sacerdotal do sumo sacerdote, e nos altares do incenso e das ofertas queimadas. Anéis também eram usados como uma espécie de artigo de trocas ou escambo.

ANÉM
No hebraico, **duas fontes**. Uma cidade de Issacar, dada aos levitas (ver I Crô. 6:73). No trecho paralelo, Jos. 19:21, essa cidade é chamada En-Ganim, isto é, «fonte dos jardins». O lugar era bem servido de água, tendo sido identificado com Anea, do século IV D.C. Tinha bons banhos e distava quinze milhas romanas de Cesaréia, para oeste. Eusébio, porém, identificou-a com Aner. Alguns arqueólogos têm identificado com a moderna Khirbet 'Anim, a três quilômetros a nordeste de Alã, ou com a própria Olá, a treze quilômetros a suleste do monte Tabor. (ND S UN Z)

ANER
No hebraico, **jovem**. 1. Aner, Escol e Manre eram três cananeus (amorreus) que uniram suas forças às de Abraão, na perseguição aos reis Quedorlaomer, Anrafel e seus aliados, que haviam pilhado Sodoma e levado Ló, sobrinho de Abraão, como prisioneiro (ver Gên. 14:13,24). Também é possível que Aner fosse o nome de um lugar, visto que Manre também é nome antigo de Hebrom (ver Gên. 23:19), e Escol é o nome de um vale perto de Hebrom (ver Núm. 13:23). Terminada a tarefa, Abraão ignorou os despojos. Mas aqueles que o ajudaram compartilharam dos mesmos. Uma décima parte (o dízimo) foi dado a Melquisedeque, rei de Salém. (Ver o artigo sobre *Melquisedeque*). O tempo era 2060 A.C.

2. Uma cidade de refúgio, no território de Manassés (ver I Crô. 6:70), de localização desconhecida. (ND S UN Z)

ANETHON
No grego significa **Endro**.

ANFÍPOLIS
Nome grego de uma cidade da Grécia, **pela qual Paulo e Silas passaram a caminho de Tessalônica, vindos de Filipos** (ver Atos 17:1). Originalmente era um centro comercial dos trácios, conhecida como *nove estradas* (ennea odoi). Ficava localizada na margem oriental do rio Estrimom (modernamente Estruma ou Karasu), onde esse rio emerge do lago Cercinitis, cerca de cinco quilômetros e meio do mar.

Era uma cidade da Macedônia, cerca de cinqüenta e três quilômetros de Filipos.

Seu nome, Anfípolis, provavelmente deriva-se do fato de que era quase completamente *circundada* por uma curva do rio (no grego, *amfi*, em redor), ou talvez, porque era conspícua por todos os lados, estando localizada sobre um terraço elevado. Thuc. 4,102,4 apresenta a primeira dessas duas razões.

O local começou a ser ocupado em 436 A.C., por colonos atenienses, sob a liderança de Hagnon, depois que tentativas anteriores haviam fracassado. O general espartano Brasidas, conquistou-a militarmente, mas depois devolveu-a a Atenas. Continuou independente até que foi ocupada por Filipe da Macedônia, em 357 A.C. Sob o domínio dos romanos, foi reconhecida como uma cidade livre, servindo de residência ao governador romano da Macedônia.

A região era próspera por causa de suas terras férteis, de seu comércio com muitos produtos, incluindo o vinho, o azeite, a lã e a madeira. Dominava uma ponta que atravessava o rio Estrimom e ficava localizada na *Via Inácia*, uma das principais estradas romanas, que ligava Roma a muitas cidades da área de Anfípolis, visto que atravessava a Macedônia desde Dirracum, porto do mar do Épiro, vinculando assim a Itália à Grécia, nos tempos antigos.

Paulo passou por essa cidade a caminho de Tessalônica, vindo de Filipos, mas não há qualquer registro histórico de que ali estacou para pregar e organizar igrejas. (A ND NTI UN Z)

ÂNGELUS
1. A oração, recitada três vezes ao dia, em honra à encarnação, composta por três Ave-Marias, com a adição de três versículos bíblicos e uma oração final.

2. Os sinos que soam para que se faça essa oração. (E)

ANGLO-CATOLICISMO
De maneira frouxa, o termo pode designar aqueles que, desde os tempos de Henrique VIII, têm favorecido o catolicismo, sem o papa. Mais comumente o termo é usado para aludir ao Movimento de Oxford (ver o artigo) e seus sucessores (nos séculos XIX e XX), por meio do qual a fé católica foi fortemente propagada dentro da comunidade anglicana. Os anglo-católicos professam a fé da Igreja antes do cisma que dividiu o Ocidente do Oriente. Acolhem (embora não sem crítica) os desenvolvimentos modernos da Igreja Católica Romana. Inspiram-se na Bíblia, nos pais da Igreja, nos eruditos carolinos (ver o artigo) e no catolicismo contemporâneo, e não nos reformadores. Usam material litúrgico anglicano comum, como o Livro da Oração Comum, embora o suplementem com fontes romanistas. A teologia do Movimento de Oxford era fundamentalista, mas muitos anglo-católicos têm sido influenciados pela crítica liberal típica dos tempos modernos. Têm encorajado ativamente a reforma social, e têm dado apoio a movimentos esquerdistas. Têm-se mostrado ativos na fundação de ordens religiosas, retiros e métodos para enriquecer a vida devocional dos anglicanos. Em anos recentes, novas ênfases dentro do próprio catolicismo-romano têm modificado o anglo-catolicismo, e o reavivamento da teologia bíblica. O movimento ecumênico tem produzido muitas modificações; e em alguns sentidos, os vários grupos da comunhão anglicana têm podido unificar-se mais. (AM C E LL)

ANGST

Um vocábulo alemão talvez melhor traduzido para o português como *angústia*. Dentro do pensamento existencialista (ver o artigo sobre o existencialismo), a palavra *angústia* presumivelmente descreve a condição humana básica. Há um pavor sem nome e sem objeto particular, mas que é um sentimento comum à humanidade, por terem os homens de enfrentar um mundo destruidor, hostil e insensato. Os comentadores a respeito têm sido Kierkegaard, Heidegger, Unamuno, Bultmann e Sartre. Essa filosofia deixa os homens «dentro do temporal», onde têm de lutar contra a aniquilamento e a não-entidade e ignora o fato de que na psique humana também há a descoberta que o homem, como ser espiritual que é, ultrapassa a tempestade e entra na compreensão espiritual de que a existência humana é finalmente boa e otimista. Em outras palavras, para além da tempestade, há um Novo Dia, no qual a existência humana, no nível espiritual, floresce em harmonia, bem-estar e propósito. A psicologia tem demonstrado a existência de ambos esses motivos na psique humana: 1. A tempestade do desespero, por enfrentar a não-entidade; e 2. o estado para além da tempestade, em que é confirmada uma existência digna. Esse segundo motivo afirma a imortalidade, sem o que a condição humana seria realmente *angustiosa*. (C P)

ANHIPOSTASIS

Ciro, Patriarca de Alexandria, c. 412, lutando contra a doutrina do Apolinarianismo (que vide), declarou que existe uma união perfeita das duas naturezas em Cristo, a ponto da humanidade de Cristo, embora completa e inteira, não ter uma existência independente. É isso que a palavra grega *anhipostasis* indica. Ver o artigo sobre *Cristologia*.

ANHOMOEANOS

Esse termo era aplicado aos arianos extremados, como Aécio e Eunômio, os quais diziam que o Filho era totalmente diferente do Pai, em sua essência natural básica. Alguns levavam esse ponto de vista ao extremo de dizer que essa diferença impedia o Filho de conhecer o Pai, visto que lhes faltaria uma natureza comum (ousia); o único relacionamento entre Eles seria a participação na vontade divina. Teodoreto criticava esses pensadores, afirmando que eles ensinavam mais tecnologia do que teologia, aplicando categorias lógicas às realidades metafísicas. Ver os artigos sobre *homoeanos* e *homoeousianos*, quanto a maiores esclarecimentos sobre essas questões. (C)

ANIÃO

No hebraico, **lamento do povo**. Foi o quarto filho de Semida, o manassita (ver I Crô. 7:19).

ANIAS

Foi chefe de uma família que totalizava cento e uma pessoas, e que retornara da Babilônia, após o cativeiro, com Zorobabel (ver I Esdras 5:16). Seu nome é omitido nos paralelos de Esd. 2:3 ss. e Nee. 7:8 ss (S Z)

ANIM

No hebraico significa **fontes**. Era uma cidade localizada na região montanhosa de Judá (ver Jos. 15:50), aparentemente localizada perto de Estemo, mais para o noroeste. Tem sido tentativamente identificada com Khirbet Ghuwein et Tahta, a quase dezoito quilômetros ao sul de Hebrom. É mencionada nas cartas de Amarna com o nome de Hawini. (SZ)

ANIMA

1. A palavra latina para alma (ver o artigo a respeito).
2. Na psicologia de Jung, aquela parte do inconsciente coletivo dentro de um indivíduo, que representa o aspecto feminino da natureza de um homem.

ANIMAIS, ADORAÇÃO AOS

A grande variedade de animais, alguns de grande beleza, e outros de muita força, tem provocado admiração nos homens. Alguns homens dedicam suas vidas aos animais, como nos zoólogos. E sempre há uma ponta de admiração da parte daqueles que escolhem essa profissão. Alguns homens sentem uma espécie de parentesco com os animais. Outros supõem que eles podem ser veículos da alma de antigos amigos e parentes, ou mesmo antepassados, que dão prosseguimento em sua evolução espiritual em um corpo animal. Essa crença faz os homens respeitarem, e, em alguns casos, reverenciarem os animais. Os sacrifícios de animais, até onde podemos recuar no passado, sempre fez parte dos sistemas de adoração dos homens. Desse modo, os animais têm estado associados aos ritos e às crenças religiosas. Não foi preciso grande salto para que certos animais fossem considerados favoritos dos deuses, ou seus instrumentos especiais e portanto, dignos de respeito e adoração. Alguns animais foram identificados com a fertilidade da terra, e outros, como pássaros, etc., com presságios, maldições e bênçãos. Surgiram cultos baseados na crença de que as almas humanas retornam à vida nos animais. Certas qualidades dos animais, como a força e a sutileza, foram vistas como dons divinos aos animais dotados desses atributos, como se estivessem em ligação com certos deuses. Entre os povos primitivos, plantas e outros objetos naturais, tidos como ancestralmente relacionados a alguma tribo particular, tornavam-se os seus *totens*, ou espíritos protetores, os quais eram representados em postes esculpidos laboriosamente.

ANIMAIS, ALMA DOS Ver Alma dos Animais.

ANIMAIS, DIREITOS DE, E MORALIDADE

A existência dos animais e o que sucede a eles envolve uma questão moral e merece um espaço dentro do pensamento teológico, moral e prático.

Argumentos em prol do respeito aos animais, e seus direitos:

1. **Os animais têm alma** e, assim sendo, estão envolvidos na evolução espiritual. Essa é uma doutrina comum das religiões orientais, usualmente em conexão com a idéia da transmigração de almas, ou então com o conceito de que dentro de cada grupo animal, há uma alma que pode crescer espiritualmente, embora faça sua jornada sempre em algum corpo animal. A evolução espiritual, no tocante aos animais, permanece como um item da fé religiosa, pois há boas evidências quanto à existência de um elemento não-material nos animais, sobretudo na forma de aparecimento de animais e formas cruas de comunicação com antigos proprietários. No campo da filosofia, Platão e outros supunham que *toda vida é espiritual*, que a matéria serve apenas de veículo, jamais sendo a

própria vida. Os estudos feitos nas auras e campos de vida demonstram, quase acima de qualquer dúvida, que além da matéria jaz uma contraparte psíquica, que aparentemente é a sede da vida. Têm sido usados voltímetros para detectar a radiação de energia de seres vivos, a qual alguns pensam constituir uma realidade psíquica por detrás do veículo físico. É possível que a fotografia kirliana da aura detecte uma radiação derivada do campo da vida. Ver os artigos sobre a *aura* e o *campo de vida*.

Nenhum tipo de vida parece simples. De fato, todos os seres vivos parecem assumir a forma que têm por causa de um *molde espiritual* que governa o desenvolvimento das células, por meio do código genético. O *campo de vida* é imaterial, sendo a força e a inteligência por detrás do desenvolvimento das entidades físicas. Se isso é verdade (atualmente há teorias a respeito, baseadas em implicações empíricas e filosóficas), então os animais, até mesmo da escala dos insetos, têm sido grandemente subestimados. Os animais exigem nosso respeito e consideração. Alguns crêem que os animais são pessoas.

2. Inteligência dos animais. Estudos recentes demonstram que pelo menos alguns animais têm a capacidade de raciocinar e resolver problemas. A humilde abelha chega a antecipar o futuro. Se lhes oferecermos água açucarada, as abelhas virão tomá-la. Se removermos a água açucarada para alguma distância, as abelhas irão atrás. Se continuarmos a remover a água cada vez mais longe, elas *anteciparão* nossos movimentos, buscando a água à maior distância que no dia anterior. Tem-se descoberto que os primatas superiores têm certa capacidade lingüística, se forem treinados a usar um teclado de computador para se comunicarem. É quase certo que se tivessem o aparelho fonador necessário, eles teriam inteligência suficiente para manipular sintaxe e gramática. Alguns animais, dotados de cérebros volumosos, são capazes de resolver problemas complexos, que requerem raciocínio, e não o mero instinto. Quanto mais a ciência descobre, mais ficamos impressionados ante a inteligência dos animais.

3. Emoções dos animais. Aqueles que têm contato com os animais, sabem que eles têm emoções. Os primatas superiores lamentam a perda de seus companheiros, com grande consternação. Um caçador que feriu um gorila e viu a agonia do animal, bem como a consternação de seus companheiros, afirmou que se sentiu quase como se tivesse cometido um homicídio.

4. Interesses dos animais. Para um animal, o que acontece com ele é importante. É impossível atribuirmos tudo ao instinto. Para os animais, a vida é preciosa. Alguns têm indagado se nós mesmos gostaríamos de ser tratados como os animais são tratados, se, porventura, alguma forma superior de vida, mais poderosa do que nós, nos reduzisse ao estado a que temos reduzido os animais. Um animal tem interesse pela vida, e bastaria isso para nos fazer respeitar os animais.

5. A sociedade primitiva e os animais. Quanto mais avança uma sociedade humana, mais respeito adquire pelos animais. As sociedades mais primitivas sentem prazer na tortura de animais, e a malignidade humana se compraz até em torturar outros seres humanos. Sempre será errado infligir dor desnecessária, mesmo que a vítima seja um animal.

Muitas indagações são levantadas por essas observações:

1. Os animais devem ser usados como alimentos? Alguns respondem negativamente, com bases morais e religiosas. Outros frisam que a carne é a melhor fonte de proteínas, e que o sistema humano não se dá bem com uma estrita dieta vegetariana. Os teólogos frisam que a Bíblia permite a ingestão de carne e condena o ascetismo que a proíbe (I Tim. 4:3,4). Mas outros retrucam que não há conhecimento que não possa ser aprimorado, no campo científico ou espiritual. Por exemplo, sabemos que qualquer quantidade de álcool na corrente sangüínea destrói células do cérebro, pelo que, eticamente, ingerir qualquer quantidade de bebida alcoólica é moralmente errado, com base em I Cor. 6:19,20. Essa parcela de conhecimento científico não era possível nos dias do Novo Testamento; mas, se o fosse, é lógico supormos que até mesmo a ingestão moderada de álcool teria sido condenada pelos autores do Novo Testamento. Ora, um conhecimento mais profundo sobre os animais poderá modificar a maneira como os tratamos. Alguns dizem, *dever-se-ia* fazê-lo. O problema moral que enfrentamos consiste em determinar a extensão desse *dever-se-ia*.

2. Os animais deveriam ser castigados e tratados como prisioneiros? Isso aplica-se aos cães, pássaros e qualquer bichinho de estimação que é tratado como virtual prisioneiro, sem ter cometido qualquer crime. Um cão tem o direito de ser livre?

3. Animais usados em experiências científicas. Até que ponto os animais podem e devem ser sujeitados às experiências científicas, a fim de melhorar a condição humana? O trecho de Mateus 10:29 mostra que Deus se importa até mesmo com os passarinhos dos campos. O pacto noaico incluía uma provisão relativa aos animais (Gên. 9:10,11). A lei sabática incluía o descanso para os animais (Êxo. 20:10).

4. Os homens devem caçar animais por puro esporte? Um homem com o refrigerador repleto e dinheiro no banco, sai ao campo para caçar veados. Isso é moral? Se o número de veados for grande demais, e deve ser reduzido, então talvez a caça por esporte seja justificada — seria certo matar simplesmente para ver quão bem a pessoa atira? As criaturas vivas devem ser reduzidas a simples alvos?

A crueldade contra os animais é uma óbvia perversidade. Um homem de moral não ultraja propositalmente a criação de Deus. Os animais destruidores são os criminosos do mundo animal e devem ser eliminados. Não é errado matar animais que propagam doenças e que são destruidores. Após dizermos isso, entretanto, ainda não ficou resolvido o problema moral levantado acima. Não há diretrizes simples de serem seguidas, mas o que foi escrito aqui sugere como devemos abordar esse problema. (H N)

ANIMAIS, NO ANTIGO E NO NOVO TESTAMENTOS

Termos usados. Animais, aves, alma vivente, criatura (ver Lev. 11:46). Eles são divididos em quatro classes: 1. Besta-fera, que são os grandes animais terrestres (ver Lev. 5:2); 2. Aquáticos (ver Lev. 11:9-10); 3. Aves (ver Lev. 11:13); 4. Insetos, roedores e répteis (ver Lev. 11:20,29,41). *Animais limpos e imundos*. Eram classificações cerimoniais, religiosas. Os limpos eram aqueles cuja carne podia ser comida; e os imundos, o contrário (ver Lev. 11 e Deu. 14:1-20). No Novo Testamento, foram removidas as proibições atinentes a animais limpos e imundos (ver I Tim. 4:4).

Uso metafórico. A suspensão da proibição acerca de animais imundos tornou-se um veículo de uma importante verdade. Pedro, em sua visão relatada em

ANIMAL CEVADO — ANIMISMO

Atos 10:9, recebeu ordem para comer animais imundos. Ele protestou, porquanto sempre observara os preceitos levíticos quanto à questão. Mas então foi informado de que Deus havia *purificado* aqueles animais, não havendo mais animais *imundos*. Porém, a questão toda precisava ser entendida metafórica ou espiritualmente. Os *gentios*, antes considerados imundos por Israel, agora com essa propriedade podiam ser evangelizados, tornando-se membros com todos os direitos da Igreja em formação. Posteriormente seria revelado que a Igreja seria composta principalmente por gentios, e que a Igreja seria o Novo Israel, um conceito inteiramente novo. A missão da Igreja entre os gentios começara antes mesmo de Pedro ter recebido aquela visão; mas logo começaria a pleno vapor, e Pedro participaria ativamente da missão, embora, no começo, seu ministério envolvesse principalmente os judeus. Há algo de significativo no fato de que Pedro (segundo diz a tradição bem confirmada) morreu em Roma, terminando assim os seus dias em meio à missão entre os gentios. Ver as notas expositivas no NTI em Atos 9:15, quanto a detalhes sobre tudo isso.

Sacrifícios de animais. Os animais que podiam ser sacrificados na adoração divina eram o boi, a vaca, a novilha, o touro (ver Lev. 22:24), o bode, a cabra, o cabrito, o carneiro, a ovelha, o cordeiro. Ver notas completas e detalhadas no artigo sobre os *sacrifícios*.

Proibições que persistiram. No princípio do cristianismo, foram suspensas as proibições concernentes aos animais (ver Rom. 14; Col. 2:16; Tito 1:15 e I Tim. 4:4). Na prática, entretanto, o concílio apostólico de Jerusalém achou de bom alvitre proibir os gentios de comerem carne de animais sufocados (ainda com seu sangue, portanto) e de usar o sangue dos animais como alimento. O concílio também recomendou a abstinência da idolatria e da imoralidade. (Ver Atos. 15:20). Essa foi uma medida tomada para manter a concórdia no seio da Igreja. Se os convertidos fizessem essas coisas (acerca dos animais proibidos), os cristãos judeus da Igreja ficariam revoltados. Assim, se não era classificada como errada em si mesma a ingestão de sangue e de carne de animais sufocados, seria errado ofender aos irmãos que se revoltassem contra tais práticas, por causa de uma observância da vida inteira, com base naquelas provisões veterotestamentárias. Quanto aos direitos dos animais e as questões morais nisso envolvidas, ver no artigo abaixo. (DE NTI MC S UN Z)

ANIMAL CEVADO

Trata-se de um animal ainda jovem, como o bezerro, o cordeiro ou o cabrito, engordado para o abate. Várias palavras hebraicas são usadas para indicar essa idéia. No Novo Testamento, em Mateus 22:4, temos a palavra grega *sitistós*, «novilha cevada». Quanto ao Antigo Testamento, ver Sal. 66:15; Isa. 5:17; II Sam. 6:13; I Reis 1:9,19 e I Sam. 15:9. Nessa última referência, embora nossa versão portuguesa diga «os animais gordos», o original diz «de segunda categoria», provavelmente por aludir à qualidade inferior, e não por serem animais cevados. Cevavam-se animais destinados ao consumo durante festas especiais. Como é evidente, os animais cevados tinham fortes implicações econômicas, porque os animais assim engordados eram valiosos na venda.

Uso metafórico. Depois do sangue, fonte da vida física, a gordura era tida como sinal de saúde e vigor. É por isso que encontramos expressões bíblicas como «gordura da terra», «gordura do trigo», «gordura do azeite» e «gordura do vinho». Ver o artigo sobre gordura. Daí, o termo adquiriu conotações de riqueza e abundância espiritual. A expressão «fartura da terra», em Gên. 45:18 e outros trechos, no hebraico diz «gordura da terra». Alude aos espécimes mais seletos de qualquer produção. Em Luc. 15:12 ss temos a parábola do filho perdido (filho pródigo), e ali o «novilho cevado» simboliza a alegria e as festas vinculadas à sua restauração espiritual. (ID NTI UN Z)

ANIMISMO

Esse termo vem do **anima** (alma, fôlego), tendo sido usado pela primeira vez por Stahl (1720), para expressar um conceito filosófico da alma do mundo. Mas foi introduzido na antropologia e na religião comparada por Taylor (*Primitive Culture*, 1871).

Tipos:

1. Os objetos físicos possuiriam vida ou espírito próprios, não havendo tal coisa como matéria inanimada. O Universo é uma presença viva.

2. Os objetos físicos, embora não animados por si mesmos, seriam habitados por espíritos que sobreviveriam mesmo quando os objetos físicos fossem destruídos.

3. Os espíritos manifestam-se esporadicamente por meio das pessoas, dos objetos físicos ou de lugares específicos. Pode tratar-se de puros espíritos, incluindo espíritos não-humanos, espíritos de antepassados e de pessoas já falecidas. Os bruxos, feiticeiros e médiuns, segundo alguns, podem entrar em contato com tais espíritos.

A terceira forma de *animismo* é virtualmente universal, e muitas pessoas supõem ser essa a base de toda crença religiosa. Alguns supõem que essa teoria surgiu do fenômeno dos sonhos, o que pode ser apenas uma explicação parcial. Mais provavelmente, lugares assombrados e fantasmas seriam a origem dessa teoria. Ver o artigo sobre os *fantasmas*.

Alguns eruditos vêem remanescentes do animismo no Antigo Testamento, como em Gên. 19:26 e 28:22, por exemplo. Certos aspectos da cristandade exibem vestígios dessa filosofia na veneração de lugares sagrados e dos espíritos ou santos que residem nesses lugares, ou, pelo menos, que se manifestam ocasionalmente nos mesmos.

A teoria filosófica chamada *pampsiquismo* (ver o artigo) na verdade é uma modalidade de psiquismo, seguindo a primeira das idéias acima expostas. Os filósofos que têm defendido uma forma ou outra dessa teoria são Empédocles, Plotino, Leibniz, Schopenhauer, Pierce, Schiller, Whitehead, Alexandre de Chardin e Waddington. As religiões orientais, ao tentarem oferecer explicações idealistas da realidade, incorporam uma forma de pampsiquismo que, naturalmente, é algo inteiramente diferente da idéia de que há espíritos ocultos em objetos físicos, embora a palavra possa ser usada para indicar ambas essas idéias, de maneira bem geral.

A idéia (embora crua) contida no animismo pagão é que existe um espírito, com o qual podemos entrar em contato, estabelecendo diferença em nossas vidas. O encontro com qualquer poder espiritual chama-se *dinamismo*. As pessoas que crêem na possibilidade do dinamismo, podem compreender a mensagem dAquele que disse: «Toda a autoridade me foi dada no céu e na terra...» (Mat. 28:18).

O discernimento com que contribui o *pampsiquismo* (sem importar seus muitos defeitos) é que, afinal, a verdadeira explicação da existência é o espírito, e não a matéria. Muitos físicos teóricos estão convencidos de que o átomo não é básico, nem mesmo para a matéria. Do átomo temos de passar para a *idéia*, supondo que o próprio átomo é uma concentração de energia psíquica. Da idéia passamos para a *Idéia*, ou princípio divino, pois a origem de toda inteligência é Deus. Não é possível que a própria matéria seja apenas um acidente do espírito? e que não tenha existência separada? (Ver o artigo sobre o *idealismo*). Se isso representa a verdade da realidade melhor do que o estrito conceito dualista da matéria-mente, então promove uma forma de animismo que nada tem a ver com a variedade pagã, e que do pampsiquismo apenas tomou por empréstimo alguns discernimentos.

O cristianismo tem mantido um *dualismo* estrito (ver o artigo a respeito): a matéria existe — o espírito existe. As duas coisas diferem quanto à espécie, e não apenas quanto à manifestação. A matéria é menos real por ser transitória, dependendo do espírito para continuar existindo, embora pertença a uma outra categoria. Porém, nada existe no dogma cristão que não possa ser adaptado a um ponto de vista *idealista* da realidade, se as evidências em favor do mesmo se tornarem suficientemente confirmadas.

No que convergem o cristianismo e o animismo. 1. Ambos distinguem entre o espírito e a matéria; 2. ambos reconhecem a existência de forças sobrenaturais que influenciam as nossas vidas; 3. ambos têm meios de entrar em contato com essas forças; 4. a oração, os holocaustos, a adoração e a conduta ética são influenciados pela crença no sobrenatural; 5. ambos aceitam o princípio do dinamismo, ou seja, do encontro de espíritos.

Pontos de divergência. 1. O cristianismo repudia a multiplicidade de divindades e de espíritos autoritários, postulados pelo animismo pagão; 2. o cristianismo repudia os métodos usados pelo animismo para produzir o dinamismo, como a bruxaria, as artes mágicas e os sacrifícios de animais; 3. os sistemas éticos do cristianismo e do animismo diferem grandemente entre si. A ética cristã baseia-se na lei do amor (ver o artigo sobre o *amor*) em Deus e no conceito de amigo e inimigo. A ética animista é essencialmente um sistema de terror, onde se evita desagradar os espíritos, a fim de que não atraiam o infortúnio sobre os homens. O cristianismo também destaca a santidade de Deus como o padrão de toda a ação moral. O animismo nada tem a ver com isso. As missões cristãs às terras onde se crê no animismo também envolvem uma questão ética, uma questão de dever e de amor (Mat. 18:19,20). (AM B E F H)

ANÍQUERES

Filósofo grego do século II A.C., da escola cirenaica (ver o artigo sobre o *cirenaicismo*). Tal escola advogava uma ética hedonista, encontrando no prazer o único alvo legítimo da vida humana. Todavia, eles propunham como ideal vários tipos de prazer, como corporal, mental, evitar a dor, usufruir a alegria, em vez de um prazer momentário qualquer. Aníqueres enfatizava os prazeres das relações sociais como os mais desejáveis, importantes e satisfatórios, e não os atos individuais de prazer. Deveríamos estar dispostos a sofrer dor, a fim de obter os prazeres da amizade, do respeito aos pais, da gratidão ao próximo e do patriotismo. Ver o artigo sobre o *hedonismo*. (MM P)

ANIQUILACIONISMO

É um ponto de vista pessimista do destino final da humanidade, em parte ou em sua inteireza. Tal nome vem do latim *nihil*, «nada». De acordo com essa teoria, o homem, em sua totalidade ou em parte, é reduzido finalmente a *nada*.

Formas:

1. *Materialismo*. O homem, para começar, é apenas uma criatura física, e a morte biológica é suficiente para pôr fim à sua existência.

2. *Exclusivismo-espiritualista*. O homem é mortal, embora possa receber a imortalidade sob certas condições. Deus outorga a alguns uma forma dependente de imortalidade, deixando de lado as outras. Isso significa que muitos deixam de existir, visto que não receberam a imortalidade. Tal coisa pode suceder quando da morte física, ou poderá ocorrer, finalmente, após a segunda ressurreição. Homens ímpios ressuscitarão por breve período, para propósitos de julgamento, mas então serão totalmente destruídos. Essa é uma doutrina fantástica ao ponto de absurdo. Se o homem tiver de ser extinto, que isso ocorra por ocasião da morte biológica. Por que trazê-lo de volta à vida por breve tempo, a fim de aterrorizá-lo, para que lamente por seus pecados, apenas para ser esmigalhado ato contínuo?

Esse ponto de vista dá apoio à idéia da *imortalidade condicional*. Somente Deus seria imortal, e os homens receberiam a imortalidade sob condição. Assim, o *condicionalismo* é comumente usado como sinônimo prático de aniquilamento. Ver o artigo sobre a *imortalidade condicional*.

3. *Cíclico-filosófico*. Os estóicos supunham que o homem teria uma imortalidade temporária. O Logos, o Fogo central, se emanaria. Todas as coisas fariam parte desse centro (panteísmo, visto que o Logos de fogo é Deus). As emanações do Logos podem durar por longo tempo, fazendo a criação passar por muitos e prolongados ciclos de existência. Porém, uma vez que o Logos deseje «recolher-se em si mesmo», todos os ciclos, o tempo e as coisas deixam de existir e o Logos torna-se tudo em tudo. Isso significa que a alma humana deixaria de existir, pelo que teríamos uma forma de *aniquilacionismo*. O Logos pode então desejar expedir outra emanação, reiniciando todo o processo; mas isso seria uma nova existência, não trazendo de volta à existência as almas antigas.

4. *A alma temporária*. Alguns filósofos têm imaginado que a alma existe e sobrevive à morte física, mas que ela não seria imortal por si mesma. Teria um período de existência mais longo que o do corpo (o quanto, varia de intérprete para intérprete). Mas, uma vez terminado o seu ciclo, a alma também morreria. Conseqüentemente, temos nisso uma variedade do conceito de aniquilamento.

5. *Absorção*. Algumas religiões orientais supõem que a alma existe e continua existindo após a morte biológica, mas que o destino remoto da alma humana é ser absorvida pela essência divina. Nesse caso, as almas humanas individuais deixarão de existir. É debatível se isso significa ou não que a alma humana é transformada para participar de uma forma de vida fantasticamente superior (a divina), ou se simplesmente desaparece e não mais tem autoconsciência. No primeiro caso, cessaria o indivíduo conforme o conhecemos, mas a vida humana da alma não, sendo transmutada em uma forma mais elevada de vida, uma existência espiritual comunitária.

6. *Budista anatta*. A escola Theravada do budismo ensina que a alma *não existe* (Anatta), e que aquilo que continua e se reencarna são as disposições mentais, e não alguma espécie de substância que se chama alma. Essas disposições mentais (desejos, atitudes, modos de agir), tendo sido criadas em um indivíduo, após a morte biológica deste podem passar

a fazer parte de outro indivíduo. Assim, o karma prossegue, mas a substância da alma, não. Ora, se a alma não existe, então a morte física decreta o aniquilamento, porquanto dificilmente poderíamos considerar as disposições mentais como a continuação do ser. Ver os artigos sobre o *budismo* e a *terminologia budista*. E ver também sobre a *reencarnação*.

Argumentos em prol do aniquilacionismo:

1. Só Deus é imortal (I Tim. 1:17; 6:16). Esse argumento também pode usualmente ser aplicado em favor da imortalidade derivada. Deus dá o dom da vida a todos, e assim lhes transmite a Sua imortalidade (João 5:25,26). O Pai dá Sua vida independente ao Filho (em Sua encarnação, como cabeça da raça humana). O Filho, por sua vez, compartilha dessa vida com os demais filhos de Deus. O trecho de Efé. 1:10 quase certamente subentende a transmissão dessa vida, embora não necessariamente em uma única forma. Em outras palavras, haverá muitos níveis de existência, mas todos participantes da mesma Fonte originadora.

2. A imortalidade é um dom especial, e não possessão de todos. Alguns vêem isso implícito em trechos bíblicos como Rom. 2:7; I Cor. 15:53,54; II Tim. 1:10. Mas aqui está em pauta o dom da vida na salvação, e não a imortalidade geral. Está em foco um *tipo* de imortalidade, a saber, a forma de vida obtida em união com Cristo, isto é, a natureza divina (II Ped. 1:4). Nem todos os homens participarão dessa espécie de vida. Os trechos de João 12:32 e Efé. 1:10,22,23 certamente subentendem formas de vida que incluem todos os seres, humanos ou não, como porções constitutivas da unidade que finalmente se estabelecerá. Esse é o mistério da vontade de Deus. Ver notas completas sobre esses conceitos no NTI, em Efé. 1:10. Romanos 5:18 por certo subentende que a missão de Cristo beneficiará a todos, sem que possamos distinguir gradações finais de glória entre eles. Até mesmo os ímpios continuarão existindo, embora sob castigo. O fato de que serão galardoados segundo as suas obras (Apo. 20:12 e Rom. 2:6 ss.) indica que eles continuarão a existir, ou como poderia haver uma diferença estabelecida em consideração às suas obras? Se todos fossem simplesmente aniquilados, de fato, todos seriam finalmente igualados. Isso labora contra o conceito do juízo por gradações.

3. Afirma-se que certos trechos bíblicos parecem falar em cessação da existência. (Rom. 6:23; Tia. 5:20; Apo. 20:14, ao usar o termo «morte»; Mat. 7:13; 10:28; II Tes. 1:9, ao usar o termo «destruição»). Porém, tais termos podem indicar uma mudança radical no modo de existência, de tal modo que a antiga forma seja virtualmente aniquilada, e não o fim absoluto da existência. Falamos de coisas arruinadas, destruídas quando suas formas são radicalmente alteradas, como um edifício, por causa de uma explosão; mas, não queremos dizer com isso que o material do edifício deixou de existir.

4. *Demonstração do amor de Deus*. Como é óbvio, seria maior demonstração de amor da parte de Deus se Ele simplesmente aniquilasse os perdidos, em vez de permitir-lhes (ou forçá-los) a continuarem para sempre em um tormento consciente. Ademais, tal condição significaria a continuidade do mal e do caos, o que, segundo pensamos, não pode caracterizar a eternidade. Em outras palavras, coisas odiosas continuariam a existir, fora de harmonia com aquilo que esperaríamos que Deus estabelecesse no estado eterno. Não podemos perceber o peso desses argumentos. Muitos intérpretes pensam que prestam a Deus um serviço mostrando versículos que afirmam essas tragédias, por estarem mantendo *ortodoxia* em torno de uma doutrina falsa. Na verdade, o aniquilamento é uma doutrina falsa, embora haja uma melhor maneira de respondermos a essas objeções. Podemos frisar que Cristo cumpriu uma missão em prol dos perdidos, no hades (I Ped. 3:18 - 4:6; ver o artigo sobre a *descida de Cristo ao hades*) e que isso tem efeitos contínuos sobre o destino humano (Efé. 4:10). Eventualmente, Cristo «encherá todas as coisas», tornando-se tudo para todos. Ele pregou o seu evangelho aos mortos desobedientes (I Ped. 4:6), como parte desse programa remidor. O *mistério da vontade de Deus* (ver o artigo) significa que haverá uma restauração final de tudo em torno de Cristo, com a unidade e a harmonia de todas as coisas. O juízo será instrumental nessa finalidade, porque há coisas que Deus só pode fazer mediante o julgamento. Isso não significa, todavia, que todos os homens serão *remidos* no sentido evangélico, mas significa que todos os homens serão *restaurados* de modo a participarem da unidade final em torno de Cristo (o Logos), como Cabeça de todas as coisas. Assim, Ele tornar-se-á tudo para todos, conferindo propósito, utilidade e glória para todas as formas de vida e de coisas. Esse é o discernimento dos trechos bíblicos que olham para além daqueles outros que falam sobre um sofrimento interminável. Esse é o *mistério* da vontade de Deus. E, quando usamos a palavra «mistério», queremos dizer que aquela idéia particular ainda não havia sido revelada até aquele momento. Esse ponto de vista do julgamento olha para além dos pontos de vista anteriores, mostrando que a própria existência é otimista, e não pessimista, como o outro ponto de vista certamente ensina. Deve-se adicionar aqui que as igrejas anglicanas e ortodoxas (igrejas orientais), por meio de muitos representantes, sempre falaram sobre o destino humano nesses termos, seguindo o ângulo de visão mais otimista dos pais gregos, em contraste com os pais latinos da Igreja. Portanto, esse ensino sempre fez parte da herança cristã. (B E NTI)

ANIUTE

Levita que ajudou Esdras a ensinar a lei ao povo (ver I Esdras 9:48). Também era chamado Anus. Em Nee. 8:7, seu nome aparece como *Bani*. (Z)

ANIVERSÁRIO NATALÍCIO

No grego, **genesia**, dia do nascimento, ou sua celebração. No hebraico é *yom huledeth* (ver Gên. 40:20). A celebração do aniversário natalício tanto é muito antiga quanto universal. A maioria das pessoas sente que o dom da vida é uma responsabilidade e um privilégio que merece ser celebrado. Na Pérsia aos aniversariantes eram dadas honras especiais, e festas eram efetuadas. Sabemos que o rei do Egito celebrava seu aniversário com grande pompa (ver Gên. 40:20). Os romanos mantinham registros exatos dos cidadãos, com suas datas de aniversário natalício e suas idades, tudo o que fazia parte das informações constantes no recenseamento. Não há qualquer alusão direta no Antigo Testamento à celebração de aniversários, mas o trecho de Jer. 20:14,15 pode ser um reflexo de tal celebração. É possível que as festas mencionadas em Jó 1:13,18 fossem festas de aniversário. Contudo, há evidências que mostram que os judeus consideravam idólatras as celebrações de aniversário. No Novo Testamento, temos o famoso incidente da comemoração do aniversário natalício de Herodes, em Mateus 14:6, provavelmente ligado a um

ANJO

costume romano. Mas, mesmo que não fossem celebrados, os aniversários natalícios eram considerados importantes. O cego foi classificado como «idade tem» (João 9:21). Foi registrado que Jesus tinha doze anos de idade quando visitou o templo (ver Luc. 2:42). Quando um judeu levita atingia os trinta anos de idade, estava qualificado para servir no sacerdócio.

Na Igreja primitiva, o termo «aniversário» era usado para comemorar os mártires, os dias em que, segundo se considerava, eles tinham *nascido* para a glória e a vida eterna. Nessa conexão, vale a pena mencionar que a experiência da própria morte se assemelha ao nascimento, quanto a vários aspectos. A pessoa sente que passa por um túnel, emergindo na luz, e vê-se cercada por seres espirituais que então cortam o fio de luz («o fio de prata» de Ecl. 12:6). Ver o artigo sobre as experiências de quase-morte. Além disso, há o «novo nascimento». (Ver Novo Nascimento e Regeneração). (E ID UN Z)

ANJO Ver o artigo separado sobre **Anjo da Guarda**.

Esboço
I. A Palavra e Seus Usos
II. Angelologia e Origens
III. Natureza dos Anjos
IV. Anjos Caídos
V. Adoração aos Anjos
VI. Homens e Anjos
VII. Os Anjos e a Espiritualidade
VIII. O Erro da Demitização
IX. Inexatidão do Termo Anjo
X. Ofícios e Poderes Especiais
XI. Tarefas dos Anjos

I. A palavra e seus usos. Gr. **aggelos** e heb. **malakh**, significam *mensageiro*. Diversos usos: o profeta (Hab. 1:13), um sacerdote (ver Mal. 2:7), ou os seres celestiais (ver Sal. 29:1 e 89:6) podem ter esse título. Um uso mais amplo ainda inclui também a coluna de nuvem (ver Êxo. 14:19), a pestilência (ver II Sam. 24:16,17), os ventos (ver Sal. 104:4), e as pragas (ver Sal. 78:49). Paulo chamou seu espinho na carne de *anjo*, isto é, «mensageiro de Satanás» (II Crô. 12:7 e Gál. 4:13,14). *Pastores* da igreja, Apo. 2:1,8,12, *et al.*

II. Angelologia e origens. Os anjos são referidos na Bíblia de Gên. ao Apocalipse, desde «os carvalhais de Manre» (Gên. 13:18) até à «ilha chamada Patmos» (Apo. 1:9). As mais antigas evidências arqueológicas em favor da crença na existência dos anjos vêm de Ur-Namus, de cerca de 2250 A.C., onde anjos são vistos a adejar por sobre a cabeça do rei, enquanto este orava. Visto que Abraão chegou àquela região pouco depois disso, é possível que ele estivesse familiarizado com a angelologia desde a juventude. Como é óbvio, a angelologia estava misturada a todas as formas mitológicas possíveis, religiões e superstições primitivas, sendo crença generalizada entre todas as religiões da antiguidade. Que nem todos os conceitos acerca dos anjos correspondem à realidade é algo óbvio, mas isso não significa que tais seres (dotados de impressionantes atributos) não existam. Durante o cativeiro babilônico, a angelologia recebeu maior atenção da parte dos judeus. O zoroastrismo (cerca de 1000 A.C.) sem dúvida muito contribuiu para a angelologia dos hebreus, mas a sua crença na existência desses seres antecede por muitos séculos ao zoroastrismo. Parece que quase todos os povos têm acreditado em seres espirituais que poderíamos chamar de «anjos», embora seus idiomas não tenham algum vocábulo que possamos traduzir em português

dessa maneira («mensageiro», ou algo similar). O Novo Testamento se inicia com anjos ocupados em serviço ativo e jamais põe em dúvida a sua existência.

O Anjo do Senhor. Em trechos bíblicos como Êxodo 23:21 (onde o Anjo do Senhor parece dotado de autoridade para perdoar a transgressão; e o nome de Deus estava sobre Ele) e Juízes 2:1, encontramos uma manifestação especial de Deus — talvez uma manifestação do Logos pré-encarnado, conforme crêem alguns intérpretes. Nesse caso, esses trechos são paralelos de Apo. 1:1. Acerca disso, entretanto, não podemos ter certeza. (Ver Também Gên. 16:7 ss; 21:17; 22:11,15 ss ; 24:7,40; 31:11-13; 32:24-30; Êxo. 3:6; 13:21,22; 14:19; Núm. 22:22; Jos. 5:14; 6:2; Juí. 2:1-5; I Crô. 21:15,18,27 e Eze. 1:10-13).

Origem da doutrina. É óbvio que tanto no Antigo como no Novo Testamentos há uma angelologia bastante elaborada. Mas muitos eruditos insistem que as culturas não-hebréias tinham crenças acerca de poderosos seres espirituais (anjos), antes dos tempos veterotestamentários. Talvez se possa achar a origem dessa doutrina na experiência humana, à parte dos Livros Sagrados. Há evidências que nos autorizam a crer na interferência, serviço e interesse, de natureza positiva ou negativa, de seres espirituais. Usualmente são invisíveis, podendo ser detectados por pessoas sensíveis, tanto quanto à sua presença como quanto à sua atuação. Porém, as angelologias formais parecem ter-se desenvolvido inicialmente na religião persa. A fé dos hebreus fez pelo menos alguns empréstimos daquela origem, e o cristianismo preservou as idéias essenciais da angelologia dos hebreus. O judaísmo desenvolveu um sistema elaborado, imaginando que há quatro (ou sete) anjos principais, ou «arcanjos», cada um dos quais tem miríades de assessores, com vários graus de inteligência e poder. Os anjos teriam funções que variam desde o serviço imediato diante do trono de Deus, até os mais variegados serviços na esfera terrestre, envolvendo nações, comunidades ou indivíduos. Os anjos são os mediadores da mensagem divina, segundo o trecho de Deu. 33:2 ss, que era entendido pelos intérpretes rabínicos. Essa idéia foi adotada pelo autor da epístola aos Hebreus, conforme nos mostra Heb. 2:2. Josefo, Ant. 15, cap. 15:3 confirmando o ponto de vista. E Gál. 3:19 mostra que a lei foi «mediada» pelos anjos. Todavia, em Cristo, temos uma mensagem do Filho (Heb. 2:3), que é superior à mediação angelical.

Os anjos também estarão envolvidos no julgamento (Mar. 8:38; 13:27), e se fazem presentes tanto no nascimento de Cristo (Luc. 2:13 ss.) como por ocasião de Sua futura *parousia* (ver o artigo a respeito). Também estiveram presentes quando da ascensão de Cristo (Mat. 24:31). Podemos entender que eles acompanhavam Jesus Cristo bem de perto, e que fazem o mesmo, posto que secundariamente, com os homens que compartilham da missão salvatícia do Redentor.

III. Natureza dos anjos. Somos informados de que eles são seres espirituais criados (Heb. 1:14). Orígenes supunha que não há diferença entre o espírito humano e os anjos, excetuando no grau de queda. Os demônios seriam espíritos caídos em grande escala, e os homens, em menor grau. Os santos anjos não participaram da revolta, e assim retiveram seu estado original, embora não fossem retratados como todos iguais. Paulo os concebia arranjados em muitas ordens, com diferentes poderes, como se vê em Efé. 1:21. Ver notas completas sobre a questão, no NTI.

Anjos guardiães. Os trechos de Mat. 26:53; Heb. 12:22; Apo. 5:11; Sal. 68:17 indicam que eles são

ANJO

muito numerosos. Outras passagens indicam que eles observam os homens, prestando serviços em prol de nações, comunidades e indivíduos. Ver Heb. 1:14; Mat. 18:10; Sal. 9:1; Dan. 10:13; 12:1; Jos. 5:14. Os trechos bíblicos que dão apoio à doutrina dos *anjos guardiães* são Jó 33:23; Dan. 10:13 (acerca de nações); Mat. 18:10 (onde ver notas completas, no NTI), Heb. 1:14 e Apo. 1:20. Uma antiga doutrina judaica ensina que o anjo guardião tem a semelhança ou aparência daquele a quem guarda, o que talvez seja refletido em Atos 12:15. Essa idéia pode estar ligada à noção oriental do eu-superior ou super-eu do indivíduo. Presumivelmente, a alma não é o elemento superior do indivíduo, mas sim é um instrumento do eu-superior, que é a verdadeira entidade. Esse super-eu é o homem em sua forma mais elevada, um poderosíssimo ser espiritual. Nesse caso, o anjo guardião seria o próprio homem, e a alma seria seu instrumento, tal como o corpo é o instrumento da alma. Há muitos mistérios, e talvez o que aqui dizemos perscrute um tanto esses mistérios, sem desvendá-los. Se esse conceito é veraz, então o indivíduo é seu próprio anjo guardião, ou pelo menos, poderia ser, embora esse anjo exista em uma outra dimensão de seu próprio ser. Isso não negaria a existência de outros espíritos elevados, que poderiam interessar-se em nossas vidas e aos quais poderíamos chamar de «anjos». O trecho de Mat. 18:10 mostra que esse anjo guardião tem acesso a Deus, um pensamento solene, porque faz Deus chegar bem perto de nós. Tal noção ensina o *teísmo* (ver o artigo), e não o *deísmo* (ver o artigo). O teísmo ensina que Deus não somente criou, mas também interessa-se por Sua criação, continuando a intervir, recompensar, punir e guiar a mesma. O deísmo ensina que a força criadora (pessoal ou impessoal) abandonou o universo, deixando que as leis naturais o governassem. Portanto, Deus é transcendental, sem qualquer contato imediato com os homens e suas vidas.

IV. Anjos caídos. Em tempos remotos, houve rebelião entre os seres espirituais, nos lugares elevados. Ver Jó. 4:18; Mat. 25:41; II Ped. 2:4; Apo. 12:9. O mais elevado dos anjos (Satanás, ver artigo a respeito) encabeçou essa rebelião. Sem dúvida, alguns *demônios* (ver o artigo) são anjos caídos, mas muitos deles são débeis demais para serem tanto. Por certo há muitas ordens de seres angelicais, algumas boas e outras más, outras boas e más (como no caso dos homens), algumas dotadas de grande poder, e outras de poder inferior aos homens, algumas elementares, talvez similares aos animais irracionais, e outras com inteligências ainda inferiores aos irracionais. Os espíritos demoníacos poderiam assaltar vindos de vários níveis, o que explicaria a grande diferença entre um poder demoníaco (e sua possessão) e outro. A redenção evidentemente inclui anjos, de tal modo que o caso dos anjos caídos não é irreversível. (Ver Efé. 1:10,23; Col. 1:16). O triunfo de Cristo inclui a derrota dos anjos caídos. (Ver Col. 2:15).

V. Adoração aos anjos. O respeito aos anjos era profundo no judaísmo, ao ponto de ver um anjo ser considerado como experiência tão grande quanto ver o próprio Deus. (Ver Gên. 16:13; 31:13; Exo. 3:4; Juí. 6:14; 13:22). Talvez certos desses casos fossem *teofanias* (ver o artigo), ou seja, Deus manifestando-se de alguma forma visível. A teologia judaica posterior encarava os anjos como mediadores entre Deus e os homens (Eze. 40:3; Zac. 3), e a posição tão elevada naturalmente fez com que alguns os adorassem. A adoração aos anjos penetrou na cristandade (ver Col. 2:18; ver notas completas a respeito, no NTI). As seitas gnósticas incorporaram essa prática (ver o artigo sobre o *gnosticismo*). Todavia, a prática não era aceitável para os verdadeiros cristãos (Apo. 19:10). Todavia, no século II D.C., Justino Mártir informa-nos que os cristãos veneravam a hoste dos anjos bons. Após o século IV D.C., o culto aos anjos tornou-se generalizado, sendo honrado especialmente o arcanjo Miguel. Os anjos figuram com destaque na arte e no culto dos cristãos medievais. Os líderes protestantes desencorajaram a prática, e os liberais relegaram os anjos ao domínio da fantasia religiosa e poética.

VI. Homens e anjos. Os textos de Efé. 1:10 e Col. 1:16 mostram que a redenção não excluiu os anjos, embora não saibamos comparar o grau de redenção deles com a redenção humana. Sabemos que a redenção humana, em seu estágio final, envolve a participação na natureza divina (II Ped. 1:4; ver notas completas no NTI), levando-os acima do estado atual dos anjos. O trecho de Heb. 1:14 certamente mostra a subordinação dos anjos aos homens que são herdeiros da salvação.

VII. Os anjos e a espiritualidade. É lógico supor que alguns entre os melhores homens têm o poder que demonstram por contarem com a proximidade de seus anjos guardiães. Desse modo, os homens entram em contato com o ser divino, outros seres espirituais servindo de mediadores entre Ele e nós. Também é provável que a iluminação ou revelação espiritual seja mediada pelos anjos. Não há como duvidar que eles não guardam apenas os homens. Deve haver uma intercomunicação de espíritos e de mensagens espirituais. É provável que *uma parte* da espiritualidade consista no desenvolvimento humano, que o capacita a entrar em comunicação mais livre com o poder espiritual a ele determinado. O poder que alguns manifestam de curar, expulsar demônios, ensinar de modo convincente, pode dever-se ao poder angelical que os acompanha.

VIII. O erro da demitização. — Muitos liberais e céticos, que não têm acompanhado de perto as manifestações espirituais que se conhecem em nossos dias, supõem que os milagres, os espíritos angelicais e outros, os mundos espirituais, etc., são invenções de imaginações muito religiosas. Porém, aqueles que estudam as manifestações espirituais de nossa época sabem da existência de uma poderosa realidade imaterial, que inclui seres imateriais. Os milagres de Satya Sai Baba, o santo homem hindu, provam isso. Ele tem sido observado de perto ao criar e transformar a matéria, a curar qualquer tipo de enfermidade, a ressuscitar os mortos; e as pesquisas dos céticos têm-nos convencido de que Sai Baba não é uma fraude. Fenômenos similares ocorrem em outras religiões, incluindo o aspecto evangélico do cristianismo. Apesar de que o milagre, o sinal, o poder nunca são provas de doutrina correta, servem para demonstrar a realidade do mundo espiritual e a importância da espiritualidade. Podemos afirmar com confiança que Jesus fez o que os evangelhos dizem que Ele fez; muitos de Seus milagres são reproduzidos hoje em dia, exatamente como Ele disse que sucederia. O mundo físico é apenas o véu que encobre as realidades espirituais, havendo imensas fronteiras espirituais que ainda precisam ser conquistadas.

IX. Inexatidão do termo anjo. É provável que os mundos espirituais sejam povoados por muitos tipos e gradações de seres. Não há razão para supormos que

Anjo da guarda, M. Weber
Cortesia, Historical Pictures Service, Chicago

Os espíritos ministradores

ANJO

só existe variedade no nosso mundo físico. É difícil supormos que as dimensões espirituais tenham menos seres que a dimensão física. Portanto, visto que falamos em seres dotados de alta inteligência, que têm interesses e missões espirituais, alguns dos quais entram em vários tipos de contato com os homens, então podemos usar o termo «anjo» como uma espécie de chavão. Porém, cumpre-nos entender que há uma vasta realidade por detrás dessa palavra simples, que ultrapassa toda a nossa imaginação.

X. Ofícios e poderes especiais

1. Alguns supõem, logicamente, que os anjos têm poderes criativos, podendo estar envolvidos em alguns aspectos da criação, no passado ou no presente. Isso parece lógico, posto que o próprio homem aparentemente é capaz de transformar a energia em matéria.

2. Elementos na adoração e no culto divinos (Apo. 4).

3. Mediadores da mensagem divina, da lei e de muitas comunicações pessoais, que visam prestar orientação aos homens. (Gên. 18:9 ss ; Juí. 13:2-24; Luc. 1:13,30; Gál. 3:19). Na qualidade de transmissores da mensagem divina, os anjos também estão provavelmente envolvidos na iluminação de homens que buscam uma maior espiritualidade. Nisso, eles ajudam o homem a desenvolver-se espiritualmente, como mestres ou guias. (Gên. 24:7,40; Êxo. 14:19).

4. Envolvimento na missão de Cristo, em Seu nascimento, morte e ascensão, e no futuro, em Sua segunda vinda. Ver as referências dadas na discussão anterior. Esse envolvimento inclui o julgamento. (Ver Apo. 20:1-4; Luc. 9:26).

5. Guardar e proteger. Ver as notas sobre as *anjos guardiães*, no NTI, em Mat. 18:10, bem como a discussão e as referências anteriores. As instâncias bíblicas incluem a experiência de Jacó (Gên. 32:4 ss), além de muitas outras (ver Êxo. 14:19 ss ; Núm. 22; Jos. 5:14; Dan. 3:28; 6:22; Sal. 91:11; Dan. 10:13; 11:1; Apo. 2:3). Essas referências mostram que essa proteção e orientação é dada a indivíduos, igrejas e nações.

6. Muitos atos de ministração física e espiritual. (Ver Heb. 1:14; Gên. 21:17 ss ; Mar. 1:13 ss ; Mat. 28:2; Atos 5:19; 12:6-11).

7. Um ministério prestado ao Senhor nos lugares celestiais, conforme se vê com abundância no Apocalipse. (Ver Apo. 4). (B C R S Z)

XI. Tarefas dos anjos. Estas são variadas, a saber:

a. Anunciar e avisar de antemão (ver Gên. 18:9 ss ; Juí. 13:2-24; Luc. 1:13,30; 2:8-15; Apo. 1-22).

b. Guiar e instruir (ver Gên. 24:7,20; 28:12-15; Êxo. 14:19; 23:20; Núm. 20:16; Atos. 7:38,53; Gál. 3:19). Os anjos também interpretam visões (ver Zac. 1:9,19; Dan. 7:16 e Apo. 17:7).

c. Guardar e defender, o que explica os anjos guardiães e seus serviços (ver Sal. 34:7; Gên. 32:24 ss ; Êxo. 14:19 ss ; Núm. 22; II Reis 6:17; I Crô. 12:22; Dan. 3:28; 6:22; Sal. 91:11; Dan. 10:13 - 11:1; Mat. 18:10 (ver nota no NTI) e Apo. 2 e 3 (onde a Igreja é assessorada, guiada, guardada e instruída por agentes angelicais especiais). Ver a afirmação de Jesus de que os anjos poderiam entrar em ação em Sua defesa, em Mat. 26:53.

d. Ministrar aos necessitados. (Ver Gên. 21:17 ss ; Êxo. 14:19 ss ; I Reis 19:5-7; Mar. 1:13; Luc. 22:43; Mat. 28:2; Atos 5:19 e 12:6-11).

e. Dar aos homens dons espirituais e ajudá-los nessa utilização (ver I Cor. 12:14). Visto que tais dons, quando genuínos, são originários do Espírito Santo, visto que há um envolvimento angelical que inclui a instrução (ver o ponto b); é possível que os dons possam ser mediados por poderes angelicais, tal como se deu no caso da lei (ver Gál. 3:19). Esse conceito também parece plausível quando consideramos que os anjos muito se atarefam no serviço em favor dos crentes individuais (ver Heb. 1:14); e isso sugere que todos os aspectos da vida dos crentes possam estar envolvidos nesse ministério. Outrossim, muitas religiões além da cristã têm atribuído aos anjos as funções de guias e instrutores espirituais, possibilitando aos homens a cumprirem suas respectivas missões.

f. Ajudar os homens a atingirem seu destino. Isso é declarado em Hebreus 1:14. Aqueles que receberem tal ministério herdarão a vida eterna. Antes disso, porém, aquilo que um homem tiver de fazer, a espiritualidade que ele tiver de atingir e as tarefas que ele tiver de cumprir, será com a ajuda dos anjos. Naturalmente, os anjos são agentes de Deus, e não poderes independentes.

g. Assessorar no julgamento, tanto o temporal quanto o escatológico, ver Atos 12:23; Mat. 16:27; 25:31; Luc. 9:26; 12:8,9; Mar. 13:27; os eleitos serão recolhidos pelos anjos; os anjos estarão envolvidos, de alguma maneira, na *parousia* - ver o artigo a respeito.

h. Os anjos estão ativos na adoração celeste, servindo tanto agora quanto no estado eterno (ver Apo. 19:1-3; Luc. 2:13 ss.).

O ministério dos Anjos

Rejeito a idéia que diz que nossos anjos guardiães apenas *protegem-nos*. O trecho de Hebreus 1:14 mostra que o ministério deles atua dentro do contexto espiritual. Também rejeito a noção de que os anjos têm algo a ver com a nossa salvação, como se fossem mediadores; mas creio que eles agem ajudando-nos a crescer espiritualmente. Anjos foram usados como mediadores na outorga da lei, e a lei serviu de aio para conduzir-nos a Cristo (ver Gál. 3:19,24). Quando Jesus foi tentado, foi ajudado por anjos, a fim de que não viesse a falhar naquela sua hora de provação (Mat. 4:11). Os anjos executam a vontade de Deus (Sal. 103:20) e até mesmo guiam na carreira das nações (Dan. 10:12,13,21; 12:1). É difícil supormos que isso se relaciona apenas com questões físicas, materiais. Declara sobre isso a obra Strong's Theology: «Não poderíamos admitir que os anjos bons influenciam as questões das nações, a fim de contrabalançarem o mal e ajudarem aos bons?» (volume II, pág. 451). Muitos intérpretes acreditam que os *anjos das sete igrejas* referidas no Apocalipse eram apenas *isso*, os anjos guardiães daquelas igrejas locais, os poderes que havia por detrás dos pastores daquelas igrejas. Nesse caso, o bem-estar espiritual daquelas comunidades cristãs era influenciado por esses anjos. O trecho de I Coríntios 11:30 diz que os anjos interessam-se pela ordem e pela adoração nas igrejas locais. Essas são questões que influenciam a nossa espiritualidade. Alford opina, acerca dos sete anjos das igrejas do Apocalipse, que eles eram *seres sobre-humanos*, nomeados para guardar e representar aquelas igrejas. A leitura daquelas cartas demonstra que o ponto em foco era o *desenvolvimento espiritual*, e não se alguma carruagem poderia atropelar e ferir a alguém, em alguma das ruas de Éfeso. «Assim como aos espíritos malignos foi permitido atuarem mais ativamente quando o cristianismo começou a atrair aos homens, assim também os anjos bons podiam ser mais freqüentemente reconhecidos como *os executores dos propósitos divinos*» (Strong, idem, pág. 453). Além disso, ouçamos o seguinte: «Assim como os

ANJO — ANJO DA GUARDA

anjos maus tentam aos homens, assim também é *provável* que os anjos bons *atraiam os homens para a santidade*» (Strong, idem, pág. 453). Em seguida, ele passa a dizer: «Recentes pesquisas desvendam possibilidades quase ilimitadas para outras mentes serem influenciadas através da sugestão. Superficiais fenômenos físicos, como o odor de uma violeta, ou como a visão de uma pétala de rosa, em uma página amassada de um livro, podem dar início a uma série inteira de pensamentos que podem mudar o rumo inteiro de uma vida. Uma palavra ou um olhar pode exercer grande fascínio sobre nós. Fisher, em seu livro, *Nature and Method of Revelation* (pág. 276), afirma: 'Os fatos do hipnotismo ilustram a possibilidade de uma mente cair sob uma estranha escravidão a outra mente'. Ora, se *outros homens* podem nos influenciar tão poderosamente, então é *perfeitamente possível* que os espíritos que não estão sujeitos às limitações da carne, possam influenciar-nos ainda mais» (*idem*, págs. 453 e 454).

Strong prossegue, referindo-se à naturalidade dos fenômenos psíquicos, após o que assevera: «A nossa natureza humana é mais ampla e mais susceptível às influências espirituais do que comumente temos acreditado». Em seguida, ele aborda a questão dos anjos malignos, que atraem os homens a pensamentos e atos maus, da mesma forma que se espera que os anjos bons façam o contrário. Strong foi um teólogo e educador batista, e a sua obra, durante muitas décadas, tem sido utilizada como um compêndio padrão de teologia sistemática. Não penso que eu preciso de qualquer autoridade maior do que essa. Ademais, as Escrituras falam por si mesmas.

Por conseguinte, sinto-me perfeitamente justificado ao afirmar que os poderes angelicais *podem* participar do nosso crescimento espiritual, chegando mesmo a inspirar algum ocasional sermão, quando o pregador eleva-se acima de seu «eu» normal (muitas vezes enfadonho).

A Evolução da Vereda Espiritual

1. *Materialismo*. Com ou sem a crença em um Ser Supremo (essa crença pode ser meramente teórica, sem qualquer praticalidade na vida diária), os homens podem atirar-se no materialismo. Então a vida é vivida egoisticamente. A alma não volve os olhos para cima, para seu futuro estágio eterno. A vida diária não é influenciada por essa visão do alto.

2. *Superstição*. Nesse segundo estágio, os homens chegam a *reconhecer* algo dos poderes sobre-humanos e espirituais, mas aí tudo conceito das coisas continua distorcido. As crenças religiosas podem ser até prejudiciais como na prática do sacrifício humano. Os supersticiosos deixam-se levar por toda forma de mitos e imaginações, mas, pelo menos, já chegaram a perceber que *existem* poderes espirituais.

3. *Fundamentalismo*. Nesse nível, as revelações divinas, preservadas em Livros Sagrados, são altamente reverenciadas; porém, a letra é posta acima do Espírito. Ver o artigo sobre *Bibliolatria*. Crenças e credos rígidos cristalizam e entravam o desenvolvimento espiritual. Credos tornam-se motivos fortes de divisão. A arrogância e o gosto pela polêmica são proeminentes nesse estágio. No caso de muitos, o amor é apenas uma questão da boca para fora. Textos de prova resolvem tudo. Tradições são ensinadas como se fossem a própria verdade. Porções dos Livros Sagrados são distorcidas no esforço de obter uma teologia sistemática infalível, que se torna mais importante que a própria verdade. Algumas pessoas, neste estágio, são capazes de atingir um bom grau de piedade e espiritualidade pessoais. Muitos, porém, substituem a espiritualidade pela mera aderência a algum credo.

4. *Filosofia*. Nesse nível do avanço, os homens já começam a pensar por si mesmos, e não são apenas mata-borrões que somente absorvem idéias alheias. Surge uma espécie de despertamento, após todo o *sono dogmático* do passado. A *tolerância* (vide) torna-se a linha mestra principal das atitudes e ações. A lei do amor começa a adquirir importância. As antigas verdades passam a ser entendidas de uma nova maneira, e novas verdades são descobertas e incorporadas. Os credos deixam de ser examinados e seguidos cegamente, conforme sucedera no estágio fundamentalista. É abandonado o *antiintelectualismo* (vide).

5. *Perseguição e Perseverança*. A alma começa a ter fome e sede de justiça e verdade. Sente-se aflita, impelida a uma inquirição espiritual mais *intensa*. Alguns experimentam, nesse estágio, uma *reconversão*. O estudo torna-se mais importante; a meditação é praticada; a iluminação é procurada; a compaixão e a simpatia substituem a antiga hostilidade. Os homens avançam para além da tolerância.

6. *A Vereda Mística*. A alma segue a Deus bem de perto; experiências conferem a iluminação. A *Presença Divina* torna-se uma realidade na vida. A união com Deus é desejada e procurada. O amor é supremo. Ver sobre *Misticismo* e *Cristo-Misticismo*.

7. *O estágio final* é, realmente, o processo da eterna *glorificação* (vide). Ver *Visão Beatífica* e *Transformação Segundo a Imagem de Cristo*.

Bibliografia: A GOT IR ID LAN NTI RO

ANJO DA GUARDA

Ver o artigo geral sobre os **Anjos**. Parte dessa doutrina, e antiqüíssima, é o conceito de que cada pessoa tem um guia espiritual, ajudador, que cuida de sua vida, oferecendo proteção, e instrução. O trecho de Heb. 1:14 mostra que um dos propósitos desse ministério é que as pessoas cheguem à salvação. Nesse caso, o anjo guardião é muito mais do que um simples protetor. O livro de Daniel reflete a antiga crença de que as nações também contam com guardiães, e mencionou Miguel como o poder angelical interessado pelo destino de Israel. (Ver Dan. 10:13,21; 12:1 e 10:20, onde aprendemos que até as demais nações têm um anjo guardião). Isso ensina-nos que as nações, e não apenas indivíduos isolados, têm um destino a cumprir. Elas podem falhar em seu destino, tal como pode suceder a indivíduos. Além disso, a humanidade, considerada como um todo, tem um destino, como uma entidade física, inteiramente à parte do destino espiritual dos indivíduos. Devemo-nos lembrar que a vida na terra é uma escola para o nosso treinamento espiritual, revestindo-se de grande importância por esse motivo. Além disso, como uma entidade física, a humanidade tem um destino importante, distinto do destino espiritual das almas. Aparentemente, faz parte do destino físico dos homens explorarem e habitarem outros lugares, dentro do sistema solar e mesmo além. Quando o homem olhar na direção do céu, obterá uma nova perspectiva de seu elevado destino, através da lição objetiva da conquista do espaço. Além disso, aquilo que fazemos neste mundo é importante, ao aprendermos a amar e a servir aos nossos semelhantes. O homem, pois, tem um duplo destino. Um deles é físico, e o outro é espiritual. Esses dois destinos estão relacionados entre si, mas a vida física não é mera preparação para a outra vida. Se isso é verdade, devemos afirmar que qualquer homem que cumpre bem o seu papel, em qualquer profissão que seguir, está servindo à vontade de Deus. Como é óbvio, os

ANJOS DAS SETE CARTAS DO APOCALIPSE — ANO SABÁTICO

ministros do evangelho não são os únicos que servem a Deus. Podemos afirmar que um cientista, por estar fazendo avançar a causa do destino físico relativo ao nosso planeta, também está servindo a Deus. Esse também tem um destino espiritual a preencher, embora, no momento, concentre-se específica e principalmente em um trabalho físico importante para si mesmo e para os outros homens. Posteriormente, ele haverá de ocupar-se de aspectos de sua tarefa espiritual (não-terrena). Ambos os aspectos são importantes, e ambos são maneiras de servir a Deus. O *conhecimento* adquirido em todos os ramos, e a respeito de todas as coisas, compõe a ciência divina, pelo que promover o conhecimento, de qualquer variedade (se não for inerentemente mau), é promover o conhecimento de Deus. Pois, afinal de contas, há somente uma grande verdade. Além disso, precisamos considerar a prática da lei do amor. E, se pudermos cumpri-la cofretamente neste mundo, então teremos aprendido tal coisa. Qualquer serviço humanitário, portanto, serve à vontade de Deus, mesmo que não esteja ligado a qualquer organização ou empreendimento religioso. Orfanatos, hospitais, escolas e organizações semelhantes servem a Deus, e não apenas igrejas. O ministério dos anjos envolve todas essas atividades, e não meramente as atividades espirituais. Um guia angelical pode inspirar um cientista a descobrir um medicamento. Tal guia pode levar alguém para trabalhar em uma escola ou hospital, ou mesmo para ser um político! A perspectiva de Deus acerca das coisas sempre é mais ampla do que a nossa, sendo errado alguém desprezar a outrem, somente por ser, digamos, um professor de escola pública de segundo grau, e não pastor de uma igreja batista.

Um ponto de vista oriental. No hinduísmo, os anjos guardiães são vistos como a porção superior do próprio ser do indivíduo, sendo chamado de super-eu (ou sobre-ser). Nesse caso, a alma é o instrumento de um elevado poder (a real entidade do ser), tal como o corpo é o instrumento da alma. A natureza humana é misteriosa, não podendo ser solucionada a sua complexidade mediante o mero uso de termos simples como *dicotomia* ou *tricotomia*. O conceito do super-eu não elimina o ministério dos anjos (como entidades espirituais separadas), mas antes, aumenta o nosso conhecimento sobre a estatura do homem, o qual, conforme a Bíblia ensina, foi criado pouco inferior aos anjos. Ver o artigo sobre o super-eu (sobre-ser). (EP HUS NTI)

ANJOS DAS SETE CARTAS DO APOCALIPSE
Ver Apo. 1:16,20,21 etc.

Os anjos em Apo. 1:16,20, são chamados de «sete estrelas». O trecho de Apo. 1:16 nos fornece explicações detalhadas que são sumariadas aqui, nos pontos abaixo discriminados.

1. Há aqui certa alusão astrológica (ver 1:16). Ver no NTI.

2. São grandes *poderes espirituais* associados às igrejas, visando a sua proteção e orientação. São instrumentos nas mãos de Cristo, seres angelicais literais, que ministram a igreja, controlando seus ministros, e, pelo menos em alguns casos, servindo de mediadores dos dons espirituais. Por extensão dessa idéia, podemos supor que todas as comunidades locais dos crentes contam com seus próprios anjos guardiães, tal qual sucede no caso das nações e dos crentes individuais.

3. Alguns pensam que estariam em foco os «pastores» humanos das igrejas, e não seres sobrenaturais. Apesar disso ser uma interpretação comum, não é provável. Os «pastores», entretanto, provavelmente seriam tidos como instrumentos especiais desses seres angelicais, seus *representantes*, nas assembléias locais.

4. Também há quem pense que seriam delegados especiais, enviados às sete comunidades cristãs, levando-lhes cópias do livro de Apocalipse. Mas isso é altamente improvável. Antes, devem ser membros «fixos» das igrejas locais ou seres permanentemente vinculados a elas, e não visitantes ocasionais de qualquer espécie.

5. Não são «bispos», de regiões diversas, que representariam o desenvolvimento «eclesiástico» da igreja.

6. Não são «missionários itinerantes» ou «instrutores», que exerceriam autoridade especial sobre as comunidades cristãs, atendendo às suas necessidades espirituais.

7. E nem são essas estrelas meros «símbolos místicos» das igrejas, como se seu intuito fosse apresentar seres vivos de qualquer modalidade. (Ver as notas expositivas, em Apo. 1:16 no NTI, onde essas idéias são mais amplamente desenvolvidas). A posição ou posições mais prováveis são a primeira e a segunda ou mesmo a combinação dessas duas posições.

O ensinamento que aqui temos, pois, é profundo — a igreja cristã não fica sozinha. Conta com a ajuda de grandes protetores espirituais, guardiães e instrutores angelicais. Isso faz parte da promessa de Cristo, em seu cumprimento: «De maneira alguma te deixarei, nunca jamais te abandonarei» (Heb. 13:5); e: «E eis que estou convosco todos os dias até à consumação do século» (Mat. 28:20). Isso, entretanto, não os transforma em mediadores da «salvação», pois somente Cristo Jesus pode ser tal mediador (ver I Tim. 2:5). Contudo, são mediadores de sua presença e de seu poder, enviados para ministrar às assembléias locais, bem como aos crentes individuais (ver Heb. 1:14). Cada um desses anjos tem seus «representantes» nas igrejas locais, a saber, pastores, mestres, etc. (A IB GOT MC NTI RO Z)

ANO
Ver **Calendário**.

ANO DO MUNDO
O ano mundial é um vasto ciclo de tempo pelo qual o mundo atravessa. Há muitos anos mundiais, ou ciclos. De acordo com Heráclito, um ano mundial consiste em 360 gerações de trinta anos cada, ou seja, um ciclo de 10.800 anos. Para os estóicos, não havia qualquer número específico de anos. O ano mundial seria apenas um dos intermináveis ciclos de imensa duração, que o mundo atravesssaria. Cada ciclo levaria a uma inevitável destruição, seguida pela renovação e pelo começo de um novo ciclo. Destruição e regeneração pelo fogo, é a idéia central. Esse ponto de vista pode ser encontrado comumente nas religiões orientais.

ANO ECLESIÁSTICO
Ver o artigo sobre **Calendário Eclesiástico**.

AN-OMOI-ANS Ver **Homoousios**.

ANO NOVO Ver **Festas (Festividades) Judaicas**.

ANO SABÁTICO
No hebraico consiste em uma única palavra. O ano sabático era o ano final em um ciclo de sete anos, dentro do calendário hebraico. Naquele ano os

ANO SABÁTICO — ANSELMO

campos eram deixados sem cultivo, para a terra descansar, para se cuidar dos pobres e dos animais, para remissão das dívidas e para os escravos israelitas saírem forros, isto é, livres. O ano após sete anos sabáticos era conhecido como ano do jubileu, em que o solo recebia mais um período anual de descanso, e no qual também havia a liberação de escravos israelitas e a reversão das propriedades, na forma de terras, aos proprietários originais ou seus herdeiros.

O livro do pacto refere-se ao ano sabático meramente como *o sétimo* (ver Êxo. 21:2; 23:11; cf. Nee. 10:31). Todos os escravos hebreus automaticamente eram deixados em liberdade (ver Êxo. 21:2). Mas isso talvez signifique apenas que um israelita só podia servir como escravo a outro israelita pelo espaço de seis anos, e que no ano seguinte ele seria colocado em liberdade, não importando se esse ano coincidisse ou não com o ano sabático.

No código sacerdotal, o sétimo ano é designado como «sábado de descanso solene para a terra, um sábado ao Senhor» (Lev. 25:4). Um israelita, naquele ano, não podia semear seu campo e nem podar seu vinhedo (ver Lev. 25:4). Também não podia fazer qualquer espécie de colheita; mas tudo quanto a terra produzisse naturalmente destinava-se ao consumo dos pobres e dos animais, tanto domésticos quanto selvagens (ver Lev. 25:5-7). Havia um paralelo bem próximo entre os regulamentos referentes ao ano sabático e os regulamentos referentes ao sábado semanal (ver Lev. 25:2-7; Êxo. 20:8-11 e Deu. 5:12-15).

O mesmo código também provia a observância especial do sétimo ano, dentro de uma série de sete anos sabáticos (ver Lev. 25:8,9), bem como a observância do qüinquagésimo ano como o ano do jubileu, no qual a terra também ficava sem cultivo, e no qual todas as propriedades voltavam aos seus proprietários originais e todos os escravos hebreus eram libertados (ver Lev. 25:10-55). As *únicas* propriedades isentas dessa lei eram aquelas casas que ficavam dentro de cidades muradas que não fossem resgatadas no espaço de um ano (ver Lev. 25:29-31), bem como aquelas pertencentes aos levitas (ver Lev. 25:32-34).

No código deuteronômico, o ano sabático é chamado de «sétimo ano» ou «ano da remissão» (ver Deu. 15:9). Ali há instruções quanto ao cancelamento de todas as dívidas que um israelita devesse a outro, no final do ano sabático (ver Deu. 15:1-3), juntamente com um aviso contra a má vontade em fazer empréstimos a alguma pessoa pobre, em vista da proximidade do ano sabático (ver Deu. 15:7-11). A instrução sobre a alforria de escravos hebreus também aparece nesse código (ver Deu. 15:12-15). Algo que só aparece nesse código é a leitura da lei por ocasião da festa dos Tabernáculos, durante o ano sabático (ver Deu. 31:10-13).

Não se sabe quão escrupulosamente os israelitas observavam os anos sabáticos, mas o trecho de II Crônicas 36:21 subentende que eles não os observaram. E foi por isso que o povo de Israel foi para o cativeiro, «...até que a terra se agradasse dos seus sábados...» (cf. também Lev. 26:34). O ajuntamento dos exilados que retornaram, a fim de ouvir a leitura da lei, por parte de Esdras, sem dúvida se deu por ocasião do cumprimento do pacto deuteronômico (ver Nee. 8:1-8), ou seja, no ano sabático. Uma das reformas instituídas por Neemias foi a execução ou a observância do ano sabático (ver Nee. 10:31).

Há provas extrabíblicas de que os judeus observaram o ano sabático após o exílio babilônico. Tanto os livros dos Macabeus quanto Josefo narram que o suprimento de alimentos da guarnição de Betezur logo se acabou, causando a rendição daquela guarnição, porque o fato ocorreu em um ano sabático (I Macabeus 6:49-54; *Ant.* XIII.8:1; *Guerras* I.2:4). E Josefo também relata que durante o governo de João Hircano os judeus não empreenderam nenhuma guerra agressiva por causa do ano sabático (Josefo, *Anti.* XIII.8:1; *Guerras* I.2:4). E também relatou o mesmo escritor que Júlio César isentou os judeus de pagarem o tributo anual nos anos sabáticos, visto que os judeus não cultivavam seus campos e nem colhiam suas frutas (*Anti.* XIV.10:6). No livro de Jubileus, lemos que Enoque «recontou os sábados de anos» (4:18). No entanto, a literatura judaica posterior, devido ao seu silêncio sobre essa observância, mostra-nos que a prática foi sendo gradualmente abandonada pelos judeus, tornando-se antiprática, sem sentido e obsoleta na própria Palestina. Os judeus da «diáspora» jamais observaram o ano sabático. (AM JE S)

ANRAFEL

No hebraico tem sentido incerto. Foi rei de Sinear, as terras baixas de aluvião do sul da Babilônia. Fazia parte da liga de quatro reis (Arioque, Tidal, Quedorlaomer e Anrafel), que combateu contra um grupo de reis palestinos (de Sodoma, Gomorra, Admá, Zeboim e Bela). Os primeiros derrotaram estes últimos (ver Gên. 14:1-11). O cabeça da liga oriental era Quedorlaomer, rei de Elão. Anrafel tem sido identificado com Hamurabi, da Babilônia; e Tidal com Tudalia I, de Hati. Mas tudo isso sem muitas evidências, pois as evidências lingüísticas e cronológicas laboram contra tais identificações. (UN Z)

ANRÃO

No hebraico, **o povo** ou **o parente é exaltado.** Nome de três pessoas no Antigo Testamento:

1. O primeiro dos filhos de Coate, um levita que se casou com a irmã de seu pai, Joquebede, e que teve com ela Miriã, Aarão e Moisés (ver Êxo. 6:18,20; Núm. 3:19 e 26:59). Os anrameus eram seus descendentes, encarregados de deveres especiais no tabernáculo, no deserto. Anrão morreu com a idade de 137 anos, provavelmente antes do Êxodo.

2. Filho de Disom, descendente de Esaú (ver I Crô. 1:41). Em Gênesis 35:26 ele é chamado Hendã, que é uma forma mais correta.

3. Filho de Bani, que casou-se com uma mulher estrangeira no tempo de Esdras (Esd. 10:34; I Esdras 9:34). Separou-se dela, de acordo com as ordens dadas pelos líderes espirituais, em cerca de 456 A.C.

ANSELMO

Filósofo e teólogo escolástico (1033-1109), nascido em Aosta (Piemonte), na Itália. Foi monge beneditino, com várias posições eclesiásticas na França e na Inglaterra. Tornou-se arcebispo de Canterbury em 1093, permanecendo no cargo até 1109. Aplicou a lógica aristotélica (herdada por meio de Boécio) aos seus argumentos teológicos, pelo que também alguns o intitulam pai do *escolasticismo* (ver o artigo).

Escritos. Proslogion; De Grammatico; Sobre a Verdade; Por que o Deus-Homem?

Idéias:

1. *O argumento ontológico.* (Ver o artigo; ver também sobre *Deus, Provas de Sua Existência*). Esse

argumento em prol da existência de Deus acha-se no *Proslogion*. Assume duas formas: a. Deus é aquele ser (realidade) maior que podemos conceber. Tal realidade deve existir, pois doutro modo poderíamos conceber algo maior ainda. Outrossim, tal realidade deve ser *perfeita*; se Deus existisse apenas como idéia, mas não na realidade, não seria perfeito e nem seria a realidade última. b. Deus é aquele ser que não podemos conceber como não-existente. Se falarmos em «não-existência divina» estaremos falando sobre uma contradição, porque o divino não pode deixar de existir. Em outras palavras, Deus é o Ser Necessário, ao passo que todas as outras coisas são contingentes. (Notas completas sobre esses conceitos aparecem nos artigos referidos acima). A oposição foi feita através da assertiva que o mero conceito de Ser Último, de Ser necessário, de Ser perfeito, dificilmente pode trazer à existência um tal ser. Há diferença entre o pensamento e a realidade. O que *existe* é meramente o *conceito* do Ser Último. Se for demonstrado que Ele existe na realidade, outras provas serão necessárias, para que não se trate de um mero dogma mental. Anselmo, entretanto, não se escudava em meros conceitos mentais. Ele partia do pressuposto de que a iluminação divina (as experiências místicas) esclarece o homem, que o homem é capaz de ter pensamentos sobre verdades genuínas, como um tipo de comunicação feita pelo Espírito. Portanto, para que o argumento ontológico de Anselmo seja derrotado, é mister que primeiro seja derrubado o princípio do conhecimento através das experiências místicas. (Ver o artigo a esse respeito).

2. *Descrições de Deus no Proslogion*. Deus é auto-existente, criador, sensível, embora incorpóreo, onipotente, compassivo, destituído de paixão, onisciente, supremamente justo, todo-amor, onipresente, embora não existente no espaço e no tempo, eterno e unitário. O *Monologion* discute sobre essas questões. Ver o artigo sobre os *atributos de Deus*.

3. O *Monologion* contém o ensino anselmiano sobre a *trindade* (ver o artigo), cuja imagem é a mente racional. Portanto, o homem tem afinidade com a divindade. A alma humana é imortal, e retornar a Deus, em bem-aventurança eterna, é o alvo da existência humana.

4. Em sua obra *Por Que o Deus-Homem?* pela primeira vez na teologia, a doutrina da expiação foi sujeitada a uma investigação sistemática, científica. O ensino que daí emerge se intitula teoria da «satisfação» da expiação. (Ver o artigo sobre a *expiação*). Ao morrer pelos homens, Cristo proveu uma satisfação proporcional à culpa humana, uma dádiva de Si mesmo que requer, a par disso, uma recompensa proporcional, a saber, a salvação do homem. A Igreja existe basicamente em função da expiação de Cristo. Deus ficou satisfeito ante a expiação de Cristo, pelo que Sua justiça e misericórdia foram ambas satisfeitas. Essa obra também explica a doutrina de Cristo, Sua missão salvatícia, Sua encarnação e a redenção que nEle há.

5. *Fé e razão* são mutuamente dependentes: «Creio para poder compreender». Mas também «compreendo, pelo que creio». A razão e a filosofia ajudam a fé ao responderem a objeções e ao proverem uma base lógica e racional para o dogma. Deus é o criador do intelecto, pelo que é impossível que o intelecto conflite com a fé. Porém, onde a razão mostra-se inadequada, a fé pode apreender verdades por meio da revelação.

6. Anselmo foi profundamente influenciado por Agostinho, tendo sido denominado de «o segundo Agostinho».

7. Quanto à questão dos *universais* (ver o artigo), Anselmo era realista. Acusou Roscelin de erro, quando este referiu-se aos universais como mera *flatus vocis* (meras palavras; *flatus*, sopro, respiração).

8. No campo da ética, Anselmo frisava a lei do amor, não apenas como um princípio ético, mas como um conceito que envolvia tanto a fé quanto o entendimento. Não podemos separar qualquer conhecimento ou inquirição do princípio do amor.

Anselmo foi um pensador original, eficaz e brilhante escritor. (AM E EP F FS GE MM)

ANSIEDADE (Ver também sobre Cuidado)

Ver o artigo sobre Angst, quanto a uma forma radical de ansiedade. A emoção da ansiedade, comum a todos os homens devido à precariedade da vida terrena, pode ser evitada pela fé, desde graus menores até um grau absoluto, dependendo da qualidade espiritual do momento. No trecho de Mat. 6:25-34, Jesus mostra razões pelas quais a ansiedade não se coaduna com a vida cristã, porque ela nega essencialmente o poder da providência de Deus. I Pedro 5:7 encerra uma afirmação bem conhecida contra a ansiedade: «lançando sobre ele toda a vossa ansiedade, porque ele tem cuidado de vós». Não temos necessidade de viver ansiosos, porque Deus anela por nós. Essa idéia reflete o *teísmo*, em contraste com o *deísmo*. O *teísmo* (ver o artigo) ensina que Deus não somente criou, mas também se faz presente em Sua criação, guiando, recompensando, punindo e alterando o curso dos eventos. Acima de tudo, Deus tem em mente a *salvação* (ver o artigo) da humanidade, a forma suprema de teísmo. O deísmo (ver o artigo) ensina que uma força cósmica, pessoal ou impessoal, criou tudo, mas abandonou sua criação, deixando-a sob o governo de leis naturais, como um relógio cuja corda permite que continue funcionando. Segundo essa posição, Deus não tem qualquer interesse pelo mundo, tendo-o abandonado, não recompensando e nem punindo, e jamais fazendo intervenções no mesmo.

A psicologia frisa que a ansiedade pode criar perturbações físicas. Realmente existem as doenças psicossomáticas. O existencialismo, dentro da filosofia, muito se vale da ansiedade, referindo-se a ela como inerente à condição humana, pois, de fato, há muita coisa que nos deixa ansiosos. O existencialismo ateu (ver o artigo) crê que a vida é uma piada da natureza, por ter sucedido por mero acidente, sem qualquer propósito ou desígnio. O homem está só, e não sabe onde. Não há Deus que o ajude, e a existência humana está cercada de ameaças, que as falsas esperanças bem pouco fazem para aliviar. O existencialismo religioso propõe haver esperança, mediante o uso do livre-arbítrio, através do qual o homem pode evitar sua condição. Além disso, na opinião de alguns existencialistas religiosos a missão de Cristo teve o propósito de injetar esperança nesse melancólico quadro. Apesar de que a morte finalmente nos ameaça, devido à nossa condição de mortalidade (daí derivando-se a nossa ansiedade), o próprio «eu», em sua liberdade, teria a consciência de transcender à consciência humana. Desse modo, «eu» torna-se mais do que um mero expectator. O próprio «eu», contemplando a dupla dimensão da realidade, a finitude (temporalidade), em contraste com a liberdade, precisa fazer sua escolha. A «ansiedade» é o concomitante inevitável do paradoxo da liberdade e da finitude, no qual o homem está envolvido, segundo dizia Niebuhr.

ANSIEDADE DA CRIAÇÃO— ANTEDILUVIANOS

A teologia cristã ensina que as grandes opções da existência são feitas em Cristo, com quem fomos identificados e cuja natureza e destino compartilhamos (Rom. 8:29; II Cor. 3:18). Portanto, apesar da ansiedade ser uma realidade, pois somos mortais e fracos, as grandes questões da vida e da morte não mais continuam pendentes, mas foram resolvidas otimisticamente em face de nossa identificação com Cristo, por meio de Sua missão salvadora e transformadora. Pesquisas feitas no campo do retorno após a morte clínica, isto é, de pessoas que penetram nos primeiros estágios da morte, mas retornam à vida, e que podem lembrar-se do que sucede nesse ínterim, emprestam uma interpretação otimista à vida. Em conseqüência, apesar da ansiedade ser um fato constante de nossa existência, sabemos que o sol haverá de raiar após o temporal, e podemos descansar nesse fato. Além disso, no tocante à vida diária, contamos com a permanente providência de Deus, o que significa que coisa alguma nos sucede fortuitamente. Ver o artigo sobre *Experiências da Quase-Morte*. (EP H KM SK)

ANSIEDADE DA CRIAÇÃO (Rom. 8:22)

1. A criação, ou seja, todas as coisas que foram criadas, animadas ou inanimadas, incluindo os anjos e até mesmo os homens não-remidos, em contraste com o «nós» (subentendido nas palavras «os filhos de Deus»), os eleitos. Existe uma ansiedade universal por contemplar a culminação do plano divino atinente à redenção do homem.

2. A criação, pois, anela por ver a «nova criação»; os remidos levados à glória, participando da família divina (ver as notas sobre a «filiação», em Rom. 8:14, no NTI, sob o título «O conceito da filiação»).

3. Pensamos que essa ansiedade (que poeticamente é chamada de «dores de parto», em Rom. 8:22) subentende os efeitos universais da missão de Cristo. A criação não se aproximará dessas dores de parto como uma parte desinteressada. Apesar de que não participará da filiação, conforme os eleitos, e nem da herança deles, não obstante ela será beneficiada por tal nascimento, de modo a ser retratada como alguém que procura ajudar a concretizar o mesmo.

4. A descida de Cristo ao hades produziu um grande efeito quanto a essa questão. Ver o artigo sobre a *Descida de Cristo ao Hades*.

5. Haverá a restauração de todas as coisas, em contraste com a redenção. Não será o nascimento de uma «nova espécie» (os filhos), e, sim, a elevação de tudo (através do julgamento), a um nível superior, onde Cristo será tudo para todos (parafraseando Efé. 1:23), de tal maneira que a existência será digna de ser vivida. Esse conceito é amplamente comentado em Efé. 1:10, no NTI, onde a unidade em redor de Cristo é descrita. (Ver também as notas em João 14:6, sobre a «missão universal de Cristo»).

6. Essa interpretação é comprovada pelo fato de que essa «criação» inteira haverá de partilhar da liberdade trazida pelo «nascimento da nova espécie» (ver Rom. 8:20,21). Antes de condenar esse ponto de vista, que o leitor examine o que se comenta nas referências dadas.

7. Verdadeiramente, grande é o amor de Deus, ilimitada a sua misericórdia, pois o seu amor alcança até os mais altos céus, bem como o mais profundo inferno. (Ver as notas a respeito em Rom. 11:32 no NTI).

Revelações dos filhos de Deus, Rom. 8:22. Esse é o grande ato de Deus que a criação inteira tanto sofre por ver, esperando-o com intensa expectação. Trata-se da mais exaltada das obras redentoras de Deus, da qual também participará, até certo ponto, a natureza inteira. É a transformação dos homens segundo a imagem de Cristo, em que muitos filhos serão conduzidos à glória, filhos que participem e compartilhem de tudo quanto Cristo é, bem como de tudo quanto ele herdará. No trecho de Rom. 8:29 no NTI, essa questão é comentada com amplitude, invocando várias outras passagens bíblicas em torno desse assunto. Esse é o «evangelho paulino», o «evangelho em profundidade», o mais elevado cume da mensagem evangélica, embora, infelizmente, seja um tema raramente ouvido na moderna igreja evangélica.

É um erro reduzirmos essa «revelação» à *parousia*, isto é, quando Cristo aparecer em companhia dos «remidos». Porquanto essa revelação dos filhos de Deus não se limita somente a esse acontecimento, e nem depende de tal explicação, porquanto tal explanação deixaria indefinido o que significa a palavra «remidos». (Comparar com I João 3:2; II Tes. 2:8 e Col. 3:4). Essa «revelação», bem ao contrário, é a «manifestação» ou *fruição completa* do plano divino, na personalidade do homem, o soerguimento dos homens àquela plenitude que pertence a Cristo, aquele que preenche tudo em todas as coisas, conforme também aprendemos em Efé. 1:23. Nessa «nova criação» é que será atingido o verdadeiro alvo da criação original, ou seja, «a formação da imagem de Deus nos homens», o que foi apenas parcialmente cumprido na criação física; e isso porque essa criação física tinha por seu grande alvo o cumprimento espiritual maior, que se seguiria. (IB LAN NTI S)

ANTEDILUVIANOS

Esse termo refere-se às pessoas que viveram antes do dilúvio de Noé. Biblicamente falando, o período é coberto de Gên. 1:1 (criação) a Gên. 7 (que historia o dilúvio).

1. Datas e controvérsias. Têm sido feitas tentativas de calcular quando ocorreu a criação, mediante a adição dos anos dados nas genealogias, o que também nos diria quando Adão veio à existência e quanto tempo se passou entre Adão e Noé. Essas manipulações resultam em 4000 A.C. (a grosso modo), como a data da criação; e 2450 A.C. (a grosso modo), como o tempo do dilúvio, o que sugere mil e seiscentos anos como o intervalo entre Adão e Noé. Alguns intérpretes continuam a insistir sobre esses números. Outros, supondo que as várias genealogias dos antediluvianos (havendo dez desses patriarcas no quinto capítulo de Gênesis) são apenas representativas, talvez até mesmo um simples esboço dos povos e raças que então existiam, afirmam que atribuir datas entre Adão e Noé é tarefa simplesmente impossível. Isso não seria contrário à maneira como as genealogias dos hebreus foram manuseadas. Por outra parte, mesmo que tivessem sido dados apenas dez nomes para representar cem gerações, o que envolveria um período dez vezes mais longo do que aquele que resulta da contagem dos anos indicados nas genealogias, isso não nos ajudaria a explicar os milhões de anos (e, de fato, bilhões) que a ciência postula como a idade da terra e nem a prolongada jornada de criaturas humanóides à face da terra.

Outras considerações. 1. Alguns intérpretes vêem um grande e indefinido intervalo de tempo entre Gên. 1:1 e Gên. 1:2, supondo que a criação descrita detalhadamente, no primeiro capítulo de Gênesis, seja uma reforma, e não a criação original. A criação

178

ANTEDILUVIANOS

original seria relegada a Gên. 1:1. Em seguida, esses intérpretes supõem que possam ter ocorrido todas as variedades de coisas pré-adâmicas naquele intervalo, inclusive qualquer número de raças de homens pré-adâmicas, pertencentes ou não à espécie *homo sapiens*. Além disso, a data da criação original poderia ser recuada o quanto queira fazê-lo qualquer ciência existente ou que venha a existir — bilhões de anos, se for o caso.

Mas, é então que a questão se levanta: O autor da narrativa da criação, no primeiro e no segundo capítulo de Gênesis, previa uma coisa dessa natureza? Isso pode ser respondido de diversas maneiras: a. Não, ele não previa. Portanto, a teoria inteira deve ser condenada. Ou então b. Não, ele não previa. Mas isso não labora em coisa alguma contra a veracidade da questão. Deus pode não se ter interessado em revelar-nos qualquer narrativa pré-adâmica, por não nos ser aplicável em qualquer sentido, exceto para nos satisfazer a curiosidade. Ou ainda: c. Não, ele não previa. E a teoria não corresponde à realidade dos fatos, inteiramente à parte do que o autor sagrado tencionou dizer. Ou mesmo: d. Sim, o autor tencionava que entendêssemos ter havido um imenso intervalo de tempo entre Gên. 1:1 e Gên. 1:2, embora não se tivesse preocupado em entrar nos detalhes da questão, por não ser de interesse vital para nós. Ou, finalmente: e. A discussão inteira é absurda, porque a narrativa da criação, em Gênesis, é apenas uma dentre muitas lendas antigas que procuram adivinhar como as coisas tiveram início. Por esse motivo, a narrativa não é, de fato, uma fonte informativa sobre a criação, mas tão somente uma lenda religiosa, dotada de valores morais, religiosos e simbólicos, mas sem nenhum valor no que tange à investigação científica. Os intérpretes têm assumido todas essas posições.

2. Uma espécie de reconciliação. Inteiramente à parte do que o autor de Gênesis pode ter querido dizer, podemos examinar o problema por um outro ângulo. Sim, há evidências científicas válidas em prol da vasta antiguidade da criação. Nossos telescópios são capazes de capturar luz que tem percorrido o universo durante pelo menos dezesseis bilhões de anos. É questão de simples cálculo matemático descobrir isso, uma vez que seja localizada uma fonte luminosa e a sua distância determinada. Conhecendo-se a distância da fonte luminosa e a velocidade da luz, o *tempo* que tem sido necessário para que a luz chegue à terra pode ser facilmente calculado. Contra isso, alguns têm afirmado que a luz realmente tem menos de seis mil anos, porque «Deus a criou a caminho». Tal declaração é tão absurda que chego a corar de vergonha quando a repito. A idade dos meteoritos, pelo método do radiocarbono, sugere que o sistema solar tem 4.700.000 anos. As medidas dos remanescentes do desgaste radioativo no solo e na poeira trazida à terra da lua, nos fornecem dados idênticos. Fósseis de microorganismos unicelulares, encontrados na praia do lago Superior (na América do Norte), em rochas pré-cambrianas (medidos pelo método do radiocarbono), aparentemente têm 1.900.000 anos. Dizer que Deus criou todas essas coisas já velhas na aparência, e em decadência, é opinião por demais absurda para ser considerada.

A verdade é que a ciência vai descobrindo mais fatos, quanto mais antiga reconhecemos ser a criação. Consideremos também isto. As reversões magnéticas das rochas sugerem que a posição dos povos tem sido modificado pelo menos por quatrocentas vezes. Na história recente, isso tem acontecido a cada poucos milhares de anos. Alguns cientistas acreditam (juntamente com teólogos e místicos) que uma outra dessas alterações está sendo esperada para nossos próprios dias, no primeiro quartel do século XXI. Cada alteração dessa, devido ao deslizamento da crosta terrestre, produz grandes inundações e explosões vulcânicas de incalculável potência. Naturalmente, cada alteração dessas é acompanhada pela quase destruição de todos os seres vivos. Se calcularmos as datas gerais (de conformidade com alguns eruditos) da última e da penúltima dessas mudanças de pólos, chegaremos perto da cronologia bíblica de Adão e Noé. Essa circunstância levanta a interessante possibilidade de que as narrativas bíblicas desses dois homens representam as duas últimas modificações nos pólos, pelo que seriam *novos começos*, e não começos absolutos. Nesse caso, Adão seria uma espécie de Noé, representando o reinício da raça, conforme atualmente a conhecemos. Naturalmente, isso não satisfaria uma estrita e literal interpretação do registro de Gênesis. Mas uma interpretação um tanto mais liberal talvez nos aproxime mais da verdade dos fatos, mesmo que outras pessoas nos julguem hereges. Importantes hereges sempre conseguiram fazer avançar a verdade. Pensemos sobre Jesus, Paulo e Lutero. Porém, ser um herege também não é garantia da posse de verdades mais profundas. Uma coisa, entretanto, é certa — a verdade deve ser buscada. Não podemos solucionar todos os nossos problemas de conhecimento simplesmente voltando-nos para algum *texto de prova* para extrair dali a interpretação que satisfaça nossas exigências de conforto mental. Pois, apesar da verdade algumas vezes vir à tona subitamente, na forma de um pacote feito, com maior freqüência assemelha-se a uma mina, que precisamos cavar para descobrir.

3. A arqueologia e as medições por radiocarbono. De modo geral, a arqueologia tem mostrado que estamos tratando com os *começos*, nas terras bíblicas. Em outras palavras, descobrimos um homem primitivo, um caçador, um nômade a recolher seu alimento, um pastor, um guerreiro, um lavrador — mas tudo em estágio primitivo. Um fator importante é que descobrimos o desenvolvimento do *alfabeto* (ver o artigo a respeito), que arma o palco (ou a possibilidade) para o desenvolvimento do conhecimento humano em todos os campos, mediante a linguagem escrita. Isso concorda com a narrativa bíblica sobre os começos. Ocasionalmente, porém, a arqueologia topa com algo que parece completamente fora de lugar, que sugere a existência, em milênios passados e perdidos, de civilizações mais adiantadas. Há fortes evidências em favor do uso da eletricidade, de aviões e do poder atômico por parte de alguns povos antigos. (Ver os últimos cinco parágrafos deste artigo). A cada vez que algo é descoberto e que dá a entender isso, os estudiosos, da Bíblia ou seculares, estipulam alguma explicação alternativa, embora inadequada para explicar as evidências. O moderno líder espiritual, Aaron Abrahamsen, tem sido usado pela Universidade de Arizona para descobrir locais arqueológicos por meio do conhecimento intuitivo e psíquico; e muitos locais têm sido assim descobertos. Ele é capaz de dizer a profundidade em que será encontrada alguma civilização perdida, e sua taxa de sucesso é de mais de noventa por cento. De certa feita, ele ajudou os pesquisadores a encontrarem uma civilização com «cento e cinqüenta mil anos de idade, que nada tem a ver com os índios», no deserto norte-americano do oeste. Isso falaria sobre raças pré-adâmicas sobre as quais não temos praticamente nenhuma informação, e sobre as quais a arqueologia tem pouquíssimo a dizer.

As misturas e as não-misturas. É verdade que animais pré-históricos, como os dinossauros, têm sido encontrados de mistura com restos humanos, no mesmo conglomerado. Isso parece dizer que esses presumíveis antiqüíssimos animais conviveram com o homem, ao mesmo tempo em que a ciência afirma que devemos falar em milhões de anos ao nos referirmos aos dinossauros, quando o homem ainda não existia. Portanto, temos em uma mesma mistura coisas aparentemente não-homogêneas, provenientes de diferentes épocas. Tal fato não constitui problema, porém, quando consideramos o seguinte: Quando ocorrem as grandes mudanças polares e a crosta terrestre desliza, é perfeitamente possível que coisas de diferentes épocas se misturem no mesmo conglomerado, embora pertencentes a épocas vastamente separadas entre si. Mas, em outros lugares, não ocorrem essas misturas; e, em conseqüência, escavando de camada em camada, vamos descobrindo diferentes eras, representadas na *não-mistura*. Nada há de estranho no fato da existência de misturas e de não-misturas, quando olhamos para a questão do ponto de vista das alterações polares.

A medição por radiocarbono. Os métodos de medição do tempo por radiocarbono e pelo argônio de potássio estão entre os mais fidedignos métodos de medição de datas. Esses métodos obtêm uma precisão com margem de erro de apenas dois a cinco por cento. Isso tem sido provado reiteradamente com a medição de antigos artefatos, ossos, etc., mediante a comparação com datas históricas *conhecidas* por outros métodos, como os registros históricos. A medição radiocarbônica é digna de confiança quando são datadas matérias orgânicas, ou seja, ex-organismos vivos, que viveram cerca de quarenta ou cinqüenta mil anos. — A precisão diminui à media que recuamos no tempo, porque a radioatividade diminui à medida que o tempo passa. — Mas, quando isso sucede, o processo faz as coisas parecerem mais novas, e não mais antigas. O fato é que ambos esses processos têm datado inúmeras coisas que antecedem, *por vastas eras*, os quatro mil anos antes de Cristo conferidos a Adão, se contarmos para trás o tempo referido nas genealogias. Temos de enfrentar esses fatos e descobrir a verdade. Se Adão representa um novo começo, após uma mudança polar, e não um começo absoluto da espécie humana, *ou* se ele foi uma criação especial de uma nova raça, tendo cessado de existir espécies humanas mais antigas (e parece que a primeira alternativa é preferível), então podemos admitir as evidências recolhidas pela ciência, sem termos de rejeitar o relato a respeito de Adão como um mito. Seja como for, muitos eruditos bíblicos de grande reputação, que se apegam aos pontos essenciais da fé cristã, têm abandonado inteiramente o método genealógico, reconhecendo a grande antiguidade da terra. Como prova disso, precisamos ler apenas a Zondervan Pictorial Encyclopedia of the Bible, sob o título *Antediluvianos*. Essa obra conclui acerca do método de medição do tempo: «O peso das evidências, de acordo com as interpretações anteriores dos informes disponíveis, claramente indicam que a história de Gênesis sobre os antediluvianos não fornece a cronologia de um número específico de anos, de Adão a Noé. Torna-se claro, pois, que não temos datas sobre quando viveram Noé e Adão».

Alguns estudiosos têm sugerido que as descrições sobre os patriarcas bíblicos na verdade são registros dos movimentos e das atividades de tribos inteiras. Termos como «filho» e «gerou» podem ser usados genérica ou metaforicamente, para mostrar as relações entre grupos étnicos, e não a sucessão de pais para filhos reais, dentro desses grupos. Naturalmente, tais considerações não afetam a questão dos povos pré-adâmicos.

4. A arqueologia e as informações sobre os antediluvianos. Muita informação tem sido recolhida por meio da arqueologia e da antropologia, acerca dos povos antigos. Podem ser encontrados detalhes em artigos nesta enciclopédia que abordam pessoas e locais específicos, associados àqueles tempos antigos.

5. Algumas evidências de avançadas civilizações pré-adâmicas. Isso pode ser ilustrado através das citações seguintes:

«Quando explodiu a primeira bomba atômica no Novo México, o deserto tornou-se um vidro fundido verde, no local da explosão. Esse fato, de acordo com a revista *Free World*, ofereceu aos arqueólogos uma pista. — Eles tinham escavado no antigo vale do rio Eufrates, e haviam desenterrado uma camada de cultura agrária, com oito mil anos de antiguidade, uma camada de cultura de criação de gado, mais antiga ainda, e uma ainda mais antiga cultura de homens das cavernas. Recentemente, eles atingiram uma outra camada — de vidro verde fundido. Pense só nisso, irmão!» (*New York Herald Tribune*, 16 de fevereiro de 1947).

«Pedacinhos de vidro verde, talvez fundidos em antigas fogueiras, é uma coisa; mas *áreas* inteiras de vidro verde já é algo inteiramente diferente. E esse não é o único local onde tal coisa tem sido encontrada. Há também áreas similares na costa ocidental da Escócia e em outros lugares, onde apenas um lado foi fundido, como se atingido por algum intenso calor, vindo do alto. Os relâmpagos ocasionalmente fundem a areia, mas sempre seguindo o modelo de uma raiz. Portanto, o que produziu uma *camada inteira* de vidro verde, em diversos lugares da Mesopotâmia?» (*Pursuit*, janeiro de 1970, Ian Sanderson).

Nas antigas lendas encontramos declarações que subentendem uma tecnologia avançadíssima, que se perdeu.

«O antiqüíssimo texto indiano *Mahabharata* menciona um relâmpago com ponta de ferro que foi enviado contra uma cidade inimiga. O mesmo *explodiu*, de acordo com o relato, com a luz de dez mil sóis, e com a força destruidora de dez mil vendavais. A quilômetros dali, elefantes foram derrubados por terra. Uma nuvem em forma de *guarda-chuva* elevou-se no céu. A cidade inimiga, bem como o seu exército, foram inteiramente destruídos. Os sobreviventes da conflagração foram instruídos a se lavarem em um rio próximo, lavando bem suas armaduras. Os cabelos caíam das cabeças das vítimas, a carne embranquecia e os objetos de argila se partiam sozinhos, depois que a poeira se depositou». (*The Lost Outpost of Atlantis*, Richard Wingate).

Há muitos mistérios, e quanto mais diligentemente buscarmos a verdade, com mente aberta, mais a verdade será descoberta. (JG ST TC WEB WHI Z)

ANTÉDON

Uma cidade da Palestina, à beira do mar Mediterrâneo, a quatro quilômetros ao sul de Gaza. Herodes o Grande deu-lhe o nome de Agripias, em honra ao rei Agripa. (S)

ANTEMA

No grego, **antifona**, uma forma de música coral sagrada, com palavras não-litúrgicas, usada em cultos anglicanos e protestantes. Nos tempos da rainha Isabel, da Inglaterra, a antema tomou o lugar do latim *motet* (ver o artigo), com a única diferença que era cantada em inglês, e não em latim. A evolução da antema incluiu composições corais mais elaboradas, coros mistos e a introdução de instrumentos de música, incluindo, finalmente, o órgão. Ver o artigo sobre *música*. (E)

ANTICRISTO

Declaração geral. O anticristo, embora personagem de suprema malignidade, será um instrumento nas mãos de Deus para ajudar a provocar a destruição necessária para reduzir a zero os sistemas político, econômico e militares do mundo. Isso possibilitará o início de um novo ciclo histórico. Sem a destruição dos antigos sistemas, seria impossível a inauguração da nova era, o milênio. Não será propósito do anticristo obter a *vitória*. Antes, ele encabeçará uma aliança ocidental, usando-a como meio para destruir o comunismo. Nesse processo, entretanto, pouco restará que ele possa usar como instrumento. Sua missão consistirá em provocar a destruição da imagem de Nabucodonosor, a fim de que Israel se erga como cabeça das nações, e seja inaugurado o reino milenial, como uma introdução ao estado eterno. Ver Dan. 2:31-45 quanto à imagem de Nabucodonosor, que representa os reinos do mundo. A Pedra cairá sobre essa imagem, transformando-a em pó. Ver o artigo sobre a *Tradição Profética e a Nossa Era*, quanto a explicações gerais concernentes ao que se espera que se suceda em futuro próximo.

A mente religiosa tem a tendência, em qualquer época, de pensar que os dias atuais são os *últimos*, e que *estes* são o objeto das profecias. A idéia de um tipo de grande opositor a Deus (como o anticristo será), *dos últimos dias* se encontra em Eze. caps. 38 e 39, e, sem dúvida, as pessoas daquela época esperavam o fim em breve. Durante o tempo da perseguição religiosa, na era dos Macabeus, muitos judeus consideraram o *seu* tempo a finalidade dos tempos. Esta crença é evidente em tais Escrituras como Dan. 7:21 e *ss*, e cap. 11, e também nas escrituras apocalípticas como Sib. Or., Livro III, e IV Esdras 5:4,6, Apoc. Bar. cap. 40, Asc. Isa. cap. IV. O Apocalipse do NT repete esta mentalidade, e até utiliza os velhos apocalipses para expressar a mesma idéia. A despeito deste fato, nosso tempo é diferente, e pode ser, realmente, a terminação do ciclo que começou há dois mil anos. Podemos estar agora em meio a uma preparação para a realização de uma *nova época*, um novo ciclo. Os velhos ciclos sempre terminam em destruição. O *anticristo* ajudará este processo.

O epíteto «anticristos» se encontra somente em I Jo. 2:18,22; 4:2 e II Jo. 7. Porém, a idéia de um notável opositor de Deus, do Messias e do bem, é perfeitamente comum na Bíblia, tanto no AT como no NT. Naturalmente, há muitas passagens que aludem à atitude própria de *anticristo*, mas que não falam sobre sua pessoa, propriamente dita. Contudo, ele incorpora em si mesmo todas as más qualidades que fazem oposição a Deus, e assim, muitas passagens que não falam diretamente sobre ele, destacam pontos de interesse acerca de sua natureza totalmente pervertida. O nome *anticristo*, sem dúvida alguma, tem a idéia moderna normal emprestada ao termo «anti», ou seja, *contra*, e não *em lugar de*, que é um sentido que o grego pode ter, mas que não é tencionado neste caso. Naturalmente, em certo sentido, também se pode aceitar a idéia de *substituição*, pois a lealdade que a nação de Israel e outros deveriam prestar a Cristo, será recebida temporariamente pelo anticristo.

Suas características. As passagens das epístolas joaninas que falam acerca do anticristo, se referem sobre muitas personagens e movimentos, e não apenas acerca de um indivíduo, já que falam sobre heresias contemporâneas, como o gnosticismo. Não obstante, as características que são supremamente reveladas como pertencentes ao anticristo, mostram-nos que, sem dúvida, há um grande escopo profético que pode ser aplicado diretamente ao anticristo, sem falarmos nas referências contemporâneas. Ver o artigo sobre *Gnosticismo*. As passagens, naquelas epístolas, que fornecem características a respeito do anticristo, são as seguintes:

1. O anticristo negará tanto ao Pai como ao Filho (ver I Jo. 2:22).

2. Ele negará o significado e a importância da encarnação de Cristo (ver I João 4:3 e II João 7). Naturalmente, isso é especificamente dito contra a heresia do gnosticismo, que negava a humanidade autêntica de Cristo, reduzindo-o a um dos «aeons» ou poderes angelicais, como se a sua «humanidade» fosse apenas um papel teatral, por ele desempenhado.

3. O anticristo promoverá um espírito anticristo no mundo, que já havia no tempo dos apóstolos, mas que foi mera prefiguração do tempo muito mais crítico que prevalecerá quando o anticristo estiver em ação.

4. Uma das principais características do anticristo será a capacidade de seduzir, de enganar (ver II João 7). Os capítulos décimo primeiro a décimo terceiro do livro de Apocalipse mostram-nos que isso incluirá maravilhas mentirosas. Essa lista de características pode ser grandemente aumentada se adicionarmos outros trechos bíblicos que falam acerca desse personagem, mas não sob a expressão «anticristo». Assim é que o livro de Apocalipse chama-o de «a besta», ao passo que o apóstolo Paulo lhe dá os nomes de «homem do pecado», e de «filho da perdição».

5. O anticristo será indivíduo caracterizado pela incorporação da mais profunda maldade, em sua própria pessoa. Também será homem dotado de sabedoria humana consumada, um verdadeiro gênio, embora um gênio do mal. Em seus olhos se poderá ver toda a sabedoria dos séculos, embora ele tudo use em prol da iniqüidade. Será, supremamente, o «homem do pecado»; e posto que assim será, também será ele, supremamente, o «filho da perdição», cuja causa e destino receberão todo o impacto da ira de Deus (ver II Tes. 3:3).

6. O anticristo será o *ateu* supremo, porquanto negará tanto a Deus Pai como a Deus Filho, opondo-se a qualquer reconhecimento dado a Deus, e exaltando-se a si mesmo como se fora um «deus». Será ele o mais convincente e inchado de todos os «ego-maníacos» que já existiram. Todos os outros homens maus, parecerão meras crianças, quando confrontados com ele, tão profunda e poderosa será sua impiedade, a sua manifestação de iniqüidade brutal. (Ver II Tes. 3:4 e os capítulos onze e treze do livro de Apocalipse).

7. O anticristo será operador de milagres—antes de tudo, da variedade *científica*. As profecias contemporâneas dos místicos indicam que ele espantará o mundo com realizações científicas que apresentará em lugar de qualquer coisa espiritual, negando a existência de qualquer real espiritualidade. Prometerá aos homens uma «utopia científica», sem Deus, e será extremamente convincente em seus argumentos. Além disso, porém, há muitas razões bíblicas para

ANTICRISTO

pensarmos que ele também realizará prodígios genuínos, embora *mentirosos*, isto é, que visam enganar e perverter, em vez de iluminar e beneficiar, conforme a natureza dos autênticos milagres de Cristo. (Ver II Tes. 2:9,10 e Apo. 13:14,15). Os homens que tiverem rejeitado a verdade se juntarão em nuvem em torno dele, e grande será o número de ateus e de blasfemadores que exaltarão o anticristo e que zombarão dos crentes, de Cristo e de Deus Pai. Seguir-se-á um julgamento judicial da parte de Deus, confirmando tais indivíduos em seu erro, para que realmente creiam que estão com a «verdade». Seguirão ao anticristo com profundo senso de *realização pessoal*, em face de sua lealdade a ele. Tomarão por empréstimo a plenitude perversa dele, a fim de encherem o seu vazio. E serão confirmados em sua ilusão por terem rejeitado voluntariamente a verdade (ver II Tes. 3:11).

8. O anticristo será uma espécie de imitação da *encarnação*, porquanto Satanás estará com ele, habitando nele; e assim será ele a personificação da mais elevada forma de maldade possível. Sua inteligência será astronômica, mas inteiramente perversa e destruidora, tal como se dá no caso de Satanás. (Ver II Tes. 3:9 e Apocalipse 13:2-5). Satanás será adorado indiretamente, por meio dele (ver Apo. 13:4).

9. O anticristo será judeu, pois somente tal homem poderá ser o verdadeiro anticristo, a quem Israel acolherá por algum tempo, embora depois venha a rejeitá-lo. (Ver João 5:43). As predições contemporâneas asseveram que ele nasceu a 2 de fevereiro de 1962, na Palestina; foi para um dos países árabes. Atualmente se encontra em Jerusalém.

10. A princípio ele se mostrará amigável para com Israel, recebendo a lealdade dos israelenses (ver Dan. 9:27). Mas, finalmente, voltar-se-á com toda a sua fúria contra a nação de Israel, instituindo uma perseguição e um genocídio sem paralelo. Impor-se-á como um rei, utilizando-se de seus apetrechos para a própria glorificação. Ele é a «abominação desoladora». (Ver esse termo, aplicado ao anticristo, em Dan. 9:27 e 12:11). Em Dan. 11:31, esse epíteto é aplicado a Antíoco Epifânio, que sacrificou uma porca sobre o altar, e, sem autorização, entrou no Santo dos Santos; mas até mesmo nesse mencionado versículo, as referências proféticas apontam para o anticristo dos últimos dias, visto que Antíoco Epifânio foi apenas o seu protótipo, uma pequena figura, em comparação com o que será o anticristo. (Ver no NTI as notas expositivas em Mat. 24:15, acerca da expressão «abominação desoladora»).

11. O aparecimento do anticristo se dará imediatamente antes do período chamado «tribulação», um período prolongado (40 anos, achamos) que envolverá agonias inenarráveis para os habitantes da terra, sem paralelo na história registrada. Muitos esperam que esse período comece na década de 1990. (Ver o artigo sobre a *Tribulação*).

12. O anticristo contará com um «profeta», um «precursor», a exemplo de João Batista (ver Apo. 13:1-8; 16:13; 19:20; 20:10). — Esse precursor possivelmente será a «besta saída do mar», ao passo que o próprio anticristo será a «besta saída da terra» (ver Apo. 13:11-17). Mas alguns intérpretes revertem essa ordem. Somente o tempo mostrará quem está com a razão. Seja como for, esse precursor, de acordo ainda com certos indícios de previsões de místicos, será um político do estado de Nova Iorque, nos Estados Unidos da América do Norte. O que parece claro é que, por meio dos modernos meios de comunicação em massa, esse político fará o anticristo tornar-se conhecido por todo o mundo, preparando o mundo para acolhê-lo de braços abertos. O mundo inteiro cortejará seus favores; mas, eventualmente, ele despedaçará o mundo e seus seguidores, reduzindo-os a nada e esmigalhando todo o bem que porventura ainda restar neles.

13. Ele obrigará a humanidade a adorar a Satanás, na tentativa de extirpar da terra o conhecimento de Deus. A igreja cristã daquela época terá de viver subterraneamente, porquanto o anticristo removerá toda e qualquer expressão visível da mesma, conforme a conhecemos atualmente. Perseguirá a *todos* quantos prestam lealdade a Deus e a seu Ungido, e grandes multidões serão martirizadas por esse motivo. (Ver Apo. 13:15). (Quanto à questão intensamente debatida, que pergunta se a Igreja passará ou não pela «grande tribulação», ver as notas expositivas sobre I Tes. 4:15 no NTI). Mas as Escrituras dão a entender que haverá uma igreja cristã que se oporá a esse indivíduo, e que um número incalculável de pessoas encontrará a Cristo, devido à oposição ao anticristo.

14. O anticristo aplicará sanções econômicas, exigindo certa marca identificadora para quem quiser comprar ou vender. Até mesmo hoje certas formas de tatuagens invisíveis já existem, que podem ser vistas sob certos raios de luz. A marca da besta pode ter algo a ver com isso, ou ser de idêntica natureza.

15. O próprio anticristo terá alguma forma de identificação numérica, a saber, seiscentos e sessenta e seis. Ver o artigo separado *Sinal* (*Marca*) *da Besta* (*Anticristo*) que apresenta detalhes. Quando ele aparecer, tornar-se-á claro o significado desse número, embora talvez ninguém consiga decifrá-lo até então. Nenhuma predição bíblica é escrita para satisfazer à curiosidade daqueles que vivem em tempos distantes do cumprimento da mesma, mas antes, para a instrução e para a ajuda daqueles que viverem no tempo em que essas profecias se cumprirem. Por conseguinte, esse número, que é tão obscuro para nós, será perfeitamente claro para aqueles que testemunharem o aparecimento do anticristo, o que servirá de identificação de sua pessoa. É interessante observar que o valor numérico de 1962 — que seria o seu ano de nascimento — é dezoito e dezoito é três de *seis*. Esse cálculo pode ser significativo ou não como fato que confirmará as predições contemporâneas dos místicos acerca da vinda do anticristo, e que muitos pensam ter nascido no ano aludido.

16. O conceito do anticristo não deve ser reduzido a um conflito «impessoal» entre o bem e o mal; antes, deve ser interpretado «pessoalmente». O anticristo será a encarnação de Satanás, um indivíduo autêntico, tal como Cristo Jesus era a encarnação de Deus, *uma pessoa real*. Não obstante, em sua própria pessoa o anticristo incorporará o conflito milenar entre o bem e o mal; e nele o mal será destroçado quando da «parousia» ou segundo advento de Cristo. Por assim dizer, o anticristo será a última e desesperadora tentativa de Satanás para levar o mal a dominar inteiramente ao mundo.

17. O *anticristo* promoverá a 3ª e a 4ª Guerras Mundiais, utilizando a aliança ocidental como seu instrumento de ação. Uma grande destruição mútua de nações resultará. Das cinzas, Israel se levantará como o chefe das nações e um *novo ciclo* começará. Por 1000 anos, Israel será o protetor da civilização e a nova capital da Igreja cristã, porque se converterá a Cristo em meio a *Grande Tribulação* (que vide).

Aspectos históricos da doutrina do anticristo. Essa doutrina tem passado por certo desenvolvimento, que

ANTICRISTO

pode ser acompanhado historicamente, o que fazemos através dos pontos abaixo determinados:

1. No Antigo Testamento. Cristo é revelado, nas páginas do A.T., através de profecias preditivas e tipos simbólicos; e isso se dá também no caso do anticristo. a. *Belial*: Havia certos indivíduos infames, devido à sua impiedade, iniqüidade e tendências destruidoras. Eram homens «inúteis», «idólatras», opositores de Deus e do bem. Caracterizavam-se pela «sodomia» e pela «violação» (ver Juí. 19:22; 20:13); pela «idolatria» (ver Deut. 13:13); pela total desconsideração por Deus e pelo bem (ver I Sam. 2:12); pelo sacrilégio (ver I Sam. 2:17,22); pelo desrespeito para com as idéias e os objetos santos, bem como para com toda e qualquer autoridade (ver I Sam. 10:27 e II Crô. 13:7); pela ausência de hospitalidade (ver I Sam. 25:17,25); pelo perjúrio (ver I Reis 21:10,13); pela má língua (ver Pro. 6:12 e 16:27). Esses são homens «vazios», vãos e ousados (ver II Crô. 13:7), os quais devem ser evitados pelos homens bons (ver Sal. 101:3). Esses indivíduos prefiguram o que será o anticristo, em sua revelação suprema. b. Os inimigos estrangeiros da nação de Israel. O anticristo será uma figura universal, mas inimigo especial de Israel, pelo que também o A.T. o tipifica mediante os inimigos históricos de Israel. As nações se insurgem contra Deus e contra o seu Ungido (ver o Salmo segundo); e isso é prefiguração da pessoa do anticristo e de suas forças ímpias. Os monarcas que usurpam o poder e lutam contra Deus perecerão (ver Isa. 14; Eze. 28; 39:1-20 e Apo. 20:7-10). O anticristo encabeçará um conflito infrutífero contra a autoridade de Deus no mundo, e contra Aquele para quem será dada verdadeira autoridade, a saber, o Senhor Jesus Cristo. c. A profecia do «pequeno chifre» (ver Dan. 7,8 e 9). Essa é uma visão sobre o domínio gentílico sobre o mundo, — até o fim. No fim levantar-se-ão dez reis, mas entre eles surgirá um que subjugará a três dos dez, tão completamente, que sua identidade separada se perderá. Sete «reis» serão então deixados; e entre eles o *pequeno chifre* surgirá, que é igualmente o oitavo. Esse é tipificado por Antíoco Epifânio (175 — 165 A.C. — ver Dan. 8:23-25). Será também o «príncipe que virá» (ver Dan. 9:26,27), o «rei» de feroz catadura (ver Dan. 11:36-45), a abominação desoladora (ver Dan. 12:11 e Mat. 24:15), o homem do pecado (ver II Tes. 2:4-8) e a «besta» (ver Apo. 13:4-10). O anticristo fará o que lhe aprouver, tão grande será a sua autoridade; exaltar-se-á acima de todo o deus, e dirá coisas maravilhosas contra Deus, prosperando até chegar o tempo de sua queda repentina (ver Dan. 11:36). Também não terá consideração alguma pelo Deus de seus pais (pois quase certamente será ele um judeu), e nem levará em conta o «desejo de mulheres», ou qualquer objeto santo, ou mesmo o conceito sagrado de Deus. Mas antes, honrará ao deus das forças, que talvez seja uma adoração natural e impessoal, através da ciência (ver Dan. 11:37,38). Porá fim às formas de adoração de Israel (ver Dan. 11:31; Mat. 24:15; Mar. 13:14 e Apo. 13:14,15).

2. No Período Intertestamental. Roma substitui a Síria como inimigo nacional da nação de Israel. Pompeu suplanta a Antíoco IV, a epítome da oposição a Deus. E Belial se torna o «espírito satânico» de impiedade que há no mundo. O «iníquo» tem sido identificado com Beliar, na tradição rabínica, sendo seu nome interpretado como «sem jugo», isto é, sem a lei, sem consideração alguma pela autoridade leis.

3. No Novo Testamento. Os evangelhos advertem contra os falsos profetas e contra os falsos cristos, que serão tão enganadores que terão o poder de enganar até mesmo aos eleitos. (Ver Mat. 24:24; Mar. 13:22). Essas advertências encontram seu ponto máximo no personagem isolado do anticristo. Um personagem terrível em sua maldade, será acolhido por algum tempo pela nação de Israel, como se fora o próprio Messias (ver João 5:43). A passagem de II Tes. 2:3 e ss é uma das mais claras da Bíblia sobre o anticristo. Será ele o «ateu» supremo, apresentando-se ao mundo como se fora ele o próprio Deus; empregado na causa do mal. O trecho de II Tes. 2:4 nos faz lembrar de Dan. 7:25 e 11:36. O anticristo será um arquienganador, e terá poder de enganar até mesmo por meio de prodígios, visto ser ele a própria encarnação de Satanás. (Ver II Tes. 2:9,10 e Apo. 13:14,15. Ver também as notas expositivas, no começo desta discussão, quanto a um estudo mais profundo sobre as características do anticristo, onde trechos neotestamentários adicionais são dados, no tocante a esse personagem).

4. Na Igreja. Naturalmente, — um tema profético como esse tem recebido muitíssimas interpretações em conflito. As interpretações corretas haverão de emergir dos próprios acontecimentos, os quais definirão a questão de modo inconfundível. Então compreenderemos perfeitamente as profecias preditivas; e isso será uma grande ajuda para aqueles que estiverem vivos naquela época, os quais compreenderão a natureza do que estão passando, e como poderão resistir às provas. Os pais da igreja primitiva, em geral, criam em um anticristo pessoal. O indivíduo para quem apontavam mais constantemente era *Nero*; havia lendas que diziam que ele reapareceria «redivivo». Essa idéia mui provavelmente se baseava em Apo. 13:3,14, literal e pessoalmente interpretada. Em séculos posteriores, Crisóstomo continuou anunciando essa interpretação; e outros, em tempos modernos, como R.H. Charles, C.A. Scott e William R. Newell, têm mantido viva essa interpretação. Irineu cria que o anticristo seria um indivíduo, e pensava que ele se levantaria da tribo de Dã, com base nos trechos de Gên. 49:17; Deut. 33:22; Jer. 8:16 (ver a omissão da tribo de Dã, em Apo. 7:5 e ss). No tempo da reforma protestante era natural, embora errôneo, que o anticristo e o falso profeta fossem equiparados ao papado, ou então, a um ou outro papa, individualmente. A Igreja Católica Romana retaliou, mediante seus eruditos, tachando os reformadores e todos os oponentes de Roma de *anticristos*. Em tempos mais modernos, muitos têm favorecido o ponto de vista «simbólico» sobre o anticristo, como se se tratasse de uma doutrina que não visa ensinar que algum indivíduo será a epítome do mal, da oposição contra Deus e seu Ungido, a perseguir a nação de Israel e a igreja cristã. Segundo esse ponto de vista, o anticristo seria o sistema mundano ímpio, ou seu elemento religioso iníquo. Mas muitos elementos, na igreja evangélica moderna, de tipo fundamentalista, continuam crendo na vinda pessoal do anticristo, e as profecias preditivas dos místicos contemporâneos confirmam esse ponto de vista, em contraste com o ponto de vista simbólico. M.R. Dehann ensinava que o anticristo seria Judas reencarnado. Também têm sido apresentadas outras identificações, usualmente Nero ou algum outro dos primeiros imperadores romanos. Alguns intérpretes acreditam que o anticristo já passou diversas reencarnações, se desenvolvendo para cumprir seu papel mais terrível e maligno. Entre esses intérpretes, há alguns que dizem que a última reencarnação do *anticristo* era *Hitler*. — Hitler, que matou seis milhões de judeus, — voltará, afinal, como seu

ANTÍFONA — ANTIGO TESTAMENTO

falso messias — Grande golpe! Hitler, que em sua batalha, lutava contra o imperialismo econômico americano, e contra o comunismo (seus dois grandes inimigos), mas perdeu; voltará para garantir o conflito entre estes dois elementos, provocando uma grande destruição dos dois. Grande golpe! Mas tudo isso permanece dentro de uma categoria duvidosa, ao passo que o próprio ensinamento sobre o anticristo, vai se tornando mais e mais claro, à medida que os acontecimentos que o cercam se avizinham de nós. (B E H NTI W Z)

ANTÍFONA

Uma frase extraída da Bíblia, contada antes e depois dos cânticos e salmos no oficio divino (ver o artigo a respeito), de acordo com o ânimo dessa festa ou período eclesiástico. O termo também é usado para indicar um salmo entoado como antifonia, pelos dois lados do coro.

ANTIGO SÍMBOLO ROMANO

No começo do atual século XX, o professor A.C. McGiffert apresentou argumentos em favor da teoria de que o inteiro Credo dos Apóstolos (ver o artigo a respeito) foi composto para combater a Márcion e suas heresias. Ali, o Deus Criador é identificado com o Pai de Jesus; Jesus é identificado com o Filho do Deus Criador. E também é ali defendida a idéia da ressurreição física dos mortos. Em 1919, Karl Holf propôs ainda uma outra interpretação, não se sentindo satisfeito com o que dissera o professor McGiffert. A fraqueza dessas teorias é que todos os elementos fazem parte dos ensinos do Novo Testamento, não se tendo derivado da oposição oferecida por Márcion. Todavia, não se deve duvidar de que a formação daquele Credo teve por propósito tentar combater qualquer forma de heresia que não concordasse com os ensinos da Igreja cristã da época.

ANTIGO TESTAMENTO

Cada livro do Antigo Testamento tem seu próprio artigo. Portanto, somente aquelas coisas que dizem respeito ao Antigo Testamento como um todo, além de um breve sumário de cada livro, são aqui consideradas.

1. Designação e Coleção dos Livros
2. Origem e Preservação
3. Principais Divisões
4. Valor
5. Relação com o Novo Testamento
6. Breve Pesquisa do Conteúdo dos Livros.

1. Designação e Coleção dos Livros

A palavra «Bíblia» vem do grego **bíblia**, forma plural de *bíblion*, «livro». Essa palavra, por sua vez, derivou-se da palavra que significa «papiro». A letra final *a*, da palavra bíbli*a* é um plural grego, que não deve ser confundido com o feminino singular latino. A palavra «Testamento» vem da LXX, *diatheke*, que pode significar ou «pacto» ou «testamento», embora o primeiro seja um nome mais apropriado, o que daria em resultado Antigo Pacto e Novo Pacto.

O Antigo Testamento consiste em trinta e nove livros, cerca de oito treze avos do volume inteiro da Bíblia. Os trinta e nove livros do cânon protestante são idênticos ao cânon hebreu da Palestina. O Antigo Testamento impresso pela Igreja Católica Romana adiciona onze dos catorze livros apócrifos da versão da LXX, a Bíblia grega dos judeus das áreas fora da Palestina. Ver o artigo sobre a *Septuaginta* (LXX). Ver também o artigo sobre o *Cânon*.

2. Origem e Preservação

Todos os livros, de qualquer natureza têm um pano de fundo terreno, próprio do seu meio ambiente, cultural, histórico e humano. Qualquer interpretação das Escrituras, portanto, deve levar em conta esses elementos. Ver o artigo sobre *Crítica da Bíblia*. Todavia, alguns livros têm-se distinguido, além disso, como dotados do poder e da inspiração de Deus. Esses são os livros da Bíblia. Ver o artigo sobre *Inspiração*. Ora, se há uma inspiração divina, há também uma autoridade especial (ver o artigo a respeito). Os trechos de II Timóteo 3:16 e II Ped. 1:20,21 declaram a inspiração do Antigo Testamento. E dentro dos próprios livros do Antigo Testamento encontramos com freqüência a frase: «Assim diz o Senhor». Essa é a base da mensagem dos profetas, que foram apenas agentes de Deus. A consciência de que dispunham de algo ímpar, levou Israel a preservar suas Escrituras com cuidado e diligência. Os escritos inspirados requerem leitores iluminados, sujeitos à orientação do Espírito. No mínimo, requerem uma leitura cuidadosa e uma avaliação justa, mesmo da parte daqueles que duvidam de sua autoridade. Livros que têm resistido ao teste de muitos séculos de exame não podem ser tratados superficialmente. Somente o valor intrínseco pode garantir tão extraordinária preservação como se dá com a Bíblia.

3. Principais Divisões

a. O Pentateuco: Gênesis, Êxodo, Levítico, Números e Deuteronômio.

b. Livros Históricos: Josué, Juízes, Rute, I e II Samuel, I e II Reis, I e II Crônicas, Esdras, Neemias e Ester.

c. Livros Poéticos: Jó, Salmos, Provérbios, Eclesiastes, Cantares de Salomão.

d. Profetas Maiores: Isaías, Jeremias, Lamentações, Ezequiel e Daniel.

e. Profetas Menores: Oséias, Joel, Amós, Obadias, Jonas, Miquéias, Naum, Habacuque, Sofonias, Ageu, Zacarias e Malaquias.

Uma divisão ainda mais simples: A Lei, os Profetas e os Salmos (ver Luc. 24:44).

Outros escritos judaicos. Os livros apócrifos e pseudepígrafos são citados ocasionalmente no Novo Testamento, o que seria apenas natural esperarmos, visto que os livros apócrifos faziam parte da LXX, e os livros pseudepígrafos eram largamente usados como fontes informativas, nas seções proféticas, porquanto ali a tradição apocalíptica dos judeus tem o seu desenvolvimento. Quanto ao valor e extensão do uso dessas obras, nas comunidades judaica e cristã, ver os artigos sobre cada uma delas.

4. Valor

Consideremos as minúsculas dimensões de Israel. No entanto, daquela pequena nação originaram-se documentos universais e imortais, que contêm uma literatura verdadeiramente grandiosa e importante. Trata-se de daqueles documentos que satisfazem ao anelo do coração humano; em caso contrário, eles jamais teriam exercido tamanha influência. Chegamos mesmo a aludir à nossa cultura como cultura judaico-cristã; e, à base dessa cultura, encontramos o Antigo e o Novo Testamentos.

5. Relação com o Novo Testamento

A Igreja cristã, em quase sua inteireza, tem considerado o Antigo Testamento como autoritário. Jesus ensinou que Moisés, os profetas e os salmos testificam a respeito Dele (ver Luc. 24:44). No Novo

ANTIGO TESTAMENTO

Testamento aparecem entre cento e cinqüenta e trezentas citações diretas, extraídas do Antigo Testamento, e há muitas alusões, sem citação direta. Incluindo as alusões, o número de trechos citados, direta ou indiretamente, chega acerca de mil. Ver o artigo *Citações no Novo Testamento*. Os autores sagrados, quase todos eles judeus, utilizaram-se do Antigo Testamento como base autoritativa para o Novo. E, como é óbvio, muitas idéias são passadas diretamente de um para o outro Testamento. Temas fundamentais vinculam entre si no Antigo e no Novo Testamentos: o ponto de vista monoteísta de Deus; o tema da redenção (ver Gên. 3:15); a expectação messiânica (ver Mal. 3:1-3); o princípio do pacto; o homem como uma raça decaída no pecado; a orientação da providência divina sobre a história da humanidade; e finalmente, a tradição profética. O Antigo Testamento sustenta uma relação vital, preparatória e inseparável para com o Novo Testamento. O Novo Testamento está contido no Antigo Testamento, e este desdobra-se no Novo Testamento. As expressões «Antigo Testamento» e «Novo Testamento» foram popularizadas pelos pais latinos da Igreja. Os dois Testamentos foram intitulados «Antigo» e «Novo» a fim de que fossem distinguidas as Escrituras cristãs das Escrituras judaicas. Mas há declarações específicas, no Novo Testamento, que afirmam a inspiração divina do Antigo Testamento (ver II Tim. 3:16 e II Ped. 1:20,21). Muitas personagens e coisas que figuram no Antigo Testamento são tipos de Cristo e, em determinados aspectos, do cristianismo neotestamentário. A epístola aos Hebreus é a declaração clássica a esse respeito. Até mesmo os eventos históricos do Antigo Testamento têm aplicação a Cristo e à Sua Igreja, como a travessia do mar Vermelho (ver I Cor. 10:1,2), a conquista de Canaã, sob a liderança de Josué, o descanso espiritual no qual entramos mediante a fé (ver Heb. 3:4), a chamada de Israel para fora do Egito, o retorno de Jesus do Egito à Palestina, após a morte de Herodes (ver Mat. 2:15), etc. Acrescenta-se a isso as inúmeras profecias do Antigo Testamento que foram cumpridas em Cristo, o que faz de Jesus a pessoa que une os dois pactos entre si. No NTI, nas notas sobre Atos 3:22, são alistadas essas profecias, com as referências correspondentes. Além disso, precisamos levar em conta a prova histórica da unidade dos dois Testamentos. Poderia ser considerado mero acaso histórico o fato de que, durante muitos séculos, o Antigo e Novo Testamentos têm sido impressos e encadernados juntos, formando um único grande livro, a *Bíblia*?

6. Breve Pesquisa do Conteúdo dos Livros
A. O Pentateuco:

a. *Gênesis*. Ali aparecem, pela primeira vez, os títulos descritivos de Deus: El, Adonai e Yahweh. Esse é o verdadeiro Deus, o Criador. Nele todas as coisas têm a sua origem. O homem foi criado por Deus e caiu no pecado. O perdão foi prometido, e teve início o tema messiânico da redenção, logo após a queda. Deus enviou o juízo do dilúvio, uma das grandes catástrofes que se abateu sobre o mundo, dentre muitas outras que não estão registradas nas páginas da Bíblia, mas cujo fim assinalou um novo começo para a humanidade, com os descendentes dos três filhos de Noé: Sem, Cão e Jafé. Abraão foi chamado de descendente de Sem. Com os descendentes de Abraão, Deus formou a nação de Israel, um dos veículos da redenção. Os primeiros descendentes de Abraão, isto é, Isaque, Jacó e seus doze filhos, são chamados de «os patriarcas». Todavia, os descendentes de Abraão terminaram escravizados no Egito. Ali, José foi a grande luz da espiritualidade, tendo salvo a sua gente da inanição.

b. *Êxodo*. Moisés, descendente de Abraão através de Levi, foi preparado para libertar o povo de Israel da servidão egípcia. Após o êxodo, Moisés foi usado por Deus para produzir uma nova expressão espiritual de grande magnitude: a lei mosaica. Israel apostatou, mas retornou ao Senhor. O sábado foi ordenado, e o tabernáculo e suas formas próprias de adoração foram instituídos.

c. *Levítico*. Esse livro descreve os muitos regulamentos cerimoniais que governam todos os aspectos da vida religiosa e civil dos israelitas. Ali aparecem seis tipos de sacrifícios cruentos, os quais retratam diversos aspectos da expiação. Também preceitua-se ali sobre animais limpos e imundos, sobre a santidade cerimonial em todos os níveis da vida, sobre a celebração do sábado, da páscoa, dos pães asmos, do Pentecoste, da festa das Trombetas e da festa dos Tabernáculos. O vigésimo sexto capítulo desse livro prediz o cativeiro assírio e o babilônico, mas sobretudo este último, porque fala no retorno, embora sem designá-lo especificamente por nome.

d. *Números*. Temos ali as jornadas de Israel desde o monte Sinai até às fronteiras de Canaã, em Cades-Barnéia. Temos ali o relato dos castigos motivados pela incredulidade; os quarenta anos de vagueação pelo deserto; a chegada às planícies de Moabe; os encontros com Balaque e Balaão; o recenseamento no começo do relato, e outro no fim (ver Lev. 26), quando então havia seiscentos mil homens em armas; o estabelecimento dos levitas como uma casta sacerdotal; os espias enviados a Canaã; as queixas e rebeldias contra Moisés; a conquista da Transjordânia; e, finalmente, como os israelitas em Moabe, foram induzidos a cair em idolatria.

e. *Deuteronômio*. Temos ali as instruções finais dadas por Moisés; a reiteração da lei (de onde vem o nome do livro = «segundo livro da lei»); diversas novas provisões, para quando Israel se estabelecesse em Canaã; a leitura pública do pacto; a invocação de testemunhas para que qualquer causa tivesse validade; cópias da lei que tiveram de ser guardadas na arca da aliança; e as admoestações finais a Israel, para que fosse leal ao pacto.

B. Livros Históricos:

a. *Josué*. A conquista da Terra Prometida é o tema principal desse livro; o cumprimento das promessas terrenas feitas a Abraão; a incomum dedicação e espírito decidido de Josué; as vitórias e os retrocessos da conquista; o estabelecimento das cidades de refúgio; a distribuição do território entre as dez tribos que ficaram na margem direita do rio Jordão; as cidades para os levitas; o desafio de Josué ao povo, para que renovasse sua lealdade a Yahweh.

b. *Juízes*. As gerações subseqüentes não completaram a conquista da Terra Prometida; fracassos morais e religiosos devido ao contato com povos pagãos; o estabelecimento de juízes para governar e libertar o povo de Israel; numerosos conflitos com povos vizinhos, com vitórias e derrotas; a tendência de cada qual fazer o que lhe parecia melhor; tempos violentos, quando ninguém tinha a sua vida segura; o bárbaro assassinato da concubina do levita, em Gibeá, o que levou à punição armada contra a tribo de Benjamim, da qual quase resultou a extinção dessa tribo.

c. *Rute*. Uma terna e romântica narrativa, durante o tempo dos juízes, que envolveu a moabita Rute e sua sogra israelita, Noemi. Tendo voltado a Belém, Noemi, não abandonada por sua nora viúva, Rute,

ANTIGO TESTAMENTO

atraiu para esta o favor de Boaz, rico solteirão e primo de Noemi. Noemi reivindicou-o como seu parente-remidor, e Rute casou-se com ele, tornando-se uma das ancestrais do futuro rei Davi, e, conseqüentemente, de Jesus de Nazaré.

d. *I e II Samuel*. Dias finais do sumo sacerdote Eli, tutor do menino Samuel, que fora dado por sua mãe ao serviço do Senhor; os filisteus derrotam Israel em Silo, e tomam a arca da aliança; uma praga força os filisteus a devolverem a arca. Samuel derrota os filisteus e coroa Saul como rei. Saul entra em inúmeras batalhas, com vitórias e derrotas. Davi desafia e derrota o herói dos filisteus, o gigante Golias. Tendo desobedecido a Deus, Saul é rejeitado. Muitas vicissitudes, através de mais de uma dezena de anos, levam Davi ao trono, depois dele ter sido forçado ao exílio. Davi expressa o desejo de edificar um templo em honra ao Senhor. As muitas conquistas militares bem-sucedidas de Davi. Revolta de Absalão, filho de Davi, a morte violenta de Absalão. Os trinta grandes heróis de Davi. O recenseamento ordenado por Davi é desaprovado e julgado por Deus.

e. *I e II Reis*. Tem prosseguimento a narrativa da monarquia hebréia, desde Salomão até Zedequias. I Reis termina com a morte de Acabe (835 A.C.). Salomão, como rei, com seus pontos fortes e fracos, levanta o templo. Fama e riquezas de Salomão; sua grosseira poligamia. Ocorre a separação permanente entre Israel, ao norte, e Judá, ao sul. Relatos dos ministérios de Elias e Eliseu. As intermináveis lutas de Israel e Judá, em conflito com povos vizinhos, com vitórias e derrotas. Os cativeiros assírio e babilônico. O retorno dos judeus à Terra Prometida. As descobertas arqueológicas têm confirmado a existência de mais de cinqüenta dos reis de Israel e Judá.

f. *I e II Crônicas*. A história de Israel é revisada, do ponto de vista de sua relação do pacto nacional com Deus. O sacerdócio divinamente determinado; a teocracia de Davi. Esses livros não tratam sobre Israel, o reino do norte, porquanto esse representa um cisma. Ênfase sobre a rica herança espiritual dos judeus. Elevados momentos de fé, confiança e vitórias de reis como Reoboão, Asa, Josafá. Também trágicos lapsos de fé e obediência, como o adultério e homicídio praticados por Davi, a grosseira poligamia de Salomão e sua permissividade quanto à idolatria. Finalmente, o cativeiro babilônico de Judá e a soltura dos judeus do cativeiro, por ordens de Ciro, imperador da Pérsia.

g. *Esdras*. Retorna à Palestina, em 537 A.C., a primeira vez leva quarenta e dois mil judeus, vindos da Babilônia. Esses fundam o segundo reino, lançam os alicerces do templo e reiniciam as atividades religiosas dos judeus. Algumas décadas mais tarde, Esdras vem da Babilônia à Palestina, com a aprovação do imperador, a fim de ajudar na restauração espiritual da pequena e desencorajada província de Judá (457 A.C.). Esdras leva os judeus a se desfazerem de suas esposas estrangeiras e dá início a uma restauração geral da lei, dos costumes e da religião.

h. *Neemias*. Ele era o copeiro do imperador persa, relatando-nos como foi autorizado a servir como governador de Judá (a partir de 446 A.C.). Liderou no reergimento das muralhas de Jerusalém e restaurou seus compatriotas a uma postura decente de defesa e auto-respeito, diante dos povos vizinhos hostis. Várias dificuldades foram enfrentadas e ultrapassadas. Neemias promoveu um reavivamento, por ocasião da festa dos Tabernáculos, e os judeus adquiriram um novo interesse pelas Escrituras e pelas tradições de sua nação. Esdras determinou a expulsão de certos estrangeiros que viviam em aposentos do templo, e insistiu sobre o pagamento de dízimos, para sustento dos ministros do templo. O sábado passou a ser novamente respeitado, e os judeus divorciaram-se de suas mulheres estrangeiras.

i. *Ester*. Nesse livro relata-se o livramento da nação judaica, na Pérsia, do genocídio arquitetado por Hamã, primeiro-ministro do imperador, que odiava os judeus. Hamã ignorava que a bela e jovem rainha de Xerxes (Assuero), de nome Ester, era prima de Mordecai. Mordecai era o judeu que recusara prestar homenagem a Hamã, o que deu início ao drama inteiro. Sem ter sido convidada à presença do imperador, Ester arriscou sua vida, intercedendo em favor de sua gente. A forca preparada para Mordecai, em vez disso, foi usada para execução de Hamã. Essa vitória é celebrada pelos judeus mediante a festa de Purim (ver o artigo a respeito).

C. Livros Poéticos:

a. *Jó*. Se o relato é real, então tudo ocorreu no norte da Arábia. Mas a ausência de qualquer genealogia indica, para alguns que o livro é uma espécie de romance filosófico, criado com o propósito de ensinar lições morais e espirituais, especialmente no que tange ao problema do mal. Por que o justo sofre? Satanás é retratado como um espírito dotado do poder de provocar toda a espécie de males contra os homens. Podemos aceitar essa exposição se supormos que Deus permite os acontecimentos tendo em vista o nosso bem, e também se lembrarmos que os judeus não sabiam explicar devidamente as causas, tendendo por esquecer-se de que há uma primeira causa (Deus), e muitas causas secundárias, que podem operar e realmente operam de modo independente de Deus. Para alguns, é motivo de perturbação saber que Deus deu ouvidos a Satanás, permitindo que um homem inocente sofresse, sob instigação do diabo. Mas isso exprime uma antiga teologia que não resiste ao teste da veracidade. Ou, alternativamente, Deus pode permitir que o crente sofra injustamente, a fim de acrisolá-lo, extraindo a escória e deixando sua fé mais pura — exatamente o que sucedeu a Jó. Apesar desse senão, o livro aborda o tema do mal e do sofrimento com grande maestria, e isso em meio à mais excelente poesia do tipo hebraico.

É interessante como alguns estudiosos ficam desapontados diante do final da história, pois tudo terminou tão bem para Jó, ao passo que a vida humana, mais freqüentemente, termina em tragédia. De fato, as tragédias gregas, nas quais o herói sofre perdas variadas e irreparáveis, são mais fiéis à realidade humana. Por causa desse «fim» benigno, alguns têm suposto que o final do livro de Jó não é autêntico aos fatos, embora não haja a menor evidência textual para tal idéia. Nem sempre as tragédias terminam tragicamente. Apesar de sua vida terrena ter terminado tragicamente, houve uma reversão mais do que compensadora, mediante Sua gloriosa ressurreição, e Jesus recomendou aos Seus seguidores: «...tende bom ânimo, eu venci o mundo» (João 16:33). Essa é a lição do livro de Jó.

b. *Salmos*. Em sua maior parte, os cento e cinqüenta salmos são orações ou cânticos de louvor e petição, que refletem as experiências diárias, com as suas muitas alegrias, tristezas, perigos e aspirações, tanto terrenas quanto espirituais. Dentre esses salmos, setenta e três são atribuídos a Davi. Mas como alguns salmos são anônimos, é possível que também tenham sido de sua autoria. Além dos salmos de natureza pessoal e humana, há aqueles de natureza

ANTIGO TESTAMENTO

teológica, reveladores da pessoa e do poder de Deus, tanto em Si mesmo como no Seu relacionamento com os homens. No Novo Testamento, o livro de Salmos é o mais citado de todos os livros do Antigo Testamento, e muitos deles têm um pronunciado caráter messiânico. Dez dos Salmos são atribuídos aos filhos de Coré (Sal. 42, 44 - 49, 84, 87 e 88), e doze a Asafe (Sal. 50, 73 - 83). O Salmo 90 é atribuído a Moisés; o Salmo 127 a Salomão; o Salmo 83 a Hamã; e o Salmo 89 a Etã. Salmos anônimos, entre outros, são os de números 103, 104 e 119. Alguns dos Salmos eram usados na liturgia veterotestamentária, e muitos deles exprimem a personalidade de Israel como uma corporação, e não apenas as emoções de alguns salmistas individuais.

c. *Provérbios*. Essa é uma grande coletânea de máximas vigorosas, de encorajamentos positivos e de advertências, por detrás da qual brilha a famosa sabedoria de Salomão, o qual falou sobre todas as situações imagináveis da vida diária. Alguns temas dizem respeito aos pais, outros à fidelidade aos votos conjugais, à honestidade nos contratos, aos sábios, aos insensatos, aos ímpios, aos presunçosos, aos bondosos e virtuosos, e outros são advertências acerca de vários vícios.

d. *Eclesiastes*. O filósofo Salomão fala do ponto de vista humano sobre a futilidade de todo esforço e empenho humanos, porquanto, à parte da providência e da orientação divinas, tudo resulta em nada. Alguns pensam que o livro teve dois autores, um dos quais totalmente negativo, que não acredita na existência da alma, ao passo que o outro seria mais esperançoso, crendo na existência e valor da alma. Mas, na conclusão, o livro termina em tom positivo, demonstrando que a finalidade da existência humana é caminhar pela senda do dever: temer a Deus e guardar os Seus mandamentos.

e. *Cantares de Salomão*. Esse é o livro poético que mais tem suscitado debates. Alguns pensam que ele não deveria fazer parte do cânon do Antigo Testamento. As interpretações do livro são duas: ele exprime o puro amor conjugal, segundo foi ordenado por Deus na criação; ou então simboliza o amor de Cristo por Sua noiva celestial, a Igreja. Todos admitem que até o esboço do livro é difícil de ser acompanhado. Porém, homens e mulheres de ilibada santidade têm encontrado nesse livro um deleite espiritual dos mais profundos. Somente as mentes de forte pendor ascético, que imaginam que o amor marital é condenável, voltam-se contra o livro como indigno de fazer parte da Bíblia.

D. Profetas Maiores:

São assim chamados porque seus livros são mais volumosos que os dos chamados «profetas menores», nada tendo a ver com a importância relativa daqueles em relação a estes últimos.

a. *Isaías*. Livro volumoso de sessenta e seis capítulos, com muitas declarações proféticas, incluindo muitas excelentes predições e descrições messiânicas. Tanto é assim que alguns o têm chamado de «Evangelho segundo Isaías». Reflete um período, na história de Israel, entre 739 e 680 A.C. Isaías era membro da família real judaica. Viveu em uma época de degeneração, pelo que Deus o levantou como Seu profeta. Houve a degeneração de Acaz, o reavivamento encabeçado por Ezequias, e a tremenda apostasia de Manassés. Isaías fala sobre a salvação oferecida por Deus e sobre o prometido Messias, o Deus encarnado. Yahweh não podia tolerar as condições em que vivia Seu povo de Israel, e baixou instruções através de Isaías. Ali é predito o cativeiro babilônico, e também a subseqüente restauração. Dali, a visão profética salta para a era da instauração do reino, que ainda jaz no futuro. O Servo de Yahweh é a grande figura messiânica, nascido virginalmente, o Emanuel ou Deus-homem, que ofereceria a Sua vida como expiação pelos nossos pecados. O Emanuel obteria completa vitória, livrando os remanescentes de seu povo de todos os inimigos internos e externos. A visão de Isaías é muito ampla, abarcando até mesmo o estado eterno futuro, quando bons e maus estarão definitivamente separados, cada qual no seu respectivo destino.

b. *Jeremias*. Um sacerdote e profeta desde a juventude, até a queda de Jerusalém diante dos caldeus, em 587 A.C., e daí até à migração de alguns sobreviventes judeus para o Egito, poucos anos mais tarde. Jeremias foi comissionado por Deus para denunciar a idolatria, a imoralidade e a autocomplacência em que Israel se atolara. Jeremias recomendava que os judeus se submetessem ao governo de Nabucodonosor, a quem Deus apontara como instrumento de disciplina; recomendava também que evitassem alianças com o Egito, na tentativa de escaparem do merecido castigo. Todas as classes sociais haviam-se corrompido, e o juízo divino era inevitável. Mas, após setenta anos de cativeiro, os judeus retornariam à sua terra, e, eventualmente, seriam libertados pelo Messias, descendente de Davi, o qual nesse livro é chamado de Renovo Justo. E os gentios também seriam julgados, no devido tempo, porquanto Deus é o Juiz de todos os homens, em todos os lugares. Muito sofreu Jeremias por sua fidelidade a Deus, tendo sido considerado por muitos judeus como um traidor. Mas Jeremias, mediante a proteção divina sobreviveu a tudo e teve a tristeza de contemplar o cumprimento de suas predições de castigo contra Judá e Jerusalém.

c. *Lamentações*. Nesse pequeno livro, Jeremias exprime a sua angústia ante a total depravação de seu povo, a perda de sua honra e privilégios, de sua liberdade e de suas possessões materiais. Mas, em contraste com isso, ele experimentou a alegria de contemplar a santidade e o eterno amor de Deus. «Grande é a tua fidelidade» (Lam. 3:23).

d. *Ezequiel*. Também era sacerdote, como Jeremias. Viu a glória de Deus, ao iniciar o Seu ministério profético (592 A.C.), e evidentemente prosseguiu profetizando entre seus companheiros de cativeiro, na Babilônia. Os primeiros vinte e quatro capítulos antecipam a queda de Jerusalém diante dos caldeus, um juízo divino contra a idolatria e todos os tipos de pecados e lapsos. Judá contava então com o exemplo negativo de Israel, o reino do norte, que fora levado cativo pelos assírios. Os capítulos vinte e cinco a trinta e dois encerram predições contra a Fenícia, o Egito e outros países vizinhos. Os capítulos trinta e três a trinta e nove predizem a restauração e a renovação espiritual de Israel. Talvez o quadro ali descrito retrate as condições do milênio; ou então um estado ideal, segundo outros estudiosos. O verdadeiro Pastor haverá de levantar-se, no futuro, derrotando as forças de Gogue, Magogue, Ros, etc. Então ressuscitarão os ossos secos. Os capítulos quarenta até o fim, falam sobre o templo durante o milênio (ver o artigo a respeito), com o tipo de adoração que ali haverá. A Terra Prometida desfrutará de grande prosperidade, dotada de uma população numerosa.

e. *Daniel*. O livro foi escrito quando seu autor vivia em cativeiro, na Babilônia, juntamente com todo o povo de Judá. Daniel e três amigos seus, igualmente príncipes da casa real de Judá, obtêm elevadas posições no governo da Babilônia. Perigos criados por

ANTIGO TESTAMENTO

circunstâncias adversas são revertidas mediante revelações dadas a Daniel. Este interpretou o sonho profético de Nabucodonosor, sobre quatro grandes impérios mundiais em sucessão: a Babilônia, a Média-Pérsia, a Grécia e Roma. Os três amigos de Daniel são miraculosamente salvos da fornalha ardente, onde haviam sido lançados por se recusarem a adorar uma estátua levantada pelo imperador. Por não ter deixado de orar a Deus, durante um período proibido de trinta dias, quando todas as orações só podiam ser dirigidas ao imperador, Daniel foi lançado na cova dos leões, mas sua vida foi miraculosamente preservada. Tempos depois, Daniel interpretou a terrível mensagem de julgamento divino contra Belsazar, a qual se cumpriu naquele mesmo dia. Os últimos seis capítulos do livro contêm predições concernentes aos futuros impérios mundiais, especialmente aquele envolvido no reinado de Antíoco Epifânio (ver o artigo a respeito), que foi um tipo do anticristo. Certas porções do livro - caps. 2 a 7 — foram escritas em aramaico; e o resto em hebraico. Daniel foi o inspirador da tradição profética judaica posterior, incluindo os livros pseudepígrafos e o Apocalipse de João, no Novo Testamento. É um dos livros mais importantes do ponto de vista escatológico. O Apocalipse de João completa aquilo que Daniel teve de «selar», isto é, de ocultar (ver Dan. 12:9).

E. Profetas Menores:

a. *Oséias*. Ele pertencia ao — reino do norte —, e ali profetizou, entre 755 e 720 A.C., antes da queda de Samaria, que ocorreu em 722 A.C. A esposa de Oséias era uma mulher adúltera. E isso proveu a ilustração espiritual de Israel como esposa adúltera de Yahweh. Os nomes dos três filhos do profeta tipificavam condições proféticas: a. Jezreel, a destruição da dinastia de Jeú; b. Lo-Ruama, que não haveria restauração nacional das dez tribos do norte; e c. Lo-Ami, que a nação do norte não seria restaurada à relação de pacto com Deus. Há muitas denúncias contra todos os tipos de pecados e crimes. Não obstante, o amor de Yahweh por Israel continuaria, e haveria um remanescente, composto por crentes verdadeiros, que herdariam as promessas do Senhor.

b. *Joel*. Um livro composto em cerca de 830 A.C., o que faz de Joel o primeiro dos profetas «escritores». Seu livro abrange tudo quanto os demais profetas disseram, embora sem entrar em detalhes, os quais foram explorados pelos demais profetas escritores. No tempo da composição do livro, o rei Joás era ainda menor de idade. Os adversários de Judá eram os fenícios, os filisteus, os idumeus e os egípcios (ver Joel 3:4,19). Uma praga de gafanhotos retrata uma futura invasão dos assírios e caldeus. Somente o arrependimento poderia fazer a maré invasora virar. Deus é capaz de derrotar os inimigos e de derramar o Seu Espírito (ver Joel 2:28-32). No dia de Pentecoste, segundo se vê em Atos 2:17, essa predição teve cumprimento parcial; e no futuro teremos o cumprimento cabal da mesma. O julgamento divino foi predito contra os opressores de Israel. Haverá triunfo e paz, afinal, durante o milênio (ver o artigo a respeito).

c. *Amós*. Amós não era profeta e nem filho de profeta, mas apenas um humilde pastor. Não obstante, o Espírito tornou-se um profeta que se opôs à classe sacerdotal, que estava abusando de seus deveres. E isso quase causou a morte de Amós. Ele enviou advertências ao reino do norte (cerca de 760 - 755 A.C.), e declarou também iminente o julgamento divino contra Damasco, Tiro, Gaza e Edom. Judá foi denunciada por estar dando ouvidos a falsos mestres.

Todos os tipos de vícios e exploração ao próximo foram denunciados. Foi predita uma destruição geral, através de vários meios, embora seguida por promessas da futura glória do milênio (ver o artigo). O trecho de Amós 7:10-17 registra um choque ocorrido entre Amós e o sacerdote do santuário real de Betel, chamado Amazias.

d. *Obadias*. Livro que tem um único capítulo, escrito em cerca de 841 A.C., durante o reinado de Jeorão, quando os filisteus e árabes invasores aparentemente foram ajudados pelos idumeus, na pilhagem de Jerusalém. Edom foi denunciado, e um severo julgamento foi proferido, devido aos abusos cometidos contra Israel.

e. *Jonas*. Foi um profeta desobediente a princípio, não querendo entregar uma mensagem divina de juízo contra Nínive. Para fugir do compromisso, tomou um navio para Társis, porto ocidental do Mediterrâneo. O navio foi vitimado por um imenso temporal. Os marinheiros lançaram-no fora, na tentativa de aplacar a ira divina. Uma baleia engoliu o profeta, e mais tarde vomitou-o. Então Jonas resolveu ir pregar em Nínive. Sua mensagem era simples, mas Deus a usou para fazer os ninivitas se arrependerem. A cidade não foi destruída e Jonas entristeceu-se diante do fato. Então Deus precisou ensinar ao profeta uma lição de compaixão, fazendo uma planta crescer e morrer em seguida, para mostrar a Jonas que assim como ele se indignara diante da perda da planta, Deus também não tinha prazer na morte do ímpio.

f. *Miquéias*. Profeta contemporâneo de Isaías, no século VII A.C. Ele foi enviado para anunciar o juízo de Deus contra os reinos do norte e do sul, Israel e Judá, em face de sua idolatria, pecados e muitos lapsos. Os assírios seriam usados como látego. Todas as classes sociais se tinham corrompido, havendo exploração do próximo e pecados morais por todos os lados; e fatalmente sobreviria o juízo. Haveria o exílio, a restauração e o futuro reino messiânico (ver as notas sobre o *Milênio*). A vida religiosa depende da fidelidade e da santidade, e o povo de Israel precisava aprender essa lição.

g. *Naum*. Um profeta que atuou em cerca de 650 - 625 A.C., proclamando a vingança de Deus contra a brutalidade de Nínive, capital da Assíria. Ele descreveu, antecipando, como os caldeus e medos derrubariam a Assíria. Deus afirmava que haveria a restauração de Israel, sob a condição de arrependimento.

h. *Habacuque*. Esse profeta entregou sua mensagem em cerca de 607 A.C., no intervalo entre as batalhas de Megido (609 A.C.) e de Carquemis (605 A.C.). O livro é uma espécie de diálogo entre o profeta e o Senhor, a respeito de Sua maneira de tratar Israel. O profeta fazia perguntas, e Deus dava as respostas. Os caldeus castigariam a pérfida Israel, mas os justos continuariam a rejubilar-se em Deus, embora perdendo suas possessões materiais anteriores e seus luxos.

i. *Sofonias*. Sua mensagem foi entregue no começo do reinado de Josias (cerca de 625 A.C.), predizendo o futuro Dia de Yahweh. A ainda recente invasão dos citas, que devastaram o Oriente Próximo e Médio, em cerca de 630 A.C., serviu de exemplo do que poderia acontecer. Os juízos divinos atingiriam Israel e seus vizinhos. Mas a era do reino seria dada ao remanescente justo. Israel e os povos gentílicos aprenderão a falar a mesma linguagem de fé (ver Sof. 3:9,10).

j. *Ageu*. Após o retorno de Judá do cativeiro babilônico, Ageu exortou o povo a reconstruir o

ANTIINTELECTUALISMO

templo. Este seria mais humilde, mas haveria de renovar as esperanças. A grande esperança prometida seria o Messias, que haveria de chegar ao Seu templo. Portanto, o povo deveria mostrar-se zeloso quanto à reconstrução do templo. E, no espaço de três anos (em 516 A.C.), o novo templo foi dedicado ao Senhor.

l. *Zacarias*. Esse profeta ajudou Ageu em seus esforços (a começar em 519 A.C.). O livro encerra oito visões, cujo intuito era encorajar o povo de Deus, mostrando a intervenção divina e o julgamento do Senhor contra os opressores de Israel; a Assíria, a Babilônia, a Grécia e Roma. Jerusalém seria reconstruída e prosperaria, sendo remida de seus erros e servindo como testemunha aos gentios. No livro há várias profecias messiânicas, como a da entrada triunfal de Jesus em Jerusalém (ver Zac. 9:9,10), inaugurando assim o propósito remidor de Deus. Israel haveria de receber seu Bom Pastor, em substituição aos pastores falsos, e também haveria de converter-se a Cristo, a quem seus antepassados haviam transpassado (ver Zac. 2:10). Portanto, o livro tem um decidido lado escatológico. A idolatria seria removida e os inimigos de Israel seriam derrotados. Jerusalém, embora cercada pelos exércitos do mundo, em situação desesperadora, seria miraculosamente livrada, dando início assim ao período do reino milenar de Cristo, o qual haverá de exercer domínio sobre o mundo inteiro (ver o artigo sobre o *Milênio*).

m. *Malaquias*. Esse foi o último profeta escritor de Judá, a menos que emprestemos algum valor aos livros apócrifos e pseudepígrafos. O uso da pseudepígrafa, pelo vidente João, parece indicar que ele pensava que ali havia material inspirado, ou, pelo menos utilizável, por conter informações precisas. Seja como for, Malaquias é o último profeta escritor do período do Antigo Testamento. Sua data é de cerca de 435 A.C. Ele convocou Judá a voltar à piedade. Sacerdotes negligentes haviam corrompido a adoração no templo, e pecados de todas as variedades corrompiam o povo. Esposas estrangeiras precisavam ser repelidas, e o povo precisava voltar a pagar seus dízimos. São preditos no livro tanto o ministério de Jesus Cristo como o de Seu precursor, João Batista. O juízo seria executado e a justiça seria restaurada.

— O estudo acima é abreviado propositalmente, tencionando apenas dar um esboço geral do Antigo Testamento. O leitor deveria examinar os artigos sobre cada um dos livros do Antigo Testamento. Ver também sobre a *Bíblia*. (E IB ID JE UN VT Z)

ANTIGO TESTAMENTO, *Uso pelos Cristãos Primitivos*. Ver *Uso do Antigo Testamento pelos Cristãos Primitivos*.

ANTIINTELECTUALISMO

1. Na filosofia. A idéia de que o intelecto humano não é suficiente ou digno de confiança para a obtenção do conhecimento, quer isolado (como no racionalismo; ver o artigo) quer combinado com a percepção dos sentidos (como no racionalismo empírico), chama-se antiintelectualismo. Nesse caso, duas posições podem ser adotadas: a. A posição de ceticismo (ver o artigo), que abandona qualquer tentativa de descobrir o verdadeiro conhecimento permitindo que a vida, de modo prático ou ético, seja governada pelo que é pragmático (ver sobre o pragmatismo). b. Ou então, uma atitude antiintelectual pode levar o indivíduo a supor que o conhecimento pode ser obtido por meio da intuição (ver o artigo), ou por meio do misticismo (ver o artigo).

2. Na religião. Temos então a idéia de que a razão humana é inadequada na pesquisa pela verdade religiosa. Assim, a atividade intelectual e o estudo são abandonados e degradados. Em alguns lugares, a ignorância populariza-se, e quase sempre com o acompanhamento da crendice de que o conhecimento obtido intuitiva e misticamente é necessariamente correto. Mas tal atitude ignora diversas coisas: a. Que as experiências intuitivas e místicas devem ser testadas pela razão, pois, do contrário, podem resultar a mistificação, a fraude e a auto-ilusão. b. Que tanto a intuição quanto o misticismo não são caminhos perfeitos para se conhecer e experimentar as coisas, e que, por si mesmos, esses caminhos nunca podem permanecer de pé sozinhos. c. Que a intuição e o misticismo podem ser absolutamente falsos, e que as experiências místicas, que permeiam todas as formas de religião (não estando limitadas a qualquer grupo ou a qualquer variedade de fé religiosa) não podem ser o único alicerce da crença e do dogma. d. Que tanto a intuição quanto o misticismo podem ser usados por poderes demoníacos, tornando-os não apenas falsos, mas até mesmo malignos. e. Que a chamada «fé» algumas vezes consiste em crer naquilo que não corresponde à verdade, e que os grupos que pensam que somente eles têm a verdade, ou que são superiores aos outros (e isso é evidenciado pelas experiências místicas que eles têm), são extremistas e concebem um Deus pequeno demais. Notemos que Paulo admitia que seus opositores gnósticos tivessem experiências místicas (ver Col. 2:18; ver notas completas no NTI). Porém, ele não se impressionava com isso como base da verdade. A verdade e a experiência religiosa nunca repousam sobre uma única coluna. Há muitas colunas que dão respaldo à verdade e ao desenvolvimento espiritual, e uma dessas colunas é o *intelecto*, por meio de sua capacidade de testar e pesquisar.

3. Definição do misticismo. A definição filosófica do misticismo diz, em sua essência, que o ser humano tem a capacidade de entrar em contato direto, de alguma maneira, com o Ser divino ou com as realidades divinas, mediante um processo de contemplação, comunhão, —através da presença do Espírito Santo, ou outra autoridade espiritual. Esse contato direto ultrapassa em importância tanto à percepção dos sentidos quanto à razão. Pode ser sutil como no caso dos impulsos intuitivos internos, ou pode ser avassalador e imposto de cima para baixo, como no caso das visões, de um sonho vívido e compelidor, de uma revelação, de uma visitação por parte de algum ser espiritual, etc. O misticismo oriental enfatiza (posto que não com exclusividade) o misticismo subjetivo. Em outras palavras, o contato com a própria alma ou o eu superior, que seria uma forma exaltada de conhecimento próprio, no qual o indivíduo descobre os segredos do universo, com o qual o «eu» está em harmonia. O misticismo ocidental salienta (posto que não exclusivamente) o misticismo objetivo. Este último é o contato com alguma entidade espiritual fora do próprio indivíduo: como um santo, um espírito, um anjo, Deus, Cristo ou o Espírito Santo. Todas as religiões estão baseadas primariamente no misticismo, porque é a visão do profeta que vem a transformar-se em um Livro Sagrado, o qual então é preservado pela organização religiosa que se forma em torno de suas idéias. As doutrinas, tanto quanto os dons do Espírito, a permanência do Espírito no crente, a regeneração e a santificação são todas doutrinas místicas, porque, dentro do sistema cristão, todas elas requerem a presença e a influência espiritual. Uma declaração mais completa dessa questão aparece sob o título *Misticismo*.

ANTILEGOMENA — ANTILÍBANO

O misticismo, pois, é a principal fonte da verdade espiritual básica, embora não deva ser usada isoladamente. A própria ciência, com suas investigações empíricas, está pesquisando a verdade de Deus, tendo produzido verdades, em muitos campos, importantes para os homens, embora não entre em contato com o Ser divino em qualquer sentido imediato. O intelecto é um dos melhores dons de Deus ao homem. Desprezá-lo é desprezar aquilo que Deus nos deu.

4. Antiintelectualismo. Um dos vícios da maioria dos movimentos religiosos de cunho místico e emocional é a degradação da porção desempenhada pelo intelecto na fé religiosa. Sempre haverá a tendência de dividir o homem, dizendo que ele se presta para isto ou para aquilo, mas não para alguma outra coisa. É absurda a declaração de que a experiência mística é inútil ou impossível com base no fato de que a fé religiosa deveria ser essencialmente racional. É igualmente absurdo dizer que o intelecto não tem serventia à fé, porque o contato místico com Deus é possível e desejável. De fato, Deus fez o homem total, com suas várias capacidades, desde a racional, à intuitiva e à mística. Deus também criou o homem com certa variedade de meios mediante os quais ele pode aproximar-se da divindade, sendo degradante para a criação de Deus enfatizar-se tanto um aspecto e degradar-se a outros. O homem conhece as coisas (incluindo Deus) através da percepção dos sentidos, da razão, da intuição e da experiência mística. Ver os artigos sobre cada um desses itens. Neste ponto, a fé hindu tem sido mais sábia em seus pronunciamentos do que muitos grupos cristãos. Há vários modos de alguém aproximar-se da espiritualidade: 1. *A vereda do amor.* Em outras palavras, o serviço ativo ao próximo e o amor contemplativo a Deus. 2. *A vereda do trabalho.* Algumas pessoas têm grandes tarefas a realizar, e assim ocupam-se com elas, mais do que com as questões intelectuais e místicas. São pessoas produtoras, e talvez até preferissem fazer a obra de Deus do que encontrar-se e conversar com o próprio Deus. 3. *A vereda do conhecimento e do intelecto.* Algumas pessoas deleitam-se no progresso e na aplicação intelectual. São pesquisadoras. O alvo delas é o conhecimento. Conhecimento acerca de tudo e de todas as espécies, visto que todo conhecimento procede de Deus, e finalmente, o conhecimento do próprio Deus, através de outras coisas e independentemente delas. 4. Finalmente, há a *vereda mística*, o caminho da contemplação, dos dons espirituais, dos milagres e do contato com a divindade por via das experiências místicas. Essa é uma maneira legítima de aproximar-se de Deus; mas a fé religiosa é apenas um dos caminhos. É um erro dizer-se que esse é o único caminho, ou mesmo o caminho preferido. Para *alguns*, esse é o caminho predileto; mas, não fale ao homem dedicado ao trabalho sobre tal caminho, e nem force o homem intelectual a passar todo o seu tempo contemplativamente.

A maturidade espiritual. O homem que realmente é maduro espiritualmente é aquele que já percorreu *todos* esses caminhos, quer na vida (ou vidas) física, quer na vida espiritual, antes ou depois da existência física, ou depois da vida física apenas, dependendo do fato da preexistência da alma ser uma realidade ou não. O homem verdadeiramente espiritual percorre a vereda do amor, a vereda do trabalho, a vereda do intelecto e a vereda do misticismo. E cada uma dessas veredas haverá de contribuir para a maturidade dele. Em qualquer vida, física ou espiritual, ele poderá misturar as diversas veredas, já que é perfeitamente possível alguém trabalhar e estudar ao mesmo tempo, e ocasionalmente ter uma experiência mística. Mas, diferentes pessoas, por causa das limitações naturais das coisas, enfatizarão uma coisa ou outra. Assim sendo, é *absurdo* pensar em qualquer dessas veredas como se fosse a única ou a melhor. O que é melhor é obter experiência em *todas as áreas*, e isso só pode ser feito através de um longo período de existência, enquanto a alma passa de um estágio de glória para outro, no processo da transformação espiritual (ver II Cor. 3:18). (E NTI)

ANTILEGOMENA

Vem do grego **antilegomena,** isto é, «disputado» ou «contradito». A palavra era usada pelos primeiros autores cristãos para denotar livros do Novo Testamento, ou relacionados ao mesmo, que, embora geralmente conhecidos entre os cristãos, algumas vezes usados em leituras nas igrejas, não eram realmente aceitos como dignos de fazer parte do cânon. Esses livros eram chamados *disputados* em contraste com os *homologoumena*, ou livros universalmente homologados ou *aceitos*. Os *antilegomena* são: II Pedro, Tiago, Judas, II e III João, Hebreus e Apocalipse. Livros que finalmente não foram incluídos no cânon do Novo Testamento, embora tivessem larga aceitação por algum tempo, foram Barnabé, o Evangelho aos Hebreus, e a Didache. Aparentemente, Orígenes foi o primeiro a usar o termo «antilegomena», e os títulos dados acima identificam os mesmos. Ele considerava como Escrituras Sagradas um certo número desses livros.

Eusébio (até 340 D.C.), de Cesaréia, proveu uma tripla, ou talvez uma quádrupla relação de livros:

1. Os *homologoumena*, os livros universalmente aceitos em sua época.

2. Os *antilegomena*, aqueles que continuavam sendo disputados, conforme mostramos acima, com diferenças.

3. Os *notha*, ou espúrios. Sob esse último título, ele alistava os Atos de Paulo, o Pastor de Hermas, o Apocalipse de Pedro, o evangelho aos Hebreus, a epístola de Barnabé, e a Didache. Nesse grupo ele também incluía o nosso livro canônico Apocalipse de João, embora comentasse que alguns não concordavam com a sua opinião.

4. Os livros totalmente *espúrios* e *ímpios*, que supostamente eram obras dos apóstolos, mas não o eram, como o evangelho de Pedro, Tomé, Matias, os Atos de André, de João e de outros apóstolos. Esses livros ele considerava criações dos hereges. (Ver Eusébio, Hist. III.25). Ver o artigo sobre o *cânon*. (B E S Z)

ANTILÍBANO

Cadeia montanhosa a leste da cadeia do Líbano, mais ou menos da mesma altura e comprimento. O cume mais ao sul é o monte Hermom, que se eleva a mais de 2.700 m. Nas Escrituras temos os nomes de Siriom (Sal. 29:6), Senir (Deu. 3:9) e «Líbano, para o nascente do sol» (Jos. 13:5), para indicar seus picos. O termo Líbano talvez designe ambas as cadeias, embora, algumas vezes, o Senir não inclua o monte Hermom (ver I Crô. 5:23 e Can. 4:8). As duas cadeias montanhosas provêm os mananciais principais do Jordão e de outros rios da região. A forma latina é *Antilibanus*, conforme se vê na Vulgata Latina, para indicar a mesma cadeia. No latim, *lebanus* significa *branco*. (Z)

ANTÍLOPE — ANTINOMIANISMO

ANTÍLOPE

Essa palavra aparece, em algumas traduções, em Deu. 14:5 e Isa. 51:20, ao passo que outras traduções falam no boi selvagem. Na nomenclatura científica, o termo *antílope* a princípio era usado como designação de uma única espécie. Gradualmente, porém, veio a indicar uma família mais genérica, envolvendo muitas espécies. O único antílope — distinguido das gazelas que parece ter sido nativo da Palestina, é o *órix* (ver o artigo a respeito). Esse animal caracteriza-se por ter chifres longos, finos e em forma de cone. Ele é branco, com um conspícuo tufo de pelos sob a garganta. Seu habitat é o Alto Egito, a Arábia e a Síria. Os Targuns traduzem a palavra hebraica como *boi selvagem*. Mas o órix ou bubale, o *antílope bubalis*, provavelmente está em foco. (ID S)

ANTINOMIA

No grego, **anti**, «contra», e **nomos**, «lei», termo usado para aludir a um par de proposições contraditórias, cada uma das quais pode-se demonstrar, derivar-se necessariamente de uma idéia ou premissa comum. Uma antinomia prova ou que a premissa comum é falsa, ou que o raciocínio é inerentemente autocontraditório. Outrossim, é possível que uma certa verdade simplesmente não seja entendida como deve, pelo que proposições contraditórias podem ser extraídas dela.

Na filosofia, temos uma discussão sobre a questão na *Crítica da Razão Pura*, de Kant, na seção sobre as «Aninomias da Razão Pura». Kant alista quatro antinomias. O filósofo budista, Nagarjuna, alista catorze. *Em Kant*, com igual coerência, podemos argumentar em favor do começo do mundo no tempo, ou sua eternidade. Não podemos saber qual a resposta, pois temos apenas fracos sentidos de percepção do mundo; e o próprio mundo é apenas um mundo de aparências, pelo que nada de absoluto pode ser dito quanto à sua natureza. No tocante a Deus, temos os argumentos tradicionais em prol de Sua existência, como os argumentos *ontológico*, *cosmológico* e *teleológico*. (Ver o artigo sobre *Deus, Provas de Sua Existência*). Para Kant, esses argumentos são falazes, pois dependem da transferência de inferências da percepção dos sentidos dentro do contexto do mundo para a área do contexto metafísico, acerca da qual não temos qualquer percepção. Os sentidos que nos falam acerca deste mundo não podem descrever para nós o outro mundo do Espírito. Kant encontrava apoio para a idéia da existência de Deus em bases morais. Ver o *Argumento moral em prol da existência de Deus*.

Considerações teológicas. A palavra **antimonia** usualmente é substituída por *paradoxo* ou *contradição*, sendo largamente aplicada à teologia, indicando vários aspectos inexplicáveis da teologia, como os problemas que envolvem a liberdade e o determinismo, a transcendência e a imanência de Deus, as naturezas divina e humana de Cristo, o julgamento como finito ou infinito, e a aparente contradição entre a lei e a graça. Em nenhum desses casos, porém, há qualquer contradição real. O Logos combina o divino e o humano em Jesus Cristo. O determinismo e o livre-arbítrio são ambos verdades, relacionados a alguma verdade maior que os combinam. Deus é ao mesmo tempo transcendental e imanente. O juízo envolve tanto o que é finito como o é infinito, porquanto produz modificações e opera o bem, jamais mostrando-se estagnado, e também estabelece eternas distinções quanto à posição na glória e na recompensa, além de níveis variados de seres espirituais — os quais chegarão ali por meio da evolução espiritual. Mas, nossa compreensão sobre esses grandes temas é por demais limitada, pelo que a nossa teologia parece cair em contradições. Assim, uma denominação evangélica nega o livre-arbítrio humano, enquanto outra nega o determinismo divino; uma denominação nega a divindade de Cristo, e outra nega a Sua humanidade, etc. A eliminação dos paradoxos, na teologia, requer que o intérprete reduza seus conceitos a categorias que possa compreender de fato. O resultado, porém, é uma teologia infantil. (E EP P)

ANTINOMIANISMO

Vem do grego, **anti**, «contra», e **nomos**, «lei», ou seja, aquilo que é contrário à lei. O termo é usado para indicar a doutrina e a atitude que promove a idéia de que a lei moral não é obrigatória aos cristãos, como regra de vida. De modo mais geral, é aplicado aos fanáticos que se recusam a reconhecer qualquer tipo de lei, exceto suas próprias noções subjetivas sobre o que é certo. Supõem tolamente que essas noções subjetivas suplantam toda e qualquer lei, como se fossem inspiradas pelo Espírito Santo. Além disso, o termo pode ser usado em sentido bem geral para aludir à idéia de que não há leis obrigatórias, e que os princípios da ética dependem do auto-interesse subjetivo.

A base teológica do antinomianismo é a noção de que o evangelho e a *lei da graça* prestam uma obediência desnecessária e mesmo indesejável à lei mosaica (isto é, como um código a ser obedecido), visto termos sido justificados por Cristo e estarmos agora sob a lei do Espírito (Rom. 6:14). Muitas declarações paulinas nas epístolas aos Romanos e aos Gálatas podem ser usadas em apoio a essa crença. Em contrário a essa crença, devemos salientar que a lei moral mosaica foi incorporada na lei do Espírito, de vários modos: 1. Na lei do amor, que requer inerentemente a obediência aos conceitos morais da lei mosaica. Rom. 13:9 ss. 2. No Novo Testamento, inclusive nos escritos de Paulo, há muitos mandamentos morais paralelos à lei moral mosaica; e daí se conclui não haver contração, mas antes, reafirmação da correção desses preceitos. Isso atua negativa e positivamente, isto é, em mandamentos *contra* pecados e em mandamentos *em favor* de virtudes. Todas as listas de vícios e virtudes do Novo Testamento mostram isso. Ver, por exemplo, Gál. 5:19-23.

Que queria dizer Paulo, portanto? Ele falava sobre a *motivação* e a *capacidade* de fazer o bem e de evitar o mal. Não estamos sob o código mosaico no sentido que nossa motivação e nossos princípios de ação (ou a capacidade inerente) sejam inspirados ou estejam contidos naquele código. Nossa motivação e nossa capacidade vêm do Espírito, e, conseqüentemente, estamos debaixo de Sua lei, conforme indica Rom. 8:2. Mas o Espírito nos capacita a fazer precisamente aquilo que Moisés incluiu em seu código. Portanto, não há qualquer contradição quanto à *essência*, mas somente sobre *como* devemos cumprir essas coisas. Paulo nos convida a entrar em comunhão com o Espírito, através da associação mística, ali encontrando nossa capacidade para praticarmos o bem. Destarte, ele nos afasta do legalismo, segundo o qual só fazemos algo em resposta a alguém que nos apresente suas demandas. O termo *legalismo*, na teologia, indica a obediência egoísta à lei, como motivo de redenção e como princípio de conduta

ANTINOMIANISMO — ANTÍOCO

ética. Nosso princípio, em Cristo, é a comunhão com o Espírito Santo. Alimentados por Seu poder, agimos e vencemos. Essa é a lei da graça.

Considerações históricas. A luta começou na mesma época do Novo Testamento. Extremistas, usando o nome de Paulo, repeliram a obediência à lei, a fim de satisfazer a si mesmos e suas paixões. A igreja em Corinto serve de exemplo. As reprimendas de Paulo aos ex-pagãos de Tessalônica, servem de um outro exemplo. Ver I Tess. 4:1-9; 5:4 ss. Algumas seitas gnósticas, os marcionitas, os maniqueus, os familistas, os adamistas e os davidistas são exemplos históricos. Wesley fez a absurda observação de que o próprio evangelho está «a um milímetro» do antinomianismo. Bem ao contrário, o evangelho nos liberta do pecado, mediante a operação do Espírito, embora suplantando o código legal como motivo das nossas ações. O evangelho não reduz ou anula nossa obrigação diante da lei moral. Muito pelo contrário, mostra-nos que até nossos pensamentos e motivos são agora incluídos na retidão moral, não estando envolvidos apenas os nossos feitos. (Ver Mat. 5:20 ss).

Falsidades do antinomianismo:

1. O Deus do Antigo Testamento não é o mesmo Deus do Novo Testamento. A lei mosaica foi dada por aquele, e o evangelho por este. Esse é um dos erros do gnosticismo.

2. A moralidade do Antigo Testamento é contradita pela moralidade do Novo Testamento. Apesar do Novo Testamento constituir um avanço, a moralidade básica é a mesma; pois o Novo Testamento leva em conta até os pensamentos e os motivos.

3. O que sucede ao corpo não é importante. O corpo físico pode ser corrompido, sendo até desejável que isso suceda, para que seja enfraquecido e finalmente pereça. A alma seria inteiramente separada do corpo, não sendo corrompida por ele, tal como um objeto de ouro mergulhado na lama não vira lama. Mas a Bíblia ensina que não só o corpo, mas também a alma se corrompe. O pecado começa no espírito e não no corpo. Há espíritos caídos, e não corpos. Os espíritos é que serão julgados e não os corpos (Apo. 20:12 *ss*).

4. O antinomianismo prejudica a unidade das Escrituras, lançando o Novo Testamento contra o Antigo. A maioria ou mesmo todos os preceitos morais do Antigo Testamento são reiterados no Novo.

5. O antinomianismo não entende a demanda moral do evangelho, distorcendo o intuito da *justificação* (ver o artigo) e ignorando a *santificação* (ver o artigo). Sem santificação, não pode haver salvação (Heb. 12:14). (B C E H NTI)

ANTÍOCO

No grego, **opositor.** Foi nome de treze reis da dinastia selêucida, de 280 D.C. em diante. Após a morte de Alexandre o Grande, em 323 A.C., seu vasto império desmembrou-se. Seleuco, um dos menos importantes generais de Alexandre, assumiu o controle das satrapias do Oriente. Após a batalha de Ipsus, em 301 A.C., ele fundou o porto de Selêucia, na Piéria (ver Atos 13:4), para servir sua própria capital ocidental, Antioquia. E o domínio dos selêucidas mais tarde ampliou-se por quase toda a Ásia Menor. Na dinastia, muitos dos monarcas tiveram o nome de Seleuco ou Antíoco; governaram seu império sediado na Síria durante dois séculos e meio, até serem destronados pelos romanos.

A região. Ásia Menor e Síria, o mais ocidental dos domínios orientais de Alexandre, uma dinastia helenista, tendo como capital Antioquia sobre o Orontes (ver o artigo a respeito). Selêucia (ver o artigo), à margem do Tigre, era uma segunda capital, que administrava as províncias orientais.

Os reis:

1. Antíoco I (Soter), 324-261 A.C. Era filho de Seleuco I (ver sobre Seleuco). Foi co-governante com seu pai de 293 a 292 A.C., mas tornou-se rei único em 281 A.C. Defendeu o império da invasão dos gauleses, de onde adquiriu o seu título de Soter (Salvador). Construiu uma grande quantidade de cidades, helenizando-as e fazendo Antioquia ser a sua capital. Perdeu, porém, os importantes distritos da Ásia Menor e da Síria a Ptolomeu II Filadelfo (ver sobre Ptolomeu). Mal começara a reinar quando quatro reis da Ásia Menor recuperaram sua independência, a saber, os reis do Ponto, da Bitínia, da Capadócia e de Pérgamo. Então os gauleses que devastavam a Grécia, a Macedônia e a Trácia também invadiram a Ásia Menor. Mataram Antíoco I. (216 A.C.) e se estabeleceram na região que veio a chamar-se Galácia.

2. Antíoco II (Theos), 286-246 A.C. Segundo filho de Antíoco I. Durante seu reinado, os partas, sob Arsaces (250 A.C.) revoltaram-se. Imediatamente após isso houve uma revolta em Báctria. Durante trinta anos, os partas continuaram a expandir-se às expensas da monarquia síria. Por outro lado, ele atacou Ptolomeu II Filadelfo, recuperando grande parte do que Antíoco I havia perdido. Essa batalha é chamada de Segunda Guerra Síria. Um brilhante golpe político ocorreu quando Ptolomeu convenceu Antíoco a casar-se com sua filha, Berenice (o que para tal divorciou-se de sua esposa Laodice), ficando entendido que o reino eventualmente ficaria na posse do filho de Berenice. Esse casamento resultou em paz. Antíoco e Ptolomeu faleceram ambos em 246 A.C., e os seus respectivos filhos não levaram avante a amizade que seus pais haviam mantido.

3. Antíoco III (o Grande), 242-187 A.C., segundo filho de Seleuco II e neto de Antíoco II e Laodice. Sucedeu a seu irmão mais velho, Seleuco III Soter, que foi assassinado em 223 A.C. O reino que ele recebeu estava fragmentado (a Báctria e a Pártia se separaram). Outras ameaças surgiram na Média-Pérsia e na Ásia Menor. Portanto, seu trabalho consistiu em consolidar-se e em expandir-se novamente. O rei atacou Ptolomeu IV, em 221 A.C., teve de retirar-se, mas fê-lo novamente, dessa vez com maior sucesso, empurrando os egípcios para o sul e capturando Selêucia (perto de Antioquia). Em 218 A.C., ele capturou Tiro e Ptolemaida, além de várias cidades no interior do continente. Porém, na Cele-Síria e na Fenícia, foi totalmente derrotado por Ptolomeu IV. Então dirigiu suas forças contra o Oriente (212-206 A.C.), adquirindo a Armênia e recuperando a Pártia e a Báctria. Foi por causa dessas muitas vitórias militares e aquisições de território que ele foi chamado de «o Grande». O império sírio ficou ao encargo de seu filho, Seleuco IV (Filopator), 187-176 A.C., acerca de quem sabe-se bem pouca coisa. Esse homem aparece no trecho de Dan. 11:20 como um «exator», isto é, cobrador de impostos.

4. Antíoco IV (Epifânio). Seleuco IV foi assassinado por um de seus cortesãos e, assim, seu irmão, Antíoco Epifânio apressou-se a ocupar o trono vago, embora o herdeiro natural, Demétrio, filho de Seleuco, estivesse vivo e estivesse hospedado em Roma. O trecho de Daniel 11:21 indica que ele obteve o reino com lisonjas e intrigas. Foi um bom político. Esse foi o rei selêucida que obteve tão má reputação por causa de sua interferência no estado e na

ANTÍOCO — ANTÍOCO DE ASCALÃO

adoração dos judeus, ao ponto de tornar-se um antigo tipo do futuro *anticristo*. Era o filho menor de Antíoco III e Laodice. Subiu ao trono em 175 A.C. Até 170 ou 169 A.C., reinou juntamente com seu sobrinho, Antíoco, o filho infante de Seleuco, que na ausência de Antíoco Epifânio foi assassinado por Andronico. Este, por sua vez também tirou a vida de Onias III, o sumo sacerdote judeu ilegalmente deposto (ver II Macabeus 4:32-38). Antíoco Epifânio tentou incorporar os judeus em seu programa de helenização, proibindo a adoração e os costumes religiosos deles, sob pena de morte. Contaminou o templo de Jerusalém com um holocausto idólatra, chegando ao extremo de oferecer uma porca como oferta sobre o altar, o insulto final aos judeus. Sua opressão contra o judaísmo reflete-se em Dan. 7:8,25; 8:11-14,24-26; 9:27; 11:31-36. Seguiu-se a isso a revolta dos judeus, e Antíoco foi militarmente derrotado pelos Macabeus. Antíoco Epifânio foi morto em uma campanha militar na Média, em 164 A.C.

O templo de Jerusalém foi purificado e redecorado, em dezembro de 165 A.C., um evento comemorado pelos judeus na festa de *Hanukkah* (ver o artigo a respeito). Ver também sobre Judas Macabeu e sobre Macabeus, Livros dos.

5. Antíoco V (Eupator), 173-162 A.C. Substituiu seu pai, Antíoco Epifânio, com nove anos de idade (Apiano, *As Guerras Sírias* 66). Em seu leito de morte, Antíoco nomeou Filipe como guardião de seu filho, bem como regente até que o menino pudesse reinar. O título dado ao menino, *Eupator*, e que significa nascido de pai nobre, não é algo com o que os judeus pudessem concordar facilmente. Judas Macabeu atacou Acra; e Lísias, com o rei menino, retirou-se para o sul, e finalmente derrotou Judas em Bete-Zacarias, a sudoeste de Jerusalém. Então Lísias cercou Jerusalém. Mas, ouvindo que Filipe marchava da Pérsia para Síria, a fim de reivindicar o trono para si mesmo, Lísias procurou entrar em uma aliança com Judas. Garantia a liberdade religiosa dos judeus e não derrubava as muralhas de Jerusalém (ver I Macabeus 6:55-63). Lísias partiu para Antioquia e derrotou Filipe. Porém, em 162 A.C., Demétrio I Soter, filho de Seleuco IV e sobrinho de Antíoco IV, primo de Antíoco V, escapou de Roma, onde era conservado como hóspede, e matou tanto Lísias quanto o rei menino (ver I Macabeus 7:1-4; II Macabeus 14:1; Josefo, *Anti*. xii. 10:1; Políbio xxxi.11; Apiano, *As Guerras Sírias* 46,47,67 e Lívio, *Epítome* 46).

6. Antíoco VI (Epifânio Dionísio), 148-142 A.C. Era filho de Alexandre Balas e Cleópatra Téia, filha de Ptolomeu VI. Ver sobre Cleópatra. Demétrio II Nicator assassinou Alexandre Balas em 145 A.C. e tomou a Síria. Era jovem e inexperiente e fez muitas concessões a Jônatas, o sumo sacerdote dos judeus. Suas muitas falhas fizeram um general de seu exército, Diódoto Trifo, apossar-se do trono, que então foi dado por esse general a Antíoco VI, em 145 A.C. Jônatas pôs-se ao lado de Trifo. Por causa disso, obteve muitos favores. No entanto, tinha ciúmes dos sucessos militares de Jônatas e, mediante ludíbrio, fê-lo prisioneiro e, finalmente, executou-o (ver I Macabeus 11:1-13:31; Josefo, *Anti*. xiii. 4.4-7.1, partes 109-219).

7. Antíoco VII (chamado Sidetes). Filho de Demétrio I Soter. Depôs Trifo em 138 A.C. e governou até 129 A.C. Por decreto, permitiu que os judeus cunhassem suas próprias moedas, para que assim evitassem a idolatria que as mesmas fomentavam (ver I Macabeus 15:1-9); mas invadiu e subjugou a Judéia, em 134 A.C., embora concedendo liberdade religiosa aos judeus.

8. Antíoco VIII (Gripo, *nariz de gancho*). Era sobrinho de Sidetes, tendo governado de 123 a 113 A.C. Foi derrubado por Antíoco IX Filopater, filho da mãe de Gripo, Cleópatra Téia e de Sidetes. Mas Gripo retornou em 111 A.C. e recuperou tudo quanto havia perdido, excetuando a Cele-Síria. Morreu em 96 A.C., assassinado por Haráclio, um ministro do rei (ver Josefo, *Anti*. xiii.13,4, par. 365). Sucedeu-o seu irmão mais velho, Seleuco VI Epifânio Nicator.

9. Antíoco IX (Cizíceno), embora recebesse o título de Filopater nas moedas. Reinou de 113 a 95 A.C. Era o segundo filho de Antíoco VII e Cleópatra, filha de Ptolomeu Filemetor. Foi criado em Cizico, na Ásia Menor, o que explica seu sobrenome. Em 116 A.C. derrotou seu meio-irmão e primo, Antíoco VIII, e tornou-se o único monarca (113-111 A.C.). Mas Antíoco VIII posteriormente obteve uma vitória, pelo que Antíoco IX reteve consigo apenas a Cele-Síria. Antíoco VIII foi capturado e morto, sendo substituído no trono por seu sobrinho, Seleuco VI Epifantes Nicator (ver Josefo, *Anti*. xiii. 13:4, par. 366).

10. Antíoco X (Eusebes = piedoso). Reinou entre 94 e 83 A.C. Os quatro filhos de Antíoco VIII (Gripo) tentaram derrubá-lo do trono, mas sem sucesso. Após conquistar a Mesopotâmia, Tigranes, rei da Armênia, obteve o controle sobre a Síria, em 83 A.C., e governou mediante um vice-rei até que foi derrotado pelos romanos, em 69 A.C. (ver Josefo, *Anti*. xiii.13.4 partes 366-371; Apiano, *As Guerras Sírias* 48). Conflitos internos debilitaram a dinastia selêucida, beneficiando os romanos. Isso também tornou possível a Alexandre Janeu (ver os Hasmoneanos) a conquistar quase toda a terra de Israel. Antíoco X morreu em 83 A.C., embora os relatos a esse respeito em muito variem. (Ver Apiano, *As Guerras Sírias* 49 e 69; Josefo, *Anti*. xiii. 13:4, parte 371).

11. Antíoco XIII (Asiático). Reinou de 69 a 65 A.C. Era filho de Antíoco X e Selene, filha de Ptolomeu Fiscom. Quando Lúculo, de Roma, derrotou Tigranes, da Armênia, em 69 A.C., entregou a Síria a Antíoco XIII. Em 65 A.C., Filipe, neto de Antíoco VIII tentou derrubá-lo, mas sem êxito. Antíoco XIII apelou para os romanos. — Em vez de ajudá-lo, Pompeu fez da Síria uma província romana, o que assinalou o fim da dinastia selêucida. (Ver Apiano, *As Guerras Sírias* 49, 70; Plutarco, *Pompeu*, 39; Estrabão x1. 1a).

12. Outro Antíoco, pai de Numênio (ver o artigo a seu respeito), mencionado em I Macabeus 12:16; 14:22; Josefo, *Anti*. xiii.5,8, parte 169; xiv. 8,5, parte 146).

13. Outro Antíoco, também chamado Epifânio, filho de Antíoco IV de Comagena. Estava noivo de Drusila, filha mais jovem de Agripa I (ver o artigo a seu respeito), mas o casamento nunca foi realizado, embora tivesse prometido a Agripa que abraçaria o judaísmo, que era uma das condições estipuladas. Entretanto, mais tarde mudou de plano, o que deu fim à possibilidade de tal casamento. (Ver Josefo, *Anti*. xix.9.1, parte 355; xx.7.1 parte 139). (BEV DAN RU Z)

ANTÍOCO DE ASCALÃO

Filósofo grego do século I A.C., discípulo de Filo de Larissa, e ao qual sucedeu como cabeça da Quarta Academia (ver o artigo sobre a *Academia de Platão*). Manteve o cargo de 88 a 68 A.C., ano de seu falecimento. O ceticismo da segunda e da terceira academias se abrandara, e Antíoco argumentou contra o *ceticismo* (ver o artigo). Ele afirmava que o próprio intelecto é teste suficiente da verdade. Isso equivale à posição do *racionalismo* (ver o artigo). Antíoco combinava as filosofias de Platão e Aristóteles à maneira dos estóicos (ver o artigo sobre o *estoicismo*). Portanto, seu sistema era a síntese de três sistemas. Ele ensinava que a felicidade completa se alcança através do bem-estar material, físico e mental. Seus escritos se perderam, mas, visto que Cícero muito se utilizou dos mesmos, citando-os com freqüência, possuímos o cerne de sua filosofia. (F P)

ANTÍOCO EPIFÂNIO

Um rei selêucida (175-163 A.C.). Os selêucidas eram membros da dinastia que governou a Síria desde 312 A.C., até à conquista romana, em 64 A.C., derivando seu nome de Seleuco Nicator, general macedônio de Alexandre o Grande, fundador da dinastia. *Antíoco* tentou incorporar os judeus em seu programa de helenização, proibindo o culto e os costumes religiosos deles, sob pena de morte. Conspurcou o templo com a idolatria, em 167 A.C., e ofereceu uma porca sobre o altar. Sua opressão contra o judaísmo se reflete em Dan. 7:8,25; 8:11-14,24-26; 9:27; 11:31-36. Foi militarmente derrotado pelos Macabeus. O templo foi purificado e redecorado, em dezembro de 165 A.C., um evento comemorado na festa do *Hanukkah* (ver o artigo). Ver também *Judas Macabeu* e *Macabeus, Livros dos*. (E WA Z)

ANTIOQUIA, CÁLICE DE

Trata-se de um grande cálice de prata, com 19 cm de altura, com doze retratos humanos em relevo. Foi dado a conhecer ao mundo em 1916, por G.A. Eisen. Pertence ao século I D.C., representando Cristo, oito apóstolos e dois evangelistas. A identificação foi apoiada por pessoas famosas, e o cálice popularmente veio a ser considerado o cálice usado realmente na última Ceia. Foi exibido na Feira Mundial de Chicago, em 1933. Testes químicos demonstram a sua antiguidade. O estilo das figuras sugere uma data como o fim do século IV ou o começo do século V D.C., pelo que a conexão com o primeiro século e com Cristo não passa de um mito. O cálice atualmente acha-se na Coleção Cloister do Museu Metropolitano de Artes, na cidade de Nova Iorque. Muita literatura tem sido produzida em torno desse cálice, pró e contra a sua identificação, envolvendo as diversas investigações feitas a respeito. (ARN EI)

ANTIOQUIA, DA PISÍDIA

Como cidade grega, Antioquia provavelmente foi fundada no local de uma aldeia-templo Frígia do deus Mem, cerca de vinte anos depois que os selêucidas tornaram-se os governantes da região, em 281 A.C.

Foi ali a primeira ocasião em que Paulo pregou a um grande número de gentios reunidos (ver Atos 13:44). O poder da comunidade judaica do lugar fica provado pelo fato de que puderam fazer um apelo contra Paulo, aos homens principais da cidade, e foram ouvidos. Paulo não invocou ali a sua cidadania romana como proteção, e apesar da amarga oposição, voltou ali por duas vezes, a fim de ajudar a crescente comunidade cristã (ver Atos 14:21 e 16:6).

Uma cidade montanhosa, erguida numa altitude de cerca de mil e duzentos metros (ver a nota expositiva no NTI em Atos 11:19). Essa cidade, realmente, não se encontrava na Pisídia, e, sim, na Frígia, mas ficava próxima da fronteira com a Pisídia. Assim sendo, veio a ser chamada Antioquia *da Pisídia* a fim de distingui-la da outra Antioquia, existente na Cária. Era uma colônia e um posto militar avançado dos romanos, sendo a cidade mais importante da Galácia do Sul. Foi uma das diversas cidades que receberam o nome de «Antioquia», fundadas por Seleuco I Nicator (312-280 A.C.), em honra a seu pai. Ficava situada em uma importante rota comercial entre Éfeso e a Cilícia, e era importante centro do helenismo. O imperador romano, Augusto, concedeu-lhe privilégios de colônia romana. As antigas ruínas dessa cidade ficam perto de Ialovaque, na Turquia moderna.

Embora romanizada e falando o latim, nos dias de Paulo, uma inscrição descoberta em Apolônia, uma cidade vizinha, datada dos séculos I ou II D.C., mostra que Antioquia da Pisídia continha algum elemento judaico em sua população. O santuário da principal divindade de Antioquia, Nem, foi escavado entre 1910 e 1913. Vários remanescentes de estruturas romanas também têm sido desenterrados, bem como canos para distribuição de água, transportada pelo aqueduto, um tabuleiro de jogo dos romanos e uma imensa basílica cristã (pertencente ao século IV D.C.), nessas pesquisas. (ND LE S Z)

ANTIOQUIA, ESCOLA TEOLÓGICA DE
Ver **Escola Teológica de Antioquia**.

ANTIOQUIA, SÍNODO DE

Houve dois sínodos em Antioquia, no ano de 340 D.C., em conexão com a controvérsia ariana. (Ver *arianismo*). O primeiro foi efetuado pelos semi-arianos ou Eusebianos, no qual Atanásio sofreu uma de suas muitas deposições. O segundo, que procurou conciliar o Ocidente, foi fortemente o niceno. (Ver *Nicéia, Credo de*). Foram redigidos quatro credos tão parecidos quanto possível ao credo niceno, sem que fosse usado o termo *homoousios* (ver o artigo a respeito), que significa «da mesma substância», ao qual os semi-arianos objetaram tanto quanto os arianos. (E)

ANTIOQUIA, sobre o Orontes (Síria)

Essa cidade, localizada às margens do rio Orontes, foi o berço das missões cristãs. Era conhecida como Antioquia da Síria, a fim de ser distinguida de Antioquia da Pisídia. Antioquia da Síria foi fundada em cerca de 300 A.C. e cresceu a ponto de contar com numerosa população nos tempos de Paulo, incluindo muitos judeus, os quais, desde tempos remotos haviam obtido o direito de cidadania. Durante o período das guerras dos Macabeus, muitas famílias judaicas se estabeleceram em Antioquia. Na época de Paulo, era a terceira maior cidade do império romano, perdendo em importância numérica apenas para Roma e Alexandria. Os romanos fizeram-na capital da província romana da Síria.

Paulo *começou e terminou* ali a sua segunda viagem missionária. Não sabemos exatamente quão grande era a cidade nos dias de Paulo, mas, à base da informação dada por Crisóstomo, deve ter contado com uma população de cerca de oitocentos mil habitantes, em 300 D.C. A atual Antikiyeh assinala o local da cidade antiga, mas é comparativamente pequena, cobrindo apenas pequena parte da área original. As escavações arqueológicas têm descoberto numerosas ruínas do passado, algumas das quais anteriores à era cristã. O circo, um dos maiores dos tempos romanos, a acrópole, numerosos banhos, vilas e cemitérios romanos, têm sido descobertos. Belos pisos de mosaico, que datam do período apostólico até o século VI D.C., também têm sido descobertos. O Caronion (busto de Caron, deus grego mitológico, que

Estrada romana perto de Antioquia da Pisídia
Cortesia, Matson Photo Service

Antioquia, Síria, ao lado do Rio Orontes
Cortesia, Matson Photo Service

transportava as almas para o outro lado do rio Estige), de cerca de 170 A.C., com cinco metros e pouco de altura, entalhado em uma penedia de pedra calcária, a nordeste da cidade, continua visível, embora bastante estragada pelas intempéries. Nos dias de Paulo certamente ainda era um marco notável. Mais de uma vintena de edifícios cristãos tem sido ali descoberta, embora nenhuma dessas construções date dos dias apostólicos. O famoso *Cálice de Antioquia* foi descoberto ali por alguns trabalhadores que cavavam um poço, em 1910. No início foi declarado pertencente à última parte do século I D.C., e alguns chegaram a imaginar que fosse o cálice original em que Cristo serviu a Ceia. Há nele gravadas efígies que representam Cristo e os apóstolos. A maioria das autoridades concorda que se trata de um produto da primitiva arte cristã, datando entre os séculos II e VI de nossa era.

Antioquia sobre o Orontes era *sede* do legado imperial da província romana da Síria e Cilícia, e aparecia como a capital do Oriente, Josefo, o historiador judeu do tempo dos apóstolos, diz-nos que era a terceira maior cidade do império romano, perdendo em importância somente para Roma e Alexandria. A grande maioria da população era síria, embora houvesse numerosa colônia judaica. Sua cultura era tipicamente greco-helenista. Seu porto era Selêucia (Atos 13:4), a qual era reputada cidade comercial e centro marítimo. Não muito distante dali ficava Dafné, quartel-general do culto de Apolo e Artêmisa, culto esse que se tornou famoso por sua degradação. Isso era tanto verdade que Juvenal, ao queixar-se da degradação moral que invadia Roma, disse que «...o Orontes sírio desaguou no Tibre» (Sátiras III. 62). O centro da igreja cristã passou de Jerusalém, seu berço original, para Antioquia da Síria, seu centro gentílico, pois a igreja cristã, cada vez mais, se foi tornando uma instituição gentílica. A tradição associa o apóstolo Pedro a essa cidade, considerando-o primeiro de seus bispos. Nomes ilustres posteriores, associados a essa cidade, foram *Inácio e João Crisóstomo*, ambos chamados bispos de Antioquia. Crisóstomo foi grande escritor de comentários bíblicos e exerceu notável influência sobre o desenvolvimento doutrinário da igreja cristã.

A cidade de Antioquia foi fundada por *Seleuco Nicator*, um dos generais de Alexandre, em 300 A.C., que lhe deu nome em honra a seu pai, Antíoco. Antíoco havia devastado e poluído a cidade de Jerusalém, mas os seus sucessores, de conformidade com o que diz Josefo (*Guerras dos Judeus*, 1:7, cap. 3 seção 3), foram mais liberais, tendo criado uma boa atmosfera para o desenvolvimento do judaísmo naquele lugar; e isso teria atraído a muitos judeus, até que, finalmente, Antioquia se tornou grande centro de erudição judaica, bem como cidade onde havia numerosa colônia judaica. (Ver Talmude Hieros, Kiddishin, fol. 64:4). Com base nessa circunstância, o caminho ficou preparado para a entrada e o crescimento do cristianismo em Antioquia. (DO LE ND NTI)

ANTIOQUIANOS

No grego, **pertencentes a Antíoco**. Nome usado para indicar uma comunidade judaica formada em Jerusalém, sob os auspícios de Antíoco Epifânio, mencionada apenas em II Macabeus 4:9. Não se sabe qual a natureza exata dessa comunidade. As idéias a respeito são as seguintes: 1. Os judeus compraram o favor de Antíoco (por meio de Jasom, o sumo sacerdote) a fim de contarem com a sua própria comunidade fechada, que seguia os modos de vida helenistas, embora nunca tivessem seguido a idolatria pagã. 2. Mui provavelmente isso incluiu a concessão da cidadania antioquense (do império selêucida) aos habitantes de Jerusalém, ou talvez limitou essa cidadania. 3. Ou simplesmente envolveu a formação de uma nova cidade chamada Antioquia, em Jerusalém, adaptada ao modo internacional de viver. A referência em II Macabeus 4:9 indica que, sem importar a natureza dessa comunidade, seus membros não participaram de sacrifícios pagãos, o que talvez sua nova posição civil implicasse. (TC)

ANTIOQUIS

Concubina de Antíoco Epifânio (ver II Macabeus 4.30). O rei a presenteou com as cidades cilicianas de Tarso e Malo, mas os habitantes das mesmas revoltaram-se em protesto. (Z)

ANTIPAPA

Falso ocupante da Santa Sé (ver sobre **Sé**), em oposição a um papa canonicamente eleito e universalmente reconhecido. Tais reivindicadores têm aparecido periodicamente na história da Igreja, com apoio de várias facções eclesiásticas ou políticas. Começando por *Novaciano* (ver o artigo), em 251 D.C., houve quase trinta desses antipapas, até ao tempo de Félix V (Amadeu de Savóia, 1439-1449). Houve ocasiões em que havia três rivais, como durante o grande cisma ocidental (ver o artigo a respeito), entre 1378 e 1417. Devido à confusão reinante na época, e à incerteza subjetiva até mesmo de cardeais, bispos e ordens religiosas, etc., Alexandre V (1409-1410), eleito por ocasião do concílio de Pisa, e João XXIII (1410-1414), não são considerados antipapas. Mas, devido ao apoio provincial e rebelião franca, Clemente VII (Robert de Gênova, 1373-1394) e Benedito XIII (Pedro de Luna, 1394-1414) são considerados antipapas. (CE E)

ÂNTIPAS

1. **Herodes Ântipas**, filho de Herodes o Grande e Maltace, uma mulher samaritana. Herdou os domínios de seu pai na Galiléia e Peréia, mas como tetrarca. Foi Herodes quem mandou decapitar João Batista. Quanto a mais detalhes, ver sob *Herodes*, onde são comentados todos os personagens desse nome.

2. Uma testemunha fiel e mártir, mencionada em Apo. 2:3, algum tempo antes de 100 D.C.

Nada se sabe de certo acerca desse personagem. Supomos que ele era líder ou pastor da igreja de Pérgamo, tendo sido escolhido para o martírio, talvez como advertência aos demais membros da «traiçoeira seita cristã». Simeão Metafrastes contava uma história lendária acerca de um certo Ântipas, bispo de Pérgamo, o qual, nos tempos do imperador Domiciano, foi fechado dentro de um boi de bronze, aquecido ao rubro. Seu corpo foi, literalmente, cozido. Diz-se que ele terminou seus últimos momentos em louvor e oração. Talvez essa lenda esteja baseada em fatos autênticos. Tertuliano, em *Adv. Gnost.* scorp. 12, menciona esse Ântipas, mas parece não ter tido conhecimento independente dele, à parte do texto do N.T. Eusébio, em sua História Eclesiástica iv.15:48; menciona a existência de mártires em Pérgamo, mas em uma época posterior, a saber, Carpo, Papilo e Agatônico.

Alguns estudiosos vêem certo significado simbólico, no nome desse homem. É perfeitamente possível entendê-lo como *contra todos* (no grego «anti pas»). Tratava-se da forma contraída de «antipater», que poderia ser reduzido à forma «antipapa», embora isso seja uma fantasia, como fantasia é a explicação anterior.

O Livro apócrifo, *Atos de Ãntipas* (que não mais existe) foi mencionado por Andreas e Aretas. Era comum que qualquer nome neotestamentário fosse usado pelos autores dos séculos II e III D.C., como base de narrativas maravilhosas, embora estas fossem inteiramente inventadas, ainda que aqui ou acolá houvesse pitadas de tradições genuínas. (ND S UN)

ANTÍPATER

Um embaixador enviado a Jônatas para renovar as relações com os romanos, com os espartanos e com outros (I Macabeus 12:16; 14:22). (Z)

ANTÍPATRIS

O antigo local dessa cidade era a cidade filistéia de Afeque (ver I Sam. 4:1 e 29:1). Herodes o Grande, construiu o local em 9 A.C., chamando a cidade por esse nome, em honra a seu pai, Antípater, o qual havia sido procurador da Judéia sob Júlio César. (Ver Josefo, *Anti*. xvi.5.2; *Guerras* i.21.9). O nome moderno corresponde as ruínas de Ras el-'Ain, a 42 km ao sul de Cesaréia, na estrada para Lida. Paulo viajou de Antípatris para Cesaréia depois de deixar Jerusalém (ver Atos 23:31). Josefo (*Guerras* iv.8.1) mostra que Vespasiano ocupou a cidade em 68 D.C., e dali deu início à sua marcha contra Jerusalém. A referência neotestamentária menciona como Paulo foi tomado até aquele lugar em uma marcha secreta, sob grande guarda militar. O lugar era um posto militar no caminho entre Jerusalém e Cesaréia, um lugar próprio para uma parada de descanso. No dia seguinte, a jornada continuou até Cesaréia. (DE ND Z)

ANTI-SEMITISMO

Termo popularmente usado para indicar os preconceitos e as perseguições contra os judeus, coletivamente, ou contra algum judeu em particular. A palavra também tem sido empregada para falar das atividades antijudaicas, em oposição ao estado de Israel. Muitos períodos da história se têm caracterizado por tais atividades, de forma mais intensa.

Três facetas do anti-semitismo:

1. *Faceta histórico-política*. Na colônia grega de Alexandria, em 220 A.C., um movimento contra a fé judaica foi um antigo incidente. Antíoco Epifânio, em sua tentativa de esmagar o judaísmo (175-163 A.C.), torna real outro desses incidentes. Mui naturalmente, Roma entrou em choque com o judaísmo, apesar de forçada a permitir-lhe a existência como religião legal, por ser impossível desarraigá-la. Assim, Roma periodicamente perseguia os judeus. Em cerca de 75 A.C., o anti-semitismo havia sido refinado por Cícero e outros líderes romanos como um princípio filosófico. O anti-semitismo histórico-político teve suas mais horrendas manifestações na era de Hitler, durante a. II Guerra Mundial, quando foram mortos seis milhões de judeus. Vários grupos árabes radicais dão prosseguimento a essa triste tradição.

2. *Faceta pseudocientífica*. Cerca de cem anos atrás, círculos acadêmicos alemães tentaram demonstrar a inferioridade dos judeus. Tal fato culminou na absurda afirmação da superioridade natural dos povos arianos, mormente dos gentios caucasianos. Nesses mesmos círculos acadêmicos surgiram amargos ataques críticos contra a integridade das Escrituras. Os ataques de Hitler contra os judeus basearam-se, pelo menos parcialmente, na filosofia dessas academias.

3. *Faceta religiosa*. A perseguição romana contra Israel tinha fundo religioso, e não apenas político, visto que os deuses oficiais, considerados protetores do império, não toleravam competição. A adoração a divindades não-oficializadas era considerada traição ao estado. Enquanto o judaísmo foi tido como religião legal tal aceitação sempre foi qualificada, originada na necessidade, e não no verdadeiro espírito de tolerância.

Visto que Jesus foi crucificado devido à influência de certos líderes judeus, e visto que a emergente Igreja cristã competia com a comunidade judaica e posto que o cristianismo era freqüentemente perseguido pelas diversas facções ou por indivíduos proeminentes do judaísmo (o livro de Atos relata alguns desses incidentes), surgiu dentro da Igreja cristã o ódio ao judaísmo. Era fácil os cristãos racionalizarem a perseguição contra os judeus como uma expressão de ódio aos ímpios (ver Sal. 45:7; Heb. 1:9), e, do ponto de vista cristão, como «uma defesa da fé». Portanto, nos próprios evangelhos aparecem alusões desprezíveis aos «judeus», sem qualquer qualificação, como «líderes dos judeus», «certos judeus», etc. Ver João 5:16-18; 6:41; 7:1, 10:31; 19:12.

O anti-semitismo penetrou na igreja no tempo do edito de Constantino (323 D.C.). Isso foi tanto uma reação contra os rabinos, cujo intuito era fazer oposição à Igreja cristã, como tentativa de proteger a Igreja em sua ascendência política e social. A medida que a Igreja foi obtendo maior poder político, o anti-semitismo foi-se entrincheirando cada vez mais.

Apesar de que os cristãos da atualidade dificilmente se considerariam anti-semitas, o exclusivismo faz muitos deles assumirem atitudes que dificilmente podem ter outra classificação. Por exemplo, dizer que «Deus não ouve as orações dos judeus», conforme fez um bem conhecido líder evangélico, certamente é uma atitude extremista que atiça os sentimentos antijudaicos.

Oficialmente, representantes tanto do catolicismo quanto do protestantismo têm condenado essa atitude e as suas manifestações. Isso é sumariado, pelo lado católico, no livro de Jacques Maritain: «A Christian Looks at the Jewish Question» (1939), e pelo lado protestante, pelo livro *Protestants Answer Anti-Semitism*», editado por Beatrice Jenney (1941).

Fanáticos religiosos, inchados de orgulho e arrogância, que inevitavelmente vêem em seus movimentos locais algo de melhor, se não mesmo de exclusivo, sempre tenderão por perseguir àqueles que não fazem parte de sua denominação. Uma das lições espirituais que precisamos aprender é que todas as denominações na realidade são seitas, com suas misturas particulares de verdade e erro, não havendo tal coisa como «Igreja verdadeira», em contraste com «igrejas falsas». Portanto, não há base moral ou teológica para que um grupo religioso persiga a outro. Nem há lugar para o sectarismo, que é orgulhoso e exclusivista. Pois a prova da espiritualidade não consiste em quão bom contendor alguém é, mas antes, quão bem alguém cumpre a lei do amor (I João 4:7). Essa lei não abre espaço para qualquer forma de anti-semitismo, individual ou coletivamente considerado. (E H HS)

ANTÍSTENES

Filósofo grego (445-360 A.C.), discípulo de Sócrates (ver o artigo a seu respeito). De suas numerosas obras, possuímos meros fragmentos. Ele foi principalmente um filósofo moral, que advogava uma vida frugal e austera. Consideram-no fundador da Escola dos Cínicos (ver o artigo sobre o *cinismo*). Influenciou Diógenes de Sinope (ver o artigo), que alguns reputam como o verdadeiro fundador do cinismo. Talvez seja melhor considerar a escola de Antístenes como socrática, embora, como é óbvio, tivesse sido cínica em seus estágios iniciais.

Escritos. Nas obras de antigos escritores há fragmentos de seus escritos sobre temas como a ética, a lógica, a política e a metafísica.

Idéias:

1. Juntamente com Sócrates. Só há um verdadeiro Deus, que não pode ser conhecido através de qualquer imagem. Um dos mais importantes alvos da filosofia é o da *definição*. O mito é um veículo apropriado da ética e do discurso filosófico geral.

2. Quanto aos *universais* (ver o artigo), ele era um *nominalista* (ver o artigo). Ele negava a validade do princípio de contradição.

3. Apesar de rejeitar o luxo (tal como o fizeram os cínicos posteriores), ele dava valor à educação, crendo no auto-aprimoramento e na ajuda prestada ao próximo (coisas que os cínicos posteriores não valorizavam). Buscava a sabedoria, sem afirmar-se sábio. Aceitava os prazeres como inerentemente bons, sobretudo aqueles que resultassem do trabalho honesto. Os cínicos posteriores repeliam o prazer, como se fosse algo mal, porquanto também desprezavam todos os valores humanos. Buscavam a virtude por amor à virtude. A virtude seria a independência essencial de todos os valores da sociedade, ou seja, uma espécie de independência tranqüila. (BE E P)

ANTÍTESE

Vem do grego, **anti**, «contra», e **tithemai**, «pôr». O vocábulo é usado no sentido de antinomia, no sentido de Kant (ver o artigo a respeito), uma contradição, ou uma proposição ou idéia que se opõe a uma *tese*. Em Fichte e Hegel, a *antítese* é o membro médio de uma tríada, que se opõe à tese. A oposição entre a tese e a antítese resulta na reconciliação, que é a *síntese*.

Hegel. Por exemplo, a religião grega frisava o fator individual (tese); a religião oriental, frisava o fator comunitário; e a unidade de tudo isso é a *antítese*. O cristianismo é a *síntese*, porque reúne o elemento individual e comunitário, atribuindo a ambos a sua devida importância. O materialismo dialético tomou por empréstimo o método hegeliano, imaginando uma longa série de tríadas que operam historicamente na direção do comunismo, o qual é a oposição ao capitalismo e ao socialismo, que fatalmente resultará no comunismo. Porém, ao que parece, a oposição entre comunismo e capitalismo está resultando em alguma outra coisa. Em nossos dias vemos a China pondo em dúvida a validade do marxismo, por razões de saúde econômica (1984). Outros países marxistas só continuam tais devido à opressão militar.

Quanto ao elaborado sistema hegeliano das tríadas, ver o artigo que versa sobre ele.

Soren Kierkegaard reagiu violentamente à aparente onisciência de Hegel, segundo a qual os opostos entram em harmonia em alguma síntese, visto que não haveria como tornar-se em algo. Pontos opostos permanecem em irreconciliável oposição. Ele também repelia a suposição aristoteliana de que duas contradições devem ser falsas. Por meio de um *paradoxo*, ambas podem ser verdadeiras. A fé cristã encerra muitos paradoxos em seu credo, como os trechos que ensinam o livre-arbítrio e os que ensinam o determinismo, os que ensinam o finito e os que ensinam o infinito, os que falam sobre o tempo e os que falam sobre a eternidade, os que vêem as coisas do ângulo da humanidade e os que as vêem do ângulo da divindade (em uma única pessoa, Jesus Cristo).

Apesar dessas objeções, é óbvio que a idéia da tríada (tese, antítese e síntese) é um princípio funcional da natureza, do intelecto e do espírito, embora não tenha aplicação universal ou onipotente. O mistério da vontade de Deus, que finalmente reunirá facções e forças contrárias, criando unidades de tudo em torno do Logos (Efé. 1:10; ver as notas a respeito no NTI), é um exemplo teológico e ontológico desse princípio em operação. (E H NTI)

ANTÍTIPO

Palavra traduzida por «figura», em Heb. 9:24 e I Ped. 3:21. O termo alude a uma correspondência de sentido, em alguma ilustração. No uso comum, afirma-se que o Antigo Testamento contém «tipos» das verdades neotestamentárias. As coisas assim tipificadas são chamadas «antítipos». Assim, o tabernáculo e seus móveis nos oferecem tipos de Cristo, e o próprio Cristo é o antítipo. Israel repousou na terra de Canaã (o tipo), e nós esperamos pelo descanso na esfera celeste (o antítipo). Adão, Abraão, José, etc., de alguma maneira são tipos de Cristo, e Cristo é o antítipo deles. (B)

ANTÔNIA, TORRE DE

Era uma fortaleza ao norte da área do templo de Jerusalém, com freqüência mencionada por Josefo em *Guerras* (ver v.4,2,5,8).

1. Pano de fundo. Originalmente fora construída pelos Macabeus, com o nome de Baris. Mas Herodes o Grande, a reconstruiu, aumentando seu resplendor e poderio. Recebeu então seu novo nome, em honra a Marco Antônio, antigo associado de forças armadas e patrono. Esse nome não aparece no Novo Testamento, aparecendo em Atos 21:34 sob a forma de «fortaleza».

Alguns supõem que Neemias construiu ali uma fortaleza, ao reedificar Jerusalém (ver Nee. 2:8), ou mesmo que Salomão tenha sido seu edificador, em data anterior. A esquina noroeste da área do templo era a única colina mais alta que a área onde estava o templo, tornando-a própria para tal construção.

2. *Descrição da Torre de Antônia*. A fortaleza estava em uma rocha ou colina com cerca de 25 m de altura, na esquina noroeste da área do templo, e as suas paredes ainda se elevavam por mais 20 m de altura. A própria fortaleza era de forma mais ou menos retangular. No sentido leste-oeste tinha cerca de 150 m e no sentido norte-sul tinha cerca de 80 m. Das quatro esquinas projetavam-se elevadas torres, com cerca de 23 m, mas a do sudeste tinha 30 m, sendo essa a torre que olhava por cima do templo. A informação que dispomos do interior da fortaleza nos vem de Josefo. Combinava um palácio com instalações militares e um quartel. Tinha apartamentos de vários tipos para os soldados, galerias, banhos, salões amplos, uma espécie de cidadela em si mesma. Havia uma passagem subterrânea que conduzia ao átrio de Israel, mas que era reservada para emergências. Tito

ANTÔNIO — ANTROPOLOGIA

fez o seu assalto contra a área do templo da torre de Antônia. Ao norte, estava separada da colina Bezeta por uma profunda trincheira, a fim de impedir qualquer aproximação vinda daquela área.

3. *Situação no Novo Testamento.* Em Atos 21:34,37 é chamada no grego de *parembola*, «fortaleza». Os romanos conservavam ali uma guarnição, tornando o poder romano conspícuo e ameaçador, como medida preservadora da boa ordem e da paz. Foi dali que o tribuno acorreu com seus soldados para arrebatar Paulo das mãos da turba de judeus, que o agarrara no templo e queria matá-lo. O lugar onde Jesus foi julgado perante Pilatos poderia ter sido ali. Alguns eruditos preferem pensar, porém, no palácio de Herodes, no extremo noroeste da cidade, perto da moderna porta de Jafa. Contudo, a maioria pensa que o local desse julgamento foi mesmo a fortaleza de Antônia. Pilatos e Jesus podem ter estado em uma das sacadas, enquanto a multidão se acotovelava no pátio. É possível que o «pavimento», referido em João 19:13, fizesse parte da fortaleza. Ver as notas no NTI em João 19:13, quanto a uma discussão sobre esse particular.

4. *Situação nos tempos modernos.* Em Jerusalém, na cidade antiga, a rua que começa na porta de Santo Estêvão passa diretamente acima dos remanescentes da torre de Antônia. Essa rua é aproximadamente eqüidistante entre seus muros do norte e do sul. O convento da Flagelação e a igreja das Irmãs de Sião foram construídos em grande parte sobre a metade norte da torre de Antônia. Sob esse último edifício, pode ser vista uma grande área do original pátio central, com cerca de 50 m quadrados. As maciças pedras originais do pavimento, com cerca de 30 centímetros de espessura, continuam no lugar. As valetas cavadas no pavimento de pedra, usadas para transportar a água da chuva para as cisternas, continuam em uso até hoje. Um jogo dos soldados pode ser visto riscado nas pedras do pavimento, mostrando que o quartel dos soldados originalmente ficava perto do local. (DE ND S Z)

ANTÔNIO, Ordem de Santo

Cinco distintas ordens monásticas vieram à existência sob o patrocínio de Santo Antônio (ver o artigo). Essas ordens são: 1. Os Discípulos de Santo Antônio (antonianos), homens que foram atraídos à sua ermida em Tebaida. Foram atraídos pela fama de sua santidade, tendo formado a primeira comunidade religiosa da cristandade. 2. Os Antoninos ou Irmãos Hospitalares de Santo Antônio, uma congregação fundada por um certo Gastão de Dauphne e seu filho, em cerca de 1095. Ocupavam uma casa e serviam em um hospital, próximo à igreja de Santo Antônio, em Saint-Didier de la Matthe. Essa ordem continuou até a Revolução Francesa. 3. Os Antonianos, nome dado a um grupo de armênios ortodoxos. O fundador dessa ordem foi Abram Atar Poresigh. Foi fundada no século XVII, quando armênios católicos sofriam perseguição. 4. Uma congregação de Santo Antônio foi fundada em Flandres, em 1615, sob a regra de Santo Agostinho. 5. Os Antonianos caldeus da congregação de Santo Hormíada, formaram um grupo fundado na Mesopotâmia, por Gabriel Dambo, em 1809. (E)

ANTÔNIO, SANTO

Suas datas: 251-356 D.C. Um abade, fundador do *monasticismo cristão* (ver o artigo a respeito). Nasceu em Como, no Egito, e morreu no monte Colzin, perto do mar Vermelho. Quando tinha vinte anos de idade, distribuiu sua herança entre os pobres e durante vinte anos viveu solitário, nos montes. Então organizou um mosteiro, para as pessoas que a ele acorriam. Em 311, visitou Alexandria, para dar apoio a cristãos que estavam sendo perseguidos; e fê-lo novamente em 350, para pregar contra os arianos. (Ver sobre o *arianismo*). Ele é o protetor dos *hospitalários* (ver o artigo), dos açougueiros, dos fabricantes de cestas, dos coveiros, dos animais domésticos, etc. A invocação de seu nome, segundo alguns crêem, tem efeitos curativos, especialmente no caso de doenças da pele, epilepsia, e várias pragas. Sua festa é celebrada a 17 de janeiro. A *Vida de Santo Antônio* foi escrita por Atanásio. Esse livro exerceu profundo efeito sobre a hagiografia posterior. Antônio não estabeleceu regras formais para a vida monástica, mas apenas seguiu o exemplo dado por ele mesmo. Ver sobre o *monasticismo*. (AM E)

ANTOTIAS

No hebraico, **pertencente a Anatote** (?). Era filho de Sasaque, na genealogia de Benjamim (ver I Crô. 8:24).

ANTROPOCENTRISMO

Vem dos termos gregos **anthropos**, **homem** e **kentron**, «centro». É o ponto de vista de que o homem é ou deve considerar-se centro de toda a realidade. A famosa afirmativa de Protágoras: «O homem é a medida de todas as coisas», reflete essa idéia. Pode significar: 1. O homem individualmente como centro; ou 2. o homem, coletivamente, como centro. Mais provavelmente a primeira alternativa. Protágoras usou aquela expressão no sentido ético. O homem é o padrão de suas próprias ações. O homem criou uma ética egoísta, relativa e individualista. Os padrões morais do homem servem aos seus interesses próprios. A teoria de Protágoras visava evitar «as regras ditadas pelas autoridades».

Alguns filósofos e teólogos têm pensado que o homem é um microcosmo, reflexo do macrocosmo, (que vide), isto é, ele é reflexo da realidade inteira, ou seja, nele podem ser descobertos os princípios essenciais da natureza, da ética e da espiritualidade.

A maioria das religiões faz do homem o centro das atenções de Deus. E esse, sem dúvida, é o ponto de vista do Novo Testamento, onde os temas dominantes são a redenção do homem e sua glória futura. Tudo mais quanto Deus estiver fazendo, permanece desconhecido para nós, visto que o volume sagrado essencialmente nada nos revela a esse respeito. É lógico supormos que há vastas atividades divinas que nada têm a ver com o homem, as quais envolvem tipos inimagináveis de seres, em inúmeras esferas da existência. Como comparar o homem a esses seres, agora e na vida vindoura, é um mistério que nem podemos começar a investigar no presente. (P)

ANTROPOLOGIA

A palavra significa **estudo do homem**. Tem certa variedade de usos, alguns dos quais importantes para a filosofia e a teologia.

1. **Ciência da antropologia.** Essa ciência estuda o homem como um organismo biológico e como um ser cultural, pelo que há duas divisões principais na antropologia: (a) Antropologia física, que aborda o

ANTROPOLOGIA — ANTROPOMORFISMO

que o homem era e é como um animal; e (b) antropologia cultural, que trata sobre o que o homem tem descoberto e inventado, aprendido e transmitido, como um ser social.

A *antropologia física* é um ramo da ciência natural, que tem várias subdisciplinas:

a. Estudo das origens, ou *antropogenia*, que inclui todas as considerações do processo evolutivo, utilizando-se das ciências geológicas e biológicas.

b. *Somatologia*, o estudo dos caracteres físicos das raças e sub-raças.

c. *Antropogeografia*, que é a distribuição geográfica das raças.

d. *Psicologia racial*, que é o estudo das diferenças entre as raças, no terreno psicológico.

e. *Fisiologia racial* e *bioquímica*.

f. *Anatomia comparada* e *morfologia*.

A maioria das subdisciplinas não interessa à filosofia ou à teologia, embora a questão das origens traga à tona o problema da *evolução* (ver o artigo), bem como o problema das *origens*, em geral. Ademais, temos o problema geral da identidade do homem. Muitos antropólogos vêem-no apenas como um animal, mas a teologia muito tem a dizer sobre isso, não vendo o homem apenas em seu corpo físico. Os pais alexandrinos criam que o homem real, a *alma*, tem uma história anterior ao corpo físico (ver o artigo sobre a *preexistência da alma*). Se isso é verdade, então a antropologia só estuda o veículo físico do homem e sua vida terrena, mas não sua verdadeira origem. Ver o artigo sobre as *origens*.

A *antropologia cultural* tem as seguintes subdivisões:

a. *Lingüística*, estudo comparativo dos idiomas.

b. *Tecnologia*, estudo comparativo das invenções materiais, antigas e modernas.

c. *Arqueologia da pré-história*, o estudo dos remanescentes de artefatos humanos, primeiras indústrias, etc.

d. *Antropologia social*, estudo comparativo dos costumes, tradições, organizações sociais, moral, governo, família, comunidade e economia.

O que interessa à filosofia e à teologia, dentro da antropologia cultural, centraliza-se em torno da ética. A maioria dos antropólogos defende o chamado relativismo cultural, isto é, a idéia que cada cultura desenvolve seus próprios conceitos éticos, dependendo das forças que atuam ali. Em aplicações extremas, qualquer padrão discernível de certo e errado se perde, quando se aceita que uma cultura é tão boa quanto outra, ou que aquilo que é bom para uma cultura, não é necessariamente bom para outra. Assim fazendo, terminamos com muitos padrões de conduta moral, sendo aprovados até mesmo os sacrifícios humanos enquanto que o adultério e a promiscuidade são socialmente sancionados. Ver o artigo sobre assuntos éticos em *Ética Relativa*.

2. Antropologia filosófica. Essa estuda o conhecimento filosófico do homem. A filosofia estuda o homem, procurando perscrutar mais fundo do que aquilo que é dito pela ciência pura. Sistemas filosóficos como a fenomenologia, o existencialismo e o personalismo (ver os artigos a respeito), geralmente são considerados como representantes dessa forma de antropologia. Isso, porém, é muito restritivo, porque qualquer filosofia que tente dizer algo sobre um homem, ou sobre a humanidade, além daquilo que a ciência estipula sobre seu corpo físico, é uma forma dessa antropologia filosófica. Portanto, a metafísica, a epistemologia, a ética, a estética, tudo tem algo a

dizer sobre essa área. A própria *antropologia* parece ter sido termo cunhado por Aristóteles, em sua obra *Ética*. Ele o usou para descrever o homem dotado de mente nobre, não dado à maledicência e nem à jactância. Aquele que assim fazia era um *antropólogo*, isto é, «falava sobre o homem», ou seja, sobre si mesmo.

3. Antropologia teológica. A doutrina do homem, mormente no que tange a Deus, à sua origem, à sua natureza presente, atividade, deveres e destino. A teologia ensina-nos que o homem foi criado para relacionar-se com Deus, para participar de Seus propósitos, e finalmente, para compartilhar da natureza divina (II Ped. 1:4), tal como originalmente foi criado à imagem de Deus. O homem desfigurou essa imagem, e a redenção tem por finalidade restaurá-la, mas também maximizá-la, por meio da criação do homem espiritual, uma realização das dimensões espirituais. Na antropologia teológica, o homem é um ser transcendental, ou pelo menos, está destinado a sê-lo. Ver o artigo sobre *Homem, Doutrina do*. (E H NI ROB)

ANTROPOMORFISMO

Vem do grego, **antropomorfos**, «de forma humana». A tribuição de qualidades humanas ao ser divino, ou a idéia de que Deus ou os deuses têm alguma espécie de formato, similar à anatomia humana.

A tendência para expressar idéias acerca de Deus, sob formas humanas, física, mental, moral ou espiritual, é tendência da maioria das religiões, sendo quase impossível de ser evitada, devido às restrições da linguagem humana. Não há entre os homens uma linguagem puramente divina, pelo que não há como falar sobre Deus sem usar termos que o antropomorfizem. Essa circunstância envolve uma severa limitação em nosso entendimento e em nossos discursos sobre Deus, refletindo nossas atuais limitações no campo do conhecimento e do entendimento espiritual.

Antigo Testamento. Ali Deus é apresentado sob forma humana (Êxo. 15:3; Núm. 12:8), com pés (Gên. 3:8; Êxo. 24:10), mãos (Êxo. 24:11; Jos. 4:24), boca (Núm. 12:8; Jer. 7:13), coração (Osé. 11:8). Além dessas formas, atribuímos a Deus qualidades e emoções humanas (Gên. 2:2; 6:6; Êxo. 20:5; Osé. 11:8). O homem foi criado à imagem de Deus (Gên. 1:27), e os teólogos usualmente são cuidadosos ao declarar que se trata de uma imagem «moral e espiritual», e não física. Mas mesmo assim, nossa compreensão de Deus fica severamente limitada, pois, no sentido estrito, quem pode comparar o homem a Deus?

Extremos pagãos. Se o Antigo Testamento sofre com o antropomorfismo, outras culturas são completamente derrotadas pelo mesmo. O politeísmo dos gregos e de outros povos pagãos é prova disso. Xenófanes (cerca de 570-480 A.C.) queixou-se que os homens criaram deuses à imagem deles. Os deuses do Olimpo não eram muito superiores aos heróis da ficção moderna. Paulo sentia-se aflito diante dos excessos da cultura pagã, quanto à idolatria (Atos 17). Xenófanes supunha que se os bois e os leões tivessem conceitos de divindade, certamente a representariam sob a forma de bois e leões. Para nós, é igualmente precário imaginarmos Deus como um grande papa. um bispo supremo, um superpastor. que naturalmente creia e pense como tais indivíduos costumam fazer. Porém, o que é mais comum do que isso nas modernas igrejas cristãs? O livro de J.B. Phillips, «Your God is too Small», é uma queixa moderna contra tal noção.

Extremos filosóficos. A fim de evitar o antropomorfismo trivial, que, de fato, pode degradar em muito o nosso conceito de Deus, os filósofos têm falado sobre Deus em termos de o infinito, o absoluto, o espírito absoluto, a alma do universo, etc. E assim eles têm criado modos de pensar sobre Deus que servem para obscurecer o quadro mediante termos abstratos. Com freqüência, Deus é personalizado por essas formas de descrição. Deus é transformado em uma mera força cósmica. Corremos o risco de pensar que Deus é totalmente diferente de nós, negando assim o conceito que, *de algum modo*, o homem foi criado à imagem de Deus. Porém, a própria Bíblia declara que nossos pensamentos não são como os pensamentos de Deus, estabelecendo assim uma radical diferença espiritual e intelectual entre o homem e Deus. (Isa. 55:8).

No Novo Testamento. Persistem ali expressões antropomórficas (Rom. 1:18 ss ; 5:12; I Cor. 1:25; Heb. 3:15; 6:17; 10:31). Contudo, as realidades espirituais *não* são vistas *diretamente*, mas imperfeitamente, no reflexo de algum antigo espelho fosco, de metal polido (I Cor. 13:2). Deus não habita em templos materiais (Atos 17:24), uma declaração que procura evitar o conceito antropomórfico.

Deus aproxima-se do homem em Cristo. Cristo é a suprema imagem de Deus (II Cor. 4:4), e tomou forma humana (Fil. 2:7). Seremos transformados à imagem de Cristo (Rom. 8:29). Desse modo, o distante Deus é aproximado de nós (Efé. 2:18), e finalmente, compartilharemos de Sua natureza (II Ped. 1:4). A visão plena de Deus é gradualmente revelada, e vai-se expandindo (I Crô. 13:8; II Tess. 1:7). Mas só completará na eternidade, falando-se em termos relativos, porque Deus, em Sua natureza total, jamais poderá ser absolutamente compreendido por ninguém que seja menor que Ele mesmo. Não obstante, jamais haverá qualquer estagnação em nossa busca pelo conhecimento de Deus. Nossa necessidade de empregar termos antropomórficos demonstra nosso atual baixo estágio no campo do conhecimento e da espiritualidade. (B E R)

ANTROPOPATISMO

Vem do grego **anthropos**, «homem» e **pathein**, «sofrer». Atribuição de sentimentos humanos a qualquer coisa não-humana, como objetos inanimados, animais, poderes da natureza, seres espirituais e Deus. Como é óbvio, algumas criaturas vivas não-humanas têm sentimentos e emoções, embora seja difícil determinar o quanto elas se aproximam dos humanos. Portanto, em alguns casos literalmente e em outros potencialmente, temos uma «falácia patética», isto é, uma errônea atribuição de emoções, sentimentos e sofrimentos humanos a coisas não-humanas. Quando dizemos que Deus se «ira», e portanto, «castiga» e «destrói», estamos praticando a *falácia patética*, a menos que qualifiquemos tal uso com explicações. Parece pelo menos razoável supor-se que Deus não se ira no mesmo sentido em que o fazem os homens.

O termo foi cunhado por João Ruskin (1819-1900), tal como a expressão «falácia patética». Ele objetava a atribuição feita pelos poetas de emoções, simpatias e aversões humanas à natureza, em vista dos acontecimentos. Deu-se ao trabalho de descobrir numerosos exemplos da falácia nos escritos de Shelley e Tennyson, parecendo não poder entender que o espírito poético naturalmente usa esse tipo de metáforas. Naturalmente, há aqueles que defendem a tese de que a natureza é uma presença viva, e não inanimada; e nesse caso, a própria natureza teria alguma forma de sentimento. Nesse caso, estaríamos diante de profundos mistérios.

Emoções humanas são atribuídas a Deus, na Bíblia: Gên. 6:6; 8:21; 11:5-6; Pro. 24:8; Zac. 1:2; Efé. 4:30; Rom. 1:18; Col. 3:6; Heb. 3:11. (E P S W A)

ANTROPOSOFIA

Um sistema de ocultismo que afirma que a chave para a sabedoria e a compreensão do universo é o próprio homem. O termo, que vem do grego, significa *sabedoria sobre o homem*. Atualmente é utilizado para indicar a filosofia de Rodolfo Steiner (1861-1925) que acredita que o cultivo das percepções espirituais do homem, em evolução, é a tarefa mais importante que cabe à humanidade.

ANU

Deus sumério do firmamento, chefe do panteão. Na Babilônia, ele era adorado em Uruque (Ereque), na Assíria, em Assur. Ver o artigo sobre as *Religiões da Mesopotâmia*.

ANUBE

No hebraico, *conferado*, *ligado a*. Era Filho de Coz, descendente de Judá por meio de Assur, pai de Tecoa (ver I Crô. 4:8), depois de 1618 A.C. (S)

ANUBIS

Ver **Hermes** e **Religiões do Egito**.

ANUNCIAÇÃO

No registro dos evangelhos, três pessoas recebem anunciações especiais: Zacarias (Luc. 1:13), José (Mat. 1:10), e Maria (Luc. 1:26 ss , através do anjo Gabriel). Mas o termo usualmente é empregado em relação a Maria. A Igreja tem uma festa religiosa em comemoração ao evento, celebrada a 25 de março.

Lucas relata a anunciação a Maria, em seu lar, em Nazaré. Mateus narra a anunciação a José, acerca do nascimento de Jesus. Destarte, a Bíblia ensina que o Espírito de Deus pode entrar nas vidas humanas, anunciando e produzindo grandes alterações. Isso reflete o *teísmo*, em contraste com o *deísmo*. O primeiro ensina que Deus pode intervir e intervém na vida humana, recompensando, punindo e produzindo modificações. Em contraste, o deísmo retrata o Criador (pessoal ou como força cósmica) que abandonou suas criaturas, permitindo que tudo fosse governado pelas leis naturais. Ver os artigos sobre esses conceitos.

Essência da mensagem da anunciação:

1. No grego, *xaire kexaritomenei*; no latim, *ave, gratia plena*. «Saudação, agraciada!» Os intérpretes protestantes vêem nisso o grande benefício da graça que Deus conferiu a Maria, ao escolhê-la para ser a mãe de Jesus. Os católicos vêem em Maria a própria fonte dessa graça, e não sua beneficiária, pelo que ela seria tanto a mãe quanto a filha da graça. As palavras: «Bendita és tu entre as mulheres...» pertencem ao vs. 42, e não ao vs. 28, conforme se vê em alguns manuscritos e versões. (Ver Luc. 1:26 ss). Seja como for, onde quer que essas palavras caibam, elas falam do singular privilégio conferido a Maria.

2. Nos vss. 30-33: «Maria, não temas...», porquanto Deus é quem a favorece, prometendo o nascimento de

ANUNCIAÇÃO, ORDENS DA — AOLIBÁ

Jesus por meio do Espírito. Deus estabeleceria a grandeza do Cristo que nasceria. Ele reinaria em Israel, e fundaria um reino que não teria fim. As obras de Deus transcendem a tudo quanto temos em mente para nós mesmos, se estamos em posição espiritual para participar dessas bênçãos.

3. Nos vss. 35-37: «Descerá sobre ti o Espírito Santo...» A gravidez de Maria foi obra do Espírito de Deus, e não causa humana. (Ver notas completas sobre o *nascimento virginal*). Essa circunstância mostra o caráter único de Jesus, o Cristo, e é teologicamente importante, conforme explica a nota referida. O vs. 37 enfatiza que as obras de Deus, inesperadas e de vastíssimo alcance como são, são possíveis por serem realizações divinas. Isso aponta para uma causa sobrenatural. Não devemos rebuscar condições biológicas incomuns, como explicação desses acontecimentos.

Adições lendárias. O livro de Tiago, uma obra apócrifa do séc. II D.C. ou *Proto-evangelho*, caps. 10 e 11, acrescenta alguns detalhes. Todos os eventos realmente grandes sofrem alguma elaboração posterior, sem importar se são sagrados ou profanos. (B E Z)

ANUNCIAÇÃO, ORDENS DA

Ordens religiosas da Igreja Católica Romana, fundadas sob o patrocínio da anunciação à bendita virgem Maria. Há seis dessas ordens:

1. Uma ordem militar, a ordem da Annunziata, fundada por Amadeu VIII, duque de Savóia, no século XV.
2. As *Anunciades*, uma ordem religiosa feminina, fundada por Jeanne de Valois, filha de Luís XII, da França, em 1501.
3. As *Annunciades celestes*, ordem fundada por Maria Vitória Fornari, em Gênova, em 1604.
4. As *Annunciades* da Lombardia, também chamadas Irmãs de Santo Ambrósio, organizadas em Pária, em 1408. Foram originalmente organizadas para atender aos enfermos.
5. A *Arconfraria da Anunciação*, estabelecida em 1460, em Roma, para prover dotes para as jovens pobres que estivessem noivas.
6. As *Annunziatas*, também chamadas Servitas. Seu mosteiro central fica em Florença, dedicado à anunciação, o que explica o nome delas.

ANZI

No hebraico, **forte** ou **minha força**. Nome de duas pessoas no Antigo Testamento:
1. Um antepassado de Etã, um cantor merarita do templo (I Crô. 6:46).
2. Filho de Zacarias, um antepassado de Adaías, um sacerdote do segundo templo (ver Nee. 11:12).

ANZOL

Ver o artigo geral sobre **peixes e pesca**. Em Isaías 19:8, lemos sobre «os pescadores... que lançam anzol ao rio». E em Jó 41:1, lemos: «Podes tu, com anzol, apanhar o crocodilo...?» E em Hab. 1:15: «a todos levanta o inimigo com o anzol...» E em Amós 4:2: «...vos levarão com anzóis e os vossos restantes com fisga de pesca». Isso fala sobre as ações dos homens que oprimem e matam. Todos esses versículos têm uma linguagem figurada, embora também mostrem (além das lições espirituais) que a pesca com o uso do anzol era uma antiga prática. Em Mat. 17:27, lemos: «...vai ao mar, lança o anzol, e o primeiro peixe que fisgar, tira-o...» Desse modo, Jesus e Pedro pagaram o imposto. Ali a referência ao anzol é literal, sendo a única referência neotestamentária à pesca com o emprego de um anzol. A pesca com anzol incluía a colocação de um chamariz no mesmo; mas também usava-se o método simples de se arrastar um anzol dentro da água, na esperança de apanhar algum peixe, em lugares onde eles formavam cardumes. A pesca com anzol podia apanhar uma cobra, em vez de um peixe; sendo provavelmente essa a idéia por detrás de Luc. 11:11, que fala na remota possibilidade de um pai dar uma cobra a seu filho, em lugar do peixe por ele pedido. (IB ID LAN NTI)

AOÁ

No hebraico, **fraternal**. Filho de Bela, filho de Benjamim (I Crô. 8:4). É chamado Aías no sétimo versículo desse mesmo capítulo. Pode ter sido o mesmo Iri, de I Crô. 7:7. Esse nome pode ter sido um erro escribal em lugar de Aías. (FA S)

AOÍ

Os tradutores variam entre «filho de Aoí» (II Sam. 23:9), «filho de um aoíta» e «o aoíta». Em I Crô. 11:12 encontramos «o aoíta». Eleazar, um dos heróis de Davi, é declarado neto de Aoí, exceto se, conforme dizem algumas traduções, ele simplesmente foi um aoíta. (UN Z)

AOÍTA

Um nome de família dos descendentes de Aoá. Esse nome é aplicado a Dodô (ver I Crô. 11:12) ou Dodai, segundo dizem algumas versões em II Sam. 23:9, embora nossa versão portuguesa também diga «Dodô», Eleazar (II Sam. 23:9), Zalmom (II Sam. 23:28) e Ilai (I Crô. 11:29). Todos eles foram heróis militares da época de Davi. Dodai foi um dos capitães de Salomão (ver I Crô. 27:4). (S)

AOLIABE

No hebraico, **tenda de seu pai**. Foi um habilidoso artífice da tribo de Dã, nomeado juntamente com Bezaleel para construir o tabernáculo (ver Êxo. 35:34). Ele era filho de Aisamaque. Cerca de 1440 A.C. (S UN)

AOLIBÁ

Trata-se de um nome simbólico, dado por Ezequiel à cidade de Jerusalém, por terem os seus habitantes se envolvido na idolatria da Babilônia. Nome similar foi dado à cidade de Samaria, e pelo mesmo motivo, embora através da influência assíria. Por essa razão, Samaria é então chamada de irmã de Jerusalém. Essas irmãs são consideradas esposas de Yahweh, mas culpadas de infidelidade conjugal (ver Eze. 23:1-48). Ver também sobre *Oolá*, o nome aplicado à cidade de Samaria, nesse mesmo trecho bíblico. A palavra «*Oolibá*», significa «minha tenda está nela» (isto é, em Jerusalém), sugerindo que Jerusalém abandonara essa habitação divina para casar-se com outrem. Todavia, alguns estudiosos pensam que esses nomes envolvem prostitutas bem conhecidas na época de Ezequiel, embora nada saibamos atualmente sobre elas. (G IB)

••• ••• •••

APAGADORES

Precisamos considerar duas palavras hebraicas, uma das quais significa, literalmente, «tomadores», e a outra «podar»? Eram instrumentos feitos de ouro (ver Êxo. 37:23) ou de bronze (ver II Reis 25:14), usados para a manutenção de chamas e lâmpadas no tabernáculo e no templo. Entre os eruditos há pouca concórdia quanto à função exata desses instrumentos. E a LXX não nos fornece grande esclarecimento. Ali, a primeira dessas palavras (em Êxo. 37:23; Núm. 4:9; II Crô. 4:22; Isa. 6:6) é traduzida por *labídas*, «agarrador», mas por duas vezes (em Êxo. 25:38 e I Reis 7:49) é traduzida por *eparustrídes*, «escumadeira». A outra palavra heb. é traduzida na LXX por duas vezes (em I Reis 7:50 e II Reis 12:13) por *eloi*, «unhas ornamentais», e por três vezes (em II Reis 25:14; II Crô. 4:22; Jer. 52:18) por Phiálas, «taça rasa».

Em Êxodo 25:38; 37:23, a primeira dessas palavras hebraicas aparece juntamente com outra palavra hebraica que significa «receptáculo» ou «travessa», mas que nossa versão portuguesa traduz por «apagadores». A primeira delas está intimamente ligada ao candeeiro de ouro. Em face do trecho de Isaías 6:6, onde esse instrumento é traduzido por «tenaz» na versão portuguesa, vemos que o mesmo foi usado para tirar uma brasa acesa do altar, aparentemente o segundo daqueles dois termos hebraicos deriva-se de um verbo que significa «podar». E isso, por sua vez, indica que era um instrumento usado para espevitar ou tirar o carvão do pavio das lâmpadas. Não obstante, o contexto da passagem não nos fornece qualquer indício de tal ação. Em adição a isso, conforme já vimos acima, a tradução da LXX nunca traduz o termo por qualquer coisa que ao menos remotamente dê a entender a ação de espevitar. A questão, pois, precisa permanecer na semi-obscuridade, até que novas investigações consigam trazer à tona maiores subsídios. (IB S)

APAGOGE

Vem do grego **apo**, «da parte de», e **agein**, «levar». Dentro da lógica aristotélica, o termo indica um silogismo ilusório. Ver o artigo sobre *abdução*. Ou então o termo pode ser usado para designar o método de demonstração indireta mediante o qual se pode demonstrar o absurdo de uma conclusão que é contrária àquela que deveria ser estabelecida. Ver o artigo sobre *Reductio ad Absurdum*. (EP P)

APAIM

No hebraico, **ventas**. Filho de Nadabe (1400 A.C.), descendente de Jerameel, fundador de uma importante família da tribo de Judá, ver I Crô. 2:30, 31. (ID S)

APARELHOS

Palavra usada para traduzir o termo grego **skeuos**, embora algumas traduções digam «velas». (Ver Atos 27:17). Essa palavra grega tem grande variedade de sentidos, desde coisas e objetos (ver Mar. 11:16), a vasos, pratos e vasilhames (ver Luc. 8:16), e até mesmo alguns vasos específicos, incluindo o corpo humano (ver I Ped. 3:7), ou a mulher, que é vaso de seu marido (ver I Tes. 4:4). Acompanhada por adjetivos, essa palavra refere-se a instrumentos usados por várias profissões, incluindo o caso de navios. A referência no livro de Atos poderia apontar para uma âncora leve.

APARÊNCIA

Na filosofia o termo é usado para indicar o contrário da realidade. Algumas vezes tem a conotação de *ilusão* ou falsidade, em contraste com aquilo que é real e verdadeiro. O *mundo das aparências*, isto é, o mundo físico, é chamado de ilusório nas religiões orientais e por alguns filósofos, e por *menos real* em Platão, por ser transitório, ao passo que o mundo eterno é imperecível e imutável. Na epistemologia, o termo refere-se às *opiniões*, em contraste com os fatos.

1. *Parmênides*. O mundo conforme é interpretado por nossos meios de conhecimento não passa de ilusão.

2. *Platão*. As aparências (através da percepção dos sentidos) fornecem-nos meras opiniões sobre a realidade, e para descobrirmos a realidade, precisamos da razão, da intuição e do misticismo, nessa ordem de poder crescente.

3. A tradição oriental de *Advaita* (ver o artigo) usa o termo. A filosofia vedanta ensina a natureza ilusória do dualismo. A tarefa da vida humana seria dissipar nossas crenças equivocadas quanto ao dualismo, incluindo nossa suposta separação de Bramá. O mundo físico seria ilusório, dando-nos a sensação de dualismo.

4. *Emanuel Kant*. O mundo físico (dos fenômenos) é contrastado com a realidade que a razão reconhece, bem como a intuição e a experiência mística, chamado *noumena*. Nossos sentidos nos transmitem informações sobre o mundo físico, que são meras conveniências, de tal modo que *a coisa em si mesma* (a verdadeira realidade) está oculta de nossos sentidos físicos. Portanto, o que sabemos sobre este mundo é mera convenção mental (as categorias), a qual pode estar relacionada ou não com a realidade.

5. *T.H. Green*. Ele reputava a distinção entre a aparência e a realidade como uma distinção entre a mente limitada e a mente absoluta.

6. *F.H. Bradley* retornou às noções de Parmênides, com as mesmas formas de expressão.

Os argumentos que provam que os sentidos nos dão apenas aparências, e não a realidade, incluem a demonstração destes pontos: 1. a debilidade inerente aos sentidos; 2. o fato de que a verdadeira realidade, ao nível dos átomos, não é sondada pelos nossos sentidos, e nem mesmo por nossos instrumentos científicos; 3. o fato de que mesmo que conhecêssemos plenamente o átomo, o mundo real ainda seria mais básico do que o átomo, por ser o domínio da mente, e não da matéria.

Uma mesa vista sob diferentes ângulos, e sob diferentes luzes, parece mudar de cor. Uma vara, posta na água em ângulo relativo à sua superfície, parece deformar-se. Os trilhos das estradas de ferro, conforme se distanciam no horizonte, parecem convergir a um mesmo ponto. Os cantos de uma sala, vistos de qualquer distância, parecem abrir-se a ter mais de 90°. Devido à razão, porém, continuamos a dizer que os ângulos são de 90°, e não notamos conscientemente a diferença. Mediante a razão, corrigimos a distorção visual. Mas não é fato que *toda* a nossa visão é uma distorção do que vemos, e *toda* a nossa audição é uma distorção do que ouvimos? Isso ocorre porque nossos órgãos de sentido são fracos, são instrumentos defeituosos, apesar do fato de serem admiráveis e práticos quanto à vida diária. Os instrumentos científicos aprimoram nossa percepção, mas não têm sido capazes de dar solução aos grandes problemas filosóficos, e nem mesmo aos maiores problemas científicos. Sabemos atualmente muito mais sobre o átomo do que o sabiam os filósofos gregos, mas novas partículas atômicas sempre estão sendo descobertas, alterando nossa compreensão do átomo. As partículas do átomo continuam para nós quase tão misteriosas quanto sempre o foram. A ciência materialista ainda põe o átomo no trono da realidade, como se o mesmo representasse tudo quanto existe; mas isso é fé, e não ciência. Estudos no campo da parapsicologia demonstram que há fenômenos mentais que não cabem dentro desse molde materialista. A experiência do retorno após a morte biológica (experiências de quase morte) mostra-nos que há um aspecto não-material no homem que não está sujeito à destruição produzida pela morte. Ver o artigo sobre *experiências de quase morte*. Essas coisas nos alertam para o fato de que vivemos em uma realidade essencialmente misteriosa, e pelo menos, parcialmente não-material, e que a maioria de nossas descrições dessa realidade tem natureza parabólica, com base nas meras *aparências*, e não com base na natureza verdadeira das coisas. Portanto, permanece verdadeira a declaração de Kant, no sentido que «Só podemos conhecer os objetos conforme eles nos *parecem* (para nossos sentidos), e não como eles são em si mesmos (isto é, em sua verdadeira natureza). (*Proleg.* 10). Apesar de que alguns filósofos ataquem esse conceito, o argumento permanece por força de necessidade, porque a debilidade de nossa percepção é notória. Ademais, nunca sabemos qual a verdadeira natureza de uma coisa enquanto não obtemos uma completa e perfeita descrição da mesma. Mas, com base em nossa ciência atômica, segundo ela existe na atualidade, isso é impossível. Acresce-se a isso que se há uma dimensão não-material da realidade, torna-se ainda mais difícil obter conhecimento da verdadeira natureza das coisas.

Importância da fé religiosa. Se a realidade não pode ser conhecida por meio da percepção dos sentidos, e se a realidade não se limita à matéria, então precisamos de outros meios de conhecimento, como a razão, a *intuição* e as *experiências místicas* (ver o artigo a respeito). Mesmo que esses meios só nos possam dar conhecimentos parabólicos da realidade, também podem ampliar e aguçar nossas descrições, de tal maneira que cheguem mais próximas da realidade do que o faz a percepção dos sentidos. Os cristãos defendem a validade da *revelação*, e a revelação é uma subcategoria do misticismo. Se pode haver tal coisa como revelações provenientes de um Poder Supremo, então podemos conhecer coisas inteiramente à parte da percepção dos sentidos, uma verdade que todas as religiões mantêm. (E EP F P PH)

APARIÇÃO

No grego, **fantasma**. O vocábulo pode ser bastante lato para incluir qualquer visitante vindo de algum mundo espiritual e sobrenatural. No contexto bíblico, porém, usualmente refere-se a um espírito desincorporado que retorna, pode ser visto, e pode transmitir alguma espécie de mensagem. Assim, temos o caso do falecido Samuel (I Sam. 28:13) e o caso em que Jesus foi equivocadamente tomado como um espírito (Mat. 14:26 e Mar. 6:49). Tais aparições eram temidas, não meramente por causa daquilo que pudessem fazer, mas porque a visão de um fantasma era considerada um mau presságio. Após a Sua ressurreição, Jesus salientou que Ele, diferentemente dos fantasmas, tinha forma sólida, composta de carne e ossos, que podiam ser tocados. Naturalmente, nesse caso temos um corpo físico ressurrecto, o qual, na ascensão e glorificação de Jesus foi necessariamente glorificado, assumindo natureza espiritual. Podemos ter a certeza de que esse corpo não continuou sendo de carne e ossos, por ser impossível tal veículo nos mundos espirituais.

Vários comentadores salientam que a crença comum na época incluía fantasmas, espíritos desincorporados e todas as modalidades de estranhas entidades espirituais. Alguns deles apressam-se em afirmar que tudo não passava de superstição. John Gill, comentando sobre Mat. 14:26, mostra que as referências no Talmude dos judeus desencorajavam a saudação a estranhos, à noite, porque poderia tratar-se de um demônio (ver *Tal. Bab. Megella*, fl. 3:1; *Sanh.* fl. 44.1). O demônio fêmea, Lilite, assustava as pessoas aparecendo-lhes com fisionomia humana. Gostava de seqüestrar ou matar crianças. Naturalmente, nesse caso temos uma crendice, uma superstição. Mas sempre será sábio não agir precipitadamente, supondo que uma questão como essa possa ser eliminada mediante meros assaltos verbais.

As pesquisas no campo psíquico demonstram que há muitas coisas que não podemos entender neste mundo. E não há que duvidar que o mundo espiritual é tão ou mais complexo que o mundo físico, havendo muitos tipos e níveis de seres espirituais. Alguns deles são responsáveis pela possessão demoníaca; e os demônios não pertencem apenas a uma classe de seres. Podem ser anjos caídos (casos raros), ou seres espirituais de níveis inferiores, incluindo espíritos humanos desencarnados. Os judeus sempre acreditaram nos espíritos, como todos os povos das antigas culturas. Essa era a idéia mais comum acerca dos demônios, até o século V D.C., quando Crisóstomo e seus comentários modificaram a opinião geral, fazendo com que os demônios fossem apenas anjos caídos. Não obstante, a doutrina de que um demônio possa ser um espírito humano desencarnado tem persistido na Igreja, sendo largamente defendida. As pesquisas modernas mostram que há níveis e poderes diversos entre os demônios. Ver o artigo sobre os *demônios* quanto a essa questão.

A Bíblia apresenta casos da volta de espíritos humanos desencarnados, segundo se viu no começo deste artigo. Ver também Mateus 17:3. Há muitas evidências na comprovação do fenômeno, nos tempos antigos e modernos. — Isso não significa, entretanto, que devamos formar uma religião que consista em entrar em contato com tais espíritos, para obter deles ensinos e conceitos religiosos, conforme faz o *espiritualismo*, também chamado *espiritismo* (ver o artigo a respeito). Algumas vezes, agrada a Deus permitir comunicações dessa forma, mas tudo depende de Sua vontade. Tais espíritos, ao que parece, às vezes, retornam *sem qualquer motivo;* e cumpre-me dizer que há evidências de que os destinos de tais espíritos ainda não foram fixados. Se uma pessoa morre em Cristo, vai estar com Ele. Em caso contrário, o destino dos espíritos permanece em fluxo, conforme o afirma I Pedro 4:6. Ver o NTI nesse versículo, quanto a uma doutrina representada na Igreja histórica, embora a mesma não faça parte das declarações de fé de muitas denominações evangélicas atuais. Parece que os espíritos humanos do hades algumas vezes podem retornar. Veja-se o caso do anticristo, que subirá do hades (ver Apo. 11:7 e 17:8). Naturalmente, o hades é um estado da existência espiritual, e não um lugar no centro do globo terrestre, como os antigos acreditavam. Parece que pelo menos alguns espíritos podem emergir desse estado e entrar em contato com os homens. Alguns casos de possessão demoníaca podem envolver esse tipo de contato.

A Natureza Humana. As pesquisas científicas no campo da antropologia metafísica demonstram que o homem é uma complexidade de pelo menos três formas de energia distintas. 1. O corpo, uma energia física. 2. A vitalidade, uma energia semifísica. 3. A alma ou espírito, uma energia espiritual, supostamente fora do campo atômico. Assim sendo, o *fantasma* pode ser a vitalidade, que antes fazia parte do complexo humano. Essa vitalidade é capaz de certos atos que exigem uma baixa inteligência e sejam de natureza mecânica. Uma vez que as energias de um indivíduo se separem por meio da morte, essa energia vital retém a capacidade de realizar certas coisas, demonstrando um tipo baixo e mecânico de inteligência. Sua tarefa, na pessoa viva, aparentemente é mediar entre as energias física e espiritual. Uma vez livre, ela torna-se uma espécie de espírito elementar, que pode persistir por algum tempo. Mas, com a passagem do tempo, a energia dissipa-se e o fenômeno cessa. Provavelmente, essa forma de energia (que não é um espírito humano, nem um demônio, e nem qualquer coisa similar) é responsável por muitas estórias de casas mal-assombradas, da atividade dos «poltergeists» e dos fenômenos ligados ao espiritismo. Porém, de outras vezes, o fantasma é um espírito humano desencarnado. As evidências mostram que tais espíritos não são necessariamente demoníacos no seu sentido verdadeiro; mas sempre são espíritos perturbados, de pequeno desenvolvimento espiritual, pelo que não são apropriados como companhia para os homens, podendo causar dificuldades, embora de tipo menos daninho do que no caso de demônios autênticos (sem importar qual natureza metafísica eles tenham). Todavia, cumpre-nos manter distância dos mesmos, porque já temos muitas dificuldades e perturbações próprias, sem termos de tomar por empréstimo mais dificuldades provenientes do mundo espiritual, sobre o qual tão pouco sabemos. A crença antiga sobre os danos que os espíritos desencarnados podem produzir sem dúvida estava baseada na observação e na experiência, e não na superstição criada em um vácuo. Quase sempre os mitos e lendas têm um cerne de verdade, rodeado por muita fantasia.

Uma quarta energia no homem. Podemos talvez encontrar aí o verdadeiro ser humano, um elevado poder espiritual, semelhante a um anjo. Seria similar ao conceito judaico-cristão do anjo guardião. O anjo guardião pode ser o verdadeiro ser do homem, e a alma pode ser o seu instrumento, da mesma maneira que o corpo é o instrumento da alma. Nas religiões orientais, essa entidade é chamada — *superego*. Imaginemos uma mão humana com seus cinco dedos. Um dedo é algo real, mas sua realidade é dependente. Um dedo não pode existir sem a palma da mão, sem a estrutura essencial da mão. A palma poderia representar o «superego», a verdadeira entidade de um homem. Trata-se de um poder elevado e inteligente. O dedo, pois, representa a alma.

Quando as formas tornam-se visíveis. Um corpo é uma forma de energia que nossos olhos físicos são capazes de ver. O fantasma é a vitalidade que, quando vista, aparece em preto e branco, sendo vista na forma de um corpo humano, embora não tenha natureza física. A alma é vista em cores, e usualmente aparece em forma humana, embora assuma essa forma por conveniência, e não por necessidade. A alma pode assumir muitas formas. Além disso, o «superego», é visto apenas como um campo de luz. Na verdade, ignoramos quase totalmente esses grandes mistérios, e o que sabemos meramente sonda a realidade humana. A realidade do *superego*, não exclui a realidade dos anjos guardiães independentes, que são seres separados do homem. Mas julgo, juntamente com Orígenes, que esse ser, o homem essencial, é um irmão para os anjos, sendo inferior a eles somente por causa dos efeitos da queda no pecado. Na redenção, porém, esse ser (nosso ser real e essencial) está destinado a compartilhar da natureza divina (ver II Ped. 1:4), de acordo com a imagem e a natureza do Filho de Deus (ver I João 3:3; Rom. 8:29; II Cor. 3:18 e Col. 2:10), sendo esse ponto o mistério e a doutrina mais profundos de todos.

Contudo, retornando às aparições, elas existem, algumas vezes são espíritos humanos desincorporados; entretanto, usualmente, são apenas a vitalidade. (Ver o artigo sobre a *alma*). (A BAY NTI)

APARIÇÕES DE JESUS, depois de sua ressurreição
I. O Registro Histórico

1. *No dia da ressurreição*. A Maria Madalena (Jo. 20:14-18). Às outras mulheres, Maria, mãe de Tiago e José, Joana, Salomé (e outras) que tinham vindo com especiarias para ungir o corpo de Jesus (Luc. 24:10, Mat. 28:7-10). Na tarde daquele mesmo dia, a Pedro (Luc. 24:10, Mat. 28:7-10). Mais tarde, ainda nesse dia, aos dois discípulos no caminho de Emaús, um dos quais se chamava Cléopas, embora desconhecamos o nome do outro. Provavelmente Cléopas forneceu a informação sobre este acontecimento que Lucas incluiu no seu Evangelho (ver Luc. 24:13,18). Pouco mais tarde, a dez discípulos, pois Judas Iscariotes já morrera e Tomé estava ausente (Luc. 24:36-43, Jo. 21:1-23).

2. *Oito dias mais tarde* (Jo. 20:26), a todos os onze apóstolos, incluindo Tomé (Jo. 20:24-29).

3. *Certo número indeterminado de dias*, depois disso, a sete discípulos, Pedro, Tomé, Natanael, Tiago, João (estes dois últimos filhos de Zebedeu), e dois outros cujos nomes não foram fornecidos (Jo. 21:2).

4. Em alguma *data indeterminada*, a quinhentos irmãos (I Cor. 15:6).

5. *Em Jerusalém* e em Betânia, *em data posterior*, para Tiago (I Cor. 15:7), e pouco mais tarde, a todos os apóstolos novamente, *ao tempo da ascensão* (I Cor. 15:7, Mat. 28:16,20, Luc. 24:33-43, Atos 1:3-12).

6. *Por meio de visões*, a Paulo (I Cor. 15:8, Atos 9:3-6), a Estêvão (Atos 7:55), e a João, na ilha de Patmos (Apo. 1:10-19).

As narrativas assim fornecidas nos dão uma base *histórica* firme sobre o fato da ressurreição, sendo um dos princípios fundamentais do NT e da fé cristã. Ver o artigo geral sobre a *Ressurreição*.

II. Comentários Gerais sobre as Aparições

As manifestações de Cristo, após a sua ressurreição são importantes porque, através delas, e foram muitas, temos provas empíricas do fato da ressurreição; e diversos pormenores das mesmas fornecem-nos algum discernimento na natureza da própria ressurreição. Um sumário dessas manifestações, com base em todas as fontes informativas, é dado em João 20:1

APARIÇÕES DE JESUS

no NTI.

As tradições que envolvem a questão, até mesmo aquelas preservadas nos evangelhos sinópticos, diferem muito quanto à ordem das manifestações e ao seu número; mas são unânimes na narrativa do grande *fato* da ressurreição. De fato, é quase impossível preparar-se uma harmonia desses acontecimentos, com qualquer certeza. Porém, até mesmo isso favorece *o fato*; pois se a igreja cristã primitiva tivesse criado a narrativa, apoiando-se mediante manifestações supostas, mas não reais, tal invenção mui provavelmente exibiria os sinais de uniformidade e harmonia. Bem pelo contrário, naquelas horas de perplexidade e espanto, o Senhor Jesus foi visto por muitas vezes, por muitas pessoas; e nenhuma das narrativas inclui todas essas manifestações, sendo bem possível que a ordem de ocorrência das mesmas apareça nos diversos livros bíblicos de maneira um tanto confusa. Esse «elemento humano», nas narrativas, é exatamente o que se poderia esperar em meio a circunstâncias tão avassaladoras, o que explica a presença de certa confusão nas narrativas. Portanto, onde sofre a harmonia, a *verdade* brilha ainda *com mais* resplendor.

A narrativa de Paulo, se deriva de uma das mais antigas tradições, embora com algumas curiosas e marcantes diferenças, quando a confrontamos com a história relatada nos evangelhos *sinópticos*, bem como com a história do evangelho de João. Pedro aparece em I Cor. 15 como a primeira pessoa para quem Jesus apareceu, ainda que o vocábulo «primeira» não seja usado; mas esse sentido é óbvio no texto. Portanto, o apóstolo dos gentios deixa de lado a belíssima narrativa da aparição de Jesus a Maria Madalena (contida exclusivamente no evangelho de João), além de sua manifestação a várias outras mulheres, conforme lemos nos evangelhos sinópticos. Por semelhante modo, é curioso que a manifestação do Senhor Jesus a Pedro não seja mencionada nos evangelhos exceto em uma referência passageira, em Luc. 24:34, ainda que haja narrativa de uma aparição do Senhor a Pedro, em João 21:7 e ss.; mas essa aparição teve lugar na Galiléia, e não em Jerusalém, que foi a cena de seus primeiros aparecimentos.

Outra curiosidade, acerca dessa questão em geral é que, conforme a narrativa dos evangelhos sinópticos, tem-se a impressão de que todos os acontecimentos d ressurreição, as aparições e a ascensão do Ser' . ocorreram em um só dia. Já o evangelho de João mostra um intervalo de uma semana (ver João 20:26) a separar algumas das aparições do Senhor; e foi após esse intervalo que a manifestação especial de Jesus a Pedro teve lugar, embora os «doze» já tivessem avistado ao Senhor pelo menos duas vezes antes disso. Todavia, esse aparecimento especial a Pedro não pode ter sido o mesmo mencionado pelo apóstolo Paulo. Antes, deve ter havido vários aparecimentos a Pedro, sob variegadas circunstâncias.

Quanto à longa permanência de quarenta dias, após a ressurreição, somente o livro de Atos (mas não qualquer dos evangelhos) nos dá tal informação, a qual, na realidade, não é deixada implícita em nenhum outro lugar. Além disso, somente Lucas (Lucas-Atos) nos fornece qualquer «narrativa» sobre a ascensão; mas até mesmo nesse caso, no tocante ao evangelho de Lucas, a narrativa é posta em dúvida devido a certas variantes textuais; e isso significa que somente no livro de Atos é que se encontra a história da ascensão do Senhor, ainda que existam muitas alusões a esse *fato*, em vários pontos do N.T. A narrativa da ascensão, no evangelho de Marcos, cai dentro do longo término disputado (existem quatro finais sobre o evangelho de Marcos, nos manuscritos antigos, provavelmente nenhum dos quais é original); pelo que também isso não faz parte da narrativa de qualquer dos evangelistas originais, mas de algum escriba subseqüente.

O aparecimento de Jesus a Pedro, conforme nos informa Paulo, é situado antes do seu aparecimento aos «doze», pelo que pode ser o mesmo aparecimento aludido de passagem em Luc. 24:34, embora em parte alguma haja narrativa detalhada acerca dessa ocorrência. Embora as várias manifestações do Senhor contenham elementos que nos fazem lembrar visões e outras experiências místicas, a linguagem prevalente de Paulo, neste ponto, bem como a linguagem usada na maioria das narrativas, mostra-nos que um aparecimento *literal* está em foco, embora o corpo de Cristo tenha sido *espiritualizado* tendo entrado nos primeiros estágios de glorificação, pela qual ele finalmente passou quando de sua ascensão, e que atingirá o seu clímax quando a igreja estiver inteiramente redimida e arrebatada aos céus. Pode-se notar o trecho de João 20:20, onde Jesus mostrou suas mãos e seu lado a seus discípulos, tendo feito ainda a mesma coisa a Tomé, nos versículos vigésimo sétimo em diante, onde devemos supor que Tomé realmente examinou e tocou nas cicatrizes. Então, conforme a narrativa do vigésimo primeiro capítulo, Jesus «comeu»; e essa é uma outra prova óbvia de sua manifestação «corporal».

A tradição cristã, pois, não se refere apenas à sobrevivência do espírito de Jesus, mas inclui a *espiritualização* de seu corpo, que estivera morto. A sobrevivência, mesmo sem a ressurreição, é uma grande verdade, porquanto a alma humana sobrevive à morte física; mas a doutrina cristã vincula grande importância à sobrevivência da personalidade humana inteira; e essa é uma verdade que as manifestações corporais do Senhor Jesus, após a sua ressurreição, bem demonstram. Sobre o que isso significa, no caso dos crentes — se os próprios elementos do antigo corpo (como no caso de Jesus Cristo) serão reorganizados e revivificados é até hoje questão intensamente disputada entre os eruditos bíblicos. Seja como for, isso certamente significa que a alma será revestida de um veículo apropriado, um *corpo glorificado*; e isso com a finalidade de contrabalançar qualquer derrota que seja reputada como inerente à morte do corpo físico. *Sim, a morte não pode matar!*

O aparecimento de Jesus, «primeiramente» a Simão Pedro, conforme a tradição utilizada por Paulo, sem dúvida tinha significação para a Igreja primitiva segundo as linhas da exaltação de Pedro, como uma autoridade superior, conforme também transparece em Mat. 16:18 e ss. Há aqui uma significação especial quanto à questão da «restauração» e da «esperança». Porquanto aquele discípulo, que tão poucos dias antes havia «negado» a seu Senhor, em temor e fraqueza, foi então completa e *imediatamente* restaurado pelo seu Senhor; que encontro deve ter sido aquele!

«O apóstolo que fora levantado, depois de sua queda, mediante as palavras de absolvição ditas pelo Cristo ressurrecto, foi o primeiro a anunciar o evangelho da ressurreição aos corações de seus colegas». (Swete).

Crisóstomo especulou que Pedro é alistado em primeiro lugar, nas aparições de Jesus, por ter sido o primeiro a confessar a sua missão messiânica, e devido ao seu tão profundo desejo de vê-lo vivo novamente. É provável que essa seja uma *lição* que a igreja cristã primitiva vinculava a esse aparecimento. E é bem provável que o próprio Pedro tenha narrado a

APARIÇÕES DE JESUS

história dessa manifestação do Senhor aos ouvidos de Paulo; e só podemos lamentar que Pedro não nos tenha contado, igualmente, essa sua experiência. Contudo, existem certas coisas por demais sagradas e delicadas para serem contadas a todos. Talvez assim é que Paulo e o próprio Pedro se sentiam acerca dessa questão. Seja como for, a experiência de Pedro um dia também será a nossa, ainda que isso possa demorar algum tempo.

e depois, aos doze, I Cor. 15:5. Todas as tradições bíblicas incluem essa manifestação (excetuando o evangelho de Marcos); mas, na realidade, houve mais de uma dessas manifestações, conforme os evangelhos o mostram. (Ver Mat. 28:16-20; Luc. 24:36 e ss. e João 20:19 e ss). Também constitui uma outra curiosidade que Marcos, o mais antigo dos quatro evangelhos, não inclui tal informação, embora narre o aparecimento do Senhor Jesus às mulheres. A narrativa dessa manifestação aparece no término «longo» do evangelho de Marcos, que começa no décimo quarto versículo de seu último capítulo; mas esse final não faz parte autêntica do evangelho original de Marcos. É perfeitamente possível, entretanto, que o final «perdido» desse evangelho (se tal teoria é correta) realmente contivesse tal narrativa. De fato, podemos até considerar isso como uma boa probabilidade, visto que esse final se encontra essencialmente contido nos demais evangelhos, de uma forma ou de outra; e os outros três evangelhos, em seus finais, contêm a narrativa (ou as narrativas) do aparecimento do Senhor Jesus aos «doze».

Por qual razão Paulo «deixou» de mencionar vários aparecimentos do Senhor Jesus? Precisamos lembrar que quando esse apóstolo escreveu a primeira epístola aos Coríntios, não tinha ele em mãos qualquer dos quatro evangelhos, porquanto ainda não haviam sido publicados. Paulo deve ter tido à sua disposição alguma tradição, oral ou escrita, ou ambas as coisas; porém, é lógico supormos que nenhuma das primitivas tradições cristãs continha todas as manifestações do Cristo ressurrecto.

É justo conjecturarmos que se Paulo contasse com informações acerca de outras manifestações do Senhor Jesus, após a sua ressurreição, teria ele apresentado tais narrativas, para tornar ainda mais convincentes os seus argumentos em prol da resurreição de Cristo. O fato de que ele não incluiu algumas dessas manifestações, que conhecemos hoje em dia, através de outros documentos do N.T., mostra-nos simplesmente que ele não tinha consciência das mesmas.

III. Os Evangelhos de Lucas e João Comparados

1. Ambas as narrativas mostram Jesus aparecendo *aos dez* porquanto Judas Iscariotes já se suicidara e Tomé não estava presente, embora Lucas não nos informe especificamente acerca disso. Porém, o evangelho de João diz *discípulos*, e menciona claramente que *Tomé* não estava presente na primeira oportunidade. (Ver João 20:24). Naturalmente a palavra «discípulos» não limita necessariamente o número de apóstolos a «dez», mas é provável que essa seja a intenção do termo, porque os apóstolos eram os discípulos especiais de Jesus, aqueles que eram focalizados nessa parte da história da ressurreição de Cristo. Porém, apesar de que estavam em foco os «dez», contudo o trecho de Luc. 24:36 indica que também se achavam presentes os dois discípulos com os quais Jesus se encontrara no caminho para Emaús, perfazendo um total de doze seguidores de Cristo.

2. A narrativa do evangelho de João registra o *tempo exato* dessa aparição. Ela teve lugar na noite do mesmo dia da ressurreição. Lucas, todavia, não nos dá essa informação.

3. O relato do quarto evangelho diz-nos que Jesus apareceu estando *fechadas as portas,* porquanto os discípulos temiam ainda aos «judeus». Já o terceiro evangelho nada nos adianta sobre essa particularidade.

4. O evangelho de Lucas dá a entender que a *repentina aparição* de Jesus aterrorizou os discípulos.

5. Ambos esses evangelhos indicam que o Senhor lhes trouxe uma mensagem de *encorajamento,* apesar de que a narrativa está vazada em termos diferentes, nos dois relatos.

6. Ambos esses evangelhos mostram como o Senhor Jesus comprovou ante seus discípulos que tinha corpo. Todavia, a narrativa de Lucas é mais gráfica e específica, como o evangelho de João se mostra mais tarde, ao narrar a revelação de Jesus a Tomé.

7. A narrativa do evangelho de Lucas menciona que Jesus *comeu pão e peixe,* o que o evangelho de João também faz mais adiante (João 21:12,13), embora não se trate da mesma aparição do Senhor.

8. A narrativa de Lucas faz alusão ao fato de que o Senhor *instruiu* os discípulos nas Escrituras do A.T., a respeito de sua própria pessoa, por ocasião desse seu aparecimento. Entretanto, o quarto evangelho faz silêncio acerca disso.

9. O relato do evangelho de João informa-nos que o Senhor soprou o *Espírito Santo* sobre os seus discípulos, investindo-os de uma autoridade especial, algo que, anteriormente, já havia sido dada graciosamente a Simão Pedro, conforme lemos em Mat. 18:18,19. Já o evangelho de Lucas não nos presta tal informação.

10. Nessa ação de Jesus, dando o Espírito Santo a seus discípulos, conforme o quarto evangelho (ver João 20:21), há uma espécie de *Grande Comissão* aos discípulos. No entanto, conforme a seqüência do tempo, no evangelho de Lucas isso é apresentado imediatamente antes da ascensão do Senhor. Todavia, no quarto evangelho essa comissão é claramente dada antes de sua subida aos lugares celestiais. Poderíamos supor, entretanto, que a ascensão, nesse quarto evangelho, é registrada no parágrafo seguinte, sem haver menção de qualquer intervalo de tempo, não tendo, portanto, qualquer intenção de servir de indício cronológico, como se tivesse de ser aceito como incidente que ocorreu logo depois do incidente anteriormente historiado. No evangelho de João figuram outros incidentes, incluindo outras aparições do Senhor Jesus, que o evangelho de Lucas omite inteiramente.

Com base nas considerações expostas acima, vemos a futilidade de tentar obter a harmonia entre as diversas narrativas evangélicas sobre as muitas aparições do Senhor Jesus aos seus seguidores. Pois houve muitas dessas aparições, preservadas por diversas tradições históricas diversas.

IV. A História e a Fé

1. Apesar de ser verdade que a fé religiosa pode ser comunicada por meio de símbolos, sem qualquer base histórica, notemos que os escritores do NT anelavam por apoiar sua doutrina sobre realidades históricas.

2. Isso pode ser confrontado com o prólogo do Evangelho de Lucas. Ver o artigo sobre a *Historicidade dos Evangelhos.*

A maioria das testemunhas oculares estava viva. Seus inimigos estavam vivos e poderiam disputar a história. As testemunhas nada tinham a ganhar, mas muito a perder se contassem a verdade. Essas evidências foram registradas cerca de 25 anos após a ocorrência dos fatos alegados. Teria sido fácil confirmar ou refutar estes fatos. O próprio NT é uma afirmação, baseada em pesquisas históricas, da verdade da ressurreição e das aparições de Jesus depois da sua morte. (I IB NTI Z)

APARTHEID

O vocábulo significa, literalmente, **separação**. É usado para indicar a estrita separação racial seguida pelo governo da África do Sul. Envolve a segregação forçada de raças, envolvendo as reservas nativas para os negros. A filosofia subjacente é que, em tais reservas, os negros têm a liberdade de desenvolverem melhor seu método de viver. Se os negros abandonam essas reservas, ficam sujeitos a muitos regulamentos e restrições. O alvo final dessas reservas é a independência dos negros, uma vez que os brancos julguem que os negros atingiram o ponto onde isso é possível.

Problemas. O maior problema surge devido à natureza daquelas reservas, que muitos reputam pequenas e pobres demais para sustentar a população negra. Elas constituem apenas treze por cento da área total do país, ao passo que os negros constituem sessenta e oito por cento da população. O resultado é que apenas metade da população negra vive nessas reservas, enquanto o resto busca ocupação em indústrias, minas, fazendas, etc., possuídas por brancos, —onde recebem, em média, salários muito inferiores aos que são pagos a empregados brancos.

Considerações cristãs. A lei do amor é o princípio moral supremo da vida (I João 4:7). Onde há injustiça social, não está sendo observada a lei do amor. Uma outra lei é a da honestidade. Se as reservas visam a conferir oportunidade de sustento razoável, sob o regime do *apartheid*, então isso deveria ser uma realidade, e não apenas uma política tencionada. Porém, pode a idéia manter-se de pé diante de trechos bíblicos como Gál. 3:28, onde as distinções raciais e outras, entre os homens, são eliminadas mediante a fé em Cristo?

Simplificações. Sempre haverá defesas e contradições relativas aos sistemas políticos, argumentos contra e a favor. Tais questões nunca são simples, pelo que também nenhuma declaração dogmática é capaz de resolver tão complicados problemas. O que aqui dizemos é apenas sugestivo, porquanto as normas políticas criam grandes questões morais, relacionadas a fé religiosa.

APATIA

Palavra latina que veio do grego **a**, «não», e **pathos**, «sofrimento», «sentimento». Os *estóicos* (ver o artigo) criam que a virtude cardeal e o primeiro princípio de ação é a «indiferença», a «não-reação», ou seja, a *apatia*, em todas as situações da vida. Assim, a tristeza não afetaria o homem, porque as causas da tristeza não têm lugar em seu espírito indiferente. Assim, se alguém deixasse cair um vaso de louça e se o mesmo se quebrasse, ou se a esposa desse alguém morresse, tudo viria a dar no mesmo, pois ambos os acontecimentos devem ser encarados com apatia. Desse modo, tranqüilizar-se-ia o espírito humano. Entre os estóicos, o conceito baseava-se na crença de que todas as coisas são determinadas (ver sobre o *determinismo*), não havendo razão, pois, para alguém lutar contra os eventos. De fato, visto que o Logos divino determina tudo, lutar contra o que Ele faz é uma impiedade e falta de sabedoria. Naturalmente, o Logos era, para os estóicos, uma espécie de força cósmica, e não uma pessoa; mas isso em nada alterava a noção deles de que todas as coisas acontecem necessariamente. Sob nosso controle há apenas uma coisa: nossa reação emocional diante das coisas, mas não as próprias coisas. Nosso *dever* é reagir sem qualquer sentimento aos acontecimentos, pois, de outro modo, estaríamos degradando o propósito do Logos. Esse dever inclui a eliminação tanto de emoções positivas quanto de emoções negativas. As emoções positivas meramente nos excitam emocionalmente, o que é o primeiro inimigo do homem. Portanto, nem sorriso e nem choro, e assim o espírito encontra descanso. (EP MM P)

APEDREJAMENTO

No hebraico há duas palavras a serem consideradas, e no grego também. No hebraico, uma das palavras significa «matar por apedrejamento», e a outra «dar à morte por apedrejamento». No grego temos *lithádzo* e *katalithádzo*. A primeira significa «apedrejar», e a segunda «apedrejar até à morte». Todas essas palavras indicavam o ato de apedrejar a alguém até à morte, como ato de castigo capital.

A forma mais comum de punição capital, prescrita pela lei bíblica, era o apedrejamento. Geralmente era executado fora dos muros das cidades (ver Lev. 24:23; Núm. 15:35,36; I Reis 21:13). As testemunhas de acusação (a lei requeria um mínimo de duas - Deu. 17:6) colocavam as mãos sobre a cabeça do ofensor (ver Lev. 24:14), transferindo assim a culpa da comunidade para o ofensor. As testemunhas jogavam as primeiras pedras, e os demais faziam o resto (ver Deu. 17:7). Tudo era feito com o intuito de expurgar da comunidade o mal ou males praticados (ver Deu. 22:21).

Havia dez formas de ofensa punidas por apedrejamento: 1. a adoração a deuses falsos ou aos astros (Deu. 17:2-7); 2. indução à adoração de deuses falsos (Deu. 13:6-11); 3. blasfêmia (Lev. 24:14-23; I Reis 21:10-15); 4. sacrifício de crianças a Moloque (Lev. 20:2-5); 5. adivinhação por meio de espíritos (Lev. 20:27); 6. quebra do sábado (Núm. 15:32-36); 7. adultério (Deu. 22:21-24); 8. desobediência filial (Deu. 21:18-21); 9. quebra de pactos públicos (Jos. 7:25; também havia o castigo da fogueira, em tais casos); 10. homicídio por meio de um boi (Êxo. 21:28-32). Esse último caso é o único que envolve um animal, embora o trecho de Êxodo 19:13 ameace tanto o homem como o seu animal com apedrejamento, se qualquer um deles tocasse no monte Sinai. Finalmente, embora o apedrejamento não seja mencionado, talvez esteja implícito quando a pena de morte é prescrita para o caso de um profeta que profetize em nome de alguma outra divindade (ver Deu. 13:1-5).

A grande abundância de pedras na Palestina fazia do apedrejamento a mais comum das punições capitais. Também era uma maneira conveniente de exprimir ira ou ódio. O Senhor Jesus foi várias vezes ameaçado de apedrejamento, com base em trechos bíblicos como Êxo. 17:4; Núm. 14:10 e I Sam. 30:6, o que também aconteceu com Paulo, conforme se vê em João 10:31-33; 11:8; Atos 14:5,19. Algumas vezes, o apedrejamento chegava mesmo a ser executado, como se deu com Adorão (I Reis 12:18), Zacarias (II Crô. 24:21) e Estêvão (Atos 7:58,59). (ND Z)

••• ••• •••

APEIRON

Termo grego que significa «sem limites», **indeterminado, indefinido**. Foi usado por Anaximandro (ver o artigo a seu respeito) a fim de indicar aquilo de onde provêm todos os seres e a própria existência, e no qual tudo será finalmente absorvido, embora seja algo desconhecido e sem dimensões. Em Pitágoras (ver o artigo a seu respeito), é um dos dois grandes princípios: o *ilimitado*, que é o contrário do *limitado* (no grego, *peras*). Esses termos são usados na filosofia na tentativa de definir o que essencialmente tem definição. Todavia, o termo não é inútil, porquanto pode significar o que é imaterial, em contraste com o que é material, que limita, que define a energia espiritual, e que é a fonte originária de tudo. (P)

APELES

Um cristão de Roma (ou de Éfeso) a quem Paulo enviou saudações (ver Rom. 16:10). Alguns supõem que o décimo sexto capítulo da epístola aos Romanos realmente é uma epístola independente, escrita como carta de apresentação de Febe, mas que foi vinculada à epístola aos Romanos para ser preservada. Se isso é verdade, então todas as saudações ali contidas são a crentes de Éfeso, e não de Roma. Ver sobre esse problema no artigo *Romanos*, sob o ponto VIII, *Integridade da Epístola*. Seja como for, o homem é ali descrito como «aprovado em Cristo», porquanto devia ser um crente provado e fiel. Orígenes pensava que ele poderia ter sido Apolo, mas isso não é provável. Há tradições que fazem dele um dos setenta discípulos especiais (ver Lucas 10), — que posteriormente ter-se-ia tornado bispo de Esmirna ou de Heracléia (Epifânio, *Contra Haeres.*, parte 20). Sua festa é observada pela Igreja grega a 31 de outubro. Porém, quanto a todas essas tradições, nada pode ser dito com confiança. O nome «Apeles» era designação comum na época, aparecendo em um trecho de Horácio, «Credat Judaeus Apella, non ego» (*Sat.* i.5). (HA S UN)

APELO

1. Uso comum. Um ato mediante o qual alguém busca a ajuda ou a opinião de outrem. Um homem *apelou* para Jesus para que tentasse persuadir seu irmão a dividir com ele a herança (ver Luc. 12:13). O Antigo Testamento não tinha um processo legal para esses casos, embora casos difíceis pudessem ser levados a julgamento (ver Êxo. 18:26 e Deu. 17:8-13).

2. *Nos tempos patriarcais.* O patriarca da tribo podia decidir questões a respeito das quais os membros da tribo não chegavam a um consenso. Não havia autoridade superior à do patriarca.

3. *Israel no deserto.* Moisés era a autoridade, embora tivesse nomeado autoridades subalternas, a fim de que lhe sobrasse tempo para fazer outras coisas (ver Êxo. 18:13-26). Mas ele julgava os casos que não podiam ser devidamente julgados por outros, ou que não fossem satisfatoriamente resolvidos.

4. *Na época dos juízes.* Os juízes tornaram-se as autoridades que resolviam os casos de apelo (ver Juí. 4:5).

5. *Sob a monarquia.* Foram estabelecidas então autoridades judiciais (ver II Crô. 19:8). Foram estabelecidos tribunais por Esdras, após o cativeiro (ver Esd. 7:25). Em tempos posteriores, o *Sinédrio* surgiu como uma espécie de tribunal superior (ver o artigo a respeito).

6. *No Novo Testamento*. Nas áreas judaicas, persistia o antigo sistema, com a inclusão do Sinédrio. Mas, nos casos sérios, como nas sentenças de morte, as questões eram expostas à autoridade romana. Os cidadãos romanos, onde quer que estivessem vivendo, podiam apelar para as autoridades romanas, inclusive para o próprio César. Se um homem apelasse a César, o governador local perdia a jurisdição sobre o caso. Esse direito se originava nas leis Valeriana, Porciana e Semproniana. Plínio (ver *Ep.* x.97) menciona que enviara alguns cristãos a Roma, e que eram cidadãos romanos, para apelarem a César. O famoso caso do Novo Testamento, nessa conexão, é o de Paulo, registrado em Atos 25:10,11,25. Um artigo separado é apresentado sobre esse caso. (Ver o *Apelo de Paulo a César*, mais abaixo). (BRU IB ID NTI S)

APELO DE PAULO A CÉSAR

I. O *provocatio*

Temos em Atos 25:11 um exemplo do *provocatio*, isto é, um direito legal, de todos os cidadãos romanos, de apelarem contra o veredicto de qualquer magistrado ou governante de província. Ante tal apelo, qualquer caso era transferido para o tribunal de César, que então constituía o que hoje chamaríamos de tribunal supremo. Essa forma de apelo existia, ainda que sob variegadas formas, desde os tempos mais remotos do império romano. Como exemplo disso, pode-se examinar o caso de Horácio, segundo o registro de Lívio I.26. O direito de *provocatio* foi garantido pela *Lex Valeria*, em 509 A.C. (Ver Lívio ii.8, U.C. 245). Esse direito foi suspenso por algum tempo, entretanto, durante o período dos «Decenviros», um conselho de dez magistrados da antiga Roma, que, em 450 A.C., preparou o primeiro código das leis romanas. Todavia, tal direito foi restabelecido após a deposição dos Decenviros, conforme Lívio também nos diz (iii.55, U.C. 305).

Nos primeiros tempos da república romana, o apelo ou *provocatio* era dirigido *ad populum*, isto é, ao povo. Posteriormente, porém, passou a ser feito aos *tribunos*, que eram os principais líderes do povo. Finalmente, entretanto, veio a ser feito ao «princeps», o mais elevado poder, isto é, ao imperador. Quando um apelo assim era feito ao imperador, isso eliminava todas as decisões legais e os processos porventura feitos até então. Foi mediante o apelo que fez a César, pois, que o apóstolo Paulo conseguiu livrar-se da vacilação incompreensível de governantes secundários, como Félix e Festo. Nos primeiros tempos, só se podia fazer tal apelo dentro da própria capital do império, Roma; e até uma distância de uma milha romana para além de suas muralhas. Entretanto, nos tempos de Paulo, esse direito se estendera a todos os cidadãos do império, em qualquer lugar onde se encontrassem.

II. Implicações

Quanta coisa estava envolvida nessa decisão de Paulo, de apelar para César? Isso é o que procuramos mostrar nos cinco pontos abaixo:

1. De modo geral, precisamos admitir que o apóstolo já entendera que a maré se voltara contra ele nesse caso, e que Festo talvez estivesse começando a acreditar em algumas das acusações dos judeus, ou pelo menos, que não se dispunha a entrar em choque com eles, por causa de um mero prisioneiro.

2. Assim sendo, é perfeitamente possível que Festo, a fim de *desembaraçar-se* de tão complicado caso, quisesse entregar Paulo à discrição do sinédrio, o que

APERCEPÇÃO — APERFEIÇOAMENTO DE CRISTO

teria sido fatal para o apóstolo.

3. Depois de ter passado por mais de dois anos aprisionado em Cesaréia, o apóstolo já *perdera* toda a esperança de encontrar justiça ali. Só lhe restava o recurso de esperar que um julgamento mais imparcial lhe fosse proporcionado em Roma, perante o tribunal supremo de César.

4. Após tão longo período de aprisionamento, o apóstolo já havia perdido a paciência. Aqueles que têm sofrido prolongados períodos de encarceramento, geralmente expressam o desespero que acompanha esses julgamentos sempre adiados. Paulo não tolerava mais adiamentos, e assim resolveu provocar alguma forma de mudança nessa situação.

5. Desde há muito o apóstolo dos gentios desejava conhecer Roma, tendo recebido a promessa, da parte do próprio Senhor Jesus, que isso sucederia finalmente. (Ver Atos 23:11). É possível que agora Paulo encarasse esse apelo como uma maneira providencial de *garantir* essa viagem, embora sem dúvida preferisse muito mais poder chegar na capital do império romano na qualidade de homem livre, e não como prisioneiro. No trecho de Atos 28:19, Paulo se refere à atitude que tomou nesta ocasião como algo a que fora *constrangido*, e não voluntariamente. Viajar a Roma, para ali ser julgado pelo tribunal de César, era financeiramente pesado, enfadonho e uma perda de tempo. Todavia, aparentemente não havia outra maneira de sair Paulo do dilema em que se encontrava.

«Essa lei (do apelo a César) era tão sagrada e imperativa que, nas perseguições contra o cristianismo que houve durante o reinado de Trajano, Plínio não se atrevia a executar os cidadãos romanos que porventura se tivessem tornado cristãos. Assim, em sua carta Trajano (*Lib. x. Ep.* 97), diz ele: '*Fuerunt alli similis amentiae, quos, quia civis Romani erant, annotavi in urbem remittendos*', cujo sentido é: 'Houve outros culpados de loucura semelhante, aos quais, descobrindo eu serem cidadãos romanos, determinei enviá-los à cidade (Roma).' Mui provavelmente esses são os que haviam feito apelo a César». (Adam Clarke, em Atos 25:11).

O imperador Nero, «...para César...» O *César* do tempo do aprisionamento do apóstolo Paulo era Nero, o qual foi imperador de 54 a 68 D.C.

Nero era o trineto de Augusto, por meio de sua mãe. Fora adotado por Cláudio, o imperador anterior, como seu herdeiro. Nero era filho de uma distinta família da antiga aristocracia romana, os *Domitii*. Foi o último *César* por hereditariedade, porquanto os imperadores que houve depois de Nero não eram membros dessa família. «César» era o sobrenome de Júlio César. E mais tarde esse nome foi aplicado como título aos outros membros dessa família que governou o gigantesco império romano, título esse que também foi adotado pelos subseqüentes imperadores romanos, ainda que não pertencessem a essa dinastia.

Nero fez chegar ao ponto final a hegemonia de sua família devido às suas inúmeras atrocidades, que destruíram o prestígio da família. Ele mesmo terminou por suicidar-se, em 68 D.C., por causa das revoltas que estouraram em Roma, por sua causa. Após a sua morte prematura, surgiram lendas em várias localidades a seu respeito, incluindo a idéia de diversas reencarnações. Alguns cristãos primitivos emitiram a opinião de que o futuro *anticristo* seria uma reencarnação de Nero, idéia essa que tem reaparecido nos tempos mais recentes, como nos escritos de um escritor como William R. Newell, autor de vários comentários sobre livros canônicos do Antigo e do Novo Testamentos. (Outros, porém, têm pensado que o anticristo será uma reencarnação de *Judas Iscariotes*, suposição essa que tem sido apoiada por uma autoridade não menor que a do dr. M.R. DeHaan). (I IB ID LAN NTI S)

APERCEPÇÃO

1. Em Leibniz, o termo refere-se aos estados internos de consciência de si mesmo, ao passo que percepção alude à consciência do que é externo.

2. Em Kant, a palavra denota a unidade do autoconsciente, em sua forma empírica ou em sua forma transcendental.

O vocábulo usualmente é definido como o processo mental que eleva nossas impressões indistintas ao nível da atenção, ao mesmo tempo que as arranja para formar uma ordem intelectual coerente. Todavia, o termo tem sido usado de forma ambígua, algumas vezes para indicar meramente a tomada de consciência, e outras vezes, para indicar os atos de concentração da atenção e assimilação. Os filósofos se têm demorado nessas distinções, desde o princípio. Aristóteles, os pais da Igreja e os escolásticos distinguiram entre noções vagas e sentimentos, por um lado, e conceitos produzidos pelo ato intelectual voluntário, por outro lado. Locke empregava o vocábulo *percepção* a fim de denotar o primeiro passo na direção do conhecimento; função essa perceptível em todos os animais. Para ele, porém, a *apercepção* significava o estado de consciência consciente e meditativa. (E F EP)

APERFEIÇOAMENTO DE CRISTO, O FILHO

I. Comentário sobre Heb. 2:10.

Em que sentido Cristo foi *aperfeiçoado*? Isso pode ser visto nos pontos abaixo considerados:

1. *Não* pode significar purificado de qualquer fraqueza moral ou pecado, pois esse livro defende a impecabilidade de Cristo (ver Heb. 4:15; ver também João 8:46; II Cor. 5:21; Heb. 7:26; I Ped. 1:19 e 2:22).

2. Mas, ao identificar-se com o homem, ele tomou sobre si mesmo as imperfeições humanas como ser, precisando ser aperfeiçoado segundo as «qualidades morais positivas» de Deus, como a fé, o amor, a bondade, a justiça, etc. (Ver Gál. 5:22,23). *Na qualidade de homem*, pois, Jesus teve de aprender a buscar as perfeições divinas, tal como todos os homens devem fazê-lo. Nessa inquirição espiritual ele se tornou o nosso grande «Líder». E então, sendo aperfeiçoado pessoalmente, veio a mostrar a outros homens como se deve buscar a perfeição. Para todos os remidos, o «estar aperfeiçoado» excede em muito à mera ausência do pecado. Significa, igualmente, a participação em todas as perfeições positivas e em todos os atributos morais de Deus. Estritamente falando, somente Deus é perfeito, embora possa haver outras criaturas que são impecáveis. Cristo, em sua humanidade, buscou e obteve as perfeições de Deus, tal como devem fazê-lo todos quantos estão remidos nele.

3. Além disso, Jesus foi *aperfeiçoado* em sua missão remidora no sentido que tudo quanto foi exigido dele foi formado nele, mediante os sofrimentos. O redentor, a fim de que pudesse remir, teve de morrer. Sua morte e ressurreição eram elementos necessários para qualificá-lo como perfeito e completo redentor. Ele não era um redentor imperfeito ou incompleto.

APERFEIÇOAMENTO — APETITES

Apesar do tema desse versículo transcender ao pensamento que o «sofrimento aperfeiçoa», esse preceito está longe de ser coisa comum e sem valor.

4. Uma vez que a missão de Cristo se completou, ele foi glorificado. Isso o aperfeiçoou, certamente. Ele estava incompleto sem tal elemento. O próprio homem, embora fique totalmente sem pecado, se não tiver obtido a total glorificação em Cristo, ainda não estará aperfeiçoado.

5. O Líder ou Autor da redenção deve possuir tudo quanto ele espera da parte dos remidos. É mister que sua *humanidade* seja aperfeiçoada; e deve ter em si mesmo toda a experiência humana, como a alegria e a tristeza, como o esforço por obter a vitória na inquirição espiritual. É mister que tenha tudo e passe por tudo quanto os remidos experimentarão. Ora, isso ocorreu na encarnação, e foi um aperfeiçoamento do Redentor. Nisso se vê quão profundamente ele está associado a nós. Ele tomou sobre si tudo quanto somos, a fim de podermos obter tudo quanto ele é, em sua glorificação, em que ele entrou, devido à sua perfeição.

6. O alvo é a própria perfeição de Deus Pai. Ao tornar-se pouco inferior aos anjos, Cristo já não era perfeito no sentido em que o Pai é perfeito. Sua encarnação tornou possível o aperfeiçoamento da humanidade. Cristo foi o primeiro homem a percorrer essa vereda; outros se seguirão, pois ele é o *Pioneiro* do caminho.

«Se alguém estranhar a idéia de que Deus aperfeiçoou a Cristo, não deverá olvidar-se do fato de que é a humanidade de Jesus que está sob discussão». (Robertson, in loc.).

II. Docetismo

Na moderna igreja evangélica a divindade de Cristo tem sido enfatizada às custas de sua humanidade. Um Cristo «docético» tem sido criado na atitude real, embora não quanto às declarações doutrinárias. Tudo quanto Cristo fez é atribuído à sua divindade, e nada, a não ser a sua morte, é deixado para a sua humanidade. Mas Jesus foi homem real, e deixou de lado suas divinas prerrogativas, embora não a sua natureza divina. O que ele fez, fê-lo como homem; o que ele sofreu e aprendeu, fê-lo como homem; suas obras poderosas eram feitas através do poder do Espírito; e esse mesmo poder o transformou e espiritualizou como homem, tal e qual deve suceder a todos os remidos. (Ver Fil. 2:7 no NTI quanto a uma discussão acerca da importância da doutrina da «humanidade de Cristo»). De maneira bem real, Jesus, como homem, precisa ser aperfeiçoado e o foi em sua experiência humana. Por semelhante modo, seus irmãos devem passar eventualmente por esse processo de aperfeiçoamento. Em sua função mais elevada, isso consiste em trazer o infinito para o que é finito, de trazer o divino para o que é humano. (AL GI IB NTI)

APERFEIÇOAMENTO DO CRISTÃO

I. Definição

Aperfeiçoamento. Uma palavra bastante comum em outros documentos escritos em grego, mas que aparece exclusivamente em Efé. 4:12 em todo o N.T. No original grego encontramos o termo «katartismos», que era usado para indicar a correção de ossos partidos, a restauração de algo ao seu estado primitivo, etc. A raiz dessa palavra é «artios», que significa «completo», «perfeito», «totalmente adaptado». A forma verbal, «katartidzo», significa «restaurar», «ajustar», «pôr em ordem», «reformar». Isso subentende o fato de ficarmos cheios da plenitude de deidade, tal como ela se encontra na pessoa de Cristo, conforme aprendemos em Col. 2:9,10, uma doutrina extraordinariamente elevada. Mas esse é o único caminho para a perfeição, pois esta, segundo a sua própria definição, só pode aplicar-se ao Senhor Deus, pois somente ele é perfeito. É a mensagem profundíssima do evangelho que essa mesma perfeição é dada aos homens, de acordo com sua transformação segundo a imagem de Cristo, o qual, na qualidade de Verbo eterno encarnado, e que se identificou com os homens eternamente, primeiramente a experimentou em si mesmo, na qualidade de Deus-homem. A idéia implica a participação na natureza divina, II Ped. 1:4.

II. Idéias diversas

Vários pontos de vista sobre a natureza exata dessa «perfeição», têm sido expostos, sumariados dentro da seguinte nota de Hodge (em Efé. 4:12): 1. Seria o número terminado dos santos, o 'número completo dos eleitos'. 2. Seria a renovação ou restauração. 3. Seria a redução dos crentes à ordem e à união, formando um único corpo organizado. 4. Seria a preparação dos santos para o serviço (ponto de vista esse compartilhado por vários comentadores bíblicos). 5. Seria o aperfeiçoamento dos santos. Este último sentido é que está em foco aqui, que é comentado no parágrafo anterior.

Para o desempenho do seu serviço, Efé. 4:12. Os dons ministeriais são dados com a finalidade de aperfeiçoar aos santos (maior definição ainda do que isso significa, aparece no décimo terceiro versículo), possibilitando o funcionamento do ministério na igreja, o que, por si só, já é um meio de aperfeiçoar aos crentes, já que produz aquela unidade acerca do que toda esta seção se refere. Pois os homens, uma vez aperfeiçoados em Cristo, certamente se unirão em torno dele e uns com os outros, na mesma atitude, buscando os mesmos alvos. (IB LAN NTI RO)

APETIÇÃO

1. Alguns usam o termo para indicar o processo de satisfação dos apetites.

2. Spinoza usava-o como sinônimo de esforço, de modo geral, o que, segundo a sua análise, seria o alvo central da vida humana.

3. Leibniz usava a palavra para indicar o escopo em que essa satisfação se estende pela realidade, referindo-se à maneira da ação e às mônadas destituídas de extensão que constituiriam o mundo.

4. Whitehead seguia Leibniz ao aceitar a apetição como uma categoria universal que descreve a atividade das unidades ontológicas mais básicas. (P)

APETITES

Vem do latim, *appetere*, «anelar», «desejar intensamente». O termo é aplicado ao aspecto dinâmico, que busca satisfação, própria da natureza humana.

1. Em Aristóteles (ver o artigo) os apetites constituíam a porção irracional da alma. O desenvolvimento da moral leva os apetites a serem controlados pela razão.

2. Tomás de Aquino exprimia praticamente a mesma idéia, com um pouco mais de desenvolvimento, tendo-se baseado em parte nas idéias de João Damasceno. Aquino e outros pensadores escolásticos distinguiam os apetites como: concupiscível, irascível e racional. (P)

ÁPIO FÓRUM

Era uma cidade-mercado na Via Ápia, a quase 64 km ao sul de Roma, uma parada de diligências no Lácio, ao longo da estrada que ia de Roma a Brundísio, construída por Ápio Cláudio (ver o artigo anterior, sobre a Via Ápia). Horácio informa-nos que vivia repleta de marinheiros, comerciantes e donos de hospedaria extorsivos, um lugar cheio de mosquitos e rãs (ver *Sat*. i.5,7). As ruínas dessa cidade continuam existentes em um local chamado Casrillo di Santa Maria, na fronteira dos alagadiços pontinos, o que explica os mosquitos e as rãs mencionadas por Horácio. A cidade ficava no término norte do canal que atravessava os alagadiços. Quando Paulo foi levado à Itália, alguns cristãos de Roma saíram ao seu encontro, e foi ali que se encontraram com ele. Três Tavernas, que também participa da narrativa, ficava a treze ou dezesseis quilômetros mais perto de Roma. (ID ND UN S)

ÁPIS

Um deus-boi egípcio, um touro negro com manchas brancas distintivas, cuja adoração estava ligada a vários outros deuses. Em Mênfis, no Egito, o boi (Ápis) era considerado o corpo do deus Ptah. Quando o deus-boi morria, era enterrado com elaborado cerimonial. Corpos embalsamados de bois, descobertos no cemitério Ápis, pertenciam ao período do Último Império até à época dos Ptolomeus. Ver o artigo sobre *Egito, Religiões do*. (E MER)

APOCALIPSE

Introdução
I. O Que é Um Apocalipse? Literatura Apocalíptica
II. Confirmação Antiga
III. Autoria
IV. Dependência Literária
V. Data
VI. Proveniência e Destino
VII. Motivo e Propósitos
VIII. O Grego do Apocalipse
IX. O Texto Grego
X. Visão Geral do Conteúdo: Análise, Conceitos de Arranjo
XI. Esboço do Conteúdo
XII. Conceitos e Métodos de Interpretação
XIII. Bibliografia

I. O que é um Apocalipse? Literatura Apocalíptica

Toda a literatura apocalíptica é escatológica. Em outras palavras, aborda a questão dos «tempos do fim», o término do mundo segundo o conhecemos, o começo de um novo ciclo, ou, em alguns casos, o estado eterno. Nem toda a literatura escatológica, porém, é apocalíptica. Pode-se falar, por exemplo, sobre a «alma» e seu destino, e isso nos levaria a tratar de certo aspecto do ensinamento escatológico normal, mas, ao mesmo tempo, nada de distintamente apocalíptico estará sendo envolvido nesse ensino. Os escritos que têm chegado até nós, que são chamados «apocalípticos», possuem características distintivas, o que é salientado na discussão que se segue. De modo bem geral, pode-se afirmar que essa forma literária trata da escatologia, pois visa dizer-nos as condições que haverá nos últimos tempos, nos tempos futuros remotos, mas sua apresentação fala daqueles acontecimentos futuros que terão lugar durante dias angustiosos, em que uma antiga era passará em meio a tempestades e agonias, iniciando-se uma era inteiramente nova, através das mais severas dores de parto. Mas isso não é uma característica normal e necessária dos escritos escatológicos.

No que concerne à atividade literária judaico-cristã, pode-se identificar o período dos escritos apocalípticos entre 165 A.C. e 120 D.C. Essa literatura antecipa o fim de um ciclo histórico, a saber, o ciclo judaico, o que se daria em meio a dores severas, antes do nascimento da era cristã. Os «apocalipses» cristãos refletem o desapontamento dos discípulos de Cristo por não se ter materializado o Reino de Deus em sua própria época. E esse desapontamento foi apenas natural, e se pensou que os acontecimentos que sempre foram tomados como necessários na inauguração do reino deveriam ser transferidos para outra época, o tempo da «volta» de Jesus Cristo, não mais sendo atribuídos ao seu «primeiro advento». Isso preencheu um vácuo psicológico, pois manteve os homens na «esperança» no estabelecimento do reino. No entanto, não há razão para crermos, meramente porque esse tipo de literatura cumpre uma necessidade psicológica, que as profecias contidas em nossos apocalipses bíblicos (os livros de Daniel e de Apocalipse) não sejam válidas.

Os apocalipses judaicos foram escritos na época de Antíoco Epifânio e posteriormente, acompanhado as perseguições que houve naquele período histórico. Essa literatura apocalíptica teve a finalidade de dar aos homens a «esperança quanto ao futuro», estando eles a passar por um presente dificílimo. Essa esperança contemplava particularmente o livramento através do vindouro Messias, bem como através do estabelecimento de seu reino. Pode-se ver facilmente que, tal como no caso dos apocalipses cristãos, a literatura apocalíptica judaica conservava a necessidade psicológica de «saltar por cima» de um presente difícil, a fim de levar os homens a terem esperança e fé firme de que se cumpriria uma nova era de vitória e realizações espirituais, embora isso não dispensasse grande agonia. Também é verdade que apesar da atividade da literatura apocalíptica nunca se ter tornado uma questão central no judaísmo, e apesar de que a maioria dos rabinos judeus a ignoravam essencialmente, contudo, esses escritos serviram ao seu propósito; e embora nunca tivessem ganho posição canônica, não há razão para supormos que não há ali certo discernimento quanto ao futuro, misticamente intuitivo, apesar de não ser diretamente inspirado pelo Espírito do Senhor.

Em contraste com isso, o espírito apocalíptico dominava a igreja primitiva. O fato de que o reino de Deus não se materializou então deu, aos primeiros discípulos de Cristo, a ardente esperança que a «breve» e mesmo «iminente» segunda volta de Cristo (a «parousia» dos escritos neotestamentários) haveria de desfazer o erro de sua «rejeição», cumprindo todas as expectativas da humanidade acerca de uma era melhor. Mas essa era melhor não haverá de iniciar-se senão através da morte agonizante e terrível da antiga era, e a literatura apocalíptica é, essencialmente, a descrição dessa morte febricitante, com descrições adicionais do glorioso nascimento da nova era, que se seguirá.

A literatura apocalíptica, pois, tem um *«propósito presente»*. Os fiéis necessitam de força espiritual para passar pelas aflições, desapontamentos e pressões

APOCALIPSE

desta era ímpia em que vivemos. Serão mais capazes disso se puderem antever a vitória, a qual, finalmente, reverterá os terrores do momento presente. Os escritos apocalípticos prometem que os adversários de Deus não escaparão ao juízo por causa daquilo que fizeram, por seus feitos ímpios que praticaram. Além disso, promete que aquilo contra o que os perversos se têm oposto, o governo de Deus sobre a terra, eventualmente cumprirá, a despeito deles. Outrossim, promete que até mesmo muitos daqueles que se têm oposto a isso, através dos juízos haverão de reconhecer a mão de Deus na história, acolhendo a seu Cristo como Senhor deles.

Há algumas características distintivas da literatura apocalíptica. O termo grego «apokalupto» significa «desvendar», «revelar». O «apokalupsis», pois, é uma «revelação» ou «desvendamento»; é uma «visão profética». Consideremos os pontos seguintes a esse respeito:

1. *Os livros apocalípticos são sempre reveladores.* Há ali atividade mística, revelações, sonhos, visões, viagens celestiais em espírito, tudo o que transcende à era presente pelos poderes da alma humana, com ou sem a ajuda divina. Cremos que até mesmo os apocalipses não-canônicos envolvem algumas experiências místicas válidas, ou seja, algum discernimento válido quanto as questões espirituais, incluindo revelações sobre as condições futuras. Os dois livros apocalípticos da Bíblia, Daniel e Apocalipse, certamente contêm o esboço dos acontecimentos futuros, a maioria dos quais tem sido confirmada pela atividade profética dos místicos atuais. Em outras palavras, as profecias de nossos dias concordam com as previsões bíblicas, de modo a narrar acontecimentos paralelos. Ver o artigo intitulado *Tradição Profética e a Nossa Época*, que apresenta uma discussão geral sobre essa questão.

2. *São imitativos e pseudopreditivos.* Apesar de haver discernimento espiritual quase certamente «válido», porquanto os poderes de pré-conhecimento dos homens funcionam quase sempre, com resultados que podem ser medidos, esses livros apocalípticos tendem por ser imitativos. O livro de Daniel servia de arquétipo original. Nesses escritos há «invenções» que não refletem qualquer atividade mística genuína, pois as «profecias de condenação», com subidas aos céus e descidas ao inferno, se tornaram artifícios literários, que visavam ensinar verdades espirituais, apresentando advertências e encorajamentos necessários. Portanto, — apesar de que algumas previsões válidas estarem contidas nos apocalipses não-canônicos, mais freqüentemente do que não, as profecias são pseudopreditivas; e essas previsões tornam-se «meios» de ensino,— em vez de serem tentativas sérias de predizer o futuro.

3. *Empregam verdades místicas e simbólicas*, em vez de verdades físicas e literais. A fé religiosa pode ser ensinada com habilidade sem base nos acontecimentos históricos reais, ou passados ou em antecipação ao futuro. O meio de transmitir a verdade, dentro do misticismo, é o símbolo. Um símbolo pode ser válido, sem importar que por detrás dele tenha ou não algum acontecimento físico e literal. As parábolas de Jesus (pelo menos algumas delas) não tinham o intuito de relacionarem-se com qualquer acontecimento real; antes, eram «boas narrativas» sobre as verdades eternas, que eram assim vividamente ilustradas. Assim sendo, um profeta podia falar sobre a descida ao inferno por parte de Enoque, e assim ensinar uma verdade acerca do estado das almas perdidas, sem isso significar que Enoque tenha, realmente, feito tal viagem. Até mesmo nos apocalipses canônicos, as «visões» com freqüência não apresentam objetos «reais» ou «físicos». Tomemos, por exemplo, o caso da imagem com os dez dedos formados de ferro e barro. Isso simboliza os reinos e federações do mundo, embora não seja uma verdade literal. Algumas obras apocalípticas chegam a extremos bizarros ao pintarem condições e expectações espirituais. Alguns dos intérpretes mais inclinados pela interpretação literal do Apocalipse de João procuram tornar literais esses simbolismos. Assim, os «gafanhotos» e «escorpiões», que são animais simbólicos do nono capítulo do livro de Apocalipse, seriam insetos literais que atacam os homens como praga. Porém, não são esses mais literais do que os «cavaleiros» do sexto capítulo do mesmo livro. Todas essas coisas simbolizam os terríveis julgamentos e as condições imediatamente antes da «parousia» ou segundo advento de Cristo. A tentativa de emprestar um caráter literal a esses símbolos redunda em fracasso, além de impedir o entendimento da própria natureza mística dessas visões. Até mesmo os sonhos ordinários nos falam por meio de «símbolos». Por exemplo, uma «criança» simboliza o trabalho realizado por algum obreiro do evangelho, pois esse trabalho, em certo sentido, é sua «criança». A água é símbolo da «fonte da vida»; sonhar sobre a «morte» indica o «fim» de algum aspecto da vida de uma pessoa, ou alguma mudança drástica, muito mais do que o falecimento — literal da mesma. Naturalmente, visões e sonhos algumas vezes falam de acontecimentos literais, mas é um erro interpretar os mesmos literalmente, «todas as vezes que se puder». Essa atitude mais provavelmente nos desviará da verdade, —em vez de aproximar-nos da mesma, pois é algo basicamente contraditório à própria natureza do misticismo.

4. *Os livros apocalípticos com freqüência são pseudônimos.* Isso significa que «em honra» a alguma antiga personalidade famosa, um livro foi escrito por outrem, aproveitando-se do prestígio do nome daquela personalidade, a fim de perpetuar sua tradição. Assim é que o livro de Enoque, escrito no segundo século A.C., não foi escrito por Enoque mas em memória sua. Nesse caso, não poderia haver qualquer tentativa séria, da parte do seu autor, de fazer passar seu livro como se realmente tivesse sido escrito por Enoque. É que os antigos não viam nada de errado nesta prática, sem importar o propósito com que isso fosse feito. Entre os livros apócrifos do Antigo e do Novo Testamentos, bem como entre seus livros pseudepígrafes, há mais de cem livros que certamente não foram escritos pelos indivíduos aos quais são atribuídos. Sem importar o que nós, como modernos, possamos pensar da prática, isso em nada altera a atitude dos antigos acerca da mesma. Em nosso N.T., por exemplo, é possível que o livro de Judas seja uma pseudepígrafe. Quanto a notas sobre isso, ver o artigo sobre *«Apocalipse»* sob o título *Autoria*. No entanto, os dois livros apocalípticos bíblicos — Daniel e Apocalipse — não pertencem a essa natureza. Não obstante, o «João» do livro de Apocalipse não é o mesmo apóstolo João, e sim, o «ancião», ou talvez um bem conhecido «vidente» crente que habitava na Ásia Menor. (Ver uma discussão a esse respeito, na seção III do presente artigo intitulado *Autoria*).

5. *Os livros apocalípticos são altamente dualistas.* Em primeiro lugar, retratam a criação como algo envolvido em «uma luta de morte» entre duas forças — uma boa e outra má. Outrossim, essas forças são «cósmicas», e não meramente humanas. A humanidade ver-se-á envolvida no conflito entre Deus e Satanás,

PORTO DE PATMOS

LUGAR DE ÉFESO

FILADÉLFIA

TIATIRA

LAODICÉIA

Vale de Megido — Cortesia, John F. Walvoord

Pisando o Lagar do Vinho, Apo. 19:15

Teatro de Éfeso   Cortesía. Matson Photo Service

entre os anjos e os demônios, entre a razão absoluta e o erro absoluto. Os homens poderão ser vitoriosos ou derrotados, dependendo do lado que tomarem. O pecado, por conseguinte, nunca será questão apenas humana. Trata-se da lealdade ao erro absoluto, da aprovação conferida a Satanás e às suas obras más.

A oposição das duas grandes forças cósmicas naturalmente envolve a oposição entre duas eras distintas. Assim é que a «era presente» é dominada por Satanás, ao passo que a «era vindoura» será governada por Deus, mediante o seu Messias. A era presente envolve pecado e degradação, com a conseqüente perdição das almas; e a era vindoura envolve o domínio da justiça e do bem-estar espiritual.

Essas forças opostas naturalmente geraram o conceito dos «dois mundos». Há um presente mundo, que é terreno e pervertido. Trata-se de algo físico e temporal, sem quaisquer valores absolutos. Mas também há o «mundo de amanhã», que até mesmo agora existe nas esferas invisíveis da realidade última. Este é um mundo de domínio espiritual, de santidade, de paz e de bem-estar espiritual. O «outro mundo», finalmente, virá a exercer controle sobre este mundo terreno, e esse é um dos aspectos do conflito entre o bem e o mal que atualmente começa a concretizar-se.

Existem, pois, duas «forças cósmicas» que se combatem, duas «eras» contrastantes que se digladiam, dois «mundos» contrastantes que se Os homens, necessariamente, «tomam partido», tornando-se associados e prestando lealdade a um lado ou outro desses contrastes. As obras apocalípticas, portanto, apresentam aos homens o desafio de escolherem a Deus e ao seu caminho, ao seu mundo, à sua era, rejeitando, ao mesmo tempo, o que Satanás tem a oferecer-lhes.

6. *Os livros apocalípticos são deterministas*. Isso significa que a vitória eventual do mundo vindouro sobre o mundo presente — o triunfo do bem sobre o mal — é algo que foi determinado pela mão de Deus. O triunfo de Deus é inevitável, embora pareça demorar-se por tempo excessivamente longo. Os livros apocalípticos, por conseguinte, expõem uma espécie de filosofia da história. Dizem-nos eles a natureza geral do que sucede e do que deverá acontecer. Apesar de que há caos, devido ao pecado, somos assegurados de que o processo histórico está do lado do bem e de Deus, e que nada pode alterar isso, pois a vontade de Deus é todo-poderosa. O seu propósito talvez precise de longo tempo para materializar-se, mas tudo está determinado. Há um horário divino predeterminado; e o fim do domínio de Satanás ocorrerá súbita e dramaticamente. A própria história é a crônica da luta entre Deus e Satanás, e como os seres inteligentes serão envolvidos até o fim da mesma. Mas a história, apesar de envolver muitos elementos de sofrimento e caos, finalmente está determinada para que sirva às finalidades divinas.

7. *Os livros apocalípticos, ao mesmo tempo, são altamente pessimistas e otimistas*. Expõem um quadro horrendamente negativo do que haverá de suceder a este mundo, o que envolverá a intensa depravação dos homens. Ao mesmo tempo, porém, uma vez que esse mundo seja apropriadamente julgado, deverá vir à existência um novo mundo de resplendente beleza e de incrível progresso. Do lado «pessimista», os livros apocalípticos são «cataclísmicos». Os eventos que porão fim ao presente mundo mau serão radicais, como se fora o decepar de um tumor canceroso. Os acontecimentos que darão início à nova era também serão cataclísmicos. As mudanças se produzem mediante acontecimentos bons ou maus, mas sempre repentinos, e não mediante algum processo gradual. As grandes alterações na história resultam de intervenções divinas.

8. *Os livros apocalípticos são intensamente éticos*. Isso significa que esses livros convocam os homens a abandonar o pecado, o qual necessariamente produzirá acontecimentos cataclísmicos. Apesar de tudo estar adredemente determinado, nada podendo derrotar facilmente ao pecado, Satanás e seu sistema, contudo, serão preservados, entre esses terríveis acontecimentos, os homens que mantiverem confiança em Deus e em seu Messias. Em caso contrário, haverão de participar imediatamente da glória de Deus mediante o martírio; ou então haverão de ser gentilmente conduzidos à sua presença, uma vez que tiverem sofrido com os homens terão de sofrer durante aquelas horas fatais. As advertências ali dadas, pois, visam «converter» os homens da maldade e da perversidade; não são meras predições de uma condenação inevitável.

9. *Os livros apocalípticos da Bíblia* — Daniel e o Apocalipse, bem como seus paralelos apócrifos, que foram produzidos pelas comunidades judaica e cristã, são *messiânicos* em sua natureza. Descrevem as mais prodigiosas tragédias, embora também narrem para nós o fato de que haverá um Messias, um Salvador, o qual corrigirá todos os erros.

A Literatura Apocalíptica. No próprio A.T. temos o livro de Daniel. A esse, ainda no A.T., podemos adicionar porções de livros proféticos, como os capítulos vigésimo quarto a vigésimo sétimo de Isaías. No tempo dos Macabeus, talvez tão cedo como 200 A.C., teve início a literatura apocalíptica. Primeiramente apareceu o primeiro livro de Enoque (em etíope), uma obra composta, que foi escrita durante os últimos dois séculos A.C. Várias porções do mesmo são usadas em nossos livros neotestamentários, como no de Judas. O livro de Jubileus data do século II A.C. A *Assunção de Moisés* (livro também usado na epístola de Judas) data dos fins do século I A.C. Os livros de IV Esdras e II Esdras e o Apocalipse de Baruque, datam dos fins do século I D.C. O segundo livro de Enoque (em eslavônico) é de data incerta, embora provavelmente pertença ao princípio da era cristã. Os Testamentos dos Doze Patriarcas (século II A.C.) contêm predições acerca de cada tribo de Israel. Vários fragmentos de apocalipses têm sido encontrados na literatura de Qumran, embora ainda não tenham sido publicados. Do lado do N.T., quanto aos livros não-canônicos, temos o Apocalipse de Pedro, do começo do século II D.C., que descreve a dor dos ímpios e a recompensa dos justos. A *Ascensão de Isaías*, uma obra composta (do século II ao século IV D.C.), é um livro parcialmente judaico e parcialmente cristão. O Pastor de Hermas é uma obra semi-apócrifa que data dos meados do século II D.C. No próprio N.T., temos os «pequenos apocalipses» dos capítulos vinte e quatro e treze dos evangelhos de Mateus e Marcos, respectivamente, ambos derivados da mesma fonte, com base em declarações proféticas do próprio Senhor Jesus. — O quinto capítulo da primeira epístola aos Tessalonicenses e o segundo capítulo da segunda epístola aos Tessalonicenses são escritos apocalípticos de Paulo. Mas o Apocalipse de João é o livro apocalíptico por excelência, tanto do ponto de vista literário como do ponto de vista das previsões proféticas.

Bibliografia AM B CH GS HEN J NTI S Z

II. Confirmação Antiga

O livro de Apocalipse de João foi escrito a fim de ser lido nas igrejas (ver Apo. 1:3). E podemos supor que, desde os tempos cristãos mais remotos, em algumas

APOCALIPSE

porções da igreja, especialmente na Ásia Menor, para quem esse livro foi dirigido, era ele tido como dotado de autoridade idêntica ao dos livros proféticos do A.T. No entanto, foi somente perto dos fins do século II D.C., que esse livro obteve alguma proeminência em qualquer segmento maior da igreja cristã. A mais antiga menção específica ao livro de Apocalipse (que também o atribui ao apóstolo João) foi feita por Justino Mártir, que viveu em Éfeso, em cerca de 135 D.C. (antes de ter-se mudado para Roma). Escrevendo pelos meados do século II D.C., disse ele: «Além disso, um homem entre nós, de nome João, um dos apóstolos de Cristo, profetizou, em uma revelação que lhe foi feita, que aqueles que tiverem confiado em nosso Cristo passarão mil anos em Jerusalém, e que após a ressurreição universal e eterna, terá lugar o julgamento». (*Diálogo com Trifo*, 81).

Não temos meios para precisar de que modo Justino determinou a «canonicidade» do livro de Apocalipse; mas o certo é que, havendo ele atribuído essa obra ao apóstolo João, ele não tinha qualquer dúvida quanto à sua «autoridade». A aceitação da «autoridade» de um livro é apenas um passo distante de sua canonização formal.

Antes da época de Justino Mártir, porém, não há qualquer citação clara e indisputável do livro de Apocalipse. Isso não se encontra nem nos escritos de Clemente de Roma (fins do século I D.C.), nem de Inácio (começo do século II D.C.), nem de Hermas (meados do século II D.C.), e nem no livro e na epístola de Barnabé (cerca de 130 D.C.). Andreas, no prólogo de seu comentário, informa-nos que Papias de Hierópolis, na Frígia (cerca de 150 D.C.), conhecia e usava o livro de Apocalipse, considerando-o divinamente inspirado. Entretanto, ele não disse qualquer coisa acerca de seu autor ter sido um «apóstolo», o que certamente teria feito, se o tivesse sabido. O próprio Eusébio, entretanto, nunca declara definidamente que Papias sabia da existência do Apocalipse. (Ver *História Eclesiástica* iii.39). Uma declaração em sua História Eclesiástica (iii.39,12), que ele atribuiu a Papias, entretanto, parece ser um reflexo do livro de Apocalipse. (Essa declaração parece refletir o vigésimo capítulo do livro de Apocalipse, o milênio e a ressurreição dentre os mortos).

Melito, bispo de Sardes (160 - 190 D.C.), escreveu um livro sobre «o diabo e a revelação de João» (o que é mencionado por Eusébio, em sua *História Eclesiástica* iv.26.2). Jerônimo compreendia que isso se referia a dois livros separados, escritos por Melito; mas, seja como for, é certo que ele conhecia e usava o Apocalipse de João. Também é significativo que Melito viveu em Sardes, uma das cidades às quais o livro de Apocalipse foi originalmente enviado (ver Apo. 3:1 e ss.); e era apenas natural, pois, que ele tivesse aceito esse livro antes do mesmo ter sido aceito em outras partes da cristandade antiga.

Irineu. Eusébio, em *História Eclesiástica* iv.18.8, mostra que Irineu (nos fins do século II D.C., em Lyons, na Gália) sustentava a autoria apostólica de todos os presentes escritos joaninos do N.T. Em seu livro, *Contra as Heresias*, Irineu refere-se ao livro de Apocalipse, em iv. 14.2; 17.6,18; 21.3; v.28.3; 34.2; iv. 20.11; v.26.1.

Teófilo, bispo de Antioquia (Síria ocidental), na última metade do século II D.C. cita o Apocalipse em suas disputas contra Hermógenes (ver Eusébio, História Eclesiástica iv.24), pelo que evidentemente ele aceitava a sua autoridade como Escritura Sagrada.

Alexandria. Clemente (200 D.C.) cita o livro de Apocalipse como Escritura Sagrada (ver Paed. ii.119), atribuindo-o ao apóstolo João (*Quis dives*, 42; *Strom*. vi.106,107). Orígenes fez a mesma coisa (em *Joann. tom*. v 3; *Lommatzsch*, i.165; Eusébio, *História Eclesiástica* vi.25.9).

Roma. O Cânon Muratoriano, que reflete o uso romano de cerca de 200 D.C. alistou o livro de Apocalipse como autoritário, tendo-o atribuído ao apóstolo João. O Apocalipse de Pedro também é favoravelmente mencionado; mas outras fontes informativas romanas mostram que essa não era a opinião de todos os segmentos da igreja cristã.

Cartago. Essa comunidade cristã, filha da igreja romana, também aceitava o livro de Apocalipse, pelos fins do segundo século de nossa era. Tertuliano, em seus vários escritos, cita trechos de dezoito entre vinte e dois capítulos. Ele o atribuía ao apóstolo João («*De Ressur.*», 38, Pud. 12). Os quiliastas e milenaristas — do segundo século de nossa era, como os montanistas, uma seita cristã que se originou na Frígia (cerca de 156 D.C.), aceitavam anelantemente o livro, porquanto oferecia vários textos de prova para suas idéias. Finalmente, essa seita contou com Tertuliano como um de seus aderentes.

Houve disputas sobre o Apocalipse, como também alguns o rejeitaram. Apesar de que pelos fins do século II D.C. o livro de Apocalipse gozava de larga aceitação, tanto quanto a de qualquer outro livro do N.T., houve aqueles que o rejeitaram. Márcion, um herege gnóstico (ver o artigo sobre o *gnosticismo*), mais ou menos pelos meados do segundo século da era cristã, aceitava como seu «cânon» neotestamentário dez epístolas paulinas e uma forma mutilada do evangelho de Lucas. Rejeitava ele o livro de Apocalipse por causa de seu caráter judaico, porquanto viera a considerar o judaísmo como oponente do cristianismo. Negava ele que qualquer apóstolo de Cristo tivesse escrito tal livro. (Ver Tertuliano, *Adv. Marc.*, iv.5; iii.14).

O grupo herege chamado de *alogoi* (dos fins do século II e de começos do século III D.C.), porquanto não aceitava a doutrina joanina do «Logos», como é óbvio, rejeitava também todos os chamados escritos joaninos, incluindo o livro de Apocalipse. Asseveravam que seu verdadeiro autor teria sido Cerinto, um herege gnóstico que viveu nos fins do primeiro século, e que atribuíra seu livro a «João» para obter prestígio para o mesmo (ver Epifânio, *Haer*. li.3; li.33). Afirmava esse grupo que o Apocalipse tem por demais simbolismos, errando quanto a questões literais, como o de haver sido escrita uma das sete cartas para Tiatira, onde não havia qualquer comunidade cristã.

Entretanto, a rejeição do livro de Apocalipse não se limitava a grupos hereges. Havia certos grupos que se opunham ao mesmo e aos quiliastas (especialmente os montanistas), os quais vieram a duvidar da autenticidade do Apocalipse, chegando mesmo a rejeitá-lo, evidentemente como resultado do fato de que algumas das suas doutrinas favoreciam aos hereges. Assim é que Caio de Roma (cerca de 210 D.C.), ao escrever contra os montanistas, terminou por rejeitar também ao livro. Hipólito (215 D.C.) replicou contra o ataque de Caio ao livro de Apocalipse; e essa obra se revestiu de tal vigor que poucos, no Ocidente, daí por diante, continuaram a duvidar da autoridade desse livro. Portanto, as traduções em Latim Antigo e da Vulgata Latina, sempre contiveram o Apocalipse, sem qualquer indicação de dúvida acerca de sua autenticidade. Vitorino (martirizado em 304 A.C.) escreveu um comentário em latim sobre o livro de Apocalipse, que posteriormente foi refeito por Jerônimo.

APOCALIPSE

Contudo, em certos lugares fora do Ocidente, continuou havendo dúvidas sobre o livro do Apocalipse. Dionísio, bispo de Alexandria (247-265 D.C.), renovou dúvidas sobre sua autenticidade, oferecendo fortes motivos para sua crença que não foi o mesmo escrito pelo apóstolo João, e certamente não pelo mesmo autor que escreveu o evangelho de João. (Ver Eusébio, *História Eclesiástica* vii.24). Muitas das linhas de raciocínio nos escritos de Dionísio, têm sido bem acolhidas por eruditos modernos, especialmente devido à qualidade vastamente diferente do grego, entre o quarto evangelho e o livro de Apocalipse. Dionísio informa-nos, igualmente, que em seus dias, muitos duvidavam do citado livro ou mesmo o rejeitavam. Ele mesmo, acreditando que o mesmo fora escrito por um certo João de Éfeso (um dos anciãos da igreja) e não pelo apóstolo João, duvidava de sua autenticidade e autoridade, porquanto o mesmo não seria «apostólico».

Eusébio (326 D.C.), o grande historiador eclesiástico, parece ter concordado com a avaliação geral de Dionísio (iii.29:6), mas deixou que cada congregação local manuseasse a questão a seu talante.

Cirilo de Jerusalém (315-386 D.C.) excluía o Apocalipse de seu «cânon», tendo inclusive proibido seu uso no culto público ou particular. (Ver *Catch.* iv.36).

O sínodo de Laodicéia (cerca de 360 D.C.) não incluiu o Apocalipse em seu «cânon» das Escrituras.

As Constituições Apostólicas (fins do século quarto da era cristã), no *cânon* 85, não contêm o livro de Apocalipse.

Gregório de Nazianzeno (falecido em 389 D.C.) também não o incluiu.

Anfilócio de Icônio (falecido em 394 D.C.) declarou que «a maioria» das autoridades rejeitava o livro de Apocalipse como canônico.

A escola de Antioquia (407 D.C.) também o omitiu. Crisóstomo (407 D.C.), que representava essa escola em Constantinopla, também o rejeitava, tal como o fez Teodoreto (386 - 456 D.C.).

As igrejas Armênia e Síria Oriental não aceitavam o Apocalipse como canônico, e não podia o mesmo ser encontrado em qualquer manuscrito do N.T. naqueles idiomas, por muitos séculos. Alguns manuscritos passaram a incluí-lo no ano de 508 D.C. Mas foram necessários séculos para que a igreja siríaca ficasse convencida acerca da autoridade do livro de Apocalipse. Não veio a participar da Bíblia armênia senão já no século XII D.C.

No século XIII, a canonicidade do apocalipse era universalmente aceita, exceto na igreja nestoriana. Até mesmo nos tempos da Reforma Protestante alguns duvidavam de sua autenticidade. Calvino, muito prolífico como escritor e comentador das Escrituras, nada disse acerca do Apocalipse. Ver o artigo sobre o *Cânon do N.T.*

III. Autoria

Duas posições extremas são tomadas quanto à questão da autoria dos livros Joaninos (que consistem do evangelho de João, de três epístolas de João e do Apocalipse), a saber: 1. Teria havido um único autor desses cinco livros, o qual foi o apóstolo João. 2. Cada um desses cinco livros teria tido um autor diferente, pelo que nenhuma conexão real com o apóstolo João pode ser demonstrada entre eles.

A resposta mais simplista a ambas essas posições extremas consiste da afirmativa de que o evangelho e as epístolas de João foram escritas por um autor (João ou um discípulo imediato seu), ao passo que o Apocalipse teria sido de autoria de um outro João, o ancião ou vidente da Ásia Menor, embora também pertencente à escola joanina. Essa declaração *simplista* está sujeita a todas as formas de objeção e disputa; mas é tão boa como qualquer outra idéia que já tenha sido apresentada. Pelo menos é certo que o evangelho de João e o livro de Apocalipse não podem ter sido escritos pelo mesmo autor. O grego do evangelho de João é simples, quase infantil, embora gramaticalmente correto. Mas o grego do livro de Apocalipse é bárbaro, com muitos desacordos quanto ao gênero, além de erros verbais. Foi escrito por algum judeu que tinha o grego como sua segunda língua, o qual não se interessava especialmente pelos casos gregos, pela concordância em gênero, etc. Pensava ele em hebraico, e algumas de suas declarações só podem ser compreendidas quando é reconstituído um «hebraico tentativo» (ou aramaico). (Ver a seção VII deste artigo intitulado *O Grego do Apocalipse*, quanto a detalhes sobre essa questão). Contudo, a despeito de todos os abusos feitos contra o idioma grego, ele se sentia à vontade em seu manuseio. Sem dúvida falava o grego e o usava em seus contactos diários. Em alguns lugares consegue momentos de eloqüência, e, a despeito da sua má gramática, ocasionalmente produz algumas das melhores porções literárias que o grego conhece. De fato, produziu ele o maior dos «apocalipses», e isso não foi realização pequena para quem usou um «segundo idioma». Podemos supor que, se ele tivesse escrito sua obra em aramaico, o resultado literário teria sido ainda maior.

Justino Mártir atribuía o livro de Apocalipse ao apóstolo João (ver *«Confirmação Antiga»*, imediatamente acima). Esse ponto de vista veio a ser largamente aceito na igreja, — conforme a seção anterior o demonstra; em alguns lugares, entretanto, essa posição era ardorosamente combatida, e até mesmo rejeitada. O próprio livro não afirma ser de autoria de João, o «apóstolo»; e poderíamos supor corretamente que se ele o tivesse realmente escrito, ter-se-ia identificado como tal. Outrossim, se João, o apóstolo, o escreveu, não há razão para supormos que não tivesse recebido reconhecimento antigo e universal, conforme sucedeu no caso das epístolas de Paulo. O fato de que somente nos meados do século II D.C. é que seu autor foi identificado como o apóstolo João, e que mesmo assim muitos continuavam a rejeitar sua autoridade, sob qualquer consideração, especialmente como livro de autoria joanina, mostra-nos que é quase impossível que o próprio apóstolo João tivesse sido o seu autor.

Se voltamos para a questão da evidência interna, — podemos observar que o autor não faz nenhuma tentativa para identificar-se com os doze apóstolos originais. Apesar de que ele se chama «João» em quatro versículos (ver Apo. 1:1,4,9, e 22:8), nunca deixa entendido que ele era o «João» do círculo original dos apóstolos. Em parte alguma ele afirma ter sido testemunha ocular da vida terrena de Jesus. Seu conhecimento de Jesus veio por revelação, e não através da história. Em Apo. 21:14, ao mencionar que a muralha da cidade tinha doze alicerces, inscritos com os nomes dos doze apóstolos originais, não parece identificar-se com qualquer deles. Em Apo. 18:20 ele fala sobre os «doze» de modo bastante objetivo, mas novamente sem dar a entender que fosse um deles.

Historicamente, bem se poderia pôr em dúvida que o apóstolo João tenha vivido até o fim do século I D.C. ou começo do segundo século, para que pudesse

APOCALIPSE

ter sido o autor do livro de Apocalipse. Há uma tradição, preservada por meio de Papias, que situa a morte de João próxima ao tempo da morte de seu irmão, Tiago, isto é, antes do ano 70 D.C. A passagem de Mar. 10:39 presumivelmente prediz isso; e notemos que Jesus se referiu a esses dois irmãos. Contudo, há outras tradições que associam o apóstolo João com a Ásia Menor, referindo-se a ele como homem *idoso*. E é possível que se aceitarmos estas últimas tradições que João tenha vivido até um tempo em que poderia ter escrito o livro de Apocalipse. Irineu foi quem nos expôs essa tradição. Mas, visto que as tradições não concordam entre si, nesse ponto, nada de certo pode ser extraído delas acerca da autoria do livro de Apocalipse. George Hamartolus, bem como um manuscrito seu (do século IX D.C.) repete essa tradição preservada por Papias, no sentido que João morreu às mãos dos judeus (decapitado), mais ou menos à época de seu irmão. Portanto, sem importar para que lado nos voltemos, historicamente falando, não podemos ter certeza de que o apóstolo João realmente teve tantas décadas de serviço em Éfeso ou não, o que significa que não sabemos se ele viveu o tempo suficiente para escrever o livro de Apocalipse, o qual, mui provavelmente, reflete as perseguições instauradas contra a igreja cristã nos tempos de Domiciano (falecido em 96 D.C.), ou posteriormente.

A maioria dos eruditos acredita, com base em citações antigas, que um certo «João» foi quem o escreveu. Um indivíduo que Papias chamou de «João, o ancião», que viveu em Éfeso, no começo do século II D.C., é identificado por alguns como seu autor. (Ver Eusébio, *História Eclesiástica* iii.39.4, quanto à identificação dos «dois Joãos», por parte de Papias). Esse autor João supostamente também teria sido discípulo do Senhor, e o seu túmulo estaria ao lado do de João, o apóstolo, na Ásia Menor. Dionísio fez a mesma sugestão, isto é, que «João, o ancião», escreveu o livro de Apocalipse (ver Eusébio, *História Eclesiástica* vii.25.16). Jerônimo também falou sobre o sepulcro desse outro João, em «Éfeso» (ver «*De viris*», illus.9). Vários escritores antigos pensam que esse «ancião» também foi o autor das epístolas joaninas; mas apesar de que João, o ancião, pode tê-las escrito, ele não poderia ter escrito também o livro de Apocalipse, porquanto aquelas estão lingüisticamente vinculadas ao evangelho de João, e não ao livro de Apocalipse. Vendo nisso a verdade, alguns intérpretes também atribuem o evangelho e as epístolas joaninas a «João, o ancião», ao passo que atribuem o Apocalipse ao «outro João», o qual também não teria sido um apóstolo de Cristo. Eusébio, ao citar Papias e Dionísio, aparentemente pensa que estes últimos estão certos: João, o ancião, é quem escreveu o livro de Apocalipse.

João, o vidente. Há ainda uma terceira possibilidade, que talvez seja mais viável que aquelas acima mencionadas, a saber, que um terceiro João está em foco, o qual foi um «profeta» (vidente), que não foi nem o «ancião» e nem o «apóstolo». No próprio livro de Apocalipse, esse João não se chama de «ancião», conforme se vê na segunda e na terceira epístolas de João; mas não se denomina «apóstolo», o que é declarado no evangelho de João, em seu epílogo (ver o seu vigésimo primeiro capítulo). Mas mui definidamente toma a posição e o direito de um profeta, conforme se vê claramente no primeiro capítulo do livro de Apocalipse. (Ver também Apo. 22:9, onde se vê que os profetas do N.T., em sentido especial, são «servos do Senhor», o que é repetido em Apo. 1:1; 10:7; 11:18 e 22:6). O autor recebeu ordem de «profetizar» (ver Apo. 1:3). E o Apocalipse é um livro de profecia (ver Apo. 1:3; 10:11 e 22:7,10,18). Mui provavelmente o autor foi um judeu da Palestina, homem dotado de grande estatura espiritual e gênio, dotado de pensamentos e de discernimento profundos. O aramaico era seu idioma natural, e o grego era apenas um idioma adquirido. (Compare-se isso com reivindicações similares e declarações de um outro profeta, *Hermas*, e o *Didache*, escrito em cerca de 100 D.C., que mostram que os profetas cristãos eram altamente estimados). O fato de que João, o vidente, conhecia e se utilizou de — obras apócrifas — e pseudepígrafes do A.T. (ver a seção IV deste artigo, intitulado *Dependência Literária*) indica, na opinião de alguns eruditos, que ele deve ter sido um João que vivia fora da Palestina, pois tais livros eram favorecidos principalmente entre os judeus da dispersão. Nesse caso, ele deve ter vivido relativamente isolado, na comunidade judaica, pois, de outra maneira, o seu grego teria sido melhor. Porque nenhum judeu alexandrino teria abusado tanto do idioma grego como o fez o autor sagrado, se porventura tivesse qualquer educação.

A escola joanina. Apesar da gramática do livro de Apocalipse mostrar que o autor sagrado não pode ser identificado com o autor do evangelho de João, há certas similaridades, em pensamento e conceito, que podem ser corretamente tidas como sinais de identificação do autor com a escola joanina de Éfeso. Consideremos os pontos seguintes: 1. Há a comparação de frases similares: João 16:2 com Apo. 2:2; 13:8 com 20:6; 3:8,21 com 22:15 e 7:37 com 22:17. 2. Há a mesma significação teológica conferida a termos teológicos como «vida», «morte», «glória», «fome» e «sede». 3. Algumas palavras e frases são mais freqüentemente usadas pelos dois autores do que em qualquer outro livro do N.T. Por exemplo «*poiéin semeion*», quatro vezes no Apocalipse e catorze vezes no evangelho de João, mas apenas quatro vezes em todo o resto do N.T.; «*terein t. entolas*», duas vezes no Apocalipse, sete vezes no evangelho de João, e cinco vezes na primeira epístola de João; «*deiknumai*», oito vezes no Apocalipse e sete vezes no evangelho de João; «*ebraisti*», duas vezes no Apocalipse e cinco vezes no evangelho de João; «*marturia*», nove vezes no Apocalipse, catorze vezes no evangelho de João e seis vezes na primeira epístola de João, além de uma vez na segunda epístola de João; «*piazein*», uma vez no Apocalipse e oito vezes na primeira epístola de João; «*semainein*», uma vez no Apocalipse e três vezes no evangelho de João; «*philein*», duas vezes no Apocalipse e treze vezes no evangelho de João; «*aphazein*», oito vezes no Apocalipse e duas vezes na primeira epístola de João. 4. Há idéias similares. Exemplos disso são que não haverá templo na Jerusalém celestial (ver Apo. 21:22); e o templo deixará de existir como centro de adoração (ver João 4:21). Figura a doutrina do Cordeiro de Deus em João 1:29,36; Apo. 5:6,8,12,13; 6:1,16; 7:9,10,14,17; 12:11; 13:8; 14:1,4, 10; 15:3; 17:14; 19:7,9; 21:9,14,22,23,27; 22:1,3. 5. O número «sete» permeia o livro de Apocalipse. Apesar de não ser isso especificamente declarado no evangelho de João, há sete «sinais» neste último, começando e terminando o mesmo com uma «semana» sagrada. Outrossim, o seu testemunho acerca de Cristo se desdobra em sete aspectos.

A conclusão que disso tudo se pode extrair é que esses cinco livros — o evangelho, as três epístolas e o Apocalipse — foram produzidos pela mesma escola, a escola joanina, de Éfeso. Consideremos ainda os três pontos abaixo: 1. O evangelho de João deve ter sido escrito por um discípulo imediato de João, que

APOCALIPSE

perpetuou sua tradição, incluindo suas narrativas e seu testemunho. O evangelho de João é corretamente chamado «de João», no mesmo sentido em que o evangelho de Marcos *poderia* ser chamado de «evangelho de Pedro», porquanto tal evangelho preservou para nós a tradição apostólica que chegou até nós, com base nas memórias de Pedro. (Ver o artigo sobre *João*, quanto a essa questão). 2. As epístolas joaninas poderiam ter sido escritas por esse mesmo autor. A primeira epístola de João certamente o foi. Seja como for, outro elemento da escola joanina esteve envolvido, se não foi o mesmo indivíduo. (Ver o artigo sobre *João*, onde se fala sobre a «autoria» dessas epístolas joaninas). 3. O Apocalipse foi escrito por João, o «vidente», e não pelo «ancião», ou pelo «apóstolo», embora tivesse sido ele, por igual modo, um membro da escola joanina.

IV. Dependência Literária

1. *O Antigo Testamento*. O autor do livro de Apocalipse nunca cita diretamente o A.T., mas, em um total de quatrocentos e quatro versículos, duzentos e setenta e oito encerram alguma forma de referência ao A.T. Muito mais que todos os demais livros do N.T., pois, o Apocalipse depende do A.T. Foi observando isso que Márcion o rejeitou como autoritário, já que cria ele que o judaísmo é opositor do cristianismo e não seu genitor. — O autor não parece ter usado a Septuaginta, mas parece ter feito suas próprias traduções e paráfrases. Parte disso, porém, provavelmente foi influenciado pela leitura comum e popular da Septuaginta. Alguns eruditos supõem que ele tenha usado um manuscrito grego ou manuscritos hebraicos do A.T. diferentes do texto padrão da Septuaginta, conforme o mesmo chegou até nós; mas isso é menos provável do que o que diz a outra posição. Uma lista quase completa de alusões e citações parciais, extraídas do A.T., existentes no livro de Apocalipse, aparece no *International Critical Commentary*, na sua introdução ao livro de Apocalipse, seções lxviii a lxxxvi. (Ver também as notas marginais do texto grego). O fato que o autor sagrado estava tão estribado no A.T. é uma das razões por que o livro de Apocalipse é tão fortemente «judaico» em seu caráter; mas isso não se deve impedir de perceber a igreja nos capítulos quinto a décimo nono, conforme afirmam, erroneamente, alguns intérpretes. Pelo contrário, o «servo» do Senhor é ali um crente, e não um judeu de raça apenas, conforme normalmente se pensa, o qual haverá de passar pela grande tribulação.

2. *As pseudepígrafes*. Uma vez mais, o autor sagrado não cita diretamente as obras pseudepígrafes. Mas é evidente que ele incorpora certas idéias e frases das mesmas, especialmente aquelas extraídas dos livros de Testamento de Levi, I Enoque e Assunção de Moisés. Em qualquer estudo completo do Novo Testamento, fica demonstrado que algumas vezes é impossível compreender o que o autor quer dizer, a menos que haja alguma alusão a idéias encontradas nas obras pseudepígrafes. Como exemplo disso temos os «querubins» (ver Apo. 4:6), uma «grande espada» (ver Apo. 6:3), os «mártires como um sacrifício a Deus» (ver Apo. 6:9), o «altar no céu» (ver Apo. 6:9), o «mundo vindouro», o qual surgirá quando completar-se o número dos mártires (ver Apo. 6:11), as «vestes brancas», que simbolizam os corpos espirituais (ver Apo. 6:11, etc.), tudo o que são idéias tomadas por empréstimo daqueles livros antigos. (Ver alguns empréstimos tirados diretamente dos livros pseudepígrafes judaicos, em Apo. 2:7 (Testamento de Levi 18:11), 2:17 (Testamento de Levi 18:14), 4:1 (I Enoque 14:15), 4:6 (II Enoque 3:3 e Testamento de Levi 2:7), 6:11 (I Enoque 47:3,4), 6:12 (Assunção de Moisés 10:5), 7:1 (um conceito geral do primeiro livro de Enoque), 8:8 (I Enoque 18:13), 9:1 (I Enoque 86:1), 9:20 (I Enoque 99:7), 14:10 (I Enoque 48:9), 14:14 (I Enoque 46:1), 17:14 (I Enoque 9:4), 19:15 (Salmos de Salomão 17:26,27), 20:8 (I Enoque 56:5-8; IV Esdras 13:5,8,9,18-35; Ber. 7b, Targum de Jer. sobre Núm. 11:26), 20:13, (I Enoque 51:1), 22:2 (I Enoque 62:3,5).

3. *Outros livros do N.T.* O livro de Apocalipse foi escrito em uma época histórica em que vários livros neotestamentários já deveriam ter sido escritos. Abaixo apresentamos uma lista de sugestões: Apo. 1:1 (Mat. 24:6 e Luc. 21:9); 1:3 (Luc. 11:28); 1:4 (Col. 1:2); 1:5 (Col. 1:18); 1:5 (Gál. 2:20); 1:6 (I Ped. 2:9); 1:7 (Mat. 24:30); 1:16 (Mat. 17:2); 1:18 (II Cor. 6:9); 2:7 (Mat. 11:15; 13:9,43; Luc. 8:8; 14:35); 2:10 (Tia. 1:12); 2:20 (Atos 15:28); 2:24 (Atos 15:28); 2:24 (I Cor. 2:10); 3:3 (Mat. 24:42); 16:15 (Mat. 24:43); 3:8 (I Cor. 16:9); 3:14 (Col. 1:18); 3:17 (Col. 1:27); 3:21 (Col. 3:1); 5:5 (Luc. 7:13 e 8:52); 6:4 (Mat. 10:34); 6:2-17; 7:1 (Mat. 24:6,7); 6:10 (Mat. 24:29); 6:15,16 (Luc. 23:30); 6:17 (Luc. 21:36); 7:3 (Efé. 4:30); 7:17 (I Ped. 2:25); 9:20 (Luc. 18:11); 11:3 (Luc. 4:25); 11:15 (Mat. 4:8); 12:9 (Luc. 10:18); 13:8 (I Ped. 1:19,20); 13:11 (Mat. 7:15); 14:4 (Luc. 9:57); 14:7 (Atos 4:24 e 14:15); 14:13 (I Tes. 4:16); 17:14 (I Tim. 6:15); 16:14 (Mat. 20:16 e 22:14); 18:4 (II Cor. 6:17 e Efé. 5:11); 18:24 (Luc. 11:50); 19:7 (Mat. 5:12); 19:9 (Luc. 14:16); 21:4,5 (II Cor. 5:17); 21:10 (Mat. 4:8); 22:21 (encerramento das epístolas paulinas e do livro aos Hebreus, ver também Efé. 6:24 e Col. 4:18).

4. *Outras fontes: astrológicas, numerológicas e cabalísticas*

O judaísmo helenista continha muitos elementos da astrologia, da numerologia e de várias formas de misticismo, em parte tomados por empréstimo de vizinhos pagãos, mas adicionados e modificados pelos místicos judeus. O intricado simbolismo dos números, no livro de Apocalipse, não pode deixar de refletir algo dessa atividade; e como explicações do que significam esses números, podemos apelar para as tradições místicas judaicas que contêm escritos dos rabinos cabalistas. A angelologia do livro de Apocalipse também envolve certas adaptações de idéias astrológicas da época. Os anjos que aparecem como governantes de nações, em esferas celestiais e terrenas, ou que governam os ventos, as estrelas e as manifestações celestes, eram conceitos comuns, que foram tirados da astrologia e adaptados. Não se tem certeza sobre o que o autor do livro de Apocalipse quer dizer com o uso que faz de anjos, etc., como se o uso fosse o mesmo que havia nos sistemas astrológicos; mas ao menos parte desse uso tem paralelos verbais com aqueles sistemas. Seja como for, o autor sagrado se valeu de certas expressões e usos que eram usuais na linguagem da astrologia da época. (Quanto à «influência astrológica que havia no judaísmo posterior», ver as notas expositivas no NTI em Col. 2:8, onde há provas disso. Como exemplos desse uso ver Apo. 1:20; 2:1, 4:4,6, 5:11; 7:1; 8:2; 12:1; 14:18; 15:1; 16:1; 16:5; 18:1 e 20:1).

Como um pregador moderno pode ilustrar um sermão com uma referência «astronômica», assim João o vidente usava, às vezes, a astronomia do tempo dele, que pelas definições modernas é a astrologia. Não é importante saber, se João aceitava certas dessas idéias como verdadeiras ou não. Elas serviam como um bom veículo de comunicação.

V. Data

É certo, com base no próprio livro, que o

APOCALIPSE

Apocalipse foi escrito durante um período de tremenda perseguição contra a igreja, por parte do império romano. No entanto, tem sido motivo de disputas qual era o imperador romano que governava quando o livro foi escrito. Abaixo apresentamos as principais idéias a respeito:

A data anterior. Alguns estudiosos têm situado a escrita deste livro já nos dias de Nero (54-68) D.C.). Porém, certas referências, Apo. 13:3,12,14 e 17:8,10, que os primeiros cristãos consideraram como predições de um «Nero redivivus» ou «Nero ressurrecto», o qual voltaria ao poder, na qualidade de anticristo, mostram que tal imperador já estava morto, quando o Apocalipse foi escrito. Tal doutrina dificilmente teria sido criada antes do falecimento de Nero, e isso exige uma data posterior ao ano 70 D.C., para a escrita deste livro.

Presumivelmente, o trecho de Apo. 17:10 nos fornece um meio de datarmos a escrita deste livro com exatidão. Quando o escritor sagrado escrevia sua obra, cinco imperadores romanos já haviam morrido, o sexto estava reinando, e se esperava um sétimo; e então surgiria um «oitavo», que seria o último imperador. O problema nisso envolvido, entretanto, é que não sabemos como se devem contar os cinco imperadores; também houve consideravelmente mais de sete ou oito imperadores, antes do império romano terminar, quanto a dúvidas sobre quando se deve começar a contá-los, deveríamos começar a contagem com Júlio César? Nesse caso poderíamos nomear Júlio César, Augusto, Tibério, Calígula, Cláudio, Nero, Galba, Oto, Vitélio, Vespasiano, Tito e Domiciano. Nesse caso, Cláudio seria o quinto, e Nero seria o imperador dos dias em que o livro foi escrito. A maioria dos intérpretes crê que os três antecessores imediatos de Vespasiano deveriam ser omitidos, porque seu governo foi breve e sem grandes acontecimentos. Nesse caso, o quinto continuaria sendo Cláudio, o sexto seria Nero, e, assim sendo, o livro deve ter sido escrito antes de 70 D.C. Outros estudiosos, porém, começam contando com Augusto, como se fora o verdadeiro primeiro imperador romano, ficando omitidos os três mencionados acima, em cujo caso chegaríamos a Vespasiano, como o sexto imperador, que então estaria governando. Nesse caso, Vespasiano aparece como o poder maligno que então reinava. Foi ele quem iniciou o cerco contra Jerusalém. E Tito, seu filho, foi aquele que terminou o cerco, sendo ele o sétimo governante do império. E Nero ressurrecto seria o «oitavo» monarca, o anticristo, presumivelmente o último dos governantes de Roma; pois a destruição do império romano, tal como a «parousia» ou segundo advento de Cristo era esperada para breve, até mesmo enquanto os crentes primitivos ainda viviam.

Pode-se ver, pois, que dependendo do modo como manuseamos a lista, Nero, Galba ou Vespasiano pode ser o sexto governante, durante o qual tempo o Apocalipse parece ter sido escrito. Os trechos de Apo. 6:9 e 11:1,2 podem indicar que o templo de Jerusalém continuava de pé quando o livro foi escrito, o que significa que este livro deve ter sido composto antes do ano 70 D.C. Epifânio (ver *Haer*. li. 12) atribuía a esse livro uma data ainda anterior, isto é, ao tempo de Cláudio.

A data posterior. A maioria dos eruditos, a despeito das razões acima expostas, baseando-se no que diz o próprio Apocalipse, apontam para Domiciano como o governador durante o tempo em que este livro foi escrito. Nesse caso, o trecho de Apo. 17:11 seria um oráculo judaico originalmente, incorporado no Apocalipse, embora ignorando qualquer contagem exata, por assim dizer, arbitrária, o que faria de Domiciano o sexto imperador, o qual então governava. Nesse caso, «Nero ressurrecto» presumivelmente seguiria o sétimo governante (cujo nome foi dado), o qual seria o anticristo. Ou ainda o Nero ressurrecto seria o sétimo, e o próprio Domiciano, que veio mais tarde, seria reputado uma reencarnação do Nero ressurrecto, o qual, apesar de «ser dos sete», seria o «oitavo». Porém, visto que Nero e Domiciano formavam uma única personalidade, uma contagem estrita resultaria em apenas sete imperadores. Pelo menos é certo que alguns dos súditos de Domiciano o chamavam de «outro Nero». (Ver Juvenal, *Sátiras* iv. 37,38; Marcial, *Epigrames* 1:33).

Por mais confuso que seja esse quadro, se Domiciano foi o imperador reinante quando este livro foi escrito, então sua data deve ser situada algum tempo antes de 96 D.C.

Ainda há uma outra proposta que apresenta Domiciano como o sexto governante, ou seja, aquele em foco quando o livro foi composto. É possível que o autor sagrado tivesse em mente somente aqueles governantes mortos, quando o senado romano os declarara deuses, objetos próprios à adoração. Nesse caso, os governantes em foco seriam César, Augusto, Cláudio, Vespasiano e Tito. Domiciano, pois, seria o sexto imperador, ao passo que o anticristo nerônico seria o sétimo.

Uma data ainda mais posterior. Também se tem sugerido o reinado de Trajano (98-117 D.C.) como o tempo em que foi escrito este livro. Sabemos que Trajano ordenou severa perseguição contra os crentes, pois isso fica claro nos escritos de Plínio, o Moço, governador da Bitínia em cerca de 111-113 D.C. Nesse caso, seria impossível apelarmos para a passagem de Apo. 17:10, porque sob hipótese alguma Trajano seria o sexto governante. Além disso, neste tempo o cristianismo se tornara uma religião «ilegal», não havendo qualquer evidência de que essa condição existia quando o Apocalipse foi composto. Os «imperadores» eram «deuses» que deviam ser adorados; mas não parece que então já havia qualquer decreto formal contra a fé cristã.

Irineu e Eusébio afirmam *categoricamente* que o Apocalipse foi escrito no tempo de Domiciano. (Ver Eusébio, *História Eclesiástica* iii.18.3 e Irineu, *Adv. Haer*. v.30.3). Esse testemunho foi aceito sem hesitação por Clemente de Alexandria, Orígenes e Jerônimo. Os trechos de Apo. 6:9 e 11:1,2 poderiam subentender que o templo e a cidade de Jerusalém continuavam de pé quando este livro foi escrito; apesar de que poderia ter havido alusões naturais ao templo e à cidade conforme eles existiam antes, sem apontar para o estado em que então existiam.

A data do Apocalipse, na história da interpretação. Os intérpretes têm favorecido três períodos, a saber: 1. O reinado de Nero. Assim pensavam Baur, Reuss, Hilgenfeld, Lightfoot, Selwyn, B.W. Henderson. A data neroniana, entretanto, dificilmente pode ser sustentada de pé, à luz do trecho de Apo. 17:10,11, segundo se aclara acima a questão. 2. Dependendo de como manusearmos a lista dos imperadores romanos, é possível a data correspondente ao imperador Vespasiano. Nada absolutamente fatal pode ser dito contra isso, exceto que não há provas históricas de que Vespasiano perseguiu os cristãos. Não tomava a sério suas próprias reivindicações de «divindade», e nem jamais compeliu alguém a adorá-lo, e nem perseguiu os que se negassem a fazê-lo. Tertuliano declara especificamente que os

APOCALIPSE

cristãos não foram perseguidos durante o reinado de Vespasiano, como também não houve grande perseguição sob Tito, seu filho. Contudo, eles começaram e terminaram o cerco de Jerusalém, sendo possível que as crueldades então perpetradas tivessem inspirado um livro como o de Apocalipse, embora isso não seja muito provável. Os «cristãos» perseguidos é que precisavam do encorajamento dado por uma «revelação». 3. Domiciano foi chamado de *Nero calvo* e de «segundo Nero», por Marcial. A história mostra a ferocidade de sua perseguição contra os cristãos. Considerando-se todos os fatores, quase todos os intérpretes, antigos e modernos, têm chegado à conclusão de que o Apocalipse foi escrito durante esse tempo, ou seja, pouco antes do término do primeiro século de nossa era. As cartas às sete igrejas do Apocalipse também confirmam uma data posterior. A cidade Esmirna não contava com nenhuma comunidade cristã ao tempo de Nero. Isso é confirmado na epístola de Policarpo *aos Filipenses* xi. O culto ao imperador (obrigatório para todos os cidadãos romanos) não parece ter sido posto em vigor até os dias de Domiciano; e o livro de Apocalipse quase certamente reflete tal circunstância. Mas nos seus dias tal culto passou a ser considerado prova de lealdade ao imperador; e por causa disso, seguiram-se perseguições intensas contra os cristãos, totalmente desconhecidas nos dias de Vespasiano.

VI. Proveniência e Destino

Proveniência. O trecho de Apo. 1:9 identifica o lugar «de onde» a epístola foi enviada, o lugar de sua posição—a ilha de Patmos. Tal informe deve ser aceito como real, a menos que se suponha que tais toques sejam meros artifícios literários. Nada há contra a idéia de que João, o vidente, um dos principais líderes da igreja cristã de Éfeso, homem bem conhecido entre todas as igrejas da Ásia Menor, tenha sido banido para Patmos devido à sua fé cristã, e que ali ele escreveu esta obra. Sua reclusão e sofrimentos, entretanto, talvez tivessem provocado suas visões. Patmos é uma ilha que fica a cinqüenta e seis quilômetros ao largo da costa sudoeste da Ásia Menor (moderna Turquia), 30º 20' leste. Essa ilha tem cerca de treze quilômetros, e em alguns lugares chega a ter seis quilômetros e meio de largura. Compõe-se de colinas vulcânicas escarpadas. Atualmente pertence à Grécia.

Destino. O destino também é claramente afirmado em Apo. 1:4, bem como em seus capítulos segundo e terceiro, a saber, as «sete igrejas» da Ásia Menor. Provavelmente uma cópia do livro foi enviada para cada uma delas, e não apenas as cópias individuais das pequenas cartas. Às igrejas foi ordenado que lessem a composição inteira (ver Apo. 1:3). Na Ásia Menor havia maior número de igrejas do que apenas aquelas sete, e podemos supor que não demoraram a receber cópias da mesma. Alguns estudiosos têm pensado que essas sete igrejas representam sete períodos distintos da história da igreja; mas isso é repelido por outros. Seja como for, representam as principais condições que podem ser encontradas na igreja universal, em qualquer período da história. É interessante a observação que o Apocalipse foi aceito como autoritário, isto é, «canônico», inicialmente na Ásia Menor. (Ver a seção II do presente artigo).

VII. Motivo e Propósitos

Motivo. Deve ser óbvio, por aquilo que foi dito nas seções I e V, que o «motivo» que provocou a escrita deste livro foi uma grande perseguição tão severa que os cristãos primitivos só poderiam pensar que viviam nos dias imediatamente anteriores à «parousia» ou segundo advento de Cristo. A maioria dos estudiosos crê que essa foi a perseguição movida por Domiciano, o «segundo Nero», que houve pouco antes do fim do primeiro século de nossa era. A literatura apocalíptica tem a característica de tentar «saltar por cima» das crises presentes a fim de dirigir a mente dos fiéis para um futuro triunfo sobre os inimigos, com o estabelecimento da retidão. A última declaração do Apocalipse promete o retorno de Cristo para «breve». Em meio à morte e à destruição, os discípulos de Cristo esperavam o breve cumprimento das promessas referentes à «parousia». Dentre o reinado de Domiciano esperavam o aparecimento do anticristo para breve. O anticristo será a concretização do mal absoluto, pois ele será o servo perfeito de Satanás (ver o décimo terceiro capítulo do Apocalipse). E os cristãos primitivos criam que uma vez que se estabelecesse seu império mundial, logo Cristo voltaria, a fim de destruir o seu ímpio império. Este livro, portanto, foi escrito a fim de encorajar os cristãos, pois o fim parecia bem próximo, ou seja, o «começo» do fim, o que eles podiam observar pessoalmente com facilidade. Este livro, pois, infunde «esperança» aos crentes que sofriam, relembrando-os sobre o «mundo eterno» que eventualmente seria estabelecido, ao passo que os reinos humanos, caracterizados pela cobiça e pelo poder, seriam reduzidos a nada.

Domiciano decretou o «culto ao imperador» de um modo que seus predecessores nunca tinham feito. Ele fez disso uma prova de lealdade ao império. Os cristãos, naturalmente, se recusavam a adorar ao imperador como se fosse um «deus», e as conseqüências disso foram desastrosas para os crentes. Desenvolveu-se até mesmo o culto à família dos Flávios, na qual se encarnaria a natureza divina da família de Domiciano. Mediante sua suposta divindade, além de sua «ascendência divina», procurou estabelecer um governo absoluto sobre os corpos e as almas dos homens. Promoveu ele a sua «divindade» através de holocaustos públicos. Os espectadores que vaiassem seus gladiadores eram executados, sob a alegação de que tinham mostrado falta de respeito, para com sua natureza divina. Os próprios cortesãos de Domiciano tinham de chamá-lo «Senhor e Deus». Ao seu próprio leito ele, ridiculamente, chamava de «leito de um deus»; as festividades por ele instituídas eram denominadas «banquetes sagrados», e até o peixe servido nesses banquetes era considerado «sagrado». (Ver o artigo de Donald MacFayden, «The Occasion of the Domitianic Persecution», *American Journal of Theology*, xxiv, 1920, pp. 46-66, quanto a detalhes a esse respeito).

A história confirma a violência de Domiciano ao pôr em vigor todos os aspectos do «culto ao imperador». Não somente perseguiu aos cristãos, mas também mandou matar e banir a políticos, filósofos e até mesmo membros de sua família que parecessem oferecer-lhe resistência. Mandou executar seu primo, o cônsul Clemente, porque este parecia haver adotado o modo de vida judaico, o que, segundo pensava Domiciano, fizera dele um «ateu». Os livros de I Clemente, escritos de Roma, e Hebreus, escrito a cristãos romanos, evidenciam claramente as tremendas perseguições dessa época da história.

Propósitos. O propósito imediato da composição deste livro foi o de contrabalançar o temor e o desespero que, naturalmente, tomou conta da igreja cristã, o que talvez conduziu alguns à apostasia. Pois este livro mostra que o Senhor Jesus Cristo é o verdadeiro governante, o qual, finalmente, haverá de

APOCALIPSE

esmagar os poderes malignos, ao estabelecer o seu reino. Naquele tempo pensava-se que esse reino seria estabelecido dentro em breve (ver Apo. 22:20); assim sendo, havia boas razões para os crentes se encorajarem a sofrer pelo bem, como espírito triunfal até. O autor sagrado assegura a seus leitores que sem importar quão negra fosse a noite, o Dia estava próximo, o qual também os vingaria das perseguições que experimentavam, porquanto o «direito» seria universalmente estabelecido, ao qual pregavam e no qual criam.

Os demais propósitos deste livro, paralelos ao principal propósito, descrito no parágrafo acima, são os seguintes:

1. Autoridade absoluta de Cristo, como o Alfa e o Ômega de toda a existência humana (ver Apo. 1:8 e 22:13). Portanto, há somente um verdadeiro objeto de nossa adoração, que não é nenhum imperador romano.

2. O autor sagrado tencionava ensinar muitas lições morais à igreja, corrigindo vários lapsos e erros, além de encorajar às igrejas da Ásia Menor, e, através disso, a igreja cristã inteira (ver os capítulos dois e três de Apocalipse). Nem mesmo os tempos de crise e perseguição podem desviar nossos olhos da absoluta necessidade de um andar santo, da lealdade pessoal a Cristo, o qual é nosso Senhor.

3. Tencionava ele, por semelhante modo, descrever os horrendos acontecimentos que terão lugar nesta terra que refletirão, especialmente, as condições dos «últimos dias», ainda que, sem dúvida alguma, isso tivesse alguma aplicação à igreja primitiva, bem como à igreja cristã de todos os séculos. Não podemos deixar de sentir que as predições deste livro aludem, essencialmente, aos verdadeiros «últimos dias», isto é, ao tempo que precederá imediatamente a segunda vinda de Cristo, que falam sobre a «grande tribulação». Portanto, o Apocalipse é um paralelo claro do vigésimo quarto capítulo do evangelho de Mateus e do décimo terceiro capítulo do evangelho de Marcos. O autor sagrado cria que vivia «imediatamente antes» do retorno de Cristo (ver Apo. 22:20), e sua mente foi focalizada sobre aqueles dias, a fim de que pudesse descrevê-los com exatidão. Mas ele cria que tudo sucederia durante seus dias ainda na carne. Nisso, porém, estava equivocado, embora isso em nada afete a validade de suas predições. Ele pensava que estava encorajando especificamente aos cristãos de seus dias; e isso certamente ele fez. No entanto, também encorajava àqueles que viverão nos verdadeiros «últimos dias», prefigurados pelo reinado de Domiciano. Os capítulos sexto a décimo nono do Apocalipse nos fornecem as predições acerca do «tempo do fim».

4. Ao expor a doutrina do segundo advento de Cristo (ver o décimo nono capítulo do Apocalipse), o autor sagrado mostrou, à vitória inteira, como é inevitável a vitória final de Deus e do seu Cristo. Pensava ele que veria pessoalmente a essa vitória, ainda em seu corpo mortal. Não sucedeu assim; mas isso não significa que sua doutrina não fosse veraz. Nós mesmos cremos, com base em predições contemporâneas, da parte dos místicos, que todos os eventos descritos no livro do Apocalipse ocorrerão até o ano de 2037, e que nossa época é, realmente, o «fim dos tempos». (Ver o artigo intitulado, *Tradição Profética e a Nossa Época*).

5. O autor sagrado fornece-nos uma breve antevisão sobre o estado eterno (ver os capítulos vigésimo a vigésimo segundo do Apocalipse). Essa visão é breve, e certamente não é definitiva. Possuímos informações surpreendentemente escassas sobre a «eternidade». Deus tem tempo suficiente para ensinar essas questões a seu povo. Aquilo que sabemos, entretanto, reveste-se de grande significação. Deus e o bem, finalmente, triunfarão. O julgamento é real; a vida eterna é magnificente em suas bênçãos.

VIII. O Grego do Apocalipse

Aqueles que já leram o livro de Apocalipse em seu original grego conhecem, em primeira mão, seu caráter ímpar, suas peculiaridades, e sua natureza freqüentemente barbárica. Sem dúvida, acima de todos os livros do N.T., demonstra desrespeito às regras da gramática grega. A despeito disso, trata-se de uma composição extremamente eloqüente, o maior de todos os «apocalipses». Consideremos os pontos seguintes:

1. *Gramática do Apocalipse*. Dionísio de Alexandria (265 D.C.), para quem o grego era língua nativa, chamado de «grande bispo de Alexandria» (por Eusébio), e de «mestre da igreja universal» (por Atanásio), o eminente pupilo de Orígenes, observou a má natureza do grego do Apocalipse, além de seus muitos barbarismos e hebraísmos. «Nenhum outro autor do Novo Testamento desrespeita tão freqüentemente os cânones de estilo, gramática e sintaxe. Contudo, em sua maior parte, esse desrespeito tem causado pouca ou nenhuma perda de clareza e inteligibilidade. Tudo isso sugere que o escritor era um cristão judeu, o qual não recebera educação segundo os moldes gregos; entretanto, disso não se deve concluir necessariamente que ele fosse nativo da Palestina, conforme alguns têm sugerido, porquanto os judeus estavam largamente disseminados pelo império (romano), havendo muitos deles na Ásia Menor» (Martin Rist, *Introduction to Revelation*, pág. 358). Isso sugere, entretanto, que o autor sagrado tinha o grego como uma segunda língua, como um idioma adquirido, e não como sua língua nativa. Isso não prova, mas sugere, a *Palestina*, como seu lugar de origem, pois se o autor tivesse sido um judeu da dispersão, certamente teria crescido sabendo o grego (tendo-o aprendido nas escolas e na rua). Nesse caso, ele saberia dominar mais perfeitamente o grego, tal como sucedeu no caso de Paulo, que sabia realmente falar dois ou três idiomas.

O leitor curioso, que souber algum grego, pode perceber alguns dos erros gramaticais do autor sagrado nas seguintes referências (embora essa lista não seja exaustiva): Apo. 1:4,5,10,15; 2:20; 3:12; 4:1,7,8; 5:6,11-13; 7:4; 9:5; 11:4,5; 12:5; 13:14; 14:3; 15:12; 17:16; 19:14,20; 20:2; 21:9. Todos esses exemplos envolvem casos de discordância em caso, gênero e número, no tocante a seus antecedentes, além de discordâncias entre os sujeitos e verbos. A maioria desses casos pode ser explicada pelo fato que o autor sagrado pensava em aramaico mas escrevia em grego; suas concordâncias não eram aquelas comuns ao idioma grego. A coisa mais completa que se tem escrito sobre o problema do grego usado no livro de Apocalipse, pode ser encontrada na introdução ao Apocalipse, no *International Critical Commentary*, de autoria de R.H. Charles. Na sua seção XIII ele apresenta uma «gramática» do grego deste livro, além de uma lista de inúmeros erros e usos duvidosos, a maioria dos quais se devem ao fato que ele pensava em aramaico e escrevia em um idioma que não lhe era nativo. Na seção X dessa citada gramática, ele mosta que, algumas vezes, o grego só pode ser compreendido se for reconstituído ao aramaico por detrás do mesmo.

APOCALIPSE

2. Hebraísmos do Apocalipse. A introdução citada acima, de autoria de R.H. Charles, fornece dez páginas repletas de hebraísmos. Essas páginas demonstram conclusivamente o quão firmada estava a mente do autor sagrado no idioma e no pensamento aramaicos. O «tipo de grego» assim produzido não é um grego «bíblico», conforme se vê no caso da tradução da Septuaginta (versão grega do original hebraico do A.T.), e, sim, um grego *sui generis*. Dentre os quatrocentos e quatro versículos que há no livro de Apocalipse, o autor sagrado faz alusão ao A.T. em duzentos e setenta e oito deles; mas seu grego não foi tomado por empréstimo da Septuaginta.

3. Caráter ímpar do Apocalipse. O Apocalipse, conforme já dissemos, não é um exemplar do «grego bíblico». O autor sagrado parece ter feito suas próprias traduções, quando aludia a trechos do A.T. As similaridades com a versão da Septuaginta se deve, provavelmente, a «empréstimos» ocasionalmente feitos pelo autor. Pensando em aramaico, mas escrevendo em grego, juntamente com seus muitos «solecismos» (Charles apresenta mais de vinte referências que contém «solecismos»), ele produziu um grego «sem-par», que não pode ser comparado ao grego daquele período, mesmo quando sujeito a influências hebraizantes. Ele produziu expressões tipicamente aramaicas com palavras gregas, conforme alguém naturalmente seria levado a fazer, ao lançar mão de um idioma estrangeiro. E é evidente que ele não mandou que a sua obra fosse «revisada» por alguém cujo idioma nativo fosse o grego, embora muitíssimas correções gramaticais possam ser encontradas em manuscritos posteriores do N.T., que a aprimoram. Ao apresentar seu estudo sobre as expressões aramaicas, existentes no livro de Apocalipse, Charles alista nove casos em que ele crê que deu ao texto sagrado um melhor sentido, reconstituindo os «pensamentos aramaicos» do autor sagrado, que escreveu em grego artificial (parte «h» da seção «x» de sua introdução ao Apocalipse).

«Ele (o autor sagrado) nunca dominou idiomaticamente o grego—nem mesmo o grego de seu próprio período. Para ele, um grande número de partículas gregas era desconhecido, e as multiformes sombras de sentido que elas expressam, nas suas diversas combinações, nunca foi entendido, ou então essas partículas foram compreendidas de forma mui parcial. Por outro lado, ele é mais exato no uso de expressões idiomáticas do grego do que o autor do quarto evangelho. Não obstante, suas muitas expressões incomuns e jamais ouvidas, o livro (de Apocalipse) não tem rival na sua própria forma literária, ao mesmo tempo que, na literatura de todos os tempos, conquistou um lugar ao sol». (R.H. Charles, pág. cxliv, *Introduction to Revelation*, The International Critical Commentary).

«Juntamente com Marcos, no nível do 'koiné' não-literário, devemos colocar o último livro do N.T. Já desde os meados do século III, Dionísio de Alexandria (conforme diz Eusébio em sua História Eclesiástica VII.25,26) dizia que o grego do livro de Apocalipse é bárbaro e não-gramatical. Desde os tempos desse pai da igreja, que estava familiarizado com os padrões de um 'bom' grego, todo erudito que tem trabalhado com o texto grego do Apocalipse tem-se admirado com suas freqüentes violações das regras da concordância da gramática e da sintaxe do grego...Outra peculiaridade lingüística é a ocasional desconsideração pelos gêneros (ver o texto grego de Apo. 1:10; 4:1,8; 11:4; 19:20, etc.). Visto que noutras passagens o autor se mostra correto na observação dos gêneros, alguns desses exemplos podem ser justificados como questões de indiferença ou descuido, ao passo que outros são devidos ao fato que ele pensava em um idioma semita, ao mesmo tempo que escrevia em grego.

A despeito da presença de tão ousada desconsideração pelas regras ordinárias da sintaxe grega, ao livro de Apocalipse não falta poder literário. Certas passagens solenes e sonoras, que são dotadas de um ritmo quase poético (ver Apo. 4:11; 5:10; 7:15-17; 11:17,18; 15:3,4; 18:2-8,19-24, etc.), têm um perceptível tom miltônico, que se assemelha à voz de um órgão, o que transparece até mesmo na sua tradução inglesa». (Bruce M. Metzger, *The Language of the New Testament*, artigo introdutório ao Novo Testamento, no *Interpreter's Bible*).

IX. O Texto Grego

A confirmação, por parte de manuscritos antigos, ao texto do livro de Apocalipse, é mais fraca que aquela relativa a qualquer outro livro do N.T. No entanto, essa confirmação ao Apocalipse original é mais forte do que aquela relativa a qualquer obra extrabíblica da antigüidade. Sabe-se bem que o N.T. é o mais bem confirmado documento dos tempos antigos. Há mais de cinco mil manuscritos gregos, mais de dez mil traduções latinas, e numerosas outras traduções e extensas citações feitas pelos primeiros pais da igreja, através das quais quase o N.T. inteiro pode ser reconstituído, e que não pertencem a data posterior ao século III D.C. Outrossim, os manuscritos pertencem a uma data bem mais próxima dos originais do que se dá no caso de qualquer outro documento antigo.

Portanto, apesar de que há muitas variantes e alguns problemas textuais difíceis, a restauração do texto original do livro de Apocalipse tem sido realizada com alto grau de exatidão. Entre os cinco principais manuscritos unciais há mais de mil seiscentos e cinqüenta variantes; e as variantes dos manuscritos cursivos posteriores, naturalmente, são muito mais numerosas do que isso. Contudo, na maioria dos casos, os textos originais podem ser restaurados com alto grau de confiança. Quando Erasmo compilou o Textus Receptus, de onde surgiu o primeiro texto impresso do N.T. grego, e de onde se tem derivado a maioria das primeiras traduções do N.T. para diversos idiomas, ele tinha a sua disposição apenas um manuscrito grego, chamado Codex 1, um minúsculo (ou cursivo) do século XII ou XIII. Esse manuscrito é ao mesmo tempo inexato e defeituoso. Não havia testemunho em favor do trecho de Apo. 22:16-21, e Erasmo foi forçado a suprir esse trecho do latim, que transcreveu para o grego. Edições posteriores do texto grego, como os de Tischendorf, Weiss, Westcott e Hort e o Texto de Nestle, além do N.T. grego das Sociedades Bíblicas Unidas, mostram-se muito mais exatas, baseadas como estão em testemunhos mais antigos.

Os principais testemunhos sobre o texto grego do livro de Apocalipse, de que dispomos em nossos dias, e que servem de fontes para os modernos textos gregos, como os de Nestle e o das Sociedades Bíblicas Unidas, são os seguintes:

P(18), um manuscrito escrito em papiro, datado dos séculos III ou IV D.C., e que contém o trecho de Apo. 1:4-7.

P(47), um manuscrito escrito em papiro, datado do século III D.C., que encerra a passagem de 9:10-17:2.

Aleph, um manuscrito escrito em pergaminho, pertencente ao século IV D.C., intitulado «Sinaítico», que é um dos testemunhos centrais de todo o N.T.

APOCALIPSE

Esse manuscrito pode ter sido um dentre cinqüenta cópias do N.T. que Eusébio produzira, por ordem de Constantino e contém o livro completo do Apocalipse. Infelizmente, o codex Vaticanus (B) não contém o texto sagrado depois da passagem de Heb. 9:14, pelo que não pode dar testemunho sobre o texto do livro de Apocalipse. Quanto a informações gerais sobre esses *manuscritos*, bem como ao estudo geral e à teoria da crítica textual, ver o artigo sobre esse tema.

Codex A. Esse manuscrito é uncial, escrito em pergaminho, e data do século V D.C. É chamado «Alexandrino». Ali o Apocalipse aparece completo. A maioria dos críticos textuais acredita que é o texto mais puro dentre todos os manuscritos do Apocalipse. Porém Aleph, os papiros e C estão em consonância essencial, formando um bloco de manuscritos que confirmam o mesmo texto geral, o mesmo tipo de texto.

Codex C. É chamado «Ephraemi», um manuscrito em pergaminho, pertencente ao século V, defeituoso em muitos lugares; mas foi restaurado em certos trechos, nos quais concorda essencialmente com os papiros, Aleph e A.

0207 é um manuscrito uncial escrito em pergaminho, pertencente ao século IV D.C., que também concorda com os testemunhos acima, pertencente ao mesmo tipo, embora não contenha o livro inteiro do Apocalipse.

Os manuscritos unciais 046 (datado dos séculos VIII ou IX D.C.) e P (datado do século X D.C.), além de grande número de manuscritos minúsculos, derivados de após o séc. IX D.C., representam o texto bizantino ou eclesiástico do livro de Apocalipse, que veio à existência mediante a mescla de vários textos, adições escribais e correções (algumas vezes feitas no mau grego do original). Esse texto mesclado, entretanto, como é óbvio, é inferior ao dos demais papiros e manuscritos unciais. Mas foi esse texto, em sua forma posterior, representada pelo codex 1, que foi usado para a compilação do Textus Receptus de Erasmo.

Variantes Textuais comentadas neste artigo. Abaixo damos os lugares onde figuram as variantes textuais mais importantes do livro de Apocalipse: Apo. 1:5,6,8,11,15, 2:2,10,13,16,20,22,23; 3:2,5,7; 5:1,4,6,9,10,13,14; 6:1-5,7,8,11,12,17; 7:12,17; 8:1, 6-8,13; 9:7,10,12,13,19-21; 10:4,5-7,10; 11:2,3,12, 15,17,19; 12:10,18; 13:1,6,7,15,17,18; 14:3,5,6,8, 13,18-20; 15:2-4,6; 16:1,4,16,18; 18:2,3,7,8,11,13, 14,17,20,22; 19:5-7,11,12,13,17; 20:2,6,9,12; 21:3-6,10; 22:5,11,14,19,21.

X. Visão Geral do Conteúdo: Análise, Conceitos de Arranjo

Análise

1. O livro de Apocalipse começa com uma declaração de sua autoridade divina (o único livro do N.T. que contém tal assertiva), copulada a uma promessa de bênção para aqueles que ouvirem a leitura pública do livro (nas igrejas locais) e para aqueles que o lerem. Essa declaração é, ao mesmo tempo, uma explicação do tema do livro, isto é, Jesus Cristo, o Alfa e o Ômega da existência de todos os seres inteligentes. (Ver Apo. 1:1-3).

2. Isso é seguido pela saudação geral às sete igrejas da Ásia Menor, que seriam as primeiras a receber o livro. O próprio Cristo é visto a saudar à igreja, juntamente com João, além de ser retratado como o Alfa e o Ômega, o verdadeiro objeto de adoração, em contraste com os imperadores romanos, como Domiciano, que requeriam tal adoração dos súditos romanos. Essa saudação promete a *parousia* ou segunda vinda de Cristo, dando a entender a conversão do povo de Israel (Ver Apo. 1:4-8; comparar com Rom. 11:26 e ss).

3. A seção seguinte localiza o lugar onde foi recebida a visão—Patmos, a cinqüenta e seis quilômetros ao largo da costa da Ásia Menor (moderna Turquia), além de descrever o aparecimento e a glória de Cristo, conforme ele se mostrou a João e conforme o Apocalipse teve início. (Ver Apo. 1:18-29).

4. Sete cartas são dirigidas às sete igrejas, que originalmente receberam o livro, cada uma das quais descreve as — condições da igreja — particularmente endereçada, com instruções, advertências e promessas. Essas cartas talvez profetizem sete períodos da história eclesiástica, mas certamente refletem as condições reais da igreja cristã, quando o livro foi escrito. (Ver Apo. 2:1-3:22).

5. A substância geral do livro de Apocalipse, que é a cena nos céus (ver seu quarto capítulo), onde se vê a glória celestial de Cristo, e em cuja mão aparece o rolo selado com sete selos, dá a substância geral das revelações a serem desdobradas nas narrativas subseqüentes. Somente o exaltado Senhor e Cordeiro, que é Cristo, é digno de quebrar os selos e publicar a sua mensagem (ver o quinto capítulo do livro). Cinco selos, que revelam horrendos juízos, são abertos (ver o sexto capítulo do livro).

6. O capítulo sete é um parêntese que explica que todo o grupo dos mártires será selado (talvez *o novo Israel* ou o «antigo Israel fiel ao Senhor»), que literalmente envolve cento e quarenta e quatro mil pessoas, ou um número representado por essa quantidade. Esses mártires são vistos em adoração e serviço celestiais. Serviram bem em sua missão terrena, e agora estão exaltados. O selo de Deus garante tanto seu martírio bem-sucedido como sua salvação e sua subseqüente glória divina. Eles «pertencem» a Deus por causa dessas coisas, e foram «selados» por causa das mesmas. O nono versículo mostra que o período de tribulação também será um período de grande número de salvações, porquanto muitíssimas pessoas encontrarão a Cristo em meio as tribulações.

7. O oitavo capítulo volta a falar sobre o partir dos selos do rolo. Do sétimo selo emerge o julgamento das sete trombetas. No oitavo capítulo são soadas quatro dessas trombetas, e terríveis julgamentos caem sobre a terra. Acerca do «tempo» em que tais julgamentos terão lugar (juntamente com tudo o que é descrito nessa análise), ver as várias formas de interpretação, na seção XII do presente artigo. O oitavo capítulo encerra o julgamento das quatro primeiras trombetas.

8. O nono capítulo encerra os julgamentos da quinta e da sexta trombetas, por causa dos quais é destruído um terço da população da terra.

9. O autor interrompe sua descrição dos horrores o bastante para descrever o julgamento iminente, pior do que tudo quanto até então vinha sendo descrito, mediante o símbolo do «livrinho» ou «rolo», que é um escrito profético de total condenação para os ímpios. Era «doce» em sua boca, quando o «*comia*», porque os poderes malignos haveriam de ser transformados, o que será benéfico para toda a criação. Mas era *amargo* em seu estômago, porque falava de terrores que serão sofridos pelos homens (ver o décimo capítulo).

10. O décimo primeiro capítulo também é parentético. Descreve as duas testemunhas que atuarão durante a tribulação. Talvez simbolizem

alguma coisa, ou podem ser pessoas literais, como «Enoque e Elias», *Elias e Moisés*, etc. As duas testemunhas darão seu testemunho durante mil duzentos e sessenta dias, serão mortas e ressuscitarão. Esse incidente visa demonstrar que aqueles a quem Satanás mata, por terem sido fiéis a Cristo, deverão viver em triunfo. E isso é verdade se nos referimos às perseguições do tempo de Nero e Domiciano ou aos horrores da vindoura tribulação, ao fim da era presente, imediatamente antes da segunda vinda de Cristo.

11. O trecho de Apo. 11:15-19 encerra o soar da sétima trombeta, do que resultarão os juízos finais das taças de ira, com suas sete condenações ou «ais».

12. Os capítulos doze e treze descrevem sete personagens de grande importância para os futuros acontecimentos, descritos no Apocalipse. Esses personagens são: Israel (a mulher); Satanás (o destruidor); Cristo (o filho de Israel); o arcanjo Miguel e sua luta nos céus, em favor do bem, o que provocará a queda de Satanás e seus poderes angelicais; a descendência de Israel, o remanescente judaico, que, figuradamente, talvez também inclua o *novo Israel*; e a «besta que saiu do mar» e a «besta que saiu da terra», ou seja, o anticristo e seu falso profeta, já no décimo terceiro capítulo. É interessante que profecias místicas confirmam que esses dois personagens já estão vivos. De acordo com essas mesmas previsões, veremos o início de sua manifestação por volta do ano de 1993. (Ver o artigo sobre o *Anticristo*).

13. O capítulo catorze encerra um outro parêntese. Contrasta os adoradores da besta; o anticristo, com os discípulos fiéis de Cristo, o Cordeiro.— Em vez de adorarem ao imperador (Domiciano) e, profeticamente, ao anticristo, eles adoram ao Filho de Deus. Esses, embora tenham morte terrível, serão abençoados com a vida eterna, em contraste com os adoradores do anticristo, que aguardam a segunda morte. Antes disso, terão de sofrer os terrores do Armagedom.

14. O décimo quinto capítulo introduz os juízos das sete taças, com uma cena celeste que preparará o caminho para tais julgamentos. Nos céus são vistos aqueles que triunfaram sobre a besta, sobre sua marca, seu número e seu aterrorizante reinado, porquanto entraram no descanso, na presença de seu Senhor.

15. O décimo sexto capítulo descreve os juízos das sete taças, bem como uma nova série indizivelmente severa de julgamentos, que sobrevirão ao mundo, em prodigiosa demonstração da ira de Deus.

16. Das sete taças emergiram as sete «condenações». A primeira, que é a da Babilônia (Roma), mas que profetiza a esfera de governo do anticristo, ocupa os capítulos dezessete e dezoito.

17. Antes do reinício das «condenações», o décimo nono capítulo descreve as quatro «aleluias» dos santos glorificados. E isso é seguido por uma visão do hino do casamento do Cordeiro e sua noiva (a igreja). Poderíamos arranjar o trecho de Apo. 17:1-19:10 em «sete visões», todas as quais envolvem «Roma», a saber: 1. a prostituta; 2. interpretação da prostituta e da fera (ou besta); 3. proclamação angelical sobre a queda de Roma; 4. exultação dos santos e lamento dos povos em face da queda de Roma; 5. lamentação final sobre a cidade; 6. as «aleluias» dos santos; 7. hino matrimonial.

18. Seguem-se sete visões sobre o fim do governo e da era de Satanás, a saber: 1. A «parousia» ou segundo advento de Cristo, a fim de julgar: o Cristo conquistador (ver Apo. 19:11-16). 2. Visão da vitória de Cristo sobre o anticristo (ver Apo. 19:17-21). 3. Visão da prisão de Satanás por mil anos (ver Apo. 20:1-3). 4. Visão do reino milenar de Cristo (ver Apo. 20:4-6). 5. Visão de Gogue e Magogue derrotados e lançados no lago de fogo, juntamente com Satanás, o que assinalará o fim de sua era e governo (ver Apo. 20:7-10). 6. Desaparecimento dos céus e da terra; o grande julgamento (ver Apo. 20:11-15). 7. Visão da nova criação e da era eterna de Deus (ver Apo. 21:1-8). Nessas visões temos a continuação das «condenações». A primeira é a destruição da Babilônia (capítulos dezessete e dezoito); a segunda é a condenação da besta; a terceira é a de seu falso profeta; a quarta é a dos reis ou apoiadores do anticristo; a quinta é a de Gogue e Magogue; a sexta é a do próprio Satanás; a sétima é a dos incrédulos aliados de Satanás e do anticristo.

19. Finalmente, chegamos à criação de novos céus e nova terra, a Jerusalém celestial, a capital da glória eterna (capítulos vinte e um e vinte e dois).

20. *Epílogo*. (Ver Apo. 22:6-21). Temos aqui a última mensagem do N.T. Cristo voltará em breve. Ele é o Alfa e o Ômega. Chamada ao arrependimento; advertência contra os abusos contra esta profecia.

Conceitos de arranjo

1. Há o conceito *telescópico*, com certa sucessão de acontecimentos:

Essa idéia encara o Apocalipse como uma crônica ordenada dos acontecimentos, com alguns poucos parênteses. Assim, ao passarmos de um capítulo para outro, supostamente avançamos para novos acontecimentos e assim passamos por uma série deles.

Telescópio da Era da Igreja

A era da igreja é:

«as cousas...que são» (Que retrata a época do autor sagrado). Contudo, trata-se de profecias simbólicas de coisas que «serão». Essas «coisas que são» foram precedidas pelas «coisas que eram», isto é, aquilo que João «vira», a visão inicial (ver Apo. 1:1-20). Após as cartas para a era da igreja aparecem as *«cousas...que hão de acontecer depois destas»*, ou seja, aquilo que deverá transpirar imediatamente antes da segunda vinda de Cristo. Portanto, temos em Apo. 1:20 um esboço bem simples do livro: coisas que foram, coisas que são e coisas que hão de acontecer. No primeiro capítulo temos o passado; nos capítulos segundo e terceiro temos o presente; nos capítulos quarto a vigésimo segundo temos o futuro, os últimos dias.

TELESCÓPIO DA ERA DA IGREJA

| Éfeso, era apostólica | Esmirna, era de perseguições —até 316 | Pérgamo, era de favor imperial —317-500 | Tiatira, era negra —500-1500 | Sardes, tempo da Reforma —1500-1700 | Filadélfia, era das missões modernas —1700-1900 | Laodicéia, era da igreja apóstata —1900 - |

APOCALIPSE

As «coisas que hão de acontecer». Esses são os «últimos dias», imediatamente antes da vinda de Cristo. Os grandes juízos do período de tribulação (ou então, conforme alguns—estão incluídos vários períodos históricos).

| Sete selos (6:1-8:6) | Sete trombetas (8:8-11:19) | Sete taças (15:1-16:21) | Sete condenações (caps. 17-20) |

2. Conceito das profecias: os «duplos»

Ao interpretar o livro de Apocalipse, alguns não crêem que esteja em foco uma contínua «sucessão» de eventos (de mistura com alguns poucos parênteses). Utilizando-se do texto de Gên. 41:14 ss como chave, pensam que há apresentações paralelas dos mesmos julgamentos, e não julgamentos sucessivos. É verdade que naquele capítulo do livro de Gênesis as sete «vacas gordas» são idênticas às sete «espigas cheias» e que as sete «vacas magras» são idênticas às sete «espigas mirradas». As vacas gordas e as espigas cheias profetizavam sobre sete anos de abundância; e as sete vacas magras e as espigas mirradas profetizavam sobre sete anos de escassez.

Aplicando-se essa *chave* ao livro de Apocalipse, teríamos o seguinte arranjo: Os sete selos e as sete trombetas seriam espiritualmente paralelos; e os sete anjos e as sete taças seriam espiritualmente paralelos. Os selos e trombetas seriam uma «visão celeste» dos mesmos acontecimentos focalizados na terra pelos anjos e taças. Nesse caso, somente sete elementos distintos seriam encontrados no livro de Apocalipse, no tocante aos juízos, e não uma série de quatro conjuntos distintos de julgamentos. Alguns encaram esses sete elementos distintos como sete épocas da história do mundo (interpretação histórica), ao passo que outros vêem sete acontecimentos ou estágios distintos acerca dos «últimos dias», o período da tribulação. Seja como for, encontramos apenas uma série de sete elementos, e não quatro séries. Mas essa série é descrita de vários modos, sob diferentes pontos de vista, seguindo a orientação do quadragésimo primeiro capítulo do livro de Gênesis, que faz a mesma coisa, com diversos simbolismos. Já que as sete trombetas constituem o sétimo selo, então treze acontecimentos gerais são descritos no livro de Apocalipse, a saber: seis selos e sete trombetas (que enfeixariam, estas últimas, o último selo). O «sétimo acontecimento» consistiria de «sete acontecimentos». Isso poderia ser uma verdade se aplicássemos os mesmos a períodos históricos antes da segunda vinda de Cristo, ou a elementos da tribulação. Assim também o povo de Israel rodeou a cidade de Jericó por treze vezes. Nos primeiros seis dias eles a rodearam apenas uma vez cada dia; mas, no sétimo dia, rodearam-na por sete vezes. Seis mais sete é igual a treze. Isso derrubou as muralhas de Jericó, com a conseqüente derrota de seus habitantes. Os treze acontecimentos retratados no livro de Apocalipse, pois, porão fim ao governo de Satanás, estabelecendo o reino de Deus, como também o reinado universal de Cristo.

OS PARALELOS:

I. *Os selos e anjos* (os selos indicam o ponto de vista celeste; os anjos indicam o ponto de vista terreno dos mesmos acontecimentos).

1. Apo. 6:2   14:6,7
2. 6:3-5   14:8
3. 6:5-6   14:9-11
4. 6:7-8   14:12-13
5. 6:9-11   14:17-20
6. 6:12-7:17   14:17-20
7. 8:1-6   15:1-16:1

II. *As trombetas e as taças* (as trombetas indicam o ponto de vista celeste; as taças indicam o ponto de vista terreno dos mesmos acontecimentos).

1. Apo. 8:7   16:2
2. 8:8-9   16:3
3. 8:10-11   16:4-7
4. 8:12-13   16:8-9
5. 9:1-12   16:10-11
6. 9:13-21   16:12-14
7. 10:7; — (11-15-19)   15:17-21

Assim sendo, teríamos o seguinte: Os selos e os anjos descrevem os mesmos acontecimentos, embora de pontos de vista diferentes; o sétimo selo se constitui das sete trombetas; as sete trombetas e os sete selos descrevem os mesmos acontecimentos de acordo com diferentes pontos de vista.

3. *A teoria sincronológica*. Essa teoria também apresenta apenas sete elementos ou acontecimentos gerais, que seriam eras ou épocas. As várias séries de «setes», como os selos, as trombetas, as taças, os anjos, seriam totalmente paralelas. Cada série de «sete» descreveria os mesmos acontecimentos, eras ou sucessões de eventos, mas de acordo com diferentes pontos de vista. Cada série de «sete» cobriria o mesmo período de tempo, estendendo-se até o fim de todas as coisas.

4. Falta de qualquer arranjo de acontecimentos ou de distinção de eras. Se o livro de Apocalipse tiver de ser interpretado apenas simbólica ou misticamente, então não faz sentido falar de «eras» de «acontecimentos sucessivos» ou de qualquer arranjo de tempo.

XI. Esboço do Conteúdo

    I. Introdução (1:1-3)
   II. Saudação (1:4-8)
  III. Origem do Apoc. (1:9-20: coisas que foram)
  IV. Cartas às Sete Igrejas (caps 2-3: coisas que são)
      1. Éfeso (2:1-7)
      2. Esmirna (2:8-11)
      3. Pérgamo (2:12-17)
      4. Tiatira (2:18-29)
      5. Sardes (3:1-6)
      6. Filadélfia (3:7-13)
      7. Laodicéia (3:14-22)
   V. Visão introdutória dos selos (4:1-22:21: coisas que hão de acontecer)
      1. Visão do trono de Deus (4:1-11)
      2. Visão do livro do Cordeiro (5:1-14)
  VI. Visão dos Sete Selos (6:1-8:6)
      1. Primeiro: o cavalo branco (6:1,2)
      2. Segundo: o cavalo vermelho (6:3,4)
      3. Terceiro: o cavalo preto (6:5,6)
      4. Quarto: o cavalo amarelo (6:7,8)
      5. Quinto: lamento dos mártires (6:9-11)
      6. Sexto: tremendos juízos (6:12-17)
      7. Parênteses (7:1-17)
        a. selagem dos mártires (7:1-8)
        b. os mártires glorificados (7:9-17)
      8. Sétimo: surgimento das sete trombetas (8:1-6)
 VII. Julgamentos das Sete Trombetas (8:7-11:19)
      1. Primeira: saraiva e fogo (8:7)
      2. Segunda: montanha em fogo (8:8,9)
      3. Terceira: a estrela de fogo (8:10,11)

APOCALIPSE

4. Quarta: enegrecem sol, lua e estrelas (8:12)
5. Parênteses: advertência da águia (8:13)
6. Quinta: terríveis gafanhotos (9:1-12)
7. Sexta: os cavaleiros (9:13-21)
8. Parênteses (10:1-11:14)
   a. o rolo doce-amargo (10:1-11)
   b. as duas testemunhas (11:1-14)
9. Sétima: Cristo em breve reinará (11:15-19)

VIII. Visões dos Sete Personagens (12:1-13:18)
1. A mulher (12:1,2)
2. Satanás (12:3,4)
3. A criança (12:5,6)
4. Miguel, o arcanjo (12:7-16)
5. A descendência da mulher (12:17)
6. A besta saída do mar (13:1-10)
7. A besta saída da terra (13:11-18)

IX. Sete visões dos adoradores do Cordeiro e da Besta (14:1-20)
1. Os mártires do cordeiro (14:1-5)
2. Ordem angelical de adoração (14:6,7)
3. Condenação de Babilônia, centro da antiadoração (14:8)
4. Condenação dos adoradores da besta (14:9-12)
5. Bem-aventurança dos mártires (14:13)
6. Armagedom, a colheita (14:14-16)
7. A vinha no lagar de Deus (14:17-20)

X. Julgamentos das Sete Taças (15:1-16:21)
1. Preparativos celestiais (cap. 15)
2. Primeira taça: praga das feridas (16:1,2)
3. Segunda taça: mar transformado em sangue (16:3)
4. Terceira taça: rios e fontes transformados em sangue (16:4-7)
5. Quarta taça: calor escaldante (16:8,9)
6. Quinta taça: trevas (16:10,11)
7. Sexta taça: preparação para o Armagedom (16:12-16)
8. Sétima taça: juízo proferido contra Babilônia (16:17-21)

XI. Sete Visões da Queda de Babilônia (17:1-19:10)
1. Babilônia, a prostituta (17:1-6a)
2. Natureza da prostituta e da besta (17:6b-18)
3. Condenação proferida (18:1-3)
4. Grande lamento pela queda de Babilônia (18:4-20)
5. Lamento final sobre a cidade (18:21-24)
6. Hino de louvor a Deus, por ter sido destruída Babilônia (19:1-5)
7. Anúncio do casamento do Cordeiro (19:6-10)

XII. Sete Visões da Queda de Satanás e o Fim de seu Reinado (19:11-21:8)
1. Cristo vencerá: a *parousia* marca o juízo de Satanás (19:11-16)
2. Cristo virá e esmagará o anticristo (19:17-21)
3. Satanás é amarrado por mil anos (20:1-3)
4. O milênio (20:4-6)
5. Revolta de Gogue e Magogue (20:7-10)
6. Desaparecimento dos céus e da terra — juízo final (20:11-15)
7. A nova criação e a era eterna (21:1-8)

XIII. Jerusalém Celestial, Capital da Nova Criação (21:9-22:5)
1. Seu aparecimento (21:9-14)
2. Suas medidas (21:15-17)
3. Sua composição (21:18-21)
4. Sua glória (21:22-27)
5. O novo jardim do Éden (22:1-5)

XIV. Epílogo: Cristo voltará em breve. Preparai-vos (22:6-21)

XII. Conceitos e Métodos de Interpretação

O livro de Apocalipse tem sido estudado segundo muitos conceitos e métodos de interpretação diferentes. Abaixo mostramos os principais dentre esses:

1. *O ponto de vista preterista*. Esse ponto de vista dá a entender que todas as ocorrências aludidas no livro de Apocalipse tiveram lugar no império romano, no primeiro século de nossa era, embora talvez haja acontecimentos referentes ao segundo século. Os eruditos liberais normalmente tomam esse ponto de vista em geral, porquanto supõem que o livro não pode ser uma profecia genuína, mas tão-somente um escrito simbólico e uma avaliação mística dos acontecimentos daquela porção do mundo para onde o livro foi originalmente enviado. Alguns estudiosos católicos romanos também favorecem esse ponto de vista, talvez porque impossibilita a interpretação protestante, que faz do papa o anticristo, além de negar a idéia de que a Igreja Católica Romana seja representada por Babilônia. Esse ponto de vista, apesar de preservar sem dúvida alguma verdade, pois certamente o livro reflete alguns acontecimentos «contemporâneos», no entanto não leva em conta que se trata de uma «profecia», e que esta contempla o tempo futuro da segunda vinda de Cristo, sem importar se isso ocorreria imediatamente ou não, e sem importar nossa idéia sobre o seu cumprimento dentro do tempo.

2. *O ponto de vista histórico*. Os intérpretes que assumem essa posição procuram encaixar todos os acontecimentos previstos no Apocalipse em várias épocas da história humana. A série de «sete» (selos, trombetas, taças e anjos) supostamente representaria sucessivos estágios da história da humanidade, até à volta de Cristo, o que dará fim ao presente ciclo geral. Naturalmente, os que assim pensam não têm podido concordar entre si sobre quais visões representam estes ou aqueles acontecimentos históricos, e muitas identificações fantásticas, de homens e eventos, no tocante às predições, têm aparecido na literatura que defende esse ponto de vista. O ponto de vista puramente histórico do livro de Apocalipse deixa-o uma obra essencialmente fechada e misteriosa.

3. *O ponto de vista futurista*. Há os «futuristas extremos», que pensam que o livro inteiro é preditivo, incluindo os capítulos dois e três (as cartas às sete igrejas), que representariam sucessivos estágios da história eclesiástica, até à vinda de Cristo. Mas há os «futuristas moderados», que admitem que os capítulos dois e três referem-se ao passado (ou ao presente); mas que a começar no quarto capítulo temos o futuro, o que deverá ocorrer imediatamente antes do segundo advento de Cristo. Isso faz este livro ser, essencialmente, uma profecia, levando em conta, a sério, as declarações de Apo. 1:19 e 4:1. A principal objeção contra esse ponto de vista é que remove do livro qualquer contexto histórico. Mas isso é respondido pela observação que apesar de refletir o tempo e os acontecimentos contemporâneos, em um sentido secundário, a verdade é que, em sentido «primário», o livro reflete os «últimos dias». Portanto, este livro tanto é orientado historicamente como é escatologicamente importante; mas a ênfase recai sobre este

APOCALIPSE — APOCALIPSE DE TIAGO

último fator. Os futuristas que falam desse modo tornam-se um tanto «ecléticos» em seus pontos de vista, mas sua ênfase recai sobre o futuro, e não sobre o passado. Os liberais, a quem falta a fé na possibilidade de um livro como o de Apocalipse ser uma profecia genuína, ou que duvidam que tal profecia possa abarcar tão grande expansão de tempo, fazem objeção ao ponto de vista futurista.

O presente artigo assume, essencialmente, o ponto de vista futurista, ao asseverar que esse livro, tal como alguns livros do V.T. é essencialmente uma profecia, e, de fato, o único livro totalmente profético do N.T. Certamente o N.T. *deve* contar com *um livro* assim, que vise dirigir, orientar e consolar aos crentes (e ao povo de Israel), quando se encontrarem em meio aos horrendos acontecimentos descritos nesse livro. Esse é o livro neotestamentário que veio à existência com esse propósito, a fim de informar-nos, com detalhes, como Cristo tomará as rédeas do governo deste mundo, como as forças do mal serão derrotadas, e como o estado eterno substituirá, por fim, os ciclos terrestres. O autor desta enciclopédia, outrossim, crê que profetas e místicos contemporâneos têm pronunciado e estão proferindo predições que são paralelas às do livro de Apocalipse. Ao compararmos essas predições, vemos que a maior parte do livro de Apocalipse pode ser focalizada no futuro, nos «últimos dias», o tempo imediatamente antes do longamente previsto segundo advento de Cristo. O livro de Apocalipse, pois, tornar-se-á progressivamente melhor compreendido quando mais próximo estiverem os eventos preditos. Os acontecimentos de maior vulto (como também os secundários) lançam suas sombras antes mesmo de chegarem em cena. Ora, as sombras daqueles horrendos acontecimentos preditos no livro de Apocalipse, já estão entre nós; e este artigo defende a «especulação» que certamente, antes de 2035, terão lugar os acontecimentos preditos no Apocalipse. O leitor deveria consultar o artigo intitulado «*Tradição Profética e a Nossa Época*». Se porventura o leitor considerar extravagantes esses pontos de vista, então que o futuro imediato os confirme ou condene. Que o leitor leia para considerar e não para condenar.

4. *A interpretação simbólica ou mística*. Alguns eruditos crêem que o livro de Apocalipse não é essencialmente profético e nem histórico, mas é uma vívida coletânea de símbolos místicos, que visam ensinar lições espirituais e morais. Isso significa que não esperamos qualquer *cronologia* de acontecimentos passados ou futuros nesse livro. Tais acontecimentos seriam puramente espirituais, podendo «acontecer» em qualquer período histórico. Naturalmente, muito há no livro de Apocalipse que pode ser visto como «misticamente instrutivo»; mas isso não pode explicar sua mensagem geral. Ele assevera ser uma profecia, e certamente assim sucede.

5. *O ponto de vista eclético*. Alguns intérpretes «misturam» todas as idéias expostas acima, de modo que nenhuma domine — as demais. Não há dúvida que devemos preservar «alguns elementos» de cada um desses pontos de vista sobre o livro de Apocalipse, em um grau ou outro. Os eventos que já sucederam, e que eram contemporâneos aos dias do autor sagrado, estão em vista, embora talvez não estejam primariamente em foco (dentro do intuito do Espírito Santo, à parte do intuito do próprio autor sagrado). Porções do Apocalipse podem subentender ou descrever partes da sucessão de eventos da história humana (como é o caso das cartas às igrejas, nos capítulos segundo e terceiro), e muitos outros acontecimentos históricos refletem, pelo menos em parte, as descrições feitas. O livro ensina-nos lições morais e místicas, aplicáveis a qualquer época. Contudo, certamente erraremos se não contemplarmos o livro de Apocalipse como obra «essencialmente» profética, e de primeira ordem. Dentre todas as gerações, a nossa e mais uma ou duas, são as que precisam mais desesperadamente da mensagem deste livro. A igreja cristã deve compreender que nos aproximamos do mais aterrorizante tempo de purificação. A igreja presente é incapaz de «voar» ou «subir». Os eventos preditos neste livro prepararão a igreja para ir ao encontro de Cristo e de Deus.

XIII. Bibliografia
(AM DE EN FA I IB LAN NTI RO SE TI UN Z)

APOCALIPSE DE DOSITEU

Esse é um documento gnóstico existente na biblioteca Nag Hammadi. (Ver o artigo sobre os livros apócrifos do Novo Testamento). Essa obra ainda não foi publicada. Constitui os últimos cinco documentos do codex VII, págs. 118:10 - 127:27. No título há referências a três *stelae* (colunas ou tabelas) de Sete, e que Doresse vincula a uma alusão em uma outra obra, o *Apocalipse de Zostriano*. Essas *stelae* são hinos, cada qual com cerca de três páginas. Nas pseudo-clementinas figura um certo Dositeu, referido como rival de Simão Mago; mas não parece haver boas razões para ligarmos esses homens como se fossem um só. Podemos encontrar detalhes sobre a questão na obra de Doresse, *Secret Books of the Egyptian Gnostics*, Londres, 1960, págs. 188 ss.). (Z)

APOCALIPSE DE ELIAS

Há três obras pseudepígrafas com esse título:

1. A obra mais antiga desse grupo é um livro conhecido somente em forma fragmentar, no copta, além de algumas poucas referências obscuras feitas por Orígenes (ver artigo), em cerca de 185-284 D.C. Diz-nos Orígenes que a bela passagem de I Coríntios 2:9: «Nem olhos viram, nem ouvidos ouviram, nem jamais penetrou em coração humano o que Deus tem preparado para aqueles que o amam», na verdade foi extraída desse antigo Apocalipse. E autoridades posteriores têm concordado com essa avaliação.

2. Um escrito pós-cristão, de cerca de 260 D.C., produzido na época em que Sapor I, rei da Pérsia, capturou o imperador romano Valeriano. Essa obra fala sobre a derrota do tirano de Palmira, Odenato, arquiinimigo dos judeus.

3. Uma terceira obra desse nome é a história do rabino Josué Ben Levi, um mestre em Lida (Lode), que viveu no século III D.C. Nessa história, somos informados de que o idoso rabino viu em visão o panorama do céu e do inferno, acompanhado por seu amigo, Elias. (J JAM JE Z)

APOCALIPSE DE PAULO Ver Paulo, Apocalipse de

APOCALIPSE DE TIAGO

Há dois documentos antigos que receberam esse título. Estão contidos no codex V da Biblioteca Nag Hammadi. Quanto a informações sobre os manuscritos de Nag Hammadi, ver o artigo sobre o *gnosticismo*. O livro Apócrifo de Tiago, no codex Jung, é uma obra distinta. Consideremos os pontos abaixo:

1. A primeira obra desse nome é uma espécie de diálogo entre Tiago e Jesus, cuja primeira parte ocorre antes da crucificação, e cuja segunda parte ocorre após a ressurreição. Vários princípios morais e

APOCALÍPTICOS, LIVROS

espirituais, bem como doutrinas místicas, são ali expostas.

2. A segunda dessas obras é uma espécie de discurso formal feito por Tiago, antes de seu martírio, no qual ele discursa sobre uma aparição de Jesus e sobre a revelação transmitida a ele por meio dessa aparição. Ambas essas obras são de natureza gnóstica, e a importância principal das mesmas é a ajuda que nos prestam para conferir-nos entendimento sobre como se relacionavam entre si o cristianismo e o gnosticismo. Isso é especialmente verdadeiro no tocante à importante posição que os cristãos judeus davam a Tiago. (J Z)

APOCALÍPTICOS, Livros (Literatura Apocalíptica)

O Termo

O vocábulo grego *apokaluptein* significa «descobrir», «desvendar». Um tipo de pensamento que floresceu no judaísmo posterior e no cristianismo antigo foi designado por esse nome (165 A.C. - 120 D.C.). Os livros apocalípticos foram escritos a fim de descrever eventos futuros preditos, que poriam fim ao domínio do mal no mundo, de maneira extremamente abrupta. Alguns deles descrevem esse fim como absoluto, com o holocausto de tudo, com a completa destruição do mundo; mas outros falam em uma grande purificação, por meio do fogo. Os justos haveriam de levantar-se para viver em um mundo renovado, em uma era áurea.

Propósito. O propósito psicológico dessas obras era de ajudar os judeus (e também os cristãos) a resistirem a tiranos terrenos e a nações abusivas, já que assim era oferecida uma solução rápida para momentosos problemas, mediante a intervenção divina. Julgava-se que os poderes políticos, como em Roma, além de outros estados estrangeiros, eram controlados por forças demoníacas — o que explicaria a malignidade dos mesmos. Mas Deus haveria de prevalecer, finalmente. Os livros apocalípticos caracteristicamente encaravam o fim como próximo, porquanto o espírito humano se impacientava debaixo das perseguições. Esses livros ofereciam «um salto» por cima das condições organizadas atuais. Tal salto dar-se-ia rápida e prontamente, e a glória da vitória sobre as forças malignas não tardaria a estabelecer-se.

I. O que é um Apocalipse?

Toda a literatura apocalíptica é escatológica. Em outras palavras, aborda a questão dos «tempos do fim», o término do mundo segundo o conhecemos, e começo de um novo ciclo, ou em alguns casos, o estado eterno. Nem toda a literatura escatológica, porém, é apocalíptica. Pode-se falar, por exemplo, sobre a *alma* e seu destino, e isso nos levaria a tratar de certo aspecto do ensinamento escatológico normal, mas, ao mesmo tempo, nada de distintamente apocalíptico estará sendo envolvido nesse ensino. Os escritos que têm chegado até nós, que são chamados «apocalípticos», possuem características distintivas, o que é salientado na discussão que se segue. De modo bem geral, pode-se afirmar que essa forma literária trata da escatologia, pois visa dizer-nos as condições que haverá nos últimos tempos, nos tempos futuros remotos, mas sua apresentação fala daqueles acontecimentos futuros que terão lugar durante dias angustiosos, em que uma antiga era passará em meio a tempestades e agonias, iniciando-se uma era inteiramente nova, através das mais severas dores de parto. Mas isso não é uma característica normal e necessária dos escritos escatológicos.

No que concerne à atividade literária judaico-cristã, pode-se identificar o período dos escritos apocalípticos entre 165 A.C. e 120 D.C. Essa literatura antecipa o fim de um ciclo histórico, a saber, o ciclo judaico, o que se daria em meio a dores severas, antes do nascimento da era cristã. Os «apocalipses» cristãos refletem o desapontamento dos discípulos de Cristo por não se ter materializado o Reino de Deus em sua própria época. E esse desapontamento foi apenas natural, e se pensou que os acontecimentos que sempre foram tomados como necessários na inauguração do reino deveriam ser transferidos para outra época, o tempo da «volta» de Jesus Cristo, não mais sendo atribuídos ao seu «primeiro advento». Isso preencheu um vácuo psicológico, pois manteve os homens na «esperança» no estabelecimento do reino. No entanto, não há razão para crermos, meramente porque esse tipo de literatura cumpre uma necessidade psicológica, que as profecias contidas em nossos apocalipses bíblicos (os livros de Daniel e de Apocalipse) não sejam válidas.

Os apocalipses judaicos foram escritos na época de Antíoco Epifânio e posteriormente, acompanhando as perseguições que houve naquele período histórico. Essa literatura apocalíptica teve a finalidade de dar aos homens a «esperança quanto ao futuro», estando eles a passar por um presente dificílimo. Essa esperança contemplava particularmente o livramento através do vindouro Messias, bem como através do estabelecimento de seu reino. Pode-se ver facilmente que, tal como no caso dos apocalipses cristãos, a literatura apocalíptica judaica conservava a necessidade psicológica de «saltar por cima» de um presente difícil, a fim de levar os homens a terem esperança e fé firme de que se cumpriria uma nova era de vitória e realizações espirituais, embora isso não dispensasse grande agonia. Também é verdade que apesar da atividade da literatura apocalíptica nunca se ter tornado uma questão central no judaísmo, e apesar de que a maioria dos rabinos judeus a ignoravam essencialmente, contudo, esses escritos serviram ao seu propósito; e embora nunca tivessem ganho posição canônica, não há razão para supormos que não há ali certo discernimento quanto ao futuro, misticamente intuitivo, apesar de não ser diretamente inspirado pelo Espírito do Senhor.

Em contraste com isso, o espírito apocalíptico dominava a igreja primitiva. O fato de que o reino de Deus não se materializou então deu, aos primeiros discípulos de Cristo, a ardente esperança que a «breve» e mesmo «iminente» segunda volta de Cristo (a «parousia» dos escritos neotestamentários) haveria de desfazer o erro de sua «rejeição», cumprindo todas as expectações da humanidade acerca de uma era melhor. Mas essa era melhor não haverá de iniciar-se senão através da morte agonizante e terrível da antiga era, e a literatura apocalíptica é essencialmente a descrição dessa morte febricitante, com descrições adicionais do glorioso nascimento da nova era, que se seguirá.

A literatura apocalíptica, pois, tem um *propósito presente*. Os fiéis necessitam de força espiritual para passar pelas aflições, desapontamentos e pressões desta era ímpia em que vivemos. Serão mais capazes disso se puderem antever a vitória, a qual, finalmente, reverterá os terrores do momento presente. Os escritos apocalípticos prometem que os adversários de Deus não escaparão ao juízo por causa daquilo que fizeram, por seus feitos ímpios que praticaram. Além disso, promete que aquilo contra o que os perversos têm-se oposto, o governo de Deus sobre a terra, eventualmente se cumprirá, a despeito deles. Outrossim, promete

227

APOCALÍPTICOS, LIVROS

que até mesmo muitos daqueles que se têm oposto a isso, através dos juízos haverão de reconhecer a mão de Deus na história, acolhendo a seu Cristo como Senhor deles.

II. Características

Há algumas características distintivas da literatura apocalíptica. O termo grego «apokalupto» significa «desvendar», «revelar». O «apokalupsis», pois, é uma «revelação», ou «desvendamento»; é uma «visão profética». Consideremos os pontos seguintes a esse respeito:

1. *Os livros apocalípticos são sempre reveladores.* Há ali atividade mística, revelações, sonhos, visões, viagens celestiais em espírito, tudo o que transcende à era presente, pelos poderes da alma humana, com ou sem a ajuda divina. Cremos que até mesmo os apocalipses não-canônicos envolvem algumas experiências místicas válidas, ou seja, algum discernimento válido quanto às questões espirituais, incluindo revelações sobre as condições futuras. Os dois livros apocalípticos da Bíblia, Daniel e Apocalipse, certamente contêm o esboço dos acontecimentos futuros, a maioria dos quais tem sido confirmada pela atividade profética dos místicos atuais. Em outras palavras, as profecias de nossos dias concordam com as previsões bíblicas, de modo a narrar acontecimentos paralelos. Ver o artigo *Tradição Profética e a Nossa Época*, que apresenta uma discussão geral sobre essa questão.

2. *São imitativos e pseudopreditivos.* Apesar de haver discernimento espiritual quase certamente «válido», porquanto, os poderes de pré-conhecimento dos homens funcionam quase sempre, com resultados que podem ser medidos, esses livros apocalípticos tendem por ser imitativos. O livro de Daniel servia de arquétipo original. Nesses escritos há «invenções» que não refletem qualquer atividade mística genuína, pois as «profecias de condenação», com subidas aos céus e descidas ao inferno, se tornaram artifícios literários, que visavam ensinar verdades espirituais, apresentando advertências e encorajamentos necessários. Portanto, apesar de algumas previsões válidas estarem contidas nos apocalipses, não-canônicos, — mais freqüentemente do que não, as profecias são pseudopreditivas; e essas previsões tornam-se «meios» de ensino — em vez de serem tentativas sérias de predizer o futuro.

3. *Empregam verdades místicas e simbólicas*, em vez de verdades físicas e literais. A fé religiosa pode ser ensinada com habilidade sem base nos acontecimentos históricos reais, ou passados ou em antecipação ao futuro. O meio de transmitir a verdade, dentro do misticismo, é o símbolo. Um símbolo pode ser válido, sem importar que por detrás dele tenha ou não algum acontecimento físico e literal. As parábolas de Jesus (pelo menos algumas delas) não tinham o intuito de relacionarem-se com qualquer acontecimento real; antes, eram «boas narrativas» sobre as verdades eternas, que eram assim vividamente ilustradas. Assim sendo, um profeta podia falar sobre a descida ao inferno por parte de Enoque, e assim ensinar uma verdade acerca do estado das almas perdidas, sem isso significar que Enoque tenha, realmente, feito tal viagem. Até mesmo nos apocalipses canônicos, as «visões» com freqüência não apresentam objetos «reais» ou «físicos». Tomemos, por exemplo, o caso da imagem com os dez dedos formados de ferro e barro. Isso simboliza os reinos e federações do mundo, embora não seja uma verdade literal. Algumas obras apocalípticas chegam a extremos bizarros ao pintarem condições e expectações espirituais. Alguns dos intérpretes mais inclinados pela interpretação literal do Apocalipse do João procuram tornar literais esses simbolismos. Assim, os «gafanhotos» e «escorpiões», que são animais simbólicos do nono capítulo do livro de Apocalipse, seriam insetos literais que atacam os homens como praga. Porém, não são esses mais literais do que os «cavaleiros» do sexto capítulo do mesmo livro. Todas essas coisas simbolizam os terríveis julgamentos e as condições imediatamente antes da «parousia» ou segundo advento de Cristo. A tentativa de emprestar um caráter literal a esses símbolos redunda em fracasso, além de impedir o entendimento da própria natureza mística dessas visões. Até mesmo os sonhos ordinários nos falam por meio de «símbolos». Por exemplo, uma «criança» simboliza o trabalho realizado por algum obreiro do evangelho, pois esse trabalho, em certo sentido, é sua «criança». A água é símbolo da «fonte da vida»; sonhar sobre a «morte» indica o «fim» de algum aspecto da vida de uma pessoa, ou alguma mudança drástica, muito mais do que o falecimento — literal da mesma. Naturalmente, visões e sonhos algumas vezes falam de acontecimentos literais, mas é um erro interpretar os mesmos literalmente, «todas as vezes que se puder». Essa atitude mais provavelmente nos desviará da verdade, em vez de aproximar-nos da mesma, pois é algo basicamente contraditório à própria natureza do misticismo.

4. *Os livros apocalípticos com freqüência são pseudônimos.* Isso significa que «em honra» a alguma antiga personalidade famosa, um livro foi escrito por outrem, aproveitando-se do prestígio do nome daquela personalidade, a fim de perpetuar sua tradição. Assim é que o livro de Enoque, escrito no segundo século A.C., não foi escrito por Enoque mas em sua memória. Nesse caso, não poderia haver qualquer tentativa séria, da parte do seu autor, de fazer passar seu livro como se realmente tivesse sido escrito por Enoque. É que os antigos não viam nada de errado nesta prática, sem importar o propósito com que isso fosse feito. Entre os livros apócrifos do Antigo e do Novo Testamentos, bem como entre seus livros pseudepígrafes, há mais de cem livros que certamente não foram escritos pelos indivíduos aos quais são atribuídos. Sem importar o que nós, como modernos, possamos pensar da prática, isso em nada altera a atitude dos antigos acerca da mesma. Em nosso N.T., por exemplo, é possível que o livro de Judas seja uma pseudepígrafe. (Quanto a notas sobre isso, ver o artigo sobre o *Apocalipse*, sob o título *«Autoria»*). No entanto, os dois livros apocalípticos bíblicos — Daniel e Apocalipse — não pertencem a essa natureza. Não obstante, o «João» do livro de Apocalipse não é o mesmo apóstolo João, e, sim, o «ancião», ou talvez um bem conhecido «vidente» crente que habitava na Ásia Menor.

5. *Os livros apocalípticos são altamente dualistas.* Em primeiro lugar, retratam a criação como algo envolvido em «uma luta de morte» entre duas forças — uma boa e outra má. Outrossim, essas forças são «cósmicas», e não meramente humanas. A humanidade ver-se-á envolvida no conflito entre Deus e Satanás, entre os anjos e os demônios, entre a razão absoluta e o erro absoluto. Os homens poderão ser vitoriosos ou derrotados, dependendo do lado que tomarem. O pecado, por conseguinte, nunca será questão apenas humana. Trata-se da lealdade ao erro absoluto, da aprovação conferida a Satanás e às suas obras más.

A oposição das duas grandes forças cósmicas naturalmente envolve a oposição entre duas eras distintas. Assim é que a «era presente» é dominada por Satanás, ao passo que a «era vindoura» será

APOCALÍPTICOS, LIVROS

governada por Deus, mediante o seu Messias. A era presente envolve pecado e degradação, com a conseqüente perdição das almas; e a era vindoura envolve o domínio da justiça e do bem-estar espiritual.

Essas forças opostas naturalmente geraram o conceito dos «dois mundos». Há um presente mundo, que é terreno e pervertido. Trata-se de algo físico e temporal, sem quaisquer valores absolutos. Mas também há o «mundo de amanhã», que até mesmo agora existe nas esferas invisíveis da realidade última. Este é um mundo de domínio espiritual, de santidade, de paz e de bem-estar espiritual. O «outro mundo», finalmente, virá a exercer controle sobre este mundo terreno, e esse é um dos aspectos do conflito entre o bem e o mal que atualmente começa a concretizar-se.

Existem, pois, duas «forças cósmicas» que se opõem, duas *eras* contrastantes que se digladiam, dois «mundos» contrastantes que se combatem. Os homens, necessariamente, «tomam partido», tornando-se associados e prestando lealdade a um lado ou outro desses contrastes. As obras apocalípticas, portanto, apresentam aos homens o desafio de escolherem a Deus e ao seu caminho, ao seu mundo, à sua era, rejeitando, ao mesmo tempo, o que Satanás tem a oferecer-lhes.

6. *Os livros apocalípticos são deterministas.* Isso significa que a vitória eventual do mundo vindouro sobre o mundo presente — o triunfo do bem sobre o mal — é algo que foi determinado pela mão de Deus. O triunfo de Deus é inevitável, embora pareça demorar-se por tempo excessivamente longo. Os livros apocalípticos, por conseguinte, expõem uma espécie de filosofia da história. Dizem-nos eles a natureza geral do que sucede e do que deverá acontecer. Apesar de que há caos, devido ao pecado, somos assegurados de que o processo histórico esta do lado do bem e de Deus, e que nada pode alterar isso, pois a vontade de Deus é todo-poderosa. O seu propósito talvez precise de longo tempo para materializar-se, mas tudo está determinado. Há um horário divino predeterminado; e o fim do domínio de Satanás ocorrerá súbita e dramaticamente. A própria história é a crônica da luta entre Deus e Satanás, e como os seres inteligentes serão envolvidos até o fim da mesma. Mas a história, apesar de envolver muitos elementos de sofrimento e caos, finalmente está determinada para que sirva às finalidades divinas.

7. *Os livros apocalípticos, ao mesmo tempo, são altamente pessimistas e otimistas.* Expõem um quadro horrendamente negativo do que haverá de suceder a este mundo, o que envolverá a intensa depravação dos homens. Ao mesmo tempo, porém, uma vez que este mundo seja apropriadamente julgado, deverá vir à existência um novo mundo de resplendente beleza e de incrível progresso. Do lado «pessimista», os livros apocalípticos são «cataclísmicos». Os eventos que porão fim ao presente mundo mau serão radicais, como se fora o decepar de um tumor canceroso. Os acontecimentos que darão início à nova era também serão cataclísmicos. As mudanças se produzem mediante acontecimentos bons ou maus, mas sempre repentinos, e não mediante algum processo gradual. As grandes alterações na história resultam de intervenções divinas.

8. *Os livros apocalípticos são intensamente éticos.* Isso significa que esses livros convocam os homens a abandonar o pecado, o qual necessiarmente produzirá acontecimentos cataclismicos. Apesar de tudo estar adredemente determinado, nada poderá derrotar facilmente o pecado, Satanás e seu sistema, contudo, serão preservados, entre esses terríveis acontecimentos, os homens que mantiverem confiança a em Deus e em seu Messias. Em caso contrário, haverão de participar imediatamente da glória de Deus mediante o martírio; ou então haverão de ser gentilmente conduzidos à sua presença, uma vez que tiverem sofrido como os homens terão de sofrer durante aquelas horas fatais. As advertências ali dadas, pois, visam *«converter»* os homens da maldade e da perversidade, não são meras predições de uma condenação inevitável.

III. Literatura Apocalíptica

Antigo Testamento:

A transição da literatura profética para a apocalíptica ocorreu em vários livros proféticos do Antigo Testamento, conforme se vê em Isa. 24-27; Eze. 38-39; Joel 2-3; Zac. 12-14. O livro de Daniel, produzido durante a crise dos Macabeus, é a obra mais importante dessa classe, pertencente ao Antigo Testamento. II Esdras, entre os livros apócrifos, também é uma obra apocalíptica. Ver o artigo sobre os *Livros Apócrifos*. Vários desses livros contêm porções apocalípticas.

I Enoque. Essa obra era atribuída a Enoque, o qual, após viver trezentos e sessenta e cinco anos, «já não era, porque Deus o tomou para si» (Gên. 5:21-24). Esse livro na verdade é uma série de livros, provenientes dos séculos II e I A.C. Acredita-se que a porção mais antiga seja os caps. 83-90, de natureza totalmente apocalíptica. Consiste em visões dadas em forma de sonhos, sobre o curso inteiro da história, desde o princípio até o presumível fim. Os caps. 1-36 têm sido chamados de *Dante judaico*, visto que descrevem as jornadas de Enoque através do submundo e dos lugares celestiais. A história da descida de Cristo ao hades (I Ped. 3:18 - 4:6) tem um fraseado evidentemente alicerçado em Enoque, mostrando que o autor sagrado tinha conhecimento desse livro, e que aprovava a idéia geral das missões misericordiosas ao hades. Os caps. 37-71 contêm as parábolas ou símiles de Enoque, retratando: 1. O julgamento dos ímpios; 2. a sorte dos incrédulos; 3. a bem-aventurança dos santos. Os caps. 72-82 são descrições astronômicas, e os caps. 91-108 formam uma coletânea de exortações religiosas. Por causa da história do pensamento religioso, ali contida, I Enoque é considerado o mais importante de todos os escritos não-canônicos. Provavelmente havia um original aramaico, o qual foi preservado em uma tradição etíope e em alguns fragmentos gregos.

Assunção de Moisés. Havia um original aramaico, escrito na Palestina durante os dias de Jesus. Supostamente apresenta as instruções finais de Moisés, antes de seu corpo ser assunto ao céu. Expõe um quadro profético da história e do futuro de Israel, começando pelos dias de Moisés e estendendo-se até o estabelecimento do reino de Deus. Aparentemente o autor foi um fariseu que aproveitou o ensejo para protestar contra a secularização do seu grupo. Essa obra atualmente só é conhecida em um fragmento latino, embora haja algumas alusões à mesma no Novo Testamento, em Judas e II Pedro.

II Enoque. Um outro título desse livro é *Livro dos Segredos de Enoque.* Foi originalmente escrito em grego, por um judeu alexandrino, na primeira metade do século I D.C. Sobrevive em uma versão eslavônica, pelo que é conhecido como Enoque Eslavônico. Descreve como o patriarca Enoque subiu aos céus — dez céus, — em vista do que foi capacitado a deixar instruções espirituais aos seus filhos. O livro ensina a preexistência da alma, de acordo com idéias platônicas e neoplatônicas, muito em voga em

229

APOCALÍPTICOS, LIVROS

Alexandria. Os chamados pais alexandrinos da Igreja, Clemente, Orígenes, e outros, ensinavam essa doutrina. Ver o artigo sobre a *alma*, sob *origens*, quanto as várias idéias concernentes a essa questão.

II Baruque. Originalmente produzido em grego, mas com freqüência chamado Apocalipse Siríaco de Baruque, por ter sido descoberta uma excelente cópia do livro nesse idioma, em 1866. A obra contém pontos de vista conflitantes e variações de estilo, sugerindo que a obra se compõe de vários autores. O presumível autor do livro foi o amanuense de Jeremias; mas, na realidade, foi escrito em cerca de 70 D.C. Descreve o tempo da queda de Jerusalém, em 586 A.C.; mas, na forma em que atualmente o livro existe, a obra só foi terminada quando da queda de Jerusalém em 70 D.C. Trata das misérias e perseguições dos judeus, do pecado original do homem, da justiça divina e da vinda do Messias e Seu reino messiânico. As porções finais do livro parecem ter sido influenciadas pelos escritos de Paulo.

III Baruque. Essa obra também se intitula Apocalipse Grego de Baruque, visto que foi originalmente escrita em grego. Foi escrita no começo do século II D.C. Aparentemente, o autor tinha conhecimento de II Enoque e de II Baruque. Novamente, o alegado autor foi o amanuense de Jeremias, que descreveu a ascensão de Jeremias através de cinco céus. O livro descreve a mediação dos anjos, que expõem os méritos humanos diante do arcanjo Miguel, para sua consideração. São dadas idéias adicionais sobre a queda de Adão. Algumas dessas idéias influenciaram a teologia cristã de data posterior.

Novo Testamento:

Generalizara-se o uso de livros apocalípticos do Antigo Testamento, os quais inspiraram vários autores da era cristã a continuarem essa forma de literatura. No próprio Novo Testamento, diversos trechos podem ser classificados como apocalípticos, como Mar. 13; Mat. 24 e II Tess. 2. Além disso, o Apocalipse de João, livro canônico do Novo Testamento, é a mais completa expressão dessa atividade no Novo Testamento, sendo também o maior de todos os apocalipses. Cita continuamente o Antigo Testamento, e contém muitas passagens que refletem a literatura apocalíptica veterotestamentária, descrita acima. Ver a Introdução ao Apocalipse, no NTI, sob as seções I e IV, — no tocante a uma plena demonstração do fato.

Abaixo damos breves descrições dos livros apocalípticos cristãos não-canônicos. Tal como os do Antigo Testamento, são escritos pseudônimos:

Apocalipse de Pedro. Esse livro contém visões nas quais Cristo mostra ao apóstolo Pedro os justos no céu, e vários níveis de pecadores em lugares de tormento. Foi escrito no começo do século II D.C., em grego, embora seja preservado essencialmente em uma versão etíope.

Testamento de Abraão. O arcanjo mostra a Abraão a dimensão dos mortos. Abraão, comovido pelo que vê, obtém perdão para os ímpios mediante sua oração intercessória, o que é um óbvio reflexo do relato de Gên. 18:22-23. Esse conceito de oportunidade de salvação ou melhoria, além da morte biológica, também aparece em I Ped. 4:6 e é sugerido em Efé. 1:10. Ver os comentários sobre essa doutrina e suas implicações no NTI, em I Ped. 4:6. É obra judaica em sua natureza, tendo sido escrita no século II D.C., ou por um judeu ou por um judeu-cristão. Provavelmente foi escrito em aramaico.

Pastor de Hermas. O livro contém visões sobre a Igreja, numerosas exortações à piedade e parábolas sobre o fim desta dispensação. Esses escritos nos fornecem importante compreensão sobre a Igreja cristã primitiva. Trata-se do mais longo dos escritos incluídos na coletânea dos pais apostólicos. Uma antiga tradição informa-nos que foi escrito em cerca de 140 D.C.; mas alguns lhe dão uma data mais antiga, pelo menos a certas porções do mesmo. O autor foi Hermas, um cristão romano que redigiu seu livro em três seções: 1. Visões; 2. mandato; 3. símiles. Presumivelmente, o material lhe foi dado pelo próprio Cristo, disfarçado de pastor. O propósito final do livro é salientar diante dos leitores a necessidade do arrependimento dos pecados cometidos após o batismo.

O original foi escrito em grego, embora não haja texto grego completo disponível. O manuscrito Aleph contém o texto até o mandato IV.111.6. — Um manuscrito do século XV, de Atos, contém a maior parte do resto da obra. E também existem cópias incompletas, algumas em grego, outras em latim, e uma em etíope, além de fragmentos em cóptico e persa.

Hermas foi instruído a dar um exemplar do livro a Clemente (aparentemente Clemente de Roma), e outro a Grapte (visão II.iv.3). E então deveria ser dado ao público.

O Pastor de Hermas e o cânon do Novo Testamento. No cânon muratoriano (cerca de 200 D.C.), temos esta declaração: «Bem recentemente, em nossa própria época, na cidade de Roma, Hermas escreveu o Pastor, quando seu irmão Pio, o bispo, sentava-se na cadeira da cidade de Roma». Pio foi bispo na década que começou em 140 D.C., coincidindo com a data do livro, embora várias porções do mesmo provavelmente fossem mais antigas. Seja como for, aquela declaração mostra que esse livro chegou a merecer lugar canônico em alguns lugares, e sua presença no manuscrito *Aleph* demonstra a mesma coisa.

A teologia dessa obra tem defeitos. Quanto ao batismo, a idéia é que o mesmo é imprescindível para a salvação. Quanto aos pecados cometidos após o batismo, é dito que Deus dá Seu perdão, mas que isso não se prolonga por muito tempo. Em outras palavras, essa demonstração da graça divina seria interrompida dentro de algum tempo, evidentemente não muito distante. No campo da ética, o livro reflete noções ascéticas, embora não estritas. Contém as virtudes cardeais cristãs estóicas, como a fé, o controle próprio, o poder, a longanimidade, a simplicidade, a retidão, a santidade, a alegria, a verdade, a compreensão, a concórdia e o amor. Um segundo matrimônio é ali permitido, após o falecimento do cônjuge, embora isso seja considerado inferior à vida celibatária. O livro destaca a necessidade de boas obras que ultrapassam os mandamentos. É uma obra essencialmente ética, que diz aos leitores o que devem fazer e o que devem evitar.

Oráculos Sibilinos Cristãos. Coletânea de predições similar à obra judaica do mesmo nome. Contém elementos judaicos e cristãos e é uma obra apologética composta. Os *oráculos* são postos nos lábios da profetisa grega de Cumae, Sibila, pelo que o livro tem a forma de uma profecia pagã. Algumas porções incorporaram espectações escatológicas do tipo apocalíptico. Nos tempos antigos, as sibilas evidentemente eram parecidas com as modernas médiuns, entrando em transe e recebendo comunicações. Eram porta-vozes de alguma divindade e assim encabeçavam formalmente, ou mesmo informalmente, algum culto. No tempo dos romanos, as sibilas eram consultadas pelas autoridades e havia livros que preservavam os seus oráculos.

A coletânea total de oráculos judaicos e cristãos desse tipo chega a quinze livros. Os livros sibilinos originais teriam sido queimados no incêndio de Roma de 82 A.C., e esses oráculos presumivelmente foram escritos para substituir aqueles. Datam entre 150 A.C. e 300 D.C. Vários pais da Igreja tinham conhecimento deles, como Hermas, Justino, Teófilo de Antioquia e Clemente de Alexandria.

Os oráculos abordam assuntos como a criação, o dilúvio, a carreira e a cruz de Cristo, a destruição de Jerusalém e várias predições sobre o futuro, impérios mundiais e o expurgo final. Esse livro foi escrito em grego.

Apocalipse de Paulo. Esse livro descreve as alegadas viagens de Paulo em vários níveis do céu e do inferno. A base do livro é a alusão de Paulo, em II Cor. 12:1-4, de ter sido «arrebatado» ao «terceiro céu». Agostinho alude a um livro desse nome, que foi condenado pelo *Decreto Gelasiano*. Provavelmente foi o primeiro dos dois livros assim intitulados. O primeiro, que estamos descrevendo, foi escrito em grego; mas foi melhor preservado em versões latinas, ou então no cóptico.

Em suas viagens, Paulo é testemunha de juízo e glória, encontra-se com Enoque e com outros, vê a cidade celeste de Cristo. No inferno, impressionado com a severidade dos castigos, obtém alívio para os habitantes do mesmo, para o dia e a noite do dia do Senhor. Em outra viagem ao paraíso, encontra-se com outros personagens famosos, como Abraão, Isaque, Jacó, Maria, etc., alguns dos quais já tinham se encontrado com ele em sua primeira viagem. O autor vale-se do Apocalipse de Pedro, do Apocalipse de Elias e de Sofonias. Também alicerça-se sobre as descrições do Apocalipse (ver Apocalipse de João, no NTI). Esse livro exerceu certa influência sobre as descrições do céu e do inferno em obras posteriores, como no *Inferno* de Dante, *Ant*, 525 ss. O livro foi aparentemente escrito perto do fim do século IV D.C. O seu propósito é essencialmente advertir contra o juízo, encorajando os leitores na prática da retidão, para que obtenham a glória celeste.

Existe um outro livro desse nome, a ele semelhante, mas evidentemente sem dependência ao mesmo. É o primeiro dos quatro Apocalipses do Codex V da biblioteca de Nag Hammadi. No «monte de Jericó», Paulo ter-se-ia encontrado com os doze apóstolos, e então foi elevado ao terceiro céu. Em seguida foi levado ao quarto céu, onde testemunhou o julgamento de uma alma, que foi condenada ante o testemunho de três pessoas (Deu. 19:15). A alma condenada foi lançada de volta à Terra, em uma reencarnação forçada. Paulo prosseguiu para outros céus, tendo chegado ao décimo. As descrições são escassas. Aparecem cenas de glória e julgamento. É uma obra posterior, que os eruditos não conseguem datar com exatidão, e aparentemente foi escrita em grego.

Apocalipse de João. Uma imitação do livro canônico do mesmo nome, mas pertencente ao século V D.C. Descreve principalmente a ressurreição, a punição dos ímpios e a recompensa dos justos. Inclui itens de tempos posteriores, referindo-se às «veneráveis e santas imagens», bem como às «gloriosas e preciosas cruzes e relíquias sagradas das igrejas». Aparentemente foi escrito em grego.

Revelações de Bartolomeu. Ali, Bartolomeu e os outros apóstolos são consagrados pelo Pai, pelo Filho e pelo Espírito Santo, e Pedro é nomeado arcebispo do universo. A literatura que traz o nome de Bartolomeu inclui o *Evangelho*, *O Livro da Ressurreição* e as *Perguntas de Bartolomeu*, obras que datam dos séculos V ou VI D.C. Originalmente escritos em grego, contam com traduções preservadas em cóptico e eslavônico, dependendo da obra em questão. Entre as *perguntas*, uma delas é apresentada a Jesus, acerca de onde se encontrava a cruz. Isso leva à narrativa do *Descensus ad Inferos*, similar ao que se vê nos *Atos de Pilatos*, e paralelo a outras narrativas parecidas, nos pseudepígrafes e na literatura apocalíptica. Outras perguntas abordam diversas revelações acerca do após-túmulo, as forças do bem e do mal, os destinos dos homens. (AM B CH GS HEN J NTI S Z)

APOCATÁSTASE

Vem do grego **apokatástasis**, que significa «total restauração». A esperança de muitos teólogos e outros, através da história da Igreja, tem sido que Deus, finalmente, venha a restaurar todos os homens. Isso pode assumir a forma de puro universalismo, isto é, que todos os homens serão restaurados à mais completa salvação. Ou pode assumir a forma de restauração como uma unidade, a idéia que todos os homens não serão salvos no sentido que cheguem a participar da natureza divina (II Ped. 1:4), mas que a restauração incluirá muitos níveis do ser metafísico, embora tudo de forma harmônica com a idéia de unidade, repleto de propósito para os seres vivos. Ver o artigo sobre o *universalismo*; e, quanto a notas explicativas completas sobre a *restauração*, ver as notas no NTI, em Efé. 1:10. Ver o artigo sobre esse assunto, na presente obra. (NTI P)

APODÍCTIO

Dentro da lógica aristotélica, um termo que indica o modo ou modalidade de uma proposição. Uma proposição que assevera que algo é necessariamente impossível, como: «Sete não pode ser mais do que nove». Vem do grego, *apó*, «da parte de» e *deiknumai*, «mostrar». No uso comum, porém, mostra algo que é necessário, em contraste com proposições problemáticas, que abordam possibilidades ou declarações contingentes. A proposição *apodíctica* é a última modalidade das três tipos de proposição, a saber: possibilidade, realidade e necessidade. O estudo dessas modalidades, na lógica, é chamado Lógica Modal (ver o artigo a respeito). (F P)

APÓDOSE

Um termo grego que significa «devolução», usada para designar a cláusula de uma sentença condicional que oferece a conclusão. A cláusula introdutória, usualmente com um *se*, é chamada *prótase*. Por exemplo: Se ele tivesse tempo (prótase), me ajudaria neste trabalho (apódose). A ordem das cláusulas pode ser invertida, sem afetar o sentido. (F P)

APOLINARIANISMO

Nome que se deriva do nome próprio Apolinário «o Jovem», bispo de Laodicéia (310?-390?), sendo usado para designar a doutrina que, em Jesus, o Logos (uma perfeita natureza divina) assumiu corpo físico, passando a exercer as funções ordinariamente realizadas pela mente humana. Apolinário opunha-se tanto à noção ariana da mutabilidade do Logos como à noção da completa união das naturezas divina e humana, em Jesus Cristo. Afirmava que, na encarnação, o Logos tornou-se carne, tomando o lugar da alma humana racional na pessoa de Cristo. Em outras palavras, ele negava que Cristo tivesse espírito humano, ensinando que o ser espiritual, o Logos, manipulava um corpo humano. Isso negava a humanidade essencial de Cristo. Estamos diante de grande *mistério* na encarnação. Concebemos Cristo em termos de plena humanidade e de plena divindade, visto Cristo ter sido a grande manifestação do Logos, o princípio do Filho, dentro da trindade. Desconhecemos como uma pessoa pode combinar, em si mesma, o divino e o humano. Doutrinas como o *apolinarianismo* tentam solucionar o que não pode ser solucionado no presente.

Após diversos sínodos locais terem condenado a doutrina, o segundo concílio geral de Constantinopla, em 381, declarou-a herética. Em vida, Apolinário atraiu muitos discípulos, e formou sua própria seita. Mas, após a sua morte, o movimento desintegrou-se rapidamente. (D E P)

APOLINÁRIO

Bispo de Laodicéia da Síria, nos fins do século IV D.C. Opôs-se ao *arianismo* (ver o artigo) e colaborou com Apolinário, O Ancião, na reprodução das Escrituras segundo modelos clássicos, para compensar a perda dos cristãos devido ao edito do imperador Juliano, que lhes negou o direito de ensinarem os clássicos. Vários sínodos finalmente declararam herética a sua cristologia, especialmente o sínodo de Constantinopla, em 381. Ver o artigo sobre o *apolinarianismo*. (AM E)

APOLIOM

No grego, equivalente a **Abadom** (ver o artigo a respeito).

APOLO

Apolo (Atos 18:24) era um judeu da cidade de Alexandria. Seu nome é uma forma abreviada de *Apolônio*. Apolo chegou em Éfeso em cerca de 52 D.C., durante a viagem confirmativa de Paulo entre as igrejas da Galácia e da Frígia. Apolo já tinha ouvido falar em Jesus Cristo, e era discípulo do Senhor; no entanto, ainda não estava bem informado sobre a mensagem cristã em sua inteireza. Seu dote natural era a eloqüência, além de um conhecimento profundo das Escrituras do A.T. Combinava, pois, esses dois elementos, e assim era um poderoso pregador da verdade espiritual de Deus. Quando Apolo chegou em Éfeso, não tinha conhecimento algum da experiência do Pentecoste, e nem havia ainda participado dela; e também ainda não conhecia o *batismo cristão*. Seu discipulado era apenas o de um seguidor de João Batista, tendo crido na mensagem pregada por este de que Jesus era o Messias judaico.

Essa falta de melhor instrução, da parte de Apolo, foi eliminada pelo esforço paciente de Priscila e Áquila (ver Atos 18:26). De Éfeso, Apolo se dirigiu para Corinto. Evidentemente era homem poderoso na apologética cristã, e deve ter obtido retumbante sucesso, tornando-se famoso como um dos principais líderes da igreja cristã. Foi devido a essa reputação que os crentes de Corinto, que tendiam para as facções, fizeram de Apolo um dos supostos cabeças dessas divisões, ou, pelo menos, um de seus heróis, que uma dessas facções se dizia seguidora. Paulo, porém, salientou o fato de que na realidade só existe um único *Herói* do evangelho, isto é, o próprio Cristo Jesus. Todos os demais são apenas servos seus. (Ver I Cor. 3:4,21-23).

O fato de que Apolo não mais retornou a Corinto, mesmo depois que Paulo lhe solicitou a sua volta (ver I Cor. 16:12), talvez indique que ele se recusou a tal a fim de abafar a controvérsia que surgira por causa de líderes cristãos, dessa maneira humilhando a si mesmo. Isso é um ponto favorável para com o seu caráter cristão, servindo, por outro lado, de lamentável comentário acerca de tantos modernos líderes cristãos, que não seguem o exemplo de Apolo, mas antes, geralmente, tudo fazem para erigir sua posição e seu conceito, preferindo a fama e o orgulho à obscuridade e à humildade.

Desde os tempos de Lutero, diversos estudiosos têm sugerido que Apolo foi o autor da epístola canônica aos *Hebreus*. Todavia, apesar disso ser perfeitamente possível, considerando-se a elevada qualidade do grego, de mistura com profundo conhecimento das Escrituras hebraicas, o que era um sinal de erudição em Alexandria, não há maneira que nos permita demonstrar o acerto ou equívoco dessa opinião. De fato, existem certos paralelismos na linguagem, no estilo e no pensamento, similares aos que se encontram nos escritos de Filo, o filósofo neoplatônico e teólogo judeu de Alexandria que fortalecem a idéia de que algum judeu alexandrino foi quem escreveu a epíst. aos Hebreus. A grande verdade, porém, é que a autoria dessa epístola deve continuar um mistério para nós. (Ver o artigo sobre *Hebreus*, sob o título *Autor*). O máximo que se pode dizer a respeito dessa questão é que o grego *koiné* em que a epístola aos Hebreus foi escrita é de superior qualidade e mais clássico que as epístolas de Paulo, e é quase impossível, do ponto de vista lingüístico, que o apóstolo Paulo tenha sido também o autor dessa epístola aos Hebreus. Um indivíduo do preparo e formação de Apolo, por outro lado, bem poderia ter sido o autor desse livro neotestamentário.

A última alusão bíblica a Apolo é a que se lê no trecho de Tito 3:13, que declara: «Encaminha com diligência a Zenas, o intérprete da lei, e a Apolo, a fim de que não lhes falte cousa alguma». *Jerônimo* (século IV D.C.) diz-nos que Apolo teria ficado em Creta até que ouviu notícias sobre a cura total das brechas facciosas que tinham surgido na igreja de Corinto. Em face disso, voltou para Corinto e posteriormente tornou-se pastor daquela localidade. Os gregos, entretanto, pensam que ele ter-se-ia tornado pastor de Duras, mas existem outros que opinam que ele foi o segundo bispo de Cólofon, na Ásia. Ferrarius assevera que ele foi bispo de Icônio, na Frígia, ao passo que outros garantem que ele foi bispo de Cesaréia. Todas essas afirmativas, entretanto, não passam de meras conjecturas, baseadas em tradições nas quais não podemos confiar. Portanto, nada de realmente seguro se sabe com respeito às atividades de Apolo, depois dos informes que encontramos nas páginas do N.T.

Apolo era homem *eloqüente*. Esse vocábulo se refere à sua erudição quanto às Escrituras do A.T., ou à sua facilidade de expressar esse conhecimento, ou, talvez ainda, a ambos esses elementos. Diz Ramsay, a respeito de Apolo: «Um bom orador, bem versado nas Escrituras».

É provável que Apolo devesse parte de sua erudição ao conhecimento e às conexões que talvez tivesse mantido com a escola de Filo, ainda que não tenhamos meios para demonstrar tal vinculação. Apolo chegou a Éfeso com algum propósito para nós desconhecido. Porém, talvez ele visasse tanto ensinar como também investigar a igreja cristã que florescia naquela localidade. Por conseguinte, talvez ele tenha chegado ali tanto como um mestre quanto como um inquiridor, o que também todos nós devemos ser, de uma maneira ou de outra, em grau maior ou menor. «Sendo possuidor de dotes extraordinários de retórica, sem dúvida era educado nas escolas alexandrinas». (Adam Clarke, em Atos 18:24).

Ao aplicar o presente texto bíblico aos pregadores, os quais são dessa maneira exortados a se entregarem ao estudo profundo das Escrituras Sagradas, fazendo-se «poderosos» nas Escrituras, diz Robertson, em Atos 18:24: «Não há como desculpar a ignorância sobre as Escrituras, da parte dos pregadores do evangelho, os professos intérpretes da Palavra de Deus. A última preleção feita na classe do Novo Testamento em inglês, no Seminário Teológico Batista do Sul, por John A. Broadus, teve por fulcro essa passagem, quando ele lançou um apelo aos seus alunos para que se tornassem poderosos nas Escrituras. Em Alexandria, Clemente de Alexandria e Orígenes ensinavam na escola teológica cristã».

A eloquência de Apolo sem dúvida alguma foi uma das grandes razões pelas quais, em Corinto, uma determinada facção da igreja cristã o elegeu como seu herói, ao passo que outros grupos davam preferência a Paulo, a Pedro, ou a qualquer outro.

Além de ser *eloqüente* (ver Atos 18:24), Apolo também era *fervoroso de espírito*, expressão esta que tem de significar uma dentre duas possibilidades, a saber:

1. Estaria em foco o fervor de seu próprio espírito (conforme pensam aquelas traduções que dizem *espírito* com letra inicial minúscula). Isso significaria que Apolo era dotado de um zelo espiritual todo especial, em que a intensidade de seus sentimentos pode ser destacada mediante uma tradução literal, «ebuliente no espírito».

2. Mas alguns intérpretes preferem pensar que a expressão *fervoroso de Espírito* seja escrita com letra inicial maiúscula, como alusão ao Espírito Santo de Deus. Nesse caso, Apolo seria aqui encarado como indivíduo que fervia com a energia do Espírito de Deus. (I ID NTI RAM)

APOLO

Um dos mais importantes deuses do Olimpo, filho de Zeus e de Leto. Representava a juventude máscula, a beleza, a poesia, a música, a cura e a sabedoria oracular. Era o deus Febo Apolo do oráculo de Delfos, sendo uma divindade que irradiava luz. Foi o primeiro deus grego a ser admitido na religião dos romanos. (OS P)

APOLOFANES

Um sírio que, com seus irmãos Timóteo e Quereas, foi morto na fortaleza de Gazara, após sua captura, no vigésimo quinto dia do cerco, por vinte jovens do exército de Judas Macabeu (ver II Macabeus 10.35,37). (Z)

APOLOGETAS (APOLOGISTAS)

O termo é usado para falar sobre aqueles pais da igreja cujas obras tiveram o intuito de defender a fé e a Igreja cristã contra os ataques. Esses ataques eram lançados pelo judaísmo, pelo paganismo, pelo estado, e também pela filosofia grega de várias escolas. Como é óbvio, muitos cristãos subseqüentes e contemporâneos podem ser chamados *apologetas*. Ver o artigo intitulado, *Apologética*, onde isso é demonstrado sob o título: *Visões históricas acerca da apologética*. Mas, quando usamos as palavras «os apologetas», estas indicam os primeiros pais da Igreja que se atarefaram nessa atividade.

1. Temos a *pregação de Pedro*, proveniente do século II D.C., de autor desconhecido, que defendeu o cristianismo diante do judaísmo e do paganismo. Teve larga distribuição e tornou-se parte do livro de Aristides (que descrevemos abaixo). Nesse livro, os crentes são denominados «terceira raça». Mas foram preservados apenas alguns fragmentos.

2. Mais ou menos da mesma época, temos o livro chamado *Quadratus*, escrito em defesa do cristianismo contra os abusos do estado romano. Foi apresentado ao imperador Adriano, na esperança de obter melhor tratamento para os cristãos, por parte das autoridades romanas. O livro foi escrito em Atenas, cerca de 125 D.C. Apenas uma sentença do mesmo foi preservada para nós.

3. *Aristides* defendeu o cristianismo contra o paganismo. Ele era ateniense e escreveu em cerca de 147 D.C. Sua apologia foi endereçada ao imperador Antônio. A «raça» cristã é ali chamada de raça superior e digna de tratamento humanitário. A obra desapareceu, excetuando uma tradução siríaca e uma reprodução livre, no grego, no romance medieval de Barlaã e Joasafe. A obra ataca as formas de adoração entre os caldeus, os gregos, os egípcios e os judeus, exaltando o cristianismo acima dessas formas, tanto quanto à própria adoração quanto à moral.

4. *Justino Mártir*. Sua apologia (escrita cerca de 150 D.C.) foi endereçada a Adriano e a Marco Aurélio. Tomava a posição de que a filosofia grega, apesar de útil, era incompleta, e que esse produto não terminado é aperfeiçoado e suplantado em Cristo e Sua revelação. Para Justino, o cristianismo era a *verdadeira filosofia*. A filosofia grega era encarada sob a mesma luz que a lei judaica — precursora de algo superior.

5. *Aristo*, meados do século II D.C., de Pela, na Peréia, escreveu um livro que não chegou até nós, mas que, de acordo com Orígenes, mostrava que as profecias judaicas cumpriram-se em Jesus. Justino fez uso dessa apologia em sua obra.

6. *Atenágoras*, fins do século II D.C., escreveu contra o paganismo, o estado romano e a filosofia grega. Endereçou seu livro a Marco Aurélio, esperando poder melhorar o tratamento conferido aos cristãos. Essa obra incluía argumentos em prol da ressurreição dos mortos.

7. *Taciano*, discípulo de Justino Mártir, exibiu considerável antagonismo contra a filosofia grega, em seus argumentos em prol da superioridade do cristianismo.

8. *Teófilo de Antioquia*, que escreveu um pouco mais tarde, seguiu o caminho trilhado por Taciano.

9. *Minúcio Félix* (fins do século II ou começo do século III D.C.), em contraste com Taciano, procurou demonstrar que os cristãos são os melhores filósofos; quando os filósofos são bons, parecem-se mais com os cristãos.

10. *Tertuliano* (falecido no século III D.C.) atacou a filosofia com argumentos filosóficos, e os filósofos nunca o perdoaram por esse motivo. Ele atacou a substância e o espírito da filosofia grega, bem como o gnosticismo e o paganismo em geral. Considerava a filosofia produto da mente pagã, julgando-a inútil como apoio à fé. Exaltava a fé na revelação, mas

falhou quando não percebeu que a fé e a filosofia devem ser sujeitas à pesquisa da razão, a fim de que o falso seja separado do verdadeiro, e que o verdadeiro seja melhor compreendido.

11. *Irineu*, bem como seu discípulo, Hipólito, defendeu o cristianismo contra os gnósticos, muito poderosos na sua época. Ver o artigo sobre o *gnosticismo*. Sua obra principal nessa linha foi *Contra as Heresias* (cerca de 180 D.C.). O original grego se perdeu, excetuando fragmentos, preservados nos escritos de Hipólito, Eusébio e Epifânio. Todavia, a obra foi preservada inteira em uma tradução latina. Trata-se da mais completa declaração acerca das fantasias gnósticas. Sua exposição pode ser chamada de primeira exposição sistemática das crenças cristãs. Irineu foi um dos mais influentes cristãos da Igreja antenicena.

12. *Arnóbio* (300 D.C.) tinha a filosofia e a razão humana em baixo conceito. Atacou a idéia platônica da preexistência da alma e defendeu o criacionismo (ver o artigo a respeito). Sua obra principal é *Adversus Gentes*.

13. *Lactâncio e Eusébio de Cesaréia* (III e IV séculos da era cristã) deram continuação à tradição apologética, exaltando o cristianismo em face do paganismo e do judaísmo. Eusébio foi um origenista da segunda geração, decidido aderente da teologia filosófica do Logos, embora tivesse várias idéias não-ortodoxas acerca da divindade de Cristo. Sua principal contribuição é a sua *História Eclesiástica*. Suas obras apologéticas, embora de menor valor, encontraram lugar na história literária cristã. (B C E EP P)

APOLOGÉTICA

Definição. A apologética é a ciência ou disciplina racional que se esforça por apresentar a defesa da fé religiosa, existindo dentro e fora da Igreja cristã. O termo é usado em contraste com *polêmica*, que é um debate efetuado entre cristãos a fim de determinar a verdadeira posição cristã sobre alguma questão específica. Presumivelmente, a apologética aborda questões defendidas por alguma fé religiosa específica, como o cristianismo, mas que são negadas pelos incrédulos. No uso comum, a palavra é usualmente empregada para indicar a defesa do cristianismo. Positivamente, a apologética tenta elaborar e defender uma visão cristã de Deus, da alma e do mundo, uma visão apoiada por raciocínios reputados capazes de convencer os não-cristãos da veracidade das doutrinas envolvidas. Negativamente, trata-se de um esforço para antecipar possíveis pontos de ataque, defendendo as doutrinas cristãs contra tais ataques.

A palavra. O termo vem do grego, *apologia*, «defesa», uma resposta ao ataque (Atos 26:1; I Ped. 3:16). O famoso diálogo de Platão, *a Apologia*, expõe a *defesa* de Sócrates diante de seus acusadores.

Base bíblica. Alguns fazem oposição a qualquer defesa da fé cristã, supondo que o conhecimento da verdade por meio da revelação é perfeito, e não requer qualquer raciocínio humano em sua defesa. Porém, a idéia que a revelação, coada por mentes humanas, é perfeita, capaz assim de produzir um perfeito corpo de verdades conhecidas, não passa de um dogma formulado pelo homem, e não uma doutrina da própria Bíblia. De fato, essa idéia é uma *apologia* em favor de um dos modos de se obter conhecimento. Em qualquer instância em que algum argumento é apresentado nas Escrituras, não diretamente alicerçado sobre algum texto de prova, dentro da Bíblia, é uma apologia dentro dos livros sacros. Tomemos como exemplo o primeiro capítulo da epístola aos Romanos. Paulo mostra a culpa e a impossibilidade de defesa dos pagãos, diante da mente divina. Ele erige uma apologia em favor de certas idéias básicas, e muitos capítulos das epístolas de Paulo podem ser encarados por esse prisma.

Motivos bíblicos em favor da apologética. 1. O trecho de I Ped. 3:15 faz esta declaração direta. «...estando sempre preparados para responder a todo aquele que vos pedir razão da esperança que há em vós». Fica entendido que tal resposta conterá raciocínios acerca da fé, e não apenas textos de prova extraídos da Bíblia. 2. Segundo salientamos acima, no Novo Testamento há muita apologia, e em certo sentido, o próprio volume sagrado é uma *apologia* em prol da nova religião, em conflito com o antigo judaísmo e com o paganismo. O cristianismo enfrentou um sistema helenizador, no qual a filosofia tinha grande peso. No décimo sétimo capítulo de Atos, Paulo não hesitou em apelar diretamente à apologética, utilizando argumentos filosóficos, procurando convencer os atenienses. O evangelho de Lucas é uma *apologia* escrita para um oficial romano, a fim de procurar conquistar posição oficial para a nova fé, fazendo assim estacar a perseguição. «...para que tenhas plena certeza das verdades em que foste instruído» (Luc. 1:4). Essa era a certeza que Lucas procurou transmitir aos seus leitores.

As próprias denominações cristãs são atividades apologéticas. — Alguns têm imaginado que a apologia é uma espécie de «ausência de fé», e não de defesa de fé. Tais pessoas partem do pressuposto que a fé não precisa ser defendida. Mas com isso olvidam-se que os homens interpretam a fé das mais variegadas maneiras. *Qual é a fé que não precisa ser defendida?* Se alguém retrucar que é a fé bíblica, devemo-nos lembrar que as denominações que se utilizam da Bíblia como autoritária estão longe de concordar com a natureza exata da fé que emerge das páginas da Bíblia. Muito mais se verifica quando saímos para fora das fronteiras da Igreja cristã e conversamos com incrédulos bem-informados acerca da «fé». Eles têm informações suficientes para saber que tal fé, em qualquer forma que ela assuma, tem tal forma precisamente por causa de uma apologia por detrás da mesma e que caracteriza alguma denominação particular. Cada denominação tem sua própria apologia que dá forma às suas doutrinas e ao seu sistema, a despeito da reivindicação de que aquilo que é exposto é apenas a fé bíblica. Esses fatos não anulam nem a fé e nem a verdade, mas requerem uma cuidadosa apologia a respeito da fé, examinando-a, definindo-a e promovendo-a.

A natureza do conhecimento força-nos a apelar para a apologética. O conhecimento não tem uma única origem. Antes, pode ser adquirido por estes meios: 1. A observação empírica, baseada nos sentidos; 2. a intuição, visto que o homem é um ser que tem ciência, e que mesmo sem investigação sabe de certas coisas, tal como sucede com Deus; 3. a razão, com a qual o homem foi dotado, pode penetrar em enigmas e desencavar a verdade, à parte da experiência prática ou empírica formal; 4. a revelação, que é conhecimento outorgado com dom de Deus. A revelação é uma subcategoria do misticismo. Deus dá conhecimento por meio de homens santos, através de visões, profecias, sonhos, etc. (experiência mística), reduzidas à forma escrita, tornando-se um Livro Sagrado. Tudo isso se sucede, mas o conhecimento é mais amplo do que isso,

APOLOGÉTICA

derivando-se de mais de uma direção. Ademais, a razão e a intuição nunca cessam de examinar o conhecimento que nos chega através da revelação, porquanto há revelações incompletas, havendo até mesmo revelações que não são válidas. Em outras palavras, na busca pela verdade, precisamos de muitas fontes, de muitos meios. O fato de que o conhecimento chega até nós através de grande diversidade de meios, demonstra a nossa necessidade de uma apologia mediante a qual possamos testar, avaliar e defender a verdade. Ver os artigos separados como o *empirismo*, a *intuição*, o *racionalismo*, o *misticismo e conhecimento*, *fontes de*. O palácio do conhecimento tem muitas portas e janelas através das quais as informações entram e saem. Limitar esse palácio a uma única porta (a revelação, e a fé baseada na revelação) é contar com uma casa muito estranha, de fato.

Visões históricas acerca da apologética:

Deve-se entender desde o princípio que a apologética necessariamente envolve o investigador na filosofia, formal e erudita, ou popular e individualista. Assim é que, quando alguém começa a apresentar um argumento baseado em raciocínio, já está falando como um filósofo, quer queira quer não queira. Tertuliano conhecia a filosofia, e usava argumentos filosóficos contra os filósofos incrédulos. Portanto, ele era um filósofo que argumentava contra a filosofia. Porém, se descrevermos pontos de vista históricos relativos à apologética, para todos os propósitos práticos isso equivalerá a descrever aquilo que vários pais da Igreja e cristãos posteriores pensavam sobre a filosofia. Quanto mais uma pessoa distanciar-se da filosofia, menos valor dará à apologética, como uma atividade legítima para os cristãos.

1. *Tertuliano*. Supunha que a filosofia é produto da mente pagã, e conseqüentemente, inútil para defender a fé cristã. Isso equivale a ignorar: a. A base bíblica da apologética; e b. que não há razão pela qual não possa haver uma atividade filosófica cristã. Se a razão vem da parte de Deus, e se alguém a usa de maneira sistemática, já estará agindo como um filósofo, utilizando-se de um dom divinamente outorgado. Podemos evitar os abusos. Houve pais latinos, como Arnóbio, Lactâncio e outros, que seguiram a idéia de Tertuliano.

2. *Os pais alexandrinos*. Clemente, Orígenes, etc. Proposital e habilidosamente eles usavam a filosofia platônica e estóica para dar à fé cristã uma expressão filosófica. A filosofia pode aguçar os conceitos teológicos. Qualquer pessoa que tenha estudado filosofia pode usá-la para definir, aclarar e aprimorar seus conhecimentos teológicos. Um teólogo que tenha estudado filosofia pode tornar-se um melhor teólogo. Podemos evitar os abusos.

3. *Agostinho* ensinava que a filosofia é uma criada útil que pode ser empregada em favor da fé religiosa, esclarecendo-a e defendendo-a.

4. Tomás de Aquino foi um apologeta refinado. Sua obra *Suma contra Gentiles* defendeu a fé cristã contra a maneira materialista e não-espiritual como certos filósofos árabes (como Averróis) utilizavam a filosofia de Aristóteles. A apologética de Tomás de Aquino foi tão bem-sucedida que se transformou em uma força dominante durante séculos, na Igreja ocidental.

5. Os ataques desfechados por deístas e racionalistas contra a fé cristã produziram apologetas modernos como o bispo Joseph Butler, da Igreja anglicana. Sua famosa obra, *Analogia da Religião*, é uma obra apologética.

6. *Karl Barth* e sua escola (início e meados do século XX) tomaram uma posição negativa em relação à apologética, argumentando que tal atividade reflete uma espécie de «falta de fé», porquanto a fé não requeriria defesa, por não estar alicerçada sobre a razão humana e a filosofia. Porém, ao expressar-se assim, Barth fazia a apologia de seu ponto de vista particular do conhecimento e da fé. Muitas pessoas, outrossim, não tinham certeza se a fé de Barth era adequada, ou representasse qualquer acúmulo considerável de verdade, pelo que se tornou necessária toda a forma de atividade apologética para esclarecer as coisas.

7. *Rudolf Bultmann* resolveu redefinir a *kerugma* (pregação) do Novo Testamento, erigindo uma apologética elaborada a fim de levar avante o seu propósito. Alguns pensam que ele chegou ao ponto de querer satisfazer todas as categorias do pensamento moderno, assim debilitando a mensagem que vem mediante a revelação, ao admitir dúvidas demais e ao promover revisões evidentemente desnecessárias.

Quando a Igreja enfrenta os ataques dos ateus, dos agnósticos, dos empiristas radicais, dos positivistas, dos relativistas, então torna-se mister que a apologética continue sendo considerada um ramo da teologia cristã. Nunca é bastante dizer «fé somente», porque a própria fé é definida por uma atividade apologética, consciente ou inconscientemente.

Principais Temas da Apologética:

1. *Natureza da própria revelação*. Não basta dizer que Deus se revela mediante visões e experiências místicas dadas a homens santos, que registram a mensagem em Livros Sagrados. Uma visão pode ser falsa ou parcial. A apologética examina o problema inteiro da revelação como fonte de conhecimento. Descobrimos que muitos dogmas se têm desenvolvido em redor da idéia básica de que Deus se revela mediante a revelação. Há quem diga que não pode haver erro nisso, mas essa declaração é apenas um dogma humano, baseada em considerações *a priori*. Os próprios Livros Sagrados não reivindicam tal coisa para si mesmos. Mas os homens, anelando sentir-se mentalmente tranqüilos, criam um tipo de conhecimento que dispensa exame. Esse é um conhecimento infantil e nada tem a ver com a séria busca e investigação da verdade. Além disso, a revelação divina chega até nós de diversas maneiras. Há revelação através da natureza (Rom. 1). A *religião natural* (ver o artigo) encontra alguma verdade nessa forma de revelação, inteiramente à parte de visões, sonhos e ditados. A teologia natural não contradiz a teologia revelada, mas a suplementa. Os próprios Livros Sagrados não foram inteiramente ditados sob a forma de visões. Há história, poesia, ensinamento racional, discernimento intuitivo que parte das profundezas da alma. Também dispõe de meios, muitos meios; os meios de que Ele dispõe são inúmeros e não podem ser reduzidos a apenas um. O dogma humano que tenta dizer de que maneira Deus precisa revelar-se. A própria ciência, quando corretamente entendida, é uma das revelações divinas, porque, afinal, só existe uma verdade, a verdade de Deus em Seus muitos modos e atividades.

2. *Relação entre a filosofia e a fé*. Conforme vimos, o homem que tenta *explicar* a sua fé já está fazendo apologia, embora destreinado nesse campo. E, como apologeta, está pensando filosoficamente. *Como* os pais da Igreja e os cristãos de séculos posteriores manusearam o problema é algo sobre o qual já comentamos.

3. *Provas racionalistas e científicas* da existência de

APOLOGÉTICA — APOLÔNIA

Deus e da alma. Não quero demorar-me aqui sobre esse assunto porque em outros lugares desta publicação tenho-o abordado longamente. Ver o artigo sobre *Deus, Provas de Sua Existência,* e sobre a *Alma, provas de sua existência.* Apesar de que essas provas não são absolutas, muito têm para dizer, a fim de edificar-nos a fé. Tomás de Aquino considerava que as provas racionalistas são adequadas para demonstrar a simples existência de Deus, embora não para descrevê-Lo. É verdade. Quem pode descrever a Deus? A posição dele concorda com a declaração de Rom. 1. Outros pensadores, como Mullins ou Hodge, encaram essas evidências como críveis, embora não como provas absolutas. Mas outros, como Pascal, Kierkegaard, Brunner, etc., consideram tais provas como parte da irreligiosidade do homem, e como logicamente inválidas. Creio que a própria ciência já ultrapassou essa posição extremista, pelo menos no tocante à existência da alma. O homem, como *imagem* de Deus, tem em si mesmo a estampa da mente divina, podendo descobrir muita coisa por meio da investigação, se esta for disciplinada pela razão e essa investigação regulamenta e define a fé.

4. *Extensão da validade da teologia natural.* Deus revela-se através da natureza (Rom. 1; Atos 17; ver os salmos da natureza, como o Sal. 19). Todavia, é questão de debate a extensão do valor desse tipo de revelação. Há aqueles que dizem que ela é adequada para a piedade e a vida diária, não havendo necessidade de qualquer revelação franca. Calvino admitiu que Deus revela assim a Si mesmo; mas também pensava que o homem, por causa de seu pecado, não é capaz de extrair daí muitos subsídios. Paulo via valor suficiente na revelação mediante a natureza para a condenação do homem, mas não suficiente para salvá-lo. Há uma lei no coração, e sabemos o que é certo e o que é errado, mas nem por isso sabemos aproximar-nos de Deus. Ora, a missão de Cristo teve por alvo transpor esse abismo. O relato da descida de Cristo ao hades (I Ped. 3:18 - 4:6) mostra-nos que a missão de Cristo envolveu aqueles que tinham tido apenas a revelação da natureza, conferindo-lhes um contato direto com o Redentor, mesmo que isso não estivesse ao alcance deles enquanto jornadeavam em seu corpo físico.

5. *Natureza da fé.* Não basta alguém dizer «creio». Precisamos perceber, mediante a razão e a investigação, no que consiste a fé, no que ela está alicerçada. Outrossim, uma das funções do intelecto consiste em produzir a fé que busca a verdade. Não erramos quando nos dedicamos a um robusto intelectualismo cristão. Todavia, essa não deve ser a nossa única dedicação. Devemos também dedicar-nos a conhecer o que Deus pode e quer dar-nos através das experiências místicas, e o que Ele implantou em nós, o que pode ser sondado por meio da intuição. Multiplicidade é a resposta pela nossa busca pela verdade.

6. *A ciência.* Nenhuma ciência verdadeira contradiz a fé verdadeira. Entretanto, é inevitável que a ciência vá se tornando mais religiosa (conforme vai penetrando em áreas que antes eram consideradas como privilégio exclusivo da fé, como a questão da existência da alma), e que a religião vá se tornando mais científica (admitindo que alguns dogmas estavam equivocados e contradiziam os fatos, como as questões da origem, da antiguidade da Terra, da história passada do homem, tudo o que continua ainda envolto nas brumas de muitos mistérios). Mas a ciência pode ajudar-nos a dissipar esses pontos nebulosos. A apologética cristã não pode mostrar-se insensível diante da investigação científica. De fato, é a ciência que atualmente está às vésperas de dar-nos provas da existência e sobrevivência da alma humana, o que se revestirá de incalculável importância para a fé. Ver o artigo sobre a *alma,* sob *provas* de sua existência e sobrevivência.

7. *Natureza dos milagres.* Até mesmo alguns homens de fé negam categoricamente que exista tal coisa como os milagres. Em primeiro lugar, precisamos definir o que entendemos por *milagre.* Se dissermos que um milagre envolve um processo que vá além do que é natural, então algumas pessoas terão dificuldade para crer em milagres. Até mesmo teólogos têm procurado desmitologizar o Novo Testamento, atribuindo todos os milagres a meros mitos, interpretações distorcidas, mal-entendidos e relatos falsos. Se dissermos que os milagres envolvem leis naturais mais elevadas, embora desconhecidas, então um número maior de pessoas crerá em milagres, embora, filosoficamente falando, com isso não estejamos explicando melhor os milagres. Pois, se um processo for chamado de natural, mas permanecer desconhecido, então teremos uma designação, mas não uma descrição, o que não resulta em conhecimento. O que se pode demonstrar é que sucedem-se coisas realmente fantásticas, que não podemos explicar, nem cientificamente nem de outro modo qualquer. O santo homem hindu, Satya Sai Baba está reproduzindo atualmente muitos milagres realizados por Jesus, desde a cura à criação da matéria, e pode ser observado bem de perto. (*Journal of Religion and Psychical Research, Proceedings,* 1981, Bloomfield, Conn., USA). A maior parte do esforço de desmitologização do Novo Testamento tem sido um desperdício total de tempo. Nossos esforços deveriam concentrar-se na tentativa de aprender o propósito dos milagres e de explicar o que se sucedeu, em vez de dizermos que tudo é impossível. Penso que nos *aproximamos* da verdade quando dizemos que um milagre pode ser a manifestação de uma lei natural superior, ou pode resultar de um *novo* ato criador, que nenhuma de nossas categorias científicas pode explicar. Estaremos dizendo a verdade, se afirmarmos que praticamente nada sabemos sobre essas questões. Os *apologetas* nos conclamam a continuar investigando, e mostram que na fé religiosa há uma realidade substancial que requer nossa atenção e dedicação.

O constante desafio. A fé de uma pessoa está sujeita a um ataque permanente, do lado de fora e do lado de dentro. O indivíduo contempla seus constantes fracassos e pecados (e quanto mais iluminado for ele, mais verá); observa o problema do mal operando no mundo, a desumanidade do homem para com seus semelhantes, a destruição da natureza e o caos resultante; ouve os argumentos dos ateus, dos empiristas radicais, e chega a indagar: «De que vale a minha fé, afinal?» Em suas reflexões, ele se torna um apologeta, quanto a si mesmo e quanto a outras pessoas. Portanto, faz-se necessária uma clara defesa da fé, diante de nós mesmos e dos outros. Até mesmo o indivíduo que diz: «A fé é suficiente», está oferecendo uma *breve apologia,* baseada em uma tonelada de idéias teológicas aceitas sem investigação pessoal — mas que *outras pessoas,* antigas e modernas, produziram mediante esforço e uma interminável apologética. (B C E JR P R)

APOLOGISTAS Ver **Apologetas (Apologistas)**

APOLÔNIA

Várias cidades eram chamadas por esse nome, mas a mais conhecida é aquela mencionada no Novo Testamento (ver Atos 17:1), Apolônia da Ilíria, ponto terminal da Via Inácia. Era uma cidade da Macedônia, na província da Migdônia (ver Plínio, iv.17), situada entre Anfípolis e Tessalônica, cerca de sessenta e um quilômetros da primeira e a cinqüenta e três quilômetros da segunda. Paulo e Silas passaram pela cidade a caminho de Tessalônica. César fez dessa cidade a sua base, quando Pompeu foi cercado em Dirráquio. (ID UN S)

APOLONIANO

Era um dos elementos da explicação de Nietzche sobre a natureza das tragédias gregas. O elemento apoloniano representa a proporção, a ordem e a harmonia. Contrasta com o elemento dionisiano, que ressalta a paixão e a irracionalidade. (P)

APOLÔNIO

Nos livros apócrifos do Antigo Testamento há três homens com esse nome.

1. Um general a quem Antíoco Epifânio enviou à Judéia para conquistar Jerusalém, mas que finalmente foi derrotado e morto por Judas Macabeu (ver I Macabeus 3.10,11), em cerca de 166 A.C. No grego ele chamava-se Misarques (ver II Macabeus 5.24).

2. Um governador da Cele-Síria, general de Demétrio Nicanor, derrotado por Jônatas em favor de Alexandre Balas (ver I Macabeus 10.69-76), em cerca de 148 A.C.

3. Filho de Geneu, um dos governadores a quem Lísias deixara na Judéia, após o tratado estabelecido entre os judeus e o jovem rei Antíoco Eupator, e que conseguiu compelir os judeus a romperem o pacto (ver II Macabeus 12.2). (S)

APOLÔNIO DE TIANA

Filósofo grego do século I de nossa era, um neopitagoreano. Viajou muito, e estabeleceu uma escola de filosofia em Éfeso. Salienta a idéia pitagoreana de que o homem é um cidadão do universo. Ensina a existência de um Deus supremo, acima de todos os demais deuses, que está fora do alcance da razão, e não se interessa por holocaustos. Seus principais escritos foram: *Vida de Pitágoras* e *Sobre o Sacrifício*. Ver o artigo sobre o *pitagoreanismo*.

APOSENTO

Há uma boa variedade de palavras hebraicas e gregas, variegadamente traduzidas, como «aposento», «câmara», «cenáculo», etc. O que dizemos abaixo transmite boa idéia a respeito:

1. As câmaras usadas em conexão com o templo, onde eram conservadas as ofertas (Esd. 8:29; Nee. 10:37-39, para exemplificar, palavra hebraica usada por quarenta e sete vezes). Mas essa palavra indica outros tipos de aposento, como certas salas do templo de Ezequiel (ver Eze. 40 - 46). Essas salas eram ocupadas pelos serviçais do templo, ao cumprirem os seus deveres.

2. Quarto. Temos nesse caso uma saleta particular (ver Gên. 43:21), um lugar de proteção, reclusão e meditação (ver Isa. 26:20), e também a «recâmara» de um noivo (ver Can. 1:4). Mas essa palavra hebraica também é traduzida por «sala de verão», em Juí. 3:20. Essa palavra hebraica aparece por trinta e quatro vezes no Antigo Testamento.

3. Uma outra palavra hebraica que nossa versão portuguesa também traduz por «câmara», é usada por doze vezes, em Eze. 40:7-36. Alguns estudiosos pensam que a palavra hebraica significa «lugar separado».

4. «Câmaras laterais» é tradução da palavra hebraica que aparece por quarenta e duas vezes, sobretudo no caso de Eze. 41:5 - 26. Mas a palavra é traduzida em português de outras maneiras também.

5. Uma palavra usada apenas por três vezes no hebraico, figura em I Reis 6:5,6,10. Mas nossa versão portuguesa omite a palavra na tradução nos versículos 6 e 10; e, no quinto versículo, a traduz por «câmaras laterais», expressão que já fora usada para traduzir a palavra hebraica anterior.

6. Uma palavra traduzida por «sala», em II Sam. 18:33, e por «morada» em Sal. 104:3,13, é usada por dezessete vezes no Antigo Testamento. Uma boa tradução seria «quarto elevado» ou «quarto de primeiro andar».

7. Uma palavra grega usada por quatro vezes é *tameîon*, «despensa» (ver Mat. 6:6; 24:26; Luc. 12:3,24).

8. Outra palavra grega, usada também por quatro vezes é *uperôon*, sempre no livro de Atos (ver 1:13; 9:37,39 e 20:8), traduzida por «cenáculo». Em nossa versão portuguesa quer dizer «quarto elevado».

APOSTA DE PASCAL Ver **Pascal, Blaise**, ponto 6.

APOSTASIA

Vem do grego **apostasia**, «afastamento». Aponta para o abandono deliberado da crença na fé cristã (ou em qualquer fé, anteriormente defendida), por alguém que dizia seguir essa fé. No catolicismo romano, indica a total deserção da fé, ou das santas ordens, ou do estado monástico. O apóstata formal está sujeito à exclusão. Em sentido menos amplo, a palavra é usada para indicar pessoas que deslizam para o descuido e o abandono no tocante à sua fé religiosa, embora, teoricamente falando, continuem crendo em algumas das suas doutrinas.

1. *Usos do termo*. Em forma nominal, encontra-se somente por duas vezes no Novo Testamento: Atos 21:21 e II Tess. 2:3. É uma forma posterior do grego *apóstasis*, «manter-se longe de». Foi usada por Plutarco para indicar revolta política, sendo usada na Septuaginta, no sentido de revolta contra Deus (Jos. 22:22). É dito sobre Antíoco Epifânio que ele favorecia a apostasia do judaísmo para o helenismo (I Mac. 2:15).

2. *No Novo Testamento*. Indica um «afastamento», talvez indicando uma «revolta», com o abandono dos princípios básicos do cristianismo. (II Tess. 2:3). É a dissolução de qualquer vínculo sério com Deus e com Cristo, paralelamente à rebeldia e à hostilidade para com esses vínculos. Dentro do ponto de vista cristão, a apostasia envolve mais do que a mudança de idéias sobre doutrinas reveladas. A princípio, é a outorga da alma a alguma causa maligna, e não o mero abandono daquilo que antes era professado.

3. *A apostasia*. O trecho de II Tess. 2 e certas descrições no Apocalipse indicam que, no fim dos tempos, antes da *parousia* (ver o artigo), isto é, da segunda vinda de Cristo, ou do início da era áurea do *milênio* (ver o artigo a respeito), haverá um afastamento especialmente radical de muitos, que abandonarão a fé cristã. Essa rebelião será encabeçada pelo *anticristo* (ver o artigo). Visto que o anticristo será o «filho» da trindade maligna (Satanás, o anticristo e o falso profeta), por meio dele será adorado o pai dele, Satanás. Quanto a trechos bíblicos que dão informações sobre vários aspectos

APOSTASIA — APÓSTOLO

desse ensino, ver Mat. 24:4,5; 10:13; Mar. 13:5,6,22; Luc. 21:8; I Tim. 4:1 ss ; II Tim. 3:1 ss ; Apo. 13:8,15. A apostasia promovida pelo anticristo será especialmente maligna, porque ele encabeçará uma forma espúria de cristianismo, dentro do arcabouço de uma religião do mundo. No seio da cristandade, os homens deixarão de prestar lealdade ao Senhorio de Cristo, e não mais haverão de considerá-Lo único e sem-par(Col. 2:18; I João 4:1-3; II Ped. 2:1). Quanto a descrições dos líderes apóstatas (os gnósticos dos tempos neotestamentários), ver II Tim. 4:3; II Ped. 2:1-19; Judas 4,8,11,13,16. «Eles saíram de nosso meio, entretanto não eram dos nossos» (I João 2:19), uma outra declaração a respeito dos gnósticos, é aplicável em espírito a esses desertores. Ramos que antes pareciam participar da vida da vinha, perderão a vitalidade, porque sua união com a vinha será decepada. Por conseguinte, serão lançados fora (ver João 15:6).

4. *Aspectos históricos da apostasia*:
No Novo Testamento, faz-se a distinção entre o apóstata e o herege. Aos crentes é ensinado que tentem preservar a comunhão com os hereges (Tito 3:10), mas a condição dos apóstatas parece ser irreversível (II Tess. 2:10-12; II Ped. 2:17,21; Jud. 11-15; Heb. 6:1-6). Naturalmente, essa irreversibilidade não é teórica, porque somente um pecado é considerado imperdoável (Mat. 12:31). Portanto, trata-se de uma irreversibilidade prática. Pode-se dizer com plena confiança: «Um apóstata não volta». O herege, por outra parte, é alguém que caiu em algum tipo de erro doutrinário; mas, de modo geral, ele é discípulo de Cristo e pode ser restaurado. Como é óbvio, devemos lembrar que a definição do que é um herege pode ser restringida a idéias denominacionais de ortodoxia doutrinária, de tal modo que um membro em regular situação perante uma denominação pode ser tido como herege perante outra denominação. Além disso, os grandes hereges, como Jesus, Paulo e Lutero, para citar alguns poucos, foram aqueles que trouxeram grandes avanços espirituais. Portanto, devemos usar esses termos com extrema cautela. A palavra «ortodoxia» nem sempre é sinônima de «verdade», pois esse termo com demasiada freqüência é empregado para indicar «o que eu creio», e não, necessariamente, «o que, de fato, é verdade».

Na Igreja pós-apostólica, havia três modos segundo os quais uma pessoa ou uma igreja podiam ser considerados apóstatas: 1. mediante a renúncia da fé (uma das definições usuais); 2. mediante lapso moral, por haver o indivíduo cometido os grandes pecados de adultério ou homicídio (sem arrepender-se dos mesmos). Os cristãos não recebiam de volta à comunhão aos que assim transgredissem. Porém, na Idade Média, a palavra apostasia parece que era aplicada somente àqueles que renunciavam inteiramente à fé cristã (Tomás de Aquino, *Summa Theologica* IIa-IIae, gg. 11,12).

Nos primeiros séculos, a apostasia podia ser punida não apenas pela Igreja, mas também pelo governo secular, e muitos apóstatas perderam assim a vida. As leis civis também puniam os apóstatas cortando-os de seus empregos, de suas posições e confiscando-lhes as propriedades, conforme sucedeu na época do rei Guilherme III, da Inglaterra. Esses costumes, porém, foram abandonados.

Nos tempos modernos, igrejas e denominações inteiras têm sido chamadas apóstatas, e não apenas indivíduos isolados, devido ao liberalismo teológico ou à presença de atividades políticas ou outras, incompatíveis com os ideais cristãos. Quanto a outras notas bastante completas sobre a *apostasia*, salientando o problema especial levantado no sexto capítulo da epístola aos Hebreus, ver o *NTI* em II Tess. 2:3 e Heb. 6:4. Ver o artigo *Segurança Eterna do Crente* que apresenta detalhes sobre a controvérsia. (AM B C E H NTI R Z).

A POSTERIORI
Ver sobre **A Priori, A Posteriori**.

APOSTOLADO
Termo usado para designar a dignidade e o ofício dos apóstolos de Cristo. Mais tarde, foi usado para indicar o ofício episcopal. Porém, chegou a designar o ofício papal, por ser ele considerado nos círculos católicos romanos como o principal «enviado», para benefício da Igreja. Ver **Apóstolos (Apostolado)**, IV.

APOSTOLICIDADE
A **apostolicidade** é uma das quatro características da Igreja, conforme o Credo Niceno. Tertuliano, no fim do século II D.C., usou a palavra a fim de referir-se à Igreja «edificada sobre os apóstolos» (Efé. 2:19 ss). Tal Igreja deve manter sua doutrina e sua prática. Só assim ela permanece primitiva e apostólica (*de Praes*. 20). Agostinho empregou o termo em controvérsia com os donatistas, aos quais reputava cismáticos. Tal termo tem sido usado ao longo da história da teologia a fim de distinguir a verdadeira Igreja das facções. A doutrina paralela da *sucessão apostólica* (ver o artigo a respeito) entrou na questão. Segundo o dogma católico romano, a *apostolicidade* inclui o reconhecimento do papa como herdeiro do trono de Pedro. No vocabulário dos teólogos protestantes, a palavra tem sido usada com o sentido de primitivo ou original, e portanto, livre de erros e corrupções posteriores, que invadiram a Igreja cristã. Atualmente, o termo é usado para aludir à participação na missão da Igreja. (C)

APOSTOLICUM = Credo dos Apóstolos (vide)

APÓSTOLO
Ver o artigo sobre **Apóstolos**, a seguir. O termo *apóstolo* vem do grego *apóstolos*, cujo significado mais comum é simplesmente *delegado*, *mensageiro*. A palavra é usada em sentido religioso para designar os mensageiros de Deus, de uma maneira bastante geral, como mensageiros ou delegados de oficiais, Fil. 2:25, II Cor. 8:23, e pode ter a noção de *missionário*. No grego clássico, entre uma variedade de usos, a palavra foi usada para designar os *mensageiros de Deus*, Epict. 3,22,23, como os *sábios* da filosofia. No Novo Testamento, o termo é usado para designar o maior desses mensageiros, *Cristo*, Heb. 3:1. Este documento continua o uso amplo da palavra. Barnabé, Atos 4:14, Andrônico, Júnias, Rom. 16:7, Tiago, o irmão do Senhor, Gál. 1:19, são chamados de *apóstolos*. Mas o uso mais comum no Novo Testamento é a designação dos *Doze Apóstolos*, os primeiros missionários da Igreja Cristã. Numa maneira especial trouxeram a Nova Mensagem e trabalharam como operadores de milagres, doutores poderosos da palavra, de bispos, e como alicerces da Igreja, Efé. 2:20.

Depois da era apostólica, o termo tem sido empregado para designar os primeiros missionários cristãos que levaram a mensagem para países que nunca a tinham recebido. Por exemplo, Bonifácio (680-754) se chama o *Apóstolo da Alemanha*.

APÓSTOLOS

A Evolução da Vereda Espiritual

1. *Materialismo*. Com ou sem a crença em um Ser supremo (essa crença pode ser meramente teórica, sem qualquer praticidade na vida diária), os homens podem atirar-se no materialismo. Então a vida é vivida egoisticamente. Para aqueles que se acham nesse estágio, a vida presente reveste-se de suprema importância. A alma não volve os olhos para cima, para seu futuro estágio eterno, e a vida diária não é influenciada por essa visão do alto.

2. *Superstição*. Nesse segundo estágio, os homens chegam a reconhecer algo dos poderes sobre-humanos e espirituais, mas aí todo conceito das coisas continua distorcido. As crenças religiosas, nesse estágio, podem até levar as pessoas a ocuparem-se em realizações prejudiciais, como é o caso dos sacrifícios humanos. Os supersticiosos deixam-se levar por toda forma de mitos e de imaginações, mas, pelo menos, já chegaram a perceber que existem os poderes espirituais.

3. *Fundamentalismo*. Nesse nível, as revelações divinas, preservadas em Livros Sagrados, são altamente reverenciadas; porém, a letra é posta acima do Espírito. Ver o artigo *Bibliolatria*. Crenças e credos rígidos cristalizam e entravam o desenvolvimento espiritual, e com freqüência os credos tornam-se motivos fortes de divisão, que separam as pessoas religiosas em campos que se hostilizam. A arrogância e o gosto pela polêmica são proeminentes nesse estágio. No caso de muitos, o amor é apenas uma questão da boca para fora. Todas as questões religiosas ficam dependentes de textos de prova, via de regra interpretados de forma a eliminar idéias contrárias e fortalecer as idéias que se coadunem com a visão limitada das doutrinas desta ou daquela denominação. Tradições começam a ser ensinadas como se fossem a própria verdade. Até mesmo porções dos Livros Sagrados são distorcidas ou omitidas, no esforço de obter uma teologia sistemática infalível, que geralmente se torna mais importante que a própria verdade. Apesar das desvantagens evidentes desse estágio, algumas pessoas são capazes de atingir um bom grau de piedade e espiritualidade pessoais. Porém, muitos substituem essa piedade e espiritualidade pela mera aderência a algum credo.

APÓSTOLOS (APOSTOLADO)

I. A Palavra e o Ofício
II. Nomes, Características e Listas
III. Observações Sobre as Listas
IV. O Apostolado
V. As Qualificações Especiais dos Apóstolos
VI. A Autoridade dos Apóstolos
VII. A Importância do Ofício Apostólico
VIII. Sucessão Apostólica

I. A Palavra e o Ofício

1. O termo vem do grego **apóstolos**, «enviado». A forma verbal é *apostello*, «enviar», e era aplicada a todas as variedades da ação, enviar um navio, uma expedição naval, um comandante, uma pessoa, etc. No Antigo Testamento, a idéia de Deus enviar Seus servos é de uso freqüente, e a forma verbal é empregada na Septuaginta em relação a Moisés, Elias, Eliseu e Ezequiel. A forma nominal é usada com o sentido de «agente credenciado».

No Novo Testamento. Cristo é o supremo *apóstolo* (Heb. 3:1). Seus mensageiros especiais são outros «apóstolos», incluindo, acima de todos, os doze apóstolos originais e Paulo.

4. *Filosofia*. Nesse nível do avanço, os homens já começam a pensar por si mesmos, e não são apenas mata-borrões que somente absorvem idéias alheias. Surge uma espécie de despertamento, após todo o sono dogmático do passado. A *tolerância* (vide) torna-se a linha mestra principal das atitudes e ações. A lei do amor começa a adquirir importância. As antigas verdades passam a ser entendidas de uma nova maneira, e novas verdades são descobertas e incorporadas. Os credos deixam de ser examinados e seguidos cegamente, conforme sucedera no estágio fundamentalista. Mais do que meros textos de prova escriturísticos são exigidos, para que a pessoa aceite uma idéia como expressão da verdade. Verdades antes negligenciadas, agora são descobertas e valorizadas. É abandonado o *antiintelectualismo* (vide). As reivindicações dos místicos são investigadas.

5. *Perseguição e Perseverança*. A alma começa a ter fome e sede de justiça e verdade. A alma sente-se aflita, impelida a uma inquirição espiritual mais intensa. Alguns experimentam, nesse estágio, uma espécie de reconversão. — Tornam-se comuns uma leitura mais constante, uma vida de estudo e de oração mais permanente e vigorosa. Os homens buscam então a companhia de outros, que compartilhem dessa mesma intensidade, talvez até mudando de organização religiosa. Outros buscam a meditação, para receber maior iluminação. A compaixão e a simpatia vêm substituir a antiga hostilidade. Os homens avançam para além da tolerância, chegando à compreensão e à compaixão.

6. *A Vereda Mística*. A alma segue a Deus bem de perto, e busca a iluminação pessoal. As experiências místicas conferem a iluminação buscada, e a Presença Divina torna-se uma realidade na vida. É buscada a união com Deus. O amor reveste-se de grande importância. Ver os artigos intitulados *Misticismo* e *Cristo-Misticismo*.

7. *O estágio final* é, realmente, o processo da eterna *glorificação* (vide). Ver os artigos *Visão Beatífica* e *Transformação Segundo a Imagem de Cristo*.

Ora, o ofício apostólico tinha por finalidade ajudar-nos na evolução na vereda espiritual.

2. *Apostolado*. Houve uma missão especial que envolveu os doze e Paulo. Os apóstolos foram dotados de poderes e autoridade especiais, agindo como agentes pessoais de Cristo. Mesmo depois de Sua morte e ressurreição, continuaram ativos nessa capacidade. Tinham o dever de pregar, de curar, de administrar a Igreja e de serem os representantes especiais da missão e da pessoa de Cristo, para darem prosseguimento à Sua autoridade. (Ver Atos 2:42; 5:1-11; 6:1-6; 8:14; 9:32, quanto a alguns desses deveres). E então, através deles, era ministrado o Espírito (Atos 8:15-17). Foram-lhes dados dons e poderes extraordinários, como emblemas de sua divina autoridade (Atos 5:12; 2 Cor. 12:12). Eram eles que lideravam, — na solução de problemas difíceis que surgiam na igreja (Atos 15:6; ver também Atos 6:3). A nomeação de Paulo ao apostolado teve a chancela da autoridade divina (Gál. 1:1; Rom. 5:1).

O termo «apóstolos» figura pela primeira vez no Novo Testamento em Mat. 10:2. Ver trechos paralelos como Mar. 3:13-19 e Luc. 6:12-16. Porém, um *uso mais amplo* do termo inclui o próprio Senhor Jesus (Heb. 3:1), Barnabé (Atos 14:14), Tiago, irmão do Senhor (Gál. 1:19), e talvez Silvano e Timóteo (Tess. 2:6). Ver também Efé. 4:11. Atualmente há apóstolos

APÓSTOLOS (APOSTOLADO)

na Igreja, no sentido secundário de alguém que Deus superdistinguiu em seus serviços, ou que seja dotado de significativa autoridade e poder espiritual. Mas muitos põem em sérias dúvidas se eles devem ser considerados parte do ministério oficial da igreja.

3. *Sinais do apostolado.* 1. Os apóstolos precisavam ser testemunhas oculares (Atos 1:21,22; I Cor. 9:1). 2. Eram dotados de poderes especiais (até mesmo miraculosos), como credenciais de seu ofício (Mat. 10:1; Atos 5:15,16; II Cor. 12:12). 3. Eram os agentes especiais do reino, em sua autoridade e administração (Mt. 10:5,6; Efé. 2:20). 4. Recebiam um serviço e uma missão definidos, tanto para os dias de Jesus como para o futuro (Mat. 19:28). Portanto, torna-se problemático determinar se, fora da era apostólica, algum homem pode ser qualificado como apóstolo, no sentido primário. A *autoridade* deles pode ser transferida a terceiros? Ver o artigo sobre a *Sucessão Apostólica.*

Pano de fundo histórico. Os apóstolos foram enviados por Jesus, e acompanharam-no em sua segunda viagem pela Galiléia. Cumpria-lhes duplicar o tipo de ministério que Jesus tivera em Sua primeira viagem por aquele território. Esse ministério envolvia autoridade sobre os demônios e exorcismo, cura de enfermidades e a pregação da mensagem espiritual, sobretudo como preparação para a chegada do reino de Deus (Mat. 10:1 ss). Mais tarde, receberam autoridade relativa da Igreja (Mat. 16:17 ss ; João 20:21-23; Atos 1:8 ss ; Efé. 2:20 ss ; 4:11).

Paulo dá a entender que aos vários apóstolos foram determinadas áreas específicas de atividade: Tiago, Pedro e João tinham um ministério entre os judeus, e Paulo, entre os gentios. Os doze foram removidos de Jerusalém devido às perseguições, e o alcance do ministério deles expandiu-se por causa disso. (Ver Gál. 2:7-10; Atos 8:1).

II. Nomes, Características e Listas

Nomes e Características

Simão, também chamado Pedro (em grego, pedra) ou Cefas (pedra, palavra de origem caldaica) por Jesus. Era filho de Jonas (Mat. 16:17), pescador por profissão. Betsaida era sua cidade natal (João 1:47), mas também residia em Cafarnaum, na Galiléia (Marc. 1:21,29). Existem cerca de outros oito «Simões» nas páginas do N.T. Alguns desses são o «cananeu», em Mat. 10:4; um dos irmãos de Jesus, em Mat. 13:55; um leproso de Betânia, em Mat. 13:55; um homem de Cirene, que foi compelido a ajudar a carregar a cruz de Cristo, em Marc. 15:21, identificado por alguns como Simão, que aparece em Atos 13:1; um fariseu (Luc. 7:40), que alguns identificam com Simão, o leproso, aludido acima; Simão Iscariotes, pai de Judas Iscariotes; um curtidor de Jope, que Pedro visitou (Atos 9:40). As tradições antigas dizem que Pedro morreu crucificado em Roma, de cabeça para baixo.

André, irmão de Simão Pedro, cujo nome é grego, «másculo». Originalmente, era discípulo de João Batista. Subseqüentemente conheceu a Cristo e passou a segui-lo, tendo-lhe apresentado Pedro. Era sócio de Pedro na indústria de pesca. Diz-se que foi crucificado na Acaia.

Filipe e André aparecem juntos nos trechos de João 1:45 e 6:7,8, parecendo-nos que havia um laço especial de amizade entre esses dois apóstolos; razão pela qual Filipe transmitiu o recado a André, provavelmente a fim de solicitar o seu parecer sobre a questão do pedido dos *gregos.* E então os dois transmitiram a solicitação ao Senhor Jesus.

André, como as escrituras afirmam, era irmão de Pedro, e foi um dos doze apóstolos. Evidentemente foi o primeiro de todos os discípulos de Jesus, tendo passado a seguir a Cristo mediante o testemunho de João Batista. Subseqüentemente, conduziu seu irmão, Simão Pedro, à presença de Jesus. (Quanto a notas sobre essa questão, e as lições por ela ensinadas, ver João 1:35-42, no NTI). O «outro» discípulo, entre os primeiros que seguiram a Jesus (juntamente com André) mui provavelmente era João. (Ver os comentários relativos a João 1:35,40 no NTI, sobre essa questão). André se distinguia pelo seu zelo ao ganhar outros para Cristo, através de sua fé eminentemente prática. (Ver João 6:8 e 12:21,22). Foi ele um dos discípulos a indagar ao Senhor acerca do julgamento que sobreviria a Jerusalém. (Ver Marc. 13:3,4). É digno de nossa atenção que, na passagem de João 1:42, ele foi o primeiro missionário entre seus compatriotas; e também se vê, neste texto do décimo segundo capítulo de João, que ele foi o primeiro missionário no estrangeiro.

William Temple (*Readings in St. John's Gospel,* pág. 29) diz: «Talvez seja esse um grande serviço à igreja, tão notável como o que qualquer outro homem prestou». É evidente que esse autor se referia ao zelo de André por ajudar tão decisivamente na formação do núcleo primitivo dos discípulos de Jesus, tendo trazido aos pés do Senhor o seu próprio irmão, Simão Pedro.

Parece-nos que André assumiu a liderança da iniciativa, neste episódio em foco, e que, juntamente com Filipe, levou a questão à apreciação do Senhor. Alguns estudiosos supõem que assim aconteceu por ser ele mais íntimo de Jesus do que o era Filipe; no entanto, não temos qualquer prova sobre essa opinião. Adam Clarke (*in loc.*) percebe nesse episódio uma ilustração de como os ministros deveriam concordar entre si, unindo seus esforços num propósito comum, ao dizer: «Quão agradável a Deus é essa unidade, quando os ministros de seu evangelho entram em harmonia e se unem no esforço comum de conduzir as almas a Cristo. Porém, onde prevalecem o amor-próprio e os interesses pessoais, e onde não é buscada a honra que vem exclusivamente de Deus, essa unidade jamais passa a existir. Os preconceitos com freqüência arruínam todos os sentimentos generosos que porventura existam entre as diferentes denominações do povo de Deus». Essa observação foi feita há mais de cento e cinqüenta anos atrás, — mas é óbvio que tem aplicação moderna.

Tiago, um dos filhos de Zebedeu, um pescador da Galiléia, que pertencia ao grupo selecionado dos três mais íntimos, entre os doze apóstolos. Foi morto pela espada de Herodes Agripa I (ver Atos 12:2). Precisa ser distinguido de Tiago, filho de Alfeu, outro dos doze apóstolos (Mat. 10:3); e também de certo irmão de Jesus (Mat. 13:55); e, igualmente, de um irmão do apóstolo Judas (Atos 1:13). Alguns crêem, entretanto, que a expressão indica que esse Judas é realmente filho do Tiago aqui mencionado.

João, outro dos filhos de Zebedeu, irmão do Tiago mencionado em primeiro lugar entre os Tiagos. À base de Marc. 16:1 e de Mat. 27:56, parece que a Salomé mencionada era mãe desses dois apóstolos. Acredita-se comumente que Salomé era irmã de Maria, mãe de Jesus. Se assim realmente foi, então Tiago e João eram primos de Jesus. A família provavelmente tinha recursos, obtidos com a indústria da pesca. Salomé é uma das mulheres que contribuíam para a subsistência de Jesus e seus discípulos (ver Luc. 8:3; Marc. 15:40). Tiago e João foram chamados de «filhos do trovão» pelo Senhor Jesus (Marc. 3:17), provavelmente por causa de seu

APÓSTOLOS (APOSTOLADO)

espírito exaltado e indisciplinado, que talvez fosse uma das características dos homens de sua profissão. Esse João era um dos três apóstolos do círculo mais íntimo (Pedro, Tiago e João). Só esses três foram testemunhas oculares da ressurreição da filha de Jairo (Marc. 5:37), da transfiguração de Jesus (Marc. 9:2) e só eles tiveram permissão de estar com Jesus no jardim de Getsêmani (Marc. 14:33). João é o discípulo a quem Jesus amara, autor do evangelho de João. Diversas histórias sobre seu martírio não têm sido consideradas conclusivas. Deve ser distinguido de João Batista e de João Marcos.

Filipe, chamado para seguir a Jesus no dia seguinte ao do chamamento de Pedro e André. Ele trouxe Natanael a Cristo. Era de Betsaida, de onde também eram Pedro e André. (Ver João 1:44). É incerto se o túmulo que há em Hierápolis é o desse Filipe ou do «diácono» Filipe. O apóstolo Filipe deve ser distinguido de certo Filipe, filho de Herodes o Grande e de Mariamne, filha do sumo sacerdote Simão; e de um filho de Herodes o Grande e sua quinta esposa, Cleópatra de Jerusalém; e, igualmente, de Filipe, diácono e evangelista, um dos sete escolhidos para um serviço especial na igreja de Jerusalém (Atos 6:5).

Bartolomeu, que é mencionado exclusivamente nas listas dos doze apóstolos. Sua identificação com Natanael é incerta (João 1:45). Se Bartolomeu e Natanael são a mesma pessoa, então sabemos que ele veio de Caná da Galiléia. Foi ele que viu a Cristo, no dia de sua ressurreição, à beira do mar de Tiberíades. (Ver João 21:2).

Mateus, filho de Alfeu, não o Alfeu, pai de Tiago, o menor, também conhecido pelo nome de Levi. Era «publicano» ou cobrador de impostos por profissão. (Ver Mat. 10:3). Existem indicações de que após a ressurreição de Jesus, ele pregou primeiro na Judéia, e então em países estrangeiros. Tradicionalmente aceito como autor do evangelho que traz o seu nome, embora esse evangelho não tenha provas internas de quem fora o seu autor. Papias diz-nos que Mateus compilou oráculos, mas de forma alguma se tem certeza se isso se refere ao livro que chamamos de evangelho segundo Mateus. Nas listas dos apóstolos, vê-se no evangelho de Mat. que o seu nome aparece depois do de Tomé, ao passo que nos outros evangelhos é alistado antes do de Tomé. Isso tem sido reputado como um sinal interno da autoria de Mateus, como sinal de humildade pessoal.

Tomé, cujo nome significa *gêmeo*, embora não tenhamos qualquer informação acerca de algum irmão ou irmã de quem era gêmeo. Somente o evangelho de João contém algumas referências pessoais a Tomé. Mostrou-se disposto a morrer junto com Jesus (João 11:16), mas fraquejou quanto à fé, deixando-se assaltar pelas dúvidas (João 20:25), embora mais tarde tivesse sido o grande confessor da deidade de Cristo (João 20:28). É evidente que Tomé também era pescador de profissão, posto ser mencionado na companhia de Pedro, entre sete discípulos, à beira do mar da Galiléia (João 21:2). As tradições informam-nos que posteriormente ele labutou na Síria, na Pártia, na Pérsia e na Índia. Ver outras notas em João 11:16 no NTI.

Tiago, filho de Alfeu. Com freqüência é identificado com «Tiago, o menor», nome esse que talvez fosse melhor traduzido como «Tiago, o pequeno». Obviamente essa designação se refere à sua estatura física, em comparação com Tiago, filho de Alfeu, ou talvez se refira à sua idade, por ser mais jovem que este. Era filho de uma das Marias mencionadas no N.T. (Ver Marc. 15:40). A tradição revela-nos que ele pregou na Palestina e no Egito. Não há evidência alguma de que esse homem fosse parente do Senhor.

Simão, chamado o Zelote. Também é chamado de «o cananeu», embora seja uma tradução um tanto deficiente. Deveria ser «cananeano», que é referência a um partido político, posteriormente apelidado de «zelotes» (como se vê em Luc. 6:15). Esse partido se opunha à tentativa de pôr a Judéia sob o domínio de Roma, e posteriormente se opôs amargamente ao governo romano sobre a Judéia, em qualquer de suas formas. Esse apodo, aplicado a Simão, poderia ser uma referência ao seu zelo religioso, embora a outra explanação pareça ser mais provável. Ver o artigo sobre os *Zelotes*.

Judas, irmão de Tiago, também chamado Tadeu (em Marc. 3:18). Alguns acreditam que «irmão de Tiago» poderia ser traduzido mais corretamente por «filho de Tiago». O grego, literalmente traduzido, diz simplesmente «de Tiago». Ele também é chamado «Labeu» (Mat. 10:3). Acreditam muitos que ele tenha sido o autor da epístola de Judas. Tradicionalmente, teria sido pregador em Edessa, na Síria, na Arábia e na Mesopotâmia.

Judas Iscariotes. As tentativas para fazer o nome «Iscariotes» significar «assassino», relacionando-o a uma palavra aramaica similar, parecem fúteis. A referência mais provável é a Queriote, lugar localizado em Moabe (ver Jer. 48:24), ou então a Queriote-Hesrom (ver Jos. 15:25), acerca de vinte quilômetros ao sul de Hebrom. Esse Judas sempre aparece em último lugar nas listas dos apóstolos, e sempre é identificado pelo adjetivo, «traidor». Era o tesoureiro do grupo apostólico. Sua carreira levou-o à apostasia e ao suicídio final. (Ver Atos 1:25; Mat. 27:5; Atos 1:18). Sendo originário da Judéia, foi o único apóstolo que não era da Galiléia.

Matias, sucessor de Judas Iscariotes. (Ver Atos 1:15,26). Eusébio, o primeiro historiador eclesiástico, revela-nos que ele pertencera antes ao grupo dos setenta, e que, por isso mesmo, era uma testemunha ocular. Mas nada de certo se sabe com respeito à sua vida posterior. Ver outras notas sobre ele em Atos 1:23 no NTI.

Paulo. No princípio de sua vida, era um jovem aristocrata de Tarso, embora tivesse sido criado em Jerusalém, sob a direção do famoso mestre, Gamaliel. Evidentemente esteve afastado de Jerusalém durante o ministério de Jesus, porquanto nunca o vira pessoalmente, até à visão que lhe foi dada na estrada de Damasco. (Ver Atos 9). Sua reivindicação ao apostolado era autêntica, posto ter visto o Senhor após a sua ressurreição, por meio de visões; então foi nomeado apóstolo e enviado especialmente aos gentios, tendo sido aceito como tal pelos demais apóstolos. (Ver Gál. 1:1,15,16,17; 2.6-9). Ver o artigo sobre Paulo.

Há quatro listas dos apóstolos: em Mat. 10:2-4; em Mar. 3:16-19; em Luc. 6:14-16 e em Atos 1:13,16,26. Pedro encabeça a lista em todas as instâncias. Assumiu o primado *interpares* entre eles, segundo está registrado no segundo e terceiro capítulos do livro de Atos. Judas Iscariotes sempre aparece em último lugar nas listas dos apóstolos, exceto no livro de Atos, onde o seu nome é omitido. Mateus dá os nomes dos apóstolos aos pares, provavelmente na mesma ordem em que foram enviados em sua missão, de dois em dois.

Ver os artigos separados sobre cada um dos Apóstolos.

APÓSTOLOS (APOSTOLADO)

MAT. 10:4	MAR. 3:16-19	LUC. 6:14-16	ATOS 1:13
1. Simão Pedro	Simão Pedro	Simão Pedro	Simão Pedro
2. André	Tiago	André	Tiago
3. Tiago	João	Tiago	João
4. João	André	João	André
5. Filipe	Filipe	Filipe	Filipe
6. Bartolomeu	Bartolomeu	Bartolomeu	Tomé
7. Tomé	Mateus	Mateus	Bartolomeu
8. Mateus	Tomé	Tomé	Mateus
9. Tiago, de Alfeu	Tiago, de Alfeu	Tiago, de Alfeu	Tiago, de Alfeu
10. Tadeu	Tadeu	Simão, o Zelote	Simão, o Zelote
11. Simão, o Zelote	Simão	Judas, de Tiago	Judas, de Tiago
12. Judas Iscariotes	Judas Iscariotes	Judas Iscariotes	(em branco)

III. Observações sobre as Listas

1. *Mateus* apresenta sua lista aos pares: Simão e André, Tiago e João, Filipe e Bartolomeu, Tomé e Mateus, Tiago e Tadeu, Simão e Judas. Sabe-se que Jesus enviou esses homens aos pares a fim de evangelizarem. Provavelmente a lista de Mateus mostra-nos os pares conforme foram enviados.

2. Entre os apóstolos havia *pares de irmãos*: Simão e André, Tiago e João. Alguns intérpretes acham que Mateus e Tomé eram irmãos, como também Filipe e Bartolomeu. Mas talvez somente Simão e André, e Tiago e João fossem irmãos, porquanto o texto não menciona que os demais o eram, mas identifica claramente aqueles dois pares como compostos de irmãos carnais, com as palavras «seu irmão». Não é provável que o autor, tendo feito isso em dois casos, não acrescentasse também essas palavras no caso dos outros, se realmente tivessem sido irmãos. Outrossim, não há na tradição qualquer indicação de que houvesse outros pares de irmãos entre os doze apóstolos.

3. É provável que Salomé, mãe de Tiago e João (Marc. 16:1; Mat. 27:56) fosse *irmã* de Maria, mãe de Jesus. Assim sendo, aqueles apóstolos eram primos de Jesus, como talvez João Batista também o fosse.

4. Nas listas há *três classes*, cada qual com quatro pessoas, cada classe com os mesmos nomes, ainda que em ordem diversa, ou seja: primeira classe, Pedro, André, Tiago e João; segunda classe, Filipe, Bartolomeu, Tomé e Mateus; terceira classe, Tiago, filho de Alfeu, Tadeu, Simão, o Zelote e Judas Iscariotes.

5. Em todas as listas, os nomes de Pedro, Filipe, Tiago (de Alfeu) e Judas Iscariotes ocupam o *mesmo lugar* na ordem de apresentação. Pedro sempre aparece em primeiro lugar, o que mostra que não só foi chamado antes dos outros, era discípulo há mais tempo, mas também gozava de primazia entre os doze. Isso não significa, porém, que fosse uma modalidade de papa. Ver notas sobre Mat. 16:16 no NTI, que explicam a posição ocupada por Pedro. Em todas as listas Judas Iscariotes é o último e não há que duvidar que tal posição lhe foi dada propositalmente nas listas, para indicar sua posição inferior, por haver traído ao Senhor Jesus.

6. O maior problema é o da *identificação* de certos nomes com os indivíduos, como, por exemplo, os nomes Labeu, Tadeu e Judas (irmão ou filho de Tiago), que parecem referir-se à mesma pessoa. Ver Mat. 10:3 na tradução AC, comparando com Luc. 6:16 e Atos 1:13. Levi e Mateus são a mesma pessoa.

Bartolomeu pode ser identificado com o Natanael de João 1:45. Simão Cananita, de Marc. 3:18 deve ser identificado com Simão, o Zelote, em Luc. 6:15. Ambos os apelidos se referiam ao partido político de Simão. Ver a nota em Luc. 6:12 no NTI.

7. Judas Iscariotes, da cidade de Queriote, em Judá, filho de Simão (João 6:71), era o *único* que não era natural da Galiléia. Todos os demais apóstolos eram galileus. Ver outros detalhes sobre os doze, em Luc. 6:12 no NTI.

Os antigos, na igreja primitiva, consideravam os doze como tipos dos doze filhos de Israel, no V.T.; também eram comparados simbolicamente às doze fontes de Elim (Êx. 12:27), às doze pedras de Urim e Tumim, no peitoral do sumo sacerdote, aos doze pães de Ex. 25:30, aos doze espias enviados à terra prometida (Jos. 2:1,6,23), às doze pedras tiradas do rio Jordão, como lembrando do poder de Deus entre eles (Jos. 4:3-9). Outros acham que há referência aos doze apóstolos em Apo. 12:1, no N.T., que fala das doze estrelas na cabeça da mulher vestida de sol. E certamente eles são representados pelos doze fundamentos das muralhas da nova Jerusalém (Apo. 21:14).

IV. O Apostolado

Apóstolo. Palavra que significa **enviado**, mas que também subentende aquele que faz serviço especial, em nome e pela autoridade de quem o enviou. É empregada por Mateus, pela primeira vez (10:2), mas os trechos paralelos (Marc. 3:13-19 e Luc. 6:12-16) mostram que foram escolhidos antes do Sermão do Monte, depois que Jesus passou a noite inteira em oração. O termo não é usado exclusivamente para fazer alusão aos doze, mas também se refere a Jesus, em Heb. 3:1. Mais tarde alude a Paulo, em numerosas ocorrências; alude a Barnabé, em Atos 14:14; alude a Matias, escolhido para ocupar o lugar de Judas Iscariotes, em Atos 1:16-26. Em seu sentido mais restrito, aplica-se ao ofício especial do apostolado (ver Efé. 4:11). Os sinais confirmatórios do apostolado são: 1. Tinham de ser testemunhas oculares (Atos 1:21,22; I Cor. 9:1) escolhidas pelo próprio Cristo. 2. Eram dotados de poderes miraculosos, como suas credenciais (Mat. 10:1; Atos 5:15,16). 3. Eram *preceptores especiais*, tanto do reino como da igreja (Mat. 10:5,6; Efé. 2:20). 4. Um serviço definido esperava-os no futuro (Mat. 19:28).

De modo geral, isto é, quanto aos que recebem postos elevados, há apóstolos na igreja até hoje e em todos os tempos. No sentido mais restrito, quanto ao ofício propriamente dito, não há provas de que o apostolado perdure na igreja até hoje e os que tomam

APÓSTOLOS (APOSTOLADO)

esse título não apresentam as qualificações ou credenciais do apostolado. A sucessão apostólica é pura imaginação e tradição, sem base nas Escrituras e na experiência humana, isto é, a experiência humana demonstra que àqueles que se fazem apóstolos faltam as qualificações apostólicas.

V. As Qualificações Especiais dos Apóstolos

1. Ter sido **testemunha ocular** das obras, da vida, da morte e da ressurreição do Senhor Jesus. (Ver Atos 1:16-26; e também João 15:27, onde o Senhor aborda a mesma necessidade).

2. Ter sido *escolhido* pelo próprio Cristo. (Ver I Cor. 9:1 e Gál. 1:1).

3. *Obras miraculosas* e um ministério especial autenticavam a validade do ofício apostólico. (Ver Mat. 10:1 e Atos 5:15,16).

4. Os apóstolos seriam os *precursores*, tanto da igreja cristã como do reino de Deus. (Ver Mat. 10:5,6 e Efé. 2:20).

5. Teriam os apóstolos um *ofício especial*, de tal modo que até mesmo no futuro aguarda-os um serviço especial, que nenhum dos outros pode preencher. (Ver Mat. 19:28).

Deveria tornar-se óbvio para nós, com base nessas qualificações, que não pode haver transferência do ofício apostólico para terceiros. Em sentido secundário, todavia, outros têm sido e podem ser chamados de «apóstolos», como, por exemplo, foi o caso de Barnabé. (Ver Atos 14:14). No entanto, há um apostolado que pertence exclusivamente *aos doze*, ofício esse contrastado com os ofícios menores da igreja, tais como os de profetas, evangelistas, pastores e mestres, etc. (Ver Efé. 4:11).

VI. A Autoridade dos Apóstolos. Ver o artigo geral sobre Autoridade.

A autoridade religiosa que antes estivera investida no sinédrio, que entre os judeus da época apostólica inicial era considerado como a autoridade religiosa máxima, entre os cristãos estava investida nos apóstolos e profetas. O evangelho de Mateus, que provavelmente foi escrito após a destruição de Jerusalém (no ano 70 D.C.), ao procurar uma autoridade que suplantasse o poder então desaparecido do sinédrio, encontrou-o em Pedro, «primus interpares» dos apóstolos (ver Mat. 16:18 e *ss*). Todavia, o evangelho de João refletiu um ponto de vista mais amplo, investindo todos os apóstolos, e não somente Simão Pedro, dessa autoridade (ver João 20:22,23). E a epístola aos Efésios amplia ainda mais a visão nesse sentido, incluindo os «apóstolos e profetas» nesse quadro (ver Efé. 2:20). Todavia, referindo-se somente aos apóstolos, consideremos os pontos seguintes:

1. Os apóstolos são chamados *fundamento* da igreja (ver Efé. 2:20).

2. Os apóstolos foram os receptadores originais da revelação cristã distintiva (ver Efé. 3:5).

3. Portanto, devido à sua natureza e caráter sem-par, esse ofício apostólico não pode ser transferido. Portanto, a noção de «sucessão apostólica» é um dogma humano, e não uma doutrina do N.T. Entretanto, em sentido secundário, ainda há apóstolos, homens de elevada autoridade conferida por Deus, os quais têm a cumprir serviços especiais de grande importância na igreja.

Os apóstolos originais, porém, eram: 1. Testemunhas especiais da ressurreição de Cristo. 2. Ministros especiais que agiam como representantes de Cristo, efetuando sua obra. 3. Estavam dotados de poderes especiais, tanto na organização como na edificação da igreja cristã, sendo poderosas figuras evangelizadoras cujo trabalho tendia a multiplicar o número dos participantes da igreja.

As marcas distintivas de um apóstolo eram: uma comissão direta da parte de Cristo; eram testemunhas da ressurreição; inspiração especial; autoridade suprema; confirmação por milagres; comissão ilimitada para pregar e fundar igrejas.

Suas características eram a chamada da parte do próprio Cristo (ver Gál. 1:1); a operação de milagres (ver II Cor. 12:12); a superintendência das igrejas em todas as terras (ver Mat. 28:19 e II Cor. 11:28); e, principalmente, o fato de serem testemunhas oculares da ressurreição de Cristo (ver Atos 1:22 e I Cor. 9:1).

Todo o testemunho da igreja cristã, toda a crença no Jesus histórico e no que significava a sua vida, a sua morte e a sua ressurreição para a humanidade, repousaria, em última análise, sobre a palavra daqueles «doze» apóstolos, porquanto deles é que procederia todo o material básico e os evangelhos, que são o progenitor do livro de Atos e das epístolas, bem como de todas as revelações subseqüentes de Deus.

VII. A Importância do Ofício Apostólico

1. Embora não existisse igreja cristã desde o princípio do ministério de Cristo, é óbvio, com base nos evangelhos, que aqueles doze homens ocuparam um tipo de posição oficial entre a comunidade dos seguidores de Jesus, pois até mesmo no princípio foram dotados de dons e poderes *especiais*, a fim de poderem desempenhar o seu ministério especial.

2. Embora na igreja cristã primitiva não houvesse qualquer espécie de *colégio oficial*, conforme atualmente pensaríamos no sentido dessa expressão, contudo, os apóstolos constituíam a autoridade básica da igreja. Isso é subentendido até mesmo por este texto, posto que os apóstolos permaneceram juntos, como um grupo, sentindo ser necessário fazer o seu número ser mantido como «doze».

3. O sinédrio foi destruído, juntamente com a cidade de Jerusalém, no ano 70 D.C. Ora, esse tribunal de setenta homens, que constituíam a autoridade civil e religiosa que governava Israel, desde há muito era reputado como a autoridade religiosa da nação. A destruição do sinédrio, pois, deixou um grande hiato no terreno da autoridade religiosa oficial. No tocante à destruição de Jerusalém, — ver o trecho de Luc. 2:41. O décimo sexto capítulo de Mateus mostra uma primeira tentativa de preencher essa ausência de autoridade, e a Pedro foi concedido o sinal de uma autoridade especial. Não obstante, essa autoridade foi posteriormente expandida, incluindo todos os demais apóstolos, segundo vemos em João 20:19-23. Todavia, essa autoridade não era absoluta, no sentido de que nenhum cristão individual tinha opinião a dar a respeito do que os apóstolos tratassem, porquanto o décimo oitavo capítulo do evangelho de Mateus mostra uma forma de processo democrático na solução dos problemas da igreja cristã.

4. Como grupo, os apóstolos formavam o *núcleo* da igreja primitiva, e deles é que procedeu a doutrina oficial da igreja cristã, por meio de pronunciamentos individuais, — da interpretação das Escrituras do A.T., e de seus próprios escritos, uma porção dos quais se encontra atualmente como parte integrante de nosso Novo Testamento. De fato, um dos mais importantes testes aplicados aos livros que deveriam ser aceitos como Escritura, isto é, que deveriam ser reputados «canônicos», no que diz respeito ao N.T., é que estivessem alicerçados sobre a autoridade apostólica, baseados em seu testemunho, direto ou

APÓSTOLOS, EPÍSTOLA DOS — APÓSTOLOS FALSOS

indireto e gozassem de sua aprovação; porquanto não se poderia mesmo esperar que alguém estivesse qualificado como aqueles homens, que estiveram tão intimamente associados com o próprio Senhor Jesus, a escrever de forma autorizada.

5. Os apóstolos foram nomeados *testemunhas especiais* da ressurreição de Jesus, sendo essa a doutrina central da fé cristã, bem como a demonstração irretorquível da verdade das reivindicações messiânicas de Jesus, bem como a grande prova do poder espiritual de sua pessoa, o selo do testemunho de sua vida inteira. Na boca daqueles doze homens, pois, toda palavra foi confirmada, e através deles a recém-formada comunidade cristã tinha a sua autoridade religiosa. Assim, pois, em todos os séculos, incluindo os nossos tempos modernos, a autoridade da igreja cristã repousa, em última análise, sobre os apóstolos. É por essa razão que eles formam o alicerce ou fundamento da igreja cristã, segundo nos mostra Efé. 2:20.

VIII. Sucessão Apostólica
Ver o artigo sobre este assunto (I IB ND NTI Z)

APÓSTOLOS, EPÍSTOLA DOS

Essa é uma carta presumivelmente escrita por todos os apóstolos, incluindo Natanael e Cefas, como uma pessoa separada de Simão Pedro, dirigida às igrejas das quatro regiões do mundo. Essa obra, aparentemente desconhecida para os pais da Igreja, foi descoberta em 1895, na forma de um manuscrito cóptico muito mutilado. Atualmente existe uma completa versão etíope e alguns fragmentos em latim.

Conteúdo. Há uma introdução, seguida por uma enfática declaração de fé em Jesus, como Senhor e Salvador. Há narrativas extraídas dos evangelhos canônicos, com elementos tomados por empréstimo do Evangelho da Infância, de Tomé. Um relato da ressurreição evolui na forma de um diálogo elaborado entre Jesus e os discípulos, com perguntas e respostas. Curiosamente, essa seção contém uma profecia sobre o sucesso das atividades missionárias de Paulo, prevendo sua conversão e zelo fanático. (Cap. 31 ss). Aparece então uma interpretação da parábola das virgens prudentes e das virgens insensatas (43 ss), com várias admoestações atinentes à conduta cristã.

Há uma revelação, dada como um discurso pós-ressurreição, similar ao Apócrifon de João, com afinidades e com idéias *gnósticas* (ver o artigo a esse respeito), embora não realmente gnósticas em sua natureza. De fato, os «hereges» são severamente repreendidos, sendo chamados inimigos de nosso Senhor Jesus Cristo (caps. 1,7). A realidade do corpo de Jesus (combatendo uma doutrina gnóstica) é enfatizada (caps. 11 e 12). Porém, em vários sentidos, a obra está muito aquém da tradição canônica evangélica.

Seu autor conhecia o Novo Testamento, usava o testemunho dos evangelhos e dava uma posição especial a João. Mas misturava isso com material de evangelhos não-canônicos. A Paulo é dado um lugar proeminente, embora suas doutrinas não fossem incluídas no corpo da obra.

Aparentemente a obra originou-se no século II D.C., composta na Ásia Menor, embora alguns prefiram pensar no Egito. Há algum paralelismo com a literatura encontrada nas cavernas de Qumran. O fato de que há um misto de material canônico e não-canônico nessa obra, quase certamente demonstra que, quando a mesma foi escrita, ainda não tinha sido fixado o cânon do NT, nem mesmo no que diz respeito aos evangelhos. (MH Z)

APÓSTOLOS, EVANGELHO DOS DOZE

Ver o artigo **Livros Apócrifos**, sob **Novo Testamento**. Esse evangelho foi mencionado pela primeira vez por Orígenes, em *Luc.* Hom. 1, onde é mencionado imediatamente depois do Evangelho dos Egípcios, e antes dos evangelhos de Basilides, Tomás e Matias. Comentando sobre Lucas (1:1), ele observava que a Igreja dispunha de quatro evangelhos, mas que os hereges tinham muitos evangelhos. Com base nessa observação, concluímos que ele pensava que o *Evangelho dos Doze Apóstolos* era um livro herético. Esse documento tem sido identificado como o evangelho dos ebionitas; mas, se essa identificação não corresponde aos fatos, então nada sabemos sobre o Evangelho dos Doze Apóstolos.

Esse título foi dado a vários outros evangelhos não-canônicos, a saber: 1. O evangelho Cuqueano dos Doze, que pode ter sido o evangelho ebionita; 2. um documento maniqueu, sobre o qual nada se sabe; 3. um documento sírio de data posterior, publicado por R. Rendel Harris; e 4. um alegado evangelho, publicado por Revillout, mas que é apenas uma coletânea de fragmentos cópticos. (Z)

APÓSTOLOS FALSOS

A expressão específica, «falsos apóstolos», aparece no Novo Testamento somente em II Coríntios 11:13. O próprio fato de que Paulo usou tal expressão mostra que na época, o conceito inteiro do apostolado ainda estava sendo definido. Houve doze deles, que se tornaram onze; e então Matias foi adicionado. E, finalmente, Paulo tornou-se o apóstolo dos gentios. É inteiramente possível que alguns dos oponentes de Paulo, em Corinto, realmente se considerassem figuras apostólicas, e de maior valor e estatura que o próprio Paulo.

Características dos falsos apóstolos. 1. Judeus que queriam ver o cristianismo ser transformado em mero ramo do judaísmo, que enfatizavam as obras da lei como necessárias à salvação (ver II Cor. 11:4,12). 2. Eles fingiam-se apóstolos de Cristo, mas estavam introduzindo um evangelho diferente daquele que fora entregue a Paulo (ver Cor. 11:4,13,22 ss). 3. Eram arrogantes e cobiçavam dinheiro e atenção (ver II Cor. 11:9 *ss*, 20). 4. Tacharam Paulo de inferior e cru, pois eram difamadores e competiam com a autoridade estabelecida de Paulo (ver II Cor. 11,5,6). 5. Afastavam-se da pura espiritualidade (ver II Cor. 11:3). 6. Os judaizantes (aqueles que enfatizavam a obtenção da salvação mediante a guarda da lei de Moisés e rejeitavam a doutrina da graça) reivindicavam contar com a autoridade de Tiago (ver Gál. 2:12), embora fosse uma falsa reivindicação (ver Atos 15:24). Ver o artigo sobre os *judaizantes*. 7. Eram falsos por serem autonomeados. Eles tinham uma *missão*, mas não divinamente apontada (ver Atos 15:12). 8. Eram obreiros fraudulentos, desonestos em suas atividades e motivos, buscando apenas seus próprios interesses (ver Atos 15:13). 9. A transformação espiritual deles era apenas superficial, e sua chamada ao ofício apostólico não era autêntica (ver Atos 15:3).

Bode de Judas. Conta-se a história de como certa companhia da cidade de Nova Iorque, nos E.U.A., de nome «Butchers' Dressed Meat Company», criava um animal que veio a ser conhecido pelo nome de *Bode de Judas.* Seu trabalho era o de escolher as ovelhas dos vagões que as desembarcavam na beira do rio, onde havia um matadouro à espera delas. Esse bode começava a trabalhar bem cedo toda manhã, e continuava agindo até altas horas, enquanto houvesse ovelhas a serem conduzidas ao matadouro. Fazia nada menos de dez viagens por dia. Calcula-se que durante sua carreira conduziu quatro milhões e meio de ovelhas para a morte. Isso era possível porque as ovelhas, diferentemente do gado ou dos porcos, seguem um líder, não tendo a necessidade de serem tangidas. E seguem melhor o líder, se tratar-se de um animal branco. Aquele bode era inteligente, bonito e de porte altivo, e assim desincumbia sua tarefa com grande habilidade. Os falsos líderes religiosos podem ser atraentes, inteligentes e eloqüentes. As ovelhas espirituais podem ser enganadas por eles, em detrimento próprio. (I IB LAN NTI)

APÓSTOLOS, Sucessão Dos
Ver **Sucessão Apostólica**.

APOTEOSE
Vem do grego **apó**, «da parte de», e **theoun**, «deificar». É a elevação de um ser mortal à classe dos deuses. Virtualmente todas as culturas dão evidências da transformação de governantes ou heróis a alguma categoria divina. Com o declínio dos costumes republicanos, tornou-se comum a prática no império romano, a saber, a deificação dos césares, enquanto ainda viviam. A perseguição contra os cristãos era estimulada por essa prática, porque os cristãos negavam-se a reconhecer o imperador como um deus. Na teologia grega e na teologia mística posterior, afirmou-se que os crentes, mediante a sua união com Cristo, tornam-se participantes da natureza divina, o que é explicitamente ensinado em II Ped. 1:4, o que também fica subentendido na doutrina da transformação do crente à imagem de Cristo (Rom. 8:29; II Cor. 3:18). Sobre o crente é dito que ele pode participar da plenitude de Deus, por intermédio de Cristo (Col. 2:10), expressão essa que quase certamente implica nessa doutrina. Ver essas referências no NTI, quanto a completas explicações. Há religiões que concebem a salvação, em seus estágios finais, como uma participação finita na divindade, embora sem qualquer estagnação, de tal maneira que não se pode estabelecer um limite à glorificação, que seria um eterno processo.

APRENDIZADO, PARADOXO DE
Um antigo problema levantado nos diálogos socráticos de Platão, e mais tarde encontrados em alguns escritos sobre educação e em certos exames medievais sobre o conhecimento da natureza de Deus. Uma pessoa só pode aprender aquilo que ainda não sabe. Mas, se ela não o sabe, como sabe o que está procurando aprender? Esse paradoxo, na verdade, não passa de um sofisma. (F)

A PRIORI, A POSTERIORI
Palavras latinas que significam «vem antes» e «vem depois». São usadas para fazer distinções entre tipos de declarações ou proposições baseadas no modo como alguém adquire conhecimento das suas verdades. *A priori* indica idéias já aceitas, sem investigação e provas empíricas. *A posteriori* indica verdades obtidas através da investigação empírica. Essas expressões foram introduzidas na filosofia por meio dos escolásticos.

1. Em uma proposição *a priori* sabemos o que é falso ou verdadeiro sem apelar para a experiência, exceto, naturalmente, até onde a experiência se faz necessária para a compreensão dos vocábulos. As proposições analíticas (ver o artigo) são proposições a priori, pelo que todas as fórmulas matemáticas devem ser assim classificadas. Não precisamos fazer nenhum teste para saber que $2+2=4$. Nossa razão nos demonstra isso, e qualquer experiência que declare que isso é falso, teria de ser chamada falsa. Se um animal sempre e necessariamente é negro, podemos dizer que «todos os animais dessa espécie são negros», e a cor negra torna-se parte da própria definição daquele animal. Portanto, não é necessária qualquer investigação para saber se a cor negra é uma característica necessária de tal animal. Se um suposto animal daquela espécie fosse encontrado, que não fosse negro, declararíamos que não se trata daquela espécie, porque a cor negra é essencial àquele animal. Assim sendo, dizer «todos os animais de tal espécie são negros», é uma proposição analítica, *a priori*.

2. A expressão *a priori* também tem sido usada para denotar os meios através dos quais apreendemos alguma *verdade transcendental* que não está sujeita às nossas investigações, e nem precisa disso. José Marechal (1878-1944) acreditava que apreendemos a realidade (o mundo noumenal) com nossos juízos necessários, ou *a priori*. O intelecto tem uma afinidade natural com o Ser Absoluto, ou Ato Puro, e pode apreendê-lo por sua própria natureza, sem qualquer esforço empírico. Os juízos *a priori*, que apreendem verdades transcendentais, têm natureza tanto metafísica quanto psicológica.

3. A expressão também tem sido usada para aludir a qualquer apelo às *probabilidades antecedentes*, ou seja, considerações de teoria geral, em contraste com *informes* mais ou menos diretamente envolvidos com a questão particular em pauta.

Hume supunha que todas essas são idéias derivadas da experiência, ou seja, idéias *a posteriori*. Porém, Platão e Leibniz argumentaram que conceitos importantes, como substância, igualdade, semelhança e diferença são idéias *a priori*, existentes na mente à parte de qualquer investigação. Kant argumentava que esses juízos *a priori* são necessários para a própria realização da experiência e para suas conseqüentes proposições *a posteriori*. Portanto, há categorias mentais *a priori* que então são experimentadas e testadas por meio de uma operação *a posteriori*. Isso equivale a dizer que as *proposições analíticas* podem ser *a posteriori*.

O que é *a priori* está ligado àquilo que é *necessário*, ou não-dependente, ao passo que o que é *a posteriori* está associado àquilo que é *contingente*. Porém, leis *a priori* podem ser detectadas e descritas mediante investigações *a posteriori*. Outrossim, as proposições *a priori* podem ser apenas imaginações ou aproximações, não representando totalmente a verdade, necessária ou não, como, por exemplo, o elaborado sistema hegeliano das tríades, que presumivelmente descreve a natureza intrínseca da realidade. (E EP F P)

APRIORISMO
É a posição filosófica, oposta ao **empirismo** (ver o artigo a respeito), que afirma que a mente traz *idéias inatas* (ver o artigo) embutidas, e que o conhecimento genuíno é e pode ser obtido pela razão, pela intuição e pela experiência mística, inteiramente à parte de qualquer investigação empírica. (F)

APRISIONAMENTO DE PAULO EM ROMA — UMA OU DUAS VEZES?
Ver Julgamento de Paulo perante César e o artigo

sobre Paulo.

APROPRIAÇÃO

1. Em **Kierkegaard**, esse termo aponta para a abordagem subjetiva da verdade. Ele contrastava seu ponto de vista com a abordagem objetiva da ciência, que ele chamava de «aproximação interminável», à qual objetava. A abordagem subjetiva pode envolver a razão, a intuição e as experiências místicas.

2. Na *teologia*, o termo é usado para indicar o modo de proceder lingüístico mediante o qual um atributo que pertence apropriadamente à deidade inteira é atribuído preeminentemente a uma das três pessoas, não por pertencer exclusivamente a ela, mas porque mais se aproxima de Suas propriedades especiais. Assim, Agostinho apropriava unidade ao Pai, igualdade ao Filho e conexão (como laço de amor) ao Espírito. Um antigo exemplo de apropriação se encontra em Rom. 11:36, por meio da interpretação cristã: *Todas as coisas são provenientes* dEle (o Pai), *através* dEle (o Filho) e *nEle* (o Espírito Santo). Idêntico princípio é aplicado às operações da Trindade. Assim, a criação vem do Pai, a redenção vem do Filho, e a santificação vem do Espírito, embora, estritamente falando, todas essas funções sejam operações de cada membro da Trindade. (C)

3. *Do Ensino*. A *apropriação* do ensino é o ato de o tomar como propriedade. Isto se faz de duas maneiras: a. *Aprendizagem*. Pouco vale o ensino se as pessoas que o recebem não são encorajadas ou **forçadas a aprender**. Alguém queixou-se que a *escola dominical* é a única escola que não exige alguma coisa das pessoas, existindo sem provas, sem níveis para passar e sem castigos se os ensinos não são dominados. b. *Prática*. Ensinos dominados pouco valem se a pessoa que os recebe não se interessa em praticá-los. Em qualquer profissão ou trabalho, nada se ganha sem a *prática*. O trabalho do arquiteto só tem valor se um construtor aplica, praticamente, seu trabalho. A verdade da praticalidade dos ensinos foi enfatizada por Tiago: «Sede cumpridores da palavra e não somente ouvintes, enganando-vos a vós mesmos. Pois se alguém é ouvinte da palavra e não cumpridor, é semelhante a um homem que contempla no espelho o seu rosto natural; porque se contempla a si mesmo e vai-se e logo se esquece de como era. Entretanto, aquele que atenta bem para a lei perfeita, e da liberdade, e nela persevera, não sendo ouvinte esquecido, mas executor da obra, *este* será bem-aventurado no que fizer».

APSE

Vem do grego **apsis**, «arco» ou «cúpula». Uma projeção semicilíndrica, coberta por uma meia-cúpula. Derivou-se de um modelo anterior usado pelos romanos, tendo sido uma característica constante das primeiras basílicas cristãs. Evoluiu mais ainda durante a idade média, no estilo gótico.

AQUEDUTOS ANTIGOS

Consideremos estes pontos a respeito:

1. Senaqueribe, de Nínive (em cerca de 700 A.C.), construiu o primeiro aqueduto de que se tem notícia na história. Ele construiu um grande canal de irrigação através de um tributário do Atrus-Gomel, perto da moderna Jerwan. Esse canal foi posto em uma ponte com 30 m de comprimento, com cerca de 10 m de altura, feito com cubos de meio metro, fechados com argamassa.

2. Ezequias construiu um túnel, chamado Siloé (cerca de 650 A.C.), que era um aqueduto.

3. Polícrates de Samos (século II A.C.) construiu eficientes aquedutos.

4. Os aquedutos eram uma das especializações dos romanos. Suas grandiosas obras nesse campo podem ser encontradas em todos os lugares onde dominaram. Eles elevavam seus aquedutos de concreto, com um telhado encimando os mesmos, em uma fileira de elevadas colunas de pedra ou de tijolos. Algumas vezes, por sobre alguma depressão ou ravina, eles construíam arcos sobre arcos. Em Segóvia, em Tarragona e em Esmirna vêem-se duas ou três fileiras de arcos superpostos. O aqueduto de Nemauso (moderna Pont du Gard at Nimes) tinha três dessas arcadas. Mas também havia aquedutos de superfície e aquedutos subterrâneos. De um total de 418 km de aquedutos construídos pelos romanos, 48 km consistem em aquedutos elevados. A *Aqua Appia* foi construída por Ápio Cláudio Caecus, o mesmo que construiu a Via Ápia. Era um aqueduto subterrâneo, levando água do Anio, a 16 km de Roma. Parece ter sido a primeira dessas construções feitas pelos romanos. Há estimativas que dizem que cerca de 750 milhões de litros de água eram trazidos a Roma, diariamente, por meio de aquedutos, para suprir as necessidades de cerca de um milhão de pessoas. Vários escritores queixaram-se do elevado custo de tais construções (ver Plínio, *Ep*. 10:37). Na Palestina, um aqueduto usado para suprir Cesaréia de água deixou alguns traços, o que também se dá com o aqueduto que Pilatos construiu em Jerusalém. Ele usou parte do *corbã* (ver o artigo a respeito), um fundo financeiro dos judeus, o que lhe causou dificuldades com os judeus (ver Josefo, *Guerras* II.ix.4). (CA Z)

AQUENATOM

No egípcio significa **bendito espírito de Atom** ou **benéfico a Atom**. Foi o fundador de Tell El-Amarna (ver o artigo), rei do Egito entre 1370 e 1353 A.C. Também era chamado Amen-hotep IV. Esse nome significa *Amom está satisfeito*. Consideremos estes pontos a seu respeito:

1. Quando adolescente, governou como co-regente de seu pai, a quem substituiu mais tarde como único monarca. Tornou-se herdeiro de um vasto exército e de um estado burocrático governado por sacerdotes. Sua mãe, Tiy, estava investida de grande autoridade, mas não a ponto de ser dominadora. Casou-se com Nefertiti.

2. Negligenciou muitos deveres, preferindo concentrar esforços na reforma religiosa. Em conseqüência declinaram os poderes militar e político do Egito. Seu império no continente asiático perdeu-se, e diminuiu a sua influência em outros lugares.

3. Pelo sexto ano de seu reinado, construiu um grande templo dedicado a Atom, o sol deificado, em Tebas. Mudou a capital de Tebas para Aquenatom, atualmente Tell El-Amarna, que se tornou o centro de sua revolução religiosa. Mudou então seu nome para Aquenatom, e começou a derrubar as divindades mais antigas, destruindo seus monumentos.

4. Sua reforma fracassou em seu propósito essencial, e os sacerdotes das divindades desonradas recusaram-se a reconciliar-se com o rei. Terminou seu

reinado com dificuldades, e sua memória foi obscurecida por seus adversários. Alguns dizem que seu corpo, após a morte, foi vilipendiado.

5. Alguns estudiosos associam esse Faraó com o êxodo dos israelitas, referindo-se à sua débil posição política, o que teria permitido aquele acontecimento. Contudo, ele não pareceu fraco quando teve de fazer coisas religiosas. Mas não pareceu capaz de manter a grandeza do Egito quanto a outros aspectos. Alguns místicos modernos supõem que esse rei é um antepassado remoto do futuro *anticristo* (ver o artigo a respeito), literal ou espiritualmente falando. O anticristo será o grande rei herege do Egito, que virá mudar os sistemas de adoração do mundo, e obliterar o nome de Cristo deste mundo. (DI Z)

ÁQUILA, PRISCILA

Os Nomes. Áquila é o termo grego que significa *águia*. Priscila é o nome grego que significa *pequena idosa senhora*, diminutivo de Prisca, a forma empregada por Paulo. Eles eram marido e mulher, e Paulo sempre os menciona juntos. Eram amigos achegados de Paulo. Áquila era judeu, nativo da província asiática do Ponto (ver Atos 18:2). O nome era comum em seu tempo.

Referências no Novo Testamento. Atos 18:1-3,18, 26; Rom. 16:3-5; I Cor. 16:19; II Tim. 4:19.

Honrados pela Igreja. A Igreja Ortodoxa Grega considera Áquila bispo e apóstolo, honrando sua data a 12 de julho. A festa de Áquila e Priscila cai a 8 de julho, dentro do calendário romano, onde ele é considerado bispo de Heracléia.

Atos 18:2: *E encontrando um judeu por nome Áquila, natural do Ponto, que pouco antes viera da Itália, e Priscila, sua mulher (porque Cláudio tinha decretado que todos os judeus saíssem de Roma), foi ter com eles*

Áquila...com Priscila. Tratava-se de um casal de judeus cuja profissão era a de fabricantes de tendas, o que também pode significar trabalhos diversos em couro, não indicando meramente a fabricação de tendas, as quais, na época, eram feitas de peles de animais. (Ver Atos 18:3).

Áquila era natural do Ponto (que vide), mas o casal evidentemente residia na cidade de Roma até pouco tempo atrás, quando Cláudio baixou um decreto (em cerca de 49 D.C.) que obrigava todos os judeus a abandonarem aquela cidade. Com base nas diversas narrativas que existem a respeito deles, é muito difícil determinarmos se já eram cristãos, quando conheceram o apóstolo Paulo. Existem bons intérpretes de ambos os lados da questão, alguns pensando que a resposta é positiva, e outros, negativa.

Ora, Paulo ficou em companhia deles, em Corinto, por ter a *mesma profissão* que eles, porquanto era costumeiro, entre os judeus, procurarem pessoas de seu próprio meio, não envolvendo apenas a questão racial, mas também a profissão. (Ver as notas expositivas no NTI acerca do versículo três do capítulo 18 de Atos, na parte que versa sobre essa questão). É bem provável que quando estavam em Corinto, em companhia de Paulo é que Áquila e Priscila «arriscaram as suas próprias cabeças», conforme lemos no trecho de Rom. 16:4. (Ver as notas expositivas nessa passagem no NTI). É possível que por intermédio deles é que Paulo sentiu responsabilidade por Roma, como um lugar até onde deveria alcançar o seu ministério.

Quando Paulo partiu de Corinto, esse casal o acompanhou até Éfeso; e nessa viagem foi estabelecido um contato com essa cidade que produziu diversos resultados posteriores para eles. Estando eles ali, foram capazes de instruir melhor ao poderoso e influente pregador Apolo, orientando-o melhor no caminho de Cristo. (Ver Atos 18:18-28). Áquila e Priscila tinham uma congregação que se reunia em sua casa, quando foi escrita a primeira epístola aos crentes de Corinto (ver I Cor. 16:19). É fora de dúvida que desse centro o evangelho se propagou a outros lugares, e em parte, a igreja cristã de Éfeso se tornou poderosa, assim fazendo daquela congregação local um centro do cristianismo.

Algum tempo depois esse casal obviamente regressou a Roma, pois o decreto de Cláudio deve ter sido um tanto afrouxado em seu rigor. (Ver Rom. 16:3). O trecho de II Tim. 4:19 parece indicar uma renovação subseqüente da residência do casal em Éfeso. Alguns estudiosos têm pensado que a referência a Áquila e Priscila, no décimo sexto capítulo da epístola aos Romanos seja uma confirmação da suposição de que esse capítulo, originalmente, era uma pequena epístola escrita para os cristãos de Éfeso, mas que acabou sendo vinculada à epístola maior aos Romanos. (Ver o livro de K. Lake, *The Earlier Epistles of St. Paul*, vol. 1, 1911, pág. 327 e ss). Contudo, não dispomos de qualquer meio para confirmarmos essa conjetura, a não ser que a última porção da epístola aos Romanos realmente não pareça fazer parte original dessa epístola.

É deveras interessante a observação de que o nome de Priscila aparece antes do de seu marido, nas passagens de Atos 18:18, Rom. 16:3 e II Tim. 4:9. Com base nesse fator, alguns eruditos têm pensado que era ela alguma dama romana de categoria social superior à de seu marido. (Ver Ramsay, *Cities and Bishoprics of Phrygia*, 1895-1897, pág. 637). Todavia, esse fenômeno talvez indique que Priscila era elemento de maior proeminência na igreja local. As tentativas para demonstrar que Áquila era membro ou liberto da «*gens Pontia*» ou da «*gens Acilia*», são inconclusivas, tal como também a tentativa de identificar Priscila com os «Prisci», outro clã de nobres. Paulo usava a forma *Prisca*, como nome dela (o que aparece nos melhores manuscritos quando Paulo faz alusão a ela, como em Rom. 16:4), ao passo que Lucas prefere usar a forma diminutiva, isto é, «Priscila».

A. Harnack, em sua obra *Zeitschrift fur die Neutestamentliche Wissenschaft* (I, 900, págs. 16 e s.), conjetura que Áquila e Priscila juntos, mas sob a liderança desta última, teriam escrito a epístola canônica aos Hebreus. Todavia, outros estudiosos têm pensado que o seu autor tenha sido Apolo. Na realidade, porém, não há como averiguarmos o acerto ou não dessas opiniões, que são tão válidas, por isso mesmo, como quaisquer outras. (I IB G NTI)

AQUIM

Forma abreviada de Jeoaquim, que significa **O Senhor estabelecerá**; antepassado de Jesus e descendente de Zorobabel (Mat. 1:14). (S)

AQUINO, TOMÁS DE (TOMISMO)

Viveu entre 1224? e 1274. Teólogo, filósofo e monge dominicano. Nasceu na Itália, filho do conde de Aquino (daí o seu nome) e da condessa de Teatre. Em criança, foi educado pelos beneditinos (ver o artigo), no monte Cassino, em Nápoles. Aos vinte anos, uniu-se à ordem dominicana (ver o artigo a respeito),

AQUINO, TOMÁS DE

e por muitos anos estudou em Paris e em Colônia, sob Alberto o Grande. Aos trinta e dois anos, obteve permissão para ensinar em Paris e desde então foi professor ali e na Cúria Papal em Roma e em Nápoles. Suas obras escritas são volumosas, embora as principais sejam estas: 1. Um *comentário* sobre as *Sentenças* de Pedro Lombardo; 2. *Summa contra Gentiles*, um ataque contra os erros dos incrédulos, principalmente islamitas, mas que contém muitos elementos filosóficos e teológicos, à parte da controvérsia; 3. *Suma Theologiae*, sua obra-prima, sendo um compêndio de exposições breves, sistemáticas, abrangentes e bem pensadas das principais verdades da fé cristã. Desenvolveu-se a partir dos livros de sentenças do último período patrístico e do começo do período medieval, que a princípio eram coletâneas impessoais de extratos (*sententiae*) dos escritos dos pais da Igreja. As *Sententiae* de Pedro Lombardo, sobre as quais Aquino comentou, era um desses esforços. A *Suma Teológica* foi escrita entre 1267 e 1273, estando dividida em três partes. A primeira parte trata de Deus, a segunda do homem e suas relações com Deus, e a terceira trata de Cristo, Sua encarnação e Sua continuação por meio da Igreja e seus sacramentos. 4. *Questiones Disputatae*, discussões sobre temas como verdade, poder de Deus, o mal, etc.

1. *Influências sofridas por Aquino*, e sua influência sobre outros. A princípio ele foi influenciado principalmente por Agostinho, e até certo ponto, sua filosofia-teologia sempre permaneceu atrelada à daquele. Platão sempre havia dominado a cena teológica, pelo menos até onde os teólogos usavam a filosofia para exprimir os seus dogmas. Porém, Tomás de Aquino introduziu Aristóteles como filósofo cujas obras podiam ser usadas para emprestar apoio racional à teologia. Em Aquino, Aristóteles é chamado de «o filósofo». Até a época de Aquino, a maioria dos teólogos ou ignoravam ou se opunham a Aristóteles, e os islamitas usavam-no para expor um ponto de vista do mundo de sabor materialista. Aquino, ao usar as idéias de Aristóteles, levou seus discípulos, outros mestres e as universidades, a se familiarizarem com essas idéias. E elas vieram a tornar-se um permanente veículo para exprimir idéias cristãs.

2. *Com adaptações, Aristóteles torna-se um teólogo cristão*. Tomás de Aquino usava, adaptava e modificava as idéias de Aristóteles, e assim tornou-se muito endividado para com «o filósofo». Em sua abordagem ética geral, na *Suma Teológica*, ele aborda a felicidade, a virtude, as ações e emoções humanas. É fortíssima a influência aristoteliana.

Na metafísica, Aquino aplicava a distinção aristoteliana entre a realidade e a potencialidade (ver o artigo a respeito) a uma larga gama de tópicos e problemas. A madeira, como uma substância, é o que ela é (em sua realidade), mas pode sofrer modificações como quando se aquece e se queima. Essas modificações são chamadas *potencialidade*. As realidades envolvidas nas alterações chamam-se *formas*. Há dois tipos: 1. Formas acidentais, que envolvem mudanças acidentais; 2. formas substanciais, que envolvem alterações na própria substância. A palavra *matéria* foi usada para designar aquilo que tem a capacidade de sofrer modificações substanciais. Todos os objetos terrestres consistem em matéria e forma. Mas, além das entidades *compostas*, também há *formas puras*, como se dá com os anjos, que não têm vínculo com a matéria, e que, por isso mesmo, são todos membros de uma mesma espécie. As coisas e os seres terrestres, por possuírem matéria, podem, e de fato, devem ser de diferentes tipos. Para que haja diferenças entre os anjos, é necessário que pertençam a mais de uma espécie, cada qual com sua forma individual.

A existência de todas as coisas, com a única exceção de Deus, é uma questão de atualização de potencialidade. Todas as criaturas são essências em potencial. Mas Deus combina essência e existência em Um só, pois a Sua existência é *necessária* em sentido ímpar, pelo que Ele é distinto de todas as criaturas, não tendo resultado de qualquer processo, conforme se dá com elas.

Provas da existência de Deus. Neste ponto, Tomás de Aquino também deve muito a Aristóteles. Assim, em sua maneira de pensar sobre Deus, através de «cinco vias» (*quinque viae*), vemos que ele usou idéias filosóficas aristotélicas:

a. Precisamos postular Deus, a fim de explicar os *movimentos* no mundo. Tais movimentos não consistem apenas na mudança de lugar dos objetos, mas também em todos os desenvolvimentos, como se dá com as criaturas vivas, ao que chamamos de crescimento. Se Tomás de Aquino tivesse tido conhecimento dos movimentos dos átomos, sem dúvida teria incluído a idéia. Para explicar os movimentos, temos a idéia aristoteliana de Movedor Inamovível, aquela força cósmica que faz todas as coisas se movimentarem, por serem amadas. E esse Movedor primário é Deus.

b. Argumento *etiológico*. Esse é necessário para postularmos uma «causa» (no grego, *aitios*). Existem causas intermediárias, mas finalmente precisamos admitir uma causa primária, como também o princípio de causa, que faz todas as coisas continuarem ocorrendo. O coração pulsa, mas deve haver muitos fatores contribuintes, incluindo o de natureza cósmica (as condições favoráveis da Terra, dentro do sistema solar), para que essas pulsações continuem. Deus também é esse tipo de causa (sustentadora), e não apenas a Causa primária. Sem a causa não poderia haver o efeito, e portanto, nem a vida e nem a existência de qualquer tipo.

c. Argumento baseado na *contingência* e na *necessidade*. Sem um Ser necessário, outros seres, por serem contingentes, necessariamente desapareceriam da existência. O conceito do ser, por si mesmo, conduz-nos ao seu corolário, o conceito do Ser Necessário. Esse ser é Deus. Esse argumento pode haver sido sugerido pela abordagem aristoteliana da realidade e da substância eterna, o Movedor Inamovível.

d. *Argumento axiológico*. Há graus de bondade, verdade, nobreza e valores morais. Para que nossos juízos sobre essas coisas façam sentido, precisamos postular a Bondade Absoluta, a Verdade Absoluta ou um Ser Supremo em quem estão incorporados todos os valores, o qual é, ao mesmo tempo, o alvo de toda a verdade e ação morais, bem como o inspirador das mesmas.

e. *Argumento teleológico*. Todas as coisas têm um alvo, bem como um propósito demonstrável. O estudo das ciências, em um importante sentido, é o estudo do desígnio que há na natureza, completo com suas invariabilidades. Sem esse fator, não poderia haver ciência. Se há desígnio, então deve haver um supremo Planejador, cuja inteligência garante a teleologia (no grego, *telos*, «fim», «finalidade»). A filosofia de Aristóteles repisa o conceito de desígnio, e Tomás de Aquino inspirava-se no filósofo ao formular esse conceito, embora não tivesse sido o primeiro a utilizar-se desses argumentos racionais. Quanto a uma mais completa exposição da questão, quanto às suas provas, ver o artigo sobre *Deus*, sob «Deus, Provas de Sua Existência».

3. *Abordagem Geral*. Nos parágrafos acima vimos como Aquino aplicava as idéias de Aristóteles. Isso demonstra em parte a sua abordagem, que visava incluir a filosofia aristoteliana dentro do arcabouço da fé cristã. Aquino dizia que a filosofia e a religião se complementam uma à outra. A filosofia enfatiza o exercício da razão, que é saudável à fé, pois Deus, afinal, é o Intelecto Supremo, e as almas humanas são intelectuais, tendo afinidade com Deus (idéias aristotélicas em essência). A fé pode aceitar muitas das doutrinas aceitas pela razão, mas também pode ultrapassar a razão, porquanto a fé religiosa também obtém informações por meio da intuição e das experiências místicas (por meio da revelação e de outras formas). Assim, a fé vai além da razão, embora não a contradiga. Algumas doutrinas repousam sobre a fé e a razão; e outras sobre a fé somente, por meio da revelação cristã, segundo se dá com as doutrinas da trindade e da encarnação, com seus mistérios e implicações. Essas doutrinas dependem da sabedoria de Deus, podendo ser conhecidas apenas imperfeitamente por meio da razão humana.

4. *Teoria Moral*. Tomás de Aquino deu ao catolicismo romano sua teoria ética básica, onde ele também dependeu em muito de Aristóteles. Aquino mostrou sua capacidade de razão e analogia, dando à sua ética uma maciça estrutura, grande gama de idéias, análises completas, e rica interpretação, filosófica e teologicamente falando. Esses desenvolvimentos podem ser encontrados em sua *Suma Teológica*.

Sumário:

a. O homem foi criado como ser moralmente responsável, uma criatura racional cuja própria racionalidade é uma afinidade com o divino, outorgada por Deus. O homem está a meio caminho entre os animais e os anjos, dentro da escala do ser. À semelhança dos anjos, ele possui alma racional; à semelhança dos animais, tem um corpo físico. Seus impulsos e desejos físicos são derivados de suas faculdades apetitivas, sendo essencialmente animais em sua natureza. Mas sua racionalidade lhe fornece os meios para combater as paixões e desenvolver as virtudes. O homem busca o bem segundo sua razão preceitua. Sua razão deveria ser grande e boa, por ter sido criada e inspirada por Deus. Alvos retos são selecionados por Deus, e o homem, se seu aspecto racional for desenvolvido, naturalmente seguirá esses alvos. A queda no pecado não diminuiu essa qualidade em grande escala, embora tenha debilitado moralmente o homem. Não obstante, retém uma digna maneira de pensar. Com base em Aristóteles, Aquino acrescenta aqui o fator teleológico. Há finalidades apropriadas a serem obtidas na ética, e o homem foi programado para isso. O homem possui livre-arbítrio, podendo fazer escolhas genuínas, pelas quais também torna-se responsável. A vontade de Deus é ativa quanto ao homem, e ajuda-o a fazer as escolhas certas. Sem isso, o homem nada poderia fazer. Contudo, há um esforço cooperativo envolvido em toda a ética. O homem não é um autômato.

b. *Os alvos podem ser alcançados*. As quatro virtudes cardeais são a *prudência*, a *retidão*, o *controle-próprio* e a *força de caráter* (influências aristotélicas). Todos os homens, como seres racionais que são, compreendem essas virtudes e podem buscá-las mediante o ato do livre-arbítrio. A razão deve governar essas escolhas. A *prudência*, que é a virtude intelectual, mostra-se proeminente como força diretriz em toda a ação moral. Bons hábitos morais resultam da prática diária, de contínuas boas escolhas. Seu alvo é a *felicidade* (filosofia *eudemonística*, como em Aristóteles). Porém, esse bem-estar não equivale ao prazer (filosofia hedonista), embora tenha seus aprazimentos. Às quatro virtudes aristotélicas, Aquino adicionava as virtudes cristãs básicas: a fé, a esperança e o amor. A origem destas seria a revelação divina. Há necessidade da graça sobrenatural para que essas virtudes sejam constantes no indivíduo. Mas a fé opera em união com a razão, e a razão fortalece a fé. A esperança é criada pela vontade, que assinala o alvo como algo exeqüível. A fé, ajudada pelo intelecto, apossa-se dos princípios transcendentais que precisam ser cridos. O amor fala sobre a união espiritual mediante a qual a vontade é transformada em um esforço sobrenatural. O amor é a mais excelente das virtudes, derivado do amor de Deus.

c. *Ajuda divina*. O homem não pode atingir a busca moral e sua mais alta realização sem a ajuda de Deus. Há diversas ajudas: 1. A lei eterna, na mente de Deus, transmitida à mente humana; 2. a lei natural que prevalece no mundo, e que aponta para os mesmos alvos; 3. leis humanas e decretadas, baixadas pelos governos humanos, que precisam ser obedecidas; 4. a lei divina, conforme é encontrada na Bíblia. Esta última concorda com a lei natural, embora vá além da mesma. O Espírito Santo grava essa lei no coração humano, conferindo ao homem as corretas disposições internas.

5. *Influência de Tomás de Aquino*. Sua influência foi grande, em sua época. Ele fez com que as universidades européias estudassem e aplicassem a filosofia aristotélica. Proveu uma síntese de filosofia e fé, na verdade, uma síntese de tudo quanto se conhecia na época. Destarte, ele figura como um dos grandes pensadores universais, um dos principais teólogos e filósofos, havendo poucos que se rivalizassem a ele. Sua influência continuou poderosa, mesmo após a sua morte. Foi declarado santo pelo papa João XXII, a 18 de julho de 1323, e doutor da Igreja universal pelo papa Pio V, em 1567; e patrono de todas as escolas católicas pelo papa Leão XIII, em 1880, fazendo com que a sua filosofia se tornasse a filosofia universal da Igreja de Roma. Em 1918, o *Codex Juris Canonici* (Código da Lei Canônica) determinou que essa filosofia fosse ensinada nos seminários eclesiásticos.

6. *Controvérsias, e para além das controvérsias*. Vários teólogos, principalmente protestantes, têm objetado à idéia da inteira abordagem filosófica da fé religiosa. Muitas doutrinas tipicamente tomistas têm sido atacadas, mormente aquilo que parece ser uma mui débil ênfase sobre a fé evangélica, a graça e a conversão sobrenatural, e ênfase demasiada sobre a razão e suas realizações. Porém, no caso de um homem como Tomás de Aquino, temos de ir além das controvérsias. Em primeiro lugar, porque ele foi homem de grande piedade pessoal, o que a história inteira confirma. Em segundo lugar, porque ele foi homem de raciocínio profundo, de grande poder de análise; e suas maciças obras contêm tanto bem que se duvida que possam ser rejeitadas sem grande perda. Diz-se que poucos meses antes de sua morte, ao entrar na capela, recebeu poderosa iluminação em uma visão extática. Daí por diante nada mais escreveu, afirmando que seus escritos eram apenas palha, tão grande foi a iluminação que ele recebeu naquela experiência. Assim, a palha de Tomás de Aquino foi maior que o ouro de muitos homens, e sua iluminação foi tão divina que os outros homens só

podiam esperar que a graça divina lhes proviesse igual iluminação, quando estivessem preparados para isso, por meio do desenvolvimento da alma. Durante alguns meses, pois, ele pôs de lado as suas atividades como escritor de pensamentos de palha, penetrando na luz celeste, após ter vislumbrado, de antemão, aquela glória. Sobre isso podemos estar certos.

Bibliografia: AM BENT C E EP P MM

AQUIOR

No hebraico, **irmão da luz**, general dos amonitas que se aliou a Holofernes com tropas auxiliares, em sua expedição ao Egito. Betúlia fechou as portas a Holofernes, e este ficou furioso. Chamou os príncipes de Moabe e Amom para descobrir quem era aquela gente que se opunha à sua passagem. Aquior informou-o que aqueles hebreus vieram da Caldéia, mas deixaram aquele país. E relatou as conquistas deles em Canaã. Assegurou que eles eram invencíveis, enquanto obedecessem a seu Deus. Caso contrário, poderiam ser facilmente derrotados, pelo que a sabedoria no combate a eles dependia de como estivessem andando diante de seu Deus. Altivamente, Holofernes ameaçou de morte a todos, incluindo Aquior, proclamando que Nabucodonosor era o rei do mundo inteiro. Então Aquior foi abandonado amarrado. Os habitantes levaram-no para dentro da cidade, e ele declarou-lhes a questão inteira. O povo implorou a ajuda divina para vindicar o Seu nome. O cerco começou, e Aquior ficou na casa de Ozias, um dos líderes do povo. Holofernes foi morto e todo o seu exército debandou. Vendo isso, Aquior abandonou suas superstições e converteu-se à fé dos hebreus.

AQUIS

No hebraico, **o rei dá**, talvez também chamado Abimeleque, no título de Salmo 134. Foi o rei filisteu de Gate, onde Davi se refugiou por duas vezes, enquanto fugia de Saul (ver I Sam. 21:10-15; 27:1-3). Da primeira vez, Davi correu perigo, pois não havia sido amigável com os filisteus. Para escapar do perigo, fingiu-se insano e foi para Adulão. Da segunda vez, foi bem recebido. Davi recebeu a cidade de Ziclague (na fronteira Israel-Filístia), para nela habitar, garantindo a Aquis que embora assediasse cidades, só era hostil a Judá (ver I Sam. 27:2-12). Após a morte de Samuel, quando os filisteus reuniram um exército para atacar Israel, Aquis convocou a ajuda de Davi, mas os homens de Aquis objetaram, e Davi e seus homens foram enviados de volta (ver I Sam. 28:1,2; 29:2-9).

Outros grandes homens que se fingiram loucos para escapar ao perigo foram Ulisses (Cic. *Off.* iii.26), Higino (f:95, *Schol. ad Lycophr.* 818), o astrônomo Metom (Aelian, *Hist.* xiii:12), L. Junius Brutus (*Liv.* 1:56; Dion. *Hal.* iv. 68), e o rei árabe Baca (Schultens, *Anth. Vet. Hamasa,* par. 535). (ND S UN Z)

A QUO

Vem do latim, **a «da parte de»**, e **quo**, «que». O termo, que faz parte do vocabulário da filosofia escolástica, refere-se à origem de um argumento, ou seja, aos princípios pressupostos e definições de onde se deriva aquele argumento. Deve ser contrastado com *ad quem* (ver o artigo a respeito). (P)

AR

No grego, **aer**. Designava a atmosfera, em contraste com o éter, ou pura região do firmamento (ver Atos 22:23; I Tess. 4:17 e Apo. 9:2; 16:17).

Usos Espirituais e Simbólicos:

1. O céu, de onde desce o julgamento (ver II Reis 1:10, «desça fogo do céu»; no hebraico temos «desça fogo do ar»). As pestilências também viriam dali (ver Deu. 27:22), como também camadas de ar quente, que destroem as colheitas (ver I Reis 8:37).

2. Figuradamente, «bater no ar» ou «falar com o ar» significa agir e falar sem juízo ou compreensão (ver I Cor. 9:26; 14:9).

3. *As potestades do ar.* A expressão, que se acha em Efésios 2:2, indica as várias hierarquias de poderes satânicos, invisíveis para os homens, que existem em grandes números e em muitas esferas, incluindo aquelas próximas da superfície da terra. Satanás é o príncipe dessas potestades ou poderes. No dizer de Efé. 6:12, há «...dominadores deste mundo tenebroso... as forças espirituais do mal, nas regiões celestes...» contra os quais lutamos. Alguns estudiosos vêem aqui referências à antiga astrologia, pensando que a mesma é pelo menos aludida, envolvendo os poderes demoníacos que controlam os ventos, as tempestades, etc. (ver Jó. 1:7). Talvez o uso que Paulo faz da expressão seja uma acomodação a antigas idéias. Nesse caso, ele usou as palavras, mas de modo algum em sentido astrológico. Os antigos acreditavam em muitas esferas satânicas de poderes espirituais, algumas das quais invadiriam o nosso mundo e causariam dificuldades. Paulo certamente compartilhava desse ponto de vista, conforme nos mostram esses trechos da epístola aos Efésios. Ver o artigo sobre *Satanás.* Quanto a mais detalhes sobre as potestades do ar, ver o NTI em Efé. 2:2 e 6:12. (NTI S Z)

AR

No hebraico o seu sentido é incerto, embora talvez signifique *cidade*. Era a principal cidade de Moabe (ver Núm. 21:28; Deu. 2:9,18,29), perto do rio Arnom (Núm. 21:13-15). Ficava localizada a leste do mar Morto. A Septuaginta usa o nome *Seir* para indicar o lugar. Os trechos de Núm. 21:15 e Deu. 2:9,28 usam a palavra como uma espécie de paralelo da própria Moabe, o que significa que a palavra *Ar* talvez fosse usada como outro nome para Moabe. O rei Seom aparentemente a incendiou (ver Núm. 21:38), e Isaías predisse sua ruína (ver Isa. 15:1). Seu nome grego era Areópolis. Ver as declarações de Isaías 17:17.

Quando Israel apossou-se da Terra Santa, Israel foi proibido de ocupar essa área, porquanto não figurava como parte da terra dada por Deus, visto que pertencia aos descendentes de Ló, por decreto divino (ver Deu. 2:9,18,29). O antigo local não é conhecido com certeza atualmente, embora el-Misna seja uma sugestão plausível. (FA ND S Z)

ARA

No hebraico, **caminhante**. Nome de três pessoas do Antigo Testamento e de um lugar.

1. Um dos três filhos de Ula, da tribo de Aser (ver I Crô. 7:39), em cerca de 1500 A.C.

2. Um antepassado da família que retornou do exílio com Zorobabel (ver Êxo. 2:5; Nee. 7:10; I Esdras 5:10), em cerca de 536 A.C. Acerca de quantos retornaram, esse número varia.

3. Um judeu, cujo filho, Secanias, foi sogro de

ARÃ — ARÃ, VÁRIOS POVOS

Tobias (ver Nee. 7:18), em cerca de 536 A.C.
4. Em Josué 13:4, a nossa versão portuguesa diz «Meara», que corresponde a uma expressão hebraica, «de Ara». Esse lugar tem sido identificado com a moderna Khirbet 'Arah. (ID S Z)

ARÃ

Embora em português se escreva sob a mesma forma que no verbete acima, em hebraico significa *cabra selvagem*. O homem desse nome era membro de um clã dos horeus, filho de Disã e irmão de Uz (ver Gên. 36:28 e I Crô. 1:43), em cerca de 1963 A.C. Alguns supõem que há uma conexão entre esse nome e um certo Orém, referido em I Crô. 2:25.

ARÃ (ARAMEUS)

No hebraico, provavelmente **elevado** ou **exaltado**. A palavra tem um sentido amplo, pelo que refere-se a várias coisas.

1. *Um povo*. A palavra refere-se aos *arameus* (ver o artigo a respeito), um povo semítico que vivia nas regiões da Mesopotâmia e da Síria, em várias tribos. Por essa razão, nossa versão portuguesa quase sempre diz «sírios», excetuando em I Crô. 2:23, onde diz «Arã». Ver II Sam. 8:5,6; I Reis 20:20,21; I Crô. 2:23; 19:10,12; Amós 1:5; 9:7; Isa. 7:2,4,5,8; 9:12; 17:3; Jer. 35:11; Eze. 16:57 e 27:16. O nome «Arã» aparece pela primeira vez no século XXIII A.C., em inscrições cuneiformes de Acade. Desde o terceiro milênio A.C., há evidências arqueológicas em relação a nômades chamados Sutú, mencionados nas cartas de Amarna, juntamente com os Ahlamú. Estes últimos são mencionados em alusão ao rei da Babilônia. A presença deles é confirmada na Assíria, em Nipur, em Dilmum e em Salmaneser (1274 - 1245 A.C.). Aparentemente há alguma conexão entre os Sutú e os Aramu, os Kalju e os Ahlamú, embora não se possa determinar a precisa relação entre eles.

2. *Os arameus na história do Antigo Testamento*:
a. *Listas do Antigo Testamento*. O trecho de Gênesis 10 alista Arã como filho de Sem e pai de Uz, Hul, Geter e Más. A porção noroeste da Mesopotâmia é chamada na Bíblia pelo nome de Arã-Naaraim (Gên. 24:10) e Padã-Arã (ver Gên. 25:20; 28:5). Os patriarcas são associados aos arameus (ver Gên. 24:3-10; 25:20,27,43 e Deu. 26:5).

b. Por volta do século XI, os arameus tinham conseguido estabelecer um pequeno reino de vários estados, tendo atingido certa importância ante o declínio da Assíria. Adade-apal-idina (1067 - 1046 A.C.), um arameu, foi levado ao trono da Babilônia pelos assírios, talvez esperando fazer cessar, com essa providência, o avanço dos arameus na direção do sul do Iraque. Os arameus também expandiram-se para o Ocidente, e ali organizaram, na Cilícia, o estado de Samal. Vários outros estados foram formados, alguns deles nas fronteiras de Israel. Sabemos acerca de dois desses, Zobá e Damasco, nas páginas da Bíblia. Davi conquistou a ambos, mas, quando Israel se dividiu em dois, eles obtiveram a sua independência. Saul, Davi e Salomão combateram os arameus, visto que eles ocupavam a distante fronteira norte de Israel. Havia nos estados de Arã-Zorá (título do Salmo 60, que nossa versão portuguesa diz «sírios de Zobá»), Bete-Reobe (II Sam. 10:6, que nossa versão portuguesa diz «sírios de Reobe»), Arã-Naaraim (título do Salmo 60, que nossa versão portuguesa diz «sírios da Mesopotâmia»), e Gesur (I Crô. 2:23). O reino-estado de Damasco era o mais importante deles.

Após o declínio do império de Salomão, as hostilidades entre Israel e esses povos continuaram por mais cento e cinqüenta anos. Ben-Hadade I de Damasco consolidou a força deles e por duas vezes tentou dominar Israel, mas sem obter sucesso. Em seguida, ele estabeleceu um pacto com Acabe, que se uniu à coalizão antiassíria, unindo doze reinos daquela área. — Quando a tarefa imediata estava realizada, e a Assíria foi derrotada, a aliança não se manteve, e Ben-Hadade novamente atacou Israel; mas novamente foi derrotado pelas forças combinadas de Israel e Judá, em Ramote de Gileade, em 852 A.C. (ver I Reis 22:1-35).

Seguiram-se vários ataques assírios contra os arameus, com bons resultados. Disso seguiu-se um grande declínio do reino de Damasco e de suas forças, daí resultando que Damasco eventualmente tornar-se-ia uma província assíria, em 732 A.C. Hana, após uma última tentativa de rebelião, foi derrotado por Sargão II, em 705 A.C. Israel caiu perante os assírios não muito tempo depois, em 721 A.C.

3. *O idioma aramaico*. Os arameus não contribuíram com qualquer coisa de especial para a civilização do Oriente Próximo, exceetuando seu idioma. Esse idioma tem tido uma contínua tradição, - até os nossos dias. Ver o artigo abaixo, sobre o idioma aramaico. (BN ID UN (1957) Z)

ARÃ, O POVO E A TERRA

Ver o artigo geral sobre **Arã (Arameus)** e sobre *Arã, Terra dos Arameus*, abaixo. Algumas vezes, esse termo é usado para designar tanto a terra quanto o povo, como um nome composto. Ver Juí. 10:6 e Isa. 7:1.

ARÃ, TERRA DOS ARAMEUS

Ver o artigo anterior, sobre os **Arameus**. O termo *Arã* refere-se à terra dos arameus, e como tal, é indefinido. Mas, pelas referências bíblicas, parece que a terra começa a nordeste de Israel, incluindo o que atualmente é Damasco e uma grande porção da atual Síria, prolongando-se pelo vale dos altos rios Tigre e Eufrates. No tempo dos patriarcas, o termo aplicava-se mais particularmente à região da Mesopotâmia. No tempo da monarquia, referia-se a Damasco e à área circundante. No Antigo Testamento, o termo é usado em nomes compostos como Arã-Bete-Reobe, Arã-Damasco, Arã-Maaca, Arã-Naaraim, Arã-Zobá e Padã-Arã. (Ver Núm. 23:7; II Sam. 15:8; Osé. 12:12). (ID ND Z)

ARÃ, VÁRIOS POVOS

1. Um dos cinco filhos de Sem. Era pai de Uz, Hul, Geter e Más, na lista das nações, em Gên. 10:22,23. Ver também I Crô. 1:17. Portanto, ele foi o progenitor de um dos povos semitas.

2. Filho de Quemuel, filho de Naor, irmão ou sobrinho (conforme dizem alguns) de Abraão (ver Gên. 22:21), em cerca de 1838 A.C.

3. Um dos três filhos de Semer, da tribo de Judá, na genealogia de Aser (I Crô. 7:34). Ver também Mat.

ARABÁ — ARÁBIA (ÁRABES)

1:13; Luc. 3:33, a genealogia de Jesus. (ID BN UN (157) Z)

ARABÁ
No hebraico, **ermo, deserto**. A Arabá estende-se por mais de 320 km e ocupa partes de três regiões geográficas: a. o vale do Jordão; b. a região do mar Morto e c. a área do sul do mar Morto, até o golfo de Ácaba.

Usos da palavra:
1. *Significado da raiz*. «Seco» ou «queimado», e portanto, um termo que descreve lugares desolados ou desertos (ver Jó 24:5; 39:6; 33:9; 35:1,6; Jer. 51:43).
2. *Usado com o artigo*, vem a significar uma região específica, conforme mostramos acima. No Velho Testamento, quando usada dessa maneira, está associada ao lago de Tiberíades (ver Deu. 2:7; Jos. 11:2; 12:3), e até o mar Vermelho e Elate, ao sul (ver Deu. 1:1; 3:8). O Mar Morto é chamado mar de Arabá, em Jos. 3:16; 12:3; Deu. 4:49; II Reis 14:25.
3. *No plural*. A palavra hebraica *Araboth*, sem o artigo, refere-se às terras desoladas dentro da Arabá propriamente dita, especialmente em redor de Jericó (ver Jos. 4:10; II Reis 25:5; Jer. 39:5), e no deserto de Moabe. Esse território, mediante o uso dessa palavra, é distinguido das terras cultivadas e do platô acima do vale chamado Sede-Moabe (ver Núm. 22:1; 26:3,63; 31:12).
4. Bete-Arabá (que significa «casa de Arabá»), refere-se a um povoado localizado perto de Ain El-Gharba, em Jos. 15:6,61 e 18:22.

Detalhes da Arabá:
1. A região fica abaixo do nível do mar em maior parte de sua extensão a começar com cerca de 209 m de altitude e descendo até 394 m abaixo do mar Morto. O local é o lugar mais baixo que há na face da terra.
2. É o famoso local de Khirbet Qumran, onde foram encontrados os manuscritos do Mar Morto.
3. *Geologia*. Geologicamente, a Arabá é parte de uma enorme falha na crosta da terra, que se estende desde o norte da Síria, na direção sul, entre as montanhas do Líbano e do Antilíbano. Em certo ponto, pode-se notar que houve uma falha (subida ou descida na superfície) da camada geológica, entre seiscentos e mil metros, sendo que a camada separada é visível dos lados opostos da Arabá. Alguma força gigantesca causou isso, talvez um ou mais gigantescos terremotos.
4. *Comércio e riquezas*. A porção da Arabá ao norte do mar Morto era atravessada por várias estradas, especialmente no norte, onde ficava o território de Manassés, em ambos os lados do rio Jordão. O território tornou-se comercialmente importante por causa disso, bem como por seu porto, Eziom-Geber, a porta de entrada principal para a terra de Canaã. Por ali movimentavam-se as caravanas e os negociantes em direção à Arábia, da Índia ou da África. Não há potencial agrícola na área, embora haja depósitos de ferro e cobre por ali. Provavelmente foi por causa desse fato que diz o trecho de Deu. 8:9: «...terra cujas pedras são ferro, e de cujos montes cavarás o cobre». Têm sido encontradas ruínas de diversas refinarias. Havia minas ali desde os dias de Abraão. Salomão edificou uma fundição de cobre e um centro manufatureiro em Eziom-Geber, o maior centro que já foi encontrado nas cercanias.
5. *Pontos históricos de interesse*. A parte sul da Arabá figura nas vagueações de Israel, antes mesmo do povo de Deus entrar na Terra Prometida. Parece que jornadearam de Cades-Barnéia na direção de Eziom-Geber, atravessando uma porção considerável da Arabá. As estações no deserto, alistadas em Núm. 33:37-49, referem-se a uma rota direta através de Edom e Moabe, ficando implícito que o povo de Israel atravessou a Arabá cerca de 32 km ao sul do Mar Morto. Os homens de Israel corromperam-se com as mulheres moabitas em Abel-Sitim (ver Núm. 25), uma parte da Arabá. Abner fugiu e cruzou uma parte da Arabá (ver I Sam. 2:29). Os assassinos de Isbosete atravessaram uma parte da Arabá a fim de trazerem a cabeça da vítima a Davi, em Hebrom (ver II Sam. 4:7). Zedequias, antes de ser levado para a Babilônia, fugiu em direção a Arabá, tendo partido de Jerusalém (ver II Reis 25:4 e Jer. 39:4). O trecho de Ezequiel 47:1-12 prediz que haverá tempo quando um rio fluirá através da Arabá, tornando a região produtiva. Comparar Joel 3:18 com Zac. 14:8. (BAL GL ND Z)

ARABE
No hebraico, **emboscada** ou **corte**. Uma cidade na região montanhosa de Judá, perto de Hebrom (ver Jos. 15:52). Tem sido tentativamente identificada com Khirbet er-Rabiyeh, ruínas existentes a leste de Dumá. (S UN)

ARÁBIA (ÁRABES)
No hebraico, **deserto**. Palavra usada para designar uma grande península no sudoeste da Ásia. Trata-se da maior península do mundo, consiste em uma área desértica com cerca de um terço da área do Brasil. Essa área é mais ou menos retangular em sua forma.

Nos tempos antigos se distinguiam três Arábias, a saber: a Arábia *Pétrea*, que se limitava a O com parte do Egito, ao norte com a Judéia e parte da Síria, ao sul com o mar Vermelho, e a oriente com a Arábia Félix. A segunda era designada pelo nome de Arábia *Deserta*, se limitava ao norte com uma parte da Mesopotâmia, a leste com a Babilônia, ao sul com a Arábia Félix, e a oeste com a Síria e a Arábia Pétrea. A terceira era conhecida por Arábia *Félix*, limitando-se ao norte com as fronteiras sulistas das Arábias Pétrea e Deserta e com a porção mais sulina do golfo persa. (Ptolomeu, Geografia 1.5, caps. 17 e 19, e 1.6, cap. 7). Havia judeus que habitavam em diversas dessas regiões onde se falava o árabe.

Por conseguinte, Lucas, em Atos 2:11, fornece-nos uma descrição, em pinceladas gerais, do mundo antigo que ele conhecia, ou, conforme ele diz no quinto versículo deste mesmo capítulo, «...todas as nações debaixo do céu...» Com isso ele mostrou que muitos povos, dessas tão diversas regiões, ou tinham subido a Jerusalém, para se fazerem presentes à festa do Pentecoste, ou então eram residentes em Jerusalém, embora tivessem vindo originalmente desses países. Eram judeus de raça e religião, ou então eram convertidos à fé judaica, apesar de descendentes de povos gentílicos. Como um agrupamento humano, representavam muitas nacionalidades, idiomas e grupos étnicos.

1. *Restrições bíblicas*. Na Bíblia, a palavra não denota a península inteira entre o Mar Vermelho e o golfo Pérsico, mas apenas a porção norte dessa

ARÁBIA (ÁRABES)

península, ladeando a Palestina (ver Isa. 21:13; Jer. 25:24 e Eze. 27:21). Portanto, a palavra *árabe* (ver Isa. 13:20) denota um habitante dos prados e desertos do norte. Porém, nos livros posteriores do Antigo Testamento — ver II Crô. 21:16 e Nee. 2:19 — bem como no Novo Testamento — ver Atos 2:11; Gál. 1:17; 4:25 — o nome parece ter um sentido mais amplo. Na epístola aos Gálatas a referência provável é ao reino nabateano ao sul de Damasco. Paulo segue a geografia de sua época, ao incluir o monte Sinai na Arábia (ver Gál. 4:25). O reino de Sabá, no sul da Arábia é chamado «reino do sul», em Mat. 12:42 e Luc. 11:31.

2. *Dimensões e localizações modernas.* A Arábia está limitada a oeste pelo Mar Vermelho, ao sul pelo golfo de Áden e pelo oceano Índico, a leste pelo golfo de Omã e pelo golfo Pérsico, e ao norte pelo deserto da Síria. Portanto, a Arábia está cercada por três lados de água, e os árabes a chamam de Jazirat al-'Arab, *ilha dos árabes.* No país que atualmente se chama Arábia, a área forma quase um retângulo, com 2.333 km no sentido do maior comprimento, e com 2.011 km no sentido da largura, ou seja, um terço da área do Brasil.

Os modernos estados árabes. Há a Arábia Saudita que ocupa a maior parte da península, especialmente nas suas partes noroeste e central, e que é riquíssima em petróleo; há o Iemem (na esquina sudoeste); há o Iemem do Sul, Muscate e Omã, ao sul; e há Qatar, Kuwait e outras nações dirigidas por xeques, no leste. Algumas áreas no noroeste, que já foram parte da antiga Arábia, agora pertencem à Síria, à Jordânia e a Israel.

3. *Divisões antigas.* Arábia Petra (na parte noroeste); a Arábia Félix ou Iemem (na parte sul) e a Arábia Deserta (a parte norte).

4. *Rica em minerais.* a. *Ouro* (ver I Reis 10:2,10,15,22; II Crô. 9:1,9); ouro de Ofir (ver I Reis 9:28; Jó. 22:24; Isa. 13:13); em Sabá (ver Sal. 72:15; Isa. 60:6); em Ramá (ver Eze. 27:22); em Parvaim (ver II Crô. 3:6). b. *Prata* (ver I Reis 10:22; II Crô. 9:14,21). c. *Pedras preciosas* (ver Eze. 27:22). d. *Coral* (ver Jó 28:18; Lam. 4:7). e. *Pérolas* (ver Jó 28:18; Mat. 7:6; 13:45; I Tim. 2:9; Apo. 17:4 e 18:12). L. Aristéas diz-nos que a península da Arábia era rica em cobre e em ferro e que ali havia uma intensa mineração.

5. *Esboço da história da Arábia.* a. *História secular.* No segundo milênio A.C., chegaram tribos de fala semítica nessa área, vindas do norte, tendo-se estabelecido nas regiões atualmente ocupadas pelo moderno Iemem e pelo Áden Ocidental. Foi assim que veio à existência o reino de *Sabá* (ver sobre esse reino). A área tornou-se rica por causa de seu comércio. Em investigações arqueológicas têm sido encontradas inscrições provenientes do século VIII A.C. O reino dos sabeus pagava tributo a Tiglate-Pileser III (740 A.C.), rei da Assíria (ver o artigo a seu respeito), o que nos mostra a razão de sua contínua prosperidade. Em cerca de 400 A.C., chegou à proeminência o reino de Maim, ocupando grande parte do reino de Sabá. Foi fundada uma monarquia em Catabá. Em seguida, os quatro reinos de Sabá, Maim, Catabá e Hadramaute flutuaram em poder relativo, até que a área inteira ficou sob o domínio dos himiaritas. Espalharam-se colônias até Omã e norte da Arábia, tendo sido encontradas inscrições que ilustram a vida deles. Na última porção do século IV A.C., o reino árabe dos nabateus, que falava o aramaico, prosperou como um estado dado ao comércio. Isso continuou até bem dentro do período romano. A capital deles era *Petra* (ver o artigo). Para o sul, durante esse mesmo tempo, o reino lianita de *Dedã* se formou (ver sobre Dedã). No primeiro século A.C. formou-se um outro estado árabe, com sua capital em Palmira (ver sobre Tadmor). E na era cristã, esse lugar ultrapassou em muito a Petra como centro comercial, — chegando a rivalizar até mesmo com Roma. b. *Em relação ao Antigo Testamento.* A Arábia é alistada na tabela de nações, em Gênesis 10, onde são mencionados os descendentes de Joctã (ver o artigo) e de Cus (ver o artigo). Tribos do norte da Arábia descendiam de Abraão, através de Quetura e Hagar (ver Gên. 15). No tempo de Jacó, temos dois grupos de descendentes de Abraão, os ismaelitas (ver sobre Ismael) e os midianitas (ver o artigo a respeito). Eram caravaneiros (ver Gên. 37:25,26). Ver o artigo sobre os *nômades.* A Arábia era importante para Salomão, por causa de relações comerciais, mormente no tocante ao porto de Eziom-Geber, no Mar Vermelho, salientada no relato da visita da rainha de Sabá (ver I Reis 9:26-28). Tributo era recebido da Arábia (ver II Crô. 9:14). Josafá, de Judá (no século IX A.C.), em II Crônicas 17:11, recebia tributo dos árabes. Seu sucessor, Jeorão, sofreu um ataque da parte dos árabes, e sua esposa e seus filhos foram aprisionados (ver 2 Crô. 21:16,17), tendo-lhe restado somente Acazias, o mais jovem (ver II Crô. 22:1). No século VIII A.C., Uzias reverteu a situação e reconquistou Elate (ver II Reis 14:22). Os reis do sul da Arábia eram conhecidos por Joel (ver Joel 3:8). Ezequias fez negociações com esses povos (ver Isa. 13:20 e 21:13). Alguns árabes serviram como mercenários na defesa de Jerusalém contra Senaqueribe. Nos dias finais do reino de Judá, os árabes estavam alcançando posição importante como negociantes (ver Jer. 25:23,24; Eze. 28). Gesém, o árabe, tentou impedir Neemias de reconstruir as muralhas de Jerusalém (ver Nee. 2:19 e 6:1), provavelmente porque temia rivais nos negócios. O reino nabateano elevou-se à posição de proeminência, e quando os trechos de I Macabeus 5:39 e II Macabeus 5:8 falam sobre os *Árabes,* referem-se aos nabateus. c. *Em relação ao Novo Testamento.* O trecho de Gálatas 1:17 provavelmente refere-se ao reino dos nabateus, ao sul de Damasco. Paulo segue antigas referências geográficas quando ele situa o Sinai na Arábia (ver Gál. 4:25). O reino de Sabá, no sul da Arábia, é chamado de «sul», em Mat. 12:42 e Luc. 11:31. A rainha «do sul» condenará àqueles que tiveram a oportunidade de ouvir a mensagem espiritual, mas a rejeitaram, porquanto ela veio dos «confins da terra» (a Arábia) a fim de ouvir a sabedoria de Salomão, mas Jesus, que era o grande Mensageiro da mensagem espiritual, era maior que Salomão, e foi rejeitado pelos judeus.

6. *Características da cultura árabe, segundo os indícios do Antigo Testamento e da arqueologia.* Os árabes viviam em tendas (ver Sal. 8:6; 120:5). Usavam camelos para os transportes (ver Gên. 37:25). Eram negociantes que mercadejavam com muitos produtos, como especiarias, ouro, pedras preciosas (ver I Reis 10:2). Vendiam cabras e ovelhas (ver Eze. 27:20-22). Transportavam mercadorias da África para a Índia e para as terras ao redor do Mediterrâneo (ver I Reis

ARADE — ARAMAICO

10:22). Negociavam com escravos (ver Joel 3:8). Aparavam as pontas dos cabelos e deixavam um topete, conforme fazem os beduínos até hoje. Os midianitas usavam brincos de ouro (ver Juí. 8:24). Penduravam correntes nos pescoços de seus camelos, conforme fazem alguns beduínos até hoje (ver Juí. 8:21). Dentre eles surgiram homens dotados de grande sabedoria, como as declarações de Agus e Lemuel, declarações proverbiais típicas do norte da Arábia, algumas das quais foram preservadas nos dois últimos capítulos do livro canônico de Provérbios. Os filhos de Hagar (os ismaelitas) eram chamados «buscadores da sabedoria» (ver Bar. 3:23). Escavações recentes têm descoberto vários monumentos impressionantes, como o templo sabeu do deus-lua Iluncu, em Maribe, grandes represas, canais de irrigação, estátuas em pedra e bronze e excelente trabalho de joalheria. Nos monumentos de pedra do sul da Arábia milhares de inscrições memoriais, históricas e religiosas foram esculpidas. Os nabateus erigiam túmulos espetaculares e templos no estilo greco-romano. Produziam excelente faiança.

7. *A religião árabe*. Os mais antigos árabes eram politeístas. Usavam a palavra Il (similar ao El dos hebreus) em combinações, para designar os seus deuses. Uma importante divindade era o deus-lua, chamado Iluncu, um deus dos sabeus. Além disso, havia o deus Wadd, dos mineanos, o deus Amm dos catabanianos, e o deus Sin dos hadramautianos. A esposa do deus-lua era Sansi, a deusa-sol, e eles tinham um filho, Atitar, a estrela da manhã. No século VII A.C. havia outros deuses como Atarcuruma, Atarsamaim, e talvez a deusa Alilate de Her. I. 131. No século V AC., o nome *hanilat* aparece em uma incrição do Quedar. O Talmude babilônico (Taanith 5b) diz que os habitantes de Quedar adoravam a água, o que talvez seja uma alusão às fontes sagradas, e não à água como uma substância. Os nabateus tinham o deus Dushara, o deus supremo, Alate, a deusa-mãe, e Gade, o deus da sorte. Inscrições safaíticas trazem os nomes Dusara, Alate, Gad-'Avidh e Ba'alsamin. Os deuses pagãos dos árabes incluem al-Lat, al-Uza e Maná, três filhas de Alá, o deus supremo (ver o Alcorão 53:19,20). Os árabes temiam um demônio chamado Jinn (ver Alcorão 72).

Os ritos e as práticas religiosas dos antigos árabes eram similares às que prevaleciam entre os hebreus, incluindo a prática da circuncisão, os sacrifícios de animais, a adivinhação para determinar a vontade divina, com freqüência mediante o lançamento de sortes (comparar *o Urim e o Tumim* dos hebreus, ver o artigo a respeito). Eles usavam incenso e tinham sacerdotes.

Os árabes modernos, naturalmente, são monoteístas estritos, adorando a Alá, o único e supremo Deus. (Ver sobre *o islamismo*). (HIT MON ND REN Z)

ARADE

No hebraico talvez signifique **fuga**, nome de uma cidade e de dois homens.

1. Uma cidade que ficava no sul do território de Judá, no nordeste do Neguebe, cerca de 27 km do sul de Hebrom. Tendo avançado pelo território de Canaã, o rei de Arade fez oposição à passagem deles. Ele os derrotou e inicialmente tomou algum despojo; mas então os israelitas tornaram-se donos do território (ver Núm. 21:1). Há indicações de que Arade era um centro de civilização desde o século IV A.C., e mesmo desde os dias de Abraão. A arqueologia tem demonstrado que Arade era uma cidade de pedras e tijolos, fortificada quase inexpugnavelmente por volta do século X A.C. Referências bíblicas a Arade: Núm. 21:1; 33:40; Jos. 12:14; Juí. 1:16.

2. Um rei que combateu os israelitas perto do monte Hor, mas foi derrotado (ver Núm. 21:1; 33:33,40), em cerca de 1452 A.C. Algumas traduções, entretanto, não trazem esse nome associado ao rei, mas somente ao lugar de onde ele era rei. É o que sucede à nossa versão portuguesa, que o chama de «o cananeu».

3. Um dos filhos de Beriá, um benjamita, um vulto importante em Aijalom (ver I Crô. 8:15), em cerca de 1400 A.C. (AH GL ND S Z)

ARADO

Instrumento usado para arar o solo. Ver o artigo geral sobre a Agricultura. A forma nominal da palavra designa o instrumento. Os arados eram fabricados de diferentes formas, um deles semelhante à enxada. Isso está envolvido na expressão: «...estes converterão as suas espadas em relhas de arados, e suas lanças em podadeiras...» (Isa. 2:4; cf. Miq. 4:3; Joel 3:10). Mas havia arados de formas mais complexas, como aqueles puxados por animais e guiados por um homem, que seguia atrás. A princípio os arados eram feitos de madeira, mas, na época de Davi, começaram a ser fabricados de metal. Acredita-se que o arado foi inventado no Egito, embora tal assertiva seja impossível de demonstrar. Em tempos posteriores, os arados da Palestina consistiam em duas barras que se cruzavam perto do solo. A barra mais próxima dos bois era presa ao jugo, e a outra barra servia de alça onde a pessoa segurava. Arados assim tão primitivos precisavam trabalhar em terra úmida (ver Jer. 14:4), e a área a ser trabalhada teria de ser pequena. Os arados mais sofisticados, porém, utilizavam uma peça de metal que fazia o trabalho.

Usos metafóricos. 1. Paz em contraste com a guerra. A agricultura no lugar da guerra (ver Isa. 2:4). 2. O dever de atarefar-se diligentemente no serviço cristão é simbolizado pelo homem que pega no arado e não olha para trás (ver Luc. 9:62). 3. Também é representado pelo trabalho árduo e servil, como o cativeiro (ver Osé. 10:11), com sua correspondente opressão psicológica. 4. A diligência na prática do mal (ver Jó 4:8; Osé. 10:13). 5. A destruição. Pois Sião seria arada como um campo (ver Miq. 3:12; Jer. 26:18). (S UN Z)

ARADUS

Ver **Arvade**. Aradus é a forma grega desse nome.

ARAMAICO

Um dialeto semita do noroeste, inexatamente chamado caldaico, porquanto era falado pelos caldeus, no livro de Daniel (ver Dan. 2:4 - 7:28). Porém, sabe-se atualmente que os caldeus falavam o acadiano, e assim o termo caldaico foi abandonado, para indicar o aramaico.

1. *Arqueologia*. Os registros históricos dos assírios têm muitas referências a esse idioma, a partir do século XIV A.C. em diante. Várias inscrições

monumentais têm sido encontradas em aramaico, como o selo votivo de Ben-Hadade II, estabelecido em cerca de 840 A.C., descoberto em 1941 perto de Alepo, na Síria. Outros monumentos inscritos em aramaico têm sido encontrados pertencentes ao período persa. Nesse tempo, o aramaico tornou-se a língua franca de todo o sudoeste da Ásia, porque os negociantes a levavam por toda a parte. A partir do século VIII A.C. até o século V A.C., muitos documentos de todos os tipos, falando sobre negócios, pesos, medidas, etc., têm vindo à luz, mediante as descobertas arqueológicas. Porém, a fonte informativa mais rica é a coleção de papiros encontrada em Elefantina, no Alto Egito, com data entre 500 e 400 A.C.

2. *A língua dos judeus*. Após o exílio, os judeus usavam a escrita aramaica para escrever em hebraico, e o conhecimento e o uso do próprio aramaico aumentou. Finalmente, o aramaico suplantou o hebraico, e traduções do hebraico para o aramaico tornaram-se necessárias. A princípio, essas traduções eram feitas oralmente, nas sinagogas; mas finalmente vieram a assumir forma escrita, nos Targumim. Foi então que o aramaico tornou-se a língua comum do judaísmo pós-veterotestamentário, podendo ser visto nos comentários judaicos, como a Mishnah, a Midrash e o Talmude.

3. *Parte do Antigo Testamento*. Os trechos de Daniel 2:4 - 7:28; Esdras 4:8 - 6:18; 7:12-26 e Jer. 10:11 (uma glosa?), foram escritos em aramaico.

4. *O aramaico e o cristianismo*. O cristianismo começou na Palestina, na época em que ali se falava o aramaico. Os gregos chamavam Arã de *Síria*, pelo que o idioma ali falado tornou-se conhecido como siríaco. Jesus e os apóstolos falavam o aramaico típico da Galiléia. As igrejas cristãs da Ásia, como a igreja nestoriana, produziram muita literatura em siríaco (uma forma do aramaico), havendo muitas traduções do Novo Testamento grego para essa língua, as quais fazem parte do testemunho do texto neotestamentário. Ver o artigo sobre os *Manuscritos da Bíblia*.

5. *Nos tempos modernos*. O moderno aramaico ocidental é usado como língua doméstica em algumas poucas aldeias cristãs na área do Antilíbano. O moderno siríaco oriental sobrevive sob a forma de dialetos em alguns poucos e pequenos centros nos montes do Curdistão e em áreas próximas, perto do lago Urmia, embora sob forte influência do árabe. Isso significa que o aramaico é uma das línguas de mais longa tradição contínua na face da terra. (BN ID UN (1957) Z)

ARANHA

Precisamos considerar duas palavras hebraicas, uma das quais aparece em Jó 8:14 e Isa. 59:5, a qual é corretamente traduzida por *aranha* em nossa versão portuguesa; e a outra palavra, que figura somente em Pro. 30:28, que nossa versão corretamente a traduz por «geco», embora haja traduções que erroneamente a traduzem por «aranha». Ver *Geco*.

A aranha é o nome dado a uma classe numerosa e bem definida de artrópodes (animais com pés e com juntas), diferentes dos insetos por terem quatro pares de pernas e serem sem asas. Todas as aranhas são possuidoras de glândulas especiais para a produção de seda. Os fios assim produzidos são usados por esses animais para fazer ninhos, casulos, etc., além de teias, no caso de certas famílias de aranhas, algumas das quais tecem teias bastante complexas. É evidente que o termo hebraico em pauta alude a uma dessas espécies: Isa. 59:5: «Chocam ovos de áspide e tecem teias de aranha...»; e Jó 8:14: «...a sua confiança é teia de aranha»: A palavra aqui traduzida por «teia» é uma palavra hebraica que comumente significa «casa». Seu uso poderia alterar um tanto a metáfora, podendo aludir a diferentes espécies, uma das quais faz um ninho um tanto mais óbvio.

Em Jó 27:18 temos a frase: «Ele edifica a sua casa como a da *traça*, e com a choça que o vigia constrói». Tal tradução reflete a LXX, e o siríaco. Há outras traduções que consideram o texto indefinido, necessitando de reconstituição, alterando a palavra «traça» para «teia de aranha», dando a entender que o perverso é como uma aranha que espreita a sua vítima, prestes a ficar presa em sua armadilha. (Ver Traça). (ID S UN)

ARARATE

No hebraico, **deserto**. Nome aplicado à região entre o rio Tigre e as montanhas do Cáucaso, conhecida como Armênia, mas chamada Urarti nas inscrições assírias. O nome veio a ser aplicado à cadeia montanhosa, e especialmente ao duplo pico em forma de cone, a pouco mais de onze quilômetros separados um do outro, respectivamente com 5.182 m e 4.265 m de altura. O pico de maior altura é chamado Massis pelos nativos, ou então Varaz-Baris; e os persas lhe dão o nome de Kuhi-Nuh, «monte de Noé». Seu cume é perpetuamente coberto de neve. Tradições nativas dizem que a arca repousou sobre sua vertente sul. Mas as inscrições assírias identificam um pico um tanto mais ao sul, a saber, o monte Nish'r, com 2.745 m de altura, comumente identificado com o Pir Omar Gudrun. Há relatos sobre o dilúvio por todo o Oriente, alguns dependentes da narrativa bíblica. Outras, porém, são independentes da mesma. Outrossim, essas narrativas sobre o dilúvio são universais, e supomos que a maioria delas, independentes do relato bíblico. Os sacerdotes egípcios disseram a Heródoto: «Vocês, gregos, são apenas crianças. Sabemos apenas sobre um dilúvio, mas temos registros sobre muitos dilúvios». Os registros geológicos, como a reversão do magnetismo das rochas, indicam que não apenas por uma vez, mas por muitas vezes (talvez até quatrocentas vezes) os pólos têm mudado de lugar, com deslizes conseqüentes da crosta terrestre, produzindo, obviamente, grande destruição e imensos dilúvios. Pensamos que o dilúvio de Noé foi a última dessas grandes catástrofes, e que ainda haverá outras, no futuro. Ver o artigo sobre o *dilúvio*.

No Oriente existem vários montes sagrados, assim feitos pelas tradições, que os identificam com o lugar onde a arca teria repousado, terminado o dilúvio. Portanto, além dos montes de Ararate, há outros picos que são assim considerados, como o Sufued Koh (Monte Branco), onde os afegãos dizem que a arca descansou. O pico de Adão, na ilha de Ceilão é outro desses lugares, sendo curioso que em Gên. 8:4 o Pentateuco Samaritano diga *Sarandib*, nome árabe para Ceilão. Os versos sibilinos afirmam que as montanhas do Ararate ficavam na Frígia. Outros situam-nas na porção oriental da cadeia montanhosa antigamente chamada Cáucaso e Imaus, que termina nos montes do Himalaia, no norte da Índia. As descrições bíblicas, porém, parecem eliminar regiões relacionadas ao Afeganistão, ao Ceilão e ao norte da

Índia, embora alguns advoguem esses lugares como região onde a arca ficou, ao terminar o dilúvio.

1. *Localizando o Ararate*. As únicas outras passagens bíblicas (além do livro de Gênesis) onde a palavra «Ararate» ocorre são II Reis 19:37 (Isa. 37:38) e Jer. 51:27. Nas duas primeiras, faz-se referência à terra para onde fugiram os filhos de Senaqueribe, rei da Assíria, depois que o assassinaram. Tobias 1:21 diz que eles fugiram para «as montanhas de Ararate». Isso indicaria um lugar, e não uma região dominada pela Assíria, embora não muito distante. A descrição adapta-se à antiga Armênia, que agora faz parte da Turquia moderna, em sua porção oriental. A antiga Armênia era um reino a nordeste da Ásia Menor, incluindo o leste da Turquia e da moderna Armênia, que faz parte da União de Repúblicas Socialistas Soviéticas. Se o dilúvio começou quando Noé estava em algum lugar da Mesopotâmia, então as mais elevadas montanhas das vizinhanças, quando baixaram o suficiente as águas do dilúvio, teriam sido as de Urartu (Ararate), correspondendo à informação dada acima.

2. *Descrição do Ararate*. O monte e seu satélite, o pequeno Ararate, mais para suleste, são vulcões extintos, que se elevam espetacularmente em meio à planície plana. O Ararate é um cone irregular, com ombros proeminentes e com um profundo abismo do alto ao sopé do monte, em seu lado nordeste. Seu cume é perpetuamente recoberto de neve, mas a natureza porosa e cheia de cinzas do solo impede a formação de rios, pelo que o monte é quase desnudo de árvores da base ao cume. É ligado ao Pequeno Ararate por uma longa cadeia de quase 13 km de extensão. Tratados de fronteira entre a Rússia e a Turquia (parte da qual era a antiga Armênia) deixaram o Ararate em território turco.

3. *O reino de Ararate*. «Ararate» é a forma hebraica do assírio *Urartu*, nome de um reino fundado no século IX A.C. A região continuou sendo chamada por esse nome muito tempo depois de tornar-se ela Armênia, nos fins do século VII A.C. O reino de *Urartu* floresceu no tempo do império assírio, nas vizinhanças do lago Vã, na Armênia. Esse reino é freqüentemente mencionado nas inscrições assírias como um vizinho perturbador do norte. Sua cultura foi muito influenciada pela civilização da Mesopotâmia, e, no século IX D.C., foi adotada e modificada a escrita cuneiforme para se escrever a língua urartiana, também chamada vânica e caldiana, que não deve ser confundida com o caldeu. A língua urartiana não estava relacionada à acadiana. Cerca de duzentas inscrições em urartiano têm sido encontradas pela arqueologia. Nessas inscrições, a terra é chamada de BIAI-NAE, e sua população é chamada de «filhos de Haldi», uma das principais divindades de sua religião. Exemplares de sua arte e arquitetura têm sido descobertos em Toprak Kale. A antiga capital, Tuspa, era perto do lago Vã, e, nos tempos modernos, em Karmir Blur, uma aldeia próxima de Erivan, na União de Repúblicas Socialistas Soviéticas.

As inscrições de Salmaneser I mencionam Urartu pela primeira vez no século XIII A.C. O reino começou como um pequeno estado entre os lagos Vã e Urmia. Então cresceu até tornar-se uma séria ameaça à Assíria, pelo século IX A.C. Em cerca de 830 A.C., Sardur I encabeçou uma dinastia ali, estabelecendo sua capital em Tuspa. Pelos fins do século VIII A.C., houve a invasão dos cimérios (ver o artigo sobre *Gômer*), e o reino de Urartu praticamente terminou. Houve um breve reavivamento em meados do século VII A.C., sendo possível que o rei Rusa II, daquela época, fosse o hospedeiro dos assassinos de Senaqueribe (ver Isa. 37:38). Não se sabe com certeza como terminou esse reino, mas isso parece ter ocorrido na primeira metade do século VI A.C. Antigas inscrições cuneiformes em persa antigo chamam o lugar de *Armênia*, uma designação indo-européia, mostrando que os povos de raça jafetita provavelmente tinham tomado conta da região, pelo século VI A.C., data dessas inscrições. (AM NA ND UN WHI Z)

ARATES

Rei da Capadócia em 163-130 A.C., derrotado pelo rei sírio Demétrio Soter. Demétrio assim vingou-se do que pensou ser um insulto, quando Arates recusou-se a casar-se com sua irmã. Em 158 A.C., Arates fugiu para Roma, e um pouco mais tarde foi restaurado ao seu trono, na Capadócia. Os romanos escreveram cartas a ele e a outros reis orientais em favor dos judeus, em 139 A.C. (I Macabeus 15:22). Isso ocorreu através da mediação de Simão Macabeu, que enviou uma embaixada a Roma com esse propósito. (Z)

ARATO

No grego, **pedido em oração**. Foi um poeta grego que nasceu no fim do século IV A.C., em Soli (provavelmente Tarso), na Cilícia. Estudou em Atenas e foi amigo de Zeno, fundador do estoicismo. Escreveu o *Phaenonmena*, um tratado de astronomia, popular nos tempos do Novo Testamento. Em Atenas, Paulo citou a primeira linha desse tratado (ver Atos 17:28). Mas essa frase foi tomada emprestada por Arato de Cleantes, um outro poeta estóico. (Ver os comentários sobre Atos 17:28 no NTI, que oferece detalhes, incluindo a poesia aqui aludida). (NTI Z)

ARAÚNA

No hebraico, **forte, heról** ou **senhor**. Um jebuseu que vivia em Jerusalém e era dono de uma eira, onde mais tarde foi construído o templo (ver II Crô. 3:1 e II Sam. 24:16). Davi comprou a eira de Araúna por causa do anjo destruidor que fora enviado para desolar a nação, em conseqüência do pecado de Davi por haver feito o recenseamento do povo (devido ao orgulho). Davi queria o local a fim de erigir ali um altar, na esperança de que um holocausto fizesse cessar a praga (ver II Sam. 24:16 ss e I Crô. 21:18 ss).

A princípio, Araúna recusou-se a vender a sua eira, oferecendo-a gratuitamente, juntamente com bois para o sacrifício e lenha para servir de combustível. Mas Davi objetou ao presente, dizendo que não ofereceria ao Senhor aquilo que nada lhe custara. Assim sendo, Davi pagou seiscentos siclos de ouro pelo lugar e cinqüenta siclos de prata pelos bois (ver II Sam. 24:24; I Crô. 21:25). Os holocaustos foram oferecidos e a praga cessou. Josefo afirma que Araúna era um bom amigo de Davi, que havia poupado a sua vida quando ele fugira de certa feita de Saul (ver *Anti*. vii.13, parte 9). O trecho de II Sam. 24:23 tem sido interpretado por alguns como se dissesse que Araúna era rei por seus próprios direitos. (FA GOR S UN Z)

Representação da Arca do Pacto
Cortesia, Matson Photo Service

ALTAR DO HOLOCAUSTO

A BACIA DE BRONZE PERTENCENTE AO TABERNÁCULO

A MESA DOS PÃES DA PROPOSIÇÃO

ARCA DA ALIANÇA COM O PROPICIATÓRIO

Equipamento do Tabernáculo

ARAUTO Ver **Mensageiro**.

ARBA

Ancestral dos anaquins, e o maior herói da raça. Era um gigante, pai de Anaque. Foi dele que a cidade de Hebrom derivou o seu primeiro nome, Quiriate-Arba, isto é, «cidade de Arba» (ver Gên. 35:27; Jos. 14:15; 15:13; 21:11). Arba «foi o maior homem entre os Anaquins» (Jos. 14:15). Fundou uma cidade que tinha o seu nome, onde mais tarde foi edificada Hebrom. Josué deu a Calebe a cidade de Hebrom como sua herança, por causa de sua confiança em que Deus o capacitaria a expulsar dali os gigantes (ver Jos. 14:6-15). Ver o artigo sobre Anaque (Anaquins). (FA UN Z)

ARBATA

Uma região da Palestina de onde Simão Macabeu trouxe para Jerusalém alguns judeus que corriam o perigo de serem atacados por uma força gentílica (ver I Macabeus 5:21 ss). O sítio moderno é desconhecido, mas alguns têm sugerido a planície onde o Jordão despeja suas águas no lago da Galiléia, a oeste de Samaria, na fronteira com a Galiléia. (Z)

ARBATITA

Gentílico de quem nasceu Abi-Albom (ver II Sam. 23:31), em Bete-Arabá (Arba), também chamado Abiel, em I Crô. 11:32; ele era um dos trinta principais guerreiros de Davi.

ARBITA

Provavelmente um habitante ou natural de Arabe, na região montanhosa de Judá (ver Jos. 15:52). Era epíteto de Paarai, um dos poderosos guerreiros de Davi (ver II Sam. 23:35). A lista paralela diz «Naarai, filho de Ezbai», em I Crô. 11:37. (UN Z)

ARBÍTRIO

Termo associado à solução negociada de disputas, a fim de restaurar a harmonia entre partidos contrários. Nas disputas trabalhistas, isso normalmente assume a forma de convocação de uma terceira parte interessada, como mediadora das negociações. No arbítrio voluntário, as duas partes envolvidas concordam que a terceira parte terá autoridade para estabelecer os detalhes do acordo. No arbítrio compulsório, usualmente o envolvimento das autoridades se faz necessário, para forçar um acordo, por estarem em jogo os interesses vitais da sociedade. O governo intervém quando estão envolvidas questões de segurança ou saúde pública, ou segurança nacional, de tal modo que a tensão se torna intolerável. A interferência governamental é garantida quando umas poucas pessoas, relativamente falando, podem ser causa de caos e confusão para muitas. O arbítrio é a maneira mais satisfatória de solucionar disputas, evitando a violência que a maior parte dos golpes envolve. Reforça o lado da argumentação, e não o espírito partidário. O arbítrio só é empregado após terem começado negociações adequadas entre as partes interessadas, tendo estabelecido então um impasse.

No tocante a ética cristã. O arbítrio é uma aplicação pública do princípio envolvido em Mat. 18:15 ss. Jesus instruiu-nos que primeiro tentássemos resolver nossas divergências a nível pessoal. Se isso não funciona, duas ou três pessoas devem ser chamadas a intervir. Se isso fracassasse, o caso devia ser levado à igreja. No tocante às questões eclesiásticas, Paulo recomendou que as disputas fossem solucionadas sem o recurso de pessoas *estranhas*, sobretudo se essas fossem advogados que resolveriam o caso diante de algum tribunal secular. (Ver I Cor. 6:1 ss.). (H)

ÁRBITRO

No hebraico temos uma palavra usada por mais de sessenta vezes, e que tem sido traduzida de diversas maneiras, como «reprovar», «disputar», «argumentar», «convencer», «julgar». Em Jó 9:33 (onde a palavra é traduzida pelo termo português «árbitro»), o patriarca expressava o desejo de que surgisse alguém que servisse de — mediador — do conflito entre ele e Deus. Ora, esse anelo do coração humano cumpriu-se por ocasião da encarnação. Cristo é o nosso Mediador. «Porquanto há um só Deus e um só Mediador entre Deus e os homens, Cristo Jesus, homem» (I Tim. 2:5).

Na Bíblia portuguesa, em Colossenses 2:18, encontramos a palavra «árbitro», dentro da expressão: «Ninguém se faça árbitro contra vós outros...» Mas ali não temos a palavra *árbitro*, no grego, que é *kpités*, usada por dezessete vezes no Novo Testamento (por exemplo, Mat. 5:25; Luc. 11:19; Atos 10:42; II Tim. 4:8; Heb. 12:23; Tia. 5:9). Antes, naquela expressão, na epístola aos Colossenses, encontramos o presente imperativo do verbo *katabrabeúo*, «decidir desfavoravelmente». Portanto, uma tradução mais correta da expressão seria: «Ninguém decida desfavoravelmente a vosso respeito...»

ARCABOUÇO

Várias palavras hebraicas assim traduzidas referem-se a certas porções do tabernáculo ou do templo, ou às coisas que haviam dentro deles: a. Uma trave ou armação onde ficavam suspensos o candeeiro e os vasos usados no serviço do tabernáculo, quando estavam sendo transportados (ver Núm. 4:10,12). b. Uma braçadeira ao redor da mesa dos pães da proposição, que mantinha as pernas da mesa firmes em seu lugar (ver Êxo. 25:25,27; 37:12). c. Painéis para os suportes das bacias de lavar, no templo (ver I Reis 7:28-36; II Reis 16:17). d. A armação de madeira do tabernáculo por cima da qual as cortinas e as cobertas de peles de animais eram estendidas (ver Êxo. 26:15-29; Núm.3:36). e. Uma referência às janelas e seu madeiramento (ver I Reis 7:4,5; Eze. 41:16). (Z)

ARCA DA ALIANÇA

A **arca sagrada**, tida como lugar da manifestação de Yahweh. Era chamada «arca da aliança», servindo de símbolo visível da presença de Yahweh. O vocábulo hebraico traduzido em português por «arca» significava apenas *caixa* ou cofre. Era transportada pelos sacerdotes em expedições militares, pois julgava-se que ela era motivo de proteção para os israelitas (Núm. 10:33; Deu. 1:33). Essa caixa era feita de madeira de acácia, de forma retangular, com cerca de 1,10 m de comprimento por cerca de 0,70 m de largura e de altura (Êxo. 25:10 - ver especificações e descrições da arca, nesse capítulo). Era forrada de ouro por dentro e por fora, com uma beirada de ouro. Tinha quatro pés, cada qual com uma argola de ouro (vs. 12), onde eram permanentemente inseridas varas de madeira de acácia recobertas de ouro (vs. 13-15).

ARCA DE NOÉ

Vários povos da antiguidade tiveram caixas sagradas, onde eram guardados os ídolos, símbolos dos ídolos ou outras relíquias sagradas. Naturalmente, várias nações circunvizinhas consideravam a arca como o deus de Israel, ou associada a alguma forma de idolatria física (I Sam. 4:6,7). A arca foi capturada pelos filisteus na segunda batalha de Ebenezer, o que só trouxe infortúnios para eles, de tal modo que a devolveram aos israelitas (ver I Sam. 4-6). Ficou em Quiriate-Jearim até que Davi a instalou no novo santuário de Jerusalém. Subseqüentemente, foi transferida para o templo de Salomão e colocada no Santo dos Santos (ver II Sam. 6 e I Reis 8:1-11). Nela estavam guardadas as duas tábuas de pedra, onde haviam sido escritos os dez mandamentos, as condições do pacto divino. Daí deriva-se o nome dessa caixa: arca da aliança. Os outros objetos guardados na arca, como o vaso de ouro com maná e a vara de Aarão, que florescera (ver Heb. 9:4), talvez pertencessem a uma outra época, tendo-se perdido ou perecido de alguma outra maneira, antes da construção do templo de Salomão. O trecho de I Reis 8:9 declara que só as tábuas do decálogo eram guardadas na arca.

A tampa da arca era o propiciatório, lugar onde era aspergido o sangue no Dia da Expiação (ver Êxo. 25:17 e 26:34), uma das mais importantes instituições de Israel. A arca, nesse período de sua história, era vista somente pelo sumo sacerdote, e somente uma vez por ano. Sobre o propiciatório havia os querubins, um em cada extremidade. Em certo sentido, ali ficava o trono místico de Yahweh.

O que sucedeu mais tarde à arca, não se sabe. A tradição afirma que não havia arca no segundo templo (*Menahot* 27b; Josefo, *Guerras*, V.5). No judaísmo há «arcas» que são caixas onde são guardados os rolos da Torah, ou lei. Seja como for, Jeremias predisse que chegariam dias quando não mais se buscaria a arca (Jer. 3:16), porquanto Jerusalém inteira tornar-se-ia o trono de Yahweh.

Símbolos espirituais envolvidos na arca:

1. Era sinal do pacto entre Deus e os homens, ratificado pela lei e inaugurado pelo sacrifício expiatório (Lev. 16:2). Em termos cristãos, representa Cristo, o nosso sacrifício (João 1:29; Heb. 9:24). Há um novo pacto, ou novo testamento (Heb. 7:22 e 9:15).

2. Representava a presença e proteção de Deus (Jos. 3:3; 4:10). Em termos cristãos, isso se concretiza em nosso favor através da missão de Cristo. A providência divina nos é estendida em Cristo (Efé. 1:7).

3. As *teofanias*. Deus pode aparecer e realmente aparece ao homem, comunicando-se com ele (ver o artigo sobre o misticismo). Jeremias percebeu isso quando viu que Jerusalém inteira tornar-se-ia o lugar da manifestação de Deus, mostrando a descontinuação da arca material. Agora Cristo é a teofania de Deus (João 1:14). Em Cristo há *revelação*, porque nEle Deus comunica-se com os homens. No contexto do Antigo Testamento, ver Êxo. 24:22 e Núm. 7:89. No contexto do Novo Testamento, ver João 1:18. O fato de que Deus se revela, prova a verdade que há no *teísmo* (ver o artigo), isto é, que Deus criou, comunica-se, intervém e está interessado em Sua criação. Isso contrasta com o *deísmo* (ver o artigo), ou seja, que há um Deus ou uma força cósmica criativa, mas que teria abandonado a criação, deixando-a ao encargo das leis naturais. (E FA UN WOU Z)

ARCA DE NOÉ

No hebraico temos as palavras **tebbah** e **aron**. A primeira designa a embarcação construída por Noé; e a segunda, a arca da aliança (ver o artigo seguinte). Talvez a palavra original seja o termo egípcio *db't*, que significa caixa (ver Gên. 6 - 9). No livro de Gênesis, *tebbah* designa a embarcação que Noé construiu por mandato divino, a fim de que ele e sua família fossem salvos do dilúvio. Tinha 137 m de comprimento, 23 m de largura e 14 m de altura. Foi construída com madeira de cipreste, embora alguns estudiosos pensem no pinho ou no cedro. Havia três andares e estava dividida em compartimentos. Possuía um respiradouro e uma porta em um dos lados. Foi construída estanque interna e externamente, com o uso de piche (ver Gên. 6:14 - 8:16). O trecho de Gênesis 6:14 tem sido interpretado como se as tábuas fossem mantidas no lugar por meio de ripas (se alguém ler *qanim* em lugar de *qinnim* - ninhos). Se assim sucedeu, então o conjunto inteiro recebeu uma cobertura de betume. No tocante aos três *andares*, alguns têm entendido que isso refere-se a três camadas de tábuas, cruzando-se, formando os lados da embarcação. O respiradouro aparentemente foi feito no teto, para deixar entrar luz e ar. Aparentemente, a arca foi feita apenas para flutuar, sem qualquer meio de propulsão ou controle. Noé recebeu instruções cento e vinte anos antes do tempo do dilúvio (ver Gên. 6:3,13,14; II Ped. 2:5). É possível que o dilúvio tenha sido a última ocasião em que a posição dos pólos se alterou, com o conseqüente desastre ecológico do dilúvio, devido às mudanças de posição na crosta terrestre. Quanto a detalhes sobre essa idéia, e outras informações gerais, ver o artigo sobre o *dilúvio*.

Simbolismo da arca de Noé. Ela simboliza a segurança ante a destruição, ou a salvação em vista do julgamento, provisões da misericórdia e da graça de Deus. Assim Jesus empregou a narrativa sobre a arca, em Mat. 24:38,39; Luc. 17:27. O trecho de Hebreus 11:7 usa a arca como símbolo e exemplo de fé. A passagem de II Pedro 2:5 usa o símbolo da mesma maneira que Jesus. Portanto, a arca é símbolo ou tipo de Cristo, o Salvador.

Sua carga. Noé e sua família, oito pessoas ao todo (ver Gên. 7:7; II Ped. 2:5) e uma parte dos animais imundos, além de sete pares de animais limpos, sete pares de aves e alguns pares de répteis. Alguns têm indagado, com certa razão, se uma embarcação de dimensões bastante modestas, poderia conter representantes de todas as espécies de animais da terra. Dizer tal coisa é um manifesto absurdo, pelo que devemos supor que os animais mencionados são os animais nativos da área onde Noé vivia. As pessoas que têm procurado demonstrar que a arca de Noé poderia conter todos os animais da terra, cada espécie representada aos pares, não têm noção do fantástico número de espécies de animais que existem. Um zoólogo coraria de vergonha se tivesse que declarar que uma embarcação das dimensões da arca poderia conter todas as espécies de animais. Mas, as pessoas que ignoram o fato, também não coram de vergonha.

Há evidências significativas que indicam que o dilúvio foi parcial, apesar de vasto. A China, por exemplo, permaneceu seca, o que explicaria o imenso número de chineses e outros povos amarelos, hoje em dia. Quando ocorrem os grandes cataclismos, eles rearranjam a posição dos continentes. Vastas áreas, antes ocupadas pelos homens, tornam-se fundo de oceanos, e oceanos tornam-se regiões habitadas.

ARCANJO — ARCTURUS

Portanto, esses desastres, embora de proporções gigantescas, nunca são absolutos. Fenômenos dessa natureza são mais amplamente comentados no artigo sobre o *dilúvio*. A arca trazia uma carga simbólica, mostrando o interesse de Deus por *toda* espécie de vida. Ele desejava a preservação e a propagação de todas essas formas de vida, e não apenas da vida humana. Isso fala sobre o amor de Deus como absolutamente universal. Se Deus queria salvar meros ursos e porcos, certamente devia estar interessado por cada ser humano, sem qualquer exceção. Isso é o que afirmam os textos de I João 2:2; João 3:16 e I Timóteo 2:4. Alguns pontos de vista teológicos, entretanto, têm preferido limitar o ilimitado, rebaixar aquilo que é moral e espiritualmente elevado, estabelecendo fronteiras naquilo que não pode ser medido. Uma desgraça! Notemos que o relato sobre a descida de Cristo ao hades, a fim de anunciar a Sua mensagem aos espíritos dos mortos (ver I Pedro 3:18 - 4:6), é dada em conexão com a narrativa do dilúvio. Isso serve para ilustrar ainda mais a qualidade da misericórdia e do amor divinos, aumentando nossa compreensão sobre as dimensões do evangelho. Ver o artigo sobre a *Descida de Cristo ao Hades*. (AM IB ID NTI UN WHI Z)

ARCANJO Ver sobre **Anjo** e **Rafael** (que inclui informação sobre o conceito de **Arcanjos**).

ARCEBISPO, Arcipreste, Arquidiácono
Ver **Bispo** e **Ofícios Eclesiásticos**.

ARCESILAU
Filósofo grego (315-241 A.C.). Nasceu na Eólia, tornou-se chefe da academia platônica (ver *Academia de Platão*), após Crates. Foi fundador da Segunda Academia. Foi um cético moderado e atacou a reivindicação estóica da possibilidade de se obter conhecimento universal. Sua regra, intitulada *eulogon*, asseverava que na vida devemo-nos guiar pela *probabilidade*. O indivíduo deve adotar a mais provável entre opiniões contrárias ou cursos de ação contrários. Foi poderoso apologista, tendo atacado mormente os estóicos. Não dispomos de qualquer de seus escritos, exceto sob a forma de citações em outros autores, principalmente Cícero e Sexto Empírico (ver os artigos sobre eles). (AM E P)

ARCHE
Palavra grega que significa «começo», «origem», «primeira causa» ou «no começo».

1. Entre os filósofos jônios, a primeira substância ou elemento primário.
2. Para os pitagoreanos, aludia à origem da série dos números.
3. Quanto a Platão, ver sob *arquétipo*.
4. Em Aristóteles, o termo refere-se aos princípios de ação, em sentido causal, e aos princípios demonstrativos.
5. No evangelho de João, a palavra refere-se ao Verbo ou Logos, no tocante ao começo absoluto das coisas. Ver sobre o *Logos* no NTI, em João 1:1.

ARCO
Um termo próprio da arquitetura (ver Eze. 40:16,22,26,29). Mas alguns estudiosos entendem que a palavra hebraica, *elam*, talvez signifique *vestíbulo* ou *pórtico*. A área coberta e semifechada diante do templo de Salomão (ver I Reis 6:3) era assim chamada, como também dois pórticos (ver I Reis 7:6,7). Outros pensam que essa palavra aponta para tipos de paredes laterais que se projetam, contendo janelas. Não há nenhuma palavra específica no hebraico com o sentido de *arco*. Era conhecida no Egito desde tempos remotos, e é uma palavra tomada por empréstimo pelos judeus, mas nenhum exemplo foi encontrado até hoje na Palestina ocupada por Israel. (S UN Z)

ARCO DE GUERRA
Ver sobre **Armas, Armadura**.

ARCO-ÍRIS
Refração prismática da luz do sol, refletida nas nuvens, durante ou imediatamente após uma chuva. De um avião, essa refração é vista como círculos concêntricos, mas para quem está no solo é vista como arcos. As palavras de Gên. 9:13, «porei nas nuvens o meu arco», sem paralelo no hebraico e no resto da Bíblia, têm sido interpretadas como o arco-íris. Os rabinos adicionaram o comentário de que o arco já existia, mas que daquela ocasião em diante passou a ser o sinal do pacto firmado com a humanidade, após o dilúvio. Todavia, há alguma evidência de que o termo acádico *gastu*, com o determinativo *kakkab*, é cognato da palavra hebraica que significa «estrela arco», nome que, na literatura, é aplicado à estrela Sírius, o que confunde um tanto a questão.

Os termos do pacto (Gên. 9:8-17) e a menção do relâmpago juntamente com o termo «arco» (Lam. 2:4 e Hab. 3:9-11), empresta peso ao sentido tradicional de «arco-íris». É interessante notar que o arco-íris é indicado pela mesma palavra hebraica que aponta para o arco de um guerreiro (*geset*). Se o arco de Yahweh simboliza a Sua ira, o arco-íris é símbolo de Sua graça. Deve haver alguma relação entre as duas idéias. O arco de Yahweh voltar-se-ia contra as águas, que haviam sido adversárias da humanidade.

O arco-íris caracteriza a cena celeste (Eze. 1:28), noção essa reiterada em Apo. 4:3 e 10:1, onde o termo grego *íris* nunca teve outro sentido além de «arco-íris».

ARCTURUS
Forma latina do grego **arktouros**, que significa *cauda* ou *guarda do urso*, podendo referir-se à constelação da Ursa Maior, ou a uma estrela que parece haver em sua cauda.

Na Bíblia, essa palavra (no hebraico *awsh*) aparece somente em Jó 38:32, onde faz parte de uma lista de constelações, juntamente com o Órion e as Plêiades. A referência é um tanto obscura, pelo que as traduções variam. A Septuaginta diz «estrela vespertina», o que é seguido pela Vulgata Latina; mas essa tradução é apenas uma tentativa. Não há maneira segura de recuperar o que Jó quis dizer, e nem de saber qual cosmologia estava sendo seguida. A melhor opinião, entretanto, parece ser a constelação da Grande Ursa, ou talvez, Albedarã. Posteriormente desenvolveu-se uma elaborada astrologia, embora não saibamos dizer o quanto, ou qual taxa de diferença havia na astrologia dos dias de Jó. A Grande Ursa gira em torno do pólo, e nunca aparece abaixo da linha do horizonte. Os caldeus e os árabes desde tempos remotos davam nomes às estrelas, reunindo-as em constelações. Isso era usado para efeitos de navegação, tendo também assumido sentidos religiosos, com base na idéia de que as estrelas e constelações influenciam os homens e seus destinos. Ver sobre a *astrologia*. (ID FA ND S UN)

ARDATE

Um campo onde Esdras se comunicava com Deus e recebeu uma visão (ver I Esdras 9:26).

ARDE

No hebraico talvez signifique **fugitivo**. Era filho de Bela e neto de Benjamim (ver Gên. 46:21 e Núm. 26:40). Viveu em cerca de 1660 A.C. Em Gênesis 46:21 são nomeados dez filhos de Benjamim. Em Números 26:38,39, há cinco filhos alistados e no versículo seguinte (vs. 40), Arde aparece como filho de Bela. (S Z)

ARDITAS

Pertencentes a Arde, por serem seus descendentes (Núm. 26:40). (S)

ARDOM

No hebraico, descendente. Era filho de Calebe, filho de Hezrom, através de Azuba, sua mulher (ver I Crô. 2:18), em cerca de 1560 A.C. (S)

AREIA

No hebraico e no grego temos apenas uma palavra em cada idioma, para indicar *areia*. E embora as referências à areia sejam numerosas na Bíblia, a areia do Oriente Médio figura apenas por uma vez no registro sagrado - quando Moisés sepultou o egípcio que havia assassinado, na esperança de manter secreto o crime (ver Êxo. 2:12). Todas as outras referências são figuradas, indicando, principalmente, a idéia de um número incalculável.

A área geográfica onde ocorreram os acontecimentos bíblicos contém muitas regiões cobertas de areia ou de dunas. Ao saírem do Egito, e ao atravessarem o deserto do Sinai, os israelitas devem ter marchado sobre a areia durante boa parte do trajeto. Embora o deserto do Sinai seja rochoso, e não arenoso, podem ser encontrados com bastante freqüência, trechos de areia solta. E na Terra Prometida, havia e continua havendo um largo cinturão de dunas de areia costeiras, ao longo das praias do mar Mediterrâneo, no sul da Palestina. Essas dunas tendem por introduzir-se pelo continente, a menos que sejam barradas com florestas plantadas ou com capim alto. Doutra forma, haverá a invasão de uma autêntica «areia do mar».

Sem considerarmos essas areias costeiras, também deveríamos lembrar que, em um clima seco, cada rio ou torrente que lava a superfície nua da terra fica prontamente carregada de areia e entulho, os quais deposita em suas margens, nas áreas planas. Isso nos permite entender melhor a parábola de Jesus, sobre a casa edificada sobre a areia (ver Mat. 7:26). É de presumir-se que tal casa tivesse sido edificada sobre esses depósitos de areia, em algum vale ao lado de um rio, onde facilmente a água chegava, por ocasião de uma enchente.

As referências à areia, como símbolo de um número incalculável ocorrem de Gênesis 22:17 em diante. Não apenas os futuros descendentes de Abraão foram assim descritos, mas também o cereal recolhido e guardado por José, no Egito (ver Gên. 41:49), e mui curiosamente, a sabedoria de Salomão e a amplitude de seus interesses (ver I Reis 4:29). Naturalmente, em Mateus 7:26 a areia também serve de símbolo de instabilidade, por falta de alicerces.

ARELI

Filho de Gade (Gên. 46:16 e Núm. 26:17), antepassado dos arelitas. Cerca de 1700 A.C. Ele foi um dos sete filhos de seu pai. (UN)

AREÓPAGO

No grego, **Colina de Marte** (Ares), o deus da guerra. Trata-se de uma volumosa projeção de pedra calcária, com cerca de 115 m de altura, a noroeste da Acrópolis de Atenas, à qual está ligada por uma estreita língua de terreno mais baixo. Dá frente para o Agorá, o mercado é o centro legal de Atenas dos tempos clássicos e helenistas. O termo Colina de Marte é uma designação latina. Degraus escavados na rocha conduzem ao cume. Ali ainda podem ser vistos bancos, escavados na rocha. Reunia-se ali o tribunal do Areópago. Temos conhecimento desse lugar através de muitas referências literárias e de algumas evidências arqueológicas. Há evidências do alicerce de um edifício, ou, talvez, de restos de altares que ali foram deixados. Na vertente nordeste, quatro túmulos posteriores (da civilização pré-grega) foram escavados na rocha relativamente macia. Certa quantidade de material votivo sugere que a colina a princípio era usada como santuário de algum culto religioso, talvez de *Areia*, e alguns estudiosos supõem que o nome do lugar originalmente se derivou desse designativo. Os latinos chamavam o lugar de *Scopolus Martis, Curia Martis* (Juvenal Sat. ix.101), ou *Areum Judicium* (Tácito, Annais ii.55).

Desde tempos remotos, reunia-se ali o tribunal do Areópago. No começo era uma espécie de concílio da cidade, que cuidava dos negócios da cidade; mas, antes disso, parece que era um lugar onde eram julgados os casos de homicídio. Havia duas pedras lavradas no cume. Uma delas era a *pedra do ultraje*, onde o acusador se punha de pé para expor a sua acusação. A outra era a *pedra da violência*, onde ficava o acusado. Nos dias de Péricles, era essencialmente um tribunal criminal; mas, nos tempos romanos, reverteu a uma gama maior de atividades, incluindo questões de educação e religião. O *tribunal*, composto por um corpo representativo de anciãos e dos cidadãos mais importantes, algumas vezes reunia-se no Stoá Basileios, ou Pórtico Real. É possível que Paulo tenha feito sua exposição do evangelho diante do tribunal no Pórtico, embora possa tê-lo feito na própria colina. A multidão reunida (ver Atos 17:19-22,33), sugere o primeiro caso (ver Atos 17:15-34). Seja como for, Paulo, como apresentador de idéias novas, estava sujeito à censura. Mas também havia a imensa curiosidade da mente grega, que queria ser melhor informada a respeito de estranhas doutrinas, como a ressurreição, advogada por Paulo. O relato parece indicar mais uma investigação do que um julgamento, pelo que não parece que Paulo estivesse correndo qualquer perigo. A narrativa não nos informa acerca de qualquer

AREÓPAGO — Cortesia, Matson Photo Service

ΟΤΙΑΥΤΟΙΤΟΝ·ΘΝ·ΟΨΟΝΤΑΙ·
ΜΑΚΑΡΙΟΙΟΙΕΙΡΗΝΟΠΟΙΟΙ·ΟΤΙ
ΑΥΤΟΙΥΙΟΙ‧ΘΥ‧ΚΛΗΘΗCΟΝΤΑΙ
ΜΑΚΑΡΙΟΙΟΙΔΕΔΙΩΓΜΕΝΟΙΕ
ΝΕΚΕΝΔΙΚΑΙΟCΥΝΗC·ΟΤΙΑΥ
ΤΩΝΕCΤΙΝΗΒΑCΙΛΕΙΑΤΩΝ
ΟΥΝΩΝ· ΜΑΚΑΡΙΟΙΕCΤΕ
ΟΤΑΝΟΝΕΙΔΙCΩCΙΝΥΜΑC·
ΔΙΩΞΩCΙΝΚΑΙΕΙΠΩCΙΝΠΑΝ
ΠΟΝΗΡΟΝΡΗΜΑΚΑΘ’ ΥΜΩΝ
ΨΕΥΔΟΜΕΝΟΙΕΝΕΚΕΝΕΜΟΥ·
ΧΑΙΡΕΤΕΚΑΙΑΓΑΛΛΙΑCΘΕ·ΟΤΙ
ΟΜΙCΘΟCΥΜΩΝΠΟΛΥCΕΝ
ΤΟΙCΟΥΝΟΙC·ΟΥΤΩCΓΑΡ
ΕΔΙΩΞΑΝΤΟΥCΠΡΟΦΗΤΑC
ΠΡΟΥΜΩΝ· ΥΜΕΙCΕCΤΕΤΟ
ΑΛΑCΤΗCΓΗC· ΕΑΝΔΕΤΟΑΛΑC
ΜΩΡΑΝΘΗ·ΕΝΤΙΝΙΑΛΙCΘΗ
CΕΤΑΙ·ΕΙCΟΥΔΕΝΙCΧΥΕΙΕΤΙ
ΕΙΜΗΚΑΝΘΗΝΑΙΕΞΩ·ΚΑΙ
ΚΑΤΑΠΑΤΕΙCΘΑΙΥΠΟΤΩΝ

AREÓPAGO

decisão formal, e isso também sugere que os gregos estavam apenas se divertindo, se envolvendo em mais **alguma especulação filosófica, o que os filósofos gostam de fazer, em vez de jogarem golfe.**

Paulo tomou como seu ponto de partida a inscrição em um altar onde leu: «Ao Deus Desconhecido». E procurou levar seus ouvintes a uma mais decente concepção de Deus, especialmente sobre como Ele se relaciona com o homem. Ele é o Criador e Juiz de todos os homens, e eles Lhe são responsáveis. Em seguida, Paulo expôs a porção distintivamente cristã, citando Jesus Cristo como o Juiz, o que fica comprovado pelo fato de que Deus o ressuscitara dentre os mortos, o que sem dúvida não era um sinal comum. Paulo entregou uma mensagem religiosa sob roupagem filosófica, tendo mesmo citado um poeta grego. Mas obteve apenas uns poucos convertidos, como Dionísio, membro do tribunal, e uma mulher, Damaris, além de uns poucos outros cujos nomes não são dados. A tradição faz de Dionísio, o areopagita, o primeiro bispo de Atenas. A tradição apresenta Damaris como esposa de Dionísio, embora isso seja apenas uma opinião. Alguns comentadores acham que os resultados foram parcos, criticando o uso que Paulo fez da abordagem filosófica. Porém, considerando a difícil audiência que ele teve de enfrentar, os resultados foram espetaculares, tanto mais porque, se a tradição está certa sobre a vida de Dionísio, a ocasião marcou o começo da igreja cristã de Atenas. Justino Mártir, um filósofo grego, nunca abandonou a sua *toga*, sinal da profissão, e obteve grande sucesso na pregação de Cristo por meio de termos e idéias filosóficas. Ele acreditava que assim como a lei serviu de aio para Israel, a fim de conduzir os descendentes de Abraão a Cristo, assim também a porção melhor da filosofia grega, especialmente a de Platão, teve a mesma função no caso dos gregos. Os pais alexandrinos concordavam com essa posição, e ninguém pode negar o poder do ministério de Clemente e de Orígenes. Ver o artigo sobre a filosofia.

Algumas traduções dizem, em Atos 17:22, «colina de Marte». Todavia, o deus «Ares» equivalia a «Marte», o deus romano da guerra. Isso quer dizer que os dois termos podiam ser trocados um pelo outro. Porém, isso só é normalmente conhecido por aqueles que estão familiarizados com a mitologia clássica. A palavra *Areópago*, considerada por si mesma, é ambígua, porquanto pode referir-se tanto ao tribunal judicial como à colina onde se encontrava esse tribunal, e onde os juízes se reuniam. Por isso é que alguns intérpretes têm suposto que Paulo foi levado ali como um réu, para ser julgado em sentido formal. No entanto, o contexto bíblico não indica isso. Pelo contrário, amigavelmente conduziram-no àquele lugar, até às vertentes da colina, onde pudesse estar longe do ruído e da confusão provocada normalmente pelo povo do mercado, a fim de esclarecer com mais vagar o que ele tinha a dizer.

Outrossim, não há qualquer indício na narrativa bíblica de que se tratava de juízes apenas; antes, eram principalmente filósofos, que ansiavam por apresentar a sua argumentação e debate diários, do que os filósofos viviam, como bem se sabe que era costume nos tempos antigos, sobretudo em cidades como Atenas. É possível, entretanto, que o conselho municipal também tivesse sido envolvido na discussão, porquanto parece-nos que esses funcionários tivessem igualmente por função examinar as credenciais dos conferencistas ambulantes. Todavia, Paulo,

sendo um cidadão romano, como também um judeu de raça e formação, embora não estivesse pregando o judaísmo puro, dificilmente seria passível de qualquer acusação ou julgamento formal, porquanto o judaísmo era uma religião oficialmente reconhecida pelas autoridades romanas. Ainda que em *Atenas* se tivesse podido estabelecer alguma distinção entre o cristianismo e o judaísmo, no próprio texto sagrado não há qualquer indicação de que os ouvintes de Paulo se tivessem mostrado hostis para com ele, ou que tivessem tentado levá-lo a juízo.

O conselho municipal do Areópago tinha sua sede na «Stoá Basileios» ou seja, no átrio do rei Arcon; e supervisionava as questões de ordem educacional e religiosa.

Essa colina, chamada *Areópago*, com 115 metros de altura, era o local onde se reunia o tribunal ateniense. Seu nome significa «Colina de Ares». Ora, Ares era o deus da guerra para os gregos. Até hoje se percebem bem os degraus escavados na rocha, bem como bancos cortados na própria rocha, formando três lados de um quadrado. Essa estrutura servia de tribunal e antecede o século V A.C. Essa colina ficava por detrás da «agorá» ou mercado, a noroeste da Acrópole.

O conselho que originalmente ali se reunia, tinha por designação o mesmo nome do lugar, embora em tempos posteriores, e talvez já nos dias em que Paulo ali esteve, — se reunisse no «Pórtico Real» (*Stoa Basileios*, também chamado de «Átrio do Rei»), que ficava no mercado ateniense. Portanto, paira certa incerteza sobre o lugar exato para onde Paulo foi levado, a fim de prestar aquela entrevista. Teria ele sido levado para a colina, ou meramente para um outro lugar do próprio mercado?

O conselho era a instituição mais venerada de Atenas, porquanto a sua base histórica remontava aos tempos lendários. Já havia perdido grande parte de sua autoridade, porém, ainda tinha notável prestígio. Sua jurisdição especial fora transferida para as questões da moral e da religião. Por conseguinte, teria sido perfeitamente natural que um «expositor de deuses estranhos», conforme Paulo lhes parecera ser, fosse chamado à presença desse conselho. Não obstante, tal convocação não parece ter sido formal, e o próprio contexto neotestamentário mostra-nos que ninguém tomou muito a sério o apóstolo. Realmente, como poderiam eles ter levado a sério tal coisa, visto que Atenas era a cidade onde havia mais deuses do que seres humanos?

O *Areópago* recebeu seu nome da lenda que dizia que, naquela colina, Ares fora julgado por haver assassinado ao filho de Poseidom, o deus dos mares, que a mitologia romana identificava com Netuno. De conformidade com essa lenda, Habirrótio, filho de Poseidom, havia deflorado Alcipe, filha de Ares, o qual, prontamente, o matou. Ares teria sido julgado por um tribunal composto de doze deuses, os quais o isentaram de culpa. (Ver *Apolledorus de deorum origine*, 1,3, pág. 193).

Originalmente, quando o tribunal funcionava na própria colina, os juízes costumavam assentar-se ao ar livre, sobre assentos escavados na rocha, em uma plataforma para a qual se subia por um lance de degraus de pedra, que partia diretamente do mercado, evidências dos quais são visíveis até hoje. Um templo de Marte estava situado na entrada do edifício, e o santuário das Fúrias se encontrava em uma fenda partida na rocha, imediatamente abaixo dos assentos dos juízes. A Acrópole se elevava por cima desse conjunto, com o Partenon e a colossal estátua de Atena.

«Foi uma cena vinculada a memórias espantosas de séculos. Aqueles que retrocediam do Areópago para o mercado, como que chegavam à presença de um poder mais elevado. Nenhum outro lugar de Atenas parecia tão apropriado para um discurso sobre os mistérios da religião». (Conybeare and Howson, *The Life and Epistles of St. Paul*).

«Poderemos saber que nova doutrina é essa que ensinas?» Que tremendo contraste entre esse polido tratamento e o brutal tratamento que Paulo recebera às mãos das multidões ululantes de Filipos e de Tessalônica!

«O tribunal dos refinados e polidos atenienses era muito diferente dos magistrados provincianos e grosseiros de Filipos; e os filósofos que procuraram conhecer a Paulo eram muito diferentes das multidões dos tessalonicenses». (Rackham, em Atos 17:19).

Alguns intérpretes pensam que a pergunta feita pelos interlocutores do apóstolo Paulo foi polida, ainda que tinta com uma ponta de sarcasmo e ironia. Seja como for, é óbvio que não houve nessa ocasião qualquer acusação formal. Pelo contrário, houve mais uma demonstração proverbial da curiosidade dos atenienses, o que já os tornara famosos. (I IB ND NTI UN Z)

ARETAS

Nome comum de diversos reis árabes (nabateus) do norte da Arábia:

1. O primeiro desse nome, de que temos notícia, foi contemporâneo de Jasom, o sumo sacerdote judeu e de Antíoco Epifânio, em cerca de 170 A.C. (Ver II Macabeus 5:8).

2. Josefo (*Antiq.* xiii.13,3) menciona um certo Aretas, rei dos árabes, também chamado Obedas (xiii.13.5), contemporâneo de Alexandre Janeu (falecido em 79 A.C.), e seus filhos. Após ter derrotado Antíoco Dionísio, ele reinou sobre a Cele-Síria, tendo sido chamado a governar por aqueles que dominavam Damasco. Juntamente com Hircano, ele entrou na luta em prol da soberania de seu irmão, Aristóbulo, e lançou cerco a Jerusalém. Mas, ante a aproximação do general romano Escauro, ele recuou para Filadélfia (ver Josefo, *Guerras* 1.6,3). Hercano e Aretas foram perseguidos e derrotados por Aristóbulo, em um lugar chamado Papirom, tendo perdido mais de seis mil homens. Escauro mais tarde invadiu Petra, mas teve dificuldades em arranjar provisões e aceitou a oferta que Aretas lhe fizera em dinheiro, a fim de abandonar o lugar (ver Josefo, *Guerras* xiv.5,1). Ao que parece, a gravação feita em uma moeda de um denário mostra Aretas fazendo súplicas quanto a essa questão.

3. Aretas, originalmente chamado Enéas IV, chamado também de Filopatrio, o último dos reis nabateus. Era sogro de Herodes Ântipas. Herodes fez propostas de casamento à esposa de seu meio-irmão, Herodes-Filipe, chamada Herodias, filha de Aristóbulo — irmão deles — e irmã de Agripa o Grande. Em conseqüência disso, a filha de Aretas retornou à companhia de seu pai, e seguiu-se a guerra entre Herodes e Aretas. Esse não foi o único resultado, mas, seja como for, Aretas derrotou Herodes (36 D.C.). Todavia, Roma tomou o partido de Herodes e enviou uma expedição dirigida por Vitélio, governador da Síria. Porém, foi exatamente nessa ocasião que morreu o imperador, Tibério, em 37 D.C., e a expedição foi abandonada. As fronteiras dos nabateus expandiram-se e, finalmente, chegaram desde o rio Eufrates até o Mar Vermelho. O trecho de II Coríntios 11:32 informa-nos que Aretas também tinha autoridade em Damasco, a antiga capital Síria. Portanto, Roma não controlava aquele lugar, e também não sabemos dizer por quanto tempo Aretas ali governou. Não obstante, a região certamente era uma província romana, e nos é impossível pôr em ordem esse quebra-cabeça histórico, porquanto faltam-nos detalhes para preencher os espaços em branco. É possível que o imperador Calígula, que sucedeu a Tibério, tenha dado Damasco a Aretas, o que concordava com sua norma de promover reis vassalos. Seja como for, um de seus primeiros atos foi depor Herodes Ântipas, um antigo inimigo de Aretas, o que pode ter feito parte do acordo. Porém, a data de 37 D.C. (o que significa que isso ocorreu quando Calígula subiu ao trono), é muito tardia para a conversão de Paulo (cuja ocorrência está vinculada ao trecho de II Coríntios 11:32). Os historiadores têm debatido a questão, mas sem atinarem com uma resposta indiscutível, embora pareça provável que Aretas exercia autoridade em Damasco antes de Calígula ter-se tornado imperador; e então, é possível que Calígula simplesmente tenha reconhecido uma situação que já existia. Ver o artigo sobre os *nabateus*. (ID S UN Z)

ARETE

Termo grego que significa «virtude». Para alguns filósofos (como Aristóteles), a vida humana tem seu alvo na *virtude*, isto é, na função perfeita. O termo é usado em grande variedade de modos. (Ver sob *Virtude*). (P)

ARFAXADE

1. Um dos filhos de Sem, pai de Salá. Nasceu um ano após o dilúvio, e faleceu com a idade de 438 anos (ver Gên. 11:12), cerca de 2075 A.C. Foi o avô de Éber, que alguns consideravam o antepassado dos hebreus, embora a questão ainda não esteja resolvida. Alguns vêem as letras finais *ksd* como sugestão aos casdim ou caldeus, mas outros identificam o nome com Arraphka, na Assíria. Uma etimologia iraniana tem sido sugerida, e isso, subseqüentemente, vinculado ao Arfaxade referido em Judite 1:1. Esse homem, de acordo com aquele livro apócrifo, governou os medos. Isso favorece a essa última idéia, embora muitos estudiosos não aceitem a opinião. Portanto, é possível que esse nome seja inteiramente desconhecido fora da Bíblia.

2. Rei da Média, de acordo com Judite 1:1. Cerca de 592 A.C. Todavia, não há certeza de que a narrativa não seja fictícia.

ARGAMASSA Ver o artigo sobre **Cimento**.

ARGANAZ

No hebraico temos uma palavra, **shafan**, que aparece por quatro vezes no Antigo Testamento (ver Lev. 11:5; Deu. 14:7; Sal. 104:18 e Pro. 30:26). Sendo um dos animais referidos na Bíblia, e visto que os judeus não davam nomes científicos à fauna e à flora, isso torna muito difícil a sua identificação. Nossa versão portuguesa opta pelo arganaz, um dos pequenos roedores tipo esquilo, que viviam em árvores, comuns no mundo antigo, pertencente à família dos *Gliridae*. Há versões que preferem o

Hyrax, nome científico de um animal pertencente à família dos coelhos. As descrições em Levítico 11:5 e Salmos 104:18, isto é, que ele rumina, mas não tem as unhas fendidas, e que as rochas são lugares onde se refugiam esses animais, confirmam a opinião dessas outras versões. Os animais da família do coelho não ruminam, mas movem continuamente o queixo, dando a impressão de que ruminam. Esse fato mostra que as descrições bíblicas são singelas, baseadas na observação prática, sem qualquer rigor científico.

ARGILA

Argila é um termo usado para aludir a certo grupo de minerais e rochas, essencialmente compostos de minérios de argila com tamanho de grão de até 4 mm. São silicatos de alumínio hidroso, com uma estrutura de camadas semelhante ao cristal. Aparecem em três classes gerais: 1. kaolinita, eletricamente neutra, composta de duas camadas diferentes, usada na cerâmica, porcelana e vasos de barro. 2. Montmorilonita, com três camadas, não-neutras eletricamente, com certa quantidade de moléculas de água e íons cambiáveis nos interstícios entre as camadas, usadas nas farmácias e na cosmetologia. 3. Ilita, própria para o fabrico de tijolos.

Referências bíblicas. A argila do oleiro (ver Isa. 29:16); a unção de olhos (ver João 9:6); o fabrico de tijolos (ver Gên. 11:3). Os vários tipos de argila, acima mencionados, têm essas diversas aplicações.

Uma vez misturada com água, a argila torna-se plástica, e a menos que a água seja em excesso, essa qualidade não se perde. Em caso contrário, tal propriedade perde-se, e então temos o que nossa versão portuguesa chama de «tremedal de lama» (Sal. 40:2). O aquecimento expulsa a água, resultando disso a dureza da argila. Então podem ser feitos do material tijolos ou cerâmica. As argilas são uma importante porção dos registros arqueológicos, preservando toda espécie de estrutura, inscrições e artefatos.

Os minérios de argila formam-se mediante a alteração das rochas, devido à ação da água e das intempéries. Argila em quantidades residuais é transportada pela água, tornando-se importante elemento na fertilidade dos solos. É com base nesse fato, que talvez tenha surgido a idéia de que o homem teve origem no barro (ver Jó 33:6). As mais recentes descobertas científicas sugerem que as primitivas moléculas orgânicas, que deram origem às moléculas vivas, formaram-se na superfície das camadas de argila, e não nos oceanos, conforme antes se pensava.

ARGOBE

Um distrito em Basã, a leste do lago de Genezaré, dado à meia-tribo de Manassés (ver Deu. 3,4,13; I Reis 14:12; II Reis 15:25). Mas alguns pensam que a referência de II Reis 15:25 alude a uma pessoa, um cúmplice de Peca no assassinato de Pecaías, ou então a Arié, um príncipe de Pecaías, cuja influência Peca temia, pelo que o matou juntamente com o rei. Um texto incerto que deixa a questão em dúvida. Se essa opinião é verdadeira, então o nome Argobe servia para designar tanto uma pessoa quanto um lugar. Que era usado para indicar um lugar é evidente, com base nas outras referências. Antes da invasão israelita, a região era governada por Ogue.

Descrição. Era um planalto elevado, uma espécie de ilha, com cerca de 54 × 32 km de extensão. No trecho de Lucas 3:1, a região é chamada Traconites. Quando foi dada à meia-tribo de Manassés, contava com cerca de sessenta cidades; e as descobertas arqueológicas têm confirmado a informação. Essas descobertas demonstram que havia ali uma maciça arquitetura, com paredes de 1,20 m de espessura, pedra colocada sobre pedra, sem cimento, com enormes tábuas de rocha basáltica, portas e portões de pedra de 45 cm de espessura com gigantescas trancas. Tudo isso dá a impressão que se tratava de lugares habitados por uma raça de gigantes.

As sessenta cidades da área devem ser distinguidas das aldeias de Jair, que pertenciam a Gileade. O trecho de Deuteronômio 3:14 equivocadamente localiza as aldeias de Jair «em Basã», pelo que alguns estudiosos pensam que ali o texto foi corrompido por copistas, embora possa ter sido um erro do autor original, ainda que a possibilidade seja remota. (ID ND S SI Z)

ARGUEIRO

Palavra usada por Jesus para simbolizar uma pequenina falta, em contraste com uma «trave», que simboliza uma falta grave. A palavra grega envolvida refere-se a qualquer *cisco* que o vento pode soprar, e que cai na vista de quem passa (ver Mat. 7:3 ss e Luc. 6:41 ss). A *trave*, também referida por Jesus, era uma peça de madeira de bom tamanho, usada para escorar o telhado de uma casa ou edifício. Jesus referia-se à tendência humana de ver e criticar no próximo as menores falhas, ao mesmo tempo em que se ignora as falhas graves nele próprio. Uma pequena falta é irritante, tal como um cisco que se aloja no olho de alguém; mas torna-se como nada, em comparação com uma grande trave, enfiada grotescamente na órbita da pessoa, um absurdo para indicar uma situação absurda de crítica. (ID S Z)

ARGUMENTO AD HOMINEM

Vem do latim: «argumento dirigido a um homem».

1. Um ataque pessoal contra a opinião de alguém, a fim de mostrar, por exemplo, seu caráter distorcido, ou talvez, sua falta de conhecimento e qualificações, a fim de contradizer qualquer argumento que ele apresente. Nada fica demonstrado contra a sua tese propriamente dita. Tal argumento é falaz.

2. A fim de mostrar que um oponente tem uma opinião, ou opiniões que logicamente sugerem certas conseqüências que ele não quer reconhecer. Em outras palavras, o uso do argumento contra o argumentador, mediante alguma aplicação do mesmo. Esse argumento pode ser válido. Por exemplo: Um político denuncia alguma forma de nepotismo. Mas, uma vez eleito, fica demonstrado que seus associados íntimos guindaram a postos do governo parentes e amigos de todos os graus. Visto que é de se esperar que o político exerça controle sobre seus companheiros de partido, que o ajudaram a ganhar a eleição, ele pode ser responsabilizado pelo nepotismo que originalmente condenara.

ARGUMENTO AXIOLÓGICO

Os graus de perfeição na ética, na estética ou em qualquer ciência ou condição humana sugerem o grau máximo, a saber, o grau divino, a origem de toda perfeição. (Ver o artigo sobre Deus, II. Provas da Existência de Deus, quanto a detalhes).

ARGUMENTO BASEADO NO DESÍGNIO

ARGUMENTO BASEADO NO DESÍGNIO
Ver **Argumento Teleológico**.

ARGUMENTO CLÁSSICO DO RELÓGIO
Ver **Paley, William**.

ARGUMENTO COSMOLÓGICO

Uma completa discussão sobre os vários argumentos em prol da existência de Deus aparece no artigo sobre *Deus*. Os mais importantes entre eles são descritos individualmente. Filósofos e teólogos têm compilado um grande número desses argumentos, mas o que passamos a considerar talvez seja um dos três mais importantes. Os outros dois são o argumento ontológico e o argumento teleológico, cada qual com seu artigo distinto. Ver o artigo sobre o Ambiente, sob o primeiro ponto.

O princípio. O *argumento cosmológico* parte do pressuposto básico de que o mundo (cosmos, criação) não se explica por si mesmo. A idéia grega de que a criação é eterna e não requer explicação, é rejeitada nesse argumento.

1. A própria existência de tanta questão, impulsiona-nos a buscar alguma forma de explicação sobre como o mundo veio à existência. A maciça quantidade e extensão da criação (ver o artigo sobre a *astronomia*) sugere-nos uma *Causa* grandiosa e inteligente, além de explicações que parecem adequadas somente quando usamos o termo *Deus* para falar sobre essa causa.

2. Tudo quanto vemos na natureza desintegra-se e parece *contingente*, e não é autocausado e nem se sustenta por si mesmo. Portanto, buscamos uma espécie de existência de ser separada dessa contingência, que seja permanente e possa agir como causa dessa contingência. E descobrimos a resposta em Deus. É difícil imaginar uma infinita série de substâncias contingentes, cada uma delas, em sucessão, causando outra substância contingente. Quando cessamos de retroceder, encontramos Deus como a Causa da primeira substância contingente. Um Ser necessário e não-contingente, pois, torna-se a base de um argumento separado, que recebe esse nome.

3. Observamos *movimento* na natureza, mas vemos que todo o movimento, como a própria matéria, é contingente. Ao buscar a causa do movimento, Aristóteles postulou um Movedor Inabalável. Nas mãos de Tomás de Aquino, esse conceito tornou-se outro argumento em favor da existência de Deus, uma subcategoria do argumento cosmológico. Deve haver uma Primeira Causa de todo o movimento. O movimento é uma parte integrante da matéria, conforme a ciência moderna nos tem demonstrado em suas investigações sobre o átomo. Então indagamos: Como se iniciou todo esse movimento? Em seu diálogo, *Leis*, Platão argumentou com base na insuficiência dos movimentos derivados para explicar a idéia de automovimentação. A automovimentação é identificada com o conceito divino, ou Deus.

4. Então queremos saber como as coisas podem continuar existindo. Isso envolve uma outra forma de causa e movimento. Deve haver uma causa que sustenta todas as coisas, através da preservação de uma espécie de movimento, a qual envolve desenvolvimento e propósito. A *causa sustentadora* é um aspecto do argumento cosmológico. Descartes desenvolveu esse aspecto do argumento. O trecho de Colossenses 1:17 leva em consideração a necessidade de uma causa preservadora. Deve haver uma hierarquia de causas presentes, e não apenas uma causa primária, a fim de que a vida possa ser sustentada. Quanto a uma declaração mais ampla desse aspecto, ver o artigo sobre o *Ambiente*, 1.

5. *Razão suficiente.* Leibniz indagava: «Por que existe alguma coisa, e não o nada?» Um homem acorda, olha ao seu redor, e sua mente refrescada pelo repouso, maravilha-se de tudo quanto vê. Então crê que deve haver um Deus, em algum lugar, que esteve envolvido em trazer à existência toda essa misteriosa e imensa criação. Para ele, todos os raciocínios negativos, filosóficos e ateus são apenas argumentos astutos, e não explicações das maravilhas e milagres da existência que ele vê ao seu redor. Então sua mente volta-se para algum conceito de Deus como a Causa. Ele quer alguma forma de *razão suficiente*, pois percebe que nisso ele encontrará Deus. O próprio universo parece ser um fato contingente, e não uma explicação da existência. Deus, como razão suficiente nos fornece o *como*. A razão suficiente deve ser encontrada fora do terreno das contingências físicas. Logicamente, pois, chegamos a Deus como O Ser Necessário, e isso, por sua vez, torna-se um argumento separado.

6. *Objeções.* Hume, Kant e J.S. Mill encontraram razões para rejeitar o argumento cosmológico. Hume e Mill pensavam que o infinito retrocesso de causas finitas e de causas contingentes seria um conceito superior ao conceito de uma Causa primária e necessária. Kant sentia que não podemos passar dos fenômenos observáveis para o mundo das noumenas, ou seja, entidades espirituais e não-materiais. Todo o nosso conhecimento dos fenômenos vem através da percepção de nossos sentidos, e segundo ele pensava, não possuímos sentido perceptivo algum sobre o mundo noumenal. Nisso, ele ignorava que o misticismo dá apoio à idéia de que a percepção dos sentidos físicos pode estar envolvida nas experiências espirituais, como uma espécie de mediação. A dicotomia de Kant, portanto, é por demais rigorosa. Outrossim, há outras maneiras de se tomar conhecimento das coisas, através da razão e da intuição, que podem transmitir-nos conhecimentos extra-sensoriais. Seja como for, Kant produziu um poderoso argumento em prol da existência de Deus com o seu *Argumento Moral* (ver o artigo a esse respeito). A existência e a continuação de um princípio moral requer que postulemos a existência de Deus. (EP F P)

ARGUMENTO DE GRAUS DE PERFEIÇÃO
Ver **Argumento Axiológico**.

ARGUMENTO DO MUNDO EXTERIOR DE DESCARTES
Ver **Mundo Exterior, Argumento do**

ARGUMENTO ESPECULATIVO

O argumento especulativo é considerado uma falácia, embora seja livremente empregado na argumentação. Trata-se da adoção de alguma hipótese contrária aos fatos, para que então se edifique alguma forma de argumento ou declaração com base nessa hipótese. Por exemplo: «Se Florence Nightingale não tivesse dado início à Cruz Vermelha, muitas vítimas de desastres não seriam tratadas atualmente». Essa declaração pode ser verdadeira ou não, embora nunca se possa demonstrar sua veracidade ou falsidade. (P)

••• ••• •••

ARGUMENTO FÍSICO-TELEOLÓGICO — ARGUMENTO ONTOLÓGICO

ARGUMENTO FÍSICO-TELEOLÓGICO

Trata-se apenas de um outro nome para o Argumento Teleológico, de Emanuel Kant. Ver o artigo geral sobre Kant, e ver o tratamento sobre esse argumento sob *Argumento Teleológico*. Kant dava a entender, mediante esse argumento, que Deus deveria ser concebido no máximo como um arquiteto, e não como um criador, pressupondo ainda que a validade desse argumento poderia ser posta em dúvida com base no fato de que não temos qualquer percepção de sentidos que capte um Planejador dentro de nosso sistema mundial, e que nos dê o direito de transferir esse Planejador para fora de nosso universo, transformando-o no Deus transcendental, o Deus do céu, o Deus das religiões, de modo geral. Mas Kant estava supondo que o *conhecimento*, sob a forma de proposições, nos chega através da percepção dos sentidos; e através disso, realmente não temos tal Deus. Mas esse **pressuposto** kantiano ignora diversos fatores, a saber: a. Deus pode ser imanente, e não *apenas* transcendental, o que significa que Ele pode ser conhecido neste mundo através dos sentidos. Algumas manifestações de Deus podem afetar nossa percepção. b. Também podemos conhecer a Deus através da razão, da intuição e do misticismo, tudo mediado através dos sentidos. Ora, esses meios pelos quais obtemos conhecimentos são tão bons, se não mesmo melhores, que a simples percepção dos sentidos. É por demais rígida a dicotomia de Kant, dentro de sua teoria do conhecimento. Ele distinguia agudamente os vários sentidos de se obter conhecimento. Chamava o conhecimento obtido através da percepção de sentidos de «proposições», ao passo que o conhecimento obtido através da razão, da intuição e das experiências místicas de *postulados*. Ver o artigo sobre Deus, no item «Provas de Sua Existência», que oferece um extenso sumário sobre esses argumentos. Sob o título de *Argumento*, vários dos argumentos tradicionais sobre Deus são apresentados com maiores detalhes, incluindo o argumento ora em pauta. (EP MM P)

ARGUMENTO HENOLÓGICO

Vem da palavra grega que significa **estudo** ou *raciocínio* sobre o *Um*, que nesse caso é Deus. Trata-se de um nome alternativo para aquele argumento que usualmente chama-se «Argumento de Grau de Perfeição», ou «Argumento Axiológico». Os graus de perfeição sugerem o mais elevado grau ou qualidade de perfeição, do qual todos os demais se derivam. Essa perfeição última é Deus. Ver o artigo geral sobre *Deus*, sob *Provas da Existência de Deus*, quanto a uma discussão detalhada, incluindo aquilo que está envolvido nesse argumento. (F NTI)

ARGUMENTO MORAL

A mais bem conhecida formulação do argumento moral é a de Kant. Mediante a mesma, ele tentou provar a existência de Deus e da alma humana. Valor e bondade só podem ser preservados na presença de uma estrita moralidade, que inclui recompensa e castigo absolutos para o bem e o mal praticados. Faz sentido buscar o bem somente dentro do contexto de um mundo criado e controlado pelo princípio moral. Um homem bom terá de ser finalmente recompensado e um homem mau, terá de ser finalmente punido. Provavelmente isso não sucederá, e nem mesmo ocorrerá nesta vida física em qualquer grau satisfatório. Portanto, deve haver uma alma que continuará existindo, pelo menos até que as contas sejam ajustadas, e deve haver um Juiz de estatura, poder e inteligência suficientes para garantir que a justiça seja feita. A esse Juiz chamamos Deus. Se isso não é um fato, então a única alternativa filosófica será o *caos*. Em um mundo caótico, os homens fariam o que bem entendessem, sem jamais serem chamados a prestar contas, e todo o bem que alguém praticasse nada significaria, em absoluto. A escolha, pois, dá-se entre Deus e a alma, por uma parte, e o acaso e o caos, por outra parte. Não é difícil perceber qual é a escolha mais sábia. Alguns filósofos têm preferido o acaso e o caos, pensando que isso representa a verdade, e que a outra escolha não passa de um pensamento firmado apenas no desejo. Porém, há lógica suficiente no argumento moral, bem como evidências suficientes em prol do desígnio que se percebe na criação, para resguardar-nos de fazer aquela insensata escolha, mesmo que não contássemos com a fé na revelação divina. (EP F P)

ARGUMENTO ONTOLÓGICO de Anselmo

Anselmo, 1033-1109, (vide), arcebispo de Canterbury e que foi o mais importante filósofo do século XI, é mais conhecido na atualidade como o criador do *Argumento Ontológico*. O *Proslogium* foi escrito entre os anos de 1077 e 1078.

A porção que oferecemos aqui foi extraída da obra de Anselmo, intitulada *Proslogium*, *Monologium*, *Apêndice em Favor do Insensato*, por Gaulinon; e *Cur Deus Homo*, traduzidos por S.N. Deane (1903), capítulos II a V.

Capítulo II

Deus existe verdadeiramente, embora o insensato tenha dito em seu coração que *Não há Deus*.

E assim, Senhor, tu que dás entendimento à fé, concede-me, até onde sabes ser proveitoso, que eu compreenda que és conforme cremos; e que és aquilo que cremos seres. Realmente, cremos que és um ser como nada maior pode ser concebido. Ou não existirá tal natureza, somente por que o insensato disse em seu coração que «Não há Deus» (Salmos 14:1)? Seja como for, porém, esse mesmo indivíduo insensato, quando ouve falar naquele ser ao qual me refiro—um ser como nada maior pode ser concebido—compreende aquilo que ouve, e aquilo que compreende faz parte de sua compreensão, embora ele não compreenda que isso existe.

É uma coisa, contemplar um objeto como uma imaginação mental; é outra coisa compreender que tal objeto realmente existe. Quando um pintor concebe inicialmente o quadro que mais tarde pintará, já o tem em seu entendimento, mas ainda não compreende que o mesmo já existe, porquanto ainda não o executou. Entretanto, depois da pintura executada, o pintor tanto tem o quadro em seu entendimento como também compreende que o mesmo existe, porque já o executou.

Por conseguinte, até mesmo o insensato fica convencido de que existe algo no entendimento como nada maior pode ser concebido. Quando ouve falar sobre isso o insensato o compreende. Ora, tudo quanto pode ser compreendido, existe no entendimento. E é evidente que aquilo como nada maior pode ser concebido não pode existir somente no entendimento. Pois, supondo que isso exista exclusivamente no entendimento, então pode ser concebido como existente na realidade; e isso ainda é maior.

Portanto, se aquilo como nada maior pode ser concebido existe exclusivamente no entendimento, o

ARGUMENTO ONTOLÓGICO

próprio ser, como nada maior pode ser concebido, seria um ser como outro maior pode ser concebido. É óbvio, porém, que isso é impossível. Donde se conclui que não há que duvidar que existe um ser como nada maior pode ser concebido, o qual existe tanto no entendimento como na realidade.

Capítulo III
Não se pode conceber que Deus não existe—pois Deus é aquilo como nada maior pode ser concebido. Aquilo que pode ser concebido como não existente não é Deus.

E certamente Deus existe tão verdadeiramente que não pode ser concebido como não existente. Pois não é possível conceber-se um ser que não pode ser concebido como não existente; e isso é maior do que algo que pode ser concebido como não existente. Assim, pois, se aquilo como nada maior pode ser concebido, puder ser concebido como não existente, então já não será aquilo como nada maior pode ser concebido. Isso, todavia, é uma contradição irreconciliável. Portanto, existe tão verdadeiramente um ser como nada maior pode ser concebido como existente, que o mesmo nem mesmo pode ser concebido como não existente; e esse ser és tu, ó Senhor, nosso Deus.

Desse modo, existes verdadeiramente, ó Senhor, meu Deus, de maneira a não se poder conceber que não existes; e com toda a razão. Pois se a mente pudesse conceber um ser superior a ti, tal criatura se elevaria acima do próprio Criador; e isso é absurdo ao extremo. De fato, tudo o mais quanto existe, excetuando somente a tua pessoa, pode ser concebido como não existente. Somente a ti, pois, cabe a posição de existir mais verdadeiramente que todos os outros seres; o que significa que pertences a uma categoria superior à de todos os outros. Pois, tudo o mais quanto existe, não existe tão verdadeiramente como tua pessoa, e, portanto, pertence a uma categoria inferior da existência. Por conseguinte, por que o insensato disse em seu coração que *Não há Deus?* (Salmos 14:1), posto ser tão evidente, para qualquer mente racional, que existes na mais alta categoria da existência? Por que, exceto que tal indivíduo é embotado e é um insensato?

Capítulo IV
Como o insensato tem dito em seu coração aquilo que não pode ser concebido. Uma coisa pode ser concebida de duas maneiras: 1. Quando o vocábulo que a exprime é concebido; 2. e quando a própria coisa é compreendida. No que tange ao vocábulo, Deus não pode ser concebido como não existente; na realidade ele não pode sê-lo.

No entanto, o insensato tem dito em seu coração aquilo que ele mesmo não pode conceber; pois como é que ele poderia ter deixado de conceber aquilo que disse em seu coração? porquanto é a mesma coisa conceber ou dizer no coração.

Mas, se realmente, ou melhor, posto que realmente ele tanto concebeu, visto que disse em seu coração como também não disse em seu coração, porque não podia concebê-lo, então há mais de uma maneira em que uma coisa é concebida ou dita no coração. Pois, em certo sentido, um objeto qualquer é concebido quando é concebido o vocábulo que o exprime; e, por outro lado, quando é compreendida a própria entidade que é o citado objeto.

No primeiro desses sentidos, pois, Deus pode ser concebido como não existente; mas, no segundo, sob hipótese nenhuma. Porque todo aquele que compreende o que é a água e o que é o fogo jamais poderá conceber o fogo como água, de conformidade com a natureza dos próprios fatos, embora tal confusão seja possível de acordo com os meros vocábulos. Por semelhante modo, ninguém que compreenda o que Deus é, poderá conceber que Deus não existe; embora diga tal coisa em seu coração, com ou sem qualquer significação estranha. Pois Deus é aquilo como nada maior pode ser concebido. E aquele que realmente compreende isso, certamente entende que esse ser existe tão verdadeiramente que nem ao menos pode concebê-lo como não existente. Por conseguinte, aquele que compreende que Deus existe dessa maneira, não pode conceber que ele não existe.

Agradeço-te, gracioso Senhor, agradeço-te, porque aquilo que eu anteriormente cria mediante a tua abundância, agora o entendo pela tua iluminação, de forma que se eu me inclinasse por descrer que existes verdadeiramente, eu não seria capaz de compreender que assim pode ser a verdade.

Capítulo V
Deus é tudo quanto é melhor ser do que não ser, e ele, na qualidade de único ser auto-existente, criou todas as coisas do nada.

Portanto, que és tu, Senhor Deus, senão aquele como nada maior pode ser concebido? Mas que és tu, exceto aquilo que, como o mais elevado de todos os seres, é o único que existe por si mesmo e que cria todas as outras coisas do nada? Pois qualquer coisa que não é assim, é menos do que algo que pode ser concebido. Isso, entretanto, não pode ser concebido a teu respeito. Portanto, que bem faz falta ao Deus supremo, através de quem vem todo o bem? Assim sendo, tu és justo, veraz, bendito, e tudo quanto é melhor existir do que não existir. Pois é melhor ser *justo* do que ser não justo; é melhor ser *bendito* do que ser não bendito.

ARGUMENTO ONTOLÓGICO
por Russell N. Champlin

«Deus é tudo que é melhor ser do que não ser».
(Anselmo)

1. Sua definição
2. Sua refutação
3. O erro básico de seus oponentes
4. Sua afirmação

Introdução:

Para a mentalidade religiosa há algo de atrativo na declaração aparentemente absurda de Agostinho: «*Credo ut intelligam*» («Creio para que possa compreender»). Com isso ele queria dizer que o conhecimento começa pela fé, e a fé é um exercício da alma. O indivíduo que não tem fé permanece entre as tenazes das trevas da ignorância, porquanto ainda não atingiu a esfera do acolhimento mental que lhe permitiria apreender qualquer verdade realmente importante. Participa e se ufana tão-somente daquela realidade de nível inferior e é conhecida apenas através da percepção dos sentidos, mas que ignora e até mesmo põe em ridículo as verdadeiras e sublimes realidades, como Deus e a alma.

Mas a alma religiosa, impulsionada por um tipo delicioso de preconceito, virtualmente salta de alegria quando lê as proposições ainda mais indefensáveis de Tertuliano: «Credo quia absurdum» («Creio porque é absurdo»), ou conforme lemos essa afirmativa de forma mais completa em «De Carne Christi», 5: «É crível porque é absurdo; é certo, porque é impossível». Tertuliano podia fazer tais asseverações porque tinha a confiança de que as verdades mais elevadas não se conformam à razão humana, e muito menos, com a

ARGUMENTO ONTOLÓGICO

percepção dos nossos sentidos, percepção essa que nos confere um conhecimento meramente provincial, mas jamais pode alçar-se aos lugares celestiais para dali trazer-nos Deus, não podendo afirmar qualquer coisa de significativo a seu respeito. Por essa razão é que, para as mentes humanas ordinárias, uma grande verdade geralmente é reputada como um absurdo; mas esse próprio absurdo é um ponto em favor da mesma. Alfred North Whitehead disse: «Se voltarmos a nossa atenção para as novidades de pensamento, durante nosso tempo de vida terrena, observaremos que quase todas as idéias realmente novas se revestem de um certo aspecto de insensatez quando são expostas pela primeira vez». Ora, se isso é verdade no que toca a novas idéias ordinárias, que dizem respeito às coisas materiais, quanto mais poderíamos aplicar tal declaração à «idéia divina», que é um conceito que se eleva muito acima de qualquer possibilidade de investigação humana, investigação essa que se orienta apenas «cientificamente»?

Mas, para mostrarmos que todas essas declarações aparentemente insensatas não pertencem somente aos pais da igreja cristã, e nem à Idade Média, eis que Kierkegaard impingiu ao mundo filosófico a sua tão distorcida declaração: «Deus é o mais ridículo de todos os seres», com o que, segundo nos parece, ele quis dar a entender que o entendimento humano, sem importar como impelido, na realidade não pode avançar muito no caminho da descrição da idéia divina.

Todavia, para pessoas dotadas de sentimentalidade religiosa, essas declarações, longe de serem repelentes, são motivos de júbilo, de mescla com um pouco de ufania, pois enquanto os outros homens tentam encontrar solução para os problemas contando meramente com a percepção dos sentidos, os quais, por sua própria admissão não sabem realmente muito acerca da natureza de tais problemas, por outro lado existem algumas pessoas, *homens de fé*, que receberam um outro meio de conhecer até mesmo as verdades mais profundas, tais como a existência e a natureza de Deus e a imortalidade.

É possível que o encanto de tais declarações de fé, que tão ousadamente solapam a ciência, o ceticismo e o ateísmo, seja o mesmo encanto que cerca o argumento ontológico. Esse argumento apela exclusivamente para a razão, ao fazer as suas assertivas, deixando de lado os chamados testemunhos precisos das provas experimentais, que ocupam de tal modo os pensamentos do mundo moderno. Aqueles que se aferram ao argumento ontológico são dotados de um espírito agostiniano—estão convencidos de que dizer que o conhecimento só nos pode ser transmitido através da percepção dos sentidos é cerrar as portas e janelas da casa do conhecimento; e visto que essa casa da razão foi assim fechada, o ar puro da razão se tornou pesado, e os homens se sentem virtualmente sufocados por suas proposições empíricas, que não nos conduzem a parte alguma, exceto para um mais profundo ateísmo e desespero. Portanto, abramos de par em par a casa do conhecimento e respiremos o ar fresco da razão, para que assim possamos subir até Deus.

1. Definição

Na tentativa de ajudar-nos na aproximação a Deus, Anselmo buscou criar um argumento em favor de sua existência, que também pode ajudar-nos na sua descrição, que possa originar-se da razão pura, onde nenhuma falácia baseada na percepção dos sentidos venha a distorcer o quadro. Essa tentativa, pois, resultou na formulação da seguinte declaração: Por definição, Deus é o mais perfeito dos seres, de tal modo que é impossível conceber outro ser mais perfeito; porém, se supuséssemos que ele existe apenas como uma proposição intelectual, e não na realidade, então seria claro, por essa mesma circunstância, que seria possível imaginarmos um ser mais perfeito do que o nosso suposto ser perfeito, a saber, um que realmente existisse. Portanto, Deus, o ser perfeito, deve realmente existir.

Essa asseveração de Anselmo se baseou em sua observação que os homens não têm meramente a idéia da perfeição, nem a idéia de ser, tão-somente, mas que entretemos a idéia de «um ser perfeito», de um *ens realissimum*. Esse argumento de Anselmo, na realidade, é uma faceta do argumento «axiológico» a respeito de Deus, isto é, o argumento baseado no valor, visto que se chega ao mesmo mediante uma consideração de valores. Pois temos a idéia de valores maiores e menores, aqueles valores mais ou menos completos e perfeitos que há na natureza. Essa idéia força-nos a chegar a uma dentre duas conclusões: Poderíamos dar início a uma pesquisa acerca daquilo que é mais elevado e absolutamente perfeito, indo de uma coisa para outra, ou chegando até o infinito, numa tentativa interminável e infrutífera de encontrar aquele ser mais elevado de todos; ou podemos fazer essa jornada abreviar-se e simplificar-se, dizendo que tal ser de fato existe, e que sabemos de sua existência pela *razão pura*.

2. Refutação

O mundo não teve de esperar por muito tempo até alguém tentar refutar esse argumento. Gaunilo salientou que o argumento de Anselmo necessariamente nos pode levar a uma «idéia» acerca de algum ser perfeito, subseqüente poderia acrescentar coisa alguma à sua grandiosidade, mas que isso não nos força, necessariamente, a tirar a conclusão de que tal idéia deve ter o seu paralelo no mundo objetivo. Assim também poderíamos imaginar alguma ilha perfeita no meio do oceano; porém, nenhum esforço de pensamento ou de imaginação pode trazer tal ilha à existência real. A idéia de um ser perfeito simplesmente não implica na existência de um ser perfeito. Esse contra-argumento parece suficientemente convincente; mas prossigamos até a «afirmação» do argumento de Anselmo.

Outros indivíduos têm procurado demonstrar que não podemos atribuir existência a qualquer coisa, visto que todas as atribuições se alicerçam na experiência ou nas «proposições sintéticas». As proposições sintéticas fundam sua verdade sobre a experiência, e não sobre meras idéias especulativas. Portanto, a existência não poderia ser concebida; antes, é um fato que se pode experimentar. A existência de qualquer e de todos os sujeitos juntamente, com seus predicados (se forem concebidos meramente pela razão) pode ser negada, sem qualquer autocontradição. Por conseguinte, nenhuma idéia, que meramente é uma parte da imaginação ou faculdade da razão, tem necessariamente o seu paralelo no mundo dos seres reais. Em conseqüência, para que o *ens realissimum* seja conhecido é mister que seja experimentado, e isso através da faculdade da percepção dos sentidos, a fim de que possa ser reconhecido como real; e nenhuma proposição lógica pode concretizar isso na realidade. É claro, entretanto, que não possuímos qualquer «experiência» acerca de *ens realissimum*, o que significa que não podemos afirmar a sua existência. Não podemos transferir as nossas proposições lógicas para o terreno da realidade. Sabemos o que é real tão-somente através da experiência, e as afirmações sobre a realidade sempre devem proceder dos juízos sintéticos, isto é, daqueles derivados da percepção dos sentidos. A existência não é uma idéia, mas é um fato que pode ser experimentado. Parece que esse contra-argumento destrói a validade do argumento ontológico, mas devemos continuar pensando e esperar pela afirmação do argumento de Anselmo.

3. O erro básico de seus oponentes

Esta porção da discussão na realidade é uma parte da «afirmação» do argumento ontológico; é apresentada aqui, em separado, ocupando uma posição anterior por causa de sua importância, visto que nos ajuda a afirmar que o argumento ontológico se reveste de algum valor, não podendo ser eliminado facilmente.

O erro fundamental dos oponentes de Anselmo, em seu argumento, é que eles não percebem que tudo se alicerça sobre a «suposição ontológica». Disso consiste a declaração básica do racionalismo, o qual assevera que a natureza da inteligência humana corresponde à natureza da realidade final, e que a inteligência divina é duplicada na inteligência humana, parcial e imperfeitamente, ainda que na realidade. Há, portanto, certa «afinidade» entre inteligência humana (através da alma, da criação ou emanação de Deus) e a realidade final, a realidade espiritual, também chamada Deus. Portanto, como fragmento da inteligência divina, o homem naturalmente sabe, através da razão pura, alguma coisa acerca da Inteligência Última a qual designamos pelo nome de Deus. Não existe meramente uma comunicação natural entre os dois, embora isso também seja uma verdade, mas o menor é, na realidade, uma expressão do maior. A primeira parte completa do Proslogium de Anselmo está permeada desse conceito.

Segue-se, portanto, que o argumento ontológico não é uma mera «proposição lógica», pelo menos para os seus defensores. Aqueles que o refutam, ordinariamente fazem-no sobre a suposição de que Anselmo, tendo criado uma proposição lógica, habilmente formulada, automaticamente teve o impulso de supor que essa proposição deveria ter o seu paralelo no mundo das realidades. Pelo contrário, Anselmo supunha a transmissão da Inteligência Superior para as inteligências inferiores, na forma tanto da transmissão ou comunicação de conhecimento como na forma de uma expressão natural de conhecimento àquele ser íntimo que tem algo da própria natureza daquilo que se descreve por esta proposição. O argumento ontológico, pois, torna-se tanto uma proposição racional como uma proposição mística, e não apenas uma proposição lógica. Para destruí-la, por conseguinte, é necessário que seus opositores mostrem ser falsas tanto a proposição do racionalismo (seu tipo de conhecimento *a priori*) como a proposição do misticismo (com sua idéia de comunicações divinas). Assim, pois, para provar que o argumento ontológico não pode ser verdadeiro, é necessário que o opositor consiga o feito extraordinário de refutar as idéias básicas de Platão, bem como da maioria das religiões, que dependem, essencialmente, do misticismo, como base para as suas idéias. E isso, como é óbvio, não é uma tarefa fácil.

4. Afirmação

Com base na «suposição ontológica», afirmamos que enquanto os sistemas filosóficos do racionalismo, da intuição e do misticismo não tiverem sido refutados, revestindo-se de algum valor em potencial, o *argumento ontológico* pode ser igualmente veraz.

Note-se que não dizemos que «deve» ser veraz. Se realmente existe uma realidade superior, e se essa realidade prefere comunicar-se com alguma inteligência inferior, por suas próprias faculdades, pode reconhecer a seu progenitor, então o argumento ontológico permanece como um argumento possivelmente verdadeiro. Se a «intuição» é possível para a personalidade humana, deixando de lado a percepção dos sentidos a fim de obter conhecimento, através de algum meio misterioso e ainda desconhecido (conforme os estudos no ramo da parapsicologia parecem mostrar-nos) então o argumento ontológico continua sendo um meio que nos capacita a conhecer realidades superiores, ainda que não de um modo «comprovado».

Para derrubar por terra, completa e finalmente, o argumento ontológico, seria necessário provar, além de qualquer dúvida possível, que a «intuição» é uma idéia falsa. Portanto, aquele que se arroga ao direito de entrar em batalha contra o argumento ontológico, na realidade está enfrentando Platão, os intuicionistas e os místicos, pois se, em última análise, puder mostrar-se que há algum valor nesses sistemas, então também residirá valor no argumento ontológico. Assim, pois, o argumento ontológico não tenta concretizar a existência, mas meramente afirma que a Realidade Última é um fato e que sabemos desse fato porque a própria Realidade Última o transmite para nós, tanto através da transferência de conhecimento como através da função natural da razão, a qual, visto fazer parte da Razão Suprema, mediante certo raciocínio disciplinado, pelo menos conseguirá afirmar a existência de seu progenitor. Anselmo, pois, tomou a posição que quando se punha a fazer uma afirmação lógica concernente à existência de Deus, meramente expressava o que devia expressar, por causa da própria natureza de seu ser interior, que naturalmente reconhecia e agora declarava algo sobre o seu 'Criador', porque sua natureza íntima tinha afinidade com o seu Criador. O conhecimento, pois, da categoria mais profunda, não precisa alicerçar-se sobre a experiência, mas pode derivar-se da razão pura, que é uma propriedade inerente à personalidade humana.

Parece-nos, por conseguinte, que o argumento ontológico se alicerça sobre certos pontos de vista metafísicos fundamentais, acerca da natureza da personalidade humana; e para ab-rogá-lo completamente, seria necessário comprovar a existência de uma personalidade humana totalmente diversa daquilo que Anselmo supunha ser. A verdade é que não podemos desfazer-nos com facilidade das idéias de Anselmo acerca da natureza da personalidade humana, porquanto certo número de mentes universais tem descrito a essência humana com termos similares. Quanto mais ficamos sabendo acerca da personalidade humana, tanto mais ficamos preparados para admitir que um grande mistério nos circunda; sendo perfeitamente possível que a ciência do século XXI venha a refutar o obstinado materialismo do século XX, e que a imortalidade, por exemplo, venha a ser aceita como um fato científico simples acerca do que compõe o homem; e se isso for confirmado, então qualquer coisa que Anselmo postulou se tornará facilmente possível.

Através do argumento apresentado nos parágrafos acima, a objeção de Gaunilo é refutada, porquanto, na verdade, não estamos tratando de uma mera «idéia» de ser perfeito, mas, estamos manuseando com uma suposição ontológica, que repousa sobre a validade possível do racionalismo e de certas formas de misticismo, bem como sobre a possível descrição correta acerca da personalidade humana, capaz de entrar em contacto com uma realidade superior, já que essa mesma personalidade humana faz parte dessa realidade superior. Outrossim, uma ilha perfeita, criada pela imaginação, na realidade é uma ficção arbitrária contingente, que envolve uma contradição, e não um ser necessário, não podendo mesmo ser algo posto na mesma categoria de um ser existente. Além disso, uma Realidade Suprema, que transmite algo de si mesma para a inteligência humana é uma realidade possível, ao passo que uma ficção arbitrária contingente dificilmente pode ser classificada nessa categoria.

O argumento fundamental sobre «proposições sintéticas» não é um argumento válido, porquanto supõe que tudo quanto o homem pode vir a saber, terá de chegar ao seu conhecimento através da função dos sentidos, isto é, através da experiência. Isso declara que a razão, como função mais elevada da personalidade humana, é um mito, que a intuição que ultrapassa aos cinco sentidos é uma ficção, e que todas as reivindicações do misticismo, acerca da obtenção de conhecimento, são *ipso facto*, falsas. Ao contrário, os estudos modernos no campo da parapsicologia, como no caso do «efeito de Backster», que demonstrou que existe uma espécie de comunicação telepática entre todas as coisas vivas, envolvendo até mesmo animais unicelulares, plantas, etc., que se torna possível através de alguma forma ainda desconhecida e indescritível de energia, que não depende da percepção dos sentidos, mas que é um veículo da inteligência, a despeito disso, parece servir de demonstração do fato de que o conhecimento não se limita à percepção dos sentidos, no tocante à sua obtenção.

As fotografias psíquicas (fotografias feitas mediante a energia mental) conforme os estudos demonstrados por Jule Eisenbud, da Universidade de Colorado, nos Estados Unidos da América do Norte, são um outro fator que nos mostra que há outro veículo da inteligência, além da percepção dos sentidos. Limitar toda a capacidade de obtenção de conhecimento aos cinco sentidos é, na realidade, fechar as janelas da casa do conhecimento, ignorando, propositadamente, todos os outros meios possíveis e reais de que dispomos para obter conhecimentos. A afirmação de que o conhecimento pode ser obtido extra-sensorialmente, é uma declaração de que o argumento ontológico se reveste de certa verdade, ainda que não declare que o mesmo seja realmente verdadeiro. Esta discussão, em sua inteireza, procura declarar que o argumento ontológico tem sido parcialmente mal compreendido, e que há certas coisas que podem ser ditas em seu favor; e que, embora esse argumento não seja necessariamente verdadeiro, pode envolver alguma verdade.

Enquanto esse argumento «puder» ser verdadeiro, sem importar se o é ou não, realmente, permanecerá entre nós, com seu encanto inerente, como parte da caçada dos mundos filosófico e religioso. Parte dessa caçada consistirá do fato de que determinados filósofos, que se mostram simpáticos para com os meios intuitivos, racionais e místicos de obter o conhecimento, quando não tiverem mais nada com o que ocupar o seu tempo, continuarão a escrever acerca do assunto.

Quem és tu, Senhor Deus, senão aquele que nada pode ser concebido como maior? Mas que és tu, exceto aquilo que, como o mais elevado de todos os seres, é o único que pode *existir por si mesmo*, que cria todas as outras coisas do *nada*? Pois tudo quanto não chega a isso é menor do que algo que possa ser concebido. Mas isso não pode ser concebido a teu respeito. Por conseguinte, que bem falta ao *Deus Supremo*, através de quem fluem todos os bens? Assim, pois, és justo, veraz, bendito, bem como *tudo que é melhor ser do que não ser*. Pois é *melhor* ser *justo* do que não justo; e é melhor ser *bendito* do que não bendito. (Anselmo, *Proslogium* Capítulo V). (EP MM REA)

ARGUMENTO TELEOLÓGICO

1. *Base.* Tudo quanto há no mundo foi designado por Deus, contribuindo para beneficiar o homem, embora esse aspecto possa ser exagerado.

2. *Ciência.* Toda ciência repousa sobre a necessidade de constância e coerência. Se não houvesse tais condições, seria impossível qualquer experiência, pois cada nova experiência daria um resultado diferente. Se não houver *leis* (alicerçadas sobre o desígnio), não poderá haver ciência. *Invariabilidade*. Se há alguma idéia que com razão pode ser considerada como aquela que exerce o controle máximo sobre a moderna maneira de pensar, que integra as preocupações da existência diária com os interesses da ciência, da arte e da filosofia, então essa idéia chama-se *invariabilidade*. O que consideramos como *real*? Certamente não alterações nas coisas, no formato e nas dimensões das coisas, ou a desintegração das coisas. O tempo real é determinado pelo tique-taque dos segundos, que se transforma em minutos e horas, e isso não se altera só porque me sinto entediado, embora assim me pareça ser. Consideramos o átomo e falamos da existência e da ação das partículas atômicas, tudo o que obedece a leis, embora não possamos ver qualquer Mente que as controle. Se existe algo de real acerca do átomo, essa realidade repousa sobre a invariabilidade que encontramos nele. Os cientistas, ademais, admiram-se de como o universo é testado por nossas mentes, como a mente e o mundo correspondem um ao outro, como podemos investigar as leis da natureza e descobrir coisas. Nada disso poderia ser verdadeiro sem a invariabilidade, a qual, por sua vez, depende de *desígnio*, isto é, da teleologia.

3. *A palavra em questão.* O termo *teleologia* vem do grego, e tem o sentido de estudo ou raciocínio sobre finalidades, ou sobre o desígnio que produz resultados ou finalidades. Trata-se da ciência das *causas finais*, o que necessariamente inclui a realidade do princípio de desígnio. Todos os processos, desde o atômico ao biológico, desde o moral ao espiritual, seguem pela vereda do propósito, a fim de atingir resultados específicos. O estudo da biologia, para exemplificar, é um estudo de teleologia.

4. *Os fenômenos observados.* Todos os aspectos da vida demonstram algum desígnio complexo e eficiente. De fato, a vida não poderia prosseguir sem esse princípio. Cada órgão do corpo existe, e, por sua vez, faz o corpo existir, porque há o cumprimento de desígnio. A complexidade de desígnio é tão vasta que requer o conceito que somente uma Grande Mente pode estar por detrás de sua existência, pois é impossível que o mero acaso produza aquilo que vemos. E o mero acaso não adquire maior prestígio só porque o designamos de *seleção natural*. A complexidade e ação inteligente do olho humano deixa admirada a ciência inteira; mas, quando falamos sobre o cérebro, não há palavras que possam começar a exprimir a nossa admiração. É dificílimo imaginar tal desígnio sem se levar em conta aquele Planejador que chamamos de Deus. Paulo partia da idéia de que a própria criação é suficiente para conduzir os homens a Deus, embora os homens, em sua

ARGUMENTO TRANSCENDENTAL

perversidade, resistam a esse testemunho da natureza (ver Rom. 1:20 ss). A criação fornece-nos amplas evidências do poder e da inteligência em uma maciça escala; e nisso encontramos Deus como o Planejador, Criador e Sustentador inteligente e onipotente.

5. *O argumento teleológico e os filósofos.* *Anaxágoras*, com o seu conceito de *nous* (mente), que controla todas as coisas de forma ordeira, plantou as sementes desse argumento. Porém, a primeira declaração formal do mesmo encontra-se no diálogo *Leis*, de autoria de *Platão*, onde ele cita o desígnio da natureza, juntamente com o argumento do automovimento, o que necessariamente requer a idéia de Deus. O ponto de vista de *Aristóteles* era encarar a existência inteira com base no conceito teleológico. Ele incluía as idéias de movimento, contingência e ordem, em seus raciocínios. Ver o artigo sobre Aristóteles, que fornece detalhes sobre essas questões. *Agostinho* incluiu esses argumentos em sua teologia filosófica, e assim influenciou o fluxo do pensamento cristão. *Tomás de Aquino* incluiu esse argumento como uma das cinco razões demonstrativas da existência de Deus. Ver o artigo sobre ele, e sobre os seus *Cinco Caminhos*. *Newton* invocou um *ordenador*, a fim de explicar a estabilidade e a continuação do universo. *Leibniz* achava que é necessário um ordenador para se explicar a harmonia que impera na natureza, sobretudo diante do fato de que as suas mônadas (partículas elementares) não têm janelas. O *bispo Butler* usou o princípio de um desígnio providencial como base de sua fé no cristianismo. *Hume*, entretanto, pensava que, quando muito, uma deidade finita e imperfeita poderia ser concebida por meio desse argumento. *Kant*, ao usar o termo argumento físico-teológico, pensava que poderíamos conceber um planejador ou arquiteto, mediante esse argumento, mas não um criador. Além disso, ele não acreditava que podemos partir da percepção dos sentidos e aterrissar na descrição do mundo espiritual ou noumenal. Quanto a uma expansão desses conceitos, ver o artigo sobre o Argumento Cosmológico, onde se aplicam as mesmas objeções. Não obstante, Kant mostrou ter grande apreciação pelo Argumento Teleológico. *Paley*, com sua instrução do relógio, proveu uma aplicação elaborada e provocadora desse argumento. Ver o argumento a seu respeito, que contém informações sobre isso. *Mill* concluiu que esse argumento é válido para demonstrar uma deidade finita.

6. *O argumento teleológico e Darwin.* Para efeito de ênfase, destaco essa questão como se fosse uma categoria separada. A mágica expressão cunhada por Darwin, *seleção natural*, para alguns, substitui o conceito de um Planejador. Porém, a própria idéia de seleção natural, devido ao próprio uso que faz do vocábulo *seleção*, não tem qualquer sentido a menos que pensemos em termos de inteligência. Pois com toda a razão poderíamos indagar: Como é que o mero acaso ou o caos poderiam selecionar qualquer coisa? Não é mister haver alguma forma de inteligência para fazer seleções? Porém, se admitirmos que, de alguma maneira misteriosa, o mero acaso cego, destituído de razão, pode selecionar e assim dar vida e curso livre para o desenvolvimento, ainda assim nos restará resolver o problema igualmente complicado da *matéria inanimada*, que também se reveste de um imenso desígnio. Deveríamos supor que, de alguma maneira, a matéria veio a ser o que ela é, com seus átomos, partículas e potencialidades, por meio de alguma forma de seleção natural? Teólogos e filósofos entretanto, têm argumentado que pode ter havido uma evolução teisticamente orientada. Pelo menos, parece haver alguma espécie de lei natural (divinamente instituída), que pode operar e trazer coisas à existência ou transformá-las, sem a intervenção direta de Deus. Isso explicaria a existência de muitas formas de vida, que pareceriam inúteis ou destrutivas. *Sementes de razão*, que se derivam da Razão Divina (mas agora estão separadas dela), poderiam desenvolver-se em todas as espécies de seres e existências, sem qualquer intervenção divina, de acordo com esse ponto de vista. Porém, coisa alguma poderia suceder sem um desígnio original, que faz parte da Mente Divina.

Recomendamos agora que o leitor examine o grupo inteiro de argumentos em prol da existência de Deus, que faz parte do artigo sobre Deus, sob o subtítulo *Provas da Existência de Deus*. (EP F NTI P)

ARGUMENTO TRANSCENDENTAL

1. Emanuel Kant considerava todo conhecimento transcendental, mas ele pensava mais em nossa maneira de tomar conhecimento das coisas, um conhecimento *a priori*, mas não a coisa conhecida, propriamente dita. Um argumento transcendental, portanto, esclarece qual é o sentido preciso de uma proposição conhecida como verdadeira. Por exemplo, sabemos que as proposições da geometria euclideana são verdadeiras. Mas, para Kant, isso só era possível se a mente já tivesse tais conceitos, em si mesma, e que então aplicasse ao mundo exterior e experimental. A própria mente, por exemplo, determina relações especiais que existem no mundo exterior. Ela seria mera observadora dessas condições. Todos os conceitos geométricos são idéias *a priori* da mente, e não meramente coisas que podemos descobrir neste mundo. O argumento transcendental deixa bem claro esse ponto. (EP F MM)

2. No campo da teologia, o argumento transcendental pode ser uma subcategoria dos argumentos cosmológico ou teleológico (ver ambos os artigos). A fim de explicar o mundo, precisamos depender do conceito de causa. Não pode haver efeitos sem causa, e nem pode haver causas sem uma Primeira Causa. Essa causa original, pois, é transcendental. Portanto, para explicar o desígnio que se vê no mundo, precisamos depender da existência de um Planejador transcendental, que é Deus. Esses argumentos são transcendentais porque envolvem a pessoa de Deus, que é transcendental. (EP F MM)

ARGUMENTOS DE BOM SENSO

Os argumentos alicerçados sobre crenças quase universais são chamados argumentos de bom senso. As idéias a respeito, desde os tempos mais remotos, são: a crença em Deus, a crença na existência e sobrevivência da alma, a crença na existência dos espíritos, a aceitação de certos princípios morais, como a utilidade e correção da lei do amor. As dificuldades filosóficas e lógicas incluem estes pontos: 1. Até que ponto essas crenças são universais? 2. Mesmo que elas sejam absolutamente universais, são verdadeiras? No passado, quase todos os homens acreditavam que o sol girava ao redor da terra, e que a terra era chata. Mas agora sabemos que essas idéias laboram em equívoco. 3. Se essas crenças são verdadeiras, em qual grau e de que maneira elas são verdadeiras? *Defesa*. Embora muitos argumentos possam ser expostos, e muitas objeções possam ser formadas, há uma certa lógica na aceitação dessas idéias como verdadeiras; idéias essas que têm sido cultivadas em diferentes e independentes culturas,

ARGUMENTOS EM PROL DA EXISTÊNCIA DE DEUS — ARIEL

sem haver intercomunicação entre elas. Se não são absolutamente verdadeiras, falhas quanto a detalhes, é quase certo que tais idéias *contêm* importantes verdades. Precisamos pressupor que o homem, mediante a razão (ver o artigo) e a intuição (ver o artigo) tem acesso a verdades básicas, à parte das experiências científicas, é da revelação divina. O primeiro capítulo da epístola aos Romanos expõe essa idéia. Os próprios povos pagãos sabem que Deus existe, conhecendo Suas leis básicas sem terem qualquer revelação divina. Esse argumento também pode ser chamado *consensus gentium* (consenso do povo).

ARGUMENTOS EM PROL DA EXISTÊNCIA DE DEUS

Esta enciclopédia apresenta grande variedade de artigos sobre esse assunto, a saber: Argumento Axiológico, Argumento Cosmológico, Argumento do Bom Senso, Argumento Moral, Argumento Ontológico e Argumento Teleológico.

DEUS (*que vide*)
O artigo geral inclui um sumário de argumentos em número considerável, a saber:
Cinco Argumentos em Prol da Existência de Deus, por Tomás de Aquino. Comentário sobre os Cinco Argumentos de Aquino, por F.C. Copleston. O Argumento Clássico do Relógio, de William Paley, um artigo que aparece após o material biográfico de Paley. Reafirmação Contemporânea de Argumentos Tradicionais em Prol da Existência de Deus, por A.E. Taylor.

ARIANISMO

O conjunto de ensinos de **Ário** (ver o artigo), que viveu em cerca de 265-356 D.C. Ele e seus seguidores negavam a divindade própria de Cristo. Ário desenvolveu sua doutrina com base em especulações teológicas gregas, que floresceram no gnosticismo. Foi uma elaborada tentativa de definir a relação de Cristo para com Deus, segundo a razão natural. (Ver o artigo sobre *Cristologia*). Essa atividade racional e especulativa teve lugar principalmente em Alexandria e Antioquia, sobretudo no século IV D.C., tendo obtido o apoio do imperador romano e de teólogos notáveis. Exercia poderosa atração para as mentes bem-informadas da época.

Doutrina. Estes são seus pontos principais: 1. Deus é ímpar e não-gerado (*agennetos*). Fora de Deus, tudo o mais foi criado *ex nihilo* (do nada), através da vontade de Deus. 2. O Logos (Cristo) é um intermediário entre Deus e o homem. Ele começou antes do tempo, mas não seria eterno, o que significa que houve tempo em que o Logos não existia, embora Deus já existisse. 3. Segue-se daí que o próprio Logos foi criado por Deus (o Logos foi *genetos*). Ele também nasceu (*gennetos*), o que aponta para a *filiação por adoção*. 4. O Logos encarnado (Jesus Cristo), é assim inferior a Deus, embora seja objeto próprio da adoração, por causa de Sua elevada posição, estando acima de todas as demais criaturas. Nessa exaltação, Ele é tanto Senhor quanto Redentor.

Formas de arianismo. 1. Arianismo intransigente, que mantinha que o Filho era *diferente* (*anomois*) do Pai. 2. O segundo grupo proclamou em um sínodo de Ancira (358) que o Filho é *semelhante* em substância (*homoiousia*) ao Pai. São os homoiousianos ou semi-arianos. 3. O terceiro grupo repelia os termos *homoousia* (da mesma substância) e *homoiousia* (de substância similar), como também *ousia* (ser, substância, essência), simplesmente declarando que o Filho era como o Pai.

Os homoiousianos tendiam em favor da ortodoxia, conforme determinada pelo concílio de Nicéia (325), e foram bem recebidos por Atanásio, no concílio de Alexandria (362). Os pais capadócios tentaram mostrar que o problema poderia ser solucionado pelo reconhecimento de *uma natureza* e três pessoas ou *hipóstases*. Apesar da fanática oposição do imperador ariano Valente, prevaleceu a ortodoxia defendida por Nicéia, no Ocidente, abrindo caminho para sua vitória final no Oriente. O Oriente inteiro subscreveu as doutrinas proferidas em Roma (378 e 379), e o imperador Teodósio mostrou ser um ardente defensor da fé nicena. Ver o artigo sobre o *Credo Niceno*. O sínodo de Constantinopla (381), reconhecido como segundo concílio ecumênico, reafirmou o credo niceno com leves modificações, completando-se assim a vitória em prol da plena divindade do Filho. O arianismo foi ultrapassado, embora tivesse prevalecido ainda durante algum tempo entre os povos bárbaros. A conversão de Clóvis, rei dos francos, à fé ortodoxa, em 496, assinalou um grande declínio do arianismo entre os povos teutônicos.

Eusébio, o famoso historiador eclesiástico, após o próprio Ário, foi o mais bem conhecido defensor do arianismo. (AM B E)

ARIDAI

No hebraico o sentido da palavra é incerto. Era o nono filho de Hamã, enforcado com seu pai (ver Ester 9:9), morto pelos judeus que habitavam na Babilônia. (UN)

ARIDATA

No hebraico, **forte**, sexto filho de Hamã, morto pelos judeus da Babilônia (ver Ester 9:8), em cerca de 510 A.C. (S)

ARIÉ

No hebraico, **leão**, cúmplice de Peca na conspiração contra Pecaías, ou um dos príncipes de Pecaías, morto juntamente com este (ver II Reis 15:25), em cerca de 761 A.C. (UN)

ARIEL

No hebraico, **leão de Deus**. No Antigo Testamento é um nome que tem vários empregos, a saber:

1. Pode significar «semelhante a leão», um epíteto para pessoas corajosas e aguerridas, tal como entre os árabes se usa o apelido Ali (leão de Deus). (Ver II Samuel 23:20; I Crô. 11:22 quanto a esse uso). Nessa conexão há um guerreiro de Davi, que matou os filhos de um moabita.

2. Nome de uma pessoa, um dos homens entendidos enviados a Ido, chefe do lugar chamado Casifia, juntamente com seus irmãos, servidores do templo, para que trouxessem ministros à casa de Deus (ver Esd. 8:16,17). Seu nome significa «leão de El (Deus)».

3. Sob a forma variante, «Areli», a palavra também pode significar «altar de terra». Com esse sentido, ou com o sentido de leonino, serviu como designação

simbólica de Jerusalém (ver Isa. 29:1 e 2:7). O altar de Deus é como a Sua terra. O fogo sagrado ardia ali sobre o altar. As discussões acerca do significado ali não são conclusivas, mas a maioria prefere a idéia de *terra*. (ND S UN Z)

ARÍETE

Os antigos, embora lhes faltassem os instrumentos de guerra, devido à sua tecnologia pouco avançada, eram suficientemente providos de armas que facilitavam o ato de matar. O *aríete* era, essencialmente, um forte poste dotado de ponta de metal. Era manuseado por soldados em posição horizontal, embora também houvesse aríetes montados sobre rodas. Alguns tinham protusões que protegiam os soldados de objetos que voavam, quando se tentava derrubar alguma muralha. Alguns aríetes tinham cabeças chatas, e outros tinham pontas aguçadas como as de uma lança. As esculturas assírias mostram vários tipos desses objetos. Alguns supõem que o trecho de II Sam. 20:15 alude a um instrumento dessa natureza. O profeta Ezequiel recebeu instruções divinas para representar o assédio de Jerusalém com aríetes (ver Eze. 4:2), pois esses instrumentos seriam usados no futuro cerco da cidade (ver Eze. 21:22). Foi predito que Nabucodonosor, rei da Babilônia, atacaria Tiro com essas máquinas (ver Eze. 26:9). Quanto a outros detalhes, referentes a esse e a outros instrumentos de guerra, ver o título *Máquinas de Guerra*. Ver também sobre *Armadura; Fortificação* e *Assédios*. (ND NTI Z)

ARIMATÉIA

Arimatéia foi identificado por Eusébio e Jerônimo como *Ramá* ou Ramataim, lugar do nascimento de Samuel (I Sam. 1:19). Isso é mais provável do que sua identificação com Ramá, de Benjamim. Em I Sam. 1:1, o nome é dado em sua forma completa, não-contraída, Ramataim-Zofim; enquanto que na LXX ele aparece sempre sob a forma «Armathaim»; nos escritos de Josefo como *Armatha*; e em I Macabeus 11:34 como «ramathem». Era uma cidade dos judeus que, no sentido mais estrito significaria da Judéia (ver Luc. 23:51). Alguns têm identificado a localização com a moderna Nebby Samuel, cerca de seis quilômetros e meio a noroeste de Jerusalém; todavia, sua localização exata não pode ser afirmada sem qualquer sombra de dúvida.

Esse lugar é mencionado somente no Novo Testamento, em conexão com a história de José de Arimatéia, natural daquela cidade, o qual era membro do Sinédrio. Após a crucificação, ele obteve o corpo de Jesus e o pôs em um túmulo nunca antes usado (ver Mat. 27:57-60). Quanto a notas completas sobre o incidente, ver o NTI *in loc*. Ver também o artigo sobre *José de Arimatéia*. (I IB ID NTI)

ÁRIO

Presbítero de Alexandria (256-336 D.C.), cujo desafio ao bispo Alexandre, de Alexandria, deu início à controvérsia ariana. Ver o artigo sobre o *arianismo*. Crê-se que ele nasceu na Líbia. Era diácono quando foi excluído em 313, por Pedro, patriarca de Alexandria, por haver dado apoio aos pontos de vista cismáticos de Melétio de Licópoles. Foi reinstalado pelo sucessor de Pedro, Aquiles, em 313. Tornou-se presbítero de Baucalis, onde passou a ensinar a sua doutrina que o Logos (Cristo) era um ser criado, não da mesma substância e nem co-eterno com o Pai. Ário foi censurado em 318, mas persistiu em suas atividades. Foi excluído em 321. Eusébio, bispo de Cesaréia (263-340) endossou o arianismo, que também obteve apoio em altos escalões. Com isso dividiu a Igreja no Oriente, deixando desolado o imperador Constantino. O imperador convocou o concílio de Nicéia, em 352, onde Ário foi anatematizado e banido. Então ele compôs um credo rival ao niceno (ver sobre o *credo niceno*). Constantino ficou impressionado com o contracredo de Ário, e o recebeu em 331, ordenando que Atanásio, campeão da ortodoxia nicena, recebesse Ário em comunhão. Atanásio recusou-se, e foi deposto pelo sínodo de Tiro (335), tendo sido exilado para a Gália. Constantino então ordenou que o bispo de Constantinopla restaurasse Ário à comunhão, mas este faleceu no mesmo dia da cerimônia. (AM)

ARIOQUE

No hebraico, **semelhante a leão**. Mas outros estudiosos pensam que a palavra é sumeriana, com o sentido de *servo do deus-lua*.

1. Esse era o nome de um rei de Elasar (Larsa, Senqueré, uma cidade-estado do sul da Babilônia), que estabeleceu uma aliança com Quedorlaomer, quando ele invadiu o vale do rio Jordão (ver Gên. 14:1,9). A guerra teve o propósito de punir os reis de Sodoma, Gomorra, Admá, Zeboim e Bela. Os primeiros saíram-se vitoriosos, mas foram postos em fuga por Abraão, quando este foi combater contra eles, porquanto haviam levado Ló — seu sobrinho — como cativo. Alguns estudiosos ligam o nome Arioque com Warad-Sin (Eri-aku) (cerca de 1836-1824 A.C.), ou com Rim-Sin (cerca de 1824-1763 A.C.), ambos filhos de Kudur-Maduk de Larsa, nomes comuns nos textos do segundo milênio A.C., conforme se vê nos textos de Mari (ver o artigo a respeito). Porém, isso daria a Abraão uma data mais recente. Seja como for, a cronologia da época é precária. A cidade de Elasar tem sido identificada com Ilanzura, mencionada nos textos hititas e nos arquivos de Mari, localizados entre Carquemis e Harã. Alguma confirmação para essa conjectura talvez se ache no Apócrifo do Mar Morto, que diz que o reino de Arioque era Kptwk (talvez a Capadócia). E então, se o rei Tidal, mencionado na Bíblia, puder ser identificado com Tudhaliya, dois daqueles quatro reis poderiam ser nativos de Anatólia, embora tudo isso seja muito incerto.

2. Um outro Arioque era capitão da guarda pessoal de Nabucodonosor (ver Dan. 2:14,15,24). A ele foi ordenado que executasse os mágicos que não tinham podido interpretar o sonho real. Alguns supõem que o nome fosse um *título* do ofício ocupado, e não o nome pessoal do indivíduo. Isso ocorreu em cerca de 605-562 A.C. (ID ND UN Z)

ARISAI

No hebraico, **flecha de Ária**. Era o oitavo filho de Hamã, morto pelos judeus babilônios (ver Est. 9:9), em cerca de 480 A.C. (S UN)

ARISTARCO

No grego, **melhor líder**. Era fiel seguidor de Paulo, seu cooperador, um crente de Tessalônica. Referências no Novo Testamento: Atos 19:29; 20:4; 27:2; Col. 4:10; File. 24. Atuou em cerca de 51-57 D.C. Encontramo-lo em Atos 19:29 como companheiro de viagens de Paulo, em sua terceira viagem missionária. Ele foi agarrado e quase morto no tumulto provocado pelos ourives de Éfeso. Saiu daquela cidade e continuou viajando com Paulo; primeiro a outras cidades da Grécia, e então pela Ásia Menor (ver Atos 20:4 ss.), e daí partiu para Jerusalém, provavelmente como um delegado oficial da igreja em Tessalônica, no tocante à oferta que Paulo levou aos crentes pobres de Jerusalém. Finalmente, ele foi com Paulo a Roma, depois que o apóstolo foi detido. Não há certeza de que ele tenha prosseguido tal viagem até Roma, nessa ocasião. Talvez tenha ficado em Mira (ver Atos 27:5). Seja como for, finalmente ele chegou em Roma, aparentemente como companheiro de prisão de Paulo (ver Col. 4:10). Um outro companheiro de prisão foi Epafras (ver File. 23), sendo possível que eles tivessem se revezado nos cuidados a Paulo, como prisioneiros voluntários. O trecho de Colossenses 4:10,11, parece sugerir que ele era de origem judaica. (I IB NTI)

ARISTÉIAS

Título de um documento cujo autor afirma ter sido testemunha ocular de como o Antigo Testamento hebraico foi traduzido para o grego, do que resultou a Septuaginta. Presumivelmente foi obra escrita por um oficial da corte de Ptolomeu II Filadelfo (285-246 A.C.). Esse documento comumente é chamado «Epístola de Aristéias», mas os próprios manuscritos dizem apenas *Aristéias a Filocrates*. O autor, que fala na primeira pessoa do singular, relata como ele, como um emissário do rei do Egito, dirigiu-se a Eleazar (sumo sacerdote dos judeus) para pedir-lhe permissão para traduzir a «lei judaica» para o idioma grego, tradução essa que seria incluída na biblioteca de Alexandria. Dessa maneira, setenta e dois tradutores competentes foram arranjados. Primeiramente, houve um banquete de sete noites. Aos tradutores foi exigido que respondessem a setenta e duas perguntas, feitas a eles pelo rei. Então, de modo fantástico, a tradução foi terminada em setenta e dois dias, o que explica o nome Septuaginta (no grego, setenta). Algumas variações falam em setenta tradutores e setenta dias de tradução. É justamente esse detalhe, que transmite a idéia de que o Antigo Testamento poderia ser traduzido em tão pouco tempo, o que nos mostra que o relato é fictício. Também sabemos que o autor daquela obra nunca havia traduzido qualquer trabalho. Além disso, cometeu vários anacronismos, mostrando-nos assim que ele viveu em uma época posterior. O autor da obra foi um judeu alexandrino, que escreveu sob pseudônimo, o que era bastante comum na época. As datas atribuídas a esse livro oscilam entre 200 A.C. e 50 D.C., sendo provável que a data mais correta aproxime-se mais desta última. O propósito do livro provavelmente era elogiar o judaísmo e sua maneira de viver diante dos gentios, como demonstração da superioridade do sistema judaico. (CH HAD JEL)

ARISTIDES

Apologeta cristão (ver sobre os **apologetas**) do séc. II D.C. Aparentemente nasceu e viveu em Atenas. Dirigiu sua *Apologia* ao imperador Adriano. Afirmava que somente os cristãos possuem verdade digna de confiança sobre Deus, asseverando que os cristãos constituem uma raça especial, originária de Cristo. Visto que os cristãos são tão especiais e são dotados de uma verdade especial, podem viver vidas santas. Caldeus, egípcios e gregos, devido à ausência de tais qualidades, tinham vivido no erro, tinham dado crédito ao erro. Os judeus podiam ser elogiados por seu *monoteísmo* (ver o artigo), mas, infelizmente, retiveram muitas superstições relativas aos seus ritos e cerimônias. Por muito tempo considerou-se perdida a sua *Apologia*, mas, em 1878, apareceu uma edição de um fragmento armênio em Veneza. Em 1889 foi encontrada uma versão completa em siríaco, no mosteiro do Monte Sinai. Sua publicação levou à descoberta de um texto grego que durante séculos existira no romance religioso *Barlaão e Josafate*. Porções do texto grego foram publicadas em 1922 e 1924. A *Apologia* procura demonstrar quão razoável é o cristianismo, mediante um apelo a um conjunto de fatos. Trata-se de uma obra simples e breve, mas vazada em linguagem exaltada. (AM P)

ARÍSTION (ARISTO)

Ele é mencionado como fonte informativa sobre as Declarações do Senhor por Eusébio, em *História* III.39.3. Essa informação aparece nos escritos de Papias, o qual disse: «Se chegasse alguém dentre os seguidores dos anciãos, eu costumava indagar acerca das declarações dos anciãos, o que André ou Pedro havia dito, ou Filipe, ou Tomé, ou Tiago, ou João, ou Mateus ou qualquer outro dos discípulos do Senhor; e o que Arístion e o ancião João, o discípulo do Senhor, dizem». O significado preciso dessa declaração tem sido disputado, especialmente se os dois homens de nome João, ali mencionados, não forem a mesma pessoa. Seja como for, Arístion aparece como alguém associado a João, o ancião, e, portanto, contemporâneo de Papias. Pelo menos Papias mostra que Arístion foi um discípulo de Jesus, e que algum material concernente às declarações de Jesus lhe havia sido transmitido por outros, e que assim muito ele pôde aprender sobre essas declarações. Mas não diz que obteve essa informação diretamente de Arístion, embora isso possa ser subentendido. Isso é tudo quanto sabemos sobre Arístion. Contudo, um manuscrito do Novo Testamento em armênio traz uma nota, em Marcos 16:8, antes do *término longo* daquele evangelho (pois a maioria dos manuscritos antigos termina no vs. 8), afirmando que *Arístion* provera aquele término para o evangelho de Marcos. Não há como determinar se essa informação é correta ou não; mas a data tardia da nota não encoraja sua autenticidade. (GU Z)

ARISTIPO

Filósofo grego (435-356 A.C.). Nasceu e viveu em Cirene. Foi discípulo de Sócrates. Ele iniciou sua própria escola de filosofia, chamada Escola Cirenaica (ver o artigo sobre o *cirenaicismo*). Essa foi uma das três grandes escolas resultantes dos esforços de alunos de Sócrates. Aristipo foi, acima de tudo, um filósofo moral que defendia a idéia de que o *prazer* é o alvo da existência humana inteira (ver sobre o *hedonismo*). Bem e mal poderiam ser descritos em termos de prazer e dor, o primeiro a ser obtido, e o segundo a ser evitado. Aristipo ressaltava o prazer imediato, embora com algum controle por parte da razão. A *virtude* seria obtida quando alguém alcança o prazer, ao mesmo tempo em que evita a dor. A felicidade consistiria em prazer contínuo. A satisfação imediata seria o ideal. (AM BE P)

ARISTÓBULO

No grego, **melhor consolador**. É nome de vários homens ligados à narrativa bíblica. O nome é grego, mas veio a ser adotado pelos romanos, entre os quais passou a ser comumente usado. Também era utilizado pelos judeus, resultando daí as várias pessoas das famílias Macabeu e Herodes com esse nome.

1. Um sacerdote judeu, professor de Ptolomeu, rei a quem Judas Macabeu enviou cartas (ver II Macabeus 1:10). Talvez ele deva ser identificado com Aristóbulo, o filósofo peripatético, tutor de Ptolomeu VI Filometer (180-146 A.C.). Era o chefe da comunidade judaica de Alexandria, conforme somos informados por Eusébio (Praep. Ev. VIII.10; XIII.12). Esse homem tentou mostrar que as melhores porções da filosofia de Aristóteles dependiam do judaísmo (absurdo), e preparou um livro para os gentios, explicando-lhes os princípios do judaísmo.

2. Aristóbulo I, filho mais velho de João Hircano I, o primeiro dos Macabeus a assumir o título de rei, governando assim sobre Israel. Quando João Hircano faleceu, ele passou o reino à sua esposa, e o sumo sacerdócio a Aristóbulo. Esse homem fez sua mãe morrer de fome, matou seu irmão, Antígono, aprisionou três outros irmãos, usurpou o governo, compeliu os itureanos a tornarem-se judeus. Mas, após um ano, ele faleceu tendo morte muito dolorosa (105-104 A.C.).

3. Aristóbulo II, filho mais jovem de Alexandre Janeu. Ao morrer seu pai, em 78 A.C., o trono ficou com sua esposa, Alexandra, tendo ela continuado a reinar até 69 A.C. Então revoltou-se Aristóbulo II. Após a morte de sua mãe, ele entrou em competição com Hircano II, seu irmão. Mas Antípater, pai de Herodes o Grande, e Aretas, o rei árabe, favoreciam Hircano. Ambos os irmãos tentaram obter o apoio dos romanos por meio de suborno. A maioria dos judeus não queria nem um e nem outro. Aristóbulo mostrou-se impaciente e não esperou pela decisão de Pompeu. Em vista disso, Pompeu capturou Jerusalém, aprisionou Aristóbulo e tornou o país um tributário de Roma. Isso pôs fim à independência judaica sob os Macabeus. Hircano II foi nomeado em seguida. Aristóbulo e seus familiares foram tomados cativos, para Roma. Assim terminou a dinastia dos Macabeus após cerca de oitenta anos (142-63 A.C.). Em 57 A.C., Aristóbulo escapou de Roma e tentou recuperar o seu reino, mas foi recapturado e aprisionado em Roma. Ao começar a guerra civil em Roma, Aristóbulo foi libertado e enviado para a Síria por Júlio César, a fim de combater contra Pompeu. Mas o plano foi descoberto, e Aristóbulo foi feito prisioneiro, tendo morrido em 49 A.C.

4. Um neto de Aristóbulo II e irmão de Mariamne, esposa de Herodes o Grande. Herodes nomeou-o sumo sacerdote; mas Herodes notou que Aristóbulo era muito popular entre os judeus, e «acidentalmente» matou-o afogado, quando ele se banhava, em 35 A.C.

5. O filho mais jovem dentre os dois de Herodes o Grande e Mariamne. Herodes mandou executar sua esposa em 29 A.C., e, depois, enviou seus dois filhos para Roma, a fim de serem educados. Quando eles retornaram, Herodes sentiu que eles eram perigosos para ele, desejando vingar-se da morte da mãe, pelo que os matou sufocados. Aristóbulo teve quatro filhos. Um deles, também chamado Herodes, tornou-se rei de Cálcis; um outro, Herodes Agripa I, tornou-se rei de toda a Palestina (41-44 A.C.); uma filha era Herodias, a esposa do tetrarca Herodes Ántipas. E o quarto foi o Aristóbulo que aparece como o número (6), nesta lista.

6. Esse Aristóbulo era o filho do anterior, alistado como número (5). Sabemos que ele entrou em conluio contra seu irmão, Herodes Agripa I (Josefo, *Anti*. XVIII.vi.3), e que tentou convencer o governador da Síria a não erigir uma estátua do imperador Calígula no templo de Jerusalém (Josefo, *Anti*. XVIII.viii.4), mas essa é toda a informação que temos a respeito dele.

7. O Aristóbulo do Novo Testamento é um homem à cuja família Paulo enviou saudações. Ele residiria em Roma, se o último capítulo da epístola aos Romanos sempre fez parte integral dessa epístola, homem é saudado em Rom. 16:10). Ou então, se o décimo sexto capítulo de Romanos na realidade era originalmente uma carta de apresentação de Febe, e enviada à Ásia Menor, então talvez esse Aristóbulo fosse um efésio. Quanto a esse problema, ver o artigo sobre *Romanos*, sob VIII, Integridade da Epístola. Seja como for, a data dessas ocorrências é cerca de 60 D.C. A tradição faz desse homem um irmão de Barnabé, dizendo que ele trabalhou e morreu em Bretanha. Usualmente, tais tradições são fantasias puras. Ramsey, em *St. Paul the Traveller*, pág. 353, faz dele um filho de Herodes o Grande, o que é uma opinião muito difícil de ser aceita. (AM ID JO NTI RAM UN Z)

ARISTOCRACIA

Termo grego que significa «governo dos melhores». A aristocracia é uma categoria de classe social, que durante muitos séculos da história humana conhecida, baseou-se em direito de nascimento, enobrecendo famílias possuidoras de títulos hereditários, como duque, barão e conde. A aristocracia se mantinha mediante a riqueza na forma de dinheiro ou terras. Seguiam costumes sociais afetados, além de formas de vestuário, linguagem e adoração diferentes das outras classes sociais. Usualmente governavam as classes inferiores. Ocupavam, naturalmente, as posições de liderança, na Igreja e no estado, e eram patrocinadores das artes, da educação e da arquitetura.

Desde o surgimento dos ideais democráticos, a aristocracia tradicional foi relegada a uma posição mais periférica. As *novas elites*, uma outra forma de aristocracia, são formadas pelos meramente ricos (sem títulos nobiliárquicos), intelectuais (como os cientistas, escritores, etc.), artistas e atletas, a maioria dos quais são ricos, venerados pelo público quase como heróis. Clubes de fãs promovem a adulação.

Ética cristã. Deus não tem respeito humano (Rom. 2:11), e os homens espirituais não seguem idolatrias envolvidas nas modernas formas de aristocracia. O trecho de Tia. 2:1 ensina-nos a termos fé em nosso Senhor sem respeitar as distinções de classes. Tiago frisa que usualmente os pobres, e não os ricos, é que aceitam o evangelho (2:5). Ele recomenda a obediência à lei «real», ou seja, a lei do amor. Desse modo a pessoa torna-se membro da verdadeira elite, onde o valor é medido pela qualidade e pelo desenvolvimento espirituais. Por outro lado, não é errado alguém ser rico e culto, se isso for obtido

ARISTÓTELES

Aristóteles — 384-322 A.C.

O aluno mais brilhante de Platão
Professor de Alexandre, O Grande
Chamado *o intelecto* por
seu mestre, Platão

••• ••• •••

ARISTÓTELES

••• ••• •••

Aristóteles, o aluno mais brilhante de Platão. Assistiu sua Academia por 20 anos, mas desenvolveu sua própria filosofia que em muitos pontos era longe da filosofia do mestre, Platão.

Aristóteles era chamado *O Intelecto* por seu professor Platão, e era, de fato, um dos maiores gênios da história humana. Era o pai da lógica, um dos seis sistemas tradicionais da filosofia. Aristóteles era um cientista brilhante cuja ciência dominou o pensamento humano quase até os tempos modernos. Todavia, ele escreveu sobre a filosofia de modo geral, e fez valiosas contribuições para todos os seus ramos.

Para ele, o alvo do conhecimento é *ação*, e *virtude* é o cumprimento pleno de missão.

•••

∞

honestamente e for *devidamente utilizado*. A verdadeira aristocracia consiste nos eleitos, espiritualmente falando. Devemos buscar primeiro o reino de Deus, e todas as coisas físicas necessárias nos serão acrescentadas.

Na filosofia. 1. Dentro da política platônica, a aristocracia, o governo da elite, é considerado a estrutura social ideal, em contraste com outras formas, consideradas degeneradas. 2. Para Aristóteles, a aristocracia — juntamente com a monarquia e a política — era considerada uma das três modalidades desejáveis de governo. 3. Para Hobbes, o termo designava o governo de uns poucos, presumivelmente das classes mais ricas. (H P)

ARISTON DE ALEXANDRIA

Filósofo helenista do século I A.C. Inicialmente foi membro da academia (ver sobre a Academia de Platão), sob Antíoco (ver o artigo a seu respeito). Mais tarde, uniu-se à recém-reavivada escola aristotélica de Alexandria, quando Andrônico de Rodes (ver o artigo a seu respeito) era o seu cabeça. Escreveu um comentário sobre as *Categorias* de Aristóteles, atualmente perdido.

ARISTON DE QUIOS

Filósofo grego do século III A.C. Foi membro do Liceu (escola de Aristóteles, sobre o que, ver o artigo). Depois de Lícon (ver o artigo a seu respeito), tornou-se o cabeça dessa escola, em cerca de 228 A.C.

ARISTÓTELES

Filósofo grego (384-322 A.C.). Nasceu em Estagira, na Macedônia, filho de Nicômaco, médico do rei. Com dezoito anos ingressou na Academia de Platão e ali estudou durante cerca de vinte anos. Foi o mais brilhante aluno de Platão, tendo sido por ele apodado de «o intelecto». Por ocasião da morte de Platão, um parente deste, e rival de Aristóteles, foi nomeado para chefiar a Academia e Aristóteles abandonou Atenas. Tornou-se então tutor de Alexandre o Grande, filho do rei da Macedônia. Alexandre tinha treze anos na ocasião. Em cerca de 335 A.C., Aristóteles regressou a Atenas e fundou o seu Liceu, a Escola Peripatética (ver o artigo sobre o *Liceu*). Quando Alexandre tornou-se rei, Aristóteles recebeu apoio financeiro e moral. Porém, quando Alexandre morreu, em 323 A.C., houve uma onda de antimacedonismo, e Aristóteles exilou-se voluntariamente, para que um outro mártir, como Sócrates, não viesse a pesar sobre a consciência dos atenienses. Morreu pouco depois disso, em 322 A.C.

Escritos. No campo da lógica, o *Organon* e as *Categorias*; *Sobre Refutações Sofistas*; *Física*; *Sobre os Céus*; *Geração e Corrupção*; *História dos Animais*; *Sobre as Partes dos Animais*; *Sobre o Movimento dos Animais*; *Sobre a Progressão dos Animais*; *Sobre a Alma*; *Parva Naturalia*; *Metafísica*; *Ética Nicomaqueana*; *Magna Moralis*; *Constituição de Atenas*; *Retórica e Poética*.

Esboço de suas idéias:
I. A filosofia e as ciências. Ele aceitava os princípios teleológicos e idealistas de Platão. O Universo é um mundo ideal, um todo orgânico inter-relacionado, um sistema de idéias (formas) eternas e imutáveis. As idéias (formas) dão ao mundo dos sentidos (o mundo físico) sua forma e sua vida. O conhecimento genuíno inclui o conhecimento das bases dos fatos: a filosofia inclui todo o conhecimento raciocinado, e as diferentes ciências interessam-se por porções ou fases do ser.

Tipos de ciência. a. Teóricas: Matemática, física e metafísica. b. Práticas: Ética e política. c. Criativas: Mecânica e produção artística. As duas principais divisões da filosofia seriam: *Metafísica*, ou *primeira filosofia*, que se interessa pelo ser e estuda a causa primária ou causa última das coisas; e a *segunda filosofia*, que englobaria as ciências parciais, que abrangem porções ou fases do ser.

II. Conhecimento, epistemologia. Aristóteles percebia o escopo do conhecimento, mais do que outros antes dele, sendo capaz de discernir o papel da definição da indução e da dedução, no desenvolvimento das ciências. Sua classificação das diversas ciências (práticas e teóricas) foi útil para a filosofia. Ele advogava o que atualmente é chamado de teoria correspondente da verdade. Ver o artigo sobre a *Verdade, Teorias da*. Foi um realista engenhoso, supondo que uma completa descrição de um objeto qualquer (um pleno desenvolvimento do *juízo* formado sobre esse objeto) corresponderia à verdade desse objeto. Não antecipou a teoria atômica, segundo a qual a matéria permanece essencialmente misteriosa, a despeito da crescente ciência das partículas atômicas, mesmo em sua época. Ele considerava que o conhecimento é possível, contrastando nisso com o *ceticismo* (ver o artigo).

O processo. a. O conhecimento é possível. b. O homem tem capacidades intuitivas, podendo receber lampejos de compreensão. c. Mas o conhecimento consiste, essencialmente, em juízo com uma descrição, se essa descrição for completa, teremos chegado à verdade. d. Como cientista que era, em contraste com Platão, ele ressaltava essencialmente o conhecimento científico, o qual examina os objetos do mundo físico. e. As faculdades dos sentidos são nossos instrumentos para chegarmos ao conhecimento, embora não exclusivamente, pois também atuam a razão e a intuição. f. Por meio de nossas descrições, atingimos o universal. Ele defendia o que agora se conhece por *realismo moderado*: o universal é real, mas só pode ser encontrado no particular (algum objeto físico). Ver sobre os *universais*. g. A descrição do universal é o propósito mesmo do conhecimento.

Lógica. Aristóteles foi o fundador da lógica científica. Sua função foi descrever o método pelo qual se obtém o conhecimento. Sua lógica centraliza-se em torno de dois fatores essenciais: a. Definição; b. Silogismo, os processos da prova.

Silogismo:
1. A ciência é um autêntico conhecimento, um pensar correto.

a. Passa do particular para o universal, mediante o raciocínio dedutivo. O universal reside no particular. b. O alvo do conhecimento é a demonstração completa, através de uma série de silogismos, onde as conclusões dependem das premissas. c. Esse processo continua até que se atinja um princípio que não possa ser provado pela indução, por ser inerente à razão, e por precisar ser averiguada mediante a *dedução*.

2. O conhecimento começa pela percepção dos sentidos, que prossegue em suas descrições do particular para o universal. O conhecimento esforça-se por entender o universal.

3. As *dez categorias* ou *propriedades* universais das coisas. Essas são as formas dos *predicados* com que costumamos descrever as coisas.

a. O que é (ilustração: um homem; trata-se da *substância* a ser considerada)

b. Como ela se constitui (branco: uma *qualidade*)
c. Quão grande é (dois metros: *quantidade*)
d. Como está relacionada (maior, dobro: *relação*)
e. Onde está (lugar: *espaço*)
f. Quando é (ontem: *tempo*)
g. Postura assumida: (sentado: *posição*)
h. Seu estado (vestido: *provisão*)
i. O que faz (queima: *atividade*)
j. O que sofre (é queimado: *passividade*)

4. *Processo de raciocínio*. a. Passa do universal para o particular. b. Forma juízos. c. Com base nos juízos, tira inferências. Essas inferências são chamadas proposições. d. Os juízos compõem-se de *conceitos* expressos por meio de *termos*.

III. Metafísica (descoberta dos princípios fundamentais)

1. Para Platão, a realidade é espiritual (as idéias, formas, universais), ao passo que os objetos terrenos (os particulares) são apenas cópias inferiores do que é «real». A *forma* é a substância real de alguma coisa. *Idéia* e *forma* são termos intercambiáveis. Essa realidade é mais real que a realidade física. Na filosofia, esse conceito chama-se *realismo radical*.

2. Para Aristóteles, as coisas particulares (objetos terrenos) são substâncias reais. A forma ou universal sempre se encontra no particular. A forma é real, mas não independente do particular. Na filosofia, essa posição chama-se *realismo moderado*. Ver o artigo sobre os *universais*.

3. A matéria assume diferentes formas, mas persiste a idéia ou forma. A matéria é o princípio da probabilidade. A forma é o princípio da realidade (atualidade).

4. A *substância* de uma coisa é a sua totalidade. Essa é a primeira categoria aristotélica. Sócrates é um homem; mas ele é mais do que o seu corpo material. Ele também inclui um princípio não-material, juntamente com muitas alterações em série, que se dirigem a algum alvo. Cresceu e foi educado em Atenas, e terminou sendo um grande filósofo. Tudo isso tem a ver com a sua substância. A substância de qualquer coisa inclui sua forma e sua matéria.

5. A matéria une-se à forma. Para que ela se torne no que deve, de conformidade com um *desígnio* (o princípio da teleologia), deve haver várias *causas*.

As quatro causas: a. *Causa material*. Matéria mais potencialidade, tendo em mira o desenvolvimento, conforme foi explicado acima. b. *Causa formal*. Para que algo venha a ser como deve, deve haver um padrão, desígnio ou plano. c. *Causa eficiente*. Para que o desígnio se concretize, deve haver um agente, uma força que efetiva o propósito. d. *Causa final*. É o alvo na direção do que algo se move; o desígnio em seu cumprimento. *Ilustração*: Construção de um muro. Para que se construa um muro, deve haver a matéria e sua potencialidade (a argila que será cozida: a causa material). Em seguida, deve haver um plano para a edificação do muro. Isso determinará quem fará a obra e como esta deverá ser feita (causa formal). Então deve haver um agente, o pedreiro que construirá o muro (causa eficiente). Quando o muro tiver sido construído, seu desígnio estará cumprido (causa final).

6. Para que qualquer coisa suceda, ou seja levada a bom termo, deve haver *movimento*. Se existe o movimento, deve haver um Movedor Primário (a Causa Primária do movimento). Essa entidade chama-se -Movedor Primário ou Movedor Inabalável. Trata-se de uma força cosmológica, na realidade, o Deus da concepção aristotélica, que seria uma força impessoal, e não uma pessoa. Esse Movedor Primário movimenta todas as outras coisas «sendo amado», o que é um evidente termo poético para indicar uma força de atração. Esse Movedor não tem consciência das outras coisas, por ser puro pensamento, capaz de pensar por si mesmo. Deus é a forma pura, a idéia da realidade. Deus (o Movedor Inabalável), como forma pura, existe independentemente da matéria, havendo outras formas celestiais que não são materiais. Em todos os demais casos, forma e matéria compõem as substâncias individuais, e são os acidentes da matéria que constituem um objeto particular, como uma cadeira. Por exemplo, a cor é um acidente de alguma coisa, mas não, necessariamente, o seu ser. Ver o artigo sobre *acidente*. Os acidentes não são uma das categorias aristotélicas. Ver o artigo sobre as *categorias*.

Os *quatro movimentos* (excluído o Movedor Inabalável):
a. Movimento substancial (origem e decadência). b. Movimento quantitativo (alterações no volume de um corpo). c. Movimento qualitativo (transformação de uma coisa em outra). d. Movimento local (mudança de posição no espaço, ou mudança de lugar). Devido aos fatores de causa, desígnio e movimento, a natureza não é apenas mecânica. -Antes, é dinâmica, teleológica, ativa e eivada de propósito.

A filosofia medieval, árabe ou cristã, utilizava-se de muitos dos conceitos aristotélicos em suas expressões teológicas e científicas. Ver os artigos sobre o *aristotelianismo* e sobre o *escolasticismo*.

IV. Biologia. Aristóteles é o fundador da zoologia sistemática e comparada. Ver sob seus escritos, no começo da discussão sobre os diversos livros que ele escreveu acerca dos animais. Ele se opunha aos conceitos puramente quantitativos-mecânicos-causais. Em todos os animais, a alma é a forma do corpo. O corpo é apenas um instrumento, mas a alma é o princípio normativo. Onde houver vida, haverá alma, o poder por detrás do desígnio, o princípio teleológico. A alma humana é a entelequia do corpo. Não obstante, Aristóteles aparentemente não cria (ou, pelo menos, mostrava-se agnóstico a esse respeito) na sobrevivência da alma. Todavia, o ponto é disputado.

V. Psicologia. 1. O homem é o alvo final da natureza, diferindo ele dos animais inferiores devido à sua capacidade de raciocinar. 2. Os órgãos dos sentidos informam a alma sobre as qualidades das coisas. 3. A alma humana é capaz de raciocínio conceitualizante, isto é, de capacidade de discernir o que é universal, assim descobrindo a essência necessária das coisas. 4. A razão passiva é a matéria a partir da qual atua a razão criativa e ativa. Está vinculada ao corpo, e juntamente com este, perece, tal como sucedem à imaginação e à memória. 5. A razão ativa ou criativa é pura realidade, mediante a qual chegamos aos conceitos. Existe antes mesmo do corpo. Essa alma é imaterial, imperecível e imortal. Contudo, não é claro se Aristóteles aplicava esses atributos às almas individuais, ou somente ao princípio da alma, ou alma do mundo. Averróis interpretava Aristóteles como se ele tivesse querido dizer que somente uma forma pura, ou alma, existe para a humanidade inteira, e que tal pensamento não dá apoio à idéia da sobrevivência da alma.

Três tipos de alma. a. Nutritiva-vegetativa: tem as potencialidades de assimilação e reprodução. b. Sensível: como nos animais, com capacidade de movimento e de desejos. c. Humana: além das capacidades acima, tem a capacidade de raciocinar, de rebuscar pela verdade.

ARISTÓTELES

VI. Ética. 1. O principal bem é a felicidade (eudemonia). 2. A felicidade vem através da auto-realização. 3. A virtude é o cumprimento da auto-realização da melhor maneira possível. É a função cheia de propósito de alguma coisa específica. 4. Visto que o homem tem uma razão —que busca a verdade, é desejável que ele use essa capacidade como sua principal virtude. A descoberta da verdade é a mais alta felicidade do homem. 5. O alvo da vida humana não é o prazer (ver sobre o hedonismo), mas a virtude, que deve tornar-se um hábito. 6. A virtude habitual vem através do disciplinamento da razão, a faculdade especial do homem. Uma alma virtuosa é uma razão ordeira e disciplinada, que evita extremismos. Observa o *meio-termo áureo* (a moderação). Exemplo: A coragem é o meio-termo entre a impetuosidade e a covardia. A temperança ou controle próprio é o meio-termo entre a inapetência e a glutonaria. A justiça é o meio-termo áureo entre deixar-se abusar por outros e o ato de espezinhar os direitos alheios. Ver o artigo sobre o *meio-termo áureo*. Esse artigo expõe diante do leitor as doze virtudes principais aristotélicas, juntamente com suas deficiências, excessos e meios-termos (ou virtudes). 7. As virtudes intelectuais buscam a verdade e os meios usados para isso são as artes, as ciências, a prudência, a sabedoria, a iniciativa e a razão. A sabedoria consiste na razão que aborda o que é invariável. A razão ao agir em relação ao que é variável, constitui a prudência. 8. A vida contemplativa é a mais elevada e feliz. Somos mais parecidos com Deus quando nos pomos a contemplar.

VII. Política. 1. O estado existe visando ao bem do homem. 2. A vida social é o alvo da existência humana. 3. O estado deve produzir e nutrir bons cidadãos. 4. A constituição do estado deve ser adaptada ao caráter e aos requisitos do povo, pelo que pode variar de um lugar para outro, sem a necessidade de estruturas rígidas. 5. Visto que os indivíduos diferem em suas habilidades, a justiça requer que sejam tratados de acordo com essas diferenças. 6. Cada cidadão deve exercer a sua *virtude*, ou função específica em favor da comunidade, ou estado. 7. A família é a unidade básica do estado. O homem, se isolar-se, não será auto-suficiente. 8. Há três formas aceitáveis de governo: a. monarquia; b. aristocracia; c. política, algo aparentado com a democracia constitucional. Ele preferia essa terceira opção. 9. Há três formas inaceitáveis de governo: a. tirania; b. oligarquia; c. democracia popular. Essas são deformações das formas aceitáveis.

VIII. Estética. Essa é desenvolvida na obra de Aristóteles, *Poética*. 1. A arte é a imitação do possível ou do provável na natureza, e não somente do que é real. 2. A poesia trata do *universal* (ver o artigo). 3. A beleza é a unidade na variedade, sem quaisquer características não-essenciais. 4. A tragédia provê a catarse das emoções do terror e da compaixão. 5. A participação nas artes enobrece e enriquece o homem.

Aristóteles foi um dos maiores filósofos do mundo, o qual exerceu duradoura influência sobre a teologia e sobre as ciências. A Igreja ocidental, por meio de filósofos como Tomás de Aquino, incorporou a filosofia aristotélica como uma característica permanente, bem como meio de expressar certo número de conceitos cristãos. Uma das fontes fundamentais do escolasticismo (ver o artigo a respeito) foi a filosofia de Aristóteles. (AM BE DR E EP F P)

Realizações. Platão chamou Aristóteles de *o intelecto*, sendo ele o mais brilhante de seus alunos. Suas realizações justificaram o título. Ele foi o maior cientista de seu tempo, cuja influência, neste campo, perdurou muitos séculos. Foi o pai da biologia, embora seu método, por falta de instrumentos, tenha sido essencialmente descritivo. Também foi o fundador da lógica científica, e com esta realização, tornou-se o primeiro filósofo a incorporar todos os seis ramos tradicionais da filosofia em seu sistema. Sua importância se manifesta no ditado que declara: Todos os homens são *platônicos* ou *aristotélicos* nas suas aproximações com relação ao problema do conhecimento: a aproximação *empírica-científica* = Aristóteles; a aproximação *racional-intuitiva-mística* = Platão.

O artigo que segue sobre *Aristotelianismo* ilustra alguns aspectos de sua vasta influência no mundo das idéias, especialmente no campo da religião.

* * *

ARISTOTELIANISMO Ver sobre **Aristóteles**.

A filosofia de Aristóteles é importante para a teologia e para a fé cristãs devido ao fato de que Tomás de Aquino (e os filósofos tomistas) a têm usado como meio de expressar sua fé, e vastas multidões de cristãos têm sido influenciadas por essa atividade. Ver o artigo sobre *Aquino, Tomás de*, quanto a uma descrição dessa atividade e influência.

Um dos mais importantes e extraordinários desenvolvimentos na história das idéias européias foi a adaptação da filosofia de Aristóteles para consumo cristão. O filósofo grego Aristóteles (384-322 A.C.) estudou com Platão e por este era chamado de «o intelecto», tendo-se tornado um brilhante filósofo. Tomás de Aquino encontrou em suas idéias um meio apropriado para exprimir sua teologia. Os filósofos árabes foram os primeiros a usar suas obras (ver *averroísmo*), embora interpretando materialisticamente o seu pensamento. O pensamento judaico medieval, em Maimônides e seus discípulos (ver o artigo a respeito) também foi influenciado pelo filósofo (Aristóteles, conforme Aquino o apodou). Após séculos de dominação platônica entre os filósofos cristãos (por exemplo, os pais alexandrinos e a escola de Agostinho), a «nova lógica» (a filosofia aristotélica) tomou conta das universidades da cristandade, notavelmente Paris e Oxford. Tomás de Aquino mostrou que a razão humana, conforme Aristóteles sugerira, não é adversária da fé cristã; antes, pode ser usada para compor uma teologia natural capaz de ajudar a fé. As verdades da revelação recebem assim um alicerce racional. Afinal de contas, tudo isso faz parte do nosso conhecimento de Deus e das realidades espirituais, pois Ele é o supremo Intelecto, do qual todos os outros, como intelectos. Pode-se supor a existência de uma afinidade entre os intelectos e o Intelecto, e que a razão humana pode descobrir a verdade, disciplinando sua busca.

Aspectos históricos. Platão e Aristóteles, embora fossem mestre e aluno, defendiam idéias bem diversas. Platão era o racionalista místico influenciado pelas religiões orientais, e Aristóteles era o cientista, que enfatizava o método empírico. Suas idéias filosóficas também se chocaram após a morte de ambos; mas, nos círculos religiosos, os homens usavam as idéias de Platão com mais facilidade. Assim, o *neoplatonismo* (ver o artigo a respeito) era uma expressão religiosa de Platão, que exerceu vasta influência no mundo religioso por muitos séculos, incluindo a Igreja cristã, através dos pais alexandrinos. Plotino (204-270 D.C.), o neoplatonista, encontrou alguns subsídios em Aristóteles, como a teoria do Intelecto separado e o contraste entre a matéria e a forma; mas, em tudo o mais, conflitava com ele. Porfírio de Tiro (234-cerca de 305 D.C.), discípulo de Plotino, escreveu uma introdução (*Isagoge*) a cinco conceitos: espécie, gênero, diferenças, propriedade e acidente, demonstrando nela grande influência aristotélica. Essa obra foi incorporada em seu *Organon*, tendo sido canonizada para as gerações futuras como obra de inspiração aristotélica. Foi usada por Boethius (ver o artigo a seu respeito), cuja intenção era reconciliar o neoplatonismo e o aristotelianismo. Ele produziu um comentário sobre a Isagoge, que originou a grande controvérsia sobre *os universais* (ver o artigo) e que teve muita importância para o pensamento teológico da Idade Média e depois. As obras de Aristóteles sobre a *lógica* atraíram mais atenção na Idade Média, e os teólogos cristãos começaram a desenvolver contrastes aristotélicos como substância e acidente.

Porém, no século XIII, aumentou imensamente o interesse por Aristóteles — sobretudo através de Tomás de Aquino, embora não com exclusividade. Comentários árabes sobre suas obras proviram a força que espalhou as idéias de Aristóteles por toda a parte. Eles abordavam materialisticamente as idéias dele, embora de modo atrativo para a mente religiosa. Averróis (1126-1198) era mais respeitado no ocidente latino do que em sua pátria, tendo atraído a atenção de Alberto Magno (cerca de 1200-1280), mestre de Tomás de Aquino. Foi na Universidade de Paris que Alberto Magno tomou conhecimento dos escritos de Averróis. Tomás de Aquino (1225-1274) entrou em contato com esse material quando estudava em Nápoles. Averróis emprestou um mau nome ao aristotelianismo; mas não demorou que uma nova maneira de encará-lo e manuseá-lo, em favor da fé religiosa, se tivesse desenvolvido, por meio de Tomás de Aquino. Muitos teólogos sentiam-se inquietos ante os acontecimentos. Tal fato resultou na proscrição do aristotelianismo, por diversas vezes durante o século XIII, a começar pelo ano de 1210. Esse desenvolvimento culminou na condenação do bispo de Paris, Estêvão Tempier, a 7 de março de 1277.

Esse recuo do aristotelianismo latino foi temporário. O estudo mais cuidadoso dos escritos de Aquino, bem como sua canonização em 1323, produziu a total reabilitação dessa filosofia. O grande teólogo Duns Scoto (cerca de 1266-1308), como também William de Ockham (cerca de 1285-1347), foram influenciados por essa forma de teologia-filosofia.

Os séculos XVI-XVIII testemunharam uma outra reação, parcialmente porque Copérnico (1473-1543) mostrou que algumas das idéias científicas básicas de Aristóteles estavam equivocadas. Apesar disso, por meio de Tomás de Aquino, Aristóteles continuou exercendo grande influência no mundo religioso. O papa Leão XIII (1880) decretou que essa filosofia era a posição oficial da Igreja de Roma, como meio filosófico de contemplar a religião.

Apesar de que alguns evangélicos abordam sua fé filosoficamente, nenhuma das denominações protestantes ou evangélicas têm desenvolvido um estudo sistemático e filosófico da religião. Os protestantes, sob a influência de Kant, que situava a fé e seus sujeitos dentro do mundo noumenal, dependente da intuição e do misticismo, têm subestimado a abordagem racional-filosófica da fé. Alguns deles chegam francamente a ser hostis, julgando que a filosofia é contrária à revelação e à fé. Conheço pessoalmente o caso de um pregador-filósofo, um ministro do evangelho, mas estudioso da filosofia, que foi severamente criticado por ter apresentado as provas tradicionais e racionais da existência de Deus. Alguns chegaram a exprimir a opinião que «aquele filósofo» não mais deveria ser convidado. Sem dúvida isso reflete ignorância dos fatos. Deus nos concedeu a capacidade de raciocinar. Ele é o Intelecto, e nós somos os intelectos secundários, que temos afinidade com Ele — pois fomos criados à Sua imagem. Portanto, a razão muito tem para contribuir para a inquirição espiritual. (AM C E EP)

ARLES, SÍNODO DE

O primeiro concílio geral da Igreja ocidental reuniu-se em Arles, sudeste da França, em 314 D.C. Foi convocado pelo imperador Constantino a fim de encontrar solução para disputas entre os *donatistas* (ver o artigo a respeito) e os católicos do Norte da África, que não tinham sido resolvidas pelo sínodo de Roma, em 313. Estiveram presentes representantes de bispados da Europa ocidental (incluindo a Bretanha) e do Norte da África. Vinte e dois cânones condenaram os donatistas e suas principais contenções, abordando questões de disciplina eclesiástica que haviam surgido desde a perseguição desfechada por Diocleciano. (E)

ARMAÇÃO DO NAVIO
(Ver **Navios e Embarcações**)

ARMADILHA

Certo número de termos hebraicos é usado para denotar métodos para apanhar animais ou seres humanos. Esses termos significam *amarrar, prender com uma corda* (Jó 18:10), *cilada* (Êxo. 10:7), *armadilha* (Jer. 5:26). Termos menos usados no hebraico são traduzidos por «rede», como em Eze. 12:13. Em Jó 18:9 encontramos um termo raro no hebraico, mas que em nossa versão portuguesa tem a forma de «armadilha». Apontava para uma armadilha de ferro, embora nossa versão portuguesa a traduza por «laço», em Jos. 23:13. Nas páginas do Novo Testamento encontramos dois vocábulos gregos, *bróchos*, corda, (somente em I Cor. 7:35) e *págis*, armadilha, (Rom. 11:9, I Tim. 3:7, 6:9, 2 Tim. 2:26).

Ver o artigo sobre *Rede* (*Armadilha, Laço*).

ARMADURA, ARMAS

Esboço
I. Armaduras, Armas Antigas
II. A Luta: A necessidade da armadura
III. O Inimigo: não carne e sangue
IV. Preparação para Batalhar
V. Peças Principais: Lições morais e espirituais

Quanto a uma descrição das antigas armaduras, cujas peças principais são alistadas em Efé. 6:13 ss, ver a exposição no NTI, naquele trecho.

Um item desta natureza devia figurar em uma enciclopédia religiosa, mesmo que não apareça em uma enciclopédia bíblica, — devido às suas implicações morais. Paulo empregou algumas metáforas militares, usando as peças de uma armadura antiga como símbolos de virtudes espirituais, segundo se vê na exposição em Efé. 6:13 ss. No Antigo Testamento, há menção às armaduras, usadas na vida militar, em relação a Israel e suas muitas guerras. A

ARMADURA, ARMAS

presença de uma matança organizada, nas páginas do Antigo Testamento, cria problemas morais ventilados pelo *pacifismo* (ver o artigo). Poderia isso ser correto, mesmo quando os homens apresentam Deus, nos próprios Livros Sagrados, como líder de atividades militares? Será correto os governos organizarem exércitos e enviarem-nos em expedições contra países e povos, especificamente com a finalidade de provocar sofrimentos e mortes?

I. Armadura, Armas Antigas

A armadura inteira consistia de escudo, espada, lança, capacete e armadura das pernas (que cobria as coxas até os joelhos), segundo Políbio e outros escritores antigos. (Ver Thuc. iii,14; Isócr. 352 D; Heród. i.60; Platão, *Leis* vii. par. 796 B; Políbio vi. 23,2). O soldado romano mui provavelmente está em vista aqui; mas as armaduras gregas e romanas não diferiam muito entre si. Paulo era homem intensamente viajado pelo império romano, tendo sido encarcerado e solto por muitas vezes, e estaria bem familiarizado com as armaduras de seu tempo. Os museus modernos contêm exemplares dessa armadura. O apóstolo acrescenta o cinturão e a espada em sua lista; e apesar desses dois objetos realmente não fazerem parte da armadura, eram necessários para o soldado antigo, muito apropriados para o propósito de ilustrar o equipamento espiritual necessário para derrotar o mal. Abaixo oferecemos uma descrição detalhada das armaduras antigas:

Armas de Defesa

1. *Perikephalaia*, é «capacete», que protegia a cabeça. Era feito de várias formas e de vários metais, e com freqüência era decorado com grande variedade de figuras. Alguns capacetes possuíam uma crista, ou como ornamento ou com a finalidade de aterrorizar, com figuras de leões, corvos, grifos, etc. Este último era um animal lendário, com corpo e pernas traseiras de leão, e cabeça e asas de águia. Paulo faz o capacete representar a «salvação».

2. *Zoma*, o «cinturão», posto em torno da cintura, útil para apertar a armadura em volta do corpo, mas também para sustentar as adagas, as espadas curtas ou quaisquer outras armas que ali pudessem ser penduradas. Paulo faz do cinturão símbolo da «verdade».

3. *Thoraks*, o «peitoral», que consistia de duas partes, chamadas «asas». Uma delas cobria a região inteira do peito, a parte frontal do tórax, protegendo os órgãos principais da vida, ali contidos. E a outra parte cobria uma parte das costas. Paulo faz isso representar a «justiça» ou «retidão».

4. *Knemides*, as «grevas», que serviam para proteger as canelas, isto é, do joelho para baixo, e com freqüência com uma extensão de couro que também protegia o pé.

5. *Cheirides*, uma espécie de «luvas» que serviam para proteger as mãos, bem como o antebraço, até o cotovelo.

6. *Vários tipos de escudo*, que Paulo usa como símbolo da «fé» (ver Efés. 6:16). Era o «aspis» ou o «chiled». Havia várias formas, feitas de diferentes metais. O escudo de Aquiles, que teria sido feito por Vulcano, seria circular, composto de cinco chapas de metal, sendo duas de bronze, duas de estanho e uma de ouro. Ver *Ilíada*, Upsilon, v. 270:

*Cinco chapas de vários metais, vários moldes,
Compunham o escudo; de bronze cada um se dobrava
  para fora,
De estanho, cada um para dentro; e o do meio, de ouro.*

Gerron, ou «guerra», um pequeno escudo quadrado, que a princípio foi usado pelos persas.

Laiseion, o escudo de forma oblonga, coberto com couros ásperos, ainda com os pêlos.

Pelte, o «escudo leve», na forma de uma lua crescente, com um pequeno ornamento similar às pétalas recurvas de uma flor *de luce*, no centro de uma linha diagonal reta, que passava perto de uma das beiradas. Esse era o escudo amazônico.

Thureos, o «scutum» ou «escudo oblongo», feito de madeira e recoberto de couro, mas já sem os pêlos. Tinha o formato do «laiseion» (descrito acima), embora fosse muito maior. Seu nome se deriva da palavra «thura», que significa «porta», visto que se assemelhava a portas de tamanho comum, quanto à sua forma.

Nos dias de Paulo, o «aspis» e o «thureos» eram os escudos mais usados. O primeiro se destinava a soldados levemente armados, e o último para soldados pesadamente armados.

Armas de Ataque

1. *Egchos*, a «lança», usualmente munida de ponta de bronze ou de ferro, com uma longa haste de madeira dura, geralmente de «freixo», árvore pertencente ao grupo da oliveira, mas dotada de uma madeira dura e elástica.

2. *Doru*, o «dardo», menor e mais leve que a «lança», que era atirado contra o inimigo ainda a distância.

3. *Ziphos*, a «espada», que tinha várias formas e dimensões. As primeiras eram feitas de bronze, e mais tarde começaram a ser feitas de outros materiais. Todas as espadas referidas nos escritos de Homero são de bronze. Esse é o símbolo usado por Paulo para indicar a presença do Espírito Santo.

4. *Machaira*, palavra que também significa «espada». Mas era um pouco mais curta, freqüentemente usada pelos gladiadores. Contudo, esta e a palavra anterior com freqüência eram usadas como sinônimas, sem diferenças apreciáveis.

5. *Aksine*, a «acha de armas» ou «machado de guerra».

6. *Pelekus*, a dupla «acha de armas», com uma folha afiada para cada lado.

7. *Korune*, a maça, feita de ferro, muito usada pelos persas e gregos.

8. *Tokson*, o «arco», completo com a «pharetta» (a aljava) e as flechas, que no grego têm o nome de «beie» (ver Efé. 6:16).

9. *Sphendone*, a «funda», muito usada pelos hebreus e muitos outros povos, com grande habilidade.

10. *Akontion*, o «dardo», outro tipo de lança, mais leve que o «ecchos».

11. *Belos*, «flecha».

*Enquanto a crueldade não foi melhorada pela arte,
E a fúria não forneceu espada ou dardo,
Com os punhos, ou ramos, ou pedras lutavam os
  homens,
Essas eram as únicas armas ensinadas pela Natureza:
Mas quando chamas queimavam árvores e crestavam
  o solo,
Então apareceu o bronze, e foi preparado o ferro para
  ferir,
O bronze foi usado primeiro, por ser mais fácil de
  trabalhar,
E visto que as veias da terra o continham em maior
  dose.*

(Lucrécio, *De Rerum Nat.*, lib. v. 1282)

••• ••• •••

ARMADURA, ARMAS

Tipos de Capacetes
1. de plantas 2. egípcio 3. e 4. asiáticos
5. cariano 6. e 7. egípcios 8. assírio 9. grego
10. jônio 11. parto 12. e 13. tribos da Ásia

Espada persa

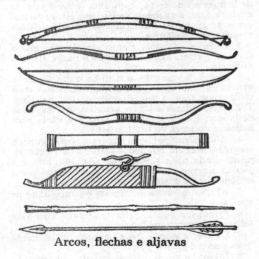

Arcos, flechas e aljavas

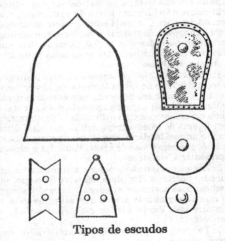

Tipos de escudos

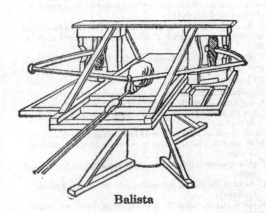

Balista

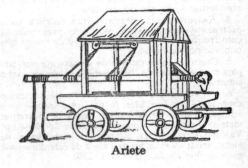

Ariete

ARMADURA, ARMAS

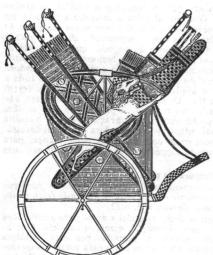

Carro de batalha, egípcio

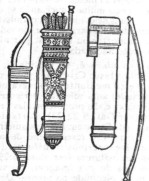

Flechas e arcos egípcios

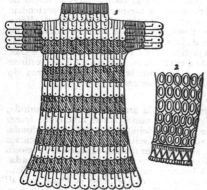

Cota de malha egípcia e jônia

Máquinas de guerra assírias

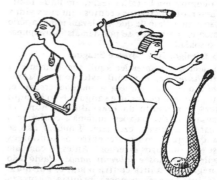

Estilingues egípcios

Roupa de guerra
1, 2. grega muito antiga 3. grega
4, 5. romana 6. bárbara

ARMADURA, ARMAS

II. A Luta: A Necessidade da Armadura

Pois não é contra carne e sangue que temos que lutar, mas sim contra os principados, contra as potestades, contra os príncipes do mundo destas trevas, contra os hostes espirituais da iniqüidade nas regiões celestes. Efé. 6:2.

Nosso conflito contra o mal exige preparação, força e coragem. No grego original temos a palavra «pale», que ordinariamente indicava a «luta romana», embora também pudesse indicar um conflito qualquer. A forma verbal significa «lançar», «projetar». Tal vocábulo é usado exclusivamente aqui, em todo o N.T. Com o sentido de «combate», essa palavra é encontrada nos escritos de vários poetas, como Ésquilo, *Cho.* 866, e Eurípedes, *Herácl.* 159. O apóstolo Paulo provavelmente a emprega no seu sentido geral, porquanto, de outro modo, ter-se-ia desviado momentaneamente de sua metáfora de uma guerra, passando a pintar o conflito cristão contra o mal como uma luta de corpo a corpo. Seja como for, é focalizada a intensidade do combate, e para o que o soldado cristão deve ter a preparação e a força necessárias. A luta contra o mal, assim sendo, deve ser vista como uma batalha séria, em nada fácil. Talvez a derrota de tantos crentes, em suas vidas morais, se deva ao fato de que não levam muito a sério esse combate, mostrando-se por demais indisciplinados como soldados.

III. O Inimigo: Não Carne e Sangue

Paulo quer dar a entender aqui, simplesmente, a *natureza humana*, em contraste com os *seres espirituais*, que não possuem a matéria crassa, e, portanto, não são de carne e sangue. Não há aqui qualquer pensamento da «carnalidade humana pecaminosa», ou das paixões humanas, conforme o termo «carne» algumas vezes tem. Também não se verifica qualquer contraste entre os «inimigos internos» e os «inimigos externos». Antes, o combate se dá entre *humanos e sobre-humanos*. Paulo não queria negar que a luta contra o mal é, por igual modo, a luta contra a nossa própria natureza pecaminosa, e nem que os «inimigos internos» não sejam também nossos inimigos (pois o sexto capítulo da epístola aos Romanos afirma ambas as coisas); mas neste ponto ele mostra que poderes malignos e externos tornam esse conflito tão intenso que facilmente o crente se sai perdedor na refrega, a menos que esteja equipado com o próprio poder de Deus.

A debilidade humana fica subentendida na expressão «sangue e carne», ao passo que o poder fica subentendido na menção que se segue sobre as entidades espirituais.

Principados e potestades. (Comparar com o trecho de Efé. 1:21. Referem-se particularmente a poderes angelicais santos, ao passo que aqui estão em foco seres espirituais do mal, embora de ordem superior). Tanto os seres espirituais de índole boa como aqueles de má índole, habitam nos «lugares celestiais» (ver Efé. 1:20 e 6:12), sem isso querer dizer que habitam exatamente nos mesmos lugares ou campos celestiais, pois existem muitas dessas dimensões, algumas ocupadas por seres benignos, e outras ocupadas por seres malignos, embora todos pertençam à categoria «espiritual». Supõe-se que o termo *principados* se refere às ordens angelicais superiores, que possuem autoridade sobre grandes regiões e sobre muitíssimos seres. Já o vocábulo *potestades* se referia a governantes subordinados.

Ciladas do diabo, Efé. 6:11. No grego, *ciladas* é «methodeia», que quer dizer «astúcias», «planos», «esquemas», ou, em linguagem militar, «estratagemas». Quando tal palavra se aplica a Satanás, no N.T., porém, sempre indica seus maus desígnios. O comandante das forças malignas é o *diabo*, o grande mestre do ludíbrio e do engodo, que capitaneia as forças do mal contra o bem. Sendo ele o comandante das forças malignas, é óbvio que toda a armadura espiritual é necessária para o crente, com toda a oração e súplica, para que essas forças sejam derrotadas. O fato de que tantos crentes são derrotados na refrega, é prova que não se têm preocupado com a preparação para a batalha espiritual, adquirindo a armadura espiritual necessária; e nem oram com suficiente perseverança, para que o mestre supremo do mal seja vencido em suas vidas.

IV. Preparação para Batalhar

Portanto tomai toda a armadura de Deus, para que possais resistir no dia mau, e havendo feito tudo, permanecer firmes. Efé. 6:13.

Tomai, ou seja, «estendei a mão» para a armadura posta à vossa disposição, e revesti-vos dela. Que as realidades espirituais pintadas por esta metáfora sejam postas em prática em vossas vidas, porquanto isso será vossa proteção e vitória. A ordem de Paulo é que nos apropriemos do poder espiritual a nós oferecido. Os antigos soldados, quando não eram apropriadamente disciplinados e se encontravam em condições físicas deficientes, mostravam-se menos dispostos e eram menos capazes de suportar as fadigas de seu duro serviço militar, queixando-se do peso da armadura; e alguns deles obtinham permissão para pôr de lado parte da armadura, ou mesmo toda. E muitos eram assim mortos ou feridos, por não contarem com a proteção adequada.

A *colocação da armadura* é, na realidade, o revestimento do Senhor Jesus Cristo por parte do crente, e isso é expresso mediante uma metáfora poética. Todas as virtudes aqui referidas pertencem supremamente ao Senhor, e são proporcionadas pelo seu Santo Espírito (ver Gál. 5:22,23). Portanto, revestir-se da armadura de Cristo equivale a assumir a natureza moral de Cristo; e o revestimento de sua natureza moral envolve o sermos transformados metafisicamente em sua natureza (ver Rom. 8:29), para que participemos de sua imagem, de sua plenitude, e também da plenitude do próprio Deus Pai (ver Efé. 1:23 e 3:19). Nisso é que consiste a vida cristã, verdadeiramente, o que é retratado mediante uma metáfora baseada na vida militar. E isso porque é a participação na natureza de Cristo que nos outorga verdadeira defesa contra todas as forças do mal e vitória sobre as mesmas, as quais pretendem impedir o progresso da alma de volta a Deus. (Ver o trecho de Rom. 13:12 acerca da colocação da «armadura da luz», bem como II Cor. 6:7, acerca das «armas da justiça». Ver o NTI em Rom. 13:14 e Gál. 3:27 quanto a notas expositivas acerca do «revestir-se de Cristo», e finalmente, Efé. 4:24, acerca do «revestir-se do novo homem»).

Toda a Armadura

Nenhuma porção da armadura pode ser omitida, pois o adversário de nossas almas sabe como tomar partido de qualquer debilidade; sendo ele profundamente maligno, aproveitar-se-á disso. Os recursos humanos, as resoluções morais, os sistemas religiosos e filosóficos, não nos servirão de ajuda em nada, porquanto somente um toque real da mão de Deus nos pode garantir a vitória nesse combate mortal. Devemos dar atenção ao fato de que em tudo isso, alguma forma de preparação espiritual autêntica,

ARMADURA, ARMAS

como a comunhão completa com o Espírito de Deus, é ordenada aos crentes, nos usos metafóricos que aparecem em seguida. Portanto, não basta o conselho que geralmente se dá aos novos convertidos: «Leia a sua Bíblia e ore», embora isso constitua um bom exercício. Pois deve haver o contacto pessoal do crente com o Senhor, a comunhão mística com ele. E o revestimento da completa armadura de Deus se faz através da busca, através dessa comunhão.

V. Peças principais: Lições Morais e Espirituais.
A Descrição Paulina—Efé. 6:14.

«A *panóplia* romana consiste primeiramente de um escudo de superfície convexa, de 0,75 cm de altura; na beirada, sua espessura é da largura de u'a mão... Juntamente com o escudo há a espada; e esta o soldado leva em sua coxa direita, chamada 'espada espanhola'. Permite um golpe poderoso e profundo com ambos os fios, pois a lâmina é forte e firme. Além disso, o soldado leva dois dardos, um capacete de bronze e grevas...A maioria dos soldados também usa uma chapa de bronze, da largura de um palmo para cada lado, que colocam sobre o peito—chamam-na de 'protetor do coração'; e aqueles que valem mais de dez mil dracmas, em vez do protetor do coração usam uma cota de malhas». Políbio, *História*, VI.23.

1. Cinturão: A Verdade. Efé. 6:14.
Cingindo-vos com a verdade. Esse simbolismo se alicerça no trecho de Isa. 11:5, onde a verdade também é pintada como um cinturão que deve ser colocado. Consideremos ainda, a respeito disso, os pontos seguintes:

1. Talvez a alusão aqui feita seja à total verdade de Deus.

2. Devemos entender aqui a verdade cristã, isto é, segundo ela se encontra na pessoa de Cristo, ou seja, tudo quanto está envolvido desde a conversão, incluindo a conduta do crente, de acordo com padrões verdadeiramente bíblicos.

3. Alguns vêem aqui a verdade como alusão particular à «fidelidade», à «lealdade» a Cristo, conforme se vê no trecho de Isa. 11:5.

4. A harmonia com a «revelação» divina e a lealdade à mesma, em contraste com as heresias dos gnósticos, ou com outros desvios doutrinários, ou mesmo com uma conduta incorreta, também está aqui em foco. Isso pode ser comparado com o que se lê em Efé. 4:21, acerca da «verdade em Jesus».

5. Há também aqueles que vêem uma significação especial no cinto, associado à verdade, porque era essa a peça que ligava as diversas peças entre si; assim sendo, a verdade «...confere unidade às diversas virtudes, bem como confere determinação e coerência ao caráter. Todas as virtudes devem ser exercidas dentro da esfera da verdade». (Vincent *in loc.*)

A referência de Paulo mui provavelmente é lata, incluindo várias das idéias expostas nos pontos acima, e não apenas um ou outro aspecto.

2. Couraça: Justiça. Efé. 6:14.
Vestindo-vos da couraça da justiça. (Ver o trecho de Isa. 59:17, que também se refere ao simbolismo do «peitoral» de uma armadura). Essa referência é messiânica, com toda a probabilidade, revelando-nos a preparação moral do Messias, o qual, mediante tal preparo, derrotou seus inimigos e completou sua missão e vitória. No trecho de I Tes. 5:8, o «peitoral» aparece composto da «fé» e do «amor», e a «fé» é também o escudo do crente.

Existiam vários tipos de *peitoral*, feitos de diferentes materiais, nas armaduras antigas. Os guerreiros levemente armados usavam um peitoral feito de linho; algumas nações bárbaras equipavam seus soldados com peitorais feitos de chifre ou osso, cortados em pedaços pequenos e pendurados como escamas, amarrados sobre um capote de couro ou de linho. Mais tarde foram introduzidas tiras flexíveis de aço, dobradas umas sobre as outras. Os lanceiros romanos usavam cotas de malha, ou armaduras flexíveis feitas de tiras de metal ligadas entre si. Virgílio menciona peitorais em que os anéis de ligação eram feitos de ouro. (*Eneida*, iii. 467). Ainda outros peitorais eram de material inteiramente rígido, ficando de pé quando postos no chão. Esse tipo de peitoral se compunha de duas partes, uma que cobria o peito e outra que cobria as costas; e essas duas metades eram ligadas entre si por tiras de couro ou tiras de metal, por cima dos ombros, amarradas na parte da frente, havendo também articulações nos lados. Esses peitorais eram fabricados de couro, de bronze, de ferro ou de outros metais. Suetônio conta-nos como Galba (imperador romano em 68-69 D.C.) foi morto pelos soldados de Oto, por haver-se protegido apenas com um peitoral de linho, em vez de usar um peitoral de material mais resistente.

O peitoral protegia os órgãos vitais do tórax e da parte superior do abdômen. O que para o soldado era uma proteção extremamente importante, assim é a «justiça» ou «retidão» para o crente. (Ver o artigo sobre a *Retidão*, que é essencial à própria salvação, como decorrência da justificação). É a própria retidão de Deus que está aqui em foco; porque ninguém pode chegar à sua presença se não possuir exatamente essa modalidade de retidão. Essa justiça tanto tem um aspecto «forense», através de um decreto divino, baixado com base no sangue expiatório de Cristo, como tem um aspecto «real», mediante a santificação, o que forma em nós a natureza moral de Cristo. Assim, pois, a perfeição da natureza moral de Deus é o próprio alvo da vida cristã (ver Mat. 5:48), e o processo que nos faz avançar nessa direção é o da santificação, que nos serve de proteção contra todos os males que fazem guerra contra a nossa alma. No dizer de Faucett (*in loc.*): «Está em pauta a própria retidão de Cristo, operada em nosso interior pelo seu Espírito». Sim, as qualidades morais da retidão estão naturalmente incluídas, porquanto essas qualidades perfazem a justiça que nos vem por intermédio da justificação, quando consideradas em seu conjunto total. E ambas essas idéias fazem parte inerente da expressão aqui usada pelo apóstolo Paulo.

3. Calçados: A preparação do Evangelho. Efé. 6:15.

O calçado do crente mui provavelmente é sugerido pela passagem de Isa. 52:7, que diz: «Quão formosos são sobre os montes os pés do que anuncia as boas-novas, que faz ouvir a paz, que anuncia cousas boas, que faz ouvir a salvação...». É possível que o calçado romano chamado «*caligae*» seja aludido nesta passagem, indicando as sandálias romanas com solas dotadas de inúmeros cravos, formando uma camada espessa. Os pés são nosso órgão de locomoção e viagem, aquele órgão que leva o mensageiro aos lugares onde ele deve anunciar a mensagem do estabelecimento da paz com Deus, o Pai celeste, bem como do estabelecimento da concórdia com os homens. (Ver em Efé. 2:14 como Cristo é a «nossa paz», através da mensagem cristã). Cristo reconciliou judeus e gentios entre si, e ambos com o Senhor Deus (ver Efé. 2:15,16), tendo-nos conferido acesso perfeito a Deus Pai (ver Efé. 2:17,18), tornando a comunidade dos crentes o próprio templo de Deus, onde ele habita mediante o seu Santo Espírito (ver Efé. 2:21,22). Sim, temos «paz com Deus» por meio de nosso Senhor Jesus

ARMADURA, ARMAS

Cristo, no evangelho, onde é narrada sua história de amor remidor (ver Rom. 5:1).

Ora, tendo obtido a paz com Deus, com seus semelhantes e consigo mesmo, o crente fica em repouso, em meio a este mundo perturbado, obtendo vitória sobre todos os inimigos, e até mesmo conduzindo-os aos pés do Senhor, onde também encontram paz. Dessa maneira as forças espirituais do mal são derrotadas, conforme se pode inferir do presente texto e do que é dito em Col. 2:15. É para idéias assim que a metáfora aqui aludida aponta.

Preparação. Para que entendamos melhor o sentido desta palavra, é mister desdobrar a explicação nos pontos dados abaixo:

1. Na versão da Septuaginta (tradução do original hebraico do A.T. para o grego, completada cerca de duzentos anos antes da era cristã), a palavra aqui empregada, «etoimasia», significa «estado de preparação» (ver Sal. 9:41 e 10:17). Portanto, fica subentendida aqui a *necessidade* de nos prepararmos para a pregação do evangelho.

2. Outros preferem traduzir esse termo grego por «equipamento». O evangelho da paz é esse equipamento, posto em nossos pés, mediante o que «avançamos» batalha adentro, obtendo a vitória através de suas virtudes.

3. Esse vocábulo também pode significar «prontidão». Há certa preparação que produz a prontidão para enfrentar o inimigo, para obter a vitória espiritual e também conferi-la a outros, o que se encontra no recebimento correto do evangelho e no seu uso correto.

4. Além disso, essa palavra também pode significar o «estabelecimento de um alicerce firme», ou uma «base firme de apoio», espiritualmente falando, o que o evangelho igualmente nos confere. Assim, pois, o crente «fica firme», tendo os seus pés «protegidos», sendo assim capaz de cumprir a sua missão. E o evangelho, que é essa proteção, confere paz tanto a ele mesmo como àqueles que dão ouvidos ao evangelho. Uma vez que os pés estão protegidos, o avanço e a atividade cristã se tornam possíveis. O crente fica «preparado em sua mente», em estado de «prontidão», por causa de seu conhecimento, de sua aceitação e de sua propagação da boa mensagem cristã. A «paz» é o objetivo colimado, e a atividade na pregação do evangelho produz esse resultado.

Naturalmente, temos aqui um paradoxo: A finalidade legítima dessa batalha é trazer a *paz*, não com os inimigos das realidades espirituais, mas com outros homens, que também estão em conflito com a impiedade existente nos «lugares celestiais». O evangelho, pois, torna-nos «prontos e dispostos» a nos atirarmos a essa batalha em prol da verdade e da retidão. Paulo aludia a tais coisas, portanto.

Dá ao Senhor o que há de melhor em ti,
Dá-lhe as tuas forças e a tua juventude;
Emprega o ardor fresco e vibrante de tua alma,
Na batalha em prol da verdade.
Jesus nos deixou o exemplo,
Intrépido ele se mostrou jovem e corajoso;
Dá-lhe a tua leal devoção,
Dá-lhe o melhor que há em ti.
......
Dá ao Senhor o que há de melhor em ti;
Dá-lhe as tuas forças e a tua juventude;
Revestido da completa armadura da salvação,
Ajunta-te à batalha em prol da verdade.

4. Escudo: A Fé. Efé. 6:16.

1. Não está aqui em foco a «fé» como um corpo de doutrinas, como um credo (objetivo e formalizado).

2. Mas devemos pensar aqui em «fé» como um princípio evangélico, o que consiste na «entrega» de alma aos braços de Cristo, mediante o que somos justificados. Essa é a fé que governa a vida do crente, já que vivemos «de fé em fé». A fé original, por conseguinte, opera a cada dia em novos atos de fé; mas, na realidade, tudo é a continuação da mesma atitude, pois entregamos sucessivamente nossa alma aos cuidados de Cristo, crescendo sempre na dedicação a ele.

3. É retratado aqui muitíssimo mais que a «crença fácil» tão generalizada nas igrejas de nossos dias, porquanto não se destaca aqui a mera aceitação de algum conjunto de doutrinas, mas antes, rebrilha neste ponto uma transação entre Cristo e a alma confiante.

4. Essa fé geral é expressa, em algumas pessoas, através do «dom da fé», algo especial, por intermédio do que empreendemos grandes realizações em favor de Cristo. Ver o artigo sobre os *Dons do Espírito* e o artigo sobre a *Fé*.

Embraçando sempre. Melhor tradução ainda dessas palavras seria, *além de todas essas coisas*, isto é, em adição àquilo que Paulo já havia ordenado.

Escudo. Segundo o original grego, temos aqui o grande escudo de forma oblonga, *thura*, por assemelhar-se muito a uma porta. Esse escudo, que era tão grande que protegia o corpo inteiro do soldado, serve de metáfora excelente para a grande proteção que nos é conferida pela fé. Normalmente, esse tipo de escudo consistia de duas camadas de madeira, recobertas de lona e então de couro, embora houvesse variações em sua fabricação. Era o escudo usado pelos soldados pesadamente armados, o que está de conformidade com a metáfora geral aqui exposta pelo apóstolo dos gentios. Esse era igualmente o escudo para o qual as mães gregas apontavam e diziam a seus filhos, que partiam para a guerra: «Volta para casa e traz esse escudo contigo, ou volta nele». Isso porque tal escudo era suficientemente grande para nele ser transportado um cadáver, como se fosse uma maca. Ver o trecho de Sal. 5:12: «...e, como escudo, o cercas da tua benevolência». (Ver também o *Anábasis*, de Xenofonte, i.8,9, onde ele descreve que os soldados egípcios usavam escudos grandes que lhes chegavam aos pés).

Apagar todos os dardos inflamados do maligno. Essas palavras aludem aos dardos munidos de uma mecha em chamas, um método de combate que se prolonga desde os tempos antigos —até os tempos modernos. (*Heródoto*, viii.52, diz, descrevendo o ataque dos persas contra uma fortaleza grega em Atenas: «...com flechas às quais haviam sido amarradas uma mecha em chamas...atiram contra as barricadas». Outro tanto diz Tucídides ii.75: «Os plateanos levantaram um arcabouço de madeira, que puseram no alto de sua própria muralha, defronte do côm oro...Também dependuraram cortinas de peles e de couros na parte da frente, tudo com o propósito de proteger o arcabouço de madeira e os trabalhadores, como se fosse um escudo contra os dardos inflamados»).

Lívio descreve o uso de um imenso dardo, quando do cerco de Sagunto. Esse dardo era atirado mediante um conjunto de cordas retorcidas. Chamava-se *falarica*. Sua haste era feita de madeira de abeto, e sua ponta era de ferro, com quase um metro de comprimento, de modo que pudesse perfurar a armadura de qualquer soldado e atravessar-lhe o corpo. No meio era munido de uma mecha inflamada,

ARMADURA, ARMAS

de tal modo que ainda que o escudo aparasse tão mortífero míssil, as chamas obrigavam o soldado a desfazer-se de seu escudo, deixando-o sem defesa e vulnerável a outro ataque. (Ver *Lívio*, xxi.8).

Tochas em chamas também eram usadas, algumas vezes com piche, juntamente com os dardos inflamados, e assim, a ala inteira do exército que avançava parecia uma grande fogueira. Tais flechas em chamas, e outros mísseis similares, fazem-nos pensar sobre as tentações lançadas pelo diabo, com toda a sua fúria. Talvez tais tentações sejam aqui retratadas como algo que vem de longa distância, mas que atacam repentinamente, com todo o vigor. No dizer de Vincent (*in loc.*): «Parece haver um indício sobre sua propagação: um pecado atrai a outro, que também ataca; a chama do dardo inflamado não tarda a espalhar-se. As tentações atuam sobre material susceptível. A autoconfiança é combustível fácil. A fé, porém, que elimina a dependência do crente de si mesmo, retira o combustível da frente do dardo. Antes, cria a sensibilidade para as influências santas, mediante as quais a força da tentação é neutralizada. A fé chama em nosso socorro a ajuda de Deus. (Ver I Cor. 10:13; Luc. 22:32; Tia. 1:2; I Ped. 4:12 e II Ped. 2:9)».

«O problema mais profundo criado pela pecaminosidade humana não consiste do 'que' se faz, e, sim, do 'por que' se faz. Por que o alcoólatra cede à tentação de beber? Por que o fariseu se mostrava orgulhoso? Por que todos nós somos vítimas dos 'dardos inflamados do maligno'? A resposta final não seria a falta de confiança em Deus? A moderna psicologia em profundidade pode sair aqui em auxílio da análise cristã. O alcoolismo se pode explicar com base na insegurança, no temor e na culpa. Esse vício oferece um meio de escape às exigências da entrevista entre Deus e o homem. E o escape, por sua vez, é um sintoma de ausência de fé. É preciso coragem para nos apresentarmos em juízo e enfrentarmos o nosso próprio 'eu'. Somente a confiança no Deus de amor—uma confiança como a que teve em seu pai o filho pródigo—pode vencer a covardia da incredulidade. E o alcoolismo é meramente uma ilustração relativamente clara de uma verdade maior. A inveja e o orgulho, por exemplo, se originam da mesma raiz de ausência de confiança. O Senhor Jesus dirigiu sua parábola sobre o fariseu e o publicano '...a alguns que confiavam em si mesmos...' (Lucas 18:9). Não há necessidade de outra comprovação mais vívida. Basta que se substitua a confiança em Deus pela confiança própria, para que o orgulho apareça como resultado necessário. Nesse caso o 'eu', julgando-se moralmente aperfeiçoado, transformou-se em um 'deus'. E esse 'deus' precisa ser protegido de todo e qualquer ataque, acima de tudo, de todo ataque contra a perda da estima própria. Daí se origina o orgulho. Mas a fé em Deus indica — a rendição do próprio 'eu'. Até mesmo da parte dos aristocratas morais, isso significa que ele deve reunir-se em coro à oração feita pelo publicano: Ó Deus, sê propício a mim, pecador». (Wedel, *in loc.*)

Prossegue esse mesmo autor: «A mesma coisa que se pode dizer acerca do orgulho, pode ser dito com relação a qualquer outro catálogo de pecados. A igreja cristã não poderia realizar um maior serviço aos homens de nosso período perturbado e desesperador, do que estender-lhes novamente a graça da 'fé'. A fé, por si mesma, é um dom. Nenhum evangelho de obras pode produzir tal resultado. A fé requer a mediação de uma estrutura de fé, a comunhão da confiança, na obediência. E é somente dentro da comunhão da fé que se pode destronar com segurança os deuses falsos do homem autônomo. Quebrar ídolos, porém, é um negócio perigoso. A fé é o tesouro supremo, confiado aos cuidados do povo de Deus, a igreja».

Sim, aprendemos que a fé é capaz de conquistar (ver I Ped. 5:9), de vencer o mundo (ver I João 5:4), e até mesmo de derrotar o «príncipe deste mundo», Satanás (ver I João 5:18).

Do maligno. Essas palavras podem ter um sentido impessoal, indicatórias do mal em geral; mas provavelmente, porém, devemos compreendê-las de maneira pessoal, como uma alusão a Satanás, o «maligno», o que é favorecido pelo contexto geral desta passagem. (Ver os trechos de Mat. 5:3 e João 17:15). O nosso conflito é contra inimigos «pessoais», contra seres maldosos, e Satanás é aqui retratado como quem lança contra nós seus dardos inflamados.

Apagar. O escudo grande, usado pelos infantes gregos e romanos, apesar de fabricado de madeira, era recoberto de couro ou com uma lona grossa, que não queimava facilmente, o que significa que quaisquer dardos inflamados eram apagados. Portanto, de maneira simbólica, os assaltos inflamados de Satanás são frustrados, e o crente é protegido pela sua fé, que se alicerça em sua fidelidade ao Senhor.

Ouvi a difamação de muitos; havia terror por todos os lados,
Mas confiei em ti, ó Jeová. Disse eu: Tu és o meu Deus!

5. O Capacete: Salvação. Efé. 6:17.

Cumpre-nos observar aqui a modificação do verbo, *tomai*, ao passo que em Efé. 6:11 é «vestindo-vos». Todas as demais peças da armadura o soldado também tomava e vestia. A armadura era posta no chão, peça por peça, e o soldado ia colocando as diversas peças de seu equipamento. Mas, agora, já protegido inteiramente por sua cota de malhas, lhe é entregue tanto o capacete como a espada, por seu escudeiro. Esse simbolismo é apropriado para mostrar a salvação e a presença inteira do Espírito Santo, conforme se entende através da teologia paulina. Pois um homem não toma e se veste dessas realidades espirituais; antes, recebe-as da parte de Deus, como se não pudesse fazê-los com as suas próprias forças. Isso é assim porque a salvação é um *dom gratuito*, recebido da parte do Senhor Deus; e o próprio Espírito Santo é dom de Cristo, «dado» àqueles que lho pedem. O Espírito Santo é conferido ao crente a fim de conferir salvação mais completa, no sentido de ser recebida mais uma bênção decorrente da expiação pelo sangue de Cristo. E a fim de cumprir isso, o Senhor também nos dá a «espada de Deus», que é a mensagem divina concernente a Cristo Jesus. E esta outorga ao soldado cristão todas as bênçãos espirituais, sendo usadas por ele para abençoar a outros, já que se trata de uma arma ofensiva. Não obstante, essa *espada do Espírito* também é arma de defesa, visto que contém aqueles preceitos que preservam a experiência da salvação, ajudando na batalha contra o mal.

A idéia de um *capacete da salvação* se alicerça em Isa. 59:17, que mui provavelmente é uma passagem messiânica, pois retrata o Messias protegido com um capacete assim, ao lançar-se em sua missão para derrotar os adversários de seu povo. O capacete protege a cabeça, e Cristo é o Cabeça. Ora, nos homens, a porção mais vulnerável e vital do corpo é exatamente a cabeça. Por conseguinte, a salvação é aquele capacete que protege o ser vital de ser desintegrado sob os efeitos condenadores do pecado. Devemos notar que, no trecho de I Tes. 5:8, o capacete aparece como «a esperança da salvação», que não pinta a salvação como incerta, mas antes, mostra-nos que seu cumprimento principal ainda é futuro, e, portanto, algo pelo que embalamos esperança. E isso está de acordo com o ponto de vista sobre a salvação. Ver o artigo sobre a *Salvação*.

Do que Consiste a Salvação?
1. Ela começa pela justificação e pela fé (ver Rom. 5:1).
2. Ela começa quando da conversão (ver João 3:3).
3. Ela começa quando do arrependimento (ver Atos 2:38).
4. Ela floresce através da santificação (ver I Tes. 4:3).
5. Alcança fruto em nosso ser transformado, segundo a imagem e natureza de Cristo, mediante as operações do Espírito (ver Rom. 8:29).
6. Ela nos conduz de um estágio de glória para outro, num processo eterno (ver II Cor. 3:18).
7. Envolve o fato de que nos tornamos co-herdeiros do Filho de Deus (ver Rom. 8:17).
8. Envolve a participação na natureza divina e seus atributos (ver II Ped. 1:4 e Efé. 3:19).

6. Espada do Espírito: A Palavra de Deus. Efé. 6:17.

Espada do Espírito...a palavra de Deus. O Espírito Santo, em nós residente, utiliza-se da *palavra* para nossa vantagem. Não podemos ignorar aqui o fato espiritual da presença íntima do Espírito de Deus (ver Efé. 2:21,22), pois é somente através do poder do Espírito Santo que a Palavra de Deus nos oferece qualquer utilidade. O Espírito Santo nos dá a Palavra e a torna eficaz em nós, dando vigor ao uso que fazemos dela. Também é o Espírito do Senhor que interpreta os preceitos da mensagem de Cristo para nós, tornando-os reais em nossas vidas. Em suma, é o Espírito Santo quem torna a Palavra de Deus uma força viva e vital em nossa vida diária. A Palavra é vitalizada pelo Espírito Santo. E isso é que eleva o cristianismo acima de todas as demais religiões, acima de qualquer filosofia, pois não consiste apenas de «conceitos», embora também envolva esse aspecto, mas é um caminho vivo e místico, segundo o qual ali temos contato genuíno com o Senhor Deus. Portanto, suas obras, em prol da vida e do poder de Deus em nós, são dadas aos crentes, no decurso da vida cristã, o que assegura o sucesso dessa vida. Por essa razão é que a Palavra é chamada de *espada do Espírito*.

A Palavra de Deus
1. Essa expressão, algumas vezes, aponta para o A.T., mas nunca para o Novo Testamento, porquanto a formação do cânon neotestamentário, só teve lugar após estar completo, como um documento escrito.
2. Usualmente, nas páginas do N.T., essa expressão indica «a mensagem oral do evangelho» (ver I Ped. 1:25). Isso também se patenteia em Rom. 10:17.
3. A palavra de Cristo, também pode indicar aquele corpo de doutrina e de conceitos que circundam a pessoa de Cristo, em seus ensinamentos, em suas instruções, etc., que algumas vezes têm algo a ver com a moralidade e a conduta de nosso viver diário.
4. Examinar as seguintes expressões paralelas:
  a. Palavra de Promessa, em Rom. 9:9
  b. Palavra de fé, em Rom. 10:8
  c. Palavra da verdade, em Efé. 1:13
  d. Palavra de Cristo, em Col. 3:16
  e. Palavra de justiça, em Heb. 5:13
  f. Palavra de profecia, em II Ped. 1:19
  g. Palavra de vida, em I João 1:1

5. A Palavra é vivificada pelo Espírito, tornando-se assim uma força impulsionadora para o bem (ver Heb. 4:12). A maioria dos usos neotestamentários é de natureza evangelística, tendo alguma referência ao evangelho pregado pelos apóstolos, à nova fé religiosa, a qual posteriormente, assumiu forma escrita no N.T. Algo como esse uso, provavelmente é o que está em pauta no presente texto. Esse vocábulo aponta para a espiritualidade, para sua criação e desenvolvimento.

É mister esclarecer aqui que os «dois gumes» da Espada do Espírito não são a *lei* e o *evangelho*, porquanto tal interpretação é totalmente contrária à mensagem do N.T. Não obstante, a lei condena, e isso tem seu devido valor, para levar os homens a se entregarem a Cristo.

A idéia que a Palavra de Deus é uma *espada* foi tomada por empréstimo da interpretação rabínica. Por exemplo, o comentário dos rabinos (a *Midrash*), diz com respeito ao trecho de Sal. 45:3: «Cinge a espada no teu flanco, herói...» que: «Isso se refere a Moisés, que recebeu a Torah, que se assemelha a uma espada». (*Rabino Judá*, 150 D.C.). E acerca da «espada de dois gumes», que figura em Sal. 149:6, o comentário rabínico diz: «Essa é a Torah, escrita e oral». E a versão da Septuaginta traduz o trecho de Isa. 11:4, que diz: «...ferirá a terra com a vara de sua boca...», como «...com a espada de sua boca...» (Isso pode ser confrontado ainda com o trecho de II Tes. 2:8).

7. Oração, Arma Ofensiva, sem um uso Metafórico: Efé. 6:18.

A oração é o sistema de comunicação que liga os soldados a seu Capitão. Assim, a ajuda dele é garantida. Era costume, entre os antigos gregos e romanos, depois de terem se revestido de suas armaduras, comeram juntos e precederam o ataque com uma súplica feita aos deuses, pedindo o sucesso. Esse costume se reflete em Efé. 6:18. Ver o artigo sobre *Oração*.

Metáforas:
1. A *armadura*, com todas as suas peças, simboliza os recursos espirituais, de tal modo que a pessoa possa lutar contra os adversários espirituais da alma (ver Efé. 6:13).
2. O *cinto* é a verdade do evangelho, a mensagem que vence o mal (ver Efé. 6:14).
3. O *peitoral* representa a retidão, a transformação da alma por meio da justiça de Cristo, mediante o que assumimos a Sua natureza moral (ver Efé. 6:14). Comparar com Isa. 59:17. Em I Tessalonicenses 5:8, o peitoral envolveria a *fé* e o *amor*.
4. Os *pés calçados* simbolizam o evangelho da paz, o qual, mediante nossos esforços é transportado a todas as nações, e assim produz a paz que resulta da reconciliação com Deus (ver Efé. 6:15).
5. O *escudo* da fé representa não somente aquilo em que cremos, mas nossa ativa confiança em Cristo, dia-a-dia, mediante a qual nos fortalecemos e cumprimos nossa missão (ver Efé. 6:16). Essa fé ajuda-nos a afastar os ataques do inimigo, que querem destruir nossa fé e nossa expressão espiritual.
6. O *capacete* da salvação, que protege nossa parte mais vital, a cabeça (ver Efé. 6:17). A salvação consiste em mais do que o perdão dos pecados e a transferência final para o céu. Envolve a transformação de nosso ser de acordo com a imagem de Cristo,

ARMADURA, ARMAS — ARMAGEDOM

incluindo, finalmente, a nossa participação na natureza divina (ver II Ped. 1:4 e II Cor. 3:18).

7. A *espada*, que é a Palavra de Deus, não meramente a Palavra escrita, a Bíblia, mas a própria mensagem de Deus, de qualquer forma que Ele prefira comunicá-la. E, no contexto do Novo Testamento, especificamente, a mensagem do evangelho, que salva a alma e fortalece o crente (ver Efé. 6:17).

8. A *oração* é apresentada como uma espada ofensiva, sem correspondência com qualquer peça específica de uma armadura, em Efésios 6:18. Através da oração comunicamo-nos com nosso General em meio à batalha, recebendo Suas instruções e Seu fortalecimento. Nos tempos modernos, a oração poderia simbolizar os *meios de comunicação*, em toda a sua complexidade. Nos tempos antigos, poderíamos pensar sobre como os soldados, antes da batalha, reuniam-se para dirigir súplicas aos deuses, para serem protegidos e obterem a vitória na batalha. Além disso, as antigas estórias retratavam a intervenção dos deuses diretamente nos campos de batalha, em resposta às preces dos soldados; e em algumas vezes, há alusão à participação direta dos deuses, nas batalhas. O Antigo Testamento refere-se a incidentes em que Deus interveio diretamente em certas batalhas, a fim de ajudar Israel. A travessia do Mar Vermelho é o incidente mais notável desse tipo de intervenções. A oração traz até nós a ajuda divina de que precisamos a fim de sermos bem-sucedidos em nossa luta contra o mal, e a fim de ultrapassar os obstáculos que tentam impedir o nosso desenvolvimento espiritual.

9. *A colocação da armadura*. A descrição paulina das várias peças de uma armadura, em Efésios 6, segue a ordem de colocação da armadura dos antigos soldados, quando se preparavam para entrar em batalha. O ato de armar-se (pôr a armadura) representa nosso uso dos vários meios de desenvolvimento espiritual, como o treinamento do intelecto através de livros sagrados e piedosos, da oração, da meditação, da santificação, da vida segundo a lei do amor e das boas obras, bem como do contato místico com o ser divino.

10. *A flecha*. Ver o artigo separado sobre essa arma.

Nota: As várias peças de uma armadura, a história e o emprego das mesmas e muitos outros detalhes, são discutidas no NTI, em Efé. 6:11-17.

11. *A metáfora da batalha*. O bom crente é um soldado que sabe enfrentar as durezas da vida cristã, alguém bem disciplinado (ver II Timóteo 2:3,4). Outrossim, ele foi chamado (convocado) pelo Comandante supremo. Daí deriva-se sua grande responsabilidade de treinar, de preparar-se e de estar pronto para lutar o bom combate da fé, acerca do que Paulo pôde dizer que se saíra bem-sucedido (ver II Tim. 4:7). Há uma batalha sobrenatural na qual estamos empenhados, e que se impõe sobre nós, embora queiramos estar envolvidos ou não (ver Efé. 6:11). Satanás encabeça a oposição, tendo ao seu dispor muitos estratagemas da astúcia, que nos poderiam derrotar, não fora a provisão divina em nosso favor. O crente carnal está perdendo batalhas dentro de si mesmo, porquanto está cheio das paixões da carne, que combatem contra a sua alma (ver I Ped. 2:11). Aqueles que foram ordenados como líderes da Igreja têm a responsabilidade especial de «combater o bom combate» (ver I Tim. 1:18), guiado por uma consciência especialmente sensível, consciência essa que, por ser negligenciada por alguns, fazem-nos naufragar (ver I Tim. 1:19). A provisão espiritual é a «armadura» de luz, porquanto procede do Pai das luzes e seu uso nos conduz à eterna iluminação (ver Rom. 13:12). (AL I IB NTI YAD)

ARMAGEDOM
Sete Visões dos Adoradores do Cordeiro e da Besta, Apo. 14:1-20.

O Armagedom, a colheita, Apo. 14:14,16.

Tendo mencionado quão «imediato» será o galardão dado aos mártires, o autor sagrado agora passa para o castigo decisivo de homens maus e irracionais, no fim do período da tribulação, a batalha do Armagedom. (Comparar com Apo. 16:16, onde esse termo é usado). O Armagedom será uma espécie de *colheita*, pelo que o simbolismo da colheita é empregado neste ponto. Em Mat. 13:24 e *ss*, o julgamento também é assemelhado a uma *colheita*; e ali também estão envolvidos os anjos, bem como na seção seguinte. (Ver também Mat. 24:31). Os anjos «recolherão» aos eleitos. A predição constante em Isa. 63:6, de que o sangue da vida das nações será derramado sobre a terra, é aqui elaborada, e o vigésimo versículo quase certamente situa isso dentro da batalha de Armagedom, talvez incluindo os eventos que conduzirão a tal ocorrência, sobretudo aquilo que tiver causado sofrimentos à igreja e à nação de Israel. Devemos supor que, originalmente, o vidente João tinha em mente o culto ao imperador e o domínio romano. E visto que o mundo inteiro se imiscuiu com essa horrenda idolatria, todas as nações terão de sofrer. João antecipou a destruição de todos os poderes ímpios, de alguma forma juntamente com a destruição de Roma. Mas, se em Apo. 17:18,19, ele esboçou elaboradamente a queda de Roma, mediante sete visões, não nos explica qual será o *modus operandi* da destruição dessas nações ímpias. Sabemos, contudo, que isso ocorrerá quando da segunda vinda de Cristo, a qual terá início no Armagedom. João esperava isso para breve, porquanto não esperava que houvesse uma longa era da igreja, conforme tem sucedido. Profeticamente falando, esta passagem fala sobre o tempo quando o anticristo houver obtido controle do —mundo inteiro—, mediante a força e os encantamentos; mas tudo terminará em uma imensa tragédia para todos, pois as nações farão oposição a Deus, por haverem dado sua lealdade ao anticristo.

Alguns estudiosos vêem a passagem diante de nós como uma «antecipação» dos juízos que ainda sobrevirão, especialmente os juízos das «taças», como se isso não tivesse nenhuma ligação com o Armagedom. Porém, a cena que temos aqui é vasta demais para harmonizar-se com quaisquer juízos preliminares. Portanto, devemos supor que aqui o autor sagrado antecipava o fim real, antes de descrever juízos secundários que o precederão. Nada de estranho há em tudo isso, no presente contexto. O vidente já descrevera o *julgamento eterno*. Agora ele descreve aquele terrível julgamento geral, portanto, é favorável à menção ao Armagedom, neste ponto.

Alguns têm considerado esta passagem como um quadro do julgamento eterno, ou seja, da *colheita final*. Mas, já que o vigésimo versículo parece fazer disso algo essencialmente terreno, alguns têm rejeitado a passagem como se fora uma interpolação, suspeitando que a mesma esteja fora de sua exata pósição original. É mais provável, entretanto, que João simplesmente tenha antecipado aqui o juízo final, para então prosseguir em suas descrições sobre os juízos decisivos contra o anticristo, em oposição ao verdadeiro Cristo, o Filho do homem. Se assim é o caso, então este trecho é paralelo a II Tes. 2:8, e até mesmo uma versão expandida daquela passagem. E, tal como naquela passagem, a derrota do anticristo faz parte da *parousia* ou segundo advento de Cristo, não sendo mero acontecimento antecipatório.

Armagedom. Essa palavra não figura em Apo. 14:14-16, mas pensamos que esta passagem é paralela ao décimo sexto capítulo do Apocalipse, onde o tema é repetido. (Ver Apo. 16:16 e seu contexto geral). Quanto à própria localização geográfica do Armagedom, os intérpretes não chegaram a um consenso geral. Alguns pensam que o vocábulo significa «monte de Megido», outros, «cidade de Megido», outros, «monte da assembléia», e ainda outros, «sua colina frutífera». O primeiro caso é a interpretação mais comum. Nos dias de João, havia um cômoro próximo de Megido, com cerca de cento e doze metros de altura, nas vizinhanças da serra do Carmelo. (Ver, em Juí. 5:19, as *águas de Megido*, e em II Crô. 35:22, «o vale da planície de Megido»). Importantes batalhas foram travadas ali, durante a história de Israel, e é perfeitamente possível que esse termo, por essa razão, se tenha tornado simbólico da grande batalha que, finalmente, libertará Israel de seus inimigos e dará o triunfo ao Messias de Israel, o Senhor Jesus Cristo, sobre o anticristo, o último e pior dos perseguidores de Israel. (Ver Eze. 39:1,4, acerca dos «montes de Israel», a cena da derrota das forças de Gogue). O termo Armagedom veio a ser aplicado a qualquer guerra ou batalha de grande força destruidora, mas, biblicamente falando, refere-se somente à batalha decisiva que porá fim, por assim dizer, ao antigo ciclo terrestre, permitindo o começo do reino milenar do Senhor Jesus.

No A.T., a planície de Esdrelom, associada ao local do Armagedom, foi o palco de várias importantes batalhas na história de Israel. Ali Baraque obteve grande vitória sobre Canaã, e Gideão sobre Midiã (ver Juí. 4,5 e 7). Saul também morreu ali, tendo sido derrotado pelos filisteus (ver I Sam. 31). Josias também morreu ali, em sua batalha contra Faraó Neco (ver II Reis 23:29,30). Apesar da palavra «Armagedom» certamente simbolizar todo o conflito final das nações, umas contra as outras, e de todas as nações contra Cristo, cremos que a área real da planície de Esdrelom será o principal campo de batalha, embora certamente não venha a ser o único, na guerra final.

Conforme se compreende a profecia, haverá uma outra Guerra Mundial, que ocorrerá em cerca de 1999, entre a federação de dez reinos, encabeçada pelo anticristo, e a União Soviética e seus aliados. A Rússia ocupará Israel e as terras circunvizinhas, a fim de pôr fim ao conflito contínuo entre Israel e os árabes, mas também para tirar benefícios próprios, inclusive o domínio do petróleo do mundo. O anticristo fará objeção a essa ocupação, e movimentará tropas de sua federação de dez reinos contra as forças russas. A União Soviética fará chover bombas atômicas nas cidades costeiras dos Estados Unidos da América, bem como em muitas cidades européias. A federação dos dez reinos fará retaliação, incluindo os Estados Unidos da América, que será um dos membros dessa federação. A humanidade temerá por sua própria existência, e não sem razão. As forças russas serão aniquiladas na Palestina. Os israelenses, vendo ali o sinal do Filho do homem, bem como o próprio Cristo, corporalmente, reconhecerão que aconteceu devido a uma *intervenção* divina, como aquela que houve no mar Vermelho. Israel haverá de converter-se em peso, como uma nação, passando a proclamar a Jesus de Nazaré, oficialmente, como o Messias. Mas isso ainda não será o Armagedom, ou, pelo menos, será somente uma parte. O Armagedom será uma matança ainda maior, uma Quarta Guerra Mundial, que também culminará na Palestina. Dessa vez, a *China*, após ter feito muitas conquistas de territórios na União Soviética e na Ásia, invadirá a Palestina com uma horda de milhões. Mas o anticristo prevalecerá novamente. Esperam os místicos contemporâneos que isso ocorra em 2020 ou mais tarde. O anticristo será destruído, e uma nova era (o milênio) será instaurada. Não sabemos muito acerca dos detalhes sobre tudo isso, mas provavelmente esse é o esboço geral dos acontecimentos finais. Será uma época terrível. Nossos filhos certamente passarão por ela, se não até mesmo nós. Terão de ser crentes melhores do que somos, se quiserem resistir incólumes, espiritualmente falando, naqueles dias horrendos. Nossa tarefa é preparálos para isso. O Armagedom assinalará o começo da *parousia* ou segundo advento de Cristo.

Pode ser que a Terceira e Quarta Guerras Mundiais possam ser consideradas *estágios* de Armagedom.

ARMEIRO

Esse era o servo que transportava armas extras para os comandantes dos exércitos. São mencionados por dezoito vezes no Antigo Testamento. Ver Juízes 9:54; I Samuel 14:7-17; 16:21; 31:4-6; II Samuel 18:15; 23:37; I Crônicas 11:39. Um outro dever dos armeiros era de matar os inimigos feridos, geralmente com cacetes. Diversos dos reis de Israel ordenaram que seus armeiros os matassem, quando sob circunstâncias muito adversas. (Z)

ARMÊNIA

Essa palavra não aparece na maioria das traduções da Bíblia, mas a área assim chamada é aludida sob os nomes de *Ararate* (ver o artigo a respeito) e *Mini* (ver Jer. 51:27), este último lugar mencionado juntamente com Ararate e Asquinaz, como um reino chamado às armas contra a Babilônia. Alguns supõem que Mini seja uma contração para Armênia. Seriam os descendentes de Togarma ou Torgama (havendo várias maneiras de grafar o nome), filho mais jovem de Gômer, o filho de Jafé (ver Gên. 10:3). Presumivelmente, os armênios descenderiam dessa linhagem, juntamente com certos outros povos. A Armênia dos tempos veterotestamentários era uma região montanhosa a leste da Ásia M., desde tempos antigos, ocupada pelo reino de Urartu (ver Ararate). Uma inscrição do fim do século VI A.C., em Behistum, mandada fazer por Dario, demonstra a transição do nome para *arminiya*, chamada *urartu*, na versão babilônica. A versão armênia de Elefantina diz *'rrt*. Algumas traduções trazem Armênia, em II Reis 19:37, mas Ararate (derivado de Urartu), é o nome preferido. O artigo sobre Ararate provê mais detalhes a respeito. (S UN Z)

ARMINIANISMO

Deriva-se do nome próprio de Jacó Hermano, no latim, Armínio (1560-1609), que foi um teólogo holandês. Ver o artigo a respeito dele. Recebeu uma

ARMINIANISMO

estrita educação reformada, tipo calvinista, embora começasse a duvidar de vários artigos de fé. Sua busca independente pela verdade levou-o a escrever um documento intitulado *Remonstrance*, que consistia de cinco artigos: 1. Deus elege ou reprova com base na fé ou na incredulidade previstas. 2. Cristo morreu por todos e por cada homem, embora somente os crentes serão salvos. 3. O homem é tão depravado que a graça divina é necessária tanto para a fé como para as boas obras. 4. Pode-se resistir à graça divina. 5. Se todos os verdadeiros regenerados perseveram com certeza na fé, é uma questão que exige maior investigação.

Esses pontos de vista causaram considerável discussão, e o sínodo de Dort (1618-1644) os condenou. Todavia, foram mantidos e chegaram a evoluir, especialmente na Holanda, mediante o esforço de pensadores como H. Uytenbogaert (1557-1644), Episcópio (1583-1643), Curcelaeus (1586-1659), Hugo Grótio (1583-1645), Limborch (1633-1712) e outros. Esses homens foram os primeiros líderes do arminianismo, noção que tomou conta de várias denominações evangélicas na época e até hoje. Quarenta e cinco ministros iniciais (apelidados *remonstrantes*; ver o artigo a respeito), iniciaram a cruzada em favor do arminianismo.

Principais doutrinas de Armínio:
1. O conhecimento que Deus tem dos atos futuros dos livres agentes não é a causa desses atos. O fato que Deus prevê não é a causa dos acontecimentos.
2. Os decretos de Deus repousam sobre Sua presciência, pelo que a eleição é baseada na fé prevista, e a reprovação é baseada na incredulidade e na desobediência dos incrédulos.
3. O homem predomina sobre criaturas inferiores porque há nele a imagem de Deus.
4. Adão foi criado na inocência, mas não em verdadeira santidade.
5. O pacto de obras foi ab-rogado após a queda.
6. O pecado consiste em atos da vontade, que se tornou rebelde.
7. A pecaminosidade é por nós herdada de Adão, mas sua culpa não é imputada aos homens.
8. A reprovação do homem, resultante da queda, não é total.
9. Portanto, o homem reteve a faculdade de autodeterminação, e sua vontade pode inclinar-se para o bem, e não para o mal.
10. A expiação se fez necessária para expor somente uma das maneiras como Deus pode manifestar Seu amor, sem prejuízo de Sua santidade.
11. A expiação é universal, mas a vontade pervertida pode rejeitar essa provisão.
12. A graça é uma só: não há graça comum que a distinga da especial.
13. Graça universal e suficiente segue a pregação do evangelho; todos podem reagir favoravelmente ou não, segundo a vontade de cada um. A graça não é irresistível em qualquer caso.
14. A regeneração origina-se no arrependimento e na fé.
15. A vontade humana é uma das causas da regeneração.
16. A fé é uma boa obra humana, base de aceitação diante de Deus.
17. A justiça de Cristo não é imputada ao crente.
18. Nesta vida, o crente pode chegar à perfeição impecável, conformando-se à vontade divina, com a cooperação de sua vontade.
19. O indivíduo pode cair da graça e perder a salvação que antes possuía.
20. O amor é o atributo supremo de Deus, a essência mesma de Seu ser.
21. O alvo da criação é a felicidade (eudaemonismo).
22. O homem foi criado naturalmente como um ser moral.
23. A expiação é rectoral ou governamental (ver o artigo sobre a *expiação*), o que significa que a expiação não é estritamente vicária e penal, e, sim, uma realização simbólica que visa a salvaguardar os interesses do governo moral de Deus, ao mesmo tempo que abre a possibilidade de salvação, alicerçada sobre a obediência evangélica.
24. Plena certeza de salvação não é possível nesta vida, exceto mediante a revelação ou iluminação individuais.

Como é óbvio, a teologia arminiana dá lugar especial ao livre-arbítrio humano, bem como à força de vontade necessária para serem feitas escolhas certas. Essa doutrina surgiu como protesto contra os dogmas da eleição incondicional e da graça irresistível. Nessas doutrinas, parece estar ausente o amor de Deus, sendo que um programa de terror envolve o mundo inteiro, pois, desde o princípio, a própria existência é maligna e trágica (exceto para o grupo numericamente insignificante dos eleitos). O calvinismo contém grande dose de *voluntarismo* (ver o artigo), isto é, algo é direito porque assim o Senhor determinou, embora nos pareça errado. Porém, poderia ser indagado se Deus faz tais coisas como uma reprovação incondicional, desde a eternidade passada, ou se os homens é que dizem que Deus assim age. O homem tem a tendência de conceber Deus segundo a sua própria imagem, e todas as teologias têm muitos elementos devidos a esse fator. Sempre se podem encontrar textos de provas para tais idéias.

O problema dos textos de prova. As doutrinas da eleição, da reprovação e da graça irresistível aparecem, realmente, nas páginas do Novo Testamento. Mas também são doutrinas neotestamentárias as noções contrárias do livre-arbítrio humano, do desejo divino de que todos os homens sejam salvos, da propiciação ilimitada, do supremo amor de Deus, e da responsabilidade humana. Encontramos nesse conflito um paradoxo, porque a verdade é mais ampla que qualquer de seus elementos constitutivos. Uma verdade mais ampla sobre o amor de Deus pode conter as idéias da eleição e do bem resultante da missão de Cristo, que beneficiará a *todos os homens*. O trecho de I Ped. 4:6 ensina que o evangelho foi pregado aos mortos, com a razão precípua de reverter seu estado de perdição, embora já se encontrassem no hades, lugar de juízo, do outro lado da fronteira da morte biológica. Assim, a morte biológica não seria o fim da oportunidade de salvação. Essa é uma verdade que o calvinismo e o arminianismo têm negligenciado, mas que era comum nos escritos dos pais gregos da Igreja, na Igreja Ortodoxa Oriental, além de ser uma doutrina comum para os anglicanos. Assim, não podemos esperar que alguma denominação evangélica chegue a exibir uma posição doutrinária que estabeleça um credo capaz de responder a todas as perguntas, fazendo com que aquela denominação seja a melhor ou a única. Todos os credos e denominações têm suas mesclas especiais de verdade e erro. A eleição incondicional pode exprimir uma verdade, se Deus também faz algo de significativo *quanto aos demais homens*. O trecho de Efé. 1:10 quase certamente alude a uma *restauração* geral. Assim, a eleição poderia ser o motivo da salvação de alguns, ao passo que a restauração destinaria seus beneficiários a uma glória secundária, envolvendo todo o resto da humanidade, mas sem que isso envolva a salvação. Tendo feito esse tipo de provisão, Deus não poderia ser considerado injusto se chamasse apenas alguns para um propósito especial, os quais chegariam a participar da natureza divina (ver II Ped. 1:4), ao passo que os demais receberiam um benefício secundário que incluísse uma glória significante.

Devemos notar que o trecho de Efé. 1:10 alude ao «mistério da vontade de Deus». A palavra *mistério* envolve algum *decreto divino*, que acabara de ser revelado. (Ver o artigo a respeito). Isso significa que até haver sido escrita a epístola aos Efésios, não fora expressa a vontade mais abrangente de Deus em algum escrito inspirado. E, sem dúvida, há inúmeros aspectos da vontade de Deus que permanecem desconhecidos para nós. Portanto, nossas doutrinas evoluem devido a acréscimos ocasionalmente feitos, e isso surpreende a muitos. Há verdades divinas que ultrapassam o calvinismo e o arminianismo. Essas verdades sempre figuraram nas páginas do Novo Testamento, tendo sido reconhecidas por outros ramos da Igreja cristã. Ver o artigo sobre a *restauração*. (AJ B E H NTI)

ARMÍNIO, JACÓ

Teólogo holandês (1560-1609), nasceu em Oudewater, no sul da Holanda. Estudou na Universidade de Leiden, então em Genebra, e foi ordenado no ano de 1588. De 1603 até sua morte, foi professor naquela universidade. Um de seus mestres foi o reformador Teodoro Beza, sucessor de Calvino. Isso posto, ele esteve sob a influência do *calvinismo* (ver o artigo), em Genebra. Sua teologia, pelo menos em parte, pode ser considerada uma revolta contra certos elementos que ele considerava contrários à razão e ao sentido teológico. Armínio conseguiu seguidores, e em breve estava florescendo uma escola de pensamento que seguia suas idéias. Após a sua morte, seus discípulos cristalizaram suas idéias em um panfleto com cinco pontos, *Remonstrance*, onde é exposta a posição arminiana. Quanto a informações gerais sobre o *arminianismo*, incluindo os cinco pontos originais, ver o artigo desse nome. Esse panfleto foi publicado a 19 de outubro de 1609. Veio à existência a Igreja Remonstrante da Teologia Reformada, que tem raízes nos ensinos de Armínio. Ver o artigo sobre os *remonstrantes*.

Tanto o calvinismo quanto o arminianismo têm textos de prova extraídos da Bíblia. É seguro afirmar-se que essa controvérsia tem origens no próprio Novo Testamento. Não se trata de mero desenvolvimento histórico, quando os dogmas estavam se desenvolvendo. O problema do *livre-arbítrio* (ver o artigo) e do *determinismo* (ver o artigo) é um *paradoxo* (ver o artigo), a saber, uma afirmação de doutrina que parece autocontraditória. Os homens, sempre inclinados a arquitetarem um sistema teológico fácil e simplista, desprezam os paradoxos. Nem por isso, estes desaparecem. O calvinismo e o arminianismo são ambos meras tentativas para evitar diversos grandes paradoxos que têm algo a ver com a natureza humana: ela é livre ou escrava? É capaz ou não de buscar a Deus mediante seus poderes inatos? Ademais, esses dois sistemas existem por causa dos problemas relativos às *intenções de Deus*. Assim, Deus deseja salvar a todos, potencialmente; ou se satisfaz em salvar apenas alguns, permitindo que os demais pereçam? Ou Ele restaurará os perdidos e remirá os eleitos? (Ver o artigo sobre a *restauração*, que aborda esses problemas). Os homens acostumaram-se a ver Deus apenas com um olho. Tanto os calvinistas quanto os arminianistas são teólogos de um olho só. A missão salvatícia de Jesus Cristo é maior que qualquer desses grupos costuma contemplar. (AM B E HR P)

ARMOM

No hebraico talvez signifique **castanheira**. Essa palavra aparece entre as varas salpicadas que Jacó pôs defronte dos bebedouros, diante das ovelhas (ver Gên. 30:37). A castanheira era uma árvore bastante grande (ver Eze. 31:8 e Eclesiástico 24:19). Porém, as descrições dessa árvore parecem deixar claro que se trata do plátano (*Platanus Orientalis*), que aparentemente é nativa da Palestina. Outros conjecturam, embora com menos plausibilidade, que seria a faia ou o bordo. (S)

ARNÃ

No hebraico, **forte, ágil**. Provavelmente foi bisneto de Zorobabel, na linhagem de Davi (ver I Crô. 3:21), identificado no trecho de Lucas 3:27 pelo nome de Joanã, um antepassado de Jesus, cerca de 536 A.C. Algumas traduções refletem o texto massorético, que diz «filhos de Arnã», mas a Septuaginta diz «Orna, seu filho». (S Z)

ARNAULD, ANTOINE

Teólogo e filósofo francês (1612-1694). Nasceu em Paris, estudou em Sorbonne, e ali ensinou desde 1643 até sua expulsão, em 1656. Isso ocorreu quando ele passou a apoiar as idéias jansenistas (ver sobre o *jansenismo*), que ele compartilhava com Pascoal. Foi perseguido devido aos seus pontos de vista, e finalmente deixou a França e se estabeleceu em Bruxelas. Continuou promovendo o jansenismo e a filosofia cartesiana até a sua morte. Ver o artigo sobre *Descartes*, René.

Escritos. A Arte de Pensar (também chamado de *Lógica de Port Royal*), 1662; *Acerca de Idéias Verdadeiras e Falsas*, 1683.

Idéias:

1. Uma lógica não-aristotélica, seguindo o método cartesiano de dividir um problema em suas partes, partindo de conceitos simples para as idéias. Ele desenvolveu várias regras para orientar nesse processo.

2. A própria idéia de Deus deriva-se de Sua existência. Portanto, diz um homem: «Creio em Deus», não porque ele esteja sendo dirigido por seus desejos, mas porque na verdade há um Deus cuja própria existência nos inspira a idéia divina.

3. Contra Malebranche (ver o artigo a seu respeito), que ensinava que as idéias que pensamos estão em Deus, e que temos consciência direta dessas idéias. Arnauld ressalta que essas idéias estão em nós (*idéias inatas*; ver o artigo), e que, quando verdadeiras, representam fielmente o mundo. (EP P)

••• ••• •••

ARNI

Um antepassado de Jesus, em Lucas 3:33, mas chamado Arão em Mateus 1:3, bisneto de Judá e ancestral de Davi (ver Rute 4:19 e I Crô. 2:9,10). (Z)

ARNÓBIO

Erudito, historiador e teólogo alemão (1666-1714). Foi professor de História Secular durante um ano, em Giessen; e então serviu como pastor em Werben e Perleburgo. Tinha veia poética, e traduziu as obras de vários místicos religiosos para a língua germânica. Também escreveu vários livros espiritualistas e uma História Eclesiástica, a primeira escrita em alemão. Defendia a interpretação espiritualista da história da Igreja cristã, e lançou um apaixonado ataque contra o cristianismo corrupto, tanto católico quanto protestante. Demonstrou como a corrupção na Igreja é um processo gradual. (E)

ARNOLD, MATTHEW

Suas datas: 1822-1888. Foi poeta e crítico literário inglês. Nasceu em Laleham e educou-se em Oxford, onde também se tornou professor. Mais tarde, tornou-se inspetor geral das escolas, cumprindo a tarefa por trinta e cinco anos. Era ardoroso proponente da cultura, o que fez por toda a sua vida.

Escritos: *Ensaios sobre a Crítica*, 1865; *Cultura e Anarquia*, 1869; *Paulo e o Protestantismo*, 1870; *Literatura e Dogma*, 1873; *Deus e a Bíblia*, 1875; *Ensaios Mistos* 1879; *Discursos na América*, 1885; *Ensaios sobre a Crítica*, 1888.

Idéias:

1. A cultura é a inquirição de nossa total perfeição, o completo conhecimento das mais elevadas idéias. A função da cultura é a crítica vinculada ao refinamento das noções e hábitos tradicionais, ou seja, «a paixão pela doçura e pela luz, a paixão para que estas prevaleçam».
2. A literatura é um dos principais fatores na promoção da cultura. A Bíblia é uma força cultural, mormente a ética cristã, que prevalece contra a crítica e reflete o espírito da cultura.
3. Ele encontrou três classes de pessoas, rotulando-as de: a. bárbaros; filisteus; c. populaça. Em cada uma dessas classes encontrou um remanescente salvável, que defenderia o espírito da cultura. Esses remanescentes devem ser encorajados por meio da educação, que é a principal tarefa do homem neste mundo.
4. Sua ética sofre forte influência por parte do cristianismo e do estoicismo.
5. Juntamente com Tennyson e Browning, ele aparece como um dos grandes poetas da era vitoriana, sendo considerado um dos quatro ou cinco maiores críticos literários da Inglaterra. A coletânea de suas obras abrange quinze volumes. (AM E P)

ARNOM

No hebraico, **murmúrio**. Um rio que formava a fronteira sul da Palestina Transjordaniana, separando-a da terra de Moabe (ver Núm. 21:13,26; Deu. 2:24; 3:8,16; Jos. 12:1; Isa. 16:2 e Jer. 48:20). Também era a fronteira sul do território de Rúben (ver Deu. 3:12). Israel atravessou o Arnom na direção sul-norte, e ali conquistou territórios; mas essa conquista foi parcial e passageira. Nos tempos antigos, esse rio deve ter sido considerado importante. Ainda há traços de uma antiga estrada romana e de uma ponte. Mas o rio secou ao ponto de tornar-se um «wadi» (ribeiro seco), começando nas colinas do norte da Arábia e fluindo por 32 km na direção oeste, até entrar no Mar Morto, diante de Engedi; chega ali através de uma garganta pedregosa e precipitada, de pedras calcárias amarelas e vermelhas. Esse nome também é aplicado ao vale ou vales conhecidos como Wady Mojib, um tipo de trincheira enorme que atravessa o platô de Moabe, cortando-o ao meio. A pedra moabita (ver o artigo a respeito) indica que os moabitas viviam ao norte do wadi, nos tempos de Onri, dando a entender que a ocupação da terra, pelos israelitas, foi parcial e passageira. (S UN Z)

ARODI

No hebraico, asno selvagem. Um filho de Gade (ver Núm. 26:17 e Gên. 46:16), em cerca de 1856 A.C. Seus descendentes eram chamados aroditas, em cerca de 1700 A.C. (ID UN)

AROER

No hebraico, **desnudo**. Era nome de várias cidades no Antigo Testamento.

1. Uma cidade na margem norte do rio Arnom e, portanto, na fronteira sul do território designado às tribos de Rúben e Gade (ver Deu. 2:36; Jos. 12:2; 13:9), mas que antes pertencia aos amorreus (ver o artigo). Antes de terem sido desapossados, eles mesmos haviam deslocado os amonitas. Jeremias 48:19 menciona Aroer como uma cidade moabita. A antiga cidade estava localizada acerca de 23 km do Mar Morto, sendo conhecida como 'Ara'ir. Ela é mencionada na vigésima sexta linha da pedra moabita, sendo evidente que a cidade continuou nas mãos dos moabitas até o tempo em que Jeremias profetizou contra ela. Isaías condenou a cidade juntamente com Damasco e Efraim (ver Isa. 17:2).
2. Uma das cidades edificadas (ou reedificadas?) pela tribo de Gade (ver Núm. 32:34). Em Josué 13:25 lemos que Aroer ficava «defronte de Raba» (de Amom), o que talvez indique que ficava para leste. O local não tem sido identificado, embora alguns estudiosos pensem que se trata da mesma cidade que a de número «1», acima.
3. Uma cidade ao sul de Judá, à qual Davi enviou presentes, após recuperar os despojos de Ziclague (ver I Sam. 30:36,38). Era uma cidade localizada no Neguebe, cerca de dezenove quilômetros a sudeste de Berseba, e que atualmente tem sido identificada com Khirbet 'Ariareh. Dois filhos de Hotão, o aroerita, estavam entre os poderosos guerreiros de Davi (ver I Crô. 11:44). (ID S Z)

AROM

Um ancestral de alguns exilados que retornaram do cativeiro em companhia de Zorobabel (ver I Esdras 5:16), cujo nome não é mencionado nas listas paralelas de Esdras e Neemias. Em Esd. 2:19 aparece o nome de Hasum, em lugar de Arom. (Z)

AROMA

No hebraico, **reach**, «odor», «fragrância». Palavra que aparece por cinqüenta e oito vezes no Antigo Testamento (por exemplo: Gên. 8:21; Êxo. 29:18,41; Lev. 1:9,13,17; Núm. 15:3; Eze. 20:41). No grego, *osmé*, «odor», palavra que figura por cinco vezes no Novo Testamento: João 12:3; II Cor. 2:14,16; Efé. 5:2; Fil. 4:18.

Está em foco qualquer fragrância, agradável ou desagradável, que afeta o sentido do olfato, embora a idéia de odor desagradável também possa ser transmitida pelo termo hebraico *tsachanah*, que aparece exclusivamente em Joel 2:20. As ofertas levíticas que não tinham coisa alguma a ver com o pecado eram chamadas ofertas de «aroma agradável» (por exemplo, Núm. 15:3). E o incenso, igualmente, com seu perfume doce e acre, era aceitável ao Senhor (ver Mal. 1:11). Figuradamente, as orações dos santos são um aroma agradável ao Senhor, como se fora incenso (Apo. 5:8). Por outra parte, a hipocrisia produz mau cheiro, espiritualmente falando (ver Amós 5:21; onde nossa versão portuguesa, em vez de fazer alusão ao fato de que o Senhor não queria cheirar as assembléias solenes de Israel, diz: «...com as vossas assembléias solenes não tenho nenhum prazer»).

ARPADE

Uma cidade síria próxima de Damasco, que tinha o seu próprio rei. O lugar tem sido identificado com Tell Refad, a 21 km ao norte de Alepo. Tinha alguma importância no tempo dos assírios, tendo sido conquistada por Adade-Nirari, em 896 A.C., por Asur-Nirari em 754 A.C., e tendo sido cercada e capturada por Tiglate-Pileser, em 742-740 A.C. Também participou dos levantes suprimidos por Sargão, em 720 A.C. Comumente é associada à cidade-estado de Hamate, nas páginas do Antigo Testamento, que não ficava muito longe (ver Gên. 11:10-13 e I Crô. 1:17,18). Tem sido identificada com a região montanhosa do alto rio Zabe, a nordeste de Nínive, sendo a mesma Arrapachitis dos geógrafos gregos. Sua história violenta tornou-se proverbial (ver II Reis 18:34; 19:13 e Isa. 36:19). (I ID UN)

ARPÃO

Vem de um termo hebraico que também significa *lança* e *fisga*. A palavra aparece na Bíblia somente em Jó 41:7. Alguns traduziam como ferro de fisga, e em adição, *lanças de pescar*. Ambos os instrumentos são declarados inúteis para combater contra o leviatã, que provavelmente é uma alusão ao crocodilo (ver Jó 41:1), ou a alguma gigantesca serpente (ver Isa. 27:1), ou a algum monstro marinho não identificado (ver Sal. 104:26). Ver o artigo sobre o leviatã. (Z)

ARQUEIRO

Ver sobre **Exército, Armadura e Armas**.

ARQUELAU

Ver sobre os **Herodes**.

••• ••• •••

ARQUELAU

Filósofo grego do século V A.C. Nasceu em Atenas ou Mileto. Foi discípulo de Anaxágoras (ver o artigo). Aparentemente sucedeu a seu mestre como chefe de sua escola. Utilizou-se do conceito da *nous* (mente) como a causa, sustentadora e inovadora do movimento. Em seus movimentos, a mente atuaria sobre a matéria primitiva e produziria o mundo que conhecemos. Ensinava uma forma de evolução. Primeiramente teria sido produzido o fogo, então a água, e, desses dois, a vida animal. Apegava-se ao convencionalismo de todos os juízos políticos e sociais. Pensava ele que o homem é superior aos animais por causa de suas aptidões morais e artísticas. Sócrates e Eurípedes figuravam entre seus alunos. (AM F P)

ARQUEOLOGIA

Esboço do Artigo:
Introdução: O termo.
I. Períodos Arqueológicos
II. Medição pelo Carbono-14 e pelo Argônio de Potássio: a Grande Antiguidade da Terra.
III. Materiais Examinados
IV. Métodos Arqueológicos
V. Usos da Arqueologia no que diz respeito à Bíblia
VI. Escavações Arqueológicas na Palestina e em Outros Locais de Interesse Bíblico
VII. Bibliografia

Introdução: O Termo

Essa palavra compõe-se de dois vocábulos gregos, *archaios* (antigo) — e *logos* (discurso, estudo), ou seja, estudo sistemático das antiguidades. É a ciência que investiga o homem e a sua cultura, desde o tempo em que ele apareceu na face da terra. Ocupava-se com aqueles remanescentes das civilizações passadas que têm sido descobertos, no sentido mais amplo, epigráfico e anepigráfico. A arqueologia geral é o estudo baseado nas escavações, deciframento e avaliação crítica dos antigos registros do passado. A arqueologia bíblica é essa ciência aplicada às questões relacionadas à Bíblia, ou diretamente mencionadas ou associadas ao registro bíblico.

I. Períodos Arqueológicos

A. A IDADE DA PEDRA

1. *Paleolítico Antigo*. Objetos de pedra têm sido encontrados na superfície na Palestina e nas regiões elevadas da Ásia Ocidental, ao passo que no Egito têm sido encontrados instrumentos de pedra quelianos e aquelianos, em formações geológicas, especialmente nos terraços do rio Nilo. Não há remanescentes humanos discutíveis antes desse período no Oriente Próximo. A medição da antiguidade é incerta, mas provavelmente corresponde à era geológica do Pleistoceno, talvez tão antiga quanto a segunda ou a primeira era interglacial na Europa, ou seja, há mais de 200 mil anos atrás, pelo menos. Importantes remanescentes têm sido encontrados em cavernas da Palestina, datados do final desse período.

2. *Paleolítico Médio*. Temos aqui os primeiros aparecimentos do *homo sapiens* na Europa (homem Cro-magnon), e o maior desenvolvimento da pintura em cavernas no sudoeste da Europa. Houve então grande avanço nas artes e nos ofícios. Os cadáveres eram sepultados com ornamentos, e aparecem as primeiras estatuetas de nudez feminina feitas de pedra, osso ou marfim. As figuras e as pinturas em cavernas provavelmente indicam um avanço nas especulações mágicas ou religiosas, cuja natureza não podemos determinar ante as evidências de que dispomos. Esse período também é representado tanto nas cavernas palestinas como na cultura Natufiana. Esses povos floresceram cerca de oito mil anos atrás, até cerca de 6000 A.C. O homem da Palestina, nesse tempo, era de pequena estatura (entre 1,52 a 1,65 m). Havia aprendido a cultivar cereais, domesticar animais, fazer bacias e cadinhos e levantar estruturas de pedra. Nos seus rituais de sepultamento encontram-se evidências suficientes de que criam na vida após a morte física.

ARQUEOLOGIA

3. *Neolítico* (Idade da Pedra Polida). Esse período escoou-se entre 7000 e 4500 A.C. Nesse período, na Europa, foi introduzida a agricultura, teve início a domesticação de animais (no Oriente Próximo, essas atividades tiveram começo mais cedo), foi inventada a cerâmica e apareceram instrumentos de pedra polida. No Oriente Próximo, a cerâmica se adiantou e foi iniciada a vida comunitária (na forma de povoados). Nesse período, houve construções de dimensões respeitáveis, em Jericó. Entre outros edifícios, há ali evidências de uma espécie de templo. O culto religioso, seja como for, estava evoluindo, conforme se vê em diversos tipos de figuras. Já se fazia presente a adoração aos deuses da fertilidade. Foram construídos monumentos megalíticos de sepultamento, tanto no Oriente Próximo quanto na Europa, embora o atraso cultural fosse notório na Europa.

B. IDADE CALCOLÍTICA (DO COBRE)

Esse período compreende de 4500 a 3000 A.C. Representa uma transição de prosperidade no Oriente Próximo, quando o cobre começou a ser usado. Cerâmica bem-feita, pintada, aparece no Crescente Fértil, e foram construídos grandes edifícios públicos. Desenvolveu-se a escrita (3500 A.C.), e floresceram a agricultura e as formas religiosas externas. Templos tornaram-se centros de organizações religiosas. As pessoas interessavam-se por deuses, pela alma, pela vida após a morte física, pela santidade, etc. Eram cultivados os cereais básicos e as frutas.

C. IDADE DO BRONZE

1. *Idade do Bronze Antiga*. As datas desse período oscilam entre 3000 e 2000 A.C. O termo é popularmente usado na arqueologia, embora alguns suponham que o bronze, no sentido moderno (liga de cobre e estanho, ou de cobre e manganês ou alumínio) ainda não existia na época. Outros eruditos, porém, insistem que o bronze, como liga de cobre e estanho, é muito antigo, e que já era usado no período chamado por esse nome. Havia minas de estanho na península da Cornualha e nas ilhas Scilly, que os fenícios obtinham e exportavam para a sua terra. Artigos de bronze eram manufaturados nas cidades púnicas (norte da África), de onde eram exportados. O bronze variava em sua composição, havendo ligas de bronze e zinco, que mais se assemelhavam ao metal amarelo. O «lustroso e fino bronze, tão precioso como o ouro» (Esd. 8:27; ver também I Esdras 8:57), pode ter pertencido a essa variedade. Minas de zinco em Laurium, na Grécia, vinham sendo exploradas desde tempos antigos. O bronze era abundante entre os hebreus e os povos vizinhos, desde tempos antiqüíssimos (ver Exo. 38; II Sam. 8:8; I Crô. 18:8; 22:3,14 e 29:7).

Foi por essa época que a organização dos primeiros estados começou, no Egito e na Mesopotâmia. Por esse motivo, esse período é referido como *o começo da história*. Nesse período tornou-se comum a arquitetura monumental, como no caso das pirâmides egípcias, com o aparecimento de muitas estátuas e inscrições. Também apareceram monumentos literários em forma de épicos, como as narrativas da criação e do dilúvio, na Suméria. Cidades construídas com tijolos (exemplificados nas aldeias canaanitas) apareceram nesse período. Houve a melhoria dos instrumentos e da cerâmica de uma forma notória. Nos itens de sepultamento dos amorreus estava incluído uma modalidade distintiva de cerâmica; e as armas multiplicaram-se. Outro tanto sucedia na Fenícia. Muitas descobertas relativas aos povos cananeus têm sido feitas, incluindo a planta do templo que havia em Ai.

2. *Idade do Bronze Média*. Esse período vai de 2000 a 1500 A.C. Foi um período de atividade internacional e intelectual, com o levantamento e a queda de reinos como o Egito, a Babilônia, os hicsos, os hititas e os mitanianos (horeus). Israel, por meio de Abraão e seus primeiros descendentes, emergiu como uma nação separada, nesse período. Também foi um tempo de grupos seminômades, – como os habiru (entre os quais podem ter vivido os patriarcas de Israel), que se infiltraram nos vales da Palestina. Têm sido encontrados túmulos desses povos, em Jericó. As cidades de Beit Mirsim, Megido e Jericó floresceram nesse período, embora aparentemente tenham sido violentamente destruídas pelos egípcios (Tutmés III), que expulsaram dali os hicsos, em cerca de 1450 A.C.

3. *Idade do Bronze Moderna*. Período que vai de 1500 a 1200 A.C. Grandes cidades foram reocupadas, somente para serem saqueadas novamente, no século XIII A.C. Os povos vagueavam pela terra como tribos selvagens, matando e sendo mortos. Houve destruição em Hazor, Betel, Beit Mirsim (Debir?) e Laquis. Ver o registro da invasão israelita na Palestina, nos dias de Josué, para se fazer idéia dos intermináveis conflitos entre os povos. Jericó parece haver sido abandonada em cerca de 1324 A.C.

— Os cananeus, na Idade do Bronze Moderna, aparentemente empregavam cinco sistemas de escrita diferentes, em diversos estágios de desenvolvimento, a saber: a. Mesopotâmio (acadiano) — tabletes inscritos em cuneiforme, encontrados em Megido, Jericó, Siquém, Taanaque, Tell el-Hesi, Gezer e Hazor. Isso inclui os tabletes de Amarna, discutidos mais adiante neste artigo. b. Hieróglifos egípcios, encontrados em lugares como Bete-Seã e Quinerote (ver os artigos a respeito). c. Proto-hebraico, descoberto em Laquis e Hazor (ver os artigos a respeito). d. Alfabeto cuneiforme ugarítico, encontrado em um tablete de Bete-Semes (ver o artigo a respeito). e. A escrita de Biblos (ver sobre Gebal). Ver o artigo sobre o *alfabeto*, quanto a detalhes sobre essas questões.

As formas religiosas dos cananeus têm sido ilustradas pelas descobertas feitas em Laquis, Megido e Siquém, onde se destacavam as adorações a Astarte e Baal (um selo cilíndrico de Betel, de cerca de 1300 A.C.).

D. IDADE DO FERRO

1. *Primeira Idade do Ferro*. Também chamada Ferro I ou Israelita I. Cerca de 1200 - 900 A.C. Foi um período de convulsões internacionais. Foi então que os israelitas expandiram-se como nação, e atingiram um estado de império, sob Davi e Salomão. O ferro tornou-se um metal de uso comum. Os filisteus foram os primeiros a usar o ferro na Palestina (por exemplo, uma adaga de ferro e uma faca encontradas em um túmulo de Tel el-Far'a). Ricas e bem construídas cidades e fortalezas canaanitas resistiram por longo tempo ao assédio dos israelitas, mas estes gradualmente conquistaram a Terra Santa, conforme se lê no livro de Josué. No tempo dos Juízes, as evidências mostram que Israel não atingiu a mesma prosperidade dos canaanitas. As casas israelitas eram essencialmente pobres, e sua cerâmica era rude e sem

ARQUEOLOGIA

sofisticação, em comparação com a dos canaanitas. Nos dias de Saul, a vida era de maneira geral, pobre e simples, embora houvesse a importação de armas de ferro e fortificações, como as cidades muradas. Salomão levou o império israelita a uma condição de prosperidade, muito maior, com o uso abundante de ferro e técnicas de construção aprimoradas. Muitos materiais eram importados, tendo servido para decorar o templo, o que assinalou um ponto culminante no desenvolvimento do culto religioso dos israelitas. Residências para os governadores distritais têm sido encontradas em meio às ruínas investigadas em Megido e Hazor. Havia imensos graneleiros para armazenar impostos, pagos na forma de grãos, em Laquis e Bete-Semes. Espaçosos estábulos, para quinhentos cavalos ou mais, foram encontrados em Megido (ver I Reis 9:15,19). Salomão fundou muitas fundições de cobre e de ferro, conforme se encontram evidências das mesmas no Wadi que vai de Eziom-Geber ao golfo de Ácaba. Ali havia um porto movimentado, que ajudava na importação de muitas mercadorias. Um vaso, encontrado em Tel Qasileh, traz a inscrição «ouro de Ofir», o que serve de testemunho confirmatório. O declínio do poder dos filisteus permitiu que os fenícios expandissem o seu comércio, o que se refletiu nos materiais usados na construção do templo de Jerusalém.

2. *Segunda Idade de Ferro*. Também é chamada Ferro II, Ferro Média ou Israelita II, com datas entre 900 e 600 A.C. Foi o período da monarquia dividida (Judá e Israel). Nesse período começou o cativeiro assírio, em 722 A.C., sob Sargão II. Foi um período de reforma profética para Israel, bem como tempo de grande expansão comercial para os fenícios. Também foi o tempo do soerguimento e da queda do império assírio. Inúmeras descobertas arqueológicas pertencem a esse período, algumas das quais são ilustradas sob o ponto «VI» deste artigo, sob o título Escavações Arqueológicas na Palestina e Outros Locais de Interesse Bíblico. Quarenta e um reis mencionados na Bíblia são confirmados pelas descobertas arqueológicas, o que mostra a abundância de evidências recolhidas.

3. *Terceira Idade do Ferro*. Também é chamada *Persa* ou *Israelita posterior*. Flutua entre 600 e 300 A.C. Esse foi o período dos impérios neobabilônico e persa, bem como o tempo do exílio e da restauração dos judeus. Nabucodonosor II capturou Jerusalém a 16 de março de 597 A.C. Muitas cidades e fortalezas dos israelitas foram destruídas, e houve destruição generalizada nas áreas circunvizinhas. Muitas cidades jamais foram ocupadas novamente. No entulho encontrado em Laquis, vinte e um pedaços de cerâmica inscrita testificam sobre as ansiedades do povo, nesse tempo, em face de um inimigo brutal, que não dava tréguas. A arqueologia tem demonstrado o estado de pobreza da Terra Santa, durante o exílio. A reocupação da terra foi lenta, e somente no século III A.C. é que Judá fora repovoada.

E. PERÍODO GRECO-ROMANO

Esse período vai de cerca de 300 A.C. a 300 D.C. Na terceira idade do ferro, aumentaram as influências persa e grega, sobretudo esta última. Alexandre o Grande conquistou a Palestina (que fizera parte do império persa), em 332 A.C., o que abriu caminho para a influência helenista. Porém, em face de sua morte, seus generais dividiram os despojos, e a Palestina ficou sob o domínio de Seleuco (ver o artigo a seu respeito). Dali por diante, os monarcas selêucidas tornaram-se os governantes do que fora Israel. A revolta dos Macabeus terminou essa fase (cerca de 161 A.C. em diante). A independência judaica, após muitas vicissitudes difíceis e batalhas sangrentas, finalmente foi estabelecida em 143 A.C. Porém, Roma tornou-se o novo poder dominante em Judá, em 63 A.C., quando Pompeu estabeleceu o protetorado romano sobre a Judéia. Em 40 A.C. Herodes foi nomeado rei de Judéia, e isso consagrou ali o domínio romano. Jerusalém foi destruída por duas vezes, em 70 e em 132 D.C. Então Israel foi esvaziada de judeus, o que deu início à grande dispersão, a qual só foi revertida em 1948, em nossa própria época. Há abundantes evidências arqueológicas acerca de todo esse período, incluindo o exílio, o retorno, o domínio selêucida, os macabeus, o domínio romano. Alguns itens desse período são mencionados no ponto «VI» deste artigo.

F. PERÍODO BIZANTINO

Esse período prolonga-se de 300 a 640 D.C., mas está fora do nosso interesse bíblico, pelo que meramente o mencionamos.

G. PERÍODO ÁRABE

Esse período começa em 640 D.C. Também está fora de nosso interesse bíblico.

II. Medição Pelo Carbono-14 e Pelo Argônio de Potássio: A Grande Antiguidade Da Terra

A arqueologia tem confirmado a total impossibilidade de se tentar datar a cronologia bíblica adicionando o número de anos mencionados nas genealogias do livro de Gênesis. Poucos arqueólogos de reputação apelariam para esse método; e a idéia de que a terra tem apenas seis mil anos cai em total descrédito uma vez que o assunto seja investigado. O problema da medição do tempo é abordado no artigo sobre os *Antediluvianos*, e, novamente, ainda mais pormenorizadamente, no artigo sobre *Astronomia*.

Medições pelo Carbono-14. Esse material é radioativo, uma forma instável de carbono, com o peso atômico 14. Está sendo constantemente formado nas camadas superiores de nossa atmosfera, devido ao bombardeio de átomos de nitrogênio-14 por parte de raios cósmicos ou nêutrons. Na atmosfera, o carbono-14 combina-se com o oxigênio a fim de formar o dióxido de carbono, que então se mistura com o dióxido de carbono, já existente na atmosfera terrestre, o qual contém carbono com doze átomos em sua estrutura molecular. Ao chegar à atmosfera, o carbono-14 entra em todas as coisas vivas, que trocam material com a atmosfera, mediante seu processo biológico. Toda matéria viva, pois, contém uma proporção constante de carbono-14, devido ao equilíbrio entre a taxa de formação do carbono-14 e a taxa de desintegração do carbono-14 contido na atmosfera, no oceano e em todos os seres vivos. Quando algum ser vivo morre, deixa de participar das trocas com a atmosfera, e assim cessa a recepção de carbono-14. Entretanto, o carbono-14 contido por ocasião da morte continua a desintegrar-se em uma taxa constante. A meia-vida do carbono-14 é de 5.568 anos. Isso significa que a quantidade de carbono-14, por ocasião da morte, é reduzida à metade nos primeiros 5.568 anos depois da morte daquele ser vivo. A quantidade restante é reduzida à metade nos

ARQUEOLOGIA

5.568 anos seguintes, e assim por diante, de tal modo que a proporção de carbono-14 restante, em um dado tempo, é proporcional ao tempo escoado desde a morte. Dessa forma, conhecendo-se a taxa de desintegração do carbono-14, é possível a determinação do tempo passado desde a morte de um espécie que anteriormente tivera vida. Essa forma de medição alcança uma taxa de exatidão de dois a cinco por cento, o que se tem confirmado através de inúmeras experiências com itens cujas datas eram conhecidas por outros meios, como os registros históricos. O teste do radiocarbono é digno de confiança quando se data matéria orgânica (antes viva) com precisão até entre 40 mil e 50 mil anos. Essa taxa de precisão cai um pouco depois disso, porque quanto mais retrocedermos no tempo, menos será a radioatividade restante. Contudo, com essa queda de taxa, as coisas datadas parecem ser mais novas do que realmente o são, e não mais antigas. E a medição através de um outro processo, intitulado argônio de potássio, pode retroceder até um milhão de anos ou mais. Seja como for, até mesmo obtidas na faixa dos bilhões de anos não são por demais distantes.

Materiais que podem ser testados. Toda matéria que antes vivia, como lã, carvão, todos os tipos de plantas, chifres, ossos queimados, couro, pele, pêlos, conchas, matéria vegetal carbonizada, excrementos e bactérias, pode ser testada.

Essa forma de medição do tempo passado foi desenvolvida no final da década de 1940, por Willard F. Libby, no Instituto de Estudos Nucleares da Universidade de Chicago. Isso revolucionou a medição do tempo na arqueologia.

Medição pelo Argônio de Potássio. Esse sistema pode datar coisas muito além do alcance do processo do carbono-14. Alicerça-se sobre o desgaste radioativo do potássio-40 em cálcio-40 e em argônio-40, utilizando proporções conhecidas em termos de taxas de troca conhecidas.

Muitos outros métodos. Também tem sido usada a *técnica da termoluminescência* para se medir a antiguidade da cerâmica. Quando a argila é queimada no forno, cada eléctron volta à sua posição estável e emite um fóton de luz. Se um fragmento da cerâmica é reaquecido em laboratório, pequenas fagulhas de luz são emitidas. A quantidade de termoluminescência indica quanto a radiação danificou cada eléctron. Portanto, a quantidade de termoluminescência é uma medida do tempo que se escoou desde que aquela peça de cerâmica foi cozida ao forno. O museu da Universidade da Pennsylvania tem-se utilizado desse processo e o tem aperfeiçoado. O método melhorado consiste em bombardear a cerâmica a ser analisada com raios-x, usando-se uma série de exemplares de pequenos pedaços de cerâmica, para cada medição do tempo.

Há um certo número de outros métodos de medição, alguns deles bastante exóticos. Novos conceitos e métodos de medição arqueológica estão sendo desenvolvidos. Um fato que certamente se destaca é o *acordo* bastante exato alcançado pelos vários métodos, quando empregados para se datar algum artefato específico, de que a terra certamente é muito antiga, talvez tendo quatro e meio bilhões de anos. Os testes aplicados a meteoritos mostram a mesma antiguidade, tal como se dá com os materiais trazidos da lua pelos astronautas norte-americanos.

Porém, a criação, fora de nosso sistema solar, é muito mais antiga. Os radiotelescópios estão atualmente captando luz que tem pelo menos dezesseis bilhões de anos de idade, e julgo que isso é apenas uma fração da idade real da criação. Quanto mais aprendemos, mais antiga ficamos sabendo ser a criação.

III. Materiais Examinados

1. *Entulho.* Os antigos locais da civilização são ricos em remanescentes jogados fora, antes associados à habitação humana, como restos de alimentos, animais mortos, fragmentos de instrumentos antigos, artefatos de túmulos, material de escrita, e até mesmo grãos de pólen e itens microscópicos como bactérias. Essas coisas estão sujeitas a sistemas de medição de tempo, descritos sob o segundo ponto, acima.

2. *Remanescentes humanos.* Os túmulos e seu conteúdo, como restos mumificados, ossos, armas, objetos de arte e indústria.

3. *Objetos de arte.* Trabalho artístico feito de pedra, de bronze, de prata, de ouro, de pedras preciosas, espelhos, desenhos em cavernas e outros materiais, cerâmica ornamental, murais. Todas essas coisas fornecem-nos algum discernimento quanto à vida e ao modo de pensar dos povos antigos.

4. *Cerâmica.* Esse é um produto quase universal da humanidade, permeando todas as civilizações, — o qual pode ser datado com grande precisão. Com freqüência, fragmentos de cerâmica provêem a data para a medição, pelo que os arqueólogos têm o cuidado de recolher e classificar a cerâmica. Alguns exemplares são toscos, e outros são incrivelmente ornamentais; mas todas as formas têm uma história a ser contada sobre as pessoas que as fabricaram.

5. *Edifícios.* O homem sempre teve a necessidade de abrigar-se a fim de proteger-se das intempéries. A maneira como ele tem feito isso revela muito sobre o seu grau de civilização. Mas também há muitas outras espécies de construções, como templos, pirâmides (e outras formas de mausoléus), acampamentos militares, estábulos, sinagogas, cabanas e mansões.

6. *Inscrições.* A arte da escrita foi uma das maiores realizações humanas, que se tornou fundamental para todas as formas de conhecimento. Ver o artigo sobre o *Alfabeto*, quanto a detalhes a esse respeito. As inscrições antigas eram feitas em tabletes de argila, em pedras, em vários metais, em cerâmicas, em peles de animais, em papiros. As coisas escritas nesses diversos materiais tornam-se uma fonte de conhecimento sobre as civilizações que as produziram, com freqüência conferindo algum conhecimento histórico sobre os povos envolvidos.

7. *Documentos escritos.* Os documentos em papiro, provenientes do Egito, pertencem desde os tempos faraônicos até à época islâmica. Era um material durável, manufaturado de uma planta aquática, que não se estragava facilmente em lugares de clima seco. Fragmentos e rolos inteiros têm sido desenterrados de túmulos, locais sagrados, cemitérios de crocodilos (dentro de crocodilos mumificados). Também há os tabletes inscritos em cuneiforme, provenientes da Babilônia e da Assíria, as famosas cartas de Tell el Amarna, que dão muitas informações sobre a Palestina antes da invasão israelita. Há os papiros de Elefantina, que lançam luz sobre o período persa no Egito e sobre o livro de Neemias. Há muitas cartas particulares que prestam informações sobre as vidas individuais e comerciais do povo. Há os manuscritos

ARQUEOLOGIA

bíblicos, do Antigo e do Novo Testamentos, como os documentos das cavernas de Qumran, descobertos em 1947, escritos em pergaminho. Ver o artigo sobre os *Manuscritos da Bíblia*.

8. *Instrumentos e armas*. Havia as armas de pedra e pederneira, muito mais antigas; mais tarde, surgiram armas de bronze e ferro, artefatos que revelam as transições envolvidas na metalurgia que identificam várias épocas. Começaram então a surgir instrumentos para uso doméstico e agrícola. A combinação das duas coisas revelam detalhes sobre a história pacífica e beligerante dos homens. Além disso, mostram a progressão em sua capacidade técnica.

9. *Moedas*. As moedas podem traçar a história dos povos, como os reinos resultantes das invasões de Alexandre o Grande, e períodos inteiros da história romana. A numismática é uma ciência em si mesma. Cobre muitos séculos e é importantíssima nessa questão de medição do tempo.

10. *Restos botânicos*. Temos nesse caso, grãos de pólen, fragmentos de madeira (petrificados ou não), restos queimados de antigas fogueiras, a dendrocronologia (medição do tempo mediante o exame dos anéis formados no crescimento das árvores) e restos da flora.

11. *Microorganismos em forma fóssil*. Podemos citar como exemplo os organismos encontrados na praia de Ontário do lago Superior, em rochas pré-cambrianas, datadas por processos radioativos de um bilhão e novecentos milhões de anos de idade.

12. *Objetos de culto*. Peças de escultura humana por razões religiosas, objetos usados para servir em cerimônias mágicas, efígies de deuses, seres humanos e animais, símbolos fálicos relativos aos deuses da fertilidade, um carneiro apanhado nos espinheiros pelos chifres, uma obra de arte suméria, provavelmente com sentidos religiosos, e inúmeros ídolos.

13. *Trabalhos com a terra*. Incluem-se aqui as fortificações, as muralhas, os terraços, as estradas, as minas, as interferências humanas com o meio ambiente, por uma razão ou por outra, tudo o que testifica a civilização humana, conferindo-nos informações.

IV. Métodos Arqueológicos

Como ciência que é, a arqueologia tem um sistema, que consiste nos seguintes itens:

1. *Preliminares*. A localização de locais promissores, com base em estudos históricos e geológicos, com auxílio da pesquisa aérea. Em nossos tempos, até mesmo os poderes psíquicos têm sido usados, como se dá com Aron Abrahamsen, que a Universidade do Arizona tem usado com grande sucesso.

2. *Organização das expedições*. Pessoas habilitadas para liderar, muitos assessores, uma tripulação de apoio — como cozinheiros, motoristas — preparação dos postos nos campos, suprimento de água, equipamento fotográfico, abrigos, armazéns, veículos de transporte.

3. *A pesquisa*. Delimitação da área a ser examinada, estabelecimento do acampamento. Divisões da área a ser examinada; registro dos indícios a serem seguidos nas escavações.

4. *Escavações e mapeamento*. As escavações começam com picaretas, enxadas, serras, brocas elétricas, material recolhido, classificação e armazenamento dos itens descobertos, selecionamento de material para maior análise em laboratório, exames por parte de técnicos de várias especialidades de apoio, como a química. A escavação continua em camadas que com freqüência passam de uma civilização para outra, comprovadas pelos processos de medição de tempo ou pelos tipos de artefatos descobertos. As áreas escavadas são cuidadosamente mapeadas, mostrando as posições de todas as áreas examinadas. No final do projeto, as escavações são enchidas novamente com terra, plantando-se uma vegetação apropriada para o local.

5. *Tratamento cuidadoso dos artefatos*. Tudo que for recolhido nas escavações é examinado por todos os métodos possíveis, se necessário; os materiais são selecionados e classificados, e tudo é registrado na história da escavação. Visto que os arqueólogos têm de tapar todas as escavações feitas, precisam incluir em seu relatório todos os detalhes inclusive fotografias.

6. *Trabalho de laboratório*. Quaisquer artefatos que exijam maior atenção são enviados ao laboratório. São feitas análises químicas ou de outra natureza. Especialistas em outros campos podem ser convocados, como historiadores, biólogos e antropólogos.

7. Finalmente, visando à preservação e o compartilhamento das informações obtidas, são feitos *relatórios* e são escritos *artigos* e *livros*. Esses relatórios incluem todos os detalhes dados acima, com fotografias, diagramas e suas respectivas interpretações. Esses relatórios são altamente técnicos, visando especialistas no campo, embora, como resultado, artigos e livros de cunho mais popular possam propagar a idéia geral das descobertas perante o público.

V. Usos da Arqueologia no que diz respeito à Bíblia

1. *A fim de ilustrar a história da Bíblia*. A arqueologia provê um testemunho secundário e confirmatório a toda a história da Bíblia, desde os dias mais remotos. Importantes colaborações e fatos adicionais acerca de cada período bíblico têm sido descobertos, desde o período adâmico, passando pelo período patriarcal, cananeu, monárquico, da dupla monarquia, exílico, pós-exílico, selêucida, helenista e - até o período romano. Da era dos patriarcas nos chegam descobertas em Ai, Siquém, Betel, Berseba, Gerar, Dotã e Jerusalém. Desse período nos chegam tabletes de Nuzi e de Mari. Muitos itens da Bíblia tornam-se mais claros por meio das descobertas arqueológicas: as bênçãos orais eram importantes para Isaque, Jacó e Esaú (ver Gên. 27:34-41). Os tabletes de Nuzi mostram que naquele tempo as bênçãos orais eram obrigatórias, tanto quanto as decisões de um tribunal. Por que Labão foi capaz de apontar para os seus netos e dizer: As filhas são minhas filhas, os filhos são meus filhos...»? (Gên. 31:43). Esses mesmos tabletes mostram que um avô exercia controle sobre seus netos. O período canaanita é bem ilustrado, tendo sido encontradas muitas ruínas de cidades em inúmeras escavações. A partir do período da monarquia, mais de quarenta reis (e as condições de Israel na época deles) têm tido suas histórias iluminadas pelas descobertas arqueológicas. Embora o Novo Testamento cubra um período histórico muito mais curto, grande tem sido a iluminação sobre as viagens de Paulo, bem como lugares, pessoas e coisas mencionados no livro de Atos.

ARQUEOLOGIA

2. *Sublinhando a realidade da inspiração divina*. Talvez os eruditos bíblicos tenham dado por demais atenção a esse aspecto, porquanto uma história digna de confiança pode ser escrita por um historiador respeitável, sem qualquer ajuda divina. Não obstante, a arqueologia provê evidências corroboradoras da exatidão dos relatos bíblicos, sendo esse um elemento que favorece (mesmo que não comprove) a inspiração divina. Em contraste, consideremos as narrativas do Livro de Mórmon, que afirma ser a *história* de certas tribos indígenas norte-americanas. Não há qualquer confirmação arqueológica acerca dessas alegadas tribos, e isso levanta muitas dúvidas sobre a autenticidade desse livro.

3. *A arqueologia empresta interesse*. A simples leitura da Bíblia pode ser vivificada mediante a referência às descobertas modernas que ilustram o texto bíblico. Isso faz a Bíblia tornar-se um livro de interessantíssima leitura. Até cerca de 1800, pouco se sabia sobre os tempos do Antigo Testamento, exceto aquilo que aparece no próprio Antigo Testamento. A situação não era tão grave no caso dos tempos neotestamentários, porque houve vários antigos historiadores seculares que comentaram sobre esses tempos. Mas a informação sobre o Antigo Testamento era praticamente inexistente. Então, começando em 1798, as ricas antiguidades do vale do Nilo foram descobertas pela expedição de Napoleão. Foi então que Paul Botta, A.H. Layard, H.C. Rawlinson e outros derramaram muita luz sobre as civilizações da Assíria e da Babilônia por meio da arqueologia. A descoberta da pedra Moabita criou sensação entre os eruditos bíblicos, por causa de sua íntima conexão com a história do Antigo Testamento, e houve um entusiasmo generalizado em favor das escavações na Palestina. Em 1901, foi encontrado o Código de Hamurabi; os papiros de Elefantina foram descobertos em 1903; os monumentos hititas de Bogazkoi foram encontrados em 1906; o túmulo de Tutancamom, em 1922; o sarcófago de Airão de Biblos, em 1923; a literatura épica religiosa de Ras Shamra em 1929-1937; as cartas de Mari e as ostraca de Oaquis, em 1935-1939; e os manuscritos do mar Morto, em Khirbet Qumran, em 1947.

4. *O valor apologético é evidente*. Esse é um ponto paralelo ao segundo item, intitulado «sublinhando a realidade da inspiração divina», embora mais amplo. Os eruditos, ao tratarem com documentos inspirados ou não, interessam-se pela exatidão do registro escrito. Querem saber se os povos e as cidades sobre as quais eles falam diante de seus estudantes, ou sobre as quais escrevem a uma audiência mais lata, realmente são históricas. A arqueologia, pois, confere-lhe um meio de autenticar o que afirma.

5. *O valor exegético*. O pregador, ao falar sobre a Bíblia, pode chamar a atenção de seus ouvintes com maior sucesso se puder falar com conhecimento sobre o seu assunto, baseado em informes extrabíblicos, que confirmam o que a Bíblia assevera. A arqueologia, além de ser ilustrativa, também é interpretativa. Muitas questões bíblicas podem ser mais acuradamente interpretadas por meio da arqueologia. Em muitos lugares, a Bíblia permanece misteriosa, não havendo iluminação por parte da arqueologia. Um pequeno exemplo pode ser visto no caso de Moisés, acerca de quem foi dito, em sua idade avançada: «...não se lhe escureceram os olhos, nem se lhe abateu o vigor» (Deu. 34:7). A palavra ali traduzida por «vigor» poderia referir-se aos *dentes* (conforme se vê na Vulgata Latina). Porém, os tabletes de Ras Shamra mostram que o vocábulo em questão tem o sentido de *vigor natural* ou *forças*, o que decide a questão da interpretação. Há muitos outros casos similares. A descoberta de material helenista tem ilustrado o vocabulário do Novo Testamento (grego koiné), em contraste com o grego clássico; e isso tem determinado muitos casos de interpretação. A descoberta de antigos manuscritos tem possibilitado a compilação de um texto bíblico mais acurado do que teria sido possível há cem anos atrás.

••• ••• •••

VI. Escavações Arqueológicas na Palestina e em Outros Locais de Interesse Bíblico

LUGAR E LOCALIZAÇÃO	DESCOBERTAS, ARQUEÓLOGOS, DATAS	REFERÊNCIAS BÍBLICAS
Abu Hawam, perto de Carmelo	R.W. Hamilton, 1932-33	
Abu Matar, SE Berseba	Centre Nat. de Recherche, 1954, Calcolith (habitações subterrâneas). França (J. Perrot)	
Ai, Et-Tel, 2 milhas SE de Betel	Exposição Rothschild, J. Marquet-Krause, 1933-35. Proto-urbano (paredes e templo). J. Callaway, Pré-urbano, 1964	Jos. 7:2, Esd. 2:28
Anatote, Anata, 3 milhas NE de Jerusalém	A. Bergman, 1936, Hellen (cerâmica)	Jos. 21:18, I Reis 2:26
Antioquia, sobre o Orontes, Síria, NO da Palestina	Universidade de Princeton. Baltimore Museum of Art, 1932. Acrópole, circo, etc.	Atos 13:1
Antioquia da Pisídia, Ásia Menor, Pisídia	G.E. Ederkin, fez escavações entre 1932 e 1939. Charles Morey fez escavações em 1933. Ruínas da cidade, templos, moedas, santuário do Deus, Men, inscrições. Francis V.J. Arudel, 1833. William Ramsey. 1910-1913. U. de Michigan.	Atos 13:14
Arade, em Canaã	David M. Robinson fez descobertas e escreveu um relatório a respeito, em 1924. R. Amiram, trabalhando para a Universidade Hebraica, em 1962.	Núm. 21:1; 33:40; Jos. 12:14; Juí. 1:16.
Asdode	M. Dothan, em escavações feitas entre 1962 e 1967.	Isa. 20:1; I Sam. 5 e Amós 3:9.
Ásia Menor – Vários lugares	Sir William Mitchell Ramsay, 1885 ss. Muitas descobertas estabeleceram a reputação de Lucas como um historiador. As publicações de Ramsay foram muitas, sobre o livro de Atos e o Apocalipse, as sete igrejas do Apocalipse, Paulo como viajante e cidadão romano. Promoveu a arqueologia em seus escritos, e incorporou suas próprias descobertas.	O livro de Atos, o livro de Apocalipse e referências paulinas.
Asquelom, Ascalon, Sarom	J. Carstang, 1920-1922, Filisteu, Romano Locais tradicionais: Acrópole, Partenon, etc. Local do julgamento de Sócrates. Theodore Shear, U. de Princeton, 1970. James Stuart, 1885; Nicholas Revett, 1885. M.E.L. Mallowan escavou o ágora, entre 1931 e 1939.	Jer. 25:20, Amós 1:8
Atenas, SE da Grécia		Atos 17:15, 16:22 e 18:1
Athlit, SE do Carmelo		
Babilônia	Hormuzd Rassam, 1878-1879. Grande quantidade de tabletes, um prisma de argila com anais de Assurbanipal e cilindros descreveram as campanhas de Senaquerib. Os jardins suspensos da Babilônia. Robert Koldewey, 1899. Muitas escavações e descobertas foram feitas, incluindo em Lagash (Telloh). E.W. Gardner, 1934-36, paleolítico; H. Richmond, 1935, Bizantino, Igreja da Natividade	II Reis 18:13; 19:16; II Crô. 32:1; 2:9,10; Isa. 36:1.
Belém, 8 km S de Jerusalém		Gên. 35:19, Rute 4:19 ; Mat. 2:1

LUGAR E LOCALIZAÇÃO	DESCOBERTAS, ARQUEÓLOGOS, DATAS	REFERÊNCIAS BÍBLICAS
Betânia, 2 km NE da área de Jerusalém	Túmulo de Lázaro, igreja memorial, 300 DC; muitos arqueólogos. Ver a lista sobre Jerusalém.	João 11, Mat. 21:17 e 26:6
Bete-Eglaim, Tell el-Ajjul,6 km SO de Gaza	Egito, F. Petrie, 1933-34; cerâmica, grande cidade hicsos, fossa, cemitério, jóias; paleolítico.	
Bete-iera, Kirbet Kerak, SO da Galiléia	B. Mazar, M. Avi-Yonah, 1944-1946; 1950-1960; Calcolítico Li-Romana (campo); islamita	
Bete-Sam, Citópolis, Tell el-Husn	Univ. de Pennsylvania Mus, 1921-23, calcolítico, nível XI; templos cananeus: nível VIII, 1350; nível VII, 1300; nível VI, 1150; nível V, 1000: todas as datas AC. A. Rowe, El I. Helênica-bizantina. Ocupação egípcia	I Sam. 31:10, II Sam. 21:12
Bete-Searim, Sheick Abreik	B. Mazar, N. Avigad: 1936-40 e 1955-1959; Helênica e I. Romana; Catacumbas; El-Romana (cidade)	
Bete-Semes – Tell er-Rumeileh, a OSO de Jerusalém	D. Mackenzie, 1911-1912; cerâmica da Palestina: Pac. School of Religion e Haverford: E. Grant; Mosteiro bizantino Cinco expedições lideradas por Elihu Grant, em 1928. Muita informação foi adicionada sobre a ocupação da terra por Israel, nos séculos XII a IX A.C. Foi, ajudado por G.E. Wright.	Jos. 21:16; I Sam. 6:15; I Crô. 6:59, II Reis 14:11,13.
Bete-Zur (Khirbet et-Tubeiqah), na região montanhosa da Judéia.	McCormick Seminary; O.R. Sellers, W.F. Albright, 1931, 1957; hicsos; helênica (fortaleza dos Macabeus)	Jos. 15:58; II Crô. 11:7; Nee. 3:16 e I Macabeus 4:28,29.
Betel, Beitin, NE de Rumallah	Pittsburg-Xênia (hicsos); W.F. Albright e J.L. Kelso, 1934; destruições pelos israelitas; moedas romanas	Gên. 12:8, Jos. 7:2
Biblos, na Fenícia	Maurice Dunand descobriu em Biblos (moderna Gegal), o antigo porto fenício de embarque de cedro e o túmulo do rei Airão, em 1919.	Atos 11:19; 15:3 e 27:12.
Cafarnaum, Tell Hûm, NO da Galiléia	Deutsch Orient-Gesellschaft Maer e Schneider, 1905-1914 Sinagoga (século III D.C.). A possível casa de Jesus, descoberta em 1983 por James F. Strange e arqueólogos franciscanos, que data de c. 60 A.C. O lugar foi marcado como importante pela construção de uma igreja sobre a localidade, que data do 3º século D.C. Ver o artigo sobre Cafarnaum, sob o título. A casa de Pedro de Jesus.	Mat. 4:18 e Marc. 1:21, 2:1
Canaã: Império hitita Ásia Menor e antiga terra de Canaã	William Wright e A.H. Sayce, que descobriram e descreveram monumentos; Hugo Winckler, que descobriu milhares de tabletes em escrita cuneiforme em Bogaz-koi, capital dos hititas, na grande curva do rio Halis, a 145 km a leste de Ancara (1906-1907). O material teve seus anais, textos religiosos e mitos em caracteres sumero-acadianos recebidos dos hurrianos (horeus), e um código de leis.	

297

LUGAR E LOCALIZAÇÃO	DESCOBERTAS, ARQUEÓLOGOS, DATAS	REFERÊNCIAS BÍBLICAS
Carmelo, Wade el-Mughara e vizinhanças	D. Garrod, 1922, Paleolítico (animais); neolítico. Univ. de Califórnia. Teodoro McCown, cemitério. R.W. Hamilton, 1932 e 1933, trabalhou em um sítio da Segunda Idade do Bronze, ao pé do monte Carmelo na planície costeira, em Tell Abu Hawam.	Jos. 12:22, I Reis 18:19
Cesaréia, Palestina, NO de Samaria, Jafo de Jos. 19:46	Aqueduto, vários edifícios, paredes, moedas. Expedição Link, 1960: Am. Philosophical Society, 1960 fragmentada de Pôncio Pilatos. Em 1956, M. Antônio Frova, em 1955, descobriu uma inscrição Avi-Yonah, descobriu ruínas de uma sinagoga. Em 1960, arqueologia subaquática, no porto romano, por A. Negev.	Atos 9:43-10:33
Cesaréia de Filipe, NO da Ituréia	Templo de Herodes, hipódromo e acrópole, ainda não foram encontrados.	Marc. 8:27
Chipre, ao longo da costa da Ásia Menor e alta Palestina	Aqueduto, 'fórum' de Deus olímpico, inscrição do templo de Afrodite. Muitos arqueólogos E. Gjersted, em 1927. Houve muito trabalho e muitas descobertas em Encomi, Paletos e Vouni.	Atos 4:36, 11:19,20, 13:4, 15:39 e 27:4
Cnossos, Creta	Sir Arthur Evans, 1894, encontrou a escrita cretense, não decifrada até 1953. Informações sobre a civilização minoana.	Atos 27:7,12,13,21; Tito 1:5.
Corinto, SL da Grécia	Agorá (mercado), templo de Apolo, estradas, portões, etc. American School of Classical Studies, 1896 até os nossos dias.	Atos 18:1, 19:1 e I Cor. 1:2
Debir (Quiriate-Sefer?), Tell Beit Mirsim, SO de Hebrom	Pitsburg-Xênia, 1926-32 (captura feita pelos israelitas); W.F. Albright e M.G. Kyle; cidade israelita; cubas de tingir	Juí. 1:11, Zac. 6:58
Deir-el-Bahri	Sir Gaston Camille Charles Maspero, 1881. Muitos sarcófagos reais em Deir-el-Bahri, e o templo de Karnak.	
Dibom, Moabe	1930, 1950-1957 (capital de Mesa) nabateus William Merton, em 1950 - 1957, com muitas descobertas.	Núm. 32:3,34;Jos. 13:9,17; Isa. 15:2; Jer. 48:18,22.
Dotã, Tell Dotha, 21 km N de Samaria	Wheaton College; J.P. Free, 1953-1960; calcolítico (cidade e portão)	Gên. 37:17 e II Reis 6:13
Ebal, Monte de, a margem ocidental do Jordão	Um antiquíssimo altar, descoberto em 1983. Perence à época de Josué (cerca de 1400 A.C.). Talvez seja o próprio altar erigido por Josué, construído depois que Israel partiu do Egito e entrou na Palestina. Adam Zartal, arqueólogo-chefe, teve confirmada a autenticidade de sua descoberta pela Universidade de Haifa.	Jos. 8:30,31 e Deu. 27:5.
Ver detalhes sobre esta descoberta no artigo intitulado, *Altar de Josué*.		

LUGAR E LOCALIZAÇÃO	DESCOBERTAS, ARQUEÓLOGOS, DATAS	REFERÊNCIAS BÍBLICAS
Éfeso, Ásia Menor, perto da costa ocidental	Templo de Artêmisa: J.D. Wood, 1869; David C. Hogart, Museu Britânico, 1905. Templo e relíquias. O.H. Benndord, Rudolf Heberdey, 1912; muitas ruínas: Anfiteatro, agora e primitivas igrejas cristãs.	Atos 18:19,21,24, 19:1,17,26,35, 20:16,17, Apoc. 2:1
Egito	Em 1922, foi descoberto o túmulo de Tutancamom, por Howard Cartar, no Vale dos Reis. O corpo mumificado foi recuperado por inteiro.	Inumerosas referências nos livros de Gênesis, Êxodo, Deut., Josué; Mat. 2:13,14; Atos 2:10; Apo. 11:8
Giza, no Egito	Sir William Matthew Flinders Petrie, 1881. As pirâmides em Giza e Tânis.	
Papiros de Chester Beatty	O Sr. A. Chester Beatty, colecionador norte-americano de manuscritos, residente em Londres, adquiriu de um negociante egípcio um grupo de folhas de papiro que pertencia a uma Bíblia em grego, escrita entre os séculos II e IV A.C., no ano de 1931. Esses manuscritos contém o Antigo e o Novo Testamentos. Consideráveis porções dos evangelhos e das epístolas de Paulo compõem a porção do Novo Testamento. Trata-se dos escritos mais antigos de Paulo, datando do começo do século III D.C. Ver sobre os *Manuscritos*.	
Papiro 52	Descoberta do papiro 52, um fragmento do evangelho de João, do século II D.C., feita em 1920. Esse é o mais antigo fragmento do Novo Testamento. Foi identificado em 1935 por C.H. Roberts. Acha-se agora na Biblioteca John Rylands, em Manchester, Inglaterra. Outros antigos fragmentos de papiro, manuscritos do Novo Testamento, sobre os quais ele escreveu são o P(52), P(32) e P(64) na *The Harvard Theological Review*, em 1953.	
Saqqara, no Egito	Walter B. Emery, em Saqqara, escavou em 1927 o túmulo intacto de Hemaka, vizir de um rei da primeira dinastia. Em Armant vários templos do boi sagrado e o túmulo do Faraó Ká, em Abidos. Foi descoberto um barco funerário, talvez do Faraó Udimu, da quinta dinastia. Em 1956, mais obras em Saqqara: foi encontrado o túmulo da rainha Her-Neite, da primeira dinastia. As explorações das ruínas de Buhen, no Sudão, nos anos de 1958 a 1960.	
Tebas, no Egito	A.E.P.B. Wiegall, em 1895. Descobriu o templo mortuário de Tutmés III, em Tebas, túmulo do Príncipe Iuha e sua esposa, Thuyu, pais da rainha de	

299

LUGAR E LOCALIZAÇÃO	DESCOBERTAS, ARQUEÓLOGOS, DATAS	REFERÊNCIAS BÍBLICAS
Tebas, cont.	Aquenaton. Daí seguiu-se seu livro sobre a vida e os tempos do Faraó Aquenaton, que se tornou um clássico e muitas edições foram vistas entre 1910 e 1934.	
Tell el-Amarna, no Egito	Descoberta acidental das cartas de Amarna, em 1887, por uma mulher aldeã que procurava fertilizantes naturais na região. Cerca de trezentos e cinquenta tabletes foram achados, suprindo informação sobre o estado da Palestina e da Síria (1400-1360 A.C.). Os tabletes iluminam a política externa do Egito e da Palestina durante o reinado do Faraó pacifista Aquenaton. As intrigas militares e os conflitos usuais com países vizinhos, as lutas pelo poder, as brutalidades e o desvario político são ali ilustrados. O conhecimento da geografia política da Palestina é aumentado. Os «habiru» que aparecem nesses textos são os hebreus, ou antes ou durante o tempo da conquista da Palestina, e mais provavelmente durante esse tempo. Laquis e Gezer estavam longe de ser destruídas, e são vistas como aliadas ativas dos «habiru». O rei de Jerusalém é chamado ali de Abdi-Hepa. Mas alguns argumentam em favor da época da invasão e logo depois.	O livro de Josué, se a data posterior for aceita.
Vale dos Reis, no Egito	M. Loret, em 1898. Ele descobriu o túmulo de Amenhotepe II, filho de Tutmés III. Foi uma interessante descoberta porque o corpo do Faraó estava intacto. — Uma geração mais tarde, foi encontrado o corpo de Tutancâmon, também intacto. Ver o artigo sobre os Faraós.	
Eglom, Tell el-Hesi, O de Laquis (erroneamente)	F. Petrie, 1890; sequência de cerâmica; armas. F.J. Bliss, 1891-93	Jos. 10:3 e Juí. 3:12
Elefantina, ilha diante de Answan, no rio Nilo	Foi descoberto um papiro em aramaico do século V A.C., com grande variedade de assuntos, mas principalmente de natureza legal, em 1906. O material foi publicado por Archibald H. Sayce e Arthur Cowley. Uma expedição do museu britânico fez outra e mais importante descoberta, no local do templo judaico na ilha, com materiais publicados em 1911. Mais papiros foram encontrados, e outras publicações se seguiram. Ver o artigo sobre o *aramaico*. Esses papiros representam as ricas fontes	

LUGAR E LOCALIZAÇÃO	DESCOBERTAS, ARQUEÓLOGOS, DATAS	REFERÊNCIAS BÍBLICAS
Elefantina cont.	de informação sobre aquele idioma, no período anterior a Cristo.	Gên. 10:10
Ereque (moderna Warka)	W.F. Loftus, 1850, escavação em Ereque.	
Eziom-Geber, Tell el-Kheleifah, Ácaba	N. Gluek, 1937-40: fortaleza de Salomão	I Reis 9:26, II Crô. 8:17 Jos. 20:7; I Reis 9:11; Mat. 2:22; 3:13;4:12; João 1:43.
Galiléia.	Uma pesquisa nas sinagogas na Galiléia, em 1907, por Herman Thiersch, Herman Kohl, Carl Watzinger e Ernest Sellin. A autoritária *Antike Synagogen in Galilaea* foi obra publicada em 1915. Ver o artigo sobre a *Galiléia*.	
Gassul, Teileilat G., 5 km L do Jordão, NE do mar Morto	Pontifical Bib. Inst., A. Mallon, R. Koeppel, 1929-1938. Calcolítico (quatro níveis principais; cerâmica, pederneiras, machados de cobre)	
Gaza; ver também *Bete-Egalim*	W.J. Phytian-Adams, 1911, 1914, 1920-1922; sondagens	Gên. 10:19 e I Sam. 6:17
Gerasa, Jerash	Yale, (1928-34); Neolítico (vila), Helênico (traços); romano (Decápolis) igreja, etc. Escavações feitas por Horsfield e Crowfoot, em Gerasa (moderna Jerash), começando em 1925. Foram nove anos de labor, com muitas descobertas. Theodore D. McCown e C.S. Fisher, em 1930.	
Gezer, Tell Abu Shusheh, 19 km S de Lida	R.A.S. Macalister, 1902-1905, 1907-1909; calcolítico, romano e bizantino. Yusif Kan'an, escavações e descobertas.	Jos. 10:33; 16:3; Juí. 1:29; I Reis 9:15; I Crô. 6:67.
Gibeá, Tell el Ful, 5 km N de Jerusalém	W.F. Albright, mediante muitas descobertas, fez grandes contribuições para o nosso conhecimento sobre a Idade do Ferro, particularmente no que diz respeito à cerâmica, 1922, 1933; vila, cidadela de Saul; torre de vigia.	Jos. 15:57; Juí. 19:12,13; 20:4; I Sam. 10:26; II Sam. 6:3; Isa. 10:29.
Gibeom, El-Jib, 15 km N de Jerusalém	Univ. Mus. Philadelphia, 1956-57; tanque e túnel, II Sam. 2:13; Church Divinity School of Pacific; J.B. Pritchard; asas de jarras inscritas; adegas; helênico (moedas)	Jos. 9:3 e II Sam. 2:12
Giza, ver sob Egito		
Hadera, Sarom	Heb. Univ.; E.L. Sukenik, 1934-1935; Calcolítico (gassuliano); ossuários	I Reis 9:15, Jer. 49:28
Hazor, Tell el Oedah, Waqqas, 8 km SO do lado Hulé	Marston, J. Garstand, 1926-27; sondagens. Heb. Univ. Rothschild; 1955-58 (Y. Yadin). Cidade dos hicsos, templo, capturado pelos israelitas; portão de Salomão, destruída em cerca de 730 A.C.	

301

LUGAR E LOCALIZAÇÃO	DESCOBERTAS, ARQUEÓLOGOS, DATAS	REFERÊNCIAS BÍBLICAS
Icônio (moderna Konia), na Grécia	James Mellaart, em escavações entre 1961 e 1963, fez muitas descobertas.	Atos 13:51; 14:1,18,21; 16:2.
Jafa	Israel, P. Guy, 1950; helênico e romano, Univ. de Leeds, J. Bowman, 1955 (cidade dos macabeus; moedas)	
Jebel-et-Tannur, a suleste do Mar Morto	Nelson Glueck escavou o cemitério dos nabateus, em 1937.	
Jemé, 9 km a SL de Gaza (erroneamente identificada com Gerar)	W.J. Phytian-Adams, 1921-1922; sondagens; estratificação continua. W.F. Petrie, 1926-27	Núm. 22:1, Deut. 33:49
Jericó (AT), Tell es-Sultan, NE de Jerusalém Jericó (NT), Tulul Abu el-Alayiq, Wade Qelt, 1 1/2 km O de Jericó	Deutsche Orient, 1869, 1907, 1909, E. Sellin, Mesolítico-neolítico; traços somente do período de Josué; Liverpool Univ. Marston. J. Garstang, 1930-36; K. Kenyon, 1952-58 Pittsburg-Xênia. J.L. Kelso, A.H. Detweiler, 1950-1951; palácio de inverno de Herodes; edifício de Herodes Arquelau John Garstang, em 1930, começou seis anos de trabalho ali, em pesquisas iniciadas por Sellin e Watzinger, em 1913. Kathleen Kenyon, em 1952-1957, deu prosseguimento ao trabalho. Garstang descobriu a primeira cultura urbana neolítica, tendo publicado seu livro *The Story of Jericho*, em 1948. Em uma caverna ao norte de Jericó, em 1961, foi descoberto um importante papiro proveniente de Samaria (722 A.C.). Nos anos de 1967 e 1968 foram feitas escavações ali por Kathleen Kenyon e W.G. Dever.	Mat. 20:29 e Luc. 10:30
Jerusalém	C. Warren, 1864-1867; estruturas, Clermont-Ganneau, 1873-1874, inscrições. C. Gordon, 1881; túmulo e Calvário de Gordon. F.J. Bliss e A.C. Dickie, 1894-1897; muro sul. Parker Mission, 1909-1911; túneis, fonte da Virgem. R. Weill Rothschild, 1913-14; ofel. R.A.S. Macalister, 1923-25; 1927-28; ofel jebusita. C.N. Johns, 1934-1948; portão dos macabeus; helênico (muros). R.W. Hamilton, 1937-38; muro norte. E.L. Sukenik e M. Dothan, 1956-60; túmulos. K. Kenyon, 1961; cidade antiga Túmulos dos reis, descobertos por F. de Saulcy, 1848. Charles Clermont-Ganneau, 1870 em diante. A pedra que proibia a entrada de gentios no templo de Jerusalém.	II Reis 8:18 e Mat. 2:1

302

LUGAR E LOCALIZAÇÃO	DESCOBERTAS, ARQUEÓLOGOS, DATAS	REFERÊNCIAS BÍBLICAS
Jerusalém cont.	Pére A.H. Vincente, em 1907. Descobriu o poço de Betesda e a torre de Antônia (ver os artigos a respeito).	João 5:2 ss.
	A guerra dos Seis Dias, em 1967, pôs a antiga Jerusalém e a península do Sinai sob o controle israelense. Em 1967, um excelente rolo do Mar Morto chegou ao conhecimento de Y. Yadin. Era um manual de regras religiosas, notas arquiteturais sobre como o templo de Jerusalém deveria ser construído, e muitas outras normas. Em 1968, B. Mazar iniciou escavações na muralha sul do monte do templo. Em Givat Ha-Mivtar, a nordeste de Jerusalém, naquele mesmo ano, foram encontrados os ossos de Yehonhanan Ha-Gaqol, um homem que fora crucificado, fornecendo informações adicionais sobre esse brutal costume. N. Avigad, em 1969, iniciou escavações no bairro judeu da antiga cidade de Jerusalém. Veio à luz uma magnífica vila helenista. Na década de 1970 os labores continuaram na esquina sudeste das muralhas da antiga Jerusalém.	
Jope	J. Kaplan, trabalhando para o Museu de Jafa, nos anos de 1948-1950, 1952 e 1955.	
Khorsabad, a leste do rio Tigre	Paulo Emile Botta, 1842. Primeira da série de descobertas que deu início à assiriologia.	II Crô. 2:16; Esd. 3:7; João 1:3; Atos 9:36,38; 10:5 e 11:5,13.
Koujunjik, na Babilônia	George Smith, 1874. Três mil tabletes e o avanço na assiriologia, com muitas descobertas em vários lugares na Babilônia.	
Laquis, Tell ed-Duweir, O de Hebrom	J. Starkey Wellcome-Marston, 1932-38; templos, sepultamentos primitivos; cidade principal, destruída em 588 A.C.; cartas em hebraico; helênica	Jos. 10:3 e II Crô. 11:9
Madaba, SO de Amam, Jordânia	A.H. Detweiler; túmulos: Macabeus-bizantino (mapa mosaico da Palestina, século VI D.C.)	
Mâmpsis, a 40 km a leste de Berseba.	Investigada por E. Robinson, em 1838; por E.H. Palmer, em 1871; por C.L. Woolley e T.E. Lawrence, que traçaram um plano das ruínas, em 1914. Uma pesquisa completa foi feita em 1937 por G.G. Kirk e P.L.O. Guy. Foi escavada por A. Negev, entre 1965 e 1968.	
Maresa, Tell Sanda, Hannah (Marisa) NO de Hebrom	R.A.S. Macalister, 1898-1900; helênico (cidade; túmulos). Ecole Biblique, Jerusalém, 1921-24. Romano (vila)	I Crô. 2:42 Miq. 1:15
Mari, ver sob Tell-Harari		

LUGAR E LOCALIZAÇÃO	DESCOBERTAS, ARQUEÓLOGOS, DATAS	REFERÊNCIAS BÍBLICAS
Leito do mar Mediterrâneo, ao longo das costas do monte Carmelo, entre Haifa e Dor.	Uma estrutura de pedra e madeira, de um antigo poço no leito do mar, em um local que já fora terra seca. Foi descoberto em 1985. Trata-se de um dos mais antigos poços jamais localizado. Fica situado acerca de 300 m da atual linha da praia. Objetos encontrados nas vizinhanças, como cabanas de pedra, ossos de ovelhas e peles de cabras, além de vários instrumentos, indicam um período neolítico posterior ou calcolítico anterior, 4500 A.C. ou mesmo antes. Restos de carvalhos mostram que a ocupação estava no meio de carvalhais. O fato de que não crescem carvalhos perto do mar, por causa da atmosfera salgada, a qual eles não resistem, mostra que a área antigamente era terra firme, e que a linha da praia foi consideravelmente alterada.	
Massada, a leste do deserto da Judéia	Heb. Univ., M. Avi-Yonah, 1955-56; Fortaleza Herodiana Um local a 80 km ao sul de Khirbet Qumran, uma fortaleza natural utilizada por Jônatas, o sumo sacerdote, que a fortificou. Em outras épocas foi utilizada por outros, como os Herodes. O local foi intensamente pesquisado por Y. Yadin, em 1963 e 1964, que publicou um livro sobre seus estudos, intitulado *Massada* (ver o artigo a respeito).	*Guerras* VIII.8.3; XIII.7-9; XIV.13.8,9, de Josefo.
Megido, Tell el-Mutesellim	Deutsche Orientges, 1903-05 I (níveis I-V). Completamente desenterrada. Oriental Inst. Chicago, 1925-39. Algumas descobertas cananéias antigas. Marfins. Y. Yadin, 1960; portão G. Shumacher, 1903. Foi descoberto o bem conhecido selo de Jeroboão. P.L.O. Guy, em 1935, descobriu os famosos marfins de Megido. C.H. Roberts também escavou na área, entre 1931 e 1933.	I Reis 4:12 e II Crô. 35:22
Mênfis a Karnak — Trinta e sete localidades	August Ferdinand François Mariette, 1850 em diante. Quinze mil monumentos. Templo de Edfu, templo de Hatsepsut, em Deir el Bahri, e templo de Abu Simbel. Pacific School of Religion. W.F. Badé, etc. 1926-35; sepultamentos; cerâmica filistéia; portão da cidade Paulo Emile Botta, 1842; M.E. Fladin, 1844; e Victor Place, 1851. Foi o início da assiriologia.	
Mispa, Tell en-Nashbeh, 15 km. N de Jerusalém		Gên. 31:49 e Nee. 3:7
Nínive, a leste do rio Tigre Cômoros de Koujunjik e Neby Yunus	M.E.L. Mallowan, trabalhou por trinta anos na região, a partir de 1931.	Gên. 10:11,12; Jonas 1:2; 3:2 e 4:11.

LUGAR E LOCALIZAÇÃO	DESCOBERTAS, ARQUEÓLOGOS, DATAS	REFERÊNCIAS BÍBLICAS
Nimrod (antiga Calá), a sudoeste da Babilônia	Austen Henry Layard. Os palácios de Assurbanipal, Salmaneser II, reconstruído por Tiglate-Pileser II, de Adadnirari e de Esar-Hadom. Foi encontrado no palácio real o obelisco negro de Salmaneser, 1842. E também vinte e cinco mil tabletes de argila da Biblioteca Real de Nínive. Hormuzd Rassam fez outras descobertas ali em 1843-1844, no palácio de Assurbanipal.	Gên. 10:11; I Crô. 1:10; Miq. 5:6.
Nipur, na Babilônia	John P. Peters, Haynes e H.V. Hilprecht, 1888. Descobriram vinte mil tabletes em Nipur, aumentando em muito o nosso conhecimento da literatura sagrada da Babilônia.	II Reis 18:13; 19:16; II Crô. 32:1; Isa. 36:1.
Nuzi (Yoghlan Tepe), a 241 km ao norte de Bagdá.	As escavações começaram em 1925 e terminaram em 1931, por uma expedição conjunta da Escola Americana de Pesquisas Orientais de Bagdá e pela Universidade de Harvard. Nuzi e os cômoros adjacentes produziram mais de vinte mil tabletes de argila com escrita cuneiforme, em um dialeto babilônico. Os tabletes incluíam arquivos completos, entre os quais os de Teipilla, príncipe Silwatesup e Tulpunaia. Os tabletes comentam sobre cada faceta da vida e ilustram muitos costumes e condições sociais dos povos na época dos patriarcas, nas narrativas bíblicas. Representam civilizações dos séculos XIV e XV A.C., quando a cidade estava sob o domínio hurriano (ver horeus). O ND ilustra alguns dos costumes abordados, que são de interesse bíblico, em seu artigo sobre a *Arqueologia*, sob o ponto VIII, Inscrições Cuneiformes, Nuzi. E. Chiera identificou os hurrianos, em 1928.	Livro de Gênesis.
Óstia, um porto do rio Tibre, na Itália	H.F. Squarciapino descobriu, em 1962, uma sinagoga do século IV D.C. Essa é a mais antiga sinagoga descoberta na parte ocidental da Europa.	
Oxyrhynchus, a 192 km do Cairo, para o sul	Bernard Pyne Grenfell e A.S. Hunt, em 1895. Descobriu a primeira página da *Logia* de Cristo. A partir de então muitos outros manuscritos em papiro foram encontrados relacionados à *Logia* ou às Declarações de Nosso Senhor, que são declarações extracanônicas de Jesus. Ver o artigo sobre as *agrafas*, quanto a detalhes. Esses dois homens deram início à ciência da papirologia. A própria palavra foi usada pela primeira vez em 1898.	
Papiros de Chester Beatty e Papiro 52. Ver sob Egito		

305

LUGAR E LOCALIZAÇÃO	DESCOBERTAS, ARQUEÓLOGOS, DATAS	REFERÊNCIAS BÍBLICAS
Pérsia	Inscrição de Dario I na rocha de Beistum, 1842, por Rawlinson, que assim proveu o alicerce de nosso conhecimento sobre a escrita cuneiforme, e conseqüentemente, a história da Babilônia e da Assíria.	II Reis 17, 20, 24, 25; Gên. 2:14; I Reis 15:19, I Crô. 5:6; Eze. 4, 5, 6; Dan. 5, 6, 9.
Petra, sudoeste do rio Jordão	Cidade antiqüíssima, do século I A.C. Johan Ludwig Burckhardt, 1784-1817. Uma cidade que tem sido uma popular atração turística, mas sem referências bíblicas diretas. A tradição diz que os cristãos fugiram para esse lugar quando da aproximação das tropas romanas, e assim escaparam completamente à destruição de Jerusalém no ano 70 D.C. George L. Robison, que descobriu o «lugar alto» de Petra. Em 1963, P. Hammond Jr. descobriu ali um teatro romano.	Mateus cap. 24 (implicado)
Qalat Jarmo, no nordeste do Iraque	Descrições da pré-história relativa aos capítulos primeiro a quarto do livro de Gênesis. Obra de Robert Braidwood, 1948-1949.	
Qasileh, El Khirbe a L de Tell Aviv	B. Mazar, 1948-49; destruída ao tempo de Davi; comércio com Chipre, Egito e Ofir	
Qumran, Ain Feshkha, a O do mar Morto	A narrativa da descoberta é contada no livro de John C. Trevers, *The Untold Story of Qumran*, 1956. Muito se tem escrito sobre os manuscritos do Mar Morto. Qumran tem sido amplamente identificada como parte de uma colônia de essênios. A descoberta de cerca de quinhentos documentos envolve material bíblico e secular. Cerca de cem rolos pertencem ao Antigo Testamento em hebraico (todos os livros do Antigo Testamento, pelo menos em parte, com exceção do livro de Ester). Datam de alguns poucos séculos A.C. até o século I D.C. Alguns fragmentos da Septuaginta também foram encontrados, e alguns poucos dos livros apócrifos, como Tobias, Eclesiástico, epístola de Jeremias (em grego), I Enoque (em aramaico), e Jubileus (em hebraico). As escavações continuam até o presente. Ver o artigo sobre *Qumran*.	Isa. 16:1 e Amós 1:5
Quir, Haraseth, Kerak, Jordânia	Sondagem (cidade de Mesa de Moabe); restos de cruzadas)	Deut. 3:11 e Eze. 21:20
Quiš (Tell-el-Uheimir), a 13 km a leste da Babilônia	Em 1923 foram feitas descobertas que desvendaram a história da Suméria. O relatório foi feito por Stephen Langdon, *Excavations at Kish*.	

LUGAR E LOCALIZAÇÃO	DESCOBERTAS, ARQUEÓLOGOS, DATAS	REFERÊNCIAS BÍBLICAS
Rabate-Amom, Aman, Jordânia (Filadélfia)	G.L. Harding, 1949. Paleolítico-calcolítico (túmulos; cerâmica); (túmulo hicso); helênico-romano (teatro)	
Roma, Itália central, perto da costa ocidental	Locais tradicionais: Coliseu, parques, banhos, edifícios, estradas, teatros, fórum, arcos (muitos arqueólogos no decorrer dos anos) Giovanni Battista de Rossi, 1864 em diante. Catacumbas de Roma.	Atos 2:10, 18:2, 19:21, 22:11, 28:14,26, Rom. 1:7
Roseta, Baixo Egito	Sete anos de escavações no cemitério sob a basílica de São Pedro, iniciados em 1950 sob a direção de Ludwig Kaas. Chave para o deciframento dos hieróglifos egípcios, em 1799, pelos franceses que estavam reparando fortificações ao norte da cidade de Roseta. Bossard foi o homem, mas sua identificação não é segura. A pedra foi levada para o Cairo, e atualmente acha-se no Museu Britânico.	
Samaria	D.G. Lyon, C.S. Fisher e G.A. Reisner, em 1910-1911. Grandes escavações em Samaria. Essa obra bem-feita e completa assinalou um ponto nevrálgico em um melhor conhecimento arqueológico da Palestina. Ver o artigo sobre a *Samaria*. Houve quatro anos de escavações, começando em 1931, iniciados pela Universidade Hebraico-Britânico-Americana, um projeto que continuou sob a liderança de J.W. Crowfoot.	I Reis 13:32; 16:24; II Reis 1:2; 2:25; II Crô. 18:2,9; Isa. 7:9; Miq. 1:1,5,6; 17:11; João 4:4,5,7,9.
Sardis	Howard C. Butler, 1910-1914, conduziu uma ótima equipe a Sardis, antiga capital da Lídia, com muitas descobertas.	Apo. 1:11; 3:1,4.
Saruem, Tell el-Far'a, SL de Gaza	Egito, W.F. Petrie, 1928-30; túmulos; cerâmica dos filisteus; hicsos; colonos fenícios; vasos persas	Jos. 19:6
Sela, Petra, a L do Arabá	Melchett Fund (C. & G. Horsfield), 1934-1938; calcolítico; helênico F.W. Albright, 1944-45; (cidade dos nabateus e portão; lugar elevado. P. Parr, etc., 1937-1957-60	Isa. 16:1
Sidom	Hugo Winckler, 1903-1904. Muitas descobertas. Expedição Palestina Dinamarquesa, A. Schmidt, 1926-29, 1932; destruída pelos filisteus; helênico-islamita (mosaicos bizantinos)	Gên. 10:15; Mat. 11:21,22; Atos 12:20.
Siló, Khirbet Seilun, S de Samaria		
Sinai	Constantin Tishendorf, 1859, que encontrou um manuscrito bíblico importantíssimo, o Codex Sinaiticus.	

307

LUGAR E LOCALIZAÇÃO	DESCOBERTAS, ARQUEÓLOGOS, DATAS	REFERÊNCIAS BÍBLICAS
Siquém, Tell Balatah	Vienna Academy, E. Sellin, 1913-34; santuário; portão leste. Drew-McCormick, G. Wright 1956-60. As descobertas mostram que Siquém (Balata) vinha sendo ocupada até 67 D.C., quando provavelmente foi destruída por Vespasiano, que também arrasou o templo adjacente dos samaritanos, no monte Gerizim.	Gên. 33:18, Núm. 26:31
Sucote, Tell Deir'alla, Rio Jaboque	Nederlands Inst., H. Francken, 1961	Gên. 49:10 e Jer. 7:12
Suméria, Baixa Babilônia	Ernest de Sarzec, 1877. Descobertas que despertaram o mundo para a arqueologia suméria. O capitão Gason Cross posteriormente participou das descobertas.	
Susa, na Pérsia	M. Dieulafoi, 1884. Escavação dos edifícios reais. J. de Morgan, 1897. Descobriu a estrela esculpida com o código de Hamurabi.	Esd. 4:9; Dan. 8:2 e Nee. 1:1
Tanque, Tell Ta'naque, 8 km a SL de Megido	Academia de Viena, E. Sellin, 1902-04; helênico (porto; tábuas do século XV A.C.; cidadela). Hetty Goldman, a começar pelo ano de 1934, fez amplos estudos, resultando na publicação de dois volumes (1950-1956), *Excavations at Gozlu Kule*.	Jos. 12:26 e I Reis 4:12
Tarso		Atos 9.11,30; 11:25; 21:39 e 22:3.
Tebas, ver sob Egito		
Teilat-el-Ghassul, no vale do Jordão	Os jesuítas efetuaram oito campanhas nessa área, até 1938, tendo feito muitas descobertas.	
Tell el-Hesi, no sudoeste da Palestina	Flinders Petrie, 1890. Estabeleceu importantes princípios arqueológicos de estratigrafia, uso de cerâmica para medição do tempo, distinção de níveis de ocupação, e portanto, de variegadas civilizações. F.J. Bliss apoiou suas teorias e a cronologia de 1894, de Petrie-Bliss, mostrou ser correta até 1500 A.C., contando para trás.	
Tell Harari, perto do rio Eufrates, no sueste da Síria.	Descobrimento de Mari (Tell Harari); a 11 km de Abu Kemal. As escavações prolongaram-se de 1933 a 1960. Foi descoberta uma imensa quantidade de tabletes de argila — mais de vinte mil — escritos em um dialeto similar ao hebraico dos tempos dos patriarcas. Provêem muita informação da geografia, da história, dos conflitos militares, da cultura e da religião do noroeste da Mesopotâmia, ilustrando coisas do período patriarcal da história bíblica. Os materiais descobertos mencionam os incursos dos *habiru* (hebreus). As mesmas escavações encontraram os templos do deus Dagon e da deusa Istar. Os tabletes foram encontrados no palácio do governante Zimri-Lim (século XVIII A.C.).	Gên. 11:23,24; 33:18; 34:1-3; Exo. 30:13,14 e Jos. 24:23.

LUGAR E LOCALIZAÇÃO	DESCOBERTAS, ARQUEÓLOGOS, DATAS	REFERÊNCIAS BÍBLICAS
Tirza, Tell Far'a, a NE de Siquém	Ecole Biblique, Jerusalém (de Vaux) 1946-47, 1950; calcolítico e proto-urbano (túmulos). Abandonada por causa de Samaria. Muros da cidade, reocupada em cerca de 700-600 A.C.	
Tróia, Ásia Menor	Heinrich Schliemann, 1870. Foi o primeiro a deixar claro que um cômoro é uma ruína com muitas descobertas arqueológicas possíveis.	
Turim, Itália, NO Sudário de Turim	Academia Francesa de Ciências, Paul Vignon, 1930. Kurt Berna (1968)	Mat. 27:40, Marc. 15:46, Luc. 23:45, João 20:5-7
Ur, na antiga Caldéia	Sir Charles Leonard Woolley, em 1922. Fez escavações que marcaram época em Ur, nas ruínas da cidade de Abraão, chamadas Al-Muqayyer. O local já havia sido investigado em 1854 por Loftus. Woolley realizou suas escavações sistemáticas de 1922 a 1934, patrocinadas pelo Museu Britânico e pela Universidade de Pennsylvania. Inúmeras descobertas foram feitas, dadas a público em seu livro, *Ur of the Chaldees*, publicado em 1929.	Gên. 11:28-31; 12:1-4; 15:7 e Nee. 9:7.
Vergina, Grécia, a 64 quilômetros de Salônica, local da antiga Aegae, sede da realeza macedônica, no século IV A.C.	Os ossos de Felipe II da Macedônia foram encontrados em um esquife de ouro, obviamente em um túmulo real. A descoberta foi feita em 1977. O ferimento foi feito por uma flechada, durante o cerco de Metone, em 354 A.C., o qual é claramente visível no crânio. Entre muitos outros objetos, cinco minúsculas esculturas em marfim foram encontradas, duas das quais são de Felipe II e de Alexandre, o Grande, seu filho. As outras três evidentemente representam a esposa de Felipe, Olímpias, e os pais de Felipe. A morte de Felipe ocorreu em Aegae, em 336 A.C. *Importância para o Novo Testamento*. Felipe unificou as cidades-estados gregas, mediante conquista militar, traçando os planos para a invasão da Pérsia. Alexandre o Grande, seu filho, efetuou essas conquistas. Então partiu para o domínio do mundo civilizado conhecido da época, propagando a língua grega a todos os rincões do império. Esse idioma tornou-se universal, sendo essa a razão pela qual o Novo Testamento foi originalmente escrito em grego. Essa descoberta arqueológica foi uma das maiores já feitas em todos os tempos. Uma figura de cera, representando o crânio de Felipe, pode ser vista no Museu de Manchester, Inglaterra.	VII. *Bibliografia* (AM ALB ALL BL BL DIR GOR HAR HARI ID KE ME ND PRE RAM UN UN (1957) UNA WR WRI YA Z)

ARQUÉTIPO — ARQUITETURA

ARQUÉTIPO
Vem do grego **arche**, «primário», e **tupos**, «figura», «padrão».

1. Em Platão, as *formas* ou *idéias* originais, das quais participam as coisas (particulares). Os particulares são cópias inferiores das formas ou idéias. Ver o artigo sobre *Formas*.
2. No escolasticismo, como em Tomás de Aquino, as formas existem na mente divina, uma idéia chamada *conceptualismo* (ver o artigo). Ver também acerca dos *Universais*.
3. Em Locke, o termo indica os originais de nossas idéias, originadas neste mundo, por meio da percepção dos sentidos.
4. Em Jung, a palavra veio a significar as formas primárias do inconsciente coletivo.
5. Na teologia cristã, o *arquétipo* de nossa existência é Cristo, visto que em Sua imagem é que estamos sendo transformados (Rom. 8:29; II Cor. 3:18). Isso nos faz participar da natureza divina com filhos (II Ped. 1:4). Trata-se do mais sublime de todos os conceitos religiosos, o cerne mesmo do evangelho. Ver o NTI em II Ped. 1:4; II Cor. 3:18; Col. 2:10 e Rom. 8:29. (NTI P)

ARQUEUS
Uma família de cananeus (ver Gên. 10:17 e I Crô. 1:15), habitantes da cidade de Arca, moderna Tell 'Arqa, cerca de 19 km a nordeste de Trípoli, na Síria. Os arqueus são mencionados na genealogia de Noé. Arca foi conquistada por Tiglate-Pileser III, em 738 A.C. O imperador Alexandre Severo nasceu nessa cidade. Esta veio a ser chamada Cesaréia do Líbano. Nas inscrições assírias, a cidade é chamada Irkatah. O lugar também é mencionado em fontes egípcias (cartas de Amarna; ver o artigo sobre *Arqueologia*, VI, Escavações Arqueológicas, sob Tell-el-Amarna). (ND Z)

ARQUEVITAS
O nome designa pessoas provenientes da cidade babilônica de Ereque (Uruque), as quais juntamente com persas, babilônios, elamitas e outras foram transplantadas por Assurbanipal, ou Osnapar, para cidades de Samaria e outras porções da província (ver Esd. 4:9,10). (Z)

ARQUIPO
Seu nome aparece na saudação da epístola de Paulo a Filemom (vs. 2). Ele também é exortado em Colossenses 4:17. Em Filemom, ele é chamado «companheiro de lutas». Isso dá a entender que ele tivera alguma associação anterior com Paulo, que labutara a seu lado. Sua associação íntima com Filemom e Áfia (provavelmente a esposa de Filemom) tem sugerido, na opinião de alguns eruditos, que ele era filho do casal. Pelo menos estava intimamente ligado a eles, na igreja de Colossos, sendo, evidentemente, um de seus líderes principais. Alguns supõem que o ministério que Arquipo foi exortado a cumprir (ver Col. 4:17) era na cidade vizinha de Laodicéia, o que pode ser verdade ou não. Porém, é extremamente improvável a idéia, aventada por alguns, que ele era o hospedeiro da igreja de Colossos, o proprietário de Onésimo e a principal personagem endereçada na nossa epístola a Filemom. Por que Paulo falaria especificamente a Filemom, se, na realidade, quisesse dirigir-se a Arquipo? A menção do nome de Filemom, em primeiro lugar, quase certamente indica que ele era a principal pessoa endereçada e que as demais pessoas são mencionadas por cortesia, pelo menos no que tange ao problema de Onésimo. É bastante improvável que o «ministério» aludido, que ele esperava cumprir, tivesse qualquer coisa a ver com a soltura de um escravo. A tradição afirma que Arquipo foi apedrejado até morrer, juntamente com Filemom e Áfia, em Cone, perto de Laodicéia, além de inclui-lo entre os setenta discípulos missionários especiais do décimo capítulo de Lucas. Usualmente, porém, tradições como essas são apenas fantasias para preencher hiatos em nosso conhecimento. (IB NTI UN)

ARQUITAS
Uma tribo mencionada em conexão com a partilha recebida pelos descendentes de José (ver Jos. 16:2). Husai, o arquita, o mais famoso personagem dessa tribo, era conselheiro de Davi, e mais tarde, de Absalão (ver II Sam. 15:32; 16:16; 17:5,14; I Crô. 27:33). A tribo estava localizada na fronteira norte de Benjamim. A data de Husai é cerca de 1050 A.C. (ID S)

ARQUITAS
Filósofo grego do século IV A.C. Viveu em Taranto. Foi pitagoreano da segunda geração, discípulo de Filolaus (ver o artigo a seu respeito). Foi amigo de Platão. Ele separou a teoria dos números dessa escola (ver sobre o *pitagoreanismo*) de seu arcabouço místico e religioso, e assim possibilitou o avanço da teoria matemática, encorajando sua aplicação científica. Defendia a idéia da infinitude do espaço, desafiando aqueles que defendiam a idéia de sua finitude, a fim de que lhe explicassem como, se ele fosse levado à beira do espaço, não poderia chegar mais além. (P)

ARQUITETÔNICO
Termo usado para descrever um sistema filosófico armado segundo um plano coerente. 1. Em Kant, essa qualidade teria sido atingida em seu plano, exemplificada nas categorias, através de distinções próprias da lógica formal. 2. A filosofia de Charles Pierce pode ser assim epitetada, devido ao fato de que ele derivou seu padrão do exame fenomenológico da experiência imediata, como também de uma pesquisa de todos os campos do conhecimento humano. (P)

ARQUITETURA
1. **O termo «arquiteto»** vem do grego **architekton**, formado por *archi*, «chefe», = *tekton*, «construtor» ou seja, o primeiro construtor, chefe-construtor. Portanto, a arquitetura é a construção de estruturas gerais e edificações que um chefe-construtor realiza.

2. **Declaração geral.** Centenas de obras arquiteturais, construídas nos tempos bíblicos têm sido desenterradas. A beleza arquitetural, conhecida e exemplificada através dos hebreus, era tomada por empréstimo principalmente dos egípcios, babilônios, assírios, fenícios, gregos e romanos. Ao deixarem o Egito, levaram consigo conceitos arquiteturais egíp-

ARQUITETURA

cios. Entrando na Palestina, adotaram o que ali encontraram, porque o que ali existia era adaptado ao clima palestino, e os materiais de construção disponíveis não incentivavam qualquer inovação. O próprio templo de Jerusalém, o ponto culminante da arquitetura de Israel, incorporava muitas idéias acerca da estrutura e do material de templos que já existiam.

3. Arquitetura egípcia. Desde tempos remotos, na primeira dinastia, entre 2900 e 2700 A.C., os ancestrais de Israel contemplavam as gigantescas pirâmides, embora já tivessem séculos de antiguidade nos dias de Abraão.

Variedades de pirâmides. Da terceira à sexta dinastia, cerca de 2700 a 2000 A.C. a. Na terceira dinastia, a pirâmide de degraus. b. Na quarta dinastia, a gigantesca pirâmide de Gizé, cuja base cobre uma área de 13 acres, com 136 m de altura. Foram usados 2.300.000 blocos de duas toneladas e meia cada. Essa era a pirâmide do Faraó Kufu. c. Seu sucessor, Cafre, construiu uma ainda mais alta, com 147 m de altura; e ele mesmo é representado na cabeça da esfinge, que foi erigida a leste dessa pirâmide. d. Então houve pirâmides com textos inscritos em seus lados, na quinta e na sexta dinastias.

Outras maravilhas arquitetônicas. a. O templo da rainha Hatsepsute, cerca de 1500 A.C., em Deir-el-Bahri, perto de Tebas, uma bela estrutura de pedra calcária branca, com terraços apoiados em colunas. b. Dois gigantescos obeliscos da rainha Hatsepsute, em Carnaque. c. O templo palacial de Amom, em Carnaque (antiga Tebas), ampliado por Tutmés III (falecido em 1450 A.C). d. O túmulo de seu vizir, Rekmire. e. Templo mortuário de Ramisés, em Tebas, um edifício estranhamente belo. f. Templo de Luxor, acrescentado por Ramisés mediante a construção de 134 tremendas colunas, uma parte do maior templo que já foi construído em toda a história da humanidade. g. Um templo completo escavado em uma rocha que contempla o rio Nilo, por Ramisés, completado por quatro estátuas desse Faraó.

4. Arquitetura na Mesopotâmia. a. Palácios (ver Isa. 39:7; II Reis 20:18) em Ereque (Uruque, Warka; ver Gên. 10:10), a 80 km a noroeste de Ur. b. Templos monumentais e a gigantesca torre de Eana, feita de tijolos de barro (cerca de 2500 a.C.). c. Uma torre palco na Babilônia (cf. Gên. 11:1-6). d. Em Ur, templos, palácios e um antigo zigurate (torre palco) (cf. Gên. 11:28,31; 15:7; Nee. 9:7). e. Na Assíria, o templo do deus Assur. cidades fortificadas com muralhas, portões e marcos. f. Na Babilônia, um espantoso número de palácios, edifícios públicos, templos e uma torre, que alguns pensam ser a torre de Babel (ver Gên. 10:10; 11:9; II Reis 17:24,30). g. Em Calné (Calá, Nimrude; ver Gên. 10:10), a 32 km a nordeste de Nínive, palácios de reis assírios do século VIII A.C., dotados de leões ornamentais com cabeças humanas. h. Em Quis, a 13 km a leste da Babilônia, palácio dos reis e o templo de Istar. i. Em Nínive, no alto rio Tigre, a norte de Assur, palácios assírios ornamentados, incluindo o palácio de Senaqueribe, cerca de 704-681 A.C., com não menos de setenta e um aposentos, três quilômetros de paredes com lajotas esculpidas. A biblioteca de Assurbanipal (669-633 A.C.). O palácio de Sargão II (721-705 A.C.), dotado de esplêndidos altos-relevos e de telhas com pinturas esmaltadas. Em Mari, um gigantesco palácio dos governantes amorreus, um templo de Istar e um zigurate. Esse palácio cobria uma área de 15 acres, dispondo de inúmeros apartamentos reais, escritórios, uma escola para escribas e uma biblioteca com mais de vinte mil tabletes de argila.

Residências particulares. Essas construções variavam em seu resplendor. Desde tempos remotos, cerca de 2000 A.C., na Mesopotâmia, as casas eram construídas de pau-a-pique. Exemplares desse tipo de construção têm sido encontrados em Ur. Também havia residências com dois pavimentos. Algumas delas tinham vários aposentos ao redor de um pátio, munido de tanques e encanamento para recolher a água da chuva. As casas dos mais abastados eram maiores, tinham muitos aposentos, todos convenientemente dispostos, com áreas de recepção e áreas privadas.

5. Arquitetura persa. As ruínas de Persépolis, a 40 km de Parsagade, para sudoeste, provêem a mais impressionante arte e arquitetura persa. As escavações descobriram o Tacara, o palácio de Dario, o Apadana, o salão de audiências de Dario e Xerxes, o salão de cem colunas, o portão de Xerxes, com gigantescas imagens de bois a guardá-lo, conforme se via também nos palácios da Assíria, o harém de Dario e Xerxes, a residência de Xerxes (486-465 A.C.), o tesouro real com magnificentes relevos. Em Susa (na Bíblia, Susã, ver Nee. 1:1; Est. 1:2 e Dan. 8:2), foi desenterrado o palácio de Dario, que tinha painéis de tijolos esmaltados lindamente coloridos, relevos de bois alados e grifos alados, e lanceiros da guarda real.

6. Arquitetura grega. Atenas é a que exibe a melhor arquitetura grega, e muitas cidades gregas contam com arquitetura similar, embora em menor extensão. No século V A.C., a idade áurea dessa arquitetura, templos soberbos e outras edificações ornavam a Grécia. O templo mais importante era aquele dedicado à deusa Atena, protetora da cidade. Muitas outras estruturas eram famosas com razão, como o Partenon, o Templo da Vitória Sem Asas, o Odeon (Salão de Música), o Erecteum, a Colunata de Eumenes II, o Tesiom, o templo de Zeus e o Ágora. Em Corinto, têm sido descobertas estruturas similares, como o Teatro, o templo de Apolo, o santuário de Esculápio e a Basílica.

O estilo dórico. Típica é a coluna de estilo dórico, cuja haste aumenta o seu diâmetro em proporção quase imperceptível, até cerca de uma quarta parte de sua altura, e então diminui levemente após isso, até o cimo. Não tinha base, mas repousava imediatamente no pedestal, sendo circundada por projeções semicirculares, encontrando-se em ângulos agudos. O capitel consistia em três partes, o pescoço da coluna, uma moldura circular, e o ábaco, um ornamento quadrangular que suportava a arquitrava, uma pedra quadrangular que se apoiava nas extremidades, em duas colunas. Acima disso havia o friso, tudo encimado pelo cornicho.

O estilo jônico. Uma coluna mais alta que a dórica, com um alargamento na base, embora menor que a dórica. A extremidade superior também tinha formato diferente, e com freqüência havia relevos ao longo de seu comprimento.

O estilo coríntio. Muito parecido com o jônico, mas com decoração de folhas e outras figuras, nas extremidades.

7. Arquitetura etrusca e romana. O etruscos (que habitavam a Itália central) apreciavam muito a

ARQUITETURA

decoração, e assim cobriam seus edifícios com ricos ornamentos entalhados. Não permanece até hoje qualquer um de seus templos, nem mesmo ruínas, porque a infraestrutura dos mesmos era construída de madeira. Suas construções são reconhecidas hoje em dia através de suas muralhas e de seus túmulos. Os portais de Volterra e Perúgia têm um verdadeiro arco feito de pedras em forma de cunha. Os esgotos de Roma, lançados no século VI A.C., foram uma impressionante demonstração de engenharia e arquitetura.

Os romanos preservaram o arco dos etruscos, elaborando-o para tornar-se no arco cruzado e na cúpula. Tomaram por empréstimo certas idéias dos gregos, preservando o estilo das colunas gregas. Foram os primeiros a construir edifícios de tijolos. No século III A.C. começou a construção das estradas, o que deu aos romanos tão justa fama. No século I A.C., a arquitetura romana tornou-se ornada e pomposa, exibida nos edifícios públicos e também nas residências dos ricos. O primeiro teatro de pedras foi erigido em Pompéia, em cerca de 55 A.C. César tomou sobre si a tarefa de erigir teatros, templos, anfiteatros, circos, basílicas e o famoso Fórum. Augusto terminou a maioria dessas obras e iniciou outras. Agripa construiu um magnificente Partenon. Até mesmo uma relativa cidade interiorana como Pompéia contava com luxuosos edifícios públicos. Vespasiano construiu o Coliseu, um gigantesco anfiteatro. E também havia os banhos de Tito e seu arco triunfal. O arquiteto de Trajano, Apolodoro de Damasco, ultrapassou em dimensões e esplendor tudo quanto havia antes dele, tendo levantado o Fórum Trianon, com sua gigantesca Basílica Ulpia, e a coluna de Trajano, que até hoje sobrevive.

8. Arquitetura dos hebreus. Originalmente, eles eram pastores e habitavam em tendas, e não tinham arquitetura. Provavelmente, devido à influência egípcia, Israel a princípio construiu cidades. Sem dúvida, foram compelidos ao trabalho escravo, edificando alguns dos grandes monumentos do Egito. Em Canaã, os hebreus habitavam em casas de pedra (ver Lev. 14:34; I Reis 7:10), a maioria das quais provavelmente eles tomaram, não as tendo construído (ver Deu. 6:10 e Núm. 13:19). Também edificaram cidades fortes, com muralhas. Aparentemente não havia uma maneira sistemática de construção, embora provavelmente predominasse o estilo de cabanas de pedras e barro, com um único aposento.

No tempo dos reis. Nesse tempo, começou realmente a arquitetura dos hebreus. Um povo que lutava para sobreviver e não tinha tempo para fantasias e grandiosidades arquitetônicas. Porém, uma vez que a prosperidade deles começou a acentuar-se, as edificações refletiram o aprimoramento da situação. Dos dias de Saul em diante, a arquitetura descoberta pela arqueologia consiste em maciças construções de pedra, como no caso das residências reais, que mais se assemelhavam a masmorras. Posteriormente, por haverem feito empréstimos dos estilos estrangeiros, passaram a ser construídas estruturas mais nobres entre os hebreus.

No tempo de Davi e Salomão. As conquistas militares trouxeram as riquezas, e havia mais para ser investido em edificações. O primeiro palácio de Davi, em Hebrom, provavelmente era uma casa de pedras de telhado chato, com as características de uma fortaleza. Ele também construiu para sua residência uma casa de madeira de cedro (ver I Sam. 7:2), a suleste do que mais tarde se tornou Jerusalém. Também fortaleceu a própria cidade com muralhas maciças. A paz e a prosperidade levaram Salomão a experimentar de tudo, e a antiga idéia da construção de um templo finalmente se concretizou. Ele dependeu muito das habilidades dos fenícios, importando inúmeros conceitos e materiais para decorar o edifício. O produto final era caracteristicamente fenício, o que também já era de se esperar, visto que foi obra de um arquiteto sírio (ver I Reis 7:13-15). Construções similares, com base em planos semelhantes, têm sido encontradas, pertencentes ao período de 1200-900 A.C., no norte da Síria e em Tell Tainat. Descrições amplas são dadas sobre *templo*, em um artigo separado, que versa sobre esse assunto.

Os impostos determinados por Davi e Salomão para financiar o extenso programa de edificações levou à construção de «cidades-armazéns». Foram construídos edifícios em Bete-Semes e Laquis, de construção bem simples, mas com paredes excepcionalmente fortes, com longos e estreitos aposentos, provavelmente para armazenar cereais. Esses aposentos tinham, inicialmente, 32 m de comprimento; e, posteriormente, 78 m de comprimento. Isso requeria residências para os encarregados, anexas aos armazéns. Em Megido e Hazor, grandes edifícios dotados de colunas foram levantados, com pátios pavimentados, que alguns estudiosos julgam ter sido estábulos, embora pudessem ser salas e escritórios para recepção ao público. Edifícios similares foram encontrados em Tanaque, Eglon e Gezer. Nesses edifícios eram usadas grandes pedras, um tanto toscas nas fieiras inferiores, mas com pedras de esquina bem formadas e perfiladas. Em seguida vinham fieiras de madeira, misturadas com tijolos cozidos ao forno. Os pátios centrais abertos e grandes, recolhiam a água da chuva em cisternas cavadas na rocha, similares àquelas encontradas em Bete-Semes, pertencentes aos séculos XIII e XIV A.C. Essas cisternas eram usadas para recolher água potável, para propósitos de lavagens e para servirem de masmorras (ver I Reis 22:38; Jer. 38:6). Algumas vezes, por baixo desses pátios centrais, profundos túneis eram cavados até à fonte mais próxima, para trazerem suprimento de água. Tais túneis têm sido encontrados em Gibeom, Gezer, Megido, Laquis e Jerusalém, demonstrando considerável técnica de engenharia. Túmulos escavados na rocha, alguns deles bastante amplos, mostram a influência egípcia.

Residências particulares. Desde tempos remotos, têm sido encontrados restos de casas próximas de Siquém (pertencentes ao século XVII A.C.). Há uma única entrada que vai dar em um pátio central, de onde há acesso para os quartos que eram usados para abrigar servos e para servir de armazéns. Esse planejamento básico parece ter sido comum em todo o antigo Oriente Próximo, para o caso de pessoas mais abastadas. As casas dos pobres eram muito austeras, tendo cobertura de palha trançada, com paredes feitas de pau-a-pique e vigas de madeira. As mais pobres contavam com um único aposento; mas dois aposentos eram comuns nessas casas. Por volta de 1500 A.C., tornaram-se comuns casas com um aposento maior na frente, e um aposento menor atrás; e naturalmente, os ricos sempre dispunham de muitos aposentos e de amplo espaço.

ARQUITETURA

9. No período intertestamental. As mais impressionantes estruturas desse período podem ser representadas pelo mausoleu da família Tobiade, em Araq'el-Emir, na Jordânia. Tinha enormes pedras e colunas com capitéis coríntios ornados com frisos e figuras de leões, mostrando a influência helenista. Porém, a influência fenícia continuava presente nesse período. Foram construídas torres redondas, em Samaria. Vários monumentos exibem uma mistura de estilos, como o túmulo de Zacarias (em Jerusalém), com seu telhado piramidal egípcio, capitéis e pilastras gregas, com colunas nas esquinas, lapidadas da rocha.

10. No Novo Testamento. Herodes e seus sucessores mostraram-se especialmente ativos em suas obra arquitetônicas, como no caso do templo de Jerusalém (ver Luc. 21:25) e de vários edifícios em Samaria e Cesaréia, bem como em cidades menores. O templo de Herodes dominava Jerusalém, no que concerne à arquitetura. De fato, era um cartão de visitas da política protecionista de Herodes ao judaísmo. Começou em cerca de 19 A.C., e foi terminado após 46 anos de labor (ver João 2:20). O trecho de Mar. 13:1,2 refere-se às suas impressionantes pedras de construção. Era uma estrutura tripla, onde o átrio inferior formava um ótimo terraço, tendo no meio um átrio interior elevado em plataforma, do qual erguia-se o santuário propriamente dito. Claustros ou pórticos parecem ter rodeado o átrio exterior, uma característica grega. Cristo ensinou ali, tal como o fizeram os Seus apóstolos (ver João 10:23; Atos 3:11 e 5:12). A área descoberta foi transformada em uma feira para vender animais para os holocaustos e em um local de troca de moedas, para os peregrinos. Jesus objetou a esse espírito de comercialização (ver João 2:13-17), algo que sempre infesta os santuários religiosos. Quanto a detalhes sobre a aparência desse edifício, ver o NTI em suas notas em João 10:23. Também pode ser visto o artigo sobre o *templo* de Jerusalém, quanto a maiores detalhes.

As Sinagogas. A estrutura das sinagogas dependia das dimensões da congregação local, mas a *posição* da estrutura era previamente determinada. Usualmente era construída em lugares elevados, e situada de tal modo que os adoradores, ao entrarem e orarem, ficassem de rosto voltado para Jerusalém. Por dentro, a construção lembrava o tabernáculo, mesmo que não fosse duplicação real dos seus elementos. Na extremidade que dava para Jerusalém, ficava a arca, a caixa que continha os livros sagrados, e essa porção da sinagoga se tornava um santuário em miniatura. Ali ficavam os *principais assentos*, que eram disputados pelos fariseus (ver Mat. 23:6). Defronte da arca ficava o candeeiro de oito ramos. Uma de suas lâmpadas ficava a arder continuamente. No meio do edifício havia uma plataforma elevada, sobre a qual várias pessoas podiam ficar em pé para fazer a leitura das Escrituras. A congregação estava dividida, os homens eram separados das mulheres, e uma repartição abaixo servia para esse propósito.

Por baixo do soalho de uma sinagoga, em Cafarnaum, pertencente ao século IV D.C., foram encontrados os remanescentes de uma edificação, que podia ser a sinagoga mencionada em Lucas 7:5, que um centurião romano presenteou aos judeus. Restos de sinagogas muito antigas não têm sido encontradas devido à total destruição das construções judaicas, no primeiro século da era cristã e no começo do século II D.C. (70 e 132 D.C., quando das invasões dos romanos sob Tito e Adriano).

Residências particulares. Conforme sempre sucedeu em todas as épocas, essas variavam segundo a abastança de cada um. As casas dos pobres daquela época, provavelmente não eram muito diferentes daquelas que hoje se vê nas vilas turcas e sírias. Os pobres tinham um aposento, talvez dois (ver Luc. 11:7). Se um homem quisesse ter privacidade ao orar, tinha de ir para a sua despensa, uma estrutura muito simples para guardar legumes, cereais e frutas (ver Mat. 6:6). As casas eram feitas de pau-a-pique, talvez com uma obra de gradil trançado e recoberta de argamassa. Isso podia ser arrombado sem muita dificuldade (ver Mat. 6:19 e as notas nesse lugar, no NTI). As pessoas mais abastadas contavam com casas mais espaçosas, construídas ao redor de um pátio, com telhado plano e vários aposentos. Havia pátios elevados sobre os telhados planos, e podiam ser estendidos ali baldaquinos para que os hóspedes e os membros da família pudessem ir ali, ao refrescar do dia (ver Atos 10:9). Os *cenáculos* (ver Atos 1.13) podiam ser o andar de cima de uma casa de dois pavimentos, ou um pavimento coberto no alto do telhado plano. Algumas vezes, uma escada externa levava a tais aposentos ou construções, no telhado plano.

11. A metáfora da arquitetura. Há várias dessas metáforas no Novo Testamento. Em primeiro lugar, temos a considerar o *alicerce* sobre o qual alguém edifica (ver Mat. 7:24,27; Luc. 6:48, 14:29; Rom. 15:20; I Cor. 3:10-12; Efé. 2:20; I Tim. 6:19; II Tim. 2:19; Heb. 11:10). Isso simboliza como o homem sábio ou espiritual preocupa-se em ter uma sólida e fidedigna base para sua fé e vida. A própria Igreja está edificada sobre o fundamento firme dos apóstolos e profetas, os líderes espirituais do Antigo e do Novo Testamentos. Naturalmente, Cristo, em certo sentido, é o único alicerce. Em outras palavras, Ele é o único fundamento como a base da salvação do indivíduo (ver I Cor. 3:10-12). Mas Ele também é a pedra de esquina, que mantém unido o alicerce e garante a simetria da construção, sendo essa uma parte importantíssima do alicerce (ver I Ped. 2:7). Paulo chamou a si mesmo de «sábio construtor», que ele designou usando o vocábulo grego *architekton*. Mas, cabe dizer que então um arquiteto não era aquele que planejava um edifício, e, sim, o mestre-de-obras, o encarregado da construção. Paulo lançava o alicerce por meio de sua prédica, e o templo cristão ia tomando forma (ver I Cor 3:10). O homem espiritual edifica com ouro, prata e pedras preciosas, materiais duradouros, que não se estragam sob os efeitos do fogo. Isso indica sua vida diária, sua espiritualidade e sua busca. O indivíduo pode construir para o tempo ou para a eternidade, pois a escolha é dele. Aqueles que edificam somente para o tempo, metaforicamente usam materiais como madeira, feno (usado na massa sobre a qual era aplicada a argamassa) e a palha, um elemento essencial no fabrico de tijolos de barro, formando um material barato, ressecado ao sol, para edificações que não tinham o propósito de ser duráveis. Espiritualmente falando, um homem pode construir como o faria um rico ou como o faria um pobre (ver I Cor. 3:12 ss). (AM BAD IB ID FRA ND UN Z)

••• ••• •••

ARQUIVOS — ARREPENDIMENTO

ARQUIVOS, CASA DOS

Em Esdras 6:1, o lugar onde eram registrados os documentos históricos da corte persa. Esses acervos eram comuns no Oriente, nos impérios assírio e babilônico (ver Est. 2:23 e 6:1). Templos, palácios ou importantes edifícios públicos tinham salas para guardar tais registros. Esdras solicitou que fossem examinados os arquivos babilônicos, quanto aos memorandos reais (ver Esd. 5:17). Algo similar foi a guarda das Escrituras no templo de Jerusalém, em Israel (ver II Reis 22:8). A câmara do escriba Elisama servia de sala de arquivo (ver Jer. 37:20). Em tempos posteriores, no Egito, havia salas especiais ou armazéns, anexos às sinagogas, para guardar e preservar os manuscritos da Bíblia. Esse cuidado foi o que preservou os manuscritos, algo tão necessário na crítica textual das Escrituras. (Z)

ARRAZOAR, RACIONAL

Temos duas palavras hebraicas e cinco palavras gregas, a saber:

1. *Yakach*, «arrazoar», palavra usada por sessenta e uma vezes (por exemplo, Isa. 1:18; Jó. 13:3; 15:3; Gên. 21:25; II Reis 19:4; Pro. 9:8; Jer. 2:19; Eze. 3:26; Osé. 4:4). É palavra que nas versões em geral, em português, tem sido traduzida por idéias diversas, por ser muito prenhe em sentido, como «arrazoar», «disputar», «corrigir», «repreender», «reprovar», etc.

2. *Shaphat*, «ser julgado», palavra que figura por duzentas e quatro vezes, com variegados sentidos, desde «vingar», «contender», «julgar», «executar», etc. Por exemplo: I Sam. 12:7; Gên. 16:5; Êxo. 5:21; Lev. 19:15; Núm. 35:24; Deu. 1:16; Juí. 4:4; 10:2,3; 11:27; 12:7-9,11,13,14; Jó. 21:22; Sal. 7:8; Pro. 29:14; Isa. 51:5; Eze. 7:3; 11:10,11; 33:20; Dan. 9:12; Joel 3:12; Miq. 3:11; 4:3.

3. *Dialégomai*, «discursar», «raciocinar». Palavra grega usada por treze vezes: Mar. 9:34; Atos 17:2,17; 18:4,19; 19:8,9; 20:7,9; 24:12,25; Heb. 12:5 e Judas 9.

4. *Dialogízomai*, «considerar», «raciocinar bem». Palavra grega usada por dezesseis vezes. E o substantivo, *dialogismós*, «consideração», «raciocínio», mais catorze vezes. Por exemplo: Mat. 16:7; Mar. 2:6,8; 8:16,17; Luc. 1:29; 3:15; 20:24—o verbo; Mat. 15:9; Mar. 7:21; Luc. 2:35; 5:22; Rom. 1:21; I Cor. 3:20; Fil. 2:14; Tia. 2:4—o substantivo.

5. *Logízomai*, «considerar». Palavra grega usada por quarenta vezes, principalmente nas epístolas de Paulo. Por exemplo: Mar. 15:28; Luc. 22:37; João 11:50; Atos 19:27; Rom. 2:3,26; 3:28; 4:3-11; I Cor. 4:1; 13:5,11; II Cor. 3:5; 12:6; Gál. 3:6; Fil. 3:13; 4:8; II Tim. 4:16; Heb. 11:19; Tia. 2:23; I Ped. 5:12.

6. *Suzetéo*, «buscar juntamente», «discutir». Palavra grega usada por oito vezes. Exemplo: Mar. 1:27; 9:10; 8:11; 12:28; Atos 6:9; Atos 15:2,7; 28:29. Daí deriva-se a palavra grega para disputante, sofista, «*suzetetés*», usada em I Cor. 1:20.

7. *Sullogízomai*, «considerar junto». Palavra grega usada por apenas uma vez, em Luc. 20:5.

«Razão» como uma faculdade humana, ou em sentido abstrato, aparece nos livros apócrifos, como Sabedoria 17:12 e Eclesiástico 37:16. Em Rom. 12:1, o «culto racional» é *logikén latreían*, «serviço racional», isto é, pertencente à razão. Os pensadores deste mundo dão excessivo valor à «razão», sem perceberem que, na queda, ficaram afetadas tanto a moral quanto a razão humanas. Por isso diz Paulo: «Visto como, na sabedoria de Deus, o mundo não o conheceu por sua própria sabedoria, aprouve a Deus salvar aos que crêem, pela loucura da pregação» (I Cor. 1:21). Todavia, se desassistida, a mente humana não atinge Deus, o Espírito Santo quer iluminar a razão humana, e o faz, conferindo-nos a mente de Cristo. «Nós, porém, temos a mente de Cristo» (I Cor. 2:16b). E essa não é uma idéia ventilada apenas no Novo Testamento. Já dizia Daniel: «...os perversos procederão perversamente, e nenhum deles entenderá, mas os sábios entenderão» (Dan. 12:10). No crente recém-regenerado, a mente de Cristo inculta lhe é dada potencialmente. Agora sua razão precisa desenvolver-se, mediante o estudo da Palavra e da meditação. Esse estudo não consiste em mera leitura aligeirada. Pedro deixa isso bem claro, ao dizer: «...nosso amado irmão Paulo vos escreveu, segundo a sabedoria que lhe foi dada, ao falar acerca destes assuntos, como de fato costuma fazer em todas as suas epístolas, nas quais há certas cousas difíceis de entender, que os ignorantes e instáveis deturpam, como também deturpam as demais Escrituras, para própria destruição deles» (II Ped. 15,16). E a epístola aos Hebreus ajunta: «Por isso, pondo de parte os princípios elementares da doutrina de Cristo, deixemo-nos levar para o que é perfeito, não lançando de novo a base do arrependimento de obras mortas, e da fé em Deus, e o ensino de batismos e da imposição de mãos, da ressurreição dos mortos e do juízo eterno» (Heb. 6:1,2). O escritor sagrado evidentemente falava em estágios da experiência cristã, cada qual representado por uma doutrina. No entanto, a maioria do povo de Deus nem chega a entender e viver a doutrina dos batismos. Não têm vivência experimental com doutrinas como imposição de mãos, ressurreição dos mortos e juízo eterno. Os grandes profetas do Antigo Testamento e os apóstolos do Novo Testamento tinham vivência com todas essas realidades espirituais. E, se buscarmos seriamente a espiritualidade, chegaremos lá, porque essa é a vontade expressa de Deus. «...até que todos cheguemos à unidade da fé e do pleno conhecimento do Filho de Deus, à perfeita varonilidade, à medida da estatura da plenitude de Cristo, para que não mais sejamos como meninos, agitados de um lado para outro, e levados ao redor por todo vento de doutrina...» (Efé. 4:13,14). (I IB ID NTL UN Z)

ARREBATAMENTO Ver Parousia.

ARRECADAS Ver Pendentes.

ARREPENDIMENTO

I. Exigência Espiritual

Essa é a principal exigência para que haja perdão de pecados. O arrependimento tem início na conversão, que é o primeiro passo da regeneração. Ver o artigo sobre *Conversão*. A conversão ainda não é a «regeneração» propriamente dita; mas antes, faz parte dela, sendo o início do novo nascimento. Sem conversão não há regeneração, embora a conversão não encerre a totalidade da regeneração. É o começo, o ponto em que o pecador abandona o pecado e o seu antigo «eu», a sua rebeldia contra Deus. A conversão, além disso, é um ato produzido pela influência do Espírito Santo, que não pode suceder sem esse poder, embora existam agitações emocionais que provocam transformações por pouco tempo, que podem imitar a conversão.

A verdadeira conversão é *uma transformação interna da alma*, e esse é exatamente o primeiro passo

O Arrependimento

O FILHO PRÓDIGO

A VOLTA DO FILHO PRÓDIGO

••• •••

ARREPENDIMENTO

•••

Versículos-Chaves
•••

Mas Deus, não tendo em conta os tempos
da ignorância, anuncia agora a todos os
homens, e em todo o lugar, que se arrependam.
(Atos 17:30)

Eu não vim a chamar os justos, mas
os pecadores ao arrependimento.
(Mat. 9:13)

•••

Porque a tristeza segundo Deus opera
arrependimento.
(II Cor. 7:10)

Digo-vos que assim haverá alegria
no céu por um pecador que se arrepende.
(Lucas 15:7)

••• •••

da regeneração. A regeneração completa consiste na total transformação do ser, segundo a imagem de Cristo, de tal modo que alguém chega a «nascer» no reino de Deus, ou seja, nos lugares celestiais, o mundo acima, o outro mundo, que também é chamado de «céu». O indivíduo totalmente regenerado é uma nova criação, de natureza moral e metafísica semelhante à de Cristo; e isso só pode suceder nos lugares celestiais, em seu grau mais elevado, que inclui a glorificação apesar de que é na esfera terrena que têm começo a conversão e a santificação.

II. Do que Consiste o Arrependimento?

1. É um ato divino que transforma o homem, mas que depende da reação positiva do homem, uma vez inspirado pela fé (ver notas completas a respeito em Heb. 11:1 no NTI).
2. É o começo do processo da santificação (ver o artigo a respeito).
3. Juntamente com a fé, perfaz a *conversão* (ver o artigo).
4. É determinado por Deus (Atos 17:30) e é conferido por ele (II Tim. 2:25).
5. Foi determinado por Cristo (Apo. 2:5,16 e 3:3).
6. É uma operação do Espírito (Zac. 12:10).
7. A bondade de Deus nos leva ao arrependimento (Rom. 2:4).
8. A tristeza segundo Deus fomenta o arrependimento (II Cor. 7:10).
9. Conduz à vida eterna (Atos 11:18).
10. É necessário para o perdão dos pecados (Atos 2:38; 3:19 e 8:22).

III. Arrependimento e Fé

Essas duas palavras aparecem freqüentemente associadas na chamada aos homens, para que venham a Cristo, a fim de receberem gratuitamente a salvação que ele oferece. O trecho de Atos 20:21 diz, concernente ao ministério de Paulo e à mensagem por ele pregada: «...arrependimento para com Deus e a fé em nosso Senhor Jesus Cristo». O anúncio feito por Jesus Cristo, em suas primeiras mensagens, logo depois de haver sido batizado por João Batista, era: «...arrependei-vos, e crede no evangelho...» Esses dois atos, na realidade, são apenas aspectos de uma mesma realidade espiritual. A fé provoca o arrependimento, e vice-versa, pois uma coisa revela a natureza da outra. No livro de Atos, Pedro mostrou aos seus ouvintes a verdadeira natureza do Messias, a quem haviam crucificado; e eles exerceram fé nele, o que imediatamente levou-os a sentir profundo golpe em seus corações e resultou em verdadeiro arrependimento.

IV. Requisitos

Quanto aos requisitos para que alguém seja aceito na comunidade cristã, pode-se dizer que era dada tal admissão quando alguém demonstrava *arrependimento*, sobretudo daquela atitude de rebeldia que havia levado aquela gente a exigir a crucificação de Cristo, o Messias. Como confissão visível de que estavam seguindo ao Senhor Jesus, e como sinal de sua lealdade a ele, tinham de receber o rito do *batismo cristão*, tal como os prosélitos do judaísmo, que tinham de submeter-se à imersão, ou como João Batista submetia ao batismo no rio Jordão os que se arrependessem através de sua prédica. Formulações completas foram proferidas, especialmente no que tange à morte de Cristo como *expiação pelo pecado*. Apesar de que tais questões tivessem sido claramente aludidas por Jesus (por exemplo, na cena da última ceia, em que o Senhor fala que estava prestes a dar a sua vida como resgate por muitos) foram mais claramente definidas através das revelações divinas concedidas ao apóstolo Paulo. Seria mesmo uma tolice esperarmos que o sermão de Pedro, nessa altura dos acontecimentos, ainda tão no começo da igreja cristã, revelasse todas as facetas possíveis da fé em Cristo, que documentos cristãos de épocas posteriores, embora ainda dos tempos apostólicos, enfatizavam. O trecho de I Ped. 1:19 certamente enfatiza a morte de Cristo como uma expiação; e é muito provável que essa ênfase fizesse parte da teologia cristã mais primitiva, sem importar se isso tenha sido destacado ou não neste sermão do apóstolo Pedro. (I IB LAN ND NTI S Z)

ARROMBAMENTO Ver **Crimes e Castigos**.

ARRUDA

No grego, *péganon*. Palavra que aparece somente em Lucas 11:42, onde Jesus diz aos fariseus: «...dais o dízimo da hortelã, da arruda e de todas as hortaliças, e desprezais a justiça e o amor de Deus...» A tradução «arruda» não labora em qualquer erro. A questão envolve a botânica, sobre a espécie a qual o Senhor Jesus referiu-se. A arruda comum, que é cultivada até nos jardins domésticos, é a *Ruta graveolens,* cujas folhas são verde-cinza e produzem um odor pungente. Poderia estar em foco essa espécie, porquanto era comum na Palestina. Todavia, também existe a *Ruta chalepensis latifolia*, espécie similar à primeira, mas com folhagem menos dividida. Tal espécie também é natural da Palestina.

ARSA

No hebraico, **mundano**. Foi governador de Tirza, em cuja casa Zinri assassinou Elá, rei de Israel (ver I Reis 16:9,10). Era o mordomo de Elá, e Zinri era um dos comandantes militares do rei. O incidente aconteceu em meio a um banquete de vinho. (ID S)

ÁRSACES

Esse é um título (no persa antigo, **herói**) que os reis partas adotavam (285-250 A.C.). Certo número de monarcas medo-persas também adotou esse nome. Um deles foi Mitrídates I Ársaces, mencionado em I Macabeus 14:1-3, embora isso nunca apareça nos livros canônicos da Bíblia. Apiano, o historiador romano, menciona suas batalhas, como também o faz Josefo (*Anti*. xiii.186). A dinastia parta dos arsácidas tornou-se uma das maiores ameaças contra as pretensões romanas no Oriente. E os dez reis de Apocalipse 17:12 provavelmente são os reis partas que Nero reencarnado traria consigo, para cometer matricídio. Na moderna interpretação profética, eles representam o reavivamento do império romano, encabeçado pelo anticristo. Ver no NTI essa referência quanto aos ensinos antigos sobre esse assunto. (NTI Z)

ARS COMBINATÓRIA

Frase latina que significa «arte combinada», que aparentemente foi usada pela primeira vez, por Leibniz (ver o artigo) a fim de denotar a prática de criar conceitos complexos a partir de conceitos simples, segundo regras especificadas. Em 1666, Leibniz escreveu *De Arte Combinatoria*, que continha o seu programa para: 1. um idioma universal; e 2. uma matemática universal. Esse alvo nunca foi atingido, embora tivesse atraído considerável atenção por parte dos filósofos. (P)

ARS MORIENDI
Conselhos para os moribundos, especialmente um guia escrito que os sacerdotes católicos usam em seu ministério entre os moribundos. Muitas *artes moriendi* apareceram nos fins da Idade Média. (E)

ARSIPURITE
Um homem cujos 112 **filhos** retornaram a Jerusalém com Zorobabel, após o cativeiro (ver I Esdras 5:16). O nome não aparece nas listas paralelas de Esdras e Neemias, mas o número é idêntico ao número mencionado em relação a Jora (Esd. 2:18) e Harife (Nee. 7:24). (Z)

ARTAXERXES
Artaxerxes I.
O seu nome deriva-se do persa, *reino de Arta*. Foi nome de três monarcas, Artaxerxes I, II e III. Evidências extrabíblicas mostram-nos quais deles estiveram envolvidos no relato bíblico. Os papiros de Elefantina mostram que, em 408 A.C., Sambalate era um homem idoso, e seu papel de governador era realmente preenchido por dois de seus filhos (Sachau, Pap. 1:29). Isso parece indicar que Artaxerxes I (464-424 A.C.), provavelmente era quem governava a Pérsia nos dias de Neemias. Isso é verdade porque Sambalate estava então no auge de seu vigor físico, não sendo ainda um homem velho. Esse Artaxerxes I era chamado Langimano. Era filho e sucessor de Xerxes I (o Assuero de Esd. 4:6 e do livro de Ester). No sétimo ano de seu reinado, ele comissionou Esdras para que retornasse a Jerusalém, conferindo-lhe extensos privilégios, juntamente com aqueles que viajaram em sua companhia (ver Esd. 7:1 ss). Isso aconteceu em cerca de 457 A.C. Cerca de treze anos depois, ele deu permissão para que Neemias assumisse o controle das questões civis de Jerusalém (ver Nee. 2:1-8). Neemias reconstruiu as muralhas e fortificações da cidade (cap. 2 de Neemias), e isso assinalou o começo das setenta semanas referidas em Daniel 9:24-27. Deveríamos observar que vários anos após os eventos registrados em Esdras 4:7-23, onde lemos que esse homem se opunha à reconstrução do templo de Jerusalém, o citado personagem mudou de parecer, tornando-se generoso para com os judeus, sobretudo no caso de Esdras e Neemias. Alguns têm pensado, por causa disso, que a Bíblia descreve duas pessoas diferentes (uma que mostrava severidade, e outra que se mostrava favorável para com os judeus), dois monarcas diversos. Mas esse ponto de vista tem sido abandonado por muitos estudiosos, embora não haja qualquer certeza quanto a esse particular.

Arcabouço Histórico

522 Dario I
Batalha de Maratona (490)   493
486 Xerxes
                               História de Ester
Batalha de Salamis (480)
                       474
465 Artaxerxes I
424 Dario II
404 Artaxerxes II.

Bibliografia. BRI OLM UN Z

ARTE
Estética. Abaixo estão as principais teorias sobre o significado da arte. A estética é um dos seis ramos tradicionais da filosofia: epistemologia (gnosiologia), lógica, política, metafísica, ética e estética. Todos os ramos da filosofia são importantes para a fé religiosa, pelo que incluímos o item que aqui está sendo considerado.

Esboço:
1. Arte eclesiástica, breve história
2. Teorias principais da estética
3. Música na Igreja

1. Arte eclesiástica, breve história

a. Desenhos nas catacumbas romanas (ver o artigo a respeito), que retratam certos aspectos da primitiva Igreja cristã, aumentando nosso conhecimento sobre certos costumes e fatos da mesma.

b. Edificações para uso da Igreja, as basílicas romanas, cujos ápices (ver o artigo) e paredes adjacentes eram decorados com mosaicos. Essa forma de templo, com suas decorações artísticas, persistiu na Itália até bem dentro da Idade Média.

c. Depois que Constantinopla tornou-se capital do império, o estilo bizantino dominou naquela cidade. Seguia precedentes orientais e romanos, caracterizando-se pelo uso da cúpula, do ápice e de profusas decorações de mármores e mosaicos coloridos. A igreja de *Santa Sofia*, em Constantinopla, construída entre os anos 532 e 562, e a igreja de São Marcos, em Veneza, de cerca do ano 1000, são exemplos notáveis desse estilo.

d. O estilo romanesco, iniciado em Lombárdia, norte da Itália, foi um novo estilo caracterizado por cúpulas cruzadas, com costelas independentes. A igreja de Santo Ambrósio, em Milão, de cerca de 1075, geralmente é considerada o monumento inicial desse estilo. O estilo romanesco toscano do centro da Itália, do qual a torre de Pisa (1063-1118) é um notável exemplo, caracteriza-se por muitos arcos externos e por mármores coloridos, mas sem interiores cobertos por cúpulas. Esse estilo floresceu no vale do Reno e em outras regiões da Alemanha, e as grandes igrejas de Mainz, Speyer e Words são exemplos representativos.

e. O estilo gótico desenvolveu-se do romanesco, na ilha de Grance, nos séculos XII e XIII, tornando-se a mais notável escola de arte de toda a história cristã. Caracteriza-se por uma escultura profusa, com vitrais coloridos. O estilo espalhou-se por todos os países europeus. Sua iconografia, — apesar de não ser profusa, tem esplêndidos exemplos. Suas catedrais, paróquias, abadias e universidades destacam-se entre as edificações do mundo, com um trabalho sem-par em vitrais coloridos.

f. Na arquitetura, a renascença começou com a cúpula de Brunelleschi, em Florença, em 1420. Teve lugar o reavivamento de todos os estilos anteriores da arquitetura européia, excetuando o estilo grego. O trabalho de Palladio (1518-1580) representa uma fase desse período, e a forma paladiana tornou-se popular na Inglaterra e influenciou o mundo de Cristóvão Wren (1632-1723). Vários templos de Londres refletem um estilo paladiano modificado. Esse estilo passou a ser chamado de georgiano.

Alguns dos templos da América do Norte refletem um estilo gótico aviltado, mas muitos seguem o estilo georgiano, especialmente do grupo anglicano. Porém, muitas capelas não-anglicanas eram simples casas de oração. A denominação episcopal reteve os antigos estilos, com torres com vários andares.

ARTE

g. O período georgiano foi seguido pelos reavivamentos grego, gótico e romanesco.

h. A partir do ano de 1900, a predominância do salão de reuniões foi cedendo lugar a casas de adoração mais apropriadas, sendo seguidos diversos estilos arquitetônicos. Tem-se destacado templos no estilo gótico, com vitrais coloridos e simbolismo abundante.

2. Principais Teorias da Estética.

A palavra *estética* vem do grego *aisthesis*, «sensação». A palavra denotava o terreno inteiro do sensível, mas como um uso especializado, veio a designar formas de beleza, derivando-se daí o sentido de teoria da beleza, ou arte. Baumgarten introduziu o termo, embora o tenha usado em sentido mais lato que a palavra recebe atualmente. Hegel aparentemente foi o primeiro a usar o termo conforme é agora empregado. As teorias concernentes à natureza da beleza, na arte e na natureza, começaram pelo menos desde Sócrates. Platão tinha uma *estética* formal, tornando-a em um dos seis ramos tradicionais da filosofia. Em vários sistemas, antigos e modernos, conceitos religiosos têm feito parte da estética, e conseqüentemente, revestem-se de importância no campo da teologia. O que a arte pretende transmitir, como a escultura, a pintura, a música, etc.? Qual é seu impulso ou origem? Qual é o significado da arte na experiência humana? Essas são questões que as teorias estéticas tentam responder.

Teorias:

1. *Platão*. A arte é uma imitação de algum aspecto do mundo caracterizado pelo espaço e pelo tempo. O próprio mundo é uma imitação do mundo ideal. A beleza consiste em simetria e proporção, mas a Beleza final, que as formas artísticas imitam, é a Forma da Beleza. Deus é a fonte de toda a beleza, como no diálogo *Simpósio*. Formas artísticas são reflexos das idéias eternas. Ver o artigo sobre as *formas*, ou idéias.

2. *Aristóteles*. A arte é a imitação de algo possível, irreal, e a beleza depende da unidade orgânica, em que cada parte contribui com sua qualidade para o todo.

3. *Plotino*. Esse filósofo neoplatônico associava a beleza com o esplendor, que resulta da qualidade da unidade, no objeto. O princípio divino, ou *o Um*, reflete-se neste mundo sob a forma de beleza, e portanto, nos objetos de arte.

4. *Tomás de Aquino*. A beleza é aquilo que dá prazer à vista, relacionada às faculdades cognitivas. A beleza se caracteriza pela integridade, pela perfeição, pela proporção, pela harmonia, pelo brilho e pela clareza.

5. *Emanuel Kant*. A beleza é aquilo que produz um senso de harmonia nas relações entre as faculdades da vontade e do entendimento.

6. *Hegel*. A beleza representa aspectos da verdade, em formas sensuais. O *Espírito Absoluto* rebrilha através dos objetos de arte. Portanto, os objetos de arte dizem-nos algo sobre a natureza do espírito, e mesmo da Realidade Última. A arte mais fundamental é a arquitetura. Vem então a escultura. A pintura é um desenvolvimento desta. Em seguida, aparecem a música e a poesia. O teatro combina todas as formas, sendo a mais alta expressão da arte. É a síntese das artes, conforme são conhecidas no mundo. Arte, filosofia e religião são as três grandes avenidas através das quais manifesta-se o Espírito Absoluto, em escala crescente.

7. *Charles W. Morris*. A arte é a linguagem do valor. Esse valor reside no próprio objeto de arte. A linguagem comunica através da semântica (ciência), da sintaxe (estética) e da pragmática (tecnologia). Conseqüentemente, a estética é um dos principais meios de comunicação. A obra de arte é sinal ou emblema de algum valor, isto é, representa aquele valor.

8. *Susana Langer*. A arte é a linguagem do valor, mas esse valor não é, principalmente, o próprio objeto, mas a reação subjetiva do indivíduo que contempla o objeto.

9. *Jacques Maritain*. Arte é beleza, mas a forma da arte nos apresenta um reflexo da beleza transcendental, como em Platão. Ela nos fala de algo divino, que pode ser apreciado pela mente humana. A beleza é uma espécie de conformidade entre a alma e a natureza. A forma é a revelação de algum princípio específico, tal como o sentido da morte é revelado por meio da tragédia. O alvo da arte tem um sentido deleitoso que transparece da unidade e do desígnio da forma de arte.

10. *Freud*. A arte é cumprimento de desejo: expressões de volições que se originam no *libido*, a profunda força instintiva da vida. Essa teoria é uma espécie de *voluntarismo hedonista*. A arte é expressão dos grandes impulsos da vida, da morte, do sexo e do senso de culpa. O artista revela esses impulsos em sua obra. O drama é cumprimento da fantasia. A tragédia é o complexo de Édipo que emerge, juntamente com o impulso da morte.

11. *Jung*. Os *arquétipos* da psique humana expressam-se através de formas artísticas. No nível consciente, o homem exibe uma representação ou máscara, não seu verdadeiro *eu*, e, sim, aquilo que ele quer projetar para os outros. Isso chama-se a *persona*. Porém, o «eu» real tem outros elementos, segundo são representados nos arquétipos. Há o arquétipo da *anima*, o aspecto feminino no homem, ou o *animus*, o aspecto masculino na mulher. Há a *sombra*, aqueles aspectos negativos e indesejáveis em um ser humano, incluindo seu desejo de autodestruição, o desejo de morrer, que é um arquétipo. O «eu» é o ideal interior que cada qual faz de si mesmo, o arquétipo ideal. Outros arquétipos incluem a serpente, o sol (cada qual com seu próprio simbolismo), e a *mandala*, um símbolo de unidade buscada do «eu», onde as porções constitutivas são mantidas juntas em unidade. Pictograficamente, esse arquétipo interior é representado na janela em rosa das catedrais da era medieval, e na pictografia das religiões orientais. As formas de arte originam-se dos arquétipos e comunicam realidades, anelos, impulsos e alvos do homem interior.

12. *Conrado Lange*. A arte é um brinquedo ilusório, cônscio de seu auto-engodo, um tipo de jogo de adultos, com base nos jogos infantis imaginários. Assim, a música é um jogo acústico, dos sentidos; a dança é um jogo de movimentos; o drama é um jogo de ilusão dramática; as artes plásticas correspondem à diversão das crianças com as bonecas; a poesia épica é o conto de histórias em nível adulto.

13. *Eugênio Véron*. A arte é expressão da emoção, a expressão maior, quanto mais sublime for a arte. A obra de arte é revelação de uma emoção ou de um complexo de emoções, que é a motivação da produção do objeto de arte, antes de mais nada.

14. *Tolstoy*. A arte é expressão de emoção, e a boa arte é uma revelação dos mais elevados e nobres sentimentos humanos. A obra de arte procura envolver outras pessoas nos mesmos sentimentos. O propósito da arte é revolucionar e elevar a alma humana.

15. *Dewey*. A arte é uma expressão da experiência.

ARTE — ARTE CULINÁRIA

A experiência tem duas fases: 1. experimental; e 2. consumatória. A arte está envolvida nessa última fase. O processo da arte é a feitura, a passagem e a percepção (ou apreciação) de uma experiência, e suas implicações na vida. A arte é um modo especial de experimentar a vida e seu significado.

16. *Henrique Bergson*. Arte é intuição, um discernimento na realidade da natureza, a dissipação das nuvens que obscurecem nosso entendimento. A arte provê uma visão direta de alguma realidade da experiência humana, que escapa à experiência empírica.

17. *Croce*. Arte é intuição. A arte é um veículo que provoca a intuição ou a visão da realidade. A arte não consiste meramente no objeto físico (pinturas, esculturas, etc.); nem é utilitária (a fim de dar prazer, ou outra coisa qualquer), e nem é conhecimento concepcional. É uma espécie de atividade espiritual, na qual intuímos o sentido da vida em seus múltiplos aspectos.

18. *Tomás Munro*. Arte no contexto científico. A pesquisa estuda a arte tal como qualquer outra atividade e ciência humana, descrevendo seu desenvolvimento e utilidade.

19. *George Lukács*. Arte marxista. A arte abstrata é uma degeneração. A arte que retrata o realismo social é a única abordagem válida da teoria e da utilidade da estética.

20. *Wittgenstein*. A filosofia analítica aplicada à arte. A arte é indefinível, tal como qualquer outro termo abrangente, como «verdade». Na arte, não se pode descobrir qualquer *essência* que a caracterize e possa servir para defini-la. Ao examinarmos as artes, só podemos descobrir coisas similares, ao passarmos de uma coisa para outra. Nenhuma definição emerge daí, embora possamos perceber como as formas de arte podem ser utilizadas para um ou outro propósito. Portanto, a arte é um empreendimento pragmático com muitos alvos.

O exame das teorias acima expostas mostra que vários filósofos têm apreciado o lado espiritual da estética. A arte pode fornecer-nos vislumbres da vida interna do homem, das qualidades e necessidades de sua alma, além de certa apreciação de princípios espirituais. A arte está envolvida nos estados metafísicos. O poeta pode intuir o sentido da morte, da realidade da imortalidade, do poder do amor, da degradação do ódio, da realidade transcendental. O mau músico pode extrair os dejetos da degradação humana, exibindo-os em sua música. O bom músico pode pintar o que é nobre, digno e espiritual. O mau artista pode fragmentar o homem em suas representações grotescas. O bom artista pode trazer a lume a beleza, a unidade e a harmonia por ele intuídas.

3. A música nas igrejas:
Reservamos uma menção especial para essa forma de arte, por causa de seu uso e influência na Igreja cristã. Ninguém precisa informar-nos que está sendo executada uma marcha militar, por exemplo, ou um coral bachiano. Nossos espíritos reagem aos acordes, e intuimos seu significado, inteiramente à parte das palavras. Quão lamentável é, portanto, que em nossos dias, uma música apropriada para os clubes noturnos, completa com seus tons discordantes e sensuais, tenha sido introduzida nas igrejas. Se as formas de arte refletem estados metafísicos, então não mais estamos tratando com acordes e escalas, quando fazemos música. Mas estamos manuseando uma força que pode influenciar a alma em seus anelos, aspirações e intenções.

Trechos bíblicos que podem ser consultados, em relação à música nas igrejas: Efé. 5:19 ss e Col. 3:16.
Ver o artigo separado sobre a *Música*.

Bibliografia. (A AM ID EP NTI P Z)

ARTE CULINÁRIA

As referências bíblicas ao assunto incluem questões que tratam de muitas variedades de alimentos, métodos de preparo, utensílios, lugares de cozimento, etc. Consideradas juntas, essas questões nos transmitem um bom conhecimento sobre a matéria, conforme ocorria nos tempos bíblicos. Um artigo separado é apresentado sob o título *Alimentos*, onde há informações extras. Ver também *Casa*, *Vasos* e *Cozinha*.

1. *Categorias básicas de alimentos*. Cereais, carnes, legumes, laticínios e cereais para o fabrico de pão, preparados mediante moagem e cozimento em forno. O termo «pão» em alguns casos, indica qualquer tipo de alimento. Os cereais usados nos tempos bíblicos eram: cevada (ver Lev. 27:16; Juí. 7:13, etc.) e trigo (ver Gên. 41:49; Êxo. 9:32; João 12:24; I Cor. 15:37; Apo. 6:6). O trigo tinha variedades, sendo o cereal preferido pelas classes abastadas, e a cevada, mais barata, era consumida pelas classes mais pobres, sendo comumente servida como forragem aos animais. (Ver Eze. 4:9). Na Palestina também era conhecido o centeio. A espelta, um cereal herbáceo, era usado. É interessante observar que em Eze. 4:9, no original, há menção a seis tipos de cereais ou condimentos, ao passo que em nossa versão portuguesa só há quatro. As outras duas são, mui provavelmente, a espelta e a noz-noscada, esta última usada como tempero. Embora algumas versões estrangeiras falem no «milho», esse cereal pertence ao continente americano, e era desconhecido nos tempos bíblicos na Palestina.

2. *Preparação dos cereais*. Estes eram preparados tostados, torrados, cozidos, assados em fornos ou caçarolas.

3. *Condimentos*. Eram usados o sal, o azeite de oliveira, o mel e certa variedade de temperos.

4. *Moagem do cereal*. Essa moagem era feita em buracos na pedra, sobre chão batido, em moinhos ou no pilão. Os moinhos tinham vários formatos. O tipo mais simples era aquele que empregava duas pedras, uma girando sobre a outra, impulsionada à mão. Essas pedras podiam variar de tamanho, de 25 cm a 45 cm de diâmetro, ou mais. Alguns moinhos tinham pernas, ou um suporte para elevar a parte do moinho que ficava mais próxima do operador. Posteriormente, apareceu o moinho circular, que consistia em duas pedras circulares de basalto, com cerca de 50 cm de diâmetro. A pedra superior tinha um cabo, para que a pessoa a fizesse girar. Havia um eixo central, e também um orifício central, que permitia que o grão fosse colocado entre as pedras. Os moinhos maiores requeriam o trabalho de duas mulheres (ver Mat. 24:21). Nos tempos romanos, moinhos com o formato de ampulhetas, tinham cerca de 1,80 m de altura e eram operados por homens escravos ou por animais. Havia uma pedra cilíndrica inferior, com topo cônico; e havia uma pedra superior, também cilíndrica, com dois funis, um como entrada e outro como saída, que levava ao centro. O cereal era vertido no funil de entrada, e o funil de saída levava o cereal moído a um receptáculo. A arqueologia tem recuperado todas as formas de moinhos. Jesus fez alusão ao tipo romano de moinho, em Mat. 18:6. Ver, quanto a detalhes, o artigo separado sobre *moinho*, *pedras de moinho*.

5. *Preparações*. A farinha de trigo era misturada

ARTE NA BÍBLIA E NAS CIVILIZAÇÕES RELACIONADAS

com água, sal, fermento e outros preparativos. A massa era colocada em gamelas de madeira. Assim eram formados os pães, que então eram cozidos ao forno ou sobre pedras quentes (ver Gên. 18:6; I Reis 19:6). Os fornos primitivos eram apenas perfurações cobertas no solo, usualmente recobertos internamente com argila cozida, pedaços de louça ou pedras. Os fornos pequenos tinham apenas cerca de 25 cm de profundidade, com 90 a 120 cm de lado. Bolos também eram preparados sobre grelhas ou em caçarolas de metal. O cozimento do pão era uma rotina diária, pois todos queriam pão fresco.

6. *Carnes.* As carnes eram consumidas pelas classes mais abastadas, pois os pobres dificilmente podiam entregar-se a tal luxo (ver I Reis 4:23), excetuando em casos muito especiais. As carnes eram de carneiro, de cabra, de gado vacum e de peixes. Carnes de aves eram preparadas como quaisquer outras carnes. Geralmente, o peixe era assado sobre brasas (ver João 21:9). Gafanhotos eram tostados e comidos (ver Lev. 11:22; Mat. 3:4).

7. *Legumes.* Esses incluíam as favas, a lentilha, a cebola, o alho e várias raízes (ver Gên. 25:39 - 34; Núm. 11:15; Jó 6:6; Mat. 5:13; Col. 4:6). Os condimentos incluíam o alho, o sal e certas sementes como o aniz, o coriandro, o cominho, o orégano, o tomilho e a hortelã. Vários tipos de castanha também eram usados na dieta.

8. *Cozimento.* Quem ocupava-se desse mister era a dona da casa e/ou as servas (ver Gên. 18:6,7). Os reis contavam com cozinheiros profissionais (ver Gên. 40:1). Cozinhava-se nas casas, em lugares fora das casas, em salas especiais ou no pátio.

9. *Utensílios.* A arqueologia nos tem fornecido um conhecimento completo a respeito dos utensílios da cozinha antiga. Havia vasos de todos os tamanhos e formatos, grelhas, caçarolas, colheres, facas, panelas, caldeirões, cestas, pratos, frigideiras, etc. Esses utensílios eram fabricados de madeira ou de metal (ver Êxo. 16:3; I Sam. 3:14; II Reis 2:20; 21:13; 25:15; II Crô. 35:13). (PRI UN Z)

ARTE NA BÍBLIA E NAS CIVILIZAÇÕES RELACIONADAS

Ver o artigo sobre a *arte*, que inclui muitas teorias sobre a estética, bem como sobre o problema das formas de arte cultivadas na Igreja, especificamente a *música*.

1. **Antes de 3000 A.C.** a. *Arte linear*, isto é, desenhos afrescos que eram formados por linhas, sem qualquer tentativa de fazer representar as duas dimensões. Foi desenterrado um esplêndido exemplo disso em Teleilat Ghassul, pertencente cerca de 3600-3400 A.C., mostrando dragões e estrelas, além de figuras geométricas. Um outro exemplo mostra um estranho pássaro, e um terceiro, uma possível cena de adoração. b. *Escultura*. Proveniente de Jericó, de 6500 A.C., foram encontradas figuras de surpreendente delicadeza, com os olhos formados por conchas coloridas, para emprestar maior realismo. Exemplos de terracota pintada também datam de tempos antiqüíssimos. Figurinhas bem executadas foram encontradas na Planície de Amuque, na Síria, provenientes dos tempos neolíticos. c. *Trabalho de entalhe*. Em objetos como cabos de osso, de instrumentos (como uma foice), com intricadas cabeças de animais, como entre os natufianos da Palestina. Esse povo também esculpia colares de considerável arte. d. *Cerâmica*. Exemplos encontrados em Jericó indicam que desde tempos remotos havia grande habilidade artística. e. *Estruturas monumentais*. Os zigurates, no topo dos quais eram construídos templos (na Suméria), túmulos e várias outras estruturas (no Egito), demonstram muito gosto artístico, sobretudo da parte dos construtores egípcios, que decoravam as paredes com cenas da vida selvagem, cortejos de adoração e de batalhas.

2. **De 3000** A.C. até a era cristã (não-hebréia). a. Egípcia. A cultura egípcia, em redor do rio Nilo, atingiu maturidade entre 2614 e 2181 A.C. Floresceram ali todos os ramos da arte, refletidos nos túmulos, templos e pirâmides. Havia decorações em paredes exibindo toda a variedade imaginável de coisas, desde cenas de batalhas até à vida animal e vegetal, e até mesmo a crença na vida após-túmulo. O corpo dos Faraós era posto em uma saleta dentro da pirâmide, supostamente para haver certeza de que ele não seria perturbado, podendo desfrutar da vida após-túmulo em paz. A escultura egípcia (feita na mais dura rocha), bem como a arquitetura eram maciças, sólidas e permanentes, servindo como obra de arte em si mesma. As formas de arte do Egito eram imitadas em outros lugares, como na Síria, sob a forma de vasos com tampa de ouro, encontrados em Biblos. Depois houve uma mudança para motivos assírios, no primeiro milênio A.C., quando a Assíria obteve a hegemonia e o poder egípcio se debilitou. b. Hitita. (Ver o artigo sobre os hititas). Na Ásia Menor e no norte da Síria, entre 2000 e 1200 A.C. Quando esse povo obteve poder, apareceu uma arte um tanto menos egípcia quanto ao estilo. c. Hurriana. Os hurrianos formavam um povo que vivia a leste dos hititas, cobrindo meio-círculo das montanhas do Taurus, desde Urquis, ao norte de Carquemis, até o país de Namar, em torno do lago Van, e até chegando tão ao sul quanto o alto rio Zabe. Ver o artigo sobre os *hurrianos*. Os reis hurrianos reinaram na Assíria em cerca de 2200 a 2000 A.C. O domínio deles introduziu uma cerâmica pintada em branco sobre negro. A arqueologia também tem descoberto estatuetas de cobre e de prata, ídolos com olhos engastados, os quais talvez originalmente eram folheados a ouro, tudo pertencente aos hurrianos. d. Creta. Após o ano de 2000 A.C., importantes civilizações apareceram nas regiões ao redor do mar Egeu, incluindo a ilha de Creta, e mais tarde, o continente grego. A primitiva arte cretense é conhecida como arte minoana, devido a Minos, um rei lendário da ilha. Houve dois períodos de grandeza, o primeiro de cerca de 1700 a 1600 A.C., e o segundo de cerca de 1600 a 1500 A.C. Então ocorreu uma misteriosa catástrofe, da qual a civilização minoana jamais se recuperou. No primeiro período, foram construídos belíssimos palácios, como aquele de Cnossos, com pinturas nas paredes, objetos religiosos e uma cerâmica característica. O segundo período reflete uma raça não-militarista, porque os habitantes parecem ter sido uma classe bastante hedonista de comerciantes. Então predominava a arte religiosa, com deusas elegantemente trajadas, mais encantadoras do que assustadoras. Os palácios eram erigidos com colunas características, com decorações suntuosas. e. Fenícia. Ali as formas de arte são um tanto cruas em sua maior parte, como as figuras de prata e as esculturas encontradas em Ugarite. Uma exceção é o busto do rei Yarim-lim de Alalaque (século XVIII A.C.), finamente executado em estilo sumeriano. f. Grega. A civilização minoana caiu em cerca de 1500 A.C. E foi então que certas cidades gregas do continente atingiram um ponto de notável realização artística. Uma dessas cidades era Micenas, que deu seu nome ao período. Seus túmulos rivalizavam com

ARTE NA BÍBLIA E NAS CIVILIZAÇÕES RELACIONADAS

os túmulos do Egito, embora construídos subterraneamente e com a forma de colméia. Os mortos eram sepultados usando máscaras de ouro, com artefatos de ouro incrivelmente trabalhados. Desse pano de fundo surgiu a arte grega, alicerce de toda a arte ocidental. De cerca de 1100 a 700 A.C., encontramos os vasos em forma geométrica, com pinturas elaboradas. Em cerca de 700 A.C. apareceu a influência oriental, o que se refletiu no desenho dos vasos, das pinturas e dos estilos de penteados femininos, retratados nas pinturas murais da Grécia. Em cerca de 650 A.C. começou o período *arcaico*, com sua soberba arte representando o corpo humano. Nesse tempo, continuou sendo mantida a típica postura egípcia, com o pé esquerdo firmemente plantado diante do pé direito, os braços rígidos ao lado do corpo. Mas, quanto a outros aspectos, a escultura atingiu uma incomum perfeição, em suas representações. Em cerca de 490 A.C., as figuras começaram a ganhar movimento e graça, tendo sido abandonada a postura rígida do período anterior. As figuras femininas da arte grega, antes do século IV A.C., aparecem vestidas, mas os homens aparecem heroicamente desnudos. O estilo clássico atingiu seu ponto culminante na escultura e na arquitetura do Partenon de Atenas (cerca de 448-432 A.C.). Os templos provêem um exemplo de arte maciça, como as pirâmides do Egito. O Partenon apresenta truques visuais para fazê-lo parecer mais perfeito do que realmente era. Os gregos tinham observado que uma linha reta horizontal parece baixar no meio, e que uma coluna com lados retos parece estreitar-se no meio. Assim sendo, os gregos faziam linhas levemente curvas nos templos, para compensar essa ilusão visual. A base dos templos se curvavam levemente na direção do centro, e os lados das colunas tornaram-se levemente bojudos. No século IV A.C., o centro da atividade política e artística da civilização grega transferiu-se de Atenas para as cidades helenizadas da Ásia Menor. As esculturas do século IV A.C. refinaram e desenvolveram conceitos pertencentes ao período clássico de Atenas. O novo estilo atingiu o clímax no grande friso do altar de Zeus, em Pérgamo, com seus grandes e musculosos deuses e seus monstruosos gigantes, empenhados em luta violenta. g. Roma. Os romanos herdaram formas artísticas dos etruscos e dos gregos. Os etruscos já tinham sido influenciados pelos gregos, embora tivessem seus próprios desenvolvimentos nos campos das ciências e das artes, sobretudo na engenharia, na planificação de cidades e na modelagem de metais. Apesar do fato de que a arte romana chegara a ser considerada um simples simulacro da arte grega, isso não diz toda a verdade sobre a questão. Houve algumas melhorias, embora também houvesse cópia e declínio. Os romanos desenvolveram a arquitetura com cúpulas, usando esse estilo para edifícios públicos, privados e religiosos. Eles perceberam a possibilidade arquitetural dos arcos e das cúpulas, e atingiram grandiosidade em suas construções, dando-nos um exemplo de arte maciça. Na escultura romana, é óbvia a influência grega, embora os romanos tenham criado uma expressão severa e poderosa, toda própria deles. No primeiro século A.C., os pintores romanos haviam desenvolvido um elaborado estilo de decoração mural, incorporando ilusões tridimensionais às figuras representadas. Isso era conseguido através de um sombreado sutil.

3. A arte em Israel. a. A influência do segundo mandamento da lei (ver Êxo. 20:4-6), contra qualquer tipo de representação de figuras vivas, evitava a idolatria. Agora podemos dizer que esse mandamento não visava proibir a arte, e, sim, o abuso de algumas formas de arte. Porém, os antigos hebreus não demonstravam paciência com esse tipo de interpretação permissiva. Para eles, aquele mandamento tinha natureza absoluta, pelo que era até uma falta de gosto fazer circular moedas estrangeiras entre os israelitas com efígies de pessoas. No entanto, havia a representação de seres angelicais, como era o caso dos querubins, no véu interior do templo de Jerusalém, e nas paredes do templo de Salomão, onde também havia a representação de palmeiras (ver I Reis 6:29). Além disso, no propiciatório, havia as figuras de dois querubins. Contudo, devemos observar que eles não eram figuras humanas, e nada tinham a ver com os «deuses» pagãos. Portanto, devemos afirmar que o segundo mandamento da legislação mosaica influenciou de forma definida, como uma influência supressiva, certas formas de arte entre o povo de Israel, como a pintura, a escultura, o desenho de figuras humanas, etc. b. Nos primeiros tempos. A arqueologia tem descoberto bem pouco do antigo Israel que demonstra interesse artístico entre os hebreus. Através da longa história de Israel, até o tempo da construção do templo de Jerusalém, encontramos uma população mista na Palestina, com suas muitas culturas, sendo quase impossível distinguir qualquer coisa que seja especificamente hebréia. Os israelitas apreciavam as jóias finas do Egito, e fabricavam as suas próprias; havia entalhe em madeira e decoração em cerâmica. Porém, a época foi de violência contínua, em que os homens matavam e eram mortos, expulsando e sendo expulsos, e condições assim não favoreciam o cultivo das artes. c. O templo. Quanto à arquitetura do templo, ver o artigo sobre o *templo*. Entre as decorações do templo havia querubins (leões com cabeça humana), grifos alados, aves, répteis, touros, leões e desenhos florais e arbóreos (ver I Reis 6:18,19). As porções de madeira entalhada, nas paredes interiores, eram ornadas com folhas de ouro, e as portas foram similarmente decoradas. Em tudo isso era forte a influência sírio-fenícia. O entalhe em madeira, recoberto de ouro, era uma das características da arte fenícia. d. Após o templo. Já desde os séculos XXXIV e XXXV A.C. temos exemplos de entalhe em osso e marfim, nos cabos das armas, em vasos e em figurinhas. Peças em marfim, encontradas em Samaria, pertencentes aos dias de Acabe, mostram a influência da arte fenícia, com os seus elementos egípcios, sirio-nititas e assírios. Algumas peças de marfim (potes, vasos, selos, etc.) eram feitas com ornatos de ouro, lápis-lazúli, contas coloridas e vidro. Outras peças também têm figuras humanas e de animais. Não há qualquer exemplar sobrevivente da pintura hebréia, pelo que não há provas diretas de que eles pintavam paisagens em paredes adubadas, conforme faziam vários outros povos, embora tenham sido encontrados pigmentos coloridos nas escavações, apesar de sabermos que o ocre vermelho era usado para colorir as paredes e a madeira (ver Jer. 22:14 e Eze. 23:14). Portanto, é possível que houvesse outras formas de pintura. Poucos exemplos de escultura têm sido encontrados no período cananeu; mas aqueles que têm sido encontrados, como a figura sentada de Baal, feita em basalto; a deusa serpente enroscada em uma estela de Beit Mirsim; e os pés muito bem esculpidos de uma estátua de Hazor (século XIII A.C.), procedem de culturas não-judaicas. O segundo mandamento que proibia a feitura de imagens em escultura, naturalmente desencorajava qualquer tipo desse labor artístico entre os hebreus. Em tempos posteriores, tal atividade continuava, mas aparentemente sem qualquer envolvimento da parte dos hebreus. *Gravações* encontradas na Palestina em cilindros, escaravelhos e selos estampam típicos motivos fenícios, como o disco alado e o escaravelho alado, — as figuras humanas e as de animais, embora representações pictográficas sejam raras nos selos dos hebreus — novamente, a influência do segundo mandamento. e. Trabalho em metais. Os hebreus sabiam trabalhar com metais, mas poucos de seus artefatos em metal têm sobrevivido. O *mar* de bronze, do templo de Salomão (para conter água), que tinha cerca de 25 toneladas, com paredes de 7,5 cm de espessura, uma taça com 5 m de diâmetro e 2,30 m de altura, e uma borda ornada, é um bom exemplo. A bacia repousava sobre as costas de doze bois moldados em separado e arranjados em quatro tríadas, como suporte (ver I Reis 7:23 ss). Continha cerca de 38 mil litros de água. De tempos posteriores, não temos quaisquer objetos de nota originados na cultura hebraica. f. Período Macabeu-hasmoneano. Nesse ponto da história, a influência grega e romana era grande. A base do candeeiro do templo é representada no arco de Tito, em Roma. Vemos dragões com rostos humanos, sabedores que somos que o seu protótipo, o templo de Apolo, em Didina, tinha rostos humanos. Josefo afirma que a mesa dos pães da proposição tinha típicas pernas de estilo grego, isto é, com patas de leão. As moedas do período mostram desenhos relativamente crus e toscos, incluindo rituais simbólicos, plantas e frutas, bem como imagens humanas. Algumas moedas estampam o templo com a arca da aliança em seu interior.

4. No Novo Testamento. Nesse tempo, a arte era imitativa e comercializada, tendendo para o realismo e para a exagerada elaboração, sem grandiosidade. Estamos informados de que o templo de Herodes era ornamentado com uma videira esculpida com cachos de uvas douradas, com 1,80 m de altura, enfeitando as portas. Formas humanas foram introduzidas nas expressões artísticas da Judéia e da Palestina, incluindo representações das divindades gregas e romanas. A escola de Hilel não fazia objeção ao uso ornamental de figuras humanas, mas outras escolas rabínicas afirmavam uma estrita interpretação do segundo mandamento. Formas arquiteturais gregas começaram a ser usadas nos sepulcros. Josefo informa-nos que o pórtico real do templo de Herodes tinha colunas de estilo coríntio, que era a sua principal característica decorativa. Internamente, o templo era abundantemente decorado, com toda a espécie de desenhos. Herodes construiu numerosas outras obras arquiteturais na Judéia, conforme se vê em Cesaréia, onde era forte a influência grega clássica. As referências neotestamentárias em Atos 17:24,29, a respeito do Areópago, e em Apo. 2:13, onde se lêem as palavras «onde está o trono de Satanás» (referindo-se ao grande altar de Zeus, com forma de trono), trazem à nossa atenção formas de arte greco-helenistas.

5. Aplicações modernas. Obviamente, a religião é relacionada a diversas formas de artes. A mais importante destas é a música. O Novo Testamento recomenda a música como um meio para inspirar a espiritualidade, Col. 3:16. Alguns filósofos acham que a música provoca estados metafísicos e estes podem ter um efeito sobre o modo de pensar e agir de uma pessoa. A experiência humana comprova este ponto de vista. A música é mais do que variações em vibrações de ondas de som. Esta forma de arte é ao mesmo tempo a mais abstrata e poderosa. É por isso que a igreja que utiliza a música mundana nos seus cultos degrada o espírito da igreja. (FEIF ROT Z)

ÁRTEMAS

No grego é contração de Artemídoro (ver Tito 3:12). Um dos estimados discípulos de Paulo, a quem este pensou enviar a Creta em substituição a Tito, ao qual convidara para vir visitá-lo em Nicópolis. Quando a epístola a Tito foi escrita, a questão dessa viagem ainda não estava resolvida. A tradição faz dele bispo de Listra, mas usualmente as tradições são meras especulações.

ÁRTEMIS

A deusa grega «Ártemis» era conhecida por **Diana**, entre os romanos. De conformidade com lendas antigas, originalmente Artemisa era filha de Zeus (para os romanos, Jove ou Júpiter) e irmã de Apolo. Era a deusa caçadora, e quando era representada entre os deuses imortais, aparecia como uma jovem equipada de arco e aljava e vestida de caçadora, sendo acompanhada por cães e veados. Acreditava-se que ela era uma destruidora, especialmente contra mulheres ofensoras, contra as quais despedia as suas flechas mortíferas. Mas também era representada como uma curadora, protetora das mulheres no seu parto. Além disso ela era deusa da lua e uma divindade feminina, cujos ministros faziam votos perpétuos de castidade.

Em suas funções, ainda que não no nome, a *Diana dos efésios* era muito diferente do que aparece na descrição acima. Essa deusa assumia mais as características de uma primitiva deusa da fertilidade, isto é, similar à deusa Cibele, dos lídios, a qual era reputada como a grande mãe dos deuses, sendo representada por um ídolo dotado de muitos seios. É bem provável que a adoração a Diana, entre os habitantes de Éfeso, combinasse, até certo ponto, as características dessas duas deusas, sob um único título. Essa deusa era o símbolo dos poderes reprodutivos da natureza; e, com base em moedas e ídolos seus que têm sido encontrados, a sua descrição é mais ou menos como segue: Era uma figura estranha, coberta de inúmeros seios. Numa das mãos brandia um tridente, e na outra trazia um cacete. Estava vestida com um traje recoberto de símbolos místicos e permanecia no interior do grande templo erigido em sua honra em Éfeso, oculta por uma cortina de púrpura. Antiquíssimas tradições pagãs asseveravam que essa imagem havia caído do céu (ver Atos 19:35), tradição essa que provavelmente se originara da queda de um meteorito qualquer, que gradualmente se desenvolveu em uma tradição popular, assumindo a forma de uma «imagem» qualquer. O seu culto se caracterizava por cerimônias orientais. Os seus sacerdotes ordinariamente eram eunucos, com os quais estavam associados outros ministrantes, especialmente sacerdotisas virgens, além de certo número de escravos, cuja categoria mais inferior era a daqueles que varriam o templo e o conservavam limpo. Essa ênfase sobre a virgindade e a castidade evidentemente resultava daquela parte da lenda que dizia que a *Artemisa grega* tinha aversão pelo matrimônio, por haver observado o horrível parto que tivera a sua própria mãe.

O templo dela servia de tesouro público e de casa bancária, onde havia também o direito de asilo. Não eram ali permitidos sacrifícios cruentos. E posto que Éfeso era a capital da Ásia, em seu sentido limitado, assim também Diana dos efésios era, naturalmente, o ídolo a quem a Ásia e o mundo inteiro adoravam. Jogos eram celebrados em Éfeso em honra a essa deusa, e a sua adoração era o laço que unia

ÁRTEMIS

politicamente a cidade de Éfeso a outras comunidades. No grande teatro de Éfeso, em uma das paredes do vestíbulo da entrada, o sr. Wood encontrou uma carta, enviada pelo imperador Adriano, aos efésios, datada de 20 de setembro de 120 D.C., além de uma inscrição concernente ao templo de Diana, que dizia respeito aos seus dotes e rituais, tais como listas de estátuas votivas de ouro e de prata, com seus respectivos pesos e as regulamentações sob as quais esses objetos deveriam ser transportados em procissão. Nesta lista há menção das muitas figuras de Diana com dois veados. Isso ilustra a menção bíblica sobre Demétrio como ourives fabricante de modelos portáteis do templo de Diana.

O templo original de Diana dos efésios foi construído no ano de 580 A.C., tendo sido inteiramente terminado em 460 A.C. No entanto, essa construção foi destruída a fogo por Erostratos, em 356 A.C., na mesma noite em que nascia Alexandre o Grande. Restou grande parte do templo incendiado, entretanto, tendo sido o mesmo reedificado ainda com maior magnificência. Esse templo restaurado (que é o templo referido no livro de Atos) foi erigido durante o reinado de Alexandre o Grande, com recursos recolhidos de todos os territórios circunvizinhos. Esse templo foi considerado uma de sete maravilhas do mundo antigo. Quanto à identificação dessas maravilhas, ver os comentários sobre Atos 21:1 no NTI. Sua forma era octogonal, e media, de maneira mais ou menos exata, 104 metros de comprimento por 49 metros de largura. Era quatro vezes mais largo que o Partenon grego, de Atenas. Contava com cento e vinte e sete colunas, com 18 metros de altura, no cimo de cada uma das quais havia a figura de um rei. As colunas tinham tambores de três metros de circunferência e quase dois metros de altura, e cada um desses era ornado com oito figuras em tamanho real, esculpidas. A *cella*, ou seja, o «santo dos santos» desse templo pagão (o santuário mais interno), tinha 21 metros de largura e era aberto para o céu. O arqueólogo J.T. Wood, após muitos anos de busca, descobriu as suas ruínas em 1869, em uma área pantanosa, ao pé do monte Aiasoluque.

Esse templo continha a imagem de Diana, que supostamente teria caído dos céus (ver Atos 19:39). Essa lenda provavelmente começou com a queda de algum *meteorito*, que a crendice popular gradualmente transformou em um culto idólatra, embora tudo houvesse começado como ocorrência natural. Plínio informa-nos que o templo de Diana dos efésios contava com uma gigantesca pedra à sua entrada, que supostamente foi deixada ali pela própria Diana. Os seus pórticos eram adornados de pinturas e esculturas feitas pelos grandes mestres das artes plásticas gregas, isto é, Fídias e Plicleto, Cálifron e Apeles. O culto à Diana dos efésios era muito elaborado, o que fica demonstrado pelo fato de que eram feitas provisões para a educação das crianças empregadas nos serviços do templo; também eram dadas pensões aos sacerdotes e sacerdotisas que eram forçados a abandonarem suas atividades. Tudo isso nos faz lembrar da regra baixada em I Tim. 5:9, a qual, segundo o pensamento de E.H. Plumptre, talvez sugira que essa prática foi incorporada no seio da igreja cristã primitiva.

Vinham *peregrinos* do mundo inteiro civilizado a fim de contemplarem as maravilhas desse templo. Na volta para seus países de origem geralmente levavam consigo uma réplica do templo ou um ídolo em miniatura, como lembrança de sua visita a Éfeso. Isso explica o lucrativo negócio dos ourives de Éfeso, segundo lemos no décimo nono capítulo do livro de Atos.

Nero pilhou o templo de Éfeso, levando dali os seus tesouros, como fez igualmente com muitos outros templos pagãos de lugares distantes, como Atenas, na Grécia. Não escaparam nem mesmo simples aldeias; e tudo isso com o propósito de adornar a sua Casa Dourada, em Roma. (Ver *Tácito*, Anais xv. 45). Trajano enviou os seus portões ricamente esculpidos, como oferta a um templo de Bizâncio. Foi por meio dessas medidas destruidoras que o antigo esplendor de Éfeso se foi empanando, ao mesmo tempo que o cristianismo ia prevalecendo por toda a parte. Quando o império romano finalmente aceitou o cristianismo como religião oficial, já nos dias de Constantino (século IV da era cristã), partes do templo de Diana em Éfeso, bem como do templo de Delfos, foram empregadas para a ereção de um templo cristão (nos tempos de Justiniano), em honra à Sabedoria divina. Atualmente esse templo é a mesquita de Santa Sofia. Os godos pilharam as ruínas do templo de Diana, sem qualquer misericórdia, em 263 D.C., e os turcos, séculos mais tarde, terminaram aquilo que os godos haviam começado. A cidade inteira de Éfeso ficou arruinada, e gradualmente foi declinando, até que se tornou inteiramente desabitada, o que continua sendo o seu estado até os nossos dias.

Desde que J.T. Wood empreendeu ali os seus esforços arqueológicos, outros pesquisadores têm estado naquela mesma região. Foi descoberto o depósito do tesouro, subterrâneo, debaixo do grande altar, por D.G. Hogarth, em 1904, descoberta essa que figura como um dos maiores romances da pesquisa arqueológica. (Ver C.M. Cobern, *The New Archeological Discoveries*, Nova Iorque, Funk & Wagnalls, 1917, págs. 468 e s).

No mundo antigo havia muitas corporações comerciais, não havendo lugar para dúvidas de que isso ocorria também em Éfeso. Demétrio provavelmente era o presidente de alguma corporação de ourives, durante o tempo em que Paulo esteve em Éfeso. Por isso é que muito se preocupou com o estado de seus negócios, ameaçados que estavam pelas atividades evangelizadoras do apóstolo, já que tanta gente se convertia ao cristianismo e abandonava as práticas idólatras. A grande festividade religiosa associada a esse culto idólatra ocorria em maio. Ora, esse mês não estava distante quando houve a perturbação em Éfeso, causada pelos ourives da cidade. Isso oferecia a esses artesãos uma espécie de «festa de Natal», durante a qual lembretes de Diana, em forma de ídolos e nichos, eram vendidos em Éfeso. Assim, pois, os ourives sentiram que alguma coisa tinha de ser feita para garantir o volume das vendas e dos lucros. Isso explica o grande zelo demonstrado por Demétrio, um zelo ditado muito mais por motivos pecuniários do que mesmo por motivos puramente religiosos. (FA I IB ND NTI VT Z)

A Grande Deusa-Mãe
Ártemis de Éfeso
(por Donald N. Wilber)

Quem foi a misteriosa Ártemis, adorada por toda a Ásia e pelo mundo? A resposta tem início 4.500 anos antes do nascimento de Cristo.

A *região* da moderna Turquia, adentrando-se desde o mar Egeu e desde há muito conhecida como Anatólia (vem do termo grego que significa *nascente do sol*) está salpicada de ruínas de renomadas cidades antigas como Sardes, Pérgamo, Hierápolis, Afrodísias e Éfeso. Dentre todas essas, Éfeso é a mais bem preservada.

Ártemis Polimastros (Ártemis dos muitos seios), Século I.

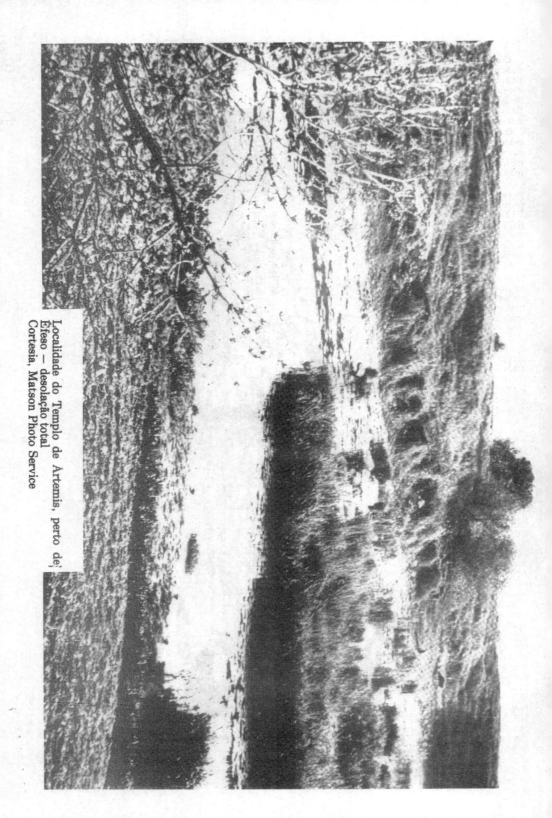

Localidade do Templo de Artemis, perto de Éfeso — desolação total
Cortesia, Matson Photo Service

ÁRTEMIS

Colonizada no século X A.C., por jônios vindos do continente grego, Éfeso logo atraiu outros colonos provenientes do interior da Anatólia. A cidade contava com um excelente porto natural, e, por volta de 200 A.C., era a cidade mais densamente povoada da região inteira. No século I A.C., tornou-se parte integrante do império romano.

O apóstolo João escreveu sobre Éfeso. «Há qualquer cidade maior do que esta? Aqueles que têm navios nos mares tornaram-se ricos por meio dela. Seus mercadores são os mais ricos do mundo e suas artes mágicas fascinam todas as nações».

Após o nascimento de Cristo, Éfeso ficou sob o governo cristão de Constantinopla e continuou a prosperar durante o reinado de Justiniano, no século VI D.C. Todavia, com a passagem dos séculos, a linha da costa foi entulhada com sedimento descido das colinas circundantes, fazendo-a afastar-se cada vez mais da cidade. A perda de seu porto apressou o declínio da cidade e, finalmente, foi abandonada.

Visto que Éfeso se espraia por uma grande área, para propósito de simplificação suas ruínas podem ser agrupadas em três sítios separados: um deles é uma elevada colônia coroada com restos de uma vasta basílica construída pelo imperador Justiniano, por sobre o *túmulo* do apóstolo João; o segundo é o sítio de Ártemis, no sopé da colina; e o terceiro é a própria cidade, situada em um vale entre montanhas que vão descendo de altitude em direção ao mar. As escavações, efetuadas por um período de mais de cem anos, têm desenterrado séculos de escombros, incluindo os profundos depósitos do subsolo que foram transportados pelas chuvas, vindos das vertentes mais altas.

Entra-se na cidade através da Porta Magnésia, que dá acesso à Avenida Curetiae. Pavimentada com lajes de mármore e flanqueada por colunas, desce de modo bastante brusco para o ocidente. Muitas estruturas, em condições relativamente boas, embora sem telhados, continuam de pé ao longo de seu curso. A maioria delas foi feita de mármore; algumas datam da época helenista e outras do período romano posterior. Essas estruturas incluem um odeon (salão de concertos), o pritanion (prefeitura), a fonte de Trajano e o templo de Adriano, que tem um vasto banho público por detrás. Espalhados pelas vertentes das colinas há os remanescentes de elegantes casas particulares. Podemos imaginar as palpitantes multidões de vendeiros, peregrinos e turistas provenientes do interior, movimentando-se ao longo da Avenida Curetiae. Esta termina na chamada Avenida Mármore, que corre na direção norte, isto é, formando um ângulo reto.

Passando pela Avenida Mármore, à direita vemos a biblioteca Celso, uma grande *agorá* (mercado) e o templo de Serepis. Não longe fica um espaçoso bordel, patronizado por marinheiros de tempos idos, que encontravam o seu caminho mediante uma série de sinais diretivos rabiscados sobre as pedras que margeiam a avenida. Então chegamos ao grande anfiteatro aberto, que acolhia 25 mil espectadores em suas sessenta e seis fileiras de bem preservados assentos. Quando havia espetáculos, um gigantesco toldo de lona era estendido por cima. Logo depois do teatro há uma larga avenida ladeada de colunas, chamada Arcadiana, que ali começa e que segue na direção do porto, para o oeste. É franqueada pelos banhos e ginásio pertencentes ao período romano. Outras estruturas na cidade, em número grande demais para serem mencionadas, incluem uma igreja do século IV, dedicada à *Virgem Maria*, que foi um edifício romano para isso adaptado.

O vasto teatro nos faz retroceder para entre 53 e 56 D.C., quando o apóstolo Paulo pregava na Ásia e passou alguns meses em Éfeso, em determinada ocasião. De acordo com Atos 19:23-30: «Por aquele tempo levantou-se não pequena agitação por causa do Caminho».

Pois um homem chamado *Demétrio*, ourives, que fazia nichos de prata de Ártemis, não dava pouco lucro aos artífices.

A esses ele reuniu, com operários de idêntica ocupação, e disse: Homens, sabeis que deste negócio derivamos nossa riqueza. E vedes e ouvis que não somente em Éfeso, mas por quase toda a Ásia esse Paulo tem persuadido e afastado a um considerável número de pessoas, dizendo que os deuses feitos com as mãos não são deuses. E há o perigo não só deste, nosso comércio cair em desprezo, mas também que o templo da grande deusa Ártemis venha a ser tido como nada e que ela venha a ser despojada de seu esplendor, ela a quem toda a Ásia e o mundo adoram.

Ao ouvirem isso, encheram-se de ira e clamaram: Grande é a Ártemis dos efésios.

E assim a cidade encheu-se de confusão; e precipitaram-se juntos para o teatro, arrastando com eles a Gaio e a Aristarco, macedônios, que eram companheiros de viagem de Paulo.

Paulo desejava entrar para o meio da multidão, mas os discípulos não lho permitiram...por cerca de duas horas, a uma voz, gritaram: *Grande é a Ártemis dos efésios*.

Quem foi a Ártemis dos efésios, a quem toda a Ásia e o mundo adoravam?

A resposta começa em tempos bem mais remotos. Escavações feitas na Turquia, em locais que datam de cerca de 4.500 A.C., têm produzido figurinhas de terracota de mulheres com pequeníssimas cabeças, nádegas enormes e bem marcados triângulos na região púbica. Representam a Deusa-Mãe considerada como a fonte da vida, naquelas épocas distantes quando não se compreendia ainda o papel do macho na procriação. Bem mais tarde, o papel desempenhado pela Deusa-Mãe foi transferido para a Ásia por Cibele, deusa da fertilidade e origem de um culto de ritos orgiásticos. Ainda mais tarde, Cibele emerge na mitologia grega como genitora de diversos deuses e como amante do deus-sol.

Estátuas de *Cibele* podem ter inspirado estátuas posteriores da Ártemis. Uma estátua de Cibele, em pedra calcária, atualmente no museu de Ancara, executada na segunda metade do século VI A.C., exibe o chamado sorriso arcaico que era comum às primitivas esculturas gregas. Acompanhada por ajudantes minúsculos—um flautista à direita e um tocador de cítara à esquerda — ela segura os seios como se os estivesse oferecendo aos adoradores. Também trazia uma altíssima coroa—provavelmente precursora daquelas coroas usadas por Ártemis.

No século VI A.C., os foceanos, ao migrarem da Grécia para a Ásia, trouxeram com eles a deusa Ártemis, a virgem caçadora e senhora dos animais selvagens. Bem mais tarde, já nos tempos romanos, Ártemis adquiriu a designação latina de Diana, continuando a ser concebida como jovem casta. Na Anatólia, entretanto, Ártemis assumiu atributos mais parecidos com os de Cibele (mais licenciosos do que castos).

Em Éfeso ela recebeu as mais altas honrarias. De acordo com uma inscrição existente no local, ela trazia todos estes títulos: Grande Mãe da Natureza, Patrocinadora dos Banquetes, Protetora dos Suplicantes, Governanta, Santíssima, Nossa Senhora,

ÁRTEMIS

Rainha, a Grande, Primeira Líder, Ouvidora, Governanta de Toda a Jônia e Salvadora. Também era chamada «Rainha Abelha».

O templo dela, o Artemision, estava localizado em um terreno baldio lamacento, talvez porque se pensasse que a sua estátua descera do céu naquele local. O local foi pela primeira vez limpo e escavado por J.T. Wood, que cavou até os alicerces e recuperou certa quanitidade de fragmentos arquiteturais, esculturas e estatuetas de marfim e de ouro.

Wood foi um arquiteto britânico que fora enviado à Turquia para desenhar e construir estações de estrada de ferro. No entanto, estava resolvido a achar o templo de Ártemis e ficou trabalhando intermitentemente de 1863 a 1874. A princípio morava em *Esmirna* (atual *Izmir*), e todas as manhãs apanhava um trem às 6:00 horas para a estação mais próxima de Éfeso, uma viagem de 80 km, que lhe tomava três horas e meia; fazia idêntica viagem de volta à tarde. Cercado de dificuldades pelas autoridades turcas, rufiões locais e trabalhadores indisciplinados, mostrou-se resoluto e cheio de recursos, e conseguiu enviar grande quantidade de esculturas para a Inglaterra em navios de guerra britânicos que aportavam em Éfeso.

A primeira estrutura encontrada no lugar foi um altar erigido por volta de 700 A.C. O templo original fora construído no início do século VI A.C., e entre 560 e 530 A.C., foi substituído por um templo que não só era o maior edifício que havia no mundo grego, como também era o único edificado inteiramente de mármore.

Em 356 A.C., um homem de nome Herostratos teve a infame idéia de imortalizar seu nome, incendiando o templo. Cerca de 20 anos mais tarde Alexandre o Grande ofereceu sacrifícios em suas ruínas, e ofereceu-se para financiar sua reconstrução, contanto que seu nome fosse inscrito na obra, como o doador. Os efésios rejeitaram o oferecimento, dizendo: «*Não convém que um deus construa um templo para um deus*».

Os próprios cidadãos lançaram-se à empreitada de reconstruir o templo. As damas chegaram a penhorar suas jóias, para ajudar a amortizar os custos. A nova estrutura seguiu o antigo plano: o *naos*, ou área central, que era uma sala triangular, estava rodeado por duas fileiras de colunas em todos os quatro lados. Com cerca de 115 metros de comprimento, e 55 de largura, o templo era maior que quatro Partenões, e com justiça ocupava posição entre as Sete Maravilhas do Mundo.

Esse templo de Ártemis foi arrasado até o chão pelos godos invasores, no século III D.C., e depois que o cristianismo se tornou dominante, foi pilhado. Algumas das suas colunas foram usadas outra vez na basílica de São João, construída nas proximidades, e outras foram levadas para a igreja de Santa Sofia, em Constantinopla. Plantas e desenhos, baseados nos alicerces restantes e nas descrições de Plínio e outros escritores clássicos têm procurado mostrar-nos a aparência original do templo. Atualmente há figuras que medram entre suas ruínas dispersas.

A Estátua de Ártemis fora colocada no **naos**, por detrás de uma cortina que era arredada somente em certas ocasiões. Se esquecermos o dito de que a estátua caíra do céu, a primeira estátua de que se tem notícia foi esculpida em madeira pelo escultor Endoios, tendo sido vestida em trajes de prata e ouro, que eram mudados com freqüência pelas donas dos trajes. As estátuas da deusa que sobreviveram são conhecidas como *Ártemis Polimastros* (Ártemis de muitos seios). Várias delas são exibidas no museu de Éfeso. Aquela que passarei a descrever foi executada no século I D.C. Longe de ser realista, é um ídolo com 5 metros de altura, decorado com incrível número de atributos.

A deusa usa uma elevada coroa de castelos superpostos. Flanqueando-lhe a cabeça há meios-discos de lua cheia, com cinco grifos cornudos de cada lado. Em redor do pescoço há pequenos adornos que representam a vida vegetal, e imediatamente abaixo da gargantilha estão os sinais do zodíaco e também o Orion. O que mais chama a atenção são os seus seios—mais de 20 deles se projetam para fora. Tem sido sugerido que essas protuberâncias não são seios, e sim, ovos, tâmaras ou abelhas (estas últimas ocupadas em fecundar a deusa). Entretanto, parece mais provável que sejam seios, o sinal da toda-cuidadosa Deusa-Mãe. Em seus braços há relevos que representam leões, carneiros, veados, touros, esfinges, grifos, serpentes e abelhas.

Da cintura para baixo, Ártemis está envolta em uma apertada faixa formada por retângulos, na qual três animais—e a rainha abelha—são repetidos. Suas mãos originalmente se apoiavam sobre cajados de ouro, e estava ladeada, à base, por estátuas de veados, reminiscência da idéia da virgem caçadora. Há uma outra estátua, pertencente ao mesmo período; falta-lhe a elevada coroa, mas restam as bases sobre as quais se apoiavam os cajados, bem como os pés dos veados.

O Artemision era o centro de uma cidade sacerdotal que atraía peregrinos de todo o mundo antigo. Vinham adorar a Deusa e pedir curas miraculosas que lhe tinham dado renome. Em adição à sua função primária, o templo era um museu, um banco e um arquivo. A deusa era reputada responsável pela prosperidade comercial da cidade. Pedras que foram postas no templo, talvez debaixo das colunas, registram a doação da cidadania para cerca de 25 pessoas. Uma delas, Filaeneto, também recebeu uma coroa de ouro, um lugar frontal vitalício nos jogos sagrados e isenção de impostos aduaneiros sobre todos os bens que ele viesse a exportar ou importar. Eram numerosas as pedras memoriais. T. Flávio Sarpedon, um menino comediante, foi reconhecido por sua excelência e pelo seu estudioso treinamento, pelo cuidado que mostrava em seu desempenho no teatro, além de sua vitória no contexto que houve quando do grande festival de Ártemis.

É provável que o *naos* fosse apinhado de estátuas e estatuetas de Ártemis. Um certo Gaio Víbio Salutário deixou sua propriedade para o templo, e, durante sua vida, despendeu grandes somas em honra à deusa. Ele doou uma estatueta de ouro de Ártemis com peso de quase um quilo e meio, com «um veado de prata e mais dois de prata com mais de cinco quilos cada um». Em dias de assembléia pública deveriam ser transportadas do templo para o teatro pelos *sacerdotes com os ornamentos dourados*, junto com os vencedores dos jogos sagrados. Ele também proveu fundos para sustento dos sacerdotes que diziam os oráculos, para os que entoavam os louvores da deusa, para os guardiães do templo, para os acrobatas e para aqueles que limpavam e purificavam as estátuas do templo.

Os «sacerdotes com os ornamentos dourados» provavelmente eram aqueles de categoria mais elevada. Através de escritos históricos ficamos sabendo que um dos **primeiros sumos sacerdotes** se chamava Megabizo, acreditando-se que é retratado por uma estatueta de marfim, achada no local do templo. Vestido com um manto sacerdotal e mitra, suas mãos parecem segurar a corrente que era o sinete de seu ofício; essa corrente bem pode ter sido de ouro.

ÁRTEMIS — ARTES E OFÍCIOS

Outros indivíduos que serviam no templo incluíam eunucos auxiliados por jovens virgens, sacerdotisas, carregadores do cetro real, tocadores de flauta, acrobatas e guardas. Uma outra estatueta de marfim, do século VI A.C., é de uma jovem sacerdotisa. Longas tranças caem sobre seus ombros, e madeixas lisas lhe escorrem pelas costas. Na mão direita traz uma pequena jarra, e na esquerda, uma bacia rasa. Fontes históricas indicam que a abertura de uma das cerimônias religiosas em honra a Ártemis consistia do derramamento de vinho em um vaso.

No calendário efésio, um dos meses recebia o nome de Ártemis, sendo inteiramente ocupado por celebrações. Os jogos atléticos tinham lugar no estádio, havia concertos no odeon e peças no teatro. Todos os cidadãos, vestidos em seus melhores trajes, apinhavam as ruas para viver o evento final, um cortejo no qual a estátua era transportada através da cidade inteira. Coros entoavam hinos, e donzelas vestidas de ninfas, em peles de corça, e brandindo arco e flecha, executavam danças eróticas.

Pode-se especular sobre o que mais ocorria durante aquele mês de Ártemis, comparando-o com os relatos do festival de Cibele, efetuado em Roma. Em um *festival de sangue*, os sacerdotes dançavam ao som de címbalos, de flautas e de tambores, ao mesmo tempo que se vergastavam nas costas com flagelos e se cortavam nos braços e nos ombros com facas afiadas. Após os sacerdotes noviços se terem emasculado com espadas sagradas, seu orgãos eram lançados contra a estátua da deusa, e então eram cuidadosamente embrulhados e sepultados. Outrossim, nos festivais de Ártemis, efetuados em outros templos, sacerdotes vestidos em peles de feras ofereciam sacrifícios humanos—mas não se acredita que isso tenha sucedido em Éfeso.

Ártemis dos efésios não era imortal. Morreu *quando triunfou o cristianismo* sobre os deuses pagãos, e seus adoradores a abandonaram. Foi substituída por uma figura feminina infinitamente mais nobre, a Virgem Maria.

Por ocasião da crucificação, Jesus entregou Sua mãe aos cuidados do apóstolo João, e segundo o evangelho deste, lê-se que «...daquela hora o discípulo a abrigou em sua casa». Já que João faleceu em Éfeso, a *Virgem Maria* bem pode ter passado ali os seus últimos anos de vida.

O Terceiro Concílio Ecumênico, levado a efeito na igreja que traz seu nome, em Éfeso, no ano de 431 D.C., aceitou o dogma de que Jesus, filho da Virgem Maria, nasceu Filho de Deus. Em 1890, uma freira alemã viu a casa da Virgem Maria em Éfeso, em uma visão, e o local, posteriormente identificado por um padre, mediante os detalhes da visão, agora é ocupado pela casa *restaurada* da Virgem. Em 1967, o papa Paulo VI visitou essa casa. Em uma cerimônia efetuada na igreja em honra a ela, ele leu a Epístola aos Efésios, de Paulo, e deu seu reconhecimento papal à autenticidade da última morada dela sobre a terra.

No entanto, Ártemis ainda vive—na antecâmara do Hotel Grandes Efes, em Izmir, pois não poderia ser mesmo noutro lugar. *Izmir* é base da flotilha norte-americana vinculada às forças da NATO, mas é provável que poucos dos marinheiros americanos, ao passarem pela grande réplica da estátua de Ártemis, lhe dêem mais do que uma rápida olhadela, apesar de ter sido ela a deusa que séculos atrás era adorada não somente em Éfeso, mas também por *toda* a Ásia.

ARTES E OFÍCIOS

As sociedades organizadas requerem um conjunto fixo de artes e ofícios, além da agricultura. Quanto mais primitiva for uma sociedade, menor a necessidade de artes e ofícios; mas as sociedades mais avançadas e complexas têm uma imensa variedade de artes e ofícios. Estamos interessados no arcabouço bíblico. Os hebreus não eram inovadores na arquitetura, — nas artes e ofícios —. Eles tomavam por empréstimo e adaptavam elementos dos povos vizinhos. Assim, o trabalho em ferro foi tomado por empréstimo dos filisteus (ver I Samuel 13:20), a indústria da tinturaria dos fenícios, que supriam os operários para projetos mais importantes, como a construção do palácio real de Davi e o templo de Jerusalém. No século I A.C., a fabricação do vidro foi importada de Tiro. Ver o artigo sobre a *arquitetura*, onde damos evidências desses empréstimos feitos pelos hebreus.

1. Materiais básicos. Geralmente, os hebreus trabalhavam com o que dispunham: aguila, madeira, pedras, metais, fios para fabricação de tecidos e outros objetos feitos de pano. Em tempos mais prósperos, outros materiais eram importados, como metais, marfim, mármore, madeiras, itens esses que foram incluídos na construção do templo (ver o artigo a respeito).

2. O comércio e as guildas. Pessoas com interesses comuns reúnem-se a fim de se ajudarem mutuamente. Isso leva, finalmente, às organizações formais, como as uniões operárias e as guildas, algumas vezes chamadas *famílias*, localizadas em lugares onde cada classe de artífice podia trabalhar na esperança de sobreviver. Assim, temos os escribas em Jabez (I Crô. 2:55), os obreiros em linhos, em Tell Beit Mirsim (Debir?) (I Crô. 4:21), o Vale dos Artífices, em Jerusalém (I Crô. 4:14 e Nee. 11:35), os oleiros (Mat. 27:7) e os lavandeiros (II Reis 18:17). Um membro de uma dessas guildas era chamado de «filho» daquela profissão (Nee. 3:8,31 — em nossa versão, «um dos ourives» e «filho de um ourives»). Nos tempos do Novo Testamento, as guildas haviam assumido um caráter político, exercendo notável influência, conforme podemos deduzir da narrativa sobre os ourives de Éfeso (Atos 19:24). O trecho de II Timóteo 4:14 fala sobre Alexandre, o *latoeiro*, podendo nós presumir que ele fazia parte de uma união de trabalhadores. Ver também sobre os artífices em metal (ver II Sam. 8:10; Isa. 40:19 e Jer. 10:9), os entalhadores de madeira (Isa. 44:13 e II Reis 12:12), os pedreiros (ver II Sam. 5:11), os gravadores em pedras preciosas (ver Êxo. 28:9,10), e, naturalmente, os fabricantes de ídolos (ver Isa. 44).

3. Instrumentos básicos. Desde os tempos pré-históricos temos provas arqueológicas do fabrico de facas de pedra lascada, raspadores, ganchos de colheita, pilões e martelos de pedra. Começando em cerca de 4000 A.C., o cobre começou a ser usado na fabricação de instrumentos; o bronze começou a ser usado em cerca de 3300 A.C. O ferro começou a ser usado em cerca de 1100 A.C. Havia abundância de instrumentos (ver I Reis 6:7). Machados de ferro eram usados para derrubar árvores. Esses machados tinham cabos de madeira (ver Deu. 191:5). Havia facas para toda espécie de finalidade (ver Pro. 30:14). Havia serras, furadeiras, enxadas, raspadeiras, puas, goivas, pregos, etc. (ver Jer. 10:3). Havia pedras de raspar, alavancas, roladoras e guinchos primitivos. Moldes de tijolos, colheres de pedreiro e picaretas têm sido encontradas, referidos nas inscrições de Siloé. Os trabalhadores em metal conheciam o malho, a bigorna, o forno, o fole, os moldes, limas, brocas, tenazes, tesouras e alicates. Os fazendeiros tinham os arados, foices, aguilhões, forcados, enxadas, pás (ver

ARTES E OFÍCIOS

I Sam. 13:21; I Reis 7:40,45 e Joel 3:13). As ferramentas eram afiadas na pedra ou com limas (ver I Sam. 13:21). O oleiro tinha sua roda, seu forno, torniquetes, pás, raspadeiras e sovelas. Outros artífices, como os tanoeiros, os tintureiros, os fabricantes de tendas, os montadores de jóias, os gravadores, os escultores, todos tinham as suas ferramentas e instrumentos especiais, muitos dos quais têm sido encontrados pelos arqueólogos, embora alguns deles não sejam especificamente mencionados nas Escrituras.

4. Alguns ofícios específicos:

a. Os oleiros. Nas terras bíblicas, a cerâmica apareceu pela primeira vez em Jericó, em cerca de 5000 A.C. Pelo menos essas são nossas primeiras evidências arqueológicas. Vasos feitos à mão persistiram até cerca de 3000 A.C. A roda do oleiro começou a ser usada no Egito e na Suméria. O trecho de Jeremias 18:3,4 descreve a obra dos antigos oleiros. Ele pisava na massa até que se formasse uma massa consistente; e então a colocava sobre a roda. As antigas rodas de oleiro eram feitas de madeira ou de pedra. Havia uma roda menor, posta sobre uma maior, que o oleiro fazia girar à mão (ver Jer. 18:3). Os vasos eram moldados sobre a roda menor, no formato desejado (ver Isa. 45:9). Estes eram então alisados, esmaltados ou queimados, decorados a gosto. A cerâmica dos hebreus era essencialmente utilitária. Exemplares de vasos e fornos têm sido encontrados pelos arqueólogos. Fora de Megido foram encontrados três fornos em forma de «U» (séculos VIII e VII A.C.). Rodas de oleiros têm sido encontradas em Jericó, Megido, Gezer, Laquis, Hazor e muitos outros locais da Palestina.

Uso metafórico. A profissão dos oleiros é usada na Bíblia em sentido simbólico para indicar: O poder de Deus sobre os homens e o destino deles (ver Sal. 2:9; Isa. 29:16; Jer. 19:11; Rom. 9:20 ss). E a fragilidade e dependência do ser humano, subentendidas nesse fato.

b. Os construtores. Esses incluem os pedreiros, os reboqueiros, os mestres construtores, etc. Os aldeões ocupavam-se na fabricação de tijolos secos ao sol. Eles usavam esses tijolos para erguer suas moradias, e então recobriam as mesmas com adobe ou palha, sobre tábuas de madeira, formando assim uma espécie de laje. Algumas vezes, os tijolos eram cozidos ao forno. Construtores especializados ou não eram usados nas construções públicas (ver II Crô. 34:11). Tais construções eram dirigidas por mestres construtores (ver I Cor. 3:10). O local da construção era medido com o uso de um cordel (ver II Sam. 8:2 e Zac. 2:1). Nos tempos helenistas, algumas vezes era usada uma vara de medir (ver Apo. 11:1 e 21:15). Para tanto, era empregado um agrimensor. O mestre construtor acompanhava o progresso da obra. Entre seus métodos de verificação eram usados o prumo — uma corda com um peso na ponta, feito de pedra ou de estanho — (ver Amós 7:7,8), para verificar as estruturas verticais. As obras complexas requeriam muitos operários especializados ou não, além dos pedreiros, carpinteiros, porteiros, trabalhadores em metal e decoradores. Ver o artigo sobre *Arte na Bíblia e Civilizações Relacionadas.*

Usos metafóricos: 1. O trabalho do mestre construtor era usado para simbolizar o juízo divino (Isa. 28:17; Jer. 31:19). Deus julga a nossa obra.

2. A medição com o prumo era usada para simbolizar a averiguação da verdade. Coisas distorcidas são desmascaradas, mediante a comparação com a retidão de Deus (ver Isa. 28:17).

3. Deus, na qualidade de Criador, é o edificador de todas as coisas (ver Heb. 3:4 e 11:10).

4. Uma construção em andamento pode simbolizar a doação de riquezas e prosperidade ao próprio filho (ver Jó. 22:23).

5. A ereção de cidades ou famílias pode significar o aumento de seu número, de suas riquezas, honra, poder ou prazer (ver I Crô. 17:10; Sal. 119:35).

6. A edificação das muralhas de Jerusalém representa o fortalecimento e a prosperidade de Israel (ver Sal. 51:18).

7. A Igreja está edificada sobre Cristo, o único alicerce espiritual, quando a questão da salvação está em pauta (ver I Cor. 3:11).

8. Entretanto, os líderes espirituais, como os apóstolos e os profetas, compõem uma espécie secundária de alicerce, sobre o qual a Igreja vai sendo edificada; e nessa metáfora, Cristo é a principal pedra angular, e não o alicerce inteiro (ver Efé. 2:21,22 e I Ped. 2:6).

9. O ato geral de edificação é um símbolo da nossa edificação espiritual, porque essa, tal como o crescimento físico, depende de uma obra gradual e de aperfeiçoamento, que tem como alvo um produto terminado (ver Jud. 20).

10. Cada crente individual tem a responsabilidade de edificar bem a sua vida espiritual, e com o material de construção apropriado, porque, em caso contrário, ele sofrerá terrível perda final, embora sua alma não se perca (ver I Cor. 3:12 ss). Isso não significa, porém, que tal perda seja permanente, pois o alvo é que todos os remidos sejam conformados à imagem de Cristo (ver Rom. 8:29), participando da natureza divina (ver II Ped. 1:4), através de uma glória que será atingida em degraus, mediante as transformações operadas pelo Espírito Santo (ver II Cor. 3:18). Não há como esse plano divino venha a falhar, pois, nesse caso, o corpo de Cristo permaneceria imperfeito e defeituoso, o que é uma hipótese ridícula e impossível.

c. Os carpinteiros. Tanto José quanto Jesus eram carpinteiros na pequena aldeia de Nazaré, e talvez os únicos dessa profissão. Objetos feitos por Jesus eram conhecidos nos tempos de Justino Mártir, no século II D.C. Os carpinteiros eram operários especializados em madeira. Trabalhavam fazendo telhados, portas, janelas, escadas e todo o tipo de móveis, como camas, cadeiras, mesas, estrados para os pés, gabinetes, etc. Mas também eram feitas tigelas, colheres e caixas. Muitos objetos assim têm sido encontrados pela arqueologia. Os carpinteiros também fabricavam tábuas (ver Isa. 28:27,28). Também faziam veículos como carroças, carros e embarcações (ver Eze. 27:5,6). Ver o artigo sobre *navios.* Os carpinteiros atarefavam-se nas construções públicas, conforme se vê nos casos do tabernáculo, do palácio de Davi e do templo de Salomão. O entalhe em madeira era uma especialização da carpintaria (ver Êxo. 31:5 e 35:33), e os carpinteiros também entalhavam osso e marfim. Os instrumentos usados por eles incluíam as lixas, as enxós, as serras, as limas, as brocas, os martelos, as sovelas, as juntas, os pregos e os formões. Objetos dessa natureza têm sido encontrados em muitos lugares da Palestina.

d. Os pedreiros. A pedra era um material dispendioso demais para ser usado na maioria das residências particulares, em cuja construção eram utilizados tijolos de barro. (Ver Amós 5:11). No templo de Jerusalém foram usadas pedras importadas do Líbano (ver I Reis 6:7), visto que a pedra calcária da região era por demais macia. Os pedreiros preparavam a pedra e a utilizavam em seu trabalho, empregando muitas das mesmas ferramentas usadas pelos carpinteiros, além da picareta e da pá. Para

ARTES E OFÍCIOS

preparar pedras nas pedreiras eram usadas cunhas de madeira, metidas entre as pedras à força; isso lascava as pedras, com a força da pressão. As pedras eram amoldadas mediante martelos de metal (ver Jer. 23:29). Os pedreiros também escavavam túmulos em cavernas naturais, ou simplesmente nas rochas (ver Isa. 22:16). As famílias sepultavam seus mortos nesses túmulos. A arqueologia tem encontrado muitos desses túmulos, desde Bete-Semes (século VIII A.C.), até Jerusalém e Bete-Searim (século I A.C. até o século II D.C.). Também havia silos e cisternas escavados na rocha, como em Jericó, Laquis e Megido. Além disso, eram escavados túneis de água, alguns dos quais envolviam muito trabalho humano. Nas construções eram usadas colunas de pedra, algumas vezes elaboradamente decoradas, especialmente nos tempos dos Herodes. As escavações têm demonstrado que, no caso do emprego de pedras, nas construções, algumas dessas pedras eram feitas com uma precisão tal que, embora não fosse usado qualquer tipo de cimento, as pedras se encaixavam tão bem que não se podia inserir uma faca entre elas. Pertencente ao século IX A.C., em Megido, há uma dessas obras dotada de tal precisão. Marcas feitas pelos pedreiros podem ser vistas nos degraus de uma sinagoga em Cafarnaum. Os pedreiros também faziam inscrições na rocha, havendo abundantes exemplos descobertos pela arqueologia. Os operários hebreus eram habilidosos no trabalho de cortar e gravar, incluindo as pedras preciosas ornamentais (ver Êxo. 35:33). Algumas vezes, porém, era mister importar operários especializados, como se deu com Davi, que os contratou com Hirão (ver II Sam. 5:11 e I Crô. 14:1). Nessa obra, ninguém se igualava aos egípcios, que usavam principalmente a pedra calcária, retirada das montanhas, produzindo com ela monumentos maciços e impressionantes, até hoje existentes. Os grandes pesos envolvidos nessas gigantescas construções requeriam considerável habilidade e engenharia. Os hieróglifos egípcios eram traçados com grande habilidade, o que seria surpreendente mesmo que os egípcios contassem com ferramentas de aço temperado (o que se acredita que eles não tinham).

e. Os ferreiros. Antes da introdução do ferro, sabemos que os palestinos mineravam, fundiam e utilizavam o ouro, a prata e o cobre. Salomão dispunha de grandes minas de cobre e ferro, no local do Wadi Arabah e em Eziom-Geber, pelo que sabemos que o ferro era usado naquele tempo (1000 A.C.). Volumosos objetos de metal eram fundidos em moldes de areia, perto das minas (ver II Crô. 4:17). O processo de fundição era ajudado por foles, que forçavam ar soprado através de tubos de argila. Por essa razão, os ferreiros comumente eram apelidados de «os sopradores». O metal fundido era derramado de baldes ou de outros receptáculos em moldes de pedra ou de argila, ou era batido na bigorna (ver Isa. 41:7). O metal era transformado em placas ou folhas a marteladas (ver Isa. 41:7). Por esse motivo, os latoeiros e os ferreiros eram também chamados «marteladores». Muitos objetos eram feitos assim, como todas as variedades de vasos e ferramentas, lâminas de arados, pontas de aguilhões, forcados, machados, alfinetes, imagens, figurinhas, facas e armas de todas as espécies (ver o artigo sobre *Armas, Armadura*). Os ferreiros trabalhavam em tempos de paz e em tempos de guerra (ver Isa. 2:4; Joel 3:10 e Miq. 4:3). Ver o artigo sobre *Mineração e Metais*. Os trabalhadores em metal tinham o malho, a bigorna (ver Isa. 41:7), os foles (ver Jer. 6:29), o cadinho (ver Pro. 17:3), e, para peças maiores, o forno (ver Eze. 22:18).

f. Os curtidores. Esses trabalhavam com couro (Atos 9:43), tratando das peles dos animais para fazer roupas de couro, tendas, odres, escudos, capacetes e calçados. É das mais antigas profissões. Os antigos hebreus tinham curtidores (ver Êxo. 25:5). Os egípcios eram habilidosos curtidores, e a literatura deles mostram como eles preparavam o couro. Havia uma preparação de três dias em que o couro era empapado com sal e farinha de trigo, a fim de ficar limpo. Um cáustico era usado para remover os pêlos. Sucos de plantas acres também eram usados nesse processo. Então a pele era secada ao sol por diversos dias, sendo tratada com cascas de árvores e folhas. Eram usados óleos para amaciá-lo (ver II Sam. 1:21 e Isa. 21:5). Os couros mais finos eram usados no fabrico de folhas de pergaminho. Esse trabalho, embora necessário, soltava fortes maus odores, e os curtidores, nas culturas judaicas, precisavam viver fora dos muros das cidades, com freqüência à beira de rios. Assim encontramos Simão, o curtidor, vivendo em Jope, perto do mar (ver Atos 9:43). Alguns animais, cujas peles eram tratadas, eram animais *imundos*, de acordo com a lei cerimonial judaica, o que era um outro motivo para os curtidores viverem extramuros. O couro usado no fabrico de tendas era raro (ver Êxo. 25:5 e Núm. 4:6), mas era comumente usado para o fabrico de equipamento militar, como capacetes, aljavas, arreios de carros de guerra, fundas, escudos, paveses, etc. (ver II Sam. 1:21 e Isa. 21:5). Sandálias feitas de peles de animais marinhos eram um luxo da época (ver Eze. 16:10). Essas peles de animais marinhos eram usadas em leitos, coberturas de cadeiras e itens de decoração. Algumas vezes, essas peles eram tingidas para adquirir ainda maior beleza.

g. Os tintureiros. Israel entrou em contato com essa profissão no Egito. A maioria das culturas antigas mostra algum sinal tanto de tecelagem quanto de tinturaria. Eram tingidos tecidos e couros. As guildas comerciais especializaram-se nesse trabalho. Fragmentos de teares de madeira e tanques para mergulhar tecidos têm sido encontrados em Laquis, no sul de Judá. Pesos de argila foram descobertos em algumas das casas destruídas por Nabucodonosor. Os cananeus, antes mesmo dos dias de Abraão, já eram habilidosos trabalhadores desse ofício, conforme se vê nas descobertas feitas pela arqueologia em Tell Beit Mirsim (Quiriate-Sefer). Muitos pesos para teares foram encontrados ali, juntamente com um elaborado sistema de fabricação de tecidos. Biblos era uma cidade famosa por sua produção de papiro e de tecidos. O Egito era bem conhecido por causa de seus excelentes linhos. Conchas de murex, em Tiro, produziam tintas de cor púrpura e vermelha. Também havia vários tipos de corantes vegetais. As cascas de romãzeiras produziam tinta de cor negra; as folhas da amendoeira davam o amarelo; a potassa e a uva davam o índigo. Essa indústria tem sido confirmada pela arqueologia em textos de Ras Shamra, de cerca de 1500 A.C. Tecidos de cor púrpura foram usados no tabernáculo (ver Êxo. 26:31 e 28:5). No véu do templo foram usados tecidos tingidos de azul, púrpura e carmesim, como variantes do mesmo corante (ver II Crô. 3:14). Os israelitas aprenderam essa indústria de operários tírios, a pedido de Salomão (ver II Crô. 2:7). A Lídia comerciava com panos tratados em Tiatira (ver Atos 16:14). Os habitantes de Tell Beit Mirsim (Debir?), perto de Neguebe, devotavam-se às indústrias de tecidos e tinturaria. Pelo menos vinte plantas usadas para o fabrico de corantes têm chamado a atenção dos arqueólogos. Tanques para imergir tecidos foram desenterrados. Em alguns casos, os fios eram tingidos

ARTES E OFÍCIOS — ARTIGOS DE FÉ

antes de serem tecidos; porém em outros casos, era tingido o tecido já pronto. Vários banhos eram dados, caso se desejasse maior fixação das cores.

h. Os lavadeiros. Estes ocupavam-se na lavagem e embranquecimento dos tecidos. Era necessário limpar as fibras de seus óleos ou gomas naturais, antes de serem tingidas. O pano tornava-se mais compacto por meio do encolhimento, um dos principais trabalhos dos lavadeiros. Algumas vezes, eles também faziam trabalho de tinturaria. Quem fazia esse trabalho precisava de um abundante suprimento de água, pelo que vivia em locais onde a água não faltava. Os lavadeiros pisavam no tecido, estendido por sobre pedras, a fim de realizarem o seu trabalho. Por essa razão, eram comumente apelidados de «pisadores». Em Jerusalém havia um local, fora da muralha leste, onde esse tipo de trabalho era realizado. Chamava-se «campo do lavadeiro» (II Reis 18:17; Isa. 7:3 e 26:2). Quando da transfiguração do Senhor Jesus, Suas vestes resplandeceram com uma brancura incomum, mais do que qualquer lavadeiro seria capaz de produzir (ver Marcos 9:3). A potassa era usada como agente embranquecedor, importado do Egito. Também eram usados sabões, argila branca e salitre, nos processos de embranquecimento (ver Pro. 25:20 e Jer. 2:22). Os álcalis, retirados de certas plantas, bem como os sabões feitos das cinzas da Salsola kali, uma planta, eram utilizados. O sabão referido no trecho de Malaquias 3:2, provavelmente era feito com cinzas de boro, visto que a nossa soda cáustica e o nitrato de sódio eram desconhecidos na Síria e na Palestina, embora tais elementos tenham sido encontrados na Babilônia.

i. Os tecelões. As donas-de-casa foram as primeiras tecelãs. Mais tarde, o ofício transformou-se em uma indústria. Tecidos eram feitos de linho, algodão, lã e pêlos. Esses pêlos eram retirados de vários animais, como a cabra e o camelo (ver Êxo. 35:25 ss ; II Reis 23:7; Pro. 31:13,19). Todos os tipos de objetos eram feitos de pano, como vestes, cortinas, tendas e coberturas de toda espécie. A profissão de tecelagem usualmente era ocupada por homens (ver Êxo. 27:16). Flores, bordados de várias cores e estampas eram entretecidos nas obras mais finas. Os filhos de Selá ocupavam-se desse mister mesmo quando Israel ainda estava no Egito (ver I Crô. 4:21). Tecelões produziam as cortinas do tabernáculo, utilizando pêlos de cabras e linho (ver Êxo. 26:1,7). Eles também produziam as vestes sacerdotais (ver Êxo. 39:1). A guilda dos tecelões existe desde os tempos do escritor ou escritores dos livros de Crônicas (ver I Crô. 6:21). Antes desse tempo, os tecidos da Babilônia eram muito prestigiados, o que se pode subentender com base em Josué 7:21, onde se lê que Acã deu grande valor a uma capa babilônica. Os egípcios eram conhecidos como produtores de excelentes tecidos de linho (ver Isa. 19:9). Os instrumentos usados pelos tecelões são mencionados no Antigo Testamento, como o tear ou seu eixo (ver I Sam. 17:7) e a lançadeira (Jó 7:6).

Uso metafórico. a. A força das armas, como a ponta da lança de Golias, era comparada com a haste de um tecelão (ver I Sam. 17:7 e II Sam. 21:19). b. A vida de um homem escoa-se mais rapidamente que a lançadeira de um tecelão (ver Jó 7:6), o que destaca a brevidade da vida física. c. A morte prematura é como um tecido terminado que é cortado do tear e enrolado (ver Isa. 38:12), mas em que as pontas dos fios continuam presos ao tear. Ver o artigo separado sobre *Enrolamento de fios e Fabrico de tecidos*.

Outros artigos interessantes, relacionados ao assunto de *Artes e Ofícios*, são Arte, Cosméticos e Perfumaria, Marfim, Enrolamento de fios e Fabrico de tecidos, e, finalmente, o Vidro. (N REIF SIN UN)

ARTÍFICE

No grego é **technites**, «artesão» ou «planejador». Palavra que se refere a um artífice em qualquer obra em pedra, madeira, metal, pedras preciosas ou argila (ver Isa. 3:3 e Apo. 18:22). A Bíblia alude a Tubalcaim como o primeiro artífice em metais (ver Gên. 4:22). Operários especializados e artífices formavam uma porção importante na sociedade hebréia, ao tempo da deportação para a Babilônia.

Ver Nee. 3:8,32; Isa. 40:19; 41:7, onde se lê sobre «ourives», os quais, tal como os que trabalhavam em prata, foram literalmente chamados, em hebraico, de refinadores ou purificadores, em Mal. 3:2,3. Os ourives batiam o ouro até tomar o formato que queriam, ou então fundiam-no em um molde. Aqueles que exerciam essa profissão usualmente eram fabricantes de ídolos de ouro (ver Jer. 10:9 e 51:17), o que significava que uma cobertura de ouro era posta sobre um ídolo de madeira. Eram usados cravos para manter a cobertura de ouro no lugar (ver Isa. 4:17). Alguns *ourives* provavelmente eram simples joalheiros (ver Nee. 3:8,31,32). Ver os artigos sobre Ouro, Artes e Ofícios. (S Z)

ARTIGOS DE ESMALCALDE (SCHMALKALD)

O nome indica uma confissão luterana, escrita pelo próprio Lutero em 1537, atendendo a um pedido do eleitor João Frederico da Saxônia, como um sumário de todo o seu ensino. Nessa declaração, encontramos uma concisa afirmativa de princípios básicos, incluindo questões como a soberania de Deus, a obra medianeira de Cristo, a justificação pela fé, a Igreja e seu ministério. Seus artigos contrastam agudamente com as doutrinas romanistas como a missa, as penitências, as relíquias, etc.,—que são ali denunciadas. O papa é atacado como se fosse o anticristo. A intenção de João Frederico era de usar esse documento para unificar os protestantes, mas ele não obteve êxito. Todavia, o documento obteve prestígio e terminou incluído no Livro da Concórdia (ver o artigo a respeito), como um credo oficial, acompanhado por um apêndice antipapal, escrito por Melanchthon (ver o artigo a respeito). Lutero dava grande importância a essa declaração, que era uma espécie de espontâneo derramamento de fé do fundador do protestantismo, e não uma exposição fria e erudita. Ver sobre o Luteranismo. (E)

ARTIGOS DE FÉ

Há declarações credais diretas no Novo Testamento. Ver I Cor. 15:3,4 e I Tim. 3:16, bem como o artigo sobre o Credo dos Apóstolos. Na Igreja primitiva, havia o desejo de se formular declarações doutrinárias exatas, embora o cânon do Novo Testamento ainda não tivesse sido terminado. Isso pode ser visto no fato de que diversos livros foram escritos, pelo menos parcialmente, para combater as heresias, especificamente o gnosticismo. As epístolas aos Efésios, Colossenses, I e II Timóteo, I, II e III João, e partes de outros livros, como o Apocalipse, foram motivados, entre outras coisas, pela necessidade de combater as heresias. A epístola aos Gálatas foi motivada pelo desejo de Paulo de preservar a pureza da revelação da graça contra os assaltos do legalismo. Era natural, pois, que a Igreja pós-apostólica desenvolvesse ainda mais a questão. Os primeiros artigos de fé foram

ARTIGOS DE FÉ — ÁRVORE DA VIDA

determinados pelos concílios eclesiásticos, usualmente em face de opiniões divergentes. Ver sobre o Credo Niceno, por exemplo. Ver o artigo sobre *credos*.

Tomás de Aquino usou a palavra *articulus* a fim de denotar uma verdade sobrenatural, revelada, distinta em si mesma, mas parte do todo orgânico do ensino cristão. Apesar de haver verdades assim, como afirmam todas as religiões, o problema tem sido a interpretação das mesmas, uma vez proferidas. E isso tem sido a tarefa dos concílios e das denominações, o que tem dividido o cristianismo em muitas seitas. O *Catecismo* do concílio de Trento chama as verdades do Credo dos Apóstolos de *artigos*. No anglicanismo há os Trinta e Nove Artigos, o padrão doutrinário oficial da Igreja da Inglaterra. Os *Artigos da Religião*, do metodismo, foram preparados por João Wesley, em 1784. Originalmente, consistiam de vinte e quatro dos trinta e nove artigos da Igreja Anglicana. Posteriormente, os metodistas norte-americanos adicionaram um artigo sobre «regras dos Estados Unidos da América». A declaração metodista elimina o calvinismo dos Trinta e Nove Artigos. Ver o artigo sobre os *Trinta e Nove Artigos*. Os luteranos têm a sua *Confissão de Augsburgo* (ver artigo). Para os protestantes ortodoxos, a Bíblia é a única regra infalível de fé e prática cristãs. Porém, nas tentativas de definir essas regras, vários credos têm surgido nos círculos protestantes, e muitas igrejas locais e missões têm sua própria declaração doutrinária.

Vantagem e desvantagem. A vantagem desses artigos é que eles unem as pessoas que se agrupam em torno dos mesmos, com base nos quais podem operar e ter comunhão. A sua desvantagem é que eles tendem por levar as pessoas a se tornarem arrogantes por sua «distinção e superioridade», dando também a impressão que «é aqui que a verdade cessa». Ademais, todas as denominações e seus credos são mesclas de verdades e erros e não há denominação ou credo que não possa ser melhorado por meio de empréstimos ou pela busca pessoal e coletiva na verdade. Essa verdade sempre é conhecida por nós apenas em parte. (B E P)

ARTIGOS DE LAMBETH

Os artigos assim chamados foram adotados a 20 de novembro de 1595. Eles expressam um sistema de predestinação, dividido em nove artigos, que chegaram a predominar na Igreja Anglicana. Nunca chegaram a obter força de lei, e uma parte daquela denominação sempre os reteve como sua posição doutrinária.

ARTIGOS DE TORGAU
Ver **Torgau, Artigos de**

ARTIGOS GALICANOS (CONFISSÃO GALICANA, CONFISSÃO DE ROCHELLE)

Esses artigos foram redigidos por Calvino (ver o artigo a respeito), tendo sido então ampliados e adotados pelo Sínodo de Paris, em 1599, como uma confissão de fé e uma ordem de disciplina. Posteriormente, essa confissão foi repetidamente revisada, sob a direção de Beza, e finalmente, foi ratificada quando do sétimo sínodo nacional em La Rochelle, em 1571, na presença da rainha de Navarra e seu filho, Henrique IV. Essa confissão, quase inteiramente compilada pessoalmente por Calvino, e por seu amigo e sucessor, Beza (ver o artigo a respeito), contém quarenta artigos que sumariam as crenças doutrinárias de Calvino. Finalmente, a confissão foi ultrapassada pela Declaração de Fé da Igreja Reformada na França, em 1872. (E)

ARTIGOS IRLANDESES

Foram adotados pela convocação da Igreja da Irlanda, em 1615, tendo sido revisados os 39 Artigos (ver o artigo a respeito), imprimindo-lhes forte tom calvinista. Embora em desuso na Irlanda, após a adoção dos 39 Artigos, em 1634, os Artigos Irlandeses foram usados como parte da fórmula da Confissão de Westminster (ver o artigo a respeito). (E)

ARUBOTE

Cidade ou distrito mencionado em I Reis 4:10, uma das doze zonas administrativas de onde eram obtidas provisões para a casa de Salomão. O intendente dessa região era Ben-Hesede, um dos oficiais da corte de Salomão. O local não é conhecido, embora seja mencionado juntamente com Socó e Hefer. E sabe-se que Hefer ficava no território de Manassés. Socó tem sido identificada com o moderno Tell er-Ras ou 'Arrabeh. Portanto, Arubote não deveria ficar muito para o norte de Samaria. É possível que Árbata fosse a forma do nome dado na época dos Macabeus (ver I Macabeus 5:23).

ARUMÁ

Esse nome significa **altura**. Era uma cidade próxima de Siquém (ver Juí. 9:41), onde foi habitar Abimeleque, filho de Gideão, depois que fora expulso de Siquém (ver Juí. 9:41). (ID S)

ARVADE, ARVADITAS

No hebraico significa lugar de fugitivos. Um lugar que figura na genealogia de Noé, na linhagem de Canaã (ver Gên. 10:18 e I Crô. 1:16). Era a cidade fenícia localizada mais ao norte, em uma ilha rochosa atualmente chamada Ruade. Os gregos chamavam-na Aruade, nome que aparece em I Macabeus 15:23. Essa ilha ficava defronte da boca do rio Eleutero, ao largo da costa da Síria, diante da ilha de Chipre. Tinha três quilômetros de uma ponta de praia à outra. Estrabão refere-se à mesma como uma rocha que se eleva em meio às ondas do mar (ver xiv. par. 753). Nos tempos antigos, era densamente povoada, apesar de suas minúsculas dimensões, tendo conseguido governar as costas próximas durante séculos. É mencionada nas cartas de Amarna de números 101, 105 e 109, onde é chamada *arwada*. Nos registros históricos de Tiglate-Pileser I (1114-1076 A.C.), ela é chamada *armada*. Cenas do local aparecem em relevos assírios (nos portões de bronze de Salmaneser III, 858-824 A.C.). Algumas moedas arvaditas retratam cenas da ilha. O lugar participava plenamente das atividades marítimas fenícias, particularmente depois que Tiro e Sidom caíram nas mãos dos reis greco-sírios. (ID ND S UN Z)

ÁRVORE DA VIDA

No hebraico temos uma expressão de duas palavras. — A LXX traduz por *to ksúlon tēs zoēs*, «a árvore da vida». Juntamente com a árvore do conhecimento do bem e do mal, a «árvore da vida» foi plantada por Deus no jardim de Éden. Deus não ordenou a Adão que ele não comesse do fruto da árvore da vida, e a tentação da serpente não envolveu a mesma. E quando Adão e Eva foram expulsos do paraíso, a razão da expulsão foi: «...para que não

ÁRVORE DE JUDAS — ÁRVORE DO CONHECIMENTO

estenda a mão, e tome também da árvore da vida, e coma e viva eternamente» (Gên. 3:22). Dois querubins, armados de espada flamejante, guardavam a árvore da vida. No relato inicial sobre o jardim do Éden, aparentemente a participação no fruto da árvore da vida, por parte do homem, era permitida por Deus; mas, por alguma razão não explicada, ele nunca participou do mesmo. Notemos que em Gênesis 2:9,10, tanto a árvore da vida quanto um rio são mencionados, embora nada ali seja esclarecido quanto à significação de uma coisa ou de outra.

Em Ezequiel 31:1-12, novamente aparece um rio, ladeado por árvores perenemente verdes, produtoras de alimento e medicamento. No Antigo Testamento, somente no livro de Provérbios aparece novamente a expressão «árvore da vida», isto é, em Pro. 3:18. O «fruto do justo» é árvore da vida, como também o desejo cumprido (em Pro. 11:30 e 13:12). E a «língua serena» participa de idêntica honraria (ver Pro. 15:4). Ao que parece, o homem é vitalizado e renovado por essas coisas, embora não haja elaboração do termo, e nem haja qualquer significação cósmica, emprestada a essas árvores da vida.

No Novo Testamento, apenas o livro de Apocalipse faz alusão à árvore da vida, e em cada caso, há um significado espiritual e cósmico. Assim, em Apocalipse 2:7 é feita a promessa de que o «vencedor» haverá de participar da árvore da vida, localizada no «paraíso de Deus». O vigésimo segundo capítulo fornece-nos ainda mais detalhes. Na Nova Jerusalém, manará o rio da vida, desde o trono de Deus. E em ambas as margens desse rio, a árvore da vida proverá tanto a vida quanto a cura para aqueles que ali viverem.

É verdade que os cultos pagãos antigos aproveitaram a idéia, embora distorcidamente, incluindo a *árvore da vida* em seus mitos. Os reis antigos também açambarcaram a idéia, associando sua imagem à da árvore da vida, geralmente sob a forma de um guardião e sacerdote sacramental que dispensa sua autoridade através do culto. Em um outro contexto, a árvore da vida aparece intimamente relacionada à deusa-mãe, que representava o princípio feminino da reprodução natural, quer nas plantações, quer no gado ou na família humana. Essa deusa-mãe também podia representar o trono, ou seja, aquela que dava vida e poder ao monarca.

Podemos concluir que a árvore da vida *representa* o poder doador de vida de Yahweh. O Senhor é a fonte de vida para o rei e para o povo de Israel, exatamente como o foi para Adão. Essas e outras idéias foram sintetizadas no livro de Apocalipse, a fim de exprimir a realidade da vida eterna e da felicidade celeste com Deus (ver Apo. 22:1-3; cf. 2:7 e 21:6). Essa evolução de idéias sugere-nos que o livro de Gênesis não se referia somente a uma situação do passado, mas a um destino definitivo que dá uma perspectiva esperançosa, e portanto, mostra-nos qual o sentido mais profundo da existência humana. Em suma, o paraíso é perdido no Gênesis mas é totalmente recuperado no Apocalipse. E todos os demais livros da Bíblia ensinam como isso ocorre. Os homens encontram vida em Jesus Cristo: «Eu sou o caminho, e a verdade, e a vida; ninguém vem ao Pai senão por mim» (João 14:6).

ÁRVORE DE JUDAS

Na Bíblia não há nenhuma árvore com esse nome. Mas a expressão é usada em relação à árvore talvez subentendida em Mat. 27:5, onde se lê: «...Judas...retirou-se, e foi enforcar-se». A lenda identifica a *Cervis siliquastrum* como a árvore em foco, que passou a ser apelidada de «árvore de Judas». Tem flores avermelhadas, nos ramos e no próprio tronco. A tradição também diz que a árvore chora sangue a cada primavera, em memória de Judas Iscariotes. As folhas têm o contorno de um coração, e representariam o duro coração de Judas. A árvore é nativa da Palestina, atingindo uma altura de cerca de nove metros. Seus ramos são suficientemente fortes para que uma pessoa se pendure em um deles, com o propósito de enforcar-se. Porém, tudo não passa de uma lenda fantástica, como acontece nas lendas que circundam figuras bíblicas. (Z)

ÁRVORE DE PORFÍRIO
Ver **Porfírio, Árvore de**

ÁRVORE DO CONHECIMENTO

A expressão, no hebraico, consiste em duas palavras, que a LXX traduz por *tó ksúlon toũ eidénai*, «a árvore do Éden». A expressão completa aparece em Gên. 2:9, «a árvore do conhecimento do bem e do mal», que designa uma das duas árvores incomuns que Deus plantou no jardim do Éden. Deus ordenou a Adão que não comesse do fruto dessa árvore, sob pena de morte (ver Gên. 2:17). A tentação de Eva, por parte da serpente, concentrou-se sobre esse mandamento. Ela cedeu à tentação, diante do argumento de que ela não morreria, mas seria «como Deus», e ela não somente comeu do tal fruto, como também deu-o ao seu marido. A expressão «do bem e do mal», que indica os pontos extremos do conhecimento, denota a idéia de conhecimento total, isto é, onisciência e poder. Segundo se depreende de Gên. 3:5, equivale a tornar-se um ser divino. Porém, ao apelar para tal fruto, buscando tornar-se divino, o homem apenas tornou-se culpado, cobrindo-se de vergonha e condenação, e foi expulso do jardim do Éden, onde comungava com Deus.

A falta de conhecimento do bem e do mal pode ser um sinal de imaturidade (ver Deu. 1:39; Isa. 7:14-17), e no trecho de II Samuel 19:35, aparece como um sinal da senilidade própria da idade muito avançada. A posse de conhecimento, por parte do rei, torna-o semelhante a um anjo de Deus, e de conformidade com I Reis 3:9, conhecimento e sabedoria era o mais almejado de todos os dons, por parte de Salomão (cf. Gên. 24:50; Núm. 24:13; Ecl. 12:14; Jer. 42:6). A árvore do conhecimento simbolizava a onisciência divina.

A árvore do conhecimento do bem e do mal ensina para o homem, simbolicamente, que o ser humano não pode fazer arbitrariamente o que quiser, e nem pode estabelecer as normas do bem e do mal. No entanto, o ato de rebeldia pecaminosa de Adão, que arrastou toda a sua descendência, fez com que o homem se arrogasse à posição de modelo ou norma, como se ele tivesse autonomia moral (ver Isa. 5:20; Amós 5:14,15). Essa arrogante auto-suficiência é freqüentemente condenada nas Escrituras, mormente nos escritos proféticos (ver Eze. 28; Isa. 14:12 ss ; cf. Gên. 11), como a característica fundamental do pecado. Portanto, profundíssimo é o ensino de Gênesis, que ensina que esse equivocado senso de auto-suficiência é a raiz e a essência do pecado, ensino esse confirmado e reforçado em todos os demais livros da Bíblia.

Qual seria a árvore do conhecimento do bem e do mal? Popularmente tratar-se-ia da macieira, e a maçã simbolizaria o contato sexual. Mas isso é produto da fantasia maliciosa. As tradições judaicas pensavam na videira, na oliveira ou em uma espiga gigantesca, ao passo que os gregos pensavam na figueira. Na verdade, porém, as Escrituras não determinam a espécie da árvore. A idéia da macieira apareceu pela primeira vez entre escritores latinos, talvez devido a uma semelhança de palavras latinas (*malum* = o mal; *malus* = macieira). Se não fosse essa similaridade de palavras, no latim, não se teria vulgarizado a idéia da maçã, que é tão tola quanto outra tolice qualquer.

ÁRVORE OLEOSA Ver Óleo, Árvore de.

ÁRVORE VERDE DA TERRA NATAL

Essa árvore é a **Laurus nobilis**, também chamada loureiro. Trata-se de uma árvore de verde perene, que cresce até cerca de 9 m de altura, embora se conheça exemplares na Palestina com até o dobro dessa altura. Por esse motivo, a espécie pode ser chamada de árvore que se alça e se espalha, devido à grandeza de sua folhagem. Suas flores são pequenas, em branco esverdeado, e com pequenas bagas negras. As folhas são fragrantes, de cor verde escura, usadas como condimento de peixes cozidos. Os gregos empregavam os ramos para fazer coroas para militares e heróis do esporte. O trecho de Salmos 37:35 alude ao ímpio que, em seu orgulho e prepotência, expande qual cedro do Líbano. No tocante a um breve sumário de espécies de árvores encontradas na Palestina, ver sob *Árvores*. Algumas versões referem-se à árvore em questão como se fosse um cedro — como se dá com nossa versão portuguesa, que a chama de «cedro do Líbano» — mas o termo hebraico indica uma árvore *nativa* da Palestina, o que não acontece no caso do cedro.

ARZARETE

No hebraico, **outra terra**. Uma região além do rio Eufrates, para onde, alegadamente, os assírios levaram as dez tribos de Israel, após a destruição do reino do norte, e de onde eles haverão de retornar nos últimos dias (ver I Esdras 13:45). Porém, o texto hebraico diz *outra terra*, o que provavelmente não deve ser entendido como um nome próprio. (Z)

ASA

Há cinco palavras hebraicas traduzidas por «asa» e uma palavra grega, *ptéruks*. As palavras hebraicas consideram a asa sob vários pontos de vista. Um deles está baseado em sua aparência de arco, outro na força exercida pela asa, um baseado na idéia de cobertura e proteção, e o outro em suas penas; embora na maioria das vezes aponte para uma flor. Anatomicamente, as asas são para as aves o que os braços são para os homens (ver Gên. 1:21), embora as asas sejam usadas pelas aves como cobertura e locomoção, e não para efeito de destreza. E é por essa razão que o uso simbólico das asas difere totalmente do uso simbólico dos braços. O desejo da esperança é expresso como segue: «Quem me dera asas como de pomba! voaria, e acharia pouso» (Sal. 55:6). E a recuperação espiritual constante dos crentes é expressa por Isaías como segue: «...os que esperam no Senhor renovam as suas forças, sobem com asas como águias, correm e não se cansam, caminham e não se fatigam» (Isa. 40:31). E Moisés escreveu: «Como a águia desperta o seu ninho, adeja sobre os filhos e, estendendo as suas asas, toma-os, e os leva sobre as suas asas, assim só o Senhor o guiou...» (Deu. 32:11,12). Rute encontrou refúgio debaixo das asas do Senhor (ver Rute 2:12). E Jesus queria recolher os habitantes de Jerusalém sob Sua proteção, dizendo: «Jerusalém, Jerusalém! que matas os profetas e apedrejas os que te foram enviados! quantas vezes quis eu reunir os teus filhos, como a galinha ajunta os seus pintinhos debaixo das asas, e vós não o quisestes!» (Mat. 23:37).

As riquezas são simbolizadas pelas asas de pombas, cobertas de prata, mas a natureza passageira das riquezas é comparada com asas de águias (ver Pro. 23:5). Oséias assemelhou a pressa com que Efraim se entregou à prostituição espiritual a alguém transportado pelo vento, que tivesse arrebatado em suas asas (ver Osé. 4:19). Das mais belas, como inspiradora imagem poética, é a declaração de Malaquias 4:2: «Mas para vós outros que temeis o meu nome, nascerá o sol da justiça, trazendo salvação nas suas asas...» Essas palavras indicam a vitória final dos seguidores do Senhor sobre os perversos, no dia do Senhor. Portanto, o simbolismo envolvido nas asas é dos mais significativos que temos na Palavra de Deus. A própria sombra de uma asa sugere o refúgio que o crente encontra no Senhor, quando perseguido pelo ímpio (ver Sal. 17:8).

Diversas personagens simbólicas aparecem dotadas de asas, como as duas mulheres referidas em Zacarias 5:9; o leão com asas de águias, em Daniel 7:4; e a mulher de Apocalipse 12:14. Nos antigos monumentos as figuras de touros e leões aparecem aladas. Os serafins, referidos por Isaías, cobriam seus rostos com duas asas, como também os seus pés, e voavam com as outras duas, enquanto adoravam ao Senhor (ver Isa. 7:1-3). E em visão similar de Ezequiel (ver 10:5), havia criaturas aladas.

Visto que Jó, por sua própria sabedoria, não sabia fazer o falcão voar ou migrar para o sul, e nem fazer a águia subir para seu ninho, no alto da montanha, ele aprendeu a virtude da humildade e a aceitar sem queixa a disciplina do Senhor. Observações ornitológicas incomuns foram feitas pelos que esperavam pela pomba que trouxera de volta à arca a folha da oliveira, e pelos que observaram a grande águia com grandes asas de Ezequiel, que transportou a ponta de um cedro para outro local (ver Eze. 17:3).

O termo grego *ptéruks* aparece por cinco vezes no Novo Testamento: Mat. 23:37; Luc. 13:34; Apo. 4:8; 9:9 e 12:14.

ASA

Nas páginas do Antigo Testamento há dois homens com esse nome:

1. Um rei de Judá.

a. *Generalidades*. No hebraico significa *cura*, ou *médico*. Foi o terceiro rei de Judá, filho de Abias e neto de Reoboão. Começou a reinar dois anos antes da morte de Jeroboão, de Israel, e reinou durante 41 anos, cerca de 915-875 A.C. Visto que ainda era muito jovem quando subiu ao trono, os negócios do estado eram administrados por sua mãe ou avó, Maacá (ver I Reis 15:1,10), a qual aparece como neta de Absalão. Ela corrompeu a terra com a idolatria.

b. *Conduta religiosa*. Zelosamente, o jovem monarca desarraigou a idolatria, chegando ao extremo de depor Maacá, a rainha-mãe, por ter ela erigido um ídolo, ao qual Asa derrubou e queimou (ver I Reis 15:13). Não obstante, os santuários das colinas (ou dos lugares altos) puderam continuar (ver I Reis 15:11-13 e II Crô. 14:2-5). Asa renovou a adoração no templo, incluindo os ritos do altar, que aparentemente haviam sido execrados ou descontinuados (ver II Crô. 15:8).

c. *Suas guerras*. Asa utilizou todos os meios disponíveis para deixar o seu reino na melhor situação militar possível. Houve paz durante os primeiros dez anos de seu reinado, e ele foi aumentando a capacidade militar do país durante esse tempo. Finalmente, conseguiu reunir uma força militar de cerca de 580 mil homens (ver II Crô. 14:6-8). No décimo primeiro ano de seu governo, atacou e derrotou as numerosas hostes do rei cuxita Zerá, que havia penetrado, através da Arábia Petrea, no vale de Zefata com um poderoso exército. Ao retornarem os judeus triunfantes, carregados com os despojos tomados, o profeta Azarias saiu ao encontro deles e declarou que a vitória fora uma provisão divina.

d. *Reformas.* Encorajado por suas vitórias militares, além de todos os bens conseguidos nas mesmas, Asa aproveitou a oportunidade para eliminar os restos de idolatria que haviam sobrevivido a outros expurgos, levando o povo a renovar sua aliança com Yahweh (ver II Crô. 15:1-15). Portanto, Asa andou nos passos de seu antepassado, Davi (ver I Reis 15:11).

e. *Problemas e declínio.* No trigésimo sexto ano (alguns dizem vigésimo sexto) seu reinado, começaram as hostilidades contra Baasa, rei de Israel. Este fortificou Ramá, a fim de impedir que seus súditos passassem para o lado de Asa. Procurando confrontar essa ameaça com maior poder ainda, Asa resolveu estabelecer aliança com Ben-Hadade I, de Damasco, e conseguiu o seu apoio entregando-lhe os tesouros do templo e da casa do rei. Ben-Hadade cumpriu a sua parte no trato, invadindo e expulsando as tropas de Israel de Ramá. Asa utilizou os despojos para edificar Geba e Mispa com os mesmos. Porém, havia desperdiçado os tesouros de Judá, pelo que foi repreendido pelo profeta Hanani. Asa irritou-se diante da reprimenda, e lançou-o na prisão. Aparentemente, nessa controvérsia, outras pessoas puseram-se também ao lado do profeta, de tal modo que também foram maltratadas (ver I Reis 15:16-22 e II Crô. 16:1-10). Nos últimos três anos de sua vida, Asa foi afligido por uma grave enfermidade em seus pés (hidropisia); mas, endurecido pelos desapontamentos da vida, além de uma tola obstinação, ele não buscou a ajuda do Senhor, mas preferiu depender inteiramente dos médicos. A doença era fatal, e ele morreu, embora ainda grandemente estimado. Foi altamente honrado por ocasião de seu magnificente sepultamento (ver I Crô. 16:11-14). Seu filho, Josafá, substituiu-o no trono. Alguns estudiosos pensam que desde quatro anos antes, Josafá já era co-regente com seu pai. Asa e Josafá aparecem na genealogia de Jesus, em Mateus 1:7.

2. Asa, um levita, filho de Elcana, pai de Berequias, que posteriormente residiu em uma das vilas dos netofatitas, após o retorno da Babilônia (ver I Crô. 9:16), em cerca de 536 A.C. (ID S UN)

••• ••• •••

ASÃ

No hebraico, **fumaça.** Era uma cidade de Judá (ver Jos. 15:42). Ficava localizada a sudoeste da Sefelá (Neguebe). Eusébio afiança que, em sua época, Bete-Asã ficava a 26 km de Jerusalém, para oeste. No trecho de I Samuel 30:30, ela é chamada «Corasã», isto é, «fornalha de fumaça». E em I Crônicas 6:59 ela é considerada uma cidade sacerdotal. Em Josué 21:16, a palavra «Aim» aparece em lugar de Asã, cidade essa que não deve ser confundida com a Aim de Núm. 34:11. Essa cidade tem sido identificada com a moderna Khirbet 'Ashan, acerca de 8 km a noroeste de Bersheba. (ID UN)

ASAEL

No hebraico, **criatura de Deus.** Foi nome de várias pessoas no Antigo Testamento.

1. Filho da irmã de Davi, Zeruia, irmão de Joabe e Abisai. Tornou-se notável pela velocidade de sua corrida. Após a batalha que houve em Gibeom, ele perseguiu e alcançou Abner, o qual, com grande relutância, a fim de salvar a própria vida, matou-o com um golpe de lança, em cerca de 1055 A.C. (ver II Sam. 2:18,23; 3:27,30,33, 34; I Crô. 9:26 e 27:7). Foi um dos trinta mais valentes guerreiros de Davi, e comandou uma divisão de vinte e quatro mil homens do exército de Davi. Finalmente, Joabe matou Abner para vingar a morte de Asael (ver II Sam. 3:26).

Em I Crônicas 27:7 é declarado que Asael era o quarto dos capitães mensais de Davi. Mas Asael morreu antes de Davi tornar-se rei. Alguns vêem nisso uma flagrante contradição; mas outros explicam que Asael foi assim honrado postumamente, na pessoa de seu filho, Zebadias (ver I Crô. 27:7).

2. Um dos levitas (cerca de 909 A.C.) durante o reinado de Josafá, o qual instruiu o povo na lei de Moisés (ver II Crô. 17:8).

3. Um levita que supervisionava o templo durante o reinado de Ezequias, cuidando das ofertas (ver II Crô. 31:13), em cerca de 727 A.C.

4. Um sacerdote, pai de Jônatas, no tempo de Esdras (ver Esd. 10:15). Em I Esdras 9:14, ele é chamado Azael (cerca de 459 A.C.). Ajudou Esdras a exigir que os judeus se desfizessem de suas mulheres estrangeiras. (ID ND S)

ASAFE

No hebraico significa coletor ou recolhedor. Nome de várias pessoas do Antigo Testamento:

1. Um levita, filho de Baraquias (ver I Crô. 6:39 e 15:17). Um músico consumado, nomeado por Davi para presidir o coral sagrado organizado pelo rei. Os filhos de Asafe posteriormente são mencionados como coristas do templo (ver I Crô. 25:1; II Crô. 20:14; 29:14; Esd. 2:41; 3:10; Nee. 6:44 e 11:22). O ofício parece ter-se tornado hereditário (ver I Crô. 25:1,2). Asafe tornou-se célebre, em tempos posteriores, como profeta e poeta (ver II Crô. 29:30 e Nee. 12:4). Os títulos de doze dos Salmos trazem o seu nome (73 a 83 e 50). Devido à cronologia sugerida nos Salmos (nos tempos de Davi, mas posteriormente no tempo do exílio para a Babilônia), alguns estudiosos pensam que houve dois Asafes envolvidos: o primeiro, da época de Davi, teria composto os Salmos 50, 73, 76 e 78, e talvez 75 e 82, e o segundo, os Salmos 74, 79 e 83, que refletem as condições do exílio. Nesse caso, os dois homens pertenceriam à mesma família.

2. Asafe, pai do cronista Joá, dos dias de Ezequias (ver II Reis 18:18; Isa. 36:3,22).

3. Um oficial de Artaxerxes Longimano, da Pérsia (465-445 A.C.). Era ele quem tomava conta das florestas do rei na Palestina (ver Nee. 2:8).

4. Asafe, em I Crô. 26:1, conforme se lê em algumas versões, como a nossa versão portuguesa, constitui um erro escribal. A verdadeira forma do nome é Ebiasafe (ver I Crô. 9:19), segundo se vê também em nossa versão portuguesa.

5. Asafe, em Mateus 1:7, corresponde à melhor variante no original grego, em lugar de Asa, na genealogia de Jesus. Contudo, no Antigo Testamento encontramos *Asa* (ver o artigo a respeito). Foi o terceiro rei de Judá. (ID S UN)

ASAÍAS

No hebraico, **realizador**, ou, então, **Yahweh fez**. Nome de várias pessoas relacionadas à narrativa do Antigo Testamento:

1. Uma das pessoas enviadas pelo rei Josias para consultar a profetisa Hulda, acerca do livro da lei, encontrado no templo (ver II Reis 22:14). Ver também II Crônicas 34:20.
2. Um dos principais líderes da tribo de Simeão, que expulsaram os pastores camitas de Gedor (ver I Crô. 4:36,39).
3. Um levita durante o reinado de Davi (ver I Crô. 6:30), o qual, com cento e vinte de seus irmãos, trouxe a arca para a cidade de Davi, em cerca de 1033 A.C. (ver I Crô. 15:6,11).
4. Um dos silonitas que retornou do cativeiro babilônico a fim de habitar em Jerusalém (ver I Crô. 9:5). Em Neemias 11:5 ele é chamado Maaséias. Cerca de 536 A.C. (ID ND)

ASANA

Vem do sânscrito, com o sentido de «sentar-se». Na ioga (ver o artigo) e em outros sistemas filosóficos hindus, a ênfase sobre a postura do corpo é uma das condições para o progresso espiritual.

ASARA

Cabeça de uma família que servia no templo, e que retornou juntamente com Zorobabel do cativeiro babilônico (ver I Esdras 5:31). Nas listas paralelas de Esd. 2:49 e Nee. 7:51, esse nome é omitido.

ASARAMEL

Nome encontrado em uma inscrição feita em memória de Simão, da família dos Macabeus (ver I Macabeus 14:28). Alguns, porém, entendem que se trata do nome de uma localidade, e não de um indivíduo ou de uma família. Pode estar relacionado à *corte* do povo ou ao *príncipe* do povo. Se a segunda alternativa é a correta, então talvez fosse um título aplicado a Simão. (Z)

ASAREEL

No hebraico quer dizer *reto de Deus* ou *preso por Yahweh*. Era filho de Jealelel, da tribo de Judá (ver I Crô. 4:16), em cerca de 1618 A.C. (S)

ASARELA

No hebraico, **Yahweh está unido**, era um dos filhos de Asafe, separado por Davi a fim de profetizar (ver I Crô. 25:2). No décimo quarto versículo desse mesmo capítulo ele é chamado Jesarela.

ASAT

Vem do sânscrito com o sentido de «não-ser», o contrário de *sat*, «ser». Uma teoria de origens, segundo a qual o ser originou-se do não-ser, que retrocede aos tempos védicos.

ASBÉIA

No hebraico, **conjuração**. Um nome pessoal ou de um lugar (ver I Crô. 4:21), cerca de 1400 A.C. Talvez se aplique aos trabalhadores em linho, embora algumas versões apliquem o nome ao lugar onde eles viviam. Seja como for, nada se sabe sobre esse lugar ou sobre essas pessoas. (S Z)

ASBEL

No hebraico, **homem de Baal**. Um dos filhos de Benjamim (ver Gên. 46:21; Núm. 26:38; I Crô. 8:1), cerca de 1856 A.C. Foi o progenitor da família denominada asbelitas. (UN)

ASCENSÃO DE CRISTO

I. Texto Principal, Atos 1:6-11

Esta breve seção é uma das mais importantes de todo o livro de Atos, porquanto registra a doutrina cardeal cristã da ascensão de Cristo. Esta seção é a principal fonte informativa sobre esse acontecimento fundamental da fé cristã. O evangelho de Lucas encerra essa mesma narrativa, posto que em forma abreviada (ver Luc. 24:50,51), embora essa narrativa contenha importantes variantes textuais, no texto *ocidental*, e que alguns consideram como representantes do evangelho original de Lucas, nesse ponto. Essas variantes poderiam talvez eliminar a narrativa da ascensão de Cristo do evangelho de Lucas, isto é, fazer com que o mesmo não a registre, sendo mesmo possível que escribas posteriores tenham modificado o texto por um par de breves adições, fazendo-o narrar a história da ascensão, ainda que em forma abreviada. A posição assumida por esta enciclopédia, a respeito, é que mesmo sem as breves adições que tendem por tornar mais clara a narrativa, essa seção do evangelho de Lucas tem por intuito registrar a história da ascensão, ainda que sob forma abreviada. Porém, mesmo que o evangelho de Lucas não preserve genuinamente essa tradição histórica para nós, o autor sagrado em sua obra em dois volumes — a história contada em Lucas-Atos, nesta seção do livro de Atos (a segunda parte dessa história), preservou enfaticamente esse acontecimento para nós.

O evangelho de Marcos contém também a história da ascensão de Cristo, ainda que o faça no duvidoso *longo final*, e que a maioria dos eruditos sobre as questões textuais acredita ser secundário, não fazendo parte do evangelho original de Marcos. Nesse caso, a história da ascensão foi registrada por um «quinto» evangelista, talvez Aristíom, um dos primeiros discípulos de Jesus, conforme declaração de um manuscrito armênio do séc. IX D.C. Porém, quanto a isso não há meios para obtermos a certeza. (Quanto ao problema inteiro do final do evangelho de Marcos, a saber, os versículos nono a vigésimo, ver no NTI as notas expositivas em Atos 1:9, que abordam com amplitude o problema, exibindo evidências em prol dos quatro finais diferentes do evangelho de Marcos, conforme os manuscritos existentes hoje em dia).

O evangelho de Mateus não conta a história da ascensão do Senhor, e isso pode sugerir que o evangelho original de Marcos, que foi empregado como esboço histórico básico e material informativo usado tanto pelo autor do evangelho de Mateus como pelo autor do evangelho de Lucas, não continha essa narrativa. Não obstante, o evangelho de Mateus contém alusões ao fato da ascensão de Cristo, segundo se observa em trechos como Mat. 22:44; 24:30; 25:14,31 e 26:64. Isso nos mostra que o autor sagrado conhecia tal tradição histórica.

O evangelho de João não tece qualquer comentário à narrativa da ascensão do Senhor, embora exista certo número de alusões ao fato nesse quarto evangelho, pelo que também é evidente que a tradição era bem conhecida pelo autor sagrado, apesar de que

ASCENSÃO DE CRISTO

não lhe deve ter parecido ser necessário registrar a própria ocorrência.

Nenhum dos quatro evangelhos indica a existência de qualquer intervalo entre a ressurreição e a ascensão do Senhor; e por esse motivo, alguns eruditos têm pensado que uma antiga tradição da ascensão dizia que a mesma ocorrera no mesmo dia da ressurreição de Cristo. João, entretanto, dá a entender que Jesus apareceu durante alguns dias aos seus discípulos, antes de sua ascensão, pois a sua aparição a Tomé é apresentada como ocorrência que teve lugar uma semana após o domingo da ressurreição. E, apesar de que João não fornece qualquer cronologia desses acontecimentos, podemos supor com segurança, com base nessa informação, que o autor do quarto evangelho considerava que a ascensão ocorreu após se terem passado alguns dias depois da ressurreição de Cristo, e não no mesmo dia.

II. Fatos a Considerar

1. O evangelho de Lucas não indica ter havido qualquer intervalo de tempo entre a ressurreição e a ascensão de Jesus. A narrativa lucana, em dois volumes, adia essa distinção para o primeiro capítulo do livro de Atos.

2. A ascensão de Jesus não é formalmente registrada em todo o resto do N.T., embora haja alusões indiretas a ela em muitos lugares, ou sua realidade fique subentendida. Em João 20:17 no NTI, há uma nota sobre como o quarto evangelho trata do assunto. Ver referências a essa doutrina nos trechos seguintes: Mat. 22:44; 24:30; 25:14,31 e 26:64; Atos 2:33,34; 3:21; Efé. 4:8-10; I Tes. 1:10; Heb. 4:14; 9:24; I Ped. 3:22 e Apo. 5:6. Há passagens na epístola aos Hebreus, que aceitam tacitamente a realidade da ascensão, com um subseqüente ministério nos céus: Heb. 4:14 e 9:24.

3. Nas páginas do N.T., a ascensão faz parte integral da glorificação de Cristo e do começo de seu ministério celeste.

4. É impossível falar-se da «ausência» desse ensino em outros livros, à parte dos dois livros de Lucas, pois, segundo já se disse, há muitas alusões «ao fato e ao significado» desse evento. Todavia, há ausência de descrições históricas fora dos escritos de Lucas. Isso tem provocado muitas dúvidas e indagações, sobretudo por parte dos intérpretes mais liberais. Os mais radicais entre eles, negam a realidade da ascensão de Jesus como um acontecimento objetivo. Seguindo damos as diversas interpretações a respeito. Essas notas incluem idéias atinentes a como ocorreu esse acontecimento.

III. Diversas Interpretações

1. *A interpretação de que houve fraude.* Segundo essa posição, os apóstolos e os primeiros cristãos teriam inventado essa história a fim de explicarem a ausência de Jesus—se de alguma maneira ele sobreviveu à cruz, mais tarde deve ter perecido por causa de seus efeitos, ou simplesmente se ausentou do país. Ora, os cristãos teriam sido forçados a explicar essa ausência, e assim inventaram a história da ascensão, apesar de saberem-na perfeitamente falsa. Resposta: Não é possível pensarmos que homens que propositalmente inventaram uma fraude, em anos subseqüentes tivessem despendido tantas energias e, finalmente, tivessem morrido em defesa daquilo que desde o princípio sabiam ser falso. Se aquilo que diziam fosse fraudulento, muito mais provavelmente teriam abandonado toda a idéia de uma nova religião, morrendo de morte natural, retornando às suas profissões anteriores, desapontados,—embora talvez considerando-se mais sábios por motivo da amarga experiência.

2. *Interpretação Mitológica.* A história da ascensão de Cristo ter-se-ia desenvolvido como um dos muitos mitos e lendas que foram criados em torno da pessoa de Jesus Cristo; e os seus discípulos originais, pelo menos, não teriam ensinado tal doutrina. Mas isso não é confirmado pelo fato de que os seus primeiros discípulos, incluindo o apóstolo Pedro, o mais primitivo de todos eles, se aferrou tenazmente a essa verdade. (Ver I Tes. 1:10 e I Ped. 3:22). O próprio livro de Atos e o evangelho de Lucas, baseados nas fontes informativas mais remotas possíveis, porquanto Lucas foi companheiro dos apóstolos originais, abordam essa questão sem rebuços, mas antes, diretamente.

3. *Interpretação simbólica.* A narrativa da ascensão de Cristo, segundo é contada nas páginas do N.T., não teria sido escrita com o intuito de narrar um fato literal, mas tão-somente para servir de símbolo de uma fé religiosa. Essa fé encararia a existência de Cristo como algo em continuação, talvez em alguma região celeste, pelo que seria dito que ele «ascendeu» aos céus, embora não sejamos obrigados a vincular a doutrina a qualquer acontecimento literal, que teria sido realmente contemplado pelos primeiros seguidores de Jesus. Porém, apesar de ser verdade que as verdades religiosas possam ser contidas na forma de símbolos, e a verdade de Deus, que é a verdade espiritual, não precisa de qualquer acompanhamento de acontecimentos históricos para ser verdadeira, porquanto a verdade divina é superior e separada dos acontecimentos históricos; é com base nas próprias narrativas do evento que nos compete contemplar alguma forma de ocorrência histórica real. A vida extraordinária de Jesus, a sua vida magnificente, a sua evidente ressurreição, vista e testemunhada por tantas pessoas, são características que poderíamos esperar de sua pessoa. E a ascensão do Senhor, embora velada por algum mistério, não obstante é outro acontecimento histórico que caracteriza a grandeza de sua pessoa.

4. *A interpretação que postula uma fraude inocente.* Jesus, após a sua ressurreição, de alguma maneira desapareceu, retirando-se para algum lugar. Os seus discípulos, ato contínuo, inventaram a história que melhor explicaria o que aconteceu a Jesus, segundo as suas mentes. Teria sido uma invenção inocente, posto que deliberada, sendo uma fraude não perpetrada com um espírito malicioso.

5. Há uma *variação* dessa interpretação que diz que apesar dos discípulos terem inventado a história, por não terem recebido qualquer prova concreta que a consubstanciasse, realmente *criam sinceramente* que Jesus subira aos céus, pensando ser essa a melhor explicação possível para o seu desaparecimento do meio dos homens. Poder-se-ia ilustrar isso com a «ascensão» de Elias, porquanto tal narrativa teria dado aos discípulos de Cristo o precedente do A.T. para a formação de tal conjectura. Porém, contrariamente a essas duas últimas interpretações, precisamos adiantar que os seguidores primitivos do Senhor Jesus certamente eram inteligentes e astutos o bastante para não criarem uma história de proporções tão gigantescas, que só poderia ser aceita pelos seus ouvintes com a maior dificuldade, e que inventaram tal fraude somente para justificar a ausência corporal de Jesus. O mais certo é que tais explicações não seriam suficientemente satisfatórias para justificar a perda das vidas, como sucedeu no caso de grande parte dos discípulos de Cristo, os quais, em muitos

NASCER DO SOL NO DIA DA RESSURREIÇÃO

G. Puermann.

A ASCENSÃO DE JESUS

casos, sofreram desmedidas agonias, em defesa de um sistema que teria sido inventado desde os seus princípios mais básicos.

6. *A interpretação mística*. O que os apóstolos teriam visto não foi a realidade palpável, mas tão-somente uma *visão* dada a eles por meio do Espírito Santo, de conformidade com a vontade de Deus, com o propósito de mostrar-lhes que Jesus fora conduzido à presença de Deus Pai, e continuava existente em uma forma altamente elevada. Em outras palavras, teriam tido uma experiência mística, isto é, receberam alguma mensagem genuína, que lhes foi dada na forma de visão. Provavelmente há nessa interpretação pelo menos, uma verdade parcial, porquanto tanto a ressurreição como a ascensão de Cristo parecem ter envolvido elementos místicos; porém quando genuína, a experiência mística é real, deixando entendido que algo mais do que o que é físico invadiu a experiência humana. Nas experiências místicas, Deus pode revelar-se de alguma maneira especial ao homem, em termos compreensíveis para este, embora as próprias experiências ultrapassem totalmente a qualquer coisa que possa ser definida em termos terrenos e físicos, pelo que também permanece essencialmente impossível transmitir a natureza real do que teve lugar, embora possamos transmitir aos outros a natureza aparente do ocorrido.

7. *A interpretação histórica*. Essa é a posição que assevera que a ascensão do Senhor Jesus foi um acontecimento histórico, literal, que ocorreu na presença dos seus discípulos, quando ele subiu espacialmente nos ares. Mas isso de forma alguma significa que sabemos qualquer coisa sobre a localização dos lugares celestiais, ou que *acima* significa qualquer coisa exceto que os céus estão em algum lugar fora de nosso planeta, considerados como a habitação de seres celestiais muito superiores a nós. Não se há de duvidar que os escritores do N.T. esperavam que pensássemos na ascensão do Senhor sob esses termos, ou, pelo menos, sob termos similares.

É muito provável que a verdade da questão seja uma mistura das posições sexta e sétima. A ascensão teria sido uma ocorrência histórica, tendo acontecido em determinado dia, e de certa maneira, apesar de também possuir elementos místicos. Ora, isso é apenas natural esperarmos, porque Jesus, em sua ressurreição, já pertencia a *uma ordem diferente* e mais elevada de ser. Ele não permaneceu na companhia constante de seus discípulos, durante o intervalo de quarenta dias que houve entre a sua ressurreição e a sua ascensão e é perfeitamente possível que ele viesse de alguma *dimensão diferente* para fazer essas suas visitas, embora, provavelmente, essa dimensão ainda não fosse a presença de Deus Pai, para onde ele ainda não havia subido. Sobre todos esses mistérios, entretanto, nada podemos definir com certeza; mas, pelo menos, é certo que Cristo, uma vez ressurrecto, já pertencia ao mundo celestial, já se encontrava em uma condição transformada, embora essa condição tenha sido grandemente transformada quando de sua ascensão aos céus.

IV. A ascensão no Evangelho de João

Ora, ninguém subiu ao céu, senão o que desceu do céu, o Filho do homem. — João 3:13.

O evangelho de João não contém a narrativa da ascensão de Jesus, que em si mesma é uma curiosidade, embora esse acontecimento fosse bem conhecido no ensino e na tradição cristã. Contudo, contém referências ou alusões àquele evento, como a este outro, diante de nós. O Filho do homem é o correto mestre das elevadas e místicas doutrinas, porquanto havia tanto descido como subido ao céu. Sabia o que sabia mediante contato especial e observação pessoal. Naturalmente, o apóstolo João pensava aqui sobre o *Logos* encarnado, acerca de quem ele explicara tão amplamente, no primeiro capítulo de seu evangelho. Esse «Logos» é o intérprete de Deus, conforme também nos diz o trecho de João 1:1,18. Por conseguinte, Jesus é o revelador dos mistérios; mas Jesus lamenta o fato de que tão poucos indivíduos tenham o *coração aberto* para tão exaltadas questões, já que encontravam tão insuperáveis dificuldades em compreender até mesmo as questões espirituais mais «terrenas».

Parece haver aqui uma referência definida à passagem de Prov. 30:4, onde se lê: *«Quem subiu ao céu e desceu? Quem encerrou os ventos nos seus punhos?* Quem amarrou as águas na sua roupa? Quem estabeleceu todas as extremidades da terra? Qual é o seu nome, e qual é o nome de seu filho, se é que o sabes? Aqui, pois, encontramos alusões ao revelador dos mistérios e àquele que estabelece os limites do firmamento. O Filho do homem, o Messias, que é o Filho de Deus, é justamente quem possui essa autoridade, e, por isso mesmo, compete-nos dar-lhe ouvidos, e à mensagem de redenção que ele veio anunciar. Era isso que Nicodemos, até aquele momento, não estava disposto a fazer, embora o tenha feito mais tarde; mas o seu exemplo não foi seguido pelos membros do sinédrio e nem pela nação de Israel em geral, e esse pensamento sem dúvida brilhava na mente do autor sagrado, quando ele registrou essas palavras. O que o autor sagrado faz aqui, portanto, é voltar às grandiosidades do primeiro capítulo, em sua descrição sobre o «Logos», fazendo referência tão especial ao vs. 18 desse primeiro capítulo, que fala especificamente do fato de ser ele o grande revelador dos conselhos de Deus.

A questão da ascensão de Cristo é usada como símbolo de seu conhecimento imediato e intuitivo sobre as coisas celestiais. E Cristo possui essa forma de conhecimento por ser um *personagem celestial*, e, na qualidade do «Logos», por ter observado, em primeira mão, todos os mistérios de Deus. E assim, na forma de Filho do homem, andando entre os homens, continuava sendo homem vindo dos céus, e continuava trazendo consigo mesmo o conhecimento de alguém que subira ao céu, e de fato, de alguém que continuava habitando no céu, embora estivesse com os pés na terra.

Essa linguagem elevadamente *mística* tem sido usada como prova contrária à autenticidade dessas palavras de Jesus, posto que vemos tão pouco da mesma nos evangelhos sinópticos. Alguns eruditos preferem acreditar que tal linguagem saiu tão-somente da pena do autor sagrado, quando ele começou a meditar sobre as maravilhas da redenção humana. Porém, não há razão alguma para supormos que o autor sagrado tivesse falado palavras de mais profunda exaltação que o próprio Jesus, embora as expressões distintas, das idéias e das palavras de Jesus, possam ter sido adaptadas pela mentalidade e pelo estilo do autor. Não obstante, o sentido permaneceria o mesmo, e isso é demonstrado como verdadeiro pelo fato de que a cristologia apresentada em outros trechos do N.T. (até mesmo nos evangelhos sinópticos) na realidade não difere grandemente do que lemos aqui. A cristologia de Paulo é especialmente similar, e nisso também se destaca o primeiro capítulo da epístola aos Hebreus. Não é provável,

ASCENSÃO DE CRISTO — ASCENSÃO DE ISAÍAS

portanto, que essas palavras tenham sido da lavra independente do autor sagrado, isto é, do autor do evangelho de João.

Que está no céu. Essas palavras se encontram nos mss. A, Theta, Fam 1, Fam 13, na maioria das versões latinas, e no SI(cp), bem como na maioria dos manuscritos gregos posteriores, da tradição bizantina. Entretanto, os mss. P(66), P(75), Aleph, B e W, além das citações de Orígenes, não trazem essa adição. Isso é uma evidência esmagadora contra a autenticidade dessas palavras, e as identifica como glosa feita por algum escriba posterior. Certo número de traduções modernas, entretanto, prefere deixá-las de fora, tais como as traduções IB, GD, RSV e WM. Outras traduções assinalam-nas como de autoridade duvidosa, tal como a tradução AA, em algumas de suas edições.

Mas, a despeito dessas palavras não serem autênticas, o sentido das mesmas fica subentendido dentro do próprio versículo em pauta. Elas significam algo como, embora habitando sobre a terra, contudo o céu estava inteiramente ao seu derredor, em virtude de sua comunhão íntima com Deus Pai. Outrossim, na qualidade de «Logos» eterno, a mente de Jesus continuava *em contato* com a realidade última, e por essa mesma razão, devido a essa comunicação, podia ele afirmar que se encontrava permanentemente no céu, apesar de fisicamente estar sobre a terra. Essa é uma doutrina joanina de alto naipe, e fica implícita no versículo, sem ou com o acréscimo em foco; e o que fica implicado nessa idéia é, provavelmente, o fator causal por detrás do fato de que o escriba posterior acrescentou tais palavras à sentença que expressa exatamente essa idéia. A passagem de João 1:18 expressa o mesmo sentido. Portanto, tais palavras expressam uma *condição de ser*, e não uma localidade.

V. Significado da Ascensão

1. A ascensão explica a **ausência** de Jesus deste mundo. Cristo saiu vivo do sepulcro, para nunca mais morrer. Em certo ponto do tempo, deixou de ser visto entre os homens. Fizera a sua transição para os lugares celestiais, tendo atravessado todas as dimensões inferiores e tendo entrado na augusta e santíssima presença de Deus Pai. Essa transição foi produzida pela sua ascensão até o Pai.

2. A ascensão significou para Cristo uma *maior transformação e glorificação*, não somente no que dizia respeito à sua posição, mas também no tocante à real transformação de seu próprio ser. Tornou-se um ser ainda mais espiritualizado, passando a pertencer a uma ordem de ser ainda mais elevada, o primeiro homem-divino-imortal, o «Logos» eterno em uma nova forma. (Ver Efé. 1:20-23).

3. A ascensão foi — *uma prova a mais* — de suas reivindicações messiânicas, porquanto somente o grande Messias, que era também o «Logos» eterno, poderia ter entrado assim até à própria presença de Deus Pai, tendo dele recebido essa exaltação. (Quanto ao tema da polêmica cristã que demonstra o ofício messiânico de Jesus, do que a ascensão aos lugares celestiais foi mais uma prova, ver as notas expositivas referentes a João 7:45 no NTI que apresentam um sumário dessa doutrina).

4. A ascensão assinalou a *inauguração do ofício* de Cristo como nosso mediador, segundo a ênfase dada pelo oitavo capítulo da epístola aos Romanos. (Ver igualmente Heb. 9:24). Esse ofício também faz parte da obra de redenção dos homens, porquanto Deus haverá de completar essa redenção, transformando totalmente os remidos, e o Senhor Jesus está prestando o seu concurso nesse labor, mediante a sua presença e as suas ações intercessórias nos lugares celestiais.

5. A ascensão era necessária como *condição da vinda* e do dom do Espírito Santo, porquanto o Espírito de Deus veio como «alter ego» de Jesus Cristo; não poderia ter dado início ao seu ofício e ao seu serviço entre os homens enquanto o Senhor Jesus não subisse a Deus Pai. Sobre esse tema, ver notas expositivas em João 16:6 no NTI.

6. A ascensão do Senhor à presença de Deus Pai é a *garantia* de nossa participação na mesma realidade espiritual, tal como a sua ressurreição é garantia de nossa participação em sua vida ressurrecta. Mediante a ascensão, o Senhor Jesus foi ainda mais intensamente glorificado, tendo sido elevado aos lugares celestiais. Quanto a nós, haveremos de participar de todas essas coisas dirigindo-nos, finalmente, para os lugares celestiais onde ele entrou como nosso precursor, ocasião em que participaremos da mesma transformação e da mesma vida que ele desfruta atualmente. Essa é exatamente a mensagem dos trechos bíblicos como Efé. 1:19-23; II Cor. 3:18 e Col. 2:8,9. Em todos os pontos, pois, seremos identificados com ele, porque ele é o cabeça de todas as coisas, preenche a tudo, e nós somos o seu corpo, e o completamos.

7. Por motivo da sua ascensão, isto é, através dos seus resultados, que lhe exaltaram a pessoa, e por causa do fato de que a sua missão terrena foi completada de maneira perfeita, o Senhor Jesus agora aguarda a *subjugação total* de todos os seus inimigos. E isso ele merece porque, acima de todos os seus companheiros, ele foi obediente e realizou perfeitamente a sua tarefa cósmica que lhe fora determinada. (Ver Heb. 1:9,13 e I Cor. 15:24-26).

8. A ascensão de Cristo foi a *grande evidência* da aprovação final de Deus Pai à sua missão terrena perfeitamente completada, na qual ele trouxe redenção perfeita aos homens. Deus aprovou isso, aceitou a sua obra, aplicou a sua obra e continua a aplicá-la e tudo isso Deus Pai demonstrou elevando a Jesus Cristo, àquele lugar que lhe pertence por direito, à sua mão direita. (Ver Heb. 10:11-14).

Tipos simbólicos da ascensão de Cristo podem ser vistos no A.T., como nas pessoas de Enoque (ver Gên. 5:24), José (ver Gên. 41:43), Moisés (ver Êxo. 19:3), Aarão (ver Lev. 16:3) e Elias (ver II Reis 2:11). (I IB LAK LE NTI)

ASCENSÃO DE ISAÍAS

Esse título foi aposto ao livro que Orígenes chamava de *O Apócrifo de Isaías*, desde os dias de Epifânio (Panar. x1.2). Também era conhecido como *O Testamento de Ezequias* ou *A Visão de Isaías*, que se aplica mais corretamente a certos segmentos do livro. Vários pais da Igreja mencionaram a obra, pelo que era conhecido na Igreja antiga. R. Laurence trouxe-o à atenção de leitores modernos quando publicou um manuscrito etíope do mesmo, E(1), como uma porção desse livro.

Aparentemente, a obra é uma compilação de várias obras mais antigas, mas cuja data de composição é o terceiro ou o quarto século D.C. A porção mais antiga, chamada *Martírio de Isaías*, evidentemente pertence ao século I A.C. Ver abaixo sobre *Unidade*.

1. *Manuscritos.* a. Em grego: G(1), do século III D.C., mas atualmente perdido. A versão etíope e uma versão latina descendem desse texto. G(2), apenas na forma de fragmentos, pertencentes aos séculos V e VI

ASCENSÃO DE ISAÍAS — ASCENSÕES DE TIAGO

D.C. O Papiro Amherst I, em fragmentos. b. Em etíope: Uma reprodução da versão grega, e o único texto completo existente, representado por três manuscritos. c. Em latim: l(1), contendo ii.14 - iii.13; vii.1-29, do século VI D.C. L(2), que contém a maior parte da Visão de Isaías, vi.1 - xi.19; xi.23-40. d. Em eslavônico, que aparentemente segue o G(2) e contém a Visão de Isaías. e. Em cóptico: fragmentos do Martírio e da Visão. A obra original era em grego.

2. *Data*. Como obra composta, não antes do século II A.C., e mais provavelmente do século III D.C., embora o Martírio possa ser do século I A.C. A visão parece pertencer ao ano 100 D.C., à qual foi acrescentada a história da ascensão, do século II D.C. O Martírio era conhecido pelos pais da Igreja Justino Mártir (*Dial. c. Trypho*, cxx.14,15), Tertuliano, Orígenes, Jerônimo. Portanto, pelo menos esse segmento da obra é bastante antigo.

3. *Autoria*. Sendo obra composta, vários autores estão envolvidos, não havendo como nos mostrarmos específicos. Porém, o Martírio parece ser de origem puramente judaica, ao passo que o Testamento de Ezequias e a Visão parecem ser de origem cristã. Mas alguns estudiosos supõem que a obra total é cristã, com um óbvio pano de fundo judaico. A questão ainda não está resolvida.

4. *Unidade*. Há muitas teorias a esse respeito, pelo que nada de certo pode ser dito que não esteja sujeito a objeções. Tem sido defendida até mesmo a unidade do livro. Porém, alguns eruditos vêem a obra como um livro composto. Abaixo damos uma sugestão (ver a bibliografia): a. Uma porção judaica, o Martírio de Isaías, do século I A.C. b. A isso foi adicionada uma porção cristã, a Visão de Isaías 3:13 - 4:18, com data de 100 D.C. e então foi adicionada a ascensão visionária de Isaías (6:11), com data do século II D.C., ou mesmo mais tarde. Alguns eruditos passam então a dividir esses segmentos em porções menores, supondo que também teriam sido compilações.

5. *Conteúdo*:

a. *O Martírio de Isaías* i.1 - iii.13a, v. 1-14. Temos aqui uma exposição sermônica da Midrash de II Reis 21:16. Isaías profetizou sobre eventos do reinado de Manassés, incluindo o seu próprio martírio. Manassés seguia a Beliar, possuído por Samael (Satanás); após a morte de Ezequias, levou o povo judeu a tornar-se idólatra. Isaías fugiu, mas Belquita, o falso profeta, deteve-o e trouxe-o à presença de Manassés. Isaías profetiza a destruição de Jerusalém, apelidando-a de Sodoma, e seus governantes de gomorritas (iii.1-12). Belquita tenta fazer Isaías retratar-se e ficar livre, mas Isaías recusa-se a isso e é martirizado, sendo serrado ao meio. Parece que foi a esse evento que Justino se referiu, como também Tertuliano e o Talmude (*Yeb*. 49b, *Sanh*. 10). O livro de IV Baruque menciona o martírio de Isaías, como também o fez Orígenes.

b. *O Testamento de Ezequias* iii.13b - iv.18. Nesse segmento, Isaías tem uma visão, na qual fala sobre a descida do Amado (o Messias) desde o sétimo céu. Ele conta a história de Ezequias. o que explica o título dessa porção. A encarnação, o ministério terreno, a crucificação, a ressurreição e a ascensão do Messias são descritos. Em seguida há pormenores sobre a era da Igreja, com o aparecimento de líderes indignos, que ignoram os profetas do Antigo Testamento, conforme realmente sucedeu no gnosticismo. Beliar mescla-se com a realeza e, em Nero reencarnado, torna-se culpado de matricídio (Roma é destruída). Beliar imita a Cristo, realizando milagres. Estabelece uma imagem de si mesmo, a fim de ser adorado, e o seu reinado perdura por três anos, sete meses e vinte e sete dias, pois a informação tira proveito do trecho de Daniel 12:12. O Senhor vem com Seus exércitos e derrota Beliar e suas hordas. É inaugurado o reino messiânico, e os que participarem da primeira ressurreição obterão os benefícios do mesmo; mas então vem uma segunda ressurreição, e o julgamento dos ímpios no fogo. Essa porção, naturalmente, assemelha-se ao vigésimo capítulo do Apocalipse, juntamente com as passagens que falam sobre o Nero redivivo (ver Apo. 17:8 ss).

c. *A Visão de Isaías* vi.1 - xi.40. Nesse ponto há um conteúdo bem mais gnóstico. Isaías é conduzido ao sétimo céu, habitação de Deus, de Cristo, do Espírito Santo e dos justos mortos, em seus corpos espirituais. Por baixo do mesmo está o firmamento onde Samael (Satanás) habita, o qual governa o mundo físico e os seres deste mundo e onde o princípio do mal habita no corpo, refletindo uma idéia gnóstica. A visão expõe um ponto de vista docético (ver sobre o *docetismo*) do nascimento de Cristo (sem trabalho de parto, após apenas dois meses de gravidez). Cristo realiza milagres; Sua morte é provocada por Beliar; Ele desce ao hades (um paralelo da história de I Ped. 3:18 - 4:6; o que demonstra que os cristãos da época conheciam e aceitavam essa doutrina; ver sobre a *Descida de Cristo ao Hades*). Em seguida vem a ressurreição, uma permanência de 545 dias na terra (uma idéia gnóstica) e a comissão entregue aos doze apóstolos. Então Cristo ascende ao sétimo céu e senta-se à mão direita de Deus, com o Espírito Santo à esquerda. Essa visão torna-se a causa da execução de Isaías, a mando de Manassés. A Visão tem muitas similaridades com as noções gnósticas, talvez da variedade orfita (Iren. 1,30). (BO BUR HCAR J Z)

ASCENSÕES DE TIAGO

Esse era um documento mencionado em conexão com os ebionitas, por parte de Epifânio (ver Pan. 30:16). De acordo com ele, nessa obra Tiago manifestou-se contra os sacrifícios no templo e contra o fogo do altar. O livro também mostra-se violentamente hostil a Paulo. Lançando mão do trecho de Atos 21:29, os ebionitas (ver o artigo sobre ele), afirmavam que Paulo era grego, filho de pais gregos, e que, estando ele em Jerusalém, queria casar-se com a filha do sumo sacerdote. A fim de tentar chegar a isso, ele tornou-se um prosélito e submeteu-se à circuncisão. Porém, ao perceber que não conseguiria obtê-la como esposa, irou-se e ficou amargurado, tendo escrito contra a circuncisão, o sábado, a lei, etc. Esse tipo de apresentação de Tiago e Paulo é similar àquela contida nas pseudoclementinas, especialmente nos capítulos finais do primeiro livro dos *Reconhecimentos*.

Alguns eruditos, por esse motivo, supõem que esteja envolvido um arquétipo comum. Eusébio, citando Hegesipo (*Hist.* II.xxiii.3-18), expõe material semelhante. É possível que Hegesipo se tenha utilizado do grande final das Ascensões de Tiago em seus comentários, conforme alguns eruditos têm sugerido. Nesse caso, as primeiras porções dessa mesma obra são aquelas que também conhecemos no livro dos *Reconhecimentos*. Não há certeza quanto à razão pela qual esse livro é chamado «Ascensões», embora talvez isso se deva ao fato de que Tiago, por muitas vezes, subiu os degraus do templo, a fim de discursar ao povo. É possível que haja alguma ligação entre essa obra e o livro ebionita atualmente perdido, *Livro de Atos*. (Z)

ASCETISMO

Vem do grego **askesis**, «exercício», «prática», «treinamento». Algumas vezes era usado com o sentido de exercícios de *autonegação*, de uma ou de outra forma. Os filósofos gregos aplicavam o termo à disciplina moral. Geralmente a palavra era usada para aludir aos exercícios e disciplina dos atletas, sendo natural que a idéia fosse metaforicamente aplicada aos atletas espirituais.

O *ascetismo* tem desempenhado um importante papel dentro da fé religiosa do Oriente e do Ocidente, embora exerça papel secundário dentro das escolas filosóficas. Normalmente, o conceito por trás da prática consiste em negar direitos ao corpo, ou mesmo castigá-lo, como se isso tivesse um efeito positivo em favor da alma, purificando-o de desejos carnais e liberando-a, para melhor progredir no caminho da salvação. A prática inclui o jejum, o celibato, a autoflagelação, a abstenção de alimentos e prazeres, a reclusão e a mendicância.

1. Na filosofia. A vida ascética era praticada pelos seguidores da escola pitagoreana (ver o artigo sobre essa filosofia), e por alguns neoplatônicos, como Plotino (ver os artigos). Nesses grupos, a filosofia adquiria forte colorido religioso, e para alguns, era uma religião. Buscava-se um meio de salvação através da filosofia, sendo apenas natural que alguns filósofos se utilizassem do ascetismo na tentativa de ajudar no avanço da alma. No cinismo (ver o artigo), isso não estava em vista. Essa escola foi uma revolta contra todas as instituições e práticas humanas, e um de seus ideais era o ascetismo usado como protesto contra os hábitos exagerados no comer, no vestir e nas condições de vida, que os cínicos consideravam fúteis. Os cínicos buscavam independência das invenções humanas, e o ascetismo era um dos meios de se obter a liberdade, o maior de todos os princípios seguidos pelos cínicos.

2. Nas religiões não-cristãs. No hinduísmo (ver o artigo) o terceiro e o quarto estágios da vida eram a renúncia, o abandono da família e a vida de mendicância, como meio de purificação. Buda procurou um meio-termo, evitando a posição radical do ascetismo, embora o ascetismo tivesse sido uma força poderosa para muitos de seus seguidores. Na ioga, que tem suas raízes no budismo (ver o artigo), as técnicas para disciplinamento do corpo são bastante rigorosas. Na *hatha-ioga*, essas técnicas são centradas na disciplina.

3. Na Bíblia:

a. **No Antigo Testamento.** Para os cristãos modernos, as intermináveis normas dietéticas (Lev. 11) e as práticas religiosas restritivas, embora naturais para os hebreus, seriam consideradas uma forma de ascetismo, para nada dizermos sobre pessoas que não seguem seriamente qualquer religião. Os trechos de Col. 2:16 e I Tim. 4:3,4 mostram que os gnósticos adotavam muitas dessas práticas. A tentativa de seguir vários preceitos do Antigo Testamento, segundo eram interpretados por eles, provavelmente também estava envolvida. Lê-se em I Tim. 4:4 que é legítima a ingestão de qualquer tipo de alimento (um ensino contrário ao gnosticismo), o que certamente foi um princípio revolucionário para a época, até onde dizia respeito à mente judaica. Outras práticas ascéticas do judaísmo eram temporárias e visavam casos especiais, como quando o povo de Israel teve de abster-se do sexo, antes da outorga da lei (ver Êxo. 19:15), ou como os nazireus tinham de abster-se de vinho, além de observarem estritas proibições de certos alimentos (Juí. 13:5). O jejum tinha suas aplicações, como ocasiões especiais no caso de indivíduos. Elias jejuou quarenta dias em sua viagem até Horebe (I Reis 19:8, como sinal de penitência e humilhação diante de Deus, Joel 2:15 ss). Ver também I Sam. 7:6 e I Reis 21:9 ss , nessa conexão. Aos sacerdotes requeria-se a abstenção de vinho antes dos holocaustos (Lev. 10:9; Eze. 44:21).

b. **No Novo Testamento.** O judaísmo da época cristã havia adotado o ascetismo como norma, mais do que se vê no Antigo Testamento. A seita dos fariseus tornou-se mais radical quanto a isso, para seus seguidores e para outros (ver Mat. 9:14; Luc. 18:12; Atos 15:10). Os essênios (ver o artigo) ainda eram mais radicais, tendo adotado o celibato como um ideal. Um outro movimento asceta entre os judeus era o dos terapêutas (ver o artigo). O ascetismo radical, porém, era estranho ao judaísmo; os grupos aqui mencionados podem ser considerados exceções. Não nos devemos olvidar, porém, que os fariseus exerciam grande autoridade sobre o povo comum, e suas formas de abstinência e rigor ascético coloriam o judaísmo inteiro dos dias de Jesus.

A prática do jejum é retida no Novo Testamento (Mat. 4:2; Luc. 2:37; Atos 13:2); mas isso visava ocasiões especiais, sendo praticado voluntariamente. Os crentes são exortados a abrirem mão de certas coisas, devido à consciência alheia (II Cor. 8:13; Rom. 14:1 ss.). Os cristãos devem suportar as aflições com ânimo forte (Mat. 10:38), quando se tornar necessário. O crente verdadeiro é um atleta espiritual, exercendo disciplina e autocontrole, para que se torne vencedor na corrida espiritual (I Cor. 9:24-27; I Tim. 4:7 ss), andando no Espírito (Gál. 5:25) e controlando a sua natureza pecaminosa (Gál. 5:17). Porém, nas páginas do Novo Testamento sempre é evidente que meros atos externos não têm valor, se desacompanhados pela correspondente virtude no íntimo (Mat. 6:2,6; 16:18; Rom. 14:17).

Principal trecho do Novo Testamento sobre o ascetismo: Colossenses 2:20-23. Essa passagem descreve e combate o ascetismo gnóstico, com suas inúmeras proibições: manuseies isto, não proves aquilo, não toques naquilo outro...» Um paralelo é o trecho de I Tim. 4:3,4, onde somos informados de que o ascetismo dos gnósticos incluía o celibato. Também havia os gnósticos libertinos (II Tim. 3:6). Era opinião dos gnósticos que qualquer coisa que tendesse por destruir o corpo era bom, visto que o corpo era material, e a matéria era tida por eles como a sede mesma do mal. Quanto mais cedo o espírito se libertasse do corpo, melhor. Os abusos contra o corpo podiam ser praticados mediante o excesso ou a abstinência, ou seja, pela licenciosidade ou pelo ascetismo.

Passagens como Mat. 5:25 ss e Luc. 14:26 não estabelecem preceitos ascéticos como condições de entrada no reino de Deus, mas apenas mostram que a inquirição espiritual é tão séria que requer nossa atenção e sacrifícios. As formas de ascetismo dos gnósticos não eram praticadas porque as coisas evitadas eram intrinsecamente más, mas porque tais práticas fariam parte da salvação. Qualquer prática ascética deve ser moderada pelo bom senso, deve ter breve duração, e deve ter algum propósito específico.

4. Tempos pós-apostólicos. O gnosticismo, que continuou até depois da época apostólica, em alguns segmentos, prosseguiu em seu ascetismo. Houve igualmente os montanistas e os maniqueus (ver os artigos). Esses movimentos tendiam por distorcer o conceito cristão da abnegação, ao ensinarem o desprezo pelo mundo material, o celibato e um severo moralismo, que negava o perdão para certos pecados. Na época de Agostinho, a vida monástica já adquirira considerável poder na Igreja, forma essa de ascetismo que tem continuado até os nossos dias, tendo-se tornado uma prática oficial em vários ramos da cristandade oriental e ocidental. Ver o artigo sobre o *Montanismo*. Inteiramente à parte dos mosteiros, a Idade Média exibiu variedades de ascetismo como a estrita observância de certos dias, ritos, jejuns, peregrinações, etc. Os reformadores rejeitaram o ascetismo medieval, considerando-o uma distorção do evangelho. Em sua obra, *Liberdade do Cristão*, Lutero lançou um ataque contra o ascetismo, asseverando que o crente tem a liberdade de usufruir de todos os dons e provisões de Deus, e que a autonegação quanto a essas coisas nada tem a ver com a salvação da alma. Não foram eliminados o asceticismo espontâneo e a autonegação, embora tivessem sido regulamentados de modo a não serem vinculados à salvação da alma. Lutero definiu a questão como segue: «Todos podem usar discreção quanto aos jejuns e às vigílias, já que todos sabem que precisam controlar o corpo. Porém, aqueles que pensam que podem tornar-se piedosos através das obras, só dão valor ao jejum como uma obra, imaginando que são piedosos por muito praticarem essas coisas. No entanto, quebram suas cabeças ou arruínam seus corpos, nessas práticas ascetas» (*Werke*, Erlanger Edition, xxvii,27,190).

5. Argumentos em prol do ascetismo:
a. Argumento bíblico. As Escrituras encorajam a —autonegação e a renúncia. Jesus é nosso modelo quanto a isso. b. O sacramento da penitência requer a renúncia quanto aos desejos carnais. c. Tomar a cruz de Cristo pode requerer uma severa autonegação. d. O ascetismo é teste da devoção do indivíduo a Deus. e. Os sofrimentos envolvidos são merecidos por causa dos nossos pecados. f. Os desejos da carne custam muito para serem satisfeitos. g. Embora alguns objetos dos desejos naturais possam ser bons, melhor ainda é a inquirição espiritual elevada. h. O desejo leva à frustração, e assim sendo, devem ser frustrados. i. O desejo merece ser aniquilado. j. Para alguns, o ascetismo faz parte do sistema de boas obras, mediante o que seria obtida a salvação. A severidade com o corpo presumivelmente liberta a alma para melhor ascender.

O moderno movimento evangélico não se tem libertado de práticas ascéticas. Isso assume uma forma de preocupação exagerada com o vestuário, regras excessivas acerca da maior parte dos entretenimentos, ou mesmo a abstinência de várias comidas e bebidas. Quanto a uma descrição detalhada das formas de ascetismo nos tempos neotestamentários, ver a exposição sobre Col. 2:20-23, no NTI, que inclui objeções à forma gnóstica, mas que podem ser aplicadas às outras variedades. (B E H LU NTI)

ASCLEPÍADES

Filósofo grego dos séculos II ou I A.C. Nasceu em Prusa (Quios, na Bitínia). Foi discípulo de Epicuro (ver o artigo a seu respeito). Derivou da academia de Heráclides (ver o artigo) a cosmologia que assevera que a natureza consiste em átomos e em espaços vagos. Também afirmava a presença apenas de diferenças quantitativas entre os átomos, e não diferenças qualitativas, segundo dizia Heráclides. Ele enfatizava a abordagem empírica da filosofia. Ver sobre o *empirismo*. (P)

••• ••• •••

ASDODE (ASDODITAS)

No hebraico, *fortaleza* ou *assediador*. Era uma das cinco mais importantes cidades dos filisteus (ver I Sam. 6:17). Localizada à beira do Mar Mediterrâneo ou próxima do mesmo, a oeste de Jerusalém. Estava localizada em um cume relvado, quase a meio caminho entre Gaza e Jope. O local era a sede da adoração a Dagom (ver I Sam. 5:1-5 e I Macabeus 11:4). Foi diante do santuário dessa divindade que foi posta a arca da aliança capturada dos israelitas, e que triunfou sobre o ídolo (ver I Sam. 5:1-9). O território ao redor, incluindo o sítio da cidade, fora dado a Judá; mas muitos séculos passaram-se antes que os seus habitantes realmente fossem subjugados por Israel. Uzias edificou aldeias nesse território (ver I Crô. 26:6). Foi mencionado, para vergonha dos judeus, que após retornarem do cativeiro, eles casaram-se com mulheres de Asdode. Isso resultou no fato de que seus filhos falavam um dialeto misto (ver Nee. 13:23,24). Antigamente era um lugar fortificado, na usual rota militar entre a Síria e o Egito. Sua possessão provocou guerras entre o Egito e as potências do norte. Por esse motivo, os assírios julgaram ser necessário conquistá-la, antes de invadirem o Egito (ver Isa. 20:1 ss). Posteriormente, a cidade foi capturada por Psamético, após um cerco de vinte e nove anos, o mais longo cerco que há na história (ver Heród.ii.157). Sua destruição foi predita por vários profetas (ver Jer. 25:20; Isa. 20:1; Amós 1:8; 3:9; Sof. 2:4; Zac. 9:6). Isso foi realizado pelos Macabeus (ver I Macabeus 5:68; 10:77-84; 11:4). Ela foi alistada entre as cidades que Pompeu uniu à província da Síria (ver Josefo, *Anti*. xiv.4,4; *Guerras* i.7,7). Gabínio ordenou a sua reconstrução (ver Josefo, *Anti*. xiv.5,3). Foi incluída nos domínios de Herodes, e foi uma das três cidades que ele doou à sua irmã Salomé (ver Josefo, *Guerras* vii.8,1). O evangelista Filipe achou-se em Asdode, depois de batizar o eunuco etíope (ver Atos 8:40). Mais tarde tornou-se sede de um bispado cristão. O lugar era chamado Azoto durante o período intertestamental e depois. No século I D.C., parece ter havido uma considerável população judaica na cidade. Vespasiano, pois, colocou ali uma guarnição romana, antes da queda de Jerusalém (ver Josefo, *Guerras* iv.iii.2). Com a queda de Jerusalém, sua história passou a ser vinculada ao cristianismo. (ID PRI S SH)

ASEITAS

Vem do latim **a se**, «ser por si mesmo», que se aplica à filosofia escolástica, em relação ao ser de Deus, contrastando com *ab alio*, «ser por meio de outro», isto é, o tipo de ser que as outras coisas possuem. Nesse contexto, as palavras *a se* significam «autocausado», ou «sem causa».

ASENATE

Em egípcio, talvez **dedicada a Neite**. A mulher desse nome era filha de Potífera, sacerdote de Om, a qual o rei do Egito deu como esposa a José. Ela se tornou mãe de Efraim e Manassés (ver Gên. 41:45,50 e 46:20). Uma lenda judaica relata como, ao casar-se com José, ela renunciou ao paganismo. O nome dela é egípcio, e literalmente significa «Ela pertence a X». Por causa disso, há várias especulações acerca de qual deus seria esse «X» (ou poderia ser uma deusa, seu pai, a ti, etc.). Tais nomes são bem confirmados na arqueologia, em seus achados do Reino Médio e do período dos hicsos (2100 - 1600 A.C.) da história do

Egito. Esse período corresponde ao período patriarcal da história de Israel. (ID ND S Z)

ASER

Forma grega de Asher (Tobias 1:2; Luc. 2:36 e Apo. 7:6). Foi um dos filhos de Jacó e Zilpa, ama de Lia (ver Gên. 30:13; 35:26; 49:20), e fundador de uma das doze tribos de Israel (ver Núm. 26:44-47). Ele teve quatro filhos e uma filha (ver Gên. 49:20). Nasceu em Padã-Arã, na Mesopotâmia, e era irmão (germano) de pai e mãe de Gade. Lia exclamou quando de seu nascimento: «É a minha felicidade! porque as filhas me terão por venturosa; e lhe chamou Aser» (Gên. 30:13). Em hebraico, Aser significa *felicidade*. Esse nome tem sido confirmado como um autêntico nome pessoal semítico do noroeste, em um papiro egípcio de cerca de 1750 A.C., embora ali seja o nome de uma escrava. A idéia de que as inscrições de Seti I (1313 - 1290 A.C.) e Ramisés II (1290 - 1224 A.C.) mencionam Aser como uma tribo conquistada na terra de Canaã, não é atualmente aceita largamente pelos eruditos, com base em que uma confusão de palavras deu origem a essa idéia. Portanto, não é válida a data do livro de Êxodo calculado com base na referência a Seti I.

A tribo de Aser. Quando Israel partiu do Egito, essa tribo contava com cerca de 41.500 homens, o que a tornava a nona tribo em número, apenas com Efraim, Manassés e Benjamin menores que ela. Antes da entrada na terra de Canaã, houve um aumento de 11.900 homens, somente excedido por Manassés; e assim, quando Israel entrou em Canaã, Aser já era a quinta tribo mais numerosa (ver Núm. 1:40,41 e 26:47).

Herança. A herança dessa tribo ficava em uma região extremamente frutífera, na costa marítima, tendo o Líbano ao norte, o Carmelo e a tribo de Issacar ao sul, e Zebulom e Naftali a leste. Esses territórios incorporavam uma larga fatia da Fenícia. Estava incluída Sidom, visto que os aseritas foram repreendidos por não terem expulsados os sidonitas (Juí. 1:31). Alguns estudiosos supõem mesmo que a verdade é que os cananeus permaneceram como a maioria da população da região de Aser.

A terra. O nome Aser também alude a uma parte de Canaã, onde a tribo habitava (ver Núm. 1:13; 2:27; 26:44; Juí. 1:31 e I Crô. 6:62,74).

Com Davi. Aser supriu guerreiros para o exército de Davi (I Crô. 12:36), fazendo parte de um distrito administrativo de Salomão (ver I Reis 4:16). Após a queda de Israel, alguns aseritas ajudaram a reavivar a páscoa, em Jerusalém de acordo com os desejos de Ezequias (ver II Crô. 30:11). Ana, uma figura do Novo Testamento, que se regozijou ao ver o infante Jesus, pertencia à tribo de Aser (Luc. 2:36).

A cidade de Aser. O trecho de Josué 17:7 pode referir-se a uma cidade com esse nome, talvez localizada no moderno local da vila de Teyasir, cerca de 18 km a nordeste de Siquém. Mas alguns eruditos insistem que ali há uma simples referência à tribo de Aser, e não a alguma cidade desse nome. (ID ND S UN)

ASFALTO (BETUME)

Essa substância era facilmente obtida na área do Mar Morto, nos tempos antigos, a fim de ser usada como material de construção. As três referências bíblicas dão-lhe o nome de «betume» (ver Gên. 6:14; Êxo. 2:3 e Isa. 34:9), indicando que era material empregado como cobertura vedante. O termo «betume» refere-se às substâncias petrolíferas que vão desde o óleo cru até formas minerais mais compactas, como a asfaltita, de cor escura, que consiste principalmente de hidrogênio e carbono, com traços de oxigênio, nitrogênio e enxofre. Os óleos com base asfáltica, nas fraturas geológicas, deixam vazar o betume natural, como o asfalto, o asfalto rochoso e outros compostos relacionados. Uma localidade bem conhecida, onde o betume pode ser obtido é o lago de Asfalto, que cobre 114 acres da ilha de Trinidade, e ainda um outro local é a área do Mar Morto. Dessa área, desde épocas remotas, era obtido o *lacus asfaltitis*. Heródoto mencionou o material, o qual era usado à guisa de cimento para assentar tijolos na Babilônia, o que até hoje pode ser averiguado nas ruínas das muralhas da Média, próximas da Babilônia. Durante o período greco-romano, a indústria do betume era controlada pelos nabateus (ver Diod. Sículo II.48 e XIX.98-100). Atualmente, o asfalto é usado na pavimentação de estradas e como material vedante para tetos, para piscinas e tanques, e conjugado com a borracha, para cobertura de canos, moldes e tintas. (S UN Z)

ASGARD

Residência dos deuses nórdicos, onde estava o trono de Odin. Ali viviam os doze deuses e as vinte e quatro deusas. Ali havia o palácio dos escolhidos mortos, o Valhala, cercado pela floresta de árvores cujas folhas eram todas de ouro vermelho. (E)

ASHRAMAS, AS QUATRO

Na Mahabharata (ver o artigo) e no hinduísmo em geral, são as quatro situações da vida e seus respectivos deveres. Ver também sobre o *código de Manu*. (P)

ASHVAGHOSA

Filósofo indiano do século I D.C. É o principal expositor do budismo mahayano, tendo procurado corrigir alegados erros de interpretação por parte do mestre, após a sua morte. Sua obra principal foi *Despertamento da Fé no Mahayana*. Ver sobre o *budismo mahayana*.

Idéias:

1. A realidade é Mesmice Absoluta, isto é, ultrapassa as categorias da compreensão humana.

2. Mas a Mesmice Absoluta é maculada pela ignorância humana, transformando-se em Mesmice Condicional. Este é o mundo de multiformes fenômenos, aparentemente composto de uma pluralidade de «eus» finitos. O oceano, tangido pelo vento, aparece como uma pluralidade de ondas, e outro tanto sucede à consciência e à realidade. As mentes finitas são apenas as ondas da grande Mente.

3. A própria razão humana é relativa e relacional, não podendo compreender a realidade, nem mesmo a realidade deste mundo de fenômenos. Portanto, precisamos transcender à razão, entrando em contato com a realidade, mediante as experiências místicas. Ver sobre o *misticismo*.

4. Os sábios buscam iluminação, ajudando outros a fazerem o mesmo, embora adiem seu próprio *nirvana* (ver o artigo), a fim de que se mostrem úteis.

5. Quando somos iluminados, tornamo-nos cônscios da Mesmice Absoluta, e nos identificamos com essa realidade auto-existente e imortal. (P)

Rochas esculpidas pelo tempo, perto de Capadócia, Ásia Menor — Cortesia, Matson Photo Service

Teatro de Éfeso — Cortesia, Matson Photo Service

ÁSIA

Os antigos desconheciam as divisões do mundo em grandes porções, como os atuais continentes. Isso não era por outra razão, senão a que não faziam idéia das dimensões do mundo. Assim, por exemplo, a África aparece na Bíblia não como um continente, mas apenas como um dos vários lugares. Como um termo abrangente, a Ásia nunca aparece em qualquer sentido no Antigo Testamento, embora apareça nos livros dos Macabeus e no Novo Testamento. Ali o termo aplica-se àquela porção peninsular da Ásia, a qual, desde o século V A.C., vem sendo chamada de Ásia Menor. Assim, nos trechos de Atos 19:26,27; 20:4,16,18 e 27:2, é bem provável que esteja em foco a inteira antiga Ásia Menor; mas, em Atos 2:9; 6:9; 19:20,22; II Tim. 1:15; Apo. 1:4,11 está em foco a Ásia proconsular da época dos romanos. Essa incorporava as províncias da Frígia, Mísia, Cária e Lídia (ver Cícero, *Pro. Flacc.* 27; e *Ep. Fam.* ii.15). Era uma das províncias romanas mais ricas, populosas e intelectualmente ativas. Era apenas natural que Paulo e Barnabé, em sua primeira viagem missionária, tivessem ido pregar nas grandes cidades da Ásia. Aparentemente, Paulo quis repetir o feito, mas foi então que recebeu a chamada para a Macedônia (ver Atos 16:6 ss). A população inteira, para todos os efeitos práticos, ouviu o evangelho (ver Atos 19:10); mas devemo-nos lembrar que, quanto às dimensões reais, a província não era muito grande, de acordo com os padrões modernos. As principais cidades da Ásia, nos dias do Novo Testamento, eram Éfeso, Esmirna, Pérgamo, Tiatira, Sardes, Filadélfia, Colossos, Mileto, Laodicéia e Tróade, ocupando uma porção da moderna Turquia. A Ásia do Novo Testamento envolvia cerca de uma terça parte da extremidade oeste e sudoeste da grande península que atualmente se chama Ásia Menor.

O domínio do território havia passado por muitas mãos; mas, em cerca do século IV A.C., o reino de Pérgamo emergiu como uma poderosa entidade, provendo cerca de duzentos anos de estabilidade na área. Os governantes, da linhagem atálida, fizeram a região prosperar em meio a demonstrações de força. Ver sobre *Átalo*. Entrementes, o poder romano ampliava-se em todas as direções. Para os romanos, a Ásia Menor parecia uma terra espaçosa, avançando ameaçadoramente na direção oeste, sobre a Europa. Mas Roma lançou alguns ataques contra esse território. Então, no ano de 133 A.C., Átalo III, o último dos reis de Pérgamo, reconhecendo como a história favorecia o domínio romano, doou o seu reino ao povo romano, e assim provavelmente poupou muita violência e derramamento de sangue. Porém, ele impôs algumas exigências. Demandou que Pérgamo e outras cidades gregas de seu reino fossem isentas de taxação e tributo. Roma aceitou as condições, pelo que a região foi transformada na província romana da Ásia. Tornou-se uma província senatorial, com um procônsul que vivia em Éfeso. Isso emprestou tranqüilidade à área. No campo religioso, a religião oficial foi adotada, segundo a qual o imperador romano era adorado como uma espécie de semideus. Muitos excelentes monumentos foram erigidos, e durante duzentos anos a Ásia talvez tenha sido a mais próspera porção do império romano. (ID JON UN Z)

ÁSIA, IGREJAS DA

Ver o artigo sobre a **Ásia** e os nomes das cidades ali mencionadas. Cada uma dessas cidades recebe um tratamento especial, com artigos separados.

ASIARCAS

Esse termo significa **governantes da Ásia**, mas na realidade, refere-se a dez superintendentes dos ritos religiosos e públicos da Ásia proconsular, os quais celebravam, por sua própria conta, os jogos em honra aos deuses e ao imperador. Somente um ricaço podia arcar com as despesas, pelo que algum cidadão abastado de cada uma das cidades da Ásia era nomeado para o ofício. Essa seleção era efetuada em assembléia pública. A pessoa escolhida era então enviada ao conselho geral da província, reunido em uma das cidades principais, como Éfeso, Esmirna, Sardes, etc. Dentre todos os delegados presentes, dez eram escolhidos. É possível que o título, uma vez ganho, se tornasse permanente, pelo que os atos e as obras daqueles que exibiam o título não representavam, necessariamente sua atuação como asiarcas. Não há certeza sobre quanto poder político eles brandiam, mas não há que duvidar que o ofício envolvia certo poder e influência, com conseqüências políticas. O trecho de Atos 19:31 relata como Paulo despertou a oposição dos idólatras ourives de Éfeso, e como a situação tornou-se violenta. Os asiarcas do lugar exortaram Paulo para que não fosse ao teatro, onde estava sendo efetuada uma demonstração pública. Essa atitude amigável mostra que a política imperial ainda não era hostil à nova fé. Provavelmente Lucas narrou a história como um elemento que combinava com a sua mensagem no livro de Atos, de que o cristianismo não era um movimento subversivo, pelo que deveria ser aceito como uma fé religiosa legal, tal como já havia sucedido ao judaísmo. Os relatos que envolvem Gálio, Félix, Festo, Agripa e os asiarcas transmitiam essa mensagem, a qual, contudo, foi finalmente rejeitada, quando grandes ondas de hostilidade e violência, por parte do governo romano, fizeram tudo quanto era possível para apagar o cristianismo da face da terra. Quanto a maiores detalhes sobre os «asiarcas», ver Atos 19:31 e as notas expositivas no NTI. (LAK NTI UN)

ASIBIAS

Um israelita que despediu sua esposa estrangeira, nos dias de Esdras (ver I Esdras 9:26), mas que não é mencionado nas passagens paralelas dos livros pertencentes ao cânon do Antigo Testamento.

ASIEL

No hebraico, **criado por Deus**. Nome de várias pessoas mencionadas nas Escrituras: 1. Bisneto de Jeú, um príncipe simionita que compartilhou da herança de Judá (ver I Crô. 4:35; Jos. 19:9), cerca de 800 A.C. 2. Um dos cinco escritores empregados por Esdras para transcrever a lei (ver II Esdras 14:24). 3. Um ancestral de Tobias (1:1), da tribo de Naftali. (Z)

ASILO

Um lugar de segurança para onde podiam fugir pessoas culpadas de homicídio acidental, de acordo com a legislação mosaica. Naturalmente, houve casos em que até mesmo criminosos procuravam refugiar-se nesses lugares. Os vingadores, de acordo com as leis escritas (que estabeleciam condições), não tinham permissão de fazer execuções nesses lugares.

1. *De acordo com a lei mosaica*. O altar dos holocaustos e o templo de Jerusalém eram santuários. Joabe fugiu para o templo e refugiou-se junto ao altar dos holocaustos, conforme se lê em I Reis 2:28,29,31. Mas Salomão, entendendo que ele não se afastaria de

perto do altar, ordenou que o matassem ali mesmo. Moisés havia ordenado (ver Êxc. 21:14) que qualquer assassino (não homicida acidental) deveria ser arrastado dali. Os santuários não existiam a fim de beneficiar assassinos propositais, mas sim, para benefício dos inocentes. Tornou-se costumeiro forçar os criminosos a se afastarem do altar deixando-os sem alimentos, ou fazendo fogueiras em redor do mesmo, forçando-os assim a se afastarem.

As cidades de refúgio não tinham o propósito de substituir esses santuários, mas eram adições aos mesmos. O conceito de asilo era humanitário, embora também tivesse uma base religiosa. O derramamento não-intencional do sangue de outra pessoa era considerado uma questão séria, que envolvia culpa. Isso exigia vingança, não podendo ser perdoado por via de resgate (ver Núm. 35:31). Coisa alguma podia expiar o homicídio acidental, salvo a morte do sumo sacerdote vigente (ver Núm. 35:25). Uma vez falecido o sumo sacerdote, então o homem que tivesse fugido para uma cidade de refúgio podia deixá-la, e ninguém tinha a permissão de tocá-lo. Naturalmente, nisso temos um excelente tipo de como qualquer pecado pode ser perdoado através da missão, da morte, da ressurreição e da contínua vida espiritual do nosso grande Sumo Sacerdote, Jesus.

2. *De acordo com o paganismo*. Há alguma evidência de que o templo da Misericórdia, em Atenas, servia de lugar de refúgio. Há tradições que dizem que os netos de Hércules foram os criadores dos lugares de refúgio na Grécia. Cadmo erigiu um lugar de refúgio em Tebas, e Rômulo fez a mesma coisa em Roma. Dafne, perto de Antioquia, era um lugar de refúgio bem conhecido (ver II Macabeus 4:34). Teseu preparou um lugar de refúgio em Atenas, especialmente para os escravos e os pobres. Os templos de Apolo, em Delfos, de Juno, em Samos, de Esculápio, em Delos, e de Baco em Éfeso, eram lugares de refúgio, havendo ainda diversos outros. A cidade inteira de Roma tornou-se um lugar de refúgio para os estrangeiros. O número de tais lugares aumentou de tal modo que o imperador Tibério foi forçado a cancelar tal direito, no caso de muitas cidades (ver Suetônio, *Tibério*; e Tácito *Annal*. liv.iii,cap. 6). Contudo, após a sua morte, seu decreto não foi mais observado à risca.

3. *De acordo com o cristianismo*. Na Igreja cristã, foi incentivado o direito de asilo, de tal modo que as edificações eclesiásticas e seus altares tornaram-se lugares de asilo. Teodósio II (431 D.C.) fez dos templos, seus pátios, jardins, banheiros, celas, etc., lugares de refúgio. Devido aos inevitáveis abusos, esse costume tornou-se menos proeminente. (GRE ID S UN Z)

ASIMA

No hebraico, talvez signifique **céu** (ver II Reis 17:30). Era o deus dos habitantes de Hamate. O Talmude babilônico e vários outros escritores judeus dizem que essa divindade era adorada sob a forma de um bode sem pêlos; mas o Talmude de Jerusalém diz cordeiro. Ainda outros referem-se a um macaco, mas a idéia do bode parece ser a preferível entre os eruditos. Não há referências extrabíblicas seguras, embora alguns associem esse deus à Aserá, uma deusa-mãe cananéia, ou ao *Semios* sírio dos papiros Elefantinos. (ND S Z)

ASÍNCRITO

Nome de um crente de Roma (ou de Éfeso), a quem Paulo enviou saudações (ver Rom. 16:14), em 55 D.C. O último capítulo da epístola aos Romanos pode ter sido originalmente uma epístola de apresentação dada a Febe, que ela deveria levar à Ásia Menor, e não uma parte da epístola original aos Romanos. Essa questão é discutida no artigo sobre Romanos, VIII.3.b. Esse nome tem sido encontrado em inscrições e documentos antigos, sendo um nome comum naquela época. (I IB NTI)

ASMITA

Termo sânscrito que significa o «eu souísmo», um falso egoísmo que confunde o «eu» sensível com o verdadeiro «eu», ou *purusha* (ver o artigo). Trata-se de um dos cinco tipos de sofrimento a serem eliminados pelo sistema da ioga. (P)

ASMODEU

Um espírito maligno, na história de Tobias (3:17), que se enamorou de Sara, filha única de Raquel de Ecbátana. Em seu ciúme, ele matou sete maridos que haviam casado com ela, cada qual na noite de núpcias. Isso teve fim quando Tobias, ajudado pelo anjo Rafael, preparou uma poção que expeliu o espírito que a assediava. Alguns estudiosos pensam que a idéia desse espírito foi tomada por empréstimo do zoroastrismo, pelos judeus, durante o exílio na Babilônia. Seja como for, nas lendas judaicas posteriores, esse espírito ocupa posição proeminente, especialmente no que concerne a Salomão. Mílton empregou a idéia em seu *Paraíso Perdido* 4.168-171.

ASMÔNIO (ASMONEANO)

Ver **Hasmoneano**.

ASNA

Cabeça de uma das famílias dos servos do templo, que retornaram do cativeiro babilônico juntamente com Zorobabel (ver Esd. 2:50 e I Esdras 5:31), em cerca de 536 A.C. (UN)

ASNÁ

No hebraico significa **fortificação** ou **brilhante**. Era uma cidade de Judá (ver Jos. 15:33), a sudoeste de Jerusalém. Tentativamente identificada com 'Aslin', perto da beira da planície marítima de Judá. Havia uma outra cidade em Judá, do mesmo nome (ver Jos. 15:43), a sudoeste de Jerusalém, que talvez seja a moderna Idna, entre Hebrom e Laquis. (Z)

ASNAPAR

Um rei mencionado somente em Esd. 4:10, chamado «o grande e afamado». Assim o considera-vam os homens, mas somente por ser um assassino sangüinário, como o foram quase todos os reis da antiguidade, conseguindo impor a sua vontade por onde quer que fosse. Seu nome tem sido inutilmente procurado nas inscrições assírias, tendo sido identificado com certa variedade de monarcas, como Esar-Hadom, Senaqueribe e Salmaneser. Mas, desde 1875, tem sido sugerido que esse nome é apenas a forma aramaica de Assurbanipal da Assíria, ponto de vista esse que atualmente é quase universalmente aceito. Ver sobre *Assurbanipal*. (UN)

ASNO

Tradução de palavras hebraicas que significam *força, resistência* ou *avermelhado*. Está em pauta o

ASNO DE BURIDAN — ASPECTO DUPLO

Equus Asinus, do qual há muitas variedades, algumas, com faixas como as zebras, com formas características que o distinguem do cavalo, com formato peculiar do corpo e dos membros, orelhas longas, crina crispada, cauda com um tufo de pêlos no fim, uma faixa ao longo da espinha dorsal, e com freqüência cruzada com outra faixa à altura das espáduas. O cavalo relincha, e o asno orneja. Os hebreus chamavam esse animal por vários nomes, distinguindo assim as espécies e as qualidades de idade e sexo; mas, naturalmente, faziam-no sem precisão científica. O *chamor* era o jumento comum de trabalho da Ásia Ocidental, pequeno em estatura, usualmente de cor avermelhada, domesticado desde tempos remotos na Arábia, na Mesopotâmia e no sul da Pérsia. Pode ser visto representado nos monumentos egípcios. Um outro nome, *orud* (ver Jó 39:5), bem como o termo caldaico *orodia* (ver Dan. 5:21), fazem alusão à voz típica do asno. Outro nome era *para*, também traduzido por asno selvagem. Vem de uma raiz hebraica que produziu *paras*, «cavalo» e *parasim* (cavaleiros), persa e parta, porquanto entre esses povos havia muitos cavaleiros. O vocábulo hebraico para designar uma espécie distinta, a mula selvagem, que os gregos denominavam *hemionos*; mas a dúvida cerca as identificações exatas.

Descrição e usos. O asno aparece como um animal importado da Líbia, para servir como pagamento de tributo, sendo ilustrado em painéis desde cerca de 2650 A.C., o que nos permite saber que desde tempos muito remotos, esse animal era domesticado e empregado para transporte de cargas. Quanto à sua coloração, havia grande variedade, como cinza, castanho, albino, negro, estriado, e também com várias manchas e sinais. O tipo que tem uma espécie de cruz formada por duas faixas que se cruzam à altura das espáduas, segundo a lenda, surgiu quando Jesus usou um jumentinho para entrar em Jerusalém, predizendo a Sua futura e breve crucificação.

O asno é dotado de passadas firmes, porquanto em tempos remotos vivia em regiões montanhosas semidesérticas. O cavalo, porém, desenvolveu-se em planícies relvadas, pelo que seus passos seriam menos seguros. Portanto, para viagens através de regiões montanhosas, o jumento sempre era escolhido, e durante muitos séculos foi o animal de carga dos pobres, e o transporte pessoal.

No Antigo Testamento. A primeira referência bíblica - Gên. 12:16 — onde se lê sobre esse animal, informa-nos que Faraó presenteou alguns deles a Abraão. Enquanto o camelo não começou a ser usado, o asno era usado nas travessias dos desertos. A capacidade desse animal sobreviver em terreno agreste e seco tornou-o valioso na Palestina e nas terras em volta do Mediterrâneo. Era usado para moer grãos (ver Mat. 24:21).

Proibições. Não se podia atrelar um asno e um boi sob uma mesma canga (ver Deu. 22:10), embora a maioria das famílias, quando pobres, seriam grandemente tentadas a fazê-lo, porque teriam, talvez, somente um asno e um boi, e isso formava um par de animais. Esse animal era considerado *imundo* pela lei cerimonial mosaica, ou seja, sua carne não servia para ser ingerida pelo homem. Ver Lev. 11:2 ss quanto a muitas dessas proibições alimentares. Tal como todos os membros da família eqüina, o asno tem um único casco nas patas, e não é ruminante. Mas os asnos eram cuidadosamente tratados, porque um proprietário pobre de um desses animais muito dependia dele para a sua sobrevivência (ver Êxo. 23:4,5,12 e Deu. 22:4). Por duas vezes, o Senhor Jesus comentou sobre o tratamento bondoso que se deve dar aos animais, incluindo os asnos (ver Luc. 13:15 e 14:5). Muitos ricos, entretanto, sentiam vergonha de montar em um simples jumento, e preferiam um cavalo para tanto. A entrada triunfal de Jesus em Jerusalém, como o Rei de Israel, foi feita no lombo de um humilde jumentinho, como condescendência do Senhor (ver Zac. 9:9). Já os reis sangüinários da terra conquistam montados a cavalo.

A palavra «asno», atualmente, é um sinônimo da idéia de «embotado na inteligência» ou «teimoso»; mas não há qualquer indício dessa idéia, no Antigo e no Novo Testamentos. (S UN Z)

ASNO DE BURIDAN

Na filosofia, a metáfora de um asno indeciso encontra-se a princípio nos escritos de Aristóteles; mas o relato acabou associado a Jean Buridan (1295-1356), um filósofo francês, o que explica a expressão «asno de Buridan». O asno estava entre dois fardos de feno igualmente apetitosos. Olhou para um fardo, e então para o outro. Sua cabeça virava-se para um lado e para o outro, sem poder tomar uma decisão quanto ao fardo que comeria. Em meio à sua indecisão, o asno terminou por morrer de fome. Um homem também pode achar-se em um dilema parecido quando tenta tomar uma decisão, mas não há razões compelidoras para preferir uma situação à outra. A símile pode ser aplicada à escolha entre duas idéias, ambas as quais podem ser defendidas com igual vigor, com argumentos aparentemente convincentes. (EP F)

ASPÁLATO

Esse é o nome dado à planta **Alhagi camelorum**. Em Eclesiástico 24:14, lê-se que a planta produzia um perfume adocicado. O arbusto é espinhento e de tamanho médio. Era usado para a produção de ungüentos e perfumes.

Vocábulo encontrado somente em Eclesiástico 24:15, que faz parte dos livros apócrifos do Antigo Testamento. Muitos pensam tratar-se de uma planta aromática da família do cinamono. Os antigos usavam-na no fabrico de perfumes ou de incenso, sendo mencionada em fontes extrabíblicas. Teofrato (ix.c.7) alista essa planta entre as substâncias aromáticas.

ASPATA

O terceiro dos filhos de Hamã, morto pelos judeus da Babilônia (ver Est. 9:7), em cerca de 510 A.C. (S)

ASPECTO DUPLO

Essa expressão, ligada ao problema do corpo-mente (ver o artigo a respeito), refere-se à distinção, quanto à essência, entre o corpo material e a alma imaterial, embora ambos sejam aspectos de alguma essência ou energia mais fundamental. Todavia, quando se manifestam, parecem separar-se, dando a impressão de uma dualidade.

Outro uso da expressão. Na doutrina do existencialismo positivo de Abbagnano (ver o artigo a respeito), essa expressão indica que cada possibilidade concreta franqueada aos homens tem um aspecto positivo e um aspecto negativo. Para exemplificar, o conhecimento de qualquer coisa tem dois lados: 1. o de saber a resposta certa; 2. e o de não se estar enganado a respeito, que é o aspecto negativo.

ASPENAZ

No hebraico talvez signifique **narina de cavalo**. Era o chefe dos eunucos do rei Nabucodonosor. Daniel e seus companheiros foram entregues aos seus cuidados, e ele lhes trocou os nomes (ver Dan. 1:3,7), cerca de 604 A.C. A petição de Daniel, no sentido de que ele não fosse compelido a comer das provisões enviadas à mesa real, foi aceita favoravelmente, bondade essa que o profeta, agradecido, registrou em Daniel 1:16. (S Y)

ASPERGES

Uma cerimônia anterior à missa principal, durante a qual o celebrante, com a ajuda dos acólitos, passa em cortejo através da congregação, aspergindo (daí o nome) os membros com água-benta e recitando palavras apropriadas do Saltério e de outras fontes. A finalidade da cerimônia é simbolizar a pureza do coração, que deveria assinalar os participantes dos santos mistérios da Igreja. (E)

ÁSPIDE

No grego é **aspis**, uma serpente venenosa, uma víbora. Ver o artigo geral sobre as *víboras*, onde são relacionadas as cobras da Bíblia. (Ver Isa. 11:8; Sal. 58:4,5 e Rom. 3:13). Hoje em dia, o termo *áspide* faz parte do nome científico de uma das víboras da areia. Os detalhes dados sobre a áspide, nas páginas da Bíblia, são os seguintes: Todas as referências aludem ao fato de ser ela peçonhenta. A serpente chamada por esse nome era usada por alguns para provocar o suicídio. O efeito de seu veneno era rápido, sendo do grupo neurotóxico, e não do grupo hemotóxico, o qual pode levar dias para matar. O trecho de Isaías 11:8 menciona o fato de que as serpentes habitam em covas. Sal. 58:4,5 reflete o mito que as serpentes podem ouvir, e que os encantadores fazem seu trabalho com as cobras por meio de sons. Porém, todas as serpentes são surdas, e o encantamento é produzido pelos movimentos do encantador, e não pelos sons por ele produzidos. Seja como for, a identificação de algumas espécies exatas, mediante os versículos da Bíblia, é um trabalho que envolve muita conjectura. (S Z)

ASQUELOM

No hebraico, **ato de pesar**. Era uma das cinco cidades dos filisteus, nas praias do mar Mediterrâneo, a 16 km ao norte de Gaza. Foi ali que Sansão matou trinta homens e tirou os despojos dos mesmos (ver Juí. 14:19). Foi dada à tribo de Judá (ver Juí. 1:18). Foi denunciada pelos profetas (ver Jer. 25:20; Amós 1:8; Sof. 2:4-7 e Zac. 9:5).

História. 1. Era a sede da deusa filistéia Astarte ou Astorete (ver o artigo a respeito). 2. É mencionada nos textos de execração da XII dinastia egípcia, no reino médio. 3. É mencionada em duas cartas em escrita cuneiforme de Amarna, números 287 e 320. A cidade revoltou-se e livrou-se do domínio do Faraó Ramisés II. E este foi obrigado a recapturá-la. Houve uma série de choques armados com os egípcios. 4. Foi dominada por filisteus, que eram indo-europeus, e permaneceu sob esse domínio até bem dentro do período da monarquia judaica (ver Jos. 13:5). 5. Os assírios conquistaram-na em 734 A.C. 6. A Pérsia passou a controlá-la mais tarde. 7. Foi atacada pelos citas em 625 A.C. (ver *Heród*. 1.105). 8. Foi helenizada, após Alexandre o Grande. 9. No tempo dos Macabeus, residia ali uma numerosa população judaica. 10. Foi o lugar do nascimento de Herodes o Grande, o qual a embelezou ao tornar-se rei. 11. Estabeleceu um acordo de paz com Roma, e foi declarada área livre. 12. Quando da rebelião dos judeus, no ano 66 D.C., os judeus atacaram-na, mas tiveram de retroceder após um furioso assalto (ver Josefo, *Guerras* 11.18.1 e III.2.1,2). 13. Sua história era de guerras contínuas, ocupações e desocupações militares durante os períodos islâmico e das cruzadas.

Deve ser identificada com a moderna Asqalon. Grandes escavações arqueológicas foram efetuadas entre 1920 e 1922. (ID PEQ)

ASQUENAZ

No hebraico o sentido da palavra é desconhecido. Foi filho de Gômer e neto de Noé (ver Gên. 10:3), antepassado dos povos associados a Ararate e Mini (ver Jer. 51:27). Provavelmente devem ser identificados com os antigos citas (*Heród*. i.103-107 e iv.1), os quais, no tempo de Jeremias, haviam-se estabelecido próximo ao lago Urmia, na região de Ararate. Nos tabletes em escrita cuneiforme há menção a uma tribo chamada *Askuza*, aliada dos Mannai em sua revolta contra a Assíria, no século VII A.C. Os citas eram aguerridos e deram muito trabalho aos assírios. O nome deles tornou-se um sinônimo de barbárie. Parece tratar-se de um povo muito disseminado pelo mundo antigo. Na Índia eles eram conhecidos como *sakas*, adversários invasores vindos do norte. As tradições judaicas afirmam que Asquenaz é o progenitor dos povos germânicos, os quais formaram países independentes no centro e no norte da Europa, na era contemporânea, embora façam parte da constituição racial de grande parte da União Soviética. Alguns estudiosos pensam que os países escandinavos, em seu nome, refletem ainda o nome de seu progenitor original. Ver Col. 3:11 e as notas no NTI, nesse ponto. (ID NTI UN)

ASQUENAZITAS

Asquenaz (Gên. 10:3), era identificado pelos hebreus medievais como ancestral dos povos germânicos. O nome asquenazitas veio a designar os judeus alemães e seus descendentes, no norte, centro e leste europeu, na Grã-Bretanha e nas Américas. Constituem mais de 90% do total dos judeus.

ASSALTOS DE TRANSPORTE

Há um seqüestro de veículos de transporte com o propósito de roubá-los. No caso de aviões, os seqüestros, inspirados por razões políticas, geralmente exigem vultosos resgates. A prática antiga consistia em assaltar caravanas. Isso tem-se tornado um tema comum nos filmes norte-americanos de Far West, porque tal prática era generalizada no século passado. Os modernos seqüestradores apenas tornaram tal crime sofisticado com as técnicas de nossos dias. Um crime não é compensado por motivos políticos. O seqüestro de caminhões, nos E.U.A., causa perdas de bilhões de dólares anuais, e no Brasil, essa prática criminosa tem-se tornado um escândalo nacional. Muitos homicídios desnecessários têm sido efetuados. Essas operações geralmente são projetadas por indivíduos e organizações que não tomam parte pessoal nos assaltos; mas contratam criminosos profissionais para a tarefa. Com freqüência negócios ilegítimos são envolvidos, recebendo as mercadorias roubadas a preços baixos, que permitem grande lucro na revenda. Paulo referiu-se aos «inventores de males»

ASSASSINATO — ASSEMBLÉIA

(Rom. 1:30). E os que se envolvem nesse tipo de crime devem ser incluídos nessa classificação. O juízo divino aguarda os pecadores de todas as modalidades, pois, do contrário, teremos de pensar que o caos é o verdadeiro deus deste mundo. O evangelho existe para salvar as pessoas desse justo e severo julgamento.

ASSASSINATO Ver **Homicídio**.

ASSASSINOS

No trecho de Atos 21:38, é usado o termo grego *sikarioi*, para indicar os seguidores de certo impostor egípcio. Noutros trechos, a palavra é usada para indicar grupos de judeus nacionalistas militantes, em meados do século I D.C., os quais armavam-se com adagas ocultas (no latim, *sicae*), o que explica o apelido que lhes era dado «homens de adaga». Eles tomavam sobre si o encargo de matar indivíduos indesejáveis, que segundo pensavam, se opunham ao movimento judeu de independência de Roma (ver Josefo, *Guerras* ii.13:3; *Anti.* xx.8.5,10). A maioria desses homens procurava promover a tradição dos Macabeus, que era seu ideal e inspiração. Eram ousados, violentos e destituídos de compaixão, misturando-se no meio do povo nos dias festivos, a fim de assassinar suas vítimas, com freqüência em plena luz do dia. Os governantes da Palestina eram forçados a se fazer acompanhar por uma guarda pessoal, cujos membros se mantinham em estado de alerta contra esses ataques súbitos. Um notável incidente que os envolveu foi o de Judas, o Galileu, em 7 D.C., o qual, com sede a seis quilômetros de Nazaré, organizou uma rebelião usando como «soldados» principalmente os *sicários*. Mas o levante foi violentamente abafado, e duzentos rebeldes foram crucificados. Quando Paulo estava sendo julgado, o capitão Lísias procurou identificá-lo com um líder egípcio que havia levado quatrocentos desses sicários ao deserto (ver Atos 21:38). Esses homens tiveram uma ativa participação na revolta de Israel contra Roma, o que produziu o desastre do ano 70 D.C. Finalmente, — eles transferiram seu teatro de operações para o Egito e Cirene, onde continuaram seus atos de terrorismo. (ID HA ND)

ASSEMBLÉIA

No hebraico há várias palavras, com diferentes implicações: 1. *Atsawraw* (Lev. 23:26), que indica uma simples reunião, especialmente usada para indicar festividades religiosas. 2. *Mikraw* (Isa. 1:13 e 4:5), que indica uma reunião pública. 3. *Asuppaw* (ver Eclesiastes 12:11), que indica uma reunião ou painel de sábios. Quanto ao Novo Testamento grego, temos: 1. *Paneguris* (ver Heb. 12:23), uma reunião popular festiva. 2. *Ekklesia* (ver Atos 19:39), que indica uma congregação reunida com o propósito de deliberar, sendo esse o vocábulo que veio a ser usado para indicar a *Igreja*, usado por cento e quinze vezes no Novo Testamento (por exemplo, Mat. 16:18; 18:17; Rom. 16:1; Gál. 1:2; Efé. 1:22; 3:10 e Col. 1:18).

Uso figurado. 1. O povo de Israel será reunido jubilosamente, quando for restaurado em Cristo (Sof. 3:18). 2. Sentir tristeza porque as reuniões solenes não são efetuadas, e desejar a restauração das mesmas, é um anseio por renovação espiritual (ver Sof. 3:18). 3. Em Cristo há aquela grande assembléia constituída por todos os povos, remidos no céu, os primogênitos, um símbolo da restauração e salvação finais, nos lugares celestiais, quando aquilo que é mortal for substituído pela imortalidade (ver Heb. 12:23).

A solene assembléia. Em Sofonias 3:18, essa idéia aparece sob as palavras «festas solenes», em nossa versão portuguesa. Isso será ocasionado pela volta do Messias, que recolherá o Seu povo e dará início à era do reino milenar. O termo também é usado para indicar um «tempo determinado» ou «estação» (ver Gên. 1:14), ou para indicar um lugar de reuniões (Sal. 74:8).

ASSEMBLÉIA DE DEUS

Uma denominação religiosa pentecostal organizada em abril de 1914, na cidade de Hot Springs, no estado de Arkansas, E.U.A. Nos Estados Unidos da América do Norte, é uma das maiores denominações pentecostais, com aproximadamente 2 milhões de membros. As igrejas locais têm um governo congregacional, mas a organização nacional incorpora elementos de governo presbiteriano. Esta denominação tem estabelecido um número de faculdades teológicas e seminários e tem seus próprios meios de publicação de literatura. Seu trabalho missionário tem sido extensivo, com campos de atividade em mais de 70 países.

Doutrina. As Assembléias de Deus são fundamentalistas e evangélicas do tipo pentecostal. A Bíblia é reconhecida como a única regra de fé e prática. A doutrina é arminiana, basicamente metodista em seu caráter. Curas divinas, o batismo do Espírito e o exercício dos dons espirituais são considerados práticas normais para a igreja moderna.

As Assembléias do Brasil. Foi o segundo ramo do pentecostismo a se instalar no Brasil, (1911), como resultado do trabalho dos missionários Gunnar Vingren e Daniel Berg, de origem sueca, mas radicados nos E.U.A. Começaram o trabalho em Belém, PA. Embora conseqüente do trabalho missionário estrangeiro, a *Assembléia* tem caráter predominantemente nacional. Constitui o maior grupo pentecostal do Brasil e realiza um crescimento fenomenal. Em 1964, tinha quase um milhão de membros, 1.000 pastores, 5.000 pregadores leigos, 1.200 igrejas, e um número considerável de faculdades e institutos teológicos.

ASSEMBLÉIA DE WESTMINSTER

O parlamento inglês, em 1640, deu aos puritanos a oportunidade de concretizarem seu alvo de reformas mais profundas, alterando assim a Igreja Anglicana. Vários teólogos e eruditos da Bíblia foram convocados, a 1º de julho de 1643, na abadia de Westminster. A tarefa deles foi alinhar melhor a Igreja Anglicana com a Igreja Escocesa (ver o artigo a respeito), e com as igrejas reformadas do continente europeu. O grupo consistia em cento e vinte e um membros, a maioria puritanos e presbiterianos (ver o artigo sobre um e sobre outro grupo), embora houvesse alguns congregacionais, rastianos e episcopais (ver os artigos sobre cada um). O documento assim produzido envolve os seguintes itens: 1. Uma forma presbiteriana de governo eclesiástico; 2. itens sobre disciplina eclesiástica; 3. regras relativas à ordenação de ministros; 4. regras de adoração, em substituição ao Livro de Oração Comum; 5. uma confissão de fé em substituição aos 39 artigos; 6. um catecismo mais completo; 7. um catecismo abreviado. Os itens de números 2, 3, 4 e 6 foram aprovados. Todavia, a autoridade do documento da assembléia foi anulada pela restauração, em 1660. Não obstante, tal documento exerceu influência sobre os presbiterianos.

ASSEMBLÉIA GERAL (UNIVERSAL)

Em todo o Novo Testamento, a expressão ocorre somente em Heb. 12:23. O acesso que temos em Cristo leva-nos a nos aproximar da cidade celestial, da incontável companhia de anjos, da assembléia geral dos primogênitos arrolados no céu, do Juiz que é Deus, dos espíritos dos justos aperfeiçoados, e do traduzido por *assembléia universal* é *paneguris*, que indica a reunião festiva de uma vasta assembléia. que indica a reunião festiva de uma vasta assembléia. Várias interpretações têm sido dadas a isso:

1. Alguns ligam a expressão à que se segue, «igreja dos primogênitos».
2. Outros ligam essa companhia à que é referida antes, as «incontáveis hostes de anjos».
3. Fazendo a referência torna-se todo-inclusiva, alguns pensam que a expressão refere-se aos anjos e à igreja, igualmente. Nas Escrituras, anjos e homens são freqüentemente vinculados, como quando se lê que os anjos servem aos homens (ver Heb. 1:14), que os anjos são mediadores da mensagem dada aos homens (ver Gál. 3:19), e que os anjos participarão do julgamento dos homens (ver Mat. 24:31 e II Tes. 1:7). Porém, o destino humano, que é a participação na natureza divina (ver II Ped. 1:4), transcende ao estado atual dos anjos (ver Rom. 8:29).

Sem importar qual seja a referência exata, a mensagem geral da passagem é clara: temos um acesso à realidades espirituais muito superior àquele que fazia parte do Antigo Testamento. De fato, no N.T. temos acesso aos lugares celestiais (ver as notas sobre Efé. 1:3, no NTI), à presença de Deus, até chegarmos a compartilhar de Sua natureza. Por essa razão, somos advertidos a não rejeitarmos a mensagem que nos vem por meio de Cristo (ver Heb. 12:25), que é precisamente a aplicação feita pelo autor do livro. (AL IB NTI)

ASSEMBLÉIA SOLENE

No hebraico temos uma única palavra, derivada de uma raiz que significa *restringir* ou *conter*. Tratava-se da reunião e da santificação da comunidade de Israel, em alguma ocasião nacional solene. É expressão (no português, «reunião solene») usada em sentido técnico para indicar o oitavo dia da festa dos Tabernáculos (ver Lev. 23:36; Núm. 29:35; 8:18) e o sétimo dia da festa da Páscoa (Deu. 16:8). Em ambos os casos, os israelitas foram instruídos a «não fazer qualquer obra», porquanto eles estavam em estado de santidade ritual. Por ocasião da dedicação do templo de Jerusalém, Salomão proclamou uma solene assembléia no oitavo dia: «...porque por sete dias já haviam celebrado a consagração do altar; a festa durava sete dias» (II Crô. 7:9). Com uma finalidade totalmente diferente, Jeú ordenou que fosse consagrada «uma assembléia solene a Baal» (II Reis 10:20). Jeú foi capaz de completar o expurgo dos adoradores de Baal da terra de Israel, mediante o massacre daqueles que se haviam reunido, por ocasião da reunião solene, para participarem do sacrifício a Baal que Jeú fingidamente oferecia.

Em contraste com as festividades acima mencionadas, a reunião solene também se reunia em dias especiais de jejum. Quando a praga dos gafanhotos ameaçava a terra, Joel exortou o povo de Israel como segue: «Promulgai um santo jejum, convocai uma assembléia solene, congregai os anciãos, todos os moradores desta terra, para a casa do Senhor vosso Deus, e clamai ao Senhor» (Joel 1:14; cf. 2:15).

Amós e Isaías zombaram de certas reuniões solenes (entre outras coisas), e disseram que algumas daquelas eram consideradas intoleráveis por Deus, (ver Isa. 1:13; Amós 5:21), porquanto o povo não agia com justiça, no trato de uns com os outros. É conforme Isaías esclareceu: «...quando multiplicais as vossas orações, não as ouço, porque as vossas mãos estão cheias de sangue» (Isa. 1:15). A mesma palavra hebraica aqui empregada é usada em Jer. 9:2, dentro da expressão «são um bando de traidores».

ASSENTO Ver o artigo sobre **Cadeira**.

ASSERTÓRICA

O termo descreve uma proposição que simplesmente assevera que algo é ou não é o caso. É usado em contraste com juízos *problemáticos* e *apodeícticos* (ver os artigos). A análise dessa modalidade retrocede ao menos a Aristóteles. As proposições assertóricas, problemáticas e apodeícticas falam sobre os modos que as proposições podem assumir. (F)

ASSIDEANOS

No hebraico quer dizer **piedosos, retos**. O nome deriva-se de uma raiz hebraica, *chasid*, palavra que denota ações muito boas ou ações muito más, embora mais geralmente o primeiro caso. Em II Macabeus, a palavra é aplicada a um grupo de homens zelosos e devotados, que se levantaram ao sinal dado por Matatias para iniciar a resistência armada. Matatias foi o pai dos Macabeus, os quais defenderam de espada na mão a doutrina da unidade de Deus, assim impedindo a helenização do povo judeu. Um termo hebraico cognato aparece em Salmos 145:10; Isaías 57:1 e Miquéias 7:2, a fim de descrever homens bons e piedosos. Em I Macabeus 2:42, eles são chamados *guerreiros valorosos*, que se ofereciam voluntariamente para servir em defesa de lei. Em II Macabeus 14:6, eles reconhecem Judas Macabeu como seu líder. Evidentemente, formaram uma espécie de partido, embora nada se saiba quanto à sua origem. A principal preocupação deles parece ter sido religiosa, e não militar. Há alguma evidência de que romperam relações com os Macabeus, por quererem estes ocupar o ofício sumo sacerdotal, o que, na opinião dos assideanos, seria uma usurpação. Alguns eruditos supõem que os fariseus, e talvez até os essênios, desenvolveram-se a partir desse grupo, formando dois ramos divergentes. (S Z)

ASSIDISMO

1. *O termo*. A palavra **hasidim** é o vocábulo hebraico plural que significa «santos». A forma singular é *hasid*, que significa uma pessoa piedosa. Tal palavra aparece freqüentemente no livro de Salmos.

2. *Um grupo religioso no tempo dos Macabeus*. Esse existiu no século II A.C. (Ver I Mac. 2:42; 7:13; II Mac. 14:6). Ver o artigo sobre os assidianos. Esse grupo opunha-se ao partido sacerdotal, que caíra sob a influência do helenismo. Liderados pelos hasmoneanos, conseguiram capturar o templo de Jerusalém. Apesar de se terem envolvido em uma revolução política, na realidade formavam um partido religioso que queria preservar os antigos valores da fé judaica. Posteriormente, romperam com os Macabeus, por causa do mundanismo deles, e assim continuaram a preservar as suas prioridades. Alguns supõem que eles foram os precursores dos fariseus e dos essênios. É mesmo possível que o vocábulo *essênio* seja uma forma variante de *hasid*. A conexão entre os essênios e

os assidianos tem sido muito disputada, sem que se tenha chegado a uma conclusão definitiva.

3. *Assidismo moderno*. Como um movimento recente, podemos datar o assidismo entre 1700 e 1760. Seu fundador foi Baal Shem To, que viveu naquele período. Tornou-se famoso como místico e operador de milagres, bem como cultor da Cabala (que vide). Era dotado de fervor evangelista e reavivalista, com o acompanhamento de dons psíquicos. Com a ajuda de seus discípulos, rabinos, Jacob Joseph Cohen, de Polonnoye, e Dov Baer, o Magido (pregador), ele exerceu larga influência, especialmente entre as pessoas menos eruditas e mais humildes. O movimento inflamou o fervor religioso de muitas pessoas. As suas reuniões eram assinaladas por exaltação emocional nas orações, a busca pela comunhão mística com Deus, isto é, o contato direto com a divindade, de alguma maneira, sem mediação do intelecto. Algumas de suas reuniões atingiam as raias do frenesi. Podemos mesmo dizer que o movimento se assemelhava ao movimento pentecostal, dentro da comunidade judaica, sem o acompanhamento de doutrinas cristãs. A principal característica deles era a ênfase que davam à imanência de Deus, do que resultava a possibilidade do contato místico de Deus com os homens. Eles buscavam milagres, alegria estática e uma fé vital e viva. O movimento não procurava aliviar a tristeza das massas pobres através da esperança messiânica, e sim, por meio de mensagens que despertavam emocionalmente os homens. Enfatizava as virtudes da mansidão e da modéstia. Seus líderes espirituais julgavam-se uma espécie de mediadores entre Deus e os homens, como uma missão a ser cumprida. Eles frisavam a salvação pela fé, e não pelas obras, e também mediante o estudo da Torah. Essa ênfase punha em perigo os alicerces do judaísmo tradicional, e o movimento acabou sofrendo oposição, tendo sido declarado herético (pelos talmudistas, em 1781), e então foi perseguido. Trata-se da mesma antiga história em que os antigos grupos «ortodoxos» manuseiam os grupos novos e diferentes, que buscam impor reformas.

Influência crescente. Apesar desse desenvolvimento, os zadiquins (líderes religiosos do grupo), continuaram a exercer grande influência sobre as massas. Durante a primeira metade do século XIX, quase a metade do povo judaico inteiro fora conquistado pelo movimento. Entretanto, a Iluminação que houve na segunda metade do século XIX, exerceu notável influência, alterando o clima intelectual da Europa. Por esse motivo, o assidismo começou a perder o seu grande poder. Elementos de excessos e superstições, dentro do movimento, tornaram-se alvos dos defensores da iluminação, o que contribuiu para o declínio gradual do movimento. Não obstante, seu poder continuou sendo considerável na Rússia, até o surgimento do comunismo. E, em outros lugares, até à Segunda Guerra Mundial. Desde então, tem continuado sendo uma força apreciável na Palestina, na América do Norte e em outras terras. Nos tempos modernos, tem sido popularizado por Martinho Buber (ver o artigo a seu respeito).

ASSINATURA

No hebraico temos uma palavra que usualmente é considerada uma forma sintética de «tau», nome da última letra do alfabeto hebraico, além de um sufixo possessivo pessoal. Significa «minha marca» ou «minhas iniciais». Aparece sem o sufixo em Eze. 9:4,6, usualmente traduzido por «marca» ou «sinal» (como faz nossa versão portuguesa). Provavelmente era um simples «X», forma da letra *tau* na antiga escrita semítica arredondada. Em Jó 31:35, onde aparece a única ocorrência com o sufixo, refere-se a um documento legal, provavelmente um tablete de argila onde alguém deixara a sua marca. Isso explica a tradução portuguesa «minha defesa assinada».

ASSIR

No hebraico, **cativo**. Consideremos os pontos abaixo:

1. Um levita, filho de Coré (ver Êx. 6:24; I Crô. 6:22), cerca de 1620 A.C. 2. Filho de Ebiasafe e neto de um outro Assir, antepassado de Samuel (ver I Crô. 6:23), em cerca de 1740 A.C. 3. Algumas versões dizem, em I Crô. 3:17, «Assir, filho de Jeconias». Mas outras preferem — conforme vemos em nossa versão portuguesa — «Jeconias, o cativo», cerca de 588 A.C. (ID S)

ASSÍRIA

Esboço do artigo:
1. Nome
2. Lugar
3. Capitais
4. Língua
5. Relações com a Babilônia
6. O povo
7. Registros escritos
8. Religião
9. Principais descobertas arqueológicas
10. História

1. Nome. Devem ser comparados Assur, a principal divindade da Assíria, e Assur, o segundo filho de Sem. Portanto, a Assíria é o país ocupado pelos descendentes desse neto de Noé. (Ver Gên. 10:22 e o artigo sobre *Assur*). A Assíria era o nome de um país; e depois de um poderoso império que dominou o mundo bíblico dos séculos IX a VII A.C. Incluía a Babilônia, o Elão, a Média, a Síria, a Palestina, a Arábia, o sul de Anatólia, a Cilícia e o Egito.

2. Lugar. Assíria era o antigo nome do distrito de ambos os lados do rio Tigre, variando em suas dimensões, dependendo da época, mas geralmente confinada à região da parte norte do moderno Iraque, entre a presente fronteira Síria e o pequeno rio Zabe. A oeste, era limitada pelo platô desértico da Mesopotâmia central, e a leste pelas montanhas do Curdistão; ao norte ficava a Armênia, e ao sul a Babilônia. Em seu zênite, incluía os lugares mencionados no primeiro ponto. O âmago da região era uma planície de aluvião muito fértil, embora a maior parte consistisse em um platô desértico com serras sucessivas de pedra calcária, com vales aráveis entre as serras. O clima desse distrito era mais fresco e mais chuvoso do que o da Babilônia, com chuvas somente no inverno. Portanto, a irrigação era imprescindível para a produção de víveres suficientes. Com a passagem do tempo, o império assírio cresceu em todas as direções, mas particularmente na direção da Síria. Devido a essa extensão para o ocidente, houve uma mudança no uso do nome, de tal modo que *Síria* passou a ser o nome usado, que se derivava do antigo nome, *Assíria*.

3. Capitais. A capital original do país, de onde também se derivava o nome do país, era Assur, modernamente Qalat Sharqat. Ficava na margem ocidental do Tigre, acima da boca do Pequeno Zabe.

ASSÍRIA

Para o norte, cerca de 97 km dali, ficava Nínive, modernamente Kuyunjik, que foi fundada muito tempo antes da cidade de Assur, mas que finalmente tornou-se capital do novo império assírio. Entre essas duas cidades ficava Calá, moderna Nimrud, que foi capital do império durante parte dos séculos IX e VII A.C. A nordeste de Nínive ficava Dur Sharrukin, modernamente Corsabade, que foi a capital durante o reinado de Sargão II (721-705 A.C.). Importantes cidades secundárias eram Arbela, modernamente Erbil ou Arbil, a sudoeste de Nínive; Harã, o principal centro do poder do novo império assírio, na parte oeste da Mesopotâmia, e última capital do império, após a queda de Nínive, em 612 A.C.

4. Língua. A Assíria e a Babilônia tiveram ambas impressionantes histórias, compartilhando de um idioma comum, conhecido como assírio-babilônico, ou acadiano.

5. Relações com a Babilônia. Uma avançada civilização se desenvolvera na Babilônia em cerca de 3000 A.C., que permaneceu o centro cultural da Mesopotâmia até o século VI A.C. A Assíria obteve o domínio militar, ocupando grande parte da mesma região, pelo que as duas civilizações muito tinham em comum, tornando-se praticamente inseparáveis. O poder político e militar oscilava para lá e para cá entre a Assíria e a Babilônia, sobretudo no período entre 900 e 600 A.C. Foi precisamente durante esse período que a Assíria passou a atuar como opressora e invasora, nas narrativas bíblicas. A Bíblia, entretanto, sempre distingue entre a Assíria e a Babilônia.

6. O povo. Eles pertenciam à raça semita, e aparentemente tinham vindo da Babilônia a fim de instalar-se como colonos. Não chegaram ali como uma raça pura (se é que existe tal coisa à face do planeta), mas já representavam uma mistura de sangue babilônico e sumério, os quais eram os habitantes originais da terra, até onde a nossa história é capaz de retroceder. Depois que chegaram a nova terra, ao norte da Babilônia (e não a grande distância de onde tinham partido, segundo os padrões modernos), continuou a mescla com povos provenientes de várias invasões, vindos do Elão e da Arábia. Mas, visto que em alguns lugares a mistura de sangue não foi tão intensa, eles jactavam-se que eram de uma raça mais pura que a dos babilônios, o que é apenas uma dentre inúmeras exibições do orgulho humano. Na verdade, não há tal coisa como uma raça pura ou um idioma puro. A arqueologia tem mostrado que eles eram de estatura média européia, de tez morena, com nariz proeminente. Usavam barbas hirsutas e despenteadas. Os registros históricos mostram que eles apreciavam muito as festas, e que tinham bom humor. Na guerra, porém, demonstravam uma ferocidade que sempre caracterizou a história da humanidade. Todavia, os assírios aparentemente inclinaram-se para a brutalidade, pois a história deles abunda em violência e derramamento de sangue.

7. Registros escritos. Os assírios não criaram um alfabeto, mas tinham um tipo de escrita em que cada sinal representava uma idéia, como o sol, uma cidade, a maderia, etc. Esses sinais chamam-se *ideogramas*. Além desses sinais, a língua escrita dos assírios tinha alguns sinais silábicos, representando fonemas como ab, ib, ub, ba, bi, bu. O resultado era capenga, embora fosse uma maneira viável de transmitir uma mensagem na forma escrita. Eles escreviam gravando sobre a argila ou a pedra com um formão. A maior parte do que conhecemos sobre a Assíria nos foi transmitida através de tabletes de argila, os quais variam muito em dimensões, alguns dos quais chegam a 40 cm de comprimento. Um pequeno instrumento de metal, com ponta triangular, era usado para deixar as marcas, em forma de cunha, o que explica o nome dessa escrita, *cuneiforme*. Muitos milhares desses tabletes têm sido descobertos pelos arqueólogos, mas a grande maioria deles ainda não foi traduzida para qualquer idioma moderno. Uma vez que esses tabletes sejam traduzidos, talvez venha-se a conhecer melhor a história da Assíria do que a de qualquer outro povo antigo, com a única exceção dos hebreus. Esses tabletes nos dão as informações mais variegadas, sobre assuntos religiosos, políticos, pessoais, orações, recibos, notas de venda, encantamentos, listas de presságios e até mesmo gramáticas que explicam como a língua dos assírios funcionava.

Os assírios estavam mais interessados pela arte militar do que pelas belas artes ou pela literatura, pelo que a Babilônia preservou sua hegemonia cultural e religiosa, mesmo quando os assírios eram o poder dominante.

8. Religião. As idéias religiosas da Assíria eram provenientes da Babilônia, desde o começo até o fim de sua história. Eles criam em muitos deuses (politeísmo), mas a divindade principal era *Assur*, honrado como fundador da nação. Divindades secundárias eram Anu, Bel e Ea, que eram divindades babilônicas, adotadas por outros povos semitas. Além dessa tríada, havia o deus-lua, Sim, o deus-sol, Shamash, e a deusa da lua crescente e rainha das estrelas, Istar, também o deus do trovão, da chuva e das tempestades, Ramã. Além desses, havia divindades de terceira categoria, além de espíritos do céu, da terra e do mar. Algumas inscrições que enfatizam a posição de algum deus específico dos assírios têm sido erroneamente interpretadas como se refletissem idéias monoteístas. É possível que, em algum período histórico, o henoteísmo fosse favorecido por alguns assírios, mas o monoteísmo jamais veio à tona naquela sociedade. Os assírios ofereciam sacrifícios pela manhã e à tardinha, nos quais empregavam vinho, leite, mel e bolos. Os tabletes de argila descobertos em Nínive contêm a história da criação, a narrativa do dilúvio, a inquirição de Gilgamés pela vida eterna; a descida de Istar ao mundo dos mortos, em busca de seu marido, Tamuz, embora, contrariamente ao que alguns têm dito, jamais se encontrou qualquer texto escrito narrando a ressurreição de Tamuz. A história de Sargão de Agade, salvo por ocasião do nascimento, ao ser posto em um cesto e deixado a flutuar no rio Eufrates, é interessante. Istar o tirou da água (conforme fez a filha de Faraó com Moisés) e o criou para que fosse rei. Além disso, há a história de Etana, que fugiu para o céu montado em uma águia. Também há uma literatura de sabedoria, semelhante à que se acha no Antigo Testamento, além de hinos, provérbios, parábolas, conselhos, etc.

9. Principais descobertas arqueológicas. A Assíria originou-se de colonos da Babilônia. O trecho de Gênesis 10:11 e a arqueologia confirmam isso. Em 1820 receberam séria atenção os cômoros de Kuyunjik e Nebi Yunus, como possíveis locais da antiga cidade de Nínive. Foi desenterrado o palácio de Assurbanipal, em 1853-1854. Quatro palácios foram descobertos em Calá. Em Corsabade, em 1843, foi encontrado o palácio de Sargão. Muitas outras expedições têm sido efetuadas, e grande massa de material informativo veio à lume. Assurbanipal, o rei-sábio, criou uma biblioteca importando ou copiando textos tanto dos arquivos reais já existentes em Nínive, Assur e Calá quanto dos centros religiosos da Babilônia. Em 1852-1853, foram encontrados mais de vinte e seis mil

ASSÍRIA

Nobre assírio

Guerreiro assírio

Carro de guerra

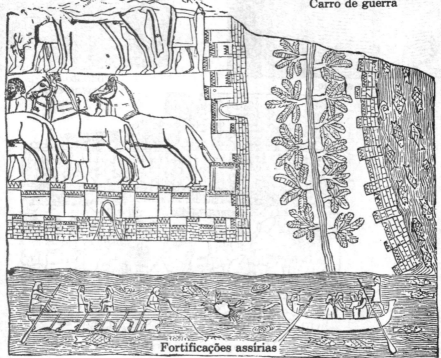

Fortificações assírias

ASSÍRIA

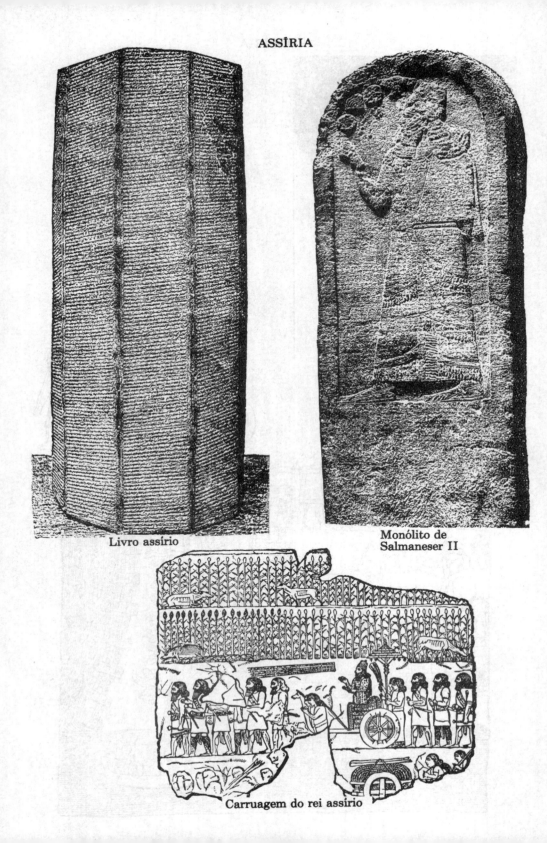

Livro assírio

Monólito de Salmaneser II

Carruagem do rei assírio

ASSÍRIA

tabletes de argila fragmentados, no palácio de Assurbanipal e no templo de Nabu, nas proximidades. Esses tabletes representam cerca de dez mil textos diferentes. Esse achado forneceu grande riqueza de informações sobre a Assíria, estabelecendo a base para o estudo de seu idioma, além de proporcionar abundante informação sobre a Babilônia. Alguns desses textos contêm traduções sumerianas interlineares, o que também ajudou na compreensão desse idioma não-semita, e que era preservado como língua religiosa na Assíria, tal como o latim, durante séculos, serviu de veículo na Europa e em outras regiões do mundo. Tal material atualmente é guardado no Museu Britânico.

10. História. a. *Primórdios.* A cerâmica foi inventada no antigo Oriente no começo do sexto milênio A.C. Restos de cerâmica do período neolítico têm sido encontrados em Nínive e outros lugares da Assíria, pertencentes à primeira metade do quinto milênio A.C. Civilizações que existiram nos tempos antigos receberam modernamente nomes de acordo com os lugares onde essas descobertas arqueológicas têm sido feitas, como Hassunã, Samarrã, Halfiã e Obeidiã. Um constante avanço na técnica pode ser notado. Nisso há provas de que foram feitos empréstimos do sul (Babilônia). As descobertas arqueológicas feitas em Assur (Tell Khuweira) e em outros lugares, mostram que a Assíria participou da primeira cultura dinástica da Babilônia do tempo dos sumérios. Mediante evidências posteriores, ficamos sabendo que a Assíria fez parte do império de Sargão, de Acade e de seu sucessor (2300-2200 A.C.). A Assíria também esteve sujeita, em parte pelo menos, aos reis babilônios da terceira dinastia de Ur (cerca de 2050-1950 A.C.). Foi descoberta uma lista de reis em Corsabade, contendo trinta e dois nomes, dos quais os últimos dezessete são considerados históricos. Mas os próprios assírios do século VIII A.C. admitiam que eles tinham pouco conhecimento dos reis de tempos mais remotos. Há confirmações arqueológicas para vários daqueles dezessete monarcas. Os primeiros quinze da lista teriam habitado em tendas, e possuíam estranhos nomes, alguns dos quais sem dúvida são mitológicos. É curioso o fato de que o segundo desses monarcas tinha o nome de *Adão*, nome do progenitor da humanidade, segundo a tradição dos hebreus.

b. *Antigo Império Assírio.* Durante o reinado de Puzur-Assur I, em cerca de 1950 A.C., chegamos a um terreno histórico indiscutível. Ele e seus sucessores, pelo espaço de cerca de duzentos anos, representavam a antiga história da Assíria, quando o poder dessa nação propagava-se em todas as direções. Os assírios ocuparam-se então do comércio e do escambo. Ilusama dominou a Babilônia em cerca de 1900 A.C. Seus quatro sucessores imediatos organizaram um extenso comércio com a Ásia Menor, o que é ilustrado por milhares de tabletes econômicos descobertos em Cânis (atual Kultepe) e na Capadócia. O idioma deles era o assírio antigo, uma língua não-semita. Porém, entre 1950 e 1750 A.C., entraram semitas ocidentais seminômades naquela região, trazendo uma língua quase idêntica à do antigo hebraico dos patriarcas. Esses povos eram chamados *amurrium* (depois, Amurru), isto é, ocidentais, pelos babilônios e assírios. Essa palavra finalmente assumiu a forma de amorreus. Em cerca de 1748 A.C., um chefe amorreu (ver o artigo a respeito dos amorreus) tornou-se rei da Assíria, sob o nome de Samsi-Adade. Ele e seu filho, Isme-Dagã governaram por duas gerações, quando então toda a região do Mediterrâneo até o Elão (sudoeste do Irã) esteve sob o poder assírio. Foram descobertos vários milhares de cartas em Mari, juntamente com outros documentos, mostrando que o lugar estava sob o hegemonia assíria.

Seguiu-se um período de anarquia, após a morte de Isme-Dagã I, e os sete governantes seguintes foram apelidados «filhos de ninguém», na lista de Corsabade de trinta e dois reis, mencionados acima. Nesse tempo, povos que haviam sido dominados pelos assírios, sacudiram o jugo. Os babilônios tomaram Mari. Parece que entre cerca de 1700 e 1500 A.C., pode ter havido um estado vassalo, dominado pelos horeus e indo-arianos vindos do leste e do norte. Durante esse período, houve uma interrupção nas inscrições assírias.

c. *Médio Império Assírio.* Começam novamente a aparecer inscrições assírias com Assurnirari I, em cerca de 1500 A.C. Há evidências de tratados feitos com os cassitas (ou cosseanos) da Babilônia, o que demonstra que a Assíria havia reconquistado a sua independência. Por esse tempo, a Assíria esteve em guerra contra o reino indo-ariano de Mitani, que ficava para oeste; mas Nínive estava subjugada pelos mitanos, sendo possível que o país inteiro estivesse sob o domínio desses indo-arianos, durante uma parte do período. Todavia, o Egito derrotou as forças mitanianas, e isso fez a Assíria mostrar-se favorável para com o Egito, enviando-lhe muitos ricos presentes. Então os hititas aplicaram o golpe de misericórdia no poder de Mitani, o que permitiu a reconstituição do império assírio, levado a efeito por Eriba-Adade (1356-1321 A.C.). Seu filho, Assur-Ubalite expandiu o império, dominando a Babilônia e outras regiões. Dispomos de parte de sua correspondência com Amenotepe IV (Aquenatom), do Egito, nas cartas de Amarna. Durante os reinados de Arique-Den-Ili (1319 A.C.) e Adade-Nirari I (1307-1275 A.C.), territórios tão para oeste quanto Carquemis, perdidos desde os dias de Samis-Adade, foram recuperados. Salmaneser I (1274-1245 A.C.) fez ataques constantes contra as tribos das colinas orientais e contra os novos inimigos, Urartu e as forças hurrianas, a nordeste. Seu filho, Tuculti-Ninurta I (1244-1206 A.C.), deu muita atenção à Babilônia, da qual também era o rei, até ser assassinado por seu próprio filho, Assurnadinapli. Pouco depois disso, a Babilônia tornou-se independente novamente. Com Tiglate-Pileser I (cerca de 1114 a 1076 A.C.), a Assíria entrou no período do império. Ele expandiu o império assírio de maneira extraordinária; mas, nos próximos dois séculos, houve um outro período de declínio, até o governo de Assurnasirpal II (883-859 A.C.), o qual inventou uma nova forma de crueldade e barbaridade diante do que os adversários da Assíria não conseguiram resistir.

d. *Novo Império Assírio* (900 a 612 A.C.). Tuculti-Ninurta II (890-885 A.C.) combateu os opressores da Assíria. Seu filho, Assurnasirpal II (885-860 A.C.), mediante uma série de campanhas militares, subjugou muitos povos, como os que estavam no médio rio Eufrates, os do Líbano, os filisteus, os do N e as colinas orientais da Babilônia. No oeste, ele entrou em conflito com Israel. Seu filho, Salmaneser III (757-824 A.C.) herdou a máquina de combate e conduziu campanhas contra a Síria-Palestina, em uma das quais lutou contra Acabe, de Israel, em Carcar, sobre o rio Orontes, em 835 A.C.; e em outra campanha recebeu tributo de Jeú, filho de Onri, rei de Judá. Esse monarca assírio fazia alta opinião de si mesmo, dizendo que ele era «o poderoso rei, rei do universo, rei sem rival, o autocrata, o poderoso dos quatro reinos do mundo, que esmigalha os príncipes do mundo inteiro, que despedaçou todos os seus adversários como potes de barro». Apesar de tanta jactância, ele morreu em meio a revoltas que seu filho, Samsi-Adade V (823-811 A.C.), teve de enfrentar. Adade-Nirari III (810-783 A.C.), deu prosseguimento à interminável guerra, com bom êxito. Mas Salmaneser IV (782-773 A.C.), Asurdan III (772-755 A.C.) e Assur-Nirari V (754-745 A.C.), não se mostraram muito bons nas matanças (ou seus adversários lhes eram superiores), o que explica o declínio do império assírio. Mas foi então que surgiu em cena o grande guerreiro e estadista, Tiglate-Pileser III, inspirado pelos feitos do grande matador em massa, Tiglate-Pileser I, do século XI A.C. Nessa inspiração sangüinária, ele reconquistou todos os territórios, incluindo a Babilônia, onde se tornou conhecido pelo nome de Pulo (na Bíblia, Pul — ver II Reis 15:19). Esse homem conquistou Israel e enviou para o cativeiro uma parte de sua população. Após a sua morte, Oséias, de Israel, revoltou-se contra a Assíria. Em face disso, Salmaneser V (726-722 A.C.) atacou Samaria, capital de Israel, o reino israelita do norte. Antes da queda de Israel consumar-se, Sarruquim II, também conhecido como Sargão II (721-705 A.C.) assumiu as rédeas do poder assírio. De fato, seu reinado foi inaugurado com a queda de Israel. O ano de 722 A.C. aparece como a data do cativeiro de Israel (ver o artigo a respeito). Sargão é mencionado no Antigo Testamento somente no trecho de Isaías 20:1. Mas as escavações feitas em seu esplêndido palácio, em Dur Sarruquim ou Corsabade, com muitas descobertas, fizeram dele um dos mais bem conhecidos reis assírios. Seu filho, Senaqueribe, sucedeu-o no trono, em 704 A.C., tendo governado a Assíria até o ano de 681 A.C. As crônicas da Babilônia informam que ele foi assassinado por seu próprio filho. Seu filho mais jovem, não envolvido no assassinato, teria perseguido seus irmãos rebeldes, presumivelmente comparsas no crime, até o sul da Armênia. Senaqueribe foi um construtor, e não apenas um guerreiro, tendo construído palácios, portões e templos em Nínive. Também construiu aquedutos e represas. Prisioneiros, entre os quais havia judeus, foram forçados a ajudar nessas obras.

O filho mais novo de Senaqueribe, ao qual acabamos de fazer menção, Esar-Hadom (680-669 A.C.), subiu ao poder e tornou-se um dos maiores conquistadores assírios de todos os tempos, distinção essa nada fácil, em meio a tão grande número de sangüinários matadores. A história da Assíria provê uma lista quase interminável de campanhas. Judá aparece entre aqueles que pagavam tributo a Esar-Hadom. A Assíria chegou a invadir o Egito, estabelecendo governadores assírios em Tebas e em Mênfis. Porém, uma vez morto Esar-Hadom, começaram as inevitáveis revoltas. O Egito libertou-se. Então coube a Assurbanipal (669-627 A.C.) recuperar o controle sobre o Egito. Esse homem também era um sábio e um humanista. (Ver o artigo sobre ele, que ilustra esse fato). As conquistas territoriais foram subseqüentemente perdidas, e o poder assírio começou a declinar radicalmente. Nabopolassar, o caldeu, expulsou os assírios da Babilônia, em 625 A.C. Os babilônios aliaram-se aos medos e capturaram a cidade de Assur, em 614 A.C., e então, em julho e agosto de 612 A.C., conforme havia sido profetizado por Naum e Sofonias, Nínive caiu. As suas muralhas foram feitas em pedaços por enchentes (Naum 1:8; Xenofonte, *Anabasis* iii. 4). Durante dois anos, Assur-Ubalite manteve-se em Harrã, mas nenhuma ajuda chegou da parte do Egito. O Faraó Neco marchou tarde demais, e assim a cidade foi conquistada pelos babilônios. Esse foi o fim de Assíria e o começo do Novo Império Babilônico, tendo início um novo período histórico. É admirável que uma potência importante e de tão longa duração pudesse ter sido conquistada com tanta rapidez. Mas assim o determina o destino humano, escapando dessa insegurança somente a estabilidade das realidades espirituais. (AM GA OLMS POE PRI UN Z)

ASSOBIAR

Som produzido pelo sopro forte e forçado entre a língua e os dentes. Esse som constitui um gesto comum nos países do Oriente Próximo, denotando derrisão, ou então, surpresa. (Ver I Reis 9:8; Jer. 19:8). Assobiar é igualmente um método para atrair a atenção de alguém (ver Isa. 5:26). No caso de assobios diante de lugares que sofreram destruição ou julgamento, ou qualquer destino adverso, talvez esse som tivesse o intuito de afastar o mal que, segundo se pensava, apegava-se ao local. Porém, a idéia central era a de zombar do lugar que merecera o castigo, em face da iniqüidade ali reinante. (Z)

ASSOCIAÇÃO DE IDÉIAS

Hume, querendo refutar certas «ficções» filosóficas, supôs que a mente tem a tendência de associar idéias correspondentes aos tipos de eventos que sempre foram observados em rápida sucessão. Em conseqüência, sempre que uma idéia do primeiro tipo de eventos se apresenta na mente, evoca a idéia e a expectação de um evento do segundo tipo. E esses dois eventos aparentemente se relacionam entre si como *causa* e *efeito*. Por esse motivo, chegamos a acreditar haver uma conexão necessária entre os dois eventos; mas, na realidade, não há qualquer fenômeno observável, e portanto, nenhuma idéia genuína de conexão necessária.

O *fenomenalismo* de J.S. Mill (ver o artigo a respeito), uma lei da *inferência* que explica a crença de alguém na existência de objetos materiais, está envolvido no conceito. Mediante a experiência, a pessoa aprende que certas sensações ocorrem juntamente com a percepção de certos objetos. O indivíduo forma um conceito de um objeto qualquer em termos de um possível grupo de sensações, associado à sua percepção.

Hobbes usava os princípios associativos a fim de explicar as operações mentais, distinguindo entre associações fortuitas e associações controladas. Locke também supunha que algumas das conexões são naturais, ao passo que outras resultaram do acaso ou do hábito. (E P)

ASSOCIAÇÃO GERAL DAS IGREJAS BATISTAS REGULARES

Um grupo de igrejas batistas, originadas no norte dos E.U.A., unidas a fim de protestarem contra as tendências liberais dentro da denominação batista, e a fim de procurar o retorno aos ideais originais, às normas e às práticas dos batistas. Tinha por intuito ser uma associação, e não uma denominação ou convenção. Suas igrejas não fazem parte de uma denominação desse nome, visto que uma igreja batista não pode ser membro de qualquer coisa fora de si mesma. Essa associação é fortemente fundamentalista em seu caráter, e muito zelosa quanto a programas missionários. Conta com um bom número de igrejas, e algumas escolas teológicas no Brasil.

ASSOCIACIONISMO

Teoria psicológica defendida por alguns filósofos, que pensam que as associações de idéias são o princípio fundamental da vida mental do homem. Foi sistematizada pela primeira vez no *Tratado* de Hume, na esperança de que vários tipos de associação entre os átomos da consciência seriam para o mundo mental o que a mecânica clássica foi para os pedaços de matéria «dura, maciça e impenetrável». A tradição prosseguiu através de Hartley, James Mill, J.S. Mill e Herbert Spencer. Usualmente a teoria tem aparecido em combinação com o *sensacionismo* (ver o artigo). Atualmente, muitos físicos estão abandonando a teoria atômica simplista, até mesmo como base para o —mundo material, quanto mais no caso do mundo mental. (F)

ASSOPRO

Esse termo é aplicado a violentos temporais da natureza, envolvendo apenas algum vendaval, ou fortes ventos com diferentes tipos de tempestade. 1. O *iroso resfolgar* do Senhor é um julgamento severo (ver II Sam. 22:16; Jó 4:9; Sal. 18:15). 2. Os homens também podem assoprar contra outros, embora Deus possa frustrar tais ataques (ver Is. 25:4). 3. Deus também pode infundir um espírito em alguém, isto é, dar um forte impulso para que esse alguém faça algo (ver II Reis 19:7 e Isa. 37:7). 4. Uma diferente palavra hebraica, que pode ser traduzida por «assopro», refere-se ao som dado pelas trombetas (ver Jos. 6:5). (Z)

ASSÓS

Uma cidade de porto marítimo da Mísia, na praia norte do golfo de Adramítio, cerca de 48 km de Tróade, seguindo pelo mar, diante de Lesbos. Paulo chegou ali caminhando a pé tendo partido de Tróade, a fim de encontrar-se com amigos seus, e apanhar uma embarcação para Mitilene (ver Atos 20:13,14). Era um ponto fortificado estratégico, que controlava a estrada costeira. Os companheiros de Paulo seguiram pelo mar, rodeando o cabo Lecto. Estrabão informa-nos que era uma cidade fortificada. Suas defesas e seus edifícios públicos ficavam em uma íngreme colina, que se erguia a 215 m de altura, formando um esquema arquitetural unificado e ligado a um porto artificial, por meio de uma longa escadaria. A arqueologia tem descoberto grandes quantidades de finas esculturas e outros objetos. No século IV A.C., esse porto era a sede de uma escola de filósofos platônicos, incluindo Aristóteles. O estoico Cleantes nasceu ali. Tornou-se parte dos domínios dos reis de Pérgamo, e, posteriormente, foi um porto da província romana da Ásia. Modernamente chama-se Rahram Koi. O antigo porto foi entulhado, formando jardins; mas um porto moderno foi construído ao lado do mesmo, protegido por um molhe artificial. (ID ND S Z)

ASSUERO

No hebraico, **homem poderoso** ou **olho poderoso**, equivalente ao vocábulo persa *khshayarsha*. A forma grega é Xerxes. O papiro aramaico elefantino exibe as consoantes *ksyrs* em lugar desse nome, quase igual à forma grega; e a versão babilônica de Xerxes, na inscrição de Behistun, é bem parecida com a forma hebraica. Foi o *título* de quatro monarcas medos e persas da Bíblia.

1. *O pai de Dario.* Ele é incidentalmente mencionado em Dan. 9:1 como o pai de Dario, o medo. É idêntico ao Astíages da história profana, embora alguns considerem incerta essa identificação. Há quem prefira Ciaxares como a pessoa em questão.

2. *O sucessor de Dario I.* É mencionado em Esd. 4:6. Xerxes I (no persa, *Khshayarsha*). Dario I (Histapes) foi o grande rei da Pérsia (cerca de 486-465 A.C.). A identificação de Assuero com Xerxes pressupõe que os vss. 6-23 do quarto capítulo de Esdras são um tanto parentéticos, provendo outra informação sobre o tópico da oposição, em um período posterior. As ruínas de Persépolis ilustram o seu reinado. Ali foi encontrada uma inscrição que alista as várias nações que ele sujeitou. Segundo o livro de Ester, ele divorciou-se de Vasti e casou-se com Ester. Isso a deixou em posição de salvar a muitos judeus de um massacre que fora planejado por Hamã. Mordecai, primo mais velho de Ester, foi uma peça fundamental na questão. Quando da morte de Hamã, Mordecai assumiu a posição governamental que antes fora do morto, tornando-se um dos ministros do monarca. Xerxes é relembrado na história secular como o monarca persa que foi derrotado em Salamis, Platea e Micale pelos gregos, em 480 - 479 A.C. Foi assassinado em sua câmara de dormir, no ano de 465 A.C.

3. Há um Assuero em Dan. 9:1, pai de *Dario, o medo* (ver o artigo), cuja identificação é incerta. Tem sido identificado com Gubaru (Gogrias), vice-rei da província da Babilônia no tempo de Ciro. Nesse caso, seu pai pode ter sido Ciaxares. Outros identificam-no com o Astíages da história profana, ou com o próprio Ciaxares.

4. O trecho de Tobias 14:15 ainda fala sobre um outro Assuero, mencionado em conexão com a destruição de Nínive, identificado por alguns com Ciaxares, conforme é mencionado por Herod. 1:106. (S UN Z)

ASSUNÇÃO DA BENDITA VIRGEM MARIA

A 1º de novembro de 1950, o papa Pio XII, na bula *Munificentissimus Deus*, decretou que «A imaculada mãe de Deus, a Maria sempre virgem, ao terminar o curso de sua vida terrena, foi arrebatada, de corpo e alma, para a glória dos céus». Essa declaração oficializou dogmaticamente uma crença que se tornara generalizada na cristandade oriental e ocidental desde o século VI D.C. Embora encontrada aqui e ali no cristianismo anterior a essa data, não aparece explicitamente nos primeiros escritos cristãos. E nas lendas que dão autoridade literária a tal noção não se vê qualquer autoridade, histórica ou doutrinária. A celebração litúrgica da *Assunção*, ou Morte da Virgem, apareceu pela primeira vez na Palestina, no século V D.C., tendo sido introduzida no Oriente pouco antes do ano 700 D.C. No Oriente, essa festividade é chamada de *Cair no Sono* (*koimesis*, *uspenie*), observada a 15 de agosto.

A definição oficial dessa doutrina não alude à questão disputada se Maria morreu ou não antes de sua assunção. Escritores recentes afirmam que o sentido dessa doutrina é que Maria acha-se onde todos os cristãos estarão após a ressurreição geral. Mas isso dificilmente pode satisfazer o intuito do decreto papal.

Os protestantes, que aceitam a regra das «Escrituras somente», ressaltam a inexistência de tal doutrina no Novo Testamento, nem mesmo como mero indício. Os católicos contra-atacam dizendo que a doutrina que afirma que só as Escrituras servem de regra de fé e prática é também um dogma, visto que a própria Bíblia não faz qualquer restrição quanto a possíveis origens da verdade revelada.

Tal doutrina provavelmente começou em face do raciocínio de que o Senhor não permitiria que o corpo sagrado, no qual Ele mesmo foi gerado, viesse a tornar-se presa da corrupção. Contra isso é alegado que tal idéia dá excessiva importância ao corpo físico, sendo o espírito o ser real e essencial, enquanto que o corpo é apenas um veículo mortal.

Fora do «raciocínio» que provavelmente lhe deu origem, a doutrina aparece pela primeira vez em escritos apócrifos do século IV D.C., como: *A morte de Maria, Livro da Morte da Bendita Virgem e Exéquias de Maria*, obras condenadas como espúrias em decretos atribuídos ao papa Gelásio, no fim do século V D.C. Gregório de Tours (falecido em 594), entretanto, aceitava-as como genuínas, e André de Creta (falecido em 740) supôs que uma passagem em *Dionísio, o Areopagita*, dá a entender que ele foi testemunha do acontecimento. No entanto, esse documento só foi escrito no século VI, e nada teve a ver com Dionísio. Portanto, essa doutrina repousa sobre a fé na autoridade papal, para interpretar e afirmar verdades extrabíblicas, uma noção negada pelos protestantes mas aceita pelos católicos. (B BO C E)

ASSUNÇÃO DE MOISÉS

Trata-se de uma obra judaica composta, que data do começo do século I D.C., e que provavelmente teve um original hebraico. Contém um discurso que supostamente Moisés fez a Josué, contendo relatos da morte do legislador e sua ascensão ao céu.

1. *Os manuscritos.* Só existe um manuscrito, um palimpsesto escrito em latim, do século V D.C. Foi descoberto na biblioteca Ambrosiana por A. M. Ceriani e publicado por ele em 1861. Parte do texto é indecifrável, e grande parte está corrompida. Há evidências de que o texto em latim foi tradução do grego, e este, por sua vez, fora traduzido do hebraico. Há expressões idiomáticas hebraicas que sobreviveram até mesmo nessa tradução latina da tradução grega.

2. *Unidade.* As listas dos livros apócrifos apresentam o Testamento de Moisés seguido pela Assunção de Moisés. Citações de antigos escritores certamente indicam que originalmente eram duas obras distintas, mas que, com o tempo, passaram a ser editadas juntamente. O *Testamento* é representado por manuscritos latinos, e a *Assunção* é representada em citações dos pais da Igreja. A obra composta atualmente é chamada de *Assunção*.

3. *Autor.* Nenhum indivíduo particular pode ser nomeado como autor, mas a obra revela um tanto da personalidade do mesmo. Parece que ele era fariseu. Fala com severidade contra os saduceus e aguarda o reino teocrático sobre a terra. Não era um zelote, porquanto fez silêncio sobre o movimento dos Macabeus. O fato de que ele demonstra interesse no futuro do templo e seus holocaustos mostra que ele não era um essênio, os quais se tinham separado da corrente central do judaísmo. O autor exalta o ideal das antigas tradições, a par de uma atitude de resignação, entregando a sua causa aos cuidados de Deus.

4. *Data.* Em Assunção 6:6 tem-se a impressão que Herodes já havia falecido, e em 6:7 o autor antecipa que seus filhos, Filipe e Ântipas, haveriam de reinar por curtos períodos. Mas, na realidade, eles reinaram por longo tempo. Isso mostra que a obra deve ter sido escrita antes de 30 D.C. Arquelau foi o único filho que reinou por menos tempo que seu pai. Visto que ele foi deposto em 6 D.C., é provável que o livro tenha sido escrito antes desse acontecimento, visto que não reflete ter conhecimento do evento.

5. *Conteúdo.* Os manuscritos latinos têm doze capítulos que devem ser divididos de acordo com o assunto tratado, como segue: a. Moisés nomeia Josué, que haveria de liderar o povo de Israel até à Terra Prometida, onde eles cairiam na idolatria (caps. 1 e 2). b. Um rei do Oriente haveria de destruir Jerusalém e impor um cativeiro de setenta anos, do qual poucos judeus retornariam (caps. 3 e 4). c. Maus sacerdotes e reis surgiriam, culminando no reinado de um tirano por trinta e quatro anos (caps. 5 e 6). Herodes é esse tirano. d. Seguir-se-ia um período agitado, envolvendo impiedade, perseguições, etc., durante o qual um herói, Taxo, preferiria a morte a ver a corrupção da lei. Finalmente, Deus faria uma intervenção, fazendo sobrevir o julgamento, e os justos seriam recompensados, com a conseqüente restauração e bênção de Israel, de maneira singular (caps. 7-12).

6. *Teologia.* O autor não demonstra qualquer afinidade com o legalismo rabínico, mas baseava-se solidamente nos ideais do Antigo Testamento, exibindo o conceito de responsabilidade moral alicerçada sobre o pacto com Deus. Não há qualquer esperança messiânica no livro. Talvez o autor rejeitasse a idéia de um Messias político e guerreiro, pelo que simplesmente não incluiu tal conceito em sua obra. O reino pelo qual ele esperava seria inaugurado mediante o arrependimento e a intervenção divina. Moisés era o homem especialmente enviado por Deus, enquanto esteve na terra; mas, mesmo tendo morrido, continuava sua obra, no mundo espiritual.

7. *Influência sobre o Novo Testamento.* Com base em citações feitas por Gelásio de Cízico (século V D.C.), e outras citações patrísticas, torna-se claro que a obra original aludia à crônica sobre a disputa entre Miguel e Satanás, acerca do corpo de Moisés, o que é aludido em Judas 9. Judas também reflete algo do Testamento de Moisés 7:7,9 e 5:5. Alguns estudiosos têm rejeitado a canonicidade de Judas, porquanto ali é utilizado esse material pseudepígrafo. (Ver a discussão sobre esse particular, no NTI, em Judas 9). Orígenes (*Quanto aos Primeiros Princípios* III.2,1) afirma especificamente que Judas empregou a Assunção nesse ponto de seu livro. Também parece haver uma alusão à Assunção no trecho de II Pedro 2:13 (Assunção de Moisés 7:5,8), e também em Atos 7:36 (Assunção de Moisés 3:11). (CH HA J Z)

ASSUR

No hebraico significa **degrau** ou **planície plana**, embora o sentido seja incerto. Consideremos estes pontos:

1. O segundo dos filhos de Sem, na ordem de sua nomeação (ver Gên. 10:22 e I Crô. 1:17), cerca de 2300 A.C. Seus descendentes ocuparam a região que veio a chamar-se Assíria. Os termos variam: Ele e seus descendentes são chamados Assur em Gên. 10:11 e Núm. 24:22-24, entre outras passagens. Assíria, em Esd. 4:2 e Sal. 83:8. Assírios, em Isa. 19:23. Assur é considerado fundador da nação assíria. O deus nacional era Assur, cujo nome ocorre em muitos nomes próprios como um elemento dos mesmos, como Assurbanipal, Esar-Hadom, etc. Provavelmente esse também era o nome da capital dessa nação.

2. A cidade de Assur, às margens do rio Tigre,

Assurnasirpal II de Ninrode, Assíria
Cortesia, British Museum

Reprodução Artística de
Darrell Steven Champlin

Arte céltica, a luta do homem contra a
serpente, evangelho de Mateus, Livro de Kells

modernamente Gala'at Sherqat, a 90 km ao sul de Mosul/Nínive. O nome tem origem acadiana, e significa *margem da água*. Por muito tempo foi a capital do distrito que tomou o nome de Assíria, até que foi substituída por Nínive. O local foi explorado por H. Rassam, em 1853, e por outros, posteriormente, em escavações que revelaram vários níveis de civilização. Primeiramente foi desenterrado o arcaico templo de Istar, do período de Sargão (2350 A.C. e depois); então a época dos medos e babilônios (614 A.C.). Nessa época, a cidade tinha importância como centro político e religioso. Um antigo santuário, um zigurate com torres gêmeas, dedicadas a Anu e Adade, era continuamente renovado. Então Samsi-Adade I edificou um templo em honra ao deus Enlil, no mesmo local. Uma biblioteca de documentos assírios do período médio, que incluíam os textos religiosos e legais de Tiglate-Pileser I (1100 A.C.), foi descoberta, prestando-nos valiosas informações sobre esse período da história. Os sepulcros dos reis do novo império assírio e a casa das festas de Ano Novo, construída para os rituais anuais fora das muralhas da cidade principal, também foram encontrados. (ID S Z)

ASSURBANIPAL

Em assírio significa **Assur criou um herdeiro**. Foi rei da Assíria, coroado príncipe em maio de 672 A.C., por seu pai, Esar-Hadom, tendo-se tornado rei por direito próprio em 669 A.C. Também era chamado Asnaper ou Osnaper. Era neto de Senaqueribe (705-681 A.C.). Foi um famoso sábio e protetor da literatura e das artes. Tinha uma imensa biblioteca em Nínive, com muitos milhares de tabletes em escrita cuneiforme, dos quais a arqueologia encontrou vinte e dois mil. Essa grande quantidade de tabletes nos tem fornecido muita informação sobre a civilização da época, sobre a Assíria e os povos vizinhos. Também falam sobre antigas versões babilônicas da criação e do dilúvio. Portanto, dessas e de outras maneiras, esses tabletes têm projetado luz sobre temas bíblicos. Assurbanipal reinou durante boa parte do longo e ímpio reinado de Manassés, em Judá (687-642 A.C.). O trecho de II Crô. 33 relata como Manassés foi deportado para a Babilônia, pelos assírios. Isso pode ter sido decretado por Assurbanipal. A autenticidade da narrativa se demonstra pelo fato de que os reis assírios daquele período passavam uma parte de seu tempo na Babilônia.

Guerras. Os reis assírios estiveram todos envolvidos em guerras e matanças; e Assurbanipal não foi exceção à regra, apesar de seus outros interesses pacíficos, conforme dissemos acima. Logo no início de seu reinado, ele guerreou contra o Egito, tendo capturado Tebas, em 663 A.C., e tendo feito ataques contra os sírios, fenícios e árabes, a fim de manter intacto o seu domínio. Provavelmente foi ele o rei que libertou Manassés do exílio. E ele ou seu pai (ou mesmo ambos) estiveram envolvidos na deportação de Judá para a Babilônia (ver II Crô. 33:13). Em 641 A.C., ele saqueou Susa, capital do Elão (ver artigo *Susã*). Portanto, acredita-se que seja ele «o grande e afamado Asnapar», o qual, de acordo com a Bíblia, trouxe para Samaria imigrantes de Susa e de Elão (ver Esd. 4:9,10). A partir de 652 A.C., Assurbanipal entrou em guerra com seu irmão gêmeo Samas-Sumukin, da Babilônia, o que fez debilitar-se o domínio assírio sobre a Palestina. Seus últimos anos de vida são obscuros. Morreu em cerca de 631 A.C.

••• ••• •••

ASSURIM

Uma tribo árabe, que deve ser distinguida dos assuritas ou aseritas (ver o artigo acerca destes últimos), que descendiam de Abraão e Quetura, juntamente com os letusim e leumim, através de Dedã (ver Gên. 25:3). Não têm qualquer ligação com os assírios, apesar da similaridade de nomes.

ASSURITAS

Não há qualquer relação com **Assur** (Assíria), e nem com os árabes *assurins*, e nem mesmo com os gesuritas. Provavelmente a referência é à tribo de Aser, sobre a qual Isbosete, filho de Saul, reinou durante seu breve reinado. Ficava na parte norte da Terra Prometida, encravada entre o mar Mediterrâneo e os territórios das tribos de Issacar, Zebulom e Naftali. (Ver II Sam. 2:9,10).

ASSURNASIRPAL II

No acadiano, **Assur guardou o herdeiro**. Foi filho de Tukulti-Ninurta I e pai de Salmaneser II. Se é possível ser o mais cruel de todos, entre incríveis matanças, torturas e barbaridades, conforme vemos nos registros dos povos antigos, relatados na Bíblia, então Assurnasirpal II foi o pior. Era um conquistador violento que espalhou o terror do império assírio por todo o sudoeste da Ásia, tornando-se uma potência temida por todos. Suas datas são 883-857 A.C. Era notório por sua barbaridade, e o seu registro histórico pouco mais é do que as jactâncias de todas as incríveis desumanidades por ele praticadas. A edição final de sua conduta destruidora ficou inscrita no pavimento da entrada do templo de Ninurta, em Calá (ver Gên. 10:11), que atualmente se chama côrnoro de Ninrode. As escavações tiveram início em 1845, por A.H. Layard, o qual descobriu quase imediatamente o palácio desse rei e um templo próximo, onde foi descoberta uma estátua dele, metade do tamanho normal de uma pessoa. Uma inscrição nessa estátua afirmava que esse rei conquistara a região inteira desde o rio Tigre até o **Grande Mar** (Mediterrâneo). Além de ser um terror militar, ele esteve ocupado nas construções de grandes muralhas, templos e um palácio em Calá (ver Gên. 10,11). Esse palácio era intensamente decorado com baixos-relevos e pinturas de batalhas e caçadas. Uma estela relata a fundação da cidade, em 879 A.C., quando mais de sessenta e cinco mil pessoas se banquetearam por dez dias de celebração. A maioria dessa gente compunha-se de cativos de guerra, que foram usados para formar o núcleo da população. Tinha cerca do tamanho da antiga cidade de Nínive, conforme calculado em Jonas 4:11. (ID UN)

ASTAROTE, ASTARTE

Essa palavra é usada como um título, usualmente com o sentido de *minha senhora* ou *minha deusa*. Um possível plural do nome aparece nos textos de Ugarite. O nome aparece em uma inscrição de Rodes e em um tablete do norte da África.

1. Uma deusa-mãe, consorte de Baal. Os dois usualmente eram adorados formando um par, conforme mostram as escavações em vilas cananéias. (Ver Juí. 2:13 e 10:6). No tempo dos Juízes, essa combinação tornou-se uma praga para Israel, produzindo idolatria e apostasia (ver I Sam. 7:4 e 12:1), sendo essa uma das razões pelas quais Israel foi derrotado em certas ocasiões, em suas campanhas militares. O texto acadiano menciona várias *Istars*₁

que provavelmente eram vários cultos em diferentes lugares. Tratava-se de uma deusa da fertilidade, humana, animal e das colheitas. Esse culto tinha seus aspectos obscenos, contrários à lei judaica. Na Mesopotâmia, Istar era identificada com a deusa-mãe dos sumérios, Inana. Esse nome aparece sob a forma *ttrt*, nos textos de Ugarite, e como *strt*, nas inscrições fenícias. Muitas figurinhas nuas de argila têm sido descobertas, pertencentes a esse culto. Seu culto prosseguiu até bem dentro da era cristã, e provavelmente só foi eliminado pela propagação do islamismo no Oriente Próximo, no início da Idade Média.

2. A forma plural do nome, Astarote (cuja forma singular é Astorete), também se refere a vários lugares no Antigo Testamento. Uma cidade com esse nome estava localizada ao norte da Transjordânia, perto da antiga Edrei, e ao norte da vila de Jair. Essa era a pátria de Ogue, rei de Basã (ver Deu. 1:4; 3:10 e Jos. 12:4). As cartas de Amarna mencionam o lugar em associação ao roubo de cavalos. Ali aparece com o nome de Astarote. Também é mencionado na inscrição da Pedra Moabita. O lugar é retratado em baixo-relevo em uma estela de Tiglate-Pileser III, encontrada em Ninrode. A meia-tribo de Manassés recebeu a área quando da divisão da Terra Prometida. Após o cativeiro assírio, o lugar passou a ser conhecido como Carnaim. Esse nome também aparece em Gênesis 14:5. Tornou-se capital da quinta satrapia persa. A cidade teve uma longa história como um centro de adoração pagã, e foi destruída pelos Macabeus, nos tempos de Judas Macabeu, em 165 A.C. (ver I Macabeus 5:44). O local tem sido identificado com o moderno Tell Ashtarah, a 32 km a leste do mar da Galiléia.

3. Essa palavra é usada em conexão com a produtividade de ovelhas (ver Gên. 31:38; 32:14 e Sal. 78:71), pelo que alguns estudiosos supõem que essa deusa era representada por uma ovelha. Porém, visto não haver provas para essa conjectura, outros têm pensado que o termo era simplesmente usado para indicar ovelhas, como uma espécie de segundo nome, da mesma forma que El, o deus supremo, é retratado como um touro entre as vacas, pelo que podia ser chamado de touro, ou um touro podia ser chamado de El. (AH ALB)

ASTARTE

Forma grega, do hebraico **Astorete**. Ver sobre *Astarote*.

No grego é *Astarte*, de onde se origina o termo em português. Em inglês é Ashtoreth, que deve ser distorção da forma grega, segundo a analogia de *Bosheth*, «vergonha». Era a deusa suprema cananéia, contraparte de Baal, e conhecida entre os babilônios como Istar (ver o artigo), e no sul da Arábia como Athtar (uma forma masculina). Virgem perene, ela era também a mãe frutífera e criadora da vida. Os filisteus (ver o artigo sobre eles) parecem haver ressaltado o caráter belicoso de Astarte (ver I Sam 31:10). As numerosas Astarotes representam várias formas sob as quais ela era adorada em diferentes lugares (Juí. 10:6; I Reis 11:33; 23:13). O nome dela foi dado à capital de Ogue, rei de Basã (Deu. 1:4). (DE E FA VT Z)

••• ••• •••

ASTERATITA

Um nativo de Astarote (ver I Crô. 11:44).

ASTEROTE=CARNAIM

No hebraico significa *Asterote dos dois chifres*, ou então *Asterote perto de Carnaim* (dois chifres). Ver Gên: 14:5. Era uma cidade habitada pelos gigantes refains. Ficava cerca de 37 km a leste do mar da Galiléia. A palavra «Carnaim» não aparece nas referências bíblicas como uma referência separada, embora figure como tal em I Macabeus 5:26, onde é descrita como uma cidade grande e fortificada. Fortificada como era, a cidade era quase inexpugnável, porquanto os vales que a cercavam eram por demais estreitos. Na época de Abraão, Asterote começou a ser ultrapassada em importância por Carnaim; e, na época dos arameus e assírios, Carnaim havia substituído Asterote como capital regional. (BAL Z)

ASTÍAGES

Foi o último rei do império medo (586-550 A.C.). Era filho de Ciaxares I. (Ver Heródoto, *Hist*. I.74). Esse autor diz que quando o pai de Astíages derrotou as forças lídias, ele fez um acordo com o rei Aliates de que o filho dele (Astíages) se casaria com a filha de Aliates, a princesa Ariene. Desse casamento nasceu uma filha, que recebeu o nome de Mandane. Com o tempo, esta casou-se com Caibises, um nobre persa de segunda categoria. Porém, Astíages temia que dessa união nascesse um filho, o que, de acordo com um sonho que ele teve, envolveria más notícias para ele. Assim, quando nasceu seu neto, chamado Ciro, Astíages resolveu tirar-lhe a vida. O infante foi deixado ao relento para morrer à míngua, mas escapou da morte. Quem o abandonou à própria sorte foi Hárpago, mordomo do rei. Mais tarde, tornou-se inimigo do rei, porque este matara um filho seu, esquartejando-o e servindo-o de comida aos animais. Entrementes, Ciro cresceu e tornou-se pastor. Quando tinha idade suficiente, Hárpago fez uma considerável porção do exército medo prestar lealdade a Ciro. Então ele derrubou seu avô, capturando a capital da Média, Ecbátana, em 550 A.C., assim cumprindo o sonho de Astíages. E então Ciro tornou-se «rei de toda a Ásia». (Ver Heródoto, *Hist*. I.117-130). (Z)

ASTIKA

Termo sânscrito que significa «ortodoxo». É usado para aludir aos sistemas baseados nos Vedas (ver o artigo), em contraste com os sistemas não-ortodoxos (*nastika*), que não têm essa base. (P)

ASTIKAYA

Palavra sânscrita que significa **físico**, usada no *jainismo* (ver o artigo a respeito), dentro da expressão *astikaya dravya*, que significa «substância física» (aplicada à matéria, ao movimento, ao repouso e ao espaço). (P)

ASTORETE

Ver **Astarote**. Astorete é a forma singular, e Astarote é a forma plural da mesma palavra.

ASTROLOGIA

Ver sobre **Adivinhação** (5).

A astrologia ocidental pode ser atribuída às teorias e práticas dos caldeus e babilônios de 2000 A.C. em diante. Em seus primórdios, a astrologia era uma

ASTROLOGIA — ASTRONOMIA

tentativa para se fazer uma aplicação prática das observações e cálculos astronômicos às atividades humanas. A astrologia esteve inseparavelmente ligada à astronomia até o tempo de Kepler. De fato, a astrologia foi a mãe da astronomia, tal como a alquimia é a mãe da química. Conceitos astrológicos (astronômicos) estão alicerçados em observações da regularidade ou periodicidade dos movimentos do sol, da lua, das estrelas e dos planetas. Os povos agrícolas associavam tais movimentos às estações, aos períodos de chuva, aos ciclos de desenvolvimento das plantas. Os caldeus e babilônios, ajudados por conceitos matemáticos mais complexos do que aqueles de que os egípcios dispunham, desenvolveram uma atividade astronômica mais refinada, completa com calendários. Isso proveu a base para o avanço da astrologia e da astronomia. Os gregos e os árabes refinaram ainda mais os seus métodos. O zodíaco reflete os conceitos astrológicos posteriores dos caldeus, os quais passaram a ser representados mitologicamente por animais. Um conjunto diferente de animais caracteriza a astrologia chinesa, que se tornou a base das idéias astrológicas no Japão, na Coréia e no sueste da Ásia. O horóscopo é um diagrama dos corpos celestes, mostrando as posições relativas do sol, da lua das estrelas e dos planetas em um dado momento. A fim de fazer um horóscopo, o astrólogo deve saber o momento exato do nascimento de uma pessoa. Eles acreditam que cada um dos doze signos do zodíaco está associado a grupos básicos de caracteres e inclinações temperamentais e psicológicas. Através do momento do nascimento de uma pessoa, tais peculiaridades poderiam ser previstas, como principais tendências de sua vida. O quadro profético geral sobre o futuro do mundo, dado pelos astrólogos, é bastante similar ao da Bíblia ou dos modernos místicos, quando se fala apenas sobre os eventos principais, sem entrar em pormenores. A mesma coisa parece aplicar-se às vidas dos indivíduos. Porém, essas predições falham lamentavelmente quando se tenta entrar em detalhes, sem importar se são vidas de indivíduos, história de nações ou de raças humanas em geral.

O fato de que os *magos* foram capazes de detectar o nascimento do Rei de Israel, com base em observações astrológicas (ver Mat. 2:1-10), mostra que, pelo menos algumas vezes, essas operações matemáticas devem ser válidas. Não há qualquer indício, na narrativa bíblica, de que aqueles homens foram divinamente orientados em seus cálculos. Tão somente eles acompanharam a *estrela*, evidentemente uma incomum combinação de planetas. Ver sobre isso no artigo intitulado *Astronomia*.

Minha avaliação. Embora superficiais, minhas observações podem ter algum valor. Se o Antigo Testamento condena a necromancia, somente degrada a astrologia. A narrativa de Mateus 2:1-10 era regularmente interpretada pelos pais da Igreja com o sentido de que a antiga sabedoria inclina-se diante da Sabedoria de Deus, em Cristo. Examinando-se o que realmente sucede nas predições astrológicas, podemos dizer o seguinte: a. Há ali verdade suficiente para que se estabeleça um esboço geral, sem detalhes, acerca dos eventos mundiais e individuais, embora o sistema fracasse se quisermos entrar em pormenores. b. Astrólogos individuais, à parte da massa geral, algumas vezes mostram-se bastante exatos em suas previsões, mesmo quanto a minúcias. Isso pode dever-se ao fato de que eles são psíquicos e usam as informações astrológicas como ponto de concentração, tal como outros usam bolas de cristal, cartas de baralho, etc. Se isso é verdade, então suas predições são quase inteiramente psíquicas, embora o crédito seja dado à astrologia. c. À parte dessas pessoas psiquicamente dotadas, a astrologia não é suficientemente exata para ser atribuída ao diabo, conforme fazem alguns religiosos, e até mesmo evangélicos. d. Nos casos especiais, de astrólogos realmente exatos, podemos ter simples poder psíquico humano, capaz de toda espécie de *prodígio*, pois o homem, afinal de contas, é um ser espiritual dotado de poderes psíquicos naturais, incluindo o conhecimento prévio. Ou, em outros casos, esses poderes podem proceder de entidades espirituais separadas, demoníacas ou não-demoníacas. Cada caso em particular deve ser examinado em seus próprios méritos, porque o assunto é por demais complexo para admitir análises simplistas. e. Por conseguinte, os astrólogos dotados de grande exatidão em suas previsões, podem ser: 1. simples psíquicos humanos naturais; 2. psíquicos inspirados por demônios; 3. psíquicos inspirados por entidades espirituais não-demoníacas. Neste último caso, quero dizer que esses indivíduos têm alguma fonte inspiradora, algum ser espiritual desconhecido, que não chamaríamos de demônio, por não estar em ligação com o diabo. Isso pressupõe uma complexidade no mundo dos espíritos, que se compõe de espíritos bons, maus e indiferentes, e *alguma* astrologia pode ser apenas preditiva, e não espiritualmente boa ou espiritualmente má. Mas a astrologia, à parte desses poucos indivíduos especiais, não é poderosa ou exata o bastante para nós atribuirmos tudo ao diabo, o qual por certo tem negócios mais importantes a dirigir do que dar aos astrólogos curiosas informações truncadas, que acertam somente em parte mas erram em muito. Isso seria uma infeliz propaganda para o Príncipe do Mal, o qual é um dos mais poderosos intelectos da criação, embora depravado no uso de seus recursos. Resta dizer que, em face dessa debilidade da astrologia, ela deve ser relegada ao seu papel de mera demonstração da curiosidade humana pelo futuro e pelo destino humano, sobretudo da parte daqueles que têm a revelação bíblica na mão e não precisam apelar para tão pobres recursos como esses.

ASTRÓLOGO

O trecho de Isaías 47:13 fala sobre os que «dissecam os céus e fitam os astros, os que em cada lua nova te predizem o que há de vir sobre ti». Jeremias advertiu Israel a não «espantar-se» diante dos sinais dos céus, simplesmente porque as nações se «atemorizavam» (ver 10:2). Os assírios eram mestres na astrologia, e a Palestina esteve sob o domínio deles por muito tempo, razão pela qual é admirável que haja tão poucas referências à astrologia, no Antigo Testamento. O trecho de Daniel 5:11 fala em «encantadores», embora algumas versões digam ali «astrólogos». Na realidade, porém, trata-se de um termo técnico acadiano que se refere ao sacerdócio dos encantadores. Mas que a astrologia estava envolvida, não se pode duvidar.

ASTRONOMIA

Esboço

1. As Teorias Geocêntrica e Heliocêntrica
2. Conceito Hebreu do Universo de sua Relação Com a Astronomia
3. A Imensa Antiguidade da Criação
4. A Vastidão da Criação
5. A Astronomia e Alguns Itens Interessantes na Bíblia
6. Vida em Outros Planetas
7. A Teoria da Grande Explosão e a Teologia

ASTRONOMIA

Quando observamos que a astrologia começou nas teorias e práticas dos caldeus e babilônios, a partir de cerca de 2000 A.C. (ver o artigo sobre a *Astrologia*), dizemos outro tanto sobre a astronomia, porque essas duas coisas estavam inseparavelmente ligadas até o tempo de Kepler (1571-1630). A astronomia é aquele ramo da ciência que inclui o estudo do universo além da terra, e tudo quanto está contido nesse universo. O astrônomo busca compreender a natureza dos objetos observados, explicando os eventos que ele vê tomarem lugar. Muitos e grandes problemas têm deixado os homens intrigados, desde os tempos pré-históricos, no tocante a essas questões. E, a despeito do avanço do conhecimento humano, muitos mistérios permanecem. Na verdade, devido às suas próprias pesquisas, a ciência vai descobrindo novos horizontes e criando novos mistérios a cada dia.

1. As teorias geocêntrica e heliocêntrica. Os primeiros estudos astronômicos registrados abordam o sol, os eclipses do sol e da lua e a rota seguida pelo sol no espaço. Os antigos, supondo que a terra seria o centro do universo, e que o sol estaria em movimento ao redor da terra, chegaram a crer, desde o começo, que esses astros exerçam alguma influência ou controle sobre vidas humanas. Os pitagoreanos propuseram a idéia de que a terra move-se ao redor do sol, sendo esse um conceito plenamente desenvolvido por Aristarco, em cerca de 300 A.C. Essa é a teoria *heliocêntrica*. Porém, ainda durante muitos séculos a teoria geocêntrica continuou sendo a preferida pelos homens. Hiparco, um famoso astrônomo do século II A.C., aceitava a teoria geocêntrica, que o astrônomo alexandrino, Ptolomeu, refinou em cerca de 150 D.C., tornando-se essa a idéia predominante até depois de 1600 D.C., quando então prevaleceu a mescla entre idéias astrológicas e astronômicas. O ponto de vista de Ptolomeu foi desafiado seriamente, pela primeira vez, por Nicolau Copérnico, em 1543, por causa do avanço do conhecimento, que mostrava quão inviável era a idéia geocêntrica. Porém, a posição central ocupada pelo homem, tanto na teologia como nas ciências, não queria ceder terreno, e houve muitas controvérsias. Todavia, era inevitável o avanço do conhecimento, e a invenção do telescópio, que posto nas mãos de Galileu, em 1608, revelou muitas coisas nunca antes observadas. Pela primeira vez, a lua foi vista como um corpo material similar à própria terra. Em 1618, João Kepler propôs as três leis dos movimentos planetários, em vista das quais as posições de Marte foram preditas com sucesso. A formulação e a prova da lei da gravidade, por Isaque Newton, um século mais tarde, removeu várias objeções à teoria heliocêntrica, incluindo uma objeção favorita, a de que uma terra em revolução, viajando através do espaço, não poderia reter em sua superfície os objetos ali existentes, porquanto seriam projetados no espaço. Contudo, o golpe de morte na teoria geocêntrica só ocorreu em 1727, quando James Bradley demonstrou que a aberração da luz das estrelas, a aparente mudança de direção da luz emanada pelas estrelas, resultava do movimento da terra, atravessando a linha de visão, e não de qualquer movimento que as próprias estrelas estivessem fazendo. Contudo, foi somente cem anos mais tarde que os cientistas começaram a perceber as vastas distâncias envolvidas no universo.

2. Conceito hebreu do universo e sua relação com a astronomia. Os hebreus acreditavam que o universo fosse uma terra chata, apoiada sobre um abismo de água. Por baixo da terra estariam os pilares da terra. Nenhuma explicação era dada sobre onde esses pilares estariam fixados, com a única exceção possível do trecho de Jó 26:7. Além disso, haveria um *firmamento* sólido em forma de cúpula, que se estenderia acima da terra. Este firmamento mantinha as águas acima da terra as quais eram vistas como um grande mar nas alturas. Os corpos celestes estariam fixados nesse firmamento. Alguns diziam que as luzes das estrelas chegavam até nós através de perfurações no firmamento, permitindo assim a passagem da luz. Uma cadeia circular de montanhas, à beira da terra chata, sustentaria o firmamento por sua beirada. O Seol, lugar dos espíritos dos mortos, que se desenvolveu na idéia de um lugar de julgamento, seria apenas um lugar onde fantasmas destituídos de mente ficariam adejando. Mais tarde, o Seol foi dividido em um compartimento bom e outro mau, onde uma autêntica vida após-túmulo era experimentada pelos justos e pelos ímpios, em seus espíritos desencorporados. Abaixo do Seol estariam os pilares.

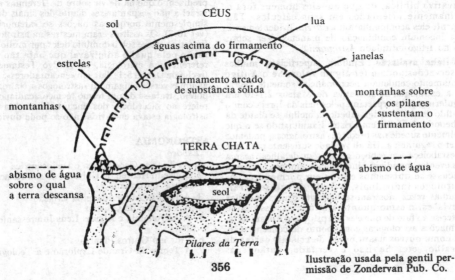

CONCEITO HEBRAICO DO UNIVERSO

Ilustração usada pela gentil permissão de Zondervan Pub. Co.

ASTRONOMIA

O estudo desse diagrama explica vários termos usados no Antigo Testamento, como *firmamento* (ver Gên. 1:6,7,8,14,15,17,20; Sal. 19:1; 150:1; Eze. 1:22,23,25,26; Dan. 12:3), *comportas* (ver Gên. 7:11; 8:2 e Isa. 24:18); o *Seol* (no grego, *hades*), como algo abaixo da superfície da terra (ver Jó 33:24 e Sal. 30:9). O Seol era visto como uma espécie de *caverna* na terra. (Ver também II Ped. 2:4). Ficaria debaixo da terra (ver Efé. 4:9 e Judas 6); seria uma espécie de abismo sem-fundo (ver Luc. 8:31 e Apoc. 9:11). O anticristo, embora anteriormente lançado no abismo, teria o poder de ascender dali, por meio do poder de Satanás, a fim de cumprir sua missão final na terra (ver Apo. 11:7 e 17:8). *Colunas* susteriam a terra em sua posição (ver I Sam. 2:8 e Jó 9:6). *Águas*. O firmamento teria sido posto como fundo e antepara das águas que haveria por cima dele (ver Gên. 1:6). Na criação, Deus teria separado as águas *de cima* das águas *de baixo*, mediante o *firmamento*. A narrativa do dilúvio inclui o detalhe de que as comportas do céu foram abertas, permitindo que as águas de cima do firmamento se despejassem sobre a terra. Também menciona que as águas do abismo, isto é, as de debaixo da terra, chegaram à superfície, pois a terra é ali retratada como descansando sobre um grande abismo de água (ver Gên. 7:11). A expressão «todas as fontes do grande abismo» aponta para o *caos* aquático subterrâneo, sobre o qual a terra repousaria. Essa idéia também é refletida em Gênesis 1:1. Esse abismo aquoso era algumas vezes retratado como que elevado acima das extremidades da terra, ameaçando-a de destruição (ver Jer. 5:22 e Sal. 104:7-9).

Esses comentários, fiéis ao que os hebreus realmente acreditavam, naturalmente provocam todo o tipo de dificuldades para aqueles que insistem em fazer da Bíblia um compêndio científico, sempre que o Livro Sagrado alude a qualquer assunto sobre o qual a ciência também se manifesta. Porém, é melhor conhecer a verdade e ensiná-la do que apoiar tradições religiosas que têm sido demonstradas como falsas e equivocadas. A *fé* dos homens espirituais não precisa de pilares de inverdade sobre os quais se possa apoiar, embora alguns insistam sobre essas coisas, por quererem obter *conforto mental*. O exame dos registros antigos mostra que os vizinhos dos hebreus compartilhavam com eles muitas de suas idéias cosmológicas, pelo que esses conceitos não surgiram do vácuo. Os escritores sagrados usaram esses conceitos para serem entendidos por seus leitores originais, a fim de ensinar verdades *espirituais* que não dependem da geologia, da astronomia e de qualquer outra ciência humana.

Os hebreus e a astronomia. Os caldeus, os chineses e os indianos têm se interessado pela astronomia-astrologia desde antes de 2000 A.C. Mas os hebreus aparentemente não devotaram tempo para estudar esses assuntos. Sabemos que eles identificaram as constelações e lhes deram nomes (ver Jó 9:9; 38:31; Isa. 13:10 e Amós 5:8), mas o mais provável é que isso tenha sido tomado por empréstimo de seus vizinhos, que tinham um ávido interesse por essas questões (ver Isa. 47:9; Jer. 27:9 e Dan. cap. 2). Provavelmente isso era verdade, considerando que a lei mosaica proibia toda a forma de adivinhação, conforme lemos em Deuteronômio 18:10,11, o que, segundo alguns intérpretes pensam, inclui a astrologia. Por outra parte, os judeus tinham licença para se ocuparem em várias outras formas de adivinhação, o que é comentado no artigo intitulado *Adivinhação*. Em contraste com isso, «os sacerdotes caldeus estavam acostumados, desde tempos remotos, a registrar em seus tabletes de argila o aspecto dos céus e as modificações que ocorriam noite após noite, a aparência das constelações, seus brilhos comparativos, os movimentos precisos de seu surgimento e desaparecimento no horizonte, a hora em que atingem o zênite, juntamente com os movimentos mais ou menos rápidos dos planetas e seus movimentos de aproximação ou afastamento uns dos outros. Foi assim que eles descobriram a revolução e os eclipses da lua, e com freqüência podiam predizer com bom êxito os eclipses do sol» (Maspero, *Dawn of Civilization*, págs. 775 ss). Se houvesse entre eles essas proibições como as que vemos em Deut. 18:10,11, essa ciência não teria sido iniciada por eles. Proibições assim tinham o intuito de evitar os abusos que algumas vezes impedem atividades legítimas. Ver o artigo sobre *Astrologia*, em seus três primeiros parágrafos, quanto a meus comentários sobre esse ponto.

A adoração do sol e das estrelas. Nos tempos de Sócrates, era uma idéia nova e revolucionária, até mesmo no caso de pessoas educadas, que a lua e as estrelas fossem similares à terra. Havia a crença generalizada de que esses astros eram entidades espirituais de alguma espécie, e a adoração aos mesmos era comum (ver Deu. 4:18; 17:3). Israel chegou a envolver-se em tal prática (ver II Reis 23:5,11 e Jer. 8:2). Os céus declaram a glória de Deus (ver Sal. 19:1), mas não são objetos próprios à adoração.

A significativa declaração de Jó. Não havia resposta popular à pergunta sobre onde as colunas da terra firmavam. Jó expôs corajosamente a idéia que diz: «Ele (Deus)...faz pairar a terra sobre o nada» (Jó 26:7). A gravidade e o magnetismo não são nada; mas pelo menos o livro de Jó demonstra uma percepção de que a terra não repousa sobre algo sólido, mas antes, permanece suspensa no espaço, de alguma maneira.

3. A imensa antiguidade da criação. A grande antiguidade da criação pode ser demonstrada de várias maneiras, dentre as quais expomos algumas representativas:

a. Os métodos de medição do tempo pelo carbono-14 e pelo argônio de potássio (juntamente com outros métodos). Uma ampla discussão sobre o assunto aparece no artigo sobre a *Arqueologia*, parte II.

b. Evidências de civilizações pré-adâmicas. Uma completa discussão sobre isso aparece no artigo sobre os *Antediluvianos*, partes 1, 2, 3 e 5. Há algumas evidências arqueológicas de considerável peso em favor desse conceito, além de algumas raras antigas referências literárias, as quais indicam o conhecimento e o uso da energia atômica em algum remoto período pré-adâmico. A segunda parte desse último artigo procura reconciliar a narrativa bíblica a esse tipo de informação.

c. Evidências geológicas da reversão dos campos magnéticos do globo terrestre, encontradas nas rochas, parecem indicar que já houve cerca de quatrocentos cataclismos como aquele da época de Noé. É possível que os relatos sobre Adão e Noé coincidam com os dois últimos grandes cataclismos da terra, representando *novos começos* da humanidade. Há algumas referências literárias, como no registros egípcios, mencionados por Heródoto, que declaram que muitos dilúvios gigantescos já aconteceram, e não apenas um. Estes cataclismos eram acompanhados, provavelmente, pela mudança dos pólos, sua verdadeira causa, com o conseqüente deslizamento da crosta terrestre para novas posições, criando vastas devastações e fazendo surgir novos continentes.

ASTRONOMIA

d. Materiais trazidos da lua e meteoritos caídos na terra têm sido datados em até quatro e meio bilhões de anos.

e. Fósseis antiqüíssimos, de microorganismos unicelulares, têm sido encontrados nas praias do lago Superior, em Ontário, em rochas da época pré-cambriana, e têm sido datados pelo método da radioatividade, em quase dois bilhões de anos de antiguidade.

f. *Luz proveniente do espaço.* Nossos radiotelescópios estão atualmente captando luz que precisou de dezesseis bilhões de anos para chegar à superfície da terra. Isso significa que quando essa luz partiu de sua fonte, o sistema solar nem ainda havia começado a existir, porque sua idade parece ser cerca de quatro e meio bilhões de anos. Devemos compreender que universos (completos com seus sistemas solares), estão vindo à existência e desaparecendo, continuamente. A criação não foi *um* acontecimento que sucedeu de uma vez para sempre. Antes, é um processo contínuo. Seja como for, é um simples cálculo matemático julgar a idade da luz que chega a terra, uma vez que se conheça a sua fonte. Afirmar que Deus criou essa luz já a caminho, de tal modo que ela já estava quase atingindo a terra quando sua fonte luminosa começou a existir, é idéia por demais ridícula para ser aceita como parte de qualquer busca séria pelo conhecimento e pela verdade.

Neste ponto, ofereci apenas um esboço de informações. Ver o último parágrafo do artigo que acrescenta outros detalhes sobre a grande antiguidade da criação.

Começos. Atualmente, os homens têm consciência da luz que chega à superfície da terra após dezesseis bilhões de anos de viagem pelo espaço. Isso, entretanto, deve ser visto como uma *minúscula* fração do número real. A ciência continuará fazendo descobertas que mostrarão que a criação ainda é mais antiga. Não há como predizer até que extremo o cálculo retrocederá.

A própria criação que conhecemos pode ter sido uma *recriação*, dentro de uma interminável série de recriações, cada qual envolvendo incontáveis bilhões de anos. Pode ter havido um número incalculável de *grandes explosões* de novas criações. Existimos no mais recente desses imensos e misteriosos ciclos.

4. A vastidão da criação. A Via Láctea, que é apenas uma galáxia entre bilhões de outras, conta com um número de estrelas (semelhantes ao nosso sol) que poderia atingir os dez bilhões, se houvesse alguma maneira de contar a todas elas. O nosso sistema solar pertence a Via Láctea. Porém, há inúmeros outros universos, muitas outras galáxias semelhantes à nossa Via Láctea. De fato, há bilhões de galáxias, cada qual com seus bilhões de estrelas. Quanto mais a ciência vai descobrindo, mais vasta a criação se torna conhecida. Aqueles que falam em limites, estão falando sobre os limites de suas próprias mentes, e não sobre os verdadeiros limites da criação. A Via Láctea é membro de um cacho de dezessete galáxias, que os astrônomos chamam de *grupo local*. Porém, fora do âmbito desse grupo de galáxias, bilhões de outras jazem dispersas através das profundezas do espaço. Parece que elas ocorrem em cachos, alguns dois quais contêm aproximadamente dez mil galáxias. Nos grandes espaços vazios, há algumas galáxias isoladas, e mesmo estrelas isoladas que não pertencem a qualquer conjunto estelar. As galáxias medem de dez a quarenta mil *persecs* em seu diâmetro. Um *persec* é 30,9 trilhões de quilômetros, ou seja, a distância que a luz percorre em um ano, à velocidade de trezentos mil quilômetros por segundo.

Portanto, um raio de luz precisaria de cento e vinte mil anos, a fim de atravessar algumas galáxias, de uma à outra extremidade, percorrendo mais de 1.225.000.000.000.000.000 de quilômetros. Para atravessar de uma ponta à outra da nossa humilde Via Láctea, a luz precisa apenas de sessenta mil anos luz. As galáxias mais próximas da nossa estão cerca de milhão de anos-luz de distância, mas outras estão muitíssimo mais distantes, afastando-se da nossa a uma incrível velocidade. Os aparelhos chamados radiotelescópios são uma das invenções mais recentes que ajudam a perscrutar o espaço. Eles estudam a radiação emitida pelos objetos celestes na faixa de rádio do espectro eletromagnético. Esses radiotelescópios têm vários formatos. Alguns se parecem com gigantescos pratos fixos no solo. Tais aparelhos têm permitido que os cientistas sondem a vastidão de nosso espaço exterior com muito mais exatidão, e a distâncias muito maiores do que era possível com os telescópios antigos, dotados de lentes.

5. A astronomia e outros itens interessantes na Bíblia.

a. *Eclipses.* Alguns percebem alusão a eclipses em Isaías 13:10 e Joel 2:31, onde é dito que o sol se escurecerá e a lua não dará a sua luz. Apocalipse 6:12 que diz, «o sol se tornou negro como saco de crina, a lua como sangue», é interpretado como tal por alguns estudiosos. Naturalmente, o *blackout* que houve por ocasião da crucificação de Jesus, em Mateus 24:29, é incluído nessa categoria. Porém, nenhum desses casos se adapta a qualquer descrição razoável de um simples eclipse. Excetuando o caso de Mateus 24:29, aqueles outros incidentes descrevem ocorrências apocalípticas de vastos juízos sob a forma de cataclismos. Não houve nenhum eclipse registrado na época da crucificação de Jesus. O mais provável é que estejamos tratando ali da passagem de uma nuvem de poeira cósmica, que atravessou o espaço, um fenômeno relativamente comum na história da astronomia. Ver comentários completos sobre a questão no NTI, em Mateus 24:29.

b. *O longo dia de Josué,* bem como o relógio em sol de Acaz. Josué ordenou que o sol estacasse em seu trajeto, até ele obter uma vitória sobre os amorreus (Jos. 10:12-14). Há várias explicações para o fenômeno. Alguns dizem que se trata de uma mera *lenda*; outros afirmam que a terra parou temporariamente de girar em torno de seu eixo, mas isso teria envolvido um cataclismo de grande magnitude. De fato, alguns dizem que o que houve, na realidade, foi uma mudança relativamente pequena dos pólos da terra; pois, quando estes mudam, a terra assume uma nova posição em relação ao sol e o horário muda, conforme as direções são alteradas, em maior ou menor grau. Essa explicação é possível, mas não lemos coisa alguma sobre algum grande cataclismo na terra nos dias de Josué. Uma outra explicação é que um outro planeta passou nas proximidades do nosso, atrasando a velocidade de rotação da terra, devido à força gravitacional. Outros tentam uma explicação mais simples, supondo ter havido uma intervenção divina que causou um *milagre de refração*. Isso significaria que a atmosfera terrestre continuou trazendo à terra a luz do sol, por meio de uma refração especial, embora o sol já tivesse mergulhado por detrás do horizonte. Essa é uma explicação *sobrenatural*, que requer o concurso da fé. Outros também se utilizam da teoria da refração a fim de explicar como o relógio de sol de Acaz retrocedeu dez graus, como sinal de que o rei Ezequias recuperaria a saúde (ver II Reis 20:9-11 e Isa. 38:8), onde temos

ASTRONOMIA

outro caso da necessidade do exercício de fé. A verdade é que não dispomos de explicações para problemas como esses.

c. *Os planetas* e a *estrela matutina*. Os antigos não tinham consciência do fato de que um planeta é um objeto celestial, tal qual a terra, que não tem sua própria luminosidade, mas que, à semelhança da lua, reflete a luz vinda do sol, parecendo brilhar. Também não sabiam que um planeta é muito menor que o sol ou alguma estrela. De fato, eles pensavam que os planetas fossem *estrelas errantes*. A palavra portuguesa *planeta* vem do vocábulo grego *planao*, que significa *vagabundar* ou *errar*. Os antigos pensavam que os planetas seriam diferentes somente por não manterem rotas regulares e constantes no firmamento, a cada noite, mas antes, vagueavam de uma maneira independente. Não compreendiam que isso era causado por suas órbitas em torno do sol. *A estrela matutina* não se trata de uma estrela, e, sim, de um planeta, ou melhor, de um dentre os vários planetas, como Mercúrio, Vênus, Marte, Júpiter ou Saturno, sem importar qual deles esteja em posição de ficar visível no oriente, imediatamente antes do nascer do sol. (Ver Isa. 14:12; II Ped. 1:19; Apo. 2:28 e 22:16). Algumas vezes, duas ou mais estrelas matutinas podem ser vistas no céu, embora usualmente esteja em pauta o planeta *Vênus*, a luz mais brilhante que aparece no céu, depois do sol e da lua, e que rebrilha o bastante para ser vista, algumas vezes, mesmo depois do surgimento do sol no horizonte. Cristo é chamado de estrela matutina, Aquele que anuncia o raiar da esperança e que resplandece em Sua glória. Ver o comentário completo, no NTI, sobre essa questão em Apo. 2:28 e 22:16. Essa estrela era símbolo de vida e imortalidade, na concepção dos antigos, podendo ser essa a mensagem central tencionada naqueles trechos do Apocalipse.

d. *Os meteoros*. As estrelas cadentes são meteoritos, mas os antigos não tinham conhecimento desse fato. Há passagens em Apocalipse 8:10; Mat. 24:29; Marcos 13:25 e Apo. 9:1 e 12:4 que podem fazer alusão a meteoros, embora o mais provável seja que se relacionem a julgamentos apocalípticos, que podem envolver, ou não, meteoros. A referência em Apo. 8:10 provavelmente fala simbolicamente de um poderoso anjo caído, porquanto esse é o pano de fundo da metáfora literária apocalíptica dos judeus. Em Apocalipse 8:8 vemos uma grande montanha em chamas que cai no mar, sendo essa, igualmente, uma referência a um ser angelical caído.

e. *A estrela de Belém*. Essa estrela tem sido interpretada de muitas maneiras. Ver no NTI em Mat. 2:2. Sumariando, as interpretações são: 1. seria uma *personalidade*, como um ser angelical. 2. Seria um mito. 3. Seria algum fenômeno divino especial, que não pode ser explicado pela ciência. 4. Alguma estrela especial, um objeto real, mas preparado por Deus para essa ocasião precípua. 5. Um cometa. 6. Uma estrela *nova* ou *supernova*. Uma estrela nova é uma que já existia, mas não de maneira visível para os olhos, até tornar-se visível de repente, quando sua luminosidade aumenta cerca de dez mil vezes, devido a alguma explosão interna. Uma estrela *supernova* é a mesma coisa, somente que sua luminosidade aumenta em centenas de milhões de vezes e então vai esmaecendo gradualmente, pelo espaço de um ano ou mais. 7. Mas a explicação favorita é a de uma *incomum conjunção de planetas*. A astronomia tem demonstrado que nos anos compatíveis com o nascimento de Cristo, houve um alinhamento ou aproximação dos planetas Vênus, Marte e Saturno, a 22 de janeiro de 12 A.C., além de um outro caso desses, envolvendo Vênus e Júpiter, a 12 de junho de 2 A.C. Em favor dessa explicação temos o fato de que os *magos*, contemplando esse evento no céu, interpretaram como o nascimento do Rei de Israel. Sabemos que os magos eram *astrólogos*, atentos a fenômenos dessa natureza. A explicação dada no NTI, em Mat. 2:2, oferece mais detalhes que favorecem essa interpretação, além de discutir os prós e os contras. De qualquer modo, essas estranhas conjunções planetárias têm ocorrido, segundo se reconhece, quando do nascimento de grandes personagens. Evidentemente, há uma espécie de inter-relação insondável e estranha entre as realidades celestes e as realidades terrestres, divinamente planejada, sem dúvida, e de tamanha magnitude que nos deixa a mente atônita.

6. Vida em outros planetas. Até o momento, todas as explorações feitas não têm revelado qualquer vida, conforme a conhecemos, em nosso sistema solar. Porém, visto que há muitos bilhões de galáxias, com bilhões de estrelas cada uma, é inevitável que existam incontáveis sistemas solares. Também é matematicamente provável que alguns desses sistemas ofereçam condições similares às do nosso mundo, que poderiam sustentar a vida biológica, além de *inúmeras* formas de vida que a nossa ciência nem imagina, tanto de natureza física quanto de natureza espiritual. Portanto, é justo dizer-se que a vida em outros universos não somente é possível, mas até *inevitável*. De fato, seria espantoso e ininteligível se Deus, tendo criado um universo tão incrivelmente vasto, tivesse criado vida somente à face da minúscula terra. As Escrituras ensinam que há muitas ordens de seres celestiais, que vivem em mundos de luz. Portanto, temos nisso uma afirmação bíblica de que há vida em outros lugares. Se isso é verdade no campo da vida espiritual, não há motivo para não supormos a mesma coisa no tocante à vida física. Um planeta em torno de uma estrela não pode ser visto com nossos atuais telescópios; mas há evidências de sua presença nas oscilações dessa estrela, devido à força gravitacional exercida pelos corpos em órbita, como no caso da estrela de Barnard, que dista apenas seis anos-luz de nosso globo. Essa estrela exibe minúsculas oscilações, as quais indicam a presença de um planeta de massa pouco maior que a de Júpiter. Sem dúvida, há inumeráveis milhões de tais estrelas, com seus próprios sistemas solares. Lá fora há vida, *muita vida*.

••• ••• •••

A criação de Deus é imensa e muito antiga.

É impossível limitar o nosso conhecimento às genealogias de Gênesis. Cada vez que lemos sobre uma *nova descoberta* no campo da astronomia, mais ficamos convencidos de que vamos levar muitas supresas ainda, e todas elas vão indicar tanto a imensa idade da criação como sua incrível magnitude. Considere isto: *Captado quasar a 12 bilhões de anos luz*. Cientistas norte-americanos de Pasadena, Cal., EUA, conseguiram determinar a distância do mais antigo objeto estelar de que se tem conhecimento no universo: um *quasar* de 12 bilhões de anos-luz, aproximadamente, denominado no catálogo astronômico de PKS 2000-300 e descoberto em 1971. Segundo os astrônomos, este quasar seria 1% mais antigo e estaria ligeiramente mais distante do que o OQ 172, que até agora era o quasar mais distante da terra já localizado. «Estamos esforçando a vista e olhando para o horizonte do universo», comentou o astrônomo Mike Klein, que trabalha para a Nasa e

ASTRONOMIA

anunciou a descoberta em Pasadena. «Este quasar é o que está mais longe de tudo o que vimos até hoje. Esta luz (que captamos) o deixou há 12 bilhões de anos e só mostra o aspecto que o quasar apresentava naquele momento». Isto significa que a lua *começou* a sua viagem muito antes de se constituir o sistema solar, há 4,6 bilhões de anos, e mesmo antes do nascimento da *Via Láctea*, há cerca de 10 bilhões de anos. Os cálculos atuais estimam que o universo nasceu há cerca de 20 bilhões de anos. O PKS 2000-300 só pode ser detectado do hemisfério sul e foi descoberto pelo radiotelescópio de Parkes, na Austrália. A primeira fonte de rádio quase estelar — definição de quasar — foi descoberta há 20 anos e consiste num centro *violentamente* ativo de galáxias. Assemelhando-se a uma estrela, ele parece emitir, porém, mais energia do que *cem milhões* de estrelas.

7. A teoria da grande explosão e a teologia. Ver o artigo sobre a Criação, VI, 8.

Existem grandes ciclos cósmicos e terrestres. As grandes explosões criam os cósmicos e as mudanças dos pólos criam os terrestres. Muitos ciclos terrestres existem dentro de cada ciclo cósmico e todos eles são de imensa duração. Portanto, a criação cósmica que conhecemos agora é realmente uma história recente. Também, o ciclo terrestre que envolve a *raça adâmica* é recente. Além destas histórias recentes, sabemos pouco sobre as obras da criação de Deus. Temos um *misterium tremendum* que as teorias dos homens, suas cosmologias e teologias são infantis demais para explicar. A história de Gênesis e a ciência moderna explicam pouco sobre os vastos *mistérios* de Deus. Todas as explicações são simplesmente gritos na noite misteriosa das obras de Deus. Mas é legítimo gritar e procurar saber mais. (AB AM BOK LY UN STR Z)

ASTRONOMIA COPÉRNICA

Nicolau Copérnico (1473-1543), astrônomo polonês, demonstrou a coerência matemática superior da crença de que a terra se movimenta ao redor do sol, que não é, portanto, estacionada no espaço, e que não é o centro do universo. Assim, ele desafiou a Astronomia Ptolemaica que, por séculos, tinha ensinado idéias contrárias as «novas» descobertas, como se fossem a própria verdade de Deus. Segundo a nova visão de Copérnico da natureza do universo, o sol tomou o lugar da terra como o centro. Mais tarde, Newton mostrou que o sol, também, não é o centro do universo. Não faz sentido falar em centros, como se o universo tivesse *um* centro. Tão cedo como 250 A.C., foi sugerida a idéia de que a terra está em movimento. Aristarco de Samos, um contemporâneo de Euclides (300 A.C.), descobriu que a terra não é o centro do universo. Copérnico usou o sistema matemático de Pitágoras (séc. 6 A.C.) para demonstrar que a terra é esférica e em moção ao redor do sol. É óbvio, então, que o serviço de Copérnico não era de *descobrir* estas verdades, mas simplesmente de demonstrá-las com mais evidências e introduzi-las na ciência, mais universalmente. A Igreja reagiu violentamente contra as *novas* idéias, supondo que faziam parte de uma decadência. A ciência e a teologia do tempo pensaram que movimento significa decadência, e de tirar a terra do centro da criação de Deus era, para elas, uma heresia imperdoável, sendo que elas tinham a *certeza* de que Deus colocou a terra exatamente *no centro* de sua criação. Textos de prova eram tirados da Bíblia para demonstrar a *centralidade* da terra. Isto demonstra que, às vezes, as certezas mais sagradas dos teólogos e dos cientistas são, de fato, mentiras ou desinformações miseráveis. De qualquer maneira, com Copérnico, a astronomia começou a ser orientada mais cientificamente, no lugar de teologicamente. Os homens sábios vêem evidências de Deus nas descobertas científicas, porque, afinal, ele é o Grande Matemático Cósmico e o Poder Universal. A ciência exalta justamente estes atributos de Deus. É inevitável que grandes e inumerosas descobertas serão feitas que revolucionarão não somente a nossa ciência atual, mas também muitos pontos da nossa teologia. Devem existir muitos tipos de seres inteligentes sobre os quais nada sabemos que têm suas maneiras para se relacionar com Deus. Existem muitos mistérios. (AM E EP F)

ASUR

Descendentes desse homem encontravam-se entre os servos do templo sob Zorobabel. Ver I Esdras 5:21. Ele é chamado *Harur* em Esd. 2:51 e Nee. 7:53.

ASVATE

Um filho de Jaflete na genealogia de Aser, I Crô. 7:33.

ATACE

No heb. significa **estalagem** ou **abrigar-se**. Um dos lugares (aldeias) da tribo de Judá, freqüentado por Davi e seus homens no tempo em que ele residia em Ziclague (I Sam. 30:30). Ficava ao sul dos sopés das montanhas de Judá. O local é desconhecido atualmente, mas alguns o identificam com *Eter* aludido em Josué 15:42, nas terras baixas de Judá.

ATADE

Não há certeza se esse nome se refere a um *indivíduo* em cuja eira os filhos de Jacó, e os egípcios que os acompanhavam, realizaram o ato final de solene despedida de Jacó, ou se se trata de uma referência à própria *eira*, como um lugar *espinhento*, que é o significado da palavra em hebraico. Seja como for, posteriormente, o local foi chamado *Abel-Mizraim*, ou seja «lamentação dos egípcios» (Gên. 50:10,11). O lugar é declarado como *além do Jordão*, isto é, na margem *oriental* do mesmo. Porém, a rota direta do Egito a Hebrom se fazia pela margem ocidental desse rio. Presume-se, pois, que as pessoas envolvidas seguiram uma antiga rota comercial, através da península do Sinai.

ATAI

No heb., **oportuno**, nome de três personagens do A.T.:

1. Neto de Sesã (c. de 1658), através de sua filha, a quem deu por esposa a Jará, seu escravo egípcio (I Crô. 2:35,36). Ele foi o pai de Natã e aparece na genealogia de Jerameel.

2. O sexto dos poderosos guerreiros de Davi (um dos trinta melhores), I Crô. 12:11, em c. 1068 A.C. Juntou-se ao exército de Davi em Ziclague.

3. Filho do rei Reobõao e Maacá, filha de Absalão, II Crô. 11:20, c. de 982 A.C.

ATAIAS

No hebraico, **Yah é ajudador**. Era descendente de

ATALHO — ATANÁSIO

Peres, filho de Judá. Após o retorno do cativeiro babilônico, ele habitou em Jerusalém (ver Nee. 11:4). Ele é chamado Utai em I Crô. 9:4, em cerca de 536 A.C.

ATALHO (Caminho Secundário)

O trecho de Juízes 5:6 fala sobre os caminhos evitados pelos viajantes, os quais preferiam os *atalhos*, as veredas e as estradas que se afastavam dos caminhos. Há uma aplicação espiritual desse termo, em Jer. 18:15. Um povo que se afasta de Deus segue por atalhos, e não pelo caminho certo. Essas pessoas contentam-se em desviar-se e vaguear ao redor, embora haja o Caminho Real para ser palmilhado. Com freqüência, aqueles que tentam evitar ser notados apelam para os atalhos, que também são preferidos por aqueles que querem evitar os assaltos comuns nos caminhos. Nesse último sentido, a palavra pode indicar proteção e bem-estar espiritual. Além disso, a palavra é simbolicamente usada para indicar uma completa investigação de um assunto qualquer. Esse é um bom sentido, porque aqueles que sempre passam por antigos e bem conhecidos caminhos, por onde passam as massas, nunca descobrem novas verdades. (ID UN Z)

ATÁLIA

No hebraico, **afligida por Yahweh**, ou então **Yah é forte**.

Era filha de Acabe, rei de Israel, provavelmente filha de Jezabel, a idólatra esposa desse rei. Em II Crônicas 22:3 ela também é chamada «filha de Onri», que foi o pai de Acabe, mas isso significa que ela era neta dele, um uso comum no hebraico.

Casamento. Ela tornou-se esposa de Jeorão, filho de Josafá, rei de Judá. Por esse motivo, Josafá, usualmente reto em sua conduta, ligou-se à casa idólatra de Israel (reino do Norte). Essa mulher herdou a falta de escrúpulos de sua mãe, daí resultando intermináveis perturbações. Ela mostrou-se ardorosa defensora do culto a Baal dos sidônios. Após oito anos, ela ficou viúva, e seu filho, Acazias, subiu ao trono (ver II Reis 8:26 e II Crô. 22:2). Dentro de menos de um ano, Jeú assassinou Acazias, juntamente com Jorão, de Israel. Por essa altura dos acontecimentos, Atália assassinou todos os seus netos, excetuando Joás, o qual foi salvo porque sua tia, Jeoseba (ver II Reis 11:2 e II Crô. 22:11), o ocultou. Entrementes, Atália foi ganhando cada vez maior autoridade, usando-a sempre para fazer o mal. Assassinou seus netos somente para usurpar para si mesma o trono de Davi. Durante seis anos governou, sem que alguém lhe pudesse barrar o caminho. Então Joiada, o sumo sacerdote, agiu contra ela. Coroou o jovem Joás como rei, e com o alvoroço popular, atraiu a rainha usurpadora para vir ver o que ocorria. A multidão aprovou os atos de Joiada, e Atália gritava: Traição! Traição! Todavia, seus gritos não conseguiram obter ajuda. Então o sumo sacerdote ordenou que os guardas a removessem do recinto sagrado e a matassem, o que foi feito (ver II Reis 11:2; II Crô. 21:6 e 22:10-12,23).

ATÁLIA

Um porto marítimo da Panfília, na Ásia Menor, perto da foz do rio Catarractes. Adquiriu tal nome de seu fundador, Átalo Filadelfo, rei de Pérgamo. (Ver Estrabão xiv. par. 667). Paulo visitou o lugar, acompanhado de Barnabé, em cerca de 45 D.C. (ver Atos 14:25). No século XII de nossa era cristã, parece que era conhecida pelo nome de Satália. Atualmente o lugar chama-se Adália. Nos tempos do Novo Testamento, era uma colônia romana, e sempre foi um importante porto marítimo, tal como o é hodiernamente na Turquia. Foi doada por Átalo III aos romanos. Ver o artigo sobre *Átalo*, quanto a essa questão. Havia uma outra Atália no norte da Lídia. (ID JON ND)

ATÁLIAS

No hebraico, **afligido por Yahweh**, ou então **Yah é forte**. Nome de dois homens referidos nas páginas do Antigo Testamento:

1. Um benjamita, filho de Jeroão, que habitava em Jerusalém (ver I Crô. 8:26), em cerca de 536 A.C.

2. Um membro da casa de Elão, e pai de Jesaías. Retornou do cativeiro babilônico junto com seu filho (ver Esd. 8:7). (ID JE)

ÁTALO

Não se sabe qual o significado desse nome. Foi o nome de vários reis de Pérgamo:

1. Em I Macabeus 15:22. O Átalo a quem os romanos escreveram, a respeito dos judeus, provavelmente era Átalo II Filadelfo (reinou entre 159 e 138 A.C.). Esse decreto parece pertencer ao ano 139 A.C., e não a um século mais tarde, conforme parece dever-se entender, com base em Josefo, *Anti*. 14.8.5.

2. Átalo I e Êumenes II, irmão do primeiro, tal como Átalo II, eram bons aliados dos romanos. Eles perceberam que o poder romano inevitavelmente controlaria grandes porções do mundo conhecido, incluindo a região deles, na Ásia Menor. Mostraram-se sábios o bastante para acompanharem as tendências da história, e assim salvaram incontáveis vidas e muita tristeza.

3. Átalo II foi um sábio governante, tendo fundado muitas cidades, incluindo Atália.

4. O sobrinho de Átalo II, que o sucedeu no trono, foi quem doou a Roma o reino de Pérgamo, o que transformou em uma província romana. Átalo III, entretanto, impôs certas condições. Ele exigiu que Pérgamo e outras cidades gregas da área ficassem isentas do pagamento de tributo. Roma aceitou as condições e a área tornou-se uma província senatorial, e um procônsul veio residir em Éfeso. Foi instituída em Pérgamo a adoração oficial ao imperador. Muitos excelentes monumentos foram edificados, e a área prosperou. Ver o artigo sobre a *Ásia*.

5. Quando, em 153 A.C., Alexandre Balas reivindicou o trono da Síria da parte de Demétrio I, e assim estabeleceu Jônatas como sumo sacerdote dos judeus (I Macabeus 10). Ele foi ativamente apoiado por Átalo II. (ID JON Z)

ATANÁSIO

Viveu de 300—373 D.C. Foi um grande teólogo cristão, oponente do arianismo, no século IV D.C. Foi Atanásio que enfatizou a interpretação do *homoousian* (da mesma substância) acerca da relação entre o Pai e o Filho, não só no concílio de Nicéia (325), mas durante toda a sua vida. Sua insistência sobre a *mesma substância* no Pai e no Filho tornou-se uma coluna da ortodoxia.

Primeiro foi diácono em Alexandria, mas depois, em 328, tornou-se bispo. Conquistou o Egito inteiro com sua interpretação, mas, no processo, sofreu no exílio por muitos anos, devido à influência de seus oponentes. Embora formalmente deposto pela maior parte do tempo entre 335 e 364, reteve notável influência na Igreja por meio de suas cartas pastorais. Morreu apenas oito anos antes do concílio de Constantinopla, que finalmente deu solução à disputa, decidindo em prol da posição de Atanásio. Permaneceu firme porque nem as intrigas arianas e nem as ameaças imperiais podiam abalá-lo. Porém, dos quarenta e cinco anos de seu episcopado, ele passou no exílio dezessete anos e meio. Faleceu a 2 de maio de 373. Sua festa é observada nessa data.

Escritos. Incluem: 1. Apologética: *Contra os Pagãos* e *Sobre a Encarnação do Verbo*. Eram duas partes de uma única obra. Então houve os *Discursos Contra os Arianos*. 2. Obras histórico-polêmicas: Foram quatro títulos, a saber: *Apologia Contra os Arianos*, *Apologia ao Imperador Constantino*, *Apologia por Sua Fuga* e *História dos Arianos*. 3. Obras exegéticas: Comentários sobre as Escrituras, conhecidas através de extratos de Gênesis, Cantares e Salmos. 4. Obras ascéticas: *Vida de Santo Antônio*, *Discurso Sobre a Virgindade*, *Sobre a Enfermidade e a Saúde* e *Amor e Autocontrole*. 5. Cartas: *Cartas Festais*, escritas anualmente aos bispos sufragâneos de Alexandria, discutindo questões eclesiásticas. Entre as mais notáveis está uma escrita em 367, que alista os vinte e sete livros do cânon neotestamentário que atualmente usamos, o primeiro assim mencionado. Outra carta importante: *Carta sobre os Decretos do Concílio de Nicéia*, dando completas informações sobre aquele acontecimento.

O *Credo* é o mais bem conhecido entre os livros pseudo-atanasianos. (AM B E P)

ATAR

Tradução de uma palavra hebraica que significa *fechar a boca*. No Oriente, o cereal era separado da palha por meio de bois que o pisavam no chão. O mandamento envolvido proibia que se atasse a boca do animal que estivesse ocupado nesse trabalho (ver Deu. 25:4). Era uma provisão humanitária. Até mesmo um animal que estivesse fazendo bem o seu trabalho tinha o direito de comer de vez em quando. Qualquer trabalho torna-se mais agradável quando se pode tirar um naco de vez em quando; e os animais certamente concordam com isso. Acresça-se que aquele que trabalha arduamente precisa alimentar-se bem, a fim de poder continuar trabalhando arduamente.

Paulo citou essa injunção para mostrar que os que labutam no evangelho devem receber devida recompensa. (Ver I Cor. 9:8-11 e I Tim. 5:17,18). Essas passagens devem ser consultadas no NTI, onde a metáfora é explicada detalhadamente. Indaga Paulo, em I Coríntios 9:9: «Acaso é de bois que Deus se preocupa?» E, como é evidente, ele esperava receber uma resposta negativa. Com isso, o apóstolo indicou que não estava em foco apenas uma provisão humanitária, mas uma provisão que nos ensina uma lição. Todavia, pensar que Deus não se importa com os animais certamente é pensar errado. Deus certamente importa-se com os animais, como importa-se até com os pequenos pardais (ver Mat. 6:26 e 10:29). Também é possível que Paulo tivesse falado jocosamente. Seja como for, o uso que Paulo faz da injunção encoraja um ministério evangélico pago, segundo se vê no Antigo Testamento. Os membros da tribo de Levi eram sustentados pelos homens das outras tribos, a fim de que pudessem ocupar-se do seu ministério. (ID NTI S Z)

ÁTARA

No hebraico significa **coroa, ornamento**. Era esposa de Jerameel e mãe de Onã (ver I Crô. 2:26), em cerca de 1568 A.C.

ATARAXIA

Vem do grego **a**, «não», e **taraktos**, «perturbado». A palavra indica o estado sereno, de prazer imperturbado. Demócrito, Epicuro, Pirro, Lucrécio e seus seguidores consideravam isso o estado mental e sentimento ideais. Com freqüência associava-se aos prazeres mentais, com a rejeição da busca pelos crassos prazeres físicos, que quase sempre perturbam a mente. É o mesmo que a *tranqüilidade mental*, obtida, segundo eles, pela repressão dos desejos, e não pela satisfação dos mesmos.

ATARGÁTIS

Nome de uma deusa síria cujo templo é mencionado em II Macabeus 12:26. Ela era a deusa da fertilidade, uma das divindades populares do período helenista, embora sua história seja muito mais antiga. Na literatura antiga ela é a *Dea Síria* ou *Deasura*, uma espécie de contraparte de Afrodite e relacionada a Astarte (ver sobre Astorete). Seu culto era generalizado, mas um dos principais centros era Hierápolis, no norte da Síria. Havia templos dedicados a ela em Carnaim, em Gileade (ver II Macabeus 12:26) e em Khirbet Tannur. Luciano presta informação sobre os ritos e cultos a ela prestados em sua obra *Deusa Síria*. Apuléias faz o mesmo em *Metamorfose*. Os sacerdotes desse culto castravam-se como parte de seu frenesi. Atargátis era associada à água, aos cereais, aos frutos, à folhagem, a todos esses aspectos diversos com conceito de fertilidade. Certas partes dos peixes representavam essa deusa, que talvez fosse a contraparte feminina de Dagom (ver o artigo a respeito), em alguns lugares. (CUM ID S Z)

ATARIAS

Um nome próprio que aparece em I Esdras 5:40. Essa palavra provavelmente é uma corrupção do título Tirsata (ver Esd. 2:63). Seja como for, esse oficial baixou ordens (tal como o fizera Neemias) aos sacerdotes, terminado o exílio babilônico. (Z)

ATARIM

No hebraico, **regiões**. Um lugar no sul da Palestina, perto do qual os israelitas, sob Moisés, passaram em sua jornada (ver Núm. 21:1). Ali os israelitas foram atacados pelo rei de Arade, e alguns deles foram tomados cativos. Algumas versões seguem a tradução siríaca Peshito, a Septuaginta, os Targuns e a Vulgata, dizendo «caminho dos espiões». Não há certeza sobre qual teria sido o texto original. (S Z)

ATAROTE

No hebraico significa **coroas**. Nome de diversos lugares, no Antigo Testamento:

1. *Atarote-Bete-Joabe*, da tribo de Judá (ver I Crô. 2:54), uma cidade fundada pelos descendentes de Salma.

2. *Atarote*, uma cidade da tribo de Gade, além do Jordão (ver Núm. 32:3, 34). Ficava perto de Gileade, a leste do Jordão, em uma fértil área de pastagens. Seu nome moderno é Khirbet Attarus.

3. Uma cidade na fronteira de Efraim (ver Jos. 16:2,7), também chamada *Atarote-Adar*, mencionada em Josué 16:5 e 18:13.

4. Atarote-Sofã, na tribo de Gade, identificada por alguns com as cidades de números (2) ou (3), acima. (ID S)

ATBACH (ATHBASH, ATBASH)

Não se trata de uma palavra verdadeira, mas de um termo cabalista fictício que denota, por suas próprias letras, a maneira de transformar uma palavra em outra, por meio de uma peculiar troca de letras. Era um artifício críptico de escrever o hebraico. Exemplos de como o esquema funcionava: A letra *alef* era substituída pela última letra, *tau*. A letra *bete* era substituída pela letra *shin*, etc. Aparentemente havia dois propósitos para se escrever dessa maneira: 1. por motivo de segredo; 2. como meio de se obter um duplo sentido. Por exemplo, temos um «atbach» nas Escrituras que tem deixado os tradutores perplexos: A palavra «caldeus», que é fielmente preservada na Septuaginta, é transformada em «o coração daqueles que se levantam contra mim». Esse texto, modificado pelo processo, tem sido seguido por diversas traduções. — O duplo sentido é que os caldeus eram aqueles que se levantavam contra o povo de Israel. O trecho de Jeremias 25:26 tem esse mesmo «atbach», mas isso pode ter sido obra de uma glosa escribal, pois a tradução da Septuaginta omite inteiramente o caso. (KEI S Z)

ATEÍSMO

Quanto às muitas idéias concernentes a Deus, ver o artigo geral sobre *Deus*, sob *Conceitos de*.

É impossível dar uma definição simples de um termo como *ateísmo*, pelo que expomos as várias formas por ele assumidas:

A palavra vem do grego *a*, «não», e *theos*, «Deus». É a descrença na existência de um deus, Deus ou deuses específicos, a descrença em conceitos que os homens têm de deus, Deus ou deuses. Ou então, é a negação de qualquer realidade sobrenatural.

1. *Descrença nos deuses populares*. Sócrates, que pendia para o monoteísmo, era um ateu (ou talvez, um agnóstico), no tocante à multidão de deuses da sociedade ateniense. Outro tanto se dava com Platão. Os pagãos chamavam os primeiros cristãos de ateus.

2. *De modo geral*, a descrença no tipo de deus, Deus ou deuses que os homens imaginam. Assim, alguém pode declarar-se ateu em relação ao Deus das batalhas, apresentado em alguns trechos do Antigo Testamento, mas não um ateu que não creia na existência de Deus, em alguma apresentação refinada.

3. A rejeição dos deuses da *superstição*, incluindo o Deus do Antigo e do Novo Testamentos, quando se pensa estar Ele em foco. Xenófanes, Heráclito e outros, nos tempos antigos, assim diziam, sem incluírem o Deus da Bíblia. Freud achava que a origem da religião é a neurose das massas, e outros têm visto na religião um instrumento para controle das massas. Tais indivíduos, é óbvio, não têm conceito de um Deus *vivo*. Pode-se incluir o marxismo dentro dessa classificação geral.

4. *No positivismo lógico*. É tolice falar sobre a existência de Deus, de modo positivo ou negativo. Não temos percepção, e portanto, não temos conhecimento de Deus. Ele pode existir ou não, mas não é um objeto de nosso conhecimento, pelo que é um desperdício de tempo participar da controvérsia do teísmo contra o ateísmo. Ambos afirmam-se conhecedores de informes que não possuem. O ateísmo diz que o conhecimento sobre Deus existe, mas é negativo. Portanto, Deus não existe. O teísmo, por sua vez, afirma que tal conhecimento existe, e é positivo. Portanto, Deus existe. O positivismo lógico diz que ambos estão equivocados, pois o conhecimento de Deus não é disponível. No positivismo temos um ateísmo *prático*, mas não teórico. Deus não teria sentido para a vida, não sendo um fator que determina as ações, e assim sendo, para todos os efeitos práticos, pode ser considerado inexistente.

5. *Ateísmo prático-moral*. Admite-se a existência teórica de Deus, um postulado necessário para explicar causa, designio, etc. Mas a existência de Deus não exerce qualquer influência sobre a vida, não sendo um fator determinante na escolha e na ação. Deus não é uma força moral. As decisões são tomadas sobre outras bases. Até mesmo alguns cristãos professos são ateus práticos.

6. *Ateísmo panteísta*. Deus é a alma do universo e o universo é o corpo de Deus. Tudo é Deus. Do ponto de vista judaico-cristão, o panteísmo é uma forma de ateísmo.

7. Deus como o *Espírito Absoluto*, como dizia Hegel. Deus é um tipo de força cósmica, que une em torno de si todas as coisas, sendo a fonte de todas as coisas, embora não seja uma pessoa, em qualquer sentido. Muito menos é uma pessoa em três: Pai, Filho e Espírito Santo. Essa forma de filosofia segue o ateísmo, a julgar pelos padrões cristãos, porquanto não reconhece o tipo de Deus que tem sentido para os cristãos. Porém, isso não nega que há discernimentos quanto à natureza de Deus, nessas especulações.

8. *Ateísmo naturalista*. Não há tal coisa como algo fora da natureza, e na natureza não encontramos deus, Deus ou deuses. Não há o *sobrenatural*, pelo que não há Deus, em termos convencionais.

9. *Ateísmo politeísta*. Se há uma multidão de deuses, então não há um verdadeiro Deus em contraste com deuses falsos. Pois, para nós, Deus indica um ser distinto de todos os outros seres, muito mais elevado. O politeísmo destrói o caráter distinto de Deus, pelo que é uma forma de ateísmo.

10. *Ateísmo absoluto*. Deus não existe, sob qualquer definição. Não há deus (ou Deus) na terminologia sofisticada da teologia ou da filosofia. Toda idéia de Deus é vã. Não há deus (ou Deus) conforme insistem que há tanto o judaísmo como o cristianismo, em suas respectivas doutrinas.

Bases do ateísmo:

1. Usualmente, o ateu é um *empirista*. Depende de seus sentidos e do acúmulo de conhecimentos através da experiência mística. Usualmente não simpatiza com outros meios de obtenção de conhecimento, como a razão, a intuição e, especialmente, as experiências místicas, que presumivelmente são contatos não-racionais e não-empíricos com um ser ou princípio divino.

2. O ateu não se deixa impressionar pelos argumentos tradicionais em favor da existência de Deus, com base na necessidade de causa, na presença de desígnio no mundo, na hierarquia de valores, que levam a um valor supremo, etc. Ver sobre *Deus, Provas de Sua Existência*, onde são expostos cerca de vinte argumentos.

3. O ateu crê que o conceito da existência de Deus é incompatível com o mal que há no mundo, sem importar se esse mal é natural (desastres, enfermidades, mortes), ou é moral (a desumanidade do homem

ATEÍSMO

contra o homem). Diz ele: «Se eu fosse Deus, com toda a inteligência e o poder que os homens dizem que Ele tem, eu teria criado um mundo melhor do que este».

4. O ateu crê que o conceito de Deus é incompatível com a dúvida que permanece no homem. Opina ele que Deus deveria comunicar Sua existência e sentido aos homens, de tal modo que a questão se tornasse óbvia para todos. O fato que assim não se sucede, mostra que não existe um Deus que esteja se comunicando.

5. *Alguns* ateus antigos e modernos têm defendido a doutrina da eternidade da matéria, eliminando assim a necessidade de um Deus criador. Em lugar de uma inteligência que guiou o desenvolvimento da vida, eles postulam a seleção natural, eliminando assim a necessidade até mesmo de um Deus sustentador.

6. *Argumento baseado na evolução*. O processo exibe muitas falhas e defeitos. Se for argumentado que o homem é o alvo desse processo, então esse argumento retruca que o homem é um produto minúsculo, considerando a suposta inteligência poderosa que os homens atribuem a Deus. Ademais, em todos os animais há resultados imperfeitos desse processo. Os órgãos, apesar de bons, com freqüência são defeituosos, sempre sujeitos a falhas. É difícil explicar por que Deus teria finalmente apresentado um produto imperfeito, tanto no mundo material e inanimado como no mundo das criaturas vivas. Naturalmente, os ateus não consideram seres acima do homem, supostos seres não-materiais e perfeitos, pois a crença nos mesmos depende da fé, e não das evidências externas.

7. Fracassos e falhas, imperfeições e elementos perturbadores, à parte da evolução. Se o teísta objeta à teoria da evolução (núm. 6), então os ateus salientam que podemos olhar para a matéria tal como ela é, extraindo daí alguns resultados. Esse mundo (inanimado) é um lugar imperfeito, sujeito aos temporais, aos terremotos, às intempéries devastadoras, etc. O reino animal está repleto de organismos imperfeitos, para nada dizermos sobre os animais francamente perigosos e daninhos, a começar pelos insetos e chegando até os grandes felinos. Podemos atribuir tal criação a um Deus inteligente, Todo-Bondoso e Todo-Poderoso?

Respostas a essas objeções, na ordem da apresentação:

1. Há modos de se obter conhecimento além dos cinco sentidos. São válidas a intuição, a razão e as experiências místicas. O terreno inteiro da parapsicologia é invocado a entrar na controvérsia, pois parece que cientistas qualificados têm encontrado modos não-empíricos de se obter conhecimentos. E há também a tradição mística, que precisa ser ouvida. Esses métodos não-empíricos de se obter conhecimento contêm a afirmação teísta. Ver os artigos sobre a *razão*, a *intuição* e o *misticismo*. No processo da morte física, vêm à tona meios não-empíricos de se obter conhecimento. Ver o artigo sobre as *experiências de quase-morte*.

2. Apesar de não serem conclusivos os tradicionais argumentos em prol da existência de Deus, como os argumentos cosmológico, etiológico, teleológico, etc., eles nos oferecem uma contra-evidência acerca do ateísmo, e que não pode ser facilmente ignorada. Não abandonamos um caso com fortes evidências só porque alguma contra-evidência forte também foi apresentada. Muitos pensadores modernos reconhecem a força desses argumentos, vendo neles bases para a manutenção das crenças teístas, ao mesmo tempo em que confessam a necessidade de reexaminar o conceito de Deus. Ver o artigo sobre *Deus, Provas de Sua Existência*.

3. O *problema do mal* (ver o artigo) é o mais difícil de ser respondido. Contudo, há respostas. Abaixo há algumas:

a. Se desistirmos da idéia de um Deus infinito, substituindo-O por um deus finito, com suas próprias dificuldades, então o mal existiria de uma maneira que ele não poderia mais controlar ou corrigir. Mas, podemos esperar a vitória final do Bem sobre o Mal. (A maioria dos religiosos, desnecessário é dizê-lo, objetam a essa abordagem, embora tenha sido adotada por muitos filósofos e por alguns poucos teólogos).

b. Precisamos redefinir o *mal*. Por exemplo, a morte (supostamente o supremo mal), não é má na maioria dos casos, pois traz um estado melhor. Mesmo nos casos onde a alma entra em julgamento, esse julgamento é remedial, e não apenas retributivo, conforme certamente ensina o trecho de I Ped. 4:6. Os sofrimentos, longe de serem prejudiciais para a alma, com freqüência são benéficos, por se tornarem instrumentos do aprendizado e da disciplina. Outrossim, os sofrimentos podem envolver dívidas da alma, provenientes da história passada da alma, ou nesta vida ou em alguma existência anterior. Isso traria uma grande bagagem, conforme ensinavam os pais alexandrinos da Igreja.

c. Também há o *problema do bem*, que faz oposição ao problema do mal. Há muitas coisas certas no mundo, como alegrias, triunfos e realizações. A vida humana não é inteiramente negra nesta esfera da existência. O ensino espiritual assegura que o que estamos adquirindo aqui é *positivo*. Essa bondade torna-se um problema para o ateu, que gostaria de ver somente o lado negativo, porque isso fortalece o seu caso. Em outras palavras, há fortes evidências em favor do desígnio desta vida, desígnio esse que inclui o bem. Esse contrabalanço do problema do mal, ainda que não resolva as dificuldades apresentadas, em sentido absoluto, pelo menos as alivia.

Uma analogia. Se alguém ler um livro biográfico, vendo que seu personagem passou por bons e maus bocados, mas que mesmo seus maus momentos contribuíram com algo, e finalmente, observar que, no fim, o personagem foi capaz de fazer o que era mister para obter grande realização e satisfação, e então morreu, o que o levou a um nível mais elevado da existência, haverá de inclinar-se a dizer que Deus não existe por causa do que sucedeu àquele homem? Se supusermos que todas as vidas finalmente se assemelharão a isso, porque assim determina o plano de Deus (Efé. 1:10), então toda a analogia dirá que um homem tem uma *longa* história da alma (com ou sem o concurso da reencarnação), e que uma vida terrena não representa senão um fragmento desse total; e, se supusermos que esse «total» finalmente produzirá um bom efeito, seremos tentados a dizer que Deus não existe por causa do mal que cerca os homens?

4. Deus comunica-se, mas o homem não escuta, necessariamente. Um homem, destituído de fé, certo de que Deus não existe, não vê qualquer prova de que Deus se comunica. O som não deixa de existir somente por causa de algumas pessoas surdas. Deus comunica-se por meio da natureza, da razão, da intuição, e principalmente, por meio das experiências místicas. Há muitos sons divinos, mas ouvidos espiritualmente surdos não os ouvem. Deus não está

ocupado em *fazer* os homens ouvirem. O desenvolvimento espiritual inclui o livre-arbítrio, e Deus permite que os homens aprendam através da dura experiência, a fim de ouvirem o divino. Alguns dos grandes líderes espirituais, homens que muito realizaram não foram necessariamente os homens bons, não foram necessariamente melhores do que os outros. Foram aqueles que estavam de ouvidos atentos.

5. Não há como defender a noção da eternidade da matéria, filosófica ou cientificamente, por não existirem evidências. Essa é uma questão de crença sem evidência. Mesmo que a matéria seja eterna, isso não é incompatível com a idéia da existência de Deus. Nesse caso, Deus não seria um criador, mas um organizador. De qualquer modo, Ele continuaria sendo Deus. Os mórmons acreditam na eternidade da matéria, mas nem por isso são ateus. Eles observam que é necessária a organização, a fim de que tenhamos o mundo que temos, pois a matéria inanimada não poderia ter adquirido as formas que tem sem uma *Inteligência* para organizá-la e utilizá-la. O termo *seleção natural* é totalmente despido de sentido, como explicação do desígnio e da adaptação que encontramos na natureza. É apenas expressão cunhada para ocultar uma profunda ignorância sobre *como* as coisas foram organizadas, eliminada a remotíssima possibilidade do acaso. É possível alguém cunhar um termo, sem conceber uma explicação correspondente. Como poderia o puro acaso fazer seleções? A *seleção* requer a razão e o desígnio. Quando usamos essas duas palavras, já estamos falando sobre alguma força divina. Além disso, essa explicação não pode dizer qualquer coisa quanto ao desígnio e à inteligência residentes na matéria *inanimada*. Nenhum processo de seleção natural poderia ter produzido isso. Alguém já afirmou tal coisa?

6 e 7. De fato, com ou sem a evolução, é óbvio que há muitas falhas nos organismos da vida animal. Além disso, há aqueles animais ferozes, que não parecem ter utilidade senão para destruir e prejudicar. O argumento padrão é que a *queda* do homem é responsável por esses problemas. Segundo essa doutrina, em sua queda o homem arrastou consigo a criação inteira, assim entrando todos os tipos de defeitos e problemas no mundo, envolvendo a natureza inanimada e as criaturas vivas. Em outras palavras, esse problema é o pecado. Esse argumento satisfaz certo segmento dos teólogos, mas outros crêem que o problema é maior do que esse. Eles suspeitam que a própria natureza simplesmente é imperfeita, e isso desde o começo, sem importar as falhas morais do homem. Admitem, contudo, que a queda do homem, sua natureza degradada, tem agravado problemas já existentes. Um outro argumento útil é aquele que afirma que Deus, no tocante ao desenvolvimento dos organismos vivos de todas as variedades, criou as *leis naturais*, permitindo que tudo opere no terreno físico. Essa lei natural existe por causa da inteligência divina. A inteligência transparece, mas isso não inclui a perfeição. Assim, um mosquito poderia ter evoluído sem a intervenção direta de Deus; e de fato, muitas espécies de seres, aparentemente desnecessários, poderiam ter vindo à existência sem a intervenção divina direta. A *mecânica* das leis naturais poderia ser a responsável por muitas coisas duvidosas, sem que Deus estivesse diretamente envolvido nessas coisas. De fato, as formas animais continuam a desenvolver-se sem a interferência divina. *Não é importante* que a vida animal seja perfeita e nem foi da vontade de Deus que assim o fosse. Os interesses primários de Deus são espirituais, e os defeitos dos organismos vivos são uma consideração trivial. As leis naturais podem atuar mediante algum arranjo, conforme propõem as *formas* concebidas por Platão, segundo as quais cada forma de vida existe e se desenvolve por causa de alguma força não-material que funciona como seu molde, e que requer sua conformidade com esse molde. Ver o artigo sobre *formas*. Deus estabeleceu as formas, mas, tendo feito isso, não tem necessidade de participar ininterruptamente do processo. Sendo esse o caso, todas as formas de imperfeição têm surgido, mas a questão não se reveste de capital importância, visto que o que importa na criação é o *espírito*, que representa a força viva real em todas as coisas.

Haverão de continuar os conflitos entre o teísmo, o ateísmo e o gnosticismo enquanto os homens se defrontarem com a tragédia, mas permanecerão em um estado essencialmente destituído de luz, devido ao seu baixo desenvolvimento espiritual, enquanto eles estiverem frente a frente com os grandes mistérios de *qualquer forma* de existência.

Hostilidade. O ateísmo mui naturalmente provoca a hostilidade por parte da mente religiosa, e com freqüência tem resultado em palavras amargas e em perseguição. O ateísmo é incompatível com a vida caracterizada pelo amor, não encontrando lugar na mente guiada pelo Deus que é amor. Um debate pode ser efetuado sem o veneno do ódio. Naturalmente, os ateus tembém podem ser hostis, e muitos deles atacam amargamente a fé religiosa. Isso, porém, não justifica mentes mais iluminadas a abrigarem hostilidade. (AM AT B C E EP F S)

ATEÍSMO METÓDICO

Essa é a idéia de que a ciência não deve usar o termo ou o conceito de Deus a fim de explicar as coisas, visto que Deus não é um objeto que a ciência possa investigar. Essa disciplina deve agir como se Deus não existisse, *etsi Deus non daretur*. Os primeiros cientistas invocavam a Deus para explicar as coisas, quando seu procedimento científico não conseguia dar explicação às mesmas. Assim foi que Newton, ao encontrar certas irregularidades nos movimentos dos corpos celestes, supôs que Deus estava intervindo diretamente, causando-as.

O conceito do ateísmo metódico é útil porque força os cientistas a continuarem as suas investigações, em vez de tomarem o atalho da ignorância, lançando a culpa sobre Deus. Porém, o fato de que os cientistas põem em prática esse conceito não significa que eles sejam meros ateus, mas apenas que eles procuram explicações científicas até onde as pesquisas e o conhecimento lhes permitem. Naturalmente, a explicação final das coisas fica com Deus. Mas a ciência humana ainda não conseguiu atingir essa explicação final em seus estudos. Os cientistas que se utilizam desse método não deveriam ser envolvidos nas discussões filosóficas e teológicas sobre o ateísmo. Eles usam um método filosófico, e não um conceito filosófico.

ATENÁGORAS

Viveu nos fins do século II D.C. Apologista cristão, que aparentemente nasceu e viveu em Atenas. Apresentou uma apologia em prol do cristianismo ao imperador Marco Aurélio. Ali ele defende o cristianismo e suas práticas, e ataca as religiões pagãs, sobretudo quanto ao seu politeísmo. Descobriu noções monoteístas em diversos poetas e filósofos gregos, e nisso, apresentou um argumento *a priori*, em favor da existência de Deus. Tratando sobre a ressurreição dos mortos, ele combinou idéias religiosas e filosóficas. Naturalmente, Platão o influenciou fortemente, pelo que sua fé religiosa geralmente foi exposta em termos platônicos. Essa era uma maneira apropriada de falar a não-cristãos, que sabiam algo das idéias de Platão e apreciavam a grandeza de seus conceitos.

Escritos: *Legatio pro Cristianis* (Apelo em Favor dos Cristãos), e *De Resurrectione* (Sobre a Ressurreição). Ver o artigo sobre os *apologetas*. (E P)

ATENAS

O mais antigo e mais obscuro período histórico da província grega denominada Acaia remonta a quase o tempo do estabelecimento final da democracia naquela cidade-república (cerca de 600 A.C.). Os alicerces de sua então futura grandeza foram lançados naqueles primeiros e remotos dias. Até mesmo o solo estéril e a atmosfera seca da Ática, em conexão com o apetite pequeno do povo, têm sido apresentados como condições favoráveis para o desenvolvimento do gênio mental que dominou aquela região, em sua idade áurea, de 450 a 350 A.C. A esterilidade da terra desencorajava outros povos a invadirem o território, naqueles primeiros dias; e isso propiciou a que ali se desenvolvesse uma sociedade homogênea, ligada por uma espécie de laço moral, em todo o território da Ática. A um certo monarca, de nome Teseu, é atribuído o crédito de haver unificado o território do qual Atenas finalmente, veio a tornar-se o principal centro populacional e capital. Esse foi o primeiro acontecimento de ordem política que é considerado digno de confiança como uma informação histórica; mas a data dessa realização ainda permanece na obscuridade, embora se possa declarar que tal tempo deve ter sido bem antes das chamadas guerras persas (500 A.C.). Essa parte da história helênica está mesclada com conceitos mitológicos e narrativas fantásticas sobre deuses e heróis. Isso concorre para que se possa distinguir facilmente a história verdadeira da mera lenda.

Até onde podemos retroceder na história e acompanhá-la, parece que a primitiva cidade de Atenas tinha um monarca e um conselho de aristocratas, juntamente com alguma modalidade de assembléia popular, que se mostrava totalmente ineficaz. O conselho, na antiga Atenas, se compunha de um grupo aristocrático denominado «Areópago», que era uma forma de desenvolvimento do conselho de anciãos, conforme lemos nos escritos de Homero. No tempo desses reis, tornou-se realidade a unificação política da Ática, o que deve ter ocorrido algum tempo antes de 700 A.C.

Diversas leis e reformas de *Sólon* (cerca de 594 A.C.) produziram modificações radicais na Ática, tendo preparado o caminho para a instalação do sistema democrático. A criação da «heliaea» ou tribunal, para o qual indivíduos de mais de trinta anos de idade, de todas as classes sociais abastadas, eram elegíveis, foi a única maior reforma isolada que preparou a cidade de Atenas para a democracia, nos dias de Sólon. Através desses tribunais, pois havia uma pluralidade dos mesmos, foram dados diversos poderes ao povo—que incluíam até mesmo o direito de remover magistrados de seu ofício, quando se tornavam culpados de conduta condenável.

Nos tempos de *Cleistenes*, através do governo do conselho, foi firmemente estabelecida uma forma de democracia (ano 500 A.C.). Pouco tempo depois disso teve início a idade áurea, com sua filosofia imortal e suas artes, que são tão bem conhecidas pelo mundo.

Um século que durou esse período, produziu Sócrates, Platão e Aristóteles, paralelamente a outros nomes um tanto menos famosos.

«Atenas era tão-somente uma parte da Ática, uma península com cerca de mil milhas quadradas, que se adentra pelo mar Egeu. Os montes Citeron, Parnes e outros dividem a Ática da Grécia central, mas esse fator adverso é compensado pelos bons portos em Maratona, e, mais perto ainda de Atenas, em Faleron e no Pireu. As pedreiras de mármore do monte Pentélico, as minas de prata em Laurium, já próximo à extremidade da península, e uma argila excelente, eram as principais riquezas naturais da Ática». (George Botsford e Charles A. Robinson, *Hellenic History*, 1956, pág. 76).

Atenas era o grande centro cultural da antiguidade, mundialmente renomada por sua filosofia, arquitetura e arte. Das três grandes cidades universitárias (Atenas, Tarso e Alexandria), Atenas era a mais famosa. Nos dias do apóstolo Paulo, Corinto havia ultrapassado Atenas em importância política e comercial. De todas as localidades do mundo antigo, Atenas é a mais bem conhecida, devido aos remanescentes arqueológicos, largamente conhecidos por meio de réplicas de muitas modalidades. Muitos desses restos antecedem a era cristã por vários séculos. O «agora» está sendo restaurado. O Odeom, onde eram efetuadas competições musicais e de oratória, projetava-se no espaço descoberto do *agorá*, no lado do sul. Mais ou menos no centro do espaço aberto do «agora» ficava a colina de Colonos, onde foram identificadas as ruínas do templo de Hefaístos, deus do fogo e da arte em metais. Na Acrópole estava construído o Partenon, o Erequiteum, o santuário de Athena Nike e outros monumentos famosos. O mais espaçoso templo da Grécia era o de Zeus Oke e outros monumentos famosos. O mais espaçoso templo da Grécia era o de Zeus Olímpio, com 108 metros de comprimento, 41 metros de largura e 27,5 metros de altura, localizado a sueste da Acrópole. Os remanescentes são tão numerosos que quatro volumes foram publicados para descrevê-los, escritos por James Stuart e Nicholas Revett, sob o título *The Antiquities of Athens*. Essa obra foi publicada em 1885, e desde então grande acúmulo de material tem sido compilado por outros autores sobre o assunto. Paulo contemplou, portanto, uma cena majestosa, ao entrar nessa notável cidade, mas ficou deprimido em seu espírito em face das evidências de trevas espirituais, conforme se via numa idolatria tão generalizada.

A arqueologia encontrou o lugar onde Sócrates foi injustamente julgado. Um recente encontro da pesquisa arqueológica trouxe à luz o lugar onde Sócrates foi condenado, em Atenas. A equipe de arqueólogos norte-americanos, chefiada por *Theodore Shear*, professor de arqueologia da Universidade de Princeton, prossegue na obra de escavações das ruínas do tribunal onde, em 399 A.C. Sócrates foi julgado e condenado à morte, sob a acusação de corromper a juventude ateniense. Essas ruínas foram encontradas numa área ao lado do antigo mercado de Atenas e perto da moderna estrada de ferro de Atenas ao Pireu, graças às informações contidas em um antiqüíssimo livro escrito por Pausânias, viajante romano que visitou aquela cidade no século II A.C. As escavações citadas, que tiveram início em outubro de 1969, foram financiadas pelo governo grego e pela Fundação Ford.

A narrativa inteira da pregação do apóstolo Paulo em Atenas, (Atos 17:16 ss), tem sido posta em dúvida,

Atenas na sua glória
Cortesia, Fate Magazine

Partenon — Cortesia, John F. Walvoord

Templo de Hepesto — Cortesia, Fate Magazine.

Acrópolis, Atenas — Cortesia,
John F. Walvoord

Templo de Adriano, 129 D.C.
Cortesia, Fate Magazine

Acrópolis e Pártenon numa colina atrás de Atenas moderna — Cortesia, Matson Photo Service

quanto à sua veracidade, por alguns eruditos liberais radicais, sob a alegação contida nas *seguintes observações*:

1. O obscuro desaparecimento de Timóteo e Silas, nessa altura dos acontecimentos, talvez sugira que na história verdadeira o autor sagrado injetou uma criação sua, que tinha por intuito associar Paulo com aquele famoso centro de erudição helênica, o que lhe daria um pouco mais de dignidade e prestígio, por ser ele o grande herói do livro de Atos.

2. A alusão ao *deus desconhecido*, embora historicamente exata, seria meramente um salto, dado pelo autor sagrado, para que pudesse compor esta seção de sua obra, esforço esse que passou a ser mais uma demonstração de apologética cristã do que realmente uma composição histórica.

3. Parece impossível supormos que Paulo teria sido *formalmente* julgado pelo tribunal do Areópago, porquanto nenhuma acusação lhe foi lançada, não tendo havido, realmente, qualquer processo e nem conclusão de processo.

Em resposta a esses argumentos dos intérpretes liberais, podemos retrucar com estas *outras considerações*:

1. Nada há de estranho no modo como Lucas manuseou o caso de Timóteo e Silas, porquanto Timóteo, por exemplo, não é ordinariamente mencionado durante a narrativa sobre a segunda viagem missionária de Paulo, embora se tivesse reunido a ele em Listra, e que, evidentemente, o ajudava durante todo o percurso da viagem. O fato de que a narrativa bíblica é um tanto vaga quanto a esse particular não pode de forma alguma lançar no descrédito a historicidade desse episódio.

2. Embora o *deus desconhecido*, ou «deuses desconhecidos» (conforme Jerônimo afirmou que estava registrado na inscrição original) fosse um fato bem sabido no mundo antigo, Paulo, tendo passado por Atenas, dificilmente poderia ter evitado fazer um sermão contra a idolatria, alicerçado nessa inscrição, do mesmo modo que Lucas, o autor sagrado, poderia ter sido inspirado a escrever essa história, centralizada em Atenas, não como uma criação sua, e, sim, como fato histórico realmente ocorrido.

3. Na própria narrativa bíblica nunca se lê qualquer indicação de que Lucas tencionou dizer que Paulo foi julgado *formalmente* no Areópago. Aqueles homens meramente quiseram ouvir o que Paulo tinha a dizer. Não estava ele sendo ouvido por motivo de qualquer crime, e nenhuma acusação foi feita contra ele; motivo também porque não esteve envolvido qualquer julgamento.

Outrossim, podemos observar que segundo todas as aparências, Paulo a princípio, não tencionava efetuar qualquer trabalho missionário em Atenas. No entanto, sentiu-se provocado a essa ação por haver observado quão assoladora era a idolatria naquela cidade. Assim sendo, talvez ele não tivesse insistido sobre a necessidade da presença de Silas e Timóteo, no decurso dessa atividade, porquanto também não a havia planejado. Outrossim, ainda que ele tivesse planejado pregar em Atenas, não é impossível supormos que ele tenha pensado que poderia fazer sozinho o trabalho de evangelização, enquanto que Silas e Timóteo continuavam no mister de fortalecer aos novos convertidos, em Tessalônica e Beréia. Não é provável, por semelhante modo, que o autor sagrado houvesse simplesmente inventado essa história, atribuindo ao esforço de Paulo tão parcos resultados. Pelo contrário, se a história tivesse sido criação de sua imaginação, a tendência seria exaltar o ministério de Paulo nessa ocasião, atribuindo-lhe resultados gloriosos. A exiguidade dos resultados, conforme foram registrados pelo autor sagrado, contribui como fator de autenticidade da história, como verdadeira narrativa de um episódio dos labores de Paulo.

Podemos notar, por igual modo, um sinal de *autenticidade* na curiosa observação que se pode ler no décimo oitavo versículo de Atos Cap. 17. Parece que a menção de Jesus e de sua ressurreição foi considerada, pelos ouvintes do apóstolo, como uma tentativa sua de introduzir uma *nova doutrina*, que expunha um novo par de deuses. Essa particularidade se assemelha em demasia à vida real e dificilmente teria sido adicionada como produto da invenção humana. Só pode tratar-se da narração de um fato histórico.

Mui provavelmente alguns dos ouvintes atenienses de Paulo consideraram-no uma espécie de sofista ambulante. Por isso mesmo lhe deram uma atenção amigável, ainda que um tanto zombeteira. Talvez tivessem querido inquirir seus pontos de vista mais por uma atitude de escárnio ou de diversão, sem que tivesse havido qualquer tentativa de fazer-lhe uma acusação formal. (DE FA HA IB ND NTI Z)

A Glória que foi Atenas
(L. Sprague de Camp)

«Todos os dias fixa teus olhos sobre a grandeza de Atenas, até que te enchas de amor por ela...» (Tucídides)

A história da maioria das cidades antigas—Atenas entre elas—começa em uma névoa de mito e lenda. Os atenienses acreditavam que sua cidade, cujo nome lhe viera de sua deusa patronisa, Atena, bem como a província circundante da Ática, tinham sido unificadas pelo herói Teseu, provavelmente personagem tão lendário quanto Hércules, seu contemporâneo. Quando, finalmente, começa sua história, no século VII A.C., a Ática já estava unida, provavelmente por meio da força, e não pela persuasão, conforme narram as lendas.

Por essa altura a Ática era uma república aristocrática oligárquica, na qual o rei fora reduzido a um magistrado secundário. O grupo mais influente era a Boule ou Concílio do Areópago, que se compunha dos cabeças das ricas famílias proprietárias de terras, que monopolizavam todos os mais importantes ofícios públicos. Os principais dentre os funcionários públicos eram os nove *arcontes*, cada um dos quais estava incumbido de certa variedade de deveres. Os *polemarcos*, por exemplo, comandavam o exército e julgavam certos casos civis. Aqueles anciãos não tinham noção de clara distinção entre os poderes legislativo, executivo e judiciário.

O povo estava organizado em famílias, clãs e tribos, e estava dividido segundo suas posses. A classe mais rica e menos numerosa apossara-se firmemente do governo. A partir do século VII A.C. em diante, porém, uma série de ameaças de levante, da parte das classes inferiores, ampliou o poder a todos os cidadãos. O reformado Clístenes, por exemplo, dividiu a cidade em grupos e distritos, formando dez novas tribos com combinações arbitrárias e distritos, e estabeleceu um Concílio dos Quinhentos, escolhidos por sorte pelas novas tribos. As comissões formadas desse concílio executavam os negócios governamentais diários.

Motivados pelas incessantes lutas entre suas próprias cidades-estado, alguns gregos europeus enviaram ajuda às cidades gregas da Ásia Menor, quando estas últimas se revoltaram contra o domínio

ATENAS

persa. Após esmagar essa revolta, o rei persa Dario o Grande, em 490 A.C., enviou uma expedição que cruzou o mar Egeu a fim de subjugar os maiores perturbadores dentre todos os atenienses.

Os persas desembarcaram em *Maratona*, a 30 km a nordeste de Atenas, diante da península Ática (as modernas maratonas se baseiam na distância percorrida pelos corredores gregos para avisarem da invasão aos atenienses). Os atenienses saíram a campo com o coração saindo pela boca. As tropas persas eram muito mais numerosas, e os soldados de Dario eram mundialmente famosos por sua habilidade em combate.

A sorte e a tecnologia, entretanto, estavam ao lado dos atenienses. Os infantes persas dependiam do apoio da cavalaria e, por algum erro de logística, os navios que traziam os cavalos persas não apareceram na cena. A mais veloz cavalaria do mundo teve de ir tropeçando a pé.

Outrossim, os ferreiros gregos tinham criado uma nova armadura para infantaria pesada, com uma couraça de bronze, um elmo de cimeira, grevas (*perneiras*) e um grande escudo circular. Aos persas faltava tal proteção. Os atenienses haviam treinado sua infantaria para marchar em formação, em vez de avançar como multidão desordenada. Quando os atenienses carregavam as couraças, as flechas dos persas eram aparadas pelas armaduras daqueles, e à pequena distância, os adversários sem armaduras dos gregos ficavam em nítida desvantagem. Após pesadas perdas, os persas fugiram para seus navios.

Dez anos depois, para vingar-se dessa derrota, Xerxes, filho de Dario, pôs-se à testa de um exército muito maior e atravessou o Helesponto em uma ponte flutuante. Dessa vez os persas invadiram a Grécia com uma força entre 150 a 180 mil combatentes, e provavelmente com três vezes esse tanto de não-combatentes—exército de número jamais ouvido, naqueles tempos. Uma força grega suicida, sob Leônidas, conseguiu entravar os persas por pouco tempo nas Termópilas. Os atenienses fugiram para a ilha de Salamina, deixando que sua cidade fosse incendiada pelos persas. Metade das cidades-estado da Grécia se bandeou para os persas, e tudo parecia indicar que seria inevitável a anexação da Grécia pelo império persa.

Foi então que a flotilha grega aliada infligiu esmagadora derrota à frota persa em Salamina. Os Persas, temendo que fossem cortadas suas comunicações com sua pátria e provavelmente tendo ouvido de insurreições em seu império, velejaram de volta com uma de suas três divisões. Os gregos aliados esmagaram uma outra divisão em Platéia, no ano seguinte, e uma terceira divisão recuou para sua terra.

Cobertos de glória, os atenienses puseram-se a reconstruir sua cidade arruinada. Fortaleceram sua marinha e construíram portos e uma base naval fortificada na península do Pireu. Junto com outras cidades gregas marítimas, Atenas formou uma confederação, a Liga de Delso, para dar prosseguimento à guerra aos persas, o que se arrastou por outros trinta anos. Para impedir que fossem privados de seu porto marítimo, os atenienses fizeram uma estrada de sete quilômetros entre sua cidade e Pireu.

Os atenienses se puseram a restaurar os templos na Acrópole (*cidade alta*). Esse imenso penhasco tinha 300 m de comprimento, 120 m de largura, elevando-se sobre abismos de 30 m. Sendo originalmente uma cidadela fortificada, a Acrópole fora transformada em um complexo de templos quando a cidade se desenvolvera. Os persas tinham destruído o antigo templo de Atena, e os atenienses resolveram edificar um novo e mais grandioso templo nas proximidades, o qual se tornou conhecido pelo nome de Partenon.

Em cerca de 460 A.C., Péricles, um jovem político descendente de aristocratas, elevou-se ao poder e obteve fama como um dos grandes estadistas da história. Seu encanto, humanidade, coragem e altruísmo, temperado com argúcia política e sagacidade eivada de extravagância, fazem-nos lembrar Henrique IV, da França, ou Franklin D. Roosevelt. Durante quase 30 anos ele foi a figura liderante de Atenas, eleito e reeleito para o cargo máximo.

Péricles tomou a resolução de fazer de Atenas a mais bela cidade da terra, bem como capital das artes e ciências. A fim de prover o dinheiro para esses planos, lançou-se a um programa de imperialismo expansivo. Os atenienses já tinham começado a transformar a Liga de Delos em um império ateniense, obrigando outros estados a unir-se à mesma pela força. Péricles mudou o tesouro da Liga de Delos da ilha de Delos para Atenas, onde, dizia, estaria mais seguramente ao abrigo dos persas. Outros membros da Liga foram persuadidos ou forçados a pagar dinheiro a Atenas sob a alegação de que não teriam de fornecer homens e navios. Embora alguns membros da Liga tenham protestado quando Péricles começou a retirar do tesouro para financiar obras públicas em Atenas, a maior parte da marinha da Liga era agora ateniense, e Atenas pôde defender suas ações.

Sem importar a moralidade ou não do uso que Péricles fez do tesouro de Delos, as obras de arte e arquitetura, disso resultantes, têm provocado a admiração de gerações. No fim do período do governo de Péricles os visitantes da Acrópole seguiam no caminho pela extremidade ocidental da Acrópole, para atravessarem a Propiléia ou vestíbulo, traçado pelo arquiteto Mnesicles. A galeria de arte municipal ficava em uma ala da Propiléia cruciforme, cujo belo teto continha vigas de mármore fortalecidas por barras internas de ferro—uma construção grega cujo método estava adiantado de sua época por muitos séculos.

Erguendo-se na fenda da Propiléia estava o *partenon*, desenhado pelos arquitetos Ictino e Calícrates. Iniciado em 474 A.C., e terminado em 432 A.C., o Partenão ocupa uma área de cerca de 31 m x 70 m, sendo considerado o ponto culminante da arquitetura grega do estilo dórico. Para esculpir as estátuas do Partenão, Péricles contratou Fídias, principal escultor da época, que já erigira o colosso de bronze de Atena, com dez metros, e que fora erguido acerca de 30 m da Propiléia. Para o salão principal do Partenão, Fídias executou uma imensa estátua de Atena em ouro e marfim, de pé, armada da cabeça aos pés e brandindo a Vitória em sua mão direita. Também esculpiu estátuas para os frontões nas extremidades do telhado e alto-relevos para os frisos, que foram brilhantemente pintados de vermelho, azul e dourado e que corriam em volta pelo lado externo das muralhas, entre as colunas e o telhado.

Durante quase *mil anos* o Partenão derramou sua glória sobre Atenas. Apesar de ter sido convertido, a princípio em uma igreja cristã e depois em uma mesquita, continuava em bom estado em 1687 quando os turcos, em guerra contra a República de Veneza, armazenaram pólvora no mesmo. Um artilheiro alemão, do exército veneziano sitiante, lançou uma granada de morteiro através do telhado, a qual fez explodir a pólvora ali armazenada, tendo feito explodir toda a parte central do templo.

Neste século, com ajuda financeira norte-americana, os gregos começaram a restaurar o Partenão.

ATENAS

Porém, os turistas que desejam ver um templo intacto dos gregos, fazem melhor se visitarem o templo de Héfaistos, chamado «Teseu», a 540 m a noroeste da Acrópole, na colina de Colono, que fronteia o antigo *agorá* (mercado) de Atenas. Esse templo dórico de mármore data de 450-440 A.C., pelo que é um tanto mais antigo que o Partenão. Sua alcunha se deriva de esculturas e frisos que retratam os feitos de Teseu, lendário herói de Atenas. Tal como diversos outros templos gregos, o Teseu foi preservado por ter sido convertido em uma igreja.

Ao lado do Partenão, na Acrópole, está o Erecteum, que também é um templo dedicado a Atena. Seu nome provém de um santuário existente atrás de um edifício dedicado a Erecteu, um rei lendário de Atenas, mencionado na *Ilíada* de Homero. Tal como o Partenão é reputado o clímax da arquitetura de estilo dórico, o Erecteum é o mais excelente exemplo do estilo jônico, um tanto posterior. A construção desse complexo, que foi feita em níveis, teve início em 421 A.C. e após adiamentos durante um período de dezesseis anos, devido a guerras contra Esparta, foi terminado em 405 A.C. Esse edifício, por igual modo, foi danificado durante as guerras turcas, mas foi cientificamente restaurado em 1909.

Muitos dos outros notáveis edifícios de Atenas foram erigidos muitos anos após a época de Péricles. Esses incluem o Teatro de Dionísio, a sueste da Acrópole, o Horologium ou Torre dos Ventos, no lado norte da Acrópole, o Templo de Zeus, completado pelo imperador romano Adriano, e numerosas outras estruturas.

Além das construções públicas e de haver ampliado o poder ateniense, Péricles ativou-se nas reformas constitucionais do governo de Atenas. Pela primeira vez foram pagos indivíduos pela prestação de serviços públicos. Antes disso, somente aqueles que eram bastante ricos para poder viver sem trabalhar eram capazes de servir como oficiais públicos. Também era pago o serviço prestado nos tribunais. Os atenienses tinham um curioso sistema judiciário, conforme nossos padrões modernos. Embora alguns casos permanecessem sob a jurisdição dos *arcontes*, a maioria dos casos era ouvida por um conselho de *dikastai*—juízes e jurados combinados—escolhidos por sorte dentre os cidadãos. Os tribunais continham de 201 a 2.501 *dicastas*, e os números esdrúxulos visavam a impedir empate nos votos. Infelizmente, a audiência perante tão grande número de pessoas encorajava os partidos a usarem apelos flagrantemente irrelevantes e emocionais.

A **Atenas de Péricles** chegou o mais perto possível do ideal de «democracia participatória», apesar do fato de que nem todos os adultos podiam votar. As mulheres não tinham voz política, e uma terça parte da população era constituída de escravos destituídos de quaisquer direitos. Uma outra fração consistia de residentes estrangeiros, que pagavam impostos e estavam sujeitos às leis, mas que não tinham representação e nem podiam vir a tornar-se cidadãos. (Era mister *um ato* especial da assembléia para naturalizar um estrangeiro, e isso ocorria raramente).

Volumes inteiros têm sido escritos acerca da vida diária na Atenas de Péricles, — que é conhecida em ricos detalhes porque muitas obras literárias dos séculos V e IV A.C. foram preservadas até hoje.

Muitas das ruas não eram pavimentadas, tinham apenas cinco metros de largura e eram ladeadas por casas de tijolos, de forma quadrada, quase todas de um pavimento só. Cinzentas, cor de barro e, algumas vezes, caiadas, essas casas tinham uma só porta no nível da rua, exibindo paredes sem janelas para o lado da rua, embora as casas de dois pavimentos contivessem, às vezes, uma pequena janela protegida com barras, bem no alto do segundo pavimento. Essa ausência de janelas servia ao propósito de impedir a entrada dos maus odores de lama e lixo, provenientes das ruas.

Ao longo dessas ruas estreitas, as pessoas apressavam-se para cá e para lá. Donas-de-casa das classes mais pobres e escravas das casas ricas carregavam jarras de água nos ombros, a caminho das fontes próximas. Citadinos de cabeça descoberta envoltos em pesadas *himatia* de lã passavam por agricultores vestidos de túnicas e chapéus de feltro, que tinham chegado do interior, trazendo jumentos carregados de produtos. Trigueiros fenícios de barbas encaracoladas, vestindo mantos soltos e com argolas nas orelhas, egípcios barbudos em roupas sujas de linho branco e alguns poucos africanos se misturavam aos gregos no *agorá*, o centro da vida da cidade. Ali os agricultores vendiam seus produtos e os vendilhões ofereciam suas quinquilharias. Todas as atividades cívicas tinham lugar nos edifícios que circundavam esse mercado.

Durante a *Idade Áurea de Péricles*, Atenas cresceu e prosperou, não somente devido às riquezas tomadas de cidades dominadas, mas também devido à prata extraída das minas do monte Laurium e ao comércio de exportação de cerâmica e azeite de oliveira. A população da Atenas de Péricles orçava entre 250 a 300 mil habitantes, rivalizando em tamanho com a Babilônia e Mênfis, que lhe eram limitadas pela logística dos alimentos importados. Quando a população não mais podia ser alimentada convenientemente pelos campos de trigo da Ática, importava-se cereal do estrangeiro, de tão longe quanto as fazendas citas, ao redor do Mar Negro.

A reputação da Atenas de Péricles repousa não somente sobre as riquezas e as artes, mas também sobre o fermento intelectual que tinha lugar. Quase todos os gêneros existentes da literatura—poesia, cenas épicas, drama, tragédia, comédia, história, conto, monografia, tese, tema, etc., o que é testemunhado por seus nomes gregos—evoluíram em Atenas durante esse período histórico. O drama evoluiu rapidamente de um único ator que atuava em conjunto com um coro que entoava uma narrativa em versos para algo bem parecido com nossos modernos espetáculos teatrais. As competições dramáticas anuais tornaram famosos os grandes mestres da tragédia: Ésquilo, Sófocles e Eurípedes, bem como o comediante Aristófanes—cujos dramas satíricos ilustram a liberdade de linguagem que prevalecia nos fins do século V A.C.

A especulação científica tinha começado durante o século anterior na Grécia Asiática e na Sicília. Homens como Tales, Pitágoras e Empédocles formularam teorias sobre o formato do globo terrestre, a natureza da matéria e a origem da vida. Filolau acendrou-se sobre a idéia de que a terra é redonda, e Anaximandro propôs uma teoria de evolução. Mais numerosos que os cientistas, entretanto eram os *sophistai*, ou «sábios», os quais especulavam sobre a política, sobre a moral, sobre a gramática e a retórica e viviam ensinando e conferenciando.

O crescimento do império ateniense provocou alarma, sobretudo na Esparta militarista, situada na extremidade do Peloponeso, cerca de 160 km a sudoeste de Atenas. A despeito de marcante contraste entre as culturas das duas cidades-estado, Esparta e

ATENAS — ÁTICO

Atenas foram atiçadas à guerra por parte de aliados beligerantes, e não tanto por uma hostilidade implacável entre elas. Certa inimizade teve início entre Corinto, aliada de Esparta, e sua colônia, Corcira, aliada de Atenas. Aumentando a hostilidade, foram feitas muitas propostas tendentes a uma solução pacífica, tendo havido até mesmo uma abortada conferência de desarmamento. Esparta, que não contava ela mesma com muralhas, propôs que outras cidades gregas derrubassem as suas muralhas. Mas essa sugestão não foi aceita com grande entusiasmo.

Finalmente irrompeu a guerra, em 431 A.C., e durante dez anos os espartanos arrasaram a Ática, enquanto os atenienses, protegidos por detrás de suas muralhas, continuavam a vida como antes. A frota ateniense, entretanto, continuamente assediava as costas marítimas de Esparta e seus aliados.

No segundo ano do conflito, Atenas foi atingida por uma *praga*. Talvez se tenha tratado de sarampo, ou, quiçá, varíola. Seja como for, isso foi mortal para os atenienses, que não tinham obtido imunização em ataques anteriores. A perda mais séria foi a de Péricles. Após sua morte, Atenas foi vitimada por uma série de temerários demagogos e aventureiros. Em 421 A.C., Esparta e Atenas assinaram um tratado de paz, e as coisas se acalmaram durante uns poucos anos. Porém, em 413 A.C., os atenienses enviaram uma numerosa expedição à Sicília, sob o pretexto de sair em defesa de um aliado, que estava sendo atacado por uma cidade próxima, aliada de Siracusa. Mas o propósito verdadeiro era o de atacar Siracusa diretamente, assim tornando Atenas a princesa do Mediterrâneo.

Em resultado de liderança *incompetente*, a força expedicionária foi destruída, e todos os seus homens capturados ou mortos. Percebendo a desorganização geral entre os atenienses, os espartanos renovaram a guerra. Dessa vez, os espartanos, apegados ao continente, construíram uma flotilha e, em 405 A.C., surpreenderam e destruíram a marinha ateniense em Egospótamos. Isso pôs fim à guerra. Embora fosse menor que muitas outras de menos fama, a Guerra do Peloponeso é relembrada principalmente por causa da detalhada narrativa feita por Tucídides, um dos grandes historiadores. Tucídides assumia uma atitude friamente pessimista em face da humanidade, e os motivos que ele atribuía aos homens podem ser vistos operando em tempos e lugares bem distantes da Grécia antiga. Ele descreve calmamente a guerra como ela é, e não como os idealistas ou militaristas gostariam que ela fosse.

Depois de haver sofrido derrota às mãos de Esparta, Atenas nunca mais gozou do poder político de que desfrutara durante os dias de Péricles. No entanto, durante séculos e séculos a cidade continuou proeminente nas lides intelectuais. No século IV A.C., Praxíteles encabeçou o movimento para a mais realista escultura da Idade Helenista. Menandro desenvolveu um novo estilo de comédia, com base em situações incongruentes, e surgiram as filosofias do cinismo, do epicurismo e do estoicismo.

O discípulo de Sócrates, *Platão*, dirigiu sua escola de um homem, no parque suburbano denominado Academia. Seu discípulo, Aristóteles, foi o tutor do jovem Alexandre da Macedônia, que depois retornou a Atenas para estabelecer uma escola rival em outro parque, o Liceu. Uma das maiores mentes de todos os tempos, Aristóteles fez mais do que qualquer outro homem para fundar o nosso método científico.

A liderança intelectual de Atenas prosseguiu sob Alexandre e os romanos. O cristianismo, entretanto, forçou o seu fim. Justiniano fechou a última das suas escolas em 529 D.C., e daí por diante Atenas foi declinando até tornar-se pequena cidade provinciana, tendo sido governada, sucessivamente, pelos bizantinos, pelos franceses, pelos espanhóis, pelos italianos e pelos turcos. A cidade só começou a recuperar a sua antiga glória depois que os gregos se libertaram do jugo turco, em 1832, quando escolheram Atenas como sua capital. Hoje em dia, uma vez mais, Atenas é uma grande cidade, com meio milhão de habitantes.

Apesar do declínio e das ignomínias que Atenas tem sofrido ao longo dos séculos, desde Péricles até seu reavivamento moderno, permanece de pé a história da Atenas de Péricles—conforme Tucídides esperava que permanecesse a sua história—«*uma possessão eterna*».

(Reimpresso por gentil permissão de *Fate Magazine*, Edição de maio de 1974).

ATENAS, ESCOLA DE
(Ver **Escola de Atenas**).

ATENÓBIO

Era amigo de Antíoco VII Sidetes, rei da Síria, o qual foi enviado a Jerusalém, por aquele rei, para discutir sobre a questão da ocupação de Jope, Gazara e a cidadela de Jerusalém. Ele exigiu que esses lugares, que haviam sido tomados pelos judeus, fossem devolvidos, ou que Simão pagasse por eles mil talentos de prata. Porém, repelindo ambas as condições, Simão ofereceu somente cem talentos de prata. Por isso, Tenóbio retornou a Antíoco sem haver conseguido realizar o seu propósito (ver I Macabeus 15:28-36). (Z)

ATER

No hebraico significa **fechado** ou **mudo**. Nome de várias personagens do Antigo Testamento:

1. Os filhos de Ater, entre os porteiros do templo, que retornaram do exílio com Zorobabel (ver Esd. 2:42; Nee. 7:45), em cerca de 536 A.C.

2. Os filhos de Ater, da família de Ezequias, que retornaram da Babilônia com Zorobabel (ver Esd. 2:16; Nee. 7:21 e I Esdras 5:28).

3. Um dos chefes do povo que assinou o pacto com Neemias (ver Nee. 10:17), em cerca de 445 A.C. (S)

ATHARVA-VEDA

Uma das quatro coleções de hinos usados nos sacrifícios védicos. Ver sobre os *vedas*. O Atharva-Veda contém muitos feitiços e encantamentos, juntamente com hinos e orações similares aos do Rig Veda. Apesar de coligidos após o Rig Veda, representa uma forma mais primitiva de fé religiosa. (E P)

ÁTICO

Filósofo platônico do século II D.C., que fazia clara distinção entre o pensamento platônico e o pensamento aristotélico, misturando idéias platônicas com o estoicismo, de tal modo que com freqüência ele é considerado um filósofo estóico. Contrariamente a Aristóteles, ele acreditava que o Universo foi criado, que as *formas* ou *idéias* existem como pensamentos da mente divina (ver *conceitualismo*). Ensinava que a alma é imortal e pode separar-se do corpo. Para ele, Deus não é um Movedor inabalável, mas capaz de intervir no mundo. (EP P)

ATITUDE

Mentalmente: envolve a forma dos pensamentos, as tendências dos mesmos e os seus impulsos; enfim, a atitude mental. Fisicamente: envolve a postura do corpo, o que, por si mesmo, subentende e exprime um estado mental, as crenças, as opiniões e os sentimentos.

1. As atitudes (postura, gesto) e a psicologia. Até mesmo a maneira de um homem andar pode revelar sobre as atitudes que ele tem para consigo mesmo e para com seus semelhantes. A psicologia tem demonstrado a importância dos gestos (ver o artigo a respeito) como reflexos dos sentimentos e atitudes. Certos gestos acompanham o ato de dizer uma mentira, pois são muito típicos. O gesto da mão pode dizer mais do que muitas palavras, revelando o que o indivíduo realmente está pensando, enquanto suas palavras dizem o que ele quer que seu ouvinte pense, e não a verdade. Os psicólogos têm investigado essa questão através de suas observações. Muitos gestos e posturas são comuns a uma raça, ou mesmo ao gênero humano, ao passo que outros são individuais. Os romanos expressavam surpresa ou consternação dando um tapinha súbito na testa, e nós ainda fazemos esse gesto, embora mais para mostrar que agora nos ocorreu uma coisa que não nos havia ocorrido antes. A futilidade é expressa pelo ato de deixar pendente os antebraços. A consternação é expressa pelo erguer súbito dos braços, algumas vezes com um gesto adicional da mão, como que para arrancar os cabelos, mas sem tocar nos mesmos. O cansaço é indicado pela colocação da palma da mão sobre a nuca. Uma pessoa que esteja dizendo uma mentira, pode cobrir parcialmente a boca com a mão, ou pode tocar no lóbulo da orelha. Usualmente, uma mudança no tom de voz (para um tom mais estridente), acompanha esse gesto. Estender as mãos, de palmas para cima, é um gesto de súplica. O punho fechado é sinal de desafio ou indicação de força. Inclinar o corpo para a frente indica reverência ou respeito. Virar o corpo para outro lado onde está uma pessoa (quando aquele que assim faz está sentado ou em pé), sem importar em que grau, com freqüência não é apenas a mudança para uma posição mais confortável. Pode indicar certa aversão. Por igual modo, o contrário, quando a pessoa volta-se para outra pessoa, indica a tentativa de comunicar-se com ela.

2. Atitudes e posturas relacionadas à Bíblia e à religião.

a. *Adoração e homenagem*. Os islamitas assumem nove posições corporais diferentes, dependentes do ato específico de homenagem que estiverem exprimindo. Essas posições vão desde o ficar de pé, em posição ereta, até à total prostração no chão.

b. *Posição ereta*. Os judeus e os primeiros cristãos punham-se de pé a fim de orarem. Tanto monumentos quanto referências literárias mostram isso (ver I Reis 8:54; Eze. 4:5; Dan. 6:10 e II Crô. 6:13).

c. *Soerguer as mãos*, a fim de suplicar (ver I Reis 8:22; II Crô. 6:12, 29 e Isa. 15). O erguer de um dos braços acompanhava um juramento proferido, como que a dizer: «Fiz um juramento». (Ver Gên. 14:22 e Deu. 32:40).

d. *Ajoelhar-se* é uma postura de adoração (ver I Reis 8:54; Eze. 9:5; Dan. 6:10; Luc. 22:41 e Atos 7:60). E, naturalmente, a oração acompanha a atitude, sobretudo quando a alma sente a necessidade de humilhar-se perante o Rei. Nas devoções islâmicas, o ato de ajoelhar-se assume três formas.

e. *Total prostração* é atitude que tem o mesmo sentido do ato de ajoelhar-se, embora seja uma forma ainda mais enfática. Expressa intensa humilhação e apelo veemente (ver Êxo. 34:18; II Crô. 29:29 e Isa. 1:15). Uma variação tipicamente islâmica consiste em pôr os joelhos, os antebraços e a cabeça no chão, mas com o resto do corpo elevado, em posição inclinada em relação ao solo.

f. *Pôr pó ou cinzas sobre a cabeça* é um ato que demonstra consternação, humilhação, penitência ou lamento (ver Jos. 7:6; Jó. 2:12; Lam. 2:10 e Apo. 18:19). Os antigos egípcios estavam acostumados ao gesto, como a maioria dos povos orientais.

g. *Bater no peito* expressa consternação, humilhação, tristeza e reconhecimento de culpa, sendo gesto comum aos povos orientais e aos egípcios (ver Heród. iii.85). Monumentos descobertos no Egito mostram pessoas de joelho, batendo no peito.

h. *Sentar-se*, ou então primeiro ajoelhar-se e então sentar-se sobre os calcanhares, é um ato de reverência. Lemos em I Crô. 17:16 que Davi veio e sentou-se diante do Senhor.

i. *Inclinar a cabeça* até encostá-la nos joelhos (ver I Reis 18:42) é ato de reverência.

j. *Estender a mão espalmada*, de pé, é um gesto de súplica, o que pode ser confirmado nos monumentos antigos e visto nas ruas, a qualquer dia, nos tempos modernos.

k. *Cair subitamente de joelhos* e cair prostrado para a frente, diante de alguém, é gesto de extrema e urgente súplica, um misto de humildade e temor. Algumas vezes, também era um ato de adoração (ver Atos 10:26).

l. *Beijar os pés* ou a fímbria das vestes de outrem (ver Mat. 9:20; Luc. 7:38,45), indicava reverência, respeito, ou mesmo adoração.

m. *Beijar a mão* de outrem indica respeito ou afeto. Beijar a própria mão era considerado um ato de homenagem aos corpos celestes (ver Jó. 31:27).

n. *Beijar na testa de outrem* era sinal de respeito ou afeto (ver I Sam. 10:1; I Reis 19:18 e Sal. 2:12).

o. Havia ainda várias maneiras de prestar homenagem, respeito, expressar tristeza ou receber uma bênção. Aquele que abençoava impunha a mão sobre a cabeça daquele que a recebia, o qual ficava em posição inclinada para a frente ou se ajoelhava (ver Gên. 48:14; ver também Gên. 18:2; 19:1; 23:7; 24:48; Êxo. 4:31; Núm. 25:2; II Sam. 14:22; I Reis 1:16; Mat. 27:29 e Rom. 11:4). Essas referências nos fornecem boa variedade de idéias acerca desses gestos de inclinação e respeito.

3. Atitudes mentais. Isso inclui os sentimentos, os humores, o modo de pensar e de crer — tudo o que é importante do ponto de vista espiritual, pois o que está na mente, determina o que uma pessoa é e faz. Há as imaginações e pensamentos, bons e maus (ver Gên. 6:5). Disse o salmista: «Examina-me, Senhor, e prova-me; sonda-me o coração e os pensamentos» (Sal. 26:2). As Escrituras ressaltam a importância dos pensamentos íntimos, das atitudes e dos sentimentos. Filipenses 4:8 recomenda: «...irmãos, tudo o que é verdadeiro, tudo o que é respeitável, tudo o que é justo, tudo o que é puro, tudo o que é amável, tudo o que é de boa fama, se alguma virtude há e se algum louvor existe, seja isso o que ocupe o vosso pensamento». Devemos levar cativo a Cristo todo o pensamento, a fim de Lhe sermos obedientes (ver I

ATITUDE INFANTIL — ATLETISMO

Cor. 10:5). A Palavra de Deus discerne os pensamentos e intenções do coração (ver Heb. 4:12). Ver os artigos sobre Coração, Mente e Alma. (NTI S Z)

ATITUDE INFANTIL

Essa atitude tem um aspecto apropriado e outro impróprio.

1. *Atitude própria.* É bom o crente ser como uma criança, no tocante à «malícia» (ver I Cor. 14:20). Quando o crente busca em Deus a sabedoria, é bom que ele seja como uma criança que não tem qualquer ilusão quanto à sua sabedoria (ver I Reis 3:8,9). Quando alguém aborda a mensagem de Deus, e potencialmente torna-se transmissor dessa mensagem, é bom que assuma a condição de uma criança (ver Jer. 1:6). São os infantes, sem ódio e sem orgulho, que podem receber a mensagem de Jesus (ver Luc. 10:21). Os crentes são reputados crianças amadas, que precisam da ajuda do Pai celeste (ver I João 2:1,12). O reino de Deus requer que os «filhos» de Deus se humilhem (ver Luc. 1:52; 6:20-26). Convém que o crente se humilhe, porque tal crente será exaltado no reino do céu (ver Mat. 18:4).

Esse princípio bíblico contradiz a ética de Aristóteles, o qual declarava que a humildade é um vício de deficiência, o oposto do espírito altivo. A missão de Jesus envolvia as «crianças» humildes e as crianças literais, motivo pelo qual devem ser respeitadas, porquanto o reino de Deus lhes pertence (ver Mat. 19:3). As pessoas dotadas das qualidades da inocência, da simplicidade e da humildade gozam de grandes vantagens diante de Deus. Deus resolveu que —coisas pequenas confundissem as sábias (ver I Cor. 1:26-29). Portanto, torna-se mister que o crente assuma tal postura, a fim de acolher como deve a mensagem espiritual e o reino de Deus (ver Mat. 18:3). Finalmente, precisamos *nascer de novo* a fim de penetrarmos nos mundos espirituais, para que cheguemos como novas criaturas na presença eterna de Deus (ver João 3:3,5). (EP H)

2. *Atitude imprópria.* Paulo declara que deixou de lado as coisas próprias de menino, ao tornar-se adulto, a fim de ilustrar que o desenvolvimento espiritual nos dota de uma atitude mais madura e entendida, e também que a nossa futura perfeição eliminará as atuais formas e veículos espirituais. Nossas formas de conhecimento, nossa prática cristã e nossos dons espirituais, etc., serão eliminados quando recebermos uma espiritualidade superior, por ocasião da «parousia» (ver artigo). (Ver I Cor. 13:11). A condição de permanente infantilidade espiritual é repreendida no sexto capítulo da epístola aos Hebreus. Pois as pessoas que não crescem, e que sempre enfatizam os «princípios elementares» da fé cristã são apenas crianças espirituais. Paulo queixou-se que alguns crentes são como infantes que nunca avançam para não mais precisar do *leite* espiritual, porquanto são crentes carnais. Também há crentes infantis que guardam no peito uma atitude ciumenta e contenciosa, um espírito sectarista (ver I Cor. 3:1 ss.). (EP H)

ATIVISMO

Ver o artigo sobre o seu contrário, o **quietismo**. O ativismo extremo seria uma vida dedicada à ação e à volição, sem consideração pelo conhecimento ou pela contemplação como diretrizes. O quietismo extremo advogaria a cessação de toda volição e desejo. Em uma possível aplicação ética, teríamos, em um lado, intelectuais de torre de marfim, cujo único propósito seria a busca pelo conhecimento, sem prestação de qualquer serviço ou trabalho. Por outro lado, teríamos os obcecados pela ação, com pouca preocupação com a contemplação e a intelectualidade. O misticismo extremo é a cessação de toda a volição e busca pela absorção em Deus, podendo representar o quietismo. (H)

ATLAI

Um dos filhos de Bebai, o qual, por desejo expresso de Esdras, despediu sua esposa estrangeira, (ver Esd. 10:28), em cerca de 459 A.C. (S)

ATLETISMO

Os clássicos gregos refletiam o ideal de mente sã em corpo são. As pesquisas científicas têm confirmado a validade do conceito. A mente funciona melhor quando o corpo é devidamente exercitado, não sendo tratado abusivamente, com excessos como a glutonaria e outros.

Considerações:

1. Até certo ponto, *a Bíblia* encoraja o atletismo. O que sucede aos nossos corpos é importante, por serem templos do Espírito Santo (I Cor. 6). O treinamento espiritual, porém, é muito mais importante, embora «o exercício corporal para pouco é proveitoso» (I Tim. 4:8, ERC). Paulo deve ter tido algum interesse por esportes, ou não teria usado metáforas esportivas (ver sobre corrida, em Fil. 3:12 ss , como um exemplo).

2. O atletismo oferece uma atividade saudável, especialmente para os jovens. Se eles praticarem atletismo, tal atividade pode substituir atividades prejudiciais, às quais se inclinam os jovens.

3. O atletismo oferece aos homens um certo *desafio*, primeiro para o desenvolvimento de habilidades específicas, para treinamento do corpo e da mente, e em segundo lugar, como uma competição, salutar como uma realização pessoal. O condicionamento mental produzido pelos esportes pode ajudar um homem a competir na vida, de modo geral, de maneira mais eficaz.

4. O atletismo promove a *saúde*, o que ajuda o indivíduo em tudo quanto ele faz, para que o faça melhor.

5. Para muitos, o *atletismo* é uma profissão; e se não houver abusos, é digna a vida de um atleta.

6. Para os espectadores, o atletismo fornece um entretenimento, mais salutar do que outras formas de entretenimento.

7. *Abusos*. Alguns esportes profissionais, como o futebol americano, o boxe, as lutas de caratê, etc., têm encorajado à violência. Mas o esqui é a modalidade mais perigosa de todas. A Associação Médica Americana tem exigido que o boxe seja descontinuado, devido aos danos cerebrais produzidos nos lutadores. Naturalmente, se o boxe se tornasse ilegal, haveria de continuar como uma atividade oculta, com pequeno público. Não seria melhor controlá-lo legalmente? Enquanto o homem for o que é, haverá quem queira lutar por causa do dinheiro ou da diversão. Os crentes não podem mostrar-se indiferentes para com essas questões, do ponto de vista moral, embora talvez não haja como solucionar os abusos no atletismo. Os jogos de azar são um outro abuso, especialmente quando escudados em organizações criminosas. (H)

Ver os artigos separados sobre *Esportes* e *Ginásio*.

ÁTMÃ — ATO HUMANO

ÁTMÃ

Termo de origem incerta que, — em seu uso mais antigo, significava «fôlego», mas que veio a significar «o eu». Nos Upanishads (ver o artigo), significa «eu universal», ou realidade final, sendo representado como Bramá-Ãtmã. Em uma das escolas filosóficas do hinduísmo (ver o artigo), era através do conhecimento da identidade do indivíduo com Bramá-Ãtmã que se alcançaria a salvação, isto é, *moksha* (ver o artigo). Essa escola filosófica é chamada *Shankara* (ver o artigo).

Nos primeiros tempos védicos, o termo significava «vento, sopro, a natureza de uma coisa». No bramanismo posterior, e mais tarde, o vocábulo passou a significar «mente», o consciente de um homem, ou a alma de um homem. Além disso, veio a significar mente cósmica, consciência cósmica, ou alma do mundo (uma unidade no agregado cósmico das almas — *purusha* — ver o artigo). (E P)

ATO

Deriva-se do latim **agere** (fazer). O grego é *energeia*.

1. Aristóteles contrastava o ato (energeia) com a potência (dynamis), associando a primeira à forma, e a última à matéria. Ver o artigo sobre *substância*, onde essas questões são aclaradas.

2. Havia esse mesmo conceito (tomado por empréstimo de Aristóteles) na teologia escolástica e na filosofia, mediante os termos *actus* e *potentia*. Fazia-se uma distinção entre o primeiro e o segundo ato. O primeiro ato é a «forma» de uma coisa (ação em potência), e o segundo é a operação real de uma coisa. «Ato» sugere, nessa terminologia, tanto realidade quanto atividade. Em contraste com outros seres, Deus é *actus purus*.

3. Gentile referia-se à sua filosofia como um ato puro, dando a entender que a atividade humana (conforme era descrita por ele) precisava ser considerada dotada de condição ontológica primária.

4. No campo da ética, ato ou ação é considerado sob o prisma moral. A intenção de agir reveste-se de qualidades morais, segundo Jesus ensinou. O pensamento mau é um mal moral, sem importar se venha ou não a exteriorizar-se na forma de atos (Mat. 5:28). Alguns filósofos supõem que o valor de uma ação depende da intenção por detrás da mesma, pois somente ali se encontra a pureza. Todos os atos são corrompidos, de algum modo, primeiramente no «ego», então em sua realização deficiente ou faltosa. Parece melhor supormos que o valor moral de um ato depende tanto da intenção quanto da realização. Ver sobre a *responsabilidade*. A ação também tem uma base ontológica. Aquilo que penso e faço, alicerça-se sobre aquilo que sou. E é nesse ponto que todas as ações devem ser modificadas. As nações que odeiam e fazem guerra contra outras nações, têm répteis em sua consciência nacional. O homem que mata é, antes de tudo, uma pessoa maligna, e assim demonstra a sua malignidade. Nessa altura o evangelho intervém a fim de transformar o indivíduo, a fim de que seus atos, como um resultado, sejam corretos.

Vontade e ação. O calvinismo radical furta do indivíduo sua capacidade de agir, ao procurar seguir textos de prova como Rom. 3:10 e ss. Mas a Bíblia, do princípio ao fim, pressupõe a responsabilidade humana, tornando o homem um ser capaz de escolha e ação apropriadas, contanto que sua vontade queira agir nessa direção. Seja como for, é claro que todas as ações dos homens acham-se em estado precário, enquanto eles não são regenerados pelo Espírito Santo. Ver o artigo sobre o *livre-arbítrio*, quanto a outros esclarecimentos. Ver também sobre o *determinismo*. (F H P NTI)

ATO HUMANO

A questão tem várias facetas, que podem ser melhor examinadas através dos seguintes pontos:

1. A ação moral de uma pessoa diante do conflito entre o desejo de satisfazer a si mesmo e o dever de servir ao próximo. Uma criança, se for amada, pode aprender a agir em favor de outras pessoas, negando a si mesma a satisfação do próprio «eu». E um adulto maduro segue essa mesma vereda de abnegação.

2. A auto-realização é um degrau mais elevado. Isso pode incluir os próprios interesses; mas, quando é correta, deve incluir algo que contribua para o bem-estar de nossos semelhantes.

3. Um verdadeiro e iluminado ato humano é aquele que vê o ser humano como um todo, e cada indivíduo como uma parte, de tal modo que aquilo que ajuda ou impede a alguém, exerce o mesmo efeito sobre a outra pessoa. Isso envolve a maturidade espiritual.

4. Uma elevada manifestação disso dá-se quando um indivíduo age voluntariamente, praticando o que é bom. Isso a pessoa faz porque sua maturidade espiritual atingiu um ponto onde ela se libertou da convicção ilusória de que o mal, de alguma maneira, produz mais prazeres e é mais vantajoso do que o bem. Tal pessoa foi libertada pelo Filho de Deus e por Sua ética.

5. Envolvida na questão encontra-se a *dignidade do indivíduo*. Um homem toma conhecimento de sua elevada posição espiritual quando é bom e pratica o bem, e não quer que em sua vida haja manifestações que degradem a sua humanidade.

6. *O dever*. O ser humano tem a responsabilidade de prestar contas a seu Criador, mostrando-se grato para com o dom da vida que lhe tem sido conferido. O dever mostra ao indivíduo certas ações que transcendem aos meros instintos animais e ao auto-interesse.

7. *A relação transcendental para com Deus*. Um ponto de vista apropriado da natureza humana, o qual assegura que o homem é um espírito, dotado de um destino espiritual, e capaz de compartilhar da própria natureza divina (ver II Ped. 1:4), influenciará tudo quanto um homem é e faz. Esse relacionamento transcendental inclui o poder transformador do Espírito, o qual atua através de meios espirituais de desenvolvimento, como a instrução da mente quanto às realidades espirituais, por meio do estudo de bons livros, dos documentos sagrados, da filosofia e de questões úteis como a oração, a meditação, a santificação, a prática da lei do amor e os toques místicos do Espírito. Estes incluem as experiências espirituais diretas, os dons do Espírito e outras experiências psíquicas e espirituais, que transcendem ao que é intelectual e físico. Mediante a aplicação desses *meios*, o homem vai sendo internamente transformado segundo a imagem de Cristo (ver Rom. 8:29), passando de um estágio de glória para o próximo, tanto nesta vida como por toda a eternidade (ver II Cor. 3:18).

8. *Uso correto do dom da vida*. O homem espiritual interessa-se sobre como está usando a sua vida, e qual será o resultado da mesma. Ele considera a vida como um dom sagrado, anelando por usar esse dom corretamente. Isso inclui o seu próprio desenvolvimento espiritual (incluindo os vários aspectos do fruto do Espírito, ver Gál. 5:22,23); mas também precisa

incluir o que o homem faz em favor de outras pessoas. A doutrina aristotélica da virtude como uma função envolve um profundo discernimento. Cada indivíduo é distinto, e está encarregado de uma distintiva e proposital *função* na sociedade, tendo em vista o aprimoramento da mesma, material e espiritualmente falando. A podadeira foi inventada para podar; as tenazes, para segurar firmemente os objetos; a chave-inglesa para apertar e afrouxar roscas; e o motor de combustão interna para impulsionar veículos. O trabalho feito por cada uma dessas ferramentas constitui a sua *virtude*. Cada indivíduo deveria interessar-se pela sua virtude funcional, estando disposto a sacrificar-se por causa da mesma. Um cientista que esteja beneficiando a humanidade é um instrumento de Deus, tanto quanto o professor de seminário teológico, que instrui os alunos nos campos da ética e da doutrina cristã. A imensa gama de atividades humanas, em que as pessoas passam de um estágio para outro, através de existências e esferas de existências, como a terrena e a celestial, tem por finalidade conferir-nos muitos tipos de experiências, muitas formas de virtudes funcionais. Tudo isso está envolvido no correto uso da vida. O terreno físico é importante, por ser o lugar onde o homem aprende a respeito de seu destino e procura concretizá-lo. Mas também há o terreno espiritual, onde um destino mais elevado é buscado. Os destinos tanto são materiais-terrenos quanto são espirituais-celestes. Esses destinos estão relacionados entre si, ainda que, em certo sentido, estejam separados um do outro.

9. *O ponto culminante do ato humano*. Do ponto de vista da ética, nada existe que se assemelhe ao amor, o qual é a raiz de todas as virtudes, bem como o elemento que empresta significação a todas as coisas. O amor é a essência e a prova da espiritualidade (ver I João 4:7,20). Cuidar dos outros e fazer por eles aquilo que fazemos por nós mesmos, devido ao cuidado que temos conosco, é o que constitui a lei do amor.

10. *A obediência à fé*. Teologicamente falando, um bom ato moral sempre será uma questão de obedecer de modo racional à fé, quando a pessoa tem consciência de que tem obrigações radicais diante de Deus, o qual proporciona fé e graça aos homens. A obediência à fé consiste no amor a Deus, o qual nos inspira fé. Por conseguinte, um ato moralmente mau é uma espécie de incredulidade e negligência acerca da fé, um tipo de arrogância e auto-asserção que desagrada a Deus, em Seu dom da graça. (NTI R)

ATO ILOCUCIONÁRIO
Ver o artigo sobre **Austin, John L.**

ATO IMPURO
O ato impuro é uma ação que em si é má, ou cuja motivação é errada ou egoísta. O homem que faz o bem, porém com motivos errados, faz um ato impuro. Alguns filósofos insistem que somente a boa vontade é realmente pura, porque todas as ações, até as mais puras, (aparentemente), sempre têm alguma corrupção no nível de motivos. Isto parece um exagero, mas, realmente, é difícil falar exageradamente sobre a corrupção dos motivos dos homens.

ATO INDIFERENTE
Este termo quer dizer que algumas ações dos homens não têm conteúdo moral ou espiritual. Nesta classificação Paulo colocou a observação de dias especiais, os ritos e cerimônias religiosas, comidas proibidas e não-proibidas, etc. Ver Rom. 14:1-10. O que é importante é que fazemos tudo em nome do Senhor, utilizando assim de coisas indiferentes para promover a espiritualidade positiva. O pragmatismo (que vide) tem sua utilidade, porque muitas coisas da vida diária, que fazemos, não são nem boas e nem más. Paulo falou da liberdade de ação que tinha e assim foi permitida ser tudo para todos os homens. Ele falou que todas as coisas eram legítimas para ele, (I Cor. 10:23 *ss*). Mas isto tem aplicação somente aos atos indiferentes. Obviamente, Paulo não quis dizer que não existem padrões morais.

ATO NECESSÁRIO, EXISTENCIAL
Este termo especifica uma ação que uma pessoa *deve* realizar como parte de seu destino. Achamos que, na vida de uma pessoa, há um número de acontecimentos necessários para a realização do seu destino. Estes acontecimentos não são muito numerosos, mas são muito importantes, porque sem eles, a alma não completa a sua missão na terra, como deve ser realizada. O ato necessário, existencial, é a realização de um acontecimento necessário. Uma *decisão existencial* é uma decisão que a pessoa faz para fazer um ato necessário.

ATO PURO
1. Eticamente falando, é um ato que seja puro em si, e na motivação que o inspira. Ver sobre *Ato impuro*.
2. Na filosofia de Tomás de Aquino (que vide), somente Deus não combina as qualidades de *actus* e *potentia*, isto é, o tipo de ser cujas ações (desenvolvimento) se dirigem para uma finalidade, através da realização de potencialidade. Deus é um ser sempre e perfeitamente auto-realizado. — Deus, considerado, deste ângulo, Aquino chamou de *Ato Puro*. Esta filosofia, naturalmente, foi baseada na discussão de Aristóteles sobre causas, especificamente sobre atualidade e potencialidade (isto é, no grego, *energeia* e *dynamis*).

ATO REDENTOR
No sentido primário, este termo significa o ato salvador de Jesus Cristo, a expiação e a ressurreição. Ver os artigos sobre estes assuntos. Ver o artigo sobre *Salvação*. Secundariamente, o termo é usado para designar o ato de um homem que compensa uma maldade ou uma falha que ele fez, efetuando uma recuperação.

ATOMISMO
Vem do grego **a**, «não», e **temno**, «cortar». Alicerça-se sobre a equivocada noção de que o átomo não pode ser dividido. O atomismo é a crença de que a matéria consiste em átomos; e em sua forma mais radical, que não há existência além do átomo, pois este explicaria todas as coisas. Seus primeiros estágios encontram-se nos filósofos gregos *Leucipo*— e *Demócrito* (século V A.C.) (ver os artigos). Essa crença repousa sobre considerações metafísicas e científicas. Pelo menos no que tange à matéria, há crescentes evidências em favor da crença que as propriedades em larga escala dos objetos podem ser

explicadas como arranjos de seus componentes fundamentais. Há um ramo da ciência que continua investigando e descobrindo novas partículas atômicas; podendo-se dizer que o átomo continuará sendo *redefinido* em sua natureza ainda por algum tempo. O fato de que não podemos dizer o que seja exatamente o átomo (de fato, o átomo continua sendo uma entidade muito misteriosa), mostra que todo o nosso conhecimento científico repousa sobre bases precárias, não passando de uma modalidade de ceticismo prático, dentro do qual a função (embora não a teoria) continua sendo o elemento principal.

Do ângulo da metafísica, é atrativa a suposição que se o nosso mundo se caracteriza pelo estado de fluxo (o que repousa sobre a instabilidade dos átomos), as partículas do átomo são elementos permanentes e inalteráveis. Os antigos gregos supunham que o próprio átomo era uma partícula indivisível, e que meras combinações de átomos produzem tudo quanto está sujeito às modificações e à dissolução. Porém, os filósofos têm procurado algo de imutável e permanente no próprio átomo.

Os físicos atômicos clássicos supunham que os átomos possuem apenas extensão espacial, forma, solidez e, talvez, peso embora sem propriedades como cor, calor e cheiro. Dessa forma, anteciparam a filosofia corpuscular de Gassendi, Boyle e Locke (ver os artigos a respeito), no século XVII, com sua ênfase sobre a diferença entre as qualidades primárias e secundárias das coisas materiais. Ver o artigo sobre *as qualidades primárias e secundárias*.

Os físicos modernos continuam pesquisando em busca de partículas cada vez menores, mas não pensam que elas têm solidez e formato, no sentido em que os têm as bolas de bilhar. Propriedades eletromagnéticas, e outras propriedades menos familiares estão sendo estudadas, e já são compreendidas, ao menos em parte. Alguns físicos teóricos têm abandonado a crença de que o átomo pode explicar a existência, incluindo os fenômenos observáveis, e estão apelando para a *mente* e a *inteligência* como fatores mais fundamentais da existência do que as partículas atômicas. De acordo com essa opinião, o átomo seria uma concentração de energias psíquicas, ou seja, resultado ou realização da Realidade, e não a própria substância da Realidade. Da mente passamos para a escala maior da *Mente Divina*. Alguns físicos têm suposto que o Universo se parece mais com uma grande idéia do que com uma grande máquina. Todas as formas de conhecimento finalmente conduzem a Deus, e assim sendo, — à medida que formos conhecendo o átomo, mais conheceremos sobre Deus. Evidências importantes frisam um conceito não-material da Realidade Última, com a provisão que há manifestações materiais dessa realidade final.

Estágios na história do atomismo:
1. Filosofia indiana do **jainismo** (ver o artigo), em cerca de 800 A.C.
2. No Ocidente, os filósofos gregos Leucipo e Demócrito (século V A.C.).
3. Epicuro (ver o artigo), século IV A.C. Entidades espaciais indivisíveis, em forma composta, constituiriam a matéria. Heráclides (ver o artigo) advogava a idéia de diferenças qualitativas nos átomos, bem como novos desenvolvimentos.
4. Estrato (ver o artigo), no século III A.C., afirmava que os átomos são infinitamente divisíveis, sujeitos às ações do frio e do calor.
5. Nas religiões e filosofias orientais, no século IV A.C., a teoria atômica nas escolas de Nyaya e Vaisesika (ver artigos). Alguns budistas do norte também eram atomistas.

6. Lucrécio, no século I A.C. (ver artigo a respeito), seguia as idéias de Demócrito e Epicuro, embora concebesse os átomos dotados de movimentos voluntários, o que teria dado início a vórtices que deram começo ao mundo.
7. A moderna teoria atômica, em Galileu (ver o artigo), é expressão do atomismo. Matéria e extensão foram identificadas pelos filósofos do século XVII, Gassendi, Berigard, Maignan e Descartes.
8. Desde o século XVII tem havido uma teoria atômica mais sofisticada, que continua evoluindo.
9. Acima das teorias atômicas, temos a idéia de *mente* (ver o artigo), como idéia fundamental, onde o átomo seria uma consideração secundária.

ÁTOMO

Uma das partículas unitárias das quais toda a matéria é composta. É considerado ser um agregado de partículas atômicas organizadas dentro e ao redor de um núcleo e que exibe características singularmente determinadas por seu número, configuração específica, movimentos e propriedades. A busca do verdadeiro átomo (isto é, uma partícula que não pode ser dividida) continua, porque o átomo que combina partículas, que podem ser separadas, não é, segundo a palavra grega, um *a - tomo* (*a + temnein*), uma coisa que não pode ser *cortada* ou dividida. O conceito do átomo é importante tanto para a teologia como para a filosofia. Ver o artigo sobre *Atomismo*.

ATORMENTADORES, VERDUGOS

Palavra que em sua forma adjetivada, **basanistés**, «atormentador», aparece somente em Mat. 18:34 (nossa versão portuguesa a traduz ali por «verdugos»). O verbo e o substantivo da mesma palavra aparecem por dezessete vezes (ver, para exemplificar, Mat. 8:6; Mar. 5:7; Luc. 8:28; Apo. 9:5; 14:11; 18:7,10,15). Uma palavra cognata é *básanos*, «tortura», que figura em Mat. 4:24 e Luc. 16:23,28. A palavra *basanistés* aponta para um carcereiro que não somente conservava presos os devedores, mas também tornava a vida deles miserável, até que pagassem a dívida. Ordinariamente, os devedores eram vendidos como escravos, se não pudessem saldar sua dívida; mas, de outras vezes, eram lançados na prisão, até que fizessem a restituição.

ATOS

De Paulo, de Pilatos, de João, de Pedro, de Tomé, etc., ver **os pseudepígrafos** do N.T.

ATOS (Novo Testamento)

Introdução

Conteúdo

I. Autor
II. Data, Proveniência e Destino
III. Caráter Literário
IV. Texto Grego do Livro de Atos
V. Contactos e Influências Literárias
VI. Fontes Informativas
VII. Ênfase Apologética; Interesses e Propósitos Teológicos
VIII. Conteúdo
IX. Tabela Cronológica dos Acontecimentos em Confronto com a História Contemporânea
X. Tabela Cronológica da Vida de Paulo
XI. Bibliografia

O livro de *Atos* é a única história da igreja cristã em existência, escrita antes do século III D.C. Bastaria esse fato isolado para que se reconhecesse universal-

ATOS

mente o valor deste livro, não o encarnado como mero documento histórico. Sem o mesmo, ficaríamos virtualmente sem qualquer registro histórico sobre o desenvolvimento inicial e a propagação do cristianismo primitivo, que o acompanha em sua rápida expansão desde a Palestina até partes distantes do mundo civilizado de então. Também é obra de grande valia na ajuda que nos presta para melhor entendermos as epístolas paulinas, que constituem uma porção avantajada do volume do Novo Testamento, posto que lhes provê valiosas informações de pano de fundo.

Não obstante, o livro de Atos não encerra uma história completa de todo o movimento cristão do primeiro século de nossa era, porquanto cobre tão-somente um período de três décadas, isto é, de cerca de 33 acerca de 63 D.C. Outrossim, se concentra sobretudo nos feitos de apenas dois dos apóstolos de Cristo: Pedro e Paulo. Cerca de metade do volume do livro se devota às atividades de Paulo, um terço às atividades de Pedro, e mais ou menos um sexto aos outros líderes cristãos primitivos de menor envergadura.

O título original do livro, *Atos dos Apóstolos*, dificilmente teria sido conferido pelo seu autor original, embora tenha sido aquele que geralmente veio a ser-lhe atribuído. De fato, não se trata de uma narrativa dos «atos dos apóstolos», visto que apenas dois apóstolos recebem alguma descrição de vulto ali. Muito menos ainda seria a história dos «atos de todos os apóstolos», segundo é denominado o livro do cânon muratoriano, certamente como exagero do conflito contra Márcion. Este havia rejeitado os demais apóstolos de Jesus à base do fato de que haviam abandonado a Cristo quando de seu injusto julgamento, tendo transformado Paulo em seu grande herói, como exclusiva autoridade da igreja cristã primitiva. Talvez um título mais apropriado fosse «História do Poder de Deus entre os Apóstolos» ou «História dos Atos do Espírito Santo», já que a presença guiadora do Espírito de Deus é um tema permanente desse livro. (Ver Atos 1:8).

O livro de Atos é a continuação da narração do levantamento e propagação do cristianismo, sendo que a primeira metade é contada pelo evangelho de Lucas. Atos 1:1 é passagem que deixa pouquíssima dúvida de que esses dois volumes—o evangelho de Lucas e o livro de Atos—resultaram de um único esforço literário. É perfeitamente possível que os manuscritos originais dessas duas obras tivessem sido postos a circular juntos; ou então que os dois volumes fossem apenas seções diversas da mesma obra. Ou então o livro de Atos pode ter sido publicado pouco depois do evangelho de Lucas, em volume separado, embora com a finalidade de ser lido e usado em conjunção com esse evangelho. Juntas, essas duas obras formam o mais completo registro histórico de como se desenvolveu a nova religião revelada, em torno da personalidade do Senhor Jesus Cristo, não como um ramo espúrio e herético do judaísmo, mas, bem ao contrário, a plena concretização dos alvos e ideais do judaísmo segundo revelado nas páginas do A.T. Pois o cristianismo bíblico preservou tudo quanto havia de bom e verdadeiro no judaísmo, embora o tenha ultrapassado em grau e em importância, de tal modo que com o cristianismo surgiu uma nova e poderosa modalidade de fé.

É exatamente o *desenvolvimento dessa nova fé* que o livro de Atos acompanha até cerca do ano 67 D.C., quando o maior herói dessa nova fé se encontrava aprisionado em Roma. Embora o autor sagrado, sem dúvida alguma, tenha vivido o bastante para ser testemunha do martírio do apóstolo Paulo, não fazia parte dos seus propósitos descrever esse último evento, mas antes, encerrar a sua narrativa com uma nota de triunfo e de otimismo, pois o sucesso do cristianismo fora espantoso, o que se deveria encarar como resultado da sua origem e propagação divinas, mediante o poder divino do Espírito Santo.

«O livro de Atos é a **pedra-chave** que vincula as duas porções principais do Novo Testamento, isto é, o 'evangelho', conforme os primeiros cristãos diziam...a única ponte de que dispomos para atravessar o abismo aparentemente intransponível que separa Jesus de Paulo, Cristo do cristianismo, o evangelho de Jesus e o evangelho sobre a pessoa de Jesus». (H.J. Cadbury, *The Making of Luke-Acts*, Nova Iorque: The Macmillan Co., pág. 2).

Os diversos títulos que têm sido atribuídos a esse livro, nos dias da antiguidade, são os seguintes: *«Atos e Transações dos Apóstolos»* (Codex Bezae) e *«Atos dos Santos Apóstolos»* (Codex Alexandrinus e outros, incluindo alguns dos primeiros pais da igreja). Os manuscritos mais antigos dizem simplesmente *«Atos dos Apóstolos»*, como o Codex Vaticanus e outros manuscritos antigos, apesar de que o ms. Aleph diga simplesmente «Atos». Alguns editores têm dado preferência a este último título, como possível representante do título original, ou, pelo menos, como aquele que mais direito tem de reivindicar originalidade. Os pais da igreja, Orígenes Tertuliano, Dídimo, Hilário, Eusébio e Epifânio também usaram meramente o título «Atos» para este livro. Já Ecumênio chamou-o de «Evangelho do Espírito Santo». E Crisóstomo apodou-se de *Livro da Demonstração da Ressurreição*.

I. Autor

Destaca-se acima de tudo a autoria comum e a unidade da obra Lucas-Atos. Isso faz de Lucas o mais extensivo autor de todo o Novo Testamento, pois, somando-se esses dois volumes, temos nessas duas obras mais de um quarto do total do volume do N.T., o que é mais do que qualquer outro autor sagrado contribuiu, a menos que consideremos paulina a epístola aos Hebreus (apesar de que isso não é muito provável), caso em que o apóstolo Paulo seria o mais copioso escritor do N.T. Assim sendo, se não considerarmos outro fator além do mero volume, Lucas-Atos serve de importantíssima consideração nos estudos do N.T. A autoria comum desse par de documentos, e o fato de que Lucas foi o autor de ambos, é algo óbvio e universalmente reconhecido, pois os dois volumes constituem duas divisões de uma mesma obra literária. O trecho de Atos 1:1 mostra que o autor sagrado tencionava que esses dois volumes fossem reputados uma unidade. Já desde o ano de 185 D.C. (em um escrito de Irineu, *«Contra as Heresias»*, 3:1,14) temos uma afirmação da autoria lucana desses dois livros. Também poderíamos acrescentar a isso o testemunho do cânon muratoriano, que pertence ao fim do século II D.C., como o fazem igualmente os testemunhos de Tertuliano (*Marc.* iv.2). Orígenes, Eusébio (*História Eclesiástica*, vi.25) e Jerônimo (*Vir. illustr.* 7). Pelos fins do segundo século, essa era a tradição corrente na igreja de Roma. Evidências linguísticas dão apoio às reivindicações do prefácio do evangelho de Lucas, bem como às declarações constantes nas tradições acima citadas.

Quase que o dobro de palavras é peculiar ao livro de Atos e ao evangelho de Lucas quando comparados entre si, do que quando se confronta o livro de Atos com os evangelhos sinópticos. Muitas palavras e expressões características do estilo do evangelho de

Lugares visitados por Paulo

— Cortesia, Dr. John F. Walvoord

Antioquia moderna (no rio Orontes)

Moeda de Derbe, da rainha
Faustina, a Jovem

Moeda de Listra, mostrando o fundador
da colônia com touro e arado

Moeda rara da cidade de Derbe,
do tempo da rainha Lucila

Pedro e Paulo, trabalhado em vidro,
das catacumbas de Roma

A Prisão *Mamertinum*, Roma, suposta localidade do aprisionamento de Paulo e Pedro

ATOS

Lucas se encontram em ambos esses documentos. Tais declarações, entretanto, têm sido desafiadas (como, por exemplo, por A.C. Clark, em sua obra *The Acts of the Apostles*), o que esse autor fez especialmente com base em considerações lingüísticas. Porém, tais desafios são quase universalmente considerados não-convincentes, sobretudo à luz de muitas evidências positivas, que consubstanciam a autoria lucana desses dois notáveis documentos do N.T.

Na história antiga existem alguns comentários desfavoráveis ao livro de Atos como livro genuíno de Lucas, especialmente entre os primeiros gnósticos, como Cerinto e a sua escola (conforme é registrado por Eusébio, em sua *História Eclesiástica* 1:4). Todavia, essas críticas não se alicerçaram em qualquer avaliação crítica, mas meramente em considerações subjetivas e doutrinárias, a saber, por causa do conteúdo geral do livro de Atos, que não concordava com os seus pontos doutrinários mais salientes. Márcion (150 D.C.) rejeitava o livro de Atos, embora Paulo fosse o seu grande herói, tendo selecionado algumas das epístolas paulinas e uma porção mutilada do livro de Lucas como seu «cânon» das Escrituras do N.T. Márcion rejeitava o livro de Atos como genuíno porque sentia que os discípulos originais haviam sido infiéis ao Senhor Jesus, pelo que também foram rejeitados; e, no entanto, o livro de Atos exalta ao apóstolo Pedro, algo que ele não podia aceitar. Mas, ao assim fazer, Márcion também rejeitava a principal autenticação das atividades apostólicas de Paulo. Também rejeitava o livro de Atos porque não somente Paulo é magnificado no livro, mas Pedro também o é (além de alguns outros indivíduos, ainda que em grau muito menos intenso). Isso não concordava com a sua opinião de que somente Paulo possuía autoridade para escrever livros sagrados, segundo as razões dadas acima. Também devemo-nos lembrar que Márcion rejeitava totalmente o A.T., tendo procurado fundar uma religião inteiramente diferente, de forma alguma alicerçada no registro do A.T., mediante o uso dos escritos de Paulo e de sua autoridade apostólica. Por semelhante modo, entre os antigos, houve outros indivíduos, como Severo, discípulo de Taciano, que rejeitavam o livro de Atos; mas, igualmente nesse caso, o verdadeiro motivo eram os preconceitos doutrinários que não tinham base em qualquer avaliação verdadeiramente crítica.

Os eruditos modernos, entretanto, quer liberais, quer conservadores, têm quase, universalmente, atribuído ambos esses livros à pena de Lucas, aquele que era o companheiro de viagens do apóstolo Paulo, o médico amado. Até mesmo os estudiosos mais radicais reconhecem a validade dessa reivindicação. Nordem e Loisy se erguem quase isolados, em sua afirmativa de que somente uma de suas fontes informativas, o diário de viagens que constitui a sua narrativa central, na realidade foi escrita pelo mesmo autor sagrado que registrou o evangelho de Lucas, pois outras fontes históricas poderiam ser também percebidas. Todavia, a evidência lingüística é poderosa em favor da conclusão de que apesar do autor sagrado ter-se valido, naturalmente, de muitas fontes informativas, tendo-as reunido em sua multicolorida narrativa, algumas das cenas não foram vistas ou testemunhadas por ele de forma alguma; mas que, a despeito disso, o mesmo autor editou e compôs o livro de Atos.

A autoria comum do evangelho de Lucas e do livro de Atos pode ser demonstrada pelas seguintes considerações:

1. *Considerações lingüísticas*—Quase o dobro de palavras é peculiar ao evangelho de Lucas, em comparação com o livro de Atos, do que ao livro de Atos em confronto com os outros evangelhos sinópticos. Muitas palavras e expressões são peculiares somente à obra Lucas-Atos. Sem dúvida alguma há mais afinidades, no vocabulário, entre esses dois livros, do que entre quaisquer outros dois escritos do N.T. Por exemplo, existem dezessete vocábulos que se encontram tanto em Mateus como no livro de Atos, embora não apareçam em nenhuma outra porção do N.T.; existem catorze dessas palavras no evangelho de Marcos e no livro de Atos, mas que não figuram em qualquer outro livro do N.T.; mas existem cerca de cinqüenta e oito dessas palavras da obra Lucas-Atos que não se encontram fora desses dois livros em nenhuma outra porção do N.T. (A obra de Vincent *Word Studies in the N.T.*, alista muito mais do que isso, nas páginas 601-611, primeiro volume).

2. O monumental *Alford's Greek New Testament* alista os seguintes sinais estilísticos que comprovam a autoria lucana e permeiam tanto o evangelho de Lucas como o livro de Atos: a. a descrição de enfermidades que subentende um homem mais versado nessas questões que os escritores ordinários do N.T., b. o emprego do termo «nós» nas passagens vazadas na primeira pessoa do plural, que são obviamente distinguidas dos trechos escritos na terceira pessoa do singular; e c. o fato de sabermos que Lucas foi um dos quase constantes companheiros de viagens do apóstolo Paulo. (Ver II Tim. 4:11). As seções que usam a primeira pessoa do plural (chamadas seções «nós», pelos estudiosos) são as seguintes: Atos 16:10-17; 20:5-15; 21:1-18 e 27:1-28:16. As comparações lingüísticas parecem demonstrar que o restante do livro foi escrito pelo mesmo autor dessas seções «nós». Idênticas considerações ligam esse autor ao evangelho de Lucas, mesmo quando não levamos em conta a clara afirmativa nesse sentido, que há no trecho de Atos 1:1. Além dessas formas de comprovação, Alford examinou diversas circunstâncias históricas que subentendem a autoria lucana, tanto do evangelho de Lucas como do livro de Atos.

3. Tanto o evangelho de Lucas como o livro de Atos foram endereçados a *Teófilo*. O trecho de Atos 1:1 esclarece-nos que ambos os livros foram escritos como duas partes de uma mesma obra literária, e a linguagem em que ambos esses volumes foram escritos, no que tange à qualidade do grego *koiné*, distingue Lucas dos autores dos outros evangelhos e de todos os demais livros do N.T. Trata-se de excelente grego «koiné» literário, superior ao grego dos demais evangelhos e no mesmo nível das melhores porções literárias dos demais livros do N.T., mostrando-se inferior somente à epístola aos Hebreus e a mais um ou dois livros. (Quanto a maiores detalhes sobre essa questão, ver o artigo intitulado *Linguagem do N.T.*, que descreve o grego usado no N.T., em termos gerais, e que também caracteriza de modo passageiro o grego *«koiné»* de cada um dos livros do N.T.). Não é por mero acidente que o mesmo excelente grego *koiné* vazado no mesmo estilo, e com o mesmo vocabulário distintivo, permeia a obra Lucas-Atos. E isso é um dos motivos que têm levado os estudiosos a concordar, quase universalmente, sobre o fato de que Lucas foi o autor de ambos esses volumes.

4. De conformidade com um tipo mais clássico de grego, podemos observar, tanto no evangelho de Lucas como no livro de Atos, o emprego do *modo*

ATOS

optativo grego, o qual figura com muito maior freqüência do que nos livros de qualquer outro dos autores do N.T., posto que ocorre ali por nada menos de vinte e oito vezes. Ora, esse é o tipo de fator que distingue não somente o estilo, como também a cultura de um autor. O modo optativo havia desaparecido quase inteiramente no grego «koiné», excetuando em certas expressões estereotipadas. No entanto, Lucas utiliza uma linguagem mais elevada, em seu caráter literário, que nos faz lembrar mais das obras clássicas do grego antigo. E o evangelho de Lucas e o livro de Atos possuem tais características.

5. O fato de que tanto o evangelho de Lucas como o livro de Atos foram escritos pelo mesmo autor é igualmente demonstrado pelo fato de que ambos enfatizam *os mesmos temas*, do princípio ao fim, alguns dos quais são os seguintes: a. A universalidade da religião cristã, que abandonou o caráter provinciano do judaísmo. Agora todas as raças e todos os povos se tornaram igualmente objetos do amor e da graça de Deus. (Comparar Lucas 2:32; 4:23-27; 10:29-37 e 17:15-18 com Atos 10:35; 13:46,47; 17:26-28 e 28:28). b. O Espírito Santo, se destaca tanto no evangelho de Lucas como no livro de Atos, muito mais do que nos evangelhos sinópticos. O evangelho de João também salienta o papel do Espírito Santo na economia cristã. (Comparar Luc. 1:15,35; 2:25-27; 4:1,18; 10:21 e 24:49 com Atos 1:2,8; 2:1-4,38; 8:14,17,29,39; 10:44-47; 13:2,4,9; 15:28; 16:7 e 19:1-7). c. Ambos esses livros demonstram uma marcante simpatia pelos pobres e pelos grupos desprezados da sociedade antiga. (Comparar Luc. 3:11; 4:18; 6:20 e 16:22 com Atos 2:44,45; 4:33-35 e 9:16,39). d. — Ambos os volumes demonstram antipatia pelos ricos. (Comparar Luc. 1:53; 6:24; 12:13-21 e 16:14,19 com Atos 8:18-24). e. Há saliência sobre o dever e o uso apropriado das riquezas. (Comparar Luc. 12:42-48; 16:1-13 e 19:12-27 com Atos 4:36,37; 5:1-11 e 20:35). f. Há ênfase em ambos os volumes sobre o papel desempenhado pelas mulheres na vida de Cristo e no desenvolvimento da igreja primitiva. (Comparar Luc. 1:39-56; 2:36-38; 7:37,38; 8:1-3; 19:49; 23:27-29 e 24:10 com Atos 1:14; 5:1; 9:36; 12:12,13; 16:13-18; 18:2; 24:24 e 25:13). g. Há em ambos os livros intensa ênfase sobre a necessidade de oração por parte do crente. (Comparar Luc. 11:5-13; 18:1-5,9-14 e 22:39-46 com Atos 1:24,25; 2:42; 4:31; 6:6; 10:2,9; 12:12; 13:3; 16:25 e 21:5). h. O tema da *graça* divina figura nessas duas obras com muito maior freqüência que nos evangelhos sinópticos, porquanto no evangelho de Lucas essa palavra aparece por oito vezes, ao passo que no livro de Atos aparece por dezesseis vezes. (Comparar Luc. 1:30; 2:40,52; 4:22; 6:32-34; 17:34 e 17:9 com Atos 2:47; 4:33; 11:43; 13:43; 14:3,26; 15:11,40; 18:27; 20:24,32; 24:27 e 25:3,9). A palavra *graça* não aparece nos evangelhos de Mateus e de Marcos, apesar de figurar por quatro vezes no evangelho de João. Aparece com maior abundância nos escritos do apóstolo Paulo, conforme também já seria de se esperar. (Por nada menos de cento e duas vezes, sem contarmos a epístola aos Hebreus). i. Há no evangelho de Lucas e no livro de Atos maior destaque ao tema do perdão dos pecados do que no caso dos evangelhos sinópticos. (Comparar Luc. 1:77; 7:47; 11:4; 15:11-32 e 24:47 com Atos 2:38; 5:31; 10:43; 13:38 e 26:18). j. Nesses dois volumes se vê, igualmente destaque sobre o quadro político, na tentativa de mostrar que o cristianismo não era subversivo, merecendo ser aceito pelo estado romano como movimento religioso legítimo. (Comparar Luc. 20:20-23 e 23:1-17,20-22,47 com Atos 13:7,12;

16:35-49; 18:12-17; 19:31,37; 23:26-30; 24:23; 25:25-27; 26:30-32; 27:43 e 28:30,31).

6. Sobre a autoria comum de Lucas-Atos, Morton Scott Enslin, em seu livro *The Literature of the Christian Movement* (Harper and Brothers, Nova Iorque, 1956, pág. 413), diz: «O livro de Atos é a continuação da história do surgimento e da propagação do cristianismo, cuja primeira metade consiste no evangelho de Lucas, o que é tão universalmente aceito que requer pouquíssimo argumento. A comum dedicação dessas obras a Teófilo; o reinício da narrativa nos últimos capítulos, precisamente no ponto onde termina o evangelho; a partida final de Jesus da presença de seus discípulos; uma sutil mas não obstante inequívoca unidade de propósitos, de atitudes, de ênfase e de fraseologia, tudo isso dificilmente poderia ter sucedido por mero acidente».

Não obstante, existem argumentos contrários à autoria lucana do livro de Atos, a saber:

1. O próprio livro de Atos é *anônimo*, isto é, em porção alguma o seu autor se desvenda, não dando qualquer indício sobre a sua identidade. Mostrar que a obra Lucas-Atos tem um autor comum é fácil; mas não há justificação alguma em identificar esse autor com Lucas, tendo sido apenas uma opinião especulativa dos primeiros pais da igreja. A essa objeção, entretanto, podemos replicar que essa é a *opinião universal* dos pais da igreja e dos séculos subseqüentes, sendo que essa declaração universal mui provavelmente estava bem alicerçada *nos fatos*, sabendo-se sobejamente, além de tudo, que Lucas foi companheiro quase constante do apóstolo Paulo em suas viagens missionárias. (Ver Col. 4:14; Fil. 24 e II Tim. 4:11). Sobre isso, ver os diversos antigos testemunhos acerca da autoria lucana, sobre o que tratamos mais abaixo.

2. Diversos eruditos têm procurado demonstrar, com base nos termos *médicos* da obra Lucas-Atos que foi um «médico» quem escreveu essa dupla obra, mas essa asseveração não tem podido resistir à luz das investigações. Acima de todos, H.J. Cadbury tem solapado essa idéia (em sua obra *The Style and Literary Method of Luke*, Cambridge: Harvard University Press, 1920, págs. 39-72; e *Lexical Notes on Luke-Acts*. The Journal of Biblical Literature, XLV, 1026, págs. 190-209). Dentre os quatrocentos termos supostamente médicos, usualmente salientados como parte do vocabulário dos médicos, nada menos de trezentos e sessenta se encontram na Septuaginta, sem que isso indique qualquer uso especializado. Outros autores, como Filo, Plutarco e Luciano (o último dos quais usa nada menos de noventa por cento dos chamados termos «médicos»), empregaram tais vocábulos, sem que quisessem dar a entender qualquer linguagem própria de médicos. Josefo e a Septuaginta, se considerados juntamente, contêm trezentos e noventa desses quatrocentos vocábulos, emergindo assim a verdade de que não havia qualquer vocabulário médico especializado nos tempos de Lucas. Por conseguinte, é justo dizermos que se alguém não tivesse feito a conexão entre o «médico» Lucas e este livro de Atos, para em seguida sair à caça de um vocabulário «médico», com a mesma facilidade o autor sagrado poderia ter sido considerado como «capitão da marinha» ou «advogado», porquanto existem ali diversos termos náuticos, além de expressões legais, sobretudo nos capítulos finais do livro de Atos.

No que tange ao argumento acima exposto, contrário à autoria lucana parece que o mesmo diz essencialmente a verdade; e isso parece eliminar um

ATOS

dos argumentos favoritos em favor da autoria lucana do livro de Atos. No entanto, esse argumento contrário não é fatal à posição geral em favor da autoria de Lucas, a qual pode facilmente sobreviver sem esse elemento relativo aos termos «médicos».

Contudo, embora nenhum vocabulário «médico» especial possa ser demonstrado na obra Lucas-Atos, muitos eruditos acreditam que ainda transparece nessa obra um *interesse desusado* pelas questões «médicas», além de um interesse todo especial pelas curas motivadas pela fé. (Ver Luc. 7:18-23; Atos 5:12-16 e 19:11, passagens cuja finalidade é a de demonstrar que o poder curador de Jesus continuava em operação através dos apóstolos, o que é especificamente salientado em Atos 3:12,13 e 4:7-10). Deve-se observar como o trecho de Luc. 8:43 modifica a passagem de Marc. 5:26, a interesse do bom nome da profissão médica. Assim sendo, apesar de que o próprio vocabulário usado na obra Lucas-Atos não possa servir de prova definitiva acerca da autoria lucana, o conteúdo desses dois livros, no que diz respeito a essa questão, parece confirmar que o autor sagrado era indivíduo extraordinariamente interessado pelas questões médicas, o que aponta fortemente para Lucas, o «médico amado».

3. É possível que o argumento favorito, contrário à autoria lucana do livro de Atos, seja a tentativa de demonstrar que o autor sagrado não poderia ter conhecido o apóstolo Paulo tão bem como se pensa, porque mui provavelmente não fora seu companheiro de viagens. O quadro que tal autor pinta do apóstolo, especialmente no que tange às suas crenças doutrinárias, *difere* tão radicalmente do que Paulo expressa, além do fato de que apresenta alguns acontecimentos históricos que não estão de acordo com o que transparece nas epístolas daquele apóstolo. E em seguida os opositores argumentam que o autor sagrado jamais teria feito isso, se realmente o tivesse conhecido bem. Segundo um ponto de vista histórico, os trechos do primeiro capítulo da epístola aos Gálatas e de Atos 9:20-30, que falam sobre as atividades de Paulo, imediatamente após a sua conversão, diferem muitíssimo, quanto aos pormenores e ao que fica implícito, do que nos diz o livro de Atos, porquanto este último não se refere aos três anos de ausência de Paulo, mas antes, faz alusão ao fato de que imediatamente ele se pôs a pregar, viajando e associando-se a outros líderes cristãos. Outras considerações difíceis são aquelas que falam de Paulo, que freqüentemente andava em conflito com o elemento judaico no seio da igreja cristã. Atos e suas epístolas não se harmonizam quando fazem referência a estes fatos. (As epístolas aos Gálatas e aos Romanos são apresentadas como escritos em harmonia contra a totalidade da narrativa de Atos, como também no que diz respeito à circuncisão de Timóteo e no que diz respeito aos votos que Paulo fez, no templo de Jerusalém—ver Atos 16:1-3 e 20:17-26), ações essas que nos parecem impossíveis pelo que sabemos de Paulo através de suas epístolas aos Gálatas e aos Romanos.

Esses problemas podem ser solucionados como segue: 1. Os trechos paulinos que parecem incandescentemente partidários foram escritos sob a pressão da controvérsia, e talvez Paulo nem sempre tivesse sido tão antijudaico, tão antilegal e tão anti-ritual como essas suas epístolas nos indicam; ou talvez tenha havido períodos em que ele demonstrou maior simpatia pelos caminhos antigos, o que, corretamente, seria apenas natural e humano. 2. Não há razão alguma para pensarmos que Lucas precisava ter *pleno conhecimento* de todos os detalhes dos—primeiros anos—da vida cristã de Paulo. É óbvio que a narrativa lucana é apenas uma apresentação *parcial* daqueles primeiros anos, onde se devem esperar alguns lapsos. No que tange às idéias doutrinárias que são tão importantes para Paulo, segundo transparece em suas epístolas, mas que não são intensamente mencionadas no livro de Atos, especialmente no que concerne à morte de Cristo, que é fato central nos escritos desse apóstolo, mas que usualmente é apresentada como horrendo crime, no livro de Atos, sem que apareça a idéia do desígnio divino em toda essa ocorrência. Pode-se responder que se por um lado Paulo enfatizou o papel divino muito mais do que aparece no livro de Atos, contudo, tanto o evangelho de Lucas como o livro de Atos contêm esse conceito, segundo se vê demonstrado nas seguintes passagens: em Luc. 22:19,20, onde se lê sobre a instituição da Ceia do Senhor e que pronuncia claramente esse tema; em Luc. 24:44-47, que alude às profecias do A.T., todas frisando o papel do Messias sofredor, que traria a remissão dos pecados aos homens, por meio de sua paixão na cruz; e Atos 2:23,27, que mostra que os sofrimentos de Cristo haviam sido adredemente determinados por Deus, pois através deles é que receberíamos a redenção, das mãos do Messias. Ver também o trecho de Atos 20:28 no NTI, onde esse tema é expresso nos termos mais definidos possíveis.

Eduard Meyer (*Ursprung und Anfange des Christentums*, Berlim: J.G. Cotta, 1921-1923), levanta objeção, em sua obra de três volumes, àquilo que ele denomina de objeções arbitrárias e de métodos arbitrários dos teólogos, que requerem uma *abordagem completa e harmoniosa*, em todos os assuntos, por parte de Lucas e de Paulo, meramente porque esses dois homens de Deus viajaram juntos. A verdade é que cada um desses autores sagrados se utilizou de seu próprio método de expressão, enfatizando certos particulares diferentes um do outro, sendo fácil para nós encontrarmos pontos de vista em aparente contradição; contudo, dificilmente isso pode ser contrário à conclusão de que esses dois homens se conheciam bem um ao outro.

Os antigos defendiam a autoria e a autoridade lucana da obra Lucas-Atos, segundo se vê nas seguintes fontes históricas:

1. *Eusébio* (testemunho e comentário na sua História Eclesiástica iii.25). 2. Epístola das igrejas de Lyons e Viena às igrejas da *Ásia Menor* e da Frígia, de 177 D.C., segundo é citada por Eusébio, em sua *História Eclesiástica* v. 2. 3. Irineu (*Contra as Heresias* iii., cap. 14). 4. Clemente de Alexandria, em 200 D.C. (*Strom*. v.12). 5. Tertuliano, em 150 D.C. (*De Baptismo*, cap. 10, vol. 12; *De jejuniis*, cap. 10, vol. 12; *Adv. Marnio*. lib. v. §2 e iv. 2). 6. Orígenes, citado por Eusébio (*História Eclesiástica vi*.26). 7. Jerônimo, (*Vir*. ilustr. 7). 8. *Cânon Muratoriano*, do fim do século segundo de nossa era, que alista o livro de Atos como canônico, de autoria lucana. (O cânon muratoriano era uma lista de livros do N.T., que eram reputados autorizados, usados e lidos na adoração pública da igreja. Evidentemente foi traduzido para o latim, com base num original grego. Reflete os usos da igreja cristã de Roma em cerca de 200 d.C. e pode ter sido escrito por Vítor, de Roma. O nome desse cânon se deriva do erudito italiano que o descobriu na biblioteca ambrosiana, em Milão, e o publicou em 1740, como exemplar de latim bárbaro).

A seção do *fragmento muratoriano* confirma a autoria lucana do evangelho de Lucas e do livro de Atos como segue: «O terceiro livro do evangelho,

ATOS

segundo Lucas, aquele médico que após a ascensão de Cristo, se tornou devoto auxiliar de Paulo, que o tomara consigo (ou talvez como 'companheiro de viagens'), foi composto por ele, em seu próprio nome, por informes recebidos de terceiros. No entanto, ele mesmo não viu ao Senhor na carne, pelo que também (?) conforme podia seguir, assim ele registrou (?), começando a falar desde a natividade de João. Mas os Atos de todos os apóstolos foram escritos em um livro. Lucas compilou, para o 'excelentíssimo Teófilo', os diversos acontecimentos ocorridos em sua presença, conforme ele claramente revela mediante a omissão da morte de Pedro e da partida de Paulo da cidade, quando viajou para a Espanha». (Fragmento muratoriano, linhas 2-8 e 34-39, conforme traduzido por Morton Scott Enslin, que procurou reproduzir na tradução o latim deficiente em que o documento foi escrito).

A personagem de Lucas. Seu nome é contração de Lucano, tal como Silas o é de Silvano. Tal apelativo provavelmente significava, a princípio, alguém originário da Lucânia, lugar da baixa Itália, e vem de «luca bos», boi lucano, isto é, elefante, pois foi justamente na Lucânia que os romanos pela primeira vez puderam conhecer os elefantes, trazidos no exército de Pirro.

Lucas é mencionado por nome no trecho de Fil. 24, como cooperador de Paulo no trabalho missionário; em Col. 4:14, como o «médico amado»; em II Tim. 4:11 como o único que permanecera junto a Paulo, em seus sofrimentos e labores. Eusébio (*História Eclesiástica* iii.4) assevera que ele era natural da cidade de Antioquia. A tradição apresenta-o como um *gentio* que falava o grego e a natureza da composição da obra Lucas-Atos confirma ter-se tratado de indivíduo bem-educado, cuja língua nativa era o grego. As passagens «nós» (assim chamadas porque o autor sagrado passa a usar a primeira pessoa do plural) do livro de Atos mostram que Lucas acompanhou o apóstolo Paulo em algumas de suas mais importantes viagens, pelo que foi testemunha ocular de grande parte daquilo que ele mesmo narra nesse livro, pois nessas oportunidades mui provavelmente fez parte do grupo de missionários viajantes. (Ver Atos 16:10-17; 20:5-15; 21:1-18 e 27:1-28:17).

Epifânio (*Haer*. 1.12, bispo de Constância ou Salames, capital de Chipre, eleito para o ofício em 367 D.C.) informa-nos que Lucas foi um dos setenta discípulos especiais que o Senhor Jesus enviara a ministrar pela Galiléia (ver o décimo capítulo do evangelho de Lucas). Mas é claro, conforme o prefácio do evangelho de Lucas, que o autor não fora testemunha ocular do ministério de Jesus, ainda que tenha tido contato com muitas dessas testemunhas oculares, o que não podemos de forma alguma duvidar. Essa tradição, transmitida por Epifânio, provavelmente teve origem na circunstância de que somente o evangelho de Lucas registra esse ministério especial dos setenta discípulos de Jesus. Os conhecimentos que Lucas tinha do fato, entretanto, não foram adquiridos em primeira mão, mas sem dúvida, resultaram de suas diversas pesquisas nessas questões que circundavam a vida e o ministério de Cristo Jesus e de seus apóstolos, às quais devemos muitos outros pormenores e narrativas sobre tais ocorrências, que os demais evangelhos nada registram.

Pelo livro de Atos aprendemos que ele se reuniu a Paulo, em Trôade (Atos 16:10), tendo-o acompanhado em sua viagem a Roma. Com base nas epístolas desse apóstolo (ver II Tim. 4:11), ficamos sabendo que ele permaneceu em companhia de Paulo, até mesmo após o seu primeiro encarceramento e soltura,

e, evidentemente, até o tempo de martírio do grande apóstolo, em cerca de 67 D.C., após um segundo encarceramento. Lucas não registrou tais acontecimentos para nós, e é possível que estivesse planejando um terceiro volume para completar a sua história, ou então, propositalmente, ignorou o fim negativo da carreira de Paulo, a fim de não entrar em antagonismo com as autoridades romanas, pois Roma, pelo tempo em que foi escrito o livro de Atos, já vinha perseguindo a igreja cristã. (Quanto a outras razões possíveis para o término abrupto mas otimista do livro de Atos, ver as notas expositivas referentes aos versículos finais desse livro no NTI).

A tradição cristã primitiva observa igualmente a fidelidade toda especial de Lucas ao apóstolo Paulo. Outras tradições existem que nos dizem que Lucas teve um longo ministério e finalmente faleceu na Boécia, na Grécia, com oitenta e quatro anos de idade. Outras tradições, ainda, indicam que ele morreu como mártir, algum tempo perto do fim do primeiro século de nossa era.

Os livros de Lucas—o evangelho de seu nome e o livro de Atos mostram que ele era um grego bem-educado, dotado de considerável habilidade literária, porquanto as suas obras em nada ficam a perder para os escritos dos melhores historiadores gregos. Sua capacidade dramática, descritiva e de narração impressionou de tal modo ao erudito francês, Ernest Renan, que este o chamava de *um novo Homero* (segundo citação de Sypherd, pág. 168). Um outro autor, Chase (págs. 185-186), também chamou a atenção para os quadros falados de Lucas, bem como para os seus episódios dramáticos. (Ver Wilbur O. Sypherd, *The Literature of the English Bible*, Nova Iorque, Oxford University Press, 1936; e *The Bible and the Common Reader*, por Mary Ellen Chave, Nova Iorque, Macmillan Co., 1952).

Pelas obras que escreveu, depreendemos que Lucas era homem humilde e disciplinado, que sempre preferiu manter-se em segundo plano, permitindo que o Senhor Jesus fulgurasse resplandecentemente, como também Pedro e Paulo, os maiores discípulos do Mestre. Entretanto, ele mostra um orgulho justificável em suas obras literárias, bem como nas pesquisas que fez para escrevê-las, porquanto, em seu prólogo ao evangelho de Lucas não hesita esse autor em afirmar que fizera um trabalho intensivo e completo de investigação, examinando todas as questões que fazem parte da produção de seus livros, tendo transmitido a nós uma narrativa inteiramente fidedigna das cenas por ele descritas.

II. Data, Proveniência, Destino
A. Data

A data aproximada da dupla obra Lucas-Atos pode ser melhor determinada mediante o exame mais do livro de Atos do que do evangelho, porquanto, em Atos pelo menos podemos determinar, com alguma exatidão, certos acontecimentos históricos, quanto à data em que ocorreram.

A data mais recuada possível é a de 60 D.C., por ser esse o tempo mais cedo em que Paulo poderia ter chegado a Roma. O livro de Atos não poderia ter sido escrito antes dos últimos incidentes ali registrados. Supondo-se que Lucas escreveu esse livro imediatamente depois do encarceramento de Paulo, então tal volume poderia ter sido escrito em cerca de 60 D.C. A data mais avançada possível é a de 150 D.C., quando Márcion fez uso bem definido do evangelho de Lucas, razão pela qual sabemos que o livro de Atos já existia por essa altura.

Entretanto, Lucas foi companheiro de viagens

missionárias de Paulo, pelo que também não podia ser homem de idade muito diferente da do apóstolo. Não é muito provável, pois, que ele tivesse vivido para além do ano 100 D.C., e isso significa que tanto o evangelho de Lucas como o livro de Atos devem ter sido escritos antes dessa data. Outrossim, não é razoável pensarmos que Lucas tivesse esperado por mais de trinta anos, antes de registrar as suas impressões, muitas das quais vividas como testemunha ocular.

Em favor daquela data mais remota, alguns eruditos, como Harnack, têm opinado que a data de 63-64 D.C. seria a correta, salientando o término abrupto do livro de Atos, o que nos deixa supor que Paulo ainda não fora executado a mando do imperador Nero (em cerca de 67 D.C.), pois, se isso já tivesse ocorrido não se há de duvidar que Lucas teria registrado tão importante acontecimento. Outrossim, não é provável que o trecho de Atos 20:25,38, segundo alguns frisam, dissesse que Paulo não mais veria os seus amigos de Éfeso, e que o autor sagrado tivesse sabido (com base nos acontecimentos subseqüentes) que de fato, ele tornou a encontrar-se com eles, conforme nos mostram as epístolas pastorais (I e II Timóteo e Tito).

Além disso, não há qualquer menção à destruição de Jerusalém (que ocorreu no ano 70 D.C.), e nem às perseguições movidas por Nero contra os cristãos. O livro de Atos termina com uma atitude de otimismo, narrando como Paulo continuou a pregar livremente em Roma, embora tolhido em seus movimentos, pois estava continuamente sob a custódia militar, encerrado em sua própria casa. Alguns estudiosos, pois, raciocinam que esse otimismo não teria sido possível se a perseguição imperial contra os cristãos já estivesse em processo há muitos anos.

A maioria do eruditos recentes, entretanto, concorda que uma data intermediária entre aqueles dois extremos, digamos 70-75 D.C., é a que tem maiores probabilidades de estar certa, como data em que foi composta a obra Lucas-Atos. Mas, contrariando a opinião desses eruditos, expomos as seguintes razões, que nos obrigam a aceitar uma data anterior a essa, para os livros de Lucas-Atos:

1. *O término abrupto* do livro de Atos, que não faz qualquer menção à soltura de Paulo, ao seu encarceramento subseqüente e à sua execução, talvez tenha tido por motivo o desejo de Lucas de evitar menção a tais ocorrências, a fim de não provocar o antagonismo das autoridades romanas, que já haviam talvez começado a perseguir a igreja cristã. Mencionar oficialmente e descrever os maus tratos contra o principal campeão do cristianismo, que certamente teria exigido um juízo negativo de alguma forma, talvez só provocasse o incremento da perseguição ao cristianismo. Contudo, alguns estudiosos têm pensado que talvez Lucas tivesse planejado escrever um outro volume, narrando os acontecimentos subseqüentes, embora tal obra nunca tivesse sido concretizada. Ainda outros intérpretes pensam ser possível que Lucas soubesse que Teófilo, para quem a dupla obra, Lucas-Atos, foi escrita, além de outros indivíduos interessados, já estivessem bem familiarizados com os acontecimentos mais recentes da vida de Paulo, pelo que seria desnecessário um terceiro volume de narrativas, para quem já as conhecia a sobejo. Outrossim, o propósito do autor sagrado—mostrar que o cristianismo não era mero ramo herético do judaísmo, mas antes, marchara triunfalmente desde Jerusalém até Roma, pelo que merecia o respeito e o reconhecimento das autoridades romanas, tal como o judaísmo obtivera esse respeito e reconhecimento, e em nada ganharia se fosse narrado qualquer final negativo da vida do apóstolo Paulo.

2. O fato de que a destruição de Jerusalém não é aludida é *mais difícil* de explicar, por parte dos que preferem uma data posterior para a composição da obra Lucas-Atos. Porém, esse silêncio pode ter sido causado simplesmente porque o autor sagrado não chegara até àquela altura das ocorrências, em sua narrativa, e qualquer menção desse evento seria um deslocamento cronológico, um anacronismo. Outrossim, o evangelho de Lucas (escrito antes do livro de Atos) parece fazer alguma alusão distante à destruição de Jerusalém. Isso pode significar que tanto o evangelho de Lucas como o livro de Atos foram escritos depois de 70 D.C. (Quanto a outras informações sobre isso ver o artigo sobre *Lucas*, sob o título «Data»). As passagens de Luc. 19:43,44 e 21:20-24 sugerem fortemente que o autor sagrado, quando registrou os acontecimentos ali narrados, sabia que a melancólica predição de Jesus já tivera cumprimento. (Note-se, igualmente, a predição de Jesus sobre o anticristo, em Mar. 13:14, que aparece como exércitos a cercarem Jerusalém, se assemelhando à indicação de que o autor desse evangelho tinha conhecimento que essa ocorrência já jazia no passado).

Não querendo ser parciais, em favor de um ponto de vista, oferecemos abaixo as evidências positivas que favorecem uma data intermediária para a composição da dupla obra Lucas-Atos:

1. O conhecimento de que a predição de Jesus se cumprira (acerca da destruição de Jerusalém), segundo se subentende pela leitura, especialmente do evangelho de Lucas, serve de evidência positiva de que essa obra foi escrita após o ano 70 D.C. (Ver dois parágrafos acima).

2. A primeira *Epístola de Clemente* indica que por aquele tempo (corria o ano de 95 D.C.) já se fizera uma coletânea preliminar das epístolas do apóstolo Paulo, as quais eram encaradas pela igreja cristã como dotadas de autoridade espiritual, isto é, haviam alcançado posição canônica. Se Lucas tivesse escrito após esse tempo, mui provavelmente teria feito várias referências ou citações a essas epístolas. Não obstante, tais referências ou citações mostram-se completamente ausentes no livro de Atos. (Ver a seção V sobre essa questão).

3. A dupla obra, Lucas-Atos, diferentemente do evangelho de João, não reflete as primitivas controvérsias dos cristãos com os gnósticos, conforme seria de esperar. Dessa maneira, a obra de Lucas foi escrita antes de ter florescido essa controvérsia, que surgiu nos fins do primeiro século da era cristã e nos princípios do segundo século. (Alguns estudiosos encaram o trecho de Atos 20:29,30 como exceção a essa declaração; porém, o que lemos nessa passagem tem natureza extremamente geral, e pode não ter essa aplicação de forma alguma).

4. *O ecumenismo* que transparece na obra Lucas-Atos parece também refletir uma data intermediária entre 60 e 150 D.C. Em outras palavras, a visão clara sobre a missão de âmbito mundial, por parte da igreja cristã, parece refletir uma época mais avançada. Por conseguinte, uma data posterior a 67 D.C., mas anterior a 90 D.C., parece ser a mais acertada conforme os pontos 2 e 3 acima, nos indicam.

5. Alguns eruditos pensam haver certa dependência do evangelho de Lucas aos escritos de Josefo (o qual escreveu depois de 90 D.C.); mas essa idéia não tem sido bem recebida por parte da maioria dos

estudiosos.

6. Não é razoável pensarmos que Lucas, tendo sido companheiro de viagens de Paulo, tivesse esperado por mais de trinta anos, antes de encetar a sua grande obra histórica. Considerando-se todos os fatores, portanto, conclui-se que Lucas escreveu entre os anos de 70-85 D.C. O evangelho de Lucas, por conseguinte, também se encaixa bem dentro desse período.

B. Proveniência

Não temos maneira certa e segura para afirmar onde o livro de Atos foi escrito (especialmente certas porções, em que o autor sagrado passa a usar a primeira pessoa do plural descrevendo cenas das quais Lucas participara pessoalmente, isto é, Atos 16:10-17; 20:5-15; 21:1-18 e 27:1-28:16. Poderiam ter sido extraídas de um diário conservado por Lucas, mais tarde incorporado no livro de Atos). Pois a narrativa poderia ter sido escrita em diversos lugares ao redor do mundo mediterrâneo. Porém isso não solucionaria o problema do local onde a obra foi composta e editada. Desde os tempos de Jerônimo, a tradição favorece Roma, como esse local; mas provavelmente isso se deve à circunstância de que é nesse ponto que a narrativa do livro de Atos nos deixa, subentendendo-se que Lucas acompanhou o apóstolo Paulo até ali. Há, igualmente, uma outra consideração que favorece essa tradição, a saber, que o autor parece ansioso por mostrar a expansão da igreja de Cristo desde Jerusalém até Roma, isto é, a *universalidade* do cristianismo. Se ele estivesse vivendo então em Roma, essa teria sido uma atitude perfeitamente compreensível. Além disso, o próprio livro de Atos salienta a reação favorável de muitos oficiais romanos para com os primeiros missionários cristãos, porquanto, na realidade, se dirigia a um membro da aristocracia romana.

Mas outros estudiosos têm sugerido Antioquia como lugar da composição e edição da obra *Lucas-Atos*, sobretudo porque há uma tradição que faz menção dessa cidade como terra natal do autor sagrado, além do interesse especial desse autor por essa cidade (ver Atos 18:24,26; 19:17-38). Porém, ambas essas condições poderiam existir nesse livro sem que Antioquia tivesse sido o lugar de sua compilação. Por falta de uma melhor idéia, Roma tem permanecido como melhor alternativa, pelo menos para o livro de Atos, ainda que isso não se aplique, necessariamente, ao evangelho de Lucas.

C. Destino

O livro de Atos, tal como o evangelho de Lucas, foi escrito para um oficial romano de nome *Teófilo* (ver o artigo). Por conseguinte, o livro foi enviado a um membro da aristocracia romana, que mui provavelmente residia em Roma. Foi escrito esse livro com a finalidade de apresentar a esse oficial, e a outras pessoas interessadas, uma defesa do cristianismo; não se tratava de um ramo herético do judaísmo, não era uma organização política, contrária ao estado romano. Segundo parece, não foi obra dirigida principalmente às comunidades cristãs, conforme sucede ao resto do Novo Testamento, mas antes, visava circular entre os lançamentos literários da época, para benefício do público leitor gentílico, visando os propósitos descritos acima. Pelo menos parcialmente, trata-se, pois, de uma apologia apresentada ao mundo gentílico pagão, sobretudo à aristocracia romana. Não é por isso, contudo, que haveríamos de eliminar o livro de Atos da lista das obras sagradas dirigidas à igreja cristã universal, como se não tencionasse explicar aos cristãos as origens e os primeiros desenvolvimentos do cristianismo, que emprestavam validade à sua missão de âmbito universal.

III. Caráter Literário

«Os Atos dos Apóstolos eleva-se bem **alto** como obra literária. Possui o mesmo brilho, o mesmo calor, a mesma ternura e o mesmo entusiasmo que se encontram como grandes características do evangelho de Lucas. O autor demonstra soberba habilidade na apresentação dos episódios dramáticos: as ocorrências do tempo do Pentecoste (Atos 2:1-41), a carreira de Filipe lado a lado com a carruagem do eunuco etíope (Atos 8:26-39), a conversão de Paulo (Atos 9:1-9) e o naufrágio de Paulo (Atos 27:14-44). Outrossim, há muitos retratos notabilíssimos de pessoas interessantes: o ousado e confiante Pedro, o astuto e oportunista Simão Mago, o enganador Ananias, e o erudito e zeloso Paulo. A narrativa prossegue suave e logicamente, de acordo com um plano adredemente traçado: o avanço do evangelho, desde Jerusalém, até lugares os mais distantes.

As habilidades dramáticas, descritivas e de narração de Lucas impressionaram de tal maneira a Ernest Renan que ele intitulou o autor do livro de Atos de *um novo Homero*.

Como narrador exato, Lucas se compara favoravelmente com Heródoto, Xenofonte, Josefo, Tito Lívio e Tácito; em questões como costumes, geografia e topografia, que podem ser averiguadas pela pesquisa histórica e arqueológica, o livro de Atos se tem mostrado extraordinariamente digno de confiança. Uma comparação do livro de Atos, de Lucas, com os 'Atos' apócrifos de diversos personagens da igreja, escritos no segundo século D.C., revela que estes últimos são meros romances, ao passo que o volume de Lucas é uma história séria». (Buckner B. Trawick, *The New Testament as Literature*, Barnes and Noble, College Outline Series, 1964).

«*A exatidão histórica* da narrativa de Lucas tem sido amplamente confirmada pelas descobertas da arqueologia. Apesar de haver em sua obra interesses apologéticos e teológicos, essas coisas em nada diminuem a sua detalhada exatidão, embora tais interesses controlem a sua seleção dos fatos a serem apresentados. Lucas encaixa a narrativa dentro do arcabouço da história contemporânea; suas páginas estão repletas de referências a magistrados das cidades, a governadores das províncias, a reis vassalos e outros vultos semelhantes. Essas alusões, uma e vez mostram-se exatamente apropriadas para o local e o período de tempo em foco. Com um mínimo de palavras ele transmite a verdadeira cor local de cidades que diferiam tanto entre si, mencionadas em sua narrativa. A sua descrição sobre a viagem de Paulo (vigésimo sétimo capítulo do livro de Atos) até o dia de hoje permanece como um dos mais importantes documentos sobre a vida marinha antiga». (*The New Bible Dictionary*: Grand Rapids, Michigan, Wm. B. Eerdmans Pub. Co., 1962, pág. 11).

O estilo de Lucas é superior ao dos autores dos evangelhos sinópticos. Ele não titubeia em polir, adornar e modificar de qualquer outro modo a linguagem utilizada no evangelho de Marcos (que Lucas usou como esboço básico, em seu evangelho). Essa mesma linguagem estilizada se evidencia no livro de Atos, com exceção de algumas seções, tais como as que falam sobre o dom do Espírito Santo, a conversão de Cornélio, a história de Filipe, o evangelista, onde se destaca o estilo mais tipicamente arcaico e redundante dos documentos escritos em hebraico. Mui provavelmente isso reflete as fontes informativas das quais ele tomou por empréstimo o seu material histórico, e onde ele quase não fez revisões literárias, permitindo que transpareça o sabor hebraico original. Outros trechos, como o que alude ao comparecimento de Paulo no areópago, são verdadeiramente vazados em grego, praticamente clássicos em sua tonalidade, sempre no melhor estilo do grego «koiné» literário. Por conseguinte, o estilo de Lucas demonstra variações, dependendo da fonte informativa que usava no momento, conforme também observou H.H. Moulton: «Ele (Lucas), firma o seu estilo na fraseologia bíblica, extraída do A.T. grego, enquanto que seu livro se desenvolve em solo palestino, onde quem falava obviamente usava um grego que para eles era um idioma estrangeiro, ao passo que se afasta instintivamente desse estilo, quando o assunto o afasta das terras e do povo bíblico». (*A Grammar of New Testament Greek*, Edinburgh: T. and T. Clark, 1919, II, págs. 7-8).

No tocante ao grego «koiné» empregado por Lucas em sua dupla obra, Lucas-Atos, podemos tecer as seguintes considerações:

Lucas, o médico amado (ver Col. 4:14), demonstrou considerável aptidão como escritor na língua grega. Suas peças literárias exibiram maior versatilidade do que qualquer outra obra do N.T. Seu prefácio, elaboradamente redigido para o evangelho (ver Luc. 1:14), pode ser comparado favoravelmente com os prefácios de famosos historiadores gregos como Heródoto e Tucídides. Lucas demonstra possuir sólida cultura ao usar um grande e bem escolhido vocabulário. Seus dois livros contêm cerca de setecentos e cinquenta vocábulos que não se encontram em nenhuma outra parte do N.T., e isso é uma grande proporção, considerando-se que o vocabulário total do N.T. é de apenas cerca de cinco mil palavras. O pensamento frequentemente repetido de que o seu vocabulário exibe um vocabulário «médico» especial não tem sido bem recebido pela maioria dos eruditos modernos, mas pelo menos essas palavras indicam uma boa educação e uma sólida cultura. Todavia, é definidamente verdadeiro que a sua posição como médico e os seus conhecimentos da medicina deixaram traços que se destacam no evangelho de Lucas e no livro de Atos. (Ver Luc. 4:38, em comparação com Mat. 8:14 e Marc. 1:30, onde Lucas dá uma descrição mais exata sobre a «febre alta»; outro tanto se verifica com respeito a Luc. 5:12, em contraste com Mat. 8:2 e Marc. 1:40, onde Lucas diz que o homem estava «coberto de lepra»).

Lucas emprega o modo *optativo* por vinte e oito vezes, embora esse modo já tivesse quase desaparecido no grego *koiné* de seus dias, e não figure nos escritos de Mateus, João, Tiago e no livro de Apocalipse. Seu emprego do idioma grego é muito diferente do grego de Políbio, Dioscórides e Josefo. Os autores dotados de boa cultura não apreciavam palavras estrangeiras de som estranho, e Lucas exibiu essa aversão. Assim é que ele omite palavras tais como «Boanerges», conforme se vê no evangelho de Marcos, além de muitas palavras distintamente aramaicas, como «Hosana», «Getsêmani», «abba», «Gólgota» e «Eloi, Eloi, lama sabachthani». Em vez do vocábulo aramaico *rabi*, que aparece por dezesseis vezes nos demais evangelhos, ele usa a palavra distintamente grega de *mestre*. Não obstante, Lucas não reescreveu completamente as narrativas de Marcos e de outras fontes menos literárias que usou, e nessas seções encontramos influências de expressões aramaicas, bem como outros elementos indesejáveis do ponto de vista literário. Por conseguinte, podem ser vistos dois níveis de qualidade. Por exemplo, no livro de Atos, a primeira porção do livro, que diz respeito a situações e testemunhos palestinos, pode-se observar um grego menos culto, que algumas vezes contém semitismos claríssimos. A última parte do livro, porém, que foi escrita acerca de situações totalmente gentílicas, foi vazada em um grego «koiné» muito mais elegante.

Classificação do Tipo Literário:

O volume de Lucas-Atos não pode ser classificado como simples *biografia*, paralelamente a outras obras antigas, como *Vidas Paralelas*, de Plutarco, *Vidas dos Césares*, de Suetônio, ou *Agrícola*, de Tácito. Tanto o evangelho de Lucas como o livro de Atos, embora incorporem características como biografias, ultrapassam esse simples plano. Por semelhante modo, essa obra lucana não pode ser reputada como uma «história» apesar do caráter definitivamente histórico desses documentos, pois, apesar de serem uma história séria, contudo são muito mais do que isso. Lucas não procurou apresentar coisa alguma similar a uma completa descrição de seus personagens, e nem tentou expor um delineamento histórico de sua época, nem ao menos no que tange aos personagens ali descritos. Tais personagens passam pelas páginas dessa dupla obra lucana mais como atores de um drama do que objetos de uma biografia formal. Naturalmente o livro de Atos consiste mais em história formal do que o evangelho de Lucas, mas até mesmo ali apenas trinta anos de acontecimentos são cobertos, e o assunto se limita mais ainda em seu escopo do que se veria nas modernas histórias. Naturalmente isso não nega que dentro das páginas do livro de Atos encontramos grande volume de história contemporânea valiosa, que não se pode encontrar em qualquer outra fonte histórica.

A verdade, entretanto, é que tanto o evangelho de Lucas como o livro de Atos fazem parte da *apologética cristã*, eivada de interesses cristãos tradicionais, o que faz dessas obras mais tratados do que mesmo histórias. À parte dessas características, há uma outra particularidade que distingue o livro de Atos dos evangelhos, biografias e histórias—é seu sabor «popular», no sentido de que não somente a obra foi escrita para as massas (o que, no caso do livro de Atos é menos óbvio do que nos evangelhos de Mateus e Marcos, por exemplo), mas também no sentido de que se desenvolveu com base na vida comum, «popular», da igreja cristã, como representante dessa comunidade e de quaisquer de seus interesses.

Pode-se perceber, portanto, que o evangelho de Lucas (como também os demais evangelhos) e o livro de Atos realmente criaram uma nova forma literária, devendo ser classificados como um grupo literário à parte. Os evangelhos e Atos apócrifos copiaram esse novo estilo literário, dando-nos outros documentos dessa natureza, posto que espúrios.

IV. Texto Grego do Livro de Atos

Não existe outro livro, em todo o N.T., que exiba tão numerosas e importantes variantes, nos manuscritos gregos existentes, bem como nas versões, como o livro de Atos dos Apóstolos. Podem-se distinguir dois níveis diferentes de texto:

1. O chamado texto *neutro* (conforme se acha nos manuscritos papiros A,B, Aleph, versões Vulgata, Peshitta siríaca e nos escritos dos pais gregos da igreja Clemente de Alexandria, Orígenes e Crisóstomo), também denominado «alexandrino» (por não ser demonstração de preferências e aberrações «locais», o que explica o seu apodo «neutro» ou *alexandrino*, porque preserva a tradição alexandrina, que geralmente é reconhecida como «mais» original do que as demais tradições). O termo que mais se tem preferido, para indicar esse tipo de texto, é «alexandrino»,

apesar de «neutro» ser a designação mais antiga.

2. O texto *ocidental* (que inclui o codex D, as antigas versões latinas e siríacas, e citações feitas pelos pais ocidentais da igreja, como Irineu, Tertuliano, Cipriano e Agostinho, o qual representa um texto mais longo, com variantes nas seguintes passagens: Atos 1:2,5; 4:18; 5:15,18,39; 6:10; 7:24; 8:24,37,39; 9:4,5,7,8; 10:25; 11:2,17,27,28; 12:10,23; 13:33,43; 14:2,7; 15:2,5,20; 16:4,35,39; 17:15; 18:21,27; 19:1,9,15; 21:16,25; 23:15,23,24,27; 24:6-8,10,24,27; 25:24,25; 27:1; 28:16,19,29,31).

Essas variantes (que não aparecem no tipo de texto «neutro» e que podem ser examinadas nas referências dadas no parágrafo acima, são tão numerosas que alguns eruditos têm pensado que o livro original de Atos circulou em duas edições—talvez ambas as edições lançadas por Lucas, ou uma como edição posterior a outra. Nesse caso, os estudiosos têm defendido o tipo de texto «alexandrino» como o mais primitivo, mas outros têm dado suas preferências ao tipo de texto «ocidental». Friedrich Wilhelm Blass era de opinião que a versão original de Lucas se assemelhava mais ao tipo de texto «ocidental», e que uma edição do mesmo, após ter passado pelas mãos da comunidade cristã de Roma, circulou francamente a partir daquele centro. Porém, Lucas teria enviado igualmente uma outra versão, revisada por ele mesmo, um tanto mais breve, a qual seria a versão «alexandrina», que esse autor designou como «alfa». As outras versões ele chamou de «beta» e «ocidental». (Ver *Acta*).

Essa teoria, entretanto, não tem sido bem acolhida pelos críticos textuais. Pois não é muito provável que um autor fizesse a revisão de seu livro, reduzindo as suas informações históricas, eliminando importantes descrições ou incidentes interessantes. O ponto de vista defendido pela maioria dos críticos modernos, portanto, é que a edição «ocidental» do livro de Atos na realidade é o tipo *neutro* revisado, corrigido e expandido por algum escritor de tempos bem remotos, ou por editores que possuíam conhecimento específico de elementos geográficos ou outros, que circundam os acontecimentos ali descritos. Parte dessa revisão «ocidental» visa efeitos de harmonização, como se vê em Atos 9:5,6 (uma expansão do texto comum), e foi tomada de empréstimo do trecho de Atos 22:10; como também as passagens de Atos 26:14 e 13:33, que são a simples adição da citação baseada em Sal. 2:7,8. O trecho de Atos 18:27 pode ter sido um empréstimo feito da passagem de I Cor. 16:12. Outras adições visam conferir maior exatidão quanto às questões de tempos e datas, como Atos 1:5, sobre o Pentecoste; Atos 5:21, que fala em «levantando-se cedo» e Atos 12:1, que diz «que pertenciam à igreja na Judéia». Mas há variantes que parecem ter sido feitas por motivo de mera alteração de estilo. Essas formas de variantes subentendem que a revisão «alexandrina» do texto é a mais primitiva.

O texto chamado *ocidental*, apesar de ocupar posição secundária, na realidade fornece-nos algumas informações históricas autênticas, muito interessantes, como os «sete degraus», em Atos 12:10; ou como os prisioneiros de «Trogílio», em Atos 20:15 («Trogílio» era uma localização geográfica) que foram entregues pelo centurião ao «stratopedarch» (ver Atos 28:16; ver no NTI as notas expositivas em todos esses versículos citados).

V. Contatos e Influências Literárias

Apesar de que em termos gerais, o livro de Atos pode ser perfeitamente encaixado dentro de uma cronologia histórica, paralelamente às epístolas do apóstolo Paulo, a maioria dos estudiosos modernos tem pronunciado a idéia de que o livro de Atos de modo algum dependeu dessas epístolas, pois Lucas não as teria usado ao escrever o mesmo. É natural que ele soubesse muitas coisas a respeito dessas epístolas, e como é óbvio, conhecia as condições de muitas igrejas que são igualmente descritas nas epístolas paulinas. Porém, a menos que ele tivesse ignorado propositalmente muitas coisas escritas nessas epístolas, parece não haver dúvida de que Lucas não lançou mão delas, como fonte informativa, em qualquer sentido, ao compilar material histórico para o seu volume de Atos.

Baseados em várias referências históricas, sabemos que as epístolas de Paulo (pelo menos algumas delas) já tinham alçado a uma posição canônica ou *quase-canônica*, pelos fins do primeiro séc. da era cristã. Geralmente se pensa, por exemplo, que a primeira epístola de Clemente fornece-nos provas de que as epístolas do apóstolo Paulo já circulavam amplamente, pelo menos em Roma e que já se fizera uma coletânea das mesmas. No entanto, o livro de Atos não mostra qualquer evidência de que punha confiança no mesmo, o que provavelmente teria sido feito se porventura houvesse sido escrito depois do ano 90 D.C. Essa é uma das razões pelas quais os estudiosos preferem datar o livro de Atos antes desse tempo. (Quanto a uma discussão sobre a data provável da escrita do livro de Atos, ver a parte II deste artigo). Se o livro de Atos tivesse dependido das epístolas de Paulo, então poderíamos esperar encontrar citações e reflexos verbais das mesmas, mas tudo isso se faz surpreendentemente ausente. Outrossim, o retrato falado que Lucas traça de Paulo é extremamente diferente daquele que obtemos da parte do próprio Paulo, sobretudo nas tendências paulinas mais radicalmente antijudaicas e antilegalistas, que se fazem notoriamente ausentes no livro de Atos.

Um exame que se faça nas epístolas mais clássicas de Paulo—Romanos 1 e II Coríntios e Gálatas—que ninguém duvida terem sido da lavra desse apóstolo, não revela (quando as comparamos com o livro de Atos) que Lucas tivesse dependido das mesmas, ou que as tivesse utilizado em qualquer sentido. No livro de Atos, a cidade de Roma parece ser o alvo final de Paulo, provavelmente por causa do interesse demonstrado pelo autor sagrado em mostrar como o evangelho se propagara desde Jerusalém até Roma, assim conquistando e mostrando-se triunfal por todo o mundo, atingindo a mais importante capital de seu tempo. No entanto, na epístola aos Romanos, vemos que o apóstolo Paulo meramente tencionava passar pela capital, a caminho da *Espanha*, fato esse que de forma alguma aparece na narrativa do livro de Atos. Nem podemos descobrir neste último se Lucas exibia qualquer conhecimento de que existisse na capital do império uma grande igreja cristã, que não era fruto do trabalho de Paulo, existência essa que se depreende facilmente da leitura da epístola aos Romanos. Pelo contrário, o livro de Atos deixa essa questão de lado, como se em Roma já não existisse uma pungente igreja cristã, quando Paulo ali chegou prisioneiro.

A primeira e a segunda epístolas aos Coríntios nos dão muitos nomes de indivíduos que residiam em Corinto, como também nos fornecem informações sobre diversas facções e dificuldades naquela comunidade cristã, embora o livro de Atos coisa alguma nos revele a respeito. A primeira epístola aos Coríntios também menciona algumas ocorrências importantes da vida de Paulo, como a sua luta contra as feras de Éfeso (I Cor. 15:32; essa primeira epístola aos Coríntios foi escrita de Éfeso), ao passo que o livro de Atos nada nos adianta sobre esse particular. Mui provavelmente, acontecimentos tão notáveis, se fossem do conhecimento do autor sagrado, mediante o seu contato com as epístolas paulinas, teriam sido inclusos na narrativa do livro de Atos. Outras expressões das severas provações experimentadas pelo apóstolo Paulo em II Cor. 1:8, também teriam sido incluídas na história do livro de Atos, se Lucas tivesse contado com as epístolas de Paulo quando escreveu esse livro.

Mas é em confronto com a epístola de Paulo aos Gálatas que se podem perceber as diferenças mais violentas, entre os escritos de Paulo e o livro de Atos. Por exemplo, na narrativa das atividades de Paulo após a sua conversão, especialmente no que diz respeito às suas visitas a Roma e à questão de sua conferência com os outros apóstolos, tudo aparece de modo diverso, entre o primeiro capítulo da epístola aos Gálatas e as passagens do livro de Atos que narram os mesmos eventos, a saber, Atos 9:20-29; 15:1-29. (Comparar essas passagens com Gál. 1:15-2:10). Parece impossível que Lucas, se tivera oportunidade de ler a epístola aos Gálatas, tivesse apresentado outro arranjo e apresentação do material, do que se encontra nessa epístola, onde Paulo conta pessoalmente quais os seus primeiros passos na carreira cristã.

Ora, tudo isso nos conduz a diversas importantíssimas conclusões, a saber:

1. A despeito do fato de que Lucas não dependeu das epístolas de Paulo ao escrever o livro de Atos, e a despeito de algumas aparentes discrepâncias assim criadas, contudo, de maneira geral, essas obras concordam entre si. Isso confirma a *exatidão histórica* geral de ambas, pois, embora tivessem sido escritas independentemente umas das outras, narram essencialmente a mesma história.

2. O fato de que Lucas não dependeu das epístolas de Paulo confirma uma data *relativamente remota* para sua composição, certamente antes do ano 90 D.C., e provavelmente entre 75 e 85 D.C.

3. De forma indireta, tudo isso confirma a autoria lucana do livro de Atos, porquanto um escritor que chegasse à cena mais tarde e que desejasse escrever uma obra como o livro de Atos, certamente teria procurado fontes informativas onde lhe fosse possível encontrá-las, — e sem dúvida, ter-se-ia valido das epístolas do apóstolo Paulo, dependendo pesadamente delas. Mas Lucas, tendo sido testemunha ocular de grande parte dos acontecimentos por ele mesmo narrados, tendo dependido, por semelhante modo, de testemunhas oculares que haviam acompanhado o apóstolo em suas andanças, antes dele mesmo ter começado a acompanhá-lo em suas viagens missionárias (antes do décimo sexto capítulo do livro de Atos), não precisou depender de tais fontes informativas. Pelo contrário, valeu-se daqueles documentos ou informações que foi recolhendo ao longo do caminho, como relatórios pessoais de outros apóstolos, do próprio Paulo, de sua *própria memória* e do conhecimento pessoal que tinha das ocorrências que ele descreve em seu livro de Atos.

No que tange à suposta dependência de Lucas aos escritos de Josefo, o grande historiador judeu, podemos considerar o seguinte: Alguns estudiosos, que favorecem uma data posterior para o evangelho de Lucas, bem como um outro autor para o livro de Atos, têm procurado demonstrar que o autor de Atos dependeu muito do historiador Josefo, na narração de vários episódios contados ali. Ora, posto que Josefo escreveu em cerca de 93 D.C., isso nos forçaria a aceitar uma data para o livro de Atos para pelo menos a partir dessa data em diante. Isso também indicaria que outro, e não Lucas foi o autor do livro de Atos, porquanto é extremamente improvável que Lucas tivesse esperado tantos anos para compilar o seu evangelho. É verdade que testes lingüísticos elaborados indicam certa afinidade, no tocante ao vocabulário, entre os escritos de Lucas e de Josefo, mas isso pode ser facilmente explicado com base na suposição de que ambos usaram certa forma de grego «koiné» literário, dependendo bastante do estilo e do vocabulário do A.T. em hebraico, como também da versão LXX (*Septuaginta*) do A.T., em suas citações.

O trecho de Atos 5:36,37 (em que Gamaliel se refere às rebeliões encabeçadas por Teudas e Judas, o Galileu), segundo esses estudiosos teria dependido de Josefo, o que faria Lucas tornar-se culpado de grosseiro anacronismo. Porém, apesar de que verdadeiramente há certas similaridades de expressão, não há razão alguma para supormos que Lucas interpretou Josefo erroneamente, registrando um acontecimento deslocado cronologicamente, de forma diversa do que de fato ocorreu. (Ver as notas expositivas sobre esse problema, em Atos 5:36,37 no NTI). Outra suposta dependência de Lucas a Josefo é quando de sua menção a Lisânias, o qual, em Lucas 1:3 aparece como tetrarca de Abilene, o que teve lugar no ano de 28 D.C. Porém o único Lisânias que se sabe ter governado ali, morreu em 36 A.C. Não obstante, as pesquisas arqueológicas têm provido evidências (na forma de uma inscrição antiga) de que um certo Lisânias (e portanto, um outro indivíduo do mesmo nome daquele que conhecíamos pela história profana) realmente recebeu o título de «tetrarca», tendo governado Abilene em algum período do primeiro século da era cristã. (Sobre essa questão, ver Josefo *Antiq.* XX.7.1). (Ver também as notas expositivas referentes a Luc. 3:1 no NTI).

Dessa maneira, as teses de alguns estudiosos, como Max Krendel, em *Josephus und Lukas*, de que o autor da dupla obra Lucas-Atos dependeu pesadamente de Josefo, o historiador judeu, o que resultaria na aceitação de uma data posterior a 93 D.C. para essa obra, Lucas-Atos, além de uma autoria provavelmente não-lucana para a mesma, não têm podido ser bem aceitas, porquanto faltam-lhes provas palpáveis e conclusivas. Essa é a opinião adversa a sua tese por parte da maioria dos eruditos modernos. (Assim diz Jackson, F.J. Foakes e Lake Kirsopp, em sua obra *Beginning of Christianity*, London; Macmillan Co., 1920-1933).

Os contatos literários de Lucas, por conseguinte provavelmente se deram todos dentro dos limites da primitiva igreja cristã, incluindo alguns registros escritos sobre ocorrências descritas em Atos antes do décimo sexto capítulo, registros esses que eram documentos estritos da comunidade cristã, que descreviam eventos do interesse da tradição cristã. Isso não significa, entretanto, que Lucas não tenha podido, ou não tenha realmente usado material histórico proveniente de outras fontes, como quando ele menciona os reinados de monarcas, reis vassalos, governadores ou magistrados locais; mas tais documentos não são suficientemente óbvios e transparentes em Lucas-Atos para que se tornem identificáveis, ainda que, por acaso, o autor sagrado tenha se utilizado de alguns documentos com os quais estamos familiarizados hoje em dia.

VI. Fontes Informativas

Alguns eruditos têm apresentado a hipótese de que somente as seções chamadas «nós» do livro de Atos (aquelas em que o autor desse livro passa a usar a primeira pessoa do plural, por ter participado pessoalmente dos fatos desenrolados), são composições originais do autor. Alguns desses eruditos dizem que essas porções são de autoria lucana, mas outros nem mesmo isso querem admitir. (Essas seções são Atos 16:10-17; 20:5-15; 21:1-18 e 27:1-28:16). Partindo desse ponto inicial, existem muitas conjecturas referentes à unidade, à autoria e às fontes informativas das demais seções do livro de Atos. A maioria desses estudiosos acredita que pelo menos essas seções foram escritas por um único autor; e a maioria dos eruditos modernos defende a idéia que o resto do livro de Atos foi escrito pelo mesmo autor, ou, pelo menos, foi compilado por ele. (Quanto a comentários sobre essa questão, ver *Autor*, neste artigo).

No que concerne às fontes informativas usadas pelo autor do livro de Atos, aceita-se de modo quase universal (embora tenham surgido exceções notáveis) que a grande fonte informativa do mesmo, a partir do décimo sexto capítulo até o fim, tenha sido o testemunho ocular do próprio autor sagrado. Naturalmente a distinção e a separação entre as duas seções do livro (antes e a partir do seu décimo sexto capítulo) não são absolutas, porquanto a conversão de Paulo, personagem que passa a dominar as cenas da segunda metade do livro, é apresentada na primeira metade, no nono capítulo; e a narração sobre o concílio cristão de Jerusalém aparece no décimo quinto capítulo. Embora esse concílio tenha ocorrido antes da primeira viagem missionária de Paulo, no livro de Atos aparece como acontecimento posterior a essa viagem.

Todavia, a maior parte dos problemas referentes às fontes informativas do livro de Atos giram em torno dos capítulos primeiro a décimo quinto, isto é, antes das chamadas seções *nós*, as quais tiveram origem no relato do próprio autor, como testemunha ocular dos fatos. Parece que não podemos fazer nada melhor do que examinar alguns desses problemas, na esperança de aprendermos algo a respeito da verdade em torno da questão.

C.H. Turner pensava que podia distinguir, no livro de Atos, *seis níveis* diferentes de fontes informativas, cada um dos quais representava alguma área geral do progresso no ministério do evangelho. O protagonista central dos três primeiros desses níveis seria Pedro e a figura principal dos três últimos seria Paulo. Dessa forma, o livro de Atos se dividiria em duas metades, de três seções cada uma. Seriam as seguintes:

1. A *igreja* cristã em *Jerusalém*. O trecho de Atos 6:7 ofereceria o sumário desse progresso, onde se lê: «Crescia a palavra de Deus e, em Jerusalém, se multiplicava o número dos discípulos; também muitíssimos sacerdotes obedeciam à lei».

2. A expansão da igreja cristã por toda a *Palestina*. O sumário dessa seção se acharia no trecho de Atos 9:31, que diz: «A igreja, na verdade, tinha paz por toda a Judéia, Galiléia e Samaria, edificando-se e caminhando no temor do Senhor e no conforto do Espírito Santo, crescia em número».

3. A expansão da igreja cristã até *Antioquia*. O sumário desse nível seria Atos 12:24: «Entretanto, a palavra do Senhor crescia e se multiplicava».

4. A expansão da igreja cristã pela *Ásia Menor* e pela *Galácia*. O sumário seria o trecho de Atos 16:5: «Assim as igrejas eram fortalecidas na fé, e aumentavam em número dia-a-dia».

5. A expansão da igreja cristã pela *Europa*. O sumário se encontraria em Atos 19:20, onde se lê: «Assim a palavra do Senhor crescia e prevalecia poderosamente».

6. A expansão da igreja cristã até *Roma*. O sumário desse último nível se acharia em Atos 28:31, que diz: «...pregando o reino de Deus, e com toda a intrepidez, sem impedimento algum, ensinava as cousas referentes ao Senhor Jesus Cristo».

Por detrás dessas diversas seções poderíamos supor a existência de alguma fonte informativa, ou mesmo de diversas delas, algumas das quais na forma de testemunhas oculares entrevistadas por Lucas, ao passo que outras seriam tradições orais ou preservadas em forma escrita. Nas seções designadas «nós» (aquelas em que o autor passa a usar a primeira pessoa do plural, por ter participado pessoalmente das ocorrências narradas) mui provavelmente temos o reflexo de anotações diárias, feitas pelo autor sagrado, enquanto vivia. Isso significa que tais passagens nos transmitem a versão direta em primeira mão, dos acontecimentos ali narrados, embora só tivessem sido incorporados no livro de Atos muitos anos mais tarde.

A maioria dos eruditos concorda atualmente que nem todo o material das seções intituladas *nós* representam o testemunho real ocular do autor sagrado, porquanto ali também encontramos o uso da terceira pessoa do plural. No entanto, há, sem dúvida alguma, certa integridade e harmonia que indica que o mesmo autor foi quem escreveu todas essas porções, e, ao mesmo tempo, que foi ele a sua principal fonte informativa.

Por causa dos motivos acima aduzidos, os editores da obra *The Beginnings of Christianity* (ver a referência na bibliografia) dizem: «De maneira geral pode-se asseverar que apesar de haver alguma diferença em estilo, entre os primeiros quinze capítulos do livro de Atos e a segunda metade desse livro, não há diferença nenhuma de estilo entre as seções 'nós' e a narrativa em que foram encaixadas». (Vol. II, pág. 158). A isso acrescenta G.H.C. Macgregor, autor da introdução ao livro de Atos na *Interpreter's Bible*: «Nem mesmo o conteúdo daquelas porções dos capítulos dezesseis a vinte e oito, que estão fora das 'seções nós' representam qualquer obstáculo insuperável, no que diz respeito à suposição de que o diarista foi a fonte informativa do todo». Isso não significa, naturalmente, que o autor sagrado tivesse estado presente a observar cada pormenor daquilo que escreveu; porém quer dizer que essas porções estavam por detrás, essencialmente, do relatório de uma testemunha ocular, pois o todo de seu livro chegou ao seu conhecimento com base em fontes informativas imediatamente disponíveis a ele, acerca de acontecimentos contemporâneos.

Assim sendo, o autor das seções chamadas **nós** sem dúvida é igualmente o autor da primeira parte do livro de Atos (capítulos primeiro a décimo quinto); mas no caso dessas seções o autor sagrado foi testemunha ocular, — como é óbvio, da maior parte dos acontecimentos. As variações de estilo confirmam a teoria que grande parte de seu trabalho, nesse caso, consistiu mais na obra de um editor e compilador, o que, em última análise, é o caso de todos os livros, com pouquíssimas exceções. O autor sagrado reuniu os seus próprios comentários, as suas elaborações, mas também partes dos quais foram copiados com pouca ou nenhuma variação. Por conseguinte, ele foi ao mesmo tempo autor e editor, como também compilador. As seções registradas com base em alguma fonte informativa oral ou escrita, que ele obteve, mui naturalmente teriam um estilo diferente do dele, quando registrada alguma ocorrência por ele pessoalmente observada. Nada existe no livro de Atos que não possa ser explicado com alicerce nessa observação, o que nos permite preservar a unidade da autoria do livro. É por esse motivo que poucos estudiosos modernos se deixam atrair pela teoria que diz ter havido uma múltipla autoria do livro de Atos.

Apesar de que provavelmente existam muitas fontes informativas individuais, pertencentes à primeira parte do livro de Atos (capítulos primeiro a décimo quinto), e algumas narrativas ou detalhes talvez dependam do relatório, oral ou escrito, de alguma testemunha isolada, parece que Harnack (*Acts of the Apostles*, págs. 162-202) mostra-se essencialmente atual quando traça as três principais fontes informativas dessa primeira parte do livro de Atos, como segue:

1. Uma fonte informativa de *Jerusalém* (capítulos primeiro a quinto).
2. Uma fonte informativa centralizada em *Jerusalém-Cesaréia*, que tem como núcleo o trecho de Atos 8:5-40.
3. Uma fonte informativa centralizada em *Antioquia*, com núcleo em Atos 11:19-30.

As seções restantes, pois, foram acrescentadas a cada um desses três núcleos, excetuando a passagem de Atos 9:1-30, que talvez tenha tido uma fonte informativa paulina em separado, preservada nas tradições de Antioquia ou de Jerusalém-Cesaréia. Não obstante, a formação de cada uma dessas seções pode ter sido complexa, e partes de muitas traduções e fontes informativas podem ter sido incluídas. Mas pelo menos poderíamos identificar, dessa maneira, o núcleo e a fonte informativa principal de cada uma dessas seções fundamentais. Harnack também divide a fonte informativa de Jerusalém em duas partes, denominando-as «Jerusalém A» e «Jerusalém B», sugerindo ainda que «Jerusalém B» poderia ser idêntica à fonte informativa centralizada em Jerusalém-Cesaréia.

Já os editores do livro *The Beginnings of Christianity* sugerem que a porção de «Jerusalém A» poderia ser continuação da fonte informativa usada pelo autor do evangelho de Marcos, e que transparece no evangelho de Lucas; mas, ainda segundo a mesma autoridade, a porção de «Jerusalém B» poderia ser a mesma fonte informativa da qual Lucas se utilizou quando escreveu o vigésimo quarto capítulo de seu evangelho, material esse que os outros evangelistas não tiveram às mãos para seu uso. (*Christian Beginnings*, II. pág. 133; ver a referência na bibliografia).

Não há meios para comprovarmos a teoria exposta, mas pelo menos ela chama a nossa atenção para blocos bem definidos de material, e esses blocos de material provavelmente foram extraídos de informações disponíveis a diversas comunidades eclesiásticas, onde as histórias foram preservadas em forma oral ou escrita. Por conseguinte, podemos traçar o diagrama dessa teoria conforme o quadro abaixo:

AS FONTES DE ATOS

1. *Jerusalém* A (Atos 3:1-5:16). Primeiras atividades apostólicas do apóstolo Paulo, em Jerusalém e cercanias.	4. *Fonte informativa paulina.* (Atos 9:1-30).

ATOS DOS APÓSTOLOS

| 2. *Jerusalém B* (Atos 1:6-2:47). Ascensão, fim das instruções aos doze, o Pentecoste, os primeiros conflitos com o judaísmo. (Atos 5:17-42). Outros conflitos com o judaísmo. | 5. *Antioquia.* Nomeação dos sete diáconos. Estêvão. (Atos 6:1-8:4). A igreja em Antioquia. (Atos 11:19-30). Paulo e Barnabé; missões a Chipre e Galácia; dificuldades em Antioquia e Jerusalém. (Atos 12:25-15:35). |
| 3. *Jerusalém-Cesaréia* (Atos 8:5-40). Filipe; os labores de Pedro; a conversão de Cornélio. (Atos 9:31-11:18). Perseguição movida por Herodes. (Atos 12:1-24). | 6. *Seções nós.* Relatos do próprio autor, como testemunha ocular, de mistura com algum outro material histórico. |

Pode haver muitas outras maneiras de explicar o problema das fontes informativas usadas na escrita do livro de Atos. C.C. Torrey (*The Composition and Date of Acts*, Cambridge; Harvard University Press, 1916), supõe que houve apenas um documento por detrás dos capítulos primeiro a décimo quinto, que teria origem em um autor qualquer que compilara o seu material em Jerusalém, documento esse traduzido pelo autor das «seções nós», incorporado em seu livro. Esse mesmo escritor postula um original em aramaico, supondo que certas seções obscuras podem ser melhor entendidas quando aceitamos que por detrás delas houve um original em aramaico. (Ver Matthew Balck, *Aramaic Approach to the Gospels and Acts*, págs. 8-12). Portanto, podemos afirmar que os estudiosos não rejeitaram definitivamente a idéia de que algumas porções das fontes informativas centralizadas em Jerusalém tiveram um original aramaico, porquanto isso teria sido apenas natural.

Apesar de que nos é impossível ter qualquer certeza no que diz respeito à questão das fontes informativas usadas pelo autor do livro de Atos, especialmente no que concerne a indivíduos particulares, que tenham prestado informações a Lucas, parece razoável pensarmos que esse material chegou às suas mãos, de uma forma ou de outra, vindo dos grandes centros do cristianismo primitivo, tais como Jerusalém, Cesaréia, Antioquia e Roma.

VII. Ênfase Apologética; Interesses e Propósitos Teológicos

1. Que o cristianismo não é um *ramo herético* do judaísmo, mas antes, uma elevação e melhoria do judaísmo, com raízes profundas no mesmo, mas retendo apenas os elementos nobres e úteis, ficando rejeitados todos os seus males, especialmente a

ATOS

apostasia para a qual havia decaído, como também o seu escopo provincial.

2. Mostrar aos líderes romanos que o cristianismo *não deveria* ser temido e perseguido, como ameaça ou movimento traiçoeiro ao estado romano; pelo contrário, que era digno da proteção romana, com permissão de funcionar livremente, tal como o judaísmo havia obtido de seus conquistadores militares.

Por este motivo é que o livro de Atos apresenta os oficiais romanos como ordinariamente favoráveis aos movimentos dos missionários cristãos. Embora Lucas houvesse escrito após Paulo haver sido martirizado, e a perseguição de Roma contra os cristãos já houvesse começado, ele não ignora e nem põe em perigo o seu propósito apologético encerrando o seu livro numa atitude negativa, a saber, narrando a execução do maior advogado do cristianismo às mãos das autoridades romanas. (Ver Atos 18:12-17, onde se expõe a idéia da proteção do cristianismo, pelas autoridades romanas, tal como o judaísmo já vinha sendo protegido pelas leis do império). Lucas, portanto, quis mostrar que os levantes e as perturbações de ordem pública que seguiam na cauda do movimento dos missionários cristãos resultavam das perseguições efetuadas pelos judeus, e não de qualquer espírito malicioso dos próprios cristãos. Lucas endereçou a sua dupla obra (Lucas-Atos) a um oficial romano, de nome *Teófilo*; por conseguinte, dirigiu seu trabalho à aristocracia romana, esperando que se os argumentos ali contidos fossem recebidos e digeridos, o novel movimento cristão viesse a ser protegido, e não perseguido. Todavia, o seu grande alvo fracassou, porque sobrevieram severas e prolongadas perseguições, desde muito tempo antes do evangelho de Lucas e do livro de Atos terem sido escritos e postos em circulação.

Interesse Teológico:

As atividades e orientações do **Espírito Santo** dominam o livro de Atos, e isso o torna diferente dos evangelhos sinópticos (com exceção parcial do evangelho de Lucas), mas o evangelho de João também possui essa característica, tal como sucede às epístolas de Paulo. As manifestações sobrenaturais que acompanharam a propagação do evangelho significavam não meramente as atividades do Espírito de Deus naquela época, mas também a inauguração de uma nova era, quando os homens haveriam de ser dirigidos diretamente, cheios e controlados pelo poder do alto—o poder do Espírito Santo. Outros interesses teológicos de menor monta, que dominam o quadro apresentado pelo livro de Atos, são a descrição acurada da ascensão do Senhor Jesus, que se faz inteiramente ausente nos quatro evangelhos, a universalidade da mensagem cristã, a ênfase posta sobre os elementos mais pobres e desprezados da sociedade, e como todos podem tornar-se beneficiários das mesmas boas novas de Deus.

Um outro interesse teológico, que na realidade incorpora a atuação do Espírito Santo no seio da igreja cristã e no mundo, é aquele que demonstra a redenção de *âmbito universal*, possibilitada pela mensagem da cruz, pregada pela igreja cristã, que exalta a pessoa de Cristo Jesus. Esse é, por semelhante modo, um elevado interesse teológico do evangelho de Lucas.

Propósitos do Livro de Atos:

1. Alvos históricos — Lucas tencionava demonstrar como a igreja cristã se propagara de seu centro, em Jerusalém até Roma: a. Em Jerusalém (Caps. 1-6). b. Por toda a Palestina (Caps. 7-10). c. Até Antioquia (Caps. 11-13). d. Até a Ásia Menor e a região da Galácia (Caps. 14-16). e. Até a Europa (Caps. 17-20). f. Até Roma (Caps. 20-28). Tudo isso implica na universalidade do cristianismo, bem como na aprovação divina ao mesmo, porquanto essa propagação do evangelho, com os seus resultados positivos acompanhantes, não era obra de homens.

2. Alvos apologéticos, segundo os apresentamos no primeiro parágrafo desta seção VII.

3. Alvos teológicos, segundo são dados nos parágrafos mais acima, sob o título «Interesses teológicos».

Além dos propósitos históricos, apologéticos, poderíamos facilmente detectar ainda outros. Parece perfeitamente óbvio que o livro de Atos foi escrito, pelo menos em parte, para aumentar a autoridade do apóstolo Paulo no seio da igreja cristã. Então, por causa disso, o cristianismo passou a movimentar-se mais de acordo com as normas paulinas. A igreja cristã em geral, de fato, foi largamente dominada pela teologia paulina até o surgimento de Tomás de Aquino, o qual mediante a sua mistura de conceitos nitidamente cristãos com outros elementos (a filosofia de *Tomás de Aquino* foi proclamada como filosofia oficial da Igreja Católica Romana, pelo papa Leão XIII), enfraqueceu o caráter paulino da igreja. O autor sagrado do livro de Atos, pois, também mostra-nos como foi que o judaísmo gradualmente se tornou indigno de ser o guardião e o propagador da verdade de Deus, e como essa verdade passou para a posse da igreja cristã, que veio a tornar-se um corpo principalmente gentílico. Ora, isso prepara o ambiente para a mensagem das epístolas, tanto de Paulo como dos demais escritores do N.T., naqueles lugares onde o judaísmo se tornara um *opressor* do cristianismo, e não seu genitor.

VIII. Conteúdo

Podem ser observados seis níveis de desenvolvimento da missão cristã, a saber: 1. Em Jerusalém (até Atos 6:7). 2. Por toda a Palestina (até Atos 9:31). 3. Em Antioquia (até Atos 12:24). 4. Na Ásia Menor e na Galácia (até Atos 16:5). 5. Até a Europa (até Atos 19:20). 6. Até Roma (até Atos 28:31). Os dois principais personagens dessas atividades são os apóstolos Pedro e Paulo. Cerca de metade do livro de Atos se devota às atividades de Paulo, e cerca de um terço às atividades de Pedro. Cronologicamente falando, o livro de Atos cobre um período de apenas cerca de trinta anos, isto é, de 33 até c. de 63 D.C.

«O conteúdo 'de Atos' se divide em seis partes distintas: 1. A fundação da igreja, em Jerusalém (Atos 1:1-6:7). 2. A dispersão dos cristãos por toda a Palestina, depois do martírio de Estêvão (Atos 6:8-9:31). 3. A propagação da igreja cristã pela Palestina e a Síria (Atos 9:32-12:25). 4. A primeira viagem missionária de Paulo à ilha de Chipre e à Ásia Menor, e seu retorno a Jerusalém (Atos 13:1-16:5). 5. As viagens de Paulo à Macedônia e à Grécia (Atos 16:6-21:14). 6. Oposição a Paulo e sua viagem a Roma (Atos 21:15-28:31)». (Buckner B. Trawick, «The New Testament as Literature», Barnes and Noble, Nova Iorque, 1964).

Cada uma dessas seções principais é sumariada por alguma forma de declaração concernente ao sucesso das diversas missões, que fala sobre o desenvolvimento da igreja cristã. Essas referências se encontram em Atos 6:7; 9:31; 12:24; 16:5; 19:20 e 28:31.

ESBOÇO DO CONTEÚDO

I. A Igreja em Jerusalém (1:1-5:42)
  1. Prefácio, 1:1—5

ATOS — ATOS DIVINOS

2. A ascensão de Cristo, 1:6-11
3. Completa-se o número de doze apóstolos, 1:12-26
4. O dom do Espírito; o nascimento da igreja, 2:1-47
5. O novo poder de Pedro, 2:14-36
6. Resultados do Pentecoste, 2:37-47
7. Ministério de Pedro em Jerusalém, 3:1-26
8. Primeiro conflito com o judaísmo, 4:1-22
9. Vida comunitária da igreja, 4:23-5:16
10. Segundo conflito com o judaísmo, 5:17-42

II. A Igreja na Palestina: Primórdios do Cristianismo Helênico (Atos 6:1-8:40)
1. Nomeação dos sete diáconos, 6:1-7
2. História de Estêvão, 6:8-8:3
3. História de Filipe, 8:4-40
   a. Em Samaria, 8:4-13
   b. Visita apostólica confirmatória, 8:14-25
   c. Filipe e o eunuco etíope, 8:26-40
4. Conversão de Saulo de Tarso, 9:1-31
5. Primeiras missões entre os gentios, 9:32-11:30
   a. Atividades de Pedro, 9:32-11:30
   b. Conversão de Cornélio, 10:11-18
   c. A igreja em Antioquia: Atividades de Paulo e Barnabé, 11:19-30
6. A perseguição movida por Herodes, 12:1-25

III. Avanço de Antioquia a Roma: Três viagens missionárias de Paulo (Atos 13:1-28:31)
1. Primeira viagem missionária: Barnabé e Paulo vão aos gentios, Atos 13:1-14:29. Missão a Chipre, 13:4-12. Missão à Galácia, 13:13-14:28. Missão de Pafos a Perge, 13:13. Missão a Antioquia da Pisídia, 13:14-52. Missão a Icônio e Listra, 14:1-18. Missão a Icônio, 14:1-7. Missão a Listra, 14:8-18. Retorno a Antioquia da Síria, 14:19-28.
2. Controvérsias acerca do legalismo, 15:1-41
   a. Dificuldades em Antioquia a Jerusalém, 15:1-5
   b. O concílio de Jerusalém, 15:1-29
   c. Paulo e Barnabé em Antioq., 15:30-41
3. Segunda viagem missionária: Paulo vai à Europa, 16:1-18:17: Galácia e A. Menor, 16:1-10. Timóteo e Paulo, 16:1-5 Missão a Trôade, 16:6-10. Trabalho na Macedônia, 16:11-17:15. Em Filipos, 16:11-50. Em Tessalônica, 17:1-9. Em Beréia, 17:10-15. Na Acaia, 17:16-18:17. Esta última fase incluiu Atenas e Corinto.
4. Terceira viagem missionária: Paulo vai à Ásia Menor, 18:18-19:41 Viagem de confirmação das igrejas, 18:18-23. Apolo, 18:24-28. Paulo em Éfeso, 19:1-41. Retorno a A. Menor, 19:1-12. Paulo e os exorcistas, 19:13-20. Planos de Paulo sobre o futuro, 19:21-22. O levante em Éfeso, 19:23-41.
5. Visita final de Paulo à Macedônia e à Acaia, 20:1-4
6. Paulo vai a Jerusalém, 20:1-6. De Filipos a Mileto, 20:5-16. Defesa de Paulo ante os anciãos de Éfeso, 20:17-38. De Mileto a Cesaréia, 21:1-14. Paulo com a igreja em Jerusalém, 21:15-26.
7. Paulo, prisioneiro em Roma, 21:27-28:31
   a. Detenção e defesa, 21:27-22:29
   b. Perante o sinédrio, 22:30-23:11
   c. Transferência para Cesaréia, 23:12-35
   d. Em Cesaréia, 24:1-26:32. Paulo e Félix, 24:1-27. Paulo e Festo, 25:1-27. Defesa de Paulo perante Agripa, 26:1-32
   d. Viagem a Roma, 27:1-28:16
   f. Paulo em Roma, 28:17-31

IX. **Tabela cronológica dos Acontecimentos de Atos em Confronto com a História Contemporânea**

Ver o artigo sobre a *Cronologia do Novo Testamento*

X. **Tabela cronológica da Vida de Paulo**

5 DC	Nascimento em Tarso, da Cilícia
20-26	Estudos em Jerusalém
26-32	Estudos em Tarso
32-37	Conversão na estrada de Damasco, Atos 9
37-39	Viagem pela Arábia, Gál. 1
35-43	Prega em Tarso e noutros lugares da Cilícia, Atos 9 e Gál. 1
43-44	Prega com Barnabé em Antioquia, Atos 11
44-45	Viagem a Jerusalém, durante a fome, Atos 11
45-47	Primeira viagem missionária, Atos 13-14
47-49	Reside em Antioquia da Síria, Atos 11
49	Faz-se presente ao concílio de Jerusalém, Atos 15
49-51	Segunda viagem missionária, Atos 15-18
51-56	Terceira viagem missionária, Atos 18-21
56	Aprisionamento em Jerusalém, Atos 21
56-58	Paulo na Prisão em Cesaréia, Atos 23
58-59	Viagem a Roma, Atos 27
59-61	Confinamento em Roma, Atos 26
61-64	Viagens à Espanha, Creta, Macedônia, Grécia, não mencionadas em Atos, embora indicadas em outros documentos como no cânon muratoriano e nas epístolas de Clemente. Algumas indicações destas viagens existem nas epístolas pastorais.
64-67	Execução em Roma, durante as perseguições movidas por Nero.

XI. **Bibliografia:** AM BRU CAD HARN IB ID NTI RAM Z

ATOS DE SALOMÃO

Um livro aludido em I Reis 11:41, uma obra atualmente perdida, mas que provavelmente historiava o reinado de Salomão, com base em documentos oficiais da época. (Z)

ATOS DIVINOS

Essa expressão refere-se àquelas ocorrências e experiências que parecem desafiar princípios e explicações ordinários de causa e efeito, usualmente eventos trágicos que produzem intenso sofrimento. São chamados assim os terremotos, as enchentes, os desastres naturais. Por assim dizer, essas ocorrências lançam a culpa sobre Deus; mas podem conter um indício de que a providência divina as controlam, embora de forma misteriosa. Esses tipos de *atos de Deus* muito têm a ver com o problema do mal, isto é, se existe um Deus onisciente, benévolo e Todo-Poderoso, como pode haver também tanto sofrimento no mundo? Ver o artigo sobre *o problema do mal*.

Essa expressão também é usada para exprimir os feitos beneficentes de Deus, inerentes à redenção, à missão de Cristo, às curas divinas, aos milagres e a todas as formas de intervenção divina, como o êxodo,

ATRAÇÃO UNIVERSAL DE CRISTO

a vinda de Cristo, o Seu segundo advento, a descida do Espírito Santo, etc. (H)

ATRAÇÃO UNIVERSAL DE CRISTO

João 12:32,33: «*E eu, quando for levantado da terra, todos atrairei a mim. Isto dizia, significando de que modo havia de morrer*».

I. Declaração notável

Encontramos aqui uma das notáveis declarações joaninas, a qual nos ensina uma importante doutrina bíblica, que vem sendo quase totalmente ignorada por muitas igrejas cristãs, a saber, *os efeitos universais* da expiação de Cristo. Sem qualquer equívoco, Cristo afirma que atrairia *todos* os homens para si mesmo; e devemos observar o fato de que a declaração se reveste de tanta importância que de modo algum podemos diminuí-la. Ao mesmo tempo, em parte alguma, e nem mesmo em João 12:32,33, o N.T. ensina um universalismo comum.

Alguns importantes manuscritos gregos dizem «todas as coisas», em vez de «todos», que é o gênero masculino interpretado como «todos os homens», conforme dizem algumas traduções. Esses manuscritos são P(66), Aleph e D, que por sua vez, são seguidos por muitas versões latinas. A grande massa de evidência textual, entretanto, dá apoio à variante *todos os homens*. Pois «todas as coisas» (que Jesus haveria de atrair para si mesmo) daria a entender um sentido universal e cósmico, e não envolveria exclusivamente aos homens; incluiria, igualmente, os seres angelicais, e até mesmo o próprio mundo físico e a natureza. Não obstante, existem passagens bíblicas que ensinam essa futura *harmonização* entre Deus e toda a sua criação, como, por exemplo, Col. 1:16,17 e também o primeiro capítulo da epístola aos Efésios. Na pessoa de Cristo nos é prometida uma total *restauração cósmica*, quando toda a criação descobrirá que seu centro e razão de existência se encontram nele. João 12:32, entretanto, ao referir-se tão só a «todos os homens», faz alusão somente a uma parte da restauração universal, posto que muito importante para nós, isto é, a restauração da humanidade remida.

II. Interpretações da declaração

1. Seria um esclarecimento no sentido de que não somente os judeus, mas também *os gentios*, participam dos benefícios da expiação no sangue de Cristo —pois o cristianismo não é de âmbito local, como o judaísmo, e sim, de aplicação universal. Isso é uma verdade, faz parte da verdade aqui ensinada, mas não inclui toda a verdade dessas palavras.

2. Outros dizem que a palavra «todos» é uma referência àqueles que *dão ouvidos* ao evangelho e não oferecem resistência ao mesmo; mas isso restringe por demais o sentido da passagem, e insufla no texto o que talvez seja tomado de empréstimo de outros lugares, assim reduzindo essa grande declaração de Jesus à estatura de um ensinamento de menor importância, furtando-a de sua significação distintiva.

3. A palavra *todo* indicaria o mundo dos *eleitos*, segundo muitos intérpretes da escola calvinista. Mas isso, novamente, restringe o sentido que se evidencia em João 12:32.

4. Pelo contrário, significa *todo* sem qualquer restrição, isto é, a expiação no sangue de Cristo tem uma aplicação universal. Assim diz Ellicott, em João 12:32: «A palavra *todo* não pode ser limitada pelas interpretações que julgam tratar-se das nações, ou aos indivíduos eleitos dentre todas as nações; porém, deve ser considerada na plenitude de sua significação, com o sentido que ela tem naturalmente—*todo*. A atração para si mesmo é a asserção de seu reinado sobre o mundo, do qual o príncipe da maldade será finalmente expulso».

III. Como Cristo atrairá a si todos os homens?

1. A operação será poderosa, nada será negado, nada será negligenciado, nada será deixado de fora, pois é o Pai quem «atrai», quem «arrasta». É impossível que alguma coisa fique fora do poder do Pai, que opera no Filho. É impossível que venha a falhar a missão do Filho, embora possa ter bom êxito de diferentes maneiras.

2. Todos os homens são potencialmente eleitos, mas os eleitos serão, finalmente poucos, devido às perversas operações da vontade humana. Mas, apesar dos eleitos virem a ser poucos, a promessa em João 12:32 não falhará. Ver os pontos abaixo.

3. Este versículo também promete que *todos* os homens serão iluminados (João 1:9). Consideramos isso um paralelo deste versículo, embora vazado de modo diferente.

4. Existe aquela atração absoluta dos eleitos (ver notas em Efé. 1:4 no NTI), e eles virão de todas as nações; portanto, haverá uma espécie de universalidade. Mas o versículo ultrapassa essa idéia.

5. Uma restauração distinta da redenção. I Ped. 3:18-4:6 ensina que houve uma obra remidora de Cristo no hades. I Ped. 4:6 requer que essa obra tenha efeitos universais. Com base em Efé. 1:10, parece patente que haverá total restauração de todas as coisas em torno de Cristo. A redenção fará parte disso; mas a restauração geral, embora fique aquém da redenção, também será parte integrante. Aos perdidos serão outorgados propósito e bem-estar em sua existência, embora isso não venha a ocorrer à revelia do julgamento. Portanto, o julgamento não terá natureza apenas retributiva; também será restaurador, naquele grau que porventura agradar a Deus. I Ped. 4:6 ensina isso, o que era uma doutrina comum na igreja antiga. Haverá uma unidade universal em torno de Cristo, e nada será deixado de fora. Somente isso poderá cumprir os requisitos de João 12:32.

6. Acima da restauração, haverá a redenção dos eleitos, poucos em número. Essa redenção envolverá a participação na própria forma de vida que Cristo tem, na sua natureza, na sua plenitude, e na plenitude do Pai (ver as notas em Rom. 8:29; II Ped. 1:4 e Col. 2:10 no NTI). A *restauração* será uma glória secundária, em comparação com a infinita *redenção* dos eleitos.

7. É impossível que a missão de Cristo possa falhar, apesar de que poderia ter bom êxito de vários modos. Ver o artigo sobre a *Restauração*.

IV. Simbolismo envolvido

O simbolismo que nos apresenta Cristo a ser *levantado*; (ver também as passagens de João 3:14 e 8:28) pode ser uma alusão a duas coisas diversas: 1. A um rei que ascende ao seu trono; e 2. às insígnias ou pendões, isto é, às bandeiras que os comandantes de regimentos elevavam em mastros longos, para que o povo pudesse ver onde se encontrava o pavilhão de seu general, e assim pudesse unir-se em torno do mesmo. Dessa maneira vemos novamente que, embora a referência primária seja à cruz, contudo essa é sempre vinculada à sua «glória», tanto porque a própria cruz é uma glória, pois através da expiação os homens recebem dos benefícios provenientes de Cristo, como também porque ele destrói as forças do mal (ver Col. 2:15) e, além disso, porque a tragédia da cruz foi seguida pela grande vitória da ressurreição, ascensão

ATRIBUTO(S) — ATRIBUTOS DE DEUS

e glorificação do Senhor Jesus. Todos esses elementos estão necessariamente vinculados entre si. (Quanto ao tema de *a cruz e a glória*, tema esse que aparece reiterado com freqüência no quarto evangelho, ver as notas referentes ao trecho em João 11:51 no NTI). (FA G IB LAN NTI)

ATRIBUTO(S)

Vem do latim **ad**, «para», e **tribuere**, «atribuir», ou seja, aquilo que é atribuído a alguma coisa. Na teologia cristã, o termo veio a ser usado para indicar aquelas qualidades ou propriedades (atributos) atribuídas a Deus, como partes de Sua natureza. Ver o artigo separado abaixo. Contrastar o termo com *acidente* (ver o artigo a respeito).

1. Para *Aristóteles* (ver o artigo), o mundo divide-se em substâncias individuais e atributos dessas substâncias. Os atributos são aquelas características predicáveis à substância, seguindo as *categorias* (ver o artigo) de tempo, lugar, relação, espaço, posição, estados ativo ou passivo, etc., dez categorias ao todo.

2. Para *Tomás de Aquino* (ver o artigo), e também no escolasticismo, isso envolvia uma adaptação das idéias aristotelianas, com elementos transcendentais adicionais, como o único, o verdadeiro, o bom atributo de tudo, e especialmente, no caso de Deus.

3. Para *Descartes* (ver o artigo), pensamento e extensão são os dois atributos contrários e mutuamente opostos da realidade.

4. *Spinoza* (ver o artigo) ampliou a noção de Descartes, ao falar sobre pensamento e extensão como os dois atributos conhecidos da realidade, mas supondo que seu número real é infinito. Os atributos são aquelas características que constituem a essência.

5. Na *teologia*, quanto à sua descrição, diferem as listas de atributos divinos; mas, no teísmo clássico, o conceito ocidental tradicional de Deus envolve atributos como onisciência, sensibilidade, qualidades morais (santidade, justiça, amor, bondade, veracidade, sabedoria), qualidade estética (beleza), vontade, onipotência, simplicidade, unidade, espiritualidade, eternidade, infinitude, imutabilidade, onipresença, soberania, independência.

ATRIBUTOS DE DEUS

Na metafísica e na teologia, um atributo é uma qualidade de uma entidade que expressa sua natureza essencial. Assim, é algo indispensável ou necessário para a integridade daquele ser. Os atributos são a *summa genera* através das quais os modos são entendidos e existem na substância. Ver os atributos tradicionais do teísmo, ponto 5. no artigo *Atributo(s)*. Ver tratamentos detalhados sobre *Onipresença*; *Onipotência*; e *Onisciência* nos artigos com estes título.

I. Atributos de Deus

O teísmo **clássico** vê Deus como uma **pessoa** transcendente e terrível, embora não apenas como uma força cósmica, que não se inter-relaciona com outros seres. Deus criou o homem à Sua própria imagem (Gên. 1:26,27), intelectual e moralmente falando, e isso implica na personalidade de Deus, embora não obtenhamos grande conhecimento real através dessa afirmativa.

1. Onisciência. Como pessoa, Deus a conhece, estando cônscio de Si mesmo e de Sua criação. Esse conhecimento desconhece limites, restrições ou defeitos. A filosofia ensina-nos que todas as palavras *omni* são realmente negativas em seu caráter, porque não temos experiência ou conhecimento, sem importar os meios de conhecimento, sobre qualquer coisa ilimitada. Para nós, portanto, os termos iniciados com omni apenas exprimem um grau superlativo daquilo que sabemos apenas de forma limitada. O conhecimento de Deus estende-se para trás por todo o tempo, até quando ainda não havia tempo, todo o presente e todo o futuro possível. Aristóteles chamava Deus de «o Intelecto», e os homens de «intelectos».

2. Sensibilidade. Deus, como pessoa, tem sentimentos racionais e morais, embora não físicos, como se dá com o homem. Vários termos antropomórficos são usados para exprimir esse aspecto de Deus, como Seu deleite ou Sua ira, Seu arrependimento ou mudança de atitude acerca de algo, Seu amor, Seu desprazer, etc. (Gên. 6:6; I Sam. 13:14; Êxo. 4:14; Rom. 9:13).

3. Qualidades morais. Dificilmente poderíamos atribuir qualidades morais a uma força cósmica impessoal. Isso exemplifica a natureza pessoal de Deus.

a. *Santidade*. Deus não peca e todas as Suas virtudes são perfeitas. (Isa. 6:3; I João 1:5; Apo. 6:10; 15:4). Nessa qualidade, Deus ocupa lugar *ímpar*, pois, embora outros seres também não pequem, não compartilham das — virtudes positivas — de Deus com a mesma extensão.

b. *Justiça*. Em Si mesmo e em Seu governo, não se acha qualquer defeito de injustiça, erro ou ação duvidosa. Ele exerce direito e autoridade absolutos sobre as Suas criaturas, embora isso repouse sobre Sua bondade, e não sobre o Seu mero poder. Uma coisa qualquer não é justa somente porque Deus a faz; mas o que Ele faz segue algum padrão de justiça, que Ele estabeleceu para os homens. (I João 1:9; I Cor. 11:31,32; Rom. 2:12-16; II Crô. 19:7; Isa. 45:21; Apo. 15:3).

c. *Amor*. Esse é o único atributo moral de Deus que também Lhe serve de nome (I João 4:8). Consiste no interesse final e em ações beneficentes baseadas nesse interesse, no que todos os homens estão envolvidos (João 3:16), e que serve de impulso motivador de todos os atos da providência e da missão salvatícia de Cristo. Os próprios juízos divinos estão baseados no amor — tendo em vista a restauração (I Ped. 4:6; Heb. 12:6-8). O amor é a base de todas as demais virtudes morais, o solo onde elas medram (Gál. 5:22 ss).

d. *Bondade*. Deus é benévolo tanto para os homens mortais como para as almas, e também para toda a Sua criação. A *misericórdia* faz parte da bondade de Deus. Ele é o «Pai de misericórdias» (II Cor. 1:3), que dispensa atos de bondade a todos. A misericórdia e a bondade, tendo em vista a salvação, são manifestações fundamentais de Deus (Efé. 2:4,5; Rom. 9:15,18; I Tim. 1:13). Todos os dons perfeitos e bons são outorgados por Deus (Tia. 1:17).

e. *Veracidade*. Em Deus não há falsidade, em Seu ser ou em Seus atos. A revelação repousa sobre esse atributo, como reflexo do mesmo, pois, sendo Ele veraz, transmite a verdade (João 1:18), por meio de Seu Filho. Deus é veraz, e todo homem é mentiroso (Rom. 3:4). Os pactos de Deus repousam sobre a Sua veracidade (Sal. 12:6; Heb. 10:23). Jamais falha tudo quanto Deus declara (Êxo. 12:41). Em Cristo, Deus manifestou a verdade, pelo que o Filho é a Verdade (João 14:6).

f. *Sabedoria*. Deus sabe o que fazer e como agir, com base em recursos ilimitados (Rom. 11:33; I Cor. 1:17 ss ; Apo. 5:12).

ATRIBUTOS DE DEUS

4. Qualidade Estética. Deus é **beleza**. O diálogo de Platão, **Simpósio**, expõe a verdade de que todos os objetos e entidades de beleza assim o são por refletirem a Beleza Suprema, que é Deus. Beleza fala de harmonia, graça, simetria em pessoa e em ato. Deus exemplifica essa qualidade em grau supremo. A missão de Cristo é uma bela obra, proveniente do Pai. Encontramos beleza em outras coisas e pessoas, quando elas têm qualidades que nos fazem lembrar a beleza divina. Aqueles que anunciam o evangelho realizam uma bela missão (Rom. 10:15). Tudo Deus fez formoso (Ecl. 3:11; Sal. 48:2). Sua santidade é uma bela qualidade (Sal. 29:2). O Senhor é a própria beleza (Sal. 27:4).

5. Vontade. Somente de uma pessoa se pode esperar a qualidade da vontade. As palavras: «...faça-se a tua vontade, assim na terra como no céu...» (Mat. 6:10), subentendem que Deus pode agir e realmente age, intervindo, recompensando, punindo e dirigindo. A vontade de Deus está detrás de seu propósito de salvar (II Ped. 3:9; I Tim. 2:4). Sua vontade é absoluta, realizando aquilo que Ele quer (Efé. 1:11). Essa é a qualidade *onipotente* da vontade de Deus. A vontade de Deus é *livre*. É argumento falso afirmar-se que a vontade de Deus não pode ser livre, que Ele *não pode* pecar, porque o pecado é a própria negação da liberdade, e não um aspecto da mesma. A vontade de Deus não faz uma coisa ser certa ou errada, arbitrariamente, conforme é sugerido pelo *voluntarismo* (ver o artigo). Antes, a vontade de Deus sempre opera segundo a justiça absoluta. Aquilo que é aprovado aos olhos de Deus, deve ser bom (Mat. 11:26).

II. Qualidades Divinas:

1. Onipotência. O poder de Deus é ilimitado, o que é ilustrado na criação e demonstrado na sustentação da mesma (Gên. 1 e 2; Col. 1:16). Ele pode cumprir todos os Seus desejos (Efé. 1:11; Rom. 9). Ele é o *Todo-Poderoso* (Gên. 17:1; Núm. 24:4, 16; Sal. 19:1; II Cor. 6:18; Apo. 1:8; 4:8; 16:7,14; 19:15 e 21:22). As objeções sofistas contidas em declarações como: «Deus pode criar um peso que Ele mesmo não pode carregar», são pseudoproblemas.

2. Simplicidade. O ser divino não é composto. Deus é puro Espírito (João 4:24), e não espírito e matéria, como os homens. Em Sua essência, propriedade e modo são uma só coisa. Ele se expressa em três Pessoas, mas todas elas são da mesma substância. Seus atributos fazem parte de Sua unidade e simplicidade, e esses atributos devem ser concebidos como porções destacadas de Sua pessoa, mediante a abstração humana.

3. Unidade. Deus tem apenas uma substância ou essência, e seus atributos compõem a sua unidade. Ele tem uma só natureza e vontade. Não há contradições em Deus, não há conflitos. Ele é triúno, mas cada Pessoa é da mesma substância. Deus é singular em Sua essência, em uma categoria toda própria (Deu. 6:4; Isa. 44:6; I Cor. 8:4). Por isso declara o Credo Atanasiano (ver o artigo a respeito): «Adoramos a um só Deus em trindade, e trindade em unidade; nem confundindo as pessoas e nem dividindo a substância».

4. Espiritualidade. Deus é Espírito puro. Se há categorias entre os espíritos (o que é provável), então Deus é a forma mais elevada de Espírito (João 4:24), a origem de toda outra existência espiritual, bem como o criador de todas as coisas físicas.

5. Eternidade. Coisa alguma criou Deus. Ele sempre existiu. Outrossim, seu tipo de existência é singular, pelo que Ele é contrastado com todos os tipos de existência, material ou outra qualquer. A palavra eternidade reveste-se dos aspectos de *não-temporalidade* e de uma *qualidade* distintiva, e ambas essas coisas podem ser ditas acerca da essência divina. Deus é o autor do tempo, mas não está condicionado ao tempo. Ele já existia antes do tempo, e sempre existirá, porquanto Ele é o auto-existente, a Causa sem causa. (Gên. 21:33; Sal. 41:13; 90:2; Hab. 1:12; Rom. 1:20; 16:26; Heb. 9:14).

6. Infinitude. Não há graus ou limitações nos atributos de Deus. Ele não está limitado ao tempo e ao espaço. Seu conhecimento desconhece fronteiras. Sua presença é sentida em todos os lugares. Seu poder não conhece restrições. Ele é o Absoluto. Ele é auto-existente pelo que não depende de ninguém e de — coisa alguma, quanto ao Seu ser. As referências bíblicas que aludem à Sua onipotência, à Sua onisciência e à Sua onipresença, falam sobre aspectos de Sua infinitude.

7. Imutabilidade. Aristóteles concebia um Movedor inabalável que, em Si mesmo não se modificaria, mas que, ao ser amado, produziria todas as alterações que ocorrem na criação. Assim, Deus não seria susceptível e nem capaz de modificações. Em Seu ser não há qualquer tipo de evolução, embora Suas obras estejam em um contínuo estágio de desenvolvimento. Ele preenche todas as coisas, e nEle todas as coisas se completam (Efé. 1:23; ver também Sal. 102:24-27; Isa. 46:9,10; Mal. 3-6). «...em quem não pode existir variação, ou sombra de mudança» (Tia. 1:17). Assim como é o Pai, é também o Filho (Heb. 13:8). Embora seja imutável, Deus não é estático, pois Suas obras nunca cessam, e estão sempre em mutação.

8. Onipresença ou Imensidade. O Espírito de Deus permeia a tudo, e Sua inteligência perscruta a todas as coisas. Ele não está confinado ao espaço, mas é imanente em tudo. Ele está acima de tudo, através de tudo e em tudo (Efé. 4:6). O Espírito habita nos crentes e está onipresente no mundo (Rom. 8:9; Sal. 139:7-12). Sua presença garante a continuação de todos os outros seres (Atos 17:28).

9. Soberania. Esse é um dos aspectos da onipotência de Deus, mas administrada através de Sua bondade e amor, ou seja, Seus atributos morais. A passagem de Rom. 9 mostra a soberania de Deus. O evangelho ensina que a mesma é administrada em bondade e amor (Efé. 1:10). Isso prova que a soberania de Deus está por detrás da *unidade* que finalmente deverá caracterizar todas as coisas em torno de Cristo, além de ensinar-nos que a soberania de Deus é uma aliada da esperança e da salvação, e não uma reprovação às mesmas. O amor de Deus controlou a missão de Cristo (João 3:16), não havendo tal coisa como soberania sem amor. O próprio julgamento final requer o controle absoluto da parte de Deus, visando propósitos beneficentes, e não destrutivos. (Ver I Ped. 4:6 e as notas no NTI).

10. Independência. Deus não tem causa. Ele é o auto-existente, e perpetua-se a Si mesmo. Ele tem vida em Si mesmo, tendo dado da mesma ao Filho; e através do Filho, aos filhos. Assim, finalmente, eles compartilhão da vida necessária e independente do Pai (João 5:25,26). Deus é o Ser necessário. Não pode deixar de existir. Esse é um profundo mistério. Mas as pessoas indagam: «Quem criou Deus?» Tais perguntas, porém, não podem ser formuladas, visto como ninguém pode formular uma resposta à mesma, ou iniciar uma investigação a respeito.

Conclusão. As descrições aqui oferecidas separaram os atributos de Deus com o propósito de discuti-los, embora se encontrem entretecidos nEle e sejam dependentes uns dos outros. A maioria, se não mesmo todos desses atributos são aquelas qualidades também presentes no homem, em grau muito menor. A debilidade da linguagem humana força-nos a usar uma linguagem antropomórfica. Isso, naturalmente, obscurece o quadro, pois, quando falamos sobre Deus, o mais profundo de todos os assuntos, a maior de todas as realidades, o mais misterioso de todos os seres, os nossos melhores esforços são fraquíssimos. Ver sobre *antropomorfismo*. (B C CHA E EP R)

ÁTRIO DA GUARDA

Excetuando o trecho de Nee. 3:25, essa expressão aparece somente no livro de Jeremias. Esse *átrio* era uma área dentro do palácio onde Jeremias ficou detido (ver Jer. 32:2), pelo que era uma espécie de prisão. Ali Jeremias recebeu visitantes, e continuou efetuando negócios (ver Jer. 32:8-12). Havia ali uma cisterna, dentro da qual Jeremias foi posto por cortesãos que queriam tirar-lhe a vida (ver Jer. 38:6). (Z)

ÁTRIO DOS GENTIOS

Ver o artigo sobre o **templo**. O átrio dos gentios era um espaço aberto, dentro do complexo do templo construído por Herodes. Era pavimentado de mármore, sendo usado para ali serem entabulados negócios, como a venda de animais destinados aos holocaustos e o câmbio de moedas. Provavelmente foi nesse lugar que Jesus derrubou as mesas dos cambistas e expulsou os que vendiam animais (ver Mat. 2:12 e João 2:14-17). Ver as notas no NTI sobre essa questão. Essa área não era considerada sagrada, pelo que os gentios podiam entrar ali. Visto que suas paredes forneciam sombra, era um lugar comum de reuniões, discussões e também como passagem. As várias divisões do templo representam os variegados graus de acesso a Deus. Em Jesus Cristo, o crente torna-se templo do Espírito Santo, o que significa que desfruta de acesso direto a Deus, porquanto as antigas barreiras foram derrubadas. Agora os gentios, mediante a fé, entram no Santo dos Santos do céu, por meio de Cristo (ver Efé. 2 e Heb. 10:19 ss).

ÁTRIOS DO TEMPLO Ver **Templo**.

ATROTE-SOFÃ Ver sobre **Sofã**.

No hebraico, **coroas**. Uma cidade pertencente a Gade (ver Núm. 32:35), mencionada juntamente com Aroer e Jazer; provavelmente deve ser entendida como uma designação composta com o nome que se segue, «Sofã», a fim de distingui-la de uma outra cidade na mesma região, de nome Atarote. Ficava em uma fértil região de pastos. (S Z)

AUGSBURGO, CONFISSÃO DE

Uma declaração de fé redigida por Melancton, com a qual concordou Lutero. Foi apresentada ao imperador Carlos V, quando da Dieta de Augsburgo, a 25 de junho de 1530, tendo-se tornado um alicerce do luteranismo. Contém 21 artigos, além de mais sete artigos acerca de abusos eclesiásticos. Foi o primeiro grande símbolo ou declaração de fé dos protestantes. Foi incorporado no livro da Concórdia, em 1580, continuando a ser reputada uma declaração autoritária, por muitos luteranos. O documento é uma franca exposição das crenças essenciais do luteranismo, mas expressão com moderação, em um tom que espera a reunião de todos os cristãos.

Os vinte e um artigos abordam crenças atinentes à natureza de Deus, itens comuns aos credos cristãos tradicionais, como os sacramentos, a transubstanciação, as boas obras, os direitos ecles., o livre arbítrio e os santos. Os sete últimos artigos condenam aquilo que se considerava abusos católicos, como a distribuição apenas de um dos elementos da comunhão, o celibato obrigatório para o clero, a aceitação de pagamento pela celebração de missas, a confissão compulsória, a ausência de disciplina nos mosteiros e o abuso de autoridade. O décimo artigo, sobre a Ceia do Senhor (eucaristia), nas primeiras edições dessa declaração, afirmava que o corpo e o sangue de Cristo estão «verdadeiramente presentes e são distribuídos» (ver o artigo *transubstanciação*). Porém, a edição de Melancton, em 1540, a sua *Confesio Augustana Variata*, alterou esse artigo para que se lesse: «estão com o pão e o vinho, verdadeiramente exibidos» (ver o artigo *consubstanciação*). (AM B C E P)

AUGUSTANA

Nome latino dado à Confissão de Augsburgo. Visto que a cidade alemã de Augsburgo, onde foi apresentada essa confissão protestante básica, derivava seu nome do imperador romano Augusto, não demorou para que essa confissão se tornasse conhecida por Augustana (em latim, «pertinente a Augusto»).

AUGUSTO (CÉSAR)

No latim, **venerável, estimado, sua reverência**. No grego era transliterado por *Augoustos*; o termo grego correspondente é *sebastos*. Esse foi o título adotado por Otávio, o qual, após ter sido adotado por Júlio César, tomou o nome de Otaviano. Ele foi o primeiro imperador pacificamente reconhecido do império romano. Otávio era o imperador por ocasião do nascimento de Jesus e durante a metade de Sua vida na terra, mas seu nome não tem qualquer conexão com os eventos bíblicos, ocorrendo somente em Lucas 2:1. Ele pertenceu ao chamado segundo triunvirato, que também envolvia Marco Antônio e Lépido. Após a remoção deste último, Otávio entrou em batalha contra Antônio, em Ácio, em 31 A.C., e o derrotou. O senado romano saudou-o como imperador, em 27 A.C., conferindo-lhe o título de *Augusto*. Augusto é mencionado no Novo Testamento em conexão com Herodes, a quem reinstalara no seu reino e honrara grandemente, embora Herodes tivesse antes apoiado a causa de Antônio. Por ocasião do falecimento de Herodes, Augusto dividiu o seu reino de acordo com a vontade expressa por Herodes e até mesmo mandou educar dois de seus filhos, visto que a relação entre o imperador e Herodes havia sido bastante amistosa. Otávio reinou durante quarenta e um anos e foi sucedido por Tibério César (ver Lucas 3:1). Os sucessores do primeiro Augusto adotaram o mesmo título, embora raramente fosse aplicado a eles pelos escritores latinos. No império romano do Oriente, o termo grego *sebastos* parece ter sido comumente usado, como se dava no caso de Nero (ver Atos 25:21). Em tempos posteriores, após Diocleciano, o título *Augusto* foi dado a um ou dois dos herdeiros presuntivos do império, ao passo que o título *César* era dado a seus colegas mais jovens e herdeiros presuntivos.

Otávio nasceu em 63 A.C., tendo sido educado

principalmente por seu tio avô, Júlio César, que o tornou seu herdeiro. Após a morte de Júlio César, a influência de Otávio aumentou, razão por que terminou sendo um dos membros do triunvirato (governo por parte de três governantes combinados). Mas as circunstâncias já descritas levaram-no a governar em lugar do triunvirato. Havia morrido a democracia romana; mas, visto que Otávio sabia como revestir o império em forma republicana, ele foi largamente apoiado. — Chamava a si mesmo de *princeps*, ou primeiro cidadão. Era intitulado imperador por ser o comandante em chefe das forças armadas. Utilizava-se das antigas magistraturas a fim de governar. Delegou autoridade ao senado, confiando ao mesmo o governo das províncias. Impôs a paz; e, de modo geral, o povo não tomou consciência das radicais mudanças no governo, por ele introduzidas. (AM BUC UN Z)

AULÉN, Gustavo Emanuel Hildebrando (1879 ---)
Teólogo sueco, professor na Universidade de Lund. Desde 1933, bispo de Strengnas. Seu trabalho explora mais o campo da dogmática e da história da doutrina, com ênfase especial sobre a conexão entre a reforma e os primeiros pais da Igreja. Também fez estudos musicais e foi editor de um dos principais periódicos teológicos da Suécia, *Svensk Theologisk Kvartalskrift*. (Ver o artigo sobre a teologia *lundensiana*).

Em suas preleções *Olaus Petri* (1930) sobre a expiação, ele desenvolveu o tema e argumentos com convicção, no sentido de que a doutrina clássica da *expiação*, desenvolvida por Lutero, era essencialmente a vitória de Cristo sobre Satanás e os poderes das trevas. Foi publicado um livro a esse respeito, com edição abreviada em inglês, com o título de *Christus Victor*. (C E)

AUMAI
No hebraico, **irmão da água**, um dos dois filhos de Jaate, um zoratita, descendente de Judá (ver I Crô. 4:2). (S)

AURA HUMANA (CAMPO DE VIDA)
É um campo luminoso, invisível ao olho humano (com exceção de algumas poucas pessoas), que circunda todos os objetos físicos, animados ou inanimados. No caso dos objetos animados, esse campo está sujeito a alterações, devido às emoções. Nas curas psíquicas, a aura de quem cura diminui, e a da pessoa curada aumenta. Outras modificações são causadas por tempestades magnéticas do sol, pela música, pelo raciocínio, além de várias outras coisas. O efeito foi descoberto fotograficamente por Semyon Kirlian, um cientista russo, no começo da década de 1930. O que atualmente se chama de fotografia kirliana é um processo eletrofotográfico. Kirlian notou que quando os seus dedos tocavam no papel fotográfico, estando sob o campo de uma corrente elétrica de alta freqüência, eram deixadas impressões sobre o filme. Isso o levou à descoberta e à fotografia do campo luminoso.

Aparentemente relacionado a isso, e talvez detectando a mesma força, houve a descoberta dos *campos de vida* que cercam todos os objetos vivos. O Dr. Harold Saxton Burr, Ph.D., professor de medicina da Universidade de Yale, detectou os campos de energia ao redor dos objetos vivos, usando voltímetros sensíveis. O campo de energia humana, segundo se tem demonstrado, eleva-se até cerca de três metros de altura, variando de pessoa para pessoa e dependendo da capacidade mental de cada uma. Esse campo eletrodinâmico, segundo seu pensamento, é um tipo de molde espiritual, psíquico, não-material, que obriga a porção física a desenvolver-se como o faz. Filosoficamente falando, isso se relaciona às *formas* ou *idéias* de Platão, que são os padrões parciais e imperfeitamente duplicados nas coisas físicas. Supostamente, a forma (campo de vida) é uma dimensão não-material do ser, que controla o desenvolvimento do código genético em sua contraparte física. O campo de vida aparentemente é a matriz que controla o desenvolvimento físico. As células não seriam especializadas, ou seja, qualquer célula poderia desenvolver-se em qualquer porção do corpo humano. Uma única célula aparentemente possui o código genético do ser inteiro, e é o campo de vida que determina quais células tornar-se-ão a cabeça, ou os braços, ou os intestinos, etc. O posicionamento do campo de vida produz isso na ordem desejada. O campo de vida persiste, mesmo quando a contraparte física é removida, como quando se corta a ponta de uma folha viva. A fotografia kirliana algumas vezes exibe claramente a presença do campo de vida, sem a correspondente porção física, que fora decepada. Assim, a ponta da folha foi cortada, mas o campo de vida correspondente à ponta continua ali. Tem sido demonstrado que essas fotografias não dependem de fatores como calor ou outras condições físicas dos objetos fotografados. Burr declara: «É impossível imaginarmos que o desenvolvimento, estágio por estágio, do sistema nervoso tenha ocorrido ao acaso, sem qualquer diretiva. Você e eu, portanto, somos produtos de um padrão de organização; ou, dizendo a mesma coisa com outras palavras, somos a conseqüência de um desígnio. E é dificílimo pensarmos que um aparelho qualquer — quer se trate de um ferro elétrico ou de um ciclotron — não tenha sido produto da mente de um *planejador* qualquer. Portanto, visto que o Universo exibe desígnio, não se trata de dar um salto muito grande no espaço, quando concluímos que o Universo é produto de um Planejador».

Burr pensa que o campo de vida é primário, obrigando a porção física a assumir as formas por ela adquiridas. Ele não pensa que há qualquer tipo de radiação que emane do corpo físico, dependente do mesmo. Se isso é verdade, então estamos nos aproximando de uma prova científica da dualidade humana. Um homem se compõe de uma porção não-material e de uma porção material, isto é, tem espírito, como seu ser essencial, e tem um corpo físico (que lhe serve de veículo). Apelando para o argumento teleológico (ver o artigo a respeito), presumimos que o campo de vida tem a Inteligência por detrás do mesmo, o Planejador Cósmico que é Deus. Ver o artigo sobre a *parapsicologia*, que aborda outras regiões das pesquisas científicas, que prometem encontrar provas científicas para a existência da alma humana. (BU EC SL)

AURA-MAZDA
Nome que no antigo persa significa **senhor sábio**. Representava o princípio bom que governava a tudo, o espírito divino nos ensinos de Zaratustra ou Zoroastro, o sábio persa. Ele era considerado o criador de tudo, o opositor do mal e do maligno, *Arimã* (ver o artigo a respeito). Esse nome tem sido encontrado nas inscrições da dinastia Acaemenida, a começar pelo reinado de Ciro (ver II Crô. 36:22 e Isa. 44:28). Dizia-se que cada rei persa fizera o que fizera pelo poder dessa divindade. «Pelo favor de Aura-Maz-

da, sou rei desta terra» (R.G. Kent em *Old Persian* 116-116, 1950). Há uma inscrição de Dario que menciona um grupo de deuses como se eles fossem um complexo de divindades, encabeçadas por Aura-Mazda. Seja como for, os persas se opunham à idolatria, o que sem dúvida foi um fator no veredito favorável a Ciro e seus sucessores, segundo se vê em Esd. 7:12-20. (KEN Z)

AURANO

Nome de um homem designado como «tão insensato quanto velho», em II Macabeus 4:40, o qual liderou uma revolta contra Lisímaco, em Jerusalém. (GD)

AUROBINDO, SRI (Aurobindo Ghose)

Filósofo indiano (1872-1950), líder da **Advaita Vedanta** (ver o artigo a respeito), uma filosofia moderna da Índia. Escritos: *Essays on the Gita*; *The Life Divine*; *The Synthesis of Yoga*; *The Supramental Manifestation upon the Earth*.

Ensinos:
1. O ilusionismo de Shankara é uma distorção das Upanishads (ver o artigo).
2. A realidade existe em uma série de gradações de entidades, a começar pela matéria e subindo ao Absoluto, ou Bramá. O poder essencial de Bramá requer sua descida ao finito.
3. O mesmo poder requer que o finito esforce-se por chegar ao infinito, o que produz a evolução de formas inferiores para superiores. O homem busca identificar-se com o Absoluto, passando além do nível de vida mental para a vida divina.
4. O meio para se atingir esse estado evolutivo é chamado de «ioga interior», que torna possível a transformação da mente, da vida e do corpo. (P)

AUSTIN, JOHN L.

Filósofo inglês (1911-1960), estudante e professor de Oxford, de 1933 a 1960, excetuando os anos da Segunda Guerra Mundial. Escritos:*Philosophical Papers;Sense and Sensibilia*; *How to Do Things with Words*.

Idéias:
1. À filosofia com freqüência, falta uma completa investigação no tocante aos próprios problemas, e como os mesmos devem ser investigados.
2. Austin filosofava por meio de um exame detalhado e exaustivo das palavras e sentenças apropriadas para a consideração de um problema qualquer.
3. *Atos de fala*: ato locucionário: é a expressão de qualquer sentença apropriada. Ato ilocucionário: é o intuito da locução, considerado até mesmo o contexto; essas intenções podem ser classificadas como afirmativas, negativas, promissórias, consentidoras, votadas, sugestivas, agradecedoras, nomeadoras, diagnosticadoras, etc. Ato perlocucionário: é o ato que a pessoa, afinal, realizou, ou o acordo sobre o que será realizado. Exemplo: «O livro está estragado» (declaração locucionária). «Peço que você o repare» (declaração ilocucionária). «Substitua-o por outro» (declaração perlocucionária).
4. Nem todas as declarações são verdadeiras ou falsas. Muitas são *performativas*, sendo elas a maior proporção das sentenças. As declarações performativas incluem promessas, consentimentos, nomeações, garantias, e vetos.

5. *Sentido e capacidade de sentir*. Percebemos diretamente os objetos, da maneira como eles são: realismo do bom senso (ver o artigo). (E P)

AUTENTICIDADE

Vem do grego **authentes**, aquele que age com autoridade, ou aquilo que se faz com as próprias mãos. Os existencialistas incluíram o termo no vocabulário corriqueiro da filosofia. É o estado de ser autêntico, autoritário ou genuíno, — dotado de verdadeira vida e de verdadeiros propósitos.
1. Jaspers: o propósito da filosofia é despertar os homens para a autenticidade.
2. Heidegger: a vereda para o Ser puro é a autenticidade de vida.
3. Ortega y Gasset: Alcançar a autenticidade é o propósito da vida.
4. Bultmann: A autenticidade só é possível através da Palavra, conforme ela é revelada em Cristo.
5. No que concerne aos livros da Bíblia: Livro autêntico é aquele que realmente foi produzido pelo autor suposto do mesmo. Esse termo deve ser contrastado com *genuinidade*, que denota a qualidade de um manuscrito original cujo conteúdo não foi corrompido. A epístola aos Romanos é uma autêntica epístola de Paulo. Mas as epístolas pastorais podem não sê-lo; nesse caso, não seriam autênticas, embora possam ser genuínas. Ver o artigo sobre I Timóteo, quanto a essa controvérsia.

AUTO-AMOR

O trecho de Efésios 5:28 mostra-nos que o auto-amor é legítimo, porquanto serve de base ou padrão do amor que um homem tem por sua esposa. Ninguém odeia a si mesmo (ver Efé. 5:20). Bem pelo contrário, cada pessoa cuida de si mesma com extremados cuidados. E isso deveria servir de padrão de como um homem deveria cuidar de sua própria esposa. Essa ordem, na epístola aos Efésios, alicerça-se sobre a analogia de Cristo e Sua Igreja, a cabeça e o corpo, porque quando um homem e uma mulher casam-se, passam a compor um só corpo, do qual o marido é o cabeça. É verdade que as pessoas podem chegar a odiar a si mesmas, mas isso é uma anormalidade, até mesmo patológica. O amor-próprio, quando exagerado, transforma-se em *egoísmo*, tornando-se então prejudicial. A amor-próprio é algo necessário para a preservação do corpo como veículo de serviço, porquanto é o templo do Espírito Santo (ver I Cor. 6), pelo que merece ser tratado com cuidado. Além disso, há o amor pelo ser inteiro, e não apenas pelo corpo físico. Esse afeto também encontra bases teológicas, porque agrada ao Pai que seus filhos andem corretamente, e também é bom para o Pai celeste. Isso posto, o crente deve perceber certa importância em sua pessoa, por haver sido exaltado pelo Pai, tendo sido feito um filho de Deus, um co-herdeiro do Filho de Deus— (ver Rom. 8:14 ss). Mais do que isso, ainda, o crente terminará por compartilhar da própria natureza divina (ver II Ped. 1:4), o que lhe conferirá exaltadíssima posição. Não obstante, ninguém é grande em si mesmo, embora assim pensem os egoístas. Somente dentro da providência divina alguém pode ser considerado grande. Cada indivíduo é ímpar, e ocupa-se, aqui e na vida vindoura, de uma missão sem-par (Apo. 2:17). Ver as notas no NTI, nesse ponto, no que tange a detalhes sobre esse conceito. Ora, sendo ímpar, o indivíduo deve respeitar a si mesmo, tanto quanto aos seus semelhantes. (NTI Z)

AUTOCÉFALO — AUTODECEPÇÃO

AUTOCÉFALO
Vem do grego, com o sentido de «independente», termo que descreve certos bispos dos tempos cristãos primitivos, que eram independentes de seus metropolitas imediatos, responsáveis somente à autoridade superior. (E)

AUTOCOMPREENSÃO
Essa expressão pode ser equivalente ao autoconhecimento (ver o artigo). Todavia, tem-lhe sido dado um sentido especial, altamente teológico, por R. Bultmann, com base em sua análise das idéias de M. Heidegger (ver os artigos sobre eles). A aceitação do *kerygma* cristão (a pregação do evangelho), produz uma modificação na compreensão do homem sobre si mesmo, libertando-o do medo da nulidade, da insignificância e da morte. Bultmann insistia que tal modificação deve envolver a conversão (ver o artigo). Essa modificação é de natureza tal que, após ter ocorrido, o indivíduo passa a viver de maneira autêntica, ao passo que antes vivia de maneira não-autêntica. A nova autenticidade, pois, faz parte da autocompreensão, fazendo parte da salvação do indivíduo. O Espírito ensina o crente sobre seu próprio «eu», sua dignidade e seu destino, pelo que também os temores, as incertezas e as futilidades da existência são apagados. Seria um acontecimento místico e espiritual que ocorreria através do *kerygma*.

AUTOCONHECIMENTO
Está em pauta o conhecimento que uma pessoa tem de si mesma, de seu valor, de sua verdadeira natureza, e das ações apropriadas que promovem o verdadeiro «eu».

1. Na opinião de *Sócrates* (ver o artigo a respeito), o *autoconhecimento* é o mais elevado alvo da filosofia, como também de seu ramo mais importante, a ética (ver o artigo a respeito). A expressão «Conhece-te a ti mesmo» era uma famosa máxima dos oráculos délficos. Diz-se que Tales (ver o artigo a seu respeito) foi quem criou a máxima. Esse conhecimento próprio envolve os mais altos alvos e aspirações do homem, com base no conhecimento de sua verdadeira natureza. Sabemos quem somos e para onde estamos indo? Quanto melhor o homem souber a resposta a essa indagação, tanto mais ele será inspirado a ter um elevado ideal na vida, percebendo a dignidade de sua pessoa. Mas o homem que forma baixa opinião sobre si mesmo não se preocupa muito com questões de nobreza e de elevadas realizações. Mas, o homem que chegar a aprender que cada indivíduo é ímpar para o Criador (ver Apo. 2:17 e o conceito do *novo nome*, nas notas do *Novo Nome*, no NTI), sentir-se-á inspirado por essa idéia a dar o máximo de si. Sócrates cria que o conhecimento ético pode ser adquirido com base na razão e na intuição, sem necessidade de instrução externa. Portanto, conhecer a si mesmo equivale a rejeitar o falso conhecimento imposto por terceiros, e também equivale a descobrir os padrões do certo e do errado, no próprio ser.

2. *Abelardo* (ver o artigo a respeito) escreveu um tratado com o título: «Conhece-te a Ti Mesmo». Sua tese fundamental era similar à de Sócrates. Todo homem dispõe de uma consciência dada por Deus; e é ali que ele pode descobrir a verdadeira ética. A moralidade não reside essencialmente no próprio ato e em suas conseqüências, mas, acima de tudo, no *intuito* humano, que pode ser puro ou corrompido, dependendo do fato de estar ele seguindo ou não os verdadeiros ditames de sua consciência. Uma consciência iluminada refletirá a vontade divina. Quando um homem age contrariamente à sua consciência, sem importar se outros homens venham a louvá-lo e sem resultar seu ato em benefício, para ele mesmo e para outras pessoas, comete pecado.

3. *Agostinho* (ver o artigo a respeito) via o autoconhecimento (essencialmente explicado em termos socráticos) como algo que leva o indivíduo não somente à felicidade, por via da ação ética correta, mas também à salvação (ver o artigo), que é o alvo de toda a ética. (EP MM P)

AUTOCONTRADIÇÃO
Trata-se da afirmação, feita por uma mesma pessoa, de duas proposições contraditórias. Algumas vezes, declarações dessa natureza podem envolver a verdade, quando estamos abordando paradoxos (ver o artigo a respeito), ou declarações polares (ver o artigo). Nem toda a verdade pode ser reduzida a proposições ou descrições do tipo «sim» ou «não». (EP)

AUTOCONTROLE
Ver os artigos sobre **Controle do Próprio Ser e Temperança**. O termo **autocontrole** não aparece em muitas versões da Bíblia, embora a idéia esteja ali. O gr. *egkráteia, continência*, indica um dos aspectos do fruto do Espírito, em Gálatas 5:23. Examinar o NTI, onde a idéia é comentada com detalhes. Ver também Atos 24:25; II Ped. 1:6, quanto ao uso desse termo grego. A forma verbal ocorre por duas vezes em I Coríntios (7:9 e 9:25), e a forma adjetivada em Tito 1:8. Algumas vezes, a idéia é simplesmente a de que o indivíduo deve controlar-se em caso de alguma tensão emocional, como quando José teve dificuldades para não irromper em lágrimas, quando conversava com seus irmãos no Egito, e queria revelar-lhes a sua verdadeira identidade (ver Gên. 43:1). Davi foi exortado a tirar a vida de Saul, no interior de uma caverna, mas refreou-se (ver I Sam. 24). No sentido moral, a ausência de autocontrole baseia-se na concupiscência, e termina em excessos. Em Seu cultivo, o Espírito produz no crente a capacidade dele refrear-se de vícios e excessos. As áreas onde essa virtude opera são as seguintes: todo tipo de apetite físico e mental, a ambição, o tipo de temperamento da pessoa, a ira, a fala, todos os atos, tanto bons quanto maus. A moderação é um importante princípio moral. Os atletas precisam treinar, controlando seu espírito e seu corpo, ou não poderiam lograr bom êxito (ver I Cor. 9:24-27). O autocontrole, moral e espiritual, requer a atitude própria de um atleta. Apesar do autocontrole ser uma questão pessoal, exerce efeitos sobre nossos semelhantes, porquanto ninguém fica irado sozinho, e nem se mostra excessivamente indulgente sozinho. A linguagem exagerada pode ferir o próximo. (H NTI)

AUTODECEPÇÃO (ENGANO)
Um estado semelhante à ignorância própria da crença falsa, embora devendo ser distinguido da mesma. Aquele que está enganando a si mesmo é motivado pela sua cegueira. E isso, por causa de fatores negativos, quando a pessoa não quer dar crédito a coisa alguma, ou por causa de fatores positivos quando o sistema de crenças de uma pessoa força-a a chegar a certas conclusões, que são ilusórias. Todos os sistemas religiosos envolvem algum elemento de

AUTODEFESA — AUTO-EXAME

autodecepção, como também se dá com a maioria das ciências. Algumas vezes, até mesmo a disponibilidade de fortes evidências em contrário é convenientemente ignorada. Por exemplo, no campo científico, a recusa de se examinar e avaliar corretamente as evidências que vão surgindo na parapsicologia, em favor da crença na existência e sobrevivência da alma. Um homem que se tenha declarado defensor do materialismo a vida inteira, não cede facilmente diante de evidências que destroem seu sistema de crenças. Dentro do campo político, podemos considerar o comunismo, que tem criado uma utopia, um ideal que nunca chega a ser concretizado; porém bem pelo contrário, o sistema econômico do comunismo trabalha com menor eficiência do que o do capitalismo, que é desprezado pelos comunistas. E no campo religioso, encontramos teorias como aquela que diz que o mundo tem apenas seis mil anos de idade, embora tal idéia tenha contra si evidências esmagadoras em contrário, a menos que a palavra «ciência» perca o seu significado. No entanto, quando as pessoas querem manter seus sistemas dogmáticos de crenças, elas são capazes de ignorar tudo e qualquer coisa. As pessoas temem que aquilo que têm crido e defendido pode laborar em erro, contendo elementos de falsidade; e é por isso que, teimosa e arbitrariamente, continua a defender certas crenças, contra todas as provas em contrário. Toda essa atitude é forçada, importando em autocegueira. Algumas vezes, porém, os homens preferem o conforto mental à verdade, o que certamente opera nos casos de autodecepção. (EP F)

AUTODEFESA

Essa é a ação que consiste em defender a própria pessoa, as propriedades, os amigos e parentes de qualquer ataque físico ou mental. Sob a lei, esse é um direito universalmente reconhecido, embora Jesus tivesse aconselhado a moderação e a submissão (ver Mat. 5:38 ss.). A lei certamente reconhecia esse princípio, conforme fica subentendido nesse texto e em seu pano de fundo veterotestamentário. (Ver Êxo. 21:19-21; Lev. 24:19-21; Deu. 19:21). Todavia, sempre será melhor sofrer a injustiça do que ser injusto, mesmo quando os auto-interesses estão em pauta. Todavia, sempre foi considerado eticamente correto alguém tirar a vida de um seu atacante. Coletivamente, esse princípio aplica-se ao caso de comunidades ou nações que estejam sendo atacadas. A lei determina matar, e não ser morto; mas esse princípio envolve muitas questões morais, que só podem ser examinadas e solucionadas por cada pessoa em particular, pois, para uma questão complexa como essa, não há respostas fáceis e perfeitas. O caminho cristão consiste em enfrentar a violência com o amor (ver Rom. 12:17-21; I Cor. 13:4-7). Ver o artigo sobre *pacifismo*. (E EP)

AUTODEPENDÊNCIA

Essa expressão pode ser variegadamente aplicada, a saber:

1. *O homem deve sustentar a si mesmo*, não dependendo de outros nesse sentido. — Paulo ensinou que quem não quer trabalhar também não deve comer (ver II Tes. 3:10). O trecho de Efésios 4:28 ensina que o homem que era ladrão antes de converter-se, não mais deveria depender de sua desonestidade, como um parasita da sociedade; antes, deveria tornar-se autodependente, a ponto de até poder contribuir para a satisfação das necessidades alheias. O trecho de II Coríntios 12:14 mostra que os pais deveriam ser autodependentes, não esperando que seus filhos os sustentassem.

2. *Ralph Waldo Emerson* (ver o artigo a seu respeito) tinha um uso especial para essa expressão. A fim de combater o materialismo e o comercialismo, ele ensinava certa forma de autoconfiança. Um homem deve voltar-se para si mesmo, e não para o mundo. Deve procurar aprender os tesouros da mente e da alma, e, dessa maneira, libertar-se da louca busca deste mundo pelas posses materiais.

3. *Henry David Thoreau* tinha uma outra aplicação para essa expressão. Um homem encontra dentro de si mesmo as expressões de integridade e espontaneidade. Se vier a descobrir isso em si mesmo, dependendo dessas virtudes, tornar-se-á confiante em si mesmo, em vez de ser como um pedaço de rolha sacudido ao léu pelo mar da vida, perdido em meio a seus valores secundários e seus alvos mesquinhos. Neste último caso, seria um homem *dependente*. Temos aí a fé religiosa introspectiva, que inevitavelmente inclui alguma forma de misticismo, sem importar se sutil ou fraco.

4. *Em um sentido ético e geral*, um homem torna-se autoconfiante quando é capaz de viver de acordo com sua própria consciência e com seus princípios espirituais, ignorando as más influências deste mundo, de seus amigos e da sociedade em geral. (NTI P)

AUTODETERMINAÇÃO

Está em foco a determinação da pessoa em agir por si mesma, sem a influência de qualquer compulsão externa. A autodeterminação é um dos direitos do homem, conferidos por Deus, porquanto a alma individual deve ser respeitada. Sem isso, não poderia haver liberdade, porquanto a liberdade (ver o artigo a respeito) nunca pode ser apenas coletiva. Uma liberdade meramente coletiva degradaria a dignidade do indivíduo. Ver o artigo sobre o *Auto-amor*, quanto a comentários sobre essa questão. A exagerada autodeterminação resulta em excessos, porquanto abusa dos direitos alheios. (P)

AUTODISCIPLINA

Ver o artigo sobre **Autocontrole**.

AUTO-EXAME

Sócrates declarou que o homem que não perscruta a sua própria vida não merece viver. Ver o artigo sobre o autocontrole, que está envolvido no princípio do auto-exame. Uma distintiva característica humana é a capacidade da introspecção, da auto-avaliação. Essa atividade pode assumir várias formas:

1. O auto-exame pode abordar perguntas básicas, como: Quem sou? Por qual razão existo? Qual é o meu destino? O homem procura encontrar dentro de si mesmo razões existenciais. As religiões orientais advogavam o misticismo subjetivo, a tentativa de encontrar nas experiências místicas a razão para o próprio ser. Além disso, o próprio misticismo é subjetivo, porquanto seu alvo é o próprio eu, e não algum poder externo.

2. Essa atividade também inclui implicações éticas. Jesus ensinou que onde estiver o coração de um homem, ali estará também o seu tesouro (ver Mat. 6:21). Somos exortados a ver se reconhecemos que os nossos corações estão centralizados ou não nas

AUTO-INTERESSE — AUTONOMIA

realidades espirituais, e isso é uma espécie de auto-exame.

3. Essa expressão tem uma aplicação específica em I Coríntios 11:28. O crente deve examinar-se, a fim de descobrir pecados secretos e motivações malignas, como também injustiças praticadas contra o próximo, antes de avizinhar-se da mesa do Senhor. Tal exame deve determinar sua ação, se ele participará ou não do pão e do vinho, dependendo do estado de sua vida e de sua alma.

4. Uma outra aplicação bíblica desse princípio diz respeito à genuinidade ou falsidade de nossa profissão cristã (ver II Cor. 13:5). «Examinai-vos a vós mesmos se realmente estais na fé; provai-vos a vós mesmos». O auto-exame serve de estímulo à fé e à vida santa (ver Heb. 12:1,2; I Ped. 2:21 ss).

5. Aplicação moral dessa idéia, por parte de Sócrates. Nossa vida deveria ser auto-examinada com o propósito de nos disciplinarmos. A vida sem disciplina moral não é digna de ser vivida. (B EP H MM NTI)

AUTO-INTERESSE

Trata-se de um outro termo para indicar o egoísmo (ver o artigo a respeito).

1. Hobbes (ver o artigo a seu respeito) pensava que o auto-interesse é o único motivo verdadeiro para a ação moral.

2. Shaftesbury (ver o artigo a seu respeito) pensava no auto-interesse como um dentre dois motivos básicos. O outro motivo seria o interesse social. O interesse social, na realidade, pode ser uma forma de auto-interesse quando é defendido meramente para benefício do próprio indivíduo. Algumas vezes, porém, o auto-interesse pode ser verdadeiramente altruísta, porque um homem é capaz de demonstrar interesse e amor ao próximo.

3. Adam Smith (ver o artigo a seu respeito) supunha que o indivíduo que segue os seus próprios interesses, ainda assim pode contribuir para a vida comunitária.

4. Holbach (ver o artigo a seu respeito) concordava com Hobbes. A única preocupação real do homem é consigo mesmo, e esse interesse sempre é regulamentado pelo princípio da dor-prazer. Ver o artigo sobre o *hedonismo*.

5. Stirner (ver o artigo a seu respeito) identificava o egoísmo com a descoberta e cumprimento da natureza do próprio indivíduo.

6. Acima de tudo isso resplandece a lei do amor, a prova da espiritualidade, que pode e deve ser a principal motivação do crente (ver I João 4:6). (NTI P)

AUTOLIMITAÇÃO

Consideremos dois pontos a esse respeito:

1. Essa expressão é aplicada a Cristo, considerado em Sua humilhação (ver o artigo a respeito), conforme se aprende em Filipenses 2:6,7. A doutrina é que o Logos, chamado Cristo, em Sua missão terrena e como o Messias dos judeus, propositai e voluntariamente limitou a Si mesmo, despindo-se de vários de Seus atributos divinos, a fim de que pudesse tornar-se carne e compartilhar da humanidade, posto que sem pecado. Isso teve por propósito elevar os remidos a uma autêntica identificação com Ele, tanto quanto à natureza como quanto às limitações. O Espírito torna-se tudo em todos. O outro propósito foi o de dar ao homem o meio para chegar a participar da imagem (ver Rom. 8:29) e da natureza do próprio Logos (ver II Ped. 1:4), o que envolve o mais exaltado conceito que é ensinado no evangelho.

2. Essa expressão aplica-se eticamente àquelas pessoas que, a fim de agradar e servir a seus semelhantes, limitam-se quanto aos seus legítimos desejos e privilégios. (E NTI)

AUTONEGAÇÃO

Jesus ensinou esse princípio ao declarar: «Se alguém quer vir após mim, a si mesmo se negue, tome a sua cruz e siga-me» (Mat. 16:24). Com isso, Ele quis dizer que mais importa alguém encontrar realização espiritual no discipulado cristão do que promover seus interesses egoístas. O evangelho também ensina que o homem que tem sua realização no discipulado cristão, ao mesmo tempo obtém a mais elevada auto-realização possível, — porquanto estará promovendo os interesses de sua alma eterna. A auto-realização egoísta é um ludíbrio que tem apanhado em suas teias a vasta maioria dos seres humanos. O verdadeiro discipulado cristão sempre consiste na autonegação, porquanto a natureza carnal não se interessa por alvos espirituais. Mas o verdadeiro discipulado cristão, segundo o sentido espiritual, é uma questão egoísta, pois promove os mais elevados interesses da pessoa. Jesus deixou-nos o exemplo de autonegação, conforme lemos em Filipenses 2:6,7. Ele deixou de lado Sua glória e Seu poder, a fim de cumprir, em dependência ao Pai, e em Sua natureza humana, a missão de que fora encarregado. (Ver o artigo sobre a *humilhação de Cristo*).

Paulo atingiu um tal estado de autonegação que pôde dizer: «...já não sou eu quem vive, mas Cristo vive em mim...» (Gál. 2:20).

Cristo é o alvo do «eu» ideal e mais elevado. Paulo exortava os crentes a sacrificarem todos os desejos e atividades inferiores, tornando-se *sacrifícios vivos* (ver Rom. 12:1,2). Ao perder o mundo, o crente ganha o eterno bem-estar de sua própria alma (ver Mar. 8:36,37). Os crentes sinceros exprimem a autonegação de várias maneiras. Um jovem casal de crentes que se dirige ao campo missionário é possuído por um desejo e por uma motivação que transcendem ao próprio «eu». Mas, se esse mesmo casal, uma vez chegado ao campo missionário, passar a gastar o seu salário a fim de manter um alto estilo de vida, que se aproxime dos luxos de que desfrutavam em sua terra, já terá perdido boa parte de sua original alta motivação. Os cristãos têm formado comunidades e ordens religiosas com o intuito de negarem coletivamente o próprio «eu» e ignorarem as atrações deste mundo. O desejo de obter a santidade tem levado alguns a se internarem em mosteiros. Quando um homem recebe de Cristo a ordem de seguir pela vereda espiritual, na verdade isso é um convite para que faça morrer o seu egoísmo. No entanto, essa abnegação redunda na expressão de uma mais elevada forma de vida, no caso daqueles que atendem ao convite de todo o coração. Esse princípio tem manifestado aspectos monásticos, ascéticos, individuais e comunitários. Alguns têm caído em excessos, mas outros têm produzido o mais belo exemplo de nobreza espiritual de que se tem notícia. (E H IB NTI)

AUTONOMIA

No grego, **autos**, «ele mesmo», e **nomos**, «lei». Conseqüentemente, aquilo que é lei por si mesmo, ou é sua própria lei.

1. *Politicamente.* Poder ou direito de autogoverno, da parte de uma cidade, estado ou nação.

2. *Kant.* Ele ensinava que a vontade do homem é autônoma quando age por seu próprio impulso. A vontade é chamada de *heterônoma*, quando aceita seus princípios da parte de alguma força ou pessoa exterior. Aparentemente, foi Kant quem introduziu essa palavra na filosofia. A vontade é sua própria legisladora. Porém, princípios éticos válidos são aqueles que atingem consenso universal. Seu axioma moral consistia na postulação da pergunta: «Estou disposto a fazer com que minhas ações, alicerçadas em minha vontade, sejam uma proposição universal, para que homens de todos os lugares a sigam?» Se essa pergunta fosse respondida negativamente, então poder-se-ia supor que o princípio ético em foco envolveria algum defeito. A proposição universal é denominada de *imperativo categórico* (ver o artigo a respeito).

De acordo com esse princípio, a ética é autônoma, com raízes na boa vontade dos homens, que cumprem seus deveres por amor ao dever. Destarte, o homem parece ser uma lei para si mesmo. Porém, é duvidoso que Kant tivesse proposto essa teoria sem pensar que a vontade humana tem uma *afinidade* natural com a vontade divina; e assim, embora agindo por si mesma, em um sentido mais profundo, fá-lo dependendo da vontade divina.

3. *No existencialismo.* Existência e ação autêntica só podem ser encontradas na absoluta liberdade de escolha. No existencialismo ateu, é impossível encontrar-se uma base divina para a vontade humana interna, pelo que, nesse caso, a autonomia leva a uma moralidade individualista. O homem estaria absolutamente preso à situação humana finita, e o certo e o errado seriam determinados pela tentativa e erro, com base em absoluta liberdade de escolha. Porém, isso faz a ética tornar-se arbitrária, por estar envolvida em uma relatividade radical. Os homens nunca concordariam quanto aos ditames da liberdade absoluta. De fato, só chegariam à conclusão de que cada indivíduo segue suas próprias decisões.

Kant pensava que somente os atos autônomos são moralmente bons; mas também dizia que os homens nunca chegarão a qualquer conclusão acerca de quais atos podem tornar-se uma lei universal. Tillich (ver o artigo) distinguia entre a ética autônoma, a ética heterônoma e a ética teônoma (regras estabelecidas por Deus). Ver os artigos sobre esses termos. Tillich recomendava a ética teônoma. A maioria das religiões, pelo menos teoricamente, alicerçam-se sobre esse conceito, visto que aceitam que Deus é a origem de suas normas, usualmente contidas em livros sagrados. (E H)

AUTOPISTA

Vem do grego, com o sentido de «fé auto-evidente». Refere-se à reivindicação feita por alguns teólogos, mormente Karl Barth, de que a luz da fé é tão brilhante que nenhuma força é capaz de debilitá-la, pois nem mesmo requer corroboração. Ademais, trata-se de um dom de Deus, implantado no indivíduo, de tal modo que se o homem a possui, é capaz de arrastar qualquer coisa, não havendo espaço para dúvidas quanto à verdade. A fé, tal como a revelação, é um dom de Deus. Por si mesmo, em face de suas capacidades naturais, o homem não pode atingir a fé. A fé brota miraculosamente no homem; mas, uma vez brotada, não mais pode ser negada. Há corroborações bíblicas para essa idéia, como o conceito joanino de Cristo, como a Luz do mundo, o qual ilumina a todos os homens, sem a qual os homens permanecem nas trevas. O trecho de Efé.2:8 também é assim interpretado por alguns. Esse conceito concorda com o *calvinismo* (ver o artigo), segundo o qual qualquer impulso espiritual digno do nome obrigatoriamente vem de Deus. (C)

AUTOPRESERVAÇÃO

Biologicamente falando, trata-se do esforço instintivo de cada organismo para conservar a sua própria existência. Essa tendência instintiva tem-se tornado a base das *doutrinas políticas* que ensinam que há um direito natural à vida. Isso inclui a autodefesa contra ataques pessoais, da parte do estado ou da comunidade. No campo da *ética*, a expressão pode significar a preservação do próprio «eu», por motivos de puro auto-interesse (ver o artigo), ou então tendo em mira o bem da comunidade, ou altruísmo (ver o artigo). Alguns estudiosos fazem da autopreservação o primeiro princípio da ética, supondo que essa deva ser a regra suprema de nossa conduta. Ver o artigo sobre o auto-amor. Virtualmente todas as filosofias e religiões reconhecem que esse direito faz parte inerente da lei. Contudo, há também a lei do amor, que deveria caracterizar o homem espiritual. Algumas vezes, o sacrifício de si mesmo por alguma outra pessoa, pela comunidade ou pela nação é uma lei superior, maior do que a lei da autopreservação. Jesus tornou-se o modelo supremo disso quando deu a Sua vida pelos Seus amigos (ver João 15:13), incluindo os Seus próprios inimigos (ver Rom. 5:8). Uma perversão da autopreservação dá-se quando a força torna-se o único direito, ou seja, quando o que é certo ou errado depende exclusivamente do argumento da força. Nesse caso, a preservação da vida (quem deveria viver e quem deveria perecer) torna-se apenas uma expressão do uso ímpio e egoísta da força. Jamais deveríamos ficar impressionados por aqueles sistemas políticos e por aqueles indivíduos que matam a fim de promover alegadas causas justas. O comunismo e o terrorismo são excelentes exemplos de tal perversão.

Visto que o indivíduo é sem igual no mundo, e pode ter um destino útil sem par, é importante que ele procure preservar-se (ver as notas sobre o *novo nome*, em Apo. 2:17, no NTI). A missão de Cristo demonstra a dignidade e a importância do indivíduo. (E NTI)

Autor Ver depois de **Auto-Suficiência**.

AUTO-REALIZAÇÃO

1. Nos escritos de *Aristóteles*, a virtude de um homem é a sua função. Essa função tanto é pessoal quanto social. O indivíduo deveria desenvolver-se ao máximo, por todos os meios possíveis, primeiramente para tornar-se uma pessoa digna em si mesma; e, em segundo lugar, para tornar-se útil à sociedade, exercendo ali a sua função especial. Esse seria o homem virtuoso, porquanto a ética pessoal jamais pode ser separada da ética social.

2. Para *T. H. Green*, o maior e o mais desejável anelo que um homem pode ter é o da auto-realização. Quanto melhor esse alvo puder ser atingido, maior será a felicidade do indivíduo. E a felicidade seria o alvo de toda a existência humana. Ver o artigo sobre o *eudemonismo*.

3. *F. H. Bradley, J. Seth* e *J. H. Muirhead* defendiam essa idéia geral de Green. A auto-realização, para eles, é um processo dinâmico em que as capacidades pessoais tornam-se reais e se organizam. Envolveria tanto a integração de todas as qualidades

AUTO-RELACIONADO — AUTORIDADE

pessoais quanto a integração do indivíduo na sociedade, de acordo com os moldes aristotélicos. Dessa maneira concretizar-se-ia a felicidade.

4. *O ponto de vista da Bíblia.* Quando afirmamos que Cristo veio trazer a salvação aos pecadores, sempre estamos falando sobre a importância da **auto-realização,** porque a salvação é uma questão tanto individual quanto comunitária. Deus amou ao mundo e ao indivíduo. Uma única alma vale mais do que todo o universo físico inteiro (ver Mar. 8:35 ss). Do ponto de vista teológico, envolvido na auto-realização acha-se a questão da morte da natureza antiga, bem como o novo nascimento do indivíduo. Pois enquanto não ocorrer essa morte-ressurreição, não poderão concretizar-se as potencialidades do indivíduo (ver João 3:3). A fé cristã, portanto, assume uma postura pessimista em relação à potencialidade humana, à parte das operações do Espírito de Deus. Porém, uma vez que se manifestem essas operações, a participação na natureza divina tornar-se-á visível no horizonte (ver II Ped. 1:4). E essa é uma fantástica realização, por não ser apenas moral, mas também real, segundo a qual os remidos participarão da natureza metafísica de Deus, ainda que em proporções finitas. O alvo é eterno, visto que a glorificação é um processo eterno, e não um único acontecimento, ocorrido por ocasião da morte física (ver II Cor. 3:18). O trecho de Apocalipse 2:17, que ensina o conceito de *novo nome* (ver o artigo a respeito), esclarece como cada ser humano é um ser sem igual, completo com um destino sem-par para cada indivíduo.

Do ponto de vista prático. Não é apenas dever, mas também privilégio de cada crente buscar o máximo desenvolvimento de seu próprio «eu» e a realização máxima, naquilo que ele faz. Por essa razão é que temos escolas, ensino secular e religioso, livros, empregos e instituições. Um homem deveria buscar a melhor educação que lhe é possível, aplicando todos os meios para obter o máximo de si mesmo. Esse cultivo envolve o próprio indivíduo, a sua família, a sua comunidade, a sua nação, tendo em vista a glória de Deus. O homem altruísta também procurará investir nas vidas de seus semelhantes, a fim de que possa prestar ajuda no desenvolvimento deles. (E P)

AUTO-RELACIONADO

Ver o artigo sobre o **auto-interesse,** que é similar à idéia que temos aqui. A ação que volta a atenção para si mesmo deriva-se da liberdade inerente do indivíduo (ver o artigo sobre a liberdade). O homem deveria ser capaz de agir segundo o princípio da *liberdade,* para o seu próprio interesse ou para o interesse de outrem, conforme o caso. Essa expressão de liberdade só deveria ser restringida quando aquilo que um homem faz é prejudicial à comunidade. Até mesmo os ditadores benevolentes (se é que eles realmente existem) são malignos, porquanto furtam os homens de sua liberdade, que é uma de nossas mais preciosas possessões. (F)

AUTO-RENDIÇÃO Ver **Autonegação.**

AUTO-SUFICIÊNCIA

Essa expressão envolve, essencialmente, a idéia de *autodependência* (ver o artigo a respeito). Em adição a isso, temos a declaração de Paulo de que ele sabia como desfrutar da abundância e da escassez de bens materiais (ver Fil. 4:12), mostrando que seu bom equilíbrio psicológico, enquanto enfrentava as vicissitudes da vida, não dependia das circunstâncias externas, mas do senso interno de paz e confiança, que já são qualidades espirituais.

AUTOR Ver também: **Salvação, Autor da.**

Tradução de várias palavras gregas. 1. *Archegos,* traduzida por líder, príncipe, supervisor e *autor,* no sentido de originador ou iniciador (ver Atos 3:15 e 5:31), ou por capitão ou pioneiro (ver Heb. 2:10 e 12:2). Esta última referência reveste-se de interesse, porquanto revela que Jesus, em Sua missão terrena, fez muito mais do que cumprir algum propósito espiritual. Ele tornou-se o Pioneiro do caminho pelo qual os Seus irmãos precisam seguir, a fim de alcançarem a mesma glória que Ele alcançou. Eles são Seus irmãos, compartilhando com Ele da natureza da família divina (ver II Ped. 1:4). Ele também é o *originador* da fé envolvida nessa inquirição, a fonte da vida que buscamos (ver João 14:6; Rom. 8:29 e II Cor. 3:18). 2. *Aitios* (ver Luc. 23:4,14,22; Atos 19:40; Heb. 5:9). Quanto a esta última referência, o seu sentido exato é debatível. O sentido básico é *causa,* pelo que «origem» transmite um bom sentido. Em Atos 3:15, vemos que Cristo é a origem de nossa vida eterna, o qual cumpriu o ideal messiânico do capítulo cinqüenta e três de Isaías. Outro tanto se dá na declaração de Hebreus 5:9. Ele é a causa originária de nossa eterna salvação. Contudo, o uso da palavra «autor», conforme se vê ali em nossa versão portuguesa e em outras traduções, não contradiz o sentido. Ver o NTI quanto a notas expositivas completas em Hebreus 5:9. (A I IB NTI)

AUTORIDADE

Definição. O termo «autoridade» vem do latim, *auctoritas,* derivada de auctor, «causa», «patrocinador», «promotor», «fiador». *Auctoritas* era o termo legal romano para indicar a fiança em uma transação, a responsabilidade por um menor de idade, ou o peso de uma opinião. O senado tinha uma autoridade que não podia ser ignorada. A autoridade *pessoal* deriva-se do reconhecimento de que alguém sabe e tem realizações em um campo específico. Autoridade *oficial* é aquela dada a uma pessoa em razão de uma função ou poder que lhe tenha sido conferido por outros, de acordo com a lei, com os costumes ou com outras convenções sociais. Os *objetos* (como um livro) podem tornar-se autoritários pelo concenso de muitos. — Ou podemos usar os termos autoridade *externa* ou autoridade *interna.* A externa é aquela conferida a uma pessoa que se tornou oficial, nomeada por outros, como um governador, um policial, um professor, etc. A interna é aquela residente em um argumento convincente ou em um importante exemplo ou em uma experiência moral ou espiritual.

Esboço

1. Autoridade da Bíblia
2. Autoridade Pós-apostólica
3. A Reforma
4. Problemas Quanto à Autoridade da Bíblia
5. Conceito Básico Emergente de Autoridade
6. Hierarquia de Autoridades
7. Autoridade de Jesus no Novo Testamento
8. O Problema da Continuação de Autoridade

1. Autoridade da Bíblia. Sua autoridade é reconhecidamente interna. A Bíblia autentica-se a si mesma. Mas, na medida em que contém provas históricas, incluindo os milagres que comprovavam a intervenção divina, ela é externamente autenticada. O poder de seus ensinamentos envolve uma autoridade

AUTORIDADE

interna. As realidades históricas sobre as quais ela se alicerça (como a vida de Cristo, as Suas palavras, ressurreição, etc.) lhe conferem uma autoridade externa ou oficial. O consenso dos crentes, através dos séculos, em favor da autoridade da Bíblia, tornou-se outro fator de autoridade externa. As declarações dos pais da Igreja e dos concílios, que resultaram na canonização formal da Bíblia, formam uma autoridade oficial e externa.

Sinais de autoridade no Novo Testamento: Cristo tinha autoridade para perdoar pecados (Luc. 5:24), para expelir demônios (Mar. 6:7), para conferir a filiação divina (João 1:12), e Suas obras eram autoritárias (Mat. 7:29). A origem da autoridade é Deus, que enviou o Filho (João 3:17; 4:34; 5:23; 6:29, etc.). Para os primitivos discípulos, a ressurreição de Jesus foi a mais potente autenticação daquilo que Jesus dissera e fizera, e por conseguinte, do que estava escrito acerca dEle, quanto à Sua pessoa e autoridade sobre os homens. Ver o artigo sobre a *ressurreição*. Assim sendo, Jesus comissionou a outros (dando-lhes autoridade), para levarem avante a Sua missão (Mat. 28:18 ss), porquanto «toda autoridade» Lhe fora dada, a fim de que, por Sua vez, Ele desse dessa autoridade a outros, para que O representassem.

Os Apóstolos possuíram extraordinária autoridade, conforme transparece, claramente, — no livro de Atos (ver Atos 5:1 ss. quanto a um notável exemplo disso; ver também Atos 15, o primeiro concílio da Igreja, que envolveu os apóstolos). Os trechos de João 20:21,22 e Mat. 16:17 provêem-nos textos que provam a autoridade dos apóstolos. Ademais, o próprio Novo Testamento é essencialmente um produto dos apóstolos e seus discípulos imediatos, servindo de declaração autoritária sobre quem era Jesus e qual o significado de Sua vida para nós outros.

2. Autoridade pós-apostólica. A organização da Igreja, com seus anciãos ou bispos e diáconos, foi uma tentativa de preencher o lugar deixado vago pelo desaparecimento das testemunhas oculares. Como essa vaga deve ser preenchida, tem sido uma questão crítica desde os primeiros tempos. A autoridade da Bíblia tem sido reputada válida para a maioria dos cristãos, mas os oficiais eclesiásticos tornaram-se novas autoridades oficiais. Por volta do século IV D.C., os escritores cristãos já falavam sobre os «pais» da Igreja, cuja autoridade era respeitada após a dos apóstolos. Também havia os concílios eclesiásticos, que exprimiam as opiniões da hierarquia religiosa; e esses pronunciamentos tornaram-se uma outra autoridade — a autoridade da comunidade cristã. Com o advento de Constantino (300 D.C. e depois), o bispo de Roma adquiriu maior prestígio que os demais bispos, e assim surgiu o ofício papal. Sua autoridade tornou-se suprema, visto que foi criada a doutrina que o papa é o vigário ou substituto de Cristo. Desenvolveu-se então a elaborada lei canônica, de tal modo que, pelos fins da Idade Média, a Igreja contava com o apoio de um vasto e variegado sistema de autoridades externas.

A doutrina da *sucessão apostólica* (ver o artigo) tornou-se um aspecto importante da autoridade, segundo encarada por muitos grupos cristãos, tanto do Oriente quanto do Ocidente. Estalaram controvérsias sobre até que ponto o Novo Testamento dá apoio a essa doutrina. Mas, segundo o ponto de vista das igrejas latina e oriental, é perfeitamente legítimo haver outras autoridades (que evoluíram na Igreja), em adição às Escrituras, pois a doutrina de que *só* as Escrituras são autoritativas repousa sobre um dogma que precisou de longo tempo para desenvolver-se. O artigo aludido presta informações mais detalhadas sobre essa questão.

3. A Reforma. Por essa altura, a ênfase foi transferida para o indivíduo e sua responsabilidade pessoal perante Deus, - paralelamente à observação de que a Igreja havia acumulado muitíssima bagagem sobre o que o Novo Testamento nada diz. E parte dessa bagagem é decididamente contrária aos princípios neotestamentários. Os pronunciamentos dos pais, concílios e papas, apesar de respeitados por certos grupos protestantes, seriam apenas históricos e sugestivos, mas não obrigatórios; -e algumas vezes laboram mesmo em erro grave. Se há uma autoridade interna, essa depende da consciência do indivíduo, governada e dirigida por considerações escriturísticas. Naturalmente, isso levou à divisão na Igreja, pois as interpretações da Bíblia variam, não tendo ainda surgido uma denominação que siga por inteiro o Novo Testamento. E ainda que aparecesse um grupo cristão que defendesse a inteira verdade bíblica, nem por isso seria uma igreja perfeita.

4. Problemas quanto à autoridade da Bíblia. 1. Não solucionamos todos os problemas meramente dizendo «às Escrituras somente». Em primeiro lugar, porque, *de fato*, — o que é autoritário nesse caso é a «interpretação bíblica da minha igreja». Há muitas denominações protestantes que dizem a mesma coisa, mas têm doutrinas bastante díspares. As denominações, em sua arrogância, negam essa declaração, mas sua veracidade transparece de qualquer modo. 2. O Verbo (ou voz) de Deus é algo maior do que os livros que vieram a ser conhecidos como a Bíblia. A Bíblia é um registro escrito de certos aspectos da Palavra de Deus. Se não fosse assim, teríamos de afirmar que tudo quanto Deus sabe, toda a Sua verdade, está contida em um livro, o que é manifestamente absurdo. A Bíblia é a regra da verdade revelada, o padrão contra o qual toda verdade precisa ser cotejada. 3. Assim, apesar de «não haver autoridade senão a que procede de Deus» (ver Rom. 13:1), fica em aberto o debate acerca de onde e de quais maneiras, e através de quais agentes, Ele distribui essa autoridade. 4. Os pais gregos tinham a certeza que uma melhor filosofia grega, como a de Platão, servia de mestre escola para conduzir os pagãos a Cristo, mais ou menos como o AT fazia para com os judeus. Se essa afirmativa encerra uma verdade, se Deus atuou de outros modos para atingir outros povos, então acaba de ser adicionada uma outra autoridade, reconhecida por alguns importantes indivíduos e movimentos até mesmo dentro da Igreja antiga. 5. Alguns teólogos acreditam que a autoridade de Deus manifesta-se mormente na pessoa e missão do *Logos*, e que Ele influencia religiões não-cristãs, além de atuar na religião cristã. Nesse caso, o Logos não se limitaria somente às Escrituras, ou à Igreja cristã, ou à autoridade dos papas e dos bispos. Naturalmente, todos esses pontos de vista são intensamente debatidos. A verdade só emerge quando nos dispomos a ouvir o debate para verificarmos se alguém não está exprimindo idéias mais de acordo com a verdade, mesmo que isso não represente a minha teologia sistemática. 6. A Igreja oriental aceitava as Escrituras, os pais da Igreja e os concílios como autoridades essenciais. A Igreja ocidental acrescentou a autoridade do papa, guindando-a à posição de autoridade suprema. 7. Além disso, há a autoridade de outras disciplinas, de natureza não-religiosa, como a autoridade científica. Imaginemos, por exemplo, que a ciência finalmente possa demonstrar, por meios empíricos, a existência da alma. Muito nos alegrará em ter essa confirmação de uma doutrina preciosa. Devemos estar dispostos a

AUTORIDADE

admitir que certas verdades, ou aspectos da verdade, podem ser-nos outorgados, podendo aprimorar nossa teologia, mesmo que os subsídios provenham de fontes de natureza inteiramente extrabíblicas. Assim, apesar desse acréscimo nunca servir de base central para a fé, verdades vitais seriam adicionadas, não obstante, por autoridades secundárias. Isso exerceria certa influência sobre minha maneira de pensar e agir, mesmo que não se comparasse, em grau de importância, com as autoridades estritamente religiosas.

5. Conceito básico emergente de autoridade. Neste artigo, temos considerado a autoridade vinculada à fé e à prática religiosas. Como é óbvio, há muitos outros tipos de autoridade. No tocante à autoridade que governa minha inquirição espiritual, afirmo que não posso honestamente crer ou declarar que somente *uma* autoridade pode ser suficiente. Não creio que Deus revela a si mesmo apenas de uma maneira, em um único lugar, em apenas uma denominação, ou em qualquer filosofia ou religião isolada. Conseqüentemente, concluo que deve haver uma *hierarquia* de autoridades, maiores e menores, cada qual contribuindo com algo para minha inquirição. Outrossim, tenho verificado que aqueles que só aceitam uma autoridade, fazem-no por terem aceito um *dogma* que se respalda sobre essa *crença*. Por exemplo, em porção alguma da Bíblia é declarado que as Escrituras são a única voz (ou Palavra) de Deus. Portanto, se eu ignorar a filosofia que se estriba somente em uma fonte de autoridade, estarei apenas ignorando um dogma humano, e não qualquer princípio divino. Posso ter grande respeito por qualquer autoridade, sem transformá-la em um ídolo que substitua a Palavra (ou voz) de Deus, no sentido mais *lato*, do que o sentido literário é *um aspecto*.

6. Hierarquia de autoridades. A lista que preparei abaixo é apenas tentativa e experimental. Não procura declarar *a* verdade sobre a questão da autoridade. Apenas procura aproximar-se do assunto de forma razoável.

a. As *Escrituras*, quando honestamente interpretadas, com mente aberta e sem servidão aos dogmas de qualquer denominação. Busco a verdade, e não um lugar seguro e confortável, dentro de alguma organização religiosa. Disponho-me a tomar por empréstimo idéias de outras denominações, quando essas idéias me parecem razoáveis, dotadas de foros da verdade. Respeitarei, honrarei e utilizarei as Escrituras por causa das verdades fundamentais ali contidas; mas não farei delas, e nem de qualquer outro livro, um ídolo. Usualmente é a isso que a Bíblia é reduzida, pois as Escrituras são vistas através dos olhos do sistema doutrinário de alguma denominação ou sistema teológico. O sistema termina sendo mais respeitado que a própria Bíblia, e esta, por sua vez, sempre encerra conceitos e ensinos que entram em choque com os sistemas teológicos, incompletos e preconceituosos como são. As denominações negam isso, mas a verdade não pode ser escondida.

b. As *interpretações dos pais e dos concílios*, o corpo de doutrinas que nos foi legado. Embora haja muitas contradições nesse material, disponho-me a selecionar e pensar por mim mesmo, para ver quais interpretações são aproveitáveis.

c. As *interpretações das várias denominações*, que vieram a ser o que são por terem seguido alguma filosofia da fé. Espero poder encontrar subsídios valiosos em todas as denominações, escapando assim da arrogância do denominacionalismo, não aderindo rigidamente a qualquer grupo isolado.

d. Reconheço que o *Logos* pode manifestar-se e realmente o faz através de homens antigos e modernos, não pertencentes à Igreja cristã, e que deles posso aprender lições valiosas, mesmo que não os considere minha principal fonte de conhecimento. As *sementes do Logos* foram plantadas em filosofias e religiões fora da fé cristã. O Logos é «...a luz verdadeira, que ilumina a todo o homem que vem ao mundo» (João 1:9). Elas podem contribuir com algo de valioso, capaz de fazer-me avançar na inquirição espiritual. Confio que Deus unirá todos esses indivíduos dignos na unidade que haverá em torno de Cristo, algum tempo no futuro, posto que distante, porque nisso está envolvido *o mistério da vontade de Deus* (Efé. 1:10; ver notas a respeito no NTI). Alguns deles chegaram a falar de Cristo, embora usando uma terminologia não-cristã.

e. Reconheço que outras disciplinas, como a *ciência*, em seus diversos segmentos, também podem contribuir para minha inquirição. Só há uma verdade, a verdade de Deus. O Universo físico, a natureza investigada pela ciência, são vestígios de Deus. Na pesquisa científica, os homens pensam os pensamentos de Deus após Ele. Aprendemos sobre Deus por meio da natureza, segundo somos informados em Rom. 1. A ciência poderá vir a demonstrar, finalmente, a sobrevivência da alma ante a morte biológica, e através da parapsicologia e dos estudos de experiências de quase-morte (ver o artigo a respeito), poderá dizer-nos algo sobre a natureza espiritual do homem, sugerindo maneiras pelas quais ela deve ser cultivada.

Usos gerais do termo autoridade (no grego, *exousia*), no *N.T.*:

1. A liberdade de escolha, o direito de agir (I Cor. 7:37; 8:9; Atos 5:4).

2. A capacidade, a aptidão ou o poder de fazer algo, da parte do homem ou de Deus (Mar. 1:22; Atos 8:19; Apo. 9:19; 11:6).

3. Autoridade, poder, comissão (Atos 26:12; Mar. 11:28,29,33; Luc. 20:2,8; Apo. 2:26; 11:6; João 1:12).

4. Poder governante, poder oficial (Mat. 8:9; Apo. 17:12 s.).

5. O domínio no qual o poder é exercido (Luc. 4:6; Col. 1:13).

6. Os que estão investidos de autoridade, o governo (Luc. 12:11; Rom. 13:1,2).

7. Poderes espirituais (Efé. 1:21; Col. 2:10; I Ped. 3:22).

8. Os meios de exercício do poder, ou os símbolos de autoridade (I Cor. 1:10). (A B C E H NTI R) Quanto a idéias concernentes à *inspiração* das Escrituras, ver o artigo sobre o assunto. Quanto à autoridade dos *governantes civis*, ver Rom. 13:1 ss., no NTI.

7. Autoridade de Jesus no Novo Testamento

Atos 4:7: ...*pondo-os no meio deles, perguntaram: Com que poder ou em nome de quem fizestes vós isto?*

As palavras *fizestes isto* dizem respeito a toda a conduta recente dos apóstolos, em que o coxo de nascença foi curado e o nome de Jesus, o Cristo, foi anunciado, o que provocou não pequena comoção popular no pórtico de Salomão, dentro dos recintos do templo de Jerusalém. Durante os julgamentos, entre os judeus, os acusados e as testemunhas de defesa e de acusação se mantinham de pé, enquanto os juízes se assentavam em volta deles, formando um semicírculo.

Um Antigo Truque

1. Apresente suas credenciais! dizem eles. Têm suas escolas e seus métodos de credenciamento. Você já foi

aprovado por eles? Em caso contrário, você não poderá ser aprovado por Deus. Mas o argumento só parece convincente para eles mesmos.

2. O credenciamento dado pelo Espírito é o único que nos deveria importar. João Batista era um ministro aprovado por Deus. Sua vida demonstrou isso, embora não estivessem os seus padrões em consonância com os padrões das autoridades religiosas de seus dias.

3. Jesus teve a vida mais poderosa que alguém já viveu, e, no entanto, as autoridades de seus dias não aceitaram nem a ele mesmo e nem a seu ministério. (Ver João 20:31 no NTI quanto à «polêmica cristã» em prol do caráter messiânico de Jesus).

4. É incrível que tenham surgido seitas que reivindicam uma autoridade exclusiva para si mesmas, mesmo quando não possuem qualquer base histórica na igreja cristã.

5. As igrejas oficiais não reconhecem as credenciais de outras denominações ou indivíduos, e consideram que seus próprios ministros são os únicos que têm autoridade de batizar, distribuir a comunhão, etc. Mas tudo não passa de frutos amargos do orgulho humano.

6. Ver estas referências quanto a notas no NTI sobre a questão da «autoridade»: Mat. 21:23; João 2:18 e 5:19-47. E sobre a «autoridade da igreja», ver Mat. 16:17.

Com que poder, ou em nome de quem? É como se tivessem perguntado: Pelo poder de Deus, ou pelo poder de Satanás? pela medicina, ou pelas artes mágicas? As autoridades religiosas já sabiam que isso tinha sido feito em nome de Jesus; mas essa pergunta foi feita como introdução formal ao processo. «Parece-nos que o concílio estava convicto de que o coxo fora miraculosamente curado; porém, é muito provável que acreditassem que o feito resultara das artes mágicas; e também por associação com os espíritos familiares (espiritismo), por meio de encantamentos e outras coisas ilegais». (Adam Clarke *in loc.*).

Sabemos, alicerçados na história daquela época, que falsos profetas, feiticeiras famosas, bruxos e outros elementos deletérios da sociedade eram conduzidos à presença do sinédrio para tais julgamentos como o deste episódio, os quais eram declarados culpados ou inocentes, de conformidade com as evidências. Provavelmente as autoridades eclesiásticas dos judeus tinham a esperança de condenar os apóstolos de conformidade com as regulamentações exaradas em Deut. 13:1-10, que impunha a pena de morte por apedrejamento a todos quantos exercessem a prática das artes ocultas, não apelando para o poder do único Deus de Israel.

8. O Problema da Continuação da Autoridade

1. Após a destruição de Jerusalém, e a autoridade por ela representada, no sinédrio judaico, foi necessário que a igreja cristã estabelecesse uma nova autoridade. Não houve uma só resposta imediata para essa necessidade, e, sim, uma espécie de crescimento da solução. Pedro exercia grande autoridade em alguns círculos, conforme fica demonstrado pelas notas de Mat. 16:16-20 no NTI.

2. Porém, a autoridade conferida a Pedro mais tarde passou a ser compartilhada pelos demais apóstolos, segundo se vê em João 20:19-23 (ver as notas no NTI quanto a explicações).

3. Entretanto, a autoridade entra em vigor com mais poder quando se alicerça sobre uma larga base; portanto, a Igreja, por si mesma (mediante o voto democrático), tornou-se uma autoridade, substituindo os sinédrios locais. (Ver Mat. 18:15-18 quanto a isso).

4. A democracia é uma base excelente para a autoridade, porquanto promove a vontade da maioria, e assim deve ser aceitável para a maioria. Portanto, há certa sabedoria na democracia. (AL DE HA IB LAN MC NTI)

AUZÃO

No hebraico, **possessão deles**. Era filho de Asur, descendente de Juá, pai ou fundador de Tecoa (ver I Crô. 4:6). (S)

AUZATE

No hebraico, **possessão**. Era amigo de Abimeleque II, de Gerar, que cuidou dele em sua visita a Isaque (ver Gên. 26:26). No seu caso encontramos a primeira instância daquela **personagem não-oficial** mas muito importante nas antigas cortes orientais, chamada *amigo* ou *favorito* do rei. No Brasil, Dom Pedro I teve o seu Cualaça, seu favorito. Provavelmente ele agia como conselheiro do rei. Jerônimo, seguido por vários intérpretes, pensava que Auzate era nome de um grupo de amigos ou conselheiros, e não de um indivíduo isolado. (DE S UN)

AVA

No hebraico significa **ruína** (ver II Reis 17:24; 18:34; 19:13 e Isa. 37:13). Era a capital de um pequeno estado monárquico, conquistado pelos assírios, e de onde o rei Salmaneser enviou colonos para a Samaria. Alguns supõem que esse nome indica um rio, e não uma cidade, o mesmo rio Aava de Esdras 8:21. A idéia de que se trata de uma cidade, porém, parece ser melhor. Nesse caso, provavelmente deve ser identificada com a cidade de Iva (ver o artigo a respeito). Todavia, o local moderno é desconhecido. Alguns identificam-no com o Tell Kafr 'Ayah, no rio Orontes, a sudoeste de Homs. (I UN)

AVALOKITESVARA

Esse é o nome dado ao Dalai Lama reencarnado do lamaísmo. Ele é o líder principal que, por meio das suas repetidas reencarnações, traz a sabedoria espiritual necessária para cuidar das necessidades religiosas da comunidade. Ver o artigo sobre *terminologia budista*. (E H)

AVATAR

Vem do sânscrito, **avatara**, que significa «descida». Denota a descida de uma deidade à Terra, e à sua encarnação como homem, para ser um líder espiritual especial, a fim de promover a fé espiritual. No *hinduísmo* (ver o artigo) ensina-se que o deus Vixnu já se manifestou assim em nove grandes «descidas», e que ainda o fará mais uma vez. No *Bhagavad Gita* (ver o artigo) encontramos a declaração: «Quando a justiça declina, quando a impiedade se fortalece, então levanto-me... assumo forma visível e movo-me entre os homens como um homem». O termo pode ser usado frouxamente para referir-se a qualquer líder religioso poderoso, que aja sob o impulso e a vontade divinos. (E H)

••• ••• •••

AVE DE RAPINA DE VÁRIAS CORES

No hebraico temos uma palavra de sentido incerto, em Jeremias 12:9: «Acaso é para mim a minha herança ave de rapina de várias cores contra a qual se ajuntam outras aves de rapina?» Sendo encontrada exclusivamente nesse trecho da Bíblia, essa palavra há muito tem sido motivo de disputa. Bodenheimer (IDB) considera que se trata de uma ave de rapina (o que é refletido por nossa versão portuguesa), Mas outros estudiosos argumentam, com base em seus derivados hebraico e árabe, que a palavra aponta para uma «hiena malhada» (que vide), animal esse que se alimenta de carniça, naquela região do mundo.

AVEIA, ESPELTA, NIGELA

A referência em Eze. 4:9 provavelmente é a espelta, que faz parte da família das Ranúnculas, produzindo grande abundância de sementes negras, usadas para dar sabor. O trecho de Isa. 28:25 refere-se à *Nigella sativa*, chamada de *nigela*. Suas flores assemelham-se às da taça de manteiga, cujo fruto contém grande quantidade de minúsculas sementes negras, com frequência usadas no pão a fim de enriquecê-lo. A tradução «aveia», porém, leva-nos a um tipo inteiramente diferente de cereal. Muitas traduções confundem a flora com a fauna, e a razão por que muitas traduções são duvidosas é que as espécies animais e vegetais da Terra Santa com frequência não correspondem às espécies conhecidas na Europa e nas Américas.

AVE MARIA

Vem do latim, «salve, Maria», ou saudação angelical a Maria, em Luc. 1:28,42, usada a partir de 513 D.C. e ao que foi acrescentada uma súplica, no fim da Idade Média. Juntamente com o Credo e o Pai Nosso, há séculos que é uma oração devocional popular (ver os artigos sobre essas outras orações). É a oração repetida do *rosário* e do *Angelus* (ver os artigos). (E)

AVEMPACE

Filósofo árabe (1138 D.C.), nascido na Espanha, onde passou a maior parte de sua vida, embora tenha morrido no Marrocos, aparentemente por envenenamento. Ele combinava as idéias de um intelecto ativo com a ascensão mística. Para ele, o alvo do homem é chegar a um estado da realidade segundo o qual não haja oposição entre matéria e forma, ou entre pensamento e ser. (P)

ÁVEN

No hebraico, **nulidade, vaidade, ídolo**.

1. Em Oséias 101:8, os *altos de Aven*, uma alusão a Bete-Áven. Mas também pode ser uma figura de linguagem indicando os centros idólatras de Dã e Betel, estabelecidos por Jeroboão. Outros lugares da Samaria, de natureza similar, também poderiam estar sendo aludidos por essa palavra. Alguns supõem que o nome original de Ai (ver o artigo) era Bete-Áven. Bete-Áven, pois, seria uma distorção proposital do nome familiar da cidade de Bete-El. (Ver I Sam. 13:5; 14:23; quanto à sua localização, ver o artigo a respeito).

2. «*Áven*» é um elemento em nomes compostos, em Josué 7:2; 18:12; I Sam. 13:5, Amós 1:5, etc., como substituição de uma forma cananéia anterior, em que a palavra Baal foi substituída por Bosete. Era o nome popular de Heliópolis, no Baixo Egito, dando-lhe o sentido de *cidade ídolo*, visto que esse vocábulo significa nulidade, vaidade ou *ídolo*. (Ver Eze. 30:17). Esse lugar também se chamava On-Heliópolis. Desde o princípio da história foi conhecido como um centro da idolatria, um dos principais locais da adoração dos egípcios ao sol, onde havia um célebre templo com seu sacerdócio de eruditos.

3. Em Amós 1:5 encontramos *Biqueate-Áven*, que alguns estudiosos pensam ser idêntica à planície de Baalbeque (ver o artigo a respeito), um antiquíssimo centro de adoração a Baal. Porém, outros associam essa designação a Awanijek, perto de Jerude, na estrada para Palmira.

AVENTAL

Nossa versão portuguesa prefere «cintas», em Gênesis 3:7, ao referir-se às toscas vestimentas que Adão e Eva fizeram com folhas de figueira. Lenços e aventais eram usados para transmitir o poder curador (ver Atos 19:12). Muitos operários usavam aventais para proteger suas roupas e enxugar as suas mãos. Como é evidente no caso das curas miraculosas, as pessoas traziam suas próprias roupas (o grande número delas assim o sugere). É possível que essas vestes fossem usadas para promover a fé, como o lodo que Jesus fez para ungir os olhos do cego. Porém, os estudos no campo da parapsicologia mostram que a energia curativa que se transfere do curador para a pessoa curada, é uma energia autêntica que pode impregnar outros objetos, pelo que é possível que haja um poder curador real em uma peça de vestuário que tenha sido abençoada por um curador autêntico. É fato que a *água benta* pode fazer as plantas crescerem mais rápida e saudavelmente, por mais que isso cheire a superstição e fanatismo. Isso tem sido provado em laboratório. Além disso, pessoas psicóticas, ao abençoarem a água, são capazes de infundir uma energia negativa na mesma, de tal modo que ao ser usada essa água para regar as plantas, o crescimento das mesmas seja prejudicado. A mesma coisa acontece às simples orações, com o intuito de abençoar ou de amaldiçoar, inteiramente à parte de qualquer agente físico. Pouco sabemos acerca desses fenômenos, mas a existência dos mesmos demonstra que algo de real sucedia em Atos 19:12. Ver o artigo sobre Vestuário, no NTI.

AVERRÓIS

Filósofo árabe (1126-1198), nascido em Córdoba, Espanha. Seu nome latino era uma corruptela de Ibn Rushd. Tal como Avicena (ver o artigo), ocupou postos importantes, como juiz e diplomata, embora sua vida também incluísse opróbrio e banimento. Sua filosofia aristotelana foi amargamente combatida por teólogos e filósofos cristãos e islamitas. No campo da filosofia, tornou-se mais bem conhecido por causa de seus comentários sobre Aristóteles, tendo-se tornado conhecido como «o comentador». Tomás de Aquino adotou seu estilo de comentar. Seus labores levaram outros a investigarem e apreciarem as idéias de Aristóteles, o que foi muito importante no sistema de Aquino.

Obras: Comentários sobre as *Categorias*, *Análise Posterior e Física*, de Aristóteles; sobre *Os Céus*; sobre *Geração e Corrupção*, sobre *A Alma*; *Breves tratados sobre a Física*; *Metafísica*; *Política*; *Retórica*;

AVERROÍSMO — AVES DA BÍBLIA

Tratado contra a Destruição da Filosofia por Al-Ghazzali; *Comentário sobre a República* de Platão; *Comentário Médio sobre o Isagoge* de Porfírio; sobre a *Harmonia Entre a Religião e a Filosofia*; e uma enciclopédia médica, *Generalidades*.

Idéias principais:
1. Deus e o mundo são eternos, mas o mundo é efeito do poder de Deus, tendo sido criado desde a eternidade, ao passo que Deus é sem causa.
2. Um esquema neoplatônico de emanações do Ser necessário. A primeira emanação é a *primeira causa*, de onde emergem as *inteligências* que guiam as esferas celestiais, em escala decrescentes até o nosso mundo. Um único e definitivo poder, derivado da primeira causa, controla todas as coisas.
3. As ciências são eternas, em virtude de sua generalidade. A inteligência é capaz de descobrir a substância de uma espécie, por via da compreensão sobre uma coisa individual. Essa capacidade é um acidente do tempo, o que possibilita o homem a descobrir e a saber.
4. Os *universais* (ver o artigo), ou idéias gerais, têm como local apropriado o campo das inteligências. O intelecto humano tem afinidade com o universal. Mas o intelecto individual do homem não é imortal. Portanto, Averróis negava a imortalidade do homem, sendo nesse particular que ele era criticado mais acerbamente pelos outros pensadores.
5. O mundo precisa de profetas e místicos a fim de melhor relacionar os homens com o mundo vindouro. O mundo também precisa de grandes filósofos que conduzem os homens a compreender o intelecto, onde reside a verdade eterna.
6. Ao procurar distinguir a religião da filosofia, mantendo-as separadas, ele falou sobre a ressurreição, quando viveremos em outros corpos, não derivados daqueles que agora possuímos, mas *representando* os mesmos. Não é muito claro como ele reconciliava essa idéia com a negação da imortalidade (quarto ponto). Talvez ele pensasse que algumas verdades que não são obtidas por meio da religião, poderiam ser obtidas por meio da filosofia, e vice-versa. Mas, seja como for, o ponto permanece obscuro.
7. Ele negava a liberdade da vontade. (E P) Ver *averroísmo*.

AVERROÍSMO

(Ver o artigo sobre **Averróis**, que inclui suas idéias principais). A influência de Averróis foi sentida na religião islâmica, na filosofia judaica e na filosofia escolástica. Suas obras foram traduzidas para o hebraico, pelo que foi crescente a sua influência entre os judeus, até o século XV. As traduções latinas apareceram entre 1130 e 1150, o que prosseguiu até 1256. E nunca antes ou depois foram tão amargamente condenadas pelos líderes eclesiásticos e pelos concílios. Foram condenadas nos anos de 1209, 1215, 1240, 1270 e 1277. Os problemas eram a eternidade da matéria, a ausência de imortalidade no homem e a suposta doutrina da *dupla verdade* (uma filosófica, e outra, religiosa). No entanto, a fim de melhor compreender Aristóteles, Alberto Magno dependeu pesadamente de Averróis. Apesar de que Tomás de Aquino criticou intensamente a Averróis, principalmente em sua *Summa Contra Gentiles*, não há que duvidar que foi Averróis, acima de tudo, quem fez Aquino estudar filosofia. Ver o artigo sobre o *aristotelianismo*, quanto à importância desse acontecimento. Na Itália, o averroísmo continuou a exercer influência até o século XVI. Aquino transformou as idéias de Aristóteles em veículo para expressar a fé cristã, uma inesperada realização. (E F P SC)

AVES DA BÍBLIA

A. *Espécies*. Há muitas espécies de aves nas terras bíblicas. Os nomes que lhes são dados na Bíblia, visto não terem sido conferidos cientificamente, com freqüência são inexatos e confusos. Portanto, nem sempre há certeza quanto às espécies indicadas pelos termos empregados. As condições geográficas e climáticas da Palestina, que variam desde o semitropical ao desértico, e o fato de que a Palestina está situada em uma das principais rotas migratórias de aves entre a África, a Europa e a Ásia Ocidental, contribuem para a existência de larga variedade de pássaros, residentes ou vistos ali apenas ocasionalmente. Só no século XIX foi iniciado o estudo mais preciso dos animais, e mesmo assim, só as espécies mais comuns têm sido estudadas. Os animais, ou mesmo as aves que se parecem umas com as outras, não foram distinguidas. Documentos antiqüíssimos como os livros de Levítico e Deuteronômio jamais serão plenamente iluminados no tocante às alusões a animais que ali se acham. Os tradutores nunca saberão como manusear com certeza as listas de aves que ali aparecem, que incluem a gaivota (shap), o gavião (nes), a coruja (tahmas), o pelicano (salak), o açor (ra'a), a poupa (dukipet), a águia marinha (ozniyya) e o cisne (tinsemet). Em face da incerteza e confusão existentes, podemos apenas discutir e identificar tentativamente as aves mais comuns.

O termo hebraico *raham* (ver Lev. 11:18 e Deu. 14:17) pode ser o abutre, embora isso dependa da tradução que alguém estiver seguindo. Provavelmente é o abutre egípcio, uma ave preta e branca que se alimenta de lixo e de cadáveres de animais.

O *peres* (Lev. 11:13) é o quebrantoso (literalmente, o quebra-ossos) que costuma deixar cair ossos de grandes alturas, a fim de quebrá-los para poder consumi-los mais facilmente.

Águias verdadeiras, no hebraico *neser*, podem ser encontradas na Palestina. É provável que essa palavra hebraica indique genericamente as águias. Porém, o trecho de Miq. 1:16 diz: «...alarga a tua calva como a águia...» E essa descrição sugere o abutre grifo, que tem uma cabeça pálida e esbranquiçada, em contraste com o resto bem colorido do corpo. O termo grego *aetós*, usado em Mat. 24:28, provavelmente também aponta para a mesma ave. Ali encontramos menção à comum revoada de aves de rapina, que se juntam para o repasto de carne podre.

O *ayya* (Jó 28:7), o *daa* (Lev. 11:14) e o *dayya* (Deu. 14:13) provavelmente são nomes que se referem ao milhano. Há espécies negras e vermelhas.

As corujas são referidas por dezesseis vezes no Antigo Testamento, mas mediante o uso de cinco palavras hebraicas diferentes. Provavelmente várias espécies de corujas são assim distinguidas.

Aparentemente a *hasida* de Jer. 8:7 é a cegonha, uma das aves migratórias mais notáveis que passam pelo vale do Jordão, ao norte, em março e abril. O *agur*, também chamado *sus*, igualmente é uma ave migratória (ver Isa. 38:14 e Jer. 8:7). Provavelmente trata-se da andorinha. Várias espécies podem ser encontradas na Palestina, em certos períodos do ano.

O pardal (no hebraico, *sippor*) é uma ave comum na Palestina, idêntica à que aparece na Europa ocidental. O termo grego *struthion* provavelmente alude a certa variedade de aves pequenas, incluindo o

AVES DA BÍBLIA — AVES DE RAPINA

pardal. Jesus, em Mat. 10:29, referiu-se a essa ave por ser considerada de pequeno valor pelos homens, mas que atrai a atenção favorável de nosso Pai celeste.

Nos selos do Egito e da Assíria, desde 1500 A.C., há gravuras com galos (no grego, *alektor*). E a menção à galinha, por Jesus, em Mat. 23:37 e em Luc. 13:34 (no grego, *ornis*), mostra que a ave era natural das terras bíblicas. O galo servia de despertador natural, posto que inexato. (Ver Mat. 26:74,75). É provável que a galinha fosse domesticada.

O pavão (no hebraico, talvez, *tukkiyyim*) era importado por Salomão (ver I Reis 10:22), sendo contado entre os animais exóticos que Salomão queria ter ao seu redor, para aumentar a beleza e o interesse de seu reino. O pavão é nativo das florestas da região indo-malaia, embora chegue a outras regiões, por meios naturais ou mediante importação. Em 450 A.C. chegou em Atenas, Grécia.

A codorniz (no hebraico, *selaw*) era uma ave caçada, limpa segundo os preceitos levíticos (ver Êxo. 16:13). É ave migratória, seguindo uma rota semelhante à rota seguida pelos israelitas no êxodo. Serviu de alimento porque essa ave voa apenas cerca de um metro acima da superfície do solo, e em grandes revoadas.

A perdiz (no hebraico, *gore*; ver I Sam. 26:20), era caçada para servir de alimento, no Oriente Médio e no suleste da Europa. A espécie envolvida é similar à perdiz de pernas vermelhas (A. rufa).

Dois membros da família do corvo são nativos da Palestina, o corvo, propriamente dito, e a gralha (no heb. *oreb*; no grego, *koraks*). Essas aves alimentam-se de carne apodrecida e eram imundas, segundo a lei levítica.

A avestruz (no hebraico, *bat yaana*), em Jó 39:13-18, em algum tempo foi ave nativa do Oriente Médio. Alguns tradutores dizem «coruja», nesse trecho; mas a maioria dos estudiosos pensa que está mesmo em vista a avestruz. Em algumas versões, o termo hebraico *hasida* é traduzido por avestruz ou por cegonha, ao passo que a *yeenim*, em Lam. 4:3, é traduzida pela avestruz (conforme faz nossa versão portuguesa).

O pelicano dificilmente viveria no deserto, mas o «deserto» referido em Sal. 102:6, associado a esse pássaro, não precisa indicar um deserto de areia, mas apenas um lugar ermo. O termo hebraico ali usado tem sentido incerto. Por isso, alguns estudiosos preferem o abutre. O pelicano branco passava pelo norte do vale do Jordão, pelo que ocasionalmente podia ser visto na Palestina. Os pelicanos são aves aquáticas que, em seu vôo de migração, fazem pausas para descansar em lugares com lagos e alagadiços.

Existem várias espécies de pombas e rolas na Palestina. O termo hebraico *yona* é usado para indicar tanto uma quanto outra dessas aves, que eram usadas nos sacrifícios (ver Gên. 15:9 e Lev. 12:6).

As aves cevadas (no hebraico, *barburim*), referidas em I Reis 4:23, eram acepipes servidos na mesa de Salomão. Isso talvez indique a domesticação de certas aves, pelos povos do Oriente Médio e pelos israelitas.

B. *Divisão Geral*. No Antigo Testamento, as aves são classificadas como «limpas» e «imundas», isto é, aquelas que podiam ser consumidas pelos israelitas, e aquelas que não o podiam, de acordo com os preceitos constantes no décimo terceiro capítulo de Levítico.

C. *Ninhos*. São freqüentes as alusões a ninhos de aves, na Bíblia. Lemos sobre ninhos no santuário (ver Sal. 84:3), nas rochas (Jó 39:27), nas árvores (Sal. 104:17; Jer. 22:23), nas ruínas (Isa. 34:15), em buracos (Jer. 47:28). E, no Novo Testamento, há alusões a ninhos em Mat. 8:20 e Luc. 9:58.

D. *Ovos*. Ver Deu. 22:6 e Jó 39:14. Lucas 11:13 acrescenta que ovos eram usados na alimentação humana.

E. *Migração*. As referências a respeito são Can. 2:11,12; Jer. 8:7 e Êxo. 19:4.

F. *Usos Metafóricos*. a. As aves usadas nos sacrifícios levíticos simbolizavam o perdão dos pecados por meio de Cristo. b. O humilde pardal não é tão pequeno que Deus não o note; e muito mais cuida Ele dos homens (ver Mat. 10:29-31). c. Os pássaros imundos eram abomináveis a Deus, e vedados aos homens como alimento. Há coisas que os crentes precisam evitar, a fim de agradarem a Deus (ver Lev. 13). d. Certas aves de rapina habitam em lugares desolados pela destruição, e assim retratam o vazio que predomina onde Deus julga ou onde a Sua presença não é sentida (ver Isa. 13:21). e. A pomba simboliza a beleza (ver Can. 1:15 e 5:12), ou então, a tristeza (ver Isa. 59:11). Além disso, sua humildade e mansidão simbolizam a humildade e o caráter inofensivo dos servos de Cristo, em contraste com aqueles que são cheios de engano e malignidade (ver Mat. 10:16). f. As aves de rapina podem simbolizar os severos julgamentos divinos (ver Mat. 24:28 e Apo. 19:17,18). g. Em todas as culturas humanas, as aves têm sido associadas a presságios, seus vôos e atos são ligados à boa sorte, ao infortúnio e às vicissitudes do destino. Alguns pensam que as aves que se aninharam nos ramos da mostarda representam os demônios, ou, pelo menos, as influências demoníacas, sob a forma de mestres falsos e suas doutrinas distorcidas, que enfeiam a árvore do reino de Deus (ver Mat. 13:31,32).

AVES DE RAPINA

A Palestina conta com certa variedade de aves que caçam de dia e de noite, incluindo o corvo, a águia, o falcão, o açor, o gavião, o açor noturno, o quebrantosso, o milhano e o abutre. Alguns desses pássaros são nativos da Palestina, ao passo que outros chegam ali somente em certos períodos do ano, principalmente na primavera (ver migração de aves). Nesse caso, a parada temporária na Palestina, em seu vôo para o norte, visa a alimentação. Várias espécies nem ao menos param, mas apenas sobrevoam a região, e até os naturalistas têm dificuldades em distinguir as espécies. Essas aves são carnívoras, e portanto, vedadas à alimentação, pelas leis levíticas. Algumas delas, como o falcão e o gavião, caçam pequenos animais, ao passo que as outras, como os abutres, vivem de carne putrefacta. As águias alimentam-se de ambas as coisas. As leis levíticas sabiamente proibiam os israelitas de comerem tais aves, porque seus hábitos alimentares tornam-nas transmissoras de enfermidades com alto risco.

Na Palestina, há quatro espécies residentes de corujas, e quatro espécies migratórias, as quais são aves de rapina de hábitos noturnos. As corujas só se alimentam de presas vivas. Há várias espécies de corvos e gralhas na Palestina. Essas também são espécies de rapina, ainda que haja espécies essencialmente vegetarianas.

Uso metafórico. Trechos bíblicos como Mateus 24:28 e Apocalipse 19:17,18 incluem a presença de aves de rapina por ocasião dos julgamentos divinos escatológicos, os desastres do tempo do fim e da batalha do Armagedom. As aves que se alimentam de carne podem passar longos períodos em jejum, e quando têm a oportunidade de se alimentarem, têm apetites vorazes. O julgamento divino também pode demorar, mas sobrevirá, finalmente, com grande poder e violência.

AVESTA

Vocábulo que significa «conhecimento», nome do livro sagrado do *zoroastrismo* (ver o artigo). Na Índia é *parsis*, e na Pérsia é *gabards*, também chamado *zend* (tradição do conhecimento). Segundo uma tradição, o Avesta original encerrava todo o conhecimento, tendo sido quase inteiramente destruído por Alexandre o Grande. Do que restou, foi compilada uma obra em vinte e um volumes, no século III D.C. Mas apenas um deles, o *Vendidad*, sobrevive completo. O *Dinkard* (em idioma palevi) dá uma lista dos outros livros. Depois do século IX, certas porções que versavam sobre a adoração, foram levadas para a Índia, até hoje existentes em cinco partes, a saber: *Yasna* (incluindo as *Gathas*), a *Vispered, Vendidad, Yashts* e a *Khorda Avesta*. Ver o artigo sobre *Pérsia, Religiões da*. (E P)

AVESTRUZ

No hebraico temos uma palavra que aparece exclusivamente em Lam. 4:3, embora uma outra palavra hebraica também tenha sido traduzida por «avestruz», apesar de mais provavelmente apontar para a coruja. Oito passagens do Antigo Testamento envolvem essa dúvida (Lev. 11:16; Deu. 14:15; Jó 30:29; Isa. 13:21; 34:13; 43:20; Jer. 50:30 e Miq. 1:8). A avestruz é uma ave bem conhecida, por ser a maior ave viva de nossa época. No Brasil temos uma espécie aparentada, a «ema», embora de menor porte. A avestruz encontra-se nos desertos da Arábia e da África. Tornou-se famosa por seu imenso apetite. Engole seixos de bom tamanho, pedaços de vidro e outros objetos duros, para ajudá-la na digestão no papo. A avestruz pode atingir 2,40 m de altura e pesar 140 kg. A fêmea faz um ninho raso e põe muitos ovos de cada vez, fazendo com que alguns deles terminem não sendo chocados. A maior parte desses ovos é coberta com areia. O sol esquenta os ovos durante o dia, e a mãe e o pai se revezam no choco, durante a noite. Essa ave pode correr a uma velocidade espantosa de 80 km por hora, podendo ultrapassar facilmente em velocidade a um cavalo. A ficção de que a avestruz esconde a cabeça na areia, quando se vê em perigo, não corresponde aos fatos. Esse pássaro é basicamente um vegetariano, embora possa comer insetos, gafanhotos, etc. A descrição que aparece em Jó 39:14-17 mostra-nos que o autor sagrado conhecia bem a espécie. Os antigos começaram a domesticar a avestruz desde algum tempo antes de 2000 A.C. A acusação de estupidez, conforme se vê naquele trecho de Jó, provavelmente, origina-se do fato de que tal ave pode assustar-se com facilidade, até mesmo por causa de pequenos e inofensivos animais, ou então porque às vezes ela engole coisas que lhe são mortíferas. Esse pássaro era usado como alimento por vários povos, e talvez pelos próprios israelitas. Seus ovos também eram usados na alimentação, e as cascas vazias, muito duras, — podendo atingir de 15 a 20 cent. de comprimento, eram usadas como receptáculos. Taças ornamentais eram feitas com ovos de avestruz, as quais têm sido encontradas em sepulcros assírios desde cerca de 3000 A.C.

AVEUS

Eram os habitantes de Ava, sendo contados entre os colonos enviados pelo rei da Assíria a fim de substituir os habitantes das cidades do reino do norte, Israel, que tinham ficado despovoadas devido ao exílio (ver II Reis 17:31). Eram idólatras, adoradores dos deuses Bibas e Tartaque. (Ver sobre *Ava*). Os aveus não devem ser confundidos com os heveus, que eram descendentes de Canaã (ver Gên. 10:17), e que a versão portuguesa que usamos grafa como «aveus», em Deuteronômio 2:23.

AVICEBRON, SALOMÃO BEN-GABIROL

Filósofo judeu (1020-1070), nascido em Málaga, mas que viveu em Saragoça. Foi teólogo, poeta e filósofo, de orientação neoplatônica. Suas idéias foram combatidas por Tomás de Aquino, embora gozasse do apoio dos franciscanos, e no século XIII, dos agostinianos. Seu pensamento independente prenunciava *Spinoza* (ver o artigo). Sua obra teve maior influência entre os gentios do que entre os judeus.

Obras: *A Fonte da Vida*; *Melhoramento das Qualidades Morais*; e um volume de poesias, *A Coroa Real*.

Idéias:

1. Todas as substâncias, terrenas e espirituais, combinam forma e matéria. A matéria é potencialidade, tendo a corporalidade como uma de suas características, pelo menos até certo nível. Portanto, a matéria não pode ser o princípio da individualização, devendo haver substâncias individuais. Em conseqüência, a *forma* deve ser o princípio da individualização.

2. Muitas formas podem residir em uma coisa individual, e elas amoldam a natureza daquela coisa.

3. O mundo procede da unidade divina por meio de uma série de emanações. O mediador entre o divino e o mundo é a vontade divina. Essa vontade tanto cria quanto sustenta o mundo. Da vontade procede a *forma*, que se une à matéria. Da natureza, conforme é conhecida neste mundo físico, procedem os corpos do mundo temporal.

4. Deus, em Sua verdadeira natureza, permanece acima da compreensão humana. Não obstante, Ele é o alvo de nossa vida, mediante o conhecimento e a devoção religiosa, que nos ajudam a dominar nossa natureza sensual. A vida não tem sentido sobre quaisquer outras bases. Seus poemas refletem a natureza pessimista da vida, sem a inquirição espiritual.

AVICENA

Filósofo e médico islamita (980-1037), cujo nome é Ibn Sina, árabe. Nasceu na Pérsia. Foi um estudante brilhante, tendo-se tornado médico com dezesseis ou dezessete anos, quando já havia dominado todo o conhecimento da época. Sua vida foi aventureira, incansável e repleta de controvérsias, na Pérsia e no Irã. Pouco antes de falecer, com cinqüenta e sete anos, deu liberdade a seus escravos. Suas obras foram traduzidas para o latim, e isso permitiu que ele influenciasse o grande reavivamento de Aristóteles nos séculos XII e XIII. Tornou-se conhecido como «o terceiro Aristóteles». Combinou idéias aristotélicas e neoplatônicas. A obra *Enneads*, de Plotino (mas que ele julgou ser obra de Aristóteles), e o comentário de Al-Farabi sobre a *Metafísica* de Aristóteles, exerceram considerável influência sobre seu pensamento. Seu tratado sobre medicina foi um dos mais influentes nas universidades européias, desde o século XII ao século XVII, embora consistisse principalmente de

AVICENA — AXIOMA

uma versão aristotélica de Galeno. Todavia, houve muitas adições feitas por ele mesmo. O cume de sua influência na Europa, no tocante às idéias filosóficas, ocorreu nos séculos XIII e XIV.

Obras: *A Cura; Cânones da Medicina* (5 volumes); *Diretivas e Observações*, uma breve declaração de suas idéias filosóficas. Além dessas obras, ele escreveu mais de cem tratados sobre vários assuntos.

Idéias:

1. A lógica aristotélica, os papéis desempenhados pelos sentidos e pela razão, definição, espécies, diferenças, propriedades, acidentes, quatro causas.
2. Opunha-se ao atomismo, e pensava que os corpos podiam ser infinitamente divididos. Considerava o mundo finito, e que para além de suas extremidades, nada havia em absoluto.
3. Psicologia aristotélica, ressaltando as diferenças entre funções vegetais, animais e racionais.
4. Foi um realista no tocante aos *universais* (ver o artigo). Nossas mentes, a fim de apreenderem o universal, precisam entrar em contato com uma inteligência superior, e não meramente observar os *particulares* (ver o artigo). Nesse ponto, ele penetra na metafísica.
5. Deus é o ser perfeito, unitário e necessário. Entre Deus e o mundo há uma hierarquia de seres, uma série de dez inteligências, que ativam as esferas celestiais, e que são consideradas como dotadas de alma. O nosso intelecto pode ter contato com a décima dessas inteligências, e a partir desse ponto pode apreender a idéia dos universais.
6. A existência de Deus pode ser provada por meio de um triplo argumento: a. A necessidade de uma *causa*, a fim de que exista alguma coisa. b. Não há uma série infinita de causas. c. A série de causas devem conduzir-nos ao ser necessário, a Causa Primária, isto é, Deus.
7. *Atributos de Deus*. Ele é o ser necessário, completo, absoluto, perfeito na verdade, na bondade e no amor. Ele é a própria essência da vida. Ele deve compartilhar de Suas perfeições, de tal necessidade proveio a criação. As *inteligências* realizam a Sua vontade, cada uma delas originária em Deus. A criação também é necessária, proveniente da eternidade. A décima inteligência provê a forma, que deve ser recebida pela matéria, e a matéria é o princípio da individualização.
8. Visto que a criação é necessária, tudo quanto acontece dentro dela também é necessário, o que reflete o *determinismo*. (Ver o artigo).
9. O mal é um acidente da existência, que flui da carência, do sofrimento físico e do pecado. O mal atinge o indivíduo, mas não a espécie. De um ponto de vista superior, o mal pode ser visto como algo bom, porque, de alguma maneira, haverá unidade e harmonia em todas as coisas.
10. A criação (individualização) da alma ocorre juntamente com a do corpo. A alma é imortal, mas não haveria ressurreição.
11. O alvo da alma é a felicidade perfeita (*eudaimonismo*).
12. Os profetas têm a capacidade de entrar em contato com a *inteligência*, sendo capaz de descobrir o conhecimento (pelo menos quanto a pontos específicos) mais rapidamente do que o intelecto humano, que precisa avançar ponto por ponto em seus raciocínios.
13. Em Deus, essência e existência são idênticos, embora não nos demais seres. Portanto, Deus é um ser necessário, ao passo que os outros seres seriam contingentes. Contudo, por terem se originado em Deus, os demais seres revestem-se de uma espécie de necessidade secundária. Não podem deixar de existir, embora isso faça parte de suas próprias naturezas. Essas considerações tornaram-se importantes na filosofia medieval posterior. (AM E P)

AVIDYA

Palavra sânscrita que significa «ignorância», usada nas Upanishads e no Bhagavad-Gita (ver os artigos a respeito). O termo é sinônimo de *maya*, referindo-se à ignorância sobre a identidade do «eu» e de Bramá, derivando-se daí a crença na natureza distinta do «eu». O conceito de identidade era advogado pelos Shunyavadins (ver o artigo sobre Shunyavada), na ioga, na Gaudapada e na Shankara (ver os artigos a respeito). (P)

AVIGNON

Cidade francesa, famosa na história por ter servido de residência dos papas, de 1305 a 1378, um período chamado «cativeiro babilônico do papado», em alusão ao cativeiro dos judeus, na narrativa do Antigo Testamento. Os papas desse período foram todos franceses: Clemente V (1305-1314), João XXII (1314-1334), Benedito XII (1334-1342), Clemente VI (1342-1352), Inocente VI (1352-1362), Urbano V (1362-1370) e Gregório XI (1370-1378). (AM E)

AVITE

No hebraico, **cabana** ou **vila**. Uma cidade dos edomitas. Era a cidade de Hadade, filho de Bedade. Este foi um dos reis edomitas que reinaram antes que houvesse rei em Israel (ver Gên. 36:35 e I Crô. 1:46).

AVYAKTA

Vem do sânscrito e significa «não-manifesto», usado nas Upanishads e no Bhagavad-Gita, juntamente com o termo Prakriti (ver os artigos), referindo-se ao poder não-manifestado de Deus ou ao Bramá antes da criação, no estado de superabundância, ou ao universo não-criado. (P)

AXIOLOGIA

Vem do grego, **axios**, «valor», e **logos**, «conhecimento». O termo pode ser limitado ao referir-se ao estudo do valor, em três sistemas básicos: *ética*, *religião* e *estética*. Porém, também pode incluir os resultados das investigações psicológicas, lógicas, epistemológicas, políticas e metafísicas. O termo evidentemente foi cunhado pelo filósofo francês, Paul Lapie, em sua *Lógica da Vontade*, 1902. Foi usado como parte do título de uma obra escrita por Eduardo von Hartmann, em 1908. As análises de valor, no século XX, envolvem em um único estudo, valores de diversas modalidades, como valores éticos, estéticos, políticos, lógicos, orgânicos, etc. Quanto a notas mais completas sobre essa atividade, na história da filosofia, ver o artigo sobre *Teoria de Valor*. (E F P)

AXIOMA

Vem do grego, *axioun*, «pensar de modo digno». O vocábulo indica proposições indemonstráveis mas necessárias, que formam o alicerce de qualquer dado sistema. Um axioma é uma proposição considerada *auto-evidente*, ou acima de qualquer dúvida. Os

AXIOMA — AYER, ALFREDO J.

axiomas matemáticos servem de exemplo clássico. O vocábulo faz parte de uma família de termos conexos: *suposição, hipótese, postulado, definição* (ver os artigos a respeito).

Idéias:

1. Aristóteles. Premissas primárias de demonstração: proposições necessárias que não podem ser demonstradas. Os postulados têm a mesma posição primária, e podem ser demonstrados, embora possam ser usados sem qualquer demonstração.

2. *Euclides*. Aos axiomas ele chamava *noções comuns*, das quais não se pode duvidar, incluindo os axiomas geométricos. Todos os seus postulados eram geométricos. Euclides estruturou sua geometria inteira baseada em somente dez axiomas coerentes e independentes. Outros teoremas podem ser deduzidos desses dez axiomas. Por exemplo: a. Uma linha reta pode ser traçada de um ponto para outro qualquer. b. Qualquer segmento finito de reta pode ser prolongado indefinidamente para se construir uma reta. c. Dado um ponto qualquer e uma distância qualquer, pode-se traçar um círculo do centro daquele ponto, de raio igual à distância dada. d. Todos os ângulos retos são iguais entre si. Outro exemplo: «O total é maior do que qualquer uma de suas partes», embora esse axioma tenha sido sujeitado ao aparente bom sucesso do ataque de certa declaração: «No caso de uma classe infinita, pode haver tantos membros na parte da classe como na classe inteira». Por exemplo, existem tantos números pares inteiros como há números pares e ímpares inteiros».

3. *Wolff*. Para ele, um *axioma* significava qualquer proposição não-demonstrável, teórica, e portanto, *universal*, ao passo que um postulado indicava uma proposição não-demonstrável, prática e *particular*.

4. *Kant*. Seguia essencialmente as idéias de Wolff, aplicando o termo à intuição, referindo-se a princípios *a priori* (ver o artigo a respeito) que envolvem puro entendimento. Por exemplo, «todos os fenômenos têm extensão».

5. *Elementos de um axioma*. 1. É indemonstrável, necessário para a construção de um sistema de pensamento. 2. Auto-evidente. 3. Subjetivamente certo e objetivamente verdadeiro. 4. Inato ao homem, invocado pela experiência, mas não precisando dela para ser demonstrado.

6. Modos como essas afirmações foram manuseadas pelos filósofos. a. Platão, Descartes, Leibniz afirmaram todos os quatro axiomas. b. Kant eliminou o terceiro. c. A Filosofia empírica elimina os dois últimos, retendo porém, os dois primeiros.

7. *Descartes* obteve seus axiomas básicos por meio da dúvida. O que sobreviveu à dúvida pôde ser visto clara e distintamente, tornando-se fundamental para qualquer pensamento, como a existência de Deus, da alma e do mundo exterior.

8. *John Locke* desafiou o quarto axioma, alterando a maneira de pensar de muitos filósofos quanto a esse elemento.

9. *Kant* opinava que a natureza contém, de forma inata, as proposições auto-evidentes e as categorias mentais.

10. A escolha de axiomas pode ser arbitrária. Mas a maioria dos filósofos parece concordar que o número dos mesmos deve ser pequeno. Um conjunto de axiomas precisa ser coerente se tiver que servir de base para qualquer sistema de pensamentos. Cada axioma deve ser independente dos demais; e nenhum deles deve ser derivado de outro.

11. *Uso secundário*. Qualquer princípio ou regra estabelecidos.

12. *Axiomas religiosos*. Deus, a primeira causa; teleologia; a alma; o destino; recompensa-punição; triunfo da bondade; responsabilidade. Desses tipos de crenças dependem todos os sistemas religiosos.

Aristóteles declarou que todas as ciências demonstráveis precisam partir de princípios não-demonstráveis. Portanto, na lógica não se permite a indagação: «Quem criou Deus?» Simplesmente começamos pelo axioma — que Deus existe. Porém, isso não significa que não há qualquer evidência. Somente significa que as evidências não constituem uma demonstração absoluta. Quanto ao axioma da alma (ver o artigo a respeito), as evidências estão se tornando tão vastas que o assunto em breve deixará de pertencer à categoria de axiomas, entrando na categoria das coisas que têm sido demonstradas. (AM E EP MI P)

AYER, ALFREDO J.

Filósofo inglês (1910---), nascido em Londres e educado em Oxford. Ensinou na Universidade de Londres, e então em Oxford. Tornou-se conhecido como um dos principais exponentes do *positivismo lógico* (ver o artigo), ou *empirismo lógico*, conforme ele preferia denominar a sua posição.

Escritos principais: *Linguagem, Verdade e Lógica*, 1936; *Fundamentos do Conhecimento Empírico*, 1940; *Ensaios Filosóficos*, 1954; *O Problema do Conhecimento*, 1956; *Filosofia e Linguagem*, 1960; *O Conceito de uma Pessoa*, 1963; *Origens do Pragmatismo*, 1968; *Russell e Moore*, 1971.

Idéias:

1. Todas as declarações genuínas são empíricas ou analíticas. A matemática e a lógica representam a posição analítica, sem conteúdo factual; mas não são declarações arbitrárias; antes, as regras da lógica são necessárias.

2. *Critérios* que se aplicam às declarações empíricas genuínas. Tais declarações são significativas quando o indivíduo sabe como verificar a proposição que a sentença expressa. Ele opinava que basta que a proposição se torne «provável por meio da experiência», e não que ela seja exaustivamente demonstrada. Uma proposição genuína factual não é necessariamente *equivalente* a uma proposição baseada na experiência. Sua abordagem mais branda do conhecimento (modificação da linha dura seguida pelos positivistas) levou-o a considerar-se um empirista lógico.

3. Em sua obra *Linguagem, Verdade e Lógica*, os critérios por ele usados tornam-se mais complexos. À parte das declarações analíticas, qualquer proposição significativa deve ser verificável direta ou indiretamente. Diretamente, quando a proposição se baseia em várias observações (experiências), averiguando-se se não há uma só observação da qual as outras podem ser deduzidas. Indiretamente, quando há pelo menos uma declaração diretamente verificável, que não pode ser deduzida de outras premissas, ou quando outras premissas existem que consistem de declarações que, ou são analíticas, diretamente verificáveis, ou indiretamente verificáveis.

4. As proposições que não satisfazem a essas exigências são consideradas *sem sentido*. Por esse motivo, ele rejeitava a metafísica, a teologia, a ética e a estética como sistemas de conhecimento válidos.

5. Portanto, no que consiste a *filosofia*? Consiste em *análise*, no aclaramento de declarações, em suas inter-relações. O modo de proceder envolve a tradução da declaração que requer esclarecimento

AZA — AZARIAS

para outras sentenças que não continham palavras-chaves, da declaração original, e sem sinônomos das mesmas.

6. As declarações dele terminam envolvendo apenas objetos materiais, conhecidos através da percepção dos sentidos. Visto que tais declarações nunca podem exaurir ou descrever plenamente tais objetos, terminamos chegando a uma forma de *ceticismo* (ver o artigo) ou *pragmatismo científico* (ver o artigo). Muitos cientistas da atualidade parecem estar-se afastando do empirismo radical, chegando mesmo a postular que a *mente* é mais fundamental para a realidade do que a matéria. Estudos no campo da parapsicologia (ver o artigo) quase certamente terminarão por demonstrar que a percepção dos sentidos não é a única maneira de se adquirir conhecimentos, e que os objetos físicos não são os únicos objetos do conhecimento. Consideremos um homem como Satya Sai Baba (ver o artigo a seu respeito), um místico indiano que está duplicando os milagres de Jesus. Os limites percebidos pelos homens usualmente são os limites de suas próprias mentes, e não os verdadeiros limites da realidade. (E EP P)

AZA

Forma alternativa para Gaza, que em algumas versões aparece nos trechos de Deu. 2:23; I Reis 4:24 e Jer. 25:20. Nossa versão portuguesa sempre grafa «Gaza».

AZÃ

No hebraico talvez signifique **espinho**. Era pai de Paltiel, príncipe da tribo de Issacar (ver Núm. 34:26). Paltiel representou a tribo de Issacar, por ocasião da divisão da Terra Prometida, em cerca de 1540 A.C. (ID S)

AZAEL

Esse nome não aparece nos livros canônicos da Bíblia. Mas, em I Esdras 9:14 e 34, aparece como apelativo de dois homens diferentes: 1. Um judeu do tempo de Esdras, que despediu sua mulher estrangeira e seus filhos após o cativeiro babilônico, no primeiro desses versículos; e 2. O pai de Jônatas, um dos investigadores que buscaram descobrir quais judeus tinham-se casado com mulheres gentias, no segundo desses versículos. (Z)

AZAI

No hebraico, **Yahweh agarrou**. Foi sacerdote no tempo de Esdras (ver Nee. 11:13). Provavelmente era o mesmo Jazera, que figura em I Crô. 9:12.

AZALIAS

No hebraico, **Yah é nobre**, ou então **aquele que Yahweh poupou** ou **separou**. Era o pai de Safã, um escriba que viveu durante o reinado de Josias (ver II Reis 22:3 e II Crô. 34:8), cerca de 625 A.C. Ele trouxe à atenção de Josias o livro da lei que o sumo sacerdote Hilquias havia encontrado no templo. (S Z)

AZANIAS

No hebraico, **Yah é ouvinte**. Era levita, pai de Jesua. Foi um dos que firmaram o pacto com Neemias, após o exílio na Babilônia (ver Nee. 10:9). (UN)

AZARAIAS

Em I Esdras 8:1, figura como um dos antepassados de Esdras. Uma forma variante de Azarias, nome de um grande número de pessoas, nas páginas do Antigo Testamento. (S Z)

AZAREEL

No hebraico significa **Deus tem ajudado**. É nome de várias pessoas do Antigo Testamento, a saber:

1. Um coraíta que se aliou a Davi, em Ziclague (ver I Crô. 12:6), em cerca de 1000 A.C.

2. Cabeça da décima primeira divisão dos músicos do templo (ver I Crô. 25:18), em cerca de 1000 A.C. Ele é chamado Uziel, em I Crônicas 25:4. Nossa versão portuguesa grafa seu nome sob a forma de «Azarel».

3. Líder da tribo de Dã, durante os dias de Davi e Salomão (ver I Crô. 27:22), em cerca de 1015 A.C.

4. Um israelita que renunciou à sua esposa estrangeira, após o cativeiro (ver Esd. 10:41), em cerca de 456 A.C.

5. O último dos chefes dos cento e vinte e oito homens valorosos entre os sacerdotes, que serviam no templo (ver Nee. 11:13), em cerca de 445 A.C.

6. Um sacerdote que soprou sua trombeta, durante o cortejo efetuado quando foram dedicadas as muralhas de Jerusalém (ver Nee. 12:36), e que talvez seja o mesmo homem referido no número 5, acima.

AZARIAS

No hebraico, **aquele a quem Yahweh ajuda**. Um nome extremamente comum nos dias do Antigo Testamento:

1. Rei de Judá, mais freqüentemente chamado Uzias (ver o artigo a respeito) (ver II Reis 14:21; 15:1,6-8,17,23,27), em cerca de 809 A.C.

2. Filho de Sadoque, o sumo sacerdote, nos dias de Davi, e um dos oficiais de Salomão (ver I Reis 4:2), em cerca de 960 A.C. Talvez se trate do mesmo que abaixo é alistado como de número 5.

3. Filho de Natã, capitão da guarda pessoal de Salomão (ver I Reis 4:5), em cerca de 1000 A.C.

4. Filho de Etã, dos filhos de Zera, filho de Judá e Tamar (I Crô. 2:8), em cerca de 1660 A.C.

5. Um sumo sacerdote, filho de Aimaás, neto de Sadoque (ver I Crô. 6:9), e talvez o mesmo que é alistado no número 2 (ver I Reis 4:2).

6. Filho de Joanã (781 A.C.), um sumo sacerdote (ver I Crô. 6:10). Alguns supõem ser o mesmo que Zacarias, filho de Joiada, morto em 840 A.C. (ver II Crô. 14:20-22).

7. Filho de Jeú, descendente de Jará, o escravo de Sesã (ver I Crô. 2:38,39), em cerca de 1330 A.C. Provavelmente é um dos capitães mencionados em II Crô. 23:1, onde ele é chamado de «filho de Obede».

8. Há um Azarias, filho de Hilquias, inserido em Hilquias e Saraías, durante o reinado de Josias. Não parece haver espaço cronológico para ele nesse ponto, sendo possível que a inserção tenha sido sugerida por Esdras 7:1. Foi morto por Nabucodonosor (ver I Crô. 6:13), em cerca de 641-610 A.C.

9. Filho de Sofonias e antepassado do profeta Samuel (ver I Crô. 6:36), talvez o mesmo Uzias do vs. 24. Cerca de 1100 A.C.

10. Homem a quem o sumo sacerdote Joiada tornou conhecido o segredo da existência do jovem príncipe Joás, e que o ajudou a elevá-lo ao trono (ver II Crô. 15:1), em cerca de 941 A.C.

AZARIAS — AZAZEL

11 e 12. Nome de dois dos filhos de Josafá, rei de Judá (ver II Crô. 21:2), em 890 A.C. Nossa versão portuguesa, a fim de distingui-los, dá o nome do primeiro como «Azarias», e do segundo, «Asarias».

13. Em II Crônicas 22:6 parece ter havido um erro clerical. O nome Azarias aparece em lugar de Acazias. Nossa versão portuguesa corrige o erro, chamando-o corretamente de «Acazias». Viveu em cerca de 885 A.C.

14. Filho de Jeroão (ver II Crô. 26:17). Era comandante de oitenta sacerdotes, que resistiram ao rei Uzias, por ter querido este queimar incenso na casa de Deus. Cerca de 765 A.C.

15. Sumo sacerdote que se opôs a Uzias, rei de Judá, por ter querido oferecer incenso ao Senhor, privilégio que cabia exclusivamente aos sacerdotes (ver II Crô. 26:17), em cerca de 765 A.C.

16. Filho de Joanã, um capitão efraimita (ver II Crô. 28:12). Fez voltar os cativos e os despojos tomados durante a invasão de Judá por parte de Peca, rei de Israel, em 726 A.C.

17. Pai de Joel, durante o reinado de Ezequias (ver II Crô. 29:12), em cerca de 726 A.C.

18. Filho de Jealelel, e contemporâneo do filho da personagem alistada acima (ver II Crô. 29:12), em cerca de 726 A.C.

19. Um sumo sacerdote do tempo de Ezequias (ver II Crô. 31:10), que cooperou zelosamente com o rei, quando da purificação do templo, em cerca de 726 A.C.

20. Filho de Maaséias, que ajudou a reparar uma porção das muralhas de Jerusalém, no tempo de Neemias (ver Nee. 3:23,24), em cerca de 445 A.C.

21. Um dos líderes que subiu da **Babilônia** em companhia de Zorobabel (ver Nee. 7:7), em cerca de 590 A.C. Em Esdras 2:2 ele é chamado Seraías.

22. Um levita que instruiu o povo na lei de Moisés, nos dias de Esdras (ver Nee. 8:7), em cerca de 445 A.C.

23. Um dos sacerdotes que solenizou o pacto com Neemias (ver Nee. 10:2), provavelmente o mesmo que ajudou na dedicação das muralhas de Jerusalém, segundo se lê em Neemias 12:33. Cerca de 445 A.C.

24. Nome alternativo para Jezanias (ver o artigo a respeito), e que em Jeremias 43:2 aparece com o nome de Azarias.

25. Nome caldaico de Abede-Nego, um dos três amigos de Daniel que foram lançados na fornalha ardente (ver Dan. 1:7 e 3:9), em cerca de 560 A.C.

AZARIAS (nos Livros Apócrifos)

Forma grega do hebraico Azariah, **Yahweh tem ajudado.**

1. Um oficial do exército de Judas Macabeu (ver I Macabeus 5:18,56,60). Quando Judas se ausentou (ver 18), ele partilhou do comando do exército judeu com Joseph ben Zacariah. Ficou inchado de orgulho e quis tornar-se famoso, convidando Górgias a combatê-lo, perto de Jamínia. Mas foi redondamente derrotado.

2. Nome do anjo Rafael, de acordo com Tobias 5:12; 6:6,13; 7:8 e 9:2.

3. Homem que deu apoio às reformas sob Esdras. (Ver I Esdras 9:43).

4. Em I Esdras 9:21, esse nome é usado, embora seu paralelo em Esdras 10:21 tenha a forma de Uzias.

5. Homem mencionado em I Esdras 9:48, mas com a forma de Azarias, no paralelo de Neemias 8:7.

6. Um homem com esse nome aparece em II Esdras 1:1, mas em I Crô. 6:13 ele é chamado de Azarias. (Z)

AZARIAS, ORAÇÃO DE

Trata-se de uma adição feita ao livro de Daniel. Juntamente com o Cântico dos Três Filhos foi inserida entre Daniel 3:23 e 3:24, na versão grega do livro. De acordo com a Vulgata Latina, essa adição foi colocada após Dan. 3:24 ss., unida ao Cântico dos Três Filhos, formando uma entidade separada. A oração foi posta nos lábios de Azarias, isto é, Abede-Nego, segundo seu nome babilônico. Alegadamente, a oração teve lugar enquanto ele e seus dois companheiros estavam dentro da fornalha ardente, onde haviam sido lançados por Nabucodonosor.

Conteúdo da oração: a. doxologia; b. declaração da justiça de Deus, devido ao que houve o cativeiro babilônico (vs. 3:10); c. um eloqüente apelo para o Senhor lembrar-se de Sua aliança, baseada na aceitação e não no sacrifício, que não mais podia ser realizado, em vista de um coração contrito (vs. 11-17); d. um voto de fidelidade e oração pedindo livramento, com a confusão lançada entre o inimigo, de tal modo que se reconhecesse que só o Senhor é Deus (vs. 18-22).

Independência. O fato de que em nenhuma porção dessa oração há ligação com o teste que imediatamente antes teria de ser experimentado, parece mostrar que a composição era uma obra literária separada, independente do livro de Daniel, e que posteriormente foi inserida nesse livro canônico, no lugar onde o editor achou mais conveniente fazê-lo. Talvez as perseguições dirigidas por Antíoco Epifânio IV (168-165 A.C.) tenham-na inspirado.

Natureza judaica. Embora escrita em grego, a obra tem atitude inteiramente judaica, com vários reflexos dos Salmos (a questão do coração contrito e do espírito humilde, Sal. 51:17) e do livro de Daniel (ver Dan. 9:4-10). Essa similaridade ao livro de Daniel talvez tenha sido a razão pela qual a obra foi inserida finalmente no livro de Daniel.

Canonicidade. Essa oração está contida no cânon da Igreja Católica Romana, que inclui a maioria dos livros apócrifos (ver o artigo a respeito), mas não faz parte do Antigo Testamento aceito pelos judeus e pelas edições protestantes da Bíblia. (CH GD J)

AZARUZ

Antepassado de uma família que retornou do exílio babilônico juntamente com Zorobabel, cujo nome aparece em I Esdras 5:15. Esse nome é omitido nos paralelos dos livros canônicos de Esdras e Neemias. (Z)

AZAZ

No hebraico significa **forte**. Foi um rubenita, pai de Bela (ver I Crô. 5:8), em cerca de 1700 A.C.

AZAZEL

Termo hebraico traduzido por «bode emissário» em Lev. 16:8, em nossa versão portuguesa. Há versões que apenas transliteram o nome, «Azazel». A palavra tem sido variegadamente compreendida:

1. Alguns supõem que está em pauta o *bode* enviado ao deserto no dia da expiação (ver o artigo). Mas o texto de Levítico 16:10 e 26 parece subentender que *Azazel* era aquilo *para o que* ou *em favor do que* o bode era solto.

2. Outros supõem que esse termo indica *o lugar para onde o bode era enviado*. Portanto, poderia indicar o lugar onde o bode era solto, ou o deserto para onde ele se dirigia por puro acaso.

3. Ainda outros pensam que a palavra refere-se a um ser pessoal, como um espírito, um demônio ou o próprio Satanás. A tradição da cabala judaica diz que Israel era salvo das astúcias do diabo quando esse bode lhe era enviado. O bode levaria todas as iniqüidades e as transgressões do povo. O bode, pois, atuaria como uma espécie de noiva, que Satanás aceitaria, permitindo que Israel escapasse sem ser atacado. (Ver Deu. 32:17; Sal. 106:37 e sobre os «sátiros», em II Crô. 11:15). Muitos eruditos têm aceitado essa idéia, embora outros considerem-na uma interpretação improvável dentro do contexto mosaico, ainda que tenha feito parte da demonologia posterior de Israel.

4. Outros estudiosos pensam que se trata de um *completo envio*, ou seja, a total remoção dos pecados do povo. Mas a erudição evangélica moderna tem favorecido a terceira dessas quatro interpretações. Não obstante, o trecho de Levítico 17:7 parece excluir a idéia de que o bode servia como um sacrifício oferecido a Azazel. Seja como for, é interessante observar que o livro de I Enoque, refletindo o judaísmo posterior, faz Azazel aparecer como o chefe dos anjos rebeldes. (MiC Z)

AZAZIAS

No hebraico significa **Yahweh é forte**. Nome de várias pessoas do Antigo Testamento:

1. Um levita, nomeado durante o reinado de Davi para tocar harpa no culto ligado ao transporte da arca da aliança da casa de Obede-Edom para seu devido lugar (ver I Crô. 15:21), em cerca de 1040 A.C.

2. Pai de Oséias, príncipe da tribo de Efraim, quando Davi fez o recenseamento do povo (ver I Crô. 27:20), em 1040 A.C.

3. Um levita que, durante o reinado de Ezequias (726 A.C.), estava encarregado de recolher os dízimos e as coisas dedicadas ao templo, sob a direção de Conanias e Simei (ver II Crô. 31:13). (S)

AZBUQUE

No hebraico significa **forte devastação** ou **perdão**. Antepassado, ou talvez pai de um certo Neemias, príncipe da metade do distrito de Bete-Zur (ver Nee. 3:16), em 445 A.C. Esse Neemias não era o mesmo Neemias que foi a principal personagem do livro desse nome, embora seu contemporâneo. Ele ajudou a reconstruir a muralha de Jerusalém. (ID)

AZECA

No hebraico, **lavrado** ou **brecha**. Uma cidade na planície de Judá (ver Jos. 15:35; I Sam. 17:1), com aldeias ao redor (ver Nee. 11:30), e que aparentemente era uma fortaleza (ver Jer. 34:7). Ali foram derrotados os reis amorreus confederados, pelas tropas de Josué. Os exércitos amorreus foram destruídos por uma saraivada (ver Jos. 10:10,11). Após a batalha de Bete-Horom, Josué perseguiu os cananeus até esse lugar. Os filisteus acamparam-se entre Azeca e Socó, antes de Davi derrotar Golias (ver I Sam. 17:1). Foi fortificada por Reoboão (ver II Crô. 11:9), e ainda era usada como fortaleza ao tempo da invasão dos babilônios (ver Jer. 34:7). Portanto, foi uma das cidades que se rendeu a Nabucodonosor, antes deste atacar Jerusalém. Após o exílio babilônico, foi um dos primeiros lugares a serem reocupados por Israel (ver Nee. 11:30). É possível que a «proteção» referida em Isaías 22:8 seja uma referência a Azeca.

Essa cidade ficava localizada a 5 km ao norte de Beit Jibrin (Eleuterópolis) e a 24 km a noroeste de Hebrom. Em um platô, no alto do cômoro, permanece até hoje um resto de muralha e torres, dessa antiga fortaleza. A cidade bizantina de Azeca talvez seja a atual Khirbet el 'Alami, imediatamente a leste do cômoro.

Tragédia. Na carta nº 4 de Laquis Hosaías, que era comandante de uma guarnição postada ao norte de Laquis, informa seu superior, Joás, em Laquis, de que não mais podia ver os sinais (de fogo ou de fumaça) emitidos por Azeca, que ficava a norte do seu posto. É que a cidade havia caído! (ID S Z)

AZEITE (ÓLEOS)

Consideremos os seguintes pontos:

1. *Termos*. No hebraico temos *shemen*, «graxa» ou «ungüento»; *yishar*, «brilhante» e «azeite claro». Está em foco o azeite de oliveira. (Ver Núm. 18:12 e Deu. 7:13). No aramaico temos *meshak*, «ungüento» (ver Esd. 6:9 e 7:22). No grego temos *elaion*, «azeite de oliveira».

2. *Produtores de azeite*. Vários animais, peixes e plantas; mais especificamente ainda, as azeitonas. Há doze tipos diferentes de óleos vegetais, entre os quais citamos a oliveira, o rícino, o babaçu, a amêndoa, etc.

3. *História do uso do azeite*. A origem do uso de azeite perde-se nas brumas da antiguidade. Há óleos mencionados nos registros históricos de todos os povos. Os egípcios tinham muitos tipos de óleos, de muitos produtos diferentes. Na Grécia o uso de oliveira remonta até onde os registros recuam. Também eram usadas gorduras animais, embora o azeite de oliveira fosse o principal óleo dos antigos. Sabemos sobre o culto da oliveira em Creta, desde 2500 A.C. O cultivo da oliveira e o uso de seu azeite, com vistas a muitos propósitos, inclusive para cozinhar, era comum nas terras que margeavam o Mediterrâneo oriental, tendo chegado a Roma desde 580 A.C. Moisés chamou a Palestina de «terra de oliveiras» (ver Deu. 8:8), o que significa que quando o povo de Israel ali chegou, já encontrou essa espécie vegetal.

4. *Manufatura*. As azeitonas eram espremidas à mão, pisadas, ou esmagadas em moinhos (ver Êxo. 27:20; 29:40; Lev. 24:2; Núm. 28:2). Ver o artigo sobre *Moinhos*, quanto a detalhes. Uma boa oliveira pode produzir nada menos de 60 litros de azeite, anualmente. As azeitonas precisavam ser esmagadas com cuidado, para que o caroço não fosse partido, o que liberaria um líquido indesejável. Para que o fruto produzisse bom óleo, a polpa devia ser ensopada em água quente, e então ser espremida uma segunda vez. Se o processo fosse repetido, haveria mais algum azeite, embora de qualidade inferior. Então deixava-se o líquido em repouso, em uma jarra ou gamela, para que as impurezas se juntassem no fundo, por decantação. Havia prensas comerciais de grandes dimensões, como aquelas que foram encontradas em Debir e Bete-Semes, em Judá, datadas dos séculos X e VI A.C.

5. *Usos do azeite*. a. Como alimento (ver I Reis 17:12; II Reis 4:2). O azeite era misturado à farinha de trigo, para o fabrico de pão (ver I Reis 17:12), ou para o fabrico de bolos (ver Lev. 2:1,4-7).

AZEITE — AZEITONA

Os gregos faziam a *maza*, uma espécie de mingau, do qual participava o azeite de oliveira. As azeitonas, sem qualquer preparação prévia, serviam de alimento para os antigos. Para os israelitas, a azeitona e seu azeite revestiam-se de primária importância (ver Sir. 39:31; Jer. 31:12; 41:8; Luc. 16:6 ss.). Sua abundância era considerada um sinal de prosperidade (ver Joel 2:19). b. Como cosmético, para ungir a pele do corpo, os cabelos, etc., ou simplesmente para efeito de beleza. (Ver Deu. 28;40; II Sam. 12:20; 14:2 e Rute 3:3). c. Para ungir os mortos. d. Como medicamento. O azeite era esfregado no corpo quando a pessoa estava febril, ou era usado em banhos e na unção de ferimentos (ver Isa. 1:6 e Luc. 10:34). Josefo fala no uso de azeite quente, em banhos, para a cura de certas enfermidades (ver *Guerras* xxxiii.5). O azeite de oliveira era usado como um rito, na unção dos enfermos, no aguardo da prometida intervenção divina (ver Tia. 5:14). e. Como sinal de hospitalidade. Pés e mãos eram lavados e ungidos com azeite, como sinal de cortesia prestada aos visitantes (ver Sal. 23:5). A negligência quanto a esses cuidados era considerada uma descortesia (ver Luc. 7:46). Esse azeite usualmente era propositalmente perfumado. f. *Para efeito de iluminação*. O azeite era o combustível usado nas antigas lâmpadas, que usavam pavios de pano torcido, de algodão ou de palha (ver Mat. 25:1-8 e Luc. 12:35).

6. *Usos religiosos*. O azeite de oliveira é usado com propósitos religiosos desde a remota antiguidade. No papiro Petersburg, à deusa-cobra são prometidos nove azeites santos, para ungir a sua estátua. Na Bíblia, o azeite da unção era uma cerimônia que envolvia reis (ver I Sam. 10:1), sacerdotes (ver Lev. 8:30), profetas (ver Isa. 61:1) e até o escudo dos guerreiros (ver II Sam. 1:21 e Isa. 21:5). O tabernáculo e seus móveis foram ungidos (ver Êxo. 30:22,23). O azeite era usado como combustível que permitia que o candeeiro permanentemente aceso no santuário (ver Êxo. 27:20). Era oferecido juntamente com o cereal (ver Lev. 2:4-6), e fazia parte do dízimo (ver Deu. 12:17). Também era oferecido aos ídolos (ver Isa. 57:9). O uso do azeite, nos sacrifícios, indicava a alegria e o júbilo, ao passo que a ausência de azeite indicava necessidade e humilhação (ver Isa. 61:3 e Joel 2:19).

7. *Valor comercial do azeite*. O azeite figurava entre os principais artigos do comércio, juntamente com os cereais e o vinho (ver Núm. 18:12; Deu. 7:13). Era largamente negociado (ver Eze. 27:17; Luc. 16:6). As riquezas de uma pessoa eram parcialmente calculadas em termos de azeite. Óleo batido (que era o melhor azeite) formava parte do pagamento anual de Salomão a Hirão, de Tiro (ver I Reis 5:11). O azeite era um produto de valor suficiente para que Eliseu aconselhasse à viúva a pagar sua dívida mediante a venda de azeite (ver II Reis 4:7). Era guardado nos tesouros reais juntamente com ouro, prata e especiarias (ver II Reis 20:13), e também era usado no pagamento do tributo (ver Osé. 12:1). Ismael poupou as vidas de dez peregrinos vindos de Siquém, quando eles lhe ofereceram azeite, juntamente com trigo e cevada. Ostraca dos dias de Jeroboão II, encontradas em Samaria, dão testemunho do comércio do azeite. Em Apocalipse 18:12,13, o azeite é alistado entre os produtos preciosos, juntamente com o marfim, os cavalos, as especiarias, o vinho e os escravos. Havia negociantes especializados no comércio do azeite (ver Mat. 25:8).

8. *Usos figurados*. a. como símbolo de abundância (ver Pro. 21:17); b. de alegria (ver Sal. 45:7); c. a ausência de azeite era evidência do desprazer divino (ver Joel 1:10); d. a sua abundância representava as bênçãos divinas (ver Joel 2:24). e. As palavras enganosas são comparadas ao azeite (ver Sal. 55:21). f. O Espírito Santo e Sua unção são representados pelo azeite (ver Lev. 8:13; I Sam. 10:1; Isa. 61:1 e Mat. 25:1,8,9). g. As palavras da mulher sedutora são comparadas ao azeite (ver Pro. 5:3). h. As consolações do evangelho assemelham-se ao azeite (ver Isa. 61:3 e Heb. 1:9). i. O azeite simbolizava a unção aprovadora de reis, profetas, e do próprio Messias (ver Heb. 1:9).

9. *Modernos usos religiosos*. O bispo católico romano consagra três óleos santos na Terça-feira Santa: 1. o óleo dos catecúmenos, derivado da prática do uso do óleo da unção, por ocasião do batismo, o qual é usado nos atos de batismo, consagração de igrejas, altares, ordenação de sacerdotes e coroação de monarcas católicos romanos. 2. Na crisma é usado o azeite de oliveira misturado com bálsamo, para unção no batismo, na confirmação, nas Santas Ordens, nas igrejas, nos altares, nos cálices, nos sinos e nas águas do batismo. 3. O óleo da extrema-unção, usado nos moribundos. (E ID UN Z)

AZEITE BATIDO

Essa expressão aparece em Êxo. 27:20; 29:40; Lev. 24:2; Núm. 28:5 e I Reis 5:11. Aparentemente refere-se ao azeite de oliveira obtido na primeira prensa, o qual seria de melhor qualidade, antes da adição do que era necessário para extração dos azeites de grau inferior. Ver Oliveira e Azeitona.

AZEITONA

No hebraico, **gargar**, «bago». No grego, **elaía**, «azeitona». O termo hebraico ocorre somente em Isa. 17:6. Sabe-se que a menção à azeitona é porque está dentro do contexto da «oliveira», mencionada no mesmo versículo. A alusão é à prática humanitária dos cultivadores israelitas, que deixavam alguns rabiscos para os pobres colherem. Isso o profeta aplica aos poucos remanescentes que restarão com vida, nos últimos dias, quando «a glória de Jacó será apoucada, e a gordura da sua carne desaparecerá» (Isa. 17:4).

A palavra grega é de ocorrência mais freqüente, quinze vezes (ver Mat. 2:1; 24:3; 26:30; Mar. 11:1; 13:3; 14:26; Luc. 19:29,37; 21:37; 23:39; João 8:1; Rom. 11:17,24; Tia. 3:12; Apo. 11:4). O termo grego também significa «oliveira».

Em notável metáfora, Paulo compara Israel com a «boa oliveira», ao passo que os gentios convertidos são ramos de «oliveira brava» enxertados na boa oliveira. Em seguida, ele mostra quão absurdo é pensar que Deus não tem mais plano relativo a Israel, quando diz: «...quanto mais não serão enxertados na sua própria oliveira aqueles que são ramos naturais!» (Rom. 11:17,24). De fato, precisamos levar em conta o futuro papel dos judeus, nos acontecimentos escatológicos preditos nas Escrituras, ou nosso quadro escatológico ficará incompleto e distorcido. O simbolismo reaparece em Apo. 11:3-13, que se refere a dois futuros grandes profetas, que são chamados de «...as duas oliveiras e dois candeeiros que se acham em pé diante do Senhor da terra». Ver as notas expositivas completas, no NTI, sobre as duas testemunhas do Apocalipse.

Tiago, ao tratar dos pecados da língua, por causa dos quais, às vezes, de uma mesma boca procedem a bênção e a maldição, mostra o quanto a maledicência é imprópria no crente, ao perguntar, de uma forma

AZEL — AZRIEL

que a resposta só pode ser negativa: «Acaso, meus irmãos, pode a figueira produzir azeitonas, ou a videira, figos?» (Tia. 3:12).

AZEL
No hebraico significa **nobre**. Era descendente de Jônatas, filho de Eleasá (ver I Crô. 8:37 ss. e 9:43 ss.), em cerca de 860 A.C.

Havia um lugar que também tinha esse nome, não muito distante de Jerusalém (ver Zac. 14:5), mas cujo local é atualmente desconhecido. (Z)

AZÉM
No grego, *Aisem*. Essa palavra significa «osso», «poderoso» e «fortaleza». Algumas traduções também grafam o nome como Ezém. (Ver Jos. 15:29; I Crô. 4:29). Era uma cidade no extremo sul da terra de Canaã. que a princípio foi dada à tribo de Judá (ver Jos. 15:29) e posteriormente à tribo de Simeão (ver Jos. 19:3). Tem sido identificada com a moderna El-Aujeh, a 24 km a sudoeste de Reobote e também com a Azmom de Números 34:4. Todavia, outros estudiosos pensam que sua localização é incerta, ao passo que ainda outros pensam que ficava acerca de vinte quilômetros a suleste de Berseba. (Z)

AZEPURITE
Forma alternativa de **Jorá** (vide).

AZETAS
Antepassado de uma família que retornou do cativeiro babilônico em companhia de Zorobabel (ver I Esdras 5:15), mas cujo nome é omitido nas passagens canônicas paralelas de Esdras 2:16 e Neemias 7:21. (Z)

AZGADE
No hebraico significa **forte na sorte**, ou então *adoração* ou *súplica*. Alguns dizem que significa *Deus é forte*. Os filhos de Azgade, em número de mil duzentos e vinte e dois, retornaram da Babilônia com Zorobabel (ver Esd. 2:12), em cerca de 536 A.C. Em Neemias 7:17 o número deles é dado como de dois mil trezentos e vinte e dois. Na segunda caravana, vieram com Esdras cento e dez homens de Azgade (ver Esd. 8:12). Esses subscreveram o pacto com Neemias (ver Nee. 10:15). (ID S)

AZIA
Forma alternativa de **Uzá** (vide).

AZIEI
Forma alternativa de **Azarias** (vide).

AZIEL
No hebraico significa **Deus é poder**. Foi um levita que tocou a harpa quando a arca da aliança foi trazida de volta a Jerusalém (ver I Crô. 15:20). É chamado Jaaziel, em I Crônicas 15:18. (Z)

AZIZA
No hebraico, o *forte*. Homem que pertencia à família de Zatu e que se casou com uma mulher estrangeira, mas que a despediu após o cativeiro babilônico, na época de Esdras (ver Esd. 10:27). Em I Esdras 9:28 é chamado Zerdaías.

AZMAVETE
No hebraico, **forte como a morte**. Nome de vários personagens do Antigo Testamento:

1. Um nativo de Baurim (ver II Sam. 23:31), provavelmente benjamita. Foi um dos trinta poderosos guerreiros de Davi. Cerca de 1050 A.C.

2. Um descendente de Mefibosete ou Meribaal (ver I Crô. 8:36 e 9:42).

3. Um benjamita, pai de Jeziel e Pelete, dois arqueiros e fundibulários habilidosos. Esse homem tem sido identificado por alguns estudiosos com o de núm. 1. Ainda outros dizem que se trata de um lugar. (Ver I Crô. 12:3). Cerca de 1050 A.C.

4. Encarregado dos tesouros reais sob Davi (I Crô. 27:25), em cerca de 1015 A.C.

5. Uma aldeia, provavelmente no território de Benjamim, identificada com a moderna el Hizmeh, cerca de 8 km a nordeste de Jerusalém. Ela é chamada Bete-Azmavete em Neemias 7:28. Quarenta e dois homens retornaram com Zorobabel, vindos do cativeiro (ver Esd. 2:24). O trecho de Neemias 12:29 informa-nos que esse lugar supriu alguns dos cantores para a dedicação do segundo templo. (ID S Z)

AZMOM
No hebraico, **parecido com um osso** ou **fortaleza**. Uma cidade no deserto de Maom, ao sul de Judá. Pertencia à tribo de Simeão (ver Núm. 34:4 e Jos. 15:4). Tem sido identificada por alguns com 'Ain el-Qaseimeh, a sudoeste de Cades-Barnéia. (S Z)

AZNOTE-TABOR
No hebraico, **cumes do Tabor**. Uma cidade ocidental do território de Naftali, entre o rio Jordão e Hucoque (ver Jos. 19:34), evidentemente na área do monte Tabor. Desconhece-se o local moderno. (S Z)

AZRICÃO
No hebraico, **ajuda contra o inimigo**, ou **a ajuda surgiu**. Nome de várias pessoas do Antigo Testamento:

1. Filho de Nearias, da linhagem real de Judá, descendente de Zorobabel (ver I Crô. 3:23), em cerca de 460 A.C.

2. Filho mais velho de Azel, descendente de Saul (ver I Crô. 8:38 e 9:44), em cerca de 860 A.C.

3. Um levita, antepassado de Semaías (ver I Crô. 8:14 e Nee. 11:15), em cerca de 470 A.C.

4. Governador do palácio de Acaz (de Judá), morto durante a invasão de Peca, rei de Israel (ver I Crô. 28:7), em cerca de 741 A.C.

AZRIEL
No hebraico, **ajuda de Deus**. Nome de várias pessoas do Antigo Testamento:

1. Chefe da casa de meia-tribo de Manassés, além do Jordão (ver I Crô. 5:24,26). Juntamente com outros, ele foi levado ao cativeiro pelos assírios.

2. Antepassado de Jerimote, um naftalita. Era chefe da tribo de Naftali ao tempo do recenseamento feito por Davi (ver I Crô. 27:19), em cerca de 1015 A.C.

3. Pai de Seraías, um dos oficiais de Jeoaquim (ver Jer. 26:26), em cerca de 606 A.C. Foi um dos emissários enviados para deter Jeremias e Baruque. (ID)

AZOR

No hebraico, **ajudador**. Era filho de Eliaquim e fez parte da genealogia de Jesus (ver Mat. 1:13,14), cerca de 400 A.C. (S)

AZOTO

Forma alternativa de **Asdode** (vide).

AZUBA

No hebraico, **ruínas** ou **esquecida**. 1. Esposa de Calebe, filho de Hezrom (ver I Crô. 2:18,19), em cerca de 1590 A.C. 2. Mãe do rei Josafá (ver I Reis 22:42 e II Crô. 20:31), em cerca de 914 A.C.

AZUL

Ver o artigo geral sobre as **cores**. 1. *Implicações espirituais*. Nos tipos simbólicos, o **azul** indica o que é celestial, a pureza e a humildade. Estudos sobre a aura humana mostram que esse conceito tem base nos fatos. Pessoas dotadas de elevada espiritualidade têm mais azul na sua aura; e quanto mais claro e brilhante for o azul, tanto maior será a espiritualidade. Ver o artigo sobre a *aura*. 2. *A ciência* tem mostrado que as diferentes cores afetam os estados de espírito, de pensamento e do corpo. As cores podem curar, porquanto controlam vibrações de luz que produzem um efeito benéfico sobre o corpo. 3. *Considerações literais*. Na Palestina, essa cor era normalmente produzida pelo uso de uma ostra, encontrada nas costas da Fenícia, atualmente denominada *Helix Ianthina*. Josefo (*Anti*. iii.7, par. 7) e Filo falaram sobre essa cor como emblema do céu. Príncipes, nobres (ver Eze. 23:6; Ecl. 40:4) e os ídolos da Babilônia (ver Jer. 10:9) vestiam-se de trajes azuis. Nas bordas das vestes dos hebreus havia um cordão azul (ver Núm. 15:38), dando a entender sua conexão espiritual. Para usos decorativos, fios eram tingidos de azul e então eram entretecidos em pano (ver Êxo. 25:4; 26:1), havendo também fazendas pintadas com várias cores. No Tabernáculo fêz-se grande uso de cores, incluindo a cor azul, e outro tanto se verificava com as vestes sacerdotais (ver Êxo. 28:5,6,28) e no interior do templo (ver II Crô. 2:7,15). Em Ecl. 6:30, temos o sentido básico de *valor*, simbolizado pela cor azul, porquanto cordas dessa cor são comparadas à sabedoria. Nos tempos antigos, Tiro era o centro produtor de corantes (ver II Crô. 2:7,14). Nos tempos romanos, Diocleciano nomeou Doroteu como superintendente da produção de corantes. Há montões de cascas de moluscos em Sidom, revelando que naquele lugar eram fabricados os corantes. (FOR I IB)

AZUR

No hebraico, **ajudador**. Nome de várias personagens do Antigo Testamento:

1. Um daqueles que assinaram o pacto com Neemias (ver Nee. 10:17), em cerca de 445 A.C. Provavelmente ele é chamado pelo nome de família.

2. Pai de Hananias, de Gibeão (ver Jer. 28:1), que foi um falso profeta no tempo de Zedequias (cerca de 596 A.C.)

3. Pai de Jaazanias (ver Eze. 11:1). Jaazanias era um líder do povo, a quem o profeta Ezequiel viu em visão traçando falsos esquemas a respeito de Jerusalém, em cerca de 593 A.C. (ID S)

Decoração barroca

1. Formas Antigas

fenício (semítico), 1000 A.C. grego ocidental, 800 A.C. latino, 50 D.C.

2. Nos Manuscritos Gregos do Novo Testamento

3. Formas Modernas

B *B* b *b*   B B b b   *B b*   B *B* b *b*

4. História

B é a segunda letra do alfabeto português. Nos idiomas semíticos, era chamada *beth*, «casa». Essa palavra começava com o fonema consonantal *b*, razão pela qual a letra «b» veio a ter, universalmente, esse som. Provavelmente essa letra desenvolveu-se a partir de um hieróglifo egípcio que representava uma casa. Os gregos adotaram a letra, chamando-a de *beta*. Finalmente, o conjunto inteiro das letras usadas em um idioma veio a chamar-se *alfabeto*, termo formado do grego *alpha* + *beta*. Essa letra passou para o latim, e daí para muitos idiomas modernos.

5. Usos e Símbolos

B é o nome da sétima nota musical, também chamada *si* na escala do Dó. Nos sistemas de gradação, essa letra representa *bom*, sendo menos do que A e melhor do que C (médio). Entretanto, pode indicar algo de qualidade inferior, como o grau B, em contraste com o grau A. Na combinação B. A., dentro dos graus acadêmicos, representa Bacharel em Artes; e B.S. indica Bacharel em Ciências. *B* é empregado como símbolo do manuscrito *Vaticano*, descrito no artigo separado *B*.

Caligrafia de Darrell Steven Champlin

B

B

Símbolo usado para designar o manuscrito bíblico *Codex Vaticanus*, que indubitavelmente é um dos melhores em existência. As objeções a essa avaliação ignoram vários fatos: a. Que muitos dos mais antigos manuscritos em *papiro* têm um texto similar ao do Vaticanus, de tal modo que em sentido algum o mesmo aparece solitário. b. Que muitos dos mais antigos *manuscritos unciais* também confirmam esse texto (chamado neutro ou alexandrino, pelos críticos textuais). c. Que várias das mais antigas *versões* (latina, boárica, saídica, etc.) confirmam esse texto. d. Que alguns dos primeiros *pais* da Igreja usaram um texto bastante similar ao do codex B (Vaticanus). Esse manuscrito data da primeira metade do século IV D.C., e poderia ter sido um dos cinqüenta manuscritos que Eusébio preparou, por ordem do imperador Constantino. No A.T., o manuscrito é completo, excetuando as primeiras trinta e nove páginas, e dez páginas dos Salmos. As porções que faltam no N.T. são Heb. 9:14 até o fim, as epístolas pastorais e o Apocalipse. O manuscrito foi escrito em finíssimo velino. Não tem iniciais em corpo maior, nem pontuação, não tem acentuação, nem divisões em capítulos ou seções, conforme se vê em manuscritos posteriores, embora tenha uma forma de divisão toda peculiar, bem como dois outros manuscritos, XI e 579. Há total ausência de ornamentação, e isso, juntamente com as diferenças acima mencionadas, confirmam sua antiqüíssima origem.

O nome desse manuscrito deriva-se do fato de que é um dos tesouros da Biblioteca do Vaticano, em Roma. Tem estado ali desde antes de 1475. Um correspondente de Erasmo, em 1533, enviou-lhe certo número de passagens selecionadas, a fim de demonstrar que esse manuscrito era superior a qualquer um que Erasmo tinha, para a compilação do seu Textus Receptus (ver o artigo); Mas o manuscrito não foi franqueado ao exame público. Por muito tempo, as autoridades do Vaticano mostraram-se muito zelosas, temendo que o manuscrito fosse danificado, e o zelo excessivo impediu seu uso. Porém, em 1889-1890, foram feitos fac-símiles fotográficos do manuscrito inteiro, de tal modo que seu estudo tornou-se possível para todos. Quanto a maiores detalhes sobre esse manuscrito e a questão inteira envolvida, tanto quanto aos documentos existentes como à teoria da crítica textual, ver o artigo sobre os *Manuscritos da Bíblia*. (KE ME)

BÃ

Um nome próprio que aparece em I Esdras 5:37, e que algumas traduções dos livros apócrifos emendam para Tobias. Um homem é chamado Bã, cujos descendentes figuram entre os exilados que retornaram da Babilônia, mas que não puderam provar que realmente pertenciam a Israel. Os trechos paralelos de Esd. 2:60 e Nee. 7:62 dizem «Tobias». (Z)

BAADER, FRANZ V.

Suas datas: 1765-1841. Foi médico praticante, professor honorário da Universidade de Munique. No campo religioso foi místico e filósofo. Seu estilo de redação, muito aforístico, com muita fantasia, analogia e etimologia, fez com que as suas obras tivessem um sentido vago. Ele combinava idéias de Jacó Boehme, Shelling e Fichte (ver os artigos a respeito deles). Afirmava que o conhecimento humano é idealmente (e possivelmente), um co-conhecimento com o conhecimento divino. Assim, sendo, o homem poderia ser receptor de conhecimento, e não criador do mesmo. Baader aderiu à doutrina católica, em consonância com as linhas traçadas por Anselmo, acusando a Reforma Protestante de ser mais uma revolução do que uma reforma. (E)

BAAL (BAALISMO)

A palavra e seu uso. Essa é a palavra hebraica que significa «proprietário», «senhor» ou «marido». É usada em I Crô. 5:5; 8:30 e 9:36 como um nome pessoal; e, de modo geral, designa a divindade cananéia desse nome. As identificações incluem aquelas com restrições a algum mero lugar de adoração, como Baal-Peor (Núm. 25:3), Baal-Gade (Jos. 11:17), Baal-Hermom (Juí. 3:3), etc. Algumas vezes, tais combinações indicam uma característica da divindade, e não algum lugar com o qual estaria associada, como Baal-Berite (Baal do pacto, em Juí. 8:33); Baal-Zebube, talvez uma corruptela de Baal-Zebul (que significa «príncipe», em II Reis 1:2). O próprio termo sugere que a divindade era considerada *proprietária* de um determinado lugar, pelo que exerceria controle ali, no tocante a certos aspectos da vida humana, mas, sobretudo, no tocante à fertilidade.

Baalismo. A adoração a Baal era, essencialmente, uma religião da natureza, cuja ênfase principal era a fertilidade. O Oriente Próximo exibiu várias formas de religião da fertilidade, e essa religião dos cananeus era a mais desenvolvida entre elas, quanto a esse aspecto. Israel deixou-se arrastar pela influência do baalismo por meio de sincretismo (os hebreus incorporaram-no, ou ao menos aspectos seus, à sua fé), tendo havido uma reação profética (os profetas que reagiram contra esses elementos corruptores).

Fontes informativas. O A.T., os tabletes de Ras Shamra (ver o artigo) e Filo Bíblio.

Idéias. *El* seria o pai dos deuses, mas não teria muito contato com os homens. Aserá era a deusa-mãe. Um filho (ou neto) de destaque deles seria Baal. Sua consorte, Astarte (que no A.T. aparece como Astarote ou Astorete), era a deusa da fertilidade (ver o artigo sobre ela). Nos tabletes de Ras Shamra, Anate aparece como a consorte de Baal. Seu maior inimigo era Mote (a morte). O clima da Síria e da Palestina contribuía para a elaboração dessa religião. As chuvas cessam em março-abril. Só começa a chover novamente em outubro-novembro; e, durante o intervalo, pouca vegetação pode crescer. A menos que as chuvas voltem, a fome é inevitável. Assim, os cananeus personificaram as forças que fazem a vegetação voltar à vida. A razão pela qual as chuvas cessariam é que Baal seria morto em uma luta feroz contra Mote. E as chuvas retornariam porque os amigos de Baal (como o Sol - Shapsh ou Shemesh) e Astarte (fertilidade), devolveriam-lhe a vida (princípio da ressurreição). A terra floresceria novamente porque Baal e Astarte copulavam. Assim, temos nisso uma forma de religião que é, essencialmente, a adoração à natureza. Quando os homens perturbam os deuses ou deixam de agradá-los, há perturbações nas condições atmosféricas, ou nas vidas das famílias e das tribos.

Festividades. A fim de promover o sentimento religioso do povo e honrar os deuses, foram instituídas festas que apelavam ao impulso procriador e a licensiosidade, incluindo a prostituição masculina e feminina, que se tornou um acompanhamento indispensável nesses cultos de fertilidade. Isso prosseguia durante os períodos de festividade e fora dos mesmos.

Influência sobre Israel. Essa religião exerceu grande influência sobre Israel, especialmente no norte (Israel, em contraste com Judá), onde as idéias e as culturas pagãs tornaram-se parte, mais rapidamente, da perspectiva religiosa dos israelitas. Isso provocou os protestos dos profetas. Sob tais circunstâncias foi que Elias e seus sucessores postularam a pergunta se o Deus de Israel era Yahweh ou Baal (ver I Reis 18). Os símbolos dessa adoração foram condenados pelos profetas, incluindo a árvore ou bosque sagrado, a coluna e os terafins (imagens, que incluíam figurinhas da deusa da fertilidade, que se tornaram populares e numerosas entre os israelitas). O protesto levantado pelos profetas contra esse tipo de religião pode ter sido um dos fatores que raramente permitia que Deus fosse chamado de *Pai*; e o A.T. não tem palavra que corresponda a *deusa*. Além disso, a expressão *filho de Deus*, aplicada ao homem, é rara no A.T. Tais termos poderiam ser erroneamente entendidos, em termos pagãos. No judaísmo havia o cuidado de se evitar a terminologia sexual no seio da família, porquanto isso era por demais comum nas religiões politeístas e de fertilidade, entre os vizinhos de Israel.

Fatores do vigor da religião de fertilidade. 1. Israel não expulsou os cananeus de suas terras, mas antes, misturou-se com eles em casamento. 2. Aqueles que tinham acabado de entrar na Terra Prometida tinham acabado de sair das experiências no deserto. Formas religiosas que fomentavam festividades e os prazeres sensuais eram alternativas tentadoras. Ou, pelo menos, elementos tomados por empréstimo dessas atividades que sem dúvida eram muito atrativos. 3. A lei de Israel era austera. Sempre será mais fácil seguir o curso de menor resistência. Assim, persistia por um lado a fé em Yahweh, e esta ia-se misturando com elementos cananeus. Esse processo sincretista é ilustrado em passagens como Juí. 2:1-5; 2:11-13,17, 19; 3:5-7; 6:25. A mesma coisa se dava com combinações de palavras, como Jerubaal (ver Juí. 7:1), Beeliada (ver I Crô. 14:7), Es-Baal e Meribe-Baal (ver I Crô. 8:33,34), que surgiram de outros nomes próprios. As ostraca de Samaria (cerca de 780 A.C.) demonstram que para cada dois nomes que envolviam o nome de Yahweh, um era uma forma qualquer composta de Baal. O trecho de I Reis 18 mostra-nos que o baalismo tornou-se tão forte em Israel que somente sete mil deles permaneceram fiéis à antiga fé. Elias conseguiu evitar o colapso total da fé judaica. Embora continuassem havendo reformas e o protesto dos profetas (ver Osé. 2:16,17), parece que foi necessário o cativeiro para impor a purificação necessária.

Dois grandes mitos de Baal. Os textos de Ras Shamra contêm esses mitos, a saber: 1. O conflito com o Príncipe do Mar e Juiz do Rio (o deus das águas obtém a ascendência e, arrogantemente, intimida os outros deuses). Baal, com a ajuda de alguns outros deuses, é capaz de derrotá-lo, confiando-o à sua devida esfera de atividade. Talvez essa luta seja simbolizada pelo leviatã da Bíblia, que poderia ser o mesmo *lotan*, a serpente enroscada, e que possivelmente seja idêntica ao Príncipe do Mar. — Alguns supõem que o Dia do Senhor (segundo originalmente concebido no judaísmo) poderia referir-se à vitória de Yahweh sobre as forças do caos. E esse conceito poderia depender do mito cananeu, acima descrito. 2. Outrossim, havia o deus que morria e ressuscitava; Baal, morto por Mote, era então ressuscitado pelo deus Sol e por Astarte. Tal suposta ressurreição era acompanhada por grandes festividades de sensualismo. Apesar de que o judaísmo, como é óbvio, nunca desenvolvesse qualquer coisa similar, excetuando casos de empréstimos diretos extraídos das religiões de seus vizinhos pagãos, alguns estudiosos supõem que o próprio conceito de ressurreição pode ter sido provocado, pelo menos em parte, por essa antiga crença. Não há como determinar até que ponto isso pode ter sido verdade. Mas a verdade do conceito da ressurreição em nada é prejudicada ainda que os povos pagãos, de maneira crua, tivessem antecipado e expressado essa idéia à sua maneira ímpia. (E ID SMIT Z)

BAAL-BERITE

No hebraico, **Senhor do pacto**. Era um deus cananeu, adorado pelo povo de Siquém, após a morte de Gideão (ver Juí. 8:33 e 9:4). Essa adoração era promovida mediante o ídolo do deus. Abimeleque, neto de Gideão, tomou setenta peças de prata da casa desse deus a fim de contratar homens para o ajudarem em sua rebelião (ver Juí. 9:4). Não se sabe como interpretar a palavra *pacto*, associada a esse deus. 1. Poderia ser um pacto geral: a aliança entre o povo e essa divindade; ou 2. poderia ser um pacto particular: a divindade chamada como testemunha do pacto de Siquém com Israel. Provavelmente devemos pensar nessa segunda alternativa. (ND S Z)

BAAL-GADE

No hebraico, **Senhor de sorte**. Nome de uma cidade no vale do Líbano, sob o monte Hermom (ver Jos. 11:17; 12:7 e 13:5). Ficava localizada no extremo norte das conquistas de Josué. A localização precisa é desconhecida, mas ficava entre o monte Líbano e o monte Hermom, talvez perto da moderna aldeia de Hasbeiya. Tell Haush, a doze quilômetros ao norte de Hasbeiya, tem sido identificado como o lugar, por alguns estudiosos. Esse lugar, de fato «todo o Líbano, na direção do pôr-do-sol, de Baal-Gade, sob o monte Hermom, até à entrada em Hamate», não foi conquistado por Israel antes da morte de Josué. Alguns têm identificado esse lugar com Baalbeque, mas tal identificação não tem resistido à investigação. (ID S)

BAAL-HAMOM

No hebraico significa «Baal das multidões». (Ver o artigo com esse título). Seja como for, era uma localidade nos montes de Efraim, perto de Samaria. Entre essa localidade e Dotã, foi sepultado o marido de Judite (ver Judite 8:3). No Antigo Testamento, o local é mencionado exclusivamente em Can. 8:11, onde se lê que ali Salomão tinha uma vinha.

BAAL-HANÃ

No hebraico, **Baal é gracioso**. Foi nome de duas pessoas, no A.T.

1. Um rei de Moabe que reinou após Saul (ver Gên. 36:38). Talvez fosse filho de Acbor, sucessor de Saul. Foi sucedido por Hadar ou Hadade (ver Gên. 37:39; Ver também I Crô. 1:49,50).

2. Um gederita, superintendente real das oliveiras e sicômoros nas planícies baixas, sob Davi (ver I Crô.

27:28), em cerca de 1015 A.C. (S)

BAAL-HAZOR

No hebraico, **Vila de Baal**. Lugar onde Absalão guardava seus rebanhos e realizou sua festa de tosquia (ver II Sam. 13:23). Não é a mesma Hazor (ver Nee. 11:33), atualmente Tell 'Asar. Por longo tempo, Absalão vinha planejando vingar-se de Amom, por haver desvirginado sua irmã, Tamar. A festa foi apenas um pretexto para que pudesse pôr as mãos sobre Amom. O plano deu certo. Absalão conseguiu matar Amom, e então foi esconder-se, durante algum tempo. É provável que o lugar onde a festa foi realizada fosse uma casa nas montanhas, sendo um lugar cerca de 1200 m acima do nível do mar. O lugar tem sido identificado com Jebel el-'Asur, a nordeste de et-Tayibeh, a pequena distância, e a leste da estrada para Siquém. (ID S)

BAAL-HERMOM

No hebraico, **Senhor de Hermom**. Tem sido identificado por alguns com Baal-Gade (ver o artigo a respeito), mas não há certeza quanto a isso. Seja como for, era um lugar onde Baal era adorado (ver o artigo a respeito), e estava localizado na Transjordânia, nas vertentes do monte Hermom. Ficava defronte da entrada para Hamate, onde habitavam os heveus (ver Juí. 3:3). Essa referência nos dá a idéia de que era uma montanha a leste do Líbano, chamada por esse nome. A atual Banjas mui provavelmente assinala o local. (Ver Jos. 13:5). (ID S UN)

BAAL-MEOM

No hebraico, **Senhor da habitação** (ver Núm. 32:38 e I Crô. 5:8). Foi uma cidade construída pelos descendentes de Rúben. Era uma das mais importantes cidades da fronteira de Moabe, juntamente com Bete-Jesimote e Quiriataim (ver Eze. 25:9). Fazia parte das possessões moabitas, ao tempo de Ezequiel (ver Eze. 25:9). Também era chamada pelo nome de Bete-Baal-Meom (ver Jos. 13:17), Bete-Meom (ver Jer. 48:23), e Beom (Núm. 32:3). Há uma inscrição na Pedra Moabita (ver o artigo a respeito) que diz que Mesa, rei de Moabe, edificou-a e ali construiu um reservatório. É provável que o lugar tivesse mudado de mãos com freqüência, entre Israel e Moabe, por diversas vezes. Ficava localizado em Ma'in, a quase quinze quilômetros a leste do mar Morto, segundo têm descoberto os arqueólogos. (ID UN)

BAAL, MEU

No hebraico, **Meu Senhor**. Um nome usado para indicar Deus (ver Os. 2:16), embora o termo fosse tipicamente pagão, e, naturalmente, trouxesse tal conotação. O povo recebeu ordem para não usar o nome, por esse motivo. Mas a referência pode significar apenas que Deus agora seria chamado *Ishi* (marido), e não Baal, porquanto essa mudança de nome estava ensinando uma lição espiritual. Israel deveria manter um correto relacionamento com Deus, como se fosse uma esposa para com seu esposo, e não meramente o relacionamento de um servo para com o seu senhor. Todavia, o desuso do nome Baal provavelmente também serviria de medida contra o paganismo. (ID)

BAAL-PEOR

No hebraico, **Senhor de Peor**. Era uma divindade adorada em Moabe, quando Balaão provocou a apostasia em Israel. Isso sucedeu quando Israel estava acampado em Sitim (ver Núm. 25:3 *ss.*). Todos os adoradores foram mortos, mediante o julgamento divino (ver Deu. 4:3). Essa apostasia particular prosseguiu, sendo relembrada muito tempo mais tarde (ver Sal. 106:28 e Osé. 9:10). Nesta última referência a adoração ao ídolo é chamada de «vergonhosa idolatria», e seus adoradores de «abomináveis». Alguns supõem que essa forma de adoração incluía excessos sexuais e perversões. Esse deus era a divindade local do monte Peor (daí o nome), e provavelmente estava vinculado ao Baal dos fenícios. (Z)

BAAL-PERAZIM

No hebraico, **Senhor dos calções**. Davi dera esse nome a um lugar, onde obteve a vitória em uma batalha contra os filisteus (ver II Sam. 5:20; I Crô. 14:11 e Isa. 28:21). Esse nome é curioso por ser o único que se compõe com o nome Baal, acerca do qual temos informações específicas sobre como o nome foi dado. O local é atualmente desconhecido, embora dois locais, próximos de Jerusalém, tenham sido sugeridos: a moderna Sheikh Bedr, a noroeste de Jerusalém, e um lugar no vale dos Gigantes, a sudoeste de Jerusalém. No trecho de Isaías 28:21, o lugar é chamado Monte Perazim. (ID S UN)

BAAL-SALISA

No hebraico, **Senhor de Salisa**. (Ver II Reis 4:42). Era um lugar no distrito de Salisa (ver I Sam. 9:4). Eusébio e Jerônimo disseram que era uma cidade a quinze milhas romanas de Dióspolis, perto do Monte Efraim. Era o lugar de nascimento do homem, de nome desconhecido, que, em tempo de fome, trouxe a Eliseu vinte pães de cevada e espigas de trigo que alimentaram cem homens. A quantidade de alimento era minúscula, para tanta gente. Mas houve um milagre de multiplicação, tornando o alimento suficiente a todos, pois ainda sobrou muito alimento após todos já estarem satisfeitos. O paralelo miraculoso de Jesus, na multiplicação dos pães e dos peixes, em Mat. 14:16 e *ss.*, é óbvio. Ambos os eventos ilustram como a provisão de Deus é surpreendente, podendo derrotar tanto a fome física quanto a fome espiritual. As pessoas sempre se surpreendem quando lhes é conferida uma provisão inesperada, e elas dizem: «Louvado seja o Senhor». Porém, em breve esquecem-se da providência divina, e tornam a surpreender-se, em futuras ocasiões. (G HA)

BAAL-TAMAR

No hebraico, **Senhor da palma**. Era um lugar perto de Gibeá, na tribo de Benjamim, onde as outras tribos lutaram com os benjamitas (ver Juí. 20:33). Eusébio chamava-a de Betamar, o que é um intercâmbio verbal com Bete e Baal. O lugar estava associado à palmeira de Débora (ver Juí. 4:5), que ficava entre Betel e Ramá, uma posição que talvez explique o nome. Israel fora à batalha para castigar o pecado de Benjamim (ver Juí. 20:33). O local atualmente é desconhecido, mas ficava perto de Gibeá, que dista seis quilômetros e meio de Jerusalém. Alguns identificam as ruínas em Erhah como o local. (UN Z)

BAAL-ZEBUBE

No heb., **Senhor das moscas**. Belzebul, segundo

se pensa, significa *deus do monturo*, que expressa repulsa ao príncipe de toda impureza moral. Todavia, alguns supõem que a palavra significa «senhor da habitação», onde se ocultariam maus espíritos. As variantes textuais nos manuscritos confundem o quadro. Baal-Zebube aparece no A.T., e Belzebu no N.T. (ver II Reis 1:2; 1:3,6; 1:16; Mat. 10:25,27; Mar. 3:33; Luc. 11:15 *ss*). Originalmente, Baal-Zebube era um deus filisteu, ao qual Acazias, filho de Acabe, rei de Israel, mandou consultar, após ter caído de seu quarto elevado, em Samaria (ver II Reis 1:2). Acazias esperava receber algum bom presságio da parte dessa divindade, acerca de sua condição, mas foi repreendido por Elias, por tal lapso. A morte foi declarada como certa, como castigo. Não se sabe porque essa divindade era chamada *das moscas*. Alguns têm sugerido que isso se deve ao fato de que ele protegia seus adoradores das moscas. Outros pensam que significa que a sua mensagem e provisões eram rápidas, como moscas. Ou então, a quase onipresença das moscas poderia sugerir uma divindade que está em todos os lugares. A forma neotestamentária varia nos manuscritos, e muita discussão se concentra em torno de seu significado e uso. Ver o artigo separado sobre Belzebul. (I IB ID)

BAAL-ZEFOM

No hebraico, **Senhor do inverno**, ou **Senhor do norte**. Uma cidade pertencente ao Egito, localizada na fronteira do mar Vermelho. (Ver Êxo. 14:2 e Núm. 33:7). Ali acampavam os filhos de Israel antes de atravessar o mar. Ao que parece, foram apanhados em uma armadilha, pelo que devia ser uma espécie de península. Ali postados, viram os exércitos egípcios que se aproximavam. Os filhos de Israel ficaram aterrorizados, queixando-se diante de Moisés por qual razão tinham sido apanhados em uma armadilha. Porém, Moisés exortou-os a que confiassem em Deus. Foi então que o povo de Israel atravessou o mar por terra seca; e os exércitos egípcios, tentando fazer a mesma coisa, foram afogados nas águas do mar, que retornaram ao seu devido lugar.

O próprio nome fala de um bem conhecido deus da literatura de Ugarite. Há evidências de que essa divindade estava associada ao porto egípcio de Tapanes. Posteriormente, Jeremias foi levado para esse porto, pelos judeus que fugiam de Jerusalém, pois recusavam-se a render-se a Nabucodonosor.

Não se sabe qual a localização exata de Baal-Zefom, mas supõe-se que ficava ao perto do mar Mediterrâneo, em Tapanes, a 35 km a suleste de Rameses, ou para o suleste daquele lugar. Tapanes é a atual Tell Defneh, na extremidade norte do istmo. (I IB SIM Z)

BAALÁ

No hebraico, **senhora**. Há variações desse nome, como Quiriate-Jearim (ver Jos. 15:9), Baalim de Judá (ver II Sam. 6:2), Quiriate-Baal, em Judá (ver Jos. 15:60 e 18:14).

1. A cidade de Quiriate-Jearim, a quase quinze quilômetros a oeste de Jerusalém, talvez a moderna Tell-el-Azhar. Ela é mencionada em conexão com as fronteiras do território de Judá (ver Jos. 15:9,10,11, 29; I Crô. 13:6).

2. Uma cidade ao sul de Judá, talvez a Baalá de Jos. 19:3, ou a Bealote de Jos. 15:24. Ficava na Sefelá, anteriormente parte do território de Simeão, tendo sido identificada com Khirbet el-Meshash, cidade no extremo sul de Judá (ver Jos. 15:29).

3. Uma cadeia montanhosa de Ecrom a Jabneel, na fronteira norte de Judá, talvez na colina atualmente conhecida como Mughar e associada a Khirbet el-Meshash (ver Jos. 15:11).

4. Baalá, uma cidade de Dã, na fronteira (ver Jos. 19:44), associada a Bel 'ain.

5. Uma cidade a oeste de Gezer, talvez a mesma mencionada no número anterior. O lugar foi construído por Salomão, para servir de cidade-armazém (ver I Reis 9:18 e II Crô. 8:6).

6. Baal, devendo ser identificada com Baalate-Beer (ver o artigo), na fronteira com Simeão (I Crô. 4:33). (Z)

BAALATE

Ver. **Baalá**, números 4 e 5.

BAALATE-BEER

No hebraico, **poço santo**, ou **Baal do poço**. Era uma cidade do território de Simeão, evidentemente o santuário de uma deusa. Deve ser identificada com «Ramá do Sul» (ver Jos. 19:8; I Crô. 4:33), a qual muitos pensam ser a mesma que a de número 6, sob o título Baalá. Não se sabe o local exato, mas pensa-se que fica no extremo sul do Neguebe, e próximo de um poço. (ID S)

BAALBEQUE

Ver *Senhor do Vale*.

Vem do sírio e significa *cidade de Baal* ou *Senhor do Vale*. Era uma antiga cidade, que separava o Líbano das montanhas do Antilíbano. Seu nome grego era Heliópolis, *cidade do sol*. Baal era um elemento comum em nomes próprios compostos, visto que o seu culto era generalizado e forte na Palestina e na Síria. Ver o artigo sobre Baal (Baalismo).

Situação. Ficava localizada no declive mais baixo das montanhas do Antilíbano, no início de um pequeno vale, dando para a planície de El-Bekaa. Através desse vale corria um riacho que se dividia em vários filetes de irrigação. Ficava localizada cerca de 65 km de Trípoli.

Importância. Antes dos tempos helenistas, era uma importante cidade, embora mais tarde tivesse declinado. Todavia, sua importância muito aumentou no período romano posterior. Josefo chama-a de Heliópolis (ver *Anti.* xiv.3,4); e o mesmo faz Plínio (ver Hist. Nat. v.22). Inscrições romanas mostram que o imperador Antônio Pio construiu um grande templo em honra a Júpiter, na cidade, o que se tornou uma das maravilhas do mundo. Isso é confirmado por João de Antioquia (Hist. Chro. lix.xi). Mediante moedas romanas, sabe-se que Heliópolis tornou-se uma colônia romana por ordem de Júlio César, e que era sede de uma guarnição romana no tempo de Augusto. Obteve o *Jus Italicum* da parte de Severo. Após a era de Constantino, os templos de Baalbeque começaram a declinar; mas, aparentemente, alguns deles foram posteriormente usados como centros de adoração cristã. A cidade continuou a ser um lugar importante até a época das invasões islâmicas, enriquecida por templos, palácios, jardins, fontes e residências luxuosas. Era bem fortificada e podia resistir a qualquer cerco. Porém, após repetidos ataques, capitulou. No ano de 1400, foi pilhada por Timour Beg. Então caiu nas mãos de uma bárbara tribo, os Metaweli. Foi conquistada por Ejezzar Pasha. O distrito inteiro terminou sob a supremacia

BAALE-JUDÁ — BABEL

turca.

Arqueologia. As ruínas da cidade cobrem uma grande área, sendo mundialmente famosas. Há alicerces de edificações antiqüíssimas, obscurecidas por templos e edifícios romanos. O templo de Júpiter era um edifício maciço, de 89 m de comprimento por 18,30 m de largura, rodeado por dezenove colunas coríntias de cada lado, e dez na frente e nos fundos. Essas colunas tinham 18,90 m de altura e 2,30 m de diâmetro. Uma parede de separação, feita de pedras, tinha 20 m de altura x 4,5 m de espessura. Um templo construído em honra a Baco está melhor preservado, localizado a 40 m ao sul do templo de Júpiter. Os restos de uma Acrópole, de pórticos e de um átrio, com várias edificações, continuam visíveis. Os edificadores romanos que originaram a glória do lugar foram Antônio Pio e Caracala. A mãe deste último era síria, e pode tê-lo influenciado a isso.

Atualmente há uma pequena e miserável aldeia, a leste das ruínas. (ID UN WIE)

BAALE-JUDÁ

No hebraico, **Senhores de Judá**. Uma cidade de Judá, de onde Davi trouxe a arca para Jerusalém (ver II Sam. 6:2), provavelmente a mesma Baalá de Jos. 15:9 e I Crô. 13:5,6. Ver o número 1 do artigo sobre Baalá (UN)

BAALINS

No hebraico, *grande Senhor*, sendo o plural de Baal. O termo encontra-se em Juí. 2:11; 3:7; I Sam. 7:4; I Reis 18:18; Jer. 2:23; Osé. 11:2 e outros trechos. Ver o artigo sobre Baal (Baalismo).

BAALIS

No hebraico, *exultação*. Foi rei dos amonitas ao tempo do cativeiro babilônico (597 A.C.) (ver Jer. 40:14). Ele enviou Ismael para matar Gedalias, que governava o remanescente dos judeus que não tinham sido levados para a Babilônia (ver Jer. 40:14). Gedalias fora nomeado por Nabucodonosor. Ele não acreditou no rumor de que Baalis tinha enviado Ismael para assassiná-lo, e essa confiança decretou a sua morte. (S Z)

BAANÃ

No hebraico, *filho de opressão*. Nome de seis personagens do A.T.

1. Um filho de Ailude, que era um dos doze oficiais que Salomão encarregara de prover alimentos para a casa real. Ele controlava os distritos de Taanaque, Medigo, Bete-Seã, perto de Zaretã, e Abel-Meolá, além de Jocmeão (ver I Reis 4:12).

2. Filho de Hisai, outro desses oficiais, cujo distrito era Aser e Bealote (ver I Reis 4:16).

3. Pai de Sadoque, que ajudou a reparar as muralhas de Jerusalém, em 470 A.C., após o cativeiro babilônico (ver Nee. 3:4). Talvez o mesmo homem de número 6, sob Baaná. Ver abaixo.

4. Filho de Rimom, o beerotita, o qual, com seu irmão, Recabe, matou Isbosete quando este estava no leito, levando sua cabeça a Davi, em Hebrom. O propósito deles era o de forçar a união dos reinos, pois então Isbosete era rei de Israel. Baaná era o capitão chefe do rei, pelo que a ação teve elementos de traição. Davi irou-se diante do acontecido, acusando os irmãos de haverem assassinado um homem inocente, quando jazia sem defesa em sua cama. Portanto, Davi ordenou que os dois fossem mortos, e seus cadáveres foram mutilados e pendurados na forca, sobre o poço de Hebrom (ver II Sam. 4:2-12), em 992 A.C.

5. Um netofatita, um dos guerreiros de Davi (ver II Sam. 23:29; I Crô. 11:30), pai de Helebe ou Helede.

6. Um dos exilados que retornou em companhia de Zorobabel, do cativeiro babilônico (ver Esd. 2:2 e Nee. 7:7). Talvez deva ser identificado com o Baaná que ocupa o terceiro lugar nesta lista, acima. Provavelmente trata-se do mesmo indivíduo que, com Neemias e outros, selou um pacto feito na época (ver Nee. 10:27). (ID S Z)

BAARA

Uma das esposas de Saaraim, um benjamita (ver I Crô. 8:8).

BAASA

O sentido desse nome é incerto no hebraico, mas talvez signifique *mau* ou *ofensivo*. Era filho de Aías, da tribo de Issacar. Foi o terceiro rei de Israel e fundador de uma dinastia (900—880 A.C.). Parece que ele não era de sangue nobre (I Reis 16:2), tendo-se levantado a uma posição de autoridade por haver assassinado a Nadabe, filho de Jeroboão I, rei de Israel. A matança envolveu a família real inteira, quando o rei estava assediando Gibetom, uma cidade dos filisteus (ver I Reis 15:27). O extermínio dessa família cumpriu a profecia de Aías (ver I Reis 16:5 ss.). Tendo começado entre homicídios, era apenas natural que ele desse prosseguimento aos maus atos de Jeroboão, e eventualmente foi punido por Deus. Foi avisado com antecedência sobre como as coisas se sucederiam (ver I Reis 16:1-5), mas isso não o impediu de prosseguir em suas ações perversas. Tentou fortificar Ramá, mas foi compelido a desistir devido a um ataque armado, desfechado por Ben-Hadade. Este era o rei sírio ao qual Asa, rei de Judá, pedira para ajudá-lo contra o reino norte, de Israel (ver I Reis 15:16-21). Romperam as hostilidades entre o sul (Judá) e o norte (Israel), durante os vinte e quatro anos do reinado de Baasa (911-888 A.C.). Seu reinado foi pontilhado de terrores, guerras e traições, e Jeú predisse o total extermínio de sua família, como castigo divino, o que de fato sucedeu (ver I Reis 16:11).

Baasa foi o instrumento divino que impôs julgamento à casa de Jeroboão (ver I Reis 16:29,30). Mas ele mesmo nada aprendeu desse fato. Acabou classificado entre dois outros reis especialmente malignos, a saber, Jeroboão (I Reis 14:11) e Acabe (I Reis 21:19). (BRI ED)

BAASÉIAS

No hebraico, **o Senhor é ousado**. Contudo, alguns manuscritos dão um nome diferente, cujo sentido é *obra do Senhor*. Foi um dos antepassados de Asafe (ver I Crô. 6:40).

BABEL (Torre e Cidade)

No hebraico, **porta de deus**. Nome de uma das principais cidades fundadas por Ninrode, em Sinear (Suméria), antiga Babilônia. — O nome figura juntamente com Ereque e Acade, em Gên. 10:10. A tradição babilônica diz-nos que foi originalmente fundada pelo deus Marduque, e que foi destruída por

BABEL

Sargão, em cerca de 2350 A.C. Ele levou terra do lugar a fim de fundar uma nova capital, a saber, Agade (ver o artigo sobre Acade). A história bíblica desse lugar, juntamente com sua torre, é relatada em Gên. 11:1-11. Ali, o termo *Babel* é explicado pela etimologia popular como o sentido de CONFUSÃO ou *mistura*. Isso é feito através de uma referência a um termo hebraico similar, *balal*, porque *babel* e essa palavra são parecidas, embora dotadas de significado diverso. Por meio dessa associação verbal, as duas palavras tornaram-se sinônimas, com o sentido de *confusão*, especificamente por causa do relato da torre de Babel, onde lemos que houve a confusão de línguas.

A expressão *torre de Babel* não se encontra no A.T., mas, em Gên. 11:4 aparece a palavra «torre». A própria torre foi feita de tijolos e asfalto, e não de pedras. É provável que a construção tivesse o intuito de ser um elevado sinal demarcatório. E visto que os antigos não faziam idéia da vastidão do espaço—pois somente na história recente da astronomia os homens chegaram a fazer boa idéia disso—talvez se pensasse que uma torre poderia atingir a habitação de um deus ou dos deuses. Contudo, a expressão «até aos céus» não indica necessariamente tal coisa. Poderia indicar apenas até bem alto no firmamento. A intenção, pois, pode ter sido simplesmente a ostentação. Eles teriam uma grande cidade, assinalada por altíssima torre, que poderia ser vista de longa distância, aumentando assim o prestígio da cidade. Naturalmente, essa torre seria usada com propósitos astrológicos, ficando assim envolvida nas suas práticas religiosas. Portanto, seria um monumento da religião pagã. Alguns supõem que a construção era um *zigurate*. (Ver o artigo a respeito). Em outras palavras, um templotorre com terraços, cada andar um tanto menor que o outro. Porém, a arqueologia não tem descoberto qualquer edifício dessa natureza antes de 4000 A.C. (a proposta data da torre de Babel), embora tais construções possam ser encontradas nas ruínas da Assíria e da Babilônia, pertencentes a datas posteriores. Por essa razão, alguns intérpretes negam que esteja em foco um zigurate, afirmando que alguma outra forma de torre deve ter sido construída. A descrição do livro de Gênesis corresponde ao que se sabe a respeito das construções usuais da Babilônia. O épico babilônico da criação, ao descrever a construção da Babilônia celestial (Tablete 6, linhas 58-61), diz: «Durante um ano inteiro eles fabricaram tijolos. Ao chegar o segundo ano, eles levantaram alto a cabeça de Esagila». Tijolos cozidos ao sol e no forno foram usados, e foi empregado asfalto como massa de ligação. A combinação de um templo torre com uma cidade era típica na construção de cidades, na Mesopotâmia. Os próprios templos eram impressionantes, tanto mais por causa de ereção de uma elevada torre, na área do templo. Porém, essas torres sempre eram zigurates, até onde a arqueologia tem sido capaz de determinar. A palavra *Esagila*, na citação acima, era o santuário de Marduque, e significa *casa cuja cabeça foi levantada alto*. E a própria torre foi chamada *Etemenanki*, que significa *casa do alicerce do céu e da terra*.

Arqueologia. O primeiro zigurate construído na Babilônia pode ser datado em cerca de 3000 A.C., ou quando muito, na última metade do século XL A.C. O mais antigo zigurate existente é o da antiga Uruque, que a Bíblia chama de Ereque (ver Gên. 10:10), moderna Warka. Mais de duas dúzias de zigurates são conhecidos pela arqueologia, todos os quais, naturalmente, vieram à existência depois de Ereque. A construção usual tinha três andares, mas pelo menos um dos zigurates tinha sete andares. Tais construções têm sido encontradas em Borsipa, a dezesseis quilômetros a sudoeste da Babilônia, em Ur, em Uruque (na Bíblia, Ereque), e em outras cidades da Mesopotâmia. Alguns supõem que o modelo original dessas construções foi a torre de Babel, que serviu de arquétipo para todas as outras torres. Mas isso é apenas uma suposição. A arqueologia não tem encontrado quaisquer evidências desse tipo de construção em um período tão antigo como aquele proposto para a torre de Babel. Outros supõem que o julgamento divino sobre a torre foi tão completo que coisa alguma restou para ser descoberta pela arqueologia. Porém, o A.T. nada diz sobre tal destruição, dando a impressão de que, quando as línguas se multiplicaram, o povo simplesmente desistiu da idéia de uma grande cidade, com sua torre magnificente. Em outras palavras, o projeto foi abandonado. (Ver Gên. 11:8).

Os zigurates na Babilônia. Se a torre de Babel foi, realmente, um zigurate, deve ter sido projetada antes de 4000 A.C. Esse tipo de construção pode ser encontrado no terceiro milênio A.C. A restauração de um zigurate, na Babilônia, teve lugar em 681-665 A.C., por Esaradom. O zigurate reconstituído, como é óbvio, era mais antigo que o tempo desse monarca, mas por quanto tempo, não sabemos dizer coisa alguma. Heródoto (460 A.C.) viu e descreveu um zigurate construído por Nebopolassar (625-605 A.C.) e por Nabucodonosor II (605-562 A.C.). Esses reis repararam um zigurate quase destruído. Um zigurate foi demolido por Xerxes, na Babilônia, em 472 A.C.

Outros zigurates. Em Ur. Esse tinha uma base de 61 m por 43 m, cujo primeiro terraço ficava a pouco mais de 15 m de altura. Um templo dotado de torre, na cidade de Borsipa, atualmente chamada Birs-Ninrode, tem sido identificado pelas tradições judaica e árabe como a torre de Babel; mas provavelmente essa opinião não é correta. Tinha sete andares, com 34 m de altura. Em *Durkurigalzu* (moderna 'Agar Quf), a 32 km de Bagdá, para oeste, com 57 m de altura, é o mais alto zigurate que se conhece.

A confusão das línguas. Um dos grandes mistérios da origem dos idiomas. 1. A Bíblia fornece-nos uma resposta teológica: Adão e Eva foram naturalmente criados com a capacidade de falar uma língua, uma língua adredemente preparada para eles. A grande variedade de idiomas é explicada pela mesma teologia com base no relato sobre a torre de Babel. Subitamente, por decreto e ato divinos, as pessoas começaram a falar em diversas línguas; e foi então que abandonaram o projeto de construir uma cidade com uma torre, na Babilônia. 2. Intérpretes liberais, céticos e científicos rejeitam ambos os relatos, como sendo mitológicos, como lendas para dar resposta a questões difíceis. 3. Uma sugestão alternativa é que assim como surgiram humanóides provenientes do reino animal inferior, assim também uma parte do processo evolutivo proveu essas criaturas com a habilidade de produzir sons que podem ser organizados em idiomas. Os substantivos teriam aparecido primeiro. As pessoas deram nomes às *coisas*. Então surgiram os verbos. As pessoas deram nomes às *ações*. Contra isso, deve-se dizer que as línguas antigas que conhecemos são extremamente complexas e matemáticas. Isso dificilmente poderia dar-se no caso de uma língua desenvolvida por esse processo ao acaso, através da simples nomeação das coisas. Qual selvagem ou semi-selvagem teria podido inventar o complexo sistema verbal e o sistema de casos que caracterizam muitas línguas antigas, e que funcionam com uma precisão matemática? 4. Outros estudiosos

BABILÔNIA

sugerem que a complexidade das línguas deve ser explicada por um longo período de desenvolvimento, antes mesmo da raça adâmica. Isso dá a entender que Adão e seus descendentes representam um novo começo, mas não um começo absoluto. Assim, a complexidade dos idiomas tem atravessado uma história que nos é totalmente desconhecida, e que já existia (por meio de um longo desenvolvimento), quando começou a raça adâmica. Contra essa idéia podemos dizer simplesmente que não há qualquer evidência em seu favor, a menos que aceitemos as declarações dos psíquicos que sustentam tal teoria. Em seu favor, pode ser declarado que, na realidade, há evidências de raças pré-adâmicas. Ver os artigos sobre os *antediluvianos*, a *agricultura* e a *astronomia*.
5. A resposta dos cientistas é que simplesmente não temos respostas para todas as perguntas. Portanto, as respostas dadas acima são as melhores conjecturas e mitos de que dispomos. (I IB ID ND)

BABILÔNIA

Esboço:
1. Nome
2. Localização da cidade e do país; descrição
3. Fundação e pré-história
4. História
5. Religião e moral
6. Principais cidades da Babilônia
7. Arqueologia

Nota: Quanto a descrições da *cidade* da Babilônia, ver o sétimo ponto, *cidades principais* (a).

1. Nome

O termo acadiano **babli, babilani** significa **porta dos deuses**. A palavra Babilônia era empregada para aludir à cidade que era capital da Babilônia. Ocupava o território que agora é o sul do Iraque. Por associação popular, o termo hebraico *balal* (confusão) (ver Gên. 11:9), foi ligado à Babilônia como o local onde houve essa confusão, causada pela impiedade. (Ver o artigo sobre a *torre de Babel*). Porém as duas palavras («porta dos deuses» e «confusão») não são a mesma coisa, exceto no conceito popular. Outros nomes da cidade que ora comentamos, nos textos babilônicos, são *tin tir ki*, «vida das árvores» ou «sede da vida», e *e-ki*, «lugar de canais». O termo «sesaque», que em algumas versões (mas não na nossa versão portuguesa), em Jer. 25:26 e 51:41, é considerado por alguns como um «atbash» (ver o artigo a respeito) que envolve o nome Babel, no qual «s» = «b», pode ser uma rara ocorrência do antigo nome da cidade, *ses-ki*.

2. Localização da cidade e do país; descrição.

A Babilônia ficava na terra de Sinear (ver Gên. 10:10), na região que agora fica no sul do Iraque, no sudoeste da Ásia. A cidade estava localizada às margens do rio Eufrates (ver Jer. 13:4,5,7 e 46:2,6). Um outro nome bíblico para ela era «a terra dos caldeus» (Jer. 24:5; Eze. 12:13). Na remota antiguidade, tinha o nome de Acade (ver Gên. 10:10). (Ver o artigo a respeito). O território posteriormente recebeu o nome de *Caldéia*, apelativo dado à região inteira, após o surgimento da dinastia caldaica (ver o artigo a respeito, e o quarto ponto do presente artigo). Assim, os babilônios também são qualificados como caldeus (ver Eze. 23:15,17,23). O país era regado pelos rios Tigre e Eufrates. A Bíblia localiza o jardim do Éden ali (ver Gên. 2:14), como também a torre de Babel, e a região para onde os judeus foram exilados (ver o cativeiro babilônico).

Descrição: De acordo com os modernos padrões de dimensão dos países, a Babilônia era pequena, pois tinha apenas cerca de 13.000 quilômetros quadrados. Era limitada ao norte pela Assíria (Samarra Jebel Hamrin, como fronteira); a leste pelas colinas da Pérsia (ver o artigo sobre *Elão*); a oeste pelo deserto da Arábia; e ao sul pelas praias do golfo Pérsico.

A cidade: A Babilônia estava localizada às margens do rio Eufrates (ver Jer. 13:4,5,7), chamado de «grande rio Eufrates», em Gên. 15:18. Era cercada por duas muralhas. A muralha externa teria sido construída por Belus e depois foi reparada por Nabucodonosor. A cidade tinha a forma de um quadrado. A extensão da circunferência das muralhas é dada com diferença, pelos diversos autores, de 7.250 m a 9.650 m. Tinham entre 18 m a 21 m de altura. **Eram suficientemente largas, no alto, para que um carro com quatro cavalos fizesse meia-volta em cima delas.** Aquelas muralhas eram uma notável defesa para a época. Não obstante, aguardava-as a destruição (ver Jer. 51:58). A própria muralha seria derrubada, e a cidade seria arrasada.

3. Fundação e Pré-História

O trecho de Gên. 10:10 informa-nos que a cidade foi fundada por Ninrode, tornando-a contemporânea de Ereque (moderna Warka) e de Acade (moderna Agade). Em comum com outras culturas, ao falar sobre sua capital ou sobre suas cidades importantes, a tradição babilônica assegura que o lugar tivera origem divina. Marduque, deus babilônico, teria sido o fundador da cidade. Porém, os próprios mitos babilônicos não exibem o nome dessa divindade senão já no século XVIII A.C. A mais antiga referência histórica é a que faz alusão a Sarcalisarri (cerca de 2250 A.C.), que nos diz como ele removeu a terra da cidade a fim de erigir Agade, um lugar próximo, que seu pai, Sargão, havia começado a construir. Essa renovada reedificação, feita por Sarcalisarri, foi efetuada a fim de preservar a santidade do local. A referência no livro de Gênesis parece indicar uma data, talvez cem anos antes disso, quando a cidade teve o seu começo.

Pré-história. O local, entretanto, vinha sendo habitado desde uma data muito mais antiga do que transparece em Gên. 10:10. Alguns estudiosos, porém, preferindo deixar de lado a marcação de datas por genealogias, presumem que essa referência em Gênesis nos faz retroceder até 4500 A.C. Seja como for, povos chamados sumérios,- antecederam os semitas, na baixa Babilônia. Há estudiosos que pensam que os sumérios seriam camitas, conforme a narrativa de Gênesis indica, — no tocante aos descendentes de Ninrode. Os sumérios desenvolveram uma elevada civilização, incluindo a escrita cuneiforme. Ver o artigo sobre a *Suméria*. Tabletes de argila desse período indicam uma linguagem não-semita. Alguns nomes, contudo, indicam certa influência semítica, o que dá a entender que talvez houvesse povos semitas na área, desde os tempos mais remotos. Esses povos construíam cidades-estados e eram politeístas. Mas, na Babilônia, alcançou particular proeminência a tríada formada por Anu (o firmamento), Enlil (a atmosfera e a terra) e Ea (as águas).

Obeide. Esse nome deriva-se de Tell-el-Obeid, um pequeno cômoro — acerca de sete quilômetros a noroeste de Ur, sendo usado para designar a mais antiga civilização conhecida na Babilônia. Implementos encontrados em Ur e em Ereque ilustram essa civilização.

Ereque (Warka). Desde tempos tão remotos quanto o quarto milênio A.C., uma outra cultura distintiva tem sido descoberta, com o mais antigo zigurate (ver o

BABILÔNIA

Cilindro em terra-cotta que relata a queda da Babilônia por Ciro, o Grande.

Inscrição de Nabucodonozor, dando direitos ao rei Ritti-Marduk

**Fragmentos de Isaías de Qumran,
Cortesia, Hebrew University**

**Fragmentos do rolo de Daniel (1:10-2:6)
primeiro século, foto por John C.
Trever — Cortesia, Dept. de
Antiguidades, Jordânia**

Os profetas viram a queda da Babilônia.

BABILÔNIA

artigo a respeito), os primeiros selos cilíndricos e o começo da escrita, como características distintivas.

Jemdet Nasr, no vale Mesopotamiano, perto da Babilônia, representa uma outra cultura, posterior (3200-3000 A.C.), com seus instrumentos de bronze, que deu origem ao surgimento de várias cidades, como Surupaque (Fara), Ewhunna (Tell Asmar) e Quis.

4. História

a. *Fundação e pré-história.* Ver o terceiro ponto, acima.

b. *O mais antigo período* dinástico (cerca de 2800-2360 A.C.).

De acordo com a lista dos reis sumérios, oito ou dez deles reinaram antes do dilúvio. Todas as coisas sucederam por divina determinação. Esses reis estiveram associados às cidades de Eridu, Badtibirra, Laraque, Sipar e Surupaque. O dirigente da última dessas cidades foi o herói sumério da história do dilúvio. Essa história é proeminente nos registros babilônicos no período de cerca de 2000 A.C. Há muitos relatos independentes sobre o dilúvio, sugerindo que Noé não foi o único que escapou desse desastre. Ver o artigo sobre o *dilúvio.*

Após o dilúvio, houve outra divina intervenção. «O reinado desceu do céu». Surgiram cidades-estados, como as de Quis, Uruque, Ur, Awan, Hamazi, Adabe, Lagase e Mari. Essas cidades-estados viviam em frequente disputa com a Babilônia, o centro das disputas. Governantes importantes foram Etana, um pastor que supostamente desceu do céu, além de doze reis, de Uruque, que teriam reinado por um total de 2310 anos, incluindo entre eles Gilgamés, um proeminente herói épico. Outro herói épico foi Aga. Esses homens podem ter sido figuras históricas, que as lendas glorificaram, de tal modo que, tal como nos relatos épicos gregos, parecem ser semideuses. O poder de Ur assinala a porção final do período dinástico. Uruque foi subjugada e Ur ganhou proeminência, através da guerra, naturalmente. A lista de reis sumérios designa quatro reis desse período, cujos reinados cobriram um período de cerca de cento e setenta e sete anos. Então Ur foi ferida por armas de guerra. Túmulos descobertos, pertencentes a esse período, revelam uma alta civilização. Escavações efetuadas em Lagase (uma outra dinastia do período posterior do antigo período dinástico) revelam grandes construções como templos, canais e outras edificações. O governante, Enanatum, derrotou seus vizinhos, a saber: Uma, Uruque, Ur, Quis e Mari. Sua batalha contra Uma é retratada na estela do Abutres. Porém, as guerras terminam e recomeçam, e assim, mais tarde Lagase foi derrotada por Uma. Lugalzagesi era o novo potentado de Uma. Ele também tornou-se o rei de Uruque e Ur, tendo-se firmado como a figura mais poderosa de todo aquele período. A fama e o poder sempre eram conquistados através da violência, naturalmente. E a espiritualidade do homem não tem melhorado muito desde então. O império de Lugalzagesi tornou-se uma espécie de protótipo dos grandes impérios que se sucederam naquela região, e que são tão importantes dentro da narrativa bíblica.

c. *Os acadianos* (2371-2191 A.C.)

Os semitas aumentaram o seu domínio na Babilônia, liderados pelo poderoso Sargão. Ele teve uma história humilde, bem como uma história de arca de juncos, semelhante à história de Moisés. Construiu um extenso império, usando novas técnicas de guerra, com arco e flecha como o principal armamento. Foi capaz de derrotar Lugalzagesi, de Uma, Quis e Uruque. A palavra *acadiano* é de origem semita, equivalente a Agade, a principal cidade dos povos semitas sobre os quais estamos discutindo. Sargão foi sucedido por Rimus-Manistusu e por Narã-Sin, seu filho e seu neto, respectivamente. Este último foi finalmente derrotado por uma coligação dirigida por Utuegal, de Uruque. Porém, esse governo teve natureza local, visto que Lagase reteve o seu poder, bem como diversas outras cidades. Gudéia, rei de Lagase, ampliou o seu poder e trouxe muitas riquezas, pelo que houve uma espécie de renascimento sumeriano, ou era áurea.

d. *Período Neo-sumeriano e a Terceira Dinastia de Ur* (2070-1960 A.C.).

Gudéia foi construtor e organizador. Ele edificou um templo famoso, trazendo madeira de cedro do monte Amanus, no norte da Síria, de uma distância imensa para a época. Salomão, mil anos mais tarde, fez a mesma coisa (ver I Reis 5:6). Gudéia foi sucedido por seu genro, e Ur, uma vez mais, tornou-se o centro do poder. Ur-Namu (2113-2096 A.C.) reconstruiu a cidadela, com seu zigurate e seus templos (ver o artigo sobre Ur). Ur ampliou o seu poder até a distante Assur e Diyala. E os governantes que vieram depois de Ur-Namu receberam poderes divinos, conforme nos mostram seus monumentos e seus selos, com uma tiara cornuda, própria da divindade. Alguns pensam que Ur-Namu teria sido também honrado dessa forma. Foi aparentemente durante essa dinastia que Abraão nasceu e mais tarde deixou a cidade. Existem muitos milhares de documentos pertencentes a esse período, confirmando-o historicamente.

e. *Invasões dos Elamitas e dos Amorreus* (1960-1830 A.C.).

Houve períodos severos de escassez de alimentos que debilitaram o império. Vieram os seminômades dos desertos ocidentais, que invadiram a região e derrubaram o governo sumério. Esses invasores vinham do Elão (elamitas) e de Mari (amorreus). Sob Ibi-Sin, Ur foi saqueada pelos elamitas. Os amorreus se estabeleceram em Isin e Larsa. Um governante elamita, Kirikiri, estabeleceu seu poder em Esnuna. O unido império sumério foi dividido em facções. Alguns supõem que foi nessa época que Abraão foi convocado a deixar o lugar (ver Gên. 11:31). A mudança das circunstâncias em Ur também modificou o destino pessoal de Abraão.

f. *Antigo Período Babilônico* (1830-1550 A.C.).

A nova Babilônia deu começo à sua ascensão, particularmente sob a liderança de Hamurabe (ver o artigo sobre ele). Os reinos amorreus continuaram lutando entre si. Essa instável situação deu a certo número de estados menores a oportunidade de obterem a independência. A Babilônia foi um desses estados menores. Hamurabe foi o sexto monarca da primeira dinastia da Babilônia. Suas datas são variegadamente estabelecidas, como 1792-1750 A.C., 1728-1686 A.C., ou 1642-1626 A.C. Hamurabe herdou pequena região para governar, mas não tardou a ampliá-la. Tabletes de Mari mostram que Hamurabe contava com dez a quinze reis a ele subordinados, embora Rim-Sin, de Larsa, Ibalpiel, de Esnuna, Amutpeil de Qatana, e Iarinlim de Yamhad também tivessem suas respectivas esferas de influência. Contudo, Hamurabe obteve uma série de vitórias, e derrotou Rim-Sin, seu rival, rei de Larsa, bem como Emutbal e Esnuna. A Assíria, bem como Mari, foram subjugadas. Finalmente, os territórios de Hamurabe espalharam-se desde o Golfo Pérsico (que na época ficava muito mais para dentro do

BABILÔNIA

continente) até Mari. Portanto, Hamurabe tornou-se o fundador da primeira dinastia babilônica, em seu sentido mais universal, como uma potência mundial. Parece que Hamurabe era de origem cassita (ver abaixo). Sua fama dependeu mais de suas atividades como legislador do que como conquistador militar. O artigo separado a seu respeito ilustra esse ponto. O código de Hamurabe, descoberto em Susa, em 1901, pertence ao período de cerca de 1700 A.C. Foi durante esse tempo, igualmente, que a famosa criação épica, *Enuma elish*, tomou a forma que veio a ser conhecida por nós (embora sua origem fosse ainda mais antiga). As descobertas feitas em Nuzu, um antigo centro hurriano, cerca de dezenove quilômetros a noroeste da moderna Kirkuk, têm derramado muita luz sobre esse período.

Hamurabe foi sucedido por uma longa linhagem de reis, acerca dos quais pouco se sabe. Um tablete encontrado alista cerca de cem nomes, embora seja impossível arranjá-los em ordem cronológica. Esses nomes eram todos semitas.

g. *Invasão e dinastia cassita* (1550-1169 A.C.)

Em cerca de 1595, o hitita Mursili I assediou a cidade da Babilônia, mas os cassitas (ou cosseanos), provenientes das colinas orientais, gradualmente assumiram o controle do país. Um deles estabeleceu uma nova capital, Dur-Kurigalzu, edificada por Kurigalzu I. Seguiu-se uma longa linha de sucessores, de tal modo que, durante certo número de séculos, eles dominaram o país. Mas então Tukulti-Ninurta, rei da Assíria, invadiu e conquistou a Babilônia (entre 1260-1232), mas, após apenas sete anos, foi dali expulso.

h. *Segunda Dinastia de Isin* (1146-1123 A.C.)

Quando terminou o predomínio cassita, pela erosão gradual provocada por vários povos invasores, surgiu uma nova dinastia na Babilônia. Esses novos monarcas eram todos babilônios nativos. Entre eles destacava-se Nabucodonosor I (1146-1123 A.C.). Ele derrotou os elamitas e os hititas, mas foi derrotado pelos assírios. Tiglate-Pileser I, da Assíria, completou a conquista da Babilônia, marchando contra o sucessor de Nabucodonosor I, Marduque-Nadin-Ahi. Entrementes, a nação judaica estava surgindo no Ocidente, e nenhuma das nações circunvizinhas (debilitadas por conflitos contínuos) pôde fazer-lhes oposição.

i. *A Dominação Assíria* (745-626 A.C.).

Desde tão cedo quanto 1100-900 A.C., tribos aramaicas e a Assíria começaram a interferir nos negócios da Babilônia. Tiglate-Pileser II (729 A.C.), o Pul referido em II Reis 15:19, conquistou a Babilônia. O artigo separado sobre a Assíria fornece os detalhes sobre esse império. Aqui damos apenas alguns poucos eventos importantes: Em 722 A.C. foi derrotada Samaria (Israel do norte), pelo que aí temos o cativeiro assírio de Israel. Esse cativeiro foi gradual, estendendo-se pelo espaço de cento e cinqüenta anos. Uma parte do mesmo ocorreu antes de 722 A.C. (ver o artigo sobre o *cativeiro*). Em 689 A.C., a Babilônia revoltou-se contra Senaqueribe, mas ele a saqueou e a incendiou até o rés do chão. Foi reconstruída por Esaradom e continuou fazendo parte do império assírio até 625 A.C.

j. *Período Neobabilônico ou caldeu* (626-539 A.C.).

A 22 de novembro de 626 A.C., Nebopolassar, governador das terras do mar (golfo Pérsico), assentou-se sobre o trono da Babilônia. Ele estabeleceu a paz com os elamitas, e então, no ano seguinte, derrotou os assírios, em Salate. Juntamente com Ciaxares, rei dos medos, o rei dos caldeus destruiu Nínive, em 612 A.C. Assim nascia o império neobabilônico ou caldeu. Seu filho, Nabucodonosor, derrotou Neco, do Egito, em Carquemis, em 605 A.C. Esse império, pois, passou a controlar todo o sudoeste da Ásia. Nabucodonosor (605-556 A.C.) teve um longo e brilhante reinado. Em seu tempo, ele destruiu Jerusalém (587 A.C.), e enviou Israel do sul (Judá) para o cativeiro. (Ver Jer. 52:12). (Ver os artigos sobre o *cativeiro* e *cativeiro babilônico*). Zedequias, o rei dos judeus, — foi capturado, cego e enviado — para Babilônia (ver Eze. 12:13). Quanto à deportação de Judá, ver Jer. 12:12-30 e II Reis 25:8-12. Foi esse mesmo Nabucodonosor quem lançou os três jovens hebreus na fornalha ardente (ver Dan. 3:13-25), embora tivesse se mostrado tão gentil para com Jeremias. Daniel interpretou os sonhos de Nabucodonosor. Esse monarca foi punido por um período de loucura; mas, posteriormente, foi exaltado e honrado por Deus (ver o quarto capítulo de Daniel). Transformou a cidade da Babilônia na mais esplendorosa das capitais, tornando-a no principal centro do mundo civilizado da época.

Nabucodonosor foi sucedido por seu filho, Amel-Marduque (na Bíblia, Evil-Merodaque) (ver II Reis 25:27 e Jer. 52:31). Seu reinado estendeu-se desde 562 a 650 A.C. Foi assassinado por Niriglissar (560-556), que o sucedeu. Mas Niriglissar também foi assassinado. Então um nobre babilônico, Nabonido, assumiu o governo. Apontou seu filho, Belsazar, como co-regente. (Ver o artigo separado sobre *Belsazar*). Nabonido foi o último rei do império babilônico. Agora surgia no horizonte o império persa.

l. *Queda da Babilônia e História Subseqüente*.

No décimo sétimo ano do governo de Nabonido (539 A.C.), Ciro II, rei da Pérsia, capturou a Babilônia. Ele penetrou na cidade quando a população inteira, dependendo das muralhas inexpugnáveis que cercavam a cidade, entregara-se à festividade e ao deboche, durante um período de festejos. Heródoto informa-nos que Ciro havia anteriormente feito secar o Palacopas, um canal que atravessava a cidade de Babilônia, levando as águas supérfluas do Eufrates para o lago de Nitocris, a fim de desviar o rio para ali. Assim, o rio baixou de nível, e os soldados puderam penetrar na cidade através do leito quase seco do rio. O registro cilíndrico de Nabonido não menciona esse fato. Além disso, o registro cilíndrico de Ciro não menciona o feito, sendo possível que a referência de Heródoto mencione uma captura posterior da Babilônia, por Dario, em 516 A.C. Alguns eruditos, porém, preferem ficar com a posição de Heródoto, sobre essa questão, supondo que houve uma omissão de evidência nesse caso, como em outros registros também. (Ver o artigo separado sobre *Ciro*).

Após haver sido capturada, a Babilônia declinou, especialmente depois que Ciro fez de Susa a sua capital. Ele adquiriu o título de «...meu pastor...» (Isa. 44:28; 45:1). Daniel prosperou, e aos judeus foi permitido retornarem a Jerusalém, pelo que cumpriu-se a profecia de Jeremias (ver Jer. 25:12; 29:10 e 33:7-14). Em 530 A.C., Ciro foi sucedido por Cambises (ver o artigo a seu respeito). A cidade da Babilônia permaneceu sob o governo persa desde 539 até 323 A.C. A morte de Cambises deu margem a uma rebelião, e pretendentes apossaram-se do trono. Em dezembro de 522 A.C., Dario I restaurou a lei e a ordem. Durante o seu reinado (522-486 A.C.), ele permitiu que os judeus reconstruíssem o templo de Jerusalém, sob Zorobabel (ver Esd. 4:5; Ageu 1:1 e Zac. 1:1). Monarcas persas continuaram governando a Babilônia, a saber: Xerxes (486-470 A.C.). Ver também sobre Assuero. Artaxerxes I (464-423 A.C.),

BABILÔNIA

Dario II (423-408 A.C.), que pode ter sido o Dario, o persa, mencionado em Nee. 12:22, a fim de ser distinguido de Dario, o medo. A Pérsia continuou dominada pela Média até o surgimento de Ciro II, o conquistador da Babilônia, que também subjugou os medos, em cerca de 549 A.C. Todavia, a Média continuou sendo uma importante província, e houve uma espécie de amálgama cultural entre os dois povos, o que explica o nome medos-persas. (Ver Dan. 5:28 e Est. 1:19). Ver também o artigo sobre a Média, quanto a esse tipo de relacionamento com a Pérsia.

A 1º de outubro de 331 A.C., Alexandre o Grande (Alexandre III) foi bem acolhido pelos babilônios ao entrar, após a sua vitória sobre os medos, em Gaugamel, perto de Ebril. Dali por diante prevaleceria o império grego. Alexandre controlou a Babilônia até o ano de 323 A.C. Ali ele efetuou algumas renovações, mas o trabalho de reconstrução cessou, por ocasião de sua morte em 13 de junho de 323 A.C. Os generais de Alexandre dividiram entre si várias áreas do império grego. Os selêucidas governaram a Babilônia entre 312 e 171 A.C. Foram sucedidos pelos partas, que governaram a região de 171 A.C. a 226 D.C. Então veio à existência a dinastia sassânida, que governou a área da Babilônia, de 226 a 641 D.C. Essa foi a dinastia nacional da antiga Pérsia. Sasã era o avô de Ardasir I, o primeiro rei sassânida, o que explica o nome dessa dinastia. Em 641 D.C., a região caiu sob o poder dos árabes islamitas.

A cidade de Babilônia declinou durante o período helênico, tendo sido abandonada antes da época de Jesus Cristo. Após a queda de Jerusalém, no ano 70 D.C., a Babilônia contou com grande população judaica, tendo-se tornado um dos quartéis da erudição judaica. No tempo de Estrabão (faleceu em 24 D.C.) e de Diodoro Selêucia (contemporâneo de Estrabão), a cidade ficou reduzida a ruínas. Jerônimo informa-nos que sabia que nesse tempo (século IV D.C.), o local da Babilônia se reduzira a um local de caçadas dos monarcas persas, e que, a fim de preservar a caça, as muralhas eram reparadas, vez por outra.

5. Religião e Moral

Visto que a história da Babilônia é muito longa, temos uma grande variedade de crenças e instituições religiosas, que procuramos sumariar aqui.

a. *Antigas divindades sumérias* foram assimiladas pelos semitas, após o tempo da primeira dinastia da Babilônia (cerca de 1800 A.C.). A versão final da biblioteca de Nínive, no século VII A.C., enumerou os deuses em mais de 2.500. Mas, em qualquer período isolado, o número desses deuses sempre foi bem menor. Contudo, isso mostra quão politeísta era aquela gente.

b. *O panteão e a tríada*. Os deuses mais importantes eram *Anu* (o An dos sumérios), o deus do céu, cujo templo principal ficava em Uruque (ver sobre Ereque). Ele era o deus semita, El. Sua esposa era Inana ou Inim, que posteriormente foi confundida com Istar. Havia também o deus do ar, *Enlil*, que acabou amalgamado com Bel (Baal) e com Marduque (ver sobre Merodaque). Sua esposa era Ninlil ou Ninusague, posteriormente também identificada com Istar. A terceira deidade dessa tríada era *Ea* (o Enki dos sumérios, senhor das águas profundas, deus da sabedoria e gentil para com os homens). Este teria permitido que o conhecimento divino fosse transmitido aos homens através do emprego da adivinhação. Seu templo, Ê.abzu, ficava em Eridu, e sua esposa tinha os nomes de Damgal, Ninma ou Damkina, sendo a esposa da terra e do céu.

c. *Divindades secundárias*. A Istar dos semitas, que a princípio era uma divindade masculina, foi depois identificada com Inana. Daí por diante, Istar foi transformada na deusa do amor, uma heroína de guerra. Também foi considerada filha de Sin, o deus-lua dos babilônios. Era adorada em templos, juntamente com a esposa de Sin, Nigal. Shamash era o deus-sol, e sua esposa, Aya, veio a ser identificada com Istar. Sumutu era o filho de Sin, e era o deus do poder, da justiça e da guerra. Tinha templos em Sipar e em Larsa. Todos os deuses principais contavam com santuários e altares separados dos templos. Adade (de origem semita) era o deus das tempestades, identificado com o deus cananeu arameu Adu ou Hadade (ver o artigo a respeito). Nergal e sua esposa, Eresquigal, governavam o submundo. Ele era o senhor das pragas, das febres e das enfermidades. Com o surgimento dos amorreus, tornou-se proeminente na Babilônia a adoração a Marduque (em sumério, amar.uto, o jovem touro do sol). Foi associado ao épico da criação (*enuma elis*). Tinha cinqüenta títulos diferentes. Nabu era o deus da ciência e da escrita, e tinha templos em diversas cidades. Assur tornou-se o deus nacional da Assíria. Amurru era uma deidade dos semitas ocidentais, que veio a ser identificada com Anu, Sin e Adade. Dagom também tinha origem semita, mas terminou exercendo vasta influência. Damuzi era um deus da vegetação, que morria, mas não ressuscitava. Ninurta era deus da guerra e da caça, e era honrado tanto pelos babilônios quanto pelos assírios.

d. *Alguns elementos teológicos*. O sistema de deuses representava uma larga distribuição de poderes e ofícios. Havia deuses dos mundos superior e inferior, e todos os reinos estavam sujeitos às leis divinas, dentre as quais mais de cem têm sido enumeradas. Os deuses eram concebidos em termos antropomórficos. Espíritos, bons e maus, eram inúmeros, com suas respectivas áreas de influência. Os deuses eram considerados imortais e poderosos, embora finitos. As questões que surgem incluem as grandes questões da origem das coisas (criação), os fundamentos do governo do mundo, e o relacionamento desses governos aos deuses. As leis eram tidas como de origem divina. Os homens interessavam-se pela busca da imortalidade. Procuravam determinar as relações entre os homens e o mundo dos espíritos.

e. *Sacerdócio*. Eles tinham um elaborado sistema sacerdotal, dentro do qual o rei era o sumo pontífice. Na época dos sumérios, o templo também era o centro financeiro. Havia sacerdotisas, tanto quanto sacerdotes, acompanhadas pela promoção da adoração a vários deuses e deusas. Havia aqueles que cuidavam da liturgia e da música. Havia exorcistas que cuidavam dos maus espíritos; e havia astrólogos que procuravam obter orientação do céu, bem como todas as variedades de adivinhos, com o mesmo propósito. Os demônios eram encarados como especialistas em tipos especiais de tentações e perturbações, e havia ritos para contrabalançar essas especialidades. A medicina estava intimamente ligada à religião. Havia um elaborado sistema de sacrifícios. Havia muitas festividades e feriados religiosos. A adoração ou o devido respeito aos deuses exercia um efeito direto sobre quão bem se poderia esperar que corressem a vida nacional e a vida dos indivíduos. O dinheiro tinha de passar pelos templos, e suas muitas atividades incluíam a comum instituição pagã da prostituição sagrada, usualmente efetuada em honra a algum deus ou deusa da fertilidade. Havia todo um complexo sistema de santuários e altares, onde o povo, à parte dos templos, podia rezar, fazer

BABILÔNIA

promessas e buscar a orientação dos deuses.

f. Ética e moral dos babilônios

Como suplemento do que diremos aqui, ver o artigo sobre *Hamurabe*, que inclui as leis de Hamurabe, e que obviamente entram no quadro na natureza da ética e da moral da Babilônia.

Visto que a Babilônia representava a mescla de muitas culturas, a ética babilônica também representa uma longa tradição de misturas. Com freqüência é impossível distinguir entre o que era de origem suméria (não-semita) e o que era semita (principalmente de origem amorréia).

Filosofia da ética. O ideal baseava-se na suposta era áurea passada, quando os homens viviam em harmonia sem qualquer necessidade ou enfermidade, unidos quanto à fé religiosa e gozando de juventude eterna. A ética refletia um hedonismo moderado; mas também era uma ética *divina*, devido ao fato de que eles pensavam que a sorte de indivíduos e de nações dependia do relacionamento mantido com os deuses. Julgava-se que o universo fosse controlado pelas leis divinas (*me*), cujas principais virtudes seriam a paz, a bondade e a justiça, e cujos principais vícios seriam a falsidade, o temor e a contenda. O mal (e, portanto, o problema do mal) era discutido, concluindo-se que fazia parte de um plano divino, posto que inescrutável. Porém, o bem era preferível ao mal, porquanto teria a promessa da vitória final sobre o mal. A ordem moral fora traçada pelo deus *Du tu* (sumério), ou *Shamash* (acadiano). Esse deus era onisciente e cuidava dos praticantes do bem, mas punia os malfeitores. Os males sociais eram a opressão dos mais fracos, os juízes inescrupulosos, os subornos, os pesos adulterados, os tiranos, os ladrões e os mentirosos. A deusa Nanshe era a protetora especial dos órfãos e das viúvas, bem como dos pobres. Eram baixadas leis sociais que procuravam evitar os abusos. O rei agia como representante especial dos deuses. Ele era responsável em transmitir um bom exemplo aos seus sucessores (*Lenda Cutereana de Narã-Sin* 1.25). Havia abundante literatura com seu acúmulo de *sabedoria*, de onde todos podiam aprender, através da mediação do rei e dos sacerdotes. Essa literatura incluía ensaios, fábulas, parábolas, dilemas, contos folclóricos, disputas e diálogos morais. O provérbio era um modo favorito de instruir nas questões morais. Essa literatura inclui títulos como: *Conselhos da Sabedoria, Aviso a um Príncipe, Instrução de Surupaque* (o mais antigo deles, 2500 A.C.). Isso formava uma coletânea de material dado após o dilúvio, visando instruir a humanidade. A obra *Conselho a Shube' awelum* descrevia a conduta apropriada para com as mulheres, os pais, a escolha de uma esposa ou a seleção de bois. Observâncias religiosas eram ditadas como uma prática diária. Os *Conselhos da Sabedoria* recomendavam adoração e sacrifícios diários e a reverência que implora o favor, os sacrifícios que prolongam a vida e as orações que expiam pela culpa. O desprazer divino e o castigo divino seguiam-se aos atos maldosos. A ética sexual dependia das leis determinadas pelo estado, mais do que de princípios religiosos. Mas, visto que toda e qualquer lei era considerada divina, essas regulamentações também eram tidas como de origem divina, de origem religiosa. As leis proibiam o comportamento sexual extramarital, o adultério, a sedução e estupro. O estupro de uma donzela noiva era punido com a morte (Lei de Esnuna 26). O mesmo documento ameaçava severa punição ao estuprador de uma jovem escrava, tanto quanto de uma mulher livre. Mulheres casadas e concubinas tinham de andar veladas em público, mas uma prostituta não precisava usar o véu (ver a discussão de Paulo, em I Cor. 11:5 ss , quanto à sua insistência sobre o uso do véu pelas mulheres crentes). O homossexualismo era considerado uma falta grave da decência social geral, mas não como um crime ou uma ofensa ao matrimônio. (Leis da Assíria Média, 19 e 20).

As leis eram melhores do que a prática diária. As leis éticas acima descritas são bastante impressionantes. Porém, sabemos, através de muitas fontes, que, na prática, os povos não se equiparavam a seus elevados ideais, como sucede em todas as culturas, e certamente até na moderna Igreja evangélica. A prostituição religiosa era uma vexação moral. Contudo, essa era uma comum instituição nas antigas religiões pagãs, e um grande problema que Paulo precisou enfrentar em Corinto. Heródoto descreve a desgraça dessa prática entre os babilônios. Os templos eram ali transformados em bordéis legais e religiosos. O dinheiro assim adquirido era dedicado às deusas do templo, pagando as despesas e aumentando os fundos de construção. A Babilônia, em seu período de exaltação, tornou-se rica. E o luxo sempre promove toda a variedade de vícios. Q. Curtius, historiador romano de meados do século I D.C. (v.1), queixou-se como segue: «Coisa alguma poderia ser mais corrupta do que a moral deles (dos babilônios) e coisa alguma é melhor ajustada para excitar e atrair aos prazeres sem moderação. Os ritos de hospitalidade eram poluídos pelas concupiscências mais grosseiras e desavergonhadas. O dinheiro dissolvia todos os laços, de parentesco, de respeito ou de estima. Os babilônios eram excessivamente dados ao vinho. As mulheres (que freqüentavam as festividades) a princípio faziam-no com algum grau de propriedade, mas iam ficando cada vez mais degradadas...e terminavam lançando fora toda a modéstia e as próprias roupas». Foi por isso que os profetas hebreus lançaram invectivas poderosas contra tal estado de coisas. (Ver Isa. 14:11; 47:1; Jer. 51:39 e Dan. 5:1).

6. Principais cidades da Babilônia

a. *Babilônia*. A história da Babilônia é, essencialmente, a história da cidade de Babilônia. Por isso, tudo que dissemos acima aplica-se, em sua maior parte, a uma e à outra. Adicionamos aqui algumas descrições específicas da cidade de Babilônia:

A cidade era tão vasta que aqueles que habitavam no centro da mesma não sabiam que seus pontos extremos haviam sido capturados (ver Jer. 51:31). Heródoto diz que a circunferência da cidade media quase cem quilômetros. A cidade tinha a forma de um quadrado, cada lado com mais de 24 quilômetros. Havia terras aráveis e de pastagem suficientes para suprir as necessidades de sua população, que era de mais de um milhão de habitantes, um número imenso, para o mundo antigo. As muralhas contavam com cem portões de bronze, vinte e cinco em cada lado (ver Isa. 45:2). A altura dessas muralhas era de 107 m, com cerca de 27 m de espessura. Um profundo e largo fosso com água circundava as muralhas, cujas partes inferiores eram cimentadas e seguras com tijolos, mantidos no lugar com asfalto. As ruas eram traçadas formando ângulos retos, e as ruas cruzadas que levavam ao Eufrates, eram fechadas em suas extremidades por portões de bronze. O templo de Belo era um zigurate com oito torres quadradas. Os jardins suspensos formavam um quadrado com 120 m de lado, construídos em terraços. A parte mais alta continha árvores. Plataformas de madeira, que se estendiam de uma pilastra à outra, feitas de pedra, formavam pontes que uniam as duas partes da cidade. Havia duzentas e cinqüenta torres nas

BABILÔNIA

muralhas, guardando a cidade de qualquer inimigo que se aproximasse. Numerosos canais cruzavam a região para efeitos de drenagem e irrigação (ver Sal. 137:1: «Às margens dos rios da Babilônia nós nos assentávamos e chorávamos...Nos salgueiros que lá havia pendurávamos as nossas harpas...»). Os maiores dentre esses canais eram navegados por embarcações, e estavam ligados aos rios Eufrates e Tigre.

Localização. Ficava às margens do rio Eufrates e cerca de 88 km ao sul da moderna cidade de Bagdá, e imediatamente ao norte da moderna Hila, no centro do atual Iraque.

Heródoto afirma que os gregos aprenderam dos babilônios o relógio de sol e a divisão do dia em 12 partes. A primeira eclipse do sol, que é contada na história, foi observada na Babilônia, em 19 de março de 721 A.C. A ciência da astronomia (via astrologia) deve sua origem aos caldeus, que conduziram tais observações desde os tempos mais remotos. Veja o artigo sobre *Astronomia*.

Divisões da cidade. Muitos detalhes dos distritos das cidades e seus templos têm sido descobertos pela arqueologia e nas referências literárias. Tanto quanto nós sabemos, havia 53 de tais distritos. Alguns dos nomes dados a eles eram algumas vezes usados para designar a cidade toda, como Shuanna, Shushan, Tuba, Tintir, Kullab.

A localização agora. A localização é agora ocultada por um número de elevações largamente espalhadas. A maior, Qasr, cobre a antiga cidadela; Merkes, um distrito da cidade; para o norte, Bawil, o palácio do norte e de verão de Nebuchadrezzar; Amram ibn 'Ali, o templo de Marduk; e Sahn, a localização do zigurate ou torre templo.

b. *Outras cidades* de importância na Babilônia. A região antigamente compreendia Sumer e Akkad. Akkad era a região norte da mais baixa planície aluvial do Tigre Eufrates, na qual estavam a Babilônia, Borsipa, Kish, Kuthah, Sippar e Agade (Acade). As principais cidades de Sumer eram Nippur, Lagash, Umma, Larsa, Erech (Uruk, Gên. 10:11), Ur, a cidade de Abraão, e Eridu. As presentes localizações de Eridu, Ur e Lagash eram provavelmente em, ou muito próximo do Golfo Pérsico, em cerca de 3000 A.C. Esta fértil planície aluvial, irrigada pelos rios Tigre e Eufrates, tornou-se o berço da civilização. Nesta parte baixa da Mesopotâmia, a 55 milhas do sul da presente Bagdá, onde uma vez ergueu-se na baía do Eufrates, a cidade tinha o altivo nome de *Babilu*, «portão de Deus», ou Babilônia. Embora a história do baixo vale não comece com esta cidade, Babilônia cedo tornou-se proeminente e seu nome é ligado principalmente à região a qual não é familiarmente conhecida como Babilônia.

O sentido figurativo da Babilônia. Nos escritos proféticos do A.T., a idéia ligada à Babilônia é *confusão*. Veja o artigo em *Torre de Babilônia*. Esta confusão é própria do paganismo, não simplesmente de línguas. Para o uso de Babilônia no N.T., veja o artigo separado em *Babilônia, Novo Testamento*.

7. Arqueologia

As descobertas arqueológicas na Babilônia têm sido extensas. Mais de vinte cidades diferentes foram descobertas e ilustradas com muitos artefatos. Abaixo damos um exemplo disso: 1. *Adabe*, a 77 km a suleste de Diwaniyah, foi descoberta a planta da cidade. 2. Al'Ubaid, a seis quilômetros e meio a noroeste de Ur, onde foram descobertos um terraço, relevos e mosaicos. 3. Babilônia, onde foram encontrados inúmeros edifícios, templos, lares particulares, um teatro grego, uma acrópole, os tabletes acaemenianos do norte da Babilônia, o portão de Istar, etc. 4. Borsipa, a onze quilômetros a sul-sudoeste de Babilônia, onde foram encontrados um zigurate, inscrições em cilindros; Ezida, ao norte de Babilônia, o palácio de Nebuchadrezar II, as muralhas da cidade. 5. Der, a 26 km a sudoeste de Bagdá, onde foram descobertos tabletes e a planta da cidade. 6. Dilbate, a 29 km a sul-suleste de Bila, Tell Dailem, onde foram encontrados tabletes do período persa. 7. Drehem, Tell Duraihim, a 5 km ao sul de Nipur, onde foram encontrados muitos tabletes. 8. Dur-Kurigalzu, a 19 km a oeste de Samawa, a capital dos cassitas, onde foram encontrados um zigurate, templos, um palácio e tabletes. 9. Ereque, a 40 km a leste de Samawa, Uruque, onde foram encontrados mosaicos, um templo e túmulos dos partas, o Anu-Antum do tempo dos selêucidas, que era um palácio parta, além de textos cuneiformes arcaicos, templos e zigurates com dezoito pisos; e em Uruque, ao norte da Babilônia, templos partas. 10. Eridu, a 39 km a sudoeste de Nasiriyah, onde foram encontrados cerâmica, instrumentos de ferro e um zigurate. 11. Esnuna, a 88,5 km a suleste de Bagdá, onde foram encontrados um palácio do período Isin, templos anteriores a Sargão, tabletes em escrita cuneiforme e estatuetas. 12. Harmal, a quilômetro e meio de Bagdá, onde foram encontradas inscrições e construções de tijolos do templo da antiga Babilônia, o templo de Hani, tabletes e o código de Esuna. 13. Jemdat Nasr, a 24 km a nordeste de Hillah, o palácio de Jemdat Nasr, cerâmica e textos arcaicos. 14. Kish, a 16 km a nordeste de Hillah, onde foram encontrados um edifício do estilo da Babilônia do norte, um templo muito antigo, vários edifícios, tabletes, cemitérios, zigurates, palácios e templos diversos. 15. Kutalla, a 40 km a sudoeste de Nasiriyah, onde foram encontrados edifícios e templos. 16. Kutha, a 32 km a nordeste da Babilônia, onde foram encontradas uma necrópole e tabletes. 17. Lagash, a 19 km a nordeste de Shatra, onde foram encontradas estátuas de Gudea, cerâmica e inscrições. 18. Larsa, a 40 km a oeste nordeste de Nasiriyah, onde foram encontrados um zigurate, um templo, mesas, palácios e inscrições. 19. Nipur, a quase 10 km a norte-nordeste de Afak, túmulos mais recentes. 20. Surupaque, a 10 km a nordeste de Shatra, restos de objetos de um período anterior a Sargão. 21. Sipar, a 29 km a suleste de Bagdá, onde foram encontrados um zigurate, um palácio e tabletes. 22. Umma, Tell Jokha, a 40 km a norte-noroeste de Shatra, onde foram encontrados muitos tabletes de Ur III, a planta da cidade, e edifícios. 23. 'Uqair, Tell 'Uqair, a 38 km a nordeste da Babilônia, perto de Uruque-Jamdat Nasr, onde foram encontrados cerâmica, mosaicos e um templo edificado sobre uma plataforma. 24. Ur, Tell Muqayyar, a mais de 22 km a oeste-sudoeste de Narisiyah, os alicerces de um zigurate, trincheiras, o templo de Eharsag, um zigurate no estilo de Ur III, do norte da Babilônia, o cemitério real, um fosso para água, templos, palácios, casa, etc. 25. Nuzi (vide), 4.000 tabletes com muita informação. (ID ND PAR SAG UN Z)

BABILÔNIA, A MERETRIZ Apocalipse 17:1-6

Não nos devemos olvidar de que o Apocalipse foi originalmente escrito para a igreja cristã primitiva, que sofria perseguições por parte do império romano. Essa perseguição era especialmente intensa porque os cristãos se recusavam a adorar o imperador romano, conforme se requeria no culto ao imperador. A besta

BABILÔNIA A MERETRIZ

saída do mar representa a Roma secular e pagã. Historicamente, representa o imperador Nero; profeticamente, o «Nero redivivo» ou anticristo. A besta saída da terra representa a Roma religiosa, o culto ao imperador (historicamente falando); mas, profeticamente, ela representa o «João Batista» do anticristo, o falso profeta, que promoverá por todo o mundo o culto ao anticristo, mediante os meios de comunicação em massa. Na antiguidade, a própria cidade de Roma fora deificada, e uma deusa, chamada «Roma», veio a ser a deusa protetora das cidades romanas da Ásia Menor. Roma era a divindade tutelar de Cartago. Em 29 A.C., foram erigidos por Otávio templos dedicados a «Dea Roma» e a «Divus Julius». Também houve templos dedicados ao próprio Otávio em Pérgamo, na Nicomédia e na Bitínia. Os remanescentes desses templos pagãos até hoje podem ser vistos em Pérgamo. Isso talvez sejam os restos do «trono de Satanás», que figura na epístola à igreja de Pérgamo, no livro de Apocalipse. Parece que o culto de Roma estava associado à adoração dos «imperadores falecidos», ao passo que o culto ao imperador dirigia-se aos imperadores reinantes. De tudo isso é que se desenvolveu uma espécie de doutrina da «Roma eterna». Não há que duvidar que o vidente João, no décimo oitavo capítulo de Apocalipse zombava dessa idéia, sendo provável também que ele fustigava todas as formas de «idolatria romana», representadas no culto a Roma e no culto ao imperador.

A **meretriz**, que figura no Apo. 17, é essa idolatria romana de muitas facetas, ainda que o culto ao imperador seja o ponto mais destacado, conforme se vê por todo o Apocalipse. Roma se tornara o centro das formas mais ousadas e horrendas de idolatria. Mas João predisse que nada disso perduraria, pois estava condenado a sofrer a mais contundente derrota que se possa imaginar. Também não se deve duvidar que João esperava que isso ocorresse em seus próprios dias, pois não antecipava a aplicação a «longo prazo» de suas predições. Nessa expectativa, que não se cumpriu em seus próprios dias, João não se mostrou diferente dos profetas do A.T., como Isaías, que esperava o reino messiânico para imediatamente depois do julgamento da Assíria (ver os capítulos dez e onze do livro de Isaías) ou como Daniel, que pensou que o fim ocorreria imediatamente após o julgamento de Antíoco IV Epifânio. Jeremias esperava o *reino* para imediatamente depois do retorno do exílio. É evidente, pois, que as visões dos profetas ultrapassavam seu próprio entendimento e as suas expectações pessoais, que tão freqüentemente ficaram sem cumprimento, ainda que Deus tenha decretado seu cumprimento para os últimos dias.

Normalmente, as predições bíblicas têm um cumprimento a curto prazo e outro a longo prazo. Portanto, nos «últimos dias», veremos o aparecimento tanto de um império político, a federação dos dez reinos, controlada pelo anticristo, que terá a cidade de Roma como seu centro, como também veremos o aparecimento de um novo «culto ao imperador», que consistirá na adoração conferida ao homem do pecado. Esse culto tornar-se-á tão forte que dominará as mentes dos homens e os tornará virtuais escravos da malignidade; pois Satanás será adorado por intermédio do anticristo (ver Apo. 13:4). A maior perseguição religiosa de todos os tempos será promovida pelos aderentes do culto ao anticristo; e essa adoração será corrupta e maligna de tal modo que fará o comunismo parecer santo comparativamente. No artigo intitulado, *A Tradição Profética e a Nossa Época*, fazemos a tentativa de reunir várias predições que ilustram as condições incrivelmente más que esperamos ver pessoalmente, ou que, pelo menos, serão vistas pelos nossos filhos. Pois acreditamos que o anticristo já está vivo. O artigo acima referido nos apresenta as razões para essa crença.

Para o vidente João, essa «idolatria», quer em seu aspecto antigo—«culto ao imperador», quer em seu aspecto futuro—«culto ao anticristo», é a «meretriz». Mas essa meretriz também será a Roma política e econômica. Não se duvida que João não pôde antecipar muitas das «implicações» dessas predições. Somente os próprios acontecimentos nos ensinarão o que precisamos saber acerca dessas coisas.

A dupla destruição. É claro que nos capítulos dezessete e dezoito do livro do Apocalipse, nas sete visões da condenação de Roma, se retrata a destruição tanto «política» quanto *religiosa* de Roma. Porém, erraríamos se fizéssemos unicamente a Igreja Católica Romana ser a Roma «religiosa». Sem dúvida, porções de todas as denominações cristãs serão atraídas para o terrível culto ao anticristo. Muitos dos chamados cristãos serão enganados, encarando o anticristo como um novo Messias. Na verdade, entretanto, o «culto» ao anticristo será uma religião inteiramente nova, combinando idéias e crenças do Oriente com as do Ocidente. Também será uma religião extremamente «antidivina» e «anticristã», por inclinar-se para as idéias do ateísmo e do agnosticismo. Tornar-se-á algo tão imensamente maligno que o comunismo parecerá algo santo, paralelamente a isso.

Não cremos que qualquer denominação verdadeiramente evangélica venha a ser enganada de tal modo que aceite esse culto ao anticristo como algo provindo do Senhor, e que dê lealdade ao anticristo. O mais provável é que as denominações evangélicas venham a ser «purificadas» pelo fogo da tribulação, que logo finalmente se formará a *unidade* de todas as denominações evangélicas, e um «movimento subterrâneo» (porquanto a igreja visível desaparecerá, tão atroz será a perseguição religiosa). Não há como chamar o «romanismo» de a meretriz tonta como o sangue dos santos e dos mártires de Jesus, quando, historicamente, reconhecemos que isso é uma referência ao «culto ao imperador». Esse culto era algo inteiramente fora dos círculos cristãos. Mas é verdade que o culto ao anticristo, em muitos lugares do mundo, se assemelhará, pelo menos no princípio, com uma espécie de «neocristianismo». Todavia, todas as denominações cristãs que realmente sejam formadas de pessoas regeneradas, e que se apegam às doutrinas centrais da Bíblia, como a «trindade», a «divindade de Cristo», etc., não poderão ficar enganadas para sempre.

Duvidamos que a Roma do décimo sétimo capítulo do Apoc. seja o «romanismo», e que a do capítulo dezoito seja a Roma secular e *comercial*. Devemos considerar esses quadros apenas como ângulos diversos de uma única coisa. Ambos retratam a «meretriz», porquanto ambos representam a Roma pagã e ímpia — uma do ponto de vista do *culto ao imperador*, e outra do ponto de vista político e econômico de Roma. Particularmente em foco, por toda a parte, está a «cidade de Roma», e isso ocorre em ambos esses citados capítulos. (Ver Apo. 17:18, onde a «meretriz» é aquela «grande cidade». Comparar com Apo. 18:7, que retrata a «rainha», o que aponta para a mesma figura feminina, mas note-se que essa rainha é uma prostituta). Isso se harmoniza com Apo. 17:2-5. Outrossim, Apo. 18:10 mostra que continua em foco a «cidade» de Roma. O décimo nono versículo reitera a idéia. Mas a cidade

BABILÔNIA DO NOVO TESTAMENTO

«subentende» o império inteiro, por ser seu centro e capital. Essa é uma interpretação que se coaduna com o qué sabemos que João atacava em seus dias; e supomos que outro tanto se dará no caso do aspecto profético dos capítulos dezessete e dezoito. Temos aqui as «sete visões» da queda de Roma, e, naturalmente, cada visão dará um ponto de vista diverso de uma mesma e única queda. Profeticamente falando, isso retrata a queda do anticristo, porquanto seu poder envolverá muitos aspectos, religioso, político, militar, etc. Em todos esses aspectos, entretanto, ele cairá; e é isso que os capítulos dezessete e dezoito do Apocalipse estão descrevendo. Notemos que em Apo. 17:9 e ss temos a Roma «política», mas imediatamente antes disso, no sexto versículo do capítulo 17, temos uma alusão inequívoca ao «culto ao imperador», que perseguia aos cristãos que não anuíam a esse culto. Portanto, não há como pôr o capítulo dezessete em contradistinção ao décimo oitavo capítulo, estabelecendo qualquer distinção básica entre eles, a não ser que ali são retratados diferentes aspectos da queda da mesma Roma.

Também não devemos ver em Apo. 17 o reavivamento da «literal cidade da Babilônia», que viria a ser a capital política e comercial do anticristo. Babilônia é apenas um código para Roma, conforme se vê nas notas expositivas sobre Apo. 14:8 no NTI, e é evidente que o vidente João escreveu contra Roma, e não contra a literal cidade da Babilônia. Isso é uma verdade histórica, e também será uma verdade profética. A profecia bíblica demonstra claramente (ver Apo. 17:9 e ss) que o centro de atividades do anticristo será a literal cidade de Roma, e não a cidade da Babilônia, reconstruída.

Para alguns intérpretes, o trecho de Apo. 17:16 fala de uma «Roma religiosa», que a Roma política se deleitará em destruir. E o décimo oitavo capítulo desse livro presumivelmente aludiria a essa Roma política, diante de cuja queda subseqüente o mundo inteiro se *lamentará*. Porém, não são retratadas aqui duas Romas, uma política e outra religiosa. Os povos oprimidos se «alegrarão» ante a queda de Roma (ver Apo. 17:16), mas, ao perceberem que isso os prejudicará, pois Roma os tornou ricos, se lamentarão. Os pequenos poderes sempre se regozijam ante a queda dos poderes maiores, mas geralmente logo descobrem que seu bem-estar está vinculado a estes últimos, pelo que têm motivos de pensar novamente, com maior sobriedade.

O décimo oitavo versículo mostra que a «cidade» de Roma está essencialmente em foco, embora ela represente o império todo. Alguns intérpretes supõem haver aqui uma clara distinção (nos capítulos dezessete e dezoito), entre a cidade de Roma e o império romano.

A razão por que alguns eruditos fazem tão radical distinção entre as duas Romas é que, nos versículos dezesseis a dezoito, há a predição de uma destruição de Roma por parte da besta e sua federação de dez reinos. O pano de fundo histórico disso é a tradição (que nunca teve lugar, historicamente falando) de que o «Nero redivivo», que era identificado com o anticristo nas antigas tradições cristãs, retornaria a Roma, à testa de um exército parta, a fim de assaltá-la, cometendo «matricídio». (Ver os Oráculos Sibilinos 5:363-369). Portanto, é fácil entender isso «historicamente». Porém, como entender isso profeticamente não é tão fácil. Os intérpretes protestantes não têm dificuldades aqui, pois supõem que o anticristo, após ter cooperado com a Igreja Católica Romana, utilizando-se dela (como também de seus aliados, as denominações protestantes apóstatas), repentinamente destruirá toda a imensa organização. Mas, apesar disso ser uma conveniente interpretação «protestante», de forma alguma é certo que isso é o que se deve ver em Apo. 17:1-6. Provavelmente haverá a unidade dos cristãos apóstatas (de todas as denominações) que prestarão lealdade ao anticristo e promoverão seu culto, os quais serão subseqüentemente perseguidos e destruídos por ele; e isso poderia cumprir o aspecto profético das descrições à nossa frente. Contudo, sentimo-nos sobre terreno precário quando começamos a «nomear as denominações». Esse «cristianismo apóstata» sem dúvida se unirá a muitíssimas *outras* religiões mundanas, porquanto a influência do anticristo será universal. É claro que o anticristo não procurará destruir o culto que o incensa, mas tão-somente um certo aspecto do mesmo, e as denominações cristãs apóstatas, por exemplo poderão cair em seu desagrado, sendo reduzidas a quase nada. A predição sobre a destruição da «meretriz» (ver Apoc. 17:16), provavelmente inclui a idéia de que todas as religiões do mundo desaparecerão, por serem destruídas, ou serão absorvidas no culto ao anticristo. Todas as religiões, excetuando seu culto imediato, terão de existir apenas subterraneamente, incluindo os membros fiéis a Cristo da igreja cristã.

BABILÔNIA NO NOVO TESTAMENTO

Há várias coisas a serem consideradas a esse respeito:

1. *Uso literal*. Babilônia é literalmente mencionada na genealogia de Jesus, quando há alusão à deportação de Judá para a Babilônia, no século VII A.C. (ver Mat. 1:11,12,17). Estêvão também aludiu ao fato, em Atos 7:43. Nesse trecho, ele alterou o fraseado de «além de Damasco», usado na LXX, para «além da Babilônia», visto que esse foi o destino do povo judeu, quando de sua deportação.

2. Em I Pedro, no fim dessa epístola, a palavra «aquela» (ver I Ped. 5:13), que envia saudações, poderia ser a esposa de Pedro. Mas, conforme dão a entender quase todas as traduções, o que está em foco é a igreja na Babilônia. Isso tem sido sujeitado a diversas interpretações: poderia estar em vista a literal cidade da Babilônia, isto é, as pessoas em reduzido número que habitavam nas redondezas; poderia estar em vista a cidade de Roma, simbolicamente descrita por Pedro como Babilônia; ou o apóstolo poderia ter-se referido ao mundo incrédulo como Babilônia, outra aplicação metafórica do termo. Vamos expandir o comentário sobre essas possibilidades:

a. *A Babilônia da Mesopotâmia*. Sabemos que a cidade da Babilônia, no século I D.C., contava com um pequeno segmento judaico, entre sua população. Os judeus foram dispersos dali, mas foi por breve período (ver Josefo, *Anti*. XVIII.ix.6-9). Trajano visitou a cidade em 115 D.C. Com base em I Pedro 5:13, a Igreja Ortodoxa pensa que Pedro realmente esteve na cidade. Apesar disso ser uma forte possibilidade, não há qualquer evidência histórica em favor da presença de Pedro naquele lugar, excetuando essa interpretação dos ortodoxos quanto a esse trecho da primeira epístola de Pedro. Muitos protestantes e evangélicos têm favorecido essa interpretação com bases dogmáticas, a fim de contradizerem a doutrina católico romana de que Pedro foi o primeiro papa. Porém, ainda que Pedro tivesse estado em Roma, isso não teria feito dele o primeiro papa. A questão do papado envolve muito mais do que a localização desse apóstolo. (Ver sobre o *papado*).

b. *A cidade de Roma*. Babilônia era um antigo

429

nome críptico para indicar a capital do império romano. Há uma antiga tradição de que Pedro terminou os seus dias de vida terrena nessa cidade, tradição essa que quase certamente corresponde à realidade dos fatos.

c. *Uma Babilônia no Egito.* Havia um posto de fronteira, pertencente aos romanos, no Egito, que tinha esse nome, de acordo com Estrabão (Geo. XVII.1.30) no século I D.C. Porém, não há qualquer evidência de que Pedro esteve ali, ou de que ali havia uma igreja cristã. Um herege alexandrino, Basílides, reivindicava autoridade petrina para os seus escritos, através de seu intérprete, Glauquias (ver Clemente de Alexandria, *Stromateis* VII.17). Todavia, coisa alguma dá apoio a essa reivindicação.

d. Poderia tratar-se de um lugar qualquer, que Pedro chamou de Babilônia, a fim de não desvendar o local onde se ocultava. Porém, em favor de tal idéia nada há, senão meras conjecturas.

Evidências em favor da cidade de Roma, capital do império romano. Não há que duvidar que as referências de Apo. 18:2-24, que falam sobre «Babilônia», aludem à cidade de Roma. No Apocalipse, Roma é caracterizada em tons mais negros: Ela é a mãe das meretrizes, fonte de todas as abominações praticadas à face da terra (ver 17:5); a cidade está cercada por muitas águas e edificada sobre sete colinas, dado este que realmente ocorre com Roma (ver 17:9); a cidade é um centro internacional de governo (ver 14:8 e 17:1); a cidade é poderosa devido ao seu comércio e à sua frota marítima (ver 18:3,11,19); a cidade é grande perseguidora dos santos do Senhor (ver 17:6 e 19:2); a cidade é notória por suas riquezas, luxo e dissipação (ver 18:11-17). Somente a cidade de Roma ajusta-se a essas descrições. Além disso, o nome Babilônia, em Apo. 17:5,7, precisa ser interpretado simbolicamente, porquanto é chamado de «mistério». Os *Oráculos Sibilinos* (v. 143) chamam Roma de Babilônia. Roma era a nova Babilônia, em contato direto com o cristianismo, tal como a antiga Babilônia estava em contato com Israel. Assim como Deus derrubou a primeira, haverá de derrubar a segunda. Finalmente, há muitas citações extraídas dos pais da Igreja que asseguram que Pedro terminou sua vida terrena em Roma. Mas, como já salientamos, isso não faz dele um papa, porque essa doutrina depende do desenvolvimento de certos dogmas e tradições, que se desenvolveram nos séculos posteriores ao cristianismo primitivo, inteiramente à parte do Novo Testamento e contradizendo os ensinamentos do mesmo. (NTI Z)

BABISMO
Ver Bahaísmo.

BACA
No hebraico significa «pranto», palavra que aparece, pela primeira vez, em Salmos 84:6, mas que nossa versão portuguesa traduz, erroneamente, por «árido»: «O qual, passando pelo vale *árido*, faz dele um manancial...» Na Bíblia, essa é a única passagem que se refere a tal vale. Mas o verbo hebraico cognato figura no Antigo Testamento por cento e catorze vezes, sendo variegadamente traduzido, como «chorar». «queixar-se», «lamentar-se», etc. Nossa versão portuguesa também labora em erro em II Sam. 5:23,24 e I Crô. 14:14,15, onde a palavra hebraica é traduzida por «amoreira». Alguns intérpretes preferem pensar no bálsamo, no álamo, ou na faia, ao passo que outros nem aceitam que se tratasse de uma árvore. A referência, pois, permanece obscura, embora se deva pensar em alguma espécie vegetal, nessas duas referências, que exudasse algo. Ver o artigo *Vale do Baca*.

BACA, Vale de
Ver o artigo sobre Baca. Como vimos ali, a palavra «Baca» não figura na nossa versão portuguesa, a qual é traduzida pelo adjetivo «árido». Os intérpretes têm pensado que a palavra hebraica «Baca» é alusão a alguma espécie de árvore, que teria dado nome ao vale, por ser ali abundante. Porém, se tal palavra realmente significa «pranto», então não teríamos de pensar em algum vale literal, mas apenas em um estado de tristeza. Nesse caso, o salmista, estando no exílio, ou, pelo menos, longe de sua pátria (dependendo das circunstâncias em que o Salmo 84 foi escrito, único lugar onde há menção a esse vale), alude à tristeza de não poder contemplar Jerusalém, o que era privilégio de outros. Mas, se realmente há referência a uma árvore, e, portanto, a um vale literal, então o mais provável é que esteja em foco o bálsamo, que exuda uma goma, a qual poderia ser comparado ao «pranto». Alguns estudiosos, diante da dificuldade, preferem substituir a palavra hebraica *hibbika* pelo que diz o texto massorético, *habbaka*, que significa «fluxo». Nesse caso, teríamos uma metáfora de alegria e plenitude, porquanto estaria em pauta um vale que flui água, por ter muitas fontes, um lugar que falava em prosperidade. (ID S Z)

BACBUQUE
No hebraico «garrafa», especialmente uma de gargalo estreito. Era chefe de uma das famílias dos netinins, que retornaram do cativeiro babilônico (ver o artigo) em companhia de Zorobabel (ver Esd. 2:51 e Nee. 7:53), em cerca de 536 A.C. (S)

BACBUQUIAS
No hebraico, «esvaziamento» ou «dilapidação por Yahweh». Parece haver duas pessoas com esse nome, nas páginas do Antigo Testamento: 1. O segundo entre vários irmãos levitas, que habitava em Jerusalém após o retorno da Babilônia (ver Nee. 11:17 e 12:9). 2. Aparentemente, na opinião de outros, o Bacbuquias referido em Nee. 12:9 seria um porteiro, também levita. Os intérpretes dizem-se capazes de encontrar dois ou três homens com esse nome; e nada de certo se sabe sobre essa questão, pois os informes bíblicos são insuficientes para lançar luz sobre a mesma. (S Z)

BACENOR
Oficial do exército de Judas Macabeu, que participou da guerra contra Górgias, governador da Iduméia (ver II Macabeus 12:35).

BACH, JOHANN SEBASTIAN
Viveu de 1685 a 1750. Foi músico e compositor alemão cujas muitas peças musicais transcendem à era barroca em que ele viveu, destacando-se o criador das mesmas como um dos mais importantes compositores de todos os tempos. Nasceu em Eisenach, a 21 de março de 1685. Ficou órfão aos dez anos de idade, deixou Eisenach e foi para Ohdruf, lugar onde nascera seu irmão mais velho, Johann Christoph. Em 1700 tornou-se membro da escola

particular da Igreja de São Miguel, em Luneiburgo. Em 1703, passou a trabalhar sob o patrocínio do duque de Weimar, e em seguida tornou-se organista da igreja de São Bonifácio, em Muhlhausen. Depois disso, envolveu-se em muitas atividades em várias cidades, o que lhe permitiu desenvolver extraordinariamente, os seus dotes musicais. Teve muitas controvérsias com associados seus; e com freqüência, sofria oposição. Excetuando suas notáveis façanhas musicais, sua vida não teve lances relevantes. A maioria de seus contemporâneos não percebia que estava ao lado de um dos compositores imortais da história da música.

As cantatas religiosas do século XVIII atingiram o seu ponto culminante nas duzentas e noventa e cinco cantatas de Bach. Em quarenta delas, ele usou apenas a voz de um solo, posto que com acompanhamento orquestral. Na maioria dos casos, as peças começam com um grande coro, prosseguindo com uma série de recitais e árias, e terminando com um simples coro, por parte de toda a congregação. As modernas cantatas apelam muito para o oratório. Bach também compôs peças corais para o órgão. Também devemos considerar as suas fugas, uma forma polifônica de composição, que usa principalmente instrumentos musicais, embora também incluindo o coro, como na sua Missa em B Menor. Bach também foi o autor de muitos hinos e missas. Seu impacto sobre a música em geral, e sobre a música religiosa em particular, não pode ser calculado. Ver os artigos sobre cada uma das formas musicais mencionadas neste parágrafo, bem como o artigo sobre a *Música*. (AM E)

BACIA

Tradução de várias palavras hebraicas e gregas, a saber:

1. *Aggan*, «bacia», usada por três vezes (ver Êxo. 24:6, em português, «bacia»; Isa. 22:24, em português, «taça»; e Can. 7:2, em português, «taça»).

2. *Kefor*, «taça», usada por seis vezes com esse sentido, e por três vezes com o sentido de «geada». Para exemplificar: I Crô. 28:17; Esd. 1:10; 8:27; e, no segundo sentido: Êxo. 16:14; Jó. 38:29 e Sal. 147:16.

3. *Mizraq*, «bacia grande». Usada por trinta e duas vezes. Para exemplificar: Êxo. 27:3; 38:3; Núm. 4:14; I Reis 7:40,45,50; Nee. 7:70; Jer. 52:18,19; Zac. 9:15 e 14:20.

4. *Saf*, «prato», mas também «porta». No primeiro sentido é palavra usada por sete vezes. Para exemplificar: Êxo. 12:22; II Sam. 17:28; Jer. 52:19.

5. No grego temos a palavra *niptér*, «jarra», usada no Novo Testamento por apenas uma vez, em João 13:5, embora seu cognato, o verbo *nípto*, «lavar», seja usado por dezessete vezes.

No tabernáculo, armado no deserto ao mandado de Deus, havia uma bacia de bronze no átrio, entre o altar dos holocaustos e a tenda (ver Êxo. 30:17,21; 38:8 e 40:30-32), onde Aarão e seus filhos lavavam as mãos e os pés, antes de entrarem na tenda da congregação, ou quando ministravam diante do altar. O simbolismo desse objeto é patente. Jesus sumariou a questão quando disse a Pedro: «Se eu não te lavar, não tens parte comigo» (João 13:8).

BACIA DE LAVAR

Expressão encontrada exclusivamente em Salmos 60:8 e 108:9, onde Deus afirma: «Moabe, porém, é a minha bacia de lavar», dando a entender que Moabe era desprezível aos olhos de Deus, como uma bacia onde as mãos e os pés sujos são lavados.

BACKUS, ISAQUE

Nasceu em 1724 e faleceu em 1806. Foi ministro congregacional, separatista, batista e historiador. Sua maior contribuição foi ser um dos campeões da liberdade religiosa, incluindo a intercessão junto a oficiais do governo norte-americano. Escreveu a história da Nova Inglaterra e certo número de outros livros. (AM F)

BACO

Ver **Dionísio**.

BACON, BENJAMIN WISNER

Suas datas são 1860-1932. Foi um pastor congregacional, erudito de Bíblia, professor de Yale do Novo Testamento. Foi um dos líderes no campo da erudição bíblica, autor de importantes livros e artigos. Seus livros incluem: *The Fourth Gospel in Research and Debate; Is Mark a Roman Gospel? The Gospel of Mark, Its Composition and Date; Studies in Matthew, the Gospel of the Hellenists.* (AM E)

BACON, FRANCIS

Nasceu em 1561 e faleceu em 1626, em Londres. Foi o precursor do empirismo britânico, descendia de uma família que já havia prestado relevantes serviços. Tendo entrado na carreira política e na advocacia, foi feito lorde por Tiago I, e posteriormente recebeu o título de visconde de São Albano. Mas, em 1621, ele foi acusado de corrupção, foi multado e banido da corte. Alexandre Pope tinha Bacon na mente quando escreveu: «...o mais brilhante, o mais sábio e o pior elemento da humanidade» (Ensaio, *Sobre o Homem*, VIII).

Como filósofo, Bacon exerceu imensa influência, tendo iniciado e influenciado a linha de pensadores que inclui Locke, Hume, Mill e Bertrand Russell. Seu ponto de vista era concreto, prático e utilitarista. Dizia-se defensor da fé cristã; mas às vezes expressava-se com tal ironia que deixava dúvidas quanto à sua real posição. Manifestou-se contra o escolasticismo, distinguindo claramente entre a razão e a revelação. Seu alvo era facilitar as investigações da ciência, por meio do método matemático, sem misturar a religião na questão. Ele equiparava o conhecimento ao poder, e antecipava um domínio tecnológico em grande escala, que resultaria em uma utopia econômica e social.

Empirismo. Bacon rejeitava a simples indução com seus valores numéricos. Antes, salientava a necessidade de averiguar as generalizações, bem como a necessidade de pesquisar instâncias negativas que contradiziam as conclusões. Talvez a sua maior debilidade consistisse no fato de que ele não entendia que um cientista, vez por outra, precisa por de lado o empirismo rígido, confiando na sua intuição acerca da verdade ou quanto a descobertas que somente mais tarde seriam comprovadas experimentalmente. Algumas vezes, um cientista tem de expor alguma hipótese bem imaginada. Quanto a essa fraqueza, Bacon foi criticado por Kant.

Em seu livro, *Novum Organum*, Bacon expôs os interesses e os motivos humanos que jazem por detrás da atitude filosófica e das conclusões de um homem. Ele chamava esses preconceitos de *ídolos mentais*. Esses preconceitos são os seguintes: 1. Os ídolos da tribo, que são os erros humanos que existem porque pertencemos à raça humana, e imaginamos que essa espécie pode ser a medida de todas as coisas. De fato, há muitas idéias falsas à solta. 2. Os ídolos da caverna são os erros que surgem devido aos preconceitos individuais. Esses erros são tão numerosos quanto as idéias que circulam nas mentes das pessoas. 3. Os ídolos do mercado, que são os erros que se originam da influência das palavras na mente, com base na idéia que a existência de uma palavra indica que deve haver uma realidade que corresponda àquela palavra. Mas a verdade é que as palavras são ambíguas e confusas, e disso resulta que a verdade tem de transpor o obstáculo formado pelos próprios idiomas. 4. Os ídolos do teatro, que são erros gerados pela influência da filosofia tradicional, devido ao exagerado respeito a heróis filósofos como Aristóteles, cuja ciência, embora boa para sua época, tornou-se obsoleta há muito tempo, embora muitos tenham deixado de perceber isso por inúmeras gerações. Hume e outros pensadores deram continuidade à campanha de Bacon contra tais ídolos.

O grande alvo de Bacon era a *Grande Restauração*, que devolveria ao homem o domínio sobre o mundo natural. Em seu livro, *The New Atlantis*, ele falou sobre a sociedade ideal, governada por princípios científicos. Essa sociedade teria um colégio intitulado Casa de Salomão, dirigido por um grupo de sábios, científica e experimentalmente orientados e motivados. Alguns supõem que essa foi a idéia que gerou a Real Sociedade Inglesa.

Principais obras. Há três ensaios: *Two Books on the Advancement of Learning; The New Organon* e *The New Atlantis*. (AM E F EP MM P)

BACON, ROGER

Nasceu em 1214 e faleceu em 1294. Foi filósofo inglês e monge franciscano. Estudou em Oxford e na Universidade de Paris. Mais tarde fez conferências em ambas essas universidades, concentrando a atenção sobre a ciência transmitida pelos escritores árabes. Foi suspeito de falta de ortodoxia, pelo que Boaventura, em 1257, proibiu suas conferências em Oxford, fazendo-o cessar as suas publicações. O papa Clemente IV liberou-o da proibição, e ele pediu para escrever um tratado sobre as ciências. Disso resultaram os seus livros *Opus Majus, Opus Minus* e *Opus Tertium*. Retornou a Oxford em 1268. Mas o infortúnio, motivado pelas perseguições religiosas, prevaleceu novamente. Suas obras foram condenadas pelo superior dos franciscanos, e Bacon foi aprisionado por catorze longos anos.

Princípios básicos. Para Bacon havia quatro grandes fontes do erro: as autoridades, os costumes, a opinião da maioria destreinada e o ocultamento da ignorância sob a máscara de sabedoria. Em segundo lugar, ele pensava que as ciências fundamentam-se na matemática, dizendo que o empirismo e a especulação jamais são suficientes para estabelecer a verdade. A ciência, portanto, precisa perscrutar tudo, jamais dependendo dos dogmas. Em terceiro lugar, as experiências devem repousar sobre a percepção dos sentidos externos. Todavia, também há a percepção interna, quando a iluminação divina faz incidir sua luz sobre algo; mas então deixamos de lado o campo das ciências e nos envolvemos na teologia. Quando isso sucede, deixamos para trás o conhecimento imperfeito e passamos a buscar ao Criador. Bacon combinava a filosofia platônico agostiniana com as especulações árabes e a ciência empírica. (BE E F EP MM P)

BADE, WILLIAM FREDERIC

Nasceu em 1871 e faleceu em 1936. Foi um erudito da Bíblia, naturalista, arqueólogo e professor de literatura do Antigo Testamento e de hebraico, no Colégio Moraviano, de 1898 a 1902. Também foi professor de literatura do Antigo Testamento e de idiomas semitas na Escola Pacífica de Religião, de 1902 a 1936. Dirigiu várias expedições arqueológicas à Palestina, e publicou o resultado das mesmas. Escreveu os livros: *Old Testament in the Light of Today* e *Life and Letters of John Muir*, além de vários documentos e artigos sobre temas bíblicos, naturais e arqueológicos. (AM E)

BAEANOS

Uma tribo que Judas Macabeu colocou em sua lista de inimigos a serem eliminados, porquanto haviam feito emboscadas contra os judeus. Essa tribo só é mencionada em I Macabeus 5:4,5, sendo a única referência que há sobre eles em toda a literatura.

BAETIL

Uma pedra sagrada, geralmente um meteorito, que era adorada como se fosse dotada de algum poder sobrenatural. Diana dos Efésios era uma pedra dessa espécie. (E)

BAGOAS

Eunuco encarregado dos negócios de Holofernes recebeu o encargo de convidar Judite a um banquete em companhia de Holofornes, conferindo a ela as cortesias reservadas aos convidados especiais. Foi Bagoas quem descobriu o corpo decapitado de seu senhor (ver Judite 12:11,13,15; 13:3 e 14:4). (Z)

BAHAÍSMO

Um movimento religioso iniciado na Pérsia, na segunda metade do século XIX por Bahaullah, como um ramo do islamismo. O caminho foi preparado por *Bab* (portão), a começar em 1844, que anunciou a vinda «daquele que Deus tornará manifesto». Em 1850, quando Bab foi martirizado, seus seguidores tomaram o seu nome, tornando-se membros da fé babi, ou seja, do *babismo*. Com o aparecimento de Baha Ullah, que se declarava o profeta prometido, nasceu a fé bahai, ou bahaísmo. Desde então tem-se transformado em uma religião internacional, com seu próprio calendário.

Crenças principais. 1. A essência de Deus está acima de nosso entendimento, pelo que conhecemos apenas as suas manifestações. 2. Essas manifestações nos são dadas principalmente através dos profetas, entre os quais poderíamos alistar Abraão, Moisés, Davi, Cristo, Maomé e Baha Ulla. 3. Essas manifestações não são independentes e nem contraditórias, mas formam uma unidade. No entanto, destinam-se a diferentes épocas e culturas, transmitindo aos homens variados graus de verdade. 4. Os principais profetas são chamados divinos, não por serem tais em si mesmos, mas porque transmitem a luz divina, aparecendo como representantes de Deus. 5. Esses profetas trabalham em prol da mesma causa, a união final da religião no mundo. 6. — Novas manifestações virão, quando isso for necessário, não podendo haver fim na série de manifestações, visto que nunca chegará o tempo em que o avanço se torne impossível. 7. O progresso individual na senda da perfeição nunca poderá parar, porque Deus é o alvo (a perfeição absoluta), e esse alvo jamais será perfeitamente atingido. Os homens, entretanto, passarão a compartilhar da natureza divina, prosseguindo sempre em direção à maior perfeição. 8: A paz mundial, a unidade de todas as religiões, a educação universal, a igualdade dos sexos são itens importantes da fé bahai. (AM EP)

BAHA ULLAH
Ver **Bahaísmo**.

BAHYA BEN JOSEPH IBN PAQUDA

Um judeu que foi juiz de um tribunal rabínico, e também filósofo que viveu na primeira metade do século XI D.C., em Saragoça, na Espanha. Ele escreveu um livro em árabe, em 1040, chamado *Guia dos Deveres do Coração*, o qual pode ser considerado como a primeira tentativa para sistematizar a ética judaica. Bahya também promoveu os estudos científicos. Inclinava-se ao ponto de vista filosófico do neoplatonismo, e apresentou vários argumentos para provar a existência de Deus. (E P)

BAIN, ALEXANDER

Filósofo e psicólogo escocês, nasceu em 1818 e faleceu em 1903. Educou-se em Aberdeen, ensinou em Glasgow e Aberdeen, e exerceu influências sobre John Stuart Mill. É considerado um utilitarista (ver o artigo sobre o *utilitarismo*). Bain salientava a introspecção, utilizando-se das leis da associação, na análise dos estados mentais. Ele aprovava as técnicas de laboratório, sendo considerado um dos fundadores da psicologia moderna. Escritos: *The Senses and the Intellect*, 1855; *The Emotions and the Will*, 1859; *Manual of Rhetoric*, 1864; *Logic, Deductive and Inductive*, 1870.

BAINHA DA ESPADA

Ver o artigo geral sobre **Armas, Armadura**. A bainha era um receptáculo para proteger a espada ou adaga, usualmente feita de couro. Ver I Sam. 17:51; II Sam. 20:8; Eze. 21:3-5,30; Jer. 47:6; João 18:11. O vocábulo hebraico figura por um total de sete vezes, *Taar*. No grego temos a palavra *théke*, que ocorre por apenas uma vez, em João 18:11.

BAIO
Ver **Cor, Cores**.

BAIO (ou Du Bay) MICHAEL

Suas datas são 1513 e 1589. É o autor de um sistema teológico que nega a gratuidade da justiça original, afirma a corrupção intrínseca da natureza humana, mediante o pecado original, e rejeita a noção da graça inerente por ocasião da justificação. O papa Pio V (ver o artigo a seu respeito) condenou o seu sistema (com suas 79 proposições), e Baio retratou-se, tendo falecido como católico romano. (E)

BAÍTE

Nome de uma cidade, em Moabe, que aparece em algumas versões em Isa. 15:2. Nossa versão portuguesa diz «templo», embora alguns estudiosos prefiram interpretar o nome como «filha».

BAITERUS

Chefe de uma família que retornou do cativeiro babilônico à Palestina (ver o artigo a respeito), em companhia de Zorobabel (ver I Esdras 5:17). O nome é omitido nos paralelos de Esd. 2:3 *ss* e Nee. 7:8 *ss*.

BAKUNIN, MIKAHIL

Filósofo russo que nasceu em 1814 e faleceu em 1876. Estudou na Alemanha e envolveu-se no levante de Dresden, em 1849, tendo sido aprisionado por oito anos na Rússia e exilado para a Sibéria. Escapou para a Europa e estabeleceu residência na Suíça, tendo sido expulso da Internacional em 1872. Seus escritos: *The State and Anarchy*, 1873; *God and the State*, 1882. *Suas idéias*: 1. Qualquer pessoa privilegiada é depravada em seu intelecto e em seu coração. Portanto, deve ser aniquilado qualquer privilégio, político ou econômico, cultivando esse aniquilamento como uma arte. Os revolucionários não deveriam deixar-se moderar pela religião, pelo patriotismo ou por qualquer outra espécie de restrição. 2. Um homem teria necessidade de obedecer somente às leis da natureza, que ele encontra dentro de si mesmo. Isso importa em total subjetivismo, sem qualquer restrição por parte da sociedade. Se os homens obedecessem à sua própria natureza, desapareceria a necessidade das organizações políticas, o que não passa de uma utopia e ilusão. (P)

BALÁ

O sentido da palavra, no hebraico, é incerto, ainda que alguns afirmem que significa «enrugado» ou «velho». Era uma cidade no território de Simeão (ver Jos. 19:3). Devido à similaridade de nomes dados na lista, presume-se que se trata da mesma cidade de Judá chamada Baalá em Jos. 15:9 e Bila, em I Crô. 4:29.

BALAÃO

No hebraico, o termo tem sentido desconhecido, embora talvez signifique «devorador», ainda que alguns digam que significa «estrangeiro». Balaão foi um adivinho pagão que vivia em Petor, cidade da Mesopotâmia (ver. Deu. 23:4), pertencente aos midianitas (ver Núm. 31:8).

1. *Pano de fundo*. Ele tinha algum conhecimento de Deus, julgando que os próprios poderes dos adivinhos, profetas e poetas derivam-se de Deus. Temia o avanço dos israelitas. Julgava que ninguém lhes poderia oferecer resistência. Eles já haviam conquistado Jericó e certas regiões dos moabitas, e os midianitas poderiam ser as próximas vítimas. A destruição ameaçava por toda a parte.

2. *Confrontos*. Balaque, rei de Moabe (1401 A.C.), firmou uma liga com os midianitas e enviou mensageiros a Balaão, para que ele viesse ajudá-lo com suas adivinhações (ver Núm. 22:5 *ss*). Balaão não se sentiu tranqüilo diante do convite, e recebeu expressa proibição da parte de Deus, ao iniciar viagem (ver Núm. 22:9 *ss*). Portanto, sentiu que não podia amaldiçoar a Israel, e despachou os mensageiros de volta a Balaque. Porém, este enviou a Balaão uma embaixada de mensageiros ainda mais honrosos, com promessas de recompensá-lo e honrá-lo. Balaão retrucou que não se deixaria tentar, mas que diria somente aquilo que Deus lhe permitisse dizer. E acompanhou os mensageiros, sob a condição de que só diria aquilo que Deus lhe permitisse dizer. A ira de

BALAÃO

Deus manifestou-se contrária a Balaão, no episódio de sua jumenta, que agiu de maneira estranha, ao sentir a presença do anjo. E a jumenta, fustigada por Balaão, falou através do poder do anjo. Ela lembrou Balaão de todo o bom serviço que lhe havia prestado, e de como ela não merecia tão brutal tratamento. Foi então que Balaão divisou o anjo, armado de espada. Ao dizer que poderia voltar, recebeu ordens para seguir caminho, e assim o fez. Ao encontrar-se com Balaque, reafirmou que só diria o que lhe fosse permitido da parte do Senhor. De acordo com suas instruções, foram preparados sete altares. Por três vezes Balaão tentou falar contra o povo de Israel, mas foi controlado a proferir bênçãos, e não maldições. (Ver Núm. 24:17). Por esse motivo, ao invés de proferir maldições, Balaão instruiu Balaque para que pusesse tropeços no caminho do povo de Deus, por meio da corrupção e da fornicação (ver Núm. 31:16). Balaão nada ganhou com sua impiedade. Houve uma batalha entre Israel e os midianitas, e Balaão foi morto durante a refrega. Todavia, Israel também recebeu o devido castigo, por ter-se deixado corromper (ver Núm. 31:16). O vigésimo quinto capítulo do livro de Números mostra-nos que essa batalha redundou em graves perdas para os midianitas.

3. *Uma lição*. A narrativa ilustra um importante princípio espiritual, que reza: «Benditos os que te abençoarem (ó Israel), e malditos os que te amaldiçoarem» (Núm. 24:9).

4. *Uso metafórico do episódio*. O ensino de Balaão. No Novo Testamento encontram-se várias interpretações dos atos de Balaão, vinculadas a lições espirituais: a. O trecho de II Pedro 2:15 refere-se ao «caminho de Balaão». Trata-se da comercialização do dom profético, ou, de maneira mais geral, o dinheiro e outras vantagens materiais exageradas, adquiridos mediante a comercialização da religião. b. Em Apocalipse 2:14 há menção à «doutrina de Balaão», que é a corrupção de pessoas piedosas, levando-as a abandonarem sua atitude separatista e a se degradarem na imoralidade e no mundanismo. Vê-se, assim, que é possível corromper àqueles que não podem ser amaldiçoados (ver Núm. 31:15,16; 22:5; 23:8). c. Em Judas 11, lemos sobre o «erro de Balaão», que consiste na suposição de que Deus deve amaldiçoar o seu povo, quando este pratica o que é errado. Deus julga, mas não amaldiçoa aos seus. A missão de Cristo protege as almas dos crentes, mas não é por isso que eles escapam ao castigo, quando merecido (ver Heb. 12:5). d. A mistura do bem com o mal. A vida de Balaão sugere-nos ainda uma outra lição, que não precisa ser salientada por algum termo especial. Em um homem, mesmo que seja profeta, pode haver a mescla do bom com o ruim, com intenções nobres e atos vis, ou a mistura da verdade com idéias do paganismo. Todos nós tornamo-nos culpados desse erro, em maior ou menor grau, pois isso faz parte daquilo que significa alguém ser um pecador. E essa mescla torna-se mais notória ainda quando envolve um presumível líder espiritual. Quanto a notas expositivas mais completas sobre «o caminho», «a doutrina» e «o erro» de Balaão, ver essas referências e a exposição das mesmas no NTI.

5. *Detalhes dos usos metafóricos*

Balaão. Sua narrativa pode ser encontrada em Núm. 22-24. Segundo as tradições judaicas, Balaão se tornou símbolo de todos quantos ensinavam ou encorajavam o povo de Israel a envolver-se na **idolatria, o que, naturalmente, incluía os vícios pagãos que acompanhavam esse sistema**, os quais eram os excessos da gula, do alcoolismo e da prostituição. (Ver Filo, *Moses* I.53-55; Josefo, *Antiq*. iv.6.6 e *Sanedrim* 106a). Balaão não foi um inimigo declarado de Deus. Professava adorar a Deus, mas traiu ao povo antigo de Deus, levando-os a aceitarem idéias e maneiras pagãs, tendo assim tentado destruir o caráter deles como um povo «separado». Os seguidores de Balaão dos tempos cristãos não possuem «integridade de alma». Podem ser indivíduos «religiosos», mas se caracterizam por defeitos vastos e sérios em sua vida espiritual, e terminam por exercer uma influência negativa sobre a maioria das pessoas, ao invés de contribuírem para a piedade.

Por não poder «amaldiçoar» ao povo de Israel, Balaão tentou corrompê-lo, e isso levando seus varões a ter relações sexuais com mulheres moabitas, assim manchando a separação deles. Assim sendo, produziu a união entre a igreja e o paganismo, exatamente o que sucedia em Pérgamo. O culto do imperador tentava os crentes a transigirem com a idolatria; mas o gnosticismo parece ter sido a principal força que buscava corromper a moral da igreja cristã. Os crentes de Pérgamo deixaram de ser «peregrinos» à face da terra. Acomodaram-se ao paganismo, até mesmo dentro dos limites da igreja. A imoralidade em seus líderes (e, por conseguinte, nos seus discípulos) era aceita como «normal» na ética cristã. Portanto, o evangelho perdeu ali o seu «imperativo moral».

No tocante a «Balaão», nas páginas do N.T., examinar as notas expositivas no NTI sobre: 1. O *caminho de Balaão*, II Ped. 2:15. 2. Sobre o *«erro de Balaão*, Jud. 11:2,3. 3. A *doutrina de Balaão*, ver Apo. 2:14. A atitude moral de Balaão na vida se tornou a doutrina oficial, a «ética cristã», em Pérgamo. A imoralidade tornou-se algo desejável, como se tivesse «finalidades boas» no seio da igreja cristã. Em outras palavras, a «mentalidade pagã», no tocante às questões sexuais e outras, tornou-se a mentalidade prática e a doutrina da igreja dali. Os gnósticos julgavam ser aconselhável contaminar o corpo, a fim de degradá-lo, o que ajudaria no sistema mundial, em sua tentativa de destruir a matéria. Tolamente imaginavam que anjos se punham a seu lado, sussurrando em seus ouvidos, procurando conduzi-los a todas as formas de deboche.

A armar ciladas diante dos filhos de Israel, Apo. 2:14. Balaão, literalmente procurou levar os israelitas a adotarem idéias pagãs, a tomarem esposas pagãs, a se envolverem na idolatria e seus vícios. Espiritualmente falando, eles estavam «caindo». O termo grego aqui usado é «skandalon», «armadilha», ou qualquer coisa que leve alguém a «tropeçar» ou «cair». O ardil de Satanás consistiu do atrativo de mulheres pagãs, dos deleites pervertidos da adoração pagã. Satanás tem suas «tentações», que agem como «armadilhas». Transformam-se então em «vícios», que são extremamente difíceis de extirpar. A mulher licenciosa tem manoplas de ferro. Suas vítimas não conseguem escapar com facilidade. O homem licencioso tem um vício de aço, que oprime o seu cérebro. Não pode ser libertado facilmente, a despeito de todas as boas influências. Esses são «ardis» das influências satânicas. Essas coisas podem cativar até mesmo aos líderes da igreja, tal como sucedeu em Pérgamo e continua a acontecer até hoje. O poder do evangelho, dessa maneira, é anulado.

para comerem coisas sacrificadas aos ídolos, Apo. 2:14. Esse era um dos maiores problemas da igreja neotestamentária. Quanto a um exame completo sobre a questão, ver as notas expositivas no NTI sobre o oitavo capítulo da primeira epístola aos Coríntios. O comer de coisas sacrificadas aos ídolos é algo que

BALAÃO — BALANÇAS

pode ocorrer em mais de uma maneira. As carnes assim oferecidas podem ser vendidas nos mercados, após terem servido a seus propósitos, nos templos pagãos. O crente pode adquirir dessa carne, sem sabê-lo, ou mesmo sabendo do fato. Para Paulo, essa possibilidade era uma «questão indiferente», enquanto algum irmão mais escrupuloso não fizesse objeção, ofendendo-se porque alguém «comia» dessa carne. Todavia, outros crentes entravam em templos pagãos, convidados por seus vizinhos para alguma festividade, em honra ao deus ou deuses, patronos do templo em questão. Esses raciocinariam como segue: «Um ídolo nada é, pelo que tudo isso não passa de uma fraude; e a carne aqui oferecida à venda é tão boa como qualquer outra». Se um crente assim agisse, sua ação se tornava muito mais questionável. Além disso, Paulo relembrou aos crentes que a adoração pagã na realidade, tem demônios por detrás da mesma. De fato, o ídolo nada é, mas é possível que, através do ídolo, algum poder espiritual negativo real esteja sendo adorado, como um «demônio». (Ver I Cor. 10:20 quanto a essa crença). Era comum a *idolatria* ser vista no judaísmo como símbolo externo e físico da adoração aos demônios, em que estes recebiam homenagem dos homens. Se esse é o caso, então nenhum crente tem o direito de entrar em um templo pagão, pois, na realidade, o «ídolo nada é», mas é um meio de entrar em contacto com os poderes malignos. Portanto, honrar a um ídolo, em qualquer sentido, também é honrar ao «poder espiritual por detrás do ídolo». Ver a progressão da censura neotestamentária ao «comer carnes oferecidas a ídolos». No oitavo capítulo da primeira epístola aos Coríntios, a questão é «indiferente». Mas I Cor. 10:25 nos fornece boa razão para condenarmos alguns aspectos dessa prática. O trecho de Rom. 14:19,22-25 é mais estrito, e Atos 15:20 é uma proibição total, o que se reitera em Apo. 2:14. A princípio, Paulo mostrou-se tão liberal quanto era possível ser. Mas a experiência mostrou não ser viável, nesse caso, a liberalidade. Portanto, gradualmente Paulo foi «fortalecendo» suas proibições e censuras. Finalmente, a igreja proibiu toda essa prática, provavelmente em todos os seus aspectos. Aquele que entrasse em um templo pagão, a fim de participar de uma festividade, também seria tentado a praticar algo da «prostituição sagrada», dando dinheiro às mulheres que, supostamente, serviam à divindade honrada, dinheiro esse que, subseqüentemente, entrava para os cofres do templo pagão. Somos informados que em Corinto, na época do apóstolo dos gentios, havia nada menos de mil «prostitutas sagradas», envolvidas nesse nojento negócio.

e praticarem a prostituição, Apo. 2:14. Tradicionalmente, a idolatria sempre esteve vinculada à prostituição. Havia «prostitutas sagradas», conforme foi descrito acima. Alguns deuses e deusas eram adorados, desvergonhadamente, em meio a orgias sexuais desenfreadas. Em I Cor. 6:9, podemos notar a lista dos vícios, em que se lê sobre os «fornicários» e «idólatras», nessa ordem. Várias listas de vícios do N.T. apresentam esses dois pecados, embora não necessariamente juntos. (Ver Apo. 22:15). (Ver o artigo sobre *Vícios*).

A festividade deleitosa. — Várias referências, nos escritos clássicos, mostram que as festas idólatras, nos templos pagãos, faziam parte importante da vida social dos antigos gregos e romanos. *Tucídides* (ii.38) mostra que tais festas (que envolviam sacrifícios), faziam parte dos entretenimentos populares. Suetônio (*Cláudio*, 33) relata como Cláudio, o imperador romano, estando certo dia no fórum, ao sentir o aroma delicioso de uma festa, que estava em preparativos no templo de Marte, deixou o tribunal e tomou lugar à mesa, ao lado dos sacerdotes, a fim de regalar-se. É claro que os crentes, muitos dos quais tinham sido criados entre tais eventos sociais, que envolviam festividades e sacrifícios, com facilidade continuariam tais práticas, embora não mais sentissem que estivessem homenageando a qualquer deidade pagã. Isso fazia parte da estrutura social da época, bem como da vida social. Aqueles que punham ponto final a todas as suas relações com os templos, não se separavam apenas religiosamente, mas até mesmo socialmente.

Em tempos de perseguição, a questão ainda se tornava mais aguda. Provar os vinhos das libações oferecidas aos deuses pagãos, ou comer das carnes a eles oferecidas, eram considerados atos de homenagem a tais divindades, em cujos templos essas festividades tinham lugar. Ao mesmo tempo, tal ação indicaria que o indivíduo renunciava ao cristianismo. (ID NTI UN)

BALADÃ
Pai de Merodaque-Baladã, rei da Babilônia (ver II Reis 20:12 e Isa. 39:1).

BALANÇAS
No hebraico, temos uma palavra que sempre aparece no plural, *moznayim*, «par de balanças», que aparece por dezesseis vezes no Antigo Testamento (ver Lev. 19:36; Jó. 6:2; 31:6; Sal. 62:9; Pro. 11:1; 16:11; 20:23; Isa. 40,12,15; Jer. 32:10; Eze. 5:1; 45:10; Dan. 5:27; Os. 12:7; Amós 8:5 e Miq. 6:11).

Os antigos hebreus tinham meios de medir os pesos, conforme somos informados em Lev. 19:36 e outros trechos. Nos primeiros tempos hebreus, o ouro e a prata eram comercializados a peso, o que requeria o uso de balanças. As balanças tinham contrapesos de valores específicos, usualmente pedras de diferentes dimensões. Naturalmente, pessoas desonestas usavam dois tipos de peso: os mais pesados, com que vendiam coisas e os pesos mais leves, com que as compravam. Isso explica as expressões em Miq. 6:11 e Osé. 12:7. «Poderei eu inocentar balanças falsas? e bolsas de pesos enganosos?» Os arqueólogos têm descoberto: desenhos de balanças, algumas menores e outras maiores, mas sempre seguindo o mesmo princípio, dois pratos bem equilibrados; em um deles punha-se a mercadoria a ser pesada, e no outro, os pesos. Algumas vezes, os dois pratos eram suspensos por meio de um anel, e de outras vezes, havia uma cruzeta horizontal, equilibrada no meio, em cima de um pino. Talvez seja por esse motivo que o trecho de Isaías 46:6 usa um outro termo hebraico, que significa «cana» ou «vara», embora nossa versão portuguesa também traduza esse outro vocábulo hebraico por «balanças».

No Novo Testamento temos a palavra grega *zugós*, «balança», em Mat. 11:29,30; Atos 15:10; Gál. 5:1; I Tim. 6:1 e Apo. 6:5.

Usos simbólicos: 1. Os homens são postos na balança, quando são julgados pela lei, ou através dos juízos divinos. É assim que o verdadeiro caráter deles é desvendado (ver Dan. 5:27; Jó. 31:6 e Sal. 62:9). 2. O povo de Deus deve ter balanças justas, o que tipifica a honestidade moral (ver Lev. 19:36; Pro. 11:1). As balanças justas são consideradas «do Senhor», porque ele é quem determina a honestidade, nas consciências humanas (ver Pro. 16:11). 3. As balanças enganosas revelam uma condição degenerada e desonesta (ver Amós 8:5 e Osé. 12:7). 4. A balança que o cavaleiro

BALAQUE — BALEIA DE JONAS

do cavalo negro brandia, em Apo. 6:5, indica a escassez de alimentos que haverá quando da Grande Tribulação, conforme se vê no versículo seguinte. 5. As nuvens postas na balança (em português, «equilíbrio das nuvens»), em Jó 37:16, evidentemente aludem à maneira como elas existem na natureza, cumprindo o propósito que Deus lhes determinou. Isso, por sua vez, significa que Deus exerce pleno controle sobre a natureza. (BAR UN WRI WRIG)

BALAQUE

Ver o artigo sobre Balaão, quanto a detalhes da história de sua associação com Balaão. Balaque era filho de Zipor, rei dos moabitas (ver Núm. 22:2, 4). Israel obtivera grande vitória sobre os amorreus; e Balaque, tomando conhecimento disso, e julgando que também seria atacado pelos israelitas, tentou impedir o avanço do povo de Deus, solicitando os serviços de Balaão, profeta pagão famoso em seus dias, a fim de amaldiçoar a Israel (ver Núm. 22:1-6). Sob instruções de Balaão, Balaque edificou três altares em diferentes lugares, com o propósito de atrair a maldição divina contra Israel. Mas disso resultaram somente bênçãos e grandes profecias preditivas. Finalmente, Balaque e suas forças foram derrotadas por Israel. No entanto, antes de ser derrotado, e seguindo instruções de Balaão, Balaque conseguiu corromper a alguns dentre o povo de Deus, mediante pecados sexuais (ver Núm. 25:1 e Apo. 2:14). Por causa desse incidente, o nome de Balaque veio a designar aqueles que são insensatos o bastante para tentarem distorcer a vontade de Yahweh (ver Jos. 24:9 e Juí. 11:25). (ID UN Z)

BALAÚSTRES

No hebraico, **mesillah**, «terraço», «caminho elevado». Na LXX, *anábasis*, «subida», «escada». Está em foco um caminho elevado, acima do nível normal do terreno, por ser este lamacento ou mesmo pantanoso. O termo aparece por vinte e sete vezes (por exemplo: Núm. 20:19; Juí. 20:31,32,45; I Sam. 20:12,13; II Reis 18:17; Isa. 7:3; 62:10; Jer. 31:21).

Figuradamente, a palavra é usada para aludir à marcha dos gafanhotos, em Joel 2:8; o curso das estrelas, em Juí. 5:20; a conduta dos retos, em Pro. 16:17; e a subida para Sião, na mente dos piedosos (Sal. 84:5).

BALDE

Um receptáculo para transportar água e retirá-la do poço. Os mais antigos eram feitos, evidentemente, de couro (Isa. 40:15). Havia uma cruzeta, posta na boca, para mantê-lo aberto. Esses baldes continuam sendo usados, até hoje, na Palestina. O avanço obtido no uso dos metais terminou produzindo vários tipos de baldes metálicos.

Metaforicamente falando, temos o balde de Deus nas nuvens, de onde ele derrama, simbolicamente, a chuva, a neve, a saraiva, etc. (Núm. 24:7). Essa bênção do derramamento torna o povo de Israel grande e numeroso. A própria nação de Israel é retratada como um homem que transporta dois baldes de água, transbordantes, o que se refere à abundância material.

BALEIA

Está em foco, principalmente, o animal que engoliu o profeta Jonas (ver Jon. 1:17 ss), e que nossa versão portuguesa traduz por «grande peixe».

Dois pontos deveriam ser enfatizados: 1. O elemento miraculoso é ressaltado desde o começo do relato: «Preparou o Senhor um grande peixe, para que tragasse a Jonas; e esteve Jonas três dias e três noites no ventre do peixe». (Jonas 1:17). 2. O Senhor Jesus declarou que o episódio era factual, e não fictício: «...assim como esteve Jonas três dias e três noites no ventre do grande peixe, assim o Filho do homem estará três dias e três noites no coração da terra» (Mat. 12:40). No hebraico, em Jonas, a palavra significa «peixe». Em Mateus, a palavra grega significa «monstro marinho».

Muita discussão tem havido sobre a natureza do animal envolvido no caso. Alguns estudiosos pensam que a tradução «peixe» não é possível e nem necessária, pois sabe-se de episódios em que homens têm sido engolidos por baleias, para serem vomitados em seguida. As baleias podem engolir até mesmo animais de maior porte e peso que um homem, como os golfinhos e focas. Todavia, o fato de que o hebraico diz «peixe» parece conclusivo, sobretudo diante do fato de que no hebraico há uma palavra especialmente reservada para indicar a baleia, a qual não é usada no episódio que vitimou Jonas.

O que realmente importa no relato, todavia, não é qual animal engoliu o profeta, se um mamífero ou um peixe, e, sim, tudo que envolveu um milagre providencial de Deus, que Jesus usaria como ilustração do período em que Ele jazeria sepultado, entre Sua morte e ressurreição.

BALEIA DE JONAS

Mat. 12:40: *Pois, como Jonas esteve três dias e três noites no ventre do grande peixe, assim estará o Filho do homem três dias e três noites no seio da terra.*

Baleia é tradução de AC e KJ; AA diz *grande peixe*. A palavra se refere a um monstro marinho, um peixe enorme. Ocorrências modernas demonstram que há peixes capazes de engolir um homem inteiro.

Será possível ser engolido por uma baleia e continuar vivo para contar a história? A ciência responde *«Não»*, mas a resposta correta é *«Sim»*. Os registros oficiais do Almirantado Britânico provêm evidências documentadas sobre a espantosa aventura de James Bartley, um marinheiro britânico que foi engolido por uma baleia, e escapou com vida para contar a história! O Sr. Bartley estava fazendo sua primeira viagem (que terminou também por ser a única), como marinheiro de um navio baleeiro, cujo nome era *Estrela do Oriente*, em fevereiro do ano de 1891. Estavam a algumas centenas de quilômetros a leste das ilhas Falkland, no Atlântico Sul.

Em certo momento foi arpoada uma grande baleia, que então mergulhou às profundezas abissais. Quando ela subiu para respirar, ocorreu que seu corpanzil esmigalhou o bote, e muitos homens caíram no mar. Dois homens não puderam ser encontrados e um deles era o Sr. Bartley. Depois de muito serem procurados, foram dados finalmente por perdidos.

Pouco antes do pôr-do-sol, naquele mesmo dia, a baleia moribunda flutuou até à superfície. A tripulação rapidamente prendeu uma corda na baleia e a arrastou até o navio-mãe. Posto que era tempo de verão, foi necessário despedaçar imediatamente o gigantesco animal. Em pedaços foi sendo cortada a baleia. Pouco depois das onze horas da noite, os exaustos tripulantes removeram o estômago e o enorme fígado da baleia. Esses pedaços foram levados para a coberta e notou-se que havia algum movimento no interior do estômago da baleia.

Fizeram uma grande incisão no estômago da baleia, e apareceu um pé humano. Era James Bartley, dobrado em dois, inconsciente, mas ainda vivo. Bartley soltava grunhidos incoerentes ao recuperar um pouco mais a consciência, e durante cerca de duas semanas pendeu entre a vida e a morte. Passou-se um mês inteiro antes que pudesse contar perfeitamente a história do que lhe acontecera.

Lembrava-se de que quando a baleia atingiu o bote, ele foi atirado ao ar. — Ao cair, foi engolfado pela gigantesca boca da baleia. Passou por fileiras de minúsculos e afiados dentes, e sentiu uma dor lancinante. Percebeu que estava escorregando por um tubo liso, e então desapareceu na escuridão. De nada mais se lembrava, senão depois de ter recuperado a consciência, uma vez libertado do estômago da baleia.

Muitos médicos de vários países vieram examiná-lo. Viveu mais *dezoito anos* depois dessa experiência. Sua pele ficara com uma desnatural coloração esbranquiçada, mas não sofreu outros maus efeitos além desse. Na lápide de seu túmulo foi escrito um breve relato de sua experiência, com o acréscimo: «James Bartley, 1870 a 1909, um moderno Jonas». (Extraído do livro *Stranger than Science*, por Frank Edwards, págs. 11-13).

BALLOU, HOSEA

Nasceu em 1796 e faleceu em 1861. Foi educador, erudito, clérigo e universalista, que ajudou a publicar as primeiras revistas universalistas. Foi autor da obra *Ancient History of Universalism*, que fornece considerável discernimento histórico quanto a esse conceito. Foi o primeiro presidente do Tufts College, de 1854 a 1861, e membro da junta de supervisores do Harvard College, de 1843 a 1858. (E)

BALMES, JAMES

Nasceu em 1810 e faleceu em 1843. Tornou-se conhecido em face de seu argumento, no livro de sua autoria, *Protestantism Compared with Catholicism*, no sentido que a tolerância parcial é apropriada, mas não a tolerância completa ou universal. Visto que não se pode falar em tolerar a verdade, esse termo só pode ser aplicado àqueles casos em que a verdade ainda está sendo disputada. É nesses casos que precisamos ser tolerantes. A tolerância divina, sem dúvida, é muito mais vasta do que isso, porque, do contrário, a humanidade inteira estaria em dificuldades diante de Deus. (P)

BALSA

Ver o artigo sobre **Embarcações e Navios**.

BÁLSAMO

No hebraico temos uma palavra que indica uma goma medicinal, usada por seis vezes no Antigo Testamento (ver Gên. 37:25; 43:11; Jer. 8:22; 46:11; 51:8 e Eze. 27:17). O «bálsamo de Gileade» aparece como tema de hinos. Talvez se trate da espécie vegetal *Commiphora opobalsamum*, que não é nativa na Palestina, embora bastante comum na Arábia. Josefo informa-nos que a rainha de Sabá trouxe sementes dessa planta e as deu a Salomão, e desde então ela passou a ser cultivada em Israel. Ao menos sabe-se com certeza que, em tempos posteriores, tornara-se uma planta comum na Palestina.

A planta que produz a goma é uma planta perenemente verdejante. Tem flores brancas, formando cachos de três flores. Dá-se um corte em seu tronco, de onde exuda a seiva. Esta transforma-se em glóbulos duros, de onde se extrai a substância. Talvez as «especiarias» referidas em II Reis 20:13 e I Reis 10:10 tenham em vista o mesmo produto.

O «bdélio», aludido em Gên. 2:12, é uma espécie diferente, que talvez seja a *Commiphora africana* ou o bdélio índico ou africano, que originalmente se pensava ser uma pedra semipreciosa. Os eruditos não têm recebido favoravelmente a identificação do «bálsamo de Gileade» com a *Melissa officinalis*, uma erva de cheiro adocicado. A referência em Jeremias 8:22, acerca do bálsamo e do médico em Gileade, tudo associado em uma única sentença, sem dúvida indica que essa substância era considerada como dotada de valor medicinal. Isso tem levado alguns eruditos a suporem que a *Silphium terebinthinaceum* está em vista, visto que é sabido que essa espécie era usada com fins medicinais. Essa espécie produz uma resina levemente fragrante. Não era espécie nativa da Palestina, embora passasse a ser cultivada ali em data desconhecida. Os árabes lhe dão grande valor, e Josefo chega a mencioná-la. Ainda outra opinião dos especialistas favorece a *Balanites aegyptiaca*. Conforme se está vendo, a planta não tem sido inequivocamente identificada.

Em Ezequiel 27:17 encontramos uma outra palavra hebraica, mas que nossa versão portuguesa também traduz por «bálsamo», seguindo a Vulgata Latina, que a traduz por «balsamum», em acordo com várias outras autoridades antigas. Essa árvore, embora não fosse nativa da Judéia, era cultivada nos jardins próximos de Jericó, nas margens do rio Jordão, conforme nos diz Josefo (*Guerras* I.7,6). A goma por ela produzida era preciosa, e seu peso valia tanto quanto a prata em peso. Trata-se da espécie *Balanites Aegyptiaca*. Sua resina era usada para curar ferimentos, e sob a forma de chá, para os problemas estomacais. Todavia, alguns estudiosos preferem pensar na *Pistacia lentiscus*, que cresce até cerca de 3 m de altura, produzindo flores e frutos. Os cortes feitos em seu tronco ou em seus ramos produzem uma goma chamada «mástique». Os glóbulos de resina são branco-amarelados, translúcidos, aromáticos e adstringentes.

A identificação exata das árvores, das plantas, dos animais e das aves mencionadas na Bíblia geralmente é problemática, ou mesmo impossível, conforme se vê no caso do bálsamo.

Uso simbólico do bálsamo. As misericórdias curadoras de Deus, que podem curar os males morais e espirituais de um homem, são simbolizadas pelo bálsamo. Em Jeremias 8:22 e 51:8, a misericórdia de Deus é que livrava potencialmente a nação de Israel das suas angústias. (ND Z)

BÁLSAMO (pessoa)

Quando Esdras leu a lei diante do povo, de acordo com os livros apócrifos (ver I Esd. 9:43), sete homens puseram-se ao seu lado direito, e Bálsamo era um deles. Em Nee. 8:4, a referência paralela, o nome é Maaséias. (Z)

BALTASAR

Essa é a forma grega de Belsazar (ver Dan. 1:7; 2:26; 5:1; 7:1; 8:1 e Baruque 1:11). Na tradição posterior, também aparece como nome de um dos magos que visitaram o menino Jesus. A tradição também declara que eles seriam três (talvez devido às três formas diferentes de presente, ouro, incenso e mirra), embora haja tradições em que esse número varia. Ver o NTI, nas suas notas sobre Mat. 2:1, bem como o artigo desta enciclopédia sobre os *magos*.

BALUARTE

Cinco palavras hebraicas estão por detrás dessa idéia, a saber:

1. *Chel*, «forte», palavra que ocorre por nove vezes (por exemplo: Isa. 26:1; Lam. 2:8; Naum 3:8).
2. *Chelah*, «fortim», palavra que aparece por apenas uma vez, em Sal. 48:13.
3. *Matsod*, «fortaleza», palavra que figura por apenas uma vez, com esse sentido, em Ecl. 9:14.
4. *Matsor*, «fortaleza», palavra que aparece por vinte e seis vezes (por exemplo: Deu. 20:20; Jer. 10:17; Miq. 7:12).
5. *Pinnah*, «esquina», palavra que figura por vinte e oito vezes (por exemplo: II Crô. 26:15; Sof. 1:16; 3:6).

Todas essas palavras envolvem a idéia de lugar de difícil acesso, indicando algum lugar dotado de defesas naturais (Deu. 20:20), de instalações militares, de rampa, etc. (Sal. 48:13), ou então, alguma fortaleza ou torre (II Crô. 8:5). A idéia básica é de lugar cercado por muralhas ou defesas. No grego temos a palavra *edraíoma*, «estabilidade», usada apenas em I Tim. 3:15, aplicada à Igreja. Nossa versão portuguesa diz ali, «baluarte», onde algumas versões em outros idiomas, dizem «base» ou «fundamento». O ministério da Igreja de Cristo garante que os homens edificam sobre o alicerce da verdade.

BAMÃ

No hebraico significa «lugar alto», exatamente conforme a palavra é traduzida na versão portuguesa, em Eze. 20:29, único trecho bíblico onde a palavra hebraica aparece. A etimologia da palavra é desconhecida, embora pareça estar relacionada ao ugarítico ou ao acádio que significa as «costas» de uma pessoa ou de um animal. (Ver Deu. 33:29, onde aparece uma palavra hebraica similar, e que nossa versão portuguesa traduz por «alteza»). Excetuando algumas poucas referências, os lugares de adoração dos gentios (como também os de Israel, quando idólatras), localizados em lugares elevados, montes, bosques, etc., são indicados por esse outro termo hebraico. A arqueologia tem comprovado a existência desses lugares altos. Uma grande plataforma oval, medindo dez metros de comprimento, oito metros de largura e seis metros de altura, foi encontrada em Megido. O alto da plataforma era atingido mediante um lance de escada, e ali eram oferecidos sacrifícios. Data do terceiro milênio A.C. Outros desses lugares altos têm sido encontrados em Nahariya, perto de Haifa (séculos XVIII ou XVII A.C.), em Malhah, a suleste de Jerusalém (séculos VII ou VI A.C.). O trecho de Ezequiel 20:29, no original hebraico, parece conter um jogo de palavras: «Que (mah) propósito tem essa vinda (ma) a este lugar alto?» E talvez essas palavras fossem proferidas zombeteiramente. Ver também o artigo sobre *Lugares Altos*. (MCC S Z)

BAMIÃ

Uma cidade situada sobre uma colina, não mencionada na Bíblia. Segundo as tradições, embora dificilmente elas se mostrem corretas, diante dessa cidade havia um rio, que desaguava no Gurjestão. A cidade não tinha jardins e nem pomares, sendo também a única cidade da região situada sobre uma colina. Teria sido a residência de Sem, filho de Noé. (S)

BAMOTE

No hebraico significa «lugares altos de Baal». Era um lugar na Transjordânia, onde os israelitas fizeram uma parada (ver Núm. 21:19,20). Ficava ao norte do rio Arnon. Talvez seja a mesma localidade chamada Bamote-Baal, em Josué 13:17. Era um lugar pertencente aos moabitas, e adquiriu tal nome devido à adoração idólatra que ali havia. Foi nesse local que o rei Balaque (ver o artigo a seu respeito) pediu para Balaão (ver o artigo a respeito) amaldiçoar o povo de Israel. A pedra Mesha, com inscrições que datam de cerca de 830 A.C., assevera que o rei Mesha erigiu o lugar, juntamente com outros similares, em Dibom, Bezer e Medeba. À tribo de Rúben foi dada essa cidade (ver Jos. 13:17), como parte de sua herança. A localização exata é desconhecida atualmente, embora seja tentativamente localizada na margem ocidental do platô da Transjordânia, ao sul do monte Nebo, perto da moderna Khirbet el-Quweiqiyeh. (AH GROL).

BANAIA

Forma do nome **Zabade** (vide), em certas obras apócrifas.

BANAS

Também grafado como Banuas, foi ancestral de alguns levitas que retornaram com Zorobabel do exílio babilônico (ver I Esdras 5:26). O nome não aparece no paralelo canônico de Esdras 2:40.

BANCO, INSTITUIÇÕES BANCÁRIAS

As Escrituras não designam especificamente qualquer instituição financeira para custear dinheiro; mas falam apenas nas *mesas* dos cambistas (ver Mat. 21:12; Mar. 11:15; João 2:15). No trecho de Luc. 19:23, entretanto, há menção de algo que se aproxima da idéia de um «banco». (Nossa versão portuguesa diz «banco», mas isso é uma interpretação, pois o grego diz apenas *trápeza*, «mesa»). A prática de empréstimo de dinheiro a juros não era aprovada dentro da economia pastoril agrícola da antiga nação de Israel (ver Êxo. 22:5; Lev. 25:37). Portanto, verdadeiros bancos, e negócios bancários, foram estabelecidos em Israel somente depois do exílio (ver sobre o *cativeiro babilônico*). Antes desse tempo, as pessoas entregavam o seu dinheiro aos cambistas, a fim de obterem algum dividendo, ou então meramente ocultavam ou enterravam o dinheiro, para guardá-lo em segurança, visto que a taxa de inflação era mínima (ver Jos. 7:21 e Mat. 13:44). Palácios e templos eram usados para guardar dinheiro, embora, como é claro, os ricos contassem com seus cofres. Na antiga nação de Israel, podia-se cobrar juros em casos de empréstimos, mas não de compatriotas israelitas, conforme se vê nas referências acima sobre Êxodo e Levítico. Os profetas condenavam as taxas de juro excessivas (ver Deu. 23:19,20).

Nos tempos romanos, os bancos tornaram-se importantes na Palestina. Geralmente as atividades bancárias eram efetuadas nas praças dos mercados, onde os banqueiros montavam uma mesa. Isso explica as referências neotestamentárias, dadas acima. O câmbio de moedas era algo necessário, além de empréstimos. Além das moedas estrangeiras que circulavam, o templo só aceitava determinado tipo de moeda; e os cambistas naturalmente enganavam àqueles que vinham cambiar seu dinheiro. Havia empréstimos de todos os tipos e para todos os propósitos: para compras, para as despesas diárias, para amortizações, etc. No mundo antigo as taxas de juros sempre eram altas, visto que a exploração do próximo é própria da natureza humana. Em Roma e Atenas, essa taxa chegava até a 48 por cento. Além de emprestar e cambiar dinheiro, os banqueiros ajudavam a outros em investimentos e na montagem de negócios, na Palestina e no exterior. Através dos séculos, os judeus tornaram-se exímios banqueiros, envolvidos no comércio interior e exterior. Até hoje, alguns dos maiores banqueiros do mundo são judeus, como os Rothchilds da Inglaterra e do continente europeu. Todos os aspectos essenciais do comércio e das instituições bancárias foram desenvolvidos já no primeiro século da era cristã. Não sentimos que estamos especulando muito quando afirmamos que o anticristo haverá de utilizar-se do sistema bancário, no futuro, para obter suas finalidades opressivas. «A todos, os pequenos e os grandes, os ricos e os pobres, os livres e os escravos, faz que lhes seja dada certa marca sobre a mão direita, ou sobre a fronte, para que ninguém possa comprar ou vender, senão aquele que tem a marca, o nome da besta, ou o número do seu nome» (Apo. 13:16,17).

BANCOS, TÁBUAS

No hebraico, **qeresh**, «tábua». Essa palavra aparece por cinquenta e uma vezes, a começar em Êxo. 26:15, e principalmente nesse livro da Bíblia, indicando as tábuas usadas na construção do tabernáculo no deserto. Mas, por uma vez, em Eze. 27:6, indica os bancos do navio simbólico que representava Tiro, onde se lê: «...os teus bancos fizeram-nos de marfim engastado em buxo da ilha dos quiteus».

BANHO

Nas Escrituras há duas classificações gerais a respeito de banhos: 1. Para efeito de higiene pessoal. 2. Como ato religioso, cerimonial.

1. *Lavagem do Corpo.* Envolvia atos como esfregar o corpo com a ajuda de água, talvez derramada de uma jarra ou balde (Lev. 15-17; Núm. 19:7,8,19, onde é usada a palavra hebraica *rachats*). Outro modo era a imersão em rios, lagos ou poços. Somente as classes mais abastadas transportavam água para tomar banho (II Sam. 11:2). Poços como os de Siloé e de Ezequias (Nee. 3:15,16), às vezes sombreados com pórticos (João 5:2), proviam lugares de banhos públicos, que tão populares tornaram-se nos tempos gregos e romanos. Josefo (*Guerras* 1:17,7) menciona que os soldados se banhavam. Havia as termas de Tiberíades (Eusébio, *Onomast.*), bem como as termas próximas às praias do mar Morto (Josefo, *Anti*. xviii.2; xvii.6). Também lemos acerca de banhos públicos entre os antigos egípcios. Os ricos tinham piscinas, que usavam tanto como balneário como para efeitos de recreação (Josefo, *Anti*. xvii.11; xv.3).

Não há muitas menções, no Antigo Testamento, a banhos com propósitos higiênicos, embora o calor e a poeira das terras orientais tornem os banhos tão necessários. Heródoto (ii.27) conta que os sacerdotes egípcios banhavam-se nada menos de quatro vezes ao dia, embora isso incluísse abluções mais de natureza ritualista. No Antigo Testamento, um sinal de hospitalidade para com os recém-chegados era prover-lhes um banho (Gên. 18:4; 19:2; I Sam. 25:41). Bate-Seba estava no banho, quando Davi a viu pela primeira vez (II Sam. 11:2). As palavras de Noemi à sua nora, Rute (Rute 3:3), sugerem que era costume as pessoas banharem-se, antes de visitarem alguém de classe superior.

2. *Banhos Cerimoniais e Ritualistas*. O ato de lavar as mãos e os pés, antes das refeições principais, era um antigo hábito em Israel, talvez vinculado às purificações religiosas. As pessoas também se banhavam após o período de lamentação pelos mortos, porquanto isso subentendia poluição (II Sam. 12:20). Os israelitas também banhavam-se antes dos cultos religiosos (Gên. 35:2; Êxo. 19:10; Jos. 3:5; I Sam. 16:5). O sumo sacerdote banhou-se por ocasião de sua instauração (Lev. 13:6), como também o fazia no dia da expiação, antes de oferecer o ato de propiciação (Lev. 16:4,24). Servir de auxiliar do banho de outrem era considerado um ato de humilhação (I Sam. 25:41). Esse costume os primitivos cristãos transferiram para o Novo Testamento, no ato do lava-pés, descrito com detalhes em João 13. Quanto às lavagens cerimoniais, ver Mar. 7:8. Acerca de como todas essas abluções foram suplantadas por princípios espirituais em Cristo, ver Heb. 9:10. As notas, no NTI, fornecem amplas informações a respeito dessas questões.

3. *Usos Simbólicos*. a. Em face do aspecto de purificação, está em foco o batismo, em seu sentido literal e espiritual (Rom. 6:3; Tito 3:5). b. Santificação (Mar. 7:8). c. Lava-pés, que simboliza a igualdade entre os irmãos, a humildade e a purificação das falhas diárias. d. As lavagens cerimoniais do Antigo Testamento simbolizavam vários tipos de purificação, tudo o que recebeu cumprimento no ofício expiatório de Cristo, em seus vários aspectos (Heb. 9:10). e. A vingança de Deus, pois, em algumas versões, é dito que a espada do Todo-poderoso banha-se de sangue, punindo os habitantes da terra (Isa. 34:6). (ED EDE ID IB NTI)

BANI

Esse nome vem de uma raiz hebraica que significa «edificar». É apelativo de várias personagens do Antigo Testamento, a saber:

1. Um dos trinta heróis guerreiros de Davi, um gadita (ver II Sam. 23:36). O paralelo, em I Crônicas 11:38, diz «filho de Hagri», que parece envolver uma corrupção do texto.

2. Um antepassado de Merari, um levita, através de Etã, cujo filho serviu no tabernáculo, ao tempo de Davi (ver I Crô. 6:46).

3. Um filho de Judá, por Utai, da tribo de Perez, um daqueles que retornaram para habitar em Jerusalém, após o exílio babilônico (ver I Crô. 9:4).

4. Antepassado de certos homens que retornaram do cativeiro babilônico em companhia de Zorobabel (ver Esd. 2:10 e I Esdras 5:12). É chamado pelo nome de Binui, em Nee. 7:15.

5. Um ancestral de Selomite, que retornou da Babilônia juntamente com Esdras (ver Esd. 8:10), conforme se vê em Esdras 8:36.

6. Um homem cujos descendentes haviam tomado mulheres estrangeiras, estando ainda no cativeiro (ver Esd. 10:29). Em I Esdras 9:30 ele é chamado Maani.

7. Um levita cujo filho ajudou a reparar as muralhas de Jerusalém (ver Nee. 3:17).

8. Um homem que assessorou a Esdras na explicação sobre a lei. Ele era levita (ver Nee. 8:7). É

BANI — BANQUETE

chamado Aniute, em I Esdras 9:48.

9. Um levita que foi um dos signatários do pacto que resultou do reavivamento do interesse pelas questões espirituais, nos dias de Neemias (ver Nee. 10:13).

10. Um dos chefes do povo que também assinou o pacto, e que talvez seja a mesma pessoa que a de número 9 (ver Nee. 10:14).

11. Pai de um oficial dos levitas em Jerusalém, que pertencia aos filhos de Asafe, que eram cantores (ver Nee. 11:22).

Esse nome tem sido confundido com Binui ou Bunã, de tal modo que é impossível garantir-se a identificação de alguns desses personagens. (ID S)

BANI (Livros apócrifos)

Um homem mencionado em I Esdras 9:34 e em Esd. 10:34 como o fundador de uma família, cujos membros foram obrigados a divorciar-se de suas esposas estrangeiras, depois do retorno do cativeiro.

BANIAS

Era uma aldeia que ficava ao sul das colinas do monte Hermom, e que os árabes modernos chamam pelo mesmo nome, embora originalmente seu nome fosse Paneion. O nome derivava-se do deus Pan, que ali era adorado. Nichos de suas estátuas até hoje podem ser vistos no local. Cesaréia de Filipe (ver o artigo a respeito), ocupava o local. O rio Jordão tem um de seus braços originadores naquele lugar.

BANQUETE

Quatro palavras hebraicas e uma grega estão envolvidas no estudo desse tema, quase sempre envolvendo a idéia básica de «beber». Em Amós 6:7 temos uma palavra que significa «grito» (de alegria ou de tristeza). Em Jó 41:6 temos uma palavra que significa «preparar». Em Cantares 2:4, a «sala de banquete» deveria ser traduzida mais apropriadamente por «sala de vinho». Em Ester 7:1, que diz «veio...Hamã para beber...», encontramos uma palavra hebraica usada por duzentas e onze vezes, exatamente com o sentido desse verbo. E uma quarta palavra hebraica é usada por quarenta e cinco vezes, com o sentido de «banquete» (por exemplo: Ester 5:4-6,8,12,14; Dan. 5:10). A palavra grega *pótos*, «bebedice», aparece somente em I Pedro 4:3.

Ocasiões para banquetes. Podemos pensar nas festividades, religiosas ou sociais, nos aniversários (ver Gên. 40:20; Mat. 14:5); no desmame de um filho e herdeiro (ver Gên. 21:8); nos casamentos (ver Gên. 29:22; Mat. 22:2-4), por ocasião da tosquia das ovelhas (ver I Sam. 25:2); e também, conforme nos parece estranho em nossa cultura, por ocasião dos sepultamentos (ver II Sam. 3:35), ainda que, na oportunidade relatada, Davi se recusasse a fazê-lo.

Horário dos banquetes. Usualmente os banquetes tinham lugar no fim do dia, à noitinha, o que corresponde ao nosso jantar (ver Isa. 5:11). Geralmente, esses banquetes continuavam por alguns dias, (ver Juí. 14:12). Lembremo-nos da festa de casamento na qual Jesus se fez presente. Houve muito vinho, e a festa durou por muito tempo. Os excessos tornavam-se inevitáveis nessas oportunidades (ver Ecl. 10:16 e Isa. 5:11).

Convites. Os servos transmitiam verbalmente os convites (ver Pro. 9:3; Mat. 22:3). O convite de última hora também era feito (ver Mat. 22:8 e Luc. 14:7), restringido àqueles que tivessem manifestado sua disposição de se fazerem presentes. Nenhuma razão trivial era aceita como recusa a um convite desses. Nos evangelhos, a questão tornou-se símbolo do convite do Senhor para que os homens recebam o reino de Deus e a salvação.

Etiqueta. Os convidados eram identificados mediante uma espécie de tabuleta ou cartão, e eram admitidos ao salão do banquete. Uma vez que todos os convidados estivessem presentes, o proprietário fechava a porta, para que ninguém mais pudesse entrar (ver Luc. 13:25; Mat. 25:10). Os convidados eram saudados com um ósculo, na entrada (ver Tobias 7:6; Luc. 7:45), e seus pés eram lavados (ver Luc. 7:44), o que era um costume generalizado no Oriente. Além disso, cabelos e barba eram ungidos (ver Sal. 23:5). Os lugares eram designados aos convidados de acordo com a importância de cada um (ver I Sam. 9:22 e Luc. 14:8). Algumas vezes, eram fornecidos trajes especiais para tais celebrações (ver Ecl. 9:8 e Apo. 3,4,5).

O *mestre-sala* (ver João 2:9 e Ecl. 32:1) usualmente era o proprietário da casa, embora nos banquetes nas cortes reais houvesse algum oficial designado para o posto. O mestre-sala tinha autoridade de admitir quem deveria fazer-se presente, e o que os convidados deveriam fazer.

Os pratos servidos durante o banquete dependiam das posses do dono da casa, pelo que um banquete podia ser simples ou muito luxuoso, com itens importados. Nunca faltava o vinho, que era servido puro, ou então misturado com água e especiarias (ver Pro. 9:2; Can. 8:2). Com freqüência havia bebedeiras, do que resultavam todos os tipos de excessos (ver Isa. 5:12 e Amós 6:5).

Sentados à mesa ou reclinados? Nos primeiros tempos de Israel, costumava-se sentar à mesa. Mas o hábito de reclinar-se em divãs, dos gregos e romanos, terminou sendo adotado em Israel, em tempos posteriores. Na época de Jesus, as refeições eram tomadas em posição reclinada. Assim, na última Ceia, compreende-se como João podia estar «aconchegado» a Jesus (ver João 13:23), e como pôde reclinar-se «sobre o peito de Jesus» (ver João 13:25).

Como se levava o alimento à boca? Garfos, colheres e facas só se tornaram de uso comum já nos fins da Idade Média. Portanto, as pessoas levavam o alimento à boca com as mãos. Se o alimento era líquido, geralmente era apanhado com um pedaço de pão, no qual era ensopado. Um prato podia ser servido para diversos comensais; o que significa que todos podiam meter juntos a mão no prato, o que é refletido em João 13:26, na cena da última Ceia. Durante o banquete, circulavam servos, salpicando as cabeças dos convidados com perfumes ou óleos.

Cozinha. Ver o artigo sobre a *arte culinária*. Os alimentos eram cozidos, assados, estufados, grelhados, preparados com molhos e especiarias. Grande número de panelas e vasos era usado nessas ocasiões.

Guardanapos. Visto que as pessoas levavam à boca o alimento com a mão, esta ficava engordurada. Pedacinhos de pão eram usados para limpar as mãos dos convivas; os mesmos tornavam-se alimentos dos cães (ver Mat. 15:27 e Luc. 16:21). Mas, nesse processo, os convivas eram ajudados pelos servos que circulavam entre eles. Esse humilde ofício era prestado por Eliseu a seu mestre, Elias (ver II Reis 3:11).

Entretenimento. Nos banquetes, muitas vezes havia músicos que tocavam instrumentos, havia dançarinos, havia mímicas e os convivas apresentavam quebra-cabeças uns aos outros. O banquete platônico mostra que os filósofos também tinham suas ocasiões festivas, com comes e bebes, antes de se formar a atmosfera apropriada para os debates filosóficos. Os excessos eram freqüentes em tais banquetes, embora a intenção dos convidados fosse boa. (Ver Isa. 28:1; Sabedoria de Salomão 2:7; II Sam. 19:35; Juí. 14:12; Nee. 8:10 e Luc. 15:25).

Uso figurado. O banquete representa o convite de Cristo, o Seu pacto, a Igreja, a comunhão íntima com o Senhor. Além disso, a rejeição por parte de convidados não qualificados e a entrada no salão do banquete por meios astutos, simbolizam a necessidade das pessoas se qualificarem para o convite do evangelho. Os banquetes satisfazem certas necessidades do corpo. O banquete oferecido por Cristo satisfaz as necessidades do espírito. Um convite a um banquete precisava ser tomado a sério. O dono da casa exercia controle sobre a porta, admitindo e rejeitando a quem ele quisesse fazê-lo (ver Mat. 22:3; Luc. 12:25 e João 2:9). As vestes especiais, fornecidas aos convivas, pintam a provisão espiritual da santidade e da preparação espiritual (ver Apo. 3,4,5). Os convidados eram ungidos, o que simboliza a unção do Espírito, com sua presença e suas graças (ver Sal. 23:5). Havia convidados mais importantes e menos importantes. Nem toda a realização espiritual está em um mesmo nível. As pessoas variam quanto à espiritualidade (ver Luc. 14:8; ver também, quanto a símbolos gerais, o trecho de Can. 2:4). O pacto do Senhor com o seu povo é simbolizado pela Ceia do Senhor (ver Mar. 14:25; comparar com Apo. 3:20). (ID ND S UN Z)

BANUAS

Uma forma alternativa do nome próprio **Banas** (vide).

BAQUEBACAR

Nome hebraico que significa «diligente procurador». Um levita que voltou do exílio babilônico em 445 A.C., em companhia de Zorobabel. Esse nome aparece somente no trecho de I Crô. 9:15, embora talvez se trate da mesma personagem chamada Bacbuquias, em Nee. 11:17. (S Z)

BAQUIDES

Era filho de Baquim, **general do rei sírio Demétrio**, e era governador da Mesopotâmia. Viveu durante o tempo de Antíoco Epifânio, e mesmo depois. Foi enviado por aquele rei sírio à Judéia, encabeçando um exército, a fim de forçar o estabelecimento de certo sumo sacerdote, em 161 A.C., chamado Álcimo. Baquides deixou um destacamento para proteger Álcimo contra Judas Macabeu. Quando, apesar disso, Álcimo se enfraqueceu, Baquides, após um ano, retornou com um exército de tropas escolhidas, tendo derrotado e morto a Judas Macabeu em Laísa (ver I Macabeus 9:18). Então Baquides conseguiu entravar Jônatas Macabeu, e fortificou Jerusalém (ver I Macabeus 9:49,50). Porém, após a morte de Álcimo, que ocorreu no ano seguinte, Baquides retirou suas tropas. No ano subseqüente, 158 A.C., Baquides retornou à Judéia, por convite de alguns judeus descontentes. Terminou firmando um acordo de paz com Jônatas Macabeu, segundo termos razoáveis, deixando-o governar o estado judeu (ver I Macabeus 9:70 *ss*). (ID S)

• • • • • • • • •

BAR (Prefixo)

Como prefixo, «bar» é um aramaísmo no hebraico. Seu uso, tão antigo quanto Salmos 2:12, mostra que vem de tempos remotos. Era prefixo vinculado ao nome do pai de alguém, como «Bar-Abas», que significa «filho de Abas». Ver Mat. 27:16. Com esse prefixo aramaico em Daniel 7:13, temos a expressão «Filho do homem». Tal prefixo também podia transmitir as idéias de «relacionado a» ou de «da classe de». (Z)

BARAITA

Termo aramaico referente a certas tradições tanaaitas (ver o artigo a respeito), não incorporadas na Mishnah (ver o artigo). Sua relação para com a Mishnah assemelha-se à relação entre os livros apócrifos (ver o artigo) e os livros canônicos do Antigo Testamento. (E)

BARAQUE

No hebraico significa «relâmpago». Era filho de Abinoão, de Quedes de Naftali (ver Juí. 4:5. Ver também Jos. 19:37 e 21:32). Ele pertencia ao distrito que mais sofreu às mãos dos cananeus. Jabim, rei de Canaã, vinha oprimindo Israel pelo espaço de vinte anos. A profetisa Débora convocou Baraque para tentar resolver a situação. Baraque organizou um exército de dez mil homens das tribos de Naftali e Zebulom, as tribos que mais haviam sofrido sob Jabim. A idéia era marchar até o monte Tabor, com promessas de que o general de Jabim, Sísera, haveria de ser derrotado. Mas Baraque recusou-se a entrar em batalha sem a presença de Débora. Ela concordou em ir, mas advertiu-o de que ela teria o crédito pela vitória e não Baraque. Houve o choque armado. Sísera contava com um grande exército. Quando a derrota de Baraque parecia certa, subitamente os cananeus foram assaltados por um pânico estranho, irracional. Disso resultou tremenda matança. A batalha teve lugar em cerca de 1120 A.C.

Após a batalha, Baraque e Débora compuseram um cântico de vitória, em louvor a Yahweh. As tribos que ajudaram na obtenção da vitória são elogiadas, mas as tribos que se mostraram indiferentes, como as de Aser, Dã e Rúben, foram censuradas (ver Juí. 4 e 5). Embora Baraque tivesse precisado da ajuda de uma mulher (e qual homem não precisa de tal ajuda, ocasionalmente!), ele obteve menção honrosa entre os heróis da fé, em Hebreus 11:32. Ver as notas adicionais a respeito de Baraque, no NTI, nesse versículo. (ID S)

BARAQUEL

No hebraico significa «Deus abençoa». Era pai de Eliú, um buzita da família de Rã, os últimos dos três «amigos» que entraram em discussão com Jó. (Ver Jó 32:2,6). (S)

BARAQUIAS

Podemos entender seu nome como «Bar Aquias», ou seja, «filho de Aquias». Era pai de Zacarias, aquele que foi assassinado entre o santuário e o altar (ver Mat. 23:35). No Novo Testamento não há qualquer narrativa sobre o martírio de Zacarias, filho de Baraquias. Alguns estudiosos sugerem que isso ocorreu, mas que não foi registrado. Outros eruditos sugerem que deveria ser algum outro Zacarias. Ver o artigo sobre *Zacarias*, como também os comentários sobre o problema, nas notas expositivas sobre Mat. 23:35, no NTI. (NTI Z)

BARAT, Stª Madalena Sofia

Nasceu em 1779 e faleceu em 1865. Foi uma freira francesa, fundadora e primeira superiora geral (1806 a 1865) da Sociedade do Sagrado Coração. Sob sua orientação, a organização propalou-se pelo mundo. Era mulher dotada de incomum energia, de profunda religiosidade e de extraordinários poderes mentais. Foi elogiada por sua sabedoria na direção do grupo, e por seus atos singulares de caridade e humildade. A espiritualidade não acompanha os apertados limites que lhe costumamos impor. (E)

BARBA

No hebraico, **zaqan**, «barba», palavra usada por dezenove vezes (por exemplo: Lev. 13:29,30; I Sam. 17:35; I Crô. 19:5; Sal. 133:2; Jer. 41:5; Eze. 5:1). *Sapham*, «bigode», usada por cinco vezes (por exemplo: II Sam. 19:24), única vez em que nossa versão portuguesa traduz a palavra como «barba». Nas outras ocorrências, a tradução é «bigode» (ver Lev. 13:45; Eze. 24:17,22 e Miq. 3:7).

A maioria dos povos antigos não compreenderiam o moderno costume de raspar a barba, enquanto que tão poucos deixam a barba crescer; pois, na antiguidade dava-se precisamente o contrário. Entre os povos semitas a barba era sinal de virilidade, de tal forma que termos cognatos para *ancião* ou *adulto* eram palavras verbais e nominais que dizem respeito à barba. (Ver Êxo. 4:29).

A arqueologia tem descoberto muitos monumentos antigos que reproduzem variegadas formas de barba, que diferiam de cultura para cultura, ou mesmo dentro de uma dada cultura. Alguns usavam a barba curta e aparada, porém, outros longa e esvoaçante. Era considerado um adorno masculino ter barba profusa. Também era sinal de honra. Se a veracidade de alguém fosse posta em dúvida, a dúvida podia ser enfrentada com as palavras: «Olhe para a barba dele!» Assim, igualmente, faziam-se juramentos pela barba. «Por minha barba juro que...» palavras que podiam ser acompanhadas pelo gesto da mão tocando a barba. O oposto também era verdadeiro. Uma censura poderia acompanhar uma declaração como esta: «Que vergonha para a sua barba!» Uma saudação podia incluir a declaração: «Que Deus preserve a sua barba!»

Tão importante era a barba, no Egito, que até mesmo mulheres, em certas festividades, relacionadas a importantes dias oficiais, usavam barbas falsas, segundo se vê em estátuas e gravuras. Em Israel, assim como os cabelos de uma mulher eram a sua glória, outro tanto dava-se com a barba de um homem. Os sacerdotes eram proibidos de aparar as beiradas de suas barbas. Raspar a barba era considerado um ato de contrição, podendo retratar mudanças radicais para o pior (Isa. 7:20). Aos prisioneiros de guerra raspava-se a barba, em sinal de zombaria. A ausência de barba, ou barba raspada era sinal de servilismo. O rei dos amorreus lançou opróbrio sobre os embaixadores de Davi cortando pela metade as suas barbas e enviando-as de volta (II Sam. 10:1-5). Muitos gregos e romanos barbeavam-se, tirando a barba totalmente; e isso, para os israelitas, era marca de paganismo, algo a ser evitado.

Uso figurado. O povo de Deus é comparado aos pêlos da barba e aos cabelos de Ezequiel, dando a entender que eram muito queridos (Eze. 4:1-5:4). Em Isaías 7:20, quando o Senhor ameaçou raspar as cabeças e as barbas dos homens de seu povo, isso deu a entender que grande número deles seria sujeitado a julgamento divino. (G ID S Z)

BÁRBARO

No grego, **bárbaros**, «estranho», «estrangeiro», e, portanto, rude, sem polidez. Nos escritos clássicos e nas páginas do Novo Testamento, o termo usualmente é usado para denotar nações que não eram gregas, às quais sua linguagem era desconhecida. Por isso, lemos em Romanos 1:14: «...sou devedor tanto a gregos como a bárbaros...» Em Colossenses 3:11 encontramos a seguinte classificação: «...grego... judeu...bárbaro, cita...» Em I Coríntios 14:11, a palavra é usada para indicar uma língua desconhecida pelo ouvinte. Em Ovídio, *Trist*. V.10,37 temos um conceito similar. Em Atos 28:2, os naturais da ilha de Malta são chamados «bárbaros» porque originalmente tinham sido uma colônia cartaginesa, e falavam o púnico. Na LXX, em Salmos 114:1, é usada a palavra para indicar povo de «língua estranha». Estrabão (xiv.2) supunha que a palavra *bárbaros* originalmente era um som imitativo, quando algum grego queria imitar um idioma que lhe fosse estrangeiro, produzindo então sons dissonantes, nessa imitação. Visto que os gregos consideravam sua cultura superior às outras culturas, gradualmente o vocábulo «bárbaro» foi adquirindo seu moderno significado de cru, incivil, ou mesmo imoral. Tal uso tinha seu paralelo entre os judeus, que se referiam aos pagãos em tons de zombaria. Os gregos referiam-se aos romanos com certo tom de desdém na voz. Assim, quando Paulo aludia aos bárbaros, deixava claro que o evangelho também se destinava a eles. Deus não escarnecia dos «bárbaros», como o faziam os gregos e outros. Até mesmo os «citas» (que para os antigos eram o que os «selvagens» são para nós) eram destinatários da prédica evangélica. O uso que o Novo Testamento faz da palavra «bárbaro» não é pejorativo, o que é típico do amor de Deus, que deseja que todos os homens sejam salvos, vindo ao conhecimento da verdade (ver I Tim. 2:4). (ID S Z)

BARBEIRO

Palavra que no hebraico é usada somente por uma vez, em Ezequiel 5:1, *gallawb*. Raspar a cabeça até hoje é costume bastante comum nos países orientais. Algumas seitas religiosas da Índia distinguem-se por essa prática. Alguns deixam apenas um tufo de cabelos no alto da cabeça, ou acima de cada orelha. Na Síria, os homens de certa idade com freqüência raspam a cabeça, permitindo que a barba cresça. Os jovens barbeiam o rosto e aparam bem curtos os cabelos da cabeça. O lábio superior nunca é raspado, exceto no sul da Índia, onde o ato é feito como sinal de luto. A ausência de bigodes é considerada por muita gente, na Síria, como sinal de ausência de virilidade. Portanto, ali os barbeiros têm sempre muito trabalho a fazer, e eles estabelecem suas barbearias em lugares convenientes para atrair fregueses. Na passagem de Ezequiel, o Senhor ordenou que o profeta usasse uma espada afiada como uma navalha de barbeiro, para cortar seus cabelos e sua barba. Os cabelos assim cortados, deveriam ser usados em vários atos simbólicos dos julgamentos divinos. Na antiguidade, as navalhas eram feitas de pedra lascada, de cobre, de bronze ou de ferro. Os arqueólogos têm encontrado pinturas em túmulos, no Egito, que mostram barbeiros trabalhando. (S Z)

Cortesia, Zondervan Publishing House

Barcos antigos de:
 Ascalom
 Síria
 Fenícia

Paulo, o rapaz, observando os navios de Tarso

Hardy

BARCLAY, ROBERT

Nasceu em 1648 e faleceu em 1690, em Ury, na Escócia. Recebeu educação teológica calvinista em Paris, mas acabou convencido da verdade dos quacres (ver o artigo a respeito). Entre 1666 e 1670 ele foi o principal teólogo sistemático dos quacres. Sua obra mais bem conhecida é a Apologia, que já foi editada e reimpressa por muitas vezes. Essa obra tem um certo tom calvinista, refletido pela Confissão de Westminster e pelo Breve Catecismo. Os quacres até hoje consideram-no uma grande autoridade de suas crenças. Ver o artigo sobre a *Sociedade dos Amigos*. (AM E)

BARCO A REMO

Ver os dois artigos sobre **Embarcações** e sobre **Navios**. Os barcos a remo eram barcos longos e baixos que enfrentavam mar alto, impulsionados por velas e remos, ou então somente por remos. Ver Isa. 33:21, onde estão em pauta navios de guerra, impulsionados por remos. A idéia ali é que o Senhor seria a defesa de Jerusalém, como se ela fosse uma grande cidade protegida por um rio, onde nenhum navio de potência hostil podia chegar. Ver também Ezequiel 27:8. O vocábulo hebraico em questão é confirmado em uma nota cananéia das cartas de Amarna, *anaya* 245.28.

BARCOS

No hebraico, «pintor». Foi cabeça de uma das famílias dos netinins (ver Esd. 2:53 e Nee. 7:35). Alguns de seus descendentes retornaram do exílio com Zorobabel, em cerca de 536 A.C.

BARCOS (NAVIOS)

Embora os israelitas fossem um povo agrícola, não voltados para as lides marítimas como os fenícios, tinham jangadas que atravessavam o rio Jordão, embora ficassem apenas subentendidas, como em II Samuel 19:18. Também tinham barcos de pesca usados no mar da Galiléia (Mar. 4:36; João 6:1,23). Davi precisou depender da marinha fenícia de Hirão (II Sam. 5:11 ss). Salomão teve sua marinha (I Reis 9:26). Os navios de Társis traziam ouro, marfim, símios e pavões, a fim de decorar o luxuosíssimo reino de Salomão, trazendo uma nova carga de três em três anos (II Crô. 9:21).

Navios de outros povos são mencionados em Pro. 31:14; Sal. 107:23 ss e 104:26. Paulo usou navios mercantes para fazer viagens pelo império romano, em suas jornadas missionárias. Sabemos que os egípcios usavam navios para fazer viagens não só pelo rio Nilo, mas também pelo Mediterrâneo. O tráfico entre a Biblos da Fenícia e o Egito era feito por mar, e os navios envolvidos eram chamados «viajantes de Biblos». O papiro era transportado nesses navios, para o Egito, para a confecção de livros (rolos) de papiro. Porém, tais navios também transportavam muitas outras mercadorias. Os egípcios também tinham embarcações de fundo chato para transporte de pedras, para suas construções pesadas. Embarcações semelhantes eram usadas nos rios Tigre e Eufrates. Jangadas de madeira, postas a flutuar com a ajuda de peles infladas de ar, também eram usadas. Havia um intenso tráfico marítimo com a Índia, através do golfo Pérsico. Porém, nenhum povo se tornou tão famoso como marinheiros quanto os fenícios. Eles velejavam por todo o Mediterrâneo, havendo quem dissesse que eles chegaram às ilhas Britânicas, propagando a sua cultura até a Espanha.

Os navios antigos usavam tanto velas quanto remos, como meio de propulsão.

Origens. Até onde a arqueologia tem podido revelar, a navegação começou desde 3500 A.C. Navios com popa indentada (para que ali fosse posto um remo leme), bem como com velas quadradas, podem ser vistos nas pinturas egípcias, ou então esculpidos sobre túmulos. Mas as embarcações egípcias geralmente eram feitas de papiro ou de madeira. Porém, por altura do reino médio (2130-1780 A.C.) o Egito já contava com navios grandes, alguns com nada menos de 54 m de comprimento. Talvez esses navios fossem de origem fenícia. Nesse período, os navios eram usados no comércio com o Chipre e com as costas gregas (Núm. 24:24).

Tipos de Embarcações. a. Havia aquelas tripuladas por marinheiros, que podiam ser grandes ou pequenas, mencionadas nos textos de Amarna com o nome de *anayi*, palavra cananéia talvez relacionada ao termo indo-europeu *naus, navis*. Ver I Reis 9:27. b. Os navios de Társis eram cargueiros que levavam pesadas cargas, como minérios. Eram navios próprios para travessias pelo mar Mediterrâneo, tendo até 60 m de comprimento. (Ver Eze. 27:25). Com freqüência esses navios tinham proas redondas e fileiras de remos, tanto quanto sessenta, além de velas. Alguns navios fenícios tinham emblemas na proa, como a cabeça de um cavalo. c. — Os navios egípcios são descritos sob *Origens*. d. O navio em que Jonas embarcou (Jon. 1:5) era grande, dotado de tombadilho, tripulado por marinheiros e comandado por um piloto (Jon. 1:6; Eze. 27:8). e. Havia as barcaças, navios de fundo chato, usados para a travessia de rios. f. Havia pequenas embarcações usadas na pesca, principalmente na Galiléia, tão pequenas que uma grande carga de peixe era capaz de fazê-las naufragar (Mat. 4:21; Mar. 1:19; João 21:3 ss). Provavelmente eram impulsionadas tanto por remos quanto por velas (Mar. 6:48; João 6:19). g. Havia navios usados no Mediterrâneo, de muitos tipos. Os navios longos, cujo comprimento era de cerca de oito vezes mais que a sua largura, eram capazes de transportar entre 15 e 75 toneladas, com remos e velas. Os navios menores permaneciam não muito longe das praias, exceto em condições muito favoráveis. É possível que as viagens de Paulo fossem feitas nessas embarcações costeiras. Mas, quando ele viajou para Roma, tomou um cargueiro de cereais, um navio bem maior. Estes últimos geralmente transitavam na rota entre Roma e o Egito, podendo ter uma tripulação entre duzentos e trezentos homens. Luciano (*Navigium* 1 ss) descreve um desses navios, em cerca de 150 D.C. Esses navios eram dotados de um mastro central, com várias velas, além de uma vela dianteira, posta em um mastro mais à frente, para emprestar ao navio maior manobrabilidade.

— No grego essa vela chamava-se *ártemon* — Na frente havia alguma figura esculpida ou pintada, representando o nome do navio (Atos 28:11) e a popa usualmente era mais elevada, como o pescoço de um cisne, onde havia uma estátua da divindade patrona do porto de origem do vaso. Dois remos grandes, à popa das embarcações, serviam de lemes, podendo ser operados independentemente ou em conjunto. Usualmente as âncoras eram feitas de madeira, com pesos de pedra ou de chumbo, e três ou mais âncoras eram levadas a bordo.

Perigos das viagens marítimas. Antes de tudo, havia o grave problema da falta de uma navegação científica, de tal modo que um navio podia perder-se em alto-mar. Os antigos navios de madeira podiam desintegrar-se facilmente por ocasião das tempestades, pois, devido à falta de algum meio poderoso de propulsão, os navios ficavam ao léu sob as intempéries. Durante o inverno, quando as tempestades tornavam-se freqüentes, a navegação era quase inteiramente suspensa. Isso ia desde meados de novembro a meados de fevereiro (Atos 20:3,6; 27:11; I Cor. 16:6 ss; II Tim. 4:21; Tito 3:12). Um mês antes disso e um mês depois disso ainda eram considerados dias perigosos para a navegação, embora houvesse quem se arriscasse (Atos 27:9). Quando o firmamento ficava enevoado, impedindo a visão do sol e das estrelas, a navegação ficava muito difícil, porque esses objetos celestiais serviam de pontos de referência quanto à direção em que se navegava.

Usos Metafóricos. a. Como um *símbolo psicológico* o navio representa a vida de uma pessoa, — a velejar ou singrar através das vicissitudes, sujeito às tempestades e à destruição, em busca de um destino. b. Um navio também pode simbolizar o corpo físico, o veículo da alma. c. Em Hebreus 6:19, há menção à *âncora* da alma, que fala sobre as provisões e poderes espirituais que nos são providos pelo acesso a Deus. Essa âncora representa, supremamente, a esperança da vida eterna, que se tornou uma realidade através da missão de Cristo, e que penetrou para além do véu do Santo dos Santos. d. O leme de um navio, embora sendo relativamente pequeno, pode fazer uma grande embarcação mudar de rumo, assemelhando-se à língua de um homem, a qual, apesar de pequena, tem enormes potencialidades para o bem ou para o mal.
(HA ID ND SMITH STOR) Tiago 3:4

BARDESANES

Suas datas são 154 e 222 D.C. Nasceu em Edessa, na Síria, onde se tornou um mestre pioneiro do cristianismo. Foi o fundador da literatura cristã siríaca, tendo sido escritor de muitos hinos cristãos em siríaco. Foi elogiado por Eusébio, mas condenado por Efraem e outros pais sírios do século IV D.C. Tentava livrar Deus de qualquer responsabilidade pela existência e atuação do mal, asseverando que Deus era *organizador*, mas não criador do mundo. Foi acusado de manifestar tendências gnósticas. (E)

BARGANHA COLETIVA Ver Negociações Coletivas.

BARIÃ

No hebraico, «fugitivo». O homem desse nome era filho de Semaías, descendente de Davi, no tempo de Salomão (I Crôn. 3:22), em cerca de 1058 A.C.

BARJESUS

Alguns eruditos têm pensado que o nome **Elimas** deve ser considerado como tradução de «Barjesus», e não como um outro apelativo; porém, nenhuma das possibilidades ventiladas pelos estudiosos parece provável. Talvez esse homem simplesmente tivesse dois nomes próprios, conforme se dava com muitos judeus daqueles dias. Nesse caso, «Barjesus» (que significa «Filho de salvação») seria o seu nome judaico. No entanto, era conhecido pela população de fala grega pelo nome de «Elimas». F.C. Burkitt sugere que Elimas talvez seja uma corruptela das palavras gregas *«oloimos»*, que significam «sujeito pestilento» (assim declara esse autor em seu artigo *The Interpretation of Bar-Jesus*, no Journal of Theological Studies, IV, 1902, págs. 127-129). Esse sentido não é muito provável, porquanto um homem considerado como representante dos espíritos ou deuses dificilmente seria assim denominado por aqueles que procuravam a sua orientação e ajuda. Portanto, Elimas, com o sentido de «sábio», com derivação de uma raiz aramaica, é a idéia mais razoável, embora isso não seja universalmente aceito pelos estudiosos do assunto.

Theodore P. Ferris (em Atos 13:6) sugere que a maldade das artes mágicas consiste no fato de que procura torcer a vontade de Deus segundo a vontade dos homens, sendo, por isso mesmo, de natureza egoísta—não adora a Deus, mas tão-somente procura utilizar-se dele. Diz esse autor: «A religião, nesse caso, torna-se o meio da obtenção de uma finalidade, e não uma finalidade em si mesma. É oferecida como uma varinha mágica, capaz de transformar gansos em cisnes, e chumbo em ouro. Com esses trajes modernos, Elimas continua percorrendo as ruas de todas as cidades modernas».

As artes mágicas também podem ser criticadas por sua tentativa de manipularem os poderes espirituais inferiores, ignorando a Cristo e a Deus Pai. Isso, portanto, faz dessas artes uma modalidade de paganismo, ao passo que o cristianismo aponta Cristo para os homens, o mais elevado poder cósmico, o Filho de Deus, e através dele a volta para Deus Pai. A preocupação de alguns indivíduos diz respeito a «como ser algo em troca de nada...Não admira que sejam solo fértil para os feiticeiros, que lhes mostram atalhos curtos. A fé é difícil; a força mágica é fácil. Elimas caminha pelo caminho fácil, e os seus seguidores formam legiões». (Theodore P. Ferris, em Atos 13:6).

No que tange às relações entre a sociedade antiga para homens como Elimas, opina Alford em Apoc. 13:6: «A aristocracia romana estava peculiarmente debaixo da influência dos astrólogos e dos mágicos, alguns dos quais eram judeus. Lemos sobre tais indivíduos em conexão com Mário, Pompeu, Crasso, César, e posteriormente, Tibério; e as queixas de Horácio e Juvenal mostram-nos quão completamente, e por quão dilatado tempo, Roma andou inundada de impostores orientais de todas as variedades. (Ver Horácio, Sat. i.2.1; e Juvental, *Sat.* iio.13-16; vi.542-546; x.93).

«As classes mais baixas dos judeus, tanto em Atos 13:6 como em Atos 19:14, parecem ter-se viciado especialmente com tais práticas. Comerciavam com o prestígio religioso de sua raça, e se ufanavam, em adição a isso, acerca dos livros sagrados de adivinhações e encantamentos que teriam chegado até eles desde os tempos de Salomão». (E.H. Plumptre, em Apo. 13:6).

Falso profeta. É um dos qualificativos que Lucas dá a Barjesus. — Não porque ele fosse fraudulento e não possuísse reais poderes psíquicos, porquanto as Escrituras do A.T. não procuram fazer tais homens sempre enganadores, mas antes, porque era impelido por um espírito mentiroso e perverso, que talvez deva ser encarado como um demônio. Sua fonte de poder era maligna, por conseguinte. Embora talvez tenha predito o futuro corretamente, em certas oportunidades, ou até mesmo efetuado curas de enfermidades e realizado muitas outras maravilhas, não era um profeta de Deus e nem possuía qualquer autoridade da parte de Cristo. Portanto, era um *falso* profeta, um líder religioso que convinha ser evitado. Era falso profeta, mágico e judeu — e isso era excelente combinação para fazer dele uma espécie de *vagabundo espiritual.*

BARJONAS

No hebraico, «filho de Jonas», o nome patronímico

do apóstolo Pedro, em Mat. 16:17. Em um trecho paralelo, João 1:42, ele é chamado «filho de Jonas». Somente o manuscrito it(aur) lhe dá o nome de *Bariona*, em João 1:42.

BAR KOCHBA, SIMEÃO

Foi um dos *líderes* da revolta dos judeus contra Roma, nos dias de Adriano (132-135 D.C.). Essa foi a segunda principal tentativa dos judeus libertarem-se de Roma, após terem sido totalmente derrotados em sua primeira tentativa, em 70 D.C. Essa segunda revolta teve por causa a tentativa de Adriano fundar uma cidade não-judaica, *Aelia Capitolina*, no mesmo local de Jerusalém. Bar Kochba, pois, proclamou um estado judaico independente e lançou moedas. Os romanos ordenaram que Júlio Severo, que fazia parte do governo da Bretanha, esmagasse a revolta. Os judeus lutaram árdua e longamente, mas após três anos foram derrotados. O quartel dos rebeldes ficava nos wadis e nos penhascos onde o deserto da Judéia termina, às margens do mar Morto. Após fazerem pesquisas fotográficas, a bordo de um helicóptero, os arqueólogos foram capazes de localizar um acampamento de comandos romanos, em um platô. Os romanos não conseguiram vencer os judeus que se ocultavam em complexas cavernas inacessíveis. Assim, — tentaram matá-los por inanição, — mas muitos judeus cometeram suicídio. As muitas descobertas arqueológicas na área também têm feito muito para iluminar a vida dos rebeldes. Uma caverna era recoberta, pelo menos em parte, com cestas cheias de ossos; além disso, foram encontrados objetos de metal, tomados dos romanos; sandálias e outros artigos de vestuário, como também contas, pentes, talcos, potezinhos de perfumes, e um jogo completo de toalete. Também foram encontrados documentos que aparentemente pertenciam ao próprio Bar Kochba. Entretanto, vários tipos de caligrafia podem ser distinguidos nesses documentos. Um desses documentos ordena o aprisionamento de um certo Tahun Ben Ishmael, bem como o confisco de seu trigo, exigindo o castigo de alguns que haviam construído moradias em desafio às normas determinadas por Bar Kochba. Finalmente, Bar Kochba morreu na batalha de Betar, em 135 D.C. Alguns o consideravam como o Messias, mas ele foi apenas mais um rebelde que lutou e morreu pelo que julgava ser uma causa justa. (E Z)

BAR MITZVAH

No hebraico, «filho de mandamento». Expressão aplicada a duas coisas: 1. A um menino judeu ao completar os treze anos de idade, quando então assume deveres e responsabilidades religiosas. 2. Solenização do acontecimento, quando, no sábado seguinte, ele é convocado como um dos sete homens que lêem a porção semanal da lei; ou como o oitavo homem, que lê a haphtarah, ou lição profética. Em algumas oportunidades, o rapazinho apresenta um discurso religioso. O evento também é celebrado pela sua família. A partir da ocasião, o rapaz ocupa lugar entre os homens, freqüentando regularmente a adoração pública e usando as filactérias durante as orações matutinas dos dias de semana. (E)

BARNABÉ

Atos 4:36: *Então José, cognominado pelos apóstolos Barnabé (que quer dizer, filho de consolação), levita, natural de Chipre.*

Essa é a primeira menção a Barnabé em todo o livro de Atos; e é provável que por um período considerável de tempo, antes da conversão e do ministério de Saulo de Tarso, Barnabé agiu como líder principal da comunidade helenista judeu-cristã e das igrejas formadas pelo mesmo grupo. Era homem de família judia, da classe sacerdotal, que se tinha fixado na ilha de Chipre. João Marcos, que era de Jerusalém, era seu primo (conforme a maioria dos modernos intérpretes acredita, e não seu sobrinho, no dizer das traduções mais antigas). Clemente de Alexandria presta-nos a informação de que Barnabé era um dos setenta discípulos (ver *Hipt.* viii; *Stromateis* ii.20.116). Os manuscritos ocidentais do livro de Atos (em 1:23), confundem-no com José Barsabás, que surge pela primeira vez quando da eleição do substituto de Judas Iscariotes. Contudo, não há evidência alguma em prol disso, e o mais certo é que tal hipótese apareceu meramente por causa da semelhança de nomes. Barnabé é descrito como homem *«bom, cheio do Espírito Santo e de fé»*, (Atos 11:24). Em diversas ocasiões, realmente, pôde demonstrar o seu excelente caráter, segundo vemos em diversos pontos da história deste livro, a saber:

1. Em Atos 9:27 podemos observar como ele agiu como *intermediário* entre Saulo de Tarso, já convertido, e os apóstolos, tendo-lhe preparado o caminho para conhecê-los pessoalmente. E isso foi uma grande intervenção, pois até pouco tempo antes Saulo de Tarso era grande perseguidor dos cristãos.

2. Foi *Barnabé* quem representou os apóstolos em Antioquia, e mediante a sua influência Saulo de Tarso se interessou por aquele trabalho, em face do que passou ali um ano inteiro, ajudando a desenvolver o trabalho da missão entre os gentios. E foi justamente em Antioquia que os discípulos do Senhor foram, pela primeira vez, chamados «cristãos». Ver Atos 11:19-30.

3. As primeiras ofertas enviadas aos santos pobres de Jerusalém foram mandadas pelas mãos de Barnabé e Saulo de Tarso, o que também evidencia o fato de que, por essa altura dos acontecimentos, os dois líderes cristãos se tinham tornado amigos íntimos e cooperadores no trabalho de Deus. (Ver Atos 11:27-30).

4. Pessoalmente, Barnabé não possuía personalidade tão rigorosa como a de Paulo, conforme aprendemos em Gál. 2:13, onde este último menciona o fato de que até mesmo Barnabé, temporariamente, interrompeu sua comunhão com os crentes gentílicos de Antioquia, por causa das pressões feitas por elementos judaizantes na primitiva igreja cristã. Nessa reprimenda de Paulo, até Pedro foi atingido, juntamente com todos os que tinham culpa na questão, por permitirem tal condição na igreja.

5. Paulo e Barnabé foram companheiros na *primeira* viagem missionária entre os gentios, o que resultou no estabelecimento de uma cadeia de igrejas cristãs, razão pela qual o cristianismo se propagou por todo o mundo então conhecido (ver Atos 13:14). Até esse ponto, Barnabé fora a figura liderante, enquanto Paulo era o seu «protegido»; mas, daqui por diante Paulo assume a liderança, por ser a personalidade dominante. Não obstante, grande parte do crédito da formação do grande missionário e apóstolo dos gentios, Paulo, deve ser atribuída a Barnabé, que foi poderoso instrumento do Espírito Santo na vida de Paulo.

6. Finalmente houve o *rompimento* de relações mais fraternais, entre Paulo e Barnabé, por causa da questão se deveriam ou não levar juntamente com eles a João Marcos, ao iniciar-se a segunda viagem missionária, por ter esse jovem desertado da missão

445

BARNABÉ — BARNABÉ, EPÍSTOLA

gentílica, quando talvez sua presença fosse mais necessária. Paulo se recusava a tomá-lo em sua companhia, mas Barnabé não queria desistir de sua ajuda, só por motivo de seu primeiro erro. Por isso, Barnabé deu continuidade ao seu ministério, levando consigo João Marcos até Chipre. (Ver Atos 15:36-41). Mas Paulo se associou a Silas, e assim teve início a segunda viagem missionária de Paulo.

Não obstante esse conflito, as referências que muito depois Paulo faz a João Marcos são cordiais e favoráveis (ver II Tim. 4:11), o que demonstra o valor de Marcos no ministério do evangelho. Outrossim, a tradição atribui a João Marcos a autoria do segundo evangelho, na ordem em que aparece em nossas Bíblias, mas que se pensa seriamente ter sido o evangelho original, no qual se escudaram os autores dos evangelhos de Mateus e Lucas—o evangelho de Marcos. Tudo isso demonstra o acerto da decisão de Barnabé ao reter Marcos em sua companhia, e talvez a decisão precipitada, negativa e intransigente de Paulo, ao rejeitá-lo. Todavia, o Espírito Santo desmantelou o mal que daí poderia proceder, para o bem de todos. Também podemos observar que as alusões posteriores de Paulo a Barnabé são amigáveis e simpáticas, o que nos permite entender que não houve grande dano, em resultado de sua discordância acerca de João Marcos. (Ver I Cor. 9:6; Gál. 2:1,9 e Col. 4:10).

Barnabé foi um dos poucos elementos a ser chamado de **apóstolo** juntamente com os doze, o que exibe a excelência geral de sua pessoa e de seu ministério. (Ver Atos 14:14). É apenas natural que em volta dele se tenham criado muitas tradições e lendas. Uma antiqüíssima epístola anônima, que figura entre os escritos patrísticos, recebeu o seu nome, embora o mais provável é que tal epístola não tenha sido de sua lavra. Tal epístola data dos primórdios do segundo século de nossa era e se caracteriza por um tom fortemente antijudaico. Mas é evidente que tal epístola foi considerada como de algum valor, em muitas igrejas cristãs antigas, sendo lida publicamente por elas e tida quase como canônica. (Ver Eusébio, *História Eclesiástica* iii.25). A chamada epístola aos Hebreus também tem sido atribuída à sua pena, por muitos estudiosos, pelo menos desde os tempos de Tertuliano (150 D.C.), e alguns deles têm mesmo pensado que a primeira epístola de Pedro tenha sido escrita por ele. No entanto, acerca de todas essas conjecturas nada se pode dizer com certeza. Há também um chamado Evangelho de Barnabé, mas trata-se de uma obra muito posterior, já dos tempos medievais.

No calendário anual da igreja anglicana, Barnabé recebe o título de «apóstolo», sendo o único dos santos, se não considerarmos os *doze*, excetuando Paulo e os evangelistas, a ser honrado com um dia marcado em vermelho no calendário, como dia de feriado.

O seu nome original era *José*, mas recebeu o nome «Barnabé» possivelmente a fim de assinalar a sua admissão à função de profeta ou mestre na igreja, mais ou menos como Simão recebeu também o nome de «Pedro», a fim de indicar algo especial em sua personalidade e função, ou como Saulo de Tarso recebeu o nome de Paulo. O epíteto «Barnabé» é proveniente de uma palavra que é usada acerca do Espírito Santo para descrever o seu ofício de Consolador, Conselheiro e Ajudador, que no original grego aparece como «paracleto». Por conseguinte, assinala Barnabé como um homem *consolador*, *exortador*, *auxiliador* ou *filho de profecia*. No grego, o vocábulo «paracleto» indica alguém chamado para o lado de outrem, a fim de ajudá-lo. (Quanto a esse termo como título do Espírito Santo, ver as notas expositivas em João 14:16, no NTI, que descrevem as cinco grandes declarações do Senhor Jesus sobre o divino «paracleto»). Alguns intérpretes, entretanto, preferem traduzir o seu nome por «filho do encorajamento», o que seria um termo suficientemente amplo para incluir as várias idéias possíveis em torno de seu nome. No entanto, Adolfo Deissman («Bible Studies», Edinburg: T. and T. Clark, 1901, págs. 307-310) prefere a derivação do seu nome de «Nebo», aparentemente um deus-demônio dos pagãos; porém, não é nada provável que Lucas houvesse usado tal nome para indicá-lo. Além disso, a própria interpretação que Lucas oferece sobre o nome de Barnabé indica-nos que, por detrás do mesmo, havia algo como o vocábulo grego *paracleto*, ou alguma outra idéia similar. O nome «Filho de profecia» se derivaria do hebraico «bar Nebi», e alguns estudiosos têm pensado que esse é o termo aramaico por detrás do nome aqui dado, no original grego. Porém, sem importar qual o nome aramaico que Lucas assim traduziu para o grego, o fato é que o próprio Lucas forneceu o sentido popular de seu nome como «Filho de consolação», ou «Filho de exortação», ou, mais geralmente ainda, «Filho de encorajamento». De fato, *encorajamento* é a idéia central do vocábulo grego *«paraklesis»*, embora essa palavra tenha sido traduzida, em diversos lugares, como consolo, exortação e consolação, conforme se vê nos trechos de Atos 9:31; 13:15; 15:31; 16:9 e 20:12.

Variante Textual. Algumas traduções mais antigas, ao invés de José, dizem aqui «Joses», seguindo os mss P, 1, 13, 31 e as versões sah e si(p), tendo sido assim também citado o seu nome por Crisóstomo. Porém, em sua grande maioria, os manuscritos mais antigos, como P(8), P(74), Aleph, ABDE vg cop si(sch) arm aeth, dizem *José*. Sem dúvida alguma «José» representa o texto original. Quanto a informações sobre os manuscritos do N.T. e seu emprego na determinação da forma correta do texto sagrado, ver o artigo sobre *Manuscritos*. Alguns poucos manuscritos minúsculos posteriores, sem qualquer importância especial, como os mss 181 e 460, dizem *Barsabás*, ao invés de Barnabé. Porém, isso é confundir Barnabé com o candidato ao apostolado José Barsabás, que figura no trecho de Atos 1:23 e foi preferido em favor de Matias, para o lugar perdido por Judas Iscariotes. Essa identificação é altamente incerta e surgiu meramente por motivo da similaridade dos nomes dessas duas personagens diversas. Seja como for, o texto correto, neste caso, é «José Barnabé». Não obstante, os escritores rabínicos com freqüência preferiam «Joses» em lugar de «José», sendo provável que se trate apenas de duas formas do mesmo nome.

BARNABÉ, EPÍSTOLA DE (e outros escritos a ele atribuídos)

Certo número de obras tem sido atribuído a Barnabé: Atos de Barnabé, Epístola de Barnabé e Evangelho de Barnabé. Tertuliano supunha que a epístola canônica aos Hebreus foi escrita por ele, mas isso envolvia mais uma opinião pessoal do que mesmo uma tradição. O livro Atos de Barnabé é apócrifo e tardio, pertencente ao século V D.C. ou mesmo mais tarde. Relata suas supostas viagens missionárias e seu martírio final.

Epístola de Barnabé:

1. *Manuscrito*. Faz parte do manuscrito do Novo Testamento intitulado Codex Sinaiticus. Sua presença ali mostra que a obra tinha um elevado prestígio,

embora seja considerada pela maioria como parte das obras apócrifas do Novo Testamento (ver o artigo sobre os livros apócrifos do Novo Testamento). Também faz parte de um codex descoberto em Constantinopla, em 1885, pelo arcebispo Bryennios. Há outros oito manuscritos gregos que o contêm, e há uma versão latina que contém os capítulos primeiro a décimo sétimo da obra. Alguns supõem que essa versão latina é mais próxima de sua forma grega original, antes que os Dois Caminhos, também chamado Ensino dos Apóstolos (caps. 18 e 21), tivessem sido adicionados. Clemente de Alexandria citava a obra como Escritura Sagrada.

2. A citação desse livro, por Clemente de Alexandria, mostra que nos fins do II séc. D.C., a obra já estava sendo bem distribuída. Provavelmente a obra foi escrita em grego, em cerca de 130 D.C. Ali há uma referência à destruição do templo de Jerusalém, que ocorreu depois do ano 70 D.C., segundo esse livro. Parece haver uma alusão às atividades de Adriano, em Jerusalém; e, se essa alusão é correta, então a data precisa ser fixada em cerca de 130 D.C.

3. *Autor.* Provavelmente o autor era alexandrino. Ele promove o ponto de vista alexandrino de que o Antigo Testamento é verdadeiro, embora precise ser compreendido alegoricamente, e não literalmente. As leis do Antigo Testamento são por ele interpretadas alegoricamente. Os seis dias da criação são interpretados como indicação de que o mundo perdurará por seis mil anos, antes da volta de Cristo, mediante o emprego do trecho de Sal. 90:4 como base: «Pois mil anos, aos teus olhos, são como o dia de ontem que se foi, e como a vigília da noite». Certas cifras são ali interpretadas de modo fantástico, como os trezentos e dezoito homens da casa de Abraão, que presumivelmente corresponderiam ao grego TIH: o T = cruz; o IH = 18, ou seja, Jesus. Tal atividade pode ser identificada com um excesso de interpretações alegóricas. Uma coisa é indiscutível: não foi Barnabé quem escreveu esse livro, embora nada de positivo possa ser dito no tocante a outro nome qualquer, como autor.

4. *Lugar de Origem.* As descrições dadas acima sob «Autor» indicam uma origem alexandrina, como também o uso que Clemente de Alexandria fez do livro como obra canônica. Orígenes aparentemente concordava com a opinião de Clemente. Mas outros (com menor taxa de probabilidade) vêem uma origem asiática (Ásia Menor), embora não haja evidências convincentes nesse sentido.

5. *Conteúdo.* Há muitas citações extraídas do Antigo Testamento, do livro de Isaías conforme a LXX, e de outros livros veterotestamentários, como também de vários livros não canônicos, como II Esdras e I Enoque. Várias passagens do Novo Testamento são ali refletidas, como Mat. 22:14; 9:13; Luc. 5:32; Rom. 2:11; I Ped. 1:17; II Tim. 1:10; Apo. 1:7, e outras. Após a saudação encontramos os TRÊS DOGMAS. Esses dogmas parecem ser os seguintes: 1. a esperança da vida; 2. a retidão; e 3. o amor da alegria e do júbilo. Os sacrifícios são ali descontinuados, e a retidão é exigida. A caridade e o cuidado pelos pobres são coisas importantes. O fim do mundo está próximo. O sangue expiatório de Jesus Cristo é enfatizado. Cristo aparece como quem foi predito pelos profetas do Antigo Testamento. A circuncisão é a do coração, e não a do prepúcio. Um anjo maligno teria desviado os judeus, para darem valor à mera circuncisão física. Outrossim, há muitos preceitos éticos que governam todos os aspectos da vida, regras dietéticas, relações sexuais, etc. O batismo e a cruz, segundo diz essa obra, seriam descritos alegoricamente no Antigo Testamento. Assim como Jacó suplantou Esaú, assim também os cristãos suplantam os judeus. O templo é o próprio povo de Deus. Seis mil anos serão a história do mundo, até à segunda vinda de Cristo.

Os dois caminhos. Os quatro capítulos finais da obra descrevem o caminho de luz e o caminho de trevas. A luz é equiparada ao amor, à simplicidade, à humildade, à pureza, à mansidão, à generosidade e à atitude pacificadora. O ódio é comparado à idolatria, à hipocrisia, ao adultério, ao homicídio, ao orgulho e a diversos vícios. E o autor conclui: «Que possais obter a salvação, filhos do amor e da paz».

6. *Teologia.* A salvação é obtida por meio dos sofrimentos de Cristo e da obediência do homem aos mandamentos, espiritualmente interpretados. O batismo e a cruz nos conferem a vida eterna. O Filho de Deus veio em carne (encarnação). Após o sábado milenial haverá um outro mundo, que será o oitavo dia. (AM GR KR Z)

BARNABÉ, EVANGELHO DE

Essa obra, que alguns estudiosos pensam que realmente nunca existiu, é aludida por diversos autores antigos especialmente no *Decreto de Gelásio* (cerca de 500 D.C.). Um longo manuscrito italiano com esse título chegou até nós. Seu conteúdo é islâmico, aparentemente escrito por algum apóstata cristão. Essa obra exprime vários pontos de vista gnósticos. Sua data fica entre o século XIII e o século XVI D.C. Tem uma forte ênfase ética, mas, tal como a maioria dos escritos patrísticos e apócrifos medievais, é altamente imaginário e contém muito material fictício. Foi preservado em manuscritos espanhóis e italianos. (AM Z)

BARNABITAS

Nome popular dado à Congregação dos Sacristãos Regulares de São Paulo, fundada em 1530 por Antônio Maria Zaccaria. O propósito da congregação é pregar, catequizar, enviar missionários, etc., dando ênfase especial às epístolas do apóstolo Paulo. Os membros fazem os três votos religiosos comuns da Igreja Católica Romana, além de mais um voto no qual afirmam que não procurarão qualquer dignidade eclesiástica, a menos que a isso sejam convidados pela Santa Sé. (E)

BARNES, ALBERT

Ministro presbiteriano norte-americano, nascido em 1789 e falecido em 1870. Deu apoio à teologia de Nathaniel W. Taylor (ver o artigo a seu respeito), que difere do calvinismo estrito e não se harmoniza com a Confissão de Westminster. Tornou-se o fulcro de uma controvérsia e foi julgado por heresia, mormente por causa do que disse em um sermão, intitulado «O Caminho da Salvação». (E)

BARODIS

Antepassado de uma família de servos de Salomão que retornou do exílio babilônico em companhia de Zorobabel (ver I Esdras 5:34). Seu nome não figura nas listas de Esdras 2:57 e Neemias 7:59.

BARONIUS, CÉSAR

Suas datas são 1538 e 1607. Foi um historiador

eclesiástico. Nasceu em Sora e foi educado em Veroli e Nápolis. Uniu-se ao Oratório, em Roma, em 1557, sob Filipe Neri, ao qual sucedeu, em 1593. Em 1596 tornou-se cardeal e bibliotecário do Vaticano. Por duas vezes, quase se tornou papa, mas a delegação espanhola barrou seu nome, por razões políticas. Tornou-se mais conhecido por causa de suas grandes obras históricas, os *Annales Ecclesiastici*, que foram escritos para refutar o *Séculos*, de Magdeburgo. Ele copiava os erros e os corrigia baseado em fontes históricas gregas. Seu trabalho foi um trabalho pioneiro no registro objetivo da história. (E)

BARRA

Na Bíblia portuguesa a palavra aparece como tradução de um termo hebraico, *metil*, que figura apenas por uma vez no Antigo Testamento, na expressão: «...o seu arcabouço como barras de ferro» (Jó 40:18), referindo-se à fortíssima constituição do hipopótamo. Uma outra palavra hebraica, que significa, literalmente, «barra», isto é, *mot*, figura por quatro vezes no Antigo Testamento (ver Núm. 13:23; traduzido por «vara» em nossa versão; Naum 1:13—traduzida por «jugo» em nossa versão; e Núm. 4:10,12—traduzida por «varais» em nossa versão). (Z)

BARRABÁS

No hebraico é uma palavra derivada do aramaico «filho do pai» ou «filho de Abas». No Talmude, esse nome é de ocorrência comum. No Novo Testamento (ver Mar. 15:7; Luc. 23:25 e Mat. 27:16-26), o nome é dado a um criminoso, culpado de sedição e homicídio, que merecia morrer por crucificação, de acordo com a lei romana. A lei judaica também requereria a sua execução, se os judeus tivessem o direito de pôr em vigor a sua lei. No entanto, ante o desejo insistentemente expresso, por parte de certos líderes judeus, que queriam livrar-se da incômoda presença de Jesus, Barrabás foi libertado em lugar de Cristo, quando Pilatos ofereceu aos judeus a escolha. A questão toda é longamente comentada no NTI, em Mat. 27:16-26. Orígenes informa-nos que o primeiro nome de Barrabás também era Jesus, algo confirmado por muitas cópias do Novo Testamento que chegaram até nós. Apesar disso representar a opinião de uma minoria em nossos dias, muitos críticos textuais consideram que isso reflete o melhor texto, mas que o primeiro nome de Barrabás foi suprimido, por julgar-se impróprio que, nos evangelhos, um criminoso também fosse chamado pelo nome de Jesus. O problema textual é detalhadamente ventilado no NTI, em Mat. 27:16. A soltura de Barrabás é registrada em todos os quatro evangelhos, o que mostra o quanto o episódio chocou aos cristãos primitivos. Ele era um prisioneiro «notório», o qual as autoridades muito gostariam de apanhar, por ser um homem violento e perigoso para ser deixado solto. No entanto, Barrabás foi solto, e não Jesus. O impacto de tal troca só pôde ser sentido por aqueles que sabiam da má reputação e dos crimes de Barrabás. Alguns estudiosos supõem que Barrabás foi um terrorista que estivera envolvido em várias tentativas de derrubar o governo romano na Palestina. Isso é sugerido pelo emprego da palavra «amotinadores», usada em Marcos 15:7.

No tocante à soltura de algum prisioneiro, por ocasião da festa da páscoa, nada sabemos dizer historicamente, embora saibamos que costumes assim eram generalizados, relacionados a festividades e feriados religiosos. Josefo (*Anti*. XX. ix.3) e Lívio (V.13) mencionam tal costume. Não passa de uma fantasia a tentativa feita por alguns, de fazerem de Barrabás filho de um rabino, somente porque o nome desse homem aparece no evangelho apócrifo dos Hebreus, com a forma de «filho de seu senhor». Coisa alguma se sabe sobre sua história subseqüente, e até mesmo as tradições orais, que usualmente preenchem os hiatos com histórias fictícias, nada dizem a seu respeito.

Barrabás como um tipo simbólico. É legítimo salientarmos que a crucificação de Jesus possibilitou a soltura de um notório criminoso. E assim, Barrabás tornou-se símbolo de todos os pecadores que são libertados através do sacrifício do Senhor Jesus. (ID NTI S UN)

BARREIRA DE COR

Trata-se da prática de barrar pessoas de seus direitos normais, como acesso a lugares públicos, a recusa de oportunidades de empregos e de educação em escolas públicas ou particulares, a certas pessoas, por motivos raciais. Modernamente, isso se dá em países onde os negros são uma minoria, ou onde os negros, embora maioria, ainda não conseguiram autonomia. Porém, não são apenas as pessoas africanas que sentem na pele o fustigar da barreira da cor. Outros povos também têm sofrido a mesma coisa, como os ciganos, os armênios e os judeus. Talvez estes últimos não exatamente por causa da cor da pele, mas por diversos outros motivos, desde religiosos até políticos. Trata-se de certo aspecto do fenômeno da segregação. Ver os artigos sobre o *Apartheid*, *Relações Raciais* e *Segregação*.

Todos reconhecem a injustiça envolvida em tais práticas; mas as soluções demoram a aparecer, devido a muitas razões, incluindo até mesmo o problema da falta de melhor educação, que prepara as pessoas a ocuparem posições mais vantajosas, mantendo-as em posições de inferioridade econômica, a questão da integração de culturas e estilos de vida em choque. Essas coisas, na verdade, nada têm a ver com preconceitos sobre tonalidade da tez.

Além disso, em alguns lugares, organizações políticas e radicais de todas as nuanças tiram vantagem do problema racial para promover a perturbação e a subversão sociais. Dessa maneira, a oposição à segregação continua sendo um meio de defesa contra os assédios das filosofias políticas estrangeiras. Porém, não há que duvidar que algumas pessoas realmente são impulsionadas por preconceitos tolos, alicerçados sobre as diferenças raciais, que são mínimas, pois todas as raças humanas são mutuamente fertilizáveis, o que mostra que a espécie humana é uma só. Isso mostra quão insensato é o racismo. Não obstante, devemos compreender que muitas pessoas temem as diferenças, e que certas características raciais são consideradas sinais de inferioridade, e que outras são tidas como sinais de superioridade. Diz Paulo, em Atos 17:26: «...de um só (Deus) fez toda raça humana para habitar sobre toda a face da terra...» As variantes raciais são potencialidades exteriorizadas que já haviam em Adão. Entre crentes, o racismo é simplesmente inconcebível. «...porque todos vós sois um em Cristo Jesus» (Gál. 3:28). (H NTI)

BARROWS, JOHN HENRY

Nasceu em 1847 e faleceu em 1902. Era natural de Medina, no estado norte-americano de Michigan. Foi ministro congregacional, formou-se no Olivet College, e estudou nos seminários de Yale, Union e Andover.

Foi pastor por várias vezes, por breves períodos. Organizou o Parlamento Mundial de Religiões e a Exposição Mundial Colombiana de Chicago, em 1893. Estimulou o interesse pelas religiões étnicas. Foi conferencista Haskell da Universidade de Chicago, em 1895, e apresentou preleções na Índia e no Japão. Foi presidente do Oberlin College, de 1898 até à sua morte. Foi autor de vários livros de interesse sobre religiões comparadas, sobre Henry Ward Beecher e de obras como *Christianity the World Religion*; *A World Pilgrimage; Spiritual Forces in American History; Christian Conquest of Asia*. (E)

BARSABÁS

No hebraico, «filho de Saba», ou então, na opinião de alguns eruditos, «filho do sábado». Era o nome patronímico de dois dos primeiros cristãos judeus, que talvez fossem irmãos: 1. José, um discípulo que foi nomeado juntamente com Matias, para ser substituto de Judas Iscariotes no apostolado. Tinha por sobrenome Justo, e se chamava José Barsabás (ver Atos 1:23). O texto indica que ele conhecera bem a Jesus, sendo testemunha ocular de tudo quanto ocorrera ao Senhor em seus anos de ministério. 2. Um certo Judas Barsabás, enviado a Antioquia em companhia de Silas, levando a decisão do concílio de Jerusalém (ver Atos 15:22). Era profeta e um dos líderes da igreja de Jerusalém (ver Atos 15:32).

BARTACO

Pai de Apame, concubina de um rei que não podemos identificar. Esse homem foi intitulado de *ilustre*, provavelmente por causa de algum elevado ofício que ocupava. Os nomes de seu pai e de sua filha sugerem uma origem persa (ver I Esdras 4:29).

BARTH, KARL Ver também, *Crise, Teologia da*.

Teólogo reformado. Nasceu em 1886, em Basel, na Suíça. Em 1911 foi pastor evangélico em Safenwyl. Em 1921, professor de teologia reformada, em Goettingen. Em 1925, professor em Muenster-in-Westphalia. Em 1930, professor em Bonn. Em 1935, foi exilado pelos nazistas, e desde então, até sua morte, foi professor em Basel.

Foi homem de caráter forte e de piedade pessoal, dotado de vigor profético e de grande intensidade de propósitos, cuja vida e obras têm despertado interesse internacional. Foi influenciado pelo neokantianismo e por Kierkegaard (ver o artigo sobre uma e outra questão), bem como pelo socialismo religioso de Ragaz e Kutter. Foi um dos principais expoentes da *teologia de crise*, que exalta a Palavra de Deus como manifestação do Inteiramente Diferente. Lembrou aos evangélicos que todas as nossas atividades teológicas são apenas tentativas hesitantes para expressar o que é inexprimível. Seus pensamentos, nessa área, foram reverberados por Emil Brunner e Eduardo Thurneysen (ver os artigos sobre um e outro). Em cerca de 1925, entrou em um estágio em que seu pensamento sofreu influências de Calvino e do calvinismo ortodoxo (ver os artigos a respeito). Ele enfatizava a teologia bíblica, e não a teologia natural, insistindo sobre a coerência e autoridade absoluta das conclusões racionais extraídas das Sagradas Escrituras. Relutava em participar do conflito na Igreja que surgiu na Alemanha, até que a Gestapo embargou a ele mesmo e a seus livros na Alemanha. Foi uma das mentes liderantes por detrás da declaração de Barmen (ver o artigo a respeito), em 1934, bem como no conflito contra a Igreja do estado nazista. Seu comentário sobre a epístola aos Romanos (1919; nova edição em 1922), foi uma espécie de manifesto de revolta contra a teologia liberal. Ele falava com vigor em favor da soberania de Deus, da finitude e pecaminosidade do homem, da prioridade divina na graça e na revelação, e do caráter escatológico da mensagem neotestamentária.

Barth demonstrou que as promessas otimistas da teologia liberal haviam falhado, e que os homens tinham de buscar esperança nos antigos princípios religiosos. Visto que fora plenamente treinado no liberalismo alemão, tendo ficado desapontado com o sistema nazista, isso deve ter sido uma das razões pelas quais procurava e expunha uma nova ortodoxia. Sua teologia tornou-se conhecida como neo-ortodoxia por estes motivos: 1. opunha-se a muitas posições liberais; 2. não acompanhava a ortodoxia tradicional quanto a várias questões. Para exemplificar, seus pontos de vista sobre as Escrituras demonstram respeito e um uso firme, embora considerasse a Bíblia eivada de erros e uma representante fragmentada da Palavra de Deus, que transcende a qualquer livro; porquanto essa Palavra consiste na comunicação de Deus na revelação, que se processa de muitas maneiras, e não apenas de forma literária. Quanto a detalhes sobre essa e questões relacionadas, ver o artigo separado sobre a *neo-ortodoxia*.

Idéias Principais. 1. O Deus transcendental. Deus seria inteiramente diferente do homem, e nossa linguagem quando muito, é uma tentativa gaguejante de dizer algo acerca dele. Isso também se aplica às nossas declarações bíblicas. Portanto, Barth deprecia-va a teologia natural. As idéias humanas de Deus, na realidade, tornam-se outros tantos *ídolos* que os homens criam. 2. A verdade é um resultado da graça, e não da busca racionalista. Sabemos de Deus e de sua existência através da *revelação*, e não através de racionalizações. Em seus esforços para estabelecer esses princípios, Barth terminou criando uma *teologia dialética*. 3. Devemos substituir a analogia do ser pela analogia da fé. 4.Aguda distinção é feita entre a revelação e a religião. A religião tem tendências nitidamente idólatras, mesmo às mãos de teólogos conservadores, que criam um Deus à sua própria imagem e transformam em ídolos as suas idéias e doutrinas. A revelação pode ser irracional ao homem, mas seus ensinos nos dão a entender tudo o quanto sabemos sobre a verdade. 5. A ênfase de Barth recaía sobre a Palavra de Deus, nas Escrituras e com base nelas, como **autoritárias**, em contraste com os outros meios de conhecimento religioso, racional e natural. Não se pode negligenciar a autoridade da Igreja, mas essa autoridade repousa sobre a autoridade da Palavra de Deus, no tocante à sua autenticidade; e, se ultrapassar isso, deve ser posta em dúvida. Também há a autoridade da erudição. As tentativas do **aprendizado e a** definição devem ser respeitadas, mas essa autoridade não é absoluta, podendo ser posta em dúvida — à medida que o nosso conhecimento avança. Outrossim, há a autoridade da *experiência religiosa*. O conhecimento espiritual vem através da oração e das experiências místicas. Tais experiências, contudo, precisam ser equilibradas e apoiadas pelas Escrituras e pela tradição cristã. Em conseqüência, a autoridade torna-se uma combinação de fatores que se fundem harmoniosamente com a fé. Ver o artigo sobre a questão da *autoridade*.

Obras Principais de Barth. *Epistle to the Romans*, 1919; *Word of God and Word of Man*, 1928; *Anselm*, 1931; *Church Dogmatics*, 4 volumes, 1923-1935; *Credo*, 1935; *Dogmatics in Outline*, 1947; *Evangelical*

BARTIMEU

Transliteração grega do hebraico, «filho de Timeu», o esmoler cego de Jericó, a quem Jesus devolveu a visão (ver Mar. 10:46; Mat. 20:29-34 e Luc. 18:34,43). Ver uma completa exposição sobre o relato, com suas implicações espirituais e morais, no texto de Mateus, no NTI. As diversas narrativas sinópticas diferem quanto a detalhes. Lucas não fornece o nome do cego. Mateus fala em dois cegos, e não em um só. Nenhuma tentativa para dar solução a essa última discrepância tem obtido total bom êxito. Além disso, há o detalhe de que a cura teve lugar antes (Lucas) ou depois (Mateus e Marcos) da visita de Jesus a Jericó. Alguns estudiosos supõem que o episódio ocorreu entre a antiga Jericó (a cidade cananéia original) e a nova Jericó (cidade erigida por Herodes). Outros supõem que dois cegos foram curados, mas que, por alguma razão desconhecida, Marcos e Lucas não mencionaram um deles, talvez porque Bartimeu era o mais vocífero dos dois, ou então tivesse se tornado um discípulo bem conhecido de Jesus. Não há necessidade de se especular desse modo. Jesus tinha o poder de curar os cegos, sem importar se fosse um, dois ou muitos; e isso é o que o relato ensina, e o que importa, afinal de contas. Além disso, devemos considerar a *lição espiritual*. Todos os homens são espiritualmente cegos e precisam da cura referida no evangelho. E uma lição adicional é a persistência do cego. Não tolerava perder a oportunidade de ter uma conversa com Jesus, e assim foi curado. A persistência espiritual nos faz avançar ao longo da estrada que conduz a Deus. (ID ND Z)

BARTOLO DE SASSOFERRATO

Suas datas são 1314 e 1347. Foi um grande jurista que tentou aplicar os princípios da jurisprudência romana às condições políticas e religiosas de sua época. Tendo sido estudante brilhante, já era advogado aos vinte anos de idade. Ensinou em Pisa (1339-1343) e em Perúgia (1343-1347). Uma opinião sua era que a Igreja e o estado devem ser parceiros iguais, contra o ensino de Agostinho, de que à Igreja compete governar o estado. (E)

BARTOLOMEU

No grego, transliteração do hebraico, «filho de Tolmai», um dos doze apóstolos originais. Ver o artigo geral sobre os *apóstolos*.

1. *Nome e família.* Alguns eruditos identificam-no com o Natanael referido no evangelho de João. Se essa identificação é falsa, então a única coisa que sabemos a seu respeito é que Jesus tinha um discípulo de nome Bartolomeu, e nada mais. Os evangelhos sinópticos nunca mencionam o nome Natanael, ao passo que o quarto evangelho nunca menciona o nome Bartolomeu. A justaposição dos nomes Filipe e Bartolomeu, nas diversas listas dos apóstolos, sugere que Natanael e Bartolomeu eram dois nomes de um mesmo homem. Todos os companheiros de Natanael, em João 1:35-51, são apóstolos conhecidos, pelo que sabemos que ele fazia parte do grupo dos apóstolos. A promessa de Cristo a Natanael, de que ele seria testemunha da vida do Filho do homem (ver João 1:50,51) sugere uma identificação apostólica. Apesar dessa identificação não poder ser comprovada, não há objeções válidas contra ela. Bartolomeu também tem sido identificado com Mateus, e com o discípulo de Emaús, cujo nome não é dado em Lucas 24:13-22, mas essas são conjecturas destituídas de apoio escriturístico.

2. *Nas listas dos apóstolos.* O nome de Bartolomeu é registrado em todas as quatro listas dos nomes dos «doze», a saber. Mat. 10:3; Mar. 3:18; Luc. 6:14 e Atos 1:13. Nos evangelhos sinópticos ele sempre figura no segundo grupo de quatro nomes, e sempre depois do de Filipe, que encabeça aquele grupo. Porém, no livro de Atos, o nome de Tomé aparece entre o de Filipe e o de Bartolomeu.

3. *História.* Bartolomeu era nativo de Caná da Galiléia (ver João 21:3) e foi apresentado a Jesus por Filipe. Nesse encontro, ao vê-lo, Jesus observou a respeito da sinceridade de Bartolomeu: Eis um verdadeiro israelita em quem não há dolo! (João 1:47). Bartolomeu foi um dos discípulos a quem o Senhor apareceu após sua ressurreição, às margens do mar de Tiberíades. Também foi testemunha ocular da ascensão (ver o artigo a respeito), e retornou com os demais discípulos a Jerusalém (ver Atos 1:4,12,13).

4. *Tradição.* Eusébio (*História Eclesiástica* v.10) afirma que quando Pantaeno (ver o artigo) saiu em missão à Índia (fins do século II D.C.), encontrou entre eles o evangelho de Mateus, em hebraico, que ali fora deixado por Bartolomeu. Jerônimo (*De Vir. Illustr.* c. 36) assevera algo similar, ajuntando que Pantaeno trouxe de volta essa cópia de Mateus para Alexandria. Mas a palavra «Índia» parece ter tido uma aplicação mais lata, nos escritos de Eusébio, do que lhe damos atualmente, pelo que os lugares onde o apóstolo Bartolomeu trabalhou continuam na dúvida. Outros autores mencionam a missão desse apóstolo na Índia. Alguns dizem que ele viajou, posteriormente, à Grande Armênia, tendo ali convertido a muitos ao cristianismo. De acordo com o Martirológio Romano, ele foi «esfolado vivo pelos bárbaros e, por ordem do rei Astíages, recebeu o golpe de misericórdia mediante decapitação». Por causa dessa lenda, com freqüência ele é apresentado na arte, como no *Julgamento Final* de Miguelângelo, como esfolado e segurando a própria pele nas mãos. É difícil determinarmos a exatidão de tradições que chegaram até nós vindas de fontes informativas tão remotas dos acontecimentos, ou seja, mais de duzentos anos depois dos acontecimentos relatados. Em todas essas tradições usualmente há mais fantasia do que verdade. A festa de São Bartolomeu cai no dia 24 de agosto. (AM BARK ID JAM S UN Z)

BARTOLOMEU, EVANGELHO (PERGUNTAS) DE

1. *Manuscritos.* Há cinco recensões dessa obra: duas em grego, duas em latim e uma em eslavônico; mas nenhuma delas é completa.

2. *Tradições.* Jerônimo (*Migne Patrologia Latina*, xxvi.17a) menciona um livro com esse nome. Uma referência ao mesmo pode haver no Decreto de Gelásio. Algumas outras poucas referências, tardias e incertas, têm sido encontradas, uma das quais vincula a obra ao evangelho hebraico de Mateus, embora isso seja improvável.

3. *Data.* Não pode ser anterior aos séculos V ou VII D.C., embora talvez esteja baseada em material mais antigo, possivelmente pertencente ao século III ou IV D.C. Alguns estudiosos supõem que uma obra mais breve foi expandida posteriormente.

4. *Conteúdo.* O apóstolo Bartolomeu faz uma pergunta a Jesus, antes de sua paixão; e então recebe a seguinte resposta: «Nada posso revelar-te, antes de ter despido este corpo de carne». Esse diálogo dá

BARTOLOMEU — BARUQUE

início ao livro. Entretanto, Bartolomeu não se deixa desencorajar, e pergunta onde Jesus foi, quando morreu. Isso provoca um relato sobre a descida de Cristo ao hades, uma história similar àquela que aparece no livro Atos de Pilatos (ver o artigo). O segundo capítulo contém a resposta de Maria à pergunta dos apóstolos, no tocante ao papel por ela desempenhado no drama sagrado. Ela fala sobre a anunciação, com típicos detalhes apócrifos. Chamas emanam de sua boca, e ela avisa aos apóstolos de possíveis más conseqüências se eles persistirem em tentar sondar os mistérios. Mas Jesus apaga as chamas e salva o dia. No terceiro capítulo, os apóstolos pedem para que lhes seja mostrado o abismo. No quarto capítulo, Pedro insiste com Maria que peça a Jesus para mostrar-lhes os céus. Mas isso não ocorre, porquanto todos relutam em exprimir o pedido, e disso resultam muitas discussões. Maria então ajunta que Pedro é a «rocha» sobre a qual a Igreja está edificada. Fica demonstrado que Maria reverteu a maldição imposta por causa da transgressão de Eva. Bartolomeu pede para ver o grande adversário dos homens. Então Beliar é trazido, seguro por seiscentos e sessenta anjos, preso a uma cadeia. E é anunciado que outros nomes de Beliar são Satanael e Satanás. Satanás então relata a história de sua queda. No último capítulo, Jesus responde à indagação de Bartolomeu no tocante ao pecado mais grave, que é o pecado contra o Espírito Santo. (JAM Z)

BARTOLOMEU, LIVRO DA RESSURREIÇÃO DE CRISTO POR

1. *Manuscritos*. Há um texto em cóptico, no Museu Britânico. Há fragmentos escritos em cóptico em Paris e Berlim, que apresentam diferentes recensões da obra. O manuscrito existente em Londres parece ser uma espécie de paráfrase do texto mais antigo, representado por esses fragmentos.

2. *Conteúdo*. Os episódios são frouxamente alinhavados, com algumas contradições, como aquela que diz que Tomé, que duvidou da ressurreição de Cristo, expôs tal dúvida depois de seu grande ato de fé, quando ressuscitou dos mortos seu filho, Siofanes, em nome de Jesus. No manuscrito existente em Londres faltam as primeiras cinco páginas onde aparece o episódio. Mas é provável que ali estivesse contida, entre outras coisas, a história de Ananias, pois mais adiante há uma alusão ao episódio, que presumivelmente já havia sido ventilado. Além disso, há o relato do sepultamento de Jesus por José de Arimatéia, a chegada da morte personificada e de seus filhos ao túmulo, e a queixa da morte diante do corpo morto de Cristo. Também há menção à descida de Jesus ao hades, onde ele cria grande agitação e liberta as almas. Ali, o Senhor também amaldiçoa a Judas Iscariotes. A narrativa sobre a ressurreição apresenta-nos o jardineiro, Filógenes, o qual, presumivelmente, foi quem cedeu seu túmulo a Jesus. Mas o texto mistura elementos do relato dos evangelhos sinópticos, confundindo Maria Madalena com a mãe de Jesus. A ascensão de Jesus ao céu é descrita, após o que aparecem oito hinos que acompanham a recepção de Jesus, na glória, por parte de Adão e dos justos. E então cada um dos apóstolos, após uma nova revelação de Jesus no monte das Oliveiras, ascende ao céu e à glória. Nesse ponto aparece o episódio de Tomé e Siofanes, referido acima. Uma declaração quase no fim do livro fornece-nos o título:«Este é o Livro da Ressurreição de Jesus, o Cristo, nosso Senhor, em alegria e júbilo».

Bartolomeu adverte a Tadeu como segue: «Não deixes este livro cair nas mãos de qualquer homem que seja incrédulo ou herege».

3. *Data*. Os estudiosos calculam que a data dessa obra é tão tardia quanto os séculos V ou VI D.C. (JAM Z)

BARTOLOMEU, MASSACRE DE SÃO

Nome dado ao grande massacre dos huguenotes (ver o artigo a respeito), na França, que começou no dia de São Bartolomeu, a 24 de agosto de 1582. Esse massacre influenciou a tendência do pensamento e da ação dos protestantes, endurecendo os mesmos. Ver sobre *Guerras da Religião*. Ver também o artigo sobre *Perseguição*.

BARUQUE

No hebraico, «bendito». Foi nome de vários personagens bíblicos:

1. Um amigo fiel e amanuense do profeta Jeremias (ver Jer. 32:12-16; 43:3 e 51:51). Pertencia à nobreza da tribo de Judá, filho de Nerias e irmão de Seraías, camareiro-mor de Zedequias (ver Jer. 51:59), em cerca de 604 A.C. No quarto ano do rei Jeoiaquim, Baruque começou a escrever todas as profecias entregues por Jeremias, a fim de lê-las diante do povo. Também leu essas profecias diante dos conselheiros do rei. O rei sentiu-se muito desgostoso diante do que ouviu, e, apanhando o rolo, cortou-o em pedaços e jogou-os no fogo. Em seguida, ordenou que Jeremias e Baruque fossem detidos, mas eles se ocultaram, e escaparam à detenção. Foi produzida uma outra cópia das profecias, sendo adicionada a predição da ruína de Jeoiaquim e sua casa (ver Jer. 36:27-32).

O próprio Baruque sentiu-se aterrorizado por causa das profecias, mas recebeu a promessa de que seria livrado das calamidades preditas contra Judá e Jerusalém. No quarto ano do rei Zedequias, em 595 A.C., segundo se supõe, Baruque teria acompanhado Seraías à Babilônia, o lugar por ele denunciado. O rolo onde estava registrada a profecia foi atado a uma pedra e lançado no rio, dando a entender a ruína de Babilônia (ver Jer. 51:61). Essa informação também é dada no livro de Baruque. Durante o cerco de Jerusalém (587 A.C.), Jeremias comprou um terreno de Hanameel, seu primo, deixando o título com Baruque (ver Jer. 32:12). Baruque foi acusado de influenciar Jeremias a tomar o partido dos caldeus (ver Jer. 43:3), e foi lançado na prisão em companhia do profeta. Ficou ali até a cidade ser capturada (ver Josefo, *Anti*. x. 9,1). Por permissão de Nabucodonosor, foi residir com Jeremias em Mispa, mas depois foi forçado por outros judeus, revoltados, a ir para o Egito (ver Jer. 43:6). Nada mais diz a Bíblia a respeito de Baruque, embora a tradição afirme que, após a morte de Jeremias, ele foi para a Babilônia, onde faleceu, doze anos após a destruição de Jerusalém. Josefo (*Anti*. x.11) menciona a grande habilidade de Baruque no idioma hebraico, afirmando também que Nabucodonosor o tratou com respeito.

2. Filho de Zabai, que ajudou Neemias a reconstruir as muralhas de Jerusalém (ver Nee. 3:10).

3. Um homem que apôs sua assinatura no pacto de Neemias (ver Nee. 10:6).

4. Um filho de Col-Hoze, descendente de Judá através de Perez (ver Nee. 11:5).

Existem duas obras apócrifas que supostamente foram escritas pelo primeiro desses quatro homens de nome Baruque. (ID ND S UN Z)

BARUQUE, LIVRO DE (apócrifo)

Ver o artigo geral sobre os **Livros Apócrifos**. Na LXX, o livro de Baruque aparece após o livro de Jeremias. Juntamente com o livro de Lamentações, esse livro aparece ali como um suplemento do livro de Jeremias, embora não figure na Bíblia hebraica.

1. *Canonicidade*. O livro de Baruque é o único dos livros deuterocanônicos a figurar no catálogo do célebre quinquagésimo nono Cânon do Concílio de Laodicéia. É citado pelos pais Irineu, Cipriano, Clemente de Alexandria, Eusébio, Ambrósio, Agostinho, Crisóstomo, Basílio, Epifânio e outros. Tão grande uso testifica o grande prestígio do livro. Alguns estudiosos supõem que esse livro figurava em outros catálogos antigos, como parte da literatura de Jeremias, pois os compiladores simplesmente nunca mencionavam o livro de Baruque como independente do livro de Jeremias. Finalmente, foi citado como um livro separado, pelo Concílio de Florença; e, ainda mais tarde, pelo Concílio de Trento, que o tornou parte integrante da Bíblia de edição católica romana. Não obstante, tem havido opositores à sua canonicidade desde o princípio, e no próprio Concílio de Trento houve quem dissentisse de sua inclusão no cânon do Antigo Testamento. Jerônimo não considerava bem o livro, tachando-o de espúrio e pseudepígrafo. Juntamente com o resto dos livros apócrifos, nunca participou dos cânones protestantes. Ver o artigo sobre o *Cânon*.

2. *Autor*. O livro apresenta-se como de autoria de Baruque, filho de Nerias, o amanuense do profeta Jeremias (ver Jer. 32:12-16 e 43:3). Ver o artigo sobre *Baruque*. Visto que o livro consiste em quatro composições distintas, dificilmente Baruque pode ter sido o seu autor. Quando muito, foram incorporadas algumas tradições que podem ser atribuídas a Baruque. O mais provável é que seja apenas uma obra pseudepígrafa. Se o original foi escrito em grego, isso seria um argumento contra a autoria de Baruque, a menos que fosse uma tradução, o que também é possível. Alguns estudiosos pensam que o verdadeiro autor do livro foi uma pessoa desconhecida que, durante o reinado de Ptolomeu Lago, desejava confirmar a verdadeira religião dos judeus, diante de pessoas dessa raça que residiam no Egito, atribuindo suas próprias idéias a Baruque, a fim de emprestar um maior prestígio à obra. Vários eruditos pensam, contudo, que o original foi escrito em hebraico, mas nem por isso supõem que seja obra da pena de Baruque.

3. *Data*. Afirma-se que o livro teria sido escrito por *Baruque*, cinco anos após a queda de Jerusalém, isto é, em 581 A.C. Mas certas discrepâncias históricas, existentes no livro, mostram que sua composição é posterior a isso. Os especialistas usualmente datam o livro entre o séc. II A.C. e o séc. I D.C., embora haja poucas informações definidas para fixar qualquer data específica. A terceira seção do livro inclui material comum aos Salmos de Salomão, uma obra pseudepígrafa do século I A.C. Todavia é possível que esta última é que tenha feito citações do livro de Baruque, pelo que isso nada nos adianta quanto à data de sua composição.

4. *Unidade, conteúdo e propósito*. O livro parece compor-se de quatro composições diferentes, com pouca relação umas com as outras. a. Introdução histórica e confissão de pecado (1:1 — 3:8); b. Louvor à sabedoria, identificada com a lei mosaica (3:9 — 4:4); c. Lamentação e consolo (4:5 — 5:9); d. Uma epístola aos exilados (6:1-72). A quarta e última parte parece ser a mais antiga (pertencente cerca de 300 A.C.), ao passo que as outras porções são mais recentes, pertencentes aos séculos I e II A.C. Em suas várias porções, o livro foi escrito para promover a fé judaica entre as comunidades da dispersão (ver o artigo a esse respeito). Por isso, ali há temas como o da culpa nacional de Israel, da perfeição da lei, da esperança de restauração e da renovação da glória de Jerusalém. O trecho de Baruque 3:37, onde é dito que a Sabedoria apareceu sobre a terra, parece ser uma interpolação cristã, embora possa ser uma personificação da lei, conforme se vê também em Eclesiástico 24:7-11. A terceira seção do livro parece ter tido um original grego, ao passo que as demais seções mais provavelmente foram escritas em hebraico. (AM CH JE Z)

BARUQUE II (APOCALIPSE SIRÍACO DE BARUQUE)

O livro foi escrito originalmente em hebraico, embora tenha chegado até nós somente através de uma tradução do siríaco. Foi compilado em cerca de 130 D.C., com base em material composto em cerca de 50-100 D.C. Expõe e defende crenças do judaísmo farisaico do período neotestamentário, e assemelha-se em alguns pontos ao livro de IV Esdras. Circulou largamente entre os primeiros cristãos. Interessante é sua assertiva de que «cada homem é o seu próprio Adão», no ponto onde o livro aborda a história da queda no pecado. Insiste sobre a justificação pelas obras, e encerra alguns curiosos paralelos com o Novo Testamento.(AM)

BARUQUE III (APOCALIPSE GREGO DE BARUQUE)

Foi escrito originalmente em hebraico, mas foi preservado até nós em uma tradução grega. Data do século II D.C. Inclui idéias judaicas, influenciadas pela mitologia oriental. Fala sobre os sete céus e sua angelologia é complexa. Algum editor cristão posterior acrescentou interpolações, a fim de tentar influenciar judeus a abraçarem o cristianismo. Essa obra só foi descoberta perto dos fins do século XIX. (AM)

BARZILAI

No hebraico, «ferro» ou «forte». Foi nome de vários homens na Bíblia.

1. Um idoso e rico gileadita de Rogelim, que se distinguiu devido à sua fidelidade a Davi, quando este fugiu para a Transjordânia, perseguido por Absalão. Enviou um suprimento liberal de alimentos para uso do rei e para aqueles que o acompanhavam (ver II Sam. 17:27 e 19:32). Após o retorno de Davi ao trono, Barzilai recusou o convite de ir residir na corte real. Entretanto, sugeriu que seu filho, Quimã, fosse em seu lugar. É que as pessoas idosas, ao sentirem que seus anos de vida aproximam-se do fim, preferem permanecer em casa. Deixam que as gerações mais jovens lancem-se a aventuras. Davi, quando fez recomendações a Salomão, pediu-lhe que mostrasse bondade para com a família de Barzilai, aceitando-os como membros da casa real (ver I Reis 2:7).

2. Progenitor de uma família de sacerdotes que vieram a Jerusalém, havendo retornado do exílio com Zorobabel, em 538 A.C. Todavia, sua família não conseguiu comprovar sua ascendência, pelo que foram proibidos de participar dos alimentos sagrados e considerados poluídos. Esse Barzilai adquirira o nome por meio de sua esposa, quando se casou com

BASÃ — BASES DO SANTUÁRIO

uma mulher que era descendente de Barzilai, o gileadita (personagem tratado acima). Essa situação de embargo teria de continuar até que um sacerdote pudesse consultar o Urim e o Tumim (ver o artigo a respeito), conforme se vê em Esd. 2:16-63 e Nee. 7:63,64. O livro de I Esdras confere-lhe o nome de Jadus.

3. Barzilai, o meolatita, sogro de Mical, filha do rei Saul (ver II Sam. 21:8,9), em cerca de 1021 A.C. Seus cinco netos foram entregues aos gibeonitas, para serem mortos em vingança contra a culpa de sangue de Saul. (S Z)

BASÃ

No hebraico, «fértil» ou «frutífero». Era uma planície destituída de pedras, no lado oriental do alto rio Jordão, ladeando o mar da Galiléia. Desconhecem-se os seus limites exatos, mas aparentemente começava no monte Hermom, no norte, Salacá, no oriente, em Gileade, no sul, e em Gesur e Maacá, no ocidente. O rio Iarmuque atravessava essa região, em sua porção sul. Incluía as regiões de Argobe (ver Deu. 3:4) e Golã (ver Deu. 4:43). Ficavam ali as cidades de Edrei (ver Deu. 3:1), Carnaim e Astarote (ver Deu. 1:4 e Jos. 9:10), e Salcá (ver Deu. 3:10). No período helênico, ficavam ali, igualmente, as cidades de Hipos, Díon, Gamala e Selêucia. Moisés descreveu as cidades ali existentes no seu tempo como «fortificadas com altos muros, portas e ferrolhos», povoadas por gigantes (ver Deu. 3:5). Ao tempo da conquista da Terra Prometida, lê-se que ali havia sessenta cidades muradas (ver Deu. 3,4,5; I Reis 4:13). Após o exílio, a região foi dividida em quatro distritos: Gaulonites ou Jaulã; Auranites ou Haurã (ver Eze. 47:16); Argobe ou Traconites e Batanéia, atualmente Ardel-Bathanhey. Todas essas províncias foram concedidas a Herodes o Grande. E, quando de sua morte, a Batanéia tornou-se parte da tetrarquia de Filipe, segundo diz Josefo (*Guerras* ii.6 e *Anti.* xviii.4,6). Quando Filipe morreu, o território foi anexado à província da Síria, pelo imperador Tibério. Mas, em 37 D.C., o território foi concedido a Herodes Agripa, filho de Aristóbulo, pelo imperador Calígula. Então Herodes Agripa recebeu o título de rei (ver Atos e Josefo, *Anti.* xvii.6.10). Após a sua morte, o território reverteu a Roma, mas, subseqüentemente, foi concedido por Cláudio a Agripa II (ver Atos 25:13).

As alusões às riquezas e à fertilidade dessa terra são freqüentes nas páginas do Antigo Testamento (ver Deu. 32:14; Eze. 39:18; Isa. 2:13; Zac. 11:2; Eze. 27:6 e Amós 4:1).

A arqueologia demonstra que a área era ocupada desde o começo da era do bronze (cerca de 3200-2300 A.C.), tendo sido continuamente habitada desde então, tendo passado por todas as vissicitudes acima descritas. O antigo nome sobrevive no árabe, **el-Bathaniyeh**, e a cidade de Golã deu nome aos territórios de Gaulanites e Jaulã. É provável que os famosos carvalhos de Basã, em Eze. 27:6, ficassem na área de Jaulã, que continua sendo uma região intensamente arborizada. (AH HP WRI Z)

BASÃ HAVOTE-JAIR

Na LXX encontramos «Basã», as vilas de Jair». A alusão é a um grupo de cidades ao norte da Transjordânia. Havia um grupo de aldeias em Basã, em Argobe, que foi conquistado por Jair, filho de Manassés (ver Núm. 32:41 e Deu. 3:14). Há uma narrativa acerca dos trinta filhos de Jair, um dos juízes de Israel que fundou essas cidades, segundo lemos em Juí. 10:4. Isso explica o nome que aparece na LXX, «vilas de Jair». Em I Crônicas 2:22, o número dessas aldeias figura como de vinte e três. O mais provável é que esse número tivesse variado, de acordo com as vicissitudes da guerra. Somente em Deu. 3:14 o nome completo é dado. Nos registros assírios de Adade-Nirari (1305-1274 A.C.), os *Iauri* podem ser uma referência ao mesmo lugar. (Z)

BASCAMA

Localidade mencionada em I Macabeus 13:23, perto da qual Jônatas Macabeu foi morto e sepultado por Trifo. É chamada «basca», por Josefo (ver *Anti.* xiii.6,6). Alguns estudiosos identificam a localidade com a moderna el-Jummeizeh, a nordeste do mar da Galiléia. (Z)

BASEL, CONCÍLIO DE

Perdurou de 1431 a 1448, convocado pelo papa Martinho V, a fim de tratar do cisma dos hussitas, entre outras coisas. As cruzadas contra os boêmios (povo formador da atual Checoslováquia), não tinham conseguido subjugá-los. Esse concílio declarou possuir uma autoridade superior à do papa; mas o sucessor de Martinho, Eugênio IV, não reconheceu a reivindicação daquele concílio. Os hussitas (ver o artigo a respeito) foram atendidos em algumas de sua exigências, incluindo o cálice por ocasião da missa, e não somente a hóstia. Mas esse direito foi posteriormente negado pelo papa Pio II. O partido calistino, entre os hussitas, foi recebido na Igreja de Roma, e a base do acordo foi decidido. Eugênio foi capaz de reafirmar a superioridade do papa sobre os concílios. Mas uma revolta, finalmente, o depôs em 1439, e foi eleito um novo papa, Félix V. Com o pontificado do papa Nicolau V, a disputa foi resolvida, tendo sido abandonado o conceito de uma autoridade superior dos concílios em relação ao papa. (E)

BASEMATE

No hebraico, «fragrante». É nome de várias mulheres do Antigo Testamento.

1. Uma das esposas de Esaú (ver Gên. 26:34), filha de Elom, o heteu. Portanto, Esaú ignorou o mandamento divino para que os membros da família escolhida não se casassem com cananeus. Tal casamento causou tristeza a Isaque e Rebeca. Ada, outra das esposas cananéias de Esaú, provavelmente era uma irmã de Basemate.

2. Outra das esposas de Esaú, filha de Ismael e irmã de Nebaiote (ver Gên. 36:3). Em Gênesis 28:6-9, ela é também chamada de Maalate. Esse novo casamento de Esaú ocorreu quando ele percebeu que o casamento de Jacó com uma jovem da parentela de Abraão havia agradado a Isaque, redundando em bênção para Jacó. Essa mulher tornou-se a mãe de Reuel. Seus vários filhos com Esaú tornaram-se figuras importantes em Edom.

3. Filha de Salomão que se tornou esposa de Aimaás, um dos oficiais do governo de Salomão, cujo trabalho era prover provisões de boca para a casa do rei durante um dos meses do ano (ver I Reis 4:15).

BASES DO SANTUÁRIO

Devido à confusão criada pelas traduções, precisamos considerar três palavras hebraicas diferentes. Uma delas, que aparece em I Reis 7:50, indicava uma dobradiça de porta (sendo assim traduzida em nossa versão portuguesa). Muitas dobradiças inscritas têm sido encontradas nas escavações feitas na Mesopotâmia. Uma outra palavra hebraica indica o posto, ao lado da folha da porta, posta na dobradiça. E a terceira palavra, devidamente traduzida em português por «base», ligava entre si os postes das cortinas e das paredes do tabernáculo. Essa palavra hebraica é usada por cinqüenta e quatro vezes no Antigo Testamento. Para exemplificar, Êxo. 26:19,21,25; Núm. 3:36,37; Can. 5:15. Algumas dessas bases eram feitas de prata, e outras de bronze. (Ver Arquitetura).

BASILIANOS

São os monges da Igreja Ortodoxa que seguem a regra de São Basílio o Grande (ver o artigo), o qual foi arcebispo em Cesaréia da Capadócia. Basílio fundou um mosteiro em cerca de 356 D.C., e desenvolveu uma regra para servir de norma aos membros da comunidade. Essa regra tornou-se o modelo para outras regras posteriores, para governar os mosteiros. Foram feitas algumas revisões por São Teodoro de Estudion (ver o artigo), e sob essa forma revisada, a regra vem sendo obedecida até o presente. Visto que os hierarcas das Igrejas Ortodoxas são escolhidos dentre os monges, o monasticismo tem exercido uma influência maior no Oriente do que no Ocidente. Até mesmo na Igreja latina há alguns mosteiros basilianos. A mente grega busca a contemplação, e a Igreja Ortodoxa sempre exibiu profundo misticismo. (E)

BASÍLICA

Nos tempos romanos, as basílicas eram os mercados. Mais tarde, o nome foi dado a edifícios para assembléias públicas, tribunais de lei, etc. Eram grandes salões com naves e coxias, separados por arcos colunares e usualmente dotados de ápices (ver o artigo), que são projeções em um edifício, em uma ou em ambas as extremidades. Os primeiros templos cristãos supostamente foram construídos tendo as basílicas por modelo. Até hoje, a Igreja Católica Romana usa o termo *basílica* para indicar uma de suas igrejas de grandes dimensões. (E)

BASÍLIDES

Um gnóstico do século II D.C., que ensinou em Alexandria, companheiro de Valentino, que talvez tenha sido o mais famoso de todos os gnósticos. Não contamos com qualquer de seus escritos, mas aparentemente ele escreveu um evangelho e uma exposição sobre o mesmo, com vinte e quatro volumes.

Idéias. 1. Deus vive inteiramente fora do mundo, sendo totalmente transcendental. 2. Deus criou uma semente, o Logos ou Palavra divina. Essa Palavra contém, em si mesma, as sementes da criação, e dela é que todas as coisas manam. 3. Ele rejeitava a idéia de que Deus criou as coisas, e em lugar dele punha essa Semente-Logos. 4. A Semente Logos encarnou-se, tornando possível o drama da salvação, incluindo a restauração de todas as coisas. 5. Os sofrimentos mostram que o pecado é uma realidade; e a transmigração da alma seria necessária para solucionar o problema, a fim de que o indivíduo possa chegar à perfeição. 6. O principal ensinamento ético de Basílides era o de que os homens precisam controlar todos os seus desejos, não amando e nem odiando a ninguém—uma espécie de apatia estóica moderada.

Ver o artigo sobre o *gnosticismo*. (E P)

BASÍLIDES, EVANGELHO DE

Basílides, proeminente mestre gnóstico do século II D.C. (ver o artigo a seu respeito), segundo se lê, escreveu um evangelho com um comentário a respeito, com vinte e quatro volumes, em cerca de 130 D.C. (ver Eusébio, *Hist. Ecl.*). Não fica claro se se tratava de um evangelho de sua própria composição, ou se era um comentário seu sobre algum evangelho canônico. Fragmentos existentes são similares aos evangelhos de Mateus e Lucas. Orígenes tinha consciência da existência de tal obra (ver Homilética 1). Alguns estudiosos supõem que a obra é uma revisão de Lucas, ou então que era uma espécie de harmonia dos evangelhos, que foi arranjada a fim de satisfazer às necessidades dos gnósticos. O próprio Basílides afirmava haver recebido ensinamentos secretos da parte de Matias, embora não se saiba se isso tem qualquer coisa a ver com o seu evangelho. (AM JAM Z)

BASILIDIANOS

Nome dado aos seguidores de Basílides (ver o artigo a respeito), o qual foi um gnóstico do segundo século da era cristã e ensinou em Alexandria. Eles afirmavam que Jesus tornou-se divino no dia do Seu batismo, por João Batista, pois, a partir daquele momento, foi possuído pelo espírito de Cristo. Segundo a doutrina deles, foi nessa oportunidade que o Salvador divino, o *Nous* (mente), deu início à sua missão, mediante a pessoa de Jesus.

Uma antiga doutrina gnóstica dizia que o batismo de Jesus foi episódio mais importante que o de Sua morte e ressurreição (Jesus teria vindo com a água). O apóstolo João, em I João 5:6, corrige: «Este é aquele que veio por meio de água e sangue, Jesus Cristo; não somente com água, mas com a água e com o sangue. E o Espírito é o que dá testemunho, porque o Espírito é a verdade». Isso escreveu João porque os gnósticos também negavam que Cristo houvesse realizado a expiação dos pecados com seu sangue. Ver as notas no NTI, nessa referência, onde a doutrina é amplamente descrita. Ver também o artigo sobre o *gnosticismo*. (E NTI P)

BASÍLIO DA CAPADÓCIA

Ver o artigo sobre a **Patrística**, item 10.

BASÍLIO O GRANDE

Suas datas são 330 e 379 D.C. Foi um eclesiástico, arcebispo de Cesaréia da Capadócia, teólogo e representante do ideal monástico. Foi instrumento da criação de fórmulas que articularam a ortodoxia da Igreja grega. Era dotado de natureza mística, desejando transcender a tudo quanto era físico e ascender a Deus no espírito. Desejava viver exclusivamente para Deus. Ver o artigo sobre os *basilianos*, *capadócios* e *cenobitas*. (E)

BASTARDO

No hebraico, **mamzare**, «poluído», «misto» (Deu. 23:3 e Zac. 9:6). O grego é *nothos*, «bastardo» (Heb. 12:8). No Antigo Testamento, o termo é aplicado a filhos ilegítimos, dentro da proibição de entrarem na congregação, na primeira referência. Isso significa que os bastardos não tinham direitos de cidadania em

Israel. Na referência de Zacarias, a referência é à nação bastarda, a Síria, que não podia compartilhar da herança de Israel quanto à terra. No Novo Testamento, o vocábulo indica alguém «nascido fora do casamento», conforme a palavra era usada desde os tempos homéricos. Descreve aqueles que são rejeitados quanto à autoridade e à disciplina de Deus.

Origens do Problema. 1. Filhos nascidos de prostitutas israelitas, ou devido a contatos com prostitutas estrangeiras. A prostituição era proibida na lei mosaica, mas isso não fez com que ela desaparecesse. (Lev. 19:29; Deu. 23:17). Os filhos de tais pessoas podiam ter pais judeus ou pais pagãos, pertencentes a países limítrofes, que residiam em Israel ou nas proximidades. 2. Filhos ilegítimos, nascidos em Israel, devido a irregularidades sexuais, embora não filhos de prostitutas. O trecho de Juízes 11:1-7 mostra que havia crianças nessa situação em Israel, apesar da rigidez da lei mosaica.

Uso Metafórico. Aponta para os pseudocrentes, que presumivelmente têm a Igreja como sua mãe, embora não na realidade. Os tais objetam à disciplina do Senhor. No grego, a palavra também era usada para indicar alguma coisa espúria, falsa.

Uso Clássico Moderno. A lei canônica da Igreja Católica Romana proíbe os filhos ilegítimos de receberem ordens menores sem uma autorização do bispo. E também não podem ser admitidos às santas ordens, exceto por autorização do papa. Na Igreja Anglicana, eles não podem ser admitidos às santas ordens exceto por autorização do soberano ou do arcebispo. As igrejas evangélicas ignoram a proibição, harmonizando-se muito mais com a graça de Deus e com o espírito do evangelho, embora isso se distancie das atitudes refletidas no Antigo Testamento. Muitos dos mais notáveis ministros do evangelho têm nascido como filhos ilegítimos. A condição deles não exerce qualquer efeito sobre sua eficiência e espiritualidade. Em Israel, uma das razões para a prevalência desse preceito era a proteção da herança das famílias, pelo que a medida era econômica e prática. O problema da ilegitimidade dos filhos existe até hoje, e a legislação varia de país para país. (ID S UN Z)

BATALHA
Ver sobre Guerra.

BATALHA DOS DEUSES E GIGANTES
Uma cena imaginária que aparece no **Sofista** de Platão, descrevendo o perene conflito entre dois tipos de pensadores. «Um dos lados arrasta após si tudo quanto existe no céu e no mundo invisível, até à terra, rudemente agarrando rochas e árvores em suas mãos. Porquanto aferram-se a essas coisas, afirmando que só existe aquilo que pode ser tocado e manuseado... (eles são) homens terríveis. Aqueles que combatem contra os tais, defendem-se cuidadosamente, postados em alguma posição no mundo invisível, assegurando que a verdadeira existência consiste em certas formas incorpóreas (mundo das *idéias* platônicas), que são objetos da mente». Na filosofia, os «deuses» são homens como Platão, que acreditam no mundo invisível e o defendem, cônscios da existência imaterial. E os «gigantes» são os materialistas, como Leucipo, Demócrito, Hobbes e Carl Marx. (EP F)

BATALHÃO
Palavra que aparece em algumas versões, em Mat. 27:27 e Mar. 15:16, e onde nossa versão portuguesa diz «coorte». A alusão é à coorte italiana, um grupo de soldados romanos com cerca de seiscentos homens. Ver as notas em Atos 10:1, no NTI.

BATANEA
Nome grego aplicado a Basã, nos tempos neotestamentários. Ver Josefo, *Vida* 11 e *Anti.* xv.10.1; xv.2.1. A LXX diz Basã.

BATE-RABIM
Esse era o nome de uma porta da cidade de Hesbom (Can. 7:4). No hebraico significa «filha da multidão». No livro de Cantares de Salomão, dois poços as proximidades simbolizavam os olhos da noiva.

BATE-SEBA
No hebraico, «filha do juramento», ou então «sétima filha». Em I Crônicas 3:5, ela é chamada Bate-Sua. Era filha de Eliã ou Amiel, e esposa de Urias, guerreiro heteu ao serviço de Davi. Davi ficou fascinado com a beleza de Bate-Seba, e não pôde resistir à tentação de seduzi-la. Obteve sucesso na sedução, o que geralmente sucedia aos reis nas sociedades primitivas. Davi chegou ao extremo de ordenar que Urias fosse deixado a combater sozinho, a fim de morrer, em campo de batalha (II Sam. 11). Bate-Seba ficou grávida, e, após a morte de Urias, tornou-se uma das esposas do monarca. Mas o menino que nasceu faleceu, por juízo divino (II Sam. 12:15-18), o que foi profundamente lamentado por Davi. Porém, subseqüentemente, houve quatro outros filhos do casamento, incluindo Salomão, que sucedeu a Davi no trono (I Crô. 3:5). Quando Davi estava em seus últimos dias de vida, Adonias reivindicou para si a sucessão ao trono de Israel, mas Bate-Seba e o profeta Natã persuadiram Davi a instalar Salomão como rei (I Reis 1:5-40). Adonias pelo menos queria ficar com a bela Abisague, que fora uma das esposas de Davi, mas que permanecera virgem, como prêmio de consolação. Apresentou o pedido a Salomão por meio de Bate-Seba. Em face disso, Adonias foi executado, provavelmente porque tentou ficar com alguém que fizera parte do harém real, o que poderia ser interpretado como tentativa de obter poderes de mando. Ou talvez Salomão meramente tenha se sentido ofendido pela proposta, livrando-se assim do inconveniente representado pelo irmão mais velho. (I Reis 2:13-25). Bate-Seba é mencionada na genealogia de Jesus, em Mateus 1:6.

Nos Escritos Rabínicos. Os rabinos descreviam Bate-Seba como mulher muito bem informada, dotada de mente brilhante, de incomum beleza física. Supunham que parte da sabedoria de Salomão fora herdada e diretamente ensinada a ele, por sua mãe. (IB ID S Z)

BATE-SUA
No hebraico, «filha de Sua», ou «filha da abundância». É nome de duas mulheres, nas páginas do Antigo Testamento:
1. Forma alternativa de Bate-Seba (ver o artigo a respeito).
2. Esposa de Judá, uma mulher cananéia, mãe de Er, Onã e Selá (I Crô. 2:3). Em algumas versões, no primeiro livro de Crônicas, encontramos a tradução «filha de Sua», e não Bate-Sua.

••• ••• •••

BATH KOL — BATISMO

BATH KOL (QOL)

No hebraico, «filha da voz» (um som, um tom, uma chamada). Termo usado no Talmude, nos Targuns e por alguns escritores rabínicos, quando indicavam alguma espécie de voz, supostamente vinda de Deus ou de um de Seus representantes, transmitindo aos homens alguma revelação. Seria uma forma de comunicação inferior àquela dada através dos profetas, aos quais o Espírito de Deus instruiria diretamente. Presumivelmente distinguia-se por uma notável qualidade de tom, algumas vezes comparado a um cicio ou sussurro. Esse tipo de comunicação teria sido feita a vários personagens do Antigo Testamento, como Abraão, Moisés, Davi e Nabucodonosor. O equivalente grego, no Novo Testamento, é *phone*, e não *echo*. A Midrash e o Talmude referem-se a Bath Kol como uma voz que desce do céu. O trecho de João 12:28 diz apenas «veio uma voz do céu». Ver também Apo. 10:4,8 e 18:4.

Possíveis incidentes do fenômeno:

1. Em muitas instâncias do Antigo Testamento, se lê que Deus falou a alguém, mas não através do ministério formal de um profeta. Isso se vê no relato sobre Adão e os primeiros patriarcas. Essa voz soaria como um trovão ou como algum outro som natural, ou então como se alguém estivesse, realmente, falando. Ver Êxo. 9:23; Jer. 10:13 e Sal. 19:3.

2. A voz que foi ouvida por Nabucodonosor (Dan. 4:31). Alguns intérpretes pensam que, nesse caso, não houve um Bath Kol.

3. João Hircano passou por tal experiência, de acordo com Josefo (*Anti*. xiii.x.3), entre 134 e 104 A.C. A voz teria sido ouvida quando ele oferecia um sacrifício no templo. No Talmude babilônico Sotah (33a), e no Talmude de Jerusalém Sotah (ix.24b), a voz é especificamente chamada Bath Kol.

4. A voz que foi ouvida quando do batismo de Jesus (Mat. 3:17; Mar. 1:11 e Luc. 3:22).

5. A voz que confortou a Jesus, quase no fim de Seu ministério terreno (João 12:28).

6. A voz que foi ouvida por Paulo, por ocasião de sua conversão (Atos 9:4 e 22:7,9).

7. A mensagem recebida por Pedro em Jope, acerca de coisas limpas e imundas, abrindo as portas à missão gentílica da Igreja primitiva (Atos 10:13,15).

8. Naturalmente, o fenômeno era abusado por alguns. Muitos rabinos queriam obter orientação pessoal através dessa voz, para solucionar de seus problemas. Mas outros rabinos opunham-se a isso, preferindo a revelação escrita, com seus muitos preceitos orientadores. (Ver Test. Doze Patriarcas, Levi 18:6 e II Baruque 13:1).

Maimônides assumia uma posição bastante cética a respeito, dizendo que a imaginação dos homens pode produzir tal fenômeno. Além disso, há a considerar o problema das alucinações, tanto nos que são mentalmente desequilibrados como nos que sofrem de tensões severas. Essas tensões mentais podem produzir tanto impressões visuais quanto auditivas, conforme a psiquiatria tem comprovado sobejamente. A despeito disso, há poderes superiores, que ocasionalmente comunicam-se de maneira estranha, nada havendo de teórico ou impossível no fenômeno do Bath Kol.

Bath Qol, João 12:29: *A multidão, pois, que ali estava, e que a ouvira, dizia ter havido um trovão; outros diziam: Um anjo lhe falou.*

As duas interpretações inferiores:

1. A dos céticos e racionalistas. Esses dão uma explicação «natural». A voz teria sido apenas um trovão.

2. Outros, de natureza mais espiritual: teria sido a voz de um anjo. Uma interpretação melhor, mas ainda aquém da realidade. Assim acontece com muito da religião, que não é cética, mas que não eleva a Cristo à posição de Senhor. A lei teve anjos como mediadores (Atos 7:53), mas a graça e a verdade vieram por meio de Jesus Cristo (João 1:17).

Sempre houve e sempre haverá indivíduos cuja mente é tão terrena, tão materialisticamente orientada, que nada podem perceber do que é divino na existência humana. Porém, contrariamente a isso, Tennyson manifestou a sua atitude, segundo vemos neste seu poema:

Flor na parede gretada
Arranco-te para fora da greta,
Seguro-te aqui, com raiz e tudo, em minha mão,
Florzinha, se ao menos eu pudesse entender
O que és, com raiz e tudo, e tudo o mais,
Saberia o que são Deus e o homem.

Mostrando ainda mais especificamente como o próprio mundo testifica sobre a existência de Deus, e como a vida, o grande milagre, testifica sobre o criador, para que não mais duvidemos que a voz divina possa reverberar do céu, e como é possível o nosso contato com Deus, temos estes versos de Whitman:

Ver, ouvir, sentir são milagres, e cada porção e partícula minha é um milagre...
O menor movimento de minha mão zomba de todo o maquinismo,
E um camundongo é milagre capaz de deixar atônitos a sextilhões de incrédulos.
(Walt Whitman, *Song of Myself*, estrofes xxiv e xxi).

Assim também, noutra conexão, o grande filósofo árabe, Al Ghazzali, divertiu-se com as explicações dadas pelos químicos e pelos médicos, acerca das enfermidades, nas quais via evidências da existência de Deus, contrariamente ao pensamento popular: «Sem dúvida estão certos, cada qual em seu ramo particular de conhecimento. Não obstante, não lhes ocorre que o *Todo-Poderoso* se interessa pelo bem-estar de minha alma, e que produziu em mim uma condição tal que me faz deixar de lado o mundo e voltar-me para ele, meu criador. Não percebem eles que a enfermidade é *um laço de amor*, através do qual Deus atrai os santos para mais perto dele mesmo. Porquanto a própria doença é uma daquelas experiências pelas quais os homens chegam ao conhecimento de Deus; conforme declarou o profeta: 'As enfermidades são minhas servas e estão atadas aos meus escolhidos». (*Confissões*, Al Ghazzali).

A descrição em João 12:29 se coaduna bem com os conceitos judaicos sobre a *Bath Qol*, que, na literatura dos judeus, era «uma voz que vem do céu, procedente do meio de outra voz, como um trovão». (*Piske Tosephot* no Talmude Bab. Sanhedrim, artigo 30). É perfeitamente possível que esse conceito judaico tenha determinado a seleção dessas palavras, por parte do evangelista; mas isso de maneira alguma tem o efeito de negar a objetividade ou realidade dessa experiência, e nem que não se trata de alguma espécie de verdadeira comunicação que vem da parte de Deus Pai. (BLA ID S Z)

BATISMO

Esboço:

Introdução - Descrições Gerais

BATISMO

1. Pano de fundo cristão: o batismo de João; o batismo judaico; o batismo de Jesus.
2. Sacramentalismo: Crasso e Sofisticado
3. Batismo Institucional
4. Batismo Simbólico (ponto de vista dos Batistas)
5. Batismo Simbólico-Místico
6. Negação da Validade do Batismo
7. Batismo Judaico
8. Batismo de João
9. Batismo de Jesus
10. Batismo dos Discípulos de Jesus
11. Batismo Cristão - Significado e Modos
12. Uso Metafórico

Neste artigo, tento expor o assunto de modo geral, deixando para artigos separados questões como: «Batismo pelos Mortos», «Batismo no Espírito Santo», «Batismo Espiritual», «Batismo Infantil» e outros tópicos de menor importância, mas relacionados ao assunto.

Introdução - Descrições Gerais:

O batismo é a aplicação de água, mediante imersão, derramamento ou aspersão, com certa variedade de propósitos predeterminados, como um rito de iniciação, como um ato de purificação cerimonial, como sinal de identificação com a comunidade, como suposto elemento dos requisitos que levam ao perdão dos pecados, e, portanto, da salvação (isto é, quando o batismo é encarado como um *sacramento*—ver o artigo a respeito), ou como um símbolo de união com Cristo, no intuito de obedecer ao seu evangelho e aos seus mandamentos.

Os ritos de iniciação e purificação são antiqüíssimos, sendo comuns praticamente a todas as religiões. As purificações estavam ligadas ao nascimento, à morte, à guerra e ao contato com os mortos ou com supostos espíritos. Nas religiões primitivas, acreditava-se que a *água* envolvia alguma espécie de vida, mormente no caso de águas que manam do solo e se movem sob a forma de ribeiros ou rios. Até mesmo lagos e oceanos, que demonstram movimento à superfície de suas águas, eram tidos pelos antigos como investidos de vida. Na religião dos antigos gregos encontramos muitas alusões poéticas a tais crenças. Na Ilíada, encontramos o rio vivo, divino e personificado de Escamander, bem como as *águas cantantes* da poesia grega. Na Índia, as águas do santo rio Ganges são especialmente valorizadas como purificadoras. No culto de Ísis, o rio Nilo figurava de forma proeminente, e suas águas eram levadas até mesmo a países estrangeiros, com o propósito de servirem em ritos religiosos. Os antigos teutões e celtas tinham ritos de iniciação e purificação que envolviam o elemento água, muito antes do cristianismo haver chegado às suas terras. Os romanos davam nomes e reconheciam a paternidade através do uso da água. Entre outros povos, era praticado um certo rito de batismo com sangue e saliva.

1. Pano de fundo cristão: o batismo de João; o batismo judaico; o batismo de Jesus.

O uso do *batismo* entre os cristãos data dos primórdios do cristianismo. (Ver Atos 2:37-42). Porém, o pano de fundo dessa cerimônia remonta ao judaísmo. João Batista imergia os convertidos no rio Jordão (ver Mar. 1:4,5), como sinal de arrependimento e identificação com o novo movimento religioso. João lançou mão da idéia do batismo judaico de prosélitos. A isso, os judeus ajuntavam a circuncisão. Destarte, julgava-se que os pagãos ficavam livres da identificação com a idolatria e o paganismo. Um convertido gentio ao judaísmo imergia a si mesmo em água, para indicar a purificação da idolatria, enquanto dois oficiais judeus ficavam do lado de fora de um recinto fechado com cortinas, recitando passagens da Torah (a lei ou Pentateuco). E isso significava que naquele momento o batizando estava assumindo a obrigação de obedecer à lei.

Não sabemos se Jesus batizou ou não os seus discípulos. O que se sabe é que a tarefa de imergir, desde o começo ou desde algum tempo mais tarde, foi delegada por Jesus aos Seus discípulos (ver João 4:1,2). O ofício de Jesus era batizar no Espírito, e aos Seus discípulos foi deixado o encargo de administrar o ato simbólico.

2. Sacramentalismo: Crasso e Sofisticado.

a. *Sacramentalismo crasso*. O décimo quinto capítulo do livro de Atos mostra-nos que os judeus acreditavam que a circuncisão era necessária à salvação. E o trecho de Colossenses 2:11,12 demonstra ter havido um antigo vínculo entre a circuncisão e o batismo. Se a circuncisão ou o batismo são, realmente, necessários à salvação, e se ambos devem ser administrados a crianças do sexo masculino, então temos de admitir que um rito ou cerimônia tornou-se necessário à salvação, e que tal rito torna-se parte da experiência de uma pessoa, inteiramente à parte de sua busca, de sua vontade e de sua própria experiência espiritual. Isso não faz sentido para mim, e nem vejo tal coisa ser preceituada nas Escrituras. Mas, para alguns, assim é que deve ser. A Igreja Católica Romana faz do batismo um de seus sacramentos, isto é, um dos meios visíveis da operação do Espírito, administrados e controlados pela hierarquia romana, e sem o que a graça divina não operaria. Ver o artigo sobre os *sacramentos*. Isso significa, por sua vez, que a Igreja de Roma julga-se árbitro da salvação, despenseira da mesma, intermediária entre Deus e o homem. Naturalmente, há católicos romanos liberais que pensam que até mesmo os pagãos, que nunca ouviram o evangelho cristão, através da obediência à luz de sua consciência, recebem a *essência* do batismo, mesmo que nunca cheguem a receber o rito administrado pelos clérigos; mas, entre os católicos, isso é a opinião de uma pequena minoria.

Popularmente, propriedades ridículas são atreladas ao ato de batismo. Muitos protestantes sentem-se seguros, somente por haverem recebido o rito do batismo na infância, da parte de algum membro reconhecido do clero. No entanto, a verdade é que não há salvação sem a transformação da alma segundo a imagem de Cristo (ver Rom. 8:20), um processo altamente espiritual, operado pelo Espírito de Deus (ver II Cor. 3:18), acompanhado por uma inegável e vital santificação (ver Heb. 12:14), porquanto, sem a santificação, ninguém verá ao Senhor. Parece-me claro, confirmado na experiência diária, que esse tipo de experiência depende de um contínuo desenvolvimento espiritual, e não do fato de que alguém foi batizado na infância, na igreja certa, por alguma autoridade eclesiástica devidamente constituída. Se a espiritualidade não consegue chegar a esse alvo, então somente um ato mágico do mais extraordinário poder conseguiria obter tal façanha.

b. *Sacramentalismo sofisticado*. Além da Igreja Católica Romana, também as Igrejas Ortodoxas, muitos grupos luteranos e anglicanos, além de vários grupos evangélicos, como a Igreja de Cristo, ou pseudocristãos, como as Testemunhas de Jeová e os Mórmons, supõem que o ato do batismo é necessário à salvação. Muitos deles pensam que o batismo é um sacramento, ou seja, é um meio direto da regeneração. Todavia, uma teologia sacramentalista mais

BATISMO

sofisticada dá a entender que o Espírito Santo realmente aplica seu poder regenerador por ocasião do ato do batismo. Assim, a Igreja de Cristo crê que a regeneração só se completa por ocasião do batismo em água. Assim, sem tal cerimônia, uma pessoa estará eternamente perdida. Isso equivale ao que os judeus acreditavam no tocante à circuncisão; mas Paulo mostra-nos, no segundo capítulo da epístola aos Romanos, que tal idéia é uma falácia, porquanto a verdadeira circuncisão é a do coração, e não a da carne. Outro tanto se dá com o batismo, que representa a identificação espiritual com Cristo. (Ver o artigo sobre o *Batismo Espiritual*, onde há maiores explicações sobre esse conceito). Lamento, mas preciso ser franco. As teologias que misturam à salvação qualquer tipo de rito, são teologias primitivas. Tais teologias não percebem que os ritos são meras representações da espiritualização; são símbolos daquilo que é realizado exclusivamente pelo Espírito de Deus, jamais servindo de causa ou agente da espiritualização da alma, no que verdadeiramente consiste a salvação. As religiões primitivas, conforme temos visto na introdução, atribuem qualidades vivas a coisas como a água, a saliva e o sangue. Essas religiões também têm um caráter sacramentalista, porquanto julgam que divindades se fazem presentes e atuam beneficamente, quando seus adoradores realizam ritos religiosos.

Há certos versículos no Novo Testamento, nas edições populares, que geralmente são usados para dar apoio ao sacramentalismo, no que tange ao batismo. Exemplos notáveis são Marcos 16:16 e Atos 2:38. A simples leitura desses versículos, conforme eles aparecem nas traduções comuns, realmente dão a entender que o ato de batismo é necessário à salvação. O fato, porém, é que Marcos 16:16 não faz parte do evangelho original de Marcos; antes, é um adendo posterior, que reflete uma opinião antiga. E por que ficaríamos surpreendidos diante de tal opinião? O décimo quinto capítulo do livro de Atos mostra-nos que mesmo na Igreja primitiva, enquanto os apóstolos ainda eram vivos, muitos pensavam que a circuncisão e a guarda da lei eram necessárias à salvação. Se, por hipótese, pudéssemos assentar-nos em companhia dos apóstolos e cristãos primitivos, talvez ouvíssemos alguém dando apoio ao ponto de vista sacramental do batismo, e outros combatendo tal idéia. Além disso, muitos grandes problemas teológicos encontram-se nas páginas do Novo Testamento, não tendo sido produzidos por gerações posteriores. A questão do batismo em água pode ter sido motivo de muitos debates entre os primitivos cristãos. Todavia, Paulo, no segundo capítulo da epístola aos Romanos, deixa claro que o que tem valor é a circuncisão do coração, e não da carne. Em todas as exposições feitas por ele sobre a salvação, Paulo jamais incluiu a questão do batismo em água. Em I Coríntios 1:17, Paulo chegou a esclarecer que Cristo não o enviou a batizar, mas antes, a pregar o evangelho. Como explicar essas suas palavras, se o batismo fazia parte integrante do evangelho? Pelo contrário, o batismo deve ser aplicado a pessoas salvas, e não a fim de salvar os perdidos. Visto que Paulo, e, por conseguinte, o grupo apostólico, mantinham uma posição não-sacramental do batismo, então não podemos ser sacramentalistas. Por outra parte, se os apóstolos porventura estavam divididos sobre a questão (alguns estudiosos opinam que há versículos no Novo Testamento que indicam isso), e se os vários segmentos da Igreja cristã estão divididos sobre o assunto, então só resta uma coisa a fazer: que o leitor assuma posição, segundo aquilo que mais lhe pareça fazer sentido espiritual, e que não se preocupe em encontrar textos de prova para todo o pensamento que lhe cruzar a mente.

Quanto a Atos 2:38, a interpretação gira em torno do sentido da preposição grega *eis*, que nossa versão portuguesa traduz por «para», dentro da frase: «...para remissão dos vossos pecados...» Todos os peritos do grego «koiné» afiançam que ali, como em outros trechos similares, temos uma preposição de causa. Vale dizer que uma tradução mais fiel ao original, diria: «...em razão da remissão dos vossos pecados...» Em outras palavras, os ouvintes de Pedro deveriam arrepender-se, em face do que seriam salvos. E então, por já estarem salvos, a fim de mostrarem publicamente a sua identidade com Cristo, deveriam deixar-se batizar. (Ver *A Manual Grammar of the Greek New Testament*, Dana & Mantey, pág. 104).

Um outro suposto versículo de tendências sacramentalistas é I Pedro 3:21, que, em nossa versão portuguesa, diz: «...água, a qual figurando o batismo, agora também vos salva». Uma tradução mais clara, de um trecho confessadamente envolvido, diria algo como: «...água que, como antítipo (do livramento de Noé, por meio da água do dilúvio), agora também vos salva, uma imersão que não consiste na remoção da **imundície da carne**, mas na indagação de uma boa consciência para com Deus...» Portanto, a salvação é simbolicamente retratada pelo batismo (uma metáfora, conforme também se vê em Rom. 6:2,6). Em todo o Novo Testamento, a única outra passagem onde é usada a palavra «antítipo» é em Heb. 9:24, onde o tabernáculo terreno é o antítipo do tabernáculo celeste, que é o tipo. Em I Pedro 3:21, o tipo é a arca onde oito pessoas foram salvas. Não é a água do batismo que salva, mas estar alguém na arca da salvação, que é Cristo. Está em foco a transformação espiritual, que inclui a santificação. Igual idéia temos em Tito 3:5: «...segundo sua misericórdia, ele nos salvou mediante o lavar regenerador e renovador do Espírito Santo». Esse «lavar» fala sobre o que sucede à alma, regenerada e renovada pelo Espírito, lavagem essa simbolizada, então, pelo ato do batismo. Quanto a detalhes sobre esses conceitos, ver a exposição desses versículos no NTI. Ver também sobre João 3:5, onde se aprende que o indivíduo precisa nascer da água e do Espírito. A água representa ali a operação do Espírito, sendo símbolo da vida divina.

3. Batismo Institucional. Certas denominações cristãs pensam que exercem monopólio sobre a salvação e seus meios. Imaginam que Deus opera somente através deles. O orgulho e a arrogância dos homens são famosos, por causa de sua irracionalidade. Pensar que a fé religiosa não tem sentido, é absurdo. Mas é igualmente absurdo pensar que qualquer grupo monopoliza a espiritualidade. Todas as denominações religiosas são seitas, com sua mescla peculiar de verdade e erro. Por esse motivo é tão fácil um grupo cristão atacar a outro. É fácil encontrarmos algo *legítimo* a ser atacado em qualquer denominação, e então supormos, com base nisso, que o grupo atacado é falso como um todo. Por sua vez quem participa de qualquer grupo cristão pode encontrar algo de irracional ou absurdo na teologia de outrem, daí chegando à conclusão que somente o seu grupo está isento de erro. As cercas que os homens levantam, em nome de Deus, jamais realmente limitam a mente do Senhor. É curioso como as denominações, que são apenas seitas, atribuem-se à posição de únicos representantes de Deus, como se seus ritos fossem os únicos que abrem as portas do

BATISMO

céu. Jamais deveríamos institucionalizar a espiritualidade. O batismo torna-se institucionalizado quando qualquer grupo cristão afirma: «Nosso batismo é legítimo e salvador, em contraste com o de vocês, que é espúrio». Esses fazem do batismo cristão uma possessão só deles, da instituição deles. Por outro lado, há pessoas que não permitem que sua teologia interfira em sua espiritualidade, porque a teologia (aquilo que cremos sobre as questões espirituais), nunca equivale totalmente à real natureza da espiritualidade e da verdade espiritual. De fato, algumas vezes a teologia nem corresponde à espiritualidade.

4. Batismo Simbólico (ponto de vista dos Batistas)

Entre muitos batistas o batismo é compreendido como uma questão espiritual, e não como um mero rito. Em outras palavras, há uma grande realidade que cerca o batismo, — e que é *simbolizada* pela água. A essência do batismo não seria o rito propriamente dito, mas aquilo que é simbolizado pelo rito. Por essa razão, trechos bíblicos como João 3:5; Tito 3:5 e I Pedro 3:21 são encarados sob o ângulo espiritual, ou seja, aquilo que o Espírito de Deus opera, quando da transformação de uma alma. Segundo essa perspectiva, a água torna-se símbolo das operações do Espírito, e não um meio, e, muito menos ainda, a causa dessas operações. O trecho de Romanos 6:3 faz esse tipo de aplicação: «...ignorais que todos nós que fomos batizados em Cristo Jesus, fomos batizados na sua morte?» Ser batizado significa ter sido *sepultado juntamente com Cristo*. E também significa ter sido ressuscitado com Ele. Isso envolve imersão, naturalmente. Descemos à água e mergulhamos, simbolizando a descida à sepultura. E então voltamos à superfície do água e saímos, simbolizando a ressurreição dentre os mortos. Espiritualmente falando, isso fala de nossa *união* com Cristo, em sua morte e ressurreição. O Espírito faz isso tornar-se uma realidade mediante a nossa transformação à imagem de Cristo. No sentido negativo, devido ao fato de que Cristo *morreu para o pecado*; e no sentido positivo, devido ao fato de que Ele *ressuscitou para uma nova vida*. Essa é a essência do *misticismo* que envolve a pessoa de Cristo (ver *Cristo-Misticismo*), de estar alguém em Cristo, expressão usada por Paulo por mais de cento e cinquenta vezes em seus escritos. O aspecto mais atrativo dessa explicação sobre o batismo é que são evitados os conceitos primitivos, que sempre promovem ritos e cerimônias, como se esses ritos e cerimônias tivessem poder por si mesmos, ou como se fossem necessários para que certas coisas acontecessem. O batismo, naturalmente, simboliza outras coisas, conforme nos ensina o Novo Testamento. Há outros significados, mas esse é o mais importante de todos. Quanto a outros significados, ver o ponto (11) deste artigo.

5. Batismo Simbólico Místico

Alguns batistas (embora não cheguem a ser a maioria) não se sentem satisfeitos em pensar que o batismo e a Ceia do Senhor têm importância meramente simbólica. Eles acreditam que o Espírito de Deus faz-se presente a esses ritos. Essas cerimônias convocam o Espírito, para que Ele realize a sua obra. Esses dizem: «Senhor, estou pensando a teu respeito e obedecendo ao teu mandamento. Faz tua obra em minha alma!» Assim, apesar do batismo não salvar e nem abrir a porta para a regeneração, torna-se um sinal de busca sincera, que convoca o Espírito Santo. E quando o Espírito vem, não atua apenas por alguns instantes, mas de forma permanente. Mas, naquele exato instante, observando a intenção do crente de seguir a Cristo, ele separa aquele homem para sua obra transformadora, e começa a agir exatamente desse modo. A palavra «místico», que aparece neste título, indica qualquer contato genuíno com o Espírito Santo, de natureza sutil ou franca, em que a alma encontra-se com Deus. Por ocasião do batismo em água, a alma encontra-se com Deus, não por causa do que o batismo é em si mesmo, mas por tornar-se uma espécie de invocação a Deus. Naturalmente, o Espírito pode ser convocado sem qualquer rito, pelo que não há, nessa posição, qualquer intuito de dizer que o batismo é *a* avenida dessa convocação. Antes, é apenas uma ocasião conspícua em que o crente pode invocar o Espírito. E uma outra ocasião importante de invocação é a Ceia do Senhor. O autor desta enciclopédia nunca deixou de sentir-se espiritualmente emocionado, ao participar da Ceia, mesmo quando o sermão que a antecede é paralizador e amortecedor. Na verdade, há ocasiões especiais em que o Espírito aproxima-se de nós, porque estamos resolvidos a nos aproximarmos dele.

6. Negação da Validade do Batismo

Algumas pessoas, que costumam espiritualizar tudo, não mostram qualquer paciência com os ritos. Os hiperdispensacionalistas, supondo que os primeiros livros do Novo Testamento refletem um período de transição, só aceitam as epístolas da prisão, de Paulo como dotadas de autoridade doutrinária. E, visto que o batismo e a Ceia do Senhor não são descritos ali, supõem que essas cerimônias não tinham a intenção de prosseguir na Igreja. Naturalmente, esse ponto de vista é extremado e arbitrário. Primeiramente, porque o material das chamadas «epístolas da prisão» é bastante pequeno, e com eles ficamos reduzidos a uma base muito pequena para nosso sistema doutrinário. Em segundo lugar, tal posição é arbitrária porque as próprias Escrituras não ensinam tal coisa. Não obstante, essa posição demonstra um certo discernimento que não deve ser ignorado. É evidente que Paulo cresceu no conhecimento e no entendimento espiritual, conforme foi avançando os anos. Por essa razão, algumas doutrinas, como a da Igreja e a questão do julgamento e do destino humano final (ver as notas no NTI sobre Efé. 1:10), são melhor definidas em suas epístolas finais. Além disso, Paulo foi-se tornando mais e mais interessado em manter a comunhão mística com Cristo do que em combater os judeus, em torno da doutrina da justificação. Por esse motivo, deixamos de lado as intermináveis controvérsias que agitaram o começo do cristianismo, e passamos a demorar-nos mais no tema do conhecimento espiritual. Porém, se pudéssemos voltar à Igreja no fim do primeiro século e do começo do segundo século da era cristã, encontraríamos os cristãos observando o batismo e a Ceia do Senhor, ao mesmo tempo em que estariam lendo a epístola aos Efésios e as epístolas posteriores de Paulo.

Além dos hiperdispensacionalistas, há os quacres, que, em sua busca religiosa mística e intuitiva, simplesmente rejeitam qualquer tipo de rito ou cerimônia, como se não fossem coisas necessárias ao nosso bem-estar espiritual.

7. Batismo Judaico (Ver o artigo separado sob esse título).

8. Batismo de João (Ver o artigo separado sob esse título).

9. Batismo de Jesus (Ver o artigo separado sob esse título).

10. Batismo dos Discípulos de Jesus.

O mais provável é que os discípulos originais de Jesus, tendo sido batizados por João Batista (por terem sido seus discípulos), não foram rebatizados quando começa-

BATISMO

ram a seguir a Jesus. Mas à medida que crescia a comunidade, havia o batismo dos novos convertidos. Não há que duvidar que o batismo aplicado pelos discípulos de Jesus era idêntico ao batismo de João, isto é, batismo de arrependidos, dando a entender que os batizandos tornavam-se parte de um novo movimento religioso e rejeitavam a apostasia que se manifestava no judaísmo. O batismo judaico de prosélitos era aplicado pelo próprio batizando, que se imergia. O batismo cristão sempre teve um sujeito que imergia e um objeto que recebia o batismo. Por exemplo: «...ambos desceram à água, e Filipe batizou o eunuco» (Atos 8:38). O batismo cristão indica: a. purificação; b. identificação com o novo movimento cristão; c. sinal de arrependimento e de que a pessoa levaria a sério sua fé religiosa, como membro de um movimento reformista. Lê-se que o próprio Jesus a ninguém batizava, e que essa tarefa era delegada por Ele a seus discípulos (ver João 4:1,2). O batismo que Jesus realizava era o batismo no Espírito (ver Mar. 1:8 e a exposição desse versículo, e de Mat. 3:11, no NTI).

11. Batismo Cristão — Significado e Modos
Significado. a. União com Cristo, em sua morte e ressurreição, ou seja, a participação em sua forma de vida (ver Rom. 6:3,4). Ver o artigo sobre o *batismo Espiritual*, que fornece amplos detalhes sobre esse conceito. b. Aquela mesma referência na epístola aos Romanos mostra-nos que o batismo deve resultar em uma *nova maneira de andar*, em santidade e desenvolvimento espiritual. c. Para alguns, o batismo é um *sacramento*, um meio direto da regeneração, conceito esse que já discutimos no segundo ponto deste esboço. d. Para outros, o batismo é o *portão* de entrada à instituição que salva, o que é discutido sob o terceiro ponto deste esboço. e. Para outros, o batismo é apenas um *símbolo* da operação espiritual do Espírito, a saber, do batismo espiritual, sobre o qual falamos algo no quarto ponto deste esboço. f. Para outros, é por ocasião do batismo em água que o Espírito aproxima-se para observar o intuito e a obediência do batizando, separando-o para nele operar de modo especial. Seria o momento em que o poder do Espírito torna-se mais evidente na vida do crente, com resultados a longo prazo. Isso foi abordado no quinto ponto deste esboço. g. Para certas denominações evangélicas, como os batistas, o batismo é considerado como algo necessário para que alguém se torne membro de uma igreja local, se não mesmo da Igreja universal e mística. Seria, portanto, um rito de iniciação no discipulado cristão, expresso mediante a comunhão com a igreja local. h. O batismo é um *ato de obediência* à ordem de Cristo para que fôssemos batizados, bem como uma declaração do *intuito* de sermos seus discípulos (ver Mat. 28:18). i. Para os presbiterianos, o batismo é um sinal e selo do pacto da graça (Confissão de Westminster, art. xxviii). Portanto, mediante esse ato, a pessoa tornar-se-ia membro daquela comunidade e compartilharia do novo pacto estabelecido entre Deus e os homens. Isso significa que o batismo cristão é o equivalente da circuncisão judaica (conforme a sugestão de Col. 2:11-13). Penso que pode ser um *sinal* do pacto da graça, mas não que a pessoa se torne um dos beneficiários desse pacto. A posição presbiteriana dá exagerada significação a sinais externos e físicos. Mas a espiritualidade beneficia a alma, sem depender de quaisquer cerimônias externas. Não obstante, a nossa espiritualidade pode ser indicada por símbolos, e estes tornam-se instrutivos. j. O *pacto noaico* (ver I Ped. 3:18-22) é a contraparte ou tipo do batismo em água, que é seu antítipo. Tal como Noé e seus familiares foram salvos na arca, assim também as águas do batismo simbolizam o ato salvador de Cristo. Noé foi salvo mediante um pacto com ele estabelecido. O Novo Pacto, por igual modo, salva o crente; e as águas do batismo simbolizam esse pacto. Porém, o que realmente salva é o «batismo espiritual», o qual consiste em nossa identificação com Cristo, em sua morte e ressurreição. l. Há um outro paralelismo, no *pacto abraâmico* (descrito sob o ponto «i»), embora não devamos forçar o ponto, de tal modo que a causa da salvação seja um mero ato físico como o é o batismo em água. Lembremo-nos que Paulo destacou que a verdadeira circuncisão não é a da carne (externa), mas é a do coração (interna) (ver Rom. 2:29). Portanto, o batismo que salva é o espiritual, e não o literal. m. Há ainda um outro paralelismo, o *pacto mosaico*. (Ver I Cor. 10). O povo de Israel esteve sob a nuvem protetora, atravessou o mar em seco e comeu de um alimento sobrenatural, também bebeu de uma rocha sobrenatural, a qual Paulo diz representar Cristo. Desse modo, os israelitas participaram do pacto mosaico, tornando-se o povo que Deus livrara da servidão e ao qual concedera vida. (Ver também sobre o *novo pacto*, nesta enciclopédia). Participamos de todas as provisões que há em Cristo, e o batismo em água simboliza a passagem pelo mar, a fim de escaparmos da escravidão ao pecado; e assim chegarmos a desfrutar da nova vida. Mas o batismo em água não *realiza*, realmente, tal coisa, como a passagem pelo mar não espiritualizou o povo de Israel. (Ver os artigos sobre os pactos). n. O batismo em água proclama que houve arrependimento e perdão de pecados (ver Mat. 3:6 e Mar. 1:4). o. O batismo em água antecipa o batismo no Espírito (ver João 1:30-34; 3:5 e Atos 2:38). p. O batismo em água simboliza o poder purificador da Palavra de Deus, e, por conseqüência, da regeneração (ver Tito 3:5). q. O batismo em água é símbolo das operações do Espírito Santo (ver João 3:5). r. Contudo, o batismo em água não garante que todos os que são batizados são possuidores das realidades por ele simbolizadas (ver I Cor. 10:1 ss , onde se lê sobre a ilustração baseada em Israel, pois esse povo atravessou o mar, mas depois caiu em idolatria; ver também Atos 8:21-23; João 13:10,11 e 15:1-6).

Modos. O termo grego **bapto**, «mergulhar», deu origem à sua forma intensiva, **baptizo**, usada no Novo Testamento, e que remonta aos tempos de Homero. Ver Odisséia ix.392, onde alude ao ato de *mergulhar* um ferro em brasa, em água, a fim de temperá-lo. *Baptizo* tem vários sentidos, incluindo o de «mergulhar», «afundar», «imergir». Pode exprimir a idéia de *lavar*, como se vê em Mar. 7:4. Qualquer pessoa que se dê ao trabalho de examinar um léxico grego descobrirá que essa palavra denota imersão, ou, pelo menos, o uso de grande quantidade de água, do que obtemos outros sentidos como «avassalar», «ensopar», etc. Tentar furtar a palavra *baptizo* de seu sentido básico, «imergir», é ridículo, uma violência à língua e à história do termo. A maioria dos eruditos admite isso, mesmo quando não são membros de denominações evangélicas que imergem. Mas então, alguns encontram outras justificativas para não imergirem, usando de argumentos como: a. o modo do batismo não é importante; b. a Igreja primitiva praticava vários modos de batismo; c. as condições de clima exercem influência sobre o modo de batizar; d. havia algum antecedente judaico para a aspersão, como as cerimônias em que o sangue era aspergido. Mas, contra tais argumentos podemos observar que todo o batismo judaico dava-se por imersão. (Ver sob o ponto «1», *Pano de fundo cristão*, neste artigo).

Somente a imersão total pode simbolizar devidamente a purificação de uma pessoa de sua antiga vida, por estar em foco uma lavagem. Ninguém pode lavar uma pessoa salpicando-lhe algumas gotas sobre a cabeça. João Batista batizava onde havia «muita água» (João 3:23). Ele lançou mão de uma corrente de água, porque as águas do batismo não devem ser estagnadas. Podemos estar certos de que ele usava o modo judaico padrão de imersão, quando batizavam prosélitos. João *lavava* os convertidos. Não fazia somente suas cabeças ficarem molhadas. Os pecadores precisam ser lavados de seus pecados, e o batismo por imersão é o modo que representa corretamente essa lavagem.

O modo de batizar é importante? Uma vez que se admita que o modo original de batismo era a imersão, conforme é deixado bem claro por Paulo, em Rom. 6:3,4, com seu símbolo de sepultamento-ressurreição, a próxima questão diz respeito à importância do modo de aplicação. Tentar mostrar, conforme faz Unger em seu Dicionário Bíblico, que: a. mergulhar não é um sentido primário de *baptizo*, mas um sentido derivado; e b. que há outros simbolismos para o batismo, que não subentendem imersão, como a morte e a crucificação (ver Rom. 6:3), o revestir-se de Cristo (ver Col. 3:27) e a circuncisão (ver Col. 2:11-14), conforme diz a Zondervan Pictorial Encyclopedia of the Bible, é por demais ridículo para levar a sério. Em primeiro lugar, a observação de Unger é completamente infundada. Em segundo lugar, é óbvio que o batismo envolve muitos simbolismos, a maioria dos quais nada diz sobre o modo, se é por aspersão, imersão ou derramamento. Porém, o próprio simbolismo que diz respeito ao *modo* é aquele que projeta a idéia de imersão. Espanta-nos ver como os homens, na promoção de seus preconceitos, que aprenderam em seus seminários e denominações, esquecem-se completamente do que é esclarecido nos dicionários e do que ocorreu no decurso da história, que são precisamente os dados que nos deveriam guiar na interpretação da questão do modo de batizar. Quão facilmente os homens apelam para os *sofismas*, quando correm o perigo de ter de alterar alguma idéia querida, mas relutam em fazê-lo. Naturalmente, isso não sucede somente no caso do batismo. Os batistas, que podem regozijar-se quanto à sua interpretação correta sobre o modo de batizar, deveriam chorar ao considerarem o que têm feito, ao interpretarem o sentido da descida de Cristo ao hades (ver I Ped. 3:18-20), ou quando eliminam o poder da missão de Cristo de salvar além do sepulcro, conforme se aprende em I Ped. 4:6, ou quando desconsideram a plena extensão da missão de Cristo (ver Efé. 1:10). Já o disse antes, e creio estar dizendo uma verdade: Todas as denominações são seitas que promovem seus sistemas particulares, que envolvem verdades e erros. Todas as denominações evangélicas podem regozijar-se e chorar, dependendo das idéias que estiverem defendendo.

Porém, voltemos à questão da *importância do modo* do batismo. Certamente não se trata de uma questão que requeira uma guerra a respeito. E nem devemos arrastar a discussões acaloradas, que geram o ódio e se esquecem da lei do amor, que é o fator mais importante na vida cristã. Tal questão também não é suficientemente importante para tornar-se motivo de orgulho, ou para a usarmos como medida para aquilatar a verdade de qualquer denominação evangélica. Posso estar equivocado aqui, como em qualquer ponto de meu credo. Porém, visto que a «imersão» concorda mais com o sentido e com o simbolismo do batismo, do que qualquer outro modo, do ponto de vista simbólico, lingüístico e histórico, não erram aqueles que batizam por imersão. Na língua portuguesa a palavra «batizar» perdeu seu sentido original de «imergir», para adquirir o sentido popular de aplicar uma cerimônia cristã, a qual recebeu esse nome. Porém, não podemos firmar doutrinas com base no sentido popular adquirido posteriormente pelas palavras. A Igreja Ortodoxa Grega, cuja Bíblia é grega, batiza por imersão, por ser esse o sentido da palavra no grego.

Conheço um ministro batista que, devido a certas circunstâncias, freqüentava uma igreja presbiteriana e a ajudava. Mostrava-se muito ativo naquela igreja, e era bom amigo do seu pastor. Quando um de seus filhos chegou à idade de entrar na universidade, ele o enviou ao mesmo seminário presbiteriano onde o pastor daquela igreja se formara. Porém, quando outros de seus filhos tiveram de ser batizados, ele pediu ao pastor presbiteriano que usasse o modo de imersão. O pastor presbiteriano concordou, e o batismo foi feito por imersão; e depois disse o pastor presbiteriano: «Essa foi uma experiência nova para mim!» A situação inteira foi muito instrutiva. Não houve nenhuma divisão por esse motivo. Foi mantida a cooperação no trabalho do evangelho. Não houve conflitos devido as implicações teológicas do modo de batismo. Mas, quando teve de ser feita uma escolha, o modo preferível foi utilizado.

Batismo Infantil. Essa questão é tratada no artigo *Batismo dos Crentes* e *Batismo Infantil*.

12. Uso Metafórico.

Sob o ponto n° 11, «Batismo Cristão—Significados e Modos», alistei dezessete significados, vários dos quais são simbólicos. Acrescento aqui mais alguns significados:

a. Josefo, em *Guerras* 4.3.3 diz que os refugiados que fugiram para Jerusalém *inundaram* a cidade. Em outras palavras, vieram **em grande número**, como se fosse um dilúvio. E para dizer isso, ele usou a palavra grega *baptizo*. Esse é um uso muito instrutivo, porquanto mostra que a palavra grega em questão indica quantidade, sem importar se aplicada à água ou metaforicamente, a alguma outra coisa.

b. O trecho de Marcos 10:38 ss (paralelo em Luc. 12:50) refere-se ao *batismo* do qual os discípulos de Cristo compartilhariam. Isso é uma alusão a seus futuros sofrimentos, que haveriam de avassalá-lo como um dilúvio. E o trecho de Salmos 42:7 diz algo similar: «...todas as tuas ondas e vagas passaram sobre mim». De forma não-expiatória, os discípulos de Cristo podem compartilhar de seus sofrimentos, conceito esse que figura em Filipenses 3:10. Ver também I Pedro 4:13.

A lei do amor. Como sucede em qualquer controvérsia, mostramos a nossa espiritualidade discutindo as idéias pacificamente e no espírito de tolerância, reconhecendo que todos nós somos culpados de nossos erros de crença e prática. (AM B BM BRO FL S UN Z)

BATISMO DE CRENTES

Consideremos cuidadosamente os pontos abaixo:

1. O batismo em água foi obviamente ordenado aos crentes (ver Mat. 28:19). Ninguém põe isso em dúvida. Há crentes que acreditam que somente o batismo deles é legítimo. Jesus ordenou que Seus discípulos fizessem discípulos e os batizassem. Nunca os ensinou a batizarem infantes ou não convertidos. (Ver o artigo sobre o *Batismo Infantil*, que apresenta argumentos favoráveis e contrários a essa doutrina).

BATISMO DE CRENTES — BATISMO DE JESUS

2. O trecho de Atos 2:38 mostra-nos que o batismo em água seguiu-se à pregação e à conversão dos ouvintes. A maioria das pessoas batizadas havia recebido a circuncisão, mas isso nem foi levado em consideração. Se o batismo equivale à circuncisão, por que o batismo foi aplicado a circuncisos? Lemos que o eunuco etíope desejou ser batizado, o qual recebeu com base em sua fé em Cristo, após ouvir a exposição do evangelho por parte de Filipe (ver Atos 8:36 ss).

3. No caso de batismos de famílias inteiras, encontramos a mesma exigência de conversão prévia. O evangelho era pregado, as pessoas criam no mesmo, e em vista disso eram batizadas. Não há qualquer menção de batismo de infantes, em todos os textos que relatam batismos de famílias inteiras. (ver Atos 10:45; 16:32 ss e I Cor. 1:16).

4. A *teologia do batismo* encontra-se em Romanos 6:3,4. É nesses trechos que chegamos a entender o sentido básico desse rito. O batismo simboliza a identificação com Cristo, em sua morte e ressurreição. O batismo deve ser aplicado a convertidos. O batismo em água só poderia ser aplicado a infantes se pudéssemos aceitar que eles já fossem convertidos e já estivessem em união com Cristo. No entanto, isso é inteiramente estranho ao contexto das declarações de Paulo. A idéia mais distante de sua mente era a que as crianças, por meio do batismo, chegavam a adquirir tais privilégios. Paulo estava falando sobre o que é mister para que os crentes professos vençam o pecado. (Quanto a comentários completos sobre essa questão, ver o artigo sobre o *Batismo Espiritual*).

5. É verdade que o trecho de Colossenses 2:11 ss vincula o sentido da circuncisão ao batismo. Mas ali Paulo fala sobre a santificação, sobre a participação na santidade e na nova vida, coisas que só se aplicam a pessoas convertidas e que estão procurando seguir a trilha do discipulado cristão. Nesse texto bíblico não há o menor indício de que tais coisas eram esperadas da parte dos infantes, e nem há ali qualquer tentativa de promoção do rito do batismo em substituição a circuncisão.

6. O interesse de Jesus pelas crianças que lhe foram trazidas, para que as abençoasse, não nos encoraja a pensar no batismo de infantes (ver Mar. 10:13 ss). Sabemos que o evangelho pode ser compreendido e aceito até mesmo por crianças; se uma criança converter-se, ante a pregação do evangelho, cremos que ela tem o direito de ser batizada. Mas um infante, que ainda nem começou a falar, e, portanto, não tem consciência de pecado e não pode converter-se, não pode ser candidato ao batismo em água.

7. *Exposição bíblica*. Fiquemos exclusivamente com as Escrituras. Que o leitor apanhe sua concordância e que examine todas as referências atinentes ao batismo. Então averiguará estes pontos: a. não há na Bíblia qualquer menção a batismo de infantes. b. O batismo em água está reservado a pessoas convertidas. É um erro supor que quando o evangelho é pregado em algum novo lugar, que então é próprio para batizar aos crentes, e que, uma vez estabelecida uma comunidade evangélica, que naturalmente envolve crianças pequenas, haja condições para a administração do batismo infantil.

8. Os argumentos baseados na história, que incluem citações dos pais da Igreja, em favor do batismo de infantes, são duvidosos, pelos seguintes motivos: a. antes de tudo, quanto à exatidão desses argumentos; e b. mesmo que esses argumentos sejam exatos, nossa fé e nossa prática deve alicerçar-se exclusivamente sobre as Escrituras Sagradas.

BATISMO DE FOGO

A expressão faz parte das palavras de João Batista, em Mateus 3:11, em alusão ao batismo no Espírito Santo, que Jesus haveria de conferir, em contraste com o batismo em água, aplicado por ele, no tocante ao seu poder e eficácia. Todavia, a expressão também é aplicada em relação ao fogo do julgamento, e é assim que a passagem em Mateus é compreendida por alguns estudiosos. Ainda outros, entretanto, têm aplicado o termo ao «purgatório», como fase preparatória para o crente entrar no céu. As Escrituras, porém, reconhecem a existência de apenas dois lugares para a alma: o céu e o hades. E, por ocasião do juízo do trono branco, o hades entregará as almas que ali se encontram; estas, uma vez reunidas a seus corpos ressurrectos, serão lançadas na geena, o verdadeiro inferno. Ver o artigo sobre o *purgatório*. Outros estudiosos, ainda, aplicam a expressão «batismo de fogo» aos sofrimentos e provações que os crentes precisam passar, em conexão com o discipulado cristão. De modo muito ridículo, grupos cristãos antigos, como os hermenianos e os seleucianos pensavam que esse fogo deveria ser compreendido de forma literal, associado ao rito do batismo em água. Valêncio fazia com que as pessoas atravessassem chamas, de forma literal. Heráclio aplicava um ferro em brasa à orelha das pessoas batizadas, marcando-as de forma permanente, para que não se esquecessem de seus votos batismais. (S)

BATISMO DE JESUS

Está aqui em vista o batismo que Jesus recebeu, administrado por João Batista (ver Mat. 3:13-17). Vários significados têm sido conferidos a esse acontecimento, a saber:

1. Ele foi feito pecado por nós, e assim teria de tomar a posição de pecador necessitado do *batismo de arrependimento*. Jesus recebeu esse rito porque tomou a posição de pecador sob a lei. Todavia, não é provável que um motivo tão complexo, teologicamente falando, fosse a idéia que Jesus tivesse em mente, ao aproximar-se de João, a fim de ser batizado.

2. Jesus fez isso para justificar e *valorizar* a mensagem de João. É possível que isso tenha feito parte de suas razões.

3. Outros intérpretes, sem base alguma, dizem que ele veio «santificar a água para servir de limpeza mística do pecado» (Inácio). E Agostinho disse que Cristo «veio para batizar a água, ao ser batizado nela».

4. Outros pensam que Cristo foi batizado para *instituir* o batismo como um rito de sua Igreja.

5. Outros pensam que Jesus foi batizado para dar *exemplo* da necessidade do batismo ao povo.

6. Para os gnósticos, o batismo de Jesus assinalou o instante em que foi possuído pelo *aeon*, ou poder angelical, ou, como alguns deles supunham, pelo Espírito de Cristo. Desde então, o corpo de Jesus passou a ser manipulado por esse elevado poder angelical, a fim de realizar a elevada missão de que fora encarregado, embora sem a identificação da pessoa entre Jesus e esse poder. Por essa razão, os gnósticos davam valor ao batismo de Jesus, mas não à expiação por meio de seu sangue (ver I João 5:6). Ainda segundo os gnósticos, esse poder teria abandonado a Jesus por ocasião de sua morte, razão pela qual ele soltou seu grito de desespero: «Pai, por que me abandonaste?» Portanto, os gnósticos rejeitavam qualquer idéia de identificação das naturezas divina e humana em Cristo Jesus, mas

BATISMO DE JOÃO BATISTA — BATISMO DO ESPÍRITO SANTO

mantinham um rígido *dualismo* (ver o artigo a respeito).

7. Os modernos teólogos liberais dizem (pelo menos alguns deles) que a idéia de que Jesus era impecável e que sempre teve consciência de seu ofício messiânico, são invenções da igreja, e não idéias ensinadas pelo próprio Cristo. Assim sendo, Jesus teria vindo receber o batismo de João pelos mesmos motivos que outras pessoas vieram, isto é, declarar-se arrependido e desejoso de identificar-se com a reforma de João.

8. Podem ser combinados vários elementos viáveis para formar uma idéia possível: O batismo de Jesus, ainda que administrado por João, não é paralelo ao batismo normal de João, exceto que Jesus *tomou o seu lugar* junto à minoria crente, mostrando que reconhecia a autoridade e a missão de João Batista. Esse batismo marca a unção e a aprovação de Jesus, da parte do Pai, tal como no caso dos sacerdotes do Antigo Testamento. Isso aprovou o ministério de Jesus, à semelhança daqueles sacerdotes (ver Êxo. 29:4-7). No rito do batismo há um aspecto que depende do batizando, e que indica que ele está abandonando a velha vida e entrando em uma nova vida. Jesus estava fazendo exatamente isso, e talvez quisesse demonstrar esse fato. A despeito de não ter uma vida pecaminosa para abandonar, estava realmente iniciando uma vida nova, com uma missão específica, sob o poder e a orientação do Espírito. (AM S UN)

BATISMO DE JOÃO BATISTA

Trataremos aqui do batismo administrado por João Batista. Alguns supõem que João Batista fazia parte do grupo dos *essênios* (ver o artigo a respeito). Sabe-se que os essênios consideravam apóstata o resto do judaísmo. João apareceu em cena como o *novo Elias*, para chamar um remanescente fiel. Ele os chamava ao arrependimento e à renovação espiritual. Pregava que em breve viria o reino de Deus (ver o artigo) e a necessidade dos homens prepararem-se para o mesmo (ver Mat. 3:1 *ss*). Também surgiu em cena como o precursor do Messias, cônscio de que teria de haver um novo movimento religioso se a missão do Messias tivesse de alcançar bom êxito. O arrependimento era atitude necessária, e era simbolizado pelo batismo em água. Não há que duvidar que João Batista imitava o batismo judaico de prosélitos, que requeria imersão em água, representando a purificação da anterior vida pecaminosa. Enquanto a pessoa se imergia na água, trechos da lei eram lidos, dando a entender que ele tencionava fazer da lei o guia da nova vida na qual a pessoa estava entrando.

O batismo de João, estritamente falando, não era cristão. O batismo cristão simboliza principalmente a nossa união com Cristo, em sua morte e ressurreição (ver Rom. 6:3,4). Os motivos pelos quais João batizava nada tinham a ver com as razões dos judeus, porque ele estava iniciando um novo movimento religioso, que eventualmente proveu o núcleo para a emergente Igreja cristã. João tratava os judeus como pagãos, requerendo um batismo condicionado à conversão a um novo caminho. João impunha esse tipo de batismo para reforçar sua mensagem de que a verdadeira espiritualidade não depende do legalismo e nem da identificação com alguma nacionalidade. João censurava os fariseus por dependerem de sua nacionalidade, como garantia da salvação. (Ver Mat. 3:8,9; Luc. 3:7,8). Por igual modo, o *batismo* cristão, sem importar o grupo cristão que o esteja administrando, se for considerado como *institucional*, não se

revestirá de qualquer valor, pois esse valor depende da espiritualidade autêntica.

Contudo, o movimento de João Batista não era apenas o rompimento com um antigo sistema. Também era um palco onde teria início um novo sistema, fundamentado sobre Jesus Cristo. Sem dúvida, João tinha consciência de que algo de extraordinário estava acontecendo, e que um povo especial precisava ser preparado para isso. João predisse o aparecimento de Alguém que viria após ele mesmo, que batizaria no fogo, e não na água; e assim antecipou um notável avanço no plano de Deus (ver Mat. 3:11 e João 1:26). Podemos estar certos de que a maioria dos discípulos de João não foi rebatizada quando começaram a seguir a Cristo. Mas aqueles que não tinham tomado conhecimento da vinda do Messias e sua obra, foram rebatizados como uma instrução no verdadeiro discipulado cristão, conforme se vê em Atos 19:1-7.

BATISMO DE SANGUE

Tertuliano dava esse nome ao martírio ocorrido antes do batismo, bem como à morte dos mártires, de forma geral. Ele e outros pais da Igreja pensavam que o martírio tinha a eficácia de purificar o pecado. Por causa disso, o martírio era recomendado entre os cristãos, e alguns deles chegavam a procurá-lo propositalmente. Gregório Nazianzeno refere-se a um batismo de martírio e sangue, com o qual o próprio Cristo foi batizado. Houve exageros que foram associados ao batismo de sangue, no caso de crentes. As pessoas tendiam por olvidar-se que somente em Cristo há perdão para nossos pecados, sem importar quão recomendável seja a disposição de morrer pelo nome de Cristo. (Ver I João 1:7; Apo. 1:5 e 7:14). (NTI S)

BATISMO DO ESPÍRITO SANTO

Esboço

I. História das Operações do Espírito
II. A Obra do Espírito e de Seu Batismo
III. O Batismo do Espírito e seu Relacionamento Com Línguas
   A. Confronto do uso das línguas em Atos e em I Coríntios
   B. Variedades antigas e modernas do falar em línguas
   C. Avaliação do fenômeno das línguas
IV. O Batismo do Espírito em I Coríntios 12:13

Atos 2:4: *E todos ficaram cheios do Espírito Santo, e começaram a falar noutras línguas, conforme o Espírito lhes concedia que falassem.*

Aqui é historiada por Lucas a doação *do dom do Espírito Santo*. O tema de que não muito depois da ressurreição de Cristo Jesus a comunidade dos discípulos foi robustecida por um derramamento especial do Espírito Santo, é um fator constante no N.T., tanto nas profecias antecipatórias, que aparecem nos diversos evangelhos, como no livro de Atos e nas epístolas dos apóstolos, com um fato realizado. (Ver Atos 10:44 e I Crô. 10:13 para tratamentos do assunto).

Os evangelhos sinópticos encerram essa promessa da descida do Espírito quase que em seus primeiros lances, através da mensagem de João Batista. (Ver Mat. 3:11,12; Mar. 1:8 e Luc. 3:16,17). O evangelho de João contém igualmente essa promessa, embora alicerçada em fonte informativa diferente. (Ver João

BATISMO DO ESPÍRITO SANTO

1:33). Quanto a explicações sobre as fontes informativas utilizadas pelos evangelhos, ver o artigo sobre cada um deles· e quanto a um tratamento especial relativo às fontes informativas usadas pelos autores sagrados dos evangelhos sinópticos, ver o artigo intitulado o *Problema Sinóptico*.

I. História das Operações do Espírito

1. Nas páginas do A.T., o Espírito Santo não era outorgado como dádiva *permanente*. Aparentemente isso sucedia até mesmo no caso dos profetas, embora seja seguro pensarmos que os homens mais profundamente espirituais daquele período possuíam o dom do Espírito por tempos mais dilatados que o comum. (Ver Mal. 2:15 e Sal. 51:11). A operação do Espírito Santo, nos tempos do A.T., era equivalente ao que sucede no período neotestamentário, pelo menos em termos gerais, exceituando o fato de que ele então não habitava permanentemente no crente, conforme sucede aos crentes do N.T., segundo é expressamente ensinado nas Escrituras. No A.T., o Espírito Santo é retratado a lutar com os homens (ver Gên. 6:3), a iluminá-los (ver Jó 32:8), a dar-lhes forças especiais (ver Juí. 14:6,19), a conceder-lhes sabedoria (ver Juí. 3:10,6:34), a outorgar-lhes revelações (ver Núm. 11:25 e II Sam. 23:2), a prestar-lhes instruções sobre a sabedoria, o entendimento, o conselho, o poder, a bondade e o temor de Deus (ver Isa. 11:2) e a administrar-lhes a sua graça (ver Zac. 12:10).

2. Durante a vida terrena do Senhor Jesus, a atuação do Espírito Santo acompanhava as linhas gerais estabelecidas no A.T., com a exceção de que houve então a promessa da vinda do Espírito Santo como *alter ego* de Cristo, como quem haveria de dar continuidade à presença e à obra de Cristo no mundo, como agente de sua personalidade. (Ver João 14:15-17,25,26; 15:27; 16:5-15). O Senhor Jesus ensinou aos seus discípulos, quando de sua presença entre os homens, que o Espírito Santo lhes seria dado em resposta às suas orações. (Ver Luc. 11:13).

3. Quando do encerramento de seu ministério terreno, Jesus prometeu que ele mesmo rogaria ao Pai, a fim de que o dom do Espírito Santo fosse *amplamente outorgado* aos seus seguidores. (Ver João 14:16,17).

4. Na noite do dia em que ressuscitou, Cristo deu aos seus discípulos, no cenáculo, um bafejo *preliminar* do Espírito Santo, como promessa e garantia do dom mais completo que se seguiria, ao soprar sobre eles, provavelmente no mesmo cenáculo. (Ver João 20:22).

5. No dia de Pentecoste, o Espírito Santo desceu sobre todos quantos estavam reunidos no mesmo cenáculo, num total de cerca de cento e vinte pessoas. Não se há de duvidar que essa dádiva do Espírito envolveu mais do que os doze apóstolos, segundo fica subentendido no trecho de Atos 2:14, como também na profecia de Joel, conforme Simão Pedro mencionou em seu sermão, como interpretação daquela extraordinária ocorrência, que acabara de suceder. (Ver Atos 2:16-21 e Joel 2:28-32). Essa profecia revela-nos como o Espírito haveria de ser derramado sobre toda a carne, de modo *pleno* e transbordante. Os cento e vinte irmãos reunidos no cenáculo, pois, foram os primeiros a experimentar isso.

6. O restante da história diz respeito a como esse dom *se expandiu* a ponto de abarcar todos os povos: tanto aos judeus (evidentemente através da imposição de mãos, como método principal — ver Atos 8:17 e 9:17) como aos gentios (sem imposição de mãos, mas assim exerceram fé — ver Atos 10:44 e 11:15-18).

7. *Todo crente* deve possuir o Espírito Santo, pois de outro modo nem crente é. Isso pelas seguintes razões: a. Todo crente é nascido do Espírito (ver João 3:3 e I João 5:1). b. Todo crente é habitado pelo Espírito (ver I Cor. 6:19; Rom. 8:9-15; I João 2:26 e Gál. 4:6), e é assim que o crente se torna templo de Deus. c. Todo crente possui o que se chama de batismo do Espírito (Ver I Cor. 12:12,13; I João 2:20,27). d. Esse batismo é o selo de Deus que lhe assegura a obra final e completa da graça divina em sua vida. (Ver Efé. 1:13 e 4:30).

8. Mas nem todo crente é *igual* aos demais, na questão da experiência da presença habitadora do Espírito Santo ou da vida espiritual que ele nos concede. (Ver Atos 2:4 em comparação com Atos 4:29-31). Esses passos bíblicos mostram-nos que até mesmo os discípulos originais, que miraculosamente receberam o Espírito Santo, no dia de Pentecoste, depois, receberam-no *novamente*, de maneira notável. Com base nessa informação, podemos supor que *não há limites* para o que o Espírito Santo pode e quer fazer na vida do crente, dependendo das circunstâncias e da obediência pessoal daquele a quem o Espírito infunde. Outrossim, nem todos os seguidores de Cristo são iguais na questão dos dons que o Espírito oferece.

II. A Obra do Espírito e Seu Batismo

A promessa da descida do Espírito Santo é mais amplamente desenvolvida no evangelho de João, nas declarações do Senhor Jesus sobre o divino *paracleto* (que vide) que se encontram nas seguintes referências: João 14:15-17,25,26; 15:26,27 e 16:5-11,12-15. Os discípulos seriam um povo especial, dotado de um poder todo particular, vindo do alto, unidos através da influência e da presença habitadora do divino Consolador, Conselheiro e Ajudador. A vinda do Espírito Santo habitador criaria as seguintes bênçãos vantajosas ao movimento cristão e a cada crente individualmente:

1. Unidade
2. Pureza
3. Santidade
4. Aumento do conhecimento espiritual
5. Observância do novo mandamento, o qual nos recomenda amarmos uns aos outros.
6. *Poder, interno e externo* — o qual conduziria os crentes à transformação de seus seres, conforme a imagem moral e metafísica de Cristo (ver as notas sobre Rom. 8:29 no NTI), transformação essa que leva o crente a participar da natureza divina (ver II Ped. 1:4); poder externo *no ministério*, que deveria ter um alcance universal entre os homens.
7. *Manifestação do variegado fruto* do Espírito Santo, conforme aprendemos em Gál. 5:22,23. Aqui se encontra o desenvolvimento prático e diário do indivíduo, no homem interior; a sua santidade pessoal, a sua transformação na natureza divina moral e ética, o que provoca a transformação metafísica.
8. *Esse enchimento do Espírito Santo* é igualmente acompanhado pela outorga de diversos *dons* do Espírito, os quais são conferidos ao crente individual para que este se torne um instrumento especial de serviço, tanto no seio da igreja como fora dela. Ver o artigo sobre os *Dons Espirituais*.

Ora, tudo isto pode ser descrito como um batismo, pois esse rito se presta admiravelmente bem para descrever a influência total do Espírito Santo na vida do crente. (Ver Atos 1:4). No batismo em água, o corpo inteiro do crente é imerso na água, e todos os seus membros são cobertos. A esse respeito, traçamos as seguintes considerações:

BATISMO DO ESPÍRITO SANTO

1. Isso simboliza quão *completa é a benéfica influência* do Espírito Santo, o que é aqui expresso pelas palavras «...cheios do Espírito Santo...» O ser inteiro do crente torna-se sujeito à influência do Espírito, e é possuído por ele. Idealmente falando, nenhum aspecto da personalidade do crente deveria ficar isento do controle do Espírito, tal como nenhuma porção de seu corpo deixa de ser imersa na água, quando do batismo.

2. Em alguns contextos bíblicos, o batismo implica em *purificação*. E essa é, igualmente, uma das funções do Espírito Santo na vida do crente.

3. Outrossim, o batismo fala da *identificação* do crente com Cristo, em tudo quanto ele fez, foi, e é. Note-se que essa identificação não envolve meramente o que Cristo fez, mas também o que ele é no presente. Começamos a fazer o que ele fez, porque nós estamos transformados no que ele é, em sua natureza moral, como também na própria composição de sua natureza essencial. Deus está duplicando Cristo nos crentes, no sentido mais literal possível. Essa completa identificação do crente com o Senhor Jesus é simbolizada pelo batismo.

4. O batismo se tornou símbolo da *vida transformada* do crente, em que ele assumiu uma perspectiva de vida inteiramente nova e está seguindo um novo destino, porquanto possui agora uma lealdade totalmente diversa. A vinda do Espírito Santo possibilitou os homens a realizarem esse elevadíssimo alvo, não apenas teoricamente, mas também na vida diária. Tais indivíduos ficam estragados para o mundo, pois são renovados, transformados e tornados cidadãos daquele outro mundo, mais elevado e melhor que o nosso.

5. O trecho de I Ped. 3:21 emprega o vocábulo «batismo» para referir-se à *totalidade da salvação*; porque assim como Noé e a sua família passaram através das águas do dilúvio (um batismo) e assim como foram preservados em vida no meio das águas (no meio de seu batismo) também em Cristo o crente é salvo em meio a este mundo turbulento, sendo conduzido à segurança e à inteira salvação que há na pessoa de Cristo. Está em foco a purificação do indivíduo; porém, mais do que isso ainda é simbolizado aqui. O trecho de I Ped. 3:22 alude à ascensão de Cristo, ficando nisso subentendido tudo quanto ele obteve, mediante a sua ascensão e subseqüente glorificação, para os seus seguidores. Nisso consiste a salvação completa, pois haveremos de participar de sua herança e de sua natureza. O batismo do Espírito Santo, pois, é o que nos garante isso. Em seu sentido mais lato, fica subentendido muito mais do que a purificação e a preparação para o serviço, pois o crente individual é permeado pelo Espírito, e nesse processo se torna uma criação inteiramente nova.

III. O Batismo do Espírito e Seu Relacionamento com Línguas

A. Confronto de uso das línguas em Atos e I Coríntios.

1. No livro de Atos, foram falados idiomas humanos, revertendo, por assim dizer, a maldição da confusão das línguas, imposta em Babel.

2. As línguas, quando do Pentecoste, tiveram um efeito evangelizador. Possibilitaram que alguns poucos ensinassem a tantos em tão pouco tempo. Todavia, também serviram de sinal da realidade da descida do Espírito.

3. É possível, entretanto, que, quando do Pentecoste samaritano (Atos 8:14 e *ss*, se línguas foram faladas naquela oportunidade) e do Pentecoste gentílico (Atos 10:44 e *ss*), que essas línguas tivessem sido um sinal de poder e de prova da descida do Espírito, pois não mais havia a necessidade de línguas com vistas à evangelização. Portanto, nesses casos, temos uma razão diferente para o fenômeno, sendo indubitável que as línguas então faladas não foram entendidas e nem interpretadas. Seu intuito não era nem evangelizar e nem ensinar.

4. Em I Coríntios, as línguas são essencialmente didáticas em sua natureza, tanto para aquele que as fala (pois assim lhe é possível aprender intuitivamente certas realidades espirituais), como para outras pessoas, quando algum intérprete explicava o que fora dito. (Ver I Cor. 14:2 e *ss*).

5. Em I Coríntios, as línguas também serviam de sinal para os incrédulos (I Cor. 12:28-31), demonstrando a presença do poder espiritual no seio da igreja, onde pode suceder o que é miraculoso e onde as vidas humanas podem ser transformadas.

6. As línguas ocupam um lugar bastante inferior em comparação com a profecia (I Cor. 14:1 e 19). Foram classificadas entre as «coisas infantis» do desenvolvimento espiritual (I Cor. 13:11). Paulo recomendava que se buscassem dons superiores a isso, I Cor. 12:31.

7. *Tipos*. a. línguas reais, Atos cap. 2; b. sons inarticulados, ou talvez uma mistura de vários idiomas, palavras e frases individuais, juntamente com sons que não podem ser identificados com qualquer idioma; c. idiomas angelicais. Abaixo oferecemos notas sobre as «línguas», na tentativa de dar descrições e avaliações mais completas.

As Línguas no Livro de Atos — A posição do fenômeno das línguas, no livro de Atos, obviamente é mais elevada do que aquela atribuída pelo apóstolo Paulo em suas epístolas. O livro de Atos parece ter sido a confirmação do recebimento do Espírito Santo (entre outros sinais), pois em cada caso em que o evangelho era anunciado em algum novo lugar, depois do Pentecoste no cenáculo, e em cada instância em que um novo grupo de pessoas recebia o evangelho, era também batizado no Espírito Santo, com o acompanhamento da experiência das línguas; pelo que também parece que o autor sagrado tencionava que entendêssemos que essa experiência era a validação visível da genuinidade do batismo do Espírito Santo. (Ver Atos 2:4; 10:46 e 19:6). Deve-se observar, por semelhante modo, e em contraste com as línguas descritas por Paulo, que no livro o fenômeno aparece como o falar em idiomas estrangeiros, que podiam ser compreendidos pelos presentes que normalmente falavam os mesmos. (Ver Atos 2:6,11). É óbvio que isso tem por intuito indicar que a *confusão das línguas*, quando da construção da torre de Babel, por causa da revolta dos homens contra Deus, foi aqui *revertida*. Por igual modo, a universalidade do cristianismo foi destacada por esse fenômeno, o que é um tema tanto dos evangelhos como também deste livro de Atos. O Espírito Santo outorgou poder à igreja cristã a fim de que a mensagem de Cristo fosse levada a todas as nações, a fim de que pudesse ser uma gloriosa realidade, a redenção da humanidade, em grande escala.

B. Variedades do falar em línguas, antigas e modernas.

1. Meios naturais (puramente humanos).

a. Transe hipnótico: tem sido demonstrado em estudos realizados, que, sob a hipnose, o indivíduo pode experimentar um grande aumento na capacidade psíquica como a telepatia, as curas, e algumas vezes, o conhecimento prévio. As línguas podem ser

BATISMO DO ESPÍRITO SANTO

faladas por efeito telepático, em que uma mente toma emprestado de outras, e a hipnose facilita tal experiência.

b. O falar simultâneo: trata-se de uma forma de telepatia. Nos anos de 1966 e 1967, apareceu um homem na **televisão norte-americana**, que podia duplicar, simultaneamente, qualquer coisa que outra pessoa falasse, mesmo que o fizesse em idioma estrangeiro ou que estivesse lendo um material inteiramente desconhecido. Além disso, a distância não fazia qualquer diferença. No momento exato em que tal material fosse lido, ou que outra pessoa falasse, sem importar em que idioma, aquele homem era capaz de duplicar tudo com perfeição. (Registrado no artigo intitulado em inglês: «Simultaneous Speaking», na revista Fate, de julho de 1967).

O autor desta enciclopédia conhece pessoalmente um caso em que certa mulher, quando de visita ao Brasil, embora nunca tivesse estudado o português, era capaz de acompanhar, cantando, hinos que fossem entoados em português, simultaneamente, embora não fizesse a menor idéia do que estava cantando, e sem entrar em qualquer estado hipnótico. Era pura telepatia, o que, conforme estudos feitos em laboratório, tem sido demonstrado ser uma propriedade comum a todas as raças humanas.

c. Estados especiais, como estados *febris*: em um relato fidedigno, contou-se como uma arrumadeira, que trabalhava em certa universidade, ao sofrer de febre alta, podia falar em grego ou latim. As investigações feitas descobriram que ela costumava trabalhar na sala ou próximo da sala onde um professor de idiomas clássicos tinha por hábito caminhar para lá e para cá, repetindo passagens de autores clássicos. Essa forma de línguas apenas trazia do subconsciente o que lá foi entesourado pelo ouvir. O estado especial da febre, podia ativar aquele estado novamente.

d. Participação na mente universal: certos estudos (apoiados por séculos de teoria filosófica), indicam que há um depósito universal de conhecimento. A mente humana individual, sob certas circunstâncias (sobretudo em estados alterados da consciência), pode tomar algo por empréstimo desse fundo comum, e ao assim fazê-lo, em alguns casos, pode falar um idioma antigo ou moderno, que nunca foi estudado.

Não sabemos dizer se a Mente Universal é pessoal (envolvendo seres inteligentes) ou impessoal, como se assumisse a forma de alguma energia que registra pensamentos, tal como um disco pode registrar sons. As especulações sobre esse fundo comum de inteligência, retrocedem até pelo menos o tempo de Anaxágoras, 500 A.C.

A história demonstra que o fenômeno das línguas com freqüência se tem manifestado inteiramente à parte da fé religiosa, e sem intuitos religiosos de qualquer espécie. Trata-se de um fenômeno estranho, que a *psique humana pode produzir* por meios puramente naturais. Os estudos feitos em laboratório, demonstram que há capacidades telepáticas no homem, e a experiência demonstra que as línguas podem não ser outra coisa além de uma espécie de ginástica mental.

e. Freud. Afirmava que algumas vezes as línguas não passam de palavreado sem sentido, produzido propositalmente com a finalidade de autoglorificar quem as fala.

2. Línguas demoníacas (desnaturais). Alguns casos, bem documentados, mostram que, nas igrejas, algumas vezes as línguas exprimem blasfêmias e obscenidades. Em alguns desses casos, pois, podemos ter línguas «naturais» que operam desde as profundezas da mente humana depravada. Em outros casos, por certo, forças espirituais estranhas se apossam dos homens (até mesmo no seio da igreja cristã), usando-os para proferirem suas blasfêmias.

3. Línguas angelicais. Se as línguas podem ser línguas de anjos — conforme nos diz I Cor. 13:1 — então parece lógica a suposição de que podem ser inspiradas pelos anjos. Isso poderia fazer parte dos ministérios angelicais mencionados em Heb. 1:14. Os anjos poderiam, nesse caso, inspirar e usar os dons espirituais. Quiçá alguns de nossos homens mais poderosos sejam aqueles que possam manter-se próximos de seus anjos guardiães, recebendo deles o impulso.

4. Línguas sobrenaturais. O Espírito Santo pode inspirar línguas nos crentes, como um sinal para os incrédulos ou com propósitos didáticos, bem como para a edificação daquele que as fala.

C. Avaliação do fenômeno das línguas

1. Não há qualquer razão dogmática para pensarmos que as línguas e outras manifestações espirituais *tenham o propósito* de desaparecer da igreja cristã, no esquema divino, ou que tais manifestações não se revistam de grande valor na igreja moderna. Esse tipo de raciocínio parece ter-se derivado da tentativa de fazer nossas doutrinas *se adaptarem* àquilo que *praticamos atualmente*, e não àquilo que deveríamos ser e praticar em nossas igrejas. Sem dúvida, tal raciocínio representa um erro, por mais comum que seja o mesmo. Entretanto, os homens agem assim, até mesmo em relação às Escrituras, que os homens afirmam ser seu guia nas questões de fé e prática. Por exemplo, as Escrituras que versam sobre o estilo das vestes e do corte de cabelos das mulheres cristãs são variegadamente interpretadas, dependendo da *prática* que o intérprete particular *aceita* ou *tolera*. Se a esposa de um pregador qualquer usa cabelos curtos (contrariamente às recomendações de I Cor. 11:6,15), tal pregador geralmente expõe alguma explicação retorcida sobre esses versículos, preferindo passar adiante, apresentando razões vazias de sentido, ao passo que, se costuma praticar outras recomendações bíblicas, expõe uma interpretação clara sobre as mesmas. Nada existe de mais comum entre os homens, incluindo os evangélicos, do que fazer Deus e as Escrituras se conformarem àquilo que é praticado, e não à prática conformar-se àquilo que Deus e as Escrituras estipulam.

I Cor. 13:8 não serve de texto de prova de que as línguas pertenciam só à época apostólica. Ver ponto 8, a seguir. Este texto fala sobre a *Parousia*, não sobre o cânon do Novo Testamento.

2. No entanto, a busca indiscriminada e ignorante do fenômeno das línguas e de outros dons miraculosos, na igreja cristã, evidentemente abre o caminho para a *invasão* por parte de *espíritos estranhos* na igreja, o que tem convertido um grande segmento da mesma em centros espíritas tão-somente, enquanto os homens, ignorantemente, atribuem tudo quanto ali sucede à influência do Espírito Santo. Isso é evidenciado pelos seguintes fatores: a. a *baixa qualidade* dos dons, que com freqüência são inferiores àquilo que geralmente se aceitaria da parte de Deus; b. em muitos casos o fato óbvio de que a *possessão demoníaca* se tem tornado — um grave problema em tais igrejas, subentendo que os espíritos que inspiram ali o fenômeno das línguas, são os mesmos que precisam ser expulsos, posteriormente.

3. Não se há de duvidar que os crentes concordam

BATISMO DO ESPÍRITO SANTO

que as línguas e outros dons espirituais seriam *desejáveis* se fossem sempre verdadeiramente dados pelo Espírito Santo, conservados dentro dos seus limites apropriados, isto é, enfatizados, quanto à sua importância, na ordem das instruções do apóstolo Paulo, nos capítulos doze e treze de sua primeira epístola aos Coríntios. Como se conseguiria realizar isso, dentro da confusão e do ludíbrio provocado pelos espíritos malignos que evidentemente estão vinculados a essas manifestações, — se empenhando em confundir as mentes e as ações dos homens, é o verdadeiro problema, e não se o dom das línguas é uma experiência válida e possível.

4. Sob as atuais circunstâncias, é proposição extremamente dúbia aquela que assevera que o batismo do Espírito Santo *só* pode ser conferido através da experiência das línguas. O batismo do Espírito Santo, segundo ensina Paulo, destina-se a todos os crentes. Todos os crentes são possuidores da presença habitadora do Espírito, de conformidade com as afirmações desse apóstolo. (Ver I Cor. 12:12,13; João 3:3,6; I João 5:1; I Cor. 6:19; Rom. 8:9-15; I João 2:26; Gál. 4:6 e I João 2:20,27). Porém, se estivermos falando sobre a mesma experiência mística especial, que *capacita* os crentes a servirem ao Senhor, ou a aumentar sua percepção e utilidade espirituais, e chamarmos a isso de «batismo», o que é um emprego perfeitamente válido do termo, então é óbvio que nem todos os crentes são assim batizados. Além disso, o livro de Atos não indica dogmaticamente que a experiência do batismo do Espírito Santo é obrigatoriamente acompanhada pelo falar em línguas (apesar de ser fácil deduzir-se isso com base nas declarações do livro); e certamente tal doutrina não é claramente ensinada em qualquer das epístolas de Paulo. *Deus pode agir como quiser*. Se ele quiser encher e outorgar poder a alguém, de acordo com o estilo historiado no livro de Atos, pode fazer tal coisa; e quem poderia opor-se ou contradizer ao Senhor? E se ele quiser agir de outro modo no caso de alguns, está no direito de fazê-lo. O que dificilmente pode ser negado é que todos nós precisamos de experiências espirituais especiais e elevadas, de conformidade com a orientação do Espírito Santo, visando tanto a nossa purificação como o nosso fortalecimento espiritual.

5. Pode-se dizer que a posse do fenômeno das línguas é uma experiência disponível para muitos membros de igrejas evangélicas atuais, porquanto o fenômeno abunda por toda a parte. Porém, ter uma experiência válida do falar em línguas, *conferida pelo Espírito Santo*, talvez seja mais difícil e raro do que ousaríamos imaginar.

6. A interpretação que indica que a compleição do «cânon» do Novo Testamento eliminou a necessidade (e a realidade dos dons do Espírito para os tempos modernos) se baseia numa interpretação *errada* de I Cor. 13:10 (Mas, quando vier o que é perfeito, então o que é em parte será aniquilado). O exame honesto do contexto, mostrará que a *parousia* é o que é «perfeito», em suas obras, i.e. «a segunda vinda» de Cristo, quando «conhecerei plenamente, como também sou plenamente conhecido» (vs. 12 do mesmo capítulo). O *«cânon»* do Novo Testamento não se encontra entre os assuntos do capítulo. A observação de que os dons, no correr da história, desapareceram, não é um argumento dos livros sagrados, nem uma prova daquilo que *«deveria ter acontecido»*. O próprio crescimento da igreja se baseia no uso dos dons segundo Efé. cap. 4. Isto implica que a igreja que precisa crescer, precisa dos dons.

7. Mas *praticamente* falando, por mais que observamos o atual movimento carismático, menos achamos que este movimento, *como um todo*, é inspirado por Deus. Tumultos e desordens dificilmente recomendam o movimento para nada falar sobre a óbvia influência maligna que muitos sofrem. Os dons miraculosos seriam desejáveis se fossem dados verdadeiramente pelo Espírito de Deus.

Conclusão

8. Embora não exista qualquer razão dogmática (como uma prova das Escrituras) para demonstrar que o dom das línguas deveria ter desaparecido da igreja, depois da era apostólica, achamos bem possível que o processo histórico espiritual tenha *ultrapassado* esta forma de expressão espiritual. I Cor. cap. 13 mostra que no tempo da *parousia* (segunda vinda de Cristo) os dons do Espírito — como manifestos no primeiro século — vão desaparecer, dando lugar para uma modalidade de espiritualidade mais elevada. Isto já pode ser o caso, em nossos tempos. Desde o princípio o dom das línguas se mostrou sujeito a uma variedade de abusos, e por causa disto, é possível que o Espírito não mais inspire este dom. Espíritos ainda podem dar estas inspirações e o espírito humano é capaz de inspirá-lo, sem a ajuda de qualquer força exterior. O problema não é se existe ou não o fenômeno das línguas. O fenômeno existe, a despeito de muitos casos de fraude. Mas a experiência do fenômeno não prova que é o Espírito Santo que inspira a prática. O fenômeno pode acompanhar uma experiência espiritual válida e *poderosa*, ou pode ser fraudulenta ou fingida. Parte do movimento carismático representa o *oculto* na igreja, parte não. As línguas podem se originar de um truque *apto* de forças malignas, ou podem partir do próprio Espírito.

9. Que a igreja precisa dos dons espirituais é óbvio. Mas estes dons podem se manifestar sem o *modus operandi* do primeiro século, que sempre foi sujeito a muitos abusos.

10. No lugar de uma *restauração* de alguma coisa duvidosa, devemos preferir um *avanço* na nossa espiritualidade que preservará os dons espirituais, mas que evitará os abusos que tinham no primeiro século. Os dons podem se manifestar sem línguas e profecias. Eles podem ser os meios de uma transformação radical da própria alma, fazendo a pessoa mais útil no seu serviço na comunidade.

11. O movimento carismático é por demais complexo para receber uma única explicação. Estamos observando o bem e o mal neste movimento: estes dois princípios estão ativos nele. Precisamos julgar cada caso individualmente. Mas o movimento *como um todo* não me impressiona como se fosse uma grande obra do Espírito.

IV. O Batismo do Espírito de I Coríntios 12:1.

Pois em um só Espírito fomos todos nós batizados em um só corpo, quer judeus, quer gregos, quer escravos, quer livres; e a todos nós foi dado beber de um só Espírito.

A. Declaração.

Do que Consiste o Batismo Referido Neste Texto?

1. Não se trata do batismo que infunde poder, aludido em Atos 2:4.

2. Não é a mesma coisa que o *batismo espiritual* de Rom. 6:3, o qual fala da identificação espiritual com Cristo, em sua morte e vida ressurrecta.

3. Não é idêntico ao batismo *em água* (que vide).

4. Também não é o batismo em água como *sacramento*. Não há poderes regeneradores no batismo em água (ver as notas sobre isso, em Atos 2:38).

BATISMO ESPIRITUAL

5. Antes, é o poder do Espírito, *o qual une a todos os homens*, sem importar sua raça ou estado anterior, escravos ou livres, pagãos ou santos, moldando-os em um só corpo. A influência do Espírito é que os *transforma e une*, conferindo-lhes uma mentalidade espiritual e um só estado metafísico. Faz deles uma só entidade espiritual.

a. Esse ato do Espírito é retratado como «imersão» em um «elemento comum», da mesma maneira que, no batismo em água o indivíduo é imerso em água literal. Essa imersão fala de «saturação». Todos aqueles que são assim batizados ficam sob a influência do Espírito, sob seu poder e suas graças.

b. Essa imersão faz Cristo tornar-se o Senhor de todos, a Pessoa em redor de quem todos estão reunidos.

c. Todos os indivíduos em quem o Espírito habita, são realmente convertidos (ver Rom. 8:9 e I Cor. 6:19). Isso lhes proporciona uma espiritualidade comum. Esse é um elemento necessário nesse batismo de união.

B. Detalhes.

Qual é o batismo referido neste texto? Existe aquele poder unificador do Espírito Santo, o qual habita em todos os crentes. (Ver Rom. 8:9 e I Cor. 6:19). Sua influência geral e preenchimento da igreja cristã inteira se chama de «batismo», porquanto nisso os crentes são imersos e completamente cobertos, tal como se verifica no caso do batismo em água. No Espírito há influência. Isso envolve todos os membros. E deve-se dizer que alguns supostos membros, que não são assim «batizados», não são convertidos a Cristo sob hipótese alguma. Esse batismo derruba por terra as fronteiras humanas ordinárias, criadas por diferenças de raça e de posição social, tornando todos os membros dotados de um só espírito, de uma só mente, de um só propósito, de um único destino, pertencentes todos ao mesmo Senhor, estando todos igualmente no processo da transformação segundo a sua imagem. Portanto, a unidade orgânica se faz completa, e o corpo começa a assumir a natureza de Cristo, aquilo que o cabeça exige do mesmo. Por causa da imersão no único Espírito, da influência e do poder de sua operação, é criada uma unidade essencial, tanto como fato quanto como expressão. Mas, onde falta isso, pode-se duvidar que houve qualquer batismo.

A interpretação *sacramental* desta passagem deve ser rejeitada. O *batismo* aqui aludido não é o batismo em água, e nem nas Escrituras há qualquer pensamento de que o batismo em água confira o Espírito. (Ver notas expositivas, no NTI, sobre o fato de que o batismo não é a fonte do dom do Espírito, ver Atos 2:38). Paulo sempre se mostrou um místico; e suas doutrinas sempre foram místicas, e não de natureza sacramental. Naturalmente, a menção de «batismo» leva-nos a pensar em água; e isso propositadamente, a fim de ilustrar a verdade focalizada com a natureza daquele rito. Por semelhante modo, a idéia de «beber de um Espírito» bem poderia ser uma alusão à Ceia do Senhor. Mas Paulo, de forma alguma dizia que esses *sinais externos* realmente transmitem as verdades simbolizadas. Assim é que um crente poderia passar eternamente sem batismo em água e sem participar da Ceia do Senhor, e continuar possuindo as coisas ali simbolizadas, a saber, a união no Espírito, com sua influência e permanência, e o seu poder transformador, que produz Cristo no íntimo. Mas tudo isso ocorre através de meios místicos, e nunca sacramentais.

BATISMO ESPIRITUAL

Temos diante de nós o **tema central** do sexto capítulo de Rom., aquele que promete a vitória sobre o pecado, a saber, o tema do *batismo espiritual*.

O batismo espiritual consiste da união espiritual com Cristo, em sua morte e ressurreição, juntamente com tudo quanto isso significa para o homem. O batismo espiritual é a «realidade simbolizada», da qual o batismo em água é o «sinal» ou símbolo externo e físico.

A fé não é uma fantasia ou uma crença cega, sem base alguma nos «fatos». Antes, une-se ao poder espiritual e vivo; e o conceito do *batismo espiritual* diz-nos «como» isso sucede.

Já declaramos, de modo geral do que consiste o batismo espiritual. Façamos agora algumas adições a isso, esclarecendo tais conceitos de maneira ainda mais específica:

O que o batismo espiritual não é:

1. *Não é a justificação*. Paulo deixa o tema de justificação no quinto capítulo desta epístola, embora, conforme mostram as notas expositivas sobre Rom. 3:24,26, a justificação não consiste apenas da declaração forense de posição aceitável diante de Deus; antes, isso envolve a semente viva daquilo que denominamos de «santificação», a saber, a glorificação. (Ver as notas expositivas em Rom. 3:24 no NTI quanto a esclarecimentos sobre essa questão). O batismo espiritual inclui a justificação mas é uma realidade mais ampla.

2. A mais comum interpretação «não-sacramental» do batismo, no sexto capítulo da epístola aos Romanos, consiste em identificá-lo com o batismo do Espírito Santo, referido em I Cor. 12:12,13. Mas aquele batismo, que consiste em «união de judeus e gentios», formando o único corpo de Cristo, não é o tema do sexto capítulo da epístola aos Romanos. A leitura das notas anteriores, onde o «batismo espiritual» é caracterizado de forma geral, nos convencerá de que o conceito do batismo espiritual é muito mais amplo e extenso do que a idéia da «união» dentro do corpo de Cristo. Naturalmente, esses conceitos estão relacionados entre si e se justapõem. Mas o batismo espiritual envolve muito mais, teológica e experimentalmente, do que o batismo que «une em um corpo» a todos os crentes.

3. Estritamente falando, não é a mesma coisa que a *regeneração*, que está em foco no sexto capítulo da epístola aos Romanos. Contudo, a regeneração é uma idéia tão *lata* que, naturalmente, inclui aspectos do que se poderia chamar de batismo espiritual; de fato, esse conceito é tão amplo que inclui quase todas as doutrinas cristãs. A fé, o arrependimento, a conversão e a glorificação são tudo idéias que naturalmente fazem parte da «regeneração», porque isso subentende não apenas o passo «inicial» da conversão, mas também tudo quanto está envolvido em nossos seres, nascidos nas esferas celestiais como filhos de Deus, para participarmos da glória do Filho. Portanto, o batismo espiritual não pode ser separado do conceito da regeneração; mas faz parte da mesma. Ou então é uma diferente maneira de contemplar essa realidade, embora expresse os mesmos conceitos gerais.

4. O batismo espiritual não é a *presença habitadora do Espírito*. Mas essa presença é a *força ativa* que possibilita a união com Cristo, em sua morte e ressurreição. Poderíamos expressar a relação entre a presença habitadora do Espírito e o batismo espiritual, afirmando que essa presença é o «modus operandi» do batismo referido no sexto capítulo da epístola aos Romanos.

BATISMO ESPIRITUAL

5. O batismo espiritual, tema que está diante de nós, neste sexto capítulo também não é a mesma coisa que o batismo *em água*. O batismo em água de modo algum poderia efetuar aquilo que Paulo diz ser realizado pela união com Cristo. Naturalmente, o batismo em água está bem definidamente em foco, neste capítulo. Pois este é o «sinal» simbólico do batismo espiritual, o qual é a «realidade simbolizada». O batismo em água aponta, em simbolismo vívido, os dois principais aspectos da nossa união espiritual com Cristo: a união em sua morte (a descida para a água, como se fora um sepulcro), e a união em sua nova vida (a saída da água, como se fora uma vida nova, que escapa do sepulcro). Alguns intérpretes ficam muito aquém do sentido tencionado neste capítulo, ao deixarem entendido ou mesmo declararem abertamente, que a ordenança do batismo «comunica» graça ao participante. Essa é a posição da «religião sacramental», a qual é tão errada quanto a «religião legalista», embora seja óbvio que muitos homens bons e santos tenham sido «sacramentalistas».

Os **teólogos sacramentalistas**, porém, evitam os excessos dos cristãos comuns de tendências sacramentalistas. Procuram evitar qualquer implicação do que é «mágico», como se tivesse isso, poder espiritual. Antes, o Espírito Santo, ao contemplar a obediência do batizando, confere-lhe as graças espirituais necessárias, embora não transmita sua graça para aqueles que repelem o batismo em água. Exceções a isso são possíveis quando o ato do batismo em água é impossível, como se deu no caso do ladrão arrependido, na cruz. Essa espécie de «sacramentalismo», na realidade é uma forma de «misticismo», contra o que não podemos levantar objeções violentas, a não ser salientar que fazer depender a transmissão das graças divinas, pelo Espírito Santo, a qualquer ato físico, como o do batismo em água, certamente não concorda com a teologia paulina em geral. Nas notas abaixo, procuramos dar uma explanação sobre o *significado do batismo*; e o leitor é convidado a examinar essas notas expositivas. (Ver também as notas expositivas sobre Atos 2:38 no NTI quanto a comentários adicionais sobre a «dificuldade sacramentalista»).

O grande sacramento do judaísmo era a circuncisão; e Paulo a equipara, de modo geral, com o batismo cristão, em Col. 2:11,12. Contudo, o segundo capítulo da epístola aos Romanos mostra-nos que o «sinal externo», ato físico, não é a verdadeira circuncisão (ver Rom. 2:28,29). A verdadeira circuncisão é a «operação espiritual», efetuada sobre a alma. Portanto, o «batismo em água» não é o batismo real, embora certamente seja seu *símbolo*, tal como a circuncisão física era o sinal da operação espiritual, no A.T., sinal de que alguém fora separado para Deus e purificado de sua velha natureza. O exame cuidadoso do trecho de Atos 15:6 e *ss* no NTI, e a consulta às notas expositivas naquele ponto, deverá ser o suficiente para convencer o leitor que apesar dos sacramentos e ritos poderem ser símbolos e veículos apropriados da fé cristã, não podem ser sua substância, e nem podem participar dessa substância. A fé paulina não é nem «legalista» e nem «sacramentalista», e, sim, «mística». Em outras palavras, as realidades da fé cristã são transmitidas mediante o contacto da alma com o Espírito de Deus. Assim, pois, apesar deste capítulo envolver definidamente o batismo em água, a verdade é que a grande vitória sobre o pecado e a participação na vida ressurrecta de Cristo não são atribuídas a isso, e, sim, àquilo que o batismo em água simboliza, isto é, o «batismo espiritual».

6. O batismo espiritual não consiste da mera *identificação federal* com Cristo, contida na declaração forense divina. O batismo espiritual é muito mais que a «imputação forense». Também envolve isso, mas inclui a «transmissão» de uma experiência real, que comunica tudo quanto é forensicamente imputado.

7. O batismo espiritual não se limita ao processo da *santificação*. Mas é verdade que o batismo espiritual *deve incluir* a santificação, porquanto, no capítulo à nossa frente, esse batismo é muito envolvido na «feitura» de homens santos; e é a isso que chamamos de santificação. Ver I Tes. 4:3 quanto à nota de sumário sobre a «santificação» no NTI. Ver também o artigo sobre *Santificação*.

Do que consiste o batismo espiritual?

1. *Sua definição básica*. O batismo espiritual é a «coisa simbolizada» pelo «sinal» do batismo em água. É a participação mística em tudo quanto está envolvido na morte e na ressurreição de Cristo. Envolve o processo de «espiritualização» do Espírito Santo, dentro do que, antes de tudo, ele transforma as nossas naturezas morais, para que venhamos a participar da vitória de Cristo sobre o pecado; e, em segundo lugar, é aquela transformação da natureza básica que nos leva a participar, de maneira bem literal, na própria forma de vida e na natureza de Cristo. Desse modo, tudo quanto a ressurreição e a glorificação de Cristo indicam e podem efetuar potencialmente, é conferido aos remidos.

2. A fim de sermos ajudados em nossa compreensão sobre o «batismo espiritual», notemos os «níveis de conceito do batismo»:

a. O ponto de vista físico-literal-mágico. Não as explicações teológicas, mas nas explanações «amadorísticas», alguns cristãos sacramentalistas expõem um conceito que nada é senão uma forma de mágica. Supõem eles que, de alguma maneira, a água literal do batismo está carregada de poder divino; e assim, de forma «mágica» (embora nunca empreguem esse vocábulo), quando alguém entra em contacto com essa água muito especial, ocorrem transformações espirituais em seu ser, ou, pelo menos, a alma é beneficiada, devido ao reconhecimento dado por Deus.

b. Indivíduos sacramentalistas de idéias mais sofisticadas deixam de lado o conceito «mágico», mas insistem que, sem o batismo literal, em água, não podem ser transmitidas pelo Espírito as graças divinas, como a da regeneração. Nossas objeções a esse ponto de vista têm sido esboçadas nas notas expositivas acima.

c. O ponto de vista *simbólico-místico* do batismo. Este artigo defende a idéia de que o batismo em água é um «símbolo» da comunhão mística interior do Espírito de Deus com a alma remida. O batismo real, tal como a circuncisão verdadeira, é a operação feita sobre a alma, nada tendo a ver com o corpo. É aquilo que o Espírito Santo faz à alma e em benefício dela—identificando-a com Cristo, em sua morte e ressurreição. Já que o batismo místico começa na fé e na conversão, as suas operações *antecedem* ao sinal simbólico, e existem separadamente do mesmo. O «sinal» se cumpre no batismo em água, não a fim de pôr em processo o movimento do batismo espiritual, mas a fim de declarar pública e particularmente, que Cristo é agora o Senhor da vida daquela pessoa.

A comunhão mística da alma humana com o Espírito *divino* faz o homem participar na *natureza divina*, II Ped. 1:4.

BATISMO ESPIRITUAL — BATISMO INFANTIL

d. Porém, se o Pai e o Filho participam infinitamente dessa forma de vida, com sua natureza e atributos, os filhos de Deus participam disso de modo *finito*. E isso significa que apesar dos filhos terem a mesma natureza do Filho, isto é, o mesmo «tipo» de natureza (exaltados muito acima da natureza angelical, por exemplo), a *extensão* em que participam disso é bem menor. Assim deverá ser para sempre, ainda que a própria eternidade sirva de meio para ir diminuindo essa diferença. O «batismo espiritual», pois, ensina-nos que devemos participar da vida de Cristo. E aqui estamos explicando o quanto está envolvido nisso. Trata-se de uma glorificação eterna, pois a ressurreição será o começo da glorificação. As notas expositivas sobre Atos 2:32,33 no NTI mostram que a menção da ressurreição, no N.T., quase sempre antecipa a glorificação subseqüente. Ver o artigo sobre a *Glorificação*.

e. Se mergulharmos um vaso no oceano, não poderá conter o oceano, mas antes, o oceano o conterá. Mas poderíamos ir aumentando as dimensões do vaso, para que vá contendo porção cada vez maior das águas do oceano. Imaginemos que esse vaso tenha a mesma natureza do oceano. O vaso poderá ir aumentando eternamente de tamanho, contendo mais e mais do oceano. Desse modo, terá a natureza do oceano, mas também irá sendo cheio do oceano. É isso que nos ensina o trecho de Efé. 3:19, de maneira não metafórica. É isso que está envolvido no lado positivo do «batismo espiritual», do ponto de vista de «longa distância».

f. *A vida ressurrecta*, por conseguinte, envolve a «transformação moral»,um viver segundo os «valores celestes», um viver conforme a inspiração celeste, já que a vida ressurrecta é a modalidade de vida que existe nas esferas celestiais. Todavia, a vida ressurrecta é, igualmente, a atual espiritualização da alma humana, e não apenas aquela imensa glorificação que ocorrerá nos mundos eternos. E tudo isso é operação do Espírito Santo, mediante seu contacto direto com a alma remida, ou seja, trata-se de *um processo místico*.

3. Prosseguindo agora, armados de uma descrição específica do que está envolvido no «batismo espiritual», salientamos que, antes de tudo, isso envolve a participação em tudo quanto é salientado na morte de Cristo, porquanto «fomos sepultados com ele».

a. Tudo quanto está envolvido na expiação (que vide), no sangue de Cristo, entra aqui em foco. Trata-se da correta posição «forense» em Cristo, mediante um decreto divino; mas também é a operação da santidade em nós, de tal maneira que a «correta posição» se torna real na experiência do crente. Portanto, envolve a «justificação», e a «santificação». Por meio da morte de Cristo vêm os meios de santificação (ver I João 1:9).

b. A morte de Cristo destruiu parcialmente, como um fato real e presente, embora tenha destruído completamente, em sentido potencial, os poderes do reino de Satanás, que são os poderes da maldade, ver Cor. 2:15.

c. A morte de Cristo destruiu o poder da lei sobre nós, como uma autoridade condenadora. Rom. 8:2 e Col. 2:14.

d. A morte de Cristo proporciona-nos *os meios da comunhão* positiva com o Senhor Deus, o que conduz à santidade e à correta exposição diante dele, por causa daquilo que somos, e não meramente por causa daquilo que Deus declara forensemente em nosso favor. (Ver Col. 1:20-22).

e. Os «meios» ou o *«modus operandi»*, que torna real para nós, tudo quanto está envolvido na morte de Cristo, são a presença habitadora e o poder transformador do Espírito Santo. Isso significa que aquilo que é dito aqui foi exposto para mostrar que a morte de Cristo é muito mais que um mero «motivo» para vivermos na santidade. Certamente, com base na gratidão pelo amor de Deus, haveremos de «esforçar-nos na direção da santidade». Mas a união mística na morte de Cristo é muito mais que uma questão de motivação. Antes, o Espírito Santo, que em nós vem habitar, transforma nossa natureza moral, levando-nos a ser santos, a vivermos vitoriosamente sobre o pecado. Ele é a tábua da lei, escrita sobre o coração (ver II Cor. 3:3). Ele é o meio espiritual da santificação (ver II Tes. 2:13). Ele é a força que nos propicia a própria natureza de Cristo, e portanto, todas as suas vitórias e a sua própria glória (ver II Cor. 3:18). Dizendo a mesma coisa, de maneira bem simples, podemos afirmar que ele faz com que deixemos de ser o que somos, e começa a tornar-nos semelhantes a ele. Finalmente, ele duplica em nós a própria natureza de Cristo, moral e metafisicamente. A morte separa a nossa relação com o mundo; e assim também, a morte «com Cristo» põe fim à nossa lealdade ao sistema deste mundo, porquanto ficamos mortos para o mesmo.

4. Mas o batismo espiritual também tem aspectos *positivos*—é a participação na vida ressurrecta de Cristo. Somos soerguidos a uma vida nova, e a nossa lealdade se centraliza, então, nos lugares celestiais.

a. Trata-se de *algo moral*. (Ver Col. 3:1 e ss). Moralmente, chegamos a participar dos próprios atributos e das perfeições de Deus (ver Mat. 5:48 e Heb. 12:14), conforme estão investidos em Cristo (ver Gál. 5:22,23). O Espírito Santo também é o agente desse processo (ver II Cor. 3:18). Se participarmos dos atributos morais de Cristo, só poderemos fazê-lo participando da natureza moral mesma de Jesus Cristo. O Espírito está duplicando Cristo em nós, pois somos filhos de Deus que estão sendo conduzidos à glória (ver Heb. 2:10). Essa duplicação deve ser de natureza moral, pois somente a própria retidão divina, compartilhada pelos remidos, poderá habitar nos céus (ver Rom. 3:25).

b. Mas é algo mais do que moral, é algo *metafísico*. Chegamos a participar da própria natureza metafísica de Cristo (ver Rom. 8:29). A potencialidade dessa participação é infinita, pelo que o processo será contínuo e eterno. Seremos cheios de «toda a plenitude de Deus» (ver Efé. 3:19 e Col. 2:10), tal como o próprio Cristo. Isso indica a participação na «natureza divina», de maneira perfeitamente real, e não apenas figurada (ver II Ped. 1:4).

c. Haveremos de participar da mesma «forma de vida» que tem Deus, através do Filho, o qual, na qualidade de homem, foi o primeiro a receber tal modalidade de vida, por ser o Cabeça federal da raça remida. (Ver João 5:25,26 e 6:57 que esclarecem esse conceito).

BATISMO INFANTIL

Este artigo está dividido em duas seções principais: Argumentos favoráveis e argumentos contrários ao batismo infantil.

Argumentos Favoráveis:

1. Argumentos com base bíblica

Desde tempos remotos, infantes eram batizados na Igreja cristã. É até mesmo possível que tal prática fosse praticada desde o começo do cristianismo, pelo

BATISMO INFANTIL

menos em alguns lugares. É verdade que é impossível a obtenção de informações detalhadas e exatas sobre a questão. Se procurarmos achar uma base bíblica para essa prática, poderíamos usar Marcos 10:14, que diz: «Deixai vir a mim os pequeninos, não os embaraceis, porque de tais é o reino de Deus». Além disso, há casos de batismos de famílias inteiras, que poderiam incluir infantes, conforme se vê em Atos 16:31 *ss* e I Coríntios 1:16. O batismo cristão tem alguns paralelos nos pactos noaico, mosaico e abraâmico, o que é discutido no artigo geral *Batismo*, sob «11», letras «j», «l» e «m». É de presumir-se que essas famílias incluíam os infantes, os quais deviam ter sido batizados, porque aqueles pactos certamente incluíam famílias inteiras. Destaca-se acima de tudo a circuncisão, sinal do pacto abraâmico. O trecho de Colossenses 2:11 *ss* estabelece o paralelo entre a circuncisão e o batismo. Se a circuncisão envolvia crianças, por que não o batismo? A aceitação de infantes, no batismo cristão, pode ser subentendido em textos como Mateus 18:3: «Em verdade vos digo que, se não vos converterdes e não vos tornardes como crianças, de modo algum entrareis no reino dos céus».

2. Argumentos com base histórica

Há evidências conclusivas de que pelo menos no segundo século cristão estava sendo praticado o batismo infantil. Orígenes (185-253 D.C.) aludiu ao batismo infantil como prática generalizada da Igreja, afirmando que a mesma havia sido ensinada pelos apóstolos. «Por essa razão, a Igreja recebeu uma tradição, da parte dos apóstolos, para aplicar o batismo até mesmo a infantes». Tertuliano (160-240 D.C.) opunha-se à prática do batismo infantil, achando ser mais conveniente adiar o batismo até mais tarde na vida, a fim de que os pecados cometidos na vida adulta pudessem ser lavados. Naturalmente, no caso de Tertuliano encontramos grande exagero quanto às funções do batismo. Justino Mártir, em sua Apologia (138 D.C.), relaciona a circuncisão ao batismo, e, como é evidente, era favorável ao batismo de infantes. É razoável supor que visto que o batismo estava assim relacionado à circuncisão, desde os tempos neotestamentários (ver Col. 2:11 *ss*)—embora os apóstolos não nos dêem qualquer informação direta a respeito—muitos cristãos batizavam infantes, da mesma maneira que os judeus circuncidavam os mesmos, embora só disponhamos de citações de pais da Igreja, em apoio à doutrina do batismo de infantes.

3. Argumentos com base teológica

Esses argumentos são os seguintes:

a. O argumento do interesse de Jesus pelas crianças, conforme se lê em Marcos 10:14 e Mateus 18:3.

b. Os argumentos baseados na Bíblia, dados acima, que foram acolhidos por certos sistemas teológicos.

c. O argumento baseado na idéia geral dos pactos, que nos permitem entender que Deus cuida da família inteira de um homem, fazendo provisão em favor da mesma, e não apenas em favor dos crentes adultos.

d. A relação do pacto encoraja os pais a orientarem seus filhos no caminho certo, e o ato do batismo faz parte desse pacto.

e. Aqueles que acreditam na *regeneração batismal* têm aí um argumento importantíssimo em favor do batismo infantil, porquanto é de extrema importância que as crianças recebam as vantagens da graça de Deus, tendo em vista o bem-estar de suas almas eternas.

f. O princípio geral da graça divina parece indicar que Deus cuida dos infantes, e não apenas dos adultos, e que, através do batismo, os infantes chegam a fazer parte do novo pacto. O amor de Deus garante benefícios às crianças, e o batismo é um sinal do amor de Deus ao indivíduo, desde a mais tenra idade.

Argumentos Contrários:

1. Argumentos com base bíblica

Contrariamente aos argumentos expostos acima, afirmamos que textos como Marcos 10:14 e Mateus 18:3 nada dizem sobre o batismo. Só aqueles que querem encontrar apoio bíblico de qualquer maneira para sua doutrina de batismo infantil podem alicerçar-se sobre trechos assim. Há, realmente, certo paralelo entre os antigos pactos e o batismo, mas isso não nos autoriza inferir sobre o batismo infantil. O paralelo entre o batismo e a circuncisão, em Colossenses 2:11 *ss* é absoluto; mas devemos tomar cuidado para não injetar no texto aquilo que ele não diz, percebendo o que ele realmente diz. O que está em foco no texto é a santificação, pondo de lado a antiga vida pecaminosa, como também a participação na nova vida espiritual, coisas essas que certamente dizem respeito a adultos convertidos, e não a infantes. Também é verdade que o Novo Testamento alude a certos casos de batismo de famílias inteiras; mas não há menção a nenhum caso de batismo de infantes. No cristianismo primitivo só eram batizadas pessoas que pudessem «crer», após terem ouvido a exposição da Palavra de Deus. O que significa isso, senão que o batismo sempre foi aplicado a pessoas convertidas? Eram batizadas pessoas com idade suficiente para tomarem decisão, diante do evangelho, no tocante às suas condições espirituais. (Ver o artigo sobre o *Batismo de Crentes*, quanto à confirmação dessa observação).

2. Argumentos com base histórica

É verdade que nos escritos dos chamados pais da Igreja há citações favoráveis ao batismo infantil. Mas, até que ponto esses escritos são fidedignos? Se, por exemplo, Orígenes sabia que os apóstolos aprovavam o batismo de infantes, por qual razão não citou algum trecho apostólico em confirmação? Replicamos que é muito mais seguro basearmos nossas doutrinas sobre declarações expressas da Bíblia do que sobre citações duvidosas de qualquer pai da Igreja. Digamos que, por analogia, os apóstolos tivessem batizado infantes (embora não haja qualquer registro bíblico a esse respeito). Nesse caso, indagaríamos: Os apóstolos estavam com a razão ao assim proceder? Será necessário supormos que os apóstolos nunca erraram? Então por que Paulo teve de repreender publicamente a Pedro? (Ver Gál. 2:11—14). Uma vez mais, é muito mais seguro alicerçarmos nossas doutrinas sobre a Palavra escrita. E a Palavra ensina que o batismo deve ser aplicado somente a convertidos. Quando os fariseus e os saduceus quiseram ser batizados, sem terem se convertido, o Batista recusou-se a aceitá-los, dizendo: «Raça de víboras, quem vos induziu a fugir da ira vindoura? Produzi, pois, fruto digno do arrependimento...» (Mat. 3:7,8). Portanto, fiquemos com a Palavra escrita, e não com supostas práticas apostólicas, *se* o batismo de infantes fazia parte da mesma. Mas, enquanto não se puder provar o ponto pelas Escrituras, o batismo infantil terá de permanecer no terreno das meras conjecturas.

3. Argumentos com base teológica

Há alguma força nesses argumentos; mas muito menos do que seus defensores supõem, porquanto a força verifica-se mais na mente dos advogados do batismo infantil do que na teologia propriamente dita. Para tanto, eles precisam aplicar vários

BATISMO JUDAICO — BATISMO PELOS MORTOS

argumentos racionalistas, fazendo aplicações desnecessárias, a fim de tentarem encontrar apoio à sua posição. É perigoso substituir as claras instruções da Bíblia por meras especulações teológicas. Quase qualquer argumento poderá ser consubstanciado, se apelarmos para esses sofismas. Permanece de pé o fato bíblico de que o batismo em água sempre era aplicado a pessoas convertidas, após ouvirem a exposição do evangelho da graça. Qualquer coisa que ultrapasse disso é interpretação maculada por grande série de dúvidas. A honestidade na exegese nos força a repelir qualquer opinião que não possa ser claramente defendida com a Bíblia aberta.

BATISMO JUDAICO

A forma nominal **baptismós** é usada no original grego, em Heb. 9:10, para indicar as muitas «abluções» dos judeus, em suas cerimônias religiosas. Todavia, tais abluções nada têm a ver com o batismo cristão. Antes, os judeus batizavam os gentios que tinham se convertido ao judaísmo, aos quais chamavam de «prosélitos». Duas coisas eram exigidas dos gentios prosélitos. Em primeiro lugar, precisavam receber o sinal do pacto abraâmico, a circuncisão. Isso simbolizava a remoção da carne ímpia. Em segundo lugar, precisavam ser batizados. Os convertidos imergiam-se totalmente na água, indicando que estavam passando por uma completa purificação dos pecados próprios do paganismo. Enquanto os gentios faziam isso, dois judeus ficavam do lado de fora do recinto fechado por cortinas, onde o batismo estava tendo lugar, recitando passagens da Tora (lei ou Pentateuco). Isso significava que aqueles gentios estavam se submetendo aos preceitos da lei mosaica como novo padrão de sua conduta. A partir daquele instante, quem assim fizesse tornava-se parte da comunidade judaica, apesar do fato de que não era descendente direto de Abraão. (AM)

BATISMO LEIGO

De acordo com a doutrina católica romana, qualquer pessoa leiga pode batizar de modo válido, e de fato, está na obrigação de fazê-lo, em ocasiões de emergência, quando o clérigo a quem compete fazê-lo não se achar presente. Um caso de emergência seria a morte próxima de uma pessoa, que ainda não fora batizada. Essa doutrina é tão liberal que afirma que até mesmo não-católicos podem batizar legitimamente, contanto que tal pessoa tenha a intenção de batizar segundo o espírito católico, ou seja, como um católico faria, se estivesse disponível. De acordo com a doutrina romanista, a água é derramada sobre a cabeça do batizando, ao mesmo tempo em que são repetidas as palavras: «Eu te batizo em nome do Pai, do Filho e do Espírito Santo».

Também há um batismo leigo não-católico, entre aqueles grupos que não dispõem de qualquer clero formal, e, portanto, não têm ministros encarregados da função distintiva de cumprir os ritos litúrgicos, entre outros deveres clericais. O próprio Novo Testamento não nos fornece exemplos de batismo válido, exceto no sentido de que um *ancião* ou pastor da igreja local o administre, a despeito do fato de que talvez não seja um ministro pago. Nesse sentido, tal pastor é um leigo, porquanto não recebe salário de sua congregação. Porém, desde tempos antigos, quando não estavam presentes ministros do evangelho, sempre houve o chamado batismo leigo. Tertuliano defendia essa prática, com base na idéia de que o sacramento é mais importante que a ordem que o governa, pelo que a ordem pode ser ignorada em ocasiões emergenciais. Naturalmente, isso já reflete um sacramentalismo incipiente. Lutero aprovou tal prática, com base no exercício do sacerdócio de todos os crentes. Porém, as igrejas reformadas, de modo geral, não têm encorajado tal costume, e, em algumas denominações cristãs a prática é ativamente suprimida, como algo contrário à ordem neotestamentária. O batismo de nascituros, por parte das parteiras, á ali especialmente criticado. A prática foi intensamente debatida na Igreja Anglicana, até ter sido eventualmente descontinuada, após a Conferência de Hampton Court, em 1604. Ver sobre o *Batismo Infantil* e sobre a *Regeneração Batismal*.

BATISMO NÃO-CRISTÃO

A eficácia da água como agente purificador levou a seu uso cerimonial como meio de remover o contágio adquirido mediante o contato com substâncias perigosas, como o sangue, a morte e coisas proibidas. Por extensão, o contágio das falhas morais e do pecado seria removido pelo batismo ritual e religioso. Os ritos batismais dividem-se em três categorias: a. Infantil, usualmente associado à outorga de um nome próprio; b. de adolescentes, como parte da cerimônia tribal de iniciação (ver o artigo); e c. de adultos, como admissão aos privilégios de alguma religião ou como um rito de iniciação ou consagração. O líquido batismal usualmente era a água, mas, em alguns lugares também eram usados fluidos como sangue, vinho, azeite, mel, saliva ou urina de vaca. Os modos de aplicação incluíam a imersão, a lavagem e o derramamento. Entre os tibetanos e budistas pratica-se a imersão trina. Usualmente, o rito é realizado por um sacerdote ou oficial religioso qualquer, embora, algumas vezes, o pai de uma família ou o chefe de uma aldeia aja como batizador. No caso de infantil, supõe-se que as impurezas próprias do nascimento são removidas, e que isso dá proteção contra forças malignas de vários tipos. O processo de doação de um nome próprio, ligado ao rito, identifica a criança como um membro legítimo da comunidade, pondo-a debaixo da proteção do clã e da família, bem como uma pessoa a quem os deuses da comunidade devem resguardar. O batismo por ocasião da puberdade assinala o fim da meninice e o início das responsabilidades da vida adulta. Essa iniciação é uma espécie de segundo nascimento, sendo considerado como início de um novo tipo de vida. Algumas vezes, incluía o recebimento de um novo nome.

As religiões misteriosas (ver o artigo a respeito), como a eleusiana, a órfica, a mitraica, a egípcia e a síria requeriam o batismo para que fosse lavado o mal moral, como preparação para participação nos ritos religiosos, mediante os quais o deus da comunidade era procurado. O alvo final de todas essas religiões misteriosas era a imortalidade. Portanto, algumas vezes esses batismos simbolizavam a morte para a vida antiga e a vida para uma nova vida. Naturalmente, vemos paralelos disso tanto no batismo judaico quanto no batismo cristão. (AM E)

BATISMO PELOS MORTOS

I Cor. 15:29: *De outra maneira, que farão os que se batizam pelos mortos? Se absolutamente os mortos não ressuscitam, por quê então se batizam por eles?*

Batismo pelos mortos.

O *Batismo vicário?* Batismo em favor dos mortos? O simples fraseado deste texto parece indicar somente que, em Corinto, com aprovação ou não do apóstolo,

BATISMO PELOS MORTOS

havia alguns que tinham dado início à prática do batismo pelos mortos, sem dúvida alguma pensando que tal rito teria algum mérito e que beneficiaria a salvação pessoal de certos indivíduos que já haviam falecido. Os intérpretes que procuram encontrar alguma outra significação, fazem-no ou à base da tese que essa prática era uma «superstição», que não poderia ter-se originado em uma igreja que Paulo iniciara, ou então, devido à ausência de evidências históricas, procuram mostrar que, naqueles tempos remotos, de fato existia tal prática.

Esse tema (isolado no N.T., pois aparece somente em I Cor. 15:29), tem provocado muita e intensa discussão. J.W. Horsley, Newbery House Magazine, Junho de 1890, alistou trinta e seis diferentes explicações. Neste ponto, examinamos onze dessas possíveis explicações.

1. Alguns estudiosos pensam que está em vista o batismo cristão ordinário, e interpretam as palavras «...por causa dos mortos...» no sentido «a interesse da ressurreição dos mortos»; isto é, na expectativa da ressurreição. Mas o original grego não pode incluir tal significado. Pois o que faríamos com a palavra grega «uper» e com o artigo «oi», isto é, «os batizandos», o que parece apontar para um grupo distinto de pessoas, atarefadas nesse rito, pessoas essas que eram excepcionais? A palavra *mortos* significaria, nesse caso «a ressurreição dos mortos». Grande número dos primeiros intérpretes do grego pensavam que essa opinião é a correta, mas mesmo assim ela não convence.

2. Outros eruditos têm pensado que pessoas pagãs, que conheciam cristãos que haviam falecido, «em respeito a elas», como que para confirmar a sua fé, quando se convertiam se submetiam ao batismo (assim se tornando crentes reconhecidos), como se fosse um gesto de confirmação da fé de seus amigos ou parentes. Assim sendo, teríamos de pensar no batismo cristão comum, embora efetuado com propósitos especiais de comemoração. Podemos supor, neste caso, que tais crentes, que haviam falecido, tinham estado especialmente interessados pela conversão daqueles que agora se batizavam; e, por causa desse interesse, os batizandos honravam-nos com esse batismo «por causa» dos mortos. Essa explicação parece harmonizar-se bem com o texto grego, mas é altamente especulativa.

3. As palavras aqui traduzidas como *por causa dos mortos*, também têm sido compreendidas no sentido de «preencher o número» daqueles que já haviam falecido; ou então no sentido de «preencher o lugar vago na igreja», deixado por tais pessoas mortas. Assim sendo, o batismo cristão ordinário estaria novamente em foco, embora aqui deva ser compreendido como um meio para multiplicar o número dos membros da igreja. Assim, estas pessoas preencheriam as vagas produzidas pelos falecimentos. Porém, essa interpretação também é improvável.

4. Uma outra opinião é aquela que diz que crentes vivos eram batizados em lugar de crentes mortos, os quais, por alguma razão desconhecida, não haviam sido batizados em água, embora crentes. É possível que alguns desses crentes tivessem falecido repentinamente, devido a alguma praga ou outra ocorrência funesta, não tendo tido oportunidade de se batizarem. Esta quarta interpretação é mais provável do que as três primeiras, mas dificilmente reflete ela a plena extensão dessa prática.

5. Alguns supõem que o *batismo*, neste caso, equivale a *martírio*, e que teríamos aqui um «batismo de sangue». E os crentes que tivessem passado por essa experiência, tê-lo-iam feito com a esperança de ressuscitarem. Mas não é muito provável essa explicação, ainda que se possa mostrar que a palavra «batismo» podia ser usada nesse sentido, conforme de fato vemos em Mat. 20:22,23.

6. Ainda outros estudiosos pensam que Paulo aludiu a alguma prática das religiões misteriosas do paganismo, as quais tinham certo rito de batismo pelos mortos, e do que os crentes de Corinto certamente tinham conhecimento. Então Paulo ter-se-ia usado dessa circunstância para comprovar o que dizia. Entretanto, uma alusão a ritos pagãos dificilmente seria reputada autoritária na igreja de Corinto, sobretudo para os membros contrários à doutrina da ressurreição.

7. Lutero pensava que se deve traduzir *por sobre os mortos*, isto é, «por sobre suas sepulturas», como se houvesse batismos efetuados dessa maneira; mas tal idéia foge muito da realidade, além de não ser uma maneira satisfatória de explicar o sentido do termo grego «uper».

8. A interpretação de alguns é que devemos compreender aqui «por causa do morto», isto é, Cristo. Porém, no original grego, encontramos o plural, «mortos», sendo extremamente difícil vermos como Cristo poderia representar uma «categoria» inteira de pessoas. Além disso, Jesus não está morto, e, sim, ressurrecto dentre os mortos.

9. Outros ainda pensam que o verbo «batizar» deve ser aqui compreendido no sentido de «ser imerso em sofrimentos», ao passo que a palavra «mortos» significaria «a ressurreição dos mortos». Isso faria de I Cor. 15:29 um paralelo da idéia expressa nos versículos trinta e trinta e um desse mesmo capítulo. Porém, isso é dar às palavras um sentido inesperado, sendo muito menos provável essa idéia do que muitas outras.

10. Alguns autores pensam que essas palavras significam: «Por que uma pessoa sofreria por si mesma, ao ser batizada, por causa dos mortos (com o sentido de pertencer a eles, formando um reino só em companhia dos mortos)?» Esse seria o caso se a vida cristã terminasse na morte, e não na ressurreição. Porém isso daria a entender que os oponentes de Paulo negavam tanto a doutrina da imortalidade como a doutrina da ressurreição. Mas essa dupla negação, conforme já temos podido observar, não é provável. Além disso, tal uso da expressão «por causa dos mortos», é altamente *artificial*.

11. Terminando a lista neste ponto—visto que todas as demais interpretações são ainda menos prováveis do que as dez anteriores—precisamos dizer que a maneira mais natural de compreender essas palavras, é tomá-las em seu sentido mais literal. Parece que na igreja de Corinto havia alguma forma de «ministério» em favor dos mortos, que recomendava o batismo para eles. E é provável que alguns crentes, que seguiam essa prática, fossem batizados tanto em prol de crentes não-batizados (visto que muitos adiavam o rito do batismo até imediatamente antes da morte, pensando que o batismo envolvesse algum mérito místico no perdão dos pecados), bem como em favor de seus amigos e parentes ainda incrédulos. Naturalmente que esse ponto de vista também tem sido combatido por objetores. Perguntam estes: Por que Paulo não condenou tal prática? Não sabemos dizê-lo; mas é possível que Paulo tivesse mencionado a questão de passagem, a fim de provar seu argumento em prol da realidade da ressurreição, sem vincular tal declaração a alguma aprovação ou desaprovação dessa prática. Não há que duvidar que isso é possível. (Ver I Cor. 11:5 em comparação com I Cor. 14:34,

como um exemplo de prática idêntica. E um exemplo mais notório ainda aparece em I Cor. 10:8, onde Paulo menciona o fato de que certos cristãos comiam em templos idólatras e não lhes faz qualquer censura. Mas a censura aparece em outro trecho, isto é, I Cor. 10:14 e *ss*).

Uma outra objeção é que não dispomos de qualquer evidência histórica em comprovação a essa prática, senão já em um período bem posterior. Tal prática, além disso, mui provavelmente se baseava no que diz I I Cor. 15:29, como texto de prova. Mas, apesar disso expressar uma verdade, não há motivo algum para supormos que não existia em Corinto alguma prática dessa natureza, talvez baseada em noções preservadas das religiões misteriosas dos pagãos. Qualquer referência histórica a isso facilmente poderia ter sido omitida em qualquer documento que chegou até às nossas mãos, porquanto quase todos os documentos históricos dessa natureza desapareceram.

Em um período posterior, todavia, encontramos evidências da prática do «batismo em favor dos mortos». Isso era praticado entre as seitas hereges dos coríntios (ver *Ephiph. Haer.* xxviii. §6, pág. 114) e dos marcionitas (Crisóstomo, Tertuliano, *de ressurr.*, 48, vol. ii. pág. 865, *adv. Marc.* v. 10, pág. 494). Tal prática, como é evidente, confere ao batismo um valor muito maior do que o apóstolo dos gentios lhe atribuía, fazendo com que o mesmo tivesse um valor vicário, podendo salvar a alma. Porém, não há razão alguma para pensarmos que alguns cristãos primitivos não davam tal valor ao batismo, certamente em resultado de suas idéias pagãs, transferidas para o cristianismo, idéias essas que davam um valor sacramental e místico aos ritos.

Crisóstomo conta-nos como esses ritos eram levados a efeito, segundo ele os conhecia: «Depois que um catecúmeno (alguém que ainda não fora batizado, mas que já estava preparado para o batismo) falecia, punham um homem vivo oculto debaixo de seu leito; então, aproximando-se do leito do morto, falavam com ele e indagavam se ele queria receber o batismo. Não dando ele resposta, o outro respondia em seu lugar. Assim batizavam 'o vivo pelo morto'». Contudo, é possível que várias outras maneiras fossem empregadas nesse rito.

Essa prática também fazia parte dos ritos observados pelos montanistas (fins do segundo século e princípios do terceiro século da era cristã), sendo praticada ainda pelos mórmons, até hoje. No mormonismo, o batismo tem certo mérito, de acordo com as idéias errôneas da regeneração batismal (ainda que ali o batismo, isoladamente, de forma alguma seja visto como um agente salvador; todavia, faz parte integrante e necessária da salvação). Os espíritos dos mortos não são forçados a aceitar o mérito oferecido a eles através desse rito, mas tal mérito lhes é posto à disposição, se desejarem tal vantagem. O livre-arbítrio de cada um desses espíritos, escolhendo ou rejeitando tal mérito, é que determinará a questão. Os mórmons procuram batismo dessa natureza para todos os seus parentes, antepassados, amigos e totais estranhos, que tenham morrido, «incrédulos». O ideal seria que todas as pessoas que tivessem morrido sem a fé correta, em todos os séculos, tivessem esse mérito à sua disposição, através do rito. Por isso mesmo os mórmons preparam elaborados registros genealógicos. De fato, essas genealogias são as mais completas do mundo, para que sejam guiados na realização desse rito, em grande escala. Seus registros genealógicos, encerrados em vastos salões escavados nas Montanhas Rochosas a leste de Salt Lake City, no estado de Utah, nos Estados Unidos da América do Norte, poderiam resistir a qualquer desastre provocado pelo homem, exceto uma explosão direta de um engenho atômico. *Oh, o poder de um único versículo das Escrituras*, na influência que exerce sobre os homens, ainda que esse versículo seja de dúbia interpretação, como é o caso deste versículo!

Sem importar qual a natureza exata do costume que Paulo alude aqui, ele usou o mesmo a fim de indicar que os próprios crentes coríntios, ou pelo menos alguns deles, indicavam a realidade da doutrina da ressurreição dos mortos, mediante seus ritos religiosos.

BATISTAS

Uma das denominações evangélicas de maior coerência em sua fé e prática, embora também haja pontos de debilidade, que poderiam ser aprimorados. Consideremos as questões principais abaixo:

1. Origem. Um grupo religioso separado; os Batistas tiveram origem no século XVII, como um ramo que se separou dos congregacionais ingleses, os quais, por sua vez, compunham-se originalmente de elementos da Igreja Anglicana e do movimento puritano. As tentativas para fazer as origens batistas retrocederem à época dos apóstolos, através de grupos mais antigos como Waldenses, Albigenses, Cátaros, e outros (ver os artigos a respeito), são histórica e teologicamente absurdas. Isso pode ser facilmente demonstrado, mediante a simples leitura das crenças de tais grupos. De imediato, podemos perceber que aqueles grupos não eram em nenhum sentido grupos Batistas. Os Batistas nem mesmo se assemelham aos Anabatistas (ver o artigo a respeito). As crenças teológicas dos Anabatistas certamente não eram batistas. De fato, qualquer grupo evangélico tradicional de nossos dias assemelha-se mais aos Batistas do que aos Anabatistas do passado. Mas, seja como for, o valor da fé religiosa de alguém, como interpretação do Novo Testamento e do evangelho de Cristo, não depende de qualquer continuação histórica que possa ser traçada. Antes, seu valor reside nos seus méritos intrínsecos, devido às idéias que ela promove e devido ao serviço que presta a Deus e aos homens.

Se a veracidade de um grupo cristão depende da antiguidade de sua continuação histórica, então teríamos de pensar sobre a Igreja Católica Romana e sobre a Igreja Ortodoxa Grega. Não há grupo cristão que se compare com eles quanto ao fator antiguidade. No entanto, esses grupos só podem jactar-se de serem os grupos cristãos mais antigos, se não recuarmos mais do que o cisma do século XI D.C., quando a anterior Igreja Católica dividiu-se nesses dois grupos. E a Igreja Católica perdurou do imperador Constantino (século IV D.C.) até o cisma de que acabamos de falar. Houve grupos dissidentes durante a Idade Média, alguns dos quais já desapareceram, e outros que continuam até hoje. Entre os que continuam, podemos falar sobre os Waldenses, até hoje numerosos no sul da França e no norte da Itália. Os grupos protestantes tiveram início somente no século XVI, a começar com os luteranos. Os grupos pentecostais começaram no início do nosso século XX. Como estamos vendo, a autenticidade cristã de um grupo qualquer não depende de sua antiguidade. A verdade e a autenticidade consiste na fidelidade à Palavra de Deus. A continuidade histórica nada significa; o que vale é a continuidade do espírito. A espiritualidade não depende de fatores humanos, mas dos movimentos do Espírito de Deus.

No entanto, os Batistas diferem de outros grupos

BATISTAS

separatistas devido a algumas das doutrinas que eles defendem: o batismo de crentes, igrejas locais formadas idealmente por pessoas convertidas e um governo eclesiástico democrático. (Ver o artigo sobre o *Batismo de Crentes*). No entanto, no início da história dos Batistas, houve os Batistas Gerais na Inglaterra, que eram arminianos e praticavam o batismo por afusão. Somente mais tarde o batismo por imersão tornou-se generalizado entre os Batistas.

Na segunda metade do século XVI, pequenos grupos de puritanos tornaram-se impacientes em relação à reforma dentro da Igreja Anglicana. Finalmente, romperam com a Igreja oficial da Inglaterra, tornando-se conhecidos como *separatistas*. Aqueles entre eles que acreditavam no batismo só de crentes tornaram-se os originadores do que, finalmente, veio a tornar-se uma denominação separada, com o nome de Batistas. Esses puritanos também defendiam uma forma de governo eclesiástico democrático, um outro típico princípio batista. John Smyth, anterior pregador anglicano de Lincoln, na Inglaterra, tornou-se um ministro separatista. A perseguição forçou-o a mudar-se para a Holanda. Ele opunha-se ao batismo infantil. Em 1609, ele e mais 36 pessoas formaram uma nova igreja. Crendo no batismo *de crentes*, Smyth batizou a si mesmo por aspersão, e então às outras pessoas, aplicando água sobre suas frontes. Por assim dizer, temos aí uma igreja pré-batista. Posteriormente, Smyth duvidou da propriedade do autobatismo, a menos que nenhuma igreja verdadeira pudesse ser encontrada. Então decidiu que os menonitas constituíam uma igreja verdadeira. (Ver sobre os *Menonitas*). Recomendou a seu grupo que se unisse aos menonitas. Mas alguns dos primeiros batistas (ou pré-batistas) recusaram-se a isso, como Thomas Helwys. Vários outros uniram suas forças a Helwys, retornaram a Londres e estabeleceram a primeira igreja batista de Londres. O grupo da Holanda não demorou a desfazer-se. As pessoas que seguiam a Smyth e Helwys assumiram uma abordagem teológica calvinista moderada, tornando-se conhecidas como igrejas Batistas Gerais, porquanto acreditavam que a expiação de Cristo era para todos os homens. Porém, em 1638, surgiu um grupo de batistas que acreditava na expiação limitada, ou seja, Cristo teria morrido somente por seus escolhidos, tendo-se organizado como Igrejas Batistas Particulares. A palavra «particular», dentro desse nome, refere-se à idéia da expiação limitada (em contraste com a expiação geral). Em 1640 houve ainda mais uma divisão, quando alguns ficaram convencidos de que a imersão é o único modo válido de batismo. Foi então que os batistas deixaram para trás o seu estágio pré-batista.

Os anos de 1640 a 1660 viram um considerável desenvolvimento entre os batistas. A liberdade religiosa tornou-se uma outra forte ênfase das igrejas batistas, e muitos crentes batistas foram aprisionados ou tiveram seus bens confiscados. John Bunyan, um pregador batista, foi confinado por doze anos em uma prisão de Bedford, na Inglaterra. Aproveitou seu período de aprisionamento para escrever um bom número de livros. O ímpeto revivalista e de missões ao estrangeiro, entre os batistas, deveu-se a homens como William Carey e Adoniram Judson (ver os artigos a respeito deles), embora tivessem sofrido oposição dentre seus próprios pares, sobretudo o primeiro. É impossível alguém exagerar a importância dos batistas dentro do movimento das missões estrangeiras. E por esse motivo que atualmente há igrejas batistas em todas as porções do mundo, inclusive atrás da Cortina de Ferro (União Soviética e países satélites).

2. Doutrinas distintivas. A democracia gera diferenças de opinião, e não há grupo mais democrático do que os batistas. Alguém, em tom de brincadeira, declarou que os batistas são tão livres como porcos sobre o gelo. Esse tipo de liberdade tende por criar diferenças e divisões, e por essa razão, há muitas variedades de crentes batistas, desde os ultraconservadores aos muito liberais. Não obstante, podemos enumerar algumas características tradicionais dos batistas:

a. Autoridade da Bíblia como única regra de fé e prática. Ver o artigo sobre AUTORIDADE, quanto a variegados pontos de vista sobre essa questão. No entanto, as igrejas batistas aceitam ter «declarações de fé», as quais, por não serem completas, deixam de lado muitos pontos doutrinários que muitos dos irmãos nem aceitam discutir. Isso constitui uma falha por omissão. O Espírito de Deus avança, e muitos batistas marcam passo.

b. Batismo de crentes, com total rejeição do batismo infantil. Imersão como modo correto de batismo. Muitas igrejas batistas rebatizam aqueles que, vindos de outras igrejas, se unem a elas, mesmo que essas outras igrejas também pratiquem o batismo por imersão. Esse extremo cheira a sectarismo. Contudo, a partir de 1900 muitas igrejas batistas têm recebido tais membros sem exigirem o rebatismo.

c. O batismo em água e a Ceia do Senhor são as únicas ordenanças da Igreja, não sendo consideradas *sacramentos* (ver o artigo a respeito).

d. A Igreja de Cristo compõe-se apenas de crentes. A maioria dos batistas acredita na Igreja mística ou universal, composta de todos os regenerados, sem importar a quais grupos evangélicos pertençam. Mas, para muitos batistas, a admissão à igreja local requer o rito do batismo por imersão. Entretanto, os batistas não crêem na regeneração batismal (ver o artigo).

e. Sacerdócio de todos os crentes. No Novo Testamento não há tal coisa como uma classe sacerdotal. Cada crente é responsável diretamente a Deus.

f. Autonomia da igreja local e governo democrático. Os batistas podem pertencer a associações e denominações, mas não aceitam autoridades hierárquicas acima da igreja local. Assim, todas as questões atinentes à igreja local são decididas pelo voto da congregação, e não por autoridades externas à mesma.

g. Ministério. Os ministros batistas usualmente são homens dotados de treinamento teológico, os quais são sustentados pelas ofertas de suas respectivas congregações. A autoridade dos pastores, porém, depende de sua espiritualidade e de seu treinamento intelectual superior, e não de alguma superioridade doutrinária conferida por dom escriturístico ou por tradição. Há pastores e mestres (embora estes não constituam um ministério), não levantados por algum sistema eclesiástico, e sim, pela autoridade providencial do Espírito. Atualmente, entre muitos batistas, nota-se um certo desconforto diante do fato de que geralmente seus pastores são homens treinados em seminários e institutos bíblicos. Esses pensam que tal sistema dá pouca margem à atuação selecionadora do Espírito. Talvez isso se deva às influências dos grupos pentecostais, talvez por impulso legítimo do Espírito. O futuro decidirá a questão.

h. Separação entre a Igreja e o estado. Via de regra, os batistas nunca se revoltaram contra o estado. De fato, os primeiros batistas contendiam em favor do direito de reis governarem, com base em textos neotestamentários como o décimo terceiro capítulo de Romanos. Também nunca aceitaram tornar-se a religião oficial de qualquer país, por defenderem o conceito da separação entre a Igreja e o estado. Esse princípio promove a liberdade cristã; havendo intervenção governamental nessa questão, surgem muitas restrições prejudiciais, e a pureza da doutrina e a vivacidade espiritual sofrem imenso retrocesso.

De algumas poucas décadas até a nossa época, têm aparecido igrejas batistas *sui generis*, que as demais igrejas batistas rotulariam de «pentecostais». Esse fenômeno veio para ficar, e ninguém pode fechar os olhos ao mesmo. De um ponto de vista estritamente intelectual, só o futuro nos dirá se isso será para melhor ou para pior, no caso dos batistas. O perigo consiste na perda de certas doutrinas bíblicas, como a «segurança dos salvos», doutrina essa que por certo não é um apanágio dos grupos pentecostais. Todavia, uma coisa não terá de se seguir necessariamente à outra. O tradutor desta valiosa obra converteu-se entre os batistas; após quinze anos, teve uma experiência mais profunda com o Espírito de Deus, isso lhe sucedeu há mais de dezenove anos. Mas, nem por isso deixou de sentir-se batista no fundo do coração, no que tange às doutrinas distintivas dos batistas; mas aprendeu a incluir em seu credo certas doutrinas neotestamentárias que geralmente não figuram nas declarações de fé batistas, e espera poder continuar ampliando seus horizontes espirituais, aberto a todas as bênçãos que Deus, em Cristo, tenha em reserva para seu povo, ensinadas na Bíblia.

3. Supostas Debilidades. O autor desta **Enciclopédia**, bem como do **Novo Testamento Interpretado** foi criado como crente batista. Seu trabalho como pastor e autor de livros evangélicos tem sido sustentado mais por igrejas e particulares batistas do que por pessoas de qualquer outro grupo evangélico. Todavia, creio que todos os grupos evangélicos, incluindo os batistas, muito têm a aprender. Sugiro que é uma debilidade batista tomar um ponto de vista bastante pessimista quanto ao resultado final do ministério do evangelho e da missão de Cristo. Os batistas geralmente ignoram o fato de que Cristo desceu ao hades e ofereceu salvação aos perdidos, mesmo após sua morte biológica. Ver I Ped. 3:18-4:6 e o artigo *Descida de Cristo ao Hades*. Não percebem que certas porções do Novo Testamento mostram-se mais agudas em sua visão espiritual do que outras, expondo uma promessa mais esperançosa acerca do que a missão de Cristo tem para oferecer-nos. Também acredito que o resultado final da missão de Cristo será maior do que os crentes batistas ordinários antecipam. O trecho de Efésios 1:10 certamente ensina uma restauração final que, mui provavelmente, incluirá os perdidos, embora não lhes conferindo os privilégios que pertencerão exclusivamente aos remidos. No que concerne a isso, devemos notar que Paulo, naquele texto, fala sobre o *mistério* da vontade de Deus. Ao usar esse termo (ver o artigo sobre «mistério»), Paulo nos diz que estava falando de algo *novo* sobre o que Deus tenciona fazer a respeito da criação em geral. Se não fosse algo novo, então também não seria para nós um «mistério». É inútil tentar limitar essa nova mensagem, apelando para versículos menos amplos do Novo Testamento, e que falam sobre o julgamento dos perdidos. De fato, esse mistério ultrapassa, em profundidade, a outros versículos, oferecendo-nos um ponto de vista altamente otimista daquilo que a missão de Cristo, finalmente, realizará. Esse aspecto do ensino bíblico geralmente é exposto pelos antigos pais gregos da Igreja, e omitido pelos pais latinos. Os pais gregos influenciaram o pensamento da Igreja Ortodoxa, dos anglicanos e dos grupos evangélicos eslavos. Os pais latinos influenciaram o cristianismo ocidental, do qual fazemos parte. A história da doutrina mostra-nos que as distorções doutrinárias devem-se a um processo de simplificação, de acordo com o qual muitos pontos doutrinários vão sendo abandonados, com a conseqüente redução do «credo». E os espaços em branco, que assim sobram, são preenchidos com noções ditadas pela tradição. Um crente esclarecido jamais pode aceitar esse empobrecimento da doutrina cristã. Portanto, aqueles cristãos orientais, quanto a certas questões, têm um credo mais completo e sábio do que o nosso, embora o credo deles não concorde cem por cento com a posição batista tradicional. Mas isso em nada detrata as realizações dos batistas através dos séculos, e nem suas doutrinas distintivas, que mostram sinais de sabedoria espiritual. Tal como em todas as questões controvertidas, a lei do amor deveria governar nossos raciocínios, quando expressamos idéias, debatemos e mostramos nossa atitude para com os irmãos na fé. A teologia do ódio e da intolerância, que fere e queima, dificilmente pode ser inspirada por Deus. (AM B C TO)

Os Batistas no Brasil. O trabalho batista no Brasil, depois de uma tentativa em 1871 (Santa Bárbara, SP), que não durou, teve início, em caráter permanente, em Salvador, onde se organizou, em 1882, a primeira igreja batista brasileira, como resultado do trabalho dos missionários William Buck Bagley, Zachary Clay Taylor e do ex-padre católico romano, Antônio Teixeira, organizando-se no Rio de Janeiro em 1884; Maceió, 1885; Recife, 1886; Juiz de Fora, 1889; Natal, 1896; Belém, 1897; São Paulo, 1899; Manaus, 1900 e em muitos outros lugares no Brasil. Mantêm, além de igrejas, faculdades e seminários teológicos, imprensas, escolas e hospitais. Em cerca de 1970, tinham 300.000 membros e 2.200 igrejas. (DL)

BATISTAS DO SÉTIMO DIA

Um pequeno grupo de batistas, sobreviventes da obra iniciada por John Conrad Beissel, o qual, em 1732, organizou a famosa Sociedade Efrata (que vide) como sociedade monástica, com base nos ideais do celibato e da comunidade de bens. Os que atualmente fazem parte do grupo não preservam esses ideais específicos do grupo original. Eles têm afinidades com os *dunkers* (que vide).

Princípios Distintivos. Observância do sábado, o sétimo dia, como dia de guarda; bênção aos infantes; não resistência; lava-pés; unção dos enfermos e imersão tríplice, para a frente.

BATISTAS GERAIS E BATISTAS PARTICULARES

Os Batistas Gerais eram aqueles batistas (que vide) que criam na expiação geral de Cristo em favor de todos os homens. Thomas Helwys, que esteve sujeito à **influência menonita em Amsterdan, fundou — em Londres, a igreja-mãe dos Batistas Gerais** (arminianos), em 1612. Posteriormente, de um centro em Southward, surgiram diversas igrejas Batistas Particulares (calvinistas). Estas últimas publicaram conjuntamente uma confissão de fé, em 1644. Somente em 1891, os dois ramos uniram-se, formando a União Batista da Grã-Bretanha e da Irlanda. O nome «particular» refere-se à idéia da expiação limitada, isto é, a noção que Cristo morreu exclusivamente pelos seus eleitos, pelo que sua expiação seria particular, e não geral. Ver os artigos sobre o *Determinismo* e o *Livre-Arbítrio*. (C E)

BATISTAS PARTICULARES

Ver o artigo sobre **Batistas Gerais e Batistas Particulares**.

BATISTÉRIO

Nos templos católicos romanos, o batistério é um lugar em que se acha a pia batismal, reservada para o ato do batismo. Algumas vezes, um edifício separado é dedicado a esse propósito. Batistas e outros, que praticam batismo por imersão, geralmente dispõem de um grande tanque, no interior do templo, que é usado com essa finalidade. No cristianismo primitivo eram utilizados os rios (o que, naturalmente, continua sendo usado por alguns). Porém, a partir do século III D.C., batistérios continuaram sendo erigidos. Durante a Idade Média, muitos templos católicos tinham uma fonte batismal localizada na nave, mas, no nosso século XX, tem-se retornado ao uso de uma sala separada, edificada para ali se realizarem batismos. (AM E)

BATIZAR (Dar Nome)

Quatro coisas diferentes estão em foco: 1. O ato de receber uma pessoa na igreja local, mediante o ato de batismo, usualmente referindo-se ao batismo infantil, quando então à criança se dá um nome próprio. 2. Nas igrejas evangélicas onde o batismo só é aplicado após a conversão, essa palavra pode referir-se à consagração dos infantes, sem que isso inclua batismo propriamente dito. 3. A palavra também pode significar dar nome por ocasião do batismo, e nada mais. 4. Ou, popularmente, simplesmente significa dar nome a um objeto, como no caso de um navio, por exemplo.

BATO

Ver **Pesos e Medidas**.

BAUMGARTEN, ALEXANDER GOTTLIEB

Filósofo alemão (1714-1762), da escola de Wolff (ver a respeito), que se tornou melhor conhecido devido à sua teoria da estética. Ele supunha que a arte fundamenta-se sobre representações mentais sensuais e vinculadas aos sentimentos, e que, quanto a isso, a *beleza* (ver o artigo) não é alguma idéia simples e intelectual, mas um complexo confuso e elaborado. Sua obra inacabada, *Aesthetica*, apresenta o conceito. Suas obras anteriores foram *Metafísica* e *Filosofia da Ética*.

BAUR, FERDINAND CHRISTIAN

Teólogo alemão (1792-1860), fundador da famosa Escola de Tubingen. A filosofia exercia grande influência sobre ele, especialmente as idéias de Hegel. Contudo, não devemos pensar nele como um simples copiador, pois ele pode ser encarado como um pioneiro no método histórico-crítico da crítica bíblica (ver o artigo). Como tal, ele foi um dos mais importantes vultos religiosos do século XIX. Ver o artigo sobre a *Escola de Tubingen*. (C HOD)

BAURIM, BARUMITA

O adjetivo gentílico «barumita», em II Sam. 23:31 e I Crô. 11:33, aponta para uma aldeia no território de Benjamim, identificada com a moderna Ras et-Tmim, a sueste de Tsawihey e a leste do monte das Oliveiras, no lado norte da estrada romana de Jericó a Jerusalém. Foi nesse lugar que Patiel foi separado de sua esposa, Mical, filha de Saul, quando Abner a fez retornar a Davi, de quem era legítima esposa (ver II Sam. 3:16, onde a aldeia é mencionada pela primeira vez na Bíblia; ver também II Sam. 16:5; 17:8; 19:16 e I Reis 2:8). Davi tomou o caminho que passava por essa aldeia, quando fugia de Absalão (ver II Sam. 16:5). Ali habitava Simei, que lançou pedras contra Davi, enquanto o amaldiçoava, porém nesse mesmo lugar Davi contava com alguns que o apoiavam (ver II Sam. 17:18 *ss*). Um dos trinta heróis de Davi, Azmavete, era barumita (ver II Sam. 23:31 e I Crô. 11:33). (SI Z)

BAUTAIN, LOUIS ABBÉ

Filósofo francês católico romano (1796-1867). Nasceu em Paris, afastou-se do catolicismo para o ceticismo, e reconverteu-se ao catolicismo em 1821. Entretanto, continuou dando apoio à contenção de Kant de que os argumentos empíricos e racionais não podem provar a existência de Deus. Em lugar de tais argumentos, ele defendia o *fideísmo*, a idéia que diz que Deus só pode ser conhecido através da *fé*. A isso ele acrescentava os outros métodos de investigação, como o dos sentimentos, o do discernimento místico, etc. Para ele, a razão é metafisicamente incompetente. O papa Gregório XVI condenou o «fideísmo» em 1840. Por esse motivo, Bautain foi forçado a retratar-se, aceitando os poderes da razão nessa tarefa. Suas obras incluem os seguintes títulos: *Filosofia do Cristianismo; Psicologia Experimental; Religião e Liberdade;* e *O Espírito Humano e Suas Faculdades*. (EP P)

BAVAI

No hebraico, «desejador». Nome de um levita, filho de Henadade, governador de metade da cidade de Queila. Bavai ajudou na reconstrução das muralhas de Jerusalém, após o exílio (Nee. 3:18). Ele é chamado Binui, no v. 24 do mesmo capítulo. Talvez o nome Bavai seja uma forma corrompida de Binui.

BAXTER, RICHARD

Eminente pregador e autor puritano (1615-1691). Não freqüentou qualquer universidade, mas foi pessoalmente instruído por John Owen e outros eruditos, além de ser um devorador de livros. Foi consagrado em 1638 como bispo de Worcester. — Finalmente, foi atraído para o partido dos não-conformistas. Teve um frutífero pastorado em Kidderminster, tendo formado ali uma associação de ministros. Durante a Guerra Civil, serviu por algum tempo como capelão do exército do parlamento inglês. Por ocasião da Restauração, declinou da oferta que lhe foi feita de um bispado, em Heredord. Durante o reinado de Carlos II foi perseguido e encarcerado por dezoito meses.

Baxter escreveu vários livros e foi um pregador eficaz. Suas obras devocionais são melhor conhecidas, mas ele também lançou obras eruditas. Podemos incluir: *O Descanso Eterno dos Santos; O Pastor Reformado* e um *Dicionário Eclesiástico*. O primeiro desses títulos é uma obra devocional extensamente usada no passado. Baxter era classificado como presbiteriano, mas ele preferia intitular-se de *verdadeiro católico*. Com o passar dos anos, tornou-se mais liberal e tolerante, tendo-se esforçado pela pacificação e cooperação entre as denominações evangélicas. Defendia a doutrina da eleição, mas sem o aspecto da reprovação negativa; e também advogava uma espécie de *universalismo hipotético*. Na política, assumia uma posição de governo pluralista, ou de monarquia com poderes limitados. Procurou reviver a proposta de um episcopado modificado, exposta por seu falecido amigo, arcebispo Usher. Porém, seus esforços nesse sentido foram inúteis. Sua tentativa de revisar a liturgia (acerca da qual argumentou em sua obra *Reforma da Liturgia*) também não obteve sucesso.

Baxter faleceu a 8 de dezembro de 1691, e em suas cerimônias fúnebres havia tanto anglicanos quanto *dissenters* (que vide). (AM C)

BAYLE, PIERRE

Filósofo francês (1647-1706). Estudou com os jesuítas em Toulousse. Tornou-se católico romano, mas depois reconverteu-se ao calvinismo. Fugindo das perseguições, terminou em Genebra, onde interessou-se especialmente pelo estudo dos escritos de Descartes (ver o artigo). Retornou à França e tornou-se professor de filosofia no colégio calvinista de Sedan. Teve de enfrentar novas perseguições e fugiu para Rotterdam, onde deu continuação à sua carreira de professor. Foi despedido dessa universidade em 1693, sob a acusação de ser agente francês e inimigo do protestantismo.

Sua principal obra é o *Dicionário Histórico e Crítico*, com original em francês. É uma espécie de argumento do ceticismo contra teorias teológicas e filosóficas. Ele chegou à conclusão de que os esforços racionais são inúteis, e que o indivíduo precisa voltar-se para a fé, quanto às suas crenças religiosas. A obra foi violentamente atacada, sob a acusação de ser profana, por conter a afirmação de que a moralidade independe da religião. Hume e Voltaire usaram alguns de seus argumentos em seus ataques contra a teologia tradicional. Os enciclopedistas e filósofos têm usado a obra como fonte, a qual reveste-se de alguma importância até os nossos dias.

BAZAR

No hebraico, **chuts**, «rua», «lado de fora». É palavra usada por cento e setenta e seis vezes, sozinha ou em combinação com prefixos. Em I Reis 20:34, a nossa versão portuguesa diz «bazar», como tradução dessa palavra. Nos países do Oriente Próximo e Médio, os bazares eram armados em plena via pública, nas ruas ou nas praças. Ben-Hadade permitiu que Acabe tivesse bazares em Damasco, em retribuição ao fato de que o pai de Ben-Hadade tivera bazares em Samaria. (Z)

BAZLITE

No hebraico, «petição» ou «nudez». Era cabeça de uma família cujos descendentes retornaram do cativeiro babilônico em companhia de Zorobabel, junto com os servidores do templo (Nee. 7:54), em cerca de 536 A.C. Em Esdras 2:52, temos uma forma variante do nome, «Bazlute». Não se sabe qual é a forma correta. (S Z)

BDÉLIO

Termo que no hebraico é **bedolach**, e que aparece somente por duas vezes: Gên. 2:12 e Núm. 11:7. Na primeira referência aparece como uma das riquezas da terra de Havilá, na segunda, como descrição da aparência do maná. O bdélio é uma resina gomosa aromática, da espécie *Commiphora*. Exuda de uma árvore similar à mirra. Era muito apreciado pelos povos antigos, para ser usado na arte do perfumista. Assemelha-se à mirra tanto quanto a cor quanto no tocante a seu gosto amargo. Por ser uma verdadeira goma, está relacionada aos açúcares e é solúvel em água. (S UN Z)

BEALIAS

No hebraico, «Yahweh é Senhor». Foi um guerreiro ambidestro, da tribo de Benjamim, que deu apoio à causa de Davi (I Crô. 12:5), em cerca de 1054 A.C.

BEALOTE

No hebraico, «cidadãos» (?); ou então, através do grego, «possuidoras» ou «senhoras». Era nome de uma cidade no extremo sul do território de Judá (ver Jos. 15:24), que talvez deva ser identificada com a Baal aludida em I Crônicas 4:33 ou com a Baalate-Beer, que era a Ramá do Neguebe (Jos. 19:8). Alguns estudiosos também pensam em Alote, referida em I Reis 4:16, como uma possível identificação.

Um distrito que, juntamente com Aser, fazia parte do distrito do nono oficial de Salomão (ver I Reis 4:16). Havia doze intendentes que forneciam mantimentos ao rei e à casa real (ID).

BEATIFICAÇÃO

Vem do latim, **beatus**, «bendito», e **facere**, «fazer». O termo refere-se àquele estágio da canonização (que vide), dentro da Igreja Católica Romana, mediante o qual um candidato à classificação de «santo» é declarado uma pessoa «bendita», com o direito de receber honras religiosas públicas. (E P)

BEBAI

No hebraico, «paternal». Na Bíblia devemos pensar em três homens com esse nome; a saber:

1. O cabeça de uma das famílias que retornou com Zorobabel, após o cativeiro (ver o artigo) (Esd. 2:11; Nee. 7:16). Dentre essa família, outras vinte e oito pessoas retornaram do exílio com Esdras. (Esd. 8:11). Alguns deles haviam-se casado com mulheres estrangeiras, das quais tiveram de divorciar-se. (Esd. 10:28). Alguns estudiosos, porém, pensam que devemos pensar, nesse caso, em um outro Bebai, líder dos vinte e oito homens que vieram com Esdras.

2. Um homem que assinou o pacto referido no décimo capítulo do livro de Neemias (Nee. 10:15), em cerca de 445 A.C.

No livro de Judite (15:4), há menção a uma cidade chamada Bebai, até hoje não identificada, cujos habitantes perseguiram as forças assírias em fuga, após a morte de Holofernes. (ID S)

BEBEDICE

Ver os artigos sobre **Alcoolismo** e **Bebida Forte**.

••• ••• •••

BEBER O SANGUE DE CRISTO

Ver **Comer a Carne e Beber o Sangue de Jesus**.

Estes termos implicam comunhão *mística* do homem com Deus. Ver *Jesus como o Pão da Vida*.

BEBIDA, BEBER — BEBIDA FORTE

BEBIDA, BEBER
Consideremos estes pontos a respeito:
1. *O uso de bebidas alcoólicas*. Ver o artigo sobre o *alcoolismo*. No hebraico temos a palavra *shekar*, usada por vinte e três vezes (por exemplo: Lev. 10:9; Núm. 6:3; Pro. 20:1; Isa. 5:11; 56:12; Miq. 2:11). No grego, temos as seguintes palavras a considerar: 1. Síkera (usada por uma vez, em Luc. 1:15), «cerveja de cevada». 2. *Óksos* (usada por cinco vezes: Mat. 27:48; Mar. 15:36; Luc. 23:36; João 19:29,30), «vinho azedo» ou «vinagre». 3. *Oînos*, «vinho» (usado por trinta e cinco vezes: Mat. 9:17; 27:34; Mar. 2:22; 15:23; Luc. 1:15; 5:37,38; 7:33; 10:34; João 2:3,9,10; 4:46; Rom. 14:21; Efé. 5:18; I Tim. 3:8; 5:23; Tito 2:3; Apo. 6:6; 14:8,10; 16:19; 17:2; 18:3,13; 19:15). 4. *Gleûkos*, «vinho novo doce» (usado apenas em Atos 2:13).

Os hebreus faziam seu vinho de uva, de romã (Can. 8:2) e de outras frutas. Além disso, vários cereais eram empregados para a produção de certo tipo de cerveja. Havia também a cidra ou vinho de maçã. Vinho de mel era preparado com vinho misturado com mel e pimenta. No Egito, também fabricava-se vinho de tâmaras. Plínio informa-nos que, em sua época, se fazia vinho de figos, de espelta e de alfarrobeira. Os antigos árabes usavam passas de uvas para fabricar uma bebida fortemente alcoólica, sendo possível que os judeus conhecessem tal tipo de bebida. Ver o artigo sobre o *Vinho*. Os judeus, como muitos povos antigos e modernos, — eram um povo que costumava beber vinho; — porém, a moderação em sua ingestão sempre foi preceituada. Esse conceito passou para as páginas do Novo Testamento. Assim, lemos Paulo recomendando a Timóteo que usasse um pouco de vinho, para ajudá-lo em seus problemas estomacais (*I Tim*. 5:23). Os líderes da Igreja cristã precisavam dar exemplo de moderação na ingestão do vinho, um item que aparece entre as qualificações essenciais aos pastores (I Tim. 3:3,8). Não obstante, o Novo Testamento sempre se volta contra as idéias ascéticas (que vide), conforme se vê, por exemplo, em Col. 2:16 ss.

Fala a Ciência. Sabe-se atualmente que qualquer dose de álcool, posta a circular na corrente sangüínea, mata células do cérebro. Isso significa que o consumo de qualquer quantidade de bebida alcoólica é um assalto contra o próprio cérebro de quem o bebe. Visto que isso é verdade, então, com base em I Cor. 3:16,17, é errado consumir qualquer quantidade de bebidas alcoólicas. Observemos, pois, que a ciência é capaz de melhorar os princípios éticos, acima daquilo que é antecipado pela fé religiosa!

2. *Outros usos de bebidas nas Escrituras*. a. A ingestão de qualquer líquido (I Cor. 10:31), o que, como todas as atividades humanas, pode redundar na glória de Deus. b. Como *símbolo* da expressão espiritual da fé de alguém em Deus (Isa. 32:6; João 6:54,55; 7:37; I Cor. 10:4). c. Beber metaforicamente do sangue de Cristo, — equivale a alimentar-se espiritualmente e participar de seu ser, compartilhando de sua natureza (Jo. 6:54). Naturalmente, há nisso uma certa alusão à Ceia do Senhor (que vide), mas, o que está em pauta é aquilo que é simbolizado pelo rito, e não o rito propriamente dito. Ver o artigo sobre o conceito de *comer a carne e beber o sangue de Cristo*, que participa dos vários sentidos vinculados à essa passagem. Ver também sobre a *transubstanciação* e sobre *Jesus como o Pão da Vida*. d. A aceitação simbólica da vontade do Pai, por parte do Filho (João 18:11). e. A participação da *Ceia do Senhor* (que vide) Mat. 26:27; I Cor. 10:21; 11:25, que inclui as idéias de participação espiritual em suas virtudes e em sua natureza, como quem festeja em sua *memória*. f. O recebimento da ira e do julgamento de Deus é como sorver uma bebida (Jó 21:20; Sal. 75:8; Apo. 14:10). g. Participação simbólica em toda a espécie de mal, por parte dos pecadores (Jó 15:16; Pro. 4:17; 26:6). h. Beber sangue simboliza provocar matança entre os inimigos (Eze. 39:18). i. O processo mediante o qual a terra é regada pelas chuvas que caem do céu é retratado pela idéia de beber (Heb. 6:7). (LAN NTI S UN Z)

BEBIDA FORTE
Várias palavras hebraicas e gregas precisam ser consideradas:

a. Uma palavra hebraica indica o suco fermentado da uva, sendo geralmente traduzida por «vinho». Essa palavra é usada por cento e quarenta e uma vezes no Antigo Testamento, com cognatos nas línguas dos povos que viviam ao redor da Palestina, embora talvez não de origem semita. O seu equivalente grego é *oînos*, «vinho». (Ver Gên. 9:21; Êxo. 29:40; Núm. 6:3; Zac. 10:7, etc.).

b. Uma outra palavra hebraica é usada por trinta e oito vezes no Antigo Testamento, também traduzida por «vinho» ou «vinho novo», esta última sendo a sua verdadeira tradução. As alusões da palavra indicam que essa bebida era tóxica quando ingerida em grande quantidade. Oséias 4:11 diz que tanto o «vinho» quanto o «mosto» (outra tradução para essa palavra) «tiram entendimento» (cf. Juí. 9:13; Atos 2:13). A LXX também traduziu essa palavra por *oînos*.

c. Outra palavra hebraica deriva-se de uma raiz que significa «fermentar». Essa é a forma poética para indicar «vinho», no hebraico (ver Deu. 32:14), aparecendo também como seu cognato aramaico (ver Esd. 6:9; 7:22; Dan. 5:1,2,4,23).

d. Um sinônimo poético da segunda dessas palavras deriva-se da raiz que significa «esmagar». É usado apenas por cinco vezes na Bíblia, em Can. 8:2; Isa. 49:26; Joel 1:5; 3:18 e Amós 9:13).

e. Uma quinta palavra hebraica usualmente é traduzida por «bebida forte», proveniente de uma raiz que significa «ficar embriagado». Essa palavra era usada para denotar qualquer bebida alcoólica feita de fruto ou cereal, embora originalmente incluísse o vinho (ver Núm. 28:7; cf. 28:14). Em Isaías 5:11, essa palavra é usada como paralelo da primeira delas, como alusão a bebidas alcoólicas em geral. Mas nossa versão portuguesa, nesse versículo, só faz alusão ao vinho. Com o tempo, essa quinta palavra veio a indicar somente bebidas intoxicantes não feitas com base na uva. Sacerdotes e nazireus não podiam consumir vinho e bebida forte (ver Lev. 10:9; Núm. 6:3; cf. Juí. 13:4,7,14; e também Luc. 1:15, «*oînon kai síkera*»). Em Pro. 20:1, lê-se que o vinho é «escarnecedor» e que a bebida forte é «alvoroçadora» (cf. Pro. 31:4,6). Quando Eli acusou Ana de estar embriagada, ela retrucou: «Não bebi nem vinho nem bebida forte; porém venho derramar a minha alma perante o Senhor» (I Sam. 1:15).

Vinho misturado. No período do Antigo Testamento, o vinho era tomado puro porque diluí-lo com água era considerado indesejável. O vinho diluído com água tornou-se símbolo de adultério espiritual (ver Isa. 1:22). Nos tempos romanos algumas vezes o vinho era misturado com água, porque alguns criam que isso melhorava a qualidade do vinho (ver II Macabeus 15:39). O vinho vermelho geralmente era considerado melhor e mais forte que o vinho branco (ver Sal. 75:8;

BEBIDA FORTE

Pro. 23:31). Os vinhos do Líbano (ver Osé. 14:7) e os de Hebrom (ver Eze. 27:18) provavelmente eram vinhos brancos. As vinhas de Hebrom eram famosas por seus imensos cachos de uvas (ver Núm. 13:23). Samaria era um centro de viticultura (ver Jer. 31:5; Miq. 1:6), e os efraimitas tinham a má reputação de serem grandes bebedores de vinhos (ver Isa. 28:1).

Também há menção ao «vinho aromático», em Can. 8:2. Eram vinhos preparados com diferentes espécies de ervas, seguindo o costume de povos não-israelitas do Oriente Próximo, e muito mais embriagadores que o vinho regular. Esse fato fazia esse tipo de vinho muito popular nos banquetes e ocasiões festivas (ver Pro. 9:2,5). A Bíblia proíbe claramente o uso desse tipo de bebida alcoólica (ver Pro. 23:29,30; em português, «bebida misturada»).

Quando o vinho era misturado com mirra, era usado como um anestésico. Foi esse tipo de bebida que ofereceram a Jesus, quando de Sua crucificação (ver Mat. 27:34; Mar. 15:23). Os rabinos, em seus escritos, referem-se a várias misturas de vinhos. Havia uma mistura de vinho velho com água cristalina e bálsamo, usada especialmente após o banho. Havia também um vinho de uvas passas e um vinho misturado com um molho de azeite e (garum?). Uma mistura popular era a de vinho com mel e pimenta. E havia muitas outras formas de mistura com vinho. Um bom vinagre era feito misturando-se cevada ao vinho.

Atitude da Bíblia para com o uso do vinho. A atitude refletida por toda a Bíblia, quanto ao uso do vinho como uma bebida, é muito bem expressa por Ben Siraque: «O vinho bebido com moderação e no tempo certo produz alegria no coração e ânimo mental» (Eclesiástico 31:28,29). Todos os israelitas consumiam regularmente o vinho, exceto – no caso dos sacerdotes que ministravam no santuário, os nazireus e os recabitas. Mas a Bíblia constantemente denuncia a incontinência no uso do vinho, pois o *excesso* era considerado pecaminoso (ver Prov. 20:1; 23:29-35; Isa. 5:11,22; 28:7,8; Osé. 4:11). Paulo recomendava moderação no uso do vinho (ver I Cor. 8:7-13 e Rom. 14:13-21).

Todavia, o vinho também é elogiado na Bíblia. Ver Juízes 9:13: «Deixaria eu o meu vinho, que agrada a Deus e aos homens...?» (Cf. Sal. 104:15; Ecl. 10:19). *Metaforicamente*, o vinho representa a essência da bondade. Algumas vezes os israelitas acompanhavam com cânticos a ingestão de vinho (ver Isa. 24:9). A boa esposa é comparada a uma «videira frutífera» (Sal. 128:3). Israel é comparada a uma vinha que Deus trouxe do Egito e plantou na terra prometida, onde «deitou profundas raízes e encheu a terra» (Sal. 80:8-11). A prosperidade algumas vezes é simbolizada pela abundância de vinho, como quando Jacó abençoou a Judá (ver Gên. 49:11). Os tempos de paz e de prosperidade são descritos como segue, em I Reis 4:25: «Judá e Israel habitavam confiados, cada um debaixo da sua videira, e debaixo da sua figueira...» Isaías utiliza-se do vinho como figura das bênçãos espirituais (ver Isa. 55:1,2).

Ao que tudo indica na Bíblia, o uso moderado de vinho não é repreensível (ver Est. 1:10; Sal. 104:15; Ecl. 10:19; Zac. 10:7). As referências bíblicas ao vinho mostram que a ingestão dessa bebida fazia parte da dieta regular dos israelitas (ver Gên. 14:18; Juí. 19:19; I Sam. 16:20; II Crô. 11:11). Se a mera ingestão de vinho fosse pecaminosa, Jesus não teria transformado água em vinho no casamento em Caná da Galiléia (ver João 2:1-11), e nem Paulo teria recomendado a Timóteo: «Não continues a beber somente água; usa um pouco de vinho, por causa do teu estômago e das tuas freqüentes enfermidades» (I Tim. 5:23). O que as Escrituras condenam não é o uso e, sim, o *abuso* de bebidas alcoólicas. «E não vos embriagueis com vinho, no qual há dissolução, mas enchei-vos do Espírito» (Efé. 5:18). Os crentes não devem assemelhar-se aos incrédulos, muitos dos quais tornam-se viciados no alcoolismo, como em vários outros vícios (ver I Ped. 4:3). Por isso mesmo, os líderes cristãos são exortados à temperança (ver I Tim. 3,3,8). Há somente uma ocasião em que Paulo veda totalmente o uso do vinho ao crente, isto é, se chegar a ser pedra de tropeço a algum irmão (ver Rom. 14:21).

A viticultura na Palestina. A produção de vinhos era importante no Oriente Próximo, sendo descrita na Bíblia com muitas referências. (Ver Gên. 40:11; Deu. 18:4; Jos. 9:4; I Crô. 27:27; Eze. 17:5-10). A viticultura era considerada tão importante em Israel que os proprietários de vinhas eram isentados do serviço militar, no tempo da colheita da uva, no mês de setembro (Jer. 25:30; 48:33). A vindima, ou colheita da uva, é referida em conexão com a festa dos tabernáculos (ver Deu. 16:13). Os pobres podiam ficar com as uvas que caíssem ao chão, como também podiam fazê-lo com todas as outras colheitas. No ano sabático, as vinhas não recebiam cultivo, tal qual sucedia a qualquer outro tipo de plantação. O vinho, enquanto fermentava, era sujeito a muitos cuidados. Um deles consistia em derramar o vinho de um receptáculo para outro, para evitar qualquer engrossamento indesejável. Jeremias 48:11 faz alusão a esse costume. Uma vez que o vinho estivesse refinado e pronto para ser guardado por longos períodos de tempo, era colocado em jarras forradas com betume, postas então em «adegas» (ver I Crô. 27:27). Vinho não-fermentado, ou suco de uva, na opinião de alguns especialistas no assunto, era impossível de ser guardado por qualquer período de tempo, na Palestina antiga. Portanto, o vinho referido no Antigo e no Novo Testamentos tinha certa dosagem alcoólica. A preservação do suco de uva é um processo moderno.

Usos do vinho no mundo bíblico. Por todo o Oriente Médio e Próximo o vinho era usado nas libações aos deuses pagãos. Os hebreus foram constantemente advertidos pelos profetas de Deus a não se deixarem envolver nesses sacrifícios (ver Deu. 32:37,38; Isa. 57:6; 65:11; Jer. 7:18; 19:13). As libações que faziam parte dos sacrifícios levíticos eram de vinho (ver Êxo. 29:40; Lev. 23:13; Núm. 15:7,10; 28:14). Os adoradores, quando ofereciam sacrifícios, geralmente levavam vinho, entre outros requisitos, (ver I Sam. 1:24; 10:3,8). Havia certo suprimento de vinho guardado no templo, para propósitos de sacrifícios (ver I Crô. 9:29).

Além disso, o vinho era usado como medicamento, para revivificar os que desmaiassem (ver II Sam. 16:2), ou como sedativo, «aos amargurados de espírito» (Pro. 31:6). Os rabinos tinham um ditado que dizia: «O vinho é o melhor dos medicamentos; quando falta o vinho, tornam-se necessárias as drogas». O vinho era até mesmo derramado sobre os ferimentos, como se vê no caso do homem vitimado pelos assaltantes, em Lucas 10:34. Finalmente, o vinho era um importante artigo comercial e também era doado como presente. Davi recebeu de Abigail «dois odres de vinho» (I Sam. 25:18), e Ziba lhe deu «um odre de vinho» (II Sam. 16:1). Quando Salomão edificou o templo de Jerusalém, pagou a Hirão, entre outras coisas, «vinte mil batos de vinho» (II Crô. 2:10), pela madeira do Líbano e pela ajuda dos operários de Hirão.

Nos tempos modernos, a viticultura tem-se tornado a mais importante atividade agrícola em Israel. (I ID LAN UN)

BEC

Famoso centro monástico de erudição, com influências sobre a Normandia e a Inglaterra. Foi fundado perto de Rouen, na França, em cerca de 1034 D.C. Foi imortalizado por causa de grandes líderes e mestres que dali saíram, como Lanfranc e Anselmo (ver artigo a respeito). Muitos teólogos, mestres, legistas e arcebispos tiveram seus nomes associados àquele lugar. (E)

BECA

Ver **Pesos e Medidas**.

BECK, JOHANN TOBIAS

Teólogo protestante (1804-1874). Foi professor do Novo Testamento em Basel, em 1842, professor em Tubingen (ver o artigo), e um dos principais representantes modernos do realismo bíblico. Beck produziu frutíferas obras exegéticas e teológicas. *Suas idéias*: Ele concebia o Espírito Santo como agente da vida criativa. Sua atuação envolveria a formação e orientação de seu povo, bem como a produção das Sagradas Escrituras. Os pontos de vista de Beck ajudaram a entravar os excessos da teologia liberal. Através de seus seguidores, especialmente Ad. Schlatter, sua influência prossegue até hoje na teologia do continente europeu. (E)

BECKET, THOMAS

Arcebispo de Canterbury e chanceler da Inglaterra (1118-1170). Nasceu em Londres e faleceu em Canterbury. Foi um dos favoritos de Henrique II, distinguiu-se como militar, estadista e eclesiástico. Porém, sua lealdade à Igreja e sua oposição às intervenções do estado, deixaram o rei inglês indignado. E isso forçou Becket a refugiar-se na França. Houve a reconciliação, e Becket retornou à Inglaterra. Porém, surgiram novas dificuldades. Então Becket foi assassinado por homens enviados por Henrique II, a sua catedral de Canterbury. Foi canonizado três anos após sua morte. O lugar de seu sepultamento tornou-se objeto de peregrinações, até que foi violado por Henrique VIII. A festa em sua honra é celebrada a 29 de dezembro. Ver o artigo sobre as Constituições de Clarendon. (AM E)

BECORATE

No hebraico, «primogênito». Era filho de Afia ou Abia, neto de Bequer, um antepassado de Saul (I Sam. 9:1). Cerca de 1225 A.C.

BECTILETE

Uma planície que havia em algum trecho entre Nínive e o norte da Cilícia (Judite 2:21). Holofernes, partindo de Nínive, chegou a essa planície, após uma marcha de três dias. Naquele livro é dito que a planície ficava próxima de um monte no norte da Cilícia Superior. Ali estabelecido, Holofernes começou a assaltar as áreas adjacentes. Alguns estudiosos pensam que Bactali, que figura nas tabelas de Peutinger, cerca de 34 km de Antioquia, é a antiga localização.

BEDÃ

No hebraico, «filho de julgamento», embora outros estudiosos prefiram dizer que o significado do nome é incerto. Era filho de Ulão, descendente de Manassés (I Crô. 7:17). Seu nome aparece entre os juízes, em I Sam. 12:11, à margem, embora nada se saiba sobre isso em qualquer trecho da Bíblia. Na LXX e na versão Peshita, aparece ali o nome Baraque (ver o artigo). Alguns eruditos pensam que o nome é a forma abreviada de Abdom (ver o artigo), filho de Hilel, que julgou Israel por oito anos, em Piratom (Juí. 12:13). Há outras identificações ainda menos prováveis. Os estudiosos confessam que não há como estabelecer uma identificação indiscutível. (S Z)

BEDADE

No hebraico, «sozinho». Um rei idumeu, pai de Hadade (Gên. 36:35 e I Crô. 1:46), que reinou em Edom antes que houvesse rei em Israel. Cerca de 1500 A.C.

BEDE, O VENERÁVEL

Monge e erudito inglês (673-735). Foi autor de uma *História Eclesiástica do Povo Inglês*. Passou a maior parte de sua vida no mosteiro de Jarrow. Era altamente respeitado em face de sua piedade e erudição, e sua fama espalhou-se por toda a Europa. Sua maior obra literária foi a história que ele escreveu, que continua sendo usada, até hoje, como obra de referência sobre a história eclesiástica de sua época para trás, embora ele tivesse escrito um total de quarenta livros. (AM E)

BEDIAS

No hebraico, «servo de Yahweh», um homem da família de Bani, que se casara com uma mulher estrangeira, estando no cativeiro, na Babilônia (Esd. 10:35), em cerca de 458 A.C.

BEDLAM

A palavra é contração do inglês Bethlehem, «Belém». A princípio foi um famoso hospital em Londres, fundado em 1247 pela ordem de Nossa Senhora de Belém. Era um hospital dedicado aos pobres. Posteriormente, tornou-se um asilo de alienados mentais (1405). Sofreu várias mudanças de localização, terminando em Southward, nos Campos de São Jorge. Tornou-se conhecido como um lugar de desespero e vergonha. No século XVIII, seus internos eram exibidos aos visitantes, que podiam entrar ali gratuitamente; e assim o nome tornou-se sinônimo de abuso e opróbrio. Atualmente, entretanto, é conhecido pelo tratamento humano e bem-sucedido oferecido aos insanos. (E)

BEECHER, HENRY WARD

Ministro congregacional (1813-1887). Nasceu em Litchfield, estado de Connecticut, nos Estados Unidos da América, filho de rev. Lyman Foote e sua esposa, Roxana. Formou-se em Amherst, em 1834, tendo estudado teologia no Seminário Lane, em Cincinnati, estado de Ohio, onde exerceu atividades pastorais. Finalmente, estabeleceu-se na Igreja Plymouth (congregacional), no Brooklyn, Nova Iorque, onde permaneceu pelo resto de sua vida. Beecher foi um dos mais brilhantes e influentes pregadores dos tempos contemporâneos. Foi líder na campanha antiescravagista, e terminou envolvendo-se em outras reformas. Ajudava a causa unionista do presidente Lincoln através de seus discursos, tendo ido à Inglaterra com esse propósito, em 1863. Caiu em desgraça através de um notório julgamento de adultério, em 1874. O juri não conseguiu chegar a um consenso. Posteriormente, Beecher foi inocentado por um concílio eclesiástico. Grandes homens, grandes vícios, *talvez*. Em seu leito de morte, foi ouvido a sussurrar: «Agora, estou indo para o Grande Desconhecido». Verdadeiramente, nosso conhecimento do após-vida não é muito grande, a despeito de nossas experiências e de nossa teologia. Mas o crente fundado na Bíblia sabe para onde está indo. O que Beecher sabia é que ele estava indo para uma outra faceta da existência, sem importar as surpresas que por ele esperavam. As pesquisas modernas demonstram que há evidências científicas da existência da alma e de sua sobrevivência ante a morte física. E, quanto mais sabemos, mais otimistas ficamos acerca de toda essa questão. (AM E)

BEELIADA

No hebraico, «o Senhor sabe», ou «conhecido por Baal». Foi um dos filhos de Davi, nascido em Jerusalém (I Crô. 14:7). Posteriormente, seu nome foi mudado para Eliada, que no hebraico significa «Deus sabe», quando o nome de Baal passou a ser evitado, devido à sua conexão com a idolatria (II Sam. 5:16), em cerca de 1045 A.C. (S)

BEEMOTE

Essa palavra transliterada do hebraico, e que é apenas a forma plural de *behamah*, «fera», não figura em nossa versão portuguesa. Mas em Jó 40:15 está em foco algum animal, que nossa versão confiantemente traduz por «hipopótamo». Nesse caso, o plural deve ter um uso intensivo. Na verdade, a passagem em Jó é figurada, e a única coisa que se pode dizer com certeza é que está em foco algum animal aquático, poderoso (vs. 23), que come erva (vs. 15).

O hipopótamo era conhecido nos tempos bíblicos, e os registros antigos mostram cenas de caça a esse animal por meio de arpões e ganchos munidos de farpa (Diod. *Siculus* 37:35). Sabemos que o hipopótamo tem seu habitat na África, e que, em tenpos antigos, existia no Egito e nos rios que desembocam no Mediterrâneo oriental. Há evidências de que havia hipopótamos no rio Orontes, na Síria, em cerca de 1500 A.C., porém, pelo século XII D.C., o hipopótamo foi extinto na Síria. Embora seu nome signifique, no grego «cavalo do rio», o hipopótamo é mais aparentado ao porco. Seu casco é dividido, mas não rumina, embora dotado de um complexo estômago com três câmaras, para digerir as massas de alimento vegetal que ele devora. (BOD WOD)

BEER

No hebraico, «poço». Um nome próprio que denota duas localidades no Antigo Testamento:

1. Um lugar em Moabe, onde Israel acampou (Núm. 21:16), do outro lado do ribeiro de Arnom. O lugar era assim chamado porque havia um poço naquele local, escavado pelos príncipes do povo. Ali Deus deu ao povo de Israel água abundante, para deleite deles. O local tem sido identificado com Beer-Elim, «poço dos heróis», referido em Isaías 15:8.

2. Uma aldeia da tribo de Judá, para onde Jotão fugiu, após haver enunciado a parábola em que denunciava seu irmão Abimeleque, por haver este se apossado sangüinariamente do poder (Juí. 9:21). O local é desconhecido, mas muitos supõem que ficava perto do monte Gerizim. (ID)

BEER-ELIM

No hebraico, «poço dos heróis», que figura somente em Isa. 15:8. Talvez se trate de outro nome do mesmo lugar chamado Beer (que vide), referido em Núm. 21:16,18, como uma das cidades moabitas.

BEER-LAAI-ROI

No hebraico, «poço do Vivo que me vê». Um poço localizado entre Cades e Berede (Gên. 16:14), onde o anjo do Senhor apareceu a Hagar, quando ela fugia de Sara, sua patroa. Ver o artigo sobre Hagar. Os arqueólogos têm identificado tentativamente esse poço a dezenove quilômetros a noroeste de Ain Kadis, em 'Ain el-Muweileh, cuja pronúncia árabe assemelha-se um pouco ao nome original e tem o mesmo significado.

BEERA

No hebraico, «o poço». Foi chefe guerreiro da tribo de Aser (I Crô. 7:37), filho de Zofa. Cerca de 1570 A.C.

Em nossa versão portuguesa aparece um outro *Beera* em I Crô. 5:6, embora o hebraico grafe o nome deste de modo levemente diferente do daquele. Este último foi um dos chefes do clã da tribo de Rúben, que foi levado ao exílio por Tiglate-Pileser, rei da Assíria, em cerca de 740 A.C. Os estudiosos afiançam que seu nome significa «expositor», embora outros discordem da interpretação.

BEERI

No hebraico, «fonte» ou «ilustre». Há duas pessoas com esse nome:

1. Um heteu, pai de Judite, uma das esposas de Esaú (Gên. 26:34) em cerca de 1963 A.C. Com toda a probabilidade, Judite é a mesma Aolibama de Gênesis 36:2. Isso faria de Beeri e Anaque a mesma pessoa.

2. Pai do profeta Oséias (Osé 1:1), em cerca de 800 A.C. (S)

BEEROTE-BENE-JACÃ

No hebraico, «poços dos filhos de Jacã». Alguns estudiosos opinam que se trata do mesmo lugar chamado algures de Beer (que vide). Mas outros negam essa identificação. Seja como for, foi uma das quatro cidades envolvidas no tratado com os gibeonitas (Jos. 9:17), que a confederação dos heveus, por meio de ludíbrio, estabeleceu com Josué (Jos. 9:7). Posteriormente, tornou-se cidade pertencente à tribo de Benjamim (Jos. 18:25; II Sam. 4:2). Após o exílio, foi repovoada (Esd. 2:25).

Um dos trinta principais guerreiros de Davi era natural dali, de nome Naarai, que foi armeiro de Joabe (II Sam. 23:27; I Crô. 11:39). Atualmente, o lugar é de localização desconhecida, embora alguns o identifiquem com a moderna el-Bireh, a treze quilômetros ao norte de Jerusalém. Porém, várias outras identificações, antigas e modernas, têm sido propostas, sem que se chegue a uma certeza indiscutível.

Em Números 33:31,32, esse nome reaparece, sob a forma Bene-Jaacã, como localidade onde os israelitas passaram por duas vezes, em suas andanças pelo deserto, com seus acampamentos de número vinte e sete e trinta e três, em sua jornada do Egito à terra de Canaã. Provavelmente ficava no vale de Arabá, um lugar distinto daquele acima mencionado. O local mencionado em Números tem sido identificado com a moderna Birein. (SI UN)

BEESTERÁ

No hebraico, «em Astarte». Essa cidade pertencia à meia-tribo de Manassés, que habitava na Transjordânia, e que foi dada aos levitas (Jos. 21:27). Na lista paralela de I Crônicas 6:71, o nome Astarote aparece, porquanto Beesterá é apenas uma forma contraída de Bete-Astarote, «casa de Astarte».

BEHAVIORISMO

O nome indica uma psicologia moderna, baseada nas idéias de Pavlov, um russo, e de J.B. Watson (ver o artigo), um norte-americano. Visto que esse sistema alicerça-se sobre pressupostos do materialismo, suas bases encontram-se em Demócrito e em Thomas Hobbes. De acordo com esse sistema, qualquer idéia de uma alma imaterial, e conseqüentes fenômenos mentais, é repudiada. O pensamento é equiparado aos movimentos do corpo, a ações e reações. O ato de pensar é chamado de fala subvocal. Mas, se o pensamento consiste apenas nisso, então a observação dos behavioristas sobre o *meu comportamento* consiste na mera observação de minha laringe em movimento! Quando a laringe é removida mediante uma intervenção cirúrgica, não há cessamento de pensamento! A fim de evitar essa conclusão lógica, os behavioristas têm expandido extraordinariamente a sua definição de pensamento, a ponto de incluírem na mesma todos os hábitos formados durante o processo do exercício das aptidões biológicas. Segundo eles dizem, não há mentes, mas tão-somente corpos dotados de cérebros físicos e reações a estímulos externos e internos. Nesse sistema, são negados os instintos e a introspecção. Todo comportamento vê-se reduzido a ações de estímulo e reação. Em outras palavras, o homem seria apenas uma máquina de carne. O papel do condicionamento (que seria tudo quanto está envolvido no *aprendizado*) é a função toda-importante dessa máquina. Isso significa, por sua vez, que todo conhecimento é reduzido ao que os sentidos do corpo físico são capazes de colher. Como uma ciência social, esse sistema é extremamente determinista, porquanto, segundo o mesmo, o homem é apenas uma vítima impotente de seu meio ambiente, não dispondo de recursos internos para alterar a sua sorte e destino. O comportamento seria apenas a soma total das influências que atuam sobre um indivíduo. Esse ponto de vista não abre espaço para as determinações da vontade e nem para a responsabilidade moral.

A falácia do sistema é que o mesmo ignora tudo quanto a filosofia, a psicologia, a ciência e a teologia têm podido recolher de informes em favor dos fenômenos não-materiais, incluindo os fenômenos da alma (ver o artigo). Ver também o artigo sobre o problema do corpo-mente. Ver também as experiências quase-morte, as quais demonstram claramente, pela experiência humana, que há uma outra dimensão da vida.

Do ponto de vista moral, o sistema behaviorista caracteriza-se por uma pobreza extrema. Segundo ele, o homem é uma vítima ao longo de sua existência, sem qualquer capacidade de vencer, triunfar e criar.

Porém, quanto mais aprendemos sobre o ser humano, tanto mais se torna evidente, mesmo sem levar em conta a teologia, que o homem é um ser criativo, e não um mero robô, que atua quando estimulado ao acaso. (H P)

BEIJO

Ninguém sabe quando os homens começaram a beijar, mas podemos estar certos de que o costume nunca terminará. Há o beijo casto, como de uma mãe em seu filhinho, ou de uma criança em outra. Há o beijo de saudação, especialmente nos tempos antigos, que tem reflexos até nas Escrituras (ver Gên. 29:11; I Cor. 16:20b). E há também o beijo sensual. O beijo boca a boca é perigoso, por causa da contaminação que pode transmitir. Ver o artigo sobre *Boca*, quanto a evidências sobre a questão. Pelo menos na Bíblia, o beijo é tão antigo quanto a própria história. E, visto que alguns animais têm uma espécie de beijo, podemos especular que o beijo deve ser tão antigo quanto os próprios corpos físicos.

1. *Modo de beijar*. O beijo é uma carícia que consiste em pressionar os lábios e sugar de leve sobre outros lábios, rosto, barba, testa, mão, pé, etc. Mas, de algumas outras vezes, as pessoas soltam beijos no ar, o que não requer qualquer contacto físico. Também são beijados objetos, como sinal de alegria ou afeto. Algumas pessoas chegam a beijar animais!

2. *Sua significação*. As ações com freqüência falam mais alto que as palavras. Assim, o ósculo é usado para expressar afeto, respeito, homenagem, saudação, despedida, gesto cerimonial, sinal de intuito pacífico, sinal de respeito religioso, ou mesmo intuito sedutor. Naturalmente, há também o beijo romântico, que Hollywood se encarregou de popularizar.

3. *Alusões bíblicas ao beijo*. O beijo era usado, nos dias patriarcais, como uma saudação (Gên. 29:13), ou como sinal de afeto (Gên. 27:26,27). Também era sinal de amizade, quando se saudava alguém na chegada ou na partida (II Sam. 20:9; Tobias 7:6; 10:12; Luc. 7:45; 15:20; Atos 20:37; Mat. 26:48). O beijo, com parecer fatal, também era usado em conexão com as práticas idólatras, como quando se osculava a um ídolo, a um altar, ou se lançava beijos aos corpos celestes, que eram venerados (I Reis 19:18; Osé. 13:2; Tácito, *Hist.* iii.24,3; Luciano, *De Salt.*, c. 17; Plínio, *Hist. Nat.* xxviii,5). Em Salmos 2:12; I Samuel 10:1 e Xenofonte *Cyrop.*, encontramos menção ao beijo de homenagem. Xenofonte informa-nos que era um costume dos persas. Beijar os pés de alguém era sinal de obediência e sujeição. Isso pode ser comparado ao beija-pé dado por alguns no papa e em outras altas figuras da hierarquia da Igreja Católica Romana. De algumas vezes, a marca deixada pelo pé no chão, recebia o beijo, e não o pé propriamente dito, o que era um ato de supremo respeito, como se o pé de uma pessoa não pudesse ser osculado devido à elevada posição que a mesma ocupava. Ver Isa. 49:23; Miq. 7:17; Sal. 77:9; Dion Cass. lix,27; Sêneca, *De Benef.* ii.12. Entre os judeus, posteriormente as instruções rabínicas limitaram o beijo a somente três categorias: o beijo de reverência, o beijo de recebimento e o beijo de despedida, *Breschith Rabba*, comentando sobre Gênesis 29:11. Nas páginas da Bíblia, o beijo se dava entre pessoas do mesmo sexo e, entre pessoas de sexos diferentes, Gên. 29:13; 45:15; 19:11; I Sam. 10:1 e 20:41.

4. *O ósculo santo do Novo Testamento*. Ver Atos 20:37; Rom. 16:16; I Cor. 16:20; II Cor. 13:12; I Tes. 5:26; I Ped. 5:14. Já aprendemos que o beijo era uma maneira das pessoas exprimirem afeto, saudação ou

despedida. Esse costume era praticado e mesmo recomendado nos dias do Novo Testamento, sendo ainda usual em alguns países do mundo, como na América Latina, incluindo o Brasil. Mas alguns povos vêem com muito maus olhos o ósculo entre homem e homem, embora ali, ocasionalmente, se veja um homem beijar uma mulher nas saudações ou nas despedidas. Quanto ao ósculo santo, recomendado no Novo Testamento, era apenas natural que a Igreja cristã primitiva incorporasse o que já era um costume social em suas congregações, onde irmãos e irmãs na fé formam uma família, algumas vezes com laços de afeto mais íntimos que as famílias de autênticos laços de sangue. O ósculo santo, em algumas denominações evangélicas, tornou-se parte da liturgia, primariamente como uma forma solene de saudação ou de despedida, e como se fosse até uma das ordenanças da Igreja. Na antiguidade, o ósculo santo tornou-se parte integrante da Ceia do Senhor, embora o próprio Novo Testamento não faça tal conexão. Geralmente, o ósculo santo era dado no final da cerimônia. Justino Mártir, *Apol.* 1, op. 65, mostra-nos que, em seus dias, o ato de beijar fazia parte da cerimônia que circundava a celebração da Ceia do Senhor. As *Constituições Apostólicas* fornecem-nos a mesma informação (século III D.C.). Na Igreja Ortodoxa Oriental, o ósculo santo é dado nos dias de festividade religiosa. Em outros lugares, mais recentemente, pessoas recém-batizadas eram osculadas, como também o eram os convertidos, por ocasião de sua profissão de fé. Os candidatos à ordenação ministerial eram osculados, como também os cadáveres dos líderes! O concílio de Auxerre, em 578 D.C., proibiu essa última prática, pelo que podemos agradecer! O ósculo de paz era um costume comum na Igreja, até durante a Idade Média. Tertuliano, em 150 D.C., refere-se a esse «beijo de paz»; e Clemente de Alexandria alude ao *ósculo místico* (século III D.C.). Não há que duvidar que esses ósculos ocorriam tanto entre pessoas do mesmo sexo como entre pessoas de ambos os sexos. Mas também é quase certo que o ósculo sempre era aplicado na testa ou em uma das mãos, e jamais sobre os lábios. Vários grupos evangélicos de hoje em dia, como a Igreja Ortodoxa Oriental, em suas festas religiosas, os Dunkers (batistas alemães), e alguns grupos evangélicos, como certos grupos de «restauração», retêm essa prática como parte da liturgia e como um ato comum de despedida ou acolhida. Em alguns lugares, em vez de serem osculadas as pessoas, era passada entre os circunstantes uma tabuinha, onde eram aplicados os ósculos, como ato meramente simbólico. Sem dúvida isso passou a ser usual devido aos abusos a que a prática se sujeita. Pensemos na teoria das infecções por germes patogênicos, e sobre essas tabuinhas! E, naturalmente, as pessoas de fortes tendências religiosas continuam a beijar os ídolos, os altares, as relíquias e também o dedão do pé do papa e dos bispos!

Costumes sociais. Alguns insistem que as referências ao ósculo santo, no Novo Testamento, fazem o mesmo tornar-se obrigatório; mas outras pessoas simplesmente não podem aceitar tal posição por causa de costumes sociais ou do senso de propriedade. Na Índia, há o costume de dois homens darem-se as mãos, quando são muito amigos. Se mulheres fazem isso, em outras culturas, nada se repara. Mas por outro lado, se dois homens se dão as mãos, imediatamente surgem dúvidas quanto a seus motivos. O espírito inglês-norte-americano jamais permitiria que homens se beijassem; mas, em outros países, como na Rússia, por exemplo, isso é praticado sem qualquer escrúpulo. Tudo depende dos costumes vigentes. Por outro lado, **um norte-americano**, quando saúda a uma mulher que não seja sua esposa, com um aperto de mão, fá-lo com vigor, pois um aperto de mão mais suave seria olhado com desprezo. No Brasil, porém, dá-se precisamente o contrário. Sei de um missionário norte-americano que foi envolvido em um escândalo porque continuou a praticar em um país estrangeiro, onde foi trabalhar no evangelho, o tipo de aperto de mão norte-americano em relação às mulheres. As referências neotestamentárias mostram que o ósculo santo era um costume generalizado entre os cristãos primitivos, podendo até mesmo ser interpretado como obrigatório, mediante o estudo dos vários trechos bíblicos que aludem à questão. Por outra parte, temos ali um costume tipicamente oriental, com o qual alguns povos modernos não se sentem à vontade. As pessoas que não se sentem bem em oscular outras pessoas, sobretudo no caso de homens com homens, naturalmente, continuarão a prática do aperto de mãos, como substituto. (G LAN NTI WAR).

BEIRA DO RIO

São as margens delimitadoras da largura de um rio. Moisés foi salvo por sua mãe ao ser posto dentro de uma cestinha calafetada, à beira do rio Nilo (ver Êxo. 2:3). O rio Jordão transbordava de suas margens durante a primavera (ver Jos. 3:15 e 4:18). *Uso figurado*: Ezequiel 47:7,12 refere-se às ribanceiras do rio, onde havia certa variedade de árvores, de frutos e folhas igualmente úteis. A Assíria é retratada como um rio que transborda de suas margens e se precipita contra Israel, para destruí-la como um dilúvio (ver Isa. 8:7). (ID S)

BEL

Cognato hebraico do semita ocidental **Baal**, que significa «senhor» ou «proprietário». O equivalente sumério era *En*, um dos títulos de Enlil, deus do vento e das tempestades, um dos participantes originais da tríada suméria de divindades. Com o tempo, o deus Marduque obteve ascendência, e Bel tornou-se um título de honra que lhe era dado, ao passo que o deus Enlil deixou de ser importante. Na Bíblia, Merodaque é mencionado somente em Jer. 50:2; Bel aparece em Isa. 46:1; Jer. 50:2; 51:44, e também na epístola de Jeremias 6:41, obra apócrifa, como parte do nome Belsazar. (Z)

Heródoto (i:181-183) refere-se a um templo em forma de pirâmide, em honra a Bel, construído na Babilônia. Os sacrifícios ali oferecidos consistiam em gado adulto e suas crias. De acordo com o livro apócrifo «Bel e o Dragão», foi a imagem de Bel (Merodaque) que Daniel e seus companheiros se recusaram a adorar. (ID S Z)

BELÁ

No hebraico, «devorado» ou «destruição». É nome de uma localidade e de várias pessoas, referidas no Antigo Testamento:

1. Um lugar onde reinava Zoar (Gên. 14:2,8).

2. O filho de Beor que reinou sobre Edom, em cerca de 1618 A.C., na cidade de Dinabá, oito gerações antes de Saul (Gên. 26:32,33; I Crô. 1:43). Em português, o nome dele é grafado como Bela, sem acento agudo na sílaba final.

3. O filho de Azaz, um rubenita (I Crô. 5:8). Seu nome também é grafado como Bela.

Gruta da Natividade, Belém
—Cortesia, Matson Photo Service

BELÉM CERCADA COM VIDEIRAS E OLIVEIRAS — Cortesia, Matson Photo Service

BELAS ARTES — BEL E O DRAGÃO

4. Filho mais velho de Benjamim, cabeça da família dos belaítas, dentre a qual Eúde foi o mais notável, em cerca de 1700 A.C. (Gên. 46:21; Núm. 26:38). Essa última referência fala sobre os belaítas.

BELAS ARTES

Ver o artigo sobre Artes, que inclui uma discussão sobre as muitas teorias filosóficas acerca da natureza da arte. Ver o artigo separado sobre a *Música*.

BELÉM

No hebraico, «casa do pão» (isto é, do alimento) Alguns estudiosos pensam que a terminação da palavra (no hebraico, *lehem*) alude a uma divindade assíria chamada Lakmu. Nesse caso, o significado do nome seria «casa de Lakmu». Porém, não há a mínima evidência de que tal divindade tivesse sido adorada na área em questão. Há duas aldeias chamadas por esse nome nas páginas do Antigo Testamento, e atualmente têm o nome árabe de *Bayt Lahm*, com sentido idêntico ao hebraico.

1. Uma cidade na Palestina, perto de onde Jacó sepultou Raquel, e que na época era conhecida como Efrata (Gên. 35:19; 48:7), razão pela qual também é denominada Belém Efrata, em Miquéias 5:2. Outros nomes que lhe foram aplicados são: Belém de Judá (I Sam. 17:12); Belém da Judéia (Mat. 2:1) e «cidade de Davi, chamada Belém» (Luc. 2:4; cf. João 7:42). O antigo nome, Efrata, continuou a ser-lhe dado por muito tempo depois que Israel ocupara o território (Rute 1:2; 4:11; I Sam. 17:12; Sal. 132:6). A cidade dá frente para a estrada principal para Hebrom e o Egito, estando situada em uma cadeia de pedra calcária, na região montanhosa da Judéia. Após a conquista, a cidade foi outorgada à tribo de Judá (Juí. 17:7). Ibsã, que era de Belém, julgou Israel após Jefté (Juí. 12:8). Elimeleque, marido de Noemi e sogro de Rute, também era belemita (Rute 1:12), o que também sucedia a Boaz (Rute 2:1,4,11). E, naturalmente, Davi era natural de Belém, onde também foi ungido por Samuel para o futuro rei de Israel (I Sam. 16:1 ss). Por isso, compreendemos o motivo pelo qual Davi anelava por água dali, quando estava no exílio (II Sam. 23:15 ss). A fonte de onde a água lhe foi trazida, aparentemente existe até hoje, juntamente com outras, no lado norte da aldeia.

Belém atingiu seu ponto culminante na história quando Jesus Cristo ali nasceu (Mat. 2:1). Herodes ordenou que todos os meninos de Belém e dos arredores, de dois anos de idade para baixo, fossem mortos, conforme estava predito nas Escrituras, em uma tentativa satânica de destruir o Rei quando ainda infante. O relato sobre os magos também gira em torno de Belém. O imperador romano Adriano mandou devastar o lugar, no século II D.C., para tentar abafar um levante dos judeus. Isso assinalou o começo do grande exílio dos judeus, que foi revertido somente a partir de 1948, com a formação do Estado de Israel. Os turistas em Belém costumam visitar a gruta da Natividade, a igreja da Natividade, mandada erigir por Helena, mãe do imperador Constantino, uma edificação que presumivelmente assinala o local do nascimento de Jesus. Além disso, o tradicional túmulo de Raquel pode ser visto ali, tal como os campos dos pastores. Ver o artigo geral sobre Arqueologia. Atualmente, Belém é um dos principais lugares de peregrinação do mundo, sagrado tanto para os judeus quanto para os cristãos. (AM AH ALB KO)

2. Belém no território de Zebulom (Jos. 19:15), mencionada juntamente com Idala. Essa tem sido identificada com a moderna Beit Lahm, a onze quilômetros a nordeste de Nazaré. Provavelmente era a terra natal de Ibsã, um dos primeiros juízes de Israel (Jos. 12:8,10), onde também ele foi sepultado. A arqueologia tem descoberto ruínas que indicam que, em tempos passados, deve ter sido lugar de alguma importância.

BELÉM, ESTRELA DE

Ver **Estrela dos Magos**, bem como o artigo sobre a **Astronomia**.

BELEMITA

Um habitante de Belém de Judá (ver o artigo) (I Sam. 16:1; Rute 1:1,2; I Sam. 17:12).

BEL E O DRAGÃO

Três trechos diferentes foram adicionados ao livro canônico de Daniel, e esse é um deles. Essas adições aparecem na tradução grega, mas não no original hebraico. Os outros dois trechos são Susana e o Cântico dos Três Mancebos. O concílio de Trento, da Igreja Católica Romana, reconheceu esses livros como inspirados, pelo que se tornaram parte dos livros apócrifos do Antigo Testamento (ver o artigo), em 1545-1563. Alguns poucos dos antigos pais da Igreja, como Orígenes, defendiam o direito desse livro em fazer parte do cânon, mas os protestantes, seguindo o cânon hebraico, têm-no rejeitado coerentemente, junto com todos os livros não reconhecidos pelos judeus. Ver o artigo sobre o *cânon*.

1. *Textos*. Em grego encontramos dois textos básicos: a. um manuscrito da LXX, o códice Chisianus, do século IX D.C.; b. o texto de Teodoreto, representado em vários manuscritos, principalmente B A Q Gamma e Delta. E há também o texto siríaco, um manuscrito do século VIII D.C., feito sobre uma *Hexapla* de Orígenes, col. 6, que segue bem de perto a versão da LXX.

2. *Versões*. a. As versões gregas, segundo dissemos acima. b. Teodoreto, segundo dissemos acima. Ele preparou o seu texto entre 100 e 130 D.C., e Bel e o Dragão faz parte desse texto. c. A versão siríaca é representada por duas versões diferentes: a sírio-a xapla e a Peshita, que mistura o texto da LXX e o de Teodoreto. d. A versão latina, no latim antigo, que se aproxima do texto de Teodoreto e da Vulgata, alicerçada principalmente sobre a tradução de Jerônimo. e. A versão aramaica, uma versão das Crônicas de Yerahmeel, que alguns estudiosos pensam representar o texto original.

3. *Língua Original*. Há evidências lingüísticas nos manuscritos existentes, como hebraísmos, traduções equivocadas em outras versões, com base no **mal-entendido quanto às** palavras hebraicas, que parecem apontar para um original em hebraico e aramaico. Todavia, os primeiros pais da Igreja nunca mencionam um original hebraico. Como não há manuscritos mais antigos, escritos em hebraico, a maioria dos eruditos antigos, como muitos de nossa época, pensam que o livro foi originalmente escrito em grego. Mas, o peso maior das opiniões favorece um original hebraico.

4. *Autor, Lugar e Data*. O lugar depende do idioma original. Se esse idioma é o hebraico, então devemos pensar na Palestina; se é o grego, então devemos pensar no Mediterrâneo oriental. Seu autor é absolutamente desconhecido e a data de sua

BELEZA — BELEZA ESPIRITUAL

composição é incerta, embora muitos falem no século II A.C.

5. *Propósito Principal*. O autor procura divertir o leitor, embora se mostre sério em sua denúncia contra a idolatria. Como um propósito secundário, o autor exalta o trabalho de detetive, efetuado por Daniel.

6. *Conteúdo*.

Acerca de Bel. A narrativa é simples. O rei adorava o ídolo Bel na Babilônia, mas Daniel recusou-se a fazê-lo. O rei relembrou Daniel acerca de como o ídolo comia diariamente as quatro (LXX) ou quarenta (Teodoreto) ovelhas, a ele oferecidas, juntamente com certos líquidos: azeite (LXX), mais vinho (Teodoreto). Daniel sabia que em tudo isso havia um engodo, pelo que o rei exigiu dos sacerdotes que provassem a contenção. Foram providas as ofertas. Foi descoberto que os sacerdotes tinham um alçapão secreto, por meio do qual vinham e levavam as ofertas ali postas. Daniel e seus servos espalharam cinzas no caminho que levava ao alçapão. Pela manhã, as ofertas haviam desaparecido — e o rei regozijou-se. Mas Daniel mostrou as pisadas nas cinzas. E assim, os sacerdotes tiveram de confessar o truque. Em face disso, tanto Bel como o seu templo foram destruídos, e o Deus criador foi vindicado.

Acerca do Dragão. Um grande dragão era adorado na Babilônia. Esse dragão tinha o costume de comer e beber. Daniel declarou que era capaz de matar o dragão sem usar a espada. O rei deu-lhe permissão para fazer a tentativa. Daniel fez um preparado com piche, gordura e cabelos, cozendo tudo e fazendo bolos com a mistura. O horrível alimento foi demais para o dragão, pois, ao ingeri-lo, explodiu pelo meio. Então o povo ameaçou matar o rei, por haver permitido que o dragão fosse tratado daquela maneira. E assim Daniel foi lançado em uma cova com sete leões. Esses leões costumavam ser bem alimentados com os corpos de pessoas condenadas à morte ou com ovelhas. Porém, quando Daniel foi posto ali, os leões passaram fome. No sexto dia, Habacuque foi trazido da Palestina por um anjo, até à Babilônia, trazendo alimentos para Daniel. Assim, Daniel banqueteou-se, ao passo que os leões passaram fome. Habacuque voltou à sua pátria e Daniel foi solto. Então o rei lançou na cova os opositores de Daniel e os leões tiveram o seu banquete. (CH J JE)

BELEZA

Na Bíblia não há qualquer filosofia estética de belo. Porém, a apreciação natural da beleza é referida por muitas vezes. Em primeiro lugar, o próprio Deus declarou sua criação «boa». «Viu Deus tudo quanto fizera e eis que era muito bom. Houve tarde e manhã, o sexto dia» (Gên. 1:31). Ver também quanto à devida apreciação da beleza, em Sal. 8; 18:1-6; 29; 65:9-13; 104; 147:8-18. O que as Escrituras exaltam, acima da beleza física, é a beleza moral. «Enganosa é a graça e vã a formosura, mas a mulher que teme ao Senhor, essa será louvada» (Pro. 31:30).

1. *Na Filosofia*. Os filósofos aludem à excelência estética, que desperta nas pessoas sensíveis um dos mais puros prazeres. De acordo com Platão, a beleza é uma propriedade intrínseca dos objetos, mensurável em termos de exemplo, pureza, integridade, harmonia de proporções ou perfeição. De acordo com a sua filosofia, somente Deus, em última análise, pode ser chamado Belo. As pessoas e os objetos apenas exibem aspectos do belo, porquanto se aproximam do ideal de Deus, de alguma maneira. Para outros filósofos, a beleza é algo *subjetivo*, ou seja, impressiona o senso estético de quem a contempla. Um objeto ou pessoa pode despertar essa percepção do espírito. Naturalmente, os filósofos analíticos salientam que um termo tão geral e vasto como «beleza» não pode ser definido com facilidade, mas tão-somente pode ser sujeito a uma série de descrições, o que corresponde à realidade dos fatos. Ver o artigo sobre a *arte*, quanto aos muitos conceitos filosóficos a respeito, onde está incluída a idéia da beleza.

2. *Na Antiga Israel*. Para eles, por mais humilde que fosse, não havia lugar como o próprio lar. Mas, nos tempos antigos, a Terra Prometida era, realmente, bela. As mudanças ocorridas desde então modificaram o aspecto da Palestina para pior, transformando-a em um lugar desértico. Tito destruiu as florestas em redor de Jerusalém, a fim de construir máquinas de guerra, durante o cerco da cidade, no ano 70 D.C. Ver a apreciação da beleza da Terra Santa, em Jer. 3:19; Lam. 2:15; Esd. 7:27, que são trechos que se referem à terra, à cidade de Jerusalém, ao povo de Israel e ao templo.

3. *Referência a Terras Não-Judaicas*. O Egito foi comparado a lindos ramos do cedro do Líbano, belo em sua grandiosidade (Eze. 31:3,7,9). O rei de Tiro, em seu resplendor, é descrito mediante os termos mais gloriosos (Eze. 28:12). Após ser julgada pelo castigo divino, Samaria é comparada a uma flor que fenece (Isa. 28:1,4).

4. *As Pessoas*. Certas mulheres são declaradas bonitas. Os cosméticos destacavam a beleza feminina, corrigindo imperfeições naturais (Isa. 3:18-24; Eze. 10:9-14). Mulheres que o Antigo Testamento declara como belas são: Sara, Rebeca, Raquel, Abigail, Abisague, Bate-Seba e Ester. Homens bonitos são José, Moisés na infância, Davi, Jônatas e Absalão.

5. *Deus*. A presença e a glória de Deus envolvem a mais pura beleza (Êxo. 16:7,10; 24:16; 40:34; Lev. 9:6; Núm. 14:10; Jos. 7:19). Deus é como um lindo diadema para o seu povo (Isa. 28:5). O Messias é um belo rei (Isa. 33:17). Porém, em sua humilhação, a beleza do Messias foi ocultada (Isa. 53:2). O livro de Apocalipse encerra muitas descrições de coisas belas pertencentes a Deus, embora não tente qualquer descrição antropomórfica do próprio Deus. Apesar de que tal conceito não é filosoficamente declarado, é óbvio que toda a beleza tem sua origem em Deus, visto ser Ele o Criador e Planejador de todas as coisas.

6. Será glorioso o estado final dos remidos, que Deus está preparando. Lemos em Apocalipse 21:2: «Vi também a cidade santa, a nova Jerusalém, que descia do céu, da parte de Deus, ornada como noiva, adornada para o seu esposo». Paulo também declara que a Noiva de Cristo, a Igreja, é adornada e gloriosa, sem qualquer distorção como mácula ou ruga, mas «santa e sem defeito» (Efé. 5:27). (EP F MONT Z)

BELEZA ESPIRITUAL

Platão, em seu diálogo, **Banquete**, identifica a mais elevada identidade metafísica (Idéia ou Forma) com a *Beleza*. Portanto, naquele diálogo, utilizando-nos de termos tipicamente cristãos, podemos dizer que Deus é a Essência da Beleza. Desse ponto de vista, a qualidade suprema de Deus é a beleza. Em outros de seus diálogos, Platão exalta a bondade como a suprema qualidade espiritual. O ensino dele no *Banquete* é que todas as formas de beleza são, na realidade, reflexos da beleza de Deus, sendo essa, exatamente, a razão pela qual desejamos coisas belas, pois sabemos, intuitivamente, que, *nelas*, Deus transparece. O anelo e apreciação do homem pela beleza procede do senso de beleza de que ele é possuidor. A criação é, principalmente, uma situação *estética*, de acordo com a definição que aparece no *Banquete* de Platão. Se a bondade é a mais alta qualidade divina, então a criação é, essencialmente, uma situação ética. Um homem assemelha-se mais a Deus quando é uma pessoa boa, e também quando é possuidor das qualidades espirituais da beleza. Essas qualidades demonstram harmonia e desígnio. Elas são ordeiras e simétricas. De certo ângulo de visão, os vários aspectos do fruto do Espírito (Gál. 5:22 *ss*), são as lindas coisas que o Espírito Santo cultiva em nós. Admiramòs a beleza de uma vida espiritual e somos inspirados a imitá-la. Detestamos a feiúra e a hediondez do pecado, mesmo quando nos envolvemos na transgressão. A feiúra caracteriza-se pela desordem, pela desarmonia e pela imperfeição.

BELIAL

No hebraico, «indignidade» ou «iniqüidade». A palavra tornou-se associada a palavras como filho, filha ou filhas *de Belial*. Isso indicava uma «pessoa indigna», embora a expressão possa assumir o sentido mais forte de «agente de Satanás».

No Novo Testamento aparece a forma alternativa Beliar. Os habitantes de Gibeá, que abusaram da esposa do levita, foram chamados «filhos de Belial» (Juí. 19:22). No Antigo Testamento, não há qualquer indicação de que a palavra era usada como nome próprio, retendo assim seu sentido simples de pessoa *ímpia*. Ver I Sam. 1:16; Deu. 17:4; Pro. 19:28; Juí. 19:22; Sal. 18:4.

Nos escritos judaicos posteriores, tal como nos livros apocalípticos judaicos de Jubileus, Ascensão de Isaías e os Oráculos Sibilinos, a palavra torna-se um nome próprio, que alude a Satanás. O uso neotestamentário envolve esse desenvolvimento. Ver II Cor. 6:15. Ali, nos melhores manuscritos do Novo Testamento, o nome é soletrado como *Beliar*. Alguns intérpretes supõem que desde o trecho de Naum 1:15 a palavra já aparece personificada. Além disso, de acordo com alguns estudiosos, Beliar, no Novo Testamento, torna-se um sinônimo de Beelzebube (ver o artigo). Nos escritos pseudepígrafos, o nome é usado para indicar o anticristo, o principal agente humano de Satanás. O termo «homem da iniqüidade» (o anticristo), usado em II Tes. 2:3, poderia ter esse título por detrás do mesmo, embora sob forma traduzida. (E IB K NTI)

BELLAMY, JOSEPH

Pupilo e intérprete de Jonathan Edwards (ver o artigo). Tornou-se famoso por suas declarações paradoxais, como: «Deus age conforme gostaria que agíssemos com ele», referindo-se ao castigo dos pecadores, por toda a eternidade. Ou então: «Quanto mais incapazes somos de amar a Deus, mais culpados somos». Suas obras principais foram: *True Religion Defined* e *The Wisdom of God in the Permission of Sin*. (AM E)

BELLARMINE, St. ROBERT

Jesuíta italiano (1542-1621). Foi arcebispo de Cápua e, depois, cardeal. Sua obra, *De Controversiis Christiannae Fidei* foi a melhor discussão católica romana sobre a posição protestante, em seus primórdios. Essa obra incorpora uma compreensão incomum sobre a antiguidade e o conhecimento da teologia tradicional. (E)

••• ••• •••

BELMAIM

Cidade que figura no livro apócrifo de Judite (4:4 e 7:3). Seria uma aldeia nas vizinhanças de Dotã, perto de onde Holofernes acampou com seu exército. Tem sido tentativamente identificada com o local de Ibleã (ver o artigo), a oito quilômetros a nordeste de Dotã. (Z)

BELOT, GUSTAVE

Filósofo francês, cujas datas são 1859-1930. Ele negava a possibilidade de qualquer especulação *a priori*, afirmando a inutilidade da metafísica como meio para se estabelecer um código e uma técnica moral. Portanto, ele se opunha à ciência da ética. Acusava Sócrates, Jesus e o socialismo, além de Tolstoy, de se terem manifestado contrários à maré da moral de suas respectivas épocas. Segundo ele pensava, a moralidade genuína resulta do desenvolvimento pessoal, e não de imposições externas. (E)

BELSAZAR

O termo hebraico deriva-se do vocábulo babilônico *Bel-sar-usur*, «o deus Bel protegeu o rei». Era filho de Nabonido e seu co-regente (556-539 A.C.), o rei caldeu ao tempo da captura da cidade da Babilônia por Dario, o medo, em 539 A.C. (Dan. 5:30;7:1). Em Daniel 5:11,18 Nabucodonosor é chamado de seu pai, mas isso significa apenas que ele pertencia à linhagem de Nabucodonosor, atribuição comum nas antigas genealogias. Seu pai, Nabonido, tornou Belsazar co-regente e comandante do exército em cerca de 550 A.C., enquanto Nabonido se ausentava para Teima', na Arábia central. Belsazar governou por cerca de dez anos, até à volta de seu pai, em 542 A.C. É possível que o rei cujo nome não é dado, que morreu quando a cidade caiu diante de Ugbaru, governador de Gutium, e líder do exército persa, tenha sido esse homem (Dan. 5:30). Mediante um decreto de Belsazar, Daniel tornou-se o terceiro maior mandatário do reino, quando o profeta interpretou corretamente o escrito na parede, durante um banquete real. Se Belsazar era o segundo homem do reino e o primeiro sendo seu pai ausente, Nabonido, isso explica por que razão Daniel é chamado de terceiro. As crônicas de Nabunaide, dos séculos VII, IX,X e XI confirmam detalhes acerca de Daniel, referindo-se à co-regência de Belsazar e à ausência de Nabonido. Daniel estava com a razão, ao apresentar Belsazar como o último rei da Babilônia. (DOU UN)

BELTESSAZAR

No hebraico significa «príncipe de Bel» ou «líder do senhor». Porém, alguns estudiosos preferem pensar em um sentido como «Bel protege a sua vida», o que representaria o babilônico *balatusu-usur*. Foi um nome babilônico dado a Daniel, na corte de Nabucodonosor (Dan. 1:7; 2:26; 4:8,9; 18:19, etc.). O nome não aparece fora do livro de Daniel.

BELTÉTMO

No livro apócrifo de I Esdras 2:16,26, aparece como nome de um oficial de Artaxerxes, na Palestina. Na verdade, porém, não é um nome próprio, mas é a transliteração para o grego do título aramaico do ofício ocupado por Reum. Em I Esdras 2:17, esse nome é traduzido por «comandante», ou então por «cronista», de acordo com outras versões.

BELZEBU — BEM-AVENTURANÇAS

BELZEBU

Ver o artigo sobre **Baalzebube**. Essa palavra significa «senhor da imundícia» ou «senhor do lixo». A mudança de Baalzebube para Belzebu ocorre na versão da Vulgata Latina. Belzebu significa «senhor das moscas». A referência é a uma divindade pagã, que era tida como o príncipe dos maus espíritos (Mat. 10:25; 12:24,27; Mar. 3:22; Luc. 11:15). O Novo Testamento adota a identificação desse nome com o nome de Satanás. O apelativo foi aplicado a Jesus por determinados líderes judeus (Mat. 10:25), a fim de tentar identificá-lo com o reino das trevas. Em Mateus 12:24, Jesus foi acusado de expulsar os demônios através da autoridade de Belzebu, príncipe dos demônios, o que Jesus, naturalmente, repeliu com um argumento irretorquível.

Não se sabe com certeza como surgiu essa variante do nome, de *Baal* para *Bel*. Mas é bem provável que as duas formas sejam sinônimas, pelo que, em qualquer de suas formas, devemos pensar numa divindade pagã, mesmo que o significado dessas formas divirja em sentido. Apesar de que, originalmente, o nome talvez fosse aplicado a algum príncipe do mal, entre as muitas gradações de espíritos malignos, é quase certo que, pelos tempos neotestamentários, tornara-se o nome apenas um outro título de Satanás, o rei de todos os espíritos malignos. Ver Mateus 12:26,27, que certamente dá a entender exatamente isso. (JE ALB PF)

BEM-AVENTURANÇA

No grego, **makarismós**, «felicidades». O substantivo aparece somente em Rom. 4:6,9 e Gál. 4:15. O verbo, em Luc. 1:48 e Tia. 5:11, e o adjetivo por cinqüenta vezes, desde Mat. 5:3 até Apo. 22:14.

1. Para os gregos antigos, ser bem-aventurado ou feliz (*makários*) era viver livre de sofrimentos e preocupações. Os judeus entendiam a bem-aventurança principalmente em termos de bem-estar material, mas também como recompensa pela observância fiel da lei. Para o crente, entretanto, a felicidade consiste na participação no reino de' Deus. Esse último conceito ajusta-se perfeitamente à doutrina de Cristo. Como em quase tudo o mais, Jesus veio ensinar-nos noções contrárias àquilo que os homens concebem, em seu estado de perdição e embotamento espiritual. Aquilo que o Senhor considerou bem-aventuranças ou felicidades invertem diametralmente o julgamento humano.

2. As bem-aventuranças foram expostas por Jesus mormente em seu sermão da montanha (Mat. 5:1-12). Embora ele e os escritores sagrados tenham voltado regularmente ao tema, é nesse trecho que temos o sumário de seu ensino a respeito. Os estudiosos hesitam entre quatro e nove bem-aventuranças. Sem importar se Jesus as proferiu todas numa só ocasião, ou se Mateus posteriormente as juntou em um bloco, se cada felicidade é indicada pelas palavras «bem-aventurados», então teremos de dizer que elas são nove. Em Mateus, cada bem-aventurança tem uma causa e um efeito: Primeira—os que reconhecem sua falência espiritual, pois deles é o reino de Deus. Segunda—os que sofrem aflições, pois receberão consolo. Terceira—os mansos, porque serão os futuros donos do mundo. Quarta—os que anelam por retidão, porque haverão de encontrá-la. Quinta—os que são misericordiosos, porque Deus terá misericórdia deles. Sexta—os dotados de impulsos puros, porque contemplarão a glória de Deus. Sétima—os pacificadores, pois isso mostra que são autênticos filhos de Deus. Oitava—os perseguidos por causa da retidão, porque isso prova que estão no reino de Deus. Nona—os vilipendiados por causa de Jesus, porque serão grandemente galardoados na vida vindoura, equiparando-se aos profetas.

Nas bem-aventuranças sempre se acentua a disposição interna do indivíduo, e não alguma condição externa. Felicidade é um estado de alma. O restante das Escrituras encarrega-se de ensinar que essa disposição interna não é natural do homem; antes, é-lhe outorgada pela operação renovadora e regeneradora do Espírito. Isso se vê desde o Antigo Testamento: «Dar-vos-ei coração novo, e porei dentro em vós espírito novo...» (Eze. 36:26). Isso é reafirmado no Novo Testamento: «Quem não nascer da água e do Espírito, não pode entrar no reino de Deus» (João 3:5).

3. Pode-se dizer que todos os aspectos da vida cristã consistem em bênçãos conferidas pelo Senhor. Assim, a felicidade consiste na apropriação da sabedoria divina (Pro. 3:13); em ouvir a Deus e ser-lhe obediente (Pro. 8:23); em ter confiança no Senhor (Pro. 16:20); em observar os seus mandamentos (Pro. 29:18). O contrário disso, só traz a infelicidade: «Os céus e a terra tomo hoje por testemunhas contra ti que te propus a vida e a morte, a bênção e a maldição: escolhe, pois, a vida, para que vivas, tu e a tua descendência» (Deu. 30:19).

4. Se a perfeição espiritual importa em felicidade, então segue-se que ninguém é mais feliz do que Jesus Cristo. De fato, ele é o Cristo, o Filho do Deus Bendito (Mar. 14:61) pois Deus é supremamente bem-aventurado e rico em bem-estar espiritual (ver I Tim. 1:11 e 6:15). O nascimento de Jesus envolveu bem-aventurança (Luc. 1:42,48). A Ceia do Senhor é chamada de «cálice da bênção» (I Cor. 10:16). O ministério de Cristo entre os homens foi bendito, superior à administração do Antigo Testamento (Heb. 7:1,6). O segundo advento de Cristo promete bênçãos singulares (Apo. 14:13; 16:15; 19:9; 22:7,14). O pacto firmado no sangue de Cristo confere-nos uma bem-aventurança especial, a saber, a participação no Espírito Santo (Gál. 3:8,13,14). O crente é bem-aventurado porque é uma pessoa que foi justificada (Rom. 4:7). Por sua vez, o crente deve invocar bênçãos até sobre os seus perseguidores (Rom. 12:14; I Cor. 4:12; Mat. 5:10-12). Os crentes servem de bênçãos uns para os outros, tanto nas coisas materiais quanto nas espirituais (Rom. 15:29 e contexto). (B C NTI)

BEM-AVENTURANÇAS

I. De Mateus 5:3-12

Introdução: Informações Gerais.

As bem-aventuranças são *promessas* feitas aos discípulos *fiéis* do reino dos céus. Apesar de Jesus ter proferido essas palavras originalmente a Israel, não há que duvidar que ele queria que se aplicassem plenamente ao Novo Israel, a igreja. O evangelho de Mateus foi escrito quando a era cristã já tinha cinqüenta anos, e não tem sentido supor que não tencionava ser um documento inteiramente «cristão». Os discípulos de Cristo devem aprender a apegar-se a ele, a confiar nele e em suas palavras explicitamente. Não pode haver reservas na dedicação à ele e às suas palavras. — As bem-aventuranças mostram como seremos abençoados se fizermos disso a regra de nossas vidas. Os crentes seriam oprimidos pelo mundo (talvez um reflexo da perseguição de Domiciano, que a igreja sofria quando o evangelho de Mateus foi escrito). Mas os oprimidos haverão de

BEM-AVENTURANÇAS

obter, finalmente, a vitória, - embora nunca sem uma clara lealdade ao seu Senhor. «...as bem-aventuranças mostram que, para Jesus, a retidão é mais do que a súmula de seus mandamentos; é uma total atitude de mente, uma forma particular de caráter». Aqueles que são louvados no evangelho são homens e mulheres humildes, amorosos, confiantes, fiéis e corajosos. Ainda não são perfeitos, mas são convertidos. Seus interesses e desejos se voltam na direção do reino de Deus. Mateus aparentemente enumera nove bem-aventuranças, embora a oitava e a nona possam constituir uma só; e se for removido o vs. 5, teremos apenas sete. Lucas 6:20-23 contém quatro bem-aventuranças, todas as quais têm paralelos aqui. «Q» provavelmente tinha as mesmas, na terceira pessoa, e não na segunda, conforme se vê em Lucas. Mateus, entretanto, adicionou termos tais como 'em espírito' (vs. 3) e 'justiça' (vs. 6). Também haveria bem-aventuranças em L e M? Nesse caso, os quatro *ais* de Lucas (Luc. 6:24-26) podem provir de L, e pelo menos algumas das bem-aventuranças de Mateus se derivam de M. (Ver informações completas sobre as fontes informativas dos evangelhos, referidas aqui pelas abreviações «Q», «L» e «M», no artigo intitulado o *Problema Sinóptico*).

A Palavra.

Bem-aventurados. Essa palavra e suas cognatas são usadas cerca de *cinqüenta* vezes no N.T., sendo uma das muitas que o uso do N.T. expandiu e dignificou quanto ao seu sentido. A raiz original, no grego clássico, parece significar «grande», e desde cedo foi usada como sinônimo de *rico*, mas quase sempre aludindo à prosperidade externa (não à espiritual). Na literatura grega primitiva, era palavra aplicada aos deuses e à sua condição de «felicidade», em contraste com a situação medíocre de homem. Os filósofos gregos usavam-na dotada de certo elemento moral, e algumas vezes indicavam, por meio dela, que a felicidade resulta da excelência do caráter. Alguns intérpretes acreditam que o uso que Jesus fez da palavra em Mat. 5:3 reflete as idéias e expressões hebraicas que se encontram, por exemplo, em Sal. 1:1; 32:1 e 112:1, onde a palavra hebraica «*ashrê*» ou «quão feliz», indica a condição de felicidade em vista. As «bem-aventuranças», portanto, declaram quem são os *felizes*, aos olhos de Deus. O uso neotestamentário tem soerguido a idéia inteira de—felicidade—até às regiões espirituais. A verdadeira felicidade inclui aquele bem-estar ou estado de bem-aventurança associado à correta relação do homem para com Deus. Esse mesmo vocábulo é aplicado aos mortos que morrem no Senhor (Apo. 14:13) e esse uso, por sua vez, é extremamente instrutivo. Poderíamos dizer com igual verdade, «Bem-aventurados os que vivem no Senhor», e é essencialmente isso que Jesus dizia, ao pronunciar as «bem-aventuranças».

O Número e Sumário de Idéias.

Os eruditos não concordam quanto ao **número** exato das bem-aventuranças. A palavra *bem-aventurados*, ou *felizes*, aparece por nove vezes, pelo que alguns intérpretes preferem esse número. Outros crêem que sete é o número tencionado, e explicam que os vss. 10 e 11 realmente formam uma única bem-aventurança, embora a palavra apareça por duas vezes, enquanto que o vs. 5 é rejeitado por alguns, como se não fosse autêntico. Aqueles que preferem o número sete evidentemente fazem-no a fim de que transpareça o simbolismo que indica algo completo, divino e santo. Outros pretendem aumentar seu número para dez, para fazer o autor expor um novo decálogo. Não é provável que o autor tivesse qualquer dessas idéias, apesar de ser justa a observação que de fato temos aqui um novo decálogo, princípios éticos perfeitos e a oitava das músicas do reino.

Antes de observarmos cada bem-aventurança de *per si*, notemos as principais idéias expostas: 1. *Humildes de espírito*: parece significar aquela humildade espiritual que percebe sua aguda necessidade de desenvolvimento. É o oposto do orgulho espiritual. 2. *Choram...serão consolados*. Embora tenhamos aqui a mesma palavra usada para indicar a lamentação feita pelos mortos, o intuito de Jesus, uma vez mais, é salientar um aspecto do exercício espiritual que se baseia na tristeza por causa do pecado; e provavelmente essa segunda bem-aventurança está vinculada à primeira porque esse choro é aquela resposta das emoções à percepção da carência espiritual dos que são «humildes de espírito». Tais pessoas, porém, receberão aquele fortalecimento infalível e o consolo que estão subentendidos na palavra «consolados». 3. *Mansos*. Os antigos não reputavam essa virtude (certa serenidade suave, algumas vezes negativa e outras vezes positiva) como virtude. O seu sentido primário é a serenidade gentil. Essa qualidade cristã tem origem na percepção que o crente tem de sua pequenez em face da grandeza de Deus. 4. *Fome e sede de justiça*, frase que se explica por si mesma, pois todos conhecem o instinto jamais satisfeito que pede alimentos e água, necessários para a sobrevivência física. Em sentido espiritual, também deveríamos possuir um instinto difícil de satisfazer, necessário para a sobrevivência espiritual verdadeira e própria. Poucos sabem o que significa ficar *cheio*, expressão usada aqui, empregada na literatura grega para a ceva do gado. Muitos estão satisfeitos, com estômagos espirituais vazios. Jesus queria que os seus discípulos estivessem cheios, pois somente esses são realmente «bem-aventurados». Assim como o estômago físico pode encolher, não sendo mais capaz de conter a nutrição apropriada, também com a faculdade espiritual isso pode acontecer. Muitos não sabem que estão em estado de inanição espiritual, incapazes de se nutrir espiritualmente como convém. Os verdadeiramente felizes entre os discípulos de Jesus são aqueles que têm grande fome e sede, e subseqüentemente são satisfeitos até na sociedade. 5. *Misericordiosos*. Indica a capacidade de sentir a miséria humana, ligada ao impulso de aliviar essa miséria. Essa combinação resulta em um ministério prestado aos outros. 6. *Limpos de coração*. Não é sinônimo de castidade (embora possa incluir essa idéia), mas antes, indica singeleza de mente, um propósito espiritual, incorrupto, inatingido pelo mundo. A essa bem-aventurança está vinculada a maior das promessas, a visão beatífica. 7. *Pacificadores*: não meramente os dotados de natureza pacífica, mas aqueles que promovem ativamente a paz e a harmonia entre os homens. 8. *Perseguidos*. Não aqueles que desfrutam de uma modalidade suave de martírio, sensíveis a qualquer menosprezo por parte de outros, e sim, o sofrimento produzido pela vida piedosa e de serviço cristão, que provoca a oposição do mundo hostil. 9. «...*vos injuriarem...disserem todo mal contra vós*». Refere-se à forma verbal de «perseguição», que ocasionalmente é mais virulenta ao indivíduo do que a violência física, e que, desafortunadamente às vezes é sofrida pelos benfeitores da parte daqueles para quem ministram.

As bem-aventuranças constituem promessas dos *benefícios* inerentes ao reino do céu, pois os que a ele pertencerem saberão o que significa ser consolado, herdar a terra, ser satisfeito, obter misericórdia. ver a Deus e ser chamado filho de Deus. As bem-aventu-

BEM-AVENTURANÇAS

ranças ilustram de imediato que a nova lei de Jesus consiste em mais do que a simples observância de determinado número de preceitos. Jesus alude aqui às atitudes da mente e do coração, e não apenas aos atos que podem ser vistos pelos homens. Os seus discípulos são homens e mulheres dotados de humildade, amor, confiança, fidelidade e coragem.

As Bem-aventuranças de Mat. 5:3-12.

1. 5:3: *Bem-aventurados os humildes de espírito, porque deles é o reino dos céus.*

Humildes de Espírito.

Não ensina em Mateus a pobreza física **literal**, embora se possa obter essa idéia pelo paralelo de Luc. 6:20. Alguns crêem que a fonte «Q», neste caso, e a declaração original de Jesus, não continham as palavras «de espírito», mas que se trata de uma adição do autor do evangelho de Matues, como interpretação do sentido da declaração. Isso não é de todo impossível, essa «interpretação» sem dúvida é a correta. Todavia, se todos os *pobres* fossem *bem-aventurados*, especialmente na Palestina dos dias de Jesus, a vasta maioria do povo estaria entre os bem-aventurados, e **ainda** que Jesus sempre tivesse demonstrado simpatia incomum pelos pobres e por outros elementos desafortunados da sociedade, não é provável que tenha incluído tão vasto número de pessoas nessa bem-aventurança. É verdade que Jesus se dirigiu aos pobres, que a maioria dos que lhe deram ouvidos pertencia a essa classe; porém, do ponto de vista judaico, jamais poderíamos afirmar que a simples pobreza física é sinal de bem-aventurança. Sabemos, pelo V.T., que o oposto é a verdade.

Também notamos, pela história *eclesiástica*, que essa bem-aventurança tem sido interpretada literalmente em alguns círculos, e que a *pobreza física* tem sido necessária para que alguém seja membro de certas ordens religiosas. Tais ordens alicerçam sua regra de pobreza voluntária em passagens como esta, mas parece que isso não passa de exagero, se não mesmo de uma perversão do texto.

Outros pensam que essa pobreza se refere à *privação mental*, como se somente os mentalmente símplices pudessem ouvir, receber e aplicar os ensinos de Jesus. Também não passa de uma perversão do sentido tencionado no texto.

Ainda que Jesus deva ter proferido essas palavras a pessoas reais e literalmente pobres, espezinhadas sob a autoridade de Roma e desprezadas por seus próprios líderes religiosos, aquela classe da sociedade verdadeiramente «pobre» em vários aspectos, e apesar de que ele possa ter derivado a lição espiritual da observação dessa pobreza «física» literal, contudo, a sua lição é de natureza *essencialmente* espiritual. Nenhuma outra interpretação seria coerente com o que sabemos da natureza intensamente espiritual de Jesus e sua doutrina. Jesus fala de certa qualidade espiritual, e a adição das palavras, «de espírito», é justa. Trata-se de uma atitude do coração, o reconhecimento da grandeza de Deus e a necessidade de desenvolvimento espiritual, tendo a sua perfeição como modelo (ver Mat. 5:48). Essa atitude é o contrário do orgulho espiritual, e todos temos podido observar esse elemento negativo, tanto em nós mesmos como nos outros. Jesus jamais usou de ostentação e nunca manifestou atitudes e ações soberbas. Quer que os seus discípulos o imitem. Requer deles simplicidade, humildade, mansidão e bondade. O orgulho é uma das raízes principais do pecado: a humildade de espírito é uma das raízes da virtude cristã.

Talvez uma das mais notáveis ilustrações derivadas de uma fonte não-bíblica sobre o que está aqui incluso se encontra na *Divina Comédia*, de Dante. Dante ter-se-ia encontrado com o anjo da humildade. O anjo tocou na testa de Dante com suas asas, apagando o sinal do orgulho. Enquanto um coro angelical entoava *«Beati pauperes spiritu»*, Dante se afastava com passos leves, porque, uma vez apagada a marca da soberba, todos os outros pecados se tornam fardos mais leves.

Pelo texto e também pelas implicações da ilustração acima, podemos dizer com verdade que essa bem-aventurança forma uma espécie de alicerce para as demais, qual pedra fundamental. O código ético de Jesus não poderia perdurar sem ela, e o valor de todos os outros preceitos teriam de ser grandemente diminuídos se essa virtude não se fizesse presente. É verdade que Jesus bem poderia estar pensando na futura dispensação, quando haverá de se manifestar o reino sobre a terra, e estivesse expressando assim as exigências éticas daquele reino; mas é igualmente verdadeiro que deve ter esperado essas qualidades em seus discípulos, e que esses seus padrões de ética se fizessem presentes a despeito do período da história em que eles vivessem.

«Porque deles é o reino dos céus». Jesus falou não só sobre o «reino no íntimo» ou sobre o reino vindouro, isto é, o céu, mas particularmente sobre o reino que ele esperava firmar sobre a terra, o reino que continuamente anunciara a partir de seu batismo, o mesmo reino que João Batista anunciara estar *próximo*. Os judeus anelavam intensamente pela esperança de livramento da opressão romana. Certamente que Jesus esperava essa libertação, e Jesus aguardava um novo governo, um «reino sobre a terra». Não obstante, a promessa continua sendo essencialmente espiritual, pois Jesus sempre manifestou intenso interesse pelas questões espirituais, e certamente pouco pensava sobre funções políticas, pelo menos no que era envolvida a sua própria pessoa. Jesus não contemplava um reino de ostentação e de glória terrena para si mesmo e para os seus seguidores (embora isso pudesse ser uma espécie de resultado natural do reino), mas pensava—no estabelecimento—de princípios religiosos justos e na obediência de seus «discípulos» a esses princípios. Tinha em mente o caráter real e principesco do desenvolvimento espiritual, a «ostentação» legítima e aceitável diante de Deus.

Neste mundo, os «pobres», quer os que o são literalmente, quer os *humildes de espírito*, nada podem esperar da glória de qualquer reino. Jesus mostrou que essa não será a condição existente em seu reino. O que tem valor ali não é a riqueza nem o poder, mas as qualidades morais e o desenvolvimento espiritual. E apesar de que Jesus pode ter esperado um reino literal que ainda será estabelecido, para incorporar os seus ensinos em cada nível da sociedade, ansiava que os seus discípulos manifestassem essas virtudes aceitáveis em seu reino, e que a posse e exibição dessas virtudes tivessem início imediatamente. Contraste-se esses elevados ideais sobre a herança de um reino espiritual com um paralelo rabínico: «Torna-te mais e mais humilde de espírito, posto que o que o homem pode esperar é tornar-se comida de vermes (J.R. Dummelow).

Aqueles que dão ouvidos a esses preceitos estão fazendo apenas aquilo que o próprio Jesus fez: «...*assumindo a forma de servo*...a si mesmo se humilhou...» (Fi. 2:7,8). «Tende em vós o mesmo sentimento que houve também em Cristo Jesus» (Fil. 2:5).

Na Igreja abundam interpretações presentes e

futurísticas sobre esse versículo. Um grande segmento da igreja ainda espera um reino literal sobre a terra, onde serão praticados esses princípios. Outros, sem esperar tal reino, em qualquer sentido literal ou político, exortam que esses princípios sejam praticados, pois para nós «o reino está no íntimo».

2. 5:4: *Bem-aventurados os que choram, porque eles serão consolados.*

Os que Choram.

Os códices D 33 565 600 Sy e o pai Clemente Alexandrino (212 D.C.), invertem a ordem dos vss. 4 e 5. Algumas autoridades sobre questões textuais aceitam essa inversão como original, mas a maioria prefere a ordem familiar. A coerência lógica das sentenças parece igualmente boa de um modo ou de outro. A maioria da evidência dada pelos mss indica que a ordem familiar era a original. Alguns acreditam que o vs. 5 tenha sido uma glosa antiga, baseada em Sal. 37:11, que provocou a variação na ordem de versículos, mas não há qualquer prova objetiva em favor disso.

Jesus falava novamente de um exercício espiritual, e não da expressão de tristeza pessoal devido a alguma perda pessoal. Aludia à tristeza devido ao pecado, à necessidade de arrependimento, ou, talvez, a alguém que sofria tristeza não merecida, por motivo de perseguição por causa da justiça. Essa bem-aventurança parece ter base em Is. 61:1-3 e 66:2. Essa segunda bem-aventurança pode ser vinculada à primeira. *O lamento* é uma expressão que toma conta da verdadeira humildade de espírito. A chegada do Messias, que é denominada «consolo de Israel» (Is. 6:12; Luc. 2:25), indica que Israel tinha razões para aguardar tal consolo. Israel, dessa forma, poderia livrar-se de adversários opressivos, nacionais ou individuais. Esse lamento não tem causa apenas no pecado, mas também nos resultados do pecado no seio da sociedade. Provavelmente Jesus inclui ambas as possibilidades. Paulo menciona a opressão exercida pelo mundo, bem como nossa ansiedade de libertação (Rom. 8:18,19; II Cor. 4:17; ver também João 14:3). Aqueles que aprendem a permitir que a opressão, pessoal ou impessoal, sirva de instrumento de instrução, que os conduz ao arrependimento e à dependência a Deus, poderão encontrar, no fim, um bom resultado de seu «choro» e assim serão verdadeiramente «bem-aventurados». Essa bem-aventurança é proveniente do *consolo divino*, consolo no perdão e na restauração, bem como na participação na «manifestação dos filhos de Deus», conforme o ensino de Paulo. Aprendemos, pois, que o dardo do—sofrimento—pode ser armado com a vida, e não com o veneno da morte. Podemos chorar de muitos modos: pelos nossos pecados; pelos pecados de nossa nação; pelos amigos e conhecidos; pelos males humanos; pelos sofrimentos alheios. Aqueles que choram não se contentam com uma vida não-examinada, que, segundo disse Sócrates, nem é digna de ser vivida.

3. 5:5: *Bem-aventurados os mansos, porque herdarão a terra.*

Os Mansos.

Serenidade, às vezes negativa e às vezes positivamente boa. Essa bem-aventurança se alicerça no Sal. 37:11. Os homens que padecem sob o mal, sem se deixarem contaminar pelo espírito de amargura, mas com paciência, possuem qualidades aprovadas por Deus. Tais homens, como Natanael, são *israelitas em quem não há dolo* (João 1:47). Na história da Inglaterra houve pessoas que, ao serem perseguidas pelo governo e pela sociedade (e até pela igreja oficial), herdaram o continente americano. O Messias mostra que a nova ordem do reino de Deus promete a—terra—a tais pessoas. Essa é uma das características dos regenerados. Talvez haja alguma alusão a profecias como a de Dan. 7:27, que fala da esperança da vinda do Messias, no reino de Deus sobre a terra e de uma nova ordem social. Na citação de Sal. 37:11 temos a idéia de que Deus removerá da terra os inimigos de Israel, e assim a terra santa será entregue ao povo de Deus. Isso seria símbolo do grande dom que é a promessa contida neste versículo. Ver o artigo sobre o *Milênio*.

4. 5:6: *Bem-aventurados os que têm fome e sede de justiça, porque eles serão fartos.*

Os que têm fome e sede da justiça

A fome e a sede deveriam ser experiências comuns para aqueles com quem Jesus falava. Lembramo-nos de certa vez em que a multidão ficou com ele *alguns dias*, quando foi preciso satisfazer-lhes a fome por meio de um notável milagre. Provavelmente muitos dentre eles nem tinham o que comer. Jesus usa esses instintos como ilustração, mostrando que devemos sentir essa necessidade espiritual. Jesus também padeceu fome (Mat. 4:2) e podia ilustrá-la com sua experiência pessoal. O desejo é tão intenso que se transforma em dor. Jesus mostra que precisamos de tal desejo em relação às coisas espirituais, relativas à justiça. O desejo físico pelo alimento impele o indivíduo a buscar comida, quase sem considerar o preço da mesma ou as dificuldades de sua obtenção. Precisamos de—atitude similar—quanto à justiça de Deus. Qualquer um concorda que o mais forte e insistente dos instintos naturais, como também o mais necessário, é o da alimentação. O alimento sustenta a vida física. A alma também têm fome e sede.

5. 5:7: *Bem-aventurados os misericordiosos, porque eles alcançarão misericórdia.*

Os Misericordiosos.

Evidentemente as palavras vêm de Sal. 18:25. Col. 3:13 e Efé. 4:32 mostram que o crente é alvo de misericórdia, precisa da misericórdia divina, e tem a obrigação de exercer essa qualidade. Deus mostra sua misericórdia, sem merecimento da parte de quem a recebe. O povo de Deus deve imitá-lo, lembrando-se especialmente que ainda precisa de algo. Mat. 18:23-35, na parábola do credor incompassivo, ensina que aqueles que recebem misericórdia estão na obrigação de demonstrá-la, e que, se assim não fizerem, receberão mais severo julgamento. (Ver Luc. 6:37 e Tia. 5:9). Bengel tem belos pensamentos sobre o reino de Deus, dado aos «humildes», como o *benigna talio*, que significa «absolvição graciosa». Aqueles que são assim absolvidos dificilmente deixam de apresentar a mesma atitude para com seus semelhantes. Os que mostram tal misericórdia para com a humanidade estão sujeitos, *ipso facto*, à mesma graça.

6. 5:8; *Bem-aventurados os limpos de coração, porque eles verão a Deus.*

Os Limpos de Coração.

Pode incluir a idéia de **castidade**, mas indica principalmente a *singeleza* de mente, o propósito sincero e puro. Sal. 24:3,4 evidentemente é trecho básico dessa bem-aventurança. Os líderes judaicos falavam com insistência sobre a pureza cerimonial, a pureza da forma, a pureza da lei. Mas Jesus mostra, aqui e noutros trechos, que Deus se interessa pelo coração, isto é, pelo homem interior, quanto ao seu caráter na sua própria condição de ser. A justiça deve ser o princípio que guia a vida e cria, no homem interior, uma condição que resulta do contato com

BEM-AVENTURANÇAS

Deus e da transformação à imagem de Cristo. Nessas palavras sentimos que isso é impossível sem a ajuda do poder e do contato do Espírito de Deus. Indicam elas—o resultado—da regeneração. A personalidade humana não tem essa inclinação por si mesma. Tais palavras provavelmente indicam, igualmente, o processo de santificação que prepara o crente, qualificando-o para receber a visão beatífica. O propósito da vida cristã é possibilitar essa experiência.

Verão a Deus. Palavras que têm duas aplicações: a primeira é *imediata*, referindo-se aos que recebem compreensão e visão interiores da natureza e da pessoa de Deus (como vemos em Efé. 1:18). A outra é que essa visão interior também têm *aperfeiçoamento no futuro*, que é a visão beatífica, a experiência mística mais elevada. Os indivíduos podem receber vários níveis dessa visão. Os trechos de I João 3:2, Apo. 22:3,4 e Rom. 8:29 apresentam o cumprimento total dessa visão. Ela inclui a idéia de transformação do ser de acordo com a imagem de Cristo, na forma de mudança de natureza, em que a mortalidade humana é transformada na imortalidade, dotada da natureza e da glória de Cristo, o que torna o homem um ser mais elevado que os anjos, capacitando-o a tornar-se um elemento especial de Deus para realizar as suas obras divinas na eternidade futura. Aqueles que receberem essa visão completa serão perfeitos como Ele é perfeito. Esse é o plano do evangelho, a consideração mais elevada nele contida. «Seremos semelhantes a ele, porque havemos de vê-lo como ele é». (I João 3:2). Significa participação na divindade, II Ped. 1:4.

Buttrick (in loc.) diz: «O que significa ver a Deus. A visão beatífica tem sido um alvo milenar, tanto do filósofo como do santo, **mas essa bem-aventurança promete mais do que mera visão**. Talvez nosso mais profundo anelo, se pudéssemos analisar os nossos desejos, consista em ver a Deus. Tennyson deixou instrução de que o seu *Atravessando a Barra* sempre deveria ser posto no fim de suas obras publicadas. Termina como segue:

Espero ver meu Piloto face a face
Quando eu tiver atravessado a barra.

No império medo-persa havia sete conselheiros e amigos íntimos que *...se avistavam pessoalmente com o rei...*' (Est. 1:14). Talvez esse costume daquela época estivesse na mente de Cristo quando fez essa promessa. Galaade viu o Santo Graal, embora outros tivessem falhado nisso, porque o seu coração era puro. O poeta Shelley insistia em que essa bem-aventurança é apenas uma *repetição metafórica* de nossa convicção comumente expressa de que 'a virtude é sua própria recompensa' *(Shelley, Memorials)*. Para Cristo, porém, Deus não era uma virtude abstrata. Deus era *Fato* e *Vida*.

7. 5:9: *Bem-aventurados os pacificadores, porque eles serão chamados filhos de Deus.*

Os Pacificadores.

Não somente os dotados de **natureza** pacífica (Tia 3:15), nem os que aceitam a paz sem protesto ou que preferem a paz ao desacordo, nem os que têm paz na alma, com Deus, como explicou *Agostinho*, e nem os que amam a paz (Grotius, Wetstein), mas aqueles que promovem ativamente a paz e procuram estabelecer a harmonia entre inimigos. O sentimento aqui referido é mais nobre que o de Rom. 12:18, que diz: «Se possível, quanto depender de vós, tendo paz com todos os homens».

«Serão chamados filhos de Deus». Significa mais do que reconhecimento. Está em foco a realidade de ser alguém filho de Deus. (Ver Rom. 8:17,28-32; I João 3:2). O versículo implica em participação na herança dos santos (Efé. 1:13,14), e, assim sendo, trata-se de filhos adultos, como Cristo, revestidos da plenitude e divindade de Cristo (Efé. 1:23, II Cor. 3:18, II Ped. 1:4).

Os rabinos também davam grande valor aos pacificadores. *Hilel*, famoso rabino contemporâneo de Jesus, escreveu: *«Sê dos discípulos de Aarão, amando a paz e seguindo a paz»* (Aboth 1:2). Tais seriam os filhos de Deus. O V.T. emprega esse termo, «filhos de Deus», referindo-se aos anjos ou aos seres divinos (Jó 38:7), e algumas vezes também a pessoas piedosas, seres humanos que são objetos do amor especial de Deus (Deut. 32:6). Aqueles que buscam a paz amando os seus inimigos agem segundo o próprio Deus, e por isso são filhos de Deus em sentido verdadeiro. (Ver os vss. 44,45 deste capítulo). A paz é uma das virtudes cardeais da ética cristã. O exclusivismo dos judeus era e é bem conhecido, e já se tornara proverbial antes dos dias de Jesus. O discípulo—autêntico—do reino não é aquele que odeia, mas aquele que ama os seus inimigos. Isso faz do exclusivismo uma impossibilidade na ética cristã. Jesus deu a sua vida a fim de trazer a paz universal no sentido mais lato possível, tanto na terra como nos lugares celestiais. (Ver Efé. 2:14-16 e Col. 1:20). Agostinho louvou altamente à sua própria genitora, Mônica, quando escreveu: «Ela mostrou ser uma pacificadora tal que, de ambos os lados ouvindo as coisas mais amargas...nunca deixou transparecer algo, para um ou para outro, senão aquilo que contribuísse para sua *reconciliação»* (*Confissões* ix.21). Haveria aplicação para algumas Mônicas hoje em dia na igreja. Suas adversárias formam multidões. Lê-se acerca de Richard Dobden que, ao ser-lhe mencionado que talvez adquirisse tanta fama a ponto de ser sepultado na abadia de Westminster, replicou que esperava que isso nunca lhe acontecesse, porque «Meu espírito não descansaria em paz entre aqueles homens de guerra». É uma tragédia que até mesmo muitos líderes cristãos sejam respeitados por serem homens *contenciosos*, e que os grandes guerreiros do mundo sejam feitos seus heróis.

8. 5:10: *Bem-aventurados os que são perseguidos por causa da justiça, porque deles é o reino dos céus.*

Os Perseguidos.

Segundo a maioria das autoridades, esta é a última bem-aventurança, porque o vs. 11 é continuação da mesma idéia, e se destaca por ter a mesma promessa que a primeira: o reino de Deus. Provavelmente Jesus, o Cristo, o Rei do reino de Deus, estivesse antecipando a mudança que será necessária para que o reino seja estabelecido. João Batista já estava na prisão, prestes a morrer. É possível que muitos outros tivessem o mesmo destino. Considerando a intensa força do mal, a força das autoridades religiosas que se oporiam ao reino e ao Rei, a luta não seria fácil e sem problemas. As velhas formas da religião e da ordem política não se renderiam sem luta. — Naturalmente, essas palavras têm uma aplicação ainda mais ampla; pode ser que em algum tempo a perseguição venha a ser por causa da «justiça». Jesus também indicou isso (ver João 16:1-4 e 17:14). Ver o artigo sobre *Reino dos Céus*. Ver o artigo sobre *Tribulação e Perseguições, Valores de*.

5:12: *Alegrai-vos e exultai, porque é grande o vosso galardão nos céus; porque assim perseguiam aos profetas que foram antes de vós.*

«Regozijai-vos e exultai».

Saltai e continuai saltando, porque essa perseguição prova que vossa religião é verdadeira, que estais realmente prestes a participar do reino. Não temos

BEM-AVENTURANÇAS

alegria por causa da perseguição em si, mas porque é sinal dos tempos (isto é, o reino chegou), e também é sinal pessoal (isto é, vossa religião não é falsa, mas autêntica). Isso nos serve de motivo de alegria. Paulo traz a mesma idéia: «...se com ele sofrermos, para que também com ele sejamos glorificados» (Rom. 8:17). Em I Ped. 4:13 lemos: «Pelo contrário, alegrai-vos na medida que **sois co-participantes dos** sofrimentos de Cristo, para que também na revelação de sua glória vos alegreis exultando», «exultai». É interessante que Pedro usa a palavra, *exultando*, e que temos aqui, «exultai». Provavelmente a passagem de Pedro é eco das palavras de Jesus. Pedro deve ter aprendido bem essa lição.

«*Assim perseguiram aos profetas*». Qualquer judeu sabia das histórias de perseguição movida contra os profetas, e qualquer um deles tomaria o partido dos profetas, e não das autoridades religiosas que moveram a perseguição. Jesus mostra aqui que ninguém deve esperar tratamento diferente das autoridades civis e eclesiásticas. Outrossim, Jesus situou seus discípulos em boa e aceitável companhia, a despeito das dificuldades de conservação de tal companhia. Mais do que isso, ao tomarem a posição dos profetas, os discípulos também receberão o galardão dos profetas, que é o céu. Lemos na história eclesiástica que tais palavras e pensamentos eram importantes para a mentalidade geral da igreja, porque a perseguição foi muito real e perdurou cerca de *duzentos* anos. Quase não houve família que não tivesse algum mártir, e quase todos foram atingidos. Em nossos dias é difícil avaliar o impacto de tais palavras.

«*Galardão*» (que vide). A idéia da possibilidade de ganhar uma recompensa espiritual e eterna, a despeito de sua forma particular, mudaria e *enriqueceria* muitas vidas. Esse galardão é dado gratuitamente, e não é obrigação de Deus, conforme vemos na parábola do cap. 20:1. A palavra «galardão» foi tomada como empréstimo da vida comercial, e é aplicada à vida espiritual para mostrar que faz grande diferença aquilo que fazemos em relação ao nosso futuro fora deste mundo, não menos que o lucro do negociante, o esforço e a diligência que este aplica em sua empresa.

«*Nos céus*». Não «no céu». Provavelmente Jesus se refere à idéia judaica da existência de três ou mesmo de sete céus. Ver nota sobre o assunto em II Cor. 12:2 no NTI. Ou talvez indique a grande incerteza do caráter definido «*dos céus*», como as «muitas moradas» de João 14:2. De fato, não sabemos muito sobre os «céus», mas sabemos que nossos galardões serão de tal envergadura que vale a pena o esforço ou o sofrimento da perseguição que acompanha a vida cristã. Os verdadeiros discípulos já são considerados cidadãos «dos céus», e apenas aguardam a manifestação da glória. (Ver Fil. 3:20). Deve-se evitar a idéia materialista sobre os céus. A principal idéia é a de mudança de natureza, de *transformação* segundo a imagem de Cristo, de elevação do ser acima do nível dos anjos, e não a simples possessão de grandes riquezas e bens.

As bem-aventuranças apresentam uma decadência aparente do indivíduo, acompanhada de um autêntico soerguimento na sua condição espiritual:

DESCIDA (aparente)	ELEVAÇÃO (verdadeira)
1. humildade de espírito	posse do reino, no coração ou em sentimento real
2. choro	consolo
3. mansidão sob injustiça	terra como herança
4. fome e sede de justiça	fartura de virtudes divinas
5. misericórdia para com os outros, levando a carga alheia	misericórdia de Deus e participação de bênçãos dadas pela misericórdia divina
6. pureza de coração, com rejeição dos benefícios do mundo	benefícios celestiais, visão de Deus agora e futura visão beatífica
7. promoção de paz entre os homens	glória, beleza e paz conferidas pela posição de filhos de Deus
8. sofrimento pelo Rei e pela justiça de seu reino	posse do reino dos céus no homem interior, do novo mundo, da herança eterna e dos galardões

II. Do Apocalipse.

1:3: *Bem-aventurado aquele* lê *e bem-aventurados os que ouvem as palavras desta profecia e guardam as coisas que nela estão escritas; porque o tempo está próximo.*

Bem-aventurados. No grego temos o termo *makarios*. Fala, basicamente, da felicidade física e dá boa sorte. Mas o N.T. eleva essa palavra, a fim de que signifique «bem-estar espiritual», bem como as boas fortunas e a felicidade que, naturalmente, **acompanha essa bem-estar**. Originalmente, essa palavra era usada **para falar sobre a** «bem-aventurança» dos deuses, em contraste com o homem mortal, o qual, por sua própria natureza, deve passar pelas misérias e incertezas da existência. O evangelho confere aos homens as boas novas e diz como os homens podem chegar a compartilhar da «divindade» (ver II Ped. 1:4), chegando a possuir toda a plenitude de Deus (ver Efé. 3:19) e seu próprio tipo de vida (ver João 5:25,26 e 6:57), por serem transformados segundo a imagem de Cristo (ver Rom. 8:29 e II Cor. 3:18), passando assim a possuir sua natureza e seus atributos.

É através desse processo transformador, pois, que os remidos chegam a receber a «felicidade divina» com base na posse da própria vida e natureza de Deus. O que os antigos gregos ousavam atribuir exclusivamente à condição dos deuses, chamando-os de *makarios*, o N.T. mostra que pode ser dito com segurança acerca dos que encontram a redenção que há em Cristo.

Chegaremos a participar de «toda a plenitude de Deus», tal como Cristo dela participa. Sua natureza e seus atributos estão envolvidos nisso. Trata-se de um elevadíssimo conceito, de nossa mais sublime revelação. Isso é que fará os homens tornarem-se **verdadeiramente** *bem-aventurados*. — Disso consiste o evangelho cristão.

O uso deste vocábulo, neste versículo, naturalmente fala daquele bem-estar espiritual que será dado aos leitores que não negligenciarem este livro, mas antes, familiarizarem-se com o seu Cristo, que é o Alfa e o Ômega da criação, sofrendo perseguições por amor a ele, enquanto esperam sua volta dos céus, dando ouvidos às predições que estavam prestes a ser feitas. *Neste livro há sete bem-aventuranças*:

1. O bem-estar espiritual dos leitores que derem ouvidos e obedecerem às predições e suas exigências (ver Apo. 1:3). Felizes são aqueles que ouvem e observam o que aqui é dito.

2. ***Bem-aventurados*** são os mortos que morrerem no Senhor. Esses agora descansam; suas boas obras os seguem e lhes servem de bênçãos; e viverão para sempre (ver Apo. 14:13).

3. **Bem-aventurados são aqueles** que, mediante pureza na vida, conservam suas vestes sem mácula, e

que esperam pelo retorno imediato do seu Senhor. As suas expectações se cumprirão e sua fidelidade será recompensada. (Ver Apo. 16:15).

4. *Bem-aventurados* são aqueles convocados à ceia das bodas do Cordeiro. (Ver Apo. 19:9).

5. *Bem-aventurados* e santos são aqueles que tiverem parte na primeira ressurreição, sobre os quais a segunda morte não exerce poder. (Ver Apo. 20:6).

6. *Bem-aventurados* são aqueles que observam e obedecem às declarações deste livro. (Ver Apo. 22:7).

7. *Bem-aventurados* são aqueles que observam os mandamentos de Deus; esses terão acesso à «árvore da vida», isto é, participarão na «vida eterna». A vida eterna consiste na mesma modalidade de vida que Cristo possui, com base no seu mesmo tipo de natureza, que é a natureza divina. Ver Apo. 22:14 no NTI. Ver o artigo sobre *Vida Eterna*.

III. De João 20:29: *Disse-lhe Jesus: Porque me viste, creste? Bem-aventurados os que não viram e creram.*

«Maravilhosa verdadeiramente, e rica em bênçãos, para nós que não temos podido contemplar a Cristo, é essa declaração final do evangelho. Pois essas palavras não se aplicam aos dez discípulos, pois eles, a exemplo de Tomé, haviam visto para crer». (Alford)

Paralelo do Judaísmo. «O rabino Simeon ben Lachesh disse que o prosélito é mais amado pelo Deus santo e bendito do que toda a multidão que se postou defronte do monte Sinai; pois a menos que tivessem ouvido os trovões e tivessem visto os relâmpagos, as colinas a estremecerem e as trombetas a retinirem, não teriam jamais recebido a lei. Porém, o prosélito não viu nada dessas coisas, e, contudo, ele entra e se consagra ao Deus santo e bendito, tomando sobre si mesmo o jugo do reino dos céus». *(Rabino Tanchum)*

Uma *felicidade* especial ou bem-estar espiritual é vinculada àquela fé que não requer qualquer tipo de evidência, mas que acredita na evidência do coração. (I IB NTI Z)

BEM E MAL, ALÉM DO

Uma obra filosófica de Friedrich Wilhelm Nietzshe (que vide), publicada em 1886. O livro examina as estruturas e propósitos de sistemas morais.

Idéias. 1. Os códigos morais absolutos não são válidos. 2. A moralidade é relativa. 3. Existem duas formas de moralidade: a. *a moralidade dos mestres* (governantes, fortes), e b. *a moralidade dos escravos* (os humildes, os governados, homens comuns). A moralidade dos governantes incorpora as virtudes esperadas dos fortes, como força e independência. A moralidade dos escravos incorpora as virtudes de pessoas fracas como humildade, dependência, mansidão. Os dois grupos rejeitam às virtudes do outro. A moralidade é um desenvolvimento natural de tipos de pessoas, não uma entidade fixa, absoluta ou eterna.

BEM COMUM   Ver o artigo sobre **Utilitarismo**.

BEM GERAL

Ver o artigo geral sobre **Utilitarismo**. A expressão «bem geral» refere-se ao princípio utilitarista de que o objetivo da ética é o maior bem para o maior número possível de pessoas, fazendo contraste com o bem que beneficia apenas a um pequeno número de interessados. A democracia, como um sistema político, visa a esse ideal. O princípio é abusivamente exagerado quando aquilo que se julga bom para as massas populares é usado para perseguir ou mesmo tentar extirpar indivíduos ou minorias. Quando Deus amou o *mundo*, estava em pauta o bem *geral*. A redenção nunca será uma questão exclusivamente individual, embora também envolva esse aspecto. Pois Cristo está redimindo o *corpo*, composto de membros individuais. (EP MM)

BEM INSTRUMENTAL

Chama-se assim a algum bem que só é tal por causa dos bons efeitos que produz. Qualquer ação que produza um resultado avaliado pode ser chamada de bem instrumental. As leis podem ser chamadas de bens instrumentais. Em uma forma extrema, a doutrina dos bens instrumentais declara que a própria definição de bondade é uma definição prática, ou seja, o que funciona bem e obtém os resultados desejados é bom, e o que não funciona e nem obtém os resultados desejados não é bom. Ver sobre o *Pragmatismo*.

BEM INTRÍNSECO

Chama-se assim a algum bem que tem valor por si mesmo, inteiramente à parte das consequências da experiência e da aplicação. Poderíamos falar sobre a lei do amor e suas implicações éticas, ou sobre o Ser divino e sua transmissão de vida. O *pragmatismo* (que vide) não reconhece como bom senão aquilo que tem bons resultados práticos. Mas existem coisas, boas em si mesmas, que, naturalmente, produzem bons resultados.

BEM (prefixo)

No hebraico, «filho de». Era prefixo usado para indicar linhagem, e não apenas filiação direta. Podem ser distinguidos os seguintes usos: 1. filiação real, o que representa o uso mais frequente. 2. Relação de homem ou de mulher para com os seus pais (Gên. 3:16). 3. Relação de descendência, sem importar quão remota. 4. O estado próprio da juventude (Pro. 7:7). 5. Participação em uma profissão ou guilda, como na expressão «filho de profeta» (Amós 7:14). 6. Cria de algum animal (Jó 39:4). 7. Um rebento de planta que medra (Gên. 49:22). 8. Metaforicamente, indicando objetos inanimados, como «filhos da chama», que significa «fagulhas» (Jó 5:7). 9. Um uso adjetivado para indicar alguma característica notável de alguma pessoa, como quando os ímpios são chamados de «filhos da maldade», em II Sam. 3:34. 10. Indicação da idade de uma pessoa, como filho de quinhentos anos, o que significa quinhentos anos de idade (Gên. 5:32). (Z)

BEN-ABINADABE

No hebraico, «filho de Abinadabe». Foi um oficial sob Salomão, cuja responsabilidade era prover os alimentos da casa real, um mês a cada ano. O seu distrito ficava em Dor (I Reis 4:11). Houve pelo menos três Abinadabes durante o período do governo de Salomão, um deles sendo um filho de Jessé (I Crô. 2:13), e um outro filho de Saul (I Crô. 8:33).

BEN-AMI

No hebraico, «filho do meu povo». Foi o progenitor dos amonitas (Gên. 19:38), filho de Ló com uma de suas filhas, conforme se vê na narrativa do décimo nono capítulo de Gênesis. Ló havia fugido de Sodoma. As filhas de Ló estavam preocupadas com o futuro da linhagem de seu pai, pois dificilmente elas poderiam casar-se naqueles ermos. Embriagaram o pai e promoveram relações incestuosas com ele, uma a cada noite. O filho que nasceu da mais velha recebeu o nome de Moabe; o filho da mais nova foi chamado Ben-Ami. As nações daí resultantes, Moabe e Amom, tornaram-se motivos de contínua irritação para o povo de Israel. Alguns intérpretes têm imaginado que a história foi criada a fim de conferir uma reputação má àqueles tradicionais adversários de Israel, mas tal conjectura não pode ser provada. As hostilidades que posteriormente surgiram envolveram direitos de terras, e não foram causa de supostas origens degradadas. (ID)

BEN-DEQUER

Nome alistado em I Reis 4:9, entre outras onze pessoas, indicando um oficial responsável pelo provimento dos alimentos da casa real de Salomão. Ele estava encarregado do segundo distrito, que correspondia, a grosso modo, ao território de Dã.

BEN-GEBER

No hebraico, «filho de Geber» ou «filho do forte». Foi um dos doze oficiais administrativos de Salomão. Cuidava do sexto distrito, ao norte da Transjordânia, cuja capital era Ramote-Gileade (I Reis 4:13). Alguns têm equiparado Geber, filho de Uri (I Reis 4:19) com Ben-Geber (I Reis 4:13), como se fossem variantes do mesmo nome, visto que ambos aparecem como prefeitos de Gileade. Porém, a LXX, o manuscrito B e o códice Lagardiano (vs. 19) frisam «território de Gade», e não de Gileade. Cinco dos doze nomes alistados, são conhecidos apenas através do patronímico de «filho de» alguma pessoa. Paralelos existentes nos textos de Ugarite, também empregam somente uma designação patronímica. Com base em tais evidências, alguns estudiosos supõem que as duas pessoas de nomes tão parecidos não devem ser identificadas uma com a outra. (Z)

BEN-HADADE

No hebraico, «filho de Hadade». Foi apelativo de três reis da Síria, em Damasco. O nome «Hadade» está relacionado ao deus sírio Adade, idêntico ao deus chamado Rimom, na Assíria.

1. *Ben-Hadade I.* Rei da Síria. Fez pacto com Asa, rei de Judá, para invadir Israel, o reino do norte. Isso compeliria Baasa, rei de Israel, que invadiria Judá, a retornar à sua capital, para defender o seu reino da invasão síria (I Reis 15:18-20; II Crô. 16:2-4), em cerca de 907 A.C. Ver o artigo sobre *Asa*. Asa obteve bom êxito no plano, mas foi repreendido pelo profeta (II Crô. 16:7-10), de nome Hanani, por haver entrado em aliança com um monarca pagão.

Ben-Hadade fez significativas incursões no território do reino do norte, Israel. Asa foi responsável pelo fortalecimento de Ben-Hadade, o qual foi responsável, pelo menos em parte, por muitos pontos débeis do reino do norte. Contudo, do ponto de vista moral, Deus tinha tudo sob seu controle, e o episódio contribuiu para o desdobramento do plano de Deus relativo às nações.

2. *Ben-Hadade II*, presumivelmente filho do anterior e rei da Síria. Tempos atrás, os eruditos distinguiam quase unanimamente entre Ben-Hadade I, filho de Tabrimom, filho de Heziom, contemporâneo de Asa e Baasa(I Reis 15:18) e Ben-Hadade II, contemporâneo de Elias e Eliseu. Somente alguns julgavam que se tratasse do mesmo indivíduo. Porém, as evidências fornecidas pela estela de Ben-Hadade I sugerem poderosamente a identidade dos dois (ver *Bulletin of Am. Schools*, nº 83, págs. 10-12). O reajuste da cronologia dos reis de Israel também sugere que uma única pessoa deve ter estado envolvida nos acontecimentos historiados. Apesar disso, muitos eruditos continuam distinguindo as duas personagens.

A história inicial de Ben-Hadade II está envolvida com a história de Acabe, rei de Israel. Esses dois monarcas viveram em contínua hostilidade mútua. Acabe terminou levando vantagem, podendo então ter imposto a sua vitória. Em lugar disso, estabeleceu um acordo de paz com Ben-Hadade II, em cerca de 900 A.C. Esse tratado foi observado por cerca de doze anos. Mas então Ben-Hadade declarou guerra contra Jeorão, filho de Acabe, e invadiu Israel. Todavia, os planos do rei sírio foram frustrados por Eliseu, o profeta (II Reis 6:8), em cerca de 893 A.C. Alguns anos mais tarde, Ben-Hadade renovou as hostilidades e cercou Jeorão em sua capital, Samaria. Ben-Hadade reduziu Israel a quase nada; mas então, conforme Eliseu havia predito, o cerco foi inexplicavelmente levantado. No ano seguinte, Ben-Hadade enviou Hazael com presentes a Eliseu, a fim de consultá-lo sobre a enfermidade que o monarca sírio contraíra. Eliseu respondeu que a enfermidade não era mortal, mas que, não obstante, seu período de vida era curto. Poucos dias mais tarde, Hazael sufocou o rei sírio em seu leito, com um cobertor molhado em água, e apossou-se do trono sírio. Medidas políticas! (Ver II Reis 8:7-15).

3. *Ben-Hadade III* (II se é que os dois primeiros Ben-Hadades foram o mesmo indivíduo). Era filho de Hazael, mencionado no segundo ponto, que assassinara Ben-Hadade I (ou II). Foi derrotado por três vezes por Jeoás, rei de Israel, que recuperou todos os territórios que haviam sido perdidos para os sírios na Transjordânia (II Reis 13:3,34,35). As Escrituras declaram que essa contínua hostilidade era punição divina contra Israel, porque o rei e o povo seguiam os caminhos iníquos de reis anteriores (II Reis 13:2,3). Todavia, Deus mostrou-se misericordioso, provendo vitória, a fim de que Israel pudesse escapar dos ataques de Ben-Hadade (II Reis 13:5). A providência divina incluiu as derrotas dos sírios por Adade-Nirari III, rei assírio que se lançou contra Damasco. Em Amós 1:4 e Jer. 49:27, também é declarado que a derrota de Ben-Hadade se devia a falhas morais e lapsos espirituais de sua parte. (BRUC UN)

BEN-HESEDE

No hebraico, «filho de Hesede», ou «filho da gentileza», um dos doze oficiais de distritos de Salomão. A seu encargo ficava o terceiro distrito administrativo, a parte ocidental da tribo de Manassés (I Reis 4:10).

BEN-HINOM, VALE DE

Ver **Hinom, Vale de**.

BEN-HUR

No hebraico, «filho de Hur» ou «filho de nobre». Um dos doze oficiais administrativos dos distritos criados por Salomão. Ele administrava o território de Efraim (I Reis 4:8).

BEN-HUR — BÊNÇÃO E MALDIÇÃO

BEN-HUR (novela)

Esse é o título de uma novela escrita por Lew Wallace, cujo subtítulo é «Um Conto Sobre Cristo». Foi publicada pela primeira vez em 1880, tendo sido reeditada por muitas vezes, como um dos sucessos de livraria mais notáveis. A narrativa gira principalmente em torno das aventuras do fictício Ben-Hur dos dias de Jesus, que juntamente com João Batista, aparece apenas incidentalmente na novela. O herói converte-se à fé cristã. Depois é falsamente acusado por Messala, seu amigo de infância, de tentar assassinar o governador romano da Judéia, em face do que é sentenciado à galé perpétua. Sua mãe e sua irmã são lançadas em uma masmorra, onde contraem a lepra. Mas Ben-Hur escapa da galé e salva a vida de um romano poderoso, o qual subseqüentemente o adota e o leva a Roma. Então Ben-Hur retorna a Jerusalém, onde se vinga de Messala em uma corrida de biga, o evento mais emocionante da novela. Posteriormente, Ben-Hur reúne-se à sua mãe e à sua irmã, às quais Jesus cura miraculosamente da horrível enfermidade.

Ben-Hur tem sido freqüentemente apresentada nos palcos, servindo de base de duas fitas cinematográficas espetaculares, rodadas em 1926 e 1959. Aquilo que, mesmo indiretamente, toca na vida do grande Mestre, adquire uma força de atração que não é fácil de ser explicada. (AM)

BENAIA

No hebraico, «Yahweh edifica». Era nome bastante comum entre os levitas, razão pela qual é o nome próprio de vários personagens do Antigo Testamento:

1. Filho de Joiada, de Cabzeel, um dos heróis de Davi, cujo total era de trinta (II Sam. 23:20,21). Benaia serviu corretamente a Davi e permaneceu fiel a ele até o fim, pelo que foi honrado ao ser escolhido para fazer os arranjos para a proclamação de Salomão como rei (II Sam. 1:32-40). Sob Salomão, ele se tornou o comandante do exército (II Sam. 2:35; 4:4), em substituição a Joabe.

2. Benaia de Piratom, outro dos trinta heróis de Davi (II Sam. 23:30), comandante de vinte e quatro mil homens.

3. Um governante alistado na genealogia da casa de Simeão (I Crô. 4:36).

4. Um levita da segunda ordem de cantores e harpistas, sob Etã (I Crô. 15:18). Davi desenvolveu a expressão musical dos sacerdotes mediante inovação, e esse homem esteve envolvido nesse esforço.

5. Um sacerdote que tinha por tarefa tocar a trombeta, diante da arca da aliança (I Crô. 15:24).

6. Pai de Joiada, sucessor de Aitofel (I Crô. 20:14).

7. Avô de Jaaziel, da casa de Asafe (II Crô. 20:24).

8. Um supervisor da preparação das câmaras do templo no tempo de Conanias (II Crô. 31:13).

9 a 12. Quatro homens diferentes que se haviam casado com mulheres estrangeiras durante o cativeiro babilônico, e que tiveram de separar-se delas, ao retornarem à Palestina (Esd. 10:25,30,35,43).

13. O pai de Pelatias, ao qual Ezequiel viu em uma visão, de pé entre os príncipes que estavam destruindo a moral do povo com maus conselhos (Eze. 11:1-4). (BRI S Z)

BÊNÇÃO

Está em foco o ato de benzer (ver o artigo) alguma pessoa ou objeto, com a finalidade de dedicar essa pessoa ou coisa. No caso de pessoas, está em foco uma intercessão em favor delas, pedindo a bênção de Deus. No caso de objetos, o ato consagra os mesmos a alguma utilidade ou roga a sua prosperidade. A palavra «bênção» vem do latim, que tem o mesmo sentido da palavra hebraica *berakah*, vocábulo que também pode significar «felicidade», além de «bênção».

No Antigo Testamento, uma bênção usualmente consistia em uma oração ou em um pronunciamento solene. Em Salmos 103 temos uma expressão pessoal de agradecimento, em face das bênçãos divinas recebidas. O Antigo Testamento encerra várias bênçãos domésticas, nas quais o pai da família invoca a bênção divina sobre seus filhos (Gên. 9:26; 27:27-29; 48:15,16). A essas bênçãos dava-se grande valor, pois as pessoas criam no Deus de Israel. Moisés proferiu uma bênção sobre o povo de Israel como um todo (Deu. 28:1-14). A bênção clássica é a bênção de Aarão (Núm. 6:24-26), que diz: «O Senhor te abençoe e te guarde; o Senhor faça resplandecer o seu rosto sobre ti, e tenha misericórdia de ti; o Senhor sobre ti levante o seu rosto, e te dê a paz».

Bênçãos eram invocadas quando da adoração pública (Lev. 9:22; Deu. 10:8). A postura física dos invocantes usualmente incluía o gesto das mãos erguidas (Lev. 9:22).

Nas páginas do Novo Testamento há bênçãos eloqüentes, em Rom. 15:3; II Cor. 13:14; Heb. 13:20,21; Judas 24; I Ped. 5:14 e III João 15, várias dentre as quais são comumente usadas nos cultos de adoração dos evangélicos. (BLA E)

BÊNÇÃO DO BENDITO SACRAMENTO

Uma devoção que data do século XIV. Consiste em hinos e orações compostos por Tomás de Aquino, empregados antes do sacramento (ver o artigo). Conclui com uma bênção com o sacramento. (E)

BÊNÇÃO E MALDIÇÃO

Desejos, expressos mediante palavras proferidas, algumas vezes apoiadas em alguma ação, podem redundar em bênção ou infortúnio. As religiões primitivas sempre confiaram em declarações emocionalmente carregadas, como causas de bênçãos ou maldições. Há evidências de que uma maldição proferida, quando não é injusta, pode causar a morte de outrem. Algumas vezes indagamos o que estará envolvido em fenômenos dessa ordem, se tudo não será mera coincidência ou se há algo de profundamente psicológico nos mesmos. Segundo esta última alternativa, os temores da pessoa amaldiçoada explicariam muita coisa.

Por outro lado, precisamos levar em conta o poder espiritual daquele que abençoa ou amaldiçoa. Jacó abençoou não somente seus netos, Efraim e Manassés, mas também convocou seus doze filhos para abençoar a cada um deles. E essas bênçãos têm feito sentir o seu poder entre os seus descendentes até hoje. (Gên. 49:1-33). Por outra parte, há pessoas malignas, que recebem a ajuda de espíritos maus, e que evidentemente podem prejudicar ou mesmo levar outras pessoas à morte. Naturalmente, não devemos ser supersticiosos ao ponto de acreditar no que o vulgo chama de «mau olhado», e coisas similares. Mas sabe-se que há pessoas más dotadas de grande poder psíquico, que podem produzir efeitos adversos nas vidas de seus semelhantes. Todavia, quem estiver sob a proteção do Senhor, não sofrerá por causa de tais influências estranhas. «Pois contra Jacó não vale encantamento, nem adivinhação contra Israel» (Núm.

BÊNÇÃO ESPIRITUAL

23:23).

O poder espiritual de grandes homens de Deus às vezes atua de modos extraordinários. Consideremos as roupas usadas para curar enfermos, segundo se lê em Atos 19:12. Notemos que essas roupas também eram usadas para efeito de exorcismo (ver o artigo). Pouco sabemos sobre essas coisas, mas não há que duvidar que por detrás delas opera uma energia real, que talvez a ciência investigue e venha a descobrir. Vê-se, no A. Testamento, que a benção paterna era muito valorizada (Gên. 27:49). As bênções proferidas no leito de morte às vezes incluem predições, conforme já vimos no caso de Jacó.

Sabemos que os judeus muito temiam as maldições proferidas por esmoleres, mulheres, escravos e pessoas oprimidas, as quais nada podiam fazer senão amaldiçoar, não lhes restando outro poder. Bênçãos e maldições também eram proferidas acerca de animais e propriedades. Muitos acreditavam que uma pessoa qualificada era capaz de contrabalançar uma maldição com outra maldição, fazendo o feitiço virar contra o feiticeiro. Um bom exemplo disso é o episódio de Balaão (Núm. 22-24). A maldição que os moabitas desejavam que recaísse sobre Israel, acabou ricocheteando neles. «Povo meu, lembra-te agora do que maquinou Balaque, rei de Moabe, e do que lhe respondeu Balaão, filho de Beor, e do que aconteceu desde Sitim até Gilgal; para que conheças os atos de justiça do Senhor» (Miq. 6:5).

O autor desta Enciclopédia teve um aluno de filosofia cuja irmã experimentou uma série de acontecimentos estranhos, em conexão com uma maldição. A jovem quase se casara com um homem estrangeiro, mas terminou rejeitando-o. O homem voltou à sua pátria. Um dia, a jovem recebeu um vestido de seda muito bonito, enviado por aquele homem. Ela começou a usá-lo. — Então uma série inexplicável de infortúnios começou a cair sobre ela e seus familiares. A jovem acabou sentindo que tudo aquilo tinha algo a ver com o presente. — Ela jogou o vestido em um rio, e os infortúnios cessaram. Coincidência? Não vale a pena fazer experiências, quando tratamos com possíveis forças diabólicas. Há muitas variedades de maldições, com muitos modos de operação. Um professor muito cético que conheci, um dia precisou revisar seu ceticismo, quando um conhecido dele faleceu sem razão aparente, presumivelmente vítima da maldição de uma garota que ele enganara e rejeitara, menos de duas semanas antes! Quem se arriscaria com as palavras de fogo de uma mulher rejeitada? Ele se arriscou! (E HA)

BÊNÇÃO ESPIRITUAL
Efésios 1:3

Bendito. Expressão rabínica comum, que indica louvor a Deus, devido aos seus muitíssimos benefícios. Lemos em Sal. 68:19: «Bendito seja o Senhor que, dia a dia, leva o nosso fardo. Deus é a nossa salvação. (Selá)». O termo hebraico *barukh* (*bendito*) figura nesse Salmo citado, aparecendo na versão da Septuaginta (tradução do original hebraico do A.T. para o grego, completada cerca de duzentos anos antes da era cristã) sob a tradução *eulogetos*», que é exatamente a palavra empregada em Efé. 1:3.

A forma verbal desta palavra, *eulogeo*, significa «abençoar», «bendizer», «dizer bem de», «louvar», «exaltar». Portanto, sua idéia é, «que Deus seja louvado», «exaltado», devido, naturalmente, àquilo que ele fez em favor dos homens por intermédio do Senhor Jesus Cristo. Um dos nomes conferidos a Deus, na cultura dos hebreus, era «o Bendito», por motivo de reverência ou talvez temor, visto que os israelitas temiam proferir os nomes santos e sagrados de Deus. Além disso, desse modo Deus era representado como o benfeitor supremo da humanidade. E aqueles que recebem de suas bênçãos espirituais também são chamados «benditos», por se encontrarem em estado de bem-estar espiritual, tal como aquele que Deus igualmente desfruta.

Um termo grego diferente é usado nas «bem-aventuranças», em Mat. 5:3, onde tal palavra é plenamente anotada, quanto à sua história e ao seu uso. O conceito subjacente difere entre aquela e esta palavra. Pois o homem jamais deve ser «louvado» ou «exaltado», embora possa vir a ser «abençoado» por motivo do amor de Deus. E os remidos haverão de participar do estado exaltado de Deus por meio de Cristo Jesus, o que significa que desfrutarão do bem-estar divino.

Nos tem abençoado. A raiz do mesmo vocábulo grego é empregada aqui para indicar nosso ato de «bendizer» a Deus, embora aqui tenha um significado diferente. Deus é «louvado», «exaltado». Mas o homem é «abençoado», «beneficiado», recebedor da «abundância e graça de Deus», conforme esse vocábulo grego nos indica. Há aqui um jogo de palavras: Deus é «bendito» porque nos «abençoa». (Quanto a outras referências bíblicas que contêm a expressão «bendito seja Deus», ver Luc. 1:68; Rom. 1:25; 9:5; II Cor. 1:3; 11:31 e I Ped. 1:3).

«Deus não é um Deus que é apenas o autor de verdades matemáticas, ou da ordem dos elementos, conforme se dá no caso do deus dos pagãos e dos epicureus. E nem é ele meramente um Deus que dispõe providencialmente da vida e da sorte dos homens, a fim de coroar seus adoradores com anos longos e felizes...Mas o Deus de Abraão, o Deus de Isaque, o Deus de Jacó, o Deus dos cristãos, é um Deus de amor e consolo, um Deus que enche as almas e os corações daqueles que lhe pertencem, um Deus que os faz sentir sua miséria íntima e a sua infinita misericórdia, que se une ao mais íntimo de seus espíritos, enchendo-os de humildade e de júbilo, de confiança e de amor, tornando-os incapazes de qualquer outra finalidade senão ele mesmo». (Blaise Pascal, *Pensamentos*, pág. 93).

Com toda sorte de bênção espiritual. Palavras que indicam uma idéia lata e indefinida, indicativa de tudo quanto somos e possuíamos em Cristo, o que também nos torna cidadãos aptos para o mundo espiritual. Essa expressão, ampla e indefinida, sugere «totalidade» e «elevado caráter», porquanto aquelas bênçãos nos são dadas inteiramente da parte do outro mundo, por serem elevadíssimas, exaltadas, divinas. As bênçãos de Deus não são parciais, e também não têm limite. Temos indicação da mesma idéia em Rom. 8:32, onde se lê: «...porventura não nos dará graciosamente com ele todas as cousas?» O mesmo conceito transparece igualmente em I Cor. 3:21: «...porque tudo é vosso...», a saber, o mundo, os ministros de Deus, este mundo, a vida inteira, tudo quanto resulta da morte física, o mundo vindouro; tudo é dos crentes; os crentes são de Cristo, e Cristo é de Deus. (Ver I Cor. 3:22,23).

De conformidade com essas bênçãos tão definidas na epístola aos Efésios, elas envolvem os seguintes pontos:

1. Cidadania no mundo celestial (ver Efé. 2:6).

2. Transformação segundo a pessoa de Cristo, a ponto de virmos a possuir a sua própria plenitude (ver Efé. 1:23).

3. Liberação das cadeias; do paganismo, do

BÊNÇÃO SACERDOTAL — BÊNÇÃOS ÀS CRIANÇAS

pecado, do princípio do pecado-morte, paralelamente à entrada na vida eterna e imortal (ver Efé. 2:1-6).

4. Fim da alienação com Deus, o que significa que nos tornamos habitação espiritual do Espírito de Deus, com a obtenção de tudo quanto Israel possuía, mas muito mais ainda (ver Efé. 2:19 e *ss*).

5. Seremos o mais exaltado tipo de ser inteligente, em Cristo (ver Efé. 1:10 e *ss*).

6. Seremos algo sem igual na criação e na utilização nas mãos de Deus, a saber, a igreja eterna, a noiva de Cristo (ver Efé. 3:1-11; 5:32).

7. Em suma, seremos tudo quanto Cristo é (compartilhando de sua natureza essencial), e teremos tudo quanto ele possui, pois seremos seus coerdeiros. (Ver Efé. 1:23 e 2:4-7). Toda a seção «doutrinária» da epístola aos Efésios (capítulos primeiro a terceiro) descreve essas bênçãos celestiais.

A palavra grega aqui traduzida por *bênção* procede da mesma raiz que o termo usado para falar sobre o *Deus bendito* e sobre o «sermos abençoados». Notemos o jogo de palavras em torno desse mesmo vocábulo, que destaca seus vários sentidos e usos possíveis. Esse termo fala de todo o grande benefício espiritual da salvação, da imortalidade, da transformação segundo a imagem de Cristo, e de tudo quanto essas realidades envolvem. (Ver o artigo sobre a *Salvação*).

BÊNÇÃO SACERDOTAL

Estamos falando sobre a bênção que os aaronitas receberam ordem de invocar sobre o povo de Israel, em Números 6:22-27. Isso era um aspecto importante do culto no templo de Jerusalém; e até hoje, faz parte do ritual de muitas sinagogas. Antes da dispersão dos judeus, os sacerdotes de Israel se descalçavam e lavavam as mãos. De rostos voltados para a congregação, eles proferiam solenemente a bênção requerida, com as mãos erguidas. Nas sinagogas modernas, onde não há descendentes de Aarão reconhecidos, essa bênção é dada pelo rabino, terminada a função religiosa. A prática também tem sido preservada em muitas igrejas cristãs, até mesmo evangélicas. (E)

BÊNÇÃOS ÀS CRIANÇAS, Mat. 19:13-15.

Esta seção tem paralelos em Mar. 10:13-16 e Luc. 18:15-17. A fonte do material é o *protomarcos*. Consultar os detalhes sobre as «fontes» informativas dos evangelhos no artigo intitulado *O Problema Sinóptico*.

Esta seção apresenta um *breve catecismo* sobre o tratamento que se deve conferir às crianças na comunidade religiosa. Observa-se, na literatura judaica, que os judeus davam grande valor à família, e entre os escritos rabínicos há passagens carinhosas sobre a questão das crianças. Exemplos disso se vêem na obra de Joseph Klausner, *Jesus of Nazareth*, the Macmillan Co., N.Y., 1925, pág. 306. Na cultura judaica era costume que as crianças pedissem a bênção de seus genitores, — e os discípulos costumavam fazer a mesma coisa a seus mestres, os rabinos. Aquele que abençoava impunha as mãos sobre os solicitadores. O A.T. também apresenta exemplos desse costume (ver Gên. 48:14,15).

Mat. 19:13: *Então lhe trouxeram algumas crianças para que lhes impusesse as mãos, e orasse; mas os discípulos os repreenderam.*

Jesus acabara de pronunciar-se acerca da santidade do matrimônio, e era mui apropriado que agora abençoasse as crianças de várias idades, como nos indicam as palavras das diversas narrativas. O paralelo de Luc. 18:15 tem a palavra grega *brephe*, que usualmente indica bebês de pouca idade e que ilustra que as crianças que foram trazidas para serem abençoadas por Jesus pertenciam a várias idades, incluindo até mesmo bebês de colo. Provavelmente, na igreja primitiva, textos como este forneciam base suficiente para a idéia de que todas as pessoas da família, até mesmo as crianças mais novas, necessitam e devem ter acesso aos benefícios dos cultos e do ministério na congregação. Alguns intérpretes, observando essa verdade e também o fato de que Lucas usou a palavra «brephe» (bebês), ensinam o batismo de bebês pelo uso desse texto, mas tal idéia, como é claro, não passa de exagero das intenções do texto, porquanto simplesmente não encontramos nessas palavras confirmação dessa doutrina. O respeito dos rabinos pelas crianças era tão grande que eles ensinavam que até mesmo os filhinhos dos pagãos teriam parte no «mundo vindouro». De maneira geral, a igreja cristã tem conservado essa doutrina, dizendo que as crianças que morrem antes de atingirem a idade da responsabilidade estão salvas. Jesus reflete, em grau elevado, o amor da sociedade judaica pelas crianças.

Trouxeram-lhe...algumas crianças. Mateus e Marcos empregam o vocábulo grego **paidía**, que em seu sentido geral indica «crianças», mas que pode incluir uma ampla gama de idades. A palavra *brephe*, em Luc. 18:15, significa, usualmente, *bebê*. Jesus, que observava as exigências próprias ao celibato (que vide), não tinha os seus próprios filhos, e por isso adotou, como Salvador que é, a todas as crianças. O celibato pode ser um bom e desejável estado civil para alguns, mas o estado matrimonial, abençoado por filhos, é o estado comum e natural aos homens. A vida em família é o ponto central nos propósitos de Deus (ver Mat. 18:1-4; 18:10-14). É óbvio que a amabilidade de Cristo atraía a atenção das mães, e elas se aproximavam dele, sem receio, confiando que ele abençoaria os seus filhos. No notável *texto das crianças*, em Mat. 18:1-9, temos outra indicação da atitude de Jesus para com as crianças.

«*Para que*». Atitude própria do ato de abençoar, entre os judeus. As mãos eram e continuam sendo símbolos de oração e bênção, e freqüentemente simbolizavam o poder da transmissão de bênçãos espirituais ou físicas, como se dá no caso das curas espirituais. A parapsicologia tem demonstrado que os que são dotados do poder de efetuar curas mediante a imposição de mãos, emitem uma forma de energia por meio delas; essa energia é capaz de deixar marcas em um filme de raios-X. Talvez a observação dos efeitos da imposição de mãos, ainda que nada se soubesse sobre os efeitos reais desse ato, tenha dado origem à idéia de que a colocação das mãos pode ocasionar benefício moral ou espiritual. Orígenes sugere que talvez as pessoas que levaram as crianças a Jesus pensassem que aquele ato *protegeria* dos maus espíritos. A imposição de mãos era símbolo de consagração e de curas físicas no V.T. Ver exemplos disso em Gên. 48:14; Êx. 29:10 e II Reis 4:34. Na história dos judeus lê-se que os dirigentes das sinagogas abençoavam as crianças mediante—a—imposição—de mãos. O trecho de I Tim. 4:14 diz: «Não te façais negligente para com o dom que há em ti, o qual te foi concedido mediante profecia, com a imposição das mãos do presbitério». Alguns intérpretes opinam que o Espírito Santo aprovava tal imposição de mãos, por parte das autoridades da igreja, pelo fato de que ao mesmo tempo eram transmitidos os «dons do Espírito», os quais seriam utilizados para benefício da igreja. Assim sendo, alguns intérpretes têm sugerido que, neste caso, a bênção dada por Jesus não consistiu de mero ato ou rito sem substância ou efeito, mas que, mediante a bênção concedida, as crianças realmente receberam um benefício moral e espiritual. O próprio texto não expõe tais detalhes, mas isso não expressa um pensamento impossível. Pelo menos ficou claro que a igreja deve cuidar das crianças, e que até mesmo crianças pequenas podem participar dos benefícios do ministério da igreja. Não obstante, este não é texto no qual alguém possa alicerçar o ensino do batismo de infantes; e, pelo fato de que tal ensino não encontra base mais ampla do que encontramos aqui, temos toda a razão em rejeitar o batismo infantil. Se o batismo infantil é válido, terá de ser ensinado à base de outros textos e argumentos, mas não à base de implicações originadas neste texto.

Mas os discípulos. Marcos dá a idéia de que os discípulos repreendiam aos pais. Pela gramática do evangelho de Mateus, a repreensão era dirigida às próprias crianças, embora seja provável que a intenção do autor fosse idêntica à de Marcos. Com freqüência a multidão se aglomerava ao redor de Jesus, aborrecendo-o ou mesmo ameaçando-o fisicamente. Os discípulos, com toda a sinceridade, pretenderam protegê-lo dessa situação. Nesse caso pode ser que houvesse crianças pequenas demais para compreenderem os ensinamentos de Jesus, e os discípulos tivessem pensado que estas não poderiam receber qualquer benefício. Jesus, entretanto, não concordou com essa avaliação.

Mat. 19:14: *Jesus, porém, disse: Deixai as crianças e não as impeçais de virem a mim, porque de tais é o reino dos céus.*

Jesus, porém, disse: Deixai os pequeninos. Marcos adiciona a idéia da condição emotiva de Jesus, quando percebeu a atitude dos discípulos: «Jesus, porém, vendo isto, *indignou-se*». Lucas não dá essa descrição; portanto, somente Marcos conservou esse detalhe (10:14). O fato de que Jesus sentiu tão forte emoção demonstra o amor genuíno que ele tinha pelas crianças; também não teria gostado de ver as mães desapontadas em seu desejo que seus filhos recebessem a bênção. Por conseguinte, erramos quando ignoramos as crianças em nossas igrejas. O ministério da igreja local deve oferecer às crianças os benefícios que o cristianismo oferece ao mundo inteiro.

Não os embaraceis de vir a mim. Nestas palavras temos uma indicação sobre a humildade e a ternura de Jesus. Ele não levantava obstáculos no caminho de quem quer que fosse, mas recebia até mesmo as pessoas mais humildes. Antes desta ocasião, Jesus usou uma criança como símbolo dos «crentes» mais humildes e fracos e, por meio das palavras «porque dos tais é o reino dos céus», proferidas neste mesmo versículo, ele repetiu as implicações desse ensino. Jesus não aprovou a atitude dos discípulos, ao ignorarem os fracos e ignorantes. A avaliação feita por Jesus não coincidia com a deles. Pelo contrário, mostrava que todos são candidatos ao benefício do reino, não somente os que podem ser reputados inteligentes, nobres ou importantes. Os detalhes deste texto dão outro exemplo da grandeza moral de Jesus ao fazer a avaliação dos homens, isto é, da humanidade em geral. No sistema metafísico de Cristo, qualquer membro da humanidade é importante. Provavelmente essa idéia tem base nos ensinos do cristianismo sobre o grande destino que Deus tem reservado para a humanidade, que, uma vez cumprido, tornará os redimidos mais elevados que os anjos, quando os crentes estiverem plenamente transformados segundo a imagem de Cristo. Esse é o ponto mais alto da mensagem evangélica. Ver o artigo sobre a *Transformação do Crente à Imagem de Cristo.*

BENDER, WILHELM

Foi professor na Universidade de Bonn, na Alemanha. Nasceu em 1845 e faleceu em 1901. Promoveu a tendência antimetafísica das idéias de Ritschl (ver o artigo), degradando a idéia de revelação a uma posição secundária. Tornou-se um dos defensores da crítica ilusionista da religião. (E)

BENE

No hebraico, «filho de». No trecho I Crônicas 15:18 aparece como um músico levita. Naquele trecho, a LXX omite o nome, e tanto a LXX quanto o texto massorético omitem-no no vigésimo versículo.

BENE-BERAQUE

No hebraico, «filhos de Baraque» ou «filhos do relâmpago» (Jos. 19:45). Era uma cidade no território de Dã, que tem sido identificada com a moderna el-Kheiriyeh, nos subúrbios a noroeste de Tel-Avive. Foi uma das cidades da Palestina conquistadas por Senaqueribe.

BENE-HAIL

No hebraico, «filho de força». Foi um dos príncipes enviados por Josafá para ensinar nas cidades de Judá (II Crô. 17:7).

BENE-HANÃ

No hebraico, «filho de graça». Era filho de Simão, da tribo de Judá (I Crô. 4:20).

BENÉ-HASÉM

No hebraico, «rico». Foi um gizonita, um dos trinta heróis militares de Davi (I Crô. 11:34). No paralelo de II Sam. 23:32, temos Bené-Jásen.

BENE-JAACÃ

No hebraico, «filhos de Jaacã» ou «filhos da inteligência». O nome aparece em Núm. 33:31; e também em Deu. 10:6, sob a forma Beerote-Bene-Jaacã, que significa «poços dos filhos de Jaacã». Aparentemente, o nome originou-se em I Crô. 1:42. Se os filhos de Jaacã eram os mesmos nomeados entre os filhos de Seir, o horeu, em Gên. 36:20-30, então os poços de Jaacã estariam localizados nos montes que circundam a Arabá. O povo em questão, finalmente foi expulso dali pelos idumeus (Deu. 2:12).

BENÉ-JÁSEN

Um dos trinta heróis de Davi. O texto hebraico de II Sam. 23:32 diz «filhos de Jásen», e o seu paralelo de I Crô. 11:34 diz «filhos de Hasém», o gizonita. A palavra «filhos» representa uma ditografia das últimas três consoantes da palavra anterior, pelo que se trata de um erro textual. A forma original, sem dúvida alguma, era Jásen ou Hasém, sem a palavra «filhos».

BENE-ZOETE

No hebraico, «filho de Zoete» ou «filho do

corpulento». Era filho ou neto de Isi, descendente de Judá através de Calebe (I Crô. 4:20). Coisa alguma se sabe acerca dele, além do seu nome.

BENEDICTUS

Uma das fases da missa (ver o artigo) da Igreja Católica Romana, imediatamente após o *Sanctus* (ver o artigo), e parte integrante daquela seção. O termo deriva-se do latim *benedicare*, «abençoar». O cântico do Benedictus segue em linhas gerais o Benedictus do Novo Testamento (Luc. 1:68-79), conforme a descrição abaixo.

No Novo Testamento. Benedictus é uma designação técnica do trecho de Lucas 1:68-79, onde se encontra a profecia de Zacarias, pai de João Batista, acerca do Redentor de Israel, e onde a primeira linha diz, segundo a Vulgata Latina: *Benedictus Dominus Deus Israel*, «bendito seja o Deus de Israel». E ao trecho de Mateus 21:9, tradicionalmente tem-se dado o título de *Benedictus Qui Vinit*, onde se lê: «Bendito o que vem em nome do Senhor!» Há antecedentes veterotestamentários em Sal. 105; Miq. 4:4 e Mal. 3:10. (E Z)

BENEDITINOS

Essa é a mais antiga ordem religiosa do Ocidente, fundada por Benedito de Núrsia, iniciada no século VI D.C.; é regida pelas Regras de São Benedito (ver o artigo). De acordo com essa regra, os monges são forçados a permanecer dentro da ordem, o que garante a estabilidade das ordens religiosas. Assim, cada uma delas torna-se um centro de atividades religiosas, culturais e de caridade. Os beneditinos têm exercido larga influência sobre o desenvolvimento da civilização, sobretudo nos primórdios da Idade Média. A ordem ajudou a estender a civilização ocidental, antes e após o colapso do Império Romano (em seus segmentos Ocidental e Oriental), quando a Europa inteira entrou em um período de turbulência. Os beneditinos têm promovido a fé religiosa, a erudição e as artes. (E)

BENEDITO DE NÚRSIA

Ver o artigo sobre o **Monasticismo**.

BENEDITO DO MONTE CASSINO (Núrsia)

Suas datas são 480-543 D.C., segundo alguns. Foi o fundador do célebre mosteiro do monte Cassino, bem como autor da *Regra* que veio a ser conhecida como a principal legislação acerca do monasticismo ocidental (ver o artigo). Através de suas próprias experiências, ele transmitia aos outros as normas da vida monástica, orientando na vereda da renúncia do que é mundano e profano. Benedito tinha o gênio organizador, em pensamento e ação, e isso inspirava a outros. Seu programa de serviço a Deus estava alicerçado sobre a adoração divina, acima de qualquer outra consideração. Os beneditinos (ver o artigo) foram os que maior proveito tiraram de seu sistema, razão pela qual ele é considerado o fundador dessa organização religiosa. (E)

BENEDITO XIV, PAPA

As datas do seu pontificado são 1749-1758. Seu nome era Prospero Lorenzo Lambertini. Nasceu em Bolonha, a 31 de março de 1675. Tornou-se cardeal em 1726, bispo de Ancona em 1727, e arcebispo de sua cidade nativa em 1731. Foi um dos mais eruditos entre os papas, um estadista moderado que fez algumas concessões com muito tato e bom humor. Tinha muitos amigos e poucos inimigos. Por causa de sua extraordinária vocação política, foi capaz de solucionar disputas em Portugal, em Nápoles, em Sardenha e na Áustria, que tinham envolvido as relações Igreja-estado. Mantinha boas relações com os protestantes e islamitas. Voltaire dedicou a ele uma obra que escreveu sobre Maomé.

Esse papa trouxe de volta à comunhão da Igreja Católica Romana duas igrejas orientais: a Igreja Grega Malquita, de Antioquia e os maronitas (ver o artigo). Benedito XIV opunha-se à maçonaria e condenou a acomodação dos católicos a ritos pagãos, em lugares onde trabalhavam os missionários católicos. Promoveu as artes liberais, bem como reformas morais das mais diferentes variedades. Aumentou as dimensões da biblioteca do Vaticano e fundou quatro academias: a. de Antiguidades (especialmente Romanas e Cristãs); b. — de Estudos das Leis Canônicas; c. de História da Igreja e dos Concílios; e d. de Liturgia Sagrada. Também enriqueceu o acervo dos museus de Roma e Bolonha, tendo promovido a causa das universidades e de outras instituições de ensino. Escreveu muito sobre vários assuntos religiosos e eclesiásticos. Suas obras foram coligidas e publicadas como uma unidade, em 1904. (E)

BENEDITO XV, PAPA

Seu pontificado foi de 1914-1922. Nasceu em uma antiga e nobre família italiana, della Chiesa, a 21 de novembro de 1854. Seu nome era Giacomo Paulo Giovanni B. della Chiesa. Formou-se advogado na Universidade de Gênova, estudou teologia na Universidade de Roma, foi ordenado padre em 1878, ocupou diversos ofícios, tornou-se Secretário de Estado sob Leão XIII (ver o artigo), tornou-se arcebispo de Bolonha em 1907, cardeal em 1914 e papa no mesmo ano. Seu pontificado deu-se durante a I Grande Guerra. Através de discursos, encíclicas, protestos, orações, atos pessoais de diplomacia, escritos, etc., tentou obter a paz, embora alguns tenham dito o contrário a seu respeito. A 1º de agosto de 1917, publicou seu *Apelo às Nações*, com catorze artigos em favor da paz, similar ao apelo adotado e proposto pelo presidente norte-americano Woodrow Wilson. Seu oferecimento de mediação foi ignorado, mas o prestígio do Vaticano aumentou, em vista desse esforço. Durante e após o choque armado, Benedito XV realizou muitas obras de caridade para com povos e nações, no esforço de curar as cicatrizes da guerra. Ele salientou que para impedir tão insensata matança e sofrimento, os homens precisam mudar desde o íntimo. Terminada a guerra, o número de representantes oficiais junto ao Vaticano aumentou.

Sua obra inclui várias peças literárias, o aprimoramento da lei canônica, a promoção das missões católicas, a melhoria das escolas. Mas, acima de qualquer outro fator, sua reputação repousa sobre sua obra durante a guerra, —que conquistou para ele o título de «Apóstolo da Paz». Foi sepultado em uma cripta da Basílica de São Pedro, em Roma, em um esquife de bronze, sobre o qual há uma placa que descreve os seus esforços em favor da paz. Uma estátua sua, em posição ajoelhada, foi posta no lado esquerdo da basílica. (AM E)

BENEFICÊNCIA

Ver o artigo sobre o **Altruísmo**. A beneficência consiste em praticar o bem ao próximo. Jesus ensinou aos crentes que permitissem que sua luz brilhasse diante dos homens, mediante boas obras que glorificam a Deus Pai (Mat. 5:16). A preocupação pelo bem-estar do próximo — foi eloqüentemente expressa por Aristides (*Apologia* 15), o qual empregou idéias do Novo Testamento.

Aquele que é beneficente evita os vícios que prejudicam tanto a ele mesmo quanto aos seus semelhantes, promovendo atos que levam em conta os interesses alheios, igualmente. Quanto mais universal se torna esse nosso interesse, tanto mais nos tornamos semelhantes a Deus, que amou ao mundo inteiro (João 3:16). Ver o artigo sobre o *Amor*, que expande muito essas idéias. (H NTI)

BENEFÍCIO DO CLERO

Está em foco a isenção dos clérigos da jurisdição dos tribunais seculares, que foi praticada em parte durante o século IV D.C., mas, especialmente durante os séculos XII e XIII. Presumia-se que um clérigo podia ser melhor manuseado por seus superiores do que pelas autoridades seculares; mas muitos buscavam fugir dos tribunais seculares, porque os tribunais eclesiásticos eram bem mais lenientes. A classificação era bem geral, incluindo os padres, os monges, os professores e os estudantes de universidades controladas pela Igreja Católica Romana. Todas as espécies de problemas eram examinadas, e não apenas os que tivessem algum reflexo sobre a fé religiosa. Essa prática foi abolida na Inglaterra, em 1827, e nos Estados Unidos da América, em 1789-1790. Ver os artigos sobre *Imunidade*, *Lei Canônica* e *Tribunais Eclesiásticos*. (E)

BENEKE, FRIEDRICH

Filósofo alemão (1798-1854). Nasceu em Berlim e educou-se em Halle e Berlim. Ensinou em Berlim e em Gottingen, como um anti-hegeliano durante o período de maior influência de Hegel. Beneke considerava-se um discípulo de Locke, e provomeu a psicologia associativa (ver o artigo, sob o ponto terceiro). Ele argumentava que toda a filosofia deriva-se de uma análise psicológica.

Suas obras. The Empirical Doctrine of the Soul as the Basis of All Knowledge; New Basis for Metaphysics. (EP P)

BENEVOLÊNCIA

Deriva-se do latim, **bene**, «bem», e **volens**, «vontade». Significa a idéia de dar apoio aos interesses alheios, em vez de deixar-se controlar pelo egoísmo (ver o artigo). Ver sobre o *Amor*, porque esse pode ser um sinônimo. Ver também sobre *Beneficência* e *Filantropia*. Está incluído nesse conceito a idéia bíblica do coração quebrantado e do espírito contrito, que evita o orgulho e o auto-interesse exagerado (Sal. 51:16,17). (H P)

BENEVOLÊNCIA DESINTERESSADA

Expressão que precisa ser compreendida de dois modos diversos: 1. Bondade expressa para com outrem, sem qualquer motivo egoísta ou expectativa de que o ato será recompensado. Trata-se, nesse caso, simplesmente do exercício da lei do amor (que vide). 2. Amor para com Deus como o supremo objeto do amor, sem qualquer idéia de compensação. O mandamento que nos ordena amar ao próximo como a nós mesmos, dá a entender amar àquela pessoa pelo valor que ela mesma tem, e não por causa de algo que se possa ganhar egoisticamente com isso. Usualmente, o ódio também é interesseiro. Em outras palavras, uma pessoa odeia a outrem por alguma razão egoísta. Ele *me* enganou! Ele *me* dirigiu palavras ofensivas. Ele *me* defraudou. Por semelhante razão, o amor e a bondade por muitas vezes alicerçam-se sobre os auto-interesses. Jesus ordenou que amássemos os nossos inimigos (Mat. 5:43 ss), àqueles que poderíamos odiar por alguma causa justa e pessoal. Longe de termos um ódio interesseiro, cumpre-nos ter um amor desinteressado para com aqueles que nos prejudicam. O samaritano fornece-nos um bom exemplo de benevolência desinteressada (Luc. 10:33 ss). O próprio uso da palavra «samaritano», nesse relato de Jesus, significa que da parte dele não se esperava qualquer ajuda. Isso pode ser contrastado com o que sucede nas grandes cidades, hoje em dia. Publicamente, em plena luz do dia, pessoas indefesas são atacadas, enquanto outras vêem tudo com indiferença, não querendo envolver-se.

Está em pauta a doutrina filosófico-teológica da ética que diz que a *verdadeira virtude* envolve os afetos e as paixões, devendo ser definida como amor altruísta. Cada ser vivo deve ser amado de acordo com sua posição na escala do ser. Por conseguinte, o amor a Deus é o mais importante princípio moral, ao passo que o pecado consiste em auto-amor, sendo o pior de todos os vícios, sobretudo porque o auto-amor exclui ou prejudica ao próximo. A espiritualidade, uma vez renovada pelo Espírito de Deus, manifesta-se através da prática da benevolência, que inclui a eliminação dos **excessos do auto-serviço**. Essa doutrina tem provido a base de muitas das atividades filantrópicas e missionárias. (E)

BENFEITOR

Palavra que passou pelo latim, procedente do grego, *euergétes*, «benfeitor», que figura somente em Lucas 22:25, onde Jesus diz: «...e os que exercem autoridade são chamados benfeitores». O título foi, realmente, conferido a monarcas como Ptolomeu II (247-242 A.C.) e Ptolomeu VI (147-117 A.C.), e, igualmente, era dado a homens importantes, como prêmio por serviços notáveis por eles prestados. Jesus repreendeu os que buscavam tal espécie de reconhecimento. No dizer de Jesus, os gentios chamavam suas autoridades de *benfeitores*. Em contraste com isso, ainda segundo o ensino do Senhor, os apóstolos deveriam ser servos humildes, e não cobiçosos de títulos pomposos; e a instrução do Senhor pode ser aplicada a todos os crentes de modo geral.

BENGEL, JOHANN ALBRECHT

Teólogo protestante (1687-1752). Nasceu em Winneden, Wurtemberg. Foi ministro ativo do evangelho, autor e mestre, tendo administrado a Igreja Luterana de Wurtemberg. Ele é considerado o pai do pietismo da Swábia. Foi muito influente como erudito do Novo Testamento. Dentro da história da crítica textual, foi o primeiro a arranjar os manuscritos em famílias. Ver o artigo sobre os manuscritos do Novo Testamento, que inclui os princípios usados pela crítica textual. Sua obra mais bem conhecida é o *Gnomen Novi Testamenti*, uma breve exposição do Novo Testamento, mas valiosa por suas observações breves e penetrantes. Muitos autores posteriores de comentários bíblicos deixaram-se influenciar por Bengel.

Infelizmente, ele predisse a «parousia» para o ano

de 1837, e assim mostrou-se equivocado quanto às suas idéias escatológicas. Contudo, seu interesse pelo assunto valeu-lhe o título de «pai do moderno pré-milenialismo» (ver o artigo sobre o *Milênio*). Seu labor na crítica textual ganhou para ele a perseguição daqueles que insistiam no uso de manuscritos menos fidedignos, que foram usados por Erasmo de Roterdão na compilação do seu Textus Receptus. As pesquisas modernas, no campo da crítica textual, têm mostrado que Bengel estava certo em sua abordagem. (E)

BENINU

No hebraico, «nosso filho». Foi um dos levitas que assinou o pacto juntamente com Esdras (Nee. 10:13).

BENJAMIM

No hebraico, «filho da mão direita», ou, como outros pensam, «filho do sul». É nome de vários personagens e de uma das tribos de Israel, a saber:

1. *Filho caçula de Jacó*, cuja mãe foi Raquel (Gên. 35:18), cerca de 1900 A.C. Raquel não resistiu ao parto e faleceu imediatamente após o nascimento de Benjamim, tendo-o chamado, no último suspiro, de Benoni, «filho de minha dor». Mas Jacó alterou-lhe o nome para Benjamim, de som similar, mas refletindo a idéia de consolo. E, se o nome realmente significa «filho da mão direita», então a idéia era que Benjamim seria o arrimo de Jacó em sua velhice.

Benjamim era irmão de pai e mãe de José, mas meio-irmão dos demais filhos do patriarca. Grande foi a relutância de Jacó em permitir que Benjamim descesse ao Egito, em companhia de outros dez irmãos quando, por força das circunstâncias, tiveram de ir novamente ao Egito buscar alimentos (Gên. 4:24). Jacó preferia conservá-lo em casa, em cuja atitude vemos um apego especial do patriarca por seu filho caçula, algo que geralmente sucede aos filhos mais novos. Jacó não queria que nenhum mal sucedesse também a Benjamim, conforme ele pensava que havia sucedido a José (Gên. 42:4). Mas, terminou anuindo, e Benjamim também desceu com os dez irmãos ao Egito.

Deus controlava o episódio inteiro, pois há coisas que não podem ser explicadas como meras coincidências. Quando José deu-se a conhecer a seus irmãos, houve muita compunção de espírito e lágrimas, mas o amor lavou uma multidão de pecados. Então José mandou buscar seu idoso pai, Jacó (Gên. 45:4 - 46:7), com todos os seus familiares e pertences. Assim, o povo de Israel deixou de ser um pequeno clã para tornar-se um numeroso e temido povo no Egito. No relato bíblico, Israel aparece como quadro simbólico da redenção, em que uma pessoa pecadora encontra-se com seu Senhor e é chamada para fora do Egito, que representa o mundo pecaminoso.

Lemos em Gênesis 46:21 que Benjamim teve dez filhos. A bênção de Jacó, em Gên. 46:21 (ver o artigo sobre *Bênção*), garantiu uma vida frutífera para Benjamim, e os seus descendentes tornaram-se uma das doze tribos de Israel.

2. *A Tribo de Benjamim*. Quando Moisés fez o recenseamento, quando da entrada do povo de Israel em Canaã, a tribo de Benjamim supria 35.400 homens na idade própria do serviço militar (Núm. 1:37). Por ocasião do segundo recenseamento, esse número aumentou para 45.600 homens (Núm. 26:41). Tendo Abdom como seu príncipe, a tribo de Benjamim ocupava seu lugar, juntamente com Efraim e Manassés, no lado ocidental do tabernáculo (Núm. 2:18-24). Quando os espias foram pesquisar a terra de Canaã, o representante da tribo de Benjamim foi Palti (Núm. 13:9). O território dado à tribo, após as bem-sucedidas conquistas militares, foi aquele entre o de Judá e o de José (Jos. 18:11). Lugares notáveis do território de Benjamim eram Jerusalém, Gibeom, Betel, o vale de Aijalom e as duas Bete-Horom. Houve representantes bons e maus dessa tribo, incluindo Eúde, o juiz canhoto, Saul, primeiro rei de Israel (I Sam. 9:1), que ajudou a defender Israel no tempo de Débora e Baraque; também havia os maus representantes da tribo que atacaram a concubina de um levita, incidente esse que provocou uma guerra civil, no decurso da qual a tribo de Benjamim quase foi aniquilada (Juí. 20:3-48).

Há uma história das dez tribos perdidas de Israel. Muitos judeus dizem que só se tem conhecimento, na atualidade, da existência de israelitas descendentes de Judá, de Levi ou de Benjamim. Se isso corresponde ou não aos fatos, não sabemos dizê-lo. Mas também sabemos que houve tribos que absorveram outras, e que, por diversas oportunidades, muitos israelitas que pertenciam às tribos do norte vieram para Judá, quando da apostasia que culminou com o cativeiro assírio. A opinião da maioria dos eruditos é que, em torno de um núcleo da tribo de Judá, há descendentes de todas as demais tribos de Israel entre os modernos judeus. Mas também é fato de que a dispersão fez muitíssimos judeus, e seus descendentes, perderem totalmente a sua identidade. Isso chega a formar um capítulo importante na história do Brasil colônia, e têm sido escritas obras eruditas em torno da questão.

3. Um bisneto de Jacó, e neto de Benjamim, também tinha esse nome (I Crô. 7:10).

4. Um homem que se casara com uma mulher estrangeira, nos dias de Esdras (Esd. 10:32).

A Arqueologia e a Tribo de Benjamim. As famosas cartas de Mari, do médio rio Eufrates, encontradas em 1933, têm sido datadas como pertencentes ao século XVIII A.C.; mencionam os *Banu Yamina*, «filhos da direita», que provavelmente significa «sulistas». Esses estavam assediando a região naqueles tempos. Alguns estudiosos supõem que alguns dos antigos benjamitas estariam envolvidos naquele grupo, embora não haja qualquer registro de que a tribo de Benjamim chegou a habitar na Mesopotâmia. O mais provável é que tudo quanto temos nesse episódio seja uma coincidência verbal, porquanto em Mari também se falava uma língua semítica. Nos documentos de Mari, parece certo que «direita» significa sul, e que «esquerda» significa norte, visto que, no antigo Oriente Médio, as direções eram tomadas com a pessoa de face voltada para o leste, na direção do pôr-do-sol. (BRI ID NO NOT)

BENJAMIM, PORTA DE

No hebraico, «porta da mão direita» ou «porta do sul». Uma porta de Jerusalém dos tempos pré-exílicos (Jer. 37:13, 38:7). Conduzia à residência de Jeremias, em Anatote (Jer. 37:12), defronte da «porta da esquina», que ficava no lado ocidental da cidade (Zac. 14:10). Corresponde à «porta superior de Benjamim», que levava ao templo (Jer. 20:2), construída pelo rei Jotão (II Reis 15:35). (Z)

BENJAMITA

Designação dada a qualquer descendente de Benjamim (ver I Sam. 9:21; 22:7; I Reis 2:8; Juí. 3:15; 19:16; II Sam. 20:1).

BENO

No hebraico, «seu filho». Esse nome aparece somente em I Crô. 24:26,27, como apelativo de um dos descendentes de Merari, filho de Levi (cerca de 1014 A.C.). Parece que ele era filho de Jaazias, que era descendente de Merari. Algumas traduções tratam a palavra não como um nome próprio, e sim, como «seu filho». No entanto, o contexto parece exigir que se entenda como um nome próprio. (Z)

BENONI

Nome que Raquel deu a Benjamim, quando do nascimento deste. O nome significa «filho de minha tristeza». Mas seu pai, Jacó, deu-lhe o nome de Benjamim, que tem um sentido mais otimista. Talvez Jacó tivesse planejado que seu filho caçula seria o filho de sua «mão direita», isto é, seria o arrimo do patriarca, quando este chegasse à idade avançada. (Gên. 35:18).

BENTES, JOÃO MARQUES

O pastor João Bentes tem feito uma singular contribuição à causa da literatura bíblica na língua portuguesa. Ele já traduziu, a partir de 1957, mais de duzentos títulos. Entre esses destacamos *O Novo Testamento Interpretado* (seis volumes) e a *Enciclopédia de Bíblia, Teologia e Filosofia* (seis volumes), a presente obra. A essas duas obras ele dedicou cerca de doze anos de sua vida.

O pastor Bentes também é co-autor desta enciclopédia, tendo contribuído com muitos artigos bíblicos e teológicos, além de haver acrescentado valiosos comentários e observações àquilo que foi escrito por mim mesmo (Russell Norman Champlin).

Destacamo-nos fisicamente e em nossa formação acadêmica. Pois enquanto tenho 1,93 m, o pastor Bentes, descendente de judeus pelo lado paterno e português e índio pelo lado materno, tem 1,73 m. Além disso, o pastor Bentes é, essencialmente, um autodidata, o que de modo algum obscurece sua reconhecida capacidade em vários campos da erudição bíblica. Espiritualmente, porém, assemelhamo-nos muito (com distinções, naturalmente), pois amamos ambos à Palavra de Deus, como remidos que somos pelo sangue expiatório de Cristo Jesus, o Logos de Deus.

Na *Introdução* à presente obra, provi um completo artigo biográfico sobre o pastor Bentes, juntamente com outro acerca de minha pessoa. Isso aparece imediatamente após a página dedicatória.

BENTHAM, JEREMY

Escritor inglês (1748-1832). Escreveu sobre jurisprudência, ética, economia, lógica e outras disciplinas. Defendia com denodo as leis e os processos legais mais simples na Inglaterra. Ele promovia a causa de certa forma de utilitarismo (ver o artigo). Para ele, o prazer seria o impulso de toda e qualquer ação, e o prazer deveria ser medido quantitativamente. Ele defendia a idéia de que o bem deve alcançar o maior número de beneficiários, e que cada pessoa deveria ser contada como uma pessoa, e não mais do que uma.

Princípios. Seriam quatro: 1. O prazer deveria ser seguido como o grande alvo da vida, ao mesmo tempo em que a dor deveria ser evitada. 2. Socialmente falando, o maior bem para o número máximo de beneficiários deveria ser a norma de todas as ações, conforme foi descrito acima. O grande alvo seria o prazer para as multidões. 3. O prazer deveria ser julgado com base em vários critérios, como intensidade, duração, certeza e incerteza, frutificação do prazer, o seu grau de pureza, se livre de dor ou misturado com a mesma, e o número de indivíduos a desfrutar desse prazer, visto que o prazer do indivíduo isolado teria de ser subserviente ao prazer coletivo. 4. Seriam ficções doutrinárias como as dos direitos naturais e as próprias leis naturais.

Escritos. A Fragment on Government; Principles of Morals and Legislation; Handbook of Political Fallacies; Outline of the New System of Logic; Deontology or the Science of Morality; Bentham's Theory of Fiction. (E EP P)

Pedras Fundamentais do Utilitarismo:

1. As questões éticas deveriam ser guiadas, acima de todas as coisas, pelo princípio da *utilidade*.

2. Esse princípio com freqüência é expresso em sua declaração «o bem (ou felicidade) maior para o maior número possível». Não há felicidade sem **prazer**.

3. Esses critérios aplicam-se a atos individuais e coletivos, igualmente, incluindo até as regras básicas que governam a conduta humana.

4. O utilitarismo é uma espécie de aritmética moral, e sua fórmula basilar é a maior felicidade para o maior número possível de pessoas.

5. Uma aplicação teísta do utilitarismo assevera que essa felicidade mais ampla só pode ocorrer mediante o concurso da vontade de Deus, com base em princípios justos, e não apenas pragmáticos.

6. A maioria dos pensadores utilitaristas, entretanto, enfatiza o *pragmatismo* (vide).

BEOR

No hebraico, «tocha». É nome de duas personagens do Antigo Testamento:

1. Pai de Bela, rei dos idumeus, antes que Israel se tornasse uma monarquia (Gên. 36:32; I Crô. 1:43).

2. Pai do vidente Balaão, ao qual Balaque convocou para vir amaldiçoar a Israel (Núm. 22:5; 24:3; Deu. 23:4; Jos. 13:22).

BEQUER

No hebraico, «primogênito», «jovem» ou «camelo novo». É nome de dois homens referidos no Antigo Testamento:

1. O segundo filho de Benjamim, filho mais novo de Jacó (Gên. 46:21). Descendia, pois, de Raquel, que descera ao Egito com Jacó e ali se estabelecera. Entre seus descendentes podemos enumerar Saul e Seba. Este último encabeçou uma revolta contra Davi (II Sam. 20).

2. Um dos filhos de Efraim, filho de José (Núm. 26:35). Esse Bequer foi o fundador de uma família que, em Números 26:35, aparece como os «bequeritas». Em I Crônicas 7:20, seu nome aparece com a forma de Berede.

BERA

No hebraico, **presente**. Era rei de Sodoma nos dias de Abraão. Pagava tributo forçado a Quedorlaomer, rei de Elão, mas depois revoltou-se, juntamente com quatro outros reis. Após várias manobras, Quedorlaomer, com mais três reis, derrotou em batalha a Bera e seus quatro aliados. No processo da luta, Ló e sua gente foram levados cativos. Tomando conhecimento do fato, Abraão reuniu trezentos e dezoito homens dos mais capazes, nascidos em sua casa, e perseguiu os captores de seu sobrinho Ló, libertando-o. Isso permite-nos ver que Abraão era chefe de um clã poderoso, embora tenhamos de levar em conta que os reis antigos eram mais chefes de cidades-estados do que mesmo de nações inteiras. (Gên. 14:1-17).

BERACA

No hebraico, «bênção». Foi um dos guerreiros, dentre a parentela de Saul. Aliou-se a Davi, durante o exílio deste em Ziclague (I Crô. 12:1-3).

Há um «Vale de Beraca», que nossa versão portuguesa traduz por «Vale da Bênção». Era um vale no deserto da Judéia, a leste de Tecoa, — que tem sido identificado com o moderno wadi Bereikut. Foi nesse vale que Josafá derrotou uma coligação formidável de amonitas e moabitas, com a miraculosa ajuda do Senhor (II Crô. 20:1-30, esp. o vs. 26).

BERAIAS

No hebraico, «Yahweh fez». Um dos chefes benjamitas, filho de Simei (I Crô. 8:21), em cerca de 1340 A.C.

BERDYAEV, NICOLAI ALEXANDROVITCH

Suas datas são 1874-1948. Eclesiástico russo que, ameaçado de expulsão da Igreja Ortodoxa Russa, tornou-se professor da Universidade de Moscou. Foi expulso da União Soviética e estabeleceu a Academia de Filosofia Religiosa, em Berlim, Alemanha. Tornou-se o principal teólogo leigo da Igreja Ortodoxa Russa. Mostrou-se ativo no desenvolvimento do aspecto ético e social da fé ortodoxa, e suas obras exibem uma crítica penetrante, com extremo racionalismo e liberalismo. Era um crítico acerbo do comunismo (ver o artigo), do escolasticismo tomista, do humanismo ateísta, da democracia e do capitalismo. Opunha-se a todos esses sistemas porque dizia que cada um deles, à sua própria maneira, reduz o homem a um mero objeto, assim distorcendo e negando sua liberdade, o que termina na perda de todo o sentido da vida humana.

As idéias de Berdyaev fazem-nos lembrar de um dos cristãos gnósticos, embora acompanhadas de um forte elemento místico. Ele acreditava que o cristianismo havia introduzido no mundo uma poderosa tensão, diante das instruções existentes, que finalmente veio a favorecer o progresso da ciência e da tecnologia.

Idéias. 1. Ã semelhança de Deus, o homem é criativo. A criação emerge do nada. 2. A liberdade humana, pois, é uma autocriação, completando a obra do Criador. 3. A criação é um processo contínuo que caracteriza tanto a Deus quanto o homem; e a satisfação e o sofrimento são elementos necessários nesse processo. 4. O mal origina-se da liberdade, sendo uma forma degenerada da mesma. A criatividade autêntica é orientada pelo amor. O egoísmo degenera a liberdade, mas o egoísmo pode ser vencido pela tragédia da cruz. 5. O tempo divino é eterno, e o mundo é uma degeneração do tempo divino 6. O homem não está sozinho no universo. Faz parte da comunidade dos seres. Essa comunidade também não está sozinha, pois deve manter comunhão com Deus.

Obras: *The Meaning of History; The Destiny of Man; Freedom and the Spirit; Slavery and Freedom; The Beginning and the End; The Russian Idea; Dream and Reality*. (E P)

BEREDE

No hebraico **saraiva**. — No Antigo Testamento, nome de um homem e de uma cidade:

1. Um filho ou descendente de Efraim (I Crô. 7:20), e talvez o mesmo que em Números 26:35 é chamado Bequer (cerca de 1856 A.C.).

2. Uma cidade de Judá, perto de Cades (Gên. 16:14), que em caldaico chamava-se Agara, e em siríaco, Gedar. Talvez se trate da mesma Arade, referida em Josué 12:14, na parte sul do território de Judá. A. Hagar parou com seu filho, Ismael, ao vir ao encontro deles o anjo, próximo ao poço de Beer-Laai-Roi. O local tem sido identificado com a moderna El-Khulassah, a dezenove quilômetros ao sul de Berseba. Mas outras identificações também têm sido propostas.

BERÉIA

Uma cidade da Macedônia (ver o artigo), às margens do rio Astreu, não muito distante de Pela, que lhe fica a sudoeste, e próxima ao monte Bérmio. Começou a ser povoada desde cerca do século V A.C. Não tinha qualquer importância especial política ou econômica; mas, nos dias do Novo Testamento, tornara-se um dos centros mais populosos da Macedônia. Contava com uma considerável colônia judaica. A famosa estrada Inácia, com trânsito entre o Ocidente e o Oriente, ou seja, entre a Itália e a Ásia Menor, passou a poucos quilômetros ao norte de Beréia.

Ao deixar para trás as agitações havidas durante o seu ministério em Tessalônica (ver o artigo), o apóstolo Paulo chegou a Beréia, em busca de refúgio. Ali, em contraste com o que acontecera em Tessalônica e na maioria de outras localidades, a comunidade judaica (pois Paulo sempre ministrava primeiramente aos judeus) mostrou-se dotada de mente aberta à mensagem cristã, rebuscando diariamente as Escrituras, para ali encontrar confirmação do que Paulo ensinava, incluindo os seus informes sobre o Messias prometido. As Escrituras asseveram que os judeus de Beréia eram «mais nobres» que os de Tessalônica, o que ressalta uma mente receptiva nas investigações, atitude essa que não se manifesta ordinariamente entre as pessoas religiosas. (Atos 17:11). Na Bíblia, a cidade só é mencionada, além desse versículo, em Atos 17:13 e 20:4.

Há uma curiosidade histórica que envolve as cidades de Beréia e Tessalônica. Cícero apresentara um férvido discurso contra Piso, e isso provocara profunda comoção em Beréia. Em vista disso, ele foi forçado a refugiar-se em Tessalônica, para onde fugiu à noite. Cícero deixou registrado que Beréia ficava fora da vereda palmilhada, em *Piso* 36. A reversão do drama, vivida pelo apóstolo dos gentios, ocorreu cerca de um século depois desse incidente. O nome helenista da cidade era Alepo (II Macabeus 13:4). Atualmente, o lugar chama-se Verria, e conta com uma bem diminuta população. (ID ND UN Z)

BERENICE

Era a filha mais velha de Herodes Agripa I, nascida em 28 A.D, que figura em Atos 25:13-27. Suas outras duas irmãs eram Drusila e Mariamne. Berenice primeiramente se casou com seu tio Herodes, rei de Calquis. Após o falecimento deste, ela evidentemente iniciou relações incestuosas com seu próprio irmão, Agripa II. Mais tarde uniu-se por matrimônio a

Pólemon, rei da Cilícia, mas não tardou a abandoná-lo a fim de voltar ao seu irmão. Posteriormente tornou-se amante de Vespasiano, e depois do filho deste, Tito. Quando Tito se tornou imperador, por causa da opinião pública que era contrária a Berenice, o imperador a expulsou. (Ver Josefo, *Antiq*. xix.5, I. xx.7,2,3; Tácito, *História* ii.81; Suetônio, *Tito* 7).

Esses dados biográficos mostram-nos que Berenice era uma mulher fascinante, ainda que totalmente devassa. Houve certa feita, entretanto, em que ela resolveu exibir um ato magnânimo. Isso sucedeu, com grande risco da própria vida, quando ela compareceu para interceder, de pés descalços, em favor de alguns judeus, a quem ela procurava defender da brutalidade do procurador Géssio Floro. (Ver Josefo, *Guerras do Judeus*, II.15.1).

O poeta romano, Juvenal, escreveu a respeito de Berenice:

> *Deinde adamas notissium, et Berenices*
> *In digito factus pretiosior: hunc dedit olim*
> *Barbarus incestae, dedit hunc Agrippa sorori.*

A tradução desse poema é a seguinte:

> *Depois, um valiosíssimo diamante, tornado ainda mais*
> *Precioso por ter sido posto no dedo de Berenice;*
> *Um bárbaro o deu a essa mulher incestuosa, anteriormente*
> *E Agripa deu o mesmo à sua irmã.*
> (Juvenal, *Sat*. vi. ver 155)

Houve um tempo em que se segregava insistentemente que ela se tornaria imperatriz; porém, a grita popular contra isso foi tanta que ficou abafada a idéia. É evidente que Berenice era ao mesmo tempo mulher de grande beleza física e de grandes dotes. Todavia, empregava essas coisas para o desperdício e a dissipação.

Assim vemos esse famoso, mas infame, par de irmãos incestuosos em visita ao governador Festo, o qual, não tardou a conceder-lhes algumas horas de diversão às expensas do apóstolo Paulo. A visita que Agripa e Berenice fizeram a Festo provavelmente era só uma visita cordial de reconhecimento, por ser ele o recém-chegado novo procurador da província da Judéia. (Quanto a notas expositivas sobre a ênfase que Lucas, o autor sagrado, dá às mulheres, dentro da tradição dos evangelhos, ver o trecho de Atos 5:14 no NTI). (ID ND)

BEREQUIAS

No hebraico, «aquele a quem Yahweh abençoou». É nome de sete personagens do Antigo Testamento.

1. Um dos principais homens da tribo de Efraim, no tempo do rei Acaz (II Crô. 28:12), em cerca de 750 A.C.

2. Um dos filhos de Zorobabel, da família real de Judá (I Crô. 3:20), em cerca de 597 A.C. Ele descendia de Jeconias, o rei que foi levado cativo para a Babilônia, por Nabucodonosor, em 597 A.C.

3. O pai de Mesulão, um sacerdote que ajudou a reparar as muralhas de Jerusalém, nos dias de Neemias. Sua área de trabalho foi próxima da porta do Peixe (Nee. 3:3,4), e também defronte de sua morada, nas proximidades da porta Oriental (Nee. 3:30), em cerca de 520 A.C.

4. Pai do profeta Zacarias (Zac. 1:1), em cerca de 500 A.C. É possível que ninguém tivesse auxiliado tanto a Josué e Zorobabel quanto Zacarias, na tarefa de reconstruir o templo de Jerusalém, após o cativeiro babilônico (ver o artigo).

5. Um dos porteiros que cuidava da arca da aliança ao tempo de Davi, quando este reestruturou as atividades dos levitas. Muitos dos que cuidavam da arca eram cantores ou músicos; mas o filhos de Berequias eram porteiros (I Crô. 15:23). Essa função foi mantida por Salomão, após a construção do templo de Jerusalém.

6. Genitor do levita Asafe, que retornara da Babilônia a Judá e estabelecera residência em Netofá ou em uma de suas vilas. Ele participou da reconstrução do templo e da cidade (I Crô. 6:31-39 e 15:16,17).

7. Um gersonita, e, portanto, levita, pai do cantor Asafe (I Crô. 6:39), em cerca de 1043 A.C. (ID UN)

BERGSON, HENRI

Suas datas são 1859-1941. Foi judeu francês. Um dos mais notáveis, brilhantes e influentes filósofos de nossa época. Ele não percebia ou não expressava as implicações religiosas de sua filosofia, senão quando da publicação de sua última obra. Bergson chegara a uma posição que se poderia classificar de posição teísta, não-escolástica, modificada, tendo abandonado a idéia de um Deus estático, de acordo com a perfeição concebida pela teologia escolástica, para um Deus que se manifesta através de eventos concretos e na história de indivíduos e organismos vivos. Rejeitava a deidade absoluta de Aristóteles, preferindo um Deus pessoal e dinâmico, que atua pelo amor.

Suas Idéias. Podemos enfocar nove pontos principais:

1. A filosofia deve formar-se de acordo com a experiência pessoal. Somos possuidores de razão e de intuição, e podemos julgar as nossas experiências. A razão tende a fornecer-nos uma visão estática das coisas; mas a intuição tende à flexibilidade e à mudança, o que é mais harmônico com a realidade.

2. A razão falsifica as experiências, conforme vemos nos paradoxos de Zeno, onde encontramos as categorias da razão a interpretar a fluidez do tempo.

3. Aprendemos a entender o significado de um objeto mediante a consciência intuitiva, por meio da qual de algum modo identificamos o próprio objeto. A razão produz um *conceito*. Mas a intuição produz uma *metáfora*, que se aproxima mais da verdade das coisas.

4. A realidade encontra-se em estado de fluxo, ou seja, está evoluindo. Deus opera nesse processo, e é a força por detrás do mesmo. Ele é o *elo vital*, que faz o processo ser o que é. Esse elo vital é o impulso primário que atua no mundo, como poder evolucionário ativo que opera e guia toda a existência.

5. A evolução é dotada de propósito, e é aventurosa. A verdade, portanto, —não fica estagnada em forma de conceitos. Os conceitos geralmente obscurecem e distorcem a verdade. Antes, nosso conhecimento da verdade está sempre em estado de fluxo, expressando-se por meio de parábolas.

6. A liberdade é uma das principais características da verdade, sendo, igualmente, a essência do ser. O homem e Deus criam as alternativas que possibilitam o futuro, e isso assegura a expressão da liberdade.

7. Matéria e espírito. O espírito mantém-se em estado de fluxo. A matéria, ao contrário, é estagnação. As duas coisas podem ser comparadas a uma fonte de água. A água mana (espírito); mas então entra em repouso (matéria). Isso também assemelha-se à razão (força estagnadora) e à intuição (o surgimento de uma idéia).

8. Falamos em termos similares a respeito do *tempo*. O passado continua a existir, fazendo parte do presente, e sendo aquilo que chamamos de memória. A questão toda parece-se com uma bola-de-neve que contém em si mesma o que ela era no começo, ao mesmo tempo em que vai adquirindo novas camadas.

9. As mesmas espécies de metáforas aplicam-se às *variedades de religião*. A religião institucionalizada é estagnada em seus conceitos. A religião mística (extática) sempre se renova, como um manancial que nunca cessa, mas antes, evolui, muda sempre e transmite vida a tudo quanto por ele é banhado. A religião mística pode ser ameaçada pela letra, a qual mata quando as pessoas insistem em obter conceitos credais, que limitam e estagnam a vida e o pensamento. As idéias religiosas são melhor expressas sob a forma de parábolas, o que lhes concede fluidez.

Sobre conceitos éticos. Há duas fontes originadoras da ética e da religião. Uma dessas fontes é *fechada*, consistindo em instintos sociais limitados por leis. Nesse caso, a verdadeira moralidade é impossível, porquanto falta-lhe a liberdade, estando estagnada como conceitos racionais. Baseia-se no auto-interesse (ou egoísmo), adquirindo importância devido aos interesses grupais ou ao egoísmo coletivo. A moralidade *aberta*, em contraste, alicerça-se sobre a compreensão intuitiva do próprio «eu», com base nos afetos, e não na fria razão. A moralidade aberta está arraigada no «eu» supra-racional. Ali é possível o altruísmo genuíno, a verdadeira moralidade. Bergson concebia os evangelhos e o cristianismo como alicerçados sobre conceitos de moralidade aberta, em contraste com o pano de fundo veterotestamentário, fechado, legalista.

Obras. *Time and Free Will; Essays on the Immediate Giving of Awareness; Creative Evolution; Introduction to Metaphysics; The Two Sources of Morality; Thought and the Moving*. (E EP H P)

BERI

Um aserita, filho de Zofa (I Crô. 7:36). Seu nome é omitido nas genealogias paralelas de Gên. 46:17 e Núm. 26:44-47. Aparentemente não há qualquer conexão com os beriitas de Núm. 26:44, ou com os beritas de II Sam. 20:14.

BERIAS

No hebraico, «proeminente», embora alguns prefiram «mau» ou «filho do mal»; ou então algo relacionado ao termo árabe *bara'a*, «excelente». É nome de quatro pessoas mencionadas no Antigo Testamento:

1. Nome do último dos filhos de Aser, pai de Heber e Malquiel (Gên. 46:17; I Crô. 7:30). Seus descendentes são chamados de beriitas, em Núm. 26:44,45.

2. Um filho de Efraim, que obteve esse nome da casa de seu pai, onde nasceu. Alguns dos filhos de Efraim foram mortos por homens de Gate, quando tentavam furtar cabeças de gado (I Crô. 7:23).

3. Um benjamita, aparentemente filho de Elpaal. Ele e seu irmão, Sema, foram os ancestrais dos habitantes de Aijalom, e expulsaram os habitantes de Gate (I Crôn. 8:13).

4. Um levita, o último dos filhos de Simei a ser nomeado em I Crô. 23:10,11. Sua posteridade não era numerosa, tendo sido contada juntamente com a de seu irmão, Jeús.

••• ••• •••

BERIGARD, CLAUDE

Filósofo francês (1578-1633). Estudou em Paris e trabalhou na Itália. Reviveu a filosofia epicurista (ver o artigo), mas com uma metafísica diferente. Seu ponto de vista sobre o vácuo era que o mesmo estaria repleto de átomos puntiformes,— cada um ocupando a dimensão de um ponto. Movimento e mutação envolveriam a transmissão de qualidades sensíveis de um átomo para outro, ou de um conjunto de átomos para outro conjunto de átomos.

Escritos: *The Circle of Pisa; Doubts Concerning the Dialogues of Galileo*.

BERIITAS

Descendentes de **Berias** (ver o artigo), mencionados somente em Núm. 26:44. Berias era filho de Aser (Gên. 46:17 e Núm. 26:45).

BERILO

Uma gema usualmente de cor verde pálido, embora também existam variedades amarelas, róseas e brancas. Desde a antiguidade o berilo era usado como pedra preciosa. Sua única menção na Bíblia é em Apocalipse 21:20. Modernamente, o termo berilo é aplicado a um tipo grosseiro de esmeralda. O berilo é o *Beryllium aluminum silicate*. Cristais de berilo são comuns, com freqüência atingindo avantajadas dimensões, feitos de prismas hexagonais, limitados por um plano basal, algumas vezes com formas piramidais hexagonais, estriados verticalmente. Os antigos geralmente davam o nome de crisólita ao tipo amarelo e verde transparente de berilo.

A antiga designação *crisópraso* (ver o artigo) indicava uma pedra preciosa verde-dourada, que, provavelmente, também era uma variedade de berilo. A substância é mais comumente encontrada em rochas graníticas, ou encobrindo a superfície de cavidades no granito ou em veios. O berilo pode ser encontrado em muitos lugares do mundo. Ver Êxo. 28:20; 39:13; Can. 5:14; Eze. 1:16; 10:9; Dan. 10:6, trechos onde, no original hebraico, aparece o termo hebraico correspondente, *tarshish*. Nossa versão portuguesa, porém, diz «jacinto», em lugar de «berilo», na referência de Cantares. (RE)

BERITAS

Um povo mencionado somente em II Sam. 20:14, na narrativa sobre a perseguição de Seba, filho de Bicri, por parte de Joabe. Parece que eles residiam no norte da Palestina, embora alguns estudiosos localizem-nos em Biria, ao norte de Safede, a qual é então identificada com Berote, uma cidade da alta Galiléia, não distante de Cadas. Ali, de acordo com Josefo (*Anti*. v.1.18), a confederação cananéia acampou em oposição a Josué. A narrativa aparece em Josué 11, onde, entretanto, lê-se que o acampamento era próximo das águas de Merom. (UN)

BERITE

No hebraico, «aliança». É nome de um ídolo adorado em Siquem. Em nossa versão portuguesa, aparece como Baal-Berite em Juí. 8:33 e como El-Berite, em Juí. 9:46.

Essa palavra também aparece no Antigo Testamento no sentido de «pacto», «acordo», «confederação», etc., por cerca de duzentas e oitenta vezes. Envolve um dos mais importantes conceitos teológicos do Antigo Testamento. Ver sobre *Testamento*. Nesse sentido, corresponde à palavra grega *diathéke*, «acordo», «testamento». Por ocasião da instituição da Ceia, disse o Senhor Jesus: «Este é o cálice da nova aliança no meu sangue, derramado em favor de vós» (Luc. 22:20).

BERITO

Antigo nome da cidade de Beirute que, nos tempos antigos, era um dos notáveis portos da costa da Fenícia, rivalizando com Biblos, ao norte, e com Sidom e Tiro, ao sul. O lugar não é mencionado no Antigo Testamento, visto que a Berota de Eze. 47:16 e a Berotai de II Sam. 8:8, não são a mesma coisa que Berito. Porém, Berito é mencionada nos registros egípcios desde o século XV A.C., nas listas de Tutmés III. Também figura nas cartas de Amarna, em cerca de 1400 A.C. Para o Egito, Berito era importante como porto exportador de cedro, e também como um posto avançado marítimo de defesa contra os hititas. Na época, a cidade estava sob controle egípcio. Operava como um porto comercial, durante todo o período da Assíria, da Babilônia, da Pérsia e dos reis selêucidas. Foi conquistada e destruída por Trifon, em suas lutas pelo trono selêucida, em cerca de 140 A.C. O representante de Augusto, Marcos Agripa, ocupou o porto de Berito em 15 A.C., transformando-o em colônia militar romana.

Herodes I adornou a cidade, onde também instaurou um tribunal que sentenciou à morte dois de seus filhos (Josefo, *Anti*. xvi.11.2). Agripa I e Agripa II construíram teatros na cidade (Josefo, *Guerras* vii.3.1). Tito celebrou a queda de Jerusalém, bem como o aniversário natalício de Vespasiano, com jogos atléticos em Berito. As forças dos exércitos orientais, que guindaram Vespasiano ao poder, em 69 D.C., tinham-se reunido em Berito (Tácito, *Hist*. 2:81). Berito tornou-se um importante local de erudição, especialmente de estudos legais. Sua antiqüíssima história praticamente terminou por causa de um desastroso terremoto que a atingiu em 521 D.C. (Z)

BERKELEY, GEORGE

Bispo irlandês (1685-1753). Foi fundador do *idealismo subjetivo* (ver o artigo). Formou-se pelo Trinity College, de Dublim. Serviu naquela instituição em várias capacidades. Viajou extensamente pela Europa. Foi capelão e tutor. Estabeleceu um colégio missionário nas Bermudas, onde residiu por cinco anos. Viveu por três anos no estado de Rhode Island, nos Estados Unidos da América. Em 1734 tornou-se bispo de Cloyne, e passou ali quase vinte anos. Em seguida, mudou-se para Oxford, onde seu filho estava estudando. E ali faleceu, em 1753.

Uma famosa declaração sua introduz a sua filosofia: «Primeiramente, levantamos uma poeira; e então queixamo-nos de que não podemos ver». Isso equivale a dizer que os filósofos criam problemas artificiais e então procuram encontrar soluções para os mesmos. É o que se dá com o materialismo e a metafísica vinculada à posição. Supomos que a matéria é real, e então lançamo-nos à tentativa de explicá-la. Mas tudo quanto existe é *idéia* (ver o artigo sobre o idealismo).

Idéias. Consideremos os nove pontos seguintes:

1. *Ser é ser percebido*. Isso porque não há existência sem idéia. Nisso encontramos o imaterialismo de Berkeley.

2. Todas as idéias originam-se na percepção dos sentidos, conforme dizia Locke. Contudo, não temos percepção imediata do mundo material; antes, todas as nossas percepções são nossas idéias, que então impomos sobre uma suposta existência exterior. A epistemologia chama isso de *idealismo subjetivo* (ver o artigo). Aquilo que existe independente de nossas idéias, continua sendo imaterial ou idéia, o que a filosofia denomina de *idealismo objetivo* (ver o artigo). Vários filósofos que advogam o idealismo subjetivo não afirmam que não existe um mundo exterior, mas apenas que tomamos conhecimento do mesmo simplesmente como uma idéia, e não como percepções reais de tal existência.

3. A matéria, considerada como independente da mente, é autocontraditória, visto que todas as suas propriedades são apenas idéias.

4. Há um fundo de informes fixos e compartilháveis, que várias mentes podem sondar (e há outras mentes). Esses informes compartilháveis nos são impostos pela mente comunitária, ou pela mente divina, algumas vezes contradizendo idéias individuais.

5. Os informes mentais dependem do próprio Deus, que nos comunica a sua linguagem.

6. Os nomes vinculados aos informes tornam-se um idioma. Berkeley agrupava as idéias, mediante o princípio de associação, substituindo a doutrina das abstrações (ver o artigo) de Locke.

7. Berkeley também negava a validade da distinção feita por Locke de qualidades primárias e secundárias. As qualidades primárias seriam: extensão, figura e movimento; as qualidades secundárias seriam: cor, paladar, olfato. Portanto, existe em foco aquelas qualidades necessárias à existência de um objeto (qualidades primárias), bem como aquelas coisas que são meros acidentes, e não são essenciais (qualidades secundárias). Berkeley reduzia tudo isso a idéias. *Ser é ser percebido*, e ser percebido é a idéia que temos de alguma coisa.

8. Até mesmo o tempo e o espaço nada são, à parte de nossa percepção mental.

9. Em sua obra final, *Siris*, Berkeley acrescentou a categoria das *noções*, ou seja, idéias de alma e de Deus.

Obras. *A New Theory of Vision; Treatise Concerning the Principles of Human Understanding; Three Dialogues Between Hylas and Philonus; The Theory of Vision or Visual Language, Vindicated and Explained; Siris*. (E EP F P MM)

BERLIN, SIR ISAIAH

Filósofo político e moral inglês (1909— ?). Também é historiador que tem argumentado vigorosamente contra tipos deterministas da filosofia da história, tendo atacado especialmente a idéia marxista da marcha inevitável da história, com seus valores e elementos predeterminados. Ele tem salientado a importância dos valores morais, que necessariamente incluem responsabilidade e liberdade. Berlin via esses valores morais solapados por um suposto processo histórico predeterminado. Antes, os seres humanos seriam pessoas livres, criadoras, motivadas e dotadas de propósito, que poderiam moldar os eventos, e não apenas ser vítimas dos mesmos.

Escritos: *Karl Marx, Historical Inevitability; Two Concepts of Liberty*. (F)

BERNARDO DE CHARTRES

Filósofo platônico, escolástico (1080?-1167). Ensinou durante cinco anos em Chartres, na França, e então tornou-se chanceler. Segundo ele, as *idéias* existem desde a eternidade na mente de Deus, embora não sejam co-eternas com Deus. As cópias dessas coisas, nas coisas (os particulares de Platão), ele intitulava de *formae nativae* (formas nativas). Ele combinava o seu realismo (ver o artigo) com um retorno aos conceitos naturais, sendo assim um dos precursores da renascença (ver o artigo). (P)

BERNARDO DE CLAIRVAUX

Suas datas são 1090-1158. Desejando separar-se do mundo, ingressou na Citeaux, em 1112. Ali, alguns poucos anos mais tarde, fundou a abadia de Clairvaux. Saindo de sua solidão, ele tornou-se um dos mais poderosos clérigos do século XII. Conselheiro e crítico de papa e reis, fundador de mosteiros, pregador de cruzadas (ele foi o organizador da segunda cruzada), e incansável defensor da ortodoxia, conforme ele a via, foi autor de muitas obras. Não era exatamente um antiintelectual mas não simpatizava com os resultados das investigações sociais que não se confinassem com os limites de sua ortodoxia. Lamenta-se que ele tenha perseguido àqueles que dele discordavam! Temia a abordagem filosófica dos problemas teológicos. Sua própria abordagem desses problemas era mística, sendo ele homem de grande piedade pessoal. Em face de sua aversão à heresia, algumas vezes mostrava-se por demais impulsivo, e sempre haverá de ser lembrado por causa de seu brutal tratamento a Abelardo (ver o artigo), por cuja condenação ele foi o grande responsável. Grandes homens, grandes vícios! Não obstante, Bernardo de Clairvaux foi um gigante espiritual, e coisa alguma que dissermos a seu respeito poderá detratar de sua grandeza.

Idéias. 1. Mesmo caído no pecado, o homem retém a sua liberdade. Doutra sorte, a culpa seria inexplicável. O homem precisa consentir com a graça de Deus que lhe é estendida, e o mérito consiste na união da graça divina com a liberdade humana.

2. A verdade é percebida *através da fé*, e a razão é eficaz apenas para esclarecer. A razão pode ajudar-nos a desembrulhar o dom da fé, quando nos é dado.

3. O conhecimento mais alto nos é outorgado através da intuição, que resulta em alguma experiência mística. O intelecto não serve de guia na inquirição espiritual. A meditação deve ser praticada como um *modus operandi*, para que o indivíduo chegue à experiência espiritual.

4. Os quatro estágios do amor. a. O amor carnal, ou auto-amor; b. o amor egoísta a Deus, que resulta do sofrimento; c. o amor altruísta a Deus; d. a união com Deus, — que resulta no aniquilamento do auto-amor.

Escritos: On the Love of God; On Grace and Free Will; On Contemplation; Sermons on the Song of Songs. (AM EP)

BERNARDO DE CLUNY (de Morlaix)

Um poeta beneditino que viveu na primeira metade do século XII. Foi o autor do poema *Sobre o Desprezo a Este Mundo*. Nesse poema, ele satirizava a vida de sua época e as figuras notáveis de seu tempo. Sua obra foi dedicada a Pedro, o Venerável, abade de Cluny. Talvez tenha exercido influência sobre a *Divina Comédia*, de Dante. Compôs numerosos hinos, e a ele é atribuído um tratado sobre a Trindade.

••• ••• •••

BERNARDO DE TOURS (B. Silvestris)

Erudito do século XII, talvez da escola de Chartres e autor da obra *De Mundi Universitate*, onde se alternam a poesia e a prosa. Apesar de Bernardo interessar-se pela teologia cristã, ele pertencia à escola dos platônicos cristãos, que procuravam suplementar a doutrina cristã com idéias e especulações filosóficas. Para exemplificar, ele modificou a narrativa da criação, no livro de Gênesis, com o diálogo platônico *Timeu*. (E)

BERODAQUE-BALADÃ

Ver **Merodaque-Baladã**.

BEROTA

No hebraico, «alimento». Palavra que aparece somente em Eze. 47:16, como uma das cidades fronteiriças do Israel restaurado, e, portanto, ainda futuro.

BEROTAI

No hebraico, «cipreste de Yahweh». Palavra que figura apenas em II Sam. 8:8, que alguns estudiosos pensam ser a mesma Berota (que vide). Nessa referência lemos que Davi levou dali e de Betá, cidades pertencentes a Hadadezer, grande quantidade de bronze. O lugar tem sido identificado como Beirute; mas os estudiosos modernos pensam estar em pauta a cidade de Bereitan, ao norte de Damasco.

BERSEBA

No hebraico, «poço do juramento» ou «poço de sete». Uma cidade que ficava na porção sul da Palestina, que tem sido identificada com a moderna Tell es-Saba, a meio caminho entre o mar Mediterrâneo e a extremidade sul do mar Morto. O nome foi dado a esse lugar por causa do poço que foi ali cavado e devido ao acordo firmado entre Abraão e Abimeleque (Gên. 21:31).

Aparentemente, era um dos lugares favoritos de Abraão, onde também ele plantou um dos bosques que chegou a ser local de um dos templos da antiguidade do povo israelita (ver Gên. 21:33). Isaque habitava ali quando Esaú vendeu a Jacó o seu direito de primogenitura. Foi do acampamento que havia nas proximidades que Jacó partiu em sua viagem à Mesopotâmia. Jacó fez uma parada em Berseba a fim de oferecer um sacrifício ao Deus de seus antepassados, quando, noutra ocasião, estava a caminho do Egito (Gên. 46:1). As disputas entre Jacó e Esaú tiveram lugar nessa região (Gên. 28:10).

Quando da distribuição do território palestino, a região foi dada à tribo de Simeão (Jos. 19:2). Porém, visto que essa tribo chegou a mesclar-se tanto com a tribo de Judá (Juí. 1:3), as cidades pertencentes a Simeão, incluindo Berseba, também aparecem entre as aldeias do distrito de Neguebe, pertencente a Judá (Jos. 15:28). Antes do estabelecimento da monarquia, Samuel deixou ali instalados os seus filhos, para atuarem como juízes (I Sam. 8:2). - Com o tempo, Berseba passou a indicar, proverbialmente, o extremo sul do território de Israel, dentro da expressão: «De Dã a Berseba», que indica a extensão total da Terra Santa (Juí. 20:1; I Sam. 3:10). Isso continuava tendo aplicação durante o reinado de Saul (II Sam. 3:10).

Elias fugiu para Berseba, que era uma cidade de refúgio no século VIII A.C., freqüentada por gente vinda do norte de Israel (Amós 5:5; 8:14). Quando os dois reinos separaram-se; no norte, Israel; no sul, Judá, a expressão «de Dã a Berseba» foi alterada para «desde Berseba até o vale de Hinom» (Nee. 11:27,30). Após o exílio babilônico, foi repovoada (Nee. 11:27). A arqueologia tem encontrado ali consideráveis ruínas. Há ali sete poços que podem ser facilmente distinguidos, e, nas colinas que circundam o vale, há várias ruínas. (ALB UN Z)

BERTOLDO DE REGENSBURG

Suas datas são 1220-1272. Foi um **pregador popular franciscano** (que vide), que demonstrou agudo senso e interesse missionário. Era um poderoso pregador ético. Seus sermões eram simples, mas eloqüentes, plenos de simpatia humana, dotados de excelente espiritualidade e de um vívido apelo. Em suma, foi um grande pregador que também fez muito trabalho missionário. (E)

BES

Nome do deus egípcio do prazer, que também teria o poder de anular a feitiçaria (ver o artigo sobre o fetichismo). Os gnósticos adotaram sua imagem como um amuleto. (E)

BESAI

No hebraico, «conquistador». Aparece nas listas de Esdras (2:49), como o pai de uma família de servos do templo que voltou do exílio. Eles estavam entre aqueles que retornaram da Babilônia em companhia de Zorobabel. Ver também Nee. 7:52.

BESCASPASMIS

Forma alternativa de **Matanias** (que vide).

BESODIAS

No hebraico, «íntimo de Yahweh» ou «no conselho secreto de Yahweh». Era o pai de Mesulão, um dos que ajudaram a reparar as muralhas de Jerusalém, nos dias de Neemias. (Nee. 3:6).

BESOR

No hebraico, «frio». Nome de um ribeiro, mencionado em I Samuel 30:9. Davi cruzou o ribeiro após ter partido de Ziclague, ao perseguir os amalequitas, um grupo de nômades das regiões do Neguebe e do Sinai, que haviam atacado Ziclague (I Sam. 30:9,10,21). Nesse wadi, Davi deixou duzentos homens, exaustos demais para prosseguirem. Provavelmente trata-se do wadi Ghazzeh, o maior dentre os vários wadis a sudoeste de Ziclague, que atualmente é chamado Tell el-Khuweilfeh. (Z)

BESSARION

Monge distinguido por sua erudição (1403-1472). Nasceu em Trapesus, no Ponto. Era dotado de grande percepção espiritual e de profundo intelecto. Estudou em Constantinopla e em Esparta, sob o filósofo grego **Gemistos**. Finalmente, tornou-se o arcebispo de **Trapesus**, onde ganhou reputação de grande mestre e pregador. Ele enfatizava a importância da ação social e do amor. Foi nomeado representante da Igreja Grega, tendo proposto então a união das igrejas cristãs (1436). Após a queda de Constantinopla, a Igreja Católica o nomeou cardeal, em reconhecimento por seus serviços. Sendo cardeal, ele procurou organizar cruzadas contra os turcos, mas fracassou na empreitada. Escreveu muitas obras teológicas, mas seu nome é mais lembrado em face de seus esforços tendentes à união das igrejas. (E)

BESTA

No hebraico precisamos considerar quatro palavras, e no grego três.

1. *Behemah*, «gado», «quadrúpede». Palavra usada por cento e oitenta e nove vezes (por exemplo: Gên. 6:7; 7:2,8; Êxo. 8:17; Lev. 7:21; Núm. 3:13; Deu. 4:17; Sal. 8:7; Jer. 7:20; Eze. 8:10; Joel 1:18; Zac. 8:10; 14:15).

2. *Beir*, «bruto», «besta». Palavra usada por seis vezes (por exemplo: Gên. 45:17; Êxo. 22:5; Núm. 20:8,11).

3. *Chaiyah*, «criatura vivente». Palavra usada por noventa e quatro vezes com o sentido de animal. Por exemplo: Gên. 1:24; Lev. 5:2; 26:22; Núm. 35:3; Jó 5:22; Sal. 50:10; Isa. 35:9; Jer. 12:9; Eze. 5:17; Dan. 2:38; 4:12-32; Ose. 2:12; Sof. 2:15.

4. *Tebach*, «animal abatido». Palavra usada por onze vezes, mas com o sentido de «animal» em Pro. 9:2.

5. *Zoon*, «criatura viva». Palavra grega usada por vinte e três vezes, a começar em Heb. 13:11, mas a maioria das vezes é usada no Apocalipse, como, por exemplo: 4:6-9; 5:6,8,11,14; 6:1-7, etc.

6. *Ktenos*, «besta de carga». Palavra grega usada por quatro vezes. Ver Luc. 10:34; Atos 23:24; I Cor. 15:39; Apo. 18:13.

7. *Therion*, «fera», «besta». Palavra grega usada por quarenta e seis vezes, a começar em Atos 28:5, mas a maioria das vezes no Apocalipse, como, por exemplo, 6:8; 11:7; e nos capítulos 13 a 20:10.

Distinções:

1. Um mamífero, distinto do homem, das aves e dos répteis (Gên. 1:29,30).

2. Animais selvagens, em distinção aos animais domesticados (Lev. 26:22; Isa. 13:21).

3. A classe dos animais inferiores, distintos dos seres humanos (Sal. 147:9; Ecl. 3:19; Atos 28:5).

Proibições Mosaicas. Os israelitas não eram vegetarianos, mas também não podiam consumir a carne de todos os animais. No décimo primeiro capítulo do livro de Levítico, os animais são distinguidos entre os que têm cascos sólidos e aqueles de cascos fendidos. Além disso, os animais são classificados em limpos e imundos, indicando, respectivamente, se podiam ou não ser usados como carnes comestíveis. A ciência tem mostrado a sabedoria de algumas dessas proibições; porém, o que realmente está envolvido são questões religiosas e cerimoniais, que ensinam lições morais e espirituais. Os peixes e as aves também eram divididos em limpos e imundos.

Usos Metafóricos. 1. As criaturas celestes (Apo. 4:6. Ver Eze. 1). 2. Os santos temerários são comparados com animais, por causa de sua vileza, ignorância e estupidez (Pro. 30:2). 3. Os homens em geral são chamados de «animais» devido à sua ignorância e má natureza (Ecl. 3:18). 4. Contudo, animais úteis, como bois, vacas, ovelhas, cordeiros e pombas podem servir de símbolos dos seres humanos, segundo se vê no décimo capítulo do evangelho de João. 5. Ursos, leões, lobos e serpentes servem como símbolos do mal (Isa. 11:6-8). 6. Certos animais poderosos como a águia, o leão, o touro, o bode, o carneiro e o leviatã (hipopótamo?) servem de símbolos de reis e governantes, os poderosos e os ricos (Eze. 31:6; Dan. 4:14). 7. Homens iníquos são chamados «feras», em face de sua iniqüidade e violência (I Cor. 15:32; II Ped. 2:12). 8. Os maiores impérios mundiais, como a Caldéia, a Pérsia, a Grécia e Roma são retratados por feras (Dan. 7:11; 8:4; Apo. 12, 13 e 18). Isso se refere a um grande poder e autoridade, posto a serviço do mal. 9. O anticristo e seu falso profeta são apresentados como a besta saída do mar (das nações) e a besta saída da terra (Israel), respectivamente (Apo. 13 e 17:3). 10. Os vingadores contra o mal são chamados águias (Apo. 19:17,18), divinamente nomeados para a tarefa. 11. A travessia do mar Vermelho e do deserto, por parte do povo de Israel, é comparada com uma besta que atravessa um vale, de maneira fácil e segura, sob a proteção divina (Isa. 43:14).

Observações. Dentre todo o mundo visível, os animais terrestres são os que aparecem em mais íntima conexão com o homem, tendo sido criados, no mesmo dia (Gên. 1:24). No início os animais consumiam os vegetais e serviam ao homem (Gên. 1:26-30; 2:20 e seu paralelo, 1:28). O fato de que Adão recebeu o direito de dar nomes aos animais pressupõe um direito de superioridade e domínio sobre eles. Talvez por essa razão, Deus tenha resolvido que seriam destruídos juntamente com a humanidade, durante o dilúvio (Gên. 7:21). A harmonia entre o homem e os animais, quebrada por causa do pecado (cf. Gên. 3:15 ss), será restabelecida por ocasião do milênio (Isa. 11:6-8; cf. Gên. 9:2,3 e Mar. 1:13).

A Bíblia não reflete qualquer hostilidade contra os animais, sendo reiterado por muitas vezes que Deus cuida deles, conforme o próprio Jesus expressou (Mat. 6:26). A legislação mosaica protegia os animais, conforme se vê em Deuteronômio 22:6. (Cf. Mat. 16:12). Todavia, o homem pode dispor dos animais, sobretudo em sua alimentação, no caso dos animais puros, quando da vigência da legislação mosaica, e no caso de qualquer animal, na era da graça, quando não mais imperam as restrições alimentares. Certos animais, além de serem considerados puros, isto é, comestíveis, também foram declarados próprios para serem oferecidos nos sacrifícios levíticos, como, por exemplo, o boi, a ovelha, a cabra, e dentre as aves, a pomba e a rola; mas, nesse caso, os animais e as aves oferecidos não podiam ter qualquer defeito físico (Lev. 3:1-6).

O conceito de que o sangue é a sede da vida biológica requeria uma maneira toda especial de abater os animais (Gên. 9:4,5; Deu. 15:23). Os animais de grande porte eram presos pelos caçadores (Pro. 7:23; Amós 3:5), mediante armadilhas (Isa. 51:20), laços ou redes (Pro. 6:5; Osé. 9:8); os pássaros eram apanhados em seus ninhos (Deu. 22:6), os animais aquáticos com anzol, rede (Hab. 1:15) ou arpão (Jó 40:26). A criação de gado era conhecida desde os tempos mais remotos (Gên. 4:2,20; 12:16, etc.). Os animais eram empregados na tração de carros (cavalo, boi), ou para servirem de montaria (camelo, cavalo, jumento, burro). Dos animais aproveita-se muita coisa, como a carne e o couro, o leite e os pêlos, os excrementos como estrume e alguns órgãos internos como medicamento, como a vesícula, o coração e os rins dos peixes. Do elefante aproveita-se o marfim.

Alguns homens estudavam os pássaros e divertiam-se com eles (Jó 40:24), observavam seus hábitos e migrações (Jer. 8:7). Espantalhos eram colocados nos campos plantados para afugentar certas aves (Jer. 10:5). Os homens conheciam certas enfermidades que afetavam os animais (Êxo. 9:2-9). Os israelitas foram proibidos da tentativa de cruzar animais diferentes (Lev. 19:19), e sobretudo, de ter relações sexuais com eles (Êxo. 22:18), sendo isso considerado uma abominação (que vide).

Às vezes, os animais eram usados por Deus como um castigo contra os homens, devido ao pecado (Êxo. 7 em diante), especialmente no caso dos animais ferozes (Lev. 26:22; II Reis 17:25). Por causa de certas características, alguns animais simbolizam certos tipos de pessoas. Por exemplo, a cerva e a camurça representam a mulher atraente (Can. 7:4). Chamar uma mulher de pomba era usar da linguagem de adulação para com ela (Can. 2:14). Muitos nomes próprios de pessoas eram apenas nomes de animais. Assim, Raquel = ovelha; Débora = abelha; Zeebe = lobo; Águila = águia. (IB ID NTI S DEB)

BESTA DA TERRA

Os intérpretes disputam sobre se o anticristo será a besta saída do «mar» ou a besta saída da *terra*, e se é a mesma personagem identificada no segundo capítulo da segunda epístola aos Tessalonicenses. Em espírito e ação geral, ambas podem ser identificadas com a figura daquele capítulo; mas o mais provável é que ali haja uma alusão específica à besta saída do «mar», pois parece ser o poder maior, recebendo a ajuda e a exaltação conferidas pela outra. A besta saída do «mar» parece que será uma figura política, ao passo que a outra será uma figura religiosa, um «falso profeta», o «João Batista» do anticristo. Alguns intérpretes, porém, preferem pensar que a segunda besta é que será o anticristo. O ponto não é muito importante. Haverá uma figura política de grande autoridade militar, um ditador mundial, mas que governará especificamente uma federação de dez nações, a qual servirá de trampolim para seu domínio mundial. Cremos que essa figura será o anticristo. Mas haverá um ajudante, que fará a propaganda do anticristo. E esse *ajudante* será a besta saída da «terra». Também é provável que «terra», neste caso, aponte para a nação de «Israel», ao passo que o *mar* alude às nações gentílicas. A primeira besta, pois, será produto das «nações», o maior e mais horrendo pagão de todos os tempos. A segunda será produzida por Israel, sendo largamente proclamada como se fosse o «Messias» ou Cristo, porquanto será considerada como um grande profeta.

As predições dos místicos contemporâneos indicam que um indivíduo do estado de Nova Iorque, nos Estados Unidos da América, agirá como uma espécie de «João Batista» do anticristo. E esses místicos afirmam que o anticristo já está vivo. O seu *João Batista* espalhará a sua fama por toda a parte, por intermédio dos meios de comunicação em massa. Parece-me que essa será, entretanto, uma «terceira figura». Essas questões são obscuras porque ainda não começaram a cumprir-se, para que as possamos entender. Os eventos lançam sombras à sua frente, e quanto mais se aproximam, mais bem definidas ficam essas sombras. Cremos que o anticristo e seu falso profeta já estão vivos, e que pelos começos da década de 1990 saberemos quem são eles. Devemos estar preparados para tal evento.

Há muita disputa, naturalmente, quanto aos símbolos usados acerca de ambas as «bestas»; e nada de dogmático dizemos sobre isso. Confiamos, porém, que quanto mais se aproximar o tempo, mais o futuro definirá as coisas. Há aqui uma trindade satânica: o próprio Satanás, a besta saída do mar e a besta saída

BESTA DA TERRA

da terra. Ou então essa trindade poderá ser formada pelo «João Batista» do anticristo (a besta saída do «mar»; a besta; e a besta saída da terra). O certo é que o texto que ora consideramos deixa claro que o papel da besta saída da *terra* será de apoiar e promover a causa da besta saída do *mar*. Não devemos ver nisso o «papa», conforme têm dito alguns intérpretes protestantes, e, sim, uma nova forma de apostasia, que terá seu falso Cristo, e que quase certamente receberá o apoio de várias denominações cristãs apóstatas, bem como o apoio de Israel, como nação.

A besta saída do mar seria o anticristo. Em favor dessa idéia, poderíamos asseverar os seguintes fatos:

1. Essa besta virá *em seu próprio nome*, conforme foi predito acerca do anticristo, segundo se lê em João 5:43. A segunda besta, porém, promoverá a primeira, e não a si mesma.

2. O trecho de Apo. 16:13 fornece-nos a trindade ímpia—o dragão (Satanás), a besta e o falso profeta. Um «profeta» fala em lugar de outrem, e não por si mesmo; e o «profeta», neste caso, definidamente é a segunda besta, dando a entender que se tratará de um subordinado. De maneira alguma poderíamos atribuir tal subordinação ao anticristo, apesar de que poderíamos atribuir tal coisa aos «anticristos» secundários, personagens satânicas de menor envergadura.

3. O segundo capítulo da segunda epístola aos Tessalonicenses fala sobre o anticristo. Ali vemos que ele será *adorado*. Isso sucederá no caso da «primeira» besta. A segunda apenas promoverá a adoração à primeira, pelo que a segunda não poderá ser «o» anticristo. Ver o décimo segundo versículo do décimo terceiro capítulo de Apocalipse.

4. É provável que a primeira besta, devido ao seu grande poder político, seja a figura focalizada em Dan. 9:27, que estabelecerá um pacto com a nação de Israel, somente a fim de desrespeitá-lo. Apesar de que poderíamos conceber aqui a segunda besta, envolvida em atividades políticas, é mais provável que esteja em pauta a primeira besta, a personagem política forte. A figura profética do anticristo, Antíoco IV Epifânio, que aparece nos capítulos oitavo e décimo primeiro do livro de Daniel, se coaduna melhor com a «primeira besta», e não com a segunda.

5. Satanás ofereceu a Cristo os *reinos* deste mundo (ver Mat. 4:8), mas o Senhor repeliu essa oferta, segundo as condições de Satanás. Esse mesmo oferecimento será feito ao «anticristo». Assim sendo, somente a besta saída do «mar» tem estatura suficiente para ser uma figura universal e para cumprir o papel previsto para o anticristo, com seu reino universal de maldade e apostasia. (Ver Apo. 19:19 no NTI onde há uma óbvia alusão à primeira besta e seu tremendo poder). Esse terá de ser «o anticristo».

6. A tradição cristã sempre viu o anticristo como quem, pelo menos, teria seu centro em Roma, embora talvez não se originasse dali. Mas não há razão para duvidarmos que ele também operará em Jerusalém **apesar de que Roma seja sua verdadeira capital**. Isso se harmoniza com a primeira, mas não com a segunda besta, pelo que esse será o anticristo. Esperava-se que «Nero redivivo» fosse o anticristo, e os trechos de Apo. 13:3 e 17:9 e *ss* quase certamente refletem essa tradição antiga.

7. Notemos, em Apo. 13:2, que é a primeira besta quem incorporará em si mesma todos os impérios pagãos anteriores. Ele será a concretização do que há de pior na humanidade, em revolta contra Deus. Portanto, esse será, específica e inequivocadamente «o anticristo», apesar de poder haver muitos outros anticristos, entre eles, o falso profeta.

Identificação da besta saída da terra. Há certo sentimento que favorece a idéia de Judas Iscariotes reencarnado como esse homem, tal como alguns pensam em «Nero reencarnado, como a besta saída do mar. A idéia acerca de Judas envolve o fato de que ele é chamado *filho da perdição*, dando a entender que ele era tal em sentido elevado ou até mesmo exclusivo. Notemos, porém, que isso é dito acerca do anticristo, em II Tes. 2:3. E alguns estudiosos, por causa disso, pensam que a segunda besta é tanto o anticristo quanto Judas Iscariotes revivido. Mas talvez não devamos dar importância demasiada a esse «título», forçando qualquer identificação por meio dele. As passagens de Luc. 22:3 e João 6:70 indicam haver uma malignidade especial em Judas, o que poderia indicar que lhe está reservada uma futura missão diabólica, tão grande seria a sua estatura maligna. Atos 1:25 fala do fato de Judas ter ido para «seu próprio lugar», o que poderia indicar que a sua alma não foi tratada como outras almas, mas foi preservada e guardada em lugar especial, a fim de ressurgir em alguma manifestação futura. Porém, isso pode ser um refinamento demasiado, estranho ao texto sagrado. Por esse motivo, é melhor dizer que simplesmente nada sabemos com certeza, ainda que a idéia da reencarnação de Judas Iscariotes, na qualidade de «besta saída da terra», não é nenhum absurdo. Alguns têm sentido que em face do «anticristo» vir a ser uma «imitação» do verdadeiro Cristo, será ele essencialmente um *profeta falso*, e não um político ou militar; e isso favorece a idéia da segunda, besta ser o anticristo. Que os próprios acontecimentos futuros definam para nós esses problemas.

Apo. 13:11: *E vi subir da terra outra besta, e tinha dois chifres semelhantes aos de um cordeiro; e falava como dragão.*

Outra besta. Será uma «fera», um ser humano mas com a disposição de um animal satanicamente inspirado, em que todos os vestígios de humanidade serão eliminados por aquela supermaligna influência. Em II Baruque 29:4 e II Esdras 7:49-52, temos duas bestas, o «leviatã», ou terrível crocodilo do mar, e o «beemote», o terrível animal terrestre. É possível que o vidente João tenha tomado dali, por empréstimo o simbolismo que se vê em todo este capítulo.

Emergir da terra. Essa terra poderia ser a «Palestina», a «terra» do povo escolhido. Mas essas palavras também poderiam indicar «de dentro da terra». Nesse último caso, talvez esteja em foco o «hades», já que os antigos pensavam que a habitação dos espíritos desencarnados ficava no centro do globo terrestre. Assim, em Apo. 11:7, temos a besta que emergiu do abismo ou «hades», a fim de matar as duas testemunhas. No caso de uma ou de outra das duas bestas, isso indicaria que teria havido uma história prévia, à face da terra, um longo período de permanência no hades, e a renovação de sua missão maligna na terra. O judaísmo helenista favoreceria esse conceito; e, teologicamente falando, nada há que possamos apresentar contra tal doutrina. Cremos que os destinos finais dos homens serão fixados quando da segunda vinda de Cristo, e não por ocasião da morte física de cada um. Portanto, o presente submundo dos espíritos se acha em estado líquido: trata-se de um estado intermediário, e não de um estado permanente. Essa idéia é comentada detalhadamente em I Ped. 4:6 no NTI. — I Ped. 3:18-20 certamente mostra que Cristo levou esperança aos habitantes do submundo; e supomos que essa esperança será válida até que ele feche as cortinas, quando de sua segunda vinda.

A primeira besta vem do mar, i.e. «das nações». Ele será o produto supremo do paganismo das nações. Para controlar a confederação das dez nações, ele terá seu centro principal em Roma. A segunda besta, da terra (da Palestina) terá o seu centro principal em Jerusalém, ou pelo menos, parece assim. Quase certamente a segunda besta será judeu e alguns acham que a primeira também será desta raça, mas outros dizem que ele será «romano» (italiano). Não temos qualquer certeza sobre estas idéias. Quando chegarmos aos acontecimentos descritos neste capítulo, tudo será esclarecido, e não temos muito tempo antes desta realização.

BESTA DO MAR
Besta do Mar — O Anticristo.

Do mar, ou seja, das nações agitadas. O anticristo será a encarnação do que há de pior entre as nações. Se estas são ímpias e violentas, ele será prodigiosamente ímpio. Se elas representam a revolta, ele será o rei dos revoltados contra Deus. Se elas perseguem à igreja, ele será o campeão de todos os perseguidores. Se, antes dele, outros homens têm emergido dentre o «mar das nações, que não têm descanso», ele fará todos aqueles outros parecerem crianças, paralelamente à sua imensa perversão moral.

«O mar representa a grande e desassossegada massa da espécie humana; ou então, conforme é expresso em Apo. 17:15, 'povos e multidões'. Tiago compara o indivíduo indeciso com uma onda impelida pelo vento (ver Tia. 1:6). Os indivíduos tal como ondas maiores e menores, compõem esse grande oceano dos homens, impelido pelas paixões impulsivas. Dentre esse mar é que surgirá a besta. Não temos aqui o mesmo vocábulo usado em Apo. 4:7...mas é uma palavra que subentende o predomínio da natureza bestial. Qualquer que seja o poder que tiver de se levantar, não governará pelo amor ou pela habilidade, mas voluntariosamente, impondo terror. É a grande força do poder mundial, que em todas as eras tem sido contra o poder da razão. As feras sempre servem de símbolo dos reinos deste mundo, isto é, dos reinos fundamentados sobre a paixão ou o egoísmo». Carpenter, em Apo. 13:1.

Besta. No grego é *therion*, «fera», palavra usada na literatura grega para indicar animais «perigosos». (Ver *Antig. Car.* 29). Assim é que Policarpo foi condenado a combater contra as feras (a mesma palavra usada neste texto: ver *Martírio de Policarpo* 2:4). Tal palavra também era utilizada para indicar seres animalescos, de natureza sobrenatural (ver Barnabé 4:5). Há o uso dessa palavra para indicar um dragão monstruoso (ver *Dam. Vi Isid.* 140; *Hv. 4,1:6; 10, 4:21*). Também era usada essa palavra para referir-se a indivíduos de natureza bestial (ver Aristófanes, *Equ.* 273; *Plutus* 439; Josefo, *Guerras dos Judeus* 1,624,627; *Antiq.* 17,117,120). Há aqui um duplo simbolismo. A «besta» é o império romano, em sua impiedade; mas também é um indivíduo, Nero reencarnado, —que morreu, desceu ao hades, mas haverá de subir dali (ver Apo. 11:7 e 17:8), esperando-se que ele volte a fim de promover outro reinado de terror.

Dez chifres e sete cabeças. Essa descrição fora dada ao dragão, Satanás, em Apo. 12:3. O trecho de Apo. 17:12 diz-nos que os «dez chifres» são «dez reis»; e aquela passagem deixa patente que estão em foco auxiliares do imperador ou dos imperadores romanos. (Há notas expositivas completas sobre os «dez chifres», que são dez reis, em Apo. 17:12, no NTI). Os «sátrapas» persas, que eram esperados vir acompanhando a «Nero redivivo», em seu assédio contra Roma (ver Apo. 17:16), conforme diziam as tradições antigas que falavam sobre esse Nero redivivo, poderiam estar em foco. Mas também poderiam estar em foco os governantes das províncias senatoriais, que a cada ano eram mudados por apontamento do senado. Profeticamente falando, porém, pensamos que se trata de uma *federação de dez reinos*, que o anticristo encabeçará nos últimos dias, e que envolverá uma área bem mais vasta e diversa do que o antigo império romano. As «sete cabeças» são «sete montes», conforme diz Apo. 17:9, o que é uma alusão velada à cidade de Roma; ao mesmo tempo, porém, são *sete imperadores romanos*. (As notas expositivas em Apo. 12:3 e 17:12 no NTI abordam essas questões detalhadamente, oferecendo interpretações alternativas).

E, sobre os chifres, dez diademas. Em Apo. 12:3, os «diademas» estão sobre as «cabeças» do dragão, mas aqui estão sobre os «chifres». Essa mudança no simbolismo provavelmente não tem qualquer significação especial. Pouca diferença faz se os diademas estão nas *cabeças* ou nos *chifres*. Seja como for, a autoridade satânica estará investida sobre o *anticristo* (que vide) de tal modo que ele governará por intermédio de seus títeres, que serão *governantes terrenos*; mas tal autoridade será realmente satânica, conforme a comparação entre essas duas passagens o demonstra. (Ver Apo. 12:3).

Fonte original do simbolismo. Não pode haver dúvidas de que o sétimo capítulo do livro de Daniel é o pano de fundo literário do simbolismo desta passagem. Naquele capítulo, várias bestas surgem do mar agitado pelo vento. Os «ventos», mui provavelmente, indicam os «poderes angelicais» que exercem controle sobre a terra, poderes angelicais malignos, bem entendido. Assim também agora o grande dragão, Satanás, põe-se de pé sobre a areia da praia do mar (ver Apo. 12:17), e convoca duas bestas horrendas, uma saída do mar e a outra saída da terra, a fim de fustigar os homens. As bestas, na visão de Daniel, representam diversos impérios mundiais, a saber: o babilônico, o medo-persa, o grego e o romano. O trecho de Apo. 7:7,24 mostra-nos que «dez chifres» surgem da quarta besta, pelo que também o aspecto «profético», do império romano dos últimos dias é dado. O «pequeno chifre» de Apo. 7:8, apesar de certamente apontar para Antíoco Epifânio (ver também Dan. 8:23-35; 9:26,27; 11:36-45), provavelmente é um símbolo profético do próprio anticristo.

Blasfêmias. Um paralelo a isso é o segundo capítulo da segunda epístola aos Tessalonicenses. O anticristo fará oposição a tudo quanto é direito; haverá de se exaltar acima de tudo quanto é chamado Deus, e exigirá adoração, tal como os antigos imperadores romanos exigiam, no «culto ao imperador». Ocupará o templo de Deus, em Jerusalém, exibindo-se como se fora uma divindade. Nele operará amplamente o «mistério da iniqüidade» (ver II Tes. 2:7). Seu aparecimento será no poder de Satanás, e ele fará muitos prodígios da mentira (ver II Tes. 2:9,10). No anticristo haverá, destilada, a própria essência da blasfêmia. Ele operará muitos «milagres científicos», os quais, supostamente, eliminarão a necessidade de crer-se ou prestar lealdade a qualquer Deus «invisível». Já que ele será o falso «cristo» de Satanás, presumivelmente ele eliminará qualquer necessidade de conhecer-se ao Cristo de Deus. Por essa razão, perseguirá à igreja cristã, conforme esta nunca antes fora perseguida; e até os judeus piedosos serão objetos de sua cólera pervertida.

A Segunda Vinda

Girando e girando em círculos cada vez maiores,
O falcão não pode ouvir o seu treinador;
As coisas se despedaçam; o centro não pode manter-se:
A maré sangrenta se abate, e por toda parte
A cerimônia da inocência é abafada.
Aos melhores falta convicção; os piores
São cheios de intensa paixão.

Certamente alguma revelação está próxima,
Certamente a segunda vinda está às portas,
A segunda vinda! Nem bem são ditas essas palavras
E a vasta imagem do espírito do mundo
Atribula minha visão: em algum deserto arenoso,
Uma forma, com corpo de leão e cabeça humana,
Com olhar vazio e sem dó como o sol,
Move-se lentamente, havendo em seu redor
Sombras revoluteantes de aves indignadas do deserto.
As trevas sobrevêm novamente; mas agora sei
Que vinte séculos de sono de pedra
Foram agitados em pesadelo por um berço que balança.
E que fera violenta, que haverá de surgir,
É essa que se avizinha de Belém?

(William Butler Yeats)

Outras Idéias Sobre A Besta do Mar.

1. O «nome» de blasfêmia, se a forma singular é a correta, poderia ser uma referência específica ao «divus» ou «augustus» dos títulos com que os imperadores romanos exaltavam a si mesmos, supondo-se que eram divindades dignas de adoração.
— Quanto a esse *nome*, outros eruditos pensam que «papa», «Sua Santidade», etc. são títulos em foco. Mas isso sai muito do centro do alvo.

2. O segundo versículo demonstra que essa «fera» incorpora as características das quatro feras do livro de Daniel, pelo que será o ponto culminante do governo humano rebelde, que vem afligindo a terra por tanto tempo.

3. Se a forma plural, «nomes», é a correta, então provavelmente o quadro de cada uma das sete cabeças, munida de um «nome» de blasfêmia, totalizando sete nomes assim, é o que se deve pensar aqui. No anticristo, as blasfêmias terão sua fruição perfeita. Além disso, historicamente falando, sete específicos imperadores romanos estão em foco, cada qual representando uma «blasfêmia».

4. Há diversas outras interpretações deste versículo e desta passagem em geral, conforme mostramos nos pontos abaixo:

a. Os intérpretes da escola histórica vêem aqui muitas coisas diferentes, pois não há acordo entre eles. A maioria não pensa em um «anticristo pessoal», isto é, um indivíduo que seria «o» anticristo. Mas pensam no «sistema romano», em certo número de imperadores romanos ou no papado romanista. Aqueles que pensam estar aqui em pauta a «Roma pagã» (posteriormente «cristianizada») procuram mostrar que havia «sete» formas principais de governo romano, desde reis e cônsules até o papa. Os «dez chifres», conforme esse sistema de interpretação, não seriam governantes contemporâneos, sob o poder de Roma, e, sim, sucessivos imperadores romanos, como Augusto, Tibério, Calígula, Cláudio, Nero, Galba, Oto, Vitélio, Vespasiano e Tito. Alguns preservam o «décimo» chifre para um governante futuro, talvez do império romano revivido. Essa interpretação faz a visão ser apenas uma revisão mambembe da antiga história romana, o que dificilmente está em consonância com a natureza profética do Apocalipse, o que tem por fito revelar-nos algo sobre as condições reinantes nos «últimos dias», isto é, aqueles tempos que precederão de imediato à segunda vinda de Cristo.

b. Alguns estudiosos vêem aqui algum anticristo pessoal, julgando que será «Nero» ou algum outro imperador romano especialmente poderoso; e diversos intérpretes protestantes pensam que se trata do «papa».

c. Outros procuram incorporar toda a «história do governo humano», como se o poder aqui focalizado fosse a incorporação de todos os principais governos, desde os tempos dos babilônios. Esse seria o «anticristo», em revolta contra Deus. Toda a autoridade humana sem Deus seria o anticristo, sem importar seu lugar no tempo e na história. Mas isso é contra o pano de fundo histórico e profético do livro de Apocalipse. Historicamente falando, o vidente João atacava o império pagão e perseguidor de Roma; mas, profeticamente falando, apontava para o «anticristo» e sua federação futura de dez reinos.

5. As «sete cabeças» são uma alusão aos «sete montes» da cidade de Roma. E o próprio número fala da culminação da sabedoria satânica no anticristo. (Ver Apo. 17:9,10).

6. O anticristo encabeçará uma espécie de «império romano revivificado», mas sua federação de dez reinos incluirá nações que não faziam parte do império romano antigo. Essas nações, provavelmente, serão os Estados Unidos da América, o Canadá, o Japão, e outras (ver as notas expositivas a respeito, em Apo. 12:3 no NTI). Os dez poderes não corresponderão exatamente a dez reis, em que um seria ocidental e outro oriental, aos pares, de acordo com o simbolismo das duas pernas da imagem visionária de Daniel. Mas seu império será universal, espalhando-se para leste e para oeste, embora não queira dizer com isso, que 5 nações serão do Oriente e outras 5 do Ocidente.

Alguns estudiosos conjecturam que os «dois» pés da imagem de Daniel (ver Dan. 2:40 e *ss*) indicam dois grandes poderes entre os dez. Os pés e os artelhos são de «ferro misturado com barro», isto é, ao mesmo tempo fortes e fracos, uma federação poderosa, embora frouxamente vinculada entre si, sobre a qual o anticristo terá completa autoridade. O império romano, dessa maneira, ressuscitará, ficando curada a sua «ferida mortal» (ver Apo. 13:3) embora essa descrição final também se aplique pessoalmente ao anticristo.

7. A adoração ao anticristo será, *ipso facto*, a adoração a Satanás, porque ele será o «falso cristo» de Satanás, o instrumento de seu poder e presença.

8. O trecho de Apo. 17:12 mostra que os dez chifres serão dez reinos que receberão sua força por se associarem ao anticristo. Seus chefes não terão qualquer reino real e nem poder, enquanto o anticristo não lhes entregar esse poder. O anticristo consolidará tal autoridade, porquanto ele será um técnico nesse mister. Também derrotará as forças comunistas, primeiramente a União Soviética (na Terceira Guerra Mundial) e então a China (na Quarta Guerra Mundial) por causa das quais a humanidade andará perto de desaparecer do nosso planeta. Esperamos que a primeira dessas guerras ocorra em cerca de 1999, ao passo que a segunda delas se dará por volta de 2020, se é que podemos confiar nas declarações dos místicos contemporâneos. O elemento tempo das predições é sempre *incerto*; mas especulamos que essas datas não estarão muito longe do alvo.

BESTA DO MAR — BESTIALIDADE

13:2: *E a besta que vi era semelhante ao leopardo, e os seus pés como os de urso, e a sua boca como a de leão, e o dragão deu-lhe o seu poder e o seu trono e grande autoridade.*

O empréstimo literário é do sétimo capítulo de Daniel, e as «quatro bestas» daquele capítulo, que representam diferentes impérios mundiais, são agora combinadas em uma estranha e aterrorizante fera, apropriada para a figura do anticristo. O vidente João evidentemente deseja dizer-nos que o anticristo e sua confederação de dez nações combinarão toda a perversidade e poder dos reinos antigos, como se fora uma espécie de paganismo supremo. O seu chefe será o homem de Satanás, tal como Jesus Cristo era o homem de Deus. Assim como Cristo foi supremamente possuído pelo Espírito Santo, para o bem, assim esse homem será supremamente possuído pelo diabo, para o mal.

As representações originais. Muitos intérpretes concordam que, originalmente, as quatro bestas do sétimo capítulo do livro de Daniel representavam a Babilônia, a Média, a Pérsia e a Grécia-Síria. O pequeno chifre, um poderoso governante do último desses impérios, foi Antíoco IV Epifânio (último nome este que significa «Deus manifesto»). Suas blasfêmias e abusos precipitaram a revolta dos Macabeus, o que, segundo pensam alguns estudiosos, exerceu certa influência nos escritos de Daniel e suas interpretações. Daniel teria prometido a queda de Epifânio para dentro de três anos e meio. É fato histórico que Epifânio não perdurou por muito tempo, e os judeus obtiveram a sua independência. Mas o soerguimento de Roma e a perda da independência mudou a interpretação sobre as «quatro bestas», de tal forma que a quarta tornou-se símbolo de Roma, seu governante, ou ambas as coisas. Isso é claramente visto no tratado talmúdico de *Abodah Zarah* 2b, e em II Baruque 36:40. Portanto, o vidente João, em Apocalipse, segue essa «reinterpretação» de Daniel, com a única diferença que agora as quatro bestas são combinadas em uma só; e esse monstro é Roma, e o anticristo, por assim dizer, é o novo e muito pior Epifânio.

O que fica implícito nos elementos da fera combinada?

1. O leopardo representa o reino grego (ver Dan. 7:6), rápido, veloz, conquistador e incansável. O anticristo terá essas qualidades em grau supremo.

2. Os pés de urso representam o império persa (ver Dan. 7:5), dando as idéias de força, estabilidade e consolidação. O anticristo também incorporará esses aspectos em seu poder.

3. A boca de leão representa a monarquia babilônica (ver Dan. 7:4), subentendendo ruína ameaçadora, rugidos de blasfêmia, despedaçamento carniceiro, perseguição e matança. O anticristo será o possuidor supremo dessas qualidades.

4. A quarta besta do livro de Daniel, terrível e feroz dotada de dez chifres, já fora incorporada nesse simbolismo em Apo. 13:1, na Besta do Mar. Notemos a ordem reversa de apresentação. A feroz besta de dez chifres, que aparece em último lugar no livro de Daniel, aparece em primeiro lugar no Apocalipse. Então seguem-se os outros três na ordem reversa de sua apresentação em Daniel, provavelmente porque o vidente olhava para trás, ao passo que Daniel olhava para a frente, historicamente falando.

«O anticristo sumariará todo o brilho (Grécia), todo o poder maciço e pesado (Pérsia), todo o domínio absoluto, real e autocrático (Babilônia) que os gentios já conheceram». (Newell, em Apo. 13:2). Mas acrescentamos que o império romano também é enfocado nesse quadro profético.

«Essa besta combina características das primeiras três feras de Dan. 7:2 e ss. A força e a brutalidade do império babilônico, medo e persa aparecem também no império romano. A vigilância felina do leopardo, o poder lento e esmagador do urso e o rugido do leão, que eram características familiares para os pastores da Palestina». (Robertson, Apo. 13:2, com uma citação de Swete).

E deu-lhe o dragão o seu poder. Já temos observado a sobejo, especialmente no estudo sobre os juízos das trombetas, que o Apocalipse promete uma imensa invasão de forças satânicas nos últimos dias, o que avassalará e aterrorizará totalmente aos homens, tornando-os corruptos e violentos de modo incrível, chegando quase a se extinguirem da face da terra. A principal manifestação satânica será o próprio anticristo, com a sabedoria de todos os séculos em seus olhos, mas dedicado ao mal. Também será o grande enganador, pois muitos, especialmente a juventude, segui-lo-ão com um senso de realização. Assim como Jesus Cristo foi Deus encarnado, assim também o anticristo será a encarnação de Satanás. Assim como Cristo foi rejeitado pela maioria, assim o anticristo será quase universalmente aceito pela humanidade. Assim como Cristo saiu a fazer o bem, do mesmo modo o anticristo sairá ao redor praticando a maldade. Cristo chamou Satanás de «príncipe deste mundo» (ver João 12:31; 14:30 e 16:11), e no tempo da tribulação, isso tornar-se-á uma verdade claríssima, porquanto Satanás virá a ser adorado diretamente, mas também indiretamente, por meio de seu anticristo.

O seu trono e grande autoridade. **O João Batista** do anticristo, que alguns místicos identificam como um político do estado de Nova Iorque, nos Estados Unidos da América, fará bem o seu trabalho. O poder que se desenvolverá rapidamente no homem de Satanás, tornar-se-á universalmente conhecido através dos meios de comunicação em massa. Seus discursos e seus arbítrios nas questões e problemas mundiais serão admiravelmente sábios. É claro que ele possuirá uma inteligência prodigiosa. Logo a sua vasta inteligência será recompensada por vasta autoridade. Ascenderá ao trono da aliança de dez reinos, e, com a ajuda do poder do diabo, derrotará a todos os adversários, até mesmo a União Soviética, em uma guerra nos fins do nosso século XX, bem como a China, na segunda década do século XXI. Por conseguinte, nem indivíduos e nem nações serão capazes de resistir-lhe, e a sua supremacia excederá a de qualquer homem que já viveu. Todos os ímpios do passado parecerão crianças inocentes em comparação com ele.

BESTIALIDADE

Um vocábulo que indica a prática de contato sexual entre seres humanos e outras formas de vida animal. O Antigo Testamento condena a prática, chamando-a de «abominação» (Lev. 18:23; Deu. 27:21). O épico de Gilgamés retrata Enkidu, o caçador de feras, a praticar atos sexuais com as feras. É possível que a expressão usada por Paulo em Rom. 1:18-27, «imundícia», inclua tais práticas antinaturais.

1. *Práticas Modernas.* O famoso relatório Kinsey, que estudou estatisticamente o comportamento sexual do povo norte-americano, afirma que entre quarenta e cinqüenta por cento dos varões daquele país, que residem em áreas rurais, têm contatos sexuais ocasionais, não-habituais, com animais das fazendas.

Betânia
Foto por Alistair Duncan

Portão de Ouro, Jerusalém
Foto de Alistair Duncan

Entre as mulheres, a porcentagem é menor que dois por cento. Nas cidades, a porcentagem de varões envolvidos na prática cai para cerca de quatro por cento. Tal prática é proibida por lei em 49 dos 50 estados norte-americanos. Se fôssemos fazer um estudo semelhante no Brasil, provavelmente as taxas encontradas não seriam muito diferentes disso.

2. *A Moralidade Cristã*. A Igreja cristã sempre assumiu a posição do Antigo Testamento, condenando tal prática. Os psicólogos afirmam que o senso de culpa que os culpados adquirem é algo muito injurioso ao bem-estar e a tranqüilidade deles.

3. Um uso sinônimo do termo «bestialidade» indica qualquer ato cruel, degradante e vil, praticado por indivíduos que agem como se fossem irracionais. (H PRI WA)

BESTIÁRIO

Vem do latim **bestia**, «fera». Era o nome que se dava a livros escritos em poesia ou prosa, ilustrados com animais, fabulosos ou reais, muito populares durante a Idade Média. Tais imagens contribuíram para a decoração dos estilos esculturais gótico e romanesco, em que se usavam animais como representações simbólicas. (E)

BETÁ

No hebraico, «confiança». Trata-se de uma cidade da Síria-Zobá, conquistada por Davi de Hadadezer (II Sam. 8:8). No trecho de I Crônicas 18:8, a mesma cidade é chamada Tibate. Desconhece-se o local da mesma.

BETÂNIA

No hebraico, «casa das tâmaras». No Novo Testamento há duas cidades com esse nome, a saber:

1. Uma localidade desconhecida, referida em João 1:28, erroneamente chamada Betabara (ver o artigo sobre Bete-Arabá), em alguns manuscritos posteriores, e onde João Batista efetuava batismos, às margens do rio Jordão. O nome poderia ter sido mudado acidentalmente, por associação verbal, pelo autor original do quarto evangelho, pelo que teríamos tanto um lugar sem nome como um lugar de localização desconhecida. Outros estudiosos dizem que Orígenes foi o autor da troca do nome, de Betânia para Betabara, apoiado em meras conjecturas.

2. Uma aldeia cerca de três quilômetros a suleste de Jerusalém (João 11:18), na vertente oriental do monte das Oliveiras, assim chamada por causa das tamareiras que ali cresciam. Ali residiam Lázaro, Maria e Marta; e Jesus com freqüência ia ali, quando estava na área de Jerusalém, porquanto eram seus amigos especiais. Ver Mat. 21:17; 26:7; Mar. 11:1,11,12; 14:3; Luc. 19:29; 24:50; João 11:1,18 e 12:1. A localidade até hoje existe, em um wadi raso, nas faldas orientais do monte das Oliveiras. Conta com uma pequena e empobrecida população de cerca de mil habitantes. Por causa da circunstância em que ali Jesus realizou um de seus maiores milagres — a ressurreição de Lázaro — seu nome moderno é el-'Aziryeh, «lugar de Lázaro». O sepulcro tradicional de Lázaro é assinalado, onde continuam florescendo figueiras, oliveiras e amendoeiras. A suposta casa de Lázaro, Maria e Marta é mostrada aos turistas; mas, de modo geral, todas as identificações dessa natureza são fictícias.

Betânia também era a terra de Simão, o leproso, em cuja casa Jesus foi ungido com o ungüento guardado no vaso de alabastro, por parte de uma mulher de reputação duvidosa, mas que teve seus pecados perdoados: «Em verdade vos digo: Onde for pregado em todo o mundo o evangelho, será também contado o que ele fez, para memória sua» (Mar. 14:3-9).

BETE

No hebraico, «casa». Era a segunda letra do alfabeto hebraico. Introduz a segunda porção de Salmos 119, onde cada verso começa, no hebraico original, com essa letra. Numericamente, representava o numeral *dois*. Também pode ser encontrada em muitos nomes compostos, como «Betel», «casa de Deus». (S Z)

BETE-ANATE

No hebraico, «casa do eco». Era uma cidade no território de Naftali (Jos. 19:38; Juí. 1:33). Os habitantes originais da cidade foram escravizados pelos israelitas invasores, contrariando a ordem divina de que todos eles deveriam ser mortos. A cidade também é mencionada em diversas inscrições egípcias. Talvez seja a moderna Safed el-Battikh.

BETE-ANOTE

No hebraico, «casa do eco». Era uma aldeia na região montanhosa de Judá (Jos. 15:59), que muitos pensam ter sido um antigo altar e santuário dos cananeus, e que também parece ter sido mencionada em várias listas egípcias de cidades da parte ocidental da Palestina. Ficava situada no distrito de Bete-Zur. Modernamente é a Khirbet Beit 'Ainum, perto de Halhul.

BETE-ARÃ

No hebraico, «casa da montanha». Era uma cidade pertencente a Gade, defronte de Jericó, a pouco mais de cinco quilômetros a leste do Jordão (Jos. 13:27), e que talvez seja a mesma Bete-Harã mencionada em Núm. 32:36. Herodes trocou-lhe o nome para Julias ou Livias, em honra à esposa de Augusto. Atualmente chama-se *er Rameh*. Ver também Bete-Harã.

BETE-ARABÁ

No hebraico, «casa da travessia». Era uma cidade na margem oriental do rio Jordão. Ver João 1:28, que fala sobre «Betânia», e que tem sido identificada como a antiga Bete-Arabá, que era onde João Batista batizava. O trecho de Josué 15:6,61 é a única passagem, em nossa Bíblia portuguesa, onde figura o nome «Bete-Arabá». Quanto a João 1:28, até mesmo manuscritos inferiores dão apoio à forma «Betânia». Ver a discussão, no NTI, sobre o problema textual envolvido. Naturalmente, essa Betânia não pode ser a mesma localidade onde habitavam Lázaro e suas irmãs, Maria e Marta, porquanto, na cidade deles não havia água em abundância. Portanto, os estudiosos opinam que deveria existir uma outra Betânia, às margens do Jordão — a que se refere o quarto evangelho. Naturalmente, o autor desse evangelho poderia ter incorrido em erro, por motivo de associação verbal, um erro comum entre autores e copistas. A mudança de Betânia para Betabara, no trecho de João, foi feita por Orígenes, — que identificou o lugar com uma aldeia que ele conhecia, na localidade em foco. No entanto, Betabara significa «casa de Arabá», ou seja, «casa do deserto», ao passo que Bete-Arabá significa «casa de travessia». Além disso, a substituição de um nome por outro precisou ser feita com base na suposição, visto que havia um lugar com esse nome às margens do Jordão, não muito longe de Jericó, na margem ocidental desse rio (ver Jos. 18:18).

Provavelmente, a localidade pode ser identificada com a moderna 'Ain-el-Gharabeth, no wadi Qelt. Entretanto, nada se sabe acerca de uma Betabara nos tempos do Novo Testamento, nem mesmo como forma alternativa para Betânia. O problema permanece sem solução. Parece que Orígenes, que foi originador de muitas distorções e equívocos, repetiu nesse caso a sua fama. (NTI)

BETE-ARBEL

No hebraico, «casa da corte de Deus». É cidade mencionada exclusivamente em Osé. 10:14. Aparentemente era uma fortaleza, que poderia ser a mesma Arbela, mencionada por Josefo (*Anti.* xii.11,1; I Macabeus 9:2). O texto de Oséias menciona Bete-Arbel, juntamente com outras cidades, como a localidade destruída por Salmã, embora esse monarca não seja mencionado e nem identificado em qualquer porção das Escrituras. Salmaneser III (858-824 A.C.), rei da Assíria, é o mais provável candidato à vaga.

Um distrito pertencente à tribo de Zebulom, na Galiléia (ver Osé. 10:14), ou uma cidade daquela região. Josefo (*Anti.* XIV.xv.4 ss; *Guerras*, 1.xvi.2 ss.) escreveu que os assaltantes que foram mortos por Herodes, que infestavam o interior da Galiléia, eram de Bete-Arbel. Eles se tinham entrincheirado em cavernas fortificadas, na baixa Galiléia (*Vida*, 37). O local moderno é desconhecido, embora tenha sido identificado com Bete-Arbel em Gileade, ou com a Khirbet Irbid da Galiléia, dando frente para o Wadi el-Hamam, a oeste do mar da Galiléia.

BETE-ASMOTE

Também grafada como Bete-Samos, uma forma helenizada de Azmavete (ver o artigo). Essa palavra aparece somente em I Esdras 5:18, como lugar de origem de um grupo de pessoas que retornou com Zorobabel, após o cativeiro babilônico.

BETE-ÁVEN

No hebraico, «casa da nulidade» (isto é, da idolatria). Uma alcunha aplicada a Betel, que lhe foi dada depois que essa cidade tornou-se a sede da adoração a bezerros de ouro. Entretanto, não muito distante, para leste, havia uma cidade que realmente tinha esse nome (ver Jos. 7:2; I Sam. 13:5). A existência dessa cidade deu origem ao apelido dado a Betel (ver artigo). Alguns supõem que se trata de um nome arcaico para Ai (ver o artigo); porém, não há qualquer evidência conclusiva para a suposição. Também havia um deserto com esse nome, ver Jos. 18:12. (ID S)

BETE-AZMAVETE

No hebraico, «casa da força da morte», forma alternativa para Azmavete (ver o artigo).

BETE-BAAL-AMOM

No hebraico, «casa do senhor da habitação». Uma localidade atribuída à tribo de Rúben, nas planícies do Jordão (Jos. 13:17), anteriormente chamada Baal-Meom (Núm. 32:38) ou então Beom (Núm. 32:3), a qual o termo Bete veio a ser prefixado. Posteriormente, a cidade foi conquistada pelos moabitas (Jos. 13:17). A cidade é mencionada por Mesa, de Moabe, em sua estela, juntamente com a cidade de Bete-Diblataim (ver o artigo). O local é identificado com a moderna Ma'in, a dez quilômetros a sudoeste de Madeba.

BETE-BARA

No hebraico, «casa do vau». Estava em um dos principais vaus do Jordão, talvez onde Jacó atravessou esse rio, conforme se lê em Gênesis 32:22. Foi bem perto dali que Gideom obteve uma grande vitória (Juí. 6:24), e foi ali, igualmente, que Jefté abateu os efraimitas (Juí. 12:4). Atualmente, não há qualquer localidade que corresponde ao lugar antigo. Alguns, porém, identificam-na com Bete-Arabá (que vide).

BETE-BASI

Um lugar mencionado em I Macabeus 9:62-64, fortificado por Jonatã e Simão Macabeu. A cidade resistiu ao cerco lançado por Baquides, governador helenista da região oeste do Eufrates, sob o rei Demétrio I. Essa mal-sucedida invasão (158—157 A.C.), levou a um tratado de paz com os judeus e ao triunfo de Jonatã. O local tem sido identificado com a moderna Khirbet Beit Bassa, no deserto da Judéia.

BETE-BIRI

No hebraico, «casa do criador» ou «casa da cidade». Uma cidade de Judá (I Crô. 4:31), no extremo sul de seu território. Tem sido identificada com a cidade pós-exílica de Bete-Lebaote (Jos. 19:6).

BETE-CAR

No hebraico, «casa das ovelhas». Era uma cidade do território de Dã (I Sam. 7:11), a oeste de Mispa. Foi ali que Israel alcançou uma grande vitória sobre os filisteus. Alguns identificam-na com a localidade árabe de Khirbet-heir, embora a maioria dos estudiosos negue essa possibilidade. Há alguma confusão nos manuscritos onde esse termo aparece, visto que a LXX substitui Bete-Horom, em Jos. 10:10, por Baithchor. E outros manuscritos seguem o texto massorético.

BETE-DAGOM

No hebraico, «casa de Dagom», ou seja, um templo edificado em honra àquele deus pagão. Há duas cidades com esse nome, mencionadas no Antigo Testamento:

1. Uma localidade nas terras baixas de Judá, mencionada em Jos. 15:41. A localização exata é desconhecida em nossos dias. Só pode ser dito que ficava nas proximidades de algum templo, ali existente, em honra a Dagom, uma divindade pagã por toda parte venerada. Ver o artigo sobre Dagom. Alguns identificam a cidade com Khirbet Degun, uma localidade romana a três quilômetros a sudoeste da moderna Beit Dagan.

2. Uma cidade fronteiriça da tribo de Aser, a leste do monte Carmelo (Jos. 19:17), cuja localização é desconhecida.

3. Um templo em Azoto (Asdode), mencionado em

I Macabeus 10:83,84.
4. Uma fortaleza mencionada por Josefo (*Anti*. XII.8.1), localizada perto de Jericó.

Essas diversas referências ao nome Bete-Dagom indicam que havia muitas aldeias e vilas onde se cultuava a Dagom. Seu nome aparece pela primeira vez na Mesopotâmia, em cerca de 2500 A.C., podendo também ser achado em documentos e inscrições em Ugarite, na Fenícia, e na terra dos filisteus. (ID Z)

BETE-DIBLATAIM

No hebraico, «casa dos círculos» (isto é, dos bolos de figos). Era uma cidade de Moabe (Jer. 48:22). O local também é mencionado na estela de Mesa (I.30), rei de Moabe, em cerca de 830 A.C. Encontra-se nas suas listas de cidades conquistadas, que chegavam acerca de cem. Uma outra forma do nome da cidade, «posto rodoviário dos bolos de figos», fala sobre uma localização mencionada em Osé. 1:3, lugar do nascimento de Gomer, esposa do profeta Oséias (em nossa versão portuguesa, Diblaim). Tem sido identificada com a moderna Deleitat-esh-Sherqiyeh, mas sem qualquer grau de certeza.

BETE-ÉDEN

No hebraico, Bete-Éden, significa **casa do deleite**. Fala sobre um principado arameu, localizado na cabeceira do rio Eufrates, que deve ser identificado com a Bit-Adini das fontes assírias. Aparentemente foi um pequeno estado arameu que prosperou, mas posteriormente sucumbiu diante de potências maiores, nos séculos IX e VIII A.C. Seus habitantes foram transportados para Quir, segundo foi profetizado por Amós (Amós 1:5). (Ver II Reis 19:12 e Isa. 37:12).

BETE EGLAIM

No hebraico, «casa dos dois bezerros». Uma antiga cidade que não é mencionada no Antigo Testamento, mas ocorre no *Onomasticon* (48:19,20) de Eusébio. A cidade tem sido identificada com um cômoro escavado pelos arqueólogos, que se chama Tell el-Ajjul, que significa «cômoro do bezerrinho». Está situada a pouco mais de seis quilômetros a sudoeste de Gaza, ao lado norte da desembocadura do wadi Ghuzzeh, perto da costa marítima. As especulações afirmam que o local pode ter estado associado com os dois bezerros de ouro, dos dias de Jeroboão (I Reis 12:28). A localidade também tem sido identificada com Gaza, a qual, finalmente, foi abandonada por causa da malária, que era endêmica ali, e afetou os trabalhadores que ali escavavam modernamente. A cidade foi então transferida para o local da moderna Gaza, no começo da Idade do Bronze Posterior. Os arqueólogos só conseguiram trabalhar ali, depois que os pântanos da região foram drenados. As escavações descobriram belos exemplos de fortificações dos hicsos, um palácio, grande quantidade de cerâmica, armas feitas de bronze, escaravelhos, objetos talhados em ouro, prata, marfim e basalto, além de muitas edificações dos mais diversos tipos.

Quando surgiu um problema de segurança durante as escavações, por causa do descobrimento de ouro, o arqueólogo chefe, Petrie, deu um espetáculo para todos os trabalhadores verem. Exibiu engradados cheios de areia, engradados esses que deveriam estar cheios de ouro. No entanto, ele já tinha escondido o ouro.

Um outro palácio escavado representava uma era posterior à dos hicsos (ver o artigo); e uma terceira edificação aparentemente era uma fortaleza egípcia. Uma quarta edificação foi encontrada, pertencente aos séculos XVI e XIII: e ainda uma quinta, pertencente ao século X ou IX A.C.

Foram encontradas evidências da prática do consumo de carne de cavalo, sob o quarto palácio, o que se coaduna com aquilo que se sabe sobre a cultura dos hicsos. Foram encontrados restos de cavalos, burros e seres humanos, sepultados todos juntos em uma vala comum. Isso apresenta um quebra-cabeças para os estudiosos. (AH PET WRI)

BETE-EMEQUE

No hebraico, «casa do vale». Uma cidade da tribo de Aser, perto de sua fronteira suleste (Jos. 19:27). Talvez deva ser identificada com o moderno Tell el-Mimas, acerca de oito quilômetros a nordeste de Aco.

BETE-EQUEDE

No hebraico, «casa da tosquia». Era uma localidade à margem da estrada entre Jezreel e Samaria, na qual Jeú, a caminho de Jezreel, encontrou quarenta e dois membros da família real de Judá, aos quais matou no poço do palácio (II Reis 10:12,14). Alguns eruditos põem, à margem dessa referência, «casa dos pastores amarrados», o que indica que não se sabe com certeza qual era o sentido do nome do lugar. Comumente o mesmo é identificado com Beit Kad, cerca de vinte e seis quilômetros a nordeste de Samaria.

BETE-EZEL

No hebraico, «casa da raiz firme». Outros estudiosos preferem «casa da descida». Trata-se de uma cidade mencionada apenas em Miq. 1:1, e que talvez não ficasse muito longe da cidade de Samaria. Alguns a identificam com Ezel ou Azel, referida em Zac. 14:5, embora o local moderno seja desconhecido. Não obstante, há quem a identifique com Deir el-Asal, cerca de três quilômetros a leste do Tell Beit Mirsim. No texto sagrado, Azel será o lugar até onde se formará um imenso vale, quando da divisão do monte das Oliveiras em duas porções, por ocasião da segunda vinda de Cristo.

BETE-GADER

No hebraico, «casa da fonte». Outros preferem pensar em «casa murada». Era uma cidade de Judá (I Crô. 2:51), talvez a mesma que, em Josué 12:13, aparece com o nome de Geder. O nome aparece em uma lista de cidades pertencentes a Judá e a Simeão.

BETE-GAMUL

No hebraico, «casa do camelo». Era uma cidade moabita, no tabuleiro de Moabe, e contra a qual foi proferido o juízo de Deus, por causa da maneira como seus habitantes haviam tratado Israel (Jer. 48:23). Alguns pensam que o local moderno é Khirbet el-Jemeil, cerca de oito quilômetros de Aroer.

BETE-GILGAL

No hebraico, «casa de Gilgal» ou «casa da recompensa». Esse nome aparece somente em Nee. 12:29. É provável que a cidade deva ser identificada com Gilgal (ver o artigo), cerca de seis quilômetros e meio a suleste de Jericó. Era uma das aldeias de onde vieram cantores para celebrar a dedicação das muralhas reconstruídas nos dias de Neemias.

BETE-HAGÃ

No hebraico, «casa do jardim». Foi por esse lugar que fugiu o rei Acazias, filho de Acabe, de Israel, quando era perseguido por Jeú. O local fica no lado sul do vale de Jezreel. Tem sido identificado com a moderna Jenin.

BETE-HANÃ

Ver **Elom**.

BETE-HAQUERÉM

No hebraico, «casa das vinhas». Figura nos trechos de Nee. 3:14 e Jer. 6:1; fora da Bíblia, em II Esdras 13:14. Era uma cidade de Benjamim, situada no topo da elevação entre Jerusalém e Tecoa, cerca de cinco quilômetros a suleste de Belém. Seu prefeito, Malquias, reparou a porta do Monturo, quando ajudava Neemias a reerguer as muralhas de Jerusalém, terminado o exílio babilônico. A arqueologia a tem identificado com a moderna Ain Karem. Contudo, parece ainda mais apropriada a localidade de Ramet Rahel, que fica em uma elevada colina entre Belém e Jerusalém.

BETE-HARÃ

No hebraico, «casa da altura». É cidade que figura apenas em Núm. 32:26, embora tálvez seja a mesma Bete-Arã de Jos. 13:27. Pertencia à tribo de Gade, na Transjordânia. Posteriormente recebeu o nome de Livias ou Júlias. Ficava defronte de Jericó. Por ocasião da conquista da Terra Santa pelos israelitas, foi tomada dos amorreus e transformada posteriormente em uma fortaleza, ficando com a tribo de Gade. Alguns crêem que se trata da cidade síria de Bete-Aramftá, mencionada por Josefo. Seu local moderno tem sido identificado com o Tell Iktanus, a quase treze quilômetros a nordeste da desembocadura do Jordão, ao sul do wadi Heshbon.

BETE-HOGLA

No hebraico, «casa da corvina» ou «casa da perdiz». Foi uma das catorze cidades entregues à tribo de Benjamim (Jos. 18:21); modernamente se chama 'Ain Hajlah, a seis quilômetros e meio a suleste de Jericó. Ficava localizada na Arabá, na fronteira sul de Benjamim (Jos. 18:19) e era a fronteira norte do território de Judá (Jos 15:6).

BETE-HOROM

No hebraico, «casa das cavernas». Dois lugares tinham esse nome, nos dias do Antigo Testamento, a «Bete-Horom de baixo» e a «Bete-Horom de cima» (Jos. 16:3,5; I Crô. 7:24). Atualmente existem as aldeias de Beit 'Ur et-Tahta, (de baixo) e de Beit-'Ur el-Faqa (de cima). A de baixo fica acerca de 335 m acima do nível do mar, e a de cima fica cerca de 550 m acima do nível do mar, sendo esta última menor que a primeira. As escavações ali efetuadas mostram que sua origem remonta pelo menos ao fim da Idade do Bronze. Havia uma estrada romana ligando uma com a outra, entre Gibeom, no leste, e o vale de Aijalom e a planície costeira a oeste. Ambas ficavam na fronteira dos territórios de Benjamim e Efraim (Jos. 16:3-5; 18:13 ss). Quando ocorreu a divisão dos reinos — Israel, ao norte e Judá ao sul — elas ficaram com Israel (Jos. 21:22). Visto que ambas essas cidades estavam localizadas em um passo montanhoso na fronteira, foram a cena de muitas batalhas sangrentas. Eram também contadas entre as cidades dos levitas. Uma famosa batalha teve lugar ali, no tempo de Josué (Jos. 10:6-15). Os egípcios também combateram no local (I Reis 9:17); e elas foram atacadas por mercenários efraimitas (II Crô. 25:12, 13). Salomão reconstruiu e fortaleceu a ambas (II Crô. 8:5). Seerá, filha de Berias, reconstruiu ambas, terminado o exílio babilônico (I Crô. 7:24). Sambalate era natural do lugar (Nee. 2:10).

A literatura pseudepígrafa e apocalíptica menciona esses lugares em várias oportunidades (Jubileus 34:4; Judite 4:4; I Macabeus 3:15,16; 7:39-43), onde há menção a outras batalhas sanguinolentas no local. Baquides fortificou o lugar, após uma batalha contra Jonatã Macabeu, no deserto de Tecoa.

BETE-HOROM, BATALHA DE (O Dia Longo de Josué)

O artigo acima, sobre as duas cidades de Bete-Horom, mostra quantas batalhas ferozes foram travadas ali, durante a longa história das mesmas. Porém, aquela que se tornou conhecida como a «batalha de Bete-Horom» foi aquela travada entre as forças israelitas de Josué e os cinco reis de Canaã, perto de Gibeom, Bete-Horom e o vale de Aijalom. A descrição desse choque aparece no décimo capítulo do livro de Josué. Jericó já havia caído, e a batalha foi apenas estratégica, visando o controle do território. Os gibeonitas, observando o esmagador avanço dos israelitas, enganaram com truques a Josué; mas o ludíbrio não tardou a ser descoberto. Então os gibeonitas foram subjugados, embora não destruídos. Em face disso, os habitantes de Gibeom foram tidos como traidores pelos demais reis cananeus, os quais atacaram aquela cidade. Foi então que os gibeonitas apelaram para Israel, pedindo ajuda. Josué atacou-os imediatamente, e os reis cananeus e suas hordas entraram em pânico. A rota da fuga deles levou-os diretamente a Bete-Horom, quando subiam na direção do passo entre as montanhas. Uma grande saraivada caiu sobre os cananeus, o que o autor do livro de Josué atribui à intervenção divina. «Mais foram os que morreram pela chuva de pedra do que os mortos à espada pelos filhos de Israel» (Jos. 10:11).

O Longo Dia de Josué. A fim de que pudesse aniquilar os adversários nessa batalha, Josué ordenou que o sol estacasse em seu curso (Jos. 10:12). E o Senhor o atendeu, e o dia foi extraordinariamente prolongado. Há muitas interpretações acerca do fenômeno: 1. Explicação mitológica. Uma grande vitória, ao ser relatada, foi emendada, incluindo os lances da saraivada e o fenômeno do longo dia. A história está recheada de lendas, e o Antigo Testamento não está isento dessas interpolações. 2. Ou então, tudo quanto sucedeu foi que as nuvens encobriram o sol escaldante, facilitando a perseguição por parte dos exércitos de Josué. Porém, os vs. 13-15 mostram que o que esteve envolvido foi a passagem do tempo, e não apenas condições atmosféricas. 3. O milagre teria envolvido apenas uma questão de reflexo, e não de real envolvimento da passagem do tempo. Deus causou condições atmosféricas abaixo do horizonte, capazes de refletir os raios solares sobre o território, mesmo após dopôr-do-sol. Tudo não teria sido causado por condições extraordinárias, mas apenas naturais. 4. Ou então, conforme diz a Bíblia,

BETE-JESIMOTE — BETE-PEOR

Deus impediu a rotação da terra por algum tempo, ou fez esse movimento tornar-se bem mais lento. Essa interpretação também tem sido sujeitada por alguns a uma adaptação natural. Esses dizem que teria havido uma leve mudança dos pólos, provocando assim o prolongamento daquele dia. Sabemos que as mudanças de pólo realmente ocorrem, embora mui raramente. Talvez uma mudança de pólos tenha ocorrido quando do dilúvio de Noé. Porém, se isso sucedeu naquele dia de Josué, então a mudança de pólo foi realmente mínima, pois, doutra sorte, teria havida destruição generalizada. Alguns estudiosos também têm dito que esse prolongamento do dia, quando da batalha de Bete-Horom, foi corrigido na época de Isaías, conforme se lê em Isaías 38:8: «Eis que farei retroceder dez graus a sombra lançada pelo sol declinante no relógio de Acaz. Assim retrocedeu o sol os dez graus que já havia declinado». 5. Finalmente, a questão inteira envolve um mistério sem explicação, não importando se o fenômeno foi natural ou sobrenatural. (WHI VE Z)

BETE-JESIMOTE

No hebraico, «casa de desolação». Era uma cidade do território de Rúben, entre os montes de Abraim e o rio Jordão (Núm. 33:49), —cerca de dezesseis quilômetros a suleste de Jericó (Jos. 12:3). Posteriormente, foi conquistada pelos moabitas (Eze. 25:9). O último acampamento dos israelitas, antes de haverem cruzado o Jordão, foi perto desse lugar (Núm. 33:49). Tem sido identificado com o Tell el-Azeimeh, perto da extremidade nordeste do mar Morto. (GL)

BETE-LE-AFRA

No hebraico, «casa da poeira», uma cidade desconhecida, mencionada exclusivamente em Miquéias 1:10. Há um jogo de palavras nesse trecho, pelo que algum lugar como Ofra ou Betel poderia estar envolvido. As identificações incluem o wadi el Ghafr, entre ed-Daweimeh e o Tell ed-Duweir e Beit-Offa, a dez quilômetros a suleste de Asdode. (SI)

BETE-LEBAOTE

No hebraico, «casa da leoa». Era uma cidade de Simeão (Jos. 19:6), que é chamada Lebaote em Josué 15:32. Muitos pensam que esse lugar é a mesma Bete-Biri, que figura em I Crô. 4:31, um nome que mui provavelmente tem sido preservado no nome de Jebel el-Biri, no deserto da Judéia.

BETE-LOMOM

Assim aparece na LXX, o nome de Belém da Judéia (ver o artigo). Em I Esdras 5:17, as pessoas que residiam na área são alistadas entre os homens da Judéia que retornaram em companhia de Zorobabel, após o exílio babilônico. Nessa conexão, ver Belém, em Esd. 2:21.

BETE-MAACÁ

Ver Abel-Bete-Maacá

BETE-MARCABOTE

No hebraico, «casa das carruagens». Era uma cidade pertencente a Simeão (Jos. 19:5; I Crô. 4:31), no extremo sul de Judá. O nome pode ter-se originado do fato de que ali era uma das paradas de carruagens que transitavam entre o Egito e Jerusalém (I Reis 10:19,29; I Crô. 8:6). Tem sido identificada com a antiga Madmana e com a moderna Khirbet Umm ed-Deimineh, cerca de 24 km a sudoeste de Hebrom, o que é também sugerido pela lista correspondente, em Josué 15:31.

BETE-MEOM

No hebraico, «casa da habitação». Aparece somente em Jer. 48:23, como uma cidade moabita, próxima de Bete-Gamul. A forma completa do nome, Bete-Baal-Meom, aparece em Jos. 13:17, como cidade moabita outorgada, após a conquista, à tribo de Rúben. Ficava na margem ocidental do rio Arnom.

BETE-MILO

No hebraico, «casa da plenitude». Está em foco algum cômoro, terraço, platô, ou coisa semelhante, provavelmente onde havia um fortim (Juí. 9:6,20). Ficava perto de Siquém. Seus habitantes estavam entre aqueles que proclamaram Abimeleque o rei. Ver o artigo sobre *Milo*.

BETE-NIMRA

No hebraico, «casa da água doce». Era uma cidade de Gade (Jos. 13:27). Com a forma de Ninra, a cidade é alistada em Núm. 32:3. Foi chamada Bete-Nabris por Eusébio, como cidade que ficava cerca de oito quilômetros ao norte de Livias. Foi edificada e fortificada pelos gaditas, tendo-se tornado lugar apropriado para a guarda de ovelhas (Jos. 13:27). O local é atualmente ocupado pelo Tell Bleibil, a 16 km a nordeste de Jericó, no lado norte do wadi Shaib. Posteriormente, a cidade foi transferida para cerca de quilômetro e meio para sudoeste, onde seu nome está preservado no Tell Nimrin. (GLU)

BETE-PAZES

No hebraico, «casa da dispersão». Era uma cidade de Issacar (Jos. 19:21), próxima do monte Tabor. Sua localização moderna é desconhecida.

BETE-PELETE

No hebraico, «casa da fuga». Uma cidade no extremo sul de Judá (Jos. 15:27), que foi outorgada àquela tribo, quando da conquista da Palestina. Terminado o exílio babilônico, foi reedificada e reocupada por Judá (Nee. 11:26). Helez, o paltita, um dos trinta heróis de Davi, provavelmente era natural do lugar. Sua localização moderna é desconhecida.

BETE-PEOR

No hebraico, «casa de Peor» ou «casa da abertura» (Deu. 3:29). No primeiro caso, talvez o nome se referisse a um templo dedicado a Baal-Peor. A cidade era moabita, mas foi outorgada à tribo de Rúben, tendo-se tornado famosa como santuário daquela divindade. (Deu. 4:46; Jos. 13:20). Estava localizada na margem oriental do Jordão, defronte de Jericó, a dez quilômetros ao norte de Livias ou Bete-Hará, conforme é afirmado por Eusébio em seu *Onomasticon*. O nome Peor provavelmente significa «abertura» ou «abismo». É possível que o profeta Moisés tenha sido sepultado naquela região (Deu. 34:6). Antes de entrarem na terra de Canaã, os israelitas acamparam no vale diante de Baal-Peor, enquanto Moisés avistava a — Terra Prometida — do alto do monte Pisga (Deu. 3:29). Na ocasião alguns preceitos foram dados a Israel (Deu. 4:46). O lugar tem sido identificado com a moderna Khirbet esh-Sheikh-Jayil, ao norte do monte Nebo e a oeste de Hesbom. (S UN Z)

BETE-RAFA

No hebraico, «casa de Rafa» ou «casa do gigante». Em I Crô. 4:12 aparece com o nome do filho de Estom, dentro da genealogia de Judá (cerca de 618 A.C.). Em I Crônicas 20:6,8, a palavra aparece com o artigo, e a tradução deve ser «dos gigantes», conforme, realmente, se vê na nossa versão portuguesa.

BETE-REOBE

No hebraico, «casa de uma rua». Era uma cidade ou distrito dos arameus, perto de Laís (em Dã) (Juí. 18:28). Havia ali um vale, formando a porção superior das terras baixas de Huleh, através das quais flui o manancial central formador do rio Jordão e perto do qual ficava a cidade de Laís-Dã (que talvez seja a atual Tell el Qadi). Naquele lugar, os amonitas obtiveram mercenários para lutarem contra Davi (II Sam. 10:6). Alguns identificam o local com a moderna Banias, a oito quilômetros a nordeste de Dã; ou então com Hunin, a oeste de Banias. Porém, não há certeza quanto à questão.

BETE-SEÃ

No hebraico, «casa da segurança» ou «casa do descanso», embora talvez haja uma alusão ao deus babilônico Shahan, ao Sha'an dos fenícios e ao deus serpente dos sumérios. Se esse era o caso, então o local era um antigo santuário dedicado a essa divindade. Seja como for, pertencia à meia-tribo de Manassés (Jos. 17:11). Ficava na margem ocidental do Jordão, fazendo fronteira a oeste, com os montes de Gilboa. Era uma antiga fortaleza, estrategicamente colocada, que dominava o vale de Esdrelom. Tem sido identificada com a moderna Tell el-Husn, que significa «cômoro da Fortaleza». Outros pensam em uma identificação com a moderna Beisan.

A cidade foi fundada em cerca de 3000 A.C. Tutmés III conquistou-a em batalha, e, durante cerca de trezentos anos, foi uma fortaleza egípcia. Duas estelas, uma de Seti I e outra de Ramisés II, foram descobertas ali pela arqueologia. Sabemos que por ocasião da invasão da Palestina, pelos israelitas, os habitantes de Bete-Seã possuíam carros de guerra feitos de ferro (Jos. 17:16), e o povo de Israel não conseguiu expulsar dali os seus habitantes. No entanto, estes ficaram na obrigação de pagar tributo (Jos. 17:12-16). Quando da batalha de Gilboa, em cerca de 1000 A.C., o lugar aparentemente estava sob o controle dos filisteus, porquanto penduraram os ossos de Saul e de seus filhos na muralha da cidade (I Sam. 31:10). O trecho de I Crônicas 10:10 alude a um segundo templo existente em Bete-Seã, chamado «casa de Dagom», onde a cabeça de Saul ficou exposta.

A arqueologia tem feito importantes descobertas ali, como o templo de Astorete, um outro templo ao sul do mesmo, e o templo de Dagom. Ali há um elevado cômoro, que tem produzido, nas escavações, vários templos egípcios, datados desde 1413 a.C. As escavações têm descoberto muitos níveis de cidades, pertencentes a diversas épocas diferentes. Durante o período grego, a cidade passou a chamar-se Citópolis, isto é, «cidade dos citas», talvez por causa da cavalaria cita que estava associada ao lugar, e compunha parte do exército de Ptolomeu II. Caiu sob o governo dos Selêucidas no século II A.C., e passou a chamar-se Nisa. O seu antigo nome é retido no nome de uma aldeia árabe próxima do cômoro, chamada Beisan. No tempo dos Hasmoneus, a cidade atingiu considerável prosperidade, sendo a única cidade da Decápolis no lado ocidental do rio Jordão (I Macabeus 12:40; Josefo Anti. xiv.5.3). Algumas poucas figurinhas, pertencentes à época dos citas, sugerem que havia um santuário no alto de alguma colina, durante o período de dominação persa. No terceiro nível, foi escavado um templo, provavelmente romano. Ao lado do mesmo havia uma cisterna, onde se encontrou a cabeça de uma estátua do deus Dionísio (ver o artigo). Os níveis segundo e primeiro correspondem aos períodos bizantino e árabe. No segundo nível foi encontrado o que restava de um templo cristão de forma circular, e também um mosteiro do século VI D.C. A cidade caiu diante dos árabes em 636 D.C. (ROWE TH UN)

BETE-SEMES

No hebraico, «casa do sol». Foi o nome de vários lugares do Antigo Testamento, sendo lugares de considerável atividade arqueológica nos nossos tempos, a saber:

1. Uma cidade sacerdotal (Jos. 21:16; I Sam. 6:15). Ficava no território da tribo de Judá, na fronteira suleste com Dã (Jos. 15:10), a terra dos filisteus (I Sam. 6:12). Eusébio a situava a dez milhas romanas de Eleuterópolis, na direção de quem vai para Nicópolis. Em tempos mais remotos, pertencia aos filisteus. No tempo de Acaz (I Reis 4:9; II Crô. 28:18), os filisteus a reconquistaram de Israel. Foi naquele lugar que a arca da aliança foi tomada pelos filisteus, e também foi ali que mais de cinquenta mil homens foram miraculosamente mortos, quando tentavam examinar irreverentemente o objeto sagrado (I Sam. 6:19). A Ir-Semes de Josué 19:41 tem sido identificada por alguns estudiosos como Bete-Semes. O local tem sido identificado com a moderna Ain-Shema, nas vertentes nordestinas das montanhas de Judá, onde há o Tell er-Rumeileh. O lugar foi habitado desde 2000 A.C., o que prosseguiu até 600 A.C., quando foi destruído pelo exército de Nabucodonosor II.

A arqueologia tem feito ali muitas descobertas. Têm sido identificados nada menos de sete níveis de ocupação, cada qual produzindo muitos artefatos. As descobertas pertencentes à Idade do Bronze Posterior revestem-se de importância especial, no que diz respeito à história da escrita, em Canaã. Há um tablete de argila com uma inscrição enigmática, similar àquela usada para se escrever na língua de Ugarite (ver o artigo). Alguns cacos de barro representam uma forma de escrita protocananéia. Da Idade do Ferro há asas de jarras estampadas, uma das quais diz: «Pertencente a Eliaquim, mordomo de Jeoaquim». Dois exemplares desse selo foram encontrados em Tell Beit Mirsim, e um outro em Ramat Rahel.

2. Havia uma outra cidade com esse nome, na fronteira sul do território de Issacar, entre o monte Tabor e o rio Jordão (Jos. 19:22), que até hoje não foi localizada.

3. Havia uma cidade de Naftali, com suas aldeias (Jos. 19:38; Juí. 1:33), dentre as quais estava a cidade de Bete-Anate, de onde os cananeus não foram expulsos, que também era chamada Bete-Semes.

4. O trecho de Jeremias 43:13 atribui esse nome a uma cidade do Egito, —que usualmente era chamada Heliópolis, conforme chegou seu nome até nós, através do grego, o termo grego também significa «casa do sol». (AH GRA YE)

BETE-SEMITA

Adjetivo gentílico para quem nasceu em Bete-Semes (I Sam. 6:14,18).

BETE-SITA

No hebraico, «casa da acácia». Foi para esse lugar que fugiu o derrotado exército midianita, diante do avanço de Gideão (Juí. 7:22). Provavelmente é a atual Shattah, cerca de quatro quilômetros a leste da moderna En-Harod, na direção de Zaretã, e talvez o moderno Tell es-Sa'idihey, que fica perto do rio Jordão, a 29 km a oeste de Jerasa. Visto que Zaretã ficava perto da cidade de Adão (Jos. 3:16), às margens do rio Jordão, é óbvio que os homens se lançaram à travessia do rio Jordão.

BETE-TAPUA

No hebraico, «casa das maçãs», uma cidade a oito quilômetros a oeste de Hebrom (Jos. 15:33). Modernamente, Taffuh. Uma outra cidade, que terminou pertencendo à tribo de Judá, também se chamava, simplesmente, Tapua (Jos. 12:17) (ver o artigo). Bete-Tapua estava associada a outras sete cidades da região montanhosa (I Crô. 2:43). O distrito era frutífero e rico. Ficava à beira da cadeia montanhosa, dando frente para os férteis terraços, mais embaixo.

BETE-TOGARMA

Ver **Togarma**.

BETE-ZACARIAS

No hebraico, «casa de Zacarias» ou «casa de Yahweh lembra». Uma cidade cerca de 16 km a sudoeste de Jerusalém. Não é mencionada nas Escrituras. Mas, de acordo com I Macabeus 6:32, foi ali que Judas Macabeu foi derrotado por Antíoco V Eupator, filho de Antíoco Epifânio. Antíoco viera à batalha bem preparado e equipado, acompanhado por elefantes, e os judeus, inferiorizados, fugiram (Josefo, *Anti.* xii.9,4). Tem sido identificada com a moderna Khirbet Beit Sakaria.

BETE-ZAÍTE

No hebraico, «casa das oliveiras». Foi o lugar onde Baquides, um dos generais do rei Demétrio, massacrou a muitos judeus, durante a guerra dos Macabeus (I Macabeus 7:19). Baquides, fingindo-se amigável, enganou Judas, levando-o a confiar nele; e isso armou o palco para a matança de sessenta homens, e, posteriormente, de muitos outros, lançando-os em um poço. O local tem sido identificado com a moderna Beit-Zeita, cerca de seis quilômetros a sudoeste de Belém, perto de Bete-Zur.

BETE-ZUR

No hebraico, «casa da rocha». Era uma cidade na região montanhosa da Judéia, fundada pelos habitantes de Meom, descendentes de Hebrom (I Crô. 2:45). Era uma fortaleza colocada em posição elevada e estratégica, entre Belém e Hebrom. O local foi escavado, tendo sido encontradas ruínas da Idade do Bronze Média, de cerca do século XVI A.C. Foi uma cidade fortificada da era dos Macabeus, quando era chamada Bete-Sura. Contava com uma numerosa população durante o período dos hicsos, na porção final da Idade de Bronze Média II. Existem algumas evidências arqueológicas referentes àquele período. Existem artefatos pertencentes ao período do Bronze Posterior, bem como aos séculos XIII e XII A.C. A ocupação israelita terminou em meio a um incêndio, em meados do século XI, talvez envolvendo guarnições filistéias. Uma outra ocupação israelita teve lugar no período dos séculos X e IX A.C., incluindo a fortificação de Reoboão. Continuava ocupada nos séculos VIII e VII A.C. A invasão feita por Nabucodonosor, bem como o período persa dos dias de Neemias (Nee. 3:16), também deixaram alguns itens, descobertos pelos arqueólogos. Os monarcas Ptolomeus são representados através de algumas moedas, 124 das quais pertencentes a Antíoco IV Epifânio, 18 aos Macabeus e 16 a João Hircano. O local foi abandonado cerca do ano 100 A.C. Foi ali que Judas Macabeu derrotou os gregos, dirigidos por Lísias. (SEL UN)

BETEL

No hebraico, «casa de Deus». Uma cidade da antiga Palestina, a quase dezoito quilômetros ao norte de Jerusalém, que originalmente se chamava Luz. Para os antigos hebreus, tratava-se de um lugar sagrado, quase tão importante quanto Jerusalém, devido à sua íntima associação com a história dos israelitas, a começar com Abraão. Foi ali que Abraão acampou de certa feita (Gên. 12:8; 13:3). Quanto ao antigo nome, Luz, que significa «amendoeira», ver Gên. 28:19. Até hoje o local é próprio para pastorear ovelhas.

A cidade chegou a adquirir o nome de Betel, «casa de Deus», porque foi nas proximidades que Jacó sonhou com uma escada que subia da terra ao céu (Gên. 28:10-22). Isso posto, veio a ser considerada uma espécie de abrigo de anjos, um lugar de comunicação entre o céu e a terra. Originalmente, era uma espécie de lugar santo dos cananeus, antes de haver sido ocupada por Israel, o que constitui uma informação interessante. A arqueologia tem demonstrado que era uma espécie de santuário ao ar livre, no período calcolítico posterior (cerca de 3200 A.C.). Uma segunda leva de ocupação pode ser datada em cerca de 2400-2200 A.C. Mas o sítio foi abandonado, e então reocupado, já no século XIX A.C. Nos séculos XVIII e XVII A.C., Betel tornou-se um forte complexo defensivo. E foi durante esse período, no começo do Período Médio do Bronze, que entraram em cena os patriarcas hebreus.

Para Jacó, Betel tornou-se um lugar especial. Ele o revisitou e ali renovou o seu pacto com Yahweh. Foi ali também que Jacó edificou um altar, e também foi ali que ele recebeu seu novo nome, Israel, que significa «dotado de poder diante de Deus».

A ausência de material pertencente à era do Bronze Posterior I sugere a destruição do local, pelos egípcios, em cerca de 1550 A.C. Foi nesse tempo que os egípcios conseguiram expulsar os hicsos do Egito e da Palestina. Porém, no período do Bronze Posterior II, isto é, nos séculos XIV e XIII A.C., Betel foi reedificada. Tornou-se então uma cidade bastante próspera, dotada de indústrias, de um sistema de esgotos e de prensas de extração de azeite de oliveira.

BETEL — BETESDA

Então os israelitas invadiram a área. A arqueologia tem descoberto evidências da destruição que ocorreu, no século XIII A.C. (cerca de 1240-1235 A.C.). Betel foi ocupada por Josué (Jos. 8:7), e outorgada à tribo de Benjamim. Após a guerra civil contra a tribo de Benjamim, Betel passou à tribo de Efraim, tendo ficado na fronteira entre Efraim e Benjamim.

Durante algum tempo, esteve ali localizada a arca da aliança, o centro da vida religiosa de Israel. Os oráculos divinos eram ali consultados (Juí. 20:18). A profetisa Débora vivia perto de Betel (Juí. 4:5). Foi em Betel que o profeta Samuel estabeleceu um de seus tribunais, em seus circuitos por todo o território de Israel (I Sam. 7:16).

O local não é mencionado por nome nos dias de Davi e Salomão, mas a arqueologia tem mostrado que foi cidade próspera durante o período. Jeroboão fez de Betel o seu extremo sul, ao passo que Dã era o seu extremo norte. E Betel foi transformada em sede da adoração aos bezerros de ouro (I Reis 12:28-33 e 13:1). Os profetas abominavam tal associação, intitulando a cidade de Bete-Áven, «cidade de ídolos» (Amós 1:5; Osé. 4:15 e 5:8). Foi conquistada por Abias, rei de Judá (II Crô. 13:19), mas posteriormente reverteu ao reino do norte, Israel (II Reis 10:28). Quando Josias marchou para o norte, após a queda da Assíria, ele não destruiu Betel, mas apenas o templo que ali havia. No entanto, a cidade foi destruída juntamente com Jerusalém, pelos babilônios, em 587 A.C. A presença de colonos babilônios, na região de Samaria, é notada em II Reis 17:24,30. Betel foi destruída mediante um grande incêndio, em 553 ou 521 A.C., talvez a mando de Nabonido da Babilônia, ou então pelos persas, imediatamente antes do reinado de Dario.

Após o exílio, Betel tornou-se uma pequena aldeia de mínima importância. O recenseamento da época de Esdras e Neemias mostra que sua população era diminuta (Esd. 2:28). Aparece entre as duas aldeias situadas mais ao norte de Benjamim (Nee. 12:31 ss). A arqueologia também tem provado que Betel foi ocupada durante o período helênico, embora não haja referências literárias a ela, durante esse período. Os trechos de I Macabeus 9:50 e Josefo (Anti. xiii.1,3) mostram que ela foi fortificada por Baquides. Era cidade florescente na época dos Macabeus. No começo da dominação romana, houve alguma destruição ali, promovida por Pompeu ou Vespasiano. Algumas construções romanas têm sido ali escavadas pelos arqueólogos. De acordo com Josefo (Guerras iv.9,9), Vespasiano capturou a cidade, deixando ali uma guarnição romana.

Não há qualquer alusão a Betel no Novo Testamento, — mas Jesus deve ter passado pela localidade, em suas viagens de Siquém a Jerusalém. Eusébio alude à localidade como uma aldeia extensa, no século IV D.C., quando então continuava sendo considerada um santuário. Foi construída uma igreja bizantina em sua extremidade oriental, talvez para assinalar o local da visão de Jacó. Uma outra igreja cristã foi erigida ali no século VI, talvez para comemorar o santuário de Abraão, que havia no lugar. Uma terceira igreja bizantina foi levantada em Betel. Em cerca de 500 D.C., foi levantada ali uma nova muralha, talvez como defesa contra os samaritanos revoltados. Interessante é que a cidade acabou desaparecendo da história, sem qualquer explicação conhecida. Perto de suas ruínas há a atual aldeia de Beitin. A história de Betel tem sido ilustrada pelas descobertas arqueológicas, que nos fazem retroceder aos tempos mais primitivos. Ver o artigo geral sobre o assunto. (ALB AM KEL UN Z)

BETEL (DEUS PAGÃO)

No hebraico, «casa de El». El era uma divindade dos semitas ocidentais, o que tem sido confirmado pelo onomástico dos papiros aramaicos de Elefantina, do Egito e dos textos cuneiformes neobabilônios, que contêm cerca de quinze nomes diferentes. Quanto ao Antigo Testamento, ver Zac. 7:2; Jer. 48:13; Amós 5:5. Na primeira dessas referências a alusão é ao templo dessa divindade, visto que a expressão encontrada no versículo seguinte é «bete Yahweh» (em nossa versão, «casa do Senhor»). Isso significa que uma tradução mais apropriada de Zacarias 7:2 diria «casa de El», em vez de Betel. Há outras combinações do nome, referindo-se àquela divindade pagã, como Bete-Eloim (cerca de cinqüenta vezes), Bete-Sharezer, e também nomes babilônicos como Bitilishezibe e Bitilisharusur. A combinação bete Yahweh ocorre por cerca de duzentas e cinqüenta vezes no Novo Testamento. Mas Betel, sem qualquer combinação, não figura no Antigo Testamento hebraico, exceto quando se refere à cidade desse nome, nunca o fazendo no caso do nome daquela divindade. Os textos Elefantinos provam, acima de qualquer dúvida, que tal nome era aplicado a uma divindade. Tanto é assim que uma outra divindade desse nome era conhecida no panteão fenício de Ugarite, que dá nomes de deuses até do segundo milênio anterior à era cristã. (ALB VI Z)

BETEL, MONTE DE

Uma cadeia montanhosa que ficava ao sul da cidade de Betel (Jos. 16:1), — que deve ser distinguida da cidade propriamente dita.

BÉTEN

No hebraico, «ventre» ou «útero». Uma cidade pertencente à tribo de Aser (Jos. 19:25). Eusébio informa-nos que ficava a oito milhas romanas a leste de Acre, e que era chamada em seus dias pelos nomes de Bebeten ou Betebeten (onomástico). Tem sido identificada com a moderna El B'aneh, embora não haja certeza absoluta quanto a isso.

BETESDA

Aparece somente em João 5:2. No grego, **Bethesdá**, é a transliteração do termo aramaico que significa «casa da misericórdia». Era o nome de um tanque ou reservatório que ficava perto da porta das Ovelhas, em Jerusalém. Ao redor desse tanque havia cinco alpendres ou pavilhões, onde muitos enfermos eram deixados, à espera do suposto benefício das águas do tanque, que vez por outra, eram agitadas, produzindo curas maravilhosas em quem primeiro se atirasse nas mesmas. O local está envolvido em um dos maiores milagres realizados por Jesus, relatado na íntegra em João 5:1-18. O quarto versículo dessa passagem não é autêntico, porquanto não figura no original grego; antes, trata-se de uma glosa escribal posterior, que procura explicar por que razão os enfermos eram deixados ali. Ver uma discussão sobre essa variante textual, in loc., no NTI. O relato fala da cura de um homem que estivera paralítico durante trinta e oito anos. Por causa dessa cura, o ódio dos judeus incrédulos contra Jesus redobrou, visto que o milagre ocorreu em um dia de sábado. Quando Jesus defendeu-se da tola acusação, explicou: «Meu Pai trabalha até agora, e eu trabalho também». E o escritor sagrado ajunta: «Por isso, pois, os judeus mais ainda procuravam matá-lo, porque não somente

TANQUE DA BETESDA — Cortesia, Matson Photo Service

TANQUE DE SILOÉ — Cortesia, Matson Photo Service

BETEZATA — BETSAIDA

violava o sábado, mas também dizia que Deus era seu próprio Pai, fazendo-se igual a Deus» (vss. 17 e 18).

O local é atualmente identificado com um tanque encontrado durante reparos feitos em 1888, próximos da igreja de Santa Ana, no bairro de Bezeta, em Jerusalém, não distante da porta das Ovelhas e da torre de Antônia. O tanque foi encontrado por debaixo da cripta do templo cristão arruinado (século IV D.C.), com um pórtico dotado de cinco arcos e com pinturas afresco muito esmaecidas, retratando a cura miraculosa do paralítico. Os cruzados consideravam que aquele era o lugar autêntico do milagre, razão pela qual construíram aquela igreja.

Orígenes e Cirilo de Jerusalém mencionaram a presença de uma fonte que jorrava de forma intermitente, com águas muito ferruginosas, parecendo sangue. Eusébio imaginava que a coloração dessas águas provinha dos sacrifícios de animais que se ofereciam no templo. Seja como for, o mais provável é que a lenda de um anjo que vinha agitar ocasionalmente as águas do tanque se devesse à ação do jorro intermitente, talvez devido às flutuações das águas freáticas. Ver a completa exposição da questão no NTI. (NTI UN)

BETEZATA
Ver o artigo sobre **Betesda**.

BETFAGÉ
Deriva-se de um termo aramaico que significa «figos verdes». Era uma aldeia existente nas faldas do monte das Oliveiras. É mencionada no relato da entrada triunfal de Jesus em Jerusalém, paralelamente à Betânia (Mat. 21:1; Mar. 11:1 e Luc. 19:29). Fica à margem ou nas proximidades da estrada de Jericó a Jerusalém. No Talmude, Betfagé é algumas vezes mencionada como separada de Jerusalém; mas, de outras vezes, como parte integrante da mesma. Uma possível identificação moderna é Kefr et Tur. Não há qualquer menção à localidade, nas páginas do Antigo Testamento.

BET HAMIDRASH
No hebraico, literalmente, «casa de estudo». Indica algum lugar onde os estudantes judeus costumam reunir-se para ouvir a Midrash (ver o artigo), ou seja, a interpretação expositiva das Escrituras. Tal expressão é freqüentemente empregada como sinônimo de sinagoga (ver o artigo), visto que a sinagoga também é uma casa de estudo. (E)

BET HILLEL E BET SHAMMAI
Duas escolas rabínicas, compostas dos discípulos de Hillel e de Shammai (ver os artigos), que floresceram durante o primeiro século da era cristã. Os discípulos levavam a seus mestres pontos debatíveis sobre a lei, as Escrituras, a ética e a política. Os discípulos de Hillel eram mais liberais e lenientes, — ao passo que os de Shammai eram inflexivelmente severos. Para exemplificar, na questão do divórcio, os discípulos de Hillel aceitavam que um casamento terminasse por certa variedade de razões; mas os discípulos de Shammai só permitiam o rompimento dos laços do matrimônio por motivo de adultério. Finalmente, prevaleceu a posição da escola de Hillel, pois, em cerca de 100 D.C., ficou decidido que, em todas as disputas legais, seriam seguidas as opiniões da Bet Hillel. (E)

BETH, KARL
Professor da Universidade de Viena, na Áustria (1872- ?). Foi investigador de fenômenos religiosos à luz da filosofia, da psicologia e da sociologia. Escreveu sobre o fenômeno dos milagres, adotando o dito de Reinhold Seeberg de que «Cristo é um milagre tão grande, que todos os outros são pequenos em comparação a ele». Beth rejeitava a crítica da religião, feita por Freud, como também a teologia dialética de Karl Barth, e, igualmente, toda forma de secularização. (E)

BETOMASTAIM
Um lugar nunca identificado, que fazia frente para a planície de Esdrelom, no lado oposto da planície, perto de Dotã (Judite 4:6). Era uma posição militar estratégica, no tocante à planície de Esdrelom. Por esse motivo, o sumo sacerdote Joaquim requereu que o local fosse bloqueado, a fim de impedir a passagem das hordas de Holofernes, o general assírio. Depois que Judite tirou a vida de Holofernes, em sua tenda, um magistrado de Betúlia (terra natal de Judite), de nome Uzias, solicitou ajuda da parte de Betomastaim (Judite 15:4), para que pudesse destruir os exércitos assírios. (Z)

BETONIM
No hebraico, «nozes de pistácia». Era uma cidade do território de Gade, bem ao norte, já na fronteira com Manassés (Jos. 13:26), — cerca de 27 km a nordeste de Jericó. A palavra aparece novamente em Gên. 43:11, onde, em português, é corretamente traduzida.

BETSAIDA (da Galiléia)
Vem do aramaico, «casa de pesca» ou «casa do pescador». Era uma cidade da Galiléia, na costa ocidental do mar de Tiberíades (João 1:44; 12:21). Ficava localizada perto de Cafarnaum (Mar. 6:45; 8:22). O lugar nunca é mencionado no Antigo Testamento. Era cidade natal de Pedro, André e Filipe. Foi freqüentemente visitada por Jesus. Pedro também possuía uma casa em Cafarnaum. Ali Jesus entrou na casa de Pedro (casa de sua sogra?), e curou a sogra dele de uma febre (Mat. 8:13,14). Foi também em Betsaida que Jesus multiplicou os pães e os peixes para os cinco mil homens (Luc. 9:10).

A narrativa do quarto evangelho lança alguma confusão ao dizer que «...atravessou Jesus o mar da Galiléia, que é o de Tiberíades» (João 6:1), e então realizou o milagre de multiplicação. Isso faria com que o local desse milagre tivesse sido no lado oriental do lago; mas, algures, lê-se que Betsaida ficava na própria Galiléia (João 12:21). Por causa disso, alguns eruditos têm imaginado a existência de duas Betsaidas, para justificar essa dificuldade, um antigo truque dos harmonistas. Plínio e Jerônimo dizem-nos que Betsaida ficava no lado oriental, o que fortaleceria o argumento dos harmonistas. A tradição localiza o sítio da multiplicação em 'Ain et-Tabighah, a dois quilômetros e meio a oeste de Cafarnaum, concordando com os evangelhos sinópticos. Portanto, há alguma coisa que não podemos compreender e harmonizar nos relatos. Se havia apenas uma Betsaida, então não podemos ter certeza de sua localização antiga, e nem de qualquer identificação moderna. As referências feitas por Josefo (ver *Anti.* xviii.2.1; e *Guerras* ii.9,1) situam a cidade no lado oriental do rio Jordão e ao norte do lago de

BETSAIDA DE GAULONITE — BEZA, THEODORE

Tiberíades. Em vista desses informes, é possível que a expressão «Betsaida da Galiléia», em João 12:21, seja uma expressão muito liberal, como designação geral, fazendo com que a Galiléia envolvesse a margem oriental do rio Jordão e o norte do lago de Tiberíades. Não obstante, a questão não se reveste de maior importância.

Após uma viagem na direção de Tiro e Sidom, Jesus retornou à Galiléia, onde curou o surdo-mudo, multiplicou pães para quatro mil homens, argumentou com os fariseus e chegou a Betsaida (Mar. 8:22). Curou um cego que lhe fora trazido da cidade, e em seguida, partiu para o norte, para Cesaréia de Filipe. Em Marcos 8:26, Jesus chamou Betsaida de «aldeia». Jesus não obteve grande sucesso em Betsaida, a despeito de seus diversos milagres na região (Mat. 11:21 ss; Luc. 10:13). Somos informados, em João 5:2, que Jesus curou um inválido à beira do tanque de Betesda (ver o artigo),— que, em alguns manuscritos latinos, bem como em certos manuscritos siríacos e etíopes é chamado de — tanque de Betsaida. Porém, melhor é a outra variante, Betesda. Ver o problema dessa variante e suas evidências, *in loc.*, no NTI. (EW KO SM)

BETSAIDA DE GAULONITE

A Betsaida mencionada em Marcos 8:22-26, de acordo com alguns estudiosos, tem sido identificada como a mesma Betsaida da Galiléia (ver o artigo). Outros eruditos, porém, pensam que se tratava de uma localidade diferente daquela, além de afirmarem que foi ali que ocorreu o milagre da multiplicação dos pães para os cinco mil homens e a cura do homem cego, na estrada para Cesaréia de Filipe. Originalmente, era uma pequena aldeia, mas o tetrarca Filipe adornou-a e deu-lhe o novo nome de Julias, em honra a Júlia, filha do imperador Augusto (Josefo, *Anti.* xviii.2.1). Filipe foi sepultado ali. Os árabes identificam-na com a moderna El Tel. Muitos estudiosos não vêem qualquer necessidade da postulação de duas cidades chamadas Betsaida; e a questão ainda não foi resolvida. (UN)

BETUEL

No hebraico, «residência de Deus» ou «residente em Deus». Era nome de um lugar e de um indivíduo, nas páginas do Antigo Testamento:

1. Uma cidade pertencente à tribo de Simeão (I Crô. 4:30). Essa forma do nome é preferida pelos eruditos, que supõem que o nome foi corrompido em sua forma variante, Betul (Jos. 19:4), ou em sua outra forma, Betel (I Sam. 30:27). Alguns estudiosos identificam-na com a Khirbet el-Qaryatein, uma ruína ao sul de Hebrom. (ALBA SP)

2. O último dos filhos de Naor, irmão de Abraão. Ele era o pai de Rebeca e de Labão (Gên. 22:22,23; 24:15,24,27; 25:20; 28:2,5). Os documentos da irmandade de Nuzu (tuppi ahatuti) explicam o importante papel desempenhado pelo irmão de Rebeca, Labão, no arranjo do casamento dela, junto ao servo de Isaque, papel esse que esperaríamos que fosse desempenhado por seu pai, Betuel. Josefo (*Anti.* I.16,2) provavelmente estava equivocado ao dizer que o pai de Rebeca estava morto na ocasião, e que, por isso, as negociações foram dirigidas por Labão, irmão da noiva.

BETÚLIA

No hebraico, «habitação de Yahweh». Uma aldeia mencionada somente no livro apócrifo de Judite (4:5; 7:1,3) e que, segundo parece, ficava perto da planície de Esdrelom, pelo lado sul, não longe de Dotaim. Essa cidade estava localizada de tal modo que o exército adversário, dirigido por Holofernes, foi impedido de penetrar na planície que levava diretamente à região montanhosa, bloqueando o acesso para a Judéia, por onde uma pessoa teria de subir a Jerusalém (Judite 4:6,7).

Essa cidade tem sido identificada com a Sheih Shibil, devido a descrição de sua localização. Do alto daquele lugar, cerca de 475 m acima do nível do mar, obtém-se uma ótima visão das colinas de Samaria e das planícies de Esdrelom. Ali foi sepultado o marido de Judite (Judite 8:3). É questão debatida se Betúlia é cidade real ou imaginária. Poderia ser um nome simbólico, porquanto o autor desse livro apócrifo estava descrevendo uma espécie de cidade ideal, fiel ao verdadeiro Deus em meio a terríveis ameaças. (SI)

BETUME

Há um termo hebraico, que aparece em Gên. 11:3; 14:10 e Êxo. 2:3, cognato da palavra egípcia e cópta, e que tem o sentido de «asfalto», «betume». No Oriente Médio, de 2500 A.C. em diante, tornou-se um artigo comerciável. Naturalmente, as ocorrências desse asfalto nativo aparecem na área da Síria-Palestina e em derredor. O material era usado para vedação e como argamassa. A tradução grega, na LXX, é *asfaltos*. Essa substância era tida pelos autores gregos, que frequentemente descreveram o mar Morto, como «limne asfálttitis», especialmente Deódoro Sículo 19.98; e Estrabão 7.5,8. Era material extremamente abundante ao sul do mar Morto, onde antes ficavam as cidades da planície (ver Gên. 18 — 19:29).

BEYSCHLAG, WILLIBALD

Nascido em 1823 e falecido em 1900. Foi um dos líderes da chamada *teologia medianeira*, que combatia tanto a ortodoxia rígida quanto o radicalismo, sobretudo quando se manifestava como ceticismo teológico. Ele também se mostrou atuante em prol da unidade da Igreja. Suas obras mais bem conhecidas são: *Life of Christ* e *New Testament Theology*. (E)

BEZA, THEODORE

Suas datas são 1519 e 1605. Foi amigo, biógrafo e sucessor de João Calvino. Foi líder e teólogo da Igreja Reformada. Vinha de uma próspera família da Burgúndia, na França, tendo sido tutorado por Melchior Womar no estudo dos clássicos, antes de ingressar na faculdade de direito de Orleães. Todavia, não se sentia feliz com a profissão de advogado, e apelou para a literatura. Mantinha benefícios eclesiásticos católicos romanos, mas havia-se casado secretamente, o que veio à luz em 1544. Uma enfermidade série levou-o à conversão a Cristo, e uniu-se à fé reformada, em 1548. Tornou-se professor de grego na academia dirigida por P. Viret, em Lausanne. Mas as condições ali ficaram difíceis, pelo que ele liderou uma migração de ministros e mestres para Genebra, onde se tornou professor de grego, em 1558. Calvino nomeou-o redator de uma recém-fundada academia, em 1559. Beza foi muito bem-sucedido ali, transformando a academia em lugar de erudição clássica e teológica, internacionalmente reconhecida. Envolveu-se também em várias funções políticas, quase sempre em defesa da causa da Reforma.

Calvino reconhecia nele um de seus mais habilidosos cooperadores, tendo empregado os seus talentos de negociador. Foi enviado ao rei Antônio, de Navarra, em Nérac, para obter a tolerância para os huguenotes (ver o artigo). Quando a guerra civil irrompeu, entre os huguenotes e os católicos da França, em 1562, ele acompanhou o príncipe de Condé como capelão, durante a guerra. E quando foi restaurada uma paz temporária, em 1563, ele retornou a Genebra, onde voltou aos seus deveres.

Quando Calvino faleceu, em 1564, Beza tornou-se uma das principais figuras políticas e religiosas em Genebra. Tornou-se então o principal teólogo da Igreja Reformada Suíça, passando a ser considerado a *verdadeira alma* da Academia de Genebra. Continuou representando a causa reformada em várias capacidades e lugares. Quando da conferência religiosa de Montplier, em 1586, Beza opôs-se à posição luterana dos teólogos de Wurtemberg. A primeira esposa de Beza faleceu em 1588 e ele casou-se, no ano seguinte, com Catarina del Plano, viúva de um cidadão de Genebra. Passou a ser assediado por calvinistas e luteranos apóstatas, bem como por padres jesuítas. Os jesuítas espalharam o rumor de que Beza falecera e retornara à Igreja de Roma antes de morrer. Isso foi ridicularizado por Beza, em um vigoroso poema. Francisco de Sales tentou muito convertê-lo de volta à Igreja de Roma, mas sem sucesso, para desapontamento do papa Clemente VIII. Beza faleceu em Genebra, a 13 de outubro de 1605.

Obras Principais. Confession of the Christian Faith; Life of Calvin; Ecclesiastical History of the Reformed Churches in France.

O nome de Beza está ligado ao manuscrito grego e latino do Novo Testamento, pertencente ao século VI D.C., chamado Códice D, que contém os evangelhos e o livro de Atos, e que foi apresentado por ele a Universidade de Cambridge, em 1581. Ver o artigo sobre os *Manuscritos*. (AM E C)

BEZAI

No hebraico, «vitória» ou «conquistador»; outros também lhe dão o sentido de «brilhante». Os descendentes de Bezai, em número de 323, estavam entre os que retornaram do exílio babilônico, em cerca de 536 A.C., sob Zorobabel (Esd. 2:17 e Nee. 7:23). Em Nee. 10:18, seu nome também aparece entre os signatários do pacto de Neemias.

BEZALEL

Nas páginas do Antigo Testamento há duas pessoas com esse nome, que, no hebraico, significa «na sombra de Deus», ou seja, sob a proteção divina:

1. Um famoso artífice, filho de Uri (Êxo. 3:30; 31:1-6), ao qual Yahweh encarregou da construção da arca, no deserto. A seu encargo estava todo o trabalho em metais, madeira e pedras, e ele atuou como supervisor geral da construção (Êxo. 31:1-5). Pertencia à tribo de Judá, descendente de Perez, através de Hezrom e Uri (I Crô. 2:5; 18:20). Além de sua habilidade como artífice, o Senhor também lhe deu o impulso de ensinar a sua arte a outros (Êxo. 35:34). Viveu em torno de 1490 A.C.

2. Um dos filhos de Paate-Moabe, um daqueles que se tinham casado com mulheres estrangeiras e foram obrigados a se divorciarem delas, terminado o exílio babilônico (Esd. 10:30), em cerca de 458 A.C.

BEZEQUE

No hebraico, «brecha», posto que alguns preferem «brilho». Era nome de dois lugares, nas páginas do Antigo Testamento:

1. Uma cidade, residência de Adoni-Bezeque (ver o artigo), pertencente a cananeus e ferezeus (Juí. 1:4,5). Tem sido tentativamente identificada com a Khirbet Bezaq, perto de Gezer.

2. Um lugar onde Saul numerou as forças de Judá e Israel, antes de sair em ajuda a Jabes-Gileade (I Sam. 11:8). Tem sido identificado com a Khirbet Ibziq, a oeste do rio Jordão e a sudoeste de Jabes-Gileade.

BEZER

No hebraico, «forte». Alguns pensam em «minério», de ouro ou de prata. No Antigo Testamento é nome de uma pessoa e de uma cidade:

1. Um filho de Zofa, da casa de Aser (I Crô. 7:37).

2. Uma cidade dos levitas, na região de Rúben (Jos. 21:36; I Crô. 6:78). Tornou-se uma das seis cidades de refúgio em Israel (Deu. 4:43; Jos. 20:8). De acordo com a pedra de Mesa, a cidade ficava situada no território de Moabe. Talvez fosse a mesma Bozra de Moabe, em distinção à Bozra de Edom. Segundo a LXX, em Jer. 48:24, aparece com o nome de Bosar. Foi uma das cidades fortificadas pelo rei Mesa, em cerca de 830 A.C., e talvez deva ser identificada com a moderna Umm el 'Amad, a nordeste de Medega e a leste do monte Nebo.

BEZERRO

Ver **Gado**.

BEZERRO DE OURO

No hebraico, «vitela fundida». Trata-se da imagem que Aarão fabricou, com as jóias que os judeus lhe entregaram, para o fabrico de uma estátua. Ver Êxo. 32; Deu. 9:16; Nee. 9:18; Sal. 106:19; Atos 7:41. Além disso, dois bezerros de ouro foram levantados por Jeroboão I (I Reis 12:28-33; II Reis 10:29; 17:16; Osé. 5:6). Os dois incidentes não tiveram relação mútua, embora ambos dissessem respeito à adoração ao touro, que Israel havia observado entre os egípcios. Ver o artigo sobre *Boi Ápis*.

1. *Êxodo 32 - O Caso de Aarão*. É por demais caridosa para com Aarão a suposição de que ele fabricou esse ídolo a fim de exibir a força de Yahweh, porque o touro (que vide) era símbolo de força para muitos povos antigos. Aarão simplesmente cedeu diante da pressão popular e resolveu agradar ao povo. Mas também é por demais severa a opinião de que Aarão fez isso de todo o coração, julgando que a estátua tivesse algum valor espiritual. Seja como for, encontramos um violento contraste: Moisés estava no monte, recebendo de Yahweh os Dez Mandamentos. Mas Aarão, no sopé do monte, fazia um bezerro de ouro. O quinto versículo parece mostrar que Aarão, de algum modo, procurou justificar o feito, como se o mesmo estivesse relacionado à adoração a Yahweh. Moisés, porém, demonstrou melhor bom senso, deixando claro a enormidade do erro e fazendo o povo *ingerir* o bezerro de ouro, o qual foi moído até tornar-se pó e dissolvido na água (vs. 20). Os levitas, por ordem do Senhor, tiraram a vida a três mil pessoas (vs. 27 *ss*), e a praga que veio em seguida causou ainda pior matança (vs. 35). Esse incidente ilustrou graficamente a seriedade do pecado de idolatria, como também a estupidez dos líderes

espirituais quando concordaram com essa prática.

2. *I Reis 12:26-33 — O Caso de Jeroboão I*. Tendo rompido com Judá e com a adoração em Jerusalém, Jeroboão instituiu dois santuários, um em Betel e outro em Dã. Talvez a fim de imitar os querubins do templo de Salomão, ele levantou dois bezerros de ouro, supondo que Yahweh haveria de manifestar a sua presença entre eles. Alguns estudiosos pensam que os bezerros visavam representar Yahweh diretamente, visto que, no Egito, era comum representar as divindades sob a figura de um touro. Alguns outros têm negado enfaticamente esse ponto, procurando mostrar que essa não era uma prática conhecida entre os povos da Síria e da Palestina, mas muitas coisas podem ter ocorrido naqueles dias sobre as quais nossa arqueologia nada sabe. O relato, mui provavelmente, não deveria ser compreendido como uma tentativa, por parte do rei de Israel, de instituir uma nova religião, e sim, de mostrar que ele foi culpado de corrupção proposital, não sendo inocente em nenhum sentido. Ver I Reis 12:28, que demonstra isso sem a menor sombra de dúvida. Jeroboão disse ao povo: «Basta de subirdes a Jerusalém; vês aqui teus deuses, ó Israel, que te fizeram subir da terra do Egito!»

Os querubins (esfinges aladas), no templo de Jerusalém, não levavam à idolatria, antes de tudo, porque eram representações de poderes espirituais, e não terrenos; e, em segundo lugar, porque não tinham paralelo nas religiões pagãs dos países vizinhos, o que poderia ter corrompido os israelitas por motivo de associação. A idolatria, na moderna Igreja cristã, é algo inteiramente descabido e incompreensível, considerando o enfático ensino bíblico a respeito, bem como a verdadeira adoração. Consideremos a declaração de Salmos 106:19-21: «Em Horebe fizeram um bezerro e adoraram o ídolo fundido. E assim trocaram a glória de Deus pelo simulacro de um novilho que come erva. Esqueceram-se de Deus, seu Salvador, que, no Egito, fizera cousas portentosas». (ALB GORD)

BHAGAVAD-GITA

Esse nome vem do sânscrito e significa «Cântico dos Benditos». É o título de um poema filosófico, no sexto livro do *Mahabharata*, um poema épico- que supostamente data do século IV A.C. Trata-se de um diálogo entre Arjuna e o deus Khrishna, que atua ali como o condutor da carruagem de Arjuna. Arjuna estava dirigindo sua família em um ataque contra uma outra família, hostil, e o diálogo acompanha as ações. Envolve principalmente problemas éticos.

Temas Principais: 1. Amor a Deus, expresso através de conhecimento, devoção e estrita atenção aos próprios deveres. 2. Essa vereda conduz à salvação ou Nirvana (ver o artigo). 3. A vereda do dever, que expressa amor e devoção, é a vereda superior, embora também haja outras veredas que levam à salvação. Na realidade, o poema é eclético, expondo muitos pontos de vista religiosos. É ali mencionado o caminho do conhecimento, o caminho do trabalho, o caminho das experiências místicas e o caminho do amor. Esses vários caminhos ajudariam o homem a ir-se libertando do «ego» e do que é material. A ênfase maior da obra recai sobre o caminho da fé ou devoção (Bhakti), mas o caminho que cada indivíduo toma depende muito das disposições pessoais e dos dotes de cada um. Naturalmente, um homem bom pode misturar métodos, ao mesmo tempo em que ressalta um deles. 4. As formas do divino são duas: *Brahman*, o conceito impessoal e absoluto de Deus, e *Krishna*, a encarnação pessoal da divindade. 5. A alma não é capaz de nascer e nem de morrer, porquanto é *eterna*. 6. Uma vez liberada de suas existências terrenas, prosseguem em sua individualidade na presença de Deus e em unidade com ele. Mas, se a salvação é encarada como a absorção pelo absoluto impessoal, então isso implica na perda da individualidade. Não obstante, a individualidade que se pede pode ser interpretada como o tipo de individualidade que atualmente conhecemos, ao passo que a individualidade que está em foco é a participação na divina consciência universal, a qual será retida. Assim, na salvação, segundo esse ponto de vista religioso oriental, a alma pode se comunicar com a *Mente Divina*, participando individualmente na essência do *Ser Absoluto*. Esses pontos têm sido debatidos, e diversas conclusões a respeito são atingidas por diferentes teólogos. 7. A doutrina de Deus assume diversas formas.

Essa obra é o livro de devoção mais popular e mais largamente distribuído na Índia, sendo a fonte principal da religião hindu. Esse é um dos três livros canônicos básicos do hinduísmo. Os outros são as *Upanishadas* e o *Brahamasutras* (vide). Há interpretações antigas e modernas a respeito. (AM P SMIT)

BHAIRAVA

No hinduísmo, um dos nomes de Shiva (ver o artigo). O nome significa «temível». Esse é o nome do terceiro membro da trindade hindu. Uma dúzia de formas desse Bhairava-Shiva manifesta-se de vários modos, cada um com um título diferente. (P)

BHAKTI

Vem do sânscrito. Significa «adorar». Esse é o nome dado ao caminho da devoção, segundo o hinduísmo (ver o artigo geral). Os três bem conhecidos caminhos da tradição religiosa hindu, que supostamente levam à união mística com Deus são o caminho das obras (Karma yoga), o caminho do conhecimento (Jnana yoga) e o caminho do amor (Bhakti yoga). Esse último nome é dado às seitas hindus que enfatizam a fé devocional como meio de se atingir a salvação ou o *Nirvana* (que vide). Qualquer pessoa supostamente pode aplicar todos esses métodos de realização, embora usualmente enfatize algum deles mais do que os demais. O hinduísmo bishnuita é aquela seita que mais salienta o caminho *Bhakti* da salvação, contando com várias centenas de milhões de aderentes. Ver o artigo sobre a *yoga* e seus caminhos. A mais recente das yogas é a Hatha Yoga, alicerçada sobre uma fantástica teoria fisiológica, que ensina a existência de uma potência divina dormente em cada pessoa, na base de sua espinha dorsal. Referimo-nos aqui à questão porque a Hatha Yoga, ou «caminho da força», tem-se tornado famosa por todo o mundo, havendo quem a pratique visando apenas supostos benefícios orgânicos e longevidade, embora o sistema se proponha ser um dos caminhos da salvação do hinduísmo. A Hatha Yoga é pouco mais antiga que a invasão islâmica na Índia (712 D.C.). Cada um desses caminhos tem o propósito declarado de permitir que um homem fuja do mundo da matéria, assim liberando sua alma da necessidade de voltar à existência terrena, em um ciclo repetitivo. A extinção é o grande alvo desses caminhos. Mas, segundo o hinduísmo, seria a derrota do egoísmo a fim de ser atingido o superego, no qual o indivíduo é absorvido, e deixa de existir. (P)

BIATAS
Ver **Pelaias**.

BÍBLIA
— Ver os artigos sobre *Antigo Testamento*, *Novo Testamento* e o tratamento sobre a *Bíblia* abaixo.
A Bíblia como *literatura*. Ver o artigo, *Literatura, A Bíblia como*.

BÍBLIA
Há um certo número de artigos, nesta Enciclopédia, diretamente relacionados à Bíblia, mas que são apresentados em separado, sob outros títulos. Ver os seguintes:
Arqueologia
Autoridade
Bíblia, Versões da
Bíblia, Implicações Éticas
Bíblia em Português
Cânon do Antigo e do Novo Testamentos
Antigo Testamento
Crítica da Bíblia
Dicionários Bíblicos
Exegese Bíblica
Historiografia Bíblica
Inspiração das Escrituras
Língua do Antigo Testamento
Língua do Novo Testamento
Livros Apócrifos, Antigo e Novo Testamentos
Introdução da Bíblia
Manuscritos, Antigo e Novo Testamentos
Novo Testamento
Pseudepígrafos, Antigo e Novo Testamentos
Teologia Bíblica

Esboço
1. Os Termos
2. As Designações Antigo e Novo Testamentos
3. A Coletânea
4. A Unidade da Coletânea
5. Línguas
6. Divisões
7. Usos da Bíblia

1. Os Termos
A palavra portuguesa Bíblia vem do grego, **biblia**, que é o plural de *bíblion*, «livro». Portanto, significa «livros». Essa palavra deriva-se originalmente da cidade fenícia de Biblos (no Antigo Testamento, Gebal), que era um dos antigos e importantes centros produtores de papiro, o papel antigo. Com o tempo, esse vocábulo terminou sendo usado para designar as Sagradas Escrituras. A palavra grega *bíblos* significa um livro, um escrito qualquer, podendo mesmo servido para indicar o livro da vida, como se vê em Apo. 3:5, isto é, um livro sagrado. Estritamente falando, *bíblos* era um livro, e *bíblion* era um livrinho.

A palavra *Bíblia*, mediante um desenvolvimento histórico divinamente dirigido, segundo cremos, veio a designar o Livro dos livros, as Escrituras Sagradas, compostas do Antigo e do Novo Testamentos, a principal fonte de ensinamentos religiosos e éticos de nossa civilização.

Por volta do século II D.C., os cristãos gregos já chamavam suas Escrituras Sagradas de *ta Bíblia*, ou seja, «os Livros». Quando esse título foi então transferido para a versão latina, foi traduzido no singular, dando a entender que «o Livro» é a Bíblia. Nos livros apócrifos do Antigo Testamento, a versão LXX usa o termo grego *bibloi*, «livros», indicando os escritos sagrados. Ver também I Macabeus 12:9. Em I Macabeus 1:57, encontramos os livros do pacto. No prólogo do livro de Eclesiástico, as Escrituras são chamadas de a lei, os profetas e outros livros (*bíblia*). No Novo Testamento encontramos o vocábulo «Escrituras», empregado para indicar o Antigo Testamento (Mat. 21:42; Mar. 14:49; Rom. 15:4), ou «Sagradas Escrituras» (Rom. 1:2), ou «a lei e os profetas» (Mat. 5:17), ou «lei» (João 10:34), ou «os oráculos de Deus» (Rom. 3:2).

2. As Designações Antigo e Novo Testamentos
Essas expressões vêm sendo usadas desde os fins do século II D.C., para distinguir entre as Escrituras judaicas e as Escrituras cristãs. Alguns preferem a palavra «pacto» (no grego, *diatheke*), — em vez de «testamento». Todavia, tornou-se generalizado o uso da palavra «testamento». Visto que os pactos dependem da morte do testador (Heb. 9:1-8,16,17; 10:19-22, especialmente 9:16,17), os dois grandes pactos das Escrituras na realidade são testamentos. Ver o artigo geral sobre os pactos que fazem parte integrante do grande Pacto entre Deus e o homem. Quanto a uma completa discussão sobre o termo «pacto», onde se discute se o mesmo é melhor ou não que o termo «testamento», ver as discussões em Heb. 9:16-18, no NT. A palavra «testamento» entrou em uso por haver sido a tradução adotada na versão latina para o vocábulo grego *diatheke*. Daí por diante, o termo passou para muitos idiomas modernos. A palavra hebraica correspondente é *berit*, que foi traduzida por *diatheke*, tanto na LXX como, mais tarde, no Novo Testamento.

3. A Coletânea
A Bíblia é uma coletânea de sessenta e seis livros: 39 no Antigo e 27 no Novo Testamento. Foram reunidos em um só volume através do processo da canonização. Ver o artigo sobre o *cânon*, quanto a plenos detalhes sobre a questão. A LXX (tradução completada cerca de duzentos anos antes da era cristã, das Escrituras judaicas para o grego) conta com catorze livros adicionais, chamados *livros apócrifos* (ver o artigo), os quais foram aceitos pela Igreja Católica Romana como parte integrante de sua Bíblia oficial, no Antigo Testamento, por ocasião do concílio de Trento (1545-1563), com a exceção de I e II Esdras e a Oração de Manassés.

O processo de canonização precisou de vários séculos para terminar. Várias autoridades antigas rejeitavam livros que atualmente aceitamos. Apesar disso, podemos estar certos de que o processo histórico estava sendo controlado pelo Espírito de Deus, de tal modo que a coletânea que possuímos é autoridade espiritual genuína, devendo ser tratada como tal, mesmo quando a nossa idéia de autoridade (ver o artigo) inclua mais do que documentos escritos em qualquer número.

4. A Unidade da Coletânea
A Bíblia, naturalmente, é muito mais heterogênea do que muitas pessoas querem admitir. Alguns chegam a pensar que a reunião do Antigo e do Novo Testamentos, em um único volume, é uma perversão; mas tal opinião é exagerada. Não obstante, precisamos reconhecer que a natureza absolutamente homogênea da Bíblia, que é defendida por aqueles que têm a Bíblia como sua única regra de fé e de prática, é um conceito imposto à coletânea sagrada pela interpretação de indivíduos ou denominações. Disso resulta que se o indivíduo ou sua denominação encontram na Bíblia algum ensino com o qual não concordam, o ensino bíblico termina sendo distorcido, para concordar com os padrões denominacionais.

BÍBLIA

O primeiro problema a ser enfrentado é a rejeição de certas porções do Antigo Testamento pelo Novo Testamento. Muitas das instituições religiosas do povo israelita, como o sistema de sacrifícios, a tentativa de justificação mediante a observância da lei, etc., foram suplantadas por novos conceitos, que figuram no Novo Testamento. Se não houvesse notáveis diferenças entre o antigo e o novo pactos, Paulo não teria sido perseguido e nem teria sido reputado um herege. Não podemos ocultar as diferenças. Podemos tentar explicar, dizendo que Deus guiava o processo, e que o antigo pacto mesclou-se com o novo, em uma evolução histórico teológica. Mas declarações como essa não explicam as grandes diferenças entre os dois testamentos. Na verdade, a *mudança* faz parte da essência ou mecanismo do nosso crescimento teológico. Sem tal mudança, jamais avançaríamos em nosso conhecimento sobre as realidades divinas. Por conseguinte, onde houver mudança e transformação, esperamos também encontrar desenvolvimento, *crescimento*.

As pessoas que se opõem às mudanças, com base em dogmas supostamente imutáveis, também se opõem ao crescimento. Nada há de errado no fato de que o Novo Testamento incorpora algumas mudanças radicais de conceito. — Isso pode suceder e, realmente, sucederá novamente, quando nosso conhecimento de Deus passar para um nível superior. Algum dia, não sabemos quando, outras revelações nos serão confiadas, que suplantarão muito daquilo que o Novo Testamento diz — embora outras coisas sejam permanentes — da mesma maneira que o Novo Testamento suplantou o Antigo Testamento. Talvez isso venha a ocorrer quando Israel tornar-se a cabeça das nações, e nosso sistema mundial tornar-se coisa do passado, quando estivermos vivendo na era do milênio. Uma das coisas que as Escrituras predizem acerca do milênio é que a lei de Deus será observada com um rigor como nem mesmo no antigo Israel se viu qualquer coisa similar. (Ver Isa. 51:4,5). Isso não representará um retrocesso, mas sim, um avanço. O milênio será uma excelente ocasião para novas revelações, embora eu diga isso especulativamente, e pense que tal especulação é razoável.

Naturalmente, mesmo em nossos dias alguns afirmam já ter recebido novas revelações, como os mórmons e os espíritas. Este artigo não pretende ventilar tal questão. Ver os artigos específicos sobre esses grupos, e também sobre os *Modernos Livros Apócrifos*.

No próprio Novo Testamento não encontramos uma **única teologia**, sempre no mesmo nível de revelação e sempre congruente. Consideremos o livro de Tiago, lado a lado com a epístola paulina aos Gálatas! Sem dúvida, de um para o outro, houve evolução na exposição da verdade divina. Mas isso não nos choca, quando levamos em conta a controvérsia que houve na Igreja primitiva, —que é refletida no décimo quinto capítulo de Atos. Por assim dizer, Tiago representava a facção legalista da Igreja, ainda sem se haver desmamado inteiramente da sinagoga, ao passo que Paulo é representante de uma nova onda de pensamento, que já se afastava radicalmente das idéias judaicas. No entanto, as idéias expostas por ambos encontram-se, lado a lado, no Novo Testamento.

A epístola a Tiago foi um dos livros disputados nos primeiros séculos da Igreja cristã, exatamente em face de sua divergência em relação a Paulo. Interpretações modernas podem tentar fazê-los dizer uma mesma coisa, mas a harmonização forçada visa muito mais o nosso conforto mental. Todavia, a fé robusta não precisa de harmonização completa entre todos os escritores sagrados. Às vezes eles estavam tratando de questões multifacetadas, sem qualquer tentativa de combinar suas idéias com as de outros escritores sagrados. Por essas razões, a fé pode florescer mesmo em meio a divergências, mistérios e controvérsias. Além disso, se há pontos duvidosos nos livros que foram rejeitados como parte integrante do Novo Testamento, não sou forçado a seguir tudo o que esses livros dizem, somente porque neles há coisas que me podem ser de proveito. É mesmo possível que o Espírito do Senhor tenha permitido essa diversidade, dentro de nossos documentos sagrados, com o propósito de alertar-nos para o fato de que, no estágio espiritual em que nos achamos, sempre nos veremos às voltas com divergências e questões teológicas não resolvidas. Isso equivale a dizer que ainda somos crianças espirituais, que ainda estamos mexendo com conceitos simples, que de modo algum esgotam *toda* a verdade divina. Há mistérios que Deus ainda não revelou. Isso vem sendo dito desde o Antigo Testamento: «As cousas encobertas pertencem ao Senhor nosso Deus; porém, as reveladas pertencem a nós e a nossos filhos para sempre...» (Deu. 29:29).

Certamente a teologia não é simples e fácil. É fácil distorcer o que o Espírito nos diz nas Escrituras. Pedro adverte-nos acerca disso, II Ped. 3:15-18. Portanto, concluo que a coletânea sagrada, embora não sejamos capazes de harmonizar cada particular com o resto, serve de seguro guia espiritual. Afinal, é a única revelação em forma escrita que temos da parte de Deus! Atrevo-me mesmo a dizer que as dificuldades são pseudodificuldades, motivadas pelo fato de que ainda estamos na fase da mamadeira, espiritualmente falando. Apesar disso, quando da formação do cânon, aquilo que entrava em divergência patente com o ensino bíblico, foi sendo rejeitado, e, em nossas mãos, restou uma coletânea de livros fidedignos.

A maior parte dos livros apócrifos do Novo Testamento envolve os primeiros escritos gnósticos. O gnosticismo foi um formidável adversário do cristianismo primitivo. Há livros inteiros escritos para combatê-lo (Gálatas, Colossenses, I João, etc.). Se o gnosticismo tivesse ganho na disputa, o cristianismo ter-se-ia transformado em mais uma das religiões misteriosas da cultura grego-romana. Ver o artigo sobre o *gnosticismo*. Mas, a despeito de algumas divergências e pontos obscuros, há uma espécie de unidade geral que vincula entre si o Antigo e o Novo Testamentos, bem como os elementos heterogêneos do próprio Novo Testamento. O Espírito de Cristo transparece em meio a tudo, o que podemos divisar no desenvolvimento histórico-teológico que nos está conduzindo cada vez mais para perto de Deus. Nessa conexão, é significativo o fato de que tanto o Antigo quanto o Novo Testamentos foram produzidos pela fé dos hebreus, em estágios distintos de crescimento, embora haja alguma mistura com idéias helenistas, o que já ocorria no próprio judaísmo do começo da era cristã. Para exemplificar o que dizemos basta-nos pensar nos muitos temas doutrinários comuns. Também há uma ética comum, embora a ética do Novo Testamento seja mais profunda e espiritualizada que a do Antigo Testamento, pois, no novo pacto leva-se mais em conta o motivo por detrás das ações, e não apenas os atos externalizados. Um laço de união é a esperança messiânica, forte tanto no Antigo quanto no Novo Testamentos. Não fora Cristo a figura central da Bíblia! Por isso mesmo, há muitíssimas citações diretas e alusões do Antigo Testamento no Novo. Westcott e Hort, em seu Novo Testamento Grego,

BÍBLIA

encontraram nada menos de cerca de 980 citações diretas (360 só no Apocalipse), algumas das quais combinando duas ou três passagens do Antigo Testamento! As alusões são simplesmente incontáveis. Ver o artigo sobre *Citações do Antigo Testamento no Novo Testamento*. Ver o artigo separado sobre *Teologia Bíblica*, que também ilustra a unidade da coletânea sagrada, do ponto de vista doutrinário.

5. Línguas

Nesta Enciclopédia há artigos separados para os idiomas em que foram escritos o Antigo e o Novo Testamentos. Portanto, aqui expomos uma breve declaração. O Antigo Testamento foi escrito em hebraico, exceituando-se unicamente os trechos de Dan. 2:4 — 7:28; Esd. 4:8-6:18; 7:12-26 e Jer. 10:11, que foram escritos em aramaico. O aramaico era um dialeto semita que os israelitas adquiriram como seu idioma quando estavam no exílio, e que gradualmente foi suplantando o hebraico. Por causa de algumas poucas citações em aramaico, postas nos lábios de Jesus, sabemos que ele falava o aramaico como seu idioma natural. O hebraico antigo (clássico) era um dialeto cananeu, bem próximo do fenício e do ugarítico. (Ver o artigo sobre o *Alfabeto*, que nos fornece discernimento quanto à relação entre o hebraico e línguas semíticas cognatas. Ver também sobre o *hebraico*).

O Novo Testamento foi integralmente escrito em grego, exceituando-se algumas expressões usadas por Jesus e por Paulo. Algumas poucas autoridades opinam que os evangelhos sinópticos tinham um original em aramaico, mas tal idéia é rejeitada pela vasta maioria dos especialistas. Naturalmente, há até mesmo expressões hebreu-aramaicas (*hebraísmos*), — incluídas no texto do Novo Testamento. O grego do Novo Testamento é, essencialmente, a linguagem comum que se falava por todo o império romano como língua franca, chamada grego «koiné» (comum). Esse foi o tipo de grego propagado pelas tropas de Alexandre o Grande, durante suas conquistas, e foi herdado pelo império romano. O latim (língua do Lácio, a região em redor da capital, Roma) só conseguiu suplantar o grego, no imenso império romano, no século IV D.C. Todavia, a linguagem do Novo Testamento sofreu influências do grego do período anterior, através da Septuaginta (LXX), que é a tradução do Antigo Testamento hebraico para o grego, terminada cerca de duzentos anos antes da era cristã, além de ter sofrido influências do pano de fundo hebreu.

6. Divisões

Entre os judeus, o Antigo Testamento era dividido como segue: a. a Lei (Torah) — os primeiros cinco livros, também chamados, coletivamente, de Pentateuco; b. os Profetas (quatro anteriores: Josué, Juízes, Samuel e Reis); (três posteriores: Isaías, Jeremias e Ezequiel); (os doze: Oséias, Joel, Amós, Obadias, Jonas, Miquéias, Naum, Habacuque, Sofonias, Ageu, Zacarias e Malaquias). Os três livros mais extensos, Isaías, Jeremias e Ezequiel são chamados de *profetas maiores*, nos comentários bíblicos modernos, enquanto que os demais livros proféticos são chamados de *profetas menores*, meramente em vista da quantidade de material que eles contêm — e não porque sejam menos importantes do que os outros. c. Os escritos (Kethumbim), que são os livros poéticos: Salmos, Provérbios e Jó; e d. os Rolos: Cantares, Rute, Lamentações, Eclesiastes, Ester e Daniel. Nas edições modernas, os livros de Samuel, Reis e Crônicas são divididos em I e II, cada um.

O *Novo Testamento* é o mesmo, no cânon protestante e no cânon católico. Os livros antigamente disputados (sobre os quais várias antigas autoridades do cristianismo tinham dúvidas), como Hebreus, Tiago, II Pedro, II e III João, Judas e Apocalipse, desde o século IV D.C. foram universalmente ou quase universalmente aceitos. Os mesmos nossos vinte e sete livros do Novo Testamento nem sempre eram arrumados na mesma ordem em que aparecem em nossas Bíblias. Assim, os evangelhos, o livro de Atos, as epístolas católicas (ou universais) e o Apocalipse eram escritos em separado. Poucos manuscritos antigos continham todos os nossos vinte e sete livros.

7. Usos da Bíblia

a. Como Literatura. Os dois testamentos constituem um dos mais importantes documentos da humanidade, totalmente à parte de seu uso teológico, porque ali encontramos tesouros preciosíssimos de história, poesia e expressão devocional. Muitas universidades, ao redor do mundo, oferecem cursos de Bíblia somente do ponto de vista literário. Visto que a Bíblia é um dos alicerces da nossa moderna civilização ocidental, uma pessoa realmente educada não pode ignorar a Bíblia, ao menos como literatura. Onde fiz especialização, pós-graduada nos clássicos e em filosofia, havia um professor de filosofia contratado para ensinar assuntos relativos ao Novo Testamento, sob o ponto de vista filosófico, em face da tremenda influência que esse documento tem exercido sobre a história das idéias humanas. Algumas das traduções da Bíblia têm exercido notável influência sobre os idiomas para os quais as Escrituras foram traduzidas. A Bíblia traduzida para o alemão por Lutero padronizou os dialetos germânicos da Alemanha e produziu o alemão moderno. Também não se pode subestimar a influência da *King James Version* da Bíblia sobre o idioma inglês. A Bíblia encerra trechos de esplêndido drama, poesia, prosa histórica, filosofia, teologia e ensinamentos éticos e morais. As composições epistolares de Paulo têm poucos paralelos tão excelentes na literatura mundial.

b. Uso particular. A Bíblia é usada para dar instruções quanto à ética, a doutrina cristã, a doutrina judaica, a história (inclusive como guia das descobertas arqueológicas), e como fonte de consolo pessoal, por muitos milhões de pessoas, inteiramente à parte de escolas e igrejas. Na antiguidade, bem poucas pessoas sabiam ler, além do que os manuscritos eram raros, confinados a bibliotecas, mosteiros e igrejas. Com a invenção da imprensa, tornou-se possível o uso particular das Escrituras. Não demorou muito para que as crianças de alguns lares soubessem mais a respeito da Bíblia do que muitos padres. Os evangélicos sempre se mostraram muito dados ao estudo particular das Escrituras. A Igreja Católica Romana limitava essa prática de forma drástica, temendo interpretações particulares que debilitassem a autoridade da Sé de Roma. De fato, em muitos lugares, o estudo particular da Bíblia tem sido proibido por Roma. É possível que esse tenha sido o pior erro do catolicismo romano, que tem produzido a ignorância quase total das Escrituras pelas massas católicas. As autoridades religiosas que assim prescrevem a Bíblia dos lares e das mãos de particulares devem ser responsabilizadas, pois as pessoas são adultas, não devendo ser tratadas como menores, incapazes de chegarem a conclusões próprias sobre uma questão tão importante quanto é o eterno bem-estar da alma. — Todavia, o Segundo Concílio do Vaticano alterou bastante a situação e as idéias dos católicos romanos a esse respeito. A posição

BÍBLIA — BIBLIA EM PORTUGUÊS

rígida, assumida quando do Concílio de Trento, contra o exame particular das Escrituras (ver *Trento, Concílio de*), foi abrandada. Atualmente, muitos segmentos da Igreja Católica Romana promovem o estudo da Bíblia, nas igrejas e nos lares. Isso só poderá resultar em grande benefício para os milhões de pessoas envolvidas.

c. Uso Litúrgico. No judaísmo, a leitura das Escrituras, nas sinagogas e em público, era um costume generalizado. Sabemos que nos primeiros séculos do cristianismo havia um lecionário para três anos, que cobria todo o Antigo Testamento. Isso significa que o volume do Antigo Testamento era dividido de tal maneira que podia ser lido publicamente, para a congregação judaica em geral, naquele período de tempo. Um lecionário era uma seção das Escrituras, para ser lida publicamente. Visto que poucas pessoas sabiam ler, e visto que poucos eram os manuscritos existentes, o conhecimento das Escrituras precisava ser divulgado mediante leituras públicas ou mediante o aprendizado particular. Todavia, não sabemos dizer qual era a prática seguida pela primitiva Igreja cristã, embora possamos ter a certeza de que se aproximava da prática judaica, incluindo trechos tanto do Antigo quanto do Novo Testamentos. Com a passagem dos séculos, surgiram os lecionários do Novo Testamento. Aqueles que chegaram até nós pertencem ao século IX D.C. Mas alguns deles contêm textos de grande antiguidade, embora tivessem sido escritos em séculos posteriores; e isso indica que a prática do uso do lecionário mui provavelmente é antiquíssima entre os cristãos. O texto do Novo Testamento Grego da *United Bible Societies* contém evidências de mais de cem desses manuscritos. As citações que aparecem nas obras dos primeiros pais da Igreja mostram que a leitura pública de um livro servia de sinal de sua aceitação como livro autoritário entre os cristãos. Outros livros de cunho religioso, que os antigos julgavam dotados de valor, eram lidos em estudos individuais, particulares. Uma dessas obras chamava-se Pastor de Hermas. Na Idade Média, parece que diminuiu sensivelmente a prática da leitura pública das Escrituras, exatamente por haver sido uma era de profundo obscurantismo, quando a prepotência papal chegou ao auge. A Renascença, iniciada no século XV, e a Reforma protestante do século XVI reacenderam a prática nobre do estudo da Bíblia, embora não por intermédio dos lecionários. Somente na Igreja Católica Romana são lidos sempre os mesmos trechos criteriosamente selecionados durante a missa, destacados dentre a Bíblia. Os evangélicos preferem ter a Bíblia em casa, folheando-a à vontade, de Gênesis ao Apocalipse.

d. Uso Teológico. A Bíblia sempre foi a principal fonte de informes teológicos, tanto no judaísmo quanto no cristianismo. Uma abundante literatura, sob a forma de comentários, teologias e estudos de tópicos tem ajudado na promoção da *teologia bíblica* (ver o artigo). Alguns supõem, erroneamente, em minha opinião, que a Bíblia precisa ser a única fonte de todas as nossas idéias teológicas. Outros, mais corretamente, dão lugar a outras fontes informativas, na consciência de que nenhum livro ou coletânea de livros pode conter tudo aquilo que Deus sabe e nos comunica. Os apóstolos não citaram exclusivamente as Escrituras do Antigo Testamento, a fim de alicerçarem ou ilustrarem alguma doutrina. Citaram tanto dos chamados livros apócrifos quanto até mesmo da literatura profana, quando isso servia para ressaltar algum ponto doutrinário. Seja como for, todos os cristãos reconhecem a absoluta necessidade de um sólido conhecimento bíblico, se tivermos de organizar qualquer sistema de teologia que mereça o nome. Isso se alicerça sob a fé de que a Bíblia nos foi dada mediante inspiração divina e que ela não é apenas mais um livro entre tantos. Ver o artigo sobre *Autoridade*, que inclui a noção de autoridade bíblica. Em qualquer debate teológico cristão, a Bíblia permanece como obra central, porquanto é o padrão da doutrina revelada; contudo, não nos devemos tornar culpados de *bibliolatria* (ver o artigo), dando à Bíblia um lugar que pertence exclusivamente a Deus.

e. Uso Ético. Os hebreus destacavam-se como homens preocupados com o que era certo e com o que era errado. Estavam dispostos a sacrificar tudo nessa inquirição, sentindo-se na contínua obrigação de agradar a Deus em tudo. Dentro da história da humanidade, os hebreus foram praticamente a única nação que, como uma comunidade, estava interessada na revelação divina. Pode-se dizer que a nação de Israel era uma sociedade religiosa. Toda a cultura judaica alicerçava-se sobre a fé e a prática religiosas. Na sociedade grega, em contraste com isso, encontramos alguns poucos filósofos e legisladores preocupados e pesadamente envolvidos com as questões éticas. Todos os aspectos da vida dos hebreus eram controlados pelos preceitos da lei mosaica. O Novo Testamento aprimorou muitos dos conceitos emitidos pelo Antigo Testamento, incluindo a questão fundamental da motivação e tendo feito da lei do amor um princípio de aplicação universal no campo da ética. A Igreja herdou de Israel esse profundo respeito pelas Escrituras. (AM B IB C E GRE GT H ME)

BÍBLIA, Comentários e Dicionários. Ver estes títulos.

BÍBLIA como Literatura. Ver *Literatura, a Bíblia como*.

BÍBLIA, Crítica da. Ver *Crítica da Bíblia*.

BÍBLIA EM PORTUGUÊS (História da)

Esboço

1. Anos de Preparação
2. Tradução da Bíblia Completa
   a. Almeida
   b. Figueiredo
   c. Rodhen
   d. Soares
   e. Brasileira
   f. Revisão de Almeida
   g. Revisão de Almeida (*Imprensa Bíblica Brasileira*)
   h. A Bíblia na Linguagem de Hoje (*Novo Testamento*)
3. A Bíblia e Os Meios de Desenvolvimento Espiritual
4. Bibliografia
5. Diagrama de Ilustração

1. Anos de Preparação

a. *O rei de Portugal.* D. Diniz (1279-1325) traduziu os vinte primeiros capítulos do livro de Gênesis usando a Vulgata Latina como base. Pode-se ver que o começo da tradução da Bíblia em português ocorreu antes da tradução da Bíblia para o inglês, por João Wycliff.

b. *O rei D. João I* (1385-1433) ordenou a tradução dos evangelhos, do livro de Atos e das epístolas de Paulo. Essa obra foi realizada por «padres» católicos, que se utilizaram da Vulgata Latina como base. Desses esforços resultou uma publicação que incluía os livros mencionados e o livro de Salmos do V.T.,

BÍBLIA EM PORTUGUÊS

traduzido pelo próprio rei.

c. *Nos anos seguintes* foram preparadas diversas traduções de porções bíblicas como os evangelhos, traduzidos do francês pela infanta Dona Filipa, filha do infante D. Pedro e neto do rei D. João I; o evangelho de Mateus e porções dos demais evangelhos, pelo frei cisterciense Bernardo de Alcobaça, que se baseou na Vulgata Latina. Este último trabalho foi publicado em Lisboa, no século XV. Valentim Fernandes publicou uma harmonia dos evangelhos, em 1495. Nesse mesmo ano foi publicada uma tradução das epístolas e dos evangelhos, feita pelo jurista Gonçalo Garcia de Santa Maria. Por ordem da rainha Leonora, dez anos mais tarde, eram traduzidos e publicados o livro de Atos e as epístolas gerais.

2. Tradução da Bíblia Completa

a. *Tradução de João Ferreira de Almeida*

Nasceu João Ferreira de Almeida em Torre de Tavares, Portugal, em 1628. Ao realizar sua obra de tradutor era pastor protestante. Aprendeu o hebraico e o grego e assim usou os mss dessas línguas como base de sua tradução, ao contrário dos outros tradutores mencionados acima, que sempre se utilizavam da Vulgata Latina como base. Todavia, aqueles que conhecem os mss, sabem que um bom texto da Vulgata Latina (a despeito das desvantagens de usar latim em vez de grego), é superior aos mss do Textus Receptus, como representante do texto original. O Textus Receptus serviu de base para a primeira tradução de Almeida. O Textus Receptus representa os mss do grupo *bizantino*, o mais fraco e mais recente entre os mss gregos. A Vulgata Latina representa o grupo de mss que se intitula «ocidental», que é superior ao «bizantino». Almeida traduziu em primeiro lugar o N.T., publicando-o em 1681, em Amsterdã na Holanda. O seu título foi: "O Novo Testamento, Isto he o Novo Concerto de Nosso Fiel Senhor e Redemptor Jesu Christo, traduzido na Língua Portuguesa», o qual por si mesmo revela o tipo de português arcaico que foi usado. Essa tradução continha numerosos erros. O próprio Almeida compilou uma lista de dois mil erros, e Ribeiro dos Santos afirmou que encontrou um número ainda maior de erros. Muitos desses erros foram feitos pela comissão holandesa, que procurou—harmonizar—a tradução de Almeida com a versão holandesa de 1637. Nota-se, igualmente, que Almeida preparou uma tradução literal, e que teve cuidado demais em harmonizá-la com as versões castelhana e holandesa. Além de se ter baseado no Textus Receptus, foi influenciado pela edição de Beza, que pertence aos mss «ocidentais». No artigo sobre os *Manuscritos*, o leitor encontrará explicações sobre os tipos de textos e os valores dos diversos mss gregos e latinos, onde será abordada a questão dos mss do N.T. Devemo-nos lembrar que ao tempo de Almeida, não existia 'nenhum papiro', e poucos eram os unciais (mss em letras maiúsculas), razão pela qual foi necessário lançar mão de fontes inferiores. Por exemplo, o Textus Receptus, feito por Erasmo, em 1516, e que foi o primeiro N.T. impresso, teve como base principal quatro mss, a saber: Ms 1 (século X), ms 2 (século XV), ms 2 (Atos e Paulo, século XIII) e ms 1 (Apocalipse, século XII). Somente o ms 1 tem algum valor, e mesmo assim Erasmo não se apoiou muito nele, por achá-lo um tanto errático. O ms 2 é, essencialmente, o Textus Receptus, pertencente, assim, ao século XV. Almeida empregou a edição de Elzevir do Textus Receptus, de 1633. E a Bíblia completa, traduzida por Almeida, só foi publicada nos primórdios do século XVIII. A despeito do texto inferior por ele usado, bem como dos muitos erros e das edições e correções, essa é a tradução que tem sido melhor aceita pelos protestantes de fala portuguesa. As edições mais modernas têm obtido notáveis progressos na melhoria do texto e da tradução em geral. Depois da *Reforma*, a tradução original de Almeida foi a décima terceira a ser feita em um idioma moderno.

b. *Tradução de Antônio Pereira de Figueiredo*

Antônio Pereira de Figueiredo, que preparou a primeira tradução da Bíblia inteira, baseada na Vulgata Latina, nasceu em Mação, Portugal, a 14 de fevereiro de 1725. Essa tradução consumiu dezoito anos de trabalho. Em 1896 foi publicada a primeira tradução de Figueiredo, em colunas paralelas da Vulgata Latina e da tradução em português. Essa tradução foi aprovada e usada pela Igreja de Roma, e também foi aprovada pela rainha D. Maria II em 1842. Penetrou em Portugal através de publicações da Sociedade Bíblica Britânica e Estrangeira. É inegável que a linguagem de Figueiredo era superior à de Almeida, porquanto era mais culto do que este último. Naturalmente que, por haver usado a Vulgata Latina, como base, tem a desvantagem de não representar o melhor texto do N.T. que conhecemos hoje em dia, mediante os mss unciais mais antigos e mediante os papiros, os quais Figueiredo desconhecia por só terem sido descobertos muito mais tarde. A tradução de Figueiredo, pois, saiu do prelo um século depois da de Almeida.

Em 1952 foi publicada uma nova edição pela Livraria Católica do Rio de Janeiro, com comentários baseados em vários teólogos católicos. No Brasil, a primeira tradução foi feita por frei Joaquim de Nossa Senhora de Nazaré, somente do N.T. Foi publicada em São Luís do Maranhão, e a impressão foi feita em Portugal.

Várias traduções de porções bíblicas ou da Bíblia inteira têm sido feitas neste século XX. Entre elas temos a tradução dos evangelhos feita por D. Duarte Leopoldo e Silva (na forma de harmonia), evangelhos e Atos traduzidos do francês pelo Colégio da Imaculada Conceição, em Botafogo, Rio de Janeiro, e os evangelhos e o livro de Atos, traduzidos da Vulgata Latina, pelos padres franciscanos, em 1909.

c. *Tradução do Padre Huberto Rodhen*

Em 1930, o padre Huberto Rodhen traduziu o N.T. inteiro diretamente do grego, o primeiro tradutor católico a fazer tal tipo de tradução na história da Bíblia portuguesa. Essa tradução foi publicada pela Cruzada de Boa Imprensa, organização católica romana. A linguagem da tradução é bela, mas, infelizmente, tal como na tradução de Almeida, foram usados textos inferiores.

d. *Tradução do Padre Matos Soares*

Essa é a versão *mais popular* entre os católicos. Foi baseada na Vulgata Latina, e em 1932 recebeu apoio papal por meio de carta dirigida ao Vaticano. Quase a metade dessa tradução contém explicações dos textos, em notas entre parênteses. Essas notas parentéticas incluem, naturalmente, dogmas da Igreja Romana, à qual pertencia o tradutor.

e. *Tradução Brasileira*

Foi preparada sob a direção do Dr. H. C. Tucker, tendo sido concluída em 1917. Essa tradução nunca foi muito popular. Em 1956, de cada cem Bíblias vendidas pela Sociedade Bíblica do Brasil, somente oito pertenciam à Tradução Brasileira. Sua grande vantagem era ter usado mss melhores do que os de Almeida, além de ter sido melhorada na ortografia portuguesa da época. A despeito desses fatos, tal tradução não é mais impressa.

BÍBLIA EM PORTUGUÊS

f. *Revisão da tradução de Almeida*—Edição Revista e Atualizada

Trabalho realizado por uma comissão que agiu sob os auspícios da Sociedade Bíblica do Brasil, trabalho esse iniciado em 1945. A linguagem foi *muito melhorada*, e não resta dúvidas que nessa revisão foram usados mss gregos dos melhores, muito superiores aos do *Textus Receptus*, que Almeida tinha à sua frente para usar na tradução original que fez. Apesar disso, em diversos lugares do texto nota-se que foram *retidas palavras inferiores*, que só figuram nos manuscritos mais recentes. Por exemplo, em Mt. 6:13, «...pois teu é o reino, o *poder* e a glória para sempre, Amém»; são palavras que só aparecem nos manuscritos gregos mais recentes, e em certas edições têm sido usadas sem qualquer sinal que indique que tais palavras não fazem parte do texto original. Algumas edições têm o cuidado de colocar tais palavras entre parênteses, a fim de indicar que não se baseiam em autoridade suficiente nos mss gregos para serem usadas. Isso provoca grande confusão entre as edições. Os textos de João 5:4; Mt. 18:11; 21:44 e Mar. 5:3, entre outros, podem ser mencionados. Todos esses versículos contêm palavras que só aparecem em mss inferiores. Não obstante, somos forçados a admitir que a base do texto grego dessa revisão é *muito superior* àquela usada por Almeida, em sua tradução original.

g. *Revisão da tradução de Almeida*—Imprensa Bíblica Brasileira

Foi publicada como Bíblia completa em 1967, no Rio de Janeiro. Essa revisão é recente e ainda não houve tempo suficiente para se notar a reação do público brasileiro quanto à linguagem e ao estilo da tradução. Só o futuro pode aprovar ou não essa tradução e mostrar a sua aceitação entre as igrejas. Porém, *facilmente* se comprova que essa tradução está mais *bem baseada* nos mss gregos do que a Almeida Revista e Atualizada. Como exemplo disso, as referências mencionadas no parágrafo acima trazem algum sinal que mostra que se trata de palavras duvidosas, baseadas em mss inferiores e não nos melhores mss. Usualmente essas palavras foram deslocadas do texto e postas em nota de rodapé. Outros exemplos que indicam que essa tradução segue os melhores mss são: Mar. 3:14, que elimina as palavras *aos quais deu também o nome de apóstolos*, palavras essas que procedem de manuscritos inferiores do grego. Mar. 7:16 foi um versículo eliminado. Entrou no texto de Marcos como uma *harmonia* com o texto de Mt. 11:15. Também foram eliminados os vss. 44 e 46 do nono capítulo do evangelho de Marcos. Tudo isso serve apenas de exemplos, dentre muitos casos nos quais essa revisão segue os melhores manuscritos. O leitor poderá notar muitos outros casos, nas notas da própria revisão. Gostaríamos que sua linguagem e estilo fossem bem acolhidos pelo povo evangélico, porquanto a sua base está nos melhores mss., devendo ser aceitável a qualquer pessoa que conheça o texto grego no Novo Testamento e os manuscritos que formam uma sólida base na qual se alicerçou essa revisão.

h. *A Bíblia Na Linguagem De Hoje* (Novo Testamento)

Essa publicação da United Bible Societies (através de seu ramo brasileiro) se baseia na segunda edição (1970) do texto grego dessa sociedade. Esse texto tem tirado proveito da *vantagem* da maior parte da pesquisa moderna, pelo que é bom representante do original. Não é diferente do texto de *Nestle* em qualquer ponto essencial, embora o «aparato crítico» que acompanha a edição de *Nestle* e a edição da United Bible Societies, em publicações técnicas. se diferencie quanto à apresentação, embora baseados nos mesmos estudos sobre os manuscritos.

Foi propósito da United Bible Societies publicar em vários idiomas, Novos Testamentos que refletem a linguagem comum e corrente. Portanto, é de se esperar que essas publicações, apesar de serem em idiomas diversos, tenham apresentações similares. Todas as novas traduções tradicionalmente são vilipendiadas por pessoas que as ouvem pela primeira vez, estando elas afeitas a ouvir o evangelho de certo modo. Usualmente, um raciocínio mais sóbrio e a passagem do tempo suavizam o tratamento inicial duro que uma nova tradução recebe. Infelizmente, a crítica com freqüência se baseia apenas na observação que, «Esta tradução é *diferente* aqui e ali», quando comparada com «esta outra tradução de que costumo usar». Raramente tais críticas se baseiam na erudição e no texto grego. Outrossim, as «formas deixadas de fora» em novas traduções normalmente são as simples excisões de adições, mudanças e harmonias feitas por escribas medievais (que distorceram o texto original), adições que não têm qualquer direito a serem reputadas originais, pois estão ausentes na maioria dos manuscritos antigos, especialmente nos papiros.

A passagem do tempo provará para nós uma avaliação adequada sobre esta nova tradução. Gostaríamos que isso se desse mediante o estudo do original, e não mediante meras comparações com as traduções já existentes.

3. A Bíblia e Os Meios do Desenvolvimento Espiritual

A Bíblia, obviamente, tem um lugar entre os meios do desenvolvimento espiritual. As pessoas que usam a Bíblia constantemente para instrução, conforto e inspiração, não a consideram um livro comum. Até as pessoas religiosas mais liberais, acham que, pelo menos em alguns lugares, a *Palavra de Deus* é contida na Bíblia. As pessoas mais conservadoras acham que a Bíblia é a Palavra de Deus escrita, e a tratam com o maior respeito. Ver o artigo sobre *Inspiração*.

Os Meios do Desenvolvimento Espiritual

a. *A leitura da Bíblia* e outros livros de natureza espiritual e inspiradora. A melhor parte da filosofia tem seu lugar como parte deste meio, se usada com a devida cautela. Os livros, de outros campos, que têm alguma relação com a vida espiritual, também têm sua importância no desenvolvimento do espírito. Este meio melhora os nossos conhecimentos e o conhecimento tem uma poderosa influência nas nossas vidas.

b. *A oração* e a *meditação*. A oração é o nosso meio de comunicarmos com o divino. A meditação é o nosso meio de escutar as instruções da *Mente Divina*.

c. *A santificação*, sem a qual, ninguém verá a Deus, Heb. 12:14.

d. *O toque místico* em comunhão com o Espírito: os dons espirituais e a *iluminação*.

e. *A prática da lei do amor* e as boas obras. Cada vez que fazemos o bem em favor de outra pessoa, melhoramos a nossa própria espiritualidade.

4. BIBLIOGRAFIA.
Enciclopédia Delta Larousse, Artigo sobre *A Bíblia*, Editora Delta, Rio de Janeiro, 1970. Mein, John, *A Bíblia e Como Chegou Até Nós*, Imprensa Bíblica Brasileira, 1972. Metzger, Bruce M. *The Text of the New Testament*, Oxford, New York, 1964.

Ver o gráfico ilustrativo a seguir:

BÍBLIA EM PORTUGUÊS

5. DIAGRAMA DE ILUSTRAÇÃO:

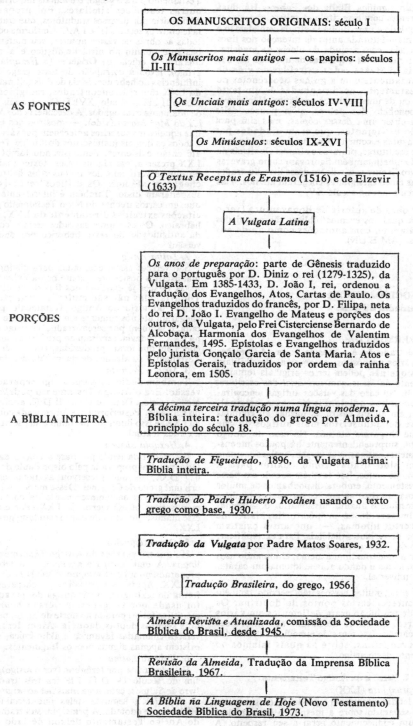

AS FONTES

- OS MANUSCRITOS ORIGINAIS: século I
- Os Manuscritos mais antigos — os papiros: séculos II-III
- Os Unciais mais antigos: séculos IV-VIII
- Os Minúsculos: séculos IX-XVI
- O Textus Receptus de Erasmo (1516) e de Elzevir (1633)
- A Vulgata Latina

PORÇÕES

Os anos de preparação: parte de Gênesis traduzido para o português por D. Diniz o rei (1279-1325), da Vulgata. Em 1385-1433, D. João I, rei, ordenou a tradução dos Evangelhos, Atos, Cartas de Paulo. Os Evangelhos traduzidos do francês, por D. Filipa, neta do rei D. João I. Evangelho de Mateus e porções dos outros, da Vulgata, pelo Frei Cisterciense Bernardo de Alcobaça. Harmonia dos Evangelhos de Valentim Fernandes, 1495. Epístolas e Evangelhos traduzidos pelo jurista Gonçalo Garcia de Santa Maria. Atos e Epístolas Gerais, traduzidos por ordem da rainha Leonora, em 1505.

A BÍBLIA INTEIRA

- A décima terceira tradução numa língua moderna. A Bíblia inteira: tradução do grego por Almeida, princípio do século 18.
- Tradução de Figueiredo, 1896, da Vulgata Latina: Bíblia inteira.
- Tradução do Padre Huberto Rodhen usando o texto grego como base, 1930.
- Tradução da Vulgata por Padre Matos Soares, 1932.
- Tradução Brasileira, do grego, 1956.
- Almeida Revista e Atualizada, comissão da Sociedade Bíblica do Brasil, desde 1945.
- Revisão da Almeida, Tradução da Imprensa Bíblica Brasileira, 1967.
- A Bíblia na Linguagem de Hoje (Novo Testamento) Sociedade Bíblica do Brasil, 1973.

BÍBLIA PAUPERUM — BÍBLIA, VERSÕES DA

BÍBLIA PAUPERUM

Esse título significa **Bíblia dos Pobres**. Há duas obras diferentes com esse título, a saber:

1. Nome dado a uma Bíblia ilustrada, em alemão e holandês, manufaturada antes da invenção dos tipos móveis, ou seja, com a ajuda de blocos de madeira. Tinha quarenta folhas impressas de um lado só, nas quais havia quarenta cenas extraídas da vida de Cristo, juntamente com algumas ocorrências do Antigo Testamento, acompanhadas de um texto ilustrativo ou de uma sentença em latim. Não visava tanto o benefício dos pobres, pois poucos deles podereiam obter uma dessas cópias, mas sim para os pregadores viajantes, que eram ajudados por aquelas gravuras e comentários. As gravuras do livro enfocavam esculturas, pinturas e altares. Os vitrais da capela de Lambeth também figuravam como gravuras naquele livro. Houve sete edições desse livro ilustrado, mas apenas cinco exemplares chegaram até nós. Tais edições circularam no século XV.

2. Uma obra de autoria de Bonaventura (ver o artigo), na qual os eventos bíblicos são arranjados alfabeticamente, com anotações como ajuda aos pregadores. (AM E UN)

••• ••• •••

BÍBLIA, SOCIEDADES DA
Ver **Sociedades Bíblicas**.

BÍBLIA, VERSÕES DA

Versão e tradução é a mesma coisa. As versões servem a vários propósitos, a saber: a. Possibilitam às pessoas que não podem ler os originais tomarem conhecimento da mensagem *universal* das escrituras Sagradas. b. No caso das versões antigas, encontramos testemunhos adicionais do texto original, porquanto, em alguns casos, as formas ali contidas derivam-se de manuscritos mais antigos do que aqueles que chegaram até nós. No caso do Antigo Testamento, surpreendentemente há poucos manuscritos realmente antigos, e as versões antigas, como a LXX, têm sido usadas como auxílio para a confirmação de textos. Isso também sucede em parte ao Novo Testamento, embora disponhamos de muitos e antigos manuscritos gregos. c. As versões também são um prestimoso auxílio missionário. d. Algumas versões têm servido ao propósito lingüístico de unificar certos idiomas, — que antes existiam sob a forma de variantes dialetais. Para exemplificar, a tradução da Bíblia para o alemão, feita por Lutero, deu origem à moderna língua alemã, eliminando usos meramente locais e dando àquele idioma um caráter unificado, universal.

Infelizmente, muitas versões têm servido também para obscurecer certos pontos de doutrina. Os critérios de tradução eram deficientes em vários particulares, ou então atendiam aos interesses denominacionais. Isso tem sido remediado através das *traduções modernas*, sobre as quais falamos no décimo ponto deste artigo.

I. Versões do Antigo Testamento

1. *A Septuaginta* (LXX)

Muitas lendas circundam a produção dessa versão. No artigo separado sobre a mesma, o leitor poderá adquirir um conhecimento geral a seu respeito. A LXX é a tradução do original hebraico do Antigo Testamento para o grego, e é a mais importante entre outras traduções similares. Foi preparada em Alexandria por diversos tradutores, que trabalharam nela entre os séculos III e I A.C. Conforme ocorre com todas as obras de vários autores, seu material difere bastante quanto ao nível lingüístico e à qualidade literária. A edição de Orígenes (a *Hexapla* — ver o artigo), levou à corrupção do texto grego mediante influências do hebraico. Mais de dois mil manuscritos da LXX têm sido encontrados, redigidos desde o século II até o século XVI D.C., os quais têm sido devidamente catalogados. A descoberta dos *Manuscritos do Mar Morto* (vide), — mostrou aos estudiosos que aqueles manuscritos antecedem por vários séculos a todos os demais manuscritos do Antigo Testamento até então existentes, demonstrando também que a LXX preserva, em alguns casos, textos mais antigos do que se verificam nos manuscritos hebraicos que chegaram até nós. Os críticos textuais sempre suspeitaram disso. Também é interessante observar que, em certos trechos do Novo Testamento grego, há citações extraídas diretamente da LXX, e não do hebraico. Os escritores sagrados teriam consciência da antiguidade do texto hebraico por detrás dessa versão?

2. *Latim Antigo*

São versões assim chamadas para distingui-las de manuscritos posteriores, como os da Vulgata Latina. Essas versões já existiam nos fins do século II D.C. Todavia, elas não são muito importantes para o estudo do texto do Antigo Testamento porquanto chegaram até nós somente em forma muito fragmentada, e também por serem traduções feitas com base na LXX. Todavia, serviram ao propósito colimado, na época em que foram produzidas, isto é, pôr o Antigo Testamento ao alcance de quem falava e lia o latim.

3. *Siríaco Peshitta*

Também dedicamos um artigo separado a essa versão. Era o Antigo Testamento padrão para os cristãos sírios. Data do século II D.C. e foi traduzida do hebraico. Posteriormente foi revisada com a ajuda da LXX, e isso diminuiu bastante a sua serventia para a crítica textual.

4. *Hexapla Siríaca*

Foi traduzida tendo por base a edição da LXX de Orígenes. Foi preparada pelo bispo Paulo de Tela, em 617 D.C., — que preservou as notas críticas do original grego de Orígenes. Desse modo, os estudiosos foram capazes de remover muito da corrupção dos manuscritos pós-Orígenes da LXX. Por essa razão, esse manuscrito tem sido muito estudado no exame da LXX.

5. *Copta* (egípcio)

Há quatro versões do Antigo Testamento nessa língua. A mais antiga é a *saídica* ou tebaica. Foi preparada no sul do Egito, no século II D.C., baseada na LXX. Ajuda os especialistas a chegarem a uma forma do texto grego mais antiga do que aquela que foi usada por Orígenes. A versão *boárica* ou menfítica foi preparada no norte do Egito, pelo menos dois séculos depois daquela. Além dessas, há as versões chamadas fayumica e akhmímica, das quais existem apenas alguns poucos fragmentos.

6. *Vulgata Latina*

Foi produzida por Jerônimo (ver o artigo), perto do fim do século IV D.C. Ele fez três traduções do livro de Salmos, cada uma mais fiel ao original hebraico mas foi a segunda delas que terminou sendo oficialmente adotada. A princípio, sua tradução geral do Antigo Testamento deixou de lado os livros

dm qm ds prior dilexnos. Siquis dixerit qm di
ligo dm et fratrem suu oderit mendax e. qui n non
diligit fratrem suu que uidet dm que non uidet quomo
do potest diligere. et hoc mandatu a do habemus ut
qui diligit dm diligat et fratrem suum
Omnis qui credit qm ihs e xps ex do natus e. et omnis
qui diligit eu qui genuit diligit et qui natus e ex do
In hoc cognouimus qm diligimus natos di cu dm dili
gamus et mandata eius faciamus. Haec e eni caritas
di ut mandata eius custodiamus et mandata eius
grauia non sunt qm omne quod natu e ex do uincit
mundu. et haec e uictoria quae uincit mundu fides
nra. quis e qui uincit mundu nisi qui credit qm ihs e
filius di. hic e qui uenit per aqua et sanguine ihs
xps. non in aqua solu sed in aqua et sanguine. et sps
est qui testificatur qm xps e ueritas. qm tres sunt
qui testimoniu dant. sps aqua et sanguis. et tres unu sunt
Si testimoniu hominu accipimus testamoniu di maius
est. qm hoc e testamoniu di quod maius e quia testi
ficatus e de filio suo. Qui credit in filiu di habet tes
tamoniu di in se. qui non credit filio mendacem facit
eum qm non credit in testimonio quod testificatus e
ds de filio suo. Et hoc testimoniu e qm uita aeterna
dedit nobis ds. et haec uita in filio eius e. qui habet fi
liu habet uita. qui non habet filiu di non habet uita
Haec scribo uobis ut sciatis qm uita habeatis aeterna
qui creditis in nomine filii di. et haec e fiducia qua

A Vulgata de Alcuino. Século IX — Cortesia, British Museum

Ms Etiópico, Século XVII, — Cortesia, British Museum

Siríaco Curetoniano, Século V, João 6:30-41, — Cortesia, British Museum

Códex Argenteus, Gótico, Século V, Marcos 5:18-24, — Cortesia, University Library, Uppsala

BÍBLIA, VERSÕES DA

apócrifos, porque ele não queria que os mesmos fossem incluídos, embora ele houvesse traduzido os livros de Judite e Tobias. Todavia, os livros apócrifos terminaram sendo adicionados, tornando-se parte da Vulgata. Essa versão foi a Bíblia oficialmente aceita na Europa ocidental durante todo o decurso da Idade Média. Atualmente existem cerca de oito mil manuscritos da Vulgata. Ela dá testemunho sobre o texto hebraico massorético. Ver sobre a *Massora*.

7. Versões Menores

Incluem manuscritos gregos não pertencentes à tradição da Septuaginta, e que foram traduzidos para o gótico, o etíope e o armênio. Todas elas datam de cerca do século IV D.C.

II. Versões do Novo Testamento

1. Latim Antigo

Originária do fim do século II D.C., e provavelmente produzida na África. Há pelo menos duas formas diversas, chamadas africana e européia. A forma européia, ou itálica, foi uma das bases da Vulgata de Jerônimo, quanto ao Novo Testamento. A forma africana foi empregada por Cipriano (ver o artigo). Ver o artigo sobre *Manuscritos, Novo Testamento*, quanto a maiores detalhes. A versão em Latim Antigo serve de importante testemunho do tipo de texto anterior ao Textus Receptus, mostrando que esse texto é de origem posterior, porquanto os manuscritos gregos que foram usados como base são mais próximos do grupo alexandrino de manuscritos gregos, representando o estágio mais antigo do tipo textual ocidental.

2. O Diatessaron

Trata-se de uma harmonia dos evangelhos de autoria de Taciano (ver o artigo), de cerca de 160 D.C. Foi preparada em grego e traduzida para o siríaco. Há uma folha do mesmo em um manuscrito grego do século III D.C. Além disso, é conhecido em uma versão armênia do comentário de Efraem, e com menos exatidão, em uma tradução árabe editada por Marmardji.

3. Siríaco Antigo

Assim chamada para distingui-la da versão Peshitta posterior. A *Peshitta* era a versão popular em siríaco, como se fosse a Vulgata daquele idioma. Essa versão existe nos manuscritos sinaítico e curetoniano. Ambos são importantes manuscritos, e o primeiro deles é o mais antigo. Representam o texto chamado ocidental.

4. Peshitta

Tradução para o siríaco, que surgiu perto do fim do século IV D.C. Essa versão suplantou as versões mais antigas, que com ela divergiam. Seu cânon consiste apenas em vinte e dois livros, com a ausência de II Pedro, II e III João, Judas e Apocalipse. Existem mais de trezentos e cinqüenta manuscritos da Peshitta. Nos evangelhos, a versão aproxima-se mais do texto bizantino, embora no livro de Atos reflita mais o texto ocidental. Vários outros manuscritos siríacos existem, sendo descritos no artigo sobre os *Manuscritos, Novo Testamento*.

5. Copta

Há cinco versões do Novo Testamento em copta ou egípcio, que chegaram até nós. A mais antiga delas é a versão saídica do sul do Egito, que apareceu já no século II D.C. A versão boárica vem do norte do Egito; mas, embora seja um texto mais recente, tornou-se a versão dominante, pelo que é representada por um número maior de manuscritos. Outras versões em copta são a fayumica, a akhmímica e a do Egito Médio, algumas das quais talvez sejam mais antigas que a versão boárica, e talvez tão antigas quanto a saídica. A versão akhmímica conta com dois manuscritos do século IV D.C. A tradição copta inteira testifica um tipo de texto anterior àquele usado no Textus Receptus de Erasmo, o que mostra que esse último foi um desenvolvimento de séculos posteriores. Foi uma espécie de amálgama dos vários tipos anteriores de texto.

6. Armênia

Foi preparada em cerca de 400 D.C., com base em uma fonte cujo texto era similar aos manuscritos gregos Theta, 565 e 700. Há cerca de 1.244 cópias dessa versão. Seu texto é de tipo cesareano e koiné (bizantino), dependendo do livro do Novo Testamento que se esteja considerando. Representa um movimento de afastamento para longe dos melhores manuscritos gregos, na direção do Textus Receptus, o que, novamente, demonstra que o Textus Receptus representa uma involução do texto, e não um representante legítimo do original.

7. Geórgia

Era a Bíblia do povo de Geórgia, uma nação do Cáucaso, um acidentado distrito montanhoso entre os mares Negro e Cáspio. Seu mais antigo manuscrito do evangelho é o Adysh, de 897 D.C. Há também o manuscrito Opiza, de 913 D.C. Alguns poucos manuscritos posteriores também representam essa tradição. O tipo de texto é o cesareano. Aparentemente, essa versão foi traduzida diretamente do armênio.

8. Vulgata Latina

Foi uma revisão e uma harmonia de manuscritos latinos mais antigos. Foi preparada por Jerônimo, algum tempo depois de 380 D.C. Nos evangelhos, os manuscritos gregos usados eram similares ao Sinaítico (Aleph). Quanto ao livro de Atos, assemelhavam-se ao manuscrito Alexandrino (A). Esse texto tornou-se o texto latino do Novo Testamento considerado oficial pela Igreja Católica Romana, desde a declaração feita quando do Concílio de Trento (ver o artigo), em 1546. Sua origem deve-se à solicitação feita pelo papa Damasco de que Sofrônio Eusébio Hierônimo, atualmente mais conhecido como Jerônimo, aceitasse a incumbência de preparar uma Bíblia Latina padrão. Os textos por detrás da Vulgata aproximam-se mais do tipo alexandrino de texto, embora a Vulgata, como um todo, represente mais o texto ocidental, ainda mais corrompido do que aquele. Há cerca de oito mil manuscritos da Vulgata, que exibem uma prodigiosa mescla de tipos textuais, em face de adições, eliminações e contaminações cruzadas, feitas por muitos escribas, através dos séculos. Seja como for, a tradição latina inteira presta testemunho sobre um texto mais antigo que aquele que serviu de base ao Textus Receptus, o qual foi o produto final de um processo de mistura, e não representante do texto original.

9. Versões Secundárias

Entre elas podemos incluir as versões gótica, etíope, eslavônica, árabe e persa, as quais são comentadas no artigo sobre os *Manuscritos do Novo Testamento*. As versões, de modo geral, mostram o avanço da Bíblia entre diversos povos; e a própria existência delas mostra-nos o poder de penetração e a importância da Bíblia, no Antigo ou no Novo Testamentos, entre todos os povos do mundo.

10. Traduções Modernas

Antes mesmo da Reforma protestante, houve traduções da Bíblia ou de porções da mesma, para o vernáculo, isto é, línguas faladas. Por exemplo, a Bíblia inglesa teve início com John Wycliff (ver o artigo), com data de 1382. A tradução dele foi feita

BÍBLIA, VERSÕES DA — BIBLIOLATRIA

com base na Vulgata Latina, e não com base no grego, pelo que também incluiu os livros apócrifos. Porções da Bíblia em português apareceram em cerca de 1280, enquanto que outras porções só apareceram em 1400. Ver o artigo separado sobre a *Bíblia em Português*. Durante a Idade Média contava com pouco apoio o movimento para tradução da Bíblia para línguas faladas. Já existia a Vulgata Latina, mas essa não era usada pelo povo, porque bem poucas pessoas tinham educação suficiente para utilizá-la, redigida como estava no latim — Em conseqüência, não foi senão quando da Reforma que a Bíblia começou a ser traduzida para idiomas modernos. E então começou a produção da Bíblia traduzida para o inglês, para o alemão, para o francês, para o italiano, para o espanhol, para o português, e para diversas outras línguas européias.

Todavia, como reflexo da época, o critério que norteava essas traduções era o critério da economia, para que as edições não fossem volumosas e o menos dispendiosas possível. Os tradutores procuravam traduzir o texto sagrado com economia de palavras. Isso resultava em Bíblias compactas, mas em que muito da riqueza de significado das línguas originais se perdia. Com o desenvolvimento da erudição bíblica entre os evangélicos, em vários países essa debilidade das primeiras traduções tem sido remediada. Os países de língua inglesa têm sido os pioneiros nessa atividade. Surgiram, pois, as chamadas traduções expandidas, nas quais a preocupação não é a economia de palavras, mas a *exploração* de todo o sentido possível dos textos sagrados, sem perda de sua riqueza. À frente deste tradutor acham-se abertos três representantes notáveis desse critério de tradução: *Amplified New Testament*, da Zondervan Publishing House; *The New Testament* de Charles B. Williams; e *The New Testament, an Expanded Translation*, de Kenneth S. Wuest.

As modernas Sociedades Bíblicas têm ajudado enormemente na divulgação das Sagradas Escrituras. A *British and Foreign Bible Society* começou em 1804, e a *American Bible Society* surgiu em 1816. Depois apareceu a *United Bible Societies*, que congrega sociedades bíblicas de muitos lugares do mundo. A Sociedade Bíblica do Brasil, também muito tem contribuído para a distribuição de Bíblias em nossa pátria, com alvos cada vez mais ambiciosos.

Foi fundada uma Sociedade Bíblica Católica Romana (Regensburgo), em 1805, mas que não foi aprovada pelo Vaticano e teve de ser fechada em 1817. Encíclicas papais opuseram-se ao funcionamento de sociedades bíblicas durante todo o século XIX, mas essa posição foi alterada quando do Concílio Vaticano II (em 1970), que deu seu apoio tácito a esse tipo de atividade. Em 1966, o papa Paulo VI ordenou que fosse estudada a possibilidade de uma futura distribuição conjunta da Bíblia, em cooperação com entidades não-católicas. Atualmente, os católicos romanos em muitos lugares estão efetuando estudos bíblicos, e a Bíblia começa a ser divulgada entre as imensas massas católicas. Isso só poderá produzir um bom resultado.

Além das sociedades bíblicas, temos de levar em conta o trabalho feito por organizações como os Gideões (ver o artigo separado) e os Wycliffe Bible Translators (ver o artigo). Pelo menos o evangelho de João tem sido traduzido para mais de 1.250 línguas e dialetos. Esses esforços promovem a leitura das Sagradas Escrituras como nunca antes se viu, ao redor do mundo. (AM BR GREE KE ME NI NTI Z)

BÍBLIAS POLIGLOTAS

Essas são as edições da Bíblia nas quais o texto original e diversas traduções aparecem em colunas paralelas. A primeira e mais famosa delas foi a Hexapla de Orígenes (que vide), que continha o texto hebraico do Antigo Testamento, com uma transliteração grega, além de quatro versões gregas. Ver o artigo Bíblia, Versões da. A Bíblia Poliglota Complutensiana, de 1514-1517, continha o Novo Testamento em grego e em latim; e o seu Antigo Testamento hebraico aparecia lado a lado com a Vulgata e a Septuaginta (que vide), juntamente com outra tradução latina e uma em caldaico. A prática de pôr duas traduções, em línguas diferentes, lado a lado, tem sido uma prática comum. As Sociedades Bíblicas têm praticado isso. Além disso, existem vários textos em grego interlineares, onde o grego é acompanhado, palavra por palavra, pelos vocábulos de algum outro idioma moderno. (E)

BIBLICISMO

É o nome que se dá à insistência de usar a Bíblia para solucionar todos os problemas teológicos, morais e filosóficos, ou, pelo menos, o uso da Bíblia para determinar o valor da verdade que há nessas questões. O *biblicismo* dá grande valor à interpretação literal da Bíblia. A forma extremada do biblicismo é a *bibliolatria* (ver o artigo).

BIBLIOLATRIA

Palavra baseada em dois vocábulos gregos, com o sentido de «adoração ao livro». O termo é usado para descrever aquelas pessoas e atividades que se utilizam da Bíblia como única regra de fé e prática, paralelamente à insistência de que a Bíblia não envolve erros de qualquer modalidade. Geralmente, isso é acompanhado pela contenção de que toda razão e ciência humanas deveriam ser sujeitadas ao cotejo com a Bíblia, interpretada literalmente. Isso posto, a Bíblia é transformada em um *papa de papel*.

A bibliolatria caracteriza-se por uma atitude pugnaz que rejeita *a priori* todo o estudo e toda e qualquer evidência que mostra que a Bíblia não é um livro perfeito. Mas, visto que a Bíblia tem um lado humano em sua produção, e visto que as produções humanas não são perfeitas, esse elemento humano impede que as Escrituras sejam perfeitas. A bibliolatria também tem a fé de que a Bíblia é a única autoridade *possível* em assuntos de fé e de moral, e que a sua ciência sempre está certa, mesmo em face de qualquer ciência secular em contrário. Mas a Bíblia não foi escrita como compêndio científico, pelo que muitas das coisas ali ditas são cientificamente ingênuas, expressando conceitos populares. Além disso, a bibliolatria também se caracteriza pela síndrome dos textos de prova, como se todo problema, de qualquer natureza, pudesse ser resolvido pela simples apresentação de um texto de prova, extraído da Bíblia.

A bibliolatria assume diferentes aspectos, dependendo de quem lança mão da Bíblia abusivamente. Assim é que, em uma denominação qualquer, a autoridade da Bíblia é usada para promover determinado conjunto de doutrinas particulares, em torno das quais gira a vida daquela denominação; mas, em uma outra denominação, os mesmos textos de prova são usados para dar apoio a idéias às vezes diametralmente contrárias. Tudo isso concorre para lançar uma nódoa sobre o uso são das Escrituras, como a nossa principal autoridade espiritual. E força sobre

BIBLIOMANCIA — BIBLIOTECAS

a Bíblia uma autoridade sobre campos que lhe são estranhos, além de limitar erroneamente o conceito de autoridade. Ver o artigo sobre *Autoridade*. (E C)

BIBLIOMANCIA

Vem de duas palavras gregas, **biblion**, «livro», e *manteia*, «adivinhação». Trata-se de uma estranha forma de adivinhação em que a pessoa primeiramente pensa sobre algum problema, e em seguida, abre o volume da Bíblia ao acaso, a fim de ver qual resposta poderá obter da mesma. Vício semelhante é aquele que envolve o uso das chamadas «caixinhas de promessas», com pequenos cartões impressos com trechos bíblicos. Toda essa prática é supersticiosa. Havia costume similar no paganismo, onde eram empregadas obras de Homero, Virgílio e outros autores profanos, com idêntico propósito.

Os judeus tinham uma forma de bibliomancia segundo a qual sempre que alguém se punha a ouvir a outrem lendo as Escrituras, as primeiras palavras a serem ouvidas eram consideradas prenhes de significado, uma espécie de voz do *céu*. Durante o tenebroso período da Idade Média, até mesmo coisas importantes eram resolvidas mediante a seleção de trechos bíblicos ao acaso, como nos casos da detecção de hereges ou da seleção de bispos. Conta-se que um crente supersticioso abriu a Bíblia ao acaso, de olhos fechados; ao abri-la, leu: «Judas foi enforcar-se». Chocado, ele fechou a Bíblia, e tentou de novo. E as primeiras palavras que leu, foram: «Vai, e procede tu de igual modo». Não há que duvidar que deve haver melhor maneira de determinarmos a vontade do Senhor! Fico pensativo diante da ação escolhida para selecionar o substituto de Judas Iscariotes, em Atos 1:26: «E os lançaram em sortes, vindo a sorte a recair sobre Matias...» (Ver o artigo sobre *Adivinhação*).

O I Ching também é uma forma de adivinhação baseada no puro acaso (ver sobre o I Ching). A crença por detrás das adivinhações dessa natureza é que existe tal coisa como coincidências significativas, um tema examinado por Carl Jung. No caso do I Ching parece haver o concurso de alguma força telepática e psicocinética da mente, — que pode forçar alguns resultados bastante surpreendentes, visto que os problemas de uma pessoa são revelados, em textos pré-impressos, com admirável exatidão. Assuntos como esses precisam ser melhor investigados. Mas, oxalá Deus sempre se comunicasse conosco através de meios superiores, embora tais meios algumas vezes produzam bons resultados! (E UN)

Outra forma de *bibliomancia* funciona assim: Uma tesoura é amarrada, com barbante, dentro de uma Bíblia, no livro de Rute, em 1:16,17. A Bíblia é suspensa no ar por duas pessoas, como segue: Os dois círculos do cabo da tesoura são suspensos pelas pessoas, cada um colocando um dedo embaixo de um dos círculos. Então, Rute 1:16,17 são lidos. Daí, uma pergunta é feita que pode ser respondida com «sim» ou «não». O livro gira segundo o relógio, ou contra, dando a resposta *sim* ou *não*, segundo a direção da giração. Para estabelecer qual é *sim* e qual é *não*, as pessoas devem experimentar com uma pergunta cuja resposta é conhecida.

A Bíblia gira mesmo, mas experiências mostram que é o poder das mentes das pessoas que controlam o movimento. Isto é, a função é um exemplo de *psicossinésia* (que vide). Se uma pessoa deseja que não funcione, a Bíblia não gira. Se uma pessoa *deseja* que a Bíblia dê uma resposta incorreta, ela obedece o comando mental. Não vou dizer que não existem exceções, mas normalmente, não há nada de sobrenatural ou demoníaco nisto. É simplesmente o poder da mente que tem efeitos sobre a matéria.

BIBLION, BIBLIA

Vem de **biblos**, «papiro». O *biblion* era uma faixa de papiro apropriada para servir de rolo de escrita. Tinha oito ou nove metros de comprimento, o que era uma dimensão conveniente para uso e capaz de acomodar um livro do tamanho do evangelho de Mateus. Esse termo acabou significando um livro, em forma de rolo, naturalmente. A forma plural, *bíblia*, dava a entender rolos de papiro, mas terminou sendo aplicada aos livros sagrados do Antigo e Novo Testamentos. Essa palavra passou para a versão latina como um feminino singular, e dali deriva-se a nossa palavra portuguesa «Bíblia», uma palavra no singular, e que se refere, coletivamente, à inteira coletânea dos livros canônicos. (E)

BIBLIOTECA DE ALEXANDRIA

Ver **Alexandria, Biblioteca de**.

BIBLIOTECAS

Consideremos os pontos abaixo:

1. *Definição*. Uma biblioteca é uma coleção de livros, sem importar se pequena ou grande, reunida com certo propósito em mira, para servir de centro de leitura e pesquisas literárias. Os livros de uma biblioteca não são oferecidos à venda, embora possam ser emprestados por certo prazo.

2. *Bibliotecas Relacionadas à Bíblia*. Não há qualquer referência específica, na Bíblia, a alguma biblioteca, embora haja referências que subentendam a existência de bibliotecas. Paulo deve ter contado com uma pequena biblioteca, para seu uso pessoal (II Tim. 4:13). O fato de que havia muitos livros, e que a produção de livros pode ser uma atividade sem-fim (Ecl. 12:12), mostra-nos que, em Israel, deve ter havido tais coleções de livros. A preparação de livros começou cedo em Israel, conforme se vê em Êxo. 14:4,7; 17:14; e Heb. 9:9. — Os sacerdotes levíticos estavam encarregados dos livros sagrados (Deu. 17:18; 31:24-26). Vários títulos foram dados aos livros sagrados dos judeus, como Livro da Lei, Livro da Aliança, etc., dos quais havia um bom número de cópias, incluindo não somente os livros canônicos do Antigo Testamento, mas até mesmo livros não-canônicos. Ver o artigo sobre os *Livros*. Ver também Isa. 30:9; Jer. 25:15; 30:3,36; 51:60. Alguns estudiosos têm pensado que essas coleções de livros eram conservadas em lugares estratégicos, como Dã, Silo, Siquém e Gibeom, e não somente em Jerusalém, e isso é uma opinião que não pode ser nem confirmada e nem negada, por absoluta falta de evidências. Além dos livros canônicos e não-canônicos (ver Núm. 21:14; Jos. 10:12,13; I Crô. 29:29 e II Crô. 33:17), provavelmente havia extensos registros genealógicos, tratados, contratos, transações comerciais registradas, tudo o que sugere coleções de livros que eram devidamente guardados. Em Esdras 5:17 temos uma referência aos arquivos (de rolos) da Babilônia, o que, quase certamente, é uma alusão à biblioteca que havia naquela cidade. A arqueologia tem descoberto grande número de bibliotecas de tabletes de argila, tanto na Babilônia quanto nas principais cidades do império assírio. A famosa biblioteca de Alexandria (ver o artigo sobre *Alexandria, Biblioteca de*), embora não fosse uma biblioteca nitidamente bíblica, teve

537

começo em 300 A.C., e continha livros sobre a erudição semita, tendo também sido a biblioteca para a qual foi preparada a versão do Antigo Testamento, intitulada **Septuaginta (ou LXX)**.

As esperanças dos arqueólogos, — de descobrirem bibliotecas nas cidades de Israel, até hoje não se concretizaram. Porém, o descobrimento de bibliotecas na Assíria, na Babilônia e no Egito, bem como os tabletes de Tell el-Amarna, do século XIV A.C., tem compensado parcialmente esse desapontamento. A biblioteca de Sargão (722-705 A.C.) compunha-se de uma grande coleção de tabletes com escrita cuneiforme, que atualmente se encontra no Museu Britânico. O número desses tabletes chega cerca de vinte e cinco mil. A Biblioteca Real de Assurbanipal (662-626 A.C.) também era muito numerosa, com cerca de vinte mil tabletes, que também encontram-se agora no Museu Britânico. Dez mil textos diferentes são ali representados, e Sir Frederic Kenyon referiu-se a essa coleção como «a primeira grande coleção particular de livros que se conhece na história». Em Nuzi (que vide), foram desenterrados cerca de vinte mil tabletes de argila, datados da primeira metade do segundo milênio A.C. A oitenta quilômetros a sueste da cidade da Babilônia, no templo de Nipur, foram encontrados cerca de cinquenta mil tabletes de argila, pertencentes aos séculos IV e V A.C.

Grandes bibliotecas gregas e romanas surgiram quase no fim do período do Antigo Testamento. Além da biblioteca de Alexandria, havia as coleções guardadas em Pérgamo e em outras cidades, embora nenhuma delas pudesse rivalizar-se com a de Alexandria, cujo intuito era contar com uma cópia de todos os livros do mundo até então conhecido.

Manuscritos do Mar Morto. Do ponto de vista bíblico, a maior descoberta isolada de manuscritos de todos os tempos se deu nos primeiros meses de 1947, quando, em diversas cavernas próximas do mar Morto, foi encontrada uma grande coleção de livros do Antigo Testamento, pseudepígrafos e algum material não-bíblico. Cerca de cem manuscritos bíblicos foram ali encontrados, alguns mais extensos, e outros apenas fragmentares. Entre esses manuscritos, há evidências acerca de todos os livros canônicos do Antigo Testamento, com a única exceção de Ester. O material data de entre 200 A.C. e 50 D.C. (AM ID FK JAS RIC Z)

BIBLOS

Cidade na Fenícia. Maurice Dunand descobriu em Biblos (moderna Gebal). o antigo porto fenício de embarque de cedro e o túmulo do rei Airão, em 1919. (Ver Atos 11:19; 15:3 e 27:12). Ver sobre *Gebal*.

BICRI

No hebraico, «jovem». Foi um homem benjamita cujo filho, Seba, incitou um levante contra Davi, após a morte de Absalão (II Sam. 20:1 ss), em cerca de 967 A.C.

BIDCAR

No hebraico, «servo de Kar» ou «filho da perfuração»? Foi um capitão de Jeú, que antes fora seu companheiro de armas (II Reis 9:25). Ele completou a sentença contra o filho de Acabe, Jeorão, lançando seu cadáver no campo de Nabote, depois que Jeú o transpassou com um dardo, em c. de 882 A.C.

••• ••• •••

BIDDLE, JOHN

Suas datas foram 1615-1662. É considerado o pai dos unitários ingleses. Nasceu em Gloucestershire, foi educado no Magdalen Hall, em Oxford, foi professor da Crypt School de Gloucester e faleceu em Londres. Foi estudioso da Bíblia, profundamente versado nas Escrituras. — Ficou convencido de que a doutrina comum da Trindade (ver o artigo) não é uma doutrina das Escrituras e nem concorda com a razão humana. Publicou então quatro pequenos folhetos, com doze argumentos, sobre o assunto, e foi acusado de heresia. Suas publicações despertaram sensação, e então apareceu uma chuva de literatura contrária, na Inglaterra e no estrangeiro. Foi perseguido por causa de suas crenças (intolerância e ódio supostamente postos a serviço de Deus), e passou os últimos dezessete anos de sua vida entrando e saindo de prisões. Quando era posto em liberdade, reunia-se com seus seguidores, nunca se tendo retratado. Seus seguidores foram os primeiros a formar uma congregação unitária. Ver o artigo sobre o *Unitarismo*. Ele acreditava que o trinitarismo termina tornando-se em *triteísmo*, uma forma de politeísmo. O próprio John Biddle era homem que exercia forte atração pessoal, caracterizado por uma piedade devota. Quando faleceu (na prisão), sua congregação dispersou-se, mas a sua influência teve prosseguimento, continuando a estimular as controvérsias trinitarianas. Disso resultou o aparecimento formal dos unitários, nas duas gerações que se seguiram. (AM E)

BIEDERMANN, ALOIS EMMANUEL

Suas datas foram 1819 a 1885. Durante muitos anos foi professor de teologia da Universidade de Zurique, na Suíça. Ele defendia a idéia que infinitude e espiritualidade são os conceitos centrais no estudo da pessoa de Deus. Consideradas juntamente, essas duas idéias formam o conceito do *espírito absoluto*. Mas, a idéia de personalidade não pode ser aplicada a esse conceito, e nisso consistia a grande fraqueza de seu sistema, pois Deus é pessoal. (E)

BIEL, GABRIEL

Escolástico alemão (1425-1495). Nasceu em Speier, ensinou em Tubingen, onde, por duas vezes, foi seu reitor. Era seguidor de Ockham e se opunha ao pelagianismo (ver o artigo). Sua exposição das idéias de Ockham (ver o artigo) expande a área da fé, no que tange à razão. Essa exposição tornou-se muito influente nas universidades alemãs, incluindo a de Wittenberg. Seus pontos de vista sobre a soberania de Deus, e sobre o poder divino absoluto e aparentemente arbitrário, sobre todos (ver sobre o *voluntarismo*), influenciaram os pensamentos de Lutero e Melanchthon. Ver sobre *predestinação* e *livre-arbítrio*. (P)

BIGAMIA

A Bíblia não condena nem a bigamia e nem a poligamia, e a legislação mosaica chega a instruir acerca dos direitos das concubinas (Êxo. 21:7-11; Deu. 21:10-14). Os reis de Israel deram um mau exemplo nesse sentido. Salomão foi o campeão da poligamia. Lemos em I Reis 11:3: «Tinha setecentas mulheres, princesas, e trezentas concubinas; e suas mulheres lhe perverteram o coração». No entanto, visto que a legislação mosaica era omissa a respeito, isso não era considerado imoral ou indecente em Israel. Incidentalmente, isso nos mostra um dos pontos onde a lei mosaica era deficiente, e por que precisou ser ultrapassada pela lei de Cristo, no Novo Testamento. No Novo Testamento, as instruções de que os ministros do evangelho devem ser maridos de uma só mulher (I Tim. 3:2; Tito 1:6), mostram-nos que pelo menos para os líderes cristãos a monogamia era considerada necessária. Jesus ensinou o conceito ideal de um-marido-uma-esposa (Mat. 19:6 *ss*), onde ele deixa claro que a legislação mosaica era uma adaptação à dureza dos corações humanos. Não obstante, Jesus legislou claramente em favor da monogamia. Quando os discípulos objetaram: «Se essa é a condição do homem relativamente à sua mulher, não convém casar», Jesus retorquiu: «Nem todos são aptos para receber este conceito, mas apenas aqueles a quem é dado» (Mat. 19:10,11). Os apóstolos secundaram o Senhor Jesus. Paulo ensinou: «...cada um tenha a sua própria esposa e cada uma o seu próprio marido» (I Cor. 7:2). Ver os artigos sobre *Matrimônio, Monogamia* e *Poligamia*.

Nos países onde a poligamia é reconhecida por lei, ou onde é prática arraigada (como em países africanos e islâmicos), a Igreja cristã encoraja a monogamia, embora não tenha sido capaz de pô-la em vigor. Nas regiões mais pobres, onde as mulheres têm poucos meios de subsistência própria, os missionários evangélicos têm descoberto que a poligamia é melhor do que a prostituição das esposas rejeitadas. Nos países onde a prática é proibida por lei, a Igreja cristã sempre a condenou. Em grande número de casos, a prática envolve, necessariamente, engano e maus-tratos.

BIGORNA

No hebraico, **batida**. Um bloco de ferro onde os ferreiros punham a peça de metal a ser moldada. Uma palavra encontrada na Bíblia somente em Isa. 41:7. A bigorna de metal era montada em madeira ou no chão, para torná-la estável, variando quanto ao formato, segundo as peças a serem ali forjadas. Geralmente tinha um bico ou chifre em uma das extremidades, para forjar peças ocas ou arredondadas. A descrição do trabalho desses artífices, em Isa. 41:6,7, é bastante similar àquilo que pode ser visto em muitos países até hoje. O trabalho geralmente era feito por dois homens, cada um de um lado da bigorna, que encorajavam e instruíam um ao outro. (HA S)

BIGTÃ, BIGTÃ

No hebraico, «dado pela fortuna». Era o nome de um dos sete eunucos do harém de Assuero ou Xerxes (Est. 1:10), em cerca de 483 A.C. É possível que se trate do mesmo homem chamado Bigtã, em Ester 2:21 e 6:2. Se isso é verdade então Bigtã ou Bigtã também entrou em conluio com outro eunuco para tirarem a vida do monarca. Essa conspiração foi descoberta por Mordecai, que a revelou a Ester. Feitas as investigações e apurada a culpa de ambos, Bigtã e Teres, os dois conluiados, foram enforcados (Est. 2:23).

BIGVAI

No hebraico, «feliz» ou «do povo». Há dois homens no Antigo Testamento com esse nome, a saber:

1. O cabeça de uma família que retornou do cativeiro babilônico (ver o artigo), em companhia de Zorobabel (Esd. 2:2; Nee. 7:7). No dizer de Nee. 7:19, nada menos de dois mil e sessenta e sete homens vieram com ele. Alguns homens desse mesmo clã vieram da Pérsia com Esdras (Esd. 8:14; I Esdras 5:14).

2. Um homem que assinou, entre outros, o pacto com Neemias (Nee. 10:16), e que, aparentemente, foi um dos chefes da expedição enviada sob as ordens de Zorobabel (Esd. 2:2; Nee. 7:7), em cerca de 410 A.C.

BILA

No hebraico, «terna», embora outros pensem em «timidez». É nome de uma mulher e de uma cidade, nas páginas do Antigo Testamento:

1. Serva de Raquel, dada por ela a Jacó para que não permanecesse sem filhos, pois até ali ela era estéril. Bila tornou-se a mãe de Dã e de Naftali (Gên. 30:1-8; 35:25; 46:25; I Crô. 7:13). Era apenas uma escrava que, dessa maneira, se tornou uma das matriarcas de Israel. E tudo por causa do ciúme de Raquel, porquanto sua irmã Lia já tinha vários filhos, enquanto ela não tinha nenhum (Gên. 29:31-35; 30:1-8). Os contratos de casamento descobertos pela arqueologia, em Nuzi, demonstram que no segundo milênio A.C., era costumeiro uma mulher estéril fazer o que Raquel fez. O fato de Raquel ter dado nome aos dois meninos assim gerados, mostra-nos que ela manteve a autoridade de mãe principal, embora não biologicamente relacionada às crianças. Posteriormente, Bila tornou-se culpada de incesto com Rúben (Gên. 35:22). Cerca de 1753 A.C.

2. Uma cidade com esse nome estava localizada no território de Simeão (I Crô. 4:29). É bem provável que essa mesma cidade apareça em Jos. 19:3, com o nome de Balá, e em Jos. 15:29, com o nome de Baalá.

BILÃ

No hebraico, «terno». Foi nome de dois homens, que aparecem no Antigo Testamento:

1. Um horeu, chefe do monte Seir, em Edom (Gên. 36:27; I Crô. 1:42). Tornou-se o progenitor de um subclã, em Edom. Cerca de 1963 A.C.

2. Um benjamita, filho de Jediael (I Crô. 7:10). Foi pai de sete filhos, os quais se tornaram cabeças de suas tribos.

BILDADE

No hebraico, «filho da contenção» ou «senhor Adade». Foi um dos confortadores molestos de Jó e segundo de seus oponentes, dentro da vívida discussão filosófica, moral e religiosa que houve entre eles (Jó 2:11; 8:1; 18:1; 25:1). Alguns supõem que, em face de ser ele chamado de «o suíta», na primeira dessas referências, ele pode ter sido descendente de Abraão e Quetura, através de Suá (Gên. 25:2), o que faria dele membro de uma tribo de nômades arameus, que vivia na região suleste da Palestina. Entretanto, outros estudiosos insistem em que, em face da total ausência de genealogias no livro de Jó, isso significa que a obra foi uma novela religiosa e filosófica, sem pretensões históricas. — Ver o artigo sobre *Jó*. As referências dadas acima mostram as intervenções de Bildade. As idéias por ele defendidas são: a. A justiça estava envolvida na triste condição a que Jó fora reduzido. b. Os filhos de Jó haviam morrido por motivo de pecado. c. Se Jó se arrependesse, Deus devolver-lhe-ia a prosperidade. d. A história mostra que Deus castiga os ímpios, fazendo prosperar os retos. e. Os pecadores nada recebem nesta vida além de miséria e de desonra após a morte. f. Finalmente, Bildade exaltou a perfeição de Deus, em contraste com a imperfeição de todas as outras coisas. Na

BILEÃ — BINITARIANISMO

verdade, porém, alguns desses argumentos de Bildade não correspondem aos fatos. Assim, os justos com freqüência sofrem, ao passo que os iníquos prosperam. Essa é uma das razões da complexidade do *problema do mal* (ver o artigo). O livro de Jó é um estudo sobre esse problema. (ID NTI)

BILEÃ

No hebraico, «lugar da conquista». Era uma cidade do território de Manassés, na parte oriental do Jordão, dada aos levitas da família de Coate (I Crô. 6:70). Em outros trechos do Antigo Testamento a cidade é chamada Ibleã (Jos. 17:11; Juí. 1:27). Tem sido identificada com o moderno Tell Bel'ameh, que fica entre Samaria e Jezreel.

BILGA

No hebraico, «rompimento». Isso seria uma alusão ao fato de que se tratava de um primogênito. Mas alguns estudiosos preferem pensar que a palavra significa «brilho». Foi nome de dois homens, nas páginas do Antigo Testamento:

1. Um sacerdote que retornou do exílio babilônico com Zorobabel (Nee. 12:5,18), e que talvez fosse o mesmo *Bilgai* que foi um dos signatários do pacto com Neemias (Nee. 10:8), em cerca de 536 A.C.

2. Um sacerdote que estava encarregado do décimo quinto turno, no serviço do templo de Jerusalém, na época de Davi (I Crô. 24:14), em cerca de 1043 A.C.

BILGAI

Provavelmente trata-se do mesmo sacerdote chamado Bilga, em Nee. 12:5,18, mas cujo nome é grafado Bilgai em Nee. 10:8. Ver *Bilga*.

BILOCAÇÃO

Esse é o nome da doutrina que diz que, visto ser dupla a personalidade humana, uma pessoa é capaz de estar em dois lugares ao mesmo tempo. Em um lugar, fisicamente, e no outro através da porção imaterial do ser. Quando isso ocorre, o indivíduo geralmente está dormindo, embora tenha havido casos em que isso não sucede. O fenômeno também é chamado *viagem astral*. Acredita-se que o corpo astral é o veículo da alma. Alguns pesquisadores supõem que todas as pessoas, quando dormem, têm essa experiência. Alguns sonhos seriam experiências reais, no nível da alma, e não meras imagens mentais ou cerebrais.

Parece haver alguma evidência em favor da idéia da multilocação, segundo a qual uma entidade pode fazer-se presente não meramente em dois lugares, mas em muitos lugares, ao mesmo tempo. Uma aplicação teológica dessa possibilidade seria a doutrina católica romana da transubstanciação (ver o artigo). Há rumores de bilocação nas religiões orientais, bem como acerca de vários santos cristãos. Os parapsicólogos modernos, os psicólogos e os psiquiatras têm feito experiências com o fenômeno, sob condições controladas, com evidências positivas em favor de sua realidade. Porém, haverá de passar-se algum tempo antes que a ciência possa confirmar tal realidade, embora as evidências colhidas já sejam promissoras. Nada existe na fé religiosa que diga que o fenômeno não pode ocorrer e há muito que o consubstancia. Seja como for, trata-se de uma experiência humana comum, que requer maior investigação.

Atualmente, é uma das principais evidências científico-empíricas em prol da existência da alma. O seu *modus operandi* é bastante parecido com aquilo que as pessoas experimentam nas experiências de quase morte (ver o artigo), as quais também são muito importantes para demonstrar empiricamente a existência da alma.

Em nossos dias, a ciência está desenvolvendo métodos para investigar e recolher evidências em favor da existência da alma. Portanto, parece perfeitamente possível que, dentro de um prazo não muito longo, a ciência venha a colher provas da existência da alma. Nessa área, pois, veremos um casamento entre a ciência e a religião e grandes serão os frutos daí resultantes. Quanto a detalhes sobre a bilocação, ver o artigo geral sobre a *Parapsicologia*, sob o título *Projeção da Psique*. (E EC)

BILSÃ

No hebraico «pesquisador (do Senhor?)». Foi um dos onze ou doze líderes judeus que retornaram do cativeiro babilônico sob a liderança de Josué e Zorobabel, em resultado do decreto de Ciro, rei da Pérsia (Esd. 2:2; Nee. 7:7). O seu nome aparece com a forma de Belsaro, em I Esdras 5:8, talvez derivado do acádico, *Belshar*, «Bel é rei».

BIMAL

No hebraico, «filho da circuncisão»? Foi um dos três filhos de Jaflete, filho de Aser, através de Berias e Héber. Foi chefe de uma família e guerreiro da tribo de Aser (I Crô. 7:33), em cerca de 1658 A.C.

BINAÇÃO

Um termo que significa de dois em dois ou dois de cada vez. Vem do latim, *binarius*, *bini*. Na Igreja Católica Romana, a palavra indica a celebração da *missa* (ver o artigo) duas vezes em um só dia, por uma mesma pessoa. Pelo menos nos dias de Agostinho (falecido em 430 D.C.), a missa era celebrada uma vez por dia. Mais tarde, duas ou três vezes por dia. Ainda mais tarde, a celebração foi novamente restringida a uma só vez por dia. Atualmente, os padres podem celebrar até duas missas aos domingos e dias santos, para que todos os católicos romanos possam fazer-se presentes. (E)

BINEÃ

No hebraico, «jorro», «fonte» ou «vagabundo». Era um benjamita, filho de Moza e pai de Rafa. Era um dos descendentes do rei Saul (I Crô. 8:37; 9:43). Viveu em cerca de 850 A.C.

BINITARIANISMO

Um termo aplicado à tendência de alguns de se referirem à Trindade de maneira dupla, e não à maneira trinitária comum. Nos dias anteriores ao concílio de Nicéia, o conceito do *Logos* incorporava as idéias e funções atualmente atribuídas ao Filho e ao Espírito Santo. Por isso, falava-se então no Pai e no Logos, e não no Pai, no Filho e no Espírito Santo. Alguns grupos reputados hereges mantinham formas de binitarianismo, como foi o caso dos monarquianos, os quais concebiam que a deidade consiste no Pai e no Filho (este último incorporando a idéia do Espírito Santo). No século IV D.C., os *tropici* do Egito negavam a divindade do Espírito. Atanásio escreveu combatendo esse grupo, em suas *Epístolas a Serapião*. Naquele mesmo século encontramos os macedônios (ver o artigo) ou pneumatomáquios (combatedores do Espírito) que também negavam a divindade do Espírito. Basílio escreveu seu tratado sobre o Espírito Santo tendo esse grupo em mira. (C)

BINUI

No hebraico, «edifício» ou «família». Foi nome de várias personagens do Antigo Testamento:

1. Um levita dos dias pós-exílicos, pai de Noadias (Esd. 8:33; I Esdras 8:63), que supervisionou a pesagem dos vasos de ouro e de prata que Esdras trouxera da Babilônia. Cerca de 536 A.C.

2. Um levita, filho de Henadade, que ajudou nos reparos das muralhas de Jerusalém, sob a supervisão de Neemias (Nee. 3:24; 10:9). Talvez deva ser identificado com o Binui mencionado em Neemias 12:8. Cerca de 446 A.C.

3. O antepassado de alguns que retornaram do exílio babilônico em companhia de Zorobabel (Nee. 7:15). É chamado pelo nome de Bani, em Esd. 2:10 e I Esdras 5:12.

4. O antepassado de alguns judeus que se tinham casado com mulheres estrangeiras, mas que tiveram de se divorciar, terminado o exílio (Esd. 10:38). Talvez deva ser identificado com o Bani de Esd. 10:34 e I Esdras 9:34.

5. Um levita que retornou do exílio, com Zorobabel (Nee. 12:8).

6. Um dos filhos de Paate-Moabe, que se casara com uma mulher estrangeira (Esd. 10:30). Ele é chamado Belnuus, em I Esdras 9:31; e talvez seja o mesmo que o alistado como o número 4, acima.

BIO DE CIRENE

Ver sobre o **Cirenaicismo**, segundo ponto.

BIOLOGIA

Vem de duas palavras gregas, **bios**, «vida» e **logia**, «conhecimento».

Esse ramo da ciência fazia parte central dos estudos do Liceu (ver o artigo) de Aristóteles, onde eram conduzidos em bases experimentais, ao passo que os estudos da física e de outras ciências permaneciam puramente especulativos e teóricos. O conhecimento dos seres vivos era obtido mediante dissecação e através do processo lógico da indução. Aristóteles, por isso mesmo, é considerado o pai da biologia.

Nos tempos modernos, essa disciplina tornou-se distinta da filosofia, embora haja uma filosofia da biologia com três interpretações principais, a saber: 1. o reducionismo (que vide); — 2. o vitalismo (ver o artigo); e c. a biologia organicista (ver o artigo).

Definições:

1. *Reducionismo*. Todos os fenômenos biológicos podem ser adequadamente explicados por meio das categorias da química e da física, através do materialismo (ver o artigo) e do mecanismo (ver o artigo).

2. *Vitalismo*. Existe uma força vital controladora, dentro das formas orgânicas, que não pode ser reduzida a uma interpretação psicoquímica. Há um elemento imaterial no material. A teoria aristotélica da *entelequia* (ver o artigo) é fator importante dentro dessa crença.

3. *Biologia organicista*. Esse sistema nega os dois anteriores, ao mesmo tempo em que encara as ações do organismo inteiro como algo que não pode ser compreendido simplesmente como a soma das ações de cada parte constituinte. Ver o artigo sobre o *Problema Corpo-Mente* (EP MM P)

BIOLOGIA ORGÂNICA

Esse título designa aquelas teorias da biologia que supõem que essa disciplina não pode ser ensinada ou descrita senão do ponto de vista dos reducionistas. Ver sobre o *Reducionismo*. A biologia, porém, envolve mais do que a física e a química. Há considerações não-materiais que precisam ser levadas em conta, — como as energias, que seriam mais básicas que os objetos materiais, e que são imateriais quanto à sua natureza. Ou então, a biologia pode ser encarada sob o ponto de vista de que as entidades biológicas são veículos de energias vitais ou formas espirituais, que não são idênticas aos veículos físicos. Ver sobre o *Vitalismo* e a *Alma*. Ver também sobre o *Holismo*. Platão supunha que a natureza inteira é dual, e que não há tais coisas como meros corpos físicos. Todas as coisas teriam uma porção correspondente, de natureza psíquica. (EP P)

BÍON DE BORÍSTENES

Filósofo grego do século III A.C. Foi discípulo do acadêmico Crates, de Teodoro de Cirene (Teodoro, o ateu) e de Teofrasto (o filósofo peripatético) (ver os artigos sobre eles). Bíon tornou-se aderente da filosofia dos cínicos. Foi ele quem popularizou essa teoria e introduziu a forma da *diatribe*. Não obstante, abrandou um tanto a doutrina cínica, afastando-se do ascetismo e aproximando-se mais do ceticismo. (AM P)

BIRAN, MAINE DE

Suas datas foram 1766-1824. Foi o mais importante psicólogo francês do século XIX. Foi profundo pensador e é considerado o santo patrono do *espiritualismo* francês. Para eles, espiritualismo era o mesmo que para nós é o *idealismo* (ver o artigo). Ele afirmava que o alicerce de nosso conhecimento é a consciência que temos de nossas próprias atividades. Para ele, a religião era definida mais como uma questão de sentimentos do que como uma questão de fé. Mostrava-se incapaz de distinguir entre a própria alma como fonte de conhecimento e o conhecimento divinamente outorgado, mediante influências externas. (E)

BIRGITTA, STª

Suas datas foram 1303-1373. Também é conhecida como Stª Bridget. Nasceu em Uppland, na Suécia, filha de uma família nobre. Casou-se com um dos conselheiros do monarca sueco e tinha acesso aos círculos sociais mais elevados. Era mulher de inclinações fortemente religiosas. Depois que seu marido faleceu, em 1344, começou a considerar-se a noiva de Cristo. Julgou ter recebido revelações da Virgem Maria, provenientes de Cristo, e que falavam especificamente de questões relativas à reforma da Igreja e ao retorno da sede papal de Avinhão, na França, para Roma. Ela trabalhou árdua e longamente em favor de uma nova ordem religiosa, o que em parte se concretizou. Várias instituições originaram-se de seus esforços ou por inspiração sua. Após uma peregrinação a Jerusalém, Birgitta morreu em Roma, em 1373. Foi canonizada em 1391. Parece que as supostas visões dela não eram tanto de natureza mística; eram antes ordens éticas a respeito da necessidade de reformar os abusos na Igreja de Roma e do estado. Seus escritos foram publicados em latim, em Lubekc, em 1492. Ela foi a fundadora da ordem das bridgetinas, tendo-se tornado a santa patrona da Suécia. Stª Catarina da Suécia foi filha de Bridget, e abadessa entre 1374 e 1375. A festa de Bridget é celebrada a oito de outubro. (AM E)

BIRSA

No hebraico, «grosso» ou «forte»; mas outros preferem pensar no sentido «filho da iniqüidade». Era o nome do rei de Gomorra, quando Quedorlaomer invadiu o lugar (Gên. 14:2), em cerca de 2080 A.C. Ele é mencionado no Gên. Apocryphon xxi.24. Birsa revoltou-se contra Quedorlaomer, rei do Elão, mas foi finalmente derrotado. Posteriormente, Abraão conseguiu derrotar as forças de Quedorlaomer, libertando os gomorritas e seu sobrinho, Ló, que havia sido levado cativo pelos elamitas. (Gên. 14:12-17).

BIRZAVITE

No hebraico, «poço de azeitonas» ou «azeite de oliveira». Pai de Malquiel e bisneto de Aser (I Crô. 7:31). É possível que a moderna cidade de Bir-Zeite, cerca de 24 km ao norte de Jerusalém, derive do nome dele, talvez por ser povoada antigamente por seus descendentes. Alguns estudiosos pensam que Birzavite era nome de uma cidade, e não nome de um homem, e que tal cidade teria sido fundada por Malquiel. A localidade tem sido identificada por alguns com Zerzeto, a aldeia onde Judas Macabeu acampou pela última vez (Josefo, *Anti*. xiii.11,1).

BISLÃO

No hebraico, «em paz». Um dos oficiais do rei da Pérsia, que escreveu a Artaxerxes, solicitando-lhe que proibisse os judeus de reconstruírem o templo (Esd. 4:7), em cerca de 522 A.C. Alguns estudiosos pensam que esse nome pode ter sido, originalmente, a palavra hebraica que significa «contra Jerusalém», e que posteriormente foi corrompido para que significasse «em paz».

BISMILÁ

Um vocábulo árabe que significa «no nome de Deus (Allah)». É uma exclamação comum entre os islamitas. (E)

BISPO

No grego, **episkopos**, «supervisor». Palavra que é aplicada, antes de tudo, a Cristo (I Ped. 2:25); em seguida, ao ofício apostólico (Atos 1:20, citando Sal. 109:8); e finalmente, aos líderes das congregações locais cristãs (Fil. 1:1). Como verbo, substantivo e adjetivo, a palavra aparece no Novo Testamento por onze vezes (Heb. 12:15; I Ped. 2:12,25; 5:2; Luc. 19:44; Atos 1:20; 20:28; I Tim. 3:1,2; Fil. 1:1, e Tito 1:7.

Origens:

Nosso termo português, «bispo», deriva-se do latim, *biscopus*, mas a palavra no Novo Testamento, é grega e designa o Senhor Jesus e os apóstolos como «supervisores», e finalmente, um dos ofícios do ministério cristão, que são os «supervisores» abaixo de Cristo. Os títulos «bispo», «ancião» e «pastor» eram sinônimos perfeitos, indicando um dos quatro ministérios cristãos: apóstolos, profetas, evangelistas e pastores/mestres (Efé. 4:11). Portanto, aqueles três títulos são intercambiáveis, conforme se vê em Atos 20:28. A palavra grega podia ser usada de maneira não-técnica, aplicada a qualquer pessoa dotada de autoridade de supervisão. Em I Pedro 2:25 é um título de Cristo. Em Filipenses 1:1 indica o grupo de autoridades liderantes de uma comunidade cristã. Tito 1:7 parece usar a palavra como sinônimo de «ancião». Talvez devêssemos dizer que «bispo», «ancião» e «pastor» eram três títulos que ressaltavam três aspectos diferentes de uma mesma função eclesiástica.

Contudo, alguns estudiosos pensam que as epístolas pastorais fornecem indícios para pensarmos de outra maneira. Pois Timóteo recebeu de Paulo o poder de consagrar anciãos para serem oficiais das igrejas da área onde ele trabalhava no evangelho. Isso parece aproximar-se ao ofício distinto de «bispo», conforme o mesmo surgiu posteriormente, o qual já tinha autoridade sobre os anciãos de alguma área geográfica. Todavia, não é necessariamente assim, pois pastores podem consagrar outros irmãos como pastores, sem que isso requeira que o presbitério consagrador componha-se de «bispos» que consagrem «pastores», como se um ofício maior desse autoridade a um menor.

Nas funções e poderes dos apóstolos, encontramos uma função similar à dos futuros «bispos», pois os apóstolos certamente tinham funções que se estendiam a áreas geográficas, e não meramente a igrejas locais isoladas. Porém, esse argumento perde muito de sua força quando consideramos que os apóstolos enfeixavam, em seu ofício, todos os demais ministérios. Em seu trabalho, os apóstolos também eram profetas, evangelistas, pastores e mestres. Portanto, não é de se admirar que fizessem coisas próprias dos deveres que, posteriormente, mas ainda dentro do período neotestamentário, eram entregues aos bispos ou anciãos.

Irineu (ver o artigo) no segundo século da era cristã, refere-se aos bispos como sucessores dos apóstolos, tanto como mestres como administradores das igrejas. Até aí, nada há de mais, pois os bispos poderiam ser os mesmos anciãos. Mas Hipólito (ver o artigo), entre 160 e 235 D.C., assevera que somente os bispos tinham a autoridade para ordenar. Torna-se claro, pois, que em sua época, um bispo era mais que um ancião. Na Síria e na Ásia Menor, cada corpo local governante era supervisionado pelos *chorepiscopoi*, ou «bispos itinerantes», os quais, por sua vez, eram responsáveis diante de um bispo fixado em alguma cidade grande mais próxima. Mas, como é evidente, isso já representa uma evolução que não existia nos tempos dos apóstolos, pelo que não deveria servir-nos de padrão. O ministério das igrejas cristãs foi sofrendo transformações que não têm base bíblica. Assim, na África do Norte, um bispo com plenos direitos era nomeado sempre que vinha à existência alguma comunidade cristã. Nos distritos em redor de Alexandria, as aldeias eram deixadas ao encargo de anciãos, os quais operavam sob a supervisão do bispo de Alexandria. A mesma coisa sucedia na Europa Ocidental, onde somente os bispos tinham o direito de ordenar a ministros locais. Naturalmente, havia muitos lugares onde o bispo era apenas o ancião ou pastor de uma igreja local. Mas, em redor das cidades maiores, surgiu a tendência de um pastor de uma cidade maior exercer influência sobre os pastores de cidades menores. E aquele passou a ser chamado «bispo». O título continuava o mesmo dos tempos do

Novo Testamento, mas as funções dos bispos ultrapassavam em tudo quanto se vê nas páginas sagradas. Esse tipo de atividade continuou até que houve a necessidade de surgirem os «arcebispos», ou «bispos-chefes»; ou então, nas igrejas orientais, os «patriarcas». Em todo esse desenvolvimento, foi surgindo o papa de Roma, que tinha maior prestígio e autoridade que a de todos os arcebispos e bispos. Isso criou toda uma hierarquia eclesiástica, ao passo que o Novo Testamento nos apresenta a idéia de um ministério diversificado, mas sem superioridades e inferioridades. Disse Jesus: «...um só é vosso Mestre, e vós todos sois irmãos» (Mat. 23:8).

Intervenção do Estado. Quando o imperador Constantino declarou-se cristão, o estado deixou de ser hostil para com o cristianismo. E, dentro do cristianismo oficializado que se formou em torno do imperador, os bispos começaram a ter poderes políticos, e não meramente eclesiásticos. Outrossim, mediante a força de decretos imperiais, o estado com freqüência conferia-lhes esses poderes. Legados e concessões de terra em vários casos transformaram os bispos em poderosos proprietários de terras, e assim sendo, governantes supremos de suas respectivas comunidades, pois combinavam muito dinheiro, autoridade eclesiástica e autoridade civil. Por essa razão é que, na Idade Média, os bispos, em muitos casos, eram cabeças de alguma comunidade feudal. Ocupavam funções políticas e geralmente eram empregados nas atividades do estado. Na igreja da Inglaterra até hoje há poderosos bispos religiosos políticos. Vinte e seis bispos anglicanos têm assento garantido no Parlamento inglês. O ofício dos bispos está muito diferente do que se vê nos dias do Novo Testamento, quando então eram apenas pastores de congregações locais!

Bispos na Cristandade Atual. Referimo-nos a bispos de grupos cristãos onde o ofício extrapola a tudo quanto o Novo Testamento lhes atribui:

a. *Na Igreja Católica Romana*, um bispo exerce autoridade sobre alguma área, havendo padres sob as suas ordens. A teologia católica romana afirma que os bispos são necessários para a própria existência da Igreja. Pois eles estão investidos de autoridade administrativa, de ensino e de ordenação de sacerdotes. Este último item é considerado o mais importante, inseparável mesmo do ofício. Os bispos católicos são considerados vice-regentes de Cristo, canais através dos quais flui a graça divina.

b. *Nas Igrejas Ortodoxas*, o direito de confirmação é regularmente delegado pelo episcopado ao clero inferior. Portanto, ali os bispos não ocupam posição tão crucial como no romanismo.

c. *Na Igreja Episcopal* a denominação é governada por bispos, que governam dioceses e congregam muitas igrejas. Somente os bispos têm o direito de consagrar, havendo três ordens no ministério episcopal: bispos, padres e diáconos.

Tanto os católicos romanos como os anglicanos insistem que seus bispos podem traçar sua sucessão desde os apóstolos de Cristo. Outros contentam-se em fazer essa sucessão retroceder até muitos séculos atrás, sem a necessidade de fazê-la remontar aos apóstolos. E ainda outros grupos cristãos abandonaram totalmente a idéia de uma real sucessão apostólica (ver o artigo), porque é impossível alguém provar tal sucessão, sem importar em qual denominação cristã estejamos pensando.

d. *Presbiterianos.* Entre eles, não é usado o título «bispo» como título separado. A distinção que fazem é entre anciãos que ensinam e anciãos que administram, tendo em mente o trecho de I Timóteo 5:17. O ancião que ensina recebe sua ordenação da parte de outros anciãos-mestres, tornando-se um pastor local, responsável por funções eclesiásticas gerais, incluindo a administração dos sacramentos (ver o artigo). Mas os anciãos administradores são escolhidos por suas respectivas congregações locais, sendo consagrados por um presbitério local, tornando-se um clérigo consagrado.

e. *Mórmons.* Entre eles o termo *bispo* refere-se à principal autoridade de uma congregação local. Não se trata de um clérigo profissional, mas apenas de alguém que se distinguiu em sua capacidade de liderança e como pessoa espiritual. Seria mais ou menos o equivalente aos pastores das igrejas evangélicas, embora sem treinamento formal e sem serem pagos por seus serviços.

Resta-nos falar sobre dois outros grupos evangélicos, que fogem desse quadro, até agora retratado, sobre o ministério dos bispos. Referimo-nos aos:

f. *Pentecostais.* Há entre eles os *pastores* (em alguns grupos se prefere o título anciãos) e os *presbíteros*. Acreditam que há uma gradação entre pastores e presbíteros. Na verdade, estes últimos não têm funções definidas. São apenas leigos esforçados. Não têm bispos como função separada. Isso torna o sistema ministerial muito ilógico. Têm pastores e presbíteros, mas não têm bispos! A lógica exigiria que, já que distinguem entre pastores e presbíteros, também deveriam distinguir entre esses dois títulos e o de bispos! Mas, como o governo eclesiástico dos pentecostais é extremamente centralizado, eles têm pastores de igrejas centrais, às quais se atrelam às vezes centenas de outras igrejas locais, formando o que eles chamam de «ministérios». Os pastores dessas igrejas centrais são virtuais bispos (aos moldes católicos romanos), embora não sejam intitulados como tais. Também têm diáconos.

g. *Congregacionais.* Os únicos oficiais eclesiásticos ali reconhecidos são os pastores e os diáconos. A ordenação efetua-se quando um grupo de pastores reúne-se com essa finalidade específica. Tal ordenação, porém, não é considerada uma transmissão de graças espirituais. Antes, é apenas o reconhecimento de que essas graças já se fazem presentes nos candidatos. Algumas igrejas congregacionais sentem-se dotadas de autoridade para efetuarem ordenações, sem necessitarem convocar igrejas congêneres para esse mister. Pois a autoridade, entre eles, repousa sobre o voto da congregação local, e não nos pastores da denominação. Os grupos batistas, quanto a esse particular, podem ser categorizados entre os congregacionais. (AM C CAR E REID)

BISPO AUXILIAR

Um bispo sem jurisdição pessoal, que atua como assistente do bispo legitimamente constituído. Tal ofício não era visto com bons olhos na Igreja antiga, embora tenha-se tornado prática regular em tempos modernos. (E)

BITIA

No hebraico, «filha de Yahweh». Ao que parece, era uma das filhas de Faraó que contraiu matrimônio com Merede, descendente de Judá (I Crô. 4:17). Todavia, não se sabe se o pai de Bitia era, realmente, um monarca egípcio, ou se se tratava de um judeu chamado Faraó. Cerca de 1658 A.C.

••• ••• •••

BITÍNIA

Uma província da Ásia Menor, com o mar Negro ao norte e o Bósforo e o Proponto (mar de Mármara) a oeste. Ao sul limitava-se com a Frígia e a Galácia, e a leste com a Paflagônia. Os bitínios, que eram de origem trácia, eram rudes e pouco civilizados; sua história começa no século VI A.C. Mas, em vista de sua força e unidade, conseguiram manter certa independência, enquanto os persas dominavam tudo. Outra coisa sucedeu durante o tempo dos Selêucidas. Formou-se ali uma dinastia, em 297 A.C., que perdurou por dois séculos, até que foi doada a Roma, em 74 A.C., pelo último dos reis trácios. Pompeu uniu a Bitínia com o Ponto, em 64 A.C., e fez do conjunto uma província senatorial. Plínio, o Moço, foi um legado imperial na Bitínia, de 110 a 112 D.C. Dessa época é que chegaram até nós as *Cartas* de Plínio para o imperador Trajano, as quais nos fornecem abundantes informações acerca de Bitínia, seus problemas administrativos, e as legislações anticristãs da época.

Não sabemos dizer como o cristianismo estabeleceu-se na Bitínia; mas, em I Pedro 1:1 a Bitínia é mencionada como um dos lugares onde havia cristãos a quem Pedro se dirigia. Paulo não teve a permissão de visitar aquela área, em certa ocasião (ver Atos 16:7). No entanto, pode tê-lo feito em outras oportunidades, sobre o que nada se sabe. As cartas de Plínio confirmam a vigorosa natureza da igreja cristã dali, requerendo considerável atenção da parte do governo romano. (ID JON)

BITROM

No hebraico, «quebrada» ou «dividida». Aparentemente era uma localidade em um vale que levava ao lado oriental do rio Jordão, através do qual Abner, comandante do exército de Isbosete, e seus homens, marcharam, após terem cruzado aquele rio, na direção de Maanaim. Isso depois da derrota a eles infligida por Joabe, general de Davi (II Sam. 2:29). Algumas traduções dizem «depois do meio-dia», como se fosse uma designação de tempo. Nossa versão portuguesa omite toda uma frase, «e atravessou toda Bitrom», o que significa que o nome do lugar não figura na Bíblia portuguesa, porquanto ela é mencionada somente nessa referência. Mas, se realmente tratava-se de uma cidade, coisa alguma se sabe a seu respeito em nossos dias. Porém, há estudiosos que acreditam que se trata de uma garganta existente na Arabá ou vale do Jordão.

BIZÂNCIO

Cidade fundada em cerca de 658 A.C. por uma colônia de megarianos, sob a liderança de Bizas, de quem a localidade tomou o nome. O imperador Constantino, em 325 D.C., escolheu-a para ser a nova capital do império romano, tendo-a reedificado para servir aos seus propósitos. A nova cidade, chamada Constantinopla, foi dedicada a 11 de maio de 330 D.C.

BIZIOTIÁ

No hebraico, «oliveiras de Yahweh». O nome aparece somente em Jos. 15:28. Aparentemente era uma vila que ficava no sul de Judá, perto de Berseba. Contudo, a LXX diz «e suas filhas», aludindo às aldeias em redor, uma tradução possível através de uma interpretação diferente do texto hebraico.

••• ••• •••

BIZTA

No hebraico, «eunuco» (?), um dos quatro eunucos do harém de Xerxes ou Assuero. Esse eunuco recebeu ordens para trazer Vasti para ser admirada pelos convidados ao banquete do rei (Esd. 1:10). Cerca de 519 A.C.

BLANSHARD, BRAND

Filósofo norte-americano (1892-?). Foi professor na Universidade de Michigan, no Swarthmore College e na Universidade de Yale.

Idéias. 1. A autonomia da razão, dotada de coerência e consistência, na busca pela verdade. 2. Idealismo. O real consiste na idéia, no espírito; e o conhecimento que temos do real é a idéia que temos, através da razão. A realidade corresponde aos universais da compreensão interna. 3. Realismo radical. O universal é uma entidade separada e real. Ver sobre o *Realismo*. 4. A teoria da coerência da verdade. Ver sobre *Teorias da Verdade*. 5. Determinismo, e não livre-arbítrio humano. 6. No campo da ética, o direito é determinado em termos de teologia, e a bondade em termos de satisfação e senso de realização. (EP P)

BLASFÊMIA Grego **blaks** (mal) + **phemi** (falar)

Há quatro palavras hebraicas e uma grega, a saber:
1. *Gadaph*, «insultar». Palavra hebraica usada por sete vezes. Por exemplo: II Reis 19:6; Sal. 44:16; Isa. 37:6,23.
2. *Naqab*, «transpassar». Usada por vinte e quatro vezes. — Por exemplo: Lev. 24:11,16; Núm. 22:11,17; 24:10.
3. *Naats*, «ferroar». Palavra usada por vinte e seis vezes. Por exemplo: II Sam. 12:14; Sal. 74:10,18; Núm. 14:11,23; Deu. 31:20.
4. *Barak*, «abençoar», quando usada negativamente. Palavra usada com o sentido de blasfemar em I Reis 21:10,13.
5. *Blaspheméo*, «blasfemar». Palavra usada por cinqüenta e seis vezes, como verbo, substantivo e adjetivo, desde Mat. 9:3 até Apo. 17:3.

Idéias envolvidas. De acordo com a mentalidade judaica, blasfemar era cometer uma ofensa séria, porquanto negava ou tratava levianamente a soberania de Deus, bem como a dignidade do homem como criatura de Deus. Além disso, os nomes de Deus eram revelações pessoais do Senhor. Difamar ou degradar o nome sagrado, o tetragrámaton—J/YHWH—equivalia a rejeitar ou tratar desprezivelmente sua soberania, sua misericórdia e seu poder.

No grego, a palavra significa dizer coisas abusivas, sendo usada para indicar ofensas contra os homens (Apo. 2:9), contra o diabo (Judas 9), contra Deus (Eze. 32:12; Mat. 26:65; Mar. 2:7; Luc. 5:21; Apo. 13:5) contra os anjos, bons ou maus (II Ped. 2:10,11; Judas 8), podendo também ser usada contra qualquer coisa pertencente a Deus. Ocasionalmente, significava difamação ou calúnia. Algumas das autoridades judaicas acusaram Jesus de blasfêmia, como quando ele afirmou que tinha autoridade para perdoar pecados (Mat. 9:3). Provavelmente, os judeus blasfemaram o nome de Cristo sob muitas circunstâncias, como, por exemplo, aquelas que envolvem a questão do sábado ou aquelas atinentes à fonte de seu poder. O perigo maior não era a blasfêmia contra o nome de Cristo; pois tal pecado, embora sério, pode ser perdoado. Todavia, a blasfêmia contra o Espírito Santo é um pecado imperdoável. Ver o artigo sobre o *pecado imperdoável*. Ver as notas sobre Mat. 12:31, no NTI.

A lei de Moisés punia os atos de blasfêmia com a pena capital (Lev. 24:10-16). Isso nos mostra a seriedade com que Deus encara esse pecado. (G ID NTI S)

BLASTO

No grego, «rebento» ou «botão». Era o nome do camareiro do rei Herodes Agripa I, mencionado exclusivamente em Atos 12:20. As pessoas íntimas de homens de grande autoridade geralmente tornam-se donas de considerável poder. Quando aquele rei se indignou contra os habitantes de Tiro e de Sidom, e proibiu a exportação de alimentos para as mesmas, chegaram dali delegações em Cesaréia, pedindo reconciliação. Os delegados procuraram a mediação de Blasto, talvez com um suborno, persuadindo-o a garantir uma audiência deles com Herodes.

BLAVATSKY, MADAME

Ver o artigo sobre a **Teosofia**.

BLONDEL, MAURICE

Um filósofo francês **espiritualista** (1891-1949). Os franceses empregam essa palavra para indicar o *idealismo* (ver o artigo), e não para indicar a religião que no Brasil chamamos de espiritismo.

Idéias. 1. A necessidade de desenvolver uma *filosofia de ação*, segundo a qual o intelecto e a vida contemplativa recebem precedência e significado, nas atividades que antecedem e resultam no pensamento. Ele buscava encontrar o equilíbrio apropriado entre a teoria e o pensamento. 2. Sem a ação apropriada, o pensamento não tem finalidade. Porém, por detrás de qualquer atividade, acha-se a *idéia*, a maior força que existe, e que provê o critério para todos os atos. 3. A análise de Blondel termina centralizando-se na idéia do trabalho puro, visto que o pensamento seria um tipo de trabalho, em si mesmo. Pensamento e trabalho são combinados em uma visão de Deus, o qual é ao mesmo tempo, o cúmulo da contemplação e uma imanência transcendental no mundo.

Obras Principais: *Action; Thought; Being and the Being; Philosophy and the Christian Spirit; Philosophical Requirements of Christianity*. (EP P)

BLONDUS, FLAVIUS

Chamado por outros de Flávio Biondo (1392-1463). Foi humanista, historiador e arqueólogo. Serviu como secretário de quatro papas diferentes. Suas obras, postumamente publicadas, a respeito de Roma e da Itália antigas, bem como acerca da era medieval, fizeram dele um dos principais fundadores da historiografia moderna. (E)

BLUMHARDTS, OS

Christoph Blumhardt (1805-1880) foi um pietista. Foi professor na Escola Missionária de Basel, pastor de uma comunidade rural no sul da Alemanha e combateu poderes demoníacos, além de ter sido o instrumento que deu início a um despertamento espiritual que incorporou elementos do cristianismo neotestamentário.

Seu filho, Cristoph Blumhardt (1842-1919), embora tenha sido, a princípio, um pastor e elemento de proa do movimento pietista, voltou sua atenção para atividades sociais e políticas, porquanto via nessas atividades a mão providencial de Deus para a criação de um mundo melhor. Ele se uniu ao Partido Democrático Social, não como membro, mas como cidadão livre, que queria promover idéias socializantes. Os dois Blumhardts, pai e filho, inspiraram outras pessoas quanto aos ideais cristãos, e eventos significativos ocorreram em Mottlingen e em Bad Roll, os lugares onde eles se mostraram mais ativos. (E)

BOÃ

No hebraico, «polegar». Foi um rubenita, em cuja honra foi erigida uma pedra que, posteriormente, serviu de marco de fronteira entre Judá e Benjamim (Jos. 15:6 e 18:17). O texto sagrado, porém, não nos esclarece se esse monumento era um marco sepulcral, ou se foi levantado para comemorar algum grande feito de Boã, quando da conquista da terra de Canaã. Cerca de 714 A.C.

BOANERGES

Uma alcunha dada por Jesus aos dois irmãos, Tiago e João, filhos de Zebedeu, um nome interpretado nas Escrituras como «filhos do trovão». (Mar. 3:17). O sentido da raiz dessa palavra é incerto, pelo que dependemos do que Marcos nos dá como seu significado. A razão pela qual essa alcunha foi dada por Jesus aos dois irmãos não é inteiramente clara, mas as idéias a respeito incluem estas explicações: 1. Eles eram dotados de grande energia física e de uma disposição explosiva. 2. Eles eram possuidores de notável eloqüência. 3. Eles eram revolucionários políticos, pois talvez fossem elementos dentre os zelotes (ver o artigo). Sabemos que um dos doze apóstolos pertencia a esse partido, a saber, Simão o Zelote (Luc. 6:15; Atos 1:13). 4. Talvez o apelido seja reflexo da antiga mitologia acerca dos Gêmeos Celestes, os *dióscuros*, filhos de Zeus, que era o deus do trovão. (ID S Z)

BOAS, GEORGE

Filósofo norte-americano (1891-1980). Estudou nas Universidades de Brown, Columbia e Harvard, tendo obtido o grau de doutor em Filosofia pela Universidade da Califórnia. Foi professor na Universidade John Hopkins, e tornou-se filósofo da história.

Idéias. 1. Os historiadores das idéias deveriam procurar determinar o papel desempenhado pelas idéias, dentro do processo histórico. O homem procura impor ao processo histórico e sua filosofia a sua lógica mas fracassa devido à existência do tempo. 2. Negou a existência dos Universais; também negou a existência dos particulares. Mas afirmou que é justamente do mundo dos particulares que tiramos as metáforas que fazem a base da nossa explicação da realidade. 3. As idéias começam como figuras de linguagem e como metáforas, e terminam transformando-se em mitos. 4. A idéia de causa, por exemplo, começou como uma metáfora, e então evoluiu até tornar-se um mito. O mesmo pode ser dito sobre o conceito de propósito. Idéias mecânicas e a teleologia, como conceitos, e depois como mitos, expandem-se para além de suas esferas legítimas. 5. Termos abstratos como beleza, verdade, lei, ordem, universo, etc., tornam-se emblemas concentrados, modelando os sentimentos, os pensamentos e os alvos humanos. 6. Todos os sistemas de idéias seguem o mesmo padrão de desenvolvimento, ficando envolvidos em

BOAS OBRAS

coisas que não podem manusear adequadamente. 7. Portanto, a *periodização* dentro da história consiste em mito e metáfora. 8. As filosofias ou a história participam do processo da mitologização, pelo que sempre são parcialmente irracionais, e a mesma coisa pode ser dita a respeito de todos os sistemas organizados de pensamento.

Obras: Primitivism and Related Ideas in Antiquity; The Happy Beast in French Thought of the 17th Century; Essays on Primitivism and Related Ideas in the Middle Ages; The History of Ideas. (EP P)

BOAS OBRAS

Convém-nos considerar os pontos abaixo:

1. Considerações Práticas. O homem espiritual foi criado a fim de praticar boas obras (Efé. 2:10). Essas são expressões da operação da lei do amor em nós, e resultam do fato de termos nascido de Deus (I João 4:7,11). As boas obras, de todas as variedades, são recomendadas aos crentes (Efé. 2:10; Tito 2:14). Elas resultam do uso apropriado das Escrituras (II Tim. 3:17). Por intermédio delas, os homens glorificam a Deus (Mat. 5:16). Há uma recompensa à espera daqueles que praticarem boas obras (I Cor. 3:14 e Apo. 22:12). As boas obras devem ser tanto sociais quanto individuais, porquanto, quando expressamos amor, devemos fazê-lo tanto em favor de indivíduos isolados como devemos ter em mira toda a sociedade humana. Fazem bem as igrejas locais que promovem programas de bem-estar social, hospitais, orfanatos e cursos práticos de instrução, que ajudam as pessoas a obterem empregos, etc. Não basta evangelizar. Nesse particular, a Igreja Católica Romana tem-se mostrado mais ativa que os evangélicos, porquanto essa igreja tem promovido caridade, escolas, hospitais, etc., e algumas de suas ordens religiosas existem com o propósito explícito de praticar boas obras. Precisamos dar-lhe o crédito por essas atividades. Deveríamos imitá-la, não nos mostrando tão pouco ativos nas boas obras sociais, somente porque não somos justificados pelas boas obras, mas pela fé. A epístola de Tiago, no seu segundo capítulo, instrui-nos quanto a essa questão. Os políticos que, com honestidade, e sem interesses egoístas, promovem o bem-estar social, estão cumprindo a vontade de Deus, e nessa medida, são servos de Deus.

2. Um dos Aspectos do Pragmatismo (que vide). Em certo sentido, a verdade pode ser equiparada às boas obras, porquanto a verdade é aquilo que produz benefícios e opera em benefício dos homens. Se não exagerarmos quanto a isso, não a transformando em uma teoria da verdade (ver sobre as *Teorias da Verdade*), então seremos possuidores de uma compreensão útil. A *verdade* não pode jamais ser apenas um conceito. É necessário que a verdade tenha manifestações práticas. Uma dessas manifestações consiste em boas obras práticas.

3. A Boa Vontade. Alguns filósofos pensam que a única coisa verdadeiramente boa é a vontade (Kant). Os atos bons que podemos realizar não serão tão bons se, por detrás dos mesmos, houver motivos egoístas. Além disso, quase sempre os próprios atos são corrompidos por motivos ulteriores, que geralmente assumem formas egoístas. Portanto, a bondade, quando pura e simples, reside na vontade de se fazer o bem. Seja como for, a boa vontade é a mola impulsionadora de onde fluem os atos bons. No sentido cristão, o Espírito Santo transforma-nos para que sejamos dotados de boa vontade, a fim de podermos praticar o bem.

4. Considerações Teológicas:

a. Em primeiro lugar, temos o *conflito em torno da causa da justificação*. Algumas denominações cristãs, e, na realidade, a maioria das religiões, misturam o que é divino com o que é humano, presumindo que a justificação vem através da combinação da fé e das boas obras. Essa era a posição dos hebreus, refletida no Antigo Testamento. Os primitivos cristãos, conforme vemos no décimo quinto capítulo do livro de Atos, tiveram de enfrentar esse ponto de vista em suas próprias fileiras, o que suscitou forte controvérsia. Além disso, o livro de Tiago reflete essa posição, parecendo uma força opositora à doutrina paulina da justificação exclusivamente pela fé. Não podemos divorciar o livro de Tiago do décimo quinto capítulo do livro de Atos, interpretando-o não-historicamente. A história da Igreja primitiva envolve essa controvérsia, — não nos devendo maravilhar que um dos livros do Novo Testamento assuma uma posição não-paulina sobre a questão. Precisamos reconhecer que uma contribuição tipicamente paulina para a compreensão da doutrina cristã é o seu princípio da graça divina. Há indícios dessa doutrina fora de Paulo, mas é inútil tentar encontrar qualquer apresentação clara da mesma antes das epístolas paulinas. Não obstante, é errônea a aplicação do princípio das boas obras dentro do *sistema de merecimento humano*, segundo o qual, mediante o acúmulo de atos corretos e feitos úteis ao próximo, uma pessoa vai acumulando crédito diante de Deus, até que chegue a merecer a salvação de sua alma, através de suas boas obras.

Essa foi a idéia que os reformadores combateram, e com toda a razão. Os escritos de Paulo são radicalmente contrários a tal noção. Ver Romanos 3-5, quanto a uma prolongada declaração cristã a esse respeito. Ver também Gál. 2:16-21 e 3:1 *ss*. Ver o artigo sobre os *Méritos Humanos*. A posição protestante é que as boas obras são o resultado natural da conversão e da justificação, e jamais a sua causa. A ordem de coisas, em Efésios 2:8-10, serve de apoio a essa contenção. O ponto de vista paulino é que o indivíduo, por si mesmo, é incapaz de agradar a Deus, pelo que suas boas obras não lhe servem de mérito. O terceiro capítulo da epístola aos Romanos é uma extensa declaração a esse respeito. O Espírito nos foi dado mediante o ouvir com fé (Gál. 3:2), e não através das obras da lei. A operação do Espírito é a nossa motivação e o nosso poder, e não a nossa tentativa, mediante as nossas próprias forças, e através de nossos próprios recursos, de acumular merecimento diante de Deus. Ver o artigo sobre a *Justificação*, para uma discussão mais completa sobre esse ponto.

b. *Reconciliação*. Há uma maneira de reconciliar os princípios das boas obras e da fé, como porções integrais da justificação. Se considerarmos que as obras realizadas são frutos e labores do Espírito em nós, e através de nós, então as obras tornam-se um termo para indicar a sua obra *transformadora* em nós, juntamente com os resultados práticos dessa transformação. Isso é algo necessário à justificação, porque o termo não é apenas uma expressão verbal. Inclui aquilo que é feito na vida do crente pelo Espírito de Deus. A justificação, em uma definição mais ampla, tanto é transformação moral e espiritual quanto é santificação. Se não fosse assim, como Paulo poderia falar sobre a justificação da vida? (Romanos 5:18). Portanto, insisto aqui que a descrição paulina da justificação é mais ampla do que a definição dos reformadores a respeito. É precisamente isso que nos ensina a epístola de Tiago! Mas, segundo a definição protestante tradicional, a justificação exclui os aspectos posteriores da santificação e da transformação do caráter do crente.

A justificação não é uma categoria isolada das demais operações do Espírito. Somente como concepção mental podemos isolá-la desse modo. Na prática, as operações do Espírito em nós são reais e simultâneas; e essa realidade e simultaneidade fazem parte da justificação. Nesse sentido, a justificação depende tanto da fé quanto das obras da fé. Não obstante, essas obras não devem ser entendidas como meritórias, como se fossem fruto da bondade humana. Antes, trata-se da atuação do Espírito de Deus em nós.

c. *O Acolhimento Humano*. A chamada ao arrependimento mostra que o homem é capaz de arrepender-se; de outro modo, tal chamada seria uma zombaria. O homem caiu no pecado, mas continua havendo uma — **graça geral** — **que o capacita a reagir** — **favoravelmente** — **a Deus**. Se não adotarmos essa posição, perderemos inteiramente o **aspecto do *livre-arbítrio* (que vide), — e tal perda é intolerável. Sem livre-arbítrio, não podem haver** requisitos éticos, e nem responsabilidade humana. Em todos os homens resta bondade suficiente para sentirem a força de atração da bondade de Deus e corresponderem à mesma. Porém, a salvação (que vide) é um ato divino, e tanto a fé quanto as obras da fé são resultantes das operações do Espírito. Contudo, o homem caracteriza-se pela inércia espiritual, e para corresponder aos reclamos do Espírito, é mister que receba o influxo da graça divina capacitadora. Desse modo o homem chega a crer e a agir em consonância com a sua fé, embora suas boas obras não sejam meritórias para a salvação.

d. *A Questão dos Galardões*. Os galardões ou recompensas incluem *aquilo que* recebemos, mas o conceito consiste, essencialmente, *naquilo em que nos tornamos*. Se um homem vier a receber a coroa da justiça (II Tim. 4:8), isso significará que ele adquiriu a natureza moral e santa de Deus. Se ele vier a receber a coroa da vida (Tia.1:12 e Apo. 2:10), isso significará que ele veio a compartilhar da vida divina, da vida eterna, da vida celestial. Por toda a parte, as Escrituras são claras no sentido de que os homens serão julgados de acordo com as suas obras, recebendo essas coroas em resultado de um *desempenho* fiel, e não meramente por haver crido em certo número de doutrinas acerca de Cristo. Ver Rom. 2:6; Apo. 20:12. O trecho de I Coríntios 3:10 *ss*, deixa claro que esse princípio aplica-se plenamente ao crente. Portanto, podemos concluir somente que a glorificação, que inclui o princípio das recompensas, dependerá das nossas obras, e não apenas da nossa fé. Ao mesmo tempo, precisamos apressar-nos a ajuntar que isso resulta das operações divinas em nós, não sendo méritos que acumulamos mediante nossos próprios esforços desassistidos. Não obstante, esse princípio mostra-nos que as obras, nesse sentido, não são meramente resultados da fé. Elas são, na sua própria essência, aquilo que o Espírito está operando em nós, em seu processo de transformação do crente. Quanto a esse aspecto, fé e obras são sinônimos. Paulo declarou sucintamente esse princípio, ao escrever: «...desenvolvei (efetuai) a vossa salvação com temor e tremor; porque Deus é quem efetua em vós tanto o querer como o realizar, segundo a sua boa vontade» (Fil. 2:12,13). Deveríamos notar que ambos os verbos portugueses, «desenvolver» e «efetuar», no original grego procedem da mesma raiz. Ninguém, por si mesmo, pode efetuar a sua salvação. Mas quando alguém, através do Espírito, torna-se capaz disso, então *está na obrigação de fazê-lo*.

e. *Contra a Crença Fácil*. Lamento, mas preciso falar como o estou fazendo. Na Igreja Católica Romana, os sacramentos tomam conta de tudo, e obtém-se a impressão de que o homem nada mais precisa fazer, se tiver sido batizado, se assistir a missa com freqüência, se participar da comunhão, etc. Tal doutrina é enganadora. Nas igrejas evangélicas, por sua vez, isso tem sido substituído pela pública confissão de fé, na qual, presumivelmente, o indivíduo confessa a Cristo e dá seu assentimento diante de certo número de doutrinas acerca de sua pessoa e de sua realização, nada mais faz, e, contudo, supostamente atinge a salvação. Trata-se de uma total insensatez. Pois contradiz todos os conceitos neotestamentários que dizem respeito ao que está envolvido na salvação: a nossa *transformação* segundo a imagem e a natureza de Cristo (Rom. 8:29), através da contínua operação do Espírito (II Cor. 3:18), mediante o *cultivo* em nós das virtudes morais e espirituais (Gál. 5:22,23). Ninguém obterá alguma coroa espiritual (ver o artigo sobre as *Coroas*), a menos que seja digno (Apo. 2:7), e ninguém verá o Senhor sem a santificação (Heb. 12:14). Todas as promessas das sete cartas do Apocalipse foram endereçadas aos vencedores. Aos vencedores é ali prometida a árvore da vida (Apo. 2:14), o escapar da segunda morte (2:11), o poder comer do maná celestial e o receber de um novo nome (2:17), o entrar no reino milenar e o receber a estrela da manhã (2:28), o andar de branco e não ter o seu nome apagado do Livro da Vida (3:5), o tornar-se uma coluna no templo celestial de Deus e ter o nome de Deus nele inscrito (3:12), e o sentar-se no trono de Deus (3:21).

f. *Essas são questões sérias*, e, em minha opinião, são tratadas com superficialidade tanto pela Igreja Católica Romana quanto por muitas igrejas protestantes e evangélicas, embora sob diferentes ângulos. Nada é mais claro para mim do que isto: A confissão de um crente é a sua vida. Sem isso, não há confissão válida. (B C H NTI)

BOAVENTURA, São

Suas datas foram 1221-1274. Nasceu em Toscana, Itália. Era frade franciscano. Foi bispo de Albano e cardeal em 1273. Era homem dotado de natureza pacífica e meditativa, sempre pronto a reconhecer os elementos de verdade contidos nas opiniões que ele rejeitava. Procurava reconciliar pontos de vista divergentes, refreando-se em tomar decisões finais, preferindo aguardar a iluminação de seu entendimento — uma pessoa realmente rara! Sua autoridade favorita era Agostinho (ver o artigo), em quem via uma útil síntese entre Platão e Aristóteles. Em suas obras religiosas e epistemológicas, ele subscrevia a teoria da iluminação. Foi um teólogo místico contemplativo, mas impelido por rigoroso voluntarismo (que vide).

Idéias. 1. A filosofia culmina no misticismo (que vide), sua mais elevada expressão. A fé é central às experiências religiosas. A razão não deve atuar independentemente da fé, visto que a razão isolada sempre cai em erro. 2. Todas as pessoas têm uma consciência e um conhecimento implícitos de Deus. A meditação encoraja o florescimento desse conhecimento. Os próprios argumentos racionais estribam-se em discernimentos intuitivos, aquele conhecimento inato que todos já trazemos conosco. 3. O melhor argumento em prol da existência de Deus é o argumento ontológico de Anselmo (que vide). 4. Há um elemento ético em todos os homens, que pode ser cultivado na busca pela felicidade. O homem é dotado de uma noção inata de virtude. Ver sobre as *idéias inatas*. 5. No tocante às experiências ordinárias, o conhecimento vem através da experiência dos sentidos, e a mente começa a operar no indivíduo como um tábula rasa. Todavia, o homem possui uma luz natural da razão, a qual lhe permite discernir a universalidade dos princípios, depois que ele já adquiriu as idéias relevantes mediante a observação. 6. A mutabilidade e as constantes alterações do mundo material não nos permitem encontrar a verdade através da observação e da percepção dos sentidos. É necessário a confiança na iluminação quanto a todo o nosso conhecimento, exceto quanto àquilo que é corriqueiro e mundano. Nossas idéias correspondem às idéias da mente de Deus, e por elas são inspiradas. 7. Todas as coisas são reflexos moldados em Deus. E o homem, como imagem de Deus, reflete a Trindade por ser um ser triúno. 8. A alma originou-se do nada, mediante um ato criador de Deus. Em sua relação com o corpo, a alma é a forma e a realidade do corpo, mas também é espiritual e transcendental, em sua natureza e destino. 9. Quando da criação, houve as *rationes seminales*, isto é, as sementes da razão que fazem as coisas serem o que são, os poderes do Logos em operação. A matéria é o canteiro das atividades dessas sementes da razão. 10. Deus é forma pura, é ato puro, o autor da matéria e da forma, e conhece todas as coisas de maneira eterna, e não como meras sucessões de formas e condições. É na direção desse tipo de ser que estamos avançando, e Nele obtemos nossa felicidade, nossa verdade, nossa realidade. Acima da nossa capacidade de percepção há trevas místicas produzidas por uma superabundante iluminação, as quais podem tornar-se uma visão de Deus do outro lado da existência. Ver sobre a *Visão Beatífica*.

Escritos: Comentário sobre as Sentenças de Pedro Lombardo; Sobre o Conhecimento de Cristo; Sobre o Mistério da Trindade; Sobre a Caridade e as Últimas Coisas; A Jornada da Mente de Deus; As Duas Vidas de São Francisco; Sobre os Sete Dons do Espírito Santo; Sobre os Seis Dias da Criação. (AM E EP P)

BOAZ

No hebraico, «felicidade» ou «rapidez». É nome de uma pessoa e de um detalhe arquitetônico do templo de Salomão, a saber:

1. Um rico belemita e parente chegado do marido falecido da moabita Rute (vide), e com quem, finalmente, se casou, sob a obrigação do casamento levirato, que ele cumpriu voluntariamente, em cerca de 1360 A.C. A conduta digna de Boaz, sua sensibilidade e seu espírito bondoso, sua piedade e suas boas maneiras, são pontos ressaltados no livro de Rute, oferecendo-nos uma boa idéia de como seriam as pessoas pertencentes à classe alta de Israel. Do matrimônio nasceu Obede, que foi pai de Jessé, que foi pai de Davi. Portanto, Boaz foi um ancestral direto de Jesus. Seu nome ocorre na genealogia de Jesus, em Mat. 1:5.

Apesar de ser proibido por lei que uma pessoa moabita fizesse parte do povo de Israel pelo decurso de dez gerações, Rute aceitou a religião e os costumes de Israel, ao seguir Noemi de volta à Terra Santa. Devido a essa circunstância, surgiu o mais bem conhecido dos versículos do livro de Rute, —que diz: «Não me instes para que te deixe, e me obrigue a não seguir-te; porque aonde quer que fores, irei eu, e onde quer que pousares, ali pousarei eu; o teu povo é o meu povo, o teu Deus é o meu Deus» (Rute 1:16). Muitas declarações devotas têm sido inspiradas por esse versículo.

2. Nome de uma das colunas de bronze postas por Salomão diante do templo de Jerusalém. Aquela que ficava no lado norte era chamada Boaz; e a que ficava no lado sul, chamava-se Jaquim. Eram adornadas com capitéis representando lírios. (I Reis 7:21 e II Crô. 3:17). (G H A ID)

••• ••• •••

BOCA

No hebraico, **peh**, palavra que aparece por cerca de quatrocentas e quarenta vezes (por exemplo: Gên. 4:11; Êxo. 4:11; Núm. 12:8; Deu. 8:3; Jos. 1:8; Juí. 7:6; I Sam. 1:12; II Sam. 1:16; I Reis 7:31; Jó 3:1; Sal. 5:9; 145:21; Pro. 2:6; 4:5; 31:36; Isa. 1:20; Jer. 1:9; Eze. 2:8; Zac. 5:8; Mal. 2:6,7). No grego, *stóma*, palavra que aparece por cerca de setenta e cinco vezes, desde Mat. 4:4 até Apo. 19:21.

A boca é a cavidade do começo do aparelho digestivo, localizada entre os maxilares superior e inferior, que conduz diretamente à faringe (garganta). Na boca estão os dentes, as gengivas e a língua. Na boca derramam-se as secreções das glândulas salivares, a saber, as parótidas, as submaxilares e as sublinguais. Essas secreções contêm enzimas que dão início à digestão dos alimentos. Na boca também está localizado o sentido do gosto, e os dentes servem para triturar os alimentos e ajudar a impregná-los com saliva. A boca também está envolvida nos processos da respiração e da articulação da fala, da expectoração e do ato de chupar. As pessoas ficam admiradas ao serem informadas de que a boca é, sem dúvida alguma, a porção mais suja do corpo humano. Consideremos estes fatos espantosos: 1. Não há líquido bucal que possa esterilizar a boca senão aqueles que são tão potentes que destróem os tecidos que recobrem internamente a boca. 2. Nem o ato mais cuidadoso de escovar os dentes é capaz de realmente esterilizar a boca. 3. Os nutrientes que colocamos na boca servem de bom meio de cultura de toda espécie de bactérias, que crescem e se reproduzem na nossa boca. 4. A saliva tende por desencorajar a multiplicação de todas as demais bactérias, excetuando aquelas que produzem enfermidades no homem. Portanto, os germens que podem causar doenças são precisamente aqueles que são ajudados pela saliva. A mordida humana é um dos ferimentos que os médicos têm maior dificuldade em curar! Até mesmo aqueles que sabem desses fatos continuam beijando-se.

Usos Metafóricos: 1. Ser pesado de boca significa falar com lentidão (Êxo. 4:1). 2. A boca macia indica a linguagem lisonjeadora, ou seja, aquele que engana o próximo (Sal. 55:21; 109:2). 3. Falar boca a boca significa comunicar-se com outrem sem a ajuda de intérprete (Núm. 12:8; I Reis 8:15). 4. Pôr palavras na boca de alguém significa sugerir o que esse alguém deve dizer (Est. 4:15, embora a figura de linguagem não apareça em português). 5. Estar na boca significa falar freqüentemente a respeito de algo (Êxo. 13:9). 6. Pôr a mão sobre a boca quer dizer guardar silêncio (Juí. 18:19; Jó 21:5). 7. Pôr um dedo sobre a boca equivale a pedir silêncio. 8. Pedir conselho da boca do Senhor é buscar informação espiritual (Jos. 9:14, outra figura de linguagem que não transparece no texto português da Bíblia). 9. Desandar a boca contra os céus é falar com extrema arrogância (Sal. 73:9). 10. A vara da boca indica a Palavra de Deus (Isa. 11:4). 11. A palavra «boca» algumas vezes indica aquilo que alguém diz (Núm. 3:16). 12. Toda a espécie de maldade procede da boca, —que é considerada a fonte de grandes males (Mat. 15:18; Rom. 3:14). 13. Entre as bocas não-humanas temos a boca de uma caverna (Jos. 10:27); a boca de um sepulcro (Sal. 141:7); a boca de um saco (Gên. 42:27); a boca de um poço (Gên. 29:10). 14. A ameaça de julgamento severo, por pronunciação de Deus, é uma *espada* que sai de Sua boca (Apo. 19:15). (AD AM BR Z)

BOCCACCIO, GIOVANNI

Poeta e novelista italiano (1313-1375), — que divide com Petrarca (ver o artigo) a honra de ser um dos primeiros humanistas. Embora tivesse estudado por toda a vida as obras de Dante (que vide) de quem era admirador, e tivesse escrito muitos poemas que mostram a influência de seu mestre, ele tornou-se mais conhecido devido ao seu *Decamerom*. Essa obra mereceu-lhe o título de criador da novela, como uma forma de arte da prosa italiana. Posteriormente, Boccaccio deplorou a licenciosidade de certas passagens de seus escritos. Ele veio a tornar-se inspirador dos anedotistas de piadas indecentes, embora seu nome seja distorcido pelo vulgo.

BOCHECHAS Ver Rosto (Bochechas).

BOCRU

No hebraico, «primogênito» ou «jovem». Foi um dos seis filhos de Azel, descendente do rei Saul (I Crô. 8:38). Cerca de 1037 A.C.

BODE EXPIATÓRIO
Ver Azazel.

BODELSCHWING, FRIEDRICH VON

Suas datas foram 1831-1910. Era filho de uma antiga família prussiana, habilidoso em questões financeiras e praticante de caridades religiosas. Foi teólogo dotado de fé singela e pastor conhecido por sua notável compaixão, que sempre se mostrou ativo em obras de caridade. Ele estabeleceu a colônia de misericórdia em Betel, em Bielefeld, na Westphalia. Ali, durante setenta anos, milhares de pessoas enfermas vieram buscar ajuda, entre as quais muitos epilépticos que viviam em grupos, formando famílias. Era uma comunidade operosa, que provia para quase todas as suas necessidades. Nas proximidades foi organizada uma colônia de trabalho para os desempregados, uma colônia agrícola, lugares onde podiam ficar trabalhadores imigrantes. Esses estabelecimentos tornaram-se modelos emulados pelo governo alemão. A igreja era um aspecto importante dessas organizações, bem como o centro do consolo que as pessoas ali encontravam. Florescia ali a lei do amor, que é um dos principais aspectos da espiritualidade autêntica. (E)

BODHI

Um termo «sânscrito que significa «sabedoria» ou «iluminação», largamente empregado na filosofia indiana. É o contrário de *avidya* (que vide), e que significa «ignorância». Ver também sobre *Bodhisattva*. (P)

BODHISATTVA

No sânscrito, trata-se da combinação de *bodhi*, «sabedoria», e *sattva*, «existência em». A palavra indica aquele que desiste de tornar-se como Buda, por amor ao próximo. Essa doutrina encontra-se tanto no budismo Hinayana como no budismo Mahayana, embora seja considerada mais importante neste último. Ver sobre o *Budismo Mahayana*. (P)

BODIN, JEAN

Filósofo político francês (1530-1596). Nasceu em Angers, educou-se em Toulouse, e tornou-se advogado. Serviu como parlamentar e posteriormente tornou-se secretário do duque de Alençon. Em 1576 foi nomeado advogado do rei da França.

Idéias. 1. O conhecimento divide-se em história humana, história natural e história divina, com os nomes de antropologia, física e teologia. O aspecto que mais chamava a sua atenção era a história humana. 2. Ele argumentava em prol da monarquia como a melhor forma de governo. A força da lei civil estaria investida no rei, dotado de poderes de vida e morte. O poder monárquico só seria limitado pelo senso de justiça. 3. Ele pensava que a geografia influencia as crenças e os costumes dos povos, incluindo as formas de governo que são estabelecidas.

Obras: *Method for the Easy Comprehension of History; The Response; The Six Books of the Republic; The Theater of Nature* (E EP)

BODMER, Papiros de. Ver Papiros de Bodmer.

BOEHM, MARTIN

Suas datas foram 1725-1812. Foi expulso do grupo menonita em face de seu zelo evangelístico. Veio a tornar-se co-fundador, juntamente com Otterbein (ver o artigo) da Igreja dos Irmãos Unidos em Cristo, tendo sido um de seus bispos, de 1800 a 1812. (E)

BOEHME, JACOB

Suas datas foram 1575-1624. Foi filósofo místico e religioso alemão. Nasceu e viveu na Saxônia. Foi criado como luterano, recebeu educação formal e exerceu notável influência sobre o pensamento posterior religioso e filosófico. Entrou em choque com pessoas que defendiam a ortodoxia e foi banido de Gorlitz, sua cidade natal, onde residia. Foi julgado por heresia, mas conseguiu retornar para o lar, sob a proteção do eleitor da Saxônia. Muitos homens eruditos visitavam-no para dialogar, em suas vívidas conversações. Era fabricante de sapatos por profissão, mas sua paixão era o misticismo religioso. Ele compôs material que continua exercendo influência até os nossos dias sobre vários sistemas. Influenciou grupos tão diversos como o pietismo alemão (que vide) e os quacres ingleses (que vide). Homens como William Law, William Blake, Hegel, Schelling, Baader e Schopenhauer muito deviam a ele. Infelizmente, seus escritos são obscurecidos pelo vocabulário que ele tomava por empréstimo da literatura da alquimia da época. Mas, todo o pesquisador de suas obras sente que ali há coisas aproveitáveis, que ainda não foram devidamente perscrutadas.

Idéias. 1. Jacob Boehme afirmava ter recebido iluminação divina acerca da natureza de Deus, da origem e estrutura do universo, de diversos mistérios das Escrituras e de discernimento quanto aos sacramentos. 2. Ele postulava que a criação inteira, em todos os seus aspectos, é manifestação de Deus, e portanto, de duas vontades: uma amorosa, e a outra, iracunda. Dessa maneira, pois, ele explicava o problema do mal (ver o artigo). 3. Por detrás de toda realidade acha-se o *Abismo*, que é o próprio Deus. Disso resultava uma certa manifestação divina, a Trindade. 4. A *Luz primária* é a essência do ser, que contém tudo quanto surgiu em seguida. 5. Da Luz derivaram-se as Trevas, uma existência contrária, que se manifesta nas pessoas sob a forma de egocentrismo e inércia. Luz e trevas seriam vontades. Quando elas entram em conflito ocorre a amargura, o descontentamento espiritual. 6. A amargura aumenta e produz o fogo, a bruxuleante luz do homem exterior. 7. O conflito pode ser resolvido pela luz, quando alguém percebe as coisas conforme elas realmente são. Em termos teológicos, Cristo é a Luz, é a própria manifestação de Deus. 8. Luz é Deus, manifesto em meio às trevas. 9. Cada indivíduo mistura os princípios da luz e das trevas: o primeiro o eleva, mas o segundo desses princípios arrasta-o para baixo. 10. Dentro do processo criativo, há o princípio de negação, existente no ser de Deus. O mundo é um reflexo da essência divina, em suas várias manifestações.

Obras: *Aurora, or the Dawn; De Tribus Principiis*, ou *Description of the Three Principles of Divine Being; Concerning the Three Divisions in the Lives of Men; The Signature of All Things; The Great Mistery, An Explanation of the First Book of Moses*. (E EP P)

BOETHIUS

Anicus Manlius Severinus Boethius, filósofo eclético romano (489-525). Ele tentou uma síntese do pensamento helenista, romano e cristão, preservando o que havia de melhor no antigo sistema, procurando engendrar um novo sistema. Tem sido chamado de último dos filósofos romanos e primeiro dos escolásticos. — Foi cônsul romano e ministro de Teodorico, rei dos ostrogodos, por quem foi acusado de traição, encarcerado e, finalmente, executado. Enquanto aguardava a execução, compôs seu livro *Sobre o Consolo da Filosofia*. Conhecia o grego, e procurou fazer as obras de Platão e Aristóteles disponíveis a leitores de latim. Todavia, não obteve grande sucesso nesse campo, embora tivesse contribuído significativamente para as artes, a filosofia e a música. Sua interpretação sobre as *Categorias*, de Aristóteles, era o único material disponível das obras aristotélicas sobre a lógica, conhecido no Ocidente, até o século XII D.C. A principal mensagem de sua obra, *Sobre o Consolo da Filosofia*, é que o mundo de valores transitórios e em mutação precisa ser contrastado com os valores eternos da filosofia e da teologia, a nós disponíveis mediante a vida contemplativa e a fé na providência de Deus.

Escritos: *Sobre o Consolo da Filosofia; Sobre a Diferença de Natureza e de Pessoa; Comentários* sobre Aristóteles, Porfírio, Cícero e Vitorino. Várias obras teológicas a ele atribuídas, antes postas em dúvida, agora são consideradas produções autênticas de Boethius.

BOFETE

No grego, **kolaphidzo**, «esmurrar», dando a entender um tratamento violento e rude. É vocábulo que figura por cinco vezes: Mat. 26:67; Mar. 14:65; I Cor. 4:11; II Cor. 12:7 e I Ped. 2:20. A ação pode envolver as idéias de várias formas de derrisão e de castigo físico, conforme se vê nas duas primeiras dessas referências, ou de aflição, como se vê em I Cor. 4:11, ou de punição, como se vê em I Ped. 2:20. Os evangelhos narram como Jesus foi moral e literalmente esmurrado pelas autoridades religiosas dos judeus. Os primitivos cristãos foram tratados com a mesma violência (I Cor. 4:11). Paulo era afligido por um espinho na carne (II Cor. 12:7). Ver o NTI quanto à natureza desse espinho na carne.

Um outro termo grego, *upopiádzo*, «bater debaixo do olho», ou produzir um olho roxo, foi usado figuradamente por Paulo, para indicar como ele disciplinava o seu corpo, com finalidades de avanço espiritual (I Cor. 9:27). A persistência na oração é uma espécie de autocastigo (desgastante), tendo em mira um bom propósito (Luc. 18:5).

BOFF, LEONARDO Ver Teologia da Libertação.

BOHMER, HEINRICH

Suas datas foram 1869-1927. Foi professor em Bonn, Marburgo e Leipzig. Foi uma das diversas mentes teológicas que contribuíram para a compreensão da Reforma protestante (que vide). Suas observações a respeito do cristianismo alemão serviram de pontos a serem discutidos por investigadores posteriores. (E)

BOICOTE

Prática de alguma recusa coletiva para fazer negócios com algum indivíduo ou com alguma organização comercial, ou mesmo com alguma nação, usualmente no sentido econômico. Isso é usado como protesto contra normas impostas, cujo intuito é alterar práticas econômicas ou políticas indesejáveis. O nome deriva-se do capitão Boycott (1832-1897), que foi alvo de uma medida dessa natureza por parte de residentes irlandeses irados, que buscavam pôr fim às explorações de Boycott, que era o proprietário de suas residências. A prática envolve implicações morais, porquanto, usualmente, é aplicada especificamente dentro de um contexto ético. Trata-se de um protesto contra os abusos daqueles que estão no poder ou exercem controle sobre outros, tendo em vista conseguir condições mais justas.

O grande problema que envolve a prática é que geralmente é difícil determinar o que é justo, porque, algumas vezes, as pessoas «oprimidas» são meramente gananciosas. Assim, indústrias têm sido fechadas por pessoas que exigem salários exageradamente altos, as quais usam de boicote para fazer valer suas demandas. Por outro lado, há alguns grandes abusos que a medida tem ajudado a eliminar. (H)

BOIEIRO

No hebraico, **boqer**, vocábulo que aparece somente por uma vez no Antigo Testamento, em Amós 7:14. Um outro termo hebraico, *noqed*, figura por duas vezes, em Amós 1:1 e II Reis 3:14. Ainda um outro termo hebraico, *raah*, «dar o pasto», é usado por mais de cento e sessenta vezes, muitas das quais traduzidas por «boieiro» ou sinônimo (por exemplo: Gên. 13:7,8; 26:20; I Sam. 21:7).

O boieiro era alguém que cuidava de bois, em contraste com o *roi*, que era quem cuidava de ovelhas. Os proprietários de rebanhos deixavam seus animais aos cuidados dos boieiros, para impedi-los de se dispersarem, para protegê-los das feras, para conduzi-los a convenientes lugares de pastagem. Usualmente, os boieiros levavam consigo uma vara dotada de ponta de ferro, o aguilhão, que podia ser usado para tanger os animais, ou como arma, se necessário fosse. Também levavam uma bolsa para provisões (ver I Sam. 17:40,43; Sal. 23:4; Miq. 7:14; Mat. 10:10). Eles usavam uma capa, com a qual envolviam o corpo (Jer. 43:12). A alimentação deles era simples e frugal (Amós 7:14; Luc. 15:15). Seu salário consistia nos produtos do rebanho (Gên. 30:32 ss; I Cor. 9:7). A ocupação deles era considerada honrosa (Gên. 47:6; I Sam. 11:15). Saul exercia esse trabalho, em seus momentos vagos (I Sam. 21:7). No Egito, os irmãos de José trabalhavam nesse mister. Os boieiros de Davi eram contados entre seus principais

BOI SELVAGEM

oficiais de estado. O profeta Amós era boieiro (Amós 1:1 e 7:14). O material encontrado em Ugarite mostra que aqueles que trabalhavam nos rebanhos reais ocupavam um ofício de grande prestígio. (S UN Z)

BOI SELVAGEM

No hebraico temos uma palavra usada por nove vezes (ver Núm. 23:22; 24:8; Deu. 33:17; Jó. 39:9,10; Sal. 22:21; 29:6; 92:10 e Isa. 34:7). Os estudiosos estão concordes que esse animal, cientificamente conhecido como *Bos Primigenius*, era um magnífico espécime, atualmente extinto, tendo sido o ancestral do moderno gado vacum. Algumas versões trazem a infeliz tradução «unicórnio», um animal imaginário dos relatos míticos.

O boi selvagem era maior que o gado domesticado de nossos dias. O touro era marrom escuro, com longos chifres voltados para frente e para cima. Nos tempos primitivos, esse animal, que em português também é conhecido por «auroque», tinha seu habitat em grande parte da Europa, da Ásia central e ocidental, e em certas porções do norte da África, incluindo o Egito, onde já estava se tornando raro, durante o reinado de Tutmés III (cerca de 1500 A.C.). A última menção ao mesmo, nos escritos egípcios, pertence à época de Ramisés III (1190). Os reis assírios também caçavam esse animal. — Interessante é que ele sobrevivia, até poucos séculos atrás, nas porções menos habitadas da Mesopotâmia. O último espécime vivo na Europa morreu em 1627. Na Palestina, porém, já havia desaparecido desde muito antes da era cristã. O auroque era o ungulado selvagem maior e mais poderoso de todos. O trecho de Isa. 34:6,7 associa esse animal a outros animais limpos. Jó 39:9,10 faz contraste entre o boi selvagem e o boi doméstico. Temos ali apenas referências figuradas que deixam entrever que os escritores sagrados estavam familiarizados com esse animal, e que ele fazia parte da fauna das terras em derredor da Palestina, senão mesmo da Palestina propriamente dita.

BOIS, HENRI

Nasceu em 1862 na França, mas a data de seu falecimento é desconhecida. Foi deão da faculdade teológica de Montaban, na França. Defendeu o teísmo pessoal (ver sobre *personalismo*). Atribuía a Deus qualidades humanas, como sentimentos, paixão e vontade, em contraste com as filosofias panteístas e agnósticas que negam esses atributos tipicamente antropomórficos. Jesus Cristo, conforme ele dizia, trouxe esclarecimentos sobre as qualidades divinas. Bois denunciava as tendências para o panteísmo e para o monismo, que furtam Deus de características pessoais. Ele estava convencido de que o personalismo neocrítico de Renouvier (que vide) fornece-nos a verdadeira solução para o problema da natureza de Deus. (E)

BOLO DE PÃO

No hebraico, **challah**, «bolo perfurado», palavra que ocorre por catorze vezes: Êxo. 29:2,23; Lev. 2:4; 7:12,13; 8:26; 24:5; Núm. 6:15; 19; 15:20; II Sam. 6:19. Nossa versão portuguesa traduz a palavra por «bolos asmos», «bolo de pão», «bolos», «pães». Alguns estudiosos pensam que há aqui menção a uma espécie de bolo de uvas passas pressionadas. Ver o artigo geral sobre *pão*. Vários itens da confeitaria antiga eram chamados *pães*, que nós chamaríamos de *bolos*.

BOLSA

Sacolas feitas de vários materiais, como couro ou fibras trançadas, de uso bastante comum nos tempos bíblicos, para transporte de todo o tipo de objetos, como dinheiro (Isa. 46:6), água e vinho (caso em que eram chamadas «odres», ver Mat. 9:17). Os pastores usavam seus surrões, onde transportavam as mais diversas coisas. No hebraico estão envolvidas quatro palavras diferentes: 1. *Khawreet*, saco, (ver II Reis 5:23; Isa. 3:22). 2. *Tserore*, literalmente, «feixe» (ver I Sam. 25:29), que era uma sacola ou saquitel para transportar dinheiro em uma viagem. 3. *Keece*, também traduzida por bolsa, em Deu. 25:13; Pro. 16:11; Isa. 46:6 e Miq. 6:11, e que indicava uma sacola para transportar pesos. 4. *Keli*, usada por nada menos de duzentas e oitenta e cinco vezes, e traduzida por «armadura», «instrumento», «jóia», «arma», «vaso», etc. (Ver, para exemplificar, I Sam. 17:40 e Zac. 11:15,16). Era usada pelos pastores, pelos médicos, para transportar lâmpadas, etc. No Novo Testamento, temos as palavras gregas *balántion*, «bolsa», em Luc. 10:4; 12:33; 22:35,36; e *glossókomon*, originalmente uma caixa para transportar uma flauta, mas depois um «receptáculo» usado para qualquer finalidade, palavra que aparece somente em João 12:6 e 13:29. (S UN)

BOM, BONDADE

Nos diálogos de Platão, exceto em seu Banquete, a Forma ou Idéia do Bom é o mais elevado princípio moral e metafísico. Portanto, usando termos cristãos, a *bondade* é a principal característica de Deus, da qual tudo o mais se originou, e na direção do que tudo se move. A vida inteira é uma inquirição ética, cujo desígnio é libertar a alma de seu cárcere do corpo mortal, devolvendo-a à liberdade do mundo das idéias (equivalente aos céus cristãos). Dali ela provém, e para ali ela está retornando. Porém, isso torna-se impossível sem a perfeição na bondade moral.

I. Idéias Filosóficas:

1. No seu diálogo, **Leis**, Platão substituiu as idéias pelo termo Deus, fazendo com que as idéias se tornassem atributos de Deus. Portanto, a bondade seria o mais elevado atributo divino. Isso é paralelo à declaração cristã e bíblica de que *Deus é amor* (ver I João 4:16). É interessante que a **palavra anglo-saxônica** para Deus, *God*, seja a palavra por detrás da palavra bom, *good*. A verdadeira bondade é uma qualidade transcendental.

2. Platão deu início à discussão sobre o que é intrinsecamente bom e sobre o que é instrumento do bem. Um bem intrínseco é aquilo que é bom em si mesmo. Um bem instrumental é aquilo que resulta no bem, mediante o seu uso.

3. O que é intrinsecamente bom mescla-se com o conceito do *bem maior*, ou *summum bonum* (que vide), uma expressão empregada pelos filósofos para referir-se a Deus, ou ao bem mais elevado possível.

4. Aristóteles pensava que a *eudaimonia* (felicidade) é o maior bem, bem como o objeto de nossa inquirição ética. Isso tem paralelo, na teologia cristã, na idéia de que a finalidade do homem consiste em glorificar a Deus e desfrutar de Deus para sempre (Confissão de Westminster, *que vide*).

5. Os filósofos epicuristas faziam do prazer o bem mais elevado, embora usualmente o compreendessem como os prazeres intelectuais ou os prazeres moderados. Os hedonistas (ver sobre o *hedonismo*) pensavam que quanto maior fosse o prazer, tanto melhor; e isso, para eles, seria o maior bem.

BOM, BONDADE — BOM VIZINHO

6. Os estóicos faziam da *apatia* ou indiferença o maior bem.

7. O confucionismo (que vide) enfatiza o *li* (que vide), isto é a propriedade ou princípio do benefício, resultante do amor, como o maior bem.

8. Alguns filósofos vêem a bondade como um conceito mais amplo do que o *direito*. O direito pode ser justo, mas a bondade aplica a misericórdia e o amor a todas as situações; pelo que a bondade é superior ao direito. Ver o contraste feito por Paulo entre o homem justo e o homem bom, em Romanos 5:7, e ver a exposição dessa idéia, no NTI.

9. Helvécio (que vide) fazia a bondade ser equivalente ao prazer coletivo.

10. Para Hegel (que vide) a bondade é a coincidência de uma vontade humana com a vontade universal, isto é, a vontade racional: a correção de vontade, e, por conseguinte, de ação, com base em princípios metafísicos.

11. Para Westermarck (que vide) a bondade equivale à aprovação da sociedade a qualquer ato ou atitude.

12. Os filósofos analíticos desistiram de definir tão importante e amplo vocábulo como é o adjetivo «bom».

13. Berdyaev (que vide) identificava o bom com a criatividade e a espontaneidade.

14. Para Blanshard (que vide) a bondade consistiria na combinação de satisfação e cumprimento.

II. Idéias Bíblicas:

1. Deus é amor, e, portanto, é o ser supremamente bom, bem como a origem de toda a bondade (I João 4:6). Através do amor, as boas obras visam o benefício do próximo. Quando Deus amou o mundo de tal maneira (ver João 3:16), ele fez a missão de seu Filho revestir-se do proveito máximo. O bem mais alto é uma qualidade transcendental, relacionado ao ser divino. (Ver Sal. 34:3 e 149:9).

2. Os homens tornam-se bons quando a bondade divina passa a ser cultivada neles, pelo Espírito Santo, pois a bondade é um dos aspectos do fruto do Espírito de Deus (ver Gál. 5:22).

3. O homem bom é superior ao homem meramente justo, porquanto, além de ser alguém dotado de ética correta, ele é generoso, demonstrando amor em sua vida (ver Rom. 5:7).

4. A criação de Deus é boa, pois ali ele manifestou suas idéias e seus atos (Gên. 3:5).

5. A prosperidade é um bem provido aos homens por Deus. Essa prosperidade pode ser material ou espiritual (ver Jos. 23:14 ss; I Reis 22:8 e Jó 2:10).

6. A lei de Deus é boa, conduzindo à alma prosperar. Ver Deu. 30:15 ss; *Pirke Aboth* 6:3: «O que é bom é simplesmente a Torah». Ver Rom. 7:12.

7. O Novo Testamento dá continuidade aos conceitos de bom exarados no Antigo Testamento. O homem é uma boa obra de Deus, criado para praticar o que é bom (Efé. 2:10). As boas obras dos crentes glorificam a Deus (Mat. 5:16).

8. A vontade predestinadora de Deus faz todas as coisas contribuírem juntamente para o bem do crente, e o propósito disso é levá-lo a compartilhar da imagem e natureza do Filho, afinal. Em outras palavras, a salvação (que vide) é o bom ato de Deus, aplicado ao homem (Rom. 8:29).

9. Todas as virtudes cristãs são boas e precisam ser cultivadas (Gál. 5:22,23; Fil. 4:8). Essas virtudes devem ser objetos constantes de nossos pensamentos, a fim de que elas se manifestem em nossas vidas. A alma é moralmente transformada por meio dessas boas qualidades, e a transformação moral nos conduz à perfeição (Mat. 5:48). E isso, finalmente, nos leva à transformação metafísica, de tal modo que os remidos compartilharão da própria natureza divina (II Cor. 3:18; II Ped. 1:4). Isso tem paralelo na idéia platônica de que o mais exaltado aspecto da inquirição ética é a transformação metafísica no mundo das *idéias*.

10. A bondade de Deus garante tanto o poder quanto o cumprimento final de seus planos cosmológicos, por meio dos quais ele chegará a restaurar todas as coisas (Efé. 1:10). O primeiro capítulo da epístola aos Efésios mostra-nos que essa bondade será reconhecida pela criação inteira, e o oitavo capítulo de Romanos contém a mesma idéia. E então o problema do mal (que vide) encontrará perfeita solução.

BOM SENSO

A questão do bom senso tem três aspectos:

1. As opiniões das massas populares, na suposição de que há coisas tão patentes e óbvias que não é preciso qualquer argumento para que as pessoas creiam nelas. Estão em foco aquelas coisas que as mentes não-filosóficas acreditam ser indiscutíveis, como a existência de Deus, a existência da alma; ou então incluem crenças equivocadas, como a idéia de uma terra plana, a de que a terra ocupa o centro do universo, ou a de que o sol gira em torno da terra, em uma órbita a cada vinte e quatro horas.

2. Em sentido secundário, temos o *realismo ingênuo* (que vide), segundo o qual a verdade é vista exatamente conforme a percepção dos nossos sentidos a vêem, em contraste com o realismo crítico, que reconhece que nossos cinco sentidos de vista, audição, olfato, paladar e tato transmitem-nos impressões débeis e distorcidas, não se podendo confiar nos mesmos, nem mesmo quando os ajudamos com instrumentos chamados de precisão. Ver o artigo sobre Thomas Reid.

3. Aristóteles usava a expressão a fim de designar a faculdade humana que integra os informes dos cinco sentidos, dando-lhes uma apreensão unificada dos objetos (EP F)

BOM VIZINHO

«Vizinho», significa alguém que nos é «próximo». Trata-se de alguém que vive nas proximidades geográficas e que, presumivelmente, é um amigo, ou, pelo menos, conhecido que nos parece importante. A boa vizinhança fazia parte importante da fé judaica, a respeito do que muitas obrigações eram impostas ao povo de Israel (Êxo. 20:16,17; Lev. 19:18). Nas cidades modernas, esse conceito perdeu-se quase inteiramente, de tal modo que, com freqüência, nem ao menos sabemos os nomes daqueles que vivem no mesmo quarteirão, ou mesmo na casa ao lado. Brigham Young, líder pioneiro dos mórmons, baixou ordens no sentido de que nenhuma cidade grande fosse edificada no estado de Utah, nos Estados Unidos da América do Norte. Apesar disso, Salt Lake City, capital daquele estado norte-americano, atualmente é uma cidade que ultrapassou a casa do meio milhão de habitantes. Young preferia cidades pequenas e bem dispersas, visto que essas comunidades têm taxas de crimes menores, e problemas menos agudos que as cidades grandes. Isso deve-se, pelo menos em parte, ao espírito de boa vizinhança, que prevalece nas comunidades menores, juntamente com a pressão imediata da boa vizinhança e da opinião pública, que se perde nas cidades grandes.

Jesus ampliou a definição de «próximo» a fim de incluir todos aqueles que precisem, porventura, de nossa ajuda (Luc. 10:25-32). Ele também ensinou que a lei pode ser sumária no preceito do amor ao próximo (Luc. 22:37-40), e Paulo reverberou o tema em Romanos 13:8: «...pois quem ama ao próximo, tem cumprido a lei». Ver o artigo sobre *o Próximo*.

Um bom vizinho é alguém que observa esses princípios espirituais e éticos. Não está limitado a condições locais, raciais ou geográficas, mas deixa-se impulsionar pela compaixão e pela lei do amor (que vide). Tiago chama o amor ao próximo de «lei régia» (Tia. 2:8). (H I NTI)

BONALD, LOUIS GABRIEL AMBROISE, VISCONDE DE

Suas datas foram 1754-1840. Ele foi o fundador, juntamente com Joseph de Maistre (que vide), do movimento *tradicionalista* do pensamento católico francês (ver o artigo). Ele supunha que todos os erros nos campos da política, da religião e da filosofia podem ser traçados como desvios da *revelação primitiva* e original, que seria melhor representada pela Igreja Católica Romana, e da qual é a guardiã suprema.

Obras: *Théorie du pouvoir politique et religieux*, em três volumes; *Legislation primitive* e *Recherches philosophiques*, em dois volumes. (E)

BONAR, HORATIUS

Suas datas foram 1808-1889. Foi um ministro presbiteriano escocês, mais famoso por causa dos hinos que compôs, alguns dos quais tornaram-se parte integrante de hinários evangélicos. O Cantor Cristão inclui seis de seus hinos, enumerados ali como hinos 197, 231, 256, 394, 486 e 510. (E)

BONHOEFFER, DIETRICH

Teólogo alemão (1906-1945). Mostrou-se ativo na resistência contra Hitler e terminou morrendo em um campo de concentração. Foi pessoa relativamente desconhecida enquanto viveu. Mas, desde sua morte, tornou-se uma das figuras centrais da Igreja contemporânea na tentativa de esclarecer o problema do discipulado e da disciplina dos crentes. O seu livro, *O Custo do Discipulado*, contém seus princípios inflexíveis de moral e de verdades espirituais. Ele opunha-se a Hitler, tachando-o de anticristo (que vide), fortalecido pelos princípios que incorporara a esse e a outros de seus livros. Sua mente brilhante estava escudada numa vida totalmente dedicada. Em última análise, é a *vida* que é a medida de um homem, porquanto não há coisas como a piedade de papel, que consiste somente em palavras escritas, mas que não se torna realidade na vida de uma pessoa. Bonhoeffer combatia a divisão comum do mundo e das experiências em duas esferas: a profana e a sagrada. Antes, ele percebia que em nossa vivência devemos viver aquilo que é sagrado. Há somente uma realidade, a saber, a realidade de Deus, e como a mesma opera em nós.

Outras idéias: 1. Bonhoeffer enfatizava o evento *histórico* da revelação de Jesus Cristo, em contraposição a filosofias de atos, que enfatizam o homem, e filosofias do ser, que enfatizam Deus, de maneira não-histórica, ou melhor, a-histórica. 2. Suas atitudes eram um tanto obscuras no tocante à filosofia. Por um lado, ele asseverava que a filosofia ajuda o homem a obter autonomia sobre si mesmo e sobre o mundo. Por outro lado, ele sentia que o crente vê-se melhor servido quando se poupa completamente das inquirições da filosofia, incluindo aquilo que está envolvido na ética e na ontologia. *Obras de Bonhoeffer*: *The Communion of Saints; Act and Being; The Cost of Discipleship; Ethics; Resistance and Submission*. (HP)

BONIFÁCIO VIII, PAPA

Suas datas foram 1294-1303, como papa. Ele procurou restabelecer a supremacia do papado (que vide), conforme fora declarada por Inocente III (ver o artigo). Seu principal conflito foi com Filipe o Belo, da França, que estava em guerra contra a Inglaterra e assim cravou o clero de impostos, recusando-se a estabelecer a paz, por ordem do papa. Bonifácio expediu a bula *Unam Sanctam* (que vide) procurando provar a supremacia papal absoluta. Mas agentes de Filipe, o Belo, detiveram o papa e levaram-no à prisão, onde morreu pouco depois, moído de desgosto. (E)

BONIFÁCIO, São (Mártir)

Suas datas foram 675-755. Apóstolo da Alemanha, nasceu em Devonshire, na Inglaterra, e faleceu em Dolkum, na Holanda. Foi educado em Exeter, uniu-se à ordem dos beneditinos e foi ordenado sacerdote em 705. Foi enviado pelo papa Gregório II (ver o artigo) para pregar aos germânicos do leste de Reno. Em 722 tornou-se bispo, quando então tomou o nome de Bonifácio, talvez uma forma latinizada de Wilfrid, seu nome original. Desferiu um golpe fatal no paganismo germânico destruindo o carvalho sagrado de Tor (que vide) em Geimar. Fundou bispados, reformou toda a igreja franca, efetuou concílios e, em 748 foi feito arcebispo de Mainz, o que ele resignou em 754, a fim de evangelizar os habitantes de Frisland. Foi morto pelos selvagens pagãos, e seus restos mortais acham-se atualmente na catedral de Fulda. Sua festa é celebrada a 5 de junho. Tendo unido a igreja alemã, tornou-se tanto seu apóstolo como seu patrono. (E)

BONOSIANOS

É o nome do bispo Bonosus de Sárdica (séculos IV e V D.C.) — que foi condenado por negar a perpétua virgindade de Maria. Esse grupo sobreviveu na Espanha e na Gália (França), até o século VII D.C.

BONS PORTOS

Nome dado a uma baía perto de Laséia, na costa sul de Creta, acerca de oito quilômetros a leste do cabo Matala. Ver Atos 27:8. Paulo, sob vigilância, velejou para oeste, partindo de Cnido, em um navio alexandrino de transportar cereais. O mau tempo forçou o barco a buscar refúgio, — que foi encontrado em Bons Portos. Porém, esse lugar era apenas uma baía aberta, pelo que o centurião que estava encarregado dos prisioneiros, bem como o capitão e o proprietário do navio, resolveram tentar velejar até Fenice, um porto mais a oeste. A tentativa fracassou, pelo que ficaram boiando ao léu, em alto-mar, durante catorze dias, até que o navio naufragou em uma praia da ilha de Malta. O episódio inteiro da viagem de Paulo a Roma, e das aventuras marítimas pelas quais passou, compõem uma das narrativas bíblicas favoritas, sobre o que muito se tem escrito.

••• ••• •••

BOODIN, JOHN ELOF

Suas datas foram 1869-1950. Filósofo norte-americano de ascendência sueca. Estudou com Royce e foi um dos exponentes do *idealismo* (que vide). Ensinou na Universidade de Harvard e na UCLA.

Idéias. 1. A criação é um processo eterno, e a evolução é um processo de espiritualização. 2. O cosmos deve ser interpretado por meio do conceito dos campos, cada um deles com seus atributos de ser, tempo, espaço, consciência própria e forma, que é a base de toda a organização e estrutura. A consciência é aquele atributo que, sob determinadas condições, *ilumina* uma porção da realidade. 3. As hierarquias, uma idéia utilizada para falar de uma evolução emergente, são campos da física, da vida orgânica, da consciência própria e da sociedade. 4. A justaposição dos campos da consciência própria possibilita o conhecimento e uma sociedade. *Deus* é aquele campo espiritual em que todos nós vivemos, movemo-nos e temos o nosso ser, ocupando tanto o espaço quanto o tempo, em toda a sua extensão.

Escritos: *Time and Reality; A Realistic Universe; Cosmic Evolution; God and Creation; A Cosmic Philosophy*. (P EP)

BOOTH, WILLIAM

Suas datas foram 1820-1912. Foi evangelista e fundador do Exército da Salvação(ver o artigo). Ele fundou esse grupo em 1865. Booth nasceu em Nottingham, na Inglaterra. Ficou órfão de pai aos treze anos, e foi treinado para trabalhar em uma casa de penhores. Em 1855, a instâncias de sua esposa, tornou-se um ministro metodista, tempo integral.
— Dez anos depois, havia iniciado o grande empreendimento de sua vida, a missão de anunciar o evangelho aos pobres. Fundou o que se chamou de Sociedade Revivalista do Leste Londrino, posteriormente intitulada Missão Cristã. Não demorou muito para que ele contasse com um grupo de ex-delinqüentes, convertidos, trabalhando em favor da causa. Em 1878, a missão mudou de nome para *Exército da Salvação*, tendo sido criada uma espécie de hierarquia militar, para estimular o progresso dos membros. Esse Exército cresceu até tornar-se uma organização internacional, conforme a vemos hoje. Tragédias domésticas entristeceram Booth. Sua esposa faleceu em 1890, e ele ficou ainda mais dependente de seu filho, Bramwell. A despeito de tudo, cresceram a sua organização e o seu poder. Além do evangelismo, ele ocupou-se em reformas sociais, empregos, programas de treinamento vocacional, colônias agrícolas, abrigos para mulheres perdidas, lares para jovens fugitivas, agências de busca a pessoas desaparecidas, e várias outras organizações que refletem a lei do amor, a essência mesma da espiritualidade. Sua última aparição em público teve lugar no Albert Hall, em Londres, no dia em que completava 83 anos de idade. Pouco depois disso, perdeu a visão e então faleceu, a 20 de agosto de 1912, em Londres.

A filha de Booth, Evangeline Booth, foi a primeira generala do Exército da Salvação. Seus filhos, Bramwell e Ballington, eram elementos ativos do movimento. Emma Moss Booth-Tucker era outra filha, também ativa no movimento. Juntamente com seu marido, Frederick Tucker, ela iniciou o movimento na Índia. Todavia, morreu ainda jovem, em um desastre ferroviário, a 28 de outubro de 1903, em Dean Lake, Missouri, nos Estados Unidos da América. Podemos louvar essa família que trabalhou pela mesma causa e cujas obras seguiram-nos até os mundos iluminados, e cujos labores humanitários provaram que neles operava a lei do Senhor: *Amai-vos uns aos outros*. Quão bom seria se Deus nos presenteasse com mais *famílias* como essa. (AM E)

BOQUIM

No hebraico, «pranto». Nome dado a um lugar, provavelmente perto de Silo, onde se encontrava o tabernáculo armado, quando um anjo do Senhor reprovou os israelitas reunidos por causa de sua desobediência, ao entrarem em liga com os habitantes da terra, e por não se terem apossado de sua herança. Isso causou profundo lamento entre o povo, o que deu nome a esse lugar. (Juí. 2:1,5).

BORDADOR, BORDADEIRA

No hebraico, o bordador era o **raqam**, palavra que ocorre por duas vezes: Êxo. 35:35 e 38:23. O bordado é expresso pelo termo hebraico *shabats*, «entretecer», usado por duas vezes: Êxo. 28:39 e 28:20.

As artes de bordar, costurar e outros trabalhos de agulha eram praticadas tanto entre os hebreus como entre os povos circunvizinhos (Exo. 28:29,32; 35:25; Juí. 5:30; Sal. 45:14). Muito antes dos dias de Abraão, os cananeus bordavam finos tecidos, empregando padrões de vívidas cores. A arqueologia tem encontrado restos de equipamentos de tinturaria, em Ugarite. Biblos e outras cidades costeiras da Fenícia tinham a reputação de produzir ótimos tecidos e vestes. Da concha do murex era extraído um pigmento púrpura avermelhado, além do que várias plantas produziam material que podiam ser usados como corantes. As descobertas arqueológicas em Tell Beit Mirsim produziram evidências de bordados muito bem-feitos, tecidos tingidos e trabalho artístico com a agulha. Mantas da Mesopotâmia eram proverbiais quanto à sua beleza. Antes mesmo da época de Abraão, governantes babilônicos tinham suas próprias fábricas de produção de bordados. O Egito também produzia excelentes produtos de linho fino, desde 2900 A.C. Foi no Egito que Israel aprendeu essa arte, e algumas famílias faziam do bordado o trabalho de suas vidas inteiras (Êxo. 35:30,35; I Crô. 4:21). O Antigo Testamento mostra-nos que era mister uma grande habilidade na produção das vestes dos sacerdotes e sumos sacerdotes, o que incluía até mesmo o uso de fios de ouro entretecido em linho fino retorcido. O trecho de Jos. 7:21 menciona vestes assírias e babilônicas. Naturalmente, esses produtos eram comercializados em alta escala (Eze. 27:24).

Usos Simbólicos. O trabalho de bordador pode simbolizar o luxo e o comércio lucrativo (Sal. 45:14; Eze. 27:16). As vestes do sumo sacerdote, em seu material e em suas cores, também teriam sentidos simbólicos. As cortinas bordadas para o portão do átrio e para a porta do tabernáculo eram símbolos de restrição ao acesso. (Ver JE, artigo sobre *Bordado*). MIL LUT.

BORLAS

No hebraico temos duas palavras envolvidas: 1. *Tsitsith*, «borlas», palavra usada por três vezes: Núm. 15:38,39. 2. *Gedilim*, palavra usada por duas vezes: Deu. 22:12 (onde nossa versão portuguesa diz «borlas») e I Reis 7:17, (onde nossa versão portuguesa diz «ornamentos torcidos»). Ambas as traduções desta última palavra fazem sentido, pois ela significa «fio torcido». Os israelitas receberam ordens de costurar na beirada de suas vestes essas borlas, a fim de lhes servirem de lembretes dos mandamentos de Deus, aos quais deveriam obedecer. Isso lhes servia de lembrete constante, pois era algo que sempre lhes sobressaía diante dos olhos. As borlas eram feitas de linho torcido azul, costuradas em cada canto das vestes. É possível que a cor azul das mesmas, simbolizasse a origem celestial dos mandamentos. Um outro lembrete eram os *tephillim*, ou *filactérias*, usadas sobre a testa, pelos homens judeus, quando da oração matinal. Eram pequenas caixas de pergaminho, com um trecho pequeno das Escrituras no interior. E também havia a *mezuzah*, uma pequena caixa oblonga que continha um trecho copiado das Escrituras, afixada às portas dos quartos de uma residência israelita.

Jesus e as Borlas. Um dos mais notáveis milagres de Jesus ocorreu quando a mulher hemorrágica tocou nas borlas de suas vestes, e seu fluxo de sangue estancou imediatamente (Mat. 9:20). O trecho de Mateus 14:36 mostra-nos que o sentimento dela, de que seria curada, se ao menos tocasse nas borlas das vestes de Jesus, era compartilhado por outras pessoas. De fato, tantos quantos tocaram ali foram curados. Os israelitas sempre tiveram as borlas das vestes em alta conta, como símbolos de poder espiritual, ou essas crenças jamais teriam surgido.

Os Fariseus e as Borlas. O Senhor Jesus condenou a ostentação dos fariseus, que mandavam fazer grandes borlas para suas vestes, a fim de chamarem a atenção alheia (Mat. 23:5). Os homens sempre gostam de receber as honras que pertencem unicamente a Deus.

Outras Referências. As borlas das vestes não tinham, necessariamente, alguma significação religiosa. Com freqüência, eram apenas itens decorativos das vestes. Monumentos provenientes do Egito e do Oriente Próximo mostram que muitos tipos de borlas eram usados, alguns deles bastante elaborados. Os babilônios também decoravam suas vestes com borlas.

Os Hebreus e as Borlas, em Tempos Posteriores. Os judeus deixavam de usar esse item externo de suas vestes em tempos de perseguição, da parte dos pagãos ou dos cristãos, a fim de não serem tão facilmente identificados. Em substituição, eles usavam uma espécie de veste íntima, que lhes cobria o peito e as costas, com borlas. Os modernos judeus ortodoxos até hoje usam borlas em suas vestes. —Xales de oração, com borlas costuradas a elas, também eram usadas. Atualmente, o fio azul retorcido não mais é considerado necessário. (ID Z)

BORNHAUSEN, KARL

Nasceu em 1882, mas a data de seu falecimento é desconhecida. Foi professor em Breslau, e então em Frankfurt, ambas na Alemanha. Foi aluno de Herrmann e de Troeltsch (que vide). Sua ênfase era sobre um cristianismo centralizado em Jesus, isento de intermináveis embaraços históricos e interpretativos. (E)

BORNHOLMIANOS

Um grupo religioso que devia seu nome à ilha dinamarquesa de Bornholm. Eles sofreram a influência do movimento revivalista dos meados do século XIX, na Suécia, sob Hedberg e Rosenius (que vide), e levaram o movimento até àquela ilha. P.L. Trandberg era o principal pregador deles. Ele rompeu com a igreja oficial dinamarquesa, e gradualmente perdeu a liderança do movimento. Vários pregadores espalharam o movimento a outras regiões, incluindo a Dinamarca e a Silésia. A ênfase deles recaía sobre o dom gratuito da graça, independente das condições do homem. (E)

BORRA DE VINHO

No hebraico, **shemarim**, «preservadores», palavra que aparece por cinco vezes (Isa. 25:6; Jer. 48:11; Sof. 1:12; Sal. 75:8). Trata-se daquele sedimento que se ajunta no fundo dos receptáculos com o vinho. Quando o vinho juntava a borra, era considerado de qualidade superior, porquanto o vinho que juntava tais sedimentos tornar-se-ia mais forte e concentrado.

Usos Metafóricos. 1. A era messiânica será um tempo de bênção especial, pois então o vinho será excelente, e por longo tempo ficará com a sua borra (Isa. 25:6). 2. Ficar repousando nas fezes (borra) do vinho indica aqueles que, devido a um longo período de prosperidade, chegaram a uma posição de força, e que, devido às distorções do ócio, terminam deleitando-se em ações corrompidas (Jer. 48:11; Zof. 1:12). 3. Sorver o vinho até às escórias indica experimentar o castigo divino até o fim (Sal. 75:8).

BOSANQUET, BERNARD

Filósofo inglês (1848-1923). Ensinou em Oxford e Stº André. Devotou-se às obras sociais, à filosofia e a escrever livros. Foi influenciado pelo idealismo hegeliano, e desenvolveu um sistema no qual o papel central era desempenhado pela idéia do indivíduo, caracterizada como o universal concreto da harmonia de princípios opostos, o que, segundo ele, é a única coisa capaz de independência, ou de permanecer de pé. Tal individualidade, entretanto, pode ser melhor vista na arte, na religião e no absoluto (que vide), que é a unidade de todas as manifestações menores, e não de indivíduos isolados. *Escritos*: *Knowledge and Reality; Logic; History of Aesthetics; The Principle of Individuality and Value*. (E F P)

BOSOR

Nome de um homem e de uma cidade referida no livro apócrifo de I Macabeus, a saber:

1. Uma forma alternativa do nome de Beor, pai de Balaão, em II Ped. 2:15. Essa forma aparece no original grego do Novo Testamento, sendo seguida por algumas versões. Mas nossa versão portuguesa atém-se à forma derivada do hebraico, *Beor*.

2. Uma cidade de Gileade cujos habitantes perseguiram seus residentes judeus, a qual, subseqüentemente, foi capturada por Judas Macabeu (I Macabeus 5:26,36). Tem sido identificada com a moderna Buar el-Hariri. Houve tempo em que essa cidade ficava dentro do território de Rúben (Jos. 20:8).

BOSORA

Uma cidade de Gileade, identificada com a moderna Busra eski Sham, a 43 km a leste de Ramote-Gileade. Também era chamada Bozra e Bostra. Porém, não devemos confundi-la com Bosor (ver o artigo), que ficava cerca de 40 km a norte-noroeste de Bosora. Também não deve ser confundida com a Bozra de Edom. Judas Macabeu derrotou os habitantes de Bosora durante a sua campanha em Gileade, em cerca de 165-162 A.C. Houve então os usuais incêndios e matanças (I

Macabeus 5:26,28; Josefo, *Anti.* xii.8.3). Nas cartas de Amarna (ver o artigo) encontramos o nome Busruna. Sob o nome de Bostra, a cidade tornou-se capital da Arábia romana. (Z)

BOSQUE Ver Floresta.

BOSSUET, JACQUES BÉNIGNE
Suas datas foram 1627-1704. Foi bispo católico romano, controversista, asceta, escritor, filósofo da história. Nasceu em Dkion, na França e foi educado pelos jesuítas, tendo sido ordenado «padre» em 1652. Mudou-se para Paris e dedicou-se, tempo integral, à prédica. Entrou em amarga controvérsia com Fénelon, sobre a questão do quietismo (que vide). (E)

BOTA
No hebraico, **seon**, «sandália» ou «sapato», embora de forma distinta das sandálias e calçados do Oriente. Aparece somente por uma vez, em Isa. 9:5. No Novo Testamento, em Efésios 6:15, temos o verbo «calçar», *upodéomai*, que também figura em Mar. 6:9 e Atos 12:8. O trecho de Isaías provavelmente refere-se à bota militar dos assírios. Mas a alusão paulina, na epístola aos Efésios, deve ser à bota cravejada dos soldados romanos, a *caliga*, da qual Gaio César derivava seu apelido, *Calígula* (que vide). Essa bota era feita de couro, com tiras de couro trançadas até à batata da perna. Os centuriões romanos tinham um calçado melhor, chamado *bardaicus calceus*, cujo nome vinha dos bardaei, uma tribo ilírica (ver Juvenal 16:13 e 3:24). Um outro nome comum para a bota, em latim, era o *calceus*, que também era usado para indicar sapatos. A Vulgata, em Efésios 6:15, diz: *et calceati pedes in praeparatione evangelii pacis*. (Z)

BOUGLÊ, Celestin Charles Alfred
Nasceu em 1870 e faleceu em 1940. Ele rejeitava as teorias econômicas, domésticas e raciais como meios de explicar o sistema de castas da Índia, tentando correlacionar a religião com algum sistema político e social. Também asseverava que um código moral jamais pode tornar-se puro e inteiramente condizente com as necessidades de uma sociedade em mutação, a menos que se desenvolva livre das sanções religiosas.

BOURDALQUE, LOUIS
Suas datas foram 1632-1704. Foi um jesuíta francês, e orador de púlpito. A sua pregação era eloqüente, mas a sua influência era devida mais ao caráter piedoso e a simplicidade de sua vida. Em outras palavras, ele vivia os princípios que anunciava em seus sermões, e nisso consistia a sua eloqüência especial. Ele apelava a todas as classes sociais e exercia uma larga influência. (E)

BOURIGNON, MADAME ANTOINETTE
Suas datas foram 1616-1680. Era uma mística francesa da escola do quietismo (ver o artigo).

BOUSSET, JOHANN FRANZ WILHELM
Nasceu em 1865 e faleceu em 1920. Ensinou nas Universidades de Gottingen e Giessen. Juntamente com Hermann Gunkel (ver o artigo) foi um dos líderes do grupo de eruditos teólogos-religiosos históricos. Mediante brilhantes investigações, ele projetou luz sobre o Novo Testamento inteiro e sobre os primeiros séculos da história da Igreja cristã. (E)

BOUTROUX, EMILE
Nasceu em Montrouge, França, em 1854, e faleceu em 1921. Foi eminente professor de filosofia da École Normale Superieur, na Sorbonne. Foi membro da escola *espiritualista* (isto é, *idealista*) da França. Bergson e M. Blondel foram alguns de seus alunos.

Idéias. 1. Ele opunha-se ao naturalismo mecanicista de sua época. 2. Foi crítico dos padrões usados pelas ciências exatas de seus dias, que ele considerava falhos em suas definições da realidade. 3. A investigação da realidade, segundo pensava, deve incluir considerações sobre os conceitos de necessidade absoluta, necessidade relativa, ser, gênero, matéria, vida e consciência. 4. Cada estágio das investigações envolve, necessariamente, um *salto*, devendo-se admitir os aspectos de contingência e da ocorrência de novidades. 5. A liberdade máxima encontra-se na vida moral, um passo necessário no caminho da vida religiosa. 6. Os ideais da beleza, do bem e da perfeição exercem uma atração sobre as hierarquias do ser, similar ao papel que Deus exerce sobre a sua criação. 7. A realidade fundamental é a liberdade. Tudo quanto sucede acontece espontaneamente e é expressão de uma atividade eternamente criativa. A liberdade é o principal atributo de Deus, o ser dotado de beleza e bondade supremas. 8. A religião existe a fim de ajudar o homem a atingir o ideal divino em si mesmo. A religião não deve guiar-se pela fé cega e crédula. Deve ser intelectualmente satisfatória.

Obras: A Contingência das Leis da Natureza; A Idéia da Lei Natural na Ciência e na Filosofia Contemporâneas; A Psicologia do Misticismo; Ciência e Religião na Filosofia Contemporânea. (AM E EP P)

BOUVIER, AMI AUGUSTE OSCAR
Teólogo natural de Genebra (1726-1893). Para ele, a personalidade de Deus é uma grande hipótese que requer ser verificada especulativamente. Quando ele falava sobre Deus, na linguagem usada pela piedade, seus termos eram pessoais. Mas, quando falava sobre Deus em termos filosóficos, usava expressões impessoais. Quando descrevia os atributos de Deus, caía em um imanentismo em que o mundo, o homem e Deus são todos idênticos. Ele se opunha às formulações tradicionais da doutrina da Trindade (que vide), usando essa palavra para indicar uma espécie de auto-evolução de Deus, — como alusão aos níveis ou fases da vida divina. Deus, para ele, é uma personalidade absoluta, que antecede o estado impessoal existente na ordem divina. Jesus seria uma personalidade relativa, sujeito exclusivo do campo religioso. O Espírito Santo, porém, seria impessoal. Ele enfatizava a paternidade divina. (E)

BOVET, PIERRE
Juntamente com E. Claparede, foi fundador do Institute de Jean Jacques Rousseau, em Genebra. Nasceu em 1878 e faleceu em data desconhecida. Para ele, as formas de vida sociais e religiosas seriam meras sublimações dos instintos sexuais e de defesa própria. Os sentimentos religiosos eram explicados por ele como uma transferência do amor filial às divindades, da mesma maneira que as crianças atribuem todas as modalidades de atributos, reais e imaginários, a seus genitores.

BOVON, JULES

Suas datas foram 1852-1904. Era nativo de Vaud, na Suíça francesa. Foi professor de teologia da Universidade de Lausanne. *Idéias*: Deus é uma personalidade infinita no que tange aos fenômenos físicos, e é uma personalidade pessoal do ponto de vista da vida espiritual. Podemos obter algumas noções sobre a personalidade divina mediante a analogia com a personalidade humana. Na qualidade de princípio do universo, Deus é infinito, mas na qualidade de Pai celeste, ele é pessoal. Deus teria dois tipos de atributos: 1. Os atributos metafísicos: Deus é infinito e está acima de todos os nossos esforços para compreendê-lo. 2. Deus é pessoal: nossas características humanas são aquelas possuídas por Deus, embora ele as tenha em grau infinito. (E)

BOWNE, BORDEN PARKER

Suas datas foram 1845-1910. Filósofo personalista norte-americano. Nasceu em Leonardsville, Nova Jérsei. Foi professor da Universidade de Boston, com estudos de aperfeiçoamento em Paris, Halle e Gottingen. Ensinava na Universidade de Boston e foi deão da Escola Graduada até seu falecimento.

Idéias. 1. Nenhuma forma de metafísica impessoal pode fazer justiça aos informes colhidos pela experiência, incluindo os conceitos impessoais do naturalismo, do materialismo e do idealismo absoluto. 2. Somente o conceito de personalidade é capaz de produzir uma explicação final da realidade. 3. A personalidade é uma explicação cuidadosa da realidade, e não uma mera abstração alicerçada sobre a experiência. 4. A descrição de um ser humano, bem como a descrição de Deus, segundo se vê no teísmo, requerem a idéia de personalidade. Nada existe de impessoal por detrás da experiência. 5. O ponto de vista resultante chama-se *personalismo* (que vide). Esse ponto de vista é uma espécie de *idealismo* (que vide), e evita os dogmas abstratos e absolutos.

Obras: *Metaphysics; Philosophy and Theism; The Theory of Thought and Knowledge; Theism; Personalism*. (E EP P)

BOXE E LUTA LIVRE

I Cor. 9:27: Antes subjugo o meu corpo, e o reduzo à submissão, para que, depois de pregar a outros, eu mesmo não venha a ficar reprovado.

Esmurro. Alguns estudiosos se têm deixado equivocar pela tradução que diz erroneamente, «mantenho meu corpo em sujeição», pensando que Paulo mudou a sua metáfora, em I Cor. 9:27, para a «luta livre». Na realidade, porém, tem prosseguindo o simbolismo do boxe, e essa palavra significa «espanco meu corpo». Originalmente, no original grego, tal vocábulo significa «bater abaixo do olho», a fim de deixar um olho inchado. Nas páginas do N.T. essa palavra grega figura apenas aqui e em Luc. 18:5, onde é usada metaforicamente com o sentido de «exaurir», «aborrecer».

No entanto, há realmente uma modificação importante dentro da metáfora, a saber, que Paulo se torna o seu próprio adversário. É como se ele dirigisse os seus golpes contra si mesmo, a fim de derrubar-se, visando seu corpo, seus apetites carnais, seus desejos desviados, que queriam derrotá-lo em sua inquirição espiritual.

A palavra *corpo*, é empregada aqui no sentido literal, porquanto a «carne» é o veículo das ações errôneas, ainda que não seja o princípio mesmo do pecado. No entanto, a natureza carnal pode ser facilmente utilizada pelo princípio do pecado, a fim de derrotar o crente em sua inquirição espiritual. Outrossim, a palavra «corpo» talvez tenha sido usada como termo metafórico para indicar a luta geral que o crente enceta consigo mesmo, contra a sua antiga natureza, a qual, na realidade, é o seu pior inimigo. As tendências do crente para o desvio, suas propensões para abandonar a Deus, à justiça e ao bem-estar da alma, uma vez atraído o homem de bem pelos espetáculos e ruídos deste mundo, pelos padrões de falsos valores, pelos pecados sensuais, é que estão aqui em foco. Assim sendo, «corpo» equivale aqui ao «velho homem», à *natureza pecaminosa*, que se utiliza do corpo físico para realizar suas ações. (Comparar essa idéia com as passagens de Rom. 6:9,11-13; 7:18,23,24 e Gál. 5:17).

O boxe praticado nos tempos antigos era esporte muito mais brutal que o seu moderno paralelo. Assim era por causa do tipo de luvas que os contendores usavam. Assim é que Virgílio (em *Eneida* v.405) descreve as luvas de Entelo dizendo que as mesmas eram formadas de sete camadas de couro de vaca, com chumbo e ferro entremeados na mesma. Algumas vezes tais luvas eram denominadas *guiotoroi*, isto é, «quebra-membros».

Rodolfo Lanziani, em sua obra intitulada *Ancient Rome in the Light of Recent Discoveries*, ao referir-se a uma estátua exumada nos alicerces do Templo do Sol, erigido por Aurélio, na cidade de Roma, e que representava um boxeador sentado, em bronze, nos dá as seguintes informações: «O nariz está inchado devido aos efeitos do último golpe recebido; as orelhas fazem lembrar — um pedaço chato e sem forma de couro; os ombros e o peito estão repletos de contusões... Os detalhes das luvas de boxe, com quatro camadas de material, também são interessantes. E nos perguntamos, admirados, como é que um ser humano, sem importar quão forte e poderoso fosse, poderia resistir aos golpes de tais instrumentos como são essas luvas, feitas de quatro ou cinco grossuras de couro, fortalecidas com articulações de bronze»?

Com base nessa descrição podemos perceber qual era o tipo de disciplina que Paulo esperava usar consigo mesmo, como achava que deveria tratar sua natureza inferior, e até que extremos ele foi, a fim de chegar ao ponto da vitória em Jesus Cristo.

Luto, I Cor. 9:26. No grego original temos aqui a palavra *pukteuo*, paralelo de *pugme*, «punho», ou seja, bater com o punho, «boxear». Dessa palavra é que se deriva o termo moderno «pugilismo» e seu derivado, «pugilista».

Desferindo golpes no ar. Diz Vincent (*in loc.*, com uma citação extraída de Virgílio): «Poder-se-ia dizer que um boxeador bate no ar quando pratica sem adversário. Esse treinamento era denominado '*skiamachia*', 'luta com sombra'. Ou poderia propositadamente bater no ar, a fim de poupar o adversário; ou talvez o adversário se desviasse de seus golpes, levando-o a desgastar suas energias no ar. Essas duas últimas idéias bem poderiam ser a combinação indicada na metáfora utilizada por Paulo. Assim, ele visaria o alvo e não pouparia, como um pugilista poderia fazer; como o versículo implica quando fala: «*...não sem meta; assim luto, não como desferindo golpes no ar*». Ele lutava objetivamente, com propósito e diligência.

BOYLE, ROBERT

Suas datas foram 1627-1692. Foi químico e físico

inglês, mas de ascendência irlandesa. Participou da promoção do ponto de vista corpuscular ou atomicista da matéria, em resultado de suas experiências com gases. Seu livro, intitulado «O Químico Cético», publicado em 1661, divorciou a química da alquimia, ao insistir que a natureza das substâncias materiais tinha de estar baseada em evidências experimentais, e não em noções gregas, que continuavam sendo respeitadas na época, as quais misturavam elementos místicos para obter explicações.

Boyle foi membro fundador da Real Sociedade Inglesa, cujo lema era *Nullius in Verba*, ou seja, «nada por mera autoridade». Interessante é observar que os físicos teóricos de nossos dias estão retornando às idéias gregas, porquanto pensam que a própria matéria consiste na concentração de energias psíquicas. Os idealistas, naturalmente, supõem que a *idéia* ou espírito ocupa posição primária, se não mesmo de importância exclusiva. Não obstante, para a ciência coisa alguma fica decidida sem a experimentação. (EP F)

BOZCATE

No hebraico, «altura». Uma cidade situada nas planícies de Judá (Jos. 15:39). Ficava no distrito de Sefelá, perto de Laquis. Era a terra natal da mãe de Josias, Jedida (II Reis 22:1).

BOZES

No hebraico, «altura» ou «brilhante». Era nome de uma das penhas íngremes que havia no desfiladeiro de Micmás. A outra penha era chamada Sené (I Sam. 14:4). Naquela área, Jônatas e seu armeiro subiram, quando atacavam um posto avançado dos filisteus. O local fica perto do moderno wadi es-Suweinit, mas nenhuma identificação exata se tem podido fazer.

BOZRA

No hebraico, «fortaleza», «recinto fechado». Era nome de dois lugares, nas páginas do Novo Testamento, a saber:

1. Uma cidade de Edom, residência de Jobabe (Gên. 36:33; I Crô. 1:44. Ver também Isa. 34:6; Jer. 49:13,22; Amós 1:12). Tem sido identificada com a moderna Buseireh, localizada no início do wadi Hamayideh, em uma escarpa isolada, cercada por três lados por profundos vales. Fica cerca de 48 km ao norte de Petra. Era a mais poderosa fortaleza no norte de Edom, controlando o acesso à Estrada do Rei, e portanto, à Arabá e ao porto de Elate, no mar Vermelho. É possível que tenha funcionado como capital de Edom, pelo menos em parte de sua história. Tornou-se famosa por causa de suas vestes tingidas (Isa. 63:1).

2. Uma localidade de Moabe (Jer. 48:24), que talvez fosse a mesma Bezer (que vide). (UM Z)

BRAÇA

No grego, **orguiá**, «braça». Palavra que figura somente em Atos 27:28, por duas vezes. Era o comprimento dos braços abertos, ou seja, cerca de 1,80 m. O verbo grego por detrás da palavra é *orégo*, «estendo», pelo que a *orguiá* é a própria medição. Antigas fontes informam-nos que equivalia a quatro côvados gregos.

BRACELETES

No hebraico encontramos várias palavras:

1. *Etsadah*, «tira de braço», «corrente», usada apenas por duas vezes: II Sam. 1:10 e Núm. 31:50.

2. *Chach*, «gancho». Palavra usada por sete vezes. Por exemplo: Êxo. 35:22; II Reis 19:28. Geralmente indicava um gancho para manter cativos homens ou animais (II Reis 19:28; Eze. 29:4), embora em Êxo. 35:22 apareça como um ornamento.

3. *Tsamid*, «bracelete». Palavra que aparece por sete vezes. Por exemplo: Gên. 24:22,30,47; Eze. 16:11; 23:42.

4. *Sheroth*, «ornamentos torcidos». Palavra que aparece por cinco vezes. Por exemplo: Isa. 3:19.

Os braceletes eram um artigo de adorno, populares nos tempos antigos e usados por homens e mulheres igualmente (Eze. 16:11). Eram fabricados de vários metais, como bronze, ferro, ouro, prata e até mesmo de vidro. A arqueologia tem trazido à luz muitos tipos de braceletes, inclusive aqueles deixados em túmulos reais, que os reis usavam com insígnias inscritas, designando a autoridade imanente em seu ofício. Alguns braceletes eram muito ornamentados com pedras preciosas incrustadas, pérolas e outras decorações.

Abraão enviou braceletes a Rebeca, através de Eleazar (Gên. 24:22). Em Números 31:50 lemos que braceletes de prata e de ouro foram dissolvidos para o fabrico de vasos para o tabernáculo. Saul usava um bracelete real, quando morreu (II Sam. 1:10). Também havia ornamentos nas mulheres de Israel usavam nos pés, que se assemelhavam a braceletes (Isa. 3:17,18,20) e dos quais o profeta zombou. O trecho de Judite 10:4 alista braceletes entre os muitos itens de enfeites que as mulheres da época costumavam usar. Ver *Ornamentos*. (UN HA)

BRAÇO

Esse vocábulo é usado por 84 vezes no Antigo Testamento e por 3 vezes no Novo Testamento. Em alguns poucos casos, refere-se a um braço humano literal (ver Juí. 15:14 e 16:12); mas, com maior freqüência, há um uso metafórico, — que inclui as seguintes idéias: 1. O braço desnudo e estendido, que representa atos que revelam o poder de Deus a fim de remir ou destruir (ver Êxo. 6:6; Isa. 51:9; 52:10 e Eze. 20:33). 2. Um símbolo de refúgio (ver Deu. 33:27). 3. A diminuição ou destruição de algum poder, quando então a idéia é a de quebrar o braço (ver Sal. 10:15; Eze. 30:21 e João 12:38). 4. O fortalecimento de grandes realizações (ver Sal. 18:34). 5. Como símbolo de grande poder (ver Jó 40:9). 6. O *braço de carne* simboliza a debilidade humana, pelo que não podemos confiar no poder humano (ver Jer. 17:5). 7. O braço mirrado indica a impotência (ver Zac. 11:17). 8. O braço simboliza proteção e preservação (ver Isa. 40:11 e Deu. 33:27). 9. Há também a representação de algum poder ou força impessoal, como os braços de um dilúvio (ver Dan. 11:22). Há um certo paralelismo com a *mão*, especialmente com a mão direita (ver Sal. 44:3). (FA ND S UN Z)

BRADLEY, FRANCIS HERBERT

Suas datas foram 1846-1924. Foi filósofo inglês, um idealista absoluto. Nasceu em Clapham, Glasbury. Educou-se em Oxford, tendo sido um atleta e erudito. Porém, desde 1871 até à sua morte, viveu na invalidez. Foi o primeiro filósofo a receber a Ordem de Mérito, uma alta honraria.

BRADWARDINE — BRAHMA SAMAJ

Idéias. 1. Sofreu a influência de Hegel e Kant, embora tivesse postulado suas próprias noções da realidade, de acordo com as quais nenhuma coisa isolada pode ser vista como o conjunto de propriedades a ela atribuídas. A unidade e o caráter de qualquer coisa lhe são conferidas pela *relação* entre a coisa e suas propriedades. 2. O *absoluto* não é apenas um sistema de aparências, mas também é aquilo que contém o sistema. 3. Toda aparência, mesmo que ilusória, no tocante à verdadeira natureza de alguma coisa, faz parte da realidade. 4. A idéia de realidade é dada através de experiências sensíveis, combinando, de forma inseparável, o sensor e a coisa sentida. 5. A noção que um indivíduo faz de si mesmo só pode ser definida em termos do que é *outrem*. 6. Somente o que satisfaz o intelecto pode ser real ou verdadeiro, e o que é mais valioso também é o que é mais real. 7. A tentativa do intelecto encontrar soluções para seus problemas é uma tentativa para ultrapassar as aparências incoerentes, relacionadas entre si e sempre mutáveis nas coisas. Dessa maneira, pois, o intelecto procura chegar ao *absoluto*, que é idêntico àquilo que é real e verdadeiro. Não podemos conhecê-lo em sua completa natureza, mas, ao menos, podemos conhecê-lo em parte. Por exemplo, o absoluto caracteriza-se por suas qualidades de coerência e permanência. O absoluto é inerentemente necessário, não sendo mera aparência, além de ser completo e harmônico. É uma unidade que inclui a diversidade. 8. Se não houver uma total experiência, acima da experiência do indivíduo, então a pessoa termina no solipsismo (que vide). Porém, a experiência de um homem pode transcender ao absoluto, que contém a total diversidade do mundo, em uma unidade. 9. No campo da *ética*, Bradley pensava que o bem mais alto, bem como a grande virtude a ser buscada, é a *auto-realização*, primeiramente no próprio indivíduo, e então naquilo em que ele se relaciona à comunidade, segundo moldes aristotélicos. A religião faz parte dessa auto-realização. Ver o artigo geral sobre o *Idealismo*.

Obras: Ethical Studies; The Principles of Logic; Appearance and Reality; Essays in Truth and Reality.

BRADWARDINE, THOMAS

Filósofo e teólogo inglês (1290-1349). Nasceu em Sussex e educou-se em Oxford. Foi chanceler da Universidade de Oxford em 1349, arcebispo de Canterbury, e foi intitulado de *doutor profundo*. Contradizia os seguidores de Pelágio (que vide), afirmando que a vontade de Deus é a primeira causa, responsável por todos os efeitos no mundo, incluindo as ações humanas. Influenciou várias figuras contemporâneas e posteriores, incluindo Wycliff, tradutor da Bíblia para o inglês. Morreu de praga, pouco depois de haver sido nomeado arcebispo de Canterbury.

Escritos: On the Divine Causality against the Pelagians; On Proportion; On Speculative Geometry. (AM E P)

BRAHE, TYCHO

Astrônomo dinamarquês (1546-1601). Nasceu em Knudstrup, estudou em Copenhague e Leipzig, Rostock e Ausburgo. Trabalhou por muitos anos como astrônomo. Kepler (que vide) serviu como seu assistente. Aprimorou imensamente as observações astronômicas, e proveu a Kepler o material que o ajudou a aperfeiçoar as revolucionárias idéias de Copérnico. (AM P)

BRAHMA (BRAMA)

Paralelamente a Vishnu (que vide) e Siva (que vide), ele compõe a Trindade da concepção hindu. Seria o Deus Criador. Atualmente, sua adoração não é muito difundida na Índia. É a personalização de Brahman. Este último desempenha um importante papel na filosofia do hinduísmo (que vide). (E P)

BRAHMAN (BRAMAN)

O vocábulo sânscrito de onde se deriva esse termo é de sentido duvidoso, embora pareça significar «mágica». Refere-se aos resultados mágicos obtidos através de ritos e sacrifícios. No Rig-Veda aparece com o sentido de oração ou de encantamento por meio de oração. Nos Upanishades, veio a indicar a realidade última. Nos Vedas (que vide), esse nome torna-se sinônimo de vento, hálito, sol e da sílaba Om (que vide), sendo considerado como a essência mística dos Vedas. Na teologia posterior hindu, o termo passou a significar a essência divina pura, imutável e eterna, na qual todos têm sua origem e destino. Esse é o conceito central das Upanishades (que vide), bem como da filosofia Vedanta (que vide). Faz-se ali uma distinção entre o Brahman Saguna (Brahman dotado de qualidades) e o Brahman Nirguna (Brahman sem qualidades). Brahman também é identificado com Atman, dentro da fórmula Brahman-Atman, onde se chega ao monismo. Todas as divindades, como Brahma, o criador, Vishnu, Siva, Krishna, e mesmo as divindades secundárias da religião popular, podem ser assimiladas por Brahman, como manifestações ou aspectos pessoais do mesmo. Entretanto, Brahman é impessoal e superpessoal. Brahman seria tanto imanente quanto transcendental. (AM E P F)

BRAHMANAS (BRAMANAS)

Escritos sacerdotais do hinduísmo, vinculados aos Vedas (que vide), produzidos, mui provavelmente, entre 800 e 600 A.C. Contêm normas relativas a sacrifícios, e tentam explicar o significado do ritual. São instruções detalhadas e repetitivas, contendo muitos mitos e teologia especulativa. Representam uma transição da fé religiosa entre as idéias dos Vedas e o hinduísmo filosófico. (E)

BRAHMANASPATI

Literalmente, «senhor da oração». Uma deidade védica abstrata, intimamente relacionada a Indra e a Agni (que vide), sendo considerada a expressão do poder misterioso que há em Brahman (que vide). (E)

BRAHMANISMO (BRAMANISMO)

Ver **Hinduísmo**.

BRAHMA SAMAJ

Um moderno movimento eclético e reformista do hinduísmo, fundado por Ram Mohan Roy (que vide), em 1828. No início foi chamado Brahma Sabha, mas depois adquiriu a nova designação. O islamismo influenciou Roy com um ponto de vista monoteísta de Deus; e ele também sofreu influência de idéias cristãs unitaristas. Vários líderes passaram a ajudá-lo, e finalmente surgiram seitas, — entre elas aquela chamada *Nova Dispensação*, iniciada por Keshub Chunder Sen, que era muito influenciado por idéias cristãs.

BRAHMINS — BREVIÁRIO

Características do Movimento. 1. Combate à idolatria. 2. Monoteísmo. 3. Adoração congregacional. 4. Reforma moral, com a aplicação da ética cristã. O grupo nunca foi numeroso, mas tem exercido grande influência sobre a religião hindu, devido ao poder carismático de alguns de seus líderes. (E)

BRAHMINS (BRAMINS)

A classe governante da tradição indiana. Ver a questão, incluída no artigo sobre o Hinduísmo.

BRANCO

Tradução de várias palavras hebraicas e gregas, dentre as quais há uma mais importante no hebraico e no grego, esta última, *leukós*. No Antigo Testamento, a palavra «branco» serve para indicar a aparência natural dos objetos de cores claras, como o linho, a madrepérola e o pão branco (ver II Crô. 5:12; Est. 1:6; Gên. 40:16), além de outros tipos de tecidos e materiais, como as cãs das pessoas idosas (ver Osé. 7:9), as cabras (ver Gên. 30:35), os dentes, a lã, o leite e a lepra (ver Lev. 13:3), ou o maná.

Pode-se obter um branco puro alvejando um tecido por longa exposição ao sol, ou usando fumaça de enxofre sobre o pano estendido. No mundo antigo, o trabalho dos alvejadores geralmente era entregue a pessoas do sexo masculino, por ser um trabalho árduo. O processo de alvejamento é aludido em Salmos 51:7, como símbolo de purificação do homem pecaminoso.

O branco, além de simbolizar a qualidade da inocência (ver Isa. 1:18) e da pureza, era também a cor das vestes dos santos, além de representar a deidade de Cristo (Mat. 17:2). Era também a cor da vitória (ver Apo. 6:2).

Nos dias de Jesus, os sepulcros eram caiados de branco, a fim de que os passantes, inadvertidamente, não pisassem sobre os mesmos, a fim de que evitassem a contaminação cerimonial (ver Mat. 23:27), de acordo com certo preceito constante no antigo pacto (ver Núm. 19:16). Ver também *Còr, Cores*.

BRASAS

Estão envolvidas duas palavras hebraicas e uma palavra grega, a saber:

1. *Pecham*, que aparece por três vezes: Pro. 26:2; Isa. 44:12 e 54:16. A LXX a traduz por *anthrakiá*.

2. *Gacheleth*, «brasa acesa». Palavra que aparece por dezoito vezes (por exemplo: Lev. 16:12; II Sam. 14:7; Jó 41:21; Sal. 18:8; Isa. 44:19; Eze. 1:13; 24:11).

3. *Anthrakiá*, «brasas vivas», usada em João 18:18 e 21:9.

No hebraico, as palavras usadas envolvem, principalmente, carvão de madeira, pois na Palestina não havia depósitos de hulha, embora alguns disputem esse ponto. Os trechos de Isa. 44:12 e 54:16 apontam para o trabalho dos ferreiros, e Pro. 26:21 alude a carvões não acesos ainda. Os trechos de Isa. 47:14 e João 18:18 mostram que carvões eram usados para cozinhar. Os montes do Líbano contêm algum carvão mineral, embora não haja evidências de que os hebreus chegaram algum dia a extraí-lo. O junípeiro e o buxo eram usados para fazer carvão de madeira (Sal. 120:4).

Alguns estudiosos pensam que a alusão a «brasas», em Isa. 6:6, na verdade indica pedras aquecidas (ver também I Reis 19:6). Em Cantares 8:6 a referência é a pedras quentes, e não a brasas de carvão. No Novo Testamento, o «braseiro» aceso tinha por intuito aquecer os circunstantes.

Usos Figurados. 1. O trecho de II Sam. 14:17 refere-se à extinção da família de alguém, quando alguém apaga uma fogueira. 2. Os «carvões», em II Sam. 22:9; Sal. 18:8,18 podem referir-se ao processo de iluminação que procede de Deus. 3. O «amontoar brasas vivas» sobre a cabeça de alguém, em Pro. 25:22 e Rom. 12:20, representa a vergonha e a confusão que os homens sentem quando a maldade que praticam é retribuída com o bem. 4. Em Cantares 8:6, os carvões servem de paralelo do «ciúme», que é tão cruel quanto a sepultura.

BRASEIRO

No hebraico **esh**, «fogo». Essa palavra é de ocorrência muito freqüente no Antigo Testamento, por cerca de trezentas e sessenta vezes. Mas, com o sentido de «braseiro», nossa versão portuguesa só a traduz em Jer. 36:22,23. Se, realmente, está em foco um braseiro, então deve ter sido um receptáculo portátil, feito de metal, onde se punham carvões acesos para aquecer um ambiente, durante os dias de inverno. Nesse caso, a casa de inverno de Jeoaquim era assim aquecida.

BRENTANO, FRANZ

Suas datas foram 1838-1917. Filósofo e psicólogo austríaco. Nasceu em Mariemburgo, ensinou em Wurzburgo, Viena e Florença. Foi professor de A. Von Meinong e E. Husserl.

Idéias. 1. Uma psicologia puramente objetiva deveria ser produzida mediante experimentação e descrição, sem pressupostos *a priori* e *posteriori*, e cujo objetivo deveria ser produzir uma nova classificação dos fenômenos psíquicos. 2. Esses fenômenos aludem a coisas acima de nós mesmos, pois os atos mentais estão relacionados a fenômenos psíquicos. O que quer que se apresente diante de nossa mente será apenas uma representação, isto é, apenas algo que se apresenta à nossa consciência. Essa representação se chama juízo, que pode ser verdadeiro ou falso. Também pode ser um fenômeno que envolve amor ou ódio, isto é, algo aceito ou rejeitado no nível das *emoções*. Em cada caso há um objeto, concreto ou abstrato, real ou imaginário, em torno do qual gira a atividade mental. 3. Todos os juízos dizem respeito a coisas. A *existência* não é um predicado, mas antes, um termo que nos capacita expressar a nossa aceitação ou rejeição das coisas. 4. Os juízos de valor repousam sobre evidências internas, no tocante às relações expressas pelo termo «melhor do que», e podem ser objetivos. 5. A alma e Deus são juízos que precisamos fazer, necessariamente. A filosofia tende por atravessar as fases de declínio e de ascensão (vitalidade). Essas fases incluem a transferência de interesses para questões práticas, com o correspondente declínio dos temas da metafísica, do ceticismo, mas que, finalmente, redunda em um renovado interesse pelo misticismo, quando o que é prático e concreto não mais consegue satisfazer os corações humanos.

Escritos: *Psychology from an Empirical Standpoint; On the Origin of Moral Knowledge; The Four Phases of Philosophy; Truth and Evidence; The Basis and Structure of Ethics*. (EP P)

BREVIÁRIO

No latim, **breviarium**, que significa «resumo» ou

compêndio, um livro que contém salmos, hinos, trechos escolhidos para leitura, orações, etc., extraído Divino Ofício (que vide), de conformidade com o rito romano. É impresso em quatro volumes, a fim de corresponder às quatro estações do ano. Antes dos séculos XII e XIII D.C., o material estava contido em diversos livros, arranjados para as diversas pessoas que participavam do Ofício Coral. (E)

BREWSTER, WILLIAM

Suas datas foram 1560-1644. Conhecido como Ancião Brewster, foi líder dos peregrinos, que chegaram à América do Norte, vindos da Inglaterra, no navio Mayflower, em 1629. Ele nasceu em Scrooby, em Nottinghamshire, e por algum tempo estudou em Cambridge. Em cerca de 1587, estabeleceu a Scrooby Manor House, passando a agir como uma espécie de hospedeiro de viajantes. Nessa casa, os separatistas (que vide) efetuavam cultos. Em 1608, Brewster mudou-se para a Holanda, onde se ocupou da publicação de literatura puritana. Em 1619, ele obteve os direitos de ocupação de um trecho do território da América do Norte. Juntamente com outros, ele atravessou o oceano; e, uma vez na América do Norte, ele se tornou o líder dirigente da colônia de Plymouth, até à sua morte, que ocorreu em 1644. Portanto, Brewster foi um dos pioneiros que ajudaram nos primórdios da nação norte-americana. (AM E)

BRIDEL, PHILIPPE

Foi professor de teologia da Universidade de Lausanne, na Suíça (1852 ?). *Idéias*. 1. Ele falava sobre o tema de Deus, como um ser pessoal, em contraste com as noções panteístas (que vide). 2. Nossa linguagem humana é insuficiente para falarmos sobre Deus, de tal modo que todos os termos que usamos são apenas relativos. 3. Reveste-se de suprema importância o tema da Paternidade de Deus. Quando aprendemos acerca de Deus, usamos muito desse conceito. 4. Ele preferia a revelação, e não a filosofia, em sua inquirição espiritual. 5. Essa revelação nos foi dada através de Jesus Cristo. (E)

BRIGHTMAN, EDGAR SHEFFIELD

Suas datas foram 1884-1952. Foi um filósofo personalista norte-americano. Nasceu em Holbrook, Massachussets. Foi professor na Universidade de Boston.
Idéias. 1. Meras categorias impessoais não podem explicar a experiência humana. 2. Precisam ser empregadas categorias pessoais. Ver sobre o *Personalismo*. Ver também o artigo sobre Bowne, Borden Parker, quanto ao desenvolvimento dessa idéia. Brightman foi o sucessor de Bowne, na Universidade de Boston. 3. As idéias da filosofia fenomenológica e existencial precisam ser levadas a sério, porquanto apóiam as idéias do personalismo. 4. O personalismo também dá apoio às noções de individualidade, pelo que não devemos permitir que a idéia do senhorio de Deus avassale o conceito de *liberdade*. Ver sobre o *livre-arbítrio*. 5. O problema do mal (que vide) pode ser resolvido se concebermos Deus como um ser finito, e não como um ser infinito. A tragédia também é um problema para Deus, acerca do qual ele está operando.
Escritos: *An Introduction to Philosophy; A Philosophy of Ideals; The Problem of God; Nature of Values; Person and Reality; The Nature of Some of Our Physical Concepts*. (AM EP P)

BRIGITTA, Ver **Birgitta, Stª**.

BRIHASPATI

Literalmente, **senhor da fala**. Trata-se de uma das divindades abstratas mencionadas na literatura védica posterior. — Estaria intimamente relacionada aos *agni* (que vide). Ver também sobre os *Vedas*.

BRINCOS

No hebraico, **nezem**, «argola de orelha ou de nariz». Essa palavra aparece por quinze vezes (para exemplificar: Gên. 24:22,30,47; 35:4; Êxo. 32:2; Juí. 8:24-26; Osé. 2:13).
O uso de brincos é um costume muito antigo, muito generalizado. Já desde os dias de Abraão há menção ao costume (Gên. 24). Em algumas culturas, tanto homens quanto mulheres usavam brincos (Êxo. 32:2, onde se aprende que, desde a época de Moisés, meninos israelitas usavam brincos). O trecho de Juí. 8:24,25 mostra-nos que os ismaelitas também costumavam usar brincos. A arqueologia tem demonstrado que as estátuas gregas tinham os lobos das orelhas perfurados, para receberem brincos. Muitos tipos de brincos egípcios têm sido descobertos nas escavações arqueológicas. As damas egípcias usavam brincos grandes, tipo argola, feitos de ouro, de quatro a cinco centímetros de diâmetro. Alguns brincos consistiam em até seis argolas soldadas umas às outras. Alguns brincos tinham o formato de vespas, mas parece que o formato limitava-se aos membros da família real. Alguns brincos tinham formatos estilizados de diversos animais. Os antigos assírios, homens e mulheres igualmente, usavam brincos de vários formatos. Entre os hebreus, havia argolas para o nariz, muito parecidas com os brincos. A argola para o nariz está em foco em Gên. 24:47; Pro. 11:22; Isa. 3:21. Algumas vezes, jóias eram vinculadas aos anéis, como decoração extra. — Aparentemente, argolas e anéis de ouro, que os israelitas tinham em sua possessão, foram usados por Aarão para o fabrico do bezerro de ouro (Êxo. 32:2,3), o que nos sugere que muitas pessoas usavam prodigiosa quantidade de jóias como adorno pessoal. É evidente que vários tipos de jóias eram usadas como talismãs e amuletos, pelo que eram usados na idolatria e em práticas supersticiosas. Provavelmente assim se dava com os brincos usados pelos familiares de Jacó, que ele enterrou, juntamente com os deuses estranhos, em Betel (Gên. 35:4). O Novo Testamento recomenda-nos moderação no uso de jóias (I Tim. 2:9,10). (G I IB S)

BRITHWAITE, R.B.

Filósofo inglês (1900- ?). Nasceu em Banbury e foi educado em Cambridge, onde passou a ensinar, a começar em 1924. Era essencialmente um filósofo da ciência, que procurava ampliar seus pensamentos até o campo da ética.
Idéias. 1. As teorias científicas envolvem vários níveis de generalização, cujos termos são interpretados apenas parcialmente pela experiência. As explicações consistem em generalizações menores, por parte de alguma generalização superior. 2. Seu ponto de vista da freqüência de probabilidades contém uma regra de rejeição, quando as freqüências relativas variam em demasia, no tocante às probabilidades inicialmente postuladas. Ele também se mostrava prudente, quando tinha de escolher entre duas hipóteses estatísticas alternativas. 3. Argumentava ele

que não há nenhum círculo vicioso no problema da indução, visto que o pensamento passa da mera crença na segurança da indução para uma crença razoável, alicerçado sobre evidências. 4. Ele aplicava os princípios da teoria dos jogos, sobretudo aqueles entre duas pessoas, aos problemas que envolvem decisões judiciais e problemas de escolhas morais difíceis.

Obras: *Scientific Explanation; An Empiricist's View of the Nature of Religious Belief; Theory of Games as a Tool of the Moral Philosopher*. (AM P)

BROAD, CHARLES DUNBAR

Nasceu em 1887, e a data do falecimento é desconhecida. Filósofo britânico, nascido em Londres. Foi professor das Universidades de St. Andrews, Dundee e Bristol, e de 1933 a 1953 foi professor de Filosofia Moral em Cambridge. Deu continuação à tradição de filósofos anteriores de Cambridge, como Russell, More, W.E. Johnson e McTaggart.

Idéias. 1. No conhecimento, nunca se chega à certeza, embora se possa adquirir um peso maior em favor de uma teoria, e não de outra, em face das experiências apropriadas e do acúmulo de evidências. 2. É necessário o desenvolvimento de uma filosofia crítica, de tal modo que essa filosofia se torne científica. 3. Após o exame de muitas teorias alternativas, Broad chegou à conclusão de que o materialismo está com a razão, isto é, que o mundo não tem componentes não-materiais, e que a consciência é criada pela combinação apropriada das condições físicas. Ver sobre o *epifenomenalismo*. 4. Ele acreditava, porém, na existência de certas condições que produzem a psique, as quais persistiriam após a morte, indefinidamente. As *sensações*, por outro lado, teriam pouca duração. Essas sensações nos proveriam a consciência. As sensações seriam os informes sobre questões imediatas como cor, formato, sons, cheiros e impressões tácteis. Portanto, para Broad, as sensações seriam o que outros chamam de percepção dos sentidos. Todavia, ele também as definia como efeitos mentais imediatos das atividades cerebrais, resultantes da excitação de algum órgão dos sentidos, por parte de estímulos externos. 5. A filosofia especulativa, embora não possa apresentar verdades demonstráveis, pode ter uma visão sinóptica que correlacione as descobertas das ciências naturais com as teorias sociais, com a religião, com a arte e com o bom senso. 6. O conceito de uma psique material, a qual, não obstante, é capaz de sobreviver à morte do corpo físico, segundo era defendido pelo estoicismo (que vide); ou conforme as idéias dos mórmons, que acreditam que todas as coisas são materiais, incluindo Deus, embora cada coisa se encontre em um nível diferente de energia material. (AM E P)

BROADUS, JOHN A.

Suas datas foram 1827-1895. Foi ministro batista e erudito do Novo Testamento. Foi presidente do Seminário Teológico de Louisville. Foi muito influente como escritor e mestre. Dirigiu as «Lyman Beecher Lectures», na Universidade de Yale. (E)

BROCHE

Ver o artigo sobre **Ornamentos**. O broche era um fecho ornamental, com fivela, exercendo a função de alfinete de segurança. Alguns deles eram objetos muito dispendiosos, por serem feitos de ouro, de prata ou de bronze. Ver Êxo. 35:22. Havia broches na Palestina, desde o século X A.C., sendo usados por ambos os sexos para manterem as vestes no seu lugar. Eram fabricados com desenhos ornamentais, sendo tanto do tipo com dobradiça como do tipo de mola.

BRONZE

O bronze é uma liga feita de cobre, com algum estanho, embora as referências ao bronze, na Bíblia, possam indicar cobre puro. O bronze é menos maleável e mais duro que o cobre, embora mais apropriado para ser fundido, devido à sua maior fusibilidade, ou seja, seu mais baixo ponto de fusão. Quanto maior for a proporção de estanho, mais baixo será esse ponto de fusão. O uso do cobre remonta de cerca de 6000-5000 A.C., e o do bronze de cerca de 3700 A.C. Esses dois metais encontram-se entre os primeiros sucessos metalúrgicos do homem. A expressão *Idade do Bronze* (que vide) denota um período da história em que começaram a ser feitos instrumentos e armas de bronze (e de cobre), e não de pedra, madeira e osso, materiais que, antes disso, eram empregados com esse propósito.

Nas referências bíblicas, as traduções confundem o latão (que vide) com o bronze, havendo a possibilidade de que, realmente, esteja em vista o cobre. Ver Jó 28:2; Êxo. 26:11; II Sam. 8:8; Isa. 26:11; Núm. 21:9; Apo. 1:15; 2:18 e 9:20. Nos tempos do Antigo Testamento, Israel usava largamente o bronze. O templo de Salomão incluía vários objetos de bronze (II Reis 7:1-51), incluindo o lavatório de bronze, também chamado «mar de fundição», que repousava em sua posição sobre as costas de doze bois de bronze, no átrio do templo. Esse objeto, segundo cálculos modernos, pesaria umas trinta toneladas, tendo sido feito por artífices fenícios. — O bronze servia para o fabrico de armaduras (I Sam. 17:5), de algemas (Juí. 16:21) e de receptáculos ocos (II Reis 25:14 e Eze. 27:13), além de servir de material de construção, como portas (Sal. 107:16), ornamentos (I Reis 7:14) e ídolos (Dan. 5:4).

Usos Figurados. 1. O bronze indica dureza e força (Lev. 26:9; Deu. 28:23). 2. Também qualidades morais, como a firmeza (Jer. 1:18), a obstinação (Isa. 48:4), etc. 3. Um firmamento tórrido e sem chuvas (Deu. 28:23), ou um solo gretado pela seca (Lev. 26:19). 4. O cativeiro (Lam. 3:7). 5. Estava associado à brutalidade, ao julgamento, ao sofrimento, etc., devido à sua associação às armas de guerra e às armaduras defensivas. Por essa razão, Homero fala no «bronze sem misericórdia». Em Apocalipse 1:15 e 2:18, o bronze está ligado ao julgamento.

Pelos fins do segundo milênio A.C., o ferro começou a substituir o bronze, naqueles objetos que requeriam maior resistência; e o mundo foi passando para a Idade do Ferro. Ver o artigo sobre a *Arqueologia*. (AM BAR ID UNA)

BROOKE, STOPFORD AUGUSTUS

Suas datas foram 1832-1916. Foi escritor e pregador de fama, autor de livros, de peças teatrais, de discursos e de poemas. Nasceu no condado de Donegal, na Irlanda, e tornou-se sacerdote da Igreja da Inglaterra. Porém, veio a tornar-se um eclesiástico independente, com simpatias unitarianas (que vide).

BRORSON, HANS ADOLF

Suas datas foram 1694-1764. Alguns consideram-no um dos três grandes compositores de hinos da Dinamarca. Foi ordenado sacerdote, em 1722, e tornou-se bispo em 1741. Porém, é relembrado por sua simplicidade pietista, o que se reflete em seus hinos simples, mas belos. Obteve o seu maior sucesso com os seus hinos de Natal. (E)

BROWNE, ROBERT

Suas datas foram 1550-1633. Nasceu em Tolethorpe, perto de Stafford, na Inglaterra. Foi educado no Corpus Christi College e em Cambridge. Reuniu uma congregação de inconformados em Norwich, e foi aprisionado, em 1581, por haver denunciado o episcopado, mas escapou para Midelburgo, na Holanda, em 1582. Foi na Holanda que ele escreveu seus dois livros: *Reformation Without Tarrying for Any* e *Free Christians*. Nesses livros, ele exibiu sua teoria de independência congregacional. Porém, mais tarde, retratou-se de seus pontos de vista separatistas (que vide), e foi ordenado ao sacerdócio anglicano. Então serviu nessa categoria durante os seus últimos quarenta e dois anos de vida. Seus pontos de vista modificados podem ser vistos em sua obra *Reproof of Certain Shismatical Persons and Their Doctrine Concerning the Teaching and Hearing of the Word of God*. Não obstante, ele continuava defendendo o ideal congregacional da independência de cada igreja local, opondo-se ao unionismo entre Igreja e estado. (E)

BROWNE, SIR THOMAS

Suas datas foram 1615-1682. Foi escritor prosaico e médico. Nasceu na Inglaterra e era místico por natureza; ensinou os princípios da meditação e da inquirição mística. Sua obra mais importante é a *Religio Medici*, de 1643, que é uma confissão de fé e uma coletânea de idéias religiosas curiosamente compostas. (E)

BROWNING, ROBERT

Nasceu em 1812 e faleceu em 1899. Foi poeta e dramatista inglês, religioso quanto ao treinamento e ao temperamento, tendo-se tornado um intérprete moderno, vital e discernidor, através da poesia e do cristianismo. Em seus poemas, intitulados *Cleon, Imperante Augusto* e *Uma Estranha Epístola*, ele tornou bem vívida a vida de Jesus. Em seus poemas *Véspera de Natal, Dia da Páscoa* e *Uma Morte no Deserto*, ele retratou, mui habilidosamente, os sentidos da encarnação e da revelação. Em sua afirmação sobre *Saul, Evelyn Hope* e *Prospício*, ele expressou a esperança de uma vida futura, póstumulo. Ele expressava a sua espiritualidade mediante a evolução, e em *Paracelso* ele emprestou à lei do desenvolvimento um sentido humanista e cristão. Browning enfatizava a importância e a natureza crítica do desenvolvimento da alma, conforme fez em seu poema *Rabino Ben Esdras*. Demonstrava profundo otimismo e confiança nos valores espirituais, em muitos dos seus poemas, tendo mostrado como esse meio pode servir aos interesses do espírito. (E)

BROWNISMO

Ver o artigo sobre *Robert Browne*, de cujo nome deriva-se esse nome. O vocábulo *brownismo* era aplicado a um agressivo separativismo que se manifestou na porção final do reinado de Isabel I, da Inglaterra. Embora o próprio Brown, posteriormente, tivesse retornado à Igreja da Inglaterra, muitos outros elementos, principalmente homens de Cambridge, tinham começado a expressar idéias semelhantes, a respeito da reforma, tendo organizado pequenos grupos separatistas. Henry Barrowe e seus aderentes, apodados de Barrowistas, ampliaram os conceitos de Browne, o que resultou em grande oposição à Igreja Anglicana. De acordo com a lei separatista de 1593, Barrowe e outros líderes separatistas foram executados. Os homens transformaram em ódio o amor de Deus, em ambos os lados da controvérsia, e ambos os grupos pensavam que estavam servindo a Deus com palavras odiosas e com punição capital. O resultado dessas execuções foi que muitos se exilaram voluntariamente na Holanda. O nome de Brown passou a ser usado para designar os separatistas, mas eles mesmos repudiavam a ligação com Brown. Esses acontecimentos foram os primórdios dos movimentos dos batistas e dos congregacionais, que, — mais tarde, se tornaram denominações separadas, consolidando assim, uma vez mais, algum grupo religioso, através de posições doutrinárias assumidas. (C)

BROWNSON, ORESTES AUGUSTUS

Suas datas foram 1803 e 1876. Um filósofo transcendentalista e pensador religioso, nascido na América do Norte. Foi discípulo do filósofo francês Victor Cousin, e intimamente relacionado, em suas idéias, ao idealista italiano, Vincenzo Gioberti (1801-1852). Brownson era um deísta (ver sobre o *deísmo*), dependendo não somente da fé, mas também do racionalismo (que vide), quanto a seus pontos de vista. Seus escritos foram publicados em um jornal chamado *Brownson's Quarterly Review*. (F)

BRUNNER, EMIL

Suas datas foram 1899-1966. Foi um teólogo protestante suíço que estudou em Berlim e Zurique, e ensinou em Zurique.

Idéias. 1. Brunner ocupava posição a meio caminho entre o protestantismo liberal e a neo-ortodoxia (e a teologia da crise) de Karl Barth (que vide). Asseverava que apesar do homem não poder prover sua própria salvação, possui determinados poderes naturais para corresponder a Deus, estando na obrigação de utilizar os mesmos. Em outras palavras, o livre-arbítrio (que vide) é uma realidade. 2. A razão não pode solucionar todos os problemas humanos, motivo pelo qual inevitavelmente surgem contradições na filosofia e na teologia. Isso, porém, meramente mostra que a revelação encerra mistérios que, por enquanto, não cedem diante do nosso conhecimento. Uma teologia sem contradições seria uma teologia falsa, porquanto teria a presunção de resolver os grandes mistérios. 3. A tecnologia e a política tendem a despersonalizar o homem. A revelação cristã visa às *pessoas*, provendo uma chave que abre a verdadeira natureza do homem e de sua comunidade. 4. Brunner eliminava de sua discussão todos os tópicos que, para ele, não dissessem respeito imediato à inquirição espiritual do indivíduo, como o nascimento virginal e a maioria dos relatos de milagres do Novo Testamento. Destarte, ele simplificava a ortodoxia, em prol da espiritualidade prática. 5. Ele se opunha ao intelectualismo teológico, e punha a pessoa de Cristo no centro da teologia. 6. Dentro do campo da ética, ele combinava a crítica de Kant com o realismo da Bíblia e do luteranismo moderno. Mostrava-se sempre interessado pelo aspecto prático da ética. Em seu livro, *Homem em Revolta*, ele via o homem como um ser estranhamente pessoal. Empregava as categorias e discernimentos de Kierkegaard (que vide), bem como o personalismo (que vide) de Ebner e Buber, filósofos que enfatizavam a relação com Deus, expressa pela fórmula do *eu-tu*. O homem é um pecador, responsável diante de Deus, mas revoltado contra Deus, mediante o seu pecado. Porém, o homem pode reagir favoravelmente, e então o Espírito faz dele uma nova criatura. A vontade de Deus opera através das ordenanças da criação, como a família, o trabalho, a Igreja, o estado e a cultura geral. O diálogo com todos os níveis da sociedade ajuda-nos a definir como a vontade de Deus opera através dessas instituições.

Escritos: *The Symbolical in Religious Knowledge; The Mystic and the Word; The Philosophy of Religion of Evangelical Theology; The Mediator; The Divine Imperative; Man in Revolt; Christianity and Civilization.*

BRUNO, GIORDANO

Nasceu em 1548 e faleceu em 1600. Foi filósofo italiano, nascido em Nápoles. Foi monge dominicano, e caiu na heresia através da astronomia, tendo sido então excomungado. A partir daí pôs-se a vaguear de universidade em universidade, como as de Genebra, Lyons, Toulouse, Paris, Londres, Oxford, Wittenburg, etc. Aventurou-se a ir a Veneza, em 1592, mas, para sua infelicidade, foi apanhado pela Inquisição, tendo sido aprisionado em Roma, de 1593 a 1599. Tendo-se recusado a retratar-se, foi executado na fogueira, por aqueles que, supostamente, «amavam» a Deus. Foi sepultado no Campo dei Fiori, a 17 de fevereiro de 1600, e, desse modo, tornou-se mártir da filosofia.

Idéias. 1. O universo é infinito em sua extensão e diversidade, não havendo tal coisa como o centro do universo, pois um lugar qualquer é tão centro do universo como qualquer outro. 2. Não há tal coisa como permanência; antes, tudo está em estado de fluxo. 3. As almas das coisas são mônadas; e Deus é a mônada das mônadas. Os átomos são a base formadora da matéria. Todos os elementos são imortais e eternos. As mônadas mais simples são animadas, e os mundos têm vidas que lhes são próprias. 4. Deus é tanto transcendente quanto imanente. O universo é Um, e esse Um é Deus—panteísmo (que vide). A consideração do universo como Um consiste em pensar na realidade como *Natura Naturans*. Considerá-lo sob o ponto de vista da diversidade é pensar na realidade como *Natura Naturata*. 5. O universo consiste na emanação e no retorno da natureza divina (emanação a moldes estóicos). Isso exibe as potencialidades divinas infinitas. Finalmente, todas as coisas haverão de retornar a Deus, antes que outro grande ciclo possa ter início. 6. O ponto culminante da busca ética, guiada pela razão e inspirada pelo amor, é a união eterna com Deus.

Escritos: *The Ash Wednesday Supper; Concerning the Cause; Principle and One; On the Infinite Universe and Worlds; On Heroic Enthusiasma; Concerning the Boundless; Summa of Metaphysical Terms*; comentários e sumários sobre a obra de Aristóteles, *Physics*. (AM RP)

BRUNSCHWIGG, LÉON

Nasceu em 1869 e faleceu em 1944. Foi filósofo francês, nascido em Paris. Educou-se na École Normale Supérieure e na Sorbonne. Ensinou na Sorbonne. Foi um idealista crítico que acreditava que a realidade é uma função do pensamento, e que a mente tem progredido através da história. No homem, a mente atinge a autoconsciência, tendo-se tornado a base de toda a ciência. Esse movimento também se dá na direção dos valores espirituais. Conhecer é impor sobre a objetividade as formas da subjetividade. O verdadeiro progresso do homem é na direção do seu interior. A filosofia nada acrescenta ao conhecimento, mas tão-somente é um reflexo seu. Ele salientava o conceito imanente de Deus, rejeitando todo antropomorfismo. (E EP P)

BRUXARIA
Ver **Adivinhação**.

BRUXARIA E MÁGICA

A mágica e a religião sempre estiveram vinculadas bem de perto, e, na maioria dos casos, assim continua sendo até os tempos modernos. Talvez assim suceda tanto por causa da tentativa de elevar o véu que separa o homem do sobrenatural como porque o espírito humano jamais se sente satisfeito com uma perspectiva puramente materialista da existência.

Além disso, tanto a religião como as artes mágicas reivindicam para si mesmas a capacidade de obter ajuda, para o homem, da parte de poderes mais elevados ou sobrenaturais, possuindo alguma forma de credo ou ritual que leva esses poderes mais altos a notarem aos homens, ajudando-os na realização de alguma coisa que porventura sintam não serem capazes de conseguir sem esse auxílio externo e sobre-humano.

Ao refletirmos pode parecer razoável afirmar que as artes mágicas são meramente uma forma disfarçada de religião, que mantém o seu próprio credo doutrinário. Diferindo grandemente de cultura, mas ordinariamente dotadas dos elementos comuns das *divindades* e dos *espíritos* bons e maus, e sempre, de alguma crença na sobrevivência da alma, que é o estofo essencial que perfaz os alicerces doutrinários de quase todas as religiões, as artes mágicas são seguidas por muitos como sua própria religião. Isso lhes satisfaz o impulso de seguirem alguma expressão religiosa qualquer, que é perfeitamente natural para a natureza humana.

As artes mágicas são de âmbito universal. Existe a *magia branca* e a *magia negra*. Esta última emprega símbolos malignos e com freqüência tenta produzir resultados maléficos através de maldições, encantamentos e bruxarias, mediante a destruição de um bonequinho que representa a vítima, e supostas alianças com os espíritos maus. Essa forma de artes mágicas pode assumir a forma de bruxaria, embora nem todas as formas de bruxaria pratiquem a magia negra—mas podem ser mais acertadamente classificadas como *magia branca*. Por sua vez a *magia branca* procura desfazer as maldições e os encantamentos por meio do uso de contra-encantamentos e encantamentos de natureza boa ou positiva, utilizando-se até mesmo de versículos e de passagens das Escrituras em suas fórmulas fundamentais. A «magia branca», por conseguinte, supostamente procura praticar o bem, e assim sendo, operaria através de espíritos ou deuses bons.

Nas páginas do A.T., a palavra traduzida por *bruxa* ou *bruxaria* mui provavelmente se deriva de uma raiz que significa *cortar* e isso se refere ao ato de cortar as ervas usadas nos encantamentos e adivinhações. (Ver os trechos de Êxo. 22:18; Deut. 18:10; Isa. 47:9,12 e Jer. 22:9). Outros termos, associados às

BRUXARIA E MÁGICA

artes mágicas ou à bruxaria, significam «sussurrar» ou *encantar*, como nas passagens de Isa. 3:20 e Sal. 58:5; «encantador», como em Deut. 18:11 e Isa. 42:9,12; ou *caldeu*, que pode significar a raça ou a classe dos mágicos daquela raça, segundo se lê em Dan. 2:2,4. Todavia, este último vocábulo pode significar *astrólogo*, conforme nos mostram diversas antigas inscrições babilônicas.

Nos livros do NT, a palavra grega **magos** e seus cognatos podem significar um mágico, um astrólogo. Originalmente, entretanto, se referia a um grupo racial da Idade Média, que assumiu posteriormente essa significação técnica. (Ver os trechos de Atos 8:9,11; 13:6,8 e Mat. 2:1). O emprego desse vocábulo, no evangelho de Mateus, certamente tem o sentido de *astrólogo*, e não de «mágico», conforme este último termo é atualmente compreendido. Lembremo-nos de que no passado a ciência astronômica era infante, empírica, e os seus cultores eram chamados «astrólogos», e não «astrônomos». — A astrologia acredita na influência dos corpos celestes sobre a existência humana; a astronomia verifica as leis que regem os movimentos desses corpos. Há uma outra palavra, no N.T., no grego *«pharmakos»*, que se deriva da idéia das poções poderosas usadas nas bruxarias, como drogas, venenos, etc. (Ver Apo. 9:21; 18:23; 21:8; 22:15; Gál. 5:20). O vocábulo grego *goes*, que aparece em II Tim. 3:13, e que em nossa tradução portuguesa aparece como «impostores», pode significar um mágico ou encantador.

Embora as artes mágicas sejam ordinariamente condenadas no A.T. (ver as diversas referências dadas mais acima, que mostram a atitude negativa a respeito), há evidências de que os israelitas praticavam *certas formas* de artes mágicas; e certamente a sociedade judaica não estava inteiramente isenta disso, ainda que, algumas vezes, tais artes fossem praticadas sob a bandeira de *Yahweh*. Ornamentos eram usados como encantamentos, uma forma disfarçada, suave, de artes mágicas (ver Isa. 3:18-23). Esses ornamentos eram na forma de argolas de orelhas, broches com o formato de serpentes e várias outras modalidades de jóias, o que, para as mulheres não serviam de meros ornamentos, mas antes, eram encantamentos que supostamente atraíam a boa sorte, que facilitavam a concepção de filhos, etc. Ou então eram objetos que as judias reputavam valiosos como preservadores contra as forças malignas, como se pudessem mantê-las à distância. O trecho de Gên. 35:4 quase sem dúvida alguma, faz alusão a objetos dessa natureza, bem como a imagens domésticas.

A passagem mais notável à bruxaria dos hebreus aparece em Eze. 13:17-23, onde vemos profetisas judias a praticarem as artes mágicas a fim de preservar ou destruir indivíduos. Nisso elas eram mais *aptas* que as suas colegas pagãs. Outras formas mais inocentes de bruxaria existiam que, aparentemente, passavam sem sofrer condenação, como o uso de *encantamentos* de ervas, usados para assegurar a concepção de filhos, por parte das mulheres. (Ver Gên. 30:14-18). O patriarca Jacó usou certa forma de artes mágicas quando usou varas de vários tipos, que supostamente fizeram o gado nascer com diversos sinais. Se o artifício realmente funcionou ou não, não vem ao caso. É altamente provável que Jacó pensou que tal método *daria certo*, porque, de outra forma não teria perdido tanto tempo com tal insensatez. (Ver Gên. 30:37 e ss).

É possível que o ato de Samuel, ao derramar água (ver I Sam. 7:6), tenha visado *induzir* uma tempestade, e que isso fosse uma forma qualquer de magia, embora alguns intérpretes muito se esforcem por *limpar* essas passagens de tal sentido possível, vendo nelas outros significados, a fim de evitar a idéia de que homens e mulheres de Deus aceitaram essas práticas sem qualquer censura. Outrossim, podemos observar o elevado poder que se dava, entre os israelitas, às bênçãos e às maldições, o que, sem dúvida alguma, eram um fator muito importante na sociedade hebréia. Os resultados disso são sempre apresentados como de conformidade autêntica ao tipo de bênção ou de maldição proferida, como se algum poder místico estivesse em operação por detrás da bênção ou da maldição. (Ver Gên. 27:33,37; Núm. 23:8,20 e II Sam. 16:10).

Na cultura egípcia, as artes mágicas, visando o bem-estar dos vivos e a segurança e o bem-estar dos mortos, — eram praticadas continuamente. Várias modalidades de artes mágicas poderiam ser classificadas como «defensivas», «produtivas», «prognosticadoras», «malévolas», «fúnebres» e «operadoras de milagres». Através de tais meios supunha-se poder ajudar os homens no controle tanto de seu ambiente físico como de suas cercanias sobrenaturais, controlando tudo, desde a ação de um escorpião, de uma serpente, de animais ferozes, até as ações dos deuses ou espíritos, no que essas coisas se relacionam aos homens. O futuro era adivinhado a fim de ajudar os homens a se defrontarem com ele, ou para que pudessem tomar decisões alicerçadas em um conhecimento prévio. Os mortos eram supostamente ajudados em seu vôo para o grande além desconhecido.

Os praticantes das artes mágicas usualmente eram homens conhecedores de certas literaturas e de determinados ritos, e quando em suas manifestações mais formais, eram construtores e chefes de templos.

Nem toda a arte mágica consiste em fraude ou truque. Embora seja óbvio que os efeitos de grande parte das artes mágicas, sobre as pessoas, dependem de suas próprias *reações psicológicas* a tais coisas — e as atitudes psicológicas podem ser *fortíssimas*, causando ou curando enfermidades, e possuindo até mesmo o poder de tirar a vida — não se pode negar que mais do que isso algumas vezes está envolvido nas artes mágicas. Não é mesmo impossível que *espíritos*, de uma ou de outra categoria, estejam em ligação com certos praticantes das artes mágicas, operando através destes últimos. Outrossim, é provável que alguns desses cultores da magia sejam pessoas psiquicamente dotadas, que podem exercer grande influência psíquica, de natureza boa ou má, possuindo poderes de clarividência, de telepatia ou de conhecimento anterior. É insensatez, portanto, classificar todas estas manifestações como fraudes ou truques. Os poderes daqueles que usam das artes mágicas podem ser perfeitamente reais, e incidentes tanto antigos como modernos confirmam isso. Isso não significa, entretanto, que a fraude não seja um elemento quase constante na magia.

As atitudes demonstradas como a de Robertson (em Atos 13:18 ss), por conseguinte, laboram em erro, como quando ele diz: «Se alguém fica surpreendido que um homem como Sérgio Paulo tivesse sido vitimado pela influência dessa *fraude*, deveria relembrar-se do que Juvenal disse sobre o imperador Tibério, 'assentado sobre a rocha de Capri, com seu grupo de caldeus ao seu derredor'». É que o professor Robertson evidentemente supõe que as artes mágicas são sempre fraudulentas. Porém, ouso afirmar que se ele pudesse ter investigado os poderes psíquicos de Barjesus e dos *«caldeus»* que guiavam Tibério, teria encontrado um poder genuíno, embora *não* proveniente de Deus. Se tal poder, desses homens e de outros que lhes seguem as pisadas, é de natureza boa ou má, já é *outra* questão. Lucas informa-nos que o poder de Barjesus era usado para o *mal*; mas esse poder era autêntico, a despeito disso. Mas os homens do nosso século XX são de uma atitude tão materialista que até mesmo comentadores bíblicos supõem que tais práticas devem ser sempre fraudulentas, baseadas em meros truques, ao passo que a parapsicologia está atualmente conseguindo definir, em termos mais científicos, os poderes psíquicos que com freqüência se encontram por detrás de tais manifestações. Ver o artigo sobre *Adivinhação*.

BRUXO
Ver **Adivinhação**.

BRYSON, FILHO DE STILPO
Ver o artigo sobre a Escola Megariana de Filosofia, onde há um comentário a respeito dele.

BUBER, MARTIM
Suas datas foram 1878-1965. Filósofo e místico judeu. Nasceu em Viena, tendo estudado em Viena e Berlim. Tornou-se professor de religião na Universidade de Frankfurt em Main, e professor de filosofia na Universidade hebraica em Jerusalém. Foi influenciado pelos ensinos dos hasidim de Kierkegaard. Apropriou-se do misticismo dos hasidim (que vide), e promoveu o misticismo no seio do judaísmo moderno. Ver sobre *misticismo*.

Idéias. 1. Seu tema dominante dizia respeito a como o indivíduo deve relacionar-se consigo mesmo, com o mundo e com Deus. Distinguia duas relações possíveis: Eu-tu e *eu-a coisa*. O tipo correto de relação é a primeira. O *tu* representa uma existência eterna de substância separada do eu. Esse tu, que pode ser chamado Deus, nunca pode ser apenas uma coisa. 2. Podemos falar sobre o Tu por meio da fé, com base nas experiências místicas, mas não podemos desenvolver uma epistemologia com base na relação dessa essência para com a existência e a experiência. 3. A inquirição espiritual visa o Tu misterioso, e isso requer a experiência mística. 4. A relação *eu-a coisa* diz respeito somente ao nosso conhecimento e uso das coisas, a manipulação dos objetos espaço-temporais. O *eu-eu* é uma relação entre sujeito e sujeito, e não entre sujeito e objeto. 5. *Tu* é o inteiramente outro, que não é observado, mas que pode ser reconhecido quando se revela a nós. 6. Buber opunha-se a todas as filosofias, teologias e sistemas políticos, como o Marxismo, que reduzem a experiência humana a uma relação de eu-a coisa, e que negam que haja um Tu a ser buscado.

Escritos: *I and Thou; Religion and Philosophy; The Kingdom of God; Between Man and Man; The Prophetic Faith; Two Types of Faith; Hasidism and Modern Man; The Eclipse of God; The Origin and Meaning of Hasidism*. (E C P)

BUCER, MARTIN
Suas datas foram 1491-1551. Foi um reformador e teólogo ecumênico de Estrasburgo, que se tornara frade dominicano (que vide) aos quinze anos de idade. Em 1518, ouviu Lutero e conversou com ele, em Heidelberg. Deixou os dominicanos e trabalhou como capelão e pregador, mas foi excomungado por haver contraído matrimônio. Então ele foi para Estrasburgo, associando-se aos reformadores protestantes. Procurou encontrar uma fórmula capaz de reconciliar os pontos de vista divergentes dos protestantes, acerca da Ceia do Senhor. Isso fez parte de seus esforços em prol da unidade cristã. Ele exibia uma atitude transigente pragmática e dinâmica, mas, por causa disso, obteve a reputação de ser dotado de poucas convicções teológicas. Procurou ser o mediador entre os católicos romanos e os reformadores, quando da dieta de Tatisbon, em 1541, bem como por ocasião do colóquio de Regensburgo, em 1546. Porém, a posição de transigência, sugerida pelo imperador Carlos V, no Interim de Augsburgo, em 1548 foi por ele rejeitada, embora algumas de suas próprias idéias tivessem sido utilizadas pelo monarca. Por causa disso, ele foi forçado a deixar Estrasburgo, e foi para a Inglaterra, a convite do arcebispo Cranmer. Então cooperou com a reforma cautelosa efetuada por Eduardo VI. Portanto, exerceu alguma influência sobre o Segundo Livro de Orações (1552), e sobre o Ordenal Anglicano (1550). A pedido de Eduardo, ele escreveu o *De regno Christi*, uma obra política sobre como cristianizar a Inglaterra. Parece que ele se saiu bem como anglicano. Faleceu em Cambridge, a 28 de fevereiro de 1551. Foi sepultado com altas honrarias, mas, posteriormente, a rainha Maria ordenou que seus restos mortais fossem exumados e queimados. A rainha Maria era católica, e isso explica o ato. Porém, no reinado de Isabel I, seu nome foi restaurado à honra. (AM C E)

BUCHMANISMO
Um movimento não-credal, de despertamento religioso, do séc. XX, também conhecido como Grupo de Oxford e Rearmamento Moral, fundado por Frank Buchman, um ministro luterano. Originalmente tinha por centro a Universidade de Oxford, donde se deriva um de seus nomes. Buscava alcançar verdadeira moralidade na dedicação cristã. Ver sobre o *Movimento de Oxford*.

BUCHNER, LUDWIG
Nasceu em 1824 e faleceu em 1899. Foi filósofo alemão, treinado em medicina, porém, escreveu sobre assuntos filosóficos.

Idéias. 1. Toda realidade é material, e a força e a matéria pertencem à mesma natureza, embora sejam aspectos distintos de uma mesma realidade. Ele negava a possibilidade da existência de Deus—ateísmo (que vide). 2. A mente e a alma são apenas funções do cérebro, e não entidades separadas. 3. A realidade material é dinâmica, seguindo linhas darwinianas, o que explica as inúmeras formas que conhecemos pela experiência diária. Isso também explica o desenvolvimento da cultura. 4. No terreno da ética, ele buscava a maior felicidade possível para todos, com base no respeito pelos direitos humanos, tanto individuais quanto comunitários. (P)

BUDDE, KARI
Suas datas foram 1850-1935. Professor do Antigo Testamento por trinta e cinco anos, em Marburgo, foi erudito, comentador, orientalista, teólogo e um prolífico escritor, que exerceu grande influência no ensino pessoal e através de suas obras escritas, sendo considerado um dos grandes mestres da erudição bíblica. (E)

BUDDHA, GAUTAMA SIDDHARTHA
Suas datas foram 560-477 A.C. É considerado o fundador da fé budista. Nasceu no sul do Nepal, na

BUDISMO

Índia, nas vertentes da cadeia dos Himalaias, filho de um rei do clã Shakya. Sua grande *renúncia* de todas as coisas materiais, parece ter sido resolvida após o nascimento de seu primeiro filho. A partir de então, ele começou a sua busca pela iluminação, mediante a meditação e certas práticas ascéticas. Por algum tempo, ele viveu como um esmoler. Intensificando sua inquirição, ele sentou-se debaixo da árvore Bo, de frente para o oriente, resolvido a não se movimentar enquanto não recebesse a iluminação buscada. Diz-se que ele ficou sentado em uma só posição, meditando, durante sete semanas. Veio, afinal, a iluminação que ele buscava, e ele tornou-se um Buda, isto é, um *iluminado*. Cinco companheiros, com os quais tinha praticado o ascetismo, tornaram-se seus primeiros monges, mas o número deles cresceu rapidamente. Mais tarde, foi adicionada uma ordem de freiras budistas. Durante muitos anos, ensinou seus discípulos e teve um ministério produtivo. Já idoso, sentindo a aproximação da morte, fez seu leito ser posto entre duas árvores, e passou suas últimas horas sendo servido por alguns discípulos, a quem deu instruções. Ficou registrado que suas palavras finais foram: «Agora, irmãos, despeço-me de vocês. Todos os componentes do ser são transitórios; operai vossa salvação com diligência». Tendo dito essas palavras, passou a um estado de transe. Presume-se que, dali, passou para o Nirvana (que vide). Naturalmente, os detalhes de sua vida e de sua morte são acompanhados por muitas lendas, conforme geralmente se dá no caso de todos os líderes, religiosos ou não, bons ou maus. Há rumores de que se sucederam estranhos eventos, quando da aproximação de seu nascimento, incluindo curas miraculosas, e também música celestial. Quando nasceu, deu um grito de vitória. É de presumir-se que a sua renúncia, bem como os grandes acontecimentos de sua vida, também foram acompanhados por eventos e sinais incomuns. Ver o artigo abaixo, sobre o *budismo*, onde são apresentados os seus pensamentos, e os desenvolvimentos posteriores do sistema por ele criado.

BUDISMO
I. A Religião: Pano de Fundo Histórico
II. As Idéias de Gautama Siddhartha Buddha
III. A Escola Hinayana (incluindo a Theraveda) do Budismo
IV. A Escola Mahayana do Budismo
V. Contrastes entre as Escolas Theravada e Mahayana
VI. O Budismo na China
VII. O Budismo no Japão

I. A Religião: Pano de Fundo Histórico

O budismo é a religião fundada por Gautama Buddha, no século VI A.C. Surgiu nas províncias orientais, longe do vale do rio Indus, o centro da cultura védica. Foi fundado no mesmo período do jainismo (que vide). O budismo tornou-se a religião oficial da Índia no século III A.C., mas, finalmente, desapareceu da cena indiana. — Posteriormente, tornou-se a religião dominante na China e em outras nações do Extremo Oriente. Naturalmente, em um sentido mais profundo, o budismo não desapareceu da Índia, mas foi assimilado pelo *hinduísmo* (que vide), pois cada um de seus pontos básicos foram aceitos por grandes números de hindus, para os quais Buddha é um dos grandes avatares (que vide), que espalharam a iluminação entre o povo. O budismo é antivédico e contrário às castas. Consiste em dois ramos principais, que são discutidos mais abaixo: o ramo Hinayana e o ramo Mahayana.

II. As Idéias de Gautama Siddhartha Buddha

Buda acreditava que muitas questões não tendem para a edificação, e, por esse motivo, evitava muitas questões metafísicas. O budismo original, por conseguinte, era, essencialmente, uma fé moral e mística. Consideremos os pontos abaixo:

1. A chave para o problema da salvação e da iluminação é a presença do sofrimento, da miséria e da dor. A dor não é apenas um dentre muitos aspectos de nossa experiência, mas é a sua característica mais marcante. Até mesmo muitas outras experiências, não essencialmente dolorosas, incluem seu elemento de sofrimento. Se alguém tiver de experimentar a iluminação, terá de descobrir como eliminar o sofrimento.

2. Tudo tem alguma causa, incluindo a dor; e, se essa *causa* puder ser eliminada, então o sofrimento cessará.

3. O sofrimento tem sua causa na originação dependente. A dor deve-se à *ignorância*, a qual nos leva a tomar decisões impróprias, que nos causam dor. Essas decisões impróprias produzem o *karma*, a bagagem de nossa experiência, que nos faz prosseguir nos ciclos da reencarnação (que vide)—pagando as nossas dívidas, porém, incorrendo em novas dívidas.

4. A chave para o sucesso consiste em saldar todas as dívidas antigas, sem com isso, incorrer em novas dívidas. Se deixarmos de ser ignorantes, poderemos conseguir o feito.

5. Se alguém puder pôr ponto final ao *karma* (que vide), com isso porá fim à consciência, o que importa no fim do *nome* e da *forma*. Isso equivale à cessação das sensações, da percepção, da intelecção e de seus correlatos físicos. Os cinco sentidos serão eliminados, juntamente com o sexto, o *sentido interno*. O desejo termina quando as percepções são eliminadas. Quando o desejo termina, então nosso louco apego ao mundo também termina; e é precisamente nisso que consiste toda a nossa busca.

6. O fim de nosso apego a este mundo significa que a própria existência (conforme a conhecemos) termina. Mediante a nossa busca, pomos fim à ignorância, e, através disso, pomos fim à própria existência.

7. *A vereda nobre e mediana*. Falando em termos práticos, a eliminação da ignorância ocorre quando seguimos a nobre e mediana vereda. Essa vereda evita todos os extremismos. Ela consiste em oito ações específicas, a saber:

a. Fé correta; b. resolução correta; c. linguagem correta; d. ações corretas; e. vida diária correta; f. esforços corretos; g. pensamentos corretos; h.- concentração correta.

Aqueles que têm treinamento filosófico vêem nessa vereda uma grande similaridade com os conceitos aristotélicos no tocante ao *meio-de-ouro*. Ver sobre *Aristóteles*. E, naturalmente, o estoicismo romano tirou proveito do grande tema grego da moderação; paralelamente, encontramos as declarações favoráveis de Paulo, acerca do mesmo tema, em Filipenses 4:5. Ver a expressão desse versículo no NTI. Buda pensava que a **auto-indulgência** e a automortificação são fúteis, e que seus oito atos específicos buscam evitar esses extremos. Portanto, temos a fé correta nas *quatro verdades nobres* (ver abaixo). Resolvemos ter motivos sãos e altruístas; usamos de linguagem correta, empregando somente palavras dignas, que são úteis; praticamos a reta conduta, que inclui o evitar tirar a vida de qualquer criatura viva. Isso também inclui a rejeição dos vícios humanos comuns e os exageros, como o furto, o ódio, a sensualidade e a

BUDISMO

intoxicação de qualquer espécie. O indivíduo *vive corretamente* quando evita o luxo e usa a sua vida para benefício do próximo (lei do amor). Um correto esforço significa evitar o mal, desvinculando-se dos desejos mundanos e enfatizando os valores positivos. A correta maneira de pensar inclui a contemplação sobre o caráter transitório da vida e a prática da meditação, de tal modo que a experiência do indivíduo inclua os estados místicos de arrebatamento e felicidade. A prática diária desses princípios éticos leva à eliminação da ignorância, e, portanto, leva à iluminação.

Talvez seja curioso que, a despeito dos ensinamentos de Buda acerca da moderação, os budistas, tanto homens quanto mulheres, geralmente tornam-se seguidores do monasticismo, o que é sinal da seriedade com que enfrentam a sua inquirição espiritual. Outrossim, essa prática foi iniciada pelo próprio Buda. Esse aspecto, pois, deve ter sido considerado um elemento da vida correta, e não um excesso.

8. *As Quatro Verdades Nobres.* a. O *sofrimento.* Esse é o fator mais importante de toda a existência humana, pois até mesmo nas situações que, essencialmente, não envolvem sofrimento, encontramos algum elemento do mesmo. Além disso, há muito sofrimento humano franco. b. — Há uma *causa do sofrimento*, que está inseparavelmente ligada ao desejo louco do homem por uma existência individual. c. Mas, há uma terceira verdade, a saber, que é possível pôr-se um *ponto final* no sofrimento, removendo-se a sua causa. d. A *vereda de oito passos*, descrita acima, é o meio para pormos fim ao sofrimento. Se alguém seguir fielmente essa vereda, poderá libertar-se totalmente do ciclo do renascimento, desenvolvimento, decadência e morte.

9. *O Nirvana.* Isso ocorre quando o karma de uma pessoa se desgasta, quando suas dívidas são pagas, quando ela não incorre em novas dívidas. Então aquela pessoa deixa de renascer, e entra no Nirvana. Contudo, a natureza do Nirvana (que vide) nunca é esclarecida, porquanto está acima das categorias da intelecção humana. Buda dizia que tudo quanto for negado acerca do Nirvana está errado, como também, tudo quanto for afirmado a seu respeito. Mediante a leitura de suas palavras, podemos respigar algumas idéias; contudo, resta um profundo mistério, que tem levado várias escolas do budismo a conjecturar sobre idéias contraditórias acerca do que seria a existência após a morte, se é que há tal existência. Abaixo damos as sugestões que se têm feito a respeito.

10. A alma ou «ego» não é uma entidade, e, estritamente falando, não existe tal coisa como identidade pessoal, porquanto trata-se de um agregado em estado de fluxo. A consciência própria é um agregado. Tal como a chama de uma tocha pode passar de um feixe para outro, sem que dois feixes sejam idênticos, assim também as *características* do próprio eu podem ser transmitidas de um agregado para outro, de tal modo que, na reencarnação, não temos uma alma que migra de um corpo para outro, mas apenas características da personalidade, as quais são transferidas para uma entidade diferente. O que passa de uma pessoa para a outra são as *skandhas*, isto é, parece ser a mesma alma que passa de um corpo para outro, embora não seja, realmente, assim. *Skandha* é um termo que significa *agregado*, referindo-se àqueles inúmeros elementos que compõem uma personalidade, suas características, desejos, vícios, virtudes, etc. Esse agregado encontra-se em estado de fluxo. Existe a identidade pessoal, mas não existe identidade *permanente*.

11. Há vida após a morte? Buda não forneceu resposta a essa pergunta. Ele não se ocupava com especulações metafísicas, porque o seu sistema era, essencialmente, ético. Naturalmente, sua ética tinha muitos elementos metafísicos, mas, a despeito disso, ele não entrou em qualquer discussão racional quanto a certas indagações específicas. Portanto, no tocante à alma, a sua proposta transferência de um corpo para outro e sua sobrevivência sempre podemos assumir diferentes posições. Consideremos a gota de orvalho. Ela termina no rio, e o rio termina no oceano. Assim, a gota de orvalho mescla-se ao oceano e deixa de existir como uma entidade individual. Porém, também podemos imaginar que o oceano entra na gota de orvalho, de tal modo que se torna uma imensidade, deixando de existir *da maneira* como vinha existindo, porquanto assumiu uma nova forma de existência, indizível e elevada. O budismo, pois, especula de ambas essas maneiras, no que diz respeito à alma.

12. *Estritamente falando*, não existe tal coisa como substância material, porque, tal como a alma, a matéria está em estado de fluxo, sendo apenas um agregado de partes em constante mutação. Neste ponto, aplicamos a doutrina budista da *transitoriedade*, que contradiz a idéia de identidade, conforme a mesma normalmente é compreendida.

III. A Escola Hinayana (incluindo a Theravada) do Budismo (500-250 A.C.). Essa foi a escola mais antiga e mais estrita do budismo. A palavra hinayana quer dizer «pequeno veículo», em contraste com o «grande veículo», chamado mahayana (que será explicado abaixo). A palavra *veículo* alude ao sistema e suas provisões. A escola hinayana desdobrou-se em quatro escolas principais: a. Theravada; b. Sarvastivada; c. Mahasanghika; d. Vaibhasika, com similares pontos de vista. A segunda dessas escolas, Sarvastivada, é a mais filosófica, sendo, para nós, a que melhor se presta para um exame de idéias.

Idéias:

1. A dor continua sendo o elemento dominante, como explicação da natureza de toda a existência humana.

Oh, é real. É a única coisa real.
A dor. Que demos nome à verdade, como homens.
Nascemos para a alegria, para que esta se torne em dor.
Nascemos na esperança, para que esta se torne em dor.
Nascemos para o amor, para que este se torne em dor.
Nascemos em dor, para que esta se torne em dor ainda maior.
E desse inexaurível superfluxo,
Possamos dar aos outros a dor, como nossa primária definição.
(Irmão aos Dragões).

2. O mesmo ensino sobre o karma, imitando Buda. Seja o karma desgastado, e não se desenvolva mais karma ainda.

3. A prática disso levará o indivíduo ao Nirvana, conforme foi descrito acima. Porém, agora, temos uma bem definida definição do Nirvana. Significa extinção, podendo ser comparada ao apagar de uma lamparina.

Exaurido o antigo anseio;
Outro não se ergue.
Libertos dos pensamentos de um futuro,
Os anseios, como sementes estéreis, não voltam,

BUDISMO

E são apagados como se apaga uma chama.
(Sutta-Nipata)

4. A doutrina das *skandhas*, ou natureza agregada da matéria e da alma, segundo se descreveu sob os ensinamentos de Buda, é retida por essa escola.

5. A idéia da transitoriedade também é retida. Tudo está em estado de fluxo.

6. A reencarnação não envolve uma alma que migra de um corpo para outro, mas é apenas a transferência das *skandhas*.

7. Deus não existe. Buda deixou o ponto muito vago, juntamente com outras idéias metafísicas. Mas essa escola Sarvastivada do budismo nega a existência de um Deus pessoal. Portanto, a responsabilidade da salvação do homem repousa exclusivamente sobre ele mesmo, sem a possibilidade de qualquer ajuda divina.

IV. A Escola Mahayana do Budismo

O seu período formativo vai de 0 a 500 D.C. Essa é a forma mais popular e elaborada das escolas budistas. Esse nome significa «grande veículo», referindo-se ao sistema que é empregado para a busca da iluminação e do Nirvana. O vocábulo «grande» é contrastado com o termo «pequeno», que dá nome ao sistema anterior. Os seguidores do grande veículo desprezam os seguidores do pequeno veículo, sentindo-se superiores àqueles, por estarem aderindo a uma interpretação mais estrita e crua dos ensinos do grande mestre deles, Buda.

Idéias:

1. A instituição da crença no **bodhisattva**, o Salvador. O indivíduo iluminado, que ama os seus semelhantes, pode adiar sua absorção pelo Nirvana com a finalidade de ajudar a outros ao longo da vereda. Naturalmente, o *bodhisattva*, é opcional. Contudo, há muitos, nessa escola, que supõem que a figura é necessária como um estágio na direção dos budas, ou iluminados. A salvação deixa, pois, de ser questão meramente pessoal. O corpo também precisa ser salvo, e não apenas os membros individuais. Isso pode ser comparado à idéia de Cristo, a Cabeça, e da Igreja, o corpo. Estritamente falando, não haveria tal coisa como uma salvação isolada, individual. Sempre fazemos parte da comunidade, e temos responsabilidade de cuidar dela, e não apenas de nós mesmos. Isso sempre corresponderá à verdade. A salvação é uma questão comunitária. Isso faz a lei do amor tornar-se muito importante, sendo um importante discernimento quanto à natureza dá espiritualidade.

2. O alvo final de toda vida, de alcance universal, é atingir a natureza de Buda, mas isso requer milênios e mesmo aeons de tempo. Nisso consistiria a salvação. Haveria dez estágios para que alguém chegasse lá: deleite; pureza; brilho intelectual; destruição de quaisquer sedimentos da ignorância e das paixões negativas; vida equânime, contemplando-se a eternidade dentro do tempo, vendo a essência interior imutável das coisas por baixo do mal que as cerca; ignorância e particularidade; obtenção da capacidade de produzir quaisquer meios necessários para a obra da salvação; inocência santa, a par de um conhecimento imediato e intuitivo; um estado mais elevado de conhecimento, que os seres sensíveis não podem seguir e, finalmente, a chegada ao cume: agora, o homem, o *bodhisattva*, é o amor e a simpatia personificados, é onisciente, é virtude, sabedoria e justiça absolutas e perfeitas.

3. O Nirvana torna-se positivo. Um sentido *secundário* é conferido ao termo, passando então a significar a concretização do amor universal e de uma profunda sabedoria, empregados em benefício do próximo. O buda é dotado de tranqüilidade mental. Ele está acima das tempestades da vida. Ele conquistou a dor e o estado de fluxo. Porém, o termo também tem o sentido *primário* de vida do além. A alma foi absorvida pelo Oceano da Vida. A existência, conforme era antes conhecida, deixou de existir. A reencarnação, embora tivesse sido a jornada real da alma, através dos aeons de tempo, terminou; e agora a alma chegou a descansar na extinção.

É verdade que os textos Mahayanas dão apoio à idéia de uma existência imortal, em uma Terra Pura. Porém, essa é apenas uma das interpretações, que não exclui a idéia de extinção.

4. *A Trindade Budista*. O Buda deve ser entendido como dotado de três manifestações: a. o corpo da transformação; b. o corpo da felicidade; e c. o corpo do Dharma. O primeiro é o Buda histórico. O segundo é uma realidade intermediária, compartilhando das qualidades do mundo físico e da realidade última, pondo em ação esquemas de salvação, em todos os lugares e em todas as épocas. O terceiro é similar aos conceitos de deidade. O Dharma é a Realidade Última, bem como o corpo cósmico de Buda, transcendendo ao que é físico. É a parte imortal que existe em nós, em Gautama Buda e em todos os outros Budas. Ver o artigo sobre aquele termo, que também tem outros significados.

V. Contrastes Entre as Escolas Theravada e Mahayana:

Theravada

a. O homem como indivíduo
b. O homem busca a emancipação pessoal por seus esforços
c. Virtude chave: a sabedoria
d. A religião é uma atividade de tempo integral
e. O ideal: o discípulo *perfeito* (o *Arhat*)
f. Buda, o santo
g. Repele as idéias metafísicas
h. Repele o ritualismo
i. Meditação apenas
j. Sempre conservador

Mahayana

a. O homem envolvido com o próximo
b. A comunidade busca a emancipação, com a ajuda do princípio da graça
c. Virtude chave: o amor (compaixão)
d. A religião é relevante a todas as vidas, incluindo os leigos
e. O ideal: o mestre Salvador (o *Bodhisattva*)
f. Buda, o Salvador
g. Inclui uma elaborada metafísica
h. Inclui rituais
i. Meditação e orações peticionárias
j. Liberal

VI. O Budismo na China

Não se sabe dizer quando o budismo atingiu a China, embora deva ter sido antes do início da era cristã. Mas, a data tradicional é 67 D.C. No primeiro século D.C., já existia lado a lado com o taoísmo (que vide), com o qual, finalmente, se misturou. Mestres indianos foram à China, livros sagrados foram escritos, regras disciplinares foram estabelecidas, e a prática da meditação foi instituída. Finalmente, nada menos de dez diferentes escolas budistas vieram à existência. Na China predomina a escola Mahayana, embora com distorções chinesas próprias. A história do budismo na China é, essencialmente, posto que não exclusivamente, a história do desenvolvimento da escola Mahayana, naquele país. Os desenvolvimentos chineses incluem o idealismo, o negativismo (nihilismo), o vazio (que vide), a dupla verdade, os três veículos, a sabedoria transcendental, um quádruplo Nirvana, a universalidade da natureza de Buda, a salvação final para todos, — a salvação pela fé, os votos, a possibilidade de uma súbita iluminação, a doutrina da transferência de méritos e missas pelos mortos. De modo geral, pode-se dizer que a postura ética de Buda tem sido enfatizada na China, e que o sistema adquiriu ali aplicações eminentemente práticas.

VII. O Budismo no Japão

Todas as dez escolas budistas chinesas penetraram no Japão, e, por volta de 573 D.C., o budismo mostrava-se florescente ali. Subseqüentemente, desenvolveram-se várias subdivisões dessas dez escolas. As características distintivamente japonesas vieram à tona. Com o Nichiren, o budismo tornou-se, para todos os efeitos práticos, a religião oficial do Japão. As escolas Singon e Zen (Meditação) salientam muito o misticismo. Ver o artigo separado sobre o *Budismo Zen*. Foram efetuadas reformas, que incluem o matrimônio dos sacerdotes. O budismo tem sofrido muito na China, devido ao advento do comunismo, de tal modo que, atualmente, o Japão é o grande centro do budismo, onde há mais de sete mil templos budistas, além de muitas escolas budistas. Eruditos de renome mundial têm emergido desse sistema. Ver o artigo sobre *Religiões Japonesas*. (AM E H HUS P)

BUDISMO CH'AN

Ver sobre o **Budismo Zen**, bem como o artigo geral sobre o **Budismo**.

BUGAEANO

Um epíteto dado a Hamã nas adições a Ester (que vide) (Est. 12:6). Parece que significa brigão ou fanfarrão, correspondente ao uso homérico em *Ilíada* xiii.824, *Odisséia* xviii. 79. Mas também poderia simplesmente significar um agagita, por causa da corrupção da palavra grega *agagaios*.

BUGIOS

No hebraico é **koph**, e no latim é **cephus**. O termo hebraico é amplo em seu sentido, podendo designar vários tipos de símios, como macacos e o babuíno. No Antigo Testamento, a palavra aparece somente em I Reis 10:22, onde alguma variedade de macacos constituía parte da carga importada pela frota mercante de Salomão. Provavelmente, esses animais eram trazidos do leste da África ou da Índia. Talvez esteja em foco o babuíno ou o macaco veludo, embora não possamos determinar o tipo exato envolvido nessa importação. Ao que parece, não havia macacos nativos da Palestina, pelo menos até recentes períodos geológicos. Atualmente, o habitat mais próximo de qualquer espécie de macaco é a costa da Arábia, onde vive o babuíno sagrado (hamardriada). Essa espécie vivia no Egito desde os tempos mais antigos, onde também era adorado. O ídolo babuíno talvez tivesse chifres de cabras, o que também fosse aplicado às figuras de leões, cavalos e elefantes, conforme as mesmas aparecem em moedas. (S UN Z)

BUL

Era o oitavo mês do calendário judaico, correspondente aos nossos meses de outubro e novembro (I Reis 6:38). Ver sobre *Calendário*.

BULA UNIGENITUS

Vem do latim **unus**, «um», e de **genitus**, «gerado».
Esse documento foi assim chamado por causa das palavras latinas *Unigenitus Dei Filius*, «o unigênito Filho de Deus», que abrem o texto do tal documento. Essa bula foi expedida pelo papa Clemente XI, a 8 de setembro de 1713, contra a doutrina jansenista de Pasquier Quesnel (que vide). Ver o artigo sobre o *jansenismo*. (E)

BULAS PAPAIS

Esse é o nome dado às missivas oficiais publicadas solenemente pelos papas da Igreja Católica Romana. Esses documentos começam com as palavras em latim Episcopus Servus Servorum Dei, «Supervisor Escravo dos Escravos de Deus», e contêm decretos sobre questões consideradas importantes pela hierarquia romana, como declarações doutrinárias, decretos de canonização, questões disciplinares, promulgação de indulgências gerais, concessões do pálio, etc. A palavra vem do termo latino *bulla*, que indica uma pequena *bola* de metal, que, durante vários séculos, foi usada como selo autenticador dos documentos papais. Tal uso remonta do século VII D.C., e os primeiros selos-bolas eram de chumbo. Até o tempo do papa Leão XIII, as bulas eram seladas com chumbo e os breves pontifícios eram selados com o *anel de pescador*. O papa Leão XIII (que vide), modificou esse costume, passando a usar o selo de chumbo em documentos como aqueles que tratam da ereção, supressão e provisão de bispados. Esses selos, atualmente, de um lado têm as effigies de Pedro e Paulo, e, do outro lado, o nome do pontífice reinante.

Classificados juntamente com as bulas papais estão os breves pontifícios, nome esse que vem do latim *breve*, «curto». Esses outros documentos abordam todas as espécies de questões, mas são de menor importância que aqueles cobertos pelas bulas. Além desses, há as semibulas solenes documentos papais expedidos por papas recentemente eleitos, antes de sua coroação. Além desses, há outros documentos chamados *motu próprio* (que vide) e *rescritos* (que vide). Os primeiros são missivas papais sem selos, preparadas pessoalmente pelo papa, abordando questões de importância secundária. O *rescrito* é um documento preparado para responder a perguntas ou petições feitas ao papa ou a alguma das congregações sagradas, sendo uma espécie de mensagem de indivíduo para indivíduo, que não afeta outras pessoas ou comunidades. (E)

BULLINGER, HEINRICH

Suas datas foram 1504-1575. Foi reformador, mestre e pastor evangélico suíço, sucessor de Zwínglio (que vide), e principal pastor de Zurique, no ano de 1531. Foi um escritor habilidoso e pensador profundo, o qual, mesmo em meio à controvérsia, era capaz de compreender a outros, ansioso por encontrar pontos de acordo com seus adversários. Um homem raro, portanto. Suas obras de controvérsia mostram dignidade e restrição! Foi um dos responsáveis pela Confissão Helvética (que vide), que influenciou o pensamento religioso inglês. (E)

BULTMANN, RUDOLF

Suas datas foram 1884-1976. Teólogo protestante alemão, nascido em Wiefelsted. Estudou em Marburgo, Tubingen e Berlim. Ensinou em Marburgo. Foi influenciado por Heidegger. Bultmann foi um teólogo existencialista. Ver sobre o *Existencialismo*.

Idéias. 1. Ele suspeitava que muitos dos relatos do

Novo Testamento são produtos de uma imaginação superativa, e/ou de elementos mitológicos que ali foram incorporados. A tarefa do intérprete seria a de *demitizar* os textos sagrados, a fim de torná-los relevantes para o mundo contemporâneo. O único aspecto isento desse processo seria a reivindicação fundamental de que Deus tem falado e continua a falar através de Cristo. Aí temos uma verdade que não requer demitologização. 2. A mensagem central evangélica da salvação, que é a pregação do Novo Testamento, o *kerygma*, deve ser reinterpretada segundo a linguagem do existencialismo, com ênfase sobre a doutrina da liberdade humana, com inclusão do elemento do *Angst*, uma espécie de temor indefinível, sem objeto, que seria um dos elementos básicos da existência humana. Ver o artigo sobre a *dimitização*, — quanto a maiores detalhes a respeito. Parece-nos que a suposta necessidade de encontrar o elemento mítico no Novo Testamento escuda-se no *ceticismo* (que vide). Algumas pessoas simplesmente não se mostram capazes de acreditar na veracidade histórica de muito do que é declarado no Novo Testamento, como se Jesus não fosse capaz de realizar as maravilhas que lhe são ali atribuídas. Entretanto, consideremos o caso contemporâneo de *Satya Sai Baba* (que vide), o qual está reproduzindo muitos dos milagres de Jesus, diante de testemunhas oculares, em plena luz do dia, e sob escrutínio cauteloso. O ceticismo ignora o fato de que há grandes maravilhas, milagres estupendos, os quais requerem um ponto de vista mundial que inclui o que é extraordinário e miraculoso. Quando alguém se põe a pensar sobre a própria maravilha da existência, não acha estranho que ocorram milagres, pois o fato das coisas existirem já é o mais admirável milagre de todos! Questões como o nascimento virginal de Cristo, os milagres do Antigo e do Novo Testamento, a ressurreição literal de Jesus Cristo, a existência de demônios, anjos, as intervenções divinas e a expiação do pecado, através do sangue de Cristo (coisas essas que Bultmann preferia eliminar, mediante seu **processo de demitização, ajustam-se facilmente em nosso mundo tão repleto de maravilhas que deixa o indivíduo que pensa inteiramente admirado.** 3. Abordagem ética: Era quanto a isso que Bultmann mais se declarava um existencialista. Para ele, a existência humana pode ser considerada à parte da fé. Um homem pode se ver dominado pelas questões carnais, pressionado pelo que é visível, concreto, tangível e grosseiro, pelo que é sensual e arrogante. Em outras palavras, pode ser esmagado por toda forma de cuidados, e pela *angústia* que isso produz. Desse modo, torna-se escravo daquilo que deveria dominar.

Não obstante, a existência humana também pode ser vivida sob o pálio da fé. A autêntica vida de fé alicerça-se sobre realidades invisíveis, intangíveis. O homem precisa abandonar toda a segurança por ele mesmo arquitetada, pois isso é apenas outra fonte de sua ansiedade. As Escrituras falam sobre a vida de fé, no Espírito (Rom. 8:13 ss; Gál. 2:20 ss; Fil. 4:6), o que não consiste em uma atitude de repúdio ascético, e, sim, em certa distância em que o indivíduo se mantém do mundo. A vida espiritual caracteriza-se pela cruz e pela ressurreição, metaforicamente compreendidas, pois Bultmann mantinha uma atitude cética para com a historicidade dos relatos sagrados como base de nossa fé. Através do evangelho, uma pessoa seria liberada de sua servidão ao mundo e aos temores no mesmo existentes. A pessoa seria liberada para amar. A fé consistiria na renúncia das obras, bem como em um ato de decisão, mediante o qual o indivíduo se entrega à graça divina. A fé libertaria o indivíduo do seu passado, conferindo-lhe liberdade para viver para um novo futuro. O imperativo fundamental de toda ética é o amor (que vide). Bultmann convida-nos a ter fé no espírito do evangelho cristão, inclusive em suas leis do amor e da liberdade, sem qualquer necessidade de uma base histórica. Pois, segundo ele, até mesmo os mitos são capazes de comunicar uma profunda mensagem àqueles que têm ouvidos para ouvir.

Escritos: *Jesus and the Word; Belief and Understanding; Theology of the New Testament; The Question of Demythologizing; History and Eschatology; Jesus Christ and Mythology*. (AM C E H P)

BUNA
No hebraico, «discreção», embora outros prefiram «entendimento». Em I Crônicas 2:25 há menção a um homem com esse nome, filho de Jerameel, da família de Perez, de Judá. Cerca de 1658 A.C.

BUNI
No hebraico, «edificado». Há três homens com esse nome, no Antigo Testamento: 1. um levita da época de Neemias (Nee. 11:15), em cerca de 410 A.C. 2. Um levita cujo descendente, Semaías, foi nomeado superintendente do templo de Jerusalém, após o retorno de Judá do exílio (Nee. 11:15), em cerca de 445 A.C. Lightfoot diz que esse era o nome judaico de Nicodemos (João 3:1-3). 3. Um levita que esteve presente quando da leitura pública da lei, por parte de Esdras (Nee. 9:4).

BUNYAN, JOHN
Nasceu em 1628 e faleceu em 1688. Foi um ministro não-conformista e escritor prosaico inglês. Escreveu «O Peregrino». A despeito de sua pobreza, falta de educação formal e de haver passado doze anos encarcerado, por causa de seus pontos de vista e de suas atividades como líder da congregação de não-conformistas de Bedford, na Inglaterra, ele produziu quase sessenta livros e tratados sobre assuntos religiosos. Seu «O Peregrino» tem merecido larga circulação em diversos idiomas. Outras obras suas são: *Grace Abounding to the Chief of Sinners; The Life and Death of Mr. Badman; The Holy War*. Ele se tornou mais conhecido por causa de suas alegorias poderosas; várias de suas figuras de linguagem têm entrado na fala comum dos povos de língua inglesa e outros, como Sábio Mundano, Sussurro do Desânimo, Rio da Morte, etc. (E P)

BUQUI
No hebraico, «dilapidador». Houve dois homens com esse nome, nas páginas do Antigo Testamento:
1. Um filho de Jogli, príncipe da tribo de Dã, um dos dez homens selecionados por Moisés para distribuir a conquistada terra de Canaã entre as doze tribos (Núm. 34:22). Cerca de 1618 A.C.
2. Um filho de Abisua, pai de Uzi, da linhagem de Aarão (I Crô. 6:5,51; Esd. 7:4). Cerca de 1618 A.C. Não sabemos se ele chegou a tornar-se sumo sacerdote. Em II Esdras 1:2, ele é chamado Borite.

BUQUIAS
No hebraico, «desgastado por Yahweh». Foi um levita coatita, filho de Hemã. Era músico no templo

de Jerusalém, e a seu cargo estava o sexto turno dos serviçais do templo (I Crô. 25:4). Cerca de 1014 A.C.

BURACO DA AGULHA
Ver **Agulha, Buraco da**.

BURGUESIA (BURGUÊS)
Nome dado à classe média, derivado do vocábulo francês que significa *citadino* ou *negociante*. Parece que a palavra surgiu quando a aristocracia feudal passou a referir-se às classes inferiores, como proprietários de lojas e negociantes, cujas maneiras eles deploravam e cujas condições de vida eles desprezavam, em termos levemente pejorativos. O vocábulo foi tomado por empréstimo por marxistas ou comunistas, como designação de empregadores aos quais atribuíam táticas ardilosas, calculadoras e opressivas. Assim sendo, o termo passou a envolver as idéias de luta de classes, ódio e sentimentos amargos, que são as sementes das revoluções. (E WA)

A aplicação da lei do amor curaria os males da sociedade mas os homens dificilmente aprendem esta lição. (E WA)

BURIDAN, JOHN
Nasceu em cerca de 1295 e deve ter falecido após 1366. Provavelmente nasceu em Béthune, na França. Foi filósofo e reitor da Universidade de Paris, de 1328 a 1340. Filosoficamente ele foi um nominalista moderado (ver sobre os *Universais*). Acreditava em uma força não-local que permearia o espaço e atuaria sobre os corpos locais. Discutiu sobre o problema da relação entre a razão e a vontade. Tornou-se conhecido por sua gráfica ilustração sobre o dilema da seleção entre idéias, quando duas ou mais boas idéias se conflitam. Quanto a essa questão ver o artigo sobre o *Asno de Buridan*. Escritos: *Summulae de Dialectica; Consequentiae; Sophismata; Questions on the Four Books of the Heavens and the Earth*. Comentários sobre Aristóteles. (E EP P)

BURKE, EDMUND
Suas datas foram 1729-1797. Foi estadista e escritor filosófico britânico, nascido em Dublim, na Irlanda. Educou-se no Trinity College, em Dublim. Teve carreira como escritor e filósofo, mas as atividades políticas tiraram-no da carreira de filósofo ativo. Entrou na Casa dos Comuns em 1766, e continuou no poder, no partido Whig, durante um quarto de século.

Idéias. 1. Ele distinguia o sublime do apenas belo. O belo é infinito, e não se mistura com elementos negativos. O sublime é infinito, mas não se mistura com elementos negativos como o terror e a dor. Suas idéias sobre o *sublime* influenciaram Moses Mendelssohn e o movimento do *Romantismo* (que vide). 2. Como político, ele defendeu a Revolução Americana, supondo que a mesma tentava defender liberdades tradicionais que estavam sendo desrespeitadas. No entanto, ele sentia que a Revolução Francesa voltava-se contra as tradições, em nome de um ideal imaginário.

Escritos: *On the Sublime and the Beautiful; Reflections on the Revolution in France*. (AM P)

BURLEIGH, WALTER
Nasceu em 1275, na Inglaterra, e faleceu em 1343. Foi monge franciscano e filósofo. Ensinou em Oxford e na Universidade de Paris. Foi um dos opositores de Ockham. Empregou e elaborou muito a teoria das suposições (ver *Suppositio*). Atualmente, sua obra seria classificada como semântica.

Idéias. Sua obra concentrou a atenção sobre as suposições próprias e impróprias, **sobre o inter-relacionamento** entre elas, suas categorias, suas descrições, etc. Sua obra aborda os tipos de relação que surgem entre termos, e o que eles designam. Tais relações são chamadas *suposições*.

Escritos: *On Aristotle; On Matter and Form; On Intention and the Remission of Form; On the Purity of the Logical Arts*. (EP P)

BUSHIDO
Vem do termo japonês **bushi**, «guerreiro», com o vocábulo *do*, «caminho» ou «princípio», uma palavra que se refere ao código dos cavaleiros (de origem confucionista e budista zen), dos cavaleiros guerreiros do Japão feudal.

BUSHNELL, HORACE
Suas datas foram 1802-1876. Foi pregador e teólogo norte-americano. Formou-se na Yale College e Divinity School. Foi pastor da North Church, em Harford, estado da Pennsylvania. Sua obra marcou o fim da teologia da Nova Inglaterra (que vide). Suas contribuições incluíram a tentativa de emancipar a Igreja do revivalismo que ignorava a lei do crescimento cristão, um conceito da Trindade que era triteísta do que trinitarista, — um ponto de vista dos milagres que ignorava as leis naturais, teorias de expiação que não levavam em conta as leis que governam a vida humana. Em lugar do revivalismo, ele preferia treinar as crianças, desde tenra idade, nos princípios da educação cristã, temendo o emocionalismo como algo superficial e ilusório na fé religiosa. Em todas as suas escritas, Bushnell desafiava os homens a adquirirem novos hábitos e modos de pensar, afastando-se de definições formais e precisas, que incorporam a letra, mas matam e ignoram o Espírito, que transmite vida. Defendia o fato de que sempre se manifestarão os elementos da intuição e do misticismo na religião, e também que é responsabilidade da teologia reconhecer e interpretar essas questões. Por outro lado, o formalismo e a letra morta como base na fé precisam ser evitados. A despeito disso, o emocionalismo destituído de bases no estudo e no treinamento deveria ser evitado. Tanto o formalismo quanto o emocionalismo são destrutivos do espírito da verdadeira fé cristã. A doutrina cristã sempre deveria ser formulada com base na *experiência* cristã, e não como mero assentimento a idéias abstratas. Bushnell foi um dos grandes pregadores do século XIX, e até hoje seus sermões são lidos com proveito. Também escreveu as seguintes obras: *Christian Nature; God in Christ; God in Theology; Nature and the Supernatural; Forgiveness and Law*. (AM C E)

BUTLER, JOSEPH
Suas datas foram 1692-1752. Bispo e filósofo britânico que, até os nossos próprios dias, tem seu nome ligado de perto às questões éticas. Nasceu em Bristol. Foi deão da catedral de São Paulo e bispo em Durham.

Idéias. O critério do certo e do errado é a nossa *consciência*. Trata-se de um princípio reflexivo e racional, que opera admiravelmente bem dentro do homem. Na qualidade de bispo, sem dúvida, ele sentia que essa faculdade de consciência era outorgada por Deus, pelo que estaria espiritualmente garantida, embora tal idéia nem sempre seja defendida pelos filósofos que falam sobre a ética de Butler. Para ele, a consciência controla todas as ações humanas, desde o auto-amor até o altruísmo, sem muita sutileza em suas maneiras de operar e não podendo ser reduzida a uma única máxima ou critério. Seria uma faculdade intuitiva, e não meramente utilitária. *Metafísica*: Butler acreditava que a verdade da existência de Deus pode ser explicada pela razão, porquanto nos cumpre conceber um Governante Moral e Autor da natureza, em nossa filosofia. Sem isso, o mundo não tem sentido. Ver o *argumento moral*, em prol da existência de Deus e da alma, um desenvolvimento especial de Emanuel Kant. Butler também defendia a revelação bíblica contra os ataques dos deístas (ver sobre o *Deísmo*). Para ele, há dois livros nos quais o homem deve confiar: o Livro da Revelação (a Bíblia), apesar de suas ambigüidades e problemas; e o Livro da Natureza. E os dois concordam em espírito, porquanto ambos têm sua origem em Deus. A razão recebe destaque, em todas as obras de Butler. Ele argumentava que todo homem racional, ao examinar o caso, teria de admitir quão razoável é a tradição cristã como fé religiosa. A ordem e a beleza, até mesmo das coisas destituídas de vida, desvendam uma inteligência criadora, que manipula todos os objetos com algum desígnio consciente em mira. Ver sobre *Argumento Cosmológico* e *Argumento Teleológico*.

Escritos: *Fifteen Sermons; The Analogy of Religion; Dissertation upon the Nature of Virtue*. (AM C E EP P)

BUXO

No hebraico, **teashshur**. A palavra ocorre apenas por duas vezes, em Isa. 41:19 e 60:13. Indica uma variedade do cedro. A árvore produz uma madeira dura, da qual são feitos muitos objetos, incluindo colheres e pentes. O nome científico da espécie é *Buxus sempervirens longifolia*. A árvore pode atingir a altura de 5,60 m. As folhas são pequenas e escuras. Há flores minúsculas, esverdeadas pálidas, com estâmens amarelos. A espécie continua abundante nas colinas da Galiléia, e era uma árvore comum nos tempos do Antigo Testamento.

BUZ, BUZITA

No hebraico, «desprezo». Foi o nome de duas pessoas, no Antigo Testamento.

1. O segundo filho de Naor e Milca (Gên. 22:21), irmão de Uz. Cerca de 1880 A.C. Sua descendência provavelmente estabeleceu-se na Arábia Pétrea. Jeremias (25:3) anunciou julgamentos contra essa tribo, e o contexto sugere-nos uma localização no deserto da Arábia.

2. Um membro da tribo de Gade (I Crô. 5:14), pai de Jado. Cerca de 1093 A.C.

O pai de Eliú, Baraquel, é chamado de buzita (Jó 32:2,6).

BUZI

No hebraico, «desprezado por Yahweh». Era pai do profeta Ezequiel (Eze. 1:3), provavelmente um sacerdote, visto que Ezequiel também o era. Cerca de 598 A.C. Coisa alguma se sabe sobre esse homem, embora possamos supor que ele era sacerdote e/ou profeta, sendo pai de alguém que era sacerdote e profeta.

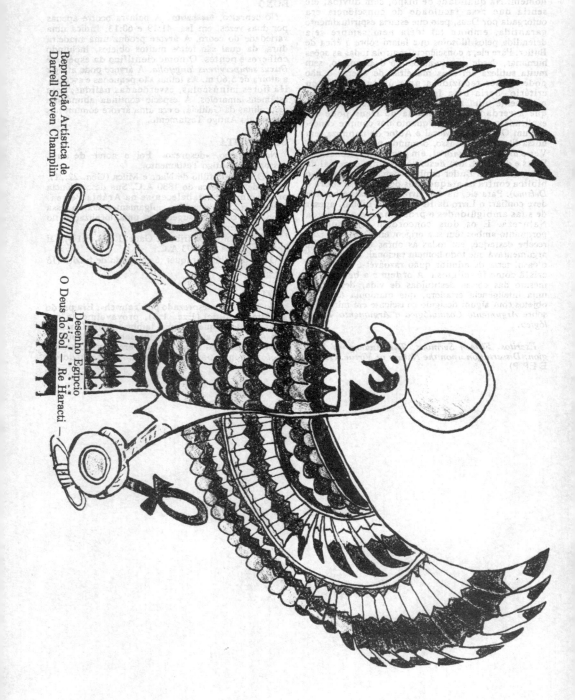

Desenho Egípcio
O Deus do Sol — Re Haracti

Reprodução Artística de
Darrell Steven Champlin

1. Formas Antigas

fenício (semítico), 1000 A.C.   grego ocidental, 800 A.C.   latino, 50 D.C.

2. Nos Manuscritos Gregos do Novo Testamento

Γ (K, C) (Formas Derivadas)

3. Formas Modernas

C C c c   C C c c   C C c c   C c

4. História

C é a terceira letra do alfabeto português. Nas antigas línguas semíticas, era chamada *gimel*, «camelo». Os gregos adotaram-na, chamando-a *gamma*. Neste último idioma a letra era pronunciada tanto como K quanto como G. No latim, o *C* deixou de ser usado como «g», embora tivesse retido o fonema «k». No português a letra tem o fonema «k» e o fonema «ss», o primeiro antes das vogais a, o, u, e o segundo antes das vogais e, i.

5. Usos e Símbolos

C é o símbolo usado para representar o numeral romano 100. Na música representa o *dó* na escala do Dó. Nos sistemas de gradação, representa *médio*. Também é a abreviação de *Celsus* (graus centígrados) e de *cerca de*. *C* é o símbolo do manuscrito *Codex Epraemi Rescriptus*, descrito no artigo separado C.

Caligrafia de Darrell Steven Champlin

C

C

Designação usada para indicar o **Codex Ephraemi**, atualmente na Biblioteca Nacional de Paris. O manuscrito, datado do século V D.C., originalmente incluía toda a Bíblia grega, mas deve sua sobrevivência ao fato de que foi usado para fazer uma cópia da obra de Efraem, da Síria. O texto bíblico foi apagado da melhor maneira possível, e as obras de Efraem foram copiadas por cima do mesmo. Tal produção chama-se *palimpsesto*. Somente sessenta e quatro folhas do Antigo Testamento grego foram assim preservadas, e cerca de cento e quarenta e cinco folhas, ou mais ou menos duzentas e trinta e oito páginas do Novo Testamento. A despeito de seus problemas (a restauração foi boa, de acordo com métodos modernos), trata-se de um dos principais manuscritos do Novo Testamento. Ver o artigo sobre os *Manuscritos*. (KE ME)

CAABA

No árabe, **kabah**, um edifício em forma de cubo, cujo nome vem da palavra *kab*, cubo. Esse nome identifica o edifício praticamente cúbico que há no átrio da grande mesquita de Meca (que vide), onde está contida a rocha negra sagrada, que os islamitas (que vide) pensam ter sido dada pelo anjo Gabriel a Abraão. Esse é um objeto de peregrinações anuais, bem como o centro da adoração para onde os islamitas se voltam, em suas orações diárias.

CABALA

No hebraico, **kabel**, «receber», isto é, tradições transmitidas e aceitas. A Cabala é o conhecimento místico esotérico do judaísmo, baseado na interpretação oculta da Bíblia, à qual foram adicionados elementos de outras religiões e sistemas. Esses materiais eram entregues aos iniciados, em sua maior parte, e não ensinados publicamente. Contudo, essas idéias espalharam-se, pelo que a Cabala veio a exercer considerável influência sobre o pensamento dos líderes do povo e até do próprio povo. Por exemplo, a crença geral na reencarnação (que vide), pelo judaísmo em geral, da época de Jesus, devia-se, pelo menos em parte, à atividade cabalística.

1. *Origem*. As origens desse sistema são obscuras, mas o tipo de atividade por ele representado (a teosofia especulativa e a taumaturgia prática) encontra-se na literatura apócrifa e na Midrash. Durante o seu desenvolvimento, muitas correntes de pensamento fluíram para a corrente principal, como as idéias do gnosticismo (que vide), do neoplatonismo (que vide), do neopitagoreanismo (que vide), do zoroastrismo (que vide) e do sufismo (que vide). A Cabala teve começo na Palestina; mas foi na Babilônia, durante o período de 550 a 1000 D.C., que experimentou seu primeiro sistemático e substancial desenvolvimento. Duas importantes obras cabalísticas surgiram ali, a saber: 1. O *Sefer Yetzirah* (o Livro da Formação), um estudo sobre os poderes criativos das letras e dos números, uma obra estudada largamente; 2. o *Shiur Komah* (a Medida de Altura), uma obra antropomórfica sobre as dimensões da deidade.

2. *Movimentos*. Começando pela Babilônia, centro da atividade cabalística, o movimento passou para a Itália, Espanha, Provença, Alemanha, nos séculos IX e X D.C. Aaron ben Samuel trouxe seus discípulos da Babilônia para a Itália. Isaque, o Cego, e Azriel desenvolveram a Cabala na Provença. A família Kalonymous transportou a Cabala da Itália para a Alemanha. Judá, o Piedoso, e Eleazar de Worms trabalharam na Alemanha, e Moisés ben Nachman (que vide) desenvolveu o sistema na Espanha. Vários novos livros foram publicados nessa época. Apareceram o *Masechet Atzilut* (Tratado sobre a Emanação), por Jacó Nazir (século XII DC.); o *Sefer Ha-Bahir* (o Livro Luminoso), do século XIII; o *Sefer Ha-Temunah* (o Livro da Imagem), do século XIII; e o *Zohar*, que se tornou conhecido por Moisés de Leon, em 1300. Esse foi o mais significativo livro cabalístico do período, que veio a ser considerado como o mais sagrado de todos os escritos similares.

O próximo período significativo de atividades cabalísticas deu-se no século XVI. Seu principal centro foi em Safede, na Palestina. A Polônia também tornou-se um importante centro cabalístico. Bem conhecidos personagens dessa época foram Moisés Cordovero (1522-1570), Isaque Luria (1533-1572), o qual é chamado de pai da moderna e *prática* Cabala. Seu discípulo, Chayim Vital (1543-1620), registrou em forma escrita os ensinamentos de Luria. Luria foi o fundador de uma escola na qual a redenção e o messianismo figuravam proeminentemente, conceitos esses que influenciaram muito as escolas subseqüentes. Esse movimento tornou-se um movimento místico popular da Europa Oriental, nos séculos XVIII e XIX, conhecido como *chasidismo* (que vide).

3. *Propagação às massas*. O *Zohar* fez os ensinos cabalísticos influenciarem as massas populares. Esses ensinos deixaram de ser as doutrinas secretas apenas dos iniciados. Naturalmente, os rabinos tradicionais atacavam as idéias cabalísticas; mas, apesar disso, elas prosperaram, florescendo paralelamente a algumas poucas boas idéias, aberrações e superstições.

4. *Propagação entre os cristãos*. Era apenas natural, devido à perene e íntima conexão entre o cristianismo e o judaísmo, que os ensinamentos cabalísticos influenciassem líderes e eruditos cristãos. Isso ocorreu mormente durante a Idade Média. Raimundo Lully, Pico della Mirandola e João Reuchlin (que vide) utilizaram tais ensinamentos, primeiramente como uma fonte de investigação de novas idéias, e então como meio de consubstanciar certas doutrinas cristãs. O misticismo (vide) tem muitos ramos, e a Cabala é apenas um deles; as informações acerca de uma das formas de misticismo naturalmente acabaram sendo aceitas por outras dessas formas.

5. *A exegese da Cabala*. Naturalmente, os cabalistas precisavam de maior espaço que os eruditos hebreus tradicionais. Porém, caíram em vários absurdos. Cada palavra da Bíblia, escrita em hebraico, que eles pensavam ser a língua do próprio Deus, bem como cada letra, e mesmo cada sinal vocálico, e todas as suas possíveis permutas e combinações, eram consideradas questões que encerravam profundos mistérios. A Bíblia era interpretada não apenas literalmente, mas também alegórica, homilética e anagogicamente, com a esperança de desvendar sentidos ocultos. As palavras eram interpretadas de acordo com seus valores numéricos, numa pseudociência chamada *gematria*. Além disso, cada letra de uma palavra sugeria outras palavras que eram iniciadas pela mesma, e disso os cabalistas extraíam certos sentidos, chamados *notarikon*. Havia ainda a substituição de algumas letras por outras, e disso emergiam supostos significados, chamados *temurah*. A despeito de toda essa manipulação, os

CABANIS — CABEÇA

cabalistas nunca sentiram o constrangimento da letra que mata. Porém, esse sistema fez contribuições significativas para o misticismo, apesar desse tipo de atividade ser tão dúbio.

6. *Idéias da Cabala*: a. Emanações de um Deus transcendental. b. A doutrina das esferas, o *sefiroth*, que seriam mediadores entre a Luz Infinita e a criação física. c. Muitas ordens de anjos e demiurgos, que facilitariam a comunhão entre Deus e o homem. d. A reencarnação (que vide). e. O pecado consiste na *separação* entre o homem e o Ser Divino, ao passo que a perfeição consiste na eliminação desse estado de separação. f. A crença no Adão Kadmon, um homem primordial, do qual se derivaria o homem terreno. g. O Adão Kadmon seria uma união dos sexos, da qual o homem e a mulher terrenos são meros reflexos. h. O homem é um microcosmos do universo. i. Um assinalado *dualismo* (que vide), expresso em termos de luz e trevas, de esquerda e direita, de pureza e impureza, de macho e fêmea, além de inúmeros outros pares. j. Amuletos, números e letras teriam significação própria, e o lançamento de sortes e outras formas de adivinhação eram empregados. Além disso, por ocasião das enfermidades ou em períodos de penitência, a pessoa podia mudar seu nome, a fim de procurar beneficiar-se da mudança de letras e de seus valores numéricos. Ver sobre a *Numerologia*. (AM BR E JE P)

CABANIS, PIERRE

Suas datas foram 1757-1808. Foi filósofo francês e professor de medicina em Paris. Foi um dos líderes dos idealistas franceses (que vide).

Idéias: 1. Não podemos ter uma idéia segura sobre os pressupostos metafísicos que estão por detrás de nossas idéias a respeito do que é físico e do que é psíquico, e de suas supostas diferenças. Talvez pertençam a uma mesma natureza, de tal modo que não há qualquer diferença essencial entre as duas coisas; mas, apesar disso, em termos práticos, é óbvio que essas duas coisas se influenciam mutuamente. Ver sobre o *Problema Corpo-Mente*, especialmente sobre o *duplo aspecto*. 2. Dependendo da ênfase posta por aqueles que o estudam, Cabanis pode ser considerado um materialista ou um crente nos fenômenos espirituais, ao manipular os mesmos fatos. 3. Seu ponto de vista tende por uma espécie de *panteísmo* (que vide). 4. A ênfase principal de Cabanis era ética. Ele acreditava no conceito do progresso, acreditando que o homem está se aproximando de uma espécie de idade áurea, quando suas grandes esperanças terão cumprimento.

Obra Principal: *The Relations of the Physical and Ethical in Man*. (EP P)

CABE

Ver sobre **Pesos e Medidas**.

CABEÇA

Há várias palavras hebraicas e uma palavra grega envolvidas neste verbete:
- 1. *Gulgoleth*, «crânio». Palavra hebraica que aparece por três vezes com esse sentido: I Crô. 10:10.

2. *Resh*, «cabeça». Palavra aramaica usada por treze vezes. Para exemplificar: Dan. 2:28,32,38; 3:27; 7:1,6,9,15,20.

3. *Rosh*, «cabeça». Palavra hebraica usada por quase trezentas e cinqüenta vezes com esse sentido. Por exemplo: Gên. 2:10; 3:15; Êxo. 6:14; 25; Lev. 1:4,8; Núm. 1:4,16; Deu. 1:15; Jos. 2:19; I Reis 2:32; II Reis 2:3; Est. 2:17; Pro. 1:9; Ecl. 2:14; Can. 2:6.

4. *Kephalé*, «cabeça». Vocábulo grego que é usado por setenta e quatro vezes no Novo Testamento, desde Mat. 5:36 até Apo. 19:12.

Esse termo inclui tanto o crânio, que abriga o cérebro, como também o rosto. Alguns antigos reconheciam a cabeça como a sede da inteligência; mas outros pensavam que essa função era ocupada pelo coração. Ou então o coração seria a sede das emoções (Gên. 3:15; Sal. 3:3). Algumas vezes, a palavra «cabeça» indica a pessoa inteira (Gên. 49:26; Pro. 10:6). A palavra também é aplicada a animais, literalmente, como a cabeça de um novilho, nas ofertas queimadas (Lev. 1:4), ou então indicava o animal inteiro. Os objetos inanimados, como um portão, teriam cabeça, em sentido metafórico, segundo se vê em Salmos 24:7, «Levantai, ó portas, as vossas cabeças...» Cabeças de animais serviam de motivo de decoração, em desenhos, pinturas e peças do mobiliário.

Ferimentos e Enfermidades da Cabeça. A principal maneira de ferir a um inimigo consistia em produzir-lhe um ferimento na cabeça (Sal. 68:21). A decapitação era uma forma de punição capital, sendo praticada na Assíria, na Babilônia, e em muitos outros países antigos. A lepra podia atingir uma pessoa na cabeça (Lev. 13:42,44). A cabeça também estava sujeita a doenças da pele (Isa. 3:17), e a doenças internas (II Reis 4:29; Isa. 1:5). Ver o artigo geral sobre as *Doenças*.

Costumes. Inclinar a cabeça diante de alguém simboliza humildade ou reverência (Gên. 24:26; Êxo. 4:31; 43:28). Cobrir a cabeça representava tristeza (II Sam. 15:30; Est. 6:12). Pôr cinza ou pó sobre a cabeça indicava consternação e tristeza (Jos. 7:6; Jó 2:12). Impor as mãos sobre a cabeça de alguém era sinal de transmissão de alguma bênção, embora também pudesse indicar tristeza (II Sam. 13:19; Jer. 2:37). Os sacerdotes e os nazireus, entre os israelitas, estavam proibidos de rapar a cabeça (Lev. 21:5,10; Núm. 6:5). As cabeças dos inimigos, em tempos de guerra, ou dos criminosos, eram decapitadas em sinal de total vitória e escárnio (Mat. 14:10; Juí. 5:36; I Sam. 17:51).

Usos Figurados. 1. Jesus Cristo é o Cabeça da Igreja (Efé. 4:15). Há um artigo separado sobre esse assunto, intitulado *Cristo, a Cabeça; a Igreja, o Corpo*. Ver também o artigo sobre o *Corpo de Cristo*.

2. *Governantes*. Ver I Sam. 15:17; Dan. 2:38.

3. Pessoas que ocupavam posições importantes (Isa. 9:14,15).

4. A cidade principal de algum reino (Isa. 7:8).

5. Deixar uma cabeça calva era julgar severamente (Isa. 3:24; 15:2).

6. Levantar a cabeça era triunfar de modo jubiloso (Sal. 3:3; Luc. 21:28).

7. Ungir a cabeça era consagrá-la ou mostrar respeito pela pessoa ungida (Êxo. 29:7; Luc. 7:46).

8. Sacudir a cabeça era um gesto de zombaria, incredulidade ou consternação (Isa. 37:22; Sal. 22:7; Jer. 18:16; Mat. 27:39).

CABEÇA (Cristo) e CORPO (Igreja)

Col. 1:18: *Também ele é a cabeça do corpo, da igreja; é o princípio, o primogênito dentre os mortos, para que em tudo tenha a preeminência*,

A Metáfora da Cabeça e do Corpo

1. A união vital entre Cristo e seu «corpo» é referida

CABEÇA (CRISTO COMO)

sob o simbolismo da cabeça e do corpo: uma união mística é assim salientada (ver as notas expositivas a respeito, em I Cor. 1:4, no NTI).

2. Estão em foco a autoridade absoluta de Cristo e seu governo ativo sobre a igreja, na qualidade de Senhor.

3. Nutrição e poder transmissor da vida são atribuídos ao Cabeça, o qual sustenta o corpo.

4. A vida sem o Cabeça é simplesmente impossível.

5. *Há união*, harmonia e amor entre o Cabeça e o corpo, em que cada qual cuida do outro, tão vital é essa união. Essas são as idéias aqui incluídas. Na epístola aos Efésios, a união da igreja é vista como prefiguração da unidade universal que será produzida, tendo Cristo como Cabeça de tudo, e não apenas da igreja. (Ver Col. 1:10, acerca do «mistério da vontade de Deus»). A igreja atualmente está vinculada a Cristo, em harmonia com ele, tal como um corpo está vinculado à sua cabeça.

6. Cristo pertence a nós, e nós a ele. Assim sendo, nossos destinos estão ligados para sempre, tal como se dá no caso de um corpo e sua respectiva cabeça.

7. A exaltação do corpo também faz parte da metáfora, pois os grandes poderes angelicais, por mais elevados que sejam, não são o corpo de Cristo, o qual é o Cabeça de todos.

8. A participação na «mesma natureza» é outro fator envolvido nessa metáfora, tal como um corpo deve ter a mesma natureza que sua cabeça. Assim também nós compartilhamos da própria essência de Cristo (ver Rom. 8:29 e II Cor. 3:18).

Cabeça da Igreja triunfante!
Alegremente te adoramos;
Até que tu apareças,
Teus membros, aqui,
Cantar-te-ão na glória!
(Charles Wesley).

(Quanto a outros trechos onde o conceito de Cristo como «Cabeça da igreja» também pode ser visto, ver Efé. 1:22,23; 4:15; 5:23 e Col. 2:19. Quanto a outras passagens onde a igreja é retratada como o «corpo de Cristo», ver Efé. 1:23; Rom. 1:4 e I Cor. 12:12-27. Notas expositivas completas sobre a igreja como «corpo» e sobre Cristo como o «Cabeça», são oferecidas em Efé. 1:22,23 no NTI).

Devemos ter cautela com aquelas denominações evangélicas, organizações religiosas ou indivíduos que exaltam de tal modo a si mesmos, à sua autoridade ou às suas doutrinas, que chegam a diminuir o conceito de Cristo como Cabeça de tudo, tanto no tocante à igreja como no que toca a Cristo no que concerne ao universo.

«...uma figura de amor, que desce do alto para baixo, que se agarra e que movimenta o que é corpóreo, elevando-o anelantemente de baixo para cima, — cuja obra consiste em transformar constantemente a natureza inferior àquela por que anseia, de tal modo que, finalmente, compartilha da natureza mais elevada que é desejada». (*Schubert*, referindo-se a Efé. 1:22).

A significação cósmica de Cristo (o logos) se estende aos homens, sendo aplicada a eles. — Os gnósticos reconheciam essa significação em pequena medida, mas tinham perdido Cristo entre os «aeons». Paulo mostra aqui que, na realidade, só há um Senhor, até onde nos diz respeito. (Ver Rom. 1:4,7 sobre o «senhorio de Cristo»). Em relação à posição de Cristo como cabeça, devemos pensar também na «nova criação». Portanto, ele é o criador tanto do mundo físico como do mundo espiritual.

Cabeça da Igreja. Em Col. 1:18, vemos a oitava superioridade de Cristo do livro de Colossenses. Cristo é o cabeça da igreja, e isso com exclusividade, pois não pode haver outro cabeça. Aqueles que adoravam os mediadores angelicais roubavam de Cristo sua posição de cabeça conforme se vê em Col. 2:18,19. A definição básica de um crente é alguém que tem a Cristo como *Cabeça*, isto é, que aceita o senhorio de Cristo. (Ver as notas expositivas completas sobre esse tema, em Rom. 1:4 no NTI). Um crente pode ter pensamentos e doutrinas errôneos; mas acerca de uma coisa ele terá plena certeza, a saber, que Cristo é seu Senhor. Outrossim, não há tal coisa como um crente que tenha Cristo como Salvador, mas não como Senhor. Isso fica perfeitamente claro em Rom. 10:9,10, onde a fé evangélica e a invocação do nome do *Senhor* aparecem como confissão daquele que é tanto o Salvador como o Senhor. A alma deve ser-lhe «entregue», pois a essência mesma da fé é a outorga da alma aos cuidados do Senhor. (Ver notas expositivas completas sobre a *fé*, em Heb. 11:1 no NTI). Tendo mostrado como o universo inteiro está relacionado com o Cristo exaltado, tanto o preexistente como o eterno e como o atual glorificado, Paulo mostra agora, particularmente, como a igreja está relacionada com Cristo (ver Col. 1:18-22). Essa mesma grandeza de Cristo, que precisa ser reconhecida pela igreja, sem o que ninguém pode ser um crente autêntico, também foi demonstrada pelo ministério apostólico (ver Col. 1:24-25).

A cabeça está vitalmente ligada ao corpo, embora seja superior a este último, sendo seu comandante e guia. Renegar à cabeça é condenar o corpo *à morte;* e nenhum corpo pode viver sem sua cabeça. Atualmente não temos problema com qualquer movimento herético, como o que assediava a igreja de Colossos; mas ainda há muitos cristãos que supõem que podem viver espiritualmente sem o Cabeça, que não aceitam o senhorio de Cristo. Esses não são cristãos verdadeiros, mas são ramos cortados e lançados no refugo, estando mortos e ressecados.

Uma definição do cristão

O que é ser cristão? O cristão é aquele que tem ao Senhor Jesus como seu *cabeça*, isto é, que não dá prioridade a ninguém acima de Cristo. A questão de «reter a Cristo como cabeça», idéia essa que figura em Col. 2:19, aparece dentro do contexto do combate de Paulo contra as noções falsas do gnosticismo, o qual postulava muitos deuses e muitos senhores, cada qual com sua província de governo; e, para os gnósticos, Cristo seria apenas um desses deuses ou senhores. Ora, esse conceito errôneo reduzia a importância e a grandeza de Cristo, onde o Senhor Jesus não aparecia realmente como Cabeça. Aquele que reputa a Cristo como Cabeça, reconhece sua autoridade absoluta sobre a alma, e assim exerce fé, que consiste da entrega da alma às mãos de Cristo. Ora, se um homem exerce essa fé, tendo a Cristo como Cabeça, como o grande objeto de sua fé, então o Espírito de Deus o converte, e ele entra no primeiro passo da regeneração. Tal homem pertence a Cristo, é um crente.

Por outro lado, pode não ser um crente uma pessoa que proclama em altas vozes a divindade de Cristo, mas a quem não entregou definitivamente a própria alma. E isso nos permite perceber, uma vez mais, que os «credos» não nos salvam. Deve haver real conversão; e existem muitos convertidos autênticos que ainda se encontram em estado de confusão mental acerca de questões doutrinárias.

Vinculação entre a cabeça e o corpo. Schubert (em Col. 2:14), comenta a esse respeito, como segue:

CABELEIRA FRISADA — CABELOS

«...temos aqui uma figura simbólica de amor, que desce do alto até nós, conquistando e movimentando o que é corpóreo, levando-o a uma longa elevação, debaixo para cima, numa obra que transforma constantemente a natureza inferior do objeto, a ponto deste último vir a compartilhar, finalmente, da natureza daquilo que o eleva». Cristo Jesus é, «...ao mesmo tempo, membro e governante do corpo». (Gerlach em Col. 2:19).

CABELEIRA FRISADA

No grego, *plégma*, derivada de *pléko*, «trançar». Vocábulo que aparece somente em I Tim. 2:9. Sob a forma *enpléko*, figura em II Ped. 2:20; I Ped. 3:3. O trançado dos cabelos era uma prática comum feminina entre os romanos e outros povos do período neotestamentário, envolvendo penteados elaborados, algumas vezes com mistura de elementos decorativos como finas argolas de ouro, pérolas e pedras preciosas. A denúncia contra essa prática, nas páginas do Novo Testamento, deve-se aos exageros que a prática envolvia, e também porque as mulheres que apreciavam o costume geralmente mostravam-se por demais preocupadas com a sua aparência pessoal atrativa, fisicamente falando, presumivelmente com uma negligência paralela às qualidades espirituais. Quanto a outras idéias sobre os versículos em questão, ver as notas no NTI. (NTI Z)

CABELOS

No hebraico, temos duas palavras; no grego, também duas, a saber:

1. *Sear*, «cabelo». Palavra que figura por vinte e quatro vezes. Por exemplo: Lev. 13:3,4,10,20,21,25, 26;30—32,36,37; Núm. 6:5; Juí. 16:22; Eze. 16:7.

2. *Saarah*, «cabelo». Palavra que aparece por sete vezes: Juí. 20:16; I Sam. 14:45; II Sam. 14:11; I Reis 1:52; Jó 4:15; Sal. 40:12; 69:4.

3. *Thríks*, «cabelo». Palavra grega que ocorre por catorze vezes: Mat. 3:4; 5:36; 10:30; Mar. 1:6; Luc. 7:38,44; 12:7; 21:18; João 11:2; 12:3; Atos 27:34; I Ped. 3:3; Apo. 1:14; 9:8.

4. *Kóme*, «cabeleira». Palavra grega usada por vinte e sete vezes: Algumas referências são: Mat. 9:35; 10:11; Mar. 6:6,36, Luc. 5:17; João 11:1, Atos 8:25.

Os cabelos são um assunto importante na Bíblia, e também na experiência humana. As mulheres estão sempre procurando ajeitar melhor os cabelos, para melhorar sua aparência, e a maioria dos homens preferiria que as mulheres deixassem seus cabelos soltos e longos. Quase todos os animais têm pêlos que podem ser chamados por diferentes nomes, como lã ou penugem. O homem utiliza-se do pêlo dos animais de muitas maneiras, tecendo-os ou não, para a fabricação de tecidos ou para rechear travesseiros ou colchões (Mar. 1:6; I Sam. 19:13).

Costumes Humanos:

1. *Entre os Egípcios*. Comentando sobre o assunto, Heródoto afirmou que os homens egípcios «só deixavam crescer o cabelo e a barba quando de luto. e que, em todas as outras ocasiões, raspavam-nos». Isso concorda com o trecho de Gênesis 41:14, onde vemos que José «barbeou-se» quando saiu da prisão para apresentar-se diante de Faraó. Parece que os motivos dos egípcios eram alguma mania de higiene exagerada. Lemos que os sacerdotes egípcios mostravam-se fanáticos quanto a isso, raspando todo o pêlo do corpo a cada três dias. Até a cabeça das crianças era raspada, sendo deixados cachos ao redor da mesma, como decoração. Entretanto, as mulheres egípcias nunca raspavam os cabelos, nem mesmo quando de luto. Pelo menos os egípcios davam seu voto ao reconhecimento universal da beleza da cabeleira feminina.

2. *Entre os Assírios e Babilônios*. As esculturas e as gravuras que os arqueólogos têm achado mostram que os assírios e babilônios usavam cabelos longos, homens e mulheres. Heródoto também diz que esses povos usavam cabelos longos. Parece que eles usavam perucas para aumentar o volume dos cabelos.

3. *Entre os Gregos e Romanos*. Desde os tempos mais remotos os gregos, tanto homens quanto mulheres, usavam seus cabelos longos, exceto quando se lamentavam pelos mortos, quando os cabelos aparados eram um sinal de luto. Algumas vezes, os cabelos eram enrolados, formando um nó, ou então seguros com um espécie de alfinete grande. Os escravos com freqüência usavam cabelos curtos e um cidadão ateniense livre jamais haveria de imitar os escravos, usando cabelos curtos. As mulheres gregas usavam cabelos longos, embelezando-os com vários penteados e enfeites, incluindo jóias e alfinetes de cabelo de muitos tipos. Esses alfinetes eram feitos de ouro, de prata, de bronze, de marfim e até de pedras preciosas. Eram usados artifícios para tingir os cabelos, quando as damas se cansavam de ver seus cabelos da mesma cor todos os dias. Entre os romanos, havia paralelos desse costume. Os homens romanos, tal como os gregos, nos tempos antigos usavam cabelos longos. Ter cabelos curtos era identificar-se com os escravos, que os usavam curtos. Porém, por volta de 300 A.C., esse costume sofreu mutações, quando apareceram os primeiros barbeiros, na Sicília. Cipião teria sido o primeiro cidadão romano a barbear-se todos os dias. As barbas ficavam em moda e saíam de moda. Por volta do século II D.C., o costume era cortar os cabelos bem curtos, segundo faziam os atletas e os filósofos estóicos. Se atentarmos ao que Paulo diz, no décimo primeiro capítulo da sua primeira epístola aos Coríntios, é quase certo que tanto os gregos quanto os romanos dos seus dias costumavam usar os cabelos curtos, no caso de homens; pois, de outra sorte, suas declarações ali não fariam sentido. Ver Rom. 11:14. Para Paulo, a própria natureza ensina que os homens deveriam usar cabelos curtos, e que as mulheres deveriam usar cabelos longos. Essa declaração seria impossível de compreender se, em sua época, os costumes fossem consideravelmente diferentes disso.

4. *Entre os Hebreus*. Os homens hebreus tinham grande respeito pela barba (que vide), imaginando toda a espécie de virtude para a mesma. Mas a calvície chegava a ser motivo de zombarias (II Reis 2:23). Os jovens de ambos os sexos usavam longos cabelos soltos (II Sam. 14:26; Can. 5:11). Os nazireus continuavam deixando seus cabelos longos (Núm. 6:5). Mas parece que outros homens hebreus, quando atingiam a idade da responsabilidade, talvez aos trinta anos, costumassem cortar seus cabelos. Naturalmente, temos o relato sobre Absalão, que continuou usando cabelos longos. E, se ele assim fazia, é razoável presumir que outros também o fizessem, mesmo que isso não fosse um regral geral (II Sam. 14:26). Na época de Paulo, de acordo com I Coríntios 11:14, o uso de cabelos curtos, por parte dos homens judeus, deve ter sido um costume universal, pois, de outra maneira, o que ele diz ali não teria o menor sentido. Mas, as mulheres judias, tal como as mulheres de outras culturas, muito se esforçavam em embelezar seus cabelos (Isa. 3:24). Esse tipo de atividade ocorria até mesmo entre os cristãos, e Paulo

CABELOS — CABRA

achou por bem censurar o exagero (I Tim. 2:9), no que foi secundado por Pedro (I Ped. 3:3). Josefo informa-nos que até mesmo homens davam-se ao trabalho de embelezar seus cabelos (*Anti.* iv.9,4). O trecho de Ezequiel 44:20 parece dar a entender que, de vez em quando, os homens aparavam seus cabelos com uma navalha. Surgiram certos profissionais que cuidavam dos cabelos das pessoas, como os barbeiros e as cabeleireiras (Eze. 5:1).

5. *Na Igreja Cristã Primitiva.* Paulo é quem nos fornece as linhas mestras, quanto a esse particular. As mulheres crentes devem usar cabelos longos, e os homens crentes, cabelos curtos (I Cor. 11). Paulo apelou para a natureza, como se esta nos desse este tipo de instrução, não parecendo depender dos costumes sociais como diretrizes. Comentei extensamente sobre a questão, no NTI, em diversos versículos daquele capítulo de I Coríntios. Visto que o costume social da época ditava que as mulheres honestas deviam usar cabelos longos, somente as prostitutas, ou, talvez, as que se lamentassem por seus mortos, contradiziam a regra geral. Nesse trecho paulino, não há como justificar cabelos curtos para as mulheres crentes. Se insistirmos que é correto que as mulheres cortem seus cabelos, então teremos de afirmar que o que Paulo ensinou sofria a influência dos costumes sociais de sua época, pelo que não seria aplicável aos nossos dias, embora tornasse a ser aplicável em alguma época futura. Outro tanto deve ser dito a respeito do uso do véu, pelas mulheres crentes. Contudo, que cada crente resolva a questão segundo a formação de sua consciência. Conheço um pregador que dividiu uma igreja local por esse motivo. Todavia, a questão não tem tanta importância assim, ainda que consideremos que essa instrução paulina seja obrigatória para todos os crentes.

6. *Usos Figurados.* Os cabelos simbolizam a virilidade e a fertilidade. Em um sonho ou visão, os cabelos podem ter esse significado. Além disso, os cabelos são um símbolo natural da beleza feminina. No entanto, os cabelos de uma pessoa podem ser cortados sem que ela sofra muito com isso. Isso posto, os cabelos também simbolizam aquilo que tem pouco valor para uma pessoa (I Sam. 14:45; I Reis 1:52; Mat. 10:30). Podemos entender muitas coisas, através das metáforas que usam os cabelos (Sal. 40:12; 69:4), como uma distância minúscula (Juí. 20:16); os cabelos grisalhos dão a idéia de honra ou autoridade (Pro. 16:31; Apo. 1:14), ou então decadência física e desintegração (Osé. 7:9). Cobrir a barba ou o rosto, de baixo até ac nariz, é sinal de lamentação (Lev. 13:45), ou então de tribulação e vergonha (Miq. 3:7; Eze. 24:17). O fato de que nossos cabelos estão todos contados na mente divina ilustra o valor da alma humana para o nosso Deus (Mat. 10:30). Quando os cabelos ficam eriçados, isso significa medo (o que, realmente, pode suceder!) (Jó 4:15). O ato de arrancar os cabelos significa consternação e tristeza (Isa. 15:2). A unção dos cabelos é sinal de alegria ou respeito, quando esse ato é realizado em favor de outras pessoas (Sal. 23:5; Luc. 7:38,44).

7. *Significação Religiosa dos Cabelos.* Os povos primitivos modificavam o estilo de seu penteado em ocasiões especiais, como no período de lamentação pelos mortos, para indicar arrependimento por erros praticados, etc. Os cabelos longos representam a força e a vitalidade físicas, como no caso de Sansão (Juí. 16:17), bem como a dedicação a Deus, como através de um voto (Juí. 13:5). Os cabelos também simbolizam as provisões de um voto feito a Deus e a sua *perpetuidade*, enquanto os cabelos permanecessem longos. Raspar os cabelos, por sua vez, indica humilhação, punição, desgraça. As ordens monásticas cristãs cortam os cabelos em sinal de iniciação. Os ascetas e eremitas hindus encontram alguma significação no arranjo ou desarranjo dos cabelos, como símbolo de seu ascetismo. Entre os hindus, algumas vezes eles cortam os cabelos e oferecem-nos a alguma divindade, como um sacrifício ou símbolo do sacrifício do corpo inteiro, na busca pelas realidades espirituais. Na Grécia antiga, os cabelos eram oferecidos pelos jovens, aos deuses, em seus ritos de iniciação. (AM E FO NTI UN)

CABET, ETIENNE
Ver o artigo sobre a **Utopia**, ponto sétimo.

CABIR Ver **Kabir**.

CABOM
O termo hebraico tem sido interpretado de várias maneiras, como «círculo», «montanhosa» ou «envolta». Era o nome de uma cidade na Sefelá, perto de Laquis (Jos. 15:40). Sua associação com Macbena (ver I Crô. 2:49), alicerça-se sobre a suposição de que ambas essas palavras procedem da mesma raiz hebraica.

CABRA
Há duas palavras hebraicas envolvidas:
1. *Ez,* «cabra». Palavra usada por sessenta vezes. Por exemplo: Gên. 27:9,16; Êxo. 12:5; 25:4; Lev. 1:10; 3:12; 4:23,28; Núm. 7:16; 15:24; Deu. 14:4; I Sam. 19:13,16; Pro. 27:27; Can. 4:1; Eze. 43:22; 45:23.

2. *Sair,* «peludo». Aparece por vinte e três vezes. Por exemplo: Lev. 4:24; 9:15; 10:16; 16:7-10,15,18, 20-22,26,27; Núm. 28:22; 29:22,28,31,34,38; Eze. 43:25.

Com freqüência, as Escrituras Sagradas associam a cabra à ovelha (Mat. 24:32,33), embora a cabra fosse considerada menos valiosa e útil. No entanto, ambas as espécies eram usadas nos sacrifícios, e a carne e o leite de ambas eram usados pelos israelitas (Lev. 3:12; 4:24; 9:15; 10:16; Núm. 15:27; 28:22). Uma das primeiras referências a esse animal, nas páginas da Bíblia (Gên. 37:31), refere-se a um desses animais que foi morto para manchar de sangue a túnica multicolorida de José, para dar a impressão de que ele fora morto por alguma fera. Isso mostra-nos que, desde os tempos mais remotos, esse animal era usado na Palestina. Muitos estudiosos supõem que a cabra foi o primeiro animal ruminante a ser domesticado. Há antepassados ainda selvagens, como a cabra de Bezoar ou a cabra cretense, *Capra aegagrus,* que tem os pêlos cor marrom avermelhado durante o verão e marrom cinza, durante o inverno. Vive desde a Índia até à ilha de Creta, embora atualmente esteja grandemente reduzida em números, em contraste com os tempos antigos. As cabras são conhecidas por seus passos firmes, mesmo sobre terreno muito acidentado. Geralmente percorrem largas áreas, buscando pasto.

Há evidências da domesticação da cabra desde a era neolítica, e seus ossos têm sido datados, pelo método do carbono, de seis a sete mil anos atrás. Houve certa variedade de cabras desde o início, mas, nos tempos modernos, o número das variedades ainda é maior. Objetos de arte antigos, encontrados no Egito, retratam a cabra.

CABRA MONTÊS — CAÇA

Usos. Nos tempos bíblicos usava-se para consumo humano a carne e o leite de cabra (Juí. 6:19). Contudo, era uma carne menos apreciada que a da ovelha ou a da vaca (Luc. 15:29 ss). As peles de cabras eram usadas para o fabrico de vestes, de tendas, de cortinas, de odres e de muitos itens de uso diário. O pêlo da cabra era torcido e tecido. Além disso, naturalmente, o sistema de sacrifícios levíticos utilizava a cabra, conforme já notamos antes.

Destruidores. Alguns afirmam que, depois do homem, a cabra é o maior destruidor de terras da história. Na área do mar Mediterrâneo, as cabras chegam a subir em árvores baixas para comer seus brotos e raminhos. Isso é ilustrado em gravuras da mais remota antiguidade. A cabra destrói tôdo tipo de vegetação. Essa destruição tem sido tão intensa, em certos lugares, que, em resultado, as cabras têm morrido de inanição.

Usos Figurados. No oitavo capítulo de Daniel, o bode representa o império grego (vs. 21). Em Mateus 25:32,33, ovelhas e bodes representam, respectivamente, os justos e os injustos. Nessa conexão, o bode talvez seja usado devido ao seu mau cheiro, teimosia e maus hábitos; mas, principalmente, porque era um animal considerado relativamente inútil e destruidor.

CABRA MONTÊS

No hebraico, **aggo**, palavra que aparece somente em Deu. 14:5. A maioria dos eruditos confessa que o sentido da palavra é desconhecido. Há também uma outra palavra hebraica, *yeelim*, usada em I Sam. 24:2; Jó 39:1 e Sal. 104:18, e que a nossa versão portuguesa traduz por «cabras monteses» nas duas primeiras dessas referências, e por «cabras montesinhas» na terceira delas.

É essencial distinguir entre essas duas espécies relacionadas, mas confundidas uma com a outra, conforme se vê também em nossa versão portuguesa. O íbex da Núbia (*Capra nubiana*) até hoje pode ser encontrado na porção oeste da Palestina. Em sentido estrito, a cabra montês é a *Capra aegagrus*, o principal antepassado selvático da cabra domesticada, ao passo que o íbex nunca foi domesticado. A cabra montês, em certo período, vivia até o sul da Palestina, onde têm sido encontrados restos e ossadas da mesma, em depósitos da idade da Pedra, embora seja improvável que os israelitas tivessem-na conhecido. A maioria dos estudiosos opina que a cabra montês era o *yeel*, que identificamos acima com o íbex. Quanto ao aqqo, temos que contentar-nos com uma espécie desconhecida, embora o trecho de Deu. 14:5 mostre-nos que era um dos animais que os israelitas podiam consumir, pois era um animal limpo.

CABRIS

No livro de Judite (6:15,16; 8:10 e 10:6), um dos livros apócrifos do Antigo Testamento, ele aparece como filho de Gotoniel, um ancião, um dos três governantes de Betúlia, a quem Judite apelou, solicitando ajuda.

CABUL

A palavra, no hebraico, significa «distrito». 1. Era o nome de uma cidade na fronteira leste de Aser (Jos. 19:27), talvez a Chabolo que aparece em Josefo, *Vida*, xliii.44. A moderna Kabul, nas colinas, cerca de catorze quilômetros e meio de Ese de Acre, é o local moderno. Porém, esse lugar nada tem a ver com a Kabura, da lista de Ramisés III, que ocupa o vigésimo terceiro lugar. Esse lugar fica um tanto mais ao sul. 2. Um distrito ao norte da Galiléia, onde havia cerca de vinte cidades, o qual Salomão cedeu a Hirão (I Reis 9:13), em pagamento parcial por havê-lo ajudado a construir o templo de Jerusalém. Hirão, entretanto, não ficou satisfeito com o pagamento, e chamou a região de *terra de Cabul*, que, provavelmente, significa, «de nada vale». É provável que Hirão, sendo um fenício, — desejava uma localização à beira-mar. Além disso, as cidades poderiam estar em mau estado, ou então faziam parte de uma região desértica. Hirão aparentemente devolveu as cidades a Salomão, e ele as reedificou. (II Crô. 8:2).

CABZEEL

No hebraico, «Deus recolhe». Uma cidade ao sul de Judá, lugar onde nasceu Benaia (Jos. 15:21; II Sam. 23:20; I Crô. 11:22). Em Neemias 11:25, esse nome aparece com a forma de Jecabzeel. Benaia (que vide) foi um dos principais oficiais do governo israelita, na época de Davi e de Salomão. O lugar foi reocupado após o exílio babilônico. O local tem sido identificado com a moderna Kirbet Horah.

CAÇA

No hebraico, **tsayid**, «caça». Esse vocábulo aparece por dezenove vezes com esse sentido. Por exemplo: Gên. 25:28; 27:5,7,19,25,31,33. Uma variante, *tsedah*, que tem o mesmo significado, aparece por nove vezes, como por exemplo, em Gên. 27:3; Êxo. 12:39; Jos. 1:11; 9:11; I Sam. 22:10.

Qualquer tipo de caça é referido pelas palavras hebraicas acima; embora, usualmente, esteja em foco alguma caça da família do veado. Os hebreus não caçavam por puro esporte, conforme faziam outros povos do Oriente Próximo e Médio. Antes, abatiam predadores e animais para consumo. Contudo, houve caçadores bem conhecidos, como Ismael (Gên. 21:20) e Esaú (Gên. 25:27). Os israelitas caçavam vários tipos de aves, como a perdiz, e de quadrúpedes, como a gazela, a corça e o veado.

Por raras vezes o Antigo Testamento menciona essa atividade da caça. O Novo Testamento nunca a menciona. As comunidades nômades e rurais, em alguns lugares, dependiam (e continuam dependendo) muito da caça, para obter alimentos. Porém, o povo de Israel era uma nação essencialmente agrícola, que provia para suas necessidades alimentares mediante o cultivo de cereais e legumes ou mediante a criação de animais domésticos. O termo «caçador» foi aplicado a Ninrode, o fundador de Babel e de outras cidades do vale da Mesopotâmia (Gên. 10:9). Os babilônios caçaram por mero esporte, capturando até mesmo leões, montados em cavalos e usando lanças. Muitos leões assim capturados tornavam-se animais de estimação ou eram usados para -echear zoológicos particulares. As referências do Antigo Testamento vinculadas à matança de animais, giram mais em torno da idéia de proteção dos rebanhos (Juí. 14:5,6; I Sam. 17:34-36), nada tendo a ver com a caça como um esporte. Visto que certos animais selvagens podiam ser consumidos, de acordo com as leis dietéticas de Israel, é possível que alguma caça fosse efetuada com essa finalidade (Lev. 17:13; Deu. 14:5).

As armas empregadas na caça eram o arco e a flecha (Gên. 27:3), as redes para apanhar aves e peixes (Pro. 1:71; Ecl. 9:12), as armadilhas (Amós 3:5), e os fossos (Sal. 35:17).

CACHORRO — CACHORRO DE LEÃO

A Questão Moral Envolvida na Caça. Os babilônios, os egípcios e os assírios caçavam por puro esporte. Muitas descobertas arqueológicas confirmam isso. No mundo moderno, a caça, quando é permitida, só cobre certos períodos do ano, e está sujeita a vários regulamentos e proibições. Os homens podem ter ótimas residências, dois automóveis, dinheiro na poupança, mas eles gostam de sair à caça, ou para conseguir alimentos diferentes, ou por puro esporte, quase sempre por esta última razão. A caça pode ser justificada sobre bases morais? Ver o artigo sobre os *Animais.* Uma das razões que justificam a caça é quando uma dada região não consegue sustentar um maior número de animais selvagens do que aquele que é mantido mediante a caça e a captura, por não haver alimento necessário para tantos. Todavia, é errado matar, até mesmo animais, por simples diversão. Ensinei meus três filhos homens a não infligirem qualquer dor desnecessária, mesmo entre os animais irracionais.

CACHORRO

No hebraico, **kehleb**, que vem de um termo que significa «uivar». No hebraico temos *kúon* e *kunárion*, «cão» e «cãozinho», respectivamente. O termo hebraico é usado por trinta e uma vezes, de Êxo. 11:7 a Jer. 15:3. *Kúon* é termo grego usado por cinco vezes: Mat. 7:5; Luc. 16:21; Fil. 3:2; II Ped. 2:22 (citando Pro. 26:11) e Apo. 22:15. *Kunárion* é usado por quatro vezes: Mat. 15:26,27; Mar. 7:27,28.

Esse animal era considerado totalmente impuro para os hebreus, o que significa que, em Israel, ninguém ficava acordado à noite porque o cão do vizinho estava latindo. Na Palestina e no Egito, o cão era animal consumidor de carniça, percorrendo as aldeias e povoados brigando e rosnando por causa de qualquer alimento que encontrasse. Um cão, embora prefira a carne, come qualquer tipo de refugo, pelo que está sujeito a muitas doenças, algumas das quais ele pode transmitir ao homem. O trecho de II Reis 9 registra como o cadáver de Jezabel foi devorado pelos cães. Na história temos provas de que, algumas vezes, os cadáveres eram lançados aos cães, para serem consumidos por eles, nas culturas antigas. No Egito, os cães eram muito apreciados. Parece evidente que o cão foi o primeiro animal a ser domesticado no Egito, onde era usado de muitos modos pelos caçadores, criadores, etc., servindo como vigias e companheiros do homem. Israel, portanto, estava bem familiarizado com o cão; mas, uma vez que escaparam do Egito, os israelitas não quiseram continuar a amizade com os cães. Mas, visto que havia cães por toda a parte, os israelitas não conseguiam livrar-se deles. Restos de corpos de cães têm sido encontrados nas camadas mais inferiores de Jericó. A arqueologia tem encontrado certa variedade do greyhound, ou cão de corrida, que já seria domesticado desde 3000 A.C. Sabemos que em toda a Mesopotâmia, os cães eram muito estimados. Relevos provenientes da Babilônia retratam cães de diferentes raças. Os historiadores informam-nos que havia matilhas de cães que viviam perto das cidades, como se fossem lobos; de fato, cães selvagens viviam nas proximidades das cidades. Isso significa que havia muitos cães semi-selvagens, vivendo perto das cidades, constituindo um perigo às pessoas. Naturalmente, também havia cães que eram criados como bichos de estimação, os quais formavam uma elite entre os cães. Em Jó 30:1 há alusão ao cão que guardava as ovelhas. Isso significa que ou esse livro foi escrito antes do aparecimento do livro de Levítico, ou então que Jó não era israelita. O trecho de Isaías 56:10, ao falar sobre os cães mudos, que não sabem ladrar, sugere a existência de cães que guardavam os rebanhos, protegendo-os dos ataques dos animais ferozes. Por conseguinte, é possível que alguns israelitas criassem cães com propósitos especiais, como esse.

As cidades do Oriente Próximo e Médio até hoje são assoladas por imensas matilhas de cães que passam a noite uivando, algo que é aludido em Salmos 59:6,14. Os visitantes dos países orientais dizem-nos que essa condição é um descalabro. Ali, os cães continuam consumidores de carniça. Os árabes evitam cães soltos pelas ruas, por serem animais imundos. Ver o artigo sobre *Limpo e Imundo.*

Usos Figurados:

1. **Pessoas cruéis são chamadas «cães»** (Sal. 22:16,20; Jer. 15:3). Estão em pauta os cães semi-selvagens que havia nas proximidades das cidades antigas, mais semelhantes aos lobos, em seus hábitos.

2. Expressões como «cão», «cabeça de cão» e «cão morto» eram usadas para indicar opróbrio ou humilhação, que as pessoas usavam contra outras ou contra si mesmas (I Sam. 24:14; II Sam. 3:8; 9:8; II Reis 8:13).

3. Os gentios, como um povo cerimonialmente impuro que eram, são chamados «cães» (Mat. 15:26,27). Temos nessa referência a história da mulher siro-fenícia. O relato mostra-nos que até mesmo pessoas humildes, consideradas impuras ou imundas, podem participar dos benefícios do evangelho.

4. Os *falsos apóstolos* foram chamados «cães» por causa de sua impureza espiritual e ganância pelo dinheiro (Fil. 3:2).

5. Aqueles que são excluídos do reino dos céus são chamados «cães» (Apo. 22:15), o que é uma referência à sua vileza espiritual, a razão mesma da exclusão deles.

6. O próprio *Satanás* é chamado «cão», por causa de sua vileza e malignidade (Sal. 22:20).

7. *O Cão nos Sonhos e nas Visões.* a. Uma pessoa fiel, em quem se pode confiar, pode ser representada como um cão. b. Uma pessoa pode apresentar-se em um sonho mediante a imagem desse animal, talvez reprendendo os seus hábitos sexuais. c. Um sonho com um cão que uma pessoa possuiu pode representar aquele período de sua vida, nada tendo de específico com o próprio cão. d. Uma caçadora, acompanhada de um cão, pode representar a Ânima, um dos arquétipos de Jung. A Ânima é a força feminina em um homem. e. Um cão pode representar apetites sexuais descontrolados, ou então os aspectos não civilizados da personalidade de uma pessoa. (CHE S UN Z)

CACHORRO DE LEÃO

No hebraico precisamos considerar três palavras:

1. *Gor*, «leãozinho». Palavra que ocorre por duas vezes: Jer. 51:38 e Naum 2:12.

2. *Gur*, «leãozinho». Palavra que aparece por sete vezes: Gên. 49:9; Deu. 32:22; Eze. 19:2,3,5; Naum 2:11; Lam. 4:3.

3. *Ben*, «filho». Palavra extremamente comum, mas que, nesse sentido, ocorre somente em Jó 4:11 e 28:8.

Está em vista um filhote de leão, embora as Escrituras usem essas palavras (*gor* e *gur*) mais no sentido figurado do que no sentido literal. O caso da palavra *ben* será comentado mais abaixo. Elifaz, no

CACO — CADEIA, CADEIAS

livro de Jó, menciona os «leõezinhos» que teriam sido dispersos, por faltar presa ao leão velho (Jó 4:11). Interessante é observar que, quanto a *gor*, nossa versão portuguesa a traduz por «filhos da leoa», em Jó 4:11, mas por «leãozinho», em Jó 28:8.

A Babilônia haveria de rugir como os leõezinhos, por ocasião de sua destruição (Jer. 51:38), e Nínive haveria de ficar desolada, onde os leões teriam capacidade de despedaçar presas suficientes para seus filhotes que viviam em covis (Naum 2:11,12). Jacó profetizou: «Judá é leãozinho» (Gên. 49:9). Isso equivale ao cumprimento feito por Moisés no caso de Dã (Deu. 33:22); e Ezequiel reverberou isso, dizendo que os príncipes de Israel eram leõezinhos apanhados nas redes e nas armadilhas (Eze. 19:2,3,5). Ver sobre *Leão*.

CACO

No hebraico, **cheres**, que significa «caco» em cinco oportunidades: Jó 2:8; Sal. 22:15; Pro. 26:23 e Isa. 45:9. Trata-se de algum pedaço de vaso de barro quebrado. Em Jó 2:8, um caco é mencionado como um objeto que aquele homem de Deus usou para raspar suas borbulhas, talvez para coçar-se ou para fazer as borbulhas estourarem e deixarem escapar o pus, embora nada haja de científico nisso que dizemos. Pedaços maiores eram usados para transportar brasas acesas, para transportar pequenas quantidades de água, ou como pesos para segurar no lugar as tampas de jarras ou panelas. Às vezes, esses fragmentos eram usados como material de escrita, em cujo caso eram chamados *ostraca*. Foi encontrado um minúsculo trecho do Novo Testamento em um caco desses; mas, afora isso, as *ostraca* têm servido de importantes evidências arqueológicas. As famosas ostraca de Laquis estavam escritas com correspondência militar, entre aquela cidade e o seu posto avançado. As ostraca samaritanas aparentemente eram recibos do governo a respeito de taxas recebidas, sob a forma de produtos da terra; mas também podem ter sido recibos ordinários. Os cacos de cerâmica podem oferecer ajuda quando se trata de determinar a antiguidade de alguma coisa, às vezes melhor, que no caso de moedas antigas. Um dos usos práticos dos antigos é que eles transformavam os cacos em pó, para serem misturados com argamassa, para que a mistura fosse usada como uma espécie de material de revestimento à prova d'água, nas cisternas (que vide). Ver o artigo separado sobre as *Ostraca*. Ver também sobre *Olaria*.

Usos figurados. Os cacos de cerâmica podem significar qualquer coisa de pequeno valor, qualquer coisa desprezível (Isa. 45:9); ou alguma coisa muito seca (Sal. 22:5); ou uma amizade fingida (Pro. 26:23).

CADÁVER

No hebraico, **geviyyah**, «corpo». O termo aparece por catorze vezes. Mas, com o sentido de *cadáver*, somente em Naum 3:3 e Sal. 110:6. E também *peger*, «carcaça», palavra usada por vinte e duas vezes (por exemplo: II Crô. 20:24,25; Jer. 31:40; 33:5; 41:9; Amós 8:3).

No grego, *ptôma*, «carcaça». Esse vocábulo aparece por sete vezes: Mat. 14:12; 24:28; Mar. 6:29; 15:45; Apo. 11:8,9.

Em português, «cadáver» indica um corpo humano sem vida. Ver II Reis 19:35; Isa. 37:36. Um cadáver insepulto significava desgraça e opróbrio, entre os antigos (Jer. 16:4). Os gregos acreditavam que a alma não pode passar para o mundo dos espíritos enquanto não haja um sepultamento condigno do corpo morto. Ver o artigo sobre *Sepultamento, Costumes de*. Na antiguidade, usualmente o sepultamento se fazia, no máximo, vinte e quatro horas após a morte, pois, se não houvesse o início imediato do processo de embalsamamento, o clima muito quente precipitava sem tardança o processo de decomposição do cadáver. Ver Marc. 6:29; Mat. 27:57,60.

Lição Espiritual Dada pelos Cadáveres. Quão pouca coisa é mister para reduzir o corpo humano a uma massa inerte, inútil, que começa a decompor-se. No entanto, antes dessa redução, provocada pela morte, quantos cuidados conferimos aos nossos corpos físicos. Quão prontamente desaparece aquilo que tanto valorizamos! Algumas estrelas do cinema têm segurado seus corpos em milhões de dólares. Depois, quando envelhecem, algumas delas passam a ter uma vida miserável, no olvido popular. Os seres humanos precisam aprender que a *pessoa real* é a alma eterna. As pessoas que têm passado pela experiência de quase morte (que vide) afirmam que, quando da aproximação da morte, pouca atenção é dada ao corpo. Muitas vezes, as pessoas só têm uma correta perspectiva da vida quando já estão moribundas. Passamos a vida inteira pensando no corpo, a menos que, em algum ponto de nosso trajeto, mediante a conversão, venhamos a compreender o valor da vida espiritual. Infelizes e dignos de lástima são aqueles que pensam que o corpo humano é o próprio ser humano.

ÇADÊ

Décima oitava letra do alfabeto hebraico (vide), e que recebeu o valor numérico de noventa, nos tempos pós-bíblicos. Essa letra encabeça os versículos 137 a 144 do Salmo 119, e também dá início a cada verso ali constante.

CADEADO Ver **Trancar (Cadeado, Fechadura, Pino)**.

CADEIA, CADEIAS

No hebraico, **noser**, «cadeias», «laços». Palavra usada por onze vezes. Por exemplo: Sal. 116:16; Jer. 5:5; 27:2; 30:8; Naum 1:13. No grego encontramos duas palavras: *álusis*, «cadeia», palavra usada por dez vezes (Mar. 5:3,4; Luc. 8:29; Atos 12:6,7; 21:33; 28:20; Efé. 6:20; II Tim. 1:16; Apo. 20:1), e *desmós*, «algemas», palavra usada por dezoito vezes (Mat. 7:35; Luc. 8:29; 13:16; Atos 16:26; 20:23; 23:29; 26:29,31; Fil. 1:7,13,14,17; Col. 4:18; II Tim. 2:9; File. 10, 13; Heb. 11:36; Judas 6).

Tanto no Antigo quanto no Novo Testamento há usos literais e metafóricos dessas palavras. 1. Com o sentido literal de cadeias, correntes ou algemas, podemos ver Atos 28:20 e Luc. 8:29. 2. O trecho de Col. 2:19 alude aos músculos e juntas que unificam o corpo humano. 3. O jugo dos animais, em Naum 1:13. 4. *Vários usos metafóricos*: a. opressão, cativeiro, aprisionamento (Naum 1:13; Sal. 116:16; Fil. 1:7). b. Obrigações morais (Núm. 30:5). c. Em Colossenses 2:19, a idéia de que o corpo místico de Cristo assemelha-se a um organismo inteiro, com suportes e ligamentos. Os antigos evidentemente pensavam que os ligamentos tinham algo a ver com a transferência de nutrientes. d. As cadeias do pecado, que prendem os homens ao mal (Atos 8:23). e. Na comunidade cristã há o vínculo da paz, que une as pessoas. f. O escrito de dívida, referido em Col. 2:14, cujos efeitos nos eram contrários. g. As justas leis de Deus, que nos restringem do mal (Jer. 5:5). (FA HA S)

CADEIA (FIO) DE PRATA

Diz Eclesiastes 12:6: «...antes que se rompa o fio de prata, e se despedace o copo de ouro, e se quebre o cântaro junto à fonte, e se desfaça a roda junto ao poço».

O autor sagrado acumula uma série de expressões poéticas que indicam a morte física. O sétimo versículo fala sobre o pó que retorna à terra e sobre o espírito que retorna a Deus. A alusão ao romper do fio de prata, conforme tem sido demonstrado por estudos sobre a natureza da morte, é mais do que meramente poética. Sabe-se atualmente que a porção **não-material** é vinculada ao corpo físico por meio de uma espécie de filamento, com cerca de cinco centímetros de espessura, e que se assemelha a um campo de energia pulsante. Enquanto esse fio de prata não se rompe, o espírito, mesmo que saia do corpo, é capaz de retornar ao mesmo. Porém, se esse fio chegar a partir-se, então a morte torna-se permanente, e o espírito não mais pode retornar. Esse fio, segundo todas as aparências, é uma espécie de conector e comunicador de energias, entre as porções material e imaterial do corpo humano. Alguns têm chamado o fio de prata de cordão umbilical do espírito. Por ocasião da morte física, a comissão de recepção que vem acompanhar a pessoa à outra dimensão da existência, algumas vezes corta esse fio, o que nos leva a entender que a morte, na realidade, é uma espécie de nascimento em uma outra dimensão da existência. Também há outros aspectos da morte física que se assemelham a um nascimento. Ver sobre as *Experiências de Quase Morte*, quanto a uma completa descrição do que significa o processo da morte, o que inclui em quais sentidos a morte se assemelha a um nascimento. Esse fio de prata, algumas vezes, pode ser visto na experiência da *projeção da psique* (que vide); enquanto o mesmo não é partido, o espírito pode retornar ao corpo sem qualquer dano. Essa experiência é uma das mais convincentes experiências, do ponto de vista empírico, da existência e da sobrevivência em potencial da morte, ante a morte física. O fato de que as experiências de quase morte também exibem uma porção imaterial, que sai da porção material, quando então, às vezes, o fio de prata torna-se visível para aquele que passa pela experiência, é um outro fator que favorece uma prova empírica da existência e da sobrevivência da alma. Ver o artigo sobre a *alma*, que inclui as diversas provas de sua existência e sobrevivência. Ver também o artigo sobre — *Abordagem Científica à Crença na Alma e em sua Sobrevivência ante a Morte Física*. Os intérpretes do Antigo Testamento percebem vários sentidos no tocante ao fio de prata, julgando que se trata de uma menção à medula óssea da espinha dorsal. Não é impossível que tal coisa esteja em foco; mas também é perfeitamente possível que o autor sagrado tenha aludido ao misterioso fio de prata, conforme acabamos de explicar. É possível que ele tivesse consciência de sua existência mediante antigas narrativas de experiências de quase morte, bem como da projeção da psique. Na literatura antiga, há evidências sobre ambas essas coisas. (G I IB)

CADEIA DO SER

Uma expressão metafórica usada na filosofia e na teologia acerca da ordem, da unidade e da abrangência do mundo criado, concebidos como uma cadeia que se estende de modo a incluir todas as possibilidades da existência, desde Deus até a mais ínfima partícula de matéria inanimada. A unidade é um dos principais fatores dessa idéia. A idéia, até onde estamos informados, entrou pela primeira vez no vocabulário filosófico no *Timaeus* de Platão. Durante a renascença (que vide), a expressão era usada para indicar o arranjo hierárquico do universo. Embora Paulo não tenha usado a expressão, certamente ele conhecia o conceito, segundo se depreende do primeiro capítulo da epístola aos Efésios, onde ele liga a cadeia do ser ao senhorio de Cristo, o Logos, com quem, e por meio de quem, todas as coisas devem, finalmente, ser restauradas. Ver sobre a *Restauração*. (F NTI)

CADEIAS

No hebraico temos duas palavras muito parecidas: *aziqqim* (usada por duas vezes: Jer. 40:1,4); e *ziqqim* (usada por cinco vezes, conforme se vê em Sal. 149:8; Isa. 45:14; Naum 3:10). Ambas essas palavras têm o sentido de «algemas». O trecho de Jer. 40:1,4 refere-se às cadeias com que foram atados os cativos, quando da queda de Jerusalém. Ver também Sal. 149:8; Isa. 45:14; Naum 3:10 quanto a um uso similar. Um estudo sobre os monumentos assírios e egípcios revela que os prisioneiros usualmente eram amarrados com cordas, embora também fossem usadas cadeias de metal, isto é, algemas.

Usos Figurados. a. Em Jó 38:31 a cadeia referida é a constelação das Plêiades. b. Qualquer coisa que cativa ou prende, no sentido figurado (Judas 6). c. Um símbolo de opressão ou castigo (Lam. 3:7; Sal. 149:8; Eze. 7:23). d. O orgulho é como uma cadeia que mantém os homens debaixo de seu poder (Sal. 73:6). e. Satanás será preso pela cadeia divina (Apo. 20:1). f. A lei de Deus é uma cadeia moral e espiritual, uma obrigação e uma força restringidora (Pro. 1:9). g. Fazer uma cadeia é preparar-se para o cativeiro e a escravidão (Eze. 7:23). (G S LAN UN)

CADEIRA (ASSENTO)

Palavras Utilizadas e Detalhes

A idéia envolve duas palavras hebraicas e três palavras gregas, a saber:

1. *Kisse*, «trono», «cadeira». Termo hebraico usado por cento e trinta e duas vezes (por exemplo: Juí. 3:20; I Sam. 1:9; 4:13,18; I Reis 2:19; Est. 3:1; Pro. 9:14).

2. *Moshab*, «assento». Palavra hebraica usada por nove vezes com esse significado, embora não seja esse seu único sentido (por exemplo: I Sam. 20:18,25; Sal. 1:1; Eze. 8:3; 28:2).

3. *Kathédra*, «cadeira», «tamborete». Palavra grega usada por três vezes: Mat. 21:12; 23:2 e Mar. 11:15.

4. *Thrónos*, «trono». Palavra grega empregada por cerca de sessenta vezes, a grande maioria das quais no livro do Apocalipse, desde Mat. 5:34 até Apo. 22:1,3.

5. *Bēma*, «assento de julgamento». Palavra grega usada por doze vezes: Mat. 27:19; João 19:13; Atos 7:5; 12:21; 18:12,16,17; 25:6,10,17; Rom. 14:10 e II Cor. 5:10.

Nas páginas do Antigo Testamento, a palavra com freqüência alude a qualquer assento ocupado por uma pessoa importante, sem importar se rei, ministro ou sacerdote, conforme se vê, para exemplificar, em Juí. 3:20; I Sam. 1:9; 4:13,18; I Reis 2:19 e Est. 3:1.

Entre os judeus, assentos considerados especialmente importantes faziam parte dos móveis das sinagogas. Jesus repreendeu os líderes religiosos de seus dias porque preferiam «o primeiro lugar nos banquetes e as primeiras cadeiras nas sinagogas» (Mat. 23:6; cf. Mar. 12:39; Luc. 11:43; 20:46). Nas

CADEIRA DE MOISÉS — CADES

sinagogas da Palestina, os assentos mais atrás eram ocupados pelas crianças e por pessoas sem importância social. Quanto mais à frente estivesse um assento, tanto maior a importância da pessoa que o ocupava. Os assentos considerados mais honrosos eram aqueles dos anciões, que sentavam-se voltados de frente para a congregação. Pois o homem que se assentava em um desses assentos podia ser visto por todos os circunstantes, e sua importância não podia ser perdida de vista. Em Alexandria, a principal sinagoga judaica tinha setenta e um desses assentos para anciãos (o que serve de testemunho sobre as dimensões daquela congregação). Esses assentos eram ocupados pelos membros do «concílio» daquela comunidade religiosa.

Em algumas instâncias do Novo Testamento, a palavra grega *bēma* é empregada para designar um trono de julgamento (ver Mat. 27:19; João 19:13; Atos 18:12,16,17; 25:6,10,17), referindo-se ao lugar ocupado por algum governador, procurador romano ou oficial que estivesse atuando como juiz. E, por duas vezes, o vocábulo é empregado para indicar Cristo, sentado para julgar (Rom. 14:10; II Cor. 5:10), pelo que alguns têm distinguido entre o juízo exercido por Cristo e o juízo exercido por Deus, em seu trono.

A palavra grega *kathédra* era usada em sentido figurado, dando a entender, simplesmente, que o lugar havia pertencido a outrem, embora a palavra desse a entender, literalmente uma banqueta ou cadeira. Assim, os fariseus são descritos como quem se assentava na cadeira de Moisés, considerando-se ser eles os sucessores legítimos de Moisés (ver Mat. 23:2). O Senhor Jesus, por sua vez, foi descrito a derrubar «as mesas dos cambistas e as cadeiras dos que vendiam pombas» (Mat. 21:12).

Dessas palavras todas, a mais comum no Novo Testamento é o termo grego *thrónos*, que dá a entender um assento real (ver Luc. 1:52; Apo. 2:13; 4:4; 11:16; 13:2; 16:10). Assim, Satanás também tem um trono, os vinte e quatro anciãos ocupam vinte e quatro tronos, e o dragão entregará ao anticristo o seu próprio trono.

CADEIRA DE MOISÉS

No grego, **Mouséos kathédras**. A expressão ocorre em Mateus 23:2. Nome dado a uma cadeira especial, muito honrosa, existente nas sinagogas, onde se assentava o mestre da lei autorizado. Tal mestre, para todos os efeitos práticos, exercia a autoridade de Moisés, o profeta considerado o originador da lei escrita e dos principais elementos das tradições orais. Não eram muitos os fariseus que também eram escribas, entre cujo número também havia saduceus. Os escribas eram tidos como os exegetas reconhecidos da lei mosaica.

CADEIRA DE SÃO PEDRO

A expressão tem três significados: 1. A cadeira episcopal ou trono que Pedro teria usado pessoalmente, como suposto cabeça da Igreja, existente primeiramente em Antioquia da Síria, e então em Roma. Essa imaginária cadeira simboliza o seu ofício episcopal em ambas essas cidades. 2. O dia de festa religiosa, estabelecido pela Igreja Católica Romana para comemorar o episcopado de Pedro em ambas essas cidades. Esse episcopado não passa de um **pseudo-episcopado**. 3. O sentido simbólico ou dogmático da expressão *ex cathedra*.

Que Pedro viveu em Roma e ali exerceu poderes eclesiásticos, é bem confirmado pelas representações existentes nas catacumbas (ver sobre as Catacumbas), pelos pais da Igreja Irineu, Cipriano, Jerônimo e pelos historiadores eclesiásticos Eusébio e Orósio. Mas isso está longe de fazer dele o primeiro papa. Uma coisa não prova a outra. Mas, onde Pedro vivia em Roma, não se sabe dizer. Há tradições que pensam em locais como Santa Pudenziana, Santa Priscila e Santa Prisca. Partes da cadeira episcopal original, ou *sedes gestatoria*, aparentemente foi usada por algum mestre ou juiz pré-cristão, mas que, presumivelmente, posteriormente foi doada a Simão Pedro. Em séculos posteriores, essa cadeira foi ornada de ouro, marfim e outro material de valor. Durante toda a Idade Média, essa cadeira foi venerada por crédulos peregrinos que vinham visitar o Altar Elevado da catedral de São Pedro, onde esse apóstolo presumivelmente teria sido sepultado. Por ordem do papa Alexandre VII (1655-1667), essa cadeira foi encerrada dentro de uma enorme caixa de bronze, desenhada por Bernini, e agora ocupa um lugar de honra, acima de um altar da atual basílica de São Pedro, conhecido como o Altar da Cadeira. Essa cadeira está apoiada sobre enormes figuras de bronze. A festa da Cadeira de São Pedro é celebrada em Antioquia, segundo a liturgia oriental, a 22 de fevereiro, e em Roma, segundo a liturgia ocidental, a 18 de janeiro. Ambas essas festividades têm origem romana. A palavra grega *káthedra* desde há muito simboliza a doutrina divina, revestida de autoridade, bem como o poder real e judicial. Por conseguinte, temos o termo *ex cathedra* aplicado aos pronunciamentos autorizados do bispo de Roma. (AM E)

CADES-BARNÉIA

No hebraico, a palavra **kades** significa «consagrado». Está em foco uma localidade onde os israelitas acamparam por duas vezes, em sua jornada do Egito para a Palestina, através do deserto de Parã. Cades-Barnéia assinalou as paradas de números dezenove e trinta e sete. O nome original do local parece ter sido Ritmá (que vide). Foi chamado de Cades, quando o tabernáculo ali foi armado. Foi desse lugar que Moisés enviou mensageiros para que explorassem a Terra Prometida. Mas os israelitas ficaram assustados diante do relatório dos espias, e desejaram retornar ao Egito, chegando ao extremo de nomearem um comandante para levá-los de volta (Núm. 14:4). Em resultado disso, Cades, o *santuário*, tornou-se En-Mispate, uma *fonte de julgamento*, por causa da incredulidade do povo de Israel, e em vista do que, eles foram sentenciados a vagar por um total de quarenta anos pelo deserto.

1. *Localização*. O local tem sido identificado com 'Ain Kadeis, cerca de quarenta e três quilômetros ao sul de Hebrom. A existência de água foi um fator determinante nessa identificação, porquanto Cades era um lugar bem servido de água, no meio do deserto, sendo essa a circunstância que permitiu que o povo permanecesse no local convenientemente.

2. *Referências bíblicas*. Em conexão com a marcha das tropas de Quedorlaomer (que vide), rei de Elão, nos dias de Abraão (Gên. 14:1-16); em conexão com a fuga de Hagar (Gên. 16:7). A água figura nessa última referência. Em relação à jornada de Abraão (Gên. 20:1). Alguns estudiosos supõem que a revolta de Coré teve lugar nessa localidade (Núm. 16:1-21). Miriã faleceu ali (Gên. 20:1), e foi ali, igualmente, que Moisés feriu a rocha, quando meramente deveria falar com ela, para obter água (Núm. 20:2-11). E foi em conexão com esse acontecimento que Cades (consagrada, santuário) tomou o nome de Meribá,

CADES — CAFARNAUM

«contenda» (Núm. 20:13).

O povo de Israel ficou em Cades-Barnéia por longo tempo e, provavelmente, viveram ali como nômades (Deu. 46:1). Eles passaram nada menos de trinta e sete anos naquela área, e não avançaram um passo sequer mais perto da conquista da Terra Prometida, durante todo aquele tempo. Essa circunstância representa uma grande lição espiritual sobre a incredulidade e a preguiça espiritual, o que nos furta grandes vitórias, que estão ao nosso alcance, mas que não são apropriadas por causa de nossa falta de fé. De Cades, — Moisés enviou os mensageiros ao rei de Edom, com a petição para passar o povo de Israel pelo seu território, a caminho de Canaã (Núm. 20:14-21). Houve um pedido similar, dirigido ao rei de Moabe (Juí. 11:16,17). (I UN)

CADES SOBRE O ORONTES

Esse é o nome de uma aldeia às margens do rio Orontes, imediatamente ao sul do lago Humus. Nesse local houve várias batalhas notáveis, incluindo aquela entre Ramisés II, do Egito, e os hititas, em 1288 A.C. No Antigo Testamento, a aldeia é mencionada como o extremo norte do território de Israel, na época de Davi (II Sam. 24:6). Porém, alguns eruditos duvidam dessa identificação, por estar demais para o norte. Tem sido identificada com o moderno Tell Nebi Mend, que fica a sessenta e quatro quilômetros ao sul de Hamate, e a oitenta quilômetros ao norte de Damasco.

CADIAS, CADIANSANOS

Seriam os habitantes de Cadias, exilados judeus que voltaram com Zorobabel (I Esdras 5:20). Seus nomes não aparecem nas listas paralelas dos livros canônicos de Esdras e Neemias. Alguns estudiosos vinculam-os ao povo de Quedes (ver Jos. 15:23), ou então de Adasa.

CADISH

Transliteração do termo aramaico que significa «santo», termo que designa uma antiga oração judaica que honra o nome de Deus e pede que o seu reino seja estabelecido na terra. Suas palavras de abertura são parecidas com as da oração do Pai Nosso, que mostra haver uma tradição da qual ambas essas orações se derivam. Essa oração funciona como uma doxologia, e originalmente, encerrava o sermão. Mas, na atual liturgia das sinagogas, ela encerra uma seção do culto. Desde a época medieval, essa oração tornou-se a declaração de fé dos lamentadores judeus.

CADMIEL

No hebraico, «Deus está na vanguarda». É palavra usada para designar dois homens, que figuram nas páginas do Antigo Testamento:

1. Um levita que, com seus familiares, retornou do cativeiro babilônico (que vide), em companhia de Zorobabel. Em outros trechos bíblicos ele é chamado Hodovias ou Judá (Esd. 2:40; Nee. 7:43; 12:8,12,24). Esteve envolvido em várias reformas que ocorreram na época.

2. Um outro levita que ajudou a dirigir as devoções do povo judeu, depois que Esdras lhes ensinara a lei (Nee. 9:4,5), o qual também assinou o pacto de Neemias. É possível que ele fosse filho do primeiro desses dois homens do mesmo nome. Cerca de 445 A.C.

CADMONEU

Esse vocábulo aparece somente em Gênesis 15:19, onde alude a uma tribo que os israelitas desapossaram. Tal palavra é um adjetivo, cujo sentido é *oriental* ou *antigo*, pelo que é possível que eles fossem os mesmos que são chamados, em Juízes 6:33, de «povos do oriente» (no hebraico, *bene-kedem*), cujo território ficava contíguo ao de Israel, na direção do nascer do sol. No livro de Gênesis, vemos que o território deles foi prometido a Abraão como uma — final possessão. Os hebreus e outros povos antigos designavam as direções voltando o rosto para o sol nascente. Isso significa que diante ou à frente era o oriente, atrás era o ocidente, a direita era o sul, e a esquerda era o norte. O território que ficava entre os rios Nilo e Eufrates, o deserto sírio a leste de Biblos (que vide), mui provavelmente era a região dos cadmoneus.

CAFARNAUM

1. *Informações Gerais*

O nome significa «cidade de Naum». Foi lugar freqüentemente mencionado em conexão com a vida de Jesus. Ficava na margem ocidental do mar da Galiléia (Mat. 4:13). Havia uma estrada que descia de Nazaré e Caná para Cafarnaum (João 2:12; Luc. 4:31). Era localidade bastante grande para ser chamada de cidade (Mat. 9:1; Mar. 1:33). Contava com a sua própria sinagoga, onde Jesus ensinou (João 6:59; Mar. 1:21), a qual foi construída pelo centurião do destacamento de soldados romanos ali estacionado (Luc. 7:1; Mat. 8:8). Também contava com um posto alfandegário (Mat. 9:9; Luc. 5:27), recebendo oficiais itinerantes (Mat. 17:24). Sendo lugar onde Jesus residia, serviu de cena de grande parte de Seus ensinamentos e milagres. Se Jesus foi criado em Nazaré, escolheu Cafarnaum como sua própria cidade (Mar. 2:1). Foi ali que Mateus ou Levi foi escolhido como um dos discípulos (Mat. 9:9). Alguns estudiosos supõem que foi nas praias do mar da Galiléia, nesse lugar, que Simão Pedro e André abandonaram tudo para seguir a Jesus (Mar. 1:16,17). Os milagres ali efetuados foram a cura do servo do centurião (Mat. 8:5), a cura da sogra de Pedro (Mat. 8:14), a restauração do paralítico (Mat. 9:1) e o livramento do endemoninhado (Mar. 1:32).

2. *Profecia de Condenação*

Grandes privilégios sempre envolvem grande responsabilidade. Cafarnaum não se mostrou à altura das expectativas. A condenação foi proferida contra ela, como a cidade incrédula que entrava à obra de Jesus (Mat. 11:23). Essa predição de Jesus tem sido notavelmente cumprida. Tell Hum, o local geralmente aceito para assinalar a antiga cidade, nada mais é que um montão de ruínas, perto de Betsaida e Tabga.

3. *Cafarnaum e a Arqueologia*

Exemplares de cerâmica romana têm sido encontrados em Tell Hum. Entre as ruínas há uma edificação de formato octogonal, referida como a casa de Pedro, embora a construção possa ter sido levantada para marcar o lugar da casa daquele apóstolo. A mais impressionante ruína é a de uma antiga sinagoga, uma edificação com cerca de vinte metros de comprimento, com dois pisos, feita de pedra calcária, com ornamentação tão rebuscada que muitos judeus podem ter ficado chocados com a mesma. Data dos séculos II ou III D.C. Pode ter sido erigida no local onde havia uma sinagoga anterior, da época de Jesus, embora isso seja apenas especulação. Uma das colunas conta com a seguinte inscrição:

CAFARSALAMA — CAFTOR

«Alfeu, filho de Zebedeu, filho de João, fez esta coluna», talvez identificando as personagens aludidas como residentes proeminentes da cidade (Mat. 4:21), como um tipo de memorial. Um pote de maná foi descoberto ali, pertencente à sinagoga.

4. *Pedro e a Casa de Jesus*. Em agosto de 1983, arqueólogos franciscanos e o arqueólogo James F. Strange noticiaram que uma casa feita de basalto negro havia sido desenterrada em Cafarnaum, e que poderia ter sido a casa que Jesus usara como lar, naquela cidade. Data de 60 A.C.; mas posteriormente foi reformada e ampliada, talvez para que pudesse ser usada como templo da Igreja cristã. No século III D.C., foi construído no local um templo cristão octogonal, obviamente assinalando o local como importante. A reforma da casa incluiu o reboco das paredes da construção. Os comuns aparelhos de cozinha, que se esperam encontrar em residências normais, estavam ausentes, ao passo que ali havia lâmpadas e jarras, indicando uma modificação radical nas atividades da casa. O reboco das paredes, medida incomum em Cafarnaum, pode ter tido a intenção de tornar a construção apropriada para abrigar reuniões públicas. Essa casa tinha as seguintes dimensões: 30 m de comprimento por 23 m de largura.

Anteriormente pensava-se em Khan Minya como a possível localização de Cafarnaum, com apoio de vários estudiosos; mas a opinião atual tende por favorecer Tell Hum, o que conta com as evidências fornecidas por antigos viajantes, como Jerônimo (340-420 D.C.).

O culto na sinagoga usualmente consistia de oração, louvor, leitura das Escrituras e exposição feita por algum rabino ou outra pessoa competente. A vida de Jesus, incluindo milagres notáveis, ofereceu-lhe capacidade para pregar, apesar de não ter recebido instrução formal que tal posição geralmente requeria. A cidade ficava a noroeste da costa. Não é mencionada no V.T., mas nos dias de Jesus era cidade importante. Era conhecida como «sua cidade» (a cidade de Jesus), porque ali ele passou a habitar. (Ver Mat. 9:1). O fato da cidade contar com um centurião provavelmente significa que era um posto militar dos romanos. «Cafarnaum» significa «vila de Naum»; mas não sabemos se essa designação se deriva do profeta do V.T., que tem esse nome. Provavelmente o nome moderno, «Tell Hum», é lembrança de seu nome original. «Tell» significa «cômoro».

A Luz de Cafarnaum

Ele nasceu em **Belém**; viveu a maior parte da sua vida em Nazaré, mas deixou Nazaré e foi habitar em Cafarnaum, à beira-mar. Ali e nas circunvizinhanças viveu a maior de todas as vidas. Ele foi a Luz de Cafarnaum.

Terra de Zebulom, terra de Naftali,
Caminho do mar, além do Jordão,
Galiléia dos gentios?
O povo que jazia em trevas
Viu grande luz,
E os que viviam na região e sombra da morte,
Resplandeceu-lhes a luz (Is. 9:1,2; Mat. 4:15,16).

As *autoridades* religiosas e os judeus de raça pura desprezavam os habitantes de Zebulom e Naftali, tribos da Galiléia, pois ali as fronteiras de Israel eram contíguas às fronteiras das terras gentílicas. Não é verdade que, durante os dias de Salomão, vinte cidades dessa região foram anexadas ao reino de Tiro? Sim, e além disso, relembramo-nos de que durante o primeiro cativeiro, os assírios removeram quase toda a população para servirem de escravos seus. E depois, quando alguns retornaram, como povo, nunca foram racial ou religiosamente puros, pois suas terras permaneceram para sempre *Galiléia dos gentios*. Portanto, tornou-se um povo independente e alienado, distante do favor e das vantagens desfrutadas pelo povo de Deus em Jerusalém. Poder-se-ia examinar a situação para ter certeza: Nada de bom poderia originar-se na Galiléia. Porventura algum profeta já saíra de lá?

Mas *eis* que à vista do profeta surge uma *visão*, resplandece «uma grande luz!». Uma grande luz irrompe em Cafarnaum, uma pequena cidade nas fronteiras de Zebulom e Naftali, na Galiléia. Então muitos séculos mais tarde, a Luz, em realidade e não em visão, **surgia à beira-mar**. Seus magníficos raios se elevavam, refletindo-se por toda parte com tanto brilho por sobre as ondas do mar, porquanto Cafarnaum ficava à beira-mar. Aquela gente, nas terras de Zebulom e Naftali, que vivia em áreas de sombra e de morte, essa gente é que contemplava a grande Luz que brilhava à beira-mar.

Jesus Cristo, Rei de eterna glória,
Nasceste para seres Príncipe-Salvador,
Se os anjos louvam Tua vitória,
Alegramo-nos em nosso Redentor.
Cantamos de Tua graça a história,
Louvamos-te com mui intenso ardor.
Ó Jesus, Luz de Cafarnaum,
Brilha sobre nós, um por um!
 (Russell Champlin)

Ver o artigo sobre **Sinagoga**, seção VII, que dá informações sobre uma sinagoga do 1º século descoberta em Cafarnaum.

CAFARSALAMA

Uma localidade, atualmente desconhecida, onde Judas Macabeu e Nicanor, oficial do rei da Síria e governador da Judéia, entraram em batalha. Antes disso, Nicanor havia tentado apoderar-se de Judas mediante astúcia, a fim de tirar-lhe a vida. Tendo o plano falhado, eles se chocaram em batalha frontal. Nicanor perdeu quinhentos homens e fugiu para evitar maior desastre. Parte do nome da localidade, *Cafar*, significa «aldeia»; e *Salama* poderia significar Siloam. Tem sido identificada com Khirbet Deirsallam, a dezenove quilômetros a oeste de Jerusalém.

CAFE

Nome da décima primeira letra do alfabeto hebraico, com o som de *k*. A palavra significa «palma da mão». A letra foi tomada por empréstimo do alfabeto grego, como *kappa*, de onde se derivou a letra *k*, latina. O valor numérico da letra era vinte (20).

— Em Salmos 119:81-88, essa letra dá início a cada verso, no original hebraico. Essa letra tem sido transliterada pelo «k» ou pelo «c».

CAFENATA

Segundo todas as aparências, essa palavra indica uma secção das muralhas de Jerusalém, no vale oriental (I Macabeus 12:37), a qual foi reparada por Jonatã Macabeu e pelos anciãos do povo. Sua localização é desconhecida.

CAFIR Ver **Kafir**.

CAFTOR, CAFTORIM

Lugar de onde vieram originalmente os filisteus

(Jer. 47:4 e Amós 9:7). Esse lugar tem sido verbalmente identificado com *Kaptara*, ou Creta, nome esse escrito em caracteres cuneiformes. As palavras que aparecem nessa referência de Amós, «e de Caftor os filisteus», atualmente, por parte de muitos estudiosos, são consideradas uma nota deslocada, realmente pertencente a Gênesis 10:14: «...a Casluim (donde saíram os filisteus) e a Caftorium», onde a frase entre parênteses, ao que parece, deveria aparecer depois da palavra «Caftorim». A identificação de Caftor com o delta do Nilo, no Egito, ou com a Capadócia, há muito tem sido abandonada. A declaração veterotestamentária que mais claramente mostra a origem dos filisteus é a que aparece em Jeremias 47:4, onde eles são declarados «...o resto de Caftor da terra do mar», o que pode ser uma alusão às costas marítimas da Palestina, embora outros estudiosos pensem que a alusão é às ilhas ou costas do Mediterrâneo. Referências bíblicas assim indiretas não podem solucionar o quebra-cabeças, e todas as identificações esbarram com problemas. A identificação com Creta também tem seus problemas, embora a própria palavra Caftor possa estar relacionada àquela ilha. Por isso, outros eruditos preferem pensar na Cilícia.

CAIADURA

Ver o artigo sobre a **Cal**. Àquele artigo adicionamos aqui as seguintes informações:

Usos do reboco. 1. A fim de renovar uma casa, cujas paredes tivessem sido infectadas pela *lepra*, era mister que um sacerdote removesse as pedras ou os tijolos da área atingida, substituí-los por novas pedras ou novos tijolos, e rebocar o reparo (Lev. 14:42,48). Nesses casos, a palavra «lepra», sem dúvida designa alguma espécie de fungo, e não a lepra que ataca os seres humanos. 2. As palavras da lei deveriam ser inscritas sobre pedras, no monte Ebal, pedras que haviam sido adredemente preparadas para esse propósito (Deu. 27:2,4; Jos. 8:32). Um processo similar era feito no Egito, para fazerem-se baixos relevos. As pedras eram polidas; defeitos e espaços eram preenchidos com argamassa; figuras eram desenhadas; a pedra em volta era desgastada, para que as figuras ficassem em alto-relevo. Então as pedras eram polidas para preservação. 3. Em certos tipos de paredes rebocadas, a mão mística traçou a sua mensagem, predizendo a queda de Belsazar (Dan. 5:5,24-28).

Usos figurados. O reboco serve para ocultar, disfarçar, enganar, para tornar uma superfície diferente do que ela é, realmente. É o que Jesus quis dizer com «paredes branqueadas», ao falar com certos hipócritas religiosos, os quais faziam coisas más parecerem boas, da mesma maneira que os homens caiam os sepulcros que, no entanto, estão cheios de ossos dos mortos (Mat. 23:27).

O reboco era largamente usado no mundo antigo. Este era produzido aquecendo-se pedras calcárias ou gesso. A simples argila misturada com palha, também formava uma espécie de reboco. O artigo sobre a *Cal* fornece maiores detalhes sobre essa questão.

CAIBARA Ver **Kaibara**.

CAIFÁS

No grego, «depressão», usado como um sobrenome. Josefo (*Anti*. xviii.2) dá-lhe o nome de *José Caifás*. Foi sumo sacerdote judeu no reinado de Tibério César (que vide) Luc. 3:2; Mat. 26:4,57; João 11:49; 18:13,14,24,28; Atos. 4:6. Ele foi o sumo sacerdote oficial durante o ministério, o julgamento, a morte e a ressurreição de Jesus. Josefo informa-nos de que ele sucedeu a Simão, filho de Camite, em cerca de 27 ou 28 D.C. Sua esposa era filha de Anás, ou Ananu, ex-sumo sacerdote, que continuou exercendo grande influência durante o sumo sacerdócio de Caifás, pelo que também é referido como sumo sacerdote, em Atos 4:6 e João 18:19,22. De acordo com a prática judaica, um sumo sacerdote tinha um ministério vitalício, embora Roma os depusesse a seu talante. Contudo, de acordo com a opinião judaica, os sumos sacerdotes depostos continuavam sendo sumos sacerdotes. Ver o artigo sobre Anás.

Caifás foi nomeado ao ofício sumo sacerdotal pelo curador Valério Grato, tendo mantido o posto durante o tempo em que Pilatos foi o procurador romano. Foi deposto pelo procônsul Vitelo, em cerca de 38 D.C., o que significa que ocupou o cargo durante cerca de nove anos. O relato do Novo Testamento informa-nos que após a ressurreição de Lázaro, Caifás procurava ativamente tirar a vida de Jesus. Ver João 11:49,50 quanto a uma notável citação a esse respeito. Quando Jesus foi detido, levaram-no primeiramente a Anás, e então a Caifás. Foram buscadas testemunhas apropriadas, mas não foram achadas; pois, para que Jesus fosse condenado, a acusação precisava ter grande gravidade. Impaciente, Caifás pôs Jesus sob juramento, perguntando-lhe se ele era o Cristo, o Filho de Deus. Sua resposta afirmativa deixou Caifás indignado, levando-o a declarar que Jesus estava *blasfemando*. (Mat. 27:57-68). Caifás não tinha autoridade para mandar executar a qualquer prisioneiro, mas conseguiu a cooperação de Roma (Mat. 26:3,57; João 18:13,28). Como saduceu que era, Caifás também se opunha ao ensino sobre a ressurreição, e, naturalmente, opunha-se aos primeiros pregadores cristãos. Em Atos 4:6, ele aparece entre aqueles que perseguiram a Igreja primitiva, especificamente a Pedro e a João. Provavelmente, ele é o sumo sacerdote não chamado por nome, que aparece em Atos 5:17-21; 7:1; 9:1; como amargo e fanático perseguidor da Igreja. (I IB LAN NTI)

CAIM

No hebraico, **lança** (?). Foi o filho mais velho de Adão e Eva (Gên. 4:1). Tragicamente, foi o primogênito da raça humana, de acordo com a narrativa sobre a raça adâmica; e também foi o primeiro assassino e fratricida. Há algo de apropriado nas circunstâncias de que o homem de quem se diz ter sido o primeiro filho produzido pelo homem, também é descrito como o primeiro homem a ser um assassino. Essa narrativa simboliza a degeneração humana desde o princípio. Nada havia no meio ambiente de Caim que o tenha levado a matar seu irmão. O ato originou-se da maldade do íntimo. Muito erra a criminologia quando busca a causa dos crimes no meio ambiente adverso das pessoas, mas não a busca no íntimo pervertido do ser humano.

1. *Nome*. Não há certeza alguma quanto à origem do nome «Caim», embora pareça estar relacionado à forja de metais, como um «ferreiro»; outros preferem dar-lhe o sentido de «lança»; e, de acordo com a etimologia popular, «adquirir». Outros ainda pensam em «inveja». *Aquisição* (Gên. 4:1), é a mais comum idéia entre os intérpretes.

2. *O Sacrifício*. Adão e Eva cultivavam o solo; Abel era pastor de ovelhas. Caim também cultivava o solo.

Caim

O ódio matou

Homicídio

Oh, Deus, que carne e sangue fossem
  tão baratos,
Que os homens odiassem e matassem,
que os homens silvassem e cortassem a outros,
Com línguas de vileza ...por causa de...
«teologia».
    (Russell Norman Champlin)

••• •••

Senhor, disse eu,
  Jamais eu poderia matar um meu semelhante;
  Crime de tal grandeza cabe a um
  selvagem somente,
  É o crescimento venenoso de
  mente maligna,
  Ato alienado do mais indigno.
Senhor, disse eu,
  Jamais eu poderia matar um meu semelhante;
  Um ato horrível de raiva sem misericórdia,
  Apunhalada irreversível de
  inclinações perversas,
  Ato não imaginável de plano ímpio.
Disse o Senhor a mim,
  Uma palavra sem afeto lançada contra
  vítima que odeias,
  É um dardo abrindo feridas de cores cruéis.
  Bisbilhotice corta o homem pelas costas,
  Um ato covarde que não podes retirar.
  Ódio no teu coração, ou inveja levantando
  sua horrível cabeça,
  É um desejo secreto de ver alguém morto.
    (Russell Norman Champlin)

••• •••

CAIM, CIDADE DE — CAINÃ

Os irmãos trouxeram suas ofertas a Deus. Caim as trouxe do fruto de seu trabalho no solo; e elas foram rejeitadas. Abel trouxe suas ofertas do rebanho; e elas foram aceitas por Deus. A maioria dos intérpretes vê nisso um prenúncio dos sacrifícios cruentos, e, naturalmente, do sacrifício de Cristo. De conformidade com isso, a oferta de Caim representa o auto-esforço, o mérito humano, que parece bom a nossos olhos, mas não é aceitável diante de Deus. Isso dá a entender a necessidade da justificação (que vide) mediante a fé, com base na expiação de Cristo (que vide). Não estão em foco apenas as ofertas de Caim e Abel, mas as próprias pessoas deles, pois lemos: «Agradou-se o Senhor de Abel e de sua oferta; ao passo que de Caim e de sua oferta não se agradou» (Gên. 4:4,5). Portanto, Deus, que lê os corações, viu as atitudes deles: a de Abel de autodesistência e confiança na expiação de outrem; a de Caim de auto-suficiência e de confiança própria.

3. *A Ira de Caim*. A ira de Caim impeliu-o a matar. A enormidade de seu crime se vê no fato de que matou a seu próprio irmão. A ira é um dos pecados cardeais. Aparece na lista das obras da carne, na lista de Paulo, em Gál. 5:20. A ira encontra-se na raiz de muitos atos irracionais, e quase sempre tem o egoísmo como sua base, e o ódio como sua motivação.

4. *O Crime de Caim*. Embora repreendido por Deus, Caim resolveu dar vazão à sua maldade mediante um ato irracional de homicídio. Desde então, os homens têm satisfeito à sua vontade tirando a vida do próximo, o que mostra a extensão da queda. Quando Deus perguntou de Caim onde estava seu irmão, Abel, Caim indagou: «Não sei; acaso sou eu tutor de meu irmão?» (Gên. 4:9). Essa pergunta de Caim, famosa desde então, usada em inúmeros contextos, mostra-nos a natureza egoísta de seu ato homicida. Pois, a lei do amor leva-nos a cuidar uns dos outros, como cuidamos, cada um, de nós mesmos. Negar que eu sou guardador de meu irmão é negar a essência da lei do amor. A voz de Abel clamava do solo. Isso demonstra que os atos pecaminosos não podem ser ocultados, pois apelam a Deus, pedindo vingança.

5. *O Castigo de Caim*. De certo modo, Caim recebeu a primeira sentença perpétua. Ele seria objeto de ódio, e outros haveriam de querer tirar-lhe a vida. Porém, ele escaparia. Em lugar disso, foi pronunciada contra ele uma maldição divina. Ele tornar-se-ia vagabundo e fugitivo à face da terra, pelo resto de seus dias, caçado e odiado pelos outros seres humanos.

6. *A Marca de Caim*. Caim seria caçado pelos outros homens. Correria o risco permanente de ser morto. Deus, entretanto, não permitiria que ele fosse executado. Para garantir isso, foi posta uma marca em Caim, como se dissesse: Vede este homem. Não o matai! Não se sabe que marca seria essa. Alguns supõem que Deus deu-lhe coloração negra à pele, pelo que a marca seria forte carga de melanina. Porém, essa interpretação, além de ser mera especulação, só serve para fomentar preconceitos raciais. Esse sinal também poderia ser uma marca tribal, alguma espécie de tatuagem ou sinal que identificasse uma pessoa dentre um grupo particular, um costume que, mais tarde, tanto se viu no Oriente Médio. Outros compreendem que o *sinal* era a promessa de Deus de que ele não seria morto, —em vez de suporem alguma marca física. Não há como determinar a questão, por ausência de maiores informes bíblicos.

7. *Posteriormente*. Caim foi enviado à terra de Node (vagueação), onde ele edificou uma cidade e tornou-se o progenitor de uma numerosa família, que se ocupou de muitas artes e ofícios. De acordo com as tradições, os primeiros residentes em tendas, metalúrgicos e músicos vieram da linhagem de Caim. Mas outras tradições antigas dizem que os deuses foram os originadores das artes e ofícios (que vide).

8. *De Onde Caim foi Buscar Sua Esposa?* Alguns críticos indagam assim, com escárnio, julgando haver encontrado uma séria discrepância no relato bíblico. É como se dissessem: se Adão e Eva geraram somente Caim, Abel e Sete, onde Caim encontrou esposa, quando se retirou para a terra de Node? Esse tipo de objeção, além de exibir uma atitude cética para com os relatos sagrados, demonstra a ausência de um exame cuidadoso dos textos bíblicos por parte de tais críticos. A Bíblia não diz que Adão e Eva geraram somente àqueles três filhos homens. Caim, Abel e Sete foram apenas três dentre os muitos filhos do primeiro casal. Seus nomes são fornecidos por causa do relato expressivo que gira em torno deles, e nada mais. Lemos em Gênesis 5:4: «Depois que gerou a Sete, viveu Adão oitocentos anos; e teve filhos e filhas». Não há informação quanto ao número desses filhos e filhas, mas essa informação é suficiente para indicar que Caim levou consigo, para Node, uma de suas irmãs. E Sete, onde quer que tenha ficado, sem dúvida fez o mesmo. Não há nenhuma dificuldade para sabermos onde Caim arranjou esposa!

9. *Referências Neotestamentárias a Caim*. a. Hebreus 11:4. Pela fé, Abel ofereceu melhor sacrifício que o de Caim. Dentro do plano de Deus, Cristo ofereceu o sacrifício final e definitivo, que substituiu a todos os outros sacrifícios, sendo essa a mensagem central da epístola aos Hebreus. b. I João 3:12 é trecho que nos relembra o crime de Caim, seu ato homicida e o fato de que suas obras eram más, e as de seu irmão Abel, boas. c. Judas 11 alude ao *caminho* de Caim. Lemos ali que os mestres gnósticos seguem esse caminho. A literatura rabínica diz que o caminho de Caim caracteriza-se pela concupiscência, pela cobiça, pela auto-indulgência e pela malignidade geral. Se juntarmos a isso a inveja e o ódio, parece que é isso o que tal caminho significa. Caim tornou-se um homem profundamente depravado. Ver Sabedoria de Salomão 10:3; Jubileus 4:1-5; Apocalipse de Moisés 3:2.(G I IB NTI S)

CAIM, CIDADE DE

Era uma localidade nas terras baixas de Judá, mencionada juntamente com Zanoa, Gibeá, Timna, etc., formando um total de dez cidades (Jos. 15:55-57). Tem sido identificada com a moderna Khirbet Yakin, a quase cinco quilômetros a suleste de Hebrom.

CAIN Ver **Queneu**.

CAINÃ

Há dois homens com esse nome, nas páginas da Bíblia, a saber:

1. O filho de Enos, bisneto de Adão, que nasceu quando seu pai tinha noventa anos de idade. Cainã viveu setenta e cinco anos e gerou a Maalaleel, e então viveu por mais oitocentos e quarenta anos (Gên. 5:9-14).

2. Filho de Arfazade, filho de Sem, e pai de Salá. Seu nome não se encontra no texto hebraico do Antigo Testamento, mas aparece na LXX, em Gên. 10:24 e 11:12, bem como em Luc. 3:36, onde o nome é encontrado na genealogia de Jesus. A informação

dada por Lucas mostra-nos que o texto hebraico sofreu alguma omissão, conforme o conhecemos agora, e que Lucas pôde encontrar o nome nos registros sagrados. A cronologia da LXX, portanto, torna-se um tanto mais longa que a da Bíblia em hebraico. É possível que o nome «Cainã» tenha sido removido propositalmente do texto hebraico, a fim de fazer as gerações, de Adão a Noé, serem um número redondo, «dez». Mas outros estudiosos dizem que Cainã e Salá foram a mesma pessoa, dotada de dois nomes; e isso significaria que a adição que aparece na LXX seria um erro. O problema não encontra solução definitiva. Pelo menos é certo que o nome «Cainã», no evangelho de Lucas, faz parte do original, ainda que tenha sido omitido em alguns manuscritos posteriores do Novo Testamento. Naturalmente, o próprio Lucas pode tê-lo registrado, por causa da influência da LXX, ao passo que poderia estar realmente ausente do texto hebraico original do Antigo Testamento.

CAIRD, EDWARD

Suas datas foram 1835-1908. Foi um filósofo e teólogo escocês, irmão de John Caird (que vide), professor de filosofia moral em Glasgow, e mestre da Balliol Oxford. Ele exercia uma incrível infuência sobre os seus alunos, tendo promovido causas sociais e reformas, incluindo a extensão da educação universitária às mulheres. Foi o fundador do neo-hegelianismo na Inglaterra, e igualmente um importante intérprete de Kant. Entre seus escritos mais importantes, temos: *A Critical Account of the Philosophy of Kant; The Social Philosophy and Religion of Comte; The Evolution of Religion; The Evolution of Theology in the Greek Philosophers*. (E)

CAIRD, JOHN

Suas datas foram 1820-1898. Um clérigo escocês de renome, irmão de Edward Caird (que vide), reitor da Universidade de Glasgow em 1873. Foi autor de *An Introduction to the Philosophy of Religion; The Fundamental Ideas of Christianity*, e de uma excelente obra sobre *Spinoza*. (E)

CAIXÃO Ver **Sepultamento, Costumes de.**

CAJADO Ver **Vara.**

CAJETANO, TOMÁS DE VIO

Cardeal da Igreja Católica Romana, cujas datas foram 1469-1534. Foi importante expositor da obra de Tomás de Aquino, *Summa Teologiae*. Na qualidade de legado papal na Alemanha, ele examinou as doutrinas de Lutero e redigiu a bula de condenação.

CAL

No hebraico há duas palavras que têm sido traduzidas como «cal».

1. *Eben gir*, «pedra de cal». Essas palavras aparecem somente em Isa. 27:9. O termo aramaico *gir*, que também significa «cal», é usado em Dan. 5:5.

2. *Sid*, «reboco», «cal». Esse termo hebraico aparece em Isa. 33:12 e Amós 2:1.

É impossível determinarmos qual a natureza exata da cal dos hebreus, ou mediante qual processo eles chegavam a produzi-la. Porém, sabe-se que o carbonato de cálcio (pedra calcária), quando aquecido, perde o seu ácido carbônico e passa para o estado de óxido de cálcio. Quando o óxido de cálcio entra em contacto com a água, combina-se com a mesma, produzindo considerável calor, formando o hidrato de cálcio, mas que gradualmente adquire dióxido de carbono, que extrai do ar, até que volta a ser carbonato de cálcio. Se alguém misturar o dióxido de carbono com areia, é produzido um tipo de argamassa que, quando endurece torna-se uma espécie de pedra artificial, bastante resistente e duradoura. O sulfato de cálcio (gesso, alabastro) contém certa quantidade de água, em uma condição conhecida como «água de cristalização». O aquecimento faz evaporar-se a água, e o resultante sulfato anídrico, quando pulverizado, torna-se gesso. Esses dois produtos têm sido usados na civilização humana desde há muito, através de vários processos.

A mistura de argila com argamassa forma uma espécie de cimento (que vide) usado na colocação de tijolos. O gesso pode ser misturado com mármore pulverizado, o que produz um material duro, para ser aplicado a superfícies, capaz de ser polido. A água de cal é feita com cal e grande quantidade de água, o que é usado como pintura barata. A pedra calcária é abundante na Palestina. Geologicamente, essa pedra calcária foi formada da compactação de conchas no leito do mar, que então foi trazido à tona mediante os movimentos da crosta terrestre. A Palestina já foi o fundo do mar por mais de uma vez, o que explica a presença ali de tanta pedra calcária. A maior parte da pedra calcária visível atualmente, em ambos os lados do vale do Jordão, pertence ao período cretáceo. (BALND UN)

CALÁ

O significado do heb. é incerto. Era uma cidade da Assíria, edificada por Ninrode, ou pelo povo dessa região (Atos 10:11). Atualmente chama-se Ninrude, estando localizada no ângulo nordeste da confluência entre os rios Zabe Superior e Tigre, cerca de trinta e nove quilômetros ao sul de Nínive, na margem oriental do rio Tigre.

Salmaneser I (cerca de 1280-1260 A.C.), rei da Assíria, foi quem tornou famoso esse lugar. A cidade havia caído em decadência na época do rei guerreiro e conquistador, Assurnasirpal II (883-859 A.C.). Mas Salmaneser I escolheu-a como sua capital e restaurou-a. As escavações arqueológicas ali iniciadas, em 1845, bem como em diversos outros lugares, têm encontrado um magnificente palácio, de Assurnasirpal II, com colossais homens alados, com cabeça de leão, que guardavam a entrada do mesmo. Em um templo pequeno, nas proximidades, encontrou-se a estátua do rei. Muitas inscrições, relativas a seu reinado, também foram trazidas à luz. O famoso obelisco negro de Salmaneser III foi encontrado ali, em 1846, onde, entre outros cativos, é referido Jeú, rei de Israel (cerca de 842-815 A.C.), trazendo ao monarca assírio o seu tributo. Muitas antiguidades valiosas de Calá atualmente encontram-se no Museu Metropolitano de Arte da cidade de Nova Iorque, ou no Museu de Belas Artes da Universidade de Boston, nos Estados Unidos da América. (MAL)

CALAFATES

No hebraico encontramos uma expressão, **chazaq** *bedeq*, «reparadores de brechas», somente em Eze. 27:9,27. Nesses versículos estão em foco os famosos construtores de navios de Gebal, na Fenícia. Os calafates eram aqueles que preenchiam as costuras entre as pranchas que formavam o casco de um navio com estopa embebida em piche, para tornar o casco à prova d'água. O retoque final consistia em pintar essas costuras com piche derretido. As rachaduras que porventura apareciam nas pranchas eram reparadas pelo mesmo processo.

CALAI

No hebraico, «ligeiro», «leve». Filho de Salai e um dos principais sacerdotes da época do sumo sacerdote Joaquim (Nee. 12:20), em cerca de 635 A.C. Ele retornou do exílio babilônico, na leva que veio com Zorobabel.

CALAM Ver Kalam.

CÁLAMO

No hebraico, **qaneh**, «cana». É uma cana aromática que atinge cerca de sessenta centímetros de altura, com um colmo com juntas e gomos, que contém um cerne mole. É desse cerne mole que o aroma ou sabor se deriva. Enquanto vai crescendo, o cálamo enche o ar de fragrância suave. Quando o cerne mole é devidamente preparado, torna-se um ingrediente para perfumes doces e fortes. Várias espécies existem, e a planta é comum na Síria, no Egito, na Judéia, em Sumatra e em outros lugares. Fazia parte do comércio tírio com os gregos (Eze. 47:19), e era um ingrediente usado no perfume sagrado dos judeus (Êxo. 30:23). (G S)

CÁLAMO AROMÁTICO

No hebraico o sentido é **cana aromática**, palavra também encontrada em Êxo. 30:23; Eze. 27:19 e Can. 4:14. Trata-se do *Andropogon aromático*, uma grama que solta um forte odor quando amassada, mas que não deve ser confundida com a cana-de-açúcar. É alimento de vacas e ovelhas, mas isso faz com que a carne e o leite desses animais fiquem tintos. Também é chamada grama de gengibre, devido ao seu gosto acre. Provavelmente era importada pelos palestinos, por meio dos árabes. Alguns supõem que a rainha de Sabá trouxe esse cálamo aromático a Salomão, isto é, a «especiaria» mencionada em I Reis 10:10, sendo isso uma possibilidade muito exeqüível, porquanto o cálamo aromático dava em abundância na Etiópia. (Z)

CALAMOLALUS

A palavra aparece em I Esdras 5:22, na Septuaginta. Os manuscritos que contêm esse estranho nome, segundo se pensa, perpetraram a corrupção combinada dos nomes de Lode e Hadide, com base nas listas de nomes em Esdras 2:33 e Neemias 7:37.

CALAUCAU

Título dado aos ritos místicos e às palavras mágicas do gnosticismo. Ver sobre o *Gnosticismo*.

CALÇADOS

Este verbete precisa ventilar duas palavras hebraicas e uma palavra grega, a saber:

1. *Naal*, «sapato». Palavra hebraica que ocorre por vinte e duas vezes (por exemplo: Êxo. 3:5; 12:11; Deu. 25:9,10; Jos. 5:15; Rute 4:7,8; Sal. 60:8; Isa. 5:27; Eze. 24:17,23; Amós 2:6 e 8:6).

2. *Minal*, «sapato». Palavra hebraica que aparece por apenas uma vez, isto é, em Deu. 33:25.

3. *Upódema*, «sandália» (literalmente, «sob os pés»). Palavra grega que aparece por dez vezes: Mat. 3:11; 10:10; Mar. 1:7; Luc. 3:16; 10:4; 15:22; 22:35; João 1:27; Atos 7:33; 13:25.

Também precisamos considerar a expressão hebraica *serok naal*, «cordões da sandália», que aparece em Gên. 14:23 e Isa. 5:27. Dentre as trinta ocorrências das palavras hebraicas, quase todas são traduzidas por «sandálias» em nossa versão portuguesa, pois, à mente moderna, uma sandália dá mais perfeitamente a idéia do formato de um antigo sapato do Oriente Próximo e Médio. No mínimo, consistia em uma sola chata feita de couro, madeira ou outro material, com um cordão em cada lado, a fim de segurar a sola ao pé. Naturalmente, havia formatos diversos, dependendo do uso que se queria dar ao calçado. Os pastores precisavam de uma sandália forte, porquanto geralmente caminhavam por lugares pedregosos e difíceis. As mulheres de elevada posição social, por outro lado, geralmente usavam um tipo leve de sandália, e mais ornamentada.

A significação simbólica dos calçados é um fenômeno bíblico bem confirmado. Podemos detectar pelo menos cinco usos figurados:

a. Os cordões das sandálias geralmente indicavam algo barato, de pouco valor. Isso se devia ao fato que tais cordões eram praticamente insignificantes. Portanto, Abraão não queria ficar com a coisa mais insignificante do rei de Sodoma (Gên. 14:23). Mas também há um uso similar do próprio calçado, em Amós 2:6: «...e condenam o necessitado por causa de um par de sandálias» (ver também Amós 8:6), dando a entender que os necessitados eram vendidos por baixíssimo preço.

b. Com base no conceito de pouco valor, a idéia de calçados retrata a parte mais humilde do corpo de uma pessoa. De conformidade com isso, João Batista afirmou-se indigno de ao menos tocar nas sandálias de Cristo (Mat. 3:11; Mar. 1:7; Luc. 3:16; João 1:27; Atos 13:25). Até mesmo a porção mais humilde da pessoa de Jesus Cristo era por demais exaltada para ser comparada com a pessoa do seu precursor.

c. O uso de sapatos com freqüência falava sobre alguma viagem ou a preparação para alguma viagem. Por esse motivo, os israelitas deveriam consumir o cordeiro pascal, calçados e preparados para partir em seguida (Êxo. 12:11). Entre eles também houve a preservação miraculosa de suas sandálias, enquanto vagueavam pelo deserto (Deu. 29:5). Por igual modo, os discípulos do Senhor não deveriam levar consigo o costumeiro par extra de sandálias, em suas jornadas de evangelização (Mat. 10:10; Luc. 10:4; 22:35).

d. A contaminação adquirida pelos calçados, durante as jornadas pelas estradas poeirentas da época, terminou resultando em um outro símbolo. É por esse motivo que os calçados com freqüência representam a contaminação espiritual. Foi precisamente por essa razão que Moisés precisou tirar as sandálias dos pés, porquanto estava em terreno santo (Êxo. 3:5; Atos 7:33). E outro tanto ocorreu com Josué (Jos. 5:15).

e. Um bem proeminente uso simbólico dos calçados era a transferência de alguma propriedade ou de alguma responsabilidade. No caso de algum hebreu que se recusasse a cumprir sua responsabilidade, no casamento levirato, sua recusa era assinalada pela remoção de seu calçado (Deu. 25:9,10; cf. Rute 4:7,8).

CALCANHAR

Há uma palavra hebraica e uma palavra grega

CALCEDÔNIA — CALDÉIA

envolvidas neste verbete:
1. *Aqueb*, «calcanhar». Palavra hebraica empregada por sete vezes com esse sentido: Gên. 3:15; 25:26; 49:17; Jó 18:9; Sal. 41:9; 49:5; Jer. 13:22.
2. *Ptérna*, «calcanhar». Vocábulo grego usado por apenas uma vez, em João 13:18, citando Sal. 41:9.

Na Bíblia, a primeira vez em que essa palavra figura em sentido literal é no relato de Jacó que, por ocasião de seu nascimento, segurou no calcanhar de seu irmão Esaú, quando ainda no ventre de Rebeca (Gên. 25:26; Osé. 12:3), o que provavelmente significa que isso foi um vexame para Esaú, e que os dois futuramente, entrariam em choque.

Usos Figurados. 1. A promessa da derrota final de Satanás. Pois, apesar de que ele haveria de ferir o calcanhar de Cristo (que o texto chama de «descendente da mulher»), contudo Cristo esmigalharia a cabeça da serpente, ou seja, Cristo haveria de cumprir sua missão remidora, derrotando as forças do mal. 2. O moribundo patriarca Jacó, ao abençoar a Dã, desejou que todo aquele que lhe quisesse fazer oposição, encontraria nele um formidável adversário, como se ele fosse uma serpente. Assim, os inimigos de Dã aparecem como um cavaleiro, cujo cavalo seria mordido nos calcanhares, fazendo com que a montaria lançasse por terra o seu cavaleiro (Gên. 49:17). Isso significa que Dã conseguiria livrar-se com sucesso de todos os seus inimigos. 3. Um dos «amigos» de Jó insinuou que este se parecia com um homem iníquo que chega à sua própria destruição quando o seu calcanhar é apanhado em uma armadilha (Jó 18:9). 4. O salmista proclamou que um certo amigo de confiança levantaria contra ele o seu calcanhar. Naturalmente, isso é uma predição da traição de Jesus por parte de Judas Iscariotes (João 13:18). 5. Na literatura profana há a história de Aquiles, cujos calcanhares eram a única porção de seu corpo que não era protegida, e, quando foi ferido ali, foi derrotado. Isso simboliza alguma fraqueza de uma pessoa, que a leva à ruína, apesar de toda a sua fortaleza, quanto a outros particulares.

CALCEDÔNIA

Deriva-se de uma palavra grega que significa «similar ao cobre». Era nome de uma pedra preciosa. O nome vem da cidade de Calcedônia, onde havia o *chalkós*, «cobre», e com cujo metal o nome daquela pedra estava associado. Essa pedra aparecia com certa variedade de cores, nas cavidades cheias de lava vulcânica, ou como nódulos encrustados nas rochas sedimentares. Suas variedades incluem o crisópraso, a ágata e o ônix. Todas elas são dotadas de grão fino, uma sílica capaz de adquirir um lustro como de cera. A pedra é mais dura que a pederneira, e geralmente semitransparente. Tem várias tonalidades de cinza, amarelo, verde, marrom ou azul. Ocorre sob a forma de massas irregulares, formando corpos grotescos. Muitos artigos decorativos são feitos dessa pedra, que pode ser encontrada em muitos lugares do mundo. (AM Z)

CALCEDÔNIA, CONCÍLIO DE

Esse foi o quarto concílio ecumênico, efetuado em 451 D.C. Foi convocado para reverter as decisões do concílio do Latrocínio, efetuado em Éfeso, em 449 D.C. Em pauta estava a heresia de Êutico (que vide), de Constantinopla, com o apoio de Dióscuro de Alexandria. Eles ensinavam que a pessoa do Filho de Deus tinha apenas uma natureza, a divina. Por conseguinte, o nome aplicado a essa idéia é *monofisistismo* (que vide). A fórmula estava alicerçada sobre o Tomo de Leão I (que vide), que só foi satisfatória porque ele expôs o problema sem enfrentar a questão. As decisões de Éfeso (431 D.C.) contra o nestorianismo (que vide), foram confirmadas, e a Roma foi conferida a primeira posição de autoridade e a Constaninopla, a segunda, e a terceira a Alexandria (contrariamente ao concílio de Nicéia). Leão I, entretanto, recusou-se a aceitar esse cânon. O concílio de Calcedônia contou com a presença de cerca de trezentos e cinqüenta bispos orientais, três legados papais e dois bispos africanos no exílio. O papa Leão I a princípio opôs-se ao lugar das reuniões; mas depois cedeu e enviou delegados. Porém, por causa do cânon 28, que dava a Constantinopla lugar de maior proeminência que a Alexandria, Leão I recusou-se a confirmar os atos desse concílio até 21 de março de 423 D.C., somente depois que houve alguma mudança de poderes. Esse concílio também afirmou que Cristo é tanto Deus quanto homem, consubstancial com o Pai e da mesma substância do homem, um ser com duas naturezas, unidas sem qualquer confusão ou alteração. (AM E)

CALÇÕES

No hebraico, **miknesayim**, «ceroulas». Essa palavra ocorre por cinco vezes: Êxo. 28:42; 39:28; Lev. 6:10; 16:4; Êxo. 44:18.

Quando os sacerdotes oficiavam no altar (que vide), precisavam usar uma espécie de pano que lhes envolvia os quadris e as coxas. Esse pano era de linho fino, tal como o resto das vestes sacerdotais. Não tinha o formato de ceroulas ou calções, conforme atualmente os conhecemos, mas lhes cobria o baixo tronco e as coxas. Ver o artigo geral sobre o Sumo Sacerdote, sob o subtítulo de *Vestes*.

Muitos estudiosos pensam que é melhor pensarmos apenas em um pano enrolado em torno da cintura e dos quadris, o que era uma vestimenta comum no Egito e no Oriente Médio, conforme já se discutiu em *Vestimentas*. No caso específico dessas referências, está em foco essa peça de vestuário que os sacerdotes deveriam usar quando estivessem ocupados em suas funções cerimoniais.

CALCOL

No hebraico, **sustento**. Foi um homem da tribo de Judá, filho dos descendentes de Zerá (I Crô. 2:6). Provavelmente deve ser identificado com o Calcol, filho de Maol, um dos quatro sábios a quem Salomão ultrapassava em sabedoria (I Reis 4:31), em cerca de 1010 A.C.

CALCONDILAS, DEMÉTRIO

Ver sobre o mesmo no artigo sobre a **Academia Florentina**.

CALDÉIA

A Caldéia é o nome de um distrito ao sul da Babilônia, que posteriormente veio a designar a Babilônia inteira. Essa designação mais ampla entrou em uso após o império neobabilônico de Nabucodonosor II (605-562 A.C.), que se estendia desde a pequena aldeia murada de Hite, à margem direita do rio Eufrates, até o golfo Pérsico. Ver o artigo geral sobre a *Babilônia*.

1. *História Primitiva*. Os caldeus eram uma tribo seminômade que ocupava os desertos entre o norte da

CALDEIRÃO — CALEBE

Arábia e o golfo Pérsico. Desde bem cedo eles estabeleceram-se em Ur dos Caldeus (Gên. 11:28; Atos 7:4). Eram um povo aparentado remotamente dos arameus. Aparentemente eram caldianos, ou habitantes de Urartu, ou seja, Ararate ou Armênia. Eles são mencionados nas inscrições babilônicas, e começam a aparecer nas crônicas assírias durante o reinado de Assurnasirpal II (883-859 A.C.), mas a existência deles como um povo retrocede até bem antes do ano 1000 A.C.

2. *A Caldéia e os Babilônios.* Quando Tiglate-Pileser III (745-727 A.C.) tornou-se rei da Assíria, ele conquistou a Babilônia. Os caldeus viviam perturbando o rei da Babilônia. Em 731 A.C., Ukinzer, que viera de uma das cidades da Caldéia, tornou-se rei da Babilônia. No entanto, não demorou a ser deposto por Tiglate-Pileser III (728 A.C.), o qual tornou-se rei da Babilônia, onde governou com o nome de Pul. No trono assírio, Pul foi sucedido por Salmaneser IV (726-722 A.C.). Este foi sucedido no trono da Babilônia por Merodaque-Baladã, um caldeu. Merodaque foi conquistado por Sargão, embora tivesse continuado a governar até 708 A.C., quando Sargão tornou-se rei tanto da Babilônia quanto da Assíria. Nos dias de Ezequias (702 A.C.), Merodaque-Baladã, filho de Baladã, governava a Babilônia. Não foi senão em cerca de 625 A.C. que o poder dos caldeus começou a fazer-se sentir sobre a Assíria.

3. *O Império Neobabilônico.* Nebopolassar revoltou-se contra a Assíria, em cerca de 625 A.C., e estabeleceu o império neobabilônico. Ele reconstruiu a cidade da Babilônia. De 625 A.C. em diante, os caldeus conseguiram obter completo controle sobre a Babilônia. No décimo quarto ano de seu reinado, isto é, em 612 D.C., juntamente com Ciaxares, o medo, e com o rei dos citas, ele capturou Nínive, deixando-a arrasada (Naum 3:1-3). Em 605 A.C., ele foi sucedido por seu filho, Nabucodonosor II. Foi na época deste que Judá e Jerusalém foram levados em cativeiro para a Babilônia, e os exércitos dos caldeus dominavam o mundo civilizado então conhecido. Em seguida, Nabucodonosor fez da Babilônia a mais esplêndida cidade do mundo (Dan. 4:30). Ele foi sucedido por seu filho, Evil-Merodaque (562-560 A.C.), mas este acabou sendo assassinado por seu cunhado, Neriglissar (560-558 A.C.). O monarca seguinte, Labashi-Marduque, reinou apenas por três meses, e então foi sucedido pelo usurpador Nabonido. Seu filho, Belsazar (Dan. 5), foi feito co-regente, até à queda do império caldeu, em 538 A.C. Os historiadores consideram uma maravilha que uma região tão pequena como a Caldéia pôde ter produzido uma raça de poder suficiente para vencer e dominar o mundo daquela época.

4. *Nos Dias de Daniel.* O termo «caldeu», nos dias de Daniel, era usado para designar a Babilônia inteira (Dan. 3:8). Lemos que Dario, o medo, governava o reino dos *caldeus* (Dan. 9:1). A linguagem dos caldeus (Dan. 1:4) provavelmente era um dialeto semítico, babilônico. A palavra *caldaico*, nos tempos modernos, é erroneamente aplicada para indicar a língua aramaica. A proeminência da classe dos sacerdotes, os quais, em Babilônia e outros centros, mantinham as antigas tradições da astrologia e da filosofia nas línguas babilônicas clássicas, fez com que a palavra *caldeu* viesse a ser aplicada aos sacerdotes (Dan. 3:8), astrólogos e pessoas educadas (Dan. 2:10; 4:7; 5:7,11).

5. *Os Astrônomos-Astrólogos Caldeus.* Os caldeus desenvolveram consideráveis habilidades matemáticas, astrológicas, astronômicas, e, de mistura com isso, conhecimentos sobre adivinhações e ritos religiosos. Desenvolveu-se ali uma casta de astrólogos. Ver o artigo geral sobre a *Astrologia*. Os trechos de Daniel 2:2,10 e 4:7 referem-se a essa casta, utilizando-se dos nomes de «magos», «encantadores», «feiticeiros» e «caldeus». Textos produzidos por essa gente foram preservados em aramaico, que muitos eruditos chamam, erroneamente, de *caldaico*. Após isso, o termo *caldeu* com freqüência passou a ser usado como vocábulo para indicar os sacerdotes e os especialistas nas antigas artes dos caldeus, sem importar a raça a que pertenciam. Vemos isso em Heródoto i.181,183, em cerca de 450 A.C.

A Babilônia era o centro das atividades daqueles homens, a qual, por sua vez, era a capital intelectual de toda a Ásia ocidental. Como cientistas que eram, os caldeus fundaram a ciência exata da astronomia, a qual, naturalmente, entre eles, sempre envolveu a adivinhação astrológica, pois, nos tempos antigos, a astronomia não era considerada uma ciência distinta da astrologia. Durante mais de trezentos e sessenta anos, eles conservaram registros astronômicos exatos e meticulosos. Um de seus mais notáveis feitos foi calcular a duração do ano solar como de 365 dias, seis horas, quinze minutos e quarenta e um segundos, que dá uma diferença de apenas trinta e três minutos e seis segundos a menos do que aquilo que é determinado pelos modernos instrumentos. Por causa da óbvia erudição desses homens, a Babilônia tornou-se famosa, não somente em face de sua ciência, mas também por causa de sua adivinhação e ocultismo. É provável que os astrólogos de Mateus 2:1 (ver o artigo sobre os *Magos*) pertencessem à tradição dos caldeus, embora o termo *Oriente*, ali usado, não nos diga o local exato da proveniência deles. A Arábia, a Babilônia e outros lugares têm sido sugeridos. (ND UN WIS)

CALDEIRÃO

No hebraico temos quatro palavras: *agmon*, «caldeirão» (Jó 41:20); *dud*, «caçarola» ou «cesto» (II Crô. 35:13); *sir*, «pote» (Jer. 52:18,19; Eze. 11:3;7,11; Êxo. 16:3; II Reis 4:38-41; Zac. 14:20,21, etc.), *qallachath*, «caldeirão» (I Sam. 2:14 e Miq. 3:3). Era um caldeirão de barro ou de metal. Vasos metálicos com vários formatos e usos têm sido encontrados pelos arqueólogos no Egito, na Babilônia, na Mesopotâmia, etc. Eram empregados em usos domésticos ou com propósitos cerimoniais (I Sam. 2:15; II Crô. 35:13; Jó 41:20; Jer. 52:18).

CALDO

Preparo culinário feito de água com carne, algumas vezes com legumes. O caldo geralmente é ralo, para ser usado com outros alimentos. Gideão serviu um caldo ao anjo que o visitara (Juí. 6:19,20). É usado figuradamente no trecho de Isaías 65:4, onde Deus acusa Israel de comer o caldo de coisas abomináveis.

CALEBE

No hebraico, «cão», isto é, «escravo». Há vários homens com esse nome, no Antigo Testamento:

1. Filho de Jefoné (que vide), o quenezeu, chefe de uma das famílias de Judá: a. Ele serviu de espia, aos quarenta anos de idade (Jos. 14:6,7), tendo sido enviado juntamente com onze outros homens, por parte de Moisés, a fim de explorar a terra de Canaã (Núm. 13:5,17-25), em cerca de 1440 A.C. b. Distinguiu-se por seu relatório fiel e encorajador

diante do homem, instando para que os israelitas obedecessem à ordem de Deus e dessem continuação à conquista. Josué concordou com ele (que vide), embora os outros dez espias mostrassem um relatório negativo e desencorajador, devido ao seu temor e incredulidade. Eles viram quão poderosos eram os habitantes da Terra Prometida, antes da conquista, percebendo que a conquista militar não seria fácil. Mas, a fé de Calebe e Josué era maior que o temor deles, e queriam tentar grandes coisas; e assim, deixaram-nos como herança uma preciosa lição moral. (Ver Núm. 13:30). Infelizmente, o povo de Israel tomou o partido dos covardes, e quase apedrejou os dois corajosos e fiéis espias (Núm. 14:10). c. Moisés percebeu claramente que aqueles dois seriam os únicos, dentre os que tinham mais de vinte anos de idade, que finalmente entrariam na Terra Prometida. De fato, em uma praga por juízo divino, que ocorreu pouco depois desse episódio, todos os demais espias morreram (Núm. 14:26-38). Calebe recebeu a promessa especial de que entraria na Terra Prometida, e que os seus descendentes prosperariam ali; e isso indica que a recompensa por sua fidelidade foi grande (Núm. 14:25). d. Não se menciona novamente Calebe nas Escrituras, senão quarenta e cinco anos mais tarde. A terra conquistada estava sendo partilhada, e ele reivindicou uma herança especial, prometida por Moisés. Isso foi cumprido por Josué. Com a idade de oitenta e cinco anos, Calebe continuava vigoroso, tendo participado de diversas batalhas (Jos. 14:6-15; 15:4). Contudo, teve dificuldades para conquistar Debir (Quiriate-Sefer), e ofereceu uma de suas filhas, como esposa, ao homem que a conquistasse. A cidade foi conquistada por Otniel, filho de Quenaz, irmão mais jovem de Calebe; e assim Acsa, filha de Calebe, tornou-se a esposa de Otniel (Jos. 15:13-19). Nada mais ouvimos sobre ele, e nem como sua vida terminou.

2. O último entre os três filhos a ser nomeado de Hezrom (I Crô. 2:18), descendente de Judá (I Crô. 2:9), onde ele é chamado Quelubai. Ele e sua esposa, Azuba, tiveram Jeser, Sobabe e Ardom. Depois que ela faleceu, Calebe casou-se com Efrate, e desse novo matrimônio nasceu Hur, e talvez outros. Calebe teve concubinas, e também outros filhos.

3. Filho de Hur, neto de Calebe anterior (I Crô. 2:50). Coisa alguma sabe-se sobre esse homem.

4. Além desses três homens de nome Calebe, há um território com esse nome, naquela porção do Neguebe ocupado por Calebe e seus descendentes (I Sam. 30:14), provavelmente a ser identificado com a grande bacia entre Hebrom e o antigo Carmelo de Judá. (S UN)

CALENDÁRIO ECLESIÁSTICO

Originalmente, o calendário eclesiástico era uma adaptação dos calendários grego e romano (que vide). Importantes eventos religiosos influenciaram o calendário, a começar pelas principais festividades religiosas judaicas e cristãs, —incluindo a celebração das mortes dos mártires. Cada igreja tinha o seu próprio calendário, não havendo uniformidade, portanto. Porém, na Idade Média, o calendário romano passou a ser utilizado por toda a Igreja Ocidental. A partir do século VIII D.C. foram feitos calendários combinados para celebrar as datas dos santos e dos mártires. E o número de observâncias desse tipo era grande. O atual Calendário dos Santos, da Igreja Católica Romana, é muito copioso. A Igreja Luterana Alemã reteve o calendário romano, completo com os dias dos santos. Um calendário evangélico, para uso das igrejas evangélicas da Alemanha, era expedido anualmente. O calendário da Igreja Anglicana foi publicado como parte do Livro de Orações. Esse calendário tem nove colunas consistindo em um número dourado, ou ciclo do mês, dias do mês em ordem numérica; letras dominicais; calendas, nones e ides (ver o calendário romano); dias santos da Igreja, vários dos quais correspondem aos dias santos católicos romanos; e os pontos de sexto a nono, porções das Escrituras e dos livros apócrifos, para serem lidos diariamente. A Igreja Ortodoxa Russa e alguns antigos calendaristas continuam celebrando as festas fixas do calendário juliano. A Igreja Ortodoxa no Oriente continua a estabelecer festas fixas, de acordo com o calendário juliano. A maioria das **Igrejas Ortodoxas não adotou a reforma gregoriana senão já em 1924. Vários grupos protestantes** eliminaram completamente o calendário religioso, e celebram somente os principais eventos religiosos, como o dia do Senhor (domingo), a páscoa, o Natal, e alguns grupos, a sexta-feira da paixão.

Principais datas do ano cristão:

Estação do Advento, do domingo mais próximo do dia de Santo André, 30 de novembro, até o Natal.

Imaculada Conceição da Virgem Maria, 8 de dezembro (21 de novembro, segundo o calendário juliano).

Estação do Natal, do Natal até 13 de janeiro.

Natal, 25 de dezembro (7 de janeiro, segundo o calendário juliano).

Festa da Circuncisão, 1º de janeiro (14 de janeiro, segundo o calendário juliano).

Epifania, 6 de janeiro (19 de janeiro, segundo o calendário juliano).

Estação da Quaresma, desde a quarta-feira de cinzas, quarenta dias antes da páscoa, até a páscoa.

Anunciação à Virgem Maria, 25 de março.

Semana Santa, desde o domingo de Ramos até à páscoa.

Estação da páscoa, desde a sexta-feira antes da páscoa.

Domingo da Páscoa, o primeiro domingo após a lua cheia, ou na próxima lua cheia após 21 de março.

Dia da Ascensão, quinta-feira, quarenta dias após a páscoa.

Domingo de Pentecoste, cinqüenta dias após a páscoa.

Domingo da Trindade, o domingo após o Pentecoste.

Corpus Christi, a quinta-feira após o domingo da Trindade.

Assunção da Virgem Maria, 15 de agosto (28 de agosto, segundo o calendário juliano).

Dia de Todos os Santos, 1º de novembro. (AM E UN)

CALENDÁRIO EGÍPCIO

Durante os primeiros estágios da civilização egípcia, há mais de dez mil anos passados, foi usado um calendário sem sofisticação, de doze meses de trinta dias cada um. Portanto, o ano tinha apenas 360 dias. Em cerca de 4000 A.C., foram adicionados cinco dias suplementares ao fim de cada ano, resultando em anos de 365 dias cada, mas que perdia para o ano solar um dia a cada quatro anos. Esse esquema era usado pelos astrônomos gregos, e continuava em uso nos dias de Copérnico, no século XVI. A fim de fazer o calendário equiparar-se com o verdadeiro ano solar,

CALENDÁRIO GREGO — CALENDÁRIO JUDAICO

um edito do rei Ptolomeu III, em 238 A.C., adicionou outro dia suplementar a cada quatro anos. Essa foi a solução também adotada pelos romanos, que se tornou conhecida como a reforma Juliana. Mas o povo egípcio não aceitou a nova regulamentação, e o método antigo prosseguiu. (AM)

CALENDÁRIO GREGO

Os antigos gregos a princípio usavam um calendário lunar, com meses alternados de trinta ou de vinte e nove dias. Por longo tempo, os ajustes do calendário corresponderam ao ciclo das estações do ano, embora considerados sem importância. O curso dos eventos agrícolas e as probabilidades de chuva ou de bom tempo eram atribuídos ao surgimento helíaco ou ao aparecimento de várias constelações facilmente reconhecíveis. Quando os gregos começaram a adicionar o décimo terceiro mês, as intercalações eram feitas arbitrariamente. Outrossim, diferentes comunidades tinham diferentes calendários. A começar pelo século VI A.C., os astrônomos gregos propuseram certo número de ciclos crescentemente precisos, que ajustavam os meses aos anos. O mais famoso ciclo era o ciclo ocenial, um período de oito anos, quando eram intercalados três meses. Esse sistema foi empregado por longo tempo. Em 433 A.C. o astrônomo ateniense Metom publicou a sua descoberta de que cada dezenove anos solares contêm 235 ciclos lunares, ou meses lunares. Os atenienses gravaram o ciclo metônico em ouro, no templo de Atena, e a unidade de cada mês, ou mesmo ciclo, tomou o nome de *número* DOURADO. Hiparco, em 130 A.C., descobriu que o ano solar não dura exatamente 365 dias e um quarto. Mas essas descobertas, embora admiradas, não foram incorporadas ao calendário grego civil. O ciclo ocenial continuou sendo utilizado.

CALENDÁRIO ISLÂMICO

Esse calendário tinha doze meses lunares de vinte e nove ou trinta dias cada, sem quaisquer meses intercalados. Nenhuma tentativa era feita para ajustar esse calendário ao ano solar. Em resultado disso, qualquer feriado fixo, como o dia do Ano Novo, passava por um completo ciclo de estações, a cada trinta e três anos. O calendário era ajustado ao exato mês lunar, mas com a intercalação de onze dias, a cada trinta anos. Assim, havia dezenove anos comuns, de 354 dias, e onze anos intercalares, de 355 dias. Os anos intercalares, a cada trinta anos, eram os anos segundo, quinto, sétimo, décimo, décimo terceiro, décimo sexto, décimo oitavo, vigésimo primeiro, vigésimo quarto, vigésimo sexto, vigésimo nono. O ciclo fixo de 360 meses lunares continha 10.361 dias, errando por apenas um dia, a cada 2.500 anos. Entretanto, esse calendário não é usado com propósitos religiosos pelos islamitas. O mês religioso tem início quando aparece o crescente da lua nova. Essa ocorrência usualmente se verifica dois dias após a ocorrência da lua nova, de acordo com o calendário lunar fixo. Os islamitas também indicam o nome do dia, juntamente com a data, de tal modo que a disparidade não se torna por demais inconveniente. O dia religioso dos islamitas começa ao pôr-do-sol. Os anos, no calendário religioso islâmico, são contados a partir da *Hegira*, a fuga de Maomé (que vide), o que ocorreu a 16 de julho de 622 D.C. O *Ramadan*, ou jejum, começa no dia 273 do calendário fixo. (AM E)

CALENDÁRIO JUDAICO (BÍBLICO)
Esboço

1. Dias
2. Semanas
3. Meses
4. Anos
5. Ciclos
6. Eras
7. Gráfico Ilustrativo

Todos os calendários dos povos antigos estavam baseados em observações astronômicas, embora os sistemas daí resultantes variassem. Os modernos calendários geralmente dependem do ano-solar, ou seja, o tempo em que a terra dá um giro completo em torno do sol. Como esse tempo envolve um resto em horas, minutos e segundos, nosso ano solar precisa de um ajuste de quatro em quatro anos, em que um dia é acrescentado no mês de fevereiro, e também de um outro ajuste, mais raro, para compensar a defasagem. Houve um desses ajustes no tempo do imperador Júlio César, no ano de 46 A.C., com a intercalação de 67 dias, entre os meses de novembro e dezembro. Isso deu origem ao calendário juliano. Mas, no século XVI (1582), houve um novo ajuste, começando então o calendário gregoriano, que foi adotado por países católicos e protestantes. Agora, quatro séculos e pouco depois, tem-se proposto um calendário internacional fixo, com um ano de 13 meses, de quatro semanas cada. Está predito que quando o anticristo aparecer, «cuidará em mudar os tempos e a lei» (Dan. 7:25). Como se vê, a mudança de calendário requer alguma elevada autoridade.

Israel seguia e segue o sistema lunissolar, com um ano de doze meses, de 29 ou 30 dias, alternadamente, e o acréscimo periódico de um mês. Todavia, ao que parece, Israel não desconhecia o ano solar. A comunidade de Qumran seguia um calendário de doze meses, de trinta dias, com um dia suplementar a cada três meses. Isso fazia com que os anos começassem sempre no mesmo dia da semana—talvez uma quarta-feira—e as próprias festas religiosas sempre caíam no mesmo dia do mês, e também no mesmo dia da semana. Há quem pense que Jesus seguia esse calendário, o que poderia explicar a diferença de data da última Ceia, entre os evangelhos sinópticos e o de João—Jesus teria seguido esse calendário na observância da última páscoa, ao passo que as autoridades religiosas de Jerusalém seguiam o calendário lunissolar. Todavia, isso é pura especulação, nada havendo para provar tal assertiva. O fato é que, segundo a Bíblia, o Senhor criou os corpos luminosos do firmamento para «sinais, para estações, para dias e anos» (Gên. 1:14). Os que cultivam a astrologia pensam encontrar aí uma base bíblica para suas idéias, mas, na verdade, o que está envolvido é a formação de um calendário.

Para melhor entendermos o que a Bíblia ensina a respeito, dividiremos nosso estudo nestes títulos: 1. Dias; 2. semanas; 3. meses; 4. anos; 5. ciclos; 6. eras.

1. Dias. A maneira de computar os dias, começou na nação judaica com base na repetida frase de Gênesis: «Houve tarde e manhã, o primeiro dia... Houve tarde e manhã, o segundo dia...» etc. (ver Gên. 1:5-31). De acordo com essas palavras, a nação judaica iniciava cada dia às 18:00 horas (ver Deu. 23:11), ao passo que para os babilônios e a maioria dos povos do Oriente Médio o dia era computado a partir do nascer do sol, às 6:00 horas da manhã. A demarcação entre um dia e outro, entre os israelitas, na verdade era o momento em que três estrelas da segunda magnitude tornavam-se visíveis, segundo se vê em Nee. 4:21: «Assim trabalhávamos na obra; e metade empunhava as lanças desde o raiar do dia até

CALENDÁRIO JUDAICO

o sair das estrelas». Os judeus não davam nomes aos dias da semana, mas eram designados como primeiro, segundo, terceiro, etc. Os dias eram divididos em horas e vigílias, embora a divisão em horas tivesse sido adotada posteriormente, pois no começo eles falavam somente em períodos indefinidos, como «tarde», «manhã», «declinar do dia», etc. (Ver Juí. 19:8). Houve aparelhos engenhosos para marcação do tempo, desde muito antes do tempo de Daniel, entre os babilônios e os egípcios. Os babilônios dividiam o dia em vinte e quatro horas, cada hora dividida em minutos, e estes em segundos. Um desses engenhos antigos aparece no trecho de Isaías 38:8 e II Reis 20:11: «Eis que farei retroceder dez graus a sombra lançada pelo sol declinante no relógio de Acaz». No Novo Testamento, lemos que o Senhor Jesus indagou: «Não são doze as horas do dia?» (João 11:9). Outro tanto se vê no relato sobre a crucificação, que menciona a terceira, a sexta e a nona horas, correspondentes às 9:00 horas, às 12:00 horas e às 15:00 horas, pois Marcos reflete a maneira romana de contar as horas, isto é, a partir das seis horas da manhã (ver Mar. 15:25,33 ss).

Os primeiros hebreus dividiam as noites em três vigílias: a «vigília da manhã (Êxo. 14:24); a «vigília média» (Juí. 7:19); e o «princípio das vigílias» (Lam. 2:19). Mas os romanos dividiam a noite em quatro vigílias, de onde Jesus extraiu uma analogia, em sua advertência escatológica sobre um tempo imprevisível: «...se à tarde, se à meia-noite, se ao cantar do galo, se pela manhã» (Mar. 13:35).

2. Semanas. A semana de sete dias é de origem semita. Os babilônios e assírios vinculavam suas semanas ao ciclo lunar, correspondentes aos quatro ciclos da lua, a começar a cada lua nova. A semana judaica tinha origem na narrativa da criação, sem ligação aos ciclos lunares ou solares, porquanto dependia da observância do sétimo dia, ou sábado. A semana egípcia tinha dez dias.

Embora Deus tivesse salientado o sétimo dia, por ocasião da criação (ver Gên. 1:2,3), o registro bíblico faz silêncio quanto à observância do sábado durante o longo intervalo entre a criação e a época de Moisés. Não há registro da observância religiosa do sábado nos tempos antediluvianos ou nos dias dos patriarcas hebreus. Todavia, há indicações bíblicas indiretas de que o sábado sempre foi tido como um dia religioso importante. Na legislação mosaica, o sábado tornou-se um dos sinais do pacto entre Deus e Israel: «Certamente guardareis os meus sábados; pois é sinal entre mim e vós nas vossas gerações...» (Êxo. 31:13). Em consonância com isso, Jesus, que veio para cumprir a lei, não se descuidava dessa observância, embora os judeus, de modo geral, se mostrassem bastante relapsos quanto à questão: «Indo para Nazaré, onde fora criado, entrou, num sábado, na sinagoga, segundo o seu costume...» (Luc. 4:16). No entanto, em face dos cruciais acontecimentos ocorridos na vida de Cristo e da Igreja, no primeiro dia da semana, os primitivos cristãos passaram a reunir-se no primeiro dia da semana, e não no sétimo. Por causa do dia da ressurreição de Cristo: «E muito cedo, no primeiro dia da semana, ao despontar do sol, foram ao túmulo...» (Mar. 16:2 ss). Os discípulos estavam reunidos quando Cristo lhes apareceu pela primeira vez, depois de ressurrecto: «Ao cair da tarde daquele dia, o primeiro da semana, trancadas as portas da casa onde estavam os discípulos, com medo dos judeus, veio Jesus, pôs-se no' meio e disse-lhes: Paz seja convosco!» (João 20:19). Por que foi em um primeiro dia da semana que teve início o ministério do Espírito Santo à Igreja: «Ao cumprir-se o dia de Pentecoste, estavam todos reunidos no mesmo lugar...» (Atos 2:1 ss). Em face desses grandes acontecimentos, os cristãos, embora ocasionalmente freqüentando a sinagoga ou o templo, em dia de sábado (sobretudo quando queriam pregar aos judeus, que se reuniam nesse dia da semana), tinham no primeiro dia da semana o seu dia normal de reuniões: «No primeiro dia da semana, estando nós reunidos com o fim de partir o pão...» (Atos 20:7). E também: «No primeiro dia da semana cada um de vós ponha de parte, em casa, conforme a sua prosperidade, e vá juntando, para que se não façam coletas quando eu for» (I Cor. 16:2). Todavia, isso não significa que o domingo tenha tomado o lugar do sábado, para os cristãos. Para nós, servos de Deus, todos os dias são santos. É sinal de pouca espiritualidade quando alguém insiste em guardar dias e estações, porquanto, tudo quanto é simbolizado pelos mesmos, foi cumprido em Cristo. «...agora que conheceis a Deus, ou antes, sendo conhecidos por Deus, como estais voltando outra vez aos rudimentos fracos e pobres, aos quais de novo quereis ainda escravizar-vos? Guardais dias, e meses, e tempos e anos. Receio de vós tenha eu trabalhado em vão para convosco» (Gál. 4:9-11). A lei e suas ordenanças foram canceladas no caso do crente: «...(Cristo Jesus)... aboliu na sua carne a lei dos mandamentos na forma de ordenanças» (Efé. 2:15). Ora, o sábado é uma das ordenanças da lei. (Ver sobre o *dia de domingo*).

3. Meses. No hebraico, a palavra é um sinônimo para «luas». Os povos antigos mediam o tempo pelas fases da lua. Assim, o termo árabe para *lua* significa «medidora». E o deus-lua dos egípcios, era também o deus da medição. Entre os judeus de gerações posteriores, três membros do sinédrio tinham a responsabilidade de vigiar e anunciar a primeira aparição da lua nova, e então a notícia do começo de um novo mês espalhava-se pelo país através de sinais de fumaça, e, mais tarde, mediante mensageiros. O calendário constante, que dispensou essa medida, pelo menos em tese, segundo se diz, foi inaugurado pelo patriarca Hilel.

Entre os israelitas, os meses eram designados com nomes tomados por empréstimo dos cananeus e fenícios. Esses nomes estavam ligados às estações do ano, segundo se vê pelos quatro nomes que sobreviveram nos antigos registros hebraicos: Abibe (Êxo. 13:4 e Deu. 16:1), correspondente ao Nisã do calendário posterior, que significa «mês das espigas maduras»; Zive (I Reis 6:1), correspondente ao posterior mês do Iyyar, que significa «mês das flores», Etanim (I Reis 8:2), correspondente ao posterior mês de Tisri, que significa «mês dos riachos perenes»; e Bul (I Reis 6:38), correspondente ao posterior mês de Marchesvam, que significa *chuvas*, sendo que o primeiro mês da estação chuvosa. No entanto, durante o período monárquico de Israel, o calendário foi reformado, e os antigos nomes dos meses foram substituídos por números ordinais, primeiro, segundo, terceiro, etc., ao mesmo tempo em que o começo do ano foi transferido para a primavera. Isso é ilustrado em I Reis 6:1 e 8:2. Citamos este último trecho: «Todos os homens de Israel se congregaram junto ao rei Salomão, na ocasião da festa, no mês de etanim, que é o sétimo». Em cerca de 520 A.C., Ageu (1:1 e 2:1,10), usou apenas números ordinais para indicar os meses, sem referir-se aos antigos nomes dos mesmos. Zacarias, um profeta contemporâneo daquele, liga o número ordinal de certo mês ao nome babilônico do mesmo, o que se tornou prática popular após o exílio. Diz Zacarias 1:7: «Aos vinte e quatro

CALENDÁRIO JUDAICO

dias do mês undécimo, que é o mês de sebate...» Todavia, esses nomes importados da Babilônia não eram usados nos registros civis e históricos dos judeus. Tais nomes tinham conotações agrícolas, ainda que vinculados a nomes de divindades pagãs da natureza, em certos casos. O chamado calendário de Gezer, que data do século X A.C., fornece-nos um interessante vislumbre sobre a vida agrícola da Palestina. Trata-se de uma inscrição que enumera operações agrícolas referentes a oito meses, e onde são mencionadas atividades como a semeadura, a colheita do linho, a colheita da cevada e a poda da videira.

4. Anos. O calendário judaico envolvia dois anos concorrentes, a saber: o ano religioso, que começava na primavera, com o mês de Nisã, e o ano civil, que começava no outono, com o mês de Tisri. O ano religioso foi instituído por Moisés, após o êxodo. Consiste em doze ou treze meses lunares de 29-1/2 dias cada. O ano civil é mais antigo, computado supostamente desde a criação, que tradicionalmente ocorreu no outono (3760 A.C.). Tornou-se popular a partir do século III D.C. Que o ano civil era observado pelo antigo povo de Israel torna-se evidente no preceito mosaico, que diz: «Guardarás a festa da sega dos primeiros frutos do teu trabalho, que houveres semeado no campo, e a festa da colheita, à saída do ano, quando recolheres do campo o fruto do teu trabalho» (Êxo. 23:16).

Os babilônios e os egípcios criaram o mês intercalado, a fim de ajustar o ano solar ao ano lunar. Os anos bissextos dos judeus, com seu ciclo de 19 anos foram fixados, com adição de um décimo terceiro mês nos anos terceiro, sexto, nono, décimo primeiro, décimo quarto, décimo sétimo e décimo nono. E se no décimo sexto dia do mês de Nisã o sol não tivesse atingido o equinócio de inverno, o mês era declarado como o segundo mês de Adar, ao passo que o mês seguinte era declarado mês de Nisã.

Conforme dissemos no começo deste artigo, grande avanço foi feito quando do calendário traçado por Júlio César, primeiro imperador romano, em 46 A.C. Mas esse ano, de 365 dias e um quarto, tinha uma defasagem de onze minutos, acima do ano solar. Por esse motivo, em 1582, o então papa Gregório XIII fez uma reforma, e o novo calendário passou a chamar-se de calendário gregoriano (sob cujo regime vivemos). Esse envolve um erro infinitesimal que se acumula para formar um dia, a cada 3.325 anos. É interessante observar que o calendário mais exato que a humanidade já criou é o dos índios maias, da América Central, que acusa um erro acumulado de um dia, a cada seis mil anos!

5. Ciclos. Em face do sétimo dia da criação, os judeus passaram a dar um elevado sentido religioso e sagrado ao número sete. Assim, as convocações solenes e as festas judaicas tinham lugar no sétimo dia, ou na sétima semana, ou no sétimo mês, ou no sétimo ano ou a cada sete vezes sete anos. A cada sete dias havia o sábado. A festa do Pentecoste caía no fim de sete semanas após a páscoa, no primeiro dia da semana seguinte. A festa das Trombetas, que introduzia o sétimo mês, envolvia uma «assembléia solene». O ano sabático impunha um solene repouso para os proprietários de terras, para as terras aráveis e até para os animais de carga. Nesse ano também eram postos em liberdade os escravos hebreus. Os anos sabático e de jubileu eram sincronizados ao ano civil ou agrícola. O ano do jubileu, que ocorria a cada cinqüenta anos, após sete vezes sete anos, tinha conotações importantíssimas na vida social judaica. (Ver Lev. 25:8-17).

6. Eras. No calendário bíblico, «eras» indicam todo o tempo que vai da criação do mundo à consumação dos séculos. Há grandes acontecimentos que são marcos terminais, com o início de alguma nova fase para a humanidade. Esses marcos, em sua seqüência cronológica, são: a criação, o dilúvio, a vida de Abraão, o êxodo, o exílio babilônico e o nascimento de Jesus. Em conseqüência, as eras bíblicas poderiam ser intituladas como: antediluviana, pós-diluviana, patriarcal, israelita, judaica e cristã. (Ver Mat. 1:2-17 e Luc. 3:23-37).

Astronomicamente falando, a fenomenal estrela que guiou os magos ao menino Jesus, dividiu a história da humanidade em Antes de Cristo (A.C.) e Depois de Cristo (D.C.). Esse é o eixo em torno do qual a história humana é datada, pondo fim a uma antiga ordem de coisas e dando início a uma nova ordem. As predições bíblicas aludem a mais duras eras, a saber: a. O milênio, logo após a Grande Tribulação, inaugurado pela segunda vinda de Cristo, quando ele instaurar o seu reino de mil anos à face da terra; e b. a era eterna, quando forem criados novos céus e nova terra. Ver acerca do *milênio* e da *era eterna*. Cf. Apo. 20:1-15 e 21:1-5.

7. GRÁFICO ILUSTRATIVO

Nomes dos Meses	Equivalentes	Festas	Estações	Tempo	Colheita
Abide ou Nisã, 30 dias. 1º mês do ano sagrado e 7º mês do ano civil	Março-abril	1. Lua Nova, Núm. 10:10. Jejum por Nadabe e Abiú, Lev. 10:1,2. 10. Seleção do cordeiro pascal, Êxo. 12:3; festa por Miriã, Núm. 20:1. 14. Abate do cordeiro pascal, à tarde, Êxo. 12:6. Começa a páscoa, Núm. 28:16. 15. Primeiro dia dos pães asmos, Núm. 28:17. 16. Primícias; molhos são oferecidos, Lev. 23:10. Começo da colheita; 50 dias para o Pentecoste, Lev. 23:6. 15 a 21. Santas convocações, Lev. 23:7. 21. Fim da páscoa; fim dos pães asmos, Lev. 23:6. 26. Jejum pela morte de Josué.	Equinócio da primavera	Ventilado; queda das últimas chuvas, Deu. 11:14. As neves se dissolvem e os rios se enchem. O Jordão extravasa, Jos. 3:15.	Cevada, maturação do trigo; aparecem as flores e hortaliças.
Zife ou Ijar, 29 dias. 2º do ano sagrado e 8º do ano civil	Abril-maio	1. Lua nova, Núm. 1:18. 6. Jejum de 3 dias por excessos da páscoa. 10. Jejum pela morte de Eli e captura da arca, I Sam. 4:11 ss. 15. Segunda páscoa, para os que não a celebraram no mês de Abide, relembrando a entrada no deserto, Êxo. 16:11. 23. Festa lembrando a captura de Gaza pelos Macabeus e a purificação do templo. 27. Festa lembrando a expulsão dos galileus de Jerusalém. 28. Jejum pela morte de Samuel, I Sam. 25:1.	Verão	Ventilado; chuvas e trovoadas, com raros temporais. Céu sem nuvens. Ventos quentes do vale do Jordão.	Colheita da cevada, Rute 1:22. O trigo amadurece; abricós.
Sivã, 30 dias, 3º do ano sagrado e 9º do ano civil	Maio-junho	1. Lua nova 2. Festa do Pentecoste ou das semanas, por ser 7 dias após a páscoa, Lev. 23:15-21. 15,16. Celebração da vitória sobre Bete-Seã, I Mac. 5:52, 12:40,41.	Verão	Ventos do noroeste e leste; vento ressecante dos desertos do sul. Céu claro.	Começa a colheita: trigo; amêndoas; uvas começam a amadurecer; mel do vale do Jordão.

Nomes dos Meses	Equivalentes	Festas	Estações	Tempo	Colheita
		22. Jejum pelos súditos de Jeroboão que levaram primícias a Jerusalém, I Reis 12:27. 25. Jejum em memória dos rabinos Simeão, Ismael e Canina. Festa lembrando o juízo de Alexandre em favor dos judeus. 27. Jejum relembrando a queima dos livros da lei.			
Tamuz, 29 dias. 4º do ano sagrado e 10º do ano civil	Junho-julho	1. Lua nova. 14. Festa comemorando a abolição de um livro dos saduceus e dos betusianos, que queriam subverter a lei oral e as tradições. 17. Jejum comemorando a quebra das tábuas da lei por Moisés, Êxo. 32:19; e tomada de Jerusalém por Tito, em 70 D.C.	Calor máximo do verão	Ventilado do norte, do oeste e do leste; calor intenso.	Colheita do trigo nas terras altas; várias frutas.
Abe, 30 dias. 5º do ano sagrado e 11º do ano civil	Julho-agosto	1. Lua nova. Jejum pela morte de Aarão. 9. Jejum em memória da declaração divina contra os murmuradores opostos à entrada em Canaã, Núm. 14:29-31. 18. Jejum por causa da lâmpada apagada, nos dias de Acaz. 21. Festa quando a madeira era empilhada no templo. 24. Festa em memória da lei, segundo a qual filhos e filhas herdavam a mesma dos seus pais.	Calor do verão	Ventos do leste; calor intenso; céu claro.	Vindima, colheita do figo, das castanhas, azeitonas, etc. Lev. 26:5.
Elul, 29 dias. 6º do ano sagrado e 12º do ano civil	Agosto-setem.	1. Lua nova. 7. Festa da dedicação dos muros de Jerusalém, por Neemias. 17. Jejum pela morte dos espiões incrédulos, Núm. 14:26. 21. Festa, oferta da madeira. 22. Festa em memória dos israelitas ímpios punidos com a morte. Durante o mês todo, soavam as trombetas, avisando sobre o ano civil próximo.	Verão quente	Ventos do norte e do leste. Calor intenso; relâmpagos, com pouca chuva.	Vindima; colheita do milho, do algodão; romãs amadurecem.

Nomes dos Meses	Equivalentes	Festas	Estações	Tempo	Colheita
Etanim ou Tisri, 30 dias, 7º do ano sagrado e 1º do ano civil	Setem.-outub.	1. Lua nova; Ano Novo; festa das Trombetas, Lev. 23:24, Núm. 29:1,2. 3. Jejum pelo assassínio de Gedalias, II Reis 25:25. O sumo sacerdote é separado para o Dia da Expiação. 7. Jejum relembrando a adoração do bezerro de ouro. 10. Dia da Expiação, Atos 27:9. Único dia de jejum exigido pela Lei; primeiro dia do Ano de Jubileu. 15-21. Festa dos Tabernáculos. 22. Santa convocação; ramos de palmeiras; oração pela chuva. 23. Festa pelo término da Lei; dedicação do templo de Salomão.	Semeadura; o grão germina	Ventos do nordeste.	Aração e semeadura começam assim que se iniciam as chuvas, Pro. 20:4. Colheita do algodão.
Bul ou Marcesvan, 29 dias, 8º do ano sagrado e 2º do ano civil	Outub.-novem.	1. Lua nova 6,7. Jejum por Nabucodonosor ter cegado Ezequias, II Reis 25:7; Jer. 52:10. 17. Orações pela chuva. 19. Jejum pelas faltas durante a festa dos Tabernáculos. 23. Pedras memoriais do altar profanado pelos gregos, I Mac. 4:44. 26. Festa em memória da recuperação, após o exílio, dos lugares ocupados pelos cutitas.	Outono	Ventilado de várias direções; muita chuva.	Semeadura do trigo e da cevada; vindima no N. Colheita do arroz; frutas cítricas florescem; figos amadurecem; desaparece quase toda a vegetação.
Quisleu, 30 dias, 9º do ano sagrado e 3º do ano civil	Novem.-dezem.	1. Lua nova. 2. Jejum de três dias, se não viessem chuvas. 3. Festa em honra aos Asmoneus que derrubaram ídolos postos no templo pelos gentios. 6. Festa em memória da queima dos rolos por Jeoaquim, Jer. 36:23. 7. Festa em memória da morte de Herodes, o Grande. 14. Jejum absoluto, se não viessem chuvas.	Começa o inverno, João 10:22.	Neve nos montes; tempestades; muita chuva.	Árvores sem folhas, mas planícies e desertos reverdecem.

Nomes dos Meses	Equivalentes	Festas	Estações	Tempo	Colheita
Tebete, 29 dias, 10º do ano sagrado e 4º do ano civil	Dezem.-janeiro	21. Festa no monte Gerizim; o monte Gerizim é arado e semeado com joio, como os samaritanos intentaram fazer com o terreno do templo. 25. Festa da dedicação do templo, ou Luzes (8 dias), em memória da restauração do templo por Judas Macabeu.	Meio-inverno	Ventos do norte, do nordeste, noroeste. No mês mais frio, saraiva e neve, Joel 10:11, nas terras altas, e, algumas vezes, em Jerusalém.	Rebanhos descem para os vales. Cultivo dos vales começa. Laranjas amadurecem. Regiões mais baixas reverdecem com o cereal.
Sebate, 30 dias, 11º do ano sagrado e 5º do ano civil	Janeiro-fev.	1. Lua nova. 2. Regozijo: Alexandre Janeu, inimigo dos fariseus, morreu. 4,5. Jejum em memória da morte dos anciãos, sucessores de Josué. 15. Começo do ano das Árvores. 22. Festa em memória da morte de Niscaleno, que ordenou a colocação de ídolos no templo, mas que morreu antes disso ser cumprido. 29. Celebração da morte de Antíoco Epifânio.	Inverno	Ventos do noroeste, norte e nordeste. Tendência para o calor.	Amêndoas e pêssegos florescem nas áreas quentes. Laranjas são colhidas.
Adar, 29 dias, 12º do ano sagrado e 6º do ano civil	Fever.-março	1. Lua nova. 7. Jejum pela morte de Moisés, Deut. 34:5. 8,9. Trombetas soam em agradecimento pelas chuvas; orações por mais chuvas. 12. Festa em memória de Holiano e Pipo, dois prosélitos que preferiram morrer a quebrar a lei. 13. Jejum de Ester, (4:6). Festa celebrada a morte de Nicanor, inimigo dos judeus I Mac. 7:44. 14. 1º Purim, festa menor das sortes, Est. 9:21. 15. Grande Festa de Purim. 17. Festa em comemoração aos sábios que fugiram de Alexandre Janeu. 20. Festa pelas chuvas em época de seca, nos dias de Alexandre Janeu. 23. Festa comemorativa da dedicação do templo de Zorobabel, Esd. 6:16. 28. Festa comemorativa por terem sido repelidos os decretos dos reis gregos proibindo a circuncisão.	Primavera, com resíduos do inverno.	Ventos do oeste; trovoadas, saraiva e neve nas terras altas. Começam as últimas chuvas, das quais dependem as plantações, para ser evitada a fome.	Nos vales, cultivo chega ao fim, e amadurece a cevada.

CALENDÁRIO ROMANO

Os antigos romanos adotavam o sistema lunar, em que os meses tinham trinta ou vinte e nove dias alternadamente. O ano civil tinha apenas dez meses, ou seja, apenas 295 dias. O primeiro mês era março. Os meses sétimo, oitavo, nono e décimo receberam nomes que indicavam a ordem numérica no calendário, de onde nos vieram os modernos meses de setembro, outubro, novembro e dezembro. De conformidade com as lendas, foi durante o reinado de Numa Pompílio, em cerca de 700 A.C., que foram acrescentados os meses de janeiro e fevereiro, para serem os meses décimo primeiro e décimo segundo. Fevereiro tinha apenas 28 dias. Posteriormente, na história romana, os meses deixaram de ser lunares. Os meses segundo, quarto, sétimo e nono passaram a ter trinta dias cada, e os demais, trinta e um dias, excetuando fevereiro, que tinha apenas vinte e oito. Os romanos dividiam os meses em unidades. Portanto, as calendas eram o primeiro dia de cada mês; os nomes eram o quinto ou o sétimo dia, e os ides eram o décimo terceiro ou o décimo quinto dia. O dia que antecedia a cada unidade era chamado de *véspera*. A maneira como os romanos manipulavam os dias, e os termos aplicados aos mesmos, eram totalmente arbitrários, e os imperadores romanos interferiam de uma maneira que muito perturbava o bom fluxo do calendário. Assim, eles podiam alongar ou encurtar as magistraturas, o que provocou a confusão geral. Ver sobre as reformas Juliana e Gregoriana: *Calendários Juliano e Gregoriano*.

CALENDÁRIOS BABILÔNIO, ASSÍRIO E CALDEU

Para as civilizações do vale do Tigre-Eufrates, o ano começava na primavera, com o mês de *Nisanu*, consistindo de doze meses lunares. Cada mês começava ao cair da tarde, assim que aparecia a lua crescente. Os meses duravam, alternadamente, 30 ou 29 dias, e o ano de 354 dias sofria uma diferença de aproximadamente um mês, em relação ao ano solar, ao fim de cada três anos. Em consequência, um mês extra usualmente era adicionado a cada três anos, por ordem do monarca reinante. O tempo de tais intercalações era determinado pela observação de uma estrela cujo aparecimento helíaco ocorria, pelo menos em princípio, em um mês designado. Infelizmente, essas intercalações eram falhas. Por isso, não era incomum que houvesse dois anos consecutivos de treze meses cada. Porém, a partir de 380 A.C., houve melhor codificação, havendo sete intercalações a cada dezenove anos, o mesmo período que o do ciclo que fora desenvolvido na Grécia, cinquenta anos antes. Não se sabe se os babilônios descobriram sozinhos o ciclo, ou se o pediram emprestado dos gregos. (AM)

CALENDÁRIOS JULIANO E GREGORIANO

Júlio César resolveu reformar o calendário romano (que vide). Convidou o astrônomo grego Sosígenes para servir de conselheiro. Foi feita uma modificação em 46 A.C., que se tornou conhecida como *o fim da confusão*. Em primeiro lugar, ficou decidido que o equinócio de inverno cairia a 25 de março. Para tanto, oitenta e cinco dias foram acrescentados ao ano 46 A.C. O ano civil, dali por diante, foi fixado em 365 dias. Os reformadores sabiam que o ano solar tinha 365 dias e um quarto, mas sentiam que o ano continuaria concordando com as estações, se um dia adicional fosse intercalado a cada quatro anos. Esse dia extra não era adicionado ao fim do mês de fevereiro, conforme sucede em nossos dias, mas após o dia 24 de fevereiro. De acordo com a terminologia romana, o dia 24 era o sexto das calendas de março (ver Calendário Romano), pelo que, na verdade, o dia intercalado era um segundo dia seis. O termo bissexto, pois, foi usado para designar esse dia extra. A reforma juliana também fez o dia 1º de janeiro ser o dia em que os cônsules davam início a seus deveres, e assim, esse tornou-se o primeiro dia do ano. O dia 1º de janeiro de 45 A.C. foi o dia da inauguração do calendário juliano. Porém, os meses de setembro, outubro, novembro e dezembro retiveram seus nomes, a despeito do fato que agora eles não eram mais o sétimo, o oitavo, o nono e o décimo meses do ano. O ano juliano de 365 dias e um quarto é ligeiramente mais longo que o verdadeiro ano solar, que, de fato, dura 365,2422 dias. Essa variação cria uma diferença que é apenas uma fração: 0,0078 de dia, a cada ano. Isso acumula-se para formar três dias a cada quatro séculos. Por causa desse pequeno desvio, que, acumulado século após século, torna-se grande, tornou-se necessária uma nova reforma, conhecida como reforma gregoriana.

Reforma Gregoriana. O calendário juliano continuou desviando-se cada vez mais do verdadeiro ano solar. A páscoa, um importante feriado da primavera, a continuar as coisas, terminaria no verão, perturbando tudo. Pela época do papa Gregório XIII, nos fins do 'século XVI, o desvio já era de dez dias. Reconhecendo que a questão estava ficando crítica, Gregório resolveu reformar o calendário. Ele cortou dez dias do ano de 1582, de tal modo que, começando pelo ano seguinte, o equinócio cairia novamente a vinte e um de março. O dia depois da sexta-feira, quatro de outubro de 1582, tornou-se assim a sexta-feira, quinze de outubro.

O calendário gregoriano requer que se cortem três dias do ano, a cada quatrocentos anos. Isso ocorreu em 1600, e terá de ocorrer novamente no ano 2000. Embora o ano solar tenha exatamente 365,2422 dias, há variações, pois a rotação da terra, em torno de seu eixo, não se dá de maneira uniforme. Portanto, é impossível predizermos quais futuros ajustes tornar-se-ão necessários, digamos, dentro de três a quatro mil anos a partir de agora. Além disso, podem ocorrer mudanças de pólo, e isso conturbará todos os cálculos. Todos os países têm adotado esse calendário para uso civil, embora existam, lado a lado com ele, os calendários religiosos. (AM)

CALEVALA Ver **Kalevala**.

CALFI

Pai de Judas, um capitão sob as ordens de Jonatã Macabeu (I Macabeu 11:70). Seu filho, Judas, juntamente com Matias, permaneceu em companhia de Jonatã, quando outros fugiram a Hazor, após terem caído em uma emboscada. Esses reuniram forças e derrotaram o inimigo, —matando três mil deles. Josefo, *Anti.* xiii.5,7 diz que seu nome era Chapseu.

CALI Ver **Kali**.

CÁLICE

No latim, **calix**; no grego, **potérion**. Palavra usada em Mateus 26:26 e paralelos, para indicar o vaso usado por Jesus para distribuir o vinho, por ocasião da instituição da Ceia do Senhor. E também indica o vaso usado na *eucaristia* (que vide), para conter o vinho a ser consagrado, segundo o uso da Igreja Católica Romana, durante a «missa». Nesta, o cálice é feito de metal precioso. Na Idade Média, os cálices tinham um maior leque de utilizações. O cálice ministerial distribuía o vinho à congregação, quando a comunhão ainda incluía tanto o pão quanto o vinho. Os vasos usados com essa finalidade usualmente eram feitos de ouro ou de prata. Materiais mais humildes eram proibidos. Grandes cálices eram postos nos templos para receber o vinho doado pelos fiéis. Nos ritos batismais, era empregado um cálice especial para misturar a bebida simbólica do candidato ao batismo, isto é, leite e mel. Cálices funerários eram disponíveis, para serem postos nos túmulos dos membros do clero. Os primeiros cálices eram modelados segundo o estilo da época. A lei canônica requer que antes que um cálice possa ser usado na Igreja Católica Romana, seja o mesmo consagrado por um bispo ou por um abade. (AM E)

CÁLICE DE BÊNÇÃO

Um título aplicado ao vinho da Ceia do Senhor, em I Coríntios 10:16. Provavelmente porque o mesmo título foi dado ao terceiro cálice de vinho, por ocasião da última páscoa festejada por Jesus; e mais ainda por ser o cálice do Senhor, um símbolo do novo pacto. Os judeus encerravam suas refeições com um cálice de bênção, símbolo de agradecimento a Deus, a fonte originária de todas as coisas boas. Quando da celebração da Ceia do Senhor, expressamos graças por aquilo que a morte de Cristo significa para nós. Para a alma remida, há um banquete espiritual, o banquete dos benditos, congraçados em torno de Jesus Cristo, o Senhor que os remiu.

CALICLES

Filósofo e político grego do século V A.C., um dos disputantes do diálogo de Platão, *Górgias*. Na qualidade de sofista (que vide), ele argumentava em prol do forte império ou governo, como lei natural, o que também seria um direito natural. Em outras palavras, poder é direito. Ele supunha que as convenções da sociedade tentam escravizar os fortes, e assim subverter a justiça natural. Ele também argumentava em favor do *prazer* como o grande alvo da vida. Ver sobre o Hedonismo. (EP P)

CALIFA

Vem de um vocábulo árabe que significa **sucessor**, título dado aos sucessores de Maomé, quanto às questões temporais e espirituais. Os quatro primeiros califas foram Aleu Bekr, Omar, Othman e Ali, todos antes intimamente associados ao profeta. Posteriormente, o califado tornou-se um prêmio muito procurado, circundado por intensa rivalidade e contenda. Ver sobre *Islamismo*.

CALÍGULA

Viveu de 12 a 41 D.C. Seu apelido, que em latim significa «botinhas», foi-lhe dado afetuosamente, pelos soldados sob o comando de seu pai. Em criança ele acompanhava seu genitor nas campanhas militares, usando suas próprias botas militares. No ano 19 D.C., seu pai teve morte prematura, e sua mãe foi detida como conspiradora, em 29 D.C. Após um breve intervalo, ele uniu-se ao imperador Tibério, que então residia na ilha de Capri. Após o ano 33 D.C., ele era o único filho sobrevivente de Germânico, tendo sido nomeado por Tibério como co-herdeiro de sua propriedade, juntamente com Tibério Gemellus, o neto mais jovem do imperador. Quando Tibério faleceu, em 37 D.C., o senado romano declarou seu testamento inválido, pelo que Calígula tornou-se seu único herdeiro, e foi declarado imperador. Seu nome completo era Gaio Júlio César Germânico.

Calígula adotou Tibério Gemellus, mas executou-o um ano mais tarde. No primeiro ano de seu governo, ficou seriamente enfermo. Quando, supostamente, recuperou-se, começou a manifestar sintomas de loucura sádica e de irresponsabilidade, que o tornaram relembrado na história. Foi assassinado em 41 D.C., para alívio de muitas pessoas de bem. Sua morte impediu uma revolta generalizada dos judeus. Ele havia ordenado que fosse erigido uma estátua sua, no Santo dos Santos do templo de Jerusalém. Sua morte, bem como a atuação diplomática do legado da Síria, impediram um desastre completo. Filo, o filósofo-teólogo-neoplatônico-judeu, de Alexandria, encabeçou uma embaixada que se dirigiu a Calígula, em 39 ou 40 D.C., e sua narrativa informa-nos sobre muitos dos horrores e das estranhezas desse imperador. De fato, ele foi a mais grotesca figura que já serviu como imperador do império romano. (AM PHI SU)

CALÍSTENES

Foi um soldado do exército de Nicanor, acusado de incendiar as portas do templo de Jerusalém, quando Antíoco Epifânio (que vide) destruiu Jerusalém, em 168 A.C. Quando os judeus obtiveram, afinal, a vitória, eles fizeram Calístenes e outros, que «haviam fugido para uma casinha» (II Mac. 8:33), perecerem em uma fogueira. Isso teve lugar em 165 A.C.

CALISTO

1586-1656. Foi um teólogo luterano que adquiriu a reputação de ser reconciliador. Porém, suas tentativas de reconciliação somente levaram-no a ser uma figura suspeitada por todos. A situação deu origem à controvérsia sincretista (que vide). (AM E)

CALISTO II, Papa
Ver **Worms, Concordata de**

CALNÉ

1. De acordo com alguns eruditos, no hebraico significaria «forte de Anu». Anu era uma das principais divindades do panteão babilônico. O local provável é a moderna Niffer, no Talmude, Nopher. Fica cerca de cem quilômetros a suleste da antiga cidade da Babilônia, à margem esquerda do rio Eufrates. A LXX refere-se a Calné ou Calno como o lugar onde foi edificada a torre famosa (Isa. 10:9). No século VIII A.C., foi conquistada por um dos reis assírios, e nunca mais reconquistou a sua prosperidade. Ela foi uma das cidades da Babilônia, fundada por Ninrode, referida em associação com Babel, Ereque e Acade (Gên. 10:10). O local acima referido tem **sido intensamente investigado** pela arqueologia. Ver sobre Nipur. Contudo, há estudiosos que a identificam com Kulunu, uma outra antiga cidade próxima da Babilônia. Ainda outros supõem que a mesma deveria ser identificada com Hursagkalama, uma cidade gêmea de Quis. Outrossim, com base em

uma compreensão diferente sobre o texto hebraico, alguns intérpretes traduzem Calné como *todas elas*, pelo que aquele versículo diria: «O princípio do seu reino foi Babel, Ereque, Acade, todas elas na terra de Sinear». Nesse caso, nunca houve uma cidade chamada Calné, e todas essas identificações, acima referidas, laboram em erro.

2. Calne (segundo nossa versão portuguesa, sem acento agudo no e final) figura em Amós 6:2, juntamente com Hamate. Poderia ser Kulani, a moderna Kallanhu, cerca de dez quilômetros de Arpade. Kullani(a) é uma aldeia mencionada em documentos assírios, em associação com Arpade.

CALOR E FRIO

No trecho de Gênesis 8:22 encontramos o contraste entre a semeadura e a colheita, entre o verão e o inverno, entre o dia e a noite, entre o calor e o frio. Tudo isso fazia parte da promessa do Senhor de que não haveria de sobrevir outro período de destruição geral no mundo, por meio de um dilúvio, de tal modo que esses estados e condições contrastantes prosseguiriam até o fim dos tempos.

A Palestina é um país bem pequeno, cuja área aproxima-se da do estado do Rio Grande do Norte, no nordeste brasileiro. Apesar de tão pequena, há ali tremendos contrastes de clima e temperatura. Todavia, ali o frio não perdura por longo tempo; e, apesar de cair alguma neve, o período de nevascas é bem curto. As variações climáticas devem-se aos diferentes tipos de terreno, à extensa costa marítima, à existência de montes, planícies e áreas desérticas. As antigas residências ali construídas não tinham qualquer proteção especial contra o frio, exceto no caso das casas dos mais abastados, onde havia uma espécie de forno onde era queimado carvão vegetal. Nos dias frios, as pessoas se acumulavam em torno das fogueiras de carvão, conforme se lê acerca de Pedro, no pátio da casa do sumo sacerdote (João 18:18). Ver o artigo sobre o *Calendário*, onde damos um gráfico que mostra que tipo de condições atmosféricas havia de mês em mês, durante os festivais e na época das diversas colheitas.

O Frio nos Sonhos e nas Visões. Pode estar em pauta alguma pessoa que quase não demonstra suas emoções; uma pessoa calculista e traiçoeira; uma pessoa sexualmente indiferente. Ficar moldando a cinzel um bloco de gelo pode significar tentar interessar uma pessoa sexualmente indiferente pelas questões sexuais. O medo também pode ser simbolizado pelo frio, se produz tremor.

O Calor nos Sonhos e nas Visões. Pode estar em foco uma advertência de esforço demasiado; ou o progresso na vida, a boa sorte, a boa produtividade, etc. Calor é energia, pelo que simboliza trabalho e realização. Ou então indica uma pessoa sexualmente intensa e ativa.

CALÚNIA

Várias palavras hebraicas e várias palavras gregas estão envolvidas na compreensão desse assunto, a saber:

1. *Dibbah*, «relatório contrário». Palavra hebraica que aparece por nove vezes: Jer. 20:10; Gên. 37:2; Núm. 13:32; 14:37; Pro. 25:10; Eze. 36:3; Núm. 14:36; Sal. 31:13; Pro. 10:18.

2. *Rakil*, «caluniador». Palavra hebraica que se encontra por três vezes: Lev. 19:16; Pro. 20:19; 11:13.

3. *Nirgan*, «sussurrador». Termo hebraico que aparece por quatro vezes: Pro. 18:8; 26:20,22; 16:18.

4. *Lashan*, «usar a língua». Palavra hebraica que figura por duas vezes: Sal. 101:5 e Pro. 30:10.

5. *Katalaléo*, «difamar», «caluniar». Vocábulo grego que aparece por cinco vezes: Tia. 4:11; I Ped. 2:12 e 3:16.

6. *Pseudomarturéo*, «dar falso testemunho». Palavra grega que figura por cinco vezes: Mat. 19:18; Mar. 10:19; 14:56,57; Luc. 18:20.

Caluniar é acusar falsamente, mormente em alguma situação judicial. Também é falar contrariamente a alguém a quem Deus defende.

O caráter básico desse pecado pode ser visto no fato de que foi incluído no decálogo (Êxo. 20:16), como também no fato de que aparece no contexto imediato do qual Jesus Cristo citou o segundo e grande mandamento (Lev. 19:15-18; cf. Mat. 19:19; 22:39; Tia. 2:8). Ali, o amor ao próximo é caracterizado pelo fato de que não o caluniamos, mas antes, mostramo-lhe justiça, sem qualquer parcialidade.

Que a calúnia é contra a retidão e a sabedoria de Deus é algo repetidamente frisado no livro de Provérbios (ver Pro. 9:13; 10:18; 18:8; 26:20-22). Quando a calúnia atinge os mensageiros de Deus, atinge ao próprio Deus, sendo punido de conformidade com isso (Núm. 14:36, onde os espias falam contra os pontos positivos da Terra Prometida; Rom. 3:8, onde uma falsa doutrina é imputada ao apóstolo Paulo). A calúnia consiste em fazer os padrões humanos sobreporem-se aos padrões divinos e ao julgamento divino, dando a entender até mesmo a blasfêmia (Tia. 4:11). Pertence àquela categoria de pecados aos quais Deus entrega os homens (Rom. 1:30, quando eles caluniam do bem e aprovam o mal; cf. II Tim. 3:3 quanto ao seu caráter escatológico).

O grande caluniador é o próprio Satanás (pois *diábolos* = acusador). Ele tentou alienar Deus de Jó, mediante falsas acusações. O livro de Apocalipse descreve Satanás como aquele que continuamente acusa aos irmãos, dia e noite (Apo. 12:10). O falso testemunho deliberado contra Cristo, por ocasião de seu julgamento, precisa ser visto dentro desse contexto (Mat. 26:59; cf. a ordem dada por Cristo para que os seus discípulos dêem um testemunho veraz a respeito dele). É por causa de Cristo que os seus seguidores são falsamente acusados (Mat. 5:11). Porém, uma vez que Deus proferiu o seu veredito acerca dos seus eleitos, justificando-os de tudo, quem ousaria acusá-los diante do Senhor? (Rom. 8:33).

A calúnia é uma atitude contrária ao caráter verdadeiramente cristão, refletindo total ausência de amor ao próximo (I Ped. 2:1). — Em vez de caluniarmos, como crentes que somos, devemos perdoar os nossos ofensores, relembrados de como Cristo nos perdoou de tudo (Efé. 4:31,32). Também devemo-nos revestir daquela nova natureza que não se caracteriza pelo espírito mentiroso, mas que se renova no conhecimento e no homem interior, de acordo com a imagem de Deus, conforme ela se acha em Cristo (Col. 3:8-10).

Ver também sobre: *Verdade;* os *Dez Mandamentos; Justificação;* e *Satanás*.

CALVÁRIO

Ver Mat. 27:33 e Luc. 23:33. O vocábulo **Calvário** vem do latim, *calvaria*, «crânio», que aparece na versão latina do Novo Testamento. Em Mateus 27:33, temos uma transliteração grega do termo aramaico *Golgotha*, que então é interpretado como «lugar da caveira». Gólgota é o caldaico ou aramaico *Gulgoleth*,

CALVÍCIE — CALVINISMO

com o sentido de crânio. Refere-se a uma elevação em forma de crânio, e não a lugares de crânios, ou a um lugar de sepulcros abertos. Também não é um lugar de execução, onde os ossos dos executados eram deixados insepultos. Alguns pais da Igreja julgaram tratar-se dessa possibilidade, mas parece não restar dúvidas de que o nome foi dado por causa de certas formações rochosas que até hoje são visíveis, fora das muralhas de Jerusalém, e que têm a aparência de um crânio humano. A versão Vulgata Latina diz *calvarius locus*, e é com base no latim que nos veio a palavra *Calvário*. O Calvário certamente não fica localizado no local tradicional do Santo Sepulcro, em Jerusalém. Deve ser algum lugar fora das muralhas da cidade, provavelmente o que atualmente se conhece como *Calvário de Gordon*, uma colina ao norte das muralhas da cidade, e que, do monte das Oliveiras, assemelha-se a um crânio, onde os túmulos escavados na rocha parecem as órbitas. Não é impossível que em um desses túmulos Jesus tenha sido sepultado.

A tradição que assinalou o atual local do Santo Sepulcro, como o lugar da crucificação de Jesus, não pode ser recuada para antes do século IV D.C., e poucos eruditos, hoje em dia, aceitam-no como a localização correta. Supostamente, estavam localizados ali os túmulos de Nicodemos e José de Arimatéia. Muitos estudiosos preferem o que agora se chama *Túmulo do Jardim*, ou Túmulo de Gordon, embora, para outros, a questão continue sujeita a debates. Esse local foi sugerido por Otto Thenius, em 1842, com o apoio do general Charles Gordon, em 1885. O local certamente ficava fora das antigas muralhas de Jerusalém, embora falte provas absolutas para essa opinião.

Pelo menos parece não haver dúvidas de que a referência a um crânio é uma alusão ao formato de uma elevação, e não a um terreno onde se faziam execuções, porquanto isso era contrário às leis judaicas. Outrossim, não é admissível que homens ricos como Nicodemos e José de Arimatéia tivessem adquirido túmulos em um terreno comumente usado para executar criminosos. O suposto local da crucificação e do sepultamento foi assinalado pela mãe do imperador Constantino, Helena, e a igreja do Santo Sepulcro foi erigida para assinalar o lugar, no princípio do século IV D.C. Porém, parece evidente que Helena se equivocou quanto à identificação, e, sem dúvida, também há muitos equívocos quanto a outras localidades, que se têm transformado em atrações turísticas. A maioria dessas identificações não tem tradição mais antiga do que aquela iniciada por Helena. (I IB PARR NTI)

CALVÍCIE

Ver também o artigo sobre os **cabelos**. Diversas palavras hebraicas são empregadas para indicar o alto da cabeça ou a calvície nas têmporas. A calvície pode ser natural ou artificial, esta última conseguida mediante o corte ou a raspagem à navalha. A calvície artificial era feita para indicar tristeza ou luto; e no caso de uma mulher, era aplicada como castigo por causa de algum lapso moral de grave natureza (ver Jer. 16:6; Amós 8:10; Miq. 1:16 e I Cor. 11:6). A proibição que se acha em Deu. 14:1: «...nem sobre a testa fareis calva por causa de algum morto»—provavelmente tinha por intuito impedir que Israel seguisse os costumes de povos pagãos, entre os quais havia esse. A calvície natural, por sua vez, não era considerada indicação de lepra ou de qualquer condição doentia, que tornasse uma pessoa cerimonialmente imunda (ver Lev. 13:40 *ss.*). Apesar disso, a calvície era desprezada por muitos em Israel, talvez como um defeito ou como uma feiúra. Por esse motivo, os calvos algumas vezes eram alvos de zombarias (ver II Reis 2:23 e Isa. 3:24). Há alguma associação de palavras que indicam que a calvície era associada, em certos casos, à lepra, ou então a úlceras de alguma espécie. O preconceito popular contra a calvície provavelmente estava alicerçado sobre essa circunstância; e talvez fosse essa a principal razão pela qual um calvo era considerado impedido de funcionar como sacerdote (ver Lev. 21:20; e também Mishnah tit Bechoroth vii.2). Seja como for, a calvície era considerada um defeito físico. (ID S)

CALVINISMO
Esboço
1. Duas Definições Latas
2. O Sínodo de Dort e os Cinco Pontos do Calvismo
3. O Sistema e Seus Advogados
4. A Doutrina da Polaridade
5. Calvinismo Como Uma Força Social, Religiosa e Política
6. O Calvinismo é uma Teologia Bíblica
7. A Ética Calvinista

1. Duas Definições Latas. a. Calvinismo é o termo que aponta para as doutrinas enfatizadas por João Calvino (que vide), bem como para suas idéias, conforme foram ressaltadas e interpretadas pelos eruditos calvinistas do século XVIII, mormente os *cinco pontos* do calvinismo (ver abaixo), estabelecidos pelo Concílio de Dort (*que vide*). b. Aplica-se, a grosso modo, às igrejas que se originaram sob a influência de Calvino, e, em conseqüência, exerceram impacto sobre o mundo religioso, a sociedade e a cultura em geral. Inicialmente, houve a ordem teocrática da Igreja-Estado de Genebra, na Suíça. Então apareceram os presbiterianos da Escócia, os puritanos da Nova Ingaterra, os huguenotes da França, a Igreja Reformada e os Batistas Particulares da Inglaterra. Karl Barth (que vide) e Emil Brunner (que vide) representam um tipo de reavivamento do pensamento calvinista.

2. O Sínodo de Dort e os Cinco Pontos do Calvinismo. O Sínodo de Dort foi convocado a 13 de novembro de 1618, pelos Estados Gerais dos Países Baixos, na tentativa de pôr fim à amarga controvérsia doutrinária acerca do arminianismo. Episcópio, sucessor de Armínio (que vide), que faleceu em 1609, e seus aderentes, foram convocados para comparecerem, não como membros, mas como réus. Os cinco pontos do arminianismo (que vide), que haviam sido formulados pelos seguidores da remonstrância (que vide), de 1610, foram condenados, e cinco pontos contrários às suas idéias foram aprovados. Esses cinco pontos foram expostos com subpontos detalhados, em quatro capítulos. Os cinco pontos são os seguintes:
a. Eleição incondicional
b. Expiação limitada aos eleitos
c. Depravação total, que envolve tanto a habilidade quanto o mérito
d. Graça irresistível
e. Perseverança, ou a segurança eterna do crente

Esses pontos têm sido variegadamente interpretados pelos calvinistas. Alguns pensam que a eleição seria *supralapsária* (como Beza), isto é, o decreto divino para eleger *antecedeu* à queda no pecado. Ou poderia ser infralapsária, ou seja, o decreto divino resultou da queda, com o intuito de curá-la. O

CALVINISMO

próprio Sínodo de Dort tomou o ponto de vista infralapsário. As igrejas calvinistas aprovaram de modo geral as decisões gerais do concílio. Alguns calvinistas modernos negam a expiação limitada em princípio, embora aceitem-na quanto a propósitos práticos. Pois enquanto, quanto à *teoria*, Cristo morreu por todos, na *prática*, somente aqueles que aceitam a obra de Cristo, sendo impulsionados pelo Espírito a fazê-lo, são beneficiados pela morte de Cristo, e essa impulsão depende da própria eleição. Pois o Espírito não impulsiona a quem não foi eleito. Portanto, apesar de haver uma *intenção* divina de que todos os homens se beneficiariam da expiação, o *ato* divino limita a expiação aos eleitos. Além disso, os calvinistas também estão divididos quanto ao problema da *reprovação* (que vide). Alguns deles dizem que a mesma é *ativa*, dando a entender que Deus condena ativamente a perdição, àqueles que não foram eleitos, os quais foram ativamente escolhidos. Outros afirmam que a reprovação é *passiva*, isto é, não haveria qualquer decreto divino para a perdição. Deus simplesmente nada faria em relação aos não-eleitos, deixando-os enfrentar os resultados naturais dos seus pecados. Seja como for, somente alguns poucos *poderiam* ser salvos, os eleitos. Mas essa conclusão é atingida mediante a observação, pois Deus não revela quantos são os seus eleitos. Realmente, apenas uma minoria dos homens toma a decisão de seguir a Cristo.

3. O Sistema e Seus Advogados. Todos os sistemas teológicos são sistemas fechados, e o calvinismo não forma exceção. Sua existência depende da escolha de corretos textos de prova, rejeitando ou distorcendo os trechos bíblicos que se discrepam. O arminianismo (*que vide*) também é um sistema fechado, agindo da mesma maneira, isto é, não levando em conta trechos bíblicos que não se harmonizam com o sistema. Todas as denominações cristãs são sistemas fechados, manipulando textos de prova selecionados. Isso acontece porque o Novo Testamento não é tão homogêneo como certos estudiosos gostariam de fazer-nos crer. Vários sistemas e denominações existem especificamente porque o próprio Novo Testamento é suficientemente amplo para dar-lhes origem. Muitos grupos cristãos afirmam que as Escrituras são a única autoridade de fé e prática, mas, na realidade, eles conseguem criar sistemas diferentes de teologia, com base nas Escrituras. Isso não ocorre por acidente. Antes, é o resultado natural da manipulação dos textos de prova, a fim de tentar provar alguma idéia ou conjunto de idéias. Aquelas idéias que fazem parte genuína da teologia neotestamentária, e que não concordam com este ou aquele sistema, são ignoradas ou distorcidas. Uma ilustração óbvia se dá no caso das doutrinas do livre-arbítrio e do determinismo. Ambas essas doutrinas encontram-se no Novo Testamento, e este não oferece reconciliação entre elas. Os arminianos preferem enfatizar o **livre-arbítrio**, distorcendo óbvios versículos que ensinam o determinismo. Os calvinistas preferem salientar a doutrina da eleição, distorcendo óbvios versículos que ensinam o **livre-arbítrio**. Os homens querem sentir-se bem e em conforto, com os seus sistemas teológicos. Não querem enfrentar qualquer paradoxo. Ver o artigo sobre o *Paradoxo*. Porém, quando reduzimos nossa teologia às idéias e à compreensão humanas, ficamos apenas com uma teologia deficiente. Essa torna-se *humano*logia, e não *teo*logia.

Os teólogos calvinistas, como B.B. Warfield, supõem que o calvinismo consiste na combinação do teísmo e do evangelicalismo como devem ser. Com isso, ele quer dar a entender que a teologia atinge no calvinismo o seu ponto de maturidade, o que dá a entender que qualquer sistema contrário é imaturo ou errôneo, em um ou em vários pontos. Os sistemas sempre mostram-se *arrogantes* com isso. Todos os sistemas biblicamente baseados reivindicam ver a verdade somente conforme as Escrituras a expõem, embora tenham o cuidado de discutir apenas aqueles versículos que podem ser usados em apoio às suas próprias idéias. A verdade é que Lázaro estava *morto*, e coisa alguma poderia dar solução à questão, exceto uma clara chamada da parte do Mestre. Assim como um homem está morto em seus pecados, assim também deve haver uma clara chamada divina. Mas, esse chamamento não pode ser limitado a um decreto que inclua uma expiação limitada ou apenas parcialmente eficaz. A expiação precisa ser alicerçada sobre o *amor universal* de Deus (João 3:16), que é a clara chamada de Deus a todos os homens, de todos os lugares. Consideremos, além disso, o trecho de Efésios 1:10. Esse versículo mostra-nos que a vontade de Deus tem um intuito *universal*, não podendo ser limitada a alguma estreita chamada eficaz. Naturalmente, há aqueles versículos que expõem essa estreita chamada eletiva. O nono capítulo da epístola aos Romanos ensina isso, incluindo a reprovação ativa. Porém, há outras porções do Novo Testamento, como o décimo capítulo da mesma epístola aos Romanos em diante, que *ultrapassam* esse estreito ponto de vista. Não pode haver ética sem responsabilidade, e não pode haver responsabilidade sem a *capacidade* de reação favorável. Essa capacidade já está incluída na chamada universal de Deus, exibida na missão de Cristo, ativada por meio do Espírito, que é o ativador universal. Podemos chamar isso pelo termo graça geral, se assim quisermos fazê-lo.

4. A Doutrina da Polaridade. Algumas verdades não podem ser compreendidas enquanto não são levados em conta os seus dois pólos, da mesma maneira que o globo terrestre não pode ser totalmente entendido enquanto for examinado apenas um de seus hemisférios. A verdade do *determinismo* (que vide) e do *livre-arbítrio* são dois pólos de uma verdade maior. Outro tanto se dá com as verdades da divindade e da humanidade de Cristo. Mas os sistemas, a fim de obterem conforto mental e de formularem um sistema fácil, destituído de problemas, costumeiramente eliminam um dos dois pólos dessas grandes verdades, não ousando levar em conta ambos os pólos. Assim, o determinismo (que inclui a eleição) é uma verdade; e outro tanto se dá com o **livre-arbítrio**. Há uma verdade maior, que não conseguimos perscrutar inteiramente, e que inclui ambos esses pólos. Além disso, há a doutrina do julgamento. A Bíblia declara que o julgamento divino é retributivo. Algumas denominações aferram-se a esse ponto. Para elas, o juízo é *apenas* retributivo. No entanto, o julgamento também é remedial (I Ped. 4:6), e isso é um outro pólo da mesma doutrina. Portanto, longe de ser um mal *final*, o julgamento é uma medida que *visa o bem* dos homens. Certamente trata-se de uma miséria e de um mal a curto prazo. Entretanto, também é um dedo da mão misericordiosa de Deus, um instrumento de reforma e restauração. Ver sobre a *Restauração*. Certamente Orígenes estava certo quando disse que contemplar o julgamento apenas como retributivo é condescendência de uma teologia inferior. Ele tinha razão quanto a esse particular, sem importar quais tenham sido os seus erros. A teologia não pode existir sem o conceito de *polaridade*. As humanologias podem existir sem esse conceito. De fato, elas desprezam esses duplos aspectos de muitas verdades.

CALVINISMO

Esses duplos aspectos existem porque há verdades que dizem respeito ao relacionamento entre Deus e o Homem—um pólo vê o lado divino, e o outro pólo vê o lado humano. Poderíamos esquecer qualquer desses lados?

5. O Calvinismo como uma Força Social, Religiosa e Política. Minhas críticas e raciocínios não têm o intuito de embotar o impacto de todo o bem que o calvinismo tem feito no mundo. Foi a grande força que desenterrou a Bíblia, sepultada debaixo de toneladas de tradições humanas. Trata-se de uma teologia bíblica; e quanto mais conhecermos e pusermos em prática as doutrinas da Bíblia, tanto melhor para nós. Isso não significa que a Bíblia seja a única *autoridade* (que vide), mas é a grande autoridade que vem sendo ignorada e continua a sê-la. Quão ignorantes a respeito da Bíblia são até mesmo pessoas que se consideram religiosas! As igrejas calvinistas têm exercido um tremendo impacto sobre o campo religioso, social e político dos últimos quatro séculos. E. Choisy chamou o calvinismo de *educador da consciência*. Faz o homem ser diretamente responsável diante de Deus, como indivíduo, desnudado dos vários sistemas meritórios por detrás dos quais as pessoas costumam ocultar-se. E.G. Léonard apodava o calvinismo de fundador de uma civilização. Não se pode ignorar essa influência, nos vários países onde o calvinismo tem exercido sua ação. Há muitas leis, muitas instituições, muitas sociedades, por causa das igrejas calvinistas. As grandes marcas do calvinismo são uma consciência ativa, a piedade pessoal e a piedade doméstica, a integridade nos negócios, a preocupação com a educação e com o fervor religioso. Não parece haver pessoa tão religiosa como o calvinista dedicado, talvez com a única exceção dos judeus religiosos; ninguém conseguiu ultrapassar os judeus, quanto ao fervor religioso.

A história da Inglaterra, da Escócia, da Holanda e dos Estados Unidos da América demonstra a influência notável do calvinismo. Muitas leis foram baixadas através da consciência calvinista. É verdade que muitos preconceitos também foram promovidos, mas isso já é outra história. Em muitos casos, o calvinismo tem suprido líderes aos movimentos que se opõem aos governantes despóticos, a despeito do fato de que o próprio calvinismo tem-se mostrado despótico, em certas fases de sua história.

Tal como sucede a todos os sistemas, encontramos no calvinismo bons e maus aspectos; mas, se tivermos de aquilatar o calvinismo em uma balança, parece que o mesmo fica do lado bom.

6. O Calvinismo é uma Teologia Bíblica. No calvinismo, a regra das **Escrituras somente** é uma regra viva. O sistema calvinista aceita o papel supremo das Escrituras, ao mesmo tempo que não se opõe às ciências seculares. O calvinismo aceita que toda e qualquer verdade procede de Deus, e, quanto à teologia, aceita exclusivamente a Bíblia. Naturalmente, o calvinismo utiliza interpretações específicas da Bíblia a fim de manter uma linha bíblica de pensamento, ao mesmo tempo em que ignora outras linhas igualmente alicerçadas sobre a Bíblia, conforme demonstrei acima. Não obstante, o calvinismo deduz suas crenças diretamente da Bíblia. Isso não significa que a razão seja ignorada, e, sim, que o calvinismo é edificado mediante a manipulação de ensinamentos bíblicos. Quanto a diferentes abordagens ao problema da *autoridade*, ver o artigo sobre esse assunto. A posição de que devemos ter a Bíblia como única regra de fé é uma boa posição, mesmo que o calvinismo faça uma busca parcial pela verdade. O calvinismo tem enfatizado supremamente essa boa regra, embora seja parcial.

7. A Ética Calvinista.

a. A base da ética, para o calvinismo, é a revelação bíblica, e não as descobertas empíricas. As Escrituras e a mensagem escrita dos profetas e apóstolos, fornecem-nos toda a instrução de que precisamos em nossa conduta ética.

b. A verdadeira conduta ética depende da renovação do Espírito, e não de qualquer habilidade inata ao homem. Somente os eleitos, afinal de contas, podem conduzir suas vidas de maneira verdadeiramente aceitável diante de Deus. Isso acontece somente porque o Espírito Santo está atuando sobre eles.

c. Os dez mandamentos são explicados do ponto de vista ampliado do cristianismo. As *Institutas* de Calvino abordam os mandamentos um por um, procurando trazer à tona um maior entendimento sobre os mesmos. Para ilustrar, consideremos o sétimo mandamento, contra o adultério. O que está incluído nesse mandamento? Os pecados proibidos são o adultério, a fornicação, o estupro, o incesto, a sodomia, todas as concupiscências naturais, todas as imaginações impuras, todos os propósitos e pensamentos sensuais, a conversação imoral, os olhares cobiçosos, o comportamento impudente e frívolo, as vestes sem modéstia, os casamentos ilegítimos, o permitir, tolerar e manter bordéis, o casamento indevidamente demorado, a poligamia, a poliandria, o divórcio injusto, o abandono do cônjuge, o ócio, a glutonaria, o alcoolismo, as companhias sem castidade, as canções lascivas, livros, gravuras, danças, peças teatrais e todas as demais provocações a atos impuros, quer em nós mesmos quer em outros. Esse tipo de atividade, que aumenta grandemente a aplicação da lei veterotestamentária, pode ser vista supremamente na exposição feita por Ezekiel Hopkins, sobre a lei mosaica, que ocupa trezentas páginas.

d. *Legalismo*. Alguns têm objetado a esse tipo de abordagem da lei, supondo que o mesmo amortece o livre fluxo da lei do Espírito (Rom. 8:2). Os evangélicos têm feito tais objeções com base naquelas inúmeras regras que nos põem debaixo de uma lei expandida, deixando-nos onde estava o judaísmo, de forma consciente ou inconsciente, isto é, esforçando-se por obter a retidão moral através da observância a meras regras. Os estudiosos liberais têm levantado objeções ao legalismo, mas com outros motivos, a saber, que nenhuma regra chega a ser tão completa que se ajuste a todos os casos. Por conseguinte, cada situação exigiria um manuseio especial, inspirado pela lei do amor. Em uma forma extrema, essa atitude tem permitido um liberalismo excessivo, quando as pessoas passam a sancionar o aborto, o homossexualismo, ou qualquer coisa na qual, supostamente, o amor esteja envolvido. O calvinismo não defende esse tipo de legalismo, o qual parte do pressuposto que um indivíduo pode merecer a salvação mediante a observância da lei; mas, em outros sentidos, o calvinismo cria uma espécie de legalismo prático, que guia a vida (não a fim de vir a obter a salvação), o que se parece muito com a atitude judaica. De fato, os reformadores, de maneira geral, têm sido criticados por haverem deixado a Igreja debaixo da lei *como um guia* da vida, embora a tenha salvado da noção de que a observância da lei é capaz de salvar a alma. Ver o artigo sobre *Legalismo*. Todavia, a lei nem salva o pecador e nem santifica o crente. Tanto uma coisa quanto a outra são realizadas pela atuação interna do Espírito. Ver I Tes. 5:23, 24 e

II Tes. 2:13. Pelo lado humano encontramos o uso de meios e a total dedicação da própria vida ao Senhor. Ver João 17:17 e Rom. 12:1,2. Ver sobre a *Santificação*. (AM B C CLA H)

CALVINISTAS, ANTIGOS (COERENTES) e MODERADOS

Todas as variações do calvinismo enfatizam o aspecto da soberania de Deus. Porém, os antigos ou coerentes calvinistas chegaram às doutrinas calvinistas sob sua forma mais extremada, reduzindo o homem a um robô; e, para todos os efeitos práticos, fazem Deus ser a causa do mal, visto ser Ele a única causa, na teologia. Naturalmente, esses calvinistas antigos também ensinam a reprovação ativa, e assim reduzem a missão de Cristo apenas a alguns poucos, muito aquém da ampla visão do Novo Testamento. Ver I Ped. 3:18-4:6 e Efé. 1:10 no NTI, onde se descortina a visão mais ampla do intuito da missão de Cristo. Os calvinistas moderados, por sua vez, defendem a idéia da reprovação passiva, e de causas secundárias dentro de — meios *divinamente determinados*. Os princípios do calvinismo moderado prevalecem entre os evangélicos calvinistas, como na Teologia de New Haven (que vide). Ver também sobre a *Teologia da Nova Inglaterra*. (E)

••• ••• •••

CALVINO, JOÃO

Suas datas foram 1509-1564. Teólogo protestante francês, líder eclesiástico e denominacional. Nasceu na Picardia, e estudou filosofia na Universidade de Paris, entre 1523 e 1527. Também estudou em Orleães e Bourges. Era uma pessoa dotada de mente brilhante, e um estudante extremamente diligente. Teodoro Beza, seu biógrafo, informa-nos que ele era um crítico severo das falhas dos seus colegas estudantes. Mas a lenda de que ele foi apelidado de *Caso Acusativo*, por seus colegas, por causa de seu espírito censurador, não pode ser traçada até antes de 1633, pelo que, provavelmente, foi-lhe dado posteriormente, embora reflita um fato histórico de sua vida. A despeito de sua austeridade, ele tinha um círculo de amigos fiéis, antes mesmo de sua conversão ao protestantismo, e vários deles continuaram sendo seus amigos, a despeito da separação religiosa. No começo de 1528, ele recebeu grau de mestre em teologia; mas então deu início ao estudo da advocacia, em Orleães. Essa não era uma idéia propriamente sua, mas de seu pai, pois Calvino nunca se sentiu atraído pela advocacia. O falecimento de seu pai, em 1531, deixou-o livre para tomar suas próprias decisões. Terminou seu curso de direito, mas dedicou-se à linguagem (grego, latim, hebraico) e à literatura. Sua primeira publicação independente foi um comentário sobre a obra de Sêneca, *De Clementia*. Essa obra mostra-nos que ele havia obtido considerável habilidade nos clássicos.

Em 1557, ele passou por súbita conversão, embora haja bem pouca descrição a esse respeito na literatura que chegou até nós. Em seu *Comentário sobre os Salmos*, diz Calvino: «Visto que eu estava mais teimosamente preso às superstições do papado do que me era possível desvencilhar-me de tão profundo lamaçal, Deus subjugou o meu coração da obstinação de minha idade para a docilidade de uma súbita conversão».

Não vendo esperança de reforma em Paris, mudou-se para Basel, na Suíça, onde escreveu e publicou suas *Institutas*, em 1536. Dali mudou-se para Genebra, em 1541, onde estabeleceu uma teocracia. Havia uma completa mistura de Igreja e estado, e regras rígidas e ferozes governavam toda vida e pensamento. Ofensas como jogos de azar, alcoolismo e até mesmo danças ou o uso de linguagem irreverente eram severamente punidas. No começo, houve oposição a Calvino, e sua posição não era muito segura. Porém, por volta de 1555, ele já havia obtido uma vitória permanente. Houve vítimas de sua duríssima liderança. Ao humanista Sebastião Castellio, professor, foi recusada a admissão ao ministério, por causa de certo ponto de vista que expressara em seu comentário sobre *Cantares de Salomão*. Finalmente, Castellio deixou Genebra. Jacques Gruet foi decapitado, acusado de blasfêmia. Jerônimo Bolsec, que havia feito oposição à rígida doutrina da predestinação, de Calvino, foi banido. O renomado antitrinitariano, Miguel Serveto, foi queimado na fogueira em 1553. Calvino e Serveto se haviam correspondido, debatendo diversos pontos. Calvino dera ordens para deter Serveto, se viesse a Genebra, já sabendo que ia o matar, se pudesse. Ele preferiu morte à espada, mas o conselho que julgou a Serveto ansiava por mostrar-se ainda mais feroz que seu mestre. Castellio escreveu um tratado contra a perseguição, mas sua voz perdeu-se em meio a gritos pedindo sangue. Calvino defendia a pena de morte para os hereges. Ele era conhecido por suas explosões de ira, que ele mesmo denominava de «a fera». Portanto, novamente temos o duo: Grandes homens, grandes vícios. A reputação de Calvino muito sofreu, e com justiça, por seu envolvimento nas execuções capitais e banimentos. Podemos dizer que ele foi um produto e uma vítima de sua época, mas o homicídio continua sendo homicídio, e o apóstolo Paulo não se sentia muito bem por haver praticado a violência, *antes* de sua conversão. Infelizmente, Calvino continuava a agir violentamente, mesmo *depois* de sua conversão.

Quando consideramos que a lei do amor é a grande prova da espiritualidade (I João 4:7), ficamos perplexos diante do fato de que judeus, cristãos ou mesmo protestantes, dedicam-se a perseguir, prejudicar ou matar ao próximo, em nome de Deus.

Oh, Deus, que carne e sangue fossem tão baratos,
Que os homens odiassem e matassem,
Que os homens silvassem e cortassem os outros,
Com línguas de vileza... por causa de...
«Teologia».

Russell Champlin

Por outra parte, a contribuição de Calvino à erudição bíblica e à reforma religiosa é algo que não pode ser negado. Eu mesmo já li o comentário de Calvino sobre o Novo Testamento, de capa a capa, e posso testificar sobre o poder de sua expressão, sobre a utilidade e proveito de suas idéias, sobre a dedicação do seu espírito. Através de seus escritos resplandece um grande intelecto; mas, desafortunadamente, não com pouca freqüência, vemos a *fera* em suas disposições, sempre em busca de vítimas.

Os conflitos, as contendas e o trabalho árduo cobraram um alto preço. Na casa dos quarenta, Calvino foi assaltado por uma série de dolorosas enfermidades, que solaparam a sua vitalidade. A despeito disso, ainda por certo número de anos, ele continuou trabalhando em suas *Institutas*, que terminaram sendo cinco vezes mais volumosas do que quando foram publicadas pela primeira vez, em 1536. Além dessa obra, temos o seu comentário sobre o Novo Testamento, uma obra clássica que tem sido traduzida para outros idiomas, sem falar em seus muitos tratados e panfletos. Calvino faleceu a 27 de maio de 1564.

Idéias principais. 1. A revelação bíblica é progressiva. O Novo Testamento ultrapassa ao Antigo, e o Novo Testamento não é homogêneo quanto a perspicácia espiritual, pois alguns autores eram mais perceptivos do que outros. Calvino também supunha que os autores limitavam-se à compreensão potencial de seus leitores. Para exemplificar: «A esse respeito temos muitas cousas que dizer, e difíceis de explicar, porquanto vos tendes tornado tardios em ouvir...» (Heb. 5:11).

2. Deus é a *causa absoluta* e não-condicionada de todas as coisas. Deus revela a Sua mente no homem e na natureza. — Visto que o homem foi cego pelo pecado, ele precisa de mais do que somente a Palavra objetiva de Deus, as Escrituras, para orientá-lo na direção correta de sua vida. Ele precisa de iluminação espiritual.

3. *Deus ordena* todas as coisas, mas sem fazer violência à liberdade de suas criaturas inteligentes, algumas delas sendo necessárias, outras contingentes e outras livres.

4. *O homem* foi criado puro e segundo a Imagem Divina, mas caiu e ficou corrompido, mediante o abandono voluntário do bem. Permanece nele, contudo, uma parte da imagem de Deus, embora isso não seja suficiente para o homem salvar a si mesmo.

5. *Cristo, o Redentor*, é a ajuda de que o homem precisa para a salvação de sua alma, pois nele encontra-se toda a graça suficiente.

6. O homem depende de Deus quanto a uma dupla predestinação: ou para a salvação ou para a perdição. Ver sobre a *Reprovação*. Ver também sobre a *Eleição*. O homem é salvo inteiramente à parte de qualquer mérito pessoal, mas é condenado por causa do pecado.

7. A *graça* de Deus renova a vontade do homem, e a reação humana é inspirada pelo Espírito Santo. Isso recupera para o homem a verdadeira liberdade.

8. Todos os crentes são iguais diante de Deus. As hierarquias criadas pelos homens são prejudiciais à espiritualidade.

9. As Escrituras, com exclusividade, são a nossa autoridade de fé e prática. Portanto, a teologia de Calvino é, acima de tudo, *bíblica*.

••• ••• •••

João Calvino e Exemplos Inquisitoriais
A Intolerância

A vida de João Calvino nos faz meditar sobre o vexatório problema da intolerância, da perseguição e do ódio entre cristãos. Um dos mais consternadores fatos da história eclesiástica é aquele de como cristãos perseguiram e mataram a outros cristãos por motivos de «teologia». Apresento aqui três exemplos comprobatórios:

1. *A Inquisição*. Tenho preparado um artigo separado sobre esse assunto, (ver *Inquisição*), pelo que não repito aqui o material. Basta dizer que esse movimento criou, promoveu e executou quarenta mil casos de perseguição, encarceramento, banimento e execução capital. A chamada *Santa Inquisição* foram quatrocentos e cinqüenta anos de terror. Em termos de torturas, Hitler não passava de um aprendiz, comparado aos padres do Santo Ofício.

2. *João Calvino*. Quero referir-me agora a um deplorável caso de *exemplo ao contrário*. Antes que eu termine esta seção, o leitor compreenderá o sentido de minha ilustração. Todos já temos ouvido falar sobre o lado bom da vida e da obra de João Calvino. Quando eu ainda estava na fase do meu treinamento teológico, Calvino era para mim um grande herói. Meu primeiro filho recebeu o nome de *Calvino Tiago*, em inglês, Calvin James. Parecia-me que era um nome difícil para meu filho viver à altura de sua fama. Porém, lamento dizer que há um lado tremendamente negativo na vida de João Calvino. As fontes informativas do que aqui digo são enciclopédias e histórias eclesiásticas (três volumes do professor Kurtz, um historiador luterano cuja obra, por muitas décadas, foi a obra padrão de história eclesiástica, usada nas universidades alemãs).

Preciso informar ao leitor, desde o começo, que tenho lido o comentário de Calvino sobre o Novo Testamento de capa a capa, tendo extraído dali muitas citações úteis, enriquecendo o meu comentário (*O Novo Testamento Interpretado*). Há na obra de Calvino muita coisa boa. Infelizmente, também há um lado negro.

Todos conhecemos bem a história de como Serveto foi executado na fogueira, em Genebra, na Suíça, porquanto negava a doutrina da Trindade. O que o leitor talvez desconheça é que a captura dele foi planejada e executada por Calvino, com o propósito específico de executá-lo. Calvino não enviou homens que apreendessem a Serveto, mas baixou uma ordem para que fosse detido, se ao menos chegasse perto de Genebra. Calvino pareceu misericordioso. Queria decapitar Serveto. Mas os discípulos dele foram mais entusiastas. E executaram Serveto na fogueira. Triste relato, mas apenas um dentre muitos.

Kurtz revela para nós que houve muitas vítimas de Calvino. Entre os anos de 1542 e 1546 (apenas quatro anos), — embora Genebra contasse com uma população de apenas vinte mil pessoas, houve nada menos de cinqüenta e sete execuções capitais, sessenta e seis banimentos e um número incalculável de encarceramentos, tudo por motivos religiosos. Tais pessoas não eram criminosos civis. Tão-somente eram indivíduos que discordavam de uma ou de outra das doutrinas ensinadas por Calvino. Ele usava textos de prova do Antigo Testamento, para encontrar autorização para as suas matanças. Convenientemente, ignorava textos neotestamentários como Lucas 9:54-56, que nos mostra qual o espírito da pessoa que se envolve em tais coisas.

Assim, Jacques Gruet foi decapitado. Jerônimo Bolsec foi encarcerado, e então banido. Sebastião Castellio, que era diretor do sistema escolar de Genebra, foi banido por duas razões: primeira, ele objetava às execuções e aos encarceramentos; em segundo lugar, ele objetava à interpretação dada por Calvino sobre a história da descida de Cristo ao hades. Calvino dizia que Cristo pregara a condenação no hades, contradizendo a passagem de I Pedro 4:6. Castellio teve de se retirar de Genebra e foi ensinar grego na Bailéia.

Kurtz ajuntou que esse período foi «um reinado inquisitorial de terror» (vol. 3, pág. 304). Calvino era conhecido por suas explosões de fúria, que ele chamava de sua «fera».

3. *Galileu Galilei*. Galileu foi um astrônomo e filósofo italiano (1564—1642). Criou-se em um

CALVINO

mosteiro, mas estudou na Universidade de Pisa. Tendo-se formado, continuou ali, como professor. Aderiu às novas idéias astronômicas que se alicerçavam sobre os ensinos de Copérnico. Por causa disso, Galileu foi atacado por teólogos do Santo Ofício, tendo sofrido uma amarga oposição da parte de cientistas *ortodoxos* de sua época. Em 1616, foi censurado pelos teólogos do Santo Ofício, tendo sido proibido de ensinar as novas idéias. Galileu concordou; mas as idéias ferviam em seu cérebro. Isso posto, ele publicou um diálogo que confrontava a antiga astronomia aristotélica ptolemaica com a variedade copérnica, mais recente. Embora supostamente uma exposição imparcial, não era difícil perceber qual era a preferência do próprio Galileu. E Galileu recebeu ordens de se apresentar em Roma, por parte da Inquisição. Foi acusado de haver desobedecido à ordem de *abandonar o ensino* de suas novas idéias.

Há um aspecto cansativo na história dos fanáticos. É que eles permanecem agrilhoados na prisão de seu exclusivismo. Na verdade, merecem compaixão a exemplo de quaisquer outros prisioneiros.

••• ••• •••

As Heresias de Galileu:

O seu aprimoramento do telescópio, permitia-lhe ver a natureza da luz da lua como um reflexo, além de ver as luas de Júpiter, as fases de Vênus, os anéis de Saturno, a ocorrência de manchas solares e a rotação do sol sobre o seu próprio eixo. Ele também obteve mais evidências sobre a rotação da Terra e sobre a sua órbita em redor do sol, como questões óbvias. Porém, a ortodoxia da época negava essas verdades, dizendo que a Terra mantinha-se imóvel no espaço (embora os gregos da época de antes de Cristo já tivessem afirmado que a Terra movia-se no espaço), e dizia que a Terra era o centro do Universo. Naquele tempo, tanto os cientistas quanto os teólogos consideravam o movimento como a causa primária da *decadência* e, naturalmente, todos sabiam que a criação de Deus não podia ser decadente, e que ele criara a Terra como o centro do Universo. Galileu solicitava dos teólogos que olhassem por meio de seu telescópio, como prova em contrário, mas eles se recusavam a isso!

Galileu, naturalmente, estava interessado em poupar a própria vida. Por esse motivo, concordou em retratar-se, reconhecendo o seu *erro*. Teve de retratar-se de joelhos. E confessou o seu «erro» para satisfação de todos os circunstantes, tendo concordado, uma vez mais, em não ensinar as novas idéias. Porém, diz-se que quando ele se levantou dos joelhos, disse em voz baixa: *E pur si si muove*, isto é: «Não obstante, ela (a terra) se move». E, durante o resto de seus dias, foi sujeitado a cárcere a domicílio.

É curioso que somente em nossa própria época, mais de quatrocentos anos depois, a Igreja, por meio do papa João Paulo II, «perdoou» a Galileu, limpando assim o seu nome.

A ignorância de nada vale. Os homens têm o direito de investigar, pesquisar e prestar relatório de suas descobertas. Os detratores nem sempre estão com a razão. Na maioria das vezes, eles são culpados de crimes que as suas vítimas nem pensam em cometer. Prejudicar os laços de união da Igreja de Cristo é um crime muito sério.

A Tolerância e o Amor:

Alguns cristãos congratulam-se quando conseguem demonstrar tolerância. Porém, muito acima de tolerância brilha a lei do amor. Há um vínculo de amor em Cristo que ultrapassa nossos grupos e denominações particulares. Podemos tolerar e até mesmo amar a outros, ao mesmo tempo em que discordamos de certos pontos de doutrina de outras pessoas. A lei da tolerância é uma lei secundária, comparativamente falando; e, no entanto, há muitos evangélicos e outros cristãos que nem são capazes disso. A lei do amor é uma lei superior àquela. Requer que amemos até mesmo aos nossos inimigos, para não dizer sobre outros cristãos, que jamais poderiam ser tidos como nossos inimigos. Ver os artigos separados sobre a *Tolerância* e o *Amor*.

Evolução da Vereda Espiritual: Estágios da Inquirição Espiritual

Duas coisas são claras no que tange a João Calvino. Em primeiro lugar, suas contribuições à Igreja cristã foram consideráveis, dotadas de efeitos duradouros. Em segundo lugar, ele atuava impelido por uma rígida mente fundamentalista, o que o levou a cometer erros grosseiros, conforme foi descrito acima. Somente Deus pode tirar a média dentre tais circunstâncias, fazendo o devido juízo. Seja como for, à medida que as almas avançam na evolução espiritual, e vão sendo transformadas segundo a imagem de Cristo, os maus aspectos vão sendo finalmente eliminados, e os bons aspectos vão sendo acentuados e santificados. Isso redunda em esperança para todos, visto que cada um de nós consiste em prodigiosas combinações do bem com o mal.

1. O mais baixo nível de espiritualidade é aquele no qual os homens são *materialistas*. Nesse estado, os homens, embora saibam melhor que isso, para todos os efeitos práticos, em teoria e em ações, estão imersos na materialidade e no egoísmo.

2. Daí os homens podem avançar para a *superstição*, quando então já receberam alguma iluminação acerca das realidades espirituais, posto que de maneira distorcida, ainda de mistura com muita ignorância.

3. Em seguida, aparece o nível *fundamentalista*, quando a letra das Escrituras é tudo. Nesse nível, predomina uma alegada correção credal, e promove-se a hostilidade contra todas as pessoas ou organizações que diferem das noções afagadas pelos fundamentalistas, mesmo que as diferenças sejam pequenas. A arrogância manifesta-se nesse estágio. Contudo, admitamos que esse nível já representa um considerável progresso espiritual.

4. Vem então o *estágio filosófico*, onde os credos já não ficam sem exame crítico. Tem lugar a ampliação das idéias e das posições assumidas. Doutrinas antigas são vistas por um outro prisma, e são acrescentados novos conceitos e novas posturas, que antes não faziam parte do quadro mental.

5. Em *um nível subseqüente* os homens chegam a ter fome e sede de conhecimento em primeira mão e de desenvolvimento espiritual. Isso pode atingir uma intensidade de agonia e concentração interior, quase uma paixão devoradora.

6. Finalmente, vem *a vereda mística*, a busca e a obtenção de iluminação individualizada, mediante estados místicos em que a alma apreende direta e pessoalmente, o Ser divino. Mui provavelmente, é nessa altura que o ministério dos *anjos* mostra-se mais vital.

Meios de Desenvolvimento Espiritual e de Evolução na Vereda Cristã

Precisamos de toda a ajuda que possamos obter. É maravilhoso contar com Livros Sagrados que nos apresentem o acúmulo do conhecimento e da inspiração espirituais. Cumpre-nos ler esses livros, bem como outras obras de valor, que nos façam espiritualmente sábios. É admirável dispor dos meios da oração e da meditação, mediante os quais podemos buscar o Poder Divino, para receber as forças pessoais de que carecemos e para cumprimento de nossas respectivas missões neste mundo. É fantástico recebermos as instruções espirituais e morais apropriadas, a fim de adquirirmos uma maior santificação, que aclare a vereda de nosso desenvolvimento espiritual. É grandioso podermo-nos ocupar em boas obras, no cumprimento da lei do amor, capaz de conferir-nos crescimento espiritual, útil não apenas em termos pessoais, mas também para ajudarmos ao próximo. Todos esses são importantes meios de crescimento espiritual. Ver o artigo intitulado *Desenvolvimento Espiritual, Meios do*.

Porém, em um nível ainda acima desses meios de desenvolvimento espiritual, precisamos do toque místico. A meditação é um meio pelo qual podemos obter iluminação. A alma humana precisa aproximar-se de Deus e ter experiências diretas com o Ser divino. Também necessitamos dos dons espirituais; e, uma vez recebidos, precisamos cultivá-los, mesmo que isso não envolva, obrigatoriamente, o *modus operandi* da Igreja primitiva. É excelente aprender, trabalhar e orar; mas faz-nos falta, igualmente, a *Presença Divina*, se nos tivermos de desenvolver espiritualmente como é mister.

Dentro da categoria mística, não vejo razão pela qual os anjos não possam ter um papel até preponderante. Os anjos são agentes de nossa instrução, auxiliares provindos de uma esfera superior, que se dignam em ajudar a seus irmãos humanos, mais fracos que eles. No dizer da Bíblia, os anjos são espíritos ministradores daqueles que são herdeiros da salvação (ver Heb. 1:14); e não há motivo algum pelo qual não possamos aceitar a idéia que eles são de prestimoso auxílio em nosso avanço e em nossas realizações espirituais.

Bibliografia. AM B C E P.

CAMA, LEITO

No hebraico temos de considerar cinco palavras, e no grego, quatro:

1. *Yatsua*, «algo estendido». Palavra hebraica que figura por cinco vezes (Gên. 49:4; I Crô. 5:1; Jó. 17:13; Sal. 63:6; 132:3).

2. *Mittah*, «lugar de reclinar». Palavra hebraica que aparece por vinte e nove vezes (por exemplo: Gên. 47:31; Êxo. 8:3; I Sam. 19:13,15; II Reis 1:4,6,16; Est. 7:8; Pro. 26:14; Cant. 3:7; Amós 6:4).

3. *Matstsa*, «algo estendido». Palavra que é usada exclusivamente em Isa. 28:20.

4. *Mishkab*, «lugar para deitar». Palavra hebraica usada por quarenta e sete vezes. Por exemplo: Gên. 49:4; Lev. 15:4,5,21-26; II Sam. 4:5; Sal. 4:4; Isa. 57:2; Eze. 23:17; Dan. 2:28; 4:5-13; Miq. 2:1.

5. *Eres*, «divã». Palavra hebraica usada por dez vezes. Por exemplo, Jó 7:13; Sal. 41:3; Pro. 7:16; Can. 1:16.

6. *Klíne*, «lugar de reclinar». Palavra grega usada por nove vezes (Mat. 9:2,6; Mar. 4:21; 7:4,30; Luc. 5:18; 8:16; 17:34; Apo. 2:2).

7. *Klinídion*, «cama pequena». Palavra grega usada somente em Luc. 5:19 e 24.

8. *Koíte*, «cama». Palavra grega usada por quatro vezes (Luc. 11:7; Rom. 9:10; 13:13 e Heb. 13:4).

9. *Krábbatos*, «colchão». Palavra grega usada por onze vezes (Mar. 2:4,9,11,12; 6:55; João 5:8-11; Atos 5:15; 9:33).

Além disso, temos de considerar o verbo grego *stronnúo*, «arrumar», que, em algumas das seis vezes em que aparece, é traduzido em português por «arrumar o leito», como em Atos 9:34.

Ver o artigo geral sobre *casa*. A maneira de se dormir, nos países quentes do Oriente Próximo e Médio, variava, e geralmente era diferente da maneira habitual dos países mais frios.

O Leito. Eram desconhecidos os colchões de penas e outros materiais fofos, como se vê atualmente. Os pobres e os viajantes usavam colchões bem leves, ou então enrolavam-se em suas próprias vestes externas. Por causa da importância dessa peça externa de roupa, ela não podia ser usada como garantia ou penhor (ver Êxo. 22:27). Às vezes, um travesseiro era apenas uma pedra coberta com algum pano dobrado (Gên. 28:11). As pessoas mais abastadas tinham colchões de lã ou algodão, como também tinham cobertas feitas do mesmo material. Os cobertores eram feitos de vários materiais, como peles de animais, ou mesmo com as vestes externas. No caso de peles de animais, para que ficassem mais grossas, elas eram estufadas com palha ou lã (I Sam. 19:13).

Divãs. É evidente que o formato das camas variava, mas também eram usados divãs, que serviam de leito, à noite, e de sofá, durante o dia. As diferentes palavras hebraicas usadas para indicar o leito talvez apontassem para estilos diferentes. O divã era uma plataforma pouco elevada acima do chão, sobre a qual se punham os colchões. Um divã dos grandes abrigava mais de uma pessoa. Havia divãs portáveis (I Sam. 19:15; em nossa versão portuguesa, «cama»), que alguns usavam, e que também serviam de sofá durante o dia (I Sam. 27:23; Amós 6:4). Os ricos decoravam seus leitos e seus dormitórios com tapetes e outros ornamentos.

Camas. Já havia camas nos dias do Antigo Testamento, conforme as conhecemos na atualidade. Elas eram feitas com uma armação de madeira, com um trançado miúdo de cordas ou de tecido, para dar apoio a um colchão ou outro tipo de base, sobre a qual a pessoa dormia. Talvez isso seja mencionado em I Sam. 19:15 e Eze. 23:41. Também havia uma armação leve, de madeira, com pés e um trançado de cordas, que podia ser transportada como uma cama portátil. Talvez seja isso que esteja em foco no quinto capítulo de João, transportado pelo aleijado curado por Jesus, e que no grego é um krábbaton (João 5:8,9). Naturalmente, os ricos tinham suas camas suntuosas, decoradas de jóias, ouro, prata e ricas colchas.

Lugares de dormir. Os pobres tinham cabanas com um único aposento, pelo que não podiam ser feitos arranjos especiais para servirem de dormitório. A família inteira dormia em um único aposento, arranjando-se cada qual como podia. Provavelmente isso é refletido em Luc. 11:7, na parábola do amigo importuno. No outro extremo, há menção a ricos e seus dormitórios suntuosamente decorados, às vezes apenas com um casal ocupante (II Reis 11:2; II Sam. 4:7; Ecl. 10:20). Algumas vezes, havia dormitórios em um primeiro andar (II Reis 1:4; Sal. 132:3). E os costumes antigos também incluíam a separação de homens e mulheres nos leitos e dormitórios. Algumas pessoas contavam apenas com um quartinho elevado,

CAMA, LEITO — CÂMARA

onde dormiam (II Reis 4:10). Salas eram usadas como se fossem dormitórios. Um dormitório era uma sala onde havia uma espécie de plataforma elevada, que às vezes ocupava metade da área da mesma, sobre a qual eram arrumados os colchões.

As armações que serviam de leito eram, às vezes, de ferro (material caríssimo, na antiguidade), ou então de ouro ou prata, com incrustações de marfim. No livro de Judite, lê-se que o leito de Holofernes tinha um dossel de púrpura trançada, com fios de ouro entretecidos e pedras preciosas incrustadas (Judite 10:21). A cama de ferro do rei Ogue era enorme (Deu. 3:11), com aproximadamente 4,5 m de comprimento por 2 m de largura. Ostentação pura, ou devido ao fato que Ogue era um dos refains, ou gigantes?

Usos. Além de servirem de lugar para dormir, era na cama que muitos israelitas meditavam (Sal. 63:6). As camas também serviam de padiola (I Sam. 19:15), de lugares onde eles buscavam comunhão com Deus (Dan. 2:28), de móveis que serviam de sofá durante o dia. Mas também era lugar onde os malignos planejavam suas astúciosas manobras (Osé. 7:14; Sal. 36:4).

Uso Metafórico. O leito podia representar alianças proibidas (Isa. 57:7,8). Ser lançado na mesma cama significa ter a mesma sorte que alguém (Eze. 32:25). O julgamento contra a iniquidade e a imoralidade é retratado em Apocalipse 2:22 como ser lançado à força em uma cama. Em Jó 17:13,14 lemos acerca do ato de lançar a cama nas trevas (no hebraico, «sheol»), como sinal de julgamento sofrido. A cama «curta» de Isaías 28:20 alude a uma situação intolerável. Deus consola os enfermos em seus leitos, lugares onde eles sofrem (Sal. 41:3). (IB ID G S)

CAMALDOLITAS

Uma ordem de *eremitas* e *cenobitas* (vide) católicos romanos, isto é, eremitas que vivem uma vida comunitária. Essa ordem foi fundada por Romualdo, no começo do século XI D.C., e a sede original dos eremitas ficava em Campo Maldoli, no Abruzzi, sob a regra beneditina. Após o falecimento de seu fundador, a ordem tornou-se cenobita. O papa Alexandre II reconheceu a ordem no ano de 1072. Originalmente, a regra dessa ordem era extremamente austera, mas, posteriormente, a regra foi modificada. e alguns conventos de freiras adotaram-na. A ordem não se tem devotado à pregação e ao ensino, pelo que não tem exercido influência sobre a teologia católica romana.

CAMALEÃO

No hebraico, **koach**, que figura apenas em Lev. 11:30. Não há certeza acerca do que significa essa palavra hebraica. Alguns eruditos supõem que se trata de uma espécie de lagarto, visto que se encontra na lista dos tais, no livro de Levítico. Essa palavra hebraica tem raízes no termo «força», o que poderia apontar para a maneira como o camaleão agarra-se com força às coisas. Diz-se que é quase impossível arrancar um camaleão de um ramo ao qual ele se tenha agarrado, apenas com as mãos nuas. A despeito disso, há versões estrangeiras, como a RSV, em inglês, que diz «crocodilo terrestre». Pelo menos sabe-se que existem várias espécies de camaleão na Palestina, e ao longo da costa norte do mar Mediterrâneo. O camaleão é um animal de aparência grotesca, de aspecto feroz, dotado de olhos que enfocam em direções independentes, com pálpebras coloridas coladas sobre os mesmos, que se movem juntamente com os globos oculares. É dotado de uma língua enrolada dentro da boca, e que, ao ser lançada como um dardo, estende-se até cerca do mesmo comprimento do corpo. A cor desse animal varia de conformidade com o meio ambiente, para adaptar-se às cores do pano de fundo, facilitando assim o mimetismo do animal, quando este está à procura de insetos para alimentar-se. A Vulgata Latina identifica o animal em questão com uma espécie de toupeira. Como se nota, não há maneira segura de se saber qual espécie de animal está em vista. (WOD)

CÂMARA

No hebraico há doze palavras envolvidas, e, no grego, quatro.

1. *Cheder*, «câmara interior». Palavra hebraica que ocorre por vinte e duas vezes (por exemplo: Gên. 43:30; Juí. 3:24; 16:12; II Sam. 13:10; Sal. 105:30; Pro. 7:27; Joel 2:16).

2. *Chuppah*, «cobertura». Palavra que aparece por duas vezes: Sal. 19:5 e Joel 2:16.

3. *Yatsia* ou *yatsua*, «câmara». Palavra usada por três vezes: I Reis 6:5, 6:10.

4. *Lishkah*, «abrigo». Palavra empregada por quarenta e sete vezes (por exemplo: II Reis 23:11; I Crô. 9:26,33; Esd. 8:29; 10:6; Nee. 10:37-39; 13:4,5,8,9; Jer. 35:2,4; Eze. 40:17,38,44-46; 46:19).

5. *Nishkah*, «abrigo». Palavra usada por três vezes: Nee. 3:30; 12:4 e 13:7.

6. *Aliyyah*, «cenáculo». Palavra que ocorre por dezessete vezes (por exemplo: II Sam. 18:33; II Reis 4:10,11; Sal. 104:3,13; Jer. 22:13,14).

7. *Illith*, «cenáculo». Palavra que aparece por apenas uma vez, sendo aramaica, em Dan. 6:10.

8. *Tsela*, «câmara lateral». Palavra que figura por onze vezes com esse sentido (por exemplo: I Reis 6:5,8; Eze. 41:5-9,11,26).

9. *Ta*, «lugar separado». Palavra que aparece por doze vezes (por exemplo: Eze. 40:7,10,12,13,16,21, 29,33,36).

10. *Ulam*. Em I Reis 7:6-8, essa palavra é traduzida como Salão das Colunas. Essa palavra hebraica aparece por trinta e quatro vezes. Ver também, para exemplificar, I Crô. 28:11; II Crô. 3:4; 8:12; Eze. 8:16; 40:7—9,15,39,40,48,49; 46:8; Joel 2:17. Salomão erigiu essa estrutura, embora não se saiba dizer por que razão. Sabemos, porém, que seu Salão de Julgamento era o lugar onde ele julgava casos, como supremo juiz da nação hebréia. Não se sabe se essa estrutura estava relacionada ou não ao templo de Jerusalém. É evidente que nem todas as ocorrências dessa palavra hebraica dizem respeito ao Salão das Colunas, de Salomão.

11. *Chatser*, «lugar fechado». Nossa versão portuguesa diz «pátio interior da casa do rei», em Ester 5:1. Sem dúvida era um lugar fechado do palácio real de Susã, a capital de inverno dos reis persas. Esse edifício era um palácio luxuoso, com material de construção importado de muitos lugares, do mais alto valor, como metais preciosos, pedras finas, marfim e ébano. Muitos artífices haviam sido empregados nessa construção. O salão de audiências do rei, onde Ester veio falar com ele, era um imenso salão com cerca de 60 m(2), com trinta e seis colunas, cada qual com quase 20 m de altura, sustentando o teto. Essa palavra hebraica é usada por 140 vezes com esse sentido. Ver, por exemplo, Êxo. 27:9,12,13,16-19; 35:17,18; 40:8,33; Núm. 3:26,37, I Reis 6:36.

CÂMARA — CÂMBIO, CAMBISTAS

12. *Baith mishteh*. Em nossa versão, essa expressão é traduzida por «casa do banquete». Figura apenas em Daniel 5:10. Foi o lugar onde o rei Belsazar viu o escrito na parede, pela mão misteriosa. Heródoto alude aos luxos da Babilônia. Havia ali três palácios reais, o mais amplo dos quais continha a sala do trono. Ver o artigo separado sobre a *Babilônia*, quanto a maiores detalhes.

13. *Aulé*, palavra grega que significa «pátio». Ocorre por doze vezes: Mat. 26:3,58,69; Mar. 14:54,66; 15:16; Luc. 11:21; 22:55; João 10:1,16; 18:15; Apo. 11:2. Algumas traduções dizem «pretório», em vários desses lugares. Ver o artigo sobre o *Pretório*, onde há detalhes completos sobre a questão.

14. Também podemos mencionar o *akroatérion*, palavra que aparece exclusivamente em Atos 25:23. No grego significa «lugar de audiência». Nossa versão portuguesa a traduz por «audiência». Está em foco o salão de audiências do procurador romano, onde Paulo compareceu à presença de Festo, e seus convidados.

15. *Tameîon*, «lugar separado», «despensa». Palavra grega que aparece por quatro vezes: Mat. 6:6; 24:26; Luc. 12,3,24.

16. *Uperôon*, «cenáculo». Palavra grega que é usada também por quatro vezes: Atos 1:13; 9:37,39; 20:8.

I. Sentidos Literais. a. Uma «despensa», como no templo (II Crô. 31:11 e Nee. 10:39). b. Lugares onde os sacrifícios eram comidos (Eze. 42:13). Tais câmaras provavelmente também serviam de residência para aqueles que se ocupavam dos deveres do templo. c. Uma *câmara interior*, em uma casa (Gên. 43:40). d. Uma recâmara de noiva (Can. 1:4). e. Um cenáculo construído com o propósito de ter um lugar de abrigo do calor do verão, à tarde ou à noite (II Sam. 18:33). f. Alcovas para uso dos guardas, no templo de Ezequiel (Eze. 40:7). g. Câmaras laterais do templo (I Reis 6:5; Eze. 41:5), para diversos usos. h. Quartos no andar superior de uma casa (II Reis 4:10), ou uma recâmara usada figuradamente, para indicar a habitação de Deus (Sal. 104:3,13). i. Uma despensa, onde alguém poderia imaginar que o anticristo se esconderia (Mat. 24:26). j. Um cenáculo, ou dependência feita no andar superior de uma casa, suficientemente grande para conter uma congregação (Atos 20:8).

II. Sentidos Figurados. a. A habitação de Deus (Sal. 104:3). b. Entrar no quarto simboliza **entregar-se à** oração privada (Isa. 26:20). c. As recâmaras do sul são as constelações ou regiões do sul, no espaço, vistas do hemisfério norte da terra (Jó 9:9). d. As câmaras de imagens (Eze. 8:12) apareceram em uma visão do profeta, acerca de práticas idólatras de elementos importantes do povo de Israel. e. Em Romanos 13:13, a palavra traduzida por «impudicícias», em nossa versão portuguesa, vem, do grego, de uma raiz que significa «cama», *koité*, dando a entender o uso de uma alcova para práticas imorais. (ID IB Z)

CÂMARAS PINTADAS DE IMAGENS

Essa expressão aparece em Eze. 8:12, referindo-se às representações pictográficas que o profeta Ezequiel viu em visão, no tocante às práticas idólatras dos israelitas. Ver todo o oitavo capítulo de Ezequiel. Foi-lhe assim mostrado por que Israel merecia o juízo divino, a saber, por causa de seu profundo envolvimento com a idolatria. Ezequiel viu espetáculos como a gigantesca estátua de Baal, com muitas pessoas em redor, munidas de muitos objetos idólatras. Também viu adoradores do sol, de costas voltadas para o templo e de rosto elevado na direção do nascer do sol. Isso simbolizava o que sucede nas práticas idólatras. Deus é abandonado pelos homens, e algo de sua criação vem tomar o lugar que a ele cabe, nos corações dos homens. Ver o artigo sobre a *Idolatria*.

CAMAREIRO

No hebraico temos uma palavra, e no grego, duas, a saber:

1. *Saris*, «camareiro» ou «eunuco». Palavra hebraica usada por quarenta e duas vezes (por exemplo: II Reis 23:11; Est. 1:10,12,15; 2:3,14,15,21; 7:9).

2. *Oikonómos*, «mordomo», palavra grega que aparece por dez vezes: — ver Lucas 12:42; 16:1,3,8; Ro. 16:23; I Cor. 4:1,2; Gál. 4:2; Tito 1:7; I Ped. 4:10.

3. *Epì toû koitônos*, «encarregado da cama». Expressão grega que aparece somente em Atos 12:20, e que nossa tradução portuguesa verte por «camarista».

O termo hebraico por detrás dessa palavra é *saris*, «eunuco», pelo que, algumas vezes, é traduzido como tal. O termo grego é *oikonómos*, «mordomo». É com base nesses dois vocábulos que encontramos os usos bíblicos. Pode indicar um eunuco empregado nos haréns dos déspotas do Oriente Próximo e Médio.

Com freqüência, os camareiros vinham a ocupar posições importantes, como conselheiros de reis ou oficiais (Est. 1:10; Gên. 39:1). Salomão parece ter-se utilizado desse tipo de oficial (I Reis 4:6; 16:9; 18:3). O dever do camareiro ou eunuco consistia em muito mais do que cuidar do harém do rei. Parece ter sido uma espécie de supervisor geral do palácio e da etiqueta real. Em alguns casos, era usado como se fosse um secretário, para selecionar aqueles a quem o rei deveria conceder entrevistas, com qualquer propósito.

Nos tempos do Novo Testamento, o *oikonómos* podia ser alguém que nada tinha a ver com as funções que anteriormente cabiam aos eunucos do palácio. É provável que nem todos os *sarisim* fossem castrados ou eunucos. Em Romanos 16:23, há menção a Erasto, o qual, em algumas traduções (como a nossa versão portuguesa) aparece como camareiro, mas que, na realidade, era o tesoureiro da cidade de Corinto, sendo esta a tradução preferida para o termo grego, nesse caso. No entanto, a palavra grega envolvida é mais geral, podendo indicar um gerente de qualquer classe. O ofício de Erasto aparentemente consistia no que os latinos chamavam de *arcarius*, ou seja, magistrados inferiores, encarregados do erário público, sujeitos à supervisão do senado. *Blasto* (que vide), camarista de Herodes (Atos 12:20; no grego *koitón*), era uma espécie de valido ou confidente do rei. Ele exercia considerável influência sobre Herodes, conforme esse trecho nos permite entrever. (I ID UN Z)

CAMAREIRO-MOR

Palavra encontrada em Jer. 51:59. Essa tradução é uma emenda feita pela RSV, seguida por nossa versão portuguesa. Mas uma expressão similar é aplicada a Davi, em I Crô. 28:2, no texto hebraico (embora não figure na nossa versão portuguesa), cujo sentido mais aproximado é «príncipe tranqüilo». Trata-se de um título nobiliárquico, embora tenha sido usado em várias relações semânticas com significados diferentes

CÂMBIO, CAMBISTAS

No grego temos três palavras que precisam ser consideradas quanto a essa questão:

CAMBISES — CAMELO

1. *Kermatistés*, derivada de *kerma*, um pedaço de cobre. Essa palavra ocorre exclusivamente em João 2:14. 2. *Kollubistés*, «cambista», que é usada em Mat. 21:12; Mar. 11:15 e João 2:15. 3. *Trapezeítes*, «mesários» (que nossa versão portuguesa traduz por «banqueiros»), que ocorre somente em Mat. 25:27.

A profissão dos cambistas era bastante comum nos dias do Novo Testamento. Nos centros mercantis, bem como no templo de Jerusalém, sempre havia a necessidade de cambiar a moeda corrente em um país por outra. Para Jerusalém convergia dinheiro de muitas procedências. Judeus da dispersão visitavam a cidade, trazendo moeda estrangeira. A taxa do templo, porém, precisava ser paga com dinheiro judaico, e isso criava um intenso comércio cambista. Além disso, havia o problema de trocar dinheiro mais graúdo por dinheiro mais miúdo. Os cambistas lucravam cobrando uma taxa por seu serviço, e, naturalmente, também havia muita desonestidade nesse processo. Contra essa desonestidade foi que Jesus lançou o seu protesto. Outrossim, ele não concordava com o fato do recinto do templo tornar-se o local para tal comércio. —em detrimento dos reais propósitos daquele logradouro. Jesus virou as mesas dos «ladrões». Ver Mat. 21:12,13; Mar. 11:15-17; João 2:13-16.

Todo israelita, sem importar se rico ou pobre, tinha a obrigação de pagar uma taxa ao tesouro sagrado (Êxo. 30:13-15). Essa taxa precisava ser paga com uma moeda judaica específica. Os registros antigos mostram que os cambistas conseguiam altas faturas com suas desonestas manipulações, ao ponto de serem contados entre os ricos. Naturalmente, na área do templo efetuavam-se outros negócios, além do câmbio de moedas. E parece que a mesma casta dos cambistas também se envolvia nesses outros negócios. E havia mais comércio, mais ludíbrio, mais desonestidade.

O termo grego *trapezeítes*, usado somente em Mat. 25:27, é uma palavra geral para indicar cambista ou banqueiro. Esse termo incluía o negócio do empréstimo a juros. Onde quer que o dinheiro seja o artigo principal, a avareza domina o ambiente. Ver o artigo separado sobre o *Dinheiro*, que é uma das raízes de todos os males. Mas outros pensam que a *falta de dinheiro* é a raiz de todos os males! (I HA UN)

CAMBISES

Esse foi o nome de dois monarcas da dinastia acamenida, da Pérsia, a saber:

1. *Cambises I*. Foi o rei de Susã, a pátria ancestral dos reis acamenidas, desde cerca de 602 até 559 A.C. Era vassalo da Média; e casou-se com a filha de Astíages, rei dos medos. Seu filho foi Ciro, o Grande.

2. *Cambises II*, rei da Pérsia (529-522), filho de Ciro, o Grande. Durante o reinado de Ciro, governou a Babilônia (538-530 A.C.). Após haver sucedido a seu pai, em 525, Cambises invadiu o Egito, conforme Ciro havia planejado. Derrotou o Faraó Psamético III, em Pelúsio, e capturou as cidades de Menfis e Heliópolis, em vista do que entrou em colapso toda a resistência dos egípcios. A princípio, Cambises tratou Psamético com leniência; mas, após uma revolta dos egípcios, mandou executá-lo. Cambises teve outras notáveis aventuras militares, mas diversas de suas expedições militares foram malsucedidas. Assim, conquistou uma parte da Etiópia, — mas teve de retroceder, em vista da falta .de suprimentos. Enviou uma força armada para conquistar o oásis de Amom, mas essa força militar pereceu em uma tempestade de areia. Tentou conquistar a cidade de Cartago, mas os marinheiros fenícios não quiseram combater seus parentes cartagineses.

Cambises e a Bíblia. Cambises II foi o conquistador da Babilônia, em outubro de 539 A.C., sendo mencionado tanto pela Crônica de Nabonido como pelo Cilindro de Ciro como filho de Ciro. Já foi confundido com o Assuero de Esdras 4:6; mas, atualmente, sabe-se que Assuero deve ser identificado com Xerxes. Cambises II não aparece no Antigo Testamento, exceto implicitamente, em Daniel 11:2, onde deve ser o primeiro dos três monarcas que se seguiram a Ciro. Quando Ciro faleceu, em campanha militar, Cambises tornou-se o único governante do imenso império persa. Conseguiu a posição de único governante mandando assassinar o seu irmão, Esmérdis (Bardia), e então deu início às aventuras militares acima mencionadas. Seu maior sucesso foi no Egito, onde tomou para si o nome real e o título dos reis egípcios, e passou a usar o costume real do Egito. A caminho de volta à Babilônia, em 522 A.C., recebeu a notícia de que um certo Gaumata (que afirmava ser o seu irmão assassinado) havia usurpado o trono, contando com forte apoio. Morreu perto do monte Carmelo, na Palestina, talvez por suicídio. Cambises II não tinha herdeiros, e Dario Histapes, um oficial do exército persa, sucedeu-o, matando o pseudo Esmérdis, no espaço de poucos meses, tendo então conseguido consolidar o império sob as suas ordens.

O reinado de Cambises coincidiu com o período da oposição de certos gentios à construção do segundo templo de Jerusalém (ver Esd. 4:5 e Ageu 1:4). Ver sobre *Ciro; Dario o Medo* e *Dario*. (AM DUB OLM)

CAMBOTAS, CAMBAS

No hebraico, **gab**. Com esse sentido, a palavra é usada somente por três vezes, duas em Eze. 1:18, dentro da visão de Ezequiel sobre as rodas cheias de olhos (onde nossa versão portuguesa diz «cambotas») e uma em I Reis 7:33, onde se fala sobre o mar de fundição, preparado a mando de Salomão, e onde a nossa versão portuguesa diz «cambas».

CAMELO

No hebraico, **gamal**, palavra que aparece por cinqüenta e quatro vezes, desde Gên. 12:16 até Zac. 14:15. Também há menção ao dromedário, no hebraico, *achashteranim*, palavra que ocorre somente em Ester 8:10,14. No grego, *kámelos*, vocábulo que aparece por seis vezes: Mat. 3:4; 19:24; 23:24; Mar. 1:6; 10:25 e Luc. 18:25.

1. *Fatos Gerais*. Aquele que disse que «o camelo é um cavalo criado por uma comissão», tinha razão ao dar a entender que as comissões com freqüência não executam um trabalho que um único indivíduo pode fazer melhor e com maior prontidão. Porém, estava equivocado quando, aparentemente, desvalorizou o camelo. O camelo é um dos mais úteis de todos os animais domesticados pelo homem, embora não seja um animal de bonito porte. Com exceção do elefante, é o maior dos animais usados pelo homem. Com freqüência atinge a altura de 2,40 m, ou mesmo mais, e é dotado de grande força e resistência. Tem um casco espalhado, que o capacita a caminhar por cima de lugares arenosos, sem afundar na areia. Seu estômago é dotado da maravilhosa capacidade de armazenar água, pelo que é capaz de viajar durante dias, sem beber uma gota de água. Além disso, sua dieta é a mais simples possível, podendo subsistir com a erva mais amarga e daninha. Pode até mesmo triturar espinhos com seus dentes, e digeri-los. É tão

CAMELO — CAMINHO

alto que precisa ajoelhar-se para receber sua carga. Uma vez carregado, embora transportando um peso de até cerca de 250 kg, pode levantar-se sobre as patas e viajar durante os dias mais quentes, através dos piores desertos imagináveis. A corcova que ele tem nas costas é um armazém de gordura, uma reserva para longos períodos de jejum. O povo de Israel foi proibido de comer a carne do camelo, mas os árabes não têm tais escrúpulos. Seu couro é usado para fabricar sandálias, e seu pêlo é empregado para tecer um pano grosseiro. O leite da camela, bem como os produtos derivados do mesmo, são alimentos primários da dieta dos beduínos do deserto.

2. *Disposição do Camelo.* O camelo é um animal muito fleumático. Troteia à velocidade de até dez quilômetros horários. Anda à velocidade de cinco quilômetros e meio.—Pode galopar até dezesseis quilômetros por hora, mas não por muito tempo. O camelo é famoso por sua estupidez e obstinação. Os machos são briguentos e mordem-se selvagemente quando brigam. A gravidez das fêmeas dura quase um ano, e só nasce um camelinho de cada vez. O intervalo natural entre os nascimentos é de dois anos. Os camelos só atingem seu pleno desenvolvimento com cerca de dezesseis anos de idade, e seu período médio de duração da vida é de vinte e cinco anos.

3. *Referências Bíblicas.* A primeira menção ao camelo dá-se na época dos patriarcas, conforme se vê em Gên. 12:16; 24:10,11,14,19, etc. Em Levítico 11:4 sua carne é proibida para consumo do povo de Israel. Ver também Êxo. 9:3; Juí. 6:5; I Sam. 27:9; Esd. 2:67; Jó 1:3; Isa. 21:7; Jer. 49:29; Eze. 25:5; Mat. 3:4; Luc. 18:25.

4. *Domesticação e Utilização.* As evidências arqueológicas asseguram-nos que a domesticação do camelo já era generalizada tão cedo quanto 1200-1000 A.C. Porém, nos dias de Abraão, isto é 2000 A.C., isso já teria acontecido, visto que há referências bíblicas com esse sentido. Alguns arqueólogos têm duvidado dessa informação. Mas o camelo tem sido domesticado desde os tempos mais remotos. A espécie floresceu até mesmo na América do Norte há cerca de dois milhões de anos atrás, e mais tarde tornou-se extinta. Há evidências de que já havia a espécie na América do Sul, na Ásia e na África há cerca de dez milhões de anos atrás. Há evidências de completa domesticação do camelo em cerca de 1800 A.C., e restos de ossadas de camelos têm sido encontrados em antigos cemitérios urbanos, em Israel, desde cerca desse tempo. A domesticação em larga escala, após o século XII A.C., expandiu enormemente o comércio através do deserto, pois para viagens por lugares áridos e quentes, não há animal que se compare em utilidade ao camelo. Continua sendo importante, com esse propósito, nos países de extensas áreas desérticas. O dromedário pode transportar até cerca de 280 kg, a uma distância de cerca de cinqüenta quilômetros por dia. O mais corpulento camelo bactriano pode levar até 450 kg de carga.

5. *Usos Figurados na Bíblia.* a. Os judeus são comparados a uma *veloz dromedária* no tempo do cio. A passagem de Isaías 40:6-8, que se refere a multidões de camelos chegando de todos os lugares, e o trecho de Isaías 46:20, que fala sobre os judeus serem trazidos em camelos, mulas, cavalos, etc., como uma oferenda ao Senhor, vindos de todas as nações, alude à futura restauração e glória de Israel. b. O trecho de Mateus 19:24 diz: «...é mais fácil passar um camelo pelo fundo de uma agulha, do que entrar um rico no reino de Deus». Essa metáfora mostra-nos como as riquezas embotam a sensibilidade de um homem para com as coisas espirituais, dificultando-lhe entrar no reino de Deus. O provérbio original provavelmente dizia «elefante», em lugar de «camelo»; mas, na Palestina, o maior animal conhecido era o camelo. Uma variante textual diz «corda», em lugar de «camelo», mas isso não corresponde ao original. A suposta referência a uma portinhola nas muralhas de Jerusalém, através da qual um camelo só podia entrar ajoelhando-se, não é muito provável, pois não há provas de que um dia existiu ali uma porta chamada buraco de agulha. Ver o NTI em Mat. 19:24, quanto a detalhes sobre a questão. (AM ALB UN Z)

CAMI Ver **Kami**.

CAMINHO

Em adição ao sentido literal do termo, a Bíblia usa essa palavra também em sentido metafórico. Por esse motivo, várias palavras hebraicas e gregas estão envolvidas nesse assunto.

1. Palavras hebraicas:

a. *Orach*, «caminho costumeiro». Termo que figura por sessenta vezes. Para exemplificar: Jó 16:22; 19:8; Sal. 44:18; 142:3; Pro. 1:19; 2:15; 4:14; 8:20; Isa. 26:7,8; 41:3.

b. *Orcha*, «caminho costumeiro». Palavra aramaica que aparece somente em Dan. 4:37 e 5:23.

c. *Derek*, «vereda». Palavra usada por quase mil e setecentas vezes. Por exemplo: Gên. 3:24; 6:12; Êxo. 4:24; 13:17; Lev. 26:22; Núm. 14:25; 20:17; Deu. 1:2,19,22,31,33,40; 2:1,8; 3:1; Jos. 1:8; 2:7; Juí. 2:17,19,22; 5:10; Rute 1:7; I Sam. 1:18; 6:9,12; II Sam. 2:24; 13:30,34; I Reis 1:49; 2:2-4; II Reis 2:23; 3:8,20; II Crô. 6:16,23,27,30,31,34; Esd. 8:21,22,31; Nee. 9:12,19; Jó 3:23; 4:6; 6:18; Sal. 1:1,6; 2:12; 5:8; 10:5; Pro. 1:15,31; 2:8,12,13,20; 3:6,17,23,31; Ecl. 10:3; Isa. 2:3; 3:12; Jer. 2:17,18,23,33,36; Lam. 1:4; Eze. 3:18,19; 7:3-9,27; 8:5; 9:2,10; Osé. 2:6; Joel 2:7; Amós 2:7; Jó 3:8,10; Miq. 4:2; Naum 1:3; Zac. 1:4,6; Mal. 3:1.

d. *Magalah*, «vereda», «curso». Palavra usada por sete vezes. Por exemplo: Pro. 5:6; 2:15,18; Sal. 17:5.

e. *Nathib*, «vereda». Palavra usada por cinco vezes: Jó 18:10; Sal. 78:50; Jó 28:7; 41:32; Sal. 119:35.

f. *Mesillah*, «estrada». Palavra usada por vinte e sete vezes. Por exemplo: Isa. 59:7; Joel 2:8; Núm. 20:19; Isa. 7:3; 11:16; Jer. 31:21.

g. *Magal*, «estrada larga (para vagões)». Palavra usada por oito vezes. Por exemplo: Sal. 23:3; Pro. 2:9; Isa. 26:7.

h. *Mishol*, «vereda estreita». Palavra usada por uma vez somente, isto é, em Núm. 22:24.

i. *Nethibah*, «trilha». Palavra usada por dezenove vezes. Para exemplificar: Jó 19:8; Sal. 119:105; Pro. 1:15; 3:17; Isa. 42:16; 43:16; Jer. 6:16; Lam. 3:9; Osé. 2:6.

j. *Shebil*, «vereda», «avanço». Palavra usada somente por duas vezes: Sal. 77:19; Jer. 18:15.

Os usos metafóricos mais comuns, no Antigo Testamento, são os seguintes:

a. Processos naturais: como o caminho do relâmpago e do trovão (Jó 28:26; 38:25), os movimentos da luz (Jó 38:19,24), a vida de uma formiga (Pro. 6:6), o comportamento das águias, das serpentes, os movimentos de uma embarcação e o namoro de um homem, etc. (Pro. 30:19).

b. A conduta moral de um homem, embora a idéia também possa ser expressa de outras maneiras, como é evidente: quanto à bondade (I Sam. 12:23; Sal. 1:6; 119:1; Pro. 2:20; 8:20); quanto à maldade (Juí. 2:19;

613

CAMINHO — CAMINHO (CRISTO)

Sal. 119:101,104; Pro. 4:14; Isa. 55:7; Eze. 3:18.19); algumas vezes, sem especificação quanto ao caráter moral de uma pessoa (Gên. 6:12; II Crô. 6:16,30; Jó. 13:5; Sal. 39:1; Pro. 12:15; 16:29); quanto às tradições boas ou más (I Sam. 8:3,5; I Reis 15:26,34; 22:52); quanto aos galardões da vida ou da morte, por causa da bondade ou da maldade praticadas (Pro. 10:17; 14:12; 15:24; 16:25; Jer. 21:8).

c. Várias facetas da vida humana, como o curso da vida de um homem (Deu. 28:29; Jó 3:23; Sal. 2:12; 37:5; Pro. 3:6; Jer. 10:23); seus planos para a sua vida (Pro. 16:9; Osé. 10:13); seus sofrimentos e provações (Sal. 142:3; Jó 23:10); o destino humano na morte (Jos. 23:14; I Reis 2:2).

d. Em muitos casos também estão em foco os caminhos ou métodos de ação seguidos por Deus, como a sua vontade e os seus mandamentos (Deu. 5:33; 8:6; 10:12; 26:17; Sal. 44:18; 119:15; Isa. 2:3); os seus juízos (Isa. 26:8); os seus propósitos (Jó 36:23; Sal. 77:13; 103:7; Isa. 55:9); o seu governo providencial (Deu. 8:2; II Sam. 22:31,33; Jó 19:8; 26:14; Sal. 18:30; Eze. 18:25).

2. Palavras gregas:

a. *Odós*, «caminho». Palavra usada por cem vezes, desde Mat. 2:12 até Apo. 16:12.

b. *Párodos*, «passagem». Palavra usada somente em I Cor. 16:7.

c. *Poreía*, «ida». Palavra usada apenas por duas vezes: Luc. 13:22 e Tia. 1:11.

d. *Trópos*, «maneira». Palavra empregada por treze vezes: Mat. 23:37; Luc. 13:34; Atos 1:11; 7:28; 15:11; 27:25; Rom. 3:2; Fil. 1:18; II Tes. 2:3; 3:16; II Tim. 3:8; Heb. 13:5,7.

e. *Ékbasis*, «saída». Palavra usada somente por duas vezes: I Cor. 10:13 e Heb. 13:7.

Além do sentido literal de «caminho», o Novo Testamento encerra os seguintes sentidos metafóricos:

a. Acerca da conduta moral (Mat. 7:13,14; 21:32; Atos 14:16; Rom. 3:16,17; Tia. 5:20; II Ped. 2:15,21).

b. Acerca da vontade, dos propósitos e da veracidade de Deus (Mat. 22:16; Mar. 12:14; Atos 13:10; 18:25,26; Rom. 11:33; I Cor. 4:17; Heb. 3:10 e Apo. 15:3).

c. No livro de Atos, a expressão «o Caminho» refere-se à fé cristã e à maneira de viver seguida pelos discípulos do Senhor, tudo o que era desprezado e até caluniado por seus adversários gratuitos (Atos 9:2; 19:9; 22:4,14; 24:22).

d. Jesus Cristo, o último e perfeito revelador, é «o Caminho» por excelência, em face do exemplo soberbo dado por sua própria pessoa e pela sua morte sacrificial. Ele é o caminho vivo e pessoal até Deus. Também estão em pauta a sua santidade e a sua salvação, pelo que ele é o mestre, o caminho da verdade (Mat. 22:16; Mar. 12:14; Luc. 1:79). Em si mesmo, Jesus é o único «caminho» para Deus (João 14:4-6). E Cristo também é Aquele que abre o caminho para o Santo dos Santos celeste, onde manifesta-se a glória plena de Deus, mediante o seu sacrifício na cruz (Heb. 9:8; 10:19,20).

Do Caminho. Aparentemente tornou-se costumeiro designar desse modo o cristianismo, em que é apresentado o «caminho da vida», sem dúvida uma designação antiqüíssima, antes de tornar-se comum o termo *cristão*. (Ver também *vida* como termo para indicar o cristianismo, em Atos 5:20). A expressão «caminho», como maneira de expressar o cristianismo e o tipo de vida (talvez incluindo também a doutrina cristã, embora isso não faça parte proeminente da idéia) é usada por nada menos de seis vezes no livro de Atos, e, mui curiosamente, sempre em alguma passagem relacionada a incidentes da vida de Paulo. (Ver Atos 9:2; 19:9,23; 22:4; 24:14,22). É bem possível que essa designação se tenha originado no modo judaico de expressar as coisas, conforme achamos em Isa. 40:3: «...o caminho do Senhor...»; em Sal. 1:6: «...o caminho dos justos...», e «...o caminho dos ímpios...», etc. Não nos devemos esquecer de que o próprio Senhor Jesus chamou-se de «...o Caminho...» (João 14:6). Os índios norte-americanos chamavam o cristianismo de *estrada de Jesus*. Meyer (em Atos 9:2) diz a respeito disso: «Trata-se da *direção característica* da vida, determinada pela fé em Jesus Cristo».

Existem certas interpretações, alicerçadas na *fantasia*, como a de Crisóstomo, que pensam tratar-se do *caminho para os céus*; porém, esse não era o emprego original do termo, por parte de incrédulos, quando usavam essa expressão, e nem é a idéia dominante quando usado pelos crentes, embora, teologicamente falando, seja esse um desenvolvimento natural da idéia. Não é impossível, entretanto, que tal designação se tenha originado do uso que o Senhor Jesus fez da palavra, referindo-se à sua própria pessoa, como «...o Caminho, e a Verdade e a Vida...». Todavia, é mais provável que se tenha originado da observação feita por algum indivíduo alheio ao movimento cristão, sobre o tipo distinto de vida que os cristãos levavam, dizendo que os mesmos eram gente *do Caminho* que difere em seus costumes e ações, bem como no modo geral de vida, daquele outro «caminho» pelo qual seguem os inconversos. Os primeiros crentes, provavelmente, também se utilizavam do termo para se identificarem a si mesmos, ainda que tal expressão talvez se tenha originado da observação de pessoas estranhas ao cristianismo.

CAMINHO, CRISTO COMO
Exclusividade de Cristo

Provavelmente essa é a melhor conhecida e a mais repetida das declarações do Senhor Jesus nas quais ele diz «Eu sou...» (Quanto a um sumário dessas declarações, no evangelho de João, ver as notas sobre o trecho de João 11:25 no NTI).

«*Sem o Caminho*, não pode haver avanço; *sem a Verdade* não pode haver conhecimento; *sem a Vida*, não pode haver vida. Eu sou o Caminho que deveis procurar; eu sou a Verdade na qual deveis crer; e eu sou a Vida, na qual deveis pôr as vossas esperanças». (Thomas a Kempis, em *Imitação de Cristo*, III.56).

Quanto à declaração de Cristo: «*Eu sou o caminho*...» poderíamos tecer as considerações seguintes:

1. Jesus é o caminho *para Deus*, o qual é o destino final da humanidade redimida.

2. Portanto, Jesus é o caminho para *os lugares celestiais*, que é onde habita a divindade. Jesus é igualmente o caminho para aquele lugar especial que está preparando, conforme está descrito nos versículos dois e três do décimo quarto capítulo do evangelho de João.

3. Jesus é o caminho para a transformação espiritual, a fim de que os homens venham a participar da forma de vida divina, a vida necessária e independente do próprio Pai (João 5:25,26), a plenitude de Deus, isto é, sua natureza e seus atributos (ver notas em Efé. 3:19 no NTI), tais seres chegarão a possuir a plenitude de Cristo. Ver o artigo sobre *Plenitude de Cristo*.

4. Jesus é o Pioneiro desse caminho, e mostra aos homens como se devem desenvolver espiritualmente,

CAMINHO (CRISTO) — CAMINHOS

pois sempre palmilhou pela vereda que os homens devem seguir. Ele é o Homem ideal a ser seguido, o Homem divino a ser duplicado. Ele é o caminho quanto ao seguinte:

a. O Logos, que revela Deus aos homens, João 1:18.

b. Em sua encarnação, ele tem a missão de conduzir os homens ao Pai, João 1:14.

c. Em sua morte, ele torna possível o caminho de volta a Deus, Rom. 5:11.

d. Em sua ascensão, ele soergue os homens até os lugares celestiais, Efé. 1:19 e ss.

e. Em sua ressurreição, ele dá aos homens a vida de Deus, Rom. 4:45.

f. Em sua glorificação, os homens são glorificados e assim penetram no mais elevado dos céus, Rom. 8:30.

A verdade que mostra que o Senhor Jesus não é somente o alvo, mas igualmente o caminho para esse alvo, é verdade importantíssima, comentada no seguinte poema de Alice Meynell:

Tu és o Caminho
Não foras tu nada, senão o alvo,
Não diria eu, nada duvidando,
Que encontraste a minha alma.

(I am the Way, Poemas, pág. 28)

Apesar do fato de o seguirmos no caminho, palmilhando pelo caminho que ele nos aponta, sendo ele mesmo o alvo para onde conduz a vereda, podemos descobrir que se trata de uma jornada rigorosa; e o próprio Senhor Jesus assegurou-nos que os discípulos não devem esperar que a nossa peregrinação não tenha suas durezas, tal como a dele mesmo foi dificílima. Samuel Rutherford refere-se exatamente a isso quando escreveu:

A estrada serpeia para cima, por todo o caminho?
Sim, até o seu próprio fim.
Os dias de jornada ocuparão o dia inteiro?
Da manhã à noite, meu amigo.

(Extraído da obra de Christina Rossetti, *Uphill*).

5. *Cristo, O Logos, o Caminho Universal*. O Logos (Cristo) planta suas sementes em filosofias e religiões não-cristãs como atos preparatórios à Restauração (que vide), como Efé. 1:10 demonstra. Portanto, sua exclusividade é ao mesmo tempo uma *universalidade*, porque opera através de uma *multiplicidade* de meios. As verdades nas religiões, nas filosofias, e nas ciências, são *todas elas*, as verdades universais do *Logos*. Seu campo de atividade é universal. Também, não é limitado pela morte biológica de cada indivíduo, sendo que a oportunidade do *Caminho* se estende além do sepulcro. Ver I Ped. 4:6.

CAMINHO DE DEUS

O Caminho de Deus é a Presença do Evangelho, nos seus Benefícios Resultantes.

1. Em tão breve período de tempo, essa verdade chegou a tornar-se conhecida pelo mundo inteiro. Essa é a verdade que o livro de Atos demonstra de forma gráfica. (Ver Col. 1:6, no que tange à declaração de Paulo sobre o fato).

2. O livro de Atos demonstra o avanço irresistível da verdade de Cristo, e a própria história da humanidade, desde então, tem sido demonstração similar.

Consideremos Estas Idéias e Referências
O Caminho Abriu-nos O Acesso
Vem de Deus (Sal. 65:4).
Por meio de Cristo (João 10:7,9; 14:6; Rom. 5:2; Efé. 2:13; 3:12; Heb. 7:19,25; 10:19; I Ped. 3:18).
Por meio do Espírito Santo (Efé. 2:18).
Obtido através da fé (Atos 14:27; Rom. 5:2; Efé. 3:12; Heb. 11:6).
Segue-se à reconciliação com Deus (Col. 1:21,22).
Na oração (Deu. 4:7; Mat. 6:6; I Ped. 1:17).
Em seu templo (Sal. 15:1; 27:4; 43:3; 65:4).
A fim de obter misericórdia e graça (Heb. 4:16).
Um privilégio dos santos (Deu. 4:7; Sal. 15; 23:6; 35:3,4).
Os santos o têm, com confiança (Efé. 3:12; Heb. 4:16; 10:19,22).
Proporcionado aos pecadores penitentes (Osé. 14:2; Joel 2:12).
Os santos o buscam ansiosamente (Sal. 27:4; 42:1,2; 43:3; 84:1,2).
Aos ímpios é ordenado que o busquem (Isa. 55:6; Tia. 4:8).
Exortemos outros a buscá-lo (Isa. 2:3; Jer. 31:6).
Promessas vinculadas ao mesmo (Sal. 145:18; Isa. 55:3; Mat. 6:6; Tia. 4:8).
Suas bênçãos (Sal. 16:11; 65:4; 73:28).
Tipificado (Lev. 16:12-15 com Heb. 10:19-22).
Exemplificado: Moisés (Êxo. 24:2; 34:4-7).

CAMINHO DE OITO ELEMENTOS

Essa idéia faz parte da doutrina budista. O **Nirvana** (que vide) poderia ser atingido pela vereda moral em oito passos, que incluem as oito virtudes cardeais, a saber: corretos pontos de vista, corretas intenções, linguagem correta, conduta correta, corretos meios de sobrevivência, esforços corretos, atenção correta e concentração correta. No artigo sobre o *Budismo* (2.7), apresentamos o desenvolvimento dessas noções.

CAMINHOS do Desenvolvimento Espiritual

Cada tarefa, para ser devidamente levada a termo, requer um modo próprio de operação. A mais nobre tarefa de todas é a do próprio desenvolvimento espiritual. Trata-se de um nobre caminho, porquanto não somente prepara o espírito para os mundos de luz, mas também envolve, necessariamente, que ajudemos a outros a atingirem o mesmo destino. Em certo sentido, cada indivíduo é uma ilha, pois cada qual é altamente responsável pelo que faz, bem como por seu futuro estado espiritual. O que cada pessoa faz agora, sempre exerce efeito sobre o futuro. Em outro sentido, porém, cada indivíduo está ligado ao continente, pelo que cada um pode ser comparado a um istmo, pois tudo quanto ele faz afeta outras vidas. O homem tem dois amplos destinos, a saber:

1. *O destino terreno*. O que acontece neste mundo é importante, inteiramente à parte do futuro estado espiritual. A terra tem um destino, e não apenas os indivíduos. Há um propósito que devemos cumprir *neste* mundo. Por esse motivo, um cientista, que esteja ajudando a comunidade humana a cumprir o seu destino terreno, está cumprindo uma missão divina. Na verdade, todos os homens, os quais vivem dentro daquilo que a vontade de Deus lhes determinou, são seus ministros, conscientes ou inconscientes, sem importar o tipo de trabalho que estiverem fazendo. Temos tarefas terrenas a cumprir, que se relacionam somente a esta vida, mas que são importantes, mesmo quando não se leva em conta a preparação de nossas almas para estados mais elevados. Cada *nação* à face da terra, e não apenas indivíduos isolados, tem um propósito a cumprir na história. Quando vemos o que está acontecendo,

CAMINHOS (MEIOS ESPIRITUAIS)

percebemos que as nações têm características que também caracterizam os indivíduos: elas são egoístas, atéias, arrogantes e preguiçosas, ou então ambiciosas, generosas e zelosas quanto às questões religiosas. As nações, e não apenas os indivíduos, podem falhar no cumprimento do que lhes foi dado para fazerem. Os propósitos combinados de todas as nações perfazem o propósito da *terra*, se todas elas cumprirem o seu papel. A antiga doutrina judaica dizia que cada nação tem seu guia angelical, tal como acontece a cada indivíduo; e essas forças espirituais ajudam as nações a atingirem os propósitos a que cada uma delas está destinada.

2. Também há o *destino espiritual, não terreno*, dos indivíduos. Na Igreja de Cristo, encontramos um destino comunitário, e nenhuma pessoa é remida como indivíduo isolado. A redenção também tem um especto comunitário. A nação de Israel também tem um destino comunitário e espiritual; e isso pode ocorrer no caso de outras nações e de outros grupos, embora as Escrituras não nos prestem informações a esse respeito.

Como é óbvio, os destinos terreno e espiritual estão inter-relacionados. Ademais, mesmo quando consideramos questões meramente terrenas, vemos que as pessoas trabalham e produzem melhor se contam com guias e influências espirituais, que as inspiram.

Quais são os meios de desenvolvimento espiritual? Consideremos os **sete pontos** abaixo:

1. *O treinamento do intelecto*, mediante o estudo de livros espirituais, filosóficos, religiosos, e sobretudo, o estudo das Escrituras Sagradas. É proveitoso o estudo das religiões não cristãs, pois aqui ou acolá encontramos jóias de grande valor, nos lugares mais inesperados. Além disso, a ignorância sobre as crenças alheias dificilmente promove a espiritualidade; a ignorância, por si só, já é prejudicial à espiritualidade.

2. *O uso da oração* (que vide). A oração é a linha de comunicação que temos com o mundo celestial, de onde derivamos ajuda e poder espirituais.

3. *O uso da meditação*. A meditação é irmã gêmea da oração. Consiste em esperar receber comunicações do Ser divino, **em vez de falar** com o Ser divino. A Igreja Ortodoxa Oriental tem-se notabilizado pelo fato de que muitos de seus vultos têm buscado iluminação espiritual através da meditação. Alguns evangélicos se têm manifestado contrariamente à meditação, mas a meditação Cristocêntrica pode ser uma grande força iluminadora. O trecho de Efé. 1:17,18 refere-se, de modo bem definido, à necessidade que temos de *iluminação*. Esse é o toque místico da nossa fé religiosa. Ver o artigo sobre o *Misticismo*. Conforme esse termo é usado nesta enciclopédia, misticismo é o contacto com algum poder superior a nós mesmos, sem importar se com a alma, com o homem espiritual ou com poderes divinos. Isso posto, doutrinas como a da regeneração, das operações do Espírito Santo, da iluminação diária, etc., são doutrinas místicas, em consonância com essa definição.

4. *A santificação*. A inquirição espiritual de alguém não pode avançar grande coisa sem o concurso da santificação (que vide). Sem a santificação, ninguém verá a Deus (Heb. 12:14); sem a santificação, o progresso espiritual do indivíduo é tolhido.

5. *As boas obras.*—Cada vez que alguém pratica o bem em favor de outrem, aprimora-se a qualidade espiritual de seu ser. Ver Efé. 2:10.

6. *A lei do amor*. Essa lei consiste em fazer pelo próximo o que gostaríamos que os outros fizessem por nós. O amor é a mais poderosa virtude de todas, o solo onde todas as demais virtudes são cultivadas. Ver Gál. 5:22. Ver o artigo sobre o *Amor*.

7. *O desenvolvimento de todas as virtudes*. Ver Gál. 5:22,23, que menciona qualidades como «amor», «alegria», «paz», «longanimidade», «benignidade», «bondade», «fidelidade», «mansidão» e «domínio próprio». Todas essas qualidades espirituais devem ser cultivadas, porquanto são necessárias ao nosso progresso espiritual.

Os Quatro Caminhos do Hinduísmo. Não prejudica ao crente examinar o que outras pessoas e religiões têm pensado. No tocante à vida espiritual, o sistema do hinduísmo tem algumas sugestões valiosas, ao menos para efeito de comparação. O hinduísmo parte da idéia de que diferentes tipos de pessoas ressaltam diferentes meios de expressão, através dos quais elas se desenvolvem espiritualmente. No hinduísmo, esses caminhos são chamados *yogas* ou *jugos*. Cada indivíduo se especializaria em um jugo diferente, embora, em algum grau, também utilize todos os outros jugos. Alguns gigantes espirituais são capazes de suportar mais de um jugo a cada vez. No hinduísmo, os *quatro caminhos* têm o intuito de separar-nos de pensamentos e atos egoístas, instalando em nós o senso de outra dimensão, da dimensão divina. Os sentidos nos transformariam em escravos. O corpo é nosso exigente senhor. Porém, há algo mais elevado a ser buscado.

*A mente sem repouso do homem
É fortemente sacudida
Nas garras dos sentidos...
Verdadeiramente, penso
Que o vento não é tão selvagem.*
(Bhagavad-Gita)

a. *O Caminho do Trabalho*. Algumas pessoas preferem trabalhar para o Senhor do que desfrutar de sua comunhão, — conforme foi tipificado por *Marta*, irmã de Maria (ver Luc. 10:38-42). A idéia do hinduísmo é que precisamos eliminar o egoísmo; e uma das maneiras para conseguirmos isso é dedicar-nos a alguma tarefa de modo absoluto. Se nos perdermos nesse afã, haveremos de tornar-nos menos egoístas, assim obtendo uma melhor qualidade espiritual. Os cientistas em geral, são pessoas que escolhem o caminho do trabalho.

b. *O Caminho do Conhecimento*. Algumas pessoas têm fome e sede de conhecimento. O caminho intelectual também pode despir-nos de muito egoísmo, melhorando a nossa qualidade espiritual. Além disso, o conhecimento é capaz de outorgar-nos horizontes espirituais mais amplos. Os intelectuais e os eruditos entram por esse caminho.

c. *O Caminho do Misticismo*. Alguns são místicos naturais, e sentem que o caminho do misticismo é muito recompensador. Que outros prefiram o trabalho ou as atividades intelectuais. Porém, sempre haverá um lugar para os místicos. Os profetas e santos são místicos, e devemos ser gratos por eles, porquanto eles nos têm dado os Documentos Sagrados, estabelecendo um elevado exemplo espiritual a ser seguido, sobretudo na senda da santidade.

d. *O Caminho do Amor*. Não existe princípio espiritual mais elevado do que a vida que segue pelo caminho do amor, segundo o qual a pessoa serve a seus semelhantes com atitude altruísta. Algumas pessoas inclinam-se, naturalmente, para esse caminho, e todos deveriam buscar esse tipo de vida. Os filantropos, os médicos, as enfermeiras, ao servirem ao próximo, geralmente sob condições desagradáveis, porque convivem com pessoas enfermas e moribundas, expressam-se através desse caminho. A Igreja cristã inteira deveria ocupar-se nesse tipo de atividade, fazendo pelo próximo, o que gostariam que se fizesse a eles.

O ser humano, que afastou-se para longe do Fogo Central, precisa de muitos modos de ajuda, que lhe facilitem recuperar sua glória perdida. (HUS NTI)

CAMISARDOS (FILHOS DE DEUS)

Um grupo de aldeões protestantes liderados por Jean Cavalier, filho adolescente de um barbeiro. Eles combatiam os católicos romanos por haver sido revogado o edito de Nantes (que vide), de 1702-1705 e depois. A bula de Clemente XI (que vide), descrevia-os como *antigos Albigenses*. Mas, por causa de seus excessos, serviam de embaraço para outros grupos protestantes, incluindo os huguenotes franceses (que vide). Em suas observações religiosas eles incluíam profecias extáticas, prodígios, vozes, luzes preternaturais vistas no firmamento, e toda a variedade de misticismo. (E)

CAMOM

Esse era o nome de uma cidade de Gileade, onde foi sepultado o juiz Jair (Juí. 10:3-5). O local é desconhecido na atualidade, embora as opiniões falem em Qamm, a sudeste do mar da Galiléia, e em Qumein, a leste-nordeste de Irbide.

CAMOS

Nome da divindade nacional dos moabitas (que vide), segundo se vê em I Reis 11:7; II Reis 23:13 e Jer. 48:7. Monumentos arqueológicos, como a Pedra Moabita (que vide), também confirmam o fato. Ocasionalmente, — ele era aplacado por sacrifícios humanos (II Reis 3:27). Está escrito que Salomão erigiu um santuário em sua honra, em Jerusalém, o qual continuou de pé até à reforma de Josias (II Reis 23:13). Por causa de sua conexão com essa divindade, algumas vezes os moabitas são chamados de «povo de Camos» (Núm. 21:29). Os amonitas, por igual modo, estavam envolvidos nesse culto idólatra (Juí. 11:24). Os profetas mostraram-se indignados contra esse desvio para a idolatria, e Jeremias predisse que seus devotos sofreriam o cativeiro (Jer. 48:7). O nome «Camos» aparece por doze vezes na Pedra Moabita. Ali aparece como um nome composto, a saber, Astar-Camos, o que sugere que ele pode ter sido um deus astral, cujo par era a deusa Istar, ou Vênus. As informações que aparecem na Pedra Moabita mostram que ele era considerado um selvagem deus da guerra. Os homens gostam de imaginar suas divindades vinculadas à guerra. Esse deus, pois, punia os homens derrotados em batalha. A tradição judaica afirma que essa divindade era adorada sob o símbolo de uma estrela negra, a qual, por sua vez, estava ligada a certas formas da idolatria dos árabes. Sua conexão com Moloque (I Reis 6:7), sugere que ele estava ligado à adoração ao planeta Saturno. As evidências apontam para a conclusão de que seu culto era bastante diversificado, assumindo várias formas, conforme a área em questão. (E S THO)

CAMPAINHA, SINO

No hebraico temos duas palavras, **paamon**, «gongo» e **metsilloth**, «campainha». A primeira palavra é usada por sete vezes (por exemplo: Êxo. 28:33); e a segunda por uma vez só, em Zac. 14:20. O gongo está ligado ao címbalo. Os gongos mais antigos, descobertos pela arqueologia, eram feitos de uma placa de metal encurvado para tomar forma oval, onde a percussão era feita ao mesmo tempo, nas duas extremidades. Havia vários modelos usados pelos assírios e chineses.

Nas Escrituras. Havia pequenas campainhas de ouro, presas à borda da sobrepeliz dos trajes oficiais do sumo sacerdote dos israelitas. Essas campainhas tinham o propósito de anunciar seus movimentos ao povo, além de servirem de ornamento (Êxo. 28:33-35).

Além disso, pode-se ler sobre os pequenos ornamentos que as mulheres de Israel usavam no pulso e nos tornozelos, a fim de atraírem a atenção, (Isa. 3:16-18), uma prática condenada pelo profeta.

No trecho de Zacarias 14:20, onde o original usa outra palavra, lê-se acerca das campainhas usadas pelos cavalos, quando do milênio, provavelmente feitas de peças côncavas de bronze. Talvez isso tivesse por motivo o adorno, ou então o fato das pessoas gostarem de ouvir sons agradáveis. Nessas campainhas estava escrita esta inscrição: «Santo ao Senhor», a mesma inscrição que havia na mitra do sumo sacerdote. Isso assim sucederá porque, durante o milênio, todas as coisas serão consagradas ao Senhor, que será o Rei de toda a terra. A arqueologia tem mostrado que os antigos assírios costumavam pôr campainhas nos pescoços dos cavalos.

Sinos. O mais antigo sino do mundo, encontrado perto da cidade da Babilônia tem, calculadamente, mais de três mil anos. A literatura grega e romana fala em sinos desde Eurípedes (cerca de 484-407 A.C.). As pesquisas feitas pelos antiquários mostram que os sinos eram usados desde os tempos mais remotos. Layard, o escavador de Nínive, quando pesquisava em Ninrode, encontrou oito sinos de mão, feitos de bronze. Esta cidade foi destruída juntamente com Nínive, pelos medos, em 612 A.C. Até mesmo no Peru, nos túmulos antigos, têm sido encontrados sinos da era pré-incaica, isto é, antes de 500 D.C., quando teve início a era dos metais naquela região.

O primeiro escritor cristão a referir-se a sinos, o que o fez com certa freqüência, foi Gregório de Tours, em cerca de 585 D.C. Ele afirma que os sinos eram tangidos ou sacudidos, e até fala de uma corda que era usada no tanger dos sinos. Mas foi Paulinus, bispo de Nola, em Campania, na Itália, que criou o sino similar a sua forma moderna (cerca de 400 D.C.). Em 752 D.C., o papa Estêvão III erigiu um campanário com três sinos. É possível que o nome *campanário* tenha levado Walafrido Estrabão a dizer que os sinos são de origem italiana, da região de Campania, idéia em que equivocou-se, conforme temos visto. O maior sino que existe no mundo é o «Tsar Kolokol», fundido em 1733. Esse sino tem 5,80 m de altura, 6,86 m de diâmetro e pesa 193 toneladas. Nunca foi tangido. Perdeu um pedaço de 11 toneladas, em um de seus lados, devido a um incêndio que causou sua queda. Os sinos postos à maior altura são os da torre da *Metropolitan Life Insurance*, em Nova Iorque, que podem ser ouvidos à distância recorde de quarenta e cinco quilômetros. Ver o artigo sobre *Instrumentos Musicais*. (ND S UN EB)

CAMPANELLA, TOMASSO

Suas datas foram 1568-1639. Filósofo italiano, nascido na Calábria. Ingressou na ordem dos monges dominicanos. Foi acusado de heresia e aprisionado em 1599-1626. Na prisão, escreveu suas principais obras. Foi condenado a encarceramento perpétuo pelo tribunal da Inquisição. Todavia, foi libertado em

1629, por haver sido julgado insano. Viveu ainda por cinco anos depois disso, até que morreu, em Paris.

Idéias: 1. A única experiência que nos fornece informes dignos de confiança é o *sentimento* da própria existência. O conhecimento deriva-se das implicações dessa experiência. Portanto, o conhecimento consiste em *notitia innata*, noções inatas. 2. O conhecimento que tenho de mim mesmo fornece-me um meio de conhecer a Deus e ao mundo (ver sobre Descartes, que disse as mesmas coisas). Se eu conheço a mim mesmo como sabedoria, poder, amor, etc., em sentido limitado, poderei saber que Deus é tudo isso, em sentido ilimitado. 3. A existência compõe-se de uma hierarquia de realidades, que se estendem desde Deus até à matéria, passando por muitas gradações, cada qual dotada de seu próprio grau de perfeição, incluindo os valores primários de conhecimento, poder e amor. Esses seriam os primeiros princípios de todas as coisas. Infundidos em tudo isso encontra-se o amor de Deus e o desejo de conhecê-lo. 4. A cidade ideal de Dampanella (política), chamada *a Cidade do Sol*, era uma imitação da República de Platão, com sua vida comunitária; o estado controlando a eugenia e dividindo-a em classes como guardiães, filósofos e sacerdotes. 5. No campo político, ele também favorecia a supremacia do papa em questões tanto espirituais quanto temporais.

Escritos: A Philosophy of Perception Demonstrated; City of the Sun; Philosophies of the Rational and Real. (EP P)

CAMPBELITAS

Um apodo dado aos **Discípulos de Cristo** (que vide). Essa designação surgiu com base em vários motivos: 1. Por ufania, pelo grupo que reverenciava os iniciadores do movimento, Thomas e Alexander Campbell. 2. Ignorantemente, pelos não Discípulos. 3. De modo pejorativo, por aqueles que se opõem às seitas, e assim identificam esse movimento como um esforço tipicamente humano, em contraste com as operações orientadoras do Espírito de Deus. (E)

CAMPBELL, ALEXANDER

Suas datas foram 1788-1866. Foi líder de um movimento reformador que esperava poder unir os cristãos, restaurando o cristianismo primitivo. Esse movimento desenvolveu-se até tornar-se nos Discípulos de Cristo (que vide). Campbell nasceu em Antrim, na Irlanda, passou um ano na Universidade de Glasgow e, em 1809, transferiu-se para a América do Norte, onde já residia seu pai. Seu pai, Thomas Campbell (que vide), foi o primeiro a defender os princípios promovidos por Alexander. Estabeleceu-se na região que atualmente é o estado de Virgínia, e deu prosseguimento à sua obra. Publicava duas revistas, pregava e organizava. Foi membro da Convenção Constitucional de Virgínia, em 1829; fundou o Colégio Betânia, do qual foi presidente durante vinte anos, e também tinha tempo para debater e para cuidar de plantações. Suas atividades agrícolas mostraram-se tão bem-sucedidas quanto a sua pregação, e ele conseguiu reunir considerável fortuna pessoal. (E)

CAMPBELL, JOHN McLEOD

Nasceu em 1800 e faleceu em 1872. Tornou-se conhecido por causa de sua teologia da expiação (ver sobre *Expiação*), de acordo com a qual afirmava que Cristo arrependeu-se em lugar da humanidade, e assim cumpriu as condições necessárias ao perdão dos pecados. Os sofrimentos de Cristo não teriam sido penais. Essa teoria pavimentou o caminho para o ponto de vista ético da expiação (que vide). Em 1830, seus pontos de vista foram condenados pela Assembléia Geral Presbiteriana, mas ele continuou a sua carreira em uma igreja não denominacional. (E)

CAMPBELL, THOMAS

Suas datas foram 1763-1854. Ministro irlandês que se separou do presbiterianismo. Era de origem escocesa e migrou para a América do Norte em 1807. Estando insatisfeito com as doutrinas de sua igreja, ele organizou a Associação Cristã de Washington, Pennsylvania, e escreveu «Uma Declaração e Discurso», incorporando os princípios de seu sistema. Com base nisso, seu filho, Alexander Campbell (que vide), deu início a um movimento que se tornou nos Discípulos de Cristo (que vide). (AM E)

CAMPINA DO JORDÃO

No hebraico, **kikkar**, «círculo». «redondo». Essa palavra era usada para descrever toda espécie de coisas, como distritos, pães e pesos. É vocábulo traduzido por campina ou vale do Jordão, em Gên. 13:10, referindo-se a uma área de formato quase oval, ao norte da bacia do mar Morto.

CAMPO

Há diversas palavras hebraicas (aramaicas) e gregas envolvidas neste verbete, a saber:

1. *Bar*, «campo aberto». Palavra aramaica usada por oito vezes: Dan. 2:38; 4:12,15,21,23,25,32.

2. *Chuts*, «lugar ao ar livre». Palavra hebraica usada por trinta vezes com esse sentido. Por exemplo: Jó 5:10; Pro. 8:26; Gên. 15:5; 19:17; Êxo. 12:56; Lev. 14:8; Deu. 23:10,12,13; 24:11; I Sam. 9:26; Eze. 34:21.

3. *Sadeh*, «campo», «lugar plano». Palavra hebraica usada por trezentas e seis vezes. Por exemplo: Gên. 2:5,19,20; 50:13; Êxo. 1:14; Lev. 14:7,53; 17:5; Núm. 16:14; Deu. 5:21; 7:22; 11:15; Jos. 8:24; Juí. 1:14; 5:4,18; Rute 2:2,3,8,9,17,22; I Sam. 4:2; 6:14,18; II Sam. 1:21; 10:8; 11:11,23; I Reis 2:26; II Reis 4:39; 7:12; I Crô. 1:46; 6:56; II Crô. 26:23; Nee. 11:25,30; Jó 5:23; Sal. 78:12,43; Pro. 23:10; Can. 2:7; Isa. 5:8; 7:3; Jer. 6:12,25; 7:20; 8:10; Eze. 7:15; 16:5,7; 17:5,24; Osé. 2:12; Joel 1:10,11,12,19,20; Miq. 1:6; 2:2,4; Zac. 10:1; Mal. 3:11.

4. *Sadai*, «lugar plano». Palavra hebraica usada por treze vezes: Deu. 32:13; Sal. 8:7; 50:11; 80:13; 96:12; 104:11; Isa. 56:9; Jer. 4:17; 18:14; Lam. 4:9; Osé. 10:4; 12:11; Joel 2:22.

5. *Shedemah*, «campo». Palavra hebraica usada por cinco vezes: Deu. 32:32; II Reis 23:4; Isa. 16:8; Hab. 3:17.

6. *Yegebim*, «campos cultivados». Palavra hebraica usada por apenas uma vez, em Jer. 39:10.

7. *Agrós*, «campo». Palavra grega que aparece por trinta e seis vezes: Mat. 6:28,30; 13:24,27,31,36,38, 44; 19:29; 22:5; 24:18,40; 27:7,8,10 (citando Zac. 11:13); Mar. 5:14; 6:36,56; 10:29,30; 11:8; 13:16; 15:21; 16:12; Luc. 8:34; 8:12; 12:28; 14:18; 15:15,25; 17:7,31,36; 28:26; Atos 4:37.

8. *Chóra*, «espaço aberto». Palavra grega que figura por vinte e oito vezes: Mat. 2:12; 4:16; 8:28; Mar. 1:5; 5:1,10; 6:55; Luc. 2:8; 3:1; 8:26; 12:16; 15:13-15; 19:12; 21:21; João 4:35; 11:54,55; Atos 8:1; 10:39; 12:20; 13:49; 16:6; 18:23; 26:20; 27:27; Tia. 5:4.

9. *Chorion*, «pequeno espaço aberto». Palavra grega usada por nove vezes: Mat. 26:36; Mar. 14:32; João 4:5; Atos 1:18,19; 4:34; 5:3,8; 28:7.

Conforme vimos acima, a palavra hebraica mais comumente usada é *sadeh*, que também pode ser traduzida por «suavidade». Geralmente está em pauta algum terreno cultivado. A própria palavra implica uma extensão de terra que não é cercada, como se dava com as cidades. Também pode indicar pastos (Gên. 29:2; 31:4; Êxo. 9:3), ou lugar arado (Gên. 37:7; 47:24). No entanto, também é palavra usada para indicar um bosque (I Sam. 24:25), o topo de um monte (Juí. 9:23), — uma área desértica (Gên. 33:19), uma vinha (Êxo. 22:5; Lev. 25:3,4), um lugar distante de casa (Gên. 4:8; 24:63) ou um campo aberto (Lev. 14:7,53; Núm. 19:16). Portanto, metaforicamente falando, o termo veio a ser associado às idéias de exposição, desolação ou deserção (Jer. 9:22; Eze. 16:5; 32:4).

Quando um campo qualquer pertencia a alguém, usualmente a posse era assinalada com uma pedra, a qual não deveria ser removida por nenhum motivo (Deu. 19:14; 27:17; Pro. 22:28). Esses campos, não sendo cercados, estavam sujeitos à invasão por parte de gado perdido (Êxo. 22:5). Isso tornava necessário o trabalho dos pastores e boiadeiros.

Nas Escrituras há menção a vários campos específicos, como o Campo das Espadas (II Sam. 2:16), o «campo do lavandeiro» (II Reis 18:17) e o «campo do oleiro» (Mat. 27:7).

Expressões Utilizadas. Campo fértil, em Isa. 10:18; regozijo do pomar, em Isa. 16:10, onde, no original hebraico, aparece a palavra *karmel*, usualmente associada a algum parque ou lugar bem conservado, em distinção a algum lugar desértico.

Usos Simbólicos. Esses usos podem ocorrer na literatura, ou então em sonhos e visões, a saber: 1. Um campo cultivado representa o trabalho ou missão de uma pessoa. 2. Um campo a ser cultivado é uma mulher que ficará grávida, ou um projeto que alguém em breve iniciará. 3. Um campo ou uma planície, é um lugar ou circunstância caracterizados pela liberdade. 4. Uma arte ou ciência, ou uma área qualquer de nosso aprendizado. 5. Campos verdejantes indicam prosperidade física e espiritual, ou já possuída, ou ainda por vir a ser possuída. 6. Um campo a ser arado representa uma tarefa a ser realizada ou uma habilidade a ser desenvolvida.

CAMPO DE VIDA Ver **Aura Humana (Campo de Vida)**
CAMPO DO OLEIRO Ver **Acéldama**.
CAMPO UNIFICADO Ver **Einstein**, ponto 4.
CAMUS, ALBERT

Suas datas foram 1913-1960. Filósofo e escritor francês, nascido na Argélia. Educou-se na Universidade de Algiers. Mudou-se para Paris, em 1940. Foi ativo na Resistência Francesa, durante a Segunda Guerra Mundial.

Idéias: 1. Ele argumentava contra o suicídio, afirmando que se trata de uma resposta inadequada ao absurdo da vida. Ele pensava que a resposta adequada consiste em continuar a viver, desenvolvendo a própria humanidade, apesar dos absurdos da existência. 2. O valor final da vida é a solidariedade humana, uma outra forma de AMOR (que vide). Toda e qualquer modificação política deveria ter esse alvo em mente. Ele rejeitava a destruição por amor à destruição, incluindo o suicídio e o nihilismo (que vide). Ele também considerava absurda a punição capital (que vide).

Escritos: *The Myth of Sisyphus; Letters to a German Friend; The Rebel; Reflections on Capital Punishment*. (E EP P)

CANA

No hebraico são usadas duas palavras diferentes; no grego, *kálamos*. A cana referida em Jer. 51:32 obviamente é um tipo especial, por ser a única vez em que uma daquelas duas palavras hebraicas é usada, a qual está vinculada à idéia de «poço», pois enfatiza o local onde medrava a cana. A outra palavra hebraica é usada em II Reis 18:21; Isa. 36:6 e Eze. 29:6, aludindo a uma cana ou mesmo a uma trave. Outro tanto pode ser dito sobre a palavra grega *kálamos*. Por exemplo, feriram Jesus na cabeça com uma cana (Mar. 15:19), e puseram uma esponja ensopada em vinagre, na ponta de uma cana, para chegá-la à boca do Senhor, na cruz (Mar. 15:36). O anjo também mediu a cidade com uma cana (Apo. 21:16).

A «cana gigante», *Arundo donax*, medrava no vale do Jordão e em redor do mar Morto. Crescia até a altura de 5,5 m, encimada por uma pluma branca. O caule, em sua base, podia ter um diâmetro de 8 cm. Esses caules, muito fortes, eram usados como bordões ou bengalas, o que explica a referência em Eze. 29:6 e II Reis 18:21, onde o imperador Senaqueribe alude ao Egito como bordão feito de uma cana esmagada.

Se a cana usada para levar a esponja à boca de Cristo, na cruz, era a *Arundo donax*, não importa. Há quem pense em uma cana diferente, capaz de atingir uma altura de 4,5 m e que cresce bem sem irrigação.

Nos dias da Bíblia, penas eram feitas de cana. Em III João 13 há alusão a uma pena feita de cana. Eram penas usadas para escrever sobre papiro. A tinta era fabricada com fuligem de lâmpadas e suco de fel.

Há várias outras espécies de canas e juncos na Terra Santa, cujo caule pode atingir até 3,60 m. O papiro (*Cypherus papyrus*) medrava no Nilo, nos alagadiços, produzindo gigantescas raízes horizontais, às vezes com 6 m de extensão. Plantas inteiras eram desenterradas, e suas raízes eram usadas para fabricar cabos de instrumentos, enquanto os caules eram usados no fabrico de sandálias, cordas, colchões e cestas. O cerne podia ser comido, cozido ou cru, ou então aproveitado para o fabrico de um tipo de papel grosseiro (ver Junco).

O fato de que o cerne do papiro podia ser comido ou transformado em papel se reflete em Eze. 3:3: «Filho do homem, dá de comer ao teu ventre, e enche as tuas entranhas deste rolo que eu te dou. Eu o comi, e na boca era doce como o mel».

A palavra «cana» é usada em conexão com o ato de medir (Eze. 40:3,5). Uma cana equivalia a seis côvados. Cada côvado tinha cerca de 46 cm. Em Eze. 40:5, cada cana media cerca de 2,75 m. O ribeiro de Caná (Jos. 16:8 e 17:9) ficava entre os territórios de Efraim e Manassés. «Caná» significa «cana» ou «possessão». Provavelmente o ribeiro era assim chamado devido a grande quantidade de cana que ali crescia, à beira do ribeiro.

CANÃ

O nome significa, no hebraico, «lugar de canas». Designa duas coisas diferentes:

1. Um riacho que deságua no mar Mediterrâneo, entre Cesaréia e Jope, e que servia de fronteira entre Efraim e Manassés (Jos. 16:8; 17:19). Alguns estudiosos identificam-no com o rio Aujeh; e outros, com a wadi Qana.

2. Nome de uma aldeia da porção norte do território de Aser (Jos. 19:28). Têm sido encontradas

CANAÃ, CANANEUS

nesse local ruínas colossais e figuras de pessoas sob a forma de estátuas, que alguns eruditos pensam ser de origem fenícia. Essa aldeia assinalava o extremo norte do território de Aser. A vila chamada atualmente Qanah marca o local, cerca de dez quilômetros a suleste de Tiro.

CANAÃ, CANANEUS
Ver o artigo separado sobre **Fenícia**.

1. *O Nome*. Canaã refere-se ao indivíduo e seus descendentes, mencionados em Gên. 10:15-18. Os cananeus eram os habitantes da terra de Canaã, o nome mais antigo da Palestina. A palavra vem do hurriano, sendo uma evidente referência à cor vermelho-púrpura, que se refere a um bem conhecido item do comércio fenício. Ver abaixo. A partir do século XIV A.C., o nome Canaã passou a ser empregado para indicar a região onde habitavam os cananeus. Eram negociantes fenícios. Um de seus principais produtos era um corante vermelho-púrpura derivado do molusco *Murex*, que havia nas costas da Palestina. Nas cartas de Amarna, a expressão «terra de Canaã» aplica-se às costas da Fenícia; os egípcios chamavam todos os sírios por esse nome. Pela época em que Israel deu início à sua conquista da Palestina, toda esta região era conhecida por terra de Canaã. Algumas referências bíblicas indicam o uso mais restrito da palavra, que significa «negociante». Ver Jó 41:6; Isa. 17:4; Osé. 12:7; Sof. 1:11 e Zac. 11:7,11.

2. *O Território*. Conforme ficou claro acima, houve uma evolução no tocante àquilo que era designado pelo nome Canaã. Em Números 34:3-12, encontramos o nome em um sentido mais lato, referindo-se à Palestina inteira, a oeste do rio Jordão. Esse território ficava localizado entre os grandes impérios antigos dos rios Tigre-Eufrates e Halis, por um lado, e do rio Nilo, por outro lado. A região formava uma espécie de ponte geográfica entre os antigos centros da civilização pagã. Os descendentes de Canaã estavam divididos em seis ou sete nações distintas, quando Israel ali entrou: os heteus, os girgaseus, os amorreus, os cananeus, os perezeus, os heveus e os jebuseus: Ver Êxo. 3:17 e Deu. 7:1. O termo geral, «cananeus», era usado para incluir todas essas nações. Além disso, havia diversas tribos cananéias que viviam nas fronteiras da Palestina, em seu lado norte, a saber, os arqueus, os sinitas, os arvaditas, os zemaritas e os hematitas (Gên. 10:17,18). Israel não entrou em contacto com essas tribos. As cartas de Amarna, do século XIV A.C., referem-se aos cananeus como um povo que ocupava todo o território sino-palestino do Egito. O papiro egípcio Anastasi IIIA, linhas 5 e 6, e IV16, linha 4, pertencente ao século XIII A.C., menciona escravos cananeus de Huru, que é a mesma coisa que a Síria-Palestina.

3. *A Civilização Cananéia*. As descobertas arqueológicas mostram que os cananeus eram bem desenvolvidos nas artes e nas ciências. Suas construções eram superiores às que Israel edificava na terra de Canaã, após tê-la conquistado. Eles destacavam-se na cerâmica, na música, em instrumentos musicais e na arquitetura, e seus artesãos e operários executaram grande parte do projeto e da construção do templo de Salomão, em Jerusalém (I Reis 7:13-51). A arqueologia tem desenterrado as fortificações cananéias, bem como seus palácios e templos, ou seus tesouros de arte trabalhados em ouro, marfim e alabastro. As descobertas feitas em Ras Shamra-Ugarite, ilustram o ponto. Todavia, a história mostra-nos que Israel entrou em contacto com os cananeus quando estes já estavam em um período de declínio. As escavações feitas na Palestina, no Líbano e na Síria têm mostrado a extensão de suas realizações. As principais cidades cananéias eram Biblos, Ugarite, Kadatu, Hamate sobre o Orontes, certos cômoros perto de Antioquia, Mari sobre o Eufrates e Alalaque. O pano de fundo cananeu dos fenícios tem sido iluminado pelas descobertas feitas em Ugarite (Ras Shamra), onde milhares de tabletes de argila secos ao sol, escritos em caracteres acadianos regulares, ou na escrita cuneiforme alfabética, têm sido encontrados. Esses tabletes têm sido decifrados, o que nos tem outorgado considerável riqueza de informações. A começar pelo ano de 1890, uma série de escavações, envolvendo Bete-Seã, Jericó, Megido, Laquis, Tell el-'Ajjul, Tell Beit Mirsim, Bete-Semes, Betel, Ai, Bete-Yerah, Hazor e Siquém, nos tem dado muito conhecimento sobre a civilização da antiga terra de Canaã. Outro tanto pode ser dito no que concerne às escavações efetuadas em Betel, Dotã, Gibeom, Hazor, Jericó, Qasileh, Siquém, Tirza e outros locais em Israel e ao longo do rio Jordão, a partir do fim da Segunda Guerra Mundial. Isso tem possibilitado a reconstituição da história da área inteira da Palestina, retrocedendo por mais de mil anos antes da conquista da Terra Prometida por parte de Israel.

4. *O Idioma dos Cananeus*. A língua cananéia pertencia ao grupo noroeste das línguas semitas, em distinção ao grupo nordeste, chamado acádico. Também havia o grupo sudoeste (árabe do norte) e o grupo suleste (árabe do sul). Esse idioma, no começo, era escrito com um número indeterminado de caracteres relacionados ao sistema hieroglífico do Egito. Diversas inscrições com essa forma têm sido encontradas, gravadas sobre metal ou pedra, em Biblos. Em Ras Shamra (Ugarite), era usado o alfabeto cuneiforme. Finalmente, o típico alfabeto semítico do noroeste substituiu todos os demais, tornando-se a forma de escrita padrão. As antigas formas escritas hebraica e fenícia estão intimamente relacionadas. O hebraico parece ser uma forma adaptada do dialeto cananeu. As origens do alfabeto proto-semítico continuam obscuras até agora. Ver sobre *Alfabeto*. Abraão encontrou o idioma hebraico já em uso na Palestina, ou ele o trouxe consigo para ali? Os patriarcas hebreus falavam um dialeto aramaico na Mesopotâmia, antes de entrarem na Palestina; entretanto, quando entraram na Palestina, adotaram o dialeto cananeu local, que não era idêntico à fala padrão dos cananeus. !O hebraico antigo, seja como for, é bem parecido com o fenício. Após cerca de 1000 A.C., o hebraico, o moabita, o fenício e o aramaico já aparecem em inscrições como línguas distintas.

5. *A História dos Cananeus*. No terceiro milênio A.C., havia povos que falavam línguas semíticas na Síria-Palestina, conforme se vê nas evidências extraídas das inscrições encontradas pela arqueologia. Quanto a um período anterior a esse, nada se sabe. As descobertas arqueológicas têm demonstrado, com algum detalhe, a história desses povos, até cerca de mil anos antes da conquista da Palestina por Israel (cerca de 1400 A.C.). As mais antigas cidades da Palestina sobre as quais chegamos a saber algo, tinham nomes cananeus, como Megido, Bete-Seã, Bete-Yerah, Jericó. Na Síria encontramos Ugarite, Gabala, Acre ('Irquatrum), Tiro (Sur), que são nomes cananeus. Os cananeus e seus parentes próximos, os amorreus, já estavam bem estabelecidos na terra por volta de 2000 A.C., e a região foi dominada por várias **cidades-estado dos cananeus e amorreus. Após o fim das invasões dos amorreus, estabeleceu-se a Idade do Bronze Médio da Palestina**, que sofria influências

nortistas. Ver o artigo sobre a *Arqueologia*. As invasões dos hicsos, entretanto, perturbaram um tanto esse quadro. Após a expulsão dos hicsos, o Egito dominou a área da Síria-Palestina, em cerca de 1570-1310 A.C., e, novamente, mais tarde, em 1310-1200 A.C. Nesse período, continuaram predominando as cidades-estado. No século XIV A.C., alguns estados, como Ugarite, caíram sob o controle dos heteus, que a história secular chama de hititas. Também houve as invasões dos habiru, após o que o Egito reobteve o controle, para então perdê-lo novamente, por causa das incursões dos povos do mar, isto é, os filisteus, em cerca de 1200 A.C. A começar em cerca de 1400 A.C., Israel começou a tomar conta da região da Palestina. As terras altas foram conquistadas prontamente, mas o progresso foi lento, e nunca se completou em outras áreas. Mas na própria Palestina, os cananeus, que nunca foram extintos, foram sendo gradualmente absorvidos pela civilização israelita, ao passo que outros foram confinados às regiões costeiras, naquilo que veio a tornar-se conhecido como a Fenícia. Esses cananeus restritos (fenícios) foram se tornando, crescentemente, uma potência marítima. Ver o artigo sobre os *Fenícios*.

6. *A Religião dos Cananeus*. O Antigo Testamento informa-nos muita coisa a respeito do *Panteão* dos cananeus. A divindade principal era *El,* a quem os outros deuses precisavam consultar sobre questões importantes. Porém, *Baal,* filho de El, tornou-se mais significativo. Ver o artigo sobre BAAL. Essa palavra significa «senhor». Havia muitas manifestações locais de Baal, como deus da fertilidade, deus da tempestade, etc. Tanto Baal quanto Dagom tinham um templo em Ugarite. *Atar* era a divindade que substituía a Baal, quando este último supostamente excursionava pelo submundo dos espíritos. Atar era filho de *Aterate,* consorte de El. Havia muitas deusas, como Anate, Aserá e Astarte (ou Astarote), deusas do sexo, da fertilidade e da guerra. — Anate era uma importante deusa para a agricultura. Os deuses *Shahru* (estrela matutina) e *Yarbu* (deus-lua), bem como Resebe, deus da pestilência e da morte, também eram adorados em Canaã. Não há certeza se o deus Yahweh era conhecido ou não pelos cananeus. Milhares de tabletes de argila, guardados em uma biblioteca existente entre dois templos, datados de cerca dos séculos XV e XIV A.C., descobertos em Ras Shamra, nos fornecem abundantes informações sobre a religião dos cananeus. Havia grosseira imoralidade de mistura com a adoração prestada a várias divindades da fertilidade, e os cananeus estavam maduros para o julgamento divino. É significativo que alguns dos nomes de Deus, no hebraico, têm paralelo nos nomes dos deuses cananeus, o que mostra que havia certo contacto e troca de idéias ali, embora a religião cananéia e a religião hebréia tanto diferissem, mormente no tocante ao monoteísmo. Os deuses cananeus não se destacavam quanto à santidade.

Templos cananeus têm sido escavados na Síria e na Palestina, e significativos modelos têm sido encontrados em Laquis (que vide), Megido, Jericó, Bete-Seãe e Hazor, pertencentes a um tempo tão remoto quanto 3000 A.C., e daí até 1900 A.C. Muitos objetos relacionados à adoração pagã têm sido desenterrados, como objetos de culto, facas, tenazes, vasos de libação e ossos de animais, o que mostra que ali se praticava o sacrifício de animais.

Em Ugarite, havia um sistema complexo de religião, talvez típico também de outras localidades. Havia um sumo sacerdote e nada menos do que doze famílias de sacerdotes. O rei exercia funções sacerdotais. Havia cantores, costureiros de vestimentas, escultores e outros especialistas. Novamente, vemos considerável correspondência entre isso e a religião de Israel. Pelo menos é verdade que, quanto às questões culturais, os cananeus eram superiores aos israelitas, que muito se aproveitaram da cultura cananéia. Já vimos como Salomão dependeu desse povo quanto aos planos e à construção do templo de Jerusalém. Era tarefa dos profetas impedir pesados empréstimos e corrupções provenientes dos pagãos, mas os profetas nem sempre mostraram-se bem-sucedidos em seus esforços. A confusão entre Baal e Yahweh destruiu a distintiva fé dos hebreus. Lembremo-nos do desafio lançado por Elias: «Se o Senhor é Deus, segui-o; se é Baal, segui-o» (I Reis 18:21). (ALB ALBR AM LAM)

CANAÃ, A PESSOA

O termo hebraico parece significar *pertencente à terra da púrpura-vermelha*. Canaã era filho de Cão e neto de Noé. A transgressão de seu pai, Cão, relatada em Gênesis 9:22-27, — na qual, segundo alguns pensam, Canaã esteve envolvido de alguma maneira, deu a Noé ocasião para proferir a condenação que sobreviria aos descendentes de Canaã. Porém, não há base nenhuma para a suposição de que os descendentes de Canaã foram amaldiçoados como uma conseqüência imediata da transgressão de Cão. De qualquer modo, ele foi o progenitor dos fenícios e do povo que vivia a oeste do rio Jordão, antes da conquista da região pelo povo de Israel. (Gên. 10:15; I Crô. 1:13).

CANA AROMÁTICA

No hebraico, a palavra **qaneh** figura por sessenta e uma vezes, mas é nos trechos de Isa. 43:24 e Jer. 6:20 que parece entrar em pauta a «cana aromática». Diz o trecho de Isaías 43:24: «Não me compraste por dinheiro cana aromática...» E Jer. 6:20 diz: «Para que pois, me vem o incenso de Sabá e a melhor cana aromática de terras longínquas?...» A cana nativa ou selvática encontra-se espalhada por toda a Palestina, **em riachos e valados.** Seu nome científico é *Saccharum biflorum,* a espécie que poderia estar em pauta nesses dois trechos. No entanto, a maior parte dos estudiosos da Bíblia sentem que a «cana aromática», na verdade, era a *Saccharum officinarum,* ou seja, a nossa comum cana-de-açúcar. O mais provável é que os antigos hebreus não fabricassem açúcar com base nessa cana; antes, ela era chupada ou usada em sua forma natural para adoçar bebidas e alimentos. Naturalmente, o mel era o adoçante mais comumente usado nos dias do Antigo Testamento.

Nas passagens de Josué 16:8 e 19:28, aparece o ribeiro de Caná, onde a cana nativa medrava com abundância. No hebraico, *qaneh* era a palavra genérica para indicar todas as plantas de tipo junco.

Alguns estudiosos têm pensado que a palavra «cálamo», em Can. 4:14, na realidade seria o «nardo» (*Nardostachys jatamansi*); mas essa opinião é extremamente improvável, porquanto a palavra «nardo» aparece no começo desse mesmo versículo, e isso seria uma redundância desnecessária. (Ver Cana).

CANÁ DA GALILÉIA

Caná vem do termo hebraico que significa «cana». Era esse o nome de certa aldeia da Galiléia, local do primeiro milagre de Jesus, quando ele transformou

CANA DE MEDIR — CANAL

água em vinho. Ver o artigo detalhado sobre esse milagre, intitulado *Água, Transformação em Vinho*. Há menção a essa localidade somente em João 2:1-11, onde o milagre é descrito. A aldeia nunca é mencionada no Antigo Testamento; mas Josefo, *Vita*, sec. 16:64, e *Guerras* i.17,5, a mencionam.

Caná era o local do nascimento de Natanael, um dos apóstolos de Jesus. Não deve, contudo, ser identificada com a Caná de Jos. 19:28, que ficava localizada perto de Tiro. A localização de Caná da Galiléia não é certa, embora tenha sido identificada com Kefr Kenna, cerca de seis quilômetros a nordeste de Nazaré, na estrada para Tiberíades. Ali foi erigida uma igreja Ortodoxa Grega, perto da estrada, e jarras de pedra, supostamente usadas naquele milagre feito por Jesus, são ali conservadas. Uma outra igreja comemorativa foi construída pelos frades franciscanos, perto do centro da aldeia. Uma pequena capela, comemorando o local da casa de Natanael, também é exibida aos turistas.

Alguns eruditos preferem Khirbet Qana como a localização moderna do antigo sítio de Caná. Fica localizada cerca de treze quilômetros ao norte de Nazaré, à margem norte da planície chamada Sahl el-Battuf. Aparentemente, os cruzados aceitaram esse lugar como o local da antiga Caná da Galiléia. E, naturalmente, os viajantes falam sobre jarras de água que eram as jarras *originalmente* empregadas no milagre de Jesus. Eusébio, citado por Jerônimo, situa Caná no território de Aser, perto de Sidom e Tiro, o que corresponderia a Khirbet Qana, e não a Kefr Kenna. O termo Caná, «cana», é apropriado a esse lugar, visto que se encontra perto de um alagadiço. Descobertas arqueológicas pertencentes ao século I D.C., mostram que ali era um lugar de habitação desde aquele tempo. Não há como resolver a questão acerca do local original. Seja como for, além de ter sido o local onde Jesus operou seu primeiro milagre, também foi o lugar onde ele curou o filho do nobre de Cafarnaum (João 4:46-54). (AM ID Z)

CANA DE MEDIR

No hebraico, **qaneh**, «cana». Palavra que ocorre por dezenove vezes. Por exemplo, I Reis 14:15; Isa. 19:6; 42:3; Eze. 29:6; 42:17-19. No grego *kálamos*, termo usado por doze vezes: Mat. 11:7; 12:20 (citando Isa. 42:3); 27:29,30,48; Mar. 15:19,36; Luc. 7:24; II João 13; Apo. 11:1; 21:15,16.

A cana era uma planta útil, cujo caule era usado para servir como material de construção, material de escrita e como medida. Tanto é assim que o termo hebraico envolvido também significava «medir». Idêntico uso lingüístico encontra-se nos idiomas indo-europeus bem como no babilônio e no assírio. Um outro termo grego, *kanon*, «vara», que deu em português «cânon», que significa «medida» ou «padrão», está relacionado ao termo hebraico *qaneh*.

A cana era preparada como varas de comprimentos específicos, usadas então para fazer medições, da mesma maneira que, em nossos dias, temos réguas e metros de madeira e de outros materiais. Uma vara comum de medir era aquela com cerca de três metros. Ver os trechos de Apo. 11:1 e 21:15,16, que parecem ser citações do trecho de Ezequiel 40:3, segundo a Septuaginta. Ver o artigo sobre *Linha de Medir*.

CANADA Ver **Kanada**.

CANAIS

Vem de uma palavra hebraica emprestada da palavra que significa o rio Nilo. Ver Êxo. 7:19, 8:4. Esta palavra mormente significa riachos, Isa. 19:6, mas também pode ter a idéia de canais artificiais. Canais foram feitos para propósitos de irrigação. Tais canais foram uma característica comum na área do Nilo, cuja água foi utilizada pela construção de canais, para transportar suas águas para as áreas ao longo do rio. A sobrevivência em Israel teria sido muito difícil sem canais artificiais.

CANAIS DE ÁGUA

No hebraico, **rahat**, «canal». Esse vocábulo aparece por quatro vezes: Gên. 30:38,41; Êxo. 2:16 e Can. 7:5. Nas duas últimas referências, nossa versão portuguesa traduz esse vocábulo, respectivamente, por «bebedouros» e «tranças». Neste último caso, acompanha uma variante na tradução, feita em certa versão estrangeira.

CANAL

Há duas palavras hebraicas envolvidas, a saber:

1. *Aphiq*, «cavidade». Palavra usada por dezesseis vezes (por exemplo:II Sam. 22:16; Sal. 18:15; Isa. 8:7).

2. *Shibboleth*, «riacho». Palavra usada por três vezes com esse sentido: Isa. 27:12; Sal. 69:2,15.

A primeira dessas palavras era usada para indicar rios, canais feitos pelos homens, sistemas de irrigação, e igualmente o leito de um rio ou do mar. (Sal. 18:15; Isa. 8:7). O trecho de Jó 40:18 tem um uso metafórico do vocábulo, referindo-se aos ossos do hipopótamo, como se fossem tubos de bronze. Jó 6:15 é passagem que alude aos ribeiros da Palestina como perigosamente instáveis. Salmos 69:2 usa esse vocábulo para indicar o ímpeto das enchentes. Em Isaías 8:7 há uma outra metáfora, que refere-se ao fato de que Israel rejeitou as águas mansas de Siloé (a saber, o reino de Davi), e assim ficou exposto à enchente destruidora do Eufrates, a saber, a Assíria. Ainda um outro uso metafórico pinta os *alicerces* do mundo desnudados pelo sopro de Deus (II Sam. 22:16; Sal. 18:15). O significado exato desses dois versículos é controvertido. Talvez haja uma alusão aos antigos conceitos equivocados de que o mundo estaria circundado pelo oceano, cujas correntes seriam guiadas por canais ocultos. Ou então a referência poderia ser ao leito do mar Vermelho, desnudado por Deus para que o povo de Israel pudesse atravessá-lo a pé enxuto. *Canal* também traduz o heb. *shibboleth* (vide), «riacho». Ver os artigos separados sobre *Giom* e *Warren*, *Canal (Escavação) de*.

CANAL SUBTERRÂNEO

Indica um conduto subterrâneo para transportar água potável desde uma nascente até alguma cidade. Há evidências arqueológicas da existência de canais subterrâneos em Jerusalém e em Megido, do período cananeu em diante. Em Jerusalém há um túnel que começa na fonte de *Giom* (vide) que transportava água para o interior da cidade. Alguns eruditos pensam que o trecho de II Samuel 5:8 refere-se a um canal dessa natureza, o que é refletido em nossa versão portuguesa. Instalações similares também têm sido encontradas em Gibeom, Etã e Ibleã. É evidente que se uma cidade contasse com um suprimento de água garantido, poderia resistir mais facilmente ao inimigo, em tempos de assédio, conforme sucedeu à cidade de Samaria, que resistiu aos assírios por dois anos, em 722 A.C., ou como se deu com Jerusalém,

que resistiu aos babilônios por 1 1/2 anos (586 A.C.)
Ver o artigo sobre *Warren, Canal (Escavação) de*.

CANALIZAÇÃO Ver **Nova Era**, pontos 3 e 4.

CANANEU, SIMÃO, O

Nas listas dos apóstolos, em Mateus 10:2-4 e Marcos 3:16-19, temos o nome «Simão, o cananeu». Mas Lucas 6:14-16 e Atos 1:13 dizem «Simão, o Zelote». O termo «cananeu» é uma transliteração da palavra aramaica que significa «zelote», isto é, «entusiasta», mas nada tem a ver com a palavra que é um adjetivo gentílico idêntico, «cananeu». Esse Simão foi assim chamado porque pertencia ao partido político dos zelotes, que buscavam livrar-se do domínio romano e defendiam ferozmente a teocracia de Israel. Nada sabemos sobre esse homem, através das páginas sagradas, embora as tradições preencham os espaços em branco. Ver sobre Simão e as informações gerais dadas no estudo sobre os *Apóstolos*.

CÂNCER
Ver sobre **Doenças e Enfermidades**.

CANCIONÁRIO

Uma coleção de músicas eclesiásticas para completa adoração litúrgica, incluindo material apropriado para o pastor, para o coro e para a congregação. Os cancionários clássicos originaram-se na Reforma luterana, tendo sido compilados nos séculos XVI e XVII. Os mais notáveis entre eles são o Spangenber (1545), o Lossius (1561), o Kralitz, e os Irmãos Boêmios (1576). A obra moderna mais completa é o Meckenburg, em quatro volumes (1868-1887). O termo cancionário tem sido usado de modo frouxo, como sinônimo de hinário. (E)

CANDACE

Nome da rainha dos etíopes, cujo tesoureiro-mor converteu-se ao cristianismo, sob a pregação do evangelista Filipe, conforme o registro de Atos 8:27. Etiópia era o reino da Núbia, no norte do Sudão. Sua capital era a cidade de Meroe. — Vários escritores clássicos referiram-se às rainhas de Meroe, dos séculos I A.C. a I D.C., que tinham o título de Candace, a saber, Estrabão XVII.1.54; Dio Cássio LIV 5:4-6; Plínio, História VI.35.186. A cidade de Meroe ficava próxima da atual cidade de Assour, cerca de trinta e dois quilômetros ao norte de Shendy. Ali há extensas ruínas, e a arqueologia tem confirmado as realizações do povo que ali habitava. Meroe era centro das artes, do comércio e da erudição entre os antigos etíopes. Mantinha contactos com a África, com o sul da Ásia e com outras regiões. As riquezas e as mercadorias da Etiópia são dadas a entender em Isaías 45:14.

A palavra «Candace» parece ter sido um título, como Faraó ou Ptolomeu, e aludia a uma série de rainhas da Etiópia. Monumentos desenterrados na Etiópia confirmam a existência de rainhas ali. Assim, temos uma grande pirâmide sepulcral perto de Assour, antiga Meroe, que retrata uma guerreira com as insígnias reais na cabeça. Ela arrasta muitos cativos, que a seguem. Essas rainhas eram conquistadoras e heroínas. A maior parte das descobertas arqueológicas sobre essas questões envolvem construções que datam de cerca de 300 A.C. até 300 D.C. Os túmulos piramidais das Candaces reinantes são os restos arquiteturais mais importantes. (ID UN)

••• ••• •••

CANDEEIRO DE OURO Ver sobre **Menorah**.

No trecho de Êxodo 25:31-39 encontramos as orientações recebidas pelos israelitas para a fabricação desse item da tenda da congregação. Uma base suportava uma haste. Três braços curvados para cima, partiam dessa haste central; esses braços terminavam em seis receptáculos, em cada um dos quais havia uma lamparina; somando-se à lamparina no alto da haste central, havia um total de sete lamparinas. O ouro foi o material usado para a construção do candeeiro. A haste central e os braços eram decorados com desenhos em alto relevo de florescências de amendoeira. As espevitadeiras para as lamparinas também eram feitas de ouro. O trecho de Êxodo 37:17-24 adiciona uma segunda instrução concernente a essa questão, para garantir a perfeição da execução da obra. O candeeiro de ouro foi posto no Lugar Santo do tabernáculo (que vide), do outro lado da mesa dos pães da proposição. Quando o templo de Jerusalém (que vide), construído por Salomão, ficou pronto, para o mesmo foram preparados dez candeeiros de ouro, de acordo com as maiores dimensões dessa estrutura permanente. Mas, no segundo templo de Jerusalém, por razões desconhecidas, havia apenas um candeeiro. Antíoco Epifânio removeu esse candeeiro de seu lugar. Quando Judas Macabeu restaurou a adoração no templo, um novo candeeiro foi provido para o mesmo. Aparentemente, o mesmo formato de candeeiro havia no templo construído por Herodes.

Simbolismo do Candeeiro de Ouro. O trecho de Apocalipse 1:12-20 exibe uma aplicação direta, ao chamar as sete igrejas de sete candeeiros. Naturalmente, em sentido primário, Cristo é o candeeiro, pois ele é a luz do mundo. E o número sete indica a perfeição de seu ofício de iluminador. Ver João 1:9. O material de que o candeeiro foi feito, o ouro, representa a preciosidade da estrutura da Igreja, bem como a divindade de Cristo (que vide). O azeite, que queima no candeeiro, representa o Espírito Santo e seu ministério iluminador. É o Espírito Santo que nos conduz a toda a verdade (João 16:13). (NTI Z)

CANDELÁRIA

Trata-se da festa religiosa da apresentação de Cristo ao templo de Jerusalém, historiada em Luc. 2:22. Na Igreja Ocidental é conhecida como Purificação da Bendita Virgem, e, na Igreja do Oriente, como Encontro com Simeão e Ana. A festa é celebrada desde o imperador Justiniano a 2 de fevereiro. Em Roma, a data coincide com as procissões penitenciais (que vide), derivadas das Amburales do paganismo, quando os oficiantes levavam luzes. Esse costume, e a referência, no cântico de Simeão, fizeram ser esse o dia da bênção das velas, com uma procissão em que os participantes levam velas acesas, o que explica o nome dessa festa. (E)

CÂNEGOS (CÔNEGOS)

Os cônegos são clérigos que ocupam posição intermediária (*a quid medium*) entre os monges e o clero secular. O trabalho deles não se assemelha nem às atividades da vida monástica e nem às atividades dos padres paroquianos; mas apenas têm o direito de celebrar os mistérios sagrados. Eles afirmam que se originaram com Agostinho. Desde o século VIII D.C., o título feminino canonisas tem sido dado a mulheres que professam uma vida em comum, embora sem seguirem a regra de Agostinho. O trabalho deles é mais de vida contemplativa, e eles dedicam-se aos cuidados aos enfermos e à educação de crianças. (E)

CÂNFORA

No hebraico, **kopher**, palavra que só aparece por duas vezes: Can. 1:4 e 4:13. O termo vem do malaio, *kapur*; sendo a hena ou *Lawsonia inermis*, largamente cultivada na Terra Santa. A cânfora é extraída de suas flores de cor creme, que dão em cachos. A planta cresce até 3 m de altura, tem folhas parecidas com as da espécie *Ligustrum vulgare*, da Europa, e massas de flores muito fragrantes, brancas e amareladas. Alguns estudiosos supõem que essas flores eram usadas na antiguidade em banhos de sais. As folhas da hena eram ressecadas e pulverizadas; e uma pasta era feita desse pó. A pasta era usada para pintar as unhas das mãos e dos pés, ou mesmo as solas dos pés e as palmas das mãos. Os homens punham o pó em suas barbas, e também nas caudas dos cavalos. No Egito, a substância era usada como um cosmético de sombrear, e as mulheres de Israel imitavam esse costume. Os trechos de Cantares 1:14 e 4:13 celebram a beleza e a atração física, dizendo: «Como um racimo de flores de hena, nas vinhas de En-Gedi, é para mim o meu amado». «Os teus renovos são um pomar de romãs, com frutos excelentes: a hena e o nardo...» (G HA I)

CANHESTRO

As pessoas canhestras, que o vulgo chama de «canhotas» possuem a mão, o braço e o ombro esquerdos mais fortes e habilidosos que os direitos. Essa palavra é usada apenas por duas vezes na Bíblia, em ambos os casos acerca dos guerreiros da tribo de Benjamim. No hebraico é usada uma expressão, *itter yad yamim*, «amarrado da mão direita». Ver Juí. 3:15 e 20:16. Eúde, filho de Gera, era canhestro. Matou o rei de Moabe e assim libertou Israel dos moabitas. Nessa última referência encontramos a informação de que dentre os vinte e seis mil benjamitas preparados para a guerra, setecentos eram canhestros, dotados de incrível pontaria com a funda.

CANIBALISMO

O canibalismo consiste em homens ingerirem a carne de outros homens. Essa prática parece ter sido quase universal nos primeiros estágios da cultura humana. O mais provável é que a fome tenha sido o motivo primário. As limitações começaram quando as leis tribais naturais contra o ato de matar um membro da tribo, foram ampliadas para que não se ingerisse a carne de alguém que tivesse morrido por qualquer causa. Porém, a antiga crença de que os poderes e virtudes de outrem podiam ser adquiridos mediante o ato de comer o corpo dessa outra pessoa, era suficientemente forte para que a prática do canibalismo nunca tivesse sido totalmente abandonada, em todos os séculos. Além disso, comer da carne de um inimigo satisfazia o desejo sádico de humilhá-lo no mais alto grau. Algumas vezes, nos sacrifícios humanos, era considerado benéfico comer a carne da pessoa sacrificada, como uma maneira de manter comunhão com a divindade a quem o sacrifício estava sendo oferecido. Além disso, há a considerar as horrendas práticas dos adivinhos, os quais, como parte de suas qualificações, eram forçados a comer a carne de cadáveres em estado de decomposição. Os poderes de fertilidade e a comunicação com os demônios também faziam parte da prática do canibalismo. Além disso, um suposto homem santo às vezes demonstrava o seu desprezo ao mundo e aos seus valores, consumindo a carne de algum corpo humano. O canibalismo continuava sendo uma prática generalizada, quando as modernas missões cristãs de evangelização chegaram a países primitivos. Os missionários cristãos têm encontrado diversas razões como justificativa do canibalismo, conforme se vê acima. Missões cristãs e governos têm reduzido grandemente essa horrível prática, mas, vez por outra, ouve-se a respeito de reiterações da prática, mesmo em nossos dias. Quem sabe o que se sucede em lugares primitivos, onde não há estranhos contemplando a cena? Ainda recentemente, Idi Amim, um déspota africano, vangloriou-se de comer a carne de seus adversários políticos! (E H)

CANÍSIO, PEDRO

Suas datas foram 1521-1597. Foi um jesuíta holandês, líder da Contra-Reforma na Alemanha. Sendo amigo de bispos e príncipes, ele exerceu grande influência na vitalização das universidades católicas alemãs, tendo fundado uma dúzia de instituições jesuítas que, durante séculos, continuaram centros culturais. Em adição a isso, ele foi infatigável pregador e escritor. Seu catecismo tornou-se o catecismo católico padrão da Alemanha. (AM E)

CANIVETE

No hebraico, as palavras **taar sopher**, «faca de escrivão», aparecem somente em Jer. 36:23. Nossa versão portuguesa, juntamente com outras, diz ali «canivete». Está em foco uma faca usada para aguçar as penas feitas de cana, ou para cortar rolos de papiro.

CÂNON

Palavra latina que significa «linha de medir», «regra», «modelo». O termo latino deriva-se do grego *kanon*, «regra», ou «vara».

1. O termo é usado frouxamente para indicar qualquer regra ou padrão.

2. Uma lista das obras de um autor qualquer, consideradas genuínas, como o cânon de Shakespeare, no pressuposto de que nem todas as obras a ele atribuídas são, realmente, de sua autoria.

3. Uma relação oficial da Igreja, contendo os nomes de santos reconhecidos ou de membros de algum de seus capítulos.

4. Uma regra de fé ou de disciplina, especialmente se houver sido expedida por algum concílio eclesiástico (dentro da Igreja Católica Romana), e ratificada pelo papa.

5. Aquela porção da missa católica romana entre o Sanctus e a oração do Padre Nosso. Consiste em um prefácio e em uma oração de ação de graças, e então vem a oração eucarística ou de consagração.

6. Na música, uma composição que tenha vozes ou partes, de acordo com a que cada voz ou parte, em sucessão, entoa a mesma melodia (chamada tema).

7. *Lei Canônica*. De conformidade com as definições mais básicas, a *lei canônica* consiste, simplesmente, no conjunto de regras da antiga Igreja, com o intuito de controlar a conduta e a fé das pessoas, além de regras disciplinares para os ministros. A princípio, essas regras consistiam em pronunciamentos *ad hoc*, feitas pelos líderes e concílios da Igreja antiga, a maioria com base em

CÂNON — CÂNON DO ANTIGO TEST.

proposições bíblicas. Particularmente importantes, foram aquelas leis que vieram de grandes centros cristãos, como os cânones adotados em Nicéia, em 325 D.C. Essas leis acumularam-se, tendo-se tornado necessário que houvesse um processo de seleção e codificação. A padronização teve lugar, no Ocidente, sob a liderança de Carlos Magno. Graciano foi o homem que levou o processo a seu ponto culminante virtual, dentro da comunhão romana, com seu famoso *Decretum*, de 1140 D.C., que se tornou o alicerce do moderno *Corpus iuris canonici*. Esse conjunto de leis tornou-se a mais autoritária lei da Igreja Católica Romana, envolvendo a autoridade das Escrituras, dos concílios e dos papas. Essas leis precisam ser distinguidas dos decretos dos bispos, das concordatas entre a Igreja e os governos seculares, e das leis eclesiásticas, as quais repousam sobre os costumes. Tais leis são consideradas divinamente conferidas, pelo que são consideradas obrigatórias e imutáveis. Todavia, não há razões para que não se façam acréscimos, conforme a necessidade surgir, visto que para tanto há a autoridade dos papas e dos concílios. O corpo das leis canônicas foi publicado em 1582, por Gregório XIII, com o nome de *Corpus Iuris Canonici*. Uma nova codificação, conhecida como *Codex Iuris Canonici*, foi promulgada sob o papa Benedito XV, em 1917. As leis canônicas cobrem quatro áreas principais, a saber: 1. Área pessoal, que trata de leis dirigidas a indivíduos, incluindo aquelas que dizem respeito ao clero. 2. Área *material*, que são leis que dizem respeito aos sacramentos, à liturgia, etc. 3. Área judicial, que são leis que dizem respeito ao casamento, etc. 4. Área penal. O código inteiro incorpora leis divinas, com base nas Escrituras, embora também seja um documento eclesiástico, que reúne as tradições e leis da Igreja. Trata-se de uma tentativa de codificar as regras da vida cristã, de doutrinas práticas e da disciplina.

As igrejas protestantes, naturalmente, repelem essa legislação, embora algumas delas contem com legislações similares, visto que a tendência das denominações é codificar suas crenças e práticas.

8. Os cânones do Antigo e do Novo Testamento. Esses incluem os livros considerados divinamente inspirados e autoritários para a fé e a prática dos cristãos. O cânon judaico ou hebreu consiste na Lei, Profetas e Escritos—um total de trinta e nove livros. O cânon do Novo Testamento consiste em vinte e sete livros. Certos segmentos da Igreja também aceitam os livros apócrifos do Antigo Testamento, que consistem em outros doze livros, os quais foram incluídos na versão Septuaginta do Antigo Testamento (que vide). Quanto a essas questões, ver os dois artigos separados: *Cânon do Antigo Testamento* e *Cânon do Novo Testamento*. (AM B E H P)

CÂNON BUDISTA

Esse cânon, chamado **Tripitaka** (no sânscrito) ou *Tipitaka* (no pali), termos esses que significam «três cestos», consiste no seguinte: 1. Os *Sutras* (no pali, *sutta*) ou *discursos* de Buda; 2. as *Vinaya* (pali e sânscrito), ou *regras*; e 3. as *Sastras* (em pali, Abhidharma) ou *tratados*. A versão pali é aceita pelo segmento Hinayana do *budismo*. Ver o artigo sobre o *Budismo*. A versão sânscrita encerra algumas consideráveis diferenças, quando comparadas à versão pali. Essa versão é seguida pelo grupo Mahayana, tendo sido traduzida para o chinês, o tibetano, o mongol e o manchu. A edição mais completa é a *Tripitaka*, em chinês. Consiste em 13.250 *chuans* (porções), em cem volumes de cerca de mil páginas cada. O cânon tibetano adiciona algumas obras tântricas, em sete partes, em um total de cento e três volumes. Há comentários sobre as obras canônicas, comentários esses chamados *Tanjur*, totalizando duzentos e cinqüenta volumes, o que dá um total de 5.102 *chuans*. Essa foi a versão traduzida para o mongol. Somente uma pequena porção desse material tem sido traduzida para as línguas ocidentais, pelo que o nosso conhecimento sobre o budismo vem, principalmente, das obras e discursos a respeito e não de alguma leitura direta de documentos sagrados do budismo. (E)

CÂNON DO ANTIGO TESTAMENTO

1. Um Processo Histórico
2. O Salto da Fé
3. Buscando uma Posição Intermediária
4. Breve Declaração do Processo Histórico do Cânon do Antigo Testamento
5. Os Livros Disputados. Evidências Colhidas nos Catálogos Cristãos
6. Os Livros Apócrifos
7. O Cânon do Antigo no Novo Testamento
8. Os Livros Apócrifos e os Cristãos Primitivos
9. Citações dos Livros Apócrifos do Antigo Testamento pelos Primeiros Pais da Igreja
10. Os Pseudepígrafos.
11. Cronologia de Literatura
12. Catálogos Cristãos dos Livros do Antigo Testamento: **Livros Disputados**

Bibliografia

1. Um Processo Histórico

Como estudante diplomado do Novo Testamento, fiz um curso de um trimestre, na Universidade de Chicago, nos Estados Unidos da América do Norte, limitado ao cânon do Novo Testamento. Fiquei impressionado diante do fato de que o processo de canonização, de qualquer coleção de Livros Sagrados, é um processo histórico que precisa de séculos para ser completado. As evidências em favor disso são esmagadoras e irrefutáveis. Contudo, podemos assumir vários pontos de vista sobre a *natureza* desse processo.

Alguns liberais supõem que a canonização é apenas uma atividade humana, e que o resultado é apenas uma espécie de seleção de livros religiosos. O extremo oposto dessa suposição é a posição dos estudiosos extremamente conservadores, os quais pensam que esse processo histórico foi tão perfeito e exatamente guiado e inspirado pelo Espírito Santo que os livros que, finalmente, foram canonizados, foram precisamente aqueles que o Espírito de Deus queria que fizessem parte do cânon, e que os livros rejeitados foram repelidos não somente pelos homens, mas também pelo Espírito Santo. Em outras palavras, estes últimos não admitem qualquer possibilidade de erro ou de inferioridade na seleção. Entre essas duas opiniões extremas, temos a posição dos muitos eruditos conservadores que supõem que o processo de canonização foi divinamente guiado, embora também tenha havido o concurso decisivo do elemento humano. Para exemplificar, temos o caso da inclusão da epístola de Tiago, um livro especificamente escrito com o propósito de atacar a idéia paulina da justificação pela fé, refletindo, historicamente, o *legalismo cristão* (que vide). Que esse legalismo foi uma realidade, vê-se obviamente no décimo quinto capítulo do livro de Atos. Diversos dos pais da Igreja e dos reformadores protestantes rejeitaram a epístola de Tiago, julgando que a mesma não merecia lugar no cânon neotestamentário, exatamente por essa razão.

CÂNON DO ANTIGO TESTAMENTO

Alguns também rejeitaram a epístola de Judas, por citar uma obra pseudepígrafa do Antigo Testamento (ver Judas 14, e o comentário no NTI, nesse versículo). Houve oito livros disputados que só foram aceitos no cânon já no século IV D.C.; mas, em algumas porções da Igreja, nem mesmo então. Precisamos reconhecer esses fatos, percebendo que o processo de canonização envolveu grandemente a história e as opiniões humanas sobre o valor dos livros. O Espírito Santo não impulsionou os corações dos homens, de modo a *concordarem completamente*, e *desde o início*, sobre quais livros deveriam ser incluídos no cânon do Novo Testamento. No caso do Antigo Testamento, devemos considerar o problema inteiro dos livros apócrifos, os quais, a começar pelos judeus da dispersão, foram aceitos ou rejeitados, dependendo, essencialmente, apenas de questões geográficas. Essa disputa prolongou-se até aos dias neotestamentários, tendo sido resolvido somente na **época da Reforma Protestante** (embora de diferentes maneiras). O Espírito Santo nunca reuniu os homens a fim de informá-los acerca do que deveriam fazer com os livros apócrifos. Homens tomaram decisões racionais a respeito deles, e diferentes segmentos da Igreja chegaram a diferentes decisões. Que os livros apócrifos revestem-se de grande valor, especialmente do ponto de vista histórico, é inegável. Mas, seriam suficientemente valiosos e dignos de serem incluídos no cânon? Os católicos romanos dizem «sim»; os protestantes dizem «não»; e os anglicanos hesitaram, antes de chegarem a qualquer decisão.

2. O Salto da Fé

Os livros apócrifos devem ser incluídos no cânon do Antigo Testamento? Indagações como essa não podem ser decididas apenas sobre bases dogmáticas, porquanto, com base em considerações dogmáticas já há preferências doutrinárias a serem levadas em conta. Ninguém pode dizer: «Este ou aquele livro é canônico, pois concorda com minha interpretação de quais doutrinas deveriam ser ensinadas». Se alguém fizer isso, já estará partindo de um pressuposto. Em outras palavras, já sabe de antemão onde quer chegar, dirigindo seus argumentos para esse ponto, desrespeitando qualquer argumentação em contrário. Por isso, o que alguém disser sobre o cânon, terá de depender, *parcialmente*, de um *salto de fé*. Os estudiosos extremamente conservadores dão seu salto de fé na dependência da sua *convicção* de que não pode ter havido erro ou inferioridade envolvidos na seleção canônica final. Esses acreditam que o resultado final do processo foi predestinado de modo absoluto, desde o começo, apesar do fato de que foram necessários séculos para que esse resultado fosse obtido. Por sua vez, os intérpretes liberais em extremo partem, em seu salto de fé, da idéia que o Espírito (se é que o Espírito existe, conforme eles pensam) não estava interessado em tal resultado, e que foram *homens*, usando todo o bom senso de que eram capazes, que fizeram uma seleção razoável de material, provendo-nos uma visão respeitável das origens judaico-cristãs de nossas crenças. Não obstante, esses extremamente liberais lamentam o que pode ter sido deixado de lado, pensando que o material rejeitado poderia fornecer-nos também uma compreensão útil sobre essas questões. Então os extremamente conservadores voltam à carga, injetando em seu princípio de canonização a noção de que os livros, tão exatamente selecionados, não podem envolver qualquer erro, sendo absolutamente autoritários, ou mesmo autoridades absolutas, conforme dizem alguns deles. Mas os extremamente liberais pensam que isso não passa de uma racionalização dogmática, partindo do pressuposto que a seleção feita, apesar de útil, tem seus pontos positivos e negativos, suas verdades e erros, e que, em nenhum sentido pode ser considerada absoluta ou exclusivamente autoritária..

Prezados leitores, sou forçado a dizer essas coisas. Em parte alguma das *próprias Escrituras* encontramos qualquer declaração acerca de qualquer seleção canônica final. Os próprios autores sagrados não tinham consciência de que os livros que estavam produzindo algum dia seriam parte de uma coletânea reverenciada como sagrada e canônica. Isso não significa que eles não tinham consciência da inspiração divina de suas obras. Mas isso já é coisa bem diferente da formação de uma coleção de *livros* divinamente inspirados. Somente o autor do Apocalipse, em todo o Novo Testamento, antecipou uma espécie de uso canônico de seu livro (ver Apo. 22:18,19). Mas, ironicamente, foi exatamente esse o livro que exigiu mais tempo para ser aprovado como canônico pela Igreja universal. É uma interpretação descabida aquela que faz o trecho de Apocalipse 22:18,19 aplicar-se à inteireza do Novo Testamento, e não somente àquele *livro profético*, pois trata-se de uma referência específica ao próprio livro de Apocalipse, e não à coletânea inteira que, quando essa declaração joanina foi escrita, nem existia ainda. Portanto, voltamos a dizer que qualquer afirmação a respeito da natureza do cânon é um *dogma* humano, e não uma afirmação feita pela própria Bíblia Sagrada. No entanto, os homens fazem de seus dogmas uma parte necessária da ortodoxia, procurando assustar aos que consideram-se hereges, por não concordarem com eles, acusando-os de manipularem a Palavra de Deus. Naturalmente, o ponto de vista dos liberais *também* constitui o seu dogma, havendo certos fatores da verdade que eles perdem de vista, em seu salto de fé.

3. Buscando uma Posição Intermediária

Usualmente, a verdade sobre as questões debatidas jaz em algum ponto entre suas interpretações exageradas. Não afirmo que isso sempre ocorre, mas tal princípio com freqüência funciona, exigindo de nós a devida atenção. Portanto, quero aplicá-lo aqui:

a. Contra os liberais extremados. Quero salientar que o curso do liberalismo está calcado sobre o *ceticismo* (que vide). Quem é liberal aborda todos os problemas com certa falta de fé. Também sente-se muito insatisfeito com os muitos dogmas que estão mesclados a tantas questões religiosas, e anela por desdogmatizar as coisas. Ele se sente como um cruzado. Mas, idêntico sentimento é compartilhado pelos extremamente conservadores. Assim, há um inevitável choque de radicais. O extremamente liberal observa que o processo de canonização precisou de séculos para completar-se; percebe como vários livros foram disputados; nota como vários segmentos da Igreja chegaram a conclusões diferentes; toma consciência de que algum *bom* material não chegou a fazer parte do cânon; e também sabe que certas obras de Paulo se perderam, e que ele supõe que eram tão boas como aquelas que foram preservadas; e, finalmente, especula que, provavelmente, havia muitos livros úteis, nos dias do Novo Testamento, que deveriam ter sido incluídos no cânon. Ele pode usar o prólogo do evangelho de Lucas, baseando-se num argumento em prol de suas suposições e usando esse prólogo como texto de prova. Ele reúne todos esses fatores e conclui que o que sucedeu foi apenas um processo humano de seleção, e que se o fator divino estivesse envolvido na questão, não teria havido tanta contorção. Como um toque final, o extremamente

CÂNON DO ANTIGO TESTAMENTO

liberal salienta que certos livros que finalmente entraram no cânon (como a epístola de Tiago), deixaram insatisfeitos alguns dos estudiosos mais conservadores (como Lutero). Sua fórmula está preparada. Segundo ele, o *cânon* foi produzido pela atividade humana, e a própria natureza dessa atividade obtém sucessos e sofre derrotas. Isso não significa que ele não veja valor naquilo que foi produzido. Ali há grandiosas idéias; ali há espiritualidade e instrução; ali há contribuições valiosas à literatura e à história. Deus talvez se mova em meio a tudo aquilo, e isso contribui para o bem. Mas, a última coisa que o extremamente liberal quer ser é culpado de *bibliolatria* (que vide).

Minha Avaliação. Penso que os estudiosos extremamente liberais, apesar de toda a boa intenção que possam ter, nos oferecem pouco demais. O que eles oferecem não é bastante para mim. Em *primeiro lugar*, quero destacar que podemos criar um bom argumento sobre como a vontade de Deus opera no e *através do processo histórico*. Que um processo qualquer precise de muito tempo em nada detrata da orientação divina, dentro desse processo. De fato, a própria inquirição espiritual está intimamente envolvida no processo histórico, sem importar se da Igreja, como uma organização (com base, desde o começo, na evolução espiritual judaica), ou se de indivíduos isolados. Todas as coisas de valor precisam de tempo para concretizar-se. Em *segundo lugar*, no tocante aos valores espirituais, não precisamos de perfeição. É como alguém já disse: «Não se joga fora o bebê, juntamente com a água de seu banho». Os liberais, em seu intuito de desdogmatizar as coisas, podem jogar fora o bebê espiritual, juntamente com a água das manipulações humanas. Eles podem aplicar um exagerado ceticismo, deixando-nos ao léu, naquele mar onde o Espírito de Deus não se move. E esse mar é totalmente estéril. Em *terceiro lugar*, é razoável supormos que visto que a literatura é a maneira mais eficaz de comunicação, Deus, ao querer comunicar-se com os homens, poderia ter usado esse método, entre outros. Penso que isso não é esperar demais. De fato, temos essa coleção de trinta e nove livros do Antigo Testamento e vinte e sete livros do Novo Testamento. E, se alguns segmentos da Igreja querem um maior número de livros, que os obtenham. Neles, poderão buscar a comunicação divina; não havendo necessidade de serem livros perfeitos, hermeticamente selados, para transmitirem esse recado. Em *quarto lugar*, o fato de que outras sociedades têm suas coletâneas sagradas, nada diz contra a coletânea judaico-cristã. Por enquanto, que outros decidam quanto ao valor que nelas encontram, porque, agora, estamos preocupados somente com o cânon da Bíblia Sagrada.

b. Contra os conservadores extremados. — Em *primeiro lugar*, eles ignoram o elemento humano que, inevitavelmente, deve atuar sobre a formação de qualquer coletânea de livros sagrados. Em *segundo lugar*, sempre precisam aplicar sua fé de modo que *não pode* haver qualquer erro, quer na coletânea como um todo, quer em qualquer livro isolado dessa coletânea. Tudo isso faz parte de seu salto de fé, tornando-se um dogma duro como o diamante. É um dogma, porque as Escrituras não contêm tal ensino. Em *terceiro lugar*, mediante um raciocínio *a priori*, eles ignoram quaisquer problemas que encontrem no caminho, porquanto partem de um pressuposto. Em *quarto lugar*, eles equiparam o que chamam de ortodoxia à verdade. Mas as duas coisas nem sempre são a mesma coisa. Ademais, eles preferem sua ortodoxia particular à verdade, mesmo quando as evidências lhes são esmagadoramente contrárias. Isso é brincar com a verdade, e não inquirir pela mesma. Em *quinto lugar*, eles demonstram grande dose de imaturidade em sua maneira de pensar, porquanto não podem tratar das questões espirituais exceto com base em livros presumivelmente perfeitos em todos os aspectos. Lamento ter de usar aqui uma antiga ilustração liberal, mas é que nela há uma certa verdade. Os extremamente conservadores defendem uma teoria que se assemelha a um balão. Se alguém perfurar o balão em qualquer lugar, todo o ar ali contido escapará inevitavelmente. A *verdade*, porém, não se assemelha a um balão, que qualquer indivíduo ou sistema possa perfurar. A verdade nunca sofre coisas desse jaez. Em *sexto lugar*, embora professando-se reverenciadores do Livro Sacro, eles criam um dogma a respeito do mesmo que chega a ter aspectos irracionais. Finalmente, tal como o ceticismo é a maldição do liberalismo, assim também o *espírito contencioso* é a maldição do conservatismo extremado. Este promove campanhas em favor de dogmas sobre as Escrituras, de uma maneira quase belicosa, utilizando-se da palavra «herege» de modo ridículo e contra quem não a merece.

c. O Meio-Termo. — Até esse ponto de minha exposição, tenho falado sobre as filosofias que circundam o problema do cânon. Tendo dito o que penso que deve ser dito sobre isso, abordarei o aspecto histórico do processo. Primeiro a filosofia e depois a história. Portanto, quais bases filosóficas são devemos utilizar em nosso estudo sobre o cânon? Alisto algumas bases filosóficas óbvias: 1. De modo geral, evitemos os dois extremos que acabamos de discutir. 2. Tenhamos a confiança de que Deus falou através da literatura, e que os nossos Antigo e Novo Testamentos representam essa comunicação. 3. Não façamos uma parte necessária da nossa fé que o cânon tem de incluir exatamente aqueles livros que possuímos na Bíblia, e que não pode incluir outros. Estou convicto de que a epístola a Tiago foi escrita para combater idéias de Paulo; mas ali há coisas boas que precisam ser ditas. Tenho ensinado sobre a epístola de Tiago, versículo após versículo, mas nunca deixei de ressaltar que existem considerações históricas que deveriam ser levadas em conta. O judaísmo antigo não desistiu facilmente de seu sistema de mérito através das obras, e essa idéia penetrou no cristianismo primitivo, conforme se vê em Atos 15, e conforme a história eclesiástica subseqüente demonstra amplamente. Portanto, ensino a epístola de Tiago com essas qualificações, e não preciso encontrar uma perfeita harmonia entre todos os livros da Bíblia, para encontrar neles coisas boas e úteis. Se eu tivesse de escolher entre Tiago e Efésios, este último livro ganharia quilômetros à frente. Não é mister contemplarmos o Novo Testamento como se cada um de seus livros tivesse igual valor: há livros mais profundos do que outros. 4. É de bom alvitre respeitar o que os pais da Igreja e os concílios antigos disseram sobre o cânon das Escrituras. O que eles fizeram produziu um bom resultado. No entanto, eles poderiam ter chegado a outras decisões, resultando em um Novo Testamento levemente diferente, sem que isso prejudicasse em nada qualquer questão de fé e práticas cristãs. 5. Acima de tudo, respeitemos a autoridade das Escrituras, mas não dogmatizemos a questão da autoridade (que vide), afirmando que não existem outras autoridades que também deveriam influenciar naquilo em que cremos e praticamos. 6. Finalmente, em todas as coisas, apliquemos a lei do amor naquilo que dizemos e naquilo que fazemos. Palavras ásperas originam-se no ódio; e é um erro ferir a outrem em defesa de pontos de vista teológicos.

CÂNON DO ANTIGO TESTAMENTO

4. Breve Declaração do Processo Histórico do Cânon do Antigo Testamento

a. *A Lei*. A piedade judaica supunha que Moisés era autor dos livros da lei, com a exceção única de algumas poucas passagens; e também julgava que, desde o começo, seus escritos foram respeitados como comunicações divinas. Isso nos daria uma data bem remota para a canonização da lei, isto é, cerca de 1500 A.C. Os eruditos liberais pensam que não houve qualquer processo real de canonização senão quando foi reencontrado — o Livro de Deuteronômio — no templo de Jerusalém, que aconteceu durante a reforma encabeçada por Josias, em 621 A.C. Esse livro ter-se-ia tornado o texto base das reformas, e, subseqüentemente, o núcleo da lei judaica, de Gênesis a Deuteronômio, que atingiu seu total desenvolvimento no começo do século IV A.C. Foi por essa altura que essa coletânea foi considerada a plena expressão da vontade divina. Quando examinamos os livros do Pentateuco, no tocante à sua autoria, observamos que o livro de Gênesis, que aborda ocorrências anteriores a Moisés, não traz qualquer informação sobre seu autor. Mas os incidentes historiados em Gênesis exibem um conhecimento de causa muito grande, devendo estar baseado em documentos escritos e cuidadosamente preparados. Portanto, embora esse livro possa ter sido escrito por Moisés, pode ter sido muito mais uma compilação de obras escritas anteriormente. Os demais livros do Pent. também não mostram qualquer indicação quanto ao seu autor, mas a principal personagem e autoridade é Moisés. Por mais de setenta e cinco vezes, somente no livro de Êxodo, é dito que «disse o Senhor a Moisés», o que mostra a consciência de que esses documentos estão alicerçados sobre a vontade revelada de Deus, sem importar quem tenha registrado em forma escrita as suas palavras. Além disso, foi Deus quem revelou essa vontade a Moisés. E o mesmo modo de expressão prossegue nos demais livros do Pentateuco. Poderíamos perguntar, com toda a razão, se foi Moisés quem escreveu diretamente esses livros, por qual motivo não se lê ali: «disse-me o Senhor», —em vez de «disse o Senhor a Moisés»? Certamente os profetas escreveram na primeira pessoa do singular. Não obstante, duas coisas devem ser ditas por esta altura: 1. A *canonicidade* não depende do autor envolvido; depende de quão digno de confiança é o registro e o propósito espirituais. 2. Mesmo que Moisés não tenha escrito esses livros, na forma como eles se acham, eles se parecem com narrativas de alguma testemunha ocular da vida e da época de Moisés. Se esses livros refletem uma revelação espiritual genuína, sobre os tempos de Moisés, é totalmente imaterial se Moisés agiu como autor, compilador ou recebedor da mensagem, ou se isso foi feito por algum outro autor. A questão da autoria, com os devidos detalhes, é abordada nos artigos sobre cada livro em particular; é ali que o leitor poderá encontrar os argumentos acerca da questão.

O resto do Antigo Testamento, bem como o Novo Testamento, consideram que o Pentateuco teve Moisés como autor. Moisés é mencionado por cinqüenta e seis vezes no livro de Josué, e sua lei escrita é ali referida por quatro vezes, segundo se vê em Jos. 1:7; 8:31,32 e 23:6. Essas alusões quase certamente garantem que o próprio Moisés escreveu ao menos o núcleo do que se encontra no Pentateuco, e que, pelo menos, ele foi o compilador de certas porções, e escritor original de outras porções. Expressões similares encontram-se em Juí. 3:4; I Reis 2:3; 8:9; II Reis 18:6. Naturalmente, em livros posteriores, como os de Crônicas, Esdras e Neemias, é simplesmente declarado que Moisés escreveu a lei. Ver Nee. 9:14; Esd. 7:6,14, etc. O trecho de João 5:46 registra que Jesus meramente declarou que Moisés escreveu a Seu respeito, e isso reflete a comum tradição, da época de Jesus, de que Moisés foi o autor do Pentateuco. Ver abaixo as referências neotestamentárias sobre essa questão.

A questão da autoria mosaica do Pentateuco é importante por ter sido ele uma grande e bem reconhecida figura espiritual, pelo que, o que ele escreveu, deve ser respeitado como divinamente inspirado. É nesse ponto que encontramos a primeira comprovação de canonicidade. Porém, essa verdade em nada se alteraria, ainda que alguma outra pessoa ou pessoas tivessem escrito o material, incorporando as experiências e revelações feitas a Moisés.

b. *Os Profetas, os Anteriores e os Posteriores*. As evidências históricas demonstram que os profetas anteriores, como Josué, Juízes, Samuel e Reis, bem como os profetas posteriores, como Isaías, Jeremias, Ezequiel e os doze profetas menores, eram considerados Escritores Sagrados pelo menos desde 250 a 175 A.C. Naturalmente, os eruditos conservadores supõem que os escritos dos profetas, desde perto da data de escrita de cada um deles, foram reconhecidos como mensagens espirituais, como se desde quase imediatamente tivessem recebido uma posição canônica. O raciocínio *a priori*, por detrás dessa suposição, é que um profeta distinguia-se de tal modo que os seus escritos não demoravam a assumir uma função autoritária. — Os eruditos liberais, por sua parte, supõem que os escritos dos profetas não foram aceitos prontamente por causa da mensagem geralmente negativa, e porque havia resistência a qualquer coisa, excetuando a autoridade de Moisés. Historicamente, não contamos, praticamente, com qualquer evidência sobre a qual podemos basear discussões a esse respeito. Mas a experiência humana mostra que uma figura profética sempre é impressionante, e que ela logo consegue um bom grupo de seguidores. Além disso, um profeta sofre oposição daqueles que preferem o *status quo*. Portanto, se a experiência nos serve de guia sobre a questão, então podemos afirmar que, desde o começo, os profetas do Antigo Testamento tinham seguidores que os aceitavam como autoridades espirituais, ao passo que o *clero* de sua própria geração, mui provavelmente não deu valor aos escritos deles. No caso do Novo Testamento, sabemos que, desde o começo, várias das epístolas de Paulo tiveram uma virtual autoridade canônica, e que, no começo do segundo século D.C., havia um pequeno Novo Testamento, em nada considerado inferior ao Antigo Testamento. No caso de Maomé, para ilustrar o ponto, em seu próprio período de vida, seus escritos já eram considerados autoritários, pelos discípulos por ele reunidos. Não há nenhuma razão suficiente para supormos que outro tanto não sucedeu aos profetas do Antigo Testamento. Pelo menos, é verdade que suas mensagens foram transmitidas como inspiradas por Deus. Há numerosas referências como «disse o Senhor», ou como «Eis que ponho na tua boca as minhas palavras» (Jer. 1:5-9). Também existem visões extáticas como as de Isaías (6:6-9), ou as de Ezequiel (3:3,4), um fenômeno comum entre os profetas, evidenciando que a tradição profética operava desde o começo.

c. *Os Escritos*. Essa é a terceira porção do cânon hebraico, constituída por certa variedade de livros. Esses livros são os Salmos, Provérbios, Jó e os cinco rolos: Cântico dos Cânticos, Rute, Lamentações, Eclesiastes e Ester, cada um dos quais era lido em uma das cinco grandes festas, da páscoa à festa de

CÂNON DO ANTIGO TESTAMENTO

Purim. Além desses, há os livros de Daniel, Esdras, Neemias, Crônicas e Eclesiastes. Dentre esses livros todos, o Cântico dos Cânticos e o Eclesiastes foram os últimos a serem aceitos como canônicos. As datas marcadas pelos estudiosos liberais ficam entre 160 e 105 A.C.

Também havia livros disputados do Antigo Testamento, o que é discutido, com a ajuda de um gráfico, no quinto ponto. Os liberais argumentam que nenhum passo consciente foi dado com vistas à formação de uma terceira divisão, até que se encerrou a segunda divisão (os profetas). Uma vez fechado o cânon, as pessoas relutariam em reabrir suas mentes à possibilidade do aparecimento de outras Escrituras. A ordem dos livros em questão é salientada como prova disso. Esdras, Neemias e Crônicas, se tivessem sido aceitos desde o começo, conforme prossegue esse raciocínio, teriam sido colocados juntamente com outros livros históricos. Antes, ficaram juntos, e isso mostra que, como uma espécie de unidade, eles apareceram posteriormente. Entretanto, não sabemos as razões da ordem dos livros do Antigo Testamento, uma vez que a cronologia histórica foi perturbada por eles, a menos que o prestígio pessoal dos autores tenha exercido algum efeito sobre esse arranjo. Alguns eruditos têm argumentado que a tradução desses livros, do hebraico para o grego, uma tradução de qualidade inferior à tradução dos livros anteriores, mostra-nos que eles eram considerados menos dignos de respeito. Porém, é possível que esses livros apenas tenham sido entregues a tradutores menos habilidosos. A maneira vaga como esse grupo de livros é referido no livro de Eclesiástico, «o resto dos livros», presumivelmente diz-nos que eles tinham menor prestígio. Contudo, isso não é mais vago do que as referências gerais que dizem «a lei e os profetas», por exemplo. É possível que Josefo tenha refletido uma antiga opinião, ao informar-nos que o cânon foi essencialmente fechado nos dias de Artaxerxes (465-425 A.C.), e que «desde aquele tempo, nenhuma alma aventurou-se a alterar uma sílaba». Ver Contra Apionem I.8. No mesmo contexto, Josefo menciona que alguns livros merecem menos confiança do que outros, e que a sucessão dos profetas não foi fixada com exatidão. Isso permite-nos ver que havia dúvidas e livros disputados, embora o sentido exato dessa citação seja incerto. Se pudermos tomar como padrão aquilo que sucedeu aos livros do Novo Testamento, então podemos asseverar que, excetuando o caso dos livros disputados, o poder de algum líder espiritual ou profeta já servia de garantia de que, pouco depois de seu tempo (quando a oposição à sua pessoa, por parte das autoridades religiosas, que procuravam manter o *status quo*, já havia passado), os seus escritos eram considerados autoritários.

Em certos sentidos, a discussão em nada redunda. Eu gostaria de salientar que os argumentos pró e contra não é tudo quanto importa. Os escritos que encerram alguma mensagem espiritual para nós, podem ser rejeitados e desprezados sem qualquer motivo real. Assim, Jesus e a sua mensagem foram francamente rejeitados pela maioria dos judeus de sua época. Isso é um fato histórico. As autoridades eclesiásticas anelavam por declarar que os escritos a seu respeito não tinham qualquer valor. Todavia, isso não correspondia à realidade do caso. Por conseguinte, um profeta do Antigo Testamento e a sua mensagem podem ter sido rejeitados injustamente. A data ou antiguidade não é a única consideração que se deve levar em conta aqui. De fato, o poder e a utilidade da própria mensagem são mais importantes do que a *data* em que uma mensagem passou a ser aceita. Não obstante, o peso da evidência, bem como a razão, parecem favorecer a aceitação do Antigo Testamento desde os primeiros tempos, em todas as suas divisões, excetuando os livros disputados. Nosso principal problema com os Escritos Sagrados é o seu *valor intrínseco*, e não a época em que os homens resolveram aceitá-los.

5. Os Livros Disputados. Evidências Colhidas nos Católogos Cristãos

A citação extraída acima, dos escritos de Josefo, mostra que, no tempo de Artaxerxes (465-425 A.C.), na época de Esdras, havia livros disputados do Antigo Testamento, e as pessoas não sabiam onde traçar a linha divisória no tocante à tradição profética autêntica. Com a tradução do Antigo Testamento hebraico para o grego, e com a inclusão dos livros apócrifos naquela obra (285-246 A.C.), outros livros duvidosos foram acrescentados à lista. Os livros que eram respeitados, embora não reputados tão valiosos quanto outros, eram Lamentações, Baruque, Ester, Eclesiástico, Sabedoria, Tobias, Judite e I e II Macabeus. Naturalmente, as dúvidas incluíam outros livros, em menor grau, e a outros livros apócrifos, em grau maior. Se excluirmos os livros apócrifos, os livros de Cantares e Eclesiastes foram os que permaneceram na dúvida por mais tempo. Mesmo após o sínodo de Jamnia, no ano 90 D.C., alguns rabinos não queriam aceitar o livro de Ester como parte das Escrituras Sagradas, talvez porque ali não é mencionado o nome de Deus nem uma vez sequer.

Ver o **gráfico ilustrativo** sob ponto 12 que ilustra este problema.

6. Os Livros Apócrifos

O cânon palestino e o cânon alexandrino. Existiam, realmente, estes dois cânones do A.T. nos tempos helenistas? Alguns eruditos negam, absolutamente, que isto seja a verdade. A argumentação deles se baseia essencialmente sobre a falta de qualquer indicação clara sobre dois cânones diferentes, em citações de pessoas daquele tempo, ou depois. Contra isto, devemos observar que a própria existência da *Septuaginta*, com seus livros extras, é prova absoluta de um cânon além daquele da Bíblia hebraica da Palestina.

O Antigo Testamento foi traduzido para o grego no reinado de Ptolomeu Filadelfo (285-246 A.C.). Ver o artigo sobre a *Septuaginta*, ou LXX, quanto a detalhes mais completos a respeito. Essa obra continha os catorze livros apócrifos do Antigo Testamento; mas, pelo menos para os judeus da dispersão, esses livros eram considerados Escrituras Sagradas. Quase a coleção inteira, através da decisão do Concílio de Trento (que vide), ao tempo da **Reforma Protestante, foi adotada pela Igreja Católica Romana,** ao passo que o cânon protestante manteve-se idêntico ao cânon palestino (ou hebraico), que consiste nos nossos trinta e nove livros do Antigo Testamento, posto que arrumados de maneira um tanto diferente. Torna-se óbvio, pois, que, nos tempos de Jesus, havia um cânon mais amplo, aceito por muitos, que ultrapassava aos nossos trinta e nove livros veterotestamentários. Ver o artigo geral sobre os *Livros Apócrifos*, quanto a detalhes sobre a questão, bem como quanto a uma descrição sobre a natureza dessa obra. O segundo ponto desse artigo ilustra o uso dos livros apócrifos no Novo Testamento. O terceiro ponto encerra uma discussão sobre o *cânon*, no que tange a essa obra.

7. O Cânon do Antigo Testamento no Novo Testamento

CÂNON DO ANTIGO TESTAMENTO

As muitas citações do Antigo Testamento no Novo, mostram a estatura canônica daquela coletânea, nas mentes daqueles que escreveram o Novo Testamento. Há um artigo separado, intitulado *Citações no Novo Testamento*, —que ilustra amplamente a questão. Vários livros do antigo pacto, a saber, Ester, Eclesiastes, Cantares de Salomão, Esdras, Neemias, Obadias, Naum e Sofonias não são citados diretamente no Novo Testamento; mas é provável que isso apenas ilustre a questão da seleção de passagens a serem usadas, nada significando contra a posição canônica dos livros assim omitidos. O termo «Escrituras» é freqüentemente usado no Novo Testamento, apontando para o Antigo Testamento. Ver Mat. 26:54; João 5:39; Atos 17:2. Além disso, temos II Tim. 3:16 que reivindica inspiração divina para esses livros; e também II Ped. 1:21 reflete isso. Jesus referiu-se à *lei* e ao fato de que Moisés escreveu a Seu respeito. Aludiu aos *profetas*, como quem escrevera acerca dele. De fato, começando por Moisés, passou por todos os profetas, encontrando referências que prediziam o seu ministério (Luc. 25:27). O trecho de Lucas 24:44 conta que quando os discípulos relataram o diálogo que tinham tido com Jesus, a caminho da aldeia de Emaús, eles incluíam Moisés, os Salmos e os Profetas como aquelas porções bíblicas que Jesus usara para mostrar-lhes o que fora previsto sobre sua pessoa. Admite-se universalmente que o cânon de trinta e nove livros do Antigo Testamento hebraico era universalmente aceito nos dias do Novo Testamento. As únicas exceções a essa aceitação eram os saduceus, os quais, provavelmente, aceitavam somente Moisés (a lei), e os céticos, que nem ao menos se deixavam impressionar pela autoridade de Moisés. Em caso contrário, por qual razão negavam até mesmo a existência dos anjos, seres comumente mencionados no Pentateuco? Ver Gên. 16:7,9,10; 19:1; Êxo. 3:2; 14:19; Núm. 20:16; 22:22, o que é apenas uma seleção representativa de referências aos anjos no Pentateuco. O trecho de Atos 23:8 revela-nos o que os saduceus criam quanto a certos particulares, mostrando o quão céticos eles eram. É difícil perceber como eles poderiam ter usado os Salmos e os Profetas como livros canônicos, incluindo os ensinos dos mesmos em suas doutrinas.

Os cânones dos dias de Jesus. É evidente, pois, que nos dias de Jesus, havia três cânones: 1. O cânon dos judeus palestinos, de tendências farisaicas, seguidos pelas massas populares: os tradicionais trinta e nove livros do Antigo Testamento hebraico. 2. O cânon da Septuaginta (chamado «alexandrino»), que incluía os livros apócrifos, aceito pelos judeus da dispersão, isto é, judeus que falavam o grego. 3. O cânon abreviado dos saduceus (a cujo partido pertenciam muitas autoridades judaicas, que dominavam a política da nação), que incluía somente o Pentateuco, com exclusão de todos os demais livros do Antigo Testamento.

Levanta-se, portanto, a indagação: os cristãos primitivos aceitavam o cânon ampliado da Septuaginta? Ver o oitavo ponto, abaixo.

8. Os Livros Apócrifos e os Cristãos Primitivos

Quando era estudante em seminário teológico, foi-me ensinado que o Novo Testamento nunca cita dos livros apócrifos do Antigo Testamento. Porém, quando escrevi *O Novo Testamento Interpretado*, e tive de repassar versículo após versículo, através de todos os capítulos do Novo Testamento, fiquei surpreso ao descobrir as muitas vezes em que ali há reverberações verbais ou mesmo citações diretas dos livros apócrifos. Visto que se sabe de modo absoluto que os escritores do Novo Testamento, como um todo, usavam a versão Septuaginta em suas citações, esse fato deixa de ser surpreendente. Se alguém não aceita os livros apócrifos do Antigo Testamento como canônicos, também inclina-se a afirmar que os escritores do Novo Testamento, igualmente, não aceitavam esses livros como inspirados. É possível que alguns dos autores do Novo Testamento tivessem os livros apócrifos em menor estima, e, de fato, eles merecem menor estima. Mas o uso que deles se faz, no Novo Testamento, quase certamente indica que os autores sagrados do Novo Testamento os respeitavam, considerando-os Escrituras. As poucas vezes, falando relativamente, em que são citados, pode indicar que eram menos favorecidos, sendo provável que o prestígio desses livros variasse de indivíduo para indivíduo, pelo que não podemos fazer qualquer declaração geral sobre essa questão, sem a devida qualificação. Também reconhecemos que os escritores do Novo Testamento citaram livros históricos e poetas seculares; e isso não faz desses livros obras inspiradas. Porém, fica de pé o fato de que os escritores do Novo Testamento citaram dos livros apócrifos. Ver o artigo sobre os *Livros Apócrifos*, segundo ponto, quanto a ilustrações de citações dessas obras, nas páginas do Novo Testamento.

9. Citações dos Livros Apócrifos do Antigo Testamento pelos Primeiros Pais da Igreja

Ver o *gráfico* sob ponto 12 que ilustra esta informação.

Também tem sido erroneamente afirmado que os primeiros pais da Igreja não citaram os livros apócrifos como Escritura. Porém, as evidências rebatem essa afirmação. Como é óbvio, a questão era debatida, e o prestígio desses livros variava de pessoa para pessoa. Alguns (como Jerônimo) rejeitavam-nos abertamente; mas outros os aceitavam. Alguns estudiosos recentes negam que houve um cânon alexandrino (dos judeus da dispersão), presumindo que até mesmo os judeus que viviam fora da Palestina aceitavam o cânon palestino em hebraico. Mas, as citações existentes no Novo Testamento e nos escritos dos pais da Igreja, refletindo a Septuaginta, mostram que tal assertiva não concorda com os fatos. O dogma mostra-se tão renitente, quanto a essa questão que, a fim dos homens livrarem-se dos livros apócrifos, alguns chegam a afirmar que a Septuaginta, em seu estado primitivo, não continha esses livros, que só mais tarde teriam sido adicionados. Mas, mesmo que isso fosse verdade, finalmente a Septuaginta chegou a incluir os livros apócrifos, e, na época de Jesus, eles se encontravam ali, sendo aceitos como parte integrante das Escrituras, como é demonstrado pelo fato de que os escritores do Novo Testamento não titubearam em citá-los. Ver uma discussão sobre as datas dos livros apócrifos, o que dá alguma idéia acerca de quando esses livros começaram a penetrar no cânon usado pelos judeus da dispersão. Naturalmente, pode-se demonstrar facilmente que vários dos pais da Igreja desprezaram ou mesmo rejeitaram os livros apócrifos. Além de Jerônimo, podemos mencionar Tertuliano e Orígenes. Mas meu gráfico, que vem abaixo, mostra que eles também citaram os livros apócrifos. Até mesmo os conservadores mais radicais admitem que esses pais citaram esses livros *de vez em quando*, e que a questão inteira está eivada de dúvidas, devido à ausência de evidências mais sólidas e definitivas. Quando imperam tais condições, os homens sempre procuram distorcer as evidências em apoio àquilo em que querem acreditar, ignorando as evidências em contrário. Uma vez mais, cumpre-me afirmar que a questão do cânon pode ser melhor examinada sob o ponto de vista do *valor intrínseco* de cada livro, e,

CÂNON DO ANTIGO TESTAMENTO

apenas secundariamente, com base em datas e aceitação histórica. Seguindo-se o correto padrão, penso que é evidente que os livros apócrifos (como um todo), não merecem a mesma aceitação que os tradicionais trinta e nove livros canônicos do Antigo Testamento hebraico têm alcançado.

É possível que a Igreja Anglicana tenha tomado a posição correta sobre a questão, ao afirmar que esses livros canônicos são bons para servir de exemplo à vida e para instruir sobre as maneiras, mas não servem de base para nossas doutrinas. A isso podemos acrescentar a grande valia histórica de alguns dos livros apócrifos, que iluminam o período intermediário entre o Antigo e o Novo Testamentos.

10. Os Pseudepígrafos

Os pseudepígrafos do Antigo Testamento são livros ainda menos conhecidos que os livros apócrifos. Ver o artigo separado sobre *Pseudepígrafe*. Na realidade, o Novo Testamento também cita esses livros, e o esquema profético geral, conforme pode ser visto no livro canônico do Novo Testamento, o Apocalipse, muito deve a eles. Porém, dificilmente alguém ouve uma declaração como essa, na grande maioria dos seminários teológicos. A ignorância sobre esses livros, entre os evangélicos, é profunda.

11. Cronologia de Literatura

CRONOLOGIA DO A. TESTAMENTO

	Eventos Históricos	Desenvolvimento dos Livros Apócrifos e Hagiógrafos				Pseudepígrafos		
		História e Lenda	*Apocalipse*	*Sermão e Ensaio*	*Sabedoria*			*Salmos*
AC 250	Palestina sob Ptolomeus (Egito)	Aikar (?) Tobias, 220 AC? Adições a Ester. c. 181-145 AC						
200	Palestina sob Selêucidas (Síria). 198 Antíoco IV contamina o templo, 167; Judas Macabeu o purifica, 164 AC.	Judite, 180-100			Sabedoria de Jesus Ben Siraque (Eclesiástico), 180 AC.			
150	Dinastia Hasmoneana	I Esdras, antes de 100 AC. I Macabeus, 105-65 AC.? II Macabeus, 100 AC 70 DC.? Susana. 80-50 AC Bel e o Dragão, 80-50 AC. Vidas dos Profetas	I Enoque, 183-80 AC. Guerra Filhos da Luz e Trevas	Testamento 12 Patriarcas I Baruque, 150 AC. Manual de Disciplina, 100 AC? Fragmentos Sadoquitas Oráculos Sibilinos III				Cântico dos Três Jovens Salmos da Seita de Qumran
63	Pompeu conquista Jerusalém, 63 AC.							
50				Epístola Jeremias Carta de Aristéias Comentário sobre Habacuque 1,2 IV Macabeus. 50 AC - 70 DC.				
DC 1	Herodes, O Grande, 40 AC Judéia sob procuradores romanos	III Macabeus, 50 AC -50 DC. Martírio de Isaías Crônicas de Jeremias Vida de Adão e Eva / Apo. de Moisés/	Assunção de Moisés, 4 AC- 28 DC.		Sabedoria de Salomão 50 AC- 10 DC			Salmos de Salomão
66	Começa a guerra judaica. 66 DC.		II Baruque /Baruque siríaco/ II Enoque /Enoque eslavônico ou Segredos de Enoque/ II Esdras, 88-117 DC. Apocalipse de Abraão III Baruque /Baruque grego/		Ditos dos Pais /Pirke Aboth, 10-100 DC?/			Oração de Manassés
100	Queda de Jerusalém, 70 DC							

CÂNON DO ANTIGO TESTAMENTO

12. Catálogos Cristãos do Antigo Testamento: Livros Disputados

N.B. A lista envolve somente os livros disputados.

CHAVE:
- * indica que o livro é expressamente reputado *Escritura Sagrada*
- \+ indica que ocupa segunda categoria
- ? indica que o livro é duvidoso

um espaço em branco marca o silêncio do autor sobre o livro em pauta

	Lam.	Bar.	Est.	Ecl.	Sab.	Tob.	Jud.	I,II Mac.	
I. Catálogos Conciliares									
Laodicéia 363 D.C.	*	*	*		*				Cânon lix
Cartago 397 (?)					*	*	*	*	III. Cânon xxxix (al. 47)
Cânones Apostólicos			+			?		+	lxxvi (al. 85)
II Catálogos Privados									
a. Escritos gregos									
Melito c. 160 (180)	*		*						Apo. Euséb. H.e. iv. 26
Orígenes c. 183-253	*	*	?					+	Apo. Euséb. H.E. vi. 25
Atanásio 296-373	*	*				+			Ep. Fest. i.767. ed. Ben.
Cirilo Jer. 315-386		*							Cat. iv.35
Sinôpse S. Escrituras					+	+	+		Credner, Zur Gresch. des Kan. 127 s.
Nicéforo, Esticomet.	*				+	+	+		Credner, a.a. O. pág. 117 ss.
Gregório Naz. 300-391								+	Carm. xii.31, ed. Par. 1840
Anfilóquio c. 380		?					?		Anf. ed. Combef. pág. 132
Epifânio c. 303-403	*	*		+					De Mensuris, pág. 162. ed. Petav.
Leôncio c. 590									De sectis. a. ii (Gal. xii:625 ss)
João Damasceno c. 750	*	*			*	?	?		De Fide orthod. iv. 17
Nicéforo Cal. c. 1330	*	+			+	?	?	+	Hody. pág. 648
Cód. Gr. Séc. X									Montfaucon, Bib. Coislin, p. 193 ss
b. Escrits. latinos									
Hilário c. 370	*	*				?			Pról. in Sal. 15
Jerônimo 329-420	*	*	?		+	+	+	+	Pról. Galea. ix; p. 547 ss, Migna
Rufino c. 380		*						*	Expos. Symb., pág. 37 s.
Agostinho 355-430				*	*	*	*	*	de Doctr. Christ. ii. 8
Cassiodoro c. 570		*		*	*	*	*	*	De Inst. Div. Litt. xiv
Isidoro c. 696	*				*	*	*	*	de Orig. vi.1
Sacram. Gálicos					*				Hody, pág. 654
Cod. Clarom. sec. VII		*		+	*	*	*	*	Ed. Tisch. pág. 468 ss

Bibliografia: CH GS HEN HRC ID J UN Z

CÂNON DO NOVO TESTAMENTO

CÂNON DO NOVO TESTAMENTO
Esboço
1. A Palavra *Cânon*
2. Influências na Formação do Cânon (*esboço*)
   a. Do Velho Testamento
   b. Da Vida e Das Palavras de Jesus
   c. Do Cristianismo
   d. Dos Apóstolos
   e. Dos Pais Apostólicos
   f. Dos Concílios
   g. A Posição Moderna
3. Resumo da História do Cânon
4. Princípios que Formaram o Cânon
5. O Problema de Autoridade para Determinar A Verdade
6. Os Livros Controvertidos Nos Pais, Concílios e Catálogos
7. Bibliografia

1. A Palavra «Cânon». — Essa palavra é uma forma latina da palavra **kanon**, que, no grego, significa *cana*. Tratava-se de uma planta usada de várias maneiras para medir e pautar. Assim sendo, o termo passou a significar «regra» ou «pauta», e, mais tarde, uma lista de coisas ou itens escritos em uma coluna. O vocábulo «kanon», por extensão, passou a significar «regra» ou «padrão». Quando falamos sobre o *cânon das Escrituras* (e, neste caso o N.T.) referimo-nos à lista de livros aceitos pela igreja em geral como livros que foram escritos sob a inspiração divina, os quais, por isso mesmo, são usados como regra de fé e da experiência prática da religião cristã. Numa análise do cânon do N.T. é mister examinarmos o desenvolvimento da autoridade e da aceitação dos vinte e sete livros que hoje em dia são reputados canônicos, e também precisamos examinar a história e a autoridade de cada um desses vinte e sete livros.

2. Influências na Formação do Cânon (esboço)

a. *O Velho Testamento*, que forneceu o impulso criador de um *Novo* Testamento.

b. A *Vida e as Palavras de Jesus Cristo* e, em conseqüência, a necessidade de criar uma autoridade além da autoridade do V.T.

c. *A Nova Religião Cristã*, que criou a necessidade de mais *Escrituras* além das Escrituras judaicas, para formar a base da nova revelação.

d. *Os Apóstolos*, primeiros grandes líderes da *Nova Religião* revelada, os quais, com seus livros e epístolas, forneceram a base das novas Escrituras.

e. *Os Pais Apostólicos*, que criaram os *cânones primitivos* e uma nova autoridade na igreja cristã primitiva.

f. *Os Concílios* da igreja primitiva e medieval.

g. **A Posição Moderna**

Os Itens Considerados Detalhadamente

a. Influência do V.T. A história do cânon do V.T. é longa e complexa, e não é tema deste estudo. É importante notar aqui apenas que, depois de alguns séculos de desenvolvimento, o cânon do V.T. foi finalmente estabelecido antes do fim do século I A.C. Grande parte da congregação judaica aceitava diversos livros apócrifos, pelo que não havia *opinião unânime* sobre o assunto. Seja como for, com ou sem esses livros apócrifos, nossa investigação sobre o cânon do N.T. em nada se modifica. *A verdade* é que então já existia o fato de comunidades religiosas que compilavam listas de livros dotados de autoridade religiosa. Aqueles que estudam a história e a literatura dos povos antigos notam que todos esses povos contaram com sua *Literatura Sagrada*. Os romanos contavam com os escritos sibilinos; os gregos tinham os escritos de Homero, de Masaio e de Orfeu. Os egípcios colecionaram os quarenta e dois livros de Hermes, o Livro dos Mortos e outros mais. Por semelhante modo, a nova religião cristã sentiu a necessidade de contar com uma fonte escrita de *autoridade*, que servisse de base à fé e à prática cristãs.

Assim é que a *Igreja* primitiva aceitava os livros do V.T. como dotados de—autoridade religiosa—e de «inspiração divina».— Estes livros formaram o *cânon* mais primitivo da igreja cristã, embora seja evidente que nesses livros estavam ausentes determinados ensinos—os ensinos distintos do cristianismo, emanados de Cristo ou dos apóstolos. Portanto, os livros que continham as palavras de Jesus e dos apóstolos facilmente foram aceitos como parte do cânon das Escrituras. Houve um processo longo e complexo antes que todos os livros que hoje temos no N.T. constituíssem, individual ou coletivamente, o N.T. Neste encontramos grande número de citações e alusões tomadas por empréstimo do V.T. Também vemos que os autores do N.T. aceitaram a idéia de que Jesus era o Cristo prometido no V.T., pelo que, os profetas do V.T. são, ao mesmo tempo, os profetas antigos da fé cristã. O cristianismo, ao usar tanto o V.T. como o N.T., para formar a «Bíblia», fez uma ligação entre as antigas e as novas revelações divinas. Dessa maneira é que se estabeleceu a base histórica do cristianismo. Contudo, essa base não foi unicamente histórica, porquanto é claro que muitas das idéias, especialmente éticas, do N.T., foram derivadas do V.T. Pode-se dizer, por conseguinte, que o V.T. foi não somente o precedente que exerceu influência na formação de um «novo» Testamento (documento escrito), mas também que exerceu notável influência no caráter e nas idéias dessa nova coleção de livros sagrados.

b. Influência da vida e das palavras de Jesus Cristo — Nunca homem algum falou como Jesus. *Ninguém jamais* viveu como ele. Considerando sua vida e suas palavras, achamos não somente uma explicação para a existência do N.T., mas também entendemos que seria impossível que, depois da vida de um homem assim, não tivessem sido escritos muitos livros acerca dele. O sentido e a ilustração desse fato pode ser observado pelo leitor na existência não só do N.T., mas também na existência dos livros apócrifos do N.T., porquanto muitos «evangelhos», «atos» e «epístolas» foram escritos por diversos indivíduos, descrevendo as vidas dos doze apóstolos ou de outros cristãos antigos. Ver o artigo sobre este assunto. — A referência que se acha em Luc. 1:1-3 mostra que muitos escreveram livros sobre Cristo e suas palavras, e que o próprio Lucas usou partes desses livros como base do evangelho que escreveu. Dizendo isto, porém, não queremos afirmar que Lucas usou livros «apócrifos», porquanto não se sabe da existência de qualquer livro apócrifo escrito antes de Lucas. Esses livros que Lucas usou são desconhecidos hoje em dia, com exceção do evangelho de Marcos. No artigo intitulado *Problema Sinóptico*, abordamos as origens dos evangelhos. Devemos notar que a vida e as palavras de Jesus não deixaram de ser observadas pelo mundo, e que até hoje o mundo continua a observá-las, e muitos continuam escrevendo a respeito do assunto.

c. Influência da nova religião cristã, e a conseqüente necessidade de novas escrituras. O cristianismo teve por berço o judaísmo, mas desde seus primórdios, os novos elementos dos ensinos de Cristo e dos apóstolos exerceram grande influência sobre os cristãos. Mui dificilmente um judeu estrito

CÂNON DO NOVO TESTAMENTO

aceitaria os ensinamentos de Cristo sobre a lei das cerimônias, sobre o divórcio, etc., mas o mais intragável seria aceitar as declarações de Cristo sobre sua própria pessoa, ou seja, a sua divindade. Jesus mesmo disse: «...edificarei a minha igreja...» Jesus, tal como Lutero, foi separado da organização religiosa, que estava nas mãos das autoridades religiosas da época, e, tal como o mesmo reformador, logo contou com uma igreja estabelecida em seu nome. Nota-se, igualmente, que nas epístolas dos apóstolos, desde o princípio penetraram elementos não-judaicos. Apesar do fato de que, a princípio, o povo cristão tivesse permanecido no seio das sinagogas judaicas, quando Cristo ressuscitou dentre os mortos já havia notáveis dissemelhanças entre os israelitas e os cristãos. A principal diferença era feita pelo próprio Cristo. Ele foi mais do que um reformador. Ele é o Deus-Homem, e com a sua ressurreição provou ser o primeiro homem imortal, tornando-se, dessa maneira, o padrão da vida e do destino de todos os cristãos. Essas explicações encontramos nas palavras de Jesus e dos apóstolos. É natural, pois, que a nova religião cristã tivesse adotado os livros e as epístolas que continham essas diferenças como suas «escrituras sagradas». Pode-se dizer, também, que bastava a existência da nova religião para que também se impusesse a existência de novas «escrituras», que servissem de base à nova religião revelada.

d. Influência dos apóstolos — Não há que duvidar que as epístolas de Paulo, como também as dos demais escritores sagrados, apresentam matéria que eles reputavam ser de inspiração divina. Por muitas vezes Paulo fala das revelações que recebeu, dando a entender que as crenças ali apresentadas não eram propriamente suas. (Ver Gál. 1:8,9,11; Efé. 1:8-11; I Cor. 15:51; II Cor. 12:7-13). Bem cedo muitos denominaram as epístolas de Paulo de *escritura* (ver II Ped. 3:15,16, em combinação com 1:21). O autor do livro de Apocalipse tinha como indiscutível que o seu livro seria considerado parte integrante das escrituras sagradas (ver Apo. 22:19,20).

O parecer de E.J. Goodspeed, de que foi feita uma coletânea de epístolas, mediante um ato excepcional (em 80-85 D.C.), parece mais razoável que a opinião de Harnack e outros, que pensam que o *corpus* dos escritos sagrados foi crescendo gradativamente. A evidência é que muitos elementos influentes da igreja cristã aceitaram pelo menos determinadas epístolas de Paulo, bem como, mui provavelmente, outros livros do N.T., como *escritura* inspirada durante o tempo dos apóstolos. Após o falecimento dos apóstolos, sua influência aumentou,— em vez de diminuir, pelo que foi natural que muitos livros tivessem sido escritos em nome deles, e também que seus escritos autênticos tivessem sido recebidos pela igreja como «escrituras» inspiradas, dotadas de não menor autoridade que o V.T.

Outros argumentos que mostram que no tempo dos apóstolos as suas epístolas já exerciam grande influência e eram extensamente usadas, são os seguintes: Paulo solicitava que as igrejas trocassem de epístolas (ver Col. 4:16). Certas epístolas mostram grande cuidado em sua preparação, como as epístolas aos Romanos e aos Hebreus. É impossível que os autores dessas epístolas pensassem que suas obras seriam lançadas no lixo pelos seus destinatários. O autor do livro de Apocalipse mostra claramente que ele queria que a igreja lesse, cresse e usasse o seu livro. (Ver Apo. 22:18,19). Não é provável que Marcos tivesse composto seu livro, contando a história de «Jesus Cristo», o Filho de Deus, pensando que a igreja haveria de lê-lo apenas por uma vez, para em seguida jogá-lo fora. Não é provável que Lucas tivesse efetuado tanto preparo e pesquisa para escrever seu livro a um oficial do governo romano com a idéia de que os próprios cristãos logo jogariam fora essa magistral obra histórica. Aquele que lê o N.T. pode sentir o forte propósito que seus autores tiveram de estabelecer, comunicar e glorificar a mensagem da nova religião revelada. *Dificilmente* alguém poderia aceitar a idéia de que tudo isso fora fruto de um impulso momentâneo, sem qualquer grande anelo ou finalidade. O fato de que Mateus e Lucas usaram o evangelho de Marcos como alicerce de seus próprios livros mostra que confiavam na veracidade da narrativa apresentada por Marcos. Assim sendo, podemos ver como a influência dos próprios apóstolos e de outras autoridades da igreja primitiva serviu de importante fator na formação do cânon do N.T.

e. Influência dos pais apostólicos, que criaram os cânones primitivos. Marciano, perto do fim do século II D.C., pregou uma doutrina de dois deuses: o Deus do V.T., que seria um Deus de juízo, e o Deus do N.T., que seria um Deus bondoso e misericordioso, e mais exaltado que o primeiro. *Marciano* rejeitava o V.T. como «escritura» autêntica para a igreja, e expôs doutrinas que não podiam ser aceitas pela igreja em geral. Pensava ele que os apóstolos (com exceção de Paulo) tinham pervertido o evangelho que haviam recebido de Jesus. Por esse motivo, Marciano aceitava somente o evangelho de Lucas (que ele modificou onde bem quis) e dez das epístolas de Paulo (ficando omissas Hebreus, I e II Timóteo, Tito e Filemom). Pode-se dizer que esse foi o primeiro cânon do N.T., ainda que não tenha sido aceito pela igreja de modo geral. Outrossim, esse cânon de Marciano foi usado como base para aqueles que se seguiram, a despeito do fato que os pais apostólicos escreveram violentamente contra Marciano. Antes dessa data é certo que algumas das epístolas de Paulo e dos evangelhos eram **usadas e reputadas** como «escritura sagrada», mas até então ninguém se pronunciara a respeito à semelhança de Marciano. Como exemplo disso temos provas de que *Clemente* conhecia os evangelhos e até mesmo os empregou em suas epístolas (90 D.C.). A epístola de II Clemente e a epístola de Barnabé usam porções das epístolas de Paulo (130 D.C.). Provavelmente já se tinham fixado opiniões diversas, entre os pais apostólicos, no tocante a determinadas porções do N.T., como «escritura»; mas foi preciso esperar que Marciano fizesse uma declaração definida e compreensível a respeito. Assim sendo, Marciano é quem forçou os pais da igreja a se pronunciarem.

Irineu de Leão (185 D.C.), em seu livro «*Sabedoria, falsamente chamada*», que refutava o gnosticismo e às vezes é intitulado de «Contra Heresias», mostra que os quatro evangelhos eram recebidos como «escritura», com a autoridade do V.T. Irineu também cita o livro de Atos dos Apóstolos como «escritura». Isso indica que ele também aceitava as epístolas de Paulo, o Apocalipse e algumas das epístolas universais como «escritura sagrada». Contudo, rejeitava a epístola aos Hebreus, por não ter sido escrita por Paulo. Em contraste com a maioria dos pais apostólicos, Irineu citou o Pastor de Hermas como parte das «escrituras» (provavelmente 200 D.C.). O cânon dele se compunha de vinte e dois livros.

Hipólito de Roma (234 D.C.) citou a maior parte do N.T. como *escritura* e também falou de dois «testamentos»—o Velho e o Novo. Também aludiu aos «quatro» evangelhos. Alguns acham que ele é quem fez a lista de livros canônicos encontrada no Fragmento Muratoriano, ainda que não haja provas dessa afirmação.

CÂNON DO NOVO TESTAMENTO

O Cânon Muratoriano (170-210 D.C.). O nome desse fragmento provém do primeiro editor do manuscrito, Ludovico Muratori. Uma lista de livros considerados canônicos foi encontrada em um manuscrito em latim, na cidade de Milão. Essa lista inclui as epístolas de Paulo, duas epístolas de João e uma de Judas, mas não menciona nenhuma das epístolas de Pedro ou a de Tiago. Outros livros aceitos pelo cânon Muratoriano, mas que não temos no cânon atual, são a Sabedoria de Salomão e o Pastor de Hermas, os quais, todavia, não eram recomendados para ser lidos publicamente na igreja. O Fragmento Muratoriano reveste-se de grande importância porque mostra diversas coisas: 1. O desenvolvimento do cânon foi grande antes dessa data. 2. A maior parte dos livros que temos em nosso N.T. já era aceita naquela época. 3. O processo do estabelecimento do cânon ainda estava em desenvolvimento. 4. Havia muitos livros que eram aceitos por alguns, mas não pela igreja em geral.

Tertuliano de Cartago (200 D.C.). Cartago foi o primeiro centro do cristianismo latino que teve um cânon quase igual ao de Irineu. Ambos aceitavam os quatro evangelhos e treze epístolas de Paulo. Em contraste com Irineu, porém, Tertuliano rejeitava o Pastor de Hermas como livro pertencente à coleção sagrada. Pode-se ver, pelos fatos mencionados, que os cânones do N.T., até o fim do século III D.C. — seja, o de Roma, o de Leão e o de Cartago — parecem ter variado um pouco entre si.

Orígenes de Alexandria (254 D.C.). Ele dividia os livros religiosos em duas categorias: os *reconhecidos* e os *discutidos*. Ele mesmo aceitava a todos, mas admitia que nem todos concordavam com a sua opinião. Os livros reconhecidos eram: os quatro evangelhos, catorze epístolas de Paulo (incluindo a epístola aos Hebreus), o livro de Atos, duas epístolas universais, I Pedro, I João e o Apocalipse de João — ao todo, vinte e dois livros. Os livros discutidos eram: a epístola de Tiago e é notável que nenhum escritor antigo tenha incluído essa epístola em seu «cânon» do N.T., o que se prolongou até o tempo da reforma, porquanto o próprio Lutero chamou-a de «epístola de palha», II e III João, II Pedro, Judas, epístola de Barnabé e o Pastor de Hermas.

O Codex Claromontano, do século VI D.C., é um manuscrito grego e latino do N.T. que tem uma lista de livros canônicos que não contém a epístola aos Hebreus, e, sim, o Pastor de Hermas, os Atos de Paulo e o Apocalipse de Pedro. As divergências nos cânones muitas vezes dependiam da geografia. Por exemplo, a igreja siríaca aceitava o livro chamado de *Evangelho segundo os Hebreus*, e também uma outra pseudoepístola de Paulo, III Coríntios; — mas o Apocalipse de João só foi aceito ali bem mais tarde. A opinião da igreja cristã de Alexandria parece ter sido idêntica à de Orígenes. A igreja de Roma e de outras regiões ocidentais provavelmente considerava que o cânon do N.T. incluía os livros que apareciam na tradução latina. Assim sendo, figuravam ali os quatro evangelhos, treze epístolas de Paulo, as três epístolas universais de João, I Pedro, Judas e o Apocalipse de João. Mais tarde a epístola aos Hebreus também veio fazer parte do «cânon», mas na antiga versão latina faltavam II Pedro e Tiago. A versão etíope contava com todos os vinte e sete livros do N.T. que temos hoje em dia, além de mais outros sete, que eram as epístolas de Clemente e outros livros que coletivamente eram chamados *Sínodo*, e que incluem o Apocalipse de Pedro. Além desses, algumas pessoas, ainda que não toda a igreja cristã, aceitavam mais oito livros, intitulados «Constituições Apostólicas», publicados em nome de Clemente, os quais continham diversas leis eclesiásticas.

Eusébio. As opiniões mantidas pela igreja em geral, até o século IV D.C., se refletem no resumo preparado por Eusébio, o pai da história eclesiástica, cuja história foi terminada em 326 D.C. Ele dividiu a lista em três porções: 1. Livros *reconhecidos* (homologoumena); 2. Livros *discutidos* (antilegomena); 3. Livros *espúrios* (notha).

Os «reconhecidos» eram — os quatro evangelhos, Atos dos Apóstolos, catorze epístolas de Paulo, I Pedro, I João, e de acordo com alguns, o Apocalipse de João.

Os «discutidos» eram — Tiago, Judas, II Pedro e II e III João.

Os «espúrios» eram — Atos de Paulo, Pastor de Hermas, Apocalipse de Pedro, a epístola de Barnabé, o Didache, o evangelho segundo os Hebreus, e de acordo com alguns, o Apocalipse de João.

Eusébio fez uma lista de livros que considerava terem sido produzidos só a interesse das opiniões hereges, que por isso mesmo não figuravam nem entre os livros espúrios. Essa última lista incluía o evangelho de Tomé, o evangelho de Pedro, o evangelho de Matias, os Atos de André e João e outros livros apócrifos.

Fixação do Cânon — Foi no século IV D.C. que o cânon *se fixou* de forma quase universal, com Atanásio de Alexandria (325 D.C.). Naquele tempo, o «cânon» passou a incluir os vinte e sete livros que temos hoje em nosso N.T. Um dos proeminentes personagens do cristianismo egípcio foi Atanásio bispo de Alexandria depois do concílio de Nicéia (325 D.C.). Ele ocupou essa posição por quase cinqüenta anos. Era costume seu enviar cartas às igrejas de sua diocese, por ocasião da Páscoa. No ano de 367 D.C. ele enviou uma carta (Carta Pascal 39) estabelecendo a lista de livros sagrados que deveriam ser lidos nas igrejas. Essa lista era exatamente a mesma que contém os atuais vinte e sete livros do N.T. Além desses livros, Atanásio «recomendava» a leitura de Ensino (Didache) dos Apóstolos e do Pastor de Hermas, mas como literatura benéfica, e não como livros inspirados divinamente como os demais. Outros livros que ele reputava como proveitosos, como literatura, foram a Sabedoria de Salomão, a Sabedoria de Siraque, Ester (com as adições gregas), Judite e Tobias (livros apócrifos do V.T.). E assim ficou firmado o «cânon» nas igrejas cristãs do Oriente.

No Ocidente e em outros lugares a fixação do «cânon» foi feita por decisão de *concílios*, em Cartago, em 397 D.C., quando uma lista, idêntica a de Atanásio, foi aprovada. Ao mesmo tempo, autores latinos mostraram interesse pelo problema e fixaram os limites do cânon como já haviam feito Atanásio e o concílio de Cartago. Esses autores latinos foram Prisciliano, na Espanha, Rufino de Aquiléia, na Gália e Agostinho, na África do Norte, cujas opiniões exerceram forte influência na decisão a que se chegou em Cartago. A versão de Jerônimo — a Vulgata Latina — tornou-se a Bíblia padrão da Europa ocidental. Essa versão continha os mesmos vinte e sete livros que hoje temos no N.T.

f. Influência dos concílios da igreja primitiva e medieval — Os concílios também exerceram influência na formação do «cânon» do N.T. Pode-se dizer que os concílios não formaram o cânon, mas tão-somente tiveram a função de declarar a opinião geral das igrejas, em diversas partes do mundo, servindo, por isso mesmo, para consolidarem e oficializarem essas opiniões.

CÂNON DO NOVO TESTAMENTO

O concílio de *Laodicéia*, 363 D.C., proibiu o uso dos livros não canônicos, pelo que é provável que uma lista determinada, como aquela que conhecemos atualmente, tenha sido aprovada. (Foram aceitos todos os nossos vinte e sete livros, com exceção do Apocalipse).

O concílio de *Hipona*, na África, 393 D.C., aceitou todos os vinte e sete livros que temos hoje em dia.

O concílio de *Cartago*, em 397 D.C., aprovou esses vinte e sete livros.

O concílio de *Cartago*, em 419 D.C. confirmou essa posição, mas separou a epístola aos Hebreus dos escritos de Paulo, não aceitando a idéia que Paulo foi quem a escrevera. Agostinho foi um dos principais personagens desses dois concílios.

O concílio de *Nicéia*, 325 D.C., aceitou o cânon de Atanásio (todos os atuais vinte e sete livros do N.T.).

Eusébio, Bispo de Cesaréia, na Palestina, aceitou essa decisão do concílio de Nicéia, mas não sem fazer algumas restrições.

Crisóstomo, patriarca de Constantinopla, autor de muitos comentários, e que foi a principal *força influenciadora* na igreja do Oriente ao seu tempo (398 D.C.), aceitava os quatro evangelhos, o livro de Atos, catorze epístolas de Paulo, três epístolas universais (mas não II Pedro, I e II João, Tiago e Judas ou o Apocalipse). Esse é o chamado «cânon» Peshitto (versão siríaca), que reflete a tradição de Antioquia. Esse era o *cânon* daquela parte do mundo, a despeito da falta de qualquer decisão oficial, tomada em concílio.

O concílio de Trento, da igreja Romana (1546) aceitou a Bíblia tal como a temos hoje em dia, mas, no V.T. incluiu vários livros apócrifos.

Os cristãos protestantes, principalmente sob a influência de Lutero e de sua tradução da Bíblia para o alemão, aceitavam a Bíblia tal como a encontramos hoje—sem os livros apócrifos do V.T. A Igreja Anglicana (1562) rejeitou oficialmente esses livros apócrifos, e aceitou todos os outros sem levantar dúvidas.

É fato bem conhecido que fora dos concílios, muitos indivíduos, em particular, incluindo entre eles até mesmo muitos líderes da igreja, durante a Idade Média e até o tempo da Reforma, não aceitavam certos livros, ou pelo menos não lhes davam o mesmo valor que emprestavam a outros. Por exemplo, *Lutero* rejeitou as epístolas de Tiago e de Judas (considerando esta última uma cópia inexata de II Pedro), e considerou que a epístola aos Hebreus não era de origem apostólica. Até mesmo entre as epístolas de Paulo ele estabeleceu categorias de valores, considerando mais as epístolas aos Romanos, aos Gálatas e aos Efésios. O evangelho de João era o que merecia sua maior consideração. *Carlstadt*, contemporâneo de Lutero e líder protestante, dividiu os livros sagrados do N.T., em três categorias diversas. *Zwinglio*, líder do protestantismo suíço, rejeitou o livro de Apocalipse mas aceitou as epístolas de Tiago e aos Hebreus. *Calvino* rejeitou II e III João e o Apocalipse, e reservava certas dúvidas quanto a II Pedro. Aceitou as epístolas de Judas e Tiago, mas aludiu ao fato que muitos nutriam dúvidas a respeito delas.

g. A posição moderna—Os grupos conservadores, tanto dentre os protestantes como dentre os católicos, aceitam o «cânon» do N.T. conforme foi estabelecido pelos antigos. Os representantes da teologia liberal, por sua vez, não estão tentando criar um novo «cânon», a despeito do fato que provavelmente nutrem dúvidas sobre a validade do cânon atual. Realmente, há toda forma de idéias sobre o «cânon» como sempre aconteceu desde o princípio de sua formação. Certos indivíduos conservadores em todos os outros pontos de vista, não aceitam determinados livros do N.T., usualmente um ou mais dos mesmos livros discutidos pelos antigos, a saber: Tiago, II Pedro, II e III João, Hebreus, Judas e Apocalipse. Muitos estudiosos, principalmente liberais, acreditam que certos livros aceitos nos tempos antigos e na Idade Média como apostólicos, em realidade não o são, como II Pedro, Hebreus, Apocalipse e Tiago. A maior parte dos conservadores aceita a epístola aos Hebreus como canônica, mas rejeita a idéia de que foi Paulo quem a escreveu. Todas as idéias modernas em realidade são muito antigas, pois toda essa variedade de opiniões surgiu desde o princípio da formação do «cânon». Porém, quando se fala de grupos religiosos ou denominações, então a *fixação* do cânon do século XVI permanece até o dia de hoje.

3. Resumo da História do Cânon

a. Durante o *tempo dos apóstolos*, algumas das epístolas de Paulo e um ou mais evangelhos já eram aceitos como *Escritura*.

b. Já no *começo do século II D.C.*, de modo geral, ainda não universal, treze epístolas de Paulo eram recebidas como Escrituras, como também os quatro evangelhos, as epístolas de I João e I Pedro, e também o livro de Apocalipse—totalizando vinte livros ou mais. Irineu aceitava vinte e dois livros (185). Alguns livros não aceitos hoje em dia foram aceitos por certos elementos dos primeiros séculos, especialmente a epístola de Barnabé, as epístolas de Clemente e o Pastor de Hermas.

c. *Durante o século III D.C.*, eram aceitos quase universalmente todos os vinte e sete livros do N.T., com a exceção da epístola de Tiago. Contudo, alguns aceitavam essa epístola também. Orígenes foi o primeiro dos pais da igreja a aceitar a epístola de Tiago (254 D.C.), mas também aceitava a epístola de Barnabé e o Pastor de Hermas, pelo que o seu N.T. constava de vinte e nove livros.

d. *No século IV D.C.*, chegou-se à fixação quase universal do *cânon do N.T.*, tal como existe hoje em dia.

e. *Os concílios*, tanto os antigos como os da Idade Média, em geral aprovaram o cânon de vinte e sete livros, tal como o conhecemos na atualidade.

f. *Indivíduos* da antiguidade, da Idade Média e dos tempos modernos retiveram e retêm diversas opiniões, especialmente com relação aos *livros discutidos*: Tiago, II Pedro, II e III João, Hebreus, Judas e Apocalipse — ao todo, *sete* livros.

4. Princípios que Formaram o Cânon

a. *Circulação universal*. Alguns livros jamais foram aceitos por falta de circulação, enquanto outros foram aceitos tariamente por falta de circulação na igreja universal, pois circulavam somente em *certos setores* da igreja.

b. *Autoria dos apóstolos* ou dos discípulos dos apóstolos. Dentre os apóstolos temos as epístolas de Paulo e Pedro, e o evangelho de João. Dentre os discípulos temos os evangelhos de Marcos e de Lucas, o livro de Atos, a epístola aos Hebreus, etc.

c. *Livros segundo a tradição e a doutrina dos Apóstolos*: Lucas, Atos, Hebreus, Apocalipse e II Pedro.

d. *Houve rejeição* de livros escritos mais tarde, após o tempo dos apóstolos. Isso explica a rejeição final das epístolas de Clemente, etc.

CÂNON DO NOVO TESTAMENTO

e. *Também foram rejeitados* os escritos ridículos ou fabulosos. Entre esses podemos enumerar a maior parte dos livros apócrifos, o evangelho de Tomé, os evangelhos de André, os Atos de Paulo, o Apocalipse de Pedro, etc.

f. *Houve rejeição* de literatura escrita que visava a propagar *heresias*, como o evangelho de Tomé, diversos outros evangelhos, epístolas falsas e apócrifas. Ver detalhes no artigo sobre *Livros Apócrifos*.

g. *Uso universal* por parte da igreja inteira. Alguns livros foram aceitos apenas por determinados setores da igreja, ou somente por alguns indivíduos. Finalmente, os vinte e sete livros atuais do N.T. foram aceitos e passaram a ser universalmente usados na igreja cristã.

5. Ó Problema da Autoridade quanto à Determinação da Verdade

A questão que envolve o *cânon* obviamente está envolvida no problema geral que investiga as autoridades nas quais alicerçamos a verdade e a busca pela mesma. Na Igreja cristã inteira, as Sagradas Escrituras ocupam o lugar primordial na hierarquia de autoridades que apóiam a verdade; e, em alguns segmentos da Igreja cristã (protestantes e evangélicos), ocupam o único lugar. Mesmo assim, é mister qualificar essa afirmativa. Provi um detalhado artigo intitulado *Autoridade*, que procura mostrar que há certa variedade de autoridades quanto à verdade, e onde enfatizei a posição das Escrituras Sagradas entre essas autoridades.

GRÁFICO QUE ILUSTRA A DIVERSIDADE DAS AUTORIDADES QUE EXISTEM

• • •   • • •   • • •

CÂNON DO NOVO TESTAMENTO

O CÂNON DO NOVO TESTAMENTO

6. Os Livros Controvertidos nos Pais, Concílios e Catálogos

CHAVE:
- = coincidência verbal
- • citação direta
- ** evidência não conclusiva
- ? expressão de dúvida quanto à posição no •cânon•
- ! clara rejeição
- ?? referência incerta

DATA	PAI	EPIS. HEBREUS	JUDAS	TIAGO	2 e 3 JOÃO	2 PED.	APOCALIPSE	EP. BARN.	PASTOR HERM.	EP. CLEM.	APOC. PEDRO
96	Clemente de Roma	= Ep. 36 etc. cf. Hieron. de vir. ill. 15									
125	Policarpo	= Apol. i:12.63		= Ep. 10.38		= Ep. 11					
150	Justino Mártir					= Ep. 3	• Dial. 81				
180	Irineu	! Eus. H.E. v:26		?? Adv. Haer. iv: 16.2	• Adv. Haer. ii:16.3			• Adv. H.v: 35. Cf. Eus. H.E. V:8	• Adv. H.iv: 20.2. Cf. Eus. H.E. V-8		
200	Clemente de Alexandria	• Strom. vi:8 par. 62. cf. Eus. H.E. vi:14	• Str.ii:? par.11. Cf. Eus. H.E. vi:13		** Cf. Eus. H.E. vi:14	** Str.15.p.66 vi:14			• Strom. ii: 6. par.31. Cf. Eus H.E. vi:13	• Strom. i:29 par.107. Cf. Eus. H.E. vi:13	• Strom.:17 par. 181	** Cf. Eus. H.E. vi:13
200	Tertuliano	? De pudic.20 Barnabé	• de Hab. mul.3					• Adv. Marc. iii:14			
225	Orígenes	•Ap. Eus. H.E. vi:25	? Comm. in Mt. x par.17 ! Id.T. xvii:3	? Comm. in Joann. xix:6 ! Sel. in Sal. xxx	** Hom. in Joss.vii:1	! Hom. in Jos. vii:1. in Lev.iv:4 Cf. Sel. in Ps.iii		• Ap. Eus.H.E. vi:25.Comm. in J. i 14	• C. Cels.i:63	• Prnc. iii:3 Comm. in Rom. xvi:14	! Sel. in Eze. viii
250	Dionísio Alexandria	•Ap. Eus. H. E. vi:41		= Comm. in Luc. xxii:46			? Ap. Eus. H.E. vii:25	• Eus. H.E. vii:10 ? H. E. vii:24			
250	Cipriano	! De exh. mart.11						• De op et eleem.14			
225	Hipólito	! Phot. 121						• De Antic. 36			
300	Metódio	= De Resur.5.p.269 Conv.:5:7						• De Resur. 9, par.315; Conv. viii:4. p.143			
325	Eusébio	• Ecl. Proph. 1:25 Cf.H.E. iii.3		? H.E. iii:25	? H.E. iii:25	? H.E. iii:25	? H.E. iii:25		! H.E. iii:25	! H.E. iii:25	! H.E. iii:25

638

CÂNON DO NOVO TESTAMENTO

O CÂNON DO NOVO TESTAMENTO

CHAVE: Ver a página anterior

OS CONCÍLIOS E CATÁLOGOS
Atinentes aos Livros Disputados

CATÁLOGO e DATA	HEBREUS	JUDAS	TIAGO	2, 3 JOÃO	2 PED.	APOCALIPSE	EPIST. BARN.	PASTOR HERMAS	EPIST. CLEM.	APOC. PEDRO
1. Catálogos Conciliares:										
Laodicéia 364	•	•	•	•	•					
Cartago 419	•	•	•	•	•	•				
II. Catálogos Orientais.										
1. SIRIA:										
Peshitto 420	•		•							
Junilio 550	•	?•	?•	?•	?•	?•				
João Damasceno 750	•	•	•	•	•	•				
Ebed Jesu 1285	•	•	•	•	•	•				
2. PALESTINA:										
Eusébio 325	•	?•	?•	?•	?•	?•				
Cirilo 360	•	•	•	•	•					
Epifânio 400	•	•	•	•	•	•				
3. ALEXANDRIA:										
Orígenes 250	•	?•	•	?•	?•	•	•	•		
Atanásio 350	•	•	•	•	•	•		•		
4. ÁSIA MENOR:										
Gregório Nazianzeno 340		•	•	•	•					
Anfilóquio 374		•	•	•	•	•				
5. CONSTANTINOPLA:										
Crisóstomo 400	•									
Leôncio 540	•	•	•	•	•	•				
Nicéforo 800		?•	?•	?•	?•	?•	?•	?•	?•	?•

CÂNON DO NOVO TESTAMENTO

O CÂNON DO NOVO TESTAMENTO

	HEBREUS	JUDAS	TIAGO	2, 3 JOÃO	APOCALIPSE	EPIST. BARN.	PASTOR HERMAS	EPIST. CLEM.	APOC. PEDRO
II. Catálogos Ocidentais:									
1. ÁFRICA									
Cód. Claromont.	??	•	•		•	•	•		•
(D. Paulus VI)									
Agostinho 400		•	•	•	•				
2. ITÁLIA:									
Cân. Murat. 170		•	•	??	•		—	—	
Filástrio 400		•	•	•	•				
Jerônimo 400		•	•	•	•				
Rufino 400		•	•	•	•				
Inocente 417		•	•	•	•				
Gelásio 470		•	•	•	•				
Cassiodoro 550		•	•	•	•				
3. ESPANHA:									
Isidoro de Sevilha 608	•		•	•	•				

7. Bibliografia: AM BLM E EN GD(1926) ND SO WIK(1958) Z

CÂNON HINDU
Ver o artigo sobre as **Shastras** e sobre os **Vedas**.

CÂNON ISLÂMICO
Ver o artigo sobre a **Sunna**.

CÂNONES
Vários artigos são apresentados com o título no plural, que se seguem.

CÂNONES ANGLICANOS
A revisão da Lei Canônica (que vide), ordenada em 1534, nunca foi terminada, embora tivesse sido publicada uma minuta da mesma, em 1571, intitulada *Reformatio legum ecclesiasticaram*. Em 1604, as Convocações Inglesas adotaram um código de cânones que abarcava as porções mais praticamente necessárias das legislações eclesiásticas das épocas medieval e posteriores. Esse código foi levemente emendado a partir de 1865; mas foi mais fortemente afetado por uma decisão legal, tomada em 1736, que negava o poder da Convocação Inglesa de tornar esse código obrigatório para os leigos. Fora da Inglaterra, as várias Igrejas Anglicanas nacionais, formando sociedades voluntárias, têm preparado os seus próprios códigos, os quais, usualmente, apelam para os cânones medievais e para o cânon de 1604, como precedentes. Os cânones norte-americanos foram publicados pela primeira vez em 1789, os quais têm sido emendados com certa freqüência. (E)

CÂNONES DE VÁRIAS IGREJAS
Podemos alistar dez deles:

1. O cânon *judaico-palestino:* os tradicionais trinta e nove livros do Antigo Testamento hebraico.
2. O cânon *alexandrino*, ou da LXX, usado pelo judaísmo da dispersão. Incluía os trinta e nove livros do Antigo Testamento e os livros apócrifos.
3. O cânon do *catolicismo romano*. Consiste, essencialmente, no cânon alexandrino, adotado em 1546 pelo concílio de Trento (que vide), além dos vinte e sete livros do Novo Testamento e da *Lei Canônica*, dos pronunciamentos dos pais da Igreja, dos papas e dos concílios.
4. O cânon *protestante*, que consiste no cânon palestino (nº 1, acima), além dos vinte e sete livros do Novo Testamento; e também várias coleções de cânones, que não são consideradas de igual importância em relação às Escrituras.
5. A *Igreja Ortodoxa Oriental*, quando do sínodo de Jerusalém, em 1672, outorgou estado canônico aos livros Sabedoria de Salomão, Eclesiástico, Tobias e Judite. O *codex Vaticanus* (ver o artigo sobre os *Manuscritos*), interpola esses quatro livros aos outros trinta e nove livros do Antigo Testamento. O codex Alexandrinus faz o mesmo, com adições aos livros de Jeremias, Daniel e Ester, além dos livros de Tobias, Judite e I-IV Macabeus. Em sua tradução para o inglês, Wyclif incluiu III Esdras, Tobias, Judite, Sabedoria de Salomão, Eclesiástico e Baruque. Os vinte e sete livros do Novo Testamento são considerados autoritários no Oriente, mas o livro de Apocalipse não é usado na adoração. Os 85 cânones dos Santos Apóstolos desfrutam de posição canônica na Igreja Ortodoxa, como também vários escritos de patriarcas ortodoxos. Também há um considerável acúmulo de leis (cânones) civis e religiosas, de várias épocas, leis essas tidas como obrigatórias para os fiéis.
6. A *Igreja Anglicana* tem por cânon o códice palestino, mas com elevado respeito pelo cânon alexandrino que, normalmente, era exibido na época pelo protestantismo. Esse respeito considera os livros apócrifos dotados de valor moral e ilustrativo, embora não doutrinário. Os vinte e sete livros do Novo Testamento são autoritários. Quando da Convocação de Canterbury, em 1604, foram aceitos como obrigatórios 141 cânones; e novos cânones podem ser adicionados por ato de duas convocações. Outras igrejas da comunidade anglicana têm traçado seus próprios cânones. Estritamente falando, a Igreja Anglicana não reconhece qualquer dos cânones anteriores à Reforma, embora tenha incorporado a substância dos mesmos em compilações mais modernas.
7. A *Igreja Etiópia* conta com um extenso cânon, verdadeiramente. Quanto ao Antigo Testamento, aceita alguns dos livros apócrifos do Antigo Testamento e os pseudepígrafos, com um total de quarenta e seis livros. Quanto ao Novo Testamento, há ali trinta e cinco livros!
8. As *Igrejas Nestoriana e Síria* não acolhem os livros de II e III João, II Pedro, Judas e Apocalipse; mas a Igreja Síria usa III Coríntios, o Testamento do Senhor e seis livros de Clemente.
9. A *Igreja Armênia*, em 1276, além do cânon alexandrino e dos vinte e sete livros do Novo Testamento, acrescentou os cinco livros de Clemente e Ananaias de Damasco, os dois livros dos cânones dos Apóstolos, três sermões de Justo, quatro livros de Dionísio, o Aeropagita, e cinco livros da Pregação de Pedro.
10. A *Igreja Cóptica* não usa o livro de Apocalipse em sua adoração, mas faz uso dos escritos dos pais apostólicos, alguns evangelhos e atos apócrifos, homilias dos pais gregos, etc. (AM E)

CANONIZAÇÃO
Dentro do catolicismo romano, esse é o nome dado ao decreto que inclui uma pessoa no catálogo ou cânon dos santos, os quais são recomendados à veneração dos fiéis. Para tanto, a pessoa precisa ter sido beatificada (que vide), e pelo menos dois de seus milagres devem ter sido confirmados, realizados através da presumível ajuda da pessoa que então é canonizada. A pessoa a ser canonizada precisa já haver falecido. E o papa proclama, oficialmente, a canonização. (E P)

CANTAR DO GALO
Na antiguidade era uma designação de tempo, a saber, a terceira vigília da noite, ou seja, da meia-noite às três horas da madrugada. Na época de Jesus, a noite era dividida em quatro vigílias, de acordo com o costume romano, designadas com os termos gerais de primeira vigília, meia-noite, cantar do galo e manhã cedo. Cada um dos evangelistas refere-se ao cantar do galo em conexão com a negação de Cristo por parte de Pedro. Ver Mat. 26:34,37; Mar. 14:30; Luc. 22:34; João 13:18. Alguns intérpretes têm pensado que o autor sagrado aponta para um cantar do galo meramente literário, como um artifício de adorno, ao passo que outros supõem que algum galo especial teria sido preparado pela providência divina para cantar na hora certa. Mas a verdade mais provável é que Jesus fez uma espécie de alusão geral ao tempo em que Pedro haveria de negá-lo. Os intérpretes não concordam quanto ao sentido exato da expressão. Ver o artigo sobre o *Galo*,

quanto a outros detalhes. Ver também o artigo sobre *Vigília*.

CANTARES DE SALOMÃO
Ver **Salomão, Cantares de**

CÂNTARO
Heb. **kad**, usada catorze vezes com esse sentido: Gên 25:14-28,43,45,46; Juí. 7:16,19,20; Ecl. 12:6. No N.T., gr. *kerámion*: Mar. 14:3 e Luc. 22:10.

A palavra hebraica deriva-se de uma raiz que significa «aprofundar», relacionada ao costume de puxar água de poços, por meio de cântaros, um costume prevalente até hoje nos países do Oriente. O cântaro geralmente tinha duas asas, uma de cada lado. Odres feitos com peles de animais eram usados com idêntico propósito. Ver Gên. 24:14-16 quanto à narrativa sobre Rebeca, e como ela foi escolhida para ser a esposa de Isaque. A narrativa envolve o uso de cântaros. A força de ataque, escolhida por Gideão, escondeu tochas dentro de cântaros, até o momento exato do ataque (Juí. 7:16-20). Puxar água de um poço era um trabalho árduo, como também era penoso transportar água dos poços até às residências. Geralmente os cântaros eram levados aos ombros ou na cabeça. Em Lamentações 4:2 é empregada uma outra palavra hebraica, *nebel*, mas que a nossa versão portuguesa prefere traduzir por «objetos de barro», em vez de dar a tradução mais certa, «jarra». Nos trechos de Marcos 14:13 e Lucas 22:10 é usado o termo grego *kerámion*, de onde provém nossa moderna palavra portuguesa «cerâmica». Portanto, temos nessas duas passagens uma alusão a cântaros de barro.

Usos Figurados. O trecho de Eclesiastes 12:6 usa a figura de um cântaro partido para indicar a cessação da vida física. Ali também encontramos o rompimento do fio de prata, que indica a mesma coisa. Ver o artigo sobre o *Fio de Prata*. Em Lam. 4:2, vasos de barro são contrastados com vasos de ouro: o ouro indica o real valor dos filhos de Sião, em contraste com a avaliação dos homens acerca deles, que fazia dos israelitas apenas vasos de barro. Os vasos de barro aludem à fragilidade do homem, sempre sujeito a danos e à morte. O nono capítulo da epístola aos Romanos tem a imagem do oleiro e seus vasos, ilustrando a soberania de Deus.

CANTATA
No século XVII, a **cantata** era uma série de árias para uma ou duas vozes em solo, acompanhadas por uma espineta ou outro instrumento musical, como o oboé, violoncelos ou alaúde. Os músicos que empregaram essa forma foram Carissimi, Alessandro, Domenico Scarlatti e Handel. As cantatas religiosas do século XVIII atingiram o seu ponto culminante nas 295 cantatas de Bach (que vide). Em cerca de quarenta delas, Bach usou somente a voz de um solo, mas também empregou um acompanhamento orquestrado. Essas obras usualmente são abertas com um numeroso coro, continuam com uma série de recitais e árias e terminam com um simples coral, do qual a congregação faz parte. A cantata moderna utiliza-se do coro em maior escala, podendo ser uma cantata sacra, como um pequeno oratório (que vide), ou secular, como um drama lírico ou uma estória, mas que não tem por intuito ser encenada. (E)

CÂNTICO, CANTORES
Ver **Música, Instrumentos Musicais e Louvor**.

CÂNTICO DOS CÂNTICOS, Ver **Salomão, Cânticos de**.

CÂNTICO DOS TRÊS JOVENS Ver **Cânticos dos Três Jovens**.

CÂNTICO GREGORIANO
Esse tipo de cântico não é simétrico, podendo ser cantado como solo ou em vozes em uníssono, com o acompanhamento ou não de instrumentos musicais. O cântico gregoriano conta com mais de seiscentas composições musicais sobre textos bíblicos. Esses cânticos foram iniciados por Ambrósio (que vide), bispo de Milão, no século IV D.C. Para os mesmos contribuiu também o papa Gregório I (que vide), nos fins do século VI D.C.

O cântico gregoriano, além de ser um estilo musical todo próprio, também contribuiu para outras composições musicais polifônicas durante todo o século XII D.C., e mesmo posteriormente. A maneira original de se executar a música gregoriana foi reavivada nos fins do século XIX, por Dom Mocquereau, na abadia beneditina de Solesmes, na França. Em 1904, o papa Pio X (que vide), ordenou o retorno do uso do cântico gregoriano na Igreja Católica Romana, embora sem a exclusão das demais formas de música sacra.

CÂNTICO SIMPLES
Uma antiga forma de cântico, usada em algum culto cristão, em uníssono e sem métrica. Muitos antigos pensavam que o ritmo, em uma música, pertencesse ao diabo, o que explicava o esforço para cantar sem qualquer ritmo. O cântico simples é apenas um outro nome para o cântico gregoriano (que vide), quanto a maiores detalhes.

CÂNTICOS
São hinos de louvor, com base em textos bíblicos, excetuando os Salmos, entoados na liturgia da Igreja Católica Romana. Entre os mais familiares cânticos temos o *Nunc dimittis* (Luc. 2:29), o *Benedicite omnia opera* (Dan. 3:27), o *Magnificat* (Luc. 1:46) e o *Benedictus Dominus Deus Israel* (Luc. 1:68).

CÂNTICOS DA BENDITA VIRGEM
Trata-se do **Magnificat** (que vide), encontrado no trecho de Lucas 1:46-55, entoado ou recitado diariamente como vespertinos (que vide).

CÂNTICOS DOS CÂNTICOS
Ver **Salomão, Cantares de**

CÂNTICOS DOS DEGRAUS
Ver sobre **Instrumentos Musicais**.

CÂNTICOS DOS TRÊS JOVENS
Uma das adições gregas ao livro de Daniel. Em grego, o título dessa adição é *Ymnos tōn triōn paídon*, «Hino das três crianças». Juntamente com a chamada Oração de Azarias, esse acréscimo não é propriamente um apêndice, mas uma inserção suplementar, entre Daniel 3:23 e 3:24, segundo a Septuaginta. Esses dois blocos de material acrescido, vinculados por uma curta ponte narrativa, formam um livro separado das obras apócrifas. Mas, na Vulgata Latina (tal como na Septuaginta), esse material encontra-se no terceiro capítulo do livro canônico de Daniel.

Após a chamada Oração de Azarias, o editor observa que o fogo dentro do qual os três jovens

CÂNTICOS — CAOS

haviam sido lançados continuou a ser atiçado, tornando-se tão intenso que queimou aqueles que estavam próximos da fornalha, mas que o anjo do Senhor veio proteger os três jovens (vs. 23-27). Alguns estudiosos, todavia, perguntam se essa porção da narrativa não faria parte do texto massorético. Em seguida, é dito sobre os três jovens que eles cantaram «como que a uma boca», em uma grandiosa doxologia.

Esse hino de louvor, após uma secção introdutória (vs. 29-34), gira em torno das palavras reiteradas, «Bendizei ao Senhor», seguidas pelo refrão «cantai-lhe louvores, e exaltai-o para sempre», o qual ocorre em um padrão idêntico por trinta e duas vezes em sucessão (excetuando uma leve variação no vs. 52). Isso faz-nos lembrar de um ritmo litúrgico em Salmos 136, onde o refrão reiterado é «porque a sua misericórdia dura para sempre». A idéia de que todas as várias obras do Senhor devem bendizê-lo ou louvá-lo bem pode ter-se derivado da mesma idéia, no Salmo 148. O Cântico dos Três Jovens encontrou lugar permanente na liturgia da cristandade, tendo sido também incluído no Livro de Oração Comum, onde aparece no Culto Matutino como alternativa do *Te Deum*.

No Cântico (vs. 66), há referência aos nomes dos três jovens israelitas, os quais louvaram ao Senhor por haverem sido libertados de morrerem na fornalha ardente. Todavia, é provável que esse versículo tenha sido uma adição feita pelo editor, o qual foi responsável pela inserção desse material no terceiro capítulo do livro canônico de Daniel. Esse jubiloso louvor do Cântico faz notável contraste com a oração penitencial que o antecede, pelo que qualquer conexão essencial entre esses dois blocos de material parece fora de cogitação. O Cântico, tal como a Oração, foi composto independentemente, ou seja, sem qualquer vinculação com a narrativa de Daniel propriamente dita, parecendo derivar-se mais de uma época em que o povo de Israel sentia-se muito grato diante das bênçãos divinas que cumulavam a sua nação. Por essa razão, alguns eruditos têm sugerido o período da restauração dos Macabeus, embora isso não passe de mera sugestão. Se a data da composição do Cântico dos Três Jovens é desconhecida, igualmente ninguém sabe dizer quem foi o seu autor, embora não seja improvável que esse autor desconhecido tenha escrito a peça, originalmente, em hebraico.

O Cântico dos Três Jovens, antecedido pela Oração de Azarias, é disponível como uma entidade separada, na coleção das obras apócrifas. O texto grego (a Septuaginta e a recensão de Teodócio concordam bem de perto um com o outro) aparece na edição comum da Septuaginta, como porção integrante do terceiro capítulo do livro de Daniel, mas também como uma das odes coligidas (edit. Alfred Rahlfs, vol. II), e que geralmente aparecem como apêndices do livro de Salmos. A Igreja Católica Romana aceita o Cântico dos Três Jovens como uma porção canônica do terceiro capítulo do livro de Daniel. Ver sobre *Azarias, Oração de*.

CANTO

Vem do latim, **cantus**. O canto é uma antiga forma de música eclesiástica simples, usada para entoar hinos e cânticos. O canto normalmente usado na Igreja latina é o canto gregoriano (que vide). Deriva o nome do papa Gregório o Grande, a quem a tradição atribui a introdução do canto. O canto anglicano é um tanto mais elaborado e métrico. Ver o artigo sobre *Música e Instrumentos Musicais*. A substância dos cantos eclesiásticos é extraída dos textos bíblicos, adaptados a essa forma de música.

CANTOR

Palavra derivada do termo assírio **hazzan**, «supervisor», e que, originalmente, entre os judeus, designava o *servo* da sinagoga. É o cantor quem lidera a congregação nas orações.

CÃO, FILHO DE NOÉ

Este artigo refere-se ao filho mais novo de Noé, aos seus descendentes e a uma cidade.

1. *Cão, Filho de Noé*. No hebraico, seu nome, *ham*, significa «queimado», «moreno». Era o mais jovem dos três filhos de Noé (Gên. 5:32). Já era casado na época do dilúvio. Juntamente com sua esposa, foi salvo da destruição, na arca. Terminado o dilúvio, provocou a ira de seu pai por um ato de indecência, tendo sido castigado por meio de uma predição de longo alcance (Gên. 9:21 ss). Segundo essa profecia, os descendentes de Cão seriam escravos dos descendentes de seus dois irmãos. A Bíblia atribui todos os povos atualmente existentes no mundo a esses três irmãos. Na tabela das nações, em Gên. 10:6-10, Cão é apresentado como o antepassado dos egípcios e dos povos sob o controle egípcio, no nordeste da África, além de certas porções da Arábia e a terra de Canaã, com a exceção de Ninrode. Por causa da conexão entre o nome de Cão e a África, alguns intérpretes têm pensado que o comércio escravagista, que envolveu os africanos já nos tempos modernos, além do fato de que os povos negros têm sido, de modo geral, subservientes a outros povos, resultam da maldição lançada contra Canaã, descendente de Cão. Outros estudiosos não podem ver nenhum sentido nisso. Os intérpretes liberais supõem que a tabela das nações, no livro de Gênesis, não passa de uma criação da imaginação piedosa dos homens, sem qualquer base na antropologia científica.

O adjetivo «camita» é usado pelos estudiosos modernos para referir-se a um grupo de idiomas, entre os quais destaca-se o egípcio. Segundo a moderna classificação antropológica, não há nenhuma raça reconhecida como camita. Mas isso é compreensível, porque os antropólogos não partem da Bíblia, e, sim, de certas distinções mais ou menos artificiais, como cor da pele, tipo de cabelo, etc. Lembremo-nos que os três filhos de Noé eram irmãos. E as variações raciais que encontramos atualmente dependem mais de certas características que se vão acentuando, devido à seleção natural e o isolamento em que os povos viveram durante milênios. Só na nossa época de transporte rápido e fácil, quando os povos podem miscigenar-se mais prontamente, esse isolamento está desaparecendo.

2. A palavra *Cão* também é usada para indicar os descendentes do homem desse nome (ver o primeiro ponto, acima) (I Crô. 4:40; Sal. 78:51; 105:23,27; 106:22).

3. Nome de uma cidade cujos habitantes, os zuzins, foram feridos por Quedorlaomer, na época de Abraão. Em nossa versão portuguesa, o nome dessa cidade aparece como «Hã» (Gên. 14:5).

CAOS

1. *Idéias Cosmológicas*. Encontramos um uso bem

antigo desse termo, «caos», na literatura grega, na *Teogonia* de Hedios, do século VIII A.C. Ele usou o vocábulo para descrever o hiato resultante do surgimento do mundo de um estado não diferenciado. Por sua vez, Aristóteles empregou o termo para descrever o conceito pré-filosófico de espaço. Os estóicos utilizavam-se do mesmo para descrever o estado aquoso que, segundo eles acreditavam, sempre ocorre após as destruições periódicas do universo por meio do fogo, e que precede a um novo ciclo. A antiga cosmologia grega sempre concebia que o mundo veio à existência através da imposição da ordem em um caos já existente. O primeiro capítulo de Gênesis, em seu começo, tem sido assim interpretado por muitos eruditos. Pelo menos, torna-se óbvio que a narrativa bíblica subentende esse estado caótico, antes de uma criação reformadora de Deus, se não mesmo existente antes de sua criação absoluta, em alguma eternidade passada nunca mencionada.

2. *O Caos Moral e Espiritual*. Quando não há qualquer orientação ou designio definido, instala-se o caos nas cenas moral e espiritual. Essa é a posição defendida pelo *pessimismo* (que vide). Segundo o pessimismo, a própria vida seria má, caótica, sem qualquer propósito. Ser alguém bom ou mau não teria, afinal, qualquer conseqüência, porquanto o mundo não estaria indo a parte alguma. Os homens esforçar-se-iam inutilmente. Os sistemas de pensamento são sem valor, pois esses próprios sistemas fazem parte do caos geral. Em Romanos 8:20, Paulo tece comentários sobre a *futilidade* a que a criação ficou sujeita, por causa do pecado. No entanto, Paulo percebeu que Deus usa até mesmo essa condição, visando aos Seus propósitos benfazejos. Quando os homens chegam ao fim de seus próprios desígnios, percebendo a futilidade da vida sem um centro composto de princípios espirituais, então têm oportunidade de voltar-se para Deus, em busca de refúgio e significação. Quanto a um desenvolvimento mais detalhado desses conceitos, ver o artigo sobre *Chance*. (EP F)

CAPA BABILÔNICA

A capa que Acã furtou, por ocasião da destruição de Jericó (ver Jos. 7:21), segundo Josefo nos informa, era um manto real tecido com fios de ouro. Contudo, não dispomos de qualquer descrição histórica exata a seu respeito. Provavelmente, era feita de tecido bordado, no que os babilônios eram famosos (ver Plínio VIII.7). A obra hebraica, Bereshith Rabba, sec. 85, fol. 75.2 diz que se tratava de uma capa púrpura, mas seu autor estava apenas conjecturando, tal como outros que comentaram sobre a questão. Seja como for, a capa envolvida deve ter-se revestido de considerável valor. Nesse caso, a ambição de Acã terminou em desastre, uma lição muito mais importante do que saber-se qual a verdadeira natureza do tecido envolvido. (S Z)

CAPACETE

Há duas palavras hebraicas e uma palavra grega envolvidas:

1. *Koba*, «capacete». Termo hebraico que aparece por seis vezes: I Sam. 17:5; II Crô. 26:14; Isa. 59:17; Jer. 46:4; Eze. 27:10 e 38:5.

2. *Qoba*, «capacete». Vocábulo hebraico usado por duas vezes: I Sam. 17:38 e Eze. 23:24.

3. *Perikefalaía*, «algo envolto na cabeça». Palavra grega empregada por duas vezes: Efé. 6:17 (citando Isa. 59:17) e I Tes. 5:8.

Ver o artigo geral sobre *Armadura, Armas*, que nos confere informações gerais. O capacete era uma peça importante da armadura, visto que servia para proteger a cabeça. Os arqueólogos têm descoberto capacetes de vários materiais e estilos, em gravuras nas muralhas de Karnak, no Egito. Ali os hititas aparecem usando capacetes em forma da parte superior de um crânio humano. A armadura de Saul incluía um capacete, feito de bronze (I Sam. 17:38). Golias também contava com um capacete (I Sam. 17:5). O capacete era parte do equipamento comum das tropas armadas de várias nações antigas (Jer. 46:4; Eze. 23:24; 27:10; 38:5). Os reis providenciavam para que seus soldados tivessem capacetes (II Crô. 26:14). Gravuras antigas mostram que os assírios e babilônios usavam capacetes que terminavam com uma ponta, o que contrastava com os capacetes dos sírios e dos hititas. Muitos capacetes eram feitos de couro; e, na verdade, parece que somente na época dos monarcas selêucidas os soldados começaram a usar, de modo geral, capacetes feitos de metal. No Novo Testamento encontramos menção ao capacete da salvação (Efé. 6:17), bem como a esperança da salvação (I Tes. 5:8). O artigo sobre *Armadura* entra em detalhes quanto aos usos metafóricos dessa palavra, conferindo informações adicionais sobre os capacetes literais.

CAPACIDADE

Essa palavra refere-se às capacidades naturais do homem, nos terrenos físico, moral e intelectual (Dan. 1:4; Mat. 25:15; I Ped. 4:11). Torna-se termo importante quando usado como sinônimo de «livre arbítrio» ou de *livre agência*. Quando assim usado, denota a capacidade que o homem tem de fazer a vontade de Deus, usualmente com base na noção de que todos os homens foram assim dotados por Deus, pela graça geral da missão de Cristo. Os calvinistas radicais negam essa capacidade, alicerçados em trechos como Rom. 3:11-12. Mas a doutrina tem de ser verdadeira, ou se o homem tiver ter qualquer responsabilidade moral, e por toda a parte a Bíblia conclama os homens a se arrependerem. Se não pudessem arrepender-se, a conclamação seria um absurdo. Ademais, o ministério do Espírito é universal e todo abrangente, segundo vemos em João 12:32 e Efé 1:10. Há notas completas sobre os problemas envolvidos em tudo isso, nos artigos sobre o «livre-arbítrio» e o «determinismo». Esse é um dos maiores problemas da filosofia e da teologia. Precisamos evitar as teologias unilaterais que consideram apenas um dos lados dessa questão, distorcendo os argumentos do outro lado para obter conforto mental. Nenhum outro assunto tem sido sujeito a abusos como o problema do livre-arbítrio e do determinismo. (B NTI)

CAPADÓCIA

Era uma antiga província da Ásia Menor, limitada ao norte pelo Ponto, a leste pelo rio Eufrates e pela Armênia Menor, ao sul pelos montes Taurus, além dos quais ficavam a Cilícia e a Síria e a oeste pela Frígia e pela Galácia. No séc. VI A.C., fazia parte do império persa, estando dividida em duas satrapias. Alexandre, o Grande, não se importou com essa região; mas, mais tarde, ela fez parte dos domínios dos reis Selêucidas. Finalmente, ficou debaixo do poder romano, no tempo do rei vassalo Ariarates IV. Ariarates V foi um súdito leal, que dava apoio à hegemonia romana.

CAPADÓCIA — CAPITALISMO

Dentro da história do Novo Testamento, ela era, essencialmente, a Armênia Menor. Posteriormente, tornou-se costume geográfico chamar sua porção norte de Ponto, ao passo que sua porção sul era a Capadócia Maior. Tibério constituiu essa região em província romana, e, no ano 70 D.C. Vespasiano unificou-a à Armênia Menor, como um dos grandes baluartes de fronteira do império romano. Sob imperadores posteriores, aumentou grandemente a área e a importância desse território. Era lugar onde se criava muito gado vacum, ovino e eqüino, e ficava na rota comercial entre a Ásia Central e o mar Negro. Atualmente, o território da Capadócia faz parte da moderna Turquia.

Referências Neotestamentárias. Habitantes desse território foram representados em Jerusalém, no dia de Pentecoste (Atos 2:9). Sabe-se que uma igreja cristã chegou a ser estabelecida ali (I Ped. 1:1), embora não se saiba por intermédio de quem.

CAPADÓCIOS, OS TRÊS (Pais Capadócios da Igreja)

Os três grandes luminares teológicos da Capadócia (que vide) foram Basílio o grande (330-379), seu irmão, Gregório de Nissa (cerca de 330-395), e Gregório Nazianzeno (329-389) (que vide). Teologicamente falando, esses três homens são relembrados por suas tentativas de explicar a doutrina da Trindade. Eles expuseram proposições essencialmente idênticas. Eles supunham que há um único ser divino com três *hipóstases*. Esta é uma palavra grega com diversos sentidos, significando, basicamente, *apoio*. Todavia, o termo era empregado nas discussões sobre a Trindade (que vide), como sinônimo de *ousia* (ser), a cujo vocábulo se dava o sentido de *substância* ou *essência*. Portanto, o termo indica a idéia dos *modos divinos* de expressão da essência divina. Esses modos seriam expressões pessoais, pelo que os três seriam uma trindade de pessoas, embora originados de uma única essência. As hipóstases teriam existência separadas, mas uma substância comum às três. Cada existência separada teria características distintivas. Haveria uma relação recíproca dentro dessa unidade.

Os três capadócios determinavam a diferença das hipóstases divinas com base em sua origem divina interna, e não com base em suas diferentes operações. As hipóstases, estranhamente, descenderiam uma da outra, o Espírito do Filho, e o Filho do Pai. Assim, eles tentariam preservar a unidade de substância, apesar da existência separada. Nisso consistia uma fraqueza da exposição dos capadócios. Eles apoiavam radicalmente a união absoluta da Trindade. Os capadócios foram os criadores da ortodoxia grega, como intérpretes, que foram, de Atanásio (que vide), no espírito de idéias modificadas de Orígenes (que vide). Talvez tivessem feito tanto bem como qualquer outro pode fazer, ao experimentar dizer coisas racionais sobre aquilo que, essencialmente, é um *mistério*.

Outras religiões, como a egípcia, o hinduísmo, o budismo, etc., têm conceitos trinitarianos de alguma espécie. Ver o artigo sobre a *Trindade* e sobre *Conceitos Trinitarianos nas Religiões Não-Cristãs*.

Esses três pais capadócios da Igreja têm sido descritos como originistas da ala direita. Eles tornaram-se os grandes líderes da reação nicena. Eles desempenharam um importante papel na reconciliação dos *homoeousianos* (que vide), bem como no desenvolvimento da doutrina do Espírito Santo. A ortodoxia dos pais capadócios foi ratificada pelo concílio de Constantinopla, em 381 D.C. Seus principais oponentes foram os arianos, os macedonianos e os sabelianos. Ver os artigos sobre cada um desses adjetivos. (C E)

CAPELA

Deriva-se do latim **capella**, uma «capa». Esse termo foi inicialmente aplicado ao lugar onde São Martinho guardava a sua capa. Veio então a significar um pequeno trecho, uma ala subordinada ao edifício principal, embora contendo o seu próprio altar (que vide). Mas também dava a entender um lugar onde se efetuava adoração particular, à parte da igreja organizada. Assim, os lugares de adoração existentes em lares, escolas e outros lugares fora de uma igreja, receberam esse nome. Em algumas traduções da Bíblia, a palavra «capela» aparece em Amós 7:13, para indicar o santuário de Jeroboão, em Betel. Foi ali que aquele monarca estabeleceu o seu culto real ao bezerro de ouro, que veio a tornar-se um culto rival daquele efetuado no templo de Jerusalém (I Reis 12:25-33). Amazias tornou-se o sacerdote desse santuário (Amós 7:10-17).

CAPELÃO

Vem do latim **capellanus**, «cabo». Dentro do contexto moderno, o termo usualmente refere-se a algum ministro religioso que serve nas forças armadas, visando à orientação espiritual dos homens. Em muitos lugares, ele é um oficial entre as tropas às quais serve. É o responsável pela vida religiosa de seus homens, e também atua como conselheiro religioso. Parece que o termo foi aplicado, pela primeira vez, ao padre que tomava conta da capa (cappela) de São Martinho de Tours. Quando desenvolveram-se vários tipos de capela, o ofício de capelão expandiu-se, e alguns capelães passaram a exercer grande poder eclesiástico. Antes da era contemporânea, esse ofício incluía homens nomeados para servir à realeza, à nobreza e a outros clérigos da hierarquia eclesiástica. Finalmente, os capelães passaram a ser nomeados para servir em quartéis, hospitais, prisões e instituições de educação. A *capelânia militar* é um antigo ofício, com amplas aplicações modernas. O ofício de capelão em hospital é antiqüíssimo. Usualmente ele faz parte do pessoal pago do hospital. Os capelães de instituições de ensino usualmente são ministros evangélicos, rabinos ou padres católicos romanos, que tomam conta de uma capela do campus ou de uma fundação religiosa denominacional, localizada perto do campus. Na sociedade moderna, encontramos o aparecimento dos *capelães industriais*. Os sacerdotes operários da França servem de exemplo desse conceito. Esses ministram enquanto trabalham, mantendo alguma posição de respeito na indústria onde servem. (AM E)

CAPILA Ver **Kapila**.

CAPITALISMO

O capitalismo é um sistema econômico baseado nas idéias de propriedade privada, lucros privados e iniciativa privada nos negócios. O socialismo (que vide), substitui o indivíduo pelo estado. Ver também os artigos sobre *Comunismo, Competição* e *Responsabilidade Coletiva*. Assuntos como esses foram incluídos nesta enciclopédia por causa de suas implicações éticas.

CAPITALISMO

1. História do Capitalismo. O capitalismo tem existido até onde a história nos faz retroceder, sempre que as pessoas tinham propriedades que consideravam exclusivamente suas, produziam bens agrícolas que trocavam e/ou comercializavam, ou então quando famílias mantinham propriedades privadas. Nas sociedades mais primitivas, como as dos indígenas do Brasil, não há propriedade privada, mas tudo pertence à coletividade. Portanto, o capitalismo já representa uma evolução. Porém, se estamos falando sobre o capitalismo que entrou em choque com outros sistemas, que atualmente fazem parte da sociedade contemporânea, então devemos começar pela forma capitalista que havia no período medieval, quando a Europa começava a adotar uma economia comercial, com laços comerciais distantes. Por volta do século XVII, o capitalismo havia substituído o feudalismo como o sistema econômico geral. O século XIX tem sido considerado a era do capitalismo clássico. Adam Smith argumentava em prol do capitalismo *laissez-faire*, o autocontrole em um mercado livre. Sua teoria foi a fórmula usada na revolução industrial (que vide), que ocorreu nos Estados Unidos da América e na Europa. A economia tomou grande vulto, vieram à existência gigantescas empresas e surgiram multimilionários, e, naturalmente, também houve grandes abusos contra os direitos individuais.

O capitalismo foi desafiado pela Revolução Russa de 1917. Marx asseverava que as desigualdades e injustiças da livre iniciativa requeriam a intervenção do estado, e que o capital deveria visar ao bem público, e não ao bem de alguns poucos privilegiados. Talvez isso fosse típico das idéias de um judeu espezinhado, mas ele era o porta-voz de milhões que pertenciam às esbulhadas classes operárias. Lenin observou que o poder econômico era controlado pelas rédeas dos governos, da Igreja e de certas estruturas sociais, e invocava uma revolução radical, para derrubar o sistema. As condições da Grande Depressão, dos fins da década de 1920 e começo da década de 1930, apresentaram um outro desafio ao capitalismo. Nos Estados Unidos da América, para exemplificar, a resposta foi a maior intervenção governamental e o controle sobre as corporações e trustes privados, bem como uma maior participação dos operários em suas respectivas companhias, mediante a venda de ações entre eles, e outros benefícios dados aos operários. Como vemos, as próprias democracias, através de seus governos, notaram que os abusos precisavam ser corrigidos. É verdade que a Alemanha Ocidental e o Japão mantêm um capitalismo essencialmente clássico, mas outras nações ocidentais atualmente têm economias mistas, onde despontam certas medidas nitidamente socialistas. Vice-versa, atualmente somos testemunhas do curioso fenômeno de que as nações comunistas, a fim de melhorarem a produção e a qualidade de seus produtos, estão injetando normas do antigo capitalismo em seu socialismo, com notáveis resultados práticos. Em 1985, o governo chinês declarou que o comunismo clássico não era mais viável, como sistema econômico, para satisfazer às necessidades chinesas atuais. É que as pessoas trabalham melhor quando está em jogo o seu interesse próprio, do que quando visam apenas um vago ideal do bem-estar coletivo ou do estado. Afinal, o que é o capitalismo, senão uma meia solução para os males sociais e econômicos da era medieval? E o que é o comunismo, senão uma meia solução para os males sociais e econômicos da era czarista? Senhores, o regime áureo só virá quando do reinado milenar de Cristo! Antes disso, todos os sistemas terão de fracassar, por estarem calcados sobre a má índole do homem perdido!

2. Questões Éticas. O capitalismo, como princípio básico, sem os seus abusos, concorda com os ideais do cristianismo. O conceito da propriedade privada era uma das vigas mestras do judaísmo. Cada família contava com a sua propriedade particular, protegida por detalhadas leis de herança. O ideal era e continua sendo que cada homem tenha a sua própria vinha e a sua própria figueira (I Reis 4:25; Miq. 4:4). Porém, é deveras instrutivo ver como a legislação mosaica também defendia os direitos dos pobres. De acordo com o cristianismo, o conceito de propriedade privada não somente é exposto como normal, mas, igualmente, como meio de proteger o indivíduo de medidas ditatoriais do estado. O sistema de propriedade privada é um incentivo ao desenvolvimento econômico e ao auto-aprimoramento O Novo Testamento defende com denodo os direitos individuais, dando grande importância à vida e ao destino do indivíduo. Ver Apo. 2:17, nas notas do NTI, quanto a comentários sobre essa noção. A experiência comunitária, na Igreja primitiva (ver Atos 4:32 *ss*) foi voluntária, motivada pela pobreza forçada, devida à perseguição. O trecho de Atos 5:4 mostra-nos que Pedro enfatizou que Ananias podia fazer o que bem entendesse com a sua propriedade. Os comentadores, de modo geral, dizem que a experiência falhou. Porém, talvez devamos dizer que a mesma foi descontinuada, por não ser mais necessária, quando a pressão da perseguição amainou. Mas a partilha de bens, sem uma produção aumentada, apenas propaga mais ainda a pobreza. Foi mister que Paulo fizesse uma coleta, entre os crentes gentios, a fim de aliviar a pobreza que continuava entre os crentes judeus (I Cor. 16:1 *ss*). O Novo Testamento, naturalmente, combate os típicos abusos do capitalismo, como a desconsideração pelos direitos do indivíduo e a escravização dos pobres pelos ricos, mediante medidas econômicas. Paulo apelou em prol da leniência e da generosidade, no caso do escravo fugido, Onésimo (ver a epístola a Filemom). Jesus, por sua vez, salientou o grande valor da alma individual (Mar. 8:36). O Novo Testamento combate a avareza e promove a lei do amor, como a própria essência da espiritualidade (I João 4:7 *ss*). Os vários aspectos do fruto do Espírito (Gál. 5:22, 23) incluem aquelas qualidades que levam um homem a cuidar do próximo; e o amor a Deus e ao próximo forma a essência das exigências da lei (Rom. 13:8). Adam Smith, que tinha um ponto de vista otimista da natureza humana, supunha que, — finalmente, surgiria do mercado livre uma espécie de *harmonia automática*, visto que o homem seria essencialmente bom em sua natureza, a qual controlaria os seus interesses pessoais. Mas o cristianismo ensina que isso só começa a ser curado com a conversão espiritual. Esse preceito, pois, volta-se tanto contra os abusos do capitalismo como contra o ateísmo do comunismo, sistema este que supõe que o mundo é governado por princípios econômicos, e não por princípios espirituais.

De certo ângulo, pode-se dizer que a Reforma Protestante foi uma revolta contra as instituições que estavam esmagando o indivíduo, na tentativa de retornar ao espírito do Novo Testamento. Quando os homens se tornam materialistas, sem importar se o fazem por motivos capitalistas ou por motivos comunistas, eles já abandonaram a essência de seu próprio ser, e seus sistemas tornam-se incapazes de satisfazer às necessidades e desejos comuns a todos os homens. Além do mais, o dinheiro nunca poderá resolver os problemas realmente imperiosos, as

CAPITÃO — CAPÍTULOS DA BÍBLIA

questões envolvidas na vida e na morte; e isso faz parte de uma inquirição que deve ser vista por seus próprios méritos. As desigualdades promovidas pelos sistemas econômicos persistem, sem importar o sistema dominante. Somente o Espírito pode dar solução a esses tipos de problemas. Outrossim, nunca nos deveríamos olvidar que o mandamento de Jesus continua sendo: «...buscai, pois, em primeiro lugar, o seu reino e a sua justiça, e todas estas cousas vos serão acrescentadas» (Mat. 6:33). Jesus declarou que os gentios são aqueles que não se preocupam com outra coisa além dos assuntos econômicos (Mat. 6:32). Qual é a vantagem de andar alguém em conforto e afluência se a sua alma está faminta, despida e podre? A igreja local que Jesus repreendeu mais fortemente foi precisamente aquela que desfrutava de mais conforto e de mais dinheiro (ver Apo. 3:14). As próprias riquezas materiais só são boas quando servem de meio para promover a vida espiritual (II Cor. 9:8). Senhor, concede-nos *esse tipo* de afluência! (AM E H)

CAPITÃO

Esse termo traduz três termos hebraicos e dois gregos, a saber:

1. *Sar*, «cabeça», «príncipe», palavra hebraica usada por cerca de quatrocentas e vinte vezes (por exemplo: Gên. 37:36; 39:1; Núm. 31:14,38,52; I Sam. 8:12; II Sam. 2:8; I Reis 1:19; II Reis 1:9; I Crô. 11:6,21; II Crô. 1:2; Jer. 40:7,13; 43:4,5). O paralelo grego é *chiliarchos*, um título militar (ver abaixo). Um outro paralelo grego é *stratopédarchos*, «capitão do acampamento», que aparece somente em Atos 28:16, mas que nossa versão portuguesa traduz por «o soldado». Este era comandante de um destacamento de soldados. No Antigo Testamento temos usos similares, como capitão de cinqüenta, capitão de mil, ou capitão do exército.

2. *Qatsin*, «árbitro», palavra que aparece por doze vezes (por exemplo: Jos. 10:24; Juí. 11:6,11), mas que pode indicar um líder civil (Isa. 1:10), ou militar (as duas primeiras referências).

3. *Shalish*, «terceiro», palavra que aparece por vinte e uma vezes (por exemplo: Êxo. 14:7; 15:4; II Reis 9:25; 10:25; 15:25; II Crô. 8:9). A posição exata de tal oficial nos é obscura, mas, evidentemente, alude a uma ordem superior de militar que combatia em carros de guerra, aludindo, especificamente, àquele elemento que controlava os cavalos, ao passo que os demais homens que estavam no carro de guerra ocupavam-se mais diretamente no combate. Entretanto, há estudiosos que pensam que a referência é a uma terceira ordem de oficiais, após o rei, ou então a comandantes de uma terça parte do exército.

4. *Chiliárchos*, «chefe de mil», palavra que aparece por vinte e duas vezes no Novo Testamento, de Marc. 6:21 a Apo. 19:18.

5. *Strategós*, «capitão», palavra que aparece por dez vezes no Novo Testamento: Luc. 22:4,52; Atos 4:1; 5:24,26; 16:20,22,35,36,38. Nas cinco primeiras referências a palavra é usada para indicar os «capitães do templo», que não eram oficiais militares, e, sim, sacerdotes que comandavam a polícia levítica do **templo. Os autores judeus chamavam-nos de «homens do monte do templo».** O dever deles era comandar os guardas noturnos, garantindo que as sentinelas estavam cumprindo os seus deveres. No entanto, nas referências do décimo sexto capítulo de Atos, nossa versão traduz essa palavra por «pretores» (que vide), que já eram oficiais gentílicos, nada tendo ver com o templo de Jerusalém.

Usos Figurados. O próprio Deus é chamado de «príncipe do exército do Senhor», isto é, da inteira congregação de Israel, ou das hostes celestiais protetoras de Israel (Jos. 5:14 e Dan. 8:11). A idéia é que Deus tomava sobre si o encargo de proteger o seu povo, liderando-o em seus conflitos gerais e em suas guerras com os inimigos. Acresça-se a isso que Jesus Cristo é o *Capitão de* nossa salvação (Heb. 2:10, onde já é usada outra palavra grega, *archegós*, «líder», palavra essa que aparece em Atos 3:15; 5:31; Heb. 2:10 e 12:2).

CAPITÃO DO EXÉRCITO

Ver o artigo sobre **Capitão**, Usos Figurados.

CAPITEL

Um capitel é um ornamento arquitetônico da parte superior de uma coluna. Os capitéis protojônicos encontrados em Megido, presumivelmente foram usados no palácio de Acabe, em Samaria, segundo pensava Albright. As principais menções a capitéis (no hebraico, *kothereth*, palavra usada por vinte e quatro vezes), nas páginas da Bíblia são as das colunas Jeoiaquim e Boaz, no templo de Salomão (que vide). Esses capitéis tinham cinco côvados de altura (cerca de 2,2 m) (I Reis 7:16), ou então 1,3 m, de acordo com II Reis 25:17, que fala em três côvados. É possível que esses capitéis estivessem divididos em duas porções, e que a porção inferior tivesse três côvados. Seja como for, esses capitéis tinham o formato de uma pétala de lírio, encimado por uma taça invertida, que recebia as telas que apoiavam as romãs. O trecho de Amós 9:1 encerra uma referência direta aos capitéis, como um lugar que podia ser ferido, para causar destruição e fazer os limiares do templo estremecerem. O quadro inteiro é uma referência ao julgamento divino. Em Sofonias 2:14, esse item da ornamentação arquitetônica é aludido como lugar onde as aves se alojavam. (Z)

CAPÍTULOS E VERSÍCULOS DA BÍBLIA

Na maioria dos livros da Bíblia, podemos distinguir divisões naturais, tencionadas pelos autores sagrados. Lucas, por exemplo, como é óbvio, tencionava que seu livro de Atos fosse dividido em sete partes, tendo assinalado o fim de cada uma dessas secções por uma fórmula literária. (Ver *Livro de Atos*). Antes da época de Jesus Cristo, a lei havia sido dividida em secções, para facilitar a sua leitura nas sinagogas. Cada uma dessas secções tinha um nome especial, como, por exemplo, *o arbusto*. Há uma alusão a isso, em Marcos 12:26. Esse sistema acabou envolvendo todo o Antigo Testamento, e as *Parashas* até hoje são assinaladas na Bíblia hebraica. Os primeiros manuscritos gregos do Novo Testamento também tinham divisões. Porém, foi somente no século XIII que Estêvão Langton (que vide), arcebispo de Canterbury, que foi o redator da Magna Carta (que vide), introduziu o sistema que agora conhecemos como capítulos da Bíblia. A Vulgata Latina foi a primeira versão da Bíblia a ser assim dividida. Os versículos foram adicionados bem mais tarde pelo impressor Estêvão, em sua edição do Novo Testamento grego, em 1551. Pouco depois disso, na Bíblia Poliglota de Antuérpia (que vide), de 1569-1572, o sistema de versículos numerados foi aplicado à Bíblia inteira. Ver o artigo separado sobre a *Divisão da Bíblia em Versículos*. Esse sistema, apesar de ser de grande ajuda no estudo do texto bíblico, também ressente-se de uma falha grave. É que, com freqüência, divide o fluxo das idéias, às vezes bem pelo meio. Disso é culpada tanto a divisão em capítulos como a divisão em versículos. Além disso, alguns versículos são muito breves, e outros muito longos. Nenhum critério de qualquer espécie serviu de guia ao sistema. Porém, consagrado pelo uso, é muito difícil que o sistema seja modificado, pelo menos em nossos dias (E).

CAPUCHINHOS

Um ramo autônomo da ordem religiosa mendicante dos católicos romanos, os franciscanos (frades menores; que vide), que data da reforma efetuada em 1525, na Itália. O fundador do grupo foi o frade Matteo di Bassi. O seu alvo era o retorno à religiosidade original e à austeridade da regra de Francisco de Assis (que vide). O capuz longo e pontudo (chamado *capuche*), deu origem ao nome da ordem, Capuchinhos, similar ao capuz usado por Francisco de Assis. Essa ordem tem se mostrado muito ativa na obra missionária, pelo mundo inteiro. Os Capuchinhos mostraram-se especialmente ativos nas missões americanas, durante os anos formativos dessa civilização. (E)

CARAATALÃ

Um nome encontrado em I Esdras 5:36, designando um líder de certa família que retornou da Babilônia em companhia de Zorobabel. Muitas variações desse nome existem nas traduções. Ver Esd. 2:29 e Nee. 7:61, quanto aos nomes dos lugares, na Babilônia, de onde Israel retornou à Palestina.

CARAÍTAS

Esse foi o nome de uma seita judaica do Oriente Médio, principalmente na Babilônia, nos séculos IX a XII D.C. Foi uma espécie de movimento *volta à Bíblia*. O termo *caraíta* significa *leitor das Escrituras*. Aceitava como autoridade religiosa *somente* as Escrituras do Antigo Testamento, rejeitando todas as interpretações rabínicas do Talmude (que vide). O movimento foi iniciado por Anan ben David.

Precisando de um melhor critério de interpretação (visto que a regra que diz *somente as Escrituras* sempre termina como *eu* e *meu grupo* interpretamos), esse grupo permitiu que a *consciência* de cada indivíduo se encarregasse do trabalho de interpretação. Como era inevitável, e conforme vem sucedendo também no *protestantismo*, isso levou à anarquia e à fragmentação. De nada adianta esperar que todas as consciências humanas, miraculosamente, de alguma maneira, chegarão todas às mesmas interpretações. As comunidades caraítas não demoraram a discordar sobre quase tudo. Não obstante, houve uma contribuição de todo esse esforço, porquanto encorajou o judaísmo a retornar ao estudo da Bíblia. Além disso, — forçou aqueles que pensavam que o *Talmude* é útil expusessem uma polêmica apropriada. O debate sempre é bom, se não termina em hostilidades. O mais bem conhecido oponente do movimento caraíta foi o brilhante Saadi ben Joseph (que vide), que viveu entre 882 e 942 D.C., o qual, subseqüentemente, tornou-se o chefe da academia rabínica de Sura, na Babilônia. Até hoje a seita existe no judaísmo, embora com pequeno número de seguidores e exercendo pouca influência sobre o pensamento dos judeus. (E P)

CARÁTER

Aquilo que caracteriza um homem, sobretudo em seu progresso espiritual, pois as Escrituras frisam o progresso do caráter no sentido do avanço dentro do processo de transformação segundo a imagem de Cristo; a quantidade e a qualidade resultantes de sua possessão de Cristo. O alvo disso é a perfeição absoluta. Os crentes se encontram em muitos pontos variados, ao longo desse caminho, mas todos os crentes autênticos estão seguindo no caminho da perfeição. O caráter, uma vez completado, será semelhante ao de Cristo, pois os remidos haverão de participar de seu ser essencial e de sua natureza moral, até que, finalmente compartilhem de sua natureza metafísica, de sua divindade, sendo ele o Deus-homem. (Ver o trecho de II Ped. 1:4). Ora, a tribulação desempenha um decisivo papel na produção desse resultado, o que nos mostra a sua importância, embora os sofrimentos sejam tão cruéis como as chamas do fogo. O homem, no ser de quem Cristo realmente está sendo formado, chega àquele estado de «aprovação divina» que, segundo tivemos ocasião de ver em muitos textos bíblicos, é a idéia básica contida na palavra «caráter». Está escrito que Deus Pai aprovou seu Filho, Jesus Cristo, declarando: «Este é o meu Filho, em quem me comprazo» (Mat. 3:17). Por igual modo, os filhos de Deus são «agradáveis» ao Pai, ou seja, são «aprovados» por ele.

CARÁTER ÍMPAR de Cada Pessoa

Ver o artigo intitulado **Novo Nome e Pedra Branca**.

CARÁTER INDELÉVEL

Ver o artigo sobre **Caráter Sacramental**. De acordo com a teologia católica romana tradicional, compartilhada pelas igrejas Anglicana e Ortodoxa Oriental, as ordens dos ministros ordenados são indeléveis, isto é, vigoram durante toda a vida do ministro. A Igreja Ortodoxa Oriental, porém, supõe que um ministro indigno perde o privilégio de sua ordenação. Seja como for, a autoridade eclesiástica cabível ao caso pode abrogar a ordem de alguém, de acordo com essa igreja. (E)

CARÁTER, MORAL E ESPIRITUAL

1. **Caráter Moral-Origem**. Por que as pessoas são como são? Elas já nascem com suas aptidões, ou desenvolvem-nas no decorrer da vida? A filosofia, a sociologia, a genética e a teologia procuram todas encontrar solução para a questão. Alguns estudiosos supõem que o caráter e as características da personalidade são frutos do desenvolvimento, com base na experiência de cada um, condicionadas pelo meio ambiente. Entretanto, os estudos sobre a mentalidade criminosa indicam que algumas crianças, desde a mais tenra idade, exibem tendências para atos criminosos, embora criadas entre outras crianças perfeitamente normais. Alguns cientistas supõem que haja o concurso de defeitos cerebrais ou genéticos que explicam esse fenômeno, ainda 'que', por enquanto, não existam sólidas evidências para servirem de base à assertiva. Aqueles que acreditam na pré-existência da alma, de mistura ou não com a reencarnação (conforme os pais alexandrinos da Igreja pensavam), falam em uma história da alma separada do corpo, tanto antes quanto depois da encarnação, os quais também dizem que a herança genética é essencialmente destituída de importância, no tocante ao caráter básico do indivíduo. Nesse caso, o caráter dependeria do desenvolvimento, embora a longo prazo, pois envolveria a própria história da alma. E a alma, ao associar-se a um corpo físico, dá continuação à sua história, melhorando ou piorando. Mas, de acordo com esse ponto de vista, o caráter é

CARÁTER, MORAL E ESPIRITUAL

trazido desde a história da alma, não sendo um desenvolvimento que ocorre somente durante esta existência terrena, e nem mesmo dependente do estágio infantil. Ian Stevenson, professor de psiquiatria e parapsicologia da Universidade de Virgínia, nos Estados Unidos da América, nunca se sentiu satisfeito com a teoria freudiana do caráter. Por essa e por outras razões, embarcou em uma carreira que o levou a investigar a reencarnação (que vide) em profundidade, com a ajuda de métodos científicos.

A *teologia*, por sua vez, admite a possibilidade da intervenção divina nessa questão da formação do caráter. Podemos meditar sobre o caso de João Batista, cheio do Espírito Santo desde o ventre materno (Luc. 1:15). Paulo dizia que sabia que havia sido separado para a sua missão, desde antes do seu nascimento (Gál. 1:15). Aqueles que acreditam na preexistência da alma não vêem nisso qualquer atuação arbitrária de Deus, — e nem mesmo uma atuação alicerçada sobre algum misterioso propósito divino. A entidade João e a entidade Paulo teriam estado atarefadas no desenvolvimento da alma por muito tempo, e já haviam atingido uma elevada posição. Precisamente por *essa razão* eles foram escolhidos para cumprir as elevadas missões de que foram encarregados. Outro tanto sucede a cada pessoa, em todas as missões de que os indivíduos são encarregados. As tarefas da vida de cada um dependem, essencialmente, do que cada qual faz a si mesmo, até aquele ponto. A teologia judaica, da época de Cristo em diante, vem ensinando que os grandes profetas de Israel teriam mais de uma missão terrena. Jeremias, por exemplo, era identificado com Moisés, como se fossem uma mesma entidade. Esse conceito tem reflexos na narrativa do Novo Testamento, como em Mateus 16:14, onde o povo judeu tentou identificar Jesus com um dos antigos profetas. Profundos mistérios circundam essas questões, mas é quase certo que o caráter não depende, essencialmente, de variações ambientais. Aqueles que têm criado filhos podem testificar que cada criança exibe seu caráter básico, desde o começo, com notáveis diferenças entre uma criança e outra. As tentativas dos pais para treinar e modificar são úteis e necessárias, e a conversão religiosa (que vide) muito transforma o indivíduo. Porém, existe um material básico sobre o qual essas forças atuam, que raramente é ultrapassado em qualquer grau mais elevado, pois esse material sempre exibirá suas qualidades inerentes. Nem mesmo a conversão religiosa transcende, de modo absoluto, essas qualidades fundamentais, porquanto existem pessoas religiosas em todos os estágios de desenvolvimento de caráter, o que não pode ser inteiramente explicado por seu desenvolvimento espiritual subseqüente à conversão.

2. Caráter Moral—Desenvolvimento. O Espírito de Deus ocupa-se da tarefa de nossa transformação espiritual. O caráter básico de cada um de nós, o nosso próprio desenvolvimento, apressa ou retarda essa atuação do Espírito. Mas, cada um de nós pode ir transcendendo a estágios anteriores, e, assim, ir-se aprimorando (II Cor. 3:18). Essa é a mensagem do evangelho. O cultivo dos vários aspectos do fruto do Espírito (Gál. 5:22,23) nos confere maior força de caráter. Portanto, deveríamos mostrar-nos otimistas sobre o que o poder do Espírito Santo pode fazer na nossa vida, a despeito da partida lenta, quanto ao caráter básico de onde todos partimos. Não há que duvidar que a conversão não deixa todas as pessoas envolvidas no mesmo nível espiritual. Existem convertidos que logo tornam-se gigantes espirituais; enquanto que outros são pigmeus espirituais.

Percebemos evidências desse fato por todos os lados. Além disso, precisamos considerar aqueles que não passaram por nenhuma clara experiência de conversão, mas que, apesar disso, tornam-se dotados de caráter vigoroso e hígido. Penso que Deus está conduzindo os tais ao longo da reta vereda, e que algum dia, aqui ou no outro lado da existência, ele reivindicará os tais, conferindo-lhes avanços adicionais e entregando-lhes importantes missões espirituais. Deus tem todo o tempo que quiser. As condições se modificam lentamente, e Cristo terminará beneficiando a todos os homens, ou com a *redenção* ou com a *restauração*, em última análise. Ver o artigo sobre a *Restauração*, quanto a esse conceito. Platão por certo estava com a razão, quando pensou que a transformação moral é necessária para que uma pessoa obtenha residência permanente nos mundos espirituais. Hebreus 12:14 ensina-nos exatamente isso; e II Coríntios 3:18 descreve o processo. Por sua parte, I Pedro 4:6 mostra, bem definidamente, que Deus está operando em todas as pessoas, levando-as pelo caminho da espiritualidade, em uma caminhada que não termina com a morte biológica. A missão de Cristo abarca mais do que esta esfera terrena. Opera em todas as dimensões da existência, não havendo ser humano, em qualquer lugar, que esteja fora do alcance de seu poder, sem importar se ainda está nesta vida física e terrena, ou não. Esse sempre foi o ponto de vista dos pais gregos da Igreja. Para mim, essa é uma posição mais razoável do que aquela que foi adotada pelo cristianismo ocidental, que concebe uma vida, uma morte, julgamento e estagnação. Não peço desculpas por declarar-me aqui aliado da Igreja Oriental, quanto a esse ponto de vista. A formação do caráter envolve tempo. Isso envolve a espiritualidade básica de cada um, envolve a própria questão do *destino* de cada um. Isso requer tempo. Deus não tem pressa quanto a isso, embora haja versículos no Novo Testamento que ensinam que, quanto a outras questões, o tempo urge.

3. O Caráter Moral e os Ataques Contra o Mesmo. O ceticismo, o hedonismo, o materialismo e muitos outros tipos de *ismos*, lançam sérios ataques contra o caráter, transformando em ídolos o erro, o pecado e a busca pelas vantagens materiais. Todavia, as pessoas dotadas de caráter forte e bem formado não parecem deixar-se abalar por esses ataques, ao passo que os débeis de caráter são sacudidos para todos os lados, por qualquer sopro do vento. Os homens dotados de caráter forte (e eles existem em todas as denominações religiosas, e até mesmo fora delas) são dotados de um forte senso de missão. Apesar de passarem por sua dose normal de tribulações e de terem suas falhas, eles conseguem fixar a mente e o coração em algum ideal, avançando sempre nessa direção. Os indivíduos dotados de caráter mal formado, por sua vez, não se sentem dotados de alguma missão a cumprir, embora isso não signifique que tal condição nunca será alterada. Essas qualidades desenvolvem-se por meio da inquirição espiritual.

4. O Desenvolvimento Espiritual e o Caráter. Os meios de desenvolvimento espiritual são diversos. Poderíamos sugerir os seguintes: a. O *treinamento da mente* nas Escrituras Sagradas e na boa literatura, religiosa ou secular, o que confere aos homens o senso do que é superior e melhor, treinando suas mentes para as coisas mais nobres. b. A *oração*, que consiste tanto na petição a Deus como na comunhão com Deus, em louvor a ele prestado. É óbvio que a oração transforma as pessoas e altera o rumo dos acontecimentos. c. A *meditação*, que consiste em sintonizar o espírito com Deus e a irmã gêmea da oração, é um outro poderoso meio de desenvolvimento espiritual. A **Igreja Oriental** sempre enfatizou esse fator, e ali muitos buscam a *iluminação* espiritual por via da meditação sistemática. Isso confere à nossa fé aquele toque místico de que ela precisa. d. A *santificação*. Esta nos conduz a Deus (Heb. 12:14), não podendo haver futura glorificação sem a presente santificação. e. A prática da *lei do amor*. Essa é a qualidade espiritual por excelência, aquela em torno da qual todas as demais qualidades espirituais se desenvolvem (Gál. 5:22,23). O amor também é a prova e a essência da espiritualidade (I João 4:7 ss). Cada vez que alguém faz o que é bom e gentil para com outrem, impelido pelo verdadeiro motivo do amor, esse alguém aprimora a sua qualidade espiritual, em sua própria alma. f. Cada um de nós deveria ter um ideal para seguir, uma missão para realizar, uma tarefa a cumprir com todas as nossas forças, com todo o zelo de nosso espírito. Isso serve de poderoso edificador do caráter. Todos esses meios desenvolvem em nós o caráter e a espiritualidade, e é com essa finalidade que estamos vivos neste mundo. (H NTI)

CARÁTER SACRAMENTAL

Muitos teólogos que acreditam no ponto de vista sacramental do batismo, da eucaristia, etc., supõem que essas cerimônias não são meros símbolos. Esses presumem que o Espírito Santo honra aos ritos quando a pessoa os recebe, *marcando* os mesmos ou conferindo-lhes a virtude do alto. É nos escritos de Agostinho que encontramos o desenvolvimento desse tipo de teologia, que recebeu o nome de *sacramentalismo*. Os escolásticos desenvolveram ainda mais o sacramentalismo. Duns Scotus (que vide) ensinava que os sacramentos comunicam *qualidade*, um conceito similar à idéia de PODER, de Aristóteles. Esse ensino foi endossado pelo concílio de Florença (1438-1445). E o concílio de Trento (1545-1563) definiu-o solenemente como segue: «Se alguém disser que nos três sacramentos, a saber, no batismo, na confirmação e nas santas ordens, não há um *caráter* impresso sobre a alma, isto é, uma certa marca (*signum*) espiritual e inapagável, pelo que esses sacramentos não podem ser repetidos, que o tal seja anátema». (Conc. Trid. Sess. ult. cânon 7). Essas são palavras fortes, realmente! Onde elas deixam quem não é católico romano?

Na prática, essa doutrina tem causado alguma dificuldade, mesmo para os católicos romanos. Visto que se pensa que o caráter dos sacramentos não se pode perder, o resultado ocasional disso tem sido os *episcopi vagantes* (bispos vagabundos). Até mesmo um bispo excomungado pela Igreja Católica Romana retém o caráter episcopal, e, por conseguinte, pode continuar a ordenar a outros.

A Igreja Ortodoxa Oriental, entretanto, repudia a idéia do caráter indelével das ordens eclesiásticas, com base no conceito que a ordenação transmite autorização, e não uma marca indelével. Portanto, ali, se uma pessoa é excomungada, ou, de outro modo torna-se indigna de ocupar um ofício eclesiástico, só com isso perdeu o direito à sua ordenação. Acresça-se a isso que alguns grupos insistem sobre o caráter moral do ministro, como fator necessário para a correta administração dos sacramentos ou ordenanças. Assim, os donatistas (que vide), seguindo a doutrina de Cipriano, mantinham que a validade dos sacramentos depende da dignidade daqueles que os administram. Contrariamente a isso, outros argumentam que a validade dos sacramentos depende de Deus, e não dos ministros humanos. Essa é a posição prevalente na Igreja Católica Romana. Uma razão para isso é que é impossível se saber, na maioria dos casos, quão digno ou indigno é um ministro.

No tocante aos grupos cristãos não cerimonialistas, a discussão inteira faz pouco ou nenhum sentido, visto que o que realmente importa é a qualidade espiritual daquele que participa dos sacramentos ou ordenanças, o que já é uma qualidade da alma, nada tendo a ver com a mecânica da religião, com os símbolos que são os ritos religiosos. De fato, essa é a posição que concorda com o espírito do Novo Testamento. Aproximamo-nos mais da verdade quando concebemos que os sinais externos, as cerimônias que os homens incorporam em seus sistemas religiosos, jamais podem servir de instrumentos da graça e da espiritualidade. Esses sinais externos podem tipificar a graça e a espiritualidade, mas não podem criá-las. O judaísmo conta com muitas cerimônias, sacrifícios, etc., atribuindo aos mesmos um valor salvatício. Consideremos o caso da circuncisão. O décimo quinto capítulo do livro de Atos mostra-nos claramente que os primitivos cristãos judeus, mesmo depois que se tornaram parte da Igreja cristã, continuaram crendo que a circuncisão é algo necessário à salvação. Os cristãos gentios, em lugar da circuncisão, pensam que o batismo é necessário à salvação. Pergunto: Se a circuncisão judaica, como um dos principais ritos judaicos, não tinha qualquer efeito salvatício, por que haveríamos de pensar que o batismo, uma outra cerimônia religiosa, tem qualquer efeito quanto à salvação da alma? Essas proposições não são conceitos religiosos primitivos? Os homens tendem por misturar o símbolo com a realidade espiritual que o mesmo representa. Ver o artigo sobre a *Lei Cerimonial* e sobre os *Sacramentos*. Se a circuncisão salvasse, ou fizesse parte da salvação, como teriam sido salvos os patriarcas anteriores a Abraão? E se o batismo salvasse, ou fizesse parte da salvação, como teriam sido salvos todos os crentes do Antigo Testamento? E como teria sido salvo o ladrão que se converteu na cruz, à direita de Jesus? (Ver Luc. 23:39,43). Paulo indaga se a bênção da justificação vem somente sobre os circuncisos ou também sobre os incircuncisos, mediante a fé. E acrescenta: «A fé foi imputada a Abraão para justiça. Como, pois, lhe foi atribuída? estando ele já circuncidado, ou ainda incircunciso? Não no regime da circuncisão, e, sim, quando incircunciso» (Rom. 4:9,10). (C E)

CARAVANA

No hebraico, **arach**, palavra usada por sete vezes (por exemplo: Gên. 37:25 e Isa. 21:13), e que significa «grupo viajante». Ver o artigo sobre o *Comércio*. O «caminho dos nômades», referido em Juí. 8:11, refere-se a uma rota caravaneira. Formavam-se caravanas por diversos motivos, como migração de povos, viajantes que seguiam em grupos como medida de proteção, e negociantes que andavam em grupos, pela mesma razão. As caravanas tinham seus animais de carga, líderes específicos, se necessário fosse, lugares de descanso e alojamentos em posições estratégicas. Albright demonstrou que desde tão cedo como a Idade do Bronze Médio I (2100-1800 A.C.), já existiam caravanas, e que eram empregados jumentos como bestas de carga, nessa época. As caravanas estabeleceram pontos de ocupação em suas jornadas, espalhados nas rotas comerciais pelo Neguebe e pela península do Sinai, ao longo do caminho interior de Sur (que vide), e desde Berseba, passando por Cades-Barnéia, até Ismailia e Suez. Os camelos mostravam-se melhores animais de carga para uso nas áreas arenosas, visto que suas patas espalhadas afundam menos facilmente na areia fofa.

Foi uma caravana de especiarias, ismaelita-midianita, que levou o jovem José, filho de Jacó, ao Egito, onde ele foi vendido como escravo (Gên. 37:25,28). Os camelos também eram melhores animais para serem usados nas viagens pelo deserto, devido à sua capacidade de armazenar água em seus estômagos. Ver o artigo sobre o *Camelo*. Os servos de Abraão seguiram em lombo de camelo (Gên. 24:10,56,61). Salomão fortificou Arade, a fim de proteger as rotas das caravanas, que iam buscar especiarias e incenso no sul da Arábia (I Reis 10:2,15). Plínio informa-nos que uma caravana de camelos precisava de sessenta e cinco dias para ir do sul da Arábia até Gaza. Ver *História Natural* xii.32. Até hoje há caravanas de camelos, algumas delas imensas, envolvidas nas peregrinações dos islamitas. (DT Z)

CARBARITAS

Uma escola de pensamento do islamismo que defende o conceito do fatalismo absoluto. Ver sobre o *Islamismo*, ponto 6.

CARBONO 14

Ou mediação pelo radiocarbono. Essa é uma técnica largamente usada para aquilatar a antiguidade dos objetos arqueológicos. O isótopo 14(C) forma-se na atmosfera, mediante o bombardeio do nitrogênio pelos raios cósmicos. Oxida-se sob a forma de dióxido de carbono e é absorvido pelas plantas. Por sua vez, as plantas são ingeridas pelos animais. Nos organismos vivos, há um equilíbrio entre a ingestão do 14(C) e a decadência do isótopo. Após a morte, a radioatividade vai-se decompondo lentamente; quando o nível, em um espécime qualquer, é comparado com o nível existente nos organismos vivos, pode ser calculado o período da morte, de acordo com a taxa de decomposição do 14(C), que tem uma meia vida de 5.700 anos. — Esse método pode ser usado com bastante exatidão por períodos de até sessenta mil anos. Para períodos mais longos do que isso, o tempo passado parece mais curto do que na realidade se passou. Nos artigos sobre a *Astronomia* e a *Arqueologia*, esse e outros métodos para medir a passagem do tempo são discutidos. (AM)

CARBÚNCULO

No hebraico temos três palavras, assim traduzidas, a saber: *Bareqeth*, «pedra brilhante» (ver Êxo. 28:17 e 39:10). Baregath, «esmeralda» (ver Eze. 28:13). *Eben eqdach*, «pedra de brilho» (Isa. 54:12). Os antigos carbúnculos eram, provavelmente, a granada, conforme algumas versões estrangeiras dizem, em Isaías 54:12. É possível que rubis (que vide), também fossem referidos por esse termo. A palavra continua sendo aplicada à granada, usualmente escavada para permitir que a cor da pedra torne-se mais conspícua. A granada de vermelho vivo compõe-se, principalmente, de silicato de alumínio ferroso, embora também possa compor-se de silicato de magnésio alumínio. (Z)

CARCA

No hebraico, «solo», «soalho». Nome de um lugar localizado entre os mares Mediterrâneo e Morto (Jos. 15:3), que veio a pertencer a Judá, na sua fronteira sul. A localização é desconhecida na atualidade.

CARCAÇA

No hebraico, precisamos considerar quatro palavras, e no grego, uma:

1. *Geviyah*, «corpo», palavra usada por nove vezes (por exemplo: Juí. 14:8,9).
2. *Mappeleth*, «coisa caída», palavra usada por quatro vezes (para exemplificar: Juí. 14:8).
3. *Nebelah*, «carcaça», palavra empregada por quarenta e seis vezes (por exemplo: Lev. 5:2; 11:8,11,24-40; Deu. 28:26; I Reis 13:24-30).
4. *Peger*, «coisa exaurida», palavra que ocorre por vinte e duas vezes (para exemplificar: Gên. 15:11; Núm. 14:29,32,33; Isa. 14:19; Naum 3:3).
5. *Ptoma*, «coisa caída», palavra grega usada por sete vezes: Mat. 14:12; 24:28; Mar. 6:29; 15:45; Apo. 11:8,9. Essas palavras aludem tanto a cadáveres humanos quanto a carcaças de animais. Ver Jos. 8:29; Isa. 14:19 e Heb. 3:17. As leis cerimoniais mosaicas a respeito de corpos mortos indicavam os seguintes pontos: 1. Um corpo morto, em uma casa ou tenda, fazia o lugar tornar-se cerimonialmente imundo. Em outras palavras, uma pessoa não podia participar da adoração ou dos ritos religiosos, enquanto essa condição persistisse. Além disso, qualquer vaso ou receptáculo aberto ficava imundo, enquanto o período de imundície perdurasse, o qual era de sete dias (Núm. 19:16,18; 31:19). 2. O contacto, em qualquer lugar, com um cadáver ou carcaça, fazia a pessoa tornar-se imunda até o cair da noite (Lev. 11:39). Ver o artigo sobre a *Imundícia Cerimonial*.

Outras Idéias: 1. As pessoas sentem um horror natural pelos cadáveres ou carcaças, o que se expressa, por muitas vezes, sob a forma de desdém (Isa. 34:3): «Os seus mortos serão lançados fora, dos seus cadáveres subirá o mau cheiro, e do sangue deles os montes se inundarão». 2. A total destruição de um inimigo qualquer ocorria quando se permitia que as feras e as aves de rapina devorassem o seu cadáver. 3. Figuradamente, destacando a sua inutilidade, os ídolos são chamados «cadáveres», em Lev. 26:30. 4. A idolatria, evidentemente, envolvia a adoração em lugares de sepultamento, o que equivalia a veneração às carcaças dos mortos (Naum 3:3; Eze. 43:7,9). 5. O trecho de Mateus 24:28 associa as carcaças com o prometido julgamento final. As águias (abutres), geralmente reúnem-se nos lugares onde há matanças, e a matança assim subentendida, é aquela que acompanhará os horrores da Grande Tribulação (que vide). (I G HA NTI)

CARCAS

Um dos sete eunucos que servia ao rei Assuero, da Pérsia, mencionado apenas em Ester 1:10. A esses eunucos foi ordenado, pelo monarca, que trouxessem a rainha Vasti, para ser admirada pelos príncipes do império, em face de sua incomum beleza física. Mas ela recusou-se a vir com os eunucos. O episódio terminou com a rejeição de Vasti como a consorte do rei. Sua substituta foi Ester, atrás do que havia a mão providencial de Deus.

CARDAN, GIROLAMO

Suas datas foram 1510-1576. Um matemático, médico e astrólogo italiano. Ele defendia o ponto de vista orgânico do mundo. Ver sobre *Organismos*, *Filosofia dos*. Isso ele explicava segundo termos míticos e panteístas. Também foi o autor dos livros: *Sobre a Sutileza das Coisas* e *Sobre a Diversidade das Coisas*.

CARDEAL

Um título e ofício eclesiástico da Igreja Católica Romana. O cardeal, originalmente título de grandes clérigos de cidades importantes, como Constantinopla, tornou-se título do mais alto de todos os prelados. As principais funções de um cardeal são: eleger o papa, aconselhá-lo e assessorá-lo no governo da Igreja, e votar em concílios ecumênicos. O ofício é honorário. Não se trata de uma extensão ou ampliação do sacramento das Santas Ordens, não tendo qualquer significação teológica em particular. Só pode ser conferido a alguém pelo papa. O código da Lei Canônica, promulgado em 1917, especificou que todos os cardeais devem ser padres ordenados. Antes desse tempo, outras pessoas, até mesmo leigas, ocasionalmente eram nomeadas cardeais. O papa João XXIII adicionou o regulamento que diz que todos os cardeais devem ter sido, primeiramente, bispos, embora o uso da palavra «bispo», nessa conexão, refira-se ao estado hierárquico, dentro do sacramento das Santas Ordens, e não às categorias de diácono, padre e bispo. Os bispos-cardeais não são responsáveis por alguma área, conforme se dá com os bispos normais. Na qualidade de conselheiros do papa, eles têm uma função semelhante à dos ministros dos governos civis. Precisam agir como chefes de departamentos da Igreja, chefes de comissões, etc. A administração diária da Igreja Católica Romana é manuseada, primariamente, pelos cardeais que são oficiais importantes da Cúria Romana. Esses cardeais residem em Roma. Os cardeais que vivem fora de Roma, ocupam posições em vários escritórios, e são consultados sobre questões de grande importância. A eleição do papa foi entregue ao colégio de cardeais, como um dever e um privilégio, pelo Terceiro Concílio Luterano, em 1179. Uma maioria de dois terços dos votos é requerida para que um novo papa seja eleito. (AM E)

CARDO

No hebraico, **choach**, «cardo». Vocábulo que aparece por doze vezes. Para exemplificar: I Sam. 13:6; Isa. 34:13. O cardo é uma das plantas daninhas da Palestina. Muitos botânicos e estudiosos pensam que se trata do *Rubus sanctus*, muito comum naquela região do mundo. É um arbusto de folhas perenes, com estames espinhentos. Suas folhas são macias como a lã na parte superior, com a superfície inferior esbranquiçada. Suas flores são róseas, brancas ou púrpura, e os frutos negros e redondos. Ver *Espinheiros*.

CAREÃ

No hebraico, «calvo». Esse era o nome do pai de Joanã e Jonatã, príncipes judeus da época de Gedalias, o governador babilônio de Jerusalém (Jer. 40:8 *ss*; 41:11 *ss*; 42:1,8; 43:2,4,5). Após a queda de Jerusalém diante dos babilônios, seus filhos juntaram-se a Gedalias, em Mispa (II Reis 25:23).

CAREM

Uma cidade de Judá, cujo nome só figura no trecho de Jos. 15:29, na LXX, ao passo que no texto seguido pela nossa versão portuguesa só encontramos os nomes de Baalá, Ilim e Azém, nesse versículo. Provavelmente, a cidade deve ser identificada com a Bete-Haquerém de Nee. 3:14 e Jer. 6:1, que fica a oito quilômetros ao norte de Tecoa.

CAREY, WILLIAM

Suas datas foram 1761-1834. Foi um ministro batista inglês, grande responsável pela formação, em 1792, da primeira sociedade missionária ao estrangeiro iniciada na Inglaterra, chamada *Baptist Missionary Society*. Foi também o primeiro missionário a ser enviado por essa sociedade. Chegou à Índia em 1794, onde permaneceu até à sua morte, cerca de quarenta anos mais tarde, dedicando-se, portanto, ao seu trabalho, de modo vitalício. Além de fazer trabalho evangelístico, Carey distinguiu-se no campo da lingüística. Ensinou o sânscrito, o bengali e o marati durante trinta anos, tendo escrito dicionários e gramáticas sobre essas línguas.

Carey acreditava que os missionários devem estudar o pano de fundo e as maneiras de pensar dos povos não-cristãos aos que servem, treinando um ministério indígena o mais prontamente possível. Assim, quando Carey faleceu, os próprios crentes indianos puderam dar continuação à obra, pois havia uma liderança formada. Para ajudar nesse mister, Carey proveu um Novo Testamento em língua bengali. Esse excelente exemplo tem sido seguido por grupos ou indivíduos crentes, enviados por várias denominações evangélicas, embora também haja exceções à regra. Há grupos fechados em si mesmos que pensam que o futuro nunca chegará, e não preparam continuadores nacionais de seu trabalho missionário. O resultado disso é uma liderança nacional deficiente, ou mesmo a total ausência de liderança por parte de crentes nacionais. Ver o artigo geral sobre os *Batistas*. (AM E)

CÁRIA

Um antigo país que ficava na extremidade sudoeste da Ásia Menor, mencionado apenas no livro apócrifo de I Macabeus 15:22,33. Era uma área fértil, dotada de bom clima, dividida por colinas costeiras que atravessavam o país, partindo da orla marítima do mar Egeu. Não dispomos de muita informação sobre os antigos habitantes de Cária, embora aparentemente, no séc. VIII A.C., fossem uma população notável, que dispunha de considerável poder marítimo. Não se sabe, contudo, por qual razão deixaram de ser um poder marítimo. Sob os persas, a região tornou-se uma satrapia distinta; e parece ter-se envolvido na revolta jônica contra o domínio persa. A região foi rapidamente helenizada, embora sempre tivesse sido uma região que os monarcas sírios Seleúcidas tiveram dificuldade em controlar. Mudou de mãos por diversas vezes, segundo mudava a maré do predomínio militar sobre a região. Em 129 A.C., tornou-se parte da província romana da Ásia. Naquela referência de I Macabeus, a região é mencionada como um território para onde Roma enviou comunicações, quando de seu apoio inicial aos judeus. (S Z)

CARIDADE

Por influência da Vulgata Latina, as traduções mais antigas estampam essa palavra em lugar de «amor». Porém, visto que modernamente esse termo tem um sentido mais restrito, dando a entender a doação de esmolas, o cuidado pelos pobres, enfermos, órfãos, etc., as traduções e versões mais modernas dão preferência ao termo «amor» como tradução do termo grego *agapé*. Apesar disso, a importância da *caridade*, em seu sentido moderno, tem sido subestimada em muitos segmentos da Igreja. Ver o artigo sobre as *Esmolas*.

652

A caridade cristã, no sentido mais restrito da palavra, tem uma nobre história no judaísmo e no cristianismo. A legislação mosaica tinha provisões favoráveis aos pobres. Os pobres, os órfãos e os estrangeiros tinham o direito de respigar o cereal, a uva e a azeitona (Lev. 19:9,10; 23:22; Deu. 24:19). Rute tirou proveito desse costume. (Ver Rute 2:2 e ss). Ver também sobre *Respigar*. Na Igreja primitiva, em Jerusalém, todas as coisas eram usadas em comum, de modo voluntário, a fim de evitar as condições difíceis criadas pela perseguição e pela escassez. Ver o artigo sobre a *Vida Comunal da Igreja Primitiva*. As igrejas gentílicas doaram uma oferta substancial, para aliviar essa situação (I Cor. 16:1 ss). Nos primeiros dias do cristianismo, os cristãos praticavam os costumes judaicos quanto aos cuidados pelos pobres e pelas viúvas. Os primeiros diáconos (que vide) foram eleitos precisamente com essa finalidade (Atos 6). Paulo estabeleceu regras para a admissão das viúvas, como pessoas sustentadas pelas igrejas locais (I Tim. 5:3 ss). Os primeiros cristãos levaram avante essas práticas, e adicionaram outras, como hospedarias para recepção de viajantes cristãos e estrangeiros. As antigas hospedarias viviam repletas de ladrões e prostitutas, e isso criou a necessidade de hospedarias cristãs. Instituições como hospitais, escolas e orfanatos chegaram a tornar-se parte do trabalho das igrejas. Várias ordens religiosas especializaram-se em trabalhos de caridade. Nessa área de atividades, a Igreja Católica Romana tem feito mais e melhor do que os evangélicos em geral. Além disso, não devemos falar sobre as extensas obras de caridade dos espíritas, pois, do contrário, ficaremos embaraçados, porque Deus não nos inspira mais ao amor ao próximo. A *caridade*, no sentido moderno e restrito, é um aspecto da lei geral do amor, a prova mesma da regeneração e da espiritualidade (I João 4:7 ss).

CARISMATA

Ver o artigo geral sobre os **Dons Espirituais**, onde o assunto é amplamente ventilado. O termo *charismata*, em grego, significa, literalmente «coisas dadas gratuitamente», ou seja, «dons». O uso especializado do termo alude aos dons do Espírito Santo (I Cor. 12:4-11). Paulo fornece-nos uma longa lista de diversos desses dons, e no artigo acima mencionado cada um desses dons é individualmente descrito. Em Efésios 4:7-16, há menção a homens espiritualmente dotados, os quais são presenteados à Igreja. Ali a lista dos dons ministeriais da Palavra é completa, estando enumerados os apóstolos, os profetas, os evangelistas e os pastores e mestres. Um detalhe da sintaxe grega dá-nos a entender que «pastores e mestres» formam um único ministério, desdobrado em dois aspectos. Há pastores que apenas pastoreiam; e há pastores que também ensinam. Ver I Tim. 5:17. Ver também Romanos 12:6 ss, onde há menção a outros dons, por serem exercidos pelos diversos *membros* do corpo. Cada membro deve ter sua função específica, e deve estar atuando bem nessa função, pois, em caso contrário, o corpo inteiro ressentir-se-á e ficará espiritualmente debilitado ou enfermo.

Ver o artigo sobre *Movimento Carismático*.

CARLSTADT, Andreas Rudolf Bodenstein

Nasceu em 1480 e faleceu em 1541. Foi notável personagem da Reforma Protestante. Ocupava posição de autoridade em Witenberg, e, quanto a alguns pontos, antecipou o desenvolvimento dado por Lutero. Era dotado de coragem e convicções fortes, embora lhe faltasse algum equilíbrio e bom senso. Em várias oportunidades, seu vigor e falta de prudência, na tentativa de aplicar alguns de seus princípios, quase provocaram o caos. Em seus anos de início de carreira, ele era conhecido como um extremista; e, em várias ocasiões, durante a vida, despertou a animosidade. Isso, finalmente, provocou o seu exílio, e muito sofrimento para ele.

Foi um erudito que ensinou na cidade de Colônia, e mais tarde, na Universidade de Wittenberg, ambas na Alemanha. Suas cadeiras eram a de filosofia e a de teologia. Sua abordagem era essencialmente tomista. Em 1515 foi a Roma, onde se formou em direito. A sua estada em Roma exerceu sobre ele o mesmo efeito que exercera sobre Lutero. Carlstadt renunciou ao tomismo e abraçou as idéias de Agostinho, com ênfase sobre a doutrina paulina-agostiniana da salvação. A 16 de setembro de 1516, ele publicou suas 151 teses, antes mesmo de Lutero haver desafiado ao sistema papal. Carlstadt e Lutero influenciavam um ao outro, embora nunca tivessem sido bons amigos.

O rei da Dinamarca, Cristiano II, convidou Carlstadt para vir ajudar na reforma daquele país. Porém, com seu temperamento, Carlstadt antagonizou o clero e a nobreza dinamarqueses. Ele denunciou a prática do celibato, casou-se e regressou a Wittenberg. Lutero chegou ali nove meses mais tarde, e os dois entraram em choque sobre como dever-se-ia aplicar as medidas da Reforma Protestante. Carlstadt tinha menos paciência do que Lutero, e sempre assumia posições mais radicais. Chegou a negar a necessidade de ordens clericais, e, por algum tempo, abandonou totalmente o ministério. Passou a porção final de sua vida no exílio, na Suíça, quase sempre na pobreza. Exerceu influência sobre o decurso da reforma, de 1518 a 1524; mas seu ardor inflamado, nunca temperado com a prudência e com o bom senso prático, terminou por abafar-lhe a influência. Faleceu em Basel, a 24 de dezembro de 1541. Penso que Carlstadt realizou o seu trabalho, a despeito dos seus problemas, e isso é mais do que podemos dizer acerca de um grande número de pessoas. (AM E)

CARLYLE, THOMAS

Suas datas foram 1795-1881. — Homem letrado, britânico, nascido em Ecclefechan, na Escócia. Educou-se na Universidade de Edimburgo, tendo-se sempre mostrado um homem impelido por intensa busca e conflito espiritual. Sua publicação, *Sartor Resartus* (1833-1834), reflete essa intensidade. Passou a residir em Londres, após o ano de 1834. Embora grande parte de sua energia se tivesse gasto em obras históricas e biográficas como *A Revolução Francesa* e *Frederico, o Grande*, tornou-se conhecido por causa de seus ensaios de crítica social e política, dos quais os principais exemplos são *Chartismo*, *Heróis*, *Adoração e os Heróis da História*, *Panfletos dos Últimos Dias* e *Sartor Resartus*, este último sendo o grande representante de seu gênio notável.

Idéias: 1. A necessidade de renúncia e de trabalho, para que o indivíduo realize o que deve, com todas as suas forças. 2. Carlyle promovia a teoria do GRANDE *homem* da história. A esperança do homem jaz em seu *ato heróico*. Esses atos despertam em nós a determinação de produzirmos o melhor de que somos capazes. À sombra dos grandes heróis, os demais homens encontram os seus respectivos lugares. Portanto, a biografia é a essência da história. 3. Ele opunha-se ao materialismo e ao utilitarismo como fatores que contribuem para a degeneração dos homens. Definia a *liberdade* como o direito dos

CARMA — CARMI

ignorantes serem governados pelos verdadeiros sábios. Essa idéia não concorda com os ideais democráticos, embora haja aí um grande conceito, *se* homens verdadeiramente sábios puderem ser encontrados para governarem. (E P)

CARMA
Ver sob **Karma**.

CARMANIANOS
Em II Esdras 15:30 há uma referência a esse povo, natural da Carmânia, uma fértil província da antiga Pérsia, na margem norte do golfo Pérsico, que modernamente se chama Kerman. Trata-se de uma região montanhosa, separada por um deserto da porção sudoeste do Irã, Persis. Além da província da Carmânia, também havia uma cidade com esse nome. Uma e outra derivavam seu nome dos Kermani ou germanos, uma tribo que ali residia. Heródoto (i.155) menciona esse povo, além de outros tribos, que formavam uma sapatria e pagavam tributo a Dario (ii.93). Posteriormente, o helenismo foi introduzido no lugar por Antíoco I Soter. Cidades gregas foram fundadas na região, como Alexandria da Carmânia. Ainda mais tarde, o sátrapa Numenio de Mesene, do sul da Babilônia, derrotou os persas, nas praias da Carmânia, no mar e na terra, segundo nos informa Plínio (vi.152). (OLM Z)

CARMELITAS
O nome todo dessa ordem mendicante católica romana é Ordem de Nossa Senhora do Monte Carmelo. Foi fundada em meados do século XII D.C., na Terra Santa. Alguns estudiosos têm procurado achar os antecedentes dessa ordem em fraternidades judaicas, anteriores à época cristã. Foi reconhecida pelas autoridades católicas romanas em 1274, por recomendação do segundo concílio de Lyons, na França. Os carmelitas adotaram sua característica manta de lã em 1287, pelo que, em inglês, a ordem é chamada de *Whitefriars*, «frades brancos». Há duas divisões na ordem: 1. A ordem *Calçada*, que é mais antiga e menos rigorosa; e 2. a ordem *Descalça*, mais numerosa, que data das reformas instituídas por Teresa de Ávila (que vide), em cerca de 1560 D.C.
— Teologicamente, eles têm-se notabilizado na sua oposição às idéias de Wycliff, e por sua pertinaz aderência ao tomismo (que vide). Ver o artigo sobre *João da Cruz*. (E)

CARMELO
No hebraico, «campo plantado», «parque» ou «jardim». É palavra que aparece por vinte e seis vezes no Antigo Testamento.

1. *Um Nome Comum*. O nome Carmelo aparece de forma indefinida, com os sentidos dados acima, em Isa. 16:10; Jer. 4:26; II Reis 19:23. Em Lev. 2:14 e 23:14, o nome aparece para indicar espigas frescas de trigo. Porém, a palavra também ocorre para indicar lugares específicos. É possível que as colinas de pedra calcária do Carmelo tenham recebido tal nome devido à vegetação arbustiva luxuriante e aos densos arvoredos que as encobriam.

2. *Uma Cadeia Montanhosa*. Essa cadeia estende-se por cerca de quarenta e oito quilômetros, na direção noroeste-sueste, desde as margens do mar Mediterrâneo, ao sul da baía de Acre, até à planície de Dotã. Em um sentido mais estrito, o monte Carmelo é o pico principal dessa curta cadeia montanhosa, que alcança um máximo de 531 m, em sua extremidade nordeste, e que fica cerca de dezenove quilômetros distante da beira-mar. Servia de um dos marcos da fronteira de Aser (Jos. 19:26). O rei de Jocneão, de Carmelo, foi um dos chefes cananeus que foram derrotados por Josué. Desde os tempos mais antigos, a paisagem de Carmelo, bela como um jardim, foi sagrada para eles, onde adoravam o Baal cananeu, além de outras divindades oraculares. A beleza natural atrai as pessoas à inquirição espiritual. Talvez os mais bem conhecidos episódios que circundaram o Carmelo foram aqueles em que Elias e Eliseu estiveram envolvidos. Foi no monte Carmelo que Elias desafiou e derrotou os profetas de Baal e Aserá, as divindades que Jezabel, esposa do rei Acabe, de Israel, havia decidido promover (I Reis 18 e 19). Ver o artigo sobre *Baal*. Foi também no monte Carmelo que Eliseu recebeu a visita da mãe cujo filho morrera, e que logo foi por ele ressuscitado (II Reis 4:25).

3. *A Cidade de Carmelo*. Era uma aldeia na região montanhosa de Judá (Jos. 15:55), terra natal de Nabel (I Sam. 25:2,5,7,40) e de Abigail, a carmelita, a qual tornou-se a esposa favorita de Davi (I Sam. 27:3). Saul estabeleceu o lugar, após sua vitória sobre os amalequitas (I Sam. 15:12). Era ali, e não na outra Carmelo, que o rei Uzias tinha as suas vinhas (II Crô. 26:10). Essa cidade atualmente chama-se Karmel, estando localizada cerca de quinze quilômetros a suleste de Hebrom. A palavra não aparece no Novo Testamento. Ao que parece, Judas Iscariotes era natural dessa região, embora isso não transpareça no Novo Testamento. (ID S UN)

CARMESIM
No hebraico temos a palavra **karmil**, que figura por três vezes no Antigo Testamento: II Crô. 2:7,14; 3:14.

Na antiguidade, os corantes eram obtidos de vegetais, minerais ou animais. Plínio descreveu a cor carmesim (no grego, *kokkinos*) como um vermelho que se aproxima do rosa escuro, quase como a púrpura de Tiro (*Hist. Natural* xxi.45,46). Esse corante derivava-se de certas substâncias extraídas do corpo de um inseto, do gênero feminino. O corante foi usado para vários itens do tabernáculo. Não parece que os hebreus faziam clara distinção entre o carmesim e o escarlate. Todavia, eles tinham um vocábulo para indicar esta última cor, a saber, *shani*, que figura por quinze vezes (para exemplificar: Jer. 4:30; Isa. 1:18). Nesta última referência, a cor indica a culpa do pecado, provavelmente porque o pecado está associado à expiação pelo sangue. Ver o artigo geral sobre as *Cores*.

CARMI
No hebraico, «frutífero» ou «nobre». Há três homens com esse nome, nas páginas do Antigo Testamento, a saber:

1. Um homem de Judá, pai de Acã, o *perturbador* de Israel (Jos. 7:1,18; I Crô. 2:7). Neste último versículo, Acã é chamado Acar. No trecho de I Crônicas 4:1, Carmi aparece como um dos filhos de Judá. A questão é difícil de deslindar, mas o mesmo indivíduo deve estar em foco.

2. Quarto filho de Rúben, fundador da família dos carmitas (Gên. 46:9; Êxo. 6:14; Núm. 26:6; I Crô. 5:3), em cerca de 1872 A.C.

3. Filho de Hezrom (neto de Judá), pai de Hur (I Crô. 4:1), que em outros textos é chamado de Calebe (I Crô. 2:18) ou de Quelubai (I Crô. 2:9). Alguns

estudiosos identificam-no com o mesmo homem do nº 1, acima.

CARMIS

Um dos três governantes de Betúlia (Judite 6:15 e 8:10), a quem Judite apelou, pedindo ajuda, quando Holofernes ameaçou a região.

CARNAL

Esse vocábulo vem do latim *caro, carnis*, «carne», tradução dos termos gregos *sarkikós* e *sárkinos*. Usualmente, esse vocábulo alude ao corpo de carne; mas também é usado metaforicamente para indicar os apetites do corpo, ou então aquilo que é mundano, fazendo contradição ao que é espiritual. Consideremos os pontos abaixo:
1. Em Romanos 7:14, indica-se a posse da natureza da carne, e isso governado por considerações e valores humanos, e não pelo Espírito de Deus (I Cor. 3:1,3). 2. O que é *carnal* também pode ser uma alusão àquilo que é inerentemente fraco (II Cor. 10:4); 3. o que é temporal (Heb. 7:16); 4. o que é débil e pecaminoso (II Cor. 1:12). 5. Também pode ser uma distinta disposição antiespiritual (Rom. 7:14). 6. Ou então aquela disposição antiespiritual que aliena os homens de Deus (Rom. 8:5-8). 7. O que é carnal também pode apontar para a imaturidade espiritual, que não conseguiu livrar-se daquilo que é inerentemente mau (I Cor. 3:3,4). 8. O poder do que é carnal pode ser tão grande que chega a alienar a mente, tornando-a inimiga de Deus (Rom. 8:7). 9. As antigas cerimônias veterotestamentárias eram carnais, no sentido que diziam respeito aos corpos dos homens e dos animais, que são entidades terrenas, e não espirituais, embora tais cerimônias tivessem um simbolismo espiritual (Heb. 7:16; 9:10). 10. As relações sexuais proibidas também são chamadas *carnais* (Lev. 18:20 e 19:20). 11. As armas usadas pelos ministros do evangelho não são carnais, e, sim, espirituais em sua natureza (II Cor. 10:4). 12. Carnais também são as substâncias necessárias para o sustento do corpo (Rom. 15:57; I Cor. 9:11), ou seja, as *coisas materiais*. 13. *Contrastes*. Existe o homem espiritual; existe o homem natural (não-regenerado); e existe o homem regenerado, mas ainda carnal. Este último é o crente que ainda não se esforçou por cumprir todo o seu potencial espiritual, que continua lançando mão de coisas carnais em muitos aspectos de sua vida, quando deveria lançar mão de realidades espirituais. Ver Rom. 7:14 e I Cor. 3:1 (homem carnal); I Cor. 2:14 (homem natural); I Cor. 2:15 e 3:1 (homem espiritual). (I IB NTI)

CARNAP, RUDOLF

Suas datas foram 1891-1970. Foi filósofo alemão, positivista (ver sobre o *Positivismo*). Foi professor de filosofia na Universidade de Chicago, bem como na UCLA. Durante muitos anos, foi um dos mais influentes lógicos positivistas, aquele que expunha a mais completa filosofia desse ponto de vista. Ele acreditava que o progresso na filosofia requer a análise científica dos conceitos envolvidos, considerando o desenvolvimento de uma linguagem formal como o primeiro passo essencial de tal análise. Ele fez contribuições importantes, mas controvertidas, no campo da semântica. Suas principais obras escritas foram: *Der Logische Aufbau der Welt; Logische Syntax der Sprache; Introduction to Semantics;*
Meaning and Necessity; Logical Foundations of Philosophy.

Idéias Principais: 1. A metafísica é destituída de significado, visto que todo o conhecimento alicerça-se sobre a percepção dos sentidos, e não existem objetos metafísicos. 2. As proposições são destituídas de sentido, a menos que tenham alguma conseqüência empírica. As proposições precisam ser testadas empiricamente. Esse teste deve envolver uma linguagem científica. 3. O conhecimento é muito mais uma questão de taxa de probabilidades, e não uma entidade completa, fixa e perfeita. De fato, o conhecimento, segundo as definições tradicionais, nem existiria. Ver sobre o *Ceticismo*. 4. O caráter do significado das idéias deve ser julgado por seus resultados práticos, com base na análise lingüística e lógica. Carnap considerava as proposições da metafísica como destituídas de sentido por serem respostas a pseudoproblemas. 5. Haveria dois tipos de probabilidades: uma delas seria a simples freqüência de probabilidade, apropriada aos problemas estatísticos. A outra seria a probabilidade de confirmação, que se aplicaria aos modos de proceder indutivos. Com base nas evidências, poderíamos afirmar a probabilidade de uma proposição qualquer, através da experiência e da análise. Nisso, vemo-nos envolvidos na lógica indutiva.

Crítica. Do ponto de vista religioso, podemos criticar o **Positivismo Lógico** (ver o artigo), quanto a certos pontos: 1. Parte do conhecimento religioso, pelo menos, pode ser mediado através dos *sentidos*, como os acontecimentos históricos, que são importantes para a fé histórica, e as experiências místicas, que também podem ser mediadas através dos sentidos. 2. As *provas racionais* da fé religiosa também podem ter sua base na observação empírica, como o raciocínio acerca da existência da alma ou de Deus, com base no exame empírico do universo, a consideração sobre seu designio, a necessidade racional de postular o princípio de causa, com base na existência de efeitos que fazem parte óbvia de nosso mundo empírico. No que tange à alma, atualmente há provas empíricas, até mesmo em forma de experiências de laboratório, que comprovam a sua existência. Há, para exemplificar, a *projeção da psique* (que vide), bem como as experiências de quase morte (que vide), para mencionarmos apenas dois dos modos mais destacados de olharmos para a alma, do ponto de vista científico. 3. É um erro limitarmos a busca pelo conhecimento somente a meios empíricos (que vide). O racionalismo (que vide), a intuição (que vide) e o misticismo (que vide), também são meios válidos para a obtenção de conhecimentos. Supor que somente o empirismo é válido como meio, revela um preconceito *a priori*, por parte de quem assim pensa. 4. O *positivismo* é uma crua tentativa de retirar o mistério de um mundo repleto de mistérios. De fato, demonstra estagnação na maneira de pensar, o que, se for seguido muito de perto, só poderá impedir a busca pelo conhecimento. As contribuições do positivismo à ciência são inegáveis, mas há outras maneiras de considerarmos o mundo e de aprendermos a seu respeito sem ser através dos sentidos. 5. Com demasiada freqüência, o positivismo tem como uma de suas bases, uma espécie de pressuposto antifé, como se qualquer coisa sujeita à fé automaticamente seja suspeita. Aqueles que promovem o positivismo não são especialistas na fé e na experiência religiosa, mas presumem saber que nada há de válido na fé e na experiência religiosa. Essa é uma típica atitude preconcebida, e, portanto, não científica. Pois a própria base da ciência é a experiência, mesmo

CARNE

quando não se espera um resultado positivo. Se os positivistas não têm experiência, como podem saber? 6. No positivismo há uma ignorância sobre o que acontece no caso dos gigantes espirituais, cujas obras ilustram que sucedem-se coisas que podem acontecer, completamente fora de toda expectação do que é natural e científico. Consideremos a vida de Jesus Cristo e suas obras. Ele estava muito acima da ciência. Consideremos ao menos o caso moderno de Satya Sai Baba (que vide), o qual, em nossos próprios dias (1985), está reproduzindo os milagres de Jesus a curta distância. Os positivistas lógicos têm-se convertido instantaneamente ao observá-lo, mesmo quando chegam à sua frente a fim de criticá-lo, pensando em poder provar que tudo não passa de uma fraude. (EP P)

CARNE

Esboço:
 I. Idéias Básicas
 II. A Carne Não é Pecaminosa
 III. A Carne é Fraca
 IV. Usos Metafóricos e Espirituais
 V. O Corpo Não-Físico
 VI. A Comunhão Mística com Cristo
 VII. Palavras Envolvidas

O termo «carne» representa certa complexidade de idéias nas Escrituras Sagradas, envolvendo sentidos literais, metafóricos e espirituais. Poderíamos sumariá-las conforme o fazemos abaixo:

I. Idéias Básicas

1. A *criação animal*, que inclui o homem e os animais irracionais (Gên. 6:13,17,19; 7:15; Mat. 24:22; I Ped. 1:24).

2. O *corpo vivo*, tanto dos homens quanto dos animais (Gên. 41:2,19; Jó 33:21; I Cor. 15:39).

3. O corpo de carne, em distinção à armação óssea (Luc. 24:39).

4. Os animais usados como alimento, e o próprio alimento (Êxo. 16:12; Lev. 7:19).

5. O corpo em distinção ao *espírito* (Jó 14:22; 19:26; Pro. 14:30; Isa. 10:18; João 6:52; I Cor. 5:5; Col. 2:5; I Ped. 4:6).

6. *Carne e sangue* indicam a natureza humana inteira (Gên. 2:23; Mat. 19:5; Efé. 5:25-31).

7. A *encarnação* de Cristo (João 1:14; 6:51; Rom. 1:3; Col. 1:22).

8. A *geração física* ou natural (Gên. 29:14; 37:27; João 1:13; Rom. 9:8; Heb. 2:11-14).

9. Um outro *homem mortal* (Isa. 58:7).

10. A *natureza sensual* do ser humano, incluindo seus desejos naturais. Isso não precisa incluir qualquer sugestão de depravação (João 1:13) ou ter tais conotações (Mat. 26:41; Mar. 14:38).

11. A *natureza humana* à parte da influência divina, e, portanto, inclinada ao pecado, mostrando-se contrária a Deus (Rom. 8:3,5,6; II Cor. 7:5; Gál. 5:16).

12. Uma expressão eufêmica para os órgãos sexuais (Gên. 17:11; Êxo. 28:42; Lev. 15:2,3; II Ped. 2:10; Jud. 7).

13. Em combinação com o sangue, ou seja, *carne e sangue*, dando a entender a fraqueza e falibilidade humanas, inclinada ao erro (Mat. 16:17; Gál. 1:16; Efé. 6:12).

II. A Carne Não é Pecaminosa

O Novo Testamento, em contraste com o gnosticismo (que vide) não ensina a pecaminosidade do corpo físico ou princípio material. Ambos podem ser usados na promoção do mal, e o corpo físico é fácil de ser tentado ao pecado; mas a matéria, por si mesma, é moral e espiritualmente neutra. Os gnósticos tinham dois pressupostos básicos que eram errôneos: 1. O espírito é puro. 2. O corpo é mau, porque o princípio do mal reside na própria matéria. O cristianismo bíblico dispõe de dois pressupostos que contradizem a posição dos gnósticos: 1. O espírito humano é decaído, pois o homem essencial é o espírito, ao passo que o corpo físico é apenas um veículo. 2. O corpo físico é moralmente neutro, embora sirva de instrumento que, naturalmente, tenta ao pecado, conforme se dá, por exemplo, nas questões sexuais, ou na glutonaria, ou seja, através dos apetites.

III. A Carne é Fraca

Platão aludiu ao corpo físico como o sepulcro ou a prisão da alma. O Novo Testamento não compartilha de tão melancólica atitude, embora valorize muito mais o espírito do que o corpo físico. — O alvo da carreira cristã é a liberdade em um corpo novo ou espiritual, em que o antigo veículo é deixado para trás (I Cor. 15:35 ss). O corpo nos sujeita a certa variedade de tentações, por causa de sua debilidade (Mat. 26:41). A lei de Deus envolve maior número de mandamentos do que podemos manusear devidamente em meio a essa fraqueza (Rom. 8:3). O corpo está sujeito a debilidades que nos servem de empecilhos (Gál. 4:13), além de ser instrumento fácil do pecado, conforme se vê no sétimo capítulo da epístola aos Romanos. O corpo físico é mortal e, portanto, fraco (II Cor. 4:11).

IV. Usos Metafóricos e Espirituais

1. Ter nascido somente segundo a carne é estar perdido (Gál. 4:29).

2. Há a natureza carnal e pecaminosa, em contraste com a natureza espiritual (Rom. 8:9).

3. A carne é a sede das tentações (Rom. 7:18,25; 8:5,12,13; I João 2:16).

4. A carne é uma natureza carnal que procura perturbar (Gál. 5:13).

5. A palavra «carnal» aponta para a natureza pecaminosa, ou então, simplesmente, para o pecado (Jud. 23).

6. Existe uma mente carnal, que é a natureza pecaminosa do homem que opera através de sua mente e de todo o seu ser (Rom. 8:7; Col. 2:18).

V. O Corpo Não-Físico

O novo corpo, ressurrecto, veículo da alma após a morte biológica, não será um corpo físico, e, sim, uma energia espiritual. Será resultado da ressurreição, que considero ser uma espécie de nova criação, e não a mera reformulação dos elementos físicos, atômicos. Alguns teólogos insistem em uma ressurreição literal do corpo físico. Ver I Cor. 15:35 ss e Fil. 3:21. Ver o artigo sobre a *Ressurreição*.

VI. A Comunhão Mística com Cristo

Essa comunhão é expressa através de expressões como comer sua carne e beber o seu sangue (João 6:53). Ver o artigo sobre esse assunto, sob o título, *Comer a Carne e Beber o Sangue de Jesus*. Ver também sobre *Jesus Como o Pão da Vida*.

VII. Palavras Envolvidas

Há três palavras hebraicas e duas palavras gregas principais, envolvidas neste verbete, a saber:

1. *Basar*, «carne». Palavra hebraica que ocorre por cerca de duzentas e sessenta vezes, começando em Gên. 2:21 e terminando em Zac. 14:12.

2. *Sheer*, «remanescentes». Palavra hebraica usada

por nove vezes com esse sentido. Por exemplo: Sal. 73:26; 78:20,27; Pro. 11:17; Jer. 51:35; Miq. 3:2,3.

3. *Besar*, «carne». Palavra aramaica usada por três vezes, sempre no livro de Daniel (2:11; 4:12; 7:5).

4. *Kréas*, «carne» (como alimento). Termo grego usado por duas vezes: Rom. 14:21 e I Cor. 8:13.

5. *Sarks*, «carne». Vocábulo grego usado por cento e trinta e seis vezes: Mat. 16:17; 19:5,6; 24:22; 26:41; Mar. 10:8; 13:20; 14:38; Luc. 3:6; 24:39; João 1:13,14; 3:6; 6:51-56,63; 8:15; 17:2; Atos 2:17,26,31; Rom. 1:3; 2:28; 3:20; 4:1; 6:19; 7:5,18,25; 8:3-9,12, 13; 9:3,5,8; 11:14; 13:14; I Cor. 1:26,29; 5:5; 6:16; 7:28; 10:18; 15:39,50; II Cor. 1:17; 4:11; 5:16; 7:1,5; 10:2,3; 11:18; 12:7; Gál. 1:16; 2:16,20; 3:3; 4:13,14,23,29; 5:13,16,17,19,24; 6:8,12,13; Efé. 2:3, 11,15; 5:29,31; 6:5,12; Fil. 1:22,24; 3:3,4; Col. 1:22,24; 2:1,5,11,13,18,23; 3:22; I Tim. 3:16; File. 16; Heb. 2:14; 5:7; 9:10,13; 10:20; 12:9; Tia. 5:3; I Ped. 1:24; 3:18,21; 4:1,2,6; II Ped. 2:10,18; I João 2:16; 4:2; II João 7; Jud. 7,8,23; Apo. 17:16; 19:18,21. (NTI RO (1952) UN Z)

CARNE OFERECIDA AOS ÍDOLOS

Ver os trechos de I Cor. 8:1 ss, 10:25,27; Apo. 2:14,20. A passagem de Atos 15:20 mostra-nos que comer carnes oferecidas aos ídolos foi uma prática vedada aos crentes, pelo concílio apostólico de Jerusalém. As carnes eram expostas diante dos ídolos para agradar aos deuses ou espíritos que esses ídolos representavam. O trecho de I Cor. 10:20 mostra que os judeus e os cristãos primitivos acreditavam que há espíritos demoníacos por detrás dos ídolos, sem importar se isso era ou não reconhecido pelos participantes dos cultos idólatras. Os alimentos oferecidos nos templos podiam então ser vendidos nos mercados. Um cristão que por ali passasse poderia comprar de tais alimentos. Se, porventura, desconhecesse a sua origem, então não poderia ser acusado de haver participado dos mesmos. Mas, se ele comprasse e comesse dos mesmos de maneira consciente, então um outro cristão poderia pensar que ele era culpado de certa forma de idolatria. Ou então, um cristão podia ser convidado a uma refeição ou banquete, participando de tais alimentos. Paulo assumia uma atitude de indiferença para com questões assim, porquanto, na verdade, o ídolo nada significa (I Cor. 8:4). Mas, a atitude que transparece em I Cor. 10:20, de que os demônios estão por detrás das práticas idólatras, pelo menos no caso de alguns serviria de indicação de que a participação em tais alimentos oferecidos a ídolos era um ato extremamente repugnante. Por esse motivo, Paulo recomendou que os crentes evitassem ofender aos outros, abstendo-se de tal prática, a menos que o fizessem totalmente em segredo. Podemos estar quase certos de que alguns dos outros apóstolos não concordariam com essa atitude *liberal* de Paulo. Antes de tudo, o concílio de Jerusalém havia condenado a prática de maneira absoluta; e a razão para tanto provavelmente não envolvia somente a tentativa de agradar aos cristãos judeus. Outrossim, o trecho de Apo. 2:14,20 mostra-nos que o autor sagrado desse último livro do Novo Testamento via tal prática com horror. Para ele, a questão não parecia ser indiferente.

Simbolismo. A questão ilustra a prática de coisas inocentes em si mesmas, mas que podem ofender a outras pessoas, como formas de entretenimento, ingestão moderada de bebidas alcoólicas, uso de jóias e enfeites pelas mulheres crentes, etc. A aplicação é que aquele que é sério em sua inquirição espiritual deveria estar disposto a sacrificar aquelas coisas que ofendem a outros crentes, ainda que ele mesmo não veja nenhum erro nessas coisas.

CARNÉADES

Nasceu em 214 e faleceu em 129 A.C. Foi um filósofo cético, nascido em Cirene, na Grécia. Foi o fundador da Terceira Academia, em 156 A.C. Ele opunha-se ao estoicismo, ao seu tipo de conhecimento e a seu sistema ético. Ver o artigo geral sobre o *Ceticismo*.

Idéias: 1. Não temos consciência das coisas, mas apenas de *nossas impressões* sobre elas. Outrossim, é impossível distinguir entre as impressões falsas e as verdadeiras. Portanto, quem é sábio suspende seu juízo, não tendo certeza de que pode ter certeza de alguma coisa. 2. Não obstante, há graus de *probabilidades*. Uma forte impressão *pode* estar certa. Além disso, há impressões que parecem harmonizar-se com aquelas de outras pessoas, que não são contraditas. Há até mesmo impressões não contraditas e confirmadas, fornecendo-nos uma mais alta taxa de probabilidades. 3. Contrariamente à idéia da providência divina, ele salientava toda a desarmonia existente nas coisas deste mundo. Pensava que a ordem que porventura existe na criação, pode ser explicada segundo termos naturais, e não sobrenaturais. 4. O *conceito de Deus* compõe-se de várias contradições, nas quais o infinito é misturado com o finito, o bem ordenado com o desordenado, a infinitude com a individualidade, a imanência com a transcendência. Deus não pode ser, ao mesmo tempo, dotado de corpo e destituído de corpo. Se ele tem corpo, então Deus deve ser simples ou composto. Se ele é simples, então é incapaz de ter vida e de pensar; se ele é composto, então está sujeito à desintegração. Se destituído de corpo, Deus não pode agir e nem sentir. Finalmente, nenhuma assertiva de qualquer espécie pode ser feita acerca de Deus. 5. Carnéades rejeitava a idéia de uma ação sem causa, que requer uma explicação extrafísica. 6. A essência do *ceticismo* é que o conhecimento, se tiver de ser reputado perfeito ou completo, é impossível, ou, pelo menos, é impossível para nós conhecê-lo. O «conhecer» somente acompanha uma taxa de probabilidades, com base em nossos débeis sentidos da percepção. (E EI P)

CARNEIRO

Ver **Ovelha**.

CARO, JOSÉ

Nasceu na Espanha, em 1488, e faleceu em Safede, na Palestina, em 1575. Tornou-se conhecido principalmente como autor da obra *Shulhan Aruk*, a qual, a partir do século XVII, tornou-se a autoridade padrão sobre a lei, o ritual e a observância judaicas. Caro era um místico, conforme transparece em seu diário, onde ele entra em discussões com seu guia celestial. (E)

CARPINTEIRO

Ver o artigo geral sobre **Artes e Ofícios**. O termo bíblico «carpinteiro», no hebraico, *harush*, «artesão», e no grego *tékton*, «artífice», é uma espécie de termo geral para indicar qualquer artífice que trabalha em pedra, metal ou madeira, e não somente em madeira. Ver II Sam. 5:11; I Crô. 14:1; Isa. 44:13; Mat. 13:55; Mar. 6:3. Nos trechos de II Sam. 5:11; II Reis 12:11; I Crô. 14:1; Isa. 44:13; Mat. 13:55 e Marc. 6:3, o termo parece limitar-se ao trabalho em madeira. O trabalho feito por vários artífices é pintado na denúncia de Isaías contra a idolatria (Isa. 41:7 e 44:9,10). Infelizmente, tais homens produzem ídolos para serem adorados (vs. 13:17); eles têm grande habilidade, mas são suficientemente embotados para não perceberem que estão produzindo algo inferior a eles mesmos, algo que simplesmente não pode ser equiparado à divindade. A passagem de Jer. 24:1 mostra-nos que a deportação para a Babilônia incluiu homens de diversas profissões. Portanto, eles tornaram-se elementos valiosos para o inimigo, ao mesmo tempo em que Judá desintegrava-se.

No Novo Testamento. Marcos 6:3 chama Jesus de «carpinteiro»; e Mateus 13:55 diz que Jesus era «o' filho do carpinteiro». Mui provavelmente, Jesus foi ambas as coisas. Supõe-se que Jesus trabalhava em companhia de José, na carpintaria, e que, após a morte de José, Jesus continuou sozinho o trabalho de carpinteiro. Visto que Nazaré era uma pequena comunidade, provavelmente José e Jesus eram os únicos carpinteiros da localidade. Justino Mártir, em seu *Diálogo com Trifo*, assevera que Jesus trabalhava como carpinteiro, e que, no segundo século D.C., objetos feitos por ele ainda existiam. Portanto, Jesus aprovou o labor comum, tornando-o honroso. Porém, também demonstrou que esse trabalho, por si só, não é suficiente. Não basta trabalhar. Deve também haver a inquirição espiritual em cada vida humana. É interessante observar que a palavra grega *tékton* pode significar um carpinteiro, mas também pode significar um construtor ou pedreiro, um artífice, ou mesmo qualquer artista em qualquer arte ou ofício, incluindo um planejador, um autor ou um poeta. A tradição apresenta José e Jesus como carpinteiros, isto é, como quem trabalhava em madeira, não havendo qualquer boa razão para contradizermos a mesma. (A FO I RO VIN)

CARPO

Provavelmente um nome derivado do termo grego *kárpos*, que significa «fruto». Esse era o nome de um homem com quem Paulo ficou hospedado, quando esteve em Trôade, e que, presumivelmente, era cristão. O trecho de II Timóteo 4:13 informa-nos que Paulo deixara ali uma capa. Provavelmente isso ocorreu quando Paulo passou pela Ásia Menor pela última vez, antes de seu martírio em Roma. O frio que Paulo experimentou na prisão, levou-o a pedir que Timóteo lhe trouxesse a tal capa. Alguns intérpretes supõem que, na ocasião, Paulo estava recolhido em uma masmorra. Carpo não é mencionado em qualquer outro trecho do Novo Testamento; mas, de conformidade com Hipólito, ele tornou-se bispo de Berito ou Beréia, na Trácia.

CARQUÊMIS

Era uma cidade hitita, à margem direita do rio Eufrates, uma grande fortaleza localizada perto dos melhores vaus daquele rio (Jer. 46:24; Isa. 10:9). Era a capital oriental dos hititas. O rei assírio, Assur-Natsupal (cerca de 885-860 A.C.) ameaçou atacá-la, mas foi comprado mediante ricos presentes. Chegou a tornar-se lugar de muito luxo e riquezas, devido a séculos de comércio com outros povos. Sargão capturou Carquêmis em 717 A.C., o que assinalou a queda do império hitita. Os hititas são chamados heteus, na Bíblia. Foi em Carquêmis que Nabucodonosor II derrotou Faraó Neco, do Egito, em 605 A.C. (ver Jer. 46:2), evento esse que marcou o início do esplêndido império neobabilônico, e que pressagiou o cativeiro babilônico (que vide), do reino israelita do sul, Judá. Após o ataque de Nabucodonosor contra Carquêmis, sua importância declinou rapidamente. Na época dos monarcas Selêucidas, uma nova cidade ocupava o local da antiga Carquêmis, chamada Europos. Esse local tem sido amplamente escavado pelos arqueólogos. Isso revelou-nos uma importante cultura hitita. As ruínas da antiga Carquêmis estão no local da moderna Jerablus, que é uma corruptela da palavra grega *Hierópolis*. (UN WIS WOO)

CARRO

No hebraico, **agalah**, «vagão», vocábulo que aparece no Antigo Testamento por vinte e cinco vezes (para exemplificar: I Sam. 6:7-14; I Sam. 7:3; Isa. 5:18; Gên. 45:19,21,27; Núm. 7:3,6,7). Essa palavra denota qualquer veículo que se movia sobre rodas e era puxado por animais. Cada contexto deve determinar o tipo de carro envolvido. Por exemplo, Faraó enviou carros para transportar para o Egito a família de Jacó e seus bens (Gên. 46:5). E, por ocasião da entrega das ofertas dos príncipes de Israel, quando da dedicação do altar, essas ofertas foram trazidas em seis carros cobertos, cada qual puxado por dois bois (Núm. 7:3,6,7). Quando Davi tentou trazer a arca de Deus desde Quiriate-Jearim, esta foi transportada em um carro novo. Nessa oportunidade, Uzá, um dos dois homens que guiava o carro, foi morto pelo Senhor, quando se atreveu a pôr a mão sobre a mesma, ao pensar que a arca poderia tombar no chão, visto que os animais haviam tropeçado (I Crô. 13:7 *ss*). E a arca terminou ficando na casa de Ovede-Edom por três meses; e ele e sua família foram abençoados pelo Senhor, por causa disso. Em I Sam. 6:7, há carros mencionados usados para remoção da arca e de outros utensílios sagrados, puxados por dois bois. Carros comuns eram usados para transportar produtos agrícolas (Amós 2:13).

A arqueologia mostra-nos que os carros eram comuns desde o alvorecer da história humana. Eram conhecidos na Babilônia e no Egito (Gên. 45:19-21; 46:5). Nos dias dos Juízes, em Israel, eram usados carros nas principais estradas das regiões montanhosas, para transportar toda espécie de coisas (I Sam. 6:1-12). Normalmente, eram puxados por dois bois ou por dois cavalos (Núm. 7:3-8; I Sam. 6:10). Pessoas e coisas eram transportadas em carros (Gên. 45:19). Os carros maiores tinham dois condutores (I Crô. 13:7). Usualmente eram fabricados de madeira, pelo que podiam ser desmantelados e queimados (I Sam. 6:14; Sal. 46:9). As rodas eram feitas sólidas ou munidas de raios, e algumas vezes, eram munidas com cambotas de metal (Isa. 28:27,28). Nos baixos relevos do Egito e da Assíria encontram-se boas representações dessas rodas. Também havia carros militares, para transporte de equipamentos ou comestíveis (Isa. 28:27,28; Sal. 46:9).

Uso Figurado. Há aqueles que puxam o pecado como com tirantes de carro (Isa. 5:18), o que indica que alguns homens escravizam-se ao pecado como se fossem carros sobrecarregados de cargas. Ou então está em foco o pecador, vergado sob as pesadas cargas de seus vícios. (G HA S UN)

CARROLL, LEWIS

Pseudônimo de Charles Lutwidge Dodgson (1832-1898), que ele empregava em seus escritos não profissionais. Formou-se com distinção em matemática, e

CARROS DO SOL — CARRUAGEM

publicou seus úteis livros chamados *Euclides I* e *Euclides II*. Além disso, ele escreveu ensaios pioneiros sobre a teoria matemática da votação. Todavia, tornou-se melhor conhecido devido a seus livros populares, como *Alice no País das Maravilhas, Através da Lente* e *Sílvia e Bruno*. O primeiro, apesar de ser famoso como história infantil, também é uma obra casual e leve sobre a lógica filosófica, guarnecida de inúmeros exemplos de inesquecíveis absurdos. Os inimigos da fé religiosa têm comparado a mesma a uma *Alice no País das Maravilhas* de natureza espiritual.

CARROS DO SOL

Essa expressão aparece em II Reis 23:11, indicando aqueles carros que Josias queimou, entre outras medidas purificadoras que tomou, quando de suas reformas religiosas em Judá. Vários versículos do Antigo Testamento informam-nos sobre a adoração ao sol, prestada por vários povos nos tempos antigos (Êxo. 24:24; Lev. 26:30; II Crô. 14:5; 34:4; Isa. 17:8; 27:9; Eze. 6:4,6). Um dos objetos usados nesse culto era precisamente o carro do sol (IICrô. 24:4,7). Também havia os cavalos dedicados à adoração ao sol, os quais puxavam os carros (II Reis 23:11). Zinjirli, nas inscrições aramaicas do século VIII A.C., aparentemente era o cocheiro do deus sol Shamash. A arqueologia tem mostrado quão generalizada era essa adoração ao sol, porquanto existia entre os assírios, entre os cananeus e entre os judeus. Até mesmo nos primeiros tempos da Roma imperial esse culto era popular. Uma das cerimônias incluía o lançamento de quatro cavalos ao mar, por ocasião da festividade anual em honra ao sol. Um outro ato comum, nessa adoração, era o costume dos reis e nobres envolverem-se na mesma. Eles levantavam-se antes da aurora e partiam em seus carros de guerra na direção do oriente, ao encontro do sol que surgia no horizonte. Essa jornada era efetuada em carros dedicados ao sol.

CARRUAGEM

Sete palavras hebraicas e duas palavras gregas estão envolvidas:

1. *Hotsen*, «carro de guerra». Essa palavra hebraica figura exclusivamente em Eze. 23:24.

2. *Merkab*, «carruagem». Palavra que aparece por somente uma vez, em I Reis 4:26.

3. *Markabah*, «carruagem». Palavra que é usada por quarenta e quatro vezes (para exemplificar:Gên. 41:43; 46:29; Êxo. 14:25; Jos. 11:6,9; I Sam. 8:11; I Reis 7:33; II Reis 5:21; II Crô. 1:17; Isa. 2:7; Jer. 4:13; Joel 2:5; Zac. 6:1-3).

4. *Agalah*, «vagão». Essa palavra ocorre por vinte e cinco vezes (para exemplificar: I Sam. 6:7-14; Isa. 5:18; Gên. 45:19,21,27; Núm. 7:3,6,7).

5. *Rekeb*, «carruagem». Palavra que aparece por cento e quinze vezes com esse sentido (por exemplo: Gên. 50:9; Êxo. 14:6-28; Deu. 11:4; Jos. 11:4; Juí. 1:19; 5:28; II Sam. 1:6; I Reis 1:5; 9:19,22; II Reis 2:11,12; 5:9; 6:14,15,17; II Crô. 1:14; Sal. 20:7; Can. 1:9; Isa. 21:7,9; 66:20; Jer. 17:25; Eze. 26:7; Dan. 11:40; Na. 2:3,4,13; Zac. 9:10).

6. *Rikbah*, «carruagem». Palavra que figura apenas em Eze. 27:20.

7. *Rekub*, «carruagem». Palavra que aparece somente em Sal. 104:3.

8. *Árma*, «carro de guerra» (com duas rodas). Palavra grega que aparece por quatro vezes: Atos 8:28,29,38; Apo. 9:9.

9. *Réde*, «vagão» (com quatro rodas). Palavra grega que é usada somente em Apo. 18:13.

As palavras envolvidas geralmente significam «carro», havendo um artigo separado para esse verbete. Salmos 46:9 refere-se a um vagão para transporte de suprimentos de guerra. A maioria das referências tem em vista veículos puxados por bois, cavalos ou asnos, sendo traduções de palavras que derivam do verbo hebraico «guiar».

1. *Carruagens Egípcias*. A arqueologia nos tem provido abundantes ilustrações das carruagens antigas. As carruagens egípcias tinham duas rodas, equipadas do lado direito com receptáculos para arcos, lanças e flechas. A construção era inteiramente de madeira, exceto que havia arcos de metal nas rodas. Os arreios e os tirantes eram de couro. O soalho era feito de um trançado de cordas, o que provia uma espécie de amortecedor para os tripulantes. A parte de trás da carruagem era aberta, por onde também entrava o condutor do veículo. — As carruagens da realeza e dos ricos eram decoradas com metais preciosos. Uma carruagem muito ornada foi encontrada intacta no túmulo de Tutancamom. Os carros de guerra do Egito tinham três tripulantes, cada qual com diferentes funções: o guerreiro, o escudeiro e o condutor. De outras vezes, porém, um único guerreiro manipulava um desses carros. É provável que os termos *cocheiro* e *cavalariano* se referiam aos tripulantes não-combatentes dos carros de guerra, ao passo que o *capitão* seria o combatente em cada carro de guerra. — Ver Êxo. 14:7,9; 15:1 quanto a essas designações. Presume-se que o capitão fosse a máquina de guerra, e que os outros apenas facilitassem o seu trabalho.

2. *Carruagens Assírias*. A arqueologia demonstra a grande similaridade entre as carruagens assírias e as carruagens dos egípcios. Assim, as primeiras carruagens de Ur da Suméria tinham rodas de madeira sólida, protegidas por um aro de cobre. Algumas carruagens eram puxadas por dois, ou mesmo por três cavalos, dependendo das dimensões das carruagens.

3. *Carruagens Cananéias*. Quando se lê que os cananeus tinham carruagens de ferro (ver Jos. 17:8), isso significa que algum ferro era usado nesses veículos, como nas rodas. O trecho de Juízes 4:3 diz-nos que Jabim, rei de Canaã, tinha novecentos carros de guerra; os filisteus, no tempo de Saul, teriam trinta mil (I Sam. 13:5), embora alguns eruditos suponham que o número real fosse de três mil, e que ali houve um erro de cópia. Davi tomou mil carros de guerra de Hadadezer, rei de Zobá (II Sam. 8:4), e, posteriormente, setecentos dos sírios (II Sam. 10:18). A fim de se recuperarem da perda, eles tomaram emprestados trinta e dois mil carros de guerra de vários países (I Crô. 19:6,7). Haveria aqui outro erro de cópia, ou os exércitos antigos eram assim tão bem equipados?

No início só havia rodas de madeira sólida, mas, posteriormente, surgiram as rodas dotadas de raios. A princípio havia seis raios; depois, oito. As primeiras carruagens tinham o eixo no meio, porém, posteriormente, quase na traseira. As rodas eram relativamente pequenas, embora também houvesse algumas carruagens gigantescas, com rodas da altura de um homem. Quando uma carruagem era impelida por três cavalos, então o terceiro animal era atrelado atrás e não na frente do veículo.

4. *Carruagens dos Hebreus*. Os israelitas mostraram-se lentos na utilização desse modo de transporte em caso de guerra, talvez devido à proibição contra a multiplicação de cavalos. Mas Salomão, que fazia

tudo em grande escala, criou muitos cavalos e contava com uma força de mil e quatrocentos carros de guerra (I Reis 10:26). Para tanto, ele teve de cobrar de seu povo pesados impostos. E importava carros e cavalos do Egito (I Reis 10:29). As carruagens eram consideradas como um símbolo de esplendor mundano, de alta posição, como hoje se dá com os carros novos (I Sam. 8:11). Porém, os carros de guerra facilitavam a matança, em caso de guerra; pelo que coisa alguma era capaz de impedir a multiplicação dos mesmos. Após certa batalha, Davi jarretou todos os cavalos tomados do inimigo, menos cem (II Sam. 8:4). Salomão, entretanto, multiplicou os cavalos em seu território. Os carros de guerra dos israelitas eram tripulados por três homens, à semelhança do que faziam os egípcios. Acabe teve de envolver-se em muitas guerras, pelo que também contava com um grande número de carros de guerra. Quando da batalha de Qarqur, em 853 A.C., ele empregou dois mil carros de guerra. Alguns arqueólogos supõem que os estábulos que geralmente são considerados pertencentes a Salomão, na realidade foram construídos por ordem de Acabe. A arqueologia tem descoberto que, em Megido, os verdadeiros estábulos de Salomão continuam sepultados sobre o cômoro ali existente. Após a divisão do reino em Israel e Judá, este último reino contava com bem menos carros de guerra do que Israel.

5. *Usos das Carruagens*. Já comentamos o suficiente sobre o uso dos carros de guerra; mas as gravuras em pinturas e relevos, descobertas pelos arqueólogos, mostram que as carruagens também eram usadas nas caçadas, nos cortejos e nas cerimônias mais diversas, incluindo as de caráter religioso. Nas ocasiões especiais de visitas de dignitários, a pessoa importante era conduzida em uma carruagem (Gên. 41:43; Est. 6:1).

6. *No Novo Testamento*. Há somente cinco referências a carruagens ou carros de guerra no Novo Testamento, a saber: no relato sobre Filipe e o eunuco etíope (Atos 8:28,29,38), e a menção a cavalos e carruagens, que faziam parte das mercadorias, em Apo. 18:13. Em Apocalipse 9:9, o ruído dos gafanhotos infernais se assemelhava ao ruído feito por muitos cavalos e carros de guerra que se dirigiam à batalha.

7. *Usos Figurados*. a. As carruagens eram símbolos de poder (Sal. 20:7; 104:3); b. de coragem, fé e poder diante de Deus (II Reis 2:12); c. das velozes agências de Deus na natureza (Sal. 68:17; Isa. 66:15); d. as carruagens dos querubins do templo retratavam a pompa com que Deus chega ao seu trono (I Crô. 28:18); e. os carros de fogo (II Reis 2:11) simbolizam qualquer brilho refulgente que alguém poderia ver; f. os carros do sol referem-se àqueles que eram dedicados ao sol, por seus adoradores, supondo que essa divindade era puxada por uma carruagem com cavalos (II Reis 23:11). Os rabinos informam-nos que o rei e seus nobres partiam em suas carruagens, quando saíam para saudar o sol matutino; g. o termo «carros de Israel» é empregado acerca dos profetas Elias e Eliseu (II Reis 2:12), aparentemente dando a entender que esses dois profetas fizeram mais por Israel que todos os seus carros e cavaleiros materiais. (GA HAL YAD)

CARSENA

Nada se sabe sobre esse homem, exceto aquilo que transparece em Ester. 1:14. Ele era um dos sete príncipes da Média-Pérsia, na época do rei Assuero. Esses príncipes tinham o privilégio de se avistarem pessoalmente com o monarca, ou seja, tinham fácil acesso à sua presença, a fim de consultá-lo. Isso ocorreu em cerca de 483 A.C.

CARTA (LETRA) Ver **Letra (Carta) e Epístola**.

CARTÃ

No hebraico, «cidade». Uma aldeia pertencente à tribo de Zebulom, e que foi atribuída aos levitas da família de Merari (Jos. 21:34). O local é desconhecido hoje em dia.

CARTÃ

No hebraico, «cidade». Era o nome de uma das cidades de refúgio (que vide). Ficava localizada no território de Naftali, e pertencia aos levitas gersonitas. Não ficava longe do mar da Galiléia (Jos. 21:32). O trecho paralelo de I Crônicas 6:76 traz o nome Quiriataim. Tem sido identificada com a moderna Khirbet el-Qureiyeh, na Alta Galiléia.

CARTA DE DIREITOS

As cartas de direitos são uma série de documentos constitucionais que enumeram as liberdades fundamentais do indivíduo, incluindo itens como liberdade de expressão, liberdade religiosa, liberdade de imprensa, liberdade de reunião, direito de votar, direitos econômicos e trabalhistas, direitos criminais, direito de ser julgado por júri, igualdade diante da lei, direitos de participação política. Ver também *Direitos Civis*, *Direitos* e *Direitos Naturais*.

História. 1. A *Magna Carta* (1215), foi a primeira das chamadas cartas de direitos. Ali estavam alistadas as liberdades tradicionais dos cidadãos ingleses, dentro do sistema feudal. Os itens mais importantes eram o governo segundo os preceitos legais, o devido processo em tribunal, o julgamento por júri, nenhuma taxação sem representação. 2. A *Carta de Direitos*, de 1689, redefinia, reconfirmava e expandia os direitos da Carta Magna, tornando-se a base do governo constitucional inglês. Muitas de suas provisões foram aproveitadas pelos redatores das constituições de vários lugares do mundo e em diferentes épocas. 3. A nova sociedade norte-americana também teve seus direitos alicerçados sobre tais provisões, bem como sobre uma expansão dessa filosofia. A primeira constituição dos estados norte-americanos começou por uma declaração dos direitos básicos dos cidadãos. A Carta Americana de Direitos eram as primeiras dez emendas feitas sobre a constituição de 1787. 4. A «Declaração dos Direitos do Homem e do Cidadão», de 1789, redigida pela Assembléia Nacional Francesa, identificava os direitos como *naturais* e *imprescritíveis*. Havia a menção de várias liberdades, como proteção de detenção arbitrária, direito de posse privada de propriedades, etc. 5. Até mesmo as democracias totalitárias, como se vê na União Soviética, têm suas cartas de direito. A carta russa data de 1936. A República Popular da China tem sua carta de direitos, como parte integrante da constituição, desde 1954. 6. A Declaração Internacional de Direitos, de 1948, redigida pela Assembléia Geral das Nações Unidas, procura enfatizar os direitos humanos universais. Os homens têm direitos por serem *pessoas*, e isso requer respeito. Esses direitos são salvaguardas da dignidade dos indivíduos, em contraste com o poder do estado e das forças da sociedade em que vivem os indivíduos. Nessas cartas de direitos são enfatizados itens como direito de emprego, de educação, de saúde, de segurança social, de descanso, de lazer e de aprazimento de benefícios culturais e da tecnologia moderna.

Em 1988, uma nova constituição foi lançada no Brasil que melhorou, significantemente, em algumas áreas, os direitos dos cidadãos. (H)

CARTA DE DIVÓRCIO
Ver **Divórcio, Carta (Termo) de**

CARTAS DE INÁCIO
Ver **Inácio, Cartas de**.

CARTESIANISMO
Esse termo está baseado no nome de Renatus Cartesius, forma latinizada do nome de René Descartes. Refere-se a todas as filosofias inspiradas pelos métodos e pressupostos de Descartes (que vide), Spinoza (que vide) e Malebranche (que vide). E também aos ocasionalistas (que vide), e mais geralmente, a qualquer sistema que enfatize a mente humana aberta para a realidade, a exatidão matemática no campo da metafísica, e o dualismo mente-corpo ou interacionismo. As demonstrações da existência de Deus, segundo esse sistema, estão vinculadas aos argumentos *a priori* de Anselmo. Ver sobre o *argumento ontológico*, um raciocínio que Descartes aprovava e utilizava. A vontade de Deus é ali considerada a razão última ou o alicerce da verdade, o que se assemelha ao voluntarismo de Ockham (que vide). (E P)

CARTUSIANOS
Uma ordem religiosa de monges católicos romanos, fundada por Bruno, no ano de 1084. A ordem foi estabelecida a princípio em Chartreuse, na diocese de Grenoble. *Cartusia* é uma forma latina posterior corrompida de Charterhouse (que vide), na Inglaterra. Os monges dessa ordem vivem como eremitas solitários, e só se reunem para a celebração de certas cerimônias religiosas. Usam um hábito branco. O estilo de vida deles não visa à produção de eruditos, embora a ordem tenha produzido alguns notáveis eruditos. Dionísio Rickel (1402-1471) preparou uma autêntica enciclopédia do pensamento escolástico anterior. Popularmente, a ordem tornou-se conhecida por sua produção de *chartreuse*, um licor de alta qualidade. As rendas obtidas com a venda desse licor são revertidas em propósitos caritativos. (E P)

CARVALHO
No hebraico, *allon*. Esse termo é usado por oito vezes: Gên. 35:8; Isa. 2:13; 6:13; 44:14; Eze. 27:6; Osé. 4:13; Amós 2:9 e Zac. 11:2. Não há dúvidas quanto ao sentido dessa palavra. Mas, dois outros termos hebraicos, *elah* e *allah*, têm sido traduzidos por «carvalho», por «terebinto» e por «olmo». Trataremos aqui somente sobre o *allon*. Ver também sobre *Terebinto* e *Olmo*.

O carvalho era considerado a mais importante árvore decídua da Palestina. Uma decídua é uma espécie vegetal que perde suas folhas durante o inverno. Por igual modo, o cedro (que vide) era tido como a mais importante espécie sempre-viva. Várias espécies de carvalho medram na Palestina. Há a espécie que cientificamente é chamada *Quercus sessiliflora*, das montanhas do Líbano e do Haurã. Há quatro outras variedades da espécie espinhenta, que se encontram no Carmelo, em Basã e em Gileade, e que podem atingir consideráveis dimensões. O carvalho Valônia encontra-se na Galiléia e em Gileade.

A mais conspícua menção ao carvalho, em todo o Antigo Testamento, encontra-se em Gênesis 35:4, onde se lê que Jacó ocultou os ídolos da família sob um certo carvalho, em Siquém. Tempos depois, Jacó sepultou Débora, a idosa ama de Rebeca, sob um carvalho (Gên. 35:8).

Associações Religiosas com os Carvalhos. O carvalho é um símbolo universal de força e durabilidade. É possível que exatamente por essa razão vários povos antigos efetuavam seus cultos idólatras em bosques de carvalho, ou em lugares de algum modo associados a carvalhos. Lemos que os druidas das ilhas Britânicas efetuavam seus cultos idólatras em bosques de carvalhos.

Simbolismo. O carvalho representa a força e a durabilidade, conforme se vê nos escritos de três profetas: Isaías (2:13), Amós (2:9) e Zacarias (11:2). Nos sonhos e nas visões, um carvalho pode significar um espírito de varão, ou a força física, ou talvez, um homem forte fisicamente. (CHE UN Z)

CARVALHO DOS ADIVINHADORES
O único lugar onde aparece essa expressão é Juízes 9:37. Porém, é possível que o sexto versículo desse mesmo capítulo, bem como o trecho de Gên. 12:6, estejam envolvidos na questão. Esse carvalho ficava localizado em um lugar proeminente, talvez em uma pequena colina. Os carvalhos eram muito estimados por serem árvores majestosas. E os idólatras costumavam praticar sua adoração debaixo de carvalhos escolhidos. Há uma variante, nesse trecho de Juízes, que diz «planície dos adivinhadores». Nesse caso, um lugar específico é destacado, e não uma árvore, onde os adivinhos viriam atuar. Ver o artigo geral sobre a *Adivinhação*.

CÃS
Há duas palavras hebraicas envolvidas:
Sebah, «cabelos brancos», «idade avançada». Esse vocábulo ocorre por dezessete vezes, como em Gên. 42:38; 44:29,31; Deu. 32:25; Osé. 7:9.
Sib, «idoso», «dotado de cabelos brancos». Ocorre por duas vezes: I Sam. 12:2; Jó 15:10.

Os cabelos negros eram apreciados em ambos os sexos; mas os cabelos grisalhos eram muito honrados entre os israelitas (cf. Lev. 19:32). O próprio Deus, em algumas oportunidades, é retratado como dotado de cabelos brancos (Dan. 7:9; Apo. 1:14). É interessante que Herodes, o Grande, preferia uma aparência juvenil, pois sabe-se que ele mandava tingir seus cabelos, depois que estes começaram a branquear. Há muitos imitadores de Herodes em nossos dias, onde a juventude é cultuada e a idade avançada é desprezada. Isso é um defeito de nossa cultura ocidental. Nas sociedades primitivas a idade avançada sempre é tida em um elevado apreço. Os ameríndios chegam a orgulhar-se de sua idade avançada, e, na tribo, todos respeitam um índio velho. Ver também os verbetes *Idade Avançada* e *Cabelos*.

Uso Figurado. Os cabelos brancos representam a idade avançada, com sua desintegração lenta das energias físicas e mentais. Nos sonhos e visões, cabelos grisalhos podem indicar dificuldades ou retrocessos, como quando alguém vê uma cortina cinza descer à sua frente. Se a cortina é negra, então está em pauta a morte física. Uma área cinzenta indica um problema não-resolvido ou uma dificuldade que surge no horizonte, ou um ato que não pode ser claramente definido como bom ou mau, mas, provavelmente, fingido. O cinza é uma cor insípida, denotando depressão ou melancolia.

CASA

No hebraico, **bayith**. Palavra usada por quase mil e oitocentas vezes no Antigo Testamento, desde Gên. 7:1 até Mal. 3:10. No grego, *oikía* e *oíkos*. A primeira dessas palavras gregas aparece por noventa e quatro vezes, de Mat. 2:11 a II João 10. E a segunda ocorre por cento e oito vezes, de Mat. 9:6 a I Ped. 4:17.

Esboço:
 I. Antes de Israel e no Começo de Israel
 II. As Casas no Oriente
 III. Desenvolvimentos Arquiteturais
 IV. Usos Metafóricos

Os antropólogos informam-nos que o homem tem vivido quase em qualquer tipo de abrigo que lhe ofereça proteção das intempéries, como cavernas, buracos por ele escavados, cabanas cruamente feitas com varas e barro, tendas de peles de animais, etc. Precisamos lembrar que é provável que o período adâmico foi uma renovação da civilização, porquanto parece ter havido civilizações pré-adâmicas, em grande número, que foram sucessivamente destruídas por cataclismos provocados pelas mudanças dos pólos magnéticos da terra. Essas mudanças provocam o deslocamento da crosta terrestre, diante do que porções inteiras de continentes desaparecem, outras terras emergem, e a configuração da porção seca é rearranjada. Os sobreviventes são destituídos de tudo quanto conseguiram juntar, tornando-se necessário recomeçar tudo, da melhor maneira possível. A tecnologia desaparece. Os homens retornam a viver como animais, fazendo uso das cavernas e caçando animais para alimentar-se e para fazer vestes. As descobertas arqueológicas que mostram que os homens habitaram em cavernas poderiam indicar não que o homem *começou* desse modo, e então progrediu até atingir um elevado nível de civilização, mas antes, que o homem foi forçado a *retroceder* a tais condições devido a algum cataclismo, pelo que teve de reunir todos os seus esforços. A história humana, desde Adão, apesar de cheia de hiatos sobre os quais pouco conhecemos, pelo menos tem sido bastante iluminada pela arqueologia. Vestígios de evidências de civilizações anteriores à época de Adão, fornecem-nos um espantoso discernimento sobre onde o homem pode ter estado, incluindo a possibilidade de que os homens já haviam possuído a energia atômica. Há algumas indicações sobre isso, em meu artigo sobre os *Antediluvianos* (que vide). Ver também o artigo sobre a *Astronomia*. Isso posto, quando falamos sobre um assunto tão vasto quanto a *casa*, só podemos oferecer algumas indicações sobre as condições a respeito, nos últimos poucos milhares de anos.

I. Antes de Israel e no Começo de Israel

Abraão deixou de lado quaisquer luxos que pudesse ter conhecido, como casas confortáveis, em Ur, quando dali saiu para tornar-se um nômade que vivia em tendas. Isso assinala a natureza precária da maneira de viver dos primeiros patriarcas de Israel. Abraão havia abandonado a cidade, em busca da cidade celestial (Heb. 11:9,10). Porém, ao que parece, mesmo durante a sua peregrinação, houve ocasiões em que ele dispôs de alguma casa para morar (Gên. 17:27). Quando os filhos de Israel desceram ao Egito, eles reiniciaram a vida de citadinos, morando novamente em casas. Na antiguidade, as casas variavam muito, de acordo com o clima, a área geográfica e as condições financeiras. Portanto, é impossível contarmos a história da casa com grande exatidão. Abaixo, porém, damos as características mais comuns das casas orientais.

II. As Casas no Oriente

1. O *pórtico* só aparece no Antigo Testamento em conexão ao templo e ao palácio de Salomão (I Reis 7:6,7; II Crô. 15:8). Porém, sabemos que, no Egito, isso era uma característica comum das casas. Com freqüência consistia em uma dupla fileira de colunas. Ver o artigo separado sobre *Câmara*. Os cinco pórticos de Betesda (João 5:2) eram uma colunata onde eram deixados os enfermos. 2. O *átrio* era uma das principais características das casas orientais. O átrio era uma espécie de área fechada, em torno da qual era construída a casa, não podendo ser visto do lado de fora. Toldos eram pendurados na casa, sombreando o átrio. Ver Sal. 104:2, que é uma alusão a esse costume. 3. O *quarto de hóspedes*, nas casas mais afluentes (Luc. 22:11,12; I Sam. 9:22), — era um lugar reservado àqueles que estivessem de passagem, em viagem, ou para algum amigo que quisesse passar ali por alguns dias. 4. As *escadas* subiam à porção superior da casa ou ao telhado. Sempre eram feitas do lado de fora. Isso parece indicar que aqueles que levaram o paralítico foram capazes de subir ao eirado pela escada, fazendo o enfermo descer pela abertura, diante de Jesus (Mar. 2:4). 5. O *teto* era feito de varas e barro, ou de arbustos e palmas, nas casas mais pobres. Nas casas mais bem feitas, o teto era feito de pedras, de telhas feitas com barro endurecido e um tipo de cimento. O teto provia uma área aberta para recreação, reuniões, um lugar fresco à noitinha, para as reuniões em família, quando o interior da casa ainda estava quente (I Sam. 8:5). Alguns desses pátios, sobre os tetos, eram suficientemente amplos e fortes para que ali houvesse cultos religiosos (Atos 10:9). Com freqüência, as pessoas dormiam nesses terraços, para evitarem o calor que ficava retido no interior das casas (II Reis 4:10). Dali também era comum fazerem-se proclamações (II Sam. 18:24,33; Mat. 10:27). Pedro recebeu uma visão de grande significação estando em um terraço (Atos 10:9). 6. A *câmara* (I Reis 20:30; 22:25) era de vários tipos, sendo usada para diversos propósitos. O número e o estilo das câmaras, em cada casa, dependia dos meios financeiros de cada família. Algumas casas da Palestina contavam apenas com um aposento, onde vivia a família inteira, conforme é sugerido pela história de Lucas 11:7. Ver o comentário no NTI, nesse versículo, quanto a maiores detalhes. 7. As *lareiras* não apareciam em todas as casas. Na maioria delas havia apenas um fogão de carvão de pedra, para prover aquecimento (Jer. 36:22). Também havia chaminés, mas eram raras (Osé. 13:3). Nas casas mais humildes, simples orifícios deixavam coar alguma luz para o seu interior, por onde também saía a fumaça. 8. As *cozinhas*, ou aposentos construídos especialmente para cocção de alimentos, são mencionadas pela primeira vez em Eze. 46:23,24. Na maioria das vezes fazia-se uma fogueira em algum pátio aberto (Luc. 22:55,56,61), embora algumas casas contassem com verdadeiras cozinhas. 9. *Cisternas*, onde a água era retida, eram uma necessidade imperiosa na Palestina. Ver o artigo separado sobre esse assunto. A água das chuvas era conservada em cisternas públicas ou privadas, algumas vezes com túneis por onde a água era transportada. 10. Os *alicerces* eram feitos com grande cuidado. Algumas vezes, os alicerces repousa-

CASA — CASA DE CÉSAR

vam diretamente sobre a rocha, após a remoção da camada de terra; ou então eram feitos alicerces com pedras (Luc. 6:48). Em uma das parábolas de Jesus, um homem insensato não se mostrou cuidadoso quanto ao alicerce de sua casa, segundo se vê nesse texto. Cristo mencionou a principal pedra de esquina, que unia paredes, em uma esquina, e que Jesus usou metaforicamente para ressaltar um detalhe da edificação de sua Igreja (Efé. 2:20). Cristo é o alicerce da Igreja, como também os apóstolos e profetas do Novo Testamento, embora só Jesus o seja soteriologicamente (I Cor. 3:11 e Efé. 2:20). Pedro, em sentido especial, foi um desses alicerces da Igreja (Mat. 16:16-19). 11. *Janelas*. Nas casas antigas não se faziam as grandes janelas que vemos nas residências modernas. Usualmente eram pequenas, protegidas por uma grade. Nas casas das pessoas pobres, as janelas eram meras perfurações em uma parede, diante das quais havia alguma pele de animal ou alguma espécie de pequena cortina. 12. As *paredes* eram feitas do que no Brasil se chama pau-a-pique, ou então de ramos. As pessoas mais abastadas faziam casas com paredes de tijolos ou de pedras, que eram materiais muito mais duráveis. Devido a precariedade dos materiais de construção das casas mais pobres, não era difícil um ladrão escavar uma parede, a fim de roubar alguma coisa do interior de uma dessas casas (Jó 4:19). Isso explica as palavras de Jesus, quando disse que as coisas materiais estão sujeitas a essas dilapidações (Mat. 6:19). Porém, também havia casas com paredes feitas de tijolos e argamassa, e então rebocadas. E também havia casas construídas com paredes de pedras, algumas delas decoradas com tapetes, pinturas e outros ornamentos. 13. As *portas*. As choupanas dos pobres tinham uma abertura na parede, com algum tipo de cortina, como uma pele de animal a proteger a entrada. Todavia, havia casas com portas de madeira, algumas vezes madeiras tão caras quanto o cedro (Can. 8:9). Também havia portas feitas de simples lajes de pedras, que tinham eixos de pedra. Algumas dessas pedras eram ricamente decoradas, ao passo que outras eram sem artifícios, tudo dependendo das riquezas materiais dos proprietários. Em Israel, costumava-se pôr alguma tabuleta escrita nas portas, a fim de atrair bênçãos e afastar perigos. 14. *Colunas*. Essa era uma das características comuns das casas antigas. As colunas eram usadas para fechar áreas, como pórticos, ou para sustentar tetos planos, toldos ou cortinas. Sansão derrubou um edifício inteiro derrubando as suas principais colunas (Juí. 16:26). 15. *Móveis*. No Oriente antigo, as casas podiam contar com móveis rústicos, feitos de pedras ou de madeira. Mas os ricos contavam com móveis luxuosos, que decoravam suas casas. Os itens comuns eram uma cama, mesa, assentos de vários tipos, a lamparina (II Reis 4:10), os vasos para cozinhar e para servir à mesa. Os mais abastados contavam com sofás, divãs, tapetes, travesseiros, mesas engastadas com marfim, vasos de metais caros (Pro. 7:16; Eze. 13:18,20; Amós 6:4; II Reis 4:10; Pro. 9:14). Quase todos os alimentos eram cozidos sobre fornos abertos, pelo que as fagulhas e a cinza chegavam a constituir um grave problema. Porém, também havia fornos devidamente ventilados, que minimizavam esse problema. 16. *Iluminação*. Vários combustíveis eram usados para alimentar as lâmpadas; mas o melhor combustível era o azeite de oliveira. Todavia também havia outros óleos, de origem vegetal. Também eram usadas tochas para iluminar o interior das casas. Ver Mat. 25:1 e 5:15 quanto a outras indicações sobre os meios de iluminação.

••• ••• •••

III. Desenvolvimentos Arquiteturais

Esse aspecto é ventilado no artigo sobre a *Arquitetura* (que vide).

IV. Usos Metafóricos

1. Uma casa indica a linhagem de uma pessoa (Luc. 1:27; 2:4). 2. Também aponta para a descendência de uma pessoa (II Sam. 8:11; Sal. 113:9). 3. Pode indicar uma família ou clã (Gên. 43:16). 4. O céu é a casa de Deus (João 14:2). 5. A sepultura é a casa dos mortos (Jó 30:23). 6. O corpo humano é a casa da alma, enquanto ela está neste mundo (II Cor. 5:1). Isso é comum nos sonhos e nas visões, quando as condições observáveis em uma casa são paralelas às condições do corpo físico. 7. Outros símbolos nos sonhos e nas visões. Uma casa pode indicar a pessoa, a sua personalidade, as suas qualidades, etc. Algo encontrado inesperadamente em uma casa, pode apontar para uma qualidade ou um defeito insuspeitados em uma pessoa. As aberturas existentes em uma casa podem corresponder aos orifícios do corpo. O andar de cima pode apontar para o cérebro. O andar de baixo ou o porão pode indicar os instintos mais básicos. A mudança de uma casa para outra pode significar mudança na vida, ou, então, a morte física. A *construção* pode apontar para a tentativa de realizar algum trabalho, de ocupar-se em algum projeto, etc. A obra de construção pode representar a missão de uma pessoa. (CHE ND UN Z)

CASA DAS ARMAS

Originalmente, essa palavra, no hebraico, indicava uma arma, cognato da *nsq*. (Ver Nee. 3:19, quanto a esse uso). Porém, o uso comum indica o lugar onde eram guardadas as armas, um arsenal. O desenvolvimento de carros de guerra mais sofisticados, e de armas mais letais, exigiu que fossem construídos armazéns especiais para guardá-los. (Ver I Reis 7:2-12; 10:16,17; II Reis 11:10; 20:13). Essas referências representam esses arsenais em diferentes lugares e ocasiões. (Z)

CASA DE CÉSAR

A casa de César era o pessoal administrativo imperial, e não os parentes do imperador. Esse pessoal incluía tanto escravos quanto cidadãos livres. Ver Filipenses 4:22. A expressão «casa de César» tem causado muita discussão entre os intérpretes. Muitos encontram ali uma alusão a membros da casa imperial, da família real, que ter-se-iam convertido ao cristianismo. Porém, as descobertas arqueológicas têm demonstrado que oficiais subalternos, membros das forças armadas romanas, e até mesmo escravos que faziam algum trabalho em prol do governo, eram chamados membros da *casa de César*. Portanto, essa frase nada comprova no sentido de Paulo encontrar-se ou não em Roma, nas circunstâncias descritas em Filipenses 4:22, e nem que aquela carta foi escrita ali. O texto também não diz que Paulo contava com convertidos entre os membros da família real. A *guarda pretoriana* estava incluída nessa terminologia, sendo perfeitamente possível que Paulo tenha podido converter a alguns de seus membros, que estivessem encarregados de vigiá-lo. Ver Filipenses 1:13, que descreve esse grupo de soldados profissionais. Por conseguinte, ainda que Paulo se encontrasse aprisionado na cidade de Roma, e embora a maioria dos **intérpretes assim acredite**, nada mais é subentendido no texto, além do fato de que vários soldados, escravos e oficiais de segunda categoria se tenham convertido ao evangelho, em Roma. Certamente, Paulo não procurava vangloriar-se de *elevadas conexões*, como é comum entre os homens. Provavelmente, as saudações especiais, da parte dos tais, indicam que aquela gente, a serviço do governo romano, tinha amigos nas províncias, igualmente pertencentes à *casa de César*. Alguns eruditos têm pensado que Sêneca (que vide) teria sido um dos membros dessa casa e que Paulo o conhecia. Porém, apesar de similaridades entre coisas que Paulo e Sêneca escreveram, isso pode ser melhor explicado pela familiaridade que ambos tinham do estoicismo (que vide) romano. As supostas epístolas de Paulo a Sêneca, e vice-versa, não são autênticas, posto que interessantes. A idéia de que se conheciam e eram amigos, é apenas uma ficção romântica, sem qualquer base histórica. (I IB NTI)

CASA DE INVERNO

No hebraico, **bayith choreph**. A expressão ocorre somente em Jer. 36:22 e Amós 3:15, exatamente com o sentido que lhe foi dado em nossa tradução portuguesa. Na Palestina, os ricos possuíam casas de verão e casas de inverno, as quais ocupavam de acordo com as condições climáticas. Isso mostra-nos que o luxo convivia com a pobreza mais abjeta. A propósito, essas desigualdades e injustiças sociais continuam em nossos dias, e prosseguirão até os últimos dias, segundo a Bíblia deixa claro, quando refere-se aos últimos dias. Jesus disse: «...os pobres sempre os tendes convosco, mas a mim nem sempre me tendes» (João 12:8). Essas suas palavras predizem que a justiça social, com oportunidades iguais para todos, só tornar-se-á uma realidade quando do reino milenar de Cristo, e nunca antes. Aliás, a tendência da diferenciação entre ricos e pobres vai-se acentuando cada vez mais, sobretudo em países subdesenvolvidos ou em desenvolvimento, como é o caso dos países da América Latina. Nos regimes socialistas há uma pobreza menos evidente, ao passo que nas democracias a pobreza é mais conspícua. Porém, verdadeiras condições de igualdade só teremos quando do milênio. Prediz o trecho de Miquéias 4:3,4: «...ele julgará entre muitos povos, e corrigirá nações poderosas e longínquas; estes converterão as suas espadas em relhas de arados, e suas lanças em podadeiras; uma nação não levantará a espada contra outra nação, nem aprenderão mais a guerra. Mas assentar-se-á cada um debaixo da sua videira, e debaixo da sua figueira, e não haverá quem os espante, porque a boca do Senhor dos Exércitos o disse».

CASA DO BOSQUE DO LÍBANO

Esse era um palácio de Salomão (I Reis 7:1-12). Ver o artigo sobre **Palácio**.

CASA DO TESOURO

Quanto a esse verbete, precisamos considerar duas palavras hebraicas:

1. *Asamim*, «celeiros». Palavra que ocorre por duas vezes: Deu. 28:8; Pro. 3:10.

2. *Bet Otsar*, «casa do tesouro». Expressão que figura por quatro vezes: I Crô. 27:25; II Crô. 11:11; Sal. 33:7 e Mal. 3:10.

No capítulo vigésimo oitavo do livro de Deuteronômio encontramos as promessas de bênção, em razão da obediência, e as promessas de castigo, em razão da desobediência do povo de Israel aos preceitos do Senhor. No oitavo versículo desse capítulo lemos que Deus cuidaria de manter cheios os celeiros do povo de Israel, se eles fossem obedientes. Em Provérbios 3, há uma promessa similar, feita aos que honrassem ao Senhor com seus bens e com as primícias de sua renda: «...e se encherão fartamente os teus celeiros, e transbordarão de vinho os teus lagares» (Pro. 3:10).

Malaquias acusou os judeus de sua época de estarem roubando a Deus, por não estarem trazendo seus dízimos à «casa do tesouro» de Deus (Mal. 3:10). De acordo com muitos eruditos, ele estaria se referindo ao tesouro do templo de Jerusalém. Nos dias de Neemias, o sumo sacerdote e os levitas deveriam receber os dízimos da parte do povo. Então os levitas deveriam levar esses dízimos «às câmaras da casa do tesouro» (Nee. 10:38). Nesta última passagem, portanto, parece estar em vista certos aposentos especiais, onde esses dízimos eram armazenados para uso futuro. Nos dias de Jeremias, Ebede-Meleque, o etíope, foi à casa do rei, «por debaixo da tesouraria», de onde tomou roupas usadas e trapos, fazendo-os descer ao fundo da cisterna onde se encontrava Jeremias, que ali havia sido posto por ordem dos príncipes, onde aparece a palavra hebraica *otsar*, ainda que não a expressão *bet otsar*, que se referia à câmaras existentes no templo de Jerusalém, e não na casa do rei, posto que algumas versões confundem esses dois lugares diferentes, chamando a ambos de «tesouro».

CASA DOS DEPÓSITOS

Estão em foco os armazéns do templo de Jerusalém (ver I Crô. 26:15; ver também Nee. 12:25, que fala em «depósitos das portas»). O termo hebraico assim traduzido significa, literalmente, «coleções», pelo que alguns pensam que a alusão é ao tesouro guardado no templo, embora a maioria dos eruditos prefira a tradução mais geral de «depósito».

CASAMENTO Ver o artigo sobre **Matrimônio**.

CASAMENTO COMUNAL

No seu diálogo intitulado **República**, Platão projetou a idéia de que a classe de elite da sociedade (os governantes) poderia desfrutar de uma forma total de comunismo, incluindo a possessão em comum de esposas e de propriedades. Aristóteles, porém, objetou a isso como prejudicial à família, que é um princípio muito mais importante do que a utopia de um casamento comunal. A prática do amor livre aproxima-se bastante do conceito do casamento comunal, do ponto de vista prático. A poligamia e a poliandria são formas de casamento comunal. A poligamia sempre fez parte do judaísmo bíblico; mas Jesus insistiu sobre a *monogamia* (que vide), como a situação ideal (Mat. 19:5). As razões para a defesa desse princípio aparecem no artigo com esse nome. Ver também o artigo geral sobre o *Matrimônio*.

CASAMENTO DA LEI COMUM

Esse é o costume que prevalece em alguns países mediante o qual homens e mulheres vivem juntos, sem os laços legais do matrimônio, mas que, após certo tempo, chegam a casar-se legalmente, embora sem cerimônia de noiva com véu e grinalda. A expressão também pode indicar um casamento consubstanciado por simples — acordo — entre os dois membros de que eles estão casados, o que pode ser afirmado através de um contrato escrito particular, ou pelo fato de que estão vivendo juntos, embora sem o

CASAMENTO — CASAMENTO INFANTIL

reconhecimento legal do estado e sem o apoio moral da Igreja. Esse tipo de aliança matrimonial era comum nos dias da conquista das fronteiras, na América do Norte; e continua sendo legal em catorze dos estados norte-americanos. A lei brasileira também reconhece a validade dessas alianças, mormente se o casal chegar a ter filhos. De fato, até mesmo o concubinato é reconhecido por lei. Na Igreja Católica Romana também há alusão a esse tipo de casamento, dentro da lei canônica do *matrimonium per verba de praesenti*, isto é, «um casamento por meio de palavras referentes ao tempo presente».

Vantagens. Tal lei tende por desencorajar os homens que pretendem aproveitar-se das mulheres, com o intuito de, finalmente, abandonarem-nas. Em alguns países, se um homem convive com uma mulher por, digamos, dois anos, então ela se torna sua esposa legal, caso ele não seja casado com outra. Um homem hesitaria em viver com uma mulher, sob tais condições, se ele soubesse que a simples passagem do tempo fosse suficiente para torná-los marido e mulher. Tal lei também permite que os filhos sejam considerados legítimos, após algum tempo. E essa lei também tem a vantagem de proteger os direitos materiais e sociais da mulher, contra exploradores que só estão atrás de aventuras amorosas.

Desvantagens. Excetuando em condições muito especiais, como na época dos pioneiros e nos lugares remotos onde o casamento legal envolve grande dispêndio de dinheiro, o casamento da lei comum pode encorajar hábitos lassos. Isso tem ocorrido, para exemplificar, nos lugares distantes do interior brasileiro, onde os casais formam-se e desmancham-se com grande facilidade, com a conseqüente queda da seriedade do matrimônio e conseqüente insegurança dos filhos. Em um país de esmagadora maioria católica romana, como é o caso do Brasil, os casamentos meramente religiosos, celebrados por padres que não têm qualquer autorização para casar legalmente a ninguém, multiplicam enormemente os casos de convivência frouxa. Em seguida, os bispos católicos romanos reúnem-se para dizer publicamente que é preciso pôr fim a esse grave problema social. Na verdade, não há qualquer razão pela qual, sob circunstâncias normais, duas pessoas que cuidem uma da outra, vivendo juntas, não possam vir a casar-se legalmente. Se não o fizeram desde o princípio, isso parece ser prova de que eles entraram na experiência indispostos a assumir a devida responsabilidade. Os testes de sangue e outros exames médicos deveriam ser requeridos da parte daqueles que se casam, com o intuito de prevenir as doenças venéreas. Os casamentos da lei comum, entretanto, desconsideram essas sábias medidas. (AM H)

CASAMENTO ENTRE PESSOAS DE RAÇAS DIFERENTES

Consideremos os seguintes pontos a respeito:

1. Do ponto de vista cristão, nada há na Bíblia que instrua sobre esse assunto. Ali, as proibições acerca do matrimônio seguem linhas espirituais, e não físicas. Os israelitas foram proibidos de casamento misto com outros povos semitas, embora eles também fossem semitas; e a razão disso era para que eles não aprendessem os costumes pagãos e nem se tornassem coniventes com os mesmos. O crente do Novo Testamento não deve casar-se com pessoa incrédula, porque isso importaria no debilitamento de sua espiritualidade, com a transferência desse problema para os filhos do casal (I Cor. 7:39; II Cor. 6:14).

2. A Bíblia, sobretudo no Novo Testamento, deixa claro que questões de raça não têm a mínima importância em Cristo (Gál. 3:28). O *homem* foi criado à imagem de Deus. Não foram criados homens de diversas raças, e todos os seres humanos estão sujeitos aos mesmos benefícios espirituais. A missão de Cristo visa o benefício de todos os homens, sem a menor consideração para com as questões raciais (Jo. 3:16; I João 2:2). Afinal, após o dilúvio, a terra foi repovoada com descendentes de Noé, através de seus três filhos homens, embora nada saibamos dizer quanto à procedência das esposas deles.

3. Portanto, as objeções aos casamentos entre pessoas de raças diferentes necessariamente repousam sobre considerações meramente humanas, e não espirituais ou éticas. Abaixo alistamos algumas dessas considerações humanas:

a. *A questão estética*. Segundo alguns pensam, as raças exibem maior graça e beleza física quando as diversas características físicas que as separam não são misturadas geneticamente. Pode parecer um pouco adverso à estética ver um filho de traços germânicos, mas com olhos nitidamente mongólicos, ou ver um irmão claramente europeu, enquanto seu irmão é essencialmente africano. Certas miscigenações podem parecer estranhas a alguns. Mas, nos países onde as raças misturam-se em grande escala, como no Brasil, há aceitação de todos os tipos físicos humanos.

b. *Condições sociais*. Nas sociedades onde a cor da pele é fator importante, os filhos de casamentos mistos sofrem efeitos adversos, mesmo que isso não atinja seus pais adultos. Por qual motivo sujeitar os filhos a esse vexame? Parece que o problema reside muito mais nos preconceitos do que em qualquer realidade palpável. Vivemos em sociedade e precisamos levar isso em conta. Mas os preconceitos raciais não devem prevalecer sobre o amor que une duas pessoas de sexo oposto e de raças diferentes. Cada casal deveria resolver o caso sem intervenção alheia.

c. *Atitudes culturais diferentes*. Cada cultura tem seus próprios valores e costumes. Pode ser motivo de brigas quando, desgastado o romance, o casal começa a enfrentar conflitos culturais. O remédio para isso é o ajustamento de um cônjuge ao outro, até que a convivência se torne menos difícil.

d. Quando um casamento entre pessoas de raças diferentes envolve a necessidade de um dos cônjuges deixar sua terra nativa, tornando-se um *estrangeiro* no país do outro cônjuge, surge um problema agudo, porquanto nem todas as pessoas conseguem tornar-se bons estrangeiros por muito tempo.

Todos os casais, de um modo ou de outro, em um grau ou outro, precisam enfrentar esses problemas, e outros parecidos. O que importa é que se disponham a pagar o preço quando o matrimônio envolve diferenças muito grandes quanto a esses aspectos, acima discutidos. Mas, para o crente, o que importa são as razões espirituais e morais. Quanto aos demais fatores, ninguém é capaz de predizer qual será o resultado específico de qualquer casamento. A experiência demonstra que alguns casais em que cada cônjuge pertence a uma raça ou a uma cultura diferente, obtêm sucesso, ao passo que outros casais fracassam. Todavia, o sucesso ou o fracasso ocorre em qualquer casamento. Os problemas raciais podem exacerbar as condições já problemáticas.

CASAMENTO, IMPEDIMENTOS Ver Impedimentos ao Casamento.

CASAMENTO INFANTIL

Isso envolve o casamento de pessoas que ainda não

atingiram a idade legal ou biológica para se casarem. A expressão é usada quando, em um casamento, está envolvida uma mulher com menos de dezoito anos de idade, ou um homem com menos de vinte e um anos de idade, o que aponta para uma fase ainda de imaturidade legal, embora não de imaturidade biológica. Com essa idade, as pessoas não podem casar-se sem o consentimento dos pais. Essa idade varia de país para país. Os judeus casavam-se bem jovens, sendo dezesseis anos a idade ideal da mulher para casar-se. O Talmude fixava a idade legal mínima para o casamento na puberdade. Na Europa, na época da Renascença (que vide), a idade de casamento mais comum para as jovens era os doze anos. Contudo, na Europa, até o século XVII, celebravam-se casamentos de pessoas que ainda não haviam chegado à puberdade, o que continuava sucedendo-se na Índia, até bem recentemente. Usualmente, porém, essas alianças só se consumavam por ocasião da puberdade, ou mesmo mais tarde.

CASAMENTO LEVIRATO Ver **Matrimônio Levirato**.

CASAMENTO MISTO

O que Paulo ensinava sobre os casamentos mistos?

1. Os casamentos «mistos» são legítimos, a despeito do que os judeus pudessem pensar a respeito. (Ver I Cor. 7:14). São legítimos ante as leis civis, e não podem ser menos legítimos aos olhos da igreja cristã. Nada existe de pecaminoso e impuro no contato físico e espiritual envolvido em tais casamentos, conforme os judeus erroneamente imaginavam. Quanto a este ponto, Paulo se desvia inteiramente da tradição judaica.

2. O crente jamais deve dar início a um processo de «divórcio», se estiver casado com um incrédulo, sobretudo por causa de supostas razões «morais» ou «religiosas». No entanto, aqueles que conhecem as Escrituras do A.T. sabem que o «divórcio», no caso dos *casamentos mistos*, (as uniões entre judeus e gentios), longe de ser desaprovado, era realmente ordenado e exigido. (Ver Esd. 10:10). Naqueles casos, após ter-se desvencilhado de seu cônjuge gentio, o judeu estava na total liberdade de casar-se novamente, pois, na realidade, ele não estivera casado legitimamente antes.

3. No caso de crentes, a iniciativa do processo de divórcio não deve ser tomada nem pelo homem e nem pela mulher. Dentro da sociedade grega, porém, uma mulher podia instaurar processo de divórcio contra seu marido, o que também se dava entre os romanos. Porém, nem o homem e nem mulher crente podem iniciar processo de divórcio contra seu cônjuge incrédulo, devendo ficar unido a ele—enquanto este não quiser desfazer os laços matrimoniais. (Ver os versículos doze e treze do sétimo capítulo de I Cor.).

4. O casamento com um incrédulo, porém, não é «obrigatório» para o crente, se é o cônjuge incrédulo quem dá início ao processo de divórcio. (Ver Isa. 7:15). A razão para tal divórcio não é declarada, o que nos permite perceber que qualquer razão levantada pelo cônjuge incrédulo pode dissolver tal casamento, embora tal iniciativa deva sempre partir do cônjuge incrédulo. Os divórcios dessa categoria, portanto, não precisam estar escudados no «adultério» como sua causa. Visto que a *sujeição* às obrigações matrimoniais é desfeita, o crente, no dizer de Paulo, está livre para casar-se novamente, com a condição única que o faça «no Senhor», isto é, com outro crente, nos termos do sexto capítulo da segunda epístola aos Coríntios e do trecho de I Cor. 7:39.

5. Nesses casos de «novas núpcias», segundo vemos no ponto anterior (4), é de supor-se que ao crente deva ser permitido ser membro de uma igreja local, sem restrição de qualquer espécie, porquanto, nesse caso, as palavras de I Tim. 3:12 não teriam jamais qualquer aplicação.

6. Os filhos dos casamentos mistos são *legítimos*, e não ilegítimos, conforme eram erroneamente considerados segundo a mentalidade tipicamente judaica. (Ver I Cor. 7:14).

7. Se for possível, é sábio *conservar* um casamento «misto», em vez de dissolvê-lo. O crente deve tolerar tal situação o máximo possível, porquanto o seu cônjuge incrédulo pode ser conduzido aos pés de Cristo, mediante a conduta piedosa do cônjuge crente. Por conseguinte, a preservação dos vínculos matrimoniais é desejável, embora isso, uma vez mais, vá de encontro aos pontos de vista israelitas sobre a questão. (Ver I Cor. 7:16).

Consente. I Cor. 7:12. No grego, literalmente traduzido, encontramos *concorda em estar contente*, numa forma composta, que subentende «acordo mútuo». Nesse caso, supõe-se que o incrédulo tem o desejo de preservar os vínculos matrimoniais, no que é correspondido pelo crente. Paulo ensina mesmo que tal desejo, por parte do cônjuge incrédulo deve ser correspondido pelo crente, o que fica entendido tanto em I Cor. 7:12 como em I Cor. 7:16.

Não a abandone, I Cor. 7:12. Não está aqui em foco somente a separação no leito conjugal, conforme essas palavras têm sido reduzidas em seu sentido por alguns intérpretes; mas está em vista o próprio *divórcio*, o que fica subentendido na idéia de «sujeição», que fala sobre as obrigações matrimoniais em geral. Pois ficar livre da «sujeição» (ver I Cor. 7:15), corresponde ao rompimento do contrato matrimonial, e não a alguma forma superficial de separação.

CASFOR

Uma das cidades fortificadas da terra de Galaade, a leste do Jordão (I Macabeus 5:26), onde os judeus refugiaram-se dos amonitas, sob Timóteo. Essa e outras cidades foram capturadas por Judas Macabeu (I Macabeus 5:36). Ali, o nome do lugar aparece como Casfom, tal como se vê a forma Caspis, em II Macabeus 12:13, embora não seja indiscutível que esteja em foco o mesmo lugar. Nos escritos de Josefo, o lugar chama-se Casfoma (*Anti.* xx.8,3).

CASIFIA

No hebraico, «branco» ou «brilhante». Esdras diz que quando retornou à Judéia, ele mandou buscar Ido, que residia em Casifia. É possível que se trate do monte Caspio, próximo do mar Cáspio, entre a Média e a Hircânia, ou então perto da Babilônia, onde se encontravam muitos cativos judeus (ver Esd. 8:17). Seja como for, o lugar permanece não-identificado. Etimologias populares levam-nos a muitas variantes como «no lugar prateado» ou «no lugar do tesouro» (ver I Esd. 8:45), e várias tradições circundam esse nome.

CASLUIM

Um povo cujo primeiro antepassado era filho de Mizraim (Gên. 10:14; I Crô. 1:12). Portanto, era um povo canita. Em ambos esses textos, onde o adjetivo pátrio aparece, a palavra aparece como se os filisteus descendessem de Casluim, e não de Caftorim, conforme se vê em Deu. 2:23. Portanto, nesses dois trechos parece ter havido uma transposição de nomes.

CASPIS — CASTAS

A única indicação que temos do lugar onde esse povo residia originalmente nos vem da posição que eles ocupam na lista dos filhos de Mizraim, entre os patrusim e os caftorim, o que sugere que, provavelmente, esse lugar era o Alto Egito.

A palavra também indica o indivíduo que foi o genitor dos filisteus, segundo se vê na referência de Gênesis 10:14. Várias conjecturas a respeito da identificação dessa tribo não têm sido favorecidas. A palavra aparece sob muitas formas variantes, o que indica a dificuldade do problema. (S Z)

CASPIS (Caspim)

Uma cidade bem fortificada, mencionada em I Macabeus 5:24-26, trecho que relata a campanha de Judas e Jônatas Macabeus na Transjordânia. Judas defrontou-se com Timóteo na área de Bosra, provavelmente a moderna Busr el-Hariri, cerca de trinta e dois quilômetros a nordeste de el-Muzeirib, e o derrotou. Em seguida, os judeus capturaram uma série de cidades, incluindo Caspis; e na conquista das mesmas houve grande matança. É possível que Caspis ou Caspim seja a Efrom de Hesbom (I Macabeus 5:46) ou el-Muzeirib, situada em um dos tributários do rio Iarmuque, onde atualmente encontram-se a antiga estrada romana, a estrada dos peregrinos islâmicos e a via férrea de Hejak. Alguns arqueólogos preferem pensar no local moderno de Khisfin. Fica acerca de dez quilômetros ao norte do rio Iarmuque e a dezesseis quilômetros a leste do mar da Galiléia. (AH Z)

CÁSSIA

Vem de uma palavra hebraica que significa *enrugada*. Aparece somente em Êxo. 30:24; Eze. 27:19 e Sal. 45:8. Essa substância era um dos ingredientes na composição do azeite do ungüento santo. Em Tiro, conforme nos mostra a referência do livro de Ezequiel, era um artigo de seu comércio. A Vulgata Latina traduz a palavra como «mirra líquida»; e a LXX diz «íris», uma espécie de espadana. Provavelmente aponta para alguma espécie de madeira ou casca de árvore. Aparece em sua forma plural em Salmos 45:8, onde é associada à mirra e ao aloés, três substâncias usadas para deixar as vestes fragrantes. Alguns estudiosos supõem que se trata de uma variedade do cinamomo, a *Cinnamomum cassia*, talvez a espécie mencionada em Can. 4:14 e Apo. 18:13 (nossa versão portuguesa diz aqui «canela de cheiro»). Outros estudiosos preferem pensar na *Saussurea lappa*, nome científico de íris. Seja como for, parece tratar-se de uma substância aromática, em cujo caso seria um pó feito da casca ou da raiz de alguma planta. (WAL)

CASSIANO, JOÃO

Nasceu em cerca de 360 e faleceu em cerca de 435 D.C. Foi um monge no sul da Gália, o qual introduziu as regras do monasticismo oriental (que vide) no ocidente. Tornou-se conhecido por seu protesto moral contra o fatalismo da doutrina agostiniana da predestinação (que vide).

CASSIODORUS, MAGNUS AURELIUS

Suas datas aproximadas são 480-575 D.C. Foi erudito, eclesiástico e administrador. Serviu como ministro do estado de Teodorico, o rei ostrogodo, em 540 D.C. Em seguida, retirou-se para o mosteiro de sua fundação, em Vivarium, no sul da Itália. Inaugurou o trabalho do escritório monástico, facilitou a aquisição de uma notável biblioteca, e de modo geral, promoveu o monasticismo (que vide), conferindo ao mesmo a tendência de buscar a erudição, o que, até então, faltava ao monasticismo. Foi autor de três obras: *A Crônica; A História Tripartite* e *História dos Godos*. (AM E)

CASSIRER, ERNST

Suas datas foram 1874-1945. Foi um filósofo alemão, nascido em Breslau. Foi professor das Universidades de Berlim e de Hamburgo. Opondo-se a Hitler, mudou-se para a Inglaterra, para a Suécia e então para os Estados Unidos da América, onde ensinou nas Universidades de Columbia e Yale. Ele representa a escola de Marburgo da filosofia neokantiana (que vide).

Idéias: 1. A realidade é mediada até nós através dos fenômenos, sob forma simbólica. 2. As formas simbólicas têm origem no que é mítico, fazendo-se sentir na arte, na matemática, nas ciências e na filosofia. Três estágios de formas simbólicas podem ser distinguidos: o estágio mimético, o estágio analógico e as expressões simbólicas propriamente ditas. 3. O estágio inicial é o próprio estágio mítico. Nesse ponto, a imagem é a realidade; por meio da imagem, a linguagem torna-se um mundo contido em si mesmo. Os nomes são realidades. Saber o nome de alguma coisa é exercer poder sobre essa coisa. À medida que avança a evolução cultural, decresce o poder do mito, ao mesmo tempo em que aumenta o poder da expressão simbólica. 4. Em primeiro lugar, temos uma *metáfora*, da qual emerge o *conceito*. O pensamento científico consiste em uma meticulosa universalização de idéias que jazem lado a lado, ou que dependem uma da outra, sob formas reconhecíveis. O pensamento religioso é essencialmente metafórico. A poesia exerce a mesma função. 5. Uma das funções da filosofia consiste em examinar os modos de conhecimento que podem ser encontrados nas formas culturais emergentes.

Escritos: The Problem of Knowledge in the Philosophy and Science of Modern Times; Substance and Function; The Individual and the Cosmos in Renaissance Philosophy; Platonic Renaissance in England; The Philosophy of Enlightenment; Determinism and Indeterminism in Modern Physics; An Essay of Man; The Myth of the Sate. (EP P)

CASTANHOLAS

Ver sobre **Instrumentos Musicais**.

CASTAS

Um sistema social melhor representado pela Índia, embora não com exclusividade. Acredita-se que o sistema veio à existência como uma espécie de superioridade racial, em que os arianos de tez mais clara dominaram as populações dravidianas de tez mais escura. Isso é confirmado pelo fato de que a palavra *casta* (no sânscrito, *varna*) significa «cor». Os arianos (que vide) vieram a compor a casta sacerdotal e guerreira, ao passo que as castas inferiores eram formadas pelas populações nativas. Sem importar qual tenha sido a origem das castas, ou formalmente, como na Índia, ou informalmente, como em outros países, é mister aceitarmos esses preconceitos raciais como um fato de todos os tempos. Quando o sistema é formal, então uma casta é algo essencialmente

CASTAS — CASTIDADE

estático, pertencente a alguma classe social exclusiva, determinada por berço. A própria palavra, em seu uso moderno, vem do termo português «casta», que significa «raça» ou «classe», indicando as diversas camadas sociais do subcontinente indiano. Naturalmente, a palavra reveste-se de um sentido geral, indicando as classes sociais em qualquer cultura ou país.

Na Índia, as castas são formadas por indivíduos de uma mesma ocupação ou dotados de costumes comuns relacionados às condições gerais de vida como casamento, tipo de alimentação e de organização social. As castas têm seus oficiais, chefes e concílios. As estimativas indicam que há nada menos de três mil castas diferentes na Índia, variando em número desde alguns poucos indivíduos até milhões de indivíduos que delas fazem parte. Originalmente, havia apenas quatro castas ou classificações. No Rig Veda (3000 A.C.), encontramos cinco divisões hierárquicas. Essas divisões eram os brâmanes (sacerdotes e eruditos); os guerreiros e governantes; os negociantes; os artesãos, agricultores, servos e escravos; e, finalmente, os intocáveis. O alimento tocado por membros desta última casta não podia ser usado por membros das demais castas. As três primeiras dessas cinco castas tinham acesso aos documentos sagrados dos indianos. Nos tempos modernos, essas cinco divisões cederam lugar a um sistema muito mais complexo. É verdade que vários indianos têm procurado descontinuar o sistema; porém, não há evidências de que o sistema de castas desaparecerá em breve naquele país. Pois, em nossos dias, as castas tendem por consolidar-se segundo distinções econômicas e políticas. Além disso, diferentes práticas religiosas também são seguidas pelas diferentes castas.

Os cristãos e os islamitas ao redor do mundo, por motivos doutrinários, repelem esse sistema de castas. Na prática, entretanto, a questão está bem viva, por toda a parte. De fato, até mesmo nossas denominações evangélicas, em certo sentido, são formas de castas, porquanto cada uma delas forma um sistema fechado que se defende das demais. Assim, os casamentos são desencorajados entre católicos e protestantes, e não somente por causa de diferenças doutrinárias, mas até mesmo por diferenças culturais e econômicas. A questão, pois, envolve um aspecto cultural e social.

O cristianismo não conseguiu desfazer o sistema de castas na Índia, nem mesmo nas igrejas evangélicas, e muito menos na sociedade indiana como um todo. Na verdade, as castas nunca se evidenciam tanto como quando há diferentes tipos de pessoas que se dizem cristãs. Consideremos os sírios caldeus, os jacobitas sírios, os católicos latinos, os católicos sírios e os ortodoxos gregos. Os islamitas, por sua vez, estão divididos em quatro classes: *sayid*, *pathan*, *sheikh* e *momim*. Os budistas contam com três seitas que se excluem mutuamente: o grupo mahayana, o grupo hinayana e o grupo thervadi. O ideal cristão de que, em Cristo Jesus, não há tal coisa como judeu ou gentio, livre ou escravo, homem ou mulher (ver Gál. 3:28), na prática nunca se concretizou nas fileiras cristãs, e nem mesmo em outras fés religiosas. A despeito disso, o mistério da vontade de Deus (ver Efé. 1:10) nos está fazendo avançar na direção da unidade final. Porém, por enquanto, os homens sempre encontram motivos que os dividem, ainda que esses motivos não sejam reais. O dinheiro e as idéias diferentes encontram-se entre os principais motivos divisores. (MA E)

••• ••• •••

CASTELO

Na Bíblia portuguesa há duas palavras hebraicas a considerar, bem como uma palavra grega, a saber:

1. *Armom*, palavra hebraica usada por trinta e duas vezes (para exemplificar, Pro. 18:19; I Reis 16:18; Sal. 48:3; Isa. 23:13; Jer. 6:5; Amós 1:4, 6:8; Miq. 5:6).

2. *Biraniyot*, «cidadelas». Palavra hebraica usada apenas por duas vezes: II Crô. 17:12; 27:4. Geralmente adjacentes a alguma fortaleza.

3. *Púrgos*, «castelo». Palavra grega usada por quatro vezes: Mat. 21:33; Mar. 12:1; Luc. 13:4 e 14:28. Nossa versão portuguesa a traduz sempre por «torre».

A palavra portuguesa «castelo» deriva-se do termo latino *castrum*, «lugar fortificado». Desde a antiguidade, as cidades eram cercadas por muralhas. Uma aldeia ou vila não contava com tal proteção. Nas cidades fortificadas havia uma «cidadela», geralmente ocupando a posição mais elevada e de mais difícil acesso. Daí derivou-se a idéia de «castelo», já no império bizantino. A diferença entre a cidadela e o castelo é que a primeira servia somente a finalidades militares, como um último refúgio contra possíveis tropas inimigas, ao passo que o castelo já era uma construção de grande porte, que servia de residência de quartel, de armazém e de arsenal. Além disso, uma cidadela geralmente ficava no interior das muralhas de alguma cidade, enquanto que um castelo geralmente era cercado pelas cabanas humildes dos vassalos dos grandes senhores de terras. Em face de todas essas considerações, talvez fosse melhor traduzirmos aquelas palavras hebraicas envolvidas por «cidadela», pois, no Antigo Testamento, a rigor não havia «castelos», no sentido que costumamos dar-lhes, quando pensamos mais nas formidáveis fortificações do período feudal. Ver *Silo*, *A torre de Davi*.

CASTIDADE

Vem do latim **castitas, castitatis**, «casto», «puro», correspondente ao termo grego *agnos*. O uso primário dessa palavra, no campo da ética, é a pureza moral. Essa conotação é óbvia em II Coríntios 11:2, onde as virgens são assim caracterizadas; e em Tito 2:5 e I Pedro 3:2, onde a palavra é usada para descrever as mulheres casadas. Ver também Filipenses 4:8, onde há uma referência geral a tudo quanto é *puro*, incluindo a pureza moral e religiosa dos rapazes (I Tim. 5:22). O trecho de I João 3:3 aplica o termo a Deus, como santo, cuja santidade espera-se que seja reproduzida em nós.

Apesar de todas as suas faltas, o povo de Israel desenvolveu o conceito de santidade de Deus, com a necessidade paralela dos homens serem, correspondentemente, santos. Do povo de Deus esperava-se que se separassem da polução moral e religiosa dos pagãos (Lev. 20:21). No Antigo Testamento, porém, a castidade nada tinha ver com a idéia de celibato, conforme a palavra veio a significar nas mentes de muitos homens modernos, talvez devido à influência das idéias católicas romanas. Na verdade, segundo o pensamento judaico, ninguém era considerado um homem espiritualmente próspero, qualificado para ser um dos líderes da sinagoga, se não fosse casado. Ver o artigo sobre o *Celibato*. No Novo Testamento, a castidade é valorizada, mas nunca confundida com o ascetismo (Col. 2:20 ss). Dos seguidores de Jesus esperava-se que fossem diferentes das demais pessoas (I Cor. 5:6-13; II Cor. 6:14-18; Tito 2:5; I Ped. 3:2).

O divórcio tornara-se uma praga no império

romano. Juvenal afirma que, durante o período da Igreja primitiva, não somente os homens, mas também as mulheres, divorciavam-se e recasavam. Era comum uma mulher ter tido oito maridos em menos de cinco anos. Os crentes deveriam respeitar as tradições da herança judaico-cristã. A própria Igreja é comparada a uma virgem casta (II Cor. 11:2). Os cristãos estão na obrigação de resistir aos padrões e às práticas do paganismo. (Ver I Tes. 4:11,12). A santidade é necessária à salvação, pois, sem a mesma, ninguém verá a Deus (Heb. 12:14). Ver o artigo geral sobre a *Santificação*.

•••

CASTIGO, CASTIGAR

Discussão Preliminar
As palavras:
1. O Princípio Bíblico
2. O Castigo como Remédio
3. Alicerces do Castigo
4. Pontos de Discussão e Debate
5. O Castigo e os Incrédulos
6. O Castigo Relativo à Perseguição e à Tribulação

Há dois substantivos envolvidos, um hebraico e um grego, como também há dois verbos, um hebraico e um grego, a saber:
1. *Musar*, «instrução», palavra hebraica usada por quarenta e nove vezes (por exemplo: Deu. 11:2; Jó 5:17; Pro. 3:11; Isa. 3:11; 53:5; Jer. 30:14).
2. *Paideía*, «instrução de criança». Palavra grega que aparece por seis vezes: Efé. 6:4; II Tim. 3:16; Heb. 12:5,7,8,11).
3. *Yasar*, «instruir». Palavra hebraica empregada por quarenta e três vezes (por exemplo: Deu. 8:5; 21:18; Sal. 6:1; 38:1; Pro. 19:18; Osé. 10:10).
4. *Paideúo*, «instruir uma criança». Palavra grega que aparece por treze vezes: Luc. 23:16,22; Atos 7:22; 22:3; I Cor. 11:32; II Cor. 6:9; I Tim. 1:20; II Tim. 2:25; Tito 2:12; Heb. 12:6,7,10 e Apo. 3:19.

Idéias Gerais. A principal palavra hebraica traduzida por «castigo» é **yasar**. Tem o sentido básico de ensinar uma lição, e apenas secundariamente o sentido de castigar ou punir. Podemos aprender lições de várias maneiras, através do exemplo, da experiência e do sofrimento (João 13:5; I Tim. 4:12; Jer. 10:24); da aceitação de instruções verbais (Sal. 16:7), da observação (Jer. 2:30). Além disso, a razão, inteiramente à parte da experiência, pode fornecer-nos informações que nos dirigem aos atos. Sócrates pensava que a moralidade pode ser alicerçada sobre princípios racionais, que a mente humana possuiria de forma inerente. Ver sobre o *Racionalismo*. Também há as informações obtidas mediante meios místicos, por meio da revelação divina ou não. Ver os artigos sobre o *Misticismo* e a *Revelação*.

O verbo grego *paideúo* (o substantivo é *paideía*), que significa «instruir uma criança», tem os sentidos secundários de treinar, educar física e mentalmente (Atos 7:22). O substantivo indica a criação de uma criança, o treinamento, a educação, e, naturalmente, a base da palavra é o vocábulo grego que significa *criança*, alguém que precisa dessa criação e treinamento. No Novo Testamento, a idéia de castigo refere-se, quase sempre, à correção que Deus dá ao Seu povo, por causa de algum desvio, pecado ou falta (I Cor. 11:32; II Cor. 6:9; Heb. 12:5-11). Assim como os pais humanos castigam os seus filhos, assim o nosso Pai celestial nos castiga. Se isso não sucede conosco, então é porque somos bastardos, e não filhos. Portanto, a disciplina e o castigo são medidas benéficas. Platão afirmava que uma das piores coisas que pode suceder a uma pessoa é praticar ela um erro, mas não ser punida por esse erro. Isso ensina a alma a corromper-se. Essa disciplina benéfica pode ser aplicada até mesmo através de Satanás (I Tim. 1:20). O décimo segundo capítulo da epístola aos Hebreus mostra-nos que os frutos da piedade resultam do castigo recebido. Parte dessa disciplina, pelo menos, envolve certa medida de retribuição, mesmo no caso dos crentes, porquanto temos de colher aquilo que semeamos (Gál. 6:7,8). Naturalmente, também há aquele treinamento que não envolve o elemento de castigo, sem importar se está em pauta o crente ou o incrédulo; mas não há retribuição que seja apenas isso. Deus simplesmente não age desse modo. Deus é o Pai de todos, e seus atos disciplinadores sempre são aplicados à luz de sua Paternidade. A disciplina aplicada por Deus prova o seu amor, porquanto há coisas que Deus pode fazer melhor dessa maneira do que de outra maneira qualquer. O castigo pode chegar ao extremo de fazer uma pessoa perder a sua vida física, visando ao seu benefício espiritual (I Cor. 11:30). Isso deveria ser um forte incentivo para vivermos no temor de Deus (Atos 5:11). Se dermos atenção à *instrução* divina, haveremos de sofrer menos castigo (II Tim. 3:16,17).

Este artigo apresenta os princípios gerais da punição. Ver os artigos separados sobre *Crime e Castigo*, *Castigo Capital* e *Castigo Eterno*, que aparece sob o título o *Julgamento de Deus dos Homens Perdidos*. Ver também o artigo sobre *Recompensas e Castigos*.

1. O Princípio Bíblico. Do princípio ao fim, a Bíblia dá a entender que o indivíduo está sujeito à sociedade dos homens e a Deus. Isso significa que os seus atos estão sujeitos a exame, e, subseqüentemente, a recompensa ou castigo. As leis levíticas eram uma elaborada declaração dessa crença. O Novo Testamento põe-nos debaixo da lei do Espírito (Rom. 8:2). A *lex talionis* (que vide) ou retaliação segundo a ofensa, requer olho por olho e dente por dente. O Novo Testamento reconhece o poder das autoridades civis, um poder delegado por Deus (Rom. 13:1 ss), e até esse ponto, dá sanção à *lex talionis*. Porém, a questão inteira da punição é alçada **até à** dimensão espiritual, onde aprendemos que aquilo que uma pessoa semeia, isso também haverá de ceifar (Gál. 6:7,8). O princípio geral da recompensa e do castigo é reafirmado por vários autores neotestamentários, como Tiago (Tia. 2:14); Paulo (Rom. 2:5; I Cor. 3:8,13-15; II Cor. 5:10; Col. 3:23-25); João (Apo. 5-6; 8 - 9; 10:7-15).

2. O Castigo como Remédio. A razão diz-nos que um castigo meramente retributivo não concorda com a natureza de Deus, como o *amor*. Alguns teólogos têm asseverado que a punição dos perdidos é final e somente retributiva. Orígenes declarou que esse ponto de vista «condescende com uma teologia inferior». Essa posição é condenada por alguns teólogos; mas ela sempre aparece de modo bem definido nos escritos dos pais gregos da Igreja, contando com muitos aderentes na Igreja Ortodoxa Oriental e entre os anglicanos. Além disso, trata-se de uma doutrina bíblica. Há o relato sobre a descida de Cristo ao hades (I Ped. 3:18-4:6). Ele foi ali pregar o evangelho aos que haviam sido desobedientes nos dias de Noé, e por extensão a todos os perdidos. I Ped. 4:6 diz-nos o motivo disso: «...pois, para este fim foi o evangelho

CASTIGO — CASTIGO FUTURO

pregado também a mortos, para que, mesmo julgados na carne, segundo os homens, vivam no espírito, segundo Deus». A passagem de Efé. 1:10 promete a restauração geral de todas as coisas, em resultado da obra divina de todos os séculos, o que incluirá os efeitos do próprio julgamento. Portanto, o julgamento ou castigo é um dedo da mão amorosa de Deus. *Aprendamos este princípio*: 'O contrário da injustiça não é a justiça; é o amor. O trecho de Efésios 4:9;10 mostra-nos que a descida de Cristo ao hades teve o mesmo propósito que a sua ascensão, porquanto os dois atos contribuem para fazer Cristo tornar-se tudo para todos, aquilo que se deve entender no fato de que ele *preenche todas as coisas*. O trecho de Hebreus 12:7 mostra-nos que a disciplina, que envolve o castigo, é uma medida do amor do Pai por seus filhos, tal como sucede na vida humana. Deus trata todos os homens como se fossem filhos, sem importar se salvos ou perdidos, através do mesmo princípio ensinado nos versículos que mencionei. Isso é o que deveríamos esperar da parte de Deus Pai.

3. Alicerces do Castigo. O homem é um ser responsável tanto diante de Deus quanto da comunidade humana. O castigo é um elemento que garante a responsabilidade ética. É melhor amar, e, portanto, obedecer; mas, o homem caído não se ajusta muito bem a isso. Contudo, — à medida que o crente vai sendo transformado segundo a imagem de Cristo, mais ele se adapta à lei do amor, porquanto Cristo é o Filho amoroso e obediente do Pai. Porém, por enquanto, o homem precisa da ameaça do castigo tanto para impedi-lo de errar como para castigá-lo, se ele chegar a errar. O castigo também é uma medida de amor necessária, para servir de remédio para o mal, e para transformar aquele que tiver praticado o mal. O Senhor pode fazer melhor certas coisas, através do juízo, do que através de outra medida qualquer. Deus é o nosso Criador, pelo que exerce autoridade sobre nós. Cristo é o Redentor e o Restaurador, pelo que também exerce autoridade legítima sobre o homem. O dever do homem é diante do Pai e do Filho, e também é diante das autoridades civis humanas, porquanto elas são delegadas de Deus para impor a disciplina nesta esfera terrestre. Nem todos os pecados revestem-se da mesma gravidade, pelo que nem todo o castigo é igual. Os homens são julgados de acordo com suas obras (Rom. 2:6). Os crentes serão julgados de acordo com as suas obras, posto que não para efeito de salvação e perdição e sim, para efeito de recebimento ou não de galardões (I Cor. 3:10 ss). Ver sobre os *Galardões dos Crentes*.

4. Pontos de Discussão e Debate. Os teólogos debatem se o castigo imposto por Deus tem apenas um efeito retributivo, ou também tem um efeito restaurador. Em grande parte, essa é uma questão que tem envolvido choques entre as porções ocidental e oriental do cristianismo. A Igreja ocidental argumenta em favor somente da idéia de retribuição. A Igreja oriental argumenta em prol do valor remedial do castigo imposto por Deus. Quanto a esse ponto, ponho-me ao lado da Igreja oriental. Os educadores modernos defendem a idéia que a *imposição positiva* de boa conduta é uma medida mais eficaz para aprimorar a conduta de um indivíduo do que o castigo. Esse é um bom princípio, que pode ser aplicado com freqüência. Porém, não pode substituir a necessidade do castigo. Alguns crimes merecem retribuição, por amor à justiça. Além disso, o castigo severo, incluindo a punição capital (que vide), é benéfico à alma, e não apenas para livrar a sociedade dos malfeitores. Freud preocupava-se com os efeitos negativos a longo prazo do castigo. Uma punição excessivamente severa pode causar um trauma duradouro, se imposta no espírito do ódio e da hostilidade. Porém, os abusos não eliminam a validade do *princípio* do castigo, com vistas à retribuição e à restauração, igualmente.

5. O Castigo e os Incrédulos. Os evangélicos geralmente estabelecem uma distinção por demais radical entre o que Deus faz com os crentes e com os incrédulos. Afinal de contas, todos os incrédulos são crentes em potencial, sendo, igualmente, objetos do amor de Deus (João 3:16). Tornou-se popular, na teologia evangélica, dizer que o julgamento divino tem apenas um aspecto retributivo, quando aplicado aos incrédulos. E, no entanto, o trecho de I Pedro 4:6 contradiz essa noção de forma enfática e específica. A missão de Cristo ao hades (ver sobre a *Descida de Cristo ao Hades*), levou até ali o seu ministério evangelístico, quando o evangelho foi pregado aos mortos (I Ped. 4:6), aos desobedientes (I Ped. 3:19,20). Então, eles foram julgados como homens que vivem na carne. Estão pagando pelo mal que praticaram. No entanto, o próprio castigo a que são sujeitados tem o propósito de dar-lhes vida, para que vivam como Deus vive, no espírito. Somente assim poderia ter cumprimento a restauração de todas as coisas (ver Efé. 1:10), que envolve o mistério da vontade de Deus. Ver o artigo sobre a *Restauração*. O julgamento é um dedo da mão amorosa de Deus, e ele pode fazer certas coisas, através desse método, como não pode fazer de outra maneira qualquer.

Inútil é falar em *justiça* somente em termos de vingança. A passagem de Romanos 5:7 estabelece a distinção entre o homem justo e o homem bom. O homem justo é eticamente correto. Ele não infringe as demandas da lei e da moralidade. Mas o homem bom, além disso, também mostra-se generoso e amoroso. Por esse tipo de pessoa, alguém poderia ousar morrer, mas, pelo indivíduo meramente justo, quem se incomodaria? É impossível supormos que a justiça de Deus é inferior às exigências impostas aos homens. O oitavo capítulo de Romanos mostra-nos que neste mundo há caos e tragédia, fazendo a vida humana tornar-se fútil. Porém, Deus usa esses elementos para atrair os homens a si mesmo, e essas são formas de castigo aplicadas a todos os homens, e não somente aos crentes. (Ver Rom. 8:20). A criação ficou sujeita à futilidade a fim de que pudéssemos obter, finalmente, a liberdade. Geralmente estreitamos demais o amor de Deus. Esse amor opera por toda a parte, em favor de todos; e essa é a grande mensagem do evangelho.

6. O Castigo Relativo à Perseguição e à Tribulação. Quanto aos resultados benéficos desse castigo, ver o artigo separado sobre *Tribulação, Valor da*.

7. O Castigo e a Lei da Colheita Conforme a Semeadura. É evidente que colhemos aquilo que semeamos (Gál. 6:7,8). A graça de Deus, em face da confissão e do arrependimento, pode livrar-nos das conseqüências; mas, usualmente, a despeito do perdão recebido, essa lei é posta em vigor, de qualquer maneira. Nem por isso o crente castigado é, por causa disso, condenado diante de Deus, conforme o trecho de Romanos 8:1 deixa perfeitamente claro.
(B H NTI W)

CASTIGO ETERNO

Ver o artigo sobre o **Julgamento de Deus dos Homens Perdidos**.

CASTIGO FUTURO

Esse castigo aponta para a punição recebida após a

morte biológica da pessoa. Kant afirmava que o conceito de um mundo justo requer que todo o bem e todo o mal praticados no mundo devam, finalmente, ser devidamente recompensados ou castigados. Em caso contrário, o *caos* seria o deus real deste mundo. A necessidade de um ajuste final de contas requer as noções da existência e da sobrevivência da alma como conceitos filosóficos, porquanto, em algum ponto da história da alma, deve haver recompensa ou castigo. Ademais, deve haver um Juiz adequado para impor essa recompensa ou esse castigo. Deus é o único que pode cumprir essa tarefa com sabedoria e justiça, pelo que também ele deve existir. Esse tipo de raciocínio é chamado, na filosofia, de *Argumento Moral* (que vide) em favor da alma e de Deus. O Novo Testamento concorda com esse princípio, acrescentando o argumento baseado na revelação (que vide). As Escrituras Sagradas asseguram-nos que haverá um castigo futuro para todos os erros praticados pelos homens. De acordo com a Bíblia, estes serão os critérios usados: a. O castigo futuro será de acordo com as obras de cada um (Rom. 2:6). b. O castigo futuro será retributivo (Apo. 20; Heb. 9:27). c. O castigo futuro também será remedial (I Ped. 4:6; Efé. 1:10). De fato, o castigo imposto por Deus é um dedo da amorosa mão de Deus. É uma medida que transforma de maneira eficaz, segundo se aprende em Efésios 1:10. Aquilo que foi dito aqui serve apenas de observações introdutórias. Ver o artigo sobre a punição futura com o título o *Julgamento de Deus dos Homens Perdidos*.

CASTOR E POLUX

Ver o artigo sobre os **Dioscuri**, que significa «filhos gêmeos».

CASUALISMO

Outro vocábulo moderno derivado de **Casus**, «caso», um termo latino. O casualismo é a doutrina que diz que todas as coisas resultam de alguma causa. O princípio de causa é importante dentro dos argumentos tradicionais em prol da existência de Deus. Ver o *Argumento Cosmológico*. O *argumento teleológico* também está envolvido na questão, tal como vários outros argumentos em favor da existência da alma e de sua sobrevivência diante da morte física.

CASUÍSMOS

Esse vocábulo deriva-se do latim **casus,** «caso», sendo termo empregado modernamente em dois sentidos principais, a saber: 1. A aplicação de princípios éticos a algum caso específico. 2. Racionalizações, sofismas e trocadilhos, usados na tentativa de justificar aquilo que não merece justificação. Teologicamente, este segundo sentido tem sido associado aos métodos empregados pelos jesuítas (que vide).

No tocante ao primeiro desses sentidos, os princípios aplicados usualmente são aqueles constantes nas Escrituras, ou na lei canônica, nas tradições eclesiásticas, — na lei da sociedade — ou à luz da razão. Nessa conexão, o termo é atualmente usado por alguns em sentido derrogatório, os quais supõem que a conduta ideal e as questões de certo e errado não podem ser solucionadas pelo mero apelo à autoridade. (E EP P)

CATACUMBAS

Essa palavra é aplicada às antigas câmaras mortuárias subterrâneas, numerosas nas vizinhanças da cidade de Roma. A vasta maioria desses cemitérios pertencia aos cristãos, que os construíram durante os séculos II, III e IV D.C. O sentido da palavra latina é incerto, embora tenham sido sugeridas interpretações como taça, barco, carteira de notas, etc. Naturalmente, a palavra vem da expressão grega *katá kymbas*. No grego, *kymbe* era um vaso oco, uma taça, um barco. Portanto, é possível que, originalmente, a palavra referia-se ao vale que acompanhava lateralmente a via Ápia (uma das principais estradas que ligam a cidade de Roma ao sul da Itália), onde foram construídas várias câmaras subterrâneas. Portanto, *o oco* (o vale), onde essas câmaras subterrâneas tinham sido cavadas, finalmente veio a indicar esse tipo de sepultamento em câmaras mortuárias. Ver sobre *Sepultamento*, quanto a completas descrições sobre os antigos costumes de sepultamento. As principais catacumbas encontram-se na área da cidade de Roma, embora também existam outras em Albano, Alexandria, Nápoles, Malta e Siracusa. As catacumbas eram escavadas em rocha mole.

Cada catacumba consistia em uma complicada rede de passagens subterrâneas, com 0,90 m a 1,20 m de largura por 1,80 m ou mais de altura. Nas paredes desses túneis eram feitos nichos, onde os corpos mortos eram postos em camadas, e então cuidadosamente selados com cimento e lajes de pedra. As catacumbas existentes em Roma estendiam-se por mais de quinhentos e sessenta quilômetros, em muitas direções, atuando como uma espécie de colchão contra os abalos sísmicos. As mais famosas catacumbas são as de São Sebastião, Santa Priscila, São Paulo, São Calisto São Pretexto e São Ponciano. Há estimativas que dizem que ali foram feitos entre 1.750.000 e 4.000.000 sepultamentos, durante um espaço de dez gerações. Isso parece indicar que a população cristã da cidade de Roma era entre 175.000 e 400.000, em cada geração. Alguns dos corredores têm vários níveis ou camadas, atingindo algumas centenas de quilômetros.

A idéia de que os cristãos antigos usavam esses lugares para se ocultarem, ou para efetuarem seus cultos religiosos, proibidos que estavam pelos romanos, não é mais favorecida entre os estudiosos. Mui provavelmente, eram apenas cemitérios reconhecidos como cristãos. Os romanos também sepultavam no chão, e a cremação era uma prática comum entre eles. Os cristãos acreditavam na ressurreição literal do corpo físico, pelo que muitos deles não seguiam o costume de cremação. É óbvio que os cristãos tinham permissão do estado para sepultar seus mortos separadamente dos pagãos.

É interessante observar que, em Roma, também havia quatro catacumbas dos judeus. O sepultamento deles não indicava que eles fossem escravos, embora a maioria deles tivesse sido trazida para Roma como escravos. Filo declarou que os judeus haviam sido trazidos à cidade como escravos, mas eles não ficaram neste estado por muito tempo (*Legatio* 23,155). Muitos dos nomes desses judeus eram latinos, sendo provável que muitos deles tivessem dois nomes, um hebraico e outro latino. (BES E LE)

CATADUPAS

No hebraico, **tsinnor**. A palavra aparece somente em II Sam. 5:8 e Sal. 42:7.

Na primeira dessas passagens, nossa versão portuguesa traduz o termo hebraico por «canal subterrâneo», e, na segunda, por «catadupa». As versões em geral têm traduzido essa palavra por «catarata», por «queda d'água», *tromba d'água*, etc. «Catadupa», palavra pouco usada em português é sinônima de *catarata*. No hebraico, essa é a idéia básica, e não «canal subterrâneo». Evidentemente, em Salmos 42:7 encontramos um uso metafórico do termo, simbólico do espírito abatido e avassalado.

CATÃO, MARCUS PORCIUS

Um filósofo estóico romano (95-46 A.C.). Tornou-se tribuno e defendeu o antigo estado livre romano, e assim incorreu na ira de outros políticos. Finalmente, cometeu suicídio sob condições heróicas. Por esse motivo, tornou-se o patrono do estoicismo romano. Os filósofos estóicos deram prosseguimento à sua agitação política contra o império romano até que, finalmente, Marco Aurélio, que também era filósofo estóico, obteve o trono imperial. Ver o artigo geral a respeito do *Estoicismo*.

CATARINA DE ALEXANDRIA

Uma virgem e mártir cuja festa religiosa é celebrada a 25 de novembro. Sua história está envolta em obscuridade, e quase nenhum detalhe dessa história tem resistido ao escrutínio da crítica. Portanto, quase tudo é mitológico. Ela é venerada como a santa protetora dos filósofos. De acordo com a tradição, ela teria derrotado cinqüenta filósofos em debate público. Se ela, realmente, fez isso, então seu feito foi extraordinário, pois até o apóstolo Paulo, no Areópago, não conseguiu grande coisa contra um número bem menor de filósofos. O próprio Sócrates foi contradito, ridicularizado e vaiado por seus contemporâneos. Na verdade, a própria existência de Catarina de Alexandria tem sido controvertida, e a estória que ela derrotou cinqüenta filósofos em debate público bem pode servir para confirmar a teoria da sua inexistência. No entanto, ela tem sido um tema favorito de pinturas e ícones.

No tocante à suposta porção histórica de sua vida, diz-se que ela pertencia a uma nobre e real família cristã de Alexandria, do Egito ou de Chipre. Imediatamente após o batismo, ela teria recebido uma visão de seu desposório místico com Cristo. Durante uma perseguição, ela foi detida em Alexandria. Foi durante seu julgamento que, supostamente, ela teria confundido os cinqüenta filósofos, precisamente em Alexandria, onde os mais aptos entre eles residiam. Mediante essa vitória, ela teria convertido à fé cristã todos esses cinqüenta filósofos, juntamente com duzentos guardas. Apesar disso, ela foi torturada na roda e deixada a morrer de inanição. Teria sido sujeitada a tudo isso por causa das conversões que produziu durante o seu julgamento. Miraculosamente, entretanto, ela escapou de tudo. Em face disso, o imperador Maximiniano, e seu filho, Maxêncio, mandaram-na decapitar, a 24 ou 25 de novembro de 305 D.C. Pelo século VIII D.C., a veneração a Catarina de Alexandria havia chegado a Roma, e, pelo século XI D.C., ela era uma das santas católicas mais populares. No entanto, a festa religiosa dessa santa, até então observada a 25 de novembro, foi descontinuada do calendário litúrgico universal, em 1969, por causa das grandes dúvidas sobre a sua existência. (AM E)

CATARINA DE MEDICI

Suas datas foram 1519-1589. Foi rainha da França, durante cujo reinado ocorreram as chamadas guerras religiosas. Destituída de senso moral, ela lançava as forças religiosas contendoras uma contra a outra, visando às suas finalidades pessoais; uma política que produziu confusão e constantes perturbações. Ela usava a guerra, o homicídio e até mesmo o massacre como armas políticas. Ver sobre o *Massacre de São Bartolomeu*. (E)

CÁTAROS

Nome alternativo dos albigenses (que vide). O vocábulo significa *puros*, o que alude à sua busca fanática pela perfeição e pela pureza.

CATARSE

Palavra que se deriva do grego **katharsis**, «purificação». Dentro da teoria estética de Aristóteles, o vocábulo indica o efeito expurgador que a tragédia supostamente exerceria sobre a mente dos espectadores, provocando neles as emoções de compaixão, temor, etc. Dentro do contexto religioso, a palavra é usada para indicar qualquer experiência que tenha um efeito purificador, que ajude o indivíduo a aprimorar suas qualidades espirituais; e, mais frouxamente, que aponte para certos aspectos da doutrina da santificação (que vide). Na medicina, a palavra refere-se a algum elemento purgativo, usado para limpar o sistema digestivo.

CATATE

Uma das aldeias de Zebulom (Jos. 19:15). Provavelmente é a mesma Quitrom, referida em Juí. 1:30. Tem sido tentativamente identificada com a moderna Khirbet Quteineh.

CATECISMO

1. *O termo*. Originalmente, esse termo referia-se à instrução oral religiosa. Posteriormente, passou a indicar os livros que continham tal instrução.

2. *Antigos Catecismos*. Os primeiros seis capítulos do Didache (que vide) eram o catecismo original da fé cristã, se não levarmos em conta as próprias Escrituras. O *Didache* apareceu entre 60 e 90 D.C. Essa obra esboçava práticas litúrgicas, os dez mandamentos, integrados com itens diversos do sermão do monte, que eram considerados os ensinamentos fundamentais da vida cristã. Por volta do terceiro século da era cristã, o *catecumenado*, uma grande comunidade de pessoas que desejava o batismo, já se havia desenvolvido. A preparação dessa gente para o batismo ocupava cerca de três anos. Além das Escrituras Sagradas, do Didache, de lições e sermões, vários credos também eram usados, parte de cujo material o candidato precisava memorizar. Agostinho escreveu o seu *Catequese dos Não-Instruídos*, que se tornou uma das obras mais influentes dessa categoria. A sua obra era muito mais complexa do que as anteriores, com narrativas bíblicas, exposições e instruções, uma apresentação dos ensinos bíblicos, desde a criação até o juízo final.

3. *O Catecismo Medieval*. Após a conversão das hordas bárbaras, no século VI D.C., o batismo infantil tornou-se a norma comum. Em conseqüência disso, a catequese passou a visar às crianças, e não aos candidatos adultos ao batismo. A isso foi adicionada a ênfase da educação paterna, como instrução suplementar. Os bispos da Idade Média compuseram manuais para os padres locais usarem em suas instruções. Esse tipo de livro de instrução era chamado catecismo.

4. *O Período da Reforma*. **A Reforma Protestante**

inspirou a renovação do interesse pelo ensino e pelo aprendizado, e isso deu origem a catecismos protestantes. Em 1529, Martinho Lutero publicou o seu Pequeno Catecismo, que exerceu notável influência em seu tempo, e que, desde então, tornou-se uma espécie de declaração da fé luterana. A Instrução e Confissão de Fé, de João Calvino, para uso da Igreja de Genebra, foi publicada em 1541, e continuava sendo usada em 1563, quando foi substituída pelo Catecismo de Heidelberg. Então este foi revisado pelo sínodo de Dort, em 1619. O Livro de Oração Comum da Igreja Anglicana inclui um catecismo, desde o ano de 1549. Esse catecismo foi escrito nos dias do rei Eduardo VI, da Inglaterra, mui provavelmente por Thomas Cranmer. A Igreja Católica Romana publicou o *Catecismo Romano* em 1556, por recomendação do concílio de Trento. Esse catecismo é muito apologético em sua natureza, e algumas de suas fórmulas são longas, muito técnicas e complicadas. O principal catecismo da Igreja Ortodoxa Oriental foi compilado por Pedro Moghlia, metropolitano de Kiev, em 1640. Chama-se *Confissão Ortodoxa*, uma obra similar ao catecismo de Pedro Canísio, de 1555, com o intuito precípuo de promover os pontos de vista distintivos da ortodoxia oriental sobre a fé cristã. Esse documento foi modificado e aprovado sob nova forma, pelo concílio de Constantinopla, em 1643.

5. *A Catequese Moderna*. Os catecismos de estilo antigo, compostos de perguntas e respostas, com seu forte tom apologético, gradualmente foi dando lugar a uma orientação bíblica e litúrgica mais positiva. Uma abordagem mais acentuadamente cristocêntrica foi encorajada pelo Segundo Concílio do Vaticano (1962-1965), em seu decreto sobre o ofício pastoral dos bispos.

Diversos grupos protestantes continuam a usar versões modificadas de antigos catecismos, embora com a suplementação de muita literatura didática. Revistas de Escola Dominical são comuns com esse propósito, as quais são bastante centralizadas na Bíblia. Alguns grupos evangélicos ignoram inteiramente os catecismos formais, mas usam a literatura de Escola Dominical, com seus comentários sobre a Bíblia, como guia de estudo. Além disso, existem inúmeros livros de estudo, que substituem o catecismo. (AM E)

CATECISMO DE HEIDELBERG
Ver **Heidelberg, Catecismo de**.

CATECISMO DE WESTMINSTER
Ver **Westminster, Catecismo de**.

CATECUMENADO
Trata-se da instituição que visa preparar os catecúmenos (que vide) para o batismo e para a sua plena aceitação como membro da Igreja. Em seu sentido mais amplo, a palavra é sinônima de educação religiosa. Ver os artigos sobre *Catecismo, Catequese* e *Catecúmeno*.

CATECÚMENO
O termo significa, literalmente, «ensinado por palavra de boca», designando um convertido ao cristianismo que estava recebendo instruções para ser preparado para o batismo e para assumir responsabilidades como membro da Igreja. É fácil alguém deixar-se arrebatar emocionalmente pelas palavras de um orador eloqüente, embora sem fazer idéia do que esteja envolvido no discipulado cristão. Portanto, desde o começo do cristianismo, sentiu-se a necessidade de fornecer instruções religiosas aos tais. O Novo Testamento mostra-nos que o batismo não era assim adiado, até que o candidato estivesse devidamente instruído. Essa instrução vinha depois, como parte da vida diária do convertido. Porém, em tempos subseqüentes, tornou-se prática adiar o ato do batismo até que as pessoas estivessem preparadas para o discipulado cristão. Essa medida impedia, pelo menos em parte, o êxodo de pessoas entusiasmadas a princípio, mas que não mantinham a sua atitude original. Referências a pessoas assim acham-se em passagens como I Cor. 14:16; Gál. 6:6. E o trecho de Atos 18:26 mostra-nos um episódio de instrução informal dada a recém-convertidos. Lucas dedicou o seu evangelho a Teófilo, referindo-se a ele como um *catecúmeno*, a quem desejava transmitir um conhecimento mais preciso sobre as crenças e tradições cristãs.

A propagação das heresias e facções, a partir do século II D.C., criou a necessidade de uma instrução cristã mais formal. As chamadas epístolas pastorais já aparecem imbuídas desse espírito. Estritamente falando, o termo aplica-se aos candidatos ao batismo, que recebiam instrução, embora também pudesse ser usado para incluir membros da igreja que estavam sendo preparados como mestres, que precisavam dominar certo conjunto de ensinamentos com esse propósito. Paulo falava sobre uma sabedoria superior, que ele comunicara a um grupo seleto em Corinto (ver I Cor. 2:6 *ss*). Sabemos que essa prática desde há muito era comum nas sinagogas judaicas. Em Alexandria desenvolveu-se uma escola catequética regular, equivalente aos modernos seminários e institutos teológicos. Entre seus mestres estavam Clemente e Orígenes. Clemente falava em arrancar os homens da idolatria, mediante a instrução. Aparentemente, pelo menos em certos lugares, essa instrução podia perdurar até por três anos. Ver Hipólito (Tradição Apostólica), em cerca de 215 D.C. (CARR E)

CÁTEDRA
Vem do termo grego que significa «cadeira». É termo aplicado ao assento oficial ou trono de um bispo, em uma igreja católica romana. Ver sobre *Cadeira de São Pedro* e sobre *Ex-Cátedra*.

CATEDRAL
Vem do termo grego **cáthedra**, «cadeira». Na Igreja Católica Romana, a palavra é usada para indicar a igreja na qual é estabelecida a autoridade do bispo, pelo que aquela é a principal igreja da diocese. A catedral tem vários altos oficiais associados ao bispo, como um deão, um capítulo e outros dignitários. O capítulo é um grupo de clérigos. Um uso mais amplo da palavra permite que esse termo seja usado para falar de qualquer igreja ampla ou importante, embora não seja sede de um bispo. Como adjetivo, a palavra significa, *pertencente* ou *similar* a uma catedral, como o coro da catedral ou um edifício parecido com uma catedral. Visto que a catedral é uma igreja importante, muitas catedrais são exemplos de impressionante arquitetura, sendo rebuscadamente decoradas.

CATEGORIA
1. *O Termo*. A palavra portuguesa deriva-se do vocábulo grego *kategoria*, o qual, originalmente, significava «acusação» ou algo predicado a uma pessoa ou coisa. Mas então veio a designar qualquer classe abrangente ou descrição de coisas, — ou uma dentre as diversas formas de concepção ou conheci-

mento que, considerados juntamente com outros, abarcam tudo quanto existe ou pode ser predicado.

2. *Na Filosofia*. a. Modos fundamentais de predicação (que vide); seria um tipo irredutível de relação gramatical, expresso na linguagem, segundo Aristóteles. b. Uma maneira fundamental de ser, com substância, quantidade, qualidade, relação, lugar, tempo, posição, estado, ação, afeto (ver Aristóteles, *Categoriae*, 4). c. Uma classificação lógica de juízos sobre qualidades essenciais do ser, o que é uma forma mais elaborada das idéias de Aristóteles, conforme se vê na *Crítica da Razão Pura*, de Kant. Ver o artigo sobre *Kant*. Esse filósofo apresentava uma Classificação Lógica das Declarações, em doze partes, onde cada parte corresponderia a uma função da compreensão humana. Filósofos como Hegel, Husserl e Pierce seguiram as idéias de Kant quanto a essas categorias. As categorias de Hegel são os princípios essenciais do ser do universo todo inclusivo, o *Absoluto*. d. Na filosofia moderna, o termo tem sido usado para indicar os *sistemas* que não podem ser isolados, como as categorias da lógica, da ética, da física, da religião, etc. e. Pierce usava a palavra para indicar termos gerais que encerram descrições da experiência humana. Ele falava em três categorias gerais: *primeira*, *segunda* e *terceira*, que corresponderiam a aspectos como qualidade, reação e generalidade. f. Whitehead pensava em trinta e sete categorias que, presumivelmente, explicariam toda a experiência. g. Nos escritos de Ryle, a palavra indica um tipo de *palavra* que realmente é capaz de descrever alguma coisa em vista. (E EP P)

CATENA

Coletânea de extratos dos primeiros escritores eclesiásticos, agrupados a fim de exibir uma interpretação uniforme e encadeada de alguma passagem bíblica. Vem do termo latino que significa «cadeia», «corrente».

CATEQUESE

A palavra vem do grego **echein**, «sondar», e **katá**, «para baixo». Portanto, a palavra é uma alusão à sondagem que um orador faz, ao dirigir-se aos seus ouvintes. O termo é usado em Lucas 1:4; Atos 18:25 e 21:21 para indicar o conhecimento transmitido através das tradições orais, ou para indicar, simplesmente, informações orais. Paulo emprega esse último uso da palavra, em Rom. 2:18 e I Cor. 14:19. O substantivo *catequese* tornou-se o termo técnico para indicar a instrução e o treinamento em preparação ao batismo, e, mais tarde ainda, para indicar toda instrução religiosa, antecedente à aceitação de pessoas como membros da igreja. O termo também é usado para indicar lições formais, como as dezoito catequeses de Cirilo de Jerusalém, ou as noventa e seis catequeses do Catecismo de Lutero. (E)

CATEQUÉTICA

Abreviação de **katechetike techné**, ou seja, a arte de transmitir conhecimento em forma oral, especialmente o conhecimento religioso, como preparação para alguém tornar-se membro de uma igreja cristã local. Portanto, a *catequética* é o nome dado à teoria e à prática da educação religiosa. Trata do desenvolvimento histórico da educação religiosa, seu propósito (aprimorar a vida espiritual do aluno), o material, o método de ensino e os alvos da educação religiosa. (REU)

CATIVEIRO (CATIVEIROS)

No hebraico várias palavras são usadas para indicar essa idéia, mas as palavras principais são: 1. *Golah*, «cativo», palavra que, em suas várias formas figura por cerca de cento e setenta vezes. 2. *Shabah*, «cativar», palavra que, em suas diversas formas aparece por cerca de setenta e duas vezes. Trechos notáveis são: de *golah* (II Reis 24:15; I Crô. 5:22; Esd. 1:11; Est. 2:6; Jer. 29:16,20,31; Eze. 3:11; 11:24,25; Zac. 6:10; 14:2); de *shabah* (Deu. 30:3; Jó 42:10; Sal. 14:7; 126:4; Jer. 29:14; 49:6,39; Lam. 2:14; Joel 3:1; Eze. 16:53; Dan. 11:33; Sof. 2:7).

No grego temos as palavras: *Aichmalotizo*, «tomar à ponta de lança», termo que figura em Luc. 21:24; Rom. 7:23; II Cor. 10:5 e II Tim. 3:6. *Aichmalotéo*, em Efé. 4:8. *Aichmálotos*, em Luc. 4:18. *Zogréo*, «apanhar vivo», em Luc. 5:10 e II Tim. 2:26.

As Escrituras descrevem muitos tipos de cativeiro, a saber: 1. O cativeiro efetuado pelo inimigo, em tempos de guerra ou de paz, mediante o qual pessoas são cativas, contra a própria vontade. Nos tempos antigos, com freqüência isso envolvia a escravidão (Deu. 28:27-48; Gên. 14:14; Jer. 52:29,30). 2. O cativeiro evangélico dá-se quando o todo poderoso amor de Cristo obtém controle sobre uma pessoa, que então dedica-se totalmente à inquirição espiritual (II Cor. 10:5). 3. O cativeiro do pecado, quando alguém é oprimido e escravizado pelo poder de Satanás, bem como por suas próprias corrupções internas, naturais (Rom. 7:23; I Sam. 30:3; II Tim. 2:26). 4. O cativeiro moral, cujo conceito contrário é a vitória sobre o pecado e os vícios. Essa vitória leva o crente ao progresso espiritual, permitindo-lhe vencer os elementos morais e espirituais prejudiciais, levando tudo a cativeiro, à vontade do Senhor (II Cor. 10:5), incluindo os próprios *pensamentos*. Não está em foco alguma pequena vitória! 5. O cativeiro do mal, que Jesus levou cativo (Efé. 4:8). Provavelmente, isso significa que as forças satânicas que escravizam as almas, especialmente aquelas que existem no hades, e ali conservam as almas cativas, por sua vez foram vencidas e cativadas por Jesus, sendo derrotadas e desativadas. Alguns interpretam isso como a transferência de almas justas, que viveram antes do ministério terreno de Jesus, para o céu. Seria a transferência da parte boa do hades (ou paraíso), para o céu. Ver a exposição no NTI, sobre Efé. 4:8, quanto a completos detalhes. 6. O cativeiro pode ser imposto como *retribuição ao mal*, de tal maneira que aqueles que levam outros em cativeiro, haverão de colher segundo semearam, sendo levados em cativeiro (Apo. 13:10). Essa é uma promessa especial àqueles crentes que sofrerão durante a Grande Tribulação. Os seus opressores, no devido tempo, serão julgados por Deus. 7. Os males morais levam-nos ao cativeiro à lei do pecado (Rom. 7:23), que em nós opera. Trata-se da escravização moral, que todos os homens experimentam, e da qual a missão de Cristo tem o intuito de livrar-nos. 8. Vários cativeiros nacionais de Israel são descritos no Antigo Testamento. Temos o cativeiro de Israel no Egito, bem como o relato da libertação deles, mediante o êxodo. Isso serve de símbolo moral e espiritual do livramento do pecado e de sua escravização, para que o homem possa entrar no mundo dos benditos, na Terra Prometida espiritual. Artigos separados são apresentados sobre o *Cativeiro Babilônico* e sobre o *Cativeiro Assírio*. 9. *Cativeiro sob os Romanos*. O que sucedeu a Israel, às mãos dos conquistadores romanos, foi a culminação dos cativeiros e das escravizações de Israel. Muitos milhares de judeus foram massacrados, e muitos outros milhares foram exilados e escravizados. Josefo

CATIVEIRO — CATIVEIRO BABILÔNICO

diz-nos que, durante o cerco de Jerusalém por Tito, no ano 70 D.C., noventa e sete mil judeus foram capturados, e um milhão e cem mil judeus foram mortos. Esse foi um número imenso, levando-se em conta a pequenez da nação judaica, de tal modo que quase cada indivíduo sofreu um ou outro desses horrores. Aqueles que tinham menos de dezessete anos foram vendidos para servir de escravos a particulares. Muitos outros foram enviados para trabalho forçado nas minas do Egito, — e outros foram enviados às províncias do império para serem mortos nos teatros, à espada ou pelos animais ferozes. Ver *Guerras* vi.9,3. Uma outra devastadora destruição da nação judaica ocorreu nos dias do imperador Adriano, em cerca de 132 D.C. Os poucos judeus que tiveram permissão de continuar na Palestina, foram finalmente levados dali, dando início à grande dispersão, que só foi revertida em nossos próprios dias, após a Segunda Guerra Mundial, quando da formação do Estado de Israel, em 1948. A partir dessa data, Israel tornou-se novamente uma nação organizada, conforme os profetas haviam predito. O milagre de Israel inclui o fato de que, a despeito da verdade que eles não tinham pátria nem território, e estavam espalhados pelo mundo inteiro, Israel foi capaz de preservar a sua cultura e religião, e portanto, a sua identidade como nação.

O Cativeiro de Israel e as Profecias Bíblicas. O Antigo Testamento predizia a restauração de Israel à sua terra, no fim dos tempos e que após algum tempo, seguir-se-ia a era milenar (Isa. 11:11). Isso refere-se à segunda restauração. A primeira foi parcial, após o cativeiro babilônico. Essa segunda e última restauração será a versão da grande dispersão ou diáspora (ver Jer. 16:14,15; Isa. 43:5-7). Seu aspecto definitivo virá após o término dos tempos dos *gentios* (Luc. 21:24), por ocasião do segundo advento de Cristo (Mat. 23:29). Isso envolverá até mesmo a reversão da incredulidade de Israel (Eze. 36:24-27). Será uma completa restauração nacional, física e espiritual (Rom. 11:25). Ver a exposição desse último versículo no NTI, quanto a detalhes completos. Então Israel tornar-se-á a cabeça das nações, e um povo sacerdotal, anunciará a mensagem de Deus a todos os demais povos, em um período de prosperidade e paz sem-igual (Zac. 3:1-12; Apo. 20:1-10, caps. 21 e 22). Israel, pois, será reenxertada na vinha divina da vida (Rom. 11:23). (I IB HA NTI)

CATIVEIRO ASSÍRIO

Ver o artigo geral sobre **Cativeiro, Cativeiros**. Esse cativeiro também é conhecido como cativeiro das dez tribos de Israel. Embora nos refiramos a esse cativeiro como um único evento, na realidade envolveu um complexo processo. A maior parte da população das tribos israelitas do norte foi levada em exílio, não para a Babilônia (que foi a experiência da tribo de Judá; ver sobre o *Cativeiro Babilônico*), mas para a Assíria (que vide). O período durante o qual essa remoção teve lugar, estendeu-se por cerca de cento e cinqüenta anos. Podemos dividir esse período em quatro fases: a. de daqueles levados cativos por Tiglate-Pileser III, nos dias de Peca, rei de Israel, em cerca de 740 A.C. Nesse exílio estiveram envolvidas as tribos transjordânicas de Israel (I Crô. 5:26), e os habitantes da Galiléia (II Reis 15:29). O destino deles foi a Assíria. b. Durante o reinado de Oséias, rei de Israel, Salmaneser, rei da Assíria, invadiu Israel por duas vezes (II Reis 17:3,5), provavelmente levando os israelitas que tinham sobrevivido na outra invasão. c. Seu sucessor, Sargão II, em 721 A.C., conquistou a capital, Samaria, e levou mais de vinte e sete mil pessoas. Isso está registrado nos anais de Corsabade. d. O que não fora levado cativo pelos reis anteriores, outros monarcas assírios, —especialmente Esar-Hadom, em cerca de 681-668 A.C., levou embora.

Atualmente, há estudiosos que acreditam que os descendentes desses exilados israelitas, em várias levas, encontram-se, muito misturados com outros povos, na região em torno do lago Vã, na porção extremo oriental da moderna Turquia, onde esse país tem fronteiras comuns com o sul da União Soviética, com o Irã ocidental e com o norte do Iraque. Se isso corresponde à realidade dos fatos, é algo que não sabemos dizer. (ALB AM BAD BAR E)

CATIVEIRO BABILÔNICO

Esse título refere-se ao período da história dos judeus que começou no ano de 597 A.C., quando foi deportado o primeiro grande grupo de judeus, juntamente com seu rei, Jeoiaquim, para Babilônia, por determinação de Nabucodonosor. Esse período terminou em 538 A.C., quando Ciro, vencedor persa da Babilônia, baixou um decreto concedendo aos judeus o direito de retornarem a Jerusalém e reconstruírem o templo (ver o artigo). No período entre essas duas datas, tiveram lugar diversas outras deportações, entre as quais aquela após a destruição do templo, em 587 A.C. As fontes informativas diferem no tocante ao número de judeus que foram exilados, conforme se vê mediante a comparação dos trechos de II Reis 24:14,16 e Jeremias 52:28-30. O certo, porém, é que pelo menos vinte mil judeus foram deportados. Os judeus, chegados a Babilônia, desfrutaram de condições relativamente favoráveis. O solo ali era mais fértil que o da Judéia, e os agricultores judeus facilmente podiam cultivá-lo. Alguns deles conseguiram enriquecer. Muitos tornaram-se tão bem-sucedidos na Babilônia que recusaram-se a retornar à Paletina, quando Ciro lhes permitiu o retorno. Contudo, ajudaram financeiramente àqueles que desejaram voltar do exílio. Cerca de quarenta e dois mil judeus retornaram à Judéia, em 538 A.C. E aqueles que permaneceram na Babilônia, formaram o núcleo de uma comunidade que, séculos mais tarde, tornou-se um importante centro da erudição e das tradições judaicas. (Ver também o artigo sobre o *cativeiro assírio*).

Tanto o cativeiro assírio quanto o babilônico haviam sido preditos pelos profetas do Antigo Testamento. Por detrás desses cativeiros havia razões morais e espirituais, e não apenas econômicas, militares e políticas, que se originam dos conflitos entre os povos. É verdade que todos esses fatores existiam; mas ao povo de Deus só sucede aquilo que Ele permite ou ordena. E assim, todas as grandes modificações, relativas a indivíduos ou nações, dependem, em última análise, da vontade de Deus. O juízo divino sobrevém aos desobedientes e interrompe, se não mesmo destrói, tudo quanto estiver sendo feito de positivo. Todavia, o juízo divino sempre é remedial, e não apenas punitivo. A apostasia pode ser revertida pelo julgamento divino; e, com freqüência, Deus pode fazer coisas boas através do juízo divino, que não podem ser realizadas de outra maneira qualquer. (Ver o artigo sobre o *julgamento divino*).

Quanto à interpretação das predições proféticas de que o cativeiro babilônico foi um juízo divino, ver os trechos de Isaías 54:9,10 e Jeremias 31:3-6. Resultados do cativeiro babilônico: Esse evento demonstrou a soberania de Deus e também o Seu interesse pelo Seu povo. A universalidade de Deus foi demonstrada, porquanto ficou provado que Ele trata com todas as nações, e não apenas com Israel. Além disso, os judeus exilados levaram o judaísmo a lugares que, doutra sorte, só teriam sido atingidos dentro de muitos séculos. E isso deu um grande avanço à mensagem espiritual. (ALB AM BAD BAR E)

CATIVEIRO BABILÔNICO DO PAPADO
Ver sobre **Avignon**.

CATIVEIRO LEVADO CATIVO
Levou cativo o cativeiro, Efé. 4:8. Posto que não há explicação sobre o que isso poderia significar, várias explicações têm sido oferecidas. Abaixo alistamos as três explanações principais e mais prováveis:

1. A alusão é à derrota dos inimigos de Deus, sobretudo os poderes angelicais malignos. Naturalmente que essa é a maneira mais simples de entendermos essas palavras, segundo seu uso normal. (Ver I Esdras 5:45 e Judite 2:9; ver também Juí. 5:12, onde se lê: «...levanta-te Baraque, e leva presos os que te prenderam, tu, filho de Abinoão...», que talvez seja origem da expressão de Sal. 68:18. O *cativeiro* nesse sentido, não tem a idéia de algo que «cativara» alguma coisa de antemão, e que agora fora por sua vez «cativado». Isso tem sido insuflado no texto, mas o original hebraico meramente alude a cativar algo, que ficou cativo. No que diz respeito à identificação dos cativos, isso também tem sido disputado. Podemos supor que o pecado, a morte e os poderes malignos de toda a sorte estão em foco, incluindo os seres inteligentes. Se essa é a correta interpretação, então Efé. 4:8 é paralelo ao trecho de Col. 2:15: «...despojando os principados e as potestades, publicamente os expôs ao desprezo, triunfando deles na cruz». No dizer de Faucett (em Efé. 4:8): «No Salmo há alusão aos inimigos cativos de Davi. Como antítipo, os inimigos de Cristo, o Filho de Davi, que são Satanás, a morte, a maldição e o pecado (ver Col. 2:15 e II Ped. 2:4), levados em processão triunfal para sua condenação final (ver Apo. 10:10,14)». Assim pensa a maioria dos eruditos.

2. Outros supõem que Efé. 4:8 ensina a remoção *dos santos* que estavam no mundo intermediário (o hades), os quais seriam transportados para os lugares celestiais. Esses cativos, portanto, seriam aqueles que anteriormente tinham estado em *cativeiro*, na porção boa do hades, mas que foram libertados dali quando da ascensão de Cristo aos céus. É verdade que várias das fontes informativas sobre a «descida de Cristo ao hades» mostram-no a levar os remidos (ou todos os homens—tanto os remidos como aqueles que estavam sendo remidos) para fora daquela «prisão» que o hades representava. É possível, por conseguinte, segundo essa tradição, compreender desse modo essas palavras. Esse uso seria contrário ao uso comum que a expressão recebe nas páginas do A.T., mas, no tocante a alguns aspectos, inclina-se para o pensamento cristão, no que diz respeito aos efeitos da ascensão de Cristo aos lugares celestiais.

3. Outros percebem um sabor *Redentor* nessa expressão, pois o «cativeiro» seria remidor e não destruidor. Por isso comentou Braune (Efé. 4:8), «...os homens...ele recebeu e levou consigo para o mesmo santuário...Pois Deus conquista, vence, leva consigo, toma para si, torna seu mesmo e não deseja reter para si mesmo, mas transforma-o, dota-o e faz dele um presente: seus cativos tornam-se seus servos, os servos de Israel. Ele faz dos inimigos e antagonistas de sua teocracia servos da mesma. Assim também, em um sentido mais elevado, Cristo fez de Saulo, o inimigo e destruidor da igreja, um apóstolo. O ato de Deus tomar e receber para si, aponta para uma doação subseqüente, a doação de Cristo a um recebimento prévio...Pela palavra *homens* devemos compreender principalmente os homens conquistados por ele, seus homens, a quem ele outorgou dons da graça, a fim de que eles mesmos sejam e possam tornar-se dons para os homens, em círculos maiores (ver Efé. 4:11 e Atos 2:33)».

4. *A restauração geral*. A realização de Cristo, em sua descida e ascensão, propiciou a restauração geral de todas as coisas. Ver Efé. 4:7 *ss* e o artigo sobre *Restauração*.

Concedeu dons aos homens. Neste ponto vemos que Cristo «dá» dons e no Salmo 68, citado nessa passagem, lemos que Cristo os «recebe». Porém, de conformidade com a interpretação rabínica, isso significa que «ele recebeu a fim de dar». Essa é a interpretação tradicional, seguida neste artigo. O original sem dúvida alguma se referia a (despojos) de guerra, ou seja, ele «tomou dons (despojos) da parte dos homens». Mas Paulo empresta a isso um alto sentido espiritual. A ascensão de Cristo envolveu a doação de dons, o que equivale às «bênçãos espirituais» referidas nessa epístola (ver Efé. 1:3).

Não estão aqui em vista, especificamente, os «dons do Espírito» (ver o décimo segundo capítulo da primeira epístola aos Coríntios), nem está em foco o próprio «dom do Espírito»; antes, devemos pensar aqui nos dons maiores da bênção espiritual e da salvação, dos quais fluem os dons do Espírito, que são usados na igreja.

Cristo é descrito como alguém que triunfa nessa batalha contra o mal; e, uma vez vencedor, torna-se muito enriquecido; e então, uma vez enriquecido, distribui sua riqueza a todos, até mesmo a aqueles que anteriormente eram seus inimigos, os quais agora tornaram-se seus amigos e irmãos. Trata-se de uma elevadíssima mensagem de esperança, semelhante àquela de Rom. 11:32.

CATOLICISMO
Ver os artigos sobre *Católico*, *Igreja Católica* e *Igreja Católica Romana*.

CATOLICISMO LIBERAL Ver **Liberalismo Católico**.

CATÓLICO
Transliteração do termo grego **kathólicos**, que significa «universal» ou «geral». Consideremos os pontos abaixo:

1. Dentro do ambiente cristão, encontramos o termo usado pela primeira vez por *Inácio* (ad Smyrn, viii.2). Disse ele: «Onde estiver Jesus Cristo, ali está a Igreja Católica». Nesse caso, o contraste é entre a Igreja universal em comparação com as igrejas locais. Justino Mártir refere-se à ressurreição católica, isto é, de todos, em *Dial*. lxxxi. No Credo Apostólico de cerca de 450 D.C., encontramos menção à «santa igreja católica». No anterior Credo Niceno, de cerca de 325 D.C., temos «uma santa igreja católica e apostólica». Orígenes referiu-se às *epístolas católicas*, isto é, àquelas que foram enviadas a audiências gerais, e não a algum indivíduo ou igreja isolado. Nessas referências é retido o sentido original de universal ou geral, sem qualquer intenção de distinguir um segmento da Igreja de outro.

2. Pelos fins do século II D.C., quando a heresia tornara-se uma ameaça, a palavra «católico» tornar-se um virtual sinônimo de «ortodoxo», indicando aquela igreja que mantinha a doutrina verdadeira, em

contraste com os novos agrupamentos cristãos que estavam formando-se. O cânon Muratoriano de cerca de 170 D.C. refere-se a certos escritos que não podiam ser recebidos pela igreja católica, da mesma maneira que ninguém pode misturar mel e fel. A universalidade é uma das provas de ortodoxia, de acordo com a opinião de muitos, visto que aquilo em que todos acreditam, por toda a parte, deve ser verdade. Isso representa a teoria da verdade chamada *consensus gentium*. Ver o artigo sobre as *Teorias da Verdade*. De acordo com essa teoria, um dos testes comprovadores da ortodoxia seria a opinião geral; e essa noção é designada pelo termo *católico*.

3. Durante a **Reforma Protestante**, a palavra *católica* veio a designar aquelas igrejas que aderiram ao papado. A designação *Católica Romana* emergiu em conexão à controvérsia entre Roma e a Igreja Anglicana. A palavra «romana», pois, foi adicionada àquele ramo da Igreja que tinha identificação histórica e continuidade com a Igreja Católica antiga, e cujo bispo mais importante era o de Roma. No decurso da história, quando esse bispo recebeu aquela autoridade que é própria dos papas, surgiu plenamente a Igreja Católica Romana. Desde então, a palavra «católica» tornou-se uma espécie de emblema de aprovação, indicando que as igrejas assim intituladas submetiam-se ao governo da hierarquia romana, sem o qual, supostamente, uma igreja não podia ser chamada de verdadeira igreja.

4. *Usos Modernos*. a. A Igreja Católica Romana, segundo se vê no terceiro ponto, acima. b. Um membro individual daquela igreja. c. Indicação de um ponto de vista amplo, em contraste com um ponto de vista restrito, sobre qualquer assunto. d. Antiga Igreja Católica é um título usado pelos historiadores para referir-se àquela fase do desenvolvimento da cristandade que se seguiu à Igreja Apostólica, mas que antecedeu a Igreja Católica Romana. e. As *Epístolas Católicas* (que vide). f. Quanto à Igreja Católica, ver o artigo separado com esse nome. (AM B E)

CATÓLICO

Um título dos patriarcas nestoriano e armênio. Originou-se na Pérsia, durante o reinado de Yazdeger I (399-420 D.C.), o qual aprovou a organização de uma Igreja Cristã Persa autônoma, e que elevou o metropolitano da capital, a Selêucia-Cetesifon, à posição de primaz, com o título de *católico*. (C)

CATÓLICOS ANTIGOS

Esse foi o nome dado a um grupo de católicos que professaram lealdade a antigos princípios católicos, repudiando as posições e práticas católicas romanas posteriores como a doutrina tridentina (que vide) além de outras. Por causa de várias disputas, o capítulo de Utrecht elegia arcebispos de forma independente de Roma, desde o ano de 1723. Após 1870, os católicos alemães e suíços, que rejeitaram o concílio do Vaticano (que vide) organizaram as Antigas Igrejas Católicas, obtendo sucessão apostólica da Holanda. A Declaração de Utrecht, de 1889, é a base doutrinária comum. Os grupos dos católicos antigos encontram-se principalmente na Holanda, na Suíça, na Alemanha, na Áustria, na Checoslováquia, na Iugoslávia e na Polônia. A Igreja Católica Nacional Polonesa, nos Estados Unidos da América, também está filiada a esse grupo de antigos católicos. Outros grupos, não associados, mas que usam essa denominação, foram repudiados em Utrecht. No movimento há ramos conservadores e liberais. O clero tem permissão para contrair matrimônio e é usada uma liturgia em línguas vernáculas, desde o ano de 1909. Eles participam dos movimentos ecumênicos e mantêm intercomunhão com os anglicanos, com base no reconhecimento mútuo. Ver sobre *Jansenismo*.

CATUA

Essa palavra aparece somente no livro de I Esdras 5:30, na LXX. Seria o nome de uma pessoa que não é mencionada na lista paralela de Esd. 2:47 e de Nee. 7:49 da Bíblia hebraica.

CAUDA

Há uma palavra hebraica e uma palavra grega envolvidas neste verbete, a saber:

1. *Zanab*, «cauda», «ré». Esse vocábulo hebraico ocorre por onze vezes: Êxo. 4:4; Deu. 28:13,44; Juí. 15:4; Jó. 40:17; Isa. 7:4,9,14,15. Essa palavra aparece tanto em sentido literal quanto em sentido figurado.

2. *Ourá*, «cauda». Termo grego que é usado por cinco vezes: Apo. 9:10,19 e 12:4. Devido à natureza das visões simbólicas do Apocalipse, onde essa palavra grega aparece com exclusividade, sempre há algum sentido simbólico nas menções a «caudas», no Novo Testamento.

A primeira menção a essa palavra, no Antigo Testamento, refere-se à cauda da serpente em que se transformou o cajado de Moisés, quando ele o atirou ao solo, por ordem do Senhor. Moisés foi instruído a não temer: «estende a mão, e pega-lhe pela cauda...» (Êxo. 4:4). Mas, se essa primeira menção refere-se a uma cauda literal, a segunda já tem sentido altamente representativo. Em Deuteronômio 28:13, lemos as palavras: «O Senhor te porá por cabeça, e não por cauda; e só estarás em cima, e não debaixo, se obedeceres aos mandamentos do Senhor teu Deus, que hoje te ordeno...» Com as tribos divididas, seis no monte Ebal e seis no monte Gerizim, Moisés desfilou diante delas as maldições e as bênçãos de Deus, decorrentes da desobediência ou da obediência do povo de Israel ao Senhor. Essa foi uma predição feita com auxílio de encenação, e tem-se cumprido fielmente na história do povo terreno de Deus. Nos dias do Antigo Testamento, sempre que os israelitas mostraram-se obedientes, o Senhor os abençoou. Houve uma série de apostasias, intercaladas com períodos de breve arrependimento, tanto antes quanto depois do estabelecimento da monarquia. Os períodos de arrependimento foram assinalados pelo levantamento de juízes, que foram, acima de tudo, «líderes militares» carismáticos, que libertaram Israel de seus opressores. E, quando o reino dividiu-se em dois, houve uma sucessão ininterrupta de monarcas ímpios no reino do norte, Israel, o qual acabou sendo castigado com um exílio sem retorno, na época do predomínio assírio por toda a região do Oriente Médio (722 A.C.). Para o reino de Israel, isso representou a redução ao estado de «cauda». No reino do sul, Judá, houve reis piedosos e ímpios. Mas Deus perdeu a paciência por causa de Manassés, o pior dos reis de Judá, no que concerne ao seu relacionamento com o Senhor. Lemos em II Reis 21:11,12 que o Senhor deu o seguinte recado, através de seus profetas: «Visto que Manassés, rei de Judá, cometeu estas abominações, fazendo pior do que quanto fizeram os amorreus antes dele, e também a Judá fez pecar com os ídolos dele, assim diz o Senhor Deus de Israel: Eis que hei de trazer tais males sobre Jerusalém e Judá, que todo o que os ouvir, lhe tinirão

CAUDA — CAUSA

ambos os ouvidos». Essa predição cumpriu-se pouco mais de cinqüenta anos depois do reinado de Manassés, quando Nabucodonosor levou os habitantes de Judá e Jerusalém para o exílio (586 A.C.). Setenta anos mais tarde, os judeus começaram a voltar à sua própria terra; mas nunca mais tiveram o seu próprio governante supremo, que se assentasse no trono de Davi.

Houve oportunidade dos judeus redimirem-se de sua humilhante situação, nos dias do Senhor Jesus. No entanto, em sua cegueira espiritual, o povo de Deus repeliu o seu próprio Messias e Rei, o Senhor Jesus, exigindo a sua crucificação, quando o próprio governante romano o havia considerado inocente de todas as acusações assacadas contra ele, pelos invejosos líderes religiosos da nação judaica. Em uma de suas parábolas, Jesus mostrou o resultado disso: «Portanto vos digo que o reino de Deus vos será tirado e será entregue a um povo que lhe produza os respectivos frutos» (Mat. 21:43). Materialmente, essa predição cumpriu-se no ano 70 D.C., quando começou ó grande exílio judeu que só terminou em 1948, por ocasião da formação do moderno Estado de Israel. Além da perda de sua nacionalidade (embora não de sua cultura e nem de sua identidade), os judeus têm sido atrozmente perseguidos nestes quase dois milênios, objetos de motejo dos povos e de abusos da parte dos poderosos e dos religiosos fanáticos. Eles têm sido a cauda das nações, cumprindo as predições de Deuteronômio 28:13,44. Todavia, o Senhor Deus jamais se mostrará infiel às promessas feitas a seu amigo, Abraão, reiteradas através dos séculos, em gerações sucessivas, por meio das Escrituras Sagradas, no tempo determinado o reino de Deus será devolvido aos judeus, no sentido material e no sentido espiritual. Isso ocorrerá por ocasião da futura restauração de Israel, que terá plena concretização durante o milênio. Ver os artigos sobre a *Restauração de Israel* e sobre o *Milênio*. E Israel voltará, então, a ser a cabeça das nações, e nunca mais a cauda.

De todas as caudas, a mais horrenda certamente é a do dragão, referido em Apocalipse 12:1-18. Lemos em 12:4 desse livro: «A sua cauda arrasta a terça parte das estrelas do céu, as quais lançou para a terra...» Dentro da visão de João, esse momento representa duas fases da história de Satanás: *a*. na eternidade passada, quando de sua rebeldia contra o Senhor Deus, em que o diabo foi acompanhado por um terço das criaturas angelicais, e *b*. quando da futura Grande Tribulação, quando Satanás invadir este mundo com seu exército demoníaco, do que dá testemunho um outro trecho do Apocalipse: «Ai da terra e do mar, pois o diabo desceu até vós, cheio de grande cólera, sabendo que pouco tempo lhe resta» (12:12).

A cauda do dragão retrata o ludíbrio vergonhoso em que caíram aqueles anjos que se deixaram envolver pelo diabo, na eternidade passada. Também podemos antever nessa cauda o triste fim desses mesmos anjos, quando forem julgados. A queda de Satanás e de seus anjos é gradual, conforme o sabe todo estudioso das Sagradas Escrituras. Na história deles há momentos de vitória fugaz, como quando da morte do Senhor Jesus (Luc. 22:53, «Esta, porém, é a vossa hora e o poder das trevas»), ou como quando da futura Grande Tribulação (que vede). Todavia, fatalmente chegará o tempo em que o diabo e seus anjos serão, realmente, a «cauda» de toda a criação, isto é, quando forem julgados e encerrados em sua perpétua prisão (ver Mat. 25:41). E Judas, versículo seis arremata: «E a anjos, os que não guardaram o seu estado original, mas abandonaram o seu próprio domicílio, ele tem guardado sob trevas, em algemas eternas, para o juízo do grande dia». Sem dúvida, não foi um bom negócio para os anjos maus, quando resolveram seguir a liderança de Lúcifer. A perda deles é eterna e irreparável. Não há qualquer provisão de salvação para os anjos que pecaram. Mas, pela graça divina, qualquer homem que está reduzido ao estado de *cauda*, espiritualmente falando, mediante a redenção que há no sangue de Cristo, e através do arrependimento e da fé, pode ser guindado à posição de cabeça, juntamente com o Filho do Deus bendito.

CAUDA GORDA

No hebraico, **alyah**. Essa palavra figura por cinco vezes: Êxo. 29:22; Lev. 3:9; 7:3; 8:25; 9:19. Somente na referência de Êxodo que nossa versão portuguesa traduz por «cauda gorda»; nas outras referências, apenas por «cauda». Isso faz alusão ao tipo de gado ovino cultivado na Palestina, cuja cauda é bem mais volumosa que a de outras espécies. Essa ovelha é também chamada de ovelha síria, cuja cauda chega a pesar quase dez quilos, sendo considerada uma das porções mais deliciosas ao paladar, depois de preparada. Os sacerdotes não podiam comer da carne da cauda dessa ovelha, quando a ofereciam em holocausto. Antes, ela era alçada diante do Senhor e inteiramente consumida como aroma suave a Yahweh.

CAUSA

Deriva-se do latim **causa** (que vide), um termo que dá a entender aquilo que ocasiona, determina, produz ou condiciona um efeito qualquer. Há várias definições específicas, dependendo do filósofo ou teólogo, a saber:

1. Aristóteles desenvolveu uma completa doutrina de causa. Ele falava em *quatro* causas: material, formal, eficiente e final. Sua discussão ocasionou um abundante tratamento posterior sobre o assunto. Essas causas podem ser ilustradas como segue: A causa *material* é o potencial de qualquer entidade. Indica a matéria de que essa entidade é feita, bem como sua natureza inerente, sem importar como a mesma tenha de ser explicada. Digamos, a *argila*. Tal entidade tem uma natureza inerente, sendo capaz de transformar-se em outras coisas. A causa *formal* é o desígnio e o potencial para a modificação que alguém tem para fazer alguma coisa da argila. É a composição característica de qualquer coisa, bem como seu potencial para o desenvolvimento. A causa *eficiente* é a capacidade que produz aquela transformação, como o fabricante de tijolos, que faz a argila tomar a forma de tijolos. Além disso, há a causa *final*, ou seja a coisa em que a matéria inicial é transformada, cumprindo assim o desígnio do planejador. Seria a parede feita pelo pedreiro, o resultado final da argila. Ver sobre *Aristóteles*.

2. Guilherme de Ockham achava que a causa eficiente é a mais útil categoria das quatro causas de Aristóteles, tendo-a desenvolvido na definição do bom senso de causa.

3. Hobbes identificava a causação com a transmissão de movimento, assim salientando a causa eficiente.

4. Para Geulincx, Deus é a causa única do universo, ao ponto de ser praticamente Ele, a única realidade.

5. Locke vê a causa tornar-se um conceito com base no controle que alguém exerce sobre seu próprio

CAUSA — CAUSA FINAL

corpo, o movimento dos seus membros, de acordo com a sua volição interna.

6. Leibniz enfatizava a causa formal em sua doutrina de razão suficiente. Precisamos ter razão suficiente para tudo, pois coisa alguma pode ter lugar exceto através desse princípio. Ver sobre Leibniz, quarto ponto.

7. Hume, em seu ceticismo, pensava que fosse impossível demonstrar o princípio de causa. Podemos apenas observar dois eventos e supor, mediante um salto de fé, que um dos eventos causou o outro. Ver sobre *Hume*, pontos 2 e 3.

8. Emanuel Kant pensava que a *causalidade* é um dos princípios mentais *a priori*, que os homens impõem sobre o mundo que os cercam. Ver *Kant*, item 3.

9. Fichte (que vide, ponto 3) supunha que a causa é um elemento postulado do mundo.

10. Trendelenburg (que vide) enfatizava as causas final e eficiente de Aristóteles, como elementos necessários à ciência.

11. John Stuart Mill (que vide, item 6), referia-se à causa como um antecedente invariável e incondicional.

12. Whitehead tinha um amplo ponto de vista de causa, percebendo que, em inúmeras causações temos uma explicação de todas as coisas que ocorrem e existem no universo. Qualquer ocorrência presente tem certa relação para com o todo, desde o começo.

13. Ducasse frisava o arranjo da mente e do corpo como uma relação de causa e relação. Ver o Problema Corpo-Mente e o *Interacionismo*. O que é material afeta o que é imaterial, e vice-versa.

14. Modernas investigações científicas dependem do reconhecimento necessário do princípio de causa, o qual, por sua vez, repousa sobre a crença na constância ou *invariabilidade* da natureza. A mesma causa produzirá continuamente o mesmo efeito ou os mesmos efeitos. Em caso contrário, a ciência seria simplesmente impossível. Muitos cientistas, em face disso, caem no absurdo de não reconhecer que deve haver uma Inteligência que supervisiona esse arranjo, pois como o caos poderia produzir o tipo de relações de causa e efeito de que todas as coisas dependem, ao menos para existir? Uma vez que aceitamos o princípio de inteligência nesse arranjo universal e todo abrangedor, já estaremos falando sobre a natureza divina.

15. O misticismo oriental fala de causa e efeito, em nosso mundo material, apenas como aparências, como partes da grande ilusão que está envolvida na materialidade. Podemos, entretanto, admitir a Realidade Suprema sem dizer que a realidade inferior e dependente seja apenas uma ilusão.

16. *Causa e as Considerações Teológicas*. O princípio de causa é o âmago do *argumento cosmológico* (que vide) em prol da existência de Deus. A causa final requer o princípio da teleologia (que vide), e isso é importante para o *argumento teleológico* (que vide), em favor da existência de Deus. A *Causa primária* é Deus, e coisa alguma pode acontecer sem a sua autorização ou permissão. Porém, também existem *causas secundárias*, que são permitidas, mas não diretamente causadas por Deus. O homem tem a capacidade de agir como causa secundária, fazendo coisas contrárias à vontade de Deus. Se assim não fosse, Deus seria a causa de tudo, incluindo do mal, e também não poderia haver sistema ético segundo o qual o homem fosse um ser responsável. O calvinismo extremado (que vide) faz de Deus a única causa, e, portanto, o autor do mal. O calvinismo moderado evita essa armadilha, falando sobre a vontade permissiva de Deus; mas também fica aquém da verdade, por não reconhecer que o homem é um ser criativo, dotado de poderes sobrenaturais, mediante sua natureza inerente e mediante os poderes divinos, dados através da graça geral, que o torna realmente passível de ser redimido, o que não foi planejado apenas para alguns poucos. Muitos sistemas cristãos também negligenciam o princípio de causa, conforme o mesmo é expresso pelo mistério da vontade de Deus (em Efésios 1:10), que promete que a *vontade ativa* de Deus deve fazer uma diferença em *todas* as coisas, para *o bem, finalmente*. Nisso, Deus torna-se a *única* causa, embora de maneira benigna e gloriosa, e não daquela maneira negativa em que ele aparece como a única causa, segundo o sistema do calvinismo extremado.

17. Deus e o Filho, o Logos, são as quatro causas: material, formal, eficiente e final. Ver ponto 1. Artigos separados são oferecidos sobre cada um destes assuntos. Ver também os artigos sobre *Primeira causa*; o *Argumento cosmológico*; o *Argumento teleológico*. (EP F MM NTI P)

CAUSA (em frases latinas)

Deriva-se da palavra latina que significa **causa** (que vide). Aparece sob várias combinações em frases latinas, cada uma delas dotada de um sentido filosófico especial, a saber:

1. *Causa cognoscendi*, a causa de nosso conhecimento sobre algum evento. 2. *Causa essendi*, a causa do próprio evento. 3. *Causa immanens*, uma modificação produzida em alguma entidade, devido à sua própria atividade. 4. *Causa transiens*, uma modificação produzida em uma entidade por meio de outra. 5. *Causa sui* (que vide), ou autocausa, referindo-se a Deus, que não tem causa exterior. O termo *causa immanens* tem o mesmo sentido. 6. *Vera causa* significa «causa verdadeira». Newton usou a expressão *verae causae*, indicando as causas que existem na natureza, e que são explicações verdadeiras e suficientes das coisas. (P)

CAUSA EFICIENTE

A causa eficiente é o agente ou poder que produz alguma coisa. O construtor é a causa de um edifício; o inventor é a causa de uma máquina. Ver o conceito de acordo com Aristóteles, no artigo sobre *Causa*, primeiro ponto. Na teologia, a causa eficiente é Deus; Deus criou os céus e a terra, como o poder que realizou o trabalho (Gên. 1:1). O trecho de Colossenses 1:16 apresenta Cristo, o Logos, como a causa eficiente da criação.

CAUSA FINAL

Ver o artigo sobre **Causa**, sob o primeiro ponto, onde discutimos sobre as quatro causas de Aristóteles: causa material, causa formal, causa eficiente e causa final.

No sentido teológico, a causa final é Deus, na direção de quem se move a criação inteira. Em Romanos 11:30 encontramos Deus como a causa material (a criação é obra *proveniente* dele); mas ele também é a causa eficiente (a criação é realização feita *por meio* dele) e ele também é a causa final (a criação foi feita *para* ele). A mesma coisa é dita, em Colossenses 1:16, a respeito do Filho, o Logos de Deus. Ali, as proposições usadas (na nossa versão portuguesa) são: *nele, por meio dele* e *para ele*. Ver a

CAUSA FORMAL — CAVALO

exposição no NTI, em Col. 1:16, quanto a descrições mais completas sobre essa doutrina.

CAUSA FORMAL

A causa formal é **o plano** mediante o qual alguma coisa foi criada, conforme se vê na doutrina platônica das *idéias* ou *universais* (que vide) onde o mundo material aparece criado de acordo com os requisitos e padrões das idéias, e em imitação às mesmas. Quanto ao tratamento que Aristóteles faz a esse respeito, ver o artigo sobre *Causa*, primeiro ponto. De acordo com a teologia, Deus é a causa formal por causa do fato de que o plano utilizado na criação de todas as coisas existe na mente de Deus. Outro tanto é dito acerca do Filho, o Logos, em Colossenses 1:16, sob a proposição *por meio*. Todas as coisas foram criadas por meio do Filho, isto é, tendo o Filho como padrão.

CAUSA MATERIAL

A causa material é o material ou materiais empregados na feitura ou criação de qualquer coisa. Deus é a causa material do universo, porque nele todas as coisas foram criadas. Quanto a amplas explicações sobre esse conceito, ver sobre *Causa*, primeiro ponto, e a breve declaração no artigo *Causa Final*.

CAUSA PRIMEIRA

Ver os artigos sobre *Primeira Causa, Argumento Cosmológico* e *Causa Secundária*.

CAUSA SECUNDÁRIA

Deus é a causa **primária**. Elementos da natureza, e os homens e outros seres inteligentes podem ser *causas secundárias*, pela direção de Deus, ou por sua permissão. Nem tudo que acontece deriva-se de Deus, e isto explica a presença do pecado no mundo, bem como o *caos* que se manifesta na criação. Existe também o *caos* que provoca acontecimentos, que castiga e ensina lições duras, mas este elemento não determina finalidades, embora seja um elemento bastante pertubante no nosso mundo. A vitória é de Deus e do bem, afinal. Pelo poder de Deus, e pela fé, podemos controlar e utilizar até o caos para o nosso bem.

CAUSA SUI

Ver sobre **Causa**. Essa expressão é latina, significando *causa de si mesmo*, ou seja, uma autocausa. A expressão é normalmente aplicada a Deus como autocausado, por parte daqueles que relutam em dizer que Deus não tem causa. Alguns pensadores tomam o mesmo ponto de vista da alma ou da matéria como *eternas* e sem causas externas.

CAVALARIA

Palavra derivada de **cavalo**, que tem seus correspondentes no hebraico (*sus*), e no grego (*úpppos*). O uso de cavalos, em grande número, nas batalhas, pode ser traçado até cerca de 1200 A.C. As vantagens do uso do cavalo, dessa maneira, eram as seguintes: 1. Velocidade. 2. Um cavaleiro podia ferir a um soldado a pé, tornando-se invulnerável, exceto em caso de ataque com flechas. 3. Um terror para os soldados que combatiam a pé, que dificilmente seriam capazes de enfrentar uma carga de cavalaria. 4. Para acompanharem carros também puxados por cavalos, aumentando o ímpeto da carga. Sabemos, através de trechos como II Sam. 8:3,4; 15:1; I Reis 4:26; 10:26, que tanto Davi quanto Salomão lançaram mão dessa estratégia. As mulas também eram usadas com esse propósito (2 Sam. 13:29). O cavaleiro, lutando como um arqueiro, guiava o cavalo mudando o peso de seu corpo, ou mediante a pressão das pernas. Um lanceiro podia operar a lança com uma das mãos, e os arreios com a outra. Sela, esporas e estribos foram inovações posteriores. Ver o artigo sobre *Exército*, *Guerra*.

CAVALEIROS DE COLOMBO

Essa é uma sociedade fraternal e beneficente de leigos católicos romanos, fundada em New Haven, estado de Connecticut, nos EUA, em 1882. O grupo original consistia em dois padres, M.J. McGinney e P.P. Lawlor, além de oito leigos católicos romanos. O propósito da sociedade era de promover a participação prática de católicos romanos em instituições de educação e caridade. A organização espalhou-se por todos os Estados Unidos e por vários países estrangeiros. Pouco antes da Primeira Grande Guerra, seus membros já haviam atingido a casa de um milhão; mas, depois disso, esse número declinou. A sociedade tem concedido doações a universidades católicas romanas, a fim de promover os seus ideais.

CAVALHEIRISMO

Vem da palavra francesa **chevalier**, «cavaleiro». O cavaleiro ideal era um homem honrado, protetor dos fracos, poderoso, mas generoso até mesmo com os inimigos. Foram as cruzadas que deram impulso à cavalaria, na qual um homem podia mesclar seu desejo de lutar e matar com o ideal religioso de recuperar a Terra Santa, então em poder dos pagãos islâmicos. Então um homem podia lutar pelo *Rei Supremo*, e não apenas por algum monarca terreno. A cavalaria exerceu certa influência sobre a ética da Idade Média. A literatura romântica, relativa ao período, forneceu-nos a palavra cavalaria, que se tornou sinônimo de uma cortesia desinteressada, de bravura, de magnanimidade, ou de *cavalheirismo galante*. Os historiadores creditam os cavaleiros por haverem infundido nas classes mais humildes da sociedade um senso maior do que é ser honroso e ético. (H WA)

CAVALO

No hebraico, **sus**. Palavra que ocorre por cento e trinta e três vezes, desde Gên. 47:17 até Zac. 14:20. No grego, *íppos*, um vocábulo que ocorre por dezessete vezes: Tia. 3:3; Apo. 6:2,4,5,8; 9:7,9,17,19; 14:20; 18:13; 19:11,14; 19:18,19,21. Ver os artigos separados sobre *Cavalaria; Cavalos, Os Quatro do Apocalipse*.

Esboço:
 I. Origens
 II. Domesticação
 III. Referências Bíblicas
 IV. Referências Figuradas

Há evidências que mostram que o *cavalo* foi o último e mais forte dos animais de transporte a ser domesticado e desenvolvido na nossa civilização. Por motivo de sua grande utilidade, espalhou-se por todas as regiões do nosso planeta, segundo a civilização foi avançando. As evidências que nos chegam das eras mais remotas, muitas delas pré-adâmicas, e que terminaram em grandes cataclismos, mostram que o cavalo já era um animal importante naquelas civilizações perdidas no passado. Mesmo então esse animal existia sob várias espécies. Alguns povos antigos comiam carne de cavalo, como parte de sua dieta ordinária. Porém, os hebreus não consumiam

CAVALO

carne de cavalo, porquanto não se ajustava às leis levíticas, que afirmavam que só podia ser comida a carne de animais que ruminassem e tivessem os cascos fendidos. Não há qualquer razão higiênica para a proibição da ingestão da carne do cavalo. É possível que o fato de que o cavalo sempre esteve tão ligado ao homem, tenha-o isentado de ser animal de consumo, o que também se aplicaria ao cão, embora, neste último caso, haja outros problemas que devem ser considerados.

I. Origens

Quando falamos a respeito de origens, em qualquer contexto, temos de relembrar que estamos falando somente da civilização mais recente, à qual podemos denominar «adâmica». Há fortes evidências em prol de civilizações pré-adâmicas, várias delas, que terminaram em grandes cataclismos com mudanças dos pólos magnéticos da terra. Essas mudanças de pólos rearranjam os continentes, produzindo destruições de grande magnitude, que requerem um novo começo. O período adâmico parece ter sido o anterior à última dessas fases; e o período de Noé, a última delas. Muitos cientistas e místicos afirmam que não estamos distantes de um outro desses tremendos cataclismos. Dentro da teologia, isso significa que o milênio só começará uma vez que nosso ciclo venha a ser demolido. Não olvidando essas coisas, no que concerne ao cavalo, devemos dizer que suas origens dizem respeito muito mais aonde ele apareceu a princípio, em sua recuperação, bem como dentro do escopo de nossa história, desde a época de Adão. Nesse caso, tem sido demonstrado que houve espécies de cavalos que podem ser atribuídas a diferentes áreas geográficas, como: 1. No leste e no sul da África, as zebras. 2. No norte e no nordeste da África, o asno (que vide). 3. No leste da Palestina até o deserto de Gobi, o asno selvagem. 4. Nas estepes da Eurásia, ao norte das grandes cadeias montanhosas. 5. Uma pequena espécie de cavalo, com cerca de 1,20 m nas espáduas, na Mongólia. 6. Na Ucrânia, havia ainda uma outra espécie, ancestral de várias estirpes, um pequeno cavalo cinzento. O último exemplar dessa espécie morreu em 1851. É interessante notar que, na América do Norte, onde o cavalo foi introduzido pelos europeus em época relativamente recente, a arqueologia tem descoberto várias espécies, ali existentes em tempos remotos. Não somente isso, mas também ali houve vários outros animais, como o leão, o camelo, além de muitas espécies agora extintas, que datam de tempos pré-adâmicos. Portanto, quando falamos em origens, estamos falando sobre como as coisas tornaram a arranjar-se recentemente. O resto está perdido nos arquivos da eternidade passada.

II. Domesticação

As evidências mostram que outros animais úteis, como a ovelha, a cabra, o touro e o asno foram os primeiros a serem domesticados pelo homem. Os fazendeiros utilizavam-se de todos eles. Com exceção do asno, todos eles também serviram para alimentar o homem. Na literatura suméria há referências ao cavalo desde o ano 2000 A.C. Porém, parece que eles não domesticavam o cavalo. Talvez tenham sido os nômades indo-europeus, a leste do mar Negro, que tiveram essa distinção. Já desde 1900 ou 1800 A.C., cavalos estavam sendo usados nas guerras entre os povos, pelo que, algum tempo antes disso, esse animal deve ter sido domesticado. O trecho de Gênesis 49:17 menciona o cavalo, o que significa que a nossa Bíblia começa praticamente na época de sua domesticação. Os guerreiros hicsos, ao que parece, foram os introdutores do cavalo no Egito. Faraó usou-os contra Israel (Êxo. 14:9; 15:19). O trecho de Deuteronômio 17:16 parece indicar que Israel foi proibido de ficar com os cavalos que fossem capturados. Porém, o cavalo era um animal por demais valioso para que essa lei ficasse em vigor por muito tempo. A multiplicação de cavalos em Israel foi rápida. Salomão tinha doze mil cavaleiros e quatro mil cavalos para puxar seus carros de guerra. Outros animais, como o asno, a mula e o camelo também eram usados nas operações militares; mas o cavalo sempre foi um marco de superioridade militar, o animal preferido acima de todos os outros. Nas trilhas, ou em terreno áspero, o asno saía-se muito melhor que o cavalo; mas, em tudo o mais, o cavalo era preferido. Naturalmente, para viagens através do deserto, nenhum animal equipara-se ao camelo.

III. Referências Bíblicas

Há muitas referências bíblicas ao cavalo (cento e cinqüenta delas, no Antigo e no Novo Testamento). Portanto, damos aqui apenas exemplos dessas referências. 1. Eram usados cavalos em Israel, desde os tempos dos patriarcas (Gên. 47:17). O cavalo era usado como montaria ou para puxar carros. 2. Somente em I Reis 20:20 há alusão direta a cavalos usados como montarias; mas é provável que essa prática então já fosse antiga. 3. Lemos em Gênesis 50:9 que tanto cavaleiros quanto vagões acompanharam o grande cortejo do sepultamento de Jacó, em Canaã, e isso implica no uso do animal como montaria, o que também se depreende do relato que o exército egípcio usava cavalos (Êxo. 14:9). 4. O Egito tornou-se um importante centro criador de cavalos; e Salomão tirou proveito dessa circunstância para obter cavalos e equipar o seu exército, pois o Egito era país que fazia fronteira com Israel (I Reis 10:28,29). 5. A multiplicação de cavalos fora proibida em Israel (Deu. 17:16). É significativo que essa proibição esteja no contexto da predição de que, algum dia, Israel exigiria um rei. Foi justamente na época dos reis de Israel que essa multiplicação de cavalos teve lugar. Naturalmente, era impossível enfrentar exércitos estrangeiros invasores sem cavalos, pelo que um mal contribuiu para outro. O trecho de II Samuel 8:4 mostra-nos que Davi contava com um pequeno número de cavalos, mas Salomão foi um campeão dos criadores de cavalos em Israel, segundo já mencionamos. Ele construiu estábulos para abrigar quatro mil cavalos (II Crô. 9:25). A menção a «quarenta mil cavalos», em I Reis 4:26, parece ser um erro escribal.

Provavelmente, foram os hicsos (1700-1600 A.C.) que trouxeram os cavalos da Ásia Menor, introduzindo-os no Egito e na terra de Canaã. Esses animais eram então usados especialmente para puxar os carros de combate. Os egípcios empregaram cavalos para perseguir os israelitas, por ocasião do *êxodo* (Êxo. 14:9). E, ao entrarem na terra de Canaã, os israelitas ali encontraram os habitantes locais empregando esse animal em suas batalhas (Jos. 11:4; Juí. 4:3; I Sam. 13:5 e II Sam. 1:6). Somente já no tempo de Salomão, os cavalos tornaram-se familiares aos hebreus em maior escala (cf. Jos. 11:9; II Sam. 8:4). Assim, as palavras *sus*, *rekes* (parelha de cavalos) e talvez até mesmo *parash*, «cavaleiro», parecem ter tido uma origem estrangeira, não-semítica. Prevaleceu ainda por muitos séculos a idéia de que o cavalo serve de símbolo das potências militares estrangeiras, e, portanto, inimigos de Deus, conforme se vê em Oséias 1:7 e Isaías 31:1-3.

Foi Salomão quem organizou a cavalaria em Israel, importando esses animais da Ásia Menor (I Reis 10:26-29; II Crô. 1:14-17). Houve a organização de

CAVALO — CAVALOS, OS QUATRO

esquadrões especiais de cavalaria e de carros de guerra (I Reis 9:19; II Crô. 9:25). Isso tem sido confirmado por descobertas feitas quando das escavações arqueológicas em Megido. No entanto, alguns estudiosos têm pensado que as estrebarias antigas, ali descobertas, pertencem a um período posterior, talvez mandadas construir pelo rei Acaz (735-731 A.C.).

Usos do Cavalo. Na Bíblia, os cavalos quase exclusivamente aparecem como cavalos de guerra, ou, pelo menos, propriedade de reis, e não de pessoas comuns. Uma referência considerada duvidosa, por muitos estudiosos, é a de cavalos usados para trilhar o grão, que aparece em Isaías 28:28. Os cavalos figuravam entre as propriedades particulares que os egípcios deram a José, em troca de cereal, durante o período de fome de sete anos (ver Gên. 47:17). Em Deuteronômio 17:16, Moisés recomendou aos possíveis futuros reis de Israel que não multiplicassem cavalos, e nem fizessem voltar o povo de Israel ao Egito para «multiplicar cavalos». Porém, essa e outras proibições não conseguiram impedir que os judeus imitassem certos costumes dos povos ao derredor, como sua idolatria e seus vícios, entre os quais a organização de cavalarias, para efeitos de conquistas militares. Nos casos de guerra, os cavalos serviam de montaria ou serviam para puxar carros de combate (ver Êxo. 14:9; Jos. 11:4; II Sam. 15:1, etc.).

Os cavalos de Salomão são mencionados em I Reis 4:26-28, e a «cevada» e a «palha», mencionados nesse último versículo, correspondem às rações empregadas pelos árabes, até os nossos próprios dias, para alimentar os seus cavalos, que figuram entre os melhores do mundo.

Se Jesus Cristo, por ocasião de sua primeira vinda, entrou em Jerusalém montado em um jumentinho, por ocasião de sua segunda vinda, ele virá montado em um cavalo branco, acompanhado por todo o seu exército de cavalarianos, igualmente montados em cavalos brancos (Apo. 19:11 ss). Isso demonstra quão diferente será o segundo advento de Cristo, em relação ao seu primeiro advento. Uma moderna noção popular é aquela que diz que, se Cristo voltar, fá-lo-á somente para ser maltratado de novo, conforme sucedeu quando de seu primeiro advento. Nada mais longe da verdade, pois Jesus voltará na qualidade de Rei dos reis e Senhor dos senhores. (Apo. 19:11-21). Quando Jesus voltar, virá a fim de conquistar o mundo, pelo que ressurgirá em nossa cena terrestre como um Cavaleiro vencedor. A cor branca, do seu cavalo, bem como dos cavalos usados pelo seu exército, de conformidade com o simbolismo bíblico sobre as cores, fala sobre a sua vitória sobre toda a oposição. Montado no cavalo branco, Jesus inaugurará o seu reino milenar.

IV. Referências Figuradas

1. Os quatro cavalos do Apocalipse são comentados em um artigo separado, prenhe de detalhes. Ver o artigo *Cavalos, os Quatro do Apocalipse*. 2. O poder que Deus tem para fazer o que quiser, pode ser simbolizado por esse animal, usado nas batalhas (Zac. 10:5). 3. Os cavalos *brancos* simbolizam a vitória, a glória e a conquista militar, segundo se vê em Apo. 6:2 e 19:11. 4. Os cavalos *vermelhos* simbolizam a destruição, o derramamento de sangue e a guerra (Apo. 6:4). 5. Os cavalos *negros* simbolizam a fome e a morte (Apo. 6:5,6). 6. Os cavalos *amarelos* simbolizam a morte, o inferno e a destruição geral (Apo. 6:8). 7. Os cavalos baios talvez simbolizem a mistura do julgamento e da misericórdia de Deus (Zac. 1:8). 8. Os cavaleiros angelicais representam o poder que Deus tem para proteger o seu povo e impor a sua vontade. 9. Os *santos* são equiparados a éguas graciosas (Can. 1:9). 10. *Símbolos nos Sonhos e nas Visões*. Um cavalo pode simbolizar a energia que as forças físicas que uma pessoa tem à sua disposição, algumas vezes, substituídas por veículos a motor, visto que esses têm tomado o lugar do cavalo, como animal de trabalho. Porém, o cavalo também pode representar o poder selvagem das paixões. Os coices de um cavalo podem indicar um ataque sexual, ou então o desejo de ser sexualmente assaltado. O cavalo negro pode representar as paixões desembestadas. O cavalo amarelo representa a morte. Um cavalo a ultrapassar obstáculos pode simbolizar a capacidade do homem vencer dificuldades; mas, negativamente, pode indicar seus impulsos inferiores em operação. Finalmente, o cavalo pode simbolizar a energia inconsciente de que alguém dispõe, se assim achar por bem. (CHE NTI UN Z)

CAVALOS DO SOL

Ver sobre o Sol.

CAVALOS, OS QUATRO DO Apocalipse

O livro de Apocalipse é representado como **selado** com sete selos. Estes selos representam o conteúdo do livro. Quando o Cordeiro abre um selo, uma porção da revelação é apresentada. Os quatro cavalos do Apocalipse são os primeiros quatro selos, e assim servem como um tipo de introdução às grandes catástrofes que o escritor esperava para os últimos dias.

I. CAVALO BRANCO

Apoc. 6:2: *Olhei, e eis um cavalo branco; e o que estava montado nele tinha um arco, e foi-lhe dada uma coroa, e saiu vencendo, e para vencer.*

O simbolismo dos quatro cavaleiros foi extraído de Zac. 1:7-17 e 6:1-8. Na primeira dessas passagens há a descrição de quatro cavalos de diferentes cores. Eles e seus cavaleiros percorrem a terra por ordem de Deus. São cavalos sobrenaturais, símbolos de verdades místicas. Nessa passagem do A.T. evidentemente prefiguram a «restauração» dos judeus a Jerusalém, após os setenta anos de exílio. Na segunda dessas passagens, vemos quatro carruagens, puxadas, respectivamente, por cavalos vermelhos, pretos, brancos e baios. O propósito desses cavalos é o de patrulhar a terra, por determinação de Deus, executando seus juízos contra as nações pagãs e rebeldes. Podem estar associados às carruagens e aos quatro ventos da teologia astral babilônica. O vidente João emprega esses mesmos símbolos, mais ou menos com a mesma intenção, embora não hesite em adicionar seus próprios significados, que ultrapassam àquilo que está implícito nos livros e nas idéias antigas.

O cavalo era comumente usado nas atividades guerreiras. Portanto, neste ponto, os cavalos representam guerra, violência, tragédia, julgamento divino, com e sem causas naturais, tudo o que envolve desastre para homens pecaminosos.

O significado do cavalo branco pode ser melhor entendido através dos pontos abaixo:

1. Há certa interpretação histórica que supõe que se trata de algum «invasor conquistador», que tivesse assediado o império romano, como os partas, muito hábeis no uso de arco e flecha e do cavalo, e que constantemente ameaçavam a paz do império. Nesse

CAVALOS, OS QUATRO DO APOC.

caso, o vidente estaria predizendo uma invasão que ajudaria a quebrar o poder da Roma perseguidora. Porém, rejeitamos a essa e a qualquer outra interpretação «histórica», embora o próprio João pudesse ter algo de histórico em mente, que recebera uma forma de cumprimento preliminar. Mas essa é uma predição a longo prazo, relativa aos últimos dias.

2. Simbolicamente, alguns intérpretes pensam que o cavalo branco significa a «vitória» obtida em Cristo, em qualquer século, ante a perseguição ou qualquer provação. A última palavra, pois, não seria dada pela Roma perseguidora ou pelas exigências do culto ao imperador—por nenhuma força maligna. A última palavra cabe a Cristo, que executa a vontade de Deus, em favor do bem. Ele sai conquistando e para conquistar, isto é, para obter a vitória final e absoluta. E a vitória dele é a nossa, contanto que exerçamos fé (ver I João 5:4).

3. Há aqueles que pensam que isso simboliza a *guerra*, de modo geral, com a idéia de que a história humana será repleta de torturas da guerra, devido aos atos pervertidos dos homens.

4. Várias interpretações «históricas» (como a invasão da Síria por Vologénus, em 61-63 D.C.) têm sido aventadas, que falam de eventos guerreiros específicos, além da ameaça imposta pelo império parta. Mas todas essas interpretações são dúbias e devem ser rejeitadas.

5. Alguns intérpretes vêem aqui o *curso vitorioso* do evangelho. Aqueles que pensam que os selos são paralelos aos anjos, pensam que Apo. 6:2 é trecho paralelo ao trecho de Apo. 14:6, onde se vê o anjo que traz o «evangelho eterno». E isso se harmoniza com a interpretação sugerida neste parágrafo. Também fazem o paralelismo com o capítulo treze do evangelho de Marcos e com o capítulo vinte e quatro do evangelho de Mateus, que falam sobre a pregação do evangelho por todo o mundo, antes dos *ais* que haverão de anteceder à segunda vinda de Cristo. Embora um grande número de intérpretes tome esse ponto de vista, nada existe de convincente a seu favor.

6. Várias outras interpretações existem, como aquela que fala sobre os conflitos sangrentos na Palestina, durante o reinado de Calígula, ou sobre a fome que houve na Síria, sob Blaudius, ou sobre as agitações que houve no império romano durante o reinado de Galba.

7. Vários intérpretes *futuristas*, que pensam que essa predição fala sobre algo que sucederá imediatamente antes da vinda de Cristo, pensam que o cavaleiro do cavalo branco é o «anticristo». Ser-lhe-ia dado o poder de fazer guerra, de conquistar o mundo inteiro. Essa é uma verdade, mas não é provável que isso é o que esteja em foco aqui. De Haan (em Apo. 6:2), entretanto, defende essa idéia, ao dizer: «O sexto capítulo fala sobre o falso cristo, o anticristo, que procura imitar o verdadeiro Cristo, e, portanto, vem sobre um cavalo branco. Ele virá prometendo paz... um período de falsa paz, estabelecendo um milênio simulado. E quando o anticristo, sobre o cavalo branco houver convencido ao mundo de que chegou a era de ouro da paz, então desfechará sua fúria contra as nações que de nada suspeitam, mergulhando o mundo na guerra. Isso é revelado no segundo selo».

8. Mas parece que esse cavalo e seu cavaleiro estão vinculados aos exércitos santos que há nos céus, pelo que o próprio Cristo está em foco. O «cavalo branco» era usado por conquistadores e heróis romanos em seus cortejos triunfais, em reconhecimento público de seu poder e êxito na guerra. O vidente João lembra a seus leitores de que não haverá triunfo genuíno fora do de Cristo. O Cristo, neste ponto, ainda não terá voltado à terra, mas ameaça a sua volta apenas, volta essa que obterá vitória completa. Os seres viventes lhe dizem: «Vem!» porque a criação inteira apela por sua vitória e pelo fim do caos provocado pelo pecado.

Com um arco. O arco é um símbolo de guerra à longa distância. A vitória de Cristo será universal. Notemos, igualmente, que o «arco» serve aqui para identificar o simbolismo como o que é usado em Hab. 3:9, onde Deus sai para vencer, em prol da salvação de seu povo. (Isso também pode ser comparado com Isa. 41:2; Zac. 9:13 e, especificamente, com Sal. 45:4,5: «As tuas setas são agudas, penetram o coração dos inimigos do Rei...»). Esse cântico é messiânico, referindo-se à segunda vinda de Cristo, o que, no presente texto, é exposto na forma de símbolo, o que será antecedido pelos «ais» que serão descritos nos demais selos que serão abertos.

Coroa. Em reconhecimento de seu direito absoluto de reinar como Rei dos reis e Senhor dos senhores, ele traz essa coroa. Agora Cristo dará início aos acontecimentos que apressarão o seu retorno à terra como Rei. (Ver Apo. 19:16, acerca desse ofício de Cristo). Pode-se notar, em Apo. 19:12, onde é retratada a segunda vinda de Cristo, que ele traz em sua cabeça «muitos diademas». Faz parte do «mistério da vontade de Deus» que Cristo seja o soberano de toda a criação. (Ver Efé. 1:10. Ver também Zac. 6:11, que é trecho paralelo). Sobre a cabeça de Josué, representante de Cristo, foram postas coroas de prata e de ouro.

Saiu vencendo e para vencer, isto é, para obter uma vitória absoluta, perfeita e final. Isso só poderia ser dito acerca de Cristo, em sua segunda vinda, quando todas as nações lhe forem sujeitadas, e, subseqüentemente, a criação inteira, conforme se vê em I Cor. 15:25 e no primeiro capítulo da epístola aos Efésios. (Ver também Fil. 2:9 e ss). A passagem de Apo. 19:16 afirma a realização de tal propósito, e Dan. 2:34 a prediz. Essa vitória não será obtida através da instrumentalidade da igreja, através de sua história, e, sim, através de uma direta intervenção divina, a segunda vinda de Cristo, que agora é prefigurada como algo que já se aproxima célere. A Grande Tribulação servirá de meio de preparação para aquela intervenção divina.

Outras idéias sobre Apo. 6:2.

1. **O cavalo branco ameaça desfechar** os «ais» que precederão a segunda vinda de Cristo. Uma vez que tenham início esses «ais», o cavalo branco estará em próximo de entrar nesta esfera terrestre, para a qual trará os exércitos dos céus, segundo se vê no décimo nono capítulo do Apo.

2. «A semelhança com o cavaleiro que figura em Apo. 19:11 e *ss*, é grande, e seu intuito é realmente esse. A diferença, contudo, é considerável. Ali, o cavaleiro é apresentado como quem já estava presente em seu triunfo, seguido pelos exércitos dos séculos; mas aqui ele opera, estando fisicamente ausente, e o cavaleiro não é o próprio Cristo, mas somente um símbolo de seu poder vitorioso, concretização de seu reino vencedor, no tocante àquele aspecto de seu avanço em que o poder terreno é derrotado, e em que os reinos deste mundo se tornam o reino de nosso Senhor e seu Cristo». (Alford em Apo. 6:2). Essa é uma interpretação comum desde os mais antigos tempos; mas é um erro pensar que isso é um evento histórico. Antes, o próprio Cristo trará os «ais»; e esses «ais» ameaçam a sua volta, volta essa antecedida por tremendos sofrimentos à face da terra. É uma ameaça de destruição, e não do avanço da bondade, através

CAVALOS, OS QUATRO DO APOC.

da igreja.

3. A cor «branca» simboliza a «vitória» (e não a «pureza», pelo menos neste caso), porquanto os cavalos romanos usados nos cortejos triunfais eram dessa cor. Há também uma certa majestade no cavalo branco, talvez um indício de realeza. «Homero pinta os cavalos de Reso como mais brancos que a neve, e mais velozes que o vento». (Vincent, em Apo. 6:2). O cavalo do Rei é branco (ver Apo. 19:11), pelo que somos relembrados da Majestade Real, ao contemplarmos esse cavalo de pura cor branca.

4. No grego, o termo aqui traduzido por *coroa* é «stephanos», que nos tempos antigos eram os *louros* dos vitoriosos, ao passo que o «diadema» era a coroa dos reis, embora essa distinção não fosse observada no grego helenista. No período do grego helenista, o «diadema» palavra grega aqui empregada, podia indicar qualquer faixa da cabeça, e não uma coroa de metal. A consulta de qualquer léxico clássico mostrará que o «stephanos» também podia ser uma «coroa» de metal, nos tempos pré-cristãos, embora, normalmente, indicasse a «coroa de louros».

II. CAVALO VERMELHO

Apo. 6:4: *E saiu outro cavalo, um cavalo vermelho; e ao que estava montado nele foi dado que tirasse a paz da terra, de modo que os homens se matassem uns aos outros; e foi-lhe dada uma grande espada.*

Marte, o planeta vermelho, era o deus da «guerra» na concepção dos antigos. O «vermelho» é a cor do sangue, dando a entender derramamento de sangue. E a «grande espada» subentende a mesma coisa. Porém, tal como no caso de todos os selos, não há acordo geral sobre exatamente o que está em foco, e nem sobre quando isso ocorrerá. Abaixo enumeramos as principais idéias apresentadas pelos intérpretes:

1. Alguns pensam que o próprio Cristo é o cavaleiro do segundo cavalo, e que por vários meios, incluindo a guerra, fará sobrevirem juízos contra a terra. Mas outros acham que o cavaleiro é o exército romano, ou então Vespasiano, Artabano, rei dos partas, ou algum outro personagem histórico qualquer.

2. Há também aqueles que pensam que os cavaleiros dos quatro cavalos não apontam para quaisquer indivíduos em particular, para qualquer guerra; antes, esses cavalos e seus cavaleiros seriam apenas conflitos civis e internacionais, que ocorreriam através da era da igreja, enquanto Cristo não voltar e estabelecer paz duradoura, por ser ele o Príncipe da paz. Há também estudiosos que pensam ser isso idêntico às «muitas guerras», aos muitos conflitos constantes, retratados em passagens como Mat. 24:7; Mar. 13:8 e Luc. 21:10. Este artigo rejeita a interpretação histórica sobre essas predições; por conseguinte, qualquer localização «passada», nas páginas da história, fica igualmente repelida, exceturando, naturalmente, aquele conflito do tempo em que foi escrito o próprio livro de Apocalipse, que foi um cumprimento preliminar e simbólico das guerras e conflitos que se realizarão imediatamente antes do segundo advento de Cristo.

3. Aqueles que pensam que os selos são paralelos aos anjos, pensam que o equivalente ao segundo selo seja a passagem de Apo. 14:8, que se refere à queda da Babilônia. Babilônia seria a representação dos «rejeitadores de Cristo», em todos os seus tipos; assim sendo, estaria em foco a cidade de «Jerusalém», de acordo com alguns outros estudiosos. Nesse caso, a destruição de Jerusalém, que ocorreu no ano 70 D.C., seria o segundo selo.

4. Sem importar o que mais seja dito, é bem provável que as guerras aqui mencionadas haverão de anteceder imediatamente a segunda vinda de Cristo. Assim é que em Jubileus 23:19; I Enoque 66:7; Esdras 5:9; 6:24; 13:31; II Baruque 48:32 e 70:3,6, temos predições acerca de tempos extremamente turbulentos, imediatamente antes da vinda do Messias, como levantes civis, guerras locais e internacionais, etc. Esse poderia ser o intuito do segundo selo.

5. Há quem creia que o segundo selo descreve as condições caóticas em geral, as agitações civis e uma anarquia em vasta escala entre todas as nações, imediatamente antes da segunda vinda de Cristo. Uma vez que a influência do Espírito Santo seja removida da face da terra, os homens exibirão a sua verdadeira natureza, como feras que são, sem Deus é sem consciência. (Ver capítulo 2 de II Tessalonicenses a esse respeito). A vida humana na terra tornar-se-á caótica, como se todos vivessem em uma selva pervertida, de paixões e violências atrozes.

6. Outros eruditos mostram-se mais específicos, determinando guerras particulares como cumprimento do segundo selo. Nesse caso, teríamos a guerra mundial que os místicos contemporâneos predizem para 1999 (havendo uma outra para o ano 2020—o verdadeiro Armagedom), como cumprimento do segundo selo. Os místicos da atualidade predizem duas guerras mundiais, com armas atômicas, antes do ano 2020. O artigo intitulado a *Tradição Profética e a Nossa Época*, apresenta detalhes sobre essas predições que concordam com o que diz o livro de Apocalipse. Os acontecimentos importantes lançam sombras à sua frente, antes de sua ocorrência; portanto, os seres humanos, que são espíritos também, podem reconhecer tais acontecimentos de antemão, mesmo que não possuam qualquer dom profético, segundo o entendemos, biblicamente falando.

7. Aqueles que interpretam o livro historicamente, vêem vários eventos que já tiveram lugar, como a perseguição contra os cristãos, ou os exércitos romanos (munidos de espada), em contraste com os partas (com o arco, de Apo. 6:1), como se fossem o cumprimento deste selo. Ou então, de modo geral, vêem aqui o conflito «entre o bem e o mal», isto é os poderes civis contra o progresso do evangelho, apelando as autoridades civis até mesmo para a perseguição contra os pregadores da mensagem cristã. Essas são interpretações bizarras. Há também aqueles que pensam que a «espada» é a do próprio Deus, com a qual ele castigaria povos hostis. Mas a quinta e a sexta dessas sete interpretações são as mais prováveis.

Grande espada. Qual o significado da mesma? 1. Alguns pensam que seria a guerra em geral; 2. outros pensam na confusão geral; 3. e há também quem estipule guerras e incidentes históricos particulares, conforme se vê nos pontos acima, sobre as interpretações acerca do segundo selo. Conforme dizemos no parágrafo acima, alguns pensam que essa é a «espada de Yahweh», seu meio de castigar às nações adversárias de Israel, segundo se vê em Isa. 27:1; 34:5; 46:10; 47:6 e Eze. 21:3 e *ss*. Não se pode duvidar que as guerras aqui aludidas são instrumentos da ira divina. Em algumas referências do A.T., como também nas obras pseudepígrafas, Israel é quem brande a espada, conforme se vê em I Enoque 90:19; 91:12, secção 34, contra os seus inimigos. Mas o presente versículo não pode fazer alusão a isso. Em I Enoque 88:2, Gabriel leva os inimigos de Deus a se destruírem uns aos outros com a espada; e essa idéia deve ser incluída como parte do significado do segundo selo, porquanto é exatamente isso que sucederá. A espada não faz referência alguma a

CAVALOS, OS QUATRO DO APOC.

Roma, exceto de maneira preliminar. E nem é ela contrastada com o «arco», que figura em Apo. 6:1, como se este fosse dos partas e a espada fosse de Roma.

Outras idéias sobre Apo. 6:4.

1. **Os homens não-regenerados só aprendem através** de erros e de violências tremendos. Essa condição de guerra e imensa destruição será utilizada por Deus para restaurar e renovar a terra para o milênio. Assim é que será elevada a qualidade total da natureza humana. Uma nova espécie de homens, mais espiritualizados, haverá de surgir daí. Mas isso só ocorrerá se primeiramente houver tremenda agonia.

2. É solene o pensamento que muitos de nós verão esses acontecimentos. E certamente nossos filhos participarão deles. O Apocalipse fala diretamente conosco.

3. Os homens «matar-se-ão uns aos outros», com armas atômicas e outras armas de incrível poder. As guerras sempre transformaram os homens em bucha para canhão, mas nunca se viu qualquer coisa que se possa comparar com a vastíssima destruição que atingirá a terra antes do fim do século XX e no começo do século XXI.

4. Consideremos as prodigiosas perversões dos homens, que produzirão condições como essas. Os homens têm rejeitado a mensagem de Deus por meio de Cristo, o Príncipe da paz. Terão de pagar um preço tremendamente alto por causa disso. Mas, finalmente, aprenderão que o bem deve ser praticado somente por ser bom; e o bem se concentra e define em Cristo.

5. *A falsa paz* que será instaurada pelo anticristo redundará em completo fracasso, devido ao pior horror que os homens poderão ver em todos os tempos, a Grande Tribulação. E isso mostrará o que o anticristo realmente é.

6. Quando os homens despertarem para o «ludíbrio» do anticristo, será tarde demais para alterar o rumo dos acontecimentos. A perversidade dos homens fará com que atuem como se estivessem totalmente enlouquecidos.

7. *O bronze sem piedade* dos escritos épicos de Homero ensinará aos homens, sem nenhuma misericórdia, algumas lições duríssimas. A história mostra que quinhentos e oitenta mil judeus morreram, quando os romanos destruíram Jerusalém e as áreas circunvizinhas, no ano de 70 D.C. Foi uma destruição aterrorizante, considerando-se a população do mundo naquela época e os instrumentos que os homens tinham para eliminar o próximo. Centenas de milhões serão mortos à espada, em um tempo relativamente curto, quando o segundo selo for rompido por Cristo.

O Comandante Sangüinário
Não é mau. Que toquem.
Que os canhões troem e os aviões bombardeiem,
Proferindo suas prodigiosas blasfêmias.
Não é mau, é chegado o tempo.
A maior violência ainda é o comandante dos valores
deste mundo.

......
Quem se lembraria do rosto de Helena,
Se lhe faltasse o terrível halo de lanças?
......
Não choreis, deixai-os tocar,
A velha violência não é antiga demais para gerar
novos valores.
(Robinson Jeffers)

III. CAVALO PRETO

Apo. 6:5: *Quando abriu o terceiro selo, ouvi o terceiro ser vivente dizer: Vem! E olhei, e eis um cavalo preto; e o que estava montado nele tinha uma balança na mão.*

Como se dá no caso de todos os quatro cavalos, muitíssimas têm sido as interpretações dadas a esses símbolos. Abaixo mostramos apenas as principais idéias:

1. Se os *selos* são paralelos aos *anjos*, então o trecho de Apoc. 6:5,6 é paralelo a 14:9-11 do mesmo livro. Neste caso, a «besta e sua imagem» estariam em foco. E, se aplicarmos isso historicamente, e não profeticamente, poderíamos supor estar em pauta a «matança da igreja», quando o cristianismo deixou de ser perseguido, tornando-se a «igreja oficial», sendo morta a sua espiritualidade. Quando Constantino se fez cristão, oficializou o cristianismo como religião do império, e, no ano de 380 D.C., Teodoro fez um edito que declarava cristãos todos os habitantes do mundo então conhecido. Isso arruinou a espiritualidade da igreja, por assim dizer, matando-a espiritualmente. Embora essa interpretação possa ser louvada por sua elástica imaginação, não é nada provável que isso é o que o autor sagrado tencionava dar a entender, como se esse fosse o cumprimento do rompimento do terceiro selo. É muito difícil perceber como Constantino poderia prefigurar a «besta» ou anticristo.

2. Os preços para o trigo e a cevada, mencionados em Apo. 6:6 (como parte do terceiro selo), são extremamente elevados. Isso fala de «escassez», ou seja, de «fome», de falta de alimentos, o que sempre ocorre na esteira das guerras. A falta de cereais será tão intensa que terão de ser medidos na mínima quantidade. Ao mesmo tempo, os ricos (possuidores de azeite e vinho) parecerão florescer a despeito de tudo, pelo menos alguns deles. Mas essa expressão bíblica nos deixa perplexos, não havendo acordo geral entre os estudiosos, acerca de seu significado. Alguns ricos conseguirão escapar, mas certamente a maioria deles sofrerá juntamente com toda a humanidade, quando as guerras tomarem conta da face inteira da terra. De modo geral, portanto, poderíamos pensar que o terceiro selo indica as fomes que se seguem às guerras, o que se repetirá nos últimos dias.

3. Preferimos pensar que a verdadeira interpretação não envolve todas as fases de escassez que se seguem às guerras em geral, mas antes, somente as condições que haverá depois de ter sido rompido o *segundo selo*. Portanto, o segundo selo está relacionado a este terceiro, bem como às interpretações quinta e sexta, sobre o *cavalo vermelho* (Apo. 6:4). Muitos conflitos violentos, o caos entre as populações e guerras gigantescas destruirão o suprimento de alimentos da humanidade, e vastas fomes terão lugar. Isso terá lugar em nosso próprio tempo, e certamente no período de vida dos nossos filhos, conforme se nota nas interpretações sobre o segundo selo.

4. As interpretações históricas, que pensam que o «terceiro selo» já teve cumprimento no decorrer da história, nos tempos do império romano, pensam que isso se refere aos dias de Domiciano, que baixou um decreto contra o luxo e ordenou que metade dos vinhedos da Ásia Menor e de outras províncias fosse desarraigada (92 D.C.). Isso visava favorecer os vinhateiros italianos e reduzir o luxo fora da Itália. Porém, não se lê acerca de nenhum período de fome severa no tempo desse imperador, e nem mesmo naquele período geral da história, que pudesse justificar essa interpretação do «terceiro selo». O sexto versículo de Apo. 6, porém, talvez aluda ao decreto de Domiciano, talvez uma elevação *antecipada* do preço de alimentos e uma possível fome; mas isso não se concretizou. É melhor pensar que o cumprimento da

profecia ainda jaz no futuro.

5. Muitas predições judaicas, ao falarem sobre os «últimos dias», mencionam a fome. (Ver *Sota* 49b e comparar isso com Mat. 24:7). Alguns pensam que esta última referência alude às muitas fomes, que sempre se seguem às guerras, através da história do mundo, até à volta de Cristo, e não aos últimos dias propriamente ditos. Na verdade, porém, o terceiro selo, como todos os demais, refere-se especificamente aos tempos do fim, estando de acordo com as predições apocalípticas judaicas acerca do fim.

6. Alguns eruditos falam da fome que houve no tempo de Cláudio, predita por Ágabo (ver Atos 11:28). Mas esse acontecimento dificilmente poderia equivaler ao prodigioso acontecimento que se espera do terceiro selo.

7. Ainda outros pensam que esse selo fala de «tribulação e agonia» em geral, e não de uma *fome*; mas essa interpretação não concorda com o simbolismo dos versículos quinto e sexto do sexto capítulo de Apo.

Com uma balança na mão, Apo. 6:5. Em períodos de escassez, os comestíveis precisam ser pesados com parcimônia. Em tempos de abundância, são distribuídos em tão grandes quantidades que não podem ser pesados com balanças de mão. A figura espectral da fome levava na mão uma balança vazia. Em Eze. 4:16 lê-se sobre o pão vendido a peso, um sinal de tempos dificultosos. É isso que o vidente João tinha em mente. O trecho de Gên. 41:49 mostra-nos que quando as coisas abundam, nenhuma medição cuidadosa se faz necessária. Lev. 26:26 é trecho que mostra a condição oposta. Duas mulheres levam o pão para ser assado em um único forno, tão escasso é o pão, o qual é distribuído a peso. Comerão, mas não ficarão satisfeitas.

Outras idéias

1. O homem colhe aquilo que tiver semeado. As guerras, que nos nossos tempos destroem objetivos civis, e não somente militares, também lançam o caos na produção agrícola, desequilibrando o suprimento normal de alimentos. Crianças inocentes sofrem por causa disso tudo. Não há limites para as perversões da mente humana, afastada que está de Deus e em hostilidade contra Cristo. Essa hostilidade será punida, quando Deus permitir que os homens se destruam a si mesmos.

2. *Preto,* a cor da lamentação e da fome. Ver Jer. 4:28; 7:21; Mal. 3:14, onde a palavra «lamento» é literalmente, «preto», conforme nos diz Vincent, em Apo. 6:5.

3. *Balança.* No grego é *zugon,* literalmente, «jugo», embora a referência seja à cruzeta da balança de pratos. Alguns intérpretes têm defendido totalmente a idéia de que aqui temos uma menção literal ao «jugo». Mas a necessidade de haver uma balança para pesar os alimentos é uma verdadeira previsão para os habitantes da terra. O trecho de Diog. Laert. 8:18 exibe essa palavra com o sentido de «balança», o que também se vê na inscrição grega 1222,4 (do século II A.C.). Ver *Inscr. gr. Rucueil D'Inscriptions grecques,* editor Ch. Michel, 1900; 1912.

4. Devemos observar que cada um dos «seres viventes» tem uma forma distintiva: leão, boi, homem e águia, respectivamente. Alguns eruditos procuram descobrir significados nessas formas, no que se aplica aos selos, porquanto, em sucessão, cada um deles abre um selo. Porém, não se deve espremer em demasia o simbolismo, pois, ao examinarmos cada símbolo, é difícil perceber qual a conexão entre sua forma e o sentido de cada selo. Por exemplo, que associação pode haver entre um «boi» e a guerra, ou entre um «rosto de homem» e a fome? Seria mais apropriado comparar a guerra ao «leão», e, no entanto, é a primeira criatura e não a segunda, que abre o primeiro selo.

IV. CAVALO AMARELO

Apo. 6:8: *E olhei, e eis um cavalo amarelo, e o que estava montada nele chamava-se Morte; e o hades seguia com ele; e foi-lhes dada autoridade sobre a quarta parte da terra, para matar com a espada, e com a fome, e com a peste, e com as feras da terra.*

O adjetivo «*chioros*», é termo grego variegadamente traduzido. Homero aplicou essa palavra ao «mel», e Sófocles à «areia». Tucídides utilizou-se da mesma para indicar pessoas atacadas de uma praga (ii.49); e Homero também a usou para indicar a «palidez» do rosto de uma pessoa atemorizada. Parece que Homero queria indicar a «ausência de cor», e não a presença de qualquer cor particular. No N.T., a cor tencionada é usualmente o «verde». (Ver Mar. 6:39; Apo. 8:7 e 9:14). A tradução de Goodspeed diz aqui «cor de cinzas». Talvez a tradução de Moffatt, «lívido», seja a melhor, porquanto trata-se de uma palavra que era utilizada para indicar a «cor exangue» dos cadáveres; e esse cavalo representa a morte. Hipócrates, *Prognost.* 2, pág. 79:18, também usa esse vocábulo para indicar isso, a carne descolorida de pessoas gravemente enfermas.

Significado do cavalo amarelo

1. O próprio autor sagrado nos dá a definição desse cavalo: a morte e o hades. Mas os intérpretes têm entendido isso de várias maneiras, como a «morte espiritual» (significado simbólico), ou como algum período específico da história antiga, quando a «morte» ameaçou grandes contingentes humanos. Vários intérpretes atribuem a esse simbolismo alguma condição histórica específica, já no passado, como no caso dos selos anteriores.

Qualquer que seja a interpretação desse cavalo, porém, podemos notar que Apo. 6:8, ao mencionar a matança específica com a espada (guerra) e com a fome, provavelmente visa incluir o que já fora dito sob os selos segundo e terceiro. Disso se conclui que os quatro primeiros selos, pelo menos, estão intimamente ligados entre si, provavelmente desdobrando desastres que sobreviriam em um dado período da história. Se antes já aplicamos os primeiros selos a algum período histórico específico, teremos de continuar a fazê-lo no caso deste selo. Essa circunstância, apesar de não ser totalmente «fatal» para o método «histórico» de apresentação, ou, pelo menos, para quase todas as interpretações propostas desse modo, chega a ameaçá-las. Em outras palavras, não se pode atribuir o segundo e o terceiro selos a um período histórico, e o quarto selo a outro período histórico, posterior ao primeiro, porquanto isso interromperia a unidade dos selos, que o autor sagrado parece ter claramente tencionado. Poder-se-ia indagar, portanto, em que período da história tiveram lugar esses acontecimentos, «como uma unidade», e com os devastadores resultados aqui descritos. É difícil situar tal coisa na história. Pois em que tempo uma quarta parte da população mundial pereceu de um golpe? Isso nos força a pensar numa interpretação «simbólica» ou *futurista*; e dentre essas duas possibilidades, preferimos a «futurista».

2. Interpretando que os selos desvendam ocorrências ainda futuras, cremos que este selo inclui a «guerra», o «caos» e a «fome» do segundo e do terceiro selos. Além disso, «grandes pragas» provavelmente fazem parte do quadro da «morte» aqui aludida, pois

CAVALOS — CAVERNA

as pragas eram comumente apelidadas de «morte» por parte dos antigos. Essas pragas se propagavam especialmente após as matanças das guerras. Isso pode ser comparado com a expressão moderna, *morte negra*, a peste bubônica, que atingiu pesadamente a Europa e a Ásia no século XIV. Essa praga era assim chamada devido às manchas negras que deixava na pele. Assim, pois, este selo fala do fato de que as horrendas batalhas do período da Grande Tribulação serão seguidas por pragas incrivelmente generalizadas. O suprimento alimentar dos seres humanos será destruído e poluído. A natureza será destruída de tal modo que os animais ferozes invadirão as áreas habitadas pelos homens, e muitos serão as suas vítimas. Tudo isso, dizem alguns, ocorrerá durante a Grande Tribulação; e, somando-se juntamente os selos de número dois, três e quatro, uma quarta parte da população da terra será destruída, numa cifra que provavelmente atingirá um bilhão de pessoas. O nome «Grande Tribulação» terá uma nova significação naqueles dias, que quase sem dúvida teremos de atravessar, e que certamente serão vividos pelos nossos filhos e netos.

3. Há certas interpretações miscelâneas que precisam ser rejeitadas: a. A destruição de Jerusalém (ano de 70 D.C.); b. os sofrimentos dos cristãos sob a Roma pagã, sobretudo durante o reinado de Domiciano, embora esses sofrimentos também tenham atingido a outros; c. as heresias que trazem a morte espiritual, a morte da igreja, por assim dizer; d. os sarracenos e outros povos específicos, que no decorrer da história causaram grandes sofrimentos a seus semelhantes.

4. Aqueles que pensam que os selos são paralelos aos anjos, assim vinculando Apo. 6:7,8 com Apo. 14:12,13, incorrem em erro. Pois se isso for aceito de modo estrito, os «mortos» teriam de ser somente crentes, porquanto o trecho de Apo. 14:13 diz: «Bem-aventurados os mortos que desde agora morrem no Senhor». Isso forma um mui duvidoso paralelo do trecho que temos aqui. Seja como for, dizer que o quarto selo representa a «Idade das Trevas», é seguir as explicações desse grupo de intérpretes, que dificilmente expõem idéias isentas de objeções difíceis de contornar. Nesse caso, a «morte» aqui referida seria a *peste bubônica* que teve lugar já perto do fim da Idade das Trevas, e que deixou uma esteira de destruição na Europa e na Ásia. Temos de admitir que a destruição de vidas, naquela oportunidade, foi verdadeiramente grande. Mas, atingiu uma quarta parte da população da terra? Certamente que não, se incluirmos regiões geográficas fora da Ásia e da Europa, as quais também precisam ser incluídas para que o quadro assuma proporções mundiais.

Morte. — O selo que aqui temos personifica a «morte». Isso pode ser confrontado com a idéia judaica do «anjo da morte», ou com Plutão, o deus grego do submundo e da morte. Alguns eruditos vêem aqui a pessoa de Satanás já que o cavalo é, ao mesmo tempo, a «morte» e o «hades». Outros concebem aqui a idéia da «praga», na morte, por ser esse um simbolismo comum na antiguidade. O símbolo, porém, provavelmente tem por intuito ser mais extenso do que isso. Trata-se da morte mediante a praga, além da morte corporal literal; mas também é a morte devido a todas as causas, como guerras, fomes, etc., já que o selo incorpora as idéias do segundo e do terceiro selos. A morte não é «simbólica», ou seja, a «morte da igreja», mediante o assédio de doutrinas falsas.

«Formas simples da morte (a guerra e a fome) foram reveladas nos primeiros selos; agora o próprio grande rei dos terrores aparece, e em sua mão estão reunidas todas as formas de morte—guerra, fome e pestilência». (Carpenter, Apo. 6:8).

No tocante à personificação da «Morte», ver Apo. 5:14 (a morte como rei) e I Cor. 15:25 (a morte como inimigo). (Comparar com Isa. 28:15). Na teologia fenícia antiga, Sanconiaton, filho de Saturno, era chamado «Morte», de forma personificada, o que os gregos imaginavam com Plutão.

Hades. O «reino da morte» é agora personificado. Originalmente, «Hades» era o deus do mundo inferior, sendo essa a origem do termo. «Hades» e «Plutão» são apelativos paralelos para o mesmo conceito mitológico, entre os gregos e os romanos. (Ver Apo. 5:13, Apo. 1:18; Mat. 16:18 e Luc. 16:23). As passagens de I Ped. 3:18-20 e 4:6 mostram que Cristo desceu àquele lugar de espíritos desencarnados, e estabeleceu certa diferença no tipo de existência que eles levam ali; e esse conceito é igualmente explicado nas notas de introdução ao Apo. 3:18 no NTI.

Há somente um cavaleiro, chamado por dois nomes. O autor sagrado não quis dizer que fossem dois cavaleiros. Há apenas um, chamado Morte e também Hades, visto que a morte é companheira inseparável do hades. (Ver Apo. 1:16 e 20:13 e *ss*). O hades «segue os passos» da morte, e para onde esta vai, vai aquele. Os intérpretes têm criado muita confusão desnecessária neste ponto, pressionando em demasia ao simbolismo, procurando solucionar o problema se o cavalo amarelo tem um ou dois cavaleiros. Os símbolos usados pelo autor sagrado são bem claros, sem necessidade de refinação exagerada.

Matar à espada, pela fome. Um quádruplo poder destrutivo é mencionado, embora não se trate de uma lista exaustiva dos meios que causarão imensa devastação no mundo nos últimos dias. Isso pode ser comparado aos quatro destruidores de Eze. 14:21, «a espada, a fome, as feras e a pestilência». Se considerarmos que a «morte» significa «pestilência», então essas duas listas serão idênticas.

CAVALOS, PORTA DOS Ver **Porta dos Cavalos**.

CAVALSILAS, NICKALOAS
Faleceu em 1371. Foi arcebispo grego da cidade de Alônica. Foi educado na Itália, tornando-se famoso como místico e filósofo. Foi um dos maiores representantes da tradição mística da Igreja Oriental, mas também teve tempo para desempenhar um importante papel na política do império bizantino. Escreveu muitos livros sobre assuntos místicos, incluindo *A União do Homem com Jesus Cristo*, tendo enfatizado o papel dos sacramentos, nessa união. Ele era oponente da Igreja Católica Romana (que vide), sendo contrário à união entre a Igreja Ortodoxa Oriental e a Igreja Católica Romana. (AM E)

CAVEIRA, LUGAR DA
Ver **Gólgota**.

CAVERNA
No hebraico temos duas palavras envolvidas, e, no grego, duas, a saber:

1. *Chor*, «buraco», palavra que figura por nove vezes (por exemplo: I Sam. 14:11; Jó 30:6; Isa. 11:8; Zac. 14:12).

2. *Mearah*, «caverna aberta», palavra que figura por trinta e nove vezes (para exemplificar: Gên. 19:30; 23:9,11,17,19,20; Jos. 10:16; I Sam. 13:6; II Sam. 23:13; I Reis 18:4,13; Sal. 57, título; Eze.

33:27).
3. *Mechilloth*, «cavernas». Palavra hebraica que ocorre por apenas uma vez, em Isa. 2:19.
4. *Oré*, «buraco», «abertura». Palavra grega que figura por duas vezes, em Heb. 11:38 e Tia. 3:11.
5. *Spélaion*, «gruta», «caverna». Palavra grega que aparece por seis vezes: Mat. 21:13; Mar. 11:17; Luc. 19:46; João 11:38; Heb. 11:38 e Apo. 6:15.

A formação geológica da Síria-Palestina favorece enormemente a formação de cavernas. Ali, usualmente, as rochas são pedras calcárias de diferentes densidades. A água, ao atravessar as rochas, deixa aberturas e fissuras que se tornam cavernas. A camada inferior ou subsolo sírio, sendo formado por arenito, giz, basalto e sódio, favorece o aparecimento de cavernas. Em conseqüência, a região inteira tem muitas cavernas, algumas das quais de grandes dimensões. Estrabão referiu-se a uma caverna, perto de Damasco, onde podiam abrigar-se quatro mil homens. As cavernas formam-se imediatamente abaixo da camada freática, nas regiões onde a água mantém-se estável por muito tempo. Usualmente, as cavernas formam-se em passagens horizontais, aparecendo diversas numa mesma área. Contudo, existem cavernas verticais. Essas passagens verticais são os pontos ativos de águas subterrâneas, escavados na pedra calcária. Formam-se assim fendas cilíndricas, que podem atingir profundezas de cem metros ou mais. O colapso do teto de uma caverna produz uma depressão na superfície. Essas depressões são tipicamente circulares, com dez a vinte metros de profundidade e, com freqüência, um diâmetro de cem metros. Quando o nível da água baixa, as cavernas, assim livres da água, tornam-se acessíveis. Devido à água que respinga do teto das cavernas e se evapora, o mineral em suspensão forma as estalactites, que vão descendo dos tetos das cavernas. As colunas que se vão elevando do chão de uma caverna, formadas pela água que pinga, são chamadas estalagmites. Quando uma estalactite e uma estalagmite, finalmente, juntam-se, forma-se uma coluna que liga o chão ao teto da caverna.

A abundância de pedra calcária, em Israel e em torno do rio Jordão, cujo vale se forma, principalmente, de maciços leitos de pedra calcária e de dolomita, com algum giz, que já é material mais mole, resulta em grande quantidade de cavernas, naquela região.

Cavernas nas Escrituras. A primeira menção a uma caverna, na Bíblia, é àquela onde se esconderam Ló suas duas filhas, após a destruição de Sodoma e Gomorra (Gên. 19:30). Além dessa, temos a caverna de Macpela, no campo de Efrom, que foi comprada por Abraão, e onde ele sepultou Sara. Posteriormente, o próprio Abraão, Isaque, Rebeca, Lia e Jacó foram ali sepultados (Gên. 49:32 e 60:13). O local, na atualidade, é conspicuamente assinalado por uma mesquita muçulmana. Não se sabe da localização da caverna de Maquedá, onde se ocultaram cinco reis dos amorreus, após terem sido derrotados por Josué (Jos. 10:16,27). Também havia cavernas artificiais, escavadas por diversas razões (Jó 6:2). A maior parte dessas cavernas artificiais eram usadas como sepulcros. Obadias escondeu cem profetas do Senhor em uma caverna, a fim de protegê-los (I Reis 18:4). Em Horebe havia uma caverna, usada por Elias (I Reis 19:8), cuja localização nos é desconhecida. Cavernas usadas como habitações são mencionadas em Núm. 24:21; Can. 2:14 e Jer. 49:16. As cavernas também eram usadas como sepulcros, conforme já vimos. Ver também João 11:38; Mat. 20:60. As cavernas eram lugares de refúgio (Juí. 6:2; I Sam. 14:1) e de habitação (Heb. 11:38; que provavelmente também inclui a idéia de refúgio). Também eram utilizadas como prisões (Isa. 24:22 e Zac. 9:11). Em tempos modernos, as cavernas servem de pontos de atração turística, porquanto algumas delas oferecem uma visão espetacular. (FAI S)

CAVERNA (Metáfora de Platão)
Ver **Metáfora da Caverna de Platão**.

CÉBERO
Na mitologia grega, seria o cão de três cabeças que guardava a entrada do hades (que vide). Nos escritos de Hesíodo, o mesmo cão já tem nada menos de cinqüenta cabeças em um único corpo. Uma monstruosidade, sem dúvida!

CEBOLA
No hebraico, **betsel**. Essa palavra ocorre exclusivamente em Núm. 11:5, juntamente com os alhos e com os legumes pelos quais os israelitas tanto desejavam, depois que deixaram o Egito. A variedade em foco provavelmente tem o nome científico de *Allum cepa*, que continua sendo plantada até hoje no Egito. Naquela época, como até hoje, a espécie era plantada às margens do rio Nilo. As cebolas eram consumidas cruas, cozidas, fritas, torradas, ou sob a forma de sopa. A cebola tornou-se símbolo de certas vantagens que o mundo oferece, e que um crente pode novamente desejar, depois de convertido. Em outras palavras, representa um item que tende ao desvio, um desejo de voltar aos antigos caminhos.

CECÍLIA
Uma virgem e mártir cristã romana, cuja festa religiosa é celebrada a 22 de novembro. Muitas lendas vieram cercar essa figura, pelo pouco do que se sabe sobre ela não está envolvido em dúvidas sombrias. As estimativas modernas pensam que ela faleceu entre 177 e 362 D.C. Pode ter sido membro da ilustre família romana dos Caecillii, e pode ter sido benfeitora dos primeiros cristãos, — tendo sido honrada por isso. A lenda que circunda a sua morte é especialmente vívida, mas o mais provável é que não passe de uma lenda. Diz-se que a tentativa para sufocá-la, a princípio, não deu certo. Então ela foi decapitada, embora tivesse continuado a viver por três dias, somente após esse prazo morreu; e então teria sido sepultada na catacumba de Calisto. O papa Pascal I transferiu os seus restos mortais para a igreja de Santa Cecília, em 821 D.C. A adoração a ela espalhou-se por muitos lugares. Ela tem sido honrada como a patrona dos músicos, e com freqüência é representada tocando um pequeno órgão, uma viola, uma harpa ou algum outro instrumento musical.

CEDRO
No hebraico, **erez**, palavra usada por setenta e duas vezes no Antigo Testamento (por exemplo: Lev. 14:4,6,49,51,52; I Reis 5:8; 6:9,10,15,16,18,20,36; Sal. 29:5; Can. 1:17; Isa. 2:13; 9:10; Jer. 22:7,14,15, 23; Eze. 17:3,22,23; Zac. 11:1,2). Como vemos, há muitas alusões ao cedro, nas Escrituras, e a maior parte dessas referências diz respeito ao cedro do Líbano. A espécie era largamente distribuída na Síria-Palestina.

1. O cedro era madeira usada nos ritos de purificação, juntamente com a escarlata e o hissopo. Parece que, nesse caso, temos uma árvore natural do deserto do Sinai, sem ligação com os cedros do Líbano. Pode ter sido o *Juniperus phoenicia*, que

também se encontra no monte Hor e circunvizinhanças. A madeira dessa variedade de cedro era queimada por um sacerdote, durante as purificações levíticas (Lev. 14:4-6, 49-52; Núm. 1:6). Alguns estudiosos supõem que a árvore em foco seja o *Juniperus oxycedrus*. Essa espécie, bem como aquela mencionada acima, dá uma fragrância agradável quando queimada a sua madeira.

2. Além disso, há menção aos cedros existentes «no jardim de Deus», em Ezequiel 31:8. Esses são contrastados com os filhos da Assíria, que são chamados cedros do Líbano, no quinto versículo do mesmo capítulo. Por esse motivo, podemos supor que há uma diferenciação de espécie em foco, embora não possamos saber quais espécies estejam em pauta.

3. O trecho de Núm. 24:6 diz «cedros junto às águas», que dificilmente podem ser os mesmos cedros do Líbano, porquanto aquele cedro sempre medra em terra firme. Alguma árvore amante da água está em foco, porém, não mais a conhecemos.

4. O *cedro do Líbano* é uma árvore conífera de grande porte, que antigamente era abundante no Líbano, mas atualmente é rara e protegida pelo governo. A sua madeira é altamente procurada devido à sua durabilidade. Foi usada na construção da casa de Davi (II Sam. 5:11), bem como do templo de Salomão (I Reis 5:6-10), e também do novo templo, após o exílio babilônico (Esd. 3:7). Salomão também usava a madeira de cedro para fabricar carruagens (Can. 3:9). Essa árvore pode atingir uma altura de até 37 metros; e, metaforicamente, nas páginas do Antigo Testamento, era usada para aludir à estatura de um homem (Eze. 31:3; Amós 2:9). Essa espécie vegetal continua abundante no Anano e no Taurus, espraiando-se desde a cadeia do Himalaia até o Atlas, e da Ásia Menor central até o Líbano. Os gregos e os romanos utilizavam a sua madeira. Assim, foi usada para a construção do teto do templo de Diana dos Efésios, como no templo de Apolo, em Utica. Algumas vezes o cedro é chamado de *rei das árvores*, mas isso só tem aplicação se estamos falando sobre as espécies vegetais conhecidas na Palestina, pois, fora dali, há muitas outras árvores maiores em altura e magnitude. O bosque sagrado em Besherri, no Líbano, ainda tem o antigo nome de *cedros do Senhor*. Os cedros verdadeiros são membros da família dos pinheiros, com um tronco muito elevado, com folhas parecidas com agulhas e cones eretos. Os cedros verdadeiros são as melhores árvores perenes para efeito de ornamentação, embora também produzam uma excelente madeira de construção. A madeira é durável e resiste bem ao efeito da água. (AM ND UN)

CEDROM

No hebraico, «turvo», «melancólico», «escuro». No grego, *kedrón*, palavra que só aparece em João 18:1, em todo o Novo Testamento. Esse é o nome de um riacho com regime de inverno, que atravessa o vale de Josafá. O termo aplica-se tanto ao riacho quanto ao vale por meio do qual flui. Em sua *Historical Geography*, Smith nos dá a seguinte descrição, à pág. 511: «Ao norte de Jerusalém começa o leito da torrente do Cedrom. Passa pelo monte do templo, por aqui que, posteriormente, veio a ser o Calvário e o Getsêmani. Deixa o monte das Oliveiras e a aldeia de Betânia para a esquerda, e Belém bem para a direita. Então precipita-se pelos terraços nus, pelos precipícios e pelas gargantas estreitas do deserto da Judéia — o deserto do bode expiatório. Esse vale fica tão estéril e ressecado, tão similar a um forno, quando desce abaixo do nível do mar, que o seu nome torna-se wadi en-Nar, ou «wadi de fogo». No mínimo, o seu curso encachoeirado leva até os precipícios imediatamente acima do mar Morto, onde deixa suas águas escassas de inverno. Porém, durante o verão inteiro, o wadi fica seco». O vale através do qual esse riacho precipita-se tem apenas cerca de 32 km de comprimento, mas, durante esse breve percurso, desce cerca de 1.120 m, do começo ao fim. O lugar onde o Cedrom deságua no Jordão é uma garganta estreita, com cerca de 366 m de profundidade.

Lemos no Antigo Testamento que Davi, quando fugia de Absalão (II Sam. 15:23,30), atravessou esse riacho. Salomão utilizou-se do mesmo para assinalar até onde Simei podia passar, e não mais (I Reis 2:37). Asa destruiu e queimou ali os ídolos de sua mãe, Maaca (I Reis 15:13). Atália foi executada ali (Josefo, *Anti*. 9:7,3; II Reis 11:16). Quando a adoração idólatra foi removida do templo de Jerusalém, esse vale tornou-se o lugar onde foram lançados os escombros e o material destruído, pelos seguidores de Yahweh (II Reis 23:4,6,12; II Crô. 29:16; 30:14). Nos dias de Josias, esse vale era usado como um cemitério comum, a serviço de Jerusalém (II Reis 23:6; Jer. 26:23; 31:40).

No vale do Cedrom há uma fonte intermitente que, na antiguidade, servia de suprimento de água para Jerusalém. Seu nome é Gihon, isto é, «jorro». Um outro nome dessa fonte é fonte da Virgem. Na antiguidade, seu fluxo foi artificialmente desviado para servir às necessidades da população de Jerusalém. Foi encontrada ali, em 1880, uma inscrição em hebraico, que menciona o túnel que foi feito a fim de transportar água dessa fonte para Jerusalém. Talvez haja uma alusão a isso em II Crônicas 32:3,4. Em nossos dias, somente quando há chuvas muito pesadas aparece ali alguma água. Um pouco mais ao sul, porém, há uma segunda fonte, onde se fundem os vales do Cedrom e de Hinom. Essa outra fonte chama-se En-Rogel.

Quando Herodes restaurou o templo, ampliou a área circundante erigindo novos alicerces para as muralhas. No seu ponto mais alto, as muralhas circundantes do templo tinham 52 m de altura, acima do vale do Cedrom. Josefo disse que quando alguém olhava para baixo, desde aquela altura, ficava tonto (*Anti*. 15:5). Foi essa grande altura que esteve associada à tentação de Jesus, em Mateus 4:5. O jardim do Getsêmani ficava na vertente ocidental do monte das Oliveiras, exatamente do outro lado do Cedrom. Jesus atravessou o vale do Cedrom, com os seus discípulos, depois que saiu do cenáculo para passar a noite no jardim do Getsêmani (João 18:1). Judas Iscariotes também atravessou o vale do Cedrom, ao guiar os soldados que foram prender a Jesus (João 18:2). Jeremias aguardava o dia quando Jerusalém seria reconstruído, quando os lugares sagrados de sepultamento, como aquele associado ao vale do Cedrom, seriam restaurados (Jer. 31:40). (FIN UN WRI Z)

CEFAS

Um apelido que Jesus deu a Simão Pedro (João 1:42). Ver também I Cor. 1:12 ss. A palavra é um termo aramaico que significa «pedra», «seixo», e que os gregos traduziam por *petros* e os latinos por *petrus*. Ver o artigos sobre *Pedro* e sobre os *Apóstolos*.

CEGONHA

No hebraico, **chasidah**, palavra que vem de uma raiz que significa «constante», «leal». Como quase

CEGUEIRA — CEIA DO SENHOR

sempre se dá com nomes pertencentes à fauna e à flora bíblicas, as traduções têm-se mostrado muito irregulares com relação a essa palavra hebraica. A Septuaginta a traduz por quatro palavras diferentes. O termo hebraico figura por seis vezes: Jó 39:13 (onde nossa versão portuguesa a traduz erroneamente por «avestruz»); Lev. 11:19; Deu. 14:18; Sal. 104:17; Jer. 8:7 e Zac. 5:9.

Os contextos bíblicos mostram que a *chasidah* dos hebreus era a mesma ave que chamamos de «cegonha», devido a três pontos confirmatórios: a. Era uma das aves imundas (Lev. 11:19). As cegonhas alimentam-se em lugares lamacentos, e, em alguns períodos do ano, alimentam-se principalmente de sapos e rãs. b. A cegonha é uma das aves migratórias, o que concorda com o que se lê em Jer. 8:7. c. Trata-se de uma ave de grande porte, o que se harmoniza com a descrição subentendida em Zacarias 5:9: «...havia vento em suas asas... e levantaram o efa entre a terra e o céu».

Cegonhas brancas e negras atravessam regularmente a Palestina, em suas migrações anuais. O marabu, que é uma cegonha de maior porte ainda, aparece ali com bastante raridade. Durante a primavera, cegonhas brancas voam desde os seus ninhos na África e no sudoeste da Arábia, para seus ninhos de postura na Europa e na Ásia, provendo um dos mais lindos espetáculos naturais. Revoadas de centenas e centenas de cegonhas chegam desde os fins de fevereiro até o mês de maio, inclusive. Ver sobre *Aves Migratórias*. Diz Salmos 104:17: «...quanto à cegonha, a sua casa é nos ciprestes». Mas, às cegonhas que não continuam seu vôo migratório, e passam o verão na Palestina, provavelmente ainda não atingiram a idade adulta, de nidificação.

Quando estão de pé, no solo, as cegonhas têm cerca de um metro de altura; e, durante o vôo, com os pescoços esticados para a frente, as patas esticadas para trás, com porções brancas e negras nas penas, essas aves são inconfundíveis. Quando pousam, a fim de descansar, imediatamente espalham-se pelos campos e pelos pântanos à caça de peixes, rãs e insetos. A cegonha negra é menor e de coloração mais escura, e não negra, realmente. Essa variedade, que passa o inverno no sul da África, aparece na Palestina em grupos bem menores, e seguem uma rota norte diferente daquela seguida pelas cegonhas brancas.

Modernamente, a cegonha é classificada dentro da ordem das Ciconiformes, paralelamente ao íbis e ao jaburu. Há dezessete espécies de cegonhas, que formam a família dos ciconídeos. Elas produzem sons que são pouco mais que piados e resmungos, mas conseguem fazer grandes ruídos quando batem as mandíbulas imensas uma na outra. O jaburu (*Jabiru mycteria*) é uma espécie que ocorre na América tropical, sendo muito comum, em nosso Brasil, tanto no pantanal matogrossense quanto na Amazônia, onde enfeitam a paisagem com seu vôo majestoso, batendo as longas asas lentamente, em vôo quase sempre rasante, embora também possam voar a grandes alturas. Se o íbis também aparece na Palestina, em certas épocas do ano, o jaburu nunca foi visto ali, pois é espécie tipicamente centro e sul-americana. **O jaburu é a maior ave dos Ciconiformes.**

CEGUEIRA

A grande incidência de cegueira, nos países do Oriente, surpreende as pessoas de outras culturas. Através dos milênios, as oftalmias têm-se mostrado epidêmicas, naqueles países. Certas enfermidades, como a varíola, e determinadas doenças venéreas também exercem esse mau efeito. Além dos germes patogênicos, há fatores como a pobreza, condições sanitárias insatisfatórias, luz solar excessiva, calor demasiado, areias sopradas pelo vento, acidentes e ferimentos de guerra.

A cegueira de nascença, nos tempos antigos e modernos, com freqüência é causada pela gonorréia, transmitida ao bebê pela vagina infectada da mãe. Porém, quando se tornou usual pingar algumas gotas anti-sépticas apropriadas nos olhos dos recém-nascidos, esse tipo de cegueira diminuiu sensivelmente. Um outro agente de infecção é um vírus que produz o tracoma. As potentes drogas de nossos dias geralmente produzem curas, em casos não muito adiantados; mas os povos antigos não dispunham de tais recursos. A sífilis congênita é uma outra causa da cegueira.

De acordo com a lei do Antigo Testamento, um homem cego ficava excluído do sacerdócio. Isso servia para ensinar uma boa metáfora espiritual. Quem pode servir espiritualmente a outros, enquanto é espiritualmente cego? (Ver Lev. 21:18; Mal. 1:13,14). Por outra parte, a legislação mosaica requeria tratamento humanitário em favor dos cegos (Lev. 19:14; Deu. 27:18).

Usos Metafóricos. 1. Aqueles que são espiritualmente ignorantes, pagãos ou não, são cegos racional e espiritualmente (Mat. 15:15; Rom. 2:19). 2. Aqueles que são destituídos de conhecimento espiritual também são classificados desse modo (Apo. 3:17). Esse mesmo versículo fala sobre aqueles que se cegam mediante a vida fácil e luxuosa, abandonando assim qualquer inquirição espiritual séria. 3. Os juízes tornam-se cegos quando influenciados pela ignorância de causa, por peitas ou por lisonjas (Êxo. 23:8). 4. Os mestres tornam-se cegos quando buscam honrarias, ou quando são espiritualmente ignorantes (Isa. 59:10; Mat. 23:16). 5. Qualquer pessoa é considerada cega quando permite que o senso de importância própria, o ódio aos seus semelhantes, ou qualquer outra atitude errada a impeça de ver as coisas do ponto de vista espiritual (I João 2:11). 6. Jesus curou a muitos cegos literais (Mat. 9:27 ss.; João 9:1 ss.). E o seu evangelho agora nos cura espiritualmente da cegueira da alma (Luc. 7:22).

CEGUEIRA JUDICIAL Ver **Julgamento que Cega**.

CEIA DO SENHOR Ver sobre Eucaristia.

As principais passagens neotestamentárias sobre a Ceia do Senhor, são o sexto capítulo do evangelho de João, I Cor. 10:16-21, e a narrativa de instituição em Mat. 26:26-29; Marc. 14:22-25 e Luc. 22:19,20. No que tange à natureza da Ceia do Senhor, conforme a prática na igreja cristã, a passagem de I Cor. 11:17-34 é a mais informativa. Nossas informações sobre a natureza exata da cerimônia da Ceia do Senhor não são muito grandes, pelo que várias coisas permanecem a respeito que continuam um tanto incertas. Também é possível que, em diferentes localidades do mundo cristão da época, diferentes práticas fossem seguidas. Quase todos os intérpretes concordam que originalmente a Ceia do Senhor consistia de uma refeição tomada à noite, não estando necessariamente vinculada ao culto dominical, mas antes, podia ser marcada para qualquer dia conveniente para a comunidade local. E a menção, em I Cor. 16:2, acerca da necessidade de separar contribuições em dinheiro no primeiro dia da semana, não significa necessariamente, que a Ceia do Senhor fazia parte das diversas atividades do primeiro dia da semana, ainda que nessa referência se possa perceber uma indicação segura de que a igreja cristã primitiva havia abandonado o sábado do judaísmo em favor do dia do Senhor, o primeiro dia da semana, como seu dia preferível de observância religiosa.(Quanto à *adoração dominical*, ver as notas expositivas em Atos 20:7 no NTI. Quanto a primeira alusão ao «Dia do Senhor», ver Apo. 1:10).

A Ceia do Senhor ou «eucaristia» original parece ter sido uma festividade, uma refeição, provavelmente em imitação à celebração da páscoa pelos judeus. Na secção bíblica de I Cor. 11:17-34, foi mister que Paulo repreendesse aos crentes de Corinto por motivo de glutonaria e bebedeira e isso, obviamente, implica em um banquete de alguma envergadura, e não em uma simples cerimônia litúrgica. A Ceia do Senhor foi reduzida a um ato litúrgico, não mais acompanhado por uma refeição real; bem provavelmente se tornou parte da adoração dominical.

É interessante que em algumas secções da igreja, a cerimônia do lava-pés era vinculada às festividades. Portanto, parece que havia três partes distintas nessas festividades: 1. A festividade (que consistia de uma *refeição comum*); 2. o lava-pés (ver João 13:2-20), que apesar de não ser universalmente praticado, era item importante para algumas comunidades (ver João 13:4,5), e 3. a Ceia do Senhor, em que se partia o pão e distribuía o suco da videira, em memória ao Senhor Jesus e à sua expiação, e em antecipação ao seu segundo advento, como sinal de fé nessa realidade futura.

A **Ceia do Senhor** ou **comunhão**, — também é chamada no N.T. original de **agape**, que significa «festa de amor». E essa porção na maioria do mundo cristão, estava destinada a ser a única coisa que sobrevivia à festa de um ritual antes tão elaborado. Essa palavra «agape» é usada pelos comentadores com alusão tanto à festa maior como à própria Ceia. No entanto, se aplica mais diretamente à festa ou banquete do que mesmo à comemoração da Ceia, que só se verificava após a refeição comum. Não há qualquer indicação de que o lava-pés fosse praticado em acompanhamento a essas festividades: de fato, nos escritos de Paulo essa ordenança nem ao menos é mencionada. (Porém, quanto ao seu caráter «obrigatório», conforme alguns estudiosos enfrentam a questão do lava-pés» a despeito dessa exigüidade de alusão nas páginas do N.T., ver as notas expositivas acima referidas). Ver o artigo sobre *Lava-pés*.

Não possuímos qualquer informação direta sobre como era providenciado o alimento para o banquete ou *agape*. É bem possível que cada família trouxesse alguma coisa; mas também podia haver um «fundo comum», usado para essa finalidade. Seja como for, de alguma maneira, os membros pobres terminavam com bem pouco ou mesmo com nada para comer, ao passo que os membros mais abastados se empanturravam e bebiam abundantemente. Ver I Cor. 11:21. Foi esse abuso que levou Paulo a recomendar a eliminação da festa, limitando as festividades ao *agape*; e finalmente, isso se tornou a ordem estabelecida. Outrossim, a Ceia do Senhor passou a ser vinculada ao culto de adoração regular, usualmente à noite, porquanto foi à noite que Jesus instituiu essa ordenança.

Não possuímos qualquer informação específica acerca de quem costumava presidir o rito da Ceia do Senhor, embora seja provável que os ministros regulares é quem dirigiam o mesmo. Entretanto, até então a Ceia do Senhor não se transformara em uma cerimônia eclesiástica, parecendo que os crentes ordinários podiam observá-la, pois, naqueles dias, a Ceia não era nenhum «profundo mistério», capaz de ser manipulado somente por um clero devidamente credenciado. Meio século mais tarde, entretanto, fixou-se a prática de somente ministros presidirem esse rito, conforme aprendemos em I Clemente 40:2-4 e Ign. Smyrn. 8:1. E é possível que a própria Ceia do Senhor se tenha tornado um dos importantes fatores no desenvolvimento do chamado «episcopado monárquico», quando o rito começou a assumir qualidades sacramentais que não possuía no começo do cristianismo. — A proporção que foram surgindo os dogmas, assim também se desenvolveram os seus campeões, isto é, o clero, composto de «sacerdotes» desses supostos mistérios.

A teologia da ceia. Ver os artigos sobre: 1. *Transubstanciação*, 2: *Consubstanciação* e *Jesus como o Pão da Vida*.

CELEIRO

Devemos pensar em três palavras hebraicas e uma palavra grega. Palavras hebraicas: 1. *Asamim*, «armazéns», usada por três vezes (ver Pro. 3:10); 2. *megurah*, «silo», usada apenas por uma vez, em Ageu 2:19; 3. *goren*, «eira» e «chão do celeiro», usada por trinta e sete vezes (ver Jó 39:12; II Reis 6:37; Gên. 50:10; Jer. 51:33, etc.). No grego temos a palavra *apotheke*, «celeiro», usada por seis vezes no Novo Testamento (ver Mat. 3:12; 6:26; 13:30; Luc. 3:17; 12:18,24). Essa palavra indica celeiros construídos acima da superfície do solo. Mas o cereal usualmente era guardado em cisternas secas, ainda que algumas vezes também fosse guardado em edifícios construídos para esse propósito.

Uso figurado. Em primeiro lugar, o celeiro simboliza bênçãos da prosperidade material. Um homem enchia seus celeiros e ocupava-se nas atividades do comércio (ver Deu. 28:8 e Luc. 12:18). Em segundo lugar, a destruição de celeiros indica escassez e tempos difíceis (ver Joel 1:17). (S)

CELESTIAL

No grego, **epouranios**, um adjetivo que ocorre por dezenove vezes: Mat. 18:35; João 3:12; I Cor. 15:40,48,49; Efé. 1:3,20; 2:6; 3:10; 6:12; Fil. 2:10; II Tim. 4:18; Heb. 3:1; 6:4; 8:5; 9:23; 11:16 e 12:22. Consideremos os pontos abaixo, que nos ajudarão a entender melhor a questão:

1. Em I Cor. 15:40,41 há alusão aos corpos celestiais, uma referência ao sol, à lua e às estrelas. De acordo com a teologia-astrologia-astronomia da época, esses seriam seres hilozoísticos, revestidos de luz. Não sabemos até que ponto Paulo compartilhava dessa opinião. Seja como for, ele usava a idéia com a finalidade de ilustrar seu conceito de que há vários tipos de corpos, e de que o corpo ressuscitado será de espécie diferente do corpo terrestre. O corpo ressurrecto da concepção paulina quase certamente é imaterial, um veículo da alma, uma entidade não-atômica. A tentativa de alguns eruditos de materializarem esse corpo, com a pequena diferença resultante entre o corpo mortal e o corpo imortal, reflete uma concepção bem inferior dos mundos espirituais. É impossível que um corpo físico, atômico de qualquer espécie, possa residir nas dimensões espirituais, porque não são formas compatíveis de energia. Devemo-nos lembrar que o corpo ressurrecto de Jesus, embora feito dos elementos do anterior corpo físico, era capaz de passar por portas fechadas, teleportando-se de um lugar para outro—exatamente

CELIBATO

aquilo que poderíamos esperar de uma entidade espiritual. Além disso, Jesus ainda não havia entrado na sua glória; quando ele o fez, seu corpo deve ter sido transformado mais profundamente ainda. A especulação dos pais gregos da Igreja, de que um corpo ressuscitado sempre estará sujeito a uma maior glorificação, enquanto ascende na escala do ser, de um estágio de glória para outro (II Cor. 3:18), é uma verdade necessária. O destino do homem remido é compartilhar da natureza divina (II Ped. 1:4), não havendo como ele possa levar consigo, nesse processo, o seu corpo físico.

2. O termo *celestial* também é aplicado a Deus (Mat. 18:35) e a Jesus Cristo (I Cor. 15:47,48), bem como aos seres celestiais (Fil. 2:10). Isso inclui o crente em seu estado glorificado (I Cor. 15:40 ss). Deus é Espírito, e o homem, finalmente, também será apenas espírito, embora a alma pareça requerer alguma espécie de veículo de expressão; e esse veículo também deverá sê-lo do espírito, se a alma tiver de habitar em uma esfera imaterial.

3. Um outro importante uso da palavra «celestial» é em referência ao céu (Efé. 1:20). A expressão paulina «lugares celestiais» limita-se à epístola aos Efésios. (Ver Efé. 1:3,20; 2:6 e 3:10). A expressão encontra-se no plural, — em consonância com a teologia judaica comum, que sempre se referiu ao mundo celestial no plural. Há muitas dimensões de seres espirituais, o que também é confirmado em João 14:2. Ver as notas expositivas a esse respeito no NTI.

4. Os teólogos judeus falavam sobre a glorificação como um processo progressivo, incluindo a passagem de uma esfera para outra, até ser atingida a esfera mais elevada, onde Deus habita. Apesar dessa idéia ser por eles cruamente exposta, aponta para uma grande verdade. Nossa glorificação (que vide) jamais poderá caracterizar-se pela estagnação, e certamente incluirá a ascensão a dimensões gloriosas cada vez mais elevadas. A cada estágio seremos revestidos de maior poder e inteligência, postos ao serviço do Senhor, de maneira sempre crescente. Naturalmente, há mistérios que circundam tudo isso; mas, esse conceito, aqui apresentado, contradiz a teologia popular sobre o *céu*, onde um homem, por ocasião da morte física, de um salto só, atinge a esfera mais elevada, onde Deus habita e manifesta sua glória e seu poder; e onde a estagnação virá caracterizar a experiência das almas remidas.

CELIBATO

Esboço:
1. Nas Culturas Antigas
2. Na Cultura dos Hebreus
3. No Período Intermediário entre o Antigo e o Novo Testamentos
4. No Novo Testamento
5. Na Igreja Cristã
6. A Reforma e o Celibato
7. Qual a Posição Atual da Igreja Católica Romana?
8. As Duas Filosofias, as Duas Lógicas
9. Conclusão e Avaliação

A palavra *celibato* vem do termo latino *caelebs*, «solteiro». O celibato pode ser voluntário ou involuntário, podendo estar apoiado ou não sobre razões religiosas.

1. Nas Culturas Antigas. Quando lemos sobre a história religiosa dos povos, impressiona-nos a preocupação dos antigos com a fertilidade, e não com o celibato. Somente sob certas condições, e por períodos limitados, era praticada a abstinência sexual. Os gregos e os romanos concebiam deusas virgens; mas, dentro da sociedade humana, esses povos mostravam desprezo pelos celibatários. Entre as mulheres, nada havia de mais importante do que o casamento e a formação de uma família. Uma exceção a isso eram as virgens vestais romanas (que vide). Vesta era a deusa romana da lareira e de suas chamas. Ela correspondia à divindade grega Héstia. Essa adoração foi introduzida por Numa Pompílio, de Lavinium. Um templo em honra a ela foi erigido em Roma, e nas proximidades foi construído o *átrio* de Vesta, onde suas sacerdotisas, que eram as virgens chamadas vestais, efetuavam o culto à mesma. Um fogo perene era conservado por elas, visto que essa era a deusa das chamas da lareira. Se essas chamas se apagassem por alguma razão, era de se esperar alguma catástrofe nacional qualquer. As mulheres homenageavam zelosamente essa deusa virgem, pois ela abençoava os lares, segundo se acreditava. A adoração a Vesta perdurou até os últimos dias do paganismo romano, tendo sido abolida pelo imperador Graciano, em 382 D.C. Mas, a despeito da existência dessas sacerdotisas virgens, por razões religiosas, que adoravam a uma divindade feminina supostamente virgem, havia muitos deuses e deusas, com seus respectivos cultos, que envolviam ritos de fertilidade, sem qualquer idéia de virgindade. Portanto, o paganismo não nos oferece precedente apenas em favor da sexualidade descontrolada, mas também em favor do celibato por motivos religiosos.

2. Na Cultura dos Hebreus. Não apenas a teologia do Antigo Testamento considerava o casamento como o melhor estado para homens e mulheres, mas também dentro da cultura hebréia, o casamento era um dever. Outrossim, nenhum homem era investido de autoridade, como líder religioso, a menos que fosse casado. Se alguma mulher permanecesse solteira e sem filhos, isso era considerado como castigo divino contra algum pecado.

3. No Período Intermediário entre o Antigo e o Novo Testamentos. Há alguma evidência de que, no período intertestamentário, as tradições judaicas foram afetadas pelas noções gnósticas e dualistas do *helenismo*. Os dualistas pensavam que o corpo humano fosse a sede e a manifestação do pecado, por fazer parte do mundo da matéria, a qual seria a depositária do princípio do mal. Os gnósticos defendiam esse dualismo. No esforço por se desvencilharem do mal, conforme este opera através da matéria, eles praticavam ou a liberalidade exagerada, procurando abusar do corpo e debilitá-lo com os vícios, ou então praticavam o ascetismo (que vide), com o mesmo propósito. Em contraste com eles, os hebreus nunca foram defensores da idéia de que o corpo físico é inerentemente mal, idéia essa eliminada pela doutrina da ressurreição final do corpo. Porém, nenhum gnóstico convicto teria qualquer interesse na ressurreição de seu corpo físico, porquanto isso seria considerado o reavivamento do princípio do mal, e somente poderia prejudicar o espírito, conforme eles pensavam.

Os *essênios* (que vide) eram uma comunidade judaica ascética que floriu no século II A.C. e permaneceu até o século II D.C. Eles compartilhavam, com os fariseus, de muitas crenças; mas, em seu ascetismo, praticavam o celibato. Muitos estudiosos têm pensado que João Batista esteve associado a esse grupo dos essênios; e que talvez até Jesus Cristo esteve entre eles. Se esse foi o caso, é possível que os primeiros avanços da doutrina do celibato, como um estado superior ao do matrimônio, tenha começado ali. Tanto João quanto Jesus eram celibatários, e Jesus

CELIBATO

recomendou o estado, em Mateus 19:12, embora sob a circunstância especial da impossibilidade de um segundo casamento, quando o primeiro fosse anulado devido a adultério da parte do cônjuge, sem que este viesse a falecer.

4. No Novo Testamento. É bem possível que as declarações favoráveis ao celibato, existentes no Novo Testamento, tivessem sido inspiradas pela filosofia dos essênios. Porém, pelo menos também é possível que as atitudes gnóstico-dualistas do helenismo tivessem levado alguns judeus (que então se tornaram cristãos) do primeiro século a suporem que havia algo de degradante no sexo. Além disso, há a considerar a óbvia circunstância de que o sexo pode envolver as pessoas em todas as formas de pecado e perversão. Por essa razão, é provável que alguns pensassem que seria melhor eliminar totalmente o sexo, na busca por uma vereda espiritual mais alta.

a. *Jesus*. Jesus nasceu de uma virgem (Mat. 1:18 *ss*; Luc. 1:34 *ss*). Esse fato deve ter exercido poderosa influência sobre as mentes de alguns, levando-os a suporem que o estado de virgindade, de alguma maneira, é superior ao estado de casado. Além disso, o próprio Jesus recomendou esse estado, para aqueles que inquirissem intensamente pelo caminho espiritual (Mat. 19:12). O fato de que ele foi capaz de afirmar que havia aqueles que praticavam o celibato por amor ao reino dos céus, mostra que isso envolvia algum ascetismo judaico. É perfeitamente possível, pois, que isso seja um reflexo direto dos essênios. Assim, se os rabinos comuns proibiam o celibato como uma idéia ética inaceitável, é possível que, juntamente com Jesus, houvesse um impulso, entre certos sérios homens de fé, em direção ao celibato.

b. *Paulo*. O apóstolo dos gentios tanto louvava quanto praticava o celibato, como um estado superior ao casamento, por razões de séria inquirição espiritual (I Cor. 7:25-35). Ele desejava mesmo que todos os crentes seguissem o seu exemplo (I Cor. 7:7), mas admitia que cada um tinha — o direito — de fazer conforme julgasse ser melhor. O trecho de I Cor. 9:5 mostra-nos, bem definidamente, que os outros apóstolos eram casados. E note-se que isso inclui os apóstolos, os irmãos do Senhor e até mesmo Cefas (Simão Pedro). De nada adianta alguém asseverar aqui que as mulheres que os acompanhavam, até mesmo nas viagens, eram irmãs virgens, e não esposas. Tal prática não seria permissível nem no contexto judaico e nem no contexto do cristianismo primitivo. Na história cristã posterior houve quem tentasse fazer-se acompanhar por alguma virgem; mas tal prática nada tinha a ver com o cristianismo do primeiro século. Desde o trecho de Marcos 1:30 somos informados de que Pedro era homem casado, e dizer-se que, após haver-se tornado um líder cristão proeminente, ele deixou de viver conjugalmente com sua esposa é puro dogma, com base em um raciocínio *a priori*. Não nos aproximamos mais da verdade mediante manipulações interpretativas. Meu interesse, neste momento, é procurar saber por qual motivo Paulo preferia o celibato. Antes de tudo, também é uma óbvia interpretação manipulada, que Paulo sugeria o celibato apenas para ocasiões de perseguição e tribulação. O trecho de I Coríntios 7:36 mostra-nos que ele tinha em vista o período de dificuldades pelo qual a Igreja estava passando. O casamento é um poderoso complicador da vida, e em tempos atribulados, pode ser melhor o homem não se casar. Não obstante, quando lemos tudo quanto Paulo tem a dizer sobre o assunto, torna-se abundantemente óbvio que o celibato era o estado que ele realmente *preferia*, com perseguições ou sem perseguições. Estamos,

portanto, supondo que a influência essênia havia afetado a Paulo, como é provável que havia afetado a Jesus. Também estou presumindo que Paulo, como judeu helenista que fora, havia absorvido algo das atitudes dos dualistas, os quais degradavam o corpo, embora isso jamais se tivesse tornado uma doutrina para Paulo. E penso que minha posição é justificada no trecho de I Coríntios 7:34. Ali Paulo recomenda a virgindade às mulheres, porquanto a crente virgem «...cuida das cousas do Senhor, para ser santa, assim no *corpo* como no espírito...» Indago, pois, por qual motivo uma mulher é mais santa no corpo, se permanecer virgem, do que se casar-se? Somente se alguém supõe que o sexo é degradante, em qualquer grau, poderá esse alguém supor que é melhor uma mulher permanecer virgem do que se ela vier a casar-se, pois assim poderá ser mais *santa*. Para mim, é claro que, inadvertidamente, Paulo mostrou uma atitude negativa para com o sexo, como parte da motivação por detrás de seu ensinamento.

Essa atitude é verdadeiramente universal. Muitas pessoas, no recesso dos seus corações, vêem algo de impuro no sexo, sem importar o que digam. Um homem religioso pode até mesmo sentir vergonha do sexo, como se fosse uma *fraqueza*. Conheço um pregador evangélico que, em meio à cerimônia de seu próprio casamento, pediu perdão a Deus, por haver cedido ante essa fraqueza! É muito comum nos seminários teológicos evangélicos encontrar rapazes que expressam o seu desejo ou intenção de não se casarem, a fim de melhor promoverem o ideal espiritual exposto por Paulo no sétimo capítulo de I Coríntios. No entanto, um por um, eles se vão casando, porque as jovens e belas mulheres têm uma maneira de ser mais convincentes do que Paulo. Além disso, o homem médio não tem a capacidade física e psicológica de ignorar o apetite sexual, que é extraordinariamente profundo e faz parte da própria textura da vida. É aqui que se encontra o verdadeiro motivo do ensino cristão e paulino sobre o casamento versus celibato. Em I Coríntios 7:7, Paulo mostra-nos que ele pensava que o crente celibatário devia ter recebido de Deus um dom, para poder permanecer nesse estado; pois, em caso contrário, ele só poderia encontrar dificuldades nesse estado, conforme se vê dois versículos adiante. As autoridades eclesiásticas de diversos grupos cristãos, como é evidente, têm dado muito pouco valor a I Coríntios 7:7. Suas legislações não podem garantir que aquele que tenta viver como celibatário foi dotado do dom espiritual, por parte do Espírito de Deus, que o ajudará a cumprir seu propósito. Efetivamente, o que via de regra sucede é que os celibatários acabam se tornando culpados de fornicação ou adultério. Também deveríamos examinar de perto o trecho de I Timóteo 3:2. Ali é recomendado que o ministro cristão (um pastor ou bispo, nesse contexto?) deve ser marido de uma só mulher. Isso demonstra, em primeiro lugar, que os ministros cristãos, no tempo dos apóstolos, eram homens casados. Em segundo lugar, que mesmo nesse estágio inicial do cristianismo já havia alguma restrição imposta ao casamento, embora não uma proibição, no tocante aos ministros da Igreja. Esse versículo quase certamente ensina que um ministro cristão faria melhor se, durante a sua vida, fosse casado apenas por uma vez. Isso aplica-se ao ministro já casado; se sua esposa viesse a falecer, ele não deveria casar-se pela segunda vez. Tal proibição nada tem a ver com a poligamia, mas tal versículo, desde o século II D.C., vinha sendo interpretado como uma proibição ao segundo casamento, no caso de ministros do evangelho. Quanto a detalhes sobre isso, ver a

CELIBATO

exposição *in loc.* no NTI. O versículo aplica-se a um possível segundo casamento de um ministro do evangelho, aplicação essa que pode ser extrapolada aos membros das igrejas. Pois verifica-se que, mesmo no caso de crentes comuns, Paulo opinava que seria melhor eles não se casarem novamente, segundo se vê em I Coríntios 7:8.

Essa doutrina é correta? Os intérpretes cristãos, incluindo muitos protestantes, têm defendido a tese paulina como correta, para ser seguida por aqueles que querem ser imitadores de Cristo *por excelência.* Outros estudiosos, entretanto, têm objetado ao conceito inteiro, excetuando que só deveriam ter o celibato como seu ideal aqueles que recebem o dom celeste para tanto. Mas repelem, peremptoriamente, a idéia de que um ministro do evangelho deveria tentar o celibato, ao mesmo tempo em que permitem que alguns indivíduos, sobre bases voluntárias, o façam, se assim forem guiados pelo Espírito. Há nisso um fator que deve ser considerado, mas que geralmente não é posto dentro do quadro. A relação do casamento é uma maravilhosa mestra, talvez podendo ensinar espiritualmente a um homem, muito mais do que se ele fosse solteiro ou celibatário. Além disso, a vida matrimonial permite que dois indivíduos—o esposo e a esposa—pratiquem, de modo todo especial, a lei do amor, que é o maior de todos os princípios espirituais (I João 4:7 *ss*). Parece-me que a lei do amor, em seus vários aspectos, é mais importante do que a opção do celibato, e que o indivíduo casado aprende mais do que se permanecesse solteiro. Isso sucede no caso de todos, excetuando, naturalmente, aqueles especificamente chamados para a vida celibatária, de acordo com o propósito divino.

5. Na Igreja Cristã. a. *Na Sua História Primitiva.* O ideal paulino começou a ser dogmatizado desde bem cedo na história da Igreja. Muitos indivíduos puseram-se a praticar o celibato, desde o começo; e o movimento monástico (século III D.C.) proveu uma prática mais formalizada do celibato, que desde então tem exercido grande influência sobre o cristianismo. Ver o artigo separado sobre o *monasticismo.* b. *Formalização.* No entanto, até o século IV D.C., não houve requisitos eclesiásticos formais sobre a questão; e nem o celibato dos ministros era universalmente exigido. A lei do celibato clerical assumiu forma definitiva, tanto no Ocidente quanto no Oriente, devido às regras estabelecidas pelos imperadores romanos cristãos Teodósio II e Justiniano I. Portanto, temos aí uma imposição feita de fora para dentro do cristianismo bíblico. c. *No Oriente.* Isso afetou a igreja oriental, cujos códigos sempre foram mais liberais do que aqueles da igreja ocidental. Assim, no Oriente, a legislação não permitia o casamento dos bispos, porém, os padres, os diáconos e os subdiáconos retiveram esse privilégio. Entretanto, nenhum clérigo podia tornar a se casar, se sua esposa viesse a falecer. As *Constituições Apostólicas* (cerca de 400 D.C.) (que vide), formam a base essencial da prática do Oriente. Por essa altura dos acontecimentos, todos os ministros, incluindo os bispos, podiam casar-se, mas apenas por uma vez. No entanto, quando do concílio de Trullo, de 692, foi exigido que os bispos fossem celibatários. Se algum deles tivesse contraído matrimônio antes de tornar-se bispo, tinha de separar-se de sua esposa quando de sua consagração ao episcopado, regra essa que continua a ser aplicada no oriente. d. *No Ocidente.* O primeiro decreto conhecido no Ocidente, acerca do celibato clerical, é o do concílio de Elvira, de cerca do ano 300 D.C. Esse decreto requeria o celibato para todos os clérigos: bispos, padres e diáconos. No entanto, essa legislação entrou em efeito somente em meados do séc. IV D.C. quando concílios e decretos papais impuseram a resolução de modo absoluto. Leão o Grande (séc. V) ampliou a obrigação aos subdiáconos. Gregório I fortaleceu a legislação no início do séc. VII. Um período de confusão e declínio moral seguiu, e muitos opuseram-se à lei do celibato. Pedro Damiano (1007-1072 D.C.) refutou as objeções em seu *Liber Gomorrhianus* bem como no *De coelibatu sacerdotum ad Nicolaum II.* Desnecessário é dizer que abusos, dentro do clero, sempre ocorreram, e vários papas procuraram corrigi-los. O papa Gregório VII, em 1075, instituiu amplas reformas, entre as quais a restauração do celibato clerical, em todas as suas formas, para todo o clero. Isso foi subseqüentemente confirmado pelo quarto concílio de Latrão, de 1215, bem como pelo concílio de Trento, em 1563.

6. A Reforma e o Celibato. Lutero não somente condenou o celibato, mas, igualmente, declarou nulo o voto de castidade de todos os padres. Calvino, menos radical, admitiu o valor do celibato, embora objetando à sua *imposição* como uma obrigação do clero. Liberdade apostólica, era o lema então usado. O indivíduo deveria seguir a sua consciência, determinando o que fazer, à luz das exigências de sua missão espiritual. Naturalmente, essa atitude tomou conta das igrejas protestantes e reformadas, bem como de seus descendentes espirituais, a saber, as inúmeras subdivisões do cristianismo que então surgiram, nos séculos que se seguiram. O concílio de Trento reagiu contra os reformadores, reafirmando a obrigação do celibato para os ministros, em 1563. Essa reafirmação foi incorporada no código da lei canônica (que vide), quando ela foi revisada, em 1917. Em sua encíclica, *Sacra virginitas,* «virgindade consagrada», de 1954, o papa Pio XII relembrou a todos os católicos, a excelência do celibato e da virgindade consagrada. O concilio Vaticano II também reafirmou a aprovação à instituição do celibato, embora tivesse permitido que a ordem dos diáconos fosse constituída de homens casados. João XXIII e Paulo VI dispensaram do voto de celibato os ministros protestantes que se tivessem convertido ao catolicismo, e que manifestassem o desejo de ordenarem-se sacerdotes católicos romanos.

7. Qual a Posição Atual da Igreja Católica Romana? O Concílio Vaticano II (que vide), produziu muitas alterações, e, naturalmente, ali houve uma renovada discussão sobre a questão do celibato. Porções representativas da Igreja Católica Romana expressaram a opinião de que o celibato deveria ser voluntário. Coube a Paulo VI tomar uma decisão sobre a questão, pelo que em sua encíclica de 24 de junho de 1967, *Sacerdotalis caelibatus,* ele reafirmou a regra tradicional do catolicismo romano. Ele refutou a opinião de que o celibato é prejudicial para o desenvolvimento físico e psicológico dos padres, e declarou que essa prática fornece ao homem a oportunidade de dedicar-se totalmente, em amor a Cristo. Ele admitiu que a virgindade não é algo requerido pela própria natureza do sacerdócio, mas afirmou que o celibato é relevante a essa natureza, sendo «uma das mais puras e nobres glórias do sacerdócio da Igreja». Essas são palavras radicais, realmente; e, apesar de uma parte considerável dos ministros católicos romanos continuar frisando a necessidade de uma regra voluntária, dificilmente alguma mudança será feita em breve. Todavia, pelo menos teoricamente há possibilidade de que a Igreja Católica Romana abandone tal prática.

8. As Duas Filosofias, As Duas Lógicas. Os

protestantes objetam à lei do celibato imposta a ministros do evangelho, afirmando que a mesma é estranha e posterior ao Novo Testamento. Eles partem do princípio de que uma doutrina que não tenha base nas Escrituras somente, não pode ser válida para os crentes. Admitem o celibato voluntário, porquanto Jesus e Paulo o encorajaram. Todavia, objetam à idéia do celibato obrigatório, para quem quer que seja, porque isso jamais foi exigido na Igreja primitiva. Bem pelo contrário, o sétimo capítulo da primeira epístola aos Coríntios favorece, claramente, o celibato voluntário. Outrossim, a questão é ali ventilada em relação a todos os membros da Igreja, incluindo donzelas, viúvos e viúvas. O Novo Testamento jamais discutiu o ponto em relação ao clero, apenas. Os protestantes e evangélicos, pois, querem que a questão fique na dependência exclusiva do próprio Novo Testamento.

Mas os católicos romanos exibem uma diferente filosofia, uma diferente lógica. A doutrina deles sobre a *autoridade* (que vide) afirma que há outras autoridades além do Novo Testamento, e que *isso* faz parte do plano de Deus. Para eles, o Novo Testamento é apenas um livro sobre primórdios, e não sobre posições definitivas. Antes de tudo, o Novo Testamento, para eles, precisa ser interpretado, pois, do contrário, penetrarão na cena religiosa muitas fantasias. Ademais, haveria a questão da evolução doutrinária. À medida que a Igreja cresce, é mister o desenvolvimento doutrinário. Para tanto, eles contam com os pais da Igreja, com os concílios e com os decretos papais. E admitem que, apesar de poder ser demonstrado que, puramente com bases no Novo Testamento, o celibato deve ser voluntário, também deveria ser respeitada a opinião dos pais da Igreja, dos concílios e dos papas. Essas também seriam autoridades. Disso eles concluem que o fato de que o celibato não se tornou obrigatório no Ocidente, senão já no século IV D.C., em nada é contrário ao fato de que deveria ser obrigatório para o clero. Presumivelmente, o celibato ajuda no desenvolvimento espiritual, antes de tudo, dos próprios clérigos, e, em segundo lugar, daqueles a quem eles ministram. Portanto, o celibato clerical seria uma instituição digna, devendo continuar a ser observada.

9. Conclusão e Avaliação. Em todas as questões controvertidas, o amor deveria predominar. Nada ganhamos promovendo o ódio e a arrogância, em nome da teologia. Devemos respeitar os pontos de vista alheios, mesmo quando não concordamos com os mesmos. Mas, quanto a mim, sinto-me forçado a lançar o meu voto em favor da idéia do celibato voluntário. Vou mesmo mais longe do que isso. Opino que é melhor a um homem física, emocional, psicológica e até mesmo espiritualmente, ter esposa e filhos. Essa é uma das melhores situações de aprendizado que existe, permitindo que um indivíduo, homem ou mulher, aprenda mais da prática da lei do amor, do que jamais poderia ser aprendido no estado celibatário, sobretudo se forçado. O que pode substituir o afeto oferecido e recebido de um filho ou de uma filha? O que pode substituir o amor que se desenvolve entre marido e mulher, dois indivíduos que crescem juntos na vida, compartilhando de tudo, *incluindo* de uma missão espiritual? Repito, que pode substituir isso? Fico impressionado diante de pessoas que buscam amar supremamente a Cristo. Porém, também fico impressionado pelo fato de que isso não pode ser plenamente conseguido exceto pelo amor ao próximo, incluindo o amor doméstico. A vida em família provê um caminho todo especial, e nada é mais importante do que o crente viver a vida do amor, que é a essência mesma da espiritualidade (I João 4:7 ss). Ora, o celibato fica muito aquém disso, meus amigos.

Nesta avaliação, acresça-se o fato de que se Paulo chegou a recomendar o celibato aos que receberam o dom especial para esse tipo de vida; ele também mostrou que uma das distorções do cristianismo consistiria na «proibição do casamento» (I Tim. 4:1-5). (AM B C LEA OS R)

CELSO

Um oponente do cristianismo, que escreveu uma obra polêmica contra os cristãos. Seu tratado anticristão, *Verdadeiro Discurso*, de cerca de 177 D.C., foi devidamente respondido por Orígenes (que vide), em sua volumosa obra intitulada *Contra-Celso*. Orígenes é o único escritor cristão que nos faz saber alguma coisa sobre Celso, mas nem mesmo ali ficamos sabendo qualquer coisa sobre a história pessoal desse homem. Porém, sua obra provê copiosas citações da obra de Celso, permitindo-nos ver como os primeiros apologistas cristãos defendiam os pontos de vista do cristianismo. O que se torna evidente é que Celso era um filósofo platônico de tendências dualistas. Ele acreditava na existência de uma hierarquia de poderes espirituais, separando o homem de Deus. Outros filósofos platônicos do período de Celso foram Ático e Nicostrato (que vide). Interessante é observar que Celso conseguiu reunir todos os argumentos que a incredulidade pagã era capaz de desfilar contra o pensamento cristão, pelo que também a resposta de Orígenes é de extraordinário valor no estudo da apologética cristã. (E P)

CEM, TORRE DOS

Essa era uma das torres da muralha norte da cidade de Jerusalém. Após o exílio babilônico, Eliasibe, o sumo sacerdote, com seus companheiros, restaurou essa torre (Nee. 3:1). Ela é mencionada no relato sobre o grande cortejo que celebrou a dedicação da nova muralha de Jerusalém (Nee. 12:39). Juntamente com a torre de Hananel, ela tinha a função de facilitar a proteção da área do templo. Ver o artigo sobre as Torres. Ver também sobre *Forte, Fortificação* e *Cidade Murada*.

CEMITÉRIO

Ver o artigo sobre **Sepultamento, Costumes de.** A palavra «cemitério» nada tem a ver com *semi*, ou parcial, como se desse a entender que somente uma parte do homem fosse sepultado, enquanto a outra se foi para as dimensões espirituais. Embora isso seja um fato (ver sobre a *Alma* e a *Imortalidade*), esse vocábulo nada tem a ver com isso. Antes, vem da raiz grega *kometrérion*, «dormitório». O verbo grego para «dormir» é *koma*. E é daí que se deriva a palavra «cemitério». Os cuidados dos cristãos pelos mortos, e a sua fé na ressurreição, emprestaram grande valor aos cemitérios, desde o começo. Ver também o artigo sobre as *Catacumbas*. Os sepultamentos normalmente tinham lugar em um terreno reservado, adjacente ao templo cristão. Em tempos posteriores, os incrédulos, os suicidas e os excluídos, não podiam ser sepultados nesses cemitérios. Os modernos cemitérios das cidades substituíram os antigos cemitérios das igrejas; mas até hoje o povo sepulta seus mortos com o acompanhamento de ritos religiosos, pondo símbolos religiosos sobre os sepulcros. (E)

CENÁCULO Ver **Sala Superior.**

CENCRÉIA

A palavra grega aparece somente em Atos 18:18 e Rom. 16:1. Era o porto oriental da cidade de Corinto. Até hoje o nome é Kenchreae, embora seu nome popular seja Kikries. Fica localizado cerca de treze quilômetros de Corinto. Em Atos 18:18 lemos que Paulo tomou um navio nesse porto. Em Rom. 16:1 ele menciona uma igreja que fora estabelecida ali. Havia uma aldeia naquele porto, o qual era essencialmente usado para transporte de mercadorias para Corinto e de Corinto, através do istmo de Corinto. A fim de evitar a rota geralmente perigosa em torno do cabo Melea, o extremo sul do Peloponeso, os navios eram arrastados por terra, de Cencréia a Lequeum, através do istmo. Se houvesse muita carga, esta era tirada do navio e transportada por meios terrestres. O nome Cencréia deriva-se do nome do filho do deus Poseidon e da deusa Pirene, e a área envolvida fora consagrada a essa divindade. O tirano de Corinto (cerca de 625-584 A.C.) planejara a construção de um canal para atravessar o istmo, e o imperador romano, Nero, deu início ao projeto. Porém, esse canal só se tornou uma realidade no ano de 1893. Foi em Cencréia que Paulo cortou os cabelos, como condição de um voto religioso judaico, e foi dali que velejou para a Síria, em companhia de Priscila e Áquila. Febe (vide) era diaconisa da igreja cristã de Cencréia (Rom. 16:1).

CENDEBEU

Foi um general do rei helenista Antíoco VIII. Foi encarregado das terras costeiras da Síria-Palestina, em cerca de 138 A.C. Ele fortificou Cedrom, uma cidade existente na planície costeira, entre Jope e Asquelom, modernamente, Qâtra. Dali ele assaltou a região montanhosa, até que Simão enviou seus filhos João Hircano e Judas contra ele, com vinte mil homens. Os judeus obtiveram a vitória, mas Judas ficou ferido na batalha. E o inimigo foi expulso daquela região. Ver I Macabeus 15:37 ss e 16:8,9, quanto a narrativa a respeito.

CENOBITA

Vem de um termo grego que significa **comum**. O termo era usado para designar monges que viviam em situação comunitária, distinguindo-os dos heremitas (que vide), ou dos ancoritas (que vide), que viviam solitários. O tipo de monasticismo cenobita foi instituído no Oriente por Basílio (que vide). Foi introduzido no Ocidente por Atanásio (que vide), em 340 D.C. O fundador do monasticismo ocidental foi Benedito (que vide). (E)

CENSOR, CENSURA

Ver o artigo, *Julgamento (Censura) de Um por Outro*.

1. Idéias Gerais. Quando alguma demanda do **id** entra em choque com o **superego**, então o ego e o superego livram-se da mesma reprimindo-a para a porção inconsciente da psique. Esse ato repressivo, dentro da psicologia freudiana, é chamado de *censor*. Ver o artigo sobre *Freud*.

Mas a palavra «censura» também é usada para indicar um examinador oficial de manuscritos, livros, filmes, atos teatrais, etc., dotado do poder de proibir a publicação ou encenação dos mesmos. Idêntica função é efetuada pelas denominações cristãs que oprimem e criticam àqueles que não concordam com suas idéias, na tentativa de impedir a propagação das mesmas. A Igreja Católica Romana tem nos censores uma de sua funções oficiais.

2. Censura Religiosa. Na Igreja Católica Romana, trata-se da supervisão da publicação de livros. A fim de preservar a unidade do pensamento católico romano, àquela Igreja reserva-se o direito de proibir a publicação de qualquer livro, ou de censurar seu conteúdo, se não concordar com os ensinamentos da mesma. Qualquer pessoa tem o direito de publicar o que quiser, mas não como um católico romano. Se desejar publicar sua obra como tal, então terá de submeter-se à censura da Igreja de Roma. Desde 1571, a Igreja Católica Romana conta com um corpo de censores que realizam esse trabalho, chamado *Congregação do Índice*. O grupo foi estabelecido pelo papa Gregório XIII (que vide).

Vem do latim, *censura*, termo derivado da lei romana, que dá a entender uma pena eclesiástica que priva alguém de algum direito, como a participação nos sacramentos. A censura é imposta a pessoas batizadas que cometeram algum ato reputado erro sério pela Igreja Católica Romana. A censura é aplicada se a pessoa envolvida não se retratar.

3. Censura. No campo da **ética**, trata-se do vício de ser habitualmente crítico, o que é atitude proibida pela Bíblia. Ver Rom. 2:1 ss. Essa referência mostra-nos que, usualmente, aquele que julga é culpado dos mesmos pecados que ele censura. Mateus 7:1 também proíbe a prática, onde é afirmado que aquele que julga a outros, será julgado com a mesma medida com que julga. Apesar disso, algumas pessoas transmutam esse vício em virtude, tachando-o de defesa da fé ou de instrução moral a inferiores. A atitude censuradora caracteriza-se pela arrogância, e esconde-se atrás de uma falsa superioridade moral. O verdadeiro amor nunca se entrega a essa baixeza. A crítica genuína, construtiva, caracteriza-se pelo amor, com o intuito de ajudar, e não de ofender. Usualmente, a atitude censuradora está escoimada sobre o motivo da auto-exaltação o que se consegue rebaixando a outra pessoa, que é considerada um rival.

4. Censura Civil. O termo «censura» vem do vocábulo latino que significa **valor ou imposto**. Refere-se a alguma restrição agressiva ou supressão de declarações, opiniões, idéias ou atos. No contexto civil, os governos censuram publicações ou pessoas, a fim de defender a ordem estabelecida. Às vezes, — a segurança nacional — está em jogo, mas, com freqüência, tudo quanto está envolvido é que tiranos ou ditadores querem preservar o seu poder, enfraquecendo ou eliminando qualquer oposição. Na questão das publicações, a censura pode ser aplicada *post facto*, isto é, após uma publicação haver sido lançada, ou então, antes do lançamento, mediante uma ordem judiciária que proíba a circulação ou a publicação do material proibido. A censura civil envolve-nos na questão dos direitos individuais, e, portanto, nas questões éticas.

Os governos modernos, sobretudo no Ocidente, têm tido de enfrentar a crescente onda de material pornográfico, que envenena as mentes das pessoas, principalmente dos jovens. De modo geral, as leis têm-se mostrado laxas quanto a essas questões, a fim de preservar os direitos individuais, os quais sempre sofrem quando os governos começam a censurar livros e revistas. Em alguns lugares, livros de texto têm sido censurados por causa de idéias contrárias à moral ou ao patriotismo. Na censura, o alvo colimado muitas vezes é o de evitar um maior mal (a injúria aos direitos pessoais, mediante regulamentações governamentais), mediante a permissão de algum mal menor, isto é, a publicação de material pornográfico, ou livros que contenham elementos antipatrióticos.

5. A Bíblia, a Religião e a Censura. Dentro da antiga teocracia veterotestamentária, censura e ações drásticas a ela vinculadas, faziam parte da legislação mosaica. Para exemplificar, qualquer indivíduo que pregasse a idolatria deveria ser executado com a pena capital (Deu. 13:18). E outros atos ou declarações malignas eram tratados com o mesmo rigor. Houve reis que censuraram a profetas, embora laborando em erro de julgamento, conforme se vê em I Reis 22:8. Em Éfeso, os cristãos queimaram muitos livros de mágica (Atos 19:19). O patriarca Teófilo, em cerca de 390 D.C., queimou uma parte da biblioteca de Alexandria (que vide), a fim de eliminar os livros pagãos; e desse modo, destruiu a muitos tesouros da literatura antiga, em seu zelo mal orientado. Em Genebra, Calvino mesclou a Igreja e o estado, passando a controlar cada minúsculo detalhe das vidas dos cidadãos. Isso o levou ao erro de executar a várias pessoas, por motivos religiosos, censurando as idéias e os escritos de outras. A censura, no campo religioso, sempre usa a máscara da piedade, mas, usualmente, é apenas uma forma de ódio.

6. Conclusão. A leitura deste artigo alertará o leitor para o fato de que o problema envolvido no espírito censurador tem aspectos religiosos e civis, extremamente complexos e que não admitem qualquer solução simples. Cada situação precisa ser examinada por seus próprios méritos. Apesar de que a total licença pode tornar-se um pretexto para que se façam e escrevam coisas perversas, quando o governo ou a Igreja legisla a respeito, é afetada a liberdade de todos. Consideremos o seguinte exemplo: Durante algum tempo os adeptos de certas religiões orientais entravam nos ônibus que partiam de São Paulo e ofereciam a sua audiência, os seus livros e revistas, ou então solicitavam donativos. Muitos passageiros sentiam-se indignados diante disso, naturalmente, e a prática era lamentada. Não sei dizer se as companhias de ônibus censuraram ou não tal prática. Mas, seja como for, de certa feita, um missionário evangélico estava em um desses ônibus, quando a prática recomeçou. Imediatamente ele se pôs de pé e disse aos passageiros que ele estava certo de que eles não queriam aqueles livros; e passou a recolher os livros e a entregá-los ao homem que os havia distribuído. À primeira vista, isso pode ser um ato corajoso e recomendável. Porém, imaginemos que aquele missionário, no dia seguinte, fosse distribuir literatura evangélica de porta em porta ou postado em uma esquina. E imaginemos que o padre, pároco daquela área, saísse atrás dele a recolher o material, garantindo ao povo que eles não querem aquela literatura. Certamente, na maioria dos casos, o padre estaria certo na suposição. Pensaríamos que o padre agiu bem? É óbvio que não. Portanto, chegamos à seguinte conclusão: A fim de proteger a *nossa* liberdade, devemos proteger a liberdade *alheia*, mesmo que pensemos que eles estejam abusando dessa liberdade. Nos países comunistas, a pornografia é severamente censurada, e os líderes daqueles governos apontam para o fato como evidência da superioridade moral de seu sistema. Porém, quando olhamos a questão mais de perto, descobrimos que muitos direitos humanos são censurados juntamente com a pornografia. Talvez seja melhor relaxar um pouco certas leis, ao mesmo tempo em que protegemos as liberdades fundamentais do homem. Nos países comunistas, por exemplo, o controle da imprensa pelo governo é básico para o sistema. Tal erro dificilmente pode ser compensado pela pornografia que não existe nos jornaleiros. (E H I NTI)

••• ••• •••

CENTO E QUARENTA E QUATRO MIL

Apo. 7:4: *E ouvi o número dos que foram assinalados com o selo, cento e quarenta e quatro mil de todas as tribos dos filhos de Israel.*

Chegamos agora à dificílima questão da identificação dos cento e quarenta e quatro mil. Há três posições extremadas, que mencionaremos em primeiro lugar, que são as de menor probabilidade de estarem com a razão:

1. A mais ridícula de todas as interpretações, que tem surgido em várias eras da história eclesiástica, é aquela que faz alguma «seita», «grupo» ou «denominação» de cristãos ser aquela companhia. Dessa forma os homens se têm glorificado estupidamente a si mesmos.

2. É também extremada a posição daqueles que pensam que os cento e quarenta e quatro mil representam *exclusivamente* a nação de Israel. Isso ignora totalmente a base histórica deste livro, pois, sem dúvida alguma, o vidente João visualizava os «mártires em potencial» como membros da igreja cristã, como o «Israel espiritual».

3. Por igual modo, é extremada a posição dos que pensam estar aqui em pauta somente a igreja, o Israel espiritual. Há muitas predições bíblicas que indicam a futura restauração de Israel, como nação, em que ela se converterá totalmente a Cristo (ver Rom. 11:26). Os místicos contemporâneos predizem a conversão da nação de Israel nos fins do nosso século XX, quando o sinal da cruz aparecer no firmamento (que seria o sinal do *Filho do homem*), o que dará início à intervenção divina que livrará Israel de adversários esmagadoramente superiores em número, que o ameaçarão de total extinção. É razoável supormos que após esse acontecimento, Israel se torne testemunha da verdade cristã, subseqüente à Terceira Guerra Mundial, mas antes da batalha do Armagedom, a qual fará parte ainda de uma outra guerra (subseqüente àquela que levará Israel à conversão). Supõe-se que primeiramente haverá a Terceira Guerra Mundial e depois, Armagedom (4ª Guerra Mundial), na primeira quarta parte do século XXI. Então se seguirá o milênio. Em algum ponto desses acontecimentos uma boa parte da nação de Israel será selada e virá a pertencer ao número dos cento e quarenta e quatro mil, sendo eles testemunhas de Cristo acerca daquele período de agonia.

4. Conjecturamos, pois, que o número «144.000» é simbólico, e não literal, envolvendo alguns elementos da igreja gentílica e outros da convertida nação de Israel, que serão instrumentos especiais da graça de Deus durante o período da Grande Tribulação, como testemunhas, embora não venham a ser necessariamente preservados do martírio, conforme parece indicar o trecho de Apo. 13:15, onde se tem a impressão de que nenhum deles escapará ao martírio.

5. O nono versículo deste capítulo pode aludir a um grupo de mártires à parte dos cento e quarenta e quatro mil. Ou então poderia estar ali em foco o mesmo grupo de pessoas, embora sob uma descrição diferente. Todavia, o fato de que se trata de uma multidão *incontável*, mostra que estão em pauta mais do que os cento e quarenta e quatro mil, embora certamente estejam inclusos naquele número. Os mártires serão mais do que o número específico de cento e quarenta e quatro mil, sendo que esse número determinado tem algum propósito especial divino para a época da Grande Tribulação. Ou então os cento e quarenta e quatro mil são um número que «simboliza» a companhia inteira dos mártires. (Ver o ponto «oitavo», mais abaixo).

6. Rejeitamos aquela interpretação que faz dos cento e quarenta e quatro mil algum «grupo seleto» de crentes, extraídos dentre todas as eras da história da igreja. Pois pertencem aos últimos dias tão-somente.

7. Historicamente falando, o vidente João deve ter tido em mente a igreja. Isso poderia ser entendido de dois modos diversos: 1. Seriam judeus cristãos, que haveriam de sofrer martírio durante o tempo dos imperadores romanos. 2. Ou seria o «Israel espiritual», sem qualquer tentativa de dividir a igreja em judeus e gentios. A última dessas posições é a mais provável e correta. Portanto, supomos que se o vidente João fosse interrogado acerca do que ele quis dizer, responderia tratar-se do «Israel espiritual». Todavia, devemos encarar o texto também de acordo com seu aspecto profético. Desse modo, devemos incluir a nação literal de Israel, em conjunção com a igreja cristã, como testemunha em favor de Cristo, naqueles horrendos tempos do fim que logo nos alcançarão.

8. O vidente João pode ter tido em mente o *número de mártires* que será preenchido antes do segundo advento de Cristo. (Ver Apo. 6:11 sobre esse conceito). Os cento e quarenta e quatro mil, pois, representariam um número místico, dotado de algum sentido simbólico, ao referir-se sobre a companhia dos mártires do fim, embora, em seu número real, em muito excedessem aos cento e quarenta quatro mil. Parece que tal cifra indica a multiplicação dos «doze» por «doze», e então por «mil», dando a idéia de «número completo». Acerca do número «doze», Lange, em sua introdução na página 15, declara: «Doze (3 X 4), número do mundo espiritual; portanto, número do 'alicerce', da 'medição' e da consumação do reino de Deus. Número da plenitude das manifestações carismáticas, bem como número da restauração terminada. Número real e celestial de algo terminado». Esse raciocínio se adapta bem ao conceito do número «necessário» de mártires, conforme se vê em Apo. 6:11.

Há ainda outros pontos de vista sobre o simbolismo desse número, a saber:

1. De acordo com alguns, esse número se derivaria do conceito de «setenta», que simbolizaria a totalidade de Israel (ver Gên. 46:27); ou se derivaria da igreja, representada em seus líderes (ver o décimo capítulo do evangelho de Lucas; e comparar com as setenta nações do décimo capítulo do livro de Gênesis). A «forma mais completa» poderia ser «setenta e dois», mas a forma mais completa desse simbolismo seria representada por 72 X 1000 X 2 = 144.000.

2. O total de «doze mil», proveniente de cada tribo, simbolizaria igual participação na graça e na proteção divinas por parte de cada tribo.

3. O doze resulta da multiplicação de três por quatro, ou seja, a idéia divina multiplicada pela idéia da extensão mundial (porquanto quatro é o número simbólico da terra, segundo se vê nas notas expositivas, no NTI, sobre o primeiro versículo deste capítulo). Doze multiplicado por doze, portanto, implicaria em fixidez e número completo. O número mil subentende um mundo perfeitamente permeado pelo ser divino, conforme se verá no «milênio» (ver o vigésimo capítulo deste livro). Pois mil também representa este mundo («dez», ver Apo. 13:1), já que é o número «dez» elevado à sua «terceira» potência (pela *força divina*).

4. Alguns estudiosos abandonam toda a idéia de um simbolismo particular, e aludem aos cento e quarenta e quatro mil apenas como um «grande número representativo»; e o nono versículo deste capítulo talvez represente exatamente isso.

5. O número «doze» representaria testemunho e autoridade: doze patriarcas, doze apóstolos. Portanto, a multiplicação de doze por doze representaria o testemunho especial daqueles futuros e privilegiados mártires.

6. Há também os intérpretes que supõem que o **número «doze» representa a igreja inteira, pelos meios dos seus principais representantes, os apóstolos**.

Esses cento e quarenta e quatro mil serão as — mesmas pessoas — que figuram no décimo quarto capítulo do Apocalipse? Cremos que sim, por motivo ali expostos (ver, no *NTI*, notas sobre Apo. 14:1), embora não possamos afirmá-lo de maneira dogmática.

CENTURIÃO

Palavra que vem de um termo latino que significa «cem». Um centurião era capitão de cem homens, portanto. Era uma espécie de oficial não comissionado. Um oficial comissionado é alguém que ocupa uma patente oficial no exército, o que, nos exércitos modernos, começa com o segundo tenente. Um centurião, embora destituído de patente oficial, tinha responsabilidades similares às dos subtenentes. Nos tempos romanos, um centurião não tinha o prestígio social dos oficiais regulares do exército, e poucos deles conseguiam promoção superior à de centurião-mor. Uma legião romana tinha sessenta centúrias, e cada uma delas tinha seu respectivo capitão ou centurião.

O emblema de sua autoridade era uma bengala de vinha. Contudo, a autoridade não era única, pois havia três classes de centuriões: 1. Havia os triarii; 2. os príncipes; e 3. os hastali. O exército romano estava dividido em legiões auxiliares, coortes e alas. Estas duas últimas divisões compunham-se de súditos das províncias, embora os judeus tivessem sido isentados desse serviço (Josefo, *Anti*. xiv.10,6). As coortes (no grego, *speira*) algumas vezes eram conhecidas por epítetos distintivos, como a coorte italiana de Atos 10:1 e a coorte imperial de Atos 27:1. Essas coortes estavam divididas em dez centúrias, ou grupos de cem homens; e, sobre cada centúria havia um capitão ou centurião.

Centuriões Referidos no Novo Testamento. Seis centuriões diferentes são aludidos nos livros do novo pacto, a saber: 1. Cornélio, o primeiro gentio convertido ao cristianismo (Atos 10:1,22). Ver o artigo separado sobre *Cornélio*. 2. O centurião de Cafarnaum, que pediu que Jesus curasse o seu criado (Mat. 8:5 ss). 3. O centurião encarregado da crucificação de Jesus (Mat. 27:54). 4. Um centurião que supervisionou o exame de Paulo sob açoites (Atos 22:25). 5. A referência a centuriões (no plural), em Atos 21:32, o que sugere que Cláudio Lísias convocou um grande número de homens para sair em socorro de Paulo, o qual, subseqüentemente, foi escoltado a Jerusalém por dois centuriões, com os seus respectivos soldados (Atos 23:23). Quando não havia guerras, os deveres de policiamento e da guarda rotineira eram entregues a esses homens. 6. Um centurião acompanhou o grupo que, de navio, levou Paulo até à cidade de Roma (Atos 27:1,6,11, etc.). (BIR ID UN)

CERA

No hebraico, **donag**. Esse termo figura por quatro vezes: Sal. 22:14; 68:2; 97:5 e Miq. 1:4.

Esse vocábulo aparece na Bíblia somente de forma poética, usado como símile para a idéia de derreter-se, de perder o ânimo. Se pensarmos

CERCA — CERTEZA E DÚVIDA

literalmente na cera de abelhas, temos a informar que os antigos usavam esse material para selar documentos e para forrar a superfície de tabuinhas de escrita, pois era então sobre essa fina camada de cera que se escrevia com um estilete. Tal uso se assemelhava muito ao uso moderno do quadro negro e do giz, onde a pessoa pode apagar tudo para escrever outra coisa qualquer.

Naquelas quatro passagens, a idéia é que o salmista, os iníquos ou a natureza dissolvem-se e dissipam-se na presença majestosa de Deus, como se a glória do Senhor fosse tão avassaladora que a própria criação fosse incapaz de manter a sua forma e unidade, mas antes, tivesse de decompor-se e desmanchar-se na organização de seus átomos.

CERÂMICA Ver Oleiro (Olaria; Cerâmica)

CERCA

A palavra hebraica **gader** é usada por doze vezes: Sal. 62:3; 80:12; Ecl. 10:8; Eze. 13:5; 22:30; Núm. 22:24; Esd. 9:9; Isa. 5:5; Eze. 42:7; Osé. 2:6; Miq. 7:11.

Na antiguidade, as cercas podiam ser feitas de vários materiais, como ramos ou pedras. As cercas eram usadas para delimitar propriedades, separar áreas para animais dentro dos quais eram guardados, etc. Nas cercas feitas de pedra, quando o trabalho era malfeito, as serpentes podiam esconder-se entre os interstícios das pedras (Ecl. 10:8; Amós 5:19).

Usos Figurados. No trecho de Sal. 62:3, os ímpios são comparados a indivíduos que pretendem derrubar o justo como se este fosse uma parede pendida ou um muro prestes a cair. Isso significa que os ímpios inclinam-se por destruir ao próximo. Os líderes de Nínive foram comparados a nuvens de gafanhotos que tivessem pousado sobre uma cerca (Naum 3:17). O trecho de Efé. 2:14 fala sobre a derrubada da parede de separação que não permitia a união, em torno de uma fé comum, entre os judeus e os gentios. Ver sobre Muro.

Símbolos nos Sonhos e Visões. Uma cerca, em um sonho ou visão, indica as coisas e instituições estabelecidas pelo homem, que contrariam e impedem. Também indica as próprias *inibições* e o *autocontrole*. Isso é especialmente verdadeiro quando, por detrás da cerca, há algum animal feroz preso, o que pode simbolizar os apetites carnais. Ou então, uma cerca pode representar os obstáculos ao progresso espiritual ou ao trabalho espiritual da pessoa. A derrubada de uma cerca significa a remoção de obstáculos.

CERCO Ver Guerra.

CÉREBRO Ver Órgãos Vitais, ponto 1.

CERÍNTIOS

Seguidores de Cerinto (que vide). Quanto às doutrinas deles, ver aquele artigo. O gnosticismo foi uma das antigas heresias que a Igreja cristã precisou combater por cerca de cento e cinqüenta anos. Vários livros do Novo Testamento, que alguns estudiosos calculam em número de oito, foram escritos, pelo menos em parte, a fim de refutar essa distorcida doutrina, a saber: João (reflexos), Colossenses, II Pedro, I, II e III João, Judas e Apocalipse (reflexos).

CERINTO

Foi o primeiro mestre gnóstico, judeu de raça, acerca de quem dispomos de informações definidas. Ele atuou por volta do ano 100 D.C., na região de Éfeso. De acordo com as tradições, ele tornou-se adversário do apóstolo João. É bem possível que a heresia denunciada em I João seja exatamente o gnosticismo (que vide) ensinado por Cerinto. De seus escritos, coisa alguma chegou até nós, pelo que, tudo quanto acerca deles sabemos, chegou a nós mediante os escritos dos primeiros pais da Igreja, além do conhecimento geral acerca do sistema gnóstico. No entanto, as declarações atinentes a Cerinto algumas vezes são vagas ou mesmo conflitantes. Seja como for, a leitura do artigo intitulado *Gnosticismo* dará ao leitor uma boa idéia sobre os ensinos gerais desse sistema pagão. Ireneu informa-nos, em sua obra *Contra Heresias*, que Cerinto operava na porção oeste da Ásia Menor; e Epifânio, falecido em 403 D.C., afirma que ele nasceu no Egito e educou-se em Alexandria. Ele ensinava um sincretismo composto de elementos gnósticos e ebionitas, com noções judaicas e cristãs. Assim, ele asseverava que a criação não fora obra do Deus Supremo, mas de um poder intermediário, inferior, o que explicaria o mundo imperfeito em que vivemos. Também ensinava a necessidade da circuncisão e da observância do sábado. Por igual modo, dizia que Jesus não nasceu de uma virgem, porquanto seria apenas um homem comum, posto que extraordinário, que o Espírito de Cristo viera possuir por ocasião do batismo, o que explicaria a vida miraculosa de Jesus. Também ensinava a usual doutrina gnóstica de que a matéria é inerentemente má, e que o espírito somente é puro. Também dizia que, por ocasião da crucificação, o Espírito de Cristo abandonara a Jesus, o que significaria que nunca houve verdadeira identificação da natureza divina com a natureza humana. No entanto, Cerinto afirmava que Jesus havia ressuscitado dos mortos. Os seguidores de Cerinto tornaram-se conhecidos como ceríntios. As idéias de Cerinto não eram originais. Ele apenas foi um dos expoentes bem conhecidos de idéias filosóficas pagãs que rivalizaram com o cristianismo em seus primeiros passos. Com todos os erros, o gnosticismo tem reaparecido em todas as eras da história da Igreja, com vários nomes. Uma de suas mais patentes manifestações modernas é o russelismo. Ver sobre as *Testemunhas de Jeová*.

CERTEZA E DÚVIDA

Esses fatores desempenham um importante papel na metodologia de Descartes. Ele supunha que um elemento necessário ao conhecimento é o da certeza, que uma pessoa alcança pondo em dúvida todas as proposições que admitem dúvida. Uma pessoa pode ter certeza, e, no entanto, ainda não saber, ou seja, estar equivocada. Não obstante, o verdadeiro conhecimento vem através do método de «duvidar de tudo para chegar à certeza». Duvidar de uma proposição dá ao indivíduo a oportunidade de aplicar à mesma todos os critérios de teste possíveis. Somente quando uma proposição qualquer resiste a esses testes, pode ser recebida como veraz. A primeira proposição que Descartes descobriu que não pode ser posta em dúvida é a da existência de Deus. Ele aceitava como válido o argumento ontológico (que vide) de Anselmo, além de aplicar idéias extraídas dos argumentos cosmológico e teleológico (que vide), como apoio. Com base nisso, ele assevera que o mundo exterior deve existir (contrariamente ao ceticismo), porquanto Deus não haveria de querer enganar-nos, fazendo-nos supor que o mesmo existe, quando, na realidade, não existe—em cujo caso, o conceito inteiro estaria baseado em uma ilusão

CERTEZA NA CRENÇA RELIGIOSA

estribada na percepção dos sentidos. Portanto, a alma existe, pois essa é uma realidade pessoal, baseada na realidade divina. Quanto a isso, Descartes desenvolveu um dualismo radical, dentro do problema corpo-mente (que vide), chamado *interacionismo*. Para chegar à alma, ele proferiu o seu famoso «Cogito, ergo sum»: *Penso, portanto existo*. Se há um processo de pensamento, deve haver um ser pensante. Isso envolve uma certa lógica, embora não sejamos capazes de postular o conhecimento.

Através do método da verdade através da dúvida, ficam estabelecidos três princípios fundamentais do conhecimento: Deus, a alma, e a existência do mundo externo. Através da teoria da coerência da verdade (ver sobre *Teorias da Verdade*), pois, conseguimos estabelecer muitas outras crenças, como alicerçadas sobre a realidade dos fatos. (AM E F P)

CERTEZA SEGUNDO A CRENÇA RELIGIOSA

Uma interessante afirmação pode estabelecer a disposição com que falamos sobre a certeza e as crenças religiosas. No tocante à teoria criacionista versus a evolução, alguém disse: «Os evolucionistas têm crenças com evidências; os criacionistas têm certeza sem evidências». É que a fé religiosa depende muito da revelação para chegar à verdade. Ver o artigo sobre as *Teorias da Verdade*. Nossas quatro maneiras básicas de chegar ao conhecimento são as seguintes: 1. A percepção dos sentidos: *empirismo* (que vide); 2. a razão: racionalismo (que vide), 3. a *intuição* (que vide), e 4. o *misticismo* (que vide). Esta última maneira, o misticismo, consiste no conhecimento que obtemos sobre um Ser ou sobre seres superiores a nós mesmos, como Deus, Cristo, o Espírito Santo, a alma, poderes angelicais, santos, espíritos humanos desencarnados, etc. Essa lista varia, dependendo do grupo religioso que esteja em pauta. O que todos os grupos religiosos têm em comum é a idéia que o conhecimento pode ser recebido como um dom divino, ou do Espírito Santo, etc. Usualmente concebe-se o conhecimento como transmitido por meio de um intermediário, como um profeta, um homem santo, um «médium», etc. Seja como for, o misticismo consiste apenas na idéia de que o conhecimento pode proceder de algum poder superior a nós mesmos, interno (segundo o misticismo oriental), ou externo a nós (segundo o misticismo ocidental).

Naturalmente, há excelentes evidências em favor da validade de *algumas* experiências místicas. A dificuldade surge quando se pensa que o conhecimento que nos é dado através desse meio, em contraste com outros métodos, automaticamente deve ser perfeito. Ora, meus amigos, preciso dizer, sem importar se vocês apreciam ou não a declaração: isso é um *dogma*. Em porção alguma as Escrituras Sagradas afirmam que esse método impossibilita o erro.

Notemos bem. Há muitos sistemas religiosos, no Ocidente e no Oriente, que afirmam que o misticismo (que inclui a *revelação*, que vide) é a base de sua fé. E quase todos esses sistemas afirmam que não há erro em seu sistema. Basta-nos ler, como exemplo disso, o artigo sobre o *Alcorão*. Ver o meu artigo sobre a *Inspiração das Escrituras*. Mas, retornando agora à citação sobre a evolução e o criacionismo, o ponto é que as pessoas que confiam na revelação embalam a idéia de que, visto ser essa uma maneira válida de obter conhecimento, como um *dom de Deus*, tal dom não pode apresentar qualquer falha. Em outras palavras, nem precisaríamos pensar e submeter a teste. Tudo quanto nos compete fazer é crer. E no entanto, até mesmo os crentes evangélicos, que têm essa crença básica, conseguem arquitetar diferentes sistemas. É possível que isso se deva ao fato de que os sistemas diferem quanto à sua abrangência (quanto mais fatores forem envolvidos em um sistema qualquer, mais este se aproximará da verdade; e, vice-versa, quanto menos fatores estiverem envolvidos, mais distante estará aquele sistema da verdade revelada). Seja como for, para contrabalançar esse fato, cada denominação tem a arrogância de dizer: «Mas o nosso grupo está com a razão, ao passo que os demais estão em erro crasso, ou expõem uma posição inferior». Isso, porém, meus amigos, é manipular a verdade. Não precisamos de perfeição para termos uma poderosa mensagem espiritual.

Aqueles que dependem somente do misticismo e exibem preconceitos antiintelectuais, desprezam a razão, bem como desprezam as descobertas da ciência. No entanto, a razão e a ciência são meios válidos de se chegar ao conhecimento, embora não sejam meios perfeitos. Ver o artigo sobre o *Antiintelectualismo*. Ver também o artigo sobre *Gnosiologia*, quanto a uma discussão geral sobre os meios do conhecimento. Deus é maior que qualquer sistema de conhecimento, mas opera através deles todos. A ciência tem conseguido alguns importantes esclarecimentos sobre a verdade. A idade ou antiguidade da terra é uma dessas questões. A idéia de que a criação teve lugar há cerca de seis mil anos (calculados com base nas genealogias do livro de Gênesis), conforme a ciência tem mostrado, é absurda. Pensemos na Via Láctea (a galáxia à qual pertence o nosso sistema solar e a nossa própria terra), que é tão vasta que a luz precisa de cem mil anos para atravessá-la. No entanto, nós, que vivemos no sistema solar, e que se encontra em um de seus extremos, podemos ver a luz que saiu da outra extremidade da galáxia, há cem mil anos atrás. Acrescente-se a isso que nossos instrumentos estão captando luz que partiu há dezesseis bilhões de anos. Portanto, a criação tem, pelo menos, essa antiguidade; e penso que estamos apenas começando a aprender quão antiga ela é. A verdadeira representação numérica da antiguidade da criação deixaria a mente atônita, tenho a certeza. Dessa maneira, a ciência nos tem ajudado a compreender um pouco melhor a grandeza de Deus. Mui provavelmente, nossa presente criação é apenas uma dentre várias outras, em uma série interminável, que surgiram e desapareceram. A criação, é verdade, é uma criação de que ouvimos no relato sagrado, é apenas um capítulo recente da história sagrada, que deve ser uma enciclopédia, e não um mero verbete. Usualmente, os limites estabelecidos pelos homens são as limitações de sua própria mente, não refletindo as dimensões da mente divina.

As pessoas religiosas com freqüência supõem que o conhecimento está além do escopo da pesquisa empírica e racional. Em seguida, professam ter uma *gnosis* que depende diretamente de Deus. Ato contínuo, elas injetam a idéia de perfeição nessa gnosis. Agostinho, porém, declarou: *Credo ut intelligam*, «Creio, para que possa compreender». Essa é uma boa declaração. O ceticismo somente nos deixa nas trevas. Cumpre-nos abordar a fé religiosa dotados do espírito da fé, e sempre será melhor crer em demasia do que crer pouco demais. Não obstante, esse conceito de VERDADE SEM QUALQUER erro é de invenção humana, e não faz parte da revelação divina. Segundo esse conceito, é como se tivéssemos café instantâneo, em forma granulada.

CERTEZA (FILOSOFIA) — CESARÉIA

Basta derramar água quente sobre o mesmo, e pronto! Aí está o café! Gostoso e perfeito! Além disso, existem aqueles crentes da mamadeira, que bebem suas fórmulas, mingaus cuidadosamente preparados pela mamãe, e que nada precisam fazer além de sugar. Jamais sentem necessidade de pesquisar pessoalmente a verdade, procurando entendê-la por si mesmos. Algumas vezes, uma pessoa pode topar acidentalmente com um tesouro, quase sem esforço. Mas freqüentemente, porém, a busca pela verdade assemelha-se mais àquele homem que procurava boas pérolas, tendo-se tornado um especialista em pérolas. Ele continuou procurando por muito tempo, antes de encontrar a pérola de grande preço. O apóstolo Paulo deixou claro que, neste lado da existência, a verdade nos é dada, por assim dizer, em doses homeopáticas: «Porque agora vemos como em espelho, obscuramente, então veremos face a face; agora conheço em parte, então conhecerei como também sou conhecido» (I Cor. 13:12).

A obtenção da verdade, além disso, é cumulativa. Nenhum indivíduo, nenhum sistema, nenhuma época da história humana pode possuir uma fatia considerável da verdade, porquanto a verdade de Deus é infinita, e todos somos finitos. Apesar disso, o tanto que nos foi revelado é preciosíssimo, importantíssimo. As reivindicações de um conhecimento superior podem ser espúrias (ver I Tim. 6:20). A verdade é superior à sabedoria humana (ver I Cor. 1:17-25), e a interpretação da mesma, sempre estará sujeita a erros, por essa precisa razão. A verdade nos é conferida mediante a condescendente vontade de Deus, e sempre encontra uma maneira de deixar de lado os arrogantes (Mat. 11:25 e I Cor. 2:9-11). Outrossim, a verdade é por demais vasta para nós; quando a acertamos em um ponto, isso não significa que já a descobrimos por inteiro. As denominações cristãs têm um jeitinho de acertar diferentes aspectos da verdade; e então supõem que a sua minúscula descoberta pode solucionar todos os problemas, na terra e fora dela. Isso é pura arrogância. De fato, nenhuma época, e, muito menos, nenhum grupo particular, consegue acertar a verdade revelada de forma abrangente. Na verdade, nenhum sistema religioso consegue sondar mais do que alguns poucos pontos da verdade. A despeito dessa debilidade de nosso conhecimento, aquilo que nos é dado entender da verdade divina é extremamente importante, são fragmentos deveras preciosos.

CERTEZA SEGUNDO A FILOSOFIA

De acordo com a filosofia, a certeza precisa ser encarada sob dois pontos de vista diferentes: 1. A certeza lógica é uma propriedade que pertence às conclusões válidas das inferências dedutivas. Em tais casos, a conclusão segue-se, necessariamente, das premissas. No entanto, ambas as premissas das quais extraímos uma conclusão, precisam ser válidas, isto é, correspondentes à realidade dos fatos, se tivermos de chegar a conclusões válidas. 2. No campo da psicologia, a certeza é um estado de crença na veracidade ou na falsidade de uma dada proposição. No entanto, esse estado de crença não assegura a veracidade das conclusões a que podemos chegar, mesmo que essas conclusões sejam obtidas mediante um raciocínio válido. (P)

CERULÁRIO, MIGUEL

Suas datas foram 1043-1058, como patriarca de Constantinopla. Ele repudiou as reivindicações do papa Leão IX (que vide), que se declarava cabeça universal da cristandade. Cerulário apoiava sua contenção sobre a antiga posição de que cada patriarca era supremo dentro de seu próprio território. Os legados papais, enviados a Constantinopla, encontraram Cerulário inflexível em seu repúdio das reivindicações papais. Em conseqüência, ele foi excomungado, juntamente com todos os seus aderentes, a 16 de julho de 1054. Em revide, o papa de Roma e todos os seus aderentes foram excomungados pelo patriarcado de Constantinopla. Se esse duplo ato de exclusão vale alguma coisa diante de Deus, então tanto o sistema papal quanto os grupos derivados do patriarcado de Constantinopla foram excluídos do reino de Deus! O fato é que isso inaugurou o *grande cisma* (vide) entre o Oriente e o Ocidente, o qual já vinha se arquitetando, durante muito tempo antes dessa data. A divisão da Igreja, em Igreja Católica Romana e Igreja Ortodoxa Oriental persiste até os nossos próprios dias. Portanto, o catolicismo antigo excomungou-se a si mesmo. (AM E)

CÉSAR

Consideremos os pontos abaixo:

1. *O Nome*. Kaisar, que se abrandou para César; quando do latim bárbaro, era um prenome pessoal masculino em latim. Tornou-se cognome da família Juliana, e acabou tornando-se uma espécie de título, como Faraó, aplicado a todos os imperadores romanos, desde Júlio César até Adriano. Em muitos idiomas modernos, o nome tem-se tornado um título para designar reis, além de servir de sinônimo de ditador ou déspota. Nas páginas do Novo Testamento, o termo é usado para indicar os imperadores romanos. Ver João 19:15 e Atos 17:7. Os judeus prestavam tributo ao imperador, porque ele era o símbolo do império romano. (Mat. 22:17; Luc. 23:2). Para ele, os judeus, na qualidade de cidadãos romanos, tinham o direito de apelar (Atos 25:11). Quando tal apelo era feito por alguém, esse alguém precisava ir a Roma para ter uma entrevista pessoal com o imperador (Atos 25:12,21). Ver a exposição desses versículos, no NTI, quanto a plenos detalhes sobre a questão.

2. *Os Césares do Novo Testamento*. a. Augusto (Luc. 2:1); b. Tibério (Luc. 3:1); c. Cláudio (Atos 11:28); d. Nero (Atos 25:8). Ver os artigos sobre cada um desses imperadores.

3. *Júlio César*. Esse homem foi um grande militar e estadista, autor e orador, um homem realmente incomum, que nasceu em 102 e faleceu em 44 A.C. Ele foi o último de uma série de comandantes que, durante um século inteiro de crises constitucionais e de agitações civis, haviam usado o poder do exército romano para impor soluções políticas. Dessa forma vinham sendo controladas as insurreições e a corrupção; mas foram exatamente essas indisciplinas que, finalmente, destruíram a república e forçaram o surgimento da ditadura. Júlio César foi assassinado em 44 A.C. Sua herança passou para Otávio, seu herdeiro adotivo, por seu sobrinho, o qual, mediante um processo legal, tornou-se Caio Otaviano César, mais tarde simplesmente chamado Augusto. Por essa altura, o termo César tornou-se o nome dinástico de todos os imperadores, até Adriano, inclusive (suas datas foram 117-138 D.C.). Palavras modernas como Tasar e Kaiser derivam-se de César. (AM UN WA)

CESARÉIA

Desde o começo é mister salientar que havia duas

CESARÉIA

Cesaréias. A Cesaréia da costa do Mediterrâneo era designada Cesaréia Palestina, em contraste com a Cesaréia de Filipe. Outros autores simplesmente chamavam de Cesaréia à cidade costeira, visto que Cesaréia de Filipe já a distinguia daquela. De fato, historicamente, essa adição foi especialmente feita a fim de distingui-la daquela outra cidade. Ambas essas cidades receberam seu nome em honra a César Augusto, o imperador romano. Filipe, o tetrarca, durante o reinado daquele imperador, adornou a cidade de Cesaréia de Filipe, razão por que seu nome foi vinculado à mesma.

No Novo Testamento há apenas duas referências a Cesaréia de Filipe: 1. Mateus 16:13, que descreve a confissão de Pedro; e 2. Marcos 8:27, que é a passagem paralela no segundo evangelho. O local ficava situado na porção norte da Palestina, a oitenta quilômetros ao sul de Damasco. Ficava perto do sopé do monte Hermom. Assinalou o limite norte das viagens de Jesus pela Terra Santa.

Cesaréia, também chamada «Cesaréia Palestina», isto é, Cesaréia da Palestina, ocupou um lugar mais importante na história, tanto bíblica quanto secular, que a sua homônima, Cesaréia de Filipe. As informações abaixo restringem-se à Cesaréia Palestina.

I. Referências Neotestamentárias a Cesaréia

Todas as referências a essa cidade, no Novo Testamento, restringem-se ao livro de Atos:

1. Atos 8:40: Filipe, o evangelista, ficou ali por algum tempo, no fim de seu torneio de pregação. Evidentemente, ele fixou residência ali, afinal.

2. Atos 9:30: Pouco depois de sua conversão, Paulo foi levado para ali, a fim de evitar certos helenistas, que procuravam matá-lo.

3. Atos 10:1 ss. até v. 24 (onde ocorre outra referência específica a essa cidade): A cidade era o lugar onde habitava o centurião Cornélio, a quem Pedro ministrou. Essa ocorrência, em certo sentido, deu o ímpeto inicial à missão entre os gentios.

4. Atos 11:1: *Pedro*, tendo retornado a Jerusalém, relatou como os gentios, em Cesaréia, haviam aceitado a Palavra de Deus.

5. Atos 12:19: Tiago foi morto e Pedro foi lançado na prisão. Entretanto, por meios miraculosos, Pedro escapou. Herodes (Agripa I) foi à prisão em busca de Pedro. Não o encontrando ali, submeteu os guardas a um exame sobre a questão, e resolveu executá-los, de acordo com um antigo costume, segundo o qual eram justiçadas as sentinelas que deixassem um prisioneiro escapar. Agripa I foi dali para Cesaréia, e, pouco depois, faleceu ali.

6. Atos 18:22: *Paulo visitou Cesaréia*, tendo partido de Éfeso, a caminho de Antioquia. Dali, o apóstolo partiu para a Galácia e a Frígia. Essas viagens fizeram parte da segunda viagem missionária de Paulo.

7. Atos 21:8: Paulo, subindo para Jerusalém, parou em Cesaréia. Ali ficou hospedado na casa de Filipe, o evangelista. Esse homem tinha quatro filhas que profetizavam. Ágabo, um profeta, desceu da Judéia e encontrou-se com Paulo em Cesaréia. Avisou graficamente ao apóstolo, para que não subisse a Jerusalém, prevendo assim o seu encarceramento. Esses eventos aconteceram na terceira viagem missionária de Paulo.

8. Atos 21:16: *Discípulos de Cesaréia* acompanharam Paulo até Jerusalém.

9. Atos 23:23,33: Paulo foi aprisionado em Jerusalém. Imediatamente, alguns judeus planejaram tirar-lhe a vida. Mas o conluio foi descoberto, e, a fim de proteger Paulo, — os oficiais romanos removeram-no para Cesaréia, e ali ele foi guardado como prisioneiro, pelo espaço de dois anos.

10. Atos 25:1,4:6: Paulo apelou para César, a fim de ser julgado, o que garantiu sua remoção de Cesaréia para Roma. Festo, que estivera em Cesaréia, foi a Jerusalém, e, estando ali, ouviu as queixas de certos oficiais do judaísmo contra Paulo. Os judeus dali queriam que Festo enviasse Paulo a Jerusalém, porquanto haviam planejado matá-lo no caminho. Mas Festo fê-los irem a Cesaréia, como testemunhas de acusação, no julgamento. Festo permaneceu em Jerusalém durante dez dias, e então retornou a Cesaréia. Em seguida, houve o julgamento de Paulo.

11. Atos 25:13: Herodes Agripa II e Berenice vieram a Cesaréia saudar a Festo. Estando eles ali, Festo convidou-os para uma entrevista pessoal com Paulo, o qual, por essa altura, era um mui famoso prisioneiro.

Cesaréia foi uma importante cidade na história da Igreja primitiva. Foi ali que Pedro obteve um mais profundo discernimento sobre a natureza do evangelho e sobre o trato de Deus para com os gentios; e isso pavimentou o caminho para a missão geral de evangelização dos gentios. Cesaréia tornou-se um importante centro do cristianismo, dotado de uma forte igreja local, que evangelizou as regiões ao derredor. Cesaréia servia de centro de onde os missionários cristãos eram enviados e para onde retornavam, refrescando-se, e então partindo novamente. O próprio Paulo passou bastante tempo ali, incluindo mais de dois anos na cidade, como prisioneiro.

II. Importantes Fatos Acerca de Cesaréia

Havia uma fortificação fenícia em Cesaréia, em tempos muito antigos. Roma reedificou ali a cidade de Cesaréia, também chamada Sebaste, que significa «de Augusto», porquanto foi em sua honra que a cidade foi construída. Durante doze anos, grande soma em dinheiro foi gasta ali (25-13 A.C.), na construção e embelezamento da cidade. Por causa da importância que César dava a essa cidade, o historiador Tácito chamou-a de «a cabeça da Judéia». Ficava na estrada que ia de Tiro ao Egito, e acerca de cento e treze quilômetros ao norte de Jerusalém. Tinha um porto com cerca de trezentos metros de extensão, e um vasto quebra-mar. Esse mole existe até hoje. Um templo com gigantescas estátuas, consagrado tanto a César quanto a Roma, foi construído ali. Cesaréia era a residência oficial dos procuradores romanos, como Félix e Festo, referidos no livro de Atos. Os reis herodianos também tinham palácios ali. E a cidade era, igualmente, o local dos principais quartéis militares da província.

Cesaréia era um importante centro comercial e marítimo. A população era mista, mas os gentios formavam um contingente mais numeroso do que a população judaica. Uma insurreição hostil em Cesaréia, assinalou o estágio inicial da grande guerra dos judeus. Todos os residentes judeus foram massacrados por ocasião dessa rebelião, que teve lugar no ano de 66 D.C. Vespasiano foi declarado imperador romano em Cesaréia. Ele a transformou em colônia romana.

Já vimos a importância dessa cidade no tocante à primitiva Igreja cristã. Em tempos posteriores, ela continuou sendo um importante centro cristão. Era a terra natal de Eusébio, bem como foi a cena de muitos dos labores de Orígenes. Sua importância como centro do cristianismo também é ilustrada pelo fato de que um distintivo texto do Novo Testamento desenvolveu-se ali, chamado «texto cesareano».

Ruínas de um aqueduto de Cesaréia, Cortesia, John F. Walvoord

Ruínas de Cesaréia, Cortesia, Dr. John F. Walvoord

Golfo de Acabá

Aqueduto de Cesaréia — Cortesia, John F. Walvoord

CESARÉIA — CESAROPAPISMO

Após o período romano, a cidade caiu em decadência. «A desgraça dos árabes caiu sobre a planície costeira, e os cruzados foram os únicos intrusos a darem atenção à restauração do porto. Suas grandes defesas são visíveis até hoje, de mistura e acima das memórias associadas à dominação romana». Antes de 640 D.C., os islamitas ocuparam o local. Cesaréia foi capturada pelos cruzados, liderados por Balduíno I, em 1101 D.C. Os cruzados reconstruíram e reergueram as muralhas de cerca de uma décima parte da antiga área. O sultão mameluco Baibars I, deixou a cidade desolada, em 1265. A moderna aldeia de Qisaya assinala atualmente o lugar onde Cesaréia antigamente floresceu. Essa aldeia está localizada cerca de trinta e cinco quilômetros ao sul da moderna cidade de Haifa.

III. Descobertas Arqueológicas em Cesaréia

1. *Um teatro romano* (em condições degeneradas) até hoje existe em Cesaréia. Josefo, o historiador e general judeu do século I D.C., aludiu ao mesmo em seus escritos, intitulando-o de «anfiteatro». Esse teatro era usado como local de reuniões de várias naturezas.

2. *Um quebra-mar* com sessenta metros de largura foi construído por causa das ondas que sopram da direção sul. Gigantescos blocos de pedra calcária, alguns deles com 15 metros de comprimento, 3 metros de largura e 2,70 metros de altura, foram usados como alicerces para um mole e um cais que ali foram construídos. Grande parte dessa construção tem sobrevivido até os nossos próprios dias.

3. Remanescentes de *outras edificações* romanas, como aquedutos, sistemas de drenagem, edifícios públicos, palácios e templos têm sido encontrados em Cesaréia. Desde 1958, a Frova, uma expedição arqueológica italiana tem descoberto as ruínas do teatro e cerca de dezesseis quilômetros de um aqueduto. Uma equipe israelense encontrou os restos de um grande templo, um pouco mais adiante daquele aqueduto, e várias fortificações dos cruzados. Foi descoberta na água uma moeda, retratando as instalações do porto de Cesaréia. Foi também encontrada uma inscrição em 1961, com o nome de Pôncio Pilatos. Ele governou a Judéia de 26-36 D.C.

Josefo (*Anti.* xv.9,6) descreveu a magnificência da original cidade de Cesaréia, mencionando seus teatros, palácios, templos, um hipódromo, aquedutos e muitas outras estruturas notáveis. Com base naquilo que ele deixou escrito, julgamos que tudo o que a arqueologia já descobriu representa apenas uma pequena fração da antiga glória da cidade de Cesaréia. (AM I IB FRE UN)

CESARÉIA DE FILIPE

À semelhança de muitas comunidades à beira do mar Mediterrâneo, nos tempos neotestamentários, sua população era muito *variegada*. Dentro da história do NT, várias decisões e acontecimentos cruciais tiveram lugar ali. — O ministério do evangelista Filipe foi que lhes levou o cristianismo, tendo havido, dessa maneira, uma forma de missão gentílica preliminar. A missão oficial de Pedro, entre os gentios, também se verificou ali; e foi igualmente ali que a Pedro foi conferido grande discernimento sobre o caráter universal da fé cristã, o que foi um desenvolvimento importantíssimo para a expansão do evangelho. Paulo também fez de Cesaréia o seu porto de desembarque, quando retornava de sua segunda e de sua terceira viagens missionárias (ver Atos 18:22 e 21:8). Ali tomou a grande decisão de visitar Jerusalém (ver Atos 21:13), que o conduziu à sua detenção e aprisionamento. Também foi nessa cidade que Paulo foi julgado por Félix (ver Atos 23:23-33). Foi ali também que apresentou a sua impressionante defesa perante Festo e Agripa, tendo sido dali, por semelhante modo, que velejou em cadeias para Roma. (Ver Atos 25:11). Durante esse período de sua história, Cesaréia era a capital romana da Judéia, sendo uma base militar romana.

Cesaréia de Filipe, por sua vez, era assim designada a fim de distingui-la daquela outra Cesaréia, descrita acima. Ambas foram assim chamadas em honra aos Césares reinantes. Cesaréia de Filipe estava localizada no sopé do monte Hermom, próxima à fonte principal do rio Jordão, uma caverna denominada atualmente Mugharet Ras en-Neba, onde estava também centralizado o culto pagão do deus Pan. Essa cidade foi erigida por Filipe, o tetrarca. Um templo magnificente foi levantado ali por Herodes, o Grande, além de outras notáveis estruturas que ainda não foram desenterradas pela arqueologia. (Ver Luc. 2:1-4 e 9:7).

Cesaréia de Filipe foi o lugar onde Pedro fez sua famosa *confissão de fé* em Cristo, conforme o registro de Mat. 16:13 e ss. Talvez seja a mesma cidade que, no A.T., é chamada de Baal-Gade. No lugar de Baal, os gregos puseram Pan, motivo pelo qual, dali por diante, a cidade passou a chamar-se Paneas, até que Filipe, o tetrarca, talvez a tenha reedificado, dando-lhe o nome de Cesaréia. Quando o monarca selêucida Antíoco III conquistou a Palestina das mãos dos ptolomeus, esse lugar foi cena de uma das batalhas decisivas desse encontro.

Essa cidade, tal como o resto do mundo conhecido na época, passou para as mãos dos romanos, e Herodes, o Grande, construiu um magnificente templo de mármore ali, dedicado a César Augusto. Filipe, posteriormente, mas ainda sob o governo do mesmo imperador, adornou o lugar. Foi por causa de sua associação com essa cidade que ela veio a ser chamada «Cesaréia de Filipe», a fim de distingui-la da Cesaréia da Palestina, que ficava perto da costa marítima do Mediterrâneo. Agripa II reconstruiu a cidade (nos tempos de Nero), tendo-lhe dado o nome de Neronias, nome esse, porém, que não tardou a ser olvidado. (I IB ID)

CESÁRIO DE ARLES

Suas datas aproximadas são 470-542 D.C. Foi um devoto monge galicano, pregador e legislador, monástico. Em adição a seu longo serviço nos mosteiros de Lerins e Arles, desde o ano de 502 até à sua morte, ele foi bispo nessa última cidade. Deixou uma *Regra* para os monges, e uma outra para as freiras. Essas regras enfatizavam a necessidade da renúncia, da disciplina, da dedicação à oração e do primado da Palavra de Deus na vida dos religiosos.

CESÁRIO DE HEISTERBACH

Faleceu em cerca de 1240. Foi um leal monge cisterciense (que vide), o qual adquiriu fama devido à sua tentativa de erradicar as corrupções sociais e econômicas de sua ordem religiosa, e também por haver escrito um valioso comentário sobre a vida e a religião da época medieval, chamado *O Diálogo sobre os Milagres*. Essa obra foi traduzida para o inglês em 1929. (E)

CESAROPAPISMO

Esse vocábulo é usado para indicar a supremacia do

estado sobre a Igreja, conforme se via no império bizantino e na Rússia, até o ano de 1917, antes do advento do comunismo. Outro tanto se tem dado nas relações entre a Igreja e o estado, na Inglaterra e na maioria dos países protestantes. Contudo, a questão real do caso não é que o estado deve dominar a Igreja, e, sim, que deve haver liberdade, tanto para a Igreja quanto para o estado, em suas respectivas esferas. Nesse sentido, o termo pode ser um sinônimo da idéia da separação da Igreja e do estado, um abençoado princípio bíblico, que nem sempre tem sido observado até mesmo por denominações evangélicas. (E)

CESTO DE JUNCO

Era um pequeno cesto,, feito de junco, tornado estanque por meio de betume e piche. Na Bíblia, a expressão encontra-se apenas no caso do barquinho feito para conter o infante Moisés, e que foi posto a flutuar à superfície do rio Nilo, para proteger-lhe a vida. Ver a narrativa em Êxodo 2:3 *ss*. Nos tempos antigos, o junco medrava abundantemente às margens do Nilo e de outros rios, mas atualmente só se encontra no baixo rio Nilo. Sabemos que essa planta era usada na construção de pequenos botes (Isa. 18:2). Esse *cesto* de Moisés, bem como a *arca* de Noé, são chamados pelo mesmo vocábulo hebraico, *tebah*, o qual, mui provavelmente, é um termo emprestado do egípcio, de uma raiz que significa *caixa* ou *esquife*. Entretanto, a arca da aliança é chamada pelo termo hebraico *aron*. Alguns intérpretes têm destacado o sentido simbólico de ambas essas arcas (a de Moisés e a de Noé), que indicam segurança e proteção. (WAL)

CESTO DE JUNCO, DE MOISÉS

O mesmo vocábulo hebraico, **tebhah**, usado para indicar a arca de Noé, é empregado para indicar o *cesto* no qual Moisés fora colocado quando criança, para flutuar nas águas do Nilo. (Ver Êxo. 2:3). Faraó baixara ordens no sentido de que todos os meninos nascidos entre os judeus fossem afogados no rio, porquanto estavam se multiplicando e se fortalecendo mais do que os egípcios. Porém, as parteiras hebréias não obedeceram à ordem. Seguiu-se então severa repressão contra os israelitas. A mãe de Moisés, temendo que seu filho fosse descoberto e morto, pô-lo em um cesto de junco e deixou-o flutuar nas águas do Nilo, esperando que alguém descobrisse a criança e a poupasse, por providência de Deus. Esse cesto fora feito de junco, que cresce naturalmente nas margens daquele rio, tendo sido recoberto com betume e piche. Plínio informa-nos que embarcações notáveis por sua rapidez eram *tecidas* com juncos. Isso é aludido em Isaías 18:2. Alguns imaginam que esse cesto era uma miniatura da arca de Noé, mas isso é por demais imaginativo. Seja como for, evidentemente era um cesto fechado, porquanto foi necessário abri-lo. (Ver Êxo. 2:6).

Somos informados que Sargão I, fundador do império semita da Babilônia, em cerca de 2400 a 2200 A.C., foi similarmente posto a flutuar, a fim de escapar de ser morto.

A fé da mãe de Moisés foi recompensada, acima de tudo quanto ela poderia ter imaginado. Moisés foi recolhido pela filha de Faraó, foi criado na corte real. E, ao tornar-se adulto, bandeou-se para a causa dos israelitas, tendo sido o instrumento usado por Deus para o livramento de Israel da servidão aos egípcios.

CETERIS PARIBUS

Expressão latina que significa «segundo iguais as outras coisas», uma expressão empregada nas discussões filosóficas.

CETICISMO

Introdução
I. Ceticismo na Filosofia
II. Ceticismo e Desobediência
III. O Ceticismo Leva à Rebelião Espiritual
IV. O Provincialismo do Ceticismo
V. Ceticismo Honesto e Ceticismo Desonesto
VI. A Utilidade do Ceticismo

«É mais fácil para mim pensar que dois professores norte-americanos disseram uma inverdade, que acreditar que pedras podem cair do céu». (Thomas Jefferson).

Ninguém está imune ao ceticismo exagerado, nem mesmo um homem sábio como foi Thomas Jefferson, ex-presidente dos Estados Unidos da América do Norte, que com as palavras acima transcritas expressou sua vigorosa objeção à possibilidade de que podem cair pedras do espaço exterior, depois que um meteorito caiu em terra, em 1807, perto da cidade de Weston, no estado de Connecticut, quando dois professores da Universidade de Yale foram recolhê-lo.

A razão para o ceticismo do ex-presidente Jefferson, de conformidade com o que nos esclarece Edward J. Olsen, encarregado da secção de mineralogia do Museu de Campo de História Natural de Chicago, pode ser atribuída à posição tomada pela prestigiosa Academia de Ciências de Paris, na França. Escrevendo no boletim de novembro daquele museu, Olsen revela que em 1772, a Academia de Ciências de Paris, que era então considerada o centro da erudição científica ocidental, declarou solenemente que 'a queda de pedras do céu é algo fisicamente *impossível*', mas que os meteoritos como tais não existem, sendo apenas pedaços de rocha terrestre que foram 'feridos por alguma descarga elétrica'.

Continua Olsen em seu relatório: «Esse pronunciamento foi assinado, entre outros, pelo brilhantíssimo Antoine Lavoisier, que hoje em dia é considerado como o pai da moderna ciência da química. O triste resultado disso é que algumas instituições e indivíduos ficaram embaraçados por causa de suas coleções de meteoritos, e as doaram ou jogaram fora.

Vemos nesse exemplo, portanto, como as opiniões **equivocadas podem ser defendidas ardorosamente** pelos homens. Mas, uma vez que tais opiniões sejam comprovadas como equivocadas, causam grande embaraço aos seus defensores. Bem podemos supor que vários daqueles cientistas franceses, da Academia de Ciências de Paris, viveram o bastante para verem que ficara comprovado que os meteoritos, em realidade, são pedras que literalmente caem do céu, o que deve ter servido para deixá-los envergonhados, em face de sua anterior atitude em que declararam ousadamente seu parecer científico.

Ora, o cristianismo evangélico, firmado nas Escrituras Sagradas, faz declarações e apresenta reivindicações ainda *mais ousadas* do que as desses ilustres cientistas, a despeito do desfavor da comunidade científica de nossa época, o que significa que sustermos tal «esperança» é correr um risco de embaraço futuro. Paulo, entretanto, estava plenamente confiante que embora a grande e estupenda esperança do cristianismo, por enquanto não pudesse ser empiricamente demonstrada, satisfazendo assim

Cestos dos tempos bíblicos
Cortesia, Zondervan Pub. House

Reprodução Artística de Darrell Steven Champlin

Arte céltica, a águia, símbolo do evangelho de João, Livro de Kells

CETICISMO

os céticos, contudo, tratava-se de uma esperança suficientemente alicerçada na Palavra de Deus, jamais se prestando para motivo de embaraço ou desilusão para os crentes, no futuro. Tal esperança jamais servirá para deixar-nos desapontados ou para humilhar-nos. É interessante observarmos que o apóstolo dos gentios não se lança a uma longa defesa de sua proposição, mas menciona tão-somente dois fatores empíricos, existentes, que servem para firmar-nos nessa confiança.

Em primeiro lugar, há a questão do fato de que esse novo amor, derramado no crente por obra do Espírito Santo, lhe cativa a alma e a mente. Trata-se, sobretudo, do amor de Deus derramado em nós; mas também envolve nosso amor a Deus, bem como nossa amizade para com os nossos semelhantes. Pois o amor de Deus, exibido por nosso intermédio, atuante em nosso homem interior, qual força ativa, não pode deixar de expressar-se em todos os aspectos de nossa vida. Em sua própria experiência, Saulo de Tarso passou do ódio e do fanatismo para o amor cristão. E o trecho de Gál. 5:22,23 mostra-nos que Paulo considerava o amor um dos aspectos do fruto do Espírito Santo. Em outras palavras, em sua verdadeira forma, o amor é uma graça espiritual, implantada no coração do crente pelo ministério íntimo do Espírito Santo.

I. Ceticismo na Filosofia

A palavra vem do gr. **skepsis**, consideração, *dúvida*. O ceticismo é a idéia de que a razão, as percepções e os outros meios que podem ser utilizados para alcançar o conhecimento, são fracos, enganadores e inadequados para este fim, se o conhecimento for considerado uma coisa perfeita, fixa ou completa. O verdadeiro conhecimento *se existe*, está simplesmente além das capacidades humanas.

1. O *ceticismo radical* cai no *niilismo* (que vide), afirmando que nem a própria existência pode ser considerada real. Górgias (que vide) declarou que «nada existe, mas mesmo se existisse seria impossível entender; e mesmo se pudéssemos entendê-lo, seria impossível expressar este entendimento».

2. *Pirreu*, 360-270 A.C., declarou-se em favor da suspensão de todos os juízos gnosiológicos. Os filósofos devem *se calar*.

3. *Timão*, seu discípulo, respondeu às críticas de seu mestre com poemas satíricos.

4. *Arcesilau* (que vide), o fundador da Segunda Academia platônica, expressou um ceticismo moderado, e interessou-se pelo desenvolvimento da teoria de *probabilidade*.

5. *Carnéades* (que vide), o fundador da Terceira Academia, enfatizou o ceticismo, utilizando de argumentos sobre a Conceito Divino e o princípio da casualidade.

6. *Cícero* continuava a tradição do ceticismo moderado como parte de seu sistema *eclético*.

7. *Sexto Empírico* (que vide), séculos II e III A.C., insistiu sobre a necessidade de critérios e definições. Nos seus sumários do assunto, temos uma rica fonte de informações sobre as idéias filosóficas céticas dos filósofos antes do tempo dele.

8. Agostinho (que vide), no quarto século D.C., argumentou que o ceticismo vence a si mesmo. Mesmo que uma pessoa seja enganada, ela deve existir para ser enganada: *Si fallor, sum*, se estou enganado, existo. Declarou também que o ceticismo é moralmente e espiritualmente uma esfera de *escuridão*, e o homem que insiste em ficar lá, nunca receberá qualquer iluminação. Neste sentido, o ceticismo também vence a si mesmo. Ele falou: Creio *para entender*, porque a crença, com sua mente aberta às realidades metafísicas, é a esfera da possibilidade de iluminação.

9. *Pico della Mirandola* (que vide), no séc. XV, utilizando os argumentos de Agostinho, numa forma desenvolvida, tentava dirigir os céticos para a fé cristã.

10. *Erasmo* (que vide), no início do séc. XVI, utilizou argumentos céticos para estabelecer sua doutrina do *livre-arbítrio* do homem.

11. *Agrippa von Nettesheim* (que vide), 1486-1535, empregou argumentos céticos para demonstrar a futilidade da ciência e assim dirigiu os homens à fé religiosa, como uma alternativa necessária.

12. *Montaigne* (que vide), 1553-92, perguntou: «O que é que sei?», e concluiu que a resposta é *nada*. Sendo que sou nada, e sei nada, devo, então, tomar refúgio na fé religiosa.

13. *Mersenne* (que vide), tomou uma posição entre o ceticismo e o dogmatismo, e estabeleceu a ciência nesta posição, declarando que a ciência está interessada somente no mundo *fenomenal*.

14. *Descartes* (que vide), 1596-1650, utilizou o método cético como um meio para adquirir o conhecimento, duvidando de tudo quanto possível, e aceitando somente aquelas proposições que não podem ser duvidadas, como Deus, alma e o mundo exterior. Através da *coerência* (que vide), construiu sua gnosiologia. Neste contexto nós temos sua declaração *Cogito ergo sum*, «Eu penso, portanto sou», porque é impossível ter um pensamento sem um pensador.

15. *Pascal* (que vide), 1623-1662, considerou o dogmatismo e o ceticismo como os pólos opostos da filosofia, e procurando escapar dos dois, achou refúgio na fé religiosa.

16. *Pierre Bayle* (que vide), 1647-1706, utilizando-se de argumentos céticos, destruiu as reivindicações da razão, e chegou a mostrar, através de sua argumentação, que devemos tolerar as opiniões dos outros.

17. *Voltaire* (que vide), 1694-1778, empregou os argumentos do ceticismo para atacar qualquer declaração sobre perguntas metafísicas e reconheceu a necessidade de tolerar as opiniões dos outros.

18. *Hume* (que vide), 1711-1776, construiu um sistema complexo, cético, pregando a *probabilidade* no lugar do conhecimento. A probabilidade se descansa sobre hábito e *fé animal*, não sobre qualquer conhecimento válido. As crenças religiosas devem ser mantidas em um nível mínimo e simples, porque quanto mais elaboradas forem, mais absurdos serão pronunciados.

19. *Kant* (que vide), influenciado por Hume, acordou-se de seu sono dogmático. A filosofia de Kant mantém a essência do ceticismo de Hume no seu tratamento sobre a *Razão Pura*, mas na sua *Razão Prática*, ele restaura tudo que o ceticismo roubou, através de seus postulados, em contraste com as *proposições da Razão Pura*.

20. *Clifford* (que vide), 1845-1879, exigiu evidências convincentes para apoiar qualquer idéia. Sem isso, devemos manter uma atitude cética.

21. *James* (que vide), 1842-1879, contra o ceticismo, enfatizou a *praticalidade* dos conceitos básicos, religiosos, e a *vontade de crer*, como uma atitude comum e inerente do homem.

22. *Royce* (que vide), 1885-1916, insistiu que a própria existência do ceticismo implica que o verdadeiro conhecimento existe, e deve ser procurado.

CETICISMO — CETRO

Existe uma verdade absoluta que o ceticismo não alcança, mas sugere.

23. *Santayana* (que vide), 1863-1952, aceitando a idéia básica do ceticismo, ensinou que devemos viver pela *fé animal*.

24. *Quando o ceticismo tem razão*. No sentido que todo nosso conhecimento é *incompleto*, seja conhecimento científico, filosófico ou teológico, o ceticismo tem razão. Não sabemos nada de modo completo. Somente Deus não compartilha esta situação. Porém, podemos saber algumas coisas, de modo completo, potencialmente, agora. Futuramente, poderemos alcançar grandes conhecimentos através da iluminação divina. Na *visão beatífica* (que vide), o ceticismo perde a batalha. Sabemos, *agora*, fragmentos extremamente importantes. Vale a pena viver em favor destes fragmentos da verdade.

II. Ceticismo e Desobediência

1. Os desobedientes foram reputados como **céticos** por terem se mostrado céticos diante da mensagem e da missão de Cristo.

2. Agostinho observou que o ceticismo é uma enfermidade espiritual, e não mera mentalidade duvidosa. Os céticos vivem em meio a trevas espirituais. A fé liberta o indivíduo desta esfera terrena e torna possível a iluminação espiritual.

3. A nós é ordenado que obedeçamos, e não meramente que creiamos no evangelho (ver II Tes. 1:8).

4. Consideremos as seguintes características da desobediência.

III. O Ceticismo Leva à Rebelião Espiritual

1. Essa rebelião é proibida por ser prejudicial ao bem-estar espiritual (ver Núm. 14:9).
2. Ela provoca Cristo (ver I Cor. 10:9).
3. Ela repele o governo divino (ver I Sam. 8:7).
4. Ela põe em dúvida o poder divino (ver Eze. 17:15).
5. Ela é um afastamento das instituições divinas (ver Êxo. 38:8,9).
6. Ela é um pecado contra a luz (ver João 15:22).
7. Ela é a preferência pelo caminho próprio, e não pelo caminho de Deus (ver Isa. 65:2).
8. A rebeldia agrava o pecado (ver Jó 34:37).
9. Ela oculta a hipocrisia (ver Osé. 7:14).
10. Leva Deus a tornar-se um inimigo (ver Isa. 63:10).
11. Produz empobrecimento (ver Sal. 68:6).
12. Deus pode perdoar a rebeldia (ver Dan. 9:9).
13. Ela é perdoada em face do arrependimento (ver Nee. 9:26,27).
14. Os ministros devem acautelar-se contra ela (ver Eze. 2:8).
15. A instrução religiosa tem por escopo impedir a rebeldia (ver Sal. 78:5,8).
16. Ela é uma obstinação espiritual, que nega a bondade de Deus (ver Êxo. 32:9).
17. Ela consiste na resistência proposital ao ministério do Espírito Santo (ver Atos 7:51).

IV. O Provincialismo do Ceticismo

1. O ceticismo se representa como se fora uma espécie de sabedoria especial. Mas tudo não passa de ilusão. Na realidade, trata-se de uma enfermidade espiritual, e não de uma iluminação mental.

2. Os céticos reconhecem somente aquilo que chega a eles por meio da percepção dos sentidos, ignorando o conhecimento adquirido pela razão, pela intuição ou pela revelação.

3. A própria ciência, em nossa época, está conseguindo ultrapassar o ceticismo. O mundo e seus fenômenos não podem ser explicados com base na mera percepção dos sentidos com suas evidências.

4. O ministério dos anjos transcende àquilo que os homens podem conhecer por meio da percepção dos sentidos. Esse é um dom de Deus. Ver Heb. 1:4.

V. Ceticismo Honesto e Ceticismo Desonesto

1. O cético honesto é aquele que não se satisfaz com supostos limites da verdade e que se dispõe a investigar além do que lhe foi ensinado. Sente-se incomodado com as cadeias impostas por qualquer sistema de pensamento.

2. Deseja avançar em seu conhecimento.

3. Está pronto a crer, uma vez que tenha as evidências.

4. Não limita seus meios de pesquisa somente à percepção dos sentidos ou ao método científico. Está preparado para receber a verdade através da razão, da intuição e do misticismo. Mas sua inteligência lhe serve de guia.

5. O cético desonesto, em contraste, tem o desejo de *não* crer, e confunde essa enfermidade espiritual como se fora a verdade. Praticamente nenhuma espécie de evidência é capaz de impressioná-lo.

6. O cético desonesto vive nas trevas, e as confunde com a luz. Praticamente, nenhuma revelação é capaz de iluminá-lo.

É somente em sentido extremamente qualificado, em questões de inquirição histórica e de pesquisa filosófica ou científica, que a dúvida pode ser chamada de progenitora do conhecimento, de acordo com o princípio exarado por Descartes: *'De omnibus dubitandum est'* (O princípio do conhecimento através da dúvida): Duvidar de tudo quanto é possível, a fim de que surja a verdade impossível de ser posta em dúvida. Essas verdades puras eram, para ele, Deus, a alma e alguma coisa sobre a verdadeira natureza do mundo. Em contraste com isso, disse Agostinho: *'Creio a fim de compreender'*, pensando ele que o espírito do ceticismo deixa o indivíduo *nas trevas* e que ali dificilmente se pode descobrir o verdadeiro conhecimento, a menos que Deus simplesmente outorgue tais coisas ao homem, através de sua pura graça, a fim de cumprir algum desígnio nessa vida e através dela.

VI. A Utilidade do Ceticismo

1. *Na Ciência*, o ceticismo é uma necessidade. O cientista só pode aceitar aquelas coisas que são baseadas em uma experimentação ampla e evidente. Sem isto não existe uma ciência física.

2. O ceticismo é uma *verdade básica* em relação ao conhecimento humano, em todos os campos, no sentido de que todo o nosso conhecimento é *parcial*. O reconhecimento deste fato nos ajuda a respeitar as idéias dos outros, e desenvolver uma atitude de tolerância. A tolerância desfaz a hostilidade e batalha contra o orgulho.

3. O ceticismo, mesmo na teologia, é uma *atitude útil*, se não se torna negativa e hostil. Devemos testar as nossas idéias, comparando-as com outras, e exigindo evidências. Não podemos aceitar idéias sem a devida investigação e comparação. O misticismo também erra, embora seja a base da crença religiosa, e deve ser controlado e examinado pela razão e pela experiência científica e prática.

CETRO

No hebraico temos duas palavras, e no grego, uma. As palavras hebraicas são *shebet*, «vara», «cetro», que

706

CETRO — CÉU

aparece por cento e noventa vezes, a grande maioria das quais com o sentido de «tribo», mas por dez vezes com o sentido claro de «cetro»: Gên. 49:10; Núm. 24:17; Sal. 45:6; Isa. 14:5; Eze. 19:11,14; Amós 1:5 e Zac. 10:11. E também *sharebit*, «cetro», palavra que figura por quatro vezes, no livro de Ester (4:11; 5:2 e 8:4). No grego temos a palavra *rábdos*, «cetro», que é usada por onze vezes no Novo Testamento: Mat. 10:10; Mar. 6:8; Luc. 9:3; I Crô. 4:21; Heb. 1:8; 9:4; 11:21; Apo. 2:27; 11:1; 12:5 e 19:15. Há uma outra palavra que algumas versões têm traduzido também como «cetro», no hebraico, *matteh*, também muito usada no Antigo Testamento, duzentas e quarenta e sete vezes, principalmente com o sentido de «tribo», mas que, em Eze. 19:11, acompanhada pela palavra que significa *força*, segundo pensam alguns estudiosos, adquire também o sentido de cetro.

Na verdade, «cetro» é um uso especializado dos termos hebraicos, pois, seu sentido comum é «vara», «bastão». Assim, elas podem indicar a «vara de correção», de ocorrência comum no livro de Provérbios, o «cacete de um pastor», em Sal. 23:4, ou mesmo um «cacete com pontas de ferro» (Sal. 2:9; Apo. 2:27; 12:5; 19:15), ou até mesmo uma vara de malhar cereais, em Isa. 28:27.

Em sentido simbólico, temos ainda a palavra hebraica *mehogeg*, usada poeticamente para indicar um «cetro», em Gên. 49:10; Núm. 21:18; Sal. 60:7 e 108:8.

Usualmente eram os reis que usavam cetros, embora oficiais menores, algumas vezes, brandissem também um cetro, como emblema de seu ofício. No Antigo Testamento há alusão aos cetros dos governantes de Israel, Moabe, Egito, Damasco, Asquelom e Judá (ver Sal. 60:7; 108:8; Jer. 48:17; Eze. 19:11; Amós 1:5,8; Zac. 10:11).

Há duas passagens geralmente consideradas messiânicas, que associam um cetro a futuros governantes de Israel, a saber: Gên. 49:10 e Núm. 24:17. Os soldados romanos que zombaram de Jesus tinham um cetro real em mente, quando puseram nas mãos de Jesus um «caniço», com o qual também davam-lhe na cabeça (Mar. 15:16-20).

Vários trechos do livro de Ester exibem um uso especial do cetro, por parte dos reis persas (Est. 4:11; 5:2 e 8:4). O cetro de Assuero é descrito como feito de ouro, ou seja, ou de ouro puro, ou então adornado com ouro, como os cetros dos reis homéricos. As gravuras que representam os reis orientais mostram-nos brandindo duas espécies de cetro. Um deles é longo, fino e muito ornamentado; o outro é curto, mais parecendo um bastão pequeno. O primeiro tipo aparece em um relevo em pedra calcária, representando Dario. Ele segura na mão um cetro, quase no alto do mesmo, ao passo que sua extremidade inferior toca no solo. O tipo curto aparece em um relevo de Esar-Hadom.

CÉU

Esboço:
1. Palavras Originais Envolvidas
2. Os Céus Materiais
3. Os Céus Não-Materiais
4. A Pluralidade dos Céus
5. Os Céus em Dois Níveis
6. Relação Entre Cristo e os Céus
7. Os Lugares Celestiais de Paulo
8. O Destino Final do Homem nos Céus.

1. Palavras Originais Envolvidas

Há uma palavra hebraica e uma palavra grega envolvidas neste verbete:

a. **Shamayim** ou *shemayin*, «coisas erguidas», «expansão». A primeira forma é hebraica e a segunda aramaica. A primeira forma aparece por quatrocentas e dezenove vezes. A segunda forma, por trinta e oito vezes. Portanto, trata-se de uma palavra de ocorrência freqüente. *Shamayim* aparece em trinta e um livros do Antigo Testamento; *shemayin* ocorre em Esdras e Daniel.

b. *Ouranós*, «céu». Termo grego que ocorre por quase duzentas e oitenta vezes, desde Mat. 3:2 até Apo. 21:10.

Há também a expressão grega *tà epouránia*, «coisas celestes», que é usada por seis vezes: João 3:12; Efé. 1:3; 2:6; 3:10; Heb. 8:5 e 9:23.

2. Os Céus Materiais

Tanto o termo hebraico quanto o termo grego podem indicar o mundo espiritual, onde residem os espíritos não-materiais, como aquilo que, em português, convencionou-se chamar de «firmamento», os céus visíveis, que inclui a nossa atmosfera terrestre e o céu estelado, a imensa expansão do universo. Os antigos eram muito ignorantes sobre as questões atinentes à *astronomia* (que vide). Isso significa que deles obtemos idéias bastante cruas, quando eles usavam a palavra traduzida por «céu» ou «céus», em português. Usualmente essa palavra aparece no plural, tanto no Antigo quanto no Novo Testamentos. Há muitas referências literárias, dos hebreus e dos cristãos antigos, que mostram que eles acreditavam na pluralidade dos céus, ou mansões celestes. Portanto, erram aqueles que dizem que não há nenhuma diferença de sentido entre essa palavra no singular e no plural.

Visto que o termo hebraico *shamayim* significa «coisas erguidas», esse vocábulo pode referir-se aos corpos celestes, aos luzeiros do céu ou ao firmamento. Os antigos pensavam que esse firmamento seria uma espécie de abóbada, que formaria um semicírculo por cima da terra, feito de material sólido, que se apoiaria sobre montanhas existentes nas extremidades da terra. O firmamento separaria o lugar onde residem Deus e os espíritos, da terra. Por sua vez, a terra estaria sustentada sobre colunas, e todo esse conjunto sobre um abismo de águas. Não se dizia, porém, onde repousavam essas águas (II Sam. 22:8; Jó 26:11). No artigo sobre a *Astronomia*, provi uma ilustração dessa cosmogonia dos hebreus, juntamente com referências bíblicas apropriadas. Também no artigo intitulado *Cosmogonia*, expomos as crenças dos hebreus e de outros povos antigos sobre essas questões. Os grandes luzeiros, como o sol, a lua e as estrelas, seriam relativamente pequenos, fixados à concavidade inferior do firmamento. Não havia conceito de distâncias e dimensões.

Também havia o *céu* simples, a expansão do espaço que era chamado firmamento ou céu atmosférico. Nesse céu estariam as nuvens, a chuva e as condições atmosféricas em geral (Sal. 146:8; Zac. 2:6; 6:5; Isa. 55:9-11). Acreditava-se que as águas existentes acima do firmamento derramavam-se através de janelas ou comportas. Essa abóbada material separaria as águas da parte de cima do firmamento das águas da parte de baixo do firmamento. Isso explica a expressão «as portas do céu» (Sal. 78:23; Gên. 28:17). É errado e desonesto fazer os antigos hebreus terem grandes conhecimentos meteorológicos e astronômicos, dizendo que os trechos bíblicos que exprimem idéias assim obsoletas são expressões meramente poéticas. Assim, quando lemos que Deus fez cair «do céu» grandes pedras (Jos. 10:11), provavelmente há uma alusão a

CÉU

um fenômeno de saraiva, juntamente com a idéia de que Deus controlava as condições atmosféricas. A angelologia dos hebreus retratava os anjos envolvidos em várias tarefas que diziam respeito à produção e controle das condições atmosféricas.

Os céus estelados. Não devemos supor que os hebreus pensassem que o sol, a lua e as estrelas, etc., estavam a tão grandes distâncias, conforme hoje sabemos. Por conseguinte, o céu das estrelas não estaria muito distante das nuvens e da atmosfera terrestre. Quando lemos que Deus pôs luzeiros no firmamento (Gên. 1:14), encontramos a noção de que os luzeiros foram preparados especificamente para iluminar a face da terra, e fica entendido que seriam de dimensões modestas. Os hebreus não tinham nenhum conceito sobre galáxias e sistemas solares. Portanto, não devemos extrapolar para a Bíblia as nossas noções astronômicas. Os céus estelados, na concepção dos hebreus, não estariam muito acima das nuvens.

3. Os Céus Não-Materiais

Aqui temos o lugar onde Deus reside, juntamente com os seres angelicais. A teologia judaica posterior era bastante coerente, ao pensar que havia uma pluralidade de céus, e que estes seriam em número de sete. Deus é o Deus dos céus (Jonas 1:9). Ali pulula um grande exército de seres espirituais (Nee. 9:6). Deus habita no mais alto e santo céu (Isa. 57:15). Segundo o mais antigo pensamento dos hebreus, esse céu habitava na luz primeva, algo distinto da luz produzida pelo sol. Por essa razão a luz já havia, na narrativa da criação da luz, antes mesmo da criação ou aparecimento do sol. Na concepção dos antigos hebreus, esse firmamento ocultaria essa luz dos olhos humanos. Mas alguns deles supunham que as estrelas seriam perfurações pelas quais resplandeceria a luminosidade do céu por cima da abóbada, ou firmamento.

4. A Pluralidade dos Céus

Os rabinos tinham como doutrina padrão o ensino de que há 7 céus. Para eles, a glorificação consiste em passar de um nível de ser para o próximo, cada nível com seu grau de transformação. Chegar à forma de vida dos anjos era considerado por eles como o clímax desse processo. Entretanto, o Novo Testamento ensina que o alvo é a participação na natureza divina, e não apenas na natureza angelical (II Ped. 1:4). Algumas indicações neotestamentárias da pluralidade dos céus são as seguintes: a. Quase sempre a palavra aparece no plural, «céus». b. Há o paraíso, ou céu inferior (Luc. 23:43), que os rabinos não concebiam como a habitação de Deus, e, sim, quando muito, a habitação de espíritos justos, no mundo intermediário. c. Jesus referiu-se a «muitas moradas», em associação às dimensões espirituais, como um lugar (aparentemente além ou inserido em) a ser preparado para os seus discípulos (João 14:2 ss). d. Além disso, haveria o *terceiro* céu, mencionado por Paulo, um elevado lugar, mas ainda não a habitação de Deus (II Cor. 12:4). e. O trecho de Hebreus 4:14 afiança que Jesus atravessou os «céus», a caminho de Deus Pai. f. Além disso, os diversos compartimentos do templo de Jerusalém seriam um retrato simbólico das divisões dos lugares celestiais, simbolizando um acesso gradual e crescente a Deus, e terminando no Santo dos Santos, o próprio lugar da habitação de Deus. O tratado aos Hebreus apresenta esses tipos de noções, no tocante ao templo e ao acesso que Jesus obteve para nós. Ver Heb. 4:14; 9:23 ss. g. Os lugares celestiais de Paulo. Não somente Paulo, mas também João e o autor da epístola aos Hebreus empregaram a expressão grega *tà epouránia*, «os lugares celestiais».

Há certas nuanças de significado, dependendo dos respectivos contextos. Na epístola aos Efésios denota a esfera dos nossos privilégios espirituais em Cristo, salvo em Efé. 6:2, onde representa o mundo espiritual invisível, onde operam tanto forças boas quanto forças más. Sempre indica a esfera que transcende ao que é terreno. Porém, em I João 3:12, os lugares celestiais são postos em contraste com as «coisas terrenas», ou seja, aquelas coisas que podem ser submetidas ao teste das experiências humanas. Na epístola aos Hebreus, como já pudemos dizer, as *cousas celestes* são os arquétipos dos quais as coisas terrestres são apenas as sombras.

5. Os Céus em Dois Níveis

Na epístola aos Hebreus temos uma perspectiva da existência em dois níveis, segundo o modelo de Platão e Filo, segundo o qual as coisas neste mundo (os particulares) são moldadas de acordo com os arquétipos, ou seja, coisas existentes nos céus (os universais). Quanto a comentários completos sobre esse conceito, ver as notas expositivas no NTI, em Heb. 9:23. Isso significa que os particulares são cópias ou imitações das realidades celestiais. Hebreus 8:5 também exprime esse conceito.

6. Relação Entre Cristo e os Céus

As Escrituras dizem que Cristo já havia habitado nessa esfera espiritual. Platão pensava que isso ocorreu no caso de todos os homens, porquanto, para ele, as almas eram preexistentes, – tendo caído de um estado primevo de utopia. Os rabinos apegaram-se a essa doutrina, ou então, chegaram independentemente à noção de que as almas já tinham tido uma vida espiritual nos lugares celestiais. O Novo Testamento, porém, faz silêncio sobre o ponto, porquanto não ensina qualquer teoria especial acerca da origem da alma. No entanto, no que concerne a Cristo, o Filho de Deus, o Logos, o ensino é claro. Antes de sua encarnação, Jesus sempre estivera nos céus (João 1:1 ss; 17:5; Fil. 2:5 ss). Jesus Cristo desceu da glória celeste e identificou-se com os homens, de tal modo que, nele, agora os homens possam ascender ao céu, juntamente com ele. A doutrina do arrebatamento é um ensino que fala em ascensão, visto que será por meio do arrebatamento que os homens participarão do evento. Naturalmente, antes disso, os remidos participarão da morte e da ressurreição de Cristo (Rom. 3:25,26; 4:24,25). A descida de Cristo ao hades mostra-nos que a missão de Cristo foi universal, suficientemente ampla para atingir todas as almas de todas as esferas, e não apenas aquelas que estivessem na esfera terrestre. O trecho de Efésios 3:8 ss, mostra-nos que a descida de Cristo ao hades teve o mesmo propósito de sua ascensão, ou seja, a fim de que ele viesse a tornar-se tudo para todos. E a passagem de Efésios 1:10 ensina-nos qual a extensão da missão universal de Cristo. Ver o artigo sobre a *Restauração*.

7. Os Lugares Celestiais de Paulo

Em seus escritos, Paulo reteve a idéia da pluralidade dos céus. A antiga cosmologia judaica não encontra lugar em seus escritos, e ele lança-se, nessa discussão sobre os lugares celestiais, a uma teologia bem mais sofisticada. Ele refere-se aos «lugares celestiais» que são o lar das almas. Essa expressão paulina aparece somente na epístola aos Efésios (ver Efé. 1:3,20; 2:6 e 3:10). Nessa mesma epístola, lemos que é o ministério total de Cristo que garante que os demais filhos de Deus compartilham desse elevadíssimo destino. Eles recebem tal privilégio mediante a bênção geral de Deus em Cristo (Efé. 1:3), com base na eleição divina (Efé. 1:4). Eles recebem total identificação com o Filho amado do Pai (Efé. 1:6), mediante o seu sangue e a sua expiação (Efé. 1:7). O próprio Cristo chegou àquela posição por haver completado com êxito a sua missão terrena (Efé. 1:20). Fomos espiritualmente ressuscitados com ele (Efé. 2:6) e chegando em sua presença, haveremos de compartilhar de suas incomensuráveis riquezas (Efé. 2:7). Portanto, a descida de Cristo ao hades e a sua ascensão ao mais alto céu garantem o sucesso do plano divino eterno (Efé. 4:8 ss).

8. O destino Final do Homem nos Céus

O céu é um lugar lindíssimo. O último capítulo do Apocalipse revela-nos que ali não haverá qualquer coisa prejudicial, não haverá lágrimas, nem tristeza, nem enfermidade e nem morte. O céu é a verdadeira utopia, real por ser criação de Deus. Porém, o céu é muito mais do que isso. De um ponto de vista mais elevado, o céu é sinônimo de *salvação* (que vide). Indica a participação na natureza divina, quando nos tornaremos autênticos filhos do Pai celeste, no mais alto sentido da palavra, bem como nos tornaremos irmãos de nosso querido Irmão Mais Velho. (Ver II Ped. 1:4). Todavia, isso não se concretizará em um único lance. Bem pelo contrário, será um processo eterno, que nos irá conduzindo de um nível de glória para o próximo, mediante o poder do Espírito (II Cor. 3:18). O céu consiste mais no que acontecerá conosco ali, do que um lugar onde habitaremos. É a mais elevada realização espiritual de Deus relativa aos remidos. Cada remido será um filho de Deus, conduzido à glória celestial (Heb. 2:10). (E NTI UN)

CÉU (Firmamento)

Uma palavra hebraica e uma palavra grega são traduzidas por «céu», com o sentido de «firmamento», ou seja, nosso céu de estrelas:

1. *Shachaq*, «nuvem tênue». Essa palavra hebraica ocorre por vinte e uma vezes (por exemplo: Deu. 33:26; II Sam. 22:12; Jó 37:18; Sal. 18:11; 77:17; Isa. 45:8; Jer. 51:9).

2. *Ouranós*, «céu». Palavra grega que ocorre por cerca de duzentas e oitenta vezes, principalmente nos evangelhos sinópticos e no livro de Apocalipse, começando em Mat. 3:2 e terminando em Apo. 21:10.

Por extensão, no Antigo Testamento, essa palavra hebraica é comumente usada com o sentido de «nuvem» (ver, para exemplificar, Deu. 33:26). Em português, tal como em grego, «céu» tanto é o lugar onde Deus habita como é a expansão celeste que abriga os corpos celestiais. O contexto de cada passagem envolvida é que decide que tipo de «céu» está em pauta.

CÉU (TERCEIRO)

Ver o artigo sobre o **Terceiro Céu**.

CÉUS NOVOS, TERRA NOVA

Ver **Nova Criação**.

CEVA

No grego, **Skeuas**. Talvez a palavra grega derive-se de *skeuos*, «utensílio». No Novo Testamento, é nome de um «sumo sacerdote» judeu que vivia em Éfeso (Atos 19:14-17). Incapaz de atuar como tal nas sinagogas de Éfeso e da Ásia Menor, ou ele exercia seu ofício em Jerusalém, ou era membro de alguma família sumo sacerdotal, ou então fora o chefe de uma das vinte e quatro turmas de sacerdotes, por causa do que continuava sendo honrado com aquele título.

Seus sete filhos percorriam muitos lugares, procurando exorcizar demônios, usando o nome de Jesus. Mas, de certa feita, um demônio negou-se a atendê-los, com a seguinte resposta: «Conheço a Jesus e sei quem é Paulo; mas vós, quem sois?» (Atos 19:15). Faltando-lhes a autoridade espiritual de Jesus ou de Paulo, os sete filhos de Ceva foram atacados pelo endemoninhado, e tiveram de fugir «desnudos e feridos». O incidente foi largamente noticiado, com o resultado que sobreveio grande reverência e temor acerca do nome do Senhor Jesus entre todos os habitantes de Éfeso. Também houve um reavivamento e uma renovação na igreja cristã. Muitos crentes confessaram que não haviam desistido de suas práticas fetichistas e ocultistas, e voluntariamente entregaram seus livros mágicos, os quais foram queimados publicamente. Desse modo, foi singularmente demonstrado o poder do evangelho, e a palavra do Senhor prevaleceu contra todas as forças malignas rivais.

CEVADA

No hebraico é uma palavra que significa «cabelos longos», e no grego é *krithé*, «pontudo». Há trinta e seis referências a esse cereal na Bíblia, das quais três no Novo Testamento (João 6:9,13 e Apo. 6:6). Era um dos principais cereais consumidos na Palestina, sendo usado como alimento dos animais, por ser o mais barato. Mas os pobres também consumiam a cevada. Era cultivada no Egito (ver Êxo. 9:31) e na Palestina (Lev. 27:16; Deu. 8:8; Rute 2:17). É mencionada na Mishnah (Pseach. fol. 3) como forragem de cavalos e asnos. Preparava-se pão de cevada para os pobres (ver Juí. 7:13 e João 6:9,13). Usualmente era plantada durante as chuvas de outono, isto é, outubro e novembro. A primeira colheita da cevada era feita na época da páscoa, no mês hebraico de abibe, isto é, março/abril. A espécie silvestre, *Hordeum spontaneum*, até hoje é comum na Palestina. Há diversas variedades cultivadas. Os pães entregues a Jesus, segundo se vê em João 6:9, eram de cevada. Eliseu esclareceu que o preço da farinha de cevada era a metade do preço da farinha de trigo (ver II Reis 7:1). A cevada era colhida trinta dias ou mais antes da colheita do trigo. Isso explica o fato de que a cevada e o linho foram feridos, ao passo que o trigo e o centeio não, quando da sétima praga, a chuva de pedras, no Egito (ver Êxo. 9:31).

Colheita da cevada. Essa era uma das mais importantes colheitas de cereais que havia na Palestina, principalmente porque a cevada era tão útil como forragem para os animais. Nas terras baixas próximas de Jericó, essa colheita começava em abril, segundo se vê em Jos. 3:16. Na região montanhosa, a colheita da cevada só ocorria em maio, ou mesmo no começo de junho. As primícias da cevada eram trazidas como oferta ao Senhor (ver Lev. 23:10).

Uso Metafórico. 1. Em Juízes 7:13, simboliza a nação de Israel reformada. 2. O pão a ser lançado sobre as águas, em Eclesiastes 7:13, era feito de cevada, onde também se promete bom retorno pela generosidade no investimento. 3. A cevada também simbolizava algo de pouco valor, pelo que era associado ao preço de uma meretriz, além de servir de oferenda oferecida pelos pobres (ver Osé. 3:2 e Núm. 5:15). 4. Os árabes chamam os judeus, nestes dias modernos, de «bolos de cevada», em tom pejorativo. Os verdadeiros seguidores de Maomé, em contraste, são chamados de «trigo». Os midianitas, em Juízes 7:13, aparentemente chamavam os judeus de «pães de cevada». (ID S Z)

CHÂLON SUR-SAONE, CONCÍLIOS DE

Os concílios nesse lugar ocorreram nos anos de 603, 649, 813, 1062 e 1129. O concílio de 649 reafirmou as decisões dos concílios de Nicéia e Calcedônia. O concílio de 813 foi importante por haver adotado sessenta e seis cânones sobre o discipulado do clero e do corpo laico, sobre o ensino, a pregação, a ordenação de sacerdotes, a confissão, a penitência, as orações em favor dos mortos, as peregrinações, etc. Châlon Sur-Saone é uma cidade no nordeste da França acerca de cento e cinqüenta quilômetros a nordeste de Paris. A soberba catedral de Santo Etienne, construída no século XIII, é uma das principais obras arquiteturais da cidade. Outro notável templo católico ali existente é o de Notre-Dame-en-Vaux, que tem quatro torres e vitrais coloridos de excepcional qualidade. (AM E)

CHAMADA

No hebraico, *qara*, «chamar», «nomear». Palavra usada por mais de setecentas e vinte vezes, desde Gên. 1:4 até Mal. 1:4. No grego, *kaléo*, «chamar», «nomear», palavra usada de Mat. 1:21 até Apo. 19:13.
Consideremos os três pontos abaixo, que nos ajudam no que precisamos saber a respeito:

1. Vários Usos Bíblicos:

a. Dar nome a uma pessoa ou a uma coisa; ser chamado por um nome, como os israelitas e suas respectivas tribos (Gên. 48:16). Além disso, há pessoas chamadas pelo nome de Deus, tanto no Antigo como no Novo Testamento, como Israel, que foi chamado filho de Deus (Isa. 52:2; Osé. 11:1), ou como os crentes, que são chamados cristãos, entre outros nomes (Atos 11:26). Ver também Tia. 2:7:

b. O ato de convidar ou solicitar (Êxo. 2:7).

c. Nomear para algum ofício (Êxo. 31:2).

d. Criar, produzir coisas mediante o poder da palavra, ou por um ato da vontade (Rom. 4:17; Eze. 36:29).

e. Convidar alguém a assumir um dever, mediante a palavra, ou através do poder impulsionador do Espírito Santo (Isa. 22:12; Pro. 1:24; Mat. 22:14).

f. *O convite feito aos pecadores* para o estado de graça, por meio da pregação do evangelho. Essa chamada harmoniza-se com o propósito divino no tocante a cada pessoa (Rom. 8:28; II Tim. 1:9). Isso conduz os homens à mais elevada glória e felicidade (Fil. 3:14), mas essa chamada não é atendida por muitos dos sábios e poderosos (I Cor. 1:26,27). Trata-se de uma chamada santa e gloriosa (II Ped. 1:3). É uma chamada celestial (Heb. 3:1). É uma chamada determinada e mantida pela vontade divina (Rom. 8:29). É universal (João 3:16; Apo. 22:7; I Tim. 2:4). Tem resultados universais (João 12:32; Efé. 1:10), nos que se salvam ou nos que se perdem (II Cor. 2:14,15).

g. Proclamar (Joel 1:3). Apelar solenemente a Deus, convocando-o para que faça o registro da alma de alguém (II Cor. 1:23). Invocar a Deus equivale a adorá-lo, particularmente no caso das orações (I Ped. 1:17).

2. Na Teologia Paulina:

Desenvolvendo algumas das idéias citadas acima, vemos que, nas epístolas de Paulo, a *chamada* quase sempre denota o decreto de Deus Pai concernente à salvação dos homens, e isso se torna eficaz mediante as operações regeneradoras e transformadoras do Espírito Santo. Essa chamada produz a reação da fé (Rom. 8:30; I Cor. 1:9; Gál. 1:15; II Tes. 2:13 *ss*; II Tim. 1:9; Heb. 9:15; I Ped. 2:9). Os teólogos falam sobre a *chamada eficaz* que ocorre por meio da pregação do evangelho. (Ver Rom. 8:28-30; 9:23-26). O nono capítulo da epístola aos Romanos realmente limita essa chamada aos eleitos, de onde os calvinistas obtêm força, em seus argumentos. Mas Paulo, no décimo capítulo dessa mesma epístola, e daí por diante, mostra que não há limite para a questão, o que concorda com a universalidade do amor de Deus. Ver sobre o *Determinismo* e o *Livre-Arbítrio*, quanto a uma discussão sobre os problemas criados e sobre o exame em separado de cada um dos lados da questão.

3. A Chamada ao Serviço. Deus às vezes chama alguém para algum serviço ou ofício especial, como no caso do apostolado (Rom. 1:1), da pregação missionária (Atos 13:2; 16:10), do sacerdócio (Heb. 5:4), ou de alguma outra ocupação específica, mediante o que certos indivíduos terão de expressar-se e desenvolver-se espiritualmente (I Cor. 7:20). O trecho de Apo. 2:17, com sua doutrina do *novo nome*, mostra-nos que cada indivíduo é sui-generis e está encarregado de missões distintivas, tanto agora quanto na eternidade. Ver esse ensino sob o título *O Novo Nome*. (B K NTI)

CHAMADOS MUITOS, ESCOLHIDOS POUCOS

Mateus 22:14: *Porque muitos são chamados, mas poucos escolhidos*.

É evidente que Jesus repetiu certas declarações ou ensinos, algumas vezes com um sentido e de outras vezes com outro sentido ou conexão, conforme qualquer mestre pode fazer. Esta é uma dessas declarações. Aqui vemos uma *distinção* entre grupos que realmente tinham ouvido e aceito o convite. Os escolhidos, neste caso, são aqueles destacados dentre o grupo dos «chamados». Essa declaração realmente expressa a intenção geral da parábola, ou das duas parábolas construídas de modo a parecerem uma só. Do princípio ao fim, o convite foi feito para muitos. A maioria rejeitara totalmente esse convite, e esse grupo, naturalmente, estaria entre os «chamados, mas não escolhidos». Todavia, dentro do grupo que correspondera afirmativamente ao convite, havia aqueles que, embora chamados, contudo, não eram escolhidos. Tinham chegado ao salão do banquete, externamente haviam obedecido à convocação para a festa de casamento, mas tinham suas próprias opiniões acerca da necessidade e do valor de alguma forma especial de *vestes nupciais* isto é, de «riquezas espirituais». Tinham tudo quanto pensavam que era mister, e a despeito das claras indicações das exigências requeridas para quem quisesse estar presente ao banquete, exigências essas determinadas pelo próprio grande rei, possuíam suas opiniões pessoais e não se prepararam convenientemente. Por esse motivo é que houve outra seleção, feita pelo rei em pessoa, o qual passou em revista os convivas. Entre os «chamados» foram encontrados aqueles que realmente não eram convidados dignos de estarem no salão de banquete, e esses foram duramente tratados, sendo expulsos. Ao empregar a palavra «escolhidos», portanto, Jesus quis indicar aqueles que realmente possuíam a «justiça», identificada pelas «vestes nupciais». Esses eram os que tinham feito uma inquirição espiritual genuína e sincera.

Talvez tenhamos neste vs. uma alusão ao costume dos romanos, ao formarem suas milícias. Todos os cidadãos eram convocados, mas somente os que estivessem realmente *aptos* eram finalmente escolhidos para desempenharem qualquer serviço real em prol da nação. «Chamados» e «escolhidos», portanto, neste caso não implica em mera diferença, mas indica uma *antítese* verdadeira. Segundo os ensinamentos de Jesus, como também acontecia com os escritos rabínicos, sempre se verifica uma rigorosa separação entre os dignos e os indignos. Alguns intérpretes encontram aqui uma idéia calvinista extremada, como se se tratasse da eleição externa e da *reprovação*; mas isso é exagerar o significado das palavras de Jesus. A idéia de «eleição» não tem alicerces dogmáticos. Quanto a essa questão, o leitor deveria ler as notas em Rom. 9:15,16 e Efé. 1:3-5 no NTI. Aqui temos antes o julgamento definido dos convidados por parte do rei, julgamento esse baseado no modo como os homens acolheram o convite, sem nada ficar subentendido acerca das ações dos indivíduos a quem foi lançado o convite. Deve-se notar, entretanto, que fica demonstrada aqui importantíssima questão doutrinária, e que a autoridade teocrática de Cristo é proclamada, bem como sua especialíssima relação para com Deus, por ser ele o filho do rei, e em face do fato de que a festa das bodas foi, ao mesmo tempo, o recebimento da noiva e a coroação do filho do rei. O autor do evangelho de Mateus, pois, ensinou que a antiga autoridade investida em Israel fora passada para os ombros de Cristo. O sinédrio portanto, tinha apenas uma aparência de autoridade. A grande verdade é que ao tempo da escrita deste evangelho, o sinédrio já havia sido destruído pelo poder romano e, em sentido muito real, a autoridade fora arrancada das mãos do povo de Israel.

— Mateus 22:14 não expressa *pessimismo* indevido; pelo contrário, **mostra a *dura realidade*.** Pouquíssimos judeus corresponderam de bom grado a Jesus e ao seu convite, e o autor deste evangelho escreveu num período quando a igreja estava sendo perseguida tanto pelos romanos como pelos judeus. Nada indicaria que haveria grande quantidade de conversões entre os judeus.

A reversão.
A Descida de Cristo ao Hades (vide) e a Restauração (vide) podem reverter qualquer situação humana.

CHAMINÉ
No trecho de Oséias 13:3 há uma palavra hebraica que também figura por outras oito vezes, *arubbah*, «janela». Essa é a tradução que aparece em nossa versão portuguesa, naquela passagem, como lugar por onde passava a fumaça. Todavia, algumas versões preferem traduzi-la, nesse trecho de Oséias, por «chaminé», embora se saiba que, naquele tempo, ainda não se faziam chaminés nas casas. Todavia, no livro apócrifo de II Esdras 6:4, segundo a Vulgata Latina, temos a palavra *caminos*, que é a raiz latina para chaminé. Ali está em foco uma lareira ou um forno, mas não uma chaminé. Esse é o sentido original da palavra latina.

CHAMPEAUX, GUILHERME DE
Suas datas foram 1070-1120. **Foi um filósofo** escolástico, discípulo de Anselmo. Estudou com Roscelin e foi mestre de Abelardo. Há artigos sobre cada uma dessas personagens. Champeaux foi bispo de Châlon-sur-Marne (que vide), —desde 1113 até o seu falecimento. Foi professor de lógica na Escola Catedral de Paris. Ele fundou a casa e escola de São Vítor, em 1108. Ele defendia a posição do *realismo* *extremo* (que vide), no tocante ao problema dos *universais* (que vide), acompanhando Platão. De acordo com a aplicação feita por Champeaux acerca desse ponto de vista, todas as espécies de uma entidade qualquer têm a mesma natureza essencial, e as diferenças são meros acidentes. Abelardo, porém, criticava essa posição, pensando que a mesma inclina-se para o panteísmo, pois Deus *é* Substância, e, nesse caso, todas as coisas seriam idênticas, participantes da substância de Deus. A fim de anular essa crítica, Champeaux passou a defender uma teoria da *indiferença* dos universais. Em outras palavras, os indivíduos que são membros de uma espécie não são idênticos essencialmente, embora o sejam indiferentemente. Isso significa que as essências dos membros individuais de uma espécie são similares, e que essa similaridade provê a base do nosso conceito de *espécies*. Esse conceito aplica-se, indiferentemente, a todos os membros de uma dada espécie. Sua principal obra literária foi *Sentenças*.

CHAMPLIN, RUSSELL NORMAN
O Dr. Russell Norman Champlin foi o autor do *Novo Testamento Interpretado Versículo por Versículo* e autor principal da presente *Enciclopédia de Bíblia, Teologia e Filosofia*. O seu co-autor é o pastor João Marques Bentes. Detalhados artigos biográficos aparecem sobre ambos na introdução da presente obra, logo após a página dedicatória.

CHANCE
Esboço:
1. Definição
2. Psicológica e Cosmológica
3. Tiquismo Puro
4. A Ciência e o Tiquismo
5. O Tiquismo e a Teologia
6. A Chance e a Ética
7. O Caos e a Chance
8. O Tiquismo e o Problema do Mal
9. O Teísmo e a Chance
10. Avaliação

1. Definição. Chance é uma palavra usada em muitos contextos importantes e de certa variedade de maneiras. A idéia básica do termo é a de que algumas, ou mesmo todas as coisas, acontecem sem predeterminação da natureza, do homem ou de Deus. O conceito pode incluir causas *desconhecidas*, de tal modo que as coisas *parecem* acontecer por puro acaso. Ou então, estariam em operação probabilidades indeterminadas.

2. Psicológica e Cosmológica. Carl Jung (que vide) falava em **coincidências significativas**. Todos nós podemos ver coincidências incomuns. Consideremos o seguinte exemplo. Duas famílias vivem perto uma da outra, em certo estado de nosso país. Os dois pais de família eram bons amigos. Mas eis que uma das famílias muda-se para um outro estado. Três anos depois, a outra família também muda-se para o mesmo estado, mas sem que nenhuma das famílias tivesse conhecimento do fato. No ginásio, dois adolescentes encontram-se e logo se tornam bons amigos. Um dia, a conversa deles gira em torno do fato de que *seus pais* eram bons amigos de alguém, há muitos anos, antes deles terem nascido, em um outro estado, quando viviam no mesmo bairro, perto desse alguém. Eles não o sabiam, mas eram precisamente os filhos daqueles homens que haviam sido bons amigos na outra cidade. Isso seria mera coincidência, ou teria sentido? A opinião de Jung era que as duas ocorrências nada tinham a ver uma com a outra, nem haveria relação de causa entre elas. Não obstante, elas estão relacionadas, e há algum significado em tudo isso. Jung encarava a astrologia como segue. Os planetas não exercem qualquer influência sobre os homens, por causa de qualquer energia ou força que tenham. Mas as posições dos astros podem corresponder a certos eventos da vida humana, mediante algum estranho arranjo de coincidências significativas. Assim, os acontecimentos nas vidas das pessoas e as posições dos astros sucedem conjuntamente, com algum significado, embora não haja qualquer relação direta de causa e efeito. No entanto, alguns têm pensado que aquilo que Jung chamou de coincidências significativas apenas esconde *causas reais*. Mas, visto que essas causas são para nós desconhecidas, falamos em coincidências. Esse estranho sincronismo na realidade é alguma espécie de misteriosa situação de causa e efeito.

3. Tiquismo Puro. A palavra grega que significa «chance» é *tuché*, de cujo termo Charles Peirce (que vide), cunhou a palavra *tiquismo*. A palavra indica a chance dos eventos imprevisíveis. O tiquismo puro é a noção de que coisa alguma é determinada e acontece devido a alguma causa; antes, os eventos ocorreriam inteiramente ao acaso. Ora, a ciência, a filosofia e a experiência humana contradizem essa noção, embora seja quase certo que certos eventos sejam caóticos, sem qualquer causa significativa perceptível. William James (que vide) falava sobre a chance como a negação da necessidade. É mister supor que *alguns* eventos são desnecessários, mesmo que a vida humana, de modo geral, tenha um propósito por detrás da mesma. Alguns filósofos têm defendido a idéia do tiquismo puro, como Epicuro (que vide), e também Lucrécio (que vide). Usualmente isso é feito em conexão com o problema do mal e das dificuldades criadas por esse problema.

4. A Ciência e o Tiquismo. Deus predetermina todos os acontecimentos, tanto os bons quanto os maus, bem como os destinos de todos os homens, incluindo a redenção ou a perdição deles? Os calvinistas radicais respondem com um «sim». Os calvinistas moderados respondem com um «sim» e com um «não», explicando que Deus preordenou ativamente a eleição, mas permitiu que o pecador caísse na conseqüência natural de seus pecados. A teologia arminiana, por sua vez, supõe que a eleição também é causa, não por Deus, mas pela escolha humana. Ver sobre a *Predestinação* e sobre o *Determinismo versus Livre-Arbítrio* quanto a uma completa discussão sobre esses problemas. A teologia dos hebreus mostrava-se fraca no que concerne a segundas causas, tendendo por fazer Deus estar diretamente envolvido como causa de tudo; e esse é também o erro do calvinismo extremado. Isso faz Deus ser a causa do mal, o que não é um conceito teologicamente aceitável. O ocasionalismo filosófico (que vide) também faz Deus ser a única causa, o que redunda em certos resultados absurdos, no tocante ao *problema corpo-mente* (vide). — O livre-arbítrio ao menos pressupõe a existência de alguns eventos sem causa, de tal modo que o homem torna-se livre para manipular a sua própria vida e destino, dentro das regras estabelecidas por Deus, naturalmente.

5. O Tiquismo e a Teologia. Deus determina de antemão todos os antecimentos, bons e maus? Deus determina os destinos de todos os homens, para a redenção ou para a destruição? O Calvinismo radical (que vide) afirma que *sim*. Os calvinistas moderados dizem *sim* e *não*. Eles afirmam que os eleitos são predestinados para a vida eterna, mas os incrédulos simplesmente são ultrapassados e deixados a sofrerem as conseqüências normais de seus erros. O Arminianismo (que vide) ensina que é o homem que determina o seu destino e não Deus, porque faz parte do plano divino que as coisas aconteçam assim. Ver os artigos, *Determinismo* e *Livre-arbítrio* para discussões completas sobre estes problemas. A teologia judaica foi fraca em relação às causas secundárias, e por isso, alguns de seus teólogos atribuíram todos os acontecimentos a Deus, achando ser ele a única causa. O erro do Calvinismo radical foi de seguir esta fraqueza judaica. Realmente, nisto temos mais do que uma fraqueza; temos uma blasfêmia que faz de Deus a causa do mal. *Ocasionalismo* (que vide) na filosofia, também faz de Deus a única causa, com certos resultados absurdos em relação ao problema corpomente (que vide). O livre-arbítrio, como teoria, declara que pelo menos alguns acontecimentos são sem causa (tiquismo), e sempre supõe que o homem é também uma causa de acontecimentos. Existem causas secundárias. O homem é livre para manipular. De fato, o homem é um ser criador, retendo esta característica como a imagen de Deus. Entretanto, a teologia corretamente rejeita o tiquismo radical. Paulo, em Rom. 8:20, aceita a doutrina da futilidade. O caos existe, portanto, às vezes o tiquismo se expressa. Mas, ele ensinou também que até o caos, pela manipulação de Deus, afinal, será utilizado para convencer os homens a procurá-lo, Rom. 8:22 *ss*, Efé. 1:10. Portanto, o tiquismo existe às vezes, e cria caos, mas sempre na corrida curta. Na corrida longa, Deus vai desfazer os maus resultados do tiquismo.

6. A Chance e a Ética. Se todos os homens fazem exatamente aquilo que Deus preordenou, ou se alguma outra forma de necessidade transforma o homem em um autômato, então deixou de existir a responsabilidade moral. Uma pessoa não pode ser considerada responsável se fizer aquilo que não pode evitar. Algumas pessoas pensam que Deus tem o direito de punir um homem que não exerce controle sobre suas ações e seu destino. Porém, isso apenas cria uma noção de justiça que não apenas é duvidosa, mas é até repugnante. Observemos que o trecho de Romanos 5:7 estabeleceu a diferença entre o homem *justo* e o homem *bom*. O homem justo observa todas as regras religiosas. Ele é devoto e correto mesmo em sua vida privada. Mas o homem bom, além de ter essas qualidades, também mostra-se benevolente, pondo em prática a lei do amor. Uma justiça impessoal, que apenas julga e destrói, dificilmente pode ser a justiça de Deus. A justiça também precisa incluir a bondade, assim exprimindo aquele amor de Deus que abrange a humanidade inteira (João 3:16). Portanto, não se deve falar em uma justiça impessoal, que requeira retribuição ao pé da letra. A mensagem do evangelho é precisamente a de que a justiça de Deus não opera com essa inflexibilidade, porquanto é temperada por sua misericórdia e graça. Ora, se Deus requer que um homem seja bom, e não meramente justo, poderia ele mesmo ser menos do que isso? Por conseguinte, o homem é dotado de livre-arbítrio, e é responsável. Isso não significa, entretanto, que não existam forças limitadoras, ou que sua vida não tenha qualquer desígnio. Mas significa que, dentro dos limites estabelecidos por Deus, o homem tem a liberdade de agir.

7. O Caos e a Chance. A passagem de Romanos 8:20 fala a respeito da **futilidade**. É quase certo que alguns eventos ocorrem absolutamente sem qualquer causa, e que alguns desses eventos criam tragédias.

Em vista disso, os homens podem chegar a sentir a futilidade da vida. Paulo também supunha que esses acontecimentos fortuitos podem ocorrer. Não obstante, naquele mesmo capítulo, ele afirma que Deus mantém sob seu controle todas as tais ocorrências, e que, finalmente, ele haverá de reverter tudo isso, quando da restauração geral (que vide), bem como através da redenção (que vide), por ele planejadas. Esse oitavo capítulo da epístola aos Romanos também mostra-nos que a futilidade pode ter uma importante função. Pois quando os homens descobrem que sua vida termina na futilidade, se seguirem seus próprios caminhos pecaminosos, — finalmente eles poderão buscar refúgio em Deus, porque esta vida fútil não é digna de ser vivida.

8. O Tiquismo e o Problema do Mal. Por que motivo os homens sofrem? E por que motivo o homem *bom* também sofre? Por que ocorrem dilúvios, incêndios, desastres, enfermidades, morte? Quando fazemos perguntas assim, estamos adentrando no problema do mal (que vide). Uma das respostas supostamente adequadas a essas perguntas diz que as coisas ocorrem totalmente ao acaso. Isso é tiquismo puro. Uma outra versão dessa resposta é a do *tiquismo controlado*. Apesar de muitas coisas acontecerem por puro acaso, produzindo assim muito sofrimento, em minha espiritualidade criativa posso fazer com que certos acontecimentos tenham um certo propósito. Posso usá-los como degraus para um maior desenvolvimento espiritual. Por si mesmos, esses acontecimentos são fortuitos, mas eu forço sobre os mesmos um certo significado, em minha vida diária.

9. O Teísmo e a Chance. Os teístas supõem que Deus existe, e que Deus continua interessado em sua criação. Por esse motivo, Deus intervém, julga, recompensa e guia. Se for levada a um ponto extremo, essa doutrina transformar-se-á no ensino de que Deus é apenas imanente. Se for inteiramente negada, isso fará Deus tornar-se apenas um Ser transcendental. É então que caímos no *deísmo* (que vide). Os deístas supõem que Deus criou todas as coisas, mas que, ato contínuo, abandonou a sua criação, deixando-a sob o governo das leis naturais. Em conseqüência, Deus não recompensaria e nem castigaria (embora isso seja feito pelas leis naturais). Realmente, precisamos do consolo que o governo de Deus nos proporciona; mas também precisamos da responsabilidade moral decorrente do fato de sermos seres livres.

10. Avaliação. É fato que há coisas que acontecem por puro acaso, e isso inclui mais do que a taxa de probabilidades de coisas triviais, como o jogo. A chance ou sorte pode produzir tragédias, e ninguém está isento delas. A futilidade criada por essa possibilidade direciona as nossas mentes para Deus, como o nosso refúgio. De modo geral, porém, o desígnio controla os acontecimentos deste mundo, mesmo que, na maioria das vezes, não sejamos capazes de percebê-lo. Ver o artigo sobre a *Teleologia*. O homem tem a liberdade de agir, e assim desenvolver a sua espiritualidade e o seu destino. No entanto, ele só é capaz disso dentro dos limites estabelecidos por Deus, ou pela sua própria alma. Alguns eventos de nossas vidas são determinados de modo absoluto, embora não sem propósito e sem desígnio. E os eventos que foram predeterminados, foram de conformidade com um plano benevolente. O homem espiritual e bem desenvolvido, através de sua alma preexistente, determina pessoalmente esses eventos, pois sabe o que precisa enfrentar e experimentar, a fim de poder crescer. A alma pouco desenvolvida sofre sob a imposição de certos eventos necessários, como medidas de aprendizado e de disciplina. Dentro do arcabouço de alguns poucos eventos determinados de antemão, temos absoluta liberdade para agir, para crescer e para nos desenvolvermos. A chance pura é uma realidade, mas uma realidade meramente periférica. As experiências de quase morte (que vide), demonstram que a vida de cada um de nós é governada pelo desígnio divino, e não pelo puro acaso. A filosofia e a teologia sempre nos asseguraram isso. (EP H MM NTI)

CHANG TSAI

Suas datas foram 1020-1077. Foi um filósofo chinês neoconfucionista, nativo de Chang-An, Shense, filho de um magistrado. Formou-se como Erudito Apresentado em 1057 e empregou-se na biblioteca imperial. Ocupou várias posições importantes, mas sua predileção era sobre a filosofia e a religião. Sua busca pessoal pela verdade levou-o do confucionismo, ao budismo, ao taoísmo, e daí de volta ao confucionismo.

Idéias: 1. As forças materiais devem ser identificadas ao grande princípio do *Yin* e do *Yang* (forças positivas e negativas), que são aspectos da força material, com base em oposições, constituindo um dinamismo e um equilíbrio, como os principais fatores da natureza do universo. O desenvolvimento espiritual também acompanharia essas forças positivas e negativas. 2. Chang eliminava as idéias espiritualistas, como seres espirituais ou espíritos dos mortos, como guias de sua filosofia e religião. Além disso, repelia as idéias do aniquilamento budista e da cessação do ser do taoísmo. 3. Em seu livro, *A Inscrição Ocidental*, ele identificou o amor como o maior de todos os princípios éticos, e situou todas as relações humanas dentro do arcabouço cósmico do respeito e da piedade filiais. 4. O seu ideal ético era a *moderação*. O mau resultaria da própria natureza do homem, que, em si mesmo, tem a possibilidade de cair em excessos. Afastar-se da moderação, pois, seria agir com maldade.

Escritos: *A Inscrição Ocidental* e *Corrigindo a Ignorância Juvenil*.

CHANG TUNG-SUN

Nasceu em 1886 e faleceu em 1979. Foi um filósofo chinês, nativo de Chekiang. — Era um autodidata, editor de jornais e revistas, professor universitário em Xangai, Cantão e Pequim. Era líder do Partido do Estado Socialista quando foi aprisionado pelos japoneses, durante a Segunda Guerra Mundial. Terminada a guerra, juntou-se à Liga Democrática Esquerdista e tornou-se membro do Comitê Central do Governo Popular, em Pequim.

Idéias: 1. Ele era um pluralista epistemológico, pois supunha que tanto o mundo que conhecemos como a mente cognoscente são resultados de construção, apesar de que haveria alguns elementos de ordem e conteúdo que não resultariam da construção. 2. A síntese ocorreria continuamente, tanto no nível das sensações quanto no nível da concepção. Ele distinguia quatro categorias dentro desse processo: a. sensação; b. concepção; c. unificação; d. regulamentação, quando as idéias tornam-se categorias universais. 3. Haveria uma progressão natural das sensações para os outros níveis do processo do conhecimento. A percepção levaria a um traço; o traço tornar-se-ia um sinal; e o sinal, transferido para várias coisas, tornar-se-ia um símbolo. Esse símbolo já seria um conceito. Os conceitos envolveriam uma capacidade normalizadora. Essas capacidades criariam tipos epistemológicos. Além disso, haveria grupos de conceitos relacionados entre si, que já formam categorias. 4. Dentro de cada categoria, o indivíduo descobriria que as sensações (percepções dos sentidos) não são o único controle dos nossos conceitos. As necessidades sociais também desempenhariam o seu papel. Assim, Deus, a substância, o absoluto são categorias que provêem à sociedade as suas forças de coesão. Portanto, nossas idéias mais gerais refletem não somente o mundo, mas, igualmente, as necessidades e os conflitos da sociedade em que vivemos.

Escritos: *Pluralismo Epistemológico* e *Conhecimento e Cultura*.

CHANNING, WILLIAM ELLERY

Suas datas foram 1780-1842. Foi um líder religioso norte-americano. Educou-se em Harvard. Era um unitariano (que vide). Ele considerava o calvinismo um sistema imoral, por causa de sua ênfase sobre a ira de Deus, com a negação do amor de Deus pelo mundo inteiro, em qualquer sentido eficaz. Também ensinava que a doutrina da Trindade (que vide) não é bíblica e nem filosófica. Ele tem sido contado entre os transcendentalistas da Nova Inglaterra (que vide). Ver também o artigo sobre *Transcendental*. (AM P)

CHAPÉU

Ver o artigo geral sobre **Vestimentas**.

CHARACTERISTICA UNIVERSALIS

A expressão foi usada por Leibniz para indicar as *verdades da razão*, as quais ele considerava mais básicas ainda do que as verdades de fato, que nos chegam à consciência através da percepção dos sentidos. Ele acreditava no primado da razão. Ver sobre o *Racionalismo*. Todas as verdadeiras proposições são analíticas, e qualquer proposição falsa é uma contradição. Ver sobre *Leibniz*, décimo primeiro ponto.

CHARISMATA

Ver os dois artigos: *Dons Espirituais* e *Movimento Carismático*.

CHARTISMO

Termo usado para descrever o movimento criado por uma petição parlamentar intitulada, em inglês, *Peoples! Charter*. Esse documento foi traçado em 1836, e exigia o sufrágio dos homens, parlamentos anualmente convocados, voto por cédula secreta, abolição de qualificações para se ter o direito a propriedades, e o pagamento aos membros da Casa dos Comuns, da Inglaterra. A petição foi esmagadoramente derrotada na oportunidade; mas, pouco a pouco, todas as suas provisões tornaram-se parte da legislação inglesa. Foi esse o primeiro protesto do proletariado da Revolução Industrial. O movimento chartista também promoveu greves, e, embora alguns de seus membros tivessem sido deportados, isso deu margem ao começo das organizações radicais e progressistas que tão fortemente chegaram a influenciar o desenvolvimento da política britânica, na segunda metade do século XIX. (E)

CHARTRES

Uma notável escola na França, fundada nos fins do século X, por Fulbert (que vide), bispo de Chartres.

Outros líderes dessa escola foram Bernardo de Chartres, falecido em cerca de 1130, seu irmão mais novo Thierry, e Bernardo Silvestris, chanceler de Chartres, em cerca de 1156. E também Guilherme de Conches (que vide), cujas datas foram cerca de 1080-1145, Walter de Mortagne (que vide), bispo de Laon, falecido em 1174; e Gilberto de la Porrée (que vide), bispo de Poitiers e chanceler de Chartres em cerca de 1154. Quanto à teologia, essa escola seguia Boetius, e, quanto à filosofia, Platão. Os tratados lógicos de Aristóteles também eram muito valorizados nessa escola. Essa escola tornou-se conhecida por sua dedicação às ciências naturais. Muito estudo foi dedicado a Hipócrates, a Galeno e aos tratados médicos dos árabes. Uma das características dessa escola era seu grande amor aos clássicos e às obras humanistas do passado. (AM E)

CHARVAKA

Um sistema filosófico indiano do **materialismo** (que vide), derivado do *Rig Veda* (que vide). Teve seu desenvolvimento inicial no escrito não mais existente, *Brhaspati Sutra*. No sânscrito, o princípio materialista é chamado *Lokayata*.

Idéias: 1. Os princípios de todas as coisas podem ser encontrados nos elementos básicos: a terra, o ar, o fogo e a água. 2. Aquilo que não pode ser percebido não existe, pois ser percebido é existir. 3. A inteligência é uma propriedade do corpo físico e de suas manipulações, e não de uma alma imaterial. 4. O propósito do homem, na vida, é encontrar o prazer. Ver sobre o *Hedonismo*. O céu e o inferno são invenções humanas, e são estúpidos e destituídos de significado. 5. A prática da religião é apenas um ganha pão dos religiosos. Os autores dos Vedas foram uns bufões, velhacos e demônios. 6. Os universais são apenas nomes de coisas que vemos e enumeramos. 7. Causa e efeito são apenas imagens da percepção, de uma coisa que antecede a outra. Não há base real para esse conceito. 8. Não podemos afirmar, com absoluta certeza, nem a existência e nem a não-existência. Ver sobre o *Ceticismo*.

CHASIDISMO

Ver sobre o **Assidismo**.

CHAVE (Ver também sobre **Chaves**).

No hebraico, **maphteach**, «abridor». Esse termo figura por três vezes: Juí. 3:25; Isa. 22:22 e I Crô. 9:27 (nesta última referência, o termo é traduzido pelo verbo «abrir»). No grego, *kleís*, vocábulo que aparece por dezesseis vezes: Mat. 6:6; 23:14; 25:10; Luc. 4:25; 11:7; João 20:19,26; Atos 5:23; 21:30; I João 3:17; Apo. 3:7,8; 11:6; 20:3; 21:25. A *chave* movimentava o pino da fechadura ou da trave.

A chave é um instrumento que, na antiguidade, usualmente era feito de madeira, embora também houvesse chaves de metal. Geralmente, as chaves antigas eram volumosas. Com freqüência era levada ao ombro, como símbolo de autoridade (Isa. 22:22; Apo. 3:7). Sempre é um símbolo de autoridade, nas Escrituras, indicando o direito de realizar alguma tarefa ou de exercer algum ofício. No sentido espiritual, Cristo é quem leva as chaves (Apo. 1:8). Há anjos que têm uma autoridade representada por alguma chave, como aquele que tem a chave do abismo ou hades (Apo. 9:1 e 20:1).

As chaves estão associadas ao conhecimento e à interpretação, como se segredos, instruções e informa-

CHAVE — CHAVES

ções fossem guardadas sob autoridade, mas pudessem ser abertas pelos ministros autorizados (Luc. 11:52). Aos apóstolos foram confiadas as «chaves do reino», visto que lhes foram dados o poder e a autoridade para abrirem o novo caminho espiritual, anunciando ao mundo a mensagem de Jesus (Mat. 16:18,19). As portas da Igreja foram abertas por Pedro, no dia de Pentecoste (Atos 2), e em Cesaréia (Atos 10), e por Paulo e Barnabé, na Ásia Menor (Atos 14:27).

O simbolismo da chave é apropriado porque os povos antigos imaginavam as dimensões espirituais guardadas por portas que só poderiam ser abertas por deuses ou por anjos. As regiões inferiores, como o hades, estariam sob a autoridade de forças demoníacas. Várias forças espirituais, divinas, ou demoníacas, eram retratadas nas culturas antigas como dotadas de chaves espirituais e metafísicas, como Shamash, entre os babilônios, Dike, entre os gregos, Jânus, entre os romanos, Aion-Cronos, no mitraísmo, Hélios, no período neoplatônico, etc. Nadu era uma divindade babilônica que guardava o mundo inferior. Além desses, temos Plutão, Aiacos, Persefone e Selena-Hecate, que seriam autoridades existentes no hades, além de Ísis, das religiões misteriosas.

Brandir uma chave equivalia a ter recebido autoridade e uma missão. Dar uma chave a alguém simbolizava conferir-lhe poder ou missão especiais.

CHAVES

I. Declaração Geral.

A idéia da *chave* é biblicamente ligada com o poder de *ligar* e *desligar*, como em Mat. 16:19. Poderes espirituais, delegados de Deus, determinam como a oportunidade espiritual é dada aos homens. O uso das chaves espirituais abre o caminho da oportunidade para o benefício dos homens. Os desobedientes encontram uma porta fechada, porque aquele que entra na porta deve obedecer às regras O *poder das chaves*, em Mat. 16:19, é associado com a autoridade de excomungar ou de receber pessoas na Igreja. Este assunto é comentado, com detalhes, no ponto II.

A metáfora. Muitos povos antigos pensaram nos lugares celestiais como protegidos pelo poder dos deuses (ou Deus), situados atrás de *portas*. Somente as autoridades espirituais superiores têm as chaves que podem ser usadas para abrir estas portas. Na religião babilônica o deus Shamash tinha as chaves; na religião grega, era Dike; na Romana, era Janus; em hades era Plutão, *Aiaco*, Persefone e Selena-Hecate. Na religião judaica, Deus ou um dos mais altos anjos, como Miguel, têm as chaves. O Talmude Babilônico fala sobre o relâmpago, o trovão, as chuvas, etc., como controlados pelas chaves dos anjos. Ver nesta conexão, Jer. 745.

No Novo Testamento. Pontos II e III falam sobre usos importantes do conceito de *chaves* no NT. Além deles, temos a *chave do conhecimento* em Luc. 11:52. As autoridades religiosas roubaram o conhecimento do povo, utilizando-se erradamente destas chaves. O livro da revelação ficou fechado pela perversidade dos homens.

As chaves que abrem o reino. Ver Mat. 16:19; 23:13. Os judeus imaginaram que Deus segurava quatro chaves: da chuva, da concepção, da ressurreição dos mortos e das ceifas. Mais importante, e relacionada com a ressurreição, é a chave do reino, pela qual, seus benefícios, na salvação, tornam-se disponíveis para os homens. Existem também as chaves do hades, que finalmente, os maiores anjos, como Miguel, utilizarão para libertar seres humanos, e anjos decaídos. Apocalipse 9:1 e 20:1 refletem estas idéias. Em Apoc. 11:6 temos o uso da chave dos céus, para fechar as fontes das águas, não permitindo chuva. Esta é uma velha idéia do judaísmo. Naquela fé, são os anjos que seguram as chaves que controlam os diversos elementos do tempo.

II. As Chaves e Pedro, Mat. 16:19.

«**Dar-te-ei** chaves...» As «chaves» simbolizam o poder e a autoridade, o encargo especial e privilegiado. Talvez a menção de «portas» e a implicação do símbolo de um castelo tenham provocado o emprego desse outro símbolo—*chaves*. Cristo tem um castelo, o castelo do reino dos céus e da igreja. Esse castelo também tem «portas», e para alguém nele entrar é mister que outrem abra essas portas. Ora, para abri-las, é necessário usar as «chaves». «As 'chaves' são símbolos da capacidade de abrir e explicar as verdades do evangelho, e também uma missão e comissão, dadas por Cristo, para que alguém as use» (John Gill, em Mat. 16:19). Pedro fez uso das chaves, pregando o evangelho primeiramente aos judeus (Atos 2), e *depois* aos gentios (Atos 10 e 15:7,14).

A passagem de Isa. 22:20-22 ilustra os pensamentos de Mat. 16:19. «E será naquele dia que chamarei a meu servo Eliaquim, filho de Hilquias, e revesti-lo-ei da tua túnica, e esforçá-lo-ei com o teu talabarte, e entregarei nas suas mãos o teu domínio, e será como pai para os moradores de Jerusalém e para a casa de Judá. E porei a chave da casa de Davi sobre o seu ombro, e abrirá, e ninguém fechará, e fechará e ninguém abrirá». O palácio do grande rei subentende a existência de alguém, de um oficial subordinado ao rei, que tenha autoridade no palácio especialmente no tocante ao tesouro, mas cujos serviços não estariam limitados a essa função. O trecho de Apo. 3:7 usa o mesmo símbolo, relacionado à ampla pregação do evangelho, pregação essa que arrostará todos os obstáculos. A expressão *pedra* alude ao *núcleo* da igreja, como se deu no caso de Pedro; as *chaves* referem-se ao *exercício* do ofício apostólico na igreja.

Alford diz: «Eis outra promessa pessoal feita a Pedro, cumprida de maneira notável na sua atitude pioneira de admitir tanto os judeus como os gentios na igreja, assim ele usou o poder das chaves para abrir as portas da salvação». Alguns intérpretes, como Wordsworth, aplicam essa promessa principalmente a Pedro, mas, por extensão da idéia, a todos quantos pregam o evangelho ou exercem outras funções na igreja, incluindo as funções relacionadas à disciplina.

Tenho as chaves da morte e do inferno... «chave»: Essa palavra indica o controle sobre algo, a fim de «abri-lo» ou «fechá-lo». É assim indicado o poder sobre a morte e o inferno. Tal expressão é típica da linguagem rabínica, podendo ser comparada aos termos de Mat. 16:19. A «chave» é o sinal de autoridade, do poder de uso, de instrumento de controle.

Morte. Estão em foco os aspectos físico e espiritual da morte. Nas mãos de Cristo se acham as grandes «finalidades» da criação. Ele venceu à morte física através de sua ressurreição; e isso indica um começo da conquista da morte espiritual, por semelhante modo. Cristo tem autoridade para infringir a morte espiritual, bem como o poder de livrar dela. A morte transforma tudo; mas Cristo veio alterar o conceito inteiro da morte; ela resulta, finalmente, em vida, devido ao seu poder remidor. A morte física separa a alma do corpo; a morte física separa o espírito humano de Deus, mas Cristo transformou a morte em portal da vida eterna.

A chave do hades. Essa expressão pode significar

(conforme era freqüente na linguagem dos rabinos judeus) o poder de produzir a ressurreição, sem qualquer alusão aos «espíritos vivos», confinados ao «hades». — O contexto cristão entretanto, inclui, forçosamente, a idéia de que Cristo é poderoso para livrar as almas da prisão do «hades», bem como é poderoso para conferir aos remidos corpos ressurrectos. Naturalmente, a chave pode «fechar», tanto quanto abrir. E isso fala do fato de que Cristo tem autoridade para encerrar almas no hades, como castigo por sua maldade e impenitência.

As chaves, que representam o poder sobre a morte e o hades, de acordo com o Targum de Jeremias, em Gên. 30:22, pertencem exclusivamente a Deus. Elias teria solicitado essas chaves (ver *Sanhedrin*, Fol. 113), mas foi informado de que três chaves não são entregues a um mensageiro: — em nascimento da chuva e a da «ressurreição dos mortos» (e, portanto, do «hades»). A *midrash Tehillin*, sobre o Salmo 93, mostra-nos que o Messias possuiria as «chaves da morte e do hades», porquanto possuiria o poder que ressuscitaria os mortos. Há um provérbio rabínico que expande isso até certo ponto: «Há quatro chaves aninhadas na mão de Deus, que ele não outorga nem a anjo e nem a serafim—a chave da chuva, a chave do alimento, a chave dos túmulos e a chave de uma mulher estéril».

Cristo, por ser o portador das chaves, consolou a João, o vidente, juntamente com seus companheiros perseguidos. Toda a autoridade «final» reside com Jesus Cristo. Êle usará as chaves (sua autoridade) para nosso benefício, e nunca para dano nosso. O dano que porventura possamos sofrer da parte dos homens, quando muito, é temporário. Deus triunfará, finalmente.

«Tragada foi a morte pela vitória. Onde está, ó morte, a tua vitória? onde está, ó morte, o teu aguilhão?» (I Cor. 15:54,55).

A morte e as trevas arrumam-te as malas para partires,
Pois agora nada mais falta ao homem;
Todos os teus triunfos agora terminaram,
E aquilo que Adão maculou, foi corrigido;
As sepulturas agora são leitos para os cansados,
E a morte é um cochilo para mais nos alegrarmos.
(Henry Vaughan, «*An Easter Hymn*»)

III. Chaves de Davi, Apo. 3:7.

Tem a chave de Davi. Aqui também precisamos considerar quatro particularidades, a saber:

1. A alusão é ao trecho de Isa. 22:22, uma predição sobre a subida de Eliaquim ao ofício de governador do palácio. A «chave de Davi» era símbolo do poder e da autoridade de seu ofício monárquico. Há certa autoridade, própria do palácio real, que é dada a Cristo, por ele brandir a chave de Davi.

2. Alguns intérpretes também vêem o uso das chaves reais para finalidade de ser aberto o tesouro real, pois Eliaquim era o mordomo principal da casa real. Aquele que possui a chave de Davi, pois, tem na ponta dos dedos as riquezas do reino. O Rei benévolo dará essa riqueza aos fiéis.

3. O vidente João, sem dúvida, nos faz uma promessa escatológica: a. O Cristo, que tem as chaves, dará ao mundo os benefícios do seu evangelho, e tornará os homens seus súditos, b. Aqueles que lhe estiverem sujeitos receberão acesso ao reino de Deus, bem como aos mundos eternos.

4. O poder de Cristo, para abrir o reino de Deus aos homens, seria administrado, pelo menos em parte, através da porta aberta de serviço (ver Apo. 3:10), que ele dará à sua igreja missionária, porquanto através dos esforços desta última é que muitos homens serão trazidos ao reino do Filho amado (ver Col. 1:13).

«Davi é tipo simbólico de Cristo, o governante supremo do reino dos céus. (Ver Jer. 30:9; Eze. 34:23 e 37:24). A casa de Davi é a designação típica do reino de Jesus Cristo (ver Sal. 122:5). O fato que Cristo brande as chaves, símbolo de autoridade, mostra que esse é um direito que lhe cabe, por ser Senhor do reino e da Igreja de Deus. (Ver Mat. 16:19). Ele admite e exclui conforme quer». (Vincent, Apo. 3:7).

«Cristo tem o poder de admitir e de excluir, segundo a sua vontade própria (ver Mat. 25:10 e ss; Efé. 1:22; Apo. 3:21; 19:11-16)». (Robertson, Apo. 3:7).

Que abre e ninguém fechará, e que fecha e ninguém abre. Essas palavras dão a entender o senhorio absoluto de Cristo. (Isso pode ser confrontado com a passagem de Mat. 28:18, onde se lê: «Toda a autoridade me foi dada no céu e na terra...» O prazer de Cristo é o de abrir a porta para todas as nações, para que ouçam o evangelho, e o Apocalipse mostra que isso se realizará. Cristo tem o poder de trazer a muitos para o reino de Deus; e isso ele fará. Os rebeldes, entretanto, perderão esse destino, que foi planejado para os homens, sem importar o tipo de restauração que venham a receber, conforme nos mostra o primeiro capítulo da epístola aos Efésios. Não obstante, há um elevadíssimo destino para o homem remido—a participação em toda a plenitude de Deus e na natureza divina (ver Efé. 3:19; Col. 2:10 e II Ped. 1:4). Nem todos os homens, todavia, atingirão essa bênção; e isso por terem sido excluídos pelo uso das chaves, por causa de sua rebelião e infidelidade. Apo. 3:7 pode ser comparado ao trecho de Apo. 1:8, onde Cristo é visto como quem possui as chaves da Morte e do Hades; e também ao trecho de Mat. 16:19, onde a Pedro foram entregues as chaves do reino dos céus.

As chaves de Davi visam um fim beneficente. O senhorio de Cristo, o Salvador, nunca se transforma, voluntariamente, em motivo da «exclusão», de homens, e para detrimento destes. Arrependendo-se, eles serão lançados nos braços abertos de Cristo, para serem acolhidos.

Nada, senão o arrependimento, poderá absolver;
E embora os pecados sejam horríveis, tão abertos são seus braços,
Com uma bondade infinita, que eles recebem
A todos quantos para eles se voltam.
(Dante)

CHEFE

Essa palavra e seus sinônimos, que dão a idéia de algum líder, precisa ser desdobrada quanto às palavras hebraicas e gregas que estão por detrás do conceito, e que, aliás, são muitas, a saber:

1. *Magen*, «escudo», palavra usada por sessenta vezes, uma das quais com o sentido de «chefe», em Oséias 4:18. A versão portuguesa diz «príncipe».

2. *Mashal*, «governante». Palavra usada por noventa e nove vezes (por exemplo: Gên. 45:8; Juí. 15:11; Sal. 105:20,21; Pro. 6:7; Isa. 14:5; Hab. 1:14).

3. *Nagid*, «líder». Palavra usada por quarenta e duas vezes (por exemplo: I Sam. 25:30; II Sam. 6:21; I Crô. 5:2; 28:4; Nee. 11:11).

4. *Nasi*, «exaltado». Palavra usada por cento e vinte e cinco vezes com o sentido de príncipe, chefe, etc., e por quatro vezes com o sentido de nuvem. No sentido que nos interessa aqui, ver, por exemplo: Êxo. 16:22;

CHEFE — CHIBOLETE

Lev. 4:22; Núm. 13:2; Jos. 9:15,18,19,21; Eze. 7:27; 12:10,12; 48:21,22.

5. *Qatsin*, «capitão». Palavra usada por doze vezes. Por exemplo: Isa. 1:10; 3:6,7; Pro. 25:15; Dan. 11:18; Miq. 3:1,9.

6. *Rosh*, «cabeça». Palavra usada por cerca de seiscentas vezes, das quais por doze vezes com o sentido de «fel». Por exemplo: Deu. 1:13; Isa. 29:10; Deu. 1:15; 5:23; Jos. 11:10; 14:1; Isa. 7:8,9,20; 9:14, etc.

7. *Sar*, «controlador». Palavra usada por quatrocentas e dezoito vezes. Por exemplo: Gên. 47:6; Êxo. 18:21,25; Juí. 9:30; II Reis 10:1; I Crô. 21:2; Esd. 10:14; Nee. 3:9,14,15,19; Est. 3:12; 89:9; 9:3, etc.

8. *Seganim*, «prefeitos». Palavra usada por dezessete vezes. Por exemplo: Esd. 9:2; Nee. 2:16; 4:14,19; 5:7,17; Jer. 51:23,28; Eze. 23:6,12,23, etc. Todas essas últimas sete palavras hebraicas são traduzidas de variegadas maneiras em nossa versão portuguesa, o que é apenas natural, face o elevado número de vezes em que todas elas são usadas.

9. *Razan*, «príncipe», palavra usada por seis vezes. Ver Sal. 2:2; Juí. 5:3; Pro. 8:15; 31:4; Isa. 40:23; Hab. 1:10.

10. *Shatar*, «supervisor». Palavra usada por vinte e cinco vezes. Por exemplo: II Crô. 26:11; Êxo. 5:6,10,14; Núm. 11:16; Deu. 1:15; Jos. 24:1; II Crô. 19:11; 34:13.

11. *Shilton*, «autoridade». Palavra usada por duas vezes: Dan. 3:2,3.

12. *Shallit*, «governo». Palavra usada por catorze vezes, com diversas traduções em português. Por exemplo: Ecl. 10:5; Dan. 2:10; 5:29, etc.

13. *Radah*, «príncipe». Palavra usada por vinte e quatro vezes, também traduzida em português de diversos modos. Por exemplo: Sal. 68:27; Núm. 24:19; Gên. 1:26; Nee. 9:28; Juí. 5:13.

Em grego, precisamos pensar em três palavras:

1. *Árxon*, «líder». Palavra usada por trinta e sete vezes. Por exemplo: Mat. 9:18,23,34; Mar. 3:22; Luc. 8:41; 24:20; João 3:11; 16:11; Atos 3:17; 23:5; Rom. 13:3; I Cor. 2:6; 8:1; Efé. 2:2; Apo. 1:5.

2. *Hegemón*, «guia». Palavra usada por dezenove vezes. Para exemplificar: Mat. 2:6; 10:18; Mar. 13:9; Luc. 20:20; Atos 23:24,26,33; I Ped. 2:14.

3. *Kosmokrátor*, «ditador do mundo». Palavra usada somente em Efé. 6:12. Há outras palavras gregas que indicam posições de chefia, mas que serão tratadas quando os verbetes a respeito dessas posições forem abordados.

CHEFE DA SINAGOGA

No grego é *archisinagogos* (ver Luc. 8:41 e Mat. 9:18). Nas sinagogas maiores, parece que havia uma espécie de colégio ou concílio de anciãos (ver Luc. 7:3), a quem eram entregues vários aspectos do governo e dos cuidados da sinagoga. O termo em discussão aparentemente se aplicava a todos esses líderes (ver Mar. 5:22 e Atos 13:15), mas algumas vezes aplicava-se somente ao presidente desse concílio, visto que tinha uma jurisdição geral, superior à dos demais.

CHEIRO Ver Odor.

CHEMNITZ, MARTIM

Nasceu em 1522 e faleceu em 1586. Foi um teólogo luterano alemão, chamado o *príncipe* dos teólogos da Confissão de Augsburgo (que vide). Era perito na matemática, na astrologia e na teologia. Sabia debater com maestria, pelo que deu grande vivacidade às controvérsias do tempo. Na qualidade de superintendente de Brunswick, ele tornou-se o líder da Igreja luterana da Baixa Saxônia, tendo exercido grande influência na unificação dos luteranos da Saxônia e da Suábia, com base na Fórmula da Concórdia (que vide), e da qual ele foi um dos principais autores. Seu *Loci Theologici*, publicado postumamente em 1591, é um comentário sobre o *Loci Communes* (que vide) de Melanchton, seu mestre. Contra os criptocalvinistas (que vide), ele escreveu a obra *De Duabus Naturis in Christo*, em 1570. Sua obra-prima, entretanto, foi o *Exame dos Concílios Tridentinos*, em catorze volumes (1565-1573), que foi uma incisiva análise dos pontos de vista católicos romanos, adotados pelo Concílio de Trento (que vide). Essa obra é uma apologia em favor do protestantismo. (AM E)

CH'ENG I

Suas datas foram 1033-1107. — Foi um filósofo chinês, nascido em Honan. Ele era neoconfucionista, o mais jovem dos irmãos Ch'eng. Recebeu seu grau de *Erudito Apresentado* em 1059. Era homem de espírito humilde, mas resoluto, que declinou de muitos ofícios elevados, preferindo trabalhar pela propagação de idéias e ideais. Expôs uma série de preleções, perante o imperador, acerca dos princípios de Confúcio, por um período de vinte meses. Tornou-se supervisor da Diretoria de Educação, em 1087, 1092 e 1100. Entre seus muitos discípulos estava Chu Hsi.

Idéias: 1. Ele enfatizava o princípio chamado *li* (que vide). Na filosofia, esse princípio é o princípio racional do universo, que permeia a todas as coisas, algo semelhante ao *Logos* dos gregos. Trata-se do princípio unitário com uma pluralidade de manifestações. 2. O universo é *produtivo*, princípio esse chamado *jen*. Esse princípio inclui as virtudes de retidão, propriedade, sabedoria e fidelidade, como guias e essências básicas da produção. Seguindo o princípio *jen*, o homem atinge a unidade com todas as coisas, tornando-se capaz de dominar o mal. 3. A obtenção da unidade requer a compreensão sobre todos os princípios, que incluem o autoconhecimento, o autocultivo e a investigação de todas as coisas, como um empreendimento científico.

Escritos: *Surviving Works*; *Additional Works*; *Collection of Literary Works by Ch'eng I*; *Commentary on the Book of Changes*; *Explanations of the Classics*; *Pure Words*. (P)

CHENOBOSKION

Ver **Nag Hamade, Manuscritos de**.

CHESTER BEATTY, Papiros de. Ver Papiros de Chester Beatty.

CHESTERTON, GILBERT KEITH

Suas datas foram 1874-1936. Foi um autor e jornalista inglês que produziu ensaios brilhantes, como *Heréticos* e *Ortodoxia*. Ele interpretava o cristianismo do ponto de vista do catolicismo. Muitas de suas opiniões e expressões vívidas são utilizadas largamente em nossos dias. — Ele escrevia de modo espirituoso, poderoso e em tom de debate. Além de ensaios, ele compunha poesia e escrevia novelas e peças teatrais. Muitas de suas obras tinham o intuito de servir de crítica social. Em 1922 ele converteu-se ao catolicismo romano, e, desde então, as suas obras passaram a incorporar a promoção de sua nova fé; mas ele nunca apenas repetiu idéias já existentes.

CHIBOLETE, SIBOLETE

No hebraico, «riacho fluente». Embora a palavra

hebraica apareça em trechos como Sal. 69:2; Jó 24:24; Gên. 41:5-7; Rute 2:2 e Zac. 4:12, em nossa versão portuguesa essa palavra, em suas duas formas, aparece somente no trecho de Juí. 12:6. A questão toda gira em torno da pronúncia que os efraimitas davam a essa palavra hebraica. Eles diziam «sibolete», em vez de «chibolete». Com isso, podiam ser identificados e mortos pelos gileaditas. Os gileaditas, que eram os homens de Jefté, mataram naquele dia quarenta e dois mil efraimitas. O episódio, por sua vez, mostra que mesmo nesse estágio inicial do povo de Israel, já haviam surgido regionalismos e diferenças de dicção, entre as diversas tribos de Israel. Essas diferenças de pronúncia dos fonemas de um idioma devem-se a vários fatores. Os gramáticos e outros dizem que as pessoas que se criam nas planícies falam de modo diferente dos que se criam nas regiões montanhosas, e que os que vivem nos climas quentes pronunciam os fonemas de maneira diferente dos que vivem nos climas frios.

CHIFRES

No hebraico, **queren**. Ocorre por setenta e oito vezes, de Gên. 22:13 até Zac. 1:21. O termo aramaico *queren* ocorre por sete vezes, sempre no sétimo capítulo do livro de Daniel (vs. 7,8,11,20,21,24). No grego, *kéras*, «chifre», palavra que aparece por onze vezes no Novo Testamento: Luc. 1:69; Apo. 5:6; 9:13; 12:3; 13:1,11; 17:3,7,12,16.

O chifre de um animal servia de símbolo de sua força física. O touro com a sua enorme força física, domesticado pelo homem desde tempos tão remotos, fornecia um bom exemplo disso. E muitos animais selvagens usam seus chifres como sua principal arma de defesa e ataque. Visto que os chifres simbolizavam poder, muitas divindades do Oriente Médio eram retratadas como se fossem dotadas de chifres. Além disso, os capacetes dos reis, sacerdotes e guerreiros com freqüência tinham chifres.

Visto que o touro era um animal sagrado para vários povos, os chifres tornaram-se símbolos do poder divino, bem como da fertilidade. Por causa dessa conexão com a idéia de fertilidade, os chifres também vieram a indicar prosperidade e saúde. As pessoas costumavam pôr chifres nos lugares que queriam proteger, por causa de sua imaginária vinculação com os poderes divinos. Da idéia de abundância proveio o símbolo da *cornucópia*, o chifre da abundância, representado como um chifre que deixa extravasar frutos e legumes. Uma espécie de trombeta também era feita pelos antigos, mediante o uso de um chifre (ver sobre *Instrumentos Musicais*). Essa trombeta era usada para alertar as pessoas à ação, para fazer anúncios, etc. Além disso, muitos acreditavam que o sonido da trombeta de chifres era capaz de espantar maus espíritos e outros perigos, incluindo enfermidades.

Usos Bíblicos. 1. Na antiga nação de Israel, os chifres de boi eram usados como receptáculos para o azeite empregado nas unções cerimoniais (I Sam. 16:1, 13; I Reis 1:39). Um chifre de carneiro era usado como instrumento musical (Jos. 6:5). 2. Os chifres do altar são mencionados em Êxo. 27:2 e Lev. 4:7,18,25,30,34; 8:15; 9:9; 16:18. Os hebreus besuntavam-nos de sangue, porquanto é no poder da expiação que encontramos a proteção divina. O fato de que esses chifres eram lugares de proteção e refúgio é mencionado em I Reis 1:50 *ss*; 2:28 *ss*. 3. Quanto a um símbolo de poder, no Antigo Testamento, ver I Reis 22:11. *Usos Metafóricos*: a. Deus exalta o chifre dos justos mas decepa os chifres dos ímpios (Sal. 75:10), o que aponta para os poderes e para o bem-estar desses dois tipos de pessoas. b. O chifre de Davi seria levado a brotar, dando a entender poder e prosperidade. c. Há menção ao chifre da salvação, o que alude aos efeitos do poder expiatório de Deus (II Sam. 22:3; Sal. 18:2; Luc. 1:69). d. Nos capítulos sete e oito do livro de Cantares e nos capítulos treze e dezessete do Apocalipse, os chifres existentes em certas criaturas que apareceram nas visões representam governantes individuais de cada império mundial. Ver o artigo separado sobre os *Sete Chifres*.

CHIFRES DO ALTAR

No hebraico, **qeren**, «chifre». Essa palavra, que tanto pode ser hebraica como aramaica, ocorre em um total de oitenta e cinco vezes, embora raramente em relação aos chifres do altar. Ver Êxo. 27:2.

Os «chifres do altar» eram as quatro protrusões nos cantos do altar de pedra, que se assemelhavam a chifres, o que lhes explica o nome. Essa era uma característica dos altares antigos, em Israel e em outras nações. A descrição desses chifres aparece em Êxodo 27:2. O altar de bronze conferia abrigo a quem se refugiasse ali. Quem segurasse o altar pelos chifres não podia ser atacado por quem quer que fosse (I Reis 1:50). Esse é um lindo símbolo sobre como há provisão sagrada para o pecador em necessidade, sem importar se ele merece ou não essa proteção. Ver sobre as *Cidades de Refúgio*.

CHIH TAO-LIN

Suas datas foram 314-366. Um filósofo budista chinês. Ver o artigo sobre o *Budismo*. Ver também *Filosofia Chinesa* e *Religiões Chinesas*.

CHI-I

Suas datas foram 538-597. Foi um filósofo chinês, nativo de Chequiam. Foi o fundador da escola T-ien-Tai do budismo. Seu nome provinha do monte onde ele ensinava. Foi o mais notável sacerdote budista de sua época. Ele fazia muitas conferências, recebendo convites da parte de governantes dinásticos, com esse propósito. Ele adotava a comum idéia oriental de que a realidade física é ilusória. A imaginação cria as formas físicas que tomamos como reais. Porém, a realidade verdadeira seria a *Mente Pura*, chamada o Assim Verdadeiro. Essa realidade existiria sem sofrer qualquer modificação, sem qualquer diferenciação. A iluminação leva-nos à consciência de nossa unidade com a Mente Pura. Naturalmente, isso reflete uma filosofia idealista. Ver sobre o *Idealismo*.

CHINA, Religião e Filosofia da.
Ver **Religião e Filosofia Chinesas**.

CHIPRE

No Antigo Testamento, parece que a única menção a essa grande ilha do mar Mediterrâneo está em Ezequiel 27:6 (onde a nossa versão portuguesa diz «ilha dos quiteus»). A ilha de Chipre fica ao largo das costas da Síria. Tem cerca de 225 km de comprimento por 80 km de largura. A princípio foi habitada pelos fenícios. Em cerca de 447 A.C., os gregos passaram a controlá-la. Após o falecimento de Alexandre, passou a ser governada pelos reis Ptolomeus, juntamente com o Egito. Em 58 A.C., os romanos apossaram-se dela.

Igreja de São Pedro e São Paulo, Chipre
—Cortesia, Matson Photo Service

Reprodução Artística de
Darrell Steven Champlin

Arte céltica — o leão, símbolo do evangelho
de Marcos, Livro de Kells

Em 27 A.C., foi feita uma província imperial. Chipre é mencionada no Novo Testamento somente no livro de Atos (4:36; 11:19,20; 13:4; 15:39; 21:3,16; 27:4). No décimo primeiro capítulo de Atos, em conexão com a propagação do cristianismo. Paulo e Barnabé estiveram na ilha em cerca de 44 D.C. Por certo, foi o primeiro campo missionário do apóstolo Paulo (Atos 13:4-13). Os «Quitim», referidos em Gênesis 10:4, referem-se aos cipriotas. Os «quitim» são os mesmos «quiteus» de Eze. 27:6. Nossa versão portuguesa interpreta o «quitim», também referidos em Isaías 23:1, como a «terra de Chipre».

Outros Detalhes.

Na antiguidade, essa ilha era recoberta de densas florestas; mas acabou desnudada das mesmas, devido à intensa exploração da madeira. Além da madeira ali existente, Chipre era importante produtora de cobre e estanho. De fato, o seu nome grego, *Kúpros*, significa «cobre». Navios fenícios eram usados nesse comércio. Nossa palavra «cobre» deriva-se do termo latino *cyprium*, relacionado ao grego *kúpros*. Talvez esse fosse o antigo nome dado ao cobre; mas também é possível que essa palavra seja de origem incerta, e que o «cobre» veio a ser associado a esse nome porque havia muito cobre naquela ilha. A localidade chamada antigamente de Kítion, de onde vem «quitim», foi fundada em torno da indústria da extração do cobre. O termo cronológico, Era do Bronze (3200-1200 A.C.), tem vinculação com o início da extração do cobre, visto que, naquela época, o cobre era misturado com o estanho, a fim de ser produzido o bronze.

No século XV A.C., a civilização minoana penetrou em Creta, e no século seguinte, houve pontos ali, colonizados pelos micenos. Têm sido encontradas inscrições arqueológicas que nos prestam alguma informação sobre a história de Creta, entre os séculos XV e XII A.C. Nos séculos IX e VIII A.C., os fenícios vieram estabelecer-se em Chipre. Daí por diante, inscrições bilíngües, em fenício e em grego, de mistura com o cipro-minoano clássico (atualmente denominado cipriota clássico), contam a história subseqüente. No século VI A.C., os egípcios passaram a dominar a ilha de Chipre, e as coisas continuaram assim até que se tornou parte do império persa, na época de Cambises, em 525 A.C. Em 333 A.C., foi conquistada por Alexandre; e, sob Antígono, passou para o domínio dos monarcas Ptolomeus. Em 58 A.C., tornou-se uma província romana.

CHISHOLM, RODERIC

Nasceu em 1916. É um filósofo norte-americano, educado em Harvard. Ensinou nas Universidades de Pennsylvania e de Brown.

Idéias. 1. *Existência intencional*. Haveria existências psíquicas, expressas através de sentenças intencionais. Essas sentenças nem afirmam e nem negam essas existências. Chisholm critica tanto o positivismo quanto o behaviorismo, por não serem capazes de manusear tais sentenças. 2. Ao enfatizar a idéia de *intencionalidade*, Chisholm aceitava o ponto de vista platônico das entidades abstratas. 3. Quanto às *declarações sobre as aparências*, precisaríamos tanto das observações apropriadas quanto das condições que descrevem as coisas percebidas. Mas, no caso das sentenças intencionais, não precisamos dessas coisas. Há outros meios de obtenção de conhecimento, além da percepção dos sentidos. 4. *Critério de conhecimento*. Para que consideremos algo verdadeiro, precisamos de uma crença a respeito que seja sem defeitos, justificada, autêntica. 5. No campo da *ética*, quando encontramos aquelas situações que são contrárias aos imperativos do dever, precisamos agir com base nas impressões *prima facie*. Essa expressão latina significa «primeiras impressões». Quando surgem tais conflitos, quando um dever parece opor-se a outro, devemos fazer o que nos parece melhor, *à primeira vista*. A reflexão pode alterar isso, mas o princípio é aplicado de modo geral. Ver o artigo sobre *Prima Facie* (*deveres*).

Escritos: Perceiving; Realism and the Background of Phenomenology; Contrary to Duty Imperative and Deontic Logic; Theory of Knowledge; The Problem of Criterion; Empirical Knowledge. (EP P)

CHI-TSANG

Suas datas foram 549-623. Ele foi um filósofo chinês, nativo de Nanquim. Era monge budista e foi um dos principais filósofos budistas. Ele sistematizou a obra de Seng-Chao, desenvolvendo ainda mais os Três Tratados ou Escola Mahayana do budismo. Essa escola dominou na China entre os séculos IV e VII D.C., mas declinou a partir do século IX.

Idéias. 1. Seguindo a posição intermediária das oito veredas negativas de Agarjuna, ele argumentava que os Dharmas (elementos da existência) não são instâncias de ser ou de não ser, e nem das duas coisas misturadas. 2. O ponto construtivo a ser atingido é o conceito do *vazio*, livre de nomes e de caráter, incapaz de ser verbalizado ou imaginado.

Escritos: Tratado sobre os Dois Níveis da Verdade; Sentido Profundo dos Três Tratados. (P)

CHOBA

Essa é uma aldeia mencionada em Judite 4:4. Aparentemente ficava situada na porção central da Palestina, e provavelmente é a mesma cidade chamada algures de Chobai. Foi uma das cidades que os judeus fortaleceram, quando Holofernes invadiu a Palestina, em cerca de 350 A.C. Com sua astúcia, Judite conseguiu decapitar Holofernes em sua tenda, o que causou considerável consternação entre os assírios, que terminaram fugindo. Os judeus perseguiram os assírios até Choba. A localização desse lugar é desconhecida em nossos dias, embora ela tenha sido confundida com Choba, na Mauritânia Sifitensis, na costa norte da África. Alguns estudiosos identificam-na com Cobais, visto que ela é mencionada com Jericó, no mesmo versículo. Ou poderia ser a Choba da Síria. Ver Gên. 14:15. Alguns estudiosos têm sugerido el-Mekhubbi, — cerca de dezoito quilômetros de Tubass e a cinco quilômetros de Besan.

CHOLA

Um lugar mencionado em Juízes 15:4, juntamente com Betomastaim, Bebai e Choba. Tem sido identificado com o Holóm mencionado em Josué 15:51, embora não passe isso de uma suposição.

CHOMSKY, A. NOAM

Ele nasceu em 1928. Trata-se de um filósofo-lingüista norte-americano, nascido na cidade de Filadélfia. Educou-se na Universidade da Pennsylvania, e tornou-se então mestre na M.I.T. A obra geral e as idéias desse filósofo estão fora do escopo da presente enciclopédia. Entretanto, parte de sua teoria de linguagem reveste-se de importância para nossos propósitos. Suas idéias entram na disputa entre os empiristas e os racionalistas. Ele argumenta que os idiomas revestem-se de similaridades estruturais subjacentes, afirmando que devemos nascer dotados de certa compreensão de uma espécie de gramática universal. Em outras palavras, as *idéias inatas* (que vide) estão envolvidas na questão, sendo essa uma idéia favorita dos racionalistas. Ele também supõe que, quando somos crianças, usamos dessa capacidade inata para analisar as declarações que ouvimos. Somente com base nessa idéia poderíamos explicar como, após termos ouvido algumas poucas declarações, somos quase imediatamente capazes de produzir e entender novas declarações. Ora, isso é contra a contenção dos empiristas, —que dizem que todo o conhecimento deriva-se das experiências pós-natais. Estudos recentes, com alguns animais, têm demonstrado que eles também são capazes de certa espécie de linguagem, embora lhes falte o aparelho fonador necessário à fala. Os chimpanzés e os símios podem comunicar-se através de um teclado com letras, ou mediante a linguagem de sinais, usada pelos surdos-mudos. No caso desses animais, por igual modo, é aparente a capacidade de melhorarem, após terem aprendido alguns poucos símbolos básicos. Indicações como essas elevam a nossa estimativa sobre a vida em geral, e obtemos maior respeito pela inteligência, onde quer que ela se manifeste. (F P)

CHORO

Muitas palavras hebraicas e duas palavras gregas estão envolvidas, com o sentido de «clamar», «chorar», «proclamar», etc. Porém, aqui queremos considerar a idéia do choro humano. É interessante observar que, no relato da vida de Jesus, nunca é mencionado que ele riu ou gargalhou. Mas lemos que «Jesus chorou» (João 11:35). Aí é usado o vocábulo grego mais típico, *dakrúo*, «chorar», «derramar lágrimas», usado somente nesse versículo.

O choro humano pode expressar diversas emoções, desde a angústia até o júbilo, passando pela raiva. A Bíblia reflete isso de vários modos:

1. O clamor de Jesus, em sua humanidade, quando ele implorou com lágrimas, em meio a súplicas e orações, mostrando a debilidade de sua natureza humana, e como ele compartilhava de nossa humilhação (Heb. 5:7). Nisso encontramos o típico choro humano de impotência, em meio ao conflito espiritual.

2. Os clamores proferidos na cruz, literais e simbólicos (Mat. 27:46; Luc. 23:46), porquanto Jesus sofreu agonias reais, simbolizando as nossas agonias. Ver o artigo sobre as *Sete Declarações da Cruz*.

3. O clamor da oração (Sal. 39:12), que mostra a sinceridade e o senso de urgência então expressos.

4. O clamor de muitas emoções, como a aflição (Êxo. 2:23; Mat. 27:46); o medo (Mat. 14:26); a alegria (Isa. 54:1; Gál. 4:27); a dúvida e a incerteza (Êxo. 17:4); o apelo (I Sam. 7:9); a tristeza (I Sam. 15:11; Mar. 15:34); a agonia (Jó 30:24; Mat. 27:46); a petição (Mat. 9:27).

CHOU TUN-I

Suas datas foram 1017-1073. — Foi um filósofo não confuciano chinês, nativo de Tau-Chou, em Hunã. Foi mestre dos famosos irmãos Ch'eng.

Idéias. 1. O Grande Ultimato, através de suas atividades, geraria o *yang*. No limite dessa atividade a tranqüilidade vem à existência, a qual é chamada *yin*. Quando esses dois modos se intercambiam, vêm à existência elementos como a água, o fogo, a madeira, o metal e o ar. Então surgem o céu e a terra, que são, respectivamente, os aspectos macho e fêmea da existência. Esses dois elementos produzem uma interminável produção e transformação, e o homem faz parte dessa produção. 2. *Idéias Morais*. O homem teria cinco princípios morais: a atitude humanitária, a propriedade, a retidão, a sabedoria e a fidelidade. O homem sábio conduz sua vida seguindo a moderação, quando da aplicação apropriada das principais virtudes. 3. Os muitos elementos existentes no mundo equilibram-se, mediante compensação. Esses muitos elementos, em última análise, reduzem-se a apenas um, e esse um vem a ser diferenciado em muitos. E cada uma dessas coisas ocupa um papel importante no esquema das coisas.

Escritos: *Uma Explicação do Diagrama do Último; Penetrando no Livro das Transformações*. (AM P)

CHUANG TZU

Filósofo chinês da escola taoísta. Nasceu em 399 e faleceu em 295 A.C. A seu respeito bem pouca coisa se sabe. Evidentemente, ele era um oficial subalterno do governo chinês. Também sabemos que ele não aceitou tornar-se o primeiro ministro na China por não sacrificar a sua liberdade pessoal. Exerceu notável influência sobre o taoísmo e sobre o budismo zen.

Idéias:

1. *Paradoxos*. A relatividade de todo o nosso conhecimento torna possível que supostos opostos sejam ambos verdadeiros. De fato, os conceitos opostos podem produzir, subentender e ser idênticos entre si. Ver o artigo sobre o conceito de *Polaridade*.

2. A totalidade da natureza exprime um fluxo contínuo em todas as coisas, as quais desenvolvem-se de formas mais simples em formas mais complexas. De acordo com um ponto de vista mais profundo, embora exista uma miríade de coisas, a ordem delas é apenas uma.

3. Tao (o *caminho*, ou a *estrada*, o princípio fundamental do cosmos, de onde todas as coisas procedem) seria o princípio básico que existe em todas as coisas. Para que possa operar sobre uma pessoa, esse princípio deve relacionar-se tanto às muitas coisas quanto à única coisa, dando margem a certa polaridade de atitudes. As atitudes mentais e éticas específicas que se fazem necessárias para esse equilíbrio na vida são as seguintes: vacuidade, tranqüilidade, brandura, quietude e sabedoria nas ações, ou *wu wei*, quando tal sabedoria faz-se necessária.

4. O começo de todas as coisas consiste no não-ser. Daí é que teria emergido o Um; e desse Um é que teria surgido a pluralidade, em que cada coisa tem o seu próprio caráter e virtude. O Um é a operação do destino, estando dividido nos princípios do *Yin* e do *Yang*, que seriam opostos cósmicos que produzem todas as coisas, mediante o movimento ou o repouso. Quando alguém cultiva as suas próprias virtudes, então retorna à Virtude. Através da virtude, o indivíduo vincula-se ao Um. A virtude é o caminho para a grandeza. Platão ensinava esse princípio, embora usando outra terminologia. E isso corresponde ao avanço metafísico e à transformação da alma. Naturalmente, de acordo com o sistema cristão e bíblico, essa transformação se processa segundo o nosso grande modelo, o próprio Jesus Cristo.

Escritos: *O Chuang Tzu*, por Chuang Tzu e seus seguidores. (P)

••• ••• •••

CHUBB, THOMAS

Deísta inglês, nascido em East Harnham, em 1679. Essencialmente, foi um auto-ditada. Defendia o cristianismo natural, a ética cristã e o livre-arbítrio. Porém, mostrava-se cético quanto à profecia, os milagres, a revelação especial e a eficácia da oração. Voltaire aludiu às suas obras, considerando-o o mais lógico de sua escola. Jonathan Edwards refutou seus pontos de vista sobre o livre-arbítrio. Suas obras deixam entrever as deficiências de muitos autodidatas, e com freqüência, eram desprezadas por controversalistas teológicos mais eruditos. Seus folhetos tendiam por limitar a religião cristã a três características fundamentais: a crença na lei moral, divinamente ordenada; a crença na necessidade de arrependimento sincero diante do pecado; e a crença em recompensas ou punições futuras. Faleceu em Salisbury, a 8 de fevereiro de 1747.

Escritos: *The Supremacy of the Father Asserted; A Discourse Concerning Reason; The True Gospel of Jesus Christ Asserted; The True Gospel of Jesus Christ Vindicated*. (AM P)

CHU HSI

Suas datas foram 1130-1200 D.C. Foi um filósofo chinês confuciano. Era nativo de Anhui. Foi homem dotado de pensamentos poderosos, com soberbas expressões, cujos escritos dominaram o pensamento chinês, coreano e japonês durante séculos.

Idéias:

1. Hsi sintetizou as doutrinas básicas do confucionismo (que vide), sistematizando-as. Ele enfatizou os analectos, o livro de Mêncio, a Grande Erudição e a Doutrina da Moderação. Os elementos de sua síntese consistiam no Grande Final, no princípio, na força material, na natureza, na investigação e na humanidade.

2. O *Grande Final* seria o princípio fundamental em sua totalidade. O princípio e a concretização precisam um do outro. A concretização envolveria tanto um princípio quanto uma força material. O primeiro desses aspectos teria relação com a universalidade das coisas, ao passo que o último desses aspectos teria relação com a individualidade das coisas. A natureza de alguma coisa física seria o seu princípio, mais a sua força material. A *investigação* resultaria da observação e da intuição. O sucesso na investigação obtém-se quando a mente do indivíduo entra em harmonia com a Mente do universo. A compreensão mais elevada depende do princípio de *jen*. Como uma substância, o *jen* é o caráter da mente do homem. Como uma função, o *jen* consiste em *amor*. O amor é a base de toda virtude e bondade. Por conseguinte, a verdadeira substância da mente e as expressões de benevolência sempre estão associadas entre si.

3. O sistema de Chu Hsi detinha a doutrina chinesa tradicional de *Yin* e do *Yang* (que vide). De acordo com o seu sistema, o Grande Final requer ambos esses princípios.

4. O princípio sempre tem prioridade sobre as funções; e sempre estão unidos a mente humana e os princípios. Para que alguém aja corretamente, é mister que esclareça, para si mesmo, a sua verdadeira natureza. Nessa conexão, recomendava Sócrates: «Conhece-te a ti mesmo». Se nos mostrarmos sérios para conosco mesmos, observando a nossa natureza e suas potencialidades, a razão da nossa existência, e o nosso destino, então haveremos de agir corretamente, em consonância com esse conhecimento. Precisamos permitir que nossa mente nos esclareça no que diz respeito à nossa própria natureza, e, por esse intermédio, precisamos criar a inspiração necessária para vivermos a lei do amor. (P)

CHUMBO

No hebraico, **ophereth**, «chumbo». Esse vocábulo é usado por nove vezes: Êxo. 15:10; Núm. 31:22; Jó 19:24; Jer. 6:29; Eze. 22:18,20; 27:12; Zac. 5:7,8.

O chumbo é um metal mole, com densidade onze vezes maior que a da água. Seu ponto de fusão é 327 graus centígrados. Forma ligas com a prata (Eze. 22:18,20) e com o estanho (então chamado solda). Preenchia espaços esculpidos na rocha, para formar letras (Jó 19:24). Quando é absolutamente puro, o chumbo tem cor branca prateada, mas as impurezas fazem com que escureça. O minério do chumbo é a galena (sulfeto de chumbo) que é encontrado associado ao zinco, com pequenos vestígios de prata. Os depósitos de chumbo mais exploráveis ocorrem em veios que se depositam através de rochas sedimentares ou as substituem. Ninguém sabe quando os homens descobriram o chumbo, mas tem sido encontrado nos mais antigos lugares examinados pelos arqueólogos. Moedas de chumbo já eram feitas no antigo Egito. Era um dos componentes usados no esmaltamento de cerâmica; e também era usado como solda. Os famosos Jardins Suspensos da Babilônia estavam ancorados sobre lâminas de chumbo, soldadas umas às outras. Os fenícios comerciavam com o chumbo, explorando minas de chumbo no rio Tinto, na Espanha. Os gregos extraíam chumbo em Laurion, na Grécia.

Referências Bíblicas. O chumbo era conhecido por sua grande densidade (Êxo. 15:19) e também por sua rápida dissipação, devido à oxidação, às altas temperaturas (Jer. 6:29). O chumbo era menos valorizado que o estanho, sendo usado no fabrico de pesos (Zac. 5:8), e também para preencher inscrições esculpidas na rocha (Jó 19:24). No trecho de Zacarias 4:10, o «prumo» era um peso de estanho; mas, em Zacarias 5:8, o peso era de chumbo. Isaías 41:7 diz que o chumbo era usado na solda. O chumbo também era usado como material para o fabrico de tabletes de escrever, ou como material de construção, especialmente no preenchimento dos interstícios entre pedras desiguais. A arqueologia tem descoberto esse uso nas escavações feitas em Nínive. Também era usado para esmaltar cerâmica, um processo usado no Egito e em outros lugares. Isso significa que muita gente ficou intoxicada com o chumbo! Ver o artigo geral sobre *Minas, Mineração*.

CHUVA

A grande importância da chuva para os habitantes de uma região onde chove pouco torna-se clara pela variedade de palavras hebraicas que a descrevem. O hebraico distingue a *chuva* do *chuvisco* (este último em Deu. 32:2). E também registra a ocorrência das chuvas próprias das estações do ano (ver abaixo).

As taxas anuais de chuva, em várias regiões da Palestina, são descritas no artigo *Palestina, Clima da* (que vide). Mas as taxas médias geralmente enganam, visto que os totais variam muito de ano para ano. Por exemplo, em Jerusalém, a média a longo prazo é de 66,3 cm anuais. Mas o máximo recebido em um ano foi de 1,01 m e o mínimo de 30,5 cm. Havendo flutuações dessa grandeza, o impacto sobre a sociedade que depende das chuvas para sobreviver facilmente pode ser imaginado.

Para os agricultores, o que mais importa é a distribuição das chuvas durante o ano. Essa distribuição é muito desigual, realmente. Nenhuma chuva cai durante os quatro meses mais quentes do ano, de junho a setembro. Isso é equilibrado por um inverno fresco e chuvoso; mas, do ponto de vista do agricultor, os dois períodos críticos são o começo e o fim da estação chuvosa, quando as temperaturas são altas o bastante para promover o crescimento das plantações, e o solo ainda está bastante úmido para o cultivo.

Portanto, as atividades dos agricultores prendem-se diretamente ao regime das chuvas, dependendo de seu início. As chuvas começam em outubro, geralmente com uma série de temporais, e a aragem e a semeadura podem então começar no solo compactado. Se o começo da estação chuvosa se adia, a produção anual sofre; e se o adiamento é muito grande, pode nem haver colheita. Portanto, essas «primeiras» chuvas são importantíssimas. Na outra extremidade do inverno, as chuvas continuam até abril e maio, quando as temperaturas são elevadas, sendo mais valiosas do que as chuvas de janeiro e fevereiro, quando as temperaturas são mais baixas; aquelas chuvas aumentam a produção por cada dia que elas se prolongam. Por isso é que os agricultores esperam ansiosos pelas «últimas» chuvas.

Essa combinação de primeiras e últimas chuvas é freqüentemente aludida na Bíblia (por exemplo, Deu. 11:14; Jer. 5:24; Osé. 6:3; Joel 2:23; Tia. 5:7). Muito temida é a ausência de chuvas, pois isso importa em fome, um evento que nunca se distancia muito dos pensamentos dos habitantes da Palestina, desde os dias de Abraão até os nossos próprios dias. Ver *Palestina, Clima da*. Em conclusão, a agricultura é mais bem servida com chuvas oportunas—tanto as primeiras, no hebraico, *yoreh* ou *moreh*; como as últimas, no hebraico, *malkos*—do que com chuvas pesadas.

CHUVAS ANTERIORES E POSTERIORES
Ver o artigo sobre **Chuva**.

CHUVAS DA PRIMAVERA
Ver sobre **Chuva**.

CIAMOM
Um lugar defronte de Esdrelom, de acordo com Judite 8:3. Talvez seja a mesma Camom, que Eusébio disse estar situada na grande planície, cerca de dez quilômetros de Légio, um pouco mais para o norte. Alguns supõem que esse nome seria uma corruptela de Jocneão, porquanto os dois nomes parecem referir-se ao mesmo lugar, mas tal identificação é dúbia. Jocneão foi uma cidade cananéia, conquistada por Josué (Jos. 12:22), então entregue ao território de Zebulom (Jos. 19:11) e posteriormente, entregue aos levitas (Lev. 21:34). O moderno Tell Qeimum identifica o antigo local.

CIBELE-ÁTIS
Ver sob **Religiões Misteriosas**, segundo ponto.

CIBERNÉTICA
Vem do grego **kubernetes**, «piloto». O vocábulo «cibernética» foi cunhado por Norbert Wiener e Arturo Rosenblueth, para indicar o estudo das máquinas em termos de mecanismos de realimentação. O termo veio a indicar a ciência do controle e da comunicação, sem importar se na sociedade humana, entre indivíduos ou máquinas dotadas de inteligência artificial. Mecanismos de auto-regulagem, sistemas de sinalização e computadores são exemplos típicos de aparelhos cibernéticos.

Essa ciência levanta sérias questões religiosas e filosóficas, razão pela qual o verbete aparece em nossa enciclopédia, a saber:

1. Até qual ponto o cérebro humano é similar às máquinas «inteligentes»? Poderia a teologia desenvolver, finalmente, máquinas que possam ser superiores ao cérebro humano, e assim remover a inteligência da suposta esfera exclusiva das propriedades da alma?

2. O comportamento humano seria tão mecanicista como o das máquinas «inteligentes», o que removeria o comportamento da esfera da ética *propositat*? O homem seria apenas uma máquina programada, cuja conduta poderia ser explicada mediante elementos de sua herança genética, de mistura com fatores ambientais?

3. O desenvolvimento de computadores fantasticamente complexos poderá, algum dia, remover a necessidade de controle humano, visto que as máquinas poderiam, quem sabe, ser planejadas para interagir com o meio ambiente, aceitar ordens verbais, ser capazes de telepatia, captando assim o pensamento das pessoas, calcular o futuro e autoprogramar-se inteiramente. De nada adianta tentarmos limitar o escopo das possibilidades da ciência. Aqueles que o fazem, acabam se surpreendendo. Os aparelhos e computadores, que funcionam ciberneticamente, têm sido comparados aos mecanismos mentais e físicos do ser humano. A aparelhagem eletrônica assemelhar-se-ia ao aspecto mental do homem; o computador assemelhar-se-ia ao aspecto físico do homem. Porém, a sofisticação ainda maior das máquinas poderia eliminar até mesmo isso. Não há que duvidar que o cérebro físico tem funções que se assemelham às de um computador; mas o próprio cérebro é apenas um instrumento da mente. Ver o meu artigo sobre o *Problema Corpo-Mente*.

Comentários. Oponho-me a qualquer noção de que alguma máquina supersofisticada, dotada de superinteligência artificial, possa duplicar a natureza humana, pelas seguintes razões:

1. Embora os criadores de computadores possam insuflar em uma máquina uma inteligência superior até mesmo à do homem, as qualidades da alma, como a vontade moral, a autoconsciência e o propósito espiritual não podem tornar-se propriedades de uma simples máquina. Por maior que seja a inteligência de uma máquina, tais qualidades jamais poderão ser duplicadas. Uma máquina fantasticamente sofisticada haverá de *amar* a alguém?

2. A ciência está fazendo progressos em muitas direções, e não apenas no campo da inteligência artificial. Ela está às vésperas de provar até mesmo a existência da alma e sua sobrevivência ante a morte física. Ver o artigo sobre a *Alma* quanto às diversas evidências a respeito, bem como o artigo intitulado, *Abordagem Científica à Crença na Alma e em sua Sobrevivência ante a Morte Física*. Esse artigo aparece, entre outros, sob o título geral de a *Imortalidade da Alma*. Ver também o artigo sobre *Experiências Perto da Morte*, que provê evidências acerca da realidade da sobrevivência da alma. Meu argumento, quanto a este ponto é esse particular, é que apesar da ciência produzir certa inteligência artificial, que ultrapassa a capacidade de inteligência do ser

humano, ela também está provando a realidade da alma e de sua sobrevivência diante da morte. Isso significa que a espiritualidade do homem também é um assunto que pode ser demonstrado pela ciência, o que salvaguarda a importância da religião e da filosofia, como disciplinas que se aplicam ao homem.

3. As experiências religiosas e místicas levam-nos totalmente para fora do escopo das máquinas. Existem seres espirituais inteligentes que, algumas vezes, entram em contacto com o homem. O homem não é apenas um ser não-mecânico. Ver o artigo sobre o *Misticismo*. Ver também sobre *Satya Sai Baba*, quanto a evidências sobre poderes acima do que é meramente mecânico.

CÍCERO, MARCUS TULLIUS

Suas datas foram 106-43 A.C. Foi um filósofo eclético e estadista romano. Mediante as traduções que fez e suas exposições da filosofia grega, ele nos concedeu muitos discernimentos quanto a Platão, Aristóteles e as principais escolas filosóficas, como a dos céticos, a dos estóicos e a dos epicúreos. Seu gracioso estilo literário empresta um certo encanto aos seus comentários. Além de suas realizações no campo da filosofia, Cícero tornou-se conhecido como orador eloquente e estadista poderoso. Ele pertencia à classe eqüestre, um nível abaixo da classe senatorial. Era estudioso ávido e incansável, tendo-se tornado um erudito em muitos ramos do saber. Seus talentos na oratória conferiram-lhe rápida ascensão na política romana. Suas muitas vicissitudes políticas, com momentos de vitória e de derrota, levaram-no até os tempos da guerra civil romana, quando César e Pompeu tomaram lados opostos. Isso levou Cícero a um dilema. Ele não simpatizava com a causa de César, embora contasse com amigos íntimos que apoiavam a César. Turbulências políticas, e a perda de uma filha, que sempre lhe fora querida, fizeram-no passar tempos difíceis, durante a ditadura de César. Cícero não teve qualquer participação no assassinato de César; mas regozijou-se com a morte do ditador. Posteriormente, Cícero colaborou com os assassinos de César, Bruto e Cássio, a fim de restaurar a república romana. Isso fê-lo entrar em choque com Marco Antônio, contra quem fez catorze escaldantes discursos, chamados de as Filípicas, e por causa dos quais obteve grande apoio da parte do senado. Porém, as inevitáveis mudanças de poder terminaram entregando a Antônio as rédeas do poder e o nome de Cícero apareceu na lista daqueles que precisavam ser mortos. Os homens de Antonio puseram-se a caçá-lo, e a 7 de dezembro de 43 A.C., tiraram-lhe a vida. Sua cabeça e suas mãos foram decepadas e expostas na entrada do Fórum de Roma.

Idéias Filosóficas:

1. O princípio ético e tipicamente estóico da *moderação* é importante na filosofia de Cícero. Essa idéia ele aplicou tanto em sua ética quanto em sua epistemologia (gnosiologia). Ele advogava o ceticismo moderado (que vide), rejeitando tanto o dogmatismo quanto o ceticismo extremo. No campo da ética ele opunha-se ao ascetismo e ao hedonismo. Ele defendia as tradições, mas também promovia as mudanças. No terreno da política, pelo menos teoricamente, ele promovia a modificação pacífica, sem violências. O princípio estóico da moderação veio a tornar-se um dos grandes princípios cristãos, por meio de Paulo, cujos escritos éticos demonstram que ele conhecia e aprovava várias idéias daquela escola filosófica. Ver Filipenses 4:5: «Seja a vossa moderação conhecida de todos os homens. Perto está o Senhor». A palavra grega aqui traduzida por moderação, *sophrosúne*, tornou-se um lema importante na Igreja Oriental.

2. No campo da metafísica, Cícero concebia uma divindade racional, cujos princípios foram incorporados no universo, sob a forma de leis naturais. Essas leis transcendem às leis e tradições dos homens, e os homens são considerados responsáveis diante delas. Essas leis naturais são, igualmente, os padrões segundo os quais os homens devem estabelecer as suas leis.

3. Cícero ensinava que a *retórica* tanto é a arte de falar bem quanto é a arte de expor os pensamentos de uma forma organizada e eficaz, estando necessariamente relacionada a todas as ciências, e, sobretudo, à filosofia, onde seu emprego é tão importante. Todavia, ele também ensinava que um bom orador também deve ser um homem bom, pois, do contrário, a sua habilidade será aplicada de maneira errada.

CICÍLIO Ver Saco.

CICLO DO TEMPO

Há várias maneiras de encararmos a história. Uma delas é a *linear*. Esse termo significa que o tempo é visto dotado de um começo, continuação e fim, como se os eventos ocorressem ao longo de uma linha, mas não se repetissem formando um ciclo. O ponto de vista hebreu da história era linear. Os pais latinos da Igreja também interpretavam a história desse modo. Isso fornece-nos a desencorajadora visão do destino humano segundo a qual um homem nasce, recebe uma alma nessa oportunidade, leva uma vida terrena de alguns poucos anos, morre biologicamente, e então é julgado; e o seu estado fica estagnado no céu ou no inferno. Em contraste com isso, os pais gregos da Igreja falavam sobre a preexistência da alma, desde algum tempo remoto que não sabemos determinar. Dali, a alma passaria pelo perímetro de um círculo, e não de uma linha reta. Em nenhum ponto desse círculo poder-se-ia assinalar um ponto onde cessa a oportunidade de salvação da alma. Um círculo não tem começo e nem fim. Isso posto, a visão grega da vida e do destino humano é circular. Em minha opinião, isso não somente é otimista, mas também parece assemelhar-se mais à realidade dos fatos, em contraposição ao derrotismo e melancolia do ponto de vista linear dos pais latinos da Igreja. Esse ponto de vista circular também ensina que o progresso espiritual do homem é interminável, o que concorda com o conceito de que o homem precisa participar, finalmente, da natureza divina. Visto que há uma infinitude nessa participação, também deverá haver um preenchimento e uma transformação infinitos (II Cor. 3:18; II Ped. 1:4).

Os estóicos pensavam que há grandes ciclos repetitivos, supondo que o *Logos* emanava-se, mas depois recolhia-se em si mesmo. Nesse recolhimento, cessaria a individualidade, porquanto tudo seria reabsorvido pelo Logos; mas, devido a uma nova emanação, tudo seria restaurado à existência. A teoria do «big bang» da astronomia moderna é uma teoria similar, quando supõe a existência de vastos ciclos no universo. A grande explosão criaria um ciclo de vida. Porém, quando o universo volta a concentrar-se em si mesmo, isso seria o fim do mesmo. Mas, eis que ocorreria uma nova explosão, dando início a um outro ciclo de vida. É presumível que isso já se teria repetido por inúmeras vezes, e que os dezesseis bilhões de anos do presente representam uma minúscula porção da expansão total do tempo em que as coisas têm existido. O conceito de grandiosos ciclos exalta o Deus eterno, ao passo que a

CIDADANIA

declaração de que todas as coisas começaram somente há cerca de seis mil anos, além de não ser científica, é absurda e degrada a grandiosidade de Deus.

Ciclos Dentro de Ciclos e Vastos Ciclos Cósmicos. Por toda a natureza podemos observar os ciclos do começo ou nascimento, florescimento, declínio, decadência e destruição. Hesíodo falava sobre ciclos que terminam no declínio, tendo postulado as quatro eras do ouro, da prata, do bronze e do ferro, cada área pior que a anterior. Por igual modo, o zoroastrismo (que vide) dividia a duração do mundo em quatro eras de três mil anos cada. O hinduísmo antigo concebia que as eras do mundo perdurariam por um total de doze mil anos divinos, e que equivaleria a 4.320.000 anos humanos. Intérpretes posteriores ampliaram isso enormemente, adicionando ciclos noturnos entre os ciclos diurnos, e igualmente de vasta duração cada um. Os ciclos budistas começam com a destruição e avançam para a perfeição, em quatro vastos períodos, recuando novamente para a destruição. Grandes cataclismos cósmicos poriam fim aos ciclos, uma idéia não muito diferente das teorias estóica e do *big bang*. Parece haver uma grande verdade nessa filosofia dos ciclos, mas somente Deus sabe o que está envolvido na questão.

Os Ciclos do Destino. As vidas dotadas de propósito parecem passar por ciclos de florescimento e de declínio, cada qual com sua própria importância para o bem da vida total. Há desígnio por detrás de tudo, pois a vida assemelha-se a uma história com muitos capítulos, cada qual com seu propósito próprio, ao mesmo tempo em que todos esses capítulos, em seu conjunto, mostram a razão da existência. Essa história teria começado em tempos remotíssimos, e continuará se desenrolando interminavelmente. A vida presente, com os seus próprios pequenos ciclos, faz parte do total, que inclui um ciclo de existência interminável. O otimismo permeia a tudo, embora certos subciclos específicos possam ser períodos escuros, períodos noturnos. O próprio Deus é o Senhor dos ciclos, controlando-os para o bem do homem. Tudo aponta na direção da *restauração* final (que vide) conforme se vê em Efésios 1:10.

CIDADANIA

1. *Entre os Hebreus*. Os israelitas tinham uma feroz identificação nacional, o que tem resistido à passagem do tempo, com todas as suas vicissitudes, guerras, exílios e caos. Entre os hebreus, a cidadania contava com várias instituições que a fortaleciam. Antes de tudo, desde o começo a consolidação da nação de Israel requeria muito trabalho e sofrimento. O que é ganho com esforço, não se larga com facilidade. Em segundo lugar, havia a suposição geral de que Yahweh estava executando a sua vontade através da nação de Israel, e coisa alguma era considerada mais importante do que a vontade divina. Em terceiro lugar, um complexo código legal, considerado divinamente transmitido, dava estabilidade e propósito ao povo de Israel. Essas leis eram bastante generosas até no caso de estrangeiros, exigindo plena proteção para os estranhos que habitavam dentro dos portões das cidades de Israel (Êxo. 12:19; Lev. 24:22; Núm. 15:15; 35:15; Deu. 1:16; 24:17). A única lei que discriminava os estrangeiros era a lei da usura. Os estrangeiros tinham de pagar juros sobre dívidas e empréstimos (Deu. 23:20), o que não era cobrado da parte dos israelitas. Havia provisões especiais para os órfãos, os pobres, etc. Estes compartilhavam dos dízimos e das ofertas feitas na época da colheita, e também eram beneficiados pelo ano do jubileu (Deu. 14:29; 16:10,14; 26:11; Lev. 25:6). Em quarto lugar, em Israel a cidadania nunca foi considerada uma questão meramente terrena. Ali acreditava-se que o homem é criatura de Deus, dotada de um destino em Deus e na espiritualidade. Enquanto que outras nações têm sido povos religiosos, ninguém pode comparar-se a Israel como uma *teocracia*, onde a vida religiosa e a vida civil confundiam-se, e onde os líderes religiosos eram, *ipso facto*, os governantes civis. Ser alguém cidadão de Israel era participar do plano de Deus para a nação, pois, doutra sorte, nem haveria razão para a existência dessa nação.

2. *No Novo Testamento*: *a Cidadania Romana*. A cidadania romana (ver Atos 27:38), a *jus civitatis civitas*, era concedida ocasionalmente, pelos imperadores, a cidades ou mesmo a províncias inteiras (Dion Cass. 41:25; Suet. *Aug.* 47), como também a indivíduos, como recompensa por algum serviço especial prestado ao estado ou à família imperial (Suet. *Aug.* 47). O trecho de Atos 22:28 indica que a cidadania romana podia ser adquirida a dinheiro. Paulo já nasceu cidadão romano porque, antes dele, algum membro de sua família, embora de sólidas tradições judaicas, adquirira esse direito. Ele usou sua cidadania romana para protestar por haver sido punido fisicamente, e também para apelar para César, mediante o que ele tinha o direito de ser julgado pelo próprio imperador, a fim de que o seu caso fosse decidido. Ver Atos 25:11 e 28:19.

A cidadania romana dependia, primariamente, de alguém nascer em algum lugar que fazia parte do império romano, cujos habitantes tinham esse direito. Porém, conforme vimos, Roma era bastante liberal nessa questão de conferir a cidadania a quem não tivesse essa qualificação básica. Por causa dessa liberalidade, os cidadãos romanos ocupavam, em grandes números, a maior parte do mundo civilizado da época. Todavia, não havia regras fixas para esse processo; tudo dependia do governante e das circunstâncias do momento, o que o tornava mais lento ou mais rápido. Júlio César tinha o desejo de estender a cidadania como medida consolidadora do império. A cidadania de Paulo tornara-se realidade por motivo de alguma medida liberal, mediante a qual os judeus da cidade de Tarso passaram a ser reputados cidadãos romanos, embora nos seja impossível determinar quando isso sucedeu. Algumas cidades eram favorecidas, como Filipos, que mantinha posição distinta e bastante cobiçada no começo do império romano, em contraste com outras cidades e províncias. De modo geral, o desenvolvimento da cidadania romana pode ser traçada historicamente. Parte disso, naturalmente, devia-se ao crescimento populacional. Ao fim da guerra púnica, em 240 A.C., os cidadãos de sexo masculino atingiam o número de 260 mil. Em 124 A.C., esse número crescera para mais de 390 mil. Em 85 A.C., eles já eram 963 mil. E isso era assim porque uma larga porção da Itália havia sido incorporada, quando o privilégio não continuou limitado à cidade de Roma e suas cercanias imediatas. Sob Augusto (quando houve recenseamentos em 28 A.C., 8 A.C. e 14 D.C.), as estatísticas falavam, respectivamente, em 4.063.000, 4.233.000 e 4.937.000. Em 47 D.C., o recenseamento feito na época do imperador Cláudio, deu 5.984.072 cidadãos.

3. *Condições*. Um cidadão tinha direitos (*iura*), privilégios (*honores*) e deveres (*numera*). Entre os direitos havia o *ius provocationis*, o direito de apelo ao imperador, nos casos de julgamento. Esse foi o direito

CIDADE

que Paulo usou, referido acima. Os deveres incluíam o *munus militare*, ou dever de serviço militar, e o *ius suffragii*, o direito de voto. Os *honores* eram privilégios especiais conferidos pelo senado a cidadãos notáveis. As referências neotestamentárias à cidadania romana (Atos 16:37,39; 22:25-27,29) mostram que, nos dias de Paulo, esse direito era muito cobiçado e respeitado. Em tempos posteriores, entretanto, a instituição inteira começou a degenerar.

4. *A Cidadania Espiritual, Celestial*. Temos o exemplo de Abraão, que buscava a cidadania celeste, confessando-se um estrangeiro neste mundo (Heb. 11:10). Paulo, em Filipenses 3:20, alude à cidadania espiritual e celeste dos membros da Igreja, onde Cristo é o Senhor absoluto. Isso subentende um novo e elevado destino. Isso também empresta uma nova perspectiva ao crente, sobre como ele deve usar apropriadamente a sua vida. Paulo exortou aos crentes de Filipos que vivessem de uma maneira digna do evangelho (Fil. 1:27). Os crentes filipenses, que tinham direito à cidadania romana, sem dúvida compreenderam bem a metáfora usada pelo apóstolo. O trecho de Colossenses 1:13 não usa a palavra «cidadania», mas fala sobre o crente como pertencente ao *reino* do amado Filho de Deus, o que subentende a nossa cidadania no mundo transcendental. (ID MOF NTI)

CIDADE

Esboço:
1. As Palavras
2. Primeiras Referências Bíblicas
3. A Cidade: a Segunda Grande Revolução
4. Antigas Cidades Hebréias
5. Cidades Não-Israelitas
6. Nos Dias do Novo Testamento

1. As Palavras

Várias palavras hebraicas e gregas estão envolvidas neste verbete:

1. *Ir*, «cidade». Essa palavra aparece cerca de mil e cem vezes no Antigo Testamento. Se alguém seguir as referências bíblicas, notará que a nossa distinção moderna entre cidade e aldeia ou vila, baseada em número de habitantes, não fazia parte inerente das palavras hebraicas. Ver Gên. 4:17; 19:29; 24:10; Êxo. 1:11; Lev. 25:29,31; I Sam. 15:5; 20:6; II Reis 17:6; Jer. 51:42,43; Jon. 3:3; Naum 3:1. Unger, grande erudito presbiteriano moderno, supõe que se possa fazer distinção entre uma cidade e uma aldeia com base nas muralhas. Se havia uma muralha circundando a comunidade, então esta se chamava cidade; em caso negativo, a comunidade era chamada aldeia. Ver Lev. 25:29-31; I Sam. 6:18; Eze. 38:11.

2. *Qereth*, «cidade». Ver Jó 29:7; Pro. 8:3; 11:11. Cinco ocorrências.

3. *Qirya*, «cidade». Ver Núm. 21:28; Deu. 2:36; I Reis 1:41; Jó 39:7; Sal. 48:2; Pro. 10:15; 11:10; 18:11; Isa. 1:21, 26; 22:2; Jer. 49:25; Osé. 6:8; Hab. 2:8,12; Esd. 4:12-21. A palavra ocorre em um total de vinte e nove vezes.

4. *Saar*, «portão», mas que serve como sinônimo de cidade em Deu. 5:14; 12:14 e 14:27,28.

5. *Chatser*, palavra hebraica que, por quarenta e seis vezes, parece indicar uma vila sem qualquer proteção, em distinção às cidades fechadas com muralhas, segundo se vê, por exemplo, em Êxo. 8:13; Jos. 13:23,28; 19:6-8,15,16,22,30,31,38,48; I Crô. 4:32, 33; Nee. 11:25,30; Sal. 10:8.

As cidades fortificadas eram chamadas, em hebraico, *ir nibtsar*, conforme se vê, por exemplo, em Núm. 13:39; II Sam. 24:7; II Reis 8:12; Sal. 80:40.

6. *Pólis*, «cidade». Palavra grega que aparece por um total de cento e sessenta e quatro vezes, em todos os tipos de conexões. É termo de larga aplicação, podendo indicar tanto uma cidade quanto uma aldeia. Ver Mat. 8:33; 21:7; Mar. 11:19; Atos 8:9. Se acompanhada do artigo definido, «a cidade», então está em foco uma cidade principal, ou uma capital, como em Atos 8:5; Apo. 21:15. Na literatura secular, a palavra também era usada para indicar os habitantes de uma cidade, conforme se vê em Josefo (*Anti*. 1.200). Também foi usada para indicar a Cidade Celeste, a *Nova Jerusalém* (Apo. 21:2,10, etc).

Metrópolis é uma combinação de palavras gregas que indica uma cidade principal, e que, no Novo Testamento, aparece somente no subtítulo de I Timóteo. Mas há palavras cognatas, que expressam questões relacionadas, como *politarches*, «magistrado civil»; *politeia*, «cidadania» (que vide); *politeuma*, «comunidade» ou estado; *polites*, «cidadão»; *politeuomai*, o verbo, sem paralelo em português, mas que significa ter a cidadania, ou então governar, viver, conduzir-se.

2. Primeiras Referências Bíblicas

A mais antiga alusão bíblica à ereção de cidades fala sobre como Caim edificou a cidade de Enoque, em Gênesis 4:17. Após a confusão das línguas, surgiram muitas cidades. Assim, Ninrode construiu Babel, Ereque e outras. Assur edificou Nínive e Reobote (Gênesis 10:10-12,19). A arqueologia tem descoberto coisas inumeráveis relativas a muitas grandes cidades antigas. Escavações arqueológicas importantes têm sido feitas em Ur, Nipur, Quis, Eridu, Lagase, Nínive, Assur, etc. Oferecemos artigos sobre essas cidades, e no artigo sobre a *Arqueologia* damos um gráfico, em ordem alfabética, que fornecerá ao leitor alguma idéia sobre as descobertas feitas nesses locais antigos. A mais antiga descrição bíblica sobre uma cidade envolve Sodoma; mas a arqueologia tem retrocedido na história muito mais do que isso.

3. A Cidade: a Segunda Grande Revolução

A domesticação de certas plantas e animais, na agricultura neolítica, foi a primeira grande revolução cultural. Isso possibilitou a vida comunitária, e, em seguida, as cidades. As cidades representaram a segunda grande revolução cultural, um passo decisivo na civilização. As cidades tornaram possível todas as formas de avanço tecnológico, que a cultura meramente agrícola não requeria e nem podia prover. Entretanto, a vida citadina também traz problemas sociais, incluindo a questão quase insolúvel da criminalidade, que o meio ambiente agrícola não provoca. As cidades iniciam todo um novo conjunto de problemas, relacionados à interação social, à necessidade de leis mais complexas e completas, etc. Então, uma vez que as necessidades básicas da sociedade agrícola são satisfeitas, os habitantes das cidades têm tempo de seguir muitas veredas de erudição e conhecimentos técnicos. Foi assim que se verificou o desenvolvimento da filosofia e da ciência. Negócios e profissões desenvolveram-se que não seriam necessários nas sociedades agrícolas. Torna-se evidente, pois, que a cidade foi um desenvolvimento revolucionário, que explica a civilização e a cultura conforme a conhecemos. A cidade confere ao homem a oportunidade de diversificar o seu conhecimento, utilizando a sua inteligência de novas maneiras. Atualmente, os homens estão contemplando o espaço sideral, como passo inicial de uma nova grande área de exploração humana, o que representa ainda uma outra revolução cultural. É claro que cada novo

CIDADE

desenvolvimento traz consigo novos meios de explorar as potencialidades humanas. Alguns estudiosos olham de volta à vida agrícola não somente como a única forma de vida desejável para o homem, mas também como a única que está em consonância com o plano divino para o homem. Eles supõem que a vida citadina representa, para o homem, uma aberração quanto ao seu estilo de vida. Tal argumento, entretanto, não pode manter-se de pé. Os homens nunca poderiam ter desenvolvido a sua inteligência sem o advento da vida nas cidades.

4. Antigas Cidades Hebréias

Josué mencionou muitas cidades na Palestina. A julgar pela pequena população de Israel, podemos supor com segurança que as cidades eram bem pequenas. Seriam como muitas cidades orientais de nossos próprios dias, com ruas estreitas e tortuosas (Ecl. 12:4; Can. 3:2), com muitas praças perto dos portões das cidades, onde havia mercados e tribunais (Gên. 23:10; Rute 4:1; Mat. 6:5). Poucas ruas eram pavimentadas no interior das cidades, e menos estradas ainda eram pavimentadas fora das cidades. Mas somos informados por Josefo (*Anti.* 8,7) que Salomão pavimentou as estradas que conduziam a Jerusalém com pedras negras. Posteriormente, quando os romanos ensinaram aos homens quão vantajoso era pavimentar as vias públicas, foram pavimentadas as ruas de algumas cidades. Herodes o Grande pavimentou as ruas principais de Antioquia; e Herodes Agripa pavimentou com pedras brancas várias das ruas de Jerusalém. Muitas cidades **contavam com muralhas, portões fortes com barras de bronze ou de ferro, — visando uma maior segurança** para seus habitantes (Deu. 3:5; I Reis 4:13). As cidades maiores também contavam com torres de vigia. Nas capitais, como Jerusalém, as muralhas eram espessas e altas (II Crô. 26:6 ss; Zac. 1:16). Havia torres elevadas por sobre os portões das cidades (II Sam. 18:24). As cidades maiores tinham cidadelas (que vide), no interior das muralhas principais, como medida de proteção extra. O número de portões variava, geralmente dependendo das dimensões das cidades. A cidade ideal de Ezequiel tinha doze portões (Eze. 48:30-35), o que se vê também na Nova Jerusalém do Apocalipse (Apo. 21:12,13).

Governo. O conselho da cidade era a unidade governante das cidades hebréias. O conselho compunha-se dos importantes anciãos e juízes (Deu. 16:18). Eles precisavam ser sacerdotes. Nos tempos dos reis, emergiu a figura do governador (I Reis 22:26; II Crô. 18:25). Após o cativeiro babilônico, continuou a prevalecer o tipo de governo mediante um conselho (Eze. 7:25).

Jerusalém. Essa cidade representou um importante desenvolvimento, pois ali temos uma capital que enfeixava grande poder, como centro da lei, da religião e da potência militar da nação de Israel. Adicionemos a isso a veneração especial de que a cidade era alvo, como lugar onde Deus manifestava a sua presença de maneira especial. Ela teve origem na fortaleza dos jebuseus que Davi capturara. Isso posto, sua localização era neutra, não pertencendo a qualquer tribo particular de Israel. Jerusalém era a única cidade israelita que podia começar a comparar-se com outras grandes cidades não-judaicas da antiguidade, como Nínive e Babilônia. A cidade de Davi era bem pequena, talvez tendo três mil habitantes. Há muita incerteza acerca da história física de Jerusalém. Ela sofria tantos desastres periódicos que nunca pôde expandir-se muito. Apesar disso, gozou de significativa expansão na época dos reis. As ilustrações acerca da antiga Jerusalém mostram uma cidade relativamente pequena. Sabemos que a Jerusalém reconstruída após o exílio, sob Neemias, não diferia muito quanto às dimensões territoriais da época da monarquia dividida. Algumas linhas defensivas foram acrescentadas, cobrindo algum território a mais; mas a população não pode ter ultrapassado doze mil habitantes. Ver o artigo separado sobre *Jerusalém*.

Características das Cidades Bíblicas. Há quatro características que não podemos olvidar, a saber: 1. Em face dos constantes conflitos armados, uma cidade de qualquer tamanho, nos tempos bíblicos, era uma *fortaleza*, com muralhas, portões, torres e cidadelas internas. 2. As ruas eram estreitas e tortuosas, e as casas eram baixas; havia nas proximidades dos portões mercados, do tipo que hoje chamaríamos de feiras livres e também era ali que se faziam negócios e funcionavam os tribunais. 3. As cidades incorporavam lugares sagrados, como santuários e lugares de sacrifício e adoração. Ver sobre Betel (Juí. 20:18) e Silo (I Sam. 7:16 e 10:2). Havia templos tipo fortaleza, designados pela palavra hebraica *migdal* (ver Gên. 32:30-32; Êxo. 14:2; Jos. 15:37). 4. As cidades ficavam perto de algum bom suprimento de água, como rios ou fontes. As cisternas (que vide), eram uma parte essencial das cidades. Havia tanto cisternas públicas quanto cisternas particulares, onde se guardava água para as estações secas. Em certos lugares havia grandes sistemas de irrigação e de condução de água. Túneis e outras instalações para transporte de água eram características comuns nas fortalezas da Idade do Ferro, como se via em Megido, Siquém e Jerusalém. Algumas dessas instalações cobriam impressionantes distâncias, trazendo água desde rios ou mananciais.

Na antiguidade, esses agrupamentos humanos eram classificados com base, acima de tudo, se eram protegidos ou não por muralhas. Isso reflete-se tanto no hebraico quanto no grego, no tocante aos termos usados na Bíblia para indicar essas comunidades. Há diversas palavras hebraicas e gregas que precisamos considerar neste verbete.

A. Cidades Muradas:

1. *Qir*, «cidade». Palavra hebraica que figura por setenta vezes, e que, realmente, refere-se mais às muralhas do que à cidade propriamente dita. Para exemplificar: Lev. 14:37,39; Núm. 22:25; 35:4; I Sam. 18:11; 19:10; 1 Reis 4:33; Jos. 2:15.

2. *Pólis*, «cidade». Palavra grega que aparece por cento e sessenta vezes no Novo Testamento, principalmente nos evangelhos sinópticos, no livro de Atos e no Apocalipse, desde Mat. 2:23 até Apo. 22:19.

B. Cidades Sem Muros:

1. *Bath*, «filha». Com o sentido de «aldeia» ou «vila», a palavra ocorre por quarenta e quatro vezes. Por exemplo: Jos. 15:45,47; 17:11,16; Juí. 11:26; I Crô. 2:23; 7:28; 8:12; II Crô. 13:19.

2. *Chavvoth*, «povoado». Palavra hebraica que aparece por quatro vezes: Núm. 32:41; Jos. 13:30; I Reis 4:13 e I Crô. 2:23.

3. *Chatser*, «vila». Palavra hebraica que ocorre por quarenta e seis vezes, por exemplo: Êxo. 8:13; Lev. 25:31; Jos. 13:23,28; 15:32,36,41,44-47,51,54,57,59, 60,62; 18:24,28; I Crô. 4:32,33; Nee. 11:25,30; Sal. 10:8; Isa. 42:11.

4. *Ir*, «cidade», «lugar agitado». Palavra hebraica extremamente comum, que ocorre por quase mil e cem vezes, desde Gên. 13:12 até Zac. 14:2.

5. *Perazoth*, «aldeias abertas». Palavra hebraica que aparece por três vezes apenas: Zac. 2:4; Est. 9:19

CIDADE

e Eze. 38:11.

6. *Kóme*, «aldeia». Palavra grega que ocorre por vinte e sete vezes: Mat. 9:35; 10:11; 14:15; 21:2; Mar. 6:6,36,56; 8:23,26,27; 11:2; Luc. 5:17; 8:1; 9:6,12,52, 56; 10:38; 13:22; 17:12; 19:30; 24:13,28; João 7:42; 11:1,30; Atos 8:25.

7. *Komópolis*, uma combinação de *kóme* e *pólis*, dando a entender uma comunidade ainda sem muralhas, mas de dimensões bastante grandes. Essa palavra grega aparece por apenas uma vez, em Mar. 1:38.

Conforme indicamos acima, duas categorias básicas de cidades aparecem nas Escrituras Sagradas. Em Lev. 25:31, onde é empregada a palavra hebraica *chatser*, a vila é caracterizada pela ausência de muralhas; e, além disso, estava sujeita a uma diferente lei de redenção. Nas vilas sem muros, as casas precisavam ser devolvidas a seus proprietários originais, quando vendidas, ao chegar o ano do jubileu, ao passo que, nas cidades muradas, as casas não podiam ser redimidas se se passasse mais de um ano após o tempo da venda das mesmas. Conforme foi demonstrado no ponto A. 1, acima, o termo *qir* geralmente era usado juntamente com adjetivos qualificativos, indicando a presença ou ausência de muralhas, o que nos mostra que essa palavra não estava especificamente limitada ao sentido de cidade murada. Podia estar em foco até mesmo uma parede de uma construção qualquer.

No período do Antigo Testamento, — uma cidade murada era distinguida não somente por possuir muralhas, mas também por ser um centro defensivo, comercial e industrial; e, em alguns casos, era também onde residia o governador local. Já no período do Novo Testamento, a diferença essencial entre uma cidade e uma aldeia não era tanto a presença ou ausência de muralhas, e, sim, a posse de constituições e de leis que diferiam das leis referentes ao interior, porquanto essa legislação seguia as leis da coroa. Após os dias neotestamentários, uma cidade era assim chamada se se tivesse tornado sede de um bispado. A Mishna fazia uma tríplice distinção: a. cidade grande; b. cidade pequena; c. aldeia. Ver sobre *Vila*. Quando a palavra *bath*, «filha» era usada com o sentido de aldeia, e não com o seu sentido primário de «filha», — então indicava uma aldeia dependente de alguma cidade maior, murada. Essas aldeias eram, principalmente, centros agrícolas interioranos, dependentes das cidades muradas para sua proteção militar, onde também eram colocados os produtos agrícolas e outros. Nas aldeias, as edificações geralmente eram de qualidade inferior, geralmente cruas, sem ornamentações arquiteturais. Há evidências arqueológicas acerca de muitas centenas de aldeias e vilas pertencentes desde a época de Jeremias para trás. Porém, a maioria delas não chegou a ser repovoada, após o exílio babilônico. Rute e Davi, em suas atividades, ilustram a vida campesina da época.

Precisamos ainda considerar os topônimos hebraicos *kafar* e *haçor*. O primeiro aparece em locativos como Quefar-Amonai, «aldeia dos amonitas» (Jos. 18:24) ou Cafarnaum (Mat. 4:13, etc.). E o segundo como em Azor (Jos. 11:1). O primeiro desses topônimos significa «aldeia». Mas o segundo deles, *haçor*, merece um estudo mais detalhado. Essa palavra era usada principalmente para indicar os povoados que ficavam no limite entre a terra cultivada e o deserto. Os povos assim classificados geralmente eram protegidos por uma espessa sebe de plantas espinhosas ou por um muro de pedras, como proteção contra as feras, e dentro da qual os habitantes viviam em tendas, e não em casas de material mais permanente. Portanto, se *kafar* indicava uma população sedentária, *haçor* indicava uma população seminômade. Resta dizer somente que a cultura não era tão desenvolvida nas aldeias, vilas e povoados de qualquer categoria, como sucedia nas cidades muradas. No caso do povo de Israel, nesse particular, nenhuma outra cidade comparava-se às duas capitais: Jerusalém, do reino do sul, ou Judá; e Samaria, do reino do norte, Israel. Ver também sobre Vilas e sobre *Povoados*.

5. Cidades Não-Israelitas

A maioria das descrições das cidades de Israel se ajustaria à descrição de cidades estrangeiras. Houve muitas idéias tomadas por empréstimo. Em primeiro lugar, quando da conquista da Palestina, os israelitas simplesmente adaptaram muitas das idéias já existentes para nelas habitarem. Porém, no mundo antigo houve alguns notáveis exemplos de cidades diferentes e maiores que aquelas da Palestina, como Nínive e Babilônia. Há artigos separados sobre essas cidades, onde o leitor poderá obter novas informações.

6. Nos Dias do Novo Testamento

Quanto a uma discussão sobre as palavras gregas envolvidas, ver o começo deste artigo. Consideremos os pontos abaixo:

a. Muitas das cidades da Palestina foram destruídas total ou parcialmente durante as guerras dos Macabeus. Aquelas que foram reedificadas antes do domínio romano, eram similares àquelas que já foram descritas. Os romanos tomaram a região em cerca de 63 A.C. O rei Herodes governou sob os romanos entre 37 e 34 A.C. Ele foi um grande construtor de cidades. Reformou a muitas delas e edificou outras. A influência arquitetônica dos romanos foi grande. Um exemplo é a cidade de Samaria, que recebeu o nome novo de Sebaste (palavra grega correspondente a Augusto). A cidade recebeu novas torres, circundando a cidade com um formato oval irregular, de cerca de um quilômetro de lado a lado. Um gigantesco templo em estilo romano foi ali construído. Tinha 69 m de comprimento, com um fórum tipo romano no seu lado oriental. Cesaréia foi construída em cerca de 12 anos (25 a 13 A.C.). Os arqueólogos têm examinado detalhadamente essa cidade, onde há típicos remanescentes arquitetônicos romanos. Essa cidade era a sede do governo romano na Palestina. Foi ali que Paulo foi julgado diante de Festo e de Herodes Agripa (Atos 25:23 ss), e onde o centurião Cornélio foi envolvido, no estabelecimento de um igreja cristã gentílica, no começo da missão da Igreja ali. Ver Atos 10:18-22. Josefo informa-nos que o porto de Cesaréia era similar, se não mesmo maior que o de Atenas, na Grécia. Ali havia uma arena ligeiramente maior que o Coliseu de Roma.

b. Jerusalém cresceu em sua área com dois novos portões, muralhas e fortificações. Um magnificente templo foi construído na cidade. Herodes foi o grande responsável por isso. Expandiu o átrio, cuja porção suleste era sustentada por colunas e imensas abóbadas, chamadas Abóbadas de Salomão. Uma gigantesca muralha de retenção foi construída, que é a atual Muralha das Lamentações. Esse templo foi um dos mais magnificentes edifícios do mundo do século I D.C. Uma predição de Jesus anunciava a destruição de Jerusalém, em vista da rejeição ao Messias. E Tito, ao pôr fim à revolta dos judeus contra Roma, cumpriu a profecia de Jesus no ano 70 D.C. Em 132 D.C., Jerusalém foi reconstruída, embora não mais no grandioso estilo de antes, e

CIDADE — CIDADE BAIXA

recebeu o novo nome de Aélia Capitolina. Cobria então uma área de apenas cerca de 320 mil metros quadrados, com uma população de, talvez, entre dez e dezoito mil habitantes.

Para os cristãos dos dias de Jesus e posteriormente, Jerusalém continou a ser considerada uma cidade santa. Jesus chamou-a de «cidade do grande Rei» (Mat. 5:35). Até a sua destruição, em 70 D.C., Jerusalém era o principal centro cristão, o lugar de onde partiram as primeiras missões cristãs de evangelismo. Porém, o tratamento dado pela cidade ao Messias amargurou a muitos cristãos contra ela. O escritor do Apocalipse chamou-a de Sodoma e Egito, porquanto foi ali que o Senhor Jesus foi crucificado (Apo. 11:8). A tradição profética, bíblica e moderna, prediz que a Igreja terá novamente Jerusalém como seu grande centro, após a conversão dos judeus, o que se espera para um futuro não muito distante. Então Jerusalém tornar-se-á o centro e a protetora da civilização por um período de mil anos, tal como sucedeu a Roma, durante a Idade Média. Ver o artigo separado sobre *Jerusalém*. Os capítulos vinte e um e vinte e dois do Apocalipse encerram descrições da Nova Jerusalém, o que muitos intérpretes aceitam como descrições simbólicas da própria Igreja. Outros estudiosos pensam sobre uma habitação celestial literal, que descerá do céu à terra, ou ficará suspensa sobre a terra. A interpretação metafórica ajusta-se melhor à natureza do Apocalipse, de acordo com a qual, **condições mileniais**, utópicas, provavelmente devem ser entendidas. Os comentários sobre esses capítulos, no NTI, fornecem as muitas interpretações que estão envolvidas na questão.

c. Herodes, o Grande, edificou certo número de esplêndidos palácios e fortalezas na Palestina, como em Ascalom, Herodion (sul de Belém), Massada, Maquero, Qarn, Sartabé (norte de Jericó) e Jericó. Nessas cidades havia muitas coisas de estilo romano, como mosaicos, construções de pedra, com evidências de riquezas e prosperidade.

d. Um distinto grupo de cidades neotestamentárias são as cidades helenistas que vieram à existência nos séculos III e II A.C., na Transjordânia e em Citópolis (Bete-Seã). Essas cidades foram reunidas em um grupo, chamado Decápolis (que vide) e então postas sob o governo do governador romano da Síria. Entre elas havia as cidades de Gerasa, Filadélfia e Gadara, a última das quais é a única que faz parte do grupo, que teve qualquer importância dentro do ministério de Jesus. Essas cidades eram tão típicas quanto as demais cidades helenistas, mostrando a influência combinada da Grécia, de Roma, da Ásia Menor e da Síria.

e. Uma outra característica distintiva, refletida nas cidades da Palestina, era o caráter da Judéia que, segundo sabemos, reteve o sistema ptolemaico de vilas, com grupos ou distritos chamados toparquias. Cada toparquia tinha seus oficiais locais, incluindo o juiz, quase inteiramente autônomo (em contraste com os sistemas grego e romano, bem mais ordeiros, segundo se vê em Mat. 5:25). Esse juiz era responsável diante de algum rei vassalo. Uma vila maior atuava como centro administrativo da toparquia. A parábola dos talentos, em Lucas 19:17-20, alude a um sistema de distritos sob o controle de alguma vila maior. O tirano vassalo fazia parte do mundo das satrapias e de outros governos menores. Por essa razão, os aldeões judeus foram governados por uma sucessão de conquistadores.

f. No livro de Atos transparece muito mais a maneira romana de fazer as coisas, em parte modelada segundo os padrões gregos. Havia a *pólis*, dirigida por seu próprio governo municipal, dentro de um território específico. Os conselhos das cidades tinham muitos membros, talvez quinhentos ou seiscentos. Nenhuma pessoa, nem mesmo juiz, tinha autoridade sem controle. Os cidadãos tinham direitos, e havia sistemas legislativos bem desenvolvidos. Quanto mais nos aproximamos da cidade de Roma, mais as cidades seguiam o estilo romano. Porém, nas cidades mais distantes, prevalecia o modelo grego. E também havia cidades helenizadas, um amálgama desses dois estilos. Foi entre as cidades helenizadas que o evangelho se propagou com maior liberdade, ao passo que a situação judaica era quase impossível de se modificar em qualquer grau mais significativo.

g. *As Cidades Gregas*. Quando o evangelho penetrou na Europa, os pregadores cristãos encontraram cidades gregas com influência romana. Ver os artigos separados sobre Corinto, Atenas, Tessalônica e Beréia, para exemplificar.

h. *Caráter Diversificado das Cidades*. A discussão acima demonstra que as cidades do Novo Testamento tinham uma natureza muito mais diversificada do que as cidades do Antigo Testamento. O antigo estilo hebreu sofreu a influência ptolemaica, como também das cidades militares e das cidades-colônias de Roma, ao mesmo tempo em que as cidades-estado dos gregos continuavam a reter grande parcela de seu típico estilo grego. As sete cartas do Apocalipse, dirigidas a sete igrejas em sete cidades diferentes, exibem uma natureza diferente de cada uma dessas cidades. Com a passagem do tempo, as cidades tornaram-se maiores, melhor planejadas, muitas delas dotadas de verdadeiros monumentos arquiteturais e grandes feitos da engenharia. (ADA AH(1967) ND RAM Z)

CIDADE BAIXA

Essa é a tradução, em nossa versão portuguesa, da palavra hebraica que aparece em Sofonias 1:10. O hebraico diz apenas *mishneh*, «segundo». Os intérpretes, entretanto, pensam que isso significa «segundo distrito», onde a palavra «distrito» fica entendida. Ver também II Reis 22:14 e II Crô. 34:22. Ali é dito que a profetisa Hulda habitava nesse segundo distrito da cidade de Jerusalém. Esse distrito ficava em um ângulo formado pela muralha ocidental do templo e pela antiga muralha norte da cidade. Posteriormente, foi incluído dentro da muralha mandada construir por Neemias.

Josefo nos dá a entender que esse distrito, que ele chamou Acra (ver *Guerras* i.1,4; 5,4 e 6:1), era, realmente a parte mais baixa da cidade, embora contígua à colina onde estava edificado o templo. Acra é a transliteração da palavra grega que significa «fortaleza». Essa fortaleza fora edificada por Antíoco Epifânio (168 A.C.). Nos dias de Simão Macabeu, não somente a fortaleza foi arrasada, mas até mesmo a colina sobre a qual ela ficava foi nivelada (ver Josefo, *Anti.* xiii.6,7; *Guerras* v.4,1). Mas, no Antigo Testamento hebraico, a expressão «cidade baixa» nunca aparece, pois o nome que ali é dado a essa porção da cidade é «Cidade de Davi». Portanto, o nome deve ter aparecido após o nivelamento daquela colina, nos dias dos Macabeus. Isso significa que a versão portuguesa nos apresenta uma interpretação, e não uma tradução do texto hebraico.

No seu sentido mais amplo, a «Cidade Baixa» incluía não somente aquela seção da cidade onde habitavam os mais abastados, mas também o trecho do vale do Tiropoeon, desde Siloé até à «Casa do Concílio», que ficava perto da «primeira muralha», a muralha norte da cidade, onde, sem dúvida, residiam muitos pobres de Jerusalém. Quanto a uma descrição mais completa sobre a topografia de Jerusalém, ver sobre *Jerusalém*, na secção sobre *Topografia*.

CIDADE CERCADA

Essa expressão serve de tradução para várias palavras hebraicas diversas:

1. *Bitstsarom*, «lugar cercado». Palavra usada somente em Zac. 9:12.

2. *Mibtsar*, «lugar cercado». Palavra usada por dezoito vezes. Por exemplo: Núm. 13:19; II Sam. 24:7; II Reis 8:12; Sal. 89:40; Jer. 48:18; Dan. 11:24; Miq. 5:11; Naum 3:12,14; Hab. 1:10.

3. *Maoz*, «fortim». Palavra usada por trinta e duas vezes. Por exemplo: Isa. 23:11; Naum 1:7.

4. *Metsad*, «fortaleza». Palavra empregada por sete vezes. Por exemplo: Juí. 6:2; I Sam. 23:14,19,29; Jer. 48:41.

5. *Metsudah*, «fortaleza». Palavra usada por dezessete vezes com esse sentido. Por exemplo: II Sam. 5:7; 22:2; Sal. 18:2; 31:3; 144:2.

6. *Matsor*, «rampa». Palavra usada por oito vezes com esse sentido: Zac. 9:3; Jer. 10:17; Miq. 7:2; Deu. 20:20.

7. *Metsurah*, «fortim». Palavra usada por duas vezes: II Crô. 11:11; Isa. 29:3.

Há uma clara distinção, no Antigo Testamento, entre uma cidade e uma aldeia. Uma cidade contava com uma muralha, e uma aldeia, não. Nesse particular, encontramos uma tríplice divisão: a. cidades; b. aldeias sem muralhas, c. aldeias com castelos ou torres (I Crô. 27:25). Ver o artigo sobre as *Cidades*. Sabemos, mediante a história, que o distrito a leste do rio Jordão, que formava os reinos de Moabe e Basã, contava com muitos castelos e fortalezas, construídos com o intuito de proteger os animais e desencorajar os inimigos (Deu. 3:5; II Crô. 26:10). Quando Israel invadiu a Palestina, encontraram muitas cidades muradas (Núm. 13:28; 32:17; Jos. 11:12,13; Juí. 1:27-33). As fortificações permitiam que os habitantes de uma cidade resistissem ao assédio de exércitos inimigos por muito tempo. Assim, Jerusalém foi mantida em poder dos jebuseus até os dias de Davi (II Sam. 5:6; I Crô. 11:5).

CIDADE DA DESTRUIÇÃO

Ver sobre **Heliópolis**.

CIDADE DAS PALMEIRAS

Esse título foi usado para indicar Jericó, em Deu. 34:2 e II Crô. 28:15. Fora uma cidade ocupada pelos queneus (Juí. 1:16), tendo sido capturada pelo rei de Moabe, Eglom (Juí. 3:13). Josefo descreve-a como local dotado de muitas palmeiras, incluindo certa variedade de espécies.

CIDADE DE DAVI

Ver sobre **Sião**.

CIDADE DE DEUS

Nome de uma obra literária de Agostinho (354-430 D.C.), onde ele expôs a sua teoria básica da história. Ele dá a entender que cada indivíduo é cidadão de duas cidades, que representam dois princípios fundamentais. Uma delas é a cidade de Deus, e a outra é a cidade do homem. A primeira é Jerusalém (a Igreja), e a outra é Roma (o estado secular). Das duas, a cidade de Deus deve ser considerada superior, permanente, mestra da cidade do homem. Essa filosofia exerceu importante influência na maneira como os homens vieram a pensar sobre as relações entre *a Igreja e o estado*. Ver o artigo separado sobre esse assunto. De conformidade com a concepção agostiniana, a Igreja é superior ao estado. Agostinho foi parcialmente impelido a escrever sua grande obra devido ao saque de Roma, em 410 D.C., pelas tropas do godo Alarico. Nesse episódio, Agostinho percebeu a natureza passageira do estado secular, contrastando isso com a permanência da Igreja, contra a qual nem mesmo as portas do inferno jamais prevalecerão. Em face da tensão entre a Igreja e o Estado, vem à tona uma terceira alternativa, a saber, o Estado moldado pela Igreja. E isso corresponde ao ideal político de Agostinho, o qual influenciou tremendamente a doutrina do papado, no que concerne ao poder secular. Quanto a outros detalhes a respeito, ver o artigo sobre Agostinho.

A expressão «cidade de Deus» também aparece no Antigo Testamento para dar nome a Jerusalém, em algumas poucas passagens. Ver Sal. 46:4, em comparação com Sal. 48:1,8. O trecho de Deuteronômio 12:5 diz: «...buscareis o lugar que o Senhor vosso Deus escolher de todas as vossas tribos, para ali pôr o seu nome, e sua habitação; e para lá ireis».

CIDADE DE ENOQUE

Ver **Enoque, Cidade de**.

CIDADE DE MOABE

Ver Números 22:36. Essa cidade ficava situada perto do rio Arnom, onde Balaque foi visitado por Balaão. Ela pode ser identificada com Ar, uma cidade moabita. Comparar com Núm. 21:15,28 e Isaías 15:1.

CIDADE DO SAL

Uma cidade existente na região desértica de Judá (Jos. 15:62). Supõe-se que essa cidade estava na extremidade sudoeste do mar Morto, onde certas colinas são formadas de sal puro, de onde lhe provém o nome. Alguns a localizam no vale do Sal, uma ravina na fronteira entre os territórios de Judá e de Edom, ao sul do mar Morto. A região foi cena de várias batalhas registradas nas Escrituras, conforme se vê em II Samuel 8:13; II Reis 14:7; I Crônicas 18:12 e II Crônicas 25:11.

CIDADE DO SOL

Assim diz a nossa versão portuguesa em Isaías 19:18. No original hebraico temos a expressão *ir haheres*, «cidade da derrubada», que algumas versões traduzem por «cidade da destruição». A Vulgata Latina é que traduz a expressão por «cidade do sol». Contudo, alguns eruditos textuais pensam que «sol» fazia parte do texto original, palavra que teria sido finalmente eliminada do texto, porquanto não há qualquer referência ao sol em um contexto onde vemos pagãos abandonando a idolatria e voltando-se para a adoração a Yahweh.

Contudo, se a alusão é a uma «cidade do sol», então estaria em foco a cidade de Heliópolis, no Egito. No grego, «heliópolis» significa «cidade do sol». Na antiguidade, essa cidade era um centro da adoração egípcia ao sol, onde eram honradas divindades solares como Ré e Atom. Da quinta dinastia egípcia em

CIDADELA — CIDADES DA CAMPINA

diante, os Faraós do Egito eram conhecidos como «filhos de Ré». Na Bíblia, a cidade de Heliópolis é chamada de «Om», que aparece em Gên. 41:45,50 e 46:20. José, filho de Jacó, quando se tornou o primeiro ministro de Faraó, casou-se com a filha do sacerdote de Om. Quanto a outros detalhes, ver o artigo sobre *Heliópolis*.

CIDADELA

No hebraico, **migdal**, «torre forte». Palavra que aparece por cinqüenta vezes como, por exemplo, em Gên. 11:4,5; Juí. 8:9,17; 9:46,47,49; 9:51,52; I Crô. 14:7; Nee. 3:1,11,25-27; Sal. 48:12; Can. 4:1; Isa. 2:15; Eze. 26:4,9; Miq. 4:8; Zac. 14:10. Umà outra forma da palavra é *migdol*, que figura por treze vezes, como, por exemplo, II Sam. 22:51; Eze. 29:10; 30:6.

A palavra hebraica aplica-se a uma defesa final, interior, em algum ponto de uma cidade. Essa idéia transparece logo na primeira menção, Gên. 11:4,5, onde os construtores da torre de Babel não pensaram em edificar uma torre isolada em campo aberto, conforme se vê em muitas gravuras de concepção artística moderna, mas disseram: «...edifiquemos para nós uma cidade, e uma torre cujo topo chegue até aos céus...» A idéia também transparece claramente na terceira passagem, Juízes 9:46,47,49, 51,52.

Com a passagem dos séculos, o termo hebraico passou a indicar todo o complexo de defesa interna de uma cidade, incluindo o palácio, o templo e quaisquer edifícios anexos. Sempre que possível, as cidadelas ou torres fortes eram construídas em uma colina íngreme, de acesso difícil, a fim de facilitar a defesa. Isso posto, a cidadela era uma espécie de cidade fortificada em miniatura, dentro da cidade, podendo ter sua própria muralha, portão e até fosso. Havia até mesmo cidadelas sem portões. As pessoas subiam até o alto das torres fortes por meio de uma escadaria.

CIDADES ARMAZÉNS

No hebraico, **ir miskenoth**, «cidade armazém». A expressão ocorre no Antigo Testamento por sete vezes: Êxo. 1:11; I Reis 9:19; II Crô. 8:4,6; 16:4; 17:12 e 32:28.

Sob as fustigadas dos chicotes dos feitores de obras, os israelitas, escravizados no Egito poucas gerações após a época de José, tiveram de construir as «cidades celeiros» (conforme diz a nossa versão portuguesa na primeira dessas referências) de Pitom e Ramessés. Pitom tem sido identificada com o moderno Tell et-Retabah, e Ramessés com a antiga Tânis.

Salomão construiu certo número de cidades armazéns em Hamate (I Reis 9:19), bem como em outros lugares dispersos pelo seu reino, não registrados na Bíblia (I Reis 9:19; II Crô. 8:4,6). Durante o reinado de Baasa, do reino do norte, Israel, Ben-Hadade, da Síria, concentrou seus ataques sobre as «cidades armazéns», terminando por conquistá-las, no território de Naftali, juntamente com outras cidades (II Crô. 16:4). O rei Josafá, em seu programa de fortalecimento do reino de Judá, construiu tanto fortalezas quanto «cidades armazéns» (II Crô. 17:12). Ezequias também promoveu a construção de «cidades armazéns» (II Crô. 32:28).

As «cidades armazéns» aparentemente tiveram a sua origem na prática egípcia de prover armazenamento para as colheitas excessivas, durante os sete anos de abundância, como reserva para os sete anos de escassez, o que ocorreu na época em que José foi o primeiro ministro de Faraó. É possível que essas chamadas «cidades armazéns» fossem como grandes silos, com estruturas longas, retangulares, em forma de salão, encontradas em Bete-Semes, Laquis e outros lugares no território de Israel. A começar pelo reinado de Salomão, e continuando durante os governos de reis posteriores, essas cidades armazéns eram usadas para armazenar cereais e azeite de oliveira, para uso posterior nas cortes reais de Judá e de Israel. (Quanto a Jerusalém, ver I Reis 4:7,22,23). Esses produtos eram também recolhidos como parte dos impostos pagos ao governo, conforme se tem conhecimento através das ostracas encontradas em Samaria e outras localidades.

Alguns estudiosos pensam que esses armazéns não eram usados somente como depósitos de mantimentos, mas isso não pode ser defendido e nem desmentido por meio das Escrituras Sagradas, que nada revelam a esse respeito.

CIDADES DA CAMPINA

Ver Gênesis 13:12 e 19:29 quanto a essa expressão. As palavras hebraicas envolvidas são comumente usadas para designar uma unidade monetária e também certo formato de pão. Seu sentido básico é «redondeza» ou «nivelamento». Ao referir-se a algum território, parece que prevalece a idéia de lugar plano. Todavia, a palavra também pode significar «oval», como no caso em foco, que se refere a uma região que vai da extremidade sul do mar da Galiléia até à extremidade norte do mar Morto, região essa que tem uma forma ovalada. Também se tem considerado que a área ia desde o ponto imediatamente acima de Jericó (I Reis 7:46; II Crô. 4:17), até à extremidade sul do mar Morto (Deu. 34:4). Seja como for, as cidades da campina, como Sodoma e Gomorra, além de outras estão em foco, segundo se vê em Gên. 13:10. Os nomes de Admá, Zeboim e Bela também fazem parte do texto sagrado. Todavia, os trechos de Gên. 17,25,28,29 parecem ampliar a área em consideração. Antes do aparecimento de cidades naquela área, compreendemos, com base em Gênesis 13:10, que a terra era fértil de tal modo que merecia comparação com o jardim do Éden ou com o delta do Nilo, no Egito. As descobertas arqueológicas confirmam a fertilidade da região. As condições climáticas têm-se modificado com a passagem dos séculos, e a região não é hoje tão fértil quanto antigamente. O trecho de Gênesis 19 narra a súbita destruição que sobreveio a quatro das cinco cidades mencionadas na área. Zoar, para onde Ló e suas filhas fugiram, foi poupada. Algum tipo de cataclismo natural atingiu a área. Talvez tivesse havido um abalo sísmico que liberou chamas resultantes da combustão de gás ou petróleo de depósitos naturais subterrâneos. Até hoje o betume aflora à superfície das águas do mar Morto. E, desde 1953, Israel tem bombeado petróleo e gás desse lugar.

Supõe-se que a área antiga está agora parcialmente coberta pelas águas do mar Morto, que tem uma área maior que na antiguidade. Em Bab edh-Dhra', um sítio arqueológico da região, tem-se encontrado peças de cerâmica de 2300 a 1900 A.C., confirmando a importância do lugar e os seus ritos religiosos. A região foi abandonada no começo do século XIX, quando as cidades da região deixaram de ser ocupadas. O trecho de Isaías 34:9,10 parece ter uma descrição gráfica de uma erupção de betume, o que poderia ser uma alusão à destruição das cidades da campina, embora usada em outra conexão. Naturalmente, alguns intérpretes preferem pensar em uma

CIDADES — CIDADES E COLÔNIAS ROMANAS

explicação totalmente sobrenatural para a destruição ali havida. Seja como for, os habitantes daquelas cidades pecaminosas chegaram a um fim repentino. Diz-se que houve planos de reconstruir a área, com cassinos e lugares de prazer. Mas tais planos foram abandonados quando alguém objetou dizendo: «Oh, não comecemos tudo de novo!» Mas, na sociedade moderna, o estilo de vida de Sodoma e Gomorra tem-se tornado quase universal. Muitos homossexuais têm-se vangloriado disso. Por certo, o juízo divino não anda longe. (CLAP KY)

CIDADES DE REFÚGIO

Ver o artigo separado sobre Cidade. As cidades de refúgio dos países antigos eram, essencialmente, medidas judiciais auxiliares, para ajudar o escape dos homicidas involuntários. Visto que o código de vingança era forte, os parentes de uma pessoa morta por outrem matavam sem misericórdia ao culpado pelo homicídio, sem temer qualquer ação da parte da lei. A lei da retribuição, em Israel, requeria punição igual ao crime (Gên. 9:6; Êxo. 21:12-14; Lev. 24:17; Eze. 18:20). Lemos que era considerado um *dever* o parente de um homem morto justiçar o assassino, mesmo que o homicídio tivesse sido feito involuntariamente, mesmo que com razão, em defesa própria. Os lugares de refúgio incluíam os templos, os santuários e os lugares santos de todas as variedades. No território de Israel, seis cidades levitas foram separadas com essa finalidade. Mas elas visavam somente os casos de homicídio acidental. Os criminosos não eram protegidos nessas cidades. Essas cidades serviam para modificar a inflexibilidade das leis vigentes. Ver as seis cidades de refúgio mencionadas em Josué 20:7,8. Essas cidades eram as seguintes:

1. Cades, cerca de 25 km ao norte do mar da Galiléia. 2. Siquém, — localidade no fim do vale que tinha um formato de «V», na linha leste-oeste, entre o monte Ebal e o monte Gerizim. 3. Hebrom (Quiriate-Arba), em Judá, cerca de 32 km ao sul de Jerusalém. 4. Bezer, nas terras altas orientais a leste de onde o rio Jordão deságua no mar Morto. 5. Ramote, cerca de oitenta quilômetros mais para o norte, nas terras altas de Gileade. 6. Golã, nas terras altas a leste do mar da Galiléia. A exata localização desta última é desconhecida. Essas cidades estavam localizadas em lugares estratégicos, dando aos habitantes de cada tribo um lugar de refúgio, não muito distante.

O trecho de Êxodo 21:14 dá a entender que um assassino proposital não podia esperar proteção em frente do altar; mas um homicida acidental podia fazê-lo, por algum tempo. As leis de Israel não proviam a remoção da culpa pelo homicídio, mas a morte do sumo sacerdote então atuante permitia que o homicida circulasse livremente, sem temor de retaliação. Alguns supõem que a morte do principal sacerdote da área tinha o mesmo efeito. Requeria-se que as estradas que levavam às cidades de refúgio fossem mantidas em boas condições (Deu. 4:41-43; 19:1-13). Havia qualificações específicas para aqueles que buscassem as cidades de refúgio, e os anciãos das cidades tomavam decisões referentes a cada caso. As cidades de refúgio provavelmente eram lugares de grande atividade; mas, curiosamente, não temos qualquer relato no Antigo Testamento que ilustre o costume.

Se os anciãos de uma cidade decidissem de modo favorável ao homicida, ainda assim este precisava confinar-se na cidade de refúgio, até à morte do sumo sacerdote (Núm. 35:25 *ss*), tornando tal refúgio um virtual aprisionamento. Em outras palavras, os homicidas involuntários ainda assim pagavam uma pena.

Tipologia. Como é óbvio, as cidades de refúgio representam o refúgio que temos em Cristo, o qual é nosso sumo sacerdote. A sua morte livrou-nos do temor ou retaliação do pecado, até onde está envolvido o destino da alma. A lei de Moisés era um código de justiça, e a misericórdia não era então um conceito tão patente como se vê em nossos dias. Apesar disso, as cidades de refúgio envolviam certa medida de misericórdia. Porém, em Cristo o pecador perdoado fica inteiramente livre de culpa e das conseqüências eternas de seu pecado.

Contrapartes Modernas. Antes do advento do cristianismo, lugares santos, templos, santuários, etc., agiam como asilos. Pelo menos desde os dias do imperador Constantino, os templos cristãos exerciam essa função. Teodósio, em 413 D.C., ampliou esse privilégio às casas, jardins e outros anexos de um templo cristão. O sínodo de Toledo, no século VII D.C., estendeu o privilégio de asilo a trinta lugares associados a cada templo cristão, quando cada igreja determinaria quais seriam esses trinta lugares. Na Idade Média, quando o poder papal tornou-se grande, esses costumes continuavam prevalecendo. Porém, — à medida que o estado se fortalecia e a Igreja se enfraquecia, os princípios de asilo foram-se tornando sujeitos mais à legislação secular, e menos à legislação eclesiástica. A maioria dos governos conta, atualmente, com uma legislação que cobre todos os casos possíveis dessa natureza, de tal modo que a Igreja não mais se envolve na questão. Às pessoas tidas como criminosas por razões políticas, ou consideradas culpadas por suas convicções políticas ou religiosas, com freqüência se permite o asilo em consulados estrangeiros que existam no país onde a perseguição esteja sendo efetuada. Entre as nações mais civilizadas, esse direito de asilo é respeitado. (AM E GREEN LAN)

CIDADES E COLÔNIAS ROMANAS

«As cidades romanas pertenciam a duas classes: Havia as 'municipia' ou 'cidades livres' e as *colônias*. Essa distinção, entretanto, nem sempre era mantida inflexivelmente, de tal modo que, em alguns casos, encontramos uma mesma cidade chamada pelos dois títulos. Esses dois nomes, todavia, não envolviam qualquer diferença no tocante aos direitos ou privilégios. A diferença histórica entre colônia e uma cidade livre era que as cidades livres eram incluídas no estado, vindas de fora, ao passo que as colônias eram rebentos vindos de dentro. 'As cidades municipais insensivelmente se foram tornando iguais, em posição e esplendor, às colônias; e, no reinado de Adriano, passou a ser motivo de disputa qual era a condição preferível; a daquelas sociedades que haviam sido derivadas de Roma, ou à daquelas que haviam sido recebidas no seio de Roma'. (Giddon, *Decline and Fall*)». Vincent.

As colônias romanas serviam a três propósitos, a saber: 1. Eram postos avançados fortificados, em algum país conquistado. 2. Serviam de meios de subsistência dos pobres de Roma, porquanto dessas áreas eram levados produtos agrícolas, etc. 3. Eram lugares onde se estabeleciam os veteranos que haviam servido ali no exército durante um certo período; e isso fez com que se tornassem lugares onde se estabeleceram vários outros povos. Ora, Filipos pertencia essencialmente ao terceiro tipo de colônia.

A sociedade romana dividiu o mundo em duas grandes classes: os «estrangeiros» e os *cidadãos*. As colônias eram reputadas habitadas por «cidadãos». A idéia geral envolvida em uma «colônia» é que para os seus habitantes, Roma transferia a sua cidadania e os seus direitos. Algumas colônias foram formadas mediante a expulsão de todos os seus habitantes.

As colônias romanas desfrutaram de três notáveis direitos (de *libertas*, *immunitas*, e *jus italicum*), o que significa governo próprio, isenção de impostos imperiais e direitos iguais aos dos cidadãos italianos.

CIDADES LEVÍTICAS Ver **Levitas, Cidades de**.

CIÊNCIA Ver **Religião e a Ciência**.

CIÊNCIA CRISTÃ

1. *O Termo*. De acordo com o atual uso da expressão, Ciência Cristã designa uma denominação que, desde o ano de 1875, vem ocupando espaço no campo das denominações cristãs-históricas. Trata-se de um movimento centralmente organizado, com igrejas locais com seus próprios edifícios, líderes e *leitores*, períodos determinados e formas de adoração próprias. Portanto, não erramos quando falamos em *Igreja da Ciência Cristã*, e seus corpos locais como igrejas da Ciência Cristã. A igreja mãe, em Boston, entretanto, ocupa uma posição ímpar dentro da organização.

2. *Origens*. A fundadora do movimento, Mary Baker Eddy, chegou às suas crenças e práticas através de uma longa série de acontecimentos, experiências e influências de diversas filosofias, através de um certo número de anos. Ela mesma foi criada em um lar de tradição extremamente calvinista, no congregacionalismo da Nova Inglaterra. Porém, ela mostrou-se rebelde desde tenra idade. Ela ficou chocada diante das implicações da doutrina da predestinação, com seus poucos eleitos à salvação e com sua reprovação positiva, em que a vasta maioria dos seres humanos termina em um castigo eterno e aterrorizante. Desde bem cedo na vida, ela foi perseguida por tragédias e enfermidades. Esses foram os elementos que inspiraram sua independência de pensamento, enquanto ela buscava tanto respostas teológicas quanto cura para seus males físicos. No entanto, ela estava ficando rapidamente inválida. A ciência médica ortodoxa não lhe oferecia qualquer ajuda, e ela tentou a homeopatia e a sugestão mental. Em 1866, quando ela estava com quarenta e cinco anos de idade, Mary Baker Eddy passou por uma experiência decisiva. Ela obteve uma notável cura mediante a inspiração espiritual, que lhe veio quando lia a narrativa contida em Mateus 9:1-9, onde é descrita a cura de um paralítico por Jesus. Ao mesmo tempo, ela passou por uma experiência mística que lhe iluminou a mente, no tocante à *vida no e do Espírito*. Ela acreditava que a iluminação espiritual foi responsável pela sua cura física, pelo que a cura mental (espiritual) tornou-se uma das práticas mais salientes que a Igreja da Ciência Cristã não tardou a desenvolver.

3. *Primórdios da Igreja da Ciência Cristã*. A maioria de seus primeiros membros eram membros de igrejas evangélicas, a maioria dos quais continuou freqüentando as reuniões de suas igrejas, e que, paralelamente, freqüentavam classes e reuniões do movimento da Ciência Cristã. Porém, em 1879, foi estabelecida uma distinta organização eclesiástica. Seu propósito original era o seguinte: «Organizar uma igreja cujo designio é comemorar as palavras e as obras de nosso Mestre, que reinstale o cristianismo primitivo e seu elemento perdido da cura» (Manual da Igreja, pág. 17). Em cerca de 1892, a organização havia expandido enormemente suas atividades, a partir de sua origem, em Boston, estado norte-americano de Massachussets. No ano de 1970, havia cerca de três mil e trezentas igrejas, dois terços das quais nos Estados Unidos, e o resto em muitos outros países do mundo.

4. *Idéias*: a. A teologia básica da Ciência Cristã defende um *idealismo* puro (que vide), que parte do pressuposto que o mundo material é uma ilusão, resultado da *idéia* ou espírito. O que é verdadeiramente *real* é Deus e o seu ideal. O termo «mente» é usado como um sinônimo de Espírito, de Alma e de Vida. Esse princípio, pleno de verdade e de amor, é tudo quanto existe. b. *O mal é ilusório*, pois a perfeita vontade de Deus, que emerge da mente divina, não pode incorrer em erro. O mal está associado à matéria, e, entre os seus efeitos, encontram-se as enfermidades. A morte é uma ilusão dos sentidos mortais, podendo continuar a ser real, até ser destruída pelo sentido espiritual. c. *O pecado é a crença* que resulta em aceitarmos a existência real de outras mentes, quando, na realidade, só existe a mente divina e a nossa participação na mente divina. O pecado pois, consiste em *crença falsa*. A enfermidade é uma crença falsa. d. A cura ocorre quando a ilusão da enfermidade é corrigida pelo pensamento iluminado, inspirado pelo Espírito. e. A doutrina primária desse sistema é a *regeneração do pensamento humano*, através da compreensão espiritual. A cura física segue-se facilmente a essa percepção. f. *O homem é o ideal espiritual* de Deus, e pertence, por direito, a uma ordem na qual não existe nem enfermidades, nem pecado, nem tristeza e nem morte. Essas coisas são meras ilusões da mente mortal. Elas não têm existência real exceto para aqueles que pensam que elas são reais. g. Jesus é mais do que um homem bom. Ele é o Cristo encarnado.

5. *Autoridades Espirituais*. A Bíblia, conforme eles a interpretam, é a principal autoridade dos cientistas cristãos. A outra obra autoritária é a obra da sra. Eddy, intitulada *Ciência e Saúde*, publicada pela primeira vez em 1875, e que foi subseqüentemente expandida, tendo passado por muitas edições. A Igreja da Ciência Cristã não tem clero formal. A lição-sermão toma o lugar dos sermões do pastor. Eles têm hinos, a oração do Pai Nosso, a leitura de trechos bíblicos selecionados, e também lêem trechos da Ciência e Saúde. Não há sacramentos, mas o espírito do que eles representam faz parte do ensino. (AM C E)

CIÊNCIA E A RELIGIÃO Ver **Religião e a Ciência**.

CIÊNCIA E ÉTICA Ver **Ética e a Ciência**

CIÊNCIA, FILOSOFIA DA Ver **Filosofia da Ciência**.

CIÊNCIA NA BÍBLIA

Pode-se definir «ciência» como o conhecimento organizado de leis naturais gerais, sobretudo aquelas obtidas através do método científico. E o método científico pode ser definido como os princípios e modos de proceder em busca do conhecimento sistemático, envolvendo o reconhecimento e a formulação de um problema, o recolhimento de informes através da observação e das experiências, e a formulação e comprovação das hipóteses.

I. A Bíblia e o Método Científico

O método científico, no sentido que lhe damos hodiernamente, surgiu nos séculos XVII e XVIII.

CIÊNCIA NA BÍBLIA

Antes disso, a coisa mais próxima do método científico era a especulação e a postulação, com pouca ou nenhuma referência a experiências e testes. A Bíblia, entretanto, é singularmente isenta de especulações e postulações acerca de verdades gerais e da operação das leis gerais, mormente no que concerne à natureza. Sempre que alguma questão científica é aludida na Bíblia, pois, deve haver alguma significação especial, porquanto tal conhecimento não foi obtido e nem testado através do método científico. O caso específico das ciências naturais será abordado em primeiro lugar, após o que consideraremos o caso geral de toda realidade sujeita a experiências.

II. Ciência Natural

A ciência natural pode ser descrita como o conhecimento dos padrões estruturais e comportamentais que se vêem na natureza.

A. Propósito, Plano e Padrão. A Bíblia, em suas referências à natureza, interessa-se primariamente pela questão do propósito. A idéia de padrão relaciona-se à idéia de propósito, através da idéia de plano. Portanto, a Bíblia muito tem a dizer sobre a questão de propósito, plano e padrão na natureza. As Escrituras reconhecem a existência do universo físico, criado por Deus (Gên. 1:1). A criação, um assunto muito debatido pelos cientistas e teólogos do século XX, é o tema dominante das referências bíblicas à natureza. É explicitamente catalogada no primeiro capítulo de Gênesis e é repetidamente invocada tanto no Antigo quanto no Novo Testamentos, a fim de identificar o único e verdadeiro Deus, e a fim de confirmar seu poder e sabedoria. Realizada como um ato da vontade de Deus (Sal. 33:9), a criação tem um propósito: Deus criou todas as coisas para si mesmo (Pro. 16:4; Col. 1:16; Apo. 4:11), e criou o homem para a sua glória (Isa. 43:7). O propósito coroador da criação é a salvação do homem através da fé em Cristo (II Cor. 5:17; Efé. 3:12,17; II Tim. 1:9,10). Esse propósito será cumprido quando a Igreja de Cristo tiver sido aperfeiçoada, e os inimigos de Cristo tiverem sido anulados (I Cor. 15:20-28). Quando esse propósito tiver cumprimento, então o próprio universo físico será destruído e um novo universo será criado (Isa. 65:17; II Ped. 3:10-13; Apo. 20:11; 21:1).

A fim de que esse propósito tivesse cumprimento, a criação foi cuidadosamente planejada (Pro. 8:22-31). O planejamento e a sabedoria evidenciada nesse planejamento são revelados na própria natureza (Jó 38-41; Sal. 19). Parte desse plano determina que o homem domine a natureza (Gên. 1:26,28; Sal. 8:6-8), explore a natureza a seu próprio benefício (Gên. 1:29,30; 9:1-4; Deu. 12:15), estude a natureza como algo que revela a glória (Sal. 19), o poder (Rom. 1:20), a providência (Sal. 104), e a constância de Deus (Sal. 89:2; Jer. 31:35-37; 33:20-26), derivando, da compreensão da natureza, uma grande sabedoria (Pro. 14:8) e uma grande recompensa (Sal. 19:7-11).

Faz parte do ensino bíblico que o universo seja organizado de forma inteligente, de acordo com o padrão divino completo, engenhoso e autocoerente, operando agora de acordo com as leis ou princípios divinamente determinados, invioláveis, de tal modo que o padrão básico e as leis de operação não se alteram com o tempo. A Bíblia também ensina que esses padrões e leis são inteligíveis para o homem, e que o bem-estar dos homens depende da correta compreensão desses padrões e leis. Esses conceitos básicos sobre a natureza contrastam violentamente com as noções e ensinos de outras culturas antigas, as quais retratavam as origens físicas como produtos de conflitos entre divindades em luta, e os fenômenos naturais como tão imprevisíveis como os caprichos dessas divindades voluntariosas.

B. Os Alicerces da Ciência Moderna. A origem da ciência moderna repousa sobre alguns poucos pressupostos básicos, que a experiência tem tornado auto-evidentes. Entre esses pressupostos podemos incluir a uniformidade da natureza quanto ao espaço e ao tempo, a inviolabilidade das leis naturais e o conceito de um universo mecanicista. Esses pressupostos só parecem auto-evidentes porque têm recebido credencial da parte das descobertas científicas. Não há necessidade e nem prova de que esses pressupostos sejam universalmente válidos na natureza. A menos que sejam aceitos pela fé, não há qualquer base para os esforços da ciência, no descobrimento dos mesmos. Contudo, não se pode dizer que o homem jamais teria chegado a tais pressupostos, à parte da cultura monoteísta dos antigos hebreus. Está historiado que esses pressupostos faziam parte da fé religiosa da cultura judaico-cristã; e sabe-se que a ciência moderna foi nutrida na cultura cristã da Europa Ocidental. Assim, a maioria dos homens que lançaram os fundamentos da ciência moderna também foram homens de vigorosa fé cristã. Entre eles podemos mencionar Copérnico, Galileu, Kepler, Newton, Francisco Bacon e René Descartes. Para eles, a uniformidade da natureza e a inviolabilidade das leis naturais faziam parte da fé religiosa. A idéia de um universo mecanicista foi postulada a fim de mostrar a perfeição da criação feita por Deus, bem como a fim de mostrar que não havia necessidade de um Deus que «preenchesse o vazio» para explicar os fenômenos naturais que a ciência fosse incapaz de explicar.

Uma conclusão razoável é que a ciência moderna muito deve à Bíblia. Seus principais conceitos de origem encontram-se na Bíblia, seus pressupostos fundamentais fazem parte da fé religiosa, e a inquirição das pesquisas científicas é algo encorajado nas Escrituras Sagradas.

C. A Criação. A Bíblia devota bem pouco espaço para a maneira como ocorreu a criação. A afirmação simples: «Pois ele falou, e tudo se fez» (Sal. 33:9), percorre o volume sagrado, do começo ao fim, como um fio de prata. Alguns poucos conceitos latos são oferecidos no primeiro capítulo do livro de Gênesis. Esse capítulo ensina-nos que a criação teve lugar mediante uma série de passos ou fases, cada qual levando avante o que fora feito na fase anterior, em preparação para o que se seguiria. Assim, a vida vegetal teria antecedido à vida animal. Diferentes formas de vida animal parecem ter sido criadas em diferentes ocasiões, dando a entender que a vida animal apareceu primeiramente, nos oceanos. O homem foi uma criação especial, subseqüente à criação de todas as demais coisas vivas. Todos esses ensinamentos coadunam-se com as observações científicas modernas, embora não necessariamente com as interpretações dadas a essas observações, por parte de determinados cientistas modernos.

D. Padrão. A Bíblia contém muitas referências aos padrões comumente observáveis na natureza. E isso não tanto para revelar os padrões, mas, sim, para chamar nossa atenção para o significado dos mesmos, pois testificam sobre a sabedoria e a providência de Deus. Assim, a garantida regularidade das estações, da semeadura e da colheita, ou dos dias e das noites, faz parte desse padrão. (Ver Gên. 8:22; Jer. 3:19; 5:24). Os mares, os montes e os vales são conservados em seus respectivos lugares por decreto divino (Jó

CIÊNCIA NA BÍBLIA

38:8-11; Sal. 104:8,9; Pro. 8:29; Jer. 5:22). A natureza foi posta em boa ordem pela sabedoria do Senhor (Pro. 8:1-4). A sabedoria de Deus é percebida até mesmo nos instintos dos pássaros (Jer. 8:7). Os relâmpagos e a chuva têm seus trajetos determinados pelas leis divinas (Jó 28:26). A interdependência entre as diferentes porções da natureza pode ser vista na alimentação da vida selvagem (Sal. 104:27 e 145:15). O reconhecimento desses fenômenos, em seus aspectos facilmente observáveis, atualmente é comum, de tal maneira que as maravilhas dos padrões da natureza são aceitas sem discussão. As relações de causa e efeito mais sutis, mediante as quais os padrões estruturais e comportamentais da natureza são cientificamente explanados, parecem mais desafiadoras para a ciência moderna. No entanto, a Bíblia é totalmente silente sobre esse aspecto da questão. Deus deixou que o homem procurasse descobrir tais relações, as quais, na verdade, são discerníveis e inteligíveis para a mente humana.

No relato da criação (Gênesis 1), a Bíblia oferece-nos um esboço geral de padrão que parece muito significativo para a ciência moderna. É feita a distinção entre radiação (luz), espaço (firmamento ou expansão) e matéria (águas, terras, mares, terras secas). Também se estabelece a distinção entre matéria bruta e matéria viva. A matéria viva é dividida em cinco grandes categorias. Essas categorias são: plantas (Gên. 1:12,13), animais marinhos e aves (Gên. 1:20,21), animais terrestres (Gên. 1:24,25) e o homem (Gên. 1:26,27; I Cor. 15:39). Dentro de cada uma dessas principais categorias, a matéria teve origem e agora persiste em classes invioláveis. A inviolabilidade de cada categoria fica entendida através da outorga, a cada classe, de um mecanismo hereditário que garante a perpetuação da espécie (Gên. 1; Mat. 7:16; I Cor. 15:37,38), protegendo cada espécie da mistura com outras classes e da consequente degeneração de todas as classes de seres vivos a um único conglomerado, composto de todas as características. Essas características gerais do padrão da natureza mostram-se coerentes com as observações científicas modernas.

Uma outra generalização de grande significação científica é o conceito do universo como uma peça de vestuário antiga, que se envelhece (Sal. 102:25,26; Isa. 34:4). Isso parece corresponder ao princípio científico da entropia crescente, dentro de um sistema fechado, conhecido como a segunda lei da termodinâmica. Entretanto, a aplicabilidade desse princípio ao universo, como um sistema, é uma questão debatida entre os cientistas.

E. Antecipações da Ciência Moderna. Alguns escritores têm encontrado trechos bíblicos nos quais vêem antecipações das modernas descobertas científicas. A teoria ondulatória da matéria pode ser vista em Gên. 1:2. A telegrafia sem fio, em Jó 38:35. O conceito de *parallage* é visto em Tiago 1:17. A teoria atômica da matéria figura em Hebreus 11:3, e a força de coesão atômica em Hebreus 1:3. A luz, como base de todas as substâncias, é vista em Gênesis 1:3; a fissão nuclear, em Gênesis 1:4, e a reação final em cadeia em Isaías 34:4 e Luc. 21:25-28. Um universo em expansão pode ser visto em Isaías 40:22. Veículos a motor, em Joel 2:3,4; aeroplanos em Isaías 31:5 e 60:8, e submarinos em Apocalipse 9:1-11. O rádio pode ser visto em Eclesiastes 10:20, e a televisão em Apocalipse 11:3-12. A esfericidade da terra é vista em Jó. 22:14; Provérbios 8:27; Isaías 40:22 e Marcos 13:35-37. A suspensão da terra no espaço é vista em Jó 26:7. O conceito do ar dotado de peso é visto em Jó 28:25. O ciclo da água, reconhecido pela ciência moderna, é visto em Jó 36:27,28; Salmos 104:10,13; Provérbios 8:28 e Eclesiastes 1:6,7. Ainda um outro grupo de escritores afirma que, em cada um desses casos, o contexto bíblico exclui interpretações que insuflam descobertas científicas modernas nesses significados. Entretanto, pode haver significação antecipatória em Jó 38:22,23, onde Deus fala com Jó a respeito dos tesouros (armazéns) da neve e da saraiva, em reserva para o dia de batalha e guerra. À luz do moderno conhecimento de armas, pode-se ver nisso uma alusão à constituição química da água e da neve, isto é, oxigênio e hidrogênio, daí inferindo a importância dos armamentos com base química, no oxigênio, ou com base no hidrogênio (bombas termonucleares), na grande guerra que porá fim à nossa dispensação.

F. Planejamento Versus Acaso. Na natureza, o planejamento pode dar lugar ao padrão, ou então este pode ser devido ao processo das meras chances. A validade da interpretação das observações científicas algumas vezes repousa sobre qual dessas alternativas se toma como pressuposto. A área das teorias da evolução orgânica provê muitos exemplos onde a direção das investigações e a interpretação dos informes podem depender, em grau significativo, do pressuposto de uma chance fortuita ou de uma criação proposital, como fator dominante, por detrás da formação dos padrões básicos. Mas, se por um lado, as Escrituras não eliminam o processo fortuito da chance dentre a cadeia de causas, por outro lado elas insistem em uma criação proposital e consciente da parte de Deus, como a verdadeira origem do universo e dos padrões fundamentais, estruturais e comportamentais, bem como em uma contínua providência divina como a base final da estabilidade das leis naturais.

III. Toda a Realidade que Pode ser Experimentada. Em seu sentido mais amplo, a ciência pode ser descrita como o conhecimento sistematizado da verdade, onde toda e cada verdade pode ser identificada. Ora, a Bíblia é um manancial prolífico de informações sobre a verdade (Sal. 119:160; João 17:17) e sobre a sua identificação (Mat. 7:15-20; João 14:6; I João 4:1-6).

A. Sobre a Dimensão Espiritual. A Bíblia ensina que o reino físico não compraz a realidade inteira, porquanto coexiste com uma dimensão espiritual (João 4:24; Apo. 16:14). A Bíblia ensina que a dimensão física é permeada pela dimensão espiritual (Gên. 2:7; Efé. 6:12; I Ped. 5:8), e que essas duas dimensões ou reinos atuam mutuamente um sobre o outro (Mat. 17:19,20; João 13:2; Atos 2:2-4). As Escrituras também ensinam que a dimensão espiritual é eterna, ao passo que a dimensão física é temporal (Mat. 24:35), e que a fonte final de todo o conhecimento e poder encontra-se na dimensão espiritual (Sal. 111:10; Mat. 28:18; Rom. 11:33-36).

B. Sobre as Interações entre o Espírito e o Físico. Os pagãos, tanto na antiguidade quanto em nossos dias, com freqüência atribuem os fenômenos naturais a uma atividade espiritual imprevisível. Os escritores bíblicos atribuem os fenômenos naturais às atividades de Deus. Em ambos os casos, a corrente natural de causas incluem agentes sobrenaturais. — À media que a ciência nos foi conferindo uma compreensão sempre crescente dos padrões do comportamento natural, as forças espirituais foram sendo eliminadas das cogitações científicas como elementos reconhecidos, dentro da corrente de causas e efeitos. Se os processos naturais tivessem de ser temporariamente modificados pela intervenção sobrenatural, as leis naturais pareceriam estar sendo violadas, e tal acontecimento seria considerado miraculoso. Não obstante, a Bíblia contém muitos relatos sobre milagres e prodígios.

Em alguns casos, como o longo dia de Josué (Jos. 10:12), e o relógio de sol de Acaz (II Reis 20:11 e Isa. 38:8), uma interpretação não-crítica daria margem a ocorrências catastróficas, que teriam ficado registradas na história, mas acerca das quais nada encontramos nas crônicas mundiais. No entanto, de acordo com certos pensadores, o exame crítico dos textos bíblicos e a sua interpretação, à luz dos contextos sagrados, produz incerteza acerca de quais perturbações naturais, teriam realmente acontecido, além de diminuir grandemente a conseqüência das pesquisas em busca de explicações científicas. Em outros casos, nas páginas do Antigo Testamento, os milagres atribuídos a testemunhas de Deus são, na verdade, atribuídos ao próprio Deus, a fim de confirmar o testemunho de seus servos, parecendo ser casos evidentes da interação entre o físico e o espiritual.

Os milagres registrados no Novo Testamento, realizados durante o ministério de Jesus Cristo, demonstram claramente o poder espiritual sobre os fenômenos naturais (Mar. 4:39; 6:41-44,48; João 2:1-11; 11:44), exibindo para nós o poder que a fé tem para controlar as forças espirituais (Mat. 9:22; Tia. 5:16). Os milagres do nascimento virginal de Jesus (Mat. 1:18-25; Luc. 1:26-2:7) e o da ressurreição do Senhor Jesus (I Cor. 15:12-23) são questões centrais para a fé cristã.

IV. A Ciência e a Teologia

A busca pelo conhecimento, dentro do campo da ciência e dentro do campo da teologia, desde há muito vem sendo considerada como duas atividades separadas, sem nenhuma relação uma com a outra. Entretanto, se a ciência procura descobrir «com o que Deus fez» alguma coisa, ao passo que a teologia aborda o «por que Deus fez» as coisas, então parece-nos que a combinação dessas duas atividades, em uma busca interdisciplinar pela verdade, beneficiaria profundamente a humanidade. Da mesma maneira que a combinação da filosofia e da tecnologia, na época de Newton, produziu a revolução científica que conduziu o mundo à revolução industrial, porventura a junção da teologia e da ciência, em nossos próprios dias, não produziria um «conhecimento da verdade» realmente revolucionário, conferindo aos homens uma compreensão sobre as forças espirituais que levariam a humanidade a uma autêntica revolução espiritual? Por conseguinte, assim como a revolução industrial libertou o homem da dependência ao trabalho estafante e da dependência às suas próprias pequenas forças físicas, a revolução espiritual libertaria o homem da servidão ao temor e da dependência ao seu próprio débil poder espiritual. Porventura, não prevalecerão, durante o milênio, condições similares às que estamos aqui antecipando? Ver sobre o *Milênio*.

CILÍCIA

Esse é o nome clássico da região costeira da Ásia Menor, na porção oriental do mar Mediterrâneo. Correspondia às atuais províncias turcas de Icel e Adana. A região está separada do planalto central da Anatólia pela elevada serra das montanhas do Taurus. Em sua porção oriental, a região vai-se alargando gradualmente, transformando-se em uma fértil planície, regada por diversos rios. As montanhas de Amano, da Síria, formam a fronteira leste da região. A despeito desse confinamento geográfico, a Cilícia nunca se mostrou culturalmente isolada. As antigas cidades de Mersim, Adana e Tarso até hoje retêm a sua importância.

História. A mais antiga menção histórica à Cilícia data de cerca do século XIV A.C., quando a região foi chamada pelo nome de *Kizzuwatna*, como um estado hitita vassalo. Descobertas arqueológicas, principalmente de peças de cerâmica, confirmam as influências gregas, que ali chegavam por via marítima. Em 715 A.C., a área foi conquistada pelos assírios, que lhe deram o nome de *Que*. Quando os persas dominaram o lugar, no século VI A.C., ela se transformou em uma **satrapia semi-independente** do império persa. Após a derrota de Dario, por Alexandre o Grande, em 333 A.C., os herdeiros políticos deste último, os Selêucidas da Síria e os Ptolomeus do Egito, dividiram a região. Quando a autoridade deles declinou, muitas cidades da Anatólia obtiveram a sua independência. Os romanos enviaram uma expedição à Cilícia, sob o comando de Pompeu, em 67 A.C., **a fim de pôr fim** às atividades dos piratas e ladrões da região montanhosa ocidental. Finalmente, a Cilícia foi absorvida pelo império romano, passando a ser governada pela Síria, até tornar-se uma província separada, em 74 D.C.

A Cilícia e o Cristianismo. Os habitantes da região converteram-se ao cristianismo. Ela é melhor lembrada pelos cristãos como a região onde Paulo nasceu, visto que ele era natural de Tarso, uma das principais cidades cilicianas. Posteriormente, a Cilícia tornou-se uma das províncias bizantinas. Mas os árabes apossaram-se da região no século IX D.C. No século XI D.C. os armênios, expulsos do oriente da Turquia, fundaram ali o estado da Pequena Armênia. Esta acabou nas mãos dos mamelucos egípcios, nos fins do século XIV D.C. Os turcos otomanos tomaram deles a região, em 1516.

Outros Detalhes. Nos dias do apóstolo Paulo, os judeus tinham uma sinagoga na Cilícia (Atos 6:9). Paulo aprendeu ali o seu ofício de fabricante de tendas. Ele visitou a região após a sua conversão (Gál. 1:21 e Atos 9:30). Cícero (que vide), atuou como cônsul na Cilícia. Seu bom clima e seus luxos atraíam residentes gregos (Atos 15:41 e 21:39).

A Cidadania Romana. Paulo nasceu como cidadão romano, e ufanava-se de sua cidade nativa (Atos 21:39). A cidadania romana, conferida a uma porção da comunidade judaica de Tarso, provavelmente data da época em que Pompeu estabeleceu na parte leste da Cilícia uma colônia judaica, em 65 ou 64 A.C.

O Evangelho na Cilícia. Não sabemos como o evangelho chegou até aquela região. É possível que Paulo o tenha levado até ali, embora as Escrituras nada nos informem quanto a isso. A região cresceu até tornar-se um dos centros do cristianismo. Catorze centros principais de atividade cristã já haviam sido estabelecidos na Cilícia, pelos fins do século III D.C. (AM UN Z)

CÍMBALO

Ver sobre **Música e Instrumentos Musicais**.

CIMENTO (ARGAMASSA)

De acordo com uma definição lata, o cimento é qualquer substância usada para ligar as coisas entre si, incluindo os tijolos ou as pedras usadas na construção de qualquer edifício. Até recentemente, os estudiosos tinham quase a certeza de que os antigos não conheciam um verdadeiro cimento, no sentido moderno de concreto. No entanto, há estudiosos que

CIMÉRIOS — CINCO ARGUMENTOS

atualmente estão dizendo que as pirâmides do Egito não foram feitas de imensas rochas, mas antes, essas pedras foram montadas no local, mediante o uso de certa forma de cimento. Seja como for, a Bíblia refere-se claramente a certos materiais de ligação, conforme se vê abaixo:

1. O trecho de Gênesis 11:3 fala sobre o betume ou asfalto. No hebraico, *chemar*. Ver também Gên. 14:10 e Êxo. 2:3. Esse material foi usado na construção da torre de Babel. A mesma palavra é usada para indicar o material empregado para tornar estanque a arca de Moisés, onde ele foi posto em pequenino. Ver o artigo separado sobre *Asfalto*.

2. Os filhos de Israel usaram «barro» (em hebraico, *chomer*, usado por quinze vezes com esse sentido; por exemplo: Gên. 11:3; Êxo. 1:14; Isa. 41:25; Naum 3:14). O barro era pisado sob os pés para amaciá-lo (Naum 3:14). Os conquistadores pisavam sobre governantes como se fossem barro (Isa. 41:25). Essa mesma palavra hebraica é usada para indicar a argila usada pelos oleiros. De fato, essa palavra hebraica é usada na Bíblia de maneira frouxa, de tal modo que pode dar a entender tanto a argila usada pelos oleiros como a lama comum. A argila dos oleiros era trabalhada até que adquirisse a consistência certa, com a evaporação gradual da água. Ver o artigo separado sobre a *Argila*.

3. *Sentidos Figurados*. Nos sonhos e nas visões, o cimento ou qualquer material de ligação indica fatores que vinculam, dando continuidade e força a uma pessoa ou situação. Também podem estar em foco as realidades ou coisas que estiverem sendo empregadas em algum empreendimento em fases. No trecho de Isaías 41:25, a ação de conquistadores militares é retratada como se estivessem pisando o barro. Há paredes que os insensatos constroem e rebocam; e os profetas e mestres falsos podem rebocar as coisas que as pessoas constroem com cumprimento e predições, mas sem qualquer base na realidade, conforme se vê em Ezequiel 13:10 ss. Portanto, o ato de rebocar simboliza a hipocrisia ou a lisonja enganosa (Mat. 23:27; Atos 23:3). Aquilo que é sensaborão ou tolo é como um reboco (Jó 6:6; Lam. 2:14).

CIMÉRIOS

Esse é o nome grego para o povo que o AT chama de Gômer, em Gên. 10:2,3 e Eze. 38:6. Gômer foi o filho mais velho de Jafé, o qual foi pai de Asquenaz, Rifá e Togarma. O povo chamado Gômer é visto como aliado do povo chamado Togarma, no exército de Gogue, na profecia de Eze. 38. Alguns teólogos modernos supõem que essa predição retrata a Terceira Guerra Mundial, com o envolvimento da União Soviética. Historicamente, o povo de Gômer pode ter sido o mesmo que as inscrições assírias do séc. VIII A.C. chamam de Gimirrai. A localidade desse povo era a atual Ucrânia. Dali eles migraram para o sul, para a antiga Urartu, que atualmente faz parte da porção ocidental da Turquia. Ali, pois, tornaram-se adversários dos assírios.

Gômer também era o nome da filha de Diblaim, que se tornou esposa do profeta Oséias, e que lhe deu três filhos, 1:3.

CINAMOMO

Há uma palavra hebraica e uma palavra grega envolvidas, a saber:

1. *Quinnamom*, «casca do cinamomo», que aparece por três vezes: Êxo. 30:23; Pro. 7:16 e Can. 4:14.

2. *Kinámomon*, «cinamomo», palavra grega que aparece somente em Apo. 18:13.

O nome científico dessa árvore é *Cinnamomum zeylanicum*, que cresce até cerca de nove metros de altura, produzindo pequenas flores brancas. O melhor cinamomo vem de ramos com cerca de três anos de idade. Um óleo é extraído do material, que é suavizado mediante mergulho em água salgada, e de onde a substância é fabricada. Os hebreus pensavam que o odor do cinamomo é *glorioso*, conforme afirma uma das minhas fontes informativas; mas muitas pessoas de nossos dias simplesmente não concordam com esse parecer. Por essa razão, a substância não continua sendo usada como perfume, como nos dias antigos, embora continue sendo uma útil especiaria.

CINCO ARGUMENTOS DE TOMÁS DE AQUINO EM FAVOR DA EXISTÊNCIA DE DEUS

Comentário de F.C. Copleston.

F.C. Copleston (1907), membro da ordem religiosa dos jesuítas, é mais conhecido por causa de sua obra em muitos volumes *History of Philosophy*, que está se tornando rapidamente uma obra padrão na língua inglesa. Esse autor se tem mostrado muito ativo, formando elos de ligação entre o tomismo e as demais áreas do pensamento.

Extraído da obra de F.C. Copleston AQUINAS (1955), *capítulo iii*.

Naturalmente, Tomás de Aquino não negava que os homens podem chegar a saber que Deus existe por outros meios que não pelas reflexões filosóficas. E nem jamais ele asseverou que a crença da maioria das pessoas, que aceitam a proposição que Deus existe, resulta de seus elaborados argumentos metafísicos que criaram por si mesmos, ou dos argumentos metafísicos alheios sobre os quais meditaram. *E nem também confundia* ele o assentimento puramente intelectual ante a conclusão a que se chega por tais argumentos metafísicos com a fé cristã viva e o amor de Deus. Mas pensava ele que a meditação sobre características perfeitamente familiares do mundo concedem-nos amplas evidências em prol da existência de Deus. A própria reflexão, sustentada e desenvolvida no nível metafísico, é difícil, e Aquino explicitamente reconheceu e confessou essa dificuldade: certamente não considerava ele que todos são capazes de reflexões metafísicas contínuas. Ao mesmo tempo, os fatos empíricos sobre os quais se fundamentavam suas reflexões eram, para ele, fatos perfeitamente familiares. A fim de ver as relações entre as coisas finitas e o ser da qual elas dependem, não é mister que alguém apele para pesquisas científicas, descobrindo assim fatos empíricos até então desconhecidos. E nem o metafísico descobre a Deus de maneira análoga à do explorador que subitamente descobre uma ilha ou uma flor até então desconhecidas. O que o investigador metafísico precisa é de atenção e de reflexão, e não de pesquisa ou exploração.

Quais, pois, são os fatos familiares que para Tomás de Aquino lhe davam a entender a existência de Deus? A menção desses fatos pode ser encontrada nos famosos «Cinco Argumentos» que provam a existência de Deus, esboçados em sua obra *Summa Theologica* la, 2,3. No primeiro argumento, Aquino começa por dizer que 'É certo, evidente para os nossos sentidos, que certas coisas do mundo se encontram em movimento'. Precisamos relembrar que ele, à semelhança de Aristóteles, entendia que o termo *movimento* tem o sentido lato de modificação, de

CINCO ARGUMENTOS DE T. DE AQUINO

redução de um estado de potencialidade para o estado de ação; não se referia exclusivamente a um movimento local. No segundo argumento, ele começa com a observação que 'Neste mundo de coisas palpáveis descobrimos que há uma ordem de causas eficientes'. Em outras palavras, dentro da nossa experiência com as coisas e com suas relações mútuas, tomamos consciência de causalidade eficiente. Assim, ao passo que no primeiro argumento ele começa pelo fato de que algumas coisas sofrem a ação de outras, sendo assim modificadas, no segundo argumento ele se estriba sobre o fato de que algumas coisas agem sobre outras, como causas eficientes. No terceiro argumento, ele começa por dizer que 'Na natureza encontramos coisas que são possíveis serem e não serem; pois são geradas, podendo ser corrompidas; e, conseqüentemente — é possível que algumas coisas venham à existência e desapareçam'. Em outras palavras, percebemos que algumas coisas são corruptíveis ou perecíveis. Na quarta prova Aquino observa que 'Entre os seres existem alguns que são mais e outros menos bons, verazes, etc.' Finalmente, ele diz quanto ao quinto argumento que 'Percebemos que as coisas às quais falta o conhecimento, tal como os corpos naturais, atuam visando uma finalidade qualquer, o que se evidencia em todas as suas ações; o que fazem sempre da mesma maneira, de modo a obterem os melhores resultados».

Penso que pouca é a dificuldade encontrada na aceitação dos fatos empíricos que dão início aos três primeiros argumentos. Pois ninguém realmente duvida que algumas coisas sofrem a ação de outras, sendo modificadas ou 'movimentadas', que algumas coisas agem sobre outras, e que algumas coisas são perecíveis. Cada um de nós tem consciência, por exemplo, que ele sofre ações e é modificado, que algumas vezes ele age como causa eficiente, e que ele é perecível. E ainda que alguém zombasse da asseveração que ele tem consciência que nasceu e que morrerá, o fato é que sabe muito bem que outras pessoas nasceram e morreram. No entanto, os pontos iniciais dos dois argumentos finais de Aquino podem causar alguma dificuldade. Pois a proposição de que existem diferentes *graus de perfeição* nas coisas requer uma análise muito mais completa do que Aquino oferece em seu breve esboço sobre seu quarto argumento. E isso porque o esboço esquemático das cinco provas de existência de Deus não visava a satisfazer mentes críticas como é a mentalidade dos filósofos sazonados, mas como material introdutório dirigido aos 'novatos' nos estudos teológicos. Além disso, seja como for, Aquino pôde naturalmente apelar para idéias familiares de seus contemporâneos do século XIII, idéias essas que ainda não haviam sido sujeitas às críticas radicais que as assediariam posteriormente. Ao mesmo tempo, não é muito difícil compreendermos o que ele queria dizer. Estamos todos acostumados a pensar e a falar como se, por exemplo, houvesse diferentes graus de inteligência e de capacidade intelectual. A fim de calcularmos os diferentes graus, precisamos, como é lógico, de pontos fixos ou padronizados de referência. Porém, uma vez dados esses pontos de referência, estamos acostumados a fazer declarações que subentendem diferentes graus de perfeição. E embora essas declarações necessitem passar por uma análise mais íntima, referem-se a algo que cabe dentro da experiência ordinária, e que tem expressão na linguagem diária. No que diz respeito ao quinto argumento, o leitor moderno pode encontrar grande dificuldade ao tentar descobrir o que Aquino queria dizer, se porventura confinar sua atenção à relevante passagem da Summa Theologica. Porém, se o mesmo leitor examinar a *Summa contra Gentiles* (1,13), descobrirá que Aquino asseverava que vemos coisas de diferentes naturezas cooperando na produção e manutenção de uma ordem ou sistema relativamente estável. Quando Aquino afirma que vemos coisas puramente materiais a agirem visando a uma finalidade qualquer, não queria dizer que agem de forma análoga à dos seres humanos, os quais agem conscientemente visando a propósitos definidos. De fato, o ponto chave do argumento é que não o fazem assim. O que ele queria dizer é que diferentes modalidades de coisas, como o fogo e a água, cujos comportamentos são determinados pelas suas diversas formas, cooperam, não conscientemente, mas como algo automático, de tal modo que surge uma ordem ou sistema relativamente estável. E novamente, embora muito mais pudesse ser dito, se tivéssemos de esperar uma discussão completa sobre essa questão, a idéia básica não encerra nada de particularmente extraordinário, e nem encerra qualquer coisa contrária às nossas experiências e expectativas ordinárias.

Também não devemos perder de vista o fato de que Aquino fala com considerável disciplina: ele evita generalizações largas. Assim é que no seu primeiro argumento ele não afirma que todas as coisas materiais são movidas, mas sim, que vemos que algumas coisas, neste mundo, segundo percebemos, são movidas ou modificadas. Quanto ao seu terceiro argumento, ele não assevera que *todas* as coisas finitas são contingentes, e sim, que estamos cônscios de que *algumas coisas* vêm à existência e desaparecem. E, no tocante ao seu *quinto* argumento, ele não assevera que há uma ordem ou sistema mundial invariável, mas ante, que vemos corpos naturais que agem sempre ou quase sempre da mesma maneira. Portanto, a dificuldade que pode ser experimentada, no tocante às provas expostas por Tomás de Aquino sobre a existência de Deus, não diz tanto respeito aos fatos empíricos ou aos alegados fatos empíricos com que ele dá início aos seus argumentos, mas diz respeito à percepção como esses fatos dão a entender a existência de Deus.

Talvez se deva dizer imediatamente alguma coisa sobre essa idéia de **implicação**. Na realidade, Tomás de Aquino jamais usa essa palavra quando fala sobre os cinco argumentos, mas se refere a *prova* e *demonstração*. E pelo vocábulo *demonstração* ele quer dar a entender, nesse contexto, aquilo que ele denomina de *demonstratio quia*, a saber, uma prova causal da existência de Deus, procedente da afirmação de algum fato empírico, como, por exemplo, que existem coisas que se alteram, partindo daí para a afirmação de uma causa transcendental. Na realidade, é o segundo argumento que apresenta uma prova estritamente causal, no sentido que aborda explicitamente a ordem de causalidade eficiente; porém, em cada um de seus argumentos, transparece, de uma forma ou de outra, a idéia da dependência ontológica a uma causa transcendental. A convicção de Tomás de Aquino era que a plena compreensão dos fatos empíricos que foram selecionados para serem considerados naqueles cinco argumentos envolve a percepção da dependência desses fatos a alguma causa transcendental. A existência de coisas que se modificam, por exemplo, segundo a sua opinião, não se explica por si mesma: ela só pode tornar-se inteligível quando vista como dependente de uma causa transcendental, uma causa, por assim dizer, que não pertence à ordem das coisas que se modificam.

CINCO ARGUMENTOS DE AQUINO

Para o leitor moderno, isso pode sugerir que Tomás de Aquino se preocupava com explicações causais no sentido que ele procurava formular uma hipótese empírica a fim de explicar determinados fatos. Porém, ele não considerava a proposição que afirma a existência de Deus como uma hipótese causal no sentido de ser revisável em princípio, como uma hipótese, ou seja, em outras palavras, que concebivelmente pode ser sujeita à revisão, à luz de novos informes empíricos, ou como uma hipótese que pode ser suplantada por uma hipótese mais econômica. Essa particularidade talvez possa ser percebida com maior clareza no caso de seu terceiro argumento, que se baseia sobre o fato de que existem coisas que podem vir à existência e desaparecer. Segundo a opinião de Aquino, nenhum novo conhecimento científico acerca da constituição física dessas coisas poderia afetar a validade do seu argumento. Ele não olhava para uma *demonstração* da existência de Deus como uma hipótese empírica no sentido em que a teoria eletrônica, por exemplo, é declarada como uma hipótese empírica. Naturalmente, todos podem objetar que, conforme a sua própria opinião, os argumentos cosmológicos em favor da existência de Deus na realidade são análogos às hipóteses empíricas das ciências e que esses argumentos se revestem de uma função preditiva; mas não se pode dizer daí que essa interpretação pode ser atribuída legitimamente a Tomás de Aquino. Não nos devemos deixar iludir pelas ilustrações que ele algumas vezes oferece com base em teorias científicas de sua época. Porquanto essas ilustrações são meras tentativas para elucidar um ponto qualquer em termos facilmente acessíveis à compreensão dos seus leitores: têm por intuito indicar que as provas acerca da existência de Deus eram, para ele, hipóteses empíricas, conforme o sentido moderno desse vocábulo.

Significaria isso, por conseguinte, que Tomás de Aquino reputava a existência de Deus como algo logicamente vinculado a fatos como as transformações ou o vir à existência e ao desaparecimento? Naturalmente que ele não considerava a proposição que diz que «é possível que algumas coisas venham à existência e desapareçam» como se essa proposição indicasse necessariamente aquela outra que afirma que «existe um ser absolutamente necessário ou independente», no sentido de que a afirmação de uma dessas proposições e a negação da outra envolvam alguém em contradição verbal ou em contradição lingüística formal. Mas ele pensava que a análise *metafísica* do que significa objetivamente ser uma coisa que vem à existência e desaparece mostra-nos que tal coisa deve depender existencialmente de um ser absolutamente necessário. E também pensava ele que a análise metafísica daquilo que significa objetivamente ser uma coisa em mutação, mostra-nos que tal coisa depende de um ser movimentador supremo, o qual não pode ser abalado. Segue-se daí que, para Tomás de Aquino, qualquer pessoa é envolvida em uma contradição se chegar a afirmar as proposições que «é possível c e algumas coisas venham à existência e desapareçam», e que «existem coisas que se modificam», ao mesmo tempo que nega as proposições que afiançam que «existe um ser absolutamente necessário» e «existe um movimentador supremo, que não pode ser abalado». No entanto, essa contradição só se patenteia através da análise metafísica. E o envolvimento em questão é, fundamentalmente, um envolvimento ontológico ou causal.

Não são poucos os filósofos (certamente todos os *empiristas*) que poderiam comentar que se isso representa realmente a mentalidade de Tomás de Aquino, então é claro que ele confundia a relação causal com o envolvimento lógico. Devemo-nos lembrar, entretanto, que embora Aquino estivesse convencido de que a proposição que assevera que tudo quanto começa a existir tem *uma* causa, por outro lado é absolutamente certo que ele não pensava que a existência de qualquer coisa finita envolve a existência de qualquer outra coisa finita, no sentido de que a existência de qualquer objeto finito pode ser declarado como algo que envolve logicamente a existência de Deus. Dentro da linguagem teológica, uma vez que admitimos que existe um Criador onipotente, podemos daí dizer que ele pode criar e pode manter em existência qualquer coisa finita, mesmo sem a existência de qualquer outra coisa finita. Mas não se segue disso que possa existir qualquer coisa finita independentemente de Deus. Em outras palavras, Tomás de Aquino não estava na obrigação de apresentar outros exemplos do envolvimento ontológico que ele assevera haver entre a existência das coisas finitas e a existência de Deus. E embora as relações entre as criaturas e Deus sejam análogas, quanto a certos particulares, às relações entre uma coisa finita e outra, quanto à dependência causal, aquelas relações anteriores, se as considerarmos como tais, são sem paralelo. Tomás de Aquino não confundia relações causais em geral com envolvimentos lógicos; pelo contrário, asseverava a existência de uma relação sem-par entre as coisas finitas e a causa transfinita transcendental da qual todas elas dependem.

Talvez seja digno de ênfase que não se segue necessariamente, com base nos pontos de vista de Tomás de Aquino, que a abordagem metafísica da existência de Deus é uma questão fácil. É verdade que ele confiava no poder da razão humana para atingir o conhecimento da existência de Deus; e, além disso, ele não considerava que os seus argumentos precisavam do apoio da retórica ou do apelo emocional. E na «Summa Theologica», na qual escrevia para novatos nos meandros teológicos, ele afirmava seus argumentos de forma ousada e talvez de maneira desconcertantemente impessoal. Porém, não podemos concluir legitimamente que ele pensasse que é fácil para um homem chegar ao conhecimento da existência de Deus mediante as meditações filosóficas isoladas. Na realidade, ele faz uma declaração explícita com o sentido oposto. Pois estava bem consciente de que, na vida humana, outros fatores além das reflexões metafísicas exercem uma poderosa influência. Outrossim, é evidente que ele concordaria que é sempre possível estacarmos o processo da reflexão em um ponto particular qualquer.

Para Tomás de Aquino, todo ser, até onde é ou tem vida, é uma entidade inteligente. Porém, podemos considerar as coisas partindo de ângulos diversos, quando então observamos aspectos diferentes de uma mesma verdade. Por exemplo, posso considerar o vir à existência e o desaparecimento simplesmente em relação a exemplos definidos e com base em um ponto de vista subjetivo. Entristece-me pensar que alguém a quem amo, provavelmente falecerá antes de mim, deixando, por assim dizer, um hiato em minha vida. Ou entristece-me pensar que poderei morrer, ficando incapacitado de completar a obra que iniciei. Ou posso considerar o vir à existência e o desaparecimento com base em algum ponto de vista científico. Quais serão as causas fenomenais finitas da decomposição orgânica ou da geração de um organismo? Porém, também pode considerar o *vir à existência* e o desaparecimento puramente como tais, objetivamen-

CINCO ARGUMENTOS DE AQUINO

te, adotando um ponto de vista metafísico e dirigindo a minha atenção para o tipo de ser, considerado como tal, que é capaz de vir à existência e de desaparecer da existência. E ninguém poderá compelir-me a adotar este ou aquele ponto de vista. Se eu estiver resolvido a permanecer no nível, digamos, de alguma ciência particular, ali permanecerei; e todas as discussões terão de terminar ali. As reflexões metafísicas, nesse caso, não terão qualquer sentido para mim. No entanto, o ponto de vista metafísico é um ponto de vista possível, e a reflexão metafísica pertence a uma completa compreensão das coisas, tanto quanto isso é possível para as mentes finitas. E se porventura eu adotar esse ponto de vista e me conservar em um estado de reflexão contínua, segundo Tomás de Aquino estava convencido, tornar-se-á claro para mim uma relação existencial de dependência, o que não se tornaria claro para mim se eu permanecesse em um nível diferente de reflexão. Porém, tal como os fatores estranhos (tal como a influência da perspectiva geral promovida por uma civilização técnica) podem ajudar-me a produzir a minha decisão de permanecer em um nível não metafísico de reflexão, assim também podem os fatores estranhos influenciar as *minhas reflexões* dentro do nível metafísico. Para mim parece ser um erro crasso a sugestão de que Tomás de Aquino não reputava as reflexões metafísicas como uma maneira possível do indivíduo tomar consciência da existência de Deus, e que ele considerava tais reflexões, segundo têm sugerido alguns escritores, como mera justificação racional a uma certeza é necessariamente atingida através de algum outro meio. Pois, se isso constitui uma justificação racional em qualquer sentido, então penso que essa é uma maneira possível de tomarmos consciência da existência de Deus. Não se pode concluir daí necessariamente, entretanto, que essa seja uma forma fácil ou comum de se chegar a tal conhecimento.

Após essas observações de natureza geral, volto-me para os cinco argumentos expostos por Tomás de Aquino acerca da existência de Deus. Quando de seu primeiro argumento ele asseverava que *movimento* ou alteração significa a redução de uma coisa que passa do estado de potencialidade para o estado de ação, e que uma coisa qualquer não pode ser reduzida da potencialidade para a ação exceto devido à influência de um agente que já se encontra em estado de ação. Nesse sentido, 'tudo quanto se movimenta é movido por outra coisa'. E argumenta ele, finalmente, que a fim de ser evitado o *retrocesso infinito* na cadeia de movimentadores, deve-se admitir a existência de um movimentador primário que não pode ser abalado. E todos compreendem que esse é Deus.

Uma declaração qualquer, como «todos compreendem que esse é Deus» ou como «a esse ser todos chamam de Deus», ocorre no fim de cada argumento, embora eu prefira adiar aqui as considerações a respeito para outra ocasião. Quanto à eliminação de um retrocesso infinito, explicarei o que Tomás de Aquino quis dizer ao usar a palavra *retirar*, após esboçar a sua segunda prova, que é similar à primeira, quanto à sua estrutura.

Ao passo que no primeiro argumento Tomás de Aquino considera uma coisa como a sofrer a ação de outra, como algo que é modificado ou *movimentado*, em seu segundo argumento ele as considera como agentes ativos, como causas eficientes. Argumenta ele que existe uma hierarquia de causas eficientes, em que uma causa subordinada é dependente da causa acima dela, dentro da hierarquia das causas eficientes. E, depois de excluir a hipótese de um retrocesso infinito, ele passa a tirar a conclusão de que deve haver uma primeira causa eficiente, — à qual chamamos de Deus.

Ora, é obviamente impossível discutirmos sobre esses argumentos de forma proveitosa a menos que eles sejam primeiramente compreendidos. E compreendê-los erroneamente é por demais fácil, posto que os termos e as frases empregadas nos são ou não familiares ou capazes de serem tomados em um sentido diferente do sentido tencionado pelo seu autor. Em primeiro lugar, é essencial compreendermos que, em seu primeiro argumento, Tomás de Aquino supôs que o movimento ou modificação depende de um *movimentador* que age aqui e agora, como também supôs, em seu segundo argumento, que existem causas eficientes no mundo que até mesmo em sua atividade causal são aqui e agora dependentes da atividade causal de outras causas. É por essa razão que falei sobre uma *hierarquia*, referindo esse vocábulo ao termo *série*. Aquilo sobre o que Tomás de Aquino pensava pode ser ilustrado da seguinte maneira. Um filho depende de seu pai, no sentido que não teria existido não fora a atividade causal de seu pai. Porém, quando o filho age por si mesmo, já não se mostra dependente, aqui e agora, de seu — genitor. Não obstante, é dependente aqui e agora quanto a outros fatores. Sem a atividade do ar, por exemplo, ele não poderia agir por si mesmo; e a atividade preservadora da vida do ar, por sua vez, depende, aqui e agora, de outros fatores, e estes, por sua vez, ainda dependem de outros fatores. *Não digo* que esta ilustração é adequada em todos os pontos, para o propósito aqui colimado; mas pelo menos ilustra o fato de que quando Aquino fala sobre uma *ordem* de causas eficientes, ele não pensava em uma série que retrocedia passado adentro, e, sim, pensava sobre uma hierarquia de causas, na qual um membro subordinado é aqui e agora dependente da atividade causal de um membro superior. Pois, se eu der corda ao meu relógio, durante a noite, o mesmo continuará funcionando sem qualquer outra interferência da minha parte. No entanto, a atividade da pena, que traça estas palavras sobre a página, é aqui e agora dependente da atividade de minha mão, o que, agora e aqui depende ainda de outros fatores.

O sentido do repúdio à idéia de um retrocesso infinito, por esta altura, deve estar claro para os leitores. Tomás de Aquino não rejeitava a possibilidade de uma série infinita como tal. Já pudemos demonstrar que ele não pensava que alguém já tivesse obtido sucesso na demonstração da impossibilidade de uma série infinita de acontecimentos que se estendesse passado adentro. Por conseguinte, ele não dava a entender que queria eliminar a possibilidade de uma série infinita de causas e efeitos, em que um dado membro dependia de um membro anterior, digamos *x* ou *y*, mas que não dependa, uma vez tendo vindo à existência, aqui e agora, da presente atividade causal do membro anterior. Por assim dizer, não convém que imaginemos uma série linear ou horizontal, e, sim, uma hierarquia vertical, em que um membro inferior dependa, aqui e agora, da presente atividade causal do membro imediatamente superior, e assim por diante. É esse tipo vertical de série, prolongado ao infinito, que Tomás de Aquino rejeitou. E ele rejeitou essa idéia à base do fato de que a menos que exista um membro *primeiro*, um movimentador que por sua vez não é abalado, que por sua vez é uma causa que não depende da atividade causal de qualquer outra causa superior, não seria possível explicarmos o *movimento* ou atividade causal do membro inferior. Esse é o seu ponto de vista.

CINCO ARGUMENTOS DE AQUINO

Suprima-se o primeiro movimentador que não pode ser abalado, e não haverá qualquer movimento ou alteração aqui e agora. Suprima-se a primeira causa eficiente e não haverá qualquer atividade causal aqui e agora. Por conseguinte, se descobrirmos que algumas coisas do mundo são modificadas, deve haver necessariamente um movimentador que não é abalado por qualquer outra causa. E se existem causas eficientes no mundo, deve haver uma primeira causa eficiente, totalmente independente de quaisquer outras causas. E a palavra *primeira* (ou sua cognata, primária) não indica primeiro quanto à ordem temporal, e, sim, suprema ou primeira dentro da ordem ontológica.

Uma observação sobre a palavra «causa» cabe bem aqui. O que Tomás de Aquino teria dito precisamente sobre os 'Davis Humes' do século XIV ou da era moderna, obviamente é impossível dizermos. Mas é indubitável que ele cria em eficácias causais reais, bem como em relações causais reais. Naturalmente que ele tinha consciência de que a eficácia causal não é objeto da visão, no sentido em que manchas coloridas são objetos da visão; mas ele considerava que o ser humano tem a consciência de relações causais reais; e, se ele realmente compreendia a palavra *percepção* como algo que envolve a cooperação dos sentidos e do intelecto, podemos dizer que 'percebemos' a causalidade. E é de presumir-se que ele teria dito que a suficiência de uma interpretação fenomenalista da causalidade, visando propósitos da ciência física, nada comprova contra a validade de uma noção metafísica de causalidade. É óbvio que é possível disputar a sua análise acerca de modificações ou «movimentos» e acerca da causalidade eficiente, se é válida ou inválida, bem como se realmente existe tal coisa como uma hierarquia de causas. E a nossa opinião acerca da validade ou invalidade dos argumentos de Tomás de Aquino sobre a existência de Deus depende extensamente de nossas respostas a essas questões. No entanto, a menção de uma série matemática de infinitos é irrelevante para a discussão sobre os argumentos desse teólogo. E é justamente esse o ponto que tenho procurado esclarecer.

No seu terceiro argumento, Tomás de Aquino parte do fato de que algumas coisas vêm à existência e perecem, de onde também conclui que é possível para essas mesmas coisas existirem ou não existirem: elas não existem *necessariamente*. Em seguida ele argumenta que é impossível para as coisas que pertencem a essa categoria existirem sempre, pois «aquilo que pode não ser, em algum período de tempo não existe». Ora, se todas as coisas pertencessem a essa categoria, em algum tempo nada existiria. É claro que Aquino estava supondo, por causa de seu argumento, a hipótese de um tempo infinito, e a sua prova tem por desígnio cobrir essa hipótese. Ele não diz que o tempo infinito é impossível—o que diz é que se o tempo é infinito, e se todas as coisas são capazes de não existirem, então essa potencialidade seria inevitavelmente cumprida no tempo infinito. Nesse caso, houve tempo em que nada existia. Mas, se realmente houve um tempo em que nada havia, também nada agora existiria. Porquanto nenhuma coisa pode trazer a si mesma à existência. No entanto, é patente que existem as coisas. Por conseguinte, jamais se poderia dizer em verdade que houve tempo em que nada existia. E, por conseguinte, é impossível que todas as coisas sejam capazes de existir ou de não existir. Deve haver, portanto, algum ser necessário. Mas quiçá esse ser seja necessário no sentido de que o mesmo deve existir se todas as demais coisas existem; em outras palavras, sua necessidade pode ser meramente hipotética. Todavia, não podemos prosseguir até o infinito, dentro da série ou hierarquia dos seres necessários. Se o fizermos, não explicaremos a presença aqui e agora, de seres capazes de existirem ou de não existirem. Portanto, devemos asseverar a existência de um ser que é absolutamente necessário (*per se necessarium*) e totalmente independente. E a esse ser chamamos de *Deus*.

Esse argumento pode parecer ser bem desnecessariamente complicado e obscuro; porém, é mister que o vejamos em seu contexto histórico. Conforme já tivemos ocasião de mencionar, Tomás de Aquino formulou o seu argumento de tal maneira que se tornasse independente das questões se o mundo existe ou não desde a eternidade. Mas quis mostrar que em qualquer dessas hipóteses deve ter havido um ser necessário. Quanto à introdução de hipotéticos seres necessários, ele queria mostrar que ainda que existam tais seres, talvez dentro dos limites do universo, que não são corruptíveis no sentido em que uma flor é corruptível, ainda assim deve existir um ser absolutamente independente. Finalmente, no que diz respeito à terminologia, Tomás de Aquino se utilizou da comum expressão medieval «ser necessário». Na realidade ele não usa o termo *ser contingente* no argumento, e em lugar disso, fala sobre seres *possíveis*, mas tudo resulta na mesma coisa. E embora os vocábulos *contingente* e *necessário* sejam atualmente empregados para indicar proposições, e não seres, tenho preferido reter a maneira de falar de Tomás de Aquino. Sem importar se alguém aceita ou não o seu argumento, não penso que exista uma dificuldade insuperável para que esse alguém entenda a sua linha de pensamento.

Precisamos admitir que o quarto argumento de Tomás de Aquino é de difícil apreensão. Aquino argumenta que existem graus de *perfeição* nas coisas. Tipos diferentes de coisas finitas possuem perfeições diferentes em diversos graus limitados. Em seguida ele argumentou não somente que se existem diferentes graus de uma perfeição como é a bondade, então é que existe um bem supremo do qual as outras coisas boas se aproximam, e também que todos os graus limitados de bondade são causados pelo bem supremo. E visto que a *bondade* é um termo intercambiável da palavra *ser*, até onde uma coisa é boa como o ser, o bem supremo é o ser supremo, bem como a causa de ser de todas as outras coisas. Por conseguinte, deve haver algo que, para todos os seres, é a causa do ser de todos eles, de sua bondade e de todas as suas outras perfeições; e a isso chamamos de *Deus*.

Tomás de Aquino se refere a algumas observações de Aristóteles de sua obra *Metafísica*; mas esse argumento nos faz lembrar imediatamente das obras de Platão intituladas *Symposium e República*. E parece estar envolvida a doutrina platônica da participação. Tomás de Aquino não estava imediatamente familiarizado com qualquer dessas obras de Platão, mas a linha do pensamento platônico lhe era familiar através de outros escritores. E tal pensamento jamais desapareceu da filosofia. De fato, alguns daqueles teístas que rejeitam ou duvidam da validade dos argumentos *cosmológicos* parecem sentir uma marcante atração por certa variedade do quarto argumento de Tomás de Aquino, argumentando que no reconhecimento dos valores objetivos reconhecemos implicitamente a Deus como valor supremo. Porém, se a linha de pensamento, representado pelo quarto desses argumentos de Aquino tiver de significar alguma coisa para o leitor moderno médio, é mister que seja apresentado de forma bastante

CINCO ARGUMENTOS DE T. DE AQUINO

diferente daquela como foi expressa por Tomás de Aquino, que foi capaz de supor que os seus leitores embalavam idéias e pontos de vista que não mais podem ser pressupostos.

Finalmente, o quinto argumento de Tomás de Aquino, se consideramos o apresentado na *Summa Theologica*, juntamente com o que ele diz na *Summa contra Gentiles*, pode ser expresso mais ou menos como segue: A atividade e o comportamento de cada coisa podem ser determinados por sua forma. Porém, observamos coisas materiais de tipos extremamente diferentes a cooperarem entre si de tal modo a produzirem e manterem uma ordem ou um sistema mundial relativamente estável. Obtêm uma *finalidade*, isto é, a produção e a manutenção de uma ordem cósmica. Entretanto, coisas materiais e sem inteligência certamente não cooperam conscientemente, tendo em vista algum propósito. Se porventura dissermos que cooperam na realização de uma finalidade ou propósito, isso não significa que tencionam a realização de tal ordem de forma análoga àquela como um homem pode agir conscientemente, tendo em vista a concretização de um propósito seu. Por semelhante modo, quando Tomás de Aquino fala sobre a operação «visando uma finalidade», nessa conexão, ele pensava mais sobre a utilidade de certas coisas para a raça humana. Não queria dizer, por exemplo, que a erva cresce a fim de alimentar as ovelhas, e que as ovelhas existem a fim de servirem de alimento e material para vestuário dos seres humanos. Antes, ele pensava sobre a cooperação inconsciente de diferentes espécies de coisas materiais, na produção e manutenção de um sistema cósmico relativamente estável, e não sobre os benefícios que nos advêm do uso que fazemos de determinados objetos. E o *seu argumento* tinha por intuito mostrar que essa cooperação, por parte de coisas materiais heterogêneas, mostra claramente a existência de um autor extrinsecamente inteligente dessa cooperação, o qual atua tendo em vista os seus propósitos. Se porventura Tomás de Aquino tivesse vivido nos dias da hipótese evolucionária, sem dúvida teria argumentado que essa hipótese evolucionária dá apoio e não invalida a conclusão de seu quinto argumento.

Nenhum desses cinco argumentos era inteiramente novo, conforme também o próprio Aquino estava perfeitamente consciente. Não obstante, ele os desenvolveu e os organizou para que formassem um todo coerente. Com isso não quero dizer, entretanto, que ele considerava que a validade de alguns desses argumentos em particular dependa da validade dos outros quatro. Pois pouca dúvida pode haver que ele pensava que cada argumento é válido por seu *próprio direito*. Entretanto, segundo já tive oportunidade de observar, conformam-se a um determinado padrão, e se complementam mutuamente no sentido que, em cada argumento, as coisas são consideradas de um ponto de vista diferente, ou sob um aspecto diferente. Existem *tantas formas* diversas de abordarmos a questão de Deus.

CINCO ARGUMENTOS EM PROL DA EXISTÊNCIA DE DEUS

Tomás de Aquino (que vide), 1225-1274, é o mais famoso dos filósofos cristãos da era medieval. O seu grande empreendimento intelectual foi a expressão de uma filosofia cristã vazada em termos aristotélicos, ainda que anteriormente Aristóteles houvesse sido reputado como uma *ameaça* à fé cristã. Nos séculos que se passaram desde então, Tomás de Aquino veio a ser o virtual filósofo oficial da Igreja Católica Romana.

A *existência de Deus pode ser provada de cinco modos*.

A primeira e mais manifesta dessas maneiras é o argumento baseado no movimento. É certo, evidente para os nossos sentidos, que certas coisas do mundo se encontram em movimento. Ora, tudo quanto se movimenta é movido por outra coisa, pois nada pode mover-se exceto em potencialidade relativa àquilo na direção do que se movimenta; ao passo que uma coisa se move enquanto está em ação. Pois o movimento nada mais é senão a redução de algo da potencialidade para a realidade. Porém, nada pode ser reduzido da potencialidade para a realidade, a não ser por meio de algo que esteja em estado de realidade. Assim sendo, aquilo que é realmente quente, como o fogo, faz com que a madeira, que é potencialmente quente, torna-se realmente quente, e assim movimenta e modifica a madeira. Ora, *não é possível* que a mesma coisa fosse, ao mesmo tempo, real e potencialmente capaz acerca de algum aspecto, mas somente no que toca a aspectos diferentes. Pois aquilo que é realmente quente não pode, simultaneamente, ser potencialmente quente; mas potencialmente é simultaneamente frio. Portanto, é impossível que, quanto a um mesmo aspecto e da mesma maneira, uma coisa seja tanto o objeto movedor como o objeto movido, isto é, que possa mover a si mesma. Por conseguinte, tudo quanto se move, deve ser movido por outra coisa. E se aquilo pelo que um objeto é movido também se movimenta, então é mister que igualmente tenha sido movimentado por outro objeto, e assim por diante. Porém, isso não pode prosseguir até o infinito, porque nesse caso não haveria o movimentador primário, posto que os movimentadores subseqüentes se movimentam somente quando são movimentados pelo primeiro movimentador; tal como um cajado se move somente porque é movimentado pela mão. Por essa razão, pois, é necessário chegarmos a um primeiro movimentador, que não é movido por qualquer outra coisa; e todos compreendem que esse é Deus.

A segunda dessas maneiras se baseia na natureza das causas eficientes. Neste mundo de coisas palpáveis descobrimos que há uma ordem de causas eficientes. Não há nenhum caso conhecido (e nem mesmo isso seria possível) em que uma coisa qualquer é a causa eficiente de si mesma; pois, nesse caso, seria anterior a si mesma, o que é simplesmente impossível. Ora, no terreno de causas eficientes, não é possível retrocedermos *até o infinito*, porque em todas as causas eficientes que se sucedem por ordem, a primeira é a causa da causa intermediária, e esta causa intermediária é a causa da causa final, sem importar se a causa intermediária é uma só ou são diversas. Ora, retirar a causa é retirar o seu efeito. Portanto, se não há qualquer causa primária entre as causas eficientes, não haverá causa final, e nem haverá causa intermediária. Por outro lado, se fosse possível, quanto às causas eficientes, *retrocedermos até o infinito*, não haveria nenhuma causa primária eficiente, e nem haveria efeito final, como também não haveria qualquer causa eficiente intermediária. Mas tudo isso é claramente falso. Assim, pois, é necessário admitirmos uma primeira causa eficiente, à qual todos aplicam o nome de Deus.

A terceira maneira de provar a existência de Deus se alicerça na possibilidade e na necessidade, podendo ser exposta como segue. Na natureza encontramos coisas que são possíveis de ser e não ser, pois são geradas, podendo ser corrompidas; e, conseqüente-

CINCO PILARES DO DEÍSMO — CINCO PONTOS DO CALVINISMO

mente, é possível serem ou não serem. Mas é impossível que essas condições perdurem para sempre, porque aquilo que pode não ser, em algum período de tempo não existirá. Portanto, se tudo pode não ser, então, em algum período de tempo coisa alguma havia em existência. Ora, se isso expressa uma verdade, então até mesmo agora nada haveria em existência, porque aquilo que não existe começa a existir somente através de algo já existente. Portanto, se houve tempo em que nada existia, seria impossível para qualquer coisa começar a existir; e assim sendo, até mesmo agora nada haveria em existência—o que é um absurdo. Por conseguinte, não é que todos os seres sejam meramente possíveis, mas também deve haver algo cuja existência é necessária. Porém, *toda a coisa necessária* necessariamente é causada por outra, ou não. Ora, é impossível retrocedermos até o infinito quanto às coisas necessárias, que têm sua necessidade causada por outra, conforme também já se descobriu ser impossível no que tange às causas eficientes. E assim sendo, não podemos deixar de admitir a existência de algum ser que tem em si mesmo a sua própria necessidade, não tendo recebido essa necessidade de outro, mas antes que é a causa da necessidade de tudo o mais. E a esse ser todos os homens chamam de Deus.

A quarta maneira de provar a existência de Deus se firma no sistema de gradação que se encontra em todas as coisas. Entre os seres existem alguns que são mais e outros menos bons, verazes, nobres, etc. Porém, *mais* ou *menos* são atribuídos a diferentes coisas, conforme se assemelham, de diferentes modos, a algo que é o máximo, do mesmo modo que se diz que algo está mais quente, em relação àquilo que é menos quente. Assim sendo, existe algo que é o mais veraz, que é o melhor, que é o mais nobre, e, conseqüentemente, algo que é mais ser que os outros seres, porquanto aquelas coisas que são maiores na verdade são maiores em seu próprio ser, conforme está escrito em *Metaph.* II Metaph 1a, 1 (993b 30). Ora, o máximo dentro de qualquer gênero é a causa de tudo quanto existe nesse gênero, da mesma forma que o fogo, que é o máximo do calor, é a causa de todas as coisas quentes, conforme também é dito naquele mesmo livro. Idem (993b 25). Por conseguinte, deve haver algo que, para todos os seres, é a causa do ser de todos eles, de sua bondade e de todas as suas outras perfeições; e a isso chamamos de Deus.

A quinta maneira de ser provada a existência de Deus se alicerça no governo do mundo. Percebemos que as coisas às quais falta o conhecimento, tal como os corpos naturais, atuam visando a uma finalidade qualquer, o que se evidencia em todas as suas ações, o que fazem quase sempre da mesma maneira, de modo a obterem os melhores resultados. Por conseguinte, é patente que obtêm o seu alvo não fortuitamente, e, sim, por meio de algum desígnio. Ora, tudo aquilo ao que falta o conhecimento não pode dirigir-se a uma finalidade, a menos que seja orientado por algum ser dotado de conhecimento e inteligência; tal como a flecha é orientada pelo arqueiro. Portanto, existe algum ser inteligente por meio de quem todas as coisas naturais são dirigidas às suas respectivas finalidades. E a esse ser chamamos de *Deus*.

(Extraído da obra de Tomás de Aquino, *Summa Theologica*, na obra intitulada *The Basic Writings of St. Thomas Aquinas* (1945), editada por A.C Pegis, parte 1, Q.2, artigo 3).

CINCO PILARES DO DEÍSMO

Ver o artigo geral sobre o **Deísmo**. Herbert de Cherbury (que vide) (1583-1648) ofereceu-nos a sua opinião sobre os cinco ensinamentos centrais do deísmo, a saber: 1. A existência de um *Ser Supremo*. 2. Esse Ser Supremo é digno da nossa adoração. 3. Precisamos relacionar-nos com o Ser Supremo mediante a virtude e a piedade. 4. O pecado é expiado por meio do arrependimento. 5. A justiça requer que recebamos recompensa ou punição, após a morte, de conformidade com as nossas obras. Essas proposições, naturalmente, pressupõem a existência da alma e a sua sobrevivência diante da morte. Entretanto, elas não nos fornecem a distinção fundamental entre o deísmo e o teísmo. O *deísmo* supõe que Deus, após haver criado todas as coisas, deixou a sua criação aos cuidados das leis naturais, não intervindo na história da humanidade, nem para recompensar e nem para castigar. O *teísmo*, por sua vez, assume a posição que Deus continua interessado na sua criação, continua dirigindo todas as coisas e haverá de recompensar ou castigar os homens, de acordo com seus atos.

CINCO PONTOS DO ARMINIANISMO

Em 1610, os arminianos dirigiram ao governo holandês um protesto, contido em **cinco artigos**, chamados a *Remonstração*. Esses artigos foram escritos em oposição aos cinco pontos do *calvinismo* (que vide). Foram preparados por Uytenbogaert e foram assinados por quarenta e cinco ministros, que foram chamados de os *Remonstrantes* (que vide).

Os Cinco Pontos

1. A *eleição* de condenação estão *condicionadas* à fé ou incredulidade do indivíduo, não sendo incondicionalmente determinadas pela vontade divina.

2. A *expiação é universal*, e seus benefícios foram postos à disposição de todos os homens, mas somente os crentes são os beneficiários.

3. O homem, sem a ajuda do Espírito Santo, é incapaz de vir a Deus. Mas *todos* os homens estão sujeitos a essa ajuda. Há uma graça geral que não exclui a qualquer indivíduo, e todo impulso humano na direção de Deus é automaticamente ajudado pelo Espírito.

4. A graça *não é* irresistível.

5. A doutrina da perseverança dos convertidos está sujeita a maiores inquirições. Um homem pode cair do estado de graça obtido antes. Ver os artigos sobre *Armínio* e sobre o *Arminianismo*. Ver abaixo os *Cinco Pontos do Calvinismo*, ao fim de cujo artigo há uma avaliação dos dois pontos de vista oferecidos neste e naquele artigo.

CINCO PONTOS DO CALVINISMO

Esses pontos emergiram nos debates que tiveram lugar entre os arminianos e os calvinistas. Ver os artigos sobre *Calvino, João* e sobre *Calvinismo*.

Os Cinco Pontos:

1. *A Eleição é incondicional*. A eleição não está alicerçada nem sobre a fé e nem sobre as obras previstas. Origina-se na graça divina, inteiramente dependente da vontade divina, sem quaisquer condições.

2. *A expiação é limitada*. O calvinismo estrito afirma que Deus, desde o começo, não tinha qualquer intenção de fazer qualquer coisa acerca dos não-eleitos, reprovando-os ativamente ou deixando-os de lado. Isso posto, a expiação jamais tivera qualquer intenção de beneficiar aos não-eleitos. E isso, por sua vez, significa que Cristo não morreu pelo mundo, mas somente pelos eleitos. E também significa que o amor

não envolve o mundo inteiro. Isso seria apenas um gesto inútil.

3. O homem é totalmente depravado. Apesar de que o homem pode mostrar algum impulso para o bem, ele não pode ser considerado como dotado de qualquer mérito diante de Deus, exceto que um homem pode receber um julgamento menos severo. As fagulhas de bondade do homem de nada servem, no tocante à salvação da alma, embora essas fagulhas possam impressionar a outros homens. A depravação do homem envolve os seus pensamentos, os seus motivos e as suas ações. Ele não é capaz de agir de uma maneira que agrade a Deus, e seus pensamentos são sempre maus.

4. A graça divina é irresistível. De acordo com qualquer definição prática, a graça divina beneficia somente os eleitos. Visto que o decreto da eleição é totalmente incondicional, tendo sido divinamente ordenado e garantido, segue-se que os eleitos não têm poder e nem desejo de resistir à graça divina, que lhes confere a concretização da eleição.

5. Há uma perseverança absoluta. Os eleitos não deixam de responder à chamada divina, visto que, do começo ao fim, a questão é divinamente impulsionada, não dependendo somente do homem. Uma vez que atenda à chamada, a pessoa eleita pode desviar-se, mas não poderá perder a sua salvação. Em outras palavras, uma pessoa eleita perseverará na fé, até a plena concretização de sua salvação, quando ela estiver na presença do Senhor.

Avaliação dos cinco pontos do arminianismo e dos cinco pontos do calvinismo. O que digo abaixo é um breve sumário, porquanto nos artigos intitulados *Arminianismo* e *Calvinismo* abordo os méritos de ambos esses sistemas. Minhas atuais observações, pois, limitam-se ao seguinte:

1. Ambos esses sistemas, mediante a **manipulação de textos de prova**, podem provar, adequada e biblicamente, as suas respectivas posições. Se os apóstolos e outros líderes cristãos primitivos se unissem em torno de uma grande mesa, e se os pontos acima fossem trazidos à tona, para discussão, haveria debate, e não concórdia quanto a todos os pontos. O próprio Novo Testamento não se mostra homogêneo quanto a essas questões; e os autores sagrados ora mostravam-se calvinistas, ora mostravam-se arminianos. Essas questões já haviam sido debatidas no judaísmo, antes do advento do cristianismo.

2. O princípio de paradoxo. As grandes idéias da teologia sempre se revestem de uma aura de paradoxo, quando seus elementos são examinados. E isso porque alguns de seus elementos aparentemente contradizem a outros. Quando um ensino qualquer parece contradizer a si mesmo, isso é chamado de paradoxo. Assim, o livre-arbítrio parece contradizer o determinismo; mas, de alguma maneira, para nós incompreensível, esses são elementos de alguma verdade maior. Por igual modo, chamamos o Logos, Cristo Jesus, de divino e humano; mas não há como explicar que um ser divino possa ser humano, ou como um ser humano possa ser divino. Essas definições não se ajustam bem uma à outra, pelo que temos aí um paradoxo.

3. O princípio de polaridade. Dentro de nosso assunto, o calvinismo é o pólo norte, e o arminianismo é o pólo sul. As suas posições jamais poderão ser totalmente harmonizadas uma à outra. Mas, assim como há dois pólos no globo terrestre, assim também a verdade bíblica apresenta um lado divino e um lado humano, destacados, respectivamente, pela posição calvinista e pela posição arminiana. Algumas grandes idéias não podem ser discutidas de maneira completa e significativa, a menos que reconheçamos que há pólos aparentemente contraditórios, mas que precisam ser igualmente levados em conta. O determinismo é um pólo, e o livre arbítrio humano é o outro pólo de uma verdade maior. Deus usa o livre arbítrio humano, sem destruí-lo, embora não saibamos dizê-lo *como*. Ver os artigos separados sobre *Paradoxos* e *Polaridade*.

4. Quanto ao problema da perseverança dos santos, penso que podemos dar, pelo menos, uma solução parcial a esse paradoxo. Suponho que uma pessoa realmente convertida pode cair da graça. Esse é um dos cinco pontos do arminianismo. Por outra parte, também suponho que toda pessoa realmente convertida, mesmo nesse caso, será trazida de volta ao estado da graça. E, de acordo com minhas crenças pessoais, isso pode ocorrer antes ou depois da morte biológica da pessoa. A missão de Cristo estendeu-se ao hades, mediante a sua descida ali, e a salvação tornou-se possível para além da morte biológica. Ver I Ped. 4:6. A doutrina da restauração (que vide) também abarca os longos ciclos da eternidade futura (ver Efé. 1:10). Isso significa que as almas tanto podem ser salvas quanto restauradas, após a morte biológica. Isso posto, depois que alguém realmente se converte ao Senhor, mas vem a desviar-se da fé, haverá de ser devolvida à posição certa, ao longo da história da alma, sem importar se antes ou se depois da morte biológica. Filosoficamente, isso concorda com um dos pontos básicos do calvinismo, o quinto. Isso significa que a perseverança final ou segurança eterna do crente (que vide), finalmente tornar-se-á uma realidade. Isso pode suceder e caracterizar uma pessoa que se convertera mas que se desviara, passando-se depois disso um período menor ou maior. Mas a segurança eterna do crente é uma verdade *absoluta*. Isso caracterizará, final e absolutamente, os crentes regenerados. Por outro lado, o desvio pode ser uma experiência desagradável para a alma, com conseqüências a longo prazo. Muito sofrimento, vagueação e vexação podem ser experimentados pela alma, em seu caminho de volta ao favor divino. Por essa razão, não devemos minimizar a questão, simplesmente porque, em última análise, seremos levados de volta à segurança. Se eu tivesse um filho que tivesse de passar quarenta anos encarcerado, por haver cometido algum crime grave, eu não haveria de minimizar a sua experiência, dizendo que, finalmente, ele seria posto em liberdade, algum dia.

5. O orgulho e a arrogância dos sistemas teológicos. A verdade nunca se beneficia mediante atitudes arrogantes e polêmicas. As denominações com freqüência orgulham-se de sua *verdade*, atacando amargamente aqueles de quem discordam. Todavia, a «verdade» defendida pelas denominações geralmente — é parcial, se não mesmo equivocada. Sempre podemos aprender coisas de outras pessoas. As denominações sempre poderão aprimorar-se comparando-se com outras, devido às modificações resultantes do confronto. Contudo, isso não acontece com muita freqüência, pois as denominações recusam-se a fazer tais comparações; mas, pelo menos, isso pode suceder no caso de *indivíduos* que não se contentam em seguir a linha teológica de qualquer sistema ou denominação isolada. Quando muito, até os mais aptos teólogos possuem verdades limitadas e parcialmente compreendidas. A busca pela verdade divina é um processo eterno. Todos nós nos encontramos em diferentes estágios da compreensão da verdade, ao longo do caminho; e, por isso, deveríamos estar dispostos a ouvir os outros, a fim de podermos

CINGIR — CINTO

aprender e melhorar. Acima de tudo, há a lei do amor, que deveria governar todas as nossas ações e todos os nossos debates. Essa é a lei real da espiritualidade, bem como a sua própria essência, conforme aprende-se em I João 4:7 ss. Aquele que ama *nasceu* de Deus. Aquele que não, não nasceu de Deus.

CINGIR O NAVIO
Ver sobre **Navios e Embarcações**.

CÍNICOS, CINISMO
Esses nomes fazem-nos pensar em uma poderosa corrente filosófica que perdurou do século V A.C., ao século V D.C. Tais vocábulos vêm da palavra grega *kúnikos*, que significa «parecido com um cão». O edifício onde essa escola funcionou a princípio chamava-se *Cynosarges*, um nome relacionado àquele. A designação proveio de Diógenes de Sinope (que vide) por causa de sua conduta vergonhosa, semelhante à de um cão. De fato, ele chegou a ser chamado de *kyon*, cão. Ele foi uma espécie de *hippie* antigo, que pensava que a felicidade consiste em viver o homem de acordo com a natureza. Ele considerava desnaturais quaisquer desejos que não visassem de imediato à satisfação das simples necessidades do corpo. Tal como um cão na sociedade, ele opunha-se aos padrões de vida e de conduta usuais. Dessa circunstância é que se desenvolveu o moderno termo, «cínico», que significa que a pessoa é maliciosa, desconfiando de tudo, pondo em dúvida os motivos alheios e inclinada ao ceticismo e ao negativismo. Os cínicos modernos são pessoas amargas; mas, os antigos cínicos simplesmente não viam utilidade para a sociedade e seus padrões, preferindo viver, conforme eles diziam, mais de acordo com a natureza.

Idéias:
1. O prazer não seria o alvo da vida, conforme ensinavam os hedonistas. Antes, a virtude, por amor à virtude, seria esse alvo. A *virtude*, porém, consistiria em viver de acordo com a natureza, da maneira mais simples, satisfazendo os desejos naturais sem as peias ou floreios exagerados da sociedade.

2. Diógenes de Sinope era realmente um «cão», e muito esforçou-se para provar a sua contenção. Os antigos, da mesma forma que os modernos, apreciavam muito o sexo, como se fosse a melhor porção do hedonismo. Diógenes, ansioso por demonstrar o seu prazer diante das convenções sociais, masturbava-se em público a fim de mostrar quão fácil e naturalmente uma pessoa pode satisfazer seus impulsos sexuais.

3. A *virtude* seria o *único* bem, pelo que a filosofia inteira seria uma especulação ociosa, excetuando o aspecto da ética; e a ética teria apenas um alvo, a virtude. A virtude desenvolver-se-ia melhor por meio da vida ascética, porque as pessoas que se excitam diante das vantagens do mundo, envolvem-se em todas as formas de atividades inúteis. Todas essas atividades custam mais do que um homem sábio estaria disposto a pagar. Porém, os insensatos sempre haverão de pagar muito pelo nada. A *independência* do indivíduo das normas sociais resulta da busca apropriada pela virtude. A independência é muito desejável.

4. A *felicidade* seria o alvo da vida, alvo esse que seria atingido através da virtude, conforme foi acima descrito. Antístenes (que vide), que os estóicos de tempos posteriores consideravam o verdadeiro fundador do cinismo, desprezava o prazer. Ele dizia que preferia ficar demente a experimentar qualquer prazer. Pensava que a dor é o grande meio onde se desenvolve a virtude; e que o prazer só é capaz de corromper o homem. — Um homem sentir-se-ia feliz ao perceber a falsidade dos valores da sociedade, especialmente aqueles que exaltam os prazeres como algo desejável.

5. *Antístenes* foi um personagem interessante. Além de preferir a dor ao prazer, ele declarava que a pobreza também é boa para o desenvolvimento da virtude. Podemos entender isso. No entanto, ele também dizia que a má reputação é boa para o homem, porquanto os hipócritas, os ricos, os prósperos e os falsos da sociedade é que têm boa reputação, preocupando-se com coisas como o prazer. Um homem sábio não se importaria com o que os outros pensam a seu respeito, visto que os outros sempre pensam errado, afinal de contas. Antístenes também era um antiintelectual. A virtude seria obtida por meio de ações, e não por meio de palavras, do estudo e dos livros. Alguns cínicos consideravam qualquer prazer como errado e mau, até mesmo os prazeres mentais, como o estudo da filosofia.

Alguns cínicos praticavam o que pregavam. Diógenes percorria as ruas de Atenas levando uma lamparina acesa, em pleno meio-dia, em busca de um homem honesto e virtuoso. Ele conseguiu converter a sua causa a Crates de Tebas, que era homem riquíssimo, e que, depois disso, abandonou todas as suas riquezas e tornou-se um cínico mendicante. O que admira é que a esposa de Crates, Hipárquia, e o irmão dela, Metrocles, tenham seguido o exemplo de Crates.

Diógenes era discípulo de Antístenes, tendo levado a sério o seu mestre. Chegou mesmo a ultrapassá-lo quanto à busca ascética pela virtude. Outros cínicos importantes foram Crates de Tebas, Menipo de Gadara, Bíon de Borístenes, Demétrio, Díon Crisóstomo, Enomaus de Gadara, Demonax de Chipre, Luciano de Samosata, Peregrino Proteu, Máximo de Alexandria (que foi um cínico cristão, bispo de Constantinopla). Apresentamos artigos sobre cada um desses homens. No século V D.C., Salústio (que vide) combinou o cinismo com o misticismo e o neoplatonismo. O estoicismo sofreu a influência de Crates de Tebas, através do seu discípulo, Zeno de Cítium (que vide) o qual foi o fundador do estoicismo (que vide). (AM E EP MM P)

CINTAS
No hebraico, **gishshurim**. Essa palavra hebraica aparece somente por duas vezes em todo o Antigo Testamento: Isa. 3:20 e Jer. 2:32. Em nossa versão portuguesa, ela aparece, respectivamente, como «cintas» e «cinto». No hebraico, a palavra está no plural. Os estudiosos pensam que está em foco alguma peça de pano, na forma de tira, que cobria a cabeça. Algumas versões fazem alguma confusão com a «venda» que o profeta pôs sobre o rosto, em I Reis 20:38. A natureza exata dessa peça do vestuário é desconhecida. Tudo quanto se pode dizer é que era uma peça para ser posta na cabeça. Ver o artigo geral sobre *Vestimentas*.

CINTO
Há cinco palavras hebraicas e uma palavra grega envolvidas neste verbete:

1. *Abnet*, «faixa», «cinto». Palavra hebraica usada por nove vezes, como em Êxo. 28:4,39,40; Lev.

CINZAS — CÍRCULO

8:7,13; Isa. 22:21.

2. *Ezor*, «cinto». Palavra hebraica usada por catorze vezes. Por exemplo: II Reis 1:8; Isa. 5:27; 11:5; Jer. 13:1,2,4,6,10,11.

3. *Chagor*, «cinto». Termo hebraico usado por quatro vezes: I Sam. 18:4; II Sam. 20:8; Pro. 31:24; Eze. 23:15.

4. *Chagorah*, «cinto». Palavra hebraica usada por três vezes com esse sentido: II Sam. 18:11; I Reis 2:5; Isa. 3:24.

5. *Mezach*, «cinto», «faixa». Palavra hebraica que ocorre por uma vez com esse sentido, em Sal. 109:19.

6. *Zóne*, «cinto». Palavra grega que aparece por oito vezes: Mat. 3:4; 10:9; Mar. 1:6; 6:8; Atos 21:11; Apo. 1:13; 15:6.

Está em foco uma faixa de pano para ser usada à altura da cintura, como também certa variedade de cinturões. Os cintos eram usados para ajustar à cintura a roupa de baixo e a túnica. Alguns cinturões eram feitos de couro (II Reis 1:8; Mat. 3:4); outros eram feitos de tecido (Lev. 16:4; Jer. 13:1). O cinturão de alto luxo era de ouro (Dan. 10:5; Apo. 1:13). O cinto do sumo sacerdote de Israel era altamente decorativo, completo com bordados (Êxo. 28:39; 39:29). Além de deixar no lugar as peças de roupa, em torno do corpo, um cinto também era lugar conveniente para segurar uma espada ou outro instrumento.

Usos Figurados. «Cingir os lombos» significa preparar-se para o serviço (Luc. 12:35; I Ped. 1:13). Se um cinto era feito de pano grosso, isso indicava humildade ou tristeza (Isa. 3:24; 22:12). Também era símbolo de força, atividade ou poder. De fato, na lista de vocábulos hebraicos acima, a quinta dessas palavras, «mezach», em duas ocorrências significa «força» (Jó 12:21 e Isa. 23:10). O cinto do Messias refere-se à sua retidão e fidelidade (Isa. 11:5). Na metáfora da armadura, no sexto capítulo da epístola aos Efésios, o cinto simboliza a *verdade* (vs. 14).

CINZAS

Há duas palavras no hebraico, *eper*, «poeira», e *desen*, «gordura». As cinzas do altar das ofertas queimadas, nos dias de grande festividade, podiam acumular-se para serem retiradas somente no dia seguinte por um sacerdote escolhido por sorte para fazer o trabalho. Uma espécie de lixívia era feita com as cinzas da novilha sacrificada no grande dia da expiação, usada para as purificações cerimoniais (ver Núm. 19:17,18). As cinzas resultantes de holocaustos especiais eram guardadas e misturadas com água corrente, para purificação das poluções e como sinal de jejum (ver Isa. 58:5 e Jon. 3:6).

Usos figurados. 1. A fragilidade humana (ver Gên. 18:27). 2. A humilhação (ver Est. 4:1; Jon. 3:6; Mat. 11:21; Luc. 10:13). 3. Assentar-se sobre cinzas era sinal de lamentação e luto (ver Jó 1:8; Lam. 3:16; Eze. 27:30). Outro tanto era indicado pelo ato de lançar cinzas sobre a própria cabeça (ver II Sam. 13:10; Isa. 41:3). 4. Alimentar-se de cinzas, misturando-as com o próprio alimento, representava a tristeza (ver Sal. 102:9). Porém, Isaías 45:20, aparentemente denota o labor que resulta em nada, porque não há nutrientes nas cinzas. 5. Total destruição (ver Eze. 28:18 e II Ped. 2:6). 6. Indignidade (ver Gên. 18:27). 7. Redução dos inimigos a nada (ver Mal. 4:3).

No cristianismo. Tertuliano usava cinzas nas cerimônias públicas de confissão e penitência (século II D.C.). Os penitentes punham cinzas sobre suas cabeças, e ficavam à porta dos templos, esperando readmissão à comunhão. Isso haveria de evoluir para tornar-se na formal Quarta-feira de Cinzas, largamente observada pela cristandade. Ver o artigo sobre esse assunto. (E ID S UN)

CIPRESTE

No hebraico, **tirzah**. Esse vocábulo aparece somente por uma vez na Bíblia, em Isaías 44:14, onde também são mencionadas espécies vegetais como o cedro, o carvalho e o pinheiro. Alguns pensam que a *tirzah* seria o *Quercus ilex*, que é uma sempre-viva. Mas outros preferem pensar no *Platanus orientalis*. Todavia, poderia estar em foco o verdadeiro cipreste, cujo nome científico é *Cupressus semprevive*. Era uma árvore bem conhecida na Palestina, porque ali havia grandes áreas cobertas de florestas. Sua madeira era usada no fabrico de muitas coisas, incluindo ataúdes. Os arqueólogos têm descoberto ataúdes feitos dessa madeira, contendo múmias, o que demonstra a grande duração dessa madeira. É possível que, em Gênesis 6:14, esteja em foco a madeira de cipreste (onde a nossa versão portuguesa traduz o termo hebraico *gopher*, por «cipreste»), visto que a madeira de cipreste é muito resinosa.

CIPRIANO DE CARTAGO

Suas datas foram 200-258 D.C. Foi o maior eclesiástico do século III D.C. Nasceu em Cartago, de família nobre e rica. Em cerca de 245 D.C., converteu-se a uma variedade ascética da vida cristã. Tornou-se bispo de Cartago e líder do clero cristão do Norte da África. Foi martirizado na época do imperador Valeriano, a 14 de setembro de 258 D.C. Suas principais contribuições foram em favor da teoria e da prática da administração eclesiástica e do discipulado cristão, e não em prol da teologia. Ele defendia a doutrina católica radical de que não há salvação fora dos limites da Igreja, e que a Igreja atua através dos bispos. Ele contribuiu para a doutrina da super-rogação (que vide) a qual desempenhou, mais tarde, um importante papel no sistema de penitências da Igreja Católica Romana. (E)

CÍRCULO

No hebraico, **chug**, «círculo», «circuito». Palavra usada por três vezes: Isa. 40:22; Jó. 22:14 e 26:10. Somente nesta última referência a nossa versão portuguesa traduz o termo por «círculo». Na outra referência de Jó é usada a palavra portuguesa «abóbada», e em Isaías 40:22 é usada a palavra «redondeza».

No grego temos apenas o verbo *kukleúo*, usado em João 10:24 e Apo. 20:9. Mas os cognatos são usados por mais quinze vezes, de Marcos ao Apocalipse.

Os gregos deixavam-se fascinar pelo círculo. O mesmo não tem começo e nem fim, e a sua simetria é perfeita. Entre eles, o círculo era símbolo da eternidade. Talvez não tenha sido por acidente que a Igreja Oriental, seguindo os pais alexandrinos da Igreja (que vide), pensava que a alma é eterna, ou, pelo menos, de origem antiquíssima, e também que o seu drama sagrado não é impedido e nem limitado pelo nascimento ou pela morte física. O círculo simboliza a eternidade passada e a eternidade futura; e, segundo aqueles pais da Igreja, nenhuma linha pode assinalar um tempo em que a oportunidade de salvação não estaria aberta. Em contraste com isso, a Igreja Latina pensa em termos de linha. A alma

CIRCUM — CIRCUNCISÃO

progrediria segundo uma linha. Essa linha teria começo no que se chama de nascimento biológico. E o julgamento começaria e terminaria com um ponto denominado morte biológica, além do que ocorreria a estagnação, pois fronteiras eternas estariam fixadas por esse ponto final. Quanto a esse particular, prefiro ficar com os pais gregos da Igreja. A teologia circular parece-me preferível à teologia linear. A engenharia não poderia existir sem o conceito do círculo, e a teologia é severamente empobrecida sem esse conceito circular. O Deus eterno ainda não terminou a sua obra; ele nunca fica plenamente satisfeito com o estado de uma alma humana. E o amor de Deus concorda com o conceito circular, sendo exatamente essa a idéia que defendo.

Uso entre os Hebreus:

Os hebreus às vezes usavam a palavra **chug** para dar a idéia do horizonte. Alguns estudiosos, usando a referência de Isaías 40:22, pensam que pelo menos alguns de Israel pensavam que a terra fosse redonda. Porém, aqueles que supostamente sabem essas coisas, informam-nos que o conceito da redondeza da terra nunca fez parte da cosmologia dos hebreus. Quanto a uma descrição acerca disso, ver o artigo sobre a *Astronomia*, onde comento detalhadamente o que os hebreus concebiam acerca da terra, do céu, do sheol, etc. Porém, sabemos que o conceito de um globo terrestre era conhecido entre os gregos desde muito antes de Cristo, pelo que tal idéia não é um desenvolvimento moderno. Os escritos deixados pelos hebreus mostram-nos que eles pensavam que o céu estrelado fosse um firmamento sólido, encurvado acima da terra; e talvez isso é o que esteja em foco em Isaías 40:22. No artigo sobre *Astronomia*, que tenho à minha frente, há um desenho onde aparece esse arco, ainda com outros detalhes típicos da cosmologia dos hebreus.

CÍRCULO DE VIENA Ver **Viena, Círculo de.**

CÍRCULO MÁGICO Ver **Magia, Círculo da.**

CIRCUM-AMBULAÇÃO

A palavra não aparece na Bíblia. Ela indica a cerimônia mediante a qual pessoas faziam círculos em torno de um objeto ou de alguém. O rito usualmente envolvia três circuitos, em que as pessoas envolvidas sempre mantinham o lado direito do corpo voltado para o objeto a ser circum-ambulado.

Usos do rito. Para demonstrar respeito, oferecer proteção, consagrar, garantir a boa sorte, tentar estabelecer comunhão com o objeto circum-ambulado, extrair poder do mesmo, declará-lo como sagrado, ou tentar estabelecer comunhão com tal objeto ou pessoa. Fazer círculos na direção oposta, isto é, com o lado esquerdo do corpo de frente para o objeto ou indivíduo circum-ambulado, segundo se acreditava, tinha o sentido precisamente oposto, mostrando desrespeito, ou tencionando transmitir alguma maldição ou influência maligna para o mesmo. Ver sobre *Magia, Círculo da.* Com freqüência, os costumes antigos têm algum significado que está por detrás da cerimônia ou rito. É possível que haja alguma forma de transferência de energias envolvida na circum-ambulação. Talvez algum dia a questão seja melhor examinada pela ciência.

CIRCUNCISÃO

Esboço
I. A Palavra
II. Antiguidade e Uso Largamente Espalhado
III. Origem e Propósitos
IV. No Judaísmo
V. Considerações no Novo Testamento

I. A Palavra

O vocábulo português deriva-se do latim, que significa, literalmente, «cortar em redor», referindo-se à pequena operação cirúrgica mediante a qual o prepúcio do pênis masculino é removido.

II. Antiguidade e Uso Largamente Espalhado

A **circuncisão** é a amputação do prepúcio masculino, sendo um dos mais antigos costumes da antiguidade, praticado por diversos povos. É, ou era, prática a circuncisão (embora com muitas variações quanto ao método, a idade e a realização do rito etc.), entre os judeus, islamitas, egípcios, polinésios e indígenas do Novo Mundo, bem como por muitas tribos primitivas da África e da Austrália. De fato, calcula-se que um sétimo da população masculina do mundo é circuncidada.

III. Origem e Propósitos

Diversas teorias têm sido apresentados como explicação da origem e do propósito dessa medida, a saber: a. teria finalidades higiênicas; b. seria um sinal de afiliação tribal; c. seria uma preparação para a vida sexual; d. seria um teste iniciatório da coragem, antes de um jovem ser aceito pela tribo; e seria um meio que santifica as faculdades geradoras; f. seria uma sacrifício que redime o varão do deus que lhe outorgou a vida.

IV. No Judaísmo

1. O Pacto com Abraão

Para os judeus, a circuncisão é um dos mais importantes dos seus seiscentos e treze mandamentos. Geralmente é interpretada como sinal de pacto entre Deus e a nação de Israel, e, por conseguinte, indispensável como sinal característico de que alguém pertence à mesma. (Conf. com Gên. 17:10-14 e Êxo. 12:44-49).

No Talmude, coletânea de comentários rabínicos, muitas prescrições são estabelecidas, regulando o ato da circuncisão. Podia ser realizada a circuncisão até mesmo em dia de sábado, se isso coincidisse com o oitavo dia após o nascimento da criança. Conforme dizem os judeus, a circuncisão consiste dos seguintes passos: a. O *«milah»*, ou seja, a amputação do prepúcio; b. o *«periah»*, em que a glande é descoberta, e c. o *«metizitzah»*, em que o fluxo de sangue é estancado. Bênçãos apropriadas eram recitadas antes e depois da circuncisão da criança, após o que o menino recebia o seu nome próprio. A cerimônia da circuncisão usualmente é acompanhada por uma refeição festiva, em que uma ação de graças especial é recitada, em alusão ao acontecimento. (*Encyclopedia of Religion*, editada por Vergilius Ferm, pág. 175).

O pacto abraâmico estava vinculado bem de perto ao símbolo da circuncisão, o que era, com efeito, a eliminação da natureza carnal (Gên. 17:11), apontando para o propósito ético de Deus, separando a nação israelita para si mesmo. Parte do destino do homem é que seja transformado moralmente, para que finalmente venha a participar das perfeições morais da natureza divina, mediante a presença habitadora do Espírito Santo, no íntimo do crente. (Ver Gál. 5:22,23 e Mat. 5:48).

O pacto abraâmico, pois, prometia a inauguração de uma nova nação, uma nação santa, para a qual Deus pudesse revelar os seus caminhos, e através da qual pudesse enviar o seu Messias ou Ungido. Ora, esse propósito divino só poderia ser perfeitamente

CIRCUNCISÃO

concretizado se essa nação viesse a participar da santidade de Deus; e isso envolve a necessidade da remoção da natureza carnal. Assim, pois, a circuncisão verdadeira, de natureza espiritual, é a do coração, não sendo apenas um ato externo, segundo também o apóstolo Paulo nos informa (ver Rom. 2:28). E isso, naturalmente, fala da expressão total do ser do crente, sendo equivalente à regeneração, pelo menos no que diz respeito aos seus aspectos morais. Para os judeus, como é claro, era um sinal nacional de identidade como povo de Deus, como uma nação separada para Deus, subentendendo o que Paulo escreve no segundo capítulo de sua epístola aos Romanos. Portanto, esse rito subentendia a operação da graça, mediante a qual Deus seleciona e assinala homens como seus.

O próprio ato físico da circuncisão era realizado em obediência a uma ordem divina; porém, por si mesmo, não tinha qualquer mérito e nem efeito espiritual, conforme Paulo demonstrou em Atos 7:8. Era um «sinal», ao passo que a *verdade simbolizada* era a diferença real que a graça de Deus faz no ser essencial do indivíduo. No trecho de Col. 2:11,12 encontramos uma vinculação um tanto frouxa entre o rito da circuncisão e o batismo cristão, de tal modo que, pelo menos em sentido bastante limitado, o batismo cristão tomou o lugar da circuncisão judaica. Isso nos é muito instrutivo, porque deixa óbvio, com base nas asseverações de Paulo, em Rom. 2:28 e *ss*, que os sinais externos, tal como o da circuncisão, não são agentes da graça, *mas tão-somente* símbolos daquela graça que verdadeiramente transforma o homem interior. E essa graça interior aparece como operação do Espírito Santo.

Contudo, o exagero posto nessa vinculação entre a circuncisão judaica e o batismo cristão têm criado a errônea doutrina do «batismo infantil», porquanto eram as crianças judias, — aos oito dias de idade, (quando do sexo masculino), que eram circuncidadas. Seja como for, a ausência da realidade espiritual torna inútil tal «sinal».

2. Considerações Específicas

a. Em Gênesis 17:10-14, Yahweh é declarado introdutor da circuncisão, como sinal do pacto estabelecido com Abraão. Naquele texto, parece estar indicado que Deus cedeu a Abraão novos poderes procriativos, no meio de sua esterilidade de velhice, para que ele pudesse tornar-se o pai de muitas nações, especificamente de Israel, através da qual a mensagem espiritual haveria de ser comunicada. Em outras culturas, encontramos a circuncisão como algo sacramental, talvez para identificar alguma casta sacerdotal. É possível que o povo de Israel compartilhasse dessa noção. A ciência moderna tem-nos ensinado que a circuncisão é uma medida higiênica. O homem circuncidado apanha menos infecções em seu aparelho genital, e, conseqüentemente, corre menor risco de ficar canceroso. A lavagem diária do pênis, sobretudo com um sabão desinfetante, produz o mesmo benefício, e isso poupa à mulher muitas infecções vaginais, visto que mais de trinta variedades de infecção podem ser transmitidas sexualmente, do homem para a mulher. Apesar de que os hebreus não conheciam essas coisas por vias científicas, podem tê-las conhecido mediante a observação e a prática. Por essa razão, é bem possível que, para eles, a circuncisão fosse um ato higiênico, e não apenas religioso. Heródoto informa-nos que os egípcios praticavam a circuncisão com finalidades de higiene. O prepúcio atua como incubador e transportador de bactérias; e, se os antigos não tinham uma teoria sobre germes, eles eram perfeitamente capazes de calcular por que tantas infecções estavam se espalhando.

b. *A marca tribal*. Entre os antigos, essa era uma das razões comuns para a prática da circuncisão, sendo possível que isso fizesse parte dos motivos da prática, entre os israelitas.

c. *Sinal de maturidade*. Um menino termina por tornar-se um homem. Em várias culturas antigas, a circuncisão assinalava a transição. Mas a idéia dificilmente poderia ser aplicada a Israel, visto que ali era praticada a circuncisão de infantes, idealmente aos oito dias de idade. Os convertidos ao judaísmo, vindos do paganismo, eram circuncidados; mas isso marcava a participação deles na aliança com Deus, e não qualquer maturidade física.

d. *Sacrifício humano*. — Em vez de sacrificar a pessoa inteira, um homem podia ser sacrificado simbolicamente, mediante a perda de uma pequena porção do seu corpo físico, como o prepúcio. Apesar dessa ser a razão da circuncisão em algumas culturas antigas, não parece haver motivo para pensarmos que a idéia tivesse qualquer coisa a ver com o povo de Israel.

V. Considerações No Novo Testamento
1. Considerações Sobre Valores

«No que diz respeito ao valor espiritual deste ato, o N.T. é taxativo: sem a obediência, a circuncisão se transforma em incircuncisão (ver Rom. 2:25-29). Esse sinal externo se reduz à insignificância, quando confrontado com as realidades da observância dos mandamentos (ver I Cor. 7:18,19), da fé que opera por meio do amor (ver Gál. 5:6), e da nova criação (ver Gál. 6:15). Não obstante, o crente não tem a liberdade de escarnecer desse antigo símbolo. Embora o crente deva evitar a circuncisão (ver Gál. 5:2 até o fim), no que diz respeito à expressão da suposta salvação através das obras (ver Col. 2:13; conf. com Isa. 52:1), contudo, segundo nos mostram estas passagens, ele precisa de seu significado interno. Em conseqüência, existe uma 'circuncisão de Cristo', o *despir* do corpo (mas não somente de uma parte—o prepúcio) da carne, em uma transação espiritual que não é realizada por mãos humanas, mas que consiste da relação com Cristo Jesus, em sua morte e ressurreição, selada pela ordenação iniciatória do novo pacto (ver Col. 2:11,12). Em resultado disso, os crentes são 'a circuncisão' (ver Fil. 3:3)». (Extraído de *The New Bible Dictionary*, Douglas, pág. 234).

O décimo quinto capítulo do livro de Atos mostra-nos claramente que até mesmo muitos cristãos primitivos, e, portanto, especialmente os judeus ordinários, eram da opinião de que a circuncisão era uma medida *necessária* para a salvação. Conforme a mentalidade judaica raciocinava, a circuncisão fazia parte do pacto abraâmico, e qualquer indivíduo que de alguma forma não fosse beneficiário do mesmo, não poderia ter esperança de que seria salvo. Ver o artigo sobre o *Pacto Abraâmico*. Quanto a comentários sobre o chamado «partido da circuncisão», os legalistas da igreja cristã primitiva, cujas atividades provocaram a escrita das epístolas aos Romanos e aos Gálatas, ver Atos 11:2 no NTI.

A circuncisão tem valor, Rom. 2:25. Qual era o valor autêntico da circuncisão? De acordo com o que diziam os judeus, tinha um valor absoluto, isto é, era uma garantia virtual da salvação, porquanto entre eles se pensava que todos os circuncidados, que eram israelitas por nascimento, já estariam automaticamente absolvidos de todo o julgamento. Entretanto, no dizer das Escrituras, qual era o real valor da circuncisão?

747

CIRCUNCISÃO, PARTIDO DA

a. A circuncisão era o sinal do pacto abraâmico (ver notas no NTI em Atos 3:25), além de ser um dos muitos privilégios de Israel, o que fazia deles uma sociedade superior. (Ver Rom. 9:4,5).

b. Tinha valor como preparação para melhores coisas vindouras. Também falava sobre a santificação. Isso teria lugar em Cristo. Falava de identificação com a geração de Abraão, e isso, por sua vez, tipificava o que Deus faria através do filho de Abraão, Jesus, o Messias.

c. Falava de um povo que seria *separado* para a santidade e a salvação. Tornava os homens cônscios de que existiam esses privilégios, e, sabendo-o, talvez os buscassem, se ao menos fossem suficientemente sábios.

d. A circuncisão afetava o órgão gerador, e isso simbolizava a produção de vida. A vida eterna está em Cristo e os homens, por darem atenção à mensagem de Deus e tomando parte em seu conceito, podem aprender acerca da real fonte da vida.

e. Há uma real circuncisão, de ordem absoluta, isto é, a circuncisão do coração. A santificação genuína leva os homens à salvação. Isso Paulo mostra no vs. 29 do segundo capítulo da epístola aos Romanos.

f. A circuncisão era mero sinal. A verdade simbolizada era a salvação. Por semelhante modo, o batismo é apenas um sinal, um símbolo, e não a substância, ou qualquer parte da substância essencial da salvação. (Ver as notas no NTI em Col. 2:11).

2. Buscando A Realidade

a. A lei podia ter um efeito ilusório, conforme se vê em Rom. 7:11. Os homens esperavam demais da lei. Dela esperavam aquilo que ela não podia fazer, libertá-los. Afirmavam eles: «A vida vem pela lei», e isso com apoio de certos versículos do A.T. Mas Paulo demonstra que tudo isso é pura imaginação.

b. A circuncisão simbolizava todos os privilégios dos judeus, por ser o sinal do pacto abraâmico. Portanto, também fazia tropeçar os homens que eram superficiais em seu entendimento espiritual.

c. O caminho da lei era difícil por demais. Requeria a perfeição, mas não tinha o poder para conferir essa perfeição. — Conferia altos privilégios, mas os homens, observando as coisas externas, e substituindo por elas as verdades que haveriam de seguir-se, terminaram possuidores de uma espiritualidade inferior e inadequada.

d. A lei apontava para a realidade em Cristo.

3. Externalidades na Religião

«O ponto aqui focalizado é simples, mas importante. Certos indivíduos vivem sujeitos à tentação constante de confundirem as externalidades incidentais com as *realidades essenciais*. Têm a confiança de ocupar um lugar, dentro da comunidade cristã, por terem sido batizados ou por serem membros nominais de alguma igreja local; e ficam altamente indignados quando alguém sugere que realmente não são crentes. Em adição a essa suposição superficial de que os sinais externos são suficientes como substitutos da participação ativa na vida da fé, é mister observarmos uma forma paralela assumida pela confiança nos sinais externos, conforme tal coisa freqüentemente ocorre. Usualmente é a pessoa que confia em suas realizações religiosas externas, que sente que os sinais visíveis da religiosidade são importantes. Não é necessário que isso seja produto de algum orgulho humano; pode, simplesmente, resultar de um ponto de vista limitado, que não leva em conta a distinção que há entre as verdades essenciais e as coisas inconseqüentes». (Gerald R. Cragg em Rom. 2:25).

«O sinal característico, que destacava os judeus, tinha dois lados; um era externo e formal, e o outro era interno e real. Sua essência dependia desse último aspecto, porquanto, sem essa circuncisão interna, tudo quanto era externo nada valia. Não é necessário alguém ter nascido judeu para possuir essa verdade essencial. Precisamente a mesma linguagem pode ser aplicada no caso dos sacramentos cristãos». (W. Sanday, em Rom. 2:25).

4. O Partido da Circuncisão, Facções e Lutas

Ver o artigo separado sobre a *Circuncisão, Partido da*. Esse artigo apresenta o argumento em favor da circuncisão, do ponto de vista do judaísmo antigo, o que nos confere a compreensão do motivo pelo qual o assunto revestia-se de tanta importância para a Igreja primitiva. Também são apresentados ali os modernos substitutos. Os homens continuam confiando em meras externalidades religiosas. Os homens confiam em ritos e cerimônias, atribuindo aos mesmos um valor atinente à eterna salvação da alma. Muitas denominações evangélicas ainda não conseguiram deixar esse sinal de primitivismo, em sua fé religiosa. Muitos homens ainda não chegaram a entender que a salvação, em todos os seus aspectos, está envolvida na transformação da alma por meio do Espírito de Deus. Esses aspectos podem ser *simbolizados* por meio de cerimônias, mas *nenhum* deles torna-se uma realidade por meios ritualísticos. Não admira que certos autores do Novo Testamento ainda se aferravam a certos primitivismos em sua fé, como a idéia da regeneração batismal, que, quase certamente, reflete-se em passagens como Atos 2:38 e Marcos 16:16. Creio, porém, que a teologia paulina afastou-se em muito de tal conceito. O trecho de Colossenses 2:11 subentende certo elo entre o batismo e a circuncisão, pelo que aquilo que a circuncisão significava para os judeus, o batismo continua a significar para alguns cristãos. Porém, tanto a circuncisão quanto o batismo em água são externalidades, são meros símbolos. Ver o artigo sobre o *Batismo*. (AM B BULT E ID NTI Z)

CIRCUNCISÃO, FESTA DA

O dia primeiro de janeiro assinala o dia da celebração do sinal da circuncisão, que confirmava o pacto estabelecido entre Deus e a nação de Israel. Essa festa comemora a reverência de Cristo pela lei, ao submeter-se ele ao rito da circuncisão, oito dias após o seu nascimento. Tal festa tinha por intuito ajudar a substituir os excessos imorais do paganismo, vinculados à adoração ao deus Janus, naquele mesmo dia. Ver também *Celebrações do Ano Novo*.

CIRCUNCISÃO, PARTIDO DA

Atos 15:1: *Então alguns que tinham descido da Judéia ensinavam aos irmãos: Se não vos circuncidardes, segundo o rito de Moisés, não podeis ser salvos*.

Ver o artigo sobre *Circuncisão*.

Neste ponto vemos o *partido da circuncisão* em operação, uma vez mais. É quase fora de dúvida que os *indivíduos* envolvidos foram os mesmos que causaram dificuldades para o apóstolo Pedro, conforme a narrativa do décimo primeiro capítulo deste livro de Atos, onde são chamados de «os que eram da circuncisão». O vocábulo *circuncisão*, se refere, como é óbvio, a algum grupo de *crentes judeus*, que se mostravam especialmente zelosos pelas leis cerimoniais do judaísmo, os quais estavam plenamente convictos de que a salvação, à parte das observâncias rituais, sobretudo da circuncisão, era simplesmente impossível. Esse mesmo termo é usado, em sentido mais lato ainda, na passagem de Gál. 2:12, a fim de indicar os judeus cristãos como uma classe, mas esse emprego é mais amplo do que o encontrado no décimo primeiro capítulo deste livro, ou do que aqui, em Atos 15:1.

Como parte integrante desse estrito grupo legalista, sobressaíam os convertidos dentre o farisaísmo, os quais não eram capazes de ver a religião, à parte de formas cerimoniais e ritualistas, embora estivessem convencidos do fato de que Jesus era realmente o Messias. Isso significa que, apesar de serem cristãos, pertenciam a uma variedade judaica, de inclinações *legalistas*.

Qual é a argumentação em prol da circuncisão?
Não se pode ocultar a verdade que, nas sinagogas, ensinava-se que a salvação é obtida mediante a observância da lei mosaica e que um dos mais importantes princípios dessa lei é a circuncisão. Disso podemos deduzir os seguintes pontos:

1. Não deixar alguém circuncidar-se era, segundo o ponto de vista judaico, uma *transgressão voluntária*, que impedia os homens de receberem a *salvação* que buscavam. Essa salvação, para os judeus, estava óbvia e necessariamente vinculada ao *pacto eterno*, estabelecido com seu antepassado, Abraão. (Ver Gên. 17:13).

2. Não se há de duvidar que salientavam vigorosamente, com suas Bíblias abertas e *citando* versículos do A.T., que esse pacto fora «estabelecido por Deus»; sendo parte da tradição seguida por todos os patriarcas.

3. Também deveriam ter procurado mostrar que esse sinal do pacto — a circuncisão — jamais fora ab-rogado, e que, por isso mesmo, os novos «meios» e «ensinamentos» de Pedro, de Paulo e de outros mestres cristãos, eram contrários à verdadeira «doutrina e prática», o que tornava o ensino desses apóstolos uma *heresia*.

4. Devem, por semelhante modo, ter salientado a magna importância da circuncisão, segundo pensavám, e sua necessidade para que os interessados obtivessem a *salvação* de Deus, mediante o fato de que antecedia à lei, tendo sido dada a Abraão como parte integrante da aliança que fora estabelecida entre ele e Deus, muito antes da entrega formal da lei mosaica. Portanto, tentar modificar essa instituição seria o mesmo que negar o valor e a importância do pacto abraâmico.

5. Além disso, segundo devem ter argumentado os legalistas, apesar de muitos haverem rejeitado Jesus, assim se separando da graça que só vem por intermédio dele, no ministério do Espírito Santo, os verdadeiros filhos de Abraão o haviam reconhecido como o Messias, e, esses, acima de todas as pessoas, deveriam estar ansiosos por «defender a fé» de quaisquer inovações heréticas.

6. Também certamente mostravam-se hábeis em demonstrar que a nova doutrina, que eliminava a circuncisão (pelo menos como necessária no caso dos convertidos dentre os gentios), era contrária à doutrina bíblica. Por conseguinte, era uma doutrina não meramente suspeita, mas também falsa.

7. Também devem ter exigido, da parte de Pedro e de Paulo, alguma *prova bíblica* para aquilo que lhes parecia uma inovação imposta à igreja cristã, que exercia influência deletéria entre os crentes.

8. Por semelhante modo, teriam exortado a outros a repreenderem aquela «nova doutrina», fazendo campanha contra ela, tanto nas igrejas como nos lares, em favor daquilo que pensavam ser a *verdadeira doutrina*.

9. Finalmente salientavam, supondo com isso pôr ponto final a toda a argumentação, que o próprio Senhor Jesus fora circuncidado, tendo dito que viera, não para destruir a lei, e, sim, para cumpri-la.

O argumento dos membros do partido legalista deve ter tido *forte* efeito de persuasão, e as indicações que nos são dadas, nas páginas do N.T., é que eles conseguiram persuadir grande número de pessoas, o que explica a grande controvérsia daí resultante, o que também levou o apóstolo Paulo a escrever sua epístola aos Gálatas. Todavia, embora convincentes e aparentemente alicerçados no A.T., esses argumentos do partido legalista **continham duas falhas seriíssimas**. a saber:

1. A circuncisão, apesar de ser sinal do pacto abraâmico, jamais foi dada como medida para *salvar* a alma.

2. Tendo servido de *sinal* de um dos pactos estabelecidos por Deus, durante o período de tempo determinado pelo Senhor, uma vez que suas relações com os homens sofreram modificações, esse sinal pôde também ser completamente eliminado. Assim argumentou Paulo no segundo capítulo de sua epístola aos Romanos. (Deve-se observar sobretudo os vss. 25-29 desse mesmo capítulo).

O argumento de Paulo se alicerça sobre o princípio fundamental de que coisa alguma, de natureza externa, serve de instrumento da salvação.

Ora, se um sinal ou rito não tem qualquer *mérito* por si mesmo, segue-se que Deus pode alterar esses símbolos e sua forma exterior, ao mesmo tempo que em nada ele precisa modificar a substância da espiritualidade. É exatamente isso que o cristianismo, às mãos dos apóstolos, e sob a orientação do Espírito Santo, se lançou a fazer. Todavia, era extremamente difícil aos homens libertarem suas mentes das cadeias às tradições e crenças que lhes haviam sido implantadas profundamente, tinham florescido por tantos e tantos anos e possuíam base na cultura e na tradição inteiras da nação em que viviam. A maioria dos homens dos primeiros tempos do cristianismo não compreendia de forma alguma o princípio espiritual, exarado por Paulo, do homem piedoso no íntimo, a despeito e sem importar as formas religiosas externas. Por isso mesmo, é admirável, não que tivesse havido uma controvérsia, e, sim, que a igreja cristã tivesse podido emergir desse tipo de mentalidade fixa, imóvel e inflexível.

Substituições Modernas

1. Hoje em dia, os homens dizem que o batismo é necessário à salvação, como se o batismo substituísse a circuncisão do A.T. Ver o artigo, *Regeneração Batismal*.

2. Outros expõem como substitutos os ritos e requisitos de várias denominações cristãs, mormente a eucaristia.

3. Os homens, num erro incurável, precisam de algo *externo*, como algum rito, alguma cerimônia, algo que lhes pareça valioso, mais ou menos como os pagãos têm seus ritos mágicos. Salvação? Pela fé somente!

John Gill mostra-nos como é que muitíssimos judeus acreditavam que nenhum homem pode ir para o inferno, se está circuncidado, e como todos os incircuncisos não escapam das penas eternas (ver Shemot Rabba, sec. 19, fol. 104.4). Na literatura judaica existem ensinos que contradizem esse parecer, especialmente no caso dos prosélitos do portão (os quais não eram circuncidados). Contudo, a outra idéia, sem dúvida alguma, era mais vigorosa na teologia judaica.

CIRCUNCISÃO — CIRCUNCISÃO FALSA

No tocante aos legalistas, Robertson (*in loc.*), nos brinda com uma descrição muito apta: «Eram homens de convicções sinceras, não se há de duvidar; mas eram obscurantistas, *incapazes* de receber *novas luzes* da parte do Senhor, em qualquer questão que envolvesse os seus preconceitos raciais e sociais. Lembravam-se de que o próprio Jesus fora circuncidado, e que ele dissera à mulher siro-fenícia que tinha vindo a fim de salvar somente as ovelhas perdidas da casa de Israel... (ver Mat. 15:24 e *ss*). Por semelhante modo, argumentavam que Cristo não havia repelido o rito da circuncisão. Desse modo teve início uma das maiores controvérsias religiosas entre todos os homens, isto é, aquela entre a religião espiritual e a religião ritualista e cerimoniosa. Continua entre nós até hoje, e o *batismo* em água tomou o lugar da circuncisão».

«A despeito das revelações especiais que haviam acompanhado o acolhimento dos primeiros gentios convertidos no seio da igreja cristã, o poderoso *partido judaizante* aderiu aos seus *antigos* preconceitos, atinentes à necessidade de conformação à lei de Moisés. Com esse partido, o apóstolo Paulo entrou em conflito durante todo o seu ministério, e mesmo depois de seu falecimento, encontramos esse partido a levantar novamente a cabeça, nas seitas dos ebionitas e dos nazarenos». (Alford).

«Observemos que existe em nós uma estranha inclinação para fazermos, das nossas próprias opiniões e práticas, uma regra e uma lei para todos os outros homens, para julgar tudo ao nosso derredor segundo nossos próprios padrões e para concluir que, porque agimos bem, todos os outros incorrem em erro, se não agem exatamente como nós». (Matthew Henry).

CIRCUNCISÃO DE TIMÓTEO

Paulo, revelador de grandes mistérios em Cristo, pressionado, voltou para uma forma mais primitiva de religião, e circuncidou Timóteo, Atos 16:3. Fez bem ou mal? Os intérpretes se divertem e brigam sobre o assunto.

Procurando solucionar o dilema.

1. Timóteo era cinqüenta por cento judeu, pelo que, incircunciso que era, servia de ofensa aos judeus. Os decretos de Jerusalém (Atos 15) relaxaram o cumprimento da lei mosaica quanto aos gentios, mas isso não se aplicava a Timóteo, à luz do fato de que ele tinha sangue parcialmente judeu.

2. A recusa de Paulo por permitir a circuncisão de Tito se fez com base no fato de que ele era gentio puro, e que os legalistas não tinham o direito de exigir sua circuncisão.

3. Paulo agiu assim para que, de todas as maneiras, pudesse ganhar para Cristo alguns judeus (ver I Cor. 9:20). Paulo afirmou que faria tudo (quanto não fosse pecaminoso) contanto que ganhasse alguns judeus; mas, por esse motivo, alguns criticavam acerbamente.

4. A maioria dos intérpretes, entretanto, opina que sua atitude era um pragmatismo justificável.

5. Alguns chegam mesmo ao extremo de pensar que Paulo nunca realmente agiu desse modo, mas que somente criou uma estória a fim de suavizar as duras atitudes judaicas contra a sua pessoa. Mas tal idéia não é provável!

6. Outros supõem que ele estivesse exausto de tantos labores, e que simplesmente não resistiu à pressão; e assim permitiu a realização de uma operação que, de outra sorte, jamais teria sido tolerada por ele.

7. Precisamos lembrar-nos de que o N.T. reflete um período de transição. Ao judaísmo foi permitido fenecer honrosamente, no seio da igreja cristã. Abaixo expomos as opiniões de alguns intérpretes.

«Paulo circuncidou Timóteo a fim de abolir a circuncisão» (Crisóstomo, em Atos 16:3). O que esse grande escritor e pregador sacro do passado quis dizer é que a circuncisão de Timóteo abria uma porta de serviço entre os judeus, na expectativa da conversão dos mesmos ao cristianismo.

«Seria a mesma coisa que se agora eu fosse viver entre os judeus, a fim de pregar-lhes o evangelho, e descobrisse que eles estavam fracos; e, nesse caso, poderia eu, voluntariamente, submeter-me à circuncisão, e comer ou fazer abstenção de alimentos, tal e qual eles fazem. Porém, eu não agiria assim sob nenhuma outra hipótese e não por mais tempo do que me fosse necessário estar com eles, a fim de entre eles trabalhar em prol do evangelho». (Lutero, em Atos 16:3).

Referindo-se à mesma questão, Calvino expressou a idéia de que apesar do fato de que seria contrário à boa consciência realizar sacrifícios de animais, após o sacrifício de Cristo, a prática da circuncisão para os judeus, sobretudo durante aquele período de *transição*, era uma questão *indiferente*. Outrossim, declara esse mesmo autor: «Tudo isso foi melhor e mais verdadeiramente dito naquele antigo provérbio: 'A sinagoga deveria ser sepultada *honrosamente*'».

«A circuncisão de Timóteo foi uma medida ditada meramente pela *prudência*; uma medida tornada imperiosamente necessária, devido às circunstâncias do momento; e, visto que essa circuncisão foi realizada meramente a fim de atender a isso, Timóteo nem por isso ficou obrigado a observar o ritual mosaico». (Adam Clarke, em Atos 16:3).

«Não houve qualquer concessão de doutrina, e nem qualquer referência ao dever que Timóteo teria ante essa questão». (Alford, em Atos 16:3).

Brown chama a isso de *passo indispensável* para que a viagem missionária prestes a ter início fosse um sucesso. E o mesmo escritor assevera que a recusa de circuncidar a Tito, diferentemente do caso de Timóteo, se fundamentou sobre princípios doutrinários, com a finalidade de impedir que os judaizantes pensassem que Paulo concordara com a sua norma de «circuncisão para os crentes gentios», norma essa que incluía o conceito de que a circuncisão era necessária para a salvação.

••• ••• •••

CIRCUNCISÃO FALSA

A expressão aparece na nossa versão portuguesa da Bíblia, em Filipenses 3:2. Outras traduções dizem «mutilação» ou algum sinônimo. Paulo empregou a expressão dentro de um jogo de palavras com o termo «circuncisão», a fim de estigmatizar o «partido da circuncisão», que procurava tornar a circuncisão uma norma obrigatória dentro da Igreja cristã. No Antigo Testamento grego (Septuaginta), o vocábulo grego em questão, *katatomé*, é usado para indicar as lacerações feitas no corpo, como no caso dos profetas de Baal (I Reis 18:28). O argumento de Paulo é que, *em Cristo*, a circuncisão foi abolida. Portanto, aqueles que insistem sobre a circuncisão tornam-se mutiladores da carne. Aquele que está em Cristo já recebeu a circuncisão espiritual, e não pode derivar qualquer vantagem da mutilação da carne literal. Ver Col. 2:11. Paulo escreveu essas palavras com ironia e desgosto, em uma das passagens bíblicas onde seu espírito mostra-se indignado. (B NTI)

CIRCUNSTÂNCIAS

Essa palavra é importante dentro da **ética relativa**. Alguns supõem que as nossas ações deveriam ser determinadas pelas *circunstâncias* específicas do momento, e não mediante fixações predeterminadas, que presumivelmente devem aplicar-se a todos os casos. Pessoas e circunstâncias são diferentes, e ambas estão sujeitas a modificações. Isso posto, a conduta humana deveria ser algo humano, e a conduta deveria variar segundo as circunstâncias. Em conseqüência disso, o que é bom para mim, não é necessariamente bom para outrem. De fato, aquilo que é bom para mim, devido a diferentes circunstâncias, amanhã, pode não ser bom para mim. Contrastemos a ética relativa à ética absoluta, que ensina que existem regras fixas, espirituais e eternas, que deveriam guiar a conduta humana. A ética teísta usualmente é absolutista em seu caráter. Ver o artigo geral sobre a *Ética*.

CIRENAICOS, CIRENAÍSMO

Houve três escolas filosóficas que se desenvolveram com base nas idéias de Sócrates (que vide), a saber: o cirenaísmo, o cinismo e o megarianismo (ver os artigos separados sobre essas três posições). O cirenaísmo deriva seu nome de Cirene da Líbia, lugar do nascimento de Aristipo (que vide), o qual foi o fundador dessa escola filosófica.

Idéias:

1. A felicidade é o alvo da conduta moral; mas, como alguém poderia ser feliz sem os prazeres? Ademais, os prazeres precisam ser intensos e freqüentes. Os prazeres mentais não seriam errados, mas nada se assemelharia aos intensos prazeres físicos.

2. Naturalmente, os prazeres podem redundar em dor, e a busca pelos prazeres pode ser dolorosa. Portanto, o verdadeiro critério da vida diária deveria ser: «Obtenha o máximo de prazer, com o mínimo de dor». Quando alguém obtém mais prazeres do que sofrimentos, então triunfa; e as pessoas que triunfam são felizes.

3. O único conhecimento que vale a pena é aquele que promove a busca pelos prazeres. O conhecimento vem através da percepção dos sentidos, e não nos deveríamos interessar pelo conhecimento tipo especulativo.

4. *Hegesias* (que vide) frisava mais a necessidade de evitar a dor do que a de cultivar os prazeres, como o alvo mais elevado da vida; mas ele não era avesso aos prazeres que pudessem ser obtidos sem o acompanhamento da dor.

5. *Anníkeris* (que vide) também buscava os prazeres, mas preferia aqueles da gracilidade social no lugar dos crassos prazeres físicos.

6. *Teodoro*, o Ateu (que vide) negava a existência de todos os seres divinos, afirmando que a finalidade da vida consiste na permanente emoção da alegria, que é o maior de todos os prazeres. Ele não se interessava muito por prazeres momentâneos e fugidios. Mas acreditava que o maior prazer consiste em alguém fazer o que quer, mesmo que seja errado, sem ser pilhado. A dor residiria em ser apanhado. Ver o artigo geral sobre o *Hedonismo*. (AM E EP MM P)

CIRENE

Nome de uma cidade no norte da Líbia, nas costas africanas, fundada em cerca de 632 A.C. por uma colônia de gregos vindos de Tera (Antonini), uma pequena ilha do mar Egeu. É mencionada somente no Novo Testamento: Mat. 27:32; Atos 2:10; 11:20 e 13:1. O adjetivo pátrio, «cireneu», também só aparece no Novo Testamento: Mar. 15:21; Luc. 23:26 e Atos 6:9.

Cirene tornou-se a principal cidade do antigo distrito da África do Norte chamado Cirenaica ou Pentápolis. Ficava localizada a 27 km do mar, sobre um planalto. Seu nome, segundo supõe-se, ter-se-ia derivado de uma fonte (Justino Mártir falava em um *monte*), chamada *kure* (Cyre), que ficava nas proximidades. A região da qual essa cidade era a capital, Cirenaica (Barca), ia desde o golfo de Platéia (Bomba) até à Grande Sirtes (golfo de Sidra). As cinco cidades de Pentápolis gozavam de considerável prosperidade, até que essa sofreu devido à competição das cidades ptolomaicas, às revoltas internas e ao abuso do solo. Em seu ponto culminante, tinham cerca de cem mil habitantes. Mas, aí por volta do século V D.C., não passavam de grandes ruínas.

A cidade de Cirene esteve sob o governo dos Batiadas até o estabelecimento da democracia, já no século IV A.C. Alexandre, o Grande conquistou-a em cerca de 331 A.C., e, mais tarde, passou para o império dos Ptolomeus. Nos tempos helênicos e romanos, havia ali uma numerosa população judaica, que falava o grego. A cidade foi doada aos romanos em cerca de 96 A.C., tendo-se tornado uma província senatorial romana, juntamente com Creta, em 27 A.C. Os trechos de Atos 2:10 e 6:9 mostram que Jerusalém contava com um bom contingente de pessoas provenientes de Cirene, juntamente com outros estrangeiros, ao ponto dos judeus cireneus terem uma sinagoga toda sua. Os cidadãos judeus de Cirene revoltaram-se em 115 e 116 D.C., derrubando monumentos pagãos e misturando-se nas batalhas que se seguiram. Dio Cássio informa-nos que cerca de duzentas mil pessoas morreram durante esse conflito. Adriano reconstruiu a cidade mas seu porto, em Apolônia, ultrapassava a cidade, quanto à importância.

No Novo Testamento. Simão, que levou a cruz de Jesus por um certo trajeto do caminho, era cireneu (Mat. 27:32; Mar. 15:21). Lúcio, um profeta e mestre da igreja cristã de Antioquia, era nativo de Cirene. A sinagoga com a qual Estêvão entrou em dificuldades, que estava em Jerusalém, e por cujos membros foi injustamente executado, tinha alguns membros que eram de Cirene (Atos 2:10 e 6:9). Os judeus cireneus convertidos ao cristianismo foram dispersos pelas perseguições, e chegaram a pregar o evangelho aos gentios, em Antioquia (Atos 11:20).

Outras pessoas famosas de Cirene. O poeta Calímaco, Carnéades, fundador da Nova Academia de Atenas, Aristipo, fundador da escola cirenaica de filosofia (ver *Cirenaicos, Cirenaísmo*), além de Eratóstenes, o historiador, eram naturais de Cirene. (AM ND Z)

CIRILO DE ALEXANDRIA

Suas datas foram 376-444 D.C. Foi patriarca de Alexandria de 414 D.C. até à sua morte. Advogava a veneração à Virgem Maria, e opunha-se vigorosamente à heresia de Nestor. Ver sobre o *Nestorianismo*. Foi principalmente graças à sua oposição que esse sistema foi condenado, quando dos concílios de Éfeso e de Calcedônia. Cirilo era um homem muito combatido, difícil de se manter convivência pacífica com ele, amante das controvérsias. Sua rivalidade tipicamente alexandrina com os antioqueanos (que vide) fê-lo entrar em oposição ativa contra Crisóstomo (que vide). Foi um polemista influente, embora não usasse de métodos inescrupulosos. Nem sempre os cristãos mais eminentes agem como cristãos. É conforme alguém já disse: «Os grandes pregadores algumas vezes são pequenos cristãos». (E P)

CIRILO DE JERUSALÉM

Suas datas foram, aproximadamente, 315-386 D.C. Foi um influente cristão em sua época. Tornou-se bispo de Jerusalém em cerca de 350 D.C. De 357 a 381 D.C., esteve envolvido na controvérsia com os arianos (ver sobre o *Arianismo*), em defesa da fé nicena. Ver sobre o *Credo Niceno*. Cirilo era suficientemente liberal para ter comunhão e para cooperar, até certo ponto, com os bispos cristãos semi-arianos. Contribuiu de modo significativo para a doutrina dos sacramentos e para a liturgia católica romana. Tornou-se mais conhecido devido à sua série de discursos catequéticos, feitos durante a Quaresma, para aqueles que tivessem de ser batizados durante a páscoa. Esses discursos consistem na *Procatequese*, as calorosas boas vindas aos candidatos, e nas dezoito instruções *catequéticas* dadas aos candidatos. Cinco dessas catequeses falam sobre as exigências para o batismo e sobre certos aspectos da fé cristã; e as outras treze catequeses explicam os artigos do Credo de Jerusalém (que vide). (AM E)

CIRO

Chamado Ciro II, o Grande. Foi conquistador da Babilônia, que governou desde 539 A.C. até a sua morte, em 530 A.C. Calcula-se que ele nasceu em cerca do ano 600 A.C. Foi o fundador do império persa. Heródoto informa-nos que ele foi o terceiro de sua linhagem a ter esse nome. Assim sendo, ele deveria ter sido intitulado Ciro III, e não Ciro II, mas foi com este último título que ele se tornou conhecido na história. Ele era filho de Cambises II, e neto de Ciro II. Seu bisavô foi Teispes II, que foi antecedido por Ciro I, Cambises I, Teispes I e Acaemenes. O nome Ciro vem do persa antigo, com o sentido de *cão jovem, kurush*.

1. *Conquistas.* Ciro herdou o trono de Ansã. Reuniu uma força armada dentre os persis (moderna província iraniana de Fars) e revoltou-se contra seu suserano medo, Astíages. Aliado com Nabonido, da Babilônia, dele derrotou Astíages, em cerca de 549 A.C., e assim ocupou a capital da Média, Ecbátana, moderna Hamadã. Em cerca de 547 A.C., ele marchou contra Creso, da Lídia, assediou sua capital, Sardes (perto da moderna Izmir), e assim aprisionou Creso. Então fez campanhas na direção do Oriente, entre muitas tribos, e ampliou os seus territórios até o rio Indo e até o sopé das montanhas do Hinducuxe. Retornando para o Ocidente, ele conquistou sua antiga aliada, a Babilônia, aparentemente sem encontrar resistência armada. Isso sucedeu em 539 A.C. Não demorou a controlar a Síria inteira, bem como a Palestina. Honrava o deus babilônico, Marduque, e também os deuses de vários povos capturados. Ele permitiu que exilados de lugares estrangeiros retornassem às suas terras, e isso incluiu os judeus exilados. Portanto, foi ele quem lançou os fundamentos do vasto império persa, sob cujo domínio a Judéia permaneceu província durante os próximos dois séculos. Ciro estabeleceu a sua capital em Pasárgade, na terra de Parsa. Ali têm sido descobertas pela arqueologia as ruínas de um palácio com a seguinte inscrição: «Eu, Ciro, o rei, o acamenida». Desse palácio nos vem a mais antiga peça em relevo da arte persa, um gênio com quatro asas, talvez representando o Ciro deificado.

2. *Seu Reinado.* Ecbátana foi a primeira capital acamenida, mas ruínas provenientes de Pasárgade mostram que Ciro edificou ali palácios e uma cidade. Ele tomou por empréstimo certos costumes e instituições dos medos. Em certo sentido, os medos eram aliados dos persas, e não tinham de pagar impostos, embora estivessem sob o controle persa. Os outros povos, portanto, chamavam o império de medo-persa. Ciro era tolerante para com os povos e suas religiões, conquistando o respeito e o apoio deles.

Heródoto informa-nos que Ciro faleceu em cerca de 530 A.C., quando combatia os massagetai, na Ásia central. Embora um homem de suaves maneiras, chamado pelos persas de *pai*, tal como a maioria dos reis, ele encontrou tempo suficiente para guerras e matanças.

A Saga de Ciro

Xenofonte escreveu e idealizou um livro didático sobre Ciro, chamando esse volume de Ciropédia, onde Ciro aparece como um soberano modelo. Xenofonte, Ctésias e Heródoto registraram a sua história. Muitos mitos têm surgido em redor dele. O épico nacional persa, o *Shah Nameh*, ou Livro dos Reis, registra muitas histórias míticas a respeito de Ciro. Vários motivos da lenda de Ciro tornaram-se parte do legado dessa história dos reis da Pérsia. As virtudes e a simplicidade de Ciro tornaram-se lições para outros seguirem. Isso significa que Ciro não somente fundou o multinacional império acamenida e lançou a base para o primeiro império realmente mundial, desde o rio Indo até o mar Egeu, mas também tornou-se o herói de uma saga que ainda sobrevive na época persa nacional. Ele deixou o seu nome em uma cidade central da Ásia, chamada Kureskhata, perto de Kurkath, não longe de Khojert, modernamente Leinabade, no sul da União Soviética.

3. *Seu Decreto.* Os trechos de II Crônicas 36:22,23 e Esdras 1:2,3 informam-nos que Ciro deu permissão aos cativos hebreus da Babilônia para retornarem à Palestina e reconstruírem o templo. A liberalidade de Ciro, no tocante às religiões, sem dúvida foi um fator em tudo isso. *O cilindro de Ciro*. Esse cilindro, descoberto no século XIX, retrata Ciro como um político politeísta, embora também demonstre paralelos com o ponto de vista bíblico a seu respeito, como um homem benévolo, que tinha misericórdia dos cativos. Esse cilindro fala sobre o deus Marduque, que teria procurado um governante justo e encontrou Ciro; o qual assim poupou as cidades e santuários sagrados, e os restaurou.

4. *Ciro e a Profecia Bíblica.* A profecia de Isaías, acerca de Ciro, começa em 41:2,25 e termina em 46:11 e 48:15. Isaías previu que Ciro não somente ordenaria a reconstrução do templo, mas também a reconstrução da própria cidade (Isa. 45:13; 44:28). Seu sucessor, Artaxerxes I, levou adiante o trabalho de reconstrução. O decreto de Ciro, mui provavelmente, incluiu a reconstrução da cidade, embora isso não seja dito especificamente. No trecho de Isaías 44:28-45:8, Ciro é chamado pelo nome, e assim os céticos têm pensado que as profecias envolvidas foram escritas após os eventos, e não antes dos mesmos.

5. *Ciro e as Inscrições.* A arqueologia tem descoberto certo número de inscrições que concordam com as declarações do Antigo Testamento quanto ao governo e às atitudes benevolentes de Ciro. O cilindro de Ciro (ver acima) demonstra isso com declarações ali inscritas. Visto que os judeus não tinham imagens de escultura, receberam permissão de restaurar o seu

templo, em Jerusalém. O édito real, registrado em II Crônicas 36:22,23 e Esdras 1:2,3, reflete o espírito daquele cilindro. Dessa maneira, Israel elogiou o homem que Deus determinara como libertador de seu povo (Isa. 45:1-4). O próprio Ciro, entretanto, afirmava-se inspirado pela divindade babilônica, Marduque. As inscrições naquele cilindro mostram a consciência que Ciro tinha de ser um homem do destino, divinamente nomeado para a sua tarefa. Essa incrível verdade, porém, aplica-se a muitos outros. Na verdade aplica-se a todos os homens, embora à vontade de Deus sejam necessários muitos séculos para levar todos os homens a se ajustarem ao plano de Deus. Para nós, os crentes, pela graça de Deus, essa oportunidade é chegada. (AM ND UN Z)

CIRURGIA
Ver sobre **Medicina**.

CISCO E REFUGO
No hebraico, **sechi**, que aparece somente por uma vez em todo o Antigo Testamento, em Lamentações 3:45. A outra palavra, que nossa versão portuguesa traduz por «refugo», aparece por nove vezes: I Sam. 16:7; Jó 34:33; Sal. 78:67; 118:22; Isa. 7:15,16; 8:6; Lam. 3:45; Eze. 5:6.

O termo grego *perípsema*, «varrido para o lado», e que nossa versão portuguesa traduz por «escória», aparece somente em I Cor. 4:13.

Está em foco algo que se desprende por abrasão, por lavagem, ou simplesmente a sujeira ou o lixo. As pessoas pensam que certos indivíduos são a escória da sociedade, mas nem sempre esse juízo humano está correto. A sociedade romana pensava que os primeiros cristãos não tinham nenhum valor, pelo que os seguidores de Cristo eram comparados com a escória. Em certo país comunista, não faz muito tempo, os ministros e missionários cristãos foram classificados como inferiores às prostitutas, dentro da gradação da cidadania. Muitos evangélicos modernos orgulham-se de seus templos luxuosos, com grandes áreas de estacionamento para seus veículos automotores. As condições externas têm-se modificado, mas o espírito não avançou muito. Bem pelo contrário.

CISMA
No grego, **schisma**, «rasgadura». O substantivo aparece por oito vezes no Novo Testamento: Mat. 9:16; Mar. 2:21; João 7:43; 9:16; I Cor. 1:10; 11:18 e 12:25. O verbo cognato, *schízo*, «rasgar», aparece por onze vezes, desde Mat. 27:51 até Atos 23:7.

Nas três referências do quarto evangelho, quando os judeus estavam em disputa sobre quem seria Jesus, houve uma «divisão» entre eles. Na parábola de Jesus sobre o remendo de pano novo em pano velho, aparece mais a idéia de «rasgar». Na reprovação paulina às contendas e divisões que haviam surgido na igreja cristã de Corinto, nossa versão portuguesa a traduz por «divisão». No vocabulário moderno, um «cisma» é uma divisão eclesiástica, uma separação provocada por falta de harmonia e coordenação, por bons ou maus motivos. Historicamente, há dois grandes cismas: o do século XI, entre as porções Ocidental e Oriental da Igreja Católica, fundada por Constantino, o primeiro imperador romano «cristão»; e o *grande cisma* de 1378-1417, quando houve dois ou até mesmo três papas eleitos, cada qual excomungando um ao outro, uma condição que só foi sanada com a eleição de Martinho V, em novembro de 1417, quando, novamente, houve um só Papa.

A *Reforma Protestante* (vide) foi outro *grande cisma*. — Os Protestantes são considerados pelos Católicos tanto como *cismáticos* como *hereges*. Para os Protestantes, os Católicos são os hereges.

Ver o artigo separado sobre *Grandes Cismas* que contém mais detalhes do que este presente artigo sobre *cismas*.

CISTERCIENSES
Essa ordem religiosa católica romana tornou-se uma realidade mediante o rígido reavivamento da *regra beneditina* (que vide), segundo a qual a erudição era substituída pelo trabalho manual. A ordem foi fundada por Roberto de Thierry, abade de Citeux, no latim, *Cistercium*, o que explica o nome da ordem. A ordem insiste sobre a simplicidade de suas igrejas, residências e vestes. O hábito consiste em uma batina branca com capuz da mesma cor, sobre um casaco negro. Uma capa negra era usada pelos monges, fora dos seus mosteiros. Os membros da ordem que se tornaram melhor conhecidos foram Estêvão Harding, seu terceiro abade (que vede), e Bernardo (que vide). A ordem espalhou-se rapidamente, tendo chegado até a Rússia, na direção leste, e até Jerusalém e a Inglaterra. Neste último país, os santuários da ordem testificam sobre a riqueza material que essa ordem, finalmente, adquiriu. Nos dias do rei Henrique VIII, setenta e cinco casas e vinte e seis conventos da ordem foram suprimidos na Inglaterra. (AM E)

CISTERNA
No hebraico, **bor**, «lugar cavado», «poço». O termo hebraico é usado por sessenta e sete vezes. Por exemplo: Gên. 37:20-29; Êxo. 21:33,34; Lev. 11:36; I Sam. 13:6; II Reis 18:31; Pro. 5:15; Ecl. 12:6; Isa. 36:16; Jer. 2:13.

Uma cisterna era um lugar onde era guardada água potável (Pro. 5:15; Ecl. 12:6; Isa. 36:16; Jer. 2:13). A maioria das cisternas consistia em reservatórios cobertos, escavados na terra ou na rocha, para onde escorria o excesso de águas da chuva, das fontes ou dos riachos, que eram para ali canalizadas e guardadas. As chuvas tornavam-se raras entre maio e setembro na Palestina e as cisternas tornavam-se o principal meio de se contar com um bom suprimento de água, naqueles meses. As cisternas comuns eram apenas um grande poço, mas, sobre muitas delas foram construídas grandes abóbadas. Visto que a água ali contida era valiosa nos meses de seca, muitas cisternas eram cobertas e disfarçadas, de modo a não serem facilmente descobertas. Em Cantares 4:12 encontramos a expressão «fonte selada», a qual, provavelmente, alude a uma cisterna coberta. A cobertura também era uma medida de segurança, visto que a lama acumulava-se no fundo das cisternas, e qualquer pessoa que ali caísse corria o perigo de afundar na lama, não sendo capaz de dali sair sem falarmos na imensa dificuldade em subir pelas paredes internas da cisterna. Ver Jer. 38:6 e Sal. 40:2. Algumas cisternas de grande tamanho serviam às cidades, as quais eram mais cuidadosamente preparadas, escavadas na rocha ou forradas com tijolos. Cisternas complexamente construídas têm sido encontradas em Jerusalém, Samaria, Marasa, Massada e outros locais antes populados, pelos arqueólogos. Visto que a água era escassa, algumas vezes as cisternas eram causa de conflitos. Uma cisterna seca e

CITA — CITAÇÕES NO NOVO TEST.

abandonada podia ser usada como cárcere, conforme vemos nos casos de José e Jeremias (Gên. 37:22 e Jer. 38:6).

Por ocasião da conquista da Palestina por Israel, cisternas foram tomadas (Deu. 6:11). Governos progressistas eram assinalados por muitas cisternas que eram feitas, tal como, nos nossos dias, os governos de áreas secas constroem reservatórios e represas. As cisternas eram objetos das obras públicas (II Crô. 26:10). Além de serem usadas como cárceres, as cisternas secas ou abandonadas eram utilizadas como silos, onde eram guardados cereais ou outros bens; e também eram empregadas como túmulos.

Usos Figurados. 1. A quebra da roda que era usada para puxar o balde do fundo do poço (ver Ecl. 12:6), serve de símbolo da perda da vitalidade do corpo físico, do que resulta a morte. 2. Tomar água da própria cisterna indica desfrutar de prazeres legítimos (Pro. 5:15). 3. As «cisternas rotas» de Jer. 2:13 indicam as maneiras vãs dos homens tentarem satisfazer suas necessidades espirituais. Deus é a fonte das águas vivas, mas o homem, em sua ignorância e rebeldia, volta-se para meras cisternas rotas.

CITA

Esse é um termo sânscrito que significa «material mental». Trata-se de um vocábulo chave na interpretação do «ego», dentro do sistema da ioga. O ego de uma pessoa desenvolver-se-ia com base no cita. Mas ambos, o ego e o cita, não teriam realidade última. Resultariam da confusão do não-eterno com o eterno. O cita parece ser uma espécie de estado intermediário entre o espírito e o ego. Os homens identificam, equivocadamente, o próprio «eu» como o corpo e a mente. Quando nos libertamos do cita, isso destrói o ego e revela a verdadeira personalidade. Ver o artigo sobre a Ioga, quanto a seus complexos conceitos acerca da natureza humana. (P)

CITA (POVO) Ver **União em Cristo**, Seção I. c. **Cita**.

CITAÇÕES NO NOVO TESTAMENTO

1. Número e tipos.
2. Afinidades textuais.
3. Estilo das citações do A.T.
4. Propósitos das citações do A.T.
5. Citações de fontes externas ao A.T.

1. Números e Tipos

A maior parte das citações existentes no N.T. é extraída do A.T. A maioria delas ocorre nos evangelhos sinópticos, nas epístolas de Paulo, em Hebreus e no Apocalipse. Quantas delas são dependentes do número de citações alusivas ao A.T.?—essa é uma questão delicada. O número de citações explícitas do A.T. tem sido variegadamente calculado entre 150 e 300; e o número de citações alusivas, mais de mil. O livro de Apocalipse contém muitas citações alusivas, mas nenhuma explícita.

As citações explícitas do A.T. são de fácil identificação. São introduzidas, por muitas vezes, com fórmulas de citação. As citações alusivas são cláusulas, frases e, algumas vezes, palavras isoladas, que facilmente podem escapar à nossa atenção. Por exemplo, o leitor desatento pode perder de vista as palavras saídas da nuvem, por ocasião da transfiguração de Jesus (Mat. 17:5), que procedem de três trechos diferentes do A.T.: «Este é o meu Filho amado» (Sal. 2:7), «em quem me comprazo» (Isa. 42:1), «a ele ouvi» (Deu. 18:15). Mais facilmente negligenciadas ainda são as palavras mediante as quais *Mateus* descreveu José de Arimatéia. Em Mar.

15:43 ele é um «ilustre membro do Sinédrio», e em Mat. 27:57 ele é «um homem rico», a fim de ajustar-se à predição de Isaías, sobre o Servo Sofredor, que «com o rico esteve na sua morte» (53:9).

É possível que algumas coincidências de palavras e de fraseados entre o A.T. e o N.T. tenham sido fortuitas, como é provável no caso do relato das fugas para o Egito por parte de Jeroboão (I Reis 11:40) e da sagrada família (Mat. 2:13-15). Na maioria dos casos, porém, houve alusões conscientes, pois a educação judaica alicerçava-se sobre os relatos do A.T. Por força da memória, muitos dos rabinos eram «concordâncias vivas». Uma prática literária comum, da época do N.T., era a mescla da fraseologia do A.T. com a própria fraseologia dos autores sagrados.

2. Afinidades Textuais

Ao citarem o A.T., os escritores do N.T. ocasionalmente transliteraram o hebraico (ou aramaico) original. Por exemplo, «Emanuel» (Mat. 1:23), e «Eli, Eli, lama sabachtani» (Mar. 15:34). Usualmente, eles seguiram o texto da Septuaginta, mesmo quando esta tradução diferia do texto massorético. Todavia, o N.T. pode discordar da LXX por uma citação inteira, ou apenas por parte de uma citação. Algumas vezes, essa discordância com a Septuaginta exibe concordância com o texto massorético, os Targuns, o A.T. Peshita, Teodócio e até com textos variantes dos manuscritos hebraicos da tradição rabínica e com Josefo. E, noutras ocasiões, exibe total independência de qualquer tradição textual conhecida do A.T. Às vezes ocorrem combinações de diferentes tradições textuais, dentro de uma única citação do A.T. Isso ocorre principalmente no caso das chamadas *fórmulas de citação*, em Mateus, introduzidas por alguma declaração como «para cumprir-se o que o Senhor dissera pelo profeta».

Essas mesclas dificilmente derivam-se de citações inexatas, feitas de memória (como muitos dizem). Isso é improvável devido às numerosas concordâncias com várias tradições textuais e pela harmonia entre diferentes escritores do N.T., em contraposição a todas as outras fontes (ver Mat. 11:10; Mar. 1:2; Luc. 7:27 com Mar. 3:1; Rom. 9:33; I Ped. 2:6 com Isa. 28:16). Por isso, os estudiosos têm exposto várias hipóteses para explicar o fenômeno. A idéia tem sido parcialmente confirmada pelos textos messiânicos descobertos na caverna de Qumran. Outros pensam que houve uma espécie de «atualização» de certos trechos citados, como no caso do comentário de Habacuque, encontrado em Qumran.

3. Estilo das Citações do A.T.

As fórmulas introdutórias de citações são várias. «Está escrito» é fórmula que frisa a validade permanente das revelações do A.T. «Para que se cumprisse» aponta para a consumação de alguma revelação veterotestamentária nos eventos do N.T. Outras fórmulas são «diz a Escritura», «diz Deus», «diz o Senhor», «diz o Espírito Santo», etc. Todas essas introduções refletem o conceito de inspiração da parte de Jesus e dos escritores do N.T. Deus aparece como autor das Escrituras, ao ponto destas, às vezes, serem personificadas, embora também transpareça o elemento humano, nas referências a Moisés, a Davi, a Isaías e a outros.

Deve-se destacar o método *haraz* de citar dois ou três trechos do cânon hebraico. Por exemplo, Rom. 11:8-10, que cita Is. 29:10; Deu. 29:43 e Sal. 68:23 ss. Também há combinações baseadas em alguma palavra-chave, entre as quais destaca-se a citação sobre a «pedra», em Rom. 9:33 (Isa. 8:14 e 28:16), e em I Ped. 2:6-8 (Isa. 28:16; Sal. 118:22 e

CITAÇÕES NO NOVO TESTAMENTO

Isa. 8:14).

Também há problemas de atribuição. Na citação de Mat. 27:9, sobre as trinta moedas de prata, a citação é atribuída a Jeremias, embora baseada em Zac. 11:13. Há tentativas de explicação desses casos, mas não são definitivas. E também há casos notórios de atribuição difícil, como nos casos de Mat. 2:23; João 7:38 e Efé. 5:14, pois por muitas vezes há citações sem a indicação da fonte. O que valia para os autores sagrados era o *sentido* tencionado, e não a fraseologia exata.

Os autores do N.T. são acusados de terem interpretado erroneamente o texto do A.T. Mas é que às vezes está em foco a tipologia de alguma passagem, sem ser negado o seu sentido original dentro do seu arcabouço histórico.

4. Propósitos das Citações do A.T.

É fortíssimo o motivo de cumprimento nas citações do A.T. As citações que cabem dentro da categoria de cumprimento dizem respeito tanto a predições diretas de eventos futuros quanto a significação tipológica por detrás do intuito dos escritores do A.T. No N.T., os principais motivos dessas citações são estes: Jesus age como o próprio Yahweh. Ele é o Rei messiânico que fora predito; o Servo de Yahweh, de Isaías; o Filho do homem, de Daniel. Ele culmina a linha profética, a sucessão dos sofredores justos do A.T. e a dinastia davídica. Ele reverte o efeito do pecado de Adão, cumpre as promessas divinas feitas a Abraão e recapitula a história de Israel.

Os sacerdócios de Aarão e Melquisedeque prefiguram (o primeiro, algumas vezes, contrasta com o segundo), o sacerdócio de Cristo. O cordeiro pascal e outros sacrifícios representavam a morte sacrificial e remidora de Jesus, e também o serviço cristão. Jesus é o pão transmissor de vida, como o maná, a rocha de onde mana a água viva, a serpente que fora levantada no deserto e o templo-tabernáculo onde Deus habitava entre os homens.

João Batista foi o precursor profético predito. Jesus inaugurou o período escatológico de salvação, que fora predito, bem como a nova aliança. Judas Iscariotes cumpriu o papel dos ímpios que foram oponentes dos sofredores justos do A.T. A Igreja (ou mesmo os crentes individuais) é a nova criação, a semente espiritual de Abraão, por motivo de sua incorporação em Cristo, o novo Israel e o novo templo. A lei mosaica prefigurava a graça positiva e negativamente. O dilúvio representava o juízo final e o batismo cristão. A passagem pelo mar Vermelho e a circuncisão também retratavam o batismo. Jerusalém representa a cidade celeste. — A entrada em Canaã prefigurava a entrada dos crentes no descanso espiritual. A proclamação do evangelho a todos os homens cumpre as promessas feitas a Abraão e as predições proféticas de salvação a todos os povos. As citações do A.T., pois, cabem dentro de um limitado conjunto de temas bem reconhecidos, o que contrasta com o tratamento confuso dos textos do A.T., nos escritos rabínicos. Os crentes primitivos devem ter aprendido a hermenêutica do A.T. com o próprio Jesus (cf. Luc. 24:27,32).

O conceito de «história da salvação» sublinha o cumprimento que aparece nas citações do A.T. Deus dirige a história segundo o seu propósito remidor. Ele revela o que fará através dos seus profetas. As predições deles têm o poder de produzir o seu próprio cumprimento, pois derivam-se do Senhor da história.

As citações do N.T., relativas a Jesus e à Igreja, derivam-se de enredos veterotestamentários bastante limitados:

a. Textos apocalíptico-escatológicos: Joel 2 e 3; Zac. 9-14; Dan. 7 (primários). Mal. 3:1-6; Dan. 12 (suplementares).

b. Textos sobre o novo Israel. Osé 13:9 e *ss*. Isa. 6:1-9:7; 11:1-10; 28:16; 40:1-11; Jer. 31:10-34 (primários). Isa. 29:9-14; Jer. 7:1-15; Hab. 1 e 2 (suplementares).

c. Textos sobre o Servo do Senhor e o Justo Sofredor: Isa. 42:1-44:5; 49:1-13; 50:4-11; 52:13—53: 12-61; Sal. 69:22; 31; 38; 88; 34; 118; 41; 42 e 43; 80 (primários). Isa. 58:6-10 (suplementares).

d. Textos miscelâneos. Sal. 8; 110; 2; Gên. 12:3; 22:18; Deu. 18:15,19 (primários). Sal. 132; 16; II Sam. 7:13,14; Isa. 55:3; Amós 9:11,12 (suplementares).

A isso pode-se adicionar Êxo. 1-4; 24; 34; Núm. 23 e 24; II Reis 1; Sal. 78; Dan. 2; a porção final de Dan. 11 e Dan. 12; Isa. 13; 34 e 35; e os últimos capítulos de Isaías; Miq. 4; 5; 7; Zac. 1-6; e o restante de Malaquias (além de 3:6).

O A.T. é a base de comentários (como no ensino de Jesus sobre o matrimônio e o divórcio, em Mar. 10:2-9 e paralelos). Ou a base de algum argumento (como no debate de Jesus com os saduceus acerca da ressurreição, em Mar. 12:18-27 e paralelos). Ou o A.T. é citado preceitualmente (cf. a reiteração de nove dentre os dez mandamentos, em passagens dispersas pelo N.T.).

5. Citações de Fontes Externas ao A.T.

À parte das citações do A.T., Mateus e Lucas citaram Marcos, e talvez, «Q» e outras fontes (ver o artigo *Problema Sinóptico*, e *cf*. Luc. 1:1-4). Nas epístolas há citações alusivas aos Ditos de Jesus. Paulo citou, em Atos 20:35, uma declaração de Jesus que não é registrada em qualquer outro lugar. Lucas cita, em Atos, certo número de sermões e discursos de cristãos. Os ensinos de Jesus foram citados pelos evangelistas, porém, nem sempre ao pé da letra. A diferença de estilo dos discursos de Jesus, em João e nos sinópticos, deve-se a pelo menos três fatores: a. Na tradução do aramaico e do hebraico para o grego, o pesado estilo grego de João fez-se sentir mais do que no caso dos sinópticos; b. João parafraseou mais vezes do que os sinópticos; c. João preservou deliberadamente uma linha de tradição que não transparece nos sinópticos. Mas, o fato de que Jesus falou no estilo joanino é indicado em Mat. 11:25-27 e Luc. 10:21,22.

Em uma classe inferior, situaríamos as citações de orações, hinos cristãos, credos e outro material tradicional. Alguns ajuntam a isso hinos litúrgicos, fórmulas credais, exortações para momentos de perseguição, extratos catequéticos, etc. Paulo pode ter citado trechos de suas epístolas anteriores, e os autores sagrados citaram-se mutuamente.

Há possíveis citações de livros apócrifos, como, por exemplo, em Mat. 11:28-30 (Eclesiástico 51:23 *ss*). Rom. 2:4 (Sabedoria de Salomão 11:23); Heb. 1:1-3 (Sabedoria de Salomão 7:25-27); 11:35-37 (II Macabeus 6 e 7). Judas 14 e 15 cita o pseudepígrafo de I Enoque 1:9, e, aparentemente, uma porção atualmente perdida da Assunção de Moisés (Jud. 9). A descida de Cristo ao Hades, I Ped. 3:18-4:6 é dependente de I Enoque. Muitas frases do Apocalipse têm sido atribuídas à literatura apocalíptica judaica extracanônica. Material vindo de escritores pagãos, como Epimênides, Arato, Cleantes, Calímaco e Menandro é citado em Atos 17:28; I Cor. 15:33; Tito 1:12. Paulo parece ter citado «slogans» de seus adversários em I Cor. 6:12; 8:1 e II Cor. 10:10.

••• ••• •••

CITÓPOLIS

No grego, **Skuthópolis;** cf. **Skuthon pólis**, «cidade dos citas», em II Macabeus 12:29, e *Skuthopolítai*, em II Macabeus 12:30. Esse era o nome grego de Bete-Seã, atual Beisan. Na época de Cristo, era uma das cidades da Decápolis (que vide). O nome talvez relembre as invasões dos citas, nos fins do século VII A.C.

CIÚME, ÁGUA DE
Ver **Água Amarga**.

CIÚMES

É estranho que o ciúme geralmente venha acompanhar um intenso amor entre as pessoas. Alguém já disse que o ciúme é o mau cheiro do amor. Seria assim mesmo? No hebraico temos a palavra *qinah*, «ciúme», «zelo», que figura por quarenta e uma vezes. Por exemplo: Núm. 5:14,15,18,25,29,30; Deu. 29:20; Eze. 8:3,5; 36:5,6; Zac. 1:14; 8:2. No Novo Testamento temos a palavra grega *parazelóo*, «ter muito ciúme», que ocorre por quatro vezes: Rom. 10:19 (citando Deu. 32:21); 11:11,14; I Cor. 10:22. Em Rom. 11:14, «emulação»; em I Cor. 10:22, «zelos».

A palavra hebraica envolvida salienta o rubor do rosto, uma espécie de ira reprimida, indicando ardor ou zelo, de forma positiva ou negativa. Tal palavra pode ser traduzida como «ardor», «zelo» ou «ciúme».

1. *Ciúmes Positivo*. O ciúme é um tipo de apreensão mental, quando a pessoa que o sente, sente estar sendo preterida por aquele que a ama, em favor de outrem. Seria o temor de ser substituído por um rival qualquer. Também envolve a atitude de ânsia e vigilância acerca daquilo que é considerado propriedade de quem tem ciúmes, como se essa pessoa ou objeto pudesse ser perdido ou prejudicado de alguma maneira. No caso de Deus, o ciúme sempre é positivo, porquanto o rival é o reino do mal, que só pode prejudicar os amados do Senhor. Nesse caso, não temos a manifestação de um egoísmo insensato. Por isso as Escrituras afirmam que Deus é um Deus «zeloso» (Êxo. 20:5), razão pela qual ele quer que todos os seus mandamentos sejam cumpridos. O cumprimento dos mandamentos do Senhor é benéfico para aqueles que são amados por Deus. O amor é a base do zelo ou do ciúme de Deus. Em outras palavras, trata-se de uma forma de amor. Essa emoção do ciúme também pode ser experimentada pelos homens, e pode ser genuína, embora seja muito difícil distinguir onde o amor termina e o egoísmo começa. O apóstolo Paulo manifestou esse tipo de ciúme pelos seus convertidos. Ver I Cor. 11:2.

2. *Ciúmes Negativo*. Esse tipo de ciúmes mistura o amor com o egoísmo. O critério de distinção deve ser o seguinte: sinto ciúmes porque temo que algo venha a prejudicar alguém a quem estimo, ou sinto ciúmes simplesmente porque não quero perder aquela pessoa ou coisa, com base em minha possessividade e egoísmo? Uma resposta bem pensada usualmente revela a existência desses dois elementos, que as *emoções* não conseguem separar adequadamente. Há casos em que o ciúme consiste em puro egoísmo. Um ciúme negativo foi que levou os irmãos de José a vendê-lo como escravo. Não houve qualquer motivo altruísta por detrás do ato deles. José era o suposto rival deles, que roubava todo o afeto e atenção do pai deles. Simplesmente, queriam livrar-se dele. Anos mais tarde, quando se reuniram todos no Egito, eles não choraram? É possível que, desde o início, houvesse o sentimento de amor, mas este foi afogado pela emoção mais imperiosa do ciúme. Seja como for, é impressionante como o ciúme pode transformar-se, rapidamente, em puro ódio. A razão para isso é simples: é mais fácil odiar do que continuar suportando mentalmente a forte emoção do ciúme. Acontece, portanto, que as pessoas que foram alvo do ciúme de outrem, acabam sendo o alvo do ódio dessa pessoa. O ciúme pode ser um sinônimo de «inveja». Porém, conforme já vimos, há um aspecto que pode ser positivo no ciúme, ao passo que a inveja sempre se manifesta como um sentimento negativo.

3. *Uma Obra da Carne*. Faz-nos pensar com sobriedade quando descobrimos que os ciúmes fazem parte da lista de vícios ou obras da carne, em Gálatas 5:19 e onde aparece a palavra grega *zelos*. Nesse caso, ciúmes é apenas um outro nome para egoísmo. Certamente envolve tanto o ódio quanto o ressentimento, levando a pessoa ciumenta a muitos atos desordenados. Mas tudo é feito na busca pelo conforto mental do indivíduo ciumento, e não visando ao bem da outra pessoa. O irmão do filho pródigo teve ciúmes dele e isso foi o começo de suas dificuldades (Luc. 15:25-30). As atitudes mentais impróprias são pecados (Mat. 5:21-31), além de serem a inspiração que impulsiona atos pecaminosos. O ciúme e a inveja manifestam-se tão comumente entre os homens porque o ser humano é, essencialmente, um ser egocêntrico. Amar consiste em deixar de lado o egocentrismo. O amor não arde em ciúmes (I Cor. 13:5); não ultrapassa seus legítimos direitos. O amor tem origem divina (I João 4:8), pelo que o crescimento na espiritualidade é o antídoto para todas as modalidades de vício humano.

CIVILIZAÇÃO

Consideremos os pontos abaixo, a esse respeito:

1. *A Palavra*. O termo «civilização» vem do latim *civis*, «cidadão». Originou-se na França, tendo sido usado pela primeira vez em 1756, por Mirabeau. Ele utilizou-se do termo para indicar que o homem elevou-se acima do seu estado primitivo, até chegar a um estado mais humanizado. Com freqüência, a palavra tem sido usada com o sentido de *cultura*. Spengler (que vide) distinguia entre «civilização» e «cultura», fazendo a primeira referir-se ao estágio final do desenvolvimento cultural. Alfred Weber (que vide) também fazia distinção, supondo que o processo da civilização é contínuo, mas que o processo de cultura opera esporadicamente. Seja como for, o termo envolve a idéia, de modo geral, do progresso do homem desde as formas primitivas até as formas aprimoradas.

2. *Em Emanuel Kant*. Para ele, a civilização é o sinal do homem sofisticado, que inclui considerações estéticas e morais. Porém, ele também empregou o termo para aludir ao refinamento artificial. Esse refinamento pode ser superficial e forçado. Porém, a verdadeira *cultura* (em contraste com a civilização externa) é algo que pertence ao campo moral, interior, não consistindo em mera decência externa. A cultura, pois, é o *ens humanissimum*, em contraste com o homem civilizado apenas superficialmente.

3. *De acordo com Pestalozzi*, 1797. Com toda a razão, esse filósofo (que vide) falava sobre a lei do amor como a força moral que cria a cultura.

4. *De acordo com Karl Marx*. Ele usava a palavra «civilização» mais ou menos à maneira de Kant, denunciando suas qualidades externas que não satisfazem às necessidades do verdadeiro homem.

CIVILIZAÇÃO CRISTÃ

Para ele, a civilização pode ter um efeito contrário àquilo que deveria ter. Ela pode *desumanizar* uma pessoa, em vez de humanizá-la.

5. *De acordo com Nietzsche.* Ele falava sobre o antagonismo básico entre a cultura e a civilização. Os confortos da civilização fazem muitas coisas boas tornarem-se acessíveis aos covardes. Isso também tende por desenvolver os elementos mórbidos e prejudiciais que podem causar o declínio fisiológico da raça humana. Portanto, a cultura deve visar o aprimoramento verdadeiro do homem. Esse filósofo alemão observava com preocupação os efeitos da tecnologia que está transformando cada vez mais o nosso mundo, a partir do século XIX. Ele sentia que isso não contribui para o aprimoramento verdadeiro das pessoas, como indivíduos.

6. *De acordo com Goethe.* Ele observava que a humanidade, como um todo, certamente continuará progredindo, mas que o próprio *indivíduo* sempre permanecerá o mesmo. Essa declaração tem-se revestido de uma implicação assustadora, agora que enfrentamos o aniquilamento mediante armas atômicas e químicas. Foi mister um imenso avanço tecnológico para possibilitar que um único homem levasse consigo um dispositivo atômico de pequeno volume, capaz de destruir uma cidade inteira! Quando observamos essas coisas, somos tentados a aliar-nos aos filósofos que têm estabelecido clara distinção entre civilização e cultura. É possível que os movimentos jovens, que requerem mudanças radicais e imediatas, estejam alicerçados sobre uma intuição interna, talvez mais própria da juventude, que sente que grande parte da civilização consiste apenas em decadência em meio a abastança material. A fuga para o antimundo das drogas, encetada por tantos jovens modernos, talvez seja, pelo menos em parte, resultante dessa intuição. Por outro lado, cumpre-nos considerar o problema da qualidade da alma, a qual, segundo penso, cada indivíduo já traz consigo, porque, segundo sinto, a alma é preexistente, conforme também diziam vários dos pais gregos da Igreja. As almas que são débeis, moral e espiritualmente falando, sob a pressão externa, naturalmente fogem para esse antimundo, para essa irrealidade.

7. *De acordo com Albert Einstein.* Esse grande matemático queixava-se da civilização porque a mesma dispõe de *meios perfeitos*, mas de *finalidades confusas*. A civilização produz superestradas que facilitam a viagem física, mas que negam às massas qualquer lugar para a espiritualidade. A civilização tem a mania de querer ampliar a duração da vida física, atarefando-se em uma batalha constante contra as enfermidades e a morte. Mas, ao mesmo tempo em que, presumivelmente, promove a vida, olvida-se inteiramente da vida eterna.

8. *A Dimensão Espiritual.* Nada haveria de errado com a civilização propriamente dita. Os homens cunharam a palavra «cultura», para fazer contraste com o termo «civilização», não porque há uma diferença a ser notada, mas porque os homens têm pervertido a civilização. Nada há de errado com as grandes rodovias, com os medicamentos que curam as enfermidades, e com os confortos e conveniências que nos dão tempo para nos preocuparmos com coisas além daquelas necessidades básicas. Porém, os homens perverteram essas coisas: usam o dinheiro na prática dos vícios, usam seu tempo vago com propósitos errados e gastam-no com seus prazeres ociosos. Eles usam as máquinas e a tecnologia para prejudicar e matar. Não tenho dúvidas de que o destino físico do homem tem por finalidade incluir a ciência e a tecnologia de toda variedade. Parte desse propósito é ensinar à humanidade como se aprende a controlar o avanço físico por meio de princípios espirituais. Como um todo, o homem ainda não alcançou grande progresso nesse tipo de desenvolvimento; mas as tribulações que aguardam a humanidade haverão de proporcionar um grande avanço nessa área. Uma vez que os homens compreendam que a ciência, não controlada pela espiritualidade, torna-se mortífera, eles haverão de querer desenvolver a sua espiritualidade, a fim de poderem controlar a tecnologia e a ciência.

História que Ilustra essa Tese. — Havia um idoso rabino, famoso por sua sabedoria. Certo dia, ele foi visitado por um jovem que era figadalmente contrário à ciência e à tecnologia. Este queixou-se de que a tecnologia é inútil e prejudicial, quando são levados em conta os verdadeiros valores da vida. Mas, o sábio rabino afirmava que é possível aprendermos de *todas as coisas*. Diante disso, o jovem fez várias perguntas, que foram respondidas como segue: Que podemos aprender com as estradas de ferro? Resposta: Que em um breve instante, como em um acidente, podemos perder tudo. Portanto, convém que cultivemos a nossa espiritualidade. Que podemos aprender do telégrafo? Resposta: Que cada palavra deve ser contada e levada em consideração. Que podemos aprender por meio do telefone? Resposta: Que há alguém que nos ouve à distância, atentando ao que dizemos aqui e agora, considerando-nos responsáveis pelo que dizemos. O visitante entendeu, convencido por esses argumentos, e se foi.

CIVILIZAÇÃO CRISTÃ

Quando a civilização romana da Europa ocidental foi destruída pelos bárbaros invasores (a própria cidade de Roma foi saqueada por Átila, o godo, em 410 D.C.), a Igreja Cristã tornou-se a única patrocinadora dos valores da civilização greco-romana que restaram no ocidente europeu, e, durante mil anos, ocupou esse papel. Novas invasões ameaçaram essa circunstância, até que, finalmente, a Europa ocidental foi superficialmente cristianizada, emergindo como uma nova civilização. Somente a Igreja produzia homens bem-educados, pelo que a educação formal tornou-se uma função da Igreja, e não mais do estado, como fora antes. Porém, a maioria dos líderes envolvia-se nas questões do estado e da Igreja, e as duas atividades mesclaram-se. Apesar desses tempos terem sido denominados «a Idade das Trevas», de barbarismo e de fanatismo religioso, misturados, os historiadores mais recentes nos têm fornecido uma estimativa mais favorável a respeito. As realizações no campo da filosofia, nesse período, foram óbvias e duradouras. Foram lançados os fundamentos da mecânica e da astronomia, sobre os quais Copérnico, Kepler e Galileu edificaram mais tarde. A autoridade da Igreja sobre o estado, na nova Europa, foi mantida. Ver o artigo sobre a *Cristandade*. Isso foi interrompido pelo surgimento do nacionalismo e do secularismo; e as mudanças foram consolidadas pela renascença (que vide) e pela Reforma Protestante. Dali, a civilização cristã foi passando por estágios seculares. É nessa fase que a encontramos essencialmente em nossos dias, à parte de sua expressão na própria Igreja Católica Romana. Não devemos esquecer que, além da educação em geral, escolas de todos os níveis, uma grande herança literária, hospitais e outras organizações filantrópicas foram desenvolvimentos que tiveram origem na civilização cristã da Idade Média. (C)

••• ••• •••

CLÃ

Não há nenhuma palavra hebraica ou grega que corresponda exatamente à idéia de «clã», nas páginas da Bíblia. Mas o conceito está embutido nos três vocábulos hebraicos e no vocábulo grego básico, a saber:

1. *Eleph*, «mil», em Juí. 6:15, que nossa versão portuguesa traduz por «família».

2. *Bayith*, «casa», que aparece, por exemplo, em I Crô. 13:14; II Crô. 35:5,12; Sal. 68:6. Esse vocábulo hebraico é de ocorrência bastante comum. O contexto é que decide se devemos entendê-lo literalmente, referindo-se a uma construção, ou se devemos entendê-lo metaforicamente, com o sentido de família.

3. *Mishpachah*, «família». Termo hebraico que figura por quase trezentas vezes, conforme se vê, por exemplo, em Gên. 10:5,18,20,31,32; Êxo. 6:14-25; Lev. 20:5; Núm. 1:2,18,20; 3:15 ss; 4:2,18,24,29,34-38,40,41,42,44,45,46; Jos. 7:14,17; 13:15,23,24,28, 29,31; Juí. 1:25; I Sam. 9:21; II Sam. 14:7; I Crô. 2:53,55; 7:5; Jer. 1:15; Eze. 20:32; Amós 3:1,2; Zac. 12:12-14; 14:17,18.

4. *Patriá*, «família». Palavra grega que ocorre por três vezes: Luc. 2:4; Atos 3:25 e Efé. 3:15.

Os idiomas semíticos usam palavras para indicar as relações de família de maneiras diferentes das línguas européias. Assim, podemos pensar em uma única família com laços de unidade bem definidos, ou em uma família com grande complexidade de relações e descendência. Essa complexidade podia incluir até mesmo pessoas que não tinham vínculos de sangue, como concubinas, servos, etc., e não somente os verdadeiramente aparentados por motivo de descendência ou casamento.

CLAPHAM, SEITA

Esse foi o nome dado a um grupo de abastados e influentes evangelistas anglicanos, que viveram no século XVIII. Adoravam na igreja da paróquia de Clapham, de onde lhes veio o nome. J. Venn foi o reitor dessa capela de 1792 a 1813. Talvez William Wilberforce (que vide), também pertencesse ao grupo. As ênfases específicas do grupo eram as seguintes: a. A abolição da escravatura. b. A promoção do trabalho missionário no estrangeiro. c. O socorro aos pobres. d. A ênfase sobre a leitura da Bíblia, a guarda do dia de sábado, vidas puritanas e bem disciplinadas. Portanto, eles foram cristãos sérios. Wilberforce opôs-se à guerra da Inglaterra contra a América do Norte (a chamada Revolução Americana). Também tentou obter um decreto, através do parlamento inglês, abolindo a escravidão. E ajudou a fundar a Sociedade Bíblica inglesa. (C E)

CLARIVIDÊNCIA

Esse termo significa, literalmente, «visão clara». Mas está em vista a percepção psíquica, e não uma visão física aguçada. De acordo com a definição popular, essa palavra indica a capacidade de ver coisas que não são visíveis para a visão humana normal, capacidade essa chamada de visão interior. De modo frouxo, o termo aponta para a sagacidade intuitiva. Também tem sido utilizado como sinônimo de telepatia (que vide), sem falarmos nas *habilidades psíquicas* em geral. Entretanto, a definição que lhe dá a emergente ciência da parapsicologia, contrasta essa palavra com a telepatia, restringindo-a a apenas uma habilidade psíquica especial. Nesse caso, clarividência é a capacidade psíquica de conhecer coisas não sujeitas à percepção dos sentidos, e que não envolve qualquer troca de informações entre as mentes. Para exemplificar, saber onde se encontra um objeto perdido é clarividência. Outro tanto se dá com a capacidade de localizar o lugar onde foi sepultado um cadáver, ou se o mesmo está em um rio, em um lago, etc. Ou então saber que um incêndio começou em um lugar distante, ou que houve um terremoto. Porém, uma vez que ocorre a intercomunicação entre mentes, já precisamos pensar na telepatia. Ambas essas capacidades são naturais e inerentes, conforme inúmeros testes de laboratório as têm demonstrado. Ambas as coisas operam nos nossos sonhos, o que tem sido abundantemente provado por aqueles que se dão ao trabalho de registrar e interpretar os seus sonhos. E ambos os fenômenos também estão sujeitos à atividade de espíritos estranhos, os quais, visto serem espíritos, têm essas capacidades, podendo-as impor aos espíritos humanos.

Os homens, sem importar se conscientemente ou não, empregam constantemente essa capacidade. A vinha dos sonhos é um importante fator de informações psicológicas e de instrução espiritual. Os sonhos dependem das nossas funções psíquicas. Isso faz parte da natureza humana, não sendo algo estranho à mesma. Como tal, está sujeito ao uso e orientação do Espírito de Deus. Não há homem vivo que não seja também um entidade não material, uma *psique*. E todos usamos, diariamente, nossas capacidades psíquicas. De fato, sem elas, seria impossível movermos um dedo, e muito menos trabalhar. A mente controla o corpo, em todas as coisas, mediante seus poderes psicossinéticos. Toda ação origina-se na vontade, a qual manipula a porção física do homem por meio dos poderes psíquicos intermediários. Isso se chama *psicossinésia* (que vide). A *psique* (ou espírito) usa constantemente o veículo que chamamos de corpo; e os poderes psíquicos são o *modus operandi* dessa interação.

Também há uma constante intercomunicação entre as mentes, sobretudo durante o sono. Nada existe de desnatural ou maligno nisso. Isso faz parte da natureza humana. Abusar desses poderes, porém, já é uma outra questão. Todas as coisas estão sujeitas ao abuso, por parte do homem pecaminoso, e não somente as capacidades psíquicas humanas. Mas isso não quer dizer que os poderes dos quais abusamos sejam maus por si mesmos. As pessoas que aludem a todos os poderes psíquicos como se fossem inerentemente maus, ou, pelo menos, como coisas que deveríamos evitar, não cessam de usar seus poderes psíquicos, pois isso nos é simplesmente impossível. E isso não os torna mais pecadores que o resto da humanidade. Ver o artigo sobre a *Parapsicologia*, onde apresento uma descrição geral acerca das capacidades psíquicas e de como esses fenômenos se manifestam, e onde defendo, com maiores detalhes, a tese aqui discutida. (AM CHE DRE E EC)

CLARK, GORDON HADDON

Nasceu em 1902. Autor das seguintes obras: *Readings in Ethics; A Christian View of Men and Things; Religion, Reason and Revelation*.

Idéias: 1. A tarefa da ética é prestar orientação moral. Esta deve repousar sobre leis universais, e não sobre o ceticismo moral. 2. Essa tarefa requer uma teoria de justificação moral. A fim de encontrar essa justificação, Clark olhava para as Sagradas Escrituras e para a razão. Na revelação divina, encontramos as leis universais de que precisamos. Através dessas leis universais e através do uso da razão, podemos deduzir outras leis, no caso de situações particulares que não são especificamente cobertas na Bíblia. 3. As teorias empíricas são logicamente injustificáveis, visto que lhes faltam qualquer argumento indutivo válido, capaz de derivar obrigações morais dos fenômenos observáveis. O sistema dedutivo, por outra parte, não conta com argumentos válidos baseados em princípios abstratos, que sejam então aplicados a casos específicos. A fim de evitar os problemas das teorias empíricas, Clark começava pela revelação bíblica. Em outras palavras, um teólogo bíblico escrevia sobre assuntos éticos. 4. A ética reveste-se de natureza *absoluta*. Deus estabeleceu as regras e então revelou-as nas páginas da Bíblia. Deus é soberano e estabelece leis. A honestidade é a melhor norma, precisamente porque Deus constituiu as coisas e suas relações de maneira honesta. 5. O *voluntarismo* (que vide) faz parte do pensamento desse escritor. Tudo quanto Deus faz é correto, precisamente porque Ele assim faz. (H)

CLARKE, ADAM

Autor e erudito metodista, nascido em 1760 e falecido em 1832, melhor conhecido por sua exposição da Bíblia inteira, essencialmente versículo por versículo. Ele era um escritor capaz, que incluía muitas ilustrações e observações curiosas em seus escritos, de tal modo que lê-los é como percorrer uma loja de curiosidades. Não obstante o seu estilo, há muito material sólido em seu comentário. Contudo, ele mostrava-se unilateral, fortemente arminiano. Devido à época em que foi escrito, o comentário não conta com informes arqueológicos ou com crítica textual, embora seu valor seja inegável. O próprio fato de que seu comentário continua sendo vendido em nossos dias, tendo sido reimpresso em edições modernas, serve de prova de seu valor. (SPU)

CLARKE, JAMES FREEMAN

Suas datas foram 1810-1888. Foi ministro unitário, nascido em Hanover, estado de New Hampshire, EE.UU. Formou-se pelo Harvard College and Divinity School, tendo-se tornado ministro em Louisville, Kentucky, e professor da Harvard Divinity School. Ele fundou uma igreja evangélica em Boston, livre quanto às suas crenças e costumes, tendo trabalhado em favor de reformas religiosas, morais, sociais e políticas. Ele mostrou-se ativo na igreja, na escola e nas lides políticas. Opunha-se à escravidão, promovia o sufrágio de homens e mulheres e defendia a temperança. Seus escritos mostram-se pacíficos e poderosos, exibindo vasta erudição da parte do autor.

Obras: Orthodoxy: Its Truths and Errors; Ten Great Religions; Commonsense in Religion; Vexed Questions in Theology.

CLARKE, SAMUEL

Suas datas foram 1675-1727. Filósofo e teólogo inglês, educado em Cambridge. Muito apreciava Descartes e dominava a ciência de Newton. Tomou ordens religiosas e foi reitor em várias instituições de ensino superior, tendo publicado muitos livros filosóficos, teológicos e bíblicos. Mantinha correspondência com Leibniz, a qual foi publicada sob o título *The Leibniz-Clarke Correspondence.*

Idéias: Infinitude do espaço e do tempo. Clarke defendia a idéia newtoniana da infinitude do espaço e do tempo, bem como a noção de que espaço e tempo são atributos de um Ser infinito, imaterial e espiritual. Essas idéias ele defendia, contrariamente à filosofia de Leibniz.

Prova da Existência de Deus. As seguintes suposições comprovam a existência de Deus, de acordo com Clarke: a. Algo tem existido desde a eternidade; b. esse algo é imutável e independente; c. sua essência é incompreensível para nós, mas podemos demonstrar algumas de suas evidências, como a eternidade, a infinitude, a onipresença, a unidade, a inteligência, a liberdade, a vontade, a onipotência, a onisciência, a sabedoria perfeita, a bondade, a justiça, a veracidade e as perfeições morais. Em outras palavras, isso justifica uma completa teologia bíblica.

Na Ética. Deus teria estabelecido certa *propriedade* nas coisas, o que significa que, por meio da razão, podemos saber o que é certo ou errado. Existem verdades éticas auto-evidentes visto que Deus fez as coisas desse modo. Buscamos harmonia e unidade entre os pensamentos e as ações; e essa relação pode ser descoberta, visto que o próprio Deus estabeleceu tal relação, da mesma maneira que arranjou de forma bem ordenada as leis físicas da natureza.

CLARO, CLAREZA

Quatro palavras hebraicas e três palavras gregas podem ser assim traduzidas, ou por sinônimos. Os termos geralmente são usados para aludir à luz e como a mesma manifesta-se nos objetos, como opacos, translúcidos ou transparentes, a saber:

1. *Or*, «iluminado». Palavra hebraica que aparece por cerca de cento e setenta vezes, mas, com esse sentido de claro, apenas em Amós 8:9; I Sam. 14:27,29.

2. *Bar*, «claro», «filho». Palavra hebraica que, com o sentido de «claro» aparece apenas em Can. 6:10.

3. *Yagar*, «precioso», «raro». Palavra hebraica que aparece por quarenta e seis vezes, embora apenas por duas vezes com o sentido de «claro»: Zac. 14:6 e Jó 31:26.

4. *Tsach*, «brilhante». Palavra hebraica usada por quatro vezes, mas, com o sentido que nos interessa, apenas por duas vezes: Isa. 18:4 e Can. 5:10.

5. *Agnós*, «puro». Vocábulo grego usado por oito vezes: II Cor. 7:11; 11:2; Fil. 4:8; I Tim. 5:22; Tito 2:5; Tia. 3:17; I Ped. 3:2; I João 3:3.

6. *Katharós*, «limpo». Palavra grega empregada por vinte e cinco vezes: Mat. 5:8; 23:26; 27:59; Luc. 11:41; João 13:10,11; 15:3; Atos 18:6; 20:26; Rom. 14:20; I Tim. 1:5; 3:9; II Tim. 1:3; 2:22; Tito 1:15; Heb. 10:22; Tia. 1:27; I Ped. 1:22; Apo. 15:6; 19:8,14; 21:18,21.

7. *Lambrós*, «brilhante», «iluminado». Palavra grega que aparece por dez vezes: Luc. 16:19; 23:11; Atos 10:30; Tia. 2:2,3; Apo. 15:6; 18:14; 19:8; 22:1,16.

Os céus são adjetivados como claros, em Êxo. 24:10. O resplendor do sol é enfatizado em Can. 6:10, e a clareza do dia em Amós 8:9. No Novo Testamento, a Nova Jerusalém aparece como feita de ouro puro, clara como vidro cristal, o que, aparentemente dá a entender que o ouro é de qualidade tão especial que chega a ser translúcido. Além disso, o rio da água da vida é claro como o cristal.

Implicações Morais. As palavras hebraicas e gregas dão a idéia de algo isento de toda poluição e defeito. No tocante à *consciência*, a idéia é de que esta está livre de qualquer fator condenatório, o que estaria alicerçado sobre algum defeito moral. Quando

CLASS — CLASSES SOCIAIS

aplicada à *inteligência*, a idéia subentende total compreensão sobre alguma questão. No tocante à *espiritualidade*, os termos usados referem-se a ela estar sem qualquer coisa que a obscureça ou distorça.

CLASS, GUSTAV

Suas datas foram 1836-1908. Foi professor de filosofia em Erlangen, na Alemanha. Sofria a influência de Fichte e Steffensen (que vide). Ele exprimia certa metafísica do espírito, o que empresta à religião uma significação universal.

CLASSE (na Filosofia)

A palavra portuguesa vem do latim *classis*. Uma classe consiste em certa multiplicidade de entidades que compartilham de alguma característica comum. A idéia de classes surgiu paralelamente ao desenvolvimento da lógica, estando presente em todas as culturas que atingem certo nível de raciocínio filosófico. Consideremos os três pontos abaixo:

1. Na opinião de Aristóteles, as classes aparecem sob as formas de gênero, espécie, propriedade, diferença e acidente. Isso veio a ser conhecido como qualidades *predicáveis* (que vide). Porfírio ajudou a organizar melhor tais idéias, como também o fizeram vários eruditos da era medieval.

2. Uma classe é considerada em sua *extensão* quando é definida em termos de entidades individuais em sua multiplicidade. Em outras palavras, vários objetos compartilham de alguma ou de algumas características específicas. Ver o artigo sobre *Extensão*, segundo ponto. E uma classe é considerada em sua *intensidade* (que vide) quando é definida em termos das características que a distinguem de outras classes.

3. Os desenvolvimentos posteriores, dentro do conceito de classes, deveram-se às contribuições da matemática e da lógica simbólica, incluindo as duas classificações gerais de classe, inclusão e exclusão, além de algum complemento de classe, como a negociação (que vide). (P)

CLASSES SOCIAIS

1. *Elementos de Distinção*. Há distinções que formam as classes dentro de uma sociedade, a saber: a. O montante e a qualidade da educação. b. O montante e as fontes de renda. c. Os tipos de associação, incluindo clubes e organizações, aos quais alguém se filia. d. Os tipos de ocupação que as pessoas conseguem. e. A localização: onde uma pessoa reside, local bom, intermediário ou impróprio. f. Os tipos de coisas acumuladas que facilitam a vida diária, como utensílios, veículos, artigos de luxo, facilidades de lazer, etc.

2. *Classes Principais*. a. As pessoas muito pobres, que dependem diariamente da ajuda alheia para o seu sustento. b. As pessoas pobres e mal nutridas, que sobrevivem independentemente, apenas com ocasional ajuda alheia. c. As classes baixas, independentes de outras, constituídas por pessoas que têm empregos, mas que recebem salário mínimo, chegando a padecer necessidade ocasional, mas nunca obtém mais do que o necessário para as necessidades básicas de sobrevivência. d. A classe média baixa, com melhores empregos que os indivíduos da classe anterior, melhor educação, e alguns poucos extras humildes, não absolutamente necessários para a sobrevivência. e. A classe média intermediária, com boa educação, residências respeitáveis, veículos automotores, aplicações econômicas modestas. f. A classe média alta, afluente, composta por pessoas que têm bons empregos, bons níveis de poupança econômica e muitos artigos extras, desnecessários à sobrevivência. g. Os ricos sem prestígio. Essa classe compõe-se daqueles que têm muito dinheiro, e possuem tudo quanto podem comprar; mas não fazem parte de famílias tradicionais, que lhes confiram prestígio social, do ponto de vista de estirpe. h. Os ricos prestigiosos que, além de todas as vantagens econômicas acima, também pertencem a famílias tradicionais, o que lhes confere ainda maior atenção e respeito, devido à sua grande sofisticação.

3. *As Denominações Religiosas e as Classes Sociais*. Há uma correlação geral entre as classes sociais e as denominações religiosas. Assim, as denominações pentecostais têm obtido um crescimento fenomenal entre as classes pobres, mas comparativamente pouco avanço entre as **classes média e abastada**. No outro extremo do espectro, movimentos como a Ciência Cristã, a Igreja Episcopal e algumas denominações congregacionais contam com forte representação entre as classes mais altas. Os presbiterianos, os batistas e os mórmons são denominações constituídas, principalmente, por indivíduos da classe média. O catolicismo romano, devido ao seu gigantismo, conta com seguidores pertencentes a todas as classes sociais.

4. *A Classe Média como Meio Equilibrador*. Aristóteles pensava que a classe média, em cada sociedade, pode exercer uma saudável função ética. Ele supunha que o desenvolvimento de uma forte classe média poderia modificar a pobreza e o tipo de comportamento animalesco das classes menos privilegiadas, e, ao mesmo tempo, servir de elemento de compensação dos excessos das classes abastadas. Isso posto, a classe média expressaria o seu famoso *meio equilibrador*. Isso corresponderia à ação intermediária entre dois extremos, evitando-se tanto os vícios de deficiência como os vícios do excesso. Ver o artigo sobre *Aristóteles*.

5. *O Novo Testamento e as Classes Sociais*. Para começar, o evangelho destina-se a todos aqueles a quem Deus ama (João 3:16), o que, como é óbvio, conta com pessoas pertencentes a todas as classes sociais. Apesar disso, alguns autores sagrados do Novo Testamento exibem notável prevenção contra os ricos, segundo se patenteia em trechos como Tiago 1:9 ss; 2:5,6 e 5:1. Naturalmente, na época do império romano, eram os ricos e poderosos que perseguiam os cristãos primitivos. Além disso, Tiago 2:2 ss mostra-nos que, devido ao respeito humano, os ricos eram favorecidos até mesmo entre os cristãos primitivos, às expensas dos pobres; e Tiago revolta-se contra esses atos de bajulação. Tiago 2:5 é trecho que mostra que Deus favorece especialmente aos pobres, a fim de que se tornem ricos na fé e na espiritualidade. Tiago queixou-se de que são os ricos que oprimem à Igreja, arrastando os crentes aos tribunais e abusando deles de várias maneiras (Tia. 2:6). Além de outros pecados, os ricos também costumam blasfemar da fé religiosa (Tia. 2:7). Paulo, por sua vez, em I Coríntios 1:26, mostra que geralmente os que se convertem não procedem de nobre nascimento, nem das classes abastadas e poderosas, etc. Antes, procedem das classes pobres, humildes e desprezadas, o que desencoraja todas as manifestações do orgulho humano (I Cor. 1:29).

O próprio Senhor Jesus falou sobre a imensa dificuldade dos ricos em pensar mais demoradamente sobre as necessidades da alma (Mat. 19:23). A despeito desses reparos, a mensagem geral do Novo Testamento é universal. Além disso, temos a declaração, em Efésios 1:10, concernente à restauração final (que vide), que garante que o efeito do evangelho finalmente atingirá todas as classes de modo absoluto. Entretanto, isso requererá várias eras, entrando até mesmo nos ciclos intermináveis da eternidade futura. (H NTI)

CLÁSSICO ARGUMENTO DO RELÓGIO, em favor da existência de Deus

Ver o artigo sobre *Paley, William*, onde aparece esse famoso argumento teleológico.

CLAUBERG, JOHANNES

Suas datas foram 1622-1665. Foi um filósofo alemão, um dos primeiros filósofos a usar o termo *ontologia* (que vide). Ele foi um dos filósofos ocasionalistas. Ver sobre o *Ocasionalismo*. Entre os seus escritos podemos mencionar os seguintes: *Elements of Philosophy* ou *Ontosophia* e *Cartesian Defense*.

CLAUDA

Essa pequena ilha é mencionada na Bíblia somente em Atos 27:16. Modernamente ela se chama Gaudos ou Gozo, situada acerca de oitenta quilômetros ao largo da costa de Creta. Algumas traduções lhe dão o nome de Clauda; outras, de Cauda. No livro de Atos, a ilhota aparece associada ao naufrágio sofrido por Paulo. A embarcação em que ele viajava velejava costeando a ilha de Creta, a fim de escapar do vento que soprava do sudoeste, o que não permitia o cruzamento direto do mar Egeu. Mas, quando o navio chegou à metade ocidental da longa ilha de Creta, o vento, pressionando ao norte da massa montanhosa, que forma aquela região, desceu como um tufão poderoso e desastroso para a navegação. Lutando para escapar desses fortes ventos, o navio acabou navegando a sotavento de Clauda, isto é, protegido por essa ilhota, de tal modo que os marinheiros puderam puxar o bote auxiliar para dentro, que até ali vinha sendo puxado a reboque, perturbando o direcionamento do navio.

CLAUDA

Forma alternativa de **Cauda** (que vide).

CLÁUDIA

Nas páginas da Bíblia, esse foi o nome de uma figura feminina e de uma ilha do mar Mediterrâneo.

1. *A Pessoa*. Cláudia é a forma feminina do latim, Claudius. Esse apelativo, com variações como Clodius, era o nome de uma família romana, com membros patrícios e plebeus. No latim, a palavra significa *aleijado*. Da mesma raiz nos vem o termo português «claudicante». Porém, como esse adjetivo veio a ser vinculado àquela família, é algo perdido na história. No Novo Testamento, *Cláudia* é o nome de uma crente, mencionada em II Timóteo 4:21, que enviava saudações a Timóteo. Juntamente com Êubulo, Lino e Prudente, Cláudia foi grande cooperadora de Paulo, que o ajudou durante seu segundo período de aprisionamento, em Roma. Nas *Constituições Apostólicas* (vii.46), Cláudia é considerada mãe de Lino (o genitivo simples, porém, deixa a questão em dúvida, conforme sabem os que têm estudado o grego «koiné»). Lino é conhecido como o primeiro bispo de Roma. Várias identificações têm sido propostas, situando-a entre as elites de Roma, como aquela que diz que estaria em foco Cláudia Rufina, esposa de Aulus Pudens, amigo do poeta Marcial, ou então Cláudia Quinctilla, esposa de Claudius Pudens. Esse casal deixou uma inscrição sobre o túmulo de seu filho infante, entre Roma e Óstia (CIL vi.15,066). Porém, os nomes Cláudia e Pudens eram bastante comuns, e as tentativas de identificação não passam de conjecturas. As tradições, sempre ansiosas por atribuir grandes realizações a nomes obscuros, dizem-nos que Timóteo, filho de Pudens, participou da evangelização dos bretões, visto que a romana Cláudia era bretã. (CIL FA UN Z)

2. Cláudia é o nome de uma ilha ao largo da costa de Creta, mencionada em Atos 27:16. Essa ilha é chamada Gaudos em outras fontes históricas. Ver Mela. ii.7; Plínio, Hist. Nat. iv.42. Os italianos modernos chamam essa ilhota de Gozo, uma forma corrompida do grego Claudanesa ou Gaudonesi.

CLÁUDIO

Quanto a comentários sobre o significado do nome Cláudio, ver o artigo sobre *Cláudia*.

O nome do quarto imperador romano era Tibério Nero Druso Germânico. Reinou de 41 a 54 D.C., como sucessor de Calígula. Era filho de Nero Druso. Nasceu em 9 A.C., tendo vivido na privacidade até que se tornou imperador. Isso ocorreu principalmente por causa da influência de Herodes Agripa I (Josefo, *Anti*. xix. 2, partes 1,3,4). Por sua vez, Cláudio ampliou os territórios governados por Herodes, fazendo com que incluíssem a eles a Judéia, a Samaria e parte do Líbano. Também nomeou o irmão de Herodes para governar Calcis e para ser presidente do templo de Jerusalém. Durante o seu reinado, ocorreu a fome mencionada em Atos 11:28-30, que atingiu a Palestina e a Síria, em cuja ocasião os procuradores eram Cúspio Fado e Tibério Alexandre. Suetônio (*Claud*. 25) escreveu a seu respeito: «Cláudio expulsou os judeus de Roma, visto que eles provocavam constantes perturbações, por instigação de um certo Cresto». Isso teria ocorrido entre 50 e 52 D.C. Alguns interpretam essa declaração como um exemplo de como os escritores antigos podiam ser bastante **ignorantes com relação aos fatos. Esse *Cresto* provavelmente seja Jesus *Cristo***. Os romanos antigos com freqüência não estabeleciam distinção clara entre os cristãos e os judeus. Cláudio envenenou a sua quarta esposa, Agripina, mãe de Nero, em 54 D.C. Suetônio informa-nos que ele foi um governante fraco, agindo mais como servo de outros do que como príncipe.

Cláudio e o Cristianismo. Esse imperador tomou três medidas diferentes que tiveram algum efeito sobre o cristianismo: 1. Ele expulsou os judeus de Roma por perturbarem a ordem, instigados por Cresto (Suetônio, *Claud*. 25). Os intérpretes não têm sabido exatamente como entender essa referência. *Cresto* pode ser uma alusão a Cristo, pelo que aquele historiador misturou judeus e cristãos naquela referência. Ou então, Cresto pode ter sido o nome próprio de algum agitador judeu, desconhecido em qualquer outra fonte histórica. Ou então a referência pode apontar para o messianismo judaico, sem qualquer alusão ao Cristo dos cristãos. 2. Cláudio reprimiu agitadores judeus importados da Síria para a cidade de Alexandria. Na opinião de alguns, estudiosos, entre eles haveria cristãos. 3. Houve um decreto imperial, talvez de autoria de Cláudio, que ordenava a punição dos violadores de túmulos, decreto esse que, aparentemente, foi publicado na Galiléia. Não se sabe dizer se a questão da ressurreição de Jesus teve qualquer coisa a ver com isso. (CAD (1955) FA ND Z)

CLÁUDIO DE TURIM

Sabe-se da data de sua morte, 827 D.C. Foi bispo na Espanha, tendo exercido influência sobre a **doutrina do adopcionismo** (que vide). Era favorecido pela corte carlovíngia, por causa de sua grande erudição bíblica. Escreveu um comentário bíblico de Gênesis aos livros dos Reis, e então de Mateus às epístolas paulinas. Opunha-se a várias práticas eclesiásticas, como a adoração aos santos, o uso de imagens, gravuras e crucifixos. Por causa disso, ele sofreu oposição por parte de várias figuras eclesiásticas importantes de sua época. (E)

CLÁUDIO LÍSIAS

Quanto a comentários sobre o significado do nome *Cláudio*, ver o artigo sobre Cláudia. Cláudio Lísias é mencionado no Novo Testamento, como comandante da guarnição romana em Jerusalém, na época do aprisionamento de Paulo ali. Ele ocupava a posição de tribuno militar (no grego, *chilíarchos*), dotado de autoridade sobre a coorte estacionada na fortaleza de Antônia (que vide) contígua à área do templo. Ele comprara a cidadania romana mediante polpuda soma em dinheiro, não podendo ocultar certa consternação ao saber que Paulo nasceu livre, por ser nativo de Tarso, na Cilícia. Ver o artigo sobre a *Cidadania*, onde damos descrições acerca da natureza da cidadania romana. Quanto à narrativa bíblica sobre o episódio, ver Atos 22:28. O serviço que esse homem prestou em favor de Paulo consistiu em livrá-lo da multidão furiosa, que pretendia linchá-lo (Atos 21:31-36 e 22:24). Lísias levou Paulo para um lugar seguro, no templo.

As autoridades romanas tinham sido testemunhas de vários levantes, e, na Judéia, as coisas viviam em constante turbilhão. Houve revolucionários como Judas da Galiléia e Teudas (Atos 5:36,37), e aparentemente Paulo pertencia a essa categoria de gente. Lísias também pensou ser ele um certo egípcio, talvez um dos líderes dos *sicários*, os quais ainda recentemente, e em número de quatro mil, tinham ido com ele para o deserto. Mas, quando Lísias descobriu quem Paulo realmente era, permitiu-lhe dirigir a palavra à multidão enfurecida. Em seu discurso, assim que Paulo mencionou a palavra «gentios», dentro da missão da Igreja cristã, o tumulto começou novamente. Conforme era usual na época, Lísias estava disposto a examinar Paulo sob tortura, para descobrir a verdade do caso; mas, ao descobrir que Paulo era cidadão romano, abandonou prontamente a idéia. A chamada *Lex Porcia* proibia a tortura de qualquer cidadão romano. Em vista disso, Paulo foi entregue ao Sinédrio, a fim de ser interrogado. Isso, porém, só resultou em maior tumulto e divisão sobre o caso, e certos judeus resolveram que o matariam à traição. Informado do conluio, mediante um sobrinho de Paulo, Lísias resolveu enviar Paulo, sob a proteção da noite, até Félix, governador romano, em Cesaréia, a principal sede da autoridade romana na Palestina. Ver o artigo sobre *Cesaréia*.

Lísias deve ter temido muito as consequências do conluio contra Paulo, se os perturbadores tivessem obtido sucesso. Ele não estava disposto a perder a cidadania romana. Por essa razão, deixou Paulo aos cuidados de uma forte escolta, tão forte que alguns intérpretes duvidam dos números envolvidos: duzentos infantes, setenta cavaleiros e duzentos lanceiros. O livro de Atos registra os pontos essenciais de uma carta enviada por Lísias a Félix, acerca do caso de Paulo. Ver Atos 23:26-30. Alguns estudiosos pensam que essa carta não foi redigida por Félix, porquanto contém certa contradição com o trecho de Atos 23:25-27. Mas qualquer pessoa pode incorrer em um erro, ou então exagerar um pouco. Em Atos 23:25-27 lemos que Félix livrou Paulo porque sabia que o apóstolo era cidadão romano. Porém, o trecho de Atos 22:24 mostra que ele havia ordenado que Paulo fosse açoitado, embora desistisse disso, ao descobrir que ele era um cidadão romano, não podendo ser interrogado dessa maneira violenta. (CAD (1955) Z)

CLAUSTRO

Vem do latim, **claustra**, «lugar fechado». A palavra pode significar um pátio aberto, cercado por uma calçada arcada com teto, conforme se vê em muitos mosteiros, ou mesmo em algumas catedrais. A intenção é prover um passeio sombreado para os monges e outras pessoas. Mas a palavra «claustro» também tem sido constantemente usada como sinônimo de mosteiro. Os claustros para passeio eram construídos de tal modo que os protegiam das intempéries, sendo usados para preleções, reuniões informais, recreação, etc. A origem dos claustros parece ter sido de certas construções arquiteturais dos lares dos mais abastados romanos. A Universidade Católica de São Paulo conta com claustros como se fossem corredores em torno de alguns edifícios. (AM E)

CLAVER, PEDRO

Suas datas foram 1580-1654. Foi um jesuíta espanhol que, pelo espaço de trinta e cinco anos, foi ministro e servo dos negros africanos que haviam sido trazidos para Cartagena, na Colômbia, para serem vendidos como escravos. Dessa maneira, ele realizava um trabalho de amor e solidariedade humana que poucos estariam interessados em realizar. (E)

CLEANTES

Suas datas foram 331-232 A.C., um filósofo grego estóico. Nasceu em Assôs e foi discípulo de Zeno, o fundador do estoicismo (que vide). Cleantes atuou em Atenas; e, após a morte de Zeno, tornou-se o líder daquela escola de filosofia. Crisipo (que vide) foi um de seus discípulos.

Idéias. 1. Ele dividia a filosofia em seis aspectos: dialética, retórica, ética, política, física e teologia. 2. Ele pensava que Deus residia no sol. Dali procede o fogo doador de vida, bem como a inteligência que permeia toda a existência. Também há a opinião de que ele considerava o mundo uma divindade. 3. Ele ensinava uma espécie de imortalidade condicional, afirmando que a vitalidade da alma, após a morte física, depende de sua vitalidade nesta vida. 4. No campo da ética, ele promovia a *apatia*. Os maus pensamentos seriam piores do que os atos maus, porquanto dos pensamentos originam-se todas as maldades.

Cleantes e o Novo Testamento. O **Hino a Zeus** é a composição mais substancial que dispomos dos escritos de Cleantes, os quais são altamente fragmentados. Paulo citou do mesmo, em Atos 17:28: «Pois nele vivemos e nos movemos e existimos, como alguns dos vossos poetas têm dito: Porque dele também somos geração». O pensamento central dessa citação é o do universo visto como um ser vivo, tendo Deus como sua alma e o sol como seu coração. Paulo, naturalmente, deu às palavras de Cleantes um sentido todo seu, enfatizando a personalidade, a vitalidade e a presença de Deus, contrastando essa idéia com a da idolatria estúpida, que é uma questão morta. (EP MM P)

CLEARCO

Viveu em cerca de 340 A.C. Foi um filósofo de tendências aristotélicas. Escreveu interpretações de Platão, tratados sobre as emoções humanas e sobre as ciências naturais.

CLEMENTE

A Personagem do Novo Testamento. O nome próprio vem do latim, *Clemens*, que significa «misericordioso». A palavra grega que aparece no Novo Testamento é uma forma adaptada com base no vocábulo latino. Há um homem com esse nome, mencionado em Filipenses 4:3, onde aparece como um dos cooperadores de Paulo em Filipos. Paulo estava certo de que o nome de Clemente encontrava-se no livro da vida (que vide), o que não é nenhuma declaração sem importância. É óbvio que esse homem era uma figura fiel e poderosa da Igreja primitiva, em Filipos. O contexto sugere que Paulo pensava que ele era um homem que poderia estabelecer a concórdia estremecida entre Evódia e Síntique (que vide), duas mulheres crentes que tinham trabalhado juntamente com Paulo, mas que depois entraram em alguma espécie de disputa pessoal uma contra a outra. Excetuando a sua identificação como o bispo de Roma (e, na opinião de alguns, um dos papas), ele entra na narrativa neotestamentária de forma muito humilde. Desse documento sagrado, não obtemos nenhuma maior informação a seu respeito.

Seria esse o mesmo Clemente de Roma? Que houve uma personagem com o nome de Clemente de Roma é algo indisputável. Mas, poderíamos identificá-lo com o Clemente mencionado em Filipenses 4:3? Vários dos pais da Igreja fizeram essa identificação, incluindo Tertuliano, Irineu, Orígenes e vários outros, de data posterior. Os argumentos apresentados contra essa identificação são os seguintes: 1. Tal identificação depende somente da similaridade de nomes, bem como do desejo da tradição oral de glorificar personagens do Novo Testamento, tornando-as mais poderosas e bem conhecidas, após a era apostólica. 2. Não existe tradição que possa confirmar essa identificação. 3. Não há qualquer prova de que Clemente (um nome comum) de Filipos tenha ido jamais a Roma. 4. O bispo de Roma, desse nome, só aparece associado a essa cidade, não havendo qualquer evidência de que ele tenha estado, ao menos por uma vez, em Filipos. 5. Não há o menor indício de que Clemente de Filipos tenha vivido até o final do século I D.C., ou até 110 D.C., quando Clemente de Roma, segundo se sabe, faleceu. A única coisa que podemos dizer em favor da identificação é a suposição, talvez pouco fundamentada, de que os primeiros pais da Igreja tinham maiores evidências, à sua disposição, do que nós, do século XX. Ver o artigo sobre *Clemente de Roma*.

CLEMENTE I DE ROMA, PAPA?

Segundo Tertuliano, ele foi consagrado pelo próprio Pedro. Ver os artigos sobre *Clemente* e *Clemente de Roma*.

CLEMENTE II

Seu pontificado foi de 1046 a 1047, data em que morreu. Seu nome original era Suidger. Pertencia a uma nobre família saxônica. Tornou-se o cânone de Halbestadt em 1032, e então capelão da corte imperial. O imperador nomeou-o bispo de Bamberg, em 1040. Quando o imperador expulsou o antipapa Silvestre III e o papa Gregório VI do papado, quando do sínodo de Sutri, ele nomeou Suidger para ser o novo papa. Então ele assumiu o título de Clemente II, tendo sido entronizado a 5 de dezembro de 1046. Ele coroou Henrique e sua esposa, Agens. Seu breve pontificado incluiu várias medidas reformistas. Faleceu perto de Pesaro, menos de um ano após ter sido feito papa, a 9 de outubro de 1047. Foi sepultado em Bamberg. Em 1943, seu túmulo foi aberto, e suas vestimentas foram encontradas ainda em boas condições de preservação. (AM)

CLEMENTE III

Foi papa de 1187 a 1191, quando morreu. Nasceu em Roma, com o nome de Paulo Scolari. Serviu como bispo-cardeal de Palestrina. Foi eleito papa em Pisa, a 19 de dezembro de 1187. Mostrou-se muito hábil como diplomata. Negociou um tratado com o senado romano, em 1188, pondo fim a um longo conflito e fazendo reconhecer o pontífice supremo como o senhor temporal de Roma. Ele procurou unificar os vários príncipes belicosos da Europa, em ação comum contra o sultão islamita Saladino, por ocasião da Terceira Cruzada. Sob Clemente III, a Igreja da Escócia caiu sob o controle direto de Roma. Esse papa protegia aos judeus e a outras minorias perseguidas. Faleceu a 27 de março de 1191. (AM E)

CLEMENTE III (Antipapa)

Nasceu com o nome de Wilbert de Ravena. Serviu como chanceler imperial na Itália. Deu apoio ao candidato do imperador, Cadato, como antipapa, em 1061, mas reconciliou-se com o papa Alexandre II, e foi feito arcebispo de Ravena. Juntamente com a família Cenio e com o Cardeal Ugo Cândido, ele deu apoio ao imperador Henrique IV contra o papa Gregório VII, naquilo que a história chama de Conflitos da Investidura, em razão do que foi eleito antipapa em Bressanone, a 25 de junho de 1080. Governou em Roma com o título de Clemente III, e foi apoiado pelo partido imperial italiano. Em 1098, a família Perleoni o depôs. Faleceu a 8 de setembro de 1100.

CLEMENTE IV

Governou como papa de 1265 a 1268. Nasceu com o nome de Guy le Gros Foulques, em St. Gilles, na França. Estudou advocacia na Universidade de Paris e foi nomeado conselheiro legal do rei Luís IX. Após o falecimento de sua esposa, em 1247, deu início a seus estudos clericais. Após ter sido ordenado, subiu rapidamente de padre a bispo, e daí a arcebispo de Narbone, e então a legado cardeal enviado à Inglaterra. Em 1265, foi eleito papa e convocou Carlos de Anjou para ser protetor da Santa Sé contra o avanço militar de Hohenstaufen, que vinha do norte. Obteve os chamados estados papais e estabeleceu a dinastia Angevina na Itália. Opunha-se vigorosamente à prática do nepotismo. Faleceu em Viterbo, na Itália, a 29 de novembro de 1268.

CLEMENTE V — CLEMENTE VIII

CLEMENTE V

Nasceu com o nome de Bertrando de Got, em Bordelais, na França. Estudou a lei canônica em Orleãs e em Bolonha. Tornou-se bispo de Comminges, e então arcebispo de Bordeaux, em 1299. Foi eleito papa em Perúgia, a 5 de junho de 1305, e foi coroado com o título de Clemente V, em Lyon, a 14 de novembro daquele mesmo ano. Permaneceu na França devido às múltiplas agitações e conflitos em Roma. O imperador Henrique VII estava exigindo coroação em Roma, mas os agentes papais franceses haviam sido desfavoravelmente acolhidos na Itália. A permanência de Clemente V na França deu início a uma série de papas daquele país, que não exerceram seu pontificado em Roma. A história chama esse período de Cativeiro Babilônico do Papado. Clemente V viu-se envolvido nas várias lutas e complicações políticas da época. Desaprovou as táticas de extorsão e de aprisionamento em massa, usadas por Filipe IV, em sua campanha contra os Cavaleiros Templários. Todavia, cedeu às exigências de Filipe IV e suprimiu essa ordem, quando do concílio de Viena, em 1312. Clemente V teve mais sucesso em seus conflitos com outros imperadores do Santo Império Romano, e proclamou o direito da Santa Sé de manter ascendência sobre o império, mediante seu decreto intitulado *Pastoralis cura*. No documento *Multorum Querela*, ele tentou estabelecer controle sobre a Inquisição (que vide), que por ele era desaprovada. Estabeleceu a Universidade de Perúgia, na Itália, em 1307, e criou uma cadeira de idiomas asiáticos. Procurou diligentemente centralizar a autoridade papal, mas encontrou constante resistência à idéia por parte dos monarcas europeus. Entrementes, muitos elementos de proa da Igreja Católica Romana acusavam-no de não impedir o avanço da heresia, porquanto procurava tolher o trabalho dos inquisidores. Após uma vida agitada, faleceu a 20 de abril de 1314. (AM BR)

CLEMENTE VI

Foi papa de 1342 a 1352. Nasceu como Pierre Roger, em Correze, na França. Foi monge beneditino, doutor em teologia, bispo de Arras, arcebispo de Sens, e então de Rouen. Tornou-se cardeal em 1338, e então sucedeu a Benedito VII como papa, em 1343.

Uma permanente agitação política na Itália forçou Clemente VI a permanecer em Avignon, na França, seguindo o exemplo de Clemente V, que fizera o mesmo. Esse período em que vários papas pontificaram fora de Roma é historicamente intitulado de Cativeiro Babilônico do Papado. Conseguiu estabelecer a concórdia entre a Igreja de Roma e o Santo Império Romano depondo Luís IV da Baváría, e arranjando a eleição de Carlos IV, de Luxemburgo, como imperador, em 1347. Procurou centralizar o poder da Igreja de Roma. Uma de suas medidas, nesse sentido, foi o decreto que dizia que somente o papado tinha o direito de conceder benefícios eclesiásticos, que consistiam em propriedades que rendiam largos proventos, pertencentes à Igreja. As autoridades seculares e eclesiásticas objetaram a esse decreto, em 1345. O rei Eduardo III encampou todos os benefícios que havia na Inglaterra, em mãos de poderes estrangeiros. Filipe VI fez outro tanto na França, com a única exceção dos cardeais e dos membros da família e da cúria papais. Isso em muito diminuiu os recursos financeiros do papa, prejudicando seu generoso patrocínio das artes. Muitos outros opuseram-se ao papa, dentro e fora da Igreja de Roma. Ele era homem extravagante, e sua corte vivia no luxo e na ostentação. Contudo, estamos informados de que sua *vida pessoal* era ordeira. Dava bom exemplo de moralidade e demonstrou coragem e caridade durante a praga da Morte Negra, que ocorreu durante o seu pontificado. (AM)

CLEMENTE VII

Governou como papa de 1523 a 1534. Nasceu com o nome de Giulio de Médici, em Florença, na Itália, a 26 de maio de 1478. Era filho ilegítimo de Giuliano de Médici. Seu pai foi morto durante a notória conspiração de Pazzi, pelo que foi criado por seu avô, Lorenzo, o Magnificente. Seu primo, Leão X, foi papa. Durante o pontificado deste, subiu rapidamente os degraus do poder, na Igreja. Foi eleito para ser o papa sucessor de Adriano IV, em 1523.

Foi homem moral e capaz; mas faltava-lhe a habilidade política e organizacional para manusear os problemas de seu reinado. O imperador Carlos V, da Alemanha, e o rei Francisco I, da França, estavam em conflito, cada qual procurando obter a supremacia na Europa; e Clemente VII tentava ser o árbitro da contenda. Mas, falhando na mediação, aliou-se à causa da França. Em face disso, Carlos V retaliou, saqueando Roma sem qualquer compaixão, em 1527. Então Clemente VII ficou virtualmente aprisionado no castelo de Sant'Angelo. Depois que a paz foi restabelecida, esse papa coroou Carlos V como imperador do Santo Império Romano, em 1530. Foi exatamente nesse período da história que Henrique VIII, da Inglaterra, **exigiu a anulação** de seu casamento com Catarina de Aragão. O papa, porém, procrastinava quanto a uma decisão, o que levou Henrique VIII a revoltar-se contra Roma, nomeando a si mesmo chefe da Igreja da Inglaterra. E ainda maiores dificuldades estavam à espreita. Surgiu em cena o movimento luterano, e grandes reformas da Igreja Católica Romana, que poderiam ter impedido o sucesso do luteranismo, nunca foram levadas a efeito. (AM BR)

CLEMENTE VIII

Foi papa de 1592 a 1605. Nasceu com o nome de Ippolito Aldobrandini, em Fano, na Itália, a 24 de fevereiro de 1536. Estudou advocacia; tornou-se cardeal em 1585, e foi eleito papa em 1592. Mediante vários estratagemas políticos, foi capaz de pôr fim ao domínio espanhol sobre Roma. Promoveu um tratado que pôs ponto final à luta entre a França e a Espanha, em 1598, e incorporou a cidade de Ferrara aos estados papais. Ver o artigo sobre os *Estados Papais*.

Clemente VIII foi mediador de uma controvérsia entre os frades jesuítas e os frades dominicanos acerca da natureza da *graça* divina. Clemente editou uma nova edição da Vulgata Latina. Faleceu em Roma, a 5 de março de 1605. (AM)

CLEMENTE VIII (Antipapa)

Foi antipapa, de 1424 a 1429. Nasceu com o nome de Aegidius Muñoz e foi o sucessor do antipapa Benedito VIII, o qual, durante o grande Cisma Ocidental, reinou em Avignon como rival do papado romano. Benedito VIII, embora deposto pelo concílio de Constança, recusou-se a abdicar e a reconhecer o papa Martinho V, de Roma.- **Em vez disso**, nomeou os seus próprios cardeais e insistiu que, após a sua morte, eles elegessem um sucessor seu. Foi precisamente o que fizeram, elegendo a Clemente VIII. O rei Alfonso, de Aragão, mostrou-se hostil ao papa Martinho V, pelo que coroou a Clemente VIII como papa. Posteriormente, porém, Alfonso reconciliou-se com o papa Martinho, e Clemente VIII foi obrigado a resignar. (AM)

CLEMENTE IX

Seu pontificado estendeu-se de 1667 a 1669. Nasceu com o nome de Giulio Rospigliosi, em Pistóia, na Itália, a 28 de janeiro de 1600. Ocupou cargos políticos antes de haver sido eleito papa. Obteve sucesso ao persuadir os bispos jansenistas da França a se submeterem à Santa Sé. Isso pôs fim à controvérsia jansenista, que vinha se arrastando por trinta anos. Ver o artigo sobre o *Jansenismo*. Mediou uma disputa entre a França e a Espanha. Pouco depois, procurou ajudar a defender a ilha de Creta da invasão turca, mas seus esforços foram inúteis, pois a ilha caiu diante dos turcos pouco depois de sua morte, que ocorreu em Roma, a 9 de dezembro de 1669. (AM)

CLEMENTE X

Governou como papa de 1670 a 1676. Seu nome de batismo era Emílio Altieri. Nasceu em Roma, a 13 de julho de 1590. Como ministro, serviu em várias funções eclesiásticas e diplomáticas, sob diversos papas. Chegado o tempo de sua eleição, Altieri protestou que tanto era indigno quanto era idoso demais; mas, a despeito de tudo, foi eleito, após uma longa sessão, como um candidato de transigência. Durante seu pontificado, apoiou a Polônia contra a invasão turca e deu sua ajuda a João Sobieski, que reivindicava o trono polonês. Opôs-se à política de extensão de Luís XIV, que queria ampliar os direitos da realeza e desejava promover a paz entre os estados europeus. Clemente X faleceu em Roma, a 22 de julho de 1676. (AM)

CLEMENTE XI

Governou como papa de 1700 a 1721. Seu nome era Gian Francesco Albani. Nasceu em Urbino, na Itália, a 22 de julho de 1649. Foi educado pelos jesuítas e tornou-se um notável erudito. Fez certo número de obras gregas para o latim. Serviu sob quatro papas sucessivos, e tornou-se uma figura importante e influente. Inocente XII nomeou-o cardeal. Em 1700, Albani foi eleito papa como candidato de transigência. Como papa, tentou manter posição neutra durante a guerra da Sucessão Espanhola. Durante o seu papado, reapareceu a controvérsia do jansenismo (que vide), cuja doutrina era promovida pelo teólogo francês Pasquier Quesnel (que vide). O papa publicou dois documentos que condenavam o movimento, chamados *Vineam Domini* e *Unigenitus*. Tentou conquistar Pedro, o Grande, da Rússia, para o catolicismo romano, mas fracassou, não querendo ele abandonar a Igreja Ortodoxa Russa. Mostrou-se zeloso promotor das missões ao estrangeiro, embora desaprovasse os ritos da China e do Malabar, os quais, segundo ele pensava, orientalizava em demasia o cristianismo. Faleceu em Roma, a 19 de março de 1721. (AM E)

CLEMENTE XII

Governou como papa de 1730 a 1740. Nasceu em Florença, Itália, a 7 de abril de 1662, tendo recebido o nome de Lorenzo Corsini. Estudou no Colégio Romano e na Universidade de Piza. Passou por postos eclesiásticos sérios e importantes. Ficou cego em 1732, apenas dois anos após ter-se tornado papa. Mas isso não impediu que dirigisse ativamente a causa missionária, combatesse o jansenismo (que vide) e condenasse a maçonaria. Durante seu período pontifical, o papado perdeu os direitos feudais sobre os ducados de Parma e Piancenza. Faleceu em Roma, a 6 de fevereiro de 1740. (AM)

CLEMENTE XIII

Pontificou de 1758 a 1769. Seu nome era Carlo Della Torre Rezzonico. Nasceu em Veneza, a 7 de março de 1693. Seu treinamento era a diplomacia, mas terminou servindo como eclesiástico. Foi ordenado em 1716 e foi galgando rapidamente os vários ofícios eclesiásticos. Em 1737, já era cardeal. Durante o seu papado, a Igreja Católica Romana, e especialmente os jesuítas, sofreram ataques por parte de certos membros do movimento de Iluminação, na França. A Sociedade de Jesus foi suprimida em Portugal, na França e na Espanha. Clemente procurou contrabalançar essas medidas, mas sem êxito. Ele reconheceu perigos ao ensino da Igreja de Roma nas doutrinas da filosofia francesa, pelo que condenou várias obras, sobretudo as de Diderot e de Helvétius. Mostrou-se ativo em obras de caridade, durante certo período de seca e fome na Itália. Faleceu a 2 de fevereiro de 1769. (AM)

CLEMENTE XIV

Governou como papa de 1769 a 1774. Seu nome de batismo era Giovani Ganganelli. Nasceu em Sant' Arcangelo, na Itália, a 31 de outubro de 1705. Estudou com os jesuítas e com os piaristas. Tornou-se membro da ordem dos Frades Menores e adotou o nome de Lorenzo. Tornou-se um dos líderes de sua ordem e foi nomeado consultor do Santo Ofício, por Benedito XIII. Foi feito cardeal por Clemente XIII, em 1759. O tempo de sua eleição como papa caracterizou-se pela confusão, devido às pressões para que se elegesse um papa que pudesse agradar os poderes temporais da França, da Espanha e de Nápoles. Ganganelli foi considerado o melhor homem do momento, pelo que foi eleito papa e tomou o título de Clemente XIV. Os jesuítas eram alvos de ataque, e Clemente cedeu às pressões para censurá-los, o que foi feito mediante a bula *Dominus ac Redemptor*. Clemente procurou aplacar o monarca, o que fez com sucesso parcial, restaurando à Igreja de Roma diversos territórios que haviam sido perdidos. Entre eles estavam Avignon e Venaissin, na França, e Benevento e Pontecorvo, na Itália. Também teve a satisfação de efetuar a reunião com Roma de um grupo de nestorianos. Organizou o valioso museu Pio-Clementino, no Vaticano. Faleceu a 22 de setembro de 1774. Muitos disseram que ele morrera envenenado, mas a maioria dos estudiosos pensa que tal rumor não tinha fundamento. (AM.E)

CLEMENTE, EPÍSTOLAS DE
I. Primeira Epístola de Clemente

Declaração Introdutória. Dentre os muitos escritos atribuídos a Clemente de Roma (ver o artigo anterior, sobre Clemente I, Papa), somente a primeira epístola aos Coríntios é considerada autêntica. De acordo com Ireneu (que vide), que considerava essa carta *importantíssima*, e de acordo com Eusébio (que vide), que chamou-a de *magnífica*, essa carta era lida publicamente nas assembléias da Igreja antiga, pelo que obteve uma posição canônica ou quase canônica, nos anos após a era apostólica.

CLEMENTE, EPÍSTOLAS

Esboço:
1. Autor
2. Data
3. Propósito e Conteúdo
4. Fatos Importantes sobre a Carta
5. Sua Relação com o Cânon do Novo Testamento
6. Texto

1. Autor

O nome de Clemente não aparece na carta, mas que é de autoria genuína de Clemente é fortemente confirmado pelos pais da Igreja. Nenhuma razão realmente boa tem sido encontrada para rejeitar essa confirmação. O autor não escreveu como uma grande autoridade, conforme se pensa que um papa moderno deve fazer, embora demonstrasse ser homem de conhecimento e habilidades, mesmo que não tivesse sido um filósofo ou teólogo de grande distinção. Ele viveu na geração imediatamente após aquela dos apóstolos, sendo perfeitamente possível que tivesse conhecido pessoalmente o apóstolo Pedro, mesmo que não tivesse sido consagrado por ele, como Tertuliano supunha. Quanto ao que se sabe a respeito dele, ver a declaração introdutória, acima.

2. Data

A julgar pela própria carta, parece que os oficiais nomeados pelos apóstolos continuavam atuantes nas igrejas (xliv.3). E é possível que as tribulações às quais o autor da carta se refere (I.1) eram aquelas causadas por Domiciano (81-96 D.C.), já quase no fim do seu reinado, o que nos confere uma data aproximada de 95 D.C.

3. Propósito e Conteúdo

O *propósito* da carta foi **acalmar** as perturbações e mal-entendidos que haviam surgido na igreja de Corinto, principalmente entre os ministros e os membros (1:10-16). Essa carta tinha o propósito de repreender o espírito *faccioso* da igreja cristã em Corinto, o que nos permite entender que eles não haviam aprendido muito com as epístolas de Paulo (ver I Cor. 3:1 ss). Entre eles havia «inveja e contenda». Tais condições geralmente apagam a luz de qualquer igreja cristã. A fim de combater tal situação, a origem e os efeitos da inveja e do espírito contencioso são traçados. A humildade de Cristo, por outro lado, é exaltada. Foi ele quem, pacífico como era, trouxe a paz. Na carta de Clemente, a humildade e a paz são referidas como grandes virtudes.

Outros Elementos do Conteúdo da Carta. O autor refere-se à ressurreição futura, e o símbolo clássico da ressurreição é mencionado, a fênix (que vide), como ilustração. Essa ave fictícia morre e torna-se em cinzas; mas então volta à vida, dentre as suas próprias cinzas. A carta de Clemente contém muitas exortações à santidade, à fé e às boas obras. Os crentes são comparados a um exército, que precisa obedecer às ordens dos superiores. São ordenados a boa ordem e a ajuda mútua. Ali é dito que a liderança espiritual é ordenada por Deus, pelo que deve ser respeitada pelos homens. As divisões e as contendas entre os líderes são condenadas. A deslealdade e o orgulho geralmente operam nesses casos. A lei do amor (que vide) é exaltada. O autor vê no amor cristão a solução para todos os problemas da Igreja. O princípio do amor requer sacrifícios pessoais. A carta se encerra com uma intercessão pedindo ajuda, purificação e paz, ao que uma bênção é acrescentada. Ver os detalhes abaixo, sob o ponto quatro.

4. Fatos Importantes sobre a Carta

Essa carta é o mais antigo escrito, após o Novo Testamento, cujo autor e cuja data podem ser determinados com razoável certeza. Em certo sentido, a história pós-apostólica da Igreja começa com essa missiva. Inclusos há vários dados históricos importantes, como o martírio de Pedro e de Paulo, bem como a informação de que Paulo morreu após ter chegado aos *limites do Ocidente*, uma alusão à sua viagem missionária entre os dois períodos de aprisionamento em Roma (v.7), mas sobre a qual o livro de Atos nada conta, visto que termina sua narrativa no seu primeiro aprisionamento na capital do império. A epístola de Clemente afirma a base apostólica da mensagem da Igreja. A expiação pelo sangue de Cristo é referida em 7:4; 21:6 e 49:6. O trecho de Isaías 53 é usado nessa conexão, em 16:5. A ressurreição é o tema dos capítulos 24 a 26.

Há um item que precisa ser destacado, devido à sua omissão. Se um papa escreveu uma carta à igreja de Corinto, e se ele tinha poderes especiais, conforme os papas sempre têm, então é difícil concluirmos por que Clemente não fez uso dessa autoridade, para sublinhar a mensagem contra o espírito faccioso da igreja de Corinto. Por outra parte, poderíamos indagar *por que* o bispo de Roma escreveu tal carta a Corinto, cidade que, como é óbvio, ficava fora de sua jurisdição. Estaria ele escrevendo apenas como um bom irmão universal, ou, na qualidade de bispo de *Roma*, exercia mais autoridade e tinha mais prestígio do que os bispos ordinários? Penso que, embora não tenhamos em Clemente uma figura papal, encontramos nele um bispo de Roma, investido de maior autoridade que os outros bispos, por consentimento dos demais, o que lhe permitiu escrever a uma igreja fora de sua área, esperando que a sua reprimenda fosse respeitada. O autor da carta não fala em seu próprio nome, mas em nome da Igreja. Porém, a menos que sua jurisdição fosse reconhecida como uma autoridade que ia além de sua própria cidade e cercanias, seria improvável que ele tivesse tomado sobre si mesmo a tarefa de instruir uma igreja tão distante quanto a de Corinto. Mas, sem importar tudo isso, essa carta preserva preciosas descrições da antiga vida, práticas e doutrinas do cristianismo antigo.

5. Sua Relação com o Cânon do Novo Testamento

O fato de que os escritos dos chamados pais da Igreja eram altamente considerados, e as alusões específicas ao fato de que essa carta era lida nos primeiros tempos da Igreja pós-apostólica, mostram que, na época, ela ocupava posição canônica ou quase canônica, pelo menos em alguns lugares. Devemo-nos lembrar que o cânon do Novo Testamento ainda estava em formação, e que, ao tempo do uso de I Clemente, o cânon neotestamentário consistia, essencialmente, dos quatro evangelhos e das epístolas de Paulo. Somente após alguns séculos a coletânea de vinte e sete livros do Novo Testamento recebeu aceitação universal. Ver o artigo separado sobre o *Cânon*.

6. Texto

O Codex Alexandrinus contém o texto grego inteiro de I Clemente, excetuando uma página, correspondente a 57.6-64.1. Naquele manuscrito, aparece imediatamente após o Apocalipse. Um outro manuscrito contém o texto grego em sua inteireza, o qual aparece após o *Didache* (que vide). Há várias versões no siríaco, no latim e duas versões em cóptico. Os textos latinos sofreram algumas modificações escribais, exaltando a autoridade de Roma. Em certo manuscrito siríaco de data posterior, seguem-se as epístolas católicas. Certos itens da primeira epístola de Paulo aos Coríntios aparecem refletidos na epístola de Clemente, em 42:1-4, da epístola aos Romanos, em 35:5,6; da epístola aos Hebreus em 9:3; 17:1 e 19:2; de Tito 3:1, em 2:7; e de I Pedro 4:8 em 49:5.

CLEMENTE DE ALEXANDRIA

Também é patente que o autor estava familiarizado com os evangelhos sinópticos.

II. II Clemente

Embora chamada de epístola, essa obra é muito mais um sermão, sendo o mais antigo sermão cristão, completo, à parte do Novo Testamento. O título atribui esse escrito a Clemente de Roma, embora nada exista capaz de dar apoio a essa tradição. Na antiguidade era comum atribuir livros e cartas a autores famosos, a fim de lhes conferir maior prestígio e maior circulação, ou mesmo para honrar o nome do suposto autor escolhido. Essa segunda epístola de Clemente talvez date de 150 D.C., e teve origem em Roma ou em Corinto. Hilgenfeld e Harnack atribuíam-na ao bispo Soter de Roma (166-174 D.C.); mas, até que ponto essa opinião pode estar certa é dificílimo determinar. Talvez tenha-se originado quando dos Jogos dos Istmos que parece serem aludidos em 7.1-4; mas também pode ter sido enviada de Roma para Corinto, como foi o caso de I Clemente.

O autor exorta os seus leitores a pensarem sobre Jesus Cristo como Deus (1:1), e, por conseguinte, a obedecerem aos seus mandamentos. Também relembra os seus leitores acerca da brevidade desta vida, destacando assim a importância da inquirição espiritual. Haverá a ressurreição e haverá o julgamento. Portanto, o crente deveria preservar o selo do batismo mediante uma vida santificada (6.6; 8.6). A santidade é o caminho da salvação. O amor oculta uma multidão de pecados, e a oração *liberta da morte*. Contudo, ali é dito que «o jejum é melhor que a oração, e o dar esmolas melhor do que ambos» (16.4). Esses são pontos de vista interessantes, mediante os quais voltamos à importante lei do amor cristão.

O sermão faz parte do Codex Alexandrinus, bem como de um manuscrito encontrado em 1873 por Bryennios. Também há uma versão em siríaco.

III. Outra Literatura Clementina Não-Autêntica.

Há duas epístolas *Ad Virgines* (às solteiras), que datam do século III D.C.; as *Homilias Pseudoclementinas*; as *Constituições Apostólicas*; a *Liturgia Clementina*; os *Cânones Clementinos*. Estes últimos consistem em cinco cartas, postas no começo das *Falsas Decretais de Isidoro* (que vide). (AM E GR LIG Z)

CLEMENTE DE ALEXANDRIA
1. Vida

Suas datas foram 150-215 D.C. Foi teólogo cristão, provavelmente originário de Atenas, e não de Alexandria, apesar do nome com que é conhecido. Foi pastor da igreja de Alexandria. Sucedeu a Pantaeno, como chefe da escola de catequese; foi mestre do famoso Orígenes, e de Alexandre, o qual tornou-se bispo de Jerusalém. Juntamente com Orígenes (que vide), foi o principal expositor da escola teológica alexandrina. Pouco se sabe sobre a sua vida pessoal. O que se sabe dele é colhido em informes dados em seus próprios escritos, bem como nas obras dos historiadores Eusébio e Pótio. Seu nome era Tito Flávio Clemente. Seus pais eram pagãos bem-educados e cultos, e a riqueza material deles lhe deu a oportunidade de viajar e de receber uma educação superior. Sua educação inicial foi em Atenas, onde adquiriu amor pela filosofia e pela literatura helênicas. Ali, converteu-se ao cristianismo. De volta a Alexandria, tornou-se estudante do filósofo cristão Pantaeno, um ex-filósofo estóico, que encabeçava a escola catequética cristã da cidade. Ficou em Alexandria de 175 a 202 D.C., ensinando e escrevendo. Mas teve de fugir por causa da perseguição iniciada pelo imperador Sétimo Severo. Praticamente nada sabemos sobre os anos restantes de sua vida, embora, provavelmente, tivessem sido consagrados à vida pastoral, em Jerusalém e Antioquia da Síria. Faleceu em cerca de 215 D.C.

Notável foi a sua contribuição para a erudição cristã e para a teologia. Ver sobre a *Teologia Alexandrina*.

2. Obras Principais.

No *Protrepticus* (Exortação), Clemente ataca os absurdos das divindades pagãs, exortando os seus leitores a voltarem-se para o cristianismo. No *Paedogogus* (Tutor) ele instrui os cristãos quanto à vida espiritual. Sua principal obra, o *Stromateis* (Colcha de Retalhos), nunca foi terminada, embora ali ele procurasse expor seus principais raciocínios filosófico-teológicos. Essa obra teve esse nome por tratar de assuntos diversos. Em parte, ela atacava o gnosticismo, como autor que era, um verdadeiro gnóstico (conhecedor). Ele asseverava que o conhecimento medra no terreno da fé, não sendo contrário à fé. Salientava o monoteísmo e a liberdade moral, contra a idéia do determinismo ético (que vide). Suas obras deram início à teologia especulativa da Igreja. Sua educação helenista capacitava-o a ter amplos pontos de vista, e assim ele pôde conferir à fé cristã uma teologia dotada de alicerce científico-filosófico. Esforçava-se por tirar proveito da erudição secular, de todas as fontes possíveis, a fim de melhor exprimir a sua teologia. Suas obras contêm muitas úteis referências à filosofia grega, bem como à literatura e às ciências físicas. Sua obra em oito volumes, *Stromata*, aborda basicamente a relação entre o cristianismo e a filosofia grega, de onde emergiram os princípios de seu cristianismo platônico.

3. Idéias:

a. O alvo do cristianismo, como também o da melhor filosofia grega, é uma vida mais nobre e mais santa. Aquilo que foi visto como meros vislumbres, pelos filósofos gregos, Cristo trouxe à plena luz e esclareceu.

b. Cristo é o *Logos*, o princípio divino entre os homens, o revelador de Deus, Aquele que implanta as Suas sementes por toda a parte. A verdade do Logos não pode ser limitada a qualquer filosofia ou religião isolada, visto que as suas sementes são plantadas e germinam por toda a parte, de acordo com a sua soberana vontade. Isso posto, a melhor porção da filosofia grega atuava como um mestre-escola, preparando os homens para Cristo, papel esse que a lei mosaica teve, em relação aos judeus. O Logos reveste-se de um caráter transcendental que não pode ser contido em qualquer sistema isolado; mas é no cristianismo que o Logos resplandece com maior brilho, e é para esse sistema que todos os demais apontam, como o mais excelente cultivo do plantio do Logos.

c. Deus Pai é Absoluto, a Mônada, isento de todas as características que possam ser expressas mediante a linguagem humana, porquanto ele é superior às distinções sensíveis dos seres humanos.

d. *Em Cristo*, os homens passam da fé para o conhecimento, por meio do amor. Nesse processo, eles adquirem autocontrole e poder moral, tornando-se livres das paixões comuns, desviando-se do caminho da busca pelos vãos prazeres. Os cristãos, pois, tornam-se os *verdadeiros* gnósticos (conhecedores).

e. Os indivíduos são preparados para o cristianismo e para sua mensagem superior; mas isso também sucede no caso da própria humanidade. Muito daquilo que acontece aqui, mas que não é uma expressão direta do cristianismo, continua sendo meios usados pelo Logos para preparar a salvação dos homens. Não deveríamos desprezar qualquer das operações de Deus.

f. A *filosofia* é um dom de Deus aos homens. Os gregos, mediante a razão, foram capazes de perceber muitos e grandes princípios espirituais, estando assim preparados para uma mais profunda manifestação da verdade. Há muitos níveis da verdade; mas, quanto ao propósito e à função, esses níveis tornam-se um só.

g. O grande problema da filosofia grega é que ela é *incompleta*, e não tanto que ela está essencialmente equivocada. A crença e a revelação cristãs são necessárias a fim de separar a verdade do erro. O verdadeiro gnóstico é o cristão, cujo conhecimento recebeu a iluminação provida pelo Logos. Nele encontramos uma iluminação mesclada com o amor. Portanto, há dois grandes pilares ou sustentáculos da verdade: o conhecimento e o amor. O crente, bem preparado em seu conhecimento, pode usar a dialética da filosofia para aclarar e melhor expor a verdade que ele obteve por parte da fé. Nisso, há uma elevação da simples fé em dogmas para o conhecimento sólido quanto às questões espirituais.

h. A *interpretação alegórica* (que vide). Nos Livros Sagrados há certas coisas que não se prestam para a interpretação literal. No Antigo Testamento, por exemplo, há incidentes nos quais os autores hebreus descrevem Deus a fazer coisas bastante duvidosas do ponto de vista moral. Nesses casos, vemos um sentido alegórico ou simbólico, e não um sentido literal.

i. O Logos é *a fonte* da verdade. Qualquer pessoa que encontrou a verdade em qualquer tempo, em qualquer lugar, em qualquer sistema, na verdade encontrou a verdade suprida pelo Logos. Todas as revelações, onde quer que sejam encontradas, são inferiores ao Logos, porquanto a Mente Divina nunca é acessível ao homem em sua perfeição ou inteireza, pois isso é impossível para a finitude humana. Portanto, a revelação precisa ser progressiva, exigindo a disciplina suprida pela razão.

j. A *missão do Logos* e a salvação humana. A alma é preexistente, e vasta é a sua oportunidade de salvação. A história da descida de Cristo ao hades (I Pedro 3:18-4:6) mostra-nos que ele pregou o evangelho aos perdidos, naquele lugar. E isso indica que a oportunidade prossegue, mesmo após a morte biológica. Os apóstolos teriam estado envolvidos nessa missão ao hades, após a morte deles. E isso faz do hades um campo missionário.

l. Os grupos e as filosofias arrancam algum membro da verdade, e supõem que têm toda a verdade. Mas a verdade é o composto de todos os membros, mostrando-se maior que aquela verdade contida em qualquer lugar ou grupo particular. As muitas partes constitutivas são unificadas em torno do Logos. A verdade contida na filosofia é parcial, embora real. Outro tanto pode ser dito no tocante a muitos grupos e denominações cristãs. Clemente compartilhava da noção de que os gregos tiraram proveito de certas idéias dos hebreus. Essa é uma noção que, mui provavelmente, não corresponde à verdade dos fatos. Mas é verdade que Platão tem várias idéias paralelas aos ensinos dos hebreus.

m. O *conhecimento* tanto é lógico quanto é espiritual. A visão espiritual e o raciocínio bem ordenado levam-nos à mesma verdade, através de diferentes caminhos. O conhecimento espiritual consiste no crescimento em Cristo, na consciência da presença universal de Deus e na união com ele, em amor. O conhecimento racional é o Grande Intelecto em operação, nos intelectos humanos. O conhecimento sempre será uma unidade complexa. A fé é uma unidade simples. O conhecimento, por ser complexo, requer uma abordagem complexa, para que obtenhamos um mais amplo e profundo conhecimento.

n. *O problema do mal e o destino do homem*. Deus não impede que o mal se manifeste. O sofrimento acompanha inevitavelmente a existência humana. Mas Deus faz redundar o mal em bem, visando o benefício do homem. No sofrimento há disciplina e ensino. Na vida física, Deus pode usar o sofrimento a fim de corrigir os pecadores. *Após a morte física*, Deus dá prosseguimento à mesma norma. Os pecadores são santificados por meio do sofrimento, o que Clemente chamava de — *fogo não-material, inteligente*. As chamas do juízo, pois, seriam inteligentes, e não meramente vindicatórias e arbitrárias. Elas teriam uma obra a realizar, em favor dos pecadores. Para alguns, isso poderia assemelhar-se à noção católica do *purgatório* (que vide); mas Clemente estava se referindo a todos os pecadores, e não a crentes que precisam ser purgados de pecados remanescentes. Em outras palavras, o julgamento é *remedial*, e não apenas retributivo; e essa é a única doutrina sobre o julgamento divino que faz algum sentido. É precisamente o que I Pedro 4:6 ensina. Ver os meus artigos sobre a *Restauração* e sobre o *Julgamento*. Ver também sobre o *Problema do Mal*.

o. *O destino final do homem*. Clemente falava em termos de *assimilação* final em Deus. Ele pensava que o homem, por ocasião da criação, recebeu a semelhança de Deus. Mas na redenção, por meio da assimilação, ele adquirirá a natureza divina. Platão, em seu diálogo intitulado *Theaetetus*, dissera algo similar. O homem vem a adquirir a natureza divina mediante o processo da bondade. As Escrituras fazem da santificação e da consagração elementos necessários à salvação da alma (Heb. 12:14). E o trecho de II Pedro 1:4 fala da participação do crente na natureza divina. Isso significa que Platão e Clemente concordavam com essas idéias bíblicas.

p. *Princípios éticos*. Em seu *Paedagogus*, Clemente enfatizou o autoconhecimento mencionado por Platão, bem como o conceito do mal como ignorância e da virtude como conhecimento. A virtude nos vem mediante a *disciplina* e a *busca* pela bondade, e tal busca deve ser livre dos motivos enganosos da vantagem egoísta. Clemente tomou por empréstimo de Aristóteles o princípio da virtude como uma função. Assim, um homem precisa cumprir sua função tencionada, a fim de obter a realização e o efeito da virtude. Toda ação, pois, precisa ser governada pelo intermédio áureo, que também é uma idéia aristotélica. Há certa classe de coisas que não estão sujeitas à vontade humana. O homem deveria reconhecer as coisas que ele pode modificar, bem como as coisas que ele não pode alterar, evitando assim ser dominado por paixões e desejos inúteis. Essa idéia ele tomou emprestada do estoicismo, e, naturalmente, Paulo fez o mesmo tipo de empréstimo quando falou sobre a *moderação* como um grande princípio cristão, em Filipenses 4:5. Tal como em toda a sua teologia e ética (que vide), Clemente encontrava princípios na filosofia grega, que ele ampliava e aprimorava na revelação cristã.

4. A Teologia Alexandrina e as Denominações Cristãs

Em termos bem gerais, Clemente falou sobre duas teologias que predominam no cristianismo (que vide).

CLEMENTE DE ROMA — CLÉOPAS

Uma delas é a teologia *latina*, derivada da interpretação dos pais latinos da Igreja cristã, completa com textos de prova apropriados, extraídos das Escrituras. No tocante à salvação do homem, essa teologia supõe que a alma é criada por ocasião do nascimento ou da concepção (ver sobre a *Alma, Origem da*). Assim, pois, a alma vive dotada de um corpo físico, durante uma breve vida física, neste mundo. Mas, quando o corpo físico morre, a alma é julgada e seu destino eterno é fixado. Podemos apelar para Hebreus 9:27 quanto a essa maneira de pensar. Porém, de acordo com a teologia grega (alexandrina), que emerge da interpretação dos pais gregos da Igreja, que também se alicerça sobre textos de provas bíblicos, obtemos uma visão bastante diferente acerca da questão. De acordo com os pais gregos da Igreja, a alma é preexistente, e já chega a esta vida física possuidora de certa qualidade espiritual. A origem da alma humana seria bem remota, ou na eternidade passada, antes do tempo, ou quando da criação dos seres angelicais. Então a alma humana experimenta uma vida física. Por ocasião da morte biológica, seu destino ainda não está determinado, porquanto o mesmo Logos que busca o homem aqui na terra, continua a fazê-lo nas dimensões espirituais. Isso posto, o destino não é fixado por ocasião da morte física. Via de regra, os pais alexandrinos da Igreja não acreditavam na reencarnação (que vide), mas acreditavam em múltiplas vidas no espírito, todas as quais direcionam a alma para Deus.

Como as denominações cristãs se postam diante desses dois sistemas? A Igreja Romana e as organizações dela derivadas, como as igrejas reformadas, e a maioria dos grupos evangélicos, seguem o sistema latino. As Igrejas orientais (ortodoxa, grega, eslava e russa) representam muito mais o ponto de vista dos pais gregos da Igreja. A Igreja Anglicana também tem seguido essa orientação em seus comentários e teologias oficiais. O relato da descida de Cristo ao hades é apontado como prova bíblica (ver I Ped. 3:18-4:6), como apoio bíblico para essa posição teológica, incluindo textos como o de Efésios 1:10, que aludem à restauração a longo prazo, de todas as coisas. Quando iniciei meu comentário, *O Novo Testamento Interpretado*, que acompanha o Novo Testamento versículo por versículo, minha teologia era essencialmente latina, visto que fui criado como crente batista. Mas, ao longo dos estudos que fiz, foram confirmadas as minhas *tendências* orientais. Mediante a razão e as Escrituras, tenho assumido uma filosofia tipicamente alexandrina. Nas muitas obras que consultei, fiquei surpreendido em ver quantos teólogos, dentro da Igreja histórica, têm ensinado os pontos de vista dos pais gregos da Igreja, em contraste com as opiniões dos pais latinos, quanto a certos pontos de doutrina, em torno dos quais eles concordam. Mas, no tocante à doutrina do homem, no tocante às dimensões da alma humana e de sua oportunidade de salvação, tornou-se evidente para mim que os pais gregos da Igreja mostraram-se mais sábios que os pais latinos. (AM C E EP)

CLEMENTE DE ROMA (Clemente I, Papa?)

Clemente foi um dos primeiros bispos de Roma, depois de Lino e Cleto (Anacleto), por muitos considerado o terceiro sucessor de Pedro, como papa da hierarquia romana. De acordo com Tertuliano (*De praesc.* 32), ele foi consagrado pelo próprio apóstolo Pedro. Mas essa declaração é difícil de entender, levando-se em conta que ele foi o *terceiro* sucessor de Pedro, e não o primeiro. Seu bispado foi de cerca de 92 a 101 D.C. A maioria dos eruditos modernos rejeita a identificação desse homem com aquele Clemente mencionado em Filipenses 4:3. Ver o artigo sobre Clemente (personagem do Novo Testamento), quanto à argumentação contra e a favor dessa identificação. Uma outra identificação rejeitada pela maioria dos intérpretes modernos é aquela com Tito Flávio Clemente, parente dos imperadores Flavianos. Entretanto, é possível que ele estivesse vinculado à família imperial, como filho de um liberto que vivia na corte. A tradição afirma em termos decididos que ele sofreu o martírio, embora não disponhamos de detalhes autênticos sobre a questão.

A obra Atos dos Mártires, do século IV ou V D.C., afirma que Clemente foi exilado para a península de Queronese, na área do mar Negro, e foi atirado ao mar com uma âncora amarrada ao seu pescoço. Porém, um grande milagre teria tido lugar, pouco depois. O mar retrocedeu, revelando o seu cadáver envolto em um santuário de mármore. Cirilo, apóstolo dos eslavos, encontrou alguns ossos com uma âncora amarrada aos mesmos, e proclamou que ali estavam os restos mortais de Clemente. Finalmente, esses ossos foram postos na basílica de São Clemente, em Roma. Os frades dominicanos tomam conta do lugar, onde os ossos citados são honrados. Essas fantásticas narrativas lembram-nos das longas tradições que adornam coisas sobre as quais nada sabemos. As tradições humanas não se ressentem da falta de muita imaginação! Mas as pessoas gostam de acreditar nessas coisas, pois a fé de algumas pessoas prefere depender de coisas concretas, sobre as quais pode-se apoiar.

Durante o reinado de Constantino (que vide), foi erigida uma cripta em memória de Clemente. Seja como for, Clemente é considerado o primeiro dos pais apostólicos. Usualmente ele é imaginado pelos artistas com uma âncora amarrada ao pescoço.

Sua memória é festejada a 23 de novembro, na Igreja ocidental e a 24 de novembro na Igreja grega, síria e russa.

Escritos: Um grande número de escritos tem sido atribuído a Clemente, mas os estudiosos modernos supõem que a única obra genuína é aquela que atualmente é conhecida como Primeira Epístola de Clemente. Ver o artigo abaixo. (AM E)

CLÉOPAS

Esse nome é uma contração do termo grego *Kleópatros*, cujo sentido é duvidoso, embora alguns pensem em «pai famoso». Cléopas foi um dos dois discípulos aos quais Jesus se reuniu, a caminho para Emaús, na tarde do dia de sua ressurreição (que vide). O relato, narrado no trecho de Lucas 24:13-32, é um dos mais dramáticos e comoventes dos evangelhos, tendo servido de base para muitos milhares de sermões e tendo inspirado a muitos hinos, sem falar nas muitas lágrimas vertidas por sua causa. Eu mesmo tenho me sentido profundamente comovido ao sermonar a respeito, e tenho visto reações emocionais da parte de outras pessoas. Trata-se de uma história de triunfo incomum e *inesperado*, em meio à aparente derrota. Contém trechos especiais, como: «E disseram um para o outro: Porventura não se nos *abrasava o coração*, quando pelo caminho (Jesus) nos falava e quando nos abria as Escrituras?» Somente mais tarde, quando partiam o pão na companhia de Jesus, quando o sol já estava se pondo no horizonte, eles reconheceram que o Senhor Jesus, a quem tinham considerado morto, tinha andado em companhia deles, tendo-lhes aberto o entendimento para compreenderem as Escrituras, e que sentara à mesma com eles. O texto tem todos os sinais de ser um relato de testemunhas oculares, sendo possível que o próprio Cléopas tenha contado o episódio a Lucas, que o registrou no terceiro evangelho.

Quando o grupo chegou à aldeia de Emaús, Jesus agiu como se quisesse continuar. Porém, já era o fim da tarde, e a noite aproximava-se rapidamente. Portanto, insistiram com ele para que ficasse com eles naquela noite. O coro do tabernáculo mórmon canta um glorioso hino que comemora o acontecimento:

Fica comigo, já é tarde, o dia está avançando;
Caem as sombras da noitinha, a noite se aproxima.
Em meu coração, um hóspede querido, no meu lar um descanso.
Oh! Salvador, passa esta noite comigo! já é tarde.
Fica comigo, já é tarde. O Senhor andava hoje comigo,
Meu coração em mim ardia, a comungar contigo;
Tuas palavras encheram minha alma.
Oh, Salvador, fica esta noite comigo! já é tarde.

Um outro hino dá prosseguimento ao mesmo tema:

Fica comigo; desce depressa a escura noite;
As trevas se aprofundam; Senhor, fica comigo.
Quando falham outras ajudas e o consolo foge,
Ajuda dos desamparados, oh! fica comigo.
Rápido se aproxima o fim da breve vida.
O júbilo terreno diminui, sua glória passa.
Mudança e decadência em tudo vejo ao meu redor.
Ó tu, que não mudas, fica comigo!

Somente Lucas registra o episódio, como parte da tradição que ele encontrou em suas investigações. O fim mais longo do evangelho de Marcos, não original do segundo evangelho (Mar. 16:9-20), menciona de forma breve o episódio, ao dizer: «Depois disto, manifestou-se em outra forma a dois deles que estavam de caminho para o campo» (Mar. 16:12).

Alguns identificam o Cléopas deste texto com o Clopas mencionado em João 19:25. Embora Cléopas possa ser a forma grega do hebraico ou aramaico «Clopas», transliterado, não há qualquer evidência que consubstancie essa identificação. (ID NTI)

CLEÓPATRA

Esse foi o nome de várias princesas egípcias, derivado da filha de Antíoco. A mais famosa delas foi aquela associada a Júlio César e a Marco Antônio, que ocupa o terceiro lugar, abaixo:

1. A esposa de Ptolomeu Epifânio, rei do Egito, talvez a princesa referida em Dan. 11:17 como «uma jovem».

2. Uma filha de Ptolomeu VI, Filômetro, e da Cleópatra mencionada acima, cujo primeiro casamento fora com Alexandre Balas (150 A.C.; I Macabeus 10:58). Posteriormente ela foi dada em casamento, por seu pai, a Demétrio Nicator, quando este invadiu a Síria (I Macabeus 11:12; Josefo, *Anti*. xiii.4.7). Porém, estando ele cativo na Pártia, Cleópatra teve ainda um terceiro casamento, dessa vez com o irmão de seu segundo marido, de nome Antíoco VII Sidertes. Quando o segundo marido de Cleópatra retornou do cativeiro, foi assassinado. E alguns historiadores crêem que Cleópatra esteve envolvida (Josefo, *Anti*. xxx.9,3). Mas o informe parece justificado, visto que sabemos que ela matou Seleuco, o Velho, a fim de permitir que Antíoco VIII subisse ao poder. Porém, ele não estava disposto a satisfazer as ridículas ambições dela. Por causa disso, ela tentou matá-lo por envenenamento. Mas ele percebeu o que ela estava fazendo, e forçou-a a beber a taça envenenada, e ela morreu, em cerca de 120 A.C.

3. A última da linhagem das Cleópatras da degenerada linhagem ptolomaica. Pouco mais elas faziam do que arrancar do povo o máximo de dinheiro possível, sem causar revolta. Essa Cleópatra ficou famosa por causa de seu envolvimento na história romana, em vista do que fez em seu próprio país. Ela foi uma culta e brilhante princesa macedônia, que usava seus encantos pessoais para promover seus desígnios. Ela se considerava filha do deus-sol, Ra, e levava a sério a religião do povo. Júlio César interveio na política dos Ptolomeus no fim de 48 A.C. Nesse tempo, Cleópatra estava exilada da corte de seu irmão, e tinha vinte e dois anos de idade. Conheceu César quando ele visitou o Egito. Ele resolveu torná-la sua amante. Ela lhe deu um filho e voltou a Roma com ele. Depois que César foi assassinado, Cleópatra voltou ao Egito. Em 41 A.C., Marco Antônio, membro do triunvirato do qual participavam Otávio e Lépido, convocou Cleópatra e outros governantes orientais para lhe prestarem contas. Ela viu uma segunda oportunidade de aumentar seus poderes, e voltou a sua atenção para Antônio. Eles tiveram um rápido romance. E, depois que Antônio rompeu relações com Otávio, em 37 D.C., casou-se com Cleópatra. Ela obteve poder absoluto sobre Antônio, tornando-se sua companheira e confidente. Cleópatra assassinou sua irmã mais jovem, Arsinoé, porque esta ameaçava remotamente a seu trono, e assim consolidou o seu poder. Antônio já tinha uma esposa em Roma, a irmã de Otávio. E, assim sendo, estava iniciando um perigoso ato de equilíbrio. Cleópatra teve gêmeos de Antônio. Diante disso, Antônio cuidou para que as terras e o império dela fossem imensamente aumentados. Ela recebeu territórios no centro da Síria, a ilha de Chipre, boa parte das costas da Fenícia, propriedades na Judéia, etc. Conseguiu apagar Otávio totalmente, havendo escândalos que sacudiram Roma. Isso laborava contra Antônio, que foi perdendo gradualmente os seus partidários. Mas Cleópatra acompanhava-o por onde quer que ele fosse, até mesmo ao campo de batalha. O desastre, porém, estava prestes a ocorrer. A família Otaviana declarou guerra a Antônio, a Cleópatra e ao império dela. Quando os dois comandantes encontraram-se em Ácio, no ano 31 A.C., para decidir quem haveria de governar o império romano, Antônio seguiu o plano de batalha traçado por Cleópatra. Porém, sua flotilha quase inteira o abandonou, e foi nos navios dela que Antônio fugiu, e tudo se perdeu. O exército dele, Em vez de segui-lo para Alexandria, simplesmente rendeu-se.

O sonho com Antônio havia terminado; e Cleópatra percebeu que ele não mais podia ser usado para concretizar os seus sonhos de poder. Ela provocou o suicídio dele, espalhando o falso rumor de que ela se matara. Em vista disso, Cleópatra tentou influenciar Otávio com os seus encantos, a fim de conseguir para si o máximo possível. O plano dela de oferecer a sua família inteira, como oferenda a Ra, fracassou. Porém, ela conseguiu ocultar uma áspide (símbolo de Ra) em uma cesta de figos. Cleópatra fez a áspide picá-la, e assim ela morreu em sacrifício a Ré. O último pedido dela de ser sepultada ao lado de Antônio, foi concedido. Tinha quarenta anos de idade, quando morreu. Os historiadores dizem-nos que os romanos não temiam a ninguém mais do que a Cleópatra, excetuando Aníbal.

A vida de Cleópatra tem produzido uma volumosa literatura, em prosa, verso e peças teatrais. Isso começou desde tempos antigos, porque os atos astuciosos e violentos de Cleópatra provocavam repúdio e terror entre os romanos. Foi assim que ela veio a fazer parte das *Odes* de Horácio, das *Éclogas* de Vergílio, da *Bella civilia* de Apiano, e das *Vidas* de Plutarco. Ovídio, Luciano e Plínio narram certos detalhes de sua história. A literatura e o teatro modernos têm-na retratado como uma sereia ávida por sexo, que nutria um descontrolado desejo de maior autoridade. Os historiadores, porém, dizem-nos que ela não foi tão má como a pintam; e, na verdade, nem todos os escândalos espalhados a respeito dela correspondiam à verdade. Ela tinha algumas qualidades. Era dotada de forte determinação, energia, inteligência e propósito firme. Ela é lembrada como contendora quase bem-sucedida pelo controle do mundo helênico de seus dias. Ver o artigo sobre *Ptolomeu*. (AM WEI)

CLÉRIGOS REGULARES

Esse nome indica alguma instituição religiosa masculina, como, por exemplo, os jesuítas, que combinam as atividades dos padres seculares com os votos solenes da vida monástica.

CLÉRIGOS SECULARES Ver **Ministros Seculares**.

CLERO

Essa palavra aponta para as ordens santas. Os artigos a serem examinados em conexão com as santas ordens e o clero são: *Sucessão Apostólica; Bispo; Ancião; Diácono; Diaconisa; Ordens; Ordenação; Papa; Padre; Sacramentos; Vigário.*

CLERO, CLERICAL

A origem dessa palavra é o termo grego **kléros**, que significa *porção*, herança ou *partilha*. Quando da eleição de Matias, para ocupar o ofício apostólico perdido por Judas Iscariotes, encontramos as *sortes* mediante as quais ele foi eleito. Destarte, o termo pode significar um ofício ou alguma possessão. No Antigo Testamento, o *clero* de Yahweh era a nação de Israel. Em I Pedro 5:3 os anciãos são exortados a não dominar os seus respectivos *kléroi*, ou seja, as suas esferas pastorais e o povo que a eles cabia. Daí temos a palavra grega cognata, *kleronomia*, que significa «herança». Foi dessa última palavra que se desenvolveram as palavras portuguesas *clero* e *clerical*. Esse uso começou na época de Tertuliano. Veio a significar o grupo inteiro de homens separados mediante ordenação, para serem os líderes da igreja local, em contraste com os leigos. No início da Idade Média, o clero era, praticamente, as únicas pessoas alfabetizadas, pelo que a educação passou para as mãos da Igreja e seu clero. Na Idade Média, o termo *clericatus* (em francês antigo *clergie*) incluía um largo espectro de pessoas: os bispos, os padres, os diáconos, os subdiáconos, aqueles que pertenciam às ordens religiosas menores, os porteiros, os leitores, os exorcistas e os atendentes, que se ocupavam de deveres subordinados.

Visto que, na Idade Média, o clero formava a classe dominante, seus membros, naturalmente, envolviam-se em cada função da sociedade, havendo então uma absoluta mistura de funções eclesiásticas e seculares (que vide). A Reforma Protestante (que vide) produziu a revolta contra tal envolvimento, acompanhada pelo desejo de ver a Igreja fora da política, tal como o papa João Paulo II atualmente o está expressando. Houve movimentos pró e anticlericais na Europa. A Revolução Francesa envolvia forte tendência anticlerical. Em vários grupos protestantes houve medidas para eliminar a distinção entre o clero e o corpo laico, nos quais não há um ministério treinado ou pago, mas apenas alguns poucos irmãos, entre irmãos, que assumem a liderança nas igrejas locais. (AM C WA)

CLITÔMACO

Suas datas foram 157-110 A.C. Foi um filósofo grego, nascido em Cartago, África do Norte. Estudou em Atenas, sob a orientação de Carnéades, o cético, cujas idéias ele passou a propagar, mediante cerca de quatrocentos tratados. Sucedeu a Carnéades como chefe da Nova ou Terceira Academia, em 129 A.C. Dispomos apenas de fragmentos de seus escritos. Cícero informa-nos que ele muito devia ao tratado de Clitômaco, *Sobre a Suspensão do Juízo*, quanto a algumas de suas idéias.

CLOE

No grego significa «ramo tenro» ou «erva verde», nome de uma crente de Corinto. Alguns membros de sua família forneceram a Paulo informações sobre as condições na igreja de Corinto, condições essas não muito favoráveis (I Cor. 1:11). Ela mesma vivia em Corinto ou em Éfeso. Alguns têm pensado que esse nome refere-se a um grupo pagão, associado ao culto de Demeter, mas isso parece improvável.

CLOPAS

Esse nome próprio masculino aparece somente em João 19:25. Alguns estudiosos pensam que esse nome grego, *Klopás*, é transliteração de uma palavra hebraica de onde também se deriva o apelativo masculino Alfeu. Na verdade, esses dois nomes, Cléopas e Clopas (que vide) têm sido confundidos um com o outro, o que também se dá com os dois homens diferentes que aparecem no Novo Testamento, cada qual com um desses nomes. Clopas pode ser uma forma grega de Alfeu (que vide). A forma aramaica para Alfeu é Halphai, que poderia ser transliterada para Clopas. Têm sido feitas tentativas para identificar Alfeu com o Cléopas de Lucas 24:18 ou com o Clopas de João 19:25. Alguns chegam mesmo a supor que todos esses três nomes referem-se ao mesmo indivíduo. A comparação entre João 19:25, Lucas 24:10 e Mateus 10:3 parece identificar Alfeu com Cléopas, mas muitos intérpretes resistem a essa identificação.

Clopas era marido (embora no grego possa ser entendido como *filho* ou como pai) de uma das mulheres que estiveram ao pé da cruz de Jesus, quando ele estava crucificado (João 19:25). O nome da esposa desse homem era Maria, embora distinta de Maria, mãe de Jesus, e de Maria Madalena. O texto grego não deixa claro se essa Maria aparece em aposição com a irmã de sua mãe, tornando-a tia de Jesus, ou se o autor sagrado queria que compreendêssemos que estavam presentes quatro mulheres. Tanto Mateus quanto **Marcos mencionam uma certa Maria,** «mãe de Tiago e José», entre as mulheres que estiveram próximas da cruz (Mat. 27:56; Mar. 15:40). Marcos identifica esse Tiago como «Tiago, o menor», a fim de distingui-lo de Tiago, filho de Zebedeu. Todas as quatro listas dos apóstolos mencionam um certo Tiago, filho de Alfeu. Se esse é o mesmo Tiago mencionado em Mat. 27 e Mar. 15; então Clopas e Alfeu foram, realmente, a mesma pessoa. Esse é um pequeno quebra-cabeças quase impossível de solucionar. Porém, a identificação de Clopas (Luc. 24:18)

CLÓVIS — COABITAÇÃO

com Cléopas é muito mais duvidosa. Aumentando ainda mais a confusão, vários pais da Igreja fizeram toda espécie de declarações conflitantes. Tudo o que é razoavelmente certo é que houve um certo Clopas, que tinha dois filhos, chamados Tiago e José, e que a sua esposa esteve entre as mulheres que se aproximaram da cruz de Cristo. Mas, alguns intérpretes pensam que nem mesmo quanto a isso há plena certeza. (S UN Z)

CLÓVIS

Suas datas foram 466-511 D.C. Foi o fundador do reino franco, ou germânico. Adotou o cristianismo, para si mesmo e seu povo. Ampliou os seus domínios territoriais às expensas de seus vizinhos arianos. Também lançou os alicerces de um estado forte e novo, formativo da Europa. De acordo com esse novo estado, as civilizações romana e teutônica mesclaram-se. Embora se dissesse cristão, através da guerra e do assassinato, ele removeu reis francos rivais, unindo os francos e ampliando os seus territórios. Todavia, sua conversão ao cristianismo, posto que apenas nominal, é considerada mais importante, para os historiadores, do que seus feitos militares e pessoais. Na verdade, ele não foi o primeiro chefe franco a tornar-se cristão; mas, por causa dele, estabeleceu-se um laço de união entre os francos e a Sé de Roma, que foi um dos mais duradouros e críticos elementos da história medieval, o que envolveu, ao longo da história, tanto cooperação, quanto ajuda mútua e antagonismo. Esse começo da igreja nacional dos francos, posteriormente incorporada à igreja galicana, produziu séculos de conflito entre o papado e os francos, e, posteriormente, entre o papado e o Santo Império Romano, onde muitos dos seus imperadores foram germânicos.

O controle da Igreja Católica por parte de Clóvis também foi um outro incidente histórico da mistura absoluta entre a Igreja e o Estado. (AM E)

CLUNIACENSE

Esse era o nome dos membros da ordem ou congregação de Cluny, fundada em 910 D.C. pelo abade Berno e seus sucessores imediatos. Eles buscaram reformar a vida monástica mediante uma aplicação mais disciplinada das regras beneditinas (que vide). Eles enfatizavam a pobreza, o trabalho árduo e a simplicidade. Entretanto, essa atitude foi-se modificando gradualmente, e pouco a pouco a ordem foi-se envolvendo nos meandros da política papal. Entraram privilégios pessoais e a decadência, fraquezas muito comuns na história humana. (E)

CLUNY

Um mosteiro beneditino fundado em Cluny, na França, no começo do século IX A.C., que se tornou famoso como residência e escola de muitos distinguidos personagens da era medieval, como o papa Gregório VII (que vide). Esse mosteiro adquiriu uma autoridade e uma influência extraordinárias, pois a abadia tinha a permissão de crescer sem interferências da parte de bispos ou de reis. Os abades de Cluny algumas vezes falavam com uma autoridade que era **maior até mesmo que a autoridade dos papas. Porém, à medida que seu poder e riquezas aumentavam**, seu fervor religioso declinava. O templo ali construído, chamado de igreja de São Paulo e São Pedro, foi o maior da Europa, até ser construída a catedral de São Pedro, em Roma. Era um excelente espécime de arquitetura romanesca. Após a Revolução Francesa, foi vendida a abadia, e muitos dos seus edifícios foram demolidos, com a passagem do tempo. Alguns edifícios da abadia, porém, continuam de pé, e vários itens das esculturas e dos tesouros originais encontram-se em vários museus. (AM)

CNIDO

Esse nome designa uma aldeia e uma península na antiga Cária que se projetavam da porção sudoeste da Ásia Menor, entre as ilhas de Rodes e de Cós. Nos tempos clássicos, era uma colônia grega, uma cidade comercial com conexões tanto com o Egito como com a Itália, já desde o século VI A.C. Havia ali uma escola de mágica e elaboradas instalações próprias para ritos religiosos, incluindo aquelas para a adoração à deusa Afrodite. Havia ali uma famosa estátua de Afrodite, esculpida por Praxíteles. A cidade era famosa por sua adoração idólatra, segundo nos diz Estrabão (xiv. par.965) e Plínio (*Hist. Nat.* xxxvi.15). O famoso astrônomo Eudoxo, era natural da ilha. Juntamente com a totalidade da Ásia Menor, a ilha de Cnido caiu sob o domínio persa, no século VI A.C. No século V A.C., a ilha tornou-se membro da liga de Delos, dominada por Atenas. Não é bem conhecida a sua história, nos períodos helênico e romano. Sabe-se que era uma cidade livre, na província da Ásia. Os romanos escreveram para a cidade de Cnido, em favor dos judeus, durante o tempo dos Macabeus (I Macabeus 15:23). Ali havia uma **população judaica, desde o século II A.C. Era uma importante cidade de centro marítimo**. Essa cidade, que ficava situada no fim de uma longa península, entre duas ilhas, Rodes e Cós, com seus dois portos, estava equipada para servir de ponto de partida e chegada do comércio. Paulo passou pela ilha em sua viagem para Roma, após seu período de aprisionamento em Jerusalém, Atos 27:7.

COA

Essa palavra aparece somente em Ezequiel 23:23. O profeta declara ali que o povo de Israel precisava ser punido, por haver adotado a idolatria e as noções fantásticas dos pagãos. Coa aparece entre os povos que influenciaram adversamente a Israel. Essa localidade, evidentemente, deve ser identificada com os Kutu, localizados a leste do rio Tigre e ao sul da porção inferior do rio Zabe, ou seja, a nordeste da cidade da Babilônia.

COABITAÇÃO

Essa palavra exprime a idéia de um homem e de uma mulher que convivem fora da relação matrimonial legal. De outras vezes, o termo é usado somente para referir-se ao ato sexual. Certa forma de coabitação tem aumentado dramaticamente em anos recentes, a saber, a de estudantes universitários. Uma das razões para isso é a razão econômica. É mais barato um casal alugar uma casa para viverem, do que cada qual viver separadamente, em um dormitório da universidade. Outra razão é que os padrões morais muito frouxos da sociedade moderna têm removido o estigma que antes era associado a uma situação similar, pelo que os estudantes sentem-se livres para viverem juntos, do ponto de vista da opinião pública. Uma outra razão é que estudantes que não dispõem de recursos financeiros para casarem-se, mas desenvolveram uma relação pessoal, querem viver juntos, sem as obrigações do casamento. Ainda outros simplesmente pensam que é mais interessante viver com um membro do sexo oposto, do que com alguém do mesmo sexo. Mas ainda há outra razão, a saber, o temor das enfermidades venéreas, porquanto existem várias delas que não têm cura. Os que assim pensam dizem que é melhor ter uma companhia constante, com o envolvimento de uma amizade especial, do que viver na promiscuidade, que a maioria dos estudantes universitários vêm praticando há longas décadas.

A *ética relativista*, naturalmente, afirma que a coabitação não é errada se as duas pessoas envolvidas se beneficiam mutuamente, se seu relacionamento não redunda em resultados prejudiciais para nenhum deles. Esse é o ponto de vista pragmático; e vários dos itens acima mencionados fazem a coabitação parecer benéfica, do ângulo relativista. Ver o artigo sobre o *Relativismo*.

A *ética absoluta*, isto é, a idéia de que existem padrões morais determinados por Deus, pela natureza, ou pelas demandas do próprio indivíduo, condena a prática da coabitação. A ética teísta, como também a ética da maioria das religiões, é uma forma de ética absoluta. A ética bíblica tem aspectos teístas e absolutos, pois ali fica entendido que as normas éticas procedem de Deus, e não dos atos e padrões relativistas dos homens. A fornicação é errada, sem importar o fato de que as despesas dos estudantes universitários aumentaram muito. O valor da verdade da ética teísta depende de quão fidedigna é a revelação divina, bem como de quão fidedigna é a razão. Ver sobre *Revelação*. Ver também I Cor. 6:18 quanto a um mandamento bíblico que tem aplicação a essa questão. Naturalmente, a Bíblia ensina que os mandamentos de Deus nos foram dados, não a fim de servirem de obstáculos, mas para ajudar-nos, porquanto são sempre benéficos a nós (Deu. 10:13). Pode-se mesmo argumentar que em nossos próprios dias, dentro da cena temporal, é bom negócio obedecer à Palavra de Deus, sem nada dizermos sobre o progresso da alma e sobre o julgamento vindouro. Ver o artigo geral sobre a *Ética*.

COATE, COATITAS

O termo hebraico **Kohate** significa «assembléia». Coate foi o segundo dos três filhos de Levi: Gérson, Coate e Merari (Gên. 46:11). Foi o pai de Anrão, Jizar, Hebrom e Uziel (Núm. 3:19). Acerca dele, porém, sabemos apenas que foi para o Egito, na companhia de Levi e Jacó (Gên. 46:11) e que sua irmã chamava-se Joquebede (Êxo. 6:18). Viveu em torno de 1870 A.C. Seus descendentes, os coatitas, formavam uma das três grandes divisões dos levitas, que continha a família sacerdotal que descendia Arão (Êxo. 6:18-20). Seus deveres específicos incluíam o de transportar a arca e os vasos sagrados (Núm. 4:15; 7:9). A herança deles (daqueles que não eram sacerdotes) cabia entre a meia-tribo de Manassés, em Efraim (I Crô. 6:61-70) e em Dã (Jos. 21:5,20,26).

Após a conquista da Palestina, os coatitas eram tratados conforme eram tratadas todas as famílias levíticas. Eles receberam cidades e pastagens, nada menos de dez (Jos. 21:20-26), quatro delas no território de Efraim, quatro outras no território de Dã, e duas no território da meia-tribo de Manassés. Nos dias de Davi, estiveram envolvidos no serviço da casa do Senhor. Hemã e Uriel foram os principais coatitas ocupados desse serviço. Eles ajudaram no retorno da arca a Israel, depois que a mesma fora tomada pelos filisteus (I Crô. 15:3-5). Também estiveram envolvidos em dois movimentos reformadores, a saber, aquele durante o reinado de Ezequias, entre 715 e 687 A.C. (II Crô. 29:12-16) e aquele durante o reinado de Josias, quando o templo de Jerusalém sofreu reparos. Zacarias e Mesulão eram levitas e coatitas que foram postos sobre o trabalho do templo (II Crô. 34:12).

COBERTA

No hebraico, **semikhah**, de sentido ainda incerto. A palavra aparece somente em Juí. 4:18, para indicar o artigo usado por Jael, mulher de Héber, queneu, para cobrir Sísera, general do rei cananeu Jabim, que por vinte anos vinha oprimindo duramente a Israel. Em batalha contra as forças dirigidas por Débora e Baraque, Sísera fugiu e refugiou-se na tenda de Jael. Apesar dele estar fugindo para não perder a vida, isso representava uma grande falta contra a intimidade e bom nome da esposa de um homem. Astutamente ela fingiu-se acolhedora, cobrindo-o com algum tipo de coberta. Mas, quando Sísera dormia de cansado, Jael apanhou uma estaca e cravou-a na fronte do general cananeu, o qual morreu. Os estudiosos reconhecem que a palavra hebraica em foco pode indicar um tapete, um cobertor, uma capa, etc., pelo que a tradução «coberta», usada em nossa Bíblia portuguesa, é boa, pois não define a natureza exata do artigo usado por Jael.

COBERTA PARA A CABEÇA, VÉU

A arqueologia tem descoberto muitas informações sobre as antigas cobertas para a cabeça. As evidências incluem pinturas, relevos e referências literárias. As descobertas arqueológicas mostram que os primeiros habitantes da Palestina andavam de cabeça descoberta. As primeiras cobertas para a cabeça eram simples faixas (I Reis 20:38,41; onde nossa versão portuguesa diz «venda»), ornamentadas de vários modos. As mulheres, naturalmente, usavam um véu que cobria totalmente os seus cabelos. Também punham panos na cabeça, quando transportavam cargas equilibradas no alto da cabeça. Ver o artigo sobre *Véu*. Os sacerdotes usavam turbantes de pano feitos de linho (Êxo. 39:28). Todas as cobertas dessa natureza eram tiradas em tempos de lamentação (Isa. 61:3; Eze. 24:17,23). Nessas ocasiões, a cabeça era coberta com as mãos, ou recoberta de pó ou cinzas (II Sam. 13:19; Lam. 2:10). O sumo sacerdote usava seu próprio tipo de turbante (Êxo. 28:4; 29:9; Lev. 8:13). Tanto os homens quanto as mulheres de alta classe usavam o *sanip*, uma coberta para a cabeça feita de pano retorcido.

Regulamentos Paulinos. O uso generalizado de cobertas para a cabeça, entre os homens, nos dias do Antigo Testamento, tem feito alguns questionarem os preceitos de Paulo a respeito, em I Cor. 11:4. Segundo ele, um homem não deveria orar ou profetizar com a cabeça coberta. É de presumir-se que os judeus da época apostólica não podiam participar das funções religiosas com a cabeça coberta. Porém, isso não impediria que eles usassem algum tipo de turbante, ou coisa parecida, em outras oportunidades. A regra de Paulo não estava alicerçada sobre meros costumes. Antes, ele afirma que essa regra estava baseada no fato de que o homem é a imagem de Deus, pelo que o homem não deveria desfigurar essa imagem, cobrindo-a por ocasião da adoração. Antes, essa imagem deveria ser evidente, por ocasião da adoração. Por outra parte, a mulher deve cobrir a cabeça, durante os cultos religiosos, mormente ao orar e profetizar, porque isso serve de sinal da sua sujeição ao marido. Ver o artigo geral sobre *Vestes*.

••• ••• •••

COBIÇA — COCEIRA

COBIÇA
Há várias palavras hebraicas e gregas envolvidas, a saber:

1. *Avvah*, «desejo por si mesmo». Palavra hebraica usada por quatro vezes: Deu. 5:21; Pro. 21:26; Sal. 45:11; Pro. 23:3.

2. *Chamad*, «desejar». Verbo hebraico usado por catorze vezes. Por exemplo: Êxo. 20:17; Jos. 7:21; Miq. 2:2; Deu. 5:21; 7:25; Jó 20:20; Isa. 1:29; 53:2.

3. *Batsa*, «ganhar (ilegalmente)». Palavra hebraica usada por oito vezes com o sentido de cobiçar. Por exemplo: Hab. 2:9; Pro. 1:19; 15:27.

4. *Epithuméo*, «fixar a mente sobre». Palavra grega usada por dezesseis vezes: Mat. 5:28; 13:17; Luc. 15:16; 16:21; 17:22; 22:15; Atos 20:33; Rom. 7:6; 13:9 (citando Êxo. 20:15,17); I Cor. 10:6; Gál. 5:17; I Tim. 3:1; Heb. 6:11; Tia. 4:2; I Ped. 1:12; Apo. 9:6.

5. *Orégomai*, «estender os braços para». Termo grego usado por três vezes: I Tim. 3:1; 6:10; Heb. 11:16.

6. *Pleoneksía*, «desejo de mais». Substantivo grego usado por dez vezes: Mar. 7:22; Luc. 12:15; Rom. 1:29; II Cor. 9:5; Efé. 4:19; 5:3; Col. 3:5; I Tes. 2:5; II Ped. 2:3,14. O adjetivo, *pleonéktes*, «cobiçoso», aparece por quatro vezes: I Cor. 5:10,11; 6:10; Efé. 5:5.

A cobiça pode ser definida como o desejo desordenado de adquirir coisas, posição social, fama, proeminência secular ou religiosa, etc. Pode incluir a tentativa de apossar-se do que pertence ao próximo. A cobiça geralmente aumenta com a idade, ao invés de diminuir, dando origem a certo número de males. A cobiça promove a alienação de Deus, a opressão e a crueldade contra o próximo, a traição e as manipulações e desonestidades de toda espécie. É um dos principais fatores por detrás de todas as guerras. Os indivíduos e os grupos mostram-se cobiçosos. As nações incorporam o princípio da cobiça em suas leis. Os hebreus condenavam esse pecado, que aparece como um dos dez mandamentos (que vide). Aparece em Êxodo 20:17. A mensagem é que coisa alguma pertencente a outrem, deve ser desejado. Quase sempre, o desejo desordenado da cobiça provoca alguma ação para que o cobiçoso adquira o que quer, ou para que persiga o possuidor do objeto ou da pessoa cobiçados. Esse mandamento chega perto do adultério, visto que uma das coisas que pode ser cobiçada é a esposa de outro homem.

O Novo Testamento Condena Também a Cobiça. Os cobiçosos anelam por ter mais dinheiro (Atos 20:33; I Tim. 6:9; Rom. 7:7). A cobiça pode expressar-se sob a forma de violência (II Cor. 2:11; 7:2). Mas Jesus repudiou o espírito ganancioso (Mat. 7:22). A cobiça é alistada entre os pecados frisados por Paulo, em Efésios 4:19. A cobiça é uma forma de auto-adoração que expulsa Deus de nossas vidas (Efé. 5:5; Col. 3:5). Aparece na lista dos vícios dos povos pagãos, em Romanos 1:29. Apesar de não ser especificamente alistada entre as obras da carne, em Gálatas 5:19-21, a cobiça é uma das causas de várias daquelas obras carnais, como o adultério, o ódio, as dissensões, a beligerância, etc., devendo ser incluída entre as «tais coisas» que Paulo mencionou, e que não permitem que uma pessoa chegue ao reino de Deus (Gál. 5:21).

Exemplos Bíblicos de Cobiça. Labão (Gên. 31:41); Acã (Jos. 7:21); os filhos de Eli (I Sam. 2:12); Saul (I Sam. 15:9,19); Acabe (I Reis 21:2); os nobres dos judeus (Nee. 5:7); a Babilônia (Jer. 51:13); Judas Iscariotes (Mat. 26:14,15); os fariseus (Luc. 16:14); Ananias (Atos 5:1-10); Félix (Atos 24:26); Balaão (II Ped. 2:15; Jud. 11).

A cobiça é alistada como um dos pecados mortais, pela Igreja Católica Romana. Ver o artigo sobre *Pecados Mortais e Veniais*. (TOR S)

COBRA Ver **Serpentes (Serpentes Venenosas)**.

COBRE
O cobre é um elemento metálico não ferroso que ocorre em estado metálico livre, na natureza. A arqueologia tem mostrado que o cobre já era usado em cerca de 8000 A.C. Os objetos eram moldados a marteladas. — Foi o substituto da pedra, usada pelos homens neolíticos. Talvez desde 6000 A.C. o cobre vem sendo moldado em moldes, assumindo objetos de muitos formatos. Em cerca de 5000 A.C., apareceram armas e instrumentos de muitos tipos, feitos de cobre. Muitos desses objetos têm sido encontrados pelos arqueólogos nos túmulos antigos do Egito e em outros lugares, onde, supostamente, serviriam aos falecidos. Em cerca de 3700 A.C., esse metal foi fundido juntamente com o estanho, sendo produzido o bronze (que vide). A julgar pelas observações feitas por Hesíodo e Lucrécio, a arte do fabrico de instrumentos de cobre é mais antiga que a do ferro. Era encontrado em grandes massas, podia ser fundido e moldado com maior facilidade do que o ferro, e isso o tornava uma opção preferível. O trecho de Deuteronômio 8:9 indica que havia muito cobre na Palestina. Davi deixou grande quantidade desse metal, para ser usado na construção do templo de Jerusalém (I Crô. 22:3-14). Muitos dos vasos usados nesse templo eram feitos de cobre (Lev. 6:28; Esd. 8:17), como também armas, capacetes, armaduras, escudos e lanças (I Sam. 17:5,6,38). Também havia correntes feitas desse material (Juí. 16:21).

Chipre era um dos grandes centros produtores de cobre, desde cerca de 3000 A.C. E suas minas de cobre era uma das razões pelas quais egípcios, assírios fenícios, gregos, persas e romanos tanto se interessavam por controlar a ilha. Os romanos chamavam o minério de cobre de *aes cyprium*, isto é, «minério de Chipre». Até hoje o cobre é extraído em Chipre.

A arqueologia tem mostrado que havia minas de cobre na península do Sinai, desde cerca de 3800 A.C. As condições que prevaleciam nessas minas são mencionadas em uma inscrição pertencente ao reinado de Amenemete III, de cerca de 1800 A.C.

Moisés instruiu o povo de Israel a buscar cobre (Deu. 8:9), e um dos acampamentos relacionados às vagueações por quarenta anos, no deserto, Dofca, mencionado em Números 33:12, contava com depósitos de cobre nas proximidades. Esse lugar tem sido identificado com a moderna Serabit el-Khadem. Ali os egípcios extraíam cobre e turquesas desde os tempos mais remotos. Salomão extraía cobre da Arabá. Havia fundições perto de Eziom-Geber, no começo do golfo de Áqaba, bem como em várias localidades ao longo do vale do rio Jordão. Esse metal era exportado a partir de Eziom-Geber (I Reis 9:26-28).

O cobre, em seu estado natural, tem cor vermelho-cobre, é dúctil e maleável. Algumas vezes é encontrado sob a forma de folhas ou placas, mas geralmente é descoberto sob a forma de grandes massas. (S Z)

COCEIRA
Ver sobre as **Doenças**.

••• ••• •••

COCHEIRO

Ver o artigo geral sobre as **Carruagens**. No Antigo Testamento encontramos o termo «cocheiro» (I Reis 22:34 e II Crô. 18:33; no hebraico *rakkab*), em alusão ao carro de guerra de Acabe. — Algumas vezes, um carro de guerra era tripulado por um único guerreiro ou capitão; mas, usualmente, havia um cocheiro que guiava o carro, deixando o capitão livre para a sua tarefa de matar. E também podia haver um terceiro homem, o escudeiro.

CODEX

Vem do latim, onde, a princípio, significava «tronco», depois «casca» e finalmente, uma «tábua», tanto aquela munida de uma camada de cera, como aquela usada para servir de capa de um livro. Portanto, a palavra veio a indicar um LIVRO, em contraste com um rolo. O formato de livro é bastante antigo, sendo usado para receber grande variedade de anotações, como uma caderneta, um livro de contabilidade ou um livro de estudos. Alguns intérpretes supõem que alguns dos livros originais do Novo Testamento foram preparados em forma de livro, e não em forma de rolos. O uso de livros parece ter surgido primeiramente no Ocidente. Por volta do século III D.C., esse formato passou a ser preferido, com o prejuízo do formato de rolo, e as Escrituras cristãs, a partir desse tempo, começaram a ser registradas por escrito quase exclusivamente no formato dos livros. Os códices eram manuscritos, encadernados à mão, e feitos de vários materiais, como papel, tecido ou velino. O vocábulo «codex» veio a assumir o sentido de coletânea ou código de leis, visto que esse código geralmente aparecia em uma coleção de livros.

Há muitos antigos e importantes códices das Escrituras. No artigo sobre os *Manuscritos*, oferecemos a descrição sobre vários deles. Ver sobre *Manuscritos do Novo Testamento*, III. Ali aparece uma lista, em forma de tabela, que inclui importantes detalhes, inclusive o tipo de texto. No fim daquela seção, são descritos individualmente os seguintes importantes manuscritos unciais: A, B, C, D, Aleph, I, L, W e Pi. Ver o artigo separado sobre os *Papiros Chester Beatty* e os *Papiros Bodmer*. O artigo sobre os *Manuscritos* também descreve os mais importantes códices das versões latina, siríaca, copta, etc.

CÓDIGO DE HAMURABI

Ver sobre **Hamurabi, Código de**.

CÓDIGO DE MANU

Trata-se de um poema métrico do hinduísmo, com 2.685 versos, que apresenta o ponto de vista ortodoxo do bramanismo sobre religião, leis, costumes e política. Seu conteúdo essencial distribui-se como segue:

1. São descritos os quatro estilos de vida, ou quatro ordens ou *ashramas*, a saber, os estilos do estudante, do dono-de-casa, do eremita e do asceta. Nessa lista, o melhor estilo seria o do dono-de-casa. Porém, segundo esse tratado, é aconselhável que o homem experimente algo de todos os quatro estilos de vida. Assim, o estilo do eremita é recomendado a fim de que o indivíduo possa tentar liberar-se das fortes influências que o mundo físico tem exercido sobre ele, a fim de receber iluminação espiritual.

2. Os deveres das quatro castas são esboçadas, como segue: a. Os *bramas*: ensinar, estudar, realizar sacrifícios, aceitar dádivas da parte dos homens puros. b. Os *kshatriyas*: esses seriam os protetores da sociedade. Entre os seus deveres particulares, eles devem proteger o próprio sistema de castas. c. Os *vaisyas*: esses deveriam atarefar-se na agricultura e no comércio. d. Os *sudras*: esses eram os que trabalhavam manualmente. Se servissem bem, era-lhes prometido o renascimento em uma casta superior, na próxima vez em que se reencarnassem (ver sobre a *Reencarnação*).

3. As mulheres eram honradas, mas conservadas sob a dependência dos homens, antes de tudo pelo pai, então pelo marido, e, na perda deste, pelos filhos homens. Às esposas fiéis é dada a promessa de compartilharem da sorte que seus respectivos maridos obtiveram na outra vida.

4. A maior de todas as virtudes é o respeito por todas as formas de vida, encontrando nelas algo do Grande Eu. (P)

CÓDIGO DE SANTIDADE

Ver **Santidade, Código da**.

CÓDIGO SACERDOTAL

Nas obras bíblicas em inglês, a abreviação desse código é *P*. Essa é considerada a mais recente e a mais ampla das quatro camadas literárias e legislativas principais do Pentateuco. Essas quatro camadas literárias chamam-se «J» «E» «D» e «P», supostas fontes de material histórico. No artigo sobre o Pentateuco, nesta enciclopédia, prestamos informações sobre essa questão, onde é abordada a história da alta crítica (que vide), no que concerne aos cinco primeiros livros da Bíblia. Presumivelmente, o documento «P» teria sido a fonte para os trechos de Êxo. 25—31; 35—40; Lev. 1—16; Núm. 11:1—10:28, além de porções dispersas pelo livro de Gênesis, Êxo. 1—24; Lev. 17—16; Núm. 11—36 e porções de Deu. 31—34. Alguns estudiosos também atribuem considerável porção do livro de Josué a essa fonte. O documento «P» é considerado como o mais recente dentre as fontes literárias do Pentateuco, estando inspirado pelo espírito do legalismo e do separatismo que, presumivelmente, surgiu entre os exilados judeus na Babilônia, nos séculos VI e VII A.C. Refletiria os pontos de vista de sacerdotes ativistas descendentes de Sadoque (que vide) que teriam retornado da Babilônia em 458 A.C., e depois. Foi composta na Palestina, essencialmente no quinto século A.C., e registra (falando em termos gerais) os rituais religiosos do templo em Jerusalém, de c. 400 A.C., e depois. Foram os escritores e redatores posteriores de P (S=código sacerdotal) que, antes dos outros, incorporaram o mais antigo *código de santidade* (Lev. caps. 17-26, dos séculos III a VI A.C.), nas escrituras deles, e então combinaram os documentos mais antigos, J, E e D, com seus próprios escritos, assim formando o *hexateuco* (que vide). Depois, por razões teológicas, omitiram Josué, e com isto, formaram o Pentateuco. A teoria inteira, com críticas, é discutida no artigo sobre o *Pentateuco*. Aqui eu tenho retido as abreviações inglesas, que naquele artigo são esclarecidas com seus equivalentes portugueses. Ver as abreviações separadamente: J=Jeová; E=Elohim; D=escritores-redatores de Deuteronômio; P=priestly, ou em português: S=Sacerdotal.

CODORNIZ

Embora a origem do nome seja incerta no hebraico, é quase certo que a tradução «codorniz» seja correta, porque nenhuma outra ave ajusta-se tão bem à narrativa bíblica (Êxo. 16:13; Núm. 11:31,32; Sal. 105:40). Tal ave teria de ser limpa e teria de viver em bandos. A revoada miraculosa de codornizes ocorreu por duas vezes: no deserto de Sim, a sudoeste da península do Sinai, cerca de seis semanas após a partida do Egito; e em Quibrote-Ataavá, não muito distante dali, um ano mais tarde. Na primavera e no outono, o vento leva essas pesadas aves migratórias para o Egito, e, em número mais reduzido, para a península da Arábia. A carne da codorniz é saborosa, também apreciada pelos egípcios (Heródoto 2.77; Aristóteles, *Hist.* 7:14; Plínio, *Hist. Nat.* 10.24,64). O elemento miraculoso do caso foi o momento preciso do fenômeno.

Há alguma dificuldade quanto à tradução do trecho de Núm. 11:31. Há versões que dizem que as aves ficaram espalhadas pelo arraial dos israelitas «cerca de dois côvados sobre a terra» (conforme diz nossa versão portuguesa). A RSV, em inglês, dá a entender que elas voam baixo, cerca de dois côvados (um metro) do chão, uma tradução preferível. As codornizes precisam da ajuda de vento forte para voar longas distâncias, embora possam voar vigorosamente pequenas distâncias sem tal ajuda. Isso explica a menção do «vento do Senhor», em Núm. 11:31.

COELE-SÍRIA

Esse nome vem do grego, e tem o sentido de «Síria oca», expressão usada para indicar certas porções da Síria-Palestina. Existe desde o século IV A.C., referindo-se ao grande vale que se estende desde a planície de 'Amq, ao norte, até o mar Morto, ao sul. Era expressão usada especificamente para aludir à planície de Biqâ, entre as montanhas do Líbano e do Antilíbano. Nos tempos helenistas, monarcas selêucidas e ptolomeus exerceram ali a sua autoridade. No século III A.C., os Ptolomeus controlavam a região, chamando-a simplesmente de *Síria*. Porém, em 200 A.C., os Selêucidas conquistaram essa porção da Síria, e, a fim de distingui-la de certas porções do mesmo território, que eles já controlavam, chamaram-na de Coele-Síria. Os membros da família dos Hasmoneanos usaram o termo em sentido mais restrito, aplicando-o somente à planície de Biqâ. No século II D.C., Sétimo Severo criou uma nova província que incluía a totalidade do norte da Síria, excluindo a planície de Biqâ, usando esse nome como designação. Naquele tempo, a planície de Biqâ tornou-se parte da Síria Fenícia. A Bíblia canônica não envolve o nome, mas este aparece nos livros apócrifos, em I Macabeus 10:69; II Macabeus 3:5,8; 4:4; 8:8; 10:11; I Esdras 2:17,24,27; 6:29; 7:1; 8:68, com alguns paralelos em Esdras 4:11,16,20; 6:8,13; 8:36. Em I Esdras 6:3 a área é simplesmente chamada de Síria. A Coele-Síria era uma divisão administrativa da província da Síria, após a ocupação romana, em 64 A.C. Herodes foi nomeado governador militar dessa região por Sexto César, em 47 A.C., e novamente, por Cássio, em 43 A.C. (ND S Z)

COELESTIUS

Foi o mais notável seguidor de Pelágio (que vide), promovendo a mesma doutrina. Coelestius era muito mais jovem e ousado que seu mestre. Treinado como advogado, provavelmente ele era italiano; mas abandonou a carreira de advogado para seguir uma vida de ascetismo. Quando Roma foi saqueada pelos godos (410 D.C.), os dois amigos atravessaram o mar para a África. E quando Pelágio partiu para a Palestina, Coelestius permaneceu em Cartago à espera de ordenação ao ministério. Mas ele foi acusado de certos erros graves de doutrina. E mesmo quando ele se defendeu, afirmando que ele se manifestara sobre pontos acerca dos quais a Igreja nunca se pronunciara oficialmente, foi excluído e condenado. Contudo, ele partiu para Éfeso onde foi ordenado. As datas de seu nascimento e morte não são conhecidas.

COELHO Ver sobre Lebre.

COELHO (ÁRGANAZ)

No hebraico, **shaphan**, que ocorre em Lev. 11:5; Deu. 14:7; Sal. 104:18 e Pro. 30:26.

Geralmente é difícil identificar itens da flora e da fauna, na Bíblia. Os nomes antigos não foram cunhados de acordo com alguma classificação científica. Essa palavra hebraica tem sido variegadamente traduzida, como «lebre», «texugo». Os eruditos modernos preferem pensar em um animal cuja aparência externa o classificaria juntamente com o coelho. Nossa versão portuguesa, com a tradução arganaz, dá a entender que se trataria antes de um animal parecido com o rato do campo. A determinação do animal envolvido requer a observação do que a Bíblia diz sobre sua natureza e seus hábitos, além do conhecimento se a Palestina era habitat desse animal, ou não. A espécie preferida pelos estudiosos modernos é um animal pequeno, semelhante ao coelho, dotado de cascos nas patas. Seu moderno nome científico é *Procavia*, que abriga-se nas fendas das rochas. Também há uma variedade que é arbórea, cujo nome científico é *Dendrohyrax*. Portanto, não estamos realmente tratando com algum rato ou coelho. A referência de Deu. 14:7 de que esse animal rumina mas não tem o casco fendido, e a de Sal. 104:18, que diz que ele se refugia nas rochas, concorda com os hábitos da Procavia. Embora similar ao coelho, quanto ao tamanho e ao peso, bem como à aparência externa, anatomicamente o animal é classificado como aparentado do elefante. As espécies encontradas nos jardins zoológicos modernos usualmente são da variedade síria, o animal referido na Bíblia. O Antigo Testamento proíbe o uso desse animal na alimentação humana, embora não saibamos os motivos exatos dessa proibição. Os árabes consomem esse animal, o qual também é muito caçado em certas regiões da África. Dizem que sua carne é rija e seca. Atualmente, esse animal é muito mais raro na Palestina do que nos dias antigos, mas ainda pode ser encontrado na Alta Galiléia. (WALK)

COENTRO

No hebraico, **gad**, termo que figura apenas por duas vezes: Êxo. 16:31 e Núm. 11:7. O coentro é uma semente aromática redonda. A planta do coentro (*Coriandrum sativum*) medra nativa na Palestina e em países circunvizinhos. Suas sementes são globulares, e, quando secas, são agradáveis ao paladar e ao olfato. Podem ser salpicadas com açúcar, tornando-se uma espécie de confeito. As sementes de coentro eram usadas para dar sabor aos alimentos. Estamos informados de que as partículas do maná (que vide) tinham o formato de sementes de coentro. Ver Êxo. 16:31 e Núm. 11:7. Modernamente, usa-se o coentro para dar maior sabor ao gim ou então para dar certo sabor aos doces ou ao pão.

COERÇÃO

A coerção é um ato mental ou físico que exerce uma pressão sobre alguma pessoa, ou por outra pessoa, ou pela lei ou por alguma circunstância. O

COERÊNCIA — COGITO, ERGO SUM

valor moral da coerção legítima depende dos propósitos e motivos envolvidos. A mensagem do evangelho, por si mesma, com seu código moral e espiritual, é uma coerção legítima. Porém, também há uma coerção ilegítima e criminosa, quando uma pessoa é forçada a fazer algo, ou a refrear-se de fazer alguma coisa. A extorsão é um exemplo radical de coerção não violenta, embora também haja atos violentos, envolvidos na coerção ilegítima. Ver Sal. 140:11; Luc. 3:4 quanto a menções bíblicas dessa natureza. Também existe a tirania política que cria uma variedade social de coerção, cujo alvo é atingir as massas populares, e não algum indivíduo particular. As leis injustas são um outro exemplo de coerção social ilegítima. A escravidão é outro exemplo de coerção social injusta. Essa escravidão pode manifestar-se através de meios econômicos, por parte de indivíduos contra indivíduos, ou de nações contra nações. Até mesmo crentes envolvem-se nesse erro grave, quando pagam salários inadequados aos seus empregados ou a pessoas que lhes prestam serviços. (H)

COERÊNCIA, TEORIA DA VERDADE DA

Em meu artigo sobre o **Conhecimento e a Fé Religiosa**, discuti sobre muitas teorias padronizadas da verdade, entre as quais destaco agora a teoria da verdade da coerência. De modo geral, podemos dizer que a ciência depende de teorias empíricas da verdade, como a da correspondência e a do pragmatismo. O *racionalismo*, por outra parte, depende do valor da verdade de certas idéias, que são coerentes com outras idéias. A teoria da verdade da coerência também está vinculada ao idealismo (que vide). Ela afirma que a verdade se estabelece, essencialmente, dentro do contexto de um sistema. O progresso no conhecimento é um avanço na direção de um único e completo sistema de pensamento; e a verdade só pode ser predicada a esse sistema. Aquilo que normalmente chamamos de proposições verdadeiras ou falsas poderia ser melhor intitulado de parcialmente verdadeiro e de parcialmente falso. A experiência humana faz parte do sistema. O conjunto das verdades incorpora todas as verdades individuais, e cada verdade subentende o conjunto inteiro. Uma idéia é verdadeira quando se ajusta ao sistema abrangente do universo ou da realidade. Mas, com freqüência, não conhecemos o grau de verdade de qualquer idéia que tenhamos; e essa é exatamente a razão pela qual o nosso conhecimento sempre está em estado de evolução.

Filósofos bem conhecidos que têm defendido essa teoria foram Leibniz, Spinoza, Hegel e Bradley. O cristianismo, naturalmente, concorda em essência com essa teoria, porquanto, para o cristianismo, a verdade é uma só — a verdade que se deriva de Deus, A Fonte Única onde toda a verdade é encontrada, especificamente na pessoa de Cristo, segundo ele mesmo disse: «Eu sou o caminho, e a verdade, e a vida...» (João 14:6). E os meios para descobrirmos essa verdade, segundo afirma essa teoria, são essencialmente racionais, e também através da revelação.

A Coerência como um critério da Verdade. Cumpre-nos estabelecer a distinção entre uma teoria e um critério. Uma verdade é estabelecida como um critério mediante a sua coerência com outras proposições que são tidas como verazes. Para exemplificar, comecemos por alguma verdade moral pronunciada na Bíblia. Dali poderíamos deduzir, mediante o princípio do que é coerente com essa verdade, muitas outras verdades. «Não matarás» é um mandamento. Pode apontar para a violência física, mental ou moral. Jesus considerava que esse pecado manifesta-se até mesmo nos pensamentos e nas intenções, e não apenas nos atos realizados. A maioria dos princípios morais têm corolários que se originam do princípio de coerência. (F P)

COFE

Essa é a décima nona letra do alfabeto hebraico. Em Salmos 119, a letra é usada para introduzir a décima nona porção. Ali, cada versículo começa com essa letra, no original hebraico. Ver sobre o *Alfabeto*.

COGITABILITAS, PRINCÍPIO DA

Esse é um princípio que era defendido por Christian August Crusius (que vide). Os princípios lógicos da identidade e da contradição dependem desse princípio. Aquilo que é *cogitável*, é *pensável*. Aquilo que não pode ser concebido como falso é verdadeiro; aquilo que não pode ser concebido de modo nenhum é falso. (P)

COGITATIO

Essa é a palavra latina para indicar a faculdade do pensamento ou da reflexão. Foi termo empregado por Spinoza (que vide), a fim de designar, juntamente com a extensão, os dois atributos de Deus, conforme são conhecidos pelo homem.

••• ••• •••

COGITO, ERGO SUM

Essas são as palavras latinas para «Penso, portanto existo». Foi a famosa declaração de Descartes (que vide), mediante a qual ele estabeleceu sua primeira certeza. Descartes buscava o elemento da certeza através da dúvida, ou, dizendo-se a mesma coisa, o conhecimento por via do ceticismo (que vide), assim revertendo o impacto do ceticismo. Ele pensava que devemos duvidar de tudo quanto pode ser posto em dúvida; e o que restar, depois disso, torna-se uma certeza. Ele partia do ser humano, conforme se manifestava nele mesmo. Ao dizer, «Penso, portanto existo», ele sentia que havia estabelecido a certeza de sua própria existência, pois, se existe o processo do pensamento, deve haver um ser *pensante*. Os lógicos têm objetado a essa abordagem, afirmando que ninguém pode predicar a existência. Não podemos dizer que «Isto ou aquilo existe», e, só com isso, garantir que qualquer coisa existe, exceto sob a forma de uma declaração. Apesar dessa ser uma boa regra geral, a declaração de Descartes contém uma lógica e uma convicção que é difícil de contradizer. Esse tipo de argumento havia sido antecipado por Agostinho, em sua obra *Cidade de Deus* (que vide), na qual ele afirma: «Si fallor, sum», que significa: «Se estou enganado, existo». Pois, para que haja um engano, então deve haver alguém que é enganado. Campanella (que vide) asseverou a mesma coisa quando disse: «A única certeza que pode ter é a da sua própria existência; mas, após análise, isso contém o conhecimento tanto do mundo quanto de Deus». O homem encontra em si mesmo os vestígios do Ser Divino. Esses raciocínios dependem, quanto ao seu conteúdo de valor, da validade da razão como conhecedora da verdade. Ver sobre o *Racionalismo*. (EP P)

COGNIÇÃO

Esse vocábulo vem do latim **cognitio**, «conhecimento» ou «reconhecimento». A palavra refere-se tanto ao processo de cognição quanto ao próprio conhecimento. Há várias teorias do conhecimento em competição. Provi um artigo sobre o *Conhecimento e a Fé Religiosa*, onde apresento as teorias básicas do conhecimento. Consideradas em seu conjunto, essas teorias, bem como outros dados acerca do conhecimento, são chamadas *Gnosiologia*, na filosofia, ou então *Epistemologia*, dentro do estudo científico do conhecimento. A teoria do conhecimento é um dos seis ramos tradicionais da filosofia (que vide). O termo *cognição* também envolve questões relacionadas à percepção, à memória, à intuição e ao juízo.

COGNITIVO

Um termo filosófico que significa estes pontos: 1. Os processos mentais, mormente aqueles relacionados à compreensão, à aquisição de conhecimento, aos processos volitivos, às crenças, aos desejos e intenções. 2. As declarações verazes ou falsas, em contraste com outras, que não podem ser assim classificadas, como ordens e exclamações, que, apesar de significativas, não podem ser consideradas quanto ao seu valor de verdade. Alguns filósofos céticos e positivistas vêem todas as declarações de avaliação, incluindo as de cunho moral, como destituídas de valor de verdade. Supostamente, essas declarações seriam apenas reações pessoais às situações circunstanciais com base em considerações pragmáticas. (F)

COGNOSCENDUM

Vem do latim, **cognoscere**, «conhecer». A palavra aponta para qualquer *objeto do conhecimento*, sem importar se verídico, fictício, abstrato ou ideal.

COHEN, HERMANN

Suas datas foram 1842-1918. Foi um filósofo neokantiano alemão. Nasceu em Coswig, Alemanha. Foi professor na Universidade de Marburgo, e fundador da Escola de Marburgo do neokantianismo (que vide).
Idéias:
1. Ele se opunha a qualquer conceito de conhecimento «anterior». Antes, todo o conhecimento nos chegaria através da experiência diária. Ele contradizia a idéia da coisa em si mesma, de Kant, como a entidade absoluta. Para ele, isso tem de permanecer como um dado desconhecido.
2. A filosofia e o conhecimento desenvolver-se-iam das categorias da cognição. Ele aplicava as categorias de Kant, ainda com maior elaboração. Ver o artigo sobre as *Categorias*. Ao aplicar as categorias, ele trabalhava nas três áreas específicas da lógica, da ética e da estética.
3. Para ele, a lógica é a elaboração das categorias da compreensão física e matemática.
4. A ética é uma ciência das categorias morais, dependendo da vontade pura e da idéia de obrigação.
5. A estética é a ciência das categorias do sentimento puro.
6. A religião. Após Cohen ter-se retirado da vida ativa, ele ensinou, por algum tempo, em um seminário de rabinos, em Berlim; e em seus últimos anos, modificou algumas de suas opiniões. Então ele não mais subordinava a religião à filosofia, mas chegou a crer que se trata de um fator independente da existência humana. Várias obras estabeleceram-no como a influência dominante da filosofia subseqüente dos judeus alemães.
Obras: *Kant's Theory of Experience; Kant's Foundation of Aesthetics; System of Philosophy; Logic of Pure Knowledge; Ethics of Pure Will; Aesthetics of Pure Feeling*. (EP F P)

COHEN, MORRIS RAPHAEL

Nasceu em 1880 e faleceu em 1947. Nasceu na Rússia e emigrou para a América do Norte em sua juventude. Foi professor na Faculdade da Cidade de Nova Iorque.
Idéias:
1. A fim de progredir na filosofia, o indivíduo deve formular problemas de natureza tal que possam ser manuseados de forma proveitosa. Ele se opunha ao dogmatismo, tanto no empirismo (ciência) como na razão (racionalismo).
2. Para ele, a ciência progride a cada vez em que descobre relações objetivas dentro do fluxo da experiência humana. Uma das tarefas da filosofia consistiria em prover uma base para esse movimento.
3. A lógica deveria prover regras referentes às relações invariáveis de todos os objetos possíveis (realismo lógico). As leis científicas fornecem-nos as regras invariáveis para serem aplicadas a domínios especializados.
4. Ele pensava no princípio de polaridade (que vide) é indispensável em todo raciocínio filosófico.
Escritos: *Reason and Nature; Law and the Social Order; An Introduction to Logic and Scientific Method; The Meaning of Human History; Reason and Law*. (EP P)

COINCIDÊNCIA SIGNIFICATIVA

Todos nós temos visto **aparentes** coincidências que nos surpreendam e admiram. Certo dia, eu estava lendo, em uma enciclopédia, um artigo sobre Neal Armstrong, simplesmente porque meus olhos caíram sobre o artigo a respeito dele, quando eu estava procurando por outra coisa. Armstrong foi o primeiro homem a caminhar à face da lua, pelo que o seu nome atraiu-me a atenção. Naquele mesmo dia, Armstrong estava visitando o Brasil, representando uma companhia fabricante de aviões; e, à noite, li um artigo, em um jornal, que versava sobre ele. Coincidência? Na semana passada, fiz uma viagem a outra cidade. No caminho, eu fui pensando sobre um antigo amigo. Quando cheguei àquela cidade, entre a multidão que se encontrava na rodoviária daquela cidade, totalmente por acidente, encontrei-me com meu amigo. Coincidência ou telepatia? Faz agora um mês, tive um sonho com um antigo amigo, com quem eu não entrava em contacto fazia alguns anos. À noite, três dias mais tarde, recebi um telefonema daquele amigo. (E aquele amigo, que é este tradutor, lembra-se de que telefonou para o Dr. Champlin por sentir-se impelido por forte senso de que era preciso entrar em contacto com ele. Peguei o automóvel e percorri nove quilômetros até achar um «orelhão azul», isto é, um telefone interurbano). Coincidência? Precognição por meio de sonho? A mão orientadora de Deus?

Richard Bach conta a história de como ele estava pilotando um antigo avião (algo que ele tem feito como passatempo, há muito tempo) e acabou tendo de fazer um pouso forçado, no campo de um fazendeiro. A aterrissagem foi difícil, tendo-se quebrado o suporte de uma das rodas dianteiras do aparelho. O avião, como já dissemos, era antigo, e apenas alguns exemplares tinham sido feitos. Parecia não haver como encontrar uma peça de reposição para a roda. Talvez tivesse de ser encomendada especialmente da fábrica. Quando o fazendeiro aproximou-se de Bach e seu avião, perguntou: «Posso ajudá-lo em alguma coisa?» Bach respondeu, em tom de ironia: «Sim, dê-me um suporte de roda para este antigo aeroplano!» Em seguida, Bach deu os nomes técnicos, os números e as especificações. O fazendeiro saiu quase correndo para o seu celeiro e procurou ali por uns poucos minutos. Quando chegou novamente diante de Bach, entregou-lhe a peça que ele precisava. — Isso ficou registrado no livro que Bach escreveu, intitulado «Nothing by Chance!» Todos nós, sem dúvida, temos sabido de coincidências similares, algumas simplesmente fantásticas. E então perguntamos: «Será que tudo não passou, realmente, de mera coincidência?»

Consideremos Este Caso. Meu irmão, que é missionário evangélico, é bom amigo do presidente de uma faculdade num estado do sul dos Estados Unidos da América, veio a conhecer esse homem quando visitava faculdades para promover a vocação missionária entre os estudantes. Mas eu mesmo entrei em contato com aquele presidente de faculdade. Sucedeu que, em certa época de minha vida, estive procurando por uma posição de professor em alguma escola evangélica, nos Estados Unidos; e escrevi para aquele presidente de faculdade. Um diálogo entre esse homem e meu irmão revelou o fato de que ele, nos seus dias estudantis, foi *colega de quarto* de um bom amigo meu, que vive no Brasil. Poderíamos comentar com um simples: «Como o mundo é pequeno!» Mas, não será que algo maior está em operação, em casos dessa natureza?

Quando eu estava procurando reunir fundos para a publicação de *O Novo Testamento Interpretado*, escrevi para um ministro anglicano em Londres, que era oficial de uma organização promotora de literatura, daquela denominação. Então esse oficial foi a Caracas, na Venezuela, levando minha carta consigo. Ali, ele encontrou-se com um homem, membro de uma missão evangélica interessadíssima pelo meu trabalho. Esse encontro foi inteiramente casual. Meu amigo, em Caracas, começou a falar sobre o meu projeto do comentário, tentando interessar o homem de Londres acerca do mesmo. Foi um pequeno momento dramático quando o homem de Londres puxou do bolso a carta que eu lhe enviara do Brasil! «Tremenda coincidência!» diríamos. Ali estavam três pessoas e uma carta. Uma delas vinha do Brasil, outra de Londres, e outra era de Caracas. Algo as reuniu ali. O que seria esse algo? Coincidência pura ou propósito divino?

O que é uma Coincidência? Diz um certo dicionário: «Uma notável ocorrência de acontecimentos, idéias, etc., ao mesmo tempo ou da mesma maneira, aparentemente por mero acidente». Isso informa-nos verbalmente no que consiste uma coincidência; mas não nos diz por que tais coisas sucedem, se é que há um *por quê* a ser investigado.

Idéias:
1. **Carl Jung interessou-se pelo problema.** Ele supunha que eventos não relacionados entre si, como fatores de causa e efeito, podem coincidir de maneira significativa. Embora um evento possa não estar relacionado a outro, por meio de qualquer causa, isso significa que temos aí coincidências significativas. A fim de exemplificar, ele falou em dois tipos de adivinhação. Ele supunha que os planetas e suas configurações na realidade não exercem qualquer influência sobre nós, do ponto de vista de qualquer *força física*. Todavia, ele presumia que há alguma verdade na astrologia, porque as configurações das posições dos planetas *correspondem* às vidas dos indivíduos mediante coincidências significativas. Por detrás de tais coincidências, que não ocorrem por mero acidente, deveríamos perceber alguma grande Mente planejadora e executora. Chamamos tal correspondência de coincidência, meramente porque não sabemos como essa correspondência ocorre. Um outro exemplo mencionado por Jung é o *I Ching* (que vide), o qual, presumivelmente, opera mediante a pura chance, mas que produz alguns resultados deveras chocantes.

2. *As Piadas da Natureza.* Algumas coincidências poderiam ser espécies de piadas cósmicas. Digamos que nossos anjos guardiães, ou outras forças espirituais que estão interessadas por nossas vidas, tenham um certo senso de humor. Algumas coincidências espetaculares poderiam ser algumas piadas contadas por essas forças. É como se elas dissessem para nós: «Vejam como tudo não passa de uma loucura!» Não obstante, essas piadas revestem-se de significado, pois não são *apenas* piadas. Essas entidades espirituais dizem-se através dessas aberrações: «Vocês não estão sozinhos. Há padrões e planos que estão sendo postos em execução!» Uma coincidência é apenas um pequeno sinal disso.

3. *O Tiquismo.* Essa palavra vem do termo grego que significa «acaso», «sorte». É provável que *algumas* coisas neste mundo aconteçam de modo inteiramente fortuito, não se revestindo de qualquer significação. De fato, algumas coincidências poderiam dever-se à mera chance. Entretanto, muitas dessas coincidências não nos permitem pensar que essa explicação explica tudo.

4. *Sinais de Desígnio.* Poderíamos supor, provavelmente de forma correta, que há algum intricado desígnio que nos une a outras pessoas, e que certos acontecimentos servem de sinal disso. É possível que o lema de Bach, «Nada acontece por acaso!», seja um tanto exagerado. Porém, quero afirmar a meus leitores que não penso que haja exemplos em número demasiado de tiquismo puro. Ver o artigo separado sobre *Chance*, que desenvolve mais plenamente esse assunto.

COINERÊNCIA

Essa palavra vem do latim **circumincessio**, que indica a doutrina que denota a interpenetração das três pessoas da Trindade, mediante o que uma delas invariavelmente encontra-se nas outras duas, e elas estão nela. A base neotestamentária dessa doutrina encontra-se em João 10:28-38. Novaciano (que vide) foi o desenvolvedor da idéia. E, a partir do século IV D.C., veio a estar ligada à teoria do *homoousios*. Ver o artigo sobre *Homoeanos* e *Homoeoussianos*. Essa doutrina ensina que cada pessoa pertence às outras duas (Atanásio, Cirilo de Alexandria). Os pais capadócios (que vide) favoreciam esse ensino por causa do forte pluralismo deles. Assim como o Deus onipresente permeia o universo, assim cada pessoa da Trindade interpenetra as demais. No Ocidente, Hilário e Agostinho enfatizavam esses pontos de vista. Cada pessoa da *Trindade* se relaciona com e reflete as outras. O Espírito é o laço de amor que une o Pai e o Filho (*vinculum amoris*, conforme dizia Agostinho). A base dessa doutrina é o ponto de vista místico da natureza. Não se origina de alguma manipulação lógica de conceitos. O termo grego *perichóresis*, usado para indicar a idéia de coinerência, não apareceu senão já no século VII D.C. E então era usado por Máximo, o Confessor, **para referir-se à inter-relação** entre as duas naturezas de Cristo. Porém, João Damasceno tomou por empréstimo o termo e aplicou-o à Trindade. No entanto, a *idéia* por detrás do termo é muito mais antiga, retrocedendo até Irineu, no século II D.C., embora outros vocábulos também fossem usados para exprimir tal idéia. O termo tem sido retido na teologia moderna, como nos escritos de Barth e de outros. Ver o artigo sobre a *Trindade*. (C)

COISA EM SI

Expressão que Kant usou para descrever **noumena** atrás dos *fenômenos* que podemos observar. Ver o artigo sobre *Ding-an-sich*.

COISAS CONSAGRADAS

O termo hebraico envolvido é **cherem**, usado por cinco vezes nesse sentido: Lev. 27:21,28,29; Núm. 18:4. Esse vocábulo hebraico indica algo consagrado ao serviço divino, embora também possa indicar algo maldito, ou algo determinado para a total destruição. Esse termo hebraico está relacionado à palavra árabe *haram*, «consagrado», como é o caso da área consagrada da Mesquita de Omar, em Jerusalém. É precisamente dessa palavra que nos vem o termo *harém*, o lugar consagrado à guarda das mulheres de um homem, ou o próprio grupo dessas mulheres, vedadas a qualquer outro homem que não o senhor delas. O termo hebraico é muito amplo, referindo-se a qualquer tipo de destruição, como aquele que ocorre nas guerras, ou quando são proibidas certas coisas. Ver Lev. 27:21,28,29; Núm. 18:14; Eze. 44:29, onde há o uso religioso da palavra, e onde aparecem oferendas *consagradas* a um uso santo. O trecho de Lev. 27:28 encerra a declaração geral de que todas as coisas consagradas a Deus são santas. Também havia pessoas que se consagravam ao Senhor (Lev. 27:29). Em sentido negativo, certas coisas eram separadas para serem destruídas (Lev. 27:29, onde estão em foco cativos de guerra). Os amalequitas foram postos sob interdição, a fim de serem destruídos (I Sam. 15:3-33). Apesar de ser verdade que a guerra mais total é aquela em que pode haver a destruição de inocentes, devido a uma misericórdia mal orientada (Sal. 106:34-38), também é verdade que em tudo isso estamos abordando uma sociedade constituída por homens brutais. A violência é um dos grandes sinais da degradação humana, sem importar em que época e de que maneira se manifeste essa violência.

COLA

Um lugar mencionado juntamente com Cabai, em Judite 15:4. Esse lugar nunca foi identificado, embora alguns eruditos o identifiquem com Holom, que figura em Jos. 15:51.

••• ••• •••

COLAÍAS

No hebraico, «a voz de Yahweh». Há dois homens com esse nome, nas páginas do Antigo Testamento:

1. Um antepassado de uma família benjamita, que se estabeleceu em Jerusalém, após o exílio babilônico (Nee. 11:7).

2. O pai do profeta falso, Acabe (Jer. 29:21).

COLCHAS

No hebraico, **marbaddim**. O sentido dessa palavra hebraica é incerto. Ela ocorre somente em Pro. 7:16 e 31:22. Isso não impediu, porém, que a mesma palavra hebraica fosse traduzida por «cobertas», em Pro. 31:22. Nada mais se pode dizer a respeito, além do fato de que deviam ser uma espécie de «coberta». É muito difícil que esteja em foco alguma espécie de «tapete», conforme dizem algumas versões estrangeiras, porquanto, na primeira dessas referências, está em pauta um leito: «Já cobri de colchas a minha cama...» O resto desse versículo, além disso, dá-nos a entender que se tratava de um tecido fino: «...de linho fino do Egito, de várias cores».

COLCHETES

No hebraico, **qerasim**, palavra que ocorre por dez vezes: Êxo. 26:6,11,33; 35:11; 36:13,18,33.

Seriam ganchos ou colchetes, usados no tabernáculo, armado no deserto. A LXX traduziu a palavra por *kríkoi*, anéis, mas é evidente que os tradutores se equivocaram quanto ao sentido da palavra. Havia cinquenta colchetes de ouro que juntavam cortinas de linho uma à outra; e havia cinquenta colchetes de cobre, que juntavam as cobertas de peles de cabras. Ver sobre o *Tabernáculo*.

Nesses trechos, onde a palavra ocorre, aparecem as especificações para a ereção do tabernáculo, com provisões para o seu transporte de um lugar para outro. No tocante à natureza dos colchetes, parece que estes compunham-se de uma espécie de botão que prendia um laço, que vinha da outra cortina. Talvez em um lado de cada cortina houvesse botões e do outro lado da mesma cortina houvesse laços. Quando esses laços eram presos nos respectivos botões, as cortinas ficavam unidas (Êxo. 26:4-6).

Há uma dificuldade envolvida nas orientações baixadas em Êxo. 26:33, onde se lê que o véu que separava os dois lugares — o Lugar Santo do Santo dos Santos — ficava pendurado «debaixo dos colchetes». Se supormos que os colchetes haviam sido postos na metade do comprimento total do tabernáculo, isso faria os dois lugares santos terem exatamente as mesmas dimensões, contrariamente à noção comum de que o Lugar Santo teria o dobro das dimensões do Santo dos Santos. Portanto, o termo «debaixo» deve ser interpretado com alguma latitude, ou então o conceito ordinário sobre o arranjo das cortinas, ou sobre as dimensões dos dois aposentos santos, terão de ser revisados. Na realidade, a descrição do livro de Êxodo não se refere a dimensões.

COLEÇÕES DE CÂNONES APOSTÓLICOS

Trata-se de uma antiga coletânea de decretos visando ao governo eclesiástico, supostamente estribados sobre a autoridade apostólica. Ver o artigo sobre as *Constituições e Cânones Apostólicos*.

COLÉGIO APOSTÓLICO

A primeira palavra da expressão vem do latim *collegium*, que significa grupo. O termo indica os apóstolos (que vide), que formavam um corpo. Pedro seria o *primus inter pares* do colégio apostólico. Isso não fazia dele um papa, isto é, o chefe de uma hierarquia, mas tão-somente o principal ou o mais destacado entre os apóstolos.

COLÉGIO DE CARDEAIS

O corpo de eclesiásticos mais próximo do pontífice

da Igreja Católica Romana, no tocante à dignidade e à autoridade. Desde a época do papa Xisto V (que vide), em 1586, o colégio de cardeais compõe-se de setenta membros, dos quais seis são bispos-cardeais, cinqüenta são padres-cardeais e catorze são diáconos-cardeais. Os cardeais (que vide) não são membros de algum parlamento formal, mas constituem uma espécie de concílio de conselheiros, com o dever de assistir ao papa no governo da Igreja Católica Romana. Eles têm a grande responsabilidade de administrar as questões eclesiásticas durante a vacância do trono papal. Também têm a responsabilidade de eleger dentre eles um novo papa, quando surgir a necessidade para tanto. Ver o artigo separado sobre os *Cardeais*.

COLÉGIO PONTIFICAL

Na antiga Roma, o título designava os conselheiros mais próximos do Sumo Pontífice da religião pagã, ajudando-o quanto a problemas legislativos e administrativos, incluindo aqueles de natureza religiosa.

Dentro da Igreja Católica Romana, durante o período imediatamente após a Reforma protestante, o título veio a designar qualquer colégio ou seminário em Roma ou fora dela, fundado ou dirigido pela Santa Sé. O termo chegou a ser aplicado especialmente à Sagrada Congregação da Propaganda, que visa à educação e treinamento de missionários católicos romanos destinados a servir na Inglaterra, na Escócia e na Irlanda. Colégios missionários foram estabelecidos em Douai, Pária (França), Valadolid (Espanha), Lisboa (Portugal) e outros lugares. Posteriormente, o termo também veio a ser aplicado às escolas de treinamento de missionários católicos romanos, a serem enviados a qualquer país estrangeiro. Desde a publicação do decreto papal, *Deus Scientiarum Dominus*, de 24 de maio de 1931, o título tem sido aplicado a todas as universidades e instituições de ensino importantes da Igreja Católica Romana, onde são conferidos graus acadêmicos. Se uma dessas escolas só pode conferir grau em alguma área, é chamada de Instituto Pontifício. Também há um terceiro título, *Academia Pontifícia*, que se refere àquelas escolas sob a tutela dos papas, que são associações de homens eruditos para a promoção das ciências e dos ideais religiosos. (E)

COLERIDGE, SAMUEL TAYLOR

Suas datas foram 1772 a 1834. **Poeta inglês**, educado em Cambridge. Ele atravessou diversos períodos de influência, como o do racionalismo, o do unitarismo e o da filosofia crítica e transcendental alemã, tendo prosseguido caminho em meio a vários *ismos*, influenciado por eles. Era um inquiridor da verdade; porém, após suas tortuosas jornadas mentais, ele voltou à fé cristã como a melhor solução para sua busca. Sua obra, publicada postumamente em 1840, fala de sua busca, intitulada *Confessions of an Inquiring Spirit*.

Coleridge negava qualquer contradição entre a ciência e a religião; frisava os princípios morais; cria na revelação gradual; não temia a crítica e a investigação bíblicas; acreditava na inspiração das Escrituras, pois, conforme afirmava, «A Bíblia encontra-me em um nível mais profundo do que qualquer outro livro». Essa linha de pensamento, bem como essa própria citação, tornou-se comum na moderna apologética cristã.

Tão Moderno Quanto Possível
Esta busca, este anelo, esta sede de saber,
Tão modernos quanto possível,
Apenas me levaram de volta a Ti.

Fortes inclinações, águas revoltas a correr,
Veredas distorcidas do pensar, descendo por muitas vertentes,
Apenas me fizeram esperar de novo em Ti.

De noite, de dia, em esperanças, desespero, vagueando
Por ásperas ravinas montanhosas, em cumes altíssimos e gélidos,
Em veredas estranhas, ainda ali Te achei perto.

Sorvos intoxicaram meu cérebro quando,
Desejando e aprendendo, provei da fonte Pieriana;
Mas, bebendo mais, isso me devolveu à sobriedade.
(Russell Champlin)

COLET, JOHN

Ver o artigo sobre os **Platônicos de Cambridge**.

COLETA

A palavra grega **koinonia** significa «partilha», «comunhão», bem como alguma quantia em dinheiro, dada por meio do espírito de participação e partilha. O trecho de Atos 6:1 *ss*, mostra-nos que havia considerável necessidade de cuidar das viúvas da igreja de Jerusalém. A experiência de comunidade de bens, na igreja de Jerusalém, demonstrou a mesma coisa no tocante a todos os níveis da Igreja (ver Atos 2:44,45; 4:34,35). A igreja de Antioquia compartilhou com a igreja de Jerusalém, de suas bênçãos materiais (Atos 11:27-30). Também houve a questão do sustento do ministério (I Cor. 9:8 *ss*). O Novo Testamento não ordena o dízimo, mas é natural supormos que esse princípio foi transferido do Antigo Testamento para a maioria das igrejas neotestamentárias. Mediante dízimos e ofertas é que o ministério é sustentado, e as missões de evangelismo são um dos grandes e mais importantes empreendimentos cristãos. Portanto, essa questão das coletas tornou-se muito importante. Se o Novo Testamento não determina o dízimo, e nunca se torna um dever sob o sistema da graça divina, é difícil imaginar um crente sério que contribua com menos do que essa porcentagem.

Nas páginas do Novo Testamento temos a famosa coleta feita por Paulo, para benefício dos santos pobres de Jerusalém. Em meio à fome e às perseguições, os crentes judeus haviam sido reduzidos à extrema pobreza. Nem sempre a prosperidade é sinal de espiritualidade e de aprovação divina. Quanto a essa coleta, ver os trechos de I Cor. 16:1; II Cor. 9:12; Atos 24:17; Rom. 15:25,26; II Cor. 8:1 *ss*. Paulo atribuía considerável importância à questão. Antes de tudo, era um ato de caridade e amor, demonstração da lei do amor e a prova mesma da espiritualidade. Em segundo lugar, foi um ato de diplomacia. A coleta era oferecida pelas igrejas gentílicas para as igrejas judaicas, como sinal de fraternidade, em um período em que talvez não fosse fácil aceitar tal oferta, por parte daqueles que contavam com um puro pano de fundo judaico, e para quem os gentios não eram exatamente agradáveis. É em conexão com essa coleta que encontramos a expressão «no primeiro dia da semana», provavelmente indicando que os cristãos gentios reuniam-se para cultuar no primeiro dia da semana, e não no sábado. Ver I Cor. 16:2. Esse versículo também tem sido

COLETA — COLETIVISMO

considerado como o modelo do recolhimento de ofertas. Não se fala ali nos dez por cento. Antes, a medida da doação era a prosperidade material de cada crente. O homem *espiritual*, entretanto, nunca encontrará um momento em que não dê pelo menos uma décima parte de suas rendas para o trabalho do ministério e manutenção da Igreja, embora o Novo Testamento não estabeleça qualquer especificação quanto à porcentagem a ser contribuída.

Ver a *oferta* de I Cor. 16:1,2. Este texto emprega a palavra grega *logeía*, que significa *coleta*. O princípio de dons e ofertas foi estabelecido no Antigo Testamento, para sustento do sistema religioso judaico e para ajudar os pobres. Ver II Crô. 31:3,10,12,14; Nee. 10:37,39; 12:44; 13:5; Eze. 20:40.

As Coletas na Igreja Moderna. Todas as igrejas locais precisam de coletas e contribuições para a manutenção do trabalho do ministério. A coleta recolhida por Paulo, conforme se descreveu acima, bem como alguns de seus ensinamentos específicos, como os que se encontram em I Cor. 9:9 *ss* e II Cor. 9:6 *ss*, demonstram que a coleta e a doação de coisas materiais, com o propósito de sustentar o ministério espiritual, fazem parte do ensino bíblico. No entanto, algumas igrejas não adotam o recolhimento de coletas *públicas*. Além disso, as diversas denominações cristãs não concordam quanto ao uso do dinheiro recolhido. Algumas delas não dispõem de um ministério profissional, que receba sustento da Igreja. Outras pensam que isso faz parte necessária do trabalho da igreja local. Seja como for, a Igreja e os seus projetos precisam de fundos, e todo crente sério deveria contribuir. Ver o artigo sobre a *Contribuição*. (B NTI)

COLETA

Essa é a oração breve, dos ritos cristãos ocidentais, que envolve: a. ou o *sumário* das devoções do povo; b. ou a oração e a reunião quando o povo se dirigia, em cortejo, à igreja onde a missa seria celebrada. No missal romano (que vide) a coleta anterior à epístola é chamada de *Oratio*. (E)

COLETIVISMO

A definição básica do termo é a de que a sociedade, como um todo, é mais importante do que os seus membros individuais, e que, por esse motivo, o indivíduo deve subordinar os seus interesses aos interesses da sociedade, cedendo diante dos desejos da coletividade, ou, pelo menos, dos desejos expressos pela maioria. O *coletivismo* usualmente implica que o povo, como um todo, deveria possuir e controlar os meios materiais de produção, os quais não deveriam ser deixados nas mãos de indivíduos. Contrastemos o coletivismo com o *individualismo*, o qual é enfatizado pelo capitalismo (que vide). Usualmente, essas coisas são como os lados opostos de uma mesma moeda; mas, através da história, encontramos conflito entre esses dois lados. O coletivismo olha para o individualismo como a *atomização* da sociedade, o último inimigo a ser eliminado.

Encontramos uma forma de ideal coletivista na *República* de Platão, embora limitada às classes mais elevadas, pois Platão pensava que as classes inferiores jamais atingiriam uma atitude mediante a qual todas as coisas pudessem ser compartilhadas. Alguns historiadores supõem que o mais perfeito exemplo desse conceito que jamais funcionou foi a sociedade feudal do período medieval, desenvolvido sob a autoridade da Igreja Católica Romana, cujo intuito era o estabelecimento de um reino de Deus na terra. Tal experiência, finalmente, fracassou; mas continuou sendo um magnífico exemplo histórico.

A **Reforma Protestante** exibiu elementos de coletivismo, especialmente no caso de João Calvino e sua igreja-estado policial, em Genebra, na Suíça, onde todos os membros da sociedade eram severamente controlados e forçados a uma expressão comum, embora não pudessem ser forçados a uma atitude comum. Na sociedade secular, com o aparecimento das monarquias, houve várias tentativas coletivistas nacionais. Diversos autores promoveram o coletivismo secular dentro do conceito de UTOPIA. Poderíamos mencionar Sir Thomas More, em seu livro *Utopia*, e Rousseau, em seu ideal democrático. E também o conde de Saint Simon, em sua obra *Du System Industrial*. Naturalmente, não podemos nos esquecer de Karl Marx e do seu ideal da ditadura do proletariado, uma tentativa humanista e atéia de estabelecer o coletivismo.

Um verdadeiro coletivismo requereria comunhão de idéias, de crenças, de ideais, e não meramente uma unidade organizacional. Certamente isso requereria alguma forma de governo ditatorial, de acordo com o qual a escola e todas as facetas da sociedade pudessem ser estritamente controladas. Elementos de tais noções podem ser encontrados nos livros de C. Virgil Georghiu, Aldous Huxley, George Orwell e Herbert Harcuse.

Tentativas mais recentes de estabelecer o coletivismo incluem o nazismo, na Alemanha, o fascismo, na Itália, e o comunismo internacional. Talvez a tentativa mais ambiciosa das últimas décadas tenha sido a da China Vermelha. No entanto, recentemente, foi anunciado ali, pelos círculos oficiais chineses, que o sistema funciona melhor com certa injeção de capitalismo individualista.

Princípios Éticos Envolvidos. Apesar do princípio democrático reconhecer que a vontade da maioria deveria fazer parte das decisões, como uma norma social, há algo no espírito humano que resiste ao totalitarismo, sem importar se de esquerda ou de direita. Além disso, a experiência mostra-nos que indivíduos resolutos, com o lucro como seu alvo, fazem a economia florescer muito melhor do que os burocratas impelidos por algum fantasioso ideal coletivista. A pior expressão do coletivismo é aquele modelo ateu absurdo, totalmente humanista, que oficialmente declara que Deus não existe, transformando o homem em um deus de metal. Essa modalidade de coletivismo chega mesmo a recusar-se a reconhecer o que o homem é, supondo que o homem consiste apenas em seu corpo físico, e que o maior bem possível é a prosperidade do homem físico, em um mundo material. Há algo no espírito humano que resiste a tal degradação. Por essa razão, destaca-se o fenômeno histórico que quase todos os sistemas dessa natureza têm sido inaugurados e são mantidos mediante a força militar, nunca havendo eleições livres, com escolhas genuínas, que confirmem a preferência popular quanto ao método. Essa imposição, de cima para baixo, mostra o equívoco em que se encontram os seus mentores e executores. Dizem as Escrituras Sagradas: «Diz o insensato no seu coração: Não há Deus» (Sal. 14:1).

O Coletivismo Cristão. A redenção nunca será uma questão meramente individual. É o **corpo** de Cristo que está sendo remido. A restauração (que vide) não será uma questão apenas individual. *Todas as coisas*, finalmente, haverão de encontrar seu centro na pessoa de Cristo (Efé. 1:10), e ele será tudo para todos (Efé. 1:23). Além disso, temos o ensino bíblico de que todas as coisas estão sob o governo e a autoridade de Deus, por meio do *Logos*. Ver sobre o *Verbo*. Por conseguinte, o crente precisa mostrar-se contrário ao totalitarismo e a todas as formas de coletivismo ateu; porém antes, deve promover o coletivismo espiritual. Visto que o coletivismo espiritual é criado e governado segundo normas teístas, e que forças espirituais e benfazejas é que o criam e governam. Essa modalidade merece nossa total dedicação e apoio. O coletivismo só funciona quando o ideal que o inspira cativa o espírito humano. (H)

COLETIVO

No tratamento das **probabilidades** (vide), por von Mises, essa palavra indica uma infinita seqüência de elementos, alguns dos quais correspondentes a certo atributo ou resultado, que satisfaz as condições de convergência e imprevisto (que vide). Ver também os artigos sobre *Chance* e sobre as *Coincidências Significativas*.

COLETORES DE IMPOSTOS

No grego, **telónes**, vocábulo que aparece por vinte e duas vezes, somente nos evangelhos sinópticos: Mat. 5:46; 9:10,11; 10:3; 11:19; 17:17; 21,31,32; Mar. 2:15,16; Luc. 3:12; 5:27,29,30; 7:29,34; 15:1; 18:10,11,13.

Essa palavra grega é incorretamente traduzida por «publicanos», em nossa versão portuguesa, como em outras versões estrangeiras. Os *publicani* (palavra latina) eram homens ricos, geralmente romanos, que pagavam pelo privilégio de fazer a cobrança de impostos e taxas, em certas localidades. Mas nem sempre os publicanos eram romanos, pois parece que o judeu Zaqueu (Luc. 19:2-10), que é chamado *architelónes*, «maioral dos publicanos», era um *publicanus*, no sentido real do termo latino.

Os publicanos empregavam os serviços de judeus locais para fazerem o trabalho real de recolhimento de impostos, em lugar deles. Estes últimos eram indicados pelo termo grego *telónes*, pelo que é preferível a tradução «cobrador de imposto», e não «publicano».

Os impostos cobrados pelo governo romano, aos habitantes do império, eram muitos e variegados. O principal de todos era o *tributum capitis*, que tinha de ser pago por toda pessoa do sexo masculino acima de catorze anos, e por toda pessoa do sexo feminino acima de doze anos (os idosos estavam isentos). Havia um imposto territorial (*tributum agri*), que precisava ser pago em espécie. Ambos esses impostos eram diretamente coletados por oficiais romanos, residentes na Palestina.

Em adição a isso, havia muitas formas de taxação indireta. Eram feitas cobranças sobre todas as mercadorias importadas e exportadas, incluindo até mesmo o transporte de escravos. Essas cobranças eram feitas pelos *telônai* dos evangelhos. Eles examinavam as mercadorias e cobravam taxas nas estradas e nas pontes. Herodes também introduziu um mercado de cobrança de impostos, em Jerusalém.

Há estudiosos que opinam que os impostos cobrados em Cafarnaum, na Galiléia, eram enviados para o tesouro de Herodes Ântipas. Nas províncias administradas pelo senado romano, este é que cuidava do dinheiro recolhido. No entanto, a Judéia era uma província imperial, pelo que todo o dinheiro assim recolhido seguia diretamente para os cofres do imperador. Essa foi a base da pergunta que dirigiram, astuciosamente, ao Senhor Jesus: «Dize-nos, pois, que te parece? É lícito pagar tributo a César ou não?» (Mat. 22:17; Mar. 12:14 e Luc. 20:22).

Como uma classe profissional, os coletores de impostos («publicanos», em nossa versão portuguesa) eram odiados por seus compatriotas judeus. Isso era quase inevitável, pois eles representavam a dominação estrangeira de Roma sobre a Judéia. Os métodos empregados pelos cobradores de impostos eram necessariamente inquisitoriais. Geralmente eles cobravam do povo acima do que era devido, metendo no bolso o que ultrapassava disso. Isso é refletido na confissão penitente de Zaqueu: «...se nalguma cousa tenho defraudado alguém, restituo quatro vezes mais» (Luc. 19:8). Por essa razão, nos escritos rabínicos, os coletores de impostos são classificados juntamente com os ladrões. Nos evangelhos sinópticos, eles foram classificados juntamente com os «pecadores» (ver Mat. 9:10; 11:9; Mar. 2:15 e Luc. 5:30; 7:34). Isso reflete a atitude comum do povo judeu para com os cobradores de impostos. Eles eram considerados renegados, os quais vendiam os seus préstimos aos dominadores estrangeiros opressivos, enriquecendo-se às custas de seus próprios compatriotas.

Jesus reconheceu essa atitude comum, acerca dos coletores de impostos, ao observar: «Porque se amardes os que vos amam, que recompensa tendes? não fazem os publicanos também o mesmo?» (Mat. 5:46). Ao mesmo tempo, porém, o Senhor Jesus repreendeu a justiça própria dos fariseus, quando disse: «Em verdade vos digo que publicanos e meretrizes vos precedem no reino de Deus» (Mat. 21:31). Quando fez essas declarações, Jesus não estava defendendo ou justificando os erros particulares de coletores de impostos e de fariseus. O que ele estava ensinando é que há perdão disponível até para os piores pecadores, contanto que se arrependam. Por outra parte, o pecado coroador dos fariseus era a recusa deles de arrependerem-se, preferindo eles a sua justiça própria, conforme Jesus retratou tão vividamente na parábola do fariseu e do cobrador de impostos (Luc. 18:9-14).

A aceitação dos cobradores de impostos penitentes, por parte do Senhor Jesus, ficou demonstrada não somente pelo fato de que ele acolheu a Zaqueu, o qual se tornou um dos seus seguidores, mas também pelo fato de que ele escolheu o coletor de impostos, Mateus (Levi), como um de seus doze apóstolos. Quando Mateus ofereceu um banquete de despedida a seus ex-associados — momento em que, provavelmente, apresentou a eles o seu novo Senhor e Mestre — os fariseus indagaram dos discípulos de Cristo: «Por que come o vosso Mestre com os publicanos e pecadores?» (Mat. 9:11). A resposta dele pelo Senhor Jesus, a essa indagação, revelou a natureza e o propósito de sua missão neste mundo: «...não vim chamar justos, e, sim, pecadores (ao arrependimento)» (Mat. 9:13).

É muito apropriado, e até mesmo dramático, que, diante do arrependimento de Zaqueu, que se notabilizara como um odiado e desonesto coletor de impostos, o Senhor Jesus tivesse definido tão claramente a sua missão: «Porque o Filho do homem veio buscar e salvar o perdido» (Luc. 19:10).

COLETORIA

A palavra grega **telónion**, «coletoria», aparece em todos os três evangelhos sinópticos: Mat. 9:9; Mar. 2:14 e Luc. 5:27. A menção à coletoria ocorre por ocasião da chamada de Mateus, por parte do Senhor

Jesus. Foi na coletoria que estava Mateus, na ocasião. O *telónion* podia ser a barra, a mesa, a sala, etc., onde os pagadores de impostos vinham pagar seus impostos. A taxa, que no grego é *télos*, era uma das principais fontes de renda dos governos, tal e qual sucede em nossos dias. Muitas práticas abusivas entraram nessa situação, o que explica a horrenda reputação dos cobradores de impostos (que vide) os quais, erroneamente, nossas versões portuguesas chamam de publicanos. Mateus ganhava bom dinheiro nessa atividade (a maioria dos cobradores de impostos ficava rica) mas Jesus ofereceu-lhe algo muito melhor para seguir, isto é, a ele mesmo, quando lhe disse: «Segue-me!» (Mat. 9:9).

Ver sobre *Impostos, Taxação.*

COLHEITA

No hebraico, **terminar**. No grego, **therizo**. Ato de cortar e recolher o produto dos campos, usualmente no fim do verão. No litoral e no vale do Jordão, a colheita do trigo começa em abril; na região montanhosa a cevada é colhida em meados de maio, o trigo ligeiramente mais tarde. Assim, toda a colheita durava cerca de três meses. O produto da terra era cortado com uma foice, ou arrancado à mão pelas raízes. No livro de Levítico há uma legislação acerca da colheita. Os colhedores deveriam deixar intocadas as extremidades dos campos, para benefício dos pobres (Lev. 19:9; 23:22). No sétimo e no qüinquagésimo anos, não havia colheita.

A semeadura e a colheita serviam para ilustrar o investimento e sua recompensa. Para exemplificar, lemos em Pro. 22:8: «O que semeia a injustiça segará males...» Algo um tanto oposto se lê em Sal. 126:5: «Os que com lágrimas semeiam, com júbilo ceifarão». «E aquele que estava sentado sobre a nuvem passou a sua foice sobre a terra, e a terra foi ceifada», lemos em Apo. 14:16.

O Pentecoste era a festa que melhor guardava seu caráter de festa da colheita. A origem da festa dos tabernáculos ligava-se com a colheita das uvas, que começava em agosto e podia terminar em outubro. As primícias e os dízimos da colheita eram entregues no santuário de Jerusalém. Em sentido figurado, o resultado dos atos humanos é chamado de colheita (Pro. 28:8; Jó 4:8). O homem colhe o fruto de suas obras (Gál. 6:7 *ss*; I Cor. 9:11; II Cor. 9:6; João 4:36-38). Nos profetas e no N.T., a intervenção escatológica de Deus também é uma colheita, a qual torna-se símbolo do juízo, no fim de nossa dispensação (Joel 4:13; Isa. 27:11; Mat. 3:12; 13:30; Mar. 4:29 e Apo. 14:15 ss).

Ver o artigo sobre o *Calendário*, onde há um gráfico que alista as diversas colheitas que se faziam na Palestina, bem como as condições atmosféricas, etc., mês após mês. A palavra «colheita» com freqüência é usada para indicar o recolhimento dos produtos agrícolas. As principais colheitas, referidas nas Escrituras, eram as do trigo, cevada, uvas, azeitonas, figos, romãs (Deu. 8:8), linho, lentilha, sésamo, centeio, feijão, ervilha, pepino, alho, alho-porro, melão e cebola. — Das árvores frutíferas eram colhidas as amêndoas, as tâmaras, as castanhas e as nozes. Ver o artigo geral sobre a *Agricultura,* quanto a maiores detalhes.

Usos metafóricos. 1. O julgamento, Jer. 51:33; Apoc. 14:15. 2. A colheita espiritual de almas pela pregação do evangelho, Mat. 9:27; João 4:35. 3. O *fim* do mundo, Mat. 13:39. 4. *Elementos.* Orvalho, no tempo da colheita = o cuidado de Deus, Isa. 18:4. O frio neste tempo simboliza um mensageiro fiel.

Ver o artigo separado sobre *Lei Moral da Colheita Segundo a Semeadura.*

COL-HOZE

No hebraico, «vidente total». Era descendente de Judá, filho de Hazaías e pai de um homem de nome Baruque (Nee. 11:5). Viveu em cerca de 445 A.C. Teve um descendente de nome Salum, que ajudou a reparar as muralhas de Jerusalém, após o cativeiro babilônico (Née. 3:15). Mas alguns intérpretes pensam que essa palavra significa antes o nome de uma família, e não o nome de um indivíduo; ou então ambas as coisas, um nome individual e um nome coletivo.

COLIGAÇÃO

Palavra que se deriva de dois termos latinos, **col**, «junto com» e *ligare*, «ligar». Consideremos os três pontos abaixo, ligados ao assunto:

1. A colocação de alguma informação isolada, sob um título ou concepção geral.

2. O processo da indagação consiste, essencialmente, em coligação. Mas o conhecimento baseado nos poderes da intuição, embora arranjado em grupos, pode não ser chamado de indução, o que já subentende um processo formal ou científico de alguma espécie.

3. A expressão também tem sido aplicada ao processo da dedução. Nesse processo, uma pessoa coliga premissas, e então determina o que se pode derivar da comparação das duas premissas. (P)

COLÍRIO

No grego, **kolloúrion**. Aparece exclusivamente em Apo. 3:18. Era um ungüento medicinal aplicado aos olhos. Pode ter-se tratado de um pó frígio, que tornou famosa a escola de medicina de Laodicéia. O Senhor Jesus referia-se à restauração da visão espiritual, por parte dos membros da igreja de Laodicéia.

COLLINGWOOD, ROBIN GEORGE

Nasceu em 1889 e faleceu em 1943. Foi um filósofo inglês, professor em Oxford, também conhecido como estudioso no campo da arqueologia e como historiador especializado na história da Bretanha romana.

Idéias:

1. Quanto à natureza da filosofia, ele ensinava que a mesma consiste em *conhecimento humano* transmutado em uma forma sistemática de conteúdo. A filosofia diferirira da ciência porque os seus conceitos se justapõem, exigindo métodos especiais de abordagem.

2. A metafísica teria a função de trazer à luz o pressuposto fundamental do pensamento humano.

3. Cada campo da experiência humana, como as artes, a religião, a ciência, a história e a filosofia, conteriam aspectos parciais da verdade, embora cada uma delas, separadamente, seja unilateral.

Obras: Speculum Mentis; Essay on Philosophical Method; The Principles of Art; The Idea of Nature, An Essay on Metaphysics; The Idea of History. (EP P)

COLOCÍNTIDAS

No hebraico temos duas palavras, **sadeh paqquoth**, que figuram apenas em II Reis 4:39. A grande dificuldade consiste em identificar a espécie vegetal em foco.

Visto que a palavra *sadeh*, «silvestre», vem de uma raiz que significa «planície», está em foco alguma planta que cresce em lugares abertos. A nossa tradução portuguesa dá a entender que seria a espécie que, cientificamente, é denominada *Citrullus colocynthus*, uma espécie de vinha selvagem do Mediterrâneo, da família da cabaça, ou cuia. Ela produzia um pequeno fruto de gosto amargoso, que era usado como catártico. Essa espécie também era chamada de «maçã amarga».

Outros estudiosos, porém, preferem pensar em uma espécie de pepino selvagem, cujo nome científico seria o *Ecballium elatrium*. Essa espécie, efetivamente, podia ser encontrada na região referida em II Reis 4:39. No entanto, poderíamos indagar: Por qual motivo o moço que fora apanhar ervas teria preferido colher esse fruto espinhento para pôr na panela?

Por outra parte, se estava, realmente, em foco, a *Citrullus colocynthus*, isso seria confirmado pelo fato de que as «colocíntidas» foram apanhadas de uma «trepadeira selvagem», que o original hebraico chama de «vinha selvagem». Por esses motivos, parece-nos que a tradução «colocíntidas» é melhor que uma outra, preferida por algumas versões estrangeiras, que falam em pepinos silvestres. Entretanto, queremos observar que as questões que envolvem a fauna e a flora do Antigo Testamento são dificílimas de deslindar, visto que os escritores sagrados não usaram uma linguagem científica para aludir a essas espécies, o que dificulta, ou mesmo impossibilita, em vários casos, uma precisa identificação dos animais e das plantas envolvidas.

Alguns estudiosos também têm pensado na mamona, a qual, com o nome **hebraico** *qiqayon*, aparece no quarto capítulo do livro de Jonas (vs. 6,7,9,10), e onde nossa versão portuguesa prefere não arriscar uma identificação, dizendo apenas «planta». A maior dificuldade dessa identificação é que a mamona não é uma trepadeira, e sim, um arbusto da família das *Euphorbiaceae*.

COLÔNIA (COLONIALISMO)

Essas palavras derivam-se do latim **colere**, «cultivar». Um *colonus* era um agricultor, e uma *colônia* era um grupo desses agricultores. O colonialismo, fenômeno histórico típico da era contemporânea, caracteriza-se pelos seguintes pontos: 1. Os países ou impérios têm espalhado sua população, adquirindo assim novas terras e novas riquezas. 2. Postos avançados militares e entrepostos comerciais são estabelecidos. 3. Cidadãos menos desejáveis, incluindo criminosos condenados pela justiça, são exilados para os novos territórios, para todos os propósitos práticos. 4. A proteção das fronteiras ou das posições estratégicas nas colônias é garantida, visando ao bem da mãe pátria. 5. Dessa maneira realiza-se a satisfação do desejo de aventura. 6. Novos empregos e novas oportunidades para a iniciativa privada são criados.

A história universal informa-nos que os romanos, dentro da Itália, colonizaram lugares como Óstia, Âncio e Terracina, no século IV A.C. Por volta de 200 A.C., essas colônias romanas costeiras já eram numerosas. Fora da Itália, Caio Graco tentou estabelecer uma colônia em Junônia. A tentativa fracassou, mas, posteriormente, Júlio César e Augusto lograram bom êxito ali.

As primeiras colônias extensas, fora da Itália, foram criadas, pelo menos em parte, para solucionar o problema de desemprego dentro da bota italina. Muitos legionários veteranos, retirados da vida ativa, estavam desempregados e agitados. Foram então enviados para colonizar o mundo mediterrâneo. Em certo sentido, eles formavam uma força militar que consolidava o poder romano sobre os seus territórios que abrigavam tantas raças diferentes.

Colônias romanas como as de Filipos, Antioquia da Pisídia, Listra, Corinto e, talvez, Icônio, tornaram-se realidades pela razão acima. No Novo Testamento só encontramos um uso específico da palavra «colônia», ou seja, em conexão com Filipos, em Atos 16:12. Para ali, Augusto havia enviado um grupo de veteranos desmobilizados, em 30 A.C. Isso resultou em uma espécie de posto militar que deu a Roma um pouco mais de segurança. Cidadãos romanos, em tais lugares, formavam uma espécie de pequena elite, porquanto tinham mais privilégios e poder que os habitantes locais. Eles também tinham certos direitos de que outros não desfrutavam, como a isenção da supervisão dos governadores locais, a imunidade de vários impostos, incluindo aqueles que incidiam sobre as propriedades, e os direitos judiciais próprios dos cidadãos romanos. A narrativa lucana demonstra o zelo com que eram resguardados esses privilégios. As autoridades locais de Filipos ficaram muito preocupadas e temerosas pelo fato de que Paulo, cidadão romano que era, fora maltratado naquela cidade (Atos 16:37 ss). Os colonos estavam isentos do serviço militar, porque ter ido para uma colônia equivalia a estar prestando serviço ao exército.

O Colonialismo e a Autodeterminação. Algumas colônias romanas alcançaram a condição de estados livres. A tendência das colônias é desenvolverem-se em entidades separadas, desejando ser livres do domínio do país de origem. Os problemas econômicos, geralmente são os fatores mais decisivos. Assim, as colônias inglesas na América do Norte objetavam à taxação sem a devida representação americana no parlamento inglês. Geralmente os habitantes das colônias, quando muito, tornam-se cidadãos de segunda classe. Acresça-se a isso o fato de que, nas colônias, a população que ali se desenvolve deve-se à miscigenação de raças, bem como a diferenças culturais e geográficas. Torna-se difícil as pátrias de origem governarem as suas colônias; e revoluções acabam aparecendo. Isso sucedeu no caso da Revolução Americana, bem como no caso de todos os países da América Latina, incluindo o Brasil. Aqui, graças à argúcia política de Dom Pedro I, não houve necessidade de uma longa guerra de libertação; mas, mesmo assim, houve lutas entre forças portuguesas fiéis a coroa portuguesa e tropas brasileiras, fiéis a Dom Pedro.

A maioria das pessoas prefere ser mal governada por si mesma do que ser governada por estrangeiros, mesmo que esse governo seja justo e progressista. Esse fato tem sido novamente demonstrado por várias vezes; na história recente, na África, o último bolsão do colonialismo moderno. A autodeterminação harmoniza-se com a dignidade do homem, pois não há tesouro tão grande quanto a *liberdade*. Até mesmo o governo estrangeiro, quando este existe, deveria trabalhar com vistas à autodeterminação do povo que estiver sendo colonizado. Por igual modo, as missões evangélicas no estrangeiro devem trabalhar com o intuito de criar igrejas nacionais. (H Z)

COLOSSENSES

I. Autoria
II. Data e Proveniência
III. Motivo e Propósitos
IV. Integridade da Epístola
V. Temas Principais
VI. Confirmação Antiga e Aceitação

COLOSSENSES

    da Epístola
VII.   Estado do Texto Grego
VIII. Conteúdo
IX.   Bibliografia

Com base em estilo gramatical e literário e no uso de palavras e de temas, as epístolas aos Romanos, I e II aos Coríntios e Gálatas são universalmente aceitas como clássicos paulinos. A aceitação de uma delas como paulina requer a aceitação de todas, e vice-versa, a rejeição de uma delas requer a rejeição de todas, tão convincente é a evidência interna de que procedem da mesma pena. Por isso mesmo é que pouquíssimos têm sido os críticos que se têm aventurado a negar a origem e a natureza autenticamente paulinas dessas quatro epístolas. Outras cinco epístolas têm sido acrescentadas a essa lista, com pouca hesitação, por estudiosos liberais e conservadores, antigos e modernos. São elas Filipenses, Colossenses, I e II aos Tessalonicenses e Filemom. Sobre o *corpus paulino*, ver o artigo sobre Romanos, primeiros parágrafos, e seção II.

Dentre as treze epístolas comumente atribuídas a Paulo, sete são reputadas «epístolas da prisão», ou seja, aquelas que supostamente o apóstolo dos gentios teria escrito quando era prisioneiro. Desde os tempos antigos, tornou-se costume supor que todas essas epístolas foram escritas em Roma, lugar onde Paulo passou seu mais prolongado e famoso período de encarceramento. Os eruditos modernos, entretanto, têm pensado ser possível, ou até mesmo provável, que algumas das chamadas «epístolas da prisão» foram escritas em outros lugares onde Paulo esteve aprisionado, como Cesaréia ou Éfeso. As *epístolas da prisão* são Filipenses, Efésios, Colossenses, Filemom, I e II a Timóteo e Tito. Quando se investiga de perto o conteúdo das mesmas, especialmente observando-se os companheiros de Paulo, além de algumas circunstâncias prevalentes, parece quase certo que nem todas essas epístolas foram escritas na mesma cidade, sob as mesmas circunstâncias, e nem na mesma época em geral.

Uma coisa, porém, é certa — as epístolas aos Colossenses, Efésios e Filemom formam uma unidade distinta, tendo sido escritas na mesma época, sob as mesmas circunstâncias, ou seja, foram compostas na mesma localidade. Essa questão é discutida no artigo sobre cada uma dessas epístolas, mas, especialmente, na seção II do presente artigo, sob o título *Proveniência*. Dentre essas três epístolas, Colossenses é ordinariamente considerada como a de maior importância e autoridade, a despeito do fato que a epístola aos Efésios, na realidade, é mais sublime. As dúvidas, entretanto, que alguns têm lançado sobre sua autoria paulina, de acordo com o parecer de alguns eruditos, têm-na feito perder o lugar de primeira importância entre as três, e de fato, entre a coletânea paulina inteira, o que, de outra maneira, certamente teria desfrutado. Este artigo defende a autoria paulina da epístola aos Efésios, por razões declaradas no artigo sobre aquele livro, sob o título *Autoria*. Com ou sem essa afirmação, a epístola aos Efésios é um livro sem comparação. Contudo, a epístola aos Colossenses compartilha de alguns de seus mais profundos raciocínios no tocante à redenção humana. Pelo menos no tocante a certas questões, ela apresenta uma visão mais elevada da pessoa de Cristo do que o faz a epístola aos Efésios ou qualquer outro livro do N.T. Melhor é a epístola que mais exalta a Cristo; por essa razão, pois, os capítulos primeiro e segundo da epístola aos Colossenses e o primeiro capítulo da epístola aos Efésios, são os «melhores».

Colossos era uma cidade pertencente à província romana da Ásia, na parte ocidental do que agora é a Turquia Asiática, situada cerca de dezesseis quilômetros do vale de Lico, partindo-se de Laodicéia, às margens da estrada principal de Éfeso para o oriente. Originalmente, ocupava o ponto onde se dividiam as estradas para Sardes e Pérgamo. Nos tempos antigos foi uma importante cidade do reino Lídio e, posteriormente, do reino de Pérgamo. Quando Roma construiu uma estrada até Pérgamo, que ficava um pouco mais a leste, deixando de lado Colossos, esta perdeu muito de sua anterior importância. Foi nessa época que Laodicéia tornou-se cidade maior e mais próspera. O local da antiga cidade de Colossos é, atualmente, desabitado. Essa cidade ficava situada a dezesseis quilômetros a leste da moderna aldeia de Denizli.

Evidentemente Paulo não foi o fundador da igreja de Colossos, segundo se depreende de Col. 1:4 e 2:1, passagens que subentendem que ele não conhecia pessoalmente a maior parte de seus leitores. É provável que o evangelho tenha chegado até eles quando Paulo vivia em Éfeso (ver Atos 19:10); e isso talvez mediante os serviços de Epafras, que era colossense (ver Col. 1:7 e 4:12,13). É patente que o desejo que Paulo tinha de visitar esse lugar se cumpriu (ver File. 12), em algum tempo posterior. Filemom e seu escravo, Onésimo, também eram membros dessa igreja (ver File. 1:10 e Col. 4:9).

A grande cidade de Éfeso ficava cerca de cento e setenta quilômetros para oeste; Laodicéia ficava a dezesseis quilômetros para oeste e ambas essas cidades vizinhas vieram a eclipsar Colossos antes dos tempos de Paulo, embora todas elas ainda estivessem intimamente associadas entre si pelos laços do comércio, especialmente vinhos, fazendas tingidas e lã, que eram seus principais produtos de exportação. Colossos mui provavelmente, era a cidade de menor importância para onde Paulo escreveu uma de suas epístolas.

A maior parte dos crentes de Colossos se compunha de gentios (ver Col. 1:27 e 2:13); porém, desde os tempos de Antíoco, o Grande, havia uma numerosa e influente população judaica ali. Contudo, os problemas que vieram a afligir a comunidade cristã ali existente não eram de origem judaica. Esta epístola foi escrita para combater o gnosticismo (ver o artigo sobre *Gnosticismo*) ensinamento esse que tinha base nas religiões orientais misteriosas, de invenção gentílica. Oito livros do N.T. foram escritos como defesa da fé cristã, diante dos assédios do *gnosticismo*. São eles: essa epístola, as três epístolas pastorais, as três epístolas joaninas e a epístola de Judas. O evangelho de João, o livro de Apocalipse e a epístola aos Efésios também aludem a essa antiga heresia, embora não tivessem sido primariamente escritos a fim de combatê-la.

I. AUTORIA

(Quanto a comentários gerais sobre a autoria da *coletânea paulina*, ver as notas preliminares anteriores). A epístola aos Colossenses cabe dentro do «segundo grupo» de cinco epístolas, após os quatro «clássicos» (Romanos, Gálatas e I e II aos Coríntios). Essas cinco epístolas do «segundo grupo» são Filipenses, Colossenses, I e II aos Tessalonicenses e Filemom, as quais são normalmente aceitas como de autoria paulina, sem qualquer disputa séria. Entretanto, no caso desta epístola aos Colossenses, tem-se duvidado de sua autoria paulina, pelos seguintes motivos:

COLOSSENSES

1. *O tipo de heresia atacada*. Certa forma de gnosticismo, conforme pensam alguns, pertenceria a um período posterior; pelo que não seria algo que Paulo pudesse combater, em seus dias. O trecho de Col. 1:15 e ss e a maior parte do segundo capítulo, mostram que Paulo (ou o autor, que escreveu em nome de Paulo, conforme alguns pensam) atacava alguma forma de heresia gnóstica. As características doutrinárias distintivas da epístola aos Colossenses foram dadas especificamente como repreensões contra a crença errônea. Essa epístola foi escrita com o propósito de revelar a natureza da verdadeira cristologia e da ética cristã, em contraste com as idéias gnósticas, que tinham impressionado alguns membros da comunidade cristã de Colossos.

2. *A exaltada cristologia* desta epístola é considerada, por alguns estudiosos, como por demais «avançada» para a teologia paulina normal, o que, uma vez mais, refletiria um período posterior, em que Cristo se tornou tão elevado, acima de todo outro nome, e até mesmo acima de todos os poderes angelicais. (Ver Col. 1:15 e *ss*, e 2:9 quanto aos principais exemplos dessa *cristologia*).

3. *Considerações literárias e de estilo*. Ainda uma outra dificuldade para a aceitação da autoria paulina desta epístola (de acordo com o que dizem alguns eruditos) reside em seu caráter literário. Os estudiosos procuram demonstrar que o estilo desta epístola aos Colossenses não é paulino, se tomarmos em consideração os quatro escritos «clássicos» de Paulo, Gálatas, Romanos e I e II aos Coríntios, como modelos da expressão e do vocabulário básico do apóstolo dos gentios. Esses eruditos argumentam que o vocabulário desta epístola é diferente, faltando-lhe as frases curtas e azedas de Paulo. Seu estilo é mais expansivo, mais semelhante ao da epístola aos Efésios. Algumas vezes o original grego é mau e ocasionalmente, é virtualmente ininteligível, conforme se vê em Col. 2:18,19.

Retornando às objeções levantadas pelos eruditos, procuramos respondê-las uma por uma, *nos pontos seguintes*:

1. *O primeiro argumento* contra a autoria paulina é o mais fácil de ser rebatido. A maior parte dos estudiosos modernos admite agora que o gnosticismo é anterior ao cristianismo. Em outras palavras, havia idéias gnósticas no mundo helênico, antes mesmo do advento de Cristo. Apesar de ser verdade, naturalmente que «combinações» de pensamentos religiosos e filosóficos tornaram-se diferentes, devido ao surgimento da teologia cristã — de tal modo que os gnósticos pré-cristãos eram diferentes em seus conceitos daqueles que apareceram dentro da era cristã — o fato é que tudo quanto podemos identificar como essencialmente gnóstico, já existia antes de Cristo. O gnosticismo combinava o misticismo oriental, a filosofia, a mitologia, a astrologia e o neoplatonismo gregos, elementos do judaísmo, além do que, inseria, nessa mistura já confusa, elementos da fé cristã. Cristo, para eles, era apenas um dos «aeons» (emanações angelicais de Deus); mas esses «aeons» já existiam como idéias gnósticas antes de «Cristo» ser considerado como um deles. Em alguns lugares, a ética cristã tornava-se *ascética* pelos gnósticos, embora o ascetismo já fizesse parte do gnosticismo, antes do advento de Cristo. Em outros lugares, a ética cristã se tornava licenciosa; mas a licenciosidade já fazia parte do gnosticismo, antes mesmo do aparecimento do cristianismo no mundo. Os gnósticos «cristãos» de tempos posteriores adoravam anjos; mas outro tanto faziam os de tempos anteriores. Os gnósticos «cristãos» não tinham idéia de «expiação pelo sangue», mas a mesma coisa ocorria entre os da época anterior ao cristianismo. Os gnósticos «cristãos» falavam sobre a grande hierarquia de poderes angelicais, os «aeons» sombrios, que seriam mediadores entre Deus e os homens; mas os gnósticos pré-cristãos eram «deístas», dependendo desses «aeons» para obter um conhecimento secundário de Deus. Os gnósticos «cristãos» elevavam o «conhecimento», em contraste com a «fé», como meio de «salvação», mas outro tanto faziam os gnósticos mais antigos. O judaísmo helenista já ensinava a existência de muitas ordens de poderes angelicais e o próprio Paulo, evidentemente, aceitava esse ponto de vista sobre os anjos (ver Fil. 2:5-10). O neoplatonismo também defendia essa posição, o que fazia parte da atmosfera do pensamento religioso do primeiro século de nossa era, muito antes de Paulo começar a escrever suas epístolas. Paulo meramente insistiu que tais ordens angelicais, sem importar sua natureza, estavam todas sujeitas a Cristo, porque, na realidade, fazem parte de sua criação, estando isso longe da idéia de que o próprio Cristo era apenas um dentre muitos *aeons*, que recebera uma incumbência terrena. Deveria ser claro, portanto, que coisa alguma, nesta epístola aos Colossenses, precisa ser atribuída a tempos pós-paulinos; de fato, a maior parte de seus elementos poderia ter precedido à época de Paulo. Por essas razões, a maior parte dos eruditos de nossos dias admite que todas as *condições religiosas* e todos os «elementos teológicos», refletidos nessa epístola, facilmente poderiam ter existido na época de Paulo, pelo que também poderiam ter sido combatidos em uma epístola como esta de Paulo aos Colossenses.

2. *É verdade que a epístola aos Colossenses* contém a mais exaltada cristologia que aparece em qualquer livro do N.T. Todavia, seus conceitos sob hipótese alguma se limitam a esta epístola. Não nos devemos esquecer que, para Paulo, o Cristo sempre foi o Cristo exaltado à mão direita de Deus Pai, e jamais o mero Jesus histórico (embora, de forma alguma, ele o rejeitasse como homem, e nem tivesse jamais lançado qualquer dúvida sobre a sua missão terrena); o Cristo de Paulo é o Senhor da glória, que ele conheceu mediante experiências místicas. Apesar de que, em suas outras epístolas, sua ênfase sobre a exaltada posição de Cristo seja menor, de fato, isso é básico em sua teologia inteira. (Ver Rom. 1:4; observar o uso que ele faz do termo *Senhor*, apontando para Cristo, bem como citações suas em que o nome de Cristo substitui a Yahweh, nas passagens do A.T.). Notemos, por igual modo, quão freqüentemente, por todos os escritos de Paulo (sobretudo nas introduções, doxologias e conclusões de suas epístolas), o Filho (Cristo) é posto em justaposição a Deus Pai. Certamente nenhuma mera criatura poderia ocupar tal posição. Graça e paz são sempre derivadas de Deus Pai e do Senhor Jesus Cristo; e quase todas as introduções e conclusões incluem esse elemento. Notemos como o Espírito de Deus é igualmente chamado «Espírito de Cristo» (ver Rom. 8:9; ver também os versículos chamados «trinitários», onde os três nomes divinos aparecem juntos, em funções variadas, I Cor. 12:3 e 15:24,27). De alguma maneira especial e elevada, Deus é o Pai de Cristo (ver II Cor. 1:3). Então, em Fil. 2:6, fica claro que o Filho possui igualdade inerente ao Pai, ainda que, devido à sua encarnação, ele tenha posto de lado essa igualdade. O nono versículo daquele mesmo capítulo declara que ele é exaltado acima de todo nome. E esse é o tema central da epístola aos Colossenses, que alguns estudiosos supõem que seja reflexo da teologia cristã

posterior, e não conceitos genuinamente pertencentes a Paulo. Porém, a mera leitura da coletânea paulina mostra que transparece ali um único Cristo. A ênfase maior acerca da exaltada posição de Cristo, nesta epístola aos Colossenses, tornou-se necessária porque o apóstolo dos gentios se opunha a uma heresia que degradava tanto a pessoa como a missão do Filho de Deus. Mas essa ênfase está em perfeita consonância com a teologia paulina básica, conforme é refletido em todas as suas demais epístolas, em nada contrária ao que ali se aprende. «Assim sendo, é perfeitamente natural que vejamos Paulo a frisar tão elaboradamente, e até com extravagância, a completa supremacia e natureza adequada de Cristo. Não há qualquer necessidade de adoração aos anjos ou a quaisquer outros espíritos. Tal ato não somente seria absurdo, mas também seria ultrajante: pois Cristo é o Senhor de todos». (Morton Enslin, «The Literature of the Christian Movement», pág. 291).

3. **Admite-se que o estilo** desta epístola aos Colossenses seja muito semelhante ao da epístola aos Efésios, isto é, mais expansivo, com sentenças mais longas que noutras epístolas, faltando-lhe aquelas frases mais curtas e cáusticas, e sem os parênteses abruptos e interrupções na seqüência de pensamentos. Mas isso poderia ser explicado com base no «desenvolvimento» do estilo, e *não* supondo-se que isso seja *contraditório* às expressões tipicamente paulinas. Outrossim, a eloqüência paulina aparece em Colossenses e Efésios, sendo base das expressões fluentes e poderosas, e não contraditória a essas coisas. O oitavo capítulo da epístola aos Romanos é similar, em estilo, ao primeiro capítulo das epístolas aos Efésios e aos Colossenses. Esse capítulo é um dos «clássicos» paulinos, o qual mostra que Paulo, quando impelido pela inspiração e por ondas de pensamento poderoso, produzia sentenças elevadas e expansivas, em vez das sentenças curtas, desligadas e azedas das suas passagens «polêmicas», que se vêem nas epístolas aos Romanos e aos Gálatas. Poderíamos dizer que as epístolas aos Colossenses e aos Efésios mostram como Paulo escrevia quando se mostrava eloqüente, quando atingia os mais elevados cumes de sua expressão verbal.

É verdade que, algumas vezes, a gramática da epístola aos Colossenses é deficiente; mas até mesmo um bom autor, quando escreve apressadamente, e se não revisa o seu material, mostrará má gramática, com construções estranhas, que ocasionalmente chegam a ser ininteligíveis, segundo se vê em Col. 2:18,19. Outrossim, a qualidade da gramática e das expressões pode variar de uma época para outra, dependendo das circunstâncias, do cansaço físico e do espírito, do estado de ânimo, etc. Contudo, o grego desta epístola não é essencialmente inferior ao grego literário «koiné» que é normalmente bom nas epístolas paulinas.

Há uma certa ausência de expressões paulinas, havendo muitas palavras, na epístola aos Colossenses, que não figuram em outros escritos paulinos. Pode-se pensar em «dikaios» e seus derivados; «apokalupsis», «dokimadzein», «upakoe», «soteria», «koinonia», «nomos», «pisteuo» e conexões adverbiais, como «ara», «dio», «diote» e «gar», que são freqüentes nos escritos paulinos «clássicos», mas que são menos freqüentes ou mesmo totalmente ausentes na epístola aos Colossenses. Tais considerações (a menos que sejam muito pronunciadas), porém, não são necessariamente convincentes em favor de um autor «diferente». Deve-se notar que listas similares podem ser compiladas se fizermos o confronto até mesmo dos escritos paulinos «clássicos» entre si. O termo «dikaiosune» (um dos grandes vocábulos da epístola aos Romanos) aparece apenas por uma vez na primeira epístola aos Coríntios; e *dikaios* não figura ali nem uma vez sequer. O vocábulo «soteria» não é usado nessa referida epístola e nem em Gálatas. E «*sodzo*» figura apenas por uma vez na segunda epístola aos Coríntios. Já «pisteuo» ocorre apenas por uma vez nesta última (ver II Cor. 4:13). A palavra «ara» não ocorre em Filipenses; e «ara oun», tão freqüente em Romanos, não faz parte de I e II aos Coríntios. Além disso, as sentenças muito longas, comuns nesta epístola aos Colossenses, têm paralelo literário em outras epístolas paulinas, como em Rom. 1:1-7; 2:5-10,14-16; 3:23-26; Gál. 2:3-5; 6:9 e Fil. 3:8-11. É perfeitamente possível que Paulo, tendo resolvido defender a cristologia, tenha naturalmente produzido uma composição literária mais formal e polida, do que é evidente em algumas seções de suas epístolas anteriores, que possuem natureza mais espontânea. As diferenças quanto ao vocabulário (novos termos, nesta epístola, que não se acham em outras epístolas paulinas) podem ser explicadas pela simples observação de que a *matéria* abordada exige um vocabulário diferente daquele que Paulo empregara. Ao opor-se ao gnosticismo, mui naturalmente Paulo teve de usar certa variedade de vocabulário que não figura em outras epístolas. Devemo-nos lembrar que a totalidade dos escritos de Paulo que chegaram às nossas mãos utiliza-se apenas de uma pequena parte de seu vocabulário total. Se ele houvesse escrito outras epístolas, teriam palavras que não se acharíam em epístolas anteriormente escritas; e sem dúvida um grande número de novos vocábulos surgiria se ele houvesse abordado novos assuntos.

Nenhuma dúvida acerca da autenticidade da natureza paulina desta epístola aos Colossenses apareceu, até a escola de Tubingen, no século XIX. E a objeção levantada por essa escola visava, essencialmente, o conteúdo «gnóstico» deste livro. A maioria dos eruditos, porém, não mais leva a sério essa objeção. A objeção à elevada cristologia desta epístola também tem sido facilmente derrubada. Aquelas objeções com base no estilo e no vocabulário são mais sérias; mas podem ser respondidas daquela maneira sugerida acima. Filemom é livro que virtualmente não tem sido criticado quanto à sua autoria paulina, pelo que empresta sua genuinidade a esta epístola aos Colossenses, ajudando a estabelecer a autenticidade desta última (se tal for considerado necessário), já que essas epístolas são companheiras literárias e históricas. A presente epístola foi escrita à igreja de Colossos, e Filemom foi escrita a um de seus membros; e ambas foram escritas sob as mesmas circunstâncias, ao mesmo tempo, na mesma prisão, sem falar-se sobre a questão que Paulo era ajudado pelos mesmos companheiros de trabalho. Não é provável que um forjador tivesse tido tanto cuidado em fazer esta epístola concordar tão de perto com a epístola a Filemom, quanto aos próprios detalhes. Pois que necessidade teria um forjador de fazer uma falsa epístola paulina concordar sobre tantos detalhes intricados, e especialmente com uma epístola tão insignificante como é a de Filemom? (Ver a seção II, intitulada *Data e Proveniência*, quanto a provas sobre como essas duas epístolas, Colossenses e Filemom, são companheiras).

De boa fé, portanto, podemos considerar esta epístola aos Colossenses como genuinamente paulina; e muitos eruditos modernos concordam com isso.

II. DATA E PROVENIÊNCIA

As epístolas aos Efésios, aos Colossenses e a

COLOSSENSES

Filemom devem ser todas vinculadas juntamente, escritas na mesma época em geral, na mesma prisão. Talvez tivessem sido escritas em um período de encarceramento anterior ao de Roma, quiçá em Éfeso. A comparação entre Col. 4:7,8 e Efé. 6:21,22 com File. 23;24 mostra que todas elas foram escritas sob circunstâncias comuns. Paulo era ajudado pelos mesmos companheiros; Tíquico (acompanhado pelo escravo fugido de Filemom, Onésimo) foi o portador dessas epístolas (ver Col. 4:9 e File. 10-12). Todas essas três foram escritas na prisão (ver Efé. 4:1; Col. 4:18 e File. 22,23). Mas nem todos os eruditos concordam que Roma tenha sido o lugar de aprisionamento. De fato, o trecho de File. 22, ao mencionar que Paulo esperava logo ser solto, e por tencionar fazer uma viagem a Colossos, o lugar onde morava Filemom (conforme sabemos em Col. 4:9), indica, em primeiro lugar, que esse encarceramento não foi efetuado em Roma, durante o qual ele não sabia se seria morto ou solto (ver Fil. 1:20 e ss). Em segundo lugar, o lugar onde Paulo foi aprisionado provavelmente não ficava muito longe. Roma ficava a mais de mil e trezentos quilômetros de distância, ao passo que Éfeso ficava, quando muito, a cento e cinqüenta quilômetros. Sabemos que a intenção de Paulo, quando ele foi a Jerusalém, e dali para Roma, era prosseguir para o ocidente (para a Espanha), não retornando ao oriente; e não é provável que ele tivesse feito uma viagem redonda de quase três mil e duzentos quilômetros antes de cumprir sua intenção. (Ver Rom. 15:24,25). Parece mais natural, pois, supormos que a «visita» de Paulo para breve—tão breve que Paulo pediu que lhe fosse reservado um lugar de hospedagem, da parte de Filemom (ver File. 22)—significa que ele não estivesse distante, como também que ele tinha quase certeza de que seria solto em breve, nenhuma dessas condições se adapta a seu aprisionamento posterior em Roma. Por isso é que vários eruditos têm conjecturado o local próximo de Éfeso como o lugar onde ele estava encarcerado. Apesar de não contarmos com qualquer menção direta de tal aprisionamento, nas páginas do N.T., é possível que a passagem de I Cor. 15:32, que menciona o fato de que ele «combateu contra as feras em Éfeso», favoreça a conjectura de que Paulo ali fora aprisionado. Se escritas em Éfeso, as cartas, Colossenses e Filemom, devem ser datadas em cerca do verão de 54 D.C. Quando Paulo deixou a área ao redor de Éfeso, foi para a Macedônia e Corinto, e talvez tenha querido visitar novamente alguns lugares da proximidade, ou então quisesse visitar, pela primeira vez, algumas das cidades menores e menos importantes da área (como Colossos), antes de dar início a uma nova missão. Essa conjectura, pelo menos, adapta-se bem às notas que encontramos nas três epístolas sobre as quais discutimos. (Segue-se um sumário dos argumentos sobre o *aprisionamento em Éfeso*).

Alguns estudiosos identificam o lugar de encarceramento como Cesaréia (ver Atos 24:27). Porém, contrário a essa posição pode-se frisar que o trecho de File. 22 indica que Paulo planejava visitar Colossos em breve; mas o livro de Atos mostra-nos que quando Paulo estava em Cesaréia, encaminhava-se para Roma (portanto, para o ocidente, e não para o oriente), não havendo nenhuma indicação que, naquele tempo, Paulo pudesse esperar ser solto em breve. Conforme já se mencionou, naquele estágio da carreira de Paulo, planejava ele uma missão ao ocidente (Espanha, ver Rom. 15:23,24), não sendo provável que ele tivesse adiado seu desígnio ao fazer, antes disso, tão longa e cansativa viagem pelo oriente.

Além disso, não é fácil explicar por que razão Onésimo, o escravo fugido, fora para Cesaréia. Muito mais provável é que se tivesse refugiado em uma cidade grande e não muito distante, a fim de encontrar esconderijo seguro. Ou então, se porventura tivesse querido arriscar-se a uma viagem longa, mais provavelmente teria ido para a cidade de Roma, que era uma autêntica «meca» de escravos fugidos. Éfeso, a capital da província, deve ter-lhe parecido um lugar convidativo, onde poderia ocultar-se com facilidade, sem arriscar-se a ser apanhado, se tentasse executar alguma longa viagem.

Não fora posto em dúvida o aprisionamento de Paulo em Roma senão já em data recente, porque isso era aceito com unanimidade nos primeiros séculos. Tal aceitação, porém, estava alicerçada principalmente sobre a idéia de que todas as epístolas da prisão foram escritas no mesmo lugar, ao passo que, examinando-as, vemos que diversos lugares facilmente podem ter estado envolvidos, tão diferentes são as condições que houve, ligadas à sua escrita. Ainda que os trechos de Fil. 1:13 («guarda pretoriana») e Fil. 4:22 (casa de César) indiquem Roma (o que não é necessidade imperiosa), isso significaria apenas que a epístola aos Filipenses, e nenhuma outra, foi escrita ali. O argumento mais vigoroso em favor de Roma é a natureza *avançada* da cristologia da presente epístola, bem como a avançada natureza da doutrina da igreja, na epístola aos Efésios, o que talvez reflita um «período posterior» da vida de Paulo; e isso se coadunaria bem à idéia do encarceramento em Roma, e não antes, em algum outro lugar. Esse argumento, todavia, é inteiramente alicerçado sobre a conjectura de que tais idéias não tiveram pleno desenvolvimento senão quando Paulo atingiu idade avançada, apesar de não haver provas quanto a isso. Todos os elementos distintivos das epístolas aos Efésios e aos Colossenses, como a hierarquia de anjos, os «*aeons*» e as idéias éticas, existiam no mundo antigo, muito antes da época de Paulo; e teria sido apenas natural que Cristo fosse colocado como cabeça de todas essas gradações de poder e autoridade, uma vez que ele fosse aceito como Senhor e Messias. Não teria havido necessidade da passagem de muitos anos, já no fim de sua vida, para que ele chegasse a tal conclusão. É mais seguro dizer-se que Paulo, pouco depois de sua conversão, por causa de suas muitas visões e de sua iluminação espiritual, tivesse visto Cristo como o Senhor da glória; e tal ponto de vista não teria exigido qualquer grande extensão de tempo, até que se desenvolvesse. Em todos os escritos de Paulo, e não somente nas epístolas aos Efésios e aos Colossenses, Cristo figura como o Senhor de tudo; e isso nos faz saber que sua elevada cristologia não foi um desenvolvimento posterior de sua teologia. Seja como for, é tão fácil supor que a epístola aos Colossenses representa o desenvolvimento de suas idéias, ao ponto em que elas tinham chegado em cerca de 54 D.C., como é fácil dizer que isso representa um desenvolvimento de data pouco posterior, isto é, depois de 58 D.C. E ainda que datemos o aprisionamento em Roma tão tarde quanto o ano de 62 D.C. conforme fazem alguns estudiosos, contudo, haveria uma diferença de apenas oito anos entre um proposto encarceramento em Éfeso e o aprisionamento na cidade de Roma, o que não é, na realidade, tempo por demais dilatado para consubstanciar um caso em favor do «desenvolvimento posterior» da teologia paulina, o que teria dado supostamente, a Paulo, o tempo de chegar às idéias cristológicas que transparecem evidentemente na presente epístola.

O caso em favor de Éfeso pode ser expresso através

COLOSSENSES

dos seguintes pontos:

1. Teria sido apenas natural que Onésimo, o escravo fugido, tivesse buscado imediato refúgio em uma cidade grande e próxima, em vez de arriscar-se a uma longa viagem até à cidade de Roma.

2. Epafras, o principal pastor da igreja cristã de Colossos, por estar enfrentando uma heresia e a confusão na comunidade cristã de Colossos, poderia ir rapidamente à cidade próxima de Éfeso, a fim de buscar o conselho de Paulo, ao passo que a longa viagem até Roma não faria tal viagem ser viável. (Ver Col. 4:12,13, que indica que esse foi o propósito da visita de Epafras a Paulo).

3. No período do aprisionamento em Roma, parece que a Paulo faltaram amigos e apoiadores autênticos, excetuando Timóteo e Epafrodito (ver Fil. 2:20 e o seu contexto). Isso dificilmente poderia ser reconciliado com a longa lista de fiéis companheiros, conforme se vê em Col. 4:7-15, na qual estão incluídos tanto Marcos como Lucas.

4. O *pedido de hospedagem*, por parte de Paulo, preparada por Filemom, bem como a certeza que tinha o apóstolo de que logo seria solto, indicam um aprisionamento anterior e menos perigoso que aquele que mais tarde, teve lugar em Roma, além de apontar para um local não muito distante. (Ver File. 22).

5. Finalmente, sabemos que Paulo, quando estava em Roma, queria ir à Espanha (o ocidente) e não voltar ao oriente (ver Rom. 15:23,24). Não é provável que, uma vez solto da prisão, tivesse o apóstolo feito uma viagem redonda de três mil e duzentos quilômetros, saindo da rota certa, o que era viagem que consumia extremamente muito tempo naqueles dias, antes de cumprir seu longamente cultivado desejo de anunciar o evangelho no ocidente. Somente algum motivo extremamente compelidor poderia tê-lo inspirado a tanto.

Contra a teoria do aprisionamento de Paulo em Éfeso:

1. Tudo não passa de uma conjectura, porque não há qualquer informação neotestamentária certa sobre isso, excetuando, talvez, o trecho de I Cor. 15:52.

2. Não há quaisquer citações, dos primeiros pais da igreja ou da tradição cristã, em apoio a essa teoria.

3. Muitos bons eruditos modernos, considerando todos os ângulos do problema, continuam afirmando que o aprisionamento em Roma é o mais provável.

4. Uma viagem confirmatória pelas igrejas do oriente poderia ter sido efetuada antes de Paulo dirigir-se ao ocidente, pois parece ter sido costumeiro, entre os grandes pregadores do evangelho, efetuarem viagens confirmatórias a áreas mais antigas, antes de se lhes abrirem novas frentes de trabalho.

A questão inteira do *local de encarceramento* de Paulo é de importância relativamente pequena, exceto no que tange ao nosso desejo de obter mais exato conhecimento da vida dele e de questões da cronologia do N.T., em relação à produção de seus documentos formadores. Seria interessante se pudéssemos determinar, com acurácia, sob quais circunstâncias, no tocante à história do livro de Atos, é que foi escrita cada uma das epístolas paulinas. Infelizmente, não contamos com informações suficientes, dentro ou fora do N.T., acerca da vida e da correspondência do apóstolo dos gentios, para fazermos isso; portanto, toda a «reconstituição» dessas questões não passa de uma conjectura, pelo menos em parte. Se tais reconstituições pudessem ser compostas com exatidão, certamente obteríamos maior discernimento quanto àquilo que Paulo escreveu, porque então poderíamos interpretar seus escritos à luz das circunstâncias históricas. A propensão por aceitar o que os antigos pais da igreja disseram sobre essas coisas, sem que se faça qualquer investigação, não tem caracterizado a muitos dos eruditos de nossa época, pois se tem raciocinado, com razão, que grande parte do que disseram os pais da igreja, com relação a essas coisas, compunha-se de meras conjecturas, pois suas fontes de informação, em muitos casos, eram inferiores às de nossos dias. A arqueologia tem iluminado grande parte do N.T., tendo podido acrescentar diversos esclarecimentos de natureza histórica, que cercam os documentos neotestamentários.

III. MOTIVO E PROPÓSITOS:

Epafras fora falar com Paulo, a fim de narrar-lhe as dificuldades da igreja de Colossos, além de descrever seu estado geral, o que incluía certos pontos encorajadores (ver Col. 1:4-8). Sem dúvida, foi ele quem informou o apóstolo sobre a penetração da heresia gnóstica nas fileiras cristãs daquela localidade. E foi principalmente para responder a esse problema que esta epístola aos Colossenses foi escrita. Naturalmente, a epístola teve o intuito de servir de instrução positiva quanto às crenças e à ética cristãs, não servindo de mera polêmica contra o gnosticismo. Paulo combinou, habilidosamente, esses dois propósitos, neste seu escrito. A seção da epístola, composta por seus capítulos terceiro e quarto, que é de natureza essencialmente ética, está inteiramente livre de assuntos polêmicos.

Paulo conhecera Onésimo, o escravo fugido de Filemom, no cárcere; ou então alguém o trouxe à presença do apóstolo. Tendo-o conduzido a Cristo, e em seguida tendo-o conduzido à idéia de que era seu dever retornar a Filemom, Paulo enviou por seu intermédio uma missiva a Filemom, a fim de garantir a aceitação favorável do portador por parte de Filemom. Também aproveitou o ensejo para enviar uma epístola geral à igreja de Colossos (que é a nossa epístola aos Colossenses).

O erro que havia na comunidade cristã de Colossos.

A natureza de tudo quanto estava envolvido nesse erro é deixado em dúvida porque o combate a esse erro está envolvido em linguagem própria dos hereges, o que, para nós é ininteligível pelo menos em parte. Não obstante, é claro que alguma forma antiga de gnosticismo está em foco; e vários de seus elementos não são distinguidos com dificuldade. Ver o artigo sobre o *Gnosticismo*. Cada área geográfica, sem dúvida alguma, tinha certa mistura de idéias, embora tudo continuasse sendo, de modo geral, conceitos representativos do pensamento gnóstico. A heresia gnóstica assediou a igreja cristã por cerca de cento e cinquenta anos, e oito dos livros do N.T. foram escritos contra a mesma, a saber, esta epístola aos Colossenses, as três epístolas pastorais, as três epístolas joaninas e a epístola de Judas.

Quanto à situação em Colossos e o tipo de gnosticismo que prevalecia ali, podemos distinguir os elementos seguintes:

1. Grande importância era conferida aos «aeons» ou ordens de seres angelicais (emanações de Deus), com prejuízo para a posição de Cristo. Os gnósticos não viam o Cristo como a «encarnação» do Logos, mas somente como um dentre muitos «aeons», dotados de alguma missão terrena. Para eles, Cristo era apenas um dos mediadores e salvadores, um pequeno deus, e não, necessariamente, o mais elevado dos «aeons». Rejeitavam qualquer «encarnação» real para os «aeons», como se isso lhes fosse impossível. Muito menos isso poderia suceder no caso do poderoso

«Logos». Assim pensavam eles porque tinham a matéria como o princípio mesmo da maldade; e o corpo físico, como é óbvio, participa da matéria. Portanto, nenhum «aeon» santo poderia, na realidade tomar carne humana, sem contaminar-se a si mesmo.

2. *Os aeons* (poderes angelicais) eram objetos de adoração entre os gnósticos. Cristo, na qualidade de «aeon», era adorado, mas somente em pé de igualdade com muitos outros «aeons». E assim era tremendamente diminuída a estatura de Cristo, com a conseqüente degradação de sua pessoa. Certamente os gnósticos não reconheciam a existência do Deus triúno, o único que, com razão, pode ser adorado pela criatura humana; e nem reconheciam Cristo como o cabeça de toda a criação. (Ver Col. 2:18-19). O universo não era «Cristo-cêntrico», na opinião deles, conforme normalmente se aprende no cristianismo normal. (Ver Col. 1:15-19). Deus trataria indiretamente com sua criação, através de muitos mediadores e salvadores, e não apenas através de um só. O trecho de I Tim. 2:5 foi escrito em favor do caráter medianeiro e único de Cristo, em contraposição à heresia gnóstica, que propunha grande quantidade de mediadores.

3. Os gnósticos propunham a idéia de *muitos criadores*, pois os «aeons», segundo sua doutrina, tinham o poder de criar. Paulo insiste que só há um poder capaz de criar (ver Col. 1:16). Outrossim, o criador é o alvo de sua criação — esta deverá encontrar nele toda a razão de sua existência, não dirigindo sua atenção para alguma quase interminável sucessão de sombrias emanações angelicais. Paulo não nega (e nem afirma) que os anjos possuem poderes de criação. É provável que os tenham. Porém, qualquer poder que porventura possuam, segundo afirma o apóstolo, vem a eles por delegação de Cristo, que é o cabeça de todos os principados, poderes e domínios; de fato, é o criador deles. Ora, se Cristo é o criador desses poderes, é impossível que seja nomeado entre eles, como um de seus iguais.

4. Os gnósticos, em Colossos, evidentemente tinham incorporado em seu sistema alguns elementos das *leis cerimoniais judaicas*, assim encorajando as suas tendências para o ascetismo. (Ver Col. 2:16 e *ss*). Os gnósticos criam que o desígnio do sistema cósmico é destruir toda a natéria, incluindo o corpo físico, visto que a matéria seria o princípio mesmo do mal. Poderíamos cooperar com esse desígnio se abusássemos do corpo, o que poderia ser feito através do ascetismo ou da licenciosidade extremados. Os gnósticos de Colossos tinham escolhido o ascetismo como esse meio de abuso, ao passo que, em outras áreas, esse meio era a licenciosidade. E isso se tornou parte oficial do sistema de ética esposado por eles. Os demais sete livros do N.T. que foram escritos contra o gnosticismo, refletem a variedade licenciosa do gnosticismo. (Ver II Tim. 3:6 acerca disso). Os gnósticos tinham a idéia equivocada de que não importa o que fazemos com nossos corpos, pois estes, conforme pensavam, seriam veículos incuráveis do princípio do pecado; outrossim, pensavam que deveriam abusar do corpo, sem que isso em nada prejudicasse à alma, como o ouro que é mergulhado na lama não tem sua natureza modificada.

5. Os gnósticos se jactavam de uma *filosofia superior*, que incorporava certa forma de *misticismo*. O gnosticismo era um misticismo basicamente oriental, apresentado como filosofia. Se por acaso tivesse vencido a luta com o cristianismo, este último teria sido transformado em outra mera religião misteriosa greco-romana. O misticismo deles era falso, porquanto não contava com Cristo como seu objeto (ver Col. 2:4,8,18). Outrossim, o misticismo deles não os transformava moralmente, o que sucede, sem dúvida, aos místicos verdadeiros. O misticismo deles, portanto, era falso. É seguro dizermos que toda a experiência mística, quando é autêntica, transforma o homem moralmente. Os gnósticos supunham-se «fora» das questões morais, devido às suas visões e êxtases.

6. Os gnósticos eram falsamente humildes, pois guiavam-se por uma forma de verdadeira auto-exaltação, já que o *ascetismo* deles somente promovia o orgulho espiritual. Precisavam fazer de Jesus Cristo o seu grande exemplo, sem apelarem para seus costumes extremados (ver Col. 2:20-23).

7. Os gnósticos tinham uma sabedoria e um conhecimento falsos, pelo que negligenciavam a Sabedoria de Deus, o seu *mistério*, a saber, Cristo (ver Col. 2:8; 1:27 e 2:2). Para eles, a salvação deveria ser obtida através do «conhecimento», e não através da «fé». Julgavam que a fé pertenceria a espíritos menos desenvolvidos, a qual poderia levar somente a uma forma inferior de redenção, ao passo que o tipo de conhecimento que possuíam (mediado através de ritos sagrados, das artes mágicas e de misticismo) os conduziria à completa redenção, a saber, a reabsorção pelo Espírito divino, com a perda da identidade pessoal, em que o *ego* seria transformado no «super-ego».

8. Os gnósticos *rejeitavam* a expiação pelo sangue, pelo que também não viam qualquer valor na morte de Cristo. Criam eles que o «Espírito-Cristo», um dos «aeons», na realidade não se encarnara, porquanto não poderia sofrer e nem morrer. Tomara conta do corpo de Jesus, o homem, quando de seu batismo, tendo-o abandonado por ocasião de sua crucificação. Para eles, a morte de Jesus, quando muito, foi somente a morte de um mártir por uma boa causa. Não poderia ter qualquer valor expiatório. Em contraste com essa opinião, Paulo declara que a expiação de Cristo tem valor cósmico, e não meramente significação terrena (ver Col. 1:20 e *ss*).

9. Os gnósticos pensavam que os «aeons» angelicais, considerados em seu conjunto, seriam a *plenitude* de Deus, isto é, a emanação de sua natureza e dos seus atributos. Cristo, nesse caso, seria apenas um dentre muitos «aeons», podendo participar da natureza e dos atributos de Deus apenas em parte, de modo fragmentário. O pensamento de Paulo, em contraste com isso, é que Cristo encerra a «plenitude» (*pleroma*) de Deus (ver Col. 2:9).

10. Os gnósticos supunham que a redenção humana, em seu nível mais elevado, indicava a *reabsorção* pelo Espírito de Deus, com a perda da identidade pessoal. Bem ao contrário disso, a redenção do homem, em seus estágios mais elevados, indica a participação em toda a plenitude de Deus a «pleroma» total — ver Efé. 3:19 e Col. 2:10, tal como Cristo dela participa, sem qualquer perda de identidade pessoal, do mesmo modo que Jesus Cristo não perdeu sua identidade pessoal ao participar da plenitude de Deus. Isso ensina, portanto, que os homens remidos chegarão a participar da natureza divina (ver II Ped. 1:4); mas isso é declarado contra o pano de fundo da polêmica contra o gnosticismo.

11. Os gnósticos classificavam os homens em três grupos: a. Os *«hílicos»*, ou *«terrenos»*, que só se importariam com a matéria. Esses homens, que seriam a vasta maioria da humanidade, visto estarem totalmente imersos na matéria, não poderiam mesmo escapar dela, o que significa que teriam de perecer

COLOSSENSES

com ela, quando da grande conflagração que haverá.
b. Os *«psíquicos»*, ou «animae». Esse grupo, que incluiria os profetas do A.T., se comporia de homens que «através da fé» (não do «conhecimento») haveriam de atingir uma redenção inferior. c. Os *«pneumáticos»* ou verdadeiramente «espirituais» (que seriam os gnósticos), os quais, mediante o «conhecimento», haveriam de atingir à mais elevada redenção, a saber, a reabsorção pelo Espírito divino. Para os gnósticos, pois, somente alguns poucos seriam passíveis de redenção. O trecho de Col. 1:20 e ss, certamente combate essa noção; e as enfáticas declarações do segundo capítulo da primeira epístola de Timóteo, no sentido que Deus quer que «todos sejam salvos e venham ao pleno conhecimento da verdade» são ataques diretos contra o exclusivismo dos mestres gnósticos.

De modo geral, pois, pode-se dizer que o gnosticismo de Colossos pertencia à variedade ordinária, talvez com um pouco mais de mistura de judaísmo do que era normal. Também pedira por empréstimo idéias comuns às religiões misteriosas orientais e ao neoplatonismo e o resultado disso era uma horrorosa conglomeração. Foi contra essas crenças sincretistas que Paulo escreveu esta epístola aos Colossenses, pois, como é claro, os gnósticos começavam a fazer adeptos seus na Ásia Menor.

A ausência de qualquer análise direta nesta epístola, acerca das doutrinas combatidas, não nos permite maior exatidão em nossas definições do gnosticismo, se contarmos exclusivamente com o N.T. Há muitas informações sobre as crenças gnósticas em vários livros apocalípticos do N.T., como o evangelho de Tomé e o evangelho de Pedro. Na introdução ao NTI há um artigo dedicado à descrição dos livros apócrifos do N.T. Alguns dos primeiros pais da igreja também descreveram as doutrinas gnósticas; e ainda que algumas de suas descrições estivessem equivocadas, devido ao calor da controvérsia, ou devido à falta de maior compreensão, há ali muitas informações válidas. Os primeiros pais da igreja, bem como os apóstolos antes deles, reconheciam com razão a ameaça que o gnosticismo representava para a igreja. Diz-se que o apóstolo João negava-se a ir aos banhos públicos de Éfeso quando sabia que Cerinto (um dos primeiros mestres gnósticos), seu oponente, também estava naqueles banhos.

Os mestres gnósticos, evidentemente, aludiam a seu sistema como uma «filosofia», ao passo que o apóstolo Paulo preferia chamá-lo de «vãs sutilezas» (ver Col. 2:8). Evidentemente afirmavam possuir certo apoio nas «tradições», dizendo-se representantes de antigas verdades. Platão alude a certas pessoas que vendiam livros de Orfeu ou Museu, em Atenas, na sua época, as quais, por igual modo, davam continuidade a certas tradições transmitidas da parte dos deuses. (Ver *República* II.364E). No hino homérico a Demétrio, vê-se que muitos pensavam que os ritos eleusianos (originalmente celebrados em Eleusis, uma cidade que ficava a noroeste de Atenas) tinham sido ordenados pelo próprio Demétrio, preservados por tradições entregues e transmitidas pela família de Eumolpides desde tempos pré-históricos. Por igual modo, as seitas mais recentes gostam de traçar suas origens a algum tempo remoto, sendo possível que os hereges combatidos por Paulo, em Colossos, não agissem de maneira diferente. Suas «tradições» eram meramente de «homens», para o apóstolo dos gentios; não tinham qualquer autoridade divina. (Ver Col. 2:8).

Conforme já se disse, os gnósticos de Colossos não pertenciam à variedade comum de religiosos licenciosos. Parecia antes que pregavam uma doutrina de «desprendimento», o ideal estóico, embora tivessem pervertido tal ideal, levando-o a assumir o caráter negativo do ascetismo extremado. Isso fazia o sistema deles favorecer o cerimonialismo mosaico, as restrições dietéticas, os jejuns e as provisões ritualistas intermináveis. Evidentemente eram vegetarianos e celibatas. Pregavam uma doutrina que ordenava: «Não manusear», «Não provar». A primeira dessas proibições parece ter tido subentendidos sexuais. É quase certo que eles praticavam a circuncisão. Observando essas coisas, percebemos que eles se assemelhavam aos essênios quanto a certos particulares. Ver o artigo sobre os *Essênios*. Alguns estudiosos têm pensado que a heresia combatida em Colossos era apenas uma forma um tanto modificada de crenças essênias; mas essa posição não tem atraído atenções sérias em tempos recentes, por ser um substituto pobre da idéia de que Paulo combatia o *gnosticismo*. As evidências históricas, que são abundantes, favorecem a suposição de que o gnosticismo foi a heresia combatida nesta epístola. O gnosticismo, e não o essenianismo, sem dúvida alguma, foi a doutrina que ameaçou o cristianismo por tantas décadas. (Quanto às práticas «vegetarianas e celibatárias do gnosticismo», com seu ascetismo em geral, ver as notas expositivas sobre Col. 2:16,20,21 no NTI). O trecho de Col. 2:11-13 subentende que eles davam grande valor à circuncisão. Parece que tinham tomado por empréstimo — exagerando-as então — várias provisões das leis cerimoniais mosaicas.

Os gnósticos defendiam a doutrina dos «espíritos elementares» (ver Col. 2:8), as «stoicheia», os «elementos animados da natureza»; pois, para eles concordando com outros povos antigos, a matéria não era reputada «inanimada». Essa idéia pode ser confrontada com o que diziam os hilozoístas jônicos, que pensavam que a matéria é cheia de força vital, provocando todas as mudanças e desenvolvimentos na natureza, resultando no que chamamos de «vida». O termo «stoicheia» (e o que nele fica implícito) foi transferido pelos gnósticos para indicar as «essências espirituais», que seriam as «ordens angelicais». Foi assim que as «stoicheia» dos pagãos se transformaram nos anjos do conceito hebraico. Na astrologia, o termo «stoicheia» era usado para indicar os «corpos celestes», que eram então considerados os «corpos» de espíritos celestiais, ou, em alguns sistemas, os lugares onde habitavam esses espíritos. Não sabemos quanto da astrologia antiga os gnósticos incorporaram no seu sistema; mas é certo que sua observância de festividades, luas novas, sábados, ciclos anuais, etc., eram mais por empréstimos do cerimonialismo judaico. Seja como for, o judaísmo helenista estava muito envolvido na astrologia, segundo nos mostra o livro de Jubileus e outros documentos do período. Visto que as «stoicheia» teriam influência sobre os homens, era natural supor que mereciam atenção e até adoração da parte dos homens. Os gnósticos, pois, veneravam esses espíritos elementares do universo (ver Col. 2:18), que eles arranjavam em muitos grupos e ordens, nos quais haveria poderes gradualmente decrescentes, segundo se distanciavam cada vez mais do Sol central, que é Deus. Nesse particular, eles tomaram por empréstimo idéias neoplatônicas, como a das *emanações*, através das quais esses espíritos vieram a ser reputados como *«partículas»* do Espírito divino; e todos eles, em seu conjunto, seriam a «plenitude» de Deus, incluindo sua natureza e seus atributos. Os termos «principados», «domínios», «poderes», etc., descrevem as ordens descendentes dos

COLOSSENSES

«aeons» (ver Col. 1:16). Cada um desses termos representa classes existentes entre as «stoicheia».

O erro combatido nesta epístola seria o judaísmo? Alguns comentadores mais antigos, não percebendo a importância do ataque gnóstico contra a igreja primitiva, e influenciados pelo ponto de vista simplista do trecho de Col. 2:11-17, têm pensado que o erro aqui combatido é o legalismo do judaísmo. Mas a epístola aos Colossenses de modo algum é apenas uma versão diferente da epístola aos Gálatas (onde é combatido o «legalismo»). Apesar do gnosticismo incorporar certos aspectos do cerimonialismo comum ao judaísmo, era muito pior que o judaísmo normal. A moderação acerca das bebidas alcoólicas, transformou-se em abstinência absoluta; a vida sexual regulamentada foi transformada no celibato; a restrição de certas carnes transformou-se no vegetarianismo; a observância de luas novas e dias santificados, com base nos ciclos anuais, transformou-se em meios de adoração das «stoicheia». Na presente epístola, não há qualquer indício de que Paulo se opunha ao simples *legalismo*, o que teria sido importante elemento, se o judaísmo fosse o objetivo de sua polêmica. A necessidade de salientar às ordens angelicais (ver Col. 1:16), em que se assevera que Cristo é seu criador e Senhor, exigindo ele a nossa adoração, que não pode ser conferida aos anjos (ver Col. 2:18), o fato de que há alusão aos *mistérios* (ver Col. 1:26 e 2:2), o ataque contra o ascetismo exagerado (ver Col. 2:20 e *ss*), a definição de «sabedoria» e de *conhecimento* (ver Col. 2:2,3), como algo pertencente originalmente a Cristo e o fato de que a «plenitude» (*pleroma*, no grego) é dele (ver Col. 2:8,9), a necessidade de salientar que toda a criação deverá encontrar em Cristo o Alfa e o Ômega (ver Col. 1:16 e *ss*), a negação do *deísmo* (vide), em razão do fato de que Cristo é visto como a *imagem* (e, portanto, a manifestação) do Deus invisível (ver Col. 1:15), a ênfase sobre o seu senhorio universal (ver Col. 2:19), e a descrição da salvação para todos (ver Col. 1:20), além do valor da morte de Cristo como expiação (ver Col. 1:20 e *ss*), tudo aponta para o gnosticismo como a heresia aqui atacada, e não o legalismo, ou qualquer forma de essenianismo.

IV. INTEGRIDADE DA EPÍSTOLA

A palavra **integridade**, aplicada à natureza de livros e epístolas, fala de questões concernentes à sua forma atual, em contraste com sua forma original. A presente epístola, conforme a conhecemos, representa a epístola original ou foi modificada com adições ou subtrações? Foram levantadas dúvidas quanto à sua autenticidade (seria de Paulo ou não?) nos meados do século passado, o que também atingiu sua integridade. A primeira dessas questões é amplamente estudada na primeira seção deste artigo. Quanto à questão da «integridade», H.J. Holtzmann propôs a complicada teoria que uma breve e autêntica epístola de Paulo aos Colossenses foi usada por um paulinista posterior como base da composição da epístola aos Efésios, cujo resultado foi então interpolado dentro da epístola aos Colossenses. Hermann von Soden («Die Briefe and die Kilosser, Epheser, Filemom», 1891) sujeitou essa teoria a exame cuidadoso, mas sua conclusão é que a mesma é altamente exagerada, pois haveria apenas algumas poucas interpolações por parte do autor posterior. Em seu comentário, impresso alguns anos mais tarde, a única interpolação por ele identificada foi a de Col. 1:16,17. William Sanday (em artigo no «Dictionary of the Bible», editores W. Smith e J.M. Fuller) apresenta uma revisão do problema, oferecendo fortes provas em favor da integridade e da autenticidade da presente epístola. A mais completa dissertação sobre essa questão (que também inclui a epístola aos Efésios), é a de Ernst Percy, intitulada «Die Probleme der Kolosser und Epheser-briefe». Ele apresentou poderosos argumentos em favor da autenticidade e da integridade de ambas essas epístolas, com base em considerações lingüísticas e teológicas. No caso da epístola aos Colossenses, pelo menos, a maioria dos eruditos concorda que ela é autenticamente paulina, tendo-se conservado praticamente segundo a forma como foi originalmente produzida. O antigo ataque contra a epístola aos Colossenses, no sentido que a mesma representa um «milieu» religioso posterior (isto é, do segundo século de nossa era), ou seja, não poderia ter sido escrita pelo apóstolo Paulo, tem sido abandonado, conforme tem aumentado nosso conhecimento sobre as condições religiosas do primeiro século de nossa era.

V. TEMAS PRINCIPAIS

A leitura da seção terceira, intitulada «Motivo e Propósitos», exporá ao leitor muito do que pode ser dito nesta seção. Consideremos os pontos seguintes:

O seu grande tema central é a pessoa de Cristo, o Cabeça do cosmos, o Mistério de Deus; ele é divino, mas é humano, pois efetuou autêntica expiação, mediante sua morte genuína. A grandeza de Cristo é retratada de forma gráfica na presente epístola aos Colossenses, mais do que em qualquer outro livro do N.T. Isso é assim porque Cristo, em sua pessoa e estatura espiritual, estava sendo atacado pelos gnósticos nas igrejas da Ásia Menor, interna e externamente; e, assim sendo, fazia-se mister forte defesa a fim de preservar a fé dos crentes. Quanto à específica cristologia assim defendida, convém que pensemos nos elementos abaixo:

a. Cristo é o doador da graça, não sendo ela conferida por alguma linhagem sombria de mediadores angelicais;

b. Cristo aparece associado ao próprio Pai, pelo que é superior aos chamados «aeons»; 1:2;

c. Cristo é o verdadeiro objeto da fé (ver Col. 1:2,4);

d. Cristo é o doador da glória celestial, o Cabeça do reino celeste;

e. Cristo é o objeto da inquirição ética, do andar diário (ver Col. 1:10 e seus capítulos terceiro e quarto), 1:5,13;

f. Cristo é o doador da herança (ver Col. 1:12);

g. Cristo fez expiação: sua encarnação foi real, como reais foram a sua morte e a sua importância cósmica (ver Col. 1:14,20,21);

h. Cristo é o Reconciliador e isso em escala cósmica (ver Col. 1:21);

i. Cristo é a Imagem do Deus invisível, seu revelador (ver Col. 1:15); e tal ofício não pode ser atribuído aos «aeons»;

j. Cristo é o criador (até mesmo dos «aeons») e o sustentador da criação (ver Col. 1:17), o alvo mesmo da criação e de todos os seres inteligentes (ver Col. 1:16), isto é, ele é o Alfa e o Ômega;

k. Cristo é o Cabeça da Igreja, o primogênito, que ocupa o lugar de maior proeminência;

l. Em Cristo habita toda a «plenitude» («pleroma») de Deus (ver Col. 1:18,19 e 2:9);

m. Cristo, em sua missão terrena, sofreu e morreu; ele não é algum «aeon» que tornou-se possuidor do corpo humano e que agiu como se fosse tal. Podemos participar dos seus sofrimentos (ver Col. 1:24);

n. A grande realidade mística do cristianismo é a presença de Cristo em nós, mediante seu Espírito.

Isso traz o divino ao humano, pelo que é declarada falsa a posição do *deísmo* que haveria um ser supremo, mas que nada tem a ver com o seu universo, pois seria sempre transcendental (ver Col. 1:27);

o. Cristo é o alvo de toda a busca pela perfeição (ver Col. 1:28);

p. Cristo é o inspirador dos labores apostólicos (ver Col. 1:25,29), pelo que devemos lealdade ao evangelho apostólico;

q. Cristo é o mistério de Deus, em quem residem todos os tesouros da sabedoria e do conhecimento (em contraste com o pretenso conhecimento dos gnósticos) (ver Col. 2:2);

r. Cristo compartilha conosco da plenitude de Deus, pelo que chegamos a participar da natureza divina (ver II Ped. 1:4 e Col. 2:10); e assim a plenitude divina é por nós compartilhada sem a perda da identidade pessoal, conforme ensinavam erroneamente os mestres gnósticos;

s. Temos comunhão mística com Cristo, em sua morte e ressurreição; e isso é a base de toda a moralidade, pois ele é o padrão da moralidade (ver Col. 2:11-12 e seus capítulos terceiro e quarto);

t. Cristo é o vencedor de todo o mal, o qual dá liberdade à alma e aos homens, em suas observâncias religiosas (ver Col. 2:14-18);

u. Cristo é o Cabeça cósmico de tudo, devendo ser reconhecido como tal pelos homens (ver Col. 2:19);

v. Cristo não nos confere o espírito de ascetismo, mas de liberdade (ver Col. 2:20-23);

w. A vida ressurrecta de Cristo nos é transmitida misticamente, de tal modo que obtemos vitória sobre o pecado (ver Col. 3:1 e *ss*);

x. A morte de Cristo, além de ter servido como expiação pelo pecado, igualmente nos é misticamente transmitida, pois o seu Santo Espírito leva-nos a morrer para o mundo e viver para Deus (ver Col. 3:1-5);

y. Cristo vence todos os vícios pagãos que antes nos cativavam (ver Col. 3:5-10);

z. Cristo regulamenta toda a conduta cristã, pois ele é o Homem ideal (ver Col. 3:11 e *ss*).

Assim sendo, pode-se ver que todas as grandes doutrinas da presente epístola são apoiadas sobre a natureza de Cristo como Cabeça e como Deus; mas sob hipótese alguma sua humanidade autêntica ou sua missão terrena é apagada ou ignorada dentro desse elevadíssimo acontecimento. A seção prática desta epístola também se alicerça sobre a pessoa de Cristo (ver os capítulos terceiro e quarto deste livro), pois a vida piedosa, na realidade, consiste em participarmos de sua vida eterna e ressurrecta, uma vez que tenhamos morrido para o mundo (ver Col. 3:1-5). E todas as questões práticas e morais, bem como todas as questões de lealdade, têm solução em Cristo.

VI. CONFIRMAÇÃO ANTIGA E ACEITAÇÃO DA EPÍSTOLA

Já que o *cânon* do N.T. na realidade não teve começo, de modo formal, senão no tempo de Márcion (150 D.C.), que se situa bem dentro do tempo em que a epístola aos Colossenses começou a ser universalmente conhecida e usada, todos os *cânones* antigos a incluem. Ver o artigo sobre *Cânon*. O cânon mais antigo consistia dos quatro evangelhos e de dez epístolas paulinas, e a presente epístola fazia parte dessa lista. Todas as coletâneas das epístolas paulinas, desde os tempos mais remotos, incluíam a epístola aos Colossenses. Ela é alistada no «cânon» marcionita, no fragmento *Muratoriano* (o que reflete o uso da comunidade cristã de Roma, por volta do ano 200 D.C.). Também foi incluído nos mais antigos manuscritos que possuímos acerca das epístolas paulinas, inclusive o antiqüíssimo ms P(46), que talvez date dos começos do fim do século II D.C., embora a maioria dos estudiosos o situe dentro do século III D.C.

O que é surpreendente é que a confirmação e uso desta epístola, pelos pais pré-canônicos e nos escritos cristãos, é inferior ao do caso da epístola aos Efésios. Nossas fontes informativas não falam de qualquer confirmação no primeiro século; mas, nos primórdios do segundo século, a epístola já era largamente conhecida e usada. Contudo, não há qualquer evidência de que esta epístola foi lançada na suspeita, por parte da igreja antiga; e nem houve jamais qualquer sugestão de que ela não pertencesse ao 1º séc., ou de que Paulo não a tenha escrito. Não há qualquer traço desta epístola nos escritos de Clemente de Roma (primeiro século de nossa era) ou no Pastor de Hermas (140 D.C.). Nos escritos de Barnabé (começo do segundo século) parece haver uma alusão a Col. 1:16 (em xii.7); e Policarpo (155 D.C.) parece ter-se baseado nesta epístola (ver *Pol*. x.1, citando Col. 1:23). Essa mesma passagem, evidentemente, foi a base de Inácio, Efésios x.3, em 110 D.C. Inácio (*Esmirna* vi.1) parece fazer alusão ao trecho de Col. 1:16; e Pol. xi.2 parece ter sido passagem sugerida por Col. 1:23,24 e 3:5, no tocante à idolatria e à cobiça. Irineu e Tertuliano (segunda metade do segundo século de nossa era) — citaram quase cada capítulo da presente epístola; e Clemente de Alexandria, bem como Orígenes, o seu grande sucesso, citam-no como epístola de Paulo.

VII. ESTADO DO TEXTO GREGO

Possuímos os mesmos manuscritos gregos antigos de Colossenses que possuímos acerca da coletânea paulina inteira. Esses são os mss P(46) (século III D.C.), Aleph e B (século IV D.C.), AC (século V D.C.), e então os unciais posteriores, do século VI em diante, HLIPS, e um grande número de manuscritos minúsculos pertencentes ao séc. IX, e depois. (Quanto a informações completas sobre os manuscritos antigos do N.T., ver o artigo existente sobre esse assunto).

Devido à grande similaridade entre as epístolas aos Colossenses e aos Efésios (ver a lista desses pontos similares em Col. 1:1 no NTI), podem ser encontradas algumas adições e assimilações harmonísticas. (Ver Col. 1:14 quanto às questões mais famosas dessa categoria). Tal como se dá no caso de todos os livros do N.T. esta epístola tem suas dificuldades textuais, algumas das quais não podem ser satisfatoriamente solucionadas. Nesses casos, o problema não consiste de textos «perdidos», mas antes, os textos existentes são confirmados com tal equilíbrio, a favor desta ou daquela variante, que é difícil dizer quais variantes representam o original. Os principais problemas são encontrados em Col. 1:2,6,12; 2:2 e 3:16. Ver as notas textuais sobre estas referências no NTI. A restauração do texto, naturalmente, tem sido efetuada com alto grau de exatidão, o que também se dá no caso do N.T. inteiro. Conforme se sabe bem, o N.T. é o mais bem confirmado documento da antiguidade, pois conta com o maior número de manuscritos verdadeiramente antigos que o confirmam quanto a seu texto.

Apesar de que as variantes textuais realmente importantes sejam poucas, conforme é comum quanto aos livros do N.T., há muitas variantes secundárias. Ver Col. 1:2,3,7,10,12,12,12,20,22,22,23,27; 2:2,7, 10,12,13,14,18,23; 3:4,5,6,7,13,14,15,16,17,20,21,

22:; 4:8,12,23,15,18. A repetição de números inidica que naqueles versículos há mais de uma variante.

VIII. Conteúdo

I. *Introdução Geral* (1:1-14)
   1. Saudação (1:1-2)
   2. Ação de graças pela fé e amor dos irmãos, bem como pelo fruto produzido entre eles, mediante a pregação do evangelho (1:3-8)
   3. Oração em favor do crescimento dos crentes na compreensão espiritual e nas boas obras (1:9-14)

II. *A Grandeza de Cristo* — Polêmica contra os Mediadores Angelicais postulados pelos Gnósticos (1:15-3:4)
   1. As onze superioridades de Cristo (1:15-19)
      a. Imagem de Deus (vs. 15)
      b. Primogênito (vs. 15)
      c. Criador (esfera da criação: Cristo como *Alfa*, vs. 16)
      d. Criador (agente da criação: Cristo como *Alfa*, vs. 16)
      e. Criador (alvo da criação: Cristo como Ômega, vs. 16)
      f. Primeiro quanto ao tempo e à importância (vs. 17)
      g. Sustentador de tudo (vs. 17)
      h. Cabeça da Igreja (vs. 18)
      i. Princípio (vs. 18)
      j. Primogênito dentre os mortos (vs. 18)
      k. Em quem habita a plenitude de de Deus (vs. 19)
   2. Sua grandeza quanto à reconciliação — uma décima segunda superioridade; até os anjos estão sujeitos à sua redenção (1:20-23)
   3. Sua grandeza demonstrada no ministério apostólico (1:24-2:1)
      a. O ministério do sofrimento (1:24)
      b. Propagação do evangelho, no qual Cristo é visto como a grande realidade mística, o divino no humano (1:25-29)
      c. O interesse pessoal de Paulo por seus leitores (2:1)
   4. Sua grandeza como mistério de Deus (2:2,3)
   5. Sua grandeza em contraste com os ensinamentos e as práticas falsas (2:4-23)
      a. O perigo dos ensinos ludibriadores, não alicerçados em Cristo (2:4-7)
      b. Contra a filosofia e o legalismo falsos (2:8-17)
         i. A filosofia vã é um vão engano e há tradições mal alicerçadas (2:8)
         ii. Nada pode ser adicionado à perfeição (2:9-13)
         iii. A lei foi abolida em Cristo (2:14-17)
      c. Advertência contra o misticismo falso (2:18-19)
      d. Advertência contra o asceticismo (2:20-23)

III. *A Ética*. A Inquirição Espiritual — Alicerçada sobre a Grandeza de Cristo (3:1-4:6)
   1. A união espiritual do crente com Cristo, agora e para sempre (3:1-4)
   2. Fruto da união com Cristo — o andar santo (3:5-17)
   3. Deveres domésticos, submissão mútua no lar cristão (3:18-4:4)
   4. Conduta para com os pagãos (4:5,6)

IV. *Apresentações e Saudações Pessoais* (4:7-18)
   1. Tíquico e Onésimo (4:7-9)
   2. Os companheiros de Paulo saúdam os colossenses (4:10-14)
   3. Saudações a Laodicéia, instrução e bênção finais (4:15-18)

IX. Bibliografia: AM BA EN I IB MOF NTI TI TIN VIN RO Z

COLOSSOS

Uma cidade da Frígia (que vide), às margens do rio Lico, cerca de dezenove quilômetros de Laodicéia, numa região que faz parte da Turquia moderna. Presume-se que a Igreja cristã que ali existia foi fundada por Epafras (Col. 1:2,7; 4:12). O trecho de Colossenses 2:1 parece indicar que o próprio Paulo ainda não havia visitado pessoalmente o lugar, ao escrever a epístola aos Colossenses. A cidade foi destruída por um terremoto no nono ano do reinado de Nero, mas foi reconstruída. A moderna aldeia de Denizli fica próxima do local da antiga cidade de Colossos. Essa cidade ficava localizada na antiga província romana da Ásia. Colossos ficava na estrada principal que partia de Éfeso para o Oriente, e revestia-se de certa importância comercial. Ali também se dividiam as estradas para Sardes e para Pérgamo, pelo que, nos reinos lídio e pergamênio, Colossos era cidade de alguma importância. Mais tarde, porém, já nos tempos dos romanos, a estrada para Pérgamo passava um pouco mais ao oeste, daí resultando que Laodicéia se tornou maior e mais importante do que Colossos.

O evangelho chegou ao vale do rio Lico enquanto Paulo achava-se em Éfeso (Atos 19:10), provavelmente através de ministros que ele, ou seus discípulos, haviam enviado a áreas adjacentes. Filemom e Onésimo, seu ex-escravo, eram membros da igreja local para a qual Paulo escreveu (ver Col. 4:9 e File. 1 e 10). A cidade tinha uma população mista, composta por judeus, gregos e frígios, sendo provável que a Igreja cristã dali refletisse essa situação. O gnosticismo (que vide), em alguma de suas formas, ameaçava o cristianismo dali, o que, igualmente reflete uma situação cultural mista. Porções da epístola aos Colossenses têm o propósito de combater essa heresia.

Originalmente, parece que a cidade contava com várias indústrias, incluindo as que trabalhavam com lã, que era uma das atividades básicas da cidade próxima de Laodicéia, por igual modo. Nos tempos persas, Colossos tivera importância consideravelmente maior. Xerxes passou pela cidade (Her. 7:30), como também Ciro (Xenofonte, *Anab.* 1.2,6). A cidade servia de quartel de exércitos. Foi fundada cerca de duzentos e cinqüenta anos antes de Laodicéia, que terminou por se tornar sua grande rival.

Colossos conseguiu manter-se próspera até os séculos VII e VIII D.C., quando o esboroamento do poder bizantino, na Ásia Menor, deixou a cidade sujeita aos ataques de diversos inimigos. A população restante foi transferida para Conae, que atualmente chama-se Conas. A destruição final de Colossos ocorreu por ocasião da invasão turca, no século XII D.C. Atualmente, o antigo local da cidade não é ocupado. Fica cerca de dezesseis quilômetros da cidade moderna de Denizli. As escavações feitas no sítio arqueológico têm descoberto um antigo templo cristão e algumas outras coisas interessantes para os arqueólogos. (ND Z)

COLPORTAGEM

Essa palavra vem do francês **colporter**, «magarefe». As palavras formadoras são *col*, «pescoço» e *porter*, «carregar». A palavra deriva-se do fato de que os magarefes levavam uma sacola pendurada ao pescoço, onde transportavam as suas quinquilharias. Um colporter é um vendedor de livros, revistas e almanaques, em distritos interioranos. Em sentido secundário, a palavra indica um agente de viagens que distribui gratuitamente Bíblias, livretos religiosos, panfletos, folhetos, etc. Ver o artigo sobre o *Movimento de Tratados e Folhetos*. (E WA)

COLUMBANO

Suas datas foram 543-615 D.C. Foi abade de Luxeuil e de Bobbio. Era de origem irlandesa. Em cerca de 583, ele partiu para Borgonha, com doze outros companheiros de vida monástica. A convite do rei Gontram, erigiu um mosteiro em Annegray; e, mais tarde, fundou outros mosteiros, em Luxeuil e Fontaines. Preparou uma regra para esses mosteiros, incorporando costumes de mosteiros celtas. Passou vinte anos sucessivos na Borgonha, até que foi banido pelo dissoluto monarca Thierry II. Após muito vaguear, estabeleceu-se em Bobbio, localizada entre Milão e Gênova, na Itália. Ali fundou o mosteiro que, posteriormente, tornou-se famoso, e onde agora descansam os seus ossos. Escreveu uma regra para esse mosteiro; mas essa regra veio a ser substituída, mais tarde, pela regra beneditina. A festividade em honra a Columbano é celebrada a 21 de novembro. Ver o artigo geral sobre o *monasticismo*. (AM E)

COLUNA

Há oito palavras hebraicas e uma palavra grega envolvidas:

1. *Ammud*, «coluna». Termo hebraico que ocorre por cento e nove vezes. Por exemplo: Êxo. 13:21,22; Nú. 3:36,37; Juí. 16:25,26,29; II Reis 11:14; Sal. 7:53, Can. 3:10; Jer. 1:18; Eze. 40:49; 42:6.

2. *Omenoth*, «colunas». Palavra hebraica no plural que só ocorre em II Reis 18:16.

3. *Misad*, «suporte». Palavra hebraica que também só aparece por uma vez, em I Reis 10:12.

4. *Matstsebah*, «algo levantado». Palavra hebraica usada por doze vezes. Por exemplo: Gên. 28:18,22; Êxo. 24:4; II Sam. 18:18; Isa. 19:19.

5. *Matsuq*, «coisa fixa». Palavra hebraica usada, com esse sentido, apenas por uma vez, em I Sam. 2:8.

6. *Natsab*, «estabelecido». Palavra hebraica usada no A.T., apenas por uma vez, com o sentido de «coluna». Ver Juí. 9:6.

7. *Netsib*, «monumento». Palavra hebraica usada por apenas uma vez com esse sentido, em Gên. 19:26.

8. *Timeroth*, «colunas». Palavra hebraica empregada por duas vezes com esse sentido, porque geralmente significa «palmeiras»: Can. 3:6; Joel 2:30.

9. *Stúlos*, «coluna». Palavra grega usada por quatro vezes: Gál. 2:9; I Tim. 3:15; Apo. 3:12; 10:1.

Uma coluna é um poste firme, posto na posição vertical, que pode ser usado para suportar porções superiores de um edifício, embora também em posição ereta, isolada ou em grupo, sem qualquer função de apoio.

1. *Uso Antigo*. Talvez o mais antigo uso de uma coluna seja o de servir de marco, como monumento ou como sinal de voto (símbolo e função religiosos). Nesses casos, usualmente uma única coluna era usada. Poderia ser apenas uma pilha de pedras (Gên. 28:18; 31:46). A «pedra de Ezel» (I Sam. 20:19), provavelmente era alguma espécie de marco, sob a forma de uma coluna. Jacó erigiu uma espécie de coluna sobre o sepulcro de Raquel (Gên. 35:20). A coluna monolítica e os obeliscos de Petra, em Iduméia, são exemplos de uso similar. Absalão mandou levantar uma coluna monumental em memória sua (II Sam. 18:18). Embora ali seja usada a palavra hebraica *massebah*, «estátua», a nossa versão portuguesa a traduz por «coluna».

A adoração dos cananeus empregava a coluna votiva e a coluna memorial. Ao povo de Israel foi ordenado que derrubassem as colunas usadas na adoração pagã, como a dos cananeus (Êxo. 23:24). Essas colunas eram erigidas ao ar livre, ou então no interior de algum lugar de adoração (II Reis 10:26; 17:10). Essas colunas eram chamadas «colunas de Baal» (II Reis 3:2). Os arqueólogos encontraram e reergueram uma coluna que havia defronte do templo de Baal-Berite. Os israelitas não podiam usar colunas em seu culto religioso (Lev. 26:1). Contudo, era-lhes permitido usar pedras memoriais, que podiam ser empilhadas, formando uma espécie de coluna.

2. *Nas Construções*. As casas e os templos do Oriente tinham muitas colunas. Ver o artigo sobre *Casa* II.14. Ver também o artigo sobre a *Arquitetura*. Colunas eram usadas para fechar área, para sustentar tetos planos, ou para dar apoio a toldos ou cortinas. Sansão fez um templo inteiro vir abaixo, quando derrubou suas duas principais colunas de sustentação (Juí 16:26). A prática geral, nas construções orientais, de sustentar tetos planos mediante colunas, ou para cobrir espaços abertos mediante toldos estendidos em colunas, levou ao grande uso delas, nas construções antigas. As colunas eram feitas de madeira, de pedra ou de vários metais. Têm sido descobertos exemplares de colunas de madeira, em Nínive.

3. *No Templo de Jerusalém*. Salomão lançou mão de colunas, no templo e em seu palácio, em Jerusalém. Em seu palácio havia o Salão das Colunas, que era uma espécie de pórtico com colunas (I Reis 7:6). Essas colunas eram feitas de madeira de cedro, embora também houvesse colunas feitas com a rara madeira de sândalo (I Reis 10:12). As colunas gêmeas de bronze, chamadas Jaquim e Boaz, foram postas do lado de fora do templo de Jerusalém. Talvez elas sustentassem a arquitrave do vestíbulo da entrada, ou podem ter sido simples colunas memoriais, que nada sustentavam, fazendo o povo de Israel lembrar-se da coluna de nuvem e fogo que guiou o povo de Israel no deserto. Notemos que certas colunas recebiam nomes específicos (I Reis 7:15,22,41,42). As colunas referidas em Ezequiel 40:49 provavelmente eram pilastras (colunas retangulares, com capitel e base). O trecho de Ester 1:6 fala de colunas de mármore, existentes no palácio persa de Susã.

4. *Usos Figurados*. a. Jeremias postava-se como uma coluna de ferro, contra a ímpia nação de Judá (Jer. 1:18). b. A casa da sabedoria está erigida sobre sete colunas (Pro. 9:1). c. A coluna de fogo e de nuvem (que vede) representavam a orientação e os cuidados de Deus por seu povo (Êxo. 13:21,22; 33:9). d. O poder de Deus sacode as colunas da terra (Jó 9:6), e as colunas do céu estremecem diante de sua palavra (Jó 26:11; ver também I Sam. 2:8 e Sal. 75:3). e. Os membros inferiores de um ser humano são as suas colunas (Can. 5:15; Jer. 18:18), onde a idéia de força está em pauta. f. A verdade é comparada a uma coluna e a um alicerce, sobre os quais podemos edificar (I Tim. 3:15). g. As principais personagens da Igreja primitiva, como Tiago, Pedro e João, seriam colunas da fé (Gál. 2:9). h. Aqueles que vencem espiritualmente recebem a promessa de que serão feitos colunas no templo espiritual de Deus (Apo. 3:12). i. As pernas de certo anjo, visto em visão, em Apo. 10:1, eram como colunas de fogo.

COLUNA — COLUNAS

COLUNA de Apocalipse 3:12
I. A PROMESSA

Fá-lo-ei coluna no santuário do meu Deus. Apo. 3:12. Há aqui, mui provavelmente, alusão ao fato de que na área onde estava localizada a cidade de Filadélfia havia terremotos freqüentes, com o resultado que muitas construções, incluindo templos, eram abaladas, rachavam-se e, algumas vezes, tombavam. *Estrabão* escreveu nessa conexão: «E Filadélfia não deixou de sofrer em suas muralhas, mas diariamente são abaladas de algum modo, e há brechas nas mesmas. Mas os habitantes continuam a ocupar o local, a despeito de seus sofrimentos e de terem de edificar novas casas» (*xii*, pág. 868). No ano de 17 D.C., a cidade foi destruída por um terremoto, mas uma doação imperial ajudou em sua recuperação. O vidente João dizia, por conseguinte, que, em contraste com os templos dos deuses pagãos, cujas colunas eram abaladas e destruídas por terremotos, os vencedores perseverantes tornar-se-ão colunas no templo do Deus vivo, a comunidade formada de pedras vivas, que compõem o templo de Deus, isto é, o lugar onde ele manifesta a sua presença. (Ver Efé. 2:22 e I Ped. 2:5 e ss., quanto ao simbolismo da igreja cristã como um *templo*).

Deus e o Cordeiro, na qualidade de templo. O livro de Apo. 21:22 afirma que o Senhor Deus Todo-Poderoso e o Cordeiro são o templo da Nova Jerusalém. Se o vidente João tenciona dar a entender tal, então, ser alguém uma coluna nesse templo divino implica em comunhão mística íntima com Deus, como quem faz parte real da personalidade divina. Já que os filhos de Deus compartilham da vida e da natureza do Filho, eles chegam a participar da «natureza divina»; também terão toda a plenitude de Deus, ou seja, sua natureza e atributos (ver Efé. 3:19 e Col. 2:10), possuindo sua mesma «modalidade de vida». Diferem do Pai não quanto ao «tipo de vida», mas somente quanto à extensão da participação na vida divina. A eternidade inteira será a oportunidade de ir aumentando cada vez mais a «extensão» dessa participação. Já que há uma infinitude com que teremos de ser cheios, também haverá um enchimento infinito. O trecho de Heb. 2:10 e ss. mostra que haverá uma «comunidade» de natureza dentro da família divina.

II. SIGNIFICADOS DA COLUNA AQUI REFERIDA

1. *Estabilidade* (de natureza espiritual), em contraste com os templos da cidade de Filadélfia, que viviam abalados por terremotos.

2. *Glória na estabilidade*, pois a «permanência» da alma conduz à transformação divina dos homens segundo a imagem de Cristo. (Ver as notas expositivas sobre esse conceito, em II Cor. 3:18 no NTI).

3. *Comunhão mística* com Deus, mediante o que a transformação do crente é produzida. Essa é uma operação do Espírito Santo. Essa comunhão visa tanto ao presente como à eternidade, e continuará aumentando sempre.

4. *Infusão da natureza divina* na natureza humana, formando um processo eterno, pois Deus é o templo, e nós somos as colunas desse templo.

5. O conceito da «coluna» fala da mesma verdade que o faz a idéia da «âncora da alma». Em meio a um mundo atribulado, com temores íntimos e terrores externos, a alma se sente segura em seu Deus, contanto que lute, disposta a pagar o preço para ser vencedora.

6. «Encontro, união, adoração, unidade, comunhão a mais profunda, esconderijo nos mistérios, luz, manifestações imperturbáveis e aprazimentos de Deus e de nosso Salvador, são as idéias principais. A esse templo santo o vitorioso cristão chega como um adorador, a fim de abeberar-se dessa luz inefável, compartilhando da plenitude dessa bem-aventurança indescritível...Não apenas como adorador, mas como habitante perpétuo, o vitorioso cristão entrará no templo celestial, porquanto 'daí jamais sairá'» (Seiss, em Apo. 3:12).

7. Em Apo. 3:12 nos é ensinada a *segurança* do crente (que vide), mas também está envolvido muito mais do que isso. Essa segurança se verifica agora e para sempre, referindo-se à *beleza* dos santos, que farão parte do magnificente templo divino. Esses serão adornados com a natureza e os atributos do próprio Deus, pois Deus é o pináculo de toda a beleza.

8. As «colunas» da igreja são seus membros mais fortes e sustentadores. Esses dão seu apoio ao trabalho da igreja, servindo de elementos fundamentais na mesma; e assim continuará sendo, por toda a eternidade, pois o trabalho de Deus é eterno. Todos os crentes podem ser vencedores e até no próprio estado eterno não haverá qualquer estagnação no progresso.

9. Os muitos templos e festividades religiosas de Filadélfia conquistaram para ela o nome de «Atenas em miniatura». Mas o vidente João viu um templo magnificente, dotado de colunas, e muitíssimo mais atrativo para a alma remida do que toda a glória pagã de Filadélfia.

10. As colunas falam sobre a *força espiritual* mediante a qual a alma será eternamente segura e abençoada. A coluna, embora talvez seja um elemento ornamental, «reveste-se de beleza», é colocada na estrutura de um edifício a fim de ocupar certa função; e, para tanto, precisa ser forte.

COLUNAS DA TERRA

Ver os trechos de Jó 9:6; I Samuel 2:8 e Salmos 75:3. Os antigos hebreus pensavam que a terra repousa sobre gigantescas colunas, e que a terra e suas colunas, por sua vez, repousassem sobre um grande abismo de águas. A terra era imaginada como se fosse plana, com o hades abaixo de sua superfície. Como se fosse uma abóbada por cima, havia o firmamento, uma substância sólida que separava os céus da terra. Por cima do firmamento havia os céus e a luz primeva. Sob o firmamento estavam fixados os luzeiros secundários, o sol, a lua e as estrelas, especificamente para iluminar a terra. Isso é devidamente explicado no artigo sobre a *Astronomia*, onde o leitor encontrará maiores detalhes. Devemos entender que essas expressões são poéticas. Embora pudessem ser assim utilizadas, essas colunas representavam o que os hebreus antigos acreditavam. De nada adianta tentarmos modernizar essas concepções, atribuindo aos hebreus noções que só surgiram na astronomia moderna. Ver o artigo sobre as *Cosmogonias*, onde oferecemos descrições sobre as crenças de vários povos antigos, inclusive os hebreus.

COLUNAS DE FOGO E DE NUVEM

Quanto a referências bíblicas a respeito, ver Êxo. 13:18,21,22; Núm. 14:14 e também Gên. 9:12-19. Quando Israel vagueava pelo deserto, após sair do Egito, Deus passou a guiá-los, a partir de certo momento, de dia por meio de uma coluna de nuvem, e, à noite, mediante uma coluna de fogo. A nuvem fornecia tanto sombra quanto orientação, e o fogo fornecia tanto luz quanto orientação. Isso faz-nos lembrar das fogueiras que as pessoas acendem, quando viajam. Também sabemos que os persas antigos levavam fogo, que eles chamavam de *sagrado e eterno*, sobre altares de prata, à frente de seus exércitos que avançavam. Os romanos apreciavam muito cortejos liderados por tochas. Muitas tochas provocavam nuvens de fumaça. Segundo somos informados pela Bíblia, no caso de Israel, a nuvem se pôs atrás do acampamento de Israel, como proteção contra os egípcios (Êxo. 14:19,20,24).

Também há menção da coluna de nuvem que desceu e pôs-se à entrada da tenda da congregação, quando Moisés ali entrou (Êxo. 33:7-9). Quando Miriã e Arão murmuraram contra Moisés, uma nuvem apareceu em protesto. Essa visão confirmava o fato de que a presença divina acompanhava Moisés. E quando Moisés faleceu, uma nuvem apareceu, na qual manifestou-se a presença divina, a fim de fornecer instruções a Josué (Deu. 31:5). Essas passagens bíblicas têm provocado muitas interpretações, dentre as quais damos abaixo alguns exemplos:

1. *A Interpretação Naturalista*. A Bíblia encerra interpretações poéticas espiritualizadas, acerca de coisas naturais. Assim, a coluna de nuvem podia ter sido formada pela fumaça das tochas que os israelitas levavam enquanto caminhavam, o que também pode ser a explicação da coluna de fogo, à noite. Já vimos como os exércitos antigos iluminavam seu caminho mediante o uso de tochas. Ou então as colunas eram apenas postes onde se levava azeite que queimava produzindo o efeito descrito na Bíblia. Em conexão com isso, pode-se observar que as grandes colunas de bronze, postas na parte da frente do templo de Salomão em Jerusalém, parecem ter sido utilizadas como tochas, de onde subiam nuvens de fumaça. Em I Reis 7:15 são chamadas colunas; mas, essencialmente, de acordo ainda com essa interpretação, haveria no alto das mesmas, grandes taças onde era queimado óleo ou betume.

Apesar dos paralelos óbvios com outras coisas, a narrativa do Antigo Testamento não parece descrever fenômenos naturais. Tem sido argumentado, porém, que as narrativas sagradas envolvem adornos piedosos, cujo intuito seria fazer a atenção dos leitores centralizar-se mais em Deus, conferindo a essas narrativas uma significação mais religiosa. Porém, tudo quanto realmente sucedeu foi que o povo de Israel marchou através do deserto, com suas tochas, que produziam colunas de fumaça, como se fosse um antigo exército.

2. *A Interpretação Mitológica*. As mentes piedosas anelam por encontrar intervenções sobrenaturais, quando recontam as histórias de seus heróis ou deuses. Assim são criados muitos acontecimentos que, na realidade, nunca ocorreram. A literatura de quase todas as nações tem esses adornos mitológicos; e por que haveríamos de pensar que os hebreus também não criaram os seus mitos?

3. *A Interpretação Sobrenatural*. Não há como ajustar o texto sagrado a qualquer explicação meramente natural. Essas nuvens e chamas agiam como se fossem controladas por alguma mente superior, como quando o fogo ameaçou destruir aqueles que haviam murmurado. Ver Núm. 17:10, ou quando saltou sobre os rebeldes e os consumiu de todo (Lev. 10:2). A mesma ação inteligente é atribuída à conduta das colunas de nuvem e fogo, no relato sobre a caminhada pelo deserto.

COMBUSTÍVEL

Embora o petróleo seja abundante nos países árabes, até hoje Israel não dispõe de reservas ou de produção suficientes. Nas antigas terras bíblicas, os combustíveis derivavam-se de hidrocarbonos vegetais, como madeiras, cascas de árvores, palha, arbustos, raízes secas, etc. O único material animal usado como combustível era o estrume seco que, naturalmente, queimava lentamente e soltava um incrível mau cheiro. Os antigos descobriram como fabricar carvão de madeira, em cerca de 2000 A.C., o qual era usado para fundir metais. Isso deu um grande impulso à civilização. Os lares dos nobres, dos ricos e alguns templos contavam com lugares onde o carvão de madeira era queimado para produzir calor, pelo que esse carvão tornou-se um item de exportação ou importação. Quanto a referências veterotestamentárias a respeito, em algum sentido, ver Jer. 36:22; I Reis 17:10; Eze. 4:12 *ss*; Isa. 44:14-16; Mat. 3:12; 6:30. O trecho de Lam. 5:4 mostra-nos o uso comum dos combustíveis em Israel, porquanto viver sem esses combustíveis era considerado uma grande dificuldade.

COMENIUS, JOÃO AMÓS

Suas datas foram 1592-1670. Nasceu em Nivnice, no sul da Morávia, atualmente porção formativa da Checoslováquia. Educou-se na Universidade dos Irmãos, em Herbrom, em Nassau e na Universidade de Heidelberg, na Alemanha. Foi expulso da paróquia de Fulnek, no começo da Guerra dos Trinta Anos, mas encontrou refúgio em Leszno, na Polônia. Foi ali que estabeleceu sua reputação como reformador da educação superior, ao escrever sua obra intitulada *Janua linguarum reserata*. Recebeu a tarefa de reformar o sistema escolar da Suécia; e, mais tarde, o da Hungria. Tornou-se conhecido como «pai da moderna teoria e prática educacional», e suas idéias sobre o assunto acham-se no seu livro *Opera didactica omnia*.

No campo da religião ele tornou-se conhecido como advogado da união dos cristãos, em razão do que ele é chamado de profeta do ecumenismo moderno. Também foi um bem conhecido pastor evangélico. Como filósofo, ele defendia uma visão pansófica da cultura, segundo a qual várias disciplinas eram unificadas, tornando-se o guia da erudição e da prática. Ele tentou estabelecer um colégio em Londres, na Inglaterra, com a finalidade de propagar as suas idéias, porém, o irrompimento da guerra civil da Inglaterra impediu a realização desse projeto. Morreu em Amsterdã, na Holanda, em 1670. (AM E)

COMENTÁRIOS SOBRE A BÍBLIA

Esboço:
Introdução
a. Observações Preliminares
b. Utilidade
c. O Impulso para Escrever
d. O Número é Grande
e. Um Testemunho

I. Os Pais da Igreja
II. A Idade Média
III. A Reforma Protestante
IV. O Século XVII
V. O Século XVIII
VI. O Século XIX
VII. O Século XX
VIII. Comentários na Língua Portuguesa

Introdução

a. **Observações Preliminares**. Indagou o eunuco

COMENTÁRIOS SOBRE A BÍBLIA

etíope: «Como poderei entender, se alguém não me explicar?» (Atos 8:31). Ele vinha lendo o rolo do profeta Isaías. Filipe lhe perguntara se ele entendia o que estava lendo, e sua resposta foi aquela que acabamos de citar. O eunuco precisava de um *comentário* sobre o texto sagrado. Filipe expôs uma explicação verbal. Um comentário escrito é tão legítimo quanto um comentário verbal. Pregar também é comentar. Uma lição de Escola Dominical. Os judeus mostravam-se fanáticos quanto às suas Escrituras Sagradas, reverenciando-as em alto grau. Em consonância com isso, o Talmude (que vide) foi compilado como um guia sobre as Escrituras e a vida judaica. O Talmude é uma verdadeira enciclopédia de conhecimentos e tradições judaicas. Foram necessários sete séculos de desenvolvimento e compilação para ser produzido. Somente nos fins do século V D.C. é que o Talmude chegou ao seu estágio final. Apesar de versar principalmente sobre as Escrituras, inclui copiosas discussões sobre os campos da religião, da ética, das instituições sociais, da história, do folclore e da ciência.

b. *Utilidade.* No tocante a comentários sobre o Antigo ou o Novo Testamentos, coisa alguma de autoridade comparável ao Talmude tem surgido entre os cristãos. Mas, podemos estar certos de que os comentários bíblicos que existem têm exercido notável influência sobre como a Igreja tem sido e continua sendo interpretada. Há indivíduos e igrejas que degradam os comentários; e, no entanto, a cada domingo, os pastores e os mestres estão fazendo comentários, embora de forma verbal. O que esses não querem reconhecer é que aquilo que dizem poderia ser melhorado em muito se consultassem um ou mais comentários escritos. Se pensam que Deus lhes pode revelar algo, que passam a declarar verbalmente, por que haveriam de negar que o mesmo Deus pode revelar coisas a outras pessoas, que registram sob forma escrita?

O propósito deste artigo é mostrar, sob forma de esboço, a história dos comentários bíblicos.

c. *O Impulso para Escrever.* Todas as grandes vidas, bem como todas as obras literárias importantes, produzem escritos subseqüentes. Trata-se da busca pelo conhecimento e pela significação das coisas. Os comentários bíblicos variam muito quanto ao seu planejamento. Alguns deles assemelham-se muito a sermões, como os comentários de Crisóstomo, que foi um eloqüente pregador; outros são essencialmente gramaticais e críticos, como vários volumes do International Critical Commentary; e ainda outros são essencialmente devocionais, com pouco conhecimento técnico, como o de Matthew Henry.

d. *O Número é Grande.* Ninguém sabe quantos comentários já foram escritos. Mas o *Dictionary of the Holy Bible*, de Calmet (1722), afirma que, até então, havia pelo menos mil e quatrocentos comentários diferentes. Alguns comentários envolvem um único volume. Outros comentários consistem de uma série. A Enciclopédia de Strong (1867-1881) alista cento e sessenta e cinco comentários sobre a Bíblia inteira. Charles Spurgeon escreveu um livro exclusivamente sobre comentários, para servir de guia na seleção dos melhores comentários para alguém adquirir. Sua lista consistia em 1437 títulos. Até mesmo na antiguidade, os comentários eram numerosos. C.H. Turner, em um longo artigo que foi incorporado no *Hastings Dictionary of the Bible*, alista cento e quinze títulos, desde os pais da Igreja até o século VIII D.C. Entretanto, sua lista cobriu somente as epístolas paulinas, pelo que teríamos de acrescentar comentários sobre o restante do Novo Testamento, para chegarmos a uma idéia clara de quanto já havia sido produzido. Além disso, devem ter existido inúmeros comentários, escritos na antiguidade, acerca dos quais nada sabemos, por não terem chegado até nós.

e. *Um Testemunho.* Esses fatos constituem um testemunho, entre muitos outros, a respeito da grandeza da Bíblia Sagrada. Indiretamente, confirmam sua divina inspiração, porquanto nenhum livro comum poderia ter provocado tanta reação da parte dos homens.

Os comentários abaixo alistados só podem esperar representar parcialmente essa atividade.

I. Os Pais da Igreja:

1. *Herácliom.* Foi seguidor de Valentino, um mestre gnóstico do século II D.C. Escreveu um comentário sobre o evangelho de João, embora seja atualmente conhecido apenas através de citações em outros autores, como Orígenes. Ele escreveu em grego.

2. *Hipólito*, cerca de 204 D.C. Comentou sobre o livro de Daniel. Essa é a mais antiga obra cristã exegética de que dispomos. Hipólito escreveu cerca de quarenta obras sobre muitos livros bíblicos, do Antigo e do Novo Testamentos. Isso posto, sua influência foi grande. Goodspeed referia-se a ele como a mais destacada figura do cristianismo grego, no Ocidente. Ele também escreveu em grego.

3. *Orígenes.* Foi o maior erudito bíblico da Igreja antiga. Suas datas foram 185-274 D.C. A quantidade de material escrito por ele produzido é espantosa. Ele escreveu treze livros sobre Gênesis, quarenta e seis livros sobre quarenta e um Salmos, trinta livros sobre Isaías, quinze livros sobre Lucas, cinco livros sobre Gálatas, três livros sobre Efésios, além de muitos outros. Ocorre que, em certas ocasiões, ele ditava a sete diferentes amanuenses, que se revesavam, anotando o que ele interpretava, segundo três ângulos diferentes: a. o ângulo literal; b. o ângulo simbólico ou alegórico; e c. o ângulo místico, o que corresponderia ao corpo, à alma e ao espírito do ser humano. Ele mostrava-se bastante independente no manuseio das Escrituras, especialmente no caso de passagens do Antigo Testamento que retratam Deus de um modo que ele reputava ser imoral. Ver o artigo sobre a *Teologia Alexandrina*, que dá informações sobre essa questão. Ver também sobre a *Interpretação Alegórica*, bem como o artigo separado acerca de *Orígenes*. Ele escreveu na língua grega.

4. *Dionísio de Alexandria.* Faleceu em 264 D.C. Escreveu uma interpretação alegórica do Apocalipse, que desapareceu. Escreveu em grego.

5. *Vitorino.* Faleceu em 304 D.C. Escreveu vários livros de comentário, dentre os quais sobrevive até hoje aquele que versa sobre o Apocalipse. Escreveu em grego.

6. *Eusébio.* Suas datas foram 260-340 D.C. Foi autor de um volumoso comentário sobre Isaías, que Jerônimo traduziu para o latim. Também comentou sobre os livros de Lucas, Provérbios, Cantares, Daniel e outros. Objetava ao método alegórico de interpretação, muito usado em seus dias, o qual, para ele, permitia liberdade demais, obscurecendo o sentido das Escrituras. Escreveu em grego.

7. *Atanásio*, bispo de Alexandria. Suas datas foram 296-374 D.C. Escreveu um comentário sobre os Salmos, que sobrevive até nós sob a forma de fragmentos. Escreveu em grego.

8. *Dídimo, o Cego.* Suas datas foram 313-398 D.C. Escreveu comentários sobre Mateus, João, Jó, Provérbios, algumas epístolas paulinas, sobre as epístolas católicas e sobre Isaías. Foi intitulado de

COMENTÁRIOS SOBRE A BÍBLIA

o último grande mestre da Escola Catequética de Alexandria. Escreveu em grego.

9. *Hilário de Poitiers*. Viveu em torno de 350 D.C. Foi o autor do primeiro comentário produzido na Igreja Ocidental. Preparou um comentário sobre os Salmos que sofreu influências da parte de Orígenes. Jerônimo e Agostinho citaram suas obras. Escreveu em latim.

10. *Basílio, o Grande*. Suas datas foram 330-379 D.C. Escreveu comentários acerca de quase a Bíblia inteira, muito usados por intérpretes posteriores, como Ambrósio e Agostinho. Escreveu em grego.

11. *Deodoro*, bispo de Tarso. Viveu em torno de 390 D.C. Foi líder da escola teológica de Antioquia. Preparou comentários sobre Hebreus, as epístolas católicas e o Apocalipse. Escreveu em grego.

12. *Crisóstomo*. Suas datas foram 347-407 D.C. Um dos mais eloqüentes pregadores de todos os tempos. Ver o artigo separado sobre ele. Também foi autor de comentários. Escreveu a mais antiga exposição de que dispomos do evangelho de Mateus. Também contamos com cinqüenta e oito de suas homilias sobre os Salmos, e com cinqüenta e cinco homilias sobre o livro de Atos. Seu comentário sobre o livro de Atos é o único comentário completo que temos sobre esse livro, proveniente dos primeiros cinco séculos da era cristã. Não conhecia o hebraico, pelo que seus escritos refletem certas inexatidões quanto ao Antigo Testamento. Mas, ele compensava isso por ser grande conhecedor do coração humano. Seu nome significa «boca de ouro», um apodo que lhe foi dado devido à sua eloqüência. Seu verdadeiro nome era João de Antioquia. Escreveu em grego.

13. *Jerônimo*. Suas datas foram 347-420 D.C. Foi o supremo comentador da Igreja latina, e um dos maiores da Igreja universal. Comentou primeiramente sobre o livro de Obadias, e então sobre o de Daniel. Finalmente, comentou sobre Mateus, sobre as epístolas paulinas (Gálatas, Efésios, Tito e Filemom), e então sobre Ezequiel. Também escreveu um livro sobre os comentadores da Bíblia, referindo-se a cento e trinta e quatro autores diferentes. Escreveu em latim.

14. *Teodoro de Mopsuéstia*. Suas datas foram 350-428 D.C. Comentou sobre os Salmos, sobre as epístolas paulinas, sobre os profetas menores e sobre o evangelho de João. Rejeitava a interpretação alegórica e dava muita atenção à gramática e ao propósito dos autores sagrados envolvidos. Escreveu em grego.

15. *Agostinho*. Suas datas foram 354-430 D.C. Talvez foi o maior e mais influente de todos os pais da Igreja. Escreveu obras de cunho filosófico e político, confissões e comentários bíblicos. Comentou sobre alguns capítulos do livro de Gênesis, sobre os Salmos, sobre o evangelho de João e sobre a epístola aos Romanos. Descreveu os tesouros das Escrituras, — os quais considerava tão vastos e profundos que ninguém, no decurso de uma vida inteira, poderia descobri-los todos. Parte dessa sua apreciação derivou-se dos seus trabalhos de pesquisa, ao escrever os seus comentários. Suas obras foram escritas em latim.

16. *Gregório Nazianzeno*. Suas datas foram 328-389 D.C. Mas há algumas dúvidas a respeito. Foi bispo de Sásima e Constantinopla. Escreveu sobre a narrativa da criação, no livro de Gênesis, sobre os subtítulos dos Salmos, além de homilias sobre os livros de Eclesiastes e Cantares, além de outras obras de menor envergadura.

17. *Policrênio*. Faleceu em 430 D.C. Foi bispo de Apamea. Escreveu comentários sobre Jó e Ezequiel, que chegaram até nós. Mas seus comentários sobre Daniel e sobre os livros do Novo Testamento pereceram. Escreveu em grego.

18. *Cirilo de Alexandria*. Faleceu em 444 D.C. Escreveu comentários sobre Isaías, sobre os profetas menores e sobre o evangelho de João, que sobreviveram, além dos fragmentos de suas exposições sobre os Salmos e as epístolas de Paulo. Escreveu em grego.

19. *Teodoreto*. Suas datas foram 393-458 D.C. Comentou sobre Cantares, Isaías, Jeremias, os profetas menores, as epístolas de Paulo, e sobre alguns detalhes dos livros de Reis e de Crônicas. Lightfoot pensava que seus comentários a respeito dos livros de Paulo eram os melhores dentre as obras dos expositores patrísticos. Escreveu em grego.

20. *Ecumênico*, que viveu no século VI D.C. Escreveu um comentário em grego sobre o Apocalipse.

21. *Ambrosiaster*. Viveu no século IV D.C. Também é conhecido como Pseudo-Ambrósio. Escreveu comentários sobre as epístolas paulinas, de considerável valor. Não se consegue identificar a sua pessoa. Seus comentários eram incorretamente atribuídos a Ambrósio, durante a Idade Média. Escreveu em latim.

22. *Gregório, o Grande*. Suas datas foram 540-604 D.C. Foi papa. Foi o último dos doutores tradicionais da Igreja. Seu comentário sobre Jó exerceu notável influência sobre o pensamento de sua época e posteriormente. Também escreveu homilias sobre os evangelhos, além de outros comentários, que não sobreviveram até nós. Escreveu em latim.

Os escritos dos chamados pais da Igreja eram cristocêntricos, guiados pela crença na inspiração divina das Escrituras. O método alegórico era comum a muitos dentre eles, embora fosse rejeitado por outros. A escatologia foi um de seus temas preferidos. A totalidade dessas obras ilustra o profundo interesse que a Igreja antiga tinha pelo estudo das Sagradas Escrituras.

II. A Idade Média

1. *Venerável Bede*. Suas datas foram 673-735 D.C. Esse homem dedicou a sua vida inteira ao estudo das Escrituras. Preparou comentários sobre os livros de Gênesis, Samuel, Esdras, Neemias, Provérbios, Cantares, Habacuque, Marcos, Lucas, as epístolas católicas e o Apocalipse. Era autor de nota, mas dependia muito de Basílio, Ambrósio e Agostinho. Escreveu em latim.

2. *Bernardo de Clairvaux*. Suas datas foram 1090-1153 D.C. Publicou oitenta e seis sermões sobre o livro de Cantares, empregando as interpretações histórica, moral e mística. Tornou-se conhecido por seu extraordinário conhecimento sobre as Escrituras. Escreveu em latim.

3. *Hugo de São Vítor*. Suas datas foram 1097-1141 D.C. Escreveu interpretações místicas sobre alguns dos livros da Bíblia. Escreveu em latim.

4. *André de São Vítor*. Faleceu em 1175 D.C. Escreveu extensos comentários sobre os primeiros oito livros da Bíblia, e também alguns sobre Cantares e Eclesiastes. Fez muitas citações das obras de Orígenes, Agostinho e Jerônimo. Escreveu em latim.

5. *Stephen Langton*. Viveu no século XII D.C. Foi arcebispo de Canterbury. Comentou sobre os primeiros oito livros da Bíblia, sobre a maioria dos profetas e sobre Cantares. Escreveu em latim.

6. *Tomás de Aquino*. Suas datas foram 1225-1274 D.C. Escreveu extensas obras teológicas e filosóficas, através das quais o seu nome foi imortalizado. Mas também escreveu sobre os evangelhos, em cujas obras

COMENTÁRIOS SOBRE A BÍBLIA

citou vinte e dois escritores gregos — e vinte escritores latinos. Comentou sobre Isaías, Jeremias, Salmos, Jó e as epístolas paulinas. Era homem dotado de vasta erudição, de inquestionável devoção, de piedade pessoal e de poderoso intelecto. Um dos fatos mais significativos que se sabe a respeito dele é que, já perto do fim dos seus dias (faleceu com 49 anos), ele passou por uma experiência mística, quando, certo dia, caminhava pelo interior da capela. A revelação foi tão grande que ele deixou de escrever. Quando seus alunos indagaram por que ele deixara de produzir literatura, Aquino respondeu: «O que me foi revelado é tão grande que os meus escritos me parecem como palha». Talvez seja significativo que ele tenha recebido essa iluminação apenas três meses antes de sua morte. Porventura, não teria ele recebido essa revelação tão tarde, a fim de que sua missão de comentador pudesse continuar? Embora suas obras lhe parecessem como palha, quando confrontadas com a forte luz da iluminação recebida naquela experiência mística, têm resplandecido como ouro entre as composições literárias dos doutores da Igreja, a despeito de algumas coisas às quais podemos objetar. Escreveu em latim.

7. *Nicolau de Lira*. Farrar chamou-o de Jerônimo do século XIV. Lutero afirmava que preferia Nicolau de Lira a qualquer outro intérprete das Escrituras. Sua famosa obra, *Postillae Perpetuae in Universam S. Scripturam*, foi o primeiro comentário bíblico a ser impresso, o qual exerceu vasta influência. Entre ele e a Reforma Protestante não houve qualquer adição significativa à exposição da Bíblia.

III. A Reforma Protestante

1. *Martinho Lutero*. Nasceu em 1483 e faleceu em 1546. Segundo ele mesmo afirmava, sua mente estava cativa à Palavra de Deus. Ele lia a Bíblia inteira duas vezes por ano. Escreveu pouco sobre o Novo Testamento, excetuando seu famoso comentário sobre a epístola aos Gálatas, o qual tem sido traduzido para muitos idiomas, com base no seu original em alemão. Não aceitava todo o Novo Testamento sobre bases iguais, tendo chamado a epístola de Tiago de «epístola de palha», e tendo rejeitado a posição canônica do Apocalipse. Parte de suas preleções sobre Romanos e Hebreus sobrevive até hoje. Escreveu mais sobre o Antigo Testamento, tendo comentado, principalmente, sobre os livros de Gênesis e de Salmos. Rejeitava a autoridade da versão latina, e comentava com base no hebraico e no grego, em latim. Uma tradução alemã de seus escritos, apareceu em 1539.

2. *João Calvino*. Suas datas foram 1509-1564. Comentou sobre o Novo Testamento inteiro, excetuando apenas o Apocalipse. Escreveu muitas outras obras, além do comentário. Também comentou sobre o Antigo Testamento, embora não sobre os livros de II Samuel, Reis, Crônicas, Rute, Ester e Cantares. Escreveu originalmente em latim, mas suas obras têm sido traduzidas para outros idiomas; muitas delas têm aparecido em inglês desde 1578. Seus comentários demonstram sólido conhecimento sobre os escritos de Orígenes, Crisóstomo e vários outros pais da Igreja. Ele também citou escritores clássicos do grego e do latim. Seus comentários eram mais habilidosos que os de Lutero, bastante informativos, embora freqüentemente cáusticos.

IV. O Século XVII

1. *Joseph Hall*. Suas datas foram 1574-1656. Escreveu comentários sobre o Antigo e o Novo Testamentos. Escrevia em latim.

2. *Patrick Lowth*. Em parceria com Thitby e Lowman, produziu muitos volumes comentando sobre o Antigo e o Novo Testamentos. Originalmente escreveu em latim, mas depois esses escritos foram traduzidos para o inglês.

3. *Matthew Poole*. Suas datas foram 1624-1679. Escreveu comentários sobre o Antigo e o Novo Testamentos, em latim, embora o próprio Poole só tenha preparado comentários até o capítulo cinqüenta e oito de Isaías. Suas obras foram traduzidas para o inglês, sendo muito usadas por muitos. Eram altamente recomendadas por John Wesley, Cotton Mather, Doddridge, bispo Tomline, e outros.

4. *Hugo Grotius*. Suas datas foram 1583-1645. Foi um teólogo holandês que escreveu valiosos comentários sobre a Bíblia, usando o latim.

V. O Século XVIII

1. *Matthew Henry*. Seu comentário sobre o Novo Testamento foi publicado entre 1708 e 1710. Esse comentário estava dividido em parágrafos, não acompanhando versículo após versículo. Ele escreveu até o livro de Atos, antes de falecer. Outros autores, de idênticas convicções, terminaram o comentário do Novo Testamento. Esse é o mais difundido de todos os comentários bíblicos em língua inglesa. A obra continua sendo publicada, embora existam várias obras similares, em inglês, que lhe são vastamente superiores. A obra de Matthew Henry é essencialmente devocional, faltando-lhe erudição quanto a vastas áreas do estudo bíblico, incluindo o conhecimento do hebraico e do grego, das descobertas arqueológicas e dos manuscritos, tudo o que se desenvolveu muito depois de sua época. Mas Matthew Henry tem assegurado o seu lugar como pioneiro entre os comentadores da Bíblia na língua inglesa. Ele estabeleceu uma trilha que outros escritores têm alargado em auto-estrada. Se já há valor no conhecimento da trilha, muito maior é o proveito de quem pode valer-se da auto-estrada.

2. *Philip Doddridge*. Suas datas foram 1702-1751. Publicou cinco volumes de comentários sobre a Bíblia inglesa, os quais têm sido reeditados por muitas vezes.

3. *Thomas Scott*. Suas datas foram 1747-1821. Escreveu um comentário sobre a Bíblia inteira, o primeiro comentário volumoso dessa natureza a ser publicado nos Estados Unidos da América. Sua obra não é muito original ou imaginativa, pelo que pouco a tenho usado.

4. *John Gill*. Suas datas foram 1697-1771. Foi um pregador e erudito batista calvinista. Escreveu o primeiro comentário versículo por versículo da inteira Bíblia inglesa, publicado em Londres, em 1763, e reimpresso em nossos próprios dias pela Baker Book House. Essa obra é muito superior às congêneres de sua época, incluindo o trabalho de Matthew Henry. Ele era um dos grandes eruditos de sua época sobre as questões judaicas, e sua obra continua sendo de imenso valor. Geralmente comentava extensamente, e isso não agrada ao leitor moderno, que vive pressionado pela exigüidade do tempo.

5. *A.A. Calmet*. Publicou vinte e três volumes de comentários sobre as Escrituras, em francês.

6. *J.A. Bengel*. Publicou um comentário do Novo Testamento em 1742, bastante útil do ponto de vista do grego e do latim. Foi feita uma tradução do mesmo, para o inglês, em 1857.

VI. O Século XIX

Os comentários bíblicos preparados no século XIX foram tão numerosos que, abaixo, incluímos somente aqueles de importância primária.

1. *Adam Clarke*. Suas datas foram 1760-1832. Foi contemporâneo e amigo de João Wesley. Publicou seis

COMENTÁRIOS SOBRE A BÍBLIA

volumes sobre a Bíblia inglesa, de grande valor, que continuam sendo publicados. Foi o principal comentador bíblico metodista de seus dias. Sua obra se assemelha a uma loja de antiguidades, cheia de curiosidades, mas também há excelentes comentários. Escreveu em inglês.

2. *Edward Greswell*. Em 1834-1835, publicou seis volumes de comentários sobre as parábolas do décimo terceiro capítulo de Mateus. Longos, mas profundos comentários. Escreveu em inglês.

3. *Henry Alford*. Suas datas foram 1810-1871. Seu *Greek Testament and Exegetical Commentary*, em cinco volumes, com toda a justiça tem passado por muitas edições, sendo reimpresso atualmente pela Moody Press. É obra de grande importância, muito útil e informativa. Ele escreveu em inglês, comentando quase versículo por versículo o Novo Testamento grego.

4. *Bispo Lightfoot*. Suas datas foram 1828-1889. Escreveu maciços comentários sobre os livros de Gálatas, Filipenses, Colossenses e Filemom. Escreveu em inglês.

5. *C.J. Ellicott*. Suas datas foram 1819-1905. Foi editor e contribuidor de um comentário sobre a Bíblia inteira, que leva o seu nome, publicado em oito volumes. Está repleto de boas informações e é extremamente útil, sendo reimpresso até hoje. Escreveu em inglês.

6. *Albert Barnes*. Publicou doze volumes sobre as Escrituras, intitulados *Notes*. Têm sido reeditados por muitas vezes, vendendo muitíssimas cópias. Escreveu em inglês.

7. *A.R. Fausset, Robert Jamieson* e *David Brown*. Publicaram conjuntamente o seu *Commentary Critical, Experimental and Practical on the Old and New Testaments*, entre 1864 e 1870, em seis volumes. A obra tem passado por muitas edições, tendo sido reimpressa pela última vez em 1945. É obra que contém muita informação e reveste-se de grande valor. Escreveram em inglês.

8. *F.C. Cook*. Editor do *Speaker's Commentary* publicado entre 1871 e 1881, em dez volumes. Contou com notáveis contribuidores. Seu grande propósito era de defender a Bíblia de uma onda crescente de ceticismo. A obra foi escrita em inglês.

9. *Bispo Perowne* e *A.F. Kirkpatrick*. Publicaram a *Cambridge Bible for Schools and Colleges*, com dignos contribuidores. Perdurou até o nosso próprio século XX. Foi publicada em inglês.

10. *Dods, Chadwick, Kellogg, Maclaren*, etc., foram os contribuidores da obra editada por W. Robertson Nicoll, intitulada *The Expositor's Bible*, em 48 volumes. Obra muito usada, embora de difícil leitura, devido ao tipo de impressão em que foi lançada.

11. *The International Critical Commentary*. Os editores e contribuidores foram Alfred Plummer, Samuel Rolles Driver, Charles Augustus Briggs, que também se valeram da obra de muitos outros contribuidores. A obra foi iniciada em 1895, mas nunca foi terminada completamente. Os volumes são de variegada qualidade. Alguns deles são por demais gramaticais e técnicos para o leitor comum. Esses volumes com freqüência sacrificam um sólido comentário bíblico em favor de tecnicalidades. No entanto, diversos dos seus volumes sobre o Antigo e o Novo Testamentos têm servido de marcos na interpretação da Bíblia. Foram escritos em inglês.

12. *H.D.M. Spence* e *J.S. Exell*, editores dos quarenta e nove volumes do *Pulpit Commentary*, publicado entre 1880 e 1896. De natureza principalmente homilética, com grande riqueza de material.

13. *W. Robertson Nicoll*, editor, conjuntamente com vários contribuidores, produziu o *Expositor's Greek Testament*, entre 1897 e 1907. Obra não muito volumosa, mas de elevado valor. Foi escrito em inglês, comentando o Novo Testamento grego quase versículo por versículo.

Além dessas séries, temos inúmeras obras individuais sobre um ou mais dos livros da Bíblia, lançados em língua inglesa. Vários comentários em alemão foram publicados no século XIX, os quais têm sido traduzidos para o inglês, tendo exercido considerável influência, conforme alistamos abaixo:

14. *John Peter Lange*. Suas datas foram 1802-1884. Foi editor e contribuidor do *Lange's Commentary*, cuja publicação teve início em 1864. Vinte e dois volumes foram impressos sob o título *Theologische-homiletisches Biblewerk*. Philip Schaff, famoso historiador e erudito, fez anotações, juntamente com outros, para a edição inglesa. Algumas dessas notas são melhores que os comentários originais. Para mim, esse comentário tem sido um dos mais úteis, pelo qual tenho um profundo respeito. O *Novo Testamento Interpretado*, de minha autoria, tem muitas citações do mesmo (original em alemão, com tradução inglesa).

15. *J.K.F. Keil* e *Franz Delitzsch*, dois dos maiores eruditos dos costumes e das línguas semitas de sua época, produziram o *Commentary on the Old Testament*, uma obra que nunca foi ultrapassada em sua linha de ataque, que continua sendo publicada em inglês. (Alemão, com tradução para o inglês).

16. *H.W. Meyer*. Deu início, em 1828, à publicação de seu célebre *Kritischexegetischer Commentar uber das Neue Testament*, em dezesseis volumes. A obra foi terminada em 1852, tendo sido publicada uma tradução inglesa da mesma nesse mesmo ano. Contém um exaustivo tratamento do texto, mas tenho visto que é menos útil que o comentário de Lange.

VII. O Século XX

Nosso século XX tem produzido um número quase inacreditável de comentários, formando coleções ou volumes isolados, principalmente na língua inglesa.

1. *Charles R. Eerdman*, editor. Uma série de manuais sobre a Bíblia, essencialmente de caráter devocional, no começo do século XX. Escritos em inglês.

2. *R.C.H. Lenski*. Lançou um comentário sobre a Bíblia em onze volumes, no começo do século XX. Escreveu em inglês.

3. *Moffat New Testament Commentary* (1926-1950). Obra lançada em dezessete volumes. Editor e contribuidor, James Moffat. Obra escrita em inglês.

4. *The Westminster Commentary Series*. Vários contribuidores notáveis. A série teve início no começo do século XX. Ainda não foi completado o comentário sobre a Bíblia inteira. Essa obra varia em valor de autor para autor, quanto ao grau de conservatismo ou de liberalismo. Está sendo escrita em inglês.

5. *The Interpreter's Bible*. Comentário publicado em 1951, em doze volumes. Editor e contribuidor, G.A. Buttrick. Comenta a Bíblia inteira. Trinta e seis eruditos contribuíram para a obra, alguns conservadores, e outros liberais. Li pessoalmente treze comentários inteiros sobre o Novo Testamento, de Mateus ao Apocalipse, quando da produção de *O Novo Testamento Interpretado*. Posso afirmar que o mais eloqüente desses comentários é o *Interpreter's Bible*, embora eu não concorde com muitos pontos de vista expostos por alguns dos contribuidores. No entanto, há muito material de excelente qualidade

COMENTÁRIOS SOBRE A BÍBLIA

nessa obra. Uma das lições que aprendemos na mesma é que, na inquirição pelo conhecimento, muito temos a aprender até mesmo da parte daqueles com quem não concordamos completamente quanto à posição teológica, sobre vários assuntos. Uma outra coisa que ali podemos aprender é que podemos dizer coisas sem ódio e sem contenção, e, mesmo assim, asseverar o que queremos. Os autores dessa obra tentaram temperar sua linguagem, não entrando em choque desnecessário com aqueles que não pertenciam à sua linha de pensamento teológico. No mundo inteiro não há coisa alguma tão importante quanto a lei do amor. Isso deveria levar-nos a aprender a usar de moderação e gentileza naquilo que dizemos, mesmo quando sentimos que é necessário protestar contra algum parecer. Essa atitude não é tão visível em nenhuma outra série como no *Interpreter's Bible*. Tenho procurado emular esse bom exemplo, depois que li essa obra do começo ao fim. A obra foi escrita em inglês.

6. *W.F. Albright* e *David N. Freedman*, autores da *Anchor Bible*, que contém muito material valioso. Escrita em inglês.

7. *Bible Guides*, publicado em 1862. Escrito em inglês. Editores, Wm. Barclay e F.F. Bruce.

8. *Black's New Testament Commentary*, publicado em 1957. Escrito em inglês.

9. *The Clarendon Bible*. Comentário iniciado em 1929. Escrito em inglês.

10. *Everyman's Bible Commentary*. Publicado em inglês.

11. *Layman's Bible Commentary*. Publicado em inglês.

12. *The Old Testament Library*. Esse é o comentário bíblico dos Adventistas do Sétimo Dia, que inclui os comentários de Ellen G. White no final de cada capítulo.

13. *Torch Commentary*. Publicado em 1960. Editores: J. Marsh e A. Richardson. Escrito em inglês.

14. *Shield Bible Study*. Publicado em inglês.

15. *Tyndale Bible Commentaries*. Editados por R.V.G. Tasker e D.J. Wiseman, em dezenove volumes, em inglês.

Numerosos comentários em um único volume, tratando da Bíblia inteira, têm sido dados a público, conforme se vê abaixo:

16. *Commentary on the Holy Bible*, por J.R. Dummelow, 1909. Escrito em inglês.

17. *Commentary on the Bible*, por A.S. Peake. Escrito em inglês.

18. *A New Commentary on Holy Scripture*, editado pelo bispo Gore.

19. *Abingdon Century Bible Commentary*, 1929.

20. *Twentieth Century Bible Commentary*, 1955.

21. *A Concise Bible Commentary*, por W.K.L. Clarke.

22. *The New Bible Commentary*, com 140 contribuidores. Editado por J.D. Douglas, em 1962. Esse comentário editado em inglês em um só volume, foi traduzido em português e publicado em três volumes. É um excelente trabalho para as suas dimensões, mas não se pode pôr um oceano em uma taça de chá. É lamentável que melhores obras não tenham sido escolhidas para serem traduzidas em português. As razões podem ser econômicas. Porém, há coisas mais importantes do que o dinheiro. Também há coisas mais importantes do que poupar tempo. Também há coisas mais importantes do que realizar apressadamente certos projetos literários.

23. *A Catholic Commentary on the Holy Scriptures*, 1969.

24. *Wycliffe Bible Commentary*, editado por C.F. Pfeiffer e Everett H. Harrison, 1962.

25. *Interpreter's One-Volume Commentary on the Bible*, 1971. Naturalmente, é uma boa obra para um volume só, considerando os eruditos que contribuíram para a mesma. Útil para quem quer um comentário aligeirado; mas, na verdade, os comentários de um volume só geralmente dizem pouco demais.

Os livros individuais da Bíblia também têm sido comentados mediante comentários de um volume só. Em inglês há uma vasta biblioteca, que não especificamos aqui por não se revestir de interesse primário para os leitores de língua portuguesa.

VIII. Comentários na Língua Portuguesa

1. *Série Cultura Bíblica*
Sociedade Religiosa Edições Vida Nova e Associação Religiosa Editora Mundo Cristão

Gênesis, Derek Kidner; Tr. Odayr Olivette, 1979.
Êxodo, Alan Cole; Tr. Carlos Oswaldo Pinto, 1979.
Levítico, K. Harrison; Tr. Gordon Chown, 1983.
Números, Gordon J. Wenhan; Tr. Adiel Almeida de Oliveira, 1985.
Deuteronômio, J.A. Thompson; Tr. Carlos Oswaldo Pinto, 1982.
Juízes e Rute, J.A. Thompson; Tr. Carlos Oswaldo Pinto, 1982.
Esdras e Neemias, Derek Kidner; Tr. Gordon Chown, 1985.
Jó, Francis Anderson; Tr. Gordon Chown, 1984.
Salmos (1-72), Derek Kidner; Tr. Gordon Chown, 1980-1981.
Salmos (73-150), Derek Kidner; Tr. Gordon Chown, 1981.
Provérbios, Derek Kidner; Tr. Gordon Chown, 1980.
Eclesiastes, Michael A. Eaton; Tr. Gordon Chown, 1980.
Jeremias, R.K. Harrison; Tr. Hans Udo Fuchs, 1980.
Ezequiel, John R. Taylor; Tr. Gordon Chown, 1984.
Daniel, Joyce G. Baldwin; Tr. Ênio R. Mueller, 1983.
Ageu, Zacar. e Malaq., Joyce G. Baldwin; Tr. Hans Udo Fuchs, 1983.
Mateus, R.V.G. Tasker; Tr. Odayr Olivette, 1980.
Marcos, R.V.G. Tasker; Tr. Odayr Olivette, 1980.
Lucas, Leon Morris; Tr. Gordon Chown, 1983.
Atos, Howard Marshall; Tr. Gordon Chown, 1982.
Romanos, F.F. Bruce; Tr. Odayr Olivette, 1979.
I Coríntios, Leon Morris; Tr. Odayr Olivette, 1981.
Gálatas, Donald Buthrie; Tr. Gordon Chown, 1984.
Efésios, Francis Foulkes; Tr. Márcio Loureiro, 1984.
Filipen. Ralph P. Martin; Tr. Oswaldo Ramos, 1985.
Colos. e Filemom, Ralph P. Martin; Tr. Gordon Chown, 1984.
I e II Tessalon., Howard Marshall; Tr. Gordon Ghown, 1984.
I e II Tim. e Tito, J.N.D. Kelly; Tr. Gordon Chown, 1983.
Hebreus, Donald Guthrie; Tr. Gordon Chown, 1984.
Epístolas de João, John R. Stott; Tr. Odayr Olivette, 1983.
I Pedro, Ênio Mueller, 1983.
II Pedro e Judas, Michael Green; Tr. Gordon Chown, 1983.
Apocalipse, George Ladd; Tr. Hans Udo Fuchs, 1980.

2. *Comentário Bíblico Moody*
Vol. I: *Gênesis-Deuteronômio*, 1984.
Vol. II: *Josué-Cantares*, 1985.
Vol. IV: *Os Evangelhos e Atos*, 1980.
Vol. V: *Romanos à Apocalipse*, 1983.

COMENTÁRIOS SOBRE A BÍBLIA

Tradução de Yolanda M. Krievin
Imprensa Batista Regular

3. *O Novo Comentário da Bíblia*: três volumes, A.T. e N.T. Original em inglês, redator, F. Davidson; versão em português, redator, Russell P. Shedd, Edições Vida Nova, SP, 1963.

4. *Comentários Individuais*
Panorama do Novo Testamento, Roberto H. Gundry, Soc. Rel. Edições Vida Nova, 1972, 490 p.
Como Estudar os Quatro Evangelhos, W.H. Griffith Thomas, Casa Editora Presbiteriana, 1953, 61 p.
Harmonia dos Evangelhos, S.L. Watson e W.E. Allen, 4ª edição, Casa Publicadora Batista, 1964, 267 p.
Comentário do Evangelho de Mateus, John A. Broadus, 3ª edição, Casa Publicadora Batista, 1966-67, 2 vols., 368, 363 p.
Comentário do Evangelho segundo São Mateus, J.C. Ryle, Imprensa Metodista, 1959, 150 p.
Comentário...São Marcos, J.C. Ryle, Imprensa Metodista, 1958, 176 p.
Comentário...São Lucas, J.C. Ryle, Imprensa Metodista, 1955, 342 p.
O Evangelho de João, C.R. Eerdman, Casa Editora Presbiteriana, 1965, 158 p.
Evangelho segundo João, W.C. Taylor, 2ª edição, Casa Publicadora Batista, 1957, 487 p.
Atos dos Apóstolos, C.R. Eerdman, Casa Editora Presbiteriana, 1960, 180 p.
Atos dos Apóstolos, Mário Neves, Casa Editora Presbiteriana, sem data (s.d.), 384 p.
O Livro dos Atos dos Apóstolos, Frank Stagg, Casa Publicadora Batista, 1958, 397 p.
O Evangelho Segundo Paulo: um estudo da Carta aos Romanos, Clifton J. Allen, 1961, 199 p.
Estudos sobre o Livro aos Romanos, C.N. Beggs, Espada do Senhor, Portugal, s.d., 111 p.
Romanos, G.B. Wilson, Publicações Evangélicas Selecionadas, 1981, 227 p.
Comentário à Epístola de São Paulo aos Gálatas, C.R. Eerdman, Casa Editora Presbiteriana, s.d., 133 p.
A Epístola aos Gálatas, tradução e comentário, W.C. Taylor, 2ª edição, Casa Publicadora Batista, 1954, 360 p.
Epístola aos Efésios, H.E. Alexander, Ação Bíblica s.d., 159 p.
Efésios: o Evangelho das Regiões Celestiais, N.B. Harrison, 2ª edição, Emprevan Editora, 1967, 180 p.
Alegrai-vos no Senhor (Filipenses), Russell P. Shedd, Vida Nova, 1984, 128 p.
Andai nEle, (Colossenses), Russell P. Shedd, ABU Editora, 1979, 92 p.
Colossenses: Tradução e Comentário, R. Sturz, Livraria Editora Evangélica, 1956, 128 p.
As Cartas aos Tessalonicenses, C.M. Keen, Imprensa Batista Regular, 1959, 88 p.
Exposição das Epístolas Pastorais: I e II Timóteo, Tito, B.H. Carol, Casa Publicadora Batista, 1961, 178 p.

Estudos na Segunda Carta a Timóteo, L. Soares, Associação para Orientação Bíblica, 1969, 78 p.
Tu Porém, a Mensagem de II Timóteo, J.R.W. Stott, ABU Editora, 1982, 123 p.
A Carta aos Hebreus, H.H. Hobbs, Casa Publicadora Batista, 1958, 169 p.
A Epístola de Tiago: Tradução e Comentário, W.C. Taylor, Casa Publicadora Batista, s.d., 154 p.
I Epístola de Pedro, P.S. Rees, Junta Bautista de Publicaceónes, 1963, 166 p.

Estudos nas Epístolas de Pedro, R.D. Jones, Edições Cristãs, 1984, 62 p.
Epístolas de João: comunhão na família de Deus William MacDonald; Escola Bíblica Emaus, s.d., 100 p.
Apocalipse de João, C.R. Eerdman; Casa Editora Presbiteriana, 1960, 142 p.
Apocalipse Ontem e Hoje, J.A. Ferreira; Luz Para o Caminho, 1983, 184 p.
Apocalipse: O Drama dos Séculos, H. Lockyer, Editora Vida, 1982, 248 p.
A Mensagem do Apocalipse: Digno é o Cordeiro, R. Summers; Casa Publicadora Batista, 1972, 203 p.

5. **O Novo Testamento Interpretado**, seis volumes, interpretação versículo por versículo, com o texto grego do Novo Testamento e um comentário sobre as variantes principais dos manuscritos antigos; Russell N. Champlin, Tr. João Marques Bentes; 1ª edição (1979), A Soc. Relig. A Voz Bíblica Brasileria; outras edições, Milenium.

O autor deste comentário também foi o autor desta presente Enciclopédia. As duas obras tinham o mesmo tradutor.
O original em inglês consistiu em vinte mil páginas datilografadas. Foram necessários oito anos de trabalho árduo para ser produzido. Foi lançado em seis volumes, nas dimensões dos volumes da Encyclopaedia Britannica, com pouco mais de mil páginas cada volume. Foram lidos treze comentários bíblicos diversos, versículo por versículo, dos quais foram extraídos os melhores elementos. Muitas outras obras em inglês foram consultadas. Foi feita uma seleção de poemas brasileiros e portugueses pela professora Aurea Lúcia de Araújo, a qual foi incorporada nesse comentário. A revisão foi realizada, com grande dedicação, por Neusa Maria da Silva e Vera Lúcia de Oliveira. O propósito foi o de produzir um comentário do Novo Testamento grego, versículo por versículo. Recebi permissão para usar a terceira edição do texto grego do Novo Testamento editado pela United Bible Societies, como também para traduzir e incorporar no comentário o seu *Comentário Textual*. Esse comentário explica as razões para a seleção de duas mil variantes do texto do Novo Testamento. Isso significa que as duas mil mais importantes variantes textuais dos manuscritos gregos foram discutidas no meu comentário. Minha equipe e eu preparamos as páginas para impressão, mediante trabalho de fotocomposição. — Esse aspecto do trabalho requereu quatro anos de trabalho ininterruptos. Minha principal auxiliar foi minha esposa, Irene Champlin, que compôs a maior parte do texto. Ela recebeu a ajuda da irmã Zélia de Araújo. O tradutor incansável da obra e também desta Enciclopédia foi João Marques Bentes (que vide). Muitos contribuíram para as necessidades financeiras, possibilitando o lançamento do comentário. Dentre as igrejas, desejo destacar a Ajax Baptist Church of Ajax, Ontario, Canadá, que se encarregou da porção financeira mais pesada. Dentre as pessoas que contribuíram financeiramente, de seu próprio bolso, quero salientar a Sra. Margaret Hutzel, de Ann Arbor, Michigan, dos Estados Unidos da América. Na qualidade de professor do Departamento de Humanidades da Faculdade de Engenharia de Guaratinguetá, no estado de São Paulo, Brasil, fui capaz de fazer poupanças que também foram lançadas no custeio da obra. Meu distribuidor tem sido Gunther Neuwahl, da Milenium Distribuidora de São Paulo, São Paulo, que trabalhou sem reservas para finalizar esta obra. O

John Gill — 1697-1771
Pastor, escritor e doutor, batista por denominação; produziu o primeiro comentário, versículo por versículo sobre a Bíblia inteira — na língua inglesa.

Adam Clarke — nasceu em 1782
metodista por denominação, escreveu um
comentário em inglês sobre a Bíblia inteira
— de grande valor.

AGORA EM PORTUGUÊS

UM COMENTÁRIO

VERSÍCULO POR VERSÍCULO

—❧ SOBRE O NOVO TESTAMENTO ❧—

EM SEIS VOLUMES

O NOVO TESTAMENTO INTERPRETADO

(*por* Russell Norman Champlin, Ph. D.)

HOMENAGEM

ao missionário Bill Barkley

••• ••• •••

Agradeço Bill Barkley pela composição dos artigos sobre *Dicionários* e *Comentários* bíblicos. Ele é o diretor da Biblioteca Evangélica do Brasil em São Paulo e é presidente da Editora, Publicações Evangélicas Selecionadas, através da qual tem publicado 44 livros. Ele sempre me tem encorajado no trabalho de literatura bíblica. É um homem de dedicação e convicção que ele combina com tolerância e generosidade.

••• ••• •••

•••

comentário já está na quarta edição, de 1979 a esta data (janeiro de 1986).

N.B. Agradeço a gentil cooperação de *William Barkley*, diretor da Biblioteca Evangélica de São Paulo, pela preparação das informações sobre comentários bíblicos *em português*.

Bibliografia. ABB AG BULL CAM DAR SPU Z

COMER

Ver o artigo geral sobre os **Alimentos**. Quanto a aplicações espirituais dos atos de comer e beber, ver o artigo sobre *Comer a Carne e Beber o Sangue de Jesus*. Ver também sobre *Jesus como o Pão da Vida*.

COMER A CARNE e Beber o Sangue de Jesus

João 6:53: *Disse-lhes Jesus: Em verdade, em verdade vos digo: Se não comerdes a carne do Filho do homem, e não beberdes o seu sangue, não tereis vida em vós mesmos.*

Grande volume de literatura tem sido escrito com referência ao sentido deste versículo, em torno do qual a passagem encontra o seu significado central. Abaixo, as notas oferecem, em forma de sumário, as diversas interpretações.

Primeiramente consideraremos os sentidos dos termos *carne* e *sangue*:

1. A interpretação *literal* dos judeus foi rejeitada por Jesus; mas, apesar disso, alguns estudiosos vêm nisso uma indicação da doutrina da transubstanciação, embora seja óbvio que se trata de uma interpretação literal. De acordo com essa doutrina, a *substância* ou *essência* do pão e do vinho, na eucaristia, é transformada na essência do corpo e do sangue de Jesus. Os meros *acidentes* físicos, como o peso, o sabor, o odor, a contextura (ou qualquer outra coisa sujeita à observação comum ou científica, o que, na linguagem filosófica se convencionou chamar de «acidentes», em contraste com a natureza real e essencial de qualquer coisa), não se alteram. (Quanto a uma completa discussão sobre o sentido da chamada *transubstanciação*, bem como sobre os problemas que envolvem a questão, ver as notas concernentes aos trechos João 6:48, Mat. 26:26 e I Cor. 11:24 no NTI. Essas notas também abordam e discutem a doutrina similar da *consubstanciação*, que é mera variação da teoria da transubstanciação).

2. Por si mesma, nas Escrituras, *a carne* pode denotar *a natureza humana*, em suas manifestações concretas mais plenas (ver João 3:6). Não precisamos supor, com o uso desse termo (e, naturalmente, não resta dúvida alguma sobre o assunto), que nenhuma idéia de natureza pecaminosa está aqui em vista, conforme Paulo emprega o vocábulo com freqüência. (Ver, por exemplo, Rom. 7:18). A expressão «carne e sangue» pode denotar a natureza humana herdada, conforme nos mostra a passagem de Mat. 16:17. (Ver também Gál. 1:16). Assim sendo, pode-se falar de uma herança cultural, como era o caso da cultura judaica e suas associações. Porém, esse termo pode significar, tal como o vocábulo «carne», considerado isoladamente, a natureza humana terrena, em contraste com a natureza espiritual. (Ver I Cor. 15:50).

3. Combinando essas idéias, chegamos à conclusão de que a carne e o sangue de Cristo, nesta passagem bíblica, em seu sentido primário, referem-se à sua *natureza humana verdadeira*, talvez subentendendo sua descendência particular por intermédio de Israel. Ou então, o que temos aqui é o «Cristo histórico».

Nesse caso, ficaria subentendida a missão do Messias, que veio a fim de salvar a humanidade. Acreditamos em um Cristo histórico e não em meras invencionices teológicas. Mediante o Cristo histórico, real, homem que realmente viveu sobre a face desta terra, é que a humanidade recebeu o privilégio de participar da vida celestial, a «vida eterna»; e todos os benefícios atinentes ao N.T. são descritos como bênçãos conferidas àqueles que exercem fé em Cristo.

4. Não obstante, a morte de Cristo fica também aqui implicada, porquanto ele se deu a si mesmo, em favor dos homens, e isso completa a idéia de sua missão como o Messias prometido. Ninguém poderia extrair benefícios espirituais de uma missão parcial do Messias, e nem mesmo o Cristo histórico, que viveu entre os homens, não fora o fato de que ele morreu em expiação pelo pecado. A vida de Jesus foi mais importante, todavia, pois é através dela que ele participou plenamente da natureza humana, a fim de que possamos participar, —finalmente, na vida divina, tal como ele participou dessa vida. É justamente a isso que chamamos de *vida eterna*.

Não é provável que Jesus tivesse querido ensinar qualquer coisa semelhante ao que disse Aristóteles, quando falou de sua carne e de seu sangue como elementos que os homens podem comer e beber, como se, de alguma maneira, os homens pudessem compartilhar da *substância* desses elementos, mediante algum processo de transferência da essência mística para o pão e o vinho, quando da celebração da missa da Igreja Católica Romana ou quando da celebração da ceia, dentro da denominação luterana e outras. Pode haver aqui alguma alusão à eucaristia; mas não temos de compreender aqui que esses elementos do pão e do vinho são misticamente modificados ou transformados, de tal maneira que a substância do pão e do vinho venha a ser transformada na substância do corpo e do sangue de nosso Senhor. (Quanto a uma descrição dessa doutrina da «transubstanciação», ver I Cor. 11:24 no NTI. Essa nota esclarece como algumas **facções da** igreja têm tomado de empréstimo a idéia aristotélica, a fim de tentar explicar passagens difíceis como essa).

No que diz respeito às interpretações gerais, vinculadas a esta passagem do evangelho de João, damos o seguinte sumário:

1. Esta passagem visa ensinar a *morte expiatória* de Cristo. Assim opinaram muitos intérpretes, tanto antigos como modernos, a saber, Agostinho, Lutero, Melancton, Calvino, Beza, Grotius, Lucke, Meyer, Tholuck, Neander, Lange, Ebrar, Weiss e Ewald.

2. A passagem alude à *vida inteira* de Cristo, ao Cristo *histórico*, bem como aos benefícios que ele nos trouxe, por meio de seu ministério divinamente determinado. Naturalmente isso inclui a sua morte. (Assim pensavam Paulus, Frommann, De Wette, e muitos outros).

3. Alguns estudiosos, ao enfatizarem a *missão histórica* de Jesus, parecem forçar a exclusão de qualquer pensamento à transmissão de sua vida, por intermédio de sua morte. «Não à dádiva de sua carne, mas à sua própria carne, é que Jesus chamou de alimento». (Delitzsch).

4. Alguns encaram esta passagem, em sua inteireza, como um *discurso profético* que descreve a ceia do Senhor ou a eucaristia. (Assim pensavam Crisóstomo e a maioria dos pais da igreja). Muitos teólogos católicos romanos aferram-se a esse ponto de vista; mas nisso são seguidos por muitos outros, como Bengel, Olshausen, Wordsworth, etc. (todos eles intérpretes protestantes).

COMER — COMÉRCIO

5. Alguns acreditam que temos aqui um discurso *mítico* ou fabricado, destituído de qualquer base nos acontecimentos históricos, antecipando o ensino sobre a ceia do Senhor ou sobre a eucaristia. (Assim têm imaginado os intérpretes mais críticos ou racionais, como Bretschneider, Strauss e Baur).

6. Outros, finalmente, dizem que a *própria ceia* do Senhor não é aqui focalizada, e, sim, a idéia ou *realidade espiritual* (isto é, participação na vida essencial do Cristo) sobre a qual se *fundamenta a ceia do Senhor*. (Esse parecer é de Meyer, Lange, Alford e Olshausen).

Avaliação e Conclusão

O sentido parece ser **geral**, e não restrito, conforme algumas dessas interpretações nos indicam. Assim sendo, poderíamos combinar a primeira e a segunda posições, com algumas modificações da quarta e da sexta posições. Certamente o autor deste evangelho estava fazendo *uma alusão* à eucaristia, quando registrou esta passagem. Os ouvintes de Jesus estavam a caminho da festa da páscoa, quando este discurso foi proferido; por conseguinte, é como se tivesse sido dito: a verdadeira páscoa é Jesus, em sua morte expiatória. E assim, dentro do contexto da polêmica cristã, isso significaria que a verdadeira páscoa é Jesus, o que é simbolizado, no seio da cristandade, pelos ritos eclesiásticos da ceia do Senhor ou da eucaristia.

Entretanto, deve-se acrescentar que o ensino *não é* sacramental, *nem* meramente simbólico. A doutrina da «transubstanciação» está alicerçada na noção aristotélica da «substância», o mais certo é que essa noção jamais fez parte dos ensinos cristãos primitivos, e nem está em vista neste evangelho. Jesus, em sua vida histórica, levou a vida necessária para conduzir os homens a Deus. Assumiu a natureza humana, foi aperfeiçoado como homem (segundo o dizer de Heb. 5:9), e, uma vez aperfeiçoado em sua missão, tornou-se o autor da eterna salvação de todos quantos nele confiam, conforme o versículo acima referido, na epístola aos Hebreus. Portanto, a realização bem-sucedida e a consumação de sua vida terrena eram elementos necessários para que ele pudesse verdadeiramente conferir vida eterna aos homens. Ele participou da nossa natureza, para que *pudéssemos participar da dele*. A *metáfora* da assimilação de elementos de comida implica a intimidade da comunhão com Cristo, através da qual, compartilhamos a própria natureza deles. Ver II Cor. 3:18.

Participando na «vida espiritual» dele, ganhamos sua *forma de vida*, i.e., participação na sua divindade (II Ped. 1:4). Ver o artigo sobre *Jesus como o pão da vida*.

Uma vez que foi assim completamente aperfeiçoado em sua missão (sendo ele o pão de Deus, enquanto esteve entre os homens, porquanto por meio dele é que foi transmitida a mensagem da vida eterna), em seguida *ofereceu a sua vida*, em sua morte expiatória. Essa morte completou a sua missão, e por meio dela a sua carne e o seu sangue foram *dados* aos homens, posto que levou nossos pecados sobre o madeiro, em seu próprio corpo. E assim a sua natureza humana verdadeira foi levada a experimentar a morte, a fim de que nossa *natureza humana pudesse ser conduzida à vida eterna*. Nisso é que consistiu a expiação pelo pecado, que remove a barreira do pecado entre Deus e os homens e os impede de se proverem da vida que lhes é oferecida por Deus.

Como Cristo Trouxe a Vida Eterna aos Homens

1. Ele se identificou completamente com os homens, participando da humanidade deles. Ver Fil. 2:7.

2. Nessa identificação, ele mostrou aos homens o caminho do desenvolvimento espiritual. Ver Heb. 2:10. Ele também se tornou o Pioneiro nesse caminho.

3. Por igual modo, ele é o próprio Caminho. Ver o artigo sobre *Caminho, Cristo como*.

4. Na qualidade de homem representativo, em sua ressurreição, ele recebeu uma nova forma de vida, a própria vida de Deus, a qual, agora, pode transmitir aos demais filhos de Deus. Ver João 5:16,27.

5. Dessa maneira, ele sustenta toda vida que participa da forma de vida divina, por ser ele o Pão da vida. Ver João 6:48.

6. A metáfora que ele usou, de comermos sua carne e bebermos seu sangue, sem dúvida chocou seus ouvintes. Mas isso alude a quão completamente o homem *depende dele* quanto à sua *sustentação espiritual*, ao crescimento espiritual e à continuação da vida espiritual. Por igual modo, assim aprendemos que ele é a única provisão posta à disposição dos homens, o que significa que a salvação vem pela graça (ver notas em Efé. 2:8 no NTI), e isso por meio da fé, ver Heb. 11:1.

7. Agora, o homem desfruta de união espiritual com Cristo (ver notas em I Cor. 1:4 no NTI), porquanto, está «em Cristo». Essa expressão é usada por 164 vezes nas epístolas de Paulo.

8. Agora os remidos podem compartilhar da plenitude de Cristo. Ver Efé. 1:23 e Col. 2:10.

A ceia do Senhor relembra-nos essa *união e participação* na vida de Cristo; mas não precisamos pensar em alguma participação literal dos elementos místicos de seu corpo e de seu sangue. «Quando Lutero rabiscou com um pedaço de giz sobre uma mesa (em sua disputa com outros, sobre o sentido da eucaristia), 'Este é o meu corpo', como se isso fosse final e conclusivo: 'Cristo disse assim e Cristo assim quis dizer, e assim tem de ser', alguém poderia ter escrito: 'Eu sou a porta', ajuntando 'Cristo disse assim, e Cristo assim quis dizer, e assim devemos crer'. Não restam dúvidas! Mas nenhum ser humano, por causa dessa declaração, pensa em Cristo como uma porta literal, a abrir e fechar em suas dobradiças. Por que uma metáfora deve ser lida com uma atitude tão literal, enquanto todas as demais não o são?» (Arthur John Gossip, em João 6:53).

Finalmente, é instrutivo para nós notarmos que a vitalidade das relações entre Cristo e os homens é aqui enfatizada pelo fato de que essa comunhão, declaradamente, é a mesma que aquela existente entre o Pai e o Filho. (Ver o vs. 57 deste mesmo capítulo). O propósito dessa relação, da salvação que há na pessoa de Cristo, na realidade é a condução dos remidos à unidade com Deus, a fim de que venham a possuir a sua mesma natureza e santidade, a fim de que participem de sua vida divina, conforme ele se manifesta em Cristo, implicando em igualdade de natureza essencial no caso de Cristo e dos filhos adotivos que estão sendo levados à glória juntamente com ele.

COMÉRCIO, NEGÓCIOS E INTERCÂMBIO

Definição dos Termos. O intercâmbio consiste no escambo ou troca de mercadorias. Na época anterior à invenção da moeda, assim eram feitas as negociações entre indivíduos e nações. A idéia sobrevive, por exemplo, em expressões como «intercâmbio de idéias» ou «intercâmbio de tecnologias». O comércio é o intercâmbio em larga escala, sobretudo em níveis internacionais, embora não exclusivamente. Os negócios, por sua vez, envolvem um comércio

COMÉRCIO

altamente sofisticado, envolvendo questões como crédito, negociações futuras e múltiplas trocas de mercadorias, geralmente envolvendo tratados ou acordos. Passando dos conceitos mais simples para os mais complexos, estudaremos a questão na seguinte ordem de apresentação:
1. Intercâmbio Local
2. Intercâmbio nos Períodos Intertestamental e Neotestamentário
3. Comércio Internacional
4. Negócios

1. Intercâmbio Local

Os principais produtos locais, transportados pelas estradas da antiga Palestina, eram alimentos de todas as variedades. Esses produtos incluíam os cereais, mormente o trigo, a cevada e outras sementes, como as lentilhas, os feijões e o gergelim. Também devemos pensar nos frutos produzidos em diferentes estações do ano. Os habitantes das cidades consumiam tanto frutos verdes quanto frutos maduros. As uvas, a fruta mais apreciada em Israel, não somente nos tempos antigos, mas também na moderna Israel, onde é a cultura mais largamente difundida na vida agrícola do país, eram consumidas frescas, ressecadas na forma de uvas passas, fermentadas sob a forma de vinho ou vinagre, ou então cozidas até formarem uma espécie de xarope. À semelhança das uvas, os figos eram ressecados para serem usados durante os meses de inverno, e não apenas durante o verão. As tâmaras sempre foram consideradas um alimento ideal, por estarem sempre frescas e por conterem um alto teor de glicose.

No que concerne aos «adoçantes», havia o mel, tanto da variedade silvestre como da variedade cultivada em apiários cuidados pelo homem. O mel produzido na Palestina podia ser adquirido em diversos sabores, visto que as colméias eram transportadas ao redor, para as abelhas tirarem proveito das flores que apareciam em diferentes estações do ano. As azeitonas, um outro alimento que os israelitas empregavam durante o ano inteiro, eram preservadas em solução salina ou em azeite. O azeite de oliveira era utilizado de várias maneiras — na cosmetologia, na culinária ou como combustível de lâmpadas antigas, correspondendo às qualidades de primeira, segunda ou terceira categorias. Castanhas de todas as espécies—das quais a amêndoa e a castanha de pinheiro eram as mais vendidas—eram muito procuradas devido ao seu conteúdo oleoginoso, visto que a gordura animal era muito dispendiosa. Legumes de muitas variedades eram vendidas aos habitantes citadinos; em Jericó produziam-se legumes todos os meses do ano.

A maior parte das carnes, como de ovelhas e cabras, era transportada aos mercados como animais vivos. Os compradores ocupavam-se do abate dos animais. O gado vacum servia, primariamente, de animal de fazenda, ocupando o lugar que o cavalo, somente muito mais tarde, veio a ocupar nas fazendas. Somente quando um boi se tornava muito velho para trabalhar, ou quando emagrecia por causa de algum período de seca, era vendido para sua carne servir de alimento. Entretanto, os ricos sempre contavam com carne, no seu cardápio diário, para o que dispunham de gado alimentado em estábulos. Animais selvagens, como os pertencentes à família do gamo, além de grande variedade de aves, encontravam um mercado sempre ativo. Outro tanto se dava no caso dos peixes; mas, nesse caso, as distâncias percorridas pelos vendedores eram necessariamente mais curtas, pois o peixe, se não for congelado, é um alimento extremamente perecível. —E, nos dias da antiguidade, quando não havia ainda frigoríficos e congeladores, o congelamento dependia da neve e do gelo trazidos das montanhas mais altas da porção norte de Israel, pelo que a área que podia dispor dessa vantagem era bastante reduzida. O remédio era apelar para o peixe salgado, que então podia ser consumido em todas as estações do ano e em qualquer lugar. A própria cidade de Roma importava peixes apanhados no mar da Galiléia, onde a pesca tornou-se uma indústria rendosa, regularmente organizada. Os laticínios, como o leite, a coalhada e o queijo, faziam parte de um comércio rendoso.

Alimentos não facilmente perecíveis, como os cereais, o azeite e o vinho eram vendidos em pequenos armazéns, existentes nas cidades. Mas os alimentos perecíveis eram geralmente vendidos em mercados diários, semelhantes às modernas feiras, armados extramuros. Nas cidades maiores, animais de porte como ovelhas e cabras, eram talvez vendidos em alguma das portas da cidade, ao passo que legumes e frutas eram vendidos em outra das portas. Chegada a estação das frutas, os vendedores saíam a oferecer os seus produtos de rua em rua.

Tanto os ricos quanto os pobres apreciavam os condimentos e as especiarias. Naturalmente, o motivo disso era o problema da preservação dos alimentos, em uma época em que o congelamento era desconhecido, a não ser em escala muito reduzida, mediante o uso da neve e do gelo extraídos dos montes mais elevados. Entre os condimentos podemos incluir o anis, as folhas de louro, o coriandro, o cominho, a alcaparreira, várias espécies de mostarda, a hortelã, o açafrão e a arruda. Entre os artigos favoritos, dessa classe, estavam as cebolas, os alhos e os alhos porros, que os israelitas da época do êxodo tanto sentiram falta, enquanto vagueavam pelo deserto do Sinai. As especiarias empregadas pelo povo de Israel eram, usualmente, importadas do estrangeiro, principalmente da Arábia. As especiarias mais importantes eram a cássia, o cinamono e o cravo-da-índia.

Os habitantes das cidades iam buscar seu combustível, para ser usado na cozinha, ou no interior, ou nas portas da cidade, onde havia vendedores de lenha ou carvão, ou ainda algum outro material. O melhor combustível era o carvão vegetal; depois vinha a lenha; e, finalmente, os arbustos de espinheiro.

Alguns alimentos eram «mercadorias manufaturadas». Para exemplificar, uma pessoa podia ir a uma padaria comprar pães, bolos e massas, —em vez de preparar esses alimentos em casa. Também era possível comprar uma refeição em uma pequena venda, ou comprar uma bebida em uma adega. A maioria das pessoas, entretanto, pensava em mercadorias manufaturadas em outros termos. Um cozinheiro, por exemplo, precisava de jarras de barro para guardar farinha de trigo, azeite e vinho. Tal pessoa também precisava de jarras para guardar água extraída de cisternas ou poços, jarras para resfriar a água servida à mesa, e copos para servi-la às pessoas. Também eram necessários panelas e pratos, nos quais as refeições preparadas pudessem ser servidas. Objetos de cerâmica eram, quase sempre, uma manufatura local, embora a cerâmica importada atraísse os ricos, como ainda sucede em nossos dias.

Após a indústria da alimentação, a indústria do vestuário ocupava o segundo lugar na ordem de importância. Sempre houve um bom mercado, aberto para a indústria de tecidos e de roupas. As vestes mais caras sempre fizeram parte das listas dos despojos de guerra. O material mais comumente usado, na

807

COMÉRCIO

indústria do vestuário, era a lã; mas o linho era mais caro que a lã. Nos tempos do Novo Testamento, a seda era disponível para os fabricantes, como também o algodão; mas faltava a este a popularidade que se dava à seda. No inverno, usavam-se sobretudos e calçados de lã. As fundas dos pastores eram feitas de lã tecida, embora também houvesse fundas de couro.

Em Israel conhecia-se a arte de trançar talas e ramos diversos. Cestos eram os principais tipos de receptáculos, para transporte de muitos tipos de material. Tapetes de palha trançada tornaram-se uma das coberturas preferidas de pisos. Também havia cabanas feitas com esse material, especialmente no caso daquelas existentes nas vinhas e pepinais, para servirem de postos de vigia. Quando havia necessidade de guardar água, sendo que a cerâmica não era apropriada para esse propósito, usava-se o couro. As sacolas nas quais os semeadores transportavam a semente a ser semeada, eram feitas de tecido ou de couro. Mas os surrões dos pastores mais provavelmente eram feitos de couro. Os odres para vinho e os receptáculos para água eram feitos de couro.

Quando alguém tinha meios suficientes para usar calçados, então havia sandálias, sapatos e botas, todos feitos de couro. Lemos que João Batista usava um cinto de couro. Os fabricantes de artigos de couro ocupavam-se também no fabrico de selas e arreios para os animais. E, nos dias do Novo Testamento, eles também fabricavam as chamadas filactérias. Couro fino também era usado para nele serem copiados exemplares do Antigo Testamento, dos livros do Novo Testamento, que estavam sendo recopiados, além de outros escritos valiosos.

Os que sabiam trabalhar com madeira tinham muito trabalho a fazer. Fabricavam os arados, os trilhos de trilhar o grão, os enxadões e as cangas para os animais de carga. Eles também fabricavam as portas e os batentes das mesmas, as janelas e seus batentes, usados nas casas das cidades, sem falarmos em toda a mobília geralmente usada nas antigas residências.

Nas cidades maiores, era comum que todos aqueles que pertenciam a algum ofício vivessem em certa porção da cidade. Assim, havia o quarteirão dos oleiros, o quarteirão dos costureiros, a rua dos padeiros, o mercado de alimentos, etc.

Diferentes seções da Palestina faziam o escambo de seus produtos. Assim, por exemplo, os pastores e os agricultores trocavam suas ovelhas por cereal ou por legumes. Os carvoeiros encontravam um mercado nas áreas onde as florestas já haviam sido derrubadas, e onde, portanto, era muito difícil conseguir lenha. As cidades costeiras, e também Jericó, mandavam sal para as populações distantes da beira mar. Os carpinteiros, mui provavelmente, eram pagos não com dinheiro, mas com outras mercadorias, pelas pessoas para quem prestavam os mais diversos serviços.

A Palestina contava com bem poucas mercadorias a serem exportadas para as nações circunvizinhas. Na verdade, essa situação perdura até hoje, quando a moderna nação de Israel tanto depende das importações. Mas, visto que a Fenícia ressentia-se com a escassez de alimentos, os habitantes do centro e do norte da Palestina vendiam às cidades fenícias cereais, azeite de oliveira, vinho e outros alimentos animais. O Egito era rico em grãos e animais, mas faltavam-lhe o azeite de oliveira e o vinho. Na Síria e na Palestina cultivavam-se os mesmos produtos agrícolas, pelo que havia bem pouco comércio internacional, quanto a esses itens, naquela região em geral, excetuando nos períodos de seca ou de guerra.

Quando o uso do camelo generalizou-se, o comércio com a Arábia se tornou comum, e as caravanas chegavam à Palestina, de onde levavam os mais variados alimentos. Uvas passas, figos secos e tâmaras, mui provavelmente, eram produtos desse comércio internacional, porquanto eram facilmente transportados. O linho era vendido para os habitantes da Palestina e para todas as nações circunvizinhas, excetuando o Egito, que era onde se fabricava o melhor linho do mundo, na época.

Os produtos naturais que ainda não foram incluídos na relação acima, eram, primariamente, o cobre, o betume e a lã em estado bruto. Os períodos de maior prosperidade do cobre ocorreram durante a época dos patriarcas, durante o reinado de Salomão e quando da divisão do império salomônico, em sua porção sul. Os períodos intermediários não deixaram indícios em favor da exploração ou não dos grandes depósitos de cobre, nas montanhas de ambos os lados da Arabá, ao sul do mar Morto.

A campanha militar, historiada no décimo quarto capítulo de Gênesis, foi ocasionada pelo desejo de controlar os valiosos depósitos de cobre em Edom e na península do Sinai. Visto que o ferro era o metal ideal, nos dias de Salomão, além de ser relativamente barato (embora outros estudos indiquem que era muito valioso), ele vendia o cobre extraído em seu reino para os povos subdesenvolvidos que viviam em torno do mar Vermelho. Em troca, Salomão recebia ouro, incenso e especiarias raras. O betume encontrava bons compradores no Egito e nas terras adjacentes à Palestina. O betume era extraído na área do mar Morto, que tinha o nome de mar de Asfalto, durante os dias intertestamentários. Todavia, o betume dali era de excelente qualidade, embora existisse em quantidade limitada, precisamente ao contrário do que sucedia na Mesopotâmia. O enxofre também era um produto natural da área do mar Morto. A Palestina sempre produziu maior quantidade de lã do que era capaz de manufaturar, pelo que a lã em estado bruto sempre foi um produto constantemente exportado, especialmente para as áreas densamente povoadas. Moabe era o principal produtor de lã de toda aquela região. Não se sabe quando o ferro começou a ser produzido em massa na Palestina, embora saibamos que não foi antes da época de Davi. Gileade era o principal centro produtor de ferro. A Palestina também exportava resinas raras, e gomas, como a mirra e o bálsamo. O bálsamo era um produto caríssimo, tendo sido um dos principais produtos que produzia rendas a Herodes, o Grande, que possuía extensos bosques de bálsamo nas cercanias de Jericó.

A era real das manufaturas, na Palestina, começou mais ou menos na época do profeta Isaías. Devemos observar que o Pentateuco não inclui qualquer legislação referente às manufaturas. Isaías, pois, foi testemunha do começo da era manufatureira na Palestina, da mesma forma que Jeremias contemplou o ponto culminante, e então o final cataclísmico de toda a indústria manufatureira na região. Foi entre Isaías e Jeremias (792-586 A.C.) que tiveram começo as modernas técnicas de linha de montagem, quando então surgiram cidades que se especializavam na fabricação de um único produto. Os fazendeiros e agricultores passaram a migrar para as cidades industriais, onde eram absorvidos pelas diversas indústrias da época. Houve um excesso de suprimento de mão-de-obra, e os salários caíram a níveis ridículos, que praticamente nem eram suficientes para a mera sobrevivência.

Miquéias, fazendeiro contemporâneo de Isaías,

808

COMÉRCIO

atacou as cortes reais do sul e do norte, Judá e Israel, por seu crime de conivência com os crimes econômicos da nação. Em Miq. 3:1-3, o autor sagrado, usando o pano de fundo da matança de ovelhas, chama os negociantes envolvidos de magnatas, enquanto seus defensores seriam os canibais que viviam da carne de seus indefesos empregados.

Os oleiros passaram a empregar técnicas de produção em massa, utilizando-se da idéia da linha de montagem, produzindo produtos de boa qualidade a preços módicos. Aqueles antigos oleiros eram conhecedores de todas as habilidades necessárias ao seu negócio, e um ceramista moderno não pode fazer mais do que admirar tais produtos.

Porém, a maior modificação ocorreu na indústria do vestuário. Quando foi escavada pelos arqueólogos, Quiriate-Sefer mostrou que fora cidade de uma única indústria. Estava localizada em uma excelente região produtora de lã, e todos os seus habitantes dedicavam-se ao trabalho de tecer a lã e de fabricar tecidos tingidos. Cada casa contava com grandes teares e com instalações para tingimento de tecidos, tudo padronizado. A matéria bruta, por assim dizer, encontrava-se na porta da «fábrica», e ambas essas indústrias contavam com um mercado consumidor constante e sempre pronto a absorver toda a produção. Todavia, quase toda a produção dos bens manufaturados na Palestina eram vendidos na própria região manufatureira, não chegando aos mercados internacionais, o que significa que não havia produção excelente.

As principais importações da Palestina parecem ter sido mercadorias de luxo. A natureza humana sempre gostou de encontrar, nos produtos comprados, a tarjeta que diz «feito em (algum país estrangeiro)». Quanto a uma descrição detalhada sobre as rotas comerciais na Palestina e no Oriente Próximo, ver o artigo sobre — *Viagens*. Tanto Abraão quanto Salomão eram negociantes em escala internacional. As atividades deste último, nesse campo, são bem conhecidas; mas os estudiosos somente agora começaram a apreciar o fato de que Abraão era um grande negociante, de acordo com a terminologia moderna.

Abraão era um príncipe entre os negociantes, cujo território de vendas ia desde Harã até o Egito, embora ele se concentrasse em torno, especialmente, de três áreas: a porção da Palestina ao sul de Siquém, o Egito e a Arábia. Não dispomos de menção específica sobre os itens vendidos por Abraão, mas, sem dúvida eram as usuais mercadorias de luxo que eram trocadas entre os ricos de todos os países da época...Esses itens seriam especialmente proveitosos para Abraão, o qual comprava o cobre bem barato, nas minas de Edom ou da península do Sinai, e então o transportava à Fenícia ou à Síria, que eram, então, os principais centros manufatureiros. Partindo destas últimas, ele podia vender esses produtos em qualquer lugar, desde a Anatólia até o Egito ou a Arábia.

Harã foi a capital original dos negócios realizados por Abraão. Ficava localizada a meio caminho entre a costa do Mediterrâneo e a grande cidade de Nínive. Harã seria uma São Paulo em miniatura, com rotas comerciais irradiando-se em quase todas as direções. Essa cidade era um misto de duas culturas distintas, a semítica e a hurriana, ambas as quais refletem-se na narrativa do livro de Gênesis. O pai de Abraão, Terá, sem dúvida operara na venda de territórios, em Ur-Harã, em um período histórico em que Ur era a cidade comercial mais influente do mundo. A família deve ter sido muito influente, porquanto pelo menos três cidades adotaram nomes de antepassados de Abraão, especificamente, Serugue, Naor e Terá. Sara também era mulher rica, por seus próprios direitos, porquanto ela é referida como «esposa-irmã», um termo legal, usado pelos hurrianos, em Harã. Esse título identificava Sara como membro da aristocracia de Harã.

Posteriormente, Abraão concentrou seus esforços no comércio entre a Palestina e o Egito. Gerar, o coração comercial da região palestina do Neguebe, tornou-se a cidade adotiva de Abraão. Tal ação foi necessária para conferir-lhe uma base legal de suprimentos de seu comércio com o Egito.

A primeira parada de Abraão na Palestina foi em Siquém, que era um centro comercial relacionado a Harã. Essa cidade ficava localizada na Palestina central, dispondo de boas rotas comerciais em todas as direções. Abraão adquiriu ali direitos territoriais, comprando terras de pastagens na região virgem da cadeia montanhosa entre Siquém e Hebrom. Mais tarde, Jacó estendeu esse território mais para o norte, até Dotã. Somente um homem muito rico poderia controlar tão extensas pastagens. O trecho de Gênesis 13:2 menciona o gado, juntamente com muito capital, consistente em ouro e prata. Por ser ótimo negociante, Abraão aplicava seu dinheiro em empreendimentos os mais diversos. Suas caravanas sempre precisavam de alimentos para os homens, e de forragem para os animais, e Abraão supria ambas essas necessidades, com base em seus próprios projetos agrícolas.

2. Intercâmbio nos Períodos Intertestamental e Neotestamentário

Alexandre, o Grande, e seus sucessores helênicos revolucionaram parte dos negócios realizados na região da Palestina. A cultura grega tornou-se a influência dominante. Pelo mundo inteiro, pessoas de muitas nacionalidades subitamente tornaram-se gregas, chegando a tomar para si mesmas novos nomes gregos. Em Marissa, na Palestina, os túmulos mostram que, no espaço de uma única geração, muitas famílias semitas mudaram os seus nomes, helenizando-se. Algumas das piores características da vida grega apareceram na Palestina, sob os governantes ptolomeus e selêucidas da região.

Grande parte da escravidão que havia entre os israelitas, nos dias do Antigo Testamento, devia-se ao fato de que era costume um homem saldar sua dívida, contraída diante de alguém, servindo a esse alguém por certo período de tempo. Entre os gregos, porém, a escravidão dependia de fatores inteiramente diferentes. Na verdade, a cultura grega girava, em grande parte, em torno da escravidão. Um escravo não era considerado uma pessoa, mas apenas uma mercadoria, como outra qualquer. E, visto que a Palestina era uma região disputada pelos monarcas ptolomeus e pelos monarcas selêucidas, com freqüência os judeus eram feitos cativos, como despojos de guerra. E os monarcas selêucidas, nesse comércio infame da escravatura, eram os piores ofensores, porquanto vendiam os seus prisioneiros de guerra, incluindo mulheres e crianças, a preços irrisórios. Antíoco IV Epifânio, que transformou Jerusalém em uma cidade grega e pagã, tornou-se o principal culpado desse crime. A Palestina, pois, tinha duas culturas; e a revolta dos Macabeus foi o desesperado mais bem sucedido retorno dos judeus ao judaísmo, embora este, mesmo após esse triunfo, continuasse maculado por algumas características próprias da cultura grega pagã. Os líderes judeus posteriores eram gregos virtuais, pelo menos no que dizia respeito às suas ações. Não obstante, desde a época da restauração da verdadeira adoração judaica em Jerusalém, sob os primeiros líderes Macabeus, a Palestina continuou

COMÉRCIO

contando com duas culturas — uma delas judaica, e a outra judaico-grega, melhor representada pela cidade de Jerusalém, onde Herodes, o Grande, introduzira muitas características próprias da cultura helenista. A influência mais intensa dessa cultura grega evidenciava-se especialmente nas cidades da Decápolis, na Transjordânia. Samaria era um outro exemplo disso, na porção ocidental da Palestina, visto que a cidade contava com um templo dedicado ao imperador Augusto.

Não há muita informação referente ao período intertestamental, no tocante ao comércio e aos negócios na Palestina. Uma das grandes melhorias, contudo, dizia respeito à qualidade do linho, que passou então a ser confeccionado no melhor tecido, destinado ao mercado internacional. Herodes, o Grande, possuía grandes propriedades perto de Jericó, onde ele plantava o bálsamo, que era uma das gomas mais caras que havia. A indústria de pesca, ao redor do mar da Galiléia, prosperava. O peixe, ali pescado e salgado, era exportado até mesmo à capital do império, Roma.

Os negócios internacionais entre diferentes agrupamentos nacionais, era algo inevitável. Os sidônios negociavam com a cidade palestina de Marissa; e os egípcios negociavam com a cidade transjordaniana de Filadélfia, a qual não deve ser confundida com a Filadélfia da Ásia Menor, que figura no livro de Apocalipse. A influência grega podia ser percebida até mesmo no sistema de propriedades da Palestina. Marissa foi planejada como uma cidade grega, e a Samaria dos tempos neotestamentários foi arquitetada de acordo com os mesmos planos daquela. Os nabateus, com suas caravanas de camelos, efetuavam grande parte do tráfico que os egípcios transportavam, para o outro lado do mar Vermelho, com os seus navios.

Quando o mar Mediterrâneo tornou-se uma possessão romana, o comércio marítimo adquiriu um novo impulso. Os principais portos tiveram suas instalações expandidas, a fim de poderem manusear esse comércio intensificado. Os habitantes de Roma eram alimentados, em grande parte, pelo cereal plantado e colhido nos vales dos rios Orontes, Nilo (e outros rios do norte da África).

O livro de Atos faz seus leitores tomarem consciência do fato de que os judeus eram cidadãos do mundo. Por ocasião da festa de Pentecoste, ali relatada, havia judeus provenientes de dezesseis países diferentes:

«...como os ouvimos falar, cada um em nossa própria língua materna, partos, medos e elamitas e os naturais da Mesopotâmia, Judéia, Capadócia, Ponto e Ásia; da Frígia e da Panfília, do Egito e das regiões da Líbia, nas imediações de Cirene, e romanos que aqui residem, tanto judeus como prosélitos, cretenses e árabes; como os ouvimos falar em nossas próprias línguas as grandezas de Deus?»

Viajando Paulo pelo mundo Mediterrâneo oriental, ele percorria um novo mundo comercial. Grande parte desse mundo comercial era antigo, embora também houvesse novas atrações. Para exemplificar isso, Paulo tanto era homem que costumava viajar de *navio*, como costumava viajar pelas *estradas* romanas. Ver sobre *Viagens*.

Paulo fez de Antioquia sobre o Orontes o ponto central do evangelismo mundial da era apostólica. «Antioquia sobre o Orontes» era o nome completo dessa cidade, porquanto havia dezesseis cidades com esse nome, Antioquia. Nessa época, Antioquia sobre o Orontes era a mais influente cidade do mundo, embora Alexandria a ultrapassasse em número de habitantes. Antioquia era o fim da estrada de todo o comércio que se processava por terra, vindo desde a China, por meio da Pérsia, e daí até as margens do Mediterrâneo, o que significa que esse comércio atravessava todo o continente asiático. Alexandria, por sua vez, era o porto por onde escoava todo o comércio africano, sem importar se ali chegava através do rio Nilo ou do mar Vermelho. Não havia qualquer outro grande porto marítimo entre essas duas cidades, mas havia apenas um bom número de portos locais, alguns dos quais Paulo usou. Antioquia especializava-se, principalmente, no comércio de artigos de luxo, e o mundo mostrava-se tão ávido por esses artigos assim como se dá até os nossos próprios dias. Alexandria, por sua parte, concentrava-se tanto no comércio de artigos de luxo como no comércio comum, incluindo a exportação de cereais, que se destinavam à mesa dos romanos.

Tarso era a cidade natal de Paulo. Ficava na extremidade sul do melhor passo entre o grande platô da Anatólia, atravessando as agrestes montanhas do Tauro, na porção suleste da Ásia Menor, e o mar Mediterrâneo. Em nossos dias, a estrada de ferro Berlim-Bagdá usa o mesmo passo. Tarso era um grande centro comercial, porquanto também tinha acesso direto ao mar Mediterrâneo. Icônio era um dos centros chaves da vida comercial do grande platô de Anatólia. Com freqüência ela tem sido chamada pelos escritores de «a Damasco da Turquia», por causa de seu abundante suprimento de água. Quando os turcos tornaram-se os senhores do mundo oriental romano, fizeram de Icônio a sua capital. Foi dali que eles lançaram seu ataque contra Constantinopla, capital do império romano do oriente, e a capturaram. Os territórios em torno de Constantinopla são os únicos territórios europeus ainda sob o domínio dos turcos, pois a maior parte da moderna Turquia fica no lado asiático desse extenso país.

Quando Paulo quis chegar à Bitínia ele dirigiu-se na direção de Constantinopla, também chamada Bizâncio desde tempos antigos. Essa sempre foi uma grande cidade comercial, porquanto domina o comércio que se faz com o mar Negro. A moderna União Soviética chega até a margem norte do mar Negro. É possível alguém percorrer a cavalo toda a imensa planície russa, quase desde as margens do Atlântico até o Pacífico, e só ocasionalmente será interrompido por grandes massas montanhosas. Paulo, pois, deve ter compreendido que aquele centro comercial seria, no futuro, um centro evangelístico mundial. Ele sempre apreciou o arrojo dos negociantes, tendo estabelecido os principais centros da igreja cristã em importantes centros comerciais da época (ver sobre cidades como *Antioquia*, *Tessalônica*, Corinto e Éfeso).

Paulo desejava visitar a província romana da Ásia, mas o Senhor negou-lhe o privilégio de entrar ali, naquela ocasião, embora, posteriormente, ele tivesse efetuado um glorioso ministério em Éfeso, capital da província da Ásia. A Ásia era a mais populosa província do império romano. Até os nossos próprios dias, as ruínas de suas grandes cidades testificam sobre a anterior prosperidade daquela região do mundo. Essa província era a porção mais fértil da Anatólia, e, igualmente, a área mais fértil das proximidades do mar Egeu. Não é de se admirar que os gregos tanto admirassem aquela região, e a tivessem colonizado desde tempos bem remotos.

Tessalônica era a segunda maior cidade comercial a ser visitada por Paulo. Ela ficava situada na

COMÉRCIO

extremidade sul do melhor desfiladeiro entre o vale do Danúbio e o mar Mediterrâneo. O comércio que passava por aquele desfiladeiro era muito intenso, visto que as civilizações, existentes nas duas extremidades daquela rota comercial, eram tão diferentes uma da outra. O vale do Danúbio era tão valioso, comercialmente falando, que o imperador Trajano o adicionou ao império romano no século II D.C. E ele também dominou os nabateus, conferindo a Roma um acesso direto ao comércio árabe.

Nos dias de Paulo, Atenas, na Grécia, estava vivendo as glórias do seu passado. Corinto havia se tornado «a cidade» da Grécia. Seu crescimento fora tão rápido e tão espetacular quanto a moderna São Paulo, no Brasil. Júlio César havia reconhecido que essa cidade, então quase em ruínas, poderia tornar-se um dos principais centros comerciais do império romano. Contudo, foi assassinado antes que pudesse recuperar a cidade; posteriormente, porém, seu desejo foi atendido, e a cidade recebeu um nome que honrava o imperador. Corinto era o maior centro de transbordo de mercadorias do Mediterrâneo (ver sobre *Viagens*). Corinto também desenvolveu-se rapidamente em uma grande cidade manufatureira, onde quase todo o labor era realizado por escravos. As epístolas de Paulo aos Coríntios oferecem-nos a melhor descrição sobre uma cidade comercial que há no Novo Testamento.

Em Corinto, Paulo era um dos trabalhadores «livres». Por ofício, ele era fabricante de tendas, usadas nos grandes mercados, e também de velas, empregadas pelos navios que aportavam nos dois portos de Corinto, um em cada lado do istmo onde estava a cidade. Foi ali que o cristianismo obteve o seu direito legal de ser uma «religião permitida» no império romano. No império romano, toda religião precisava de uma licença do governo para poder existir legalmente. Os judeus de Corinto tentaram persuadir Gálio, procônsul da Acaia, de que o cristianismo era uma religião ilegal, diferente, portanto, da religião judaica. Gálio, entretanto, rejeitou a acusação, e assim conferiu ao cristianismo a posição de *religio licita*. Nero perseguiu à igreja cristã em Roma, mas fê-lo a fim de preservar a sua influência e autoridade como imperador. No século que se seguiu ao dele, porém, houve muita perseguição contra o cristianismo, por parte das autoridades do império. E Corinto pôde demonstrar que, naquela época, como até hoje, os portos de mar geralmente são lugares iníquos, e *Corinto* tornou-se um sinônimo de imoralidade da pior espécie. Antioquia seguia bem de perto, nessa má fama, àquela cidade grega. Não obstante, ambas essas cidades tornaram-se grandes centros de evangelismo mundial.

Em Éfeso, Paulo esteve por alguns anos na cidade que, posteriormente, era reconhecida como a capital do império romano, quando o imperador encontrava-se na sua porção oriental. A prédica paulina desafiou severamente duas das maiores indústrias dessa cidade. Os publicadores de livros sobre mágicas viram suas publicações, avaliadas em cinqüenta mil peças de prata, serem queimadas (Atos 19:19). Essa soma equivalia ao salário de um dia de trabalho pago a cinqüenta mil homens. E os fabricantes de nichos de prata da deusa Diana sofreram prejuízos tão grandes que terminaram provocando um levante popular (Atos 19:23-41).

O livro de Apocalipse encerra as sete cartas às sete igrejas da província da Ásia. O evangelho fora anunciado, com base em Éfeso, com tal ímpeto, que fortes igrejas locais haviam sido estabelecidas nas cidades adjacentes, cada uma delas, um forte centro comercial. Laodicéia (ver Apo. 3:18) era um grande centro bancário, mas os membros daquela igreja foram admoestados como segue: «Aconselho-te que de mim (de Cristo) compres ouro refinado pelo fogo para te enriqueceres...» (Apo. 3:18). Essa cidade também era famosa porque ali eram fabricadas as pesadas capas de feltro negro, de pêlos de cabra, para serem usadas durante o severo inverno do planalto da Anatólia, mas, aos membros daquela igreja foi recomendado: «Aconselho-te que de mim compres... vestiduras brancas para te vestires...» Dessa mesma cidade provinha um dos famosos «medicamentos» da antiguidade, o «colírio». Os crentes dali, pois, foram aconselhados a adquirir «colírio», a fim de que ungissem os seus olhos e pudessem ver as realidades espirituais.

3. Comércio Internacional

O principal parceiro comercial da Palestina, ao sul, era o Egito, berço de uma das grandes civilizações da antiguidade. Não é de surpreender, assim sendo, quando descobrimos a forte influência do comércio egípcio nos objetos encontrados nas escavações arqueológicas da Palestina. Da Etiópia vinha o ébano que chegava à Palestina e, pelo menos parte do marfim chegava ali através do Sudão, embora houvesse elefantes na Síria, nos primeiros tempos patriarcais.

A principal rota comercial partia do Egito, mais ou menos onde fica localizado o moderno canal de Suez. Dali essa estrada seguia ao longo da costa marítima, passando por Rafia, e dali até Gaza. Essa cidade sempre foi a maior cabeça de ponte de toda a história do Egito, até tão tarde quanto a Primeira Guerra Mundial.

O outro parceiro comercial da Palestina, mais ao sul, era a Arábia. O comércio marítimo com a Arábia processava-se através de Eziom-Geber, no golfo de Áqaba. A partir dali, as mercadorias eram transportadas em lombo de camelo que seguiam para o norte, até Macã. Uma das rotas terrestres das caravanas, provenientes da Arábia, também terminava ali. O wadi Sirhan era uma outra longa rota de caravanas vindas da Arábia; mas essa ficava a leste da Palestina propriamente dita, e seu comércio chegava até a rota comercial norte-sul, em Rabate-Amom. O comércio árabe consistia inteiramente de itens de luxo, como ouro, incenso, mirra, corais, pérolas, esmeraldas, ágatas e outras pedras preciosas. Especiarias raras e madeiras odoríferas de várias espécies, trazidas desde a Índia, também chegavam à Palestina por meio da Arábia. Durante os períodos intertestamental e do Novo Testamento, os nabateus dominavam o comércio efetuado entre a Arábia e a Palestina. Quanto ao comércio internacional, podemos observar que uma capa babilônica foi alistada entre os despojos recolhidos em Jericó (Jos. 7:21), embora Jericó fosse apenas uma pequena fortaleza, no começo da história de Israel na Terra Prometida.

Ao norte da Palestina ficava a Síria, que não servia de bom mercado para as mercadorias produzidas na Palestina, pois ambos esses países produziam as mesmas mercadorias. A Síria e a Palestina, entretanto, efetuaram algumas negociações comerciais, pois as dinastias de Onri e de Ben-Hadade contavam com feiras na capital um do outro. Importa-nos observar que a rota através da qual tanto o comércio mesopotâmico quanto o comércio hitita (ou da Anatólia) se processava com o Egito, passava através da Síria e da Ásia Menor, sendo uma das principais fontes de metais da antiguidade. Os hititas

811

e seus sucessores foram os grandes mineiros, fundidores e refinadores de cobre, de prata e de ferro do mundo antigo. Eles também manufaturavam todos os tipos de objetos de metal. Antes da época de Davi, essa área detinha um dos grandes monopólios do fabrico do ferro. O cobre era tão importante para o progresso da ilha de Chipre, que o nome dessa ilha significa «ilha do cobre». Damasco, com toda a razão, era intitulada «porto de mar de todos os habitantes do deserto», embora ficasse localizada a mais de oitenta quilômetros de distância das costas do Mediterrâneo.

A Suméria e sua sucessora, a Babilônia, eram as únicas antigas primeiras civilizações manufatureiras a rivalizarem-se com o Egito. Abraão, de certo modo representava esses dois gigantes comerciais, porquanto seu pai, Terá, percorria as rotas comerciais de Ur a Harã, à sombra da Anatólia, onde Abraão negociou, antes de chegar ao Egito. Abraão tinha um grande escritório bancário em Damasco, sob a direção de Eliezer. A rota comercial da Babilônia tinha início no golfo Pérsico, acompanhando o rio Eufrates até os montes do Taurus, na Ásia Menor, em Harã e Carquêmis. A capital assíria, Nínive, igualmente era um grande centro comercial. Não era distrito manufatureiro tão grande e importante quanto a cidade da Babilônia, que ficava mais ao sul, mas servia de local para onde convergia o comércio que vinha desde a Pérsia e de outros locais do Oriente e também servia de ponto de junção de mercadorias vindas de Urartu e de outras localidades mais ao norte. Partindo de Nínive, a rota comercial acompanhava o sopé das montanhas a oeste de Harã e de Carquêmis.

Imediatamente ao norte da Palestina, e bordejando o mar Mediterrâneo, ficava a Fenícia, cuja fronteira oriental usualmente eram as montanhas do Líbano. Os vales do Litos e do Orontes normalmente pertenciam aos sírios. A Fenícia, tal como a Inglaterra durante os seus dias de auge econômico, era tanto uma nação de marinheiros como de manufaturadores. A Fenícia foi a nação que ensinou a Grécia a tornar-se uma nação manufaturadora. Os gregos também adaptaram o seu alfabeto, copiando o alfabeto fenício, tendo aprendido a escrever com seus mestres fenícios, que lhes ensinaram a comerciar. O principal recurso natural da Fenícia eram suas florestas de cedros, cuja madeira era apreciada pelo mundo inteiro da antiguidade. A Fenícia, tal como o Japão antes da Segunda Guerra Mundial, era uma boa imitadora e modificadora de outras culturas. Seus artigos variavam desde os mais excelentes até os mais medíocres. O mais importante produto internacional, manufaturado pelos fenícios eram os tecidos tingidos de púrpura. A lã era importada do estrangeiro, mas o tecido de lã e a tintura eram de origem fenícia. Parte do comércio que seguia para a Fenícia acompanhava um trajeto terrestre, acompanhando as fontes do rio Jordão, ao norte do lago Hulé, e então penetrando na Fenícia, na cabeceira do rio Litos. Alguns negociantes acompanhavam a estrada que marginava o mar Mediterrâneo, de Aco a Tiro. Mas a maior parte do comércio provavelmente se dava por via marítima, partindo de algum porto palestino até chegar a algum porto fenício, mais ao norte. Na verdade, quase todo o frete marítimo da Palestina se dava por meio de navios fenícios. No entanto, é provável que o Egito enviasse seus próprios navios até a Palestina. Quando a Pérsia chegou a uma posição de dominação mundial, os persas utilizavam-se dos fenícios como seus marinheiros e agentes marítimos. Os sucessores de Alexandre controlavam o comércio que se processava no Mediterrâneo, até que o império romano fez desse mar um lago romano.

Grande parte da indústria manufatureira do Egito era monopólio do governo, o qual também controlava, pelo menos em parte, a produção e o comércio de cereais. Salomão exercia um bem definido monopólio sobre o cobre. Salomão também foi o grande «negociante de cavalos» da nação de Israel, o que incluía o comércio de carros de combate (I Reis 10:28,29). Salomão e Hirão, de Tiro, lançaram-se a uma aventura comercial conjunta, no mar Vermelho (I Reis 9:26-28; 10:11,12,22). Gerações mais tarde, Josafá planejou uma aventura similar, mas os seus navios naufragaram em Eziom-Geber (II Crô. 20:36,37).

4. Negócios

Quando o dinheiro torna-se um dos fatores fundamentais no comércio e nas negociações, a ênfase recai sobre os negócios, pois o denominador comum de todos negócios é o dinheiro. No Antigo Testamento havia três métodos principais de vendas: a. permuta; b. peso em ouro ou prata; e c. moedas. A venda por permuta era o método mais comum entre os povos mais pobres, embora o rei Salomão e o rei Hirão, de Tiro, também tivessem usado esse método. Hirão fornecia madeira de cedro e de cipreste a Salomão, o qual, por sua vez, entregou-lhe trigo e azeite de oliveira (I Reis 5:10,11). Esses produtos agrícolas eram as taxas que Salomão havia recolhido, pois, na época, os impostos geralmente eram recolhidos em espécie. Assim, os agricultores pagavam seus impostos com trigo, azeite de oliveira e vinho; e os pastores os pagavam com ovelhas, cabras, etc. Cada indivíduo pagava seus impostos com aquilo que produzia. Quando o governo de Israel se dividiu, o reino do sul providenciou para ter jarras de tamanho padronizado, com o selo do governo na asa. Essas jarras eram usadas para recebimento de impostos, em espécie.

Para ser bem-sucedido, o comércio nos mercados internacionais precisa de um meio básico de trocas. Era o ouro e/ou a prata, — entre os povos antigos. A segunda era a mais valiosa, pois o ouro não foi extensivamente usado, enquanto a metalurgia não conseguiu solucionar o problema da fundição e do refino do minério de ouro. Depois disso, o ouro tornou-se mais valioso, devido às propriedades superiores desse metal. Uma outra razão do encarecimento do ouro era que o ouro de aluvião estava se tornando raro, ao passo que o ouro extraído em minas era difícil de se conseguir. O ouro e a prata apareciam no mercado em várias dimensões, em forma de anéis, barras, etc. O fraseado de Deuteronômio 14:25 dá a entender que esse dinheiro tinha a forma de argolas, pois as argolas podiam ser atadas umas às outras. Devemo-nos lembrar da «língua» de ouro que Acã encontrou em Jericó. O termo hebraico para dinheiro era «prata». Se algum metal menos valioso porventura era usado para servir como dinheiro, esse metal era o cobre. Gemas raras e jóias de alta qualidade também serviam como dinheiro. Pedras preciosas e jóias proviam um meio através do qual grandes riquezas podiam ser transportadas fácil e secretamente.

Os metais preciosos eram pesados, em um ato que podia ser honesto ou desonesto. Os arqueólogos têm encontrado pesos com os quais eram comprados os itens desejados, e também pesos com os quais os mesmos itens eram vendidos. «Dois pesos e duas medidas». Essa desonestidade é referida em Deuteronômio 25:13: «Na tua bolsa não terás pesos diversos, um grande e um pequeno». No trecho de Amós 8:5, esse profeta reflete o mesmo tempo, e acrescenta que medidas para secos eram desonestamente empregadas em seus dias ('cf. Deu. 25:14).

O passo seguinte no desenvolvimento do dinheiro foi a criação da moeda. Não somente os homens mostravam-se desonestos quanto ao peso das argolas e barras de ouro, de prata, etc., mas também havia grande variedade quanto à pureza dos metais empregados, sobretudo no caso da prata. Esse problema foi resolvido quando os governos começaram a cunhar moedas, garantindo assim o peso e a pureza de cada moeda cunhada. Isso era feito apondo-se o símbolo do governo (estado ou cidade) sobre cada moeda. A primeira moeda desse tipo a ser mencionada na Bíblia é o dárico persa, de ouro (Esd. 2:69). Os persas permitiram que os judeus cunhassem suas próprias moedas de prata, ao voltarem eles à Judéia. Todavia, as moedas não se tornaram comuns na Palestina senão já na época dos monarcas Ptolomeus e Selêucidas. Quanto a detalhes sobre permutas, metais e moedas, ver o artigo sobre as *Moedas*.

Onde quer que o dinheiro seja usado — na forma de pesos de ouro ou de prata, ou na forma de moedas — os banqueiros fazem-se presentes, e o próprio dinheiro transforma-se em uma outra mercadoria. Nas páginas do Antigo Testamento não há qualquer vestígio sobre a existência de banqueiros, embora saibamos que, na Mesopotâmia, os métodos bancários já funcionavam de forma muito eficiente. Durante o exílio babilônico, os judeus aprenderam as técnicas bancárias babilônicas. Banqueiros judeus, vindos da Babilônia, foram largamente usados, posteriormente, pelos sucessores de Alexandre, o Grande. Alguns estudiosos acreditam que bons métodos bancários foram a razão mais provável pela qual os antepassados de Paulo obtiveram a cidadania romana em Tarso. O exílio assinalou o começo da ênfase tão decisiva dos judeus sobre as atividades bancárias e comerciais, em geral. Isso expandiu-se ainda mais devido às negociações feitas pelos exilados judeus durante o período intertestamental. Esses exilados haviam sido levados a Alexandria, onde chegaram a controlar grande parte das atividades comerciais na cidade. Isso significava que os judeus, contavam com filiais, em todos os portos marítimos do império romano, para os seus empreendimentos.

Na época do Novo Testamento, o sistema bancário já envolvia o império romano inteiro; e os banqueiros recebiam licença para operar, a fim de que ficassem sob o controle do governo. Naquele tempo, como agora, os banqueiros recebiam depósitos em dinheiro, pagando juros pelo uso que faziam do mesmo. Jesus referiu-se a esse costume em sua parábola dos talentos (ver Mat. 25:27). Nos dias do Senhor Jesus e dos apóstolos, uma taxa comum de juros era de oito por cento. Também segundo acontece hoje em dia, os banqueiros emprestavam dinheiro com base em propriedades hipotecadas. A primeira referência bíblica ao método das hipotecas aparece em Neemias 5:3 ss. As pessoas tomavam dinheiro emprestado a fim de pagarem as suas dívidas e impostos, tal como as pessoas fazem na atualidade. Um dos elementos exponenciais da fraternidade dos banqueiros eram os cambistas; e Cristo tratou com eles (ver sobre os *Cambistas*). Já naquele tempo, tal como hoje, havia o uso de cheques; também era possível depositar dinheiro em uma cidade, e recebê-lo em outra, o que indica que havia uma verdadeira organização bancária. O sistema bancário moderno agilizou-se muito mais nesta nossa época da eletrônica e da informática, mas as bases do sistema bancário foram lançadas desde a antiguidade. Bancos relacionados entre si estavam dispersos por todo o império romano.

Um bom sistema de contabilidade já havia antes mesmo do aparecimento do sistema bancário; pode-se perceber traços dessa técnica já no tempo dos primeiros sumérios, os quais também foram os inventores da escrita.

COMIDA — Ver **Alimentos**.

COMIDA SABOROSA

Por seis vezes, no capítulo vinte e sete do livro de Gênesis, a palavra hebraica *matamot* refere-se a uma comida saborosa que Rebeca e Jacó usaram a fim de enganar Isaque. Rebeca preparou a comida com dois cabritos (vs. 9). Em Provérbios 23:3, os delicados manjares dos governantes são descritos como «enganadores». O sexto versículo desse mesmo capítulo adverte contra comer em companhia de um homem mau, cujos alimentos deliciosos servem de atração para que as pessoas lhe façam companhia. Salmos 141:4 apresenta também a comida como uma espécie de chamariz, que atrai os homens a companhias e atos maus. Gênesis 49:20, que prediz a condição futura da tribo de Aser, no contexto das bênçãos de Jacó, diz que Aser prosperaria, o que é simbolizado pelo pão e pelos acepipes. Além disso, a glutonaria resultado da ingestão abusiva de alimentos, sempre foi uma praga para os homens. Os ímpios são dados à glutonaria (Fil. 3:19; Jud. 12). Tal pecado é proibido no caso dos crentes sérios (I Ped. 4:3). Há algo de desagradável no pastor gordo demais de tanto comer e por fazer bem pouco trabalho físico. O perigo da glutonaria é ilustrado em Lucas 12:45,46. Os homens, por pensarem que a *parousia* (que vide) ainda está distante, afrouxam em seus costumes, deixando-se arrastar pelos excessos com comidas e bebidas. Um dos aspectos do fruto do Espírito, porém, é o autocontrole, e isso, sem dúvida, inclui a questão da alimentação. A glutonaria é um dos pecados capitais, juntamente com o alcoolismo. Ver o artigo separado sobre a *Glutonaria*. Ver também sobre os *Alimentos*.

COMINHO

No hebraico **kammon**; no grego, **kyminon**. Essa planta é mencionada tanto no Antigo quanto no Novo Testamentos. Juntamente com o coentro e o anis, continua sendo cultivado até os nossos próprios dias.

O cominho produz uma semente aromática, muito usada para dar maior sabor aos alimentos. É mencionado pela primeira vez em Isaías 28:25, que indica que a espécie era intensamente cultivada na época. A erva é o *Cuminum cyminum*, da família das *Umbelíferas*. Chega a sessenta centímetros de altura na Palestina, embora fique bem mais baixa nos climas mais amenos. As sementes dessa planta são preparadas de forma a tornarem-se uma especiaria para dar sabor a carnes e pães. É um estimulante do apetite. Tem sido usada com propósitos medicinais, especialmente para os olhos. Durante a Idade Média, era usada como um condimento barato. O trecho de Mateus 23:23 mostra-nos que, nos dias de Jesus, os escribas e os fariseus eram tão criteriosos em seus dízimos que chegavam a separar a décima parte dessa semente, juntamente com o endro e a hortelã. Porém, se eles mostravam-se tão cuidadosos quanto a essas coisas triviais, omitiam as questões realmente importantes da lei, como a justiça, a misericórdia e a fé. Todas as pessoas religiosas são culpadas desse pecado, até certo ponto, porque abominam certos erros, mas toleram outros nos quais estão envolvidos, em pensamento, ação ou omissão.

COMISSÃO, A GRANDE
1. Ocasião Histórica
2. Versões Bíblicas
3. Observações sobre a Grande Comissão

1. Ocasião Histórica

O ministério de Jesus Cristo havia terminado. A ressurreição fora comprovada como uma realidade, pelos discípulos de Jesus, mediante Suas diversas aparições a eles, de tal modo que todas as possíveis dúvidas haviam sido dirimidas. Agora, a partida do Senhor para as dimensões celestes era iminente. Um novo movimento religioso havia sido inaugurado, que só esperava ser mundialmente propagado. Era preciso contar com a colaboração de obreiros para esse mister. Esses obreiros precisavam ser devidamente instruídos e comissionados. A obra missionária de Jesus precisava ter prosseguimento, pelo esforço dos apóstolos e de seus discípulos. A Grande Comissão, pois, foi a autoridade e a grande inspiração para esse imenso empreendimento.

2. Versões Bíblicas

O primeiro dos evangelhos, o de Marcos, conta com uma outra versão, segundo a qual o seu último capítulo conta com um término mais longo. O original grego de Marcos vai somente até 16:8. Mas, o término que finalmente foi consagrado pelo uso envolve até 16:20, o que significa um acréscimo de doze versículos, que procuram sumariar o que os outros evangelhos e o começo do livro de Atos historiam. Quanto a uma completa discussão sobre esse problema, ver as notas expositivas no NTI em Mar. 6:9. No evangelho de Marcos, essa comissão acha-se nos vs. 15 e 16, onde se lê: «E disse-lhes: Ide por todo o mundo e pregai o evangelho a toda criatura. Quem crer e for batizado será salvo; quem, porém, não crer, será condenado». Além dessa comissão, temos uma adição concernente aos sinais que acompanhariam aos que crêem e pregam o evangelho. Eles expulsariam demônios, falariam novas línguas, não seriam prejudicados com picadas de serpentes ou com a ingestão de algum veneno, e curariam os enfermos. Tudo isso é material adicional àquilo que encontramos no relato sobre a Grande Comissão, nos outros evangelhos e em outras porções do Novo Testamento. Todo esse acréscimo foi provido por escribas posteriores, com base naquilo que estava ocorrendo na Igreja primitiva. O autor ou autores desse acréscimo injetou na Grande Comissão a idéia de regeneração batismal (ver também Atos 2:38), para consternação de muitos intérpretes de todos os séculos, que têm procurado extrair a idéia por meio de interpretações forçadas. O problema só é resolvido, de fato, quando se reconhece que esses doze versículos finais do evangelho de Marcos não fazem parte do original grego desse evangelho. A idéia das picadas de cobras provavelmente foi tomada por empréstimo de Salmos 91:13. Certas seitas modernas têm procurado demonstrar a sua espiritualidade manuseando serpentes venenosas durante as suas reuniões, somente para ficar provado freqüentemente que eles não são imunes ao veneno dos ofícios.

Quanto à Grande Comissão a *versão de Mateus* é a mais comumente citada. Ela reza como segue: «Jesus, aproximando-se, falou-lhes, dizendo: Toda a autoridade foi dada no céu e na terra. Ide, portanto, fazei discípulos de todas as nações, batizando-os em nome do Pai e do Filho e do Espírito Santo; ensinando-os a guardar todas as cousas que vos tenho ordenado. E eis que estou convosco todos os dias, até à consumação do século» (Mat. 28:18-20). O que há de mais surpreendente no evangelho de Mateus é que ali não está registrado o relato da ascensão de Jesus. Podemos entender que a Grande Comissão é uma espécie de sumário das afirmações finais de Jesus, e não uma única declaração. Outras informações, que aparecem nos demais evangelhos e no livro de Atos, certamente confirmam essa opinião.

A versão lucana da Grande Comissão aparece em Luc. 24:46-49, vinculada à aparição de Jesus aos seus discípulos, imediatamente antes de sua ascensão. Esse evento é registrado como se tivesse ocorrido no mesmo dia da ressurreição, sem qualquer intervalo de tempo. O livro de Atos, entretanto, informa-nos que entre a ressurreição e a ascensão houve um período de quarenta dias, durante o qual Jesus apareceu por diversas vezes a seus discípulos, para instruí-los acerca do reino de Deus. Ver o artigo sobre a *Ascensão*, que discute sobre essa questão e sobre o problema de harmonia que isso envolve. No terceiro evangelho, a Grande Comissão diz como segue: «...e lhes disse: Assim está escrito que o Cristo havia de padecer, e ressuscitar dentre os mortos no terceiro dia, e que em seu nome se pregasse arrependimento para remissão de pecados, a todas as nações, começando de Jerusalém. Vós sois testemunhas destas cousas. Eis que envio sobre vós a promessa de meu Pai; permanecei, pois, na cidade, até que do alto sejais revestidos de poder». No evangelho de Mateus, pois, aprendemos que a *autoridade* divina foi investida nos apóstolos mediante o dom do Espírito. Em Marcos, essa autoridade é ilustrada mediante os feitos miraculosos que os discípulos seriam capazes de realizar. Novamente, devemos supor que todas as narrativas sumariam o conteúdo geral de diversas declarações de Jesus, provavelmente feitas em diversas ocasiões, e não em uma única oportunidade.

No evangelho de João. No quarto evangelho a Grande Comissão é bastante diferente, não se tendo apoiado sobre as mesmas fontes informativas que os evangelhos sinópticos. Ver João 20:21-23: «...Assim como o Pai me enviou, eu também vos envio. E, havendo dito isto, soprou sobre eles, e disse: Recebei o Espírito Santo. Se de alguns perdoardes os pecados, são-lhe perdoados; se lhos retiverdes, são retidos». Tal como no caso do evangelho de Lucas, encontramos menção ao Espírito, que dá poder e autoridade. Tal como no caso desse evangelho, temos também a questão do perdão dos pecados, com ênfase sobre o poder apostólico de perdoar ou de reter os pecados, mediante o ministério deles. Quanto aos problemas teológicos envolvidos na versão de João, ver no NTI, nessa referência joanina.

No Livro de Atos. Nesse livro há menção ao intervalo de quarenta dias entre a ressurreição e a ascensão de Jesus (Atos 1:3). Ali a Grande Comissão é vinculada de perto com a promessa do Espírito (Atos 1:8), mas também é associada ao diálogo entre Jesus e seus discípulos sobre os *tempos dispensacionais*, em conexão com a restauração de Israel (Atos 1:6,7). Isso é completamente diferente do que se vê no contexto dos outros registros sobre a Grande Comissão. A própria Grande Comissão está contida nestas palavras: «...mas recebereis poder, ao descer sobre vós o Espírito Santo, e sereis minhas testemunhas tanto em Jerusalém, como em toda a Judéia e Samaria, e até aos confins da terra» (Atos 1:8). A menção a Jerusalém, Judéia, Samaria, e, finalmente, os confins da terra, é peculiar ao livro de Atos. E a ascensão é registrada como se tivesse ocorrido imediatamente após Jesus haver dado instruções e anunciado a Grande Comissão.

a. Esse variegado testemunho acerca da Grande Comissão assegura-nos a sua autenticidade. b. Mas essa mesma variedade também revela-nos que as várias formas em que aparece a Grande Comissão devem corresponder a porções ou sumários de uma série de ensinos de Jesus, após a sua ressurreição. c. A porção final de tais instruções aparentemente foi dada imediatamente antes da ascensão, e isso deve ter adicionado vigor ao que Jesus dizia, pois, afinal de contas, a Grande Comissão representa as palavras finais de Cristo, selando suas instruções. d. A Grande Comissão teve por propósito encorajar a continuação de sua missão, e também ampliá-la, até tornar-se absolutamente universal. O provincialismo relativo do judaísmo foi assim deixado para trás, e o cristianismo haveria de ser uma fé realmente universal, no sentido de estar dispersa pelo mundo inteiro. e. Não há como cumprir a Grande Comissão sem o concurso do poder, da autoridade e do batismo no Espírito Santo. f. A Grande Comissão convoca os homens de todos os lugares para arrependerem-se e confiarem no evangelho. Ela tem um intuito evangelizador, e a salvação das almas encontra-se no foco das atenções. g. Uma grande responsabilidade é posta sobre os homens, porquanto a eles cumpre executar a Grande Comissão. Entretanto, o trecho de I Pedro 3:18-4:6 mostra que o próprio Cristo mostrou-se e continua mostrando-se ativo na ampliação de sua missão salvatícia, até mesmo no hades. Destarte, o Senhor é sempre o Senhor, é sempre o poder principal no evangelismo. Ele compartilha dessa tarefa com os crentes, mas nunca se ausenta dessa atividade. Portanto, o resultado será absolutamente universal, conforme Efésios 1:10 nos assegura. Os homens, em sua falsa espiritualidade e em seu orgulho, pensam que a evangelização depende inteiramente deles. Mas o Salvador sempre, e em toda parte será o Salvador. Se isso não fosse verdade, então o propósito da Grande Comissão teria falhado desde há muitos séculos. (AND FRO GLO)

COMISSÕES BÍBLICAS, AS

A **Commissio Pontificia de re biblica**, estabelecida a 30 de outubro de 1902, pelo papa Leão XIII (que vide), formada por certo número de cardeais e consultores, foi organizada com o propósito de garantir a devida interpretação e defesa das Sagradas Escrituras, do ponto de vista da Igreja Católica Romana. Essa comissão também promove pesquisas bíblicas, decide sobre controvérsias acerca de questões sérias que surgem entre os eruditos, mantém a biblioteca do Vaticano bem estocada e atualizada, publica obras sobre as Escrituras, e também tem a autoridade para conferir, àqueles que são aprovados nos exames necessários, o grau de Licenciatura ou de Doutor nas Sagradas Escrituras. (E)

COMISSÕES ECLESIÁSTICAS

Na Igreja Católica Romana há corpos jurídicos aos quais competem certas funções e deveres, a saber:
1. *Comissões Pontificais*. Essas comissões compõem-se de cardeais nomeados pelo papa, a fim de realizarem tarefas específicas. Assim, a preparação da Vulgata Latina foi feita por uma comissão dessa natureza, bem como a reforma da lei canônica.
2. *Comissões Prelaciais*. Essas comissões compõem-se de prelados, secretários e consultores, talvez sob a presidência de um cardeal. Os membros dessas comissões envolvem-se em tarefas especiais, como aquela da arqueologia sagrada.
3. *Comissões Diocesanas*. Há quatro tipos de comissões diocesanas. Elas existem em cada diocese da Igreja Católica Romana. Assim, há comissões para: a. promoção de seminários; b. o exame do clero, para evitar competição quanto aos benefícios paroquiais vagos; c. música sacra; d. supressão do modernismo (que vide). O escopo e a autoridade dessas comissões estão limitados por documentos pontificais e pelas leis eclesiásticas.

COMMUNICATIO ESSENTIAE

Essa expressão latina designa a doutrina de que o Filho recebe a sua essência da parte do Pai; e que o Espírito Santo recebe a sua essência da parte do Pai e do Filho. Mas essa comunicação teria lugar dentro do contexto da essência única da natureza de Deus. Essa doutrina reputa o Pai como a Fonte da Trindade inteira (que vide), bem como a origem das diversas relações. Calvino argumentou contra o conceito, insistindo que não há qualquer processo de derivação. Quando ele usou o termo *autotheos*, para referir-se ao Filho, foi acerbamente criticado pelos teólogos católicos romanos contemporâneos, porquanto parecia que, com isso, ele estava negando o Credo Niceno, quando o mesmo diz «Deus de Deus», ao aludir à eterna geração do Filho, por parte do Pai. Entretanto, Calvino não estava negando a doutrina da geração eterna, e nem defendia a idéia do autoteísmo, como se Cristo fosse Deus *a se ipse*, *non a Patre* (por si mesmo, independentemente do Pai). Os teólogos dividiram-se por causa de minúsculas tecnicalidades da questão, de tal modo que não se sabe o que, exatamente, Calvino e seus seguidores acreditavam sobre esse particular. Os defensores afirmam que Calvino errou quanto à escolha das palavras, mas não quanto à doutrina propriamente dita. Alguns afirmam que é uso empregar o termo *geração*, visto que uma essência nem gera e nem é gerada. Mas, se a palavra «geração» for usada como uma metáfora para indicar relacionamento, e não uma sucessão cronológica, então nada haverá de errado com esse uso. Quando usamos a palavra «eterno», já eliminamos qualquer idéia cronológica. Karl Barth frisou a natureza inefável da tentativa de exprimir origens, no tocante a qualquer discussão sobre a deidade. A idéia da *communicatio essentiae* salvaguarda a *monarquia* (ver sobre o monarquismo) do Pai como a origem da Trindade inteira. Porém, quando alguém pensa em termos de produção, em relação à comunicação de essência, termina com uma espécie de Filho criado ou produzido, subordinando-o desnecessariamente ao Pai. O protesto de Calvino teve o intuito de salvaguardar a divindade autêntica do Filho. Discussões teológicas como essas, apesar de serem interessantes e curiosas, presumem que sabemos mais do que realmente sabemos. Outrossim, não temos meios para descrever adequadamente a natureza de Deus, e nem a doutrina da Trindade. Obtemos mais sucesso quando procuramos falar sobre os atributos mais óbvios de Deus e sobre as suas obras. (C)

COMMUNICATIO IDIOMATUM

Essa expressão latina alude à participação nos atributos ou propriedades de Jesus Cristo, por parte de suas duas naturezas, mutuamente. Cristo, em sua dupla natureza, tem atributos de ambas as naturezas, os quais se comunicam entre si. Mas, de alguma maneira, permanecem atributos de uma pessoa total, sem sinal algum de dupla personalidade. A questão inteira é um aspecto da *cristologia* (que vide), a qual foi debatida durante séculos, sem que se chegasse a uma opinião de consenso. O problema consiste no fato de que não podemos entender como uma pessoa

COMMUNICATIO — COMPANHEIRO

pode ser, ao mesmo tempo, divina e humana. E qualquer tentativa no sentido de descrever essa situação ímpar, só pode gerar controvérsia e incerteza.

A controvérsia acerca do título *theótokos* (mãe de Deus), entre Cirilo de Alexandria e Nestor, estava centralizada em torno da legitimidade do princípio do *communicatio idiomatum*. A doutrina de Lutero sobre a eucaristia exigia a transferência do atributo de onipresença da natureza divina de Cristo para a sua natureza humana, a fim de que a presença de Cristo pudesse estar sob as espécies do pão e do vinho; e o princípio do *communicatio idiomatum* foi considerado um princípio conveniente a ser aplicado ao caso. Porém, outros reformadores não podiam perceber qualquer sentido nessa idéia, e os próprios luteranos a abandonaram. Pois, como pode o finito conter o infinito? (C)

COMMUNICATIO OPERATIONUM

Essa expressão indica a **participação nas operações**. Foi expressão empregada pela segunda geração de luteranos, especificamente por Cheminitz, a fim de dar a entender e delimitar a interpretação realista do *communicatio idiomatum* (que vide).

COMPACTATAS

A palavra refere-se aos acordos firmados entre o concílio de Basiléia (que vide), principalmente através de seu representante, o legado Palomar, e os partidos hussitas (que vide), da Boêmia. As negociações prolongaram-se por quatro anos. A 5 de julho de 1436, em Jihlava, tais negociações foram concluídas. Os exércitos hussitas haviam sido fragorosamente derrotados em Lipany, em 1434, e o concílio foi capaz de ditar os seus próprios termos. Embora os hussitas checos tivessem recebido a permissão de administrar os elementos do pão e do vinho na Eucaristia, entretanto, não obtiveram qualquer outra concessão importante. Porém, esse concílio revogou as anteriores condenações decretadas contra os hussitas, as calistinas, conforme foram denominadas, passando a ser considerados filhos fiéis da Igreja Católica Romana. Isso pôs fim ao conflito hussita, dentro do romanismo. (E)

COMPAIXÃO

A compaixão é o amor em ação. Forneci ao leitor desta enciclopédia um artigo suficientemente longo sobre o *Amor*, que deveria ser consultado. Para mim, o assunto é suficientemente importante para merecer este artigo mais breve sobre a *Compaixão*. Todos falamos em melhor tom do que realmente somos. Todas as religiões, e quase todas as filosofias, concordam que o amor é básico a toda a motivação e ação dos homens. No entanto, quase todos os homens estão envolvidos até o pescoço nos seus interesses egoístas.

No que consiste a compaixão? Consiste na cura dos males físicos e psicológicos. Consiste em ajudar àqueles que padecem carências, para que venham a possuir aquilo que necessitam, para que aprendam a produzir. Consiste em ajudar a carregar os fardos e em compartilhar dos mesmos. Consiste em cumprir o mandamento de Jesus, de que devemo-nos amar mutuamente (I João 3:11-18). Consiste em imitar a atitude de Jesus, da qual resultavam boas ações, como quando ele teve compaixão das multidões, pois eram como ovelhas sem pastor (Mat. 9:36). Consiste em nos envolvermos no evangelismo, cujo propósito é salvar as almas (Mat. 28:19,20). Consiste em nos interessarmos por ensinar as pessoas para que as ajudemos a crescer espiritualmente (Heb. 6:1 ss). Consiste em observarmos as cargas que outras pessoas têm de suportar, ajudando-as quanto a isso (Gál. 6:2; 5:14). Consiste em perdoar àqueles que nos têm prejudicado (Efé. 4:32; Col. 3:13). Consiste em participarmos das tristezas alheias (Luc. 7:13), o que, de alguma maneira, permite que as outras pessoas suportem melhor suas tristezas. Consiste em termos dó do próximo, a exemplo do que Deus faz (Sal. 103:13). Envolve o incentivo que o amor nos confere, com o correspondente olvido de nosso próprio egoísmo (Fil. 2:1,2). Quem se mostra compassivo, nada faz impelido pelo motivo do egoísmo, mas, em humildade, pensa sobre os outros em termos melhores do que pensa sobre si mesmo (Fil. 2:3). Quem se compadece sacrifica os seus próprios interesses, a fim de servir ao próximo (Fil. 2:5 ss), assim imitando a Cristo, em sua missão neste mundo. A pessoa compassiva mostra respeito até pelos animais, e não somente pelos seres humanos. A Bíblia mostra-nos que Deus se interessa até pela queda de um passarinho (Mat. 10:29). Até o boi mudo, que trilha o grão, tem o direito à provisão alimentar, de conformidade com a lei (Deu. 25:4). Isso envolve servirmos a outras pessoas, que talvez não sejam o nosso tipo favorito, por reconhecermos que qualquer ser humano é nosso próximo (Luc. 10:29-37), conforme se vê na história do bom samaritano.

A compaixão envolve mais do que as emoções de piedade ou de simpatia. A compaixão consiste em *um ato* que procura consolar ou melhorar a situação do nosso próximo, e não meramente porque nos sentimos mal diante dessa situação adversa. A piedade pode existir apenas nos sentimentos e na mente; mas a compaixão, por força de sua própria definição, só se manifesta por meio da ação apropriada. O trecho de I João 3:18 recomenda: «Filhinhos, não amemos de palavra, nem de língua, mas de fato e de verdade». (B H)

COMPANHEIRO

Há várias palavras hebraicas e gregas envolvidas, a saber:

1. *Chaber*, «companheiro». Palavra hebraica usada por doze vezes. Por exemplo, Sal. 119:63; Pro. 28:24; Can. 1:7; Isa. 1:23; Eze. 37:16.

2. *Chabbar*, «companheiro». Palavra hebraica usada por somente uma vez, isto é, Jó 41:6.

3. *Chabar*, «companheiro». Palavra hebraica que figura por três vezes: Dan. 2:17; 2:13,18.

4. *Chabereth*, «companheira». Palavra hebraica usada apenas por uma vez, em Mal. 2:14.

5. *Kenath*, «íntimo». Termo hebraico empregado por oito vezes, sempre no livro de Esdras (4:7,9,17,23; 5:3,6; 6:6,13).

6. *Merea*, «amigo». Palavra hebraica que ocorre por sete vezes. Por exemplo: Juí. 14:11,20; 15:2,6.

7. *Rea*, «amigo». Palavra hebraica usada por mais de cento e oitenta vezes. Por exemplo: Êxo. 32:27; I Crô. 27:33; Jó. 30:29; Sal. 122:8; Isa. 34:14; Jon. 1:7; Zac. 3:8.

8. *Raah*, «deleitar-se», «desfrutar». Verbo hebraico usado por cinco vezes, como em Pro. 13:20; 28:7; 22:24.

9. *Koinonós*, «quem tem algo em comum». Palavra grega usada por dez vezes: Mat. 23:30; Luc. 5:10; I Cor. 10:18,20; II Cor. 1:7; 8:23; File. 17; Heb. 10:33;

I Ped. 5:1; II Ped. 1:4.

10. *Sugkoinonós*, «companheiro». Palavra grega usada por quatro vezes: Rom. 11:17; I Cor. 9:23; Fil. 1:7; Apo. 1:9.

11. *Sunergós*, «companheiro de trabalho». Palavra grega que ocorre por treze vezes: Rom. 16:3,9,21; I Cor. 3:9; II Cor. 1:24; 8:23; Fil. 2:25; 4:3; Col. 4:11; I Tes. 3:2; File. 1,24; III João 8.

12. *Sunékdemos*, «companheiro de viagem». Palavra grega usada por duas vezes: Atos 19:29 e II Cor. 8:19.

Os sinônimos dessas palavras hebraicas e gregas são: «associado», «vizinho», «próximo», etc. O termo hebraico *rea* transmite a idéia de duas pessoas tecidas juntas, formando uma única entidade. Isso é paralelo ao conceito aristotélico de que a verdadeira *amizade* consiste em *uma alma com dois corpos*. No trecho de Zacarias 13:7 temos o vocábulo hebraico *amith*, «próximo», «amigo».

No grego também temos a palavra *plesíon*, «próximo», que significa, basicamente, «alguém que está perto» (ver Mat. 5:43, citando Lev. 19:18; 19:19; 22:39; Mar. 12:31,33; Luc. 10:27,29,36; João 4:5; Atos 7:27; Rom. 13:9,10; 15:2; Gál. 5:14; Efé. 4:25; Tia. 2:8; 4:12). A palavra grega mais comum para «amigo» é *phílos*, que significa «querido», «estimado», e que figura por vinte e oito vezes, de Mat. 11:19 a III João 15. Ver o artigo geral sobre *Amizade*, que desenvolve os conceitos aqui introduzidos. Ver também sobre *Comunhão*.

COMPANHEIRO DE JUGO

A rigor, a expressão aparece somente em Filipenses 4:3, onde o original grego diz *súnzugos*, «companheiro de jugo». Lemos ali: «A ti, fiel companheiro de jugo, também peço que as auxilies...» Paulo dirigia-se a quem? As conjecturas chegam a formar uma legião: Lucas, Lídia, Epafrodito, Barnabé, Silas, Timóteo, e até mesmo uma possível esposa de Paulo, embora a existência dessa esposa seja pura conjectura. Devido a essa dificuldade de interpretação, alguns eruditos têm chegado a pensar que o termo grego *súnzugos* deveria ser considerado como um nome próprio, referente a um homem que, em português, teria o nome de Sínzigo. Mas isso criaria mais problemas ainda, pois nada se sabe sobre um companheiro de Paulo com esse nome. Por essa razão, outros estudiosos pensam que Paulo estaria se dirigindo ao líder da igreja cristã de Filipos.

Paulo, nesse trecho, estava recomendando a alguém que ajudasse a Evódia e a Síntique, duas mulheres que eram membros da igreja filipense, para que conseguissem sanar suas divergências.

Quanto ao que significaria «companheiro de jugo», as opiniões também variam. Alguns pensam que seria alguém que estivera aprisionado com Paulo, em Filipos. Se assim fosse, então ninguém seria melhor para ocupar o lugar do que Silas. Ver Atos 16:19 ss. Mas, se pensarmos na raiz da palavra de onde veio essa expressão, raiz essa que no grego é *zeúgos*, «jugo», talvez seja melhor pensar mesmo no líder daquela igreja. A idéia de *súnzugos*, nesse caso, estaria vinculada ao trecho de Mateus 11:29, onde lemos: «Tomai sobre vós o meu jugo...» Nesse caso, o apóstolo Paulo estaria se dirigindo a algum crente consagrado. Na verdade, porém, não há indícios bíblicos suficientes que nos capacitem identificar com certeza esse «companheiro de jugo» de Paulo.

COMPENSAÇÃO, PRINCÍPIO DE

Compensar significa retribuir, fazer emendas apropriadas, remunerar, contrabalançar, prover algo em substituição a alguma perda sofrida. O princípio de compensação é importante no campo da psicologia, bem como na experiência humana em geral. Também é importante no que se relaciona ao cumprimento de nossas missões espirituais. Ralph Waldo Emerson (que vide) fez declarações instrutivas sobre a questão. — Ele estava interessado no autodesenvolvimento do indivíduo. Acreditava que todos os homens dispõem de recursos especiais, visto que o homem é um microcosmo dentro do macrocosmo. Portanto, haveria certa correspondência entre a alma humana e tudo quanto existe no universo. Na natureza, através da providência divina, opera o *princípio de compensação*. Se a um homem falta um dote, a natureza lhe proveu um dote diferente. Faz parte de sua responsabilidade desenvolver o dote que ele possui, porquanto isso representa um investimento divino em sua pessoa. Aristóteles ensinava algo similar a isso, com sua doutrina da *virtude como função*. É óbvio que nem todos os homens possuem as mesmas capacidades ou funções em potencial; mas o que todos têm é a responsabilidade de desenvolver aqueles dotes que receberam. No corpo místico de Cristo, a Igreja, há muitos membros. Seria algo grotesco se um membro qualquer tentasse realizar as funções próprias de um outro membro. Paulo criticou aqueles que pensavam ser possuidores de todos os dons espirituais e que, por motivo de ostentação, julgavam ser necessário exibirem-se, realizando várias funções na mesma reunião. Ver I Cor. 14:26 ss. Antes, aos crentes foi recomendado que permitissem aos demais realizarem seus respectivos papéis. Ver o artigo sobre o *Corpo de Cristo*.

É importante que uma criança tenha boa saúde e equilíbrio mentais, sendo ajudada nisso por seus pais, a fim de descobrir seus pontos fortes e tirar proveito dos mesmos. Se, por exemplo, uma criança não se mostra forte quanto aos assuntos acadêmicos, deveria ser encorajada a exercer alguma outra habilidade. Se uma criança tem dificuldade com a leitura, mas é boa quanto à matemática, deveria ser encorajada a ser tão bem-sucedida na matemática que não sinta ser demasiada qualquer crítica que venha a receber no tocante à sua leitura. A auto-imagem de uma pessoa depende muito do que ela pode fazer, que a destaque entre outras pessoas. Temos a responsabilidade de conferir aos nossos semelhantes uma boa auto-imagem, ajudando-os a se destacarem em alguma coisa. No seio de uma igreja local, às vezes ocorre aquele erro fatal de competição entre os membros. Nisso, certos dons são exaltados, e outros são desprezados. Ministros entram em competição, exibindo seus dotes como itens que precisam ser admirados em uma exposição. A real necessidade é a da compensação, em que cada crente contribui com alguma coisa, sem degradar o que algum outro tem para oferecer. Todos nós conhecemos essas coisas; mas, na prática, é fácil glorificarmos a nós mesmos e humilharmos aos outros. Portanto, há duas aplicações práticas do princípio de compensação. Uma delas é de natureza *pessoal* ou individual: preciso descobrir e desenvolver minhas habilidades e dons particulares. A outra é de natureza *coletiva*: uma vez que eu tenha me destacado em algo, preciso participar da comunidade como um membro que compensa e que é compensado. (P)

COMPETÊNCIA

A **competência** consiste em se ter habilidade ou autoridade suficiente para realizar certa tarefa ou cumprir certo dever. Cada indivíduo possui qualidades inatas, que pode desenvolver de tal modo que se torne *competente* em alguma coisa. Uma triste coisa que vemos nas igrejas locais é como as pessoas passam de ano para ano sem nunca se aprimorarem, sem nunca aumentarem o seu conhecimento, sem nunca melhorarem as suas funções. Neste mundo, uma pessoa ganha mais ou menos em razão de sua competência. É verdade que os governos penalizam a competência, cobrando mais altos impostos dos que produzem e ganham mais do que dos incompetentes e preguiçosos. A despeito disso, é melhor o crente procurar ser competente, para que seja mais útil ao Senhor, em seu reino e em sua Igreja.

COMPETIÇÃO

Há vários tipos de competição, alguns bons e outros ruins. O princípio econômico do capitalismo (que vide) é a competição. Se uma pessoa tiver de competir com outras a fim de vender o seu produto, terá de procurar produzir um produto melhor, em menos tempo, com menores gastos. Se chegar a concretizar esses alvos, chegará a ganhar mais dinheiro. Em caso contrário, talvez tenha de abandonar o negócio, ou então contentar-se com menor taxa de lucro. A ausência de competição rebaixa a qualidade e eleva o preço das coisas. No entanto, a competição econômica com freqüência assume aspectos imorais ou mesmo criminosos, quando as pessoas apelam para os meios desonestos e trapaceiros. As leis foram feitas precisamente para regulamentar as práticas comerciais. Mas, infelizmente, as estatísticas falam sobre um pequeno número de negociantes honestos. A lei mosaica (Deu. 25:15) requeria a honestidade, e uma sociedade dificilmente torna-se próspera onde impera a desonestidade.

Também há uma *competição espiritual* boa ou má. É vantajoso vermos o exemplo de alguém melhor que nós mesmos, deixando-nos estimular à melhoria. Dessa maneira, disporemos de uma espécie particular de competição. Mas aquela competição pública entre ministros evangélicos ou entre membros, algo muito comum nas igrejas locais, não passa de manifestações de egoísmo, jamais produzindo resultados espirituais. A melhor e mais produtiva forma de competição espiritual é aquela que disputamos conosco mesmos. Todo crente está na obrigação moral de estabelecer elevados alvos para si mesmo, procurando corresponder ao ideal que tiver imaginado e fixado como sua meta.

COMPLEXO DE CARÁTER

Expressão usada para designar os **informes dos sentidos** (que vide), empregada no movimento do *realismo crítico* (que vide), primeiro ponto.

COMPLEXO DE ÉDIPO

Segundo as lendas gregas, Édipo era filho de Laio e Jocasta. Foi abandonado por ocasião de seu nascimento, por causa de um oráculo que predizia que, finalmente, mataria seu pai, em vingança contra algo que este último fizera.

O nome *Édipo* significa «pés inchados», porque o bebê teve seus pés atravessados, por ordem de seus pais, tendo sido deixado para morrer à míngua. Porém, o escravo que fora encarregado de cuidar da questão, poupou a criança e a entregou aos cuidados de um pastor. Esse pastor pertencia ao rei de Corinto, pelo que, finalmente, o menino acabou sendo adotado pelo rei. Foi, pois, criado pelo rei de Corinto, mas, finalmente, regressou a Tebas, lugar de onde provinha. Após ter resolvido o quebra-cabeça da esfinge, e de haver morto acidentalmente seu próprio pai, sem o saber, casou-se com sua mãe, e assim tornou-se o rei de Tebas. Porém, ao descobrir que Jocasta era sua própria mãe, cegou-se e morreu no exílio. Com base nessa circunstância, um apego forte, usualmente inconsciente, de um filho por sua mãe, é chamado de complexo de Édipo. Tal apego usualmente tem certa conotação sexual, algumas vezes de forma consciente. Pode manifestar-se sob a forma de hostilidade contra o pai, além de várias desordens neuróticas, porquanto perpetua um sentimento de culpa que não é resolvido. A expressão algumas vezes é usada de maneira muito ampla, para referir-se ao mesmo tipo de apego de uma filha por seu pai, embora, nesse caso, exista o termo mais preciso de complexo de Electra. Ver o artigo geral sobre *Freud*.

COMPLEXO DE ELECTRA

De acordo com as lendas gregas, Electra era filha de Agamenom e Clitemnestra. Ela persuadiu seu irmão, Orestes, a matar a mãe deles e o amante dela, Egisto, para vingar o assassinato do pai deles. Com base nessa circunstância, o desejo sexual compulsivo de uma filha, por seu pai, tem o nome de complexo de Electra. Trata-se do equivalente feminino do complexo de Édipo (que vide). Em sua prática, Freud (que vide) encontrou, ocasionalmente, um caso dessa natureza. Em um grau ou outro, e com diversas manifestações, esse complexo é mais comum do que gostaríamos de acreditar.

COMPRAR

Ver sobre **Comércio e Viagem**.

COMPREENSÃO

Quando o homem caiu no pecado, não foi apenas a sua moral que foi afetada, incapacitando-o a praticar o bem, no sentido de ser plenamente aprovado por Deus, mas também o seu entendimento foi afetado. Esse embotamento é universal: «Não há quem entenda, não há quem busque a Deus» (Rom. 3:11), diz o apóstolo Paulo, citando Salmos 53:1-3. Conforme se vê nessa citação, essa falta de compreensão diz respeito a Deus e às coisas relativas a Deus. No seu estado natural, pecaminoso, o homem não tem entendimento sobre as realidades das dimensões celestes: «Ora, o homem natural não aceita as cousas do Espírito de Deus, porque lhe são loucura; e não pode entendê-las, porque elas se discernem espiritualmente» (I Cor. 2:14). Isso posto, a sabedoria deste mundo, o conhecimento que os homens são capazes de adquirir, usando dos poderes de observação, raciocínio e da intuição, são reduzidos nas Escrituras, à mais perfeita nulidade: «...expomos sabedoria entre os experimentados; não, porém, a sabedoria deste século, nem a dos poderosos desta época, que se reduzem a nada» (I Cor. 2:6). Por falta de revelação divina, os homens nem ao menos sabem a resposta para as três perguntas básicas da filosofia: Quem somos? de onde viemos? para onde estamos indo? Não admira, pois, que muitos homens, nessas trevas do entendimento, cheguem à conclusão de que nada se pode saber com qualquer grau de certeza. Assim nasceu o ceticismo e o agnosticismo.

O homem moderno jacta-se dos grandes avanços de sua ciência. Isso foi até mesmo previsto nas Escrituras: «...o saber se multiplicará» (Dan. 12:4).

COMPREENSÃO

No entanto, nunca os homens se sentiram mais inseguros do que nesta nossa era de tanto avanço tecnológico. É que o conhecimento do homem, mesmo acerca das coisas naturais, pende muito mais para empreendimentos destrutivos, que infelicitam a humanidade, do que para projetos beneficentes. E, mesmo quando, mercê de Deus, alguém foge à regra, não demora para que tudo aquilo que antes visava ao bem do ser humano seja desvirtuado por uma multidão de outros, malfazejos. Destarte, todas as instituições humanas têm sido sujeitadas a esse abuso. Manipulados pela maldade humana, os valores mais sagrados têm-se tornado uma desgraça. Penso que não há exemplo mais chocante disso do que o desvirtuamento do cristianismo. Quando Deus revelava a João, e, através dele, a nós, como a Igreja de Cristo seria imitada, e como Satanás enganaria os homens com um engodo perverso, ao contemplar «a mãe das meretrizes e das abominações da terra», o apóstolo admirou-se «com grande espanto» (Apo. 17:1-6). Tudo isso é sumariado na epístola de Judas, quando ele escreve: «Estes, porém, quanto a tudo o que não entendem, difamam; e, quanto a tudo o que compreendem por instinto natural, como brutos sem razão, até nessas cousas se corrompem» (vs. 10).

Embotado em seu entendimento e dotado de tendências morais pervertidas, os homens colhem corrupção até mesmo do que entendem por instinto natural. E zombam das realidades espirituais, que não compreendem. Só o homem tiver de ter compreensão sobre as realidades espirituais, só as terá se houver intervenção da misericórdia e da graça divinas. A essa intervenção a Bíblia chama de iluminação. Se não houver iluminação, o embotamento continuará indefinidamente. «A revelação das tuas palavras esclarece, e dá entendimento aos simples» (Sal. 119:130). E também: «Naquele dia, os surdos ouvirão as palavras do livro, e os cegos, livres já da escuridão e das trevas, as verão» (Isa. 29:18). E o Novo Testamento mostra-se ainda mais claro quanto a isso: «Porque Deus que disse: De trevas resplandecerá luz — ele mesmo resplandeceu em nossos corações, para iluminação do conhecimento da glória de Deus, na face de Cristo» (II Cor. 4:6). «...o Deus de nosso Senhor Jesus Cristo, o Pai da glória, vos conceda espírito de sabedoria e de revelação, no pleno conhecimento dele, iluminados os olhos do vosso coração, para saberdes qual é a esperança do seu chamamento, qual a riqueza da glória da sua herança nos santos, e qual a suprema grandeza do seu poder para com os que cremos...» (Efé. 1:17-19).

Paulo considerava essa iluminação do entendimento algo tão importante para o crente que, em várias de suas epístolas, ele incluiu uma secção na qual ora por seus leitores, para que o Senhor lhes abra a compreensão espiritual. Além do texto acima citado, ver também II Cor. 1:10; Col. 1:9.

O entendimento iluminado do crente, pois, chega ao ponto de compreender qual o grandioso plano de Deus, e como esse plano gira em torno da pessoa de Cristo. Para os apóstolos, pois, o segredo da compreensão espiritual era ter conhecimento experimental de Cristo: «...para que os seus corações sejam confortados... e tenham toda riqueza da forte convicção do entendimento, para compreenderem plenamente o mistério de Deus, Cristo, em quem todos os tesouros da sabedoria e do conhecimento estão ocultos» (Col. 2:2,3).

Evidentemente, as Escrituras reconhecem que, por maior que seja a iluminação do nosso entendimento, neste lado da existência, somente no outro lado, já glorificados com Cristo, seremos capazes de compreendê-lo realmente, pois então teremos a mesma natureza que ele tem. Isso é lindamente expresso por João, quando ele diz: «Amados, agora somos filhos de Deus, e ainda não se manifestou o que havemos de ser. Sabemos que, quando ele se manifestar, seremos semelhantes a ele, porque havemos de vê-lo como ele é» (I João 3:2). Isso envolverá uma tremenda promoção. Os crentes glorificados serão imensamente elevados na escala do ser. Sendo agora inferiores aos anjos, tornar-se-ão semelhantes ao Filho glorioso de Deus.

Tendo chegado a este ponto em nossa exposição, resta-nos somente ficar no aguardo da volta do Senhor, quando seremos ressuscitados e glorificados, e quando nosso entendimento subirá até níveis exaltadíssimos, como agora nem podemos imaginar. Podemos aplicar aqui as palavras de I Coríntios 2:9 «...como está escrito: Nem olhos viram, nem ouvidos ouviram, nem jamais penetrou em coração humano o que Deus tem preparado para aqueles que o amam». Há infinitos tesouros de conhecimento à nossa espera, nas dimensões celestes. Essa expectação pela nossa transformação segundo a imagem de Cristo é que a Bíblia chama de virtude da esperança, uma das três virtudes cardeais da vida cristã. Ver o artigo sobre *Esperança*.

No hebraico, há várias palavras que lançam luz sobre esse assunto, a saber:

1. *Bin*, «compreender», «considerar». Palavra que aparece por cerca de cento e sessenta vezes. Trata-se de uma palavra tão rica de significado que as traduções usam muitas palavras e expressões para traduzi-la, como «considerar», «usar de sabedoria», «perceber», «usar de prudência», «discernir», etc. Para exemplificar, ver Nee. 8:8, Jó 13:1; 42:3; Sal. 19:12; 92:6; Pro. 2:5; Dan. 9:2,23; Osé. 14:9; Isa. 56:11; Sal. 119:110.

2. *Yada*, «conhecer», «estar familiarizado com». Palavra que é usada por mais de novecentas vezes. Por exemplo: Núm. 16:30; 9:3; Deu. 9:6; I Sam. 4:6; 26:4; II Sam. 3:37; Sal. 81:5; Pro. 1:2; Ecl. 1:17; Isa. 1:3; Jer. 10:23; Eze. 2:5; 5:13; Joel 3:17; Zac. 2:9; 11:11.

Há várias outras palavras hebraicas correlatas; mas, para nossas finalidades, basta-nos considerar essas principais.

No grego também há vários vocábulos que ainda lançam mais luz sobre o assunto do que as palavras hebraicas, a saber:

1. *Oida*, «conhecer (por informação)». Termo usado por mais de trezentas e quarenta vezes, desde Mat. 2:2 até Apo. 21:22. Esse vocábulo é usado principalmente nos quatro evangelhos, no livro de Atos e no Apocalipse.

2. *Ginósko*, «conhecer (por experiência própria)». Termo usado por mais de duzentas e dez vezes, desde Mat. 1:25 até Apo. 3:9. Quem mais emprega esse vocábulo é o apóstolo João, no seu evangelho e na sua primeira epístola.

3. *Noéo*, «ponderar», «pensar». Termo usado por catorze vezes: Mat. 15:16; 16:9,11; 24:15; Mar. 7:18; 8:17; 13:14; João 12:40; Rom. 1:20; Efé. 3:4,20; I Tim. 1:7; II Tim. 2:7; Heb. 11:3.

4. *Punthánomai*, «aprender por inquirição». Palavra que é usada por onze vezes: Mat. 2:4; Luc. 15:26; 18:36; João 4:52; Atos 4:7; 10:18,29; 21:33; 23:19,20,34.

5. *Suníemi*, «compreender». Palavra usada por vinte e sete vezes: Mat. 13:13,14,15,19,23,51; 15:10; 16:12; 17:13; Mar. 4:9,12; 6:52; 7:14; 8:17,21; Luc. 2:50; 8:10; 18:34; 24:45; Atos 7:25; 28:26,27; Rom.

3:11; 15:21; II Cor. 10:12; Efé. 5:17.

6. *Pronéo*, «fixar a mente ou os afetos». Vocábulo usado por vinte e seis vezes: Mat. 16:23; Mar. 8:33; Atos 28:22; Rom. 8:5; 11:20; 12:3,16; 14:6; 15:5; I Cor. 13:11; II Cor. 13:11; Gál. 5:10; Fil. 1:7; 2:2,5; 3:15,19; 4:2,10; Col. 3:2; I Tim. 6:17.

COMPULSÃO

Esse termo refere-se àquela condição em que alguém está sendo compelido ou forçado a fazer ou não alguma coisa. A compulsão pode ser errada, correta ou indiferente. Não é errado os pais forçarem seus filhos a freqüentarem a escola e estudarem. Porém, é errado forçar as crianças aprenderem o ateísmo, ou a imoralidade; é errado forçar as escolas religiosas cerrarem suas portas. Coisas assim estão ocorrendo nos países comunistas, com o apoio de leis injustas e do poder militar.

Nem toda a compulsão é física. As pessoas estão sendo forçadas a fazerem certas coisas mediante a influência psicológica. — Algumas vezes, isso se efetua mediante autocompulsão, porque uma pessoa que começa a praticar algum vício, em breve sente-se obcecada pelo mesmo. E então chegamos àquilo que os psicólogos chamam de síndrome de compulsão obsessiva; e, quando isso se instala, pouca margem resta para a correção nas ações. Alguns casos de autocompulsão são moralmente indiferentes. Conheci um homem que sentia a compulsão de pintar quadros, e ficava acordado até altas horas da noite, praticando a sua arte. — Algumas vezes, ele ficava pintando a noite inteira, e dormia durante o dia. Se, porventura, ele não estava prejudicando a outros, com sua compulsão, esta não envolvia nenhum erro. Mas, na verdade, ele não precisava agir daquele modo. Não teria incorrido em qualquer erro se deixasse inteiramente de pintar. Também existem atos compulsivos, como a lavagem exagerada das mãos ou como vários ritos pelos quais as pessoas sentem que devem passar. Quase todas as pessoas exibem algo desse tipo de compulsão, em sua conduta diária. Porém, em alguns casos, isso envolve uma enfermidade psicológica. Usualmente, por detrás dos atos compulsivos, há a ansiedade ou o temor. Tais coisas não são erradas em si mesmas, mas podem ser sinal de alguma distorção psicológica.

Finalmente, existem compulsões boas, mesmo que elas não pareçam razoáveis para outras pessoas. Um trabalhador compulsivo fará muita coisa, enquanto outros estão se divertindo na praia. É possível que a missão de um homem requeira que ele seja uma pessoa obcecada. Por outra parte, algumas pessoas ficam obcecadas com o dinheiro, e todos os seus esforços centralizam-se em torno de como ganhar mais dinheiro, por meios honestos ou desonestos. Isso é apenas uma forma de egoísmo. Outras pessoas deixam-se impulsionar por fantasias de fama e poder. Isso é pura arrogância. Outras são obcecadas pela fé religiosa e pela busca da santidade, ao ponto em que têm fome e sede dessas coisas. Isso já é espiritualidade. É que o Espírito de Deus é a força compelidora, nesses casos raros.

COMTE, AUGUSTO

Suas datas foram 1798-1857. Foi filósofo francês. Nasceu em Montpellier. Freqüentou a École Polytechnique de Paris. Foi secretário de Saint-Simom, ao qual muito influenciou, de 1817 a 1824. Foi o fundador da filosofia positivista. Ver o artigo sobre o *Positivismo Lógico*. Muitos políticos, ao redor do mundo, entre outros, têm seguido suas idéias. Getúlio Vargas, ditador do Brasil por quinze anos, e mais tarde eleito legalmente presidente, deixava-se orientar pelas idéias positivistas.

Comte costumava conferenciar sobre o tema, o que fez por dois anos, até que precisou interromper suas preleções devido ao desequilíbrio mental que sofreu. Estranhamente, ele advogava uma religião da humanidade em que o objeto de adoração era simbolizado pelas formas de um corpo humano feminino, com bustos dos benfeitores da humanidade expostos nas capelas, em cuja honra deveria haver dias festivos, de acordo com um calendário criado pelos positivistas. Mas ele não obteve sucesso, na tentativa de estabelecer essa forma de igreja. Isso representa o humanismo (que vide), em forma extremamente exagerada. Contudo, isso é levemente superior à veneração a estrelas de cinema ou a figuras políticas e militares que foram culpados da morte de milhares de pessoas. Comte teria sido o criador das palavras *altruísmo* e *positivismo*.

Idéias:

1. Todas as sociedades necessariamente passam por diversos estágios de pensamento. Haveria os estágios teológico e metafísico, mas, finalmente, chegaria o estágio do positivismo, mediante o desenvolvimento da ciência e sua influência crescente. Antigas explicações teológicas e metafísicas cederão lugar às explicações científicas.

2. As próprias ciências atravessarão desenvolvimentos progressivos, sendo purificadas de velhas maneiras de pensar, conforme se vê no primeiro ponto, acima. A ordem do desenvolvimento das ciências puras compor-se-ia da matemática, da astronomia, da física, da química, da biologia e da psicologia. Algumas dessas ciências ainda não seriam totalmente livres. A sociologia estaria se tornando uma ciência, e ainda teria de passar por certa depuração.

3. O mais importante progresso da sociedade seria o desenvolvimento intelectual. Esse desenvolvimento estaria destinado a atingir o verdadeiro altruísmo. Uma verdadeira religião humanista unirá o intelecto e os sentimentos.

4. Comte via a sociedade como um todo *orgânico* que não pode ser decomposto em individualismo, da mesma maneira que uma superfície não pode ser reduzida a meras linhas.

5. A sociedade orgânica ainda terá de tornar-se uma realidade. Os ideais gêmeos são a *ordem* e o *progresso*. (Esse é o lema da bandeira do Brasil). Vários estágios históricos têm enfatizado uma ou outra dessas duas coisas. O período feudal, por exemplo, era caracterizado pela *ordem*. A Reforma Protestante, vinculada à Revolução Francesa, criou um período de *progresso*. A ciência é que poderá unir e promover a combinação da ordem com o progresso. Em um estágio ainda mais avançado, as virtudes individuais da liberdade, da consciência individual e da tolerância, serão destiladas sob a forma de leis gerais, científicas.

6. Na *epistemologia*, Comte requeria o governo do método científico, com o abandono da metafísica, com suas especulações não verificáveis sobre as primeiras causas ou sobre as finalidades. Nesse caso, a filosofia tornar-se-ia um meio para a promoção do positivismo (que vide).

Comte e seus seguidores erraram, ao reduzir a realidade, e aquilo que pode ser conhecido, às informações que nos são dadas pela percepção dos sentidos, visto que esses são os meios utilizados pelo método científico. A razão, a intuição e o misticismo também são meios válidos para a obtenção de conhecimentos, mas esses meios não são reconhecidos pelo positivismo. E nenhuma epistemologia razoável pode estar baseada somente sobre a percepção dos sentidos. A insistência do positivismo de que todo o conhecimento nos chega através dos cinco sentidos físicos deixa de lado grandes dimensões da existência, como a doutrina de Deus, a doutrina da alma, os valores morais e espirituais, que transcendem a este mundo material, etc. Não obstante, o positivismo serviu de norma à ciência, facilitando o desenvolvimento de seu método, mesmo que não tenha ajudado quanto a outras áreas das atividades humanas.

Escritos: Course on the Positive Philosophy, em 6 volumes; *System of Positive Polity*, 4 volumes; *Catechism of Positivism; The Subjective Synthesis*. (AM F P)

COMUM

No hebraico, **chol**, palavra que ocorre por seis vezes. Por exemplo, I Sam. 21:4,5. No grego, *koinós*, «comum». Essa palavra ocorre por treze vezes: Mar. 7:2,5; Atos 2:44; 4:32; 10:14,28; 11:8; Rom. 14:14; Tito 1:4; Heb. 10:29; Jud. 3 e Apo. 21:27.

Essas palavras indicam aquilo que é comum, no sentido de que *pertence a todos*, e, por extensão, aquilo que é *profano* e *vil*. Em Atos 10:14,28 e 11:8 encontramos uma boa ilustração neotestamentária. Pedro viu o lençol descendo com todas as espécies de quadrúpedes e répteis, proibidos como alimentos humanos nas leis levíticas. Diante da ordem de matar e comer, ele exprimiu repulsa, porque, durante toda a sua vida, havia-se mantido longe de tal contaminação. A narrativa é uma metáfora concernente à aceitação dos gentios na família da fé; pois estes sempre foram considerados imundos, aos olhos dos judeus. Às traduções refletem corretamente a forte ênfase judaica sobre a pureza ou sobre a impureza cerimoniais. Em Marcos 7:2 temos a tradução «impuras»; em Romanos 14:14, por duas vezes; «impura». O verbo grego *koinoo* pode ter o sentido de *contaminar*, embora signifique, literalmente, «fazer comum». O outro uso do termo grego acha-se em Tito 1:4, dentro da expressão «a fé comum»; ou em Judas 3, «nossa comum salvação». Quanto a detalhes completos sobre essa questão, juntamente com descrições sobre a legislação veterotestamentária, do assunto, ver o artigo sobre *Puro e Impuro*.

COMUNHÃO

Esboço:
1. Definição
2. Comunhão Prática
3. Tipos Específicos de Comunhão
4. Koinonía

1. Definição

A comunhão consiste em um acordo em que diversas pessoas unem-se e chegam a participar juntas de uma determinada coisa (II Cor. 6:14 e I João 1:3). A união de propósitos e interesses em torno da Ceia do Senhor é um exemplo disso; e, por essa razão, a Eucaristia (que vide) é também chamada de *comunhão*. Também há a *comunhão geral dos santos*, acerca da qual há um artigo separado nesta enciclopédia. O termo grego *koinonía* envolve as idéias de participação, comunhão, companheirismo e *contribuição*, pois essa é uma maneira de compartilharmos com outras pessoas de nossas posses materiais.

No grego, a idéia é expressa por um verbo e um substantivo, a saber:

1. *Omiléo*, «comungar com». Esse verbo aparece em Luc. 24:14,15; Atos 20:11 e 24:26.
2. *koinonía*, «comunhão». Esse substantivo ocorre por dezoito vezes: Atos 2:42; Rom. 15:26; I Cor. 1:9; 10:16; II Cor. 6:14; 8:4; 9:13; 13:13; Gál. 2:9; Fil. 1:5; 2:1; 3:10; File. 6; Heb. 13:16; I João 1:3,6,7.

Elementos Importantes da Comunhão:

a. A comunhão começa com o Pai e com o Filho, e amplia-se para os filhos de Deus (João 17:3,6,10,11, 14).

b. Quando da restauração, haverá a comunhão universal (Efé. 1:10,23).

c. Ela nos é conferida, com base na oração feita por Cristo (João 17:20,21).

d. A nossa comunhão é com Deus (I João 1:3).

e. Também é com os santos no céu (Heb. 12:22-24).

f. Também com os outros crentes (Gál. 2:9).

g. É desfrutada em torno de Cristo (Mat. 18:20).

h. Em torno da ordenança da Ceia do Senhor (I Cor. 10:17).

i. Mediante a oração (II Cor. 1:11; Efé. 6:18).

j. Mediante as exortações cristãs (Col. 3:16).

l. Foi ordenada (Efé. 4:1-3).

m. Não devemos manter comunhão com os ímpios (II Cor. 6:14-17).

n. A reconciliação deve preceder a nossa comunhão com Deus (Amós 3:3).

o. A comunhão com Deus é prometida aos obedientes (João 14:23).

p. Exemplos bíblicos de comunhão: Jônatas (I Sam. 23:16); Davi (Sal. 119:63); Daniel (Dan. 2:17,18); os apóstolos (Atos 1:14); a Igreja primitiva (Atos 2:42); Paulo (Atos 20:36-38).

2. Comunhão Prática

O homem é um ser comunitário. Somente alguns poucos indivíduos apreciam a solidão, preferindo viver sem a ajuda, o consolo e a amizade de outras pessoas. Até mesmo os indivíduos mais introvertidos precisam de algumas pessoas. Por essa razão temos a unidade básica, a *família*. E esta oferece uma forma muito básica de comunhão, sem a qual a raça humana dificilmente teria sobrevivido. Além disso, há o clã, e também a tribo. Segue-se a aldeia, o estado, e, finalmente, a nação. Tudo isso apresenta formas de comunhão. No seio de um povo, surgem organizações de toda a espécie, algumas das quais poderíamos classificar de comunhões. Trata-se das organizações que se expressam de forma cooperativa. As organizações religiosas destacam-se acima de todas, como comunhões. Uma igreja, uma associação religiosa ou uma denominação evangélica são tipos de comunhão. É precisamente nisso que se encontra um dos grandes poderes das igrejas e denominações: elas atraem pessoas para a atmosfera reconfortante de uma comunhão, pela qual anela o espírito humano.

3. Tipos Específicos de Comunhão

a. **Comunhão festiva**. Até onde a história nos faz retroceder, encontramos pessoas reunindo-se para comer. É agradável participarmos de uma boa refeição; e é ainda mais agradável compartilhá-la com amigos e entes queridos, o que provê oportunidade para discutirmos idéias, compartilharmos de ideais e sonhos, divertir-nos, ou simplesmente, estarmos juntos com eles, desfrutando de sua companhia. Na minha própria família, isso sempre foi importante, e a hora do almoço sempre foi uma oportunidade para trocarmos idéias, sobre os mais

COMUNHÃO — COMUNHÃO ANGLICANA

variados assuntos. É provável que eu tenha participado de mais ensino religioso e de debate filosófico, à hora do almoço, com os membros de minha família, do que na hora do culto, na igreja. Sinto que isso tem redundado em bem para a minha família. No mínimo, muita informação foi trocada entre nós, e o desenvolvimento do conhecimento é algo muito importante.

A história mostra-nos que as tribos primitivas reuniam-se para festejar, e que essas festividades usualmente estavam associadas a algum acontecimento importante, religioso ou secular, relacionado à vida da tribo. Também havia a comunhão das famílias. Abraão, em consonância com os bons costumes sociais de sua época, convidou os três estranhos a comerem em sua companhia; e, sem saber, recebeu seres celestes como hóspedes (Gên. 18:1-8; Heb. 13:2). O Novo Testamento afirma que a hospitalidade é um dos requisitos necessários aos bons pastores ou diáconos da igreja (Tito 1:8).

A *páscoa* (que vide) era uma forma ímpar de comunhão. Tornou-se uma instituição nacional em Israel (Êxo. 23:15), a comemoração do livramento do povo de Israel da servidão sofrida-no Egito, bem como da escravidão ao pecado. A Ceia do Senhor é um equivalente cristão (I Cor. 5:7). Sabe-se que os essênios, em Qumran, tinham refeições rituais que envolviam a participação de toda a comunidade. Eles também contavam com grupos menores, de dez homens, que se reuniam em companhia de um sacerdote, o qual fazia uma oração de agradecimento, enquanto um dos membros da comunidade lia uma passagem da lei. O *agapé* dos cristãos primitivos era uma ocasião de comunhão especial. Tinha lugar em conexão com a Ceia do Senhor, mas era uma comemoração que envolvia uma refeição e o lava-pés. Entraram abusos, conforme se vê mediante I Coríntios 11:20-22 e Judas 12. Finalmente, devido a esses abusos, a refeição foi descontinuada, mas a participação nos elementos do pão e do vinho continuou.

b. *Comunhão fiscal.* — Algumas vezes, o motivo para se efetuar uma refeição comunal era a falta de fundos. Desse modo, os participantes contribuíam com algo, e preparavam refeições em comum. Compreendemos, por meio da história, que a pobreza material foi um dos principais fatores na prática das refeições comunais entre os essênios de Qumran. O livro de Atos mostra-nos que a Igreja primitiva praticou isso por razões financeiras, ao menos temporariamente (Atos 2). Os fundos comunais, recolhidos em Jerusalém, eram espontâneos e voluntários, tendo atendido a uma necessidade específica, por algum tempo.

c. *A comunhão de contribuição.* O vocábulo grego *koinonía* pode significar «contribuição». Ver Romanos 15:26, onde esse termo refere-se à contribuição das igrejas gentílicas para os crentes pobres de Jerusalém. Um bom membro da comunidade cristã compartilhava de sua abundância material com aqueles que possuíam menos; e isso era um tipo de comunhão.

d. *A Ceia do Senhor.* Para muitos cristãos, os termos «comunhão» e «Ceia do Senhor» são sinônimos. A Ceia do Senhor foi originalmente instituída por ocasião da celebração da páscoa, quando Jesus tornou-se a nossa páscoa (I Cor. 5:7). O pão e o vinho tornaram-se símbolos de seu corpo e de seu sangue. Misticamente falando, é através da comunhão com seu corpo e com seu sangue que temos a redenção. Jesus tornou-se o Pão da Vida. Ver o artigo sobre *Jesus, o Pão da Vida*, que apresenta completos detalhes sobre essa doutrina. Ver as passagens do Novo Testamento sobre a Ceia do Senhor, em Mat. 26:26-28; Mar. 14:22-24; Luc. 22:14-19; I Cor. 11:23-26. Ver também o artigo sobre a *Eucaristia*. O cálice da bênção que abençoamos, porventura não é a comunhão em torno do sangue de Cristo? E o pão que partimos, porventura não é a comunhão em torno do corpo de Cristo? Visto que há somente um pão, nós, que somos muitos, formamos um único corpo, porquanto todos participamos do pão único, que Cristo (I Cor. 10:16 ss).

e. *A comunhão da congregação.* As igrejas locais dispõem de certa variedade de meios para fomentar a comunhão entre os seus membros. Há a Ceia do Senhor, há as reuniões para a prédica da Palavra, para oração, para louvor e para recolhimento de dízimos e ofertas. A Igreja une todas as classes sociais, e declara que elas são *uma só* (Gál. 3:28). Cada membro da Igreja de Cristo faz parte do corpo místico, como um de seus membros (Rom. 12:4,5). Cada membro é como um pedra que faz parte da superestrutura do edifício que foi fundado e está sendo edificado por Cristo (I Ped. 2:5). Escreveu o salmista: «Companheiro sou de todos os que te temem, e dos que guardam os teus preceitos» (Sal. 119:63). Paulo adverte-nos que a comunhão inerente na Igreja — pode ser debilitada se permitirmos associações prejudiciais, que intervenham com o nosso companheirismo (II Cor. 6:14 ss).

f. *A comunhão espiritual.* Há uma comunhão com Deus, por meio do Espírito. O espírito humano é capaz de ter comunhão com o Espírito Santo. Paulo, por mais de cento e sessenta vezes, falou em estarmos «em Cristo», retratando, com essas duas palavras, a nossa comunhão mística. Ver I Cor. 1:4. As notas expositivas, no NTI, sobre aquele versículo, detalham essa doutrina. A comunhão não tem apenas a dimensão humana, do homem com homem; também tem a dimensão divina, do homem com Deus. O trecho de Efésios 4:1-6, e vários trechos paralelos, dão-nos esse ensino. Diz I João 1:3: «...a nossa comunhão é com o Pai e com seu Filho, Jesus Cristo». O Espírito Santo reside em nós e nos confere comunhão divina (João 14:16 ss). Cristo é a vinha, e nós somos os ramos, pelo que devemos pensar em uma comunhão orgânica (João 15). Há a comunhão do Espírito (Fil. 2:1 ss). «A graça do Senhor Jesus Cristo, e o amor de Deus, e a comunhão do Espírito Santo sejam com todos vós» (II Cor. 13:13).

4. Koinonia

A comunhão indica «partilhar» de alguma coisa (II Cor. 8:23; Rom. 11:7; Fil. 1:7; I Ped. 5:1). Também indica participar com algo (II Cor. 9:13; Fil. 1:5; Rom. 15:26; Atos 2:44; 4:32). Também indica partilhar (Atos 2:42; Gál. 2:9; I João 1:3 ss). (DAV GEO NTI Z)

COMUNHÃO, ABERTA OU FECHADA

Ver o artigo sobre a **Comunhão Fechada**.

COMUNHÃO ANGLICANA

Nome dado, desde o século XIX, ao grupo de igrejas autônomas, reformadas, de governo episcopal, em comunhão com a fé de Canterbury e reconhecendo seu primado. O grupo inclui algumas poucas dioceses missionárias. Base da fé delas: A Bíblia e o credo Niceno. Seus bispos afirmam estar na sucessão apostólica, derivada do episcopado inglês do século

XVI. Tem havido um esforço consciente para combinar o que se aceita como o melhor dentro das tradições católica e protestante, paralelamente à tolerância de larga gama de crenças. A organização se compõe de mais de 340 dioceses, agrupadas em dezoito igrejas nacionais ou províncias regionais.

História da formação. O cristianismo romano-britânico, que data do século II D.C., espalhou-se pelo País de Gales, Irlanda, Escócia, Inglaterra, embora não com grande vitalidade. A conversão da Inglaterra começou com a missão de Agostinho a Canterbury, em 597. Vários grupos de igrejas unificaram-se sob a liderança do arcebispo Teodoro de Tarso (668-690). Após o ano 1000, as duas províncias de Canterbury e York funcionavam como parte da Igreja ocidental, mas havia lutas de poder entre o papa, o rei e oficiais locais. A Carta Magna de 1215 estipulava a liberdade da Igreja da Inglaterra. O rei tinha autoridade para nomear oficiais eclesiásticos, usualmente dentro de uma lista apresentada pelo papa.

A política e a vida pessoal de Henrique VIII forçaram o repúdio da autoridade papal, e começou o cisma (1531 em diante). Sob Eduardo VI (1547-1553) houve um rápido movimento em prol do protestantismo, com uma breve contra-reforma sob a rainha Maria (1553-1558). Isabel rejeitou ambos os extremos da controvérsia católico-protestante, e isso assinalou a natureza da comunidade anglicana nos séculos seguintes. A denominação mantém o governo episcopal e a adoração litúrgica. O puritanismo e o metodismo exerceram vasta influência, como também os evangélicos, após 1760, e os anglo-católicos após 1833.

Tradição literária e teológica do anglicanismo: Ela se declara nem católica e nem protestante, embora alguns grupos dentro da comunidade possam ser classificados como uma ou outra coisa. Há uma longa tradição de erudição anglicana, que tem provido a maioria das obras de referência de peso na Inglaterra, e por meio da Inglaterra, para outros idiomas. As contribuições e os contribuidores dessa tradição são por demais numerosos para serem alistados. Grande respeito se dá aos pais da Igreja como intérpretes da Bíblia, e os pais gregos têm exercido forte influência sobre o pensamento anglicano que diz respeito ao destino humano final. O anglicanismo usualmente vê oportunidade de salvação para além da morte biológica, que era a posição comum dos pais gregos. Muitos representantes da Igreja oriental (ortodoxa, eslava, etc.) também têm mantido essa posição otimista sobre aquilo que a missão de Cristo tenciona realizar. Talvez a maior lição a ser aprendida dos anglicanos seja a disposição deles em evitar extremos, não hesitando em fazer empréstimos e combinar tradições na busca por um mais profundo conhecimento. Ver também sobre *Anglo-catolicismo* e *Episcopalismo*.

COMUNHÃO DO ALTAR

Termo usado pelos luteranos para aludir à participação na eucaristia, a fim de indicar a unidade da fé. «Comunhão mista do altar» alude à comunhão aberta. «Comunhão singela do altar» alude à comunhão fechada. Ver o artigo sobre *Comunhão, aberta e fechada*. (E)

COMUNHÃO DOS SANTOS

A expressão específica, **communio sanctorum**, aparentemente apareceu, pela primeira vez, em um sermão de Nicetas de Remesiana, que faleceu em cerca de 414 D.C. Tal expressão não se encontra nas páginas do Novo Testamento, embora a idéia certamente esteja ali. Ver Col. 1:12 e I João 1:3 *ss*. A comunhão dos santos está baseada e envolvida na comunhão com Deus. O trecho de II Coríntios 13:13 mostra que a comunhão é no Espírito.

A **sanctorum communionem** tornou-se a segunda cláusula do nono artigo do Credo Apostólico; e essa pode ser traçada ao uso mencionado acima, feito por Nicetas. Seu próprio uso foi uma expansão da cláusula anterior, a *santa igreja católica*, dando a entender aquela comunhão que existe entre os membros dessa igreja. A Reforma Protestante enfatizou a comunhão dos crentes, dentro da Igreja na terra. Os teólogos católicos romanos, com razão, têm enfatizado a comunhão dos santos como algo que envolve TODOS os santos de todos os lugares, sobre a terra, no céu e até mesmo no purgatório. Naturalmente, quanto aos supostos santos no purgatório, não concordamos. Não obstante, alguns pensem que nisso há um certo fundo de verdade, pois alguns eleitos já passaram pela morte biológica, mas ainda não foram chamados à companhia dos crentes, embora finalmente o façam, porquanto a missão de Cristo envolve até mesmo os que se encontram no hades, sempre sob a condição de arrependimento e fé (ver I Ped. 3:18-4:6). Portanto, até mesmo aqueles crentes em potencial fazem parte da comunhão universal dos santos. Esse conceito pode ser novamente ampliado, incluindo a comunhão com todos os seres espirituais, como os anjos, que não pertencem à espécie humana, pois Deus é o Pai de muitas *famílias*, segundo se aprende em Efésios 3:15. Na Idade Média, essa expressão era usada para designar aquela comunhão criada pela comum participação nos sacramentos, tendo sido assim empregada por Tomás de Aquino, por Abelardo e pelo concílio de Nimes. Karl Barth combinou essa idéia com a do companheirismo geral dos crentes, formando um único corpo místico.

O conceito justifica, para muitos teólogos, a doutrina da *mediação* das orações dos crentes por almas humanas glorificadas. (B C E)

COMUNHÃO FECHADA

Expressão usada para descrever a prática de admitir à mesa da Ceia do Senhor somente aqueles que fazem parte do rol de membros da igreja local que celebra o rito. Essa é a prática da Igreja Católica Romana, bem como de vários grupos não-católicos, como alguns grupos batistas e dos Irmãos. Usualmente, a prática envolve três princípios, a saber: *Primeiro*, somente os membros (de acordo com a definição denominacional) da igreja fazem parte do corpo de Cristo, e assim têm o *direito* de participar da comunhão, pois os demais não seriam membros da verdadeira Igreja. *Segundo*, quando a arrogância denominacional não é uma consideração, então a comunhão fechada é usada como uma medida disciplinar. Aqueles que não fazem parte da igreja local podem ser bons crentes, mas suas vidas não são conhecidas por parte daquela igreja local, pelo que a mesma não se deve arriscar. Além disso, a menos que alguém seja membro da igreja local, haverá alguma dúvida acerca dessa pessoa, pelo que seria mais aconselhável excluí-la do rito. *Terceiro*, é uma atitude altruísta, e não apenas uma medida preservadora da pureza da cerimônia que está em pauta. O trecho de I Coríntios 11:29 profere uma severa advertência contra aqueles que participam indignamente da Ceia do Senhor. Portanto, estranhos à igreja local, se chegarem a participar do rito, poderiam adoecer, ou mesmo morrer; e a igreja local não quer arriscar-se, juntando uma atitude exclusivista e disciplinadora à observância da Ceia do Senhor. Esses grupos argumentam que a primeira Ceia do Senhor, que envolveu Jesus e os seus apóstolos, certamente foi fechada. Contrariamente a isso, aqueles que não são praticantes da comunhão fechada dizem que a Ceia é *do Senhor*, e não da Igreja, pelo que a Igreja não teria o direito de torná-la uma cerimônia exclusivista, permitindo a participação de todos os regenerados, sem importar a quais igrejas locais pertençam. Esses opinam que a Ceia do Senhor deveria ser franqueada a todos quantos estão *instruídos* quanto à santidade da cerimônia, em cujo caso cada pessoa, de acordo com a sua própria consciência, deveria decidir se participará ou não do rito.

COMUNHÃO SANTA
Ver o artigo sobre a **Eucaristia**.

COMUNICAÇÃO INDIRETA
Trata-se de um processo que, gradualmente, vai eliminando as alternativas que envolvem uma questão qualquer, até que resta somente uma solução possível. A solução restante exprime a verdade daquela questão. Ver o artigo sobre *Kierkegaard*, quarto ponto, onde há uma ilustração a respeito. Mas, uma comunicação por meio de símbolos ou de impulsos intuitivos, e não através de conceitos expressos, também é chamada de comunicação indireta. Ver o artigo sobre *Jaspers*, quinto ponto. Desse modo podemos aprender sobre o Ser e a transcendência, embora estejam acima de nosso conhecimento conceptual.

COMUNIDADE
Essa palavra indica o povo de um estado, o próprio estado, ou um grupo de pessoas unidas em torno de algum interesse comum. O termo é usado para designar dois períodos distintos da história de Israel, quando essa nação tinha uma organização governamental independente, dotada de autoridade. O primeiro desses períodos foi o dos reis, de Saul a Jeoaquim (1075-597). O segundo foi o do governo sob Zorobabel, após o cativeiro babilônico, e daí até à queda de Jerusalém, de 537 A.C. até 70 D.C.

No Novo Testamento, encontramos a palavra grega *politeía*, que pode ter esse significado, conforme se vê em Efé. 2:12 ém nossa Bíblia portuguesa. Ali a comunidade de Israel é aludida, dando a entender Israel como o depósito e a fonte originadora das bênçãos e dos privilégios espirituais. Os gentios estavam alienados dessas bênçãos e privilégios, até que Cristo possibilitou que se tornassem em uma comunidade espiritual. O trecho de Filipenses 3:20, no original grego, traz a palavra *políteuma*, um *hapax legomenon* (palavra usada somente por uma vez em um documento, nesse caso, o Novo Testamento), que significa «comunidade», pois é apenas um sinônimo de *politeía*. Essa referência bíblica alude à comunidade celeste, à qual pertencemos espiritualmente. O trecho aponta para o aspecto comunal e coletivo das operações do evangelho, porquanto a redenção nunca aparece como uma questão meramente individual. Devemos pensar na redenção do corpo inteiro dos crentes, que se tornam cidadãos da pátria celestial; e também haverá a restauração final de todas as coisas, conforme se aprende em Efésios 1:10. Neste mundo, a Igreja de Cristo funciona como uma espécie de comunidade espiritual, entre as nações.

••• ••• •••

COMUNIDADE
Ver o artigo sobre a **Civilização**.

COMUNIDADE DE BENS
Vários tipos dessa prática são encontrados nas páginas do NT. O principal episódio foi o da experiência de comunhão de bens de Jerusalém, em bases voluntárias. Ver o artigo geral sobre *Comunismo*, ponto sexto: *O Comunismo e a Igreja*. a. A experiência de Jerusalém; e b. Estabelecimentos religiosos comunistas. Ali são descritas as tentativas, feitas através da história da Igreja, de pôr em prática essa teoria social e política. Ver os trechos de Atos 2:42-46 e 5:32-6:4. A partilha informal, naturalmente alicerçada sobre o amor de um crente por outro, é o padrão das virtudes cristãs; mas isso não precisa transformar-se em uma partilha formal e obrigatória de bens. Ver o artigo sobre o *Amor Cristão*. Tiago salientou enfaticamente esse princípio básico. Não basta que sejamos ouvintes da palavra de Deus (Tia. 1:22). A religião pura inclui a ajuda prestada aos necessitados (Tia. 1:27). Há aquela *lei real* que consiste no amor ao próximo. Não basta desejarmos uma bênção para os que padecem necessidades. O amor existe quando há uma aplicação prática, quando provemos para as necessidades básicas dos que sofrem (Tia. 2:16). Esse princípio sempre foi valorizado no judaísmo, e foi emprestado, intacto, pelo Novo Testamento. O Manual da seita do mar Morto mostra-nos que eles praticavam total comunhão de bens, banindo os fraudulentos. Filo louvou os essênios por causa da *koinonía* deles, o que incluía a comunhão de casas, vestes, alimentos e salários (Q. O. P. L., partes 84 e 91). Josefo informa-nos que vários grupos, em muitas cidades, estiveram envolvidos nessa prática.

Jesus alimentou a multidão, valendo-se de uma bolsa comum (João 12:6). E os seus discípulos também viviam com base em fundos comuns, aceitando doações de várias pessoas, que os sustentavam (Luc. 8:3). Na Igreja primitiva de Jerusalém, a fim de manter a *koinonía* descrita no segundo capítulo de Atos, muitos vendiam as suas possessões (Atos 4:36,57 e 5:1). Vários foram os fatores envolvidos nessa prática: 1. Os cristãos estavam enfrentando uma crise, provocada pela perseguição e pela fome. 2. Eles estavam esperando uma *parousia* imediata (que vide), porquanto não antecipavam a longa era da graça em que vivemos, entre a primeira e a segunda vindas de Cristo. 3. Eles foram inspirados pela lei do amor, ao ponto em que suas possessões materiais pessoais não eram consideradas importantes. A *koinonía* não demorou a dar lugar à *diakonía* organizada (Atos 6:1,2), ou seja, a ajuda da Igreja inteira aos pobres, provavelmente através de um fundo comum, controlado pelos apóstolos, sem a necessidade das pessoas disporem de tudo quanto possuíam. Isso fez a Igreja cristã retornar à prática judaica tradicional. No caso das igrejas gentílicas, Paulo exortava os seus convertidos a porem em prática o sistema da *diakonía*. Paulo também encorajava as igrejas gentílicas a ajudarem os crentes pobres de Jerusalém; e, dentre elas, recolheu uma oferta com essa finalidade (Rom. 15:25). Deveríamos notar que mesmo em meio à experiência de Jerusalém, foi mantido o princípio da propriedade privada (Atos 5:4). Paulo ensinava que os crentes individuais são os *mordomos* responsáveis por aquilo que possuem; e, em lugar algum, encorajou as igrejas gentílicas a emularem a experiência de Jerusalém. Ver I Cor. 4:1,2. O princípio de propriedade privada

COMUNIDADE — COMUNISMO

também era um princípio posto em prática no judaísmo. O judaísmo ensinava a santidade do indivíduo e de suas propriedades (Êxo. 20:15; 21:26—22:13). O ideal profético é que todos terão sua própria vinha e sua própria figueira, para suprimento de suas necessidades básicas, segundo se aprende em Zacarias 3:10. (B Z)

COMUNIDADE DE INQUIRIÇÃO

Charles Sanders Peirce (que vide) reconheceu a natureza incompleta de toda a nossa inquirição, e também a interdependência de todos os meios de que dispomos na busca do conhecimento. Contudo, ele sentia que não devemos desistir dos valores absolutos atinentes à verdade, à beleza, à bondade, etc., pois a inquirição é autocorretiva. Sem importar quão tola seja a nossa maneira de pensar no momento, podem ser encontrados meios de detectarmos os absurdos nos quais nos envolvemos. Ele acreditava que o homem, finalmente, está destinado a conhecer a verdade. Os princípios gerais da inquirição podem ser vistos nas disciplinas da lógica, da ética e da estética, segundo ele. A estética deve fazer-se presente no *ideal* da vida; a lógica deve prover-nos as *regras* racionais da inquirição. E essas duas disciplinas, consideradas juntamente, conferem-nos o *ideal racional* da conduta, ao que chamamos de *ética*. Isso posto, seria através dessa ilimitada comunidade de inquirição que os homens podem chegar à verdade. A experiência da humanidade é vasta, e deve obter resultados. A verdade, pois, não é apenas uma questão individual. Também é um empreendimento comunal.

Um aspecto dessa busca seria o *agapismo*, aquela tendência objetiva para o estabelecimento de relações humanas apropriadas na sociedade, alicerçadas sobre a lei do amor, que é fundamental. O indivíduo que busca a verdade e o ideal, através de um ou de um limitado número de meios, está condenado a obter uma forma distorcida da verdade. Mas os homens, coletivamente falando, atingirão tanto a verdade quanto o amor. Naturalmente, nesse conceito há uma grande verdade, porquanto as próprias Escrituras Sagradas ensinam que a *redenção* (que vide) é algo comunal, sendo da vontade de Deus a restauração de toda a humanidade, e não apenas de indivíduos isolados (Efé. 1:10). Deus amou o *mundo*, e o *Logos* implanta as suas sementes do conhecimento por toda a parte. Portanto, de várias maneiras, a comunidade está envolvida na inquirição pela verdade, embora de muitos pontos de vista diferentes. (P)

COMUNIDADE DE INTERPRETAÇÃO

Josiah Royce (que vide), empregou e ampliou o conceito de *comunidade de inquirição* (que vide), de Charles Sanders Peirce. Em seu livro, *The Problem of Christianity*, ele encara o mundo como uma única *comunidade de interpretação*. Todas as instituições existentes no mundo, incluindo seus objetos materiais, estariam relacionados uns aos outros de maneiras significativas. Essa comunidade teria qualidades espirituais como a esperança, a fé e o amor; e, coletivamente, teria a memória. Haveria uma graça remidora, operando através da comunidade. A nossa tarefa consistiria em trabalhar com e em favor dessa comunidade. Deus seria o grande Espírito dessa comunidade, bem como a própria essência da lealdade. Portanto, a comunidade requer a nossa lealdade. Cada segmento da comunidade interpenetra os demais segmentos sociais. Se todos esses segmentos forem considerados em seu conjunto, chegaremos a uma interpretação do conhecimento e da verdade que é muito superior àquilo que pode ser obtido por algum

indivíduo ou grupo isolado. Os indivíduos são apenas interpretações fragmentares, e as organizações isoladas não são muito melhores do que isso. A súmula só aparece quando somamos todas as porções constitutivas. O infinito é uma entidade auto-interpretativa; mas os seus fragmentos são pesados na balança e são achados em falta. Esses princípios, naturalmente, correspondem à verdade. Podemos perceber como, no cristianismo, as várias denominações cristãs, em sua arrogância, apresentam-se como melhores, se não mesmo exclusivamente corretas. As seitas religiosas quase sempre surgem devido à arrogância e ao senso da auto-importância. Todas as formas de mitos religiosos são inventadas na tentativa de consubstanciar a superioridade de cada grupo, em contraste com os demais. Porém, chegamos mais perto da verdade quando levamos em conta a comunidade cristã inteira, e não apenas uma parte da mesma. Não deveríamos considerar apenas o testemunho de cada denominação cristã isolada, mas também o testemunho das religiões não-cristãs, em nossa busca pela verdade. É verdade que Deus se revela em Cristo, através das Sagradas Escrituras, mas, às vezes, as jóias mais preciosas podem ser descobertas em lugares os mais inesperados. Os pais gregos da Igreja pensavam que o *Logos* implanta suas sementes por toda a parte; e isso expressa um conceito verdadeiro.

COMUNIDADE ILIMITADA

Ver **Peirce, Charles S.** pontos 13 e 14.

COMUNISMO

Esboço:
1. Definição
2. Origens
3. Platão
4. Incidentes Históricos
5. Marx e Engels
6. O Comunismo e a Igreja
7. O Comunismo e a Ética
8. O Comunismo e os Mártires
9. Os Serviços do Comunismo
10. O Comunismo e a Tradição Profética

Quanto aos avanços do comunismo na Igreja cristã moderna, ver o artigo sobre a *Teologia da Libertação*.

1. Definição.

Essa palavra vem do latim, **communis**, que significa «comum», «universal», «público». Quanto ao uso, o termo designa uma espécie de estrutura social ou estado político, onde todas as coisas são desfrutadas em comum, incluindo os meios de produção e os seus resultados. Os sistemas comunistas usualmente requerem a abolição da propriedade privada, bem como o controle da comunidade sobre todas as fontes de riqueza e sobre as questões econômicas.

2. Origens

A doutrina política comunista supõe que, no começo, a humanidade vivia sob condições similares às do comunismo, e que esse é o alvo da existência da humanidade. Porém, não há quaisquer evidências históricas quanto a isso, e como todos os sistemas, o comunismo tem os seus mitos. Historicamente, dispomos da declaração de Aristóteles, no sentido de que os filósofos pré-socráticos Faléias de Calcedônia e Hipódamo de Mileto, tinham idéias comunistas.

3. Platão

A primeira discussão sistemática de certa modalidade de comunismo aparece no diálogo *República*, de Platão. Ele dividia o estado em diversas classes sociais

COMUNISMO

ou categorias, cada qual com seus próprios deveres e privilégios. Havia os *produtores*: agricultores, artesãos, negociantes, produtores de bens de consumo, que são pintados como a classe mais baixa, correspondendo aos apetites inferiores do indivíduo. Havia os *protetores:* soldados e policiais, que encarregavam-se da proteção da sociedade, correspondendo à vontade, ao elemento dotado de espírito do indivíduo. E havia os *governantes*, os quais deveriam ser *filósofos* longamente treinados, que correspondem ao espírito imortal do indivíduo. Esses governantes deveriam preparar-se, mediante muitos anos de treinamento, em várias esferas de conhecimento, incluindo a política. Também deveriam ser submetidos a muitos testes. Deveriam ser não somente os mais sábios dentre os homens, mas também os mais morais e espirituais. Platão considerava o ateísmo uma ofensa contra o estado, dizendo que os ateus deveriam ser punidos. Os filósofos, que, na linguagem de Platão deveriam ser não somente os sábios, mas também os indivíduos da mais alta moralidade e espiritualidade, deveriam ser os dirigentes, formadores de uma espécie de elite social. Era entre esses, segundo Platão pensava, que o comunismo funcionaria, havendo comunidade de bens e até de esposas entre eles. Ele pensava que tal sistema não funcionaria entre as classes inferiores, cujo egoísmo sempre se mostra uma força muito poderosa. Aristóteles, entretanto, objetava ao ponto de vista social de Platão, com base no fato de que o mesmo debilita a família, a unidade fundamental do estado, com o conseqüente debilitamento do próprio estado. Dentro do diálogo de Platão, *Leis*, esse filósofo modifica o seu ponto de vista, promovendo um tanto mais o ideal democrático, mediante o senso de liberdade, cuja força impulsionadora deriva-se da fibra moral.

4. Incidentes Históricos

Antes do surgimento do comunismo na Rússia, houve várias figuras que, em diversos países, promoveram essa doutrina política. Foi advogada por François Babeuf (1760-1797), durante a Revolução Francesa. Por isso, por algum tempo essa doutrina política foi conhecida por *babouvismo*. Antes mesmo dele, foi expressa por Sir Thomas More, em sua *Utopia*, na primeira metade do século XVI. Isso tornou-se a base de uma teoria política idealista e pacífica, na obra de Étienne Cabet, *Voyage en Icarie*, 1840. Porém, as idéias de um comunismo *revolucionário* podem ser traçadas a partir da Revolução Francesa, conforme dissemos acima. Foram as crenças políticas de Babeuf, de que essa revolução seria seguida ainda por uma outra, que emanciparia o proletariado, que deram forças a essa doutrina. Tal noção foi propagada por Luis Auguste Blanqui, entre 1836 e 1849, em sociedades secretas em Paris, e foi então que o termo COMUNISMO foi cunhado. Os operários foram exortados a se rebelarem, estabelecendo uma ditadura com a finalidade de reorganizar a França segundo moldes comunistas.

5. Marx e Engels

A fundação teórica do comunismo moderno foi lançada pelos alemães Karl Marx (que vide) e Friedrich Engels, em seu *Manifesto Comunista*, de 1848. Eles aproveitaram as idéias que já haviam sido expostas e misturaram-nas com a noção hegeliana da tese, antítese e síntese, mediante o que predisseram que o processo histórico finalmente produziria um estado comunista mundial. O processo seria como segue: O estado original da antiga utopia comunista cederia lugar à escravidão segundo a qual alguns homens tornavam-se propriedade de outros. O feudalismo medieval modificaria e melhoraria um pouco a situação. O próximo passo evolutivo foi quando o capitalismo modificou o feudalismo. Então o socialismo modificou o capitalismo. Finalmente, o comunismo supostamente veio a substituir tanto o socialismo como o capitalismo, como a síntese final. De acordo com a teoria de Marx, esse processo dialético é determinado mormente por fatores econômicos, o que significa que temos um materialismo determinista e dialético. O capitalismo funciona com base na exploração dos trabalhadores, de tal modo que o proprietário se enriquece à custa do trabalho dos operários. Essa contradição moral, segundo o comunismo, condena o sistema, porquanto resulta na miséria do trabalhador. O que não foi antecipado foi que o mesmo operário está condenado a *permanecer* em sua miséria pela ausência de competição, inerente ao comunismo, o que rebaixa as taxas tanto de produção quanto de qualidade. Um outro fator que não foi considerado é o espiritual. Enquanto o homem continuar sendo o que é, se não experimentar a regeneração moral, sempre haverá de trabalhar e produzir melhor se puder fazê-lo impulsionado pelo *auto-interesse*, e não motivado por um vago ideal do bem-estar comum. Atualmente, o comunismo está reconhecendo a natureza egoísta geral do homem, injetando em sua sociedade o motivo impulsionador do lucro. Em outras palavras, estamos contemplando o espetáculo de um comunismo modificado pelo capitalismo! Isso foi algo que os teóricos originais do comunismo não haviam antecipado. Mas qualquer teólogo cristão poderia ter antecipado o fenômeno, com base no que se sabe sobre a natureza humana. Um outro ideal comunista diz que a ditadura formada para garantir a aplicação da idéia, haveria de ir-se dissolvendo, de tal modo que uma verdadeira ditadura do proletariado tomaria o seu lugar. Isso ainda não sucedeu em qualquer estado comunista. Aqueles que conservam as rédeas do poder, nos países comunistas, adiam indefinidamente a decisão, dizendo que as massas ainda não estão prontas para se autogovernarem. Em vez disso, as mais brutais ditaduras, que ignoram os direitos humanos, operam em nossos dias por causa do comunismo. Além disso, os políticos comunistas indagam se esse ideal final da ditadura do proletariado é mesmo desejável. A classe operária será capaz de dirigir o estado?

A questão da miséria. É uma miséria alguém ser pobre; e é mister admitir que a esmagadora maioria das classes trabalhadoras vive na pobreza. Porém, maior ainda é a miséria do indivíduo quando lhe falta a liberdade individual. E o pior estado de todos é o estado de pobreza espiritual. O comunismo tem promovido aberta e ativamente essa pior forma de miséria, reprimindo e perseguindo a Igreja e proibindo a liberdade religiosa.

6. O Comunismo e a Igreja

a. A Experiência de Jerusalém. O trecho de Atos 2:44 *ss*, mostra-nos que a igreja de Jerusalém passou por uma experiência de comunhão de bens, voluntária, por razões econômicas. A pobreza extrema dos cristãos judeus, devido à perseguição religiosa e a fome, forçaram esse estado de coisas. Porém, não há qualquer dogma, no Novo Testamento, no sentido de que a experiência deveria ser universal, compulsória e permanente. Antes, foi uma medida em momento de crise, e não a concretização de alguma teoria política. A maior parte dos comentadores da Bíblia pensa que essa experiência fracassou. A Bíblia também não diz isso; mas o fato é que as igrejas gentílicas, fora de Jerusalém, não

COMUNISMO

adotaram a prática. E, até mesmo entre os judeus cristãos de Jerusalém, a experiência era voluntária. Além disso, foi efetuada em meio à mais total liberdade religiosa, e, em segundo lugar, tinha por finalidade a inquirição pela espiritualidade. Por causa desses elementos, é impossível usarmos esse episódio como antecedente para um sistema ateu, que persegue à Igreja cristã. Alguns dos primeiros pais da Igreja pensaram que a experiência de Jerusalém poderia ser reiterada em outros lugares; e várias seitas hereges fizeram a tentativa. Mas, o grupo maior de cristãos pensou ser mais acertado não adotar a prática.

b. Estabelecimentos Religiosos Comunistas. A história revela um número bastante elevado de grupos, muitos deles com alguma espécie de profissão cristã, que experimentaram um estilo de governo comunista. A maior parte desses grupos tem salientado a comunhão de bens entre seus membros, tendo organizado comunidades segundo os ideais comunistas. Usualmente, porém, não têm feito qualquer modificação nos campos da família e da religião, permitindo que as relações sexuais sejam regulamentadas pelos valores bíblicos e tradicionais, e não tentando impor o ateísmo.

Os Maniqueus do Século III D.C. Eles consideravam que as possessões particulares eram uma corrupção, em si mesmas, pelo que desfrutavam de tudo em comum. Os *beneditinos*, do século VI D.C., foram a primeira ordem monástica a reintroduzir o comunismo no cristianismo ortodoxo. Os *anabatistas*, durante a Reforma Protestante alemã no século XVI, seguiam a vida comunitária. Os *jesuítas*, no Paraguai, entre 1602 e 1767, quando foram expulsos da Espanha, tinham uma forma de vida comunista em suas comunidades. Eles cultivavam «os campos comuns de Deus» e recebiam partilhas privadas de bens materiais, de acordo com suas necessidades. Nessas comunidades estavam envolvidos cerca de cem mil índios, distribuídos em cerca de trinta comunidades agrícolas.

Vários grupos cristãos, considerados hereges por alguns, como os *waldenses*, os *albigenses* e os *cátaros* (que vide), seguiram o ideal comunista. Também houve a seita *apostolicana* de Alanzo, na Itália e na França, os *beghards* da França e da Alemanha, os *lolardos* da Inglaterra, a *Sociedade Holandesa de Vida Comum*, os *taboritas* boêmios e os *irmãos morávios*.

Um bom número de comunidades dessa ordem chegou a existir nos Estados Unidos da América, como os *labadistas*, no estado de Maryland, cujo fundador foi um padre jesuíta. Essa colônia praticava um ascetismo extremado (que vide), quanto às questões sexuais, opunha-se à escravatura e ao uso do tabaco; mas, por questões de sobrevivência econômica, finalmente acabou aceitando ambas essas práticas. Um de seus líderes de época posterior tornou-se um capitalista, subordinando o bem comum aos seus interesses particulares, e faleceu como homem riquíssimo. A natureza humana nunca deixará de manifestar-se.

George Rapp, um pietista luterano, formou um grupo de separatistas, que chegou a contar com cerca de duzentas famílias. Foram perseguidos, de tal forma que Rapp e seu grupo mudaram-se para o solo norte-americano. A colônia estabeleceu-se em Butler County, no estado da Pennsylvania, e prosperou. O próprio Rapp continuou em sua séria inquirição religiosa. Porém, o movimento desintegrou-se na época de seus sucessores, tendo-se dissolvido totalmente em 1906. Os *amaritas* foram uma outra seita de vida comunal, um grupo de pietistas alemães que emigrou para os Estados Unidos da América. Eles organizaram-se como a Sociedade Ebenezer e se estabeleceram no estado de Nova Iorque. Alguns canadenses vieram juntar-se a eles. Levavam uma vida simples e austera, com muitas práticas ascéticas; mas, com o tempo, essas práticas foram abandonadas. Além disso, o movimento se foi secularizando. Em 1932, o grupo reorganizou-se como uma companhia de ações, cujos acionistas eram tanto os proprietários quanto os empregados. O movimento começou sendo semicapitalista, o qual existe até hoje. Outras comunidades formaram-se em Betel, no estado de Missouri, e em Aurora, no estado de Oregon, com imigrantes alemães. Em Bishop Hill, estado de Illinóis, formou-se uma colônia comunal luterana, com base em imigrantes escandinavos. Eles sofreram muitas dificuldades. Então, em cerca de 1848, muitos abandonaram o grupo, visto que o líder do grupo, na época, Eric Jansen, afirmava ser a reencarnação de Jesus Cristo. Finalmente, Jansen foi assassinado, e, quando ele não ressuscitou ao terceiro dia, conforme seus seguidores esperavam, muitos ficaram totalmente desiludidos. Contudo, o grupo arrastou-se até 1862. Houve também as comunidades dos *Shakers*, que tomaram o nome de Sociedade Unida dos Crentes na Segunda Vinda de Cristo. O fundador do grupo foi a mãe Ana Lee (1736-1784), que muitos aceitavam como uma reencarnação de Cristo. A seita originou-se entre alguns quacres ingleses. Seguindo visões da fundadora, a seita estabeleceu-se e floresceu no estado de Nova Iorque, e, finalmente, em outros estados norte-americanos. Eles obtiveram sucesso econômico, chegando a contar com seis mil membros, em 1840, exercendo até mesmo alguma influência na política norte-americana. No entanto, atualmente a seita praticamente desapareceu. As fraternidades das comunidades *huteritas* foram fundadas por Jacot Huter, um menonita do começo do século XVI (que vide). Eles emigraram da Alemanha e da Rússia e estabeleceram-se em South Dakota, nos Estados Unidos da América. Alguns deles entraram no Canadá, em 1917. A colônia ainda existe. mas o seu número tem sido grandemente reduzido. Eles se abstinham de toda a tentativa de lucro, de usura e de todas as atividades políticas, além de serem pacifistas.

O Comunismo Mórmon. Joseph Smith (que vide) dizia ter recebido uma visão que ordenava aos seus seguidores que consagrassem todas as suas propriedades para que fossem gerenciadas por ele; e então cada indivíduo tornar-se-ia um cooperador. Em resultado disso, formou-se a *Ordem Unida de Enoque*, tendo operado, no começo, no condado de Thompson, estado de Ohio, e no condado de Jackson, no estado de Missouri. Porém, a perseguição expulsou-os dali. Quando eles se estabeleceram no estado de Utah, várias comunidades tentaram praticar os princípios da Ordem Unida. Mas, simplesmente isso não funcionou bem em Utah; e, após uma experiência de dez anos, a idéia foi abandonada e as propriedades foram distribuídas entre os membros. O movimento nunca progrediu muito entre os mórmons, e, em nossos dias, esse grupo é radicalmente anticomunista. Um certo número de seitas de importância secundária também desenvolveu-se nos Estados Unidos da América; e a Alemanha tem tido uma longa história de tais seitas, que se têm derramado, até certo ponto, para outros países europeus. Conferi os detalhes acima para mostrar que o ideal comunista tem exercido alguma influência, mas muito mais entre os grupos heréticos, que se têm separado de outros grupos religiosos, mas nunca em qualquer grande denominação cristã.

c. A Teologia da Libertação. O movimento comunista sempre foi ínfimo na Igreja cristã, e sempre se manifestou-se em grupos separatistas, secundários. No entanto, não ocorre o mesmo no caso da Teologia da Libertação, que vai obtendo ímpeto nos **países latino-americanos** e até mesmo na Europa. Alguns estudiosos supõem que a ameaça representada por esse movimento, contra a Igreja, sobretudo contra a Igreja Católica Romana, é maior do que aquela representada pela **Reforma Protestante**. Portanto, se o ideal comunista tem exercido alguma influência sobre o pensamento cristão, através de sua história, agora essa influência é mais definida, e vai-se agigantando. O leitor pode consultar o artigo separado sobre esse tema, quanto a detalhes mais completos. Talvez não exista nenhum outro problema isolado tão grande, para a Igreja Católica Romana, como a influência que vem sendo exercida por esse movimento teológico. Conforme declarou o papa João Paulo II, a Teologia da Libertação na realidade é a secularização da teologia.

7. O Comunismo e a Ética

A base abertamente declarada de toda a ação ética, dentro do sistema comunista, é a base material e econômica. Ao assim dizer, naturalmente estou olvidando aquelas formas que têm sido praticadas por pessoas religiosas que não representam o comunismo político, internacional. A base ética do comunismo internacional é certa forma de humanismo materialista. Assim sendo, devemos entender, desde o começo, que nem Deus e nem a alma humana são centrais para esse sistema. De acordo com essa ética, temos a presunção de dizer que o cristianismo é aliado das classes exploradas. Isso tem sido declarado até mesmo por padres e bispos da Igreja Católica Romana que são os propugnadores da Teologia da Libertação. Outrossim, a religião, de modo geral, tida chamada de «ópio do povo», é considerada um empecilho para o avanço do sistema comunista. Todos os sistemas éticos são encarados como sistemas que promovem os interesses especiais de grupos, e as mudanças de classes só ocorrem mediante a luta de classes. Os padrões éticos dominantes em qualquer período histórico são aqueles defendidos pelas classes privilegiadas. No campo da ética, tanto quanto no campo da teoria histórica, estaria em operação a dialética hegeliana com sua tese, antítese e síntese. Portanto, novas sínteses produzem a percepção de uma ética superior. E assim, no comunismo acredita-se que somente no triunfo do mesmo poderemos atingir a perspectiva ética apropriada. Porém, no que consiste essa perspectiva, se for algum dia atingida? Ela está baseada na prosperidade material das massas. Para o comunismo, não há nenhum Deus que estabeleça as regras éticas, e não há qualquer alma humana a ser julgada ou recompensada de acordo com a sua conduta, após a morte biológica. Indago: Toda essa luta na vida tem algum valor se, no fim de tudo, o que ganhamos é apenas mais riquezas materiais, somente para morrermos após alguns breves anos, perdendo tudo quanto se ganhou em meio a tantos esforços? Esse *pouco* justifica o terrorismo, as guerras e as **perseguições, que se têm feito em nome do comunismo?**

O que dizer sobre a luta de classes? Quando examinamos o que realmente sucede no comunismo, vemos claramente que uma nova classe substitui a antiga classe dominante. Essa nova classe é a dos chefes do partido, que usam de tirania, abusam dos direitos humanos e lançam mão do homicídio para impor-se. O comunismo não obtém uma sociedade sem classes. Bem pelo contrário, o comunismo é a forma mais bem-sucedida de fascismo. Essa nova classe dominante é apoiada pelo poder militar. Qualquer resistência aos chefes do partido não somente produz reprimenda, mas também repressão mediante períodos de encarceramento, de exílio e até mesmo confinamento em hospitais psiquiátricos. A liberdade pessoal, essencial em qualquer sistema ético, simplesmente desaparece.

O lema de Karl Marx. Disse ele: «De cada um segundo a sua habilidade, a cada um segundo a sua necessidade». Esse é um alvo desprezível. Há um Deus que dá ricamente aos homens, através de Jesus Cristo (Efé. 1:3), e é nisso que consiste o evangelho. Há uma evolução espiritual, baseada na transformação ética, a qual nos torna participantes da natureza divina, e não meramente a uma melhor participação no que este mundo material pode suprir-nos. Essas declarações poderão ser consideradas «ingênuas» por alguns; mas a própria ciência está produzindo evidências convincentes acerca da existência da alma e sua sobrevivência ante a morte física. O momento da morte reveste-se de alto significado *espiritual*, quando a ética, a fé e a teologia operam poderosamente. Ver o artigo sobre *Experiências de Quase Morte*, quanto a demonstrações acerca disso.

8. O Comunismo e os Mártires.

Penso que é útil salientarmos, neste ponto, que o comunismo tem produzido mártires cristãos em maior número que qualquer outro sistema político da história. As matanças, por motivos religiosos, que têm tido lugar na Rússia, na China e nos países asiáticos, são espantosas. No entanto, alguns oficiais cristãos de países não comunistas, em nossos dias, estão apelando para esse sistema, como guia sobre como devem conduzir sua ética e suas atividades. Isso envolve uma cegueira quase inacreditável. E também devemos pensar nas perseguições que não terminam em assassinato. A liberdade pessoal de muitos indivíduos é tolhida, a liberdade de imprensa é destruída, igrejas cristãs são fechadas ou restringidas em suas atividades. Escolas evangélicas e cristãs em geral são simplesmente eliminadas, e as crianças são forçadas a receber doutrinamento comunista ateu, sem qualquer voz de protesto, a não ser aquela que se processa nos lares, em secreto. O próprio frade Leonardo Boff, o padre e teólogo brasileiro criador da Teologia da Libertação, disse em Campinas, em 1985, que ele não queria ver o Brasil tornar-se um país comunista. Tudo quanto ele quer é tomar por empréstimo alguns discernimentos extraídos dos dogmas comunistas, referentes à teoria política e social. Ele não quer um Brasil comunista, por tudo aquilo que esse sistema faz à liberdade pessoal e à liberdade religiosa. No entanto, ele tem se esforçado vigorosamente para aproximar o Brasil do comunismo mediante sua influência, no seio da Igreja Católica Romana e fora dela. Um grande número de pessoas que dão apoio ao padre Boff também dão apoio ao comunismo, no Brasil.

A Igreja cubana e o comunismo — Uma Ilustração

Fidel Castro destruiu a Igreja Católica em Cuba. Em 1958, havia 90% de cubanos batizados, numa população de 10 milhões. Hoje a porcentagem é de 39%. Em 1958, 24% dos católicos praticavam ali a religião, indo à missa aos domingos. Hoje esta prática tombou a 0,5% e vai descendo sem cessar. Em Cuba havia, em 1958, algumas centenas de colégios católicos. Hoje não resta um só. Havia, em 1958, mais de 700 sacerdotes. Hoje há 211. Em 1958, a Igreja cubana dispunha de jornais, revistas, emissoras de rádio e programas de TV, para difundir a fé. Hoje tudo isto lhe foi arrebatado violentamente. Desde 1961, Castro ignorou os bispos cubanos e se recusou a recebê-los. O gelo só rompido em setembro de 1985, e uma segunda visita já teve lugar em novembro de 1985, porque agora é o «degelo da simpatia tática». Durante 25 anos, toda a infância e juventude cubanas, privadas de ensino religioso (a não ser dentro dos templos, e sob o controle do Partido) foram endoutrinadas, encharcadas de materialismo e de marxismo. Agora, Castro quer entender-se com a Igreja — com uma pobre Igreja totalmente marginalizada da sociedade. Da qual tudo nos levaria a dizer que está moribunda, se não soubéssemos que, quanto à Igreja de Cristo, «suas portas nunca se fecharão» (Apoc. 21:25). *O Estado de SP*, 26 de jan. de 1986.

A Revolução Cubana produziu dez mil execuções, a detenção de 90 mil pessoas em campos de concentração e a fuga, para Miami, de 500 mil cubanos (aos quais se juntaram os 125 mil que se haviam refugiado, antes, na Embaixada do Peru em Havana. Isto aconteceu em 1980, portanto não há muito tempo). Todavia, as execuções sumárias, conforme documento do chamado Comitê Cubano de Defesa dos Direitos Humanos, prosseguiram em 1984 e 1985, enquanto os julgamentos de crimes políticos permanecem clandestinos, precedidos de torturas, e mantendo-se ainda o antigo costume de reter os condenados políticos na prisão mesmo após a expiação de suas penas. Amigos e familiares de pessoas recém-detidas correm riscos ao tentar descobrir seus paradeiros. E, nas prisões cubanas, a situação, como antes, é também agora extremamente deplorável. Citam-se casos em que o pessoal médico participa de sessões de tortura, havendo sérias suspeitas de que se realizam experiências médicas em prisioneiros sem seu consentimento. O escritor e poeta Armando Valladares qualificou, aliás, as prisões cubanas de «Gulag das Américas», afirmando que a tortura é ali praticada, sistematicamente, como meio de forçar os detentos a aceitar o comunismo. Os prisioneiros políticos que resistem à mudança — conhecidos como *plantados* — são enquadrados como presos comuns, tornando-se alvo de abusos especiais. (O Estado de São Paulo, de 15 de fevereiro de 1986).

9. Os Serviços do Comunismo

Haveria alguma coisa no comunismo que poderíamos usar de modo proveitoso? Naturalmente, sim. Em primeiro lugar, não deveríamos permitir que esse sistema político pense que é dono dos pobres. E a oposição ao comunismo deveria forçar os homens de todos os lugares a buscarem melhores soluções para a pobreza. Também não deveríamos esquecer que, a despeito de todas as falhas da Igreja Católica Romana, ela tem prestado bons serviços aos pobres, mediante hospitais, orfanatos e escolas de todas as modalidades. Ela não merece todas as críticas que lhe são dirigidas. Ademais, consideramos o seguinte: Deve haver uma maneira de servirmos aos pobres, aprimorando as condições deles, sem alguma luta de classes que promova o ódio, o conflito e as matanças. Deve haver alguma maneira melhor de servirmos aos pobres além de dizer-lhes que tudo quanto eles podem almejar é a melhoria nas condições materiais. Que dizer sobre as riquezas da alma? Um homem não é rico em vista daquilo que possui, mas em vista daquilo que ele é. Somente Deus, operando na alma humana, pode infundir valor em um homem. Ninguém faz um homem pobre tornar-se verdadeiramente rico cercando o seu corpo físico de confortos, ao mesmo tempo em que lhe sufoca a alma. Isso posto, a própria existência do sistema comunista alerta-nos para o fato de que o capitalismo explora, que os proprietários são egoístas, que muitas pessoas são economicamente oprimidas. Esses são fatos sem os quais o comunismo nunca teria vindo à existência. Os governos também são egoístas e são agências exploradoras; pois, de outra sorte, ninguém se revoltaria contra eles. Nem tudo é bom, simplesmente por não ser comunista. Finalmente, há líderes comunistas que interessam-se genuinamente pelo bem-estar dos homens. Convém que imitemos o zelo deles, dedicando-nos mais intensamente à nossa fé e às coisas a que essa fé nos inspira.

10. O Comunismo e a Tradição Profética.

Os comunistas têm a certeza de que Hegel (adaptado segundo a maneira de pensar do comunismo) disse o que sucederá no futuro: o mundo inteiro terminará aceitando os ideais do comunismo! Mas, o que a *tradição profética* assevera? a. O conflito entre o comunismo e as forças que lhe fazem oposição não terminará com a vitória do comunismo. Antes, terminará em devastadora destruição para ambos os lados em luta. As grandes potências comunistas não triunfarão e governarão, afinal. Antes, serão destruídas por aqueles que tiverem destruído, em uma destruição mútua. b. Primeiramente, os Estados Unidos da América e a União Soviética quase aniquilar-se-ão mutuamente. A China levantar-se-á maciçamente em armas. Então o anticristo, com sua aliança de países ocidentais, enfrentará os chineses e os derrotará. c. Dentre as cinzas, para surpresa de todos, *Israel*, uma vez convertida ao cristianismo, tornar-se-á a cabeça das nações. d. Jerusalém será a nova capital da civilização, tal como Roma o foi, até o fim da Idade Média. O centro da Igreja cristã voltará a orbitar em torno de Jerusalém. e. Seguir-se-á uma notável era de prosperidade, com base em princípios espirituais, e não materialistas. Isso significa que a própria filosofia que deu origem ao comunismo desaparecerá, e ideais muito superiores e verdadeiros tomarão o lugar do comunismo e de todos os sistemas de governo que têm tido a chance de atuar e têm fracassado. Estamos falando sobre o governo de Jesus Cristo na terra, durante o milênio. (AM BE E H JL P)

COMUTAÇÃO DA PENITÊNCIA

Essa expressão indica a alteração da penitência prescrita (que vide), usualmente mediante o abreviamento do período da disciplina, com a intensificação correspondente da mesma, mas, às vezes, com a total liberação da penitência. Naturalmente, estamos falando sobre a doutrina da Igreja Católica Romana. (E)

CONA

Esse é o nome de uma cidade mencionada em Judite 4:4. Nas traduções dos livros apócrifos, seguindo um texto diferente, aparece como o nome de uma vila. Todavia, o local é desconhecido.

CONANIAS

No hebraico, «Yahweh está fundando». Há dois homens com esse nome, no Antigo Testamento, a saber:

1. Nome do principal oficial e levita, que

administrou as coletas feitas durante o reinado de Ezequias (II Crô. 31:12,13). Há uma certa confusão textual no tocante ao seu nome, e aparecem variantes, como *Jeconias*.

2. Um líder levita que esteve associado à administração do rei Josias (II Crô. 35:9).

CONATO

Esse adjetivo vem do verbo lat. **conari**, «tentar». O vocábulo refere-se ao desejo inato ou impulso para realizar alguma coisa. Na filosofia de Spinoza, todas as coisas são assistidas por esse impulso, que é o desejo de qualquer criatura de perpetuar a sua espécie. Ver o artigo sobre *Spinoza*.

CONCEIÇÃO IMACULADA

Ver **Imaculada Conceição**.

CONCEITO

Vocábulo derivado das palavras latinas *con*, «junto», e *capere*, «agarrar» ou «amansar»; em outras palavras, uma *idéia* (que vide) distinguida de uma percepção (que vide) ou de uma sensação (que vide). O termo percepção usualmente é empregado para indicar a união das sensações com as percepções. No uso real, é difícil distinguir entre percepção e conceituação. *Locke* faz a conceituação ser mais geral do que a percepção. Hume torna a conceituação mais vívida que a percepção. Kant interpreta a conceituação como *esquemas*. Para ele, as funções da lógica e da matemática são instâncias da interpretação de conceitos como esquemas de vários tipos.

Um *conceito* é aquilo a que uma pessoa chega quando entende ou é capaz de usar alguma porção de seu idioma, de maneira útil. Os critérios que nos permitem averiguarmos se chegamos a um conceito podem ser simples ou complexos. Uma criança, após ter visto cães de várias raças ou variedades, pode dizer «cão»; porque já chegou ao conceito de que é um cão. Mas um cientista, ao definir o conceito de «cão», pode chegar a escrever diversos volumes sobre o assunto.

O Conceito e a Intuição. Henri Bergson recebeu importante discernimento sobre a natureza do conceito em contraste com a natureza da intuição. Ele deu-nos a metáfora da fonte de água. A *intuição* assemelha-se a uma fonte que jorra água no espaço, como se fosse um ser vivo. O *conceito* é como a água que retornou ao solo, e se estagnou como uma poça. A intuição é viva, sempre procurando novos modos e aplicações. O conceito é um item fixo do conhecimento, que se tornou parte integrante de um sistema. Isso se aplica às mil maravilhas aos credos da fé religiosa. Esses credos estão freqüentemente contidos sob a forma de conceitos estagnados, que não podem ser revistos e nem aprimorados. Mas o Espírito é um ser vivo, sempre crescendo e renovando. (E F P)

CONCEITUALISMO

Esse é um termo que expressa uma posição particular no tocante aos *universais* (que vide). Para que o leitor entenda melhor a questão, preciso fornecer-lhe as idéias básicas. No que consistem os universais? Alguns dizem que é apenas um termo da linguagem. Por exemplo, *vermelho* é termo que uso para certa classe de cor. *Quadrado* é o termo que uso para indicar certa classe de configuração geométrica. *Justiça* é um termo que uso para descrever as ações corretas. Quando o universal é apenas um termo, temos o *nominalismo* (que vide). Porém, digamos que o universal, na realidade, seja uma *entidade*, ou um atributo de uma entidade. A *justiça* pode ser personificada e pode ser chamada de Deus, ou podemos dizer que a justiça é um dos atributos de Deus. Platão idealizava um mundo de idéias ou de universais, onde existiriam entidades de alguma espécie, que seriam os arquétipos de todas as coisas que conhecemos no mundo físico. Quando o universal é uma realidade, quando é real em si mesmo, e não meramente um termo qualquer da linguagem, ou um nome, então temos o *realismo* (que vide). Em outras palavras, o universal é alguma coisa real, e não apenas um termo que usamos para criar classes de coisas. A forma platônica do realismo é chamada de *realismo radical* porque os universais existem em si mesmos, isto é, possuem existência independente. Nas obras de Aristóteles, temos aquilo que se chama de *realismo moderado*, pois, enquanto o universal é real, nunca se encontra isolado. Sempre encontra-se nos particulares, isto é, nos objetos materiais. O *vermelho* é real, mas não é algo que exista independentemente do objeto dessa cor. Sócrates, por sua vez, pensava no universal como um *conceito* da mente divina ou universal. Dentro do cristianismo, podemos dizer que a justiça é um *conceito* da mente divina. Isso faz a justiça ser muito mais que um termo da linguagem humana. Quando um universal é chamado de conceito, quer da mente humana, quer da mente divina ou universal, então temos o *conceitualismo*. Os conceitos são universais e existem nas mentes, mas não possuem existência independente. Os filósofos que têm promovido o conceitualismo são: Sócrates, Abelardo, Tomás de Aquino, Hugo de São Vítor, João de Salisbury, Locke, Berkeley, Reid, Kant, John Stuart Mill. O cristianismo expressa tanto o realismo radical quanto o conceitualismo, que não se anulam mutuamente. (B E F P EP)

CONCÍLIO

A palavra latina **consilium** significa «assembléia», «ajuntamento». O termo grego, usado no Novo Testamento, é *synedrion*, que significa «estar sentado com», e que é empregado por vinte e duas vezes, de Mat. 5:22 a Atos 24:20.

1. *O Concílio Celestial*. Deus é freqüentemente descrito na Bíblia como quem entra em concílio com as hostes celestiais (Jó 15:8; Sal. 89:7; Jer. 23:18; Amós 3:7). Apesar de que poderíamos encarar essas declarações como expressões poéticas, quando aplicadas a Deus, elas são instrutivas porque se referem à Mente divina que põe em ordem todas as coisas, e diante da qual todos os homens são tidos por responsáveis. A existência de todas as coisas, bem como a continuação das mesmas, depende dessa organização, traçada e mantida por Deus (Col. 1:16,17).

2. *Os Conselhos dos Reis*. Em português, fazemos a distinção entre «concílio», sempre com um sentido eclesiástico, e «conselho», que é seu paralelo no mundo político e administrativo. Na antiguidade, os reis tinham seus conselhos, formados por conselheiros e nobres. Os membros desse conselho tinham o privilégio de ver sua face sempre que necessário, isto é, podiam entrar em contacto com ele, sem terem de marcar audiência prévia (II Reis 25:19; Jer. 52:25).

3. *O Sistema Judaico dos Concílios*. O tribunal superior judaico era o *Sinédrio* (que vide). Esse tribunal ficava em Jerusalém. Mas também havia as *sunedria*, ou seja, os tribunais locais (Mat. 10:17; Mar. 13:9). Havia dois desses tribunais locais em Jerusalém, e um em cada cidade de Israel. Mas, como funcionavam esses tribunais locais, e quantas pessoas estavam envolvidas nos mesmos, é algo sobre o que não há informações. Provavelmente esses detalhes

CONCÍLIO DE JERUSALÉM

eram variáveis. O número de juízes era de vinte e três, nos lugares onde a população era de cento e vinte para cima; e de três, quando a população era inferior a isso. Mishna, *Sanhedr*. I, seção 6. Josefo, porém, refere-se a cifras diferentes, ao dizer que Moisés nomeara sete juízes, cada um dos quais contava com dois levitas como assessores (Deu. 16:18; *Anti*. 4:8, seção 14). Josefo (*Guerras* 2:20, seção 5) informa-nos, igualmente, que sete era o número de juízes para os casos de crimes leves.

No Novo Testamento, qualquer grupo de pessoas reunidas para tratar de alguma questão específica é um *sumboulion* (concílio), como no caso daqueles que conspiraram contra Jesus (Mat. 12:14). Festo, o procurador romano em Cesaréia, consultou-se com um conselho, para concluir sobre o que faria com o prisioneiro Paulo. A maior parte das referências do Novo Testamento é ao sinédrio, o tribunal superior, que consistia em setenta membros, sob a presidência do sumo sacerdote.

CONCÍLIO DE JERUSALÉM

Esse primeiro concílio da Igreja cristã, que muitos estudiosos aceitam como o único realmente autoritário, por contar com a presença dos apóstolos, ocorreu em 48 ou 49 D.C. O relato está registrado no décimo quinto capítulo do livro de Atos. Embora ali não apareça a palavra grega correspondente, *sunédrion*, aparece o fato em si.

Esboço:
1. Motivos
2. Atos 15 e Gálatas 2:1-10
3. Provisões do Concílio de Jerusalém

1. Motivos

A Igreja cristã começou como um grupo religioso judaico, que observava, essencialmente, leis e costumes judaicos, e que estava começando a sofrer o influxo de membros gentios, por causa da missão gentílica da Igreja primitiva. Não havia como reconciliar o estilo pagão de vida, mesmo quando refinado pela fé cristã, ao caminho judaico cristão. Não podemos olvidar que os convertidos à fé cristã, em Jerusalém, apesar de reconhecerem Jesus como o Messias, e sabendo que um novo movimento religioso estava começando, não viram razão alguma para abandonarem seus costumes religiosos, alguns dos quais reputavam como importantíssimos. Muitos cristãos primitivos, assim sendo, continuaram crendo que a circuncisão era necessária à salvação (Atos 15:5). Esse mesmo versículo mostra-nos que muitos fariseus (que vide) convertidos ao cristianismo, vieram a fazer parte da liderança da Igreja cristã primitiva. O problema tratado pelo primeiro concílio cristão consistiu, portanto, em determinar quanto do judaísmo os convertidos gentios ao cristianismo precisavam observar, a fim de que não se rompesse a concórdia entre convertidos gentios e convertidos judeus.

2. Atos 15 e Gálatas 2:1-10

Alguns estudiosos pensam que aqueles versículos da epístola aos Gálatas aludem aos acontecimentos retratados em Atos 15, embora Paulo não tivesse observado precisão cronológica. Mas, segundo esses intérpretes, mesmo assim Paulo teria aludido a aspectos do primeiro concílio da Igreja cristã. Mas outros eruditos pensam que aquela passagem da epístola aos Gálatas deve ser associada à visita da fome, feita por Paulo a Jerusalém, registrada em Atos 11:30. Isso significaria que quando Paulo escreveu a epístola aos Gálatas, ainda não havia tido lugar o concílio de Jerusalém. Isso parece ser confirmado pelo fato de que, em seu debate com os judaizantes, Paulo poderia tê-los esmagado mediante a simples evocação às decisões do concílio de Jerusalém, claramente contrárias às pretensões dos líderes judaizantes, e, no entanto, não o fez. Sem importar qual tenha sido a seqüência exata dos acontecimentos, aquela passagem na epístola aos Gálatas fornece-nos o discernimento para perceber as lutas pelo poder e as transigências que ocorreram na Igreja, ocasionadas pela entrada de convertidos gentios no cristianismo primitivo. A narrativa do livro de Atos, por sua vez, ignora essencialmente a severidade do conflito, nada nos adiantando sobre o choque entre Paulo e Pedro. A epístola aos Gálatas, de 2:11 até o fim, revela-nos que certos conflitos persistiram, apesar de acordos prévios. Portanto, de nada nos adianta tentar minimizar a controvérsia legalista, que houve na Igreja cristã primitiva. A questão era importante e manteve-se ativa por muito tempo, mais do que poderíamos compreender se contássemos apenas com o livro de Atos como fonte informativa. Exatamente por esse motivo, era urgente que houvesse um concílio. Vários delegados reuniram-se, incluindo aqueles da igreja de Antioquia, liderados por Paulo e Barnabé. Os apóstolos e anciãos da igreja de Jerusalém estavam presentes.

3. Provisões do Concílio de Jerusalém

Houve um acirrado debate. Mas Paulo, em seu apelo pela legitimidade da Igreja cristã gentílica, obteve a vitória essencial, ainda que não em todos os pormenores da questão. O próprio Tiago, pastor ou bispo de Jerusalém, foi retratado a reconhecer a obra de Deus entre os gentios, citando trechos bíblicos apropriados do Antigo Testamento, em apoio ao ponto (Amós 9:11,12; Jer. 12:15). Foi Tiago quem concluiu, mostrando quais deveriam ser as conclusões, e dirigindo a redação de uma carta que deveria propagar por todo o mundo cristão as decisões do concílio.

Provisões. a. Os gentios convertidos não deveriam ser considerados sujeitos à legislação mosaica, como condição de salvação ou como condição de fraternidade na Igreja cristã (Atos 15:19). b. Paulo e Barnabé foram reconhecidos como autênticos ministros cristãos, daí derivando-se a legitimidade da missão cristã entre os gentios (Gál. 2:9,10). c. *Proibições religiosas*. Toda a contaminação idólatra precisava ser evitada (Atos 15:20a), incluindo a ingestão de alimentos oferecidos aos ídolos (Atos 15:29). d. *Proibições morais*. Todas as formas de imoralidade foram proibidas (vs. 20b). e. *Proibições higiênicas*. Os crentes foram aconselhados a absterem-se de comer carnes de animais sufocados ou mortos de maneira indevida (Atos 15:20c). Os pagãos consideravam que a carne preparada em seu próprio sangue, além de vários pratos preparados com sangue, eram deliciosos. No Brasil temos o famoso «sarapatel» que, quando preparado segundo a receita, sempre inclui sangue. Ora, isso parecia ofensivo para os judeus, pelo que a proibição foi incluída na carta. f. *Proibições civis*. A abstinência de toda a forma de violência, crueldade, homicídio, assassínio, levantes, etc., tão comuns no mundo gentílico da época (Atos 15:20d). Isso não deve ser confundido com o sangue como parte dos alimentos. A abstenção que temos aqui, quase certamente, é uma alusão às diversas formas de violência. O texto grego ocidental diz «derramamento de sangue». Essa variante, embora uma interpretação, provavelmente expressa corretamente a idéia envolvida.

Essas provisões foram reduzidas à forma escrita, e então enviadas às igrejas gentílicas por meio de

CONCÍLIO — CONCÍLIOS

delegados de confiança, a fim de que as decisões do concílio fossem implementadas entre as igrejas cristãs gentílicas. A história subseqüente demonstrou que esses atos e provisões não solucionaram definitivamente o problema. Muita luta continuou agitando a Igreja cristã por causa dessas questões. A transição do judaísmo para o cristianismo não se fez suavemente. Além disso, conforme podemos perceber, muitas das provisões do concílio de Jerusalém tiveram o intuito de agradar aos judeus convertidos, mormente os pontos ligados a questões alimentares. No entanto, outras dessas provisões têm cunho eminentemente moral, pelo que são importantes para a espiritualidade. Ver os artigos sobre *Judaizantes* e sobre o *Partido da Circuncisão*, quanto a outros detalhes sobre a questão. Ver também sobre a *Circuncisão de Timóteo*, onde Paulo, de maneira prática, procurou manter a concórdia. (IB ID LAN NTI RAM Z)

CONCÍLIO MUNDIAL DE IGREJAS

Ver o artigo sobre **Concílios Ecumênicos**, VIII., Os Grupos Protestantes.

CONCÍLIO INTERNACIONAL DE IGREJAS CRISTÃS.
Ver o artigo sobre **Concílios Ecumênicos**, VIII., Os Grupos Protestantes.

CONCÍLIOS BUDISTAS

Vários concílios foram efetuados pelos altos oficiais dessa religião (ver sobre o *Budismo*), entre o século V A.C. e o século I D.C., com o propósito de estabelecer o cânon das escrituras budistas e para fixar questões de disciplina. O primeiro desses concílios, atendido por quinhentos monges, foi efetuado em Rajagaha, imediatamente após a morte de Buda (cerca de 483 A.C.). Prolongou-se por sete meses, e foi presidido pelo discípulo de Buda, Mahakassapa. O feito principal foi a fixação do primeiro cânon budista, o *Dhamma* e o *Vinaya*. O segundo desses concílios foi efetuado cem anos mais tarde (cerca de 383 A.C.), e contou com setecentos participantes. Reuniu-se em Vasali, tendo por finalidade condenar certas práticas ilegais que se tinham desenvolvido entre os monges. Medidas disciplinares foram baixadas. Esse concílio prolongou-se por dezoito meses. Um grupo de budistas liberais, chamado os Mahasanghikas, efetuou um concílio rival, fora da cidade, e opôs-se aos monges ortodoxos de Theravadas. Um terceiro concílio budista ocorreu em cerca de 240 A.C., do qual participaram mil oficiais budistas. Durou nove meses. Foi efetuado em Pataliputta. Nessa ocasião, foi preparada uma coletânea de tratados, a *Abhidhamma*, que foi acrescentada ao *Dhamma* e ao *Vinaya*, completando-se assim os famosos três cestos, ou seja, o cânon dos livros sagrados do budismo, também chamado de *Tripitaka*.

Todas as escolas do budismo aceitam os dois primeiros concílios como autoritários. O terceiro não é mencionado nas obras escritas em pali, ou nas obras dos Sarvastivadins. Porém, a maioria dos eruditos modernos aceita o mesmo como legítimo. A tradição do budismo nortista adiciona um quarto concílio, ocorrido em Kashmir, em cerca de 70 D.C. Nessa época, foi promulgada a doutrina mais liberal e otimista, a doutrina Mahayana, tendo sido também compilados comentários sobre as três divisões do cânon budista, usando pela primeira vez o sânscrito, como idioma, em vez do páli. (E P)

CONCÍLIOS ECUMÊNICOS

Esboço:
I. Importância dos Concílios
II. Participantes
III. Pontos de Vista Protestantes
IV. Concílios Reconhecidos pela Igreja Católica Romana
V. Concílios Plenários e Outros
VI. A Ortodoxia Oriental
VII. A Comunidade Anglicana
VIII. Os Grupos Protestantes
IX. O Antigo Problema da Autoridade

I. Importância dos Concílios

Quanto a uma apreciação mais ampla desse assunto, o leitor deveria consultar o artigo sobre a *Autoridade*. Na história eclesiástica, os concílios têm desempenhado um papel de destaque, sendo aceitos como autoritários, juntamente com as Escrituras Sagradas, as afirmativas dos pais da Igreja e os pronunciamentos *ex cathedra* (que vide) dos papas. A autoridade dos concílios pesa até mesmo sobre os papas. A interpretação de suas decisões é crítica, e sínodos (que vide) são organizados como corpos interpretativos.

As listas dos concílios ecumênicos variam, segundo dois conceitos diversos acerca do que está envolvido em um concílio ecumênico. No passado, seguindo o sentido da palavra *ecumênico*, a idéia era que um concílio era ecumênico quando contava com representantes de todos os grupos cristãos. Com o tempo, porém, desenvolveram-se outras idéias a respeito. A primeira, segue essa idéia original. Mas a segunda afirma que um concílio ecumênico consiste, essencialmente, em contar com a cabeça e os membros, isto é, o papa e outros representantes eclesiásticos. É lógico que isso representa um desvirtuamento da expressão. A função declarada, primária, é a interpretação fiel da fé tradicional. E, de acordo com a Igreja Católica Romana, nenhuma declaração conciliar é considerada válida sem a chancela papal. A verdade, porém, é que desde a divisão entre Igreja Católica Romana e Igreja Ortodoxa Oriental, e, mais tarde, com a Reforma Protestante, um concílio verdadeiramente ecumênico tornou-se muito difícil. Quando há um concílio católico romano, ortodoxos gregos e protestantes enviam apenas observadores, sem nenhuma voz ativa válida. As assembléias protestantes equivalentes também só contam com observadores de outros grupos cristãos. Não há que duvidar que um dos alvos do moderno movimento ecumênico é sarar essa situação de divisão. Mas, as divergências são muito profundas e radicais para permitir a unificação da cristandade, sobretudo porque o grupo cristão mais numeroso, a Igreja Católica Romana, só aceitaria unidade em torno do papa; e isso, pelo menos até o momento, tem sido considerado inaceitável por ortodoxos e protestantes. E ainda que, em algum futuro imprevisível, tal unidade organizacional fosse possível, podemos ter a certeza de que sempre haveria grupos cristãos dissidentes, que se aglutinariam em torno das Escrituras Sagradas cristãs, exclusivamente.

II. Participantes

Cardeais, patriarcas, primatas, arcebispos, bispos, gerais de ordens religiosas, abades e outros líderes eclesiásticos. Ainda outros podem ser convidados como conselheiros teológicos, alguns leigos importantes, e até mesmo observadores que não pertencem à Igreja Católica Romana. Os concílios da Igreja Católica Romana são convocados pelo papa, o qual os preside e lhes determina a agenda, encerra-os e promulga os decretos baixados. A moderna teologia católica romana, querendo preservar o dogma que se desenvolveu em torno dos concílios, salienta o ensino

CONCÍLIOS ECUMÊNICOS

que, juntamente com o papa, um concílio ecumênico é o órgão coletivo da Igreja, e que, juntamente com o papa, representa o ensino autoritário e infalível da Igreja Católica Romana, em questões de fé e moral.

III. Pontos de Vista Protestantes

Os vários grupos protestantes afirmam que, por mais importante que tenha sido o papel dos concílios, estes estão sujeitos ao erro. Pois, de fato, as decisões dos concílios discrepam umas das outras, em grande número de casos, sem falarmos no fato de que os grupos protestantes consideram a Bíblia como único guia infalível da fé e da moral. Não obstante, os protestantes de tendências liberais também rejeitam o conceito de uma Bíblia isenta de erros, afirmando que a verdade divina não pode ser contida em um único volume, conformando-se a escritos humanos (ainda que produzidos pela inspiração divina) ou a decisões de concílios. A busca pela infalibilidade seria apenas a busca pelo conforto mental, permitindo às pessoas que cessam na busca da verdade, — em vez de prosseguirem nessa inquirição. Entretanto, podemos ter a certeza de que se há discrepâncias bíblicas que afetam questões de números e dados históricos pormenorizados, não há contradições quanto à revelação da verdade. Quando muito, os estudiosos encontram aspectos menos ou mais avançados da revelação, que se tornam complementares, e não discordantes. Também precisamos admitir que a revelação bíblica não cobre todos os ângulos possíveis. As próprias Escrituras declaram que há coisas que não foram reveladas e que pertencem somente a Deus. (Deu. 29:29). Isso dificulta a formação de uma teologia *sistemática*. Acertamos à medida que incluímos o maior número possível de facetas; erramos à medida que nos esquecemos dos fatores revelados que devem ser levados em conta. Mas, aquilo que foi revelado, é preservado de erro pela Mente superior que é o verdadeiro autor das Escrituras. Foi por isso que o Senhor Jesus declarou: «...e a Escritura não pode falhar» (João 10:35).

IV. Concílios Reconhecidos pela Igreja Católica Romana

1. Nicéia I (325 D.C.), quando foi formulado o credo niceno (que vide), em oposição ao arianismo (que vide).
2. Constantinopla I (381 D.C.), que elaborou o credo niceno, definindo mais explicitamente a divindade do Espírito Santo.
3. Éfeso (431 D.C.), que definiu a unidade pessoal de Cristo, bem como a Virgem Maria como *Theŏtokos* (mãe de *Deus*), contra o nestorianismo (que vide).
4. Calcedônia (451 D.C.), que definiu as duas naturezas de Cristo e as relações entre elas.
5. Constantinopla II (553 D.C.), que reafirmou as decisões dos quatro concílios e condenou os erros de Orígenes e de outros.
6. Constantinopla III (680-681 D.C.), que definiu a existência de duas vontades em Cristo, em oposição ao monotelismo (que vide).
7. Nicéia II (787 D.C.), que regulamentou a veneração de imagens.
8. Constantinopla IV (869 D.C.), que tratou do cisma fotiano (que vide). O cristianismo oriental e ocidental se fez presente, mas não foi universalmente reconhecido.

Os concílios oitavo a vigésimo primeiro são considerados «ecumênicos» pela Igreja Católica Romana, com base no princípio do «papa no concílio», porquanto, desde o nono concílio em diante, nunca mais houve representação universal da cristandade. A partir desse ponto, os concílios dos outros grupos cristãos precisam ser investigados à parte. Ver os artigos separados sobre os *Concílios Lateranos*.

9. Primeiro concílio laterano (1123).
10. Segundo concílio laterano (1139).
11. Terceiro concílio laterano (1179).
12. Quarto concílio laterano (1215).
13. Lyons I (1245).
14. Lyons II (1274).
15. Viena (1311-1313).
16. Constança (1414-1418).
17. Basle-Ferrara-Florença (1431-1439).
18. Quinto concílio laterano (1512-1517).
19. Trento (1545-1563).
20. Vaticano I (1869-1870).
21. Vaticano II (1962-1965).

Ver o artigo separado sobre *Vaticano, Concílios do*. Além disso, cada um dos concílios acima alistados tem seu artigo separado.

V. Concílios Plenários e Outros

Os concílios plenários são aqueles compostos por bispos e outros oficiais eclesiásticos de diversas províncias da Igreja Católica Romana, convocados com propósitos regionais especiais e presididos por algum legado papal.

Os chamados *concílios provinciais* são aqueles constituídos pelos líderes episcopais de alguma província da Igreja Católica Romana. Esses concílios reúnem-se ao menos a cada vinte anos, sob a direção de um arcebispo metropolitano. Suas decisões precisam ser aprovadas pela Santa Sé. As conferências episcopais nacionais estão abarcando, na atualidade, quase todas as funções antes atribuídas aos concílios provinciais. Os *sínodos diocesanos* reúnem-se pelo menos uma vez a cada dez anos, atuando como corpos que aconselham e sugerem medidas. Compõem-se de representantes de cada arcebispado, de capítulo de catedral e das ordens religiosas.

VI. A Ortodoxia Oriental

Sete concílios ecumênicos são reconhecidos ali como autoritários, os mesmos primeiros sete concílios reconhecidos na lista da Igreja Católica Romana (acima). Eles aceitam aquelas decisões como irreversíveis e obrigatórias. Sínodos subseqüentes, com a representatividade de vários patriarcas, como o de Moscou (1945-1948), discutiram sobre problemas de disciplina eclesiástica ou sobre a interpretação dos primeiros concílios. Após o declínio do império bizantino, os sínodos patriarcais tornaram-se o centro das atividades conciliares.

VII. A Comunidade Anglicana

Para o anglicanismo, os órgãos sinodais tradicionais são as duas convocações de Canterbury e de York, que se reúnem por duas ou três vezes anualmente. A Assembléia da Igreja, formada em 1919, consiste em três casas, a dos bispos, a dos clérigos e a dos leigos. Esses sínodos propõem legislações eclesiásticas ao parlamento inglês. Os anglicanos que vivem fora da Grã-Bretanha têm a liberdade de formar seus próprios órgãos controladores.

VIII. Os Grupos Protestantes

Devido à grande diversidade desses grupos, os corpos controladores também são os mais diversos, desde as hierarquias denominacionais até o governo de uma única igreja local. O tipo congregacional de governo eclesiástico só reconhece a autonomia das igrejas locais, rejeitando qualquer autoridade eclesiástica superior à igreja local.

CONCÍLIOS ECUMÊNICOS

O **Concílio Mundial de Igrejas** é um corpo eclesiástico não-romanista, estabelecido em 1948, cujos membros são as denominações protestantes mais importantes, e as Igrejas Anglicanas e grupos ortodoxos orientais. Seu órgão principal é a Assembléia Geral, que se reuniu em Amsterdan, na Holanda, em 1948; em Evanston, Ill., nos Estados Unidos da América, em 1954; em Nova Déli, na Índia, em 1961; e em Upsália, na Suécia, em 1968. Esse grupo envolve corporações conservadoras e liberais, quanto aos pontos de vista teológicos. Embora afirmando acreditar oficialmente na divindade de Cristo, por meio de interpretações distorcidas tem sido capaz de assumir posições liberais, até mesmo radicais. Esse grupo eclesiástico tem promovido causas políticas duvidosas, onde a violência é o *modus operandi*. Tem condenado o governo sul-africano por causa da opressão dos negros, por parte de uma minoria branca dominante, mas tem feito virtual silêncio quanto às perseguições, matanças e abusos contra a liberdade religiosa, nos países de governo comunista. Seus envolvimentos políticos e sociais com freqüência têm anulado os esforços bíblicos e espirituais, sob a forma de evangelização e ensino, que o grupo tem envidado.

O **Concílio Americano de Igrejas Cristãs** foi formado para opor-se ao Concílio Mundial de Igrejas, provendo uma alternativa para as igrejas de tendências conservadoras, que assim podem contar com um concílio universal. Foi organizado em 1951. Defende o fundamentalismo teológico. Porém, assim como o ceticismo é a grande fraqueza do liberalismo, assim também o espírito contencioso é a fraqueza do fundamentalismo. Daí, o Concílio Americano de Igrejas Cristãs tornou-se vítima de conflitos internos, com resultantes defecções. Em seu ponto culminante, esse Concílio congregava cerca de um milhão de pessoas, em certa variedade de denominações evangélicas. O ramo internacional deste movimento foi o *Concílio Internacional de Igrejas Cristãs*.

A **Associação Nacional de Evangélicos** ocupa uma posição intermediária entre os dois concílios acima descritos. Também mostra tendências conservadoras, mas sem o radicalismo do Concílio Americano de Igrejas Cristãs. Foi formada em 1942, com o propósito de preservar a fé cristã de forma positiva, evitando a beligerância que com freqüência caracteriza o fundamentalismo (que vide). A Associação Nacional de Evangélicos enfatiza tanto o lado social quanto o lado evangelístico da ação cristã, tendo promovido organizações como a Comissão para Alívio do Após-Guerra (1944), que enviou ajuda às vítimas da guerra da Europa. Muitos dos líderes desse grupo têm defendido a teologia neo-evangélica, uma posição de meio termo entre o fundamentalismo e a neo-ortodoxia, procurando reinterpretar conceitos cristãos como a inerrância e a inspiração das Escrituras. Mas essa reinterpretação tem provocado virulentos ataques por parte dos direitistas teológicos. Ver o artigo sobre o *Protestantismo*, quanto a uma discussão sobre as várias nuanças doutrinárias que devem ser levadas em conta, no estudo do protestantismo, quanto a seus desenvolvimentos teológicos.

IX. O Antigo Problema da Autoridade

Há alguma coisa na mente religiosa, do Oriente ou do Ocidente, cristã ou não, que precisa apoiar-se sobre a segurança da inerrância e de alguma autoridade específica, que possam ser utilizadas para definir e solucionar todos os problemas. Em primeiro lugar, a maioria dos grupos religiosos que surgem não tarda a proclamar-se o melhor, se não mesmo o final, definitivo. Além disso, as escrituras sagradas que eles produzem são declaradas a *revelação final* de Deus. As crianças gostam de contar com algum ponto de segurança, correndo para as saias da mamãe ante à menor provocação. Os religiosos também exibem certa infantilidade, em sua necessidade de encontrar uma verdade final, uma autoridade final, a inerrância em assuntos religiosos. É possível que esse seja um dos imperativos da alma humana.

O **padrão de autoridade** é bastante complexo na Igreja Católica Romana e na Igreja Ortodoxa Oriental; mas, o que tem em comum é que, além dessa complexidade, eles terminam crendo em uma verdade imutável, por ser inerrante. Os grupos protestantes, por sua vez, objetam aos supostos decretos infalíveis do papado, negando que as decisões dos concílios eclesiásticos sempre estão certas. Os protestantes conservadores declaram depender exclusivamente das Escrituras Sagradas; mas, na prática, o que lhes interessa é a sua própria interpretação das Escrituras, visto que inúmeros grupos protestantes afirmam a mesma coisa, e, no entanto, exibem tão diversificadas natureza e crenças. Os protestantes de tendências liberais negam a inerrância das Escrituras, e exortam-nos a buscar a verdade mediante a preservação daquilo que é bom no antigo, mas não ignorando voluntariamente o fato de que a verdade é uma questão de conquista perene, e não uma realização única e definitiva. É bom lembrarmos que as Escrituras não reivindicam inerrância quanto a tudo quanto afirmam, mormente quando examinadas através das traduções, ou mesmo através de manuscritos que foram sujeitados, através de vários séculos, às manipulações dos copistas. A Bíblia adapta-se à linguagem e aos conceitos populares da época em que ela foi escrita; e seu propósito também não foi o de ensinar fatos científicos, e, sim, como podemos corrigir nossas relações com Deus e o próximo, dirigindo nossa alma no caminho certo para o mundo espiritual. Portanto, a idéia da inerrância da Bíblia, a respeito de tudo quanto ela afirma, é um dogma humano sobre as Escrituras. Outrossim, é impossível limitarmos a sabedoria de Deus a um livro. A própria Bíblia ensina-nos que há coisas que não nos foram reveladas. Ver Deu. 29:29. A sabedoria de Deus, pois, é infinitamente maior do que qualquer livro ou biblioteca. Isso posto, a verdade é vasta demais para ser reduzida a uma simples coleção de regras e listas de corpos interpretativos autorizados. Isso é o que procurei salientar no meu artigo sobre a questão da *Autoridade*. A busca pela verdade é uma aventura, a qual se prolongará pela eternidade. Isso não significa, porém, que mesmo neste lado da existência não possamos dispor de grandes verdades bíblicas que requerem nossa atenção e lealdade, ou que não devemos defender a revelação bíblica até o último de nossos dias na terra. A Bíblia é uma das grandes e valiosas revelações divinas. Ver II Tim. 3:16,17. Todavia, nossa busca pela verdade, em todos os seus aspectos — e não somente no religioso — não pode limitar-se às Escrituras. Isso é um dogma humano, tendo sido o grande erro de muitos eclesiásticos da Idade Média, que faziam da Bíblia o padrão até mesmo para o conhecimento científico, tendo perseguido aos que discordavam de tão grande limitação. Os que defendem os dogmas, partam eles de onde partirem, não apreciam declarações como essas. Porém, a busca autêntica pela verdade é mais importante do que ser aceito pela maioria, conformando-se aos padrões restritos dos dogmáticos. Se alguém limitar-se à verdade que *eles* aceitam, restringir-se-á à limitada verdade *deles*. Quanto a mim, busco a verdade de Deus, e não dos homens. A verdade de Deus rasga as costuras de todas as declarações denominacionais, credais, limitadas pelos sistemas religiosos dos homens.

CONCÍLIOS LATERANOS

Os concílios lateranos foram os de números nove, dez, onze, doze e dezoito, dentre os vinte e um concílios eclesiásticos reconhecidos pela Igreja Católica Romana. O nome desses cinco concílios deve-se ao fato de que foram efetuados no palácio de Latrão, dos papas de Roma. Esse palácio, por sua vez, deriva-se do fato de que, em tempos antigos, pertencia à família italiana Laterani. Alistamos abaixo esses cinco concílios:

1. Laterano I (1123), sob o papa Calisto II, que confirmou o tratado de Worms (que vide), com Henrique V, da Alemanha, pondo fim à controvérsia das investíduras (que vide).
2. Laterano II (1139), sob Inocente II, que excomungou Rogério da Sicília e os bispos nomeados pelo antipapa, Anacleto II (que vide). Esse concílio também estabilizou o *privilegium canonis*, em defesa dos clérigos, reprovando o decreto de Nicolau II, acerca da eleição dos papas.
3. Laterano III (1179), sob Alexandre III (que vide), que pôs fim às controvérsias entre o papado e o imperador Frederico I, da Alemanha, confirmando a paz de Veneza.
4. Laterano IV (1215), sob Inocente III, que confirmou o uso do termo *transubstanciação* (que vide). Também exigiu a participação na hóstia por ocasião da páscoa, com a ameaça de exclusão para os desobedientes.
5. Laterano V (1512-1517), sob o papa Júlio II, convocado para reestabelecer a paz entre os príncipes cristãos europeus, para promover a guerra contra os turcos e para determinar várias reformas «no cabeça e nos membros» da Igreja Católica Romana.

As *atas* desses concílios foram publicadas por bem conhecidos compiladores como Mansi, em seu *Conciliorum nova et amplissima collectio*, Paris (1901-1924), e Hefele, em seu *Conciliengeschichte*, Frieburgo, 1886. Além desses concílios, considerados «ecumênicos» pela Igreja Católica Romana, houve outros conclaves, de natureza local, chamados *sínodos* (que vide), também efetuados no palácio de Latrão. (AM E)

CONCÍLIOS VATICANOS

Ver **Vaticano, Concílios de**.

CONCLAVE

Essa palavra vem do latim **cum**, «com», e **clavis**, «chave». Esse termo é usado para referir-se à reunião secreta dos cardeais, ao se congregarem para eleger um novo papa. O papa Gregório X, em 1274, ordenou tal reunião secreta com esse propósito, e, de alguma maneira, a eleição dos novos papas passou a incluir a medida. A palavra *conclave* também é usada para indicar os apartamentos existentes no Vaticano onde os cardeais reúnem-se para escolher um novo papa, aposentos esses mantidos trancados até o fim da eleição do novo sumo pontífice. (E WA)

CONCOMITÂNCIA

Essa palavra significa «companheirismo»; mas é usada como termo técnico pela Igreja Católica Romana, em sua teologia, para descrever a presença tanto do corpo quanto do sangue de Cristo, em cada uma das espécies da Ceia, o pão e o vinho. A presença sagrada é usada como uma razão pela qual os leigos não podem participar do cálice. Um cuidado extremo deve ser empregado na sua manipulação, e seria desastroso qualquer derramamento do vinho. Mas o pão, segundo a doutrina católica romana, também contém o Cristo inteiro, isto é, sua divindade e sua alma humana, juntamente com seu corpo e seu sangue, em virtude da união hipostática, ou seja, aquele que participa somente do pão da Ceia, nada perdeu. A Igreja Católica Romana também afirma que Cristo, em sentido nenhum, morre durante a missa, visto que o Cristo *vivo* é a presença que se encontra nos elementos. Tomás de Aquino descreve esse detalhe teológico em sua *Summa Theologica* (3.76). A base da idéia é a comunhão mística ao nível da substância espiritual, mas nada disso tem a ver com os elementos materiais da Eucaristia (que vide), que permanecem os mesmos. Quanto a maiores explicações a respeito, ver o artigo sobre a *Transubstanciação*. (B C)

CONCORDÂNCIA (Concordâncias da Bíblia)

Uma concordância é uma tabela em ordem alfabética de palavras usadas em obras literárias, com referências, para encontrá-las nos lugares especificados. Há muitas concordâncias da Bíblia, mas também há concordância para obras de certos grandes autores, como Shakespeare, Mílton, Spenser, Tennyson, Dante, etc. A primeira concordância bíblica importante foi a do rabino Issac Nathan, que trabalhou na mesma por dez anos, de 1438 a 1448, produzindo sua obra sobre a Bíblia hebraica. Essa concordância foi posteriormente aprimorada pelo hebraísta John Buxtorf, em sua *Concordantia Bibliorum Ebraicae*, publicada em Basel, em 1632. Houve concordâncias no período medieval, da Vulgata Latina. Em 1896, Mendelkern, de Leipzig, publicou uma concordância hebraica que se tornou uma espécie de trabalho padrão, a qual foi muito usada. A melhor concordância da Septuaginta é a de Hatch e Repath, publicada em Oxford, na Inglaterra, em 1897-1900. Quanto ao Novo Testamento, temos a concordância de Moulton e Geden, publicada em 1897. Uma obra muito útil, intitulada *Greek Analytical Lexicon*, que tem algumas características de uma concordância, por causa de seu amplo sistema de referências das principais palavras, com seus derivados, foi publicada por Samuel Bagster & Sons, e continua sendo impressa, agora em edição melhorada.

No idioma inglês, o começo dessa atividade foi a concordância do Novo Testamento de autoria de Thomas Bybson, publicada em 1540. A primeira concordância em inglês da Bíblia inteira foi a de John Marbeck, publicada em 1550. Por motivo desse esforço, ele quase foi executado pelo estado! Samuel Newman, um graduado de Oxford, produziu uma concordância que foi publicada em 1672. Seu título era *Cambridge Concordance*, porquanto uma edição melhorada da mesma foi publicada em Cambridge. Provavelmente, a mais largamente usada concordância da Bíblia em língua inglesa tem sido a de Alexander Cruden, publicada em 1737, até hoje reimpressa. Ao ser lançada, afirmava-se ser *completa*, o que não corresponde à verdade, embora seja bastante abrangente. Durante cento e cinquenta anos, foi a concordância bíblica mais completa em uso. Uma concordância realmente completa é aquela de autoria de Robert Young, que foi publicada pela primeira vez em 1873, e continua sendo impressa. Tem sido

CONCORDÂNCIA — CONCÓRDIA

freqüentemente revisada. Anos depois apareceu a concordância de James Strong, publicada em 1890. Acompanha os vocábulos hebraicos e gregos, de tal modo que o leitor pode descobrir facilmente as palavras dos textos originais, por detrás da tradução para o inglês. Essa é a concordância que este autor tem usado por muitos anos, que tem servido como *sine qua non* no tocante a certos aspectos do labor da exposição das Escrituras. Paralelamente, o tradutor desta Enciclopédia, João M. Bentes, tem usado a *Young's Analytical Concordance to the Bible*, quanto a todos os verbetes sobre temas bíblicos. Isso significa que o leitor e usuário desta Enciclopédia tem o duplo benefício dessas duas excelentes concordâncias da Bíblia em inglês. Quanto aos termos gregos, usados no Novo Testamento, o tradutor tem empregado tanto o *Greek Analytical Lexicon* quanto a *Concordance to the Greek Testament*, de Moulton & Geden, obras referidas acima.

Em inglês há várias concordâncias do tipo grego-inglês, que nos dão valiosas informações sobre as palavras gregas. No *Englishman's Greek Concordance of the New Testament*, compilada por George V. Wigram, e impressa desde 1839, mil páginas apresentam ao leitor o vocabulário grego do Novo Testamento, arranjado em ordem alfabética. Uma obra similar é a de J.B. Smith, da Herald Press, de Scottdale, estado da Pennsylvania, impressa em 1955. Apresenta um gráfico de cada palavra grega, completa com todos os modos como foi traduzida na versão inglesa King James do Novo Testamento, e com referências completas onde cada palavra foi encontrada. Ainda de origem mais recente é uma obra similar, de J. Stegenga, chamada *The Greek-English Analytical Concordance of the Greek-English New Testament*, 1963.

Obras similares têm sido preparadas para o leitor inglês que deseja investigar a porção hebraica da Bíblia. Em cerca de 1876 apareceu a *A Hebrew Concordance*, de John Taylor, adaptada para a Bíblia inglesa. Aaron Pick, professor de hebraico na Universidade de Praga, publicou uma obra similar, em 1874.

No tocante a outras traduções inglesas, que não a King James Version, há uma concordância da Revised Version, de 1883, bem como uma da Revised Standard Version, de 1957. Além dessas, a New English Bible tem uma concordância, especialmente preparada para ela, que foi dada a público em 1964.

• • •   • • •

Concordâncias em Português

1. *Concordância Bíblica*, baseia-se na edição Revista e Atualizada no Brasil, da tradução de João Ferreira de Almeida. Sociedade Bíblica do Brasil.

2. *Chave Bíblica*, baseia-se na edição Revista e Atualizada no Brasil, da tradução de João Ferreira de Almeida. Sociedade Bíblica do Brasil.

3. *Concordância Bíblica Abreviada*, edição Revista e Corrigida. Editora Vida.

4. *Concordância Grega-Portuguesa*. A Editora Fiel de Atibaia, SP, está nos últimos passos (1986) na preparação de uma concordância baseada no NT grego, com definições e todas as referências onde as palavras gregas aparecem, com a estatística apropriada em relação a freqüência do uso.

N.B. Agradeço a gentil cooperação de *William Barkley*, diretor da Biblioteca Evangélica de São Paulo, pela preparação das informações sobre concordâncias *em português*. (E Z)

CONCORDATA

Uma **concordata** é um acordo feito entre os mais altos oficiais da Igreja Católica Romana e o estado a respeito das relações mútuas, feitas com o intuito de evitar fricção. Esses acordos envolvem muitos assuntos, mas, com freqüência, são feitos no interesse do papado e das propriedades da Igreja de Roma. A concordata usualmente subentende alguma forma de vitória diplomática da Igreja Católica Romana, visto que ocorre quando Roma é ameaçada de alguma maneira, e quando acontecimentos negativos são evitados mediante a diplomacia. Algumas concordatas ocorrem mediante bulas papais aceitas pelos governos. São acordos bilaterais, considerados garantias ou fianças que não podem ser rescindidas, alteradas ou abolidas, sem o consentimento de ambos os lados envolvidos. Naturalmente, se algum acordo for feito compulsoriamente, então nenhum dos lados envolvidos é considerado obrigado a observar os termos da concordata.

Três Teorias sobre Concordatas. 1. A *teoria legalista.* O estado é considerado supremo, obrigando-se a fazer algo que a Igreja solicita. Não há acordo feito entre duas partes iguais. 2. A *teoria do pacto.* O contrato seria verdadeiramente bilateral. 3. A *teoria do privilégio.* Somente o estado tem a obrigação de cumprir as condições do documento, porquanto é a Igreja que concede os privilégios envolvidos. Na prática, a teoria predominante é a segunda dentre essas três variedades.

Concordatas Históricas Importantes. A Concordata de Worms, de 1122, que pôs fim ao conflito sobre as investidores (ver *Worms...*). A concordata Constança de 1418. A Concordata Francesa, de 1516. A Concordata entre Napoleão Bonaparte e a Igreja de Roma, chamada Concordata de 1801. O Tratado e a Concordata de Latrão, de 1929, entre Pio XI e a Itália, que pôs fim à chamada Questão Romana. Desde 1926, na Alemanha e em outros países predominantemente protestantes, evangélicos e não-católicos, tem havido concordatas assinadas entre os governos e as autoridades eclesiásticas da Igreja Católica Romana. (B E)

CONCÓRDIA, FÓRMULA DE

Esse longo documento encerra a série de confissões luteranas que fazem parte do Livro da Concórdia. Foi compilado em 1577 por Jacó de Andreas, de Tubingen, em cooperação com outros. Foi aprovado pelos estados luteranos alemães, em 1580, tendo sido publicado em Dresden. Um dos propósitos da fórmula foi de eliminar as posições radicais assumidas nas controvérsias que taxavam a Igreja Luterana. Os luteranos uniram-se em oposição tanto ao papado quanto aos seguidores dos reformadores suíços; mas não estavam totalmente acordes quanto a doutrinas como a justificação pela fé, a relação entre a fé e as boas obras, a liberdade da vontade humana, a realidade da presença de Cristo nos elementos da Eucaristia. A Fórmula de Concórdia, segundo esperava-se, poria fim às controvérsias em torno dessas questões. Lutero é ali freqüentemente citado com referência, como uma autoridade, na tentativa de encerrar os debates.

Itens Importantes da Fórmula de Concórdia. Quatro itens destacam-se: 1. O pecado original corrompe totalmente, de tal modo que a vontade do homem torna-se completamente hostil a Deus e incapaz do bem, enquanto não for renovada pelo Espírito Santo. 2. A doutrina da justificação exclusivamente pela fé. 3. As boas obras resultam da salvação, não sendo a causa da salvação. 4. Aparecem as definições de Lutero a respeito da Eucaristia, da pessoa de Cristo, de sua descida ao hades, da predestinação, além de outros itens da doutrina cristã. A doutrina do *communicatio idiomatum* (que vide), aparece como um apêndice.

A Fórmula de Concórdia, juntamente com a Confissão de Augusburgo, a Apologia, os Artigos de Smalcald e os Catecismos de Lutero compunham, em 1580, o *Livro da Concórdia*, que tornou-se a constituição doutrinária da Igreja Luterana. Ver o artigo geral sobre o *Luteranismo*. (AM C)

CONCRETO UNIVERSAL

Hegel (que vide) usou a expressão para indicar seu ponto de vista de que o ato de pensar deve ser algo universal, que se origina de uma lei universal, como um dos aspectos do *absoluto*. As leis do estado, que se originam da vontade geral, seriam universais em sua forma, pelo que a vontade geral também poderia ser chamada de *universal*. Essa vontade, porém, também é a vontade de alguma comunidade histórica particular, e nesse sentido, torna-se *concreta*. (F)

CONCUBINA

Vem do lat. **con**, «com», e **combere**, «deitar». Portanto, «deitar com».

A palavra aparece somente no Antigo Testamento, havendo dois termos hebraicos envolvidos, a saber:

1. *Lechenah*, «donzela cantora». Palavra que aparece por somente três vezes: Dan. 5:2,3,23. Essa palavra aparece na porção aramaica de Daniel.

2. *Pilegesh*, «concubina». Palavra que figura por trinta e sete vezes (por exemplo, Gên. 22:24; 25:6; Juí. 8:31; 19:1,2,9,10,24,25,27,29; 20:4-6; II Sam. 3:7; 5:13; 15:16; I Reis 11:3; I Crô. 1:32; 2:46,48; II Crô. 11:21; Est. 2:14; Cant. 6:7,8).

Havia variedades de concubinas. Talvez a mais comum fosse a mulher escrava, a qual, como propriedade de seu senhor, era usada com finalidades sexuais. Quase sempre isso resultava em uma outra família, distinta da família legítima, gerada através da esposa ou esposas legítimas. Porém, de acordo com os costumes dos hebreus, tal mulher podia ser adquirida a dinheiro, ou poderia ser uma mulher cativada na guerra, ou então poderiam ser mulheres hebréias contratadas com esse propósito. Algumas vezes, quando o casamento regular não produzia os herdeiros desejados, era usada uma concubina com esse propósito, conforme se vê no bem conhecido caso de Abraão e Hagar, em Gênesis 16:2. Os pais das noivas com freqüência davam criadas às suas filhas, quando se casavam, como presente de casamento. Subseqüentemente, essas criadas tornavam-se concubinas dos maridos de suas patroas. Foi o que sucedeu a Zilpa, em Gên. 29:24, e a Bila, em Gên. 29:29. A lei mosaica protegia as concubinas (Êxo. 21:7-11; Deu. 21:10-14), embora fossem conhecidas como mulheres de posição inferior às esposas legítimas (Juí. 8:31), pelo que também os homens podiam divorciar-se delas mais facilmente (Gên. 21:10-14).

A prática era tão comum na cultura do Antigo Testamento que a concubina podia aspirar desfrutar do afeto do homem com quem estava ligada, não menos que no caso de uma esposa legítima (Juí. 19:1-3), e, por muitas vezes, desfrutava de iguais privilégios àquêles dados à esposa, no lar. Algumas concubinas eram mesmo consideradas mais importantes que as esposas legítimas, — como seria de esperar. A mente dos hebreus não via qualquer coisa de errado com certas formas de poligamia, pois ao homem era concedido grande liberdade sexual. O que era severamente punido era o adultério, quando um homem seduzia a esposa de outro. Se indagarmos por que essa prática era tão universal, há várias respostas:

1. A natureza polígama natural dos homens. 2. A questão da herança, pois nenhum homem podia deixar de ter herdeiros e ser respeitado como membro da comunidade. Havia esposas estéreis, o que exigia que o homem tomasse outras mulheres. 3. A doutrina hebréia de que ter muitos filhos era sinal do favor divino. O fruto do ventre era a *recompensa* de um homem (Sal. 127:3). Naturalmente, a prática estava sujeita a abusos. Para exemplificar, os monarcas orientais competiam uns com os outros, para ver quem conseguia o harém mais numeroso, com a maior variedade de mulheres. Houve até mesmo *princesas* que vieram a fazer parte desses haréns, aumentando a importância dos mesmos, e o gabarito dos monarcas. Portanto, é errado pensarmos nas concubinas apenas como uma segunda escolha, como mulheres de baixa envergadura, como uma escrava. Houve muitas exceções notáveis quanto a esse tipo de concubinato. O mais incrível exemplo foi dado por Salomão, nas páginas do Antigo Testamento. Ele tinha setecentas esposas, muitas delas princesas, além de trezentas concubinas (I Reis 11:3). Muitos dos homens invejavam abertamente a sua situação, a despeito do fato de que o mesmo versículo diz que essas mulheres perverteram o coração desse monarca. Sem dúvida, certas práticas idólatras foram envolvidas, para agradar as mulheres mais importantes de Salomão.

Por que o Concubinato Diminuiu nos Tempos do Novo Testamento? A primeira razão era de origem *econômica*. É preciso muito dinheiro para manter até mesmo um harém modesto. Somente os ricos e poderosos podem destacar-se. Sabemos que os mórmons, no começo da história do movimento, embora até mesmo encorajados a praticar a poligamia, por suas doutrinas religiosas, não o faziam em grandes números. A época dos pioneiros não era um tempo de dinheiro fácil para que muitos homens pudessem assumir a responsabilidade por mais de uma esposa. Além disso, Joseph Smith havia avisado a seus seguidores de que a poligamia era uma responsabilidade sagrada, não devendo ser assumida sem os recursos próprios e a atitude mental apropriada. A segunda razão era *espiritual*. Já vimos que — no caso de Salomão — a prática da poligamia havia prejudicado espiritualmente a esse rei de Israel. A terceira razão era a *voz profética*, a qual, nos últimos estágios do Antigo Testamento, tinha começado a ressaltar a monogamia como o ideal no matrimônio. Ver Mal. 2:14 ss. Jesus também frisou esse ideal (Mat. 19:8), e Paulo proibiu os casamentos plurais, no caso dos líderes da Igreja cristã (I Tim. 3:2). O próprio fato de que essa regra teve de ser determinada mostra-nos que ainda havia casamentos plurais na Igreja primitiva. A história mostra-nos, entretanto, que a monogamia tornara-se o costume padrão da sociedade hebréia, na época de Jesus, embora ainda houvesse exceções. A lei mosaica permitia a poligamia, e muitos judeus ainda seguiam tal provisão.

A Moderna Igreja Cristã tem tido problemas com a poligamia, especialmente na África, onde tal costume ainda está bem vivo. A princípio, os missionários evangélicos proibiam a poligamia para qualquer líder das igrejas. Mas, quando se descobriu que muitas das esposas rejeitadas tornavam-se prostitutas, muitos missionários mudaram de parecer, permitindo a continuação da poligamia, como algo não tão nefasto quanto a prostituição. O problema é que poucas mulheres, dentre as rejeitadas, tinham qualquer meio de sustentação, e assim voltavam-se para a prostituição, se quisessem sobreviver. Em um sínodo recente, efetuado em dezembro de 1985, efetuado para revisar algumas das medidas tomadas quando do concílio do Vaticano II (ver o artigo sobre os *Concílios da Igreja*), foi debatido o problema da poligamia na África. Um bispo católico romano da África afirmou que impor a monogamia na África é impossível. O papa João Paulo II reagiu, consternado, diante dessa declaração, erguendo as mãos ao céu, em um gesto espontâneo. É interessante observar que, durante quase o debate inteiro, o papa João Paulo II ouviu tudo em atitude quase passiva, mesmo quando problemas difíceis precisavam ser enfrentados pela Igreja Católica Romana. Porém, foi a poligamia dos africanos que produziu a reação mais emocional. Ver o artigo separado sobre a *Poligamia*. (H ND)

CONCUPISCÊNCIA

Precisamos levar em conta três palavras hebraicas e quatro palavras gregas, a saber:

1. *Nephesh*, «alma», «respiração», «desejo». Essa palavra hebraica é de ocorrência comum, mas com o sentido de «concupiscência» aparece somente por duas vezes: Êxo. 15:9; Sal. 78:18.

2. *Sheriruth*, «teimosia», «inimizade», «imaginação». Palavra hebraica usada por dez vezes, embora apenas por uma vez com o sentido de «concupiscência»: Sal. 81:12.

3. *Taavah*, «objeto de desejo». Palavra hebraica usada por quinze vezes. Por exemplo: Sal. 78:29,30; 112:10; Pro. 10:24; 21:15; Isa. 26:8.

4. *Epithumía*, «desejo forte», «concupiscência». Palavra grega usada por trinta e sete vezes. Alguns exemplos são: Mar. 4:19; Luc. 22:15; João 8:44; Rom. 1:24; Gál. 5:16,24; Efé. 2:3; Fil. 1:23; Col.3:5.

5. *Hedoné*, «prazer», «doçura». Palavra grega usada por cinco vezes: Luc. 8:14; Tito 3:3; Tia. 4:1,3; II Ped. 2:13. É desse termo que nos vem o vocábulo português «hedonismo» (que vide).

6. *Óreksis*, «desejo ansioso». Palavra grega usada por somente uma vez: Rom. 1:27.

7. *Páthos*, «sofrimento», «afeto». Palavra grega usada por três vezes: Rom. 1:26; Col. 3:5; I Tes. 4:5.

O pecado da concupiscência é combatido no *Decálogo* (que vide) de várias maneiras. Os pecados sexuais são proibidos pelo sétimo mandamento (Êxo. 20:14), e a cobiça de todas as formas é proibida em Êxodo 20:17. Porém, nenhuma outra atitude e ação é mais comum entre os homens do que a concupiscência e a cobiça. Isso harmoniza-se bem com a natureza basicamente egoísta do homem. Todavia, há palavras hebraicas e gregas que podem ser usadas em sentido negativo ou em sentido positivo. Quanto ao termo grego *epithumía*, tão importante no Novo Testamento, ele é usado em sentido positivo em Luc. 22:15 e I Tes. 2:17. Assim, Jesus *desejou* comer a páscoa com os seus discípulos; e Paulo tinha o grande desejo de visitar os crentes de Tessalônica. Mas o sentido negativo é muito mais freqüente no Novo Testamento. Os pagãos tinham desejos impuros, que os corrompiam (Rom. 1:24). Os jovens mostram a tendência de experimentar os desejos pecaminosos. Por esse motivo, Timóteo foi aconselhado a evitar as paixões da juventude (II Tim. 2:22). Paixões e maus desejos precisam ser mortificados pelos crentes (Col. 3:5). As concupiscências carnais precisam ser evitadas (I Ped. 2:11). Esses desejos distorcidos produzem toda a espécie de males e corrupções neste mundo (II Ped. 1:4; 2:10) que impedem o desenvolvimento da alma.

Os estóicos procuravam anular os desejos, mostrando que o indivíduo cai em um ciclo louco por causa dos mesmos. Primeiramente, a pessoa deseja; então obtém aquilo que quer; tendo obtido o que quer, deseja algo mais e quanto mais deseja, mais obtém, e mais deseja, *ad infinitum*. O resultado final desse ciclo vicioso é a frustração, porquanto tal ciclo não pode ser interrompido, e nem satisfaz, realmente. O estoicismo (que vide) recomendava a *apatia*, a fim de substituir os desejos. Mas o cristianismo recomenda o cultivo de desejos espirituais, em substituição aos desejos carnais.

A **concupiscência** até mesmo os apetites naturais, são classificados como concupiscência exagerada, sem falar nada sobre aquelas coisas diretamente proibidas. Algumas pessoas desejam intensamente alimentos; mas não há apetite que se possa comparar com o desejo sexual. Schopenhauer queixava-se que os jovens desperdiçam metade de seu tempo promovendo essa forma de concupiscência, supondo que tal desejo é uma *insanidade* que pode ser curada por meio do casamento. Ele percebia claramente que aquilo que quase todas as pessoas chamam de «amor», na realidade não passa de concupiscência. Contudo, ele se referia favoravelmente à simpatia, porquanto todos nos encontramos na mesma condição de miséria. Ver o artigo sobre o *Pessimismo*. Recentemente li um artigo sobre aconselhamento cristão. Ali os pastores são advertidos sobre o fato de que podem ser apanhados na teia das paixões, por causa de seus próprios *impulsos elementares*. Isso é um eufemismo, para dizer que até mesmo as pessoas mais religiosas continuam impelidas por paixões físicas, visto que todos nós somos animais sexuados. Naturalmente, há o lado espiritual do homem que combate contra o descontrole acerca dessas paixões. Paulo refere-se a esse conflito interno no sétimo capítulo da epístola aos Romanos, o que se tornou uma exposição clássica e um tanto mais impressionante, porque a questão é uma confissão feita pelo próprio apóstolo. Em Gálatas 5:16 ele alude aos desejos da carne. A Bíblia ensina que o último inimigo a ser vencido é a morte. Mas, se ele tivesse falado sobre o último vício a ser conquistado, provavelmente teria dito: «O último vício a ser conquistado é a concupiscência». Ver o artigo sobre os *Vícios*. Esse artigo mostra quantos problemas temos de enfrentar. O trecho de Efésios 5:5 informa-nos que tais vícios precisam ser conquistados, antes que possamos herdar o reino de Deus e de Cristo. Se não forem dominados, esses vícios haverão de levar-nos a juízo (Efé. 5:6). A passagem de Efésios 1:10 assegura que a vitória final espera por todos nós, mas um homem pode desviar-se para longe, e por muito tempo, antes que chegue a obter a vitória sobre as suas próprias paixões.

CONCURSO

Vem do latim *con*, «com», e *currere*, «correr», ou seja, «correr juntamente com». Na linguagem teológica, essa palavra é usada para aludir àquele aspecto da providência divina mediante o qual Deus coopera com as diversas operações da sua criação, estando envolvido, de alguma maneira, nas causas secundárias. Essa doutrina abraça a idéia de que Deus preserva e guia todas as coisas, de tal modo que a sua vontade é cumprida. No tocante à vida humana,

CONDENAÇÃO — CONDENAR

a idéia aparece mesclada ao problema da soberania divina, no tocante ao livre-arbítrio humano. Tomás de Aquino e os escolásticos muito tiveram a dizer sobre o assunto, embora continui sendo questão sujeita a muito debate. A questão envolve-nos no problema da imanência e da transcendência de Deus.

Aspectos: 1. *O concurso moral*. Esse aspecto diz respeito à relação entre a influência divina e as intenções e atos morais dos homens. 2. *O concurso físico*, que aborda a relação entre Deus e a sua criação material. Até que ponto, em ambos os casos, a vontade predestinadora de Deus está envolvida? Até que ponto as coisas acontecem impelidas pelas leis naturais, ou seja, de forma caótica? e até que ponto o homem tem a liberdade de agir? Por que existe o mal, se Deus continua agindo? Ver o artigo sobre o *Problema do Mal*. Deus usa o livre-arbítrio humano sem destruí-lo, embora não saibamos dizer *como* o faz. As duas doutrinas, da imanência e da transcendência de Deus são verdadeiras, embora não seja fácil explicar de qual maneira. (B E)

CONDENAÇÃO Ver também **Condenar**.

Rom. 8:1: *Portanto, agora nenhuma condenação há para os que estão em Cristo Jesus*.

Condenação. Está aqui em foco a sentença condenatória, segundo lemos no trecho de Rom. 5:16, o qual versículo deixa claro que se trata da condenação pronunciada contra o pecador, que o leva à morte, ou seja, especificamente, à morte eterna, ao julgamento da segunda morte, em contraste com a vida que nos tem sido proporcionada por intermédio de Cristo. Paulo dizia, por conseguinte, que o crente verdadeiro jamais poderá entrar no juízo do qual participarão os ímpios, embora, ao longo do percurso, o crente talvez tenha que experimentar castigos severos, além de juízos de outra natureza, medidas essas que têm por finalidade ensiná-lo a ser santo, a desejar receber a imagem de Cristo em sua própria alma.

Dizemos que o crente não pode participar do mesmo destino do incrédulo, ainda que, ao longo do caminho, assim pareça que ele está destinado. No entanto, finalmente, Deus haverá de trazê-lo de volta ao rebanho, sem importar até que ponto o crente se desvie. E essa recondução é feita ou através do histórico Senhor Jesus Cristo ou através do Verbo eterno, que é a mesma pessoa que aquela, posto que em ofício e em manifestação diferentes. Decair da graça, até o ponto de ficar «perdido», no caso do crente, se é que isso realmente pode acontecer (e algumas passagens bíblicas ensinam que, pelo menos como hipótese, isso pode suceder), é algo *relativo*. Em outras palavras, tal possibilidade pode ser aplicada somente a um determinado período, experimentada durante algum tempo. Porém, se falarmos em termos absolutos, conforme faz aqui o apóstolo Paulo, nenhuma das ovelhas poderá jamais vir a perder-se.

1. *Não existe condenação final*, como penalidade ou conseqüência do pecado, tanto do pecado original como dos pecados individuais, no caso dos que estão «em Cristo Jesus».

2. Mas isso não quer dizer que nada existe, na vida do crente, que seja digno de condenação; antes, essa total ausência de condenação se deve ao fato de que o crente está justificado em Cristo, já tendo sido aceito nele, achando-se, além disso, no processo da santificação, o que significa que virá a ser totalmente santo, quando então nada terá em si que seja digno de condenação.

3. Essa ausência total de condenação, portanto, aplica-se tanto à função da justificação como à função da santificação, porque é resultante de ambas essas obras do Espírito Santo.

4. Considerada essa declaração em seu sentido mais lato, não há nenhuma condenação para os que estão «em Cristo Jesus» porque o processo inteiro da salvação — a justificação e a santificação — culmina na absolvição final e na glória eterna. A ausência total de condenação, pois, antecipa o cumprimento de todas as promessas que temos na pessoa de Cristo Jesus, e a atuação interna do Espírito Santo é a garantia da fruição final e total de cada graça que Deus tem estendido aos crentes.

Condenação e os incrédulos

Algumas denominações da igreja cristã ensinam um destino fixo dos incrédulos, já determinado na hora da morte biológica. Os pais gregos ensinaram a continuação da oportunidade para fazer possível a participação na salvação, depois da morte biológica. Eles viram que a *descida de Cristo ao hades* (que vide), I Ped. 3:16-4:6, abre uma nova perspectiva para a humanidade, especialmente, porque 4:6 declara enfaticamente que, nessa descida, o evangelho foi pregado aos mortos. Com este pensamento, muitos representantes da Igreja Ocidental, e da Igreja Anglicana, têm concordado. Estes mesmos pais também entenderam que textos como Efésios 1:10, falando sobre o *mistério* da vontade de Deus, exigem o entendimento de que, afinal, a missão e o poder de Cristo, garantirão uma restauração universal. Podemos entender que esta restauração será uma tremenda obra de Cristo entre os incrédulos, ou não eleitos, e que resolverá o problema do mal (que vide). Devemos entender de Efé. 1:23, que a igreja será envolvida nesta obra, porque o corpo fará o trabalho do Cabeça, fazendo-o ser tudo para todos. Alguns teólogos entendem que o mistério da vontade de Deus exige a salvação final de todos os seres. Ver sobre Universalismo. Outros entendem que existirá uma *restauração* em contraste com a *redenção* dos eleitos. Neste caso o próprio julgamento será um instrumento (entre muitos) para efetuar esta realização, trazendo uma glória secundária para os não-eleitos. Assim, os efeitos negativos do julgamento (que vide) serão anulados, enquanto seus efeitos positivos serão aplicados. Todos os seres obterão uma glória digna do *Redentor* e *Restaurador*. Nisto, o famoso amor de Deus ganhará a vitória, e não o inimigo das almas, Satanás. Ver maiores detalhes sobre esses pensamentos no artigo sobre a *Restauração*.

CONDENAR Ver também **Condenação**.

Estão envolvidas três palavras hebraicas e cinco palavras gregas, a saber:

1. *Rasha*, «fazer ou declarar errado». Palavra hebraica usada no A.T. por quinze vezes, com o sentido de «condenar» (por exemplo: Êxo. 22:9; Deu. 25:1; Jó 9:20; 10:2; Sal. 37:33; Pro. 12:2; Isa. 50:9; 54:17).

2. *Anash*, «oprimir», «taxar». Palavra hebraica que ocorre por duas vezes com o significado de «condenar»; II Crô. 36:3 e Pro. 17:26.

3. *Shaphat*, «julgar», «agir com magistrado». Palavra hebraica usada por duzentas e três vezes. Por exemplo: Gên. 16:5; 31:53; Êxo. 5:21; 18:13; 16:22,26; Lev. 19:15; Núm. 35:24; Deu. 1:16; 16:18; Juí. 3:10; 4:4; 16:31; I Sam. 3:13; 4:18; 7:6,15,16,17; I Reis 3:9,10; II Reis 15:5; I Crô. 16:33; II Crô. 1:10,11; Jó 21:22; Sal. 7:8; 9:4,8; Pro. 29:14;

CONDIÇÕES — CONDIMENTOS

Ecl. 3:17; Isa. 1:17,23; Jer. 5:28; Lam. 3:59; Eze. 7:3,27; 11:10,11; 16:38; Dan. 9:12; Joel 3:12; Oba. 21; Miq. 3:11; 4:3.

4. *Kataginósko*, «saber algo contra». Palavra hebraica usada por três vezes: Gál. 2:11; I João 3:20,21.

5. *Katadikázo*, «julgar contra». Palavra grega que aparece por quatro vezes: Mat. 12:7,37; Luc. 6:37; Tia. 5:6.

6. *Katakríno*, «condenar». Termo grego usado por dezoito vezes: Mat. 12:41,42; 20:18; 27:3; Mar. 10:33; 14:64; 16:16; Luc. 11:31,32; João 8:10,11; Rom. 2:1; 8:3,34; 14:23; I Cor. 11:32; Heb. 11:7; II Ped. 2:6.

7. *Kríno*, «julgar». Palavra hebraica usada por cerca de cento e quinze vezes, desde Mat. 5:40 até Apo. 20:12,13.

8. *Autokatákritos*, «condenado por si mesmo». Palavra grega usada somente em Tito 3:11.

Ver o artigo geral sobre o *Julgamento*. A palavra «condenar», nas Escrituras, pode referir-se ao juízo final, quando haverá a grande condenação, ou pode referir-se à condenação comum dos homens, como em Deu. 25:1. Em Mateus 12:7, encontramos os juízos adversos que os homens fazem, maldosamente, sobre seus semelhantes. A condenação divina sobrevém aos homens que eles, em meio à luz que foi dada aos homens, preferem viver nas trevas (João 3:19). Sem essa luz divina, os pagãos estão condenados por sua própria voz interna, a consciência (Rom. 2:14,15). Aquele que dá ouvidos às palavras de Cristo escapa da condenação (João 5:24). Aqueles que estão em Cristo Jesus escaparam da condenação (Rom. 8:1). Os homens, de modo diferente do que Deus faz, condenam os inocentes (Sal. 94:21); mas, no fim, Deus reverte todos os julgamentos dessa espécie (I Reis 8:23; Sal. 109:31; Isa. 50:9). Jesus nos proíbe de condenarmos uns aos outros, mediante a atitude censuradora (Luc. 6:37; Rom. 2:1). Noé, ao agir em conformidade com as ordens de Deus, e ao pregar a retidão, condenou o mundo, tendo servido como instrumento de Deus (Mat. 12:41 ss). Um homem pode condenar a si mesmo, através de suas próprias ações e palavras (Jó 9:20; 15:6; Tito 3:11). O coração e a consciência de um homem podem condená-lo (I João 3:20). Os magistrados, como representantes de Deus, condenam àqueles que praticam a iniquidade (Rom. 13:1-5). Jesus não veio a este mundo para condenar, mas para salvar. Portanto, a condenação ocorre porque os homens, pervertidamente, negam-se a aceitar a salvação oferecida no evangelho (João 3:17). Apesar de que o julgamento é real e severo, também é remedial, o que envolve uma grande esperança para todos os seres humanos (I Ped. 4:6).

CONDIÇÕES ATMOSFÉRICAS
Ver **Palestina**.

CONDILLACE, ÉTIENNE BONNOT DE

Suas datas foram 1715-1780. Filósofo francês que, apesar de padre, associou-se às tendências secularizadoras e racionalizadoras dos enciclopedistas (que vide). Ele admirava Locke, e, em suas obras *Essai sur l'origine des connaissances humaines* e *Traité des sensations*, promoveu abertamente os pontos de vista de Locke sobre a natureza da percepção e da compreensão humanas. Chegou mesmo ao ponto de afirmar que a vontade e o entendimento dos homens são modificações do acúmulo de impressões, associa-

ções, etc., que surgem com base no estímulo dos órgãos dos sentidos. Desse modo, ele deixou sem menção considerações sobre a intuição, a razão e o misticismo, que deveriam também ser consideradas porções constitutivas da formação mental de qualquer homem religioso. Ele encontrava no *hábito* a base de todas as funções intelectuais, incluindo a atenção, a rememorização, a comparação, o juízo, a imaginação e o reconhecimento. Visto que só conhecemos os nossos próprios pensamentos, não pode haver qualquer prova absoluta de um mundo externo (ver sobre o *Nihilismo*). Porém, nossas percepções, sobretudo aquelas que envolvem sensações desagradáveis, dão-nos a entender a real existência do mundo exterior. O *ceticismo* (que vide) pode ser um interessante exercício intelectual, mas nunca ganhou coisa alguma para a alma. (F P)

CONDIMENTOS

Várias palavras hebraicas e uma grega devem ser consideradas neste verbete, a saber:

1. *Basam*, *besem* ou *bosem*, «especiaria». Essa palavra, que aparece nessas três formas, ocorre por trinta vezes. Por exemplo: Êxo. 25:6; 30:23; I Reis 10:2,10,25; II Crô. 9:1,9,24; Can. 4:10,14,16; Isa. 39:2; Eze. 27:22; Can. 5:1.

2. *Nekoth*, «arômatas». Palavra hebraica que figura por duas vezes: Gên. 37:25; 43:11.

3. *Sammim*, «substâncias odoríferas». Palavra hebraica usada por dezesseis vezes. Por exemplo: Êxo. 30:34; 37:29; Lev. 4:7; 16:12; II Crô. 2:4; 13:11.

4. *Ároma*, «aroma», «especiaria». Palavra grega que aparece por quatro vezes: Mar. 16:1; Luc. 23:56; 24:1 e João 19:40.

4. *Reqach*, «mistura aromatizada». Palavra hebraica que figura somente em Can. 8:1.

5. *Raqach*, «composto». A palavra aparece por oito vezes. Por exemplo: Eze. 24:10; Êxo. 30:25; II Crô. 16:14.

Originalmente, as especiarias aromatizantes eram usadas quase inteiramente nos cultos de adoração. Muito antes da época de Abraão, os egípcios já usavam especiarias aromatizantes. Nas escavações arqueológicas, essas especiarias têm sido encontradas em receptáculos especiais. O direito dos sacerdotes usarem especiarias aromáticas foi confirmado por Moisés (Êxo. 30:22 ss). As principais especiarias usadas eram a mirra, o cinamomo, o cálamo e a cássia. Essas especiarias, sob a forma de pó, quando misturadas, eram misturadas com puro azeite de oliveira, a fim de compor o que a Bíblia chama de «óleo da santa unção». Parece que cerca de 22 kg de especiarias aromatizantes eram misturados com cerca de 5,7 litros de azeite puro de oliveira.

O trigésimo capítulo do livro de Êxodo deve ser lido com atenção aos detalhes, para que se note as instruções que dizem que as especiarias deveriam ser preparadas por um apotecário, ou, conforme o chamaríamos atualmente, por um farmacêutico. Esses «perfumistas» não podiam preparar tais fragrâncias com qualquer outro propósito, senão aquele que visava à adoração ao Senhor. Entretanto, posteriormente, os filhos de Israel desobedeceram a essa instrução, pois, quando eles clamaram, solicitando um rei, como se dava nas nações circunvizinhas, Samuel avisou-os de que o rei, sem dúvida alguma, tomaria algumas das filhas do povo para serem perfumistas (I Sam. 8:13).

Quando um certo rei de Judá faleceu (ver II Crô. 16:14), os judeus «...puseram-no sobre um leito, que se enchera de perfumes e de várias especiarias, preparados segundo a arte dos perfumistas. Foi mui grande a queima que lhe fizeram destas cousas». É possível que assim tivesse acontecido ao rei Asa por causa de sua doença «dos pés», que era muito grave (II Crô. 16:12). É possível que essa enfermidade fosse a gangrena, que emitia um considerável mau cheiro, devido à putrefação dos pés. O uso de especiarias, nesse caso, presumivelmente poderia ser considerado um uso religioso, porquanto teve lugar em um funeral!

Bem mais tarde, já nos dias de Zedequias, o profeta Jeremias aludiu aos perfumes que seriam «queimados» por ocasião da morte desse rei (Jer. 34:5; cf. Lev. 26:31 e Eze. 20:28). É possível que haja nisso a sugestão à cremação, conforme pensam alguns estudiosos. Nesse caso, o emprego de especiarias aromáticas teria o intuito de disfarçar o mau cheiro que exalava das carnes e ossos queimados. Essa idéia quase certamente é enfatizada por Ezequiel, onde o profeta diz, segundo o original hebraico: «...cozinha a carne, põe muita especiaria...», mas onde nossa versão portuguesa diz: «...cozinha a carne, engrossa o caldo...», o que é uma tradução para a qual não encontramos razões.

As especiarias usadas em Gênesis 37:25 e em Cantares 5:1 e 6:2, provavelmente envolvem as seguintes espécies vegetais, aqui apresentadas segundo seus nomes científicos: *Astragalus tragacantha*. Disso consistiriam as «arômatas» ali mencionadas, embora em Cantares tenhamos, respectivamente, «especiaria» e «canteiros de bálsamos».

É dificílimo traduzir palavras hebraicas que dizem respeito à fauna, à flora, às pedras preciosas, etc., porque a Bíblia não foi escrita numa época de linguagem científica. Por isso, as opiniões dos eruditos e especialistas são extremamente díspares. Quanto a posteriores discussões sobre especiarias e condimentos, consultar os seguintes artigos: *Aloés; Bálsamo; Cálamo; Cana; Cássia; Cinamono; Cosmetologia; Cominho; Incenso; Goma; Hena; Mirra; Nardo; Ungüento; Perfumaria; Açafrão; Cana Aromática; Estoraque; Substâncias Odoríferas.*

CONDUTA

No latim, **con**, «com» e **ducere**, «guiar», o que dá a entender uma *maneira de agir e de viver*. O assunto reveste-se de capital importância para a ética (que vide), visto que o propósito da ética é indicar como se consegue a *conduta ideal*. Algumas respostas que têm sido propostas são as seguintes: *O prazer* (hedonismo) seria o alvo da conduta; a *felicidade* (eudaimonismo) seria esse alvo; a *virtude* (função específica de cada virtude) seria a luz orientadora; a *apatia* seria o estado ideal a ser obtido. A fé cristã situa a questão da conduta dentro da esfera da espiritualidade. A conduta do corpo visa promover o bem-estar de nossos semelhantes (o que seria viver a lei do amor), mas também visa promover a salvação de nossos semelhantes (Filipenses 2:12). Os *galardões* (que vide) dependerão de nossa conduta (I Cor. 3:10 ss). O *julgamento* final será determinado pela conduta de cada um (Rom. 2:6; Apo. 20:12). Ver os vários artigos referidos, quanto a uma completa discussão sobre o assunto.

CONDUTA IDEAL

O exemplo do apóstolo Paulo.

«Nenhum escravo romano, tangido pelo açoite ou pelo aguilhão, poderia ter trabalhado como Paulo trabalhou. Paulo exigiu o máximo de seu corpo frágil e de seu espírito sensível; e durante a vida inteira teve de enfrentar a oposição, a zombaria e a perseguição, da parte daqueles que deveriam ter sido seus amigos, e que de fato se mostraram amigáveis para com ele, até o momento em que entrou para o serviço de Jesus Cristo... Segundo o ponto de vista do mundo, ele dera muito e ganhara pouco, além das tribulações e do opróbrio. Desistira de distinguida posição na comunidade judaica, a fim de tornar-se o homem mais odiado entre aquele povo capaz de ódios apaixonados. Apesar de que seus esforços, em favor dos gentios, haverem terminado, uma terceira vez, em aprisionamento em uma prisão gentílica, da qual, segundo ele via claramente, só poderia ser libertado através da morte física... contudo, a despeito disso, o apóstolo Paulo se mostra triunfalmente exultante... É que ele media as tribulações dentro do tempo pelas glórias da eternidade. Com olhos da fé ele divisava para além de seu aparente fracasso e percebia a coroa da justiça, que o justo Juiz já tinha em reserva para ele, bem como para os milhares e milhares de outros também — a saber, para todos aqueles que tiverem aprendido a esperar anelantemente pelo tempo em que o seu Senhor voltará. Em tudo isso podemos perceber, em miniatura, a história da cristandade, desde a morte do apóstolo». (Plummer, em II Tim. 4:7).

«Nada há de sutil ou obscuro nessa afirmativa profundamente comovente; e aquilo que ele nos diz em II Tim. 4:7 é claro como o cristal. Lembra-nos que a vida cristã é um conflito contra o mal, em nós mesmos e ao nosso derredor... Lembra-nos que a carreira não está ganha enquanto não tivermos cruzado a linha da chegada, não podendo haver afrouxamento do esforço ao longo do caminho. Entre as mais penetrantes parábolas de Jesus, encontram-se aquelas nas quais ele salienta o fracasso daqueles que começaram bem, mas não foram capazes de prosseguir até o fim. (Ver Luc. 14:25-33; Mat. 13:5,6,20,21; 25:8-10). Lembra-nos que nos temos oferecido a Cristo, a quem devemos lealdade fiel». (Noyes, em II Tim. 4:7).

Completei a carreira, II Tim. 4:7. No grego, o substantivo é «dromos», que significa «pista de corrida», onde é efetuada a competição. (Quanto a essa metáfora, em sentido mais extenso, ver Fil. 3:13,14). O «prêmio» buscado é a «vida eterna», isto é, tornar-se o que Cristo é e compartilhar de sua natureza e atributos, ou perfeições, que procedem da parte de Deus Pai, mas que Cristo outorga aos homens (ver Efé. 3:19; 1:23; Col. 2:9,10; II Cor. 3:18; Rom. 8:29 e II Ped. 1:4), para que assim venham a compartilhar de sua herança e glorificação (ver Rom. 8:17,29,30). Neste caso, naturalmente, essa carreira completa aponta para o sucesso obtido no ministério; contudo, não podemos destacar disso o sucesso individual na obtenção da vida eterna (ver o trecho de I Tim. 4:16, onde o prêmio conquistado através da conduta de um autêntico ministério é a própria salvação e a de outros; e ver também a passagem de I Tim. 6:12, onde o «combater o combate da fé» é equivalente ao «apossar-se da vida eterna»).

A vida cristã é retratada como uma longa carreira, como uma maratona, repleta de obstáculos e dificuldades que esmagam os homens que não possuem a força conferida por Cristo. Nisso não pode haver vitória a menos que o corredor prossiga até à linha de chegada; mas essa linha é cruzada triunfalmente. Aprendemos que a carreira exige dedicação e coragem, bem como o poder espiritual do Espírito Santo, pois, de outro modo, será inteiramente impossível concluí-la com êxito, o que também é

CONDUTA IDEAL — CONFESSAR

comprovado pela experiência diária. Sabemos, com base de tudo quanto encontramos e sofremos, que correr com sucesso a carreira cristã não é coisa fácil. Cristo exige a total dedicação de nossas almas; a outorga da própria vida às mãos de Cristo, que é aquela atitude a que denominamos de «fé». (Ver o artigo sobre a *fé*).

«Sabes tu que em uma carreira correm todos os corredores, mas somente um pode obter o prêmio? Deves correr de tal maneira que possas obter o prêmio» (I Cor. 9:24, segundo a tradução inglesa de Williams, aqui vertida para o português).

«Porém, em nada (nos sofrimentos, nas perseguições e nos encarceramentos) considero a vida preciosa para mim mesmo, contanto que complete a minha carreira e o ministério que recebi do Senhor Jesus para testemunhar o evangelho da graça de Deus» (Atos 20:24).

Clemente de Alexandria expande essa metáfora, até seus detalhes mais completos, em seu *Quis dives salvetur*, capítulo terceiro. «Cristo já nos deu o exemplo, como o *precursor* (ver Heb. 6:20)». (Locke, em II Tim. 4:7).

Guardei a fé, II Tim. 4:7. Se porventura a metáfora tem continuação, então temos aqui o «compromisso» de um atleta de que «observaria as regras», de que «se esforçaria legitimamente» (ver II Tim. 2:5 no NTI quanto a notas a esse respeito). Em sua aplicação, isso indica: 1. Esforçar-se legitimamente, como autêntico ministro de Cristo, em obediência às suas ordens, trabalhando sob a sua autoridade. 2. Confiar na mensagem cristã, sem adições e nem corrupções. 3. Defender a fé (a doutrina e a prática paulinas ortodoxas) contra os assédios da heresia. 4. Propagar a «fé» aos perdidos. 5. Ensinar a fé em toda a sua pureza, aos novos convertidos. A fé, neste caso, é a *fé objetiva*, ou seja, o ensinamento cristão ortodoxo, especialmente como interpretado por Paulo, exibida nas *epístolas pastorais*. (Para detalhes, ver no NTI nas exposições sobre I Tim. 1:2. Ver Hebreus 11:1 quanto à *fé subjetiva*, que consiste da outorga da alma aos cuidados de Cristo). 6. Em tudo isso está envolvida a «fidelidade» pessoal para com o Senhor. É como se Paulo tivesse dito: «Tenho sido fiel às minhas promessas e ao meu compromisso com ele; tenho feito o seu trabalho e tenho sido seu servo fiel. Tenho transmitido a sua mensagem aos homens, em sua forma original e pura».

Aqui está a perseverança dos santos, os que «guardam os mandamentos de Deus e a fé em Jesus» (Apo. 14:12). A alusão que temos aqui é à dificuldade de guardar a fé, em oposição contra o anticristo, durante o negro período da Grande Tribulação.

A Conduta Ideal

Paulo terminou a sua carreira, — a sua «missão determinada», o seu destino terreno. Todos os homens têm tal curso e destino, e todos são indivíduos ímpares, sem-igual, conforme se aprende em Apo. 2:17. E o alvo final não é necessariamente a «felicidade», como também por certo não é o bem-estar físico. O texto à nossa frente ilustra isso perfeitamente. A conduta ideal consiste da tentativa de cumprirmos nossa carreira e nosso destino fixos. Para Aristóteles, a virtude consistia de *função*; e função indicava o cumprimento do designio específico para o que o indivíduo estava melhor preparado e dotado. Faz parte de nosso dever moral saber que função é essa, saber o que podemos fazer, e realizá-la ao máximo de nossas forças e de nossas habilidades. Há nisso certa verdade, se a aplicarmos às nossas vidas espirituais. Deus nos coloca na posição em que nos encontramos, e confere-nos uma tarefa, para então a realizarmos com todas as nossas forças. O N.T. não recomenda a preguiça, e nem o viver diário meramente para desfrutar dos seus prazeres. Mas é entristecedor o fato de que, nas igrejas, muitas pessoas, incluindo ministros e mestres, vão passando de um ano para outro sem nenhuma tentativa séria de se aprimorarem, em suas próprias vidas cristãs e em seu trabalho. Mas se essa atitude fosse tomada no que concerne às atividades comuns do mundo dos negócios, todos ficariam estagnados. Portanto, o que não é permitido no mundo, devido ao seu espírito competitivo, é praticado na igreja praticamente sem qualquer reprimenda. Mas é por isso mesmo que tantas pessoas sentem que a igreja é monótona e maçante, e alguns declaram-no francamente.

CÔNEGOS Ver **Cânegos (Cônegos)**.

CONFERÊNCIA DE THORN
Ver **Thorn, Conferência de**.

CONFESSAR, CONFISSÃO
Esboço:
 I. Palavras Envolvidas
 II. Usos Bíblicos
 III. Usos Eclesiásticos
 1. A Confissão Pública de Cristo
 2. Credos Formais Escritos
 3. A Confissão da Igreja Católica Romana
 4. Substituições Protestantes

I. Palavras Envolvidas

1. *Yada*, «confessar» (mediante o estender da mão). Palavra hebraica que é usada por mais de novecentas vezes, e que as traduções traduzem por muitas palavras e expressões diferentes, como «compreender», «reconhecer», «saber», «tomar conhecimento», etc. A maioria das passagens envolvidas tem algo a ver com a confissão de pecados, conforme se vê em Salmos 32:5: «Confessei-te o meu pecado e a minha iniqüidade não mais ocultei». O povo de Israel, ao sofrer tantos reveses, reconheceu a necessidade de confessar e abandonar o pecado (I Reis 8:33 ss).

2. *Homologéo*, «dizer a mesma coisa», «confessar». Palavra grega usada por vinte e cinco vezes: Mat. 7:23; 10:32; 14:7; Luc. 12:8; João 1:20; 9:22; 12:42; Atos 7:17; 23:8; 24:14; Rom. 10:9,10; I Tim. 6:12; Tito 1:16; Heb. 11:13; 13:15; I João 1:9; 2:23; 4:2,3,15; II João 7 e Apo. 3:5.

3. *Eksomologéo*, «anunciar a mesma coisa», «confessar». Palavra grega empregada por dez vezes: Mat. 3:6; 11:25; Mar. 1:5; Luc. 10:21; 22:6; Atos 19:18; Rom. 14:11 (citando Isa. 45:23); 15:9 (citando Sal. 18:50); Fil. 2:11 e Tia. 5:16.

No Novo Testamento a idéia envolvida é a de confissão ou reconhecimento do pecado. O trecho de I João 1:9 condiciona o perdão à confissão. O termo grego *homologéo* tem os sentidos básicos de promessa, acordo, reconhecimento, declaração e louvor. A forma verbal da palavra é usada por vinte e três vezes no Novo Testamento.

II. Usos Bíblicos

1. A tentativa do homem libertar-se de reveses, causados pelo pecado, faz-se mediante o arrependimento e a confissão de pecados (II Reis 8:33).

2. O perdão dos pecados é buscado mediante a confissão (I João 1:9).

3. Também há a *profissão de fé* (Fil. 2:11), que envolve o reconhecimento de Jesus Cristo em nossa vida. Isso posto, ele é declarado o Senhor da vida do crente (Rom. 10:9). Isso está envolvido na confissão batismal, quando a fé do batizando é publicamente

CONFESSAR, CONFISSÃO

declarada, quando ele passa a considerar-se um discípulo.

4. A vida geral do crente, diante dos homens, é a confissão dada mediante a sua conduta diária (I Tim. 6:12). Nesse versículo, lemos: «Toma posse da vida eterna, para a qual também foste chamado, e de que fizeste a boa confissão, perante muitas testemunhas». O próprio Jesus Cristo fez boa confissão, na presença de Pilatos, conforme o mesmo trecho afirma.

5. Por meio da confissão, Jesus é referido como o Filho de Deus (I João 4:15), e também como o Cristo, ou Ungido de Deus (João 9:22).

6. Confessar uma doutrina é concordar com a sua validade (Atos 23:8).

7. A confissão feita por Cristo, reconhecendo certos homens, é a sua confissão escatológica, confirmando que eles lhe pertencem, por terem vivido a vida espiritual, porque também o reconheceram diante dos homens (Mat. 10:32; Luc. 12:28). Naturalmente, é nesse ponto que encontramos o verdadeiro discipulado cristão, e não no mero reconhecimento verbal.

8. Nos trechos de Hebreus 3:1; 4:14 e 10:23, a confissão é sinônimo de *fé religiosa*, com a conseqüente *espiritualidade*. Ver também, nessa conexão, o trecho de II Coríntios 9:13.

9. A *confissão doxológica* consiste no louvor prestado a Deus pela sua bondade e misericórdia, com ação de graças (Sal. 42:4; Rom. 15:9; Mat. 11:25).

10. A *confissão pneumatológica* é aquela inspirada pelo Espírito Santo, que leva os homens a confessarem a Cristo (I João 4:2; I Cor. 12:3).

11. A *confissão terapêutica* é aquela feita de modo informal, segundo a qual os crentes confessam seus pecados uns aos outros, um de cujos resultados é o início do processo curador (Tia. 5:16). Os conselheiros modernos por muitas vezes ficam atônitos diante do poder físico e psicológico da confissão.

III. Usos Eclesiásticos

1. *A Confissão Pública de Cristo*. Muitas igrejas evangélicas usam a confissão pública de Cristo como meio de levar o indivíduo a declarar a sua fé em Jesus Cristo e a sua lealdade a ele. Essa confissão assinala a ocasião quando o indivíduo declarou publicamente que recebeu Cristo como seu Senhor e Salvador. Fica entendido que esse anúncio público corresponde à verdadeira conversão, embora coisa alguma garanta isso. Nesse instante, a alma estaria começando a ser uma discípula séria de Cristo.

Os Abusos: Com demasiada freqüência, a confissão é reduzida à anuência diante de um credo, com uma pública declaração do fato. Geralmente, isso assume a forma de uma cerimônia, mais ou menos paralela ao batismo católico romano, que, supostamente, teria um efeito semimágico. Por outro lado, tal confissão é aceita de modo muito superficial. Quando alguém profere uma oração de confissão de pecados, a par das palavras declaradas de que acaba de receber a Cristo como Salvador, aceita-se que aquela pessoa foi salva. Isso envolve o que se convencionou chamar de *fácil-creísmo* (que vide). Isso significa que a confissão não passa de uma afirmação credal, como se fosse uma cerimônia mágica, e não uma verdadeira conversão, que consiste em arrependimento e fé. Muitos exercem maior confiança nesse tipo de confissão do que seria razoável esperar. Seja como for, tal confissão deveria ser devidamente precedida por ensinos sobre a absoluta necessidade de arrependimento, fé correspondente e verdadeiro discipulado. Sem essas coisas, a confissão não passa de um aglomerado de palavras ocas. De nada adianta alguém afirmar que concorda com um credo que anuncie quais são as crenças aceitas. Não forçamos Deus a fazer coisa alguma, simplesmente porque dizemos: «Aceito a Jesus Cristo como meu Salvador». A salvação é dada quando outorgamos a nossa alma aos cuidados de Cristo, com os passos contemporâneos e subseqüentes do arrependimento, da verdadeira fé, da santificação e da transformação da alma segundo a imagem de Cristo. Se esses estágios não estiverem envolvidos, a confissão verbal nada significará. Ver o artigo separado sobre a *Confissão de Cristo*, quanto aos vários itens da doutrina envolvida.

Na antiga Igreja cristã, o *confessio* envolvia a profissão de fé por parte de algum mártir, que sofrera perseguição por causa de sua fé, mas não cedera, e do que resultara a mais firme convicção, publicamente professada. É interessante observarmos que essa palavra latina aparece no santuário de São Pedro, no Vaticano. Ele fez uma verdadeira confissão, cuja fé chegou a amadurecer plenamente. A mesma palavra latina tem sido encontrada no túmulo de outros mártires cristãos. A moderna Igreja cristã tem barateado o sentido da confissão; geralmente a reduz a um rito quase mágico, no qual se deposita uma exagerada confiança. Na verdade, porém, a confissão de um homem deve ser a sua vida de fé.

2. Com base na confissão oral e pública, surgiu o *credo formal escrito*. Isso posto, encontramos credos tão antigos como o credo Apostólico e o credo Niceno. Ver o artigo sobre *Credos*. As igrejas reformadas, ansiosas por reafirmarem aquilo que julgavam ser a fé apostólica, produziram uma série de confissões escritas. Houve a Confissão de Augsburg, de 1530, e a Confissão de Westminster, de 1643. Ver os artigos separados sobre as mesmas. Os decretos do Concílio de Trento (1545-1563) tinham o intuito de reafirmar a posição católica romana, combatendo certas idéias salientadas pelos reformadores protestantes. A Igreja Anglicana tem seus Trinta e Nove Artigos, que buscam reconciliar pontos de vista conflitantes nas confissões, tendo em vista a unidade da Igreja. Naturalmente, esses artigos também são uma declaração geral das crenças da comunhão anglicana. Ver o artigo separado sobre as *Confissões da Igreja Histórica*, quanto a outros detalhes.

3. *A Confissão da Igreja Católica Romana*. O título desse tipo de confissão é *confissão sacramental*. Dentro do catolicismo romano moderno, esse tipo de confissão, também chamada «confissão auricular», tornou-se a principal obra pastoral dos sacerdotes romanistas. A Igreja de Roma ensina que a confissão auricular é obrigatória antes da participação na comunhão, e que a mesma deve ser feita pelo menos uma vez por ano. Fica entendido que o padre, como suposto representante de Deus, pode reter ou perdoar os pecados, por meio de seu ofício, e que, sem essa absolvição, os pecados continuam sem perdão. A base bíblica para essa prática são os trechos de Mat. 16:19; João 20:23 e Tia. 5:16. Os teólogos evangélicos objetam ao uso das duas primeiras dessas três referências, em apoio à confissão auricular, afirmando que o que Jesus disse aplica-se aos apóstolos, e não aos padres de alguma das denominações cristãs. O trecho de Tiago nada tem a ver com alguma função eclesiástica. Em Tiago vemos uma confissão informal de pecados, entre crente e crente, que, entre outras coisas, tem o propósito de contribuir para a cura dos males físicos.

A confissão de pecados é um momento de auto-exame. Dentro da Igreja Católica Romana, o padre tem o dever de fazer certas indagações, que fazem a pessoa lembrar-se de seus pecados. Devem ser confessados tanto os pecados mortais quanto os pecados veniais, assim chamados. Se alguém que está se confessando ao padre não disser a verdade, ou não mencionar algum pecado, propositalmente, todo o processo fica automaticamente anulado.

A Confissão nas Igrejas Ortodoxa e Anglicana. A Igreja Ortodoxa Oriental recomenda a seus adeptos que se confessem anualmente. A Igreja Anglicana ensina a seus membros fazerem confissão tão freqüentemente quanto sintam ser necessário.

Requisitos da Confissão. Do penitente são requeridos estes pontos: 1. que ele se sinta contrito; 2. que faça confissão apropriada; 3. que preste *satisfação*, mediante o auto-exame, a tristeza, a correção dos erros praticados, em todos os casos possíveis. Também precisa cumprir quaisquer atos de penitência determinados pelo padre confessor.

4. *Substituições Protestantes*

Entre essas substituições devemos destacar o *aconselhamento*. O ato de aconselhamento tem surgido dentro do aconselhamento religioso e psicológico. Acredita-se que esse aconselhamento exerce um efeito terapêutico. No entanto, faz-se totalmente ausente o elemento sacramental. Não se acredita que o ministro conselheiro tenha a autoridade de reter ou de perdoar os pecados alheios. Dentro do aconselhamento pastoral, a confissão de pecados está sendo adotada novamente. E os conselheiros profissionais também pensam que a confissão de pecados é valiosa. De fato, há certo valor terapêutico na confissão dos próprios erros e pecados, se isso for acompanhado pela resolução de *mudar* a conduta. Se não houver tal resolução, os efeitos da confissão serão apenas temporários, porquanto a causa profunda dos sentimentos de ansiedade não é removida. A medicina moderna tem comprovado que a mente pode promover ou causar todas as variedades de mazelas físicas. Se a mente for restaurada, disso resultará a cura física, ou então futuras enfermidades físicas serão evitadas. O livro de Provérbios (23:7), estipula: «Porque, como imagina (o homem) em sua alma, assim ele é...» Quando alguém, mediante a confissão de seus pecados, corrige as coisas com outra pessoa ou com outras pessoas, então também se manifesta o efeito terapêutico da comunhão restaurada. Isso pode constituir *a solução para a comunhão*, conforme dizia Bonhoeffer. (AM B BOW C E)

CONFESSOR

Consideremos, a respeito, os três pontos abaixo:

1. Esse termo era aplicado aos primitivos cristãos que confessavam com denodo a sua fé em Cristo, em tempos de perseguição e martírio, estando sujeitos a todas as formas de perigos, mas que, finalmente, não foram martirizados.

2. Por extensão, esse termo veio a aplicar-se aos indivíduos dotados de especiais qualidades espirituais, embora não expostos a quaisquer testes ou perigos especiais. Por volta do século VI D.C., a Igreja começou a honrar publicamente os confessores, mesmo quando eles não sofriam o martírio. Alguns desses confessores têm sido canonizados.

3. O termo também se aplica a um padre da Igreja Católica Romana, quando, por detrás do confessionário, ouve confissões de seus paroquianos.

CONFIAR

Nas Escrituras, o ato de confiar envolve dois aspectos básicos: a. entregar-se aos cuidados de outrem; e b. deixar-se persuadir. Essas idéias fundamentais aparecem tanto no Antigo quanto no Novo Testamento, até mesmo no sentido das palavras hebraicas e gregas envolvidas. A moderna noção de «fé», apenas como crença na existência ou funcionabilidade de algo ou de alguém, é muito superficial. É extremamente comum alguém dizer que «crê em Deus», quando tudo que ele quer dizer é que sabe que Deus existe. Essas pessoas nunca se entregaram aos cuidados de Deus, quanto à segurança eterna de suas almas, nem jamais se deixaram persuadir pelas promessas e garantias dadas pela palavra de Cristo.

A. Termos Originais

Vocábulos que transmitem a idéia de outorga:

1. *Batach*, «apoiar-se em». Palavra hebraica usada por cento e vinte vezes. Por exemplo: Deu. 28:52; II Reis 18:5; 19:10; Sal. 4:5; 13:5; 49:6; Pro. 3:5; 16:20; Isa. 12:2; 26:4; Jer. 7:4; 17:5; Eze. 33:13; Amós 6:1; Sof. 3:2.

2. *Galal*, «rolar sobre». Palavra hebraica empregada por dezoito vezes. Por exemplo: Sal. 22:8; 37:5; Pro. 16:3.

3. *Chasah*, «refugiar-se». Palavra hebraica que ocorre por trinta e sete vezes. Para exemplificar: Deu. 32:37; Juí. 9:15; Rute 2:12; II Sam. 22:3; Sal. 2:12; 7:1; 31:1; 118:8,9; Pro. 30:5; Isa. 57:13; Naum 1:7; Sof. 3:12.

4. *Elpízo*, «esperar em». Palavra grega usada por trinta e uma vezes: Mat. 12:21; Luc. 6:34; 23:8; 24:21; João 5:45; Atos 24:26; 26:7; Rom. 8:24,25; 15:12,24; I Cor. 13:7; 15:19; 16:7; II Cor. 1:10,13; 5:11; 8:5; 13:6; Fil. 2:19,23; I Tim. 3:14; 4:10; 5:5; 6:17; File. 22; Heb. 11:1; I Ped. 1:13; 3:5; II João 12 e III João 14. O substantivo *elpís* «esperança», ocorre por cinqüenta e uma vezes, desde Atos 2:26 até I João 3:3.

Vocábulos que transmitem a idéia de deixar-se persuadir:

1. *Chil*, «permanecer». Palavra hebraica que figura por nove vezes. Por exemplo: Juí. 3:25; Miq. 1:12.

2. *Mibitach*, «confiança». Palavra hebraica que aparece por catorze vezes. Por exemplo: Jó 18:14; Sal. 65:5; Pro. 14:26; Jer. 2:37; Eze. 29:16.

3. *Kesel*, «firmeza». Palavra hebraica que figura por quatro vezes. Por exemplo: Pro. 3:26; Jó 8:14.

4. *Kislah*, «confiança». Palavra hebraica que, com esse sentido, aparece em Jó 4:6.

5. *Parresía*, «ousadia». Palavra grega que aparece por trinta e uma vezes: Mar. 8:32; João 7:4,13,26; 10:24; 11:14,54; 16:25,29; 18:20; Atos 2:29; 4:13,29, 31; II Cor. 3:12; 7:4; Efé. 3:12; 6:19; Fil. 1:20; Col. 2:15; I Tim. 3:13; File. 8; Heb. 3:6; 4:16; 10:19,35; I João 2:28; 3:21; 4:17; 5:14.

6. *Peítho*, «estar persuadido». Termo grego usado por cinqüenta e três vezes: Mat. 27:20,43; 28:14; Mar. 10:24; Luc. 11:22; 16:31; 18:9; 20:6; Atos 5:36,37,40; 12:20; 13:43; 14:19; 17:4; 18:4; 19:8,26; 21:14; 23:21; 22:26; 27:11; 28:23,24; Rom. 2:8,19; 8:38; 14:14; 15:14; II Cor. 1:9; 2:3; 4:11; 10:7; Gál. 1:10; 5:7,10; Fil. 1:6,14,25; 2:24; 3:3,4; II Tes. 3:4; II Tim. 1:5,12; File. 21; Heb. 2:13; 6:9; 13:17,18; Tia. 3:3; I João 3:19.

7. *Pepoíthesis*, «confiança». Substantivo grego usado por seis vezes: II Cor. 1:15; 3:4; 8:22; 10:2; Efé. 3:12 e Fil. 3:4.

A principal palavra hebraica é «batach». Alguns estudiosos, além de aceitarem para ela o sentido de «apoiar-se», também pensam que talvez, mais radicalmente, signifique *estar aberto*, o que reflete a idéia original de «confiança», dando a idéia que nada

CONFIAR — CONFIRMAR

há a ocultar da pessoa em quem se confia.

A Bíblia ensina-nos o valor da confiança (Isa. 30:15; Heb. 10:35), mas não no «ouro» (Jó 31:24), e nem no homem, por maior e mais importante que este seja (Sal. 118:8,9; Jer. 17:5). Fica excluída, das Escrituras, até mesmo a confiança própria (Pro. 14:16; Fil. 3:3). Na Bíblia, a única confiança válida é aquela posta em Deus (Sal. 65:6; Pro. 3:26; 14:26), conforme Deus se revelou na pessoa de Cristo: «...pelo qual temos ousadia e acesso com confiança, mediante a fé nele» (Efé. 3:12). «Estas cousas vos escrevi a fim de saberdes que tendes a vida eterna, a vós outros que credes em nome do Filho de Deus. E esta é a confiança que temos para com ele, que, se pedirmos alguma cousa segundo a sua vontade, ele nos ouve» (I João 5:13,14).

Tal como sempre faz, a Bíblia vai desenvolvendo o tema da confiança, desdobrando as várias idéias que fazem parte do conceito. Assim, a Bíblia tanto exorta-nos à confiança (por exemplo, Sal. 115:15), como faz promessas firmes àqueles que puserem sua confiança em Deus (por exemplo, Isa. 26:3), assim como também fornece-nos muitos exemplos de confiança em Deus. Quanto a este último aspecto, nenhum capítulo é mais eloqüente que Heb. 11:1-40. Finalmente, para desencorajar a atitude humana da incredulidade, tão natural em nós, Deus nos apresenta muitas advertências contra essa atitude que tanto desonra ao Senhor. Dessa reprimenda não escaparam nem mesmo os discípulos originais, conforme lemos em Mar. 16:14: «Finalmente, apareceu Jesus aos onze, quando estavam à mesa, e censurou-lhes a incredulidade e dureza de coração, porque não deram crédito aos que o tinham visto já ressuscitado». E o autor da epístola aos Hebreus adverte como segue, àqueles crentes judeus que pareciam dispostos a retroceder da sua nova fé em Cristo: «Tende cuidado, irmãos, jamais aconteça haver em qualquer de vós perverso coração de incredulidade que vos afaste do Deus vivo...» (Heb. 3:12).

No Novo Testamento, o ensino sobre a «confiança» no Senhor atinge o seu ponto culminante. Quanto os escritores sagrados usam o verbo *peítho*, «estar persuadido», eles mostram que a confiança, na Bíblia, nunca envolve a idéia de mera expectativa confiante. Antes, ela nos mostra que confiar é estar persuadido por argumentos celestes, usados pelo Espírito de Deus, capazes de convencer o crente sobre as realidades reveladas. «E assim, a fé vem pela pregação e a pregação pela palavra de Cristo» (Rom. 10:17). Que essa persuasão não vem apenas por meio de provas externas de qualquer espécie, lemos: «E, embora tivesse feito tantos sinais na sua presença, não creram nele; para se cumprir a palavra do profeta Isaías, que diz: Senhor, quem creu em nossa pregação? E a quem foi revelado o braço do Senhor?» (João 12:37,38). Essa persuasão vem do céu. «Certa mulher chamada Lídia, da cidade de Tiatira, vendedora de púrpura, temente a Deus, nos escutava; o Senhor lhe abriu o coração para atender às cousas que Paulo dizia» (Atos 16:14).

É por esse motivo que os crentes não se caracterizam por uma confiança tímida e hesitante. Antes, a fé deles pode crescer e fortalecer-se até tornar-se *parresía*, ou «ousadia». Talvez em nenhuma outra passagem essa ousadia transpareça tão claramente como na epístola aos Hebreus (10:19 ss), onde lemos: «Tendo, pois, irmãos, intrepidez para entrar no Santo dos Santos, pelo sangue de Jesus...aproximemo-nos com sincero coração, em plena certeza da fé... Guardemos firme a confissão da esperança, sem vacilar, pois quem fez a promessa é fiel».

CONFIRMAR, CONFIRMAÇÃO

Ver também o artigo sobre a **Iniciação Cristã**.

1. *Usos Bíblicos*. Muitas palavras hebraicas e três palavras gregas estão vinculadas a esse conceito. As palavras hebraicas, nenhuma das quais teologicamente importante, são traduzidas como «endurecer», «fortalecer», «segurar», «estabelecer», «preencher», e «confirmar». Mais importantes, teologicamente falando, são os três vocábulos gregos envolvidos, a saber:

1. *Bebaióo*, «firmar». Esse vocábulo aparece por oito vezes: Mar. 16:20; Rom. 15:8; I Cor. 1:6,8; II Cor. 1:21; Col. 2:7; Heb. 2:3; 13:9. O substantivo, *bebaíosis*, «firmeza», figura por duas vezes: Fil. 1:7; Heb. 6:16.

2. *Episteírzo*, «confirmar plenamente». Esse vocábulo aparece por três vezes: Atos 14:22; 15:32,41.

3. *Kuróo*, «validar». Essa palavra figura por duas vezes: II Cor. 2:8 e Gál. 3:15.

Usando a primeira dessas três palavras gregas, em Fil. 1:7 e Heb. 6:16, o apóstolo dos gentios fala sobre a confirmação de coisas, e não de pessoas. Em Atos 8:12-17, Lucas diz-nos que a pregação de Filipe, em Samaria, foi *confirmada* pelos apóstolos Pedro e João, que ali foram e impuseram as mãos sobre os convertidos, a fim de que recebessem o Espírito Santo. O derramamento do Espírito sobre aqueles recém-convertidos, pois, serviu de confirmação do trabalho de Filipe. Em outros trechos bíblicos, o recebimento do Espírito está vinculado ao arrependimento ou ao ato do batismo em água. Ver Atos 2:38 e 10:44-48. Há referências à confirmação dos discípulos, por parte de Paulo, em Atos 14:22; 15:32 e 18:23. No entanto, não parece ter havido algum rito eclesiástico envolvido nessas referências. Paulo simplesmente conferiu àqueles crentes ensinos e encorajamento.

2. *O Sacramento da Confirmação*. A confirmação ou crisma é um dos sete sacramentos da Igreja Católica Romana e da Igreja Ortodoxa Oriental. A primeira afirma que esse sacramento foi instituído pelo próprio Cristo, por meio de seus discípulos. Tal como no caso de outros dogmas, a história mostra-nos que a confirmação veio a transformar-se em sacramento mediante um desenvolvimento teológico. Recebeu posição de sacramento por Pedro Lombardo, no século XII D.C., e por Tomás de Aquino no século XIII D.C.

Um sacramento é um rito qualquer através do qual, segundo se crê, o Espírito de Deus confere sua graça e suas operações. O concílio de Trento, no século XVI, também pronunciou-se sobre a confirmação como um sacramento. Na Igreja Católica Romana, os bispos administram esse rito, cujo propósito é tornar os crismados fortes na fé e filhos da Igreja. É administrado a crianças, mediante a imposição de mãos e a unção, antes delas receberem a chamada primeira comunhão (que vide), mais ou menos com doze anos de idade. Tomás de Aquino comentou: «A confirmação é para o batismo, o que o crescimento é para a concepção». Em outras palavras, mediante esse rito, a graça administrada pelo Espírito levaria os cristãos a crescerem espiritualmente, encorajando-os à firmeza na fé. As palavras da crisma são as seguintes: «Assinalo-te com o sinal da cruz, e confirmo-te com a crisma da salvação». Presumivelmente, o ato confere um *caráter indelével* ao crismado, pelo que é administrado somente uma vez. Através desse rito, os sete dons do Espírito fluiriam até o crismado. Em algumas igrejas protestantes como as dos luteranos, o ato é realidade, embora não seja considerado um sacramento, ou meio de graça. Antes, o indivíduo batizado, mediante a crisma é confirmado no tocante aos votos que seus pais fizeram em seu favor, quando foi batizado. A confirmação é ministrada ao término do estudo do primeiro catecismo. Após isso, a pessoa é admitida à comunhão da Igreja Católica Romana. Na Igreja Episcopal, a confirmação é considerada um sacramento que completa o batismo em água, mediante a unção e a imposição de mãos.

Em muitas igrejas evangélicas, um equivalente geral à confirmação é a chamada ao «altar», para que a pessoa dedique sua vida a Cristo. Não há o acompanhamento de qualquer rito, mas o espírito da coisa é idêntico ao que sucede na crisma católica romana.

De acordo com o rito romano, o bispo (ou padre para isso nomeado) aplica à criança um tapinha no rosto, após haver aplicado o óleo à sua testa. Isso significa que aquele crismado deve esperar sofrimento e bofetes, se for um autêntico discípulo de Cristo. O oficiante então declara: «Defende, ó Senhor, este Teu filho (ou servo), com tua graça celestial, para que ele continue teu para sempre; e aumenta sobre ele, diariamente, o teu Santo Espírito, até que ele chegue ao teu reino eterno. Amém». Essas são belas palavras, prenhes de significado. Mas, no caso de seus escolhidos que já se converteram, o Espírito realiza essa missão, com ou sem esse rito. (AM E)

CONFISCO

Essa é a expropriação compulsória de alguma propriedade, por parte das autoridades do governo de um país, sem qualquer compensação. Mas, a *expropriação* mediante uma justa compensação não constitui confisco; todavia, se a compensação paga for abaixo do que é justo, terá havido um confisco parcial. Durante a era cristã, tem havido uma longa história dessa prática. A partir do século IV D.C., propriedades pagãs, e subseqüentemente, islâmicas, foram confiscadas pela Igreja Católica. Durante a Reforma, autoridades protestantes confiscaram propriedades da Igreja Católica Romana. Durante a Revolução Francesa, na França e em outros países europeus, propriedades eclesiásticas foram tomadas sem qualquer compensação. Durante o século XX, tem sido prática dos governos comunistas confiscar propriedades de estrangeiros e de instituições religiosas de todos os tipos. O confisco sempre foi uma das armas poderosas dos perseguidores. Freqüentes confiscos foram impostos aos judeus, em todas as épocas. Isso tem ocorrido em diversos países europeus, e o exemplo mais notável de nosso século foi aquele praticado pelo regime nazista de Adolf Hitler.

Confisco na Bíblia. Coisa alguma é dita na legislação mosaica acerca desse ato. Na prática, porém, a mesma começou em Israel com o surgimento da monarquia. O profeta Samuel predisse que, com a instituição da monarquia, os reis haveriam de confiscar propriedades privadas, para seu próprio uso e enriquecimento (I Sam. 8:14-16). Saul chegou ao poder como homem relativamente pobre; porém, não demorou muito e já tinha propriedades suficientes para distribuir terras entre seus oficiais mais diretos (I Sam. 22:7). Ao falecer, era homem rico em propriedades (II Sam. 8:7-10). Alguns textos parecem indicar que foram baixadas leis para refrear essa prática (I Reis 21:15,16; II Reis 4:12,25,26). Após o exílio, foi permitida a medida do confisco no tocante aos que desobedecessem à lei. Durante o período do governo romano, essa prática teve prosseguimento. Herodes esteve envolvido na mesma (Josefo, *Anti.* xvii.307; *Guerras* ii.3).

O trecho de Hebreus 10:34 mostra-nos que os cristãos da época apostólica, e da imediatamente depois, sofreram essa injustiça. (AM Z)

CONFISSÃO

Ver os artigos gerais sobre **Confessar, Confissão; Confissão de Cristo; e Confessões da Igreja Histórica.**

CONFISSÃO AURICULAR

Consulta religiosa particular com um clérigo ou conselheiro leigo, uma prática comum na Igreja antiga. A confissão formal, para efeito de disciplina, fazia-se publicamente; e as confissões particulares serviam de orientação. A confissão secreta de pecados ao «padre» normalmente figura nos livros penitenciais das igrejas celtas. Uma confissão anual, de natureza secreta, foi decretada como obrigatória a todos pelo quarto concílio lateranor, em 1215.

CONFISSÃO BELGA

Um credo reformado de trinta e sete artigos, preparado em 1561 por Guido de Bres, e posteriormente emendado e adotado por vários sínodos, de 1566 a 1581, e finalmente, pelo importante sínodo de Dort, em 1619. O credo tornou-se o padrão das igrejas reformadas da Holanda e da Bélgica, e então da Igreja Reformada (Holandesa) da América. (E)

CONFISSÃO DE CRISTO

Ver o artigo sobre *Confessar, Confissão*, sob o 3º ponto. *Usos Eclesiásticos da Confissão*, 1. *A Confissão Pública de Cristo*. Ali discuto sobre os *abusos* que têm caracterizado a confissão pública, na moderna Igreja cristã, incluindo o abuso do *fácil-creísmo* (que vide).

1. *Seriedade do Ato*. Em tempos de perseguição, como ocorreu durante os primeiros trezentos anos da história da Igreja cristã, é coisa séria alguém ser um discípulo sincero de Cristo. Na antiga Igreja cristã, o *confessio* indicava a profissão de fé, feita por um mártir, que resistira à perseguição e não abandonara a sua fé em Cristo. Essa mesma palavra latina tem sido encontrada nos túmulos dos mártires cristãos da antiguidade, bem como na catedral de São Pedro, no Vaticano. Em tempos de liberdade religiosa, é fácil baratear a confissão cristã, transformando-a em mera afirmação verbal, diante de um credo, sem a necessidade de reconhecer que a confissão deve ser dada pela própria vida de fé, dos discípulos sérios de Cristo. Podemos confessar a Jesus como Senhor e como Filho de Deus, sem que ele signifique isso, pessoalmente, para nós. Podemos afirmar a crença que ele se encarnou entre os homens, sem que ele se torne o Senhor e Diretor das nossas vidas.

2. *As Idéias Doutrinárias*. Não obstante, desde os próprios dias neotestamentários, quando o discipulado cristão era algo vital, a substância doutrinária da profissão cristã era considerada um fator importante. Assim, a homologia (confissão) cristã inclui os seguintes itens:

a. Jesus era o Messias (João 9:22).

b. Jesus era o Filho de Deus (I João 4:15).

c. A encarnação de Jesus foi o nascimento genuíno do Logos, em forma humana (I João 4:2).

d. Ele era o Senhor, o que ficou comprovado pela sua ressurreição (Rom. 10:9; Fil. 2:11).

e. Jesus deve ser confessado diante dos homens e seguido e obedecido com sinceridade (II João 7).

CONFISSÃO DE FÉ — CONFISSÕES

Uma confissão envolvendo esses elementos era feita, por ocasião do batismo em água, na Igreja primitiva, assinalando o começo do discipulado cristão. O arrependimento e a fé eram compreendidos como condições imprescindíveis (Atos 2:38; 20:21).

CONFISSÃO DE FÉ

Ver os artigos gerais sobre *Confissão, Confissão de Cristo* e *Confissões da Igreja Histórica*.

A princípio, a confissão era feita oralmente, como um reconhecimento público, feito diante de testemunhas (I Tim. 6:12), por ocasião do ato do batismo em água, ou em outras oportunidades. Com o tempo, essa confissão oral assumiu forma escrita, do que surgiram os credos, como o Credo Apostólico e o Credo Niceno. A Reforma protestante foi uma época em que as igrejas evangélicas, ansiosas por fixar seus credos sobre bases concretas, formularam credos escritos. Disso resultaram quase quarenta confissões formais, durante aquele agitado período da história do cristianismo. As principais confissões luteranas foram as seguintes: A Confissão de Augsburg, de 1530, que foi, essencialmente, obra de Malanchton (que vide), com a aprovação de Lutero; os artigos de Smalkald, de 1573; a Fórmula de Concórdia, de 1577; o Livro da Concórdia, de 1580. As confissões reformadas (calvinistas) chegaram a ser mais de trinta, dentre as quais as principais foram: A Confissão Helvética, de 1536; os Cânones do Sínodo de Dort, de 1618; a Confissão de Westminster, de 1646. Os decretos do Concílio de Trento (1546-1563) tiveram o intuito de reafirmar a posição da Igreja Católica Romana, em oposição a certas idéias defendidas pelos reformadores protestantes. A Igreja Anglicana tem os seus Trinta e Nove Artigos revisados em 1642. Essa confissão tem sido usada pela Igreja da Escócia desde 1647, tendo sido aprovada pelo parlamento, em 1648. A maioria dos credos acima mencionados mereceram o tratamento de um artigo separado, nesta enciclopédia. Ver também o artigo sobre *Credos*.

CONFISSÃO DE FÉ DE DORDRECHT

Essa é a confissão de fé dos menonitas holandeses. Essa confissão foi adotada em uma conferência efetuada em Dordrecht, na Holanda, a 21 abril de 1632. Essa confissão contém dezoito artigos, cada qual com o apoio de amplos textos de provas. A maior parte desses artigos consiste em proposições evangélicas comuns. Os artigos distintivos são: XI, sobre a necessidade de observar o lava-pés; XIV, que é o direito de defender-se mediante o uso da força; XV, a proibição contra os juramentos; XVII, a necessidade de evitar os excluídos. Ver o artigo geral sobre os *Credos*, bem como o artigo sobre as *Confissões de Fé*.

CONFISSÃO DE PECADOS

Ver os artigos sobre *Confessar, Confissão*, sob o segundo ponto, *Usos Bíblicos*, e sob o terceiro ponto, *Usos Eclesiásticos*, sob a., b., c. e d.

Parte da *homologia* (confissão) cristã era o reconhecimento da própria indignidade e da própria natureza pecaminosa, do que resulta uma vida em que inúmeros pecados são cometidos. Ver Lev. 26:40; Jos. 7:19 e Mat. 27:4. A confissão é uma espécie de sinal de arrependimento e fé no evangelho, e não o descarregamento psicológico do senso de culpa (Mar. 1:1-5). A confissão assim é condição para o recebimento do perdão (Sal. 32:5; I João 1:9), por ocasião da conversão ou posteriormente. A confissão de pecados é um pré-requisito para a vida de oração eficaz (I Reis 8:33; Nee. 1:6; Sal. 66:18 e Luc. 18:9-14). A lei levítica exigia confissão e restituição, em todos os casos possíveis, antes do recebimento da remissão dos pecados, de natureza individual ou coletiva (Lev. 5:5; Núm. 5:7; Lev. 16:21). E esse é um princípio que deveríamos seguir.

A confissão deve ser feita, primariamente, diante de Deus (Sal. 51:3,4; Rom. 14:10-12), mas também pode ser feita diante de outras pessoas, ou mesmo em público (Eze. 9:6; Tia. 5:16). O desvendamento, em público, de pecados secretos e escandalosos, pode ser algo muito vergonhoso (Efé. 5:12). Mas isso pode revestir-se de um valor terapêutico enorme, quando feito diante de conselheiros, de pastores, das pessoas que tivermos ofendido, etc. Em Tiago 5:16, a confissão de pecados aparece como uma ajuda terapêutica. Isso concorda com o que sabemos acerca das doenças psicossomáticas. Também há perturbações mentais que se manifestam meramente porque alguém não descarrega sua carga de senso de culpa. Se a confissão de pecados for feita com a firme resolução de *mudar* de atitude, então, algumas vezes, é admirável como a pessoa que confessa melhora. Alguns psicólogos modernos têm tentado livrar os seus pacientes de algum senso de culpa, e, ao fazê-lo, têm chamado o pecado por todo o tipo de nomes, a fim de ocultar a sua realidade. Porém, quando alguém pratica um *erro* que prejudica a si mesmo ou ao próximo, não basta chamar esse erro de fraqueza ou de mecanismo de autopreservação. Os homens são pecadores, e não apenas autopreservadores.

É medida saudável reconhecer um pecado cometido contra algum irmão a quem ofendemos ou prejudicamos de algum modo (Mat. 5:21). Isso cura não apenas o indivíduo culpado, mas também a comunidade dos crentes. De algumas vezes, uma ofensa deve ser levada ao conhecimento da Igreja inteira (Mat. 18:17). Em determinadas ocasiões, vale a pena até mesmo repreender os anciãos, quando eles praticarem algum erro, fazendo-o publicamente (I Tim. 5:20). Isso anula o mau exemplo dado.

CONFISSÃO DE WESTMINSTER
Ver **Westminster, Confissão de**.

CONFISSÃO ESCOCESA Ver **Escocesas, Confissão**

CONFISSÃO GALICANA

Também conhecida como Confissão de La Rochelle, essa confissão foi redigida por João Calvino (que vide), e ampliada e adotada pelo Sínodo de Paris, em 1559, como confissão de fé e ordem disciplinar. Depois disso, essa confissão foi reiteradamente revisada, sob a direção de Beza. Quando do sétimo sínodo nacional, em La Rochelle, em 1571, na presença da rainha de Navarra e de seu filho, Henrique IV, essa confissão foi ratificada. Ela consiste em quarenta artigos que sumariam a doutrina e a disciplina calvinista. Em 1872, essa confissão foi ultrapassada pela «Declaração de Fé da Igreja Reformada», na França. Ver os artigos gerais sobre os *Credos* e sobre outras Confissões. Ver também os *Cinco Pontos do Calvinismo*.

CONFISSÃO TETRAPOLITANA
Ver **Sacramentarianos**.

CONFISSÕES DA IGREJA HISTÓRICA

O Novo Testamento é a base principal dos credos cristãos, pois contém os artigos essenciais da fé cristã. Em face da necessidade de interpretação e ênfase,

CONFISSÕES DA IGREJA HISTÓRICA

surgiram os credos eclesiásticos. A palavra «credo» vem do latim, *credo*, que significa «creio». Em meu artigo sobre o *Credo*, apresento o pano de fundo histórico, bem como as primeiras fórmulas, pelo que tal informação não é repetida aqui. Os três grandes credos clássicos são: o Credo dos Apóstolos; o Credo Niceno, de 318 D.C., e o Credo de Atanásio (pós-agostiniano). Cada um desses é tratado nesta enciclopédia em um artigo separado. Historicamente, a maioria dos credos originou-se nos séculos IV e V D.C., e então nos séculos XVI e XVII D.C. quando a Reforma protestante foi o grande motivo da renovação dos credos. O século XX tem visto o reavivamento da preparação de credos. Os credos surgem quando há algum conflito sobre doutrinas, ou quando novos grupos cristãos estão procurando interpretar as suas doutrinas. Os credos tornam-se autoritários até certo ponto, de tal modo que tornar-se alguém membro de muitos grupos cristãos depende, de modo absoluto, da aceitação ou não deste ou daquele credo.

1. O Catolicismo Oriental. A definição da fé cristã, segundo esse segmento da Igreja cristã, é o Credo Niceno, segundo as declarações dos concílios de Éfeso (431 D.C.), Calcedônia (451 D.C.), Constantinopla (553 D.C.), Constantinopla (680 D.C.), e Nicéia (787 D.C.). A isso foram adicionados os vinte artigos da Confissão de Gonádio, em 1453. Além disso, temos as quatro respostas de Jeremias II (que vide), patriarca de Constantinopla, que criticava certos aspectos da teologia luterana de Tubingen (1547-1581), conforme os mesmos são exemplificados na Confissão de Augsburg. A confissão de Metrófanes Critópulo (1625), composta para os teólogos de Helmstaedt, publicada em 1661, reconhecia apenas o batismo, a penitência e a eucaristia como mistérios necessários. Essa confissão encerra uma polêmica contra o catolicismo romano, excluindo os livros apócrifos do cânon da Bíblia Sagrada. Também devemos levar em conta a Confissão de Cirilo Lucas (1629, 1631, 1633), que foi influenciada pelo calvinismo em dez ou dezoito parágrafos. O seu segundo parágrafo aceita a Bíblia como dotada de autoridade superior à da Igreja. Os sete sacramentos são ali reduzidos a dois; a presença real mas espiritual de Cristo substitui a doutrina da transubstanciação; o purgatório é rejeitado; e a justificação pela fé é afirmada. Entretanto, esse patriarca de Constantinopla enfrentou muitos problemas, tendo sido deposto por cinco vezes, por cinco vezes foi reinstalado, e, finalmente, foi estrangulado. Pedro Mogilas, metropolita de Kiev, pai da teologia russa, compôs, em 1638, uma confissão que se tornou canônica e padrão da Igreja russa. Essa confissão foi composta parcialmente com o propósito de repelir vários itens da confissão de Cirilo. Por ocasião do sínodo de Jerusalém, de 1672, foi expedida uma rejeição formal do credo de Cirilo Lucar, de tal modo que ficou muito reduzida a simpatia pelo calvinismo, naquele segmento do cristianismo. Doseiteu, patriarca de Jerusalém, era fanaticamente ortodoxo, e os dezoito artigos de sua confissão, bem como as quatro questões finais, fizeram a Igreja Oriental reaproximar-se novamente da posição da Igreja Católica Romana, afastando-a do calvinismo.

2. O Catolicismo Romano. Além dos antigos credos tradicionais, acima mencionados, a Igreja Católica Romana aceita as decisões de vários concílios da Igreja (que vide), os quais, pelo menos em parte, são alistados acima, nas informações dadas sobre a Igreja Oriental. Então o concílio de Trento (que vide), 1545-1563, serviu de importante meio para definir a doutrina católica romana, em oposição a certas doutrinas reformadas. Esse concílio reafirmou a declaração de alguns papas, consideradas autoritárias como confissões cristãs. O papa Pio IV reservou-se o direito de interpretar as decisões do concílio de Trento, e confirmou os decretos de duzentos e cinqüenta e cinco padres que sustentavam itens do Credo Niceno. Foram mantidas as doutrinas referentes ao pecado original, à autoridade das Escrituras, à justificação mediante a participação nos sacramentos e a doutrina do purgatório.

A confissão da fé Tridentina (que vide), que é a do papa Pio IV, de 1564, é considerada obrigatória para todos os padres e mestres públicos católicos romanos. Consiste na forma ocidental do Credo Niceno de 381 A.C., um sumário das conclusões do concílio de Trento, além de artigos adicionais e compromissos solenes de lealdade à fé católica e ao papa. O Catecismo Romano, de 1566, trata sobre o Credo dos Apóstolos, sobre os sete sacramentos, sobre o decálogo e sobre a oração do Pai Nosso.

Definições Papais. A Imaculada Conceição da Virgem Maria tornou-se doutrina oficial de Roma, em 1854. A teoria da infalibilidade papal (que vide) foi confirmada em 1870. O pontífice romano falaria *ex cathedra* ao fazer pronunciamentos específicos com base em seu ofício de vigário de Cristo, e de suprema autoridade apostólica. O papa fala como grande pastor e doutor de todos os cristãos, e, mediante seus pronunciamentos formais, seria infalível. Porém, o que ele disser em outras oportunidades, de maneira instrutiva, não tem esse caráter.

3. Confissões Protestantes. Apresentei a substância dessa questão no artigo sobre **Confissões de Fé**. O número de confissões luteranas e reformadas (calvinistas) aproxima-se de quarenta. O Livro de Concórdia, de 1580, contém nove itens básicos: o Credo dos Apóstolos, o Credo Niceno (com o *filioque*, que significa que o Espírito procede do Pai *e do Filho*), o Credo de Atanásio, a Confissão de Augsburg, a Apologia da Confissão, os Artigos de Schmalkald, os dois grandes catecismos de Lutero e a Fórmula de Concórdia. Em edições impressas na Saxônia, desde 1700, apareceram os Artigos de Visitação, de 1592. Por volta de 1530, o luteranismo foi definido essencialmente; mas os vários credos refinaram e aprimoraram essa definição. Pontos centrais da confissão luterana são a justificação pela fé e a autoridade exclusiva das Sagradas Escrituras. O sistema de penitências do catolicismo romano foi rejeitado, e o sacerdócio de todos os crentes foi asseverado. O luteranismo permaneceu ocidental em seu caráter, no tocante a doutrinas sobre as quais a Igreja ocidental e a Igreja oriental discordam uma da outra; e também tornou-se conservador e crescentemente evangélico.

As doutrinas das igrejas reformadas (calvinistas) foram afirmadas em mais de trinta credos separados, os mais importantes dos quais alistei no artigo intitulado *Confissão de Fé*.

A doutrina *batista* foi antecipada na Assembléia de Londres, ou Segunda Confissão de Londres, de 1677. A Confissão de Filadélfia, de 1677, foi muito importante para as igrejas batistas, bem como para as igrejas presbiterianas e congregacionais.

Os Trinta e Nove Artigos (que vide quanto a detalhes) apareceram como bases da teologia da Confissão de Augsburg, com algumas modificações e adaptações. Esses artigos derivam-se dos anteriores Quarenta e Dois Artigos Eduardianos, bem como dos Treze Artigos, de 1538. Forte sentimento anti-romanista transparece em alguns desses artigos. Ali é declarado que as igrejas de Jerusalém, de Alexandria, de Antioquia e de Roma erraram, tanto no tocante a questões de fé como no que concerne à conduta dos cristãos. Ver o artigo sobre *Westminster, Confissão de*.

Os anabatistas, antepassados espirituais dos menonitas, prepararam a sua confissão de fé em 1527. Pontos que são especialmente mencionados são o batismo em água, a exclusão, o partir do pão, a exclusão de pastores pecaminosos, o pacifismo e a instrução para não se fazerem juramentos. A confissão menonita de 1580 contém quarenta artigos. Cada um desses artigos é acompanhado por textos bíblicos de prova. Rejeita especificamente o batismo infantil, os juramentos e a guerra, mas reconhece um poder justo e moderado.

Grupos **evangélicos** de todas as modalidades têm aparecido, em grande proliferação de denominações e de fragmentação de denominações. Também há as igrejas bíblicas independentes, muitas das quais de tendências batistas, que seguem as confissões padronizadas dos ramos protestantes da Igreja cristã, servindo de base de interpretação e de fé. No entanto, muitas denominações evangélicas, e até mesmo igrejas locais isoladas ou missões evangélicas, sentem que devem ter suas próprias confissões de fé. A maioria dessas confissões consiste em declarações simples de doutrinas principais, acompanhadas por textos bíblicos de prova. Mas também temos a considerar as *inúmeras seitas*, muitas das quais originadas de grupos protestantes. Essas seitas têm seus próprios credos, e até mesmo livros sagrados extras. Importantes exemplos dessas seitas são os mórmons (ver sobre a Igreja de Jesus Cristo dos Santos dos Últimos Dias), os cientistas-cristãos (que vide) e os Adventistas do Sétimo Dia (que vide). Todos esses fragmentos têm suas próprias confissões. (E)

CONFISSÕES DE AGOSTINHO

Essa é uma daquelas poucas autobiografias imortais, a qual tem exercido enorme influência no mundo religioso e no mundo intelectual da civilização. Agostinho (que vide) escreveu essa obra pouco depois de tornar-se bispo de Hipona, imediatamente antes do ano 400 D.C. Na ocasião, ele tinha pouco mais de quarenta anos de idade. Pode-se dizer que as Confissões representam uma espécie de relato sobre o coração e a alma de Agostinho. Ele confessa um número razoável de pecados, em sua vida; mas a obra consiste, essencialmente, em uma declaração de louvor por tudo quanto Deus fizera por ele, através dos anos, levando-o ao estado espiritual que ele havia atingido. Na leitura da descrição dos conflitos e vitórias de Agostinho, encontramos muitos preciosos discernimentos sobre a vida humana, bem como sobre as motivações e inspirações dos homens. Naturalmente, Agostinho foi uma das mais profundas figuras intelectuais de todos os tempos, o que explica sua extraordinária capacidade de descrever essas coisas. Suas excursões no campo da psicologia infantil são interessantes. Ele nos mostra como sendo ainda criança, era impelido por definidas tendências contrárias à lei, tendências essas que nele eram naturais, não sendo fruto da influência do meio ambiente no qual vivia. Ele era negligente nos estudos, tendo aprendido valiosas lições não porque seguia regras, mas através de exemplos. Ele odiava o estudo do grego, favorecia histórias fantasiosas, queixava-se da qualidade da educação, mas, finalmente, dava crédito ao que a educação foi capaz de fazer por ele. Agostinho tinha consciência da autopiedade, pois gostava de ter pena de si mesmo, lançando sobre outras pessoas a culpa pelos seus problemas pessoais. Ele também revela o quanto o afeto pessoal significava para ele, pois, neste vasto mundo, nada se compara ao *amor*. Finalmente, foi a sua genitora quem impediu que ele continuasse semeando as sementes do mal, em sua juventude, fazendo sua mente, finalmente, voltar-se para Deus. Agostinho chegou a perceber que seu raciocínio e seus poderes intelectuais não podiam, finalmente, conferir-lhe a satisfação espiritual que ele tanto desejava. Acima disso, avulta a crença, no coração e na alma. Quando lhe perguntaram o que ele mais queria saber, Agostinho retrucou: «Deus e a alma!» E, diante da pergunta: «Nada mais?», ele respondeu: «Nada mais!» De alguma maneira, tudo deve ser encaixado dentro desse arcabouço, pois, doutra sorte, o homem fracassará naquilo que ele é requerido. Foi Agostinho quem declarou: «Creio para que possa compreender». Ele pensava que o ceticismo é prejudicial, e que somente mediante a fé uma pessoa pode aprender as grandes lições da vida. Porém, tudo quanto dissermos não pode substituir a leitura das *Confissões* de Agostinho, pelo que este artigo tem apenas o propósito de despertar a curiosidade do leitor. Quando fazia estudos de pós-graduação em Línguas Clássicas, fui forçado, pelo meu excelente professor, a ler as *Confissões* de Agostinho, em latim. Foi uma aventura difícil, mas proveitosa. (AM AUG)

CONFISSÕES HELVÉTICAS

Esse é o nome dado a dois documentos que expõem a fé comum das igrejas protestantes suíças. O primeiro desses documentos (1536) mostrou ser por demais abreviado, e exageradamente luterano para os gostos dos membros daquelas igrejas. Por esse motivo foi substituído por uma outra confissão, redigida por Bullinger (que vide) publicada em 1562 e em 1564. Essa confissão terminou sendo largamente aceita tanto na Suíça quanto na Escócia, na Hungria, na França e na Polônia. Foi uma das mais largamente reconhecidas confissões das igrejas protestantes reformadas (que vide). Ver o artigo sobre as *Confissões*, quanto a detalhes sobre essa questão. Ver também sobre os *Credos*.

CONFLITO DE DEVERES

Ver o artigo sobre **Transigência**, quanto às implicações religiosas da expressão. Dentro do jargão governamental, a expressão é usada para referir-se a oficiais que são profissionais, envolvidos em interesses particulares que interferem com o cumprimento apropriado de seus deveres, como funcionários públicos. Duas medidas são aplicadas nesses casos: Em primeiro lugar, pessoas com interesses divididos não deveriam exercer cargos públicos. Além deles não disporem de tanto tempo para dedicar aos seus deveres oficiais, estão sujeitos à tentação de usarem sua autoridade para fomentar seus interesses financeiros. Em segundo lugar, eles não deveriam aceitar presentes e nem subornos. Aqueles que presenteiam oficiais do governo podem estar esperando um tratamento especial, privilegiado, mediante o afrouxamento das sanções governamentais, mediante as autoridades envolvidas.

CONFORMIDADE

A forma verbal dessa palavra significa «tornar-se semelhante a», ou então, «seguir o padrão de». Usualmente, a conformidade refere-se ao ato de

CONFORMIDADE — CONFÚCIO

algum indivíduo, mediante o qual ele faz seus padrões de vida ou de crença, ou ambas as coisas, coincidirem com um certo conjunto de valores, de ideais ou de práticas diferentes daquilo que ele anteriormente considerava seu. O termo pode também referir-se à mesma coisa, quando envolve grupos.

1. *Quanto às Idéias*. Aquele que, mediante estudo ou influência, resolve aderir a algum sistema específico de idéias, como uma filosofia, uma religião, etc., conforma-se a esse sistema. Os discípulos de um sistema de idéias são considerados conformistas, dentro da esfera das idéias.

2. *Quanto às Práticas Éticas*. Paulo adverte-nos a não nos conformarmos com este mundo (Rom. 12:2). Aquele que não evita isso, termina por adotar os padrões éticos do mundo, tornando-se uma pessoa mundana. Para Paulo, o remédio para isso é a transformação do ser, mediante a renovação da mente. Sem dúvida isso envolve um processo espiritual, porque o homem, entregue a si mesmo, termina por amoldar-se ao mundo, em suas idéias e práticas. A fé cristã requer a denúncia do mundo, mediante uma correspondente transformação, segundo os ideais éticos e morais do evangelho.

3. *O modelo arquétipo* da transformação do crente é a imagem de Cristo (II Cor. 3:18). Esse trecho mostra-nos que passamos de um estágio de glória para o seguinte, no decurso de nossa inquirição, sendo mais e mais transformados segundo a imagem de Cristo. Essa é a transformação *metafísica*, que é um processo eterno, e não apenas temporal. O trecho de Romanos 8:29 mostra-nos que adquirir a imagem e a natureza do Filho é o alvo mesmo da salvação. Ver o artigo sobre a *Transformação Segundo a Imagem de Cristo*. Isso elimina toda a conformação com o mundo.

4. *Conformidade ao Exemplo*. Paulo exortou-nos a sermos seus seguidores, tal como ele seguia a Cristo (I Cor. 11:1. Ver também Efé. 5:1 e I Tes. 1:6, quanto a declarações similares). Desse modo, o crente amolda-se ao caminho e ao ideal cristãos. A referência em I Tessalonicenses diz que isso ocorre mediante a Palavra, o que, provavelmente, aponta para a Palavra de Deus, residente na mensagem do evangelho. Tomás a Kempis (que vide) enfatizou a verdade de que, em última análise, a homem escolhe conformar-se ou a Cristo ou ao anticristo. É praticamente impossível alguém mostrar-se neutro.

5. *Conformidade Eclesiástica*. Grupos que dissentem podem ser chamados de *não-conformistas*, visto que se recusam a conformar-se ao sistema predominante. Na Inglaterra temos o caso daqueles que, no século XVI e posteriormente, recusaram-se a conformar-se ao estilo de fé e de ritual da Igreja Anglicana. Os puritanos eram não conformistas.

6. *A Independência Mental e Espiritual*. Qualquer pessoa que gosta de pensar com independência, e não aceita cegamente qualquer sistema denominacional, e nem se deixa agrilhoar por qualquer fé religiosa, é uma pessoa não-conformista. Grande parte do conformismo deve-se ao desejo de aceitação, que é muito forte em algumas pessoas. — Algumas vezes, a conformidade a uma denominação cristã tem motivos sociais. Ninguém gosta de ser um pária. Em outras oportunidades, a razão é mais econômica. Muitas pessoas ganham a vida servindo à religião, sendo-lhes mais conveniente aquietarem-se quanto a possíveis diferenças. Mas, podemos ter a certeza de que aquele que se conforma a qualquer sistema de idéia, nisso mesmo limita o seu conhecimento, porquanto nenhum sistema é completo, e todos os sistemas têm inúmeros erros. (B H)

CONFORMIDADE NA NATUREZA
Ver **Uniformidade na Natureza**.

••• ••• •••

CONFÚCIO, CONFUCIONISMO

Ver o artigo geral sobre a **Religião e a Filosofia Chinesas**.

Confúcio (551-479 A.C.) foi um filósofo e líder religioso chinês. Nasceu no estado de Lu e na aldeia de Tsou, na porção sudoeste da província de Xantungue. Tornou-se o primeiro mestre profissional da história chinesa. Seus primeiros estudantes, que se tornaram discípulos em seu movimento religioso, segundo os registros antigos, foram vinte e quatro. Confúcio recebeu educação liberal em estudos de humanidades como poesia e literatura, havendo transmitido essa cultura aos seus discípulos. Muitos deles vieram a ocupar posições importantes no governo e na sociedade chinesas. O próprio Confúcio serviu em postos governamentais, mas ele, acima de tudo, era um mestre. Embora tenha exercido alguma influência, durante seus dias de vida, o triunfo do confucionismo não ocorreu senão já no século II A.C.

Um dos segredos de Confúcio era a ligação entre professor e estudantes, que ele cultivava, algo que veio a tornar-se um ideal chinês, muito imitado por outros. Quando foi instituído um dia do professor, na China, em nosso século XX, foi escolhida a data lendária do nascimento de Confúcio, 28 de setembro.

Idéias. Confúcio não se afirmava pensador original, mas somente transmissor de idéias que ele tomara emprestadas da antiguidade. Na realidade, porém, ele foi um pensador muito original.

1. *Alvos*. A filosofia de Confúcio centraliza-se em torno do homem e seu bem-estar, na vida presente. Ele queria instituir uma boa sociedade, caracterizada por relações sociais harmônicas.

2. As *relações sociais harmônicas* dependeriam do que Confúcio chamava de *li*, ou seja, *caminho do bom gosto*, a conduta de um cavalheiro. Se isso envolve a pessoa na realização de ritos apropriados, religiosos e outros, consiste muito mais em cumprir as próprias *funções*. Isso deve ser feito dentro das cinco relações cardeais: a. pai e filho; b. irmão mais velho e irmão mais novo; c. marido e mulher; d. amigo e amigo; e. soberano e súdito. A piedade filial é uma das importantes bases do sistema.

3. O senso de *propriedade* é um meio do desenvolvimento do caráter. Assim como uma casa dotada de alicerce sólido também precisa ter um aspecto agradável, ou um formato arquitetônico harmonioso, assim também o homem bom deve caracterizar-se por boas maneiras, mostrando-se cheio de consideração, no trato com o próximo. Isso é fomentado pelo estudo da música e da poesia. Nisso, Confúcio mesclava a ética com a estética. As qualidades humanas, segundo ele, seriam estimuladas pelas artes. A mente é despertada pela poesia para a prática do bem.

4. *Regra Áurea do Confucionismo*. «O que não quiseres que te seja feito, não o faças a outros». Naturalmente, isso corresponde à Regra Áurea ensinada por Jesus, embora afirmada negativamente. Ver Mateus 7:12. Ali Jesus declara: «...porque esta é a lei, e os profetas». E, naturalmente, temos nisso uma aplicação da lei do amor. Ver o artigo geral sobre o *Amor*. A necessidade da comunicação de um bom caráter ocupa posição central nos ensinos de Confúcio. Primeiramente o homem deve estabelecer

seu próprio bom caráter, e então deve transmitir os seus princípios a seus semelhantes.

5. *O Princípio do Jen*. O «jen» indica aquilo que é próprio e justo, mas, acima de tudo, o *amor*. Deste último fluem a retidão, o respeito, a sinceridade, a lealdade, a liberalidade, a veracidade, a diligência, a generosidade, que são virtudes cardeais. Isso pode ser comparado à declaração paulina, em Gálatas 5:22,23. O amor é o solo onde são cultivadas todas as demais virtudes cristãs.

6. *O Tao, ou «Caminho»*. A correta aplicação dos princípios leva o indivíduo a seguir o *Tao*, ou «Caminho». Isso torna o indivíduo superior em seu caráter e em suas ações. E também conduz o seu próprio ser à *dimensão cósmica*.

7. *O T'ien ou «Céu»*. Esse termo parece indicar um padrão impessoal de justiça, o qual permite que um homem, mesmo solitário, ou como parte de uma minoria, esteja correto em seus pontos de vista e em sua vida diária. O *T'ien* é uma espécie de providência ética, à qual a pessoa pode correlacionar a sua vida, e assim triunfar em espírito, mesmo que não materialmente falando. Esse T'ien parece ser o equivalente aproximado do Espírito de Deus da concepção cristã, sem quaisquer subcategorias metafísicas.

8. *Política*. Não haveria tal coisa como reforma do estado, ou realização de um elevado ideal, sem a espiritualização do indivíduo e da família. Um monarca deveria ser selecionado, por causa de seus méritos morais, e não com base no poder pessoal. Esse conceito é um paralelo do ideal platônico do *filósofo-rei*. Para Confúcio, pois, poder não é direito. O direito depende do caráter moral, e o poder real não se origina no poder militar. Ou então, dizendo a mesma coisa em termos mais modernos: «O poder não vem do cano de um fuzil», no dizer de uma outra famosa figura chinesa.

9. *Religião*. Confúcio não foi fundador de uma religião, no sentido usual. Ele acreditava na força moral universal, tendo usado as expressões «céu» e «vontade do céu» para referir-se a essa força moral. Tal como Buda, ele foi, essencialmente, um filósofo moral, e não um filósofo metafísico. Quando um de seus alunos indagou dele algo sobre a adoração aos espíritos, ele retrucou: «Ainda não sabemos como servir aos homens; e como poderemos saber como servir aos espíritos?» Quando indagado sobre a vida além-túmulo, sua resposta foi: «Ainda não sabemos muito sobre a vida. Como podemos saber muito sobre a morte?» (*Analects of Confuscius*, cap. 11, seção 2). Confúcio jamais se apresentou como profeta de Deus; mas dedicou-se ao que ele pensava ser uma missão celestial. Ele não conferenciava sobre Deus, como um ser descrito mediante proposições teológicas. Mas a história mostra-nos que ele foi homem voltado para as questões espirituais. Em períodos de tribulação, de tristeza e de busca, ele invocava o céu. Era dono de uma espiritualidade particular que não gostava de exibir diante dos homens. Na qualidade de homem piedoso, ele esperava poder desenvolver essa mesma atitude em outras pessoas.

Posso afirmar com segurança de que o *Logos* divino plantou algumas de suas sementes nos ensinamentos de Confúcio, embora possamos obter mais importantes declarações sobre questões metafísicas em outras fontes.

O Confucionismo. Os ensinamentos de Confúcio não se tornaram o ideal dominante na China, senão já no século II A.C. Finalmente, ele passou a ser considerado o mais importante entre tantas centenas de grandes filósofos da era clássica chinesa. Porém, uma vez firmado, o confucionismo teve uma longa história. Durante dois mil anos tem sido considerado como o credo ou religião oficial da China. Como fé religiosa, o confucionismo pode ser descrito como um *humanismo idealista*. Apesar de que vários aspectos de seu sonho de paz e harmonia universal nunca chegaram a concretizar-se, a China tem desfrutado de considerável unidade cultural e continuidade, até o estabelecimento do comunismo. Países circunvizinhos, como a Coréia, o Japão, o Vietnã e as ilhas Riu-Quiu também resolveram adotar Confúcio como seu principal líder e sábio religioso.

Tradições Preservadas. Um dos aspectos incomuns do confucionismo é que a linhagem de sua família pode ser acompanhada por mais de dois mil anos, até aos nossos próprios dias. Um descendente conhecido de Confúcio, da septuagésima sétima geração, estava residindo na ilha de Formosa, nos fins da década de 1960. A casa onde Confúcio viveu e ensinou continua existindo na cidade de Ch'ufu. Durante o reinado de Shih Huang, quando os tetos confucianos estavam sendo destruídos (270-221 A.C.), um descendente de Confúcio ocultou seus vários livros dentro das paredes duplas da casa. Esses livros foram recuperados durante a dinastia ocidental Han (202 A.C.), e assim prosseguiu a tradição confuciana. Essa casa recebeu o nome de *Lu-pi*, que significa «parede de Lu». Confúcio foi sepultado por seus discípulos no subúrbio nortista de Ch'ufu, perto do rio Su. O terreno inteiro do sepulcro, incluindo o túmulo mesmo de Confúcio, tem sido preservado.

Ensinamentos de Confúcio. Ver a porção deste artigo intitulado *Idéias*.

Escritos: Os escritos básicos de Confúcio são os seus próprios livros, suas declarações coligidas, chamadas *Lun Yu*, ou *Analects*. Também há aquela chamada *Ch'un-ch'iu, Anais da Primavera e do Outono*, ou *Estado de Lu*, além do *Shu Ching*, ou *Clássicos da História*, e o *Yi Ching*, ou *Clássico das Mudanças*. Um importante discípulo seu, Tseng Shen, produziu a *Grande Erudição*. Tzu Su produziu o *Chung Yung* ou *Doutrina do Homem*. O cânon confuciano coligido consiste dos *Quatro Livros* e dos *Cinco Clássicos*. (AM E HP)

CONFUSÃO DAS LÍNGUAS
Ver o artigo sobre **Babel, a Cidade e a Torre**.

CONGREGAÇÃO
Etimologicamente, essa palavra aponta para uma assembléia de pessoas. Usualmente o termo é usado em relação a atividades religiosas: 1. Uma reunião efetuada em alguma ocasião particular, com finalidade de adoração. 2. Um grupo organizado que se reúne regularmente para adorar, ou para outros propósitos religiosos. 3. Dentro do uso da Igreja Católica Romana, um ramo de uma ordem monástica, ou uma associação de um corpo administrativo, como, por exemplo, a Congregação da Propaganda (que vide).

CONGREGAÇÃO COMO TERMO BÍBLICO
1. A congregação, assembléia ou assembléia solene, são expressões que se aplicam à congregação do povo de Israel. Uma das palavras hebraicas traduzidas como «congregação», *edah*, aparece por cerca de cento e cinqüenta vezes no Antigo Testamento, a maioria no Pentateuco. Só o livro de Números tem 78 ocorrências. Encontra-se também nos livros de Josué, Juízes, I Reis, II Crônicas, Jó, Salmos, Jeremias e

CONGREGAÇÃO — CONGREGACIONALISMO

Oséias. No trecho de Êxodo 34:31, temos os líderes ou representantes escolhidos das tribos de Israel. Em Números 1:16, esses líderes são intitulados «príncipes das tribos».

2. Uma outra palavra hebraica, *qahal*, «assembléia de chamados», ocorre por cento e vinte e três vezes. Ver II Sam. 20:14, que indica aqueles convocados para a guerra; Núm. 10:7, que indica os convocados para propósitos religiosos; e Deu. 5:22, que aponta para o povo reunido para ouvir a leitura da Palavra.

3. O termo hebraico *aseret* vem de uma raiz que significa «restringir», «confinar», podendo indicar uma assembléia solene, conforme se vê em Isa. 1:13; Nee. 8:18. No Novo Testamento, o vocábulo grego *panegúris*, que aparece em Heb. 12:23, refere-se a essa palavra hebraica.

4. No Novo Testamento temos o termo grego *ekklesia*, traduzido por «igreja». Lucas o emprega em Atos 19:32, com seu sentido clássico de assembléia política convocada; e, em Atos 19:32,41, para aludir a um ajuntamento popular desordenado. O vocábulo *ekklesia* tornou-se o nome técnico da Igreja cristã, a assembléia daqueles que adoram e servem a Deus, segundo termos cristãos. Também pode estar sendo designada a Igreja universal, à qual todos os regenerados pertencem (Mat. 16:18; I Cor. 12:28), ou então alguma assembléia local formada por crentes (Atos 8:1; Rom. 16:1). Estêvão usou essa palavra, em seu discurso, ao referir-se à congregação de Israel, em Atos 7:38.

A palavra *sunagogé* tem sentido similar ao de *ekklesia*. Contudo, geralmente é aplicada às congregações locais dos judeus, ou sinagogas, e não tanto às igrejas cristãs locais. Talvez a única exceção seja Tiago 2:2, onde sinagoga é uma igreja cristã, provavelmente formada por crentes convertidos do judaísmo. Aparece também em Luc. 4:16 e Atos 13:5. Em Apocalipse 2:9 e 3:9 é usada negativamente, para indicar uma assembléia de Satanás, uma alusão a congregações religiosas apóstatas, de tendências gnósticas ou judaizantes, em contraste com a verdadeira Igreja de Deus.

5. *Usos Não-Religiosos*. Podem estar em foco: a. Um rebanho de bois (Sal. 68:30; ou um enxame de abelhas (Juí. 14:8). b. Assembléias legislativas, encabeçadas por juízes, anciãos, chefes de família, etc. (Êxo. 12:3; Deu. 31:28). c. Assembléias formadas para declarar guerra (Juí. 20:1), ou para estabelecer a paz (Juí. 21:13-20), ou para escolher governantes (I Sam. 10:17; I Reis 12:20), ou para ratificar decisões (I Sam. 11:14,15). No uso judaico posterior, o sinédrio passou a ser considerado a congregação suprema, reunida por razões religiosas ou seculares de todas as variedades.

6. *O Conceito de Congregação*. Os interesses do indivíduo são os interesses de sua comunidade; os interesses da comunidade são os do indivíduo que faz parte dela. Ninguém é uma autoridade em si mesmo. Cada pessoa está sob a autoridade da comunidade. A mensagem de Deus é dirigida à congregação. A redenção também tem um aspecto coletivo, e não apenas pessoal. Existem autoridades devidamente nomeadas para liderar a comunidade, o que envolve considerável responsabilidade.

CONGREGAÇÃO, MONTE DA

A expressão figura somente no trecho de Isaías 14:13, em todo o Antigo Testamento. Alguns intérpretes supõem que a referência original é à «congregação dos deuses», o que seria uma alusão à religiões pagãs, mencionada nos textos acádicos e ugaríticos. É possível que esteja em foco o monte Moriá. Mas, a referência ao norte, dentro desse texto de Isaías, não nos permite pensar no monte Moriá, e nem em Sião, que não ficava na porção norte de Jerusalém. Diz Delitzch, em seu comentário sobre o livro de Isaías: «O profeta faz o rei da Babilônia falar segundo a noção geral de seu povo, que localizava a sede da divindade no cume das montanhas do norte, perdidas em meio às nuvens. Outros intérpretes, para evitar a referência pagã, declaram que nada que se pareça com isso pode ser asseverado, e nem pode tal referência ser identificada com qualquer localização geográfica específica. Isso significa que não sabemos o que o autor sagrado tinha em mente.

CONGREGACIONALISMO

1. *O Termo*

A palavra aplica-se a qualquer grupo religioso autônomo em todas as questões eclesiásticas, e que usualmente toma decisões mediante o voto democrático. Quando a palavra é usada para indicar algum movimento religioso, a alusão é àquele movimento, dentro do protestantismo, que se originou na Inglaterra, nos fins do século XVI e no século XVII, cujo alvo era o de purificar (os puritanos) ou o de separar-se (os separatistas). A Igreja Anglicana foi o objeto dessa purificação, a organização da qual o movimento se separou.

2. *Situação Histórica*

Surgiu o movimento congregacional quando várias figuras religiosas da Inglaterra julgaram ser mister frisar a autonomia das congregações individuais, evitando-se assim a interferência da hierarquia eclesiástica anglicana. Os mentores do movimento buscaram textos bíblicos de prova para sua posição neotestamentária. No começo, a teologia do congregacionalismo era essencialmente calvinista. Foram perseguidos durante o reinado de Isabel I, mas floresceram no período da comunidade britânica. Oliver Cromwell, primeiro ministro do reino, considerava-se membro do movimento. Porém, depois a perseguição contra os congregacionais foi renovada. As perseguições forçaram o exílio, primeiramente para a Holanda e para Genebra, e então para a América do Norte. Os exilados puritanos estabeleceram-se na baía de Plymouth, na América do Norte, em 1620, após um período de exílio em Leiden, na Holanda.

O congregacionalismo tornou-se dominante na Nova Inglaterra, onde eles, imitando os seus perseguidores, estabeleceram uma espécie de estado teocrático, não se mostrando tolerantes para com aqueles que discordavam de seus pontos de vista. Elementos congregacionais bem conhecidos do Novo Mundo incluem elementos como Jonathan Edwards (que vide), e Cotton Mather (que vide). Com o desenvolvimento da nação norte-americana, o que envolveu intensa imigração, o congregacionalismo não conseguiu manter sua anterior preeminência. O metodismo e o unitarismo tornaram-se dominantes nos lugares onde, antes, o congregacionalismo fora poderoso. No campo teológico, tem havido uma gradual mudança do calvinismo para uma interpretação mais liberal da fé cristã. O congregacionalismo inglês, galês e norte-americano, como denominação, atualmente envolve cerca de dois milhões de membros. O ramo norte-americano uniu-se à Igreja Evangélica e Reformada, em 1961, e o novo grupo passou a ser chamado de United Church of Christ.

Períodos Históricos Distintos do Congregacionalismo. Esses períodos são seis, a saber: a. Os «dissentires», entre os anglicanos; b. exílio na Holanda e em Genebra, na Suíça; c. mudança para a América do Norte; d. predomínio numérico nas colônias da Nova Inglaterra; e. perda da preeminência, o que foi uma condição irreversível em meados do século XIX; f. liberalização doutrinária e fusão com outros grupos evangélicos.

3. *O Congregacionalismo Como Forma de Governo*
A ênfase sobre a autonomia das igrejas locais não se confinou à denominação congregacional. Os batistas, os presbiterianos (em menor escala), e muitas igrejas bíblicas independentes, além da maioria dos grupos pentecostais, em essência ou na prática, defendem um governo eclesiástico tipo congregacional, ou seja, não centralizado. Entre os pentecostais, uma notável exceção são as igrejas brasileiras, extremamente centralizadas. Um fato interessante a ser observado é que a mais antiga igreja evangélica brasileira foi uma igreja congregacional, organizada na cidade do Rio de Janeiro. (E H)

CONGRESSOS

Assembléias que promovem o bem-estar espiritual, social e intelectual dos católicos romanos. Esses congressos variam muito quanto ao seu propósito, podendo ser de natureza religiosa, política ou social, e podendo ser regionais, diocesanos, nacionais ou internacionais. O primeiro congresso de nota a ser convocado realizou-se em Mainz, na Alemanha, em 1848.

CONGRUÊNCIA, INCONGRUÊNCIA

1. *Na Gnosiologia*. Uma série de declarações mostra-se congruente, mesmo quando envolve alguma contradição ou tem conseqüências contraditórias, mas é coerente quanto a outros aspectos. Na linguagem popular, o termo é aplicado a crenças ou atos que, ao seguirem certa linha de eventos, mostram-se coerentes. Crer em uma contradição, qualquer que seja ela, é destruir a congruência. De acordo com a lógica dedutiva, mostrar-se congruente é obedecer às leis estabelecidas dos silogismos válidos. A congruência refere-se aos requisitos da teoria da *coerência* da verdade. Ver os artigos sobre *Coerência* e sobre o *Conhecimento e a Verdade Religiosa*, porção terceira, *Teorias da Verdade*.

2. *Na Ética*. As proposições éticas concordam umas com as outras, se seguirem padrões da congruência. Em outras palavras, uma proposição deriva-se lógica e naturalmente de outra, e a soma total das proposições conta com a mesma filosofia geral como sua base. Para exemplificar, se alguém acredita que os padrões das ações morais devem ser extraídos da Bíblia, é congruente crer que um indivíduo não pode agir como bem entender, ignorando as leis bíblicas. Além disso, a base bíblica dá a entender que os padrões de conduta foram revelados por Deus aos homens, não sendo produtos de experiências humanas relativas às questões éticas.

3. *Na Teologia*. Uma pessoa mostra-se congruente quando se apega a um sistema ordeiro de crenças, com base nos mesmos conceitos gerais que lhe servem de fundamento, acerca de Deus, do homem e da humanidade. Por exemplo, um Deus que seja naturalmente bom exige bondade da parte do homem, de tal modo que o padrão das ações humanas passa a ser a bondade de Deus. Na teologia, a congruência depende da formação de um sistema coerente. Para exemplificar, se Deus é considerado um ser todo-poderoso, então é coerente supor que o mundo, repleto de males como está, é governado pelo caos e está fora de controle.

Mas Isso Envolve um Paradoxo. Visto que a teologia é um estudo de realidades que ultrapassam ao nosso atual entendimento, ela envolve certos paradoxos. Assim, crer no livre-arbítrio humano e no determinismo divino, ao mesmo tempo, ou na transcendência e imanência de Deus, simultaneamente, aparentemente estabelecem contradições. No entanto, podemos raciocinar que esses conceitos são os pólos opostos de alguma verdade mais profunda, que é maior que seus elementos constitutivos. Portanto, pode parecer que alguém se mostre irracional, por crer em paradoxos (que vide), bem como no princípio da polaridade (que vide); mas esses são elementos indispensáveis na boa teologia, sob pena dela reduzir-se à *humanologia*. Os artigos sugeridos esclarecem a questão.

O Vício da Congruência. Os homens gostam de constituir sistemas teológicos inteiramente congruentes, que satisfaçam aos requisitos da *razão* humana. Entretanto, uma teologia totalmente racional terá de envolver, necessariamente, muitos erros e distorções. Com freqüência, as sutilezas da razão humana nos desviam da verdade, quando os pontos teológicos considerados não se prestam bem ao exame por parte da razão humana. Consideremos as contorções dos homens, ao procurarem formar uma cristologia (que vide), com seus argumentos que giram em torno de detalhes ínfimos. Os homens assemelham-se a um grupo de macacos, em uma árvore, quando começam a apresentar argumentos a respeito de certas verdades teológicas, que ultrapassam ao entendimento humano. A verdade é uma aventura, uma busca de fé, com muitos retrocessos e surpresas. Nesse exame, a intuição desempenha um importante papel, e não apenas a razão. A intuição assemelha-se à água que jorra de uma fonte. Ela se lança no ar e floresce. É como uma entidade viva. Mas os *conceitos* ou juízos teológicos assemelham-se à água que já se empoçou, e que ficou estagnada à superfície do solo. Os sistemas teológicos puramente conceptuais, pode aqueles que aparecem bem ordenados em compêndios, com índices intricados, são sistemas estagnados.

A Loucura das Declarações Doutrinárias. As igrejas e as instituições de ensino têm o mau hábito de alicerçar suas atividades sobre declarações doutrinárias que se tornam meios que levam à prática da exclusão e da hostilidade. O leitor já encontrou um desses sistemas que ao menos mencionasse a lei do amor? A resposta tem de ser negativa. No entanto, o amor é o maior de todos os princípios espirituais.

CONGRUIDADE

Esse termo vem do latim, **congruus**, «apto», ou «adaptado». O vocábulo subentende certa relação moral segundo a qual uma pessoa que deve receber algum direito ou privilégio não é considerada em pé de igualdade, mas inferior ou superior àquela que faz a concessão. Isso posto, o beneficiário não se sente na obrigação de retribuir ao direito ou privilégio recebido.

CONGRUÍSMO

Essa palavra vem do latim, **congruitas**, «aptidão». Na teologia, o termo é empregado para indicar a *aptidão* de alguém para receber a graça divina. A questão não envolve mérito versus graça, dentro da salvação; mas se um homem pode viver de modo a merecer a graça. Os escotistas (que vide) defendiam essa posição. Os tomistas (que vide) supunham que os

CONHECENDO A DEUS

homens podem chegar a merecer a graça, mas somente mediante a ajuda de Deus. O artigo XIII dos Trinta e Nove Artigos nega, especificamente, essa possibilidade.

Uma outra idéia teológica é aquela associada à idéia de que a graça, naturalmente, impele os eleitos a se entregarem aos cuidados de Deus, com *congruência*, isto é, movidos por sua própria livre vontade. Em outras palavras, o livre-arbítrio humano é condicionado para essa atitude pelo Espírito Santo.

CONHECENDO A DEUS

1. No V.T., **conhecer a Deus** é algo ético e prático. Os homens que fazem a vontade de Deus, o conhecem. Esta idéia continua no N.T. Mas o *Logos* é o revelador de Deus em todos os sentidos, na eternidade passada, agora e para sempre. Ver João 1:18.

2. Por meio do Espírito, o alter ego do Filho. Ver João 4:24.

3. Nas Escrituras, onde ele é revelado.

4. Intelectualmente, mas também mística e intuitivamente (ver Efé. 1:17, onde há exposição plena sobre o conceito apresentado em João 17:3).

5. Conhecer a Deus é receber a vida, se esse conhecimento for experimental e espiritual, e não apenas intelectual. Esta *vida* vem através da *transformação* da alma à imagem de Cristo (II Cor. 3:18, Rom. 8:29), e resulta na participação na *natureza divina*, II Ped. 1:4, Col. 2:10. Ver o artigo sobre *Salvação*.

6. A polêmica: a ordem para que se conheça a Deus, através de Cristo, envolve um tom polêmico. O povo de Israel pensava conhecer a Deus e ter vida nele, no entanto, rejeitava ao Filho, o que significava que não tinha conhecimento de Deus, e nem vida.

O único Deus verdadeiro, João 17:3. Temos aqui uma importantíssima frase, que nos ensina diversas grandes verdades, a saber:

1. Deus Jeová é aqui *contrastado com as divindades imaginárias* do mundo pagão (ver Rom. 16:27; Jud. 25 e Apo. 15:4). Esse tema é ventilado com clareza em I Cor. 8:5,6, onde lemos: «Porque, ainda que há também alguns que se chamem deuses, quer no céu ou sobre a terra, como há muitos deuses e muitos senhores, todavia, para nós há um só Deus, o Pai, de quem são todas as cousas e para quem existimos; e um só Senhor, Jesus Cristo, pelo qual são todas as cousas, e nós também por ele».

2. Essa declaração de Cristo também desfecha um golpe mortal no *gnosticismo*, que com freqüência anunciava que Cristo é o Deus deste mundo, embora postulasse muitos outros mundos habitados, possuidores de *seus próprios deuses*. Que possa haver outros mundos habitados por seres inteligentes não é um tema apoiado nu negado aqui, embora outros textos bíblicos subentendam uma vasta multiplicação de vidas, em outras regiões (ver, por exemplo, o primeiro capítulo da epístola de Paulo aos Efésios); mas pelo menos temos, em João 17:3 a negação da existência de outros «deuses», que exerceriam sua autoridade em outros mundos ou dimensões. Pois na realidade só existe um único Deus verdadeiro, assim chamado com toda a razão, — cuja glória não pode ser de maneira alguma empanada por qualquer rival.

3. Indiretamente, aqui também temos uma invectiva contra o *judaísmo apostatado* dos tempos de Jesus e seus apóstolos, que se foi desviando cada vez mais das verdades bíblicas do Antigo Testamento; pois, apesar do fato de que tal judaísmo reconhecia a existência de um único verdadeiro Deus, tinha rejeitado a sua mais elevada de todas as manifestações, na pessoa de Jesus Cristo. Assim, apesar de reconhecerem intelectualmente a existência de Deus, na realidade não o conheciam por experiência própria. Pois tal conhecimento chega aos homens exclusivamente por intermédio do Filho de Deus, mediante a sua encarnação; mas igualmente em seu estado posterior à encarnação, isto é, uma vez assunto aos céus, por meio do ministério do seu Espírito Santo.

4. Essa declaração de Cristo, pois, é uma das *mais claras* do N.T., em apoio e confirmação da doutrina *monoteísta*. (Quanto aos diversos conceitos de Deus, na teologia e na filosofia, ver no NTI, as notas expositivas referentes ao trecho de Atos 17:27. Ver o artigo sobre *Trindade*).

«O único Deus real, essencial...fazendo antítese com os deuses irreais, simbólicos e míticos deste mundo, e não somente do mundo gentílico, mas também do judaísmo posterior, em seu estado de apostasia da fé revelada, segundo se vê em I João 5:20; Apo. 5:7 e I Tes. 1:9. Esse é o Deus revelado na pessoa de Cristo, o Deus e Pai de nosso Senhor Jesus Cristo, na expressão de Efé. 1:3. E isso não faz antítese com a idéia de Deus segundo o Antigo Testamento, ou com a idéia de Cristo, mas antes, contrasta com toda a crença falsa e obscura sobre Deus; por conseguinte, temos aqui o verdadeiro Deus segundo ele se revela em Cristo, embora distinto quanto à sua consciência divina e distinto de Cristo» (Lange, em João 17:3).

E a Jesus Cristo, a quem enviaste. Estas palavras se relacionam à cristologia em geral, tal como aquelas primeiras estão vinculadas ao conhecimento de Deus Pai. Também estas, como aquelas, têm sido variegadamente interpretadas, e, tal como no caso daquela primeira declaração de Cristo e outras similares (como a que temos em I Cor. 8:5,6) têm servido de campo de batalha, desde a antiguidade, no que diz respeito aos conceitos de Deus e de Cristo. Podemos desdobrar suas implicações como segue:

I. Em João 17:3

1. Equivale a conhecer a Deus que é, igualmente, a fonte da vida. Esse é um tema constante do quarto evangelho. (Ver João 1:12,18; 3:16; 5:25,26 e 14:6). O conceito inclui a idéia de exclusividade. Só no Filho há vida, Atos 4:12. Essa vida é a participação na forma de vida de Deus, e não apenas existência sem fim. (Ver sobre esse conceito em II Ped. 1:4).

2. Os arianos, os seguidores das idéias de *Socínio* e os unitários têm-se utilizado com freqüência do terceiro versículo do décimo sétimo capítulo do evangelho de João para demonstrarem uma suposta diferença de natureza entre Deus Pai e Deus Filho, porque, segundo argumentam eles, há um só Deus verdadeiro, e há também o seu Filho, Jesus Cristo. Porém, isso é uma interpretação artificial, que ignora outras passagens das Escrituras, igualmente, autoritárias (como de resto, a Bíblia inteira é autoritária), e que indicam a perfeita unidade de natureza do Pai e do Filho, bem como a legítima deidade do Filho, Jesus Cristo. (Ver, por exemplo, João 1:1; 5:19,20; 10:30,33,36; 14:9,10; Heb. 1:3 e Col. 2:9).

3. Em contraste com a posição herética acima, os crentes autênticos têm deduzido ao fato de que conhecer a Deus Pai é, ao mesmo tempo, conhecer o Filho (implicando em unidade de conhecimento), que há entre Deus Pai e Deus Filho, unidade de natureza. Isso está claramente implícito no texto, ainda que não seja diretamente declarado.

4. Apesar de que o conhecimento é o mesmo, isto é,

CONHECENDO O AMOR DE CRISTO

que conhecer a Cristo é, ao mesmo tempo, conhecer a Deus Pai, contudo, fica salientada na passagem de João 17:3 a distinção de pessoas—o Pai não é o Filho, e vice-versa. Em Cristo chegamos a conhecer a Deus. Por conseguinte, em certo sentido, o Pai é conhecido tanto em Jesus como juntamente com Cristo.

5. O texto em foco *subentende* que há um *conhecimento místico* de Deus através do Espírito Santo, apesar do fato de que conhecer a Deus, no quarto evangelho, sempre é encarado do ponto de vista prático, isto é, produz resultados práticos na vida e nas ações do crente.

6. Isso quer dizer que a fé é aqui contemplada teologicamente—trata-se de um conhecimento contemplativo, com alvos e propósitos: a fé conduz ao conhecimento contemplativo, e o conhecimento contemplativo conduz à transformação do ser do crente.

Confirmando o terceiro ponto, dado mais acima, Alford observou em João 17:3: «A própria justaposição que aqui há entre Jesus Cristo e o Pai serve de prova, por implicação, da deidade de nosso Senhor. Pois conhecer a Deus e a uma criatura 'no caso, Jesus Cristo, se ele não fosse divino' não poderia ser a vida eterna, e tal associação de um com o outro, nessas condições, seria algo inconcebível».

Brown, definindo a vida eterna, escreveu: «A vida eterna da qual Jesus fala, e que, segundo ele declara, cabe a ele mesmo conferir, não consiste meramente em uma existência consciente e interminável, e, sim, de uma vida cuja característica mais distintiva é a intimidade com o Pai de nosso Senhor Jesus Cristo, bem como com o próprio Jesus, na qualidade de 'caminho' para o Pai, bem como na qualidade de 'verdade' e vida».

«Somente na Palavra 'ou Verbo' que se fez carne é que podemos ouvir a voz da misericórdia, do perdão, do amor, da paternidade; o que chega aos homens como o sopro da vida, a fim de que se tornem almas vivas» (Ellicott, em João 17:3).

Filo costumava dizer: «Fugir para o ser divino é vida eterna; mas correr para longe dele é morte». (*De Profugis*, pág. 461).

Digo que o reconhecimento de Deus, em Cristo,
Aceito pela razão, soluciona para ti
Todas as questões da terra e fora dela,
E te faz avançar de tal modo na sabedoria
Que melhorarias a ponto de reprovar o provado?
No mísero minuto da vida, com poder de usar essa prova
Deixarias o conhecimento e reverterias à sua origem?
Tu o possuis; usa-o, e avança ou morre.
Pois digo que isso é morte, e a única morte,
Quando a perda de um homem procede de seu lucro,
As trevas vindas da luz, do conhecimento para a ignorância,
E a falta de amor se manifesta dentre o próprio amor.

(Robert Browning, *A Death in the Desert*).

II. Em Efésios 4:13

Pleno conhecimento do Filho de Deus. As palavras *pleno conhecimento* traduzem um único vocábulo grego, «epignosis», mas, visto que essa palavra é uma forma intensificada (com um prefixo preposicional), é tradução correta dizer como temos aqui. Quem recebe tal conhecimento, conhece experimentalmente ao Filho de Deus. Quanto a isso, consideramos os pontos abaixo:

1. Essa palavra indica conhecimento intelectual, mas não somente isso.

2. Também significa o *conhecimento experimental* da alma, mediante a «comunhão» com o Filho de Deus, em sua natureza essencial e em suas manifestações. Paulo via Cristo como uma personalidade transcendental que, em sua grandiosidade, só pode vir a ser conhecido por métodos espirituais. E assim conhecido ele passa a transformar os homens, para que estes assumam sua natureza e suas riquezas. É por isso que Paulo declarou, em Fil. 3:10: «...para o conhecer e o poder da sua ressurreição e a comunhão dos seus sofrimentos, conformando-me com ele na sua morte...»

3. Esse conhecimento, pois, é de natureza «mística», conforme diz a teologia paulina do princípio ao fim. Em outras palavras, tal conhecimento nos chega através da «iluminação e transformação» operadas pelo Espírito Santo. (Comparar isso com Efé. 1:18, onde Paulo ora para que os crentes tenham seus olhos do entendimento «iluminados», a fim de que possam «conhecer» a esperança da nossa vocação, as riquezas da glória de herança nos santos; e assim «conheceremos» seu grande poder, que foi exercido em Cristo, e que será exercido em nós. (Ver Efé. 1:19). Conhecer e experimentar tais coisas, portanto, faz parte do que significa «conhecer» a Cristo.

A revelação, além disso, leva-nos a *conhecer ao próprio Deus*, conforme aprendemos no décimo sétimo versículo de Efésios 4. O tema da segunda oração de Paulo, neste livro, é que possamos «conhecer» o «amor de Cristo», e nesse amor se encerra o «conhecimento de tudo quanto o amor de Cristo está fazendo por nós e em nós». Pois, nas páginas do N.T., conhecer é amar, pois o «conhecimento-amor» é a «gnosis» neotestamentária, em contraste com os conceitos dos gnósticos. Sim, o amor é a real *gnosis* cristã, por ser essa a fonte originária de todas as bênçãos espirituais.

CONHECENDO O AMOR DE CRISTO

Efé. 3:19: *e conhecer o amor de Cristo, que excede todo o entendimento, para que sejais cheios até a inteira plenitude de Deus.*

Conhecer o amor de Cristo. Não temos nessas palavras o nosso amor a Cristo, pois esta oração ultrapassa tal pensamento, já que se centraliza antes no amor de Deus por nós, conferido por intermédio de Cristo—está em foco o amor divino por nós. (Ver João 3:16; II Cor. 5:14; Rom. 5:8; 9:37,39; Gál. 2:20; Efé. 2:4,5:2; I João 4:10, 11, 19 e Apo. 1:5, quanto a outras passagens neotestamentárias que enfatizam o «amor de Deus», expresso por meio de Cristo).

«...*conhecer*...» De que maneira? Vejamos os pontos abaixo:

1. Conhecer *intelectualmente*. Mas entra em jogo muito mais que a nossa capacidade intelectual, porquanto o amor de Deus em Cristo excede à razão humana, a meras fórmulas racionais.

2. Conhecer *intuitivamente*, sem quaisquer fórmulas intelectuais.

3. Conhecer *experimentalmente*, na vida diária e no nível consciente.

4. Mais particularmente, está em foco o conhecimento *místico*, como entendimento e expressão da alma, que não necessita de fórmulas verbais e racionais para existir e para impor-se.

5. Finalmente, tal «conhecimento» do amor de Cristo, tal experiência, torna-se plenamente concretizada, quando estivermos no estado eterno. (Ver I

Cor. 13:12). Por conseguinte, tanto agora como então o amor será sempre o caminho pelo qual podemos conhecer o que era impossível de ser conhecido.

O conhecimento do amor de Cristo constrange-nos a alma a amar aos nossos semelhantes. O vigésimo quinto capítulo do evangelho de Mateus mostra-nos que amar aos homens é, em certo sentido, amar a Cristo. O trecho de II Cor. 5:14 mostra-nos que o amor de Cristo por nós leva-nos a amar aos outros e a buscar o seu bem-estar eterno. A passagem de I João 4:11,12,19,20 ensina-nos que o amor é um princípio normativo da fórmula divina, e que amamos a Deus porque primeiramente ele nos amou; e assim, visto que amamos a Deus, a quem não temos visto, amamos aos irmãos, filhos de Deus, porquanto, ao amarmos a eles, estamos honrando e amando a Deus.

O amor busca o bem-estar, o bem-estar eterno do ente amado. O amor consiste em desejarmos para os outros aquilo que desejamos para nós mesmos; o amor consiste em nos interessarmos pelo próximo, como algo tão natural como quando nos interessamos por nós mesmos, sem motivos egoístas, mas por causa de um puro altruísmo. Deus também buscou o bem-estar eterno do homem, e enviou o seu Filho em sua missão terrena. O Filho de Deus, que ama ao homem com a mesma intensidade de amor que Deus Pai, levou a efeito a sua missão. E os remidos, ao receberem na alma esse amor, transmitem-no a outros homens, sendo esse o impulso inspirador da missão evangelizadora da igreja, mas também de todas as nossas ações individuais uns pelos outros, dentro da comunidade religiosa de que fazemos parte. E assim se expressa o grandioso ciclo do amor.

«Quando esse amor a Cristo enche os nossos corações e penetra até os seus recessos mais profundos, então sentimos forças para lançar fora todos os nossos preconceitos e podemos ultrapassar nossas dificuldades e limitações intelectuais. Então temos a coragem de adotar a regra simples de comunhão estabelecida por Cristo: 'Quem fizer a vontade de meu Pai, que está nos céus, esse é meu irmão, irmã e mãe'». (Findlay em Efé. 3:19).

Que excede todo entendimento. — Essas palavras mostram-nos que o amor de Cristo ultrapassa a capacidade humana de compreendê-lo intelectualmente, não podendo nós defini-lo, descrevê-lo, pô-lo dentro de uma categoria. O termo grego aqui empregado é «uperballo», que quer dizer «ultrapassar», «ir além». A mente humana, até mesmo aquilo que vai além da capacidade cerebral, não é instrumento que possa descrever quão infinito é o amor de Deus, pelo menos no presente estágio de nosso desenvolvimento. Contudo, um homem pode conhecer de maneira intuitiva, experimental e mística, os estágios mais avançados do amor de Cristo, que desafiam toda a capacidade intelectual de compreensão e de descrição. Duas idéias se mostram inerentes nessa expressão, a saber:

1. Esse amor se reveste de natureza tal que vai além de quaisquer atividades ou fórmulas cerebrais, racionais.

2. Mas o amor também ultrapassa o «conhecimento», em sua importância e qualidade.

O amor é de *qualidade superior* ao conhecimento. Os gregos davam importância demasiada ao «conhecimento», conforme o primeiro capítulo da primeira epístola aos Coríntios nos mostra. Mas o décimo terceiro capítulo dessa mesma epístola é o grande «hino ao amor», onde descobrimos que o amor é muito maior que todo o conhecimento e sabedoria, devendo ser buscado acima de todas as demais virtudes. O amor, pois, é uma espécie de «gnosis divina», preferível à «gnosis» dos gnósticos e da filosofia grega. É bem provável que Efé. 3:19 pelo menos faça alusão a essa verdade, ao exaltar tão soberanamente o «amor de Cristo». A passagem de I Cor. 8:1-3 se caracteriza pela mesma ênfase. O conhecimento infunde orgulho, mas o amor edifica. E edifica também aos outros, e não somente a nós mesmos. «Mas se alguém ama a Deus, esse é conhecido por ele» (I Cor. 8:3). Por conseguinte, o amor é melhor do que o conhecimento, embora os esforços humanos, isolados, não possam chegar até ao verdadeiro amor. Mas, visto que o amor chega até Deus e lhe presta honrarias, o amor é a maneira de conhecermos o que, de outro modo, não podia ser conhecido. O amor é a «sabedoria divina».

CONHECIMENTO, CONHECER

Dois longos artigos aparecem nesta enciclopédia que abordam o conhecimento do ponto de vista filosófico, naquilo que diz respeito à fé religiosa. Esses artigos têm o título de o *Conhecimento e a Fé Religiosa* e a *Crença Religiosa e o Problema de Verificação*. Na primeira parte, seção I, do primeiro desses artigos, expomos os principais pontos de vista sobre o conhecimento, como o empirismo, o racionalismo, a intuição, o misticismo, o ceticismo, o positivismo e o psiquismo. Na segunda parte, II, apresentamos as teorias e os critérios da verdade, como o realismo, os sentimentos, os costumes e tradições, o tempo, a intuição, a revelação, o instinto, a maioria, a pluralidade, a autoridade, a correspondência, o pragmatismo, a conformidade e a coerência. Além disso, cada uma dessas questões é abordada em separado, cada qual em seu respectivo artigo. O segundo dos artigos acima intitulados trata sobre como o conhecimento religioso pode ser averiguado. A esses artigos acrescentamos algumas observações gerais, abaixo. Ver também o artigo separado sobre *Conhecimento e Ética*.

1. A Palavra Conhecimento. O termo grego **ginoskein** significa «decidir», «determinar», «decretar», estando relacionado ao verbo português «conhecer». O vocábulo latino *cognoscere* é uma palavra cognata, de onde vem aquele verbo português. Essa palavra tem os sentidos de «familiarizar-se com», «notar», «conhecer» e «reconhecer».

2. Principais Usos da Palavra «Conhecimento». a. O resultado ou produto do processo de aprendizagem ou informação. b. O aprendizado, incluindo o conhecimento acumulado na cultura humana. c. A firme convicção da verdade. d. O ato ou processo de conhecer, de tomar conhecimento. e. O objeto de qualquer conhecimento. f. O possível alcance do conhecimento humano. g. Algum conhecimento ou informação específicos. h. Dentro da fé religiosa, os itens dados por Deus, através da razão, da intuição ou das experiências místicas, que constituem o conjunto dos conhecimentos sobre as coisas espirituais, reveladas ou adquiridas.

3. Distinções e Declarações Filosóficas

a. Platão usava a palavra **episteme** (conhecimento) em contraste com *doxa* (opinião). A opinião estaria baseada sobre a percepção dos sentidos, ao passo que o conhecimento estaria alicerçado sobre a razão, a intuição e o misticismo. O conhecimento consistiria na certeza da genuinidade de alguma coisa. A opinião consistiria na incerteza, estando sempre em fluxo. A *sofia* (sabedoria) seria a mais elevada forma de conhecimento, por ser o conhecimento da *totalidade* de alguma coisa. Ver o ponto «d» quanto a outros pontos de vista platônicos. Nos escritos de *Aristóteles*,

CONHECIMENTO E A ÉTICA

a sabedoria consiste no conhecimento dos princípios fundamentais, e a intuição participa ativamente.

b. *Aristóteles*. Para ele, o conhecimento seria científico, e seria adquirido através dos sentidos (embora não exclusivamente). O conhecimento é a completa descrição de qualquer coisa, em todas as suas porções, funções, características, etc.

c. De conformidade com *Weigel* (que vide), o conhecimento autêntico é interno e espiritual, ao passo que o conhecimento externo sobre as coisas não é autêntico.

d. *Swedenborg* (que vide) afirmava que a alma tem um conhecimento total, e que a queda no pecado tornou esse conhecimento inoperante, o que, naturalmente é um ponto de vista platônico. Platão partia do pressuposto que a alma, uma entidade eterna, pertencente ao mundo dos universais ou idéias, possuía todo o conhecimento; mas, a sua associação com o corpo terreno ocultou isso. Portanto, o conhecimento envolve recuperação ou recordação. Os estudos no campo da parapsicologia até certo ponto confirmam essa teoria, mostrando que o conhecimento de um ser humano não é apenas o acúmulo de fatos que ele consiga reunir em suas experiências diárias.

e. A *tradição empírica* tem sido destacada por Locke e pela ciência moderna em geral. Ali, a percepção dos sentidos, desassistida ou através do uso de instrumentos, é a fonte de todo o conhecimento. De acordo com o *positivismo*, esse conhecimento é visto somente como uma taxa de probabilidades, pelo que nada haveria de certo ou fixo. No *pragmatismo*, o conhecimento não é aquilo que é perfeito em sua teoria (o que não existe), mas é aquilo que é prático e funciona bem. Ver os artigos separados sobre esses assuntos.

f. Todo conhecimento está alicerçado sobre certas proposições que não podem ser investigadas. Usamos Deus para explicar muitas coisas; mas a sua natureza continua sendo misteriosa para nós. Os cientistas começam por aquilo que já existe e examinam suas características. Porém, não sabemos como explicar como as coisas vieram à existência. Ortega y Gasset (que vide) afirmava que o conhecimento precisa estar arraigado em uma crença pré-racional.

g. Algum conhecimento consiste em verdadeira e justificada crença, sem nenhum defeito. Ver sobre *Chisholm*, quarto ponto, sobre essa idéia. Também pode consistir em crença não contradita. Por exemplo, se eu morrer e então descobrir que continuo existindo, em forma espiritual, terei uma crença não contradita, embora não saiba descrever o tipo de vida que então estarei vivendo. Simplesmente estarei vivendo, sem qualquer explicação.

4. **O Conhecimento e a Fé Religiosa**. O conhecimento que as ciências adquirem vem através dos cinco sentidos físicos, com a ajuda da intuição e da razão. Porém, o conhecimento sobre as coisas espirituais vem através da *razão* (ver sobre o *racionalismo*), através da *intuição* (que vide), mas, principalmente, através do *misticismo* (que vide). A *revelação* (que vide) é uma subcategoria do misticismo. A mente religiosa busca a certeza de certas coisas e com freqüência, demonstra pouca paciência para fazer investigações. Muitas pessoas religiosas são francamente antiintelectuais em sua abordagem do conhecimento. A necessidade de segurança e conforto mental leva as pessoas religiosas a suporem que o misticismo, quando genuíno (como no caso da revelação bíblica), é perfeito. Porém, essa suposição envolve um *dogma*, estando sujeito à inquirição. Não há modo de conhecimento que nos confira um conhecimento perfeito. Antes, o conhecimento é uma busca permanente, eterna, e não um acontecimento único, divinamente conferido. Ademais, os meios de que dispomos nesta vida dão-nos um conhecimento muito elementar e primitivo, sem importar se esse conhecimento é científico ou espiritual. De nada adianta alguém mostrar-se pretencioso quanto a essa questão, pois, quanto mais pensamos que sabemos, mais absurdos e ridículos nos tornamos. Não obstante, alguns itens do conhecimento que temos são muito importantes. Entre esses itens alisto pontos como a existência de Deus; a existência, a sobrevivência ante a morte física e o destino da alma; a missão universal de Cristo, incluindo os aspectos da redenção e da restauração. Esses são temas importantíssimos, sobre os quais muito temos a aprender, sem falarmos em inúmeros outros assuntos. Além disso, há a *lei do amor*, o mais importante e poderoso de todos os princípios éticos. Todas as virtudes cristãs estão arraigadas no solo do amor cristão. O amor é a prova mesmo da espiritualidade. Ver I João 4:7 ss.

5. *O Dom da Fé*. No campo espiritual, a alma não está limitada em sua inquirição pelo conhecimento. Também há um dom de fé, operação do Espírito Santo. Certas coisas nos são dadas a conhecer pela fé, para o que não precisamos de provas. Naturalmente, há aquela fé que consiste em «crer no que não é verdade», mas que a pessoa defende tenazmente. Porém, isso é uma perversão da fé, e não uma manifestação da mesma. Agostinho insistia sobre a idéia de que o ceticismo situa o cético na área das trevas espirituais, onde a luz de Deus não pode penetrar. Mas, a atitude da fé aclara o céu e permite que a luz resplandeça. Não podemos separar o conhecimento da iluminação do Espírito (Efé. 1:17). (E EP NTI)

CONHECIMENTO E A ÉTICA

Cada sistema de conhecimento aborda o problema da ética de um ângulo diferente. Todos esses sistemas têm certo valor, e também envolvem certos problemas especiais.

1. O *empirismo* (que vide) mostra a tendência de ver a ética como uma questão *relativa*, com base nas experiências acumuladas dos homens, através da percepção dos sentidos. Nesse sistema, a ética torna-se parte do *humanismo*.

2. No *racionalismo* (que vide) acredita-se que a razão pode descobrir os mais importantes princípios éticos, inteiramente à parte da experiência. Sócrates ensinava que a alma e a mente subconsciente do homem já possuem o conhecimento do que é certo e errado, dos princípios éticos gerais, e também que a razão, quando bem disciplinada, pode trazer à tona esse conhecimento.

3. A *intuição* (que vide) parte do pressuposto que a mente e a alma são capazes de conhecer as coisas de forma imediata, sem o concurso da razão ou da percepção dos sentidos. Esse conhecimento pode provir da alma, de Deus ou de alguma outra entidade espiritual, ou então de alguma fonte desconhecida. Sabemos intuitivamente o que é certo, tal e qual Deus, porquanto somos seres dotados de intuição. O bispo Butler supunha que a consciência humana é um meio poderoso e digno de confiança para a obtenção do conhecimento, e isso aborda as funções da razão e da intuição.

4. No *misticismo* (que vide), o conhecimento ético nos seria dado como um dom de Deus, mediante as experiências místicas e a revelação divina (que vide). Simplesmente seríamos informados sobre o que é certo e o que é errado. A revelação tornar-se-ia

CONHECIMENTO E A FÉ RELIGIOSA

concreta sob a forma de livros sagrados, e a Igreja teria a função de proteger e interpretar esses livros. Eles tornam-se livros de texto da ação ética, conferindo-nos, ao menos, os grandes princípios éticos gerais, além de muitas sugestões quanto às subcategorias e normas que nos ajudam a refletir sobre outros assuntos que não são especificamente ventilados.

5. Na *razão*, na *intuição* e no *misticismo*, normalmente encontramos uma ética absoluta (e, com freqüência, teísta). As leis éticas seriam verdadeiras e absolutas, não estando sujeitas às vicissitudes das experiências humanas.

6. No *positivismo* (que vide), o único conhecimento reconhecido é o científico. E os julgamentos de valores, tal como na ética, são rejeitados por estarem além do escopo do conhecimento humano, pelo que envolveriam proposições destituídas de significado. Aquilo que não pode ser diretamente confirmado, em laboratório, é chamado de *sem significado*.

7. No *pragmatismo* (que vide) as proposições éticas são determinadas por aquilo que funciona na experiência humana, por aquilo que é *prático*, e não por aquilo que é teoricamente certo ou perfeito (cujas condições nunca existiriam). Essa forma de ética é relativa. Os pensadores pragmáticos pensam que nunca houve leis éticas eternas e imutáveis; e, se porventura existem, estão acima do alcance de nossos atuais meios de obtenção do conhecimento.

8. Dentro do *pensamento cristão*, usualmente aceita-se que as funções da razão e da intuição nos digam o que é certo. O primeiro capítulo da epístola aos Romanos dá apoio a esse pensamento, porquanto até os pagãos teriam um conhecimento básico sobre o que é certo e errado. Porém, nessa questão entra a idéia inteira do *ministério do Espírito*, o qual nos ensina o que é certo. Na Bíblia encontramos uma orientação escrita, com base na revelação divina. Apesar disso deixar muitas questões abertas a debate, temos ali um guia geral. Além disso, o ministério do Espírito preenche os detalhes. Diferentes indivíduos, partindo de pontos de vista diversos, podem interpretar essas revelações de modo diferente, mas isso não anula o método geral. O crescimento na espiritualidade vai melhorando continuamente a nossa capacidade de interpretar. Outrossim, apesar de sempre haver detalhes que precisarão ser discutidos, e problemas sociais que não são diretamente mencionados nas Escrituras, esse método é superior ao método relativista dos empiricistas e dos ateus. É uma tragédia espiritual quando alguém deixa os princípios éticos ao sabor das especulações humanas. O homem, em seu progresso espiritual, apesar de ainda ter muito para conquistar, tem obtido alguns notáveis avanços no conhecimento ético, os quais precisam ser preservados, apesar de seu conhecimento ainda ser primitivo. A idéia inteira da *responsabilidade* e do *dever* repousa sobre a admissão do homem ter atingido a um significativo estado de conhecimento ético.

CONHECIMENTO e A Fé Religiosa
Esboço
Introdução
A Filosofia e a Ciência
I. *Pontos De Vista Filosóficos Sobre A Natureza E As Fontes Do Conhecimento*
   1. Empirismo
   2. Racionalismo
   3. Intuição
   4. Misticismo
   5. Ceticismo
   6. Positivismo
   7. Psiquismo

II. *Teorias da Verdade — critérios*
   1. Realismo
   2. Sentimentos
   3. Costumes e Tradições
   4. Tempo
   5. Intuição
   6. Revelação
   7. Instinto
   8. Maioria, Pluralidade
   9. Autoridade
   10. Correspondência
   11. Pragmatismo
   12. Conformidade
   13. Coerência

III. *Bibliografia*

INTRODUÇÃO

Importância do Tema. Os religiosos estão interessados em «como sabemos as coisas», que já aceitamos como verdade, e também em «como se aprende mais». Esse interesse, para a pessoa que pensa, envolve-a naturalmente em aspectos daquilo que, na filosofia, recebeu o nome de «teoria do conhecimento» ou—gnosiologia (epistemologia). O artigo aqui apresentado procura expor, em forma de esboço, os diversos sistemas de conhecimento e as teorias de verdade, relacionando-as, de forma breve, à crença religiosa.

Conhecimento Linear. O Ocidente ficou quase tomado de obsessão pelo chamado conhecimento «linear», ou seja, o tipo de conhecimento que se baseia sobre o «pensar em uma linha», informe sobre informe, com conclusões tiradas da investigação «empírica». Essa quase obsessão tornou-se um ídolo, ao ponto de qualquer conhecimento «extra-empírico» ser tido como impossível. No Oriente, em contraste, que o conhecimento pode ser obtido através da razão, da intuição e do misticismo é tomado como algo pacífico, e o conhecimento «linear» é degradado por muitos como um tipo inferior de conhecimento.

Conhecimentos dos hemisférios esquerdo e direito do cérebro: Pesquisas recentes indicam que os tipos de conhecimento *linear* (empírico) são governados pelo hemisfério esquerdo do cérebro, ao passo que os discernimentos intuitivos ou místicos são governados pelo hemisfério direito. É possível melhorar as funções intuitivas mediante o desenvolvimento do hemisfério direito do cérebro, através do exercício e da prática. A «disposição» de um indivíduo, pois, quanto aos «modos de obter conhecimento» pode ser uma questão de desenvolvimento cerebral, ou mesmo questão de pura chance; mas isso está sujeito a modificações, para um lado ou para outro. O fato de que o «conhecimento» é governado pelo «cérebro» não prova que o conhecimento é função meramente cerebral, entretanto. As pessoas que têm experimentado os fenômenos «fora do corpo», isto é, a capacidade da alma de deixar o corpo físico temporariamente e voltar, dizem-nos que são retidas a «consciência» e a «razão», ao mesmo tempo que a faculdade intuitiva é imensamente incrementada. Isso indica, portanto, que apesar do cérebro ser um veículo do conhecimento, governando-o no complexo humano normal de alma-corpo, é tão-somente um «veículo», e não a fonte da inteligência ou do conhecimento, e que o conhecimento, na personalidade humana, no nível da alma, existe e funciona sem

CONHECIMENTO E A FÉ RELIGIOSA

o luxo do cérebro.

Este artigo expõe o tema de modo *filosófico*, porquanto a filosofia, e não a teologia, é que tem desenvolvido uma sistemática «teoria do conhecimento».

A filosofia surgiu como uma forma de pesquisa científica, na tentativa de encontrar uma explicação racional para a natureza do mundo. Os primitivos filósofos também eram cientistas; mas, como é típico na história da filosofia, foram mais do que isso, incorporavam em si mesmos o espírito do poeta e do místico.

Tales de Mileto (600 A.C.) é o filósofo mais primitivo que se conhece. Ele se interessava por explanar os processos do movimento e das alterações bem como a natureza da *multiplicidade*; e, com esse fim, criou a teoria chamada «hilozoísmo». Era uma teoria chã, terrena, que não ascendia às questões da razão universal, à primeira causa ou Deus. Não obstante, como homem, Tales tinha os olhos fitos nas estrelas. No fim de uma tarde, quando as estrelas começavam a ficar visíveis, Tales contemplava embevecido a cena, sem observar para onde ia. Subitamente, caiu em um poço. Uma espirituosa criada trácia observou imediatamente que Tales desejava tanto saber o que ocorria no firmamento, que não via onde punha os pés. Há um refrão moderno, que diz respeito especialmente às pessoas religiosas, no sentido que vivem tão absorvidas pelas coisas celestiais que não têm qualquer utilidade terrena.

Filosofia e Ciência

A filosofia e a ciência, como disso se depreende, encaram os problemas sob luz diferente, a menos, naturalmente, que a filosofia seja reduzida a mero método científico, conforme se dá no positivismo lógico. Os cientistas se preocupam com *utilidade*, «preço», «trabalho», «delito», «energia», «densidade». Os filósofos concentram seu interesse em «experiência», «conhecimento», «justiça», «significação», «verdade», «propósito», «Deus» e «alma».

O fenômeno social do furto. As ciências sociais falam da influência do ambiente, dos fatores hereditários físicos e mentais, como também dos modos e meios de correção, incluindo escolas especializadas ou instituições corretivas. A filosofia, pois, faz os seguintes tipos de aquilatação: a. Julgamentos de valores—o roubo é mau porque contradiz o que se sabe acerca da conduta ideal. b. Julgamentos morais—o roubo é uma função da consciência pervertida. c. Juízos antropológicos: o roubo é propensão de uma alma corrupta, a qual, de alguma outra existência, trouxe consigo essa má tendência. d. Julgamentos espirituais—o roubo, considerado como forma de perversão moral, provoca a função da justiça de Deus, ou de alguma elevada força cósmica; e a punição é seu resultado. e. Julgamentos metafísicos—as almas más podem sofrer punição que transcende aos limites do tempo e do espaço, ao passo que as almas boas aguardam a bem-aventurança.

Pode-se perceber facilmente, através dessa ilustração, como a filosofia é capaz de ultrapassar em muito ao campo das pesquisas da ciência, em sua inquirição por conhecer qualquer coisa, ou em suas descrições sobre a natureza de qualquer coisa. Isso se aplica à esfera da gnosiologia. A mente estritamente científica, por sua vez, não se mostra mui simpática para com grande parte do que a filosofia tem a dizer acerca do conhecimento, de seu escopo, de suas limitações, de suas possibilidades, de seus propósitos e de seus métodos.

Não há que duvidar que se a filosofia considera problemas dessa monta, sob um prisma diferente do que o faz a ciência é certo que assim também o faz a religião. A crença religiosa necessariamente apela a um «tribunal superior», em relação a qualquer problema de conhecimento e solução de problema, e não pode sentir-se restringida ao conhecimento que se deriva apenas dos sentidos (empirismo). Segundo determinado ponto de vista, a religião é um meio de conhecimento que transcende ao modo de pensar linear.

I. Pontos de Vista Filosóficos sobre a Natureza e as Fontes do Conhecimento

1. *Empirismo*. a. Acredita que todo o conhecimento humano vem através da percepção dos sentidos. b. A percepção dos sentidos é concretizada nos informes fornecidos pela «experiência». c. A experiência desenvolve a memória. d. A memória desenvolve a linguagem. e. A linguagem desenvolve a faculdade discursiva. f. A faculdade discursiva desenvolve todas as vastas sutilezas da intelecção humana, as complexidades do conhecimento humano. Tudo isso tem por alicerce a percepção dos sentidos ou a «experiência».

Empirismo é «conhecimento mediante a percepção dos sentidos». Tem-nos dado máquinas e medicamentos e outras coisas—úteis. Pode atuar como veículo para um conhecimento superior, para uma visão, por exemplo a qual pode ser «vista» ou que aparentemente pode ser vista pelos olhos. Mas a mentalidade religiosa não fica satisfeita ante tal pensamento, e com razão, pois todo o conhecimento não deve ser medido através dos cinco sentidos.

2. *Racionalismo*. Consiste na supremacia da razão. a. Esse sistema crê que o conhecimento ultrapassa a mera percepção dos sentidos, fundamentando-se em uma faculdade superior da natureza humana, usualmente equiparada com «alma» ou «mente». b. A «mente» tem afinidades com a natureza do universo. c. Existiriam idéias latentes. d. A percepção dos sentidos pode até mesmo servir de obstáculo para o conhecimento humano. e. O racionalismo se interessa por verdades «finais»—o empirismo se interessa por verdades terrenas.

Os pensadores religiosos, tanto quanto os filosóficos, supõem, e com razão, que a razão pura, inteiramente à parte dos sentidos físicos e dos informes por eles fornecidos, pode chegar a alguma verdade. O conhecimento de Deus e dos valores éticos pode ser conseguido desse modo, conforme Paulo sugere em Romanos, capítulo 1.

3. *Intuição*: a. Acredita no conhecimento imediato. b. Até mesmo sem o auxílio dos meios da experiência e da razão. c. Tal conhecimento se derivaria de uma fonte desconhecida, a «mente universal», «Deus», a «comunidade das mentes», de natureza humana ou de outra categoria. A intuição reconhece a natureza essencial de um objeto, o que a experiência pode descrever apenas parcialmente.

A intuição, que tem a forma de «conhecimento imediato», não mediado nem pelos sentidos e nem pela razão, pode chegar ao «discernimento» acerca da verdade espiritual, incluindo os problema éticos e as questões relativas à alma, sua existência, sobrevivência e destino. O exercício na meditação espiritual pode desenvolver a intuição.

4. *Misticismo*. Trata-se do conhecimento proveniente de um ser superior, de uma força cósmica, interna ou externa. Segundo o misticismo oriental, essa força seria interna, isto é, a alma. Segundo o

CONHECIMENTO E A FÉ RELIGIOSA

misticismo ocidental, seria externa, isto é, Deus, a mente cósmica, os anjos, os santos, os espíritos dos mortos, etc. «O conhecimento é dom dos deuses».

O misticismo é a verdadeira base de toda a crença religiosa, pois as «visões» e «profecias», concretizadas nas Escrituras ou «livros sagrados», dão à religião a sua autoridade. O misticismo crê que Deus pode revelar-se e realmente revela-se a si mesmo. Em outras palavras, é algo altamente «teísta», e não deísta. O teísmo ensina que Deus está interessado pelos homens e faz intervenções na história humana. Suas intervenções geralmente se dão através de indivíduos, e mediante meios místicos. Já o deísmo nega que Deus se faça presente; e mesmo que Deus exista, conforme dizem os deístas, ele trata com os homens somente através das leis naturais.

5. *Ceticismo*. Diz que o conhecimento é impossível, se nos referimos a um conhecimento certo ou infalível. O ceticismo radical segue o «nihilismo»: nada existe. Conforme diz Georgias: «Nada existe; e se algo existisse, seria incognoscível; e, mesmo que se pudesse conhecer, seria incomunicável». Já o ceticismo moderado postula um nível de probabilidade, ainda que suficiente para que «arrisquemos a vida», nessa proposição. Por exemplo, que o sol surge no oriente e se põe no ocidente. O ceticismo é resultado natural do empirismo. A percepção dos sentidos é básica nesse sistema, mas a percepção dos sentidos não é digna de confiança em sentido absoluto, sendo meramente uma «percepção mental» das coisas, e não o verdadeiro conhecimento da realidade das coisas. Por exemplo, a cor «alaranjada» pode ser descrita como certa intensidade da vibração da luz; porém, se examinarmos a natureza da luz, descobrimos que, na realidade, não sabemos o que é a luz. «Alaranjado», assim sendo, é apenas um termo conveniente que descreve uma percepção mental acerca de alguma coisa, e em nada contribui para descrever qualquer fator sobre a natureza real da luz.

De modo geral, o ceticismo é grande oponente da crença religiosa. Agostinho, sem dúvida, tinha razão quando supôs que a esfera do ceticismo é a esfera das trevas. Em outras palavras, quando um homem possui mente cética, naturalmente «habita espiritualmente» em um lugar onde sua iluminação é impossível. Somente quando abre a mente para a «crença» é que se possibilita o avanço no conhecimento espiritual. O ceticismo é freqüentemente uma «condição espiritual», e não apenas uma «atitude mental». Agostinho declarou: *Creio, para que possa entender*. Aquele que se aproxima da vida com a mente aberta da crença, embora possa cair no precipício de «crer demais», é passível de obter o «entendimento», pois tem o tipo de mente que o Espírito pode ensinar. É melhor crer demais do que pouco demais, simplesmente porque a «crença» é uma forma de busca espiritual que permite à mente receber iluminação ao nível da alma. Isso não significa que estejamos dispensados da «investigação honesta», que empregará todas as nossas faculdades do conhecimento, incluindo a empírica. Existe tal coisa como dogma morto e amortecedor, que também é adversário da verdadeira fé. O ceticismo é a maldição do liberalismo; mas o dogma amortecedor é a maldição do fundalismo.

6. *Positivismo lógico*. É uma forma de ceticismo, que limita a filosofia ao método científico empírico. Rejeita todas as proposições metafísicas como «destituídas de significação», porquanto não cabem no terreno da percepção humana. O ateísmo, portanto, incorreu em erro tanto quanto o teísmo, porque, não menos do que este, pretende fazer uma declaração de conhecimento sobre algo que nos é impossível conhecer. Até mesmo o conhecimento «científico» não passa de mero nível de probabilidade, ou seja, de «inferência lógica».

O positivismo lógico é o máximo do ceticismo, até onde vai a religião. Não acredita que os problemas religiosos sejam dignos de atenção, ou mesmo sejam sujeitos à investigação, e rejeita todo o conhecimento «empírico» por não poder ser «conhecimento certo», sobretudo qualquer outra forma de «conhecimento». Deve-se admitir que o positivismo lógico, como um «método científico», tem seu valor; mas, no tocante à religião, é apenas destrutivo. Nesse campo, é o homem exibindo a sua ignorância.

7. *Psiquismo*. Esse nome se deriva do termo grego «psuche», que quer dizer «mente» ou «alma». Esse é o campo dos estudos da parapsicologia: a telepatia, a clarividência, a psicosinésia (capacidade de mover objetos pelo poder do pensamento), a psicofotografia e o conhecimento anterior. Talvez essa habilidade seja em parte empírica (baseada em alguma energia física, posto que ainda desconhecida) e em parte intuitiva, em parte racional e em parte mística. A revolta contra o materialismo e o empirismo radical (ceticismo) é que tem provocado o intenso interesse em torno da parapsicologia.

A parapsicologia é a investigação feita sobre os temas acima mencionados. É uma ciência legítima, e deve ser tratada como tal. Contudo, existe o «oculto negro» contra o qual devemos ser advertidos, que penetra em esferas proibidas do conhecimento e em atividades espirituais de cunho negativo.

II. Teorias da Verdade—Critérios

1. Realismo:

a. *Realismo ingênuo*. Trata-se do realismo em oposição ao idealismo. Seus criadores foram James McCash, Thomas Reid e outros filósofos escoceses. A realidade seria exatamente o que parece aos sentidos, e não um concurso imperceptível de átomos em movimento, conforme os físicos atômicos afirmam. Este objeto à minha frente é uma escrivaninha, um objeto sólido e marrom, com várias configurações geométricas. Uma árvore, o firmamento, um edifício, etc., são todos exatamente o que parecem ser. Cores, dimensões, solidez, formas, peso, tudo é conforme parece ser. Os realistas ingênuos procuram eliminar tudo quanto crêem ser uma complicação desnecessária da filosofia.

Observações Acerca do Realismo Ingênuo:

1. Preserva a verdade do «bom senso», no âmbito em que todos vivemos. Embora os objetos, cientificamente falando, não sejam «sólidos», dois automóveis que colidam de frente apóiam a realidade do realismo ingênuo. Um jovem enamorado de uma bela jovem não se interessa muito pela sua estrutura atômica. Basta-lhe a beleza física evidente que ele tem.

2. Todavia, a verdade do realismo ingênuo é parcial. Nas coisas há uma natureza mais profunda, que essa escola prefere ignorar; e essa natureza pode ser o «espírito», como energia ou ser invisível, isto é, a estrutura atômica invisível das coisas, ou energias, como ondas de luz, raios-x, etc.—a verdadeira natureza das coisas.

3. O realismo ingênuo depende da percepção dos sentidos, e o faz com uma fé simples; no entanto, essa percepção pode ser enganosa, errônea, débil ou totalmente falsa. Ilustrações: Os trilhos de uma estrada de ferro, que parecem encontrar-se em um ponto distante. Um graveto fino, lançado na água, parece ondear em seguida.

CONHECIMENTO E A FÉ RELIGIOSA

b. *Realismo crítico*. Segundo essa posição, o mundo externo é real, e não depende da «mente» ou da «percepção mental», para que tenha realidade; e nem deixa de existir meramente porque nenhum ser inteligente a percebe. No entanto, não é ainda aquilo que a percepção dos sentidos nos diz. (Seus defensores são George Santayana; C.A. Strong; R.W. Sellars, Durant Drake e Bertrand Russell).

Observações sobre a Realismo Crítico:

1. Nossos sentidos nos dão uma verdade prática, embora esta fique muito aquém de qualquer noção da verdadeira essência das coisas.

2. A ciência nos fornece descrições das coisas, e se refere a átomos, eléctrons, nêutrons, prótons, quarks e outras partículas; mas essas descrições, apesar de chegarem mais perto da verdadeira natureza das coisas do que o faz a percepção dos sentidos, nos outorgam um conhecimento ainda incompleto, se, de fato, qualquer conhecimento sobre a realidade final é possível.

3. Com a expressão «fé animal» aceitamos a existência de um mundo objetivo e real, apesar de que, no momento, não contamos com meios precisos para descrevê-lo.

c. *Novo realismo*. (Defendido por E.B. Holt; W.T. Marvin e W.P. Montague). O objeto conhecido é o verdadeiro objeto, sendo real a apresentação do mesmo, e não mera representação (como se dá no caso do realismo crítico). Os objetos que podem ser percebidos são reais, e as descrições sobre os mesmos, apesar de parciais, são descrições reais.

Observações sobre o Novo Realismo:

1. Nessa escola há uma posição intermediária entre o realismo ingênuo e o realismo crítico, que preserva o «monismo» do realismo ingênuo.

2. Simplesmente tem mais «fé» do que o realismo crítico, removendo assim o elemento de ceticismo.

A maioria dos religiosos, pelo menos no Ocidente, se compõe de «realistas», no sentido que crêem que o que se vê com os olhos e se toca com os dedos, representa a realidade «objetiva». Mas nem por isso desprezam «outra realidade» que não possa ser conhecida, mas que depende de «meios» superiores de conhecimento, além dos sentidos, como sejam a «razão», a «intuição» e o «misticismo». A realidade conhecida pelos «sentidos», para os tais, é uma «realidade inferior». Desde que as coisas são exatamente assim, sem importar se as conhecemos ou não perfeitamente, e sem importar se as podemos conhecer perfeitamente, essas questões se tornam secundárias.

2. Sentimentos. Estes são usados como critério para a seleção dos alimentos; também atuam quase exclusivamente na questão da escolha do «companheiro da vida», no matrimônio. Também transparece por detrás das ações de todos os homens, de muitos modos diversos. Por igual modo, transparece por detrás de sua «escolha» das teorias: compare-se, por exemplo, Agostinho, filho de Mônica, influenciado por Ambrósio, com o filho criado por um cientista materialista e ateu; não é difícil predizer que tipo de religião, filosofia ou teoria científica os atrairá.

Observações sobre os Sentimentos:

1. Os sentimentos, como critério para averiguação da verdade, são um meio débil e ilusório, porquanto os sentimentos usualmente são vagos e mal definidos, se não entram mesmo em conflito uns com os outros; e no campo das pesquisas científicas e filosóficas os sentimentos também são estéreis.

2. Porém, nenhuma outra teoria ou base de teoria é tão poderosa na tomada de decisão sobre as coisas como os sentimentos, influenciados como vivemos por anos de condicionamento aos mesmos.

É óbvio que os «sentimentos» muito têm a ver com as crenças e o sistema religioso de uma pessoa. Contudo, a crença religiosa transcende aos sentimentos humanos, e tudo pode ser reorientado ou mesmo revolucionado por uma fonte superior de conhecimento. Os «sentimentos» são mais condicionadores da verdade do que um meio real para obtê-la. Os sentimentos, como é claro, também podem tornar-se em empecilhos à verdade, e não somente aquilo que determina a «escolha das crenças».

3. Costumes e Tradições. Os critérios para averiguação da verdade ética e para as idéias políticas e religiosas, com freqüência se baseiam em vários costumes ou tradições. Os atos diários também se alicerçam sobre os mesmos. A maioria das pessoas não chega aos princípios morais através de ações racionais ou empíricas, e, sim, seguindo costumes prevalentes na igreja, no governo, na família, na nação, na cidade ou no bairro. As mulheres se sentem particularmente embaraçadas por usarem um vestido noturno durante o dia, ao fazerem compras, sem importar quão belo e funcional seja tal vestido. E a maior parte daquilo que as pessoas fazem é similarmente obrigatório.

Observações Sobre os Costumes e Tradições:

a. Os costumes se transformam em tradições mediante o uso, com a passagem do tempo.

b. Os costumes e tradições não servem de critérios válidos para verificação da verdade no sentido absoluto, pois os costumes e tradições variam de cultura para cultura. O costume das tribos esquimós de deixarem ao relento os membros idosos do clã, ou de entregarem a mulher para passar a noite com um visitante, como parte da hospitalidade doméstica, não é exemplo aprovado em outras sociedades. No entanto, um costume pode ser um critério válido para a averiguação da verdade, quando se toma o ponto de vista pragmático sobre a verdade.

4. Tempo. Alguém poderia dizer: «Sei que o cristianismo é verdadeiro, porque tem resistido ao teste do desgaste do tempo». Porém, o judaísmo, o hinduísmo e algumas outras religiões são ainda mais antigas que o cristianismo. *Tal critério* faria de muitas superstições verdades automáticas, pois dificilmente qualquer delas é uma inovação. Apesar de virtualmente inútil como critério da verdade, o «tempo» é uma poderosa força unificadora entre os aderentes de qualquer sistema, sem importar se é de natureza religiosa, social ou política.

5. Intuição. Seus mentores foram Henri Bergson; Borden Parker Bowne; George Santayana; Carl Jung, pai da psicologia analítica. Segundo essa posição, a verdade é encarada como algo que nos chega imediatamente, sem o concurso da razão ou da experiência, através da percepção dos sentidos.

a. Intuição científica. Todo conhecimento se baseia na percepção dos sentidos; mas o cérebro pode atuar como computador, armazenando e avaliando a experiência adquirida pela percepção dos sentidos; e subitamente, sem qualquer explicação aparente, o cérebro tira uma conclusão. Um cientista pode despertar no meio da noite com a solução para seu problema, que o havia deixado perplexo durante meses. Porém, apesar desse processo ser deveras misterioso, não é mister que o consideremos «extraempírico».

b. Todavia, o sistema filosófico que se chamou de *intuição*, não pertence a esse tipo de intuição

CONHECIMENTO E A FÉ RELIGIOSA

mecânica ou empírica: o conhecimento chega imediatamente ao homem interior, no nível do subconsciente (a alma), e este é então transmitido à mente consciente. Sua origem é: 1. desconhecida; 2. a mente universal; 3. a percepção da alma; 4. Deus, os deuses, os poderes cósmicos.

Thomas Edison, inventor da lâmpada elétrica, os discos fonográficos e outras invenções, afirmava ter recebido desse modo as suas idéias. Ao receber a idéia sobre a lâmpada elétrica, isto é, de que se poderia obter iluminação, eletricamente, de uma lâmpada incandescente, também lhe sobreveio, repentinamente, a idéia como essa energia elétrica poderia ser medida e vendida comercialmente.

Observações sobre a Intuição

1. A intuição se impacienta ante o mecanismo da experiência e dos sentidos, estando convicta de que tais meios fornecem apenas descrições das coisas, e não da essência das mesmas, isto é, de sua natureza real e distintiva.

2. O conhecimento intuitivo é imediato e profundo, porque se trata de «compreensão», e não de mera fórmula. O conhecimento científico é *simbólico* e *discursivo* e, por sua própria natureza, é parcial, e, algumas vezes, superficial.

3. O conhecimento intuitivo nos faz entender as grandes «verdades», como «Deus», a «Mortalidade», os «princípios morais»; enfim, as grandes verdades metafísicas. Já o conhecimento científico nem ao menos chega à verdade completa do que seja a matéria.

Os poetas tendem por aceitar pontos de vista intuitivos sobre o conhecimento, conforme se depreende do seguinte poema de Walt Whitman:

Quando se ouvia o erudito astrônomo
Quando as provas, as cifras, foram catalogadas perante mim;
Quando me foram mostrados os mapas, os diagramas,
Para adicionar, dividir e medi-los;
Quando eu, sentado, ouvia o astrônomo que conferenciava
Sob muitos aplausos, no salão de conferências,
Quão logo, inexplicavelmente, fiquei cansado e enfadado;
Até que, levantando-me e saindo sem ruído, pus-me a vaguear,
Ao ar úmido e místico da noite, e, de vez em quando,
Olhava, em silêncio perfeito, as estrelas.

As provas astronômicas e os mapas do firmamento deixavam Walt Whitman profundamente insatisfeito. O astrônomo falava muito sobre as estrelas, mas não as mostrava. No entanto, uma contemplação silente e pacífica, desvendou muito mais para a alma do poeta.

Um impulso em um bosque primaveril
Pode ensinar-nos mais sobre o homem,
Sobre o mal ou o bem morais,
Do que todos os sábios podem fazer.
Doce é a história que nos conta a natureza;
Nosso intelecto intruso
Distorce as belas formas das coisas—
Matamos quando dissecamos.
Basta de ciência e de arte;
Fechem-se aquelas folhas estéreis;
Apresentai-vos, e trazei um coração
Que observe e que acolha.

(William Wordsworth)

4. O conhecimento intuitivo tende por ser antiintelectual; e por certo é antiempírico, sendo mesmo ocasionalmente hostil ao empirismo.

A intuição tem servido de força e fonte poderosa da verdade (ou daquilo que se julga ser a verdade) em quase todos os sistemas religiosos. Nem todos os indivíduos que aderem a um sistema religioso acham valor especial na intuição. Porém, às raízes de quase todos os sistemas religiosos avulta a crença de que a verdade pode vir através de «meios imediatos», deixando de lado a necessidade das investigações empíricas, e «ultrapassando» até mesmo o poder da razão. O indivíduo religioso usualmente crê que da parte de sua alma podem provir certas informações às quais o seu corpo não tem acesso. A alma, por ser a porção imaterial do homem, está sujeita ao contacto com as realidades imateriais, pelo que também pode receber um «dom do conhecimento» vindo da parte de Deus, sem a necessidade da compilação de informes e da avaliação dos mesmos, feitas pelo cérebro. Acredita-se que a intuição tem valor especial na apreensão das verdades «morais». «Intuimos» as ações corretas e erradas. Não dependemos do «tempo» e das «circunstâncias», para que estes nos ditem de que maneira devemos viver corretamente. Outrossim, a verdade ética reside nas realidades espirituais, e não nas considerações temporais. A verdade ética deve transformar o que é temporal, elevando-o a um nível superior de existência, e nunca ser transformada pelo mesmo em uma espécie de «licença» para nos servirmos a nós mesmos.

6. Revelação (misticismo). É a posição de Kierkegaard (do existencialismo moderno, da teologia do neo-ortodoxismo), de Agostinho, de Platão e da maioria das religiões do mundo. A verdade se derivaria de Deus, dos deuses, de forças espirituais mais elevadas que o homem, quer pessoais quer impessoais, ou então da alma interior, como um ser superior. As primeiras origens são postuladas pelo misticismo ocidental; e a última, pelo misticismo oriental. O misticismo ensina que as verdades são conferidas por Deus ou pelos deuses, sem a mediação da percepção dos sentidos (embora os sentidos possam servir de veículos), sem o concurso da razão, e até mesmo sem a presença da intuição. No entanto, há variedades do misticismo que admitem a ajuda da intuição, sobretudo em suas variedades orientais.

Observações sobre o Misticismo:

1. Diversas dessas supostas revelações são contraditórias, e a verificação das mesmas é dificílima. Algumas dessas revelações podem ser meras alucinações, ou resultantes de um sistema nervoso desequilibrado.

2. O cristianismo tradicional tem aplicado vários critérios para testar as experiências e as revelações místicas: a. Tomás de Aquino asseverava que Deus jamais daria uma revelação contrária à lógica, apesar de que as revelações possam ultrapassar os limites da lógica formal. b. Toda a revelação deve ser de natureza «moral», esse seria o teste ético. c. Poderíamos aplicar também o teste da autoridade: uma revelação qualquer concorda com o que Jesus, Pedro, o Novo Testamento, ou o papa dizem?

3. A revelação, a exemplo da intuição, tenta outorgar ao homem as verdades divinas: a natureza de Deus e suas obras, a imortalidade e o destino da alma, a conduta moral ideal, etc., e tem pouca paciência com o conhecimento que se prende às questões diárias da vida, como as invenções de maquinismos, o descobrimento de drogas ou o prolongamento e preservação da mera existência física.

4. A *fé* ocupa lugar de máxima importância no misticismo.

CONHECIMENTO E A FÉ RELIGIOSA

Fé

Oh, Mundo, não escolheste a melhor parte!
Não é sábio ser apenas sábio,
E fechar os olhos para a visão interior,
Mas é sabedoria acreditar no coração.
Colombo achou um mundo, e não tinha mapa,
Salvo o da fé, decifrado nas estrelas;
Confiar na empresa invencível da alma
Era toda sua ciência, toda a sua arte.
Nosso conhecimento é uma tocha fumegante
Que ilumina o caminho um passo de cada vez,
Através de um vazio de mistério e espanto.
Ordena, pois, que brilhe a luz terna da fé,
A única capaz de dirigir nosso coração mortal
Aos pensamentos sobre as coisas divinas.

(George Santayana)

É óbvio que o maior «meio» isolado de obtenção da verdade, até onde diz respeito ao indivíduo religioso, é o misticismo, a fonte da revelação. As Escrituras são as visões concretizadas dos profetas. Os dons espirituais, que são necessários para o desenvolvimento da igreja (Efé. 4; Rom. 12 e I Cor. 12-14) são misticamente mediados, porquanto são inspirados e dirigidos pelo Espírito Santo.

7. Instinto. (Postulado por Sigmund Freud e George Santayana). Crê que aquilo que é necessário, por determinação da natureza, representa a verdade. A sede subentende tanto a existência quanto a necessidade da água. O sono implica na verdade de um corpo que precisa de restauração e repouso. O sexo mostra a necessidade da procriação. Os impulsos ou sentimentos religiosos revelam a verdade das proposições religiosas, pelo menos em termos fundamentais e gerais. O instinto que nos faz buscar a bondade e a justiça bem como punir a má conduta e o mal, revela-nos algo sobre a verdade moral. O instinto do artista, que o leva a pintar, a compor poemas ou música, fala-nos de algo sobre a verdade estética.

Observações sobre o Instinto:

1. Os instintos, tal como os sentimentos, são vagos e muitas vezes contraditórios.

2. Grande variação de discrepâncias pode ser observada entre os instintos de pessoas diferentes.

3. Mesmo admitindo a validade dos vários instintos e das verdades que os mesmos buscam, o conhecimento religioso, filosófico e científico tem de ultrapassar os limites alcançados pelos instintos.

8. Maioria. Pluralidade, «consensus Gentium». As organizações democráticas, de ordem religiosa, política, social ou governamental, se fundamentam sobre a suposição da validade desse critério para averiguação da verdade. Cícero dizia: «Aquilo sobre o que concorda a natureza de todos os homens é necessariamente verdadeiro». (De Natura Deorum, i.16). Agostinho baseou um argumento em favor da existência de Deus e da alma imortal humana sobre a suposição de que a maioria dos homens e das culturas tem alguma forma dessa crença, a menos que sejam ensinados a não fazê-lo, tendo sido educados propositalmente de modo contrário; e isso nos levaria à forçosa conclusão de que tanto Deus quanto a alma existem.

Observações sobre a Opinião da Maioria:

1. Embora a decisão da maioria seja método desejável de resolver questões de natureza política ou social, dificilmente é adequado para solucionar problemas científicos, filosóficos ou mesmo religiosos.

2. Esse método é aplicável à verdade prática, tal como o realismo ingênuo; no entanto, é de valor dúbio no descobrimento da verdade objetiva sobre qualquer coisa. As antigas idéias cosmológicas se alicerçavam nesse método, tendo assim surgido os conceitos de que a terra é chata, que o sol gira em torno da terra, etc. Tudo era apenas a opinião da maioria, — mas finalmente se comprovou sua falsidade.

9. Autoridade. Tomás de Aquino, muitos filósofos do escolasticismo, a maioria dos teólogos e a maioria dos religiosos, aceitam certas verdades com base na autoridade. Visões e revelações estão concretizadas em escrituras santas. A verdade bíblica é uma das colunas mestras das supostas verdades da cultura ocidental. Pois da igreja, bispos, papas e organizações eclesiásticas derivam sua «verdade» da autoridade; e eles mesmos se fazem autoridades. Porém, a «ciência», segundo é atualmente interpretada, tanto para muitas pessoas não religiosas como para muitas pessoas religiosas, é uma «autoridade», da parte da qual aceitam a «verdade», sem qualquer tentativa de investigação pessoal. A autoridade é o critério usado na averiguação das verdades científicas, filosóficas, morais e religiosas. Por exemplo, o papa pronunciou-se contrariamente ao uso da pílula anticoncepcional, e milhões de pessoas, ao redor do mundo, não fazem mais indagações sobre a correta ação moral a ser tomada em relação à mesma.

Observações sobre a Autoridade:

1. A verdade que é aceita por meio da autoridade repousa sobre a premissa que as autoridades, em qualquer campo do saber humano, devem conhecer mais que os observadores externos.

2. A autoridade religiosa se alicerça sobre a validade da revelação, e se esboroa totalmente quando a suposta revelação mostra ser produto de uma ilusão ou alucinação.

3. A autoridade científica se fundamenta sobre a base claudicante da percepção dos sentidos e de um conjunto de teorias em eterna mutação. É bem possível que quase toda a verdade, com base na autoridade, seja prática e subjetiva, e não objetiva.

O mundo religioso oferece uma incrível variedade de «autoridades»; de fato, há quase tantas autoridades quanto indivíduos religiosos. Contudo, há algumas autoridades básicas que recebem aclamação quase universal, como a dos «livros sagrados». Realmente, tais autoridades possuem maior dose de verdade do que aquela que geralmente seguimos.

10. Correspondência. (Postulada por Bertrand Russell). Afirma que quando uma idéia concorda com seu objeto, isto é, corresponde ao mesmo, então essa idéia é verdadeira. Por exemplo, tenho a idéia de que choveu em São Paulo a 5 de fevereiro de 1968. Se primeiramente concordarmos sobre o que significa «chover», então mediante meios objetivos, como os registros dos jornais, as tabelas meteorológicas ou a palavra de alguém dotado de excelente memória, que diga se realmente choveu ou não nessa dia, poderei afirmar a veracidade ou falsidade dessa idéia. Todas as «idéias» científicas podem ser similarmente comprovadas, mediante a experiência e a prática reais, e as idéias comprovadas por informes e provas, que «correspondam» à realidade dos fatos são idéias verdadeiras.

Observações sobre a Posição da «Correspondência»:

1. Problemas de definição podem modificar essa questão: Qual é a natureza exata da minha «idéia»? Quão válidas são as minhas observações confirmatórias dessa idéia? Por exemplo, o que significa «chover»? O que é «São Paulo»? ou até que ponto se cumpriram as previsões da meteorologia a 5 de fevereiro de 1968?

••• ••• •••

CONHECIMENTO E A FÉ RELIGIOSA

2. Mais profundamente ainda, que tipo de *verdade* procuro demonstrar: verdade prática, absoluta ou teórica?

A teoria da correspondência da verdade é, essencialmente, a verdade do «empirismo», pelo que, quanto à crença religiosa, tem valor limitado. Sem dúvida, reveste-se de algum valor, pois algumas crenças repousam sobre «acontecimentos históricos». A ressurreição, por exemplo, do ponto de vista histórico, pode ser sujeitada à teoria da correspondência. Há registros concretos que podem corresponder ao «fato» crido.

11. Pragmatismo. (Ensinado por William James, Charles Sanders Pierce e John Dewey). Consideremos os pontos seguintes:

a. Charles Sanders Pierce ensinava certa forma de *pragmatismo científico*: uma espécie de positivismo lógico cauteloso, que reconhecia a necessidade do método científico e de que todas as proposições devem estar finalmente alicerçadas na experiência, embora também não rejeitasse algumas formas da «metafísica», como se fossem necessariamente impossíveis. Assim sendo, as proposições que se prestam à investigação talvez não sejam total e finalmente investigadas, mas o sentido de uma declaração ou idéia consiste da súmula de suas conseqüências verificáveis; e os fatos ficam necessariamente implícitos em tais conseqüências. O método de Pierce, na verificação do conhecimento, se assemelha ao do *realismo crítico*. Juntamente com o positivismo, assevera que algumas proposições não têm significação, porquanto ultrapassam as possibilidades humanas de resposta. Algumas proposições, como «Deus existe», não estão mais perto de serem demonstradas do que há mil anos passados. Todavia, o problema reside na própria proposição, e não no conhecimento humano. Algumas proposições, de fato, não estão meramente «sem solução», mas são «insolúveis». Quando Pierce vivia, a proposição «Existe uma alma imortal?» figurava entre essas proposições, segundo sua maneira de pensar. Porém, conjecturo que se ele estivesse vivo até hoje, e pudesse examinar as novas evidências comprobatórias da existência da alma, admitiria a possibilidade de comprovar, experimental e cientificamente, esse item do pensamento metafísico.

b. O pragmatismo como *algo prático* (Pensamento de William James). Segundo esse filósofo, permanece de pé a necessidade de investigação; mas o valor e a veracidade de uma idéia dependem de sua utilidade ou função, e não de sua verificação científica. Não buscamos, na verdade, aquilo que é final, e, sim, qual a diferença que as idéias fazem em nossa existência pessoal, em nosso bem-estar psicológico e em nossa conduta. Ilustração com a pessoa de Deus: Podemos estar razoavelmente certos de que, se de fato Deus existe, ele fica mais satisfeito com nossa crença em sua existência do que com o ateísmo. Posto que não podemos averiguar a validade dessa crença, ou da religião em geral, e nem podemos negar sua veracidade, podemos ao menos seguir a orientação expediente de sermos religiosos, como uma espécie de garantia para o futuro. Se porventura, em última análise, Deus realmente não existir, e nem a imortalidade—não teremos perdido coisa alguma. Mas, se pelo contrário, Deus existe e a imortalidade é fato, então só teremos a ganhar com nossa cautela. Isso é pragmatismo no mais alto nível, e se reveste de uma astúcia que ultrapassa aos limites do tempo e do espaço.

«Qualquer um que insiste que há um planejador, e está certo de que esse planejador é divino, deriva certo benefício pragmático do termo; de fato, o mesmo benefício que vimos derivar-se dos termos Deus, Espírito ou o Absoluto. O 'planejamento', por mais inútil que seja como mero princípio racionalista, posto acima ou por detrás das coisas, para a nossa admiração, se a nossa fé se concretiza em algo teísta, torna-se um termo de 'promessa'. Fazendo isso redundar em experiência, obtemos uma perspectiva mais confiante sobre o futuro...Essa vaga confiança no futuro é o único significado pragmático que se pode discernir no presente, nos termos 'planejamento' e 'planejador'...Mais do que essa significação prática não possuem as palavras 'Deus', 'livre-arbítrio', 'desígnio', etc. Entretanto, por mais obscuras que elas possam ser em si mesmas, ou por mais intelectualmente que as aceitemos, quando as pomos junto à passagem da vida, conosco, as trevas da existência tornam-se em luz ao nosso redor...Somente o pragmatismo pode infundir certa significação positiva a essas trevas, e por causa disso ela volta inteiramente as costas ao ponto de vista intelectualista» (William James, *Pragmatism*, págs. 114,115, 121 e 122).

William James pensava que se pode basear a religião sobre o **pragmatismo**. — «Quais são as conseqüências práticas de minhas crenças?» «Elas me ajudam a viver melhor» «Elas me infundem esperança diante da tragédia e da morte?» Nesse caso, elas possuem «valor veraz», simplesmente porque têm valor prático na vida, sem importar a «verdade última» acerca de qualquer questão. É óbvio que a maioria dos religiosos sente que essa maneira de buscar a verdade é muito inferior, se é que é válida. Contudo, a maior parte das pessoas religiosas apega-se «ainda mais» à sua fé religiosa porque, de fato, traz benefícios a «curto prazo», de natureza prática, e não apenas promessas a «longo prazo», que se concretizem em «mundos eternos da imortalidade». Desse modo, valorizam o pragmatismo como meio de buscar a verdade, embora não digam tal mediante alguma espécie de afirmação lógica.

c. *Pragmatismo ético* ou humanista (idealizado por F.C.S. Schiller). De acordo com essa idéia, verdadeiro e falso são apenas sinônimos de «útil» e «inútil». Quando uma pessoa declara que uma crença qualquer é verdadeira, simplesmente quer dizer que ela cabe dentro da soma total de seus interesses. As verdadeiras crenças, pois, podem modificar-se juntamente com as circunstâncias e os interesses. Ninguém procuraria uma verdade absoluta, porquanto, mesmo que ela existisse, estaria fora do alcance da pesquisa humana. A verdade se resume no «interesse humano», estando especialmente vinculada à atividade ética.

«No que tange ao fato físico da avaliação da verdade, pode-se chamar a verdade de função final de nossas atividades intelectuais. No que concerne aos objetos avaliados como 'verdadeiros', a verdade é aquela manipulação dos mesmos objetos que, sob experiência, mostram ser úteis, primariamente para alguma finalidade humana, mas, em análise final, para aquela perfeita harmonia da totalidade de nossa vida, que forma a nossa aspiração final». (*Humanism*, pág. 61). A verdade pode ser egoísta ou altruísta. Porém, de acordo com Schiller, ela é essencialmente egoísta, de tal modo que todo indivíduo tem sua própria 'verdade'. Esse sistema ignora ou subordina a verdade objetiva da ciência, e faz da verdade uma questão de interesse social.

d. Verdade *experimental* (ensinada por John Dewey). A verdade seria o êxito na inquirição, em qualquer campo da atividade humana. Determinamos o valor verdadeiro das proposições na ação real

CONHECIMENTO E A FÉ RELIGIOSA

da existência diária. Incorporamos o método científico em todas as nossas pesquisas, e absorvemos o que é melhor nas teorias tradicionais da correspondência e da coerência; mas insuflamos nisso a idéia da verdade como um «valor». Ora, os valores são humanos e precisam ser comprovados pela experiência.

«O acordo ou correspondência se verifica entre o propósito ou plano e sua própria execução ou cumprimento; entre o mapa de um curso de ação, traçado a fim de guiar nosso comportamento, e o resultado obtido ao agirmos de conformidade com as indicações desse roteiro. Exatamente até que ponto esse acordo difere do êxito?» (Essays in Experimental Logic, págs. 239 e 240). John Dewey apresenta-nos a ilustração de alguém que se perdeu em uma floresta, e que passa a utilizar-se de um mapa ou de outras indicações disponíveis, para sair da mesma. Nesse processo, pois, o indivíduo lança mão da razão, da tentativa e do erro, bem como de indicações concretas. O seu «êxito», ao conseguir sair a salvo da floresta, será a sua «verdade». De fato, seria a única forma de verdade de que ele necessitaria ou poderia vir a ter. Toda a atividade humana, incluindo as pesquisas científicas, teria esse mesmo caráter.

Observações sobre o Pragmatismo:

1. Obviamente, em relação à vida diária, os cristãos, como todos os demais homens, agem de acordo com o que é prático, quando não existem princípios morais e espirituais que devem governar as ações.

2. Mas para o cristão sincero, é impossível basear uma vida sobre tais princípios. O melhor dos sistemas pragmáticos, do ponto de vista religioso, é o de William James. Mas até o sistema dele não tem nada a ver com uma fé verdadeira. No lugar da fé ele tem colocado uma aposta piedosa. Ele aposta que Deus existe; ele aposta que a alma existe e sobreviverá, e deixa estes princípios terem alguma influência na vida dele. Isto é melhor do que o ateísmo cru, mas dificilmente pode agradar a Deus, porque somente uma verdadeira fé pode fazer isto (Heb. 11:2,6).

3. O pragmatismo, basicamente, é um tipo de agnosticismo ou ceticismo que tem abandonado qualquer busca de uma verdade fixa ou absoluta. Ora, a fé cristã declara que tal tipo de conhecimento pode ser alcançado, não por meios meramente práticos baseados nas percepções, mas através da razão, da intuição, e especialmente pela revelação.

12. Conformidade. Divide-se nas duas variedades abaixo discriminadas:

a. «Conformidade *frouxa*», que seria a mera ausência de qualquer contradição. Por exemplo: «João gosta de milho», «Hoje é quinta-feira», «O Brasil produz muito café» (o que se sabe só de viver algum tempo no Brasil). Trata-se de um critério muito fraco para averiguação da verdade, ainda que, com freqüência, se mostre correto.

b. «Conformidade *rigorosa*» (criada por Borden Parker Bowne). É o método do «vigor e rigor». As declarações ou proposições precisam ser feitas, necessária e logicamente, cada qual com base na anterior. Por exemplo: «Todos os homens são mortais. Sócrates é um homem. Portanto, Sócrates é mortal». (Lógica dedutiva). Entretanto, temos nesse caso um sistema fechado de conhecimento, que depende da validade de cada uma de suas proposições. Essa afirmativa sobre Sócrates é perfeitamente provável: mais do que isso, é certa. Porém, considere-se esta outra: «Todos os homens são racionais. Os portugueses são homens. Portanto, todos os portugueses são racionais». As religiões dogmáticas erigem seus sistemas de acordo com a idéia de «conformidade». Todavia, nem sempre seus seguidores se sentem felizes ante suas suposições fundamentais. Por exemplo, como ilustração a premissa fundamental do «teísmo».

13. Coerência (pensamento de Edgar S. Brightman e Hegel). Qualquer julgamento é verdadeiro, contanto que seja autocompatível e esteja coerentemente vinculado ao nosso sistema de juízos como um todo. «Coerência» é um dos termos técnicos para a razão; pelo que também a «coerência» é a teoria básica do racionalismo, no que tange à verdade. Em suas formas mais radicais, essa posição aceita as idéias latentes, a faculdade da razão como uma espécie de atividade da alma, e até mesmo a alma como fagulha da divindade, como também que o pensamento disciplinado leva o homem, automaticamente, às verdades essenciais da natureza. Em suas formas menos extremas, a posição tomada pela «coerência» pode incorporar os demais critérios de averiguação da verdade, aplicando aos mesmos o raciocínio coerente, em suas formulações e em sua busca pelas soluções. Mas, ordinariamente, esse sistema é mais racionalista do que científico. Como ilustração do fato, basta-nos pensar sobre a tríada de Hegel—a crença que diz que o universo, e tudo quanto nele existe, devem operar de acordo com os princípios básicos de «tese», «antítese» e «síntese». Aplicando essa tríada ao mundo das artes, teríamos: 1. Arquitetura—escultura—pintura. 2. Pintura—música—poesia. 3. Poesia epopéia—poesia lírica—poesia dramática. Assim sendo, a síntese das artes seria a arte dramática, teatro.

As pessoas religiosas dependem, mais do que imaginam, da teoria da coerência sobre a verdade. Quando ouvem alguma doutrina que não lhes «soa bem», declaram-na «falsa». E por qual motivo ela não lhes «soa bem»? Simplesmente porque não é *coerente* com o sistema que já aceitaram. É possível, naturalmente, dar início com proposições basicamente «inverídicas». Nesse caso, é tolice fazer outras proposições mostrarem-se «coerentes» com elas. Já que a teoria da coerência sobre a verdade se alicerça sobre o «racionalismo», convém supor que se «treinarmos a própria mente» para reconhecer a verdade, então poderemos obter proposições iniciais basicamente boas. Nesse caso, tais proposições serviráo de guias para a adição de outras, as quais, por sua vez, devem ser coerentes com as proposições anteriores.

Sumário:

1. É útil para cristãos sinceros saber alguma coisa sobre o que os homens pensam sobre os meios, alcance e limites do conhecimento. Este artigo tenta demonstrar o que os homens têm pensado e escrito sobre a gnosiologia. Aqui e lá, no artigo, oferecemos pequenas avaliações das idéias apresentadas, do ponto de vista religioso.

2. O homem que quer saber algo sobre a alma e Deus (os objetos verdadeiros de conhecimento significante) não vai ficar satisfeito com o que as percepções dos sentidos podem alcançar. O cristão, como qualquer outro homem, aprecia o que este tipo de conhecimento nos tem dado; isto é, máquinas, confortos, remédios, as façanhas da ciência. Mas estas coisas pertencem a este mundo, que não é o objeto principal do conhecimento do homem de fé.

3. O sistema do racionalismo tem alguma coisa para oferecer ao homem de fé. Provavelmente, filósofos como Platão e Descartes tinham razão em supor que o raciocínio, sem ajuda qualquer dos sentidos, pode fazer-nos compreender princípios

CONHECIMENTO ESPIRITUAL

éticos, aceitar a grande realidade da existência e sobrevivência da alma, e a existência de Deus, bem como suas exigências. A razão humana tem uma afinidade com a razão divina, e por si mesma alcança dados de conhecimentos que são importantes para a vida espiritual. Rom. cap. 1 indica que o homem pode conhecer a Deus, e saber quais são as exigências de seu governo, pela razão, sem a ajuda da revelação.

4. A intuição (conhecimento sem os meios da razão, ou das percepções), pode ser usada pelas forças espirituais para dar ao homem um conhecimento significante. A própria alma da pessoa, ou forças superiores (inclusive o Espírito Santo) podem ser as fontes de um «conhecimento imediato» que tem muito para nos ensinar a respeito das exigências da nossa fé. O homem, crescendo espiritualmente, será sempre mais sujeito às intuições que promovem a fé. Certamente, existe no homem uma faculdade intuitiva que pode transcender os dados do conhecimento que vem através das percepções físicas.

5. Nosso artigo tem demonstrado que a fé religiosa se baseia principalmente sobre o misticismo, ou a «revelação». Deus, na sua bondade, tem se revelado através dos profetas. As visões e mensagens dos profetas têm sido concretizadas nas Escrituras. Assim, as Escrituras foram dadas como «um dom de Deus». Nas escrituras temos a fonte principal do nosso conhecimento, e a «autoridade» da nossa fé.

6. A vida diária do homem de fé também se baseia numa forma do misticismo, isto é, no ministério do Espírito Santo. A vida cristã, verdadeiramente vivida, depende deste ministério, isto é, depende da presença e influência do Espírito. É impossível ser um verdadeiro discípulo de Cristo sem esta influência que funciona como uma força transformadora.

7. A palavra «misticismo», neste artigo, significa simplesmente «um contato verdadeiro» com uma força ou forças, com uma pessoa, ou pessoas, sobrenaturais. Segundo essa definição básica, até as doutrinas da conversão e santificação se baseiam no misticismo, porque nelas está envolvido «um contato» com o Espírito, que transcende o mero humano. Sem o «toque divino», a fé cristã seria simplesmente uma outra filosofia religiosa. É o misticismo que dá à fé sua natureza divina, e que comunica, afinal, a própria natureza metafísica de Cristo a todos os homens que têm entregado as suas almas a ele.

III. Bibliografia: (CARN CHI GE HIC RP)

CONHECIMENTO ESPIRITUAL

I. A Natureza de

1. Nas páginas do A.T., «conhecer Deus» é reconhecer a validade de seus mandamentos e obedecê-los. Esse conhecimento é ético e prático, e não essencialmente místico. O N.T. dá prosseguimento a essa maneira de pensar, mas faz-lhe muitos importantes acréscimos. Esse aspecto, entretanto, não deveria ser negligenciado por nós, porquanto é refletido em um avantajado número de ensinos éticos que figuram no N.T.

2. Além disso não nos deveríamos esquecer de que a transformação ética é o poder por detrás da transformação metafísica. A santidade resulta de uma real transformação em nossa natureza essencial, em razão de que, quanto mais santos nos tornamos, mais nos assemelhamos a Cristo em sua natureza; e, — finalmente, isso nos leva à real participação em sua natureza metafísica, em sua modalidade de vida (ver Col. 2:10).

3. Existe um assentimento místico da alma perante Deus, contemplando-o diretamente, em uma espécie de visão beatífica preliminar. Poucos homens passam por essa experiência na esfera terrena. Porém, se servirmos ao próximo, movidos pelo amor, estaremos servindo a Deus, e assim nossa qualidade espiritual é aprimorada e chegamos a «conhecer Deus» de maneira bem real. (Ver Mat. 25:35 e ss).

4. O intelecto também desempenha um papel no conhecimento de Deus. Foi-nos dada a *razão* para guiar-nos espiritualmente. A *intuição* também tem parte nisso, pois há um conhecimento intuitivo que transcende à razão. E existem, igualmente, experiências místicas, mediante as quais a alma ascende a Deus, e assim a espiritualidade é aprimorada. Esses meios são adicionados ao caminho «prático», que foi descrito acima.

II. Seu Poder e Efeitos

1. O conhecimento postulado pelos gnósticos deixava os homens agrilhoados aos seus pecados, pois presumiam que é bom para o homem abusar do próprio corpo, como meio de libertação da alma. O N.T. tacha essa noção de fantástica mentira, porquanto a verdade diz exatamente o contrário a isso. A salvação vem por meio da santificação (ver II Tes. 2:13).

2. O conhecimento ensinado pelo N.T. retém a idéia do A.T. no sentido de que, «conhecer a Deus» é algo prático e moral, desde o início. Consiste em conhecer as exigências da legislação divina, e de obedecer à mesma. Essa é a grande característica que falta aos pagãos, o que os torna pagãos.

3. O N.T. ensina que só se pode conhecer o Pai por intermédio do Filho. (Ver sobre esse conceito em João 17:3). Esse versículo também demonstra que esse conhecimento resulta na salvação.

4. Na medida que o Filho vai sendo duplicado nos filhos de Deus (em sua natureza e atributos — ver Col. 2:10), esses filhos chegam a conhecer o Pai, naquilo que está sucedendo neles, porquanto discernem a natureza do Pai tomando forma em seus próprios seres. Essa é uma elevadíssima maneira de se conhecer a Deus, e nisso está envolvido um grande poder espiritual.

5. O ministério do Espírito entra em cena em tudo isso, por ser ele tanto o iluminador (ver Efé. 1:18), quanto o transformador (ver II Cor. 3:18). A operação do conhecimento, portanto, é uma operação divina, que ultrapassa em muito às capacidades humanas. O conhecimento é sempre algo moral. Jamais poderá ser meramente informativo e intelectual. Ora, por ser algo moral, também é algo espiritual. E, sendo algo espiritual, transforma a natureza mesma do espírito humano, a ponto de ser criada uma espécie de ser totalmente diferente. Ver II Ped. 1:4, II Cor. 3:18.

III. Os Ignorantes: Heb. 5:11

Sobre isso temos muito que dizer, mas de difícil interpretação, porquanto vos tornastes tardios em ouvir.

Presumivelmente o autor sagrado queria indicar os vários aspectos do sacerdócio de Melquisedeque, como também outros aspectos da elevada glória e do serviço do Cristo ressurrecto. Esses assuntos merecem um estudo mais amplo do que foi possível ao autor sagrado expor, devido ao estado de infantilidade espiritual em que se achavam os seus leitores originais. E quão comum é essa situação! Todavia, é dever dos pastores ensinar o seu povo, tirando-os dessa situação; mas poucos são os capazes de fazê-lo ou que estão dispostos a tal esforço. Pois ensinar verdadeiramente é trabalho muito árduo.

CONHEÇO AS TUAS OBRAS

«Não damos valor suficiente ao conhecimento cristão. Evitamos o doutrinamento porque acentua diferenças de opinião, tendendo a dividir a igreja local em campos. Talvez essa 'modéstia' reflita a incerteza, a perda de convicções que caracteriza a igreja evangélica de hoje em dia. A maioria dos crentes se sente francamente embaraçada ante a oportunidade de expressar suas convicções religiosas. A força do ceticismo hostil se faz presente por toda a parte, e os membros das igrejas preferem não arriscar sua fé argumentando abertamente. Na ausência do conhecimento, propõem-se ter fé como substituto do conhecimento, com o que querem dar a entender—e essa interpretação é bastante generalizada—a crença que certas doutrinas são verdadeiras. Mas isso é uma perversão da fé neotestamentária, que sempre tem o sentido de confiança, isto é, de total entrega a Cristo. O perigo é duplo: o enfraquecimento da convicção e a intelectualização da fé». (Purdy).

Prossegue esse mesmo autor: «O N.T. nunca diminui o valor do conhecimento. O quarto evangelho apresenta Jesus a dizer: 'E a vida eterna é esta: que te conheçam a ti, o único Deus verdadeiro, e a Jesus Cristo, a quem enviaste' (João 17:3). O lamento de Jesus sobre Jerusalém, é que ela não reconhecia as coisas que lhe traziam a paz (ver Luc. 19:42). Paulo expunha a Jesus Cristo como 'a sabedoria de Deus' (ver I Cor. 1:24), tendo antecipado o dia em que não mais conheceremos 'em parte', mas antes, 'entenderemos plenamente, tal como somos conhecidos plenamente' (ver I Cor. 13:12). Assim também, nesta passagem, o escritor sagrado lamenta a falta de conhecimento por parte de seus leitores».

Infelizmente, os leitores originais deste tratado eram embotados, preguiçosos, indiferentes—intelectualmente falando. Tinham feito pouco esforço por se aprimorarem, ou por melhorarem seus conhecimentos. Pouco sabiam sobre Cristo, mesmo anos depois de sua conversão. Havia grandes e significativas coisas que poderiam ser ditas sobre ele, que poderiam parecer estranhas ou totalmente ininteligíveis. Esses não estavam preparados para avançar. Já tinham começado a desviar-se. Corriam o perigo de apostatar. A estagnação leva o indivíduo ao desvio; e o desvio leva à inutilidade, e daí, à apostasia. Quantas igrejas estagnadas vemos hoje em dia! Não admira que, em tantos lugares, seja perigoso até mesmo ensinar o N.T. em sua inteireza.

Exemplos Ruins

Tardios em ouvir. No grego temos o vocábulo *nothros*, que significa *preguiçoso*, «lento», «descuidado». As palavras, *em ouvir*, indicam o «entendimento espiritual», porquanto o ouvir e aplicar o ensinamento espiritual é aquilo que está em foco em Heb. 5:11. A expressão que aqui temos aparece na literatura grega para indicar, literalmente, «dureza de ouvir», em que a faculdade de audição é diminuída. (Ver *Heliodoro* 5:1,5). O autor sagrado fala acerca do embotamento da capacidade espiritual para receber, para compreender e para aplicar ensinamentos espirituais. Platão (*Thaet.* 144) empregava o termo *nothros* para indicar os «estudantes estúpidos». Nosso autor, pois, lamenta o embotamento espiritual que caracterizava a muitos de seus leitores originais, e que até hoje caracteriza a muitos daqueles que se dizem seguidores de Cristo.

Difíceis de explicar. Alguns estudiosos preferem aqui «difíceis de interpretar». Essa dificuldade se origina de duas razões: 1. Do embotamento espiritual e das baixas realizações espirituais dos ouvintes; 2. da dificuldade e novidade do tema — o sacerdócio segundo a ordem de Melquisedeque—que o autor sagrado desejava expor. Isso também pode basear-se na circunstância de que um mestre evangélico esteja despreparado e seja preguiçoso ou dotado de baixo nível de espiritualidade. Vemos muitos exemplos disso, também. Mas isso não é aludido em Heb. 5:11. Por essas razões, o autor sagrado abandonou seu tema momentaneamente e começou a apresentar algumas severas advertências. Finalmente, volta à sua tese e a desenvolve um pouco mais (ver Heb. 6:20 e *ss*), na esperança de que seu ensino haveria de produzir algum bem. A «incapacidade» deles não era natural; antes, fora criada pela indiferença e pela preguiça. Não foi imposta sobre eles, porquanto não tinham tido «oportunidade» de aprender; antes, toda a oportunidade fora rejeitada.

«Tardios em ouvir. Vossas almas não acompanham o passo das doutrinas e exortações que vos são feitas. Tal como 'nothres' indica a pessoa que anda pesadamente e caminha com lentidão, assim também esse termo é aqui elegantemente aplicado àqueles que são chamados para a carreira cristã, cujo caminho está claramente delineado à sua frente, cujas bênçãos a ser obtidas são enumeradas, mas que não se esforçam por avançar, mas antes, estão sempre aprendendo, nunca sendo capazes de chegar ao pleno conhecimento da verdade» (Adam Clarke).

CONHECIMENTO, Natureza Parabólica do.
Ver **Símbolos e o Conhecimento.**

CONHECIMENTO PRÉVIO Ver sobre **Precognição.**

CONHEÇO AS TUAS OBRAS

Apo. 2:2: *Conheço as tuas obras, e o teu trabalho, e a tua perseverança; sei que não podes suportar os maus, e que puseste à prova os que se dizem apóstolos e não o são e os achaste mentirosos;*

1. É salientada assim a onisciência de Cristo. Essa declaração é reiterada no caso de todas as sete igrejas.

2. O interesse de Cristo por sua igreja é focalizado, porque ele «conhece» as suas condições, a fim de louvar ou de repreender à mesma, tudo o que visa produzir modificações espirituais favoráveis.

3. As «obras» que Jesus «conhece» representam as *condições espirituais em geral* da igreja, e não apenas aquilo que chamamos de «serviço ativo». Portanto, a palavra «obra» neste caso, indica o «caráter geral», a natureza da pessoa que age, mas também aquilo que ela faz. Equivale à expressão veterotestamentária «temor do Senhor», expressão usada a fim de exprimir as condições «espirituais em geral» daquele que professava tentar agradar a Deus, reconhecendo o seu senhorio. O termo geral, «obra» é desdobrado, em Apo. 2:2, para que tenha os seguintes significados:

a. Labor (serviço ativo, prestado sob pressão).
b. Paciência (resistência nesse labor, e sob as perseguições).
c. Ódio e oposição ao mal e aos atos malignos, de homens que pervertem o evangelho e promovem a impiedade em nome de Cristo.
d. Cristo, que é o Senhor, vê através de todos os disfarces e pretensões, apresentando autêntica avaliação da condição de cada indivíduo, bem como a condição geral de cada assembléia local.

Ele não vê o que «esperamos ser», nem o que «temos feito», nem o que «pensamos que podemos fazer», e, sim, as nossas condições reais, o nosso caráter. O seu poder, que «tudo vê e tudo sabe», é, ao mesmo tempo, uma ameaça e um conforto. É uma ameaça aos

CONOTAÇÃO — CONSAGRAR

hipócritas e pretenciosos; é uma ameaça para aqueles que brincam com a fé religiosa. Mas é um conforto aos fiéis, que são perseguidos e desprezados por outros, dentro ou fora da igreja. Isso nos promete uma recompensa justa, bem como a contínua ajuda para a concretização dos ideais espirituais do cristianismo.

«Nossas tristezas, que talvez não possamos relatar, nossas tribulações, que ninguém mais conhece, nossas dificuldades, nossos reversos, os ais e as dores que jazem ocultas em nossas almas, nossas fraquezas e nossas lutas íntimas, nossos temores e dúvidas ocultos, nossa honestidade quanto a coisas que outros censuram e criticam, nossos verdadeiros motivos e esforços, que os outros não entendem, tudo é conhecido por nosso amoroso Salvador, o qual pode ser tocado com o senso de nossa debilidade, ordenando-nos que tenhamos bom ânimo, porque a sua graça nos será suficiente». (*Seiss*, em Apo. 2:2).

«O verniz de uma fé formal talvez impressionasse ao mundo, mas não pôde escapar a seu escrutínio (ver Atos 1:24). Ele também conhece, e aceita amorosamente, os atos não exibidos e nem requisitados de verdadeiro amor (ver Mat. 10:42 e 26:13), e aparecia, em meio a todas as suas falhas, a lealdade genuína a ele (ver João 2:17)». (Carpenter).

CONOTAÇÃO

Ver também o artigo sobre **Denotação**. Conotação vem do latim, *con*, «com», e *notare*, «notar» ou «marcar». Por conseguinte, a palavra refere-se ao grupo de características ou qualidades essenciais a um termo, o conjunto de coisas ao qual se refere qualquer termo da linguagem. Sinônimos de conotação são «compreensão», «intenção» e «significação». Ver os artigos separados sobre esses termos. Alguns filósofos fazem a distinção entre conotação e denotação. A primeira dessas palavras alude a alguma qualidade; e a segunda, ao objeto qualificado. Assim, na frase «cavalo branco», *branco* é a conotação, e *cavalo* é a denotação. Entretanto, outros estudiosos invertem o sentido desses termos, embora mantendo a distinção entre eles. Dentro do uso moderno, a conotação veio a indicar o conjunto de características (na forma de adjetivos), e a denotação veio a indicar o próprio conjunto. Isso posto, os nomes próprios são denotações.

CONRADO DE GELNHAUSEN

Suas datas foram 1320-1390. Foi teólogo e professor da Universidade de Paris, e, mais tarde, chanceler da Universidade de Heidelberg, na Alemanha. A sua *Epistola Concordiae*, que advogava o método conciliar de pôr fim ao grande cisma ocidental, influenciou a maneira de pensar dos teólogos conciliares posteriores, destacando-se, entre eles, Henrique de Langenstein e Jean Gérson (ver os artigos sobre eles).

CONSAGRAÇÃO DA EUCARISTIA

Trata-se de um ato solene, mediante o qual o pão e o vinho da Ceia são «santificados». A teologia católica do Oriente e do Ocidente supõe que, nesse instante, o pão e o vinho adquirem a *substância* (mas não os acidentes) do corpo e do sangue de Cristo. Ver o artigo sobre a *Transubstanciação*. No Ocidente, são proferidas as palavras da consagração: «Este é o meu corpo»; e também: «Este é o meu sangue». No Oriente, são ditas as mesmas palavras, mas juntamente com a invocação do Espírito, para que isso se realize. Alguns grupos protestantes, embora sem aceitarem que os elementos da Ceia adquiram a *substância* real do corpo e do sangue de Cristo, acham que adquirem certo caráter sagrado. Porém, a maioria dos evangélicos pensa que a cerimônia e a ocasião são solenes e sagradas, a despeito do que os elementos da Ceia continuam sendo apenas simbólicos. Esperam que a presença mística do Espírito Santo torne sagrada a ocasião. Quanto ao ponto de vista de Lutero (não seguido pela maioria dos luteranos), ver sobre a *Consubstanciação*.

CONSAGRAR, CONSAGRAÇÃO

1. Uso Geral

Como crentes, somos convidados a dedicar ou consagrar as nossas vidas a Jesus Cristo, como parte natural de nossa inquirição espiritual. Ver Romanos 12:1,2 quanto a um convite desses. A palavra *consagrar* vem do latim *consecrare*, formado por *con*, «inteiramente», e *sacer*, «santo». Portanto, «consagrar» e *santificar* são sinônimos. Os termos hebraicos usados no Antigo Testamento incluem as idéias de separação de algum uso comum ou profano e de separação para o serviço divino. Coisas e pessoas eram separadas para o serviço divino, ou seja, eram *consagradas*. Nessa separação há uma *aceitação* das coisas e das pessoas, em suas novas funções. Assim, Aarão e seus filhos usavam vestes especiais, em suas funções sacerdotais, como sinal de sua aceitação e consagração (Êxo. 29:29,33,35). Animais também eram consagrados, conforme vemos em Êxo. 29:22, 31,34. Outro tanto no caso das ofertas movidas (Lev. 8:27,28), e nas oblações de cheiro suave (Lev. 8:28).

No Novo Testamento. As palavras gregas empregadas são: 1. *Egkainízo*, «dedicar»; 2. *teleióo*, «completar» e 3. *agiázo*, «santificar». A primeira delas encontra-se em Heb. 9:18 e 10:20, em conexão com o novo e vivo caminho aberto pelo Senhor, dando acesso aos lugares e privilégios celestiais. Ele abriu e consagrou para nós esse novo caminho. Essa palavra pode significar «renovar», «inaugurar», «dedicar». O substantivo é usado para indicar a idéia de rededicação, como por exemplo, a purificação e rededicação do templo de Jerusalém, pelos Macabeus (I Macabeus 4:36-39). A segunda delas tem o sentido primário de «completar», «realizar», «levar a termo», «aperfeiçoar». Essa palavra grega era usada no vocabulário das religiões misteriosas para indicar iniciação e consagração. Aparentemente, é com base nesse uso técnico que o Novo Testamento aplica o vocábulo à consagração e iniciação de alguém em um ofício qualquer. Em Hebreus 7:28, *teleióo* é usada para descrever como o Filho de Deus, o nosso Sumo Sacerdote, foi *aperfeiçoado* em seu ofício e função. Sua eterna *dedicação* a esse ofício, fica assim salientada.

A terceira dessas palavras, *agiázo*, «santificar», «reconhecer como qualificado», é usada, por exemplo, em João 10:36; 17:17,19; I Cor. 7:14; I Tim. 4:5; II Tim. 2:21. Quando é aplicada a Jesus, a idéia envolvida é a de perfeita dotação de graça e de verdade, juntamente com a idéia de autodedicação de Jesus à sua obra remidora. No tocante a seus discípulos, o termo indica o fato de que foram separados e consagrados para essa função. Quando aplicado aos alimentos, o vocábulo indica que os mesmos são purificados para o consumo humano. No tocante ao cônjuge incrédulo, no caso de um casamento misto, o termo aponta para a legitimidade desse relacionamento.

Jesus foi aperfeiçoado quanto à sua natureza

CONSAGRAR, CONSAGRAÇÃO

humana e quanto à sua inquirição espiritual (Heb. 2:10; 5:9; 7:28). Nisso, Jesus agiu como Pioneiro, porque, como homem, tal como qualquer outro homem, ele precisou sujeitar-se ao processo do aprendizado. Isso em nada prejudica ou diminui o conceito da divindade de Jesus Cristo; mas apenas nos apresenta um paradoxo. Tal necessidade harmoniza-se à verdadeira humanidade de Jesus. Ver o artigo sobre a *Humanidade de Cristo*.

2. A Consagração Cristã

Jesus chamava os homens à renúncia (Mar. 8:34 ss). Ele não convidava os homens a *incorporarem* seus ensinamentos em sua vida e maneira de pensar. Quase todos nós estamos envolvidos no afã da incorporação, e não na tarefa da renúncia; mas isso não reflete um verdadeiro discipulado cristão. Alguns crentes deixam tudo e passam a seguir ao Senhor; mas a maioria permanece onde se acha, incorporando em suas vidas alguns elementos da fé e da prática cristãs. Paulo exortou aos crentes de Roma a repelirem toda a conformidade com o mundo, conformando-se de forma total e nova com Cristo. Isso requer a total renovação da mente, de acordo com o princípio espiritual. Ver Rom. 12:1,2. O Novo Testamento inteiro, em certo sentido, é a convocação dos homens para consagrarem suas vidas ao novo e vivo caminho. O propósito da consagração é a espiritualização. Os crentes estão envolvidos em uma evolução espiritual, no fim da qual ele deixará de ser mortal para tornar-se imortal; no fim da qual ele deixará de ser humano para revestir-se da natureza divina. Ver II Cor. 3:18 e Col. 2:10. Nesse processo, chega-se a compartilhar da imagem de Cristo, tal como ele compartilha da imagem de Deus. Entretanto, esse elevado alvo não poderá cumprir-se sem a total consagração ao Senhor. A própria vida espiritual é uma longa tentativa de consagração, onde os sucessos parciais vão-se tornando sucessos mais completos. Todos os meios espirituais de desenvolvimento estão envolvidos nesse processo, como o treinamento espiritual do intelecto, no estudo dos documentos sagrados e de outros livros, a oração, a meditação, a santificação, a prática da lei do amor e os toques místicos.

3. Consagração Eclesiástica

a. No Antigo Testamento temos a consagração de homens ao serviço religioso, e de coisas, à mesma finalidade, o que foi comentado no começo deste artigo.

b. No Novo Testamento, encontramos a consagração eclesiástica, na consagração de ministros da Palavra (Tito 1:5). Ver o artigo sobre a Ordenação. Ver também sobre os *Anciãos* quanto a uma discussão sobre o que está exatamente envolvido nos ofícios eclesiásticos do Novo Testamento.

c. No século II D.C., começamos a encontrar a ordenação de bispos, e não somente de pastores. O padrão neotestamentário inclui oração, imposição de mãos e unção com óleo. Na obra *Constituições Apostólicas* há uma indicação de alguma elaboração, que ultrapassa o método do Novo Testamento, com a inclusão de alguma forma de sacrifício, posta nas mãos do homem consagrado. Essa oferenda era então levantada no ar pelo candidato, provavelmente em imitação à lei, em Lev. 8:26,27, no trecho que aborda a questão da consagração dos sumos sacerdotes do Antigo Testamento.

d. *Uso Medieval*. O rito da ordenação de ministros do evangelho tornou-se ainda mais elaborado durante a Idade Média. No Ordo Romanus xxxvb, encontramos a seguinte descrição: a. Havia um exame moral e doutrinário do candidato. b. O candidato aprovado vestia os trajes próprios de seu ofício. c. O candidato punha suas mãos sobre uma cópia dos evangelhos. d. Eram feitas orações, juntamente com a imposição de mãos. e. Durante as orações, o candidato era ungido com óleo, primeiramente na cabeça, e depois, nas mãos. f. Atenção especial era dada à unção do polegar da mão direita, com a qual o bispo gesticulava na bênção, o que talvez indique uma influência de Lev. 8:23. g. Então era abençoado o anel que seria usado pelo bispo, e posto em seu dedo anular da mão direita. h. O cajado pastoral era abençoado e entregue ao candidato. i. Finalmente, havia o ósculo da paz.

A Igreja Ortodoxa Oriental retém um rito mais simples, mas também com os detalhes da imposição de mãos e da outorga do cajado pastoral.

e. *A Reforma Protestante*. Os reformadores do século XVI estavam interessados na simplificação da maioria das coisas, e o rito consagratório foi um dos itens afetados. Os reformadores opinavam que somente aquilo que pode ser traçado até ao Novo Testamento é necessário, devendo ser eliminados todos os acréscimos feitos pela tradição humana. Isso posto, a oração e a imposição de mãos tornaram-se os únicos elementos do rito. Na Igreja Anglicana, os ritos, determinados a partir do ano de 1550, consistiam na imposição de mãos, na colocação da Bíblia sobre a nuca do candidato (simbolizando o jugo de Cristo) e a apresentação do cajado pastoral. Porém, em 1552, o cajado passou a ser omitido, e, em seu lugar, começou a ser presenteada uma Bíblia ao candidato.

4. Consagração de Igrejas

Em I Reis 8:63 lemos sobre a dedicação do templo de Jerusalém. Isso estabeleceu o precedente para a dedicação de templos cristãos. Até o final do século VII D.C., nenhum rito especial fora criado; e a celebração da Ceia, no interior do templo, assinalava adequadamente o início das funções. Porém, no século VIII D.C., surgiu um cerimonial elaborado, que incluía os seguintes itens: a. um cortejo com relíquias; b. o bispo entrava no novo templo e seus associados traziam cimento para selar a pedra do altar; água de exorcismo era usada para lavar o altar; c. os clérigos saíam do interior do templo; d. entravam todos os envolvidos na cerimônia, e os quatro ângulos interiores da cavidade do altar eram ungidos; as relíquias eram postas sobre o altar e eram seladas; e. o templo era abençoado juntamente com todos os vasos e instrumentos de adoração; f. eram acesas as lâmpadas no interior do templo; g. era celebrada uma missa. De acordo com alguns ritos, a própria igreja era batizada por aspersão, e o bispo escrevia letras do alfabeto com seu cajado, sobre o soalho, em imitação ao antigo método romano de possessão de algum terreno, quando os limites eram traçados literal ou simbolicamente. E então as paredes do templo eram ungidas com azeite.

Nas Igrejas Ortodoxas Orientais o altar é ungido, e as paredes do templo são aspergidas e ungidas com azeite. Nenhuma cerimônia especial era seguida na Igreja Anglicana até o século XVII, e até mesmo em nossos dias cada diocese efetua ritos de acordo com seus próprios padrões. Nas igrejas protestantes e evangélicas há apenas um culto especial, sem nenhum batismo e unção do templo.

Idéias por Detrás dos Ritos. Dedicação do templo a Deus e à sua Igreja. Libertar o local de quaisquer influências demoníacas. Locais antes profanos, tornam-se consagrados em face dos ritos. Há expressão de ação de graças, e o funcionamento de uma nova igreja local é declarado. (B C LOW)

CONSALVI, ERCOLE

Nasceu em 1757 e faleceu em 1824. Foi cardeal e secretário de estado sob o papa Pio VII (que vide). Tornou-se famoso por seu entusiástico patrocínio das artes e das ciências. A Concordata (que vide), firmada entre o papado e Napoleão, deveu-se quase inteiramente aos seus grandes dotes de estadista.

CONSANGUINIDADE — Impedimento Marital

Ver outras informações nos artigos sobre *Afinidade* e *Impedimentos ao Casamento*.

As pessoas com alto grau de parentesco biológico não podem se casar, por proibição religiosa, civil, ou ambas. Esse parentesco serve de impedimento marital. E mesmo quando o casamento é contraído, propositalmente ou por ignorância dos fatos, tal aliança é anulada. A lei canônica da Igreja Católica Romana alicerça-se sobre as leis romanas (*Código de Justiniano* V.4.18,19; *Cod. Theol.* III.12.1-3), bem como sobre passagens das Escrituras, como Levítico 18:7-14, além das interpretações de pais da Igreja, como Ambrósio e Agostinho. Entre os séculos VI e XIII D.C., muitos decretos papais e conciliares proibiram o casamento entre pessoas aparentadas até o sétimo grau; mas tal rigor foi afrouxado por ocasião do quarto concílio laterano, de 1215, que limitou a proibição ao parentesco de quarto grau. Após muito debate, Alexandre II (papa entre 1061 e 1073) chegou à conclusão que, finalmente, foi aceita de modo geral. Ele mantinha que o grau de parentesco corresponde ao número de gerações entre as partes interessadas e um ancestral comum, excluindo esse ancestral. Migne, Patrologiae, 146, (1379-1381). O papa Gregório IX (1227-1241) decretou que quando as partes envolvidas estivessem aparentadas a um ancestral comum, em graus diferentes, a linhagem mais longa deveria servir de padrão determinante, quanto ao número do grau de parentesco (*Decretais* 4.14,9). O termo *afinidade* é contrastado com o termo *consangüinidade* A afinidade é afetada por relações adquiridas mediante casamento, embora sem haver qualquer relação de sangue. Aqueles que estão vinculados por relação de sangue são chamados *parentes*. Quando as pessoas estão relacionadas entre si mediante linha direta, como avô-pai-filho-neto, a linha de descendência é chamada *linear*. Se as pessoas estiverem aparentadas por descenderem de um ancestral comum, mas não linearmente, como um tio e seu sobrinho, a descendência é chamada *colateral*. (AM E)

CONSCIÊNCIA

Essa palavra vem do latim *con*, «com», e *scire*, «saber». O equivalente grego é *suneídesis*, que ocorre por trinta vezes: Atos 23:1; 24:16; Rom. 2:15; 9:1; 13:5; I Cor. 8:7,10,12; 10:25,27-29; II Cor. 1:12; 4:2; 5:11; I Tim. 1:5,19; 3:9; 4:2; II Tim. 1:3; Tito 1:15; Heb. 9:9,14; 10:2,22; 13:18; I Ped. 2:19; 3:16,21.

Em sua evolução, esse termo tem servido de sinônimo de consciência, no sentido de «percepção», conforme se dá com o francês e o português. Geralmente, porém, o vocábulo «consciência» tem assumido a idéia da faculdade de distinguir entre o certo e o errado. Na filosofia e na teologia há muitas idéias acerca da natureza da consciência, conforme se vê abaixo:

1. Sócrates falava sobre a consciência como uma espécie de voz interna de advertência, que ele reputava originar-se no ser divino. Talvez ele pensasse na consciência como uma entidade pessoal, como no caso de seu próprio «demônio», que sempre o aconselhava a não fazer certas coisas. Ver o artigo sobre *Sócrates*.

2. Nos escritos dos *estóicos*, a consciência aparece como a voz da Razão (Logos), uma fagulha do ser divino no homem, derivada da razão universal, que serve de força orientadora do ser humano.

3. *Jerônimo*, bem como certos teólogos e filósofos da Idade Média, referiam-se à *sundéresis* (que vide) como aquela faculdade humana que torna o homem instintivamente cônscio das regras universais e obrigatórias de conduta. O termo latino *conscientia* era usado para indicar a aplicação de regras gerais a casos específicos. Nessa conexão, o termo *scintilla conscientias*, «fagulha da consciência», era empregado. A ciência do *casuísmo* veio à existência como o exercício segundo o qual as leis morais são aplicadas a situações concretas.

4. Na terminologia moderna, os termos *sundéresis* e *casuísmo* entraram em desuso (exceto na literatura, e, quanto à última, na política), ao passo que a palavra *consciência* passou a incluir tanto as leis universais quanto os casos particulares.

5. O *bispo Butler* (que vide), um grande filósofo moral e teólogo, via a consciência como uma faculdade mental, e, de fato, *a* faculdade da razão que é capaz de distinguir entre o certo e o errado, uma faculdade inerente, divinamente outorgada.

6. *John Henry Newman* pensava que a consciência é uma espécie de visão luminosa, concedida por Deus à sensibilidade humana, mediante a qual a pessoa concorda que certas coisas são erradas. Segundo esse ponto de vista, a consciência é uma forma de elo entre Deus e o homem, inerente, uma qualidade do espírito.

7. Para *Freud*, a consciência é o *superego* do homem, a internalização das admoestações e requisitos da sociedade em que convive o indivíduo. De acordo com esse ponto de vista, Deus fica fora da questão. Uma criança, por temer castigo, adota essencialmente as proibições de seus pais, sentindo-se culpada se não adotar as mesmas.

8. Os *naturalistas sociólogos* afirmam que a consciência resulta da pressão da sociedade sobre o indivíduo, o que seria uma espécie de reflexo de costumes.

9. *No Novo Testamento*. «Consciência» é um termo que não aparece no Antigo Testamento, embora haja trechos como I Samuel 24:5 e II Sam. 24:10, onde lemos que «sentiu Davi bater-lhe o coração», quando ele fez o que sabia estar errado. Por igual modo, em Jeremias 31:33 lemos que a lei no coração é escrita por Deus. Nos evangelhos sinópticos, não figura a palavra «consciência»; mas sabemos das funções da consciência nos mandamentos obedecidos de todo o coração e de acordo com a luz do entendimento (Mat. 6:22,23). Várias descrições sobre a consciência mostram-nos a sua natureza geral, embora o Novo Testamento não nos ofereça alguma definição metafísica, ao gosto da filosofia.

A Consciência no Novo Testamento:

Dependendo de como o espírito humano reage ao Espírito de Deus, a consciência pode ser descrita das seguintes maneiras: 1. Fraca (I Cor. 8:7,12). 2. Má ou contaminada (Heb. 10:22; Tito 1:15). 3. Cauterizada (I Tim. 4:2). 4. Pura (II Tim. 1:5). 5. Livre de ofensa (Atos 24:6). 6. Boa ou honrada (Heb. 13:7; I Ped. 3:16). 7. Ativada por ocasião da conversão, e ativa durante a vida inteira (João 2:1 *ss*; Fil. 2:12 *ss.*).

CONSCIÊNCIA

Paulo confiava, pois, que o crente, dotado de uma faculdade interna e devidamente treinada, que reconhece *instintivamente* o bem e o mal, dando preferência ao bem, agirá de acordo com a vontade de Deus. O trecho de Romanos 2:14,15, referindo-se aos gentios, afirma que até os pagãos podem fazer, *por natureza*, aquilo que Deus requer. Portanto, Paulo não pensava que a consciência é implantada no homem por ocasião da conversão. Porém, o desenvolvimento espiritual confere à consciência maior sensibilidade e exatidão. O Novo Testamento não afirma abertamente, mas deixa entendido que a consciência é uma faculdade da alma, uma qualidade inerente mediante a qual o indivíduo reconhece o bem ou o mal, devido à própria natureza de seu ser. Portanto, a consciência pode ser melhorada, piorada ou modificada pela experiência, mas existe antes da experiência e independentemente dela. Quer dizer que o homem é um *espírito*, e esse espírito é dotado de inteligência, independente das experiências do corpo físico. Alguns teólogos, como os pais alexandrinos da Igreja, supõem que o espírito é preexistente, dotado de larga experiência de vida antes de associar-se ao corpo físico. Parte desse conhecimento sobre o bem e o mal, ou quando o espírito se utiliza de suas faculdades mentais e espirituais de modo ético, é aquilo que chamamos de *consciência*. Com ou sem a idéia de preexistência, dentro do sistema cristão, supomos que a consciência é uma qualidade espiritual, inerente ao espírito humano, e não algo que se desenvolve à medida que o cérebro cresce.

No sentido cristão, naturalmente, a consciência humana nunca se manifesta isolada. Supõe-se que o Espírito de Deus tem acesso à consciência, capaz de influenciá-la. As várias referências que Paulo alista, no tocante à sua própria experiência, mostram-nos que ele pensava que o *Espírito* concedera-lhe as convicções apropriadas (I Cor. 2:4 ss; I Tes. 1:5). A conversão começa pela obra do Espírito, e o processo continua sob a sua influência (Fil. 2:12 ss; João 3:1 ss, Efé. 2:1 ss). O Espírito abre o coração (Atos 16:14) e ilumina o entendimento do homem (Efé. 1:17 ss).

10. Citações Notáveis

«Consciência e reputação são duas coisas diferentes. A consciência deve-se a nós mesmos; a reputação deve-se ao próximo» (Agostinho).

«Há um outro homem, dentro de mim, que se ira contra mim» (Sir Thomas Browne, *Religio Medici*).

«Trata-se de voz suave e calma» (William Cowper, *The Task*).

«Uma boa consciência é um Natal permanente» (Benjamim Franklin).

«Aquela coisa feroz, que costumeiramente chamamos de consciência» (Thomas Hood, *Lamia*).

«Não há testemunha tão terrível e nem acusador tão poderoso, como a consciência, que habita no peito de todo homem» (Políbio, *Histórias*).

«O verme da consciência observa as mesmas horas que a coruja» (Schiller, *Kabale und Liebe*).

«Não confie em coisa alguma, sobretudo no homem sem consciência» (Lawrence Sterne, *Tristam Shandy*). (AM B C E NTI)

CONSCIÊNCIA (COMO PERCEPÇÃO)

Essa palavra vem do latim con, «com», e scire, «saber». O termo tem sido usado na filosofia como sinônimo de «consciência», como a capacidade inata de distinguir entre o certo e o errado. Mas tem chegado a representar diversos conceitos, a saber:

1. *A Escola da Consciência Apenas*. Também é chamada de *Caminho da Ioga*, estabelecido por Asanga (que vide), e que foi sistematizada por Vasubandhu (que vide). Essa posição encontra a própria existência na consciência, mas afirma que se trata de uma consciência pura, que não se manifesta mediante objetos externos ou mediante o ego humano empírico. O homem pode chegar a participar dessa consciência mediante a liberação. Esse conceito é uma descrição do ser divino, pois somente em Deus há uma consciência imortal.

2. *Galluppi* (que vide), ao argumentar contra o *solipsismo* (que vide), ensinou que a consciência envolve a percepção simultânea tanto do próprio eu, denominado *ego*, quanto das coisas objetivas, das quais tomamos consciência.

3. *William James* opinava que a consciência não é uma entidade, mas uma função. Ele afirmava que se trata de uma corrente da inteligência que toma conhecimento das coisas, cujos estados posteriores são capazes de perceber os seus antecedentes.

4. *Locke* referia-se à consciência como um senso de *autoconhecimento*, adquirido em virtude da capacidade que a mente humana tem de refletir sobre si mesma, em atos de introspecção. Essa posição supõe que essa é uma propriedade geral dos estados mentais.

5. A função do *autoconsciente* distingue um homem, ou um animal, de um objeto inanimado; e, segundo alguns estudiosos, isso dá a entender a existência da *alma*. Isso é uma evidência, pois evidentemente é impossível explicar o autoconsciente com base em qualquer teoria materialista. Como poderia uma máquina ter consciência de si mesma?

6. Na *psicologia*, a consciência é frisada como indicação de que existem estados mentais que não estão sujeitos à consciência ordinária; e nisso encontramos um outro uso do termo. Isso nos envolve na consciência e na mente subconsciente. Portanto, a consciência consiste naquilo em que nos apercebemos, em estados normais. A mente subconsciente é aquele aspecto do autoconhecimento que se oculta nos estados normais, mas no qual entramos nos sonhos, nos estados hipnóticos, nas experiências místicas, e que, mediante a análise, traz à tona indícios de sua existência.

7. *A Consciência e o Superconsciente*. O superconsciente é aquele estado mental que transcende ao conhecimento ordinário do homem. O termo pode aludir ao nosso «eu superior», às dimensões mais elevadas de nosso próprio ser. Pode, igualmente, referir-se aos poderes acima do que é meramente humano, incluindo capacidades divinas.

8. A palavra *consciência* pode ser sinônimo de mente ou de alma; ou pode ser considerada como a função cognitiva da mente ou da alma. A menos que incluamos a idéia de alma, em algum ponto de nossos conceitos, como uma *entidade capaz de conhecer*, será extremamente difícil, ou mesmo impossível, falar em consciência. Pois, como poderia uma mera combinação de átomos em movimento produzir essa função cognitiva, — percebendo a si mesma, e tendo conhecimento das coisas externas, conforme sabemos que o ser humano faz?

9. *Experiências que Expandem a Consciência*. É claro que o homem ordinário vive *desperto* apenas em parte. O homem tem pouca consciência de si mesmo e da realidade de cerca. Mas a consciência pode ser ampliada mediante as experiências místicas, nos sonhos, sob hipnose, ou com o uso de certas drogas. Realidades superiores e inferiores podem ser percebidas, e podemos obter uma iluminação que nos

permita tomar consciência de uma realidade superior, capacitando-nos a avaliar a mesma. Aqueles que buscam iluminação buscam uma consciência superior das coisas. Paulo falou da iluminação mediante o Espírito, através das experiências místicas (Efé. 1:17 ss). Alguns supõem que os eventos que expandem a consciência podem não passar de alucinações, destituídos de real valor, sem qualquer realidade espiritual. As experiências clínicas mostram que aqueles que usam drogas quase sempre sofrem alucinações. Com freqüência, as perturbações mentais são um corolário dessas experiências; o resultado pode ser o suicídio ou muitas outras tragédias. Isso não significa que as drogas nunca possam expandir a consciência. Há mesmo razões para crermos que as drogas podem produzir mais do que meras alucinações, expandindo a percepção mental das pessoas, embora não em um sentido moral e correto. Os meios artificiais, mesmo que, ocasionalmente, sirvam para expandir a percepção, não são lícitos aos homens espirituais.

A fé cristã supõe que um profeta pode ter uma consciência que ultrapassa à percepção do homem ordinário. Isso pode ser parcialmente inerente, e parcialmente produzido pelo Espírito de Deus. Espera-se que todos os crentes vão crescendo na iluminação, porquanto estamos sendo transformados segundo a consciência de Cristo. Lemos que possuímos a sua *mente*, em I Coríntios 2:16.

10. *A Consciência Final*. No processo de transformação do crente segundo a imagem de Cristo (Rom. 8:29; II Cor. 3:18), que envolve a participação na natureza divina (II Ped. 1:4), chegamos a compartilhar da consciência divina, de modo finito, mas realmente admirável. O conhecimento que Deus tem torna-se nosso. Essa percepção final das coisas faz parte do destino humano. Então deixará de existir a separação de mente, e o homem virá a participar integralmente da *mente divina*. (AM EP P F)

CONSCIÊNCIA CÓSMICA

O que está implícito nessa expressão é que a pessoa pode vir a participar da mente universal, e não apenas na mente individual. Ver o artigo sobre a *Mente Universal*. A expressão também dá a entender que há uma espécie de depósito universal de inteligência, no qual a mente individual pode penetrar. Sabemos que Deus é possuidor de uma mente universal ou cósmica. Deus sabe de tudo ao mesmo tempo. O espírito humano, mesmo agora, é capaz de uma elevada, embora finita participação na mente cósmica. As experiências místicas conferem iluminação em graus variegados, o que se relaciona à consciência cósmica. De algumas vezes, uma pessoa recebe uma súbita e inesperada experiência mística, na qual a sua mente penetra na mente cósmica, e sua consciência é assim grandemente expandida. Isso significa que tal pessoa está participando da consciência cósmica, até certo ponto. Algumas pessoas são capazes de ter repetidas experiências dessa natureza, tornando-se pessoas dotadas de notável experiência espiritual. Entretanto, a maioria das pessoas faz apenas visitas ocasionais à mente cósmica, enquanto que outras passam apenas por uma experiência dessas. Naturalmente, a maioria das pessoas, durante a vida inteira nunca passa por qualquer experiência dessa ordem. Somos informados que Sócrates, buscando solução para algum problema ético, e desejando conhecer a verdadeira natureza da justiça, da bondade, etc., algumas vezes passava um dia inteiro meditando, em um alterado estado de consciência. Diz-se que ele obteve consciência cósmica até certo grau. Algumas das informações assim obtidas por ele aparecem nos diálogos platônicos. O mesmo tipo de busca ética era a substância mesma da vida de Buda (que vide). Ele não especulou sobre temas metafísicos, pouco tendo falado sobre a natureza da alma ou de Deus. Quanto a essas questões, precisamos buscar informações em outras fontes. Porém, no campo da ética podemos aprender algumas preciosas verdades, ao lermos o que esse homem descobriu em sua inquirição. Penso que o Logos divino plantou algumas das suas sementes no budismo. Ver o artigo sobre *Cristo Como a Verdade*, onde é declarado que um dos aspectos da missão do Logos, chamado Jesus Cristo em sua encarnação, foi o de plantar sementes em todas as esferas da atividade humana, como na filosofia, na religião e na ciência. Nessa conexão, ver também o artigo sobre a Missão *Universal do Logos* (Cristo).

Certos momentos de consciência cósmica ocorrem às pessoas sob a forma de sonhos ou visões; e de outras vezes, por meio da hipnose. A iluminação (que vide) é uma das principais fontes informativas. A expressão *Cristo-consciência* (que vide), refere-se ao avanço do crente no campo da consciência cósmica, através do poder do Espírito Santo, e em união com Cristo. Em nossa época, muitas pessoas têm experimentado as drogas, a fim de tentarem expandir a mente e receber algo da consciência cósmica. Usualmente, essa prática produz meras alucinações, embora pareça haver casos em que há mais do que isso. Com freqüência, as *viagens* ao inconsciente obtêm resultados apenas negativos, quando então os experimentadores recebem vislumbres da real natureza do mal, e ficam aterrorizados. Quando essas viagens são «positivas» (quando então, não consistem apenas em alucinações), são vistas algumas coisas notáveis. Não obstante, preciso tachar enfaticamente essa busca de *imoral*, sem importar os resultados obtidos. Os registros médicos demonstram claramente a confusão que isso tem trazido para muitas pessoas. Ademais, não temos o direito de usar meios artificiais, potencialmente perigosos, para provocar experiências místicas. Isso é uma depravação, sem importar quais sejam os resultados. Satanás sempre tem substitutos fáceis para as experiências espirituais genuínas e benéficas. Os dons cristãos espirituais do conhecimento, do ensino e da profecia podem participar em certos aspectos da consciência cósmica; mas essas experiências, embora relacionadas a isso, em alguns casos, não são a mesma coisa que as experiências legítimas, e nem o mecanismo é idêntico. Místicos cristãos do Oriente e do Ocidente têm falado sobre experiências de consciência cósmica, segundo termos cristãos, nos casos de experiências místicas superiores pelas quais têm passado. Ver o artigo sobre o *Misticismo*.

CONSCIÊNCIA DE CRISTO

Há duas maneiras possível de compreender a questão: 1. Como Cristo, em sua vida terrena, pensava sobre si mesmo e sua missão. 2. Como o homem pode participar da mente de Cristo. Quanto a este segundo aspecto, o leitor deveria examinar o artigo intitulado *Cristo-Consciência*. O presente artigo aborda o primeiro desses dois sentidos possíveis.

1. **Declaração Introdutória**. O que Jesus pensava sobre sua natureza e missão envolve-nos na antiga controvérsia sobre as naturezas divina e humana residentes em uma única pessoa. Visto que isso constitui um *mistério*, e visto que aquilo que Jesus

CONSCIÊNCIA DE CRISTO

pensava sobre si mesmo e sobre sua missão é uma subcategoria desse mistério, a *consciência de Cristo* também é um mistério. Isso posto, apesar de podermos dizer algumas coisas úteis a respeito, não podemos integrar todos os trechos bíblicos que aludem ao assunto, e nem podemos satisfazer à curiosidade dos homens que têm tratado de tais questões. Aqueles que tentam chegar a esse ponto, sentem-se forçados a distorcer alguma coisa, em algum lugar. Para exemplificar: se eu lançar mão somente dos evangelhos sinópticos, terei a impressão de um Jesus que procurava entender e que, apenas gradualmente, chegou à consciência da natureza de sua elevada missão. Porém, se usarmos também o evangelho de João, então desde o começo terei um Cristo divino que não conhece conflitos íntimos e nem embala dúvidas. Esses dois pontos de vista são simplesmente opostos. Um deles vê as coisas do ângulo da humanidade de Jesus Cristo; e o outro vê as coisas pela perspectiva da divindade de Cristo Jesus.

2. Fontes Informativas. Alguns intérpretes supõem que é quase impossível recuperarmos a **ipsíssima** *verba* de Jesus, ou seja, suas palavras literais. E isso significa que todas as declarações chegaram até nós já coloridas pelos dogmas da Igreja cristã. Parte do problema, supostamente, reside no fato de que, desde o começo, as palavras de Jesus chegaram até nós como textos gregos traduzidos do aramaico. Apesar de admitirmos que tudo isso constitui um problema, não há razão para supormos que aquilo que temos no Novo Testamento não seja uma correta representação do que Jesus realmente disse e experimentou. Aqueles que foram os autores sagrados do Novo Testamento conviveram com o próprio Senhor. Não podemos supor que eles o malentenderam excessivamente.

3. Testemunho dos Evangelhos Sinópticos. Para começar, temos Jesus, homem nascido de mulher. Portanto, o elemento humano está presente. O trecho de Hebreus 2:10 mostra-nos que Jesus precisou ser aperfeiçoado. Isso não alude ao pecado, em nenhum sentido. Antes, está em foco o aperfeiçoamento espiritual, no conhecimento e nas virtudes divinas. Além disso, Jesus precisou aprender, conforme lemos em Hebreus 5:9. Jesus aprendeu a obedecer, mediante aquilo que sofreu. Os estudiosos liberais têm salientado corretamente que havia um *segredo messiânico*, embora isso seja peremptoriamente negado pelos eruditos conservadores. Ver Mar. 5:43; 9:9; 7:36; Mat. 8:4; 9:26; 16:15 *ss*, e 17:9. A referência de Marcos 9:9 parece dar a entender que a primeira declaração evidente do caráter messiânico de Jesus só foi feita após a ressurreição. O trecho de Mat. 16:15 *ss*, onde há a confissão de Pedro de que Jesus era o Ungido de Deus, aparece quase no fim do ministério de Jesus. Notemos que a história de sua transfiguração vem imediatamente após a confissão de Pedro. Jesus proibiu aos seus discípulos de falarem sobre a questão, antes de sua ressurreição (Mat. 17:9). Com base nessas referências, parece que Jesus, como homem, chegou a perceber apenas gradualmente as dimensões de sua missão, da mesma forma que qualquer homem espiritual recebe o desvendamento de sua missão apenas *gradualmente*. Naturalmente, desde os doze anos de idade, pelo menos, Jesus sabia que não era uma pessoa comum; porquanto ninguém podia confundir os doutores na lei e ser um homem comum, e muito menos, ser um garoto qualquer. (Ver Luc. 2:41 *ss*). Lucas fornece-nos uma significativa declaração ao final dessa narrativa: «E crescia Jesus em sabedoria, estatura e graça, diante de Deus e dos homens» (Luc. 2:52). É precisamente isso que estou procurando salientar neste parágrafo. Como ser humano, Jesus cresceu na estatura do Messias, e, tanto para ele como para outros, o segredo nisso envolvido foi aclarado: Jesus, realmente, era o Messias, o Filho de Deus unigênito, em sentido todo especial.

Em outros trechos bíblicos, porém, não temos a idéia de crescimento, aprendizado, revelação do segredo messiânico, e idéias paralelas. Assim sendo, Marcos começa com a ousada declaração de que Jesus é o Filho de Deus, em 'sentido especial. Mas até mesmo em Mateus 5:1 vemos Jesus Cristo como o Novo Moisés, o novo Legislador, que teve a coragem de dizer: «Moisés disse... Eu, porém, vos digo...» Não há que duvidar que Jesus falou com elevadíssima autoridade, desde o começo de seu ministério, embora, gradualmente, ele viesse a compreender, mais e mais, a plena implicação de seu caráter messiânico. A questão inteira dos milagres também é muito significativa. Jesus era dotado de imenso poder, e nunca encontrou quem se lhe igualasse. Ele deve ter compreendido que o Espírito Santo operava nele de forma singular. Com base nisso, naturalmente, ele tinha consciência de seu caráter messiânico, embora tal consciência também se tenha desenvolvido. Ele tinha plena consciência do supremo propósito que nele operava (Luc. 9:51). Ver também as explícitas *declarações soteriológicas* de Mar. 10:45; 14:24; Mt. 20:28. Ele tinha consciência de seu ofício como profeta especial (Mat. 21:11; Mar. 7:15; 8:27,28; Luc. 7:16). E essa convicção era compartilhada por outros, conforme algumas dessas referências demonstram. Os contemporâneos de Jesus diziam ser ele um grande profeta, talvez um dos profetas do Antigo Testamento, reencarnado (Mat. 16:13 *ss*). Pedro foi além disso, tendo identificado Jesus como o Messias prometido, o maior de todos os profetas. Ademais, consideremos o termo *Senhor*, que foi freqüentemente aplicado a Jesus, por outras pessoas e por ele mesmo, conforme vemos em Marcos 11:3. A mesma coisa pode ser dita em relação ao uso do termo *Filho*. Ver Mat. 12:8; 14:33; 16:16 e 19:28. O trecho de Mateus 22:42 é especialmente significativo, nessa conexão. No que concerne ao Messias, Jesus seria apenas o filho de Davi? Essa foi a pergunta que Jesus fez aos fariseus. Mas, Davi chamou-o de *Senhor!* Como podia Jesus ser apenas o filho de Davi, se era o Senhor de Davi? Os fariseus não foram capazes de solucionar o dilema. O trecho citado do Antigo Testamento é Salmos 110:1.

4. O Testemunho do Evangelho de João. No quarto evangelho não transparece o chamado segredo messiânico. Desde o começo, Jesus é associado ao termo de Logos eterno, que é o mesmo Deus (João 1:1-3). O Logos nunca hesitou; antes, sempre soube de todas as coisas, nunca se sentiu perturbado. João é o *evangelho teológico*, do qual inúmeras referências podem ser extraídas para demonstrar a consciência que Cristo tinha de que Jesus não somente era o Messias, mas também era o próprio Deus. Não existia ele antes mesmo de Abraão, e não era ele o grande «Eu Sou» do Antigo Testamento? Ver João 8:28. Todos os grandes discursos de Jesus, como aqueles sobre a água da vida, a porta, o pão do céu, o caminho, a verdade e a vida, foram feitos do ponto de vista de sua autoridade divina, dando a entender a sua deidade, tão claramente afirmada no prólogo do quarto evangelho. Notemos que, em vez de um segredo messiânico, desde o começo da narrativa do quarto evangelho os seus discípulos tê-lo-iam reconhecido como o Messias (João 1:41). Nesse evangelho, por dezessete vezes Jesus chamou-se de «Filho» ou de «Filho de Deus». Acrescente-se a isso a percepção sempre consciente de sua relação especial com o Pai

CONSELHEIRO (ACONSELHAMENTO)

(João 5:19; 6:57; 8:29; 12:49). Ele é o Filho a quem o Pai haveria de ressuscitar para atingir a glória eterna (João 17:1,5). A missão divina do Filho é enfatizada, porquanto é dito que Cristo foi enviado pelo Pai, nesse evangelho, por mais de quarenta vezes. Isso subentende a sua preexistência, a sua missão divina e messiânica, a sua união com o Pai em propósito e ações, o seu caráter representativo. Ele pertence às dimensões eternas, e estava realizando uma missão sobre a terra. Ver o artigo sobre Cristo, *Enviado do Pai*.

Torna-se patente, com base no contraste entre os evangelhos sinópticos e o evangelho de João que, por detrás das declarações relativas à consciência que Jesus tinha de si mesmo e de sua missão, que havia fatores divinos e humanos em operação. Entretanto, não há como harmonizar com sucesso esses fatores. No entanto, é certo que ele tinha consciência de seu caráter messiânico e de sua divindade, talvez desde bem cedo em sua vida terrena, a despeito das limitações da sua natureza humana. Quanto a isso, porém, precisou haver crescimento, conforme indicam os próprios evangelhos.

5. O Testemunho dos Gigantes Espirituais. Aqueles dotados de menor estatura espiritual, especialmente quando influenciados pelo ceticismo (que vide), dificilmente poderiam pensar nos mesmos termos que os gigantes espirituais. Os céticos, ao abordarem os elementos, temas da natureza messiânica de Cristo e de sua natureza divina, sempre que podem negam essas realidades. Dotados de mentalidade negativa, mui naturalmente eles tentam dizer-nos que o próprio Jesus nunca reivindicou a divindade ou a natureza messiânica para si mesmo. Segundo dizem os céticos, teria sido a Igreja que fez tais afirmativas, para então construir toda uma teologia de apoio, que o próprio Jesus não teria apoiado. Porém, isso é encarar a questão com olhos de anões espirituais. Os gigantes espirituais sempre se mostram muito conscientes da missão que eles possuem. Eles têm consciência da presença divina em suas vidas. Mostram-se crentes firmes na missão e no destino que desempenham em tudo isso. Jesus não era diferente deles quanto a esse particular.

6. O Testemunho de Satya Sai Baba. Ver o artigo sobre esse homem. Ele é um homem santo do hinduísmo, que está duplicando os milagres de Jesus, diante dos olhos de todos, em plena luz do dia, até mesmo na presença de cientistas. Esse homem diz-se dotado de uma elevada missão, afirmando ser um *Avatar* (que vide). Não é meu propósito defender aqui as reivindicações dele. Mas quero salientar o fato de que, como um elevado poder espiritual (alguns pensam que ele é positivo, e outros que ele é um poder negativo — que Deus resolva), ele tem plena consciência do elevado poder espiritual que nele opera. Não há que duvidar que Jesus, o Cristo, fez reivindicações acerca de sua pessoa; e os evangelhos assim afirmam. Uma vez que admitamos que Jesus fez essas reivindicações, e que a Igreja não inventou a história toda, cabe a cada indivíduo ajustar-se às mesmas. Há muitas coisas na consciência de Jesus, no tocante à sua própria natureza e missão, que os céticos jamais conseguirão compreender. Quanto a nós, é melhor confiarmos no poder que Deus tem manifestado neste mundo e na natureza humana, do que nos envolvermos na futilidade da incredulidade dos céticos. (BARC FA NTI Z)

CONSELHEIRO (ACONSELHAMENTO)

Os ministros evangélicos com freqüência são chamados a dar conselhos, de maneira formal ou informal. Em anos recentes, o aconselhamento cristão tem recebido um renovado impulso e interesse, com o surgimento de especialistas, dotados de bom treinamento nesse campo de atividades. Considerável literatura tem surgido sobre o assunto. Mas também tem havido muito *abuso*, por parte de ministros que pouco ensinam da Bíblia, porquanto eles se tornaram mais psicólogos do que pastores e mestres, e sua prédica está eivada do vocabulário usado na psicologia. Outro tanto tem sucedido a conferências onde, antes, a Bíblia era o centro das atenções. Mas agora elas se assemelham mais a sessões psicológicas populares, com algum verniz de religiosidade. Por outra parte, é bom que os ministros do evangelho tenham algumas noções básicas sobre o assunto, sabendo também como outros ministros, que se tornaram especialistas nesse campo, manipulam essas questões. Assim, são melhor capazes de examinar, expressar e manipular idéias. A ignorância nunca é recomendável. Um ministro do evangelho deve estar bem informado em muitas áreas, e quanto mais, melhor, ao mesmo tempo em que jamais deve olvidar-se dos requisitos de seu alto chamamento como pregador do evangelho de Cristo.

Em nosso moderno e complexo mundo, o ministro é uma pessoa que se dispõe a ajudar a outros, e cuja ajuda não seja dispendiosa em termos econômicos. Portanto, um pastor será procurado para aconselhar e ajudar quanto a muitos problemas, como aqueles envolvidos no matrimônio, no vício com drogas, nos casos de ansiedade, de tristezas, de aspirações, de necessidade de orientação, ou de qualquer coisa que aborde a vida humana diária. Ocasionalmente, um ministro do evangelho não se sentirá apto a aconselhar sobre determinados problemas, pelo que deveria ser capaz de encaminhar as pessoas a médicos, advogados, etc. Naturalmente, no campo das questões religiosas, um pastor jamais poderá desistir de suas funções, deixando o bem-estar das almas entregue aos cuidados de quem não entende que o principal problema humano é como corrigir seu relacionamento com Deus e com os nossos semelhantes. Infelizmente, isso tem sucedido.

Um dos mais bem conhecidos conselheiros cristãos da atualidade, um pastor presbiteriano, surpreendeu-se quando descobriu, na universidade onde estava estudando psicologia, que a melhor técnica de aconselhamento é aquela que segue os moldes bíblicos, ou seja, fazendo os pacientes enfrentarem sua realidade moral, diante de Deus, dos homens e de si mesmos. A esse método ele chamou de aconselhamento *noutético*, ou seja, alicerçado sobre a iluminação da mente do paciente, com o uso da Palavra de Deus. Esse conselheiro cristão, Jay E. Adams, evoca trechos bíblicos como Rom. 15:14 e Col. 3:16, entre outros, como base bíblica de sua contenção.

O ministro evangélico que busca aconselhar, deve dispor-se a enfrentar certo número de responsabilidades. Em primeiro lugar, ele precisa ser um homem de sólidos conhecimentos. A ignorância, oculta por detrás de citações bíblicas, não é grande ajuda. Além disso, ele precisa ser um exemplo de espiritualidade, a fim de que suas palavras tenham peso. Também é mister que entenda a linguagem das emoções. Nunca deveria devolver hostilidade pela hostilidade recebida, prestando conselhos com termos aceitáveis. Haverá de tratar com mulheres, casadas, viúvas e solteiras, que enfrentam muitos problemas com homens, mas têm sede de afeição. Isso posto, será objeto de tentativas de sedução. No caso de mulheres especialmente atraentes, será tentado a seduzi-las, porquanto um pastor é uma pessoa como outra qualquer, impulsionado por impulsos irracionais, como qualquer outra pessoa. Um dos piores escândalos que envolvem o tratamento psiquiátrico é a freqüência das relações sexuais entre os médicos e suas pacientes.

Acrescente-se a isso que um ministro do evangelho, tal e qual um médico ou um advogado, deve saber guardar segredos, sempre que as pessoas aconselhadas solicitarem segredo, e sempre que o senso de propriedade do pastor assim mostrar que deve ser. Há aquele velho escândalo da esposa do pastor que espalha tudo quanto ouve. E um ministro também não deve usar os casos que trata como ilustrações em seus sermões. As pessoas não terão dificuldade em perceberem a quem ele se refere.

Quando um ministro torna-se conselheiro profissional, deve cuidar para não promover sua igreja ou sua denominação, embora, necessariamente, promova princípios bíblicos e espirituais. Em todo o seu envolvimento no campo da psicologia, sempre deveria conferir suprema importância à espiritualidade do homem, tratando com as pessoas como almas necessitadas, e não apenas como mentes perturbadas. Um pastor sabe que o Senhor Jesus é o médico da mente, das emoções, do espírito, e não apenas do corpo! (H)

CONSELHO, CONSELHEIRO

No hebraico, **etsah**, «conselho», palavra que ocorre por oitenta e seis vezes, como, por exemplo, Deu. 32:28; Juí. 20:7; II Sam. 15:31,34; 16:20,23; I Reis 1:12; II Crô. 10:8,13; Esd. 10:3,8; Nee. 4:15; Jó 5:13; 10:3; 12:13; Sal. 1:1; 13:2; 14:6; Pro. 1:25,30; 8:14; 12:15; 19:20,21; Isa. 5:19; 11:2; Jer. 18:18,23; Eze. 7:26; Zac. 6:13. As idéias envolvidas nesse termo e seus cognatos são «sessão», «assembléia», «julgar», «defensor», «conselheiro».

Os pensamentos das pessoas transparecem em suas reuniões, e isso empresta autoridade às suas palavras, de uma maneira como não se verifica quando alguém fala isoladamente. No entanto, também há conselhos ímpios, negativos, e também aqueles conselhos que são desobedecidos e ignorados (Sal. 33:10,11; II Sam. 15:34; Isa. 49:19; 19:3).

O Messias como Conselheiro. Isaías previu a vinda do grande Conselheiro (Isa. 9:6; 11:2). O conselho da paz seria estabelecido entre o Messias vindouro e o sumo sacerdócio (Zac. 6:13). Um conselheiro sugeria soluções sábias sobre qualquer questão, sendo esse um conceito geral do Antigo Testamento (Pro. 11:14; II Crô. 25:16; II Sam. 15:12; Eze. 7:28). Porém, o Messias é o maior de todos os conselheiros, cujos conselhos exerceriam um impacto universal.

No Novo Testamento, entre os judeus os conselheiros usualmente eram membros do Sinédrio (que vide) segundo se vê em Mar. 15:43 e Luc. 23:50. José de Arimatéia foi chamado de *bouleutēs*, isto é, membro do concílio, e era um conselheiro. O conselho de Deus é imutável, pois exprime o seu propósito eterno (Heb. 6:17). O julgamento de Deus, quanto à validade ou não de nossas ações, é mais importante do que a nossa própria consciência (I Cor. 4:4). Nenhuma determinação humana pode ser ocultada de Deus; e os juízos divinos ultrapassam e frustram todas as racionalizações humanas (Rom. 11:33).

CONSELHO PLENÁRIO

Dentro do vocabulário da Igreja Católica Romana, um conselho plenário é um concílio de bispos e arcebispos de uma região, com um representante papal que atua como presidente. Sua jurisdição alcança somente questões de disciplina e de governo eclesiástico de uma determinada região.

CONSELHOS EVANGÉLICOS

Essa expressão indica os principais mandamentos e requisitos da vida cristã, conforme estão contidos na fé evangélica. O evangelho de Cristo não deixa de ter os seus requisitos. A doutrina do fácil creísmo (que vide) tem distorcido a mensagem do evangelho. O fácil creísmo dá ênfase demasiada à correção do credo, às expensas do ensino neotestamentário sobre a santificação, as boas obras e a vida segundo os ditames da lei do amor. O evangelho cristão é uma força transformadora do caráter, e não uma lista de doutrinas que devem ser cridas (Rom. 8:29). Os seus preceitos morais, mormente a lei do amor, recebem impulso da parte do ministério do Espírito Santo, através de cujo ministério a transformação moral deve ocorrer. Visto que a participação na natureza divina é o alvo mesmo da vida cristã (Col. 2:10; II Ped. 1:4), podemos estar certos de que há uma imensa transformação da alma a ser conseguida. E, visto que há uma infinitude que nos deverá encher, também deve haver um enchimento infinito (Efé. 1:23; II Cor. 3:18). O Novo Testamento tem um sistema de *amor conhecimento*. O nome grego para isso é *gnosis*. O amor e o conhecimento são os dois grandes alicerces da espiritualidade. O amor é a virtude cardeal sobre a qual se alicerçam todas as demais virtudes, a prova mesma da espiritualidade de alguém (I João 4:8 ss). Os conselhos evangélicos, pois, exortam-nos a reconhecer esses fatos, envolvendo-nos em uma ativa vida espiritual, não meramente em uma afirmação de algum credo específico, posto por escrito no papel. É nesse ponto que podemos aprender algo do budismo, ainda que não nos queiramos tornar budistas. Consideremos o seu *Caminho de Oito Elementos* (que vide). Somente um desses elementos dá atenção à crença em doutrinas. Os demais elementos abordam a espiritualidade prática, de todos os dias. As crenças são importantes, mas a transformação da alma, mediante a atuação do Espírito de Deus, é a própria substância da nossa fé cristã.

CONSENSO COMUM, ARGUMENTOS DE

Esses são argumentos alicerçados sobre a aceitação quase universal de certas crenças. A expressão latina é *consensus gentium* (que vide), que significa «concórdia dos povos». Um argumento de consenso comum é um critério da verdade. Por exemplo: Deus deve existir, porquanto todos os povos e culturas crêem em um ser ou em seres divinos. Esse argumento não requer acordo quanto a detalhes e quanto ao caráter, mas apenas o conceito de um poder ou ser acima dos homens. Por igual modo, a alma deve existir, visto que todos os povos e culturas têm essa crença de alguma maneira. Naturalmente, também há exemplos diametralmente opostos. Somente um pequeno número de pessoas, na antiguidade, acreditava que a terra era redonda. A crença em uma terra chata, porém, não fazia a terra ser chata. Os povos antigos pensavam que o sol girava em torno da terra, e não o contrário; mas isso em nada alterou as leis que regem o universo. Apesar de que, logicamente falando, os argumentos baseados na crença comum não provam um caso qualquer, contudo aquelas crenças que persistem entre todas as culturas, não podem ser facilmente desconsideradas como meros erros. Usualmente há alguma *verdade* em tais noções.

CONSENSUS

O Consenso Comum e a Existência de Deus. Se aplicarmos esse argumento especificamente à existência de Deus, teremos as seguintes declarações específicas:

1. A crença em Deus é uma *herança comum* da humanidade. Os homens crêem porque Deus, realmente, existe. Eles crêem em face da existência de Deus, e não porque essa é uma idéia consoladora, apenas. A idéia de Deus é *inata* ao ser humano. Sendo essa a verdade, todos os homens crêem na existência de Deus, até mesmo os ateus, os quais, em seu nível consciente, afirmam que não crêem. No nível subconsciente, pois, todos os homens crêem na existência de Deus, bem como nas verdades metafísicas básicas da alma.

2. A crença do homem na existência de Deus, portanto, é *instintiva*, e não empírica, embora possamos encontrar *consubstanciação* para essa crença nas coisas que observamos na natureza e em nós mesmos. Mediante o raciocínio filosófico, podemos tanto consubstanciar quanto descrever essa crença inerente.

3. No ser humano há um *anelo inerente* por Deus. Todos os homens buscam a Deus a seu modo, embora essa busca seja inepta e incompleta. Paulo pressupõe essa crença como verdadeira, nos capítulos primeiro e segundo da epístola aos Romanos, embora não se mostre bem impressionado com o resultado final dessa inquirição natural. Para que essa inquirição produza os resultados almejados, torna-se mister a missão de Cristo e do Espírito.

4. As instituições de ensino encorajam o *ceticismo*. Os homens, naturalmente, crêem na existência de Deus, mas as escolas e as suas filosofias ensinam-nos a duvidar. Chega mesmo a ser um sinal de intelectualidade quando um estudante afirma: «Sou ateu». Os cientistas são culpados da promoção dessa falácia e ilusão. Apesar de que o *ateísmo prático*, dentro da ciência, é útil, o ateísmo teórico é destrutivo. O ateísmo prático consiste na recusa de explicar fenômenos físicos misteriosos dizendo-se que *Deus assim fez*. Uma declaração desse tipo impede os cientistas de buscarem soluções para problemas que a ciência é capaz de resolver, sem ter de apelar para a teologia. Mas o ateísmo teórico, que nega o conceito de Deus, é destrutivo porque deixa o homem apenas com um universo mecânico. Os homens, por disposição inata, voltam-se contra esse conceito.

5. O problema da *malignidade*. A Bíblia ensina que existem forças satânicas que afetam as mentes dos homens. Os incrédulos, em certo sentido, são anormais. Eles ficaram sujeitos às forças negativas que lhes furtam até mesmo da crença básica correta. Eles chegam a negar a si mesmos, porquanto o homem é um espírito, ao passo que o corpo físico é apenas o seu veículo de expressão. Porém, certos incrédulos fazem com que o corpo físico seja o próprio âmago da pessoa, o que é uma noção absurda. As experiências de quase morte, entretanto, mostram que os ateus, bem como aqueles que negam a realidade da alma, para a própria surpresa deles, descobrem que a morte física não põe um ponto final à existência. A.H. Strong, em sua *Systematic Theology*, vol. I, pág 46, oferece uma ilustração gráfica, ao dizer que o carvalho não deve ser julgado pelas espécimes atrofiadas que aparecem perto do círculo polar Ártico. Por semelhante modo, não podemos julgar a *natureza humana* através das perversões que têm sido introduzidas pelos céticos.

6. A *moralidade* está baseada na crença teísta. É a existência e a influência moral de Deus que nos conferem um senso moral. A maioria das pessoas deseja ver o direito imperar, embora lhes falte a força para garantir isso. Até mesmo os ateus que são indivíduos morais e altruístas (e isso existe), são tais por que contam com o testemunho teísta em seu espírito, embora, com a sua mente consciente, neguem essa realidade de modo enfático.

CONSENSUS GENTIUM

A expressão latina significa «opinião geral do povo». Esse é um dos critérios que muitos homens usam para determinação da verdade. Ver o artigo sobre *Conhecimento e a Fé Religiosa*, na porção II, *Teorias da Verdade*. Essa expressão refere-se à doutrina que supõe que quando o povo em geral, uma civilização ou todos os homens da terra, coletivamente, *concordam* sobre alguma questão, esse consenso mostra onde está a verdade. Para exemplificar, a maioria das culturas acredita na existência de Deus e na existência da alma humana. A maioria das culturas acredita no poder da lei do amor. Isso posto, essas idéias devem ser verdadeiras. A opinião unânime sobre alguma coisa qualquer, porém, é algo que jamais será conseguido; e isso quer dizer que tal argumento perde a sua validade. Por isso mesmo, esse conceito tem sido atacado por alguns filósofos, que têm investigado a questão, e têm encontrado diversas opiniões, até mesmo no tocante a questões como a existência de Deus e da alma. Mas essas doutrinas, apesar da discordância de alguns poucos, são *quase* universalmente cridas e defendidas. Cícero deixou escrito: «Aquilo sobre o que todos os homens concordam, deve ser verdadeiro» (*De Natura Deorum*, 1.16). Outros objetam a esse argumento salientando que a maioria dos homens antigos ignorava totalmente a esfericidade da terra, usualmente imaginando-a chata; e, no entanto, estavam equivocados. A maioria dos antigos também pensava que o sol gira em torno de uma terra plana; mas eles estavam redondamente enganados (sem nenhum trocadilho!) Essas razões mostram que o *consensus gentium* é um critério apenas sugestivo, mas não válido para todos os casos.

Em favor do argumento do *consensus gentium*, porém, temos as idéias do racionalismo e da intuição. O homem possui intelecto porque participa da inteligência do grande *Intelecto*, que é Deus. Além disso, à semelhança de Deus, o homem sabe de certas coisas sem investigação prévia, simplesmente por ser um ente que sabe das coisas. A intuição é capaz de dar ao homem o conhecimento de certas verdades sem que ele utilize os seus cinco sentidos, ou mesmo além do poder da razão. Portanto, certas idéias que os homens generalizam como verdadeiras, são verdadeiras, realmente, sendo generalizadas como tais.

Concluo dizendo que o critério do *consensus gentium*, apesar de fraco, reveste-se de algum valor. Mas, cada caso precisa ser julgado em separado. Nunca podemos usar esse critério de modo absoluto; e esse argumento só pode servir de fator de apoio a outro argumento, mais definitivo. (E EP RP)

CONSENSUS PATRUM

No latim, «consenso dos pais». A expressão alude ao acordo sobre questões de fé e moral, entre os pais da Igreja, que então se tornam obrigatórias para todos os cristãos. Além disso, aquilo que, em voz uníssona, eles declaram como heresia, deve ser considerado como tal por todos os cristãos. Outrossim, as conclusões lógicas que eles extraíram unanimemente das doutrinas principais, devem exprimir a verdade. No entanto, quando os pais da Igreja abordavam questões filosóficas e científicas, a autoridade deles em muito se reduzia, embora continuasse respeitada. O *consensus patrum* faz parte do conceito de autoridade (que vide), na Igreja Católica Romana. Os reformadores protestantes repeliram a autoridade dos pais da Igreja, alçando bem alto o lema: «Somente as Escrituras». A despeito de tratar-se de um nobre ideal, o lema é deficiente, pelas seguintes razões: em primeiro lugar, nunca houve uma ocasião em que não houvesse alguma *interpretação* das Escrituras. Portanto, na prática, mesmo que não na teoria, esse lema, na verdade, significa: «As Escrituras somente, conforme eu ou minha denominação particular as interpreta». Isso nos leva de volta à filosofia do *consensus patrum*, cuja regra é: as Escrituras, conforme os pais da Igreja as interpretavam. Em segundo lugar, ninguém pode afirmar, sob pena de cair em ridículo, que qualquer livro pode conter toda a verdade de Deus. Essa crença não é um ensino da própria Bíblia, mas um dogma humano que, naturalmente, não pode ser imposto à consciência livre dos homens.

Estabelecido esse ponto, devemos indagar: devemos preferir a interpretação de quem? A minha e a de minha denominação cristã, ou a dos pais da Igreja? Todavia, é mister frisar que nem mesmo uma correta resposta a essa indagação (se é que alguém pode dá-la) pode resolver o problema da *autoridade*. Minha conclusão é a seguinte: a verdade, por ser algo extremamente complexo, requer uma complexa regra de autoridade. Outrossim, é regra óbvia que ninguém pode formular um critério que jamais se modifique, porquanto a verdade é algo dinâmico, e a nossa compreensão a respeito da verdade está sempre em estado de evolução. Portanto, nossas regras sobre a questão da autoridade, se tiverem de continuar valendo alguma coisa, também devem sofrer um contínuo processo de evolução.

CONSENTIMENTO

O termo indica a concordância **voluntária**, a cooperação ou o assentimento diante de uma proposta ou de um ato. O consentimento é o contrário da *coerção* (que vide). O consentimento não subentende um completo acordo, mas anula totalmente a imposição. Todavia, não elimina os argumentos racionais, as trocas de idéias, e o consenso em torno de algum terreno comum. Assim, um crente consente com as leis, com as situações e com as forças externas, guiado pela consciência do seu homem espiritual. Por sua parte, o homem natural consente com as práticas erradas, porque tais práticas moram, latentemente, em seu coração.

Áreas Específicas Importantes. Podemos pensar em questões como o matrimônio, o divórcio, as situações de trabalho, os envolvimentos militares, todas as formas de contrato e acordo, bem como as leis do estado ou da comunidade, quando democraticamente estabelecidas. (H)

CONSEQÜÊNCIALISMO

Esse é um termo muito geral para indicar qualquer e todas as teorias morais que afirmam que um ato está certo ou errado, ou então é bom ou mau, dependendo exclusivamente dos *resultados* produzidos. Esses resultados podem envolver conseqüências imediatas ou reais de nossos atos, ou podem incluir conseqüências tencionadas de atos, pensamentos, etc., que nunca, realmente, chegam a concretizar-se. Além disso, há resultados de *classes* de atos, conseqüências a longo prazo, e não apenas resultados imediatos. Isso significa que a teoria se torna extremamente complexa. Seja como for, esse é um dos principais conceitos do *pragmatismo* (que vide) e do *utilitarismo* (que vide). Sem dúvida, aquilo que acontece é importante, mas há muitos fatores morais e espirituais que transcendem a tudo isso. Jesus interessava-se pelo que um homem pensa, e não meramente pelo que ele termina fazendo. Dizemos popularmente que o que vale são as intenções; e, em alguns casos, isso corresponde à verdade dos fatos. Mas também precisamos levar em conta a qualidade espiritual de cada indivíduo, se ela é boa ou má, qualidade essa que poderá manifestar-se ou não mediante atos externos. (F)

CONSERVAÇÃO DE VALOR

A expressão foi cunhada por Harold Hoffding (que vide), em seu livro intitulado *Philosophy of Religion*. Ele tinha em mente a teoria científica da conservação de energias e por analogia, tentou mostrar que há uma *lei ética* que corresponde àquela teoria. A teoria diz que nos sistemas éticos e religiosos há uma espécie de função inerente de preservação de valores, a despeito das alterações sofridas. O contínuo aumento do valor é uma medida que salvaguarda contra a desintegração. A fé é então definida como a contínua percepção dos valores mais altos que podem ser atingidos acima das limitações que a experiência e a história humanas tendem por nos impor. Dentro desse sistema, as fórmulas de fé variam, em consonância com a teologia dos pensadores envolvidos. Para alguns, o próprio Deus é a origem dos valores, e os conceitos humanos sobre os valores derivam-se da mente divina. Para outros, porém, Deus é o sistema impessoal e objetivo de valores. Os nomes associados a essa teoria, além do próprio Hoffding, são W.R. Sorley (que vide) e E.S. Brightman (que vide).

CONSERVANTISMO ÉTICO

O termo indica a crença que os padrões éticos de conduta precisam ser lentamente modificados, se é que devem ser modificados, de tal modo que possam ser preservados os valores estabelecidos. Podemos encarar essa doutrina como negativa ou positiva, dependendo das circunstâncias e das perspectivas históricas. A Igreja primitiva, ao recusar-se a cooperar com os padrões da sociedade romana, cuja moral era lassa e pagã, poderia ser tachada de inovadora, ou seja, contrária ao conservantismo ético. Porém, no seio da própria Igreja cristã há um conservantismo ético que é defendido tenazmente, pois ali as inovações são consideradas prejudiciais ao cristianismo. Essa atitude alicerça-se principalmente sobre os ensinamentos bíblicos, que são considerados bons para qualquer época. Naturalmente, as interpretações dão margem a modificações, de tal modo que as pessoas chamadas cristãs, na realidade podem ser inovadoras. Ver o artigo geral sobre a *Ética*. O conservantismo ético harmoniza-se melhor com a *ética formal*, também conhecida como *ética absoluta*, a qual parte do pressuposto de que os valores éticos não são apenas humanos e são constantes e perfeitos, não estando sujeitos a modificações devidas às vicissitudes da experiência humana. Ver o artigo sobre o *Liberalismo Ético*. (H)

••• ••• •••

CONSISTÓRIO

O termo tem sentido genérico, indicando uma assembléia de oficiais eclesiásticos, que se reúnem a negócios. Dentro do uso da Igreja Católica Romana, indica uma reunião de cardeais, sob a presidência do papa. Ali, os consistórios podem ser públicos, semipúblicos ou particulares. Nas igrejas reformadas, um consistório geralmente compõe-se de um pastor e da junta de anciãos e diáconos. Esses têm autoridade sobre uma congregação. Tal grupo também pode ser chamado de *sessão* (que vide). No luteranismo, o consistório compõe-se de um corpo administrativo de clérigos e leigos. Nos primeiros anos do luteranismo, as autoridades civis tinham o direito de fazer nomeações; mas, no luteranismo posterior, isso foi descontinuado. Na Igreja Anglicana, permanecem os tribunais consistoriais das dioceses, o que se deriva da prática medieval, quando os bispos administravam suas dioceses mediante um tribunal consistorial.

Origem do Termo. Esse vocábulo originalmente referia-se à antecâmara dos palácios imperiais, onde o imperador se sentava para dispensar justiça, e onde era ajudado por assessores chamados *consistentes*.

CONSOLAÇÃO Ver Consolo, Consolação.

CONSOLADOR

No sentido geral, qualquer pessoa que age como tal. A palavra grega, *parákletos*, também pode significar advogado e exortador. Ver o artigo sobre *Consolo*.

Em um sentido especial, esse é um dos títulos do Espírito Santo. Ver o artigo geral sobre esse assunto, e também sobre o *Paracleto*.

CONSOLAMENTUM

A palavra refere-se a um rito purificador associado ao batismo em água, administrado pelos cátaros, um grupo cristão dissidente, anterior à Reforma protestante. O intuito era liberar a alma do crente dos poderes da carne, visando ao seu bem espiritual, com o perdão de seus pecados. Esse rito era efetuado mediante a imposição de mãos, por alguém que já havia recebido os supostos benefícios da cerimônia. Além disso, uma cópia do evangelho de João era posta sobre a cabeça da pessoa beneficiada. A *consolação* era usada em conexão com a ordenação de ministros, dentro do sistema da *sucessão apostólica* (que vide). Ver sobre os *Cátaros*.

CONSOLO, CONSOLAÇÃO

O consolo consiste nestes pontos:
1. Alívio em face da tristeza, com desafogo em face do desapontamento e da consternação. Na literatura ascética e devocional, o termo é usado para denotar a felicidade que se segue a períodos de depressão espiritual ou de aridez nas orações. 2. O termo também é empregado para denotar a refeição vespertina dos monges, após a refeição diária normal. Geralmente era tomada altas horas da noite. Essa refeição extra era uma espécie de compensação pelas tensões dos tempos de oração e trabalho diligentes. Alimentos mais substanciais e ricos geralmente eram oferecidos na ocasião. 3. Quanto aos usos bíblicos, ver a continuação deste artigo.

No hebraico temos três palavras, e no grego, uma:
1. *Tanchumim*, «consolos». Palavra hebraica usada por três vezes: Sal. 94:19; Isa. 66:11; e Jer. 16:7.

2. *Tanchumoth*, «consolos». Palavra hebraica usada por duas vezes: Jó 15:11 e 21:2.

3. *Nacham*, «consolo». Palavra hebraica usada por cento e três vezes (para exemplificar: Gên. 5:29; 37:35; Rute 2:13; II Sam. 10:2,3; I Crô. 7:22; Jó 2:2,11; 7:13; Sal. 23:4; Isa. 12:1; 22:4; 40:1; Jer. 16:7; Lam. 1:2,17,21; Eze. 14:23; Zac. 1:17; 10:2).

4. *Paráklesis*, «consolação». Palavra grega usada por vinte e nove vezes: Luc. 2:25; 6:24; Atos 4:36; 9:31; 13:15; 15:31; Rom. 12:8; 15:4,5; I Cor. 14:3; II Cor. 1:3-7; 7:4,7,13; 8:4,17; Fil. 2:1; I Tes. 2:3; II Tes. 2:16; I Tim. 4:13; File. 7; Heb. 6:18; 12:5; 13:22.

O nome do profeta de Israel, Neemias, vem de uma raiz hebraica que significa «consolo» (ver o número 3, acima). O vocábulo grego é usado como um dos nomes do Espírito Santo, o *Paracleto* (que vide). Essas palavras são largamente usadas para indicar todas as formas de consolo, em que a tristeza se transmuta em júbilo. Ver Isa. 40:1; 49:13; 51:3. As palavras hebraicas também podem indicar o refrigério físico ou mental (Gên. 18:5; Juí. 19:5,8). Porém, é a Palavra de Deus que, acima de tudo, aparece como o grande consolo dos crentes (Sal. 119:50). Inerente ao uso há a idéia de mudança da tristeza para a alegria. A presença de Alguém que cuida de nós e que conosco simpatiza, transparece com freqüência. Isso sucede até mesmo quando a alguém faltam as palavras próprias para consolar a outrem. De alguma maneira, a tristeza compartilhada chega a consolar, mesmo quando pensamos que isso é impossível.

No Novo Testamento, — há muitas aplicações da palavra grega e da idéia de consolo. O trecho de Mateus 5:4 promete consolo àqueles que choram. Os três membros da Trindade (que vide) envolvem-se na obra da consolação (II Cor. 1:5,6; Fil. 2:1; Atos 9:31). Jesus compartilha de nossas tristezas e é o nosso Consolador (Luc. 7:13; Heb. 2:18). O Espírito Santo, o *Alter ego* de Cristo, e perpetuador de sua missão, também é chamado de Consolador (João 14:16). Essa palavra pode significar «advogado»; e, nesse sentido, é aplicada a Jesus Cristo, em I João 2:1. O estado futuro dos remidos é descrito como um estado de consolação, para aqueles que pouco tiveram na vida terrena (Luc. 16:22). A segunda epístola aos Coríntios tem sido chamada de «epístola do consolo», porquanto contém a palavra grega *parákletos* por dez vezes. Ver II Cor. 1:3-7; 7:4,7,13; 8:4,17. No Novo Testamento, a forma nominal, *paráklesis*, é usada por vinte e nove vezes; a forma verbal, por cento e oito vezes; a forma pessoal, PARÁKLETOS, por cinco vezes, a saber, em João 14:16,26; 15:26; 16:7; I João 2:1.

Métodos de Consolo. Pode-se consolar a outrem de várias maneiras: compartilhando de sua tristeza; oferecendo simpatia; procurando modificar as condições entristecedoras; conferindo a outrem o conhecimento da salvação, que cura a tristeza da alma; oferecendo encorajamento; edificando e inspirando. E, no tocante à tristeza causada pelas privações físicas, aliviando as necessidades materiais, segundo se vê em Col. 4:11 e I Tes. 2:11.

Barnabé significa, em hebraico, «filho da consolação» (ver Atos 4:36). Ele era alguém que aconselhava de modo correto, visando ao benefício espiritual dos aconselhados. A epístola aos Hebreus é caracterizada como «palavra de exortação», refletindo a atitude demonstrada por Barnabé. A prontidão para dar apoio a quem se acha atribulado deveria ser uma das principais virtudes cristãs, no conceito dos crentes (I Tes. 2:11; Rom. 1:12; Col. 4:11). O consolo é uma dentre as várias obras de amor, comprovação e prova da espiritualidade (I João 4:7 ss). (A B)

Ary Scheffer.   Cristo, o Consolador

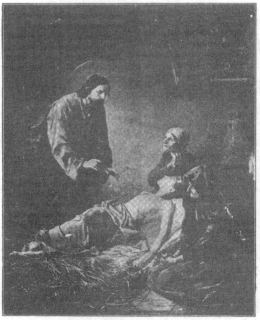

Zimmerman.   O Grande Médico

Palavras de Consolação

•••

Vinde a mim, todos os que
estais cansados e oprimidos, e
eu vos aliviarei.
 (Mat. 11:28)

Não se turbe o vosso coração;
Credes em Deus, crede
também em mim.
 (João 14:1)

...quando vier o Consolador, que eu
da parte do Pai vos hei
de enviar, aquele Espírito de
verdade, que procede do Pai,
ele testificará de mim.
 (João 15:26)

...O Espírito e a esposa dizem: Vem.
E quem ouve, diga: Vem.
E quem tem sede, venha;
e quem quiser, tome de
graça da água da vida.
 (Apo. 22:17)

••• ••• •••

CONSTÂNCIA — CONSTANTINOPLA

CONSTÂNCIA Ver **Perseverança**.

CONSTÂNCIA, CONCÍLIO DE

Ver o artigo geral sobre os **Concílios Ecumênicos**. O concílio de Constança, na Suíça, foi efetuado entre 1414 e 1418. Asseverou que a autoridade dos concílios eclesiásticos deriva-se de Cristo, e que até o papado precisa sujeitar-se a essa autoridade. Teve o intuito de pôr fim ao escândalo da existência, na época, de três papas simultâneos. Esses três papas foram: João XXIII (Pisa), Gregório XII (Roma) e Benedito XIII (Avignon). O concílio de Constança conseguiu pôr fim ao grande cisma (que vide). Outras coisas decididas durante esse concílio foram a exigência para serem feitas reformas capazes de impedir os abusos clericais, e a condenação das «heresias», como o hussismo e o wycliffismo.

Em julho de 1417, os três papas simultâneos haviam sido retirados; e, a 11 de novembro daquele mesmo ano, foi eleito o cardeal Otto Colonna como papa, — que pontificou com o título de Martinho V. João Huss foi levado a tribunal, foi condenado e executado, em 1415. Jerônimo de Praga também foi executado, e os supostos erros de Wycliffe foram anatematizados.

Também foram tomadas medidas para impedir outro cisma, incluindo a provisão de que os concílios poderiam reunir-se sem a necessidade de serem convocados sob circunstâncias extremas. Martinho V, o papa da conciliação, aceitou os decretos daquele concílio para salvaguardar a inviolabilidade do ofício papal, juntamente com a idéia de sua supremacia.

CONSTÂNCIA NA NATUREZA

Ver **Uniformidade na Natureza**.

CONSTANTINO, O GRANDE

Imperador romano cujas datas foram 280 e 337 D.C. Era filho de Constâncio Cloro. Foi, sucessivamente, César e Augusto da Gália, um soldado competente, e, acima de tudo, um governante construtivo. Sua mãe foi Helena. De 292 a 305 D.C., ele residiu na corte de Diocleciano, presumivelmente a fim de educar-se; na realidade, porém, ele era mantido ali a fim de que suas atividades fossem circunscritas. Após a abdicação de Diocleciano, Constantino fugiu da corte imperial para juntar-se ao seu pai, que se tornara Augusto. Quando seu pai faleceu, no ano seguinte (306 D.C.), Constantino foi designado Augusto, mediante o testamento de seu pai e o poder do exército, que se manifestou favorável a ele. Na Gália, os cristãos simpatizavam com ele, devido ao tratamento racional que lhes conferia. Seu poder aumentou em face da vitória militar que obteve sobre Maxêncio, na batalha da ponte Mílvia, por motivo da qual obteve total autoridade em Roma. A caminho da batalha, ele teria recebido uma visão da cruz com as palavras por cima da mesma: *In hoc signo vinces* («Com este sinal vencerás»). No ano de 313 D.C., com a ajuda de Licínio, ele expediu o célebre *Edito de Tolerância*, por meio do qual a cristandade obteve o favor imperial, com a conseqüente cessação das perseguições.

Constantino agora controlava a Gália e a Itália. Terminou declarando guerra a Licínio, em parte porque este continuava perseguindo aos cristãos. E a vitória de Constantino garantiu a total aplicação daquele decreto imperial. Em 325 D.C., Constantino convocou e participou do concílio de Nicéia (que vide). Em 326 D.C., em face de acusações feitas por sua esposa, Fausta, Constantino ordenou a execução de seu filho, Crispus; e, não muito depois, ordenou também a execução de sua esposa. Em 330 D.C., o monarca inaugurou a cidade de Constantinopla, no local da antiga Bizâncio. Depois transferiu a capital do império romano para aquela cidade. Os últimos anos de governo de Constantino foram passados em meio a conflitos armados, de mistura com atividades eclesiásticas. Foi batizado no leito de morte.

Constantino foi homem de muitas contradições, um pagão a quem o evangelho influenciou de alguma maneira. Até que ponto, é questão muito debatida. No entanto, ele estava destinado a alterar o curso da história da Igreja, a qual passou do período de perseguições imperiais para o período de favor imperial, com profundas modificações na esfera do governo eclesiástico. Disso surgiram o papado e a Igreja Católica Romana, e a civilização ocidental ficou sujeita à custódia da Igreja, e não mais à custódia do Estado, pelo espaço de mil anos, ou seja, durante toda a Idade Média. (AM E P)

CONSTANTINOPLA, CONCÍLIOS DE

1. *Concílio de* 381 D.C. Ver o artigo geral sobre os *Concílios Ecumênicos*. Esse concílio foi convocado pelo imperador romano Teodósio, tendo sido o segundo concílio geral da Igreja, e o primeiro dos três que foram efetuados em Constantinopla. Sua importância histórica jaz no fato de que pôs fim à controvérsia ariana (ver sobre o *Arianismo*). O arianismo foi condenado e o concílio endossou a fórmula do HOMOOUSIOS, que afirma que o Filho é da mesma substância do Pai. Essa fórmula foi o resultado principal do primeiro concílio geral de Nicéia (que vide). Em Constantinopla, foi melhor definida a doutrina do Espírito Santo. Foi declarado que o Espírito Santo procede *do Pai*. Na época de Carlos Magno, foi feita uma adição, com a palavra latina «filioque», que significa «e do Filho». Portanto, segundo a teologia ocidental, o Espírito Santo procede tanto do Pai quanto do Filho. Mas a Igreja Oriental rejeitou a adição do «filioque», o que provocou a grande divisão em Igreja Católica Romana e Igreja Ortodoxa Oriental. Naturalmente, essa não foi a única razão da divisão, mas foi a gota de água que entornou o balde. A razão verdadeira, porém, eram as reivindicações de superioridade e supremacia do papa de Roma, sobre todos os bispos da cristandade. Esse tem sido o grande obstáculo à conciliação entre essas duas facções da antiga Igreja Católica, iniciada pelo ato protetor de Constantino, em 313 D.C. Ver sobre *Constantino, o Grande* e sobre o *Edito de Tolerância*.

Esse concílio também determinou que o bispo de Constantinopla só perdia em honra e autoridade ao bispo de Roma, porquanto Constantinopla, por assim dizer, tornara-se a Nova Roma. Constantino, o Grande (vide), fez de Constantinopla a nova capital do império romano, em 330 D.C. Isso significa que Constantinopla ultrapassara a Alexandria em importância, um significativo acontecimento histórico.

2. *Concílio de* 553 D.C. O concílio de Constantinopla, realizado nesse ano, foi convocado pelo imperador Justiniano (527-565 D.C.), tendo sido assistido principalmente por eclesiásticos do Oriente. O imperador dirigiu as negociações, tendo conseguido declarações contra Teodoro de Mopsuéstia, contra Teodoreto de Chipre e contra o bispo Ibas, de Edessa (ver os artigos a respeito, que esclarecem as questões envolvidas). Isso foi interpretado como uma censura às provisões do concílio de Calcedônia (que vide). O papa Vigílio, que vinha sendo um virtual prisioneiro em Constantinopla, desde 547 D.C., objetou. Mas, finalmente, cedeu em 554 D.C.

3. *Concílio de* 680 D.C. O concílio que houve em Constantinopla, nesse ano, foi convocado pelo imperador Constantino IV Pogonato (668-685 D.C.). Seu propósito principal foi tratar da doutrina apelidada *monotelismo*. Essa teoria afirma que apesar de Cristo ter possuído duas naturezas - a divina e a humana — em uma única pessoa, contudo, era governado por *uma única vontade*, que dirigia ambas as Suas naturezas. Essa teoria da vontade única chegava bem perto de endossar o *monofisistismo* (que vide), o qual ensina que em Cristo há uma só natureza, a divina, visto que o Logos, encarnando-se em Jesus, transformou a carne em substância divina. Os jacobitas sírios, os coptas, os abissínios e os armênios eram monofisistas. O papa Honório, de Roma, também adotara o *monotelismo*. Mas o concílio de Constantinopla, de 680 D.C., rejeitou a teoria da vontade única e anatematizou o papa Honório. Em seguida, o concílio definiu a sua cristologia (que vide) afirmando que, em Jesus Cristo, havia duas naturezas e duas vontades, mas uma única pessoa.

Os concílios de Constantinopla foram, respectivamente, o segundo, o quinto e o sexto concílios ecumênicos. Nem o quinto e nem o sexto desses concílios decretaram quais cânones, pelo que um concílio suplementar foi efetuado em Constantinopla, em 691 D.C., que corrigiu a omissão. (E P)

CONSTELAÇÕES
Ver **Pléiades (E Outras Constelações)**

CONSTITUCIONALISMO
A idéia básica dessa palavra é que a ordem e a justiça podem ser melhor mantidas, dentro da comunidade política, mediante o império da lei. Os governos humanos tendem por ser despóticos (e demoníacos, segundo alguns pensam), e o império da lei tem a intuito de impedir os abusos de tais sistemas. Supõe-se que há um conjunto de leis que a consciência humana aprova, e que é popularmente aceito. Esse conjunto de leis, na opinião de alguns, foi divinamente conferido, estando refletido na Bíblia. Outros, porém, pensam que todos os homens podem discernir essas leis através da razão, ou das evidências da experiência humana. Entretanto, sem importar sua origem, tanto os governantes quanto os governados devem viver de acordo com esse código. Vários modelos de constitucionalismo têm influenciado as constituições dos tempos modernos, como os modelos de Platão, de Aristóteles, de Cícero e naturalmente, as leis do Antigo e do Novo Testamentos. Nos tempos modernos, as constituições começaram a aparecer no século XVI, nos estados europeus. E, através das mesmas, às minorias religiosas foram conferidos certos direitos. E outros segmentos da sociedade foram igualmente beneficiados. A Revolução Puritana, no século XVII, na Inglaterra, expandiu as demandas por maiores direitos, no caso de muitas pessoas. Isso culminou na revolução de 1688 e na Carta de Direitos, de 1689, na Inglaterra. O constitucionalismo abarcou tanto a Grã-Bretanha quanto os Estados Unidos da América, e muitos outros países aceitaram também a idéia. Essa doutrina requer a existência de constituições escritas, que limitem os poderes do governo e salvaguardem os direitos dos cidadãos individuais. Também contém provisões relativas a alterações, quando elas se fizerem necessárias. As constituições escritas impedem o aparecimento de atos governamentais arbitrários, que prejudiquem o bem-estar individual e coletivo. Muitas igrejas e instituições de ensino têm adotado esse princípio constitucionalista. (H)

CONSTITUIÇÕES E CÂNONES APOSTÓLICOS
As constituições apostólicas, das quais os Cânones são a seção final, formam um corpo de leis eclesiásticas, provavelmente do século IV D.C., embora seja chamado tradicionalmente de «apostólico». Presumivelmente são de autoria apostólica, coligidas por Clemente, mas nenhum erudito considera que isso corresponde aos fatos.

O concílio de Trullan (692) aceitou os cânones como autoritários, posto que não as *constituições*, porquanto haviam sofrido muitas interpolações não ortodoxas, muitas das quais poderiam ser dévidas a um compilador do quarto século, pertencente à igreja de Antioquia ou do norte da Síria. Aparecem afirmativas de tendências arianas, talvez pertencente ao período anteniceno (antes de 325 D.C.), quando a precisão teológica não era essencial.

Títulos e conteúdo. Por meio dos títulos, obtemos boa idéia do conteúdo geral da compilação: 1. Maneiras e hábitos dos leigos; 2. episcopado e adoração; 3. viúvas, o clero e batismo; 4. ajuda aos pobres e virgindade; 5. martírio; 6. cismáticos. Então, no sétimo livro: Caps. 1:32, baseados no Didache (ver o artigo); caps. 33-49, descrição de práticas litúrgicas. Oitavo livro: Caps. 1-2, dons espirituais; caps. 3-27, liturgia antioqueana de João Crisóstomo; caps. 28-46, cânones; cap. 47, aparentemente uma adição posterior, com 85 cânones apostólicos. Os primeiros cinqüenta desses cânones foram reconhecidos como autoritários pela Igreja ocidental. Esses cânones abordam questões como ordenação, responsabilidades e conduta moral do clero. Os cânones têm exercido um considerável poder na história da Igreja, embora não sejam reconhecidos como apostólicos. (B BA E DA S Z)

CONSTITUIÇÕES PAPAIS
Há importantes leis ou concessões papais, usadas em declarações dogmáticas e disciplinadoras. Desde o ano de 1911, as *Constituições* têm sido usadas para formar ou dividir dioceses. As Constituições podem ter a forma das antigas bulas (que vide).

••• ••• •••

CONSTRUIR, CONSTRUÇÃO
No hebraico, **banah** ou **benah**, palavra que figura por cerca de quatrocentas vezes, desde Gên. 4:17 até Mal. 1:4. No grego, *oikodoméo*, «construir uma casa», palavra que figura por quarenta vezes, desde Mat. 7:24 até I Ped. 2:7. *Oikodomé*, «construção», aparece por dezoito vezes, de Mat. 24:1 a Efé. 4:29.

Uso Literal. Esse inclui o uso de vários materiais para construir edificações ou objetos, empregando um labor habilitado (II Crô. 34:11). No caso de edificações de grande porte, o trabalho era feito sob a supervisão de um «construtor» (I Cor. 3:10). O local da construção era escolhido pelo edificador (ver Gên. 4:17, que se refere à cidade de Enoque, construída por Caim). O povo de Israel foi forçado a edificar cidades-armazéns, como Ramsés e Píton. Os gaditas reedificaram Dibom (Núm. 32:34); os rubenitas, Hesbom (Núm. 32:37). Altares foram levantados em muitos lugares (Êxo. 17:15; 32:5; Deu. 27:5). Davi construiu muito em Jerusalém (II Sam. 5:9). Salomão reconstruiu e ampliou as cidades de Milo, Hazor, Megido e Gezer, com portões e muralhas. Ele edificou Tadmor (Palmira) (II Crô. 8:4), como um posto avançado comercial. Porém, a maior obra arquitetural de Israel foi o templo de Jerusalém (que vide), erigido por Salomão, para comemorar o nome remidor de Yahweh (I Reis 6:1 ss). Nos dias de Israel e Judá, muitos palácios foram erigidos (I Reis 12:25; II Crô. 26:19; I Reis 16:23,32).

Após o exílio babilônico, Jerusalém e suas muralhas foram reconstruídas, conforme se lê nos livros de Neemias e Esdras. Durante o período intertestamentário, a Jerusalém dos hasmoneanos foi ampliada. Então foi efetuada a principal construção de Jerusalém, o templo de Herodes, em substituição ao templo de Esdras.

No antigo Israel, idéias e materiais eram importados de outros povos, sobretudo dos fenícios (Tiro) (II Sam. 5:11; I Reis 5:1 ss), o que significa que o templo de Jerusalém foi um projeto essencialmente dos fenícios. Israel nunca desenvolveu um estilo arquitetural distintivamente judaico. Os principais edificadores da história do antigo Israel foram Davi, Salomão, Uzias e Jotão. As construções feitas por Herodes seguiam o estilo romano.

Usos Metafóricos. a. Deus é o edificador de todas as coisas (Heb. 3:4, 11:10) incluindo seu grande ato de criação (Gén. 1:1), seu planejamento e sua energia, que traz à existência e empresta propósito a todas as coisas (I Cor. 8:6). b. O Filho de Deus está envolvido diretamente em cada um dos aspectos de tal criação e planejamento (João 1:1; Col. 1:16). c. Deus é o edificador de famílias, cidades e nações prósperas (I Crô. 17:10; Sal. 69:35; Jer. 18:9). d. Deus edifica o trono de Davi, tanto na nação de Israel como dentro da promessa messiânica, com alcance mundial e cósmico (Sal. 89:4). e. Deus edifica as muralhas de Jerusalém, fazendo a nação de Israel prosperar como um grande veículo espiritual (Sal. 51:18). f. A Igreja é edificada por Cristo, sobre ele mesmo, como pedra angular, e sobre os apóstolos e profetas como fundamentos (Col. 2:7; Efé. 2:21,22). Cristo é o alicerce da Igreja (I Cor. 3:11). g. Os santos são edificados em sua santíssima fé, o que os leva a prosperar espiritualmente (Judas 20). h. Os crentes são comparados a uma edificação que está sendo construída como uma entidade espiritual (I Ped. 2:4-6). i. O crescimento na graça é um processo de edificação espiritual (Col. 2:7), o que indica que se trata de um desenvolvimento gradual, passo a passo (ver Heb. 5:11-6:3). (ID S Z)

CONSUBSTANCIAÇÃO

Vem do latim, **con**, «com», e **substantia**, «substância». Indica a doutrina promovida por Lutero, como substituta da doutrina católica romana da *transubstanciação* (que vide), a qual declara que, na *eucaristia* (que vide), o corpo e o sangue de Cristo encontram-se em uma «presença real substancial» no pão e no vinho, embora a substância desses elementos não seja em nada transformada na substância do corpo e do sangue de Cristo. Tal doutrina requer a idéia monstruosa da onipresença do corpo e do sangue de Cristo. Tal doutrina tem sido rejeitada pela maioria dos luteranos. Ver o artigo sobre *Jesus, o Pão da Vida*, quanto a explicações místicas sobre a questão. (B C P)

CÔNSUL

Título igual à palavra latina que significa «deliberar», «considerar», «consultar». No latim, *consularis* é a forma adjetivada, com o sentido de relacionado a uma consulta. *Consulatus* refere-se ao ofício do cônsul, de onde vem a moderna palavra portuguesa *consulado*. O termo grego correspondente é *úpatos*, «supremo» (em seu ofício). Esse título indica os dois principais magistrados da república romana. Eles pertenciam à classe senatorial, servindo por um ano na cidade de Roma. Em conseqüência, recebiam postos administrativos nas províncias, quando eram então intitulados *procônsules*. Esse ofício teve prosseguimento durante o período imperial romano, embora tivesse sido alterado o seu caráter, passando a confinar-se a funções judiciais, à presidência do senado e à administração dos jogos públicos. Com freqüência, os imperadores nomeavam a si mesmos, ou a membros de suas famílias, a esse ofício. A idade avançada não era considerada um empecilho, e nem a pouca idade. Assim, Honório foi feito cônsul ao nascer. O ofício sobreviveu na porção ocidental do império romano até o século VI D.C.

Menções a esse ofício aparecem em I Macabeus 15:16, ao referir-se à comunicação feita pelo cônsul romano, Lúcio, provavelmente Lúcio Culpúrnio Piso, ao rei Ptolomeu. Declarava a amizade do senado romano e do povo judeu. A Septuaginta usa o termo para referir-se a um sátrapa, em Dan. 3:2,6,7. Tal palavra nunca aparece no Novo Testamento. (Z)

CONSULTAR

Vem do latim **consulere**, «aconselhar-se». Em I Reis temos o termo hebraico equivalente, onde se lê que os homens se aconselharam mutuamente. Também havia a idéia de consultar a deidade, com o propósito de determinar as ações futuras e os acontecimentos futuros. De algumas vezes, os meios usados nessa consulta são especificados; de outras vezes, não. Ver Jos. 9:14; I Sam. 14:37; 23:2. Algumas vezes, um profeta era usado para ser feita essa consulta (Jer. 38:14,27). Ou então o sumo sacerdote usava o urim e o tumim (Núm. 27:21; Esd. 2:63). Certas formas de consulta eram proibidas, como aquelas dirigidas aos espíritos ou aos ídolos (Dan. 18:11; Isa. 8:19 ss). Os pagãos costumavam fazer esse tipo de consulta (Isa. 19:3; Eze. 21:21). Também há o famoso caso de Saul (I Sam. 28:3 ss). A oração é uma forma do crente consultar a vontade do Senhor. Uma vida piedosa é um dos meios do crente consultar eficazmente a Deus. A maior parte das coisas que as pessoas buscam tem base no egoísmo. Porém, a consulta a Deus deveria ser um dos meios da promoção espiritual. As orações de Paulo buscam a iluminação e o desenvolvimento espirituais. Ver Efé. 1:17 ss.

CONSUMO CONSPÍCUO

Ver o artigo sobre **Veblen**, primeiro ponto. Ver o artigo geral sobre o *Capitalismo*.

CONTAMINAR

Mais de uma dúzia de palavras hebraicas e gregas são traduzidas por «contaminar», «contaminação» ou sinônimos: *goel*, «polução»; *chalal*, «poluir»; *chanep*, «profanar»; *tame*, «tornar imundo»; *tanaph*, «contaminar»; *alal*, «rolar»; *anah*, «humilhar». Dentre essas palavras hebraicas, a mais comumente usada é *tame*, que figura por cerca de duzentas e cinqüenta vezes, como verbo, substantivo ou adjetivo (por exemplo: Gên. 34:5,13,27; Lev. 11:44; 15:31; 20:3; Núm. 5:3; 6:9; 19:13; 35:34; II Reis 23:8,10,13; Sal. 79:1; Isa. 30:22; Jer. 2:7; 32:34; Eze. 5:11; 9:7; 18:6; 43:7,8). As palavras gregas são as seguintes: 1. *Koinóo*, «tornar comum» (usada por catorze vezes: Mat. 15:1,18,20; Mar. 7:15,18,20,23; Atos 10:15; 11:9; 21:28; Heb. 9:13). 2. *Miaíno*, «tingir», «contaminar» (usada por cinco vezes: João 18:28; Tito 1:15; Heb. 12:15; Jud. 8). 3. *Molúno*, «contaminar», «tornar imundo» (usada por três vezes: I Cor. 8:7; Apo. 3:4; 14:4). 4. *Spilóo*, «manchar», «contaminar» (usada por duas vezes: Tia 3:6; Jud. 23). 5. *Phtheíro*, «corromper», «depravar» (usada por oito vezes: I Cor.,

CONTAR — CONTEMPLAÇÃO

3:17; 15:33; II Cor. 7:2; 11:3; Efé. 4:22; II Ped. 2:12; Jud. 10; Apo. 19:2).

Contaminação entre os Judeus. 1. Contaminação física (Can. 5:3). 2. Contaminação sexual, por relações ilícitas (Lev. 18:20), ou por relações com uma mulher durante o seu período menstrual (Lev. 15:24; I Sam. 21:5). 3. Contaminação moral ou ética (Isa. 59:3; Eze. 37:23). 4. Contaminação cerimonial. Ver o artigo geral sobre *Limpo e Imundo*. A imundícia cerimonial desqualificava a pessoa, não podendo participar do culto (Lev. 11:24; 15:19; 22:6). 5. Contaminação religiosa. Esse tipo de contaminação estava envolvido com a contaminação cerimonial, mas também envolvia o coração ou espírito, porquanto é possível alguém participar de uma reunião de culto com precisão cerimonial, mas ter um espírito corrompido (Núm. 25:33; Jer. 3:1; Mal. 1:7,12). Os líderes religiosos da época de Jesus tinham feito das contaminações cerimoniais um item muito importante, alistando inúmeras coisas, o que tornava a questão uma carga insuportável (Mar. 7:2; João 18:28), esquecendo-se assim do espírito real da lei. O ensino de Jesus sobre a contaminação sempre envolve a imundícia espiritual (Mat. 15:18; Mar. 7:19; Heb. 12:15). A exaustiva lista dos vícios, no primeiro capítulo da epístola aos Romanos, mostra-nos que os apóstolos estavam interessados em combater a contaminação moral. Ver o artigo sobre os *Vícios*, quanto a uma discussão completa a esse respeito.

CONTAR, CONTO

No hebraico encontramos quatro palavras, cada uma das quais empregada apenas por uma vez:

1. *Hegeh*, «meditação», «declaração». Aparece em Sal. 90:9.
2. *Mispar*, «narração». Aparece em I Crô. 9:28.
3. *Mathkoneth*, «medida». Aparece em Êxo. 5:8.
4. *Token*, «peso», «medida». Aparece em Êxo. 5:18.

No grego encontramos a palavra *lēros*, que figura apenas em Luc. 24:11, que nossa versão portuguesa diz como segue: «Tais palavras lhes pareciam um como *delírio*, e não acreditaram nelas». A palavra em itálico corresponde ao orinal grego. Porém, a palavra grega tem mais o sentido de «absurdo», «despropósito», «disparate».

A tradução de Salmos 90:9 tem sido muito disputada. Há versões que dizem: «...como um conto que é relatado». Outras versões dizem:«...como a teia de uma aranha». Nossa versão portuguesa diz: «...como um breve pensamento». A tradução literal diria: «...como uma meditação». Portanto, nossa versão portuguesa é a que mais se aproxima da idéia.

Quando Moisés requereu permissão para entrarem os israelitas três dias de viagem deserto adentro, a fim de oferecerem sacrifícios a Yahweh, Faraó, o rei do Egito, replicou exigindo a «mesma conta» e a «mesma quantidade» de tijolos que os israelitas costumavam fabricar, e que ainda tivessem de ajuntar a palha que antes lhes era provida (Êxo. 5:8,18; ver também I Sam. 18:27 e I Crô. 9:28).

CONTEMPLAÇÃO

A contemplação é um assunto muito mais vasto e profundo que a maioria dos crentes percebe. Um número demasiadamente grande de líderes religiosos fica satisfeito com o estudo bíblico e com a oração, como meios do desenvolvimento espiritual. A ênfase sobre a correção no credo tem estagnado as inclinações naturais dos homens, que buscam o Deus vivo e procuram sentir sua presença e poder.

1. *O Termo*. Contemplação vem do latim *con*, «com», e *templum*, «lugar onde são observados sinais e portentos», o que indica lugares onde se faziam adivinhações. Partindo daí, a palavra veio a significar, em sentido religioso, «meditação», a busca pelas experiências místicas, mediante exercícios espirituais, etc. O vocábulo também pode indicar qualquer tipo de hábito religioso constante, que contenha os elementos da meditação, da oração e da expectação espiritual da presença de Deus. Por esse motivo, falamos na «vida contemplativa», que aponta para esse tipo de atividade espiritual. O *templum*, naturalmente, veio a ser «templo», em português.

2. *Como Meio de Conhecimento*. A contemplação busca o conhecimento através da meditação, da intuição e das experiências místicas, e não pelas experimentações e pela percepção dos sentidos.

3. Nos escritos de *Platão*, a contemplação envolve elevados princípios espirituais e grandes realidades, como aquilo que é verdadeiro, bom e belo. Para ele, o conhecimento tem suas formas inferiores na percepção dos sentidos. E então, como que subindo os degraus da sublimidade, chegamos à razão, à intuição e às experiências místicas, como gradações possíveis do conhecimento. Nas experiências místicas, similares à contemplação, visionamos a verdade diretamente, como se a alma contemplasse o Espírito divino. O grande alvo da contemplação é a reabsorção pelo Ser divino, o que requer a contemplação feita pela própria alma. O equivalente cristão é a *visão beatífica* (que vide).

4. Nos escritos de *Aristóteles*, é o Impulsionador Inabalável (o seu deus) quem estaria envolvido, acima de tudo, na contemplação da alma. A contemplação, segundo Aristóteles, é a mais elevada e nobre atividade em que um homem pode ocupar-se. Trata-se de uma maneira de pensar sobre o ato de pensar, uma pura atividade mental, em contraste com o que é prático e poético. O ser humano parece-se mais com Deus quando se atarefa na contemplação.

5. Nos escritos de *Plotino*, a contemplação é, ao mesmo tempo, tanto uma atividade intelectual quanto uma atividade espiritual. Seu alvo é a união com o Ser divino, visto que, nessa atividade, a alma envolve-se na absorção no Ser divino, e na sua própria transformação, segundo o modelo do objeto contemplado.

6. Nos escritos de *Hugo de São Vítor*, a *contemplatio* é considerada como o terceiro e final estágio de conhecimento, na ascensão da alma, a qual deve passar, antes disso, pela *cognitatio* e pela *meditatio*, como formas de preparação.

7. De acordo com o *quietismo* do século XVII, um momento de verdadeira contemplação era reputado como o valor de mil anos de boas obras.

8. Na *Igreja Ocidental* e na *Igreja Oriental*, durante mais de um milênio, a contemplação tem sido salientada como um meio de obtenção da iluminação. Nesse sentido, a palavra é um sinônimo de *meditação* (que vide).

9. *Fora do cristianismo*, ver as idéias que circundam o assunto, sob os títulos *Moksha* e *Satori*.

10. *Negligência quanto à contemplação*. Os grupos protestantes e evangélicos, que tanto se envolvem na correção de seus credos e na ênfase sobre as doutrinas bíblicas, como a justificação pela fé, os quais também promovem o estudo bíblico e a oração como, virtualmente, os únicos meios de desenvolvimento espiritual têm negligenciado a sábia prática da contemplação. Ocasionalmente, vê-se mesmo o espetáculo de líderes religiosos que condenam

CONTENDAS

qualquer forma de meditação ou contemplação. O que eles não entendem é que a doutrina do Espírito Santo, mediánte definição básica, é uma doutrina mística, que envolve o contacto real entre o espírito humano e o Espírito de Deus. O conceito do Espírito em nós residente é uma doutrina mística. Por definição básica, o misticismo (que vide) é o contacto da alma com alguma forma mais elevada de realidade espiritual. Esse contacto pode ocorrer com a porção mais alta da própria pessoa, ou com algum ser espiritual superior, como um anjo, Deus, o Filho ou o Espírito Santo. O Espírito do Senhor nos proporciona tanto a Luz interna quanto a Luz externa, e a contemplação é um dos meios pelos quais buscamos essa iluminação. Ver o trecho de Efésios 1:17 quanto à *iluminação*, e ver o artigo sobre esse assunto, nesta enciclopédia. Paulo usou a expressão «em Cristo», por mais de cento e sessenta vezes, em suas epístolas. Essa breve mas significativa expressão reflete o *Cristo-misticismo* (que vide).

11. *Relações Eclesiásticas*. A busca pela iluminação espiritual, por meio da meditação, tem sido honrada pela antiguidade, em muitos segmentos da Igreja Oriental. E mesmo no Ocidente encontramos as ordens monásticas contemplativas, como os cartusianos e carmelitas, cujos membros procuram levar vidas essencialmente contemplativas. Talvez os *Exercícios Espirituais* de Inácio de Loiola sejam os escritos cristãos mais bem conhecidos, dessa natureza. Nas religiões orientais não-cristãs, naturalmente, à prática da contemplação se reserva um papel importantíssimo. (C EP H P)

CONTENDAS

Há seis palavras hebraicas envolvidas e cinco palavras gregas, a saber:

1. *Din*, «contenção». Palavra hebraica que ocorre por vinte vezes. Por exemplo: Sal. 9:4; Pro. 29:7; Jer. 5:28; Pro. 22:10.

2. *Madon*, «contenda». Palavra hebraica que aparece por quinze vezes. Por exemplo: Sal. 80:6; Pro. 15:18; 29:22; Jer. 15:10; Hab. 1:3.

3. *Medanim*, «brigas», «contendas». Palavra hebraica usada por duas vezes: Pro. 10:12; 6:19.

4. *Matstsah*, «debate», «discussão». Palavra hebraica empregada por três vezes: Pro. 13:10; Isa. 58:4; Pro. 17:19.

5. *Rib*, «causa». Palavra hebraica usada por cerca de cento e quarenta vezes. Para exemplificar: Nee. 13:17,25; Jó 9:3; Isa. 49:25; Amós 7:4; Miq. 6:1; Deu. 17:8; 19:17; II Sam. 15:2; II Crô. 19:8; Jer. 25:31; Osé. 4:1; 12:2.

6. *Meribah*, «contenda», «controvérsia». Palavra hebraica usada por seis vezes: Gên. 13:8; Núm. 27:14; Sal. 106:32; Eze. 47:19; 48:28 e Sal. 95:8.

7. *Antilogía*, «contradição». Palavra grega usada por quatro vezes: Heb. 6:16; 7:7; 12:3; Jud. 11. O verbo, *antilogéo*, «contradizer», aparece por nove vezes: Luc. 2:34; 20:27; João 19:12; Atos 13:45; 28:19,22; Rom. 10:21; Tito 1:9 e 2:9.

8. *Eritheía*, «querela». Palavra grega usada por sete vezes: Rom. 2:8; II Cor. 12:20; Gál. 5:20; Fil. 1:17; 2:3; Tia. 3:14,16. O verbo, *erízo*, «querelar», aparece somente em Mat. 12:19, citando Isa. 43:2.

9. *Éris*, «briga», «contenda». Palavra grega que é empregada por nove vezes: Rom. 1:29; 13:13; I Cor. 1:11; 3:3; II Cor. 12:20; Gál. 5:20; Fil. 1:15; I Tim. 6:4; Tito 3:9.

10. *Máche*, «contenda», «batalha». Palavra grega usada por quatro vezes: II Cor. 7:5; II Tim. 2:23; Tito 3:9; Tia. 4:1. O verbo *máchomai*, «contender», também aparece por quatro vezes: João 6:52; Atos 7:26; II Tim. 2:24; Tia. 4:2.

11. *Philoneikía*, «contenda», «disputa». Palavra grega utilizada por apenas uma vez, em Luc. 22:24. O adjetivo *philóneikos*, «disputador», também só aparece por uma vez, em I Cor. 11:16.

Salomão nos dá a razão do espírito contencioso, quando diz: «Lança fora o escarnecedor, e com ele se irá a contenda; cessarão as demandas e a ignomínia» (Pro. 22:10). O espírito briguento, contencioso, é próprio dos inconformados com as coisas como elas são. Essa atitude negativa é muito bem retratada por Judas: «Estes, porém, quanto a tudo o que não entendem, difamam; e, quanto a tudo o que compreendem por instinto natural, como brutos sem razão, até nessas cousas se corrompem» (Jud. 10). Essa atitude é muito bem ilustrada no caso de Abraão, Ló e seus respectivos pastores. Estes últimos entraram em contenda, mas Abraão, que era dotado de outras atitudes, procurou entender-se com Ló, dizendo-lhe: «Não haja contenda entre mim e ti, e entre os meus pastores e os teus pastores, porque somos parentes chegados» (Gên. 13:7,8). Essa passagem, pois, mostra-nos que o afeto e a cordialidade são a vacina para o espírito contencioso. Acima de meros interesses materiais, que poderiam levar à controvérsia, Abraão punha o valor maior do parentesco.

O espírito contencioso faz parte das obras da carne. Esse espírito manifesta-se de vários modos, conforme se vê em Gálatas 5:20,21: «...inimizades, porfias, ciúmes, iras, discórdias, dissenções, facções, invejas...»

As diversas palavras hebraicas usadas no Antigo Testamento para expressar essa atitude carnal demonstram a gravidade desse pecado. Todavia, há um aspecto da questão que é pouco ventilada. É que Deus mostra-se contrário aos que lhe são desobedientes, que lhe fazem oposição. Enquanto o povo de Israel foi obediente, Deus os abençoou com sua graça providencial; no entanto, quando eles se rebelaram, Deus mostrou-se o grande opositor deles. Isso é bem expresso em Miquéias 6:2: «Ouvi, montes, a controvérsia do Senhor, e vós, duráveis fundamentos da terra; porque o Senhor tem controvérsia com o seu povo, e com Israel entrará em juízo». É que, ocasionalmente, a controvérsia está baseada em uma «causa» justa. A perversidade e maldade dos homens provocam a Deus, — que se sente forçado a defender o direito e a justiça. Nunca isso se tornará mais evidente do que nos dias finais de nossa era: «...o Senhor tem contenda com as nações, entrará em juízo contra toda carne; os perversos entregará à espada, diz o Senhor» (Jer. 25:31). Essa idéia é reiterada em Oséias 4:1: «...o Senhor tem uma contenda com os habitantes da terra; porque nela não há verdade, nem amor, nem conhecimento de Deus». Esse aspecto da questão exibe o aspecto punitivo do trato de Deus com os homens: «Ó Senhor também com Judá tem contenda, e castigará Jacó segundo o seu proceder; segundo as suas obras o recompensará» (Oséias 12:2). O remédio para esse juízo divino encontra-se quatro versículos adiante: «...converte-te a teu Deus, guarda o amor e o juízo, e no teu Deus espera sempre» (Osé. 12:6).

Talvez nenhuma passagem do Antigo Testamento seja mais ilustrativa do espírito contencioso e provocador a Deus do que o caso de Meribá, relatado em Êxodo 17:1 *ss*. Comentando a esse respeito, diz o salmista: «Não endureçais o vosso coração, como em Meribá, como no dia de Massá, no deserto; quando

CONTENDAS — CONTENTAMENTO

vossos pais me tentaram, pondo-me à prova, não obstante terem visto as minhas obras. Durante quarenta anos estive desgostoso com essa geração, e disse: «É povo de coração transviado, não conhece os meus caminhos. Por isso jurei na minha ira: Não entrarão no meu descanso» (Sal. 95:8-11). Ali vemos que o espírito contencioso equivale a submeter Deus a teste. Tal espírito merece, da parte de Deus, a atitude de repúdio e reprovação. O Espírito de Deus nos ensina, nesse Salmo, que o contencioso é assim contrário porque desconhece os caminhos do Senhor. Esse espírito de conflito com Deus só pode colher o amargo fruto que dali resulta. Os contenciosos levam Deus a resolver que eles não serão salvos.

O Espírito Contencioso no Novo Testamento. O crente aparece nas páginas do novo pacto como alguém que, mediante a autodisciplina e a ajuda do Espírito transformador, vai eliminando os vícios e cultivando as virtudes que são opostas a esses vícios. Visto que ainda trazemos bem vivo em nós a natureza adâmica, enquanto estivermos deste lado da existência haveremos de manifestar essa tendência para as querelas, dissensões, controvérsias, etc. Nos primeiros estudos sobre o temperamento, os psicólogos antigos pensavam que esse espírito contencioso se devia a um excesso de bílis, o que tornaria a pessoa amarga e negativa acima do normal. Isso é até possível, mas não como uma causa em si, e, sim, como estado resultante do espírito contencioso. A causa está na alma, podendo haver, quem sabe, um efeito *psicossomático*. O homem, em seu estado natural e de perdição, acha-se em estado de revolta contra Deus. Isso reflete-se também na dimensão horizontal, azedando e amargurando todo o relacionamento humano. Ora, não convém que o crente continue nesse estado. Daí as muitas injunções e instruções neotestamentárias a esse respeito. Existem contenções de várias espécies. Há os «debates sobre a lei» (Tito 3:9, cf. II Tim. 2:23); há a «mania por questões e contendas de palavras» (I Tim. 6:4); há as «sedições» que podem levar ao homicídio (Luc. 23:19; Atos 24:5).

Que os crentes não são curados facilmente da tendência muito humana e carnal, verifica-se através das palavras dirigidas por Paulo aos crentes, em I Cor. 11:16: «Contudo, se alguém quer ser contencioso, saiba que nós não temos tal costume, nem as igrejas de Deus».

Queremos concluir observando que se a tendência de muitos estudiosos liberais é o ceticismo diante do elemento miraculoso, a tendência de muitos estudiosos fundamentalistas é o espírito contencioso. Precisamos evitar tanto aquele quanto este extremo. A todos nós cabe atentarmos às palavras de Paulo: «Ora, é necessário que o servo do Senhor não viva a contender, e, sim, deve ser brando para com todos, apto para instruir, paciente; disciplinando com mansidão os que se opõem, na expectativa de que Deus lhes conceda não só o arrependimento, para conhecerem plenamente a verdade, mas também o retorno à sensatez...» (II Tim. 2:24-26).

De acordo com Tiago, o espírito faccioso não reflete a sabedoria que vem do alto, mas antes, é «terrena, animal e demoníaca» (Tiago 3:14,15). A atitude oposta já é uma grande virtude. Tiago a descreve com estas palavras: «A sabedoria, porém, lá do alto, é primeiramente pura; depois pacífica, indulgente, tratável, plena de misericórdia e de bons frutos, imparcial, sem fingimento» (Tia. 3:17). Quem herdará a terra? Os contenciosos? Não, os mansos. (Ver Mat. 5:5).

Um inquebrantável espírito contencioso, no dizer do apóstolo dos gentios, é sinal seguro da perdição dos que o toleram em suas vidas: «Evita o homem faccioso, depois de admoestá-lo primeira e segunda vez, pois sabes que tal pessoa está pervertida e vive pecando, e por si mesma está condenada» (Tito 3:10,11). A mansidão é sinal de fortaleza espiritual; os grandes homens de Deus foram mansos. Acerca de Moisés ficou registrado: «Era o varão Moisés mui manso, mais do que todos os homens que havia sobre a terra» (Núm. 12:3). Em contraste, o espírito contencioso reflete a falta de desenvolvimento espiritual. Portanto, evitemos o espírito contencioso e cultivemos a mansidão.

CONTENDER, CONTENDA

Há muitas palavras hebraicas e gregas por detrás dessa tradução, referindo-se a disputas e hostilidades, motivadas por desígnios egoístas, pelo orgulho e pela má vontade. As palavras hebraicas são, no mínimo, oito, com o sentido de «contender», «esforçar-se», «entrar em juízo», «preocupar-se», «contenda», «debate». Os termos gregos envolvidos são os seguintes:

1. *Diakríno*, «julgar de modo diferente». Verbo grego que ocorre por dezenove vezes: Mat. 16:3; 21:21; Mar. 11:23; Atos 10:20; 11:2,12; 15:9; Rom. 4:20; 14:23; I Cor. 4:7; 6:5; 11:29,31; 14:29; Tia. 1:6; 2:4; Jud. 9:22.

2. *Epagonízomai*, «contender». Verbo grego que aparece por apenas uma vez, em Jud. 3.

3. *Agón*, «contenda». Substantivo grego que figura por seis vezes: Fil. 1:30; Col. 2:1; I Tes. 2:2; I Tim. 6:12; II Tim. 4:7; Heb. 12:1.

4. *Éris*, «briga», «contenda». Substantivo grego que é usado por nove vezes: Rom. 1:29; 13:13; I Cor. 1:11; 3:3; II Cor. 12:20; Gál. 5:20; Fil. 1:15; I Tim. 6:4 e Tito 3:9.

5. *Eritheía*, «contenda». Substantivo grego usado por sete vezes: Rom. 2:8; II Cor. 12:20; Gál. 5:20; Fil. 1:17; 2:3; Tia. 3:14,16.

6. *Paroksusmós*, «disputa acalorada». Substantivo grego empregado por duas vezes: Atos 15:39 e Heb. 10:24.

Em Gálatas 5:19,20, esse ato é alistado entre as obras da carne, dentro da lista de vícios preparada por Paulo. Tito foi admoestado a evitar o espírito contencioso (Tito 3:9). Tal ato é pecaminoso quando impulsionado pela ira ou pelo egoísmo. No entanto, pode ter um aspecto positivo quando é usado em defesa da fé (Jud. 3). Ver o artigo geral sobre os *Vícios*. Na nossa transformação espiritual gradual, aprendemos a pôr de lado todas essas atitudes e ações, embora a lição precise de muito tempo para ser aprendida, porquanto o homem é um ser decaído, realmente muito distante de Deus. O homem chega a apresentar os seus vícios como se fossem virtudes, em autodefesa e fingida justa indignação.

CONTENTAMENTO

Há uma palavra hebraica e três palavras gregas diretamente envolvidas, a saber:

1. *Yaal*, «estar satisfeito». Palavra hebraica que aparece por onze vezes com esse sentido. Por exemplo: Êxo. 2:21; Jos. 7:7; Juí. 17:11; 19:6; II Reis 5:23; 6:3; Jó 6:28.

2. *Arkéo*, «considerar suficiente». Palavra grega que ocorre por oito vezes: Mat. 25:9; Luc. 3:14; João 6:7; 14:8; II Cor. 12:9; I Tim. 6:8; Heb. 13:5 e III João 10.

3. *Autárkes*, «auto-suficiente». Palavra grega que figura apenas por uma vez, em Fil. 4:11.

4. *Poiéo tò ikanón*, «fazer o suficiente». Expressão grega que aparece somente em Mar. 15:15.

O contentamento consiste naquela perfeita fé ou confiança que torna o crente independente das circunstâncias externas (Fil. 4:11; I Tim. 6:7,8). Assim sendo, o crente tem confiança no seu destino final, sabendo que tudo foi adredemente preparado pela providência misericordiosa de Deus. O homem destituído de fé, porém, não tem a certeza de que Deus fez provisão acerca do que ele precisa realizar. Na verdade, nem tem certeza se tem uma missão na terra, pelo que olha para este mundo como se o mesmo fosse governado pelo puro acaso e pelo caos. O contentamento também está alicerçado sobre o espírito de humildade. Algumas pessoas são por demais orgulhosas e egoístas para se contentarem com pouca coisa, dilapidando seus poderes físicos e mentais na tentativa de acumular coisas que lhes confiram segurança. O crente contente, porém, não se deixa perturbar pela inveja, pela competição e pela ansiedade (Tia. 3:16; Mat. 6:25,26). As Escrituras consideram o contentamento uma virtude, recomendando-o por diversas vezes (Luc. 3:14; Heb. 13:5). O contentamento está associado à piedade, pelo que também faz parte do desenvolvimento espiritual (I Tim. 6:6). A espiritualidade de Paulo exibia grande dose de contentamento (Fil. 4:11; I Tim. 6:8).

Convém distingamos o contentamento da inércia. Paulo conseguia estar contente e trabalhar arduamente, ao mesmo tempo. Parte do seu segredo consistia no fato de que ele não cobiçava as coisas materiais que excitam a maioria das pessoas. Os filósofos epicúreos (que vide), reputavam o contentamento como uma das principais virtudes, pois se o prazer, para eles, era o alvo da existência humana, esse prazer precisava ser apreciado em meio ao espírito contente, salientando os prazeres mentais, e não os prazeres carnais. Eles empregavam a palavra grega *ataraxia*, «tranqüilidade», «calma», para indicar uma espécie de estado mental sereno e imperturbável, o que, para eles, representava um grande prazer. Uma antiga canção popular falava sobre o homem dotado de mente contente. Os filósofos que promoveram esse ideal, foram: Demócrito, Epicuro, Pirro e Lucrécio. Cada um deles merece um artigo separado, nesta enciclopédia. A *apatia* dos estóicos ia além dos requisitos próprios da *ataraxia*, porquanto envolvia uma total liberdade de toda forma de emoção, positiva ou negativa, visto que, segundo a doutrina estóica, das emoções é que procedem todos os nossos sofrimentos.

O contentamento cristão envolve mais do que alguma emoção humana. Não depende da pessoa ajustar-se ao *status quo*. Antes, trata-se de uma convicção íntima de que nenhum mal pode sobrevir ao homem piedoso, porquanto Deus proveu para ele tudo quanto é necessário, em todas as ocorrências de sua vida, durante todos os seus dias. Trata-se também de uma influência do Espírito Santo, sobre a maneira do crente olhar para as coisas. É o contrário da petulância, do egoísmo e da ansiedade. Exclui a inveja (Tia. 3:16), a avareza (Heb. 3:5) e o espírito queixoso (I Cor. 10:10). Um crente contente não entra em pânico quando seus recursos materiais escasseiam, porquanto ele sabe que a Fonte de todos os recursos jamais perde o seu poder. Mais do que isso, Deus nunca perde o interesse por qualquer de seus filhos. O contentamento consiste em uma feliz dependência de Deus, mostrando-se humilde, isento de lutas insanas em prol das coisas materiais. Os cuidados do Pai celeste por seus filhos torna a ansiedade tanto desnecessária quanto pecaminosa (Mat. 6:25-34). Alguns indivíduos chegam a tentar obter vantagens materiais por serem religiosos (I Tim. 6:5). Mas a piedade é o maior de todos os lucros e vantagens.

CONTEXTUALISMO

Uma teoria referente à interpretação estética, que afirma que uma obra de arte deveria ser compreendida em seu contexto cultural total, e que cada obra de arte está historicamente condicionada. Esse conceito pode ser contrastado à idéia do isolacionismo (que vide).

CONTINÊNCIA

Essa palavra indica a temperança e a restrição em relação a qualquer tipo de apetite. Geralmente é usada no tocante ao apetite sexual, em tal caso refere-se à *abstinência* sexual, embora os dicionários definam de modo bastante lato a palavra, incluindo a idéia de *moderação* na atividade sexual, com vistas à manutenção da castidade. Nessa conexão, Paulo ensinou tanto a abstinência quanto a moderação. Ver o sétimo capítulo de I Coríntios. Para ele, porém, a abstinência não se reduz a alguma lei eclesiástica, mas antes, é uma prática que deve ser ditada por decisão voluntária de quem a pratica, tendo em vista o cultivo da espiritualidade. Quanto à controvérsia que gira em torno dessas idéias, ver o artigo separado sobre o *Celibato*. Não há que duvidar que Paulo considerava o celibato uma elevada virtude em potencial, contanto que levada a efeito com os propósitos corretos. Mas ele nunca fez do celibato uma obrigação para o clero. De fato, ele sugeriu o celibato para todos os cristãos, indistintamente, e não, especificamente, para a classe clerical. Em um sentido secundário, a teologia cristã tem usado a palavra «continência» para indicar a abstinência sexual, fora do casamento. E Jesus também promoveu o ideal da monogamia (Mat. 19:3 *ss*).

Em um sentido mais geral, as traduções usam a palavra «continência», e seus sinônimos, como «temperança» e «moderação», para aludirem ao autocontrole e à satisfação moderada de qualquer apetite. Paulo empregou a ilustração do atleta que desiste de muitas coisas, disciplinando-se, a fim de poder desenvolver as aptidões necessárias para triunfar na luta (I Cor. 9:25). No trecho de Gálatas 5:23, aparece, no original do Novo Testamento, o vocábulo grego *egkráteia*, «autocontrole» ou «moderação», incluindo um dos aspectos do fruto do Espírito. Com base nisso aprendemos que nossos apetites normais só podem ser devidamente controlados com a ajuda da influência e das operações do Espírito Santo.

CONTINGÊNCIA

Esse vocábulo vem do latim **contingere**, «acontecer». A palavra é usada na filosofia e na teologia de várias maneiras, a saber:

1. São contingentes aquelas entidades que não precisam existir, o que significa que sua existência deriva-se de alguma outra fonte, da qual dependem para continuar existindo. Nesse sentido, todos os seres são contingentes, com a exceção única de Deus. Essa palavra pode ser contrastada com o termo *necessário*, que designa Deus como o Ser que não pode deixar de existir.

CONTINUUM — CONTRABANDO

2. *No Tocante a Eventos*. Os acontecimentos que não precisam ocorrer são reputados como contingentes. Porém, os eventos que precisam ocorrer são chamados «necessários». Parece que na vida de cada pessoa há eventos contingentes e eventos necessários. Os acontecimentos necessários controlam o desdobrar geral da vida. Os acontecimentos contingentes podem ser simplesmente caóticos, resultantes de causas secundárias. Sobre estes últimos, exercemos algum controle. Mas os acontecimentos necessários evidentemente fazem parte das escolhas feitas, pelo menos no caso das almas mais bem desenvolvidas. Estou especulando aqui que a alma humana é preexistente, participando das decisões que determinariam o tipo de vida que ela viria a ter neste mundo, com todos os seus eventos e alvos. O desígnio divino é o grande fator controlador dos eventos necessários. E os eventos contingentes podem ser harmonizados com o desígnio divino.

3. *Quanto a Proposições*. Uma proposição contingente é aquela que não é necessariamente veraz. Alguns filósofos abandonaram totalmente a tentativa de descobrir alguma verdade necessária, supondo que esse tipo de verdade só pode ser concebido na matemática, nas proposições analíticas e nas tautologias, como: «Este quadro negro é preto». De acordo com esse ponto de vista, pois, todo o conhecimento é apenas contingente, e a própria vida deve ser vivida em consonância com princípios pragmáticos, em meio a uma atitude cética no que concerne à verdade e ao conhecimento. Ver o artigo sobre o *Ceticismo*. Ver também sobre o *Positivismo* e sobre o *Positivismo Lógico*.

4. *Quanto ao Tempo*. O futuro é considerado uma contingência, por alguns pensadores, e uma necessidade, por outros. Ver sobre o *Determinismo* e sobre o *Livre-Arbítrio*. Partindo da idéia de que o futuro é contingente, alguns supõem que ninguém, nem mesmo Deus, pode prever o futuro. Se o futuro é necessário, porém, pode ser previsto tanto pelo homem quanto por Deus. Entretanto, Agostinho demonstrou que Deus pode prever um futuro contingente, e também que, ao prever o futuro, Deus não o torna necessário. Isso é verdade porque Deus pode prever que um homem agirá livremente, e que certos acontecimentos terão lugar de forma contingente. E isso significa que a presciência de Deus está por detrás da contingência, e não dos acontecimentos necessários, inevitáveis. A verdade parece ser que certos eventos futuros são necessários, para a vida cósmica, humana e individual, ao passo que outros eventos são contingentes.

5. *Uma Prova da Existência de Deus*. Tomás de Aquino (que vide) alicerçou uma de suas cinco provas tradicionais da existência de Deus sobre os princípios da contingência e da necessidade. Ver o artigo sobre os *Cinco Caminhos* de Tomás de Aquino. Todos os seres são contingentes, com a única exceção de Deus. Isso quer dizer que todos os seres estão sujeitos à extinção final. Para que qualquer coisa exista, torna-se mister que o *Ser Necessário*, Deus, exista como fonte dos seres e coisas contingentes. Essa prova, porém, contém a falácia de fazer todas as coisas saírem da existência ao mesmo tempo, o que não precisamos supor. Por outra parte, há uma certa lógica nessa prova que é bastante sugestiva. A intuição e a razão parecem dizer-nos que para que qualquer coisa exista deve haver um Ser necessário. Os mistérios da criação simplesmente são grandes demais para que possamos supor que a contingência é a regra da vida.

6. *A Contingência, a Necessidade e o Plano de Redenção*. A questão da contingência entra no campo da soteriologia. Embora a alma humana sobreviva à morte biológica, ainda assim, pela lógica, ela poderia deixar de existir, visto que se trata de um ser contingente. Porém, quando a alma remida vem a participar da natureza divina (ver II Ped. 1:4), ela torna-se um ser necessário, devido ao próprio fato de que ela atingiu uma espécie de vida que não pode deixar de existir. O Pai deu essa vida necessária ao Filho; e o Filho dará essa vida aos filhos de Deus, por ocasião da ressurreição dos remidos (João 5:25,26). Isso ocorre mediante a transformação do homem segundo a imagem do Filho (Rom. 8:29; II Cor. 3:18). Portanto, o que é contingente, tornar-se-á necessário. Desse modo, os homens deixarão de ser apenas eternos, tornando-se verdadeiramente *imortais*. Ver o artigo geral sobre a *Imortalidade*.

7. *A Necessidade Torna Necessária a Contingência*. Alguns filósofos, como Avicena (que vide), supõem que o homem, na qualidade de ser contingente, recebe uma espécie de necessidade pelo fato que Deus, o Ser necessário, por sua soberana vontade, decreta que certas contingências não podem deixar de existir. Em conseqüência disso, apesar dessas coisas não serem necessárias por sua própria natureza, são preservadas pela vontade de Deus.

CONTINUUM

Esse é um conceito da realidade, ou uma dimensão desse conceito, que afirma que a realidade deverá continuar para sempre. A idéia pode incluir o pensamento adicional de que essa realidade sempre existiu. Os eventos que envolvem o espaço e o tempo parecem ocorrer em sucessão; mas a própria realidade não pode ser dividida dessa maneira. A expressão cunhada por Dewey (que vide), «means-end continuum» indica aquelas coisas que buscamos como alvos ou fins, mas somente enquanto não se concretizam. Uma vez atingidos, eles tornam-se novos começos, o que prossegue indefinidamente. Nesse sentido, não existem fins fixos na natureza.

O Grande Continuum. Essa expressão pode ser usada para referir-se à própria vida. Apesar da vida envolver sucessivos acontecimentos, que entram e saem de muitas crises, com suas alegrias e tristezas, como seus aparentes começos (como os nascimentos) e com seus aparentes fins (como a morte), na verdade ela constitui um grande continuum. Prossegue interminavelmente, e nós, de diferentes maneiras, sempre a acompanhamos.

CONTRABANDO

Trata-se do ato de fazer sair ou entrar de um país, estado ou território, algum item proibido por lei, ou cuja venda é controlada ou taxada, com o intuito dos contrabandistas não arcarem com as despesas alfandegárias. Todo contrabando visa aumentar os lucros das vendas dos artigos contrabandeados, mediante o não pagamento dos impostos que incidem sobre os mesmos. De outras vezes, o termo aplica-se a pessoas que se mudam de um lugar para outro, contrariamente à vontade expressa pelas autoridades do governo. Armamentos são freqüentemente contrabandeados para forças guerrilheiras ou para nações beligerantes, desobedecendo às leis dos países de onde essas armas saem e onde entram. Com freqüência, até mesmo diplomatas, e não somente criminosos comuns e fanáticos, envolvem-se nessa forma de contrabando. O termo «contrabando» vem do espanhol e do italiano, onde o sentido é «contra a lei». No italiano, *contra*, «contra», e *bando*, «lei». Mais remoto ainda é o vocábulo latino *bannum*, «lei». De acordo com o décimo terceiro capítulo da epístola aos Romanos, os crentes não podem praticar o contrabando, exceto em certos casos de abuso de autoridade, quando Bíblias são introduzidas disfarçadamente para os países onde sua publicação é proibida por lei.

CONTRACEPTIVOS

Ver os artigos sobre *Aborto* e *Controle de Natalidade*. Um contraceptivo é qualquer meio, natural ou artificial, mediante o qual o concepção é impedida. O artigo sobre o controle de natalidade aborda a moralidade envolvida nessa prática.

CONTRACONVERSÃO

Uma contraconversão ocorre quando uma pessoa, que fazia parte de um sistema qualquer, aceitando suas várias regras e doutrinas, passa a aceitar outro sistema, que ele considera mais avançado ou frutífero. Algumas vezes, essa mudança é acompanhada por grande conflito mental, ou por rejeição da pessoa envolvida, por parte de outras. As pessoas envolvidas, porém, consideram o fato um desenvolvimento religioso ou espiritual. Mas aqueles que não concordam com elas, geralmente consideram-nas hereges ou mesmo apóstatas. Alguns dos melhores líderes religiosos e dos mais produtivos escritores religiosos, têm passado por esse tipo de experiência. No entanto, certos casos parecem envolver mais um retrocesso do que um avanço, quando as pessoas passam a fazer parte de seitas exclusivistas e pessimistas, caracterizadas por atitudes mentais depressivas.

CONTRADIÇÃO

No latim, **contra**, «contra» e **dicere**, «dizer». Em outras palavras, afirmar ou fazer algo que é contra alguma coisa que outrem disse, ou é algo feito de uma maneira diferente do que seria normal esperar. Nas proposições, indica uma assertiva simultânea e negação de uma proposição qualquer, que ocorre dentre ou entre pressupostos ou assertivas em choque. Uma contradição também pode ocorrer posteriormente, em alguma declaração falada ou escrita, contradizendo algo que fora dito ou escrito em ocasião anterior. De outras vezes, o termo é usado para indicar os conflitos e as tensões. Por exemplo: «Há muitas contradições na sociedade», frase que pode significar apenas que há muitas tensões e conflitos na sociedade humana.

Contradições Bíblicas. Os céticos são capazes de encontrar algumas contradições na Bíblia, e algumas delas parecem genuínas. Os estudiosos ultraconservadores têm uma resposta engatilhada para cada uma dessas alegações, mas algumas dessas respostas envolvem falsidade. Há duas falácias envolvidas nessa questão. A primeira, é que os céticos equivocam-se ao suporem que a Bíblia deixa de ser um guia moral e espiritual, porque algumas contradições podem ser encontradas na mesma. Isso é exigir mais da Bíblia do que ela declara acerca dela mesma. A teoria do balão diz que se alguém fizer uma perfuração em um lugar do balão, todo o ar ali contido sairá pelo buraco, e que o balão entrará em colapso. Porém, a Bíblia e a fé cristã não se assemelham a um balão. A *segunda* falácia é a dos defensores fanáticos da Bíblia, que sentem ser necessário agarrarem-se a essa teoria do balão furado. No entanto, a espiritualidade não opera desse modo. Não precisamos de um livro perfeito para que o Espírito de Deus opere em nossas vidas, utilizando-se de princípios espirituais genuínos, que nos são oferecidos nas Sagradas Escrituras. Acresça-se a isso que a revelação bíblica, embora poderosíssimo meio de comunicações divinas, em nenhuma página da Bíblia é declarada perfeita, necessariamente. Os homens é que dizem tal coisa. Mas a Bíblia nunca afirma tal conceito. O conflito inteiro a respeito das contradições da Bíblia é um jogo que crianças costumam brincar. Não produz qualquer efeito sobre a fé e a espiritualidade.

Contradições Teológicas. Essa é uma porção necessária de qualquer teologia, a menos que o sistema seja tão perfeito que se torne falso, ou parcialmente falso. Para ilustrar, consideremos o caso das várias narrativas sobre a ressurreição de Jesus, nos quatro evangelhos. É impossível a harmonização das mesmas. Porém, longe disso laborar contra a veracidade do fato descrito, isso contribui para a credibilidade do relato. Se a Igreja cristã pudesse harmonizar tais narrativas, poderia tê-lo feito. Antes, os crentes primitivos deixaram esses relatos tais e quais foram escritos. Esses relatos apareceram sob forma fragmentar, porquanto foram redigidos apressadamente, com profundo senso de urgência. Isso demonstra que um evento muito incomum havia ocorrido, que não foi abordado de maneira racional ou sistemática. A própria revelação divina veio à existência dessa maneira apressada. A epístola aos Hebreus refere-se à natureza fragmentar e diversificada da revelação divina (Heb. 1:1). Qualquer teologia que seja perfeitamente sistemática e isenta de paradoxos, na realidade é uma *humano*logia. Por causa de sua própria natureza, a *teo*logia deve conter seus *paradoxos* (que vide). Muitas verdades só podem ser entendidas se considerarmos os pólos opostos da verdade, e não apenas um dos lados da questão envolvida. Muitas verdades parecem ser contraditórias com outras, como o livre-arbítrio humano e o determinismo divino, cujos lados compõem uma verdade mais ampla, embora não compreendamos exatamente como. Sucede que alguns defendem um dos pólos, como o do livre-arbítrio humano, ao passo que outros defendem o pólo do determinismo humano; porém, esses são pólos opostos de alguma verdade maior, que não foi nitidamente enfocada para nós, nas Escrituras, porquanto as coisas ocultas pertencem a nosso Deus, e as reveladas nos pertencem. A luta toda consiste em formular teologias sistemáticas que não distorçam alguma verdade, a fim de promover outra. Mas, de algumas vezes, esse conflito é simplesmente fictício, e não envolve qualquer contradição autêntica.

Contradições Morais. Essas têm lugar quando uma pessoa faz algo que contradiz seu caráter normal e aprovado, ou contradiz coisas nas quais ela afirma acreditar. Todas as pessoas, mui freqüentemente, estão envolvidas nisso, porquanto é nisso que consiste o *pecado*. Quanto mais uma pessoa sabe, e quanto maior for a experiência de um crente, mais clamorosas são as suas contradições.

CONTRA-EXEMPLO

Trata-se de algum exemplo dado para mostrar que alguma proposição é falsa, ou essencialmente falsa. Por exemplo: «Todos os cisnes são brancos». Se alguém encontrar um único cisne negro, então ficará imediatamente demonstrado que aquela proposição, supostamente universal, é falsa. Os contra-exemplos têm importância nas pesquisas científicas, a fim de refinar proposições. Uma longa série de testes pode mostrar, aparentemente, uma verdade da qual podemos depender. Mas, um único contra-exemplo pode mostrar que tal proposição é falsa ou parcialmente falsa. Por outra parte, a importância dos contra-exemplos pode ser exagerada. Uma proposição realmente veraz pode ter grande valor, não devendo ser rejeitada por causa de alguma exceção. Há necessidade de investigação, para que se verifique o porquê de tal exceção.

No campo da *teologia*, esse princípio pode operar quando abordamos trechos bíblicos aparentemente contraditórios, o que se tem tornado um instrumento para os céticos atacarem a fé religiosa. No campo da *moral*, os contra-exemplos são aqueles de natureza negativa, que *não* devem ser seguidos. Assim, no episódio do homem rico, ele estava interessado somente em obter mais e mais bens materiais; mas, subitamente, sua alma lhe foi requerida (Luc. 12:20). Esse é um exemplo que deve ser evitado, porquanto labora contra as realidades espirituais.

CONTRA-REFORMA
Ver sobre a **Reforma Católica**.

CONTRATOS

A feitura de contratos, com o intuito de controlar todas as formas de negociação, além de muitos outros atos e atividades humanas, tem uma história muito antiga. Os contratos podem envolver tratados, pactos, alianças, hipotecas, venda e compra de mercadorias, testamentos, casamentos, etc. Há várias menções bíblicas a essa prática, conforme se vê, por exemplo, em Gên. 21:27,30,31; 26:28,29; 31:50; I Sam. 11:1,2; Nee. 9:38; 10:1; Eze. 17:12-20; Luc. 6:34. A legislação mosaica proibia a quebra de um contrato (Núm. 30:2,4,12). Legalmente falando, um contrato é um acordo entre duas pessoas, que se dispõem a ganhar ou perder coisas especificadas. Um contrato impõe obrigações estipuladas a ambos os lados envolvidos. Para os crentes, um contrato põe em jogo sua honestidade e sua qualidade espiritual, porquanto fica entendido que os crentes têm a obrigação moral de agradar a Deus em qualquer empreendimento, e não somente a obrigação moral de agradar àqueles que fizerem algum contrato com eles. Um crente está na obrigação de cumprir plenamente todas as estipulações contratuais, a menos que, entrando em acordo com a outra parte, um contrato seja anulado ou modificado. Surge para os crentes um dilema, quando a outra parte não cumpre o seu lado no contrato. Um crente não tem a permissão bíblica de levar outros crentes diante dos tribunais seculares, para solucionamento de tais disputas (I Cor. 6:1 *ss*), mas essa regra não se aplica, necessariamente, no caso de contratos quebrados por pessoas incrédulas. Todavia, a longanimidade é uma boa prática cristã (Mat. 5:39,40), embora haja casos em que a perda justifica a ação legal contra aquele que fugiu de suas obrigações contratuais.

CONTRIÇÃO

As palavras hebraicas envolvidas são:

1. *Dakka*, «contrito», «ferido». Esse termo é usado por vinte e cinco vezes (por exemplo: Sal. 34:18; Isa. 57:15; Sal. 51:17).

2. *Nakeh*, «ferido». Palavra usada por apenas uma vez, com esse sentido, em Isa. 66:2. No caso de aleijado é usado por duas vezes: II Sam. 4:4; 9:3.

Em todas essas referências, menos nas do livro de II Samuel, o sentido é metafórico. Assim, o coração sente-se ferido e esmagado, sob o peso e o choque do pecado. O Espírito sente-se humilhado e quebrantado por ter-se envolvido no que é errado. A pessoa espiritualmente sensível é dotada de uma consciência ativa, que envia dardos sobre os sentimentos conscientes, quando há alguma contradição moral na vida da pessoa. O arrependimento (que vide), quando a pessoa muda inteiramente de rumo, é necessário para que haja uma contrição curadora.

Uso Eclesiástico. O vocábulo *attritio* era usado na teologia medieval para indicar o arrependimento originado no medo. Já a palavra *contritio* indicava o arrependimento acompanhado pelo amor a Deus, com o propósito de abster-se do pecado e de corrigir-se do erro ou erros praticados. Alguns estudiosos medievais caíram no erro de pensar que o *attritio* é suficiente para o perdão dos pecados, se acompanhado pela indulgência respectiva, que podia ser comprada a dinheiro. Lutero, em suas Noventa e Cinco Teses, usou a palavra latina correspondente a *contrição* com o intuito de mostrar a necessidade do verdadeiro arrependimento; e, naturalmente, ele rejeitava o sistema inteiro das indulgências (que vide). Os homens sempre anseiam por desviar-se para atalhos, quando querem chegar à espiritualidade.

De acordo com a teologia católica romana, a contrição é um dos elementos da penitência (que vide). Nessa teologia, haveria três passos. O primeiro seria a *contrição*, a tristeza pelo pecado, lado a lado com a intenção de não continuar na prática do mesmo. O segundo seria a *confissão*, o reconhecimento dos próprios pecados, aos ouvidos de um sacerdote. O terceiro seria a *satisfação*, quando a pessoa cumpre certos atos prescritos, como jejum, esmolas, rezas, reparação, a fim de pagar por seus erros.

O perdão dos pecados e atitudes diferentes. Na base de João 20:23, a Igreja Ocidental acredita que o perdão dos pecados, embora num sentido *final*, pertence somente a Deus, num sentido *secundário*, e *real*, está nas mãos do clero. Isto quer dizer que os pecados são realmente perdoados através do ministério da Igreja, e os homens precisam disto para serem perdoados, menos em casos excepcionais. Os *protestantes* negam esta possibilidade, afirmando que o perdão dos pecados se realiza somente pelo próprio ato de Deus. Afirmam também que mesmo se os apóstolos originais receberam este poder, é um pulo de fé bastante grande supor que seus sucessores receberam o mesmo. É um dogma que garante isto, não as próprias escrituras. No nível popular, pela ação de ministros não espirituais, muitos abusos têm entrado no quadro, com o resultado de que os ricos podem pecar, pagar e ser perdoados, enquanto que os pobres não têm este privilégio. Os mais esclarecidos e espirituais ministros da Igreja Ocidental também deploram os abusos. Pessoalmente, acho que a interpretação da Igreja Ocidental de João 20:23 está equivocada. Ver a exposição no NTI. Em todas as nossas atitudes, palavras e ações, devemos observar a lei do amor, que é a própria medida da nossa espiritualidade. Não observar esta lei é *pior* do que interpretar mal os versículos da Bíblia. A Bíblia exige uma reparação prática da parte da pessoa que prejudica outras pessoas. No sentido absoluto, Cristo na sua *expiação* (que vide), fez a reparação que agrada a Deus. (B E H)

CONTROLE DE NATALIDADE

Ver os artigos relacionados: aborto, anticoncepcionais, esterilização, controle da população. O tema

CONTROLE — CONTROLE DO PRÓPRIO SER

do *controle de natalidade* aparece nesta Enciclopédia porque se reveste de muitas implicações morais, e porque, ultimamente, é um assunto muito debatido por teólogos e filósofos morais. O controle da natalidade busca limitar a procriação humana por meios naturais ou mecânicos. De acordo com uma definição lata, trata-se de qualquer ato que impeça duas pessoas, capazes de procriar, de chegarem a fazê-lo. Os moralistas falam em meios naturais e desnaturais, supondo que os meios naturais são permissíveis, e que os desnaturais são condenáveis.

1. *Meios mecânicos.* Esses envolvem o uso da pílula anticoncepcional, de vários cremes ou espumas que matam os espermatozóides, lavagens vaginais, aparelhos de plástico ou arame que são inseridos na boca do útero, ou apenas as «camisinhas», etc. Todos esses meios têm sido condenados pela Igreja Católica Romana, mas não oficialmente por outras denominações cristãs, pelo que são, largamente, postos em prática entre elas. Seria errado matar os espermatozóides, embora isso em nada prejudique as pessoas que praticam tal método? Alguns dão uma resposta afirmativa, porquanto acreditam que os espermatozóides representam vidas humanas em potencial. Nesse caso, que dizer sobre a destruição dos óvulos femininos? Outros pensam que a fantástica multiplicação de espermatozóides, em que cada homem produz milhões deles a cada dia, parece indicar que o aniquilamento deles não é grande coisa, pelo menos não é algo mais grave que a matança de milhões de bactérias, que também são formas de vida. Em favor do *uso* de tais meios, podemos enumerar as seguintes razões: a. Eles diminuem a taxa dos nascimentos. b. Abrandam os sofrimentos humanos envolvidos em casos de gravidez não desejados, sem importar se dentro ou fora das relações do matrimônio. c. São medidas que ajudam economicamente as famílias, sobrecarregadas com grande número de filhos. d. Longe de serem uma ameaça à vida humana, esses meios melhoram sua qualidade, impedindo a superpopulação. e. A longo prazo, poderiam servir de grande ajuda na preservação da própria vida humana no planeta, mantendo sob controle o número de habitantes no mundo, pois, se esse número não fosse impedido de continuar crescendo, poderia resultar em fomes generalizadas, condições de emprego impossíveis, a saturação de todos os campos profissionais, deixando milhões de pessoas não somente desempregadas, mas também na impossibilidade de encontrarem ocupação. Essas condições, naturalmente, fazem-nos pensar em guerras, matanças e suicídios em massa.

Argumentos contrários a medidas anticoncepcionais. A idéia de que os espermatozóides masculinos ou os óvulos femininos representam vidas humanas, devendo ser respeitados como tais, esbarra com a seguinte consideração: o ser humano não se forma da junção de um óvulo feminino com um espermatozóide masculino? Nesse caso, enquanto não houver tal junção, também não haverá qualquer vida humana envolvida, a não ser potencialmente, mas não na realidade. Todavia, uma vez iniciado o corpo humano, mesmo que nos primeiros estágios do zigoto, então sim, a vida deve ser respeitada. Respeitar o espermatozóide isolado ou o óvulo isolado, como se já fossem seres humanos, é nada saber de biologia, tornando-se uma posição insustentável diante dos fatos. b. Por outra parte, o uso dos anticoncepcionais permite a promiscuidade. Isso é uma verdade, embora tenhamos de admitir que a promiscuidade sempre existiu, mesmo quando ninguém pensava em anticoncepcionais, embora seja melhor haver promiscuidade sem casos de gravidez, que resultarão em crianças não queridas, do que promiscuidade que resultará em grande número de crianças não desejadas. Uma pessoa promíscua é apenas um pecador, e seu uso de anticoncepcionais não a torna mais ou menos pecadora por causa disso. Contudo, tal uso torna-a mais *previdente*, impedindo muito sofrimento humano, a curto e a longo prazo. E isso parece envolver um ponto importante.

2. *Meios mecânicos mais radicais.* A esterilização de homens e mulheres, mediante processos cirúrgicos, apresenta mais perigo que outros métodos. Moralmente, porém, em nada diferem de outros meios, pelo que aquilo que dissemos acima, aplica-se também a esses meios mais radicais.

3. *Os chamados meios naturais.* Tanto a Igreja Católica Romana como qualquer grupo evangélico aceitam métodos que envolvem abstinência sexual em certos dias «críticos» da mulher. Esse método também é chamado de método do ritmo da ovulação, pois a temperatura do corpo da mulher aumenta quando se avizinham os seus dias «críticos». Todavia, o método exige abstinência sexual ao menos durante um terço dos dias de cada mês, e isso sujeita alguns homens a experiências extramaritais. Paulo proibiu a abstinência sexual senão por períodos limitados, por razões especialíssimas, como períodos de jejum e oração (I Cor. 7:5). Os outros métodos aqui mencionados são impraticáveis, a menos que o organismo de uma mulher funcione de maneira muito regular, e é exatamente por essa razão que foram criados meios mecânicos anticoncepcionais. Além disso, em muitos casos, sobretudo nas classes mais pobres e menos educadas, as pessoas não sabem como calcular um período seguro, e nem o fariam, mesmo que soubessem fazê-lo.

4. O aborto (ver o artigo) está fora de questão, por razões morais. As legislações dos países só aprovam o aborto em casos de estupro (e mesmo assim os juízes mostram-se bastante hesitantes, em alguns casos), ou quando a vida da mãe corre perigo e não há outra maneira de salvá-la (o que já depende de uma decisão médica).

5. A interrupção do coito antes da ejaculação é um método largamente praticado. Mas muitos cristãos opõem-se a esse método por ser o pecado de Onã (ver Gên. 38:8,9). Alguns voltam a evocar a questão do desperdício de espermatozóides como um mal moral. Porém, o que é importante é a relação entre a alma e o corpo, e essa questão só está envolvida quando ocorre o aborto forçado, nada tendo a ver com métodos de controle de natalidade, que atuam antes de haver qualquer união da alma com o corpo. (H SP)

CONTROLE DO PRÓPRIO SER
Ver também sobre **Autocontrole**.

No grego, *egkráteia*, «domínio próprio». Essa palavra aparece por quatro vezes no Novo Testamento: Atos 24:25; Gál. 5:23; II Ped. 1:6. O verbo, *egkrateũomai*, aparece somente em I Cor. 7:9 e 9:25. E o adjetivo, *egkratēs*, figura somente em Tito 1:8.

A palavra aparece como designação de uma das virtudes cristãs básicas. Consiste no domínio do próprio «eu», no exercício da auto-restrição, especialmente no aspecto dos prazeres sensuais. O autocontrole é o seguro humano contra a auto-indulgência na imoralidade, no alcoolismo, no espírito belicoso, na maledicência, no senso de importância pessoal e na ganância. Mediante o autocontrole, o crente consegue evitar os excessos até mesmo quanto a atividades perfeitamente legítimas, como no comer, no beber e nas suas conversações.

1. Ausência de Autocontrole. Diz um antigo provérbio bíblico: «Como cidade derribada, que não tem muros, assim é o homem que não tem domínio próprio» (Pro. 25:28). O autocontrole fortalece ao homem interior. O autocontrole levanta uma muralha de defesa em torno do crente, contra as destruidoras forças do pecado e do mal. A patética tragédia do homem vigorosamente forte, Sansão, consistiu na sua intemperança quanto aos desejos sexuais. Seu amor sexual por mulheres ímpias acabou decretando a sua destruição (Juí. 14:2 ss). O amado rei de Israel, Davi, colheu trágicos resultados devido a sua falta de autocontrole quanto aos impulsos sexuais (II Sam. 11:2 ss), e outro tanto sucedeu a seu filho, Salomão (I Reis 11:1-4). Paulo tinha plena consciência do perigo da concupiscência sexual. Em consequência disso, ao escrever à igreja cristã na devassa cidade de Corinto, ele baixou instruções específicas sobre o assunto, particularmente no que diz respeito ao casamento. Ele recomendava o autocontrole como uma salvaguarda e medida de segurança contra a imoralidade, «...para que Satanás não vos tente por causa da incontinência» (I Cor. 7:5).

2. A Prática do Autocontrole. Bons exemplos e ensinos sábios são oferecidos aos crentes, nas páginas do Novo Testamento.

Tanto João Batista quanto Jesus Cristo praticavam o autocontrole, embora seus adversários tivessem acusado João de ter um demônio, e a Jesus de ser «...um glutão e bebedor de vinho...» (Luc. 7:33,34). João seguia um curso estrito de autocontrole e abstinência, em certos aspectos similar às práticas dos essênios (que vide). E Jesus, embora sociável, homem que gostava de fazer amigos entre as classes sociais simples, deixou-nos o exemplo perfeito de autocontrole, que não depende de meras aparências externas, e, sim, da decisão de viver uma vida consagrada a Deus. Jesus desfrutava das bênçãos da natureza e dos seres humanos, mas abstinha-se dos prazeres sensuais.

O autocontrole, tal como as demais virtudes cristãs, não é uma virtude fácil de ser cultivada. Requer o exercício da vontade e a ajuda do Espírito Santo. Os pagãos mais resolutos podem ressentir-se da ausência de domínio próprio. Paulo deixou alarmado o governador romano, Félix, ao dissertar acerca «...da justiça, do domínio próprio e do juízo vindouro» (Atos 24:25). E, quando escrevia «aos solteiros e viúvos» da igreja de Corinto, sobre as questões sexuais, ele demonstrou estar plenamente consciente de quão difícil é exercer o autocontrole (ver I Cor. 7:8,9). As jovens igrejas cristãs, implantadas em meio ao paganismo, por todo o império romano, tinham de enfrentar uma grande luta contra o mundanismo. Creta era uma das piores localidades do mundo, repleta de «...mentirosos, feras terríveis, ventres preguiçosos...» e outros répobros (ver Tito 1:12). Sabendo que a igreja cristã estava em tal meio ambiente, Paulo percebia quão difícil seria, para os líderes cristãos, manterem em Creta a boa conduta cristã. Em consequência, ele determinou que Tito apontasse pastores dotados de firmes qualidades cristãs. Segundo Paulo, um bispo precisa ser «...hospitaleiro, amigo do bem, sóbrio, justo, piedoso, que tenha domínio de si» (Tito 1:8).

O autocontrole é essencial para o sucesso na busca por qualquer alvo digno do nome. «Todo atleta em tudo se domina; aqueles para alcançar uma coroa corruptível; nós, porém, a incorruptível» (I Cor. 9:25). Em seguida a essas palavras, Paulo asseverou que ele, à semelhança de um atleta, constantemente mantinha seu próprio corpo em sujeição, para benefício de seu ministério cristão. O autocontrole era um tema constante nos ensinamentos de Jesus, em relação a questões como o homicídio, a concupiscência sexual, os juramentos, a retaliação, a hipocrisia, a cobiça e a ansiedade (Mat. 5:21-6:34). Por semelhante modo, Paulo catalogou as fontes de tentação, tendo aconselhado como podemos combater e vencer as mesmas: «Ora, as obras da carne são conhecidas, e são: prostituição, impureza, lascívia, idolatria, feitiçarias, inimizades, porfias, ciúmes, iras, discórdias, dissensões, facções, invejas, bebedices; glutonarias, e cousas semelhantes a estas, a respeito das quais eu vos declaro, como já outrora vos preveni, que não herdarão o reino de Deus os que tais cousas praticam. Mas o fruto do Espírito é: amor, alegria, paz, longanimidade, benignidade, bondade, fidelidade, mansidão, domínio próprio. Contra estas cousas não há lei» (Gál. 5:19-23). E, no que concerne ao ministério cristão, Paulo encorajou Timóteo como segue: «Por esta razão, pois, te admoesto que reavives o dom de Deus, que há em ti pela imposição das minhas mãos. Porque Deus não nos tem dado espírito de covardia, mas de poder, de amor e de moderação» (II Tim. 1:6,7). Esta última palavra, «moderação», é tradução de uma outra palavra grega, *sophrosúne*, «sanidade mental», mas que pode ser considerada sinônimo de *egkráteia*. Pedro ensina que se quisermos ser participantes da natureza divina, precisamos de cultivar virtudes cristãs que se complementam umas às outras, entre as quais figura o «autocontrole» (ver II Ped. 1:4-7).

CONTROVÉRSIA

1. Considerada como um Mal Moral. O marinheiro Popeye, dos desenhos animados, declara que ele briga pelo direito e para divertir-se. Quando os homens brigam para divertir-se, isso representa um mal. Há pessoas que gostam de brigar, dentro ou fora da Igreja, e que se sentem frustrados enquanto não conseguem provocar alguma cena desagradável. Assim como o *ceticismo* é a maldição do liberalismo, assim também o *espírito de controvérsia* é a maldição do fundamentalismo. Em minha própria experiência, tenho visto muitas igrejas e denominações caírem em controvérsias, dividindo grupos e separando amigos de longa data. Esse espírito maligno também persegue as escolas teológicas, onde é muito fácil fazer os estudantes se dividirem em grupos antagônicos. Vi tal atitude destruir uma faculdade teológica. A despeito disso, os homens gostam de brigar a fim de divertir-se. É surpreendente ver quantos homens causam divisões por motivos mínimos. Sei de uma escola teológica que se dividiu em torno do debate se os dias da criação foram ou não dias literais, de vinte e quatro horas. Usualmente, por detrás da suposta «contenda pela fé», há muitas razões pessoais, egoísticas, envolvendo lutas pelo poder. Nas igrejas, todas as formas de falsas questões são levantadas, quando certas pessoas querem livrar-se de um pastor que não lhes tolera os pecados.

2. Como uma Obra da Carne. O trecho de Gálatas 5:20 usa dois termos gregos, *dichostasía* e *aíresis*, «divisões» e «rivalidades», respectivamente, e que a nossa versão portuguesa traduz por «facções» e «dissensões», —a fim de indicar os males de que estamos falando. É instrutivo notar que esses erros são chamados obras da carne, figurando entre os vícios cardeais. O homem nunca peca sozinho. Está sempre envolvido no mal cósmico. Portanto, afirmo: «Quanto erro cósmico manifesta-se na Igreja cristã, quando os crentes se envolvem nas contendas e controvérsias!» No entanto, muitos gostam de apresentar suas campanhas contenciosas e combativas mascaradas de espiritualidade e defesa da fé.

3. *Quando a Controvérsia é Boa?* Há ocasiões em que o crente deve contender pela boa teologia, ou pelas boas maneiras. Ver Judas 3. Há ocasiões em que elementos malignos precisam ser expelidos; e essa expulsão pode envolver a necessidade de contendermos. Nem sempre é possível manter a paz. Nem Cristo e nem Paulo conseguiram o feito, pois sempre encontravam adversários gratuitos. Também devemos pensar nos debates ordeiros, que estimulam as idéias e produzem mudanças necessárias ao nosso crescimento espiritual. Todos esses debates deveriam ser efetuados no espírito de fraternidade, com o propósito específico de examinar as crenças e as práticas — e não de atacar personalidades — tendo em vista a correção das mesmas. Orígenes confessou que muito havia aprendido em debates com supostos hereges! Nosso conhecimento avança aos ziguezagues; a cada reversão os debates renovam-se, e assim avançamos mais algum passo. O debate teológico, quando envolve raciocínios filosóficos bem colocados, pode ser bastante frutífero. Mas, quando os homens valem-se da oportunidade de debater a fim de destruir e causar divisões, o campo já foi inteiramente infeccionado por uma atitude carnal e pecaminosa.

A passagem de Tiago 3:16 é muito instrutiva, nessa conexão: «Pois onde há inveja e sentimento faccioso, aí há confusão e toda espécie de cousas ruins». A experiência humana mostra que essa declaração está cem por cento correta.

CONTROVÉRSIAS ICONOCLÁSTICAS

Ver os artigos sobre **Iconoclasmo (Controvérsias Iconoclásticas) e Imagens.**

CONTROVÉRSIA LAPSARIANA

Ver sobre o **Lapsarianismo.**

CONVENCER, CONVICÇÃO

No grego, **elégcho**, «convencer (do erro)», «reprovar». O vocábulo é empregado por dezoito vezes no Novo Testamento: Mat. 18:15; Luc. 3:19; João 3:20; 8:46; 16:8; I Cor. 14:24; Efé. 5:11,13; I Tim. 5:20; II Tim. 4:2; Tito 1:9,13; 2:15; Heb. 12:5 (citando Pro. 3:11); Tia. 2:9; Jud. 15,22; Apo. 3:19.

Na linguagem comum, o termo é usado em sentido forense de «demonstrar a culpa». Na teologia, além desse sentido, geralmente a palavra adquire o significado de «condenar» alguma ação errada e pecaminosa.

No Novo Testamento, às vezes é a própria consciência do indivíduo quem o convence de erro (João 8:9). Mas faz parte das atuações do Espírito Santo convencer os homens acerca do mal moral e dos requisitos espirituais (João 16:8). A autêntica convicção de pecado é seguida pelo arrependimento (que vide). Há vários meios pelos quais os homens são levados à convicção de pecado: a consciência, as circunstâncias, a verdade do evangelho, as aflições, o conhecimento das verdades morais; mas, acima de tudo, as operações do Espírito sobre o coração humano.

O *Breve Catecismo de Westminster* afirma que a convicção é obra do Espírito, sendo o primeiro passo na direção da salvação (questão 30). O ritual veterotestamentário relativo às ofertas pelo pecado, **visavam** ajudar os homens a chegarem à convicção e ao arrependimento (Lev. 16:21,22). Essa idéia foi transferida para o Novo Testamento, mediante Cristo (Heb. 13:11-13). Jesus levava as pessoas à convicção de pecado (João 4:17,29), e seus ensinamentos sempre incluem a reprimenda calculada a produzir a convicção de pecado (João 8:24,44; Mat. 21:33-45). O sermão de Pedro, no dia de Pentecoste, levou os seus ouvintes à convicção de pecado (Atos 2:37). Os psicólogos e os psiquiatras têm procurado minimizar a importância da convicção de pecado, intitulando-a de ansiedade, perplexidade e tensão, cuja causa seria algum conflito moral, geralmente desnecessário ou baseado em costumes tolos. — A Bíblia, porém, mostra-nos que a convicção de pecado é muito mais do que algum truque espiritual. A verdade é que o homem é um espírito, embora dotado de um corpo físico, razão pela qual se deixa influenciar por forças espirituais. Deus existe, e transgredir as suas leis é coisa séria. Todavia, também há o perdão divino (que vide), o qual cura a alma.

Elementos da Convicção de Pecado. Não se trata de mero truque psicológico. Antes, é uma experiência evangélica definida. Consiste na percepção do abismo que separa o pecador de Deus, juntamente com o anelo de abandonar o que é mundano e físico, a fim de buscar o que é mais nobre e espiritual. A convicção de pecado pode vir mediante a visão de Deus (Isa. 6:1-5), ou então mediante a presença e operação do Espírito Santo (João 16:7 *ss*). Inclui o remorso, mas também prepara a alma para o arrependimento (que vide), e conduz à conversão (que vide).

CONVENCIONALISMO

Palavra que vem do latim, **con**, «com», e **venire**, «vir». Na filosofia, o termo indica uma decisão que foi tomada com base no acordo comum. Mas a palavra é igualmente usada como antônimo de natural, real ou autêntico.

1. Os sofistas, como Trasímaco (que vide) e Calicles (que vide), afirmavam que os padrões morais são determinados convencionalmente, devido a meros costumes sociais, etc., e não pelas verdadeiras demandas da natureza. Rousseau (que vide) dizia que os padrões convencionais debilitam a moralidade, no que tinha toda a razão.

2. Demócrito (que vide) asseverava que questões como gosto, cores, etc., são meras convenções da nossa percepção, e que a realidade por detrás desses acidentes são os átomos e o vazio. Falando mais ou menos no mesmo tom, Locke referiu-se às qualidades *secundárias*, em contraste com as qualidades *primárias*. As qualidades secundárias seriam todos os tipos de convenção, apêndices do que é real.

3. Os filósofos sofistas Protágoras (que vide) e Górgias (que vide) faziam o contraste entre o que é real e o que é convencional. Dizia Protágoras que «o homem é a medida de todas as coisas». Para ele, portanto, não haveria verdade acima e além dessa convenção. Isso posto, a convenção seria a definição daquilo que é verdadeiro. Isso permite-nos entender que, de acordo com tal sistema filosófico, não há tal coisa como verdade absoluta. Mas Protágoras via somente metade da questão. Pois, se é verdade que «seja todo homem mentiroso» (Rom. 3:4), existe um em Quem reside a «verdade», por ser ele a própria Verdade (João 14:6). Mas Protágoras não sabia disso.

4. *A Teologia e o Convencionalismo.* Há um ditado popular que diz: «A voz do povo é a voz de Deus». Isso é convencionalismo puro. Os credos e as declarações doutrinárias vão-se tornando convencionais porque tentam sumariar as verdades teológicas mediante

algumas poucas declarações superficiais, mas em torno das quais muitos se aglutinam. Além disso, os credos e as declarações doutrinárias criam muita contenda quanto a qualquer coisa que contradiga essas afirmações convencionais. As teologias sistemáticas, como é óbvio, têm valor, embora consistam em prolongadas declarações doutrinárias convencionalizadas, que contêm elementos verídicos e falsos. Mas a espiritualidade e seu conhecimento jamais poderão ser convencionalizados com sucesso. A letra mata, e o Espírito vivifica. Porém, os homens gostam de simplificar a verdade, porque partem de um raciocínio que diz: «Até uma criança pode entender a verdade». Essa simplificação, pois, produz uma verdade infantil. Porém, nada existe de tão complexo e não-convencional quanto a verdade.

CONVENTÍCULO

Vem do latim **conventus**, «assembléia», mas na forma diminutiva da palavra. A palavra portuguesa significa uma reunião religiosa *secreta*, ou então *proibida* por lei. Assim, as reuniões dos «dissenters» protestantes, na Grã-Bretanha, eram ilegais, como também as reuniões dos «covenanters» (que vide). A palavra «conventículo» também indica o lugar onde alguma adoração ilegal estiver tendo lugar.

CONVENTOS

Essa palavra vem do termo latino **conventus**, «assembléia». A palavra pode ser empregada de três maneiras diferentes: 1. Uma comunidade religiosa de homens ou de mulheres, usualmente governada por algum superior ou superiora. A princípio, a palavra foi usada nesse sentido, a partir do século IV D.C., quando monges eremitas do Oriente começaram a formar grupos. Na Igreja ocidental, onde não havia o costume de serem formados conventos de eremitas, o termo era usado para descrever as comunidades de monges ou de freiras, sob as ordens de um superior ou superiora. 2. A palavra também é usada para designar o edifício ou edifícios onde residem as freiras. Em português, os conventos são formados por freiras, e os frades formam mosteiros; em outros idiomas, os conventos podem ser de frades ou de freiras. 3. No Brasil e outros países de língua portuguesa, os conventos sempre são formados por freiras.

A vida nos conventos varia, de acordo com os propósitos de cada sociedade religiosa. Os conventos das ordens religiosas mais antigas voltam-se mais para a vida contemplativa, para as orações, para o ascetismo. Porém, muitos conventos de ordens monásticas modernas incluem atividades como o ensino de crianças, obras de caridade, hospitais, orfanatos, asilos para velhos e instituições para crianças excepcionais. Um labor útil, voltado para as necessidades sociais, usualmente caracteriza esses conventos.

No cristianismo antigo, os conventos desempenharam importante papel na propagação da cristandade. Nos tempos modernos, continuam importantes dentro das atividades caridosas da Igreja Católica Romana. A antiga acusação, contida na declaração: «A virtude enclausurada não pode ser louvada», não mais pode ser aplicada a muitos conventos e mosteiros. Até mesmo em grupos não-católicos, a vida monástica tem seus paralelos, geralmente de variedade comunal. Ver o artigo sobre *Comunidades Comunais*.

••• ••• •••

CONVENTUAIS

Esse é o nome de um ramo autônomo da ordem mendicante dos Frades Menores (que vide), da Igreja Católica Romana. Tal designação vem sendo usada desde o ano de 1431, a fim de designar os frades que seguem a regra menos rigorosa, embora o grupo só tenha sido reconhecido oficialmente por Roma em 1517. Três papas diversos foram eleitos, antes pertencentes a essa ordem. Outras ordens que seguem uma regra similar, mas menos estrita, também têm sido chamadas pelo mesmo nome. (E)

CONVERSÃO

I. As Palavras Envolvidas. Latim, **com** (totalmente) + **vetere** (virar), portanto, fazer uma mudança radical, girar completamente. No hebraico temos *sub*, que significa girar ou voltar, que é usado em ações físicas, morais e espirituais. No grego temos *epistrepho*, que tem estes mesmos significados e usos.

II. Usos Bíblicos. As idéias bíblicas principais são o abandono da maldade e pecado, Jer. 18:8, com a dedicação do ser a Deus, Mal. 3:7. Deus é a força ativa nesta virada. Jer. 31:18. As pessoas que recusam esta operação espiritual terminam castigados, Amós 4:6-12. O Novo Testamento harmoniza-se com o Velho Testamento sobre este assunto. Ver Atos 14:15, 26:18. A verdadeira conversão envolve fé e arrependimento, Atos 3:19, 26:18. Um exemplo radical de conversão é o caso de Paulo, Atos 9:1-18. A conversão pode vir de súbito, mas normalmente tem um longo tempo de preparação.

III. Tipos de Conversão

1. *Não religiosa, política.* As pessoas são convertidas a certos sistemas políticos, às vezes de súbito, por forças humanitárias, racionais ou egoístas. Subseqüentemente, elas procuram utilizar estes sistemas para o melhoramento da sociedade ou para fins egoístas, ou os dois.

2. *Conversão biológica.* Os adolescentes, freqüentemente, são mais religiosos naquela idade do que em qualquer outra época da vida. Mais do que zelo jovem pode ser envolvido nisto. Psicólogos nos informam que há evidências que indicam que este tipo de conversão pode ser simplemente a sublimação das energias sexuais em ideais religiosos. Muitos jovens que são radicalmente religiosos nesta época, uma vez casados, cessam de ter qualquer zelo religioso. Alguns psiquiatras acham que a própria religião é somente um refinamento do libido.

3. *O nascimento de um novo ser.* Este novo ser pode ser simplesmente a entrada de um jovem na vida do adulto. Os jovens têm muito zelo natural, e muitos ideais. Aproximando-se a idade de tornarem-se adultos, eles podem expressar esta qualidade num tipo de novo nascimento, quando deixam a vida de crianças, e começam a vida de adultos. Embora esta transição possa ter elementos fortes de envolvimento na religião, ela não é necessariamente espiritual. Muitas vezes, alguma coisa permanente de valor é assim levada para a vida de adulto, mas isto, em si, não qualifica a experiência como um produto do Espírito.

4. *Uma resolução de conflito.* Paulo nos ensina que o conflito entre o bem e o mal no homem é um terror, Rom. cap. 7. A maioria das religiões procuram resolver este conflito, embora por meios diferentes. Também as filosofias, psicologias e políticas prometem resolver este conflito. Em qualquer caso, no qual alguma resolução seja alcançada, resulta em uma experiência de conversão. Os filósofos fazem «conver-

CONVERSÃO — CONVERSÃO DE PAULO

tidos» aos seus sistemas, resolvendo conflitos entre idéias. As religiões fazem a mesma coisa, e normalmente, neste caso, o problema do pecado está envolvido. Portanto, todos os tipos de religiões, cristãs ou não, produzem seus convertidos. Muitos deles tornam-se fanáticos e procuram propagar sua fé, porque, dizem eles, «isto funciona», e como prova, eles se apresentam. Tudo isto pode ter algum valor, embora não tenha nada a ver com a conversão bíblica. Naturalmente, muitos acham que todas as conversões são essencialmente iguais, sendo exercícios psicológicos, e não há razão para exaltar a variedade bíblica acima das outras.

5. *Uma revolução copernicana*. Este tipo de conversão resulta de uma evolução gradual de idéias, ideais e ambições, embora possa-se manifestar de súbito. Se a conversão for religiosa, então a pessoa, depois de uma longa busca e transformação, alcança uma posição de satisfação, da qual, pode ver claramente o avanço que foi realizado. Neste avanço, a pessoa tem ultrapassado totalmente além do tipo de ser que era antes. Na religião temos a designação *almas nascidas duas vezes*. Esta conversão pode ser biblica ou não, porque todas as religiões têm seus exemplos de pessoas cuja expressão espiritual tem passado uma revolução radical, —ou copernicana, porque a alma tem o novo centro, o Sol da Espiritualidade. Nisto, a terra cessa de ser o centro da existência. O avanço é do terrestre para o celeste.

6. *A conversão da mente sã*. Algumas pessoas que passam através de uma luta severa com doenças mentais, quando curadas, ou melhoradas significantemente, têm uma experiência de conversão. Alcançando uma mente sã, elas muitas vezes tornam-se advogadas radicais dos sistemas através dos quais elas obteram seus melhoramentos. Se a psiquiatria as ajudou, então, são convertidos psicológicos. Se a religião, em qualquer forma foi o agente, elas ficam devotas daquela religião.

7. *A conversão bíblica*. Esta conversão é espiritual e mística, porque envolve a participação do Espírito Santo que atua sobre a natureza humana, convertendo-a. Embora esta conversão possa envolver elementos dos diversos tipos discutidos, deve transcender os mesmos, ou não se qualifica como uma verdadeira conversão cristã. Ofereço maiores descrições sob os pontos II, IV e V.

•••

IV. Elementos da Conversão Bíblica

Alguns encaram o novo nascimento ou regeneração como conversão, mas isso é muito *inadequado*. A conversão, por si só, não é ainda regeneração, mas é tão-somente *parte* da regeneração. A conversão consiste em uma meia volta na vida, em que a alma se volta para Deus. Nas páginas do N.T., a palavra *epistrepho* é utilizada para expressar essa idéia, e é aplicada tanto para os desviados, que retornam à sua anterior comunhão com Deus, como para os incrédulos, ao se voltarem para Deus. (Ver os trechos de Luc. 22:32; Apo. 2:5,16; Mat. 17:3; Atos 3:19 e 26:18). A conversão é descrita como um voltar-se das trevas da idolatria, do pecado e do domínio de Satanás, para a adoração e o serviço ao verdadeiro Deus (conforme se vê nas passagens de Atos 14:15; 26:18; I Tes. 1:9) e ao seu Filho, Jesus Cristo (como se vê em I Ped. 2:25).

A conversão consiste no exercício do *arrependimento e da fé*, elementos esses que tanto o Senhor Jesus como o Apóstolo Paulo vinculam como sumários das exigências morais do evangelho. (Ver Mar. 1:15 e Atos 20:21). O arrependimento é uma mudança de mente e de coração para com Deus; a fé significa a confiança na Palavra de Deus e em seu Cristo. A conversão, pois, encerra ambas essas idéias.

1. A conversão é inspirada pela força das Escrituras, Sal. 19:7.
2. É operada pelo Espírito, Sal. 51:12.
3. Grava no coração a lei moral de Deus (ver II Cor. 3:3), e isso pelo poder do Espírito.
4. Ela é absolutamente necessária para a salvação, Mat. 18:3.
5. Prepara o caminho para o serviço espiritual, Luc. 22:32.
6. A tarefa da igreja é conduzir todos os homens à conversão, Tia. 5:19,20.
7. Ela é a base do perdão dos pecados, Atos. 3:19.
8. Ela consiste na fé e no *arrependimento*, (vide), Atos 20:21.
9. Ela prepara a alma para a união espiritual com Cristo, Rom. 6:3.
10. A conversão pode ser gradual (como no caso da maioria das pessoas), ou dramática (como no caso de Saulo). A iluminação pode ser parcial e levar aos poucos à conversão. Muitas pessoas são parcialmente iluminadas (e assim, melhoradas), embora nunca cheguem a converter-se.
11. A conversão é um ato divino, mas requer a cooperação do livre-arbítrio do homem. Portanto, é um ato divino e humano, ao mesmo tempo.
12. A conversão necessariamente resulta na santificação, pois, do contrário, não será real.

V. Bases Espirituais

Por meio de Deus (I Reis 18:37; João 6:44; Atos 21:19).
Por meio de Cristo (Atos 3:26; Rom. 15:18).
Pelo poder do Espírito Santo (Pro. 1:23).
Vem da graça (Atos 11:21 com vs. 23).
Segue-se ao arrependimento (Atos 3:19; 26:20).
Resulta da fé (Atos 11:21).
Pela instrumentalidade de:
  As Escrituras (Sal. 19:7).
  Os ministros (Atos 26:18; I Tes. 1:9).
  Auto-exame (Sal. 119:59; Lam. 3:40).
  Aflições (Sal. 78:34).
Dos pecadores, motivo de alegria:
  Para Deus (Eze. 18:23; Luc. 15:32).
  Para os santos (Atos 15:3; Gál. 1:23,24).
É necessária (Mat. 18:3).
Determinada (Jó 36:10)
Exortações atinentes (Pro. 1:23; Isa. 31:6; 55:6; Jer. 3:7; Eze. 33:11).
Promessas vinculadas à mesma (Nee. 1:9; Isa. 1:27; Jer. 3:14; Eze. 18:27).
Oremos pela mesma (Sal. 80:7; 85:4; Jer. 31:18; Lam. 5:21).
É acompanhada pela confissão de pecados e pela oração (I Reis 8:35).
Perigo de negligenciá-la (Sal. 7:12; Jer. 44:5,11; Eze. 3:19).
Dever de conduzirmos os pecadores à mesma (Sal. 51:13).
Encorajamento para conduzirmos os pecadores à mesma (Dan. 12:3; Tia. 5:19,20).
Dos gentios, predita (Isa. 2:2; 11:10; 60:5; 66:12).
De Israel, predita (Eze. 36:25-27).

CONVERSÃO DE PAULO

A Conversão de Saulo: Atos 9:1-31; 22:6-11 e 26:12-18.

CONVERSÃO

A Vida de Paulo

Paulo, apóstolo enviado aos gentios. Sabemos mais acerca do apóstolo Paulo do que sobre qualquer outra das personagens apostólicas. No N.T., as nossas fontes informativas a seu respeito são o livro de Atos e as suas próprias epístolas. Fora disso só há mais uma alusão a ele, em II Ped. 3:15, onde ele é chamado de *nosso amado irmão.*

A arqueologia fornece-nos muitas informações quanto aos locais visitados por Paulo, embora não sobre a sua pessoa. Nossos conhecimentos sobre os primeiros anos de sua vida são escassos. Desde o seu nascimento até o seu aparecimento, em Jerusalém, como perseguidor dos cristãos, possuímos informações meramente esparsas, parte das quais não passa de conjectura. Sabemos, contudo, que ele nasceu em Tarso, «...cidade não insignificante da Cilícia...» (Atos 21:39), descrição essa que as escavações arqueológicas de *Sir William Ramsay* confirmaram amplamente. Tarso da Cilícia foi incorporada à província da Síria e tivera história importante durante um período de muitos séculos. Era a principal cidade da Cilícia, e com sua região, sintetizava o Oriente e o Ocidente, isto é, as culturas grega e oriental, incluindo, por igual modo, a cultura romana. Era centro da filosofia estóica da variedade romana, onde os filósofos pregavam as suas doutrinas nos mercados e nas praças públicas, mais ou menos como os missionários de Cristo têm feito tradicionalmente. As epístolas de Paulo, em suas ilustrações e em algumas de suas idéias básicas, por isso mesmo, refletem o que há de melhor no estoicismo. É ponto muito bem conhecido e amplamente discutido que Paulo deixa transparecer muito da mesma erudição refletida por Sêneca, o importante filósofo estóico romano, que foi igualmente martirizado por Nero, à semelhança de Paulo.

1. O treinamento de Saulo, quanto à sabedoria profana, mui provavelmente incluiu a educação filosófica ordinária, a retórica e a matemática, sem falarmos em seus estudos sobre a religião judaica. (Ver Atos 22:3; 26:4 e diversas referências, em suas epístolas, a questões como coroas, jogos atléticos, lutas, etc., o que também serviam de principais ilustrações entre os filósofos estóicos para ilustrar os princípios éticos). O fato é que o grego utilizado por Paulo, em suas epístolas, é uma excelente variedade do grego literário «koiné», o que nos mostra quão bem alicerçada fora a sua educação na linguagem, além de ficar demonstrado o fato de que ele falava o grego como seu idioma nativo, provavelmente do mesmo modo que o hebraico (isto é, o aramaico). Não se há de duvidar que esse apóstolo também conhecia o latim, e, antes do fim de suas viagens missionárias, já teria aprendido mais um idioma ou dois.

2. O Testemunho pessoal de Paulo, em Gál. 1:14, mostra que ele era indivíduo intensamente religioso, desde a juventude. Costumava freqüentar regularmente as sinagogas judaicas, antes de sua conversão, e, quando já atingira idade suficiente, tornou-se seguidor fiel do farisaísmo. Esse versículo também indica que, mui provavelmente, ele era o jovem que mais se destacava em Jerusalém, sendo grande a sua fama como homem de grande zelo religioso. Sabemos também que ele estudou com o famosíssimo rabino fariseu, Gamaliel (ver Atos 22:3). (Ver o artigo sobre *Gamaliel*). A erudição maior de Paulo fora adquirida em Jerusalém, naquela escola de fariseus, o que também contribui com algo para explicar o caráter geral de sua vida e de suas crenças, alicerçadas firmemente no judaísmo tradicional.

3. Conversão de Saulo. Intensa discussão se tem centralizado em redor das razões psicológicas por detrás de sua conversão a Cristo. Saulo se tornara um intenso perseguidor de cristãos, tendo chegado ao assassínio, não poupando nem mesmo a mulheres. E no entanto, repentinamente, tornou-se igualmente zeloso defensor e propagador do evangelho de Cristo. Que ocorrência teria sido suficientemente drástica e decisiva para produzir tão notável modificação em suas atitudes? As respostas dadas por certos indivíduos são repugnantes para a fé e a sensibilidade cristãs. Porquanto alguns querem fazer-nos crer que Paulo era um esquizofrênico, ou que de outra maneira sofrera um desequilíbrio mental qualquer, o que teriam sido essas aberrações mentais que criaram as condições necessárias para suas experiências místicas. No entanto, não nos devemos admirar ante essa opinião adversa sobre Paulo, porque até mesmo pessoas moderadamente dotadas de dons psíquicos são consideradas um tanto estranhas. Quanto mais poderosos são esses dons e quanto mais elas reivindicam possuir experiências místicas, mais são consideradas fracas da cabeça. Todavia, a verdade é que tais pessoas geralmente não são *subnormais*, e sim, *supranormais.* Por isso mesmo é que os santos e homens piedosos, bem como os operadores de milagres, geralmente servem de escândalo para o mundo. Isso continuará nesse pé, até que o mundo seja suficientemente espiritualizado para compreender (se é que isso algum dia se tornará realidade) que assim deve ser a «normalidade» para a humanidade, embora, ordinariamente, os homens não passem de feras um pouco mais inteligentes de que os animais irracionais.

Outros críticos supõem que o senso de culpa, reprimido durante anos, em face de suas perseguições e assassinos contra os cristãos, teria subitamente explodido em experiências pseudomísticas, o que resultou em vir a ser ele justamente o contrário do que vinha sendo, ou seja, a sua *conversão.* Assim sendo, ainda segundo esse ponto de vista, a experiência de Saulo poderia ter sido meramente «psicológica», e não verdadeiramente mística. Ora, nesse caso, Lucas, o autor do livro de Atos, teria exagerado em suas narrativas, adornando com um colorido mais vivo a realidade da vida de Paulo.

É perfeitamente possível, entretanto, que o próprio Paulo soubesse muito bem que aquilo que lhe ocorrera era uma experiência mística da mais elevada ordem, como seja um encontro pessoal com o próprio Senhor Jesus. Nada existe no campo do bom senso ou da experiência religiosa sã que contradiga tal coisa. De fato, a maioria das doutrinas e das práticas religiosas, originalmente, se alicerça em alguma forma de experiência mística. Os modernos estudos da parapsicologia tendem a confirmar a realidade das experiências místicas válidas, embora algumas dessas experiências, como é normal, não passem de ilusões psicológicas. O fato de que a personalidade de Paulo foi transformada tão radical e permanentemente é um ponto positivo em favor da validade de sua experiência e em prol da realidade de sua origem, porquanto o Senhor Jesus está vivo, e não se há de duvidar que teve contactos pessoais, após a sua morte, ressurreição e ascensão aos céus, com Paulo, desde o momento de sua conversão, na estrada de Damasco.

4. Referências Bíblicas. A história da conversão de Saulo de Tarso é narrada em *três* lugares no livro de Atos (ver Atos 9:3,19; 33:6-21 e 26:12-18), havendo algumas variações quanto às minúcias, o que nenhuma pessoa sensata pode negar, ante a simples leitura dessas passagens (ver notas sobre estas diferenças, 22:6 no NTI). É possível que o próprio Paulo, ao narrar a história, inconscientemente tenha variado um tanto o seu conteúdo. No entanto, muitos eruditos, até mesmo da escola liberal, concordam que há uma harmonia essencial entre essas várias narrativas bíblicas, além de certas coincidências verbais que confirmam o fato de que há uma fonte informativa única para todas elas. Dessa maneira, essas narrativas são interdependentes entre si, e não narrativas independentes umas das outras. As histórias de Lucas, mui provavelmente, se basearam em narrativas pessoais, apresentadas pelo próprio Paulo, porquanto Lucas foi quase constante companheiro de viagens daquele apóstolo, em suas jornadas missionárias. Os sentimentos de temor, a luz brilhante, a purificação psicológica, a sua renovação, a sua conversão, são todos sinais de uma experiência mística genuína; e são exatamente esses os elementos que reaparecem em todas as narrativas sobre o evento da conversão de Saulo. Em sua vida posterior, Paulo recebeu outras grandes e *importantes visões*, e a sua doutrina repousa essencialmente sobre essas diversas revelações. Por que pensaríamos ser estranho que Deus se revele a alguém? De fato, o cristianismo, como revelação distintiva de Deus, se alicerça em tais revelações, sobretudo sobre as revelações outorgadas ao apóstolo Paulo, porquanto nelas é que encontramos as grandes distinções que separaram o cristianismo do judaísmo.

A *condição* original para alguém entrar no apostolado, entre outras, era que o candidato tivesse *visto* ao Senhor (ver Atos 1:21). Ora, essa exigência teve cumprimento na experiência de Saulo. Quando já apóstolo, refere-se Paulo por quatro vezes, em suas epístolas, à sua experiência de conversão; essas passagens mostram que ele estava convicto da realidade objetiva da mesma, considerando-a como equivalente a «ver» a Cristo, o que o qualificava ao ofício apostólico. (Ver Gál. 1:15,16; I Cor. 9:1; 15:8 e II Cor. 4:6). Paulo não estabeleceu distinção alguma entre essa forma de ver e aquelas que os demais apóstolos experimentaram, antes da ascensão de Cristo, porquanto todas essas aparições foram do «Senhor ressurrecto».

Importância da Conversão de Paulo

As duas grandes pedras fundamentais, que servem de características distintivas do cristianismo, são a ressurreição do Senhor Jesus e a conversão de Saulo, bem como as proposições que se seguem, coerentemente, desses dois fatos históricos.

Paulo recebeu o nome de *Saulo* ao nascer, em honra ao primeiro rei de Israel, Saul, mas posteriormente, passou a ser chamado Paulo, que se deriva do latim e significa *pequeno*. Isso talvez seja uma alusão à sua pequena estatura física. Todavia, alguns eruditos pensam que se trata antes de um reflexo de algum apelido familiar, como «nosso pequeno», ou coisa parecida. Porém, é possível que ele mesmo houvesse escolhido o nome Paulo por ser *um tanto similar* a Saulo, sem que nisso haja qualquer significação especial, como também, no mundo moderno, não damos muita significação aos nossos nomes próprios, ainda que, originalmente, todos os nomes próprios tivessem a sua respectiva significação.

CONVICÇÃO COMO CERTEZA ESPIRITUAL

Há um uso do termo «convicção» que ultrapassa aquilo que expomos no verbete chamado «Convencer, Convicção». Há oportunidades em que esse termo indica a certeza que podemos ter sobre as questões espirituais e morais. Isso sucede quando dizemos: «Estou convicto que...», com o que queremos dizer que nossas crenças sobre questões espirituais e morais são inabaláveis, afetando nossos atos. Também podemos aplicar o termo à certeza de que podemos ter sobre nossa salvação pessoal. Ver sobre *Segurança dos Salvos*.

CONVIDADO

No hebraico, **gara**, «chamar», «convidar». Verbo hebraico usado por mais de quinhentas e cinqüenta vezes, embora por poucas vezes com o sentido de «convidar». Por exemplo: I Reis 1:41,49; Pro. 9:18; Sof. 1:7.

No grego, *anákeimi*, «convidar» ou «ser convidado»: Mat. 9:10; 22:10,11; 26:7,20; Mar. 6:26; 14:18; 16:14; Luc. 22:7; João 6:11; 12:2; 13:23,28.

Ver o artigo sobre a *Hospitalidade*. Essa palavra é usada para indicar aqueles que são convidados a certos eventos, ou para passarem a noite, ou para estarem com alguém por algum tempo. Ver II Sam. 15:11; Jó 19:15. Em certos trechos, onde a palavra não é usada, a idéia está presente. A hospitalidade é recomendada como um exercício espiritual, porquanto é um ato que cumpre a lei do amor cristão. O Novo Testamento tem um ponto de vista sério sobre a questão, e faz da mesma uma das qualificações para os líderes da Igreja cristã (I Tim. 3:2). O trecho de Heb. 13:2 sugere que a hospitalidade para com os estranhos pode até levar uma pessoa a entreter involuntariamente a anjos, tal como sucedeu a Abraão e Sara (Gên. 18), ou nos casos de Ló (Gên. 19) e Manoá (Juí. 13).

No Novo Testamento, um convidado é alguém que se *reclina* à nossa mesa (o divã dos gregos e romanos), conforme a palavra grega nô-lo indica. Um convidado compartilha de nossa residência e de nossas refeições (Mat. 14:9; Mar. 6:22,26). São aqueles que freqüentam o palácio do rei e compartilham dos luxos que ali são desfrutados (Mat. 14:9). No trecho paralelo da festa de casamento (Mat. 22:10,11), encontramos um uso metafórico da palavra. Os *convidados* são aqueles que atendem ao chamado para o Reino de Deus; e a festa de casamento representa as alegrias próprias desse reino. Alguns estudiosos têm pensado que os convidados são pessoas fora da Igreja, e que a Igreja é constituída pelos *filhos*, o que significa que «convidados» seria um sinônimo dos «amigos do noivo», de João 3:29. Porém, isso é um refinamento indevido, empregado para excluir da Igreja àqueles que não pertencem a alguma denominação particular, mas que atingirão certo nível de glória. No trecho de Mateus 9:15, os discípulos de Jesus são denominados «filhos do noivo» (embora nossa versão portuguesa diga ali «convidados»).

CONVIDADOS PARA O CASAMENTO

Essa expressão encontra-se na nossa versão portuguesa em Mat. 9:15; Mar. 2:19 e Luc. 5:34, como tradução de uma expressão hebraica que, mais literalmente, significa «filhos do noivo», que indica tanto os companheiros do noivo quanto os convidados ao casamento.

CONVOCAÇÃO MILITAR

A maioria dos países do mundo moderno conta com a convocação militar obrigatória. Isso representa um problema para certas pessoas religiosas, ou então por motivos inteiramente humanitários. Abordei demoradamente as implicações éticas a respeito em meu artigo sobre *Objetores Conscientes*. Ver também

CONVOCAÇÃO SANTA — COOPERADORES DE DEUS

sobre o *Pacifismo*. Ver também o artigo sobre *Conflitos de Deveres*. Algumas vezes é difícil tomar uma decisão, porquanto isto envolve conflitos de interesses ou de deveres, de tal modo que é impossível se tomar uma decisão inteiramente livre de dúvidas.

CONVOCAÇÃO SANTA

O «ajuntamento da congregação» era a reunião do povo de Israel com a finalidade de adorar a Yahweh (Êxo. 12:6). Nesse trecho somos informados de que os primeiros sete dias da páscoa (que vide) era um tempo de «santa assembléia». Nenhum trabalho manual era permitido, com exceção da preparação de alimentos. As convocações santas eram as seguintes: 1. Os sábados (Lev. 23:2,3). 2. A páscoa, no seu primeiro e no seu sétimo dia (Êxo. 12:16; Lev. 23:7,8). 3. O dia de Pentecoste, ou festa das semanas (Lev. 23:21; Núm. 28:26). 4. A festa dos Tabernáculos, no seu primeiro e no seu último dia (Lev. 23:35,36). 5. A grande festividade, o dia da expiação, uma vez por ano (Lev. 23:27; Núm. 29:7). Nenhum trabalho manual podia ser feito nesses dias, excetuando a preparação de alimentos; mas, no caso do sábado, até mesmo a preparação de alimentos era proibida.

COOPERAÇÃO, A GRANDE

II Cor. 5:1: Em nós, cooperando com ele, também vos exortamos a que não recebais a graça de Deus em vão;

Paulo havia mostrado, em II Cor. 5:17, que a reconciliação leva o indivíduo a uma completa transformação de seu ser, não sendo isso mero termo teológico ou proposição doutrinária. Portanto, até mesmo a igreja local de Corinto ele conclamou à reconciliação com Deus (ver II Cor. 5:20), embora sem dúvida cresse que já se encontravam nesse estado por longo tempo. Porém, uma vez que lhes faltava a evidência sólida da «transformação», é possível que lhes faltasse ou tivessem perdido a graça da «reconciliação».

A Grande Cooperação

1. O Pai, sabendo da necessidade de redenção, proveu o plano necessário e enviou o seu Filho (ver João 3:16). Deus nos proveu uma ampla graça (ver notas completas a respeito, em Efé. 2:8). Ele destinou homens para que operassem de conformidade com essa graça (ver Efé. 2:10).

2. Deus enviou seu Filho na forma de um ser humano (ver Fil. 2:5 e ss), a fim de que pudesse elevar eficazmente a outros homens. Ele concedeu aos homens essa «filiação», a fim de que chegassem a ter a natureza do Filho. Ver Rom. 8:29, II Cor. 3:18 e II Ped. 1:4

3. Por meio do seu Espírito, ele inspira os homens a cooperarem para a propagação da mensagem divina, e assim exercerem um papel ativo no plano remidor (ver Mat. 28:19,20). Ora, esse não é um privilégio desprezível.

Seja como for, o fato de que Paulo falou tão prolongada e severamente sobre a necessidade da reconciliação, até mesmo para uma igreja cristã local, indica a verdade que até mesmo os crentes precisam dar cuidadosa atenção a essa questão, a fim de que não recebam a graça de Deus em vão. Essa é a única conclusão que podemos derivar desta secção, e que foi escrita para uma igreja cristã, não sendo uma epístola evangelística, dirigida aos incrédulos.

Na qualidade de cooperadores com ele. Em outras palavras: «...trabalhando juntamente com Deus, pois, nós vos rogamos que...», o que seria uma tradução mais literal, porquanto o grego tem o simples particípio. O «esforço de cooperação», que tem por alvo a reconciliação humana, é uma cooperação com Deus e o seu Cristo, conforme fica entendido nos versículos vigésimo e vigésimo primeiro. Todavia, é possível que Cristo esteja mais especificamente em foco aqui, posto que é em favor dele que agimos como embaixadores, conforme se aprende em II Cor. 5:20. No entanto, a passagem de I Cor. 3:9 fala especificamente de ser cooperadores de Deus. Portanto, cooperamos com Deus em sua missão remidora, agindo sob as suas ordens, embora não possamos excluir o Senhor Jesus do quadro, sob hipótese nenhuma. O verbo grego aqui empregado, «sunergeo», significa «trabalhar com», «auxiliar». O apóstolo Paulo, nessa qualidade, era um cooperador especial comissionado no ministério da reconciliação; e por causa disso possuía elevada autoridade, como representante de Cristo, nessa questão.

COOPERADORES DE DEUS

I Cor. 3:9: *Porque nós somos cooperadores de Deus; vós sois lavoura de Deus e edifício de Deus*.

Pequena troca na posição das palavras daria a tradução literal do grego, neste caso, a saber: «...*somos cooperadores de Deus*...», o que indica a idéia de possessão, «somos...de Deus». Há versões, entretanto, que dizem: «somos cooperadores em favor de Deus», ficando destacada mais a idéia de origem. Isso é mais ou menos o que transparece na tradução portuguesa que serve de base textual deste artigo.

Os Cooperadores de Deus

1. Eles são «de Deus», o que denota o seguinte: a. ele é a causa e a fonte da habilidade de que têm de se identificarem dessa maneira com ele (ver I Cor. 15:10). Pela graça de Deus eu sou o que sou, e faço o que faço. b. A idéia de possessão também se faz presente: «pertencemos a Deus» (Somos «de Deus»). c. Tudo quanto porventura estivermos fazendo, estará sendo feito *em cooperação* com o poder divino.

2. Outros estudiosos vêem a Deus como o objeto do labor efetuado: nosso objetivo seria servir a Deus. (Ver II Cor. 5:20). Aquilo que fazemos, fazêmo-lo para cumprir a missão que nos foi dada por Deus, a fim de glorificá-lo, cumprindo os seus desígnios.

3. Seja como for, a expressão dá a entender uma íntima associação com o Espírito Santo, na missão conferida a cada remido.

4. O resultado prático disso é que nenhum indivíduo pode jactar-se em si mesmo, pois, se lhe foi dada uma missão espiritual qualquer, Deus é a origem e o alvo da mesma. Ele inspira em nós o bem e o efetua em nós; ele inspira os nossos esforços e lhes confere bom êxito. A ele seja toda a glória, portanto!

5. Essa expressão é uma censura contra o espírito de partidarismo que havia em Corinto. Uma censura contra a adoração a ídolos humanos e contra o denominacionalismo.

Os estudiosos que pensam aqui que no original grego temos o genitivo possessivo opinam que Deus aparece nesta passagem como o principal sócio na aventura da vida de cada crente, participando de suas realizações, derrotas, alegrias e tristezas. Essa é uma verdade, embora não possamos estar certos sobre como podemos compreender o genitivo que envolve o termo «Deus». A interpretação de I Cor. 3:9 oferece várias possibilidades, cada uma das quais representa uma verdade, embora não tenhamos certeza sobre o que Paulo queria dar a entender neste ponto. (Com isso comparar os trechos de II Cor. 5:20 e 6:1). Assim sendo, alguns intérpretes sugerem a tradução «...*cooperadores uns com os outros no serviço de Deus*...» Mas essa sugestão não goza do apoio do original grego; pois se Paulo tivesse querido dizer isso, tinha meios claros para expressá-lo no grego. Contudo, essa sugestão apresenta uma verdade, embora talvez não seja aquela que o apóstolo queria dar a entender.

Ora, se os homens podem estar tão intimamente associados com Deus, a ponto de poderem ser chamados de seus «cooperadores», então dificilmente é próprio que sejam estabelecidas distinções entre eles, com o aparecimento de «heróis» deste e daquele partido, o que só serve para derrubar por terra a harmonia que deve haver na igreja cristã e entre os seus ministros. Os ministros, pois, são um com Deus, nesse serviço do evangelho, e não rivais; e ninguém tem o direito de lançar uns contra os outros.

COORTE

No grego é **speira**, «coisa torcida», «corda», «companhia». As referências bíblicas são Mat. 27:27; Mar. 15:16; João 18:3,12; Atos 10:1; 21:31 e 27:1. Ver o artigo geral sobre *Exército*.

Uma *coorte* geralmente tinha uma décima parte de uma legião romana, ou seja, seiscentos homens. Portanto, uma legião romana compunha-se de seis mil homens, ou dez coortes. As coortes, por sua vez, estavam divididas em três manípulas ou seis centúrias. A centúria tinha cem homens, comandada por um centurião. Nas províncias, o recrutamento era local, e os homens formavam unidades auxiliares. Uma unidade auxiliar podia contar com cerca de quinhentos a mil homens, e incluía tanto infantes quanto cavaleiros. Prefeitos e tributos cuidavam dessas unidades auxiliares. As traduções do Novo Testamento apresentam palavras como comandante, capitão ou chefe, para o termo grego *chiliarchos*, comandante de mil homens.

No Novo Testamento há coortes específicas, mencionadas como a «italiana», em Atos 10:1, da qual Cornélio era o centurião. Esse grupo tem sido identificado como a *Cohor ii Italica*, que os registros históricos mostram ter estado ativa na Síria, em 88 D.C. Em Atos 27:1 temos a «Coorte Imperial». Paulo foi entregue aos cuidados de Júlio, o centurião do batalhão, a fim de ser levado a Roma, como prisioneiro. Além dos seus deveres militares, a coorte era usada como tropa de guarnição e como polícia militar local, conforme se evidencia nos trechos de Mat. 27:27 e João 18:3.

COORTE IMPERIAL

Esse título aparece em Atos 27:1. Algumas versões preferem traduzir por «coorte Augusta». Sabemos que uma coorte, entre os romanos, era uma décima parte de uma legião (ver sobre o *exército*). Cada coorte era dividida em seis centúrias, cada qual comandada por um centurião. Portanto, a coorte contava com seiscentos homens, embora esse número variasse de acordo com as circunstâncias. Algumas das coortes tinham deveres especiais preestabelecidos, e algumas tomavam nomes particulares, como a coorte Italiana (ver Atos 10:1) e a coorte Imperial (ver Atos 27:1). A palavra grega *speira*, «batalhão», normalmente era traduzida pelo termo latino *manipulus*, que englobava duas coortes. (Ver Políbio xi.23.1). Porém, há alusões suficientes para nos levar a crer que alguns manipuli tinham apenas uma coorte, conforme se vê em Atos 10:1 e Josefo (*Anti*. IV.iv.2). Essas questões permanecem incertas. Permanece de pé a pergunta por que a Coorte Imperial era comandada por um centurião? Ver Atos 27:1. Alguns têm imaginado que o próprio centurião era chamado Augusto (traduzido esse nome por «Imperial», em nossa versão portuguesa), mas o original grego do versículo proíbe tal suposição. Se o centurião tinha mesmo esse nome, então Lucas teria cometido um erro de identificação. Além disso, no texto, não há qualquer indicação absoluta de que esse homem era o comandante da coorte. Ele pode ter sido apenas um centurião que pertencia à mesma. Ou, se aquela unidade do exército era nome de um corpo especial de estafetas imperiais, chamados *frumentarii*, que funcionavam como oficiais de ligação entre o imperador e suas forças armadas, segundo supunha M. Ramsay, então o centurião mencionado poderia ter sido o comandante do destacamento. Sendo assim, teríamos de supor que a coorte em foco não era uma coorte comum, mas provavelmente compunha-se de um menor número de homens. Há alguma evidência arqueológica em favor da *coorte Augusta* em operações na Síria, no tempo de César Augusto. Josefo escreveu acerca de um corpo de cavalaria intitulado *Sebastan*, forma grega para o latim *Augusto*. (ID IB RAM Z)

COPEIRO

No hebraico, **shaqah**, palavra que aparece por cerca de setenta e três vezes no Antigo Testamento, cuja raiz é «dar a beber». Com o sentido de copeiro, aparece por doze vezes (por exemplo: Gên. 40:1-23; 41:9; I Reis 10:5; Nee. 1:11).

Na corte de Salomão o «copeiro» ocupava elevada posição social, paralelamente ao ofício de copeiro do tempo dos Faraós. Era mais do que um homem que provava os líquidos a serem tomados pelos reis. Antes, era uma espécie de assessor pessoal, dotado de grande importância, devido à sua influência política junto ao monarca. Copeiros aparecem em pinturas murais nos túmulos do Egito. Os copeiros impressionaram grandemente a rainha de Sabá (I Reis 10:5). Neemias intitulou-se copeiro do rei Artaxerxes (Nee. 1:11). Esses oficiais com freqüência tornavam-se confidentes e favoritos dos reis, desfrutando da confiança dos monarcas. Algumas vezes eram por estes consultados, nas decisões importantes que precisavam fazer. Um copeiro real provava do vinho, para certificar-se de que o mesmo não estava envenenado, e assumia a posição de protetor pessoal do rei. Não há que duvidar que muitos copeiros apenas traziam o vinho ao rei, mas outros encarregavam-se de muitas espécies de deveres, em nada relacionados com esse ato relativamente simples. (IB ID Z)

COPÉRNICO, NICOLAU

Suas datas foram 1473-1543. Foi um filósofo polonês. Nasceu em Torun. Foi educado na Corcóvia, em Bolonha, em Pádua e em Ferrara, estas três últimas cidades na Itália. Ele foi o arquiteto da teoria heliocêntrica do nosso sistema solar. Ele reteve a idéia dos dezessete epiciclos de Ptolomeu (que vide), ao mesmo tempo em que supunha que as órbitas dos planetas eram perfeitamente circulares. Posteriormente, Tycho Brahe (que vide) e Kepler (que vide), abandonaram inteiramente o conceito dos epiciclos, afirmando que as órbitas dos planetas têm forma elíptica. Não obstante, as teorias de Copérnico foram revolucionárias para a sua época. Em primeiro lugar, era crença comum que a terra se mantém parada no espaço. As pessoas não podiam crer que a terra podia

COPO

movimentar-se, sem que as coisas se projetassem no espaço. Além disso, com base nas idéias de Aristóteles, o conceito da imobilidade era vinculado à perfeição. Aquilo que se move seria imperfeito e está em decadência. No dia em que Copérnico declarou que a terra se movimenta, isso foi considerado um insulto à criação de Deus. Além disso, pensava-se que a terra era o centro do universo. Reduzir o globo terrestre a uma pequena massa, comparativamente falando, que se movimenta em redor do sol, também foi considerado um insulto à *filosofia* da criação de Deus. A verdade é que, tempos depois, Newton negou até mesmo a centralidade do sistema solar; e, atualmente, sabemos que a nossa própria galáxia, a Via-Láctea, não é o centro do universo.

Uma outra questão envolvida nos ensinos de Copérnico é que a teologia ficou despida de qualquer autoridade, quando se trata de descrever a natureza e as funções do universo, o que passou a fazer parte das tarefas da matemática, da física, da astronomia, etc. Naturalmente, Deus continua sendo o grande matemático e físico cósmico; mas foi preciso muito tempo para que os teólogos se adaptassem às novas verdades da ciência. Nisso aprendemos a dura verdade que, quanto a certos aspectos, as ciências vão além da teologia, quanto ao conhecimento. E isso envolve questões importantes. Precisamos admitir que a Bíblia não foi escrita para nos ensinar fatos científicos, e, sim, para nos ensinar a corrigir nosso relacionamento com Deus e com os nossos semelhantes, e para nos guiar no destino final da alma.

Atualmente, estamos em meio a um debate sobre a antiguidade da terra, bem como sobre o criacionismo (que vide). Jamais nos deveríamos mostrar dogmáticos sobre questões como essas, especialmente diante do fato de que a ciência continua fazendo novas descobertas, mas a teologia não o está. A dificuldade é que certos teólogos, em virtude da própria estrutura fixa de seus sistemas, não querem avançar, e nem ampliar seus pontos de vista. Eles pensam que já sabem tudo quanto se pode saber. Essa posição é absurda, refletindo uma *humano*logia, e não a verdadeira *teo*logia. Já deveríamos ter aprendido a lição que a teologia, em qualquer período da história, é parcialmente determinada pelas idéias científicas ortodoxas correntes, e que, se algum pioneiro aparece em cena, ultrapassando a ortodoxia do momento, geralmente ele é rejeitado. Essa rejeição é tão grande que, às vezes, somente uma nova geração aceita novas idéias. A geração antiga fixou-se nas velhas idéias, chegando a perseguir em defesa das mesmas!

COPO

Várias palavras hebraicas poderiam ser evocadas aqui. A mais importante, porém, é o termo *kos*, «copo», usado por trinta e uma vezes. Para exemplificar: Gên. 40:11,13,21; Sal. 11:6; 116:13; Isa. 51:17; Jer. 25:15; Eze. 23:31-33; Hab. 2:16. No Novo Testamento encontramos a palavra grega *potérion*, «vaso de beber», utilizada por trinta vezes: Mat. 10:42; 20:22,23; 23:25,26; 26:27; 26:39; Mar. 7:4; 9:41; 10:38,39; 14:23,36; Luc. 11:39; 22:17,20, 42; João 18:11; I Cor. 10:16,21; 11:25,26; 11:27,28; Apo. 14:10; 16:19; 17:4; 18:6.

Usos Gerais:

1. Um vaso de beber feito de vários materiais, como ouro, prata, vidro, cerâmica, madeira, etc. (Gên. 40:13). No grego, a palavra *potérion* também pode aludir ao líquido contido no copo (I Cor. 11:27).

2. Essas palavras também eram empregadas para denotar *taças* e *bacias*. Na época do Antigo Testamento, esse vaso era uma espécie de taça. A arqueologia tem descoberto muitas informações sobre as taças, encontrando taças ou gravuras de taças em desenhos e relevos.

Em Várias Culturas:

1. *No Egito*. Eram usadas taças de muitos tipos, formatos e cores. As pinturas murais exibem copos de desenho elegante, ao passo que outros eram bastante comuns. Ouro e prata eram materiais preferidos para a confecção das taças dos ricos (Gên. 44:2; Núm. 7:84). Algumas dessas taças eram cravejadas com pedras preciosas, ou com aplicações de vidro de várias cores, ou então eram esmaltadas. Também eram feitas de pedra dura, cerâmica, vidro e porcelana.

2. *Na Assíria*. Grande variedade de formas, de desenho e de cores caracterizava as taças assírias. Eram usados os mesmos materiais que se usavam no Egito. Algumas taças da Assíria terminam com a cabeça de um leão, e têm asas. As taças festivas também eram comuns ali.

3. *Em Israel*. As taças dos hebreus refletiam os modelos egípcios e fenícios. As taças de Salomão eram de ouro (I Reis 10:21). Tal como em outras culturas antigas, as taças ou copos dos hebreus também podiam ser uma espécie de bacia (Êxo. 24:6; Can. 7:2). As taças mencionadas em I Crônicas 28:17 eram vasos de boca larga, usados nas libações (ver também Êxo. 25:28; 37:16; Núm. 4:7).

4. *No Novo Testamento*. As taças descobertas, pertencentes à época do Novo Testamento, refletem objetos idênticos de várias culturas, conforme a descrição acima; mas também incluíam modelos gregos e romanos. O termo grego *potérion* denota um vaso de beber de qualquer formato. A cerâmica era um material comum, empregado nesses vasos (Mar. 7:4), embora os ricos e os nobres contassem com seus vasos de metais preciosos. Normalmente tinham a forma de um cálice. A taça usada na Última Ceia provavelmente era uma espécie de taça de cerâmica, suficientemente grande para que todos pudessem tomar dela um pouco (Mat. 26:27).

Usos Figurados:

1. A *parte do seu cálice* (Sal. 11:6; 16:5), indicava a condição geral da vida, próspera ou cheia de carências e necessidades.

2. A *atração tentadora* (Pro. 23:31; Jer. 51:7; Eze. 17:4; 18:6) pode ser ilustrada no caso da Babilônia, atrativa, mas maligna.

3. O *copo da consolação* (Jer. 16:7) deriva-se de um costume oriental mediante o qual o consolo era oferecido aos que estivessem de luto, ou em período de lamentação, oferecendo-se aos mesmos alimentos e vinho. Ver Pro. 31:6.

4. O *cálice da salvação* (Sal. 116:13) provavelmente refere-se às ofertas de libação, em ação de graças a Deus (Núm. 15:5; 28:7), um símbolo da redenção efetuada por Deus.

5. O *cálice da bênção* (I Cor. 10:16), ou *cálice do Senhor* (I Cor. 10:21) era o cálice de vinho sobre o qual se proferia uma bênção, consagrado para uso sacro. O termo derivou-se da festa da páscoa, referindo-se à terceira taça de vinho que era tomada durante as cerimônias daquela celebração.

6. O *cálice dos demônios* (I Cor. 10:21), faz contraste com o cálice da bênção (número 5, acima).

7. O *cálice de atordoamento*, ou de intoxicação, representa o estado de insensibilidade espiritual (Isa. 51:17; Zac. 12:2).

8. O *copo de espanto e de desolação* (Eze. 23:33), aponta para o estado mental e emocional que essas palavras indicam.

9. O *cálice da ira do Senhor* (Isa. 51:17,22) indica a retribuição indignada do Senhor contra os desobedientes contumazes.

10. O *copo de adivinhações* (Gên. 44:5) pode representar poderes psíquicos, mas também pode indicar um copo literal, provavelmente cheio de água e usado como se fora uma bola de cristal. José afirma que usava um desses copos, para consternação de alguns intérpretes que supõem que a *adivinhação* (que vide) é errada por si mesma. A maior parte dos poderes psíquicos é natural, podendo ser provocada de vários modos. Ver o artigo sobre a *parapsicologia*. Naturalmente, um indivíduo psíquico pode envolver-se em poderes divinos ou em poderes demoníacos. (S UN Z)

COR Ver sobre Cores.

COR
Ver sobre Pesos e Medidas.

CORAÇÃO
I. Uso Geral
Coração. Nas páginas da Bíblia, tanto no Antigo como no Novo Testamentos, é o vocábulo mais completo para indicar todas as faculdades humanas, como os sentimentos (ver Rom. 9:2), a vontade (ver I Cor. 4:5) e o intelecto (ver Rom. 10:6). É assim apontado o homem interior, o homem essencial, aquela porção da personalidade humana que possui os meios naturais através dos quais todo o homem deveria elevar seu conhecimento de Deus a níveis mais altos, em gratidão. Todavia, é justamente o coração que se torna obscurecido. O «coração» pode ser o lar do Espírito Santo (ver Rom. 5:5), ou a maldade pode dominar ali (ver Rom. 1:24). A passagem de Mar. 7:21 e *ss*. alista os vícios que podem proceder do homem interior, ali também chamado de «coração».

II. A Perversão de
Rom. 1:21 descreve de forma abreviada como as faculdades naturais do homem, que lhe permitem vir a conhecer a Deus e a ter comunhão natural com ele, foram pervertidas, através de uma degeneração progressiva, mediante a rejeição proposital do conhecimento de Deus e da distorção da verdade, tudo o que faz parte do misterioso e primeiro deslocamento do homem para fora da harmonia original que ele desfrutava com Deus.

O homem só tem razão quando pensa corretamente, e só pensa corretamente se está em harmonia com o Criador.

Antes se tornaram nulos em seus próprios raciocínios, Rom. 1:21. A palavra *nulos*, neste caso, significa «inúteis», «vãos», «vazios». «A compreensão humana foi reduzida a trabalhar em um 'vácuo'. De certo modo se tornou *fútil*». (Godet em Rom. 1:21). Ou, conforme diz Vincent. «Suas idéias perderam o valor intrínseco, correspondente à verdade».

O vocábulo *«vaidade»*, nos contextos judaicos (o que também deve ser verdade nos escritos de Paulo), diz respeito às práticas e tendências idólatras dos homens, os quais loucamente, em lugar do Deus vivo, colocam alguma outra coisa, usualmente uma imagem de escultura, feita por seus próprios dedos, ainda que isso também possa ser expresso na forma da adoração aos corpos celestes, em lugar de adoração ao próprio criador dos corpos celestes. (Ver Jer. 2:5; II Reis 17:15 e Atos 14:15).

Raciocínios. — Alguns intérpretes preferem a tradução alternativa — *imaginações* —, o que se referia à intranqüilidade da mente depravada, que começa por inventar idéias, por especular, por raciocinar, mas tudo com resultados negativos, pervertendo tão somente qualquer luz à verdade que porventura já possua. É a «verdade humana» que os homens substituem pela «verdade de Deus». A verdade dos homens leva os homens à perversão moral, conforme se vê tão patentemente no nosso mundo atual. Os males, portanto, exercem um efeito cumulativo, e isso concorda com a experiência humana.

Tudo isso esclarece por quais razões e como os homens são *inescusáveis*. Os próprios homens fizeram descer o dilúvio sobre eles, e isso deu início a um espírito de ingratidão.

«A injustiça deles consiste nisso — imediatamente afogaram, por sua própria depravação, a semente do correto conhecimento, antes que esta pudesse amadurecer». (Calvino).

Quanto a essa verdade bíblica podemos examinar um trecho paralelo no livro apócrifo de Enoque 99:8,9, onde também se reflete a idéia e a mentalidade judaica sobre essa questão: «E eles 'os homens' tornar-se-ão ímpios em razão da insensatez de seus corações e seus olhos serão cegos pelo temor que haverá em seus corações, bem como através das visões de seus sonhos. Mediante essas coisas se tornarão ímpios e temerosos, porquanto fazem todas as suas obras na mentira, e adoram um pedra».

III. A Variedade de Usos da Palavra
1. Como paralelo de «inteligência» (ver Rom. 1:21; II Cor. 3:15; 4:6 e Efé. 1:18).

2. Como equivalente a «escolha moral» (ver I Cor. 7:37 e II Cor. 9:7).

3. Como algo que dá impulso e caráter às ações (ver Rom. 6:17; Efé. 6:6; I Cor. 3:3; I Tim. 1:5 e II Tim. 2:22). A obra da lei está escrita no coração do homem (ver Rom. 2:15). A igreja em Corinto foi inscrita como epístola de Cristo, em corações de carne (ver II Cor. 2:23).

4. Especificamente, o coração é a sede do Espírito divino (ver Gál. 4:6; Rom. 5:5; II Cor. 1:22). Essa é a esfera das diversas operações, orientações, consolos e confirmações do Espírito Santo (ver Fil. 4:7; Col. 3:15; I Tes. 3:13; II Tes. 2:17 e 3:5). O coração é igualmente a sede da fé e o órgão do louvor espiritual (ver Rom. 10:9; Efé. 5:19; Col. 3:16).

5. O coração equivale ao *homem interior* (ver Efé. 3:16,17).

Assim, pois, podemos falar sobre o homem essencial, o homem real, que é a alma humana, em contraste com o mero homem físico, o homem animal.

CORAGEM
Essa palavra vem do latim, *cor*, «coração». Um homem corajoso é aquele que não recua diante de conseqüências adversas, na realização de seu dever. A coragem é uma qualidade mental que leva o homem a enfrentar perigos ou oposição com intrepidez, calma, firmeza e propósito. Envolve ousadia, bravura, arrojo, fortaleza, temeridade, resolução. Pode ser demonstrada mediante atos físicos ou atitudes mentais independentes. O contrário da coragem não é, necessariamente, a covardia, pois também pode ser a acomodação, a aceitação dos fatos, a vacilação e a conformidade com aquilo que outros esperam de nós.

Na Filosofia. De acordo com os filósofos gregos, a coragem é uma das quatro virtudes cardeais do homem, paralelamente à sabedoria, à moderação e à justiça. Na *República* de Platão, a coragem aparece como a virtude especial da classe dos guardiães, os encarregados de proteger a sociedade. Para Aristóteles, a coragem é o meio termo entre a deficiência da covardia e os excessos da temeridade. Para Paul Tillich, a coragem é aquela qualidade que se faz necessária para nos aproximarmos da realidade última. A coragem é uma das virtudes básicas, e as virtudes são pontos fortes básicos do homem. A coragem repousa sobre a integridade e a honestidade do indivíduo, de onde se derivam os recursos mentais e espirituais de todos nós. A coragem não envolve, necessariamente, algum ato de bravura. Também pode envolver perseverança em defesa de alguma causa tida como justa, resistência diante dos reveses. É preciso coragem para alguém buscar a verdade, porquanto por todos os lados há forças que procuram fazer o homem conformar-se com algum sistema, onde a verdade supostamente foi aperfeiçoada e fixada de modo definitivo.

No Antigo Testamento, há duas palavras hebraicas que exprimem o espírito corajoso, a saber: *hazaq*, «fortaleza», e *ruah*, «espírito». O trecho de Sabedoria 8:7 apresenta a coragem como uma das virtudes fundamentais. O oposto é qualquer forma de covardia (Eclesiástico 2:12,13). Há muitos exemplos físicos de coragem em campo de batalha, no Antigo Testamento; mas também há a coragem moral e mental, como em Isa. 41:13,14; Jer. 1:8 e Eze. 2:6. A ausência da palavra «coragem», nas páginas do Novo Testamento, pode parecer surpreendente. Mas podemos vê-la exemplificada nas vidas dos grandes líderes, como Jesus, Pedro e Paulo, os quais agiram motivados pela coragem, moral e espiritual. Há também aquela coragem, que se manifesta em meio à adversidade e à oposição, que resulta em triunfo (I Cor. 15:58; 16:9).

No nosso mundo moderno, onde a degradação e a desintegração dos costumes vem aumentando de forma alarmante, até mesmo no seio da Igreja cristã, é preciso grande coragem para o crente manter-se firme em seus propósitos e em seus atos. Parece que são aqueles que praticam o erro, que odeiam, que perturbam e que matam é que são os corajosos. E, ao que parece, com grande freqüência, Deus observa compassivamente. Mas as profecias bíblicas asseguram-nos de que as condições dos últimos dias, antes do retorno de Cristo, serão caracterizadas pela violência e desrespeito dos filhos de Belial. Certo poeta conseguiu captar essa atitude, quando escreveu:

A SEGUNDA VINDA

Girando e girando, em círculos cada vez maiores,
O Falcão não pode ouvir seu treinador;
As coisas se despedaçam; o cetro não pode manter-se;
A maré sangrenta sobrevém, e, por toda parte,
A cerimônia da inocência é abafada.
Aos melhores, falta convicção;
Os piores, são cheios de paixão.

(William Butler Yeats).

CORAL

No hebraico, **ramoth**, que aparece somente por duas vezes no Antigo Testamento: Jó 28:18 e Eze. 27:16. Essa mesma palavra significa algo que cresce alto, o que indicaria o acúmulo nos recifes de corais, como aqueles encontrados nos mares Mediterrâneo e Vermelho. A palavra é mencionada em alusão às jóias egípcias. Pequenos enfeites, como contas, etc., eram feitos desse material. O coral, embora considerado uma pedra preciosa, na verdade é um esqueleto calcáreo, secretado por uma comunidade ligada de pequenos pólipos, que cercam e escondem inteiramente esse arcabouço, enquanto vivem. A espécie envolvida é o minúsculo organismo conhecido como *Anthozoa*, ou «bicho flor», conforme esse termo grego dá a entender. Eles vivem em colônias muito densas, em mares não mais frios do que a média de 20º centígrados. Há cerca de duas mil e quinhentas espécies que variam em dimensões e em formato. Os corais de cor vermelha e negra são aqueles usados como pedras preciosas. Na antiguidade, os corais eram até mesmo importados ou exportados, vindo de lugares tão distantes quanto a Índia. Alguns, na antiguidade, pensavam que o coral tem propriedades sagradas. Ver Jó. 28:28; Lam. 4:7; Eze. 27:16. A colheita de corais continua sendo uma importante indústria na parte oriental do mar Mediterrâneo.

CORAL

Hino sacro cujo estilo foi iniciado pelos reformadores luteranos. O texto sempre era cantado em alemão, e não em latim, e toda a congregação participava no cântico. As melodias eram escolhidas dentre as melhores melodias gregorianas (que vide), de canções seculares que poderiam ser adaptadas, e de obras originais de vários compositores luteranos, especialmente Johann Walther. O propósito original desse cântico era conferir à congregação uma maior participação nos cultos, do que fora possível até aquele ponto da história. As melodias eram métricas e harmoniosas, embora mais formais que os modernos hinos sacros. A melodia principal era cantada por tenores.

O coral foi usado como base para outras obras, por compositores notáveis como Bach, que compôs os chamados prelúdios para coral, ao órgão; ou por Felix Mendelssohn que usou corais familiares em suas sonatas para órgão, em suas cantatas (que vide) e em seus oratórios (que vide). Modernas composições para órgão, empregando o estilo do coral, ou outros estilos, formam uma valiosa porção de música para órgão, apropriada para uso nos cultos de adoração dos evangélicos. (E)

CORANTES Ver Tintureiros.

CORASÃ

No hebraico, «fornalha fumarenta». Uma cidade na parte sudoeste do território de Judá, mencionada somente em I Sam. 30:30, e que figura entre as localidades por onde Davi e seus homens vaguearam, antes dele tornar-se rei de Israel. Algumas versões têm emendado o nome para a forma Borasã. Talvez se trate da mesma Asã que aparece em Jos. 15:42.

CORAZIM

Uma cidade mencionada nos trechos de Mateus 11:21 e Lucas 10:12, em conexão com Betsaida e Cafarnaum, em razão do que se supõe que ela ficaria nas proximidades dessas duas outras cidades. Ficava perto do mar da Galiléia (que vide). Achava-se entre aqueles lugares que Jesus denunciou por causa de sua atitude de incredulidade contínua, a despeito da vantagem de seus habitantes terem sido testemunhas de muitas ocorrências espirituais. Excetuando essa circunstância, pouco se sabe sobre o local. Seu local tem sido identificado como Khirbet Kerazeh, a três quilômetros ao norte de Cafarnaum, o que concorda com as informações que nos são supridas por Eusébio, em seu *Onomasticon* (174). Khirbet Kerazeh fica localizada acima de Cafarnaum, em colinas de basalto. A arqueologia tem demonstrado que o local vinha sendo habitado desde a Idade da Pedra posterior. O Talmude informa-nos que a cidade era famosa pela qualidade do seu trigo, *Menahoth* 85a. Uma sinagoga feita de pedras de rocha vulcânica negra foi desenterrada ali, embora seja uma construção menos impressionante que a sinagoga achada em Cafarnaum (que vide). Entre as ruínas havia uma pedra esculpida, com uma inscrição em aramaico, onde aparece o nome de seu doador. Ali poderia ser a «cadeira de Moisés» (ver Mat. 23:2). Esse assento era usado pelos principais mestres rabinos. Os rabinos eram herdeiros de Moisés que, por assim dizer, proferiam *ex cathedra* os ensinamentos de Moisés. Quanto a notas completas sobre esses assentos e as declarações que dizem respeito aos mesmos, ver as notas expositivas no NTI, em Mat. 23:3. (KO NTI Z)

CORBÃ

A palavra é transliteração de um termo hebraico que significa «oferenda». Mas, conforme ela é usada em Marcos 7:11, alude a algo dedicado a propósitos religiosos, como o templo. Jesus frisa que os hipócritas, com uma piedade fingida, haviam descoberto um meio de desobedecer ao quinto mandamento («Honra a teu pai e a tua mãe»). Muitas pessoas acham conveniente ignorar princípios espirituais encastoados em passagens bíblicas claras, mediante algum *caso especial* ou *necessidade pessoal*, o que, para elas, transcende a claros ensinamentos espirituais. Essa tradição sobre o *corbã*, um voto proferido a respeito de alguma oferta, era tão forte que quem fizesse tal voto era proibido de usar a coisa votada, qualquer que ela fosse, para outra finalidade. No entanto, a hipocrisia desconhece limites. Os antigos judeus descobriram um modo de evitar pagarem os seus votos, tornando-os tão vagos que podiam interpretá-los como bem entendessem.

Um filho que quisesse evitar cuidar de seus idosos genitores, para que pudesse usar do dinheiro para si mesmo, poderia declarar esse dinheiro um «corbã», isto é, uma oferta pertencente ao templo. E em seguida, mediante um outro golpe de astúcia, ele podia acabar retendo o dinheiro para si mesmo. Destarte, ele apenas fingia dedicar o dinheiro ao templo. Todavia, também havia quem realmente entregasse o dinheiro ao templo, visando à promoção da religião judaica; e isso significava que os seus pais perdiam aquilo que lhes pertencia. Jesus, pois, condenou a prática, em qualquer de suas variedades.

Esse antigo costume tem paralelo, nos tempos modernos, nos grupos religiosos que exploram os sentimentos de pessoas idosas, a fim de arrancar o dinheiro delas, ou sob a forma de doações, enquanto estão vivas, ou sob a forma de testamentos, em que deixam seus bens a esses grupos. Ocasionalmente, ouvimos falar no caso de alguma família que foi deserdada, total ou parcialmente, pela intrusão de alguma igreja ou denominação cristã, que perturbou a questão de herança da família.

A palavra hebraica empregada em Lev. 1:2; 22:27 e 23:14 tem o sentido geral de oferenda. A Mishna (*Ned.* iii.6.9) afirma que qualquer coisa consagrada como *corbã* jamais podia reverter ao uso ordinário, mesmo que o voto tivesse sido feito precipitadamente. No entanto, a história revela-nos que havia toda espécie de burla, no tocante a coisas proibidas. A palavra «corbã», só é usada no Novo Testamento em Marcos 7:11, embora o mesmo incidente histórico seja ampliado em Mateus 15:1 ss. Ali o Senhor mostra que os judeus, com suas *tradições* humanas, anulavam a lei de Deus. Êles honravam a Deus com suas palavras, mas não nas suas ações (Mat. 15:8,9) o que tornava *vã* a adoração deles. Todos os sistemas religiosos e teologias, bem como as denominações cristãs que os seguem, incluem *tradições* humanas que contradizem os princípios espirituais do evangelho.

CORÇA

No hebraico, **tsebi**, «beleza». Essa palavra indica um pequeno antílope, abundante nas porções mais selvagens da Palestina. Seu nome científico é *Gazella dorcas*. É animal bem conhecido por sua velocidade, beleza e movimentos graciosos. É mencionado nos seguintes trechos: Deu. 12:15,22; 14:5; 15:22; II Sam. 2:18; I Reis 4:23; I Crô. 12:8; Pro. 6:5; Can. 2:7,9,17; 3:5; 8:14; Isa. 13:14. Esse animal era suficientemente bem distribuído pela Palestina para servir de comum fonte de alimento. É provável que esse animal estivesse envolvido no relato sobre Esaú, em Gênesis 25:28; 27:3 ss. À medida que a civilização avança, o habitat desse arisco animal vai-se encolhendo. Nos tempos modernos, escasso controle sobre os caçadores tem permitido a redução drástica da população dessa espécie. Em Israel há leis de caça, e há também reservas que estão dando oportunidade para esses animais sobreviverem, e não serem extintos definitivamente na Palestina. O nome feminino Dorcas (Atos 9:36) está baseado sobre o nome desse animal.

CORÇA DA MANHÃ

No Salmo 22, no título do mesmo, encontramos as palavras hebraicas *Ay-ye-leth Shachar*, que significa precisamente «corça da manhã». Nossa versão portuguesa interpreta o título como se esse fosse o nome de uma melodia, ao som do qual o Salmo 22 deveria ser cantado.

Todavia, há uma outra interpretação, que diz que *Shahar* e o seu irmão gêmeo, Shalem, eram filhos de El, o principal deus do panteão cananeu. Shahar seria o deus da aurora, e Shalem o deus do pôr-do-sol. Seriam similares a Castor e Pólux da mitologia clássica, que tem reflexos na lenda católica romana de Cosme e Damião, que os macumbeiros brasileiros abraçaram como dois de seus «santos». É difícil pensar que uma tradição pagã tenha penetrado no título de um dos Salmos de Davi. Por isso, optamos pela primeira interpretação, aquela que pensa no nome de uma melodia antiga, segundo é refletido em nossa versão portuguesa da Bíblia.

CORÇO

No hebraico, **yachmur**, palavra que aparece somente em Deu. 14:5 e I Reis 4:23. Seria, cientificamente, o *Alcephalus busephalus*, um tipo de veado, bem conhecido no Egito, onde têm sido encontrados espécimes mumificados, vindos do período greco-romano. Aparentemente, não era um animal nativo da Palestina. Atualmente é raro, ou mesmo extinto. O animal é mencionado como um item do cardápio de Salomão.

CORDA

No hebraico temos de considerar duas palavras, e no grego, uma, a saber:

1. *Chebel*, «corda». Essa palavra é usada por sessenta vezes, com variadas traduções em português (para exemplificar: II Sam. 17:13; I Reis 20,31,32; Jos. 2:15; Sal. 140:5; Miq. 2:5).

2. *Aboth*, «tira». Essa palavra é usada por vinte e

CORDA — CORDEIRO DE DEUS

nove vezes (para exemplificar: Juí. 15,13,14; Sal. 2:3; Isa. 5:18).

3. *Schoiníon*, «corda». Palavra grega usada por apenas duas vezes (ver João 2:15 e Atos 27:32).

Qualquer desses termos indica uma corda de qualquer espessura, feita de fibras, cabelos ou couro. Pinturas em cavernas no oriente da Espanha, pertencentes ao período paleolítico posterior (cerca de 12.000 A.C.), mostram o que parece ser uma corda usada para ajudar alguém a subir por um penhasco. No Egito, as cordas eram feitas de junco (cerca de 4000 A.C.), de fibras, de linho, de capim, de papiro ou de pêlos de camelo. Cordas de até 6,5 cm de espessura têm sido encontradas em locais do antigo Egito. As cordas eram importantíssimas no mundo antigo, porque permitiam aos homens projetos de construção. Algumas inscrições antigas (por exemplo, Rekmire, do século XV A.C.) mostram qual o processo do fabrico de cordas, no Egito.

Nas páginas da Bíblia, vemos que cordas eram usadas na guerra, para destruição de cidades (ver II Sam. 17:13), para arrear cavalos (ver Jó 39:10 e Isa 5:18), no cordoame de embarcações (ver Atos 27:32,40), para baixar pessoas que estivessem em lugares elevados (ver Jos. 2:15 e Jer. 38:6 *ss*), para armadilhas (Jó 18:10) e para amarrar pessoas (ver Juí. 15:13 *ss*).

Uma corda, — em vez de tecido ou couro, representava pobreza ou opróbrio (ver I Reis 20:31 *ss*; Isa. 3:24). O «gancho» enfiado nas bochechas do leviatã (ver Jó 41:2), talvez fosse melhor traduzido por «corda», visto que a palavra hebraica, no original, indica uma corda feita de junco. O «azorrague de cordas» que Jesus usou (ver João 2:15) para expulsar os vendedores de animais e os cambistas que infestavam o templo, e o «cabo» cortado pelos soldados para deixar o bote ir-se embora, são traduções de uma mesma palavra grega. (Ver Atos 27:32).

Usos Figurados: a. Enrolar-se com uma corda indicava tristeza e humilhação (Jó 12:18; I Reis 20:31,32). **b.** Uma herança dada era representada pelo uso de cordas, que eram usadas para medir um terreno (Sal. 105:11). De fato, o termo traduzido por «corda» podia indicar uma medida de superfície. **c.** Estender uma corda em torno de uma cidade indicava que a mesma estava destinada à destruição (Lam. 2:8). **d.** O *fio de prata*, partido por ocasião da morte física, representa o momento de não-retorno do espírito (Ecl. 12:6). Alguns estudiosos pensam que a alusão é à quebra da espinha dorsal, mas a referência é ao fio de energia que vincula o espírito ao corpo físico, como se fosse uma espécie de cordão umbilical, por meio do qual, aparentemente, há uma comunicação de energias vitais. Ocasionalmente, o fio de prata pode ser visto, quando há a projeção da psique (que vide), ou durante o processo da morte física (ver sobre *Experiências de Quase Morte*). Enquanto o fio de prata não se parte é possível o retorno do espírito ao corpo físico. Quando o mesmo é cortado, isso equivale ao *nascimento* para uma nova vida. Portanto, há algo parecido ao momento em que se corta o cordão umbilical de um recém-nascido. Ver o artigo sobre *Fio de Prata*. **e.** As *cordas de Deus* são as suas restrições aos atos humanos (Sal. 2:3). **f.** Há também as *cordas do amor* de Deus, isto é, sua boa vontade e interesse pelo bem-estar do homem (Oséi. 11:4). **g.** O poder dos pecados e dos hábitos maus, que, por assim dizer, amarram os pecadores (Pro. 5:22). **h.** Há as cordas da vaidade (Isa. 5:18) e as cordas da aflição (Jó 36:8). **i.** Nos sonhos e nas visões, uma corda pode ter vários sentidos simbólicos. Se assume uma forma circular, pode indicar a porção genital feminina. Ou pode significar o cordão umbilical e tudo quanto o mesmo representa, como proteção, apego à mãe, segurança; mas também, negativamente, falta de liberdade e senso de confinamento. Também devemos considerar uma corda pendurada, em cujo caso o simbolismo envolve alguma grave ameaça, punição ou dificuldade. Todavia, uma corda também pode simbolizar os elementos salvatícios, visto que um homem lança uma corda a uma pessoa que se está afogando, com a qual esta poderá salvar-se do afogamento. (CHE FOR)

CORDA DE PRATA Ver **Fio de Prata**.

CORDÃO

Em Núm. 15:38 lemos sobre «um cordão azul» que os filhos de Israel deveriam usar nas fímbrias de suas vestes, para atar às mesmas as borlas (que vide). O azul era símbolo de espiritualidade. Alguns estudiosos interpretam que esse cordão azul indicava que os israelitas deveriam voltar-se para as realidades espirituais, considerando como secundárias as atividades terrenas.

CORDEIRO Ver **Ovelha**.

CORDEIRO DE DEUS

I. Em João 1:29

1. Neste vs., alguns vêem o *cordeiro pascal*. (Assim pensavam Grotius, Lampe, Hofmann e Vincent): O problema que acompanha essa interpretação é que o cordeiro pascal não era encarado como lavador do pecado, mas antes, como símbolo do livramento do povo de Israel, e comemorava o livramento dos israelitas de serem mortos pelo anjo destruidor, quando este aniquilou os primogênitos no Egito. Não obstante, paralelamente ao cordeiro pascal e ao rito da aspersão do sangue, desenvolveu-se o cordeiro do sacrifício pelo pecado. (Ver I Cor. 5:7). Da maneira aventada em João 1:29, é que o apóstolo Paulo expressou a idéia, sendo perfeitamente possível que, nos dias de Jesus, tal conexão fosse comumente compreendida, provavelmente como empréstimo tirado do sentido dos cordeiros diariamente sacrificados pelos pecados, idéia essa que pelos judeus foi transferida para a festividade anual em que era sacrificado o cordeiro pascal.

2. Alguns estudiosos desviam-se inteiramente da verdade, crendo que *nenhum cordeiro sacrificial* está em foco em João 1:29, mas que estava em vista apenas a pessoa de Jesus, o Messias, como homem pleno de bondade, que pacientemente tolerou os males dos seres humanos, tendo assim participado, com toda a paciência, das dolorosas vicissitudes da existência humana (demonstrando assim qualidades de caráter que podem ser atribuídas a um cordeiro).

3. Estariam no foco da atenção as ofertas pelo pecado. (Assim opinaram Baumgarten-Crusius e Meyer). Tratar-se-ia dos cordeiros sacrificados a *cada manhã e tarde*; ou mesmo dos diversos animais (além dos cordeiros) que eram usados nesses sacrifícios. Contudo, a questão não é se tais sacrifícios serviram de tipos simbólicos ou não do sacrifício de Cristo e, sim, se João 1:29 realmente se refere a isso ou não, se João Batista tinha por escopo ou não dizer tal coisa. Sabemos, alicerçados em I Cor. 5:7; Atos 8:32 e I Ped. 1:19, que o sistema geral de sacrifícios do judaísmo chegou a ser aceito como símbolo do sacrifício de Cristo, na teologia do cristianismo primitivo.

4. Outros eruditos acreditam que Cristo, na qualidade de Cordeiro de Deus, é um cumprimento

CORDEIRO DE DEUS

profético de predições como a que lemos em Is. 53:6; e que, apesar disso assemelha-se a outros conceitos judaicos sobre os *sacrifícios cruentos*, na realidade um assunto distinto estava em consideração aqui. Dessa maneira, o conceito do Messias deveria incluir a idéia do *cordeiro conduzido ao matadouro*, segundo também expressa distintamente o trecho de Is. 53:7. Essa passagem, naturalmente, vincula o cordeiro com o tirar do pecado, o que falta essencialmente na primeira interpretação ventilada acima. Essa é, para todos os efeitos, a interpretação de Alford, e, naturalmente, conta com suas vantagens óbvias; todavia, podemos indagar por que precisaríamos excluir as demais idéias, e por que deveríamos referir-nos a esta idéia com exclusividade, se o capítulo cinqüenta e três do livro de Isaías fala do cordeiro sacrificial. Sim, por que não poderia haver mais algumas referências gerais ao sistema de sacrifícios do judaísmo, do que o cordeiro sacrificial não fazia parte. (Ver Lev. 4:32 e Núm. 5:8). O cordeiro sacrificial era um animal especialmente preparado, separado, de determinada idade, sem defeito algum. Todas essas idéias parecem exigir que o simbolismo por detrás do Cordeiro de Deus, que tira o pecado do mundo, deve ser mais lato do que aquilo que está contido em uma única passagem profética, a saber, o capítulo cinqüenta e três de Isaías.

5. Todas as considerações expostas acima parecem conduzir à necessidade de aceitarmos uma explicação mais complexa, ou pelo menos uma combinação de outras explanações. «Ele (João Batista) usou o cordeiro como símbolo *do sacrifício em geral*. É como se ele tivesse dito: Aqui está a realidade, da qual todos os sacrifícios animais eram meros símbolos». (Bruce, em João 1:29). O cordeiro pascal fala-nos acerca do livramento de Israel da escravidão; e a passagem de I Cor. 5:7 mostra-nos que a teologia cristã lançava mão desse cordeiro como tipo simbólico de Cristo, a despeito do fato de que não era assim que se achava, no pensamento judaico mais primitivo.

Efeitos do sacrifício de Jesus:
1. Foi o cumprimento de todos os tipos do A.T., no tocante ao sistema de sacrifícios.
2. A oferta da salvação plena. Ver notas completas em João 1:12 no NTI.
3. O perdão dos pecados. Ver o artigo.
4. A santificação. Ver o artigo.
5. A plena participação na vida e imagem do Logos, II Cor. 3:18.
6. A reconciliação universal, Col. 1:20 e Efé. 1:10.
7. O exemplo da humanidade dedicada a Jesus. Ver notas em Fil. 2:7 e Heb. 5:1-19 no NTI.

Que tira o pecado do mundo, João 1:29. Porque o sentido das palavras é tão elástico, existem tantas e tão variadas interpretações acerca desta declaração, dependendo do que se compreender pelo verbo aqui traduzido por «tira». No original grego, trata-se de um verbo no particípio presente, tendo por intenção esclarecer qual deve ser considerada a principal característica do «Cordeiro». As interpretações acerca dessa função ou característica do Cordeiro de Deus, são as seguintes:

1. Lançar fora. A idéia de expiação pode ser eliminada por esse termo, porquanto não se trata de uma referência necessária à morte ou sacrifício do cordeiro.
2. Outro tanto se dá quanto à idéia de *apoio*, que é defendida por alguns estudiosos.
3. Até mesmo idéias como *suportar, sofrer, tirar, levar*, etc. têm sido desnudadas, por alguns intérpretes, do conceito de sacrifício expiatório; mas sem dúvida essa posição labora contra a teologia neotestamentária sobre o assunto, e necessariamente ignora trechos bíblicos como I Cor. 5:7; Atos 8:32 e I Ped. 1:19; ou, pelo menos, assevera que tais versículos abordam um assunto inteiramente diferente daquele ventilado pelo trecho de João 1:29; mas não é provável que assim realmente aconteça. O verbo grego «aíro» pode ter, essencialmente, três significados: a. levantar ou soerguer (como se vê em João 8:59); b. suportar ou carregar (como se percebe em Mat. 16:24); c. remover ou tirar (como se lê em João 20:1). As duas últimas definições podem ser bons veículos para interpretações que favorecem a expiação, isto é, interpretações que afirmam que o tirar o pecado do mundo veio por intermédio da expiação de Cristo.

4. Assim sendo, o que está em foco na expressão «...que tira o pecado do mundo...» é ou a *remoção* ou a *expiação* do pecado, e a primeira idéia está incluída na segunda.

Podemos comparar com isso diversos versículos da primeira epístola de João, que podem ser reputados interpretações dessa idéia aqui exposta: I João 3:5: «...*ele se manifestou para tirar os pecados*...»; I João 1:7: «...*e o sangue de Jesus, seu Filho, nos purifica de todo pecado*...»; e I João 2:2, que ainda mais incisiva e exatamente declara o que temos aqui: «...*e ele é a propiciação pelos nossos pecados, e não somente pelos nossos próprios, mas ainda pelos do mundo inteiro*». Essa linguagem obviamente é de natureza sacrificial. A idéia dominante é a remoção da infecção causada pelo pecado, a fim de que os remidos possam entrar em comunhão com um Deus santo. O singular, «pecado», é empregado no trecho de João 1:29; devemos observar, entretanto, que o trecho de I João 2:2 emprega o plural, «...pecados...». O mais provável é que o singular aponte para o princípio pecaminoso, ou seja, os pecados considerados coletivamente, isto é, todos os pecados, de todos os pecadores, referidos por uma palavra só. Cristo remove ambos os tipos de pecado, tanto os atos, considerados em sua pluralidade, como o pecado, considerado como um princípio.

Cristo na qualidade de Cordeiro de Deus. Apresentamos aqui um sumário das idéias inclusas nesse simbolismo: a. A expressão «...Cordeiro de Deus, que tira o pecado...», só se encontra por duas vezes, a saber, em João 1:29 e 36; e, dessas duas ocorrências, a primeira contém, ou é uma interpretação; b. Expressões similares podem ser encontradas em Atos 8:32 e I Ped. 1:19 (as quais se referem ao cordeiro do sacrifício); c. No livro de Apocalipse se acha, com bastante freqüência, o título de Cristo, *Cordeiro*. Tal vocábulo é usado nesse livro nada menos de vinte e oito vezes. Ali, muitos conceitos adicionais sobre a pessoa de Cristo são indicados por esse título, além de o da expiação. No livro de Apocalipse ele é visto como o Cordeiro sacrificial, mas também como o elevado e transcendental Rei (Apo. 5:8 e 7:9); como a mais alta Autoridade celestial (Apo. 6:1,6 e 7:9-14); como o chefe dos exércitos celestiais (Apo. 17:14 e o cap. 19); e como o compartilhador do trono eterno (Apo. 22:1,3).

II. Em Apo. 5:5,6
Cordeiro. O Leão (aludido no versículo anterior) é agora retratado como um Cordeiro. Ambos esses animais pintam algo acerca do caráter e da missão do Cristo. Na qualidade de Leão, ele é o corajoso Rei, que defende seu povo e assume o poder universal. Na qualidade de Cordeiro, ele faz expiação e assume seu ofício de Sumo Sacerdote. (Ver João 1:29, onde Cristo aparece como Cordeiro. Ver Heb. 2:17; 4:14; 5:10 e 9:24, onde Cristo aparece como Sumo Sacerdote). No

CORÉ

Testamento de José 19:8, um leão presumivelmente de Judá, assiste ao Messias, o qual é retratado como um cordeiro. É possível que o vidente João tivesse esse simbolismo em mente, e que agora tivesse mesclado os dois símbolos em uma única pessoa. Na citada passagem do Testamento de José, o «cordeiro» é «vencedor»; mas, visto que aqui ele é «morto», sabemos que parte de sua vitória veio através da «expiação» do Cordeiro, e não meramente através de seu ofício monárquico. O vidente João, portanto, não apresenta um símbolo contrário ao do evangelho de João ou ao da tipologia judaica, —mas tão-somente suplementa o simbolismo, referindo-se aos efeitos conquistadores do sacrifício do Cordeiro. Nas páginas do A.T., conforme devemos estar lembrados, o cordeiro pascal conferiu aos israelitas a vitória sobre o Egito, não sendo apenas aquilo que forneceu a expiação. Paulo alude a Cristo como a páscoa cristã, que se sacrificou por nós (ver I Cor. 5:7).

Somente o vidente João, em todo o N.T., ao referir-se a Cristo como Cordeiro, usa o termo grego *«arnion»*. Em todas as demais passagens do N.T., é empregado o vocábulo grego «amnos». (Ver João 1:29,36; I Ped. 1:19 e Atos 8:32 quanto a essa última palavra). No Apocalipse também se pode ver o Cristo na qualidade de Cordeiro em Apo. 5:8,12,13; 6:1,16; 7:9,10,14,17; 12:11; 13:8,11; 14:1,4,10; 15:3; 17:14; 19:7,9; 21:14,22,23 e 22:1,3. O termo *arnion* é a forma diminutiva de «arnos», mas, nos tempos neotestamentários, essa palavra não tinha necessariamente esse sentido. Não há qualquer diferença de significado entre «amnos» e «arnion».

Como tinha sido morto. O Cordeiro fizera expiação (que vide), e assim obteve a vitória para os homens. Sua missão terrena conferiu-lhe a sua exaltação celestial, conforme se aprende em Heb. 1:9 e Rom. 1:3,4. A passagem de Col. 1:20 mostra que a paz com Deus e a reconciliação universal dependem desse ato de sacrifício de Cristo. Não é bastante, pois, que Cristo seja o Leão; também era mister que ele fosse o Cordeiro.

CORÉ

No hebraico, «pregoeiro» ou «perdiz». É nome de dois homens, no Antigo Testamento:

1. Um levita, filho de Ebiasafe, pai de Salum, porteiro do tabernáculo (I Crô. 9:19), chamado pai de Meselemias (Selemias), em I Crô. 26:1. Cerca de 960 A.C.

2. Um levita, filho de Imna, nomeado para ser o supervisor das ofertas voluntárias, na época de Ezequias (II Crô. 31:14). As ofertas recolhidas deveriam ser distribuídas entre os sacerdotes. Cerca de 719 A.C.

CORÉ (CORÁ)

No hebraico, «calvo». Foi nome de quatro ou cinco pessoas referidas na Bíblia, a saber:

1. O terceiro filho de Esaú e sua concubina cananéia, Aolibama (Gên. 36:5,14,18; I Crô. 1:35), em cerca de 1950 A.C. Ele nasceu em Canaã, antes que Esaú partisse para o monte Seir (Gên. 36:5-9), e se tornasse cabeça de uma tribo iduméia (Gên. 36:18).

2. O filho de Elifaz, filho de Esaú e Ada, filho de Elom, o hitita (Gên. 36:16). Entretanto, a maioria dos estudiosos pensa que esse versículo envolve um erro escribal, pois a palavra teria sido copiada, por engano, do vs. 18. A palavra não ocorre nem em Gên. 36:11 e nem em I Crô. 1:35.

3. Um filho de Hebrom (I Crô. 2:43).

4. Um neto de Coate e antepassado de um grupo de músicos sacros (filhos de Coré), aos quais são atribuídos os Salmos 42 e onze outros (I Crô. 6:22).

5. Um levita, coatita (ver *Coate, Coatitas*), da casa de Izar e que talvez deva ser identificado com o Coate de número 4, acima. Ele era filho de Jizar e neto de Coate (Êxo. 6:21,24). Esteve envolvido em uma conspiração contra Moisés e Arão, juntamente com Datã, seu irmão Abirão, um rubenita, e cerca de outros duzentos e cinqüenta homens, que lhes davam apoio. O relato aparece no décimo sexto capítulo de Números, e há alusão a isso no Novo Testamento, em Judas 11. A única coisa que sabemos sobre esse homem é aquilo que ficamos sabendo nesse incidente. É lamentável que algumas pessoas só se tornem conhecidas pelas maldades que praticam. E pior ainda é quando as pessoas vangloriam-se desse tipo de fama.

a. *As acusações*. Coré e seus associados acusaram Moisés de exaltar-se aos olhos do povo; de usurpar privilégios e poderes acima do que era próprio; e de deixar de cumprir a promessa de levá-los a uma terra prometida. Moisés defendeu-se, dizendo que os motivos deles é que eles estavam à cata de poder e queriam controlar o sacerdócio e os ministros do Senhor. Provavelmente, o antigo motivo da inveja também estivesse por detrás do caso, o que, por muitas vezes, encontra-se atrás das tentativas de obter poder e de exibir-se diante das outras pessoas.

b. *A reação*. Moisés ficou profundamente consternado diante da rebelião, e prostrou-se com o rosto em terra. Então deixou a questão aos cuidados do Senhor, desafiando os rebeldes a virem conferenciar com ele, à entrada da tenda da congregação. Cada homem deveria tomar um incensário para oferecer incenso ao Senhor. Datã e Abirão recusaram-se a ir ao encontro de Moisés. No dia seguinte, os rebeldes apresentaram-se diante do tabernáculo.

c. *A destruição*. A congregação inteira de Israel reuniu-se para ver o espetáculo, por instigação de Coré. A glória do Senhor ou *shekinah* (que vide) apareceu, e uma voz ordenou a Moisés e Arão que os dois se separassem da congregação de Israel. Todos os israelitas estavam prestes a ser destruídos, por darem apoio a uma causa injusta. Porém, Moisés ordenou que os israelitas abandonassem o lugar. E eles retrocederam. Em seguida, Moisés rogou ao Senhor para que perdoasse o povo, e também para que resolvesse a questão. Então a terra abriu-se sob as tendas de Coré, Datã e Abirão, e fechou-se em seguida. Os duzentos e cinqüenta rebelados, que provavelmente permaneceram diante do tabernáculo, foram consumidos pelo «fogo do Senhor». Subseqüentemente, os incensários usados pelos rebeldes foram transformados em placas para formarem uma cobertura exterior para o altar, como advertência acerca do fim de todos os rebeldes contra o Senhor.

d. *A rebeldia nos corações do povo*. Na manhã seguinte, a congregação inteira murmurou contra Moisés e Arão, acusando-os de terem feito morrer o povo do Senhor. Isso provocou ainda um outro desastre, uma praga que destruiu nada menos de catorze mil e setecentas pessoas. E isso bastou, como lição objetiva.

e. *Misericórdia*. Visto que os descendentes de Coré posteriormente serviram como levitas, podemos ter a certeza de que seus filhos e sua família foram poupados. Provavelmente esses viviam em tendas separadas, não se tendo envolvido no ato de rebelião.

f. *O comentário do Novo Testamento*. Em Judas 11,

Coré, juntamente com Caim e Balaão, é mencionado como um mau exemplo, cujas ações não devemos emular. Essas personagens representam os mestres desviados, presunçosos e interesseiros, que jamais deveriam ter recebido autoridade, no seio da Igreja cristã. Provavelmente, estão em foco os primeiros gnósticos. Ver o artigo sobre o *Gnosticismo*.

g. *Explicações naturais*. Alguns intérpretes supõem que a narrativa inteira acerca de Coré tenha uma explicação natural. Algum tipo de terremoto ou de ação vulcânica poderia ter ocorrido. Nesse caso, tais ocorrências foram muito seletivas, havendo atingido somente aqueles que estavam envolvidos na rebelião, apesar de haver centenas de milhares de pessoas em volta.

CORES

As Escrituras não mencionam muitas cores diferentes. A variedade de cores depende muito da tecnologia, excetuando aquela imensa variedade que a natureza nos oferece. Poderíamos presumir que a língua hebraica tinha muitos nomes de cores que não foram registrados na Bíblia. O vocabulário total do Antigo Testamento chega acerca de dez mil palavras, e devemos supor que o vocabulário ativo entre os hebreus era bem maior que isso. Seja como for, abaixo damos um sumário das cores mencionadas na Bíblia:

1. *Branco*. Em sentido plano, o branco fala dos raios do sol e daquela cor produzida pelo calor extremo, visto que todas as cores do espectro estão unidas para formar a cor branca. O trecho de Mateus 17:2 refere-se à brancura das vestes de Jesus, por ocasião da transfiguração. Os campos semeados que estavam prontos para a colheita foram chamados de «brancos», visto que o trigo maduro é branco, distinguido do trigo ainda imaturo, que é verde. O termo grego envolvido é *leukós*, que aparece por vinte e cinco vezes no Novo Testamento, por dezesseis vezes só no livro de Apocalipse (1:14; 2:17; 3:4,5,18,4:4; 6:2,11; 7:9,13; 11:11; 20:11). Esta minha lista é parcial, mas dá uma boa idéia do sentido da palavra, incluindo seu uso metafórico. No Antigo Testamento temos o termo hebraico *laban*, aplicado a muitos objetos, como ao leite (Gên. 49:12), o maná (Êxo. 16:13), a neve (Isa. 1:18), a lua (Isa. 24:23). Também temos a palavra hebraica *sah*, «ensolarado» ou «ofuscante», como em Can. 5:10. *Hiwwar* também é usado para indicar a neve ou a palidez da vergonha (Dan. 7:9 e Isa. 29:22). *Sib* é o branco das cãs de uma pessoa idosa. Outras palavras hebraicas também foram usadas, talvez primariamente como tipos de tecido, mas incluindo a sua cor, como no caso das cortinas do tabernáculo (Êxo. 28:6) e das vestes sacerdotais (Êxo. 28:6).

2. *Negro*. Essa palavra era usada para indicar as cores densas e não apenas o negro propriamente dito. Assim temos os vocábulos hebraicos *shahor*, «sombrio», «pardo», aplicado à cor dos cabelos (Lev. 13:31 e Can. 5:11); *hum*, que literalmente significa «queimado», como um tom do marrom (Gên. 30:52); *qadar*, que significa «sujo», dando a entender a cor escura que poderíamos chamar, mais apropriadamente, de «negro» (Jó 30:30, onde se aplica aos efeitos produzidos pela enfermidade ou pela tristeza). Além disso, o firmamento cheio de nuvens (I Reis 18:45), ou a noite (Miq. 3:6; Jer. 4:28), são negros. Um riacho de águas turvas, da neve dissolvida, misturada com lama (Jó 6:16), aparece descrito pela palavra hebraica que significa negro. No Novo Testamento, o termo grego *mélas*, «negro», é empregada apenas por três vezes: em Mat. 5:36, onde é dito que não temos a capacidade de tornar um cabelo nosso branco ou preto; em Apo. 6:5, que alude ao cavalo negro, referindo-se à morte como um juízo divino; e em Apo. 6:12, onde o sol é obscurecido devido a um grande terremoto.

3. *Vermelho*. O termo hebraico *adom*, usado para essa cor, refere-se ao sangue (II Reis 3:22), a uma veste tinta de sangue (Isa. 63:2), e a uma novilha dessa cor (Núm. 19:2). Também a um prato de lentilhas (Gên. 25:30), a um cavalo (Zac. 1:8; 6:2), à tez de uma pessoa (Gên. 25:25; Can. 5:10), a uma mancha leprosa (Lev. 13:19; 14:37). Uma outra palavra hebraica, *saruq*, significa «da cor de uma raposa», um tom de vermelho, de uma espécie de vinha que produz uvas púrpuras (Isa. 5:2), simbólico de derramamento de sangue (Zac. 6:2). No Novo Testamento, o termo grego *éruthros* é usado apenas por duas vezes (Atos 7:36, para indicar o mar Vermelho; e em Heb. 11:29, para indicar esse mesmo mar). A palavra grega *kókkinos*, «escarlate», porém, encontra-se por seis vezes: Mat. 27:38; Heb. 9:19; Apo. 18:12,16; 17:3,4, em várias conexões.

4. *Escarlate*. Esse é um vermelho profundo. Essa palavra figura na Bíblia em Isa. 1:18; Jer. 4:30; Gên. 38:28-30 e Êxo. 25:4. Diversas palavras hebraicas têm sido traduzidas por «escarlate». Ver também II Crô. 2:7,14 e 3:14. O termo hebraico *shani* parece envolver a idéia de «brilho». O termo hebraico *towla* fala de um *inseto* do qual se fabricava um pigmento dessa cor. A única coisa natural chamada de Escarlate, no Antigo Testamento, são os lábios, comparados a um fio escarlate (Can. 4:3). Várias peças do vestuário eram tingidas de escarlate (II Sam. 1:24; Pro. 31:21; Jer. 4:30 e Apo. 17:4). Essa cor era usada pelos gregos e romanos para indicar um túnica militar. Ver Mat. 27:38. Os livros de Marcos e João dizem «púrpura», pelo que é possível que o povo comum não tivesse uma palavra separada para isso. Porém, os dicionários clássicos falam em palavras separadas, pelo que deve haver alguma razão para essa diferença.

5. *Vermelhão*. No hebraico, *shashar*, um pigmento usado para as pinturas afresco, para representar figuras de ídolos, nas paredes e nos templos (Eze. 23:14), ou para colorir os próprios ídolos (Sab. 13:14). Também era palavra usada para indicar as decorações nas paredes e traves das casas (Jer. 22:14). Era cor muito favorecida pelos assírios, conforme a arqueologia tem demonstrado, mediante as esculturas de Ninrode e Corsabade.

6. *Amarelo*. No hebraico, *yeraqraq* (Sal. 68:13). Palavra aplicada ao ouro e a uma mancha de lepra (Lev. 13:49). Parece haver certa confusão com o verde; ou então o amarelo era considerado como um tom do verde, visto que a palavra que significa «esverdeado» também é aplicada ao ouro.

7. *Verde*. O termo hebraico *ra'anan* era usado para indicar aquilo que é vigoroso e florescente (Jó 15:32; Sal. 37:35; 52:8; Osé. 14:8). Também era usado para indicar o azeite fresco (Sal. 92:10). O termo hebraico *yerek* tem o sentido de planta que brota, sendo usado para todos os produtos alimentares (Gên. 1:30; 9:3; Êxo. 10:15). Contudo, essa cor pode também indicar uma cor doentia, a da *palidez*. No Novo Testamento, o vocábulo grego *chlóros* significa «verde» (Mar. 6:39), indicando, por exemplo, a relva onde se sentou o grupo em favor do qual Jesus multiplicou os pães e os peixinhos; a relva queimada pelos juízos divinos, em Apo. 8:7, e o verde das árvores (Apo. 9:4). Em Apocalipse 6:8, aparece como a cor de um dos quatro cavalos que trarão o juízo divino. Ali as traduções dão

amarelo ou *pálido*, como cor que representa a morte.

8. *Azul*. No hebraico, *tekeleth*. Por muito tempo, essa cor tem estado sujeita à disputa. Essa palavra tem sido variegadamente traduzida como púrpura, verde, índigo e amarelo. O Talmude (que vide) afirma que o nome dessa cor deriva-se do extrato puro de certa ostra. A origem dessa cor atualmente está identificada, de acordo com Irving Ziderman, do Instituto de Fibras de Israel, de conformidade com uma reportagem publicada na revista *Science News*. Esse animal é aparentado do caracol espinhento, chamado caramujo rajado. Se essa opinião está correta, conforme os estudiosos de Israel supõem, então a cor envolvida é o azul purpurino. Josefo (*Anti*. 3:7,7) e Filo usaram essa palavra para indicar a cor do firmamento. Porém, devemos supor que essa é uma referência inexata, a menos que o firmamento, no Oriente, seja de um azul mais escuro do que no Ocidente. Em Ester 1:6, algumas traduções dizem «violeta». Essa cor era usada nas vestimentas dos príncipes e dos nobres (Eze. 13:6; Ecl. 40:4), bem como nas vestes dos ídolos da Babilônia (Jer. 10:9).

9. *As Cores Sacerdotais*. O Antigo Testamento fala nas cores púrpura, azul, escarlate e branco, como aquelas que eram usadas em conexão com as vestes sacerdotais. As mesmas cores eram usadas no tabernáculo e nas decorações do templo de Jerusalém, nas cortinas, nos móveis, etc.

10. *Púrpura*. No hebraico, *argaman*. Essa cor era obtida de uma espécie de molusco chamado *Murex trunculus*, segundo seu nome científico moderno, especificamente de uma secreção glandular pegajosa, e não do seu sangue. Essa secreção normalmente é branca; mas, em contacto com o ar, torna-se amarela, então verde, e, finalmente, torna-se púrpura. Os fenícios quase monopolizaram a produção desse corante. Foi em Tiro que se comercializou, pela primeira vez, o produto. A arqueologia tem descoberto indícios dos lugares onde esse tipo de corante era produzido. O corante púrpura era um produto dispendioso nos dias da supremacia romana. Uma veste ou um manto colorido de púrpura era considerado um luxo que somente os ricos podiam usar. Vestes tingidas de púrpura eram usadas pelos reis (Juí. 8:26), —pelos oficiais do governo e pelos ricos em geral (Jer. 10:9; Luc. 16:19; Apo. 17:4; 18:16). Lídia, que se convertou ao evangelho, era negociante de panos tingidos dessa cor (Atos 16:14). No Apocalipse, as vestes dessa cor são mencionadas entre os itens de luxo de Roma.

11. *Tingimento*. No início do relato do Antigo Testamento, temos alusões a essa prática (Gên. 38:28 e Êxo. 26:1). Os hebreus aprenderam a arte com os egípcios e fenícios. As cores mais comumente usadas eram a púrpura, mais clara e mais carregada, o azul, o escarlate, o vermelhão. Os corantes, na sua maioria, eram extraídos de plantas e de moluscos. O corante mais caro era a púrpura extraída do *Murex*. Eram precisos cerca de duzentos e cinqüenta mil desses animais para produzir apenas 30 miligramas do corante! Isso mostra por que razão a púrpura era sinal da realeza e de grande abastança. Ver o artigo sobre *Artes e Ofícios*, 4.g, e sobre os *Tintureiros*, quanto a outros detalhes sobre a arte da tinturaria.

12. *Sentidos Metafóricos e Simbólicos das Cores*

a. *Branco*. Pureza, luz, vida, santidade, vitória. Os sacerdotes hebreus vestiam-se de branco, por serem os servos do Deus Santo. O branco era a cor básica do véu que dividia o santuário. As vestes da salvação são brancas como a luz (Sal. 27:1). Também há o branco luminoso da glória e da majestade (Dan. 7:9; Eze. 9:3). O branco é a cor das vestes dos remidos, que foram lavados no sangue do Cordeiro (Apo. 3:4,5; 7:14). A cabeça e os cabelos do Cristo exaltado eram brancos (Apo. 1:14), o qual veio para anunciar sua vitória sobre o mal, sob a forma de julgamento. O branco é também a cor do grande trono de juízo, onde a justiça é servida (Apo. 20:11).

Símbolos psicológicos e nos sonhos. O branco ou o azul claro indica o intelecto, uma das faculdades da mente, bem como a espiritualidade. É também a cor da iluminação, do autoconhecimento, da sabedoria, da mente divina, da inocência e da pureza. O branco sujo indica poluição e defloramento, oposto das vestes brancas de uma virgem.

b. *Negro*. Essa é a cor oposta ao branco, sendo vinculada à lamentação, à morte, às aflições, às calamidades (Jer. 14:2; Lam. 4:8; 5:10; Apo. 6:5). Pode indicar a humilhação (Mal. 3:14), ou um presságio de mal vindouro (Zac. 6:2).

Símbolos psicológicos e nos sonhos. A cor cinzenta pode indicar retrocessos, perturbações, escândalo, etc., mas o negro representa a morte. Também estão em foco a depressão e as premonições. As coisas que são obscuras, misteriosas, nebulosas, são simbolizadas pela cor negra. O submundo ou hades é um lugar escuro ou negro. Se alguém sonha com um animal branco e com um animal negro, ao mesmo tempo, terá sonhado com sua própria natureza boa e com sua própria natureza má. As figuras feminina e maternal são representadas pelo negro e pelo vermelho, mas o branco também pode representar a figura feminina, por estar relacionada à lua (uma luz no firmamento escuro da noite), que é uma figura feminina. O sol é um símbolo masculino.

c. *Vermelho*. Essa é a cor do fogo, e, como tal, simboliza a *vida*. Mas também é a cor do sangue, em cujo caso simboliza o sofrimento, o homicídio, o julgamento divino mediante a matança. Visto que o sangue era considerado a vida biológica de uma pessoa ou de um animal, essa cor pode simbolizar o princípio da vida (Gên. 9:4-6). Disso deriva-se o sentido metafórico de *expiação*, que liberta do pecado e provê a vida eterna (Isa. 63:2 e Heb. 9:22).

Símbolos psicológicos e nos sonhos. Sangue, fogo, vinho, emoções fortes, excitação sexual e ira são coisas comumente simbolizadas pela cor vermelha. Juntamente com o negro, pode simbolizar a feminilidade. Mas o róseo, um tipo de vermelho esbranquiçado, simboliza algo agradável, mas ilusório. Assim falamos sobre a *visão rósea* da vida, uma visão otimista, mas sem razões adequadas para tanto. As prostitutas e o sexo ilícito são simbolizados pelo vermelho. Os místicos, capazes de perceber a aura humana, dizem que as prostitutas têm uma emanação avermelhada em redor dos quadris.

d. *Verde*. Simboliza a verdura, o vigor, a prosperidade (Sal. 92:14), o desabrochar das flores (Sal. 37:35). É a cor da vida natural.

Símbolos psicológicos e nos sonhos. Tudo quanto cresce é simbolizado por essa cor, indicando o vigor e a vitalidade. A esperança, os pastos verdejantes pelos quais aguardamos, mas que ainda não obtivemos, pode ser simbolizada por essa cor. Contudo, o verde também pode simbolizar a inexperiência e a simplicidade, a necessidade de maior desenvolvimento. Além disso, a inveja também é retratada como verde. Visto que o verde pode estar associado à palidez, também pode indicar as enfermidades.

e. *Azul*. Cor do intelecto e da espiritualidade. Quanto mais apuradas forem, tanto mais claro será o azul. Os místicos dizem-nos que as pessoas especialmente inteligentes têm muito azul em suas auras. Entretanto, essa cor também representa a santidade, visto que o firmamento é azul. Para os hebreus, o azul simbolizava o divino ou o próprio Yahweh (Êxo. 24:10; Eze. 1:26), bem como as revelações divinas.

Símbolos psicológicos e nos sonhos. O intelecto, conforme dissemos acima. Essa cor simboliza a energia espiritual e a fidelidade. O azul escuro, devido à sua associação com o mar, pode indicar a intuição introvertida, bem como a compreensão intuitiva das realidades interiores e dos mistérios divinos. O azul profundo, misturado com o verde, pode indicar a liberação, a liberdade, a união de princípios opostos, como sensações e intuição.

f. *Púrpura.* Simboliza a realeza, as riquezas materiais e a majestade (Juí. 8:26; Est. 8:16; Can. 3:10; Dan. 5:7).

Símbolos psicológicos e nos sonhos. Essa cor simboliza o poder vital e a autoridade. Mas a púrpura clara representa a morte, devido à sua associação com o lilás.

Outras cores, não referidas na Bíblia. Referimo-nos abaixo aos símbolos psicológicos e nos sonhos:

g. Cores escuras, como negro, marrom, etc.: depressão, retrocesso, morte.

h. Cores brilhantes: alegria, vitalidade, esperança.

i. Mudança de cores escuras para cores claras: possibilidades de melhoria, crescimento espiritual. Mudança de cores claras para escuras: humilhação, perda, enfermidade.

j. Mudança de cores para a luz. Indica o movimento gradual do que é vil e sensual para o conhecimento e a participação na realidade superior.

l. *Marrom.* Representa os excrementos do corpo, a porção inferior do corpo humano. Visto que está associada à terra, essa cor pode indicar as sensações físicas. Porém, também pode indicar o dinheiro, visto que, nos sonhos, os excrementos geralmente simbolizam o dinheiro, os recursos materiais ou as riquezas de origem profana.

m. *Dourado.* Simboliza o sol, e, portanto, a mente consciente e a verdade. Visto que o sol representa o princípio masculino, o ouro também pode simbolizar a masculinidade. Visto que o ouro é amarelo, pode estar em foco a intuição. A combinação ouro e prata nos apresenta os princípios masculino e feminino.

n. *Amarelo.* Pode indicar a intuição e a intelectualidade. Visto que as pessoas intelectuais olham todos os lados de uma questão, podem parecer *hesitantes,* o que é injustamente associado à covardia. Um amarelo escuro ou maculado pode apontar para a morte. Visto que a urina é um líquido do corpo, e é amarela, essa cor pode simbolizar o próprio corpo.

o. *O arco-íris.* No arcoíris há a mescla das cores básicas, que formam o branco, dando a entender a esperança ou novas perspectivas. Visto que o arco-íris geralmente aparece após as tempestades, pode indicar um estado melhorado ou mais feliz, depois de um período de provação. Na Bíblia, o arco-íris é sinal da paciência de Deus, como quando resolveu que não mais destruiria a humanidade, mediante um dilúvio (Gên. 9:13 ss). (CHE GUI ID UN)

CORÍNTIOS, PRIMEIRA EPÍSTOLA AOS
Esboço
Introdução
 I. Autor
 II. Data e Proveniência
 III. A Igreja em Corinto
 IV. A Correspondência com Corinto
 V. Razão dessa Epístola
 VI. Temas Principais
 VII. Conteúdo
 VIII. Bibliografia

Introdução

Ver algumas observações gerais sobre o corpus das Epístolas Paulinas no artigo sobre Romanos, primeiros parágrafos e na secção II.

A primeira epístola aos Coríntios é um dos escritos *clássicos* de Paulo; acima de tudo ela preserva para nós não tanto a doutrina cristã, e, sim o padrão da ética cristã. Neste livro encontramos os problemas enfrentados pelos primeiros cristãos gentios, e como Paulo deu solução a esses problemas. As epístolas aos Romanos e outras revelam com maior aptidão a elevada mente de Paulo; mas nenhuma delas revela mais claramente do que I Coríntios aquilo que os psicólogos modernos gostam de chamar de «situações de vida real». Diferentemente daqueles problemas que Paulo tentou solucionar para os crentes da Galácia, que eram sobretudo questões de opinião religiosa, este livro aborda antes questões relativas à conduta cristã, questões morais da mais séria natureza. Paulo, homem de formação essencialmente judaica, tendo recebido idéias ainda mais elevadas por causa das revelações que recebeu acerca do cristianismo, ficava perplexo ante os costumes tolerados na igreja em Corinto, e que eram praticados por membros firmes da mesma.

Caráter da Primeira Epístola aos Coríntios. A fim de poder discernir o tipo de situação que o apóstolo Paulo enfrentou, o leitor faria bem em examinar as notas expositivas no NTI sobre Corinto e sobre o ministério de Paulo nessa cidade (Atos 18:1), bem como as notas introdutórias gerais sobre esse citado capítulo. Estrabão revela-nos que havia mil prostitutas religiosas oficiais associadas aos cultos religiosos daquela cidade, que tinham por principais divindades a Mãe Suprema, Melcarte, Serápis, Ísis e Afrodite. Naturalmente, isso atraía a Corinto um avantajado número de turistas. Todavia, isso não expressava toda a situação moral da cidade, porquanto muitos de seus habitantes ocupavam-se de seus empreendimentos particulares. *Viver como um coríntio* se tornou uma expressão proverbial para indicar uma vida de dissipação moral. Alcifrom escreveu em suas memórias: «Jamais estive em Corinto, porquanto sei bem qual o tipo animalesco de conduta os ricos desfrutam ali, e qual a miséria dos pobres». A população da cidade de Corinto era a mais cosmopolita dos centros gregos, e, de fato, era menos distintamente helênica do que todas as outras cidades, tendo incorporado em sua estrutura todos os vícios do paganismo, e isso de forma exagerada.

O incisivo primeiro capítulo da epístola aos Romanos foi escrito sob a influência da cultura coríntia, visto que essa epístola foi escrita em Corinto; e a simples leitura desse citado capítulo mostra-nos a atitude mental provocada no apóstolo pela observação dos espantosos vícios do paganismo que ali havia.

Embora existisse na mesma localização, a cidade que Paulo conheceu não descendia diretamente daquela que encabeçara a liga aqueana, durante o período helenístico. Aquela primeira cidade fora destruída em cerca de 146 A.C., por Lúcio Múmio, tendo ficado em ruínas por cem anos. A cidade foi então reconstruída, provavelmente por ordem de Júlio César, tendo-se tornado colônia romana. Os romanos, por conseguinte, é quem tinham reedificado a cidade de Corinto; e bastaria isso para explicar por que, dentre todas as cidades gregas, Corinto era a única que dispunha de um anfiteatro, uma das construções favoritas dos romanos. Por essa mesma razão é que muitos dos nomes pessoais, associados a Corinto, que se podem encontrar nas epístolas de Paulo aos crentes dessa cidade são de origem latina, e não grega, como Crispo, Tito Justo e Fortunato. Por semelhante modo, a maioria das inscrições atualmente achadas nessa cidade são latinas, e não gregas. A própria cidade, entretanto, não demorou a caracterizar-se como cidade cosmopolita, incluindo uma numerosa colônia judaica. Ver o artigo sobre *Corinto*.

I. Autor

Conforme lemos nas observações introdutórias, acima, existem quatro epístolas paulinas clássicas, entre aquelas que chegaram até nosso conhecimento, havendo acerca das mesmas pouquíssima desarmonia entre os estudiosos. A primeira epístola aos Coríntios ocupa lugar entre essas quatro. Questões como estilo literário, vocabulário e conteúdo confirmam a comum autoria de Romanos, Gálatas, I e II Coríntios. (Quanto às datas relativas da *coletânea* paulina, ver o artigo sobre à epístola aos Romanos, secção II, que também contém diversas comparações e observações que são úteis ao estudante). Mas, posto que a autoria da primeira epístola aos Coríntios não é posta em dúvida, talvez seja mais útil observarmos nesta altura as relações que havia entre Paulo e os crentes de Corinto.

Paulo considerava a igreja cristã de Corinto uma das provas palpáveis do seu ministério apostólico. Por causa da penetração de certos problemas ali, como práticas más e vis, contendas e divisões, que chegaram a ameaçar a sua aceitação como um apóstolo de Cristo por aquela igreja, que Paulo lhes escreveu com consternação mesclada com repreensão e demonstrações de seu afeto. (Ver I Cor. 3:10; 4:15; 9:2; II Cor. 7:3-5; 12:15; 7:8 e s; 3:1, quanto a esses diversos elementos, que demonstram a relação existente entre a igreja de Corinto e o apóstolo dos gentios).

Quantas teriam sido as visitas feitas por Paulo a Corinto? Alguns eruditos pensam que o trecho de II Cor. 12:14—13:10 subentende três visitas separadas do apóstolo, em que duas já teriam sido feitas, e uma terceira estava prestes a ter lugar. E essa suposição é mais natural do que a daqueles outros, que opinam que o apóstolo tencionara por três vezes fazer essas visitas, mas que, por algum motivo, principalmente porque sabia que o encontro seria doloroso para ele e para eles, ele ainda não os tinha realmente visitado nenhuma vez. O livro de Atos menciona apenas uma visita de Paulo a Corinto. Porém, devemos notar que o livro de Atos é notoriamente abreviado sobre tais questões, e a sua exposição sobre os ministérios de Paulo sempre é parcial, faltando-lhe muitos pormenores sobre diversas visitas que podemos depreender terem sido feitas no teor das próprias epístolas paulinas. O trecho de II Cor. 2:1 menciona que Paulo queria poupar os crentes coríntios de outra visita «dolorosa»; mas a visita descrita no livro de Atos não pode ser reputada *dolorosa*, razão pela qual precisamos postular um maior número de visitas do que aquela sobre a qual lemos no livro de Atos. (Quanto a notas expositivas sobre como o livro de Atos e as epístolas aos Coríntios se suplementam entre si, em que se destaca o fato de que mais detalhes históricos se depreendem das epístolas do que do livro de Atos, ver as notas introdutórias sobre o décimo oitavo capítulo do livro de Atos no NTI).

Paulo, portanto, já havia visitado os crentes de Corinto e permanecera algum tempo com eles, o que significa que tinha mais íntimas relações com eles do que com qualquer outra igreja cristã, com a única exceção possível da igreja em Éfeso.

A autenticidade da autoria paulina é confirmada por diversos dos pais da igreja dos primeiros anos, a saber: Clemente de Roma (Ep., cap. 47), Policarpo (Ep. aos Filipenses, cap. 11), Inácio (aos Efésios, cap. 2) e Irineu (Contra os Heréticos, iv. 27,3). Por semelhante modo fizeram Hermas (100 D.C., *Sim*. 5,7) e Barnabé (que fez alusões a I Cor. 3:16, em sua epístola, 6:16). O lugar de I Coríntios no cânon dos livros sagrados é tão antigo como o de qualquer das demais epístolas paulinas, fazendo parte integrante das primeiras coletâneas de escritos paulinos, segundo eram conhecidas pelos pais da igreja desde o ano de 150 D.C. Seu lugar no «cânon», por conseguinte, é tão antigo como qualquer dos livros do N.T., visto que algumas das epístolas de Paulo foram escritas antes de qualquer dos quatro evangelhos, e quase todas elas foram escritas antes de qualquer desses evangelhos, com a única exceção do evangelho de Marcos. Quando foi preparado o primeiro «cânon» dos livros do N.T., a primeira epístola aos Coríntios já se encontrava entre os livros selecionados. (Ver o artigo sobre o «Cânon do N.T.»). O artigo sobre o «Apóstolo Paulo» transmite-nos o que se sabe acerca do passado, da vida e das viagens missionárias de Paulo, descritas no livro de Atos, e também de seus ensinos, conforme se tem conhecimento hoje em dia sobre ele.

II. Data e Proveniência

O período da permanência de Paulo em Corinto, em contraste com suas visitas a outras localidades, pode ser determinado com grande precisão. No trecho de Atos 18:2, há menção do fato de que Priscila e Áquila chegaram a Corinto devido à expulsão dos judeus da cidade de Roma, por decreto do imperador Cláudio. (Isso é igualmente mencionado por Suetônio, em *Vida do Divinizado Cláudio*, 25:4). Ora, a data mais provável desse acontecimento é 49 D.C. Outrossim, a passagem de Atos 18:12 informa-nos como Gálio foi feito procônsul da Acaia. Sabe-se que esse personagem se chamava Lúcio Júnio Anaeu Gálio, irmão do famoso filósofo estóico romano Sêneca, que foi o tutor do terrível imperador Nero. Além disso, certa inscrição encontrada em Delfos tornou possível dar data a esse proconsulado dentro de bem estreitos limites de tal modo que se tem podido calcular que ele começou a agir nesse ofício a 1º de julho de 51 D.C.

Alguns estudiosos têm sugerido a inauguração do ofício de Gálio um ano mais tarde; porém, seja como for, podemos inferir com segurança que Gálio estava em Corinto em 50 D.C., pelo que também Paulo se encontrava ali. Mui provavelmente o apóstolo chegou àquela cidade na primavera de 50 D.C., tendo partido dali no outono de 51 D.C. Essa citada inscrição contém as palavras de uma carta de saudações enviada pelo imperador Cláudio à cidade de Delfos, na qual ele menciona a pessoa de Gálio. Com base nessa inscrição, portanto, podemos datar, com qualquer grau de certeza, a única dentre as viagens do apóstolo Paulo. (Quanto a outras notas expositivas sobre essa inscrição, ver as notas introdutórias sobre o décimo oitavo capítulo do livro de Atos no NTI).

Por conseguinte, pelo menos sabemos que a primeira epístola aos Coríntios foi escrita algum tempo depois disso. A epístola aos Gálatas já havia sido escrita, sendo muito provável que a primeira e a segunda epístolas aos Tessalonicenses foram escritas

Ainda que eu falasse as línguas dos homens e dos anjos, e não tivesse Caridade, seria como o metal que soa ou como o sino que tine. E ainda que tivesse o DOM de profecia, e conhecesse todos os mistérios e toda a ciência, e ainda tivesse toda a fé, de maneira tal que transportasse os montes, e não tivesse Caridade, NADA seria. E ainda que distribuísse toda minha fortuna para o sustento dos pobres, e ainda que entregasse o meu corpo para ser queimado, e NÃO tivesse Caridade, nada disso ME Aproveitaria.

1 aos Coríntios 13
1~3

Caligrafia de Darrell Steven Champlin

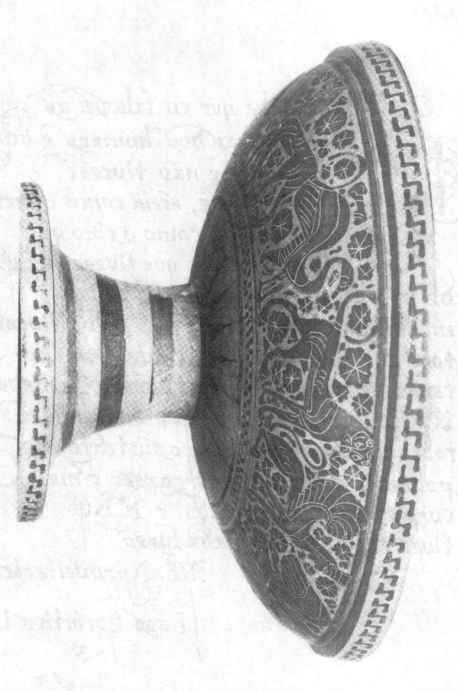

Vaso corintiano, Século VII, A.C. — Cortesia, Fogg Art Museum, Harvard University

pouco mais tarde, após a permanência de Paulo em Corinto, ou mesmo enquanto ele ainda se encontrava ali, ou seja, antes da primeira epístola aos Coríntios ter sido escrita. Porém, a primeira epístola aos Coríntios é reputada como a quarta das epístolas de Paulo, na ordem da escrita, tendo sido composta em Éfeso, durante sua permanência ali, que provavelmente se deu desde o verão de 52 até o outono de 54 D.C.

Mui provavelmente Paulo escreveu essa primeira epístola aos Coríntios poucos meses antes de deixar Éfeso, a fim de visitar novamente as igrejas que havia fundado na Macedônia e em Corinto. Podemos considerar as suas palavras em I Cor. 16:19, que dizem: «As igrejas da Ásia vos saúdam...» Ora, Éfeso era o centro de operações do apóstolo Paulo enquanto ele esteve na Ásia, pelo que é lógico supormos que ele escreveu essa epístola dessa cidade. Sua longa permanência em Éfeso, e as perturbações que estouraram quase imediatamente na igreja de Corinto servem para indicar que é natural a conclusão de que essa epístola foi escrita nessa cidade, quando Paulo ali permaneceu por cerca de três anos. Devemos notar, por semelhante modo, que esse versículo também faz alusão a Áquila e Priscila, mencionando a congregação que se reunia na casa deles; e isso subentende que ele residia onde havia um grupo de cristãos, o que, por sua vez, subentende Éfeso. Ver I Cor. 16:5, que não dá a entender que a epístola provinha da Macedônia, mas meramente que o apóstolo passaria por ali, a caminho de Corinto, com o propósito de fazer a esta cidade uma outra visita. Em contraste com isso, pode-se depreender, de II Cor. 7:5,6 que a segunda epístola aos Coríntios foi escrita da Macedônia. Porém, a referência que não mais permite lugar para disputas é a de I Cor. 16:8, que diz: «Ficarei, porém, em Éfeso até ao Pentecoste». Assim, pois, Paulo ficou em Éfeso até o festa do Pentecoste, esperando poder partir dali pouco depois; não obstante, foi inesperadamente impedido de fazê-lo, tendo de adiar sua partida, conforme nos informa o trecho de I Cor. 16:8 e s. É bem provável, pois, que Paulo tenha escrito a epístola de I Coríntios durante a primavera, pouco antes da festa de Pentecoste, em 54 D.C.

III. A Igreja em Corinto

Paulo foi o primeiro missionário cristão a chegar à Grécia, de conformidade com os registros históricos de que dispomos. Chegou ele em Corinto proveniente de Atenas, sentindo-se muito desencorajado, porquanto seus esforços ali haviam dado bem pouco fruto. Parece-nos que ele não estava nada confiante. (Ver I Cor. 2:3). Ficou em companhia de um casal de judeus, Áquila e Priscila, que eram cristãos e tinham vindo de Roma, em face da expulsão dos judeus da capital do império, por decreto do imperador Cláudio. A igreja de Corinto, por conseguinte, teve início na casa deles; e Silas e Timóteo não se demoraram a vir reunir-se a Paulo em Corinto, trazendo boas notícias sobre o ministério do evangelho na Macedônia. Assim, pois, renovado em suas forças e em seu ânimo, Paulo iniciou seu trabalho com grande intensidade em Corinto. (Ver I Tes. 3:6). Contudo, a oposição, especialmente da parte dos líderes eclesiásticos dos judeus, se tornou intensa. É possível que a esse tempo é que Priscila e Áquila arriscaram suas vidas em favor de Paulo (ver Rom. 16:3). Entretanto, Deus se pôs ao lado de seu apóstolo, primeiramente na forma de uma visitação mística, que assegurou a Paulo tanto o êxito em sua missão em Corinto como a sua segurança física pessoal. (Ver Atos 18:9 e ss). E foi assim que Paulo foi protegido por Gálio, que não se deixara influenciar pelos judeus radicais, que haviam apresentado queixa falsa contra o apóstolo.

A permanência de Paulo em Corinto se prolongou por dezoito meses, o que, para ele, representou uma longa permanência em qualquer lugar. À parte de Éfeso, onde Paulo ficou por três anos, Corinto foi o lugar onde mais o apóstolo permaneceu, durante todo o seu período de atividades missionárias. Ora, isso lhe deu a oportunidade de desenvolver um ministério mais profundo do que já pudera efetuar em outros lugares, o que também fica implícito em I Cor. 3:6. E, fazendo contraste com Atenas, parece que em Corinto o cristianismo *prosperou* grandemente, pelo menos numericamente falando, razão pela qual a cidade de Corinto se tornou um dos mais importantes centros da primitiva igreja cristã. Com os crentes de Corinto o apóstolo manteve a sua mais extensa correspondência; e da cidade de Corinto pelo menos três das epístolas de Paulo foram escritas, a saber; Romanos e I e II Tessalonicenses.

Depois da partida do apóstolo Paulo, chegaram em Corinto outros mestres do evangelho, entre os quais se destacava um outro rabino judeu, de nome Apolo, homem dotado de eloquência singular, que deu prosseguimento à obra iniciada por Paulo, não se tendo deixado envolver pessoalmente no espírito de partidarismo que afetou aquela igreja. Priscila e Áquila ajudaram a Apolo com seus dons naturais, instruindo-o com maior precisão acerca da doutrina de Cristo. (Ver Atos 18:24 e ss).

Todavia, depois do afastamento do apóstolo, a igreja de Corinto desceu de forma alarmante quanto ao seu nível moral e espiritual. Estouraram divisões amargas (ver o terceiro capítulo); permitiram os vícios mais baixos entre eles (ver o capítulo quinto e 6:9 e ss); abusaram da liberdade cristã (ver os capítulos oitavo e décimo); deixaram-se influenciar por mestres legalistas, que ensinavam de modo contrário a Paulo (ver o nono capítulo); corromperam as formas cristãs de adoração, agindo de forma ultrajante, até mesmo quando da participação na Ceia do Senhor, comendo em excesso, deixando-se embriagar e negligenciando os pobres da igreja, que ficavam famintos e esquecidos. A celebração da Ceia do Senhor, naquela época, incluía o *agape* ou «festa de amor», imitação da refeição da páscoa, o que nos explica a oportunidade de alguns terem um opíparo banquete, ao passo que outros ficavam famintos (ver o décimo primeiro capítulo). Além disso, os crentes de Corinto se mostravam extremamente ativos no uso dos dons miraculosos; no entanto, abusavam desses dons, criando a desordem nos cultos da igreja (ver os capítulos doze e catorze). Também surgiram falsas doutrinas entre eles, sendo tolerados os falsos mestres, sobretudo aqueles que pervertiam o ensino acerca da ressurreição (ver o décimo quinto capítulo). Esses se tornaram os graves vícios da igreja de Corinto, condições essas que impeliram o apóstolo a escrever a primeira epístola aos Coríntios.

IV. A Correspondência com Corinto

Trata-se este de um assunto complexo, e as investigações feitas sobre o mesmo não têm produzido qualquer coisa como resultados certos. Pode-se dizer com confiança, entretanto, que houve mais do que duas epístolas de Paulo aos crentes de Corinto, e que as próprias epístolas I e II Coríntios representam mais do que duas epístolas. Diversas reconstituições têm sido sugeridas, conforme os exemplos que damos abaixo:

CORÍNTIOS

É provável que Paulo tivesse escrito ao menos quatro epístolas ao Coríntios, partes das quais estão contidas em nossas duas epístolas tradicionais. Devemos observar que em I Cor. 5:9 há menção de alguma outra epístola que o apóstolo escreveu para eles, e que evidentemente antecedeu o material apresentado na primeira epístola aos Coríntios. Na reconstituição da correspondência com a igreja de Corinto, as sugestões têm sido como a que mostramos abaixo:

1. II Cor. 6:14-7:1 seria fragmento de uma carta que fora escrita acerca da questão do jugo desigual, mas que, mais tarde, veio a ser incorporada com outros materiais da correspondência paulina com a igreja de Corinto, tendo, finalmente, sido formulada em uma única epístola, conforme a conhecemos hoje.

2. A primeira epístola aos Coríntios representa essencialmente uma única carta, embora o sétimo capítulo da mesma possa ser uma secção separada; e o trecho de I Cor. 7:1 parece indicar uma correspondência entre os coríntios e Paulo que provavelmente consistiu da troca de várias cartas.

3. O trecho de II Cor. 10—13 parece ser uma carta separada, que alguns eruditos têm chamado de «carta amarga», por causa de seu conteúdo severo. Essa epístola parece estar um tanto *deslocada*, na presente posição em que se encontra, pois os primeiros capítulos da segunda epístola aos Coríntios expõe uma atmosfera de alívio e ações de graças, para então, subitamente, Paulo apelar para o sarcasmo e para as denúncias violentas. Parece-nos melhor pensar que tais denúncias na realidade pertençam ao tempo anterior à composição da primeira porção da segunda epístola aos Coríntios, e que elas faziam parte de outra missiva, que foi enviada antes de II Coríntios. Alguns estudiosos também têm procurado situar os capítulos décimo a décimo terceiro antes da secção dos capítulos primeiro a nono, porquanto aqueles capítulos parecem referir-se a questões futuras (ver II Cor. 10:6 e 13:2, 10), ao passo que os capítulos primeiro a nono fazem alusões ao passado (ver II Cor. 1:23 e 2:3,9), tudo o que sugere que houve deslocação de material, ou mesmo que se tratavam de duas cartas paulinas separadas, que mais tarde foram unidas, embora numa ordem cronológica revertida.

4. A passagem de II Cor. 1—9, menos a secção de II Cor. 6:14—7:1, parece formar uma unidade, escrita após a grande crise que houve entre Paulo e a igreja de Corinto. Essa passagem, pois, tem sido denominada pelos estudiosos de «carta pacífica». Mas a secção dos capítulos décimo a décimo terceiro, embora pesada e amarga, preserva para nós um bom material biográfico, que se reveste de valor porque nos permite conhecer um pouco mais da vida de Paulo. E aquela «carta amarga», a que já nos referimos (II Cor. 10:13), provavelmente foi enviada entre I Coríntios e as outras porções de II Coríntios.

Porém, outras reconstituições da correspondência paulina com os crentes de Corinto têm sido propostas, como as idéias de Johannes Weiss, *The History of Primitive Christianity*, I, págs. 356-357.

1. A carta pré-canônica, referida em I Cor. 5:9, conteria II Cor. 6:14—7:1; I Cor. 10:1-23; 6:12-20; 11:2-34, e talvez 16:7,8,20.

2. A resposta de Paulo à carta trazida de Corinto continha talvez I Cor. 7:9; 10:24—11:1, 12:1—16:6 e talvez 16:16-19.

3. Uma terceira carta, que versava sobre as facções existentes em Corinto, talvez tenha incluído os trechos de I Cor. 1:1—6:11 e 16:10-14,22-24.

Maurice Goguel, em sua obra *Introduction au Nouveau Testament*, 'Les 'epistre pauliniennes', Paris, Ernest Leroux, 1926, IV, págs. 72-86, 1926, diz essencialmente a mesma coisa, embora com alguma redistribuição de material, a saber:

1. II Cor. 6:14—7:1; 6:12-20; 10:1-22.
2. I Cor. 5:1—6:11; 7:1—8:13; 10:23—14:40; 15:1-58; 16:1-9,12.
3. I Cor. 1:10—4:21; 9:1-27; 16:10,11.

Na realidade, *não existem meios* para a defesa dessas teorias, com qualquer grau de certeza, não sendo provável que qualquer dessas opiniões represente a verdade da questão. Parece perfeitamente certo, todavia, que as duas epístolas que possuímos, escritas pelo Apóstolo Paulo aos Coríntios representam mais do que duas cartas, embora a primeira epístola aos Coríntios pareça ser uma unidade, apesar de que pequenas porções da mesma talvez tenham feito parte de alguma carta ou cartas separadas, que mais tarde foram incorporadas à mesma.

Já a segunda epístola aos Coríntios pode ser mais facilmente dividida, com muito maior grau de exatidão potencial. Pouca dúvida pode haver que a complexa situação que houve em Corinto não poderia ter sido solucionada por apenas uma epístola ou duas, o que nos explica a complexidade das duas epístolas propostas, as quais na realidade não seriam apenas duas, mas antes, representariam três ou talvez até mesmo quatro cartas diversas. E então, quando a coletânea de escritos paulinos foi recolhida, o que ele escrevera a Corinto veio a ser incorporado em apenas duas unidades, conforme as conhecemos atualmente. E também é provável que tivessem sido escritas ainda outras epístolas de Paulo a Corinto, mais curtas ou mais longas, das quais não possuímos um fragmento sequer.

As indagações que têm sido levantadas, no tocante à correspondência de Paulo com a igreja de Corinto não incluem qualquer idéia de dúvida acerca da autenticidade dessas cartas—isto é, não se põe dúvida de que o apóstolo Paulo foi o autor das mesmas—porquanto esse ponto é concordado pela maioria esmagadora dos intérpretes de todas as escolas. (Ver as notas expositivas sob o título «Autor», da secção I deste artigo). — (Quanto a fontes informativas acerca da natureza da correspondência paulina com Corinto, ver as seguintes obras: J.H. Kennedy, *The Second and Third Epistles to the Corinthians;* Kirsop Lake, *The Earlier Epistles of Paul*, 1927, págs. 144 e ss; R.V.G. Tasker, *Expository Times*, XLVII, 1935-1936, págs. 55-58; e ainda outras discussões acerca da correspondência de Paulo com Corinto, podem ser encontradas no artigo sobre à segunda epístola aos Coríntios).

V. Razão desta Epístola

A primeira epístola aos Coríntios é complexa por si mesma, e aborda muitos problemas, motivo pelo qual é extremamente difícil atribuirmos uma razão que teria levado o apóstolo Paulo a compor a mesma. E isso se torna especialmente veraz se aceitarmos a idéia de que temos na mesma, trechos reunidos de mais de uma carta. Todavia, uma declaração de âmbito geral pode ser feita, e que incorpora a maioria das muitas *razões*. A conduta ética comum em Corinto, evidenciada pelos próprios costumes da cidade, encontrara algum apoio na igreja cristã dali. Isso produziu uma espécie de ética que era uma mescla de princípios pagãos e cristãos. Esta primeira epístola, por conseguinte, trataria de situações de conduta ética, na vida diária. Além desses fatores, podemos pensar nos ataques dos legalistas, dos falsos mestres e dos detratores do apóstolo Paulo, que ameaçavam destruir não somente a obra realizada ali por Paulo, mas também a sua reputação e autoridade como apóstolo de Cristo. Essa situação, pois, é que provoca algumas das amargas refutações existentes nesse livro. Poderíamos dizer, portanto, que I e II Coríntios registram a «história de uma querela», conforme diz Kirsop Lake (*ibid*. págs. 117 e *ss*). Isso, entretanto, não tem por intuito indicar que essa querela não tivesse importância, ou que os contendores tenham entrado nela negligentemente, conforme a palavra moderna «querela» geralmente nos dá a entender.

Não muito depois de ter chegado a Éfeso, Paulo recebeu recado, da parte de elementos da família de Cloé (I Cor. 1:11 e *ss*), acerca das contenções que tinham surgido entre os crentes de Corinto, o que havia produzido facções entre eles, cada uma das quais como o seu suposto líder ou herói, como Paulo, Pedro, Apolo e Jesus Cristo. E os que trouxeram essas notícias a Paulo evidentemente foram Estéfanas, Fortunato e Acaico (ver I Cor. 16:17). E é igualmente patente que trouxeram com eles, uma carta, enviada pelos crentes de Corinto, pedindo os conselhos do apóstolo acerca de várias questões que, evidentemente, vinham sendo debatidas entre os cristãos daquela cidade. O resultado dessas indagações é a primeira epístola aos Coríntios, ou, pelo menos, partes da mesma.

A primeira porção da mesma trata das questões dos perturbadores, em que o apóstolo repreende aqueles que eram os causadores das divisões. A segunda porção responde, pela ordem, as perguntas feitas pelos crentes de Corinto, questões sobre princípios morais, matrimônio, ordem do culto na igreja, a liberdade cristã e a questão sobre a ressurreição.

Na esperança de dar melhor solução ao caso em geral, o apóstolo tencionava fazer uma outra visita àquela igreja de Corinto; mas, nesse ínterim, enviou-lhes Timóteo (ver I Cor. 4:18-21), esperando que ele fosse capaz de dar cobro à situação. Antes de escrever sua primeira epístola aos Coríntios, parece que Paulo já lhes havia escrito uma outra carta, que versava sobre questões de moral, sem dúvida por ter ouvido falar nas condições deficientes e mesmo escandalosas daquela igreja. A regra determinada por Paulo era a separação daqueles que assim se conduzissem, ficando tais elementos isolados da igreja até que se arrependessem verdadeiramente, com a modificação de suas condutas diárias. (Ver I Cor. 5:9-14). Contudo, a própria primeira epístola aos Coríntios mostra-nos que essa suposta primeira carta ainda não produzira seus esperados resultados, tendo sido necessário dar prosseguimento, nesta chamada primeira epístola aos Coríntios, às reprimendas e advertências sobre o assunto. Muitos pensam que ao menos uma parte dessa epístola não canônica é aquela representada pelo trecho de II Cor. 6:14-7:1, que contém advertências de ordem moral, parecendo bastante fora de lugar, na posição que ocupa dentro do corpo da segunda epístola aos Coríntios. É possível, portanto, que essa citada secção seja o mais antigo fragmento que possuímos da correspondência de Paulo com a igreja de Corinto.

Retornando agora à questão dos perturbadores da ordem, que pelo menos em parte provocaram a escrita da primeira epístola aos Coríntios, parece-nos que eles se tinham dividido em *quatro* grupos distintos (ver I Cor. 3:1), a saber:

1. Os que se diziam seguidores de *Apolo*, o rabino de Alexandria, o intelectual entre os líderes, e que tiveram algum desempenho no desenvolvimento da igreja cristã de Corinto. Provavelmente esse partido se compunha dos «entendidos» dentre os crentes de Corinto. Pode-se imaginar que seu pecado consistia do orgulho intelectual, juntamente com a mistura de várias filosofias com a fé cristã simples, como os bons gregos geralmente se sentiam tentados a fazer. No primeiro capítulo dessa epístola, onde Paulo diz que a sabedoria deste mundo é «loucura», provavelmente há nisso uma repreensão indireta a esse partido, embora a igreja em geral talvez estivesse envolvida em problemas dessa categoria.

2. Aqueles que eram os seguidores de Cefas, ou Pedro, e que provavelmente eram os judaizantes ou legalistas da igreja, muitos dos quais sem dúvida se haviam convertido do judaísmo, naturalmente aderiam a antigas práticas ritualistas e legalistas. O próprio apóstolo Pedro não teria encorajado tal atitude, como Apolo também não teria encorajado o partido dos «entendidos» para que o considerassem como uma espécie de herói.

3. Além desses, havia os seguidores de *Paulo*, cujo herói era o grande apóstolo dos gentios. É possível que esse grupo envolvesse aqueles que faziam forte oposição ao legalismo e ao intelectualismo, preferindo o evangelho da graça, sem as complicações da cultura judaica ou da cultura grega.

4. Além desses, havia os partidários de Cristo. Esses certamente faziam objeção ao culto aos «heróis» e seus partidários, e, acima de todos, faziam-se os grandes seguidores de Cristo. O pecado destes últimos era o do exclusivismo, tão prevalente na moderna igreja evangélica, que, nas mentes de alguns, cria a ilusão de que eles, acima de quaisquer outros, são os melhores discípulos que Cristo tem. Isso é a antítese mesma do denominacionalismo, que inevitavelmente cria outras e ainda mais estritas denominações. Em outras palavras, aqueles que se unem em combate contra as denominações, nesse processo, geralmente criam formas ainda mais estritas de denominacionalismo, embora talvez não tenham qualquer nome específico, como fazem outras denominações.

Um problema similar a esse era o dos perturbadores da ordem, exaltados aos seus próprios olhos devido ao orgulho espiritual, por exercerem dons espirituais miraculosos autênticos ou aparentes. Esses se ufanavam de tal modo de suas realizações espirituais que criavam o caos nos cultos da igreja de Corinto. Sem dúvida era difícil para outrem ter oportunidade de falar nas reuniões, porquanto estavam sempre preparados com alguma profecia, com alguma língua, com alguma exortação, com alguma mensagem, de forma alguma se envergonhando por interromper tão desabridamente aos outros, por estarem usando ininterruptamente da palavra, em qualquer das reuniões da igreja. É por esse motivo, pois, que nos capítulos décimo primeiro a décimo quarto o apóstolo dá instruções que regulamentam os dons espirituais e o seu uso. É bem provável que alguns elementos desse mesmo grupo fossem aqueles que abusavam da liberdade cristã, comprando e comendo carne de lugares onde tal carne fora apresentada às divindades, em templos pagãos; e talvez até se dispusessem a freqüentar certos ritos que eram efetuados nesses templos, em companhia de seus amigos pagãos, que os convidavam para as suas reuniões profanas. Esses crentes, pois, consolavam-se dizendo que *um ídolo nada é*, e daí concluíam que comer carne que fora apresentada aos ídolos também nada significa. Isso expressa uma verdade, até certo ponto; mas a facção legalista da igreja de Corinto, que exaltava a Pedro como seu grande herói, sem dúvida se sentia ofendida com essa forma de conduta e o

CORÍNTIOS

resultado disso eram sentimentos pesados, disputas e divisões, que ameaçavam cindir a igreja de Corinto. (Ver os capítulos sexto e oitavo dessa primeira epístola aos Coríntios).

No sétimo capítulo dessa primeira epístola aos Coríntios, Paulo se volta para as perguntas que os próprios crentes de Corinto lhe tinham feito por carta. (Ver I Cor. 7:1). A expressão reiterada, «Quanto ao que me escreveste...» (7:1). «Com respeito às virgens...» (7:15), «A respeito dos dons espirituais...» (12:1). «No que se refere às cousas sacrificadas a ídolos» (18:1), «Quanto à coleta para os santos...» (16:1) e «Acerca do irmão Apolo...» (16:12), ela provavelmente dá início às respostas às perguntas especificamente feitas pelos crentes de Corinto a Paulo. Por conseguinte, a carta que eles enviaram ao apóstolo dizia respeito aos *seguintes temas*:

1. O valor do celibato e do matrimônio, bem como seus valores relativos. Essa questão discute paralelamente o que o Senhor Jesus disse acerca dos mesmos assuntos, segundo vemos em Mat. 19:12. (Ver I Cor. 7).
2. A questão dos limites da liberdade cristã (ver I Cor. 6 e 8).
3. A questão inteira da busca, da posse e do uso dos dons espirituais. (Ver I Cor. 11-14).
4. A questão do desejo que Paulo tinha de levantar uma oferta para os crentes pobres da igreja de Jerusalém (16:1), que foi, por assim dizer, uma das obsessões do apóstolo Paulo durante sua terceira viagem missionária, cuja entrega provocou a sua última viagem a Jerusalém, onde também foi aprisionado, tendo permanecido prisioneiro por muitos anos.
5. É evidente que a carta enviada a Paulo pelos crentes de Corinto continha um pedido que Paulo lhes enviasse Apolo, a fim de que novamente lhes ministrasse ali. Paulo procurara convencer Apolo sobre essa necessidade, mas o próprio Apolo não estava disposto a fazer tal visita, provavelmente não querendo provocar ainda mais a situação que ali já prevalecia, sobretudo no que diz respeito às várias facções ali existentes, uma das quais o escolhera como seu herói.

Podemos facilmente imaginar que a epístola enviada pelos crentes de Corinto ao apóstolo Paulo lhe fizera indagações sobre a natureza da ressurreição, porquanto, em Corinto, havia alguns que pareciam negar que se deveria esperar a ressurreição, dizendo que a mesma já havia ocorrido, provavelmente querendo dar a entender com isso que a ressurreição de Cristo e outros eventos paralelos já tinham tido lugar. É que esses falsos mestres não faziam a menor idéia de como a ressurreição do Senhor Jesus garante a ressurreição de todos os remidos. Parece que haviam abandonado a idéia judaica comum de que os justos finalmente seriam ressuscitados, sem falarmos na ressurreição geral dos perdidos. Mui provavelmente esse problema doutrinário surgiu em Corinto porque, entre os gentios, a doutrina da ressurreição era um ensino estranho, embora não totalmente desconhecido em seus *mitos*; ou então porque, em Corinto havia alguns que demonstravam tendências *gnósticas*, as quais, de mistura com conceitos do judaísmo e da filosofia e mitologia gregas, além dos conceitos cristãos, aquela gente terminara por criar uma doutrina que reputava desnecessária qualquer ressurreição do corpo físico. Isso provocou a escrita do décimo quinto capítulo desta primeira epístola aos Coríntios, a mais completa e profunda declaração que existe sobre a questão, em toda a literatura mundial.

De modo geral, pois, procurando nós a razão pela qual esta epístola foi escrita, bem como suas *circunstâncias históricas*, que provocaram a sua escrita, podemos declarar o seguinte:

1. Paulo já havia escrito uma epístola anterior, mencionada em I Cor. 5:9, que tinha o propósito definido de combater a grosseira imoralidade que se abatera sobre a igreja de Corinto, que ele ouvira de alguma fonte informativa acerca da qual nada somos informados. Parte dessa epístola bem poderia ser o trecho de II Cor. 6:14-7:1.
2. Nesse ínterim, antes disso ou talvez após tais acontecimentos terem começado, Apolo levara a efeito um ministério ali; entretanto, retornara a Éfeso (I Cor. 16:12) e então começara a criar-se um partido que exaltava o seu nome.
3. Pedro também fizera uma visita à igreja de Corinto, ou pelo menos havia alguns judeus crentes que se tinham tornado membros da mesma, cujo herói era o apóstolo Pedro, os quais levaram a igreja a praticar certas normas legalistas, criando uma facção que se dizia seguidora de Cefas.
4. Uma réplica àquela primeira carta de Paulo fora enviada pela igreja, através de *Estéfanas*, *Fortunato* e *Acaico* (I Cor. 16:15-18), carta essa que continha aquelas várias perguntas, antes mencionadas. Grande parte da primeira epístola aos Coríntios, pois, constitui-se de respostas às perguntas na missiva dos coríntios a Paulo.
5. Lemos em I Cor. 1:11 que pessoas enviadas da parte de Cloé, talvez escravos daquela casa, informaram a Paulo acerca das divisões existentes na igreja de Corinto, sendo perfeitamente possível que os indivíduos, mencionados no quarto ponto (acima), tivessem sido os informantes do apóstolo, os quais não somente entregaram a epístola enviada pelos crentes de Corinto, mas que também puderam transmitir verbalmente a Paulo várias informações. Provavelmente relataram ao apóstolo até que ponto a sua reputação e autoridade apostólica foram denegridas em Corinto. E foi exatamente essa visita, acima de qualquer outro fator, que tornou necessária a continuação da correspondência entre os crentes de Corinto e o apóstolo Paulo, a começar pela maior parte da primeira epístola aos Coríntios.

Evidentemente, entretanto, houve um fim feliz no tocante aos problemas surgidos em Corinto. Pelo tempo em que foi escrita a segunda epístola aos Coríntios (ou então as cartas que foram incorporadas naquilo que hoje é chamado de II Coríntios) o pior já tinha passado. (Ver II Cor. 1 e 2). A projetada terceira visita de Paulo a Corinto, embora potencialmente dolorosa para bolsões de resistência que ainda persistiam na igreja de Corinto (ver II Cor. 10:6-11 e 13:1 e *ss*), pôde ser aludida em tons jubilosos; e a coleta para os santos pobres de Jerusalém, para o que Paulo fizera arranjos, ao projetar a sua visita mencionada em I Cor. 16:3,4, poderia ser facilmente concluída quando dessa visita adicional.

A epístola aos Romanos, que foi escrita durante a terceira visita de Paulo a Corinto, parece indicar um término feliz para a tão prolongada perturbação. Agora o apóstolo aguardava poder fazer uma visita a Roma, após muitos adiamentos e frustrações, quando estivesse de viagem para o ocidente, para a Espanha, onde tencionava desenvolver um ministério. Até onde os seus labores em Corinto estavam envolvidos, ele estava satisfeito com o progresso e o caráter dos mesmos, e agora podia partir, deixando a continuação dos trabalhos ministeriais ali a outros. (Ver II Cor. 1:10,13,15 e 15:28).

CORÍNTIOS

VI. Temas Principais

Quando abordamos a razão por detrás da escrita dessa primeira epístola aos Coríntios, já tocamos de forma suficiente sobre os temas principais. Contudo, olhando para esses temas, de forma mais particular, podemos alistar o que dizemos mais abaixo:

De maneira geral, pode-se asseverar que a primeira epístola aos Coríntios não é essencialmente uma epístola doutrinária, à semelhança de Romanos e Gálatas, ainda que sejam discutidas certas questões doutrinárias importantes, sobretudo aquilo que diz respeito à prática do governo da igreja. Seus temas, entretanto, são essencialmente éticos e práticos; e por causa dos muitos problemas acerca dos quais o apóstolo escreveu, no intuito de corrigi-los, encontramos a mais completa declaração ética da fé cristã, em todo o N.T. Em contraste com a epístola aos Romanos, por exemplo, nessa primeira epístola aos Coríntios não abordamos as relações entre o cristianismo e o judaísmo, sobre como esses dois sistemas religiosos podem ser harmonizados entre si, mas antes, lemos como a igreja cristã pode entrar em um ambiente pagão, prosperando e permanecendo pura.

Ora, isso é particularmente importante para a nossa época, porquanto não existe nenhum problema mais agudo no cristianismo atual do que esse. A maioria dos problemas que os crentes de Corinto tiveram de enfrentar são os mesmos comuns à experiência cristã hoje em dia, não havendo razão alguma para supormos que as soluções propostas pelo apóstolo Paulo não sejam igualmente válidas para os nossos próprios dias, tais como o foram para os endereçados originais dessa epístola canônica. Apresentamos, pois, os pontos prometidos acima:

1. O *Evangelho* no teor da primeira epístola aos Coríntios: Nessa epístola não há qualquer tentativa para apresentar qualquer exposição sistemática do evangelho cristão, em sua natureza e conteúdo, a menos que a primeira porção do décimo quinto capítulo seja considerada como tal; antes, por toda a parte há elementos do evangelho cristão, os quais, considerados em seu conjunto, não fornecem uma **informação suficiente sobre o assunto.** Podem-se alinhar as **seguintes razões** para isso:

a. Cristo é o centro da mensagem da epístola, do princípio ao fim (ver I Cor. 1:3).

b. Cristo é o alvo final da criação (I Cor. 8:6).

c. Cristo é o alvo supremo da vida (I Cor. 15:28).

d. Cristo é o verdadeiro Deus (I Cor. 8:4-6).

e. Cristo é o poder que sustenta a natureza (I Cor. 3:6).

f. Cristo é quem ordena providencialmente os acontecimentos entre os homens (I Cor. 4:9; 7:7 e 12:6).

g. Os homens jamais conheceram a Deus por sua própria sabedoria, mas podem vir a conhecê-lo por meio de Cristo, a própria Sabedoria de Deus (I Cor. 1:21).

h. É Deus que se achega aos homens em busca deles e não ao contrário (I Cor. 1:27).

i. Aqueles que se achegam a Deus, recebem a revelação de seus mistérios, por intermédio do Espírito Santo (I Cor. 2:10 e 4:1).

j. A vida eterna, por meio da ressurreição, nos é dada por meio de Cristo (ver I Cor. 15).

l. Cristo é o Juiz supremo, e espera a observância dos seus mandamentos (I Cor. 4:5; 5:13 e 7:19).

m. Vários aspectos da redenção nos são oferecidos: Cristo é a rocha, o sustentador, o supridor das necessidades espirituais (I Cor. 8:6 e 10:4); os poderes das trevas têm sido derrotados por meio de sua morte e ressurreição (I Cor. 2:6); a morte de Cristo significa a nossa redenção da servidão (I Cor. 6:20 e 7:23); os crentes fazem parte do corpo místico de Cristo (I Cor. 6:15 e 12:12). A ressurreição (o que provavelmente inclui as idéias da ascensão e da glorificação de Cristo, o que é comum nas páginas do N.T.) garante a verdadeira vida eterna para os crentes, e o décimo quinto capítulo desta epístola é a mais completa declaração que possuímos sobre esse tema.

2. *Os dons do Espírito Santo* no teor da primeira epístola aos Coríntios — A conduta ideal na igreja cristã, no que diz respeito a essas manifestações espirituais, também é abordada. Dentre todos os temas que há neste livro de Paulo, esse é aquele cujo tratamento recebe maior espaço. (Ver I Cor. 11-14). Vemos que os dons espirituais: a. Podem ser abusados; b. podem ser usados erroneamente; c. podem ser falsificados; e d. podem ser exercidos até mesmo por crentes carnais. Geralmente se supõe que os dons espirituais assinalam uma elevada espiritualidade; no entanto, os maiores perturbadores de todos, na igreja de Corinto, foram aqueles que se deixaram arrebatar pelo orgulho de sua suposta autoridade e desenvolvimento espirituais, pois esses, devido ao seu orgulho, produziram confusão naquela igreja.

3. A *reprimenda contra o abuso* dos dons espirituais inspirou o apóstolo a compor o magnificente décimo terceiro capítulo desta epístola, cujo grande tema é o amor cristão, o qual deve governar todas as atividades dos crentes, dentro e fora da igreja local. Nenhum outro documento sagrado sobre o amor cristão tem sido tão universalmente considerado e nem tem sido reputado tão majestático como o décimo terceiro capítulo desta epístola. E ainda que se porventura Paulo houvesse escrito uma epístola deficiente e plena de erros, a preservação de tal epístola já estaria assegurada somente por esse décimo terceiro capítulo. É interessante que embora a expressão «fruto do Espírito» não seja empregada nesta primeira epístola aos Coríntios, contudo, quase cada capítulo da mesma tem algo a ver com o poder dominante do amor cristão, em conexão com diversos aspectos da vida do crente, a qual, na realidade, é a «vida no Espírito». A igreja de Corinto sofreu com facções porque lhe faltava o amor cristão. (Ver I Cor. 3:3). Somente o amor é capaz de edificar, e não de derrubar, conforme estava sucedendo naquela igreja local. (Ver I Cor. 8:1). O amor é superior a todos os dons espirituais de que os homens se possam ufanar, sem o que o próprio uso dos dons é vazio e até mesmo perigoso. Outrossim, o amor é mais duradouro do que todos esses dons. (Ver I Cor. 13:2,8). Portanto, tudo deveria ser efetuado com o condimento preciso do amor. (Ver I Cor. 16:14).

4. *A conduta sexual* no teor da primeira epístola aos Coríntios. Os habitantes da cidade de Corinto se notabilizavam por suas práticas sexuais exageradas e pervertidas. Era inevitável que esses vícios fossem levados ao seio da igreja cristã de Corinto, por parte de alguns que se desviaram de sua profissão cristã inicial, ou que jamais haviam sido verdadeiramente regenerados, posto que tivessem o nome de cristãos. A exposição do quinto capítulo dessa primeira epístola aos Coríntios (quanto aos versículos primeiro a quinto), mostra-nos que Paulo ainda era mais estrito sobre essas questões que os rabinos judeus ordinários.

Foi em relação à conduta sexual que a questão do matrimônio foi apresentada ao apóstolo, na carta que lhe enviaram. Paulo, à semelhança do Senhor Jesus, mas contrariamente às idéias judaicas comuns (ver Mat. 19:12), reconhecia o grande valor do celibato, dando preferência ao mesmo, acima do casamento, contanto que o indivíduo envolvido houvesse sido chamado por Deus para esse estado. Portanto, podemos dizer que Paulo não procurou criar nenhum ministério eclesiástico caracterizado pelo celibato; tal exigência é antes um desenvolvimento histórico, que envolveu vários séculos, não sendo nenhuma injunção neotestamentária. Todavia, é verdade que as expectativas sobre a «parousia» ou segunda vinda de Cristo talvez tivessem algo a ver com o pensamento de Paulo expresso nessa seção; contudo, não podemos deixar de observar que Paulo expressava os seus próprios sentimentos sobre a questão, e, ao fazê-lo situou o estado do celibato acima do estado do matrimônio, como um meio de servir a Deus com uma mente mais desimpedida, livre das obrigações domésticas.

Entretanto, não peca quem se casa, mesmo que o cônjuge seja incrédulo, ficando destacado tão-somente o fato de que isso é um jugo desigual que deve ser evitado pelos crentes. Não obstante, aqueles que estiverem casados com incrédulos são legitimamente casados, e não estão vivendo em pecado. (Ver I Cor. 7:14 e II Cor. 6). Pois o cônjuge incrédulo, sem importar se o mesmo é o marido ou a mulher, é «santificado» pelo cônjuge crente. Tal matrimônio de crentes e incrédulos não é ilegítimo, conforme ensinavam os rabinos. Isso é tudo quanto o apóstolo Paulo quer dar a entender pela palavra *santifica*, nesse caso—tal casamento é legal, aos olhos de Deus e da igreja.

5. *A conduta social e eclesiástica:* as vestes e a conduta femininas. Essa é outra das questões abordadas na primeira epístola aos Coríntios. (Ver I Cor. 14:34 e *ss*). Paulo recomenda que as mulheres usem seus cabelos compridos. Entretanto, alguns estudiosos pensam que essa instrução paulina deve ser posta dentro da categoria das «situações culturalmente orientadas». Em outras palavras, Paulo teria recomendado que as mulheres crentes usassem os cabelos compridos porque, naquela época, usar cabelos curtos era sinal de prostituição, sendo um uso contrário aos costumes sociais mais nobres da época. Por semelhante modo, o véu que as mulheres devem usar, quando «oram ou profetizam», na opinião de muitos eruditos, cabe dentro dessa mesma categoria. Porquanto a grande verdade é que Paulo ordenou ambas as coisas: os cabelos compridos e o uso do véu, para as mulheres crentes. No entanto, não são muitas as igrejas evangélicas que estão obedecendo a essas injunções da Palavra de Deus. Nessa mesma passagem Paulo proíbe claramente que as mulheres crentes falem na igreja. E a maioria dos rabinos judeus teria emitido a mesma opinião, no tocante às mulheres ensinarem ou falarem nas sinagogas judaicas; e, além disso, nas culturas helenísticas distantes da Palestina, ensinarem ou falarem as mulheres nas sinagogas seria demonstração da conduta mais extremamente ímpia. E o apóstolo Paulo deixa transparecer a mesma aversão; e ele falava por inspiração divina, o que nos mostra que esse é também o parecer da mente de Deus. No entanto, muitos intérpretes dizem que essa instrução de Paulo também é «culturalmente orientada».

O máximo que podemos dizer aqui é recomendar que cada membro da igreja de Cristo examine os textos sagrados e os problemas que circundam essas questões da conduta social e eclesiástica, sobretudo no que diz respeito às mulheres crentes, a fim de chegar às suas próprias decisões honestas. Na atualidade, é difícil encontrar qualquer divisão da igreja cristã que observe essas questões, em obediência à Palavra de Deus. Há algumas denominações que insistem sobre a necessidade do uso do véu, mas que negligenciam a questão dos cabelos compridos das mulheres crentes, além de permitirem que elas usem livremente da palavra em suas reuniões, havendo casos extremos de «pastoras». Mas tudo isso é uma incoerência, em confronto com o texto sagrado. Finalmente, a grande maioria das igrejas evangélicas, não sabendo como dar solução ao caso, ignora o problema em sua inteireza, como se o mesmo não existisse.

A ordem do culto nas igrejas locais, o uso dos dons espirituais, a necessidade de haver oportunidade para todos, e a ordem necessária quando da celebração da Ceia do Senhor são os temas do décimo primeiro capítulo desta epístola. A necessidade de não abusar da liberdade cristã é o assunto dos capítulos sexto a oitavo da mesma.

6. *A segunda vinda de Cristo*, ou «parousia» é o último grande tema doutrinário desta epístola. (Ver I Cor. 15:51-58). Sobre esse tema, pois, não há explanação mais magnificente do que a que se encontra nessa seção, que tem servido de texto para inúmeros sermões e discursos escritos através da história. Ela nos ensina as verdades sublimes da imortalidade e da transformação do crente, acrescentando que certos remidos passarão para esse estado sem experimentarem a morte física, ao passo que outros chegarão ao mesmo, a despeito da morte física. Apesar de que Paulo se demorou sobre a simples imortalidade da alma (conforme fica amplamente demonstrado no quinto capítulo da segunda epístola aos Coríntios), a glorificação completa ocorrerá por meio da ressurreição, quando houver novamente a reunião da personalidade humana, em seus elementos constitutivos, bem como através da ascensão e da glorificação juntamente com Cristo, que fica implícita na doutrina da ressurreição.

VII. Conteúdo

I. *Introdução*, saudações e ação de graças (1:1-9)
II. Problema das divisões partidárias (1:10-4:21)
   1. Polêmica contra tais divisões: a. Exaltam ao homem, em detrimento de Cristo (1:10-17). b. Derivam-se do orgulho e da sabedoria humanos (1:18-2:5). Essa sabedoria é uma *loucura* para Deus. c. A cruz é a sabedoria de Deus apresentada aos homens (1:18-25). d. A comunidade cristã dos coríntios não fora chamada dentre os sábios (1:26-31). e. Paulo lhes dera exemplo de conduta humilde (2:1-5). f. A verdadeira sabedoria não é propriedade dos facciosos (2:6-3:4), cuja atitude mostra antes a ausência das influências do Espírito Santo. g. Os apóstolos não são rivais, mas labutam na mesma lavoura, regando e colhendo (3:5-23).
   2. Como o verdadeiro apóstolo deve ser julgado — secção contrária aos detratores de Paulo, que haviam causado divisões (4:1-21).
III. Imoralidade e os Padrões Éticos Gerais e Cristãos (5:1-7:40)
   1. Contra a imoralidade grosseira (5:1-13)
   2. Contra os processos legais entre crentes (6:1-8)
   3. O padrão do reino de Deus (6:9-11)
   4. A moralidade pessoal do crente (6:12-20)
   5. O casamento e o celibato (7:1-40)

IV. Liberdade Cristã (8:1-11:1)
   1. Alimentos oferecidos a ídolos e a utilização dos mesmos pelo crente (8:1-13).
   2. Paulo deu o exemplo, renunciando a seus *direitos* (9:1-23).
   3. Os perigos da *obstinação* (9:24-10:22):
      a. A necessidade de autodisciplina, ante as advertências dadas no deserto (10:1-13).
      b. O caráter destruidor da idolatria (10:14-22).
   4. Declarações finais (10:23-11:1)
V. Regulamentos sobre a Adoração Cristã (11:22-14:40).
   1. O véu das mulheres (11:2-16).
   2. A Ceia do Senhor (11:17-34).
   3. O uso dos dons espirituais (12:1-14:40).
   4. O amor governa o uso dos dons e toda a conduta cristã (13:1-13).
VI. A Ressurreição dos Mortos (15:1-58).
   1. A tradição e o fato: o *evangelho* (15:1-11).
   2. O significado da ressurreição (15:12-19).
   3. O acontecimento e a sua ordem (15:20-34).
   4. A natureza da ressurreição (15:35-50).
   5. A *parousia*: Imortalidade Final (15:51-58).
VII. Questões Pessoais (16:1-24)
   1. Coleta para os santos pobres de Jerusalém (16:1-4).
   2. Os planos de Paulo sobre o futuro (16:5-12).
   3. Exortações finais, saudação e bênção (16:13-24)
VIII. **Bibliografia**. AM EN I IB MOF NTI RO TIN VIN Z

CORÍNTIOS, SEGUNDA Epístola de Paulo aos

Introdução
I. Autor
II. Data
III. Proveniência
IV. Correspondência Paulina Com Corinto
V. Temas Centrais
VI. Conteúdo
VII. Bibliografia

Devido a questões de gramática e de estilo literário, de emprego de vocábulos, de temas dominantes, a aceitação das quatro obras *paulinas clássicas*, a saber, Romanos, I e II Coríntios e Gálatas, fica de pé ou rui juntamente. É perfeitamente óbvio que essas quatro epístolas saíram da mesma pena. Os estudiosos que têm feito objeção a esse fato são poucos, não tendo sido levados a sério pela vasta maioria dos eruditos.

No tocante a segunda epístola aos Coríntios, portanto, não existe problema algum que devamos abordar, no que diz respeito à autoria paulina; porquanto todas as considerações garantem-nos que isso não é necessário.

No tocante à coletânea geral dos escritos paulinos, acerca de particularidades sobre quando foram escritos, qual a sua interpretação, etc., o leitor pode examinar o artigo sobre *Romanos*, seção II, intitulada «As Epístolas de Paulo».

No tocante à segunda epístola aos Coríntios, encontramo-nos em terreno sólido, pois trata-se de uma das obras paulinas clássicas, embora a maioria dos estudiosos modernos pense que temos nessa epístola, na realidade, porções diversas de várias epístolas, embora todas de autoria paulina, e que chegaram até a nossa possessão como um todo composto. (Esse problema, em sua inteireza, é debatido no artigo sobre à primeira epístola aos Coríntios, em sua seção IV, discussão essa que é um tanto ampliada neste artigo, sob o ponto III).

A segunda epístola aos Coríntios, paralelamente à primeira, não consiste essencialmente de uma obra doutrinária, embora ali apareçam algumas das mais elevadas doutrinas do apóstolo Paulo, mas antes, trata-se de ventilação de problemas pessoais surgidos entre esse apóstolo e os crentes de Corinto, juntamente com problemas de ética e de conduta cristã. Portanto, nessas epístolas aos Coríntios encontramos algumas das mais profundas expressões pessoais de Paulo, sendo que nelas podemos perceber, com maior clareza, qual a personalidade e o caráter do apóstolo aos gentios. Outrossim, a segunda epístola aos Coríntios fornece-nos boa dose de material biográfico, que muito nos ajuda a conhecer melhor a vida de Paulo, em pontos que nem ao menos são aludidos no livro de Atos. Portanto, a segunda epístola aos Coríntios se reveste de grande importância, do ponto de vista histórico.

Posto que a primeira e a segunda epístolas aos Coríntios abordam essencialmente as questões relativas ao mesmo povo e às mesmas situações históricas, o leitor deveria consultar todo o artigo sobre o livro de primeiro Coríntios, porque muito daquilo que diz respeito à segunda epístola aos Coríntios aparece nos comentários relativos à primeira epístola aos Coríntios, não sendo reiterado aqui a fim de ser evitada a redundância. Como exemplo disso, a seção III sobre àquela primeira epístola descreve «a igreja de Corinto», as «razões da epístola» e a—correspondência paulina—com Corinto, temas esses que também têm aplicação a segunda epístola. Similarmente, a questão que aparece na segunda seção, «Data e Proveniência», se aplica a segunda epístola, pois Paulo, embora houvesse escrito a segunda epístola de um lugar diferente, provavelmente escreveu a epístola, ou a série de epístolas, depois de poucos meses a contar da escrita da primeira epístola aos Coríntios. Na realidade, a epístola original, escrita à igreja de Corinto, pode ser a que chamamos de I Coríntios, ou pode estar inclusa nela. Na verdade, não sabemos quantas epístolas Paulo lhes escreveu, e nem quantas visitas lhes fez (certamente houve pelo menos quatro epístolas e três visitas), mas todas elas têm bases geográficas e históricas em comum, pelo menos em termos gerais.

Supõe-se portanto, que antes de haver sido escrita a segunda epístola aos Coríntios, sem importar se a mesma se compõe de uma só ou de várias missivas que vieram a ser transformadas em uma só, já haviam sido escritas pelo menos duas outras epístolas àqueles mesmos crentes. Uma dessas epístolas é aludida no trecho de I Cor. 5:9, da qual uma parte mui provavelmente é preservada em II Cor. 6:14—7:1. Além dessa epístola, Paulo também enviou que conhecemos por I Coríntios e que essencialmente forma uma única epístola, — sobre cujo particular concordam praticamente todos os eruditos. Além disso, Paulo havia recebido pelo menos uma missiva da parte dos crentes de Corinto. Outrossim, esse apóstolo igualmente enviara Timóteo, em missão intercessória, a fim de procurar solucionar os problemas surgidos naquela igreja, missão essa que não produziu resultados positivos evidentes. O próprio Paulo já visitara aquela igreja por mais de uma vez, segundo se entende claramente de suas palavras em II Cor. 12:14: «Eis que pela terceira vez estou pronto a ir ter convosco...»

••• ••• •••

CORÍNTIOS

Não sabemos, entretanto, como situar essas visitas, porque o livro de Atos não nos ajuda nesse particular; mas certamente as visitas subseqüentes de Paulo àquela comunidade foram feitas depois que ele escrevera a primeira epístola aos Coríntios, com o propósito de encontrar solução para os dificílimos problemas existentes naquela congregação cristã. Finalmente, a combinação de sua «epístola severa» (ver II Cor. 10:10) e a obra mediatória de Tito (ver II Cor. 7:11,15), nos apresentam soluções razoáveis, que teriam sido encontradas para os problemas mais árduos daquela igreja de Corinto.

I. Autor

A liderança de Paulo é desafiada; Desígnio de Paulo e motivo da escrita dessa epístola; Autoridade dessa epístola.

Quanto a declarações sobre o consenso geral acerca da autoria paulina da segunda epístola aos Coríntios, sem importar se a mesma era uma única missiva ou uma combinação de epístolas, ver os artigos sobre às epístolas aos Romanos e I Coríntios, onde fica demonstrado que as epístolas aos Romanos, aos Gálatas e I e II Coríntios são universalmente consideradas como obras clássicas paulinas indisputadas, tendo obviamente saído da mesma pena, conforme fica demonstrado por meio da crítica literária. Portanto, a fim de evitar uma repetição desnecessária de material, que o leitor pode consultar em outros lugares, sob o título de «Autoria», damos aqui somente outro material informativo importante que diz respeito às relações entre Paulo e a igreja de Corinto.

a. A liderança de Paulo é desafiada.

— A autoridade de Paulo, na moderna igreja evangélica, e, de fato, por toda a história eclesiástica, remota da era apostólica imediata, que é tão inquestionavelmente recebida, leva os estudiosos modernos a se admirarem sobre como podiam fazer-lhe oposição no cristianismo primitivo. O fato, porém, é que os primeiros anos da igreja não se caracterizavam por tal paz, amor e unidade, conforme os cristãos modernos geralmente supõem, atribuindo tais qualidades tão precipitadamente ao caráter da igreja apostólica. Pelo contrário, os primeiros anos da igreja produziram alguns conflitos notáveis. Entre os próprios apóstolos surgiram algumas brigas feias. Sem dúvida alguma, houve casos notáveis de tal unidade; porém, antes do fim do século II D.C., o poder da personalidade de Jesus havia gerado nada menos de cem seitas diferentes, todas elas reivindicando autoridade recebida da parte de Jesus Cristo, o que, por si só, serve de poderosa prova de seu caráter transcendental.

Não é de surpreender, portanto, que no seio da própria igreja cristã houvesse tanto desassossego. Como reconciliar o judaísmo com Jesus ou com Paulo, ou com ambos? Como reconciliar Paulo com Jesus? Como explicar o profundo discernimento espiritual de Paulo, que parecia ter revolucionado os conceitos judaicos e legalistas no campo religioso? Esses não eram problemas de pouca monta e até os nossos dias muita discussão se centraliza em volta de certos aspectos dos mesmos. Entre os problemas da igreja cristã primitiva, avultava o problema «legalista». Como podia a doutrina da graça, da justificação pela fé e da transformação segundo a imagem de Cristo ser reconciliada com o legalismo centenário do antigo judaísmo? Quanto a notas expositivas sobre esse problema em geral, consultar Atos 10:9 no NTI. Os mais amargos inimigos de Paulo parecem ter sido aqueles que, tendo-se convertido a Jesus como o Messias, aferravam-se ao que Moisés ou a tradição judaica ensinavam, considerando que as obras da lei e a circuncisão eram necessárias à salvação.

Quanto a isso, pode-se consultar o décimo quinto capítulo do livro de Atos, pois o primeiro concílio universal da igreja cristã foi efetuado a fim de discutir e resolver exatamente esse problema.

Esse problema, contudo, jamais foi solucionado, nem mesmo em nossos próprios dias. Em lugar das formas mais antigas de legalismo, surgiram novas formas. Por exemplo, aquilo que os judeus atribuíam à circuncisão, muitos cristãos modernos atribuem ao batismo em água, assim pervertendo a religião mística de Paulo em um ensino sacramental ou legalista, ou uma combinação de ambas as coisas. Muitos cristãos primitivos, grande número dos quais se convertera da seita dos fariseus, conceituavam o cristianismo apenas como um judaísmo reformado, sem jamais terem apreendido realmente o fato revolucionário de que o cristianismo era uma revelação nova, não tendo percebido igualmente que Paulo fora o instrumento divino pelo qual Deus revelava essa elevada fé. Uma das razões disso é que esses judeus jamais puderam antecipar a grandeza de Paulo.

As doutrinas paulinas da graça, da justificação pela fé, da transformação segundo a imagem transcendental de Cristo, formando assim uma religião totalmente mística em sua natureza, em contraste com a religião legalista ou sacramental, não permitiam que a igreja cristã fosse uma mera forma de *judaísmo modificado*. Todavia, não é provável que o cristianismo da Palestina, nos tempos de Paulo, houvesse realmente compreendido as profundas implicações expostas por Paulo em suas epístolas. Isso sucedeu principalmente no mundo gentílico e nos processos históricos que elevaram a pessoa de Cristo ao pináculo dos poderes cósmicos. O conflito pela elevação ao platô das realidades espirituais mais altas não foi nem espontâneo e nem fácil, como de resto não pode ser espontâneo ou fácil qualquer avanço espiritual ou físico, havendo muitas covas ao longo do caminho, nas quais os homens podem cair.

Portanto, quando Paulo escreveu suas várias epístolas aos crentes de Corinto, o partido dos legalistas e fundamentalistas da velha guarda, preso em sua mentalidade rígida, fixa em leis e cerimônias, se opôs a Paulo amargamente. Esses imaginavam estar prestando um serviço a Deus, porquanto Deus havia falado a Moisés, conforme eles bem o sabiam; mas, teria Deus falado a Paulo? Não possuía ele linguagem deficiente e o seu aspecto físico não era inadequado? Não era ele apenas um outro dos seguidores de Jesus, e além de tudo herético? Não entendiam a profunda significação de Paulo, tal como seus contemporâneos haviam estado embotados para com a significação de Jesus.

A oposição a Paulo não se verificou somente em Jerusalém, mas também se deu em todos os lugares onde o judaísmo invadira o mundo gentílico. Não nos deveríamos surpreender, por conseguinte, que, em Corinto, onde viviam muitos judeus, tendo alguns desses passado para a igreja cristã, e onde outros judeus tinham vindo de Jerusalém, apresentando-se como autoridades nas questões religiosas, que a doutrina de Paulo tivesse recebido ali tão grande oposição, e que a sua autoridade apostólica tivesse sido posta em dúvida. Ver o artigo sobre *Paulo*.

Não sabemos se Pedro chegou a visitar a cidade de Corinto; mas sabemos que o seu nome era equivocadamente usado como se ele fosse representante ou líder do partido legalista. (Ver Atos 19:1 e I

CORÍNTIOS

Cor. 1:12). É possível que alguns membros da igreja de Jerusalém, amigos ou não de Paulo, houvessem exercido alguma influência na igreja de Corinto, e que uma facção houvesse sido ali criada com o propósito de *preservar a fé*, o que, para eles, era compreendido como a mescla entre o cristianismo e o legalismo mosaico, tudo posto em um molde só. Não há razão para supormos que Pedro realmente fez oposição a Paulo, porquanto isso é negado nos capítulos dez, onze e quinze do livro de Atos, bem como nos capítulos primeiro e segundo da epístola aos Gálatas.

Em face dessas razões, poucos intérpretes situam Pedro no campo legalista; pelo contrário, ele certamente se aliou a Paulo na controvérsia com os legalistas, embora não houvesse sido tão constante defensor e coluna da doutrina da graça como o era Paulo; porém, quem se assemelhava a Paulo, nesse particular? Seja como for, certos líderes, evidentemente vindos do exterior, chegaram a Corinto, trazendo cartas de recomendação (ver II Cor. 3:1), e afirmando possuir credenciais de autoridade sobre a igreja cristã (ver II Cor. 12:21).

Sendo esses legalistas inclinados a interpretar o cristianismo segundo os seus pontos de vista legalistas, conseguiram diminuir e quase anular a autoridade de Paulo entre os crentes de Corinto. Paulo tentou usar Timóteo como mediador nesse problema, mas Timóteo era tímido por natureza, e a sua missão não obteve sucesso (ver I Cor. 16:10,11, 17). Posteriormente, entretanto, Tito cuidou eficazmente da situação (ver II Cor. 7:14,15). E o próprio Paulo, entre a escrita da primeira e da segunda epístolas aos Coríntios, fez mais uma ou mais visitas a Corinto, na tentativa de solucionar os problemas ali existentes e de confirmar a sua autoridade abalada.

Sua epístola severa, partes da qual são aludidas na segunda epístola aos Coríntios, e que é especificamente mencionada em II Cor. 10:10, tem sido identificada por alguns estudiosos como certas porções dos capítulos décimo a décimo terceiro dessa segunda epístola, que os próprios adversários de Paulo consideram como eficaz. A primeira porção desta segunda epístola aos Coríntios mostra-nos que a combinação de meios, escolhida por Paulo, para cuidar da situação, foi essencialmente eficaz, tendo obtido a reconciliação entre esse apóstolo e a igreja cristã de Corinto, com a correção de muitas de suas faltas e o reestabelecimento de sua autoridade apostólica naquela comunidade cristã.

As diversas descrições que Paulo nos oferece sobre os seus oponentes, dão-nos uma boa idéia da natureza deles. Atacavam a Paulo em vários pontos. Acusavam-no de insinceridade, como se ele estivesse meramente atrás dos bens materiais dos crentes de Corinto (corrompendo assim o seu intuito de recolher uma oferta voluntária para os santos nobres de Jerusalém); de usar de engodo e ludíbrio (ver Cor. 12:16); e de não exibir os poderes manifestos de um verdadeiro apóstolo. Sua aparência pessoal era débil, não sendo ele um bom orador. (Ver II Cor. 10:10). Parece que haviam acusado ao apóstolo de ter uma linguagem obscura em sua pregação (ver II Cor. 4:3), e, embora ele manifestasse vários dons do Espírito Santo, mais do que todos eles (ver I Cor. 14:18), tendo recebido muitíssimas visões místicas (ver II Cor. 12:1 e I Cor. 9:11), para eles Paulo parecia ser um líder inadequado para a igreja cristã, e talvez até pensassem ser ele um tanto desequilibrado mentalmente. Tais eram os ataques contra a pessoa de Paulo.

A maioria desses judeus, perseguidores de Paulo, parece ter-se composto de intrujões ambulantes, representantes do partido legalista da igreja, mas violentos quanto aos seus métodos de ataque. Eles se apresentavam como os «verdadeiros apóstolos», e Paulo, zombeteiramente, chamava-os de «superapóstolos». (Ver II Cor. 11:5 e 12:11). Paulo não admitia que eles fossem verdadeiros crentes, mas intitulava-os de «falsos apóstolos», *obreiros enganadores*, que meramente se fantasiavam de apóstolos de Cristo. (Ver II Cor. 11:13). Os homens aceitavam prontamente o apoio financeiro daquela igreja de Corinto, e chegavam mesmo a insistir em receber tal ajuda. (Ver II Cor. 11:12). Faltava-lhes o coração próprio de um pastor, e eram antes ditatoriais, dominadores, cobiçosos, brutais e arrogantes. (Ver II Cor. 11:20). Paulo, pois, os acusava de pregarem a «outro Jesus» e a «outro evangelho», embora em parte alguma ele nos tenha informado sobre o que queria dizer exatamente com isso. Houve momentos em que o apóstolo parece admitir que eles deveriam ser classificados como cristãos (ver II Cor. 10:7 e 11:23), mas geralmente negava especificamente isso, classificando-os de servos de Satanás (ver II Cor. 11:13-15).

«Como, pois, Paulo retratou-se como verdadeiro apóstolo? Ele era um pecador reconciliado (II Cor. 5:18), um ser humano frágil (II Cor. 4:7), que não possuía nem os recursos espirituais e nem os recursos físicos para tal ministério. Entretanto, Deus é quem nos dá a graça e as forças necessárias (II Cor. 3:5 e 12:9), e somente pela vontade de Deus é que Paulo chegara a ser um apóstolo (II Cor. 1:1). Na qualidade de ministro do novo pacto, alicerçado no Espírito (II Cor. 3:3-6), foi-lhe conferido o poder de servir e de realizar os sinais de um apóstolo, através de milagres (II Cor. 4:7 e 12:12). Na qualidade de cativo de Cristo (II Cor. 2:14) e de embaixador de Cristo (II Cor. 5:20), por amor a Jesus (II Cor. 4:5), ele efetuou uma obra pioneira (II Cor. 10:13-16), tanto como evangelista (II Cor. 5:11) quanto como ministro da reconciliação (II Cor. 5:18,19). Ele sumariava a sua mensagem como 'Cristo Jesus, o Senhor' (II Cor. 4:5). Jamais se esqueceu das igrejas por ele fundadas: a preocupação por elas todas pesava constantemente sobre ele (II Cor. 11:28), e ele era o seu servo (II Cor. 4:5) e conselheiro. Os motivos que o impulsionavam eram a gratidão a Deus e a Cristo (II Cor. 1:3 e 5:14), o temor reverente pelo Senhor, seu Salvador e Juiz (II Cor. 5:10,11a), bem como o amor sincero pelas igrejas por ele fundadas (II Cor. 2:4 e 11:11), as quais eram o motivo de sua alegria e interesse (II Cor. 2:2,3). A integridade assinalava o seu ministério, e as cicatrizes de um labor desgastador e de sofrimentos voluntariamente aceitos eram os sinais que o identificavam como um verdadeiro apóstolo (II Cor. 1:12; 6:3-10 e 11:23,29)». (Floyd V. Filson, Introdução a II Coríntios).

A leitura e meditação dos comentários que se seguem, nesta seção, demonstrarão a profundidade do problema que Paulo teve de enfrentar, no que diz respeito aos seus oponentes, no tocante a pontos de doutrina, o que, naturalmente, tinha as suas aplicações na vida prática.

Ainda outras facções religiosas se levantaram para perseguir a Paulo acerca de outras questões, talvez principalmente por motivo de conflito de personalidades. Havia, por exemplo, o eloqüente Apolo, que punha Paulo em má luz como orador, embora não haja quaisquer indícios de que Paulo e Apolo houvessem jamais entrado pessoalmente em choque, porquanto todas as indicações de que dispomos mostram que Apolo sempre se mostrou fiel para com

CORÍNTIOS

Paulo. Contudo, em torno da forte personalidade de Apolo, desenvolveu-se uma certa facção na igreja de Corinto, que provavelmente consistia dos elementos mais inclinados para o *intelectualismo*, talvez ex-filósofos convertidos ao cristianismo, ou pelo menos, pessoas versadas na filosofia da época. Apolo era proveniente do centro importantíssimo de erudição que era Alexandria; e é bem provável que a sua mensagem fosse pregada de forma agradável para os intelectuais de então. Por conseguinte, uma certa facção da igreja de Corinto não tardou em fazer dele o seu herói.

Além disso, havia a lassidão moral da cultura e da sociedade de Corinto, o que penetrava a fundo nas barreiras da igreja cristã daquela cidade. E então, os elementos mais liberais, ou mais desavergonhadamente lassos quanto às questões morais, naturalmente se opunham ao inflexível Paulo, cuja atitude para com as questões morais se assemelhava à dos judeus, e da escola mais estrita do judaísmo, segundo se percebe em II Cor. 12:21. Não era fácil a tentativa de reunir os coríntios tão liberais quanto às questões morais, com os estritos pontos de vista judaico-cristãos. Aqueles que não podiam, ou melhor, não queriam viver de conformidade com esse padrão, eram inimigos naturais de Paulo.

Seria um otimismo exagerado de nossa parte supormos que, em qualquer dessas controvérsias, Paulo conseguiu o que queria, sendo bem possível que a igreja cristã de Corinto se tornou mais corrupta do que nunca. Em termos gerais, entretanto, a segunda epístola aos Coríntios mostra-nos que a autoridade apostólica de Paulo foi confirmada na igreja de Corinto, e que Paulo obteve boas vitórias espirituais no que se relaciona àqueles crentes. (Maiores detalhes sobre as relações entre Paulo e a igreja de Corinto podem ser vistos no artigo sobre a primeira epístola aos Coríntios, onde esse tópico ocupa toda a seção III desse artigo).

b. Designio de Paulo e motivo da escrita dessa epístola.

O propósito de Paulo era reconciliar-se com a igreja cristã de Corinto, o que envolvia o reestabelecimento de sua autoridade apostólica ali; a correção das falhas e o fim das facções. Portanto, ele enviou Timóteo como seu representante. (Ver I Cor. 16:10,11,17). Mas Timóteo obteve resultados inadequados e negativos, como também nos mostra o trecho de II Cor. 7:5 e *ss*. Por conseguinte, Paulo enviou Tito em missão similar; e dessa vez com positivos resultados. (Ver II Cor. 7:6,7,14,15). Tito parece ter permanecido em Corinto mais do que o tempo esperado, evidentemente para ajudar a Paulo em sua intenção de recolher uma oferta entre as igrejas gentílicas, para o benefício dos crentes pobres de Jerusalém. (Ver II Cor. 8:6).

Na segunda epístola aos Coríntios, Paulo explica por que razão escreveu a sua chamada «epístola severa», não o tendo feito apenas para dar vazão às suas indignações contra a oposição e as falhas morais, e, sim, em amor, tal como um pai repreende severamente a um filho seu, por saber o que é melhor para ele. (Ver II Cor. 2:1 e *ss*).

Paulo antecipava ainda outra visita à cidade de Corinto, embora não quisesse chegar ali de espírito pesado e triste, conforme se caracterizara a sua última visita. Por conseguinte, na primeira porção de II Coríntios, ele procura remover qualquer pensamento de insinceridade, de duplicidade e de instabilidade, que poderia ter sido deduzido do fato dele não ter cumprido sua anteriormente planejada visita a Corinto, mas que ele cancelara por desejar poupar, tanto a si mesmo como aos crentes de Corinto, ainda maior dor. (Ver II Cor. 1:12 e *ss*). A conduta de Paulo, entre os crentes de Corinto e de outros lugares, porém, comprovava a sua sinceridade. (Ver II Cor. 2:3 e *ss*).

Paulo se aproveita dessa ocasião da escrita da segunda epístola aos Coríntios a fim de ensinar! Ele fala sobre a obra de Satanás, isto é, um falso evangelho, em contraste com o seu próprio evangelho da verdade, conforme existia e exercia autoridade até mesmo entre os crentes de Corinto. Esse ensino, mui provavelmente, foi inspirado por várias controvérsias com falsos líderes cristãos, conforme foi previamente descrito. (Ver II Cor. 4:1-4,6). A glória futura haverá de ser o prêmio das ações dignas, e disso Paulo assegura aos seus leitores. (II Cor. 4:7 e 5:1). A mais importante seção neotestamentária sobre a *imortalidade* se encontra no décimo quinto capítulo da segunda epístola aos Coríntios, sendo uma descrição magnificente da glória futura, embora apresentada de mistura com uma severa advertência do julgamento futuro de que participarão os crentes. Serão delineados os temas da salvação e suas consequências morais, em II Cor. 5:9 e 6:10,11.

«Com base no ponto de vista geral do conteúdo dessa epístola (II Coríntios), o 'desígnio' de Paulo se torna perfeitamente claro. Tudo visou à restauração e a confirmação da autoridade desse apóstolo, que havia sido assediada tão amarga e obstinadamente, bem como a remoção de todos os empecilhos aos seus esforços, que visavam ao bem-estar espiritual de seus leitores. A maioria daqueles crentes foi conquistada para o lado do apóstolo Paulo, ficando aberto o caminho para trazê-los de volta à obediência, incluindo outros que ainda se opunham a Paulo. A fim de obter tal coisa, Paulo foi obrigado a eliminar os preconceitos que tinham surgido contra ele, desvendando a insinceridade e a perversidade daqueles que tinham seduzido àqueles crentes. É evidente que esses sedutores eram 'judaizantes' (comparar com II Cor. 11:22). Até hoje continua questão controvertida se esses pertenciam ao partido de Pedro ou ao partido de 'Cristo'. Contrariamente à opinião daqueles que mantinham que pertenciam ao primeiro (Meyer e outros), tem sido objetado como verdade, que essa epístola jamais dá a entender que Pedro era o cabeça desse partido; nem mesmo a frase *principais apóstolos* (ver II Cor. 11:5 e 12:11) pode referir-se aos apóstolos de nosso Senhor. Outros estudiosos ainda argumentam que a existência do partido de 'Cristo' parece dar a entender, em II Cor. 10:7, que haja rejeição de 'toda' a autoridade apostólica, em face dessas palavras, 'os principais apóstolos', dizendo que há certo número de indicações que mostram que eles se tinham desviado da doutrina comumente recebida, com respeito à pessoa de Jesus (ver II Cor. 11:12 e 2:17). Entretanto, parecem ter-se distinguido especialmente por sua oposição à autoridade apostólica de Paulo, bem como pelo seu zelo em favor da lei judaica e pelo cristianismo, como se este fora um mero sistema legal». (Comentário de Lange, *Introdução* a II Coríntios, pág. 5).

c. Autoridade dessa epístola.

Esta segunda epístola aos Coríntios ocupa um lugar antigo no «cânon», conforme pode ser demonstrado em favor de qualquer outro livro do N.T. Sem dúvida alguma este livro já era usado na igreja cristã desde antes do tempo em que Márcion, cujo grande herói era Paulo, incluiu-a entre as dez epístolas paulinas que ele reputava autênticas, em cerca de 140 D.C.

CORÍNTIOS

Não há razão alguma para supormos que Márcion foi quem fez a primeira coleção das epístolas de Paulo; pelo contrário, ele deve ter herdado essa coleção daquilo que já era corrente na igreja cristã, embora seja verdade que a sua aceitação dessas dez epístolas, juntamente com uma versão modificada do evangelho de Lucas, tenha provocado a canonização do N.T. O próprio Márcion rejeitava a autoridade dos livros do A.T., elevando a pessoa de Paulo à posição mais magnificente em toda a história da literatura religiosa.

Várias citações sugerem-nos que Policarpo se utilizou dessa segunda epístola aos Coríntios, e isso tão cedo como 115 D.C. (Ver a sua Ep. ad Philipp., 6, onde ele emprega as palavras de II Cor. 8:21). Clemente de Roma (91-101 D.C.), em suas citações, é um exemplo de um uso ainda anterior dessa epístola. (Ver Ep., cap. xii, onde parece bem definidamente que ele citou os trechos de II Cor. 8:21 e 11:29). Atenágoras e Atenas, em 117 D.C., em *sua obra De ressurr. mort.*, 18, evidentemente se utilizou de uma parte desta segunda epístola aos Coríntios. Por semelhante modo, Irineu de Lyons (177-202 D.C.), em seu tratado *Contra Haer*, livro ii, cap. xxx.7, menciona e comenta o fato da experiência do «terceiro céu», que Paulo teve, e que é referido no décimo segundo capítulo desta segunda epístola aos Coríntios. Clemente de Alexandria (191-202 D.C.) cita trechos da segunda epístola aos Coríntios por nada menos de vinte vezes. (Ver sua obra *Paedag.*, livro X, cap. vi: livro I, cap. vii). Nessas citações ele se refere também à experiência do «terceiro céu», citando completamente o trecho de II Cor. 2:14-16, juntamente com algumas poucas sentenças, depois de II Cor. 5:7. Conforme já se disse, outras citações dessa natureza, em número considerável, podem ser encontradas nos escritos de Clemente de Alexandria. O que falamos aqui serve apenas de exemplos.

As indicações, pois, é que por volta de 95 D.C., esta segunda epístola aos Coríntios já desfrutava de distribuição regularmente lata na igreja cristã, e que, pelo fim do século II D.C., ela deve ter sido quase universalmente conhecida. E não há qualquer evidência, até onde diz respeito à igreja, no sentido de que ela tenha jamais circulado em qualquer outra forma senão aquela que conhecemos atualmente, embora originalmente, antes de sua circulação, em Corinto, talvez tenha resultado de uma combinação de epístolas, parte da correspondência de Paulo com a igreja de Corinto. Naquele tempo, tal como hoje em dia, para nós, era uma autêntica expressão da mente, do coração e do ministério de Paulo, o grande apóstolo dos gentios.

II. Data

Podemos determinar o tempo da permanência de Paulo em Corinto com grande precisão, quando confrontamos esse caso com suas visitas a outras localidades. No trecho de Atos 18:2 encontramos a menção de que Priscila e Áquila chegaram a Corinto, vindos da cidade de Roma, porque os judeus haviam sido expulsos da capital do império por ordem do imperador Cláudio, conforme nos informa Suetônio em *Vida do Deificado Cláudio*, 25:4. A data mais provável desse acontecimento é 49 D.C. Outrossim, essa passagem de Atos 18:2 revela-nos como Gaio, que foi feito procônsul da Acaia, defendeu a causa de Paulo, negando-se a imiscuir-se numa questão religiosa, que não lhe estava afetando. Sabe-se que Gaio se chamava Lúcio Júnio Aneu Gálio, e que era irmão do famoso filósofo estóico romano, Sêneca, que fora tutor de Nero, o terrível e sádico imperador romano. Uma inscrição encontrada em Delfos possibilitou-nos datar o seu período proconsular dentro de limites bem estreitos. Isso nos tem permitido calcular que Sêneca iniciou seu encargo a 1º de julho de 51 D.C. Alguns estudiosos têm sugerido um ano mais tarde; porém, seja como for, podemos inferir com segurança que Gálio estava em Corinto, em 50 D.C., e que, portanto, Paulo ali se encontrava também. É bem provável que o apóstolo dos gentios tenha chegado ali em 50 D.C., na primavera, tendo partido no outono de 51 D.C. (Quanto a notas expositivas sobre a inscrição acima mencionada, ver as notas introdutórias sobre o décimo oitavo capítulo do livro de Atos no NTI.

Por conseguinte, a correspondência de Paulo com Corinto deve ter-se iniciado em 51 D.C., sendo provável que a primeira epístola aos Coríntios foi escrita entre 52 e 54 D.C. Mui provavelmente Paulo escreveu essa primeira epístola poucos meses antes de ter partido de Éfeso, a fim de revisitar as igrejas que havia fundado na Macedônia e Corinto. Quanto a isso, pode-se verificar o que ele diz em I Cor. 16:19: «As igrejas da Ásia vos saúdam». A cidade de Éfeso era, por assim dizer, o quartel-general de Paulo na Ásia, pelo que é lógico supormos que a primeira epístola aos Coríntios foi escrita daquela cidade. (A introdução sobre essa epístola fornece-nos outros detalhes atinentes a essa suposição).

Com base nessas considerações, podemos inferir com segurança que a segunda epístola aos Coríntios não pode ter sido escrita antes do fim de 54 D.C. E já que a segunda epístola aos Coríntios provavelmente representa uma série de epístolas, e não uma única missiva, é seguro supormos que essa correspondência poderia ter-se prolongado por um ano ou mais. Contudo, alguns estudiosos situam a escrita da primeira epístola aos Coríntios tão tarde como 56 ou 57 D.C., em vista do que a segunda dessas epístolas deve ter sido escrita algum tempo mais tarde. E a chamada «epístola severa», provavelmente a primeira das cartas que vieram a fundir-se, formando a nossa II Coríntios, provavelmente foi escrita mais ou menos nos fins de 54 D.C., depois que Paulo partira de Éfeso, tendo passado através de Trôade, até chegar na Macedônia, onde também se encontrou com Tito.

«Que esse encontro (entre Paulo e Tito) e a escrita do trecho de II Cor. 1-9 (da Macedônia) deve ter-se verificado em novembro do 54 D.C., parece provável, se pudermos depender da narrativa do livro de Atos. Na narrativa altamente condensada de Atos 20:1-6, apreendemos que Paulo passou três meses na Grécia, isto é, em Corinto, naturalmente, e que então retornou por mar de Filipos a Trôade, depois dos dias dos pães asmos. Portanto, se ele voltou para Filipos a tempo de partir após a páscoa, e se passara três meses em Corinto, parece que chegou nesta última cidade em dezembro ou janeiro, e que escrevera o trecho de II Cor. 1-9 cerca de seis semanas a dois meses antes, ou seja, novembro». (Morton Scott Enslin, «The Literature of the Christian Movement», parte II, Harper Torchbooks, Nova Iorque, 1956).

A chamada epístola severa, mencionada em diversos trechos de II Cor. 1-9, teria sido escrita antes, como é claro. Já os capítulos décimo a décimo terceiro da segunda epístola aos Coríntios contêm, ao menos, uma parte dessa «epístola severa», o que significa que esses capítulos foram escritos antes dos capítulos primeiro a nono, contanto que sejam corretas as suposições apresentadas sobre a correspondência de Paulo com Corinto, tanto aqui como na introdução à primeira epístola aos Coríntios.

III. PROVENIÊNCIA

No tocante a essa questão no que se relaciona à primeira epístola aos Coríntios, ver o artigo sobre àquela epístola, sob o título «Data e Proveniência», na seção II. A conclusão a que se pode chegar sobre esse particular é que essa segunda epístola aos Coríntios, essencialmente conforme a temos em nossa posse hoje em dia, isto é, como uma única carta, foi escrita em Éfeso. Entretanto, com base no trecho de II Cor. 7:5,6, parece que a segunda epístola aos Coríntios, ou a correspondência variegada que ela representa, foi enviada da Macedônia. Pelo menos essa citada referência parece confirmar que o trecho de II Cor. 1-9 foi escrito dali como uma única missiva. O alívio expresso por Paulo, por haver recebido boas novas através de Tito, acerca da situação que imperava agora em Corinto, parece resultado, pelo menos em parte, da «epístola severa», mencionada nos versículos oitavo e nono do sétimo capítulo da segunda epístola aos Coríntios, e também por causa da mediação pessoal de Tito, que interveio nesse problema.

Esta seção não subentende necessariamente que os capítulos décimo a décimo terceiro desta nossa segunda epístola aos Coríntios (que formam a «epístola severa» ou partes da mesma) tenham sido escritos na Macedônia. Pois essa carta poderia ter sido escrita em qualquer lugar, na rota entre Éfeso e a Macedônia. Porém, parece bem certo que nenhuma porção desta segunda epístola aos Coríntios foi escrita em Éfeso, conforme aconteceu com a primeira epístola aos Coríntios, com a possível exceção dos capítulos décimo a décimo terceiro. É provável que Filipos tenha sido a cidade de onde Paulo escreveu, sendo essa cidade um dos centros cristãos da Macedônia, tendo Paulo passado ali algum tempo, após ter partido de Éfeso, conforme se pensa com grandes probabilidades.

Goodspeed, em sua introdução à segunda epístola aos Coríntios, supõe que a citada «epístola severa» (supostamente II Cor. 10-13) foi escrita em *Éfeso*, tendo sido enviada aos crentes de Corinto por mãos de Tito. Então, após ter ficado por algum tempo em Éfeso, Paulo viajou para a Macedônia, tendo escrito o resto da correspondência atualmente chamada de segunda epístola aos Coríntios. Tendo-se encontrado com Tito na Macedônia, e tendo recebido boas notícias da parte dele, acerca da situação na igreja de Corinto, Paulo então compôs as outras porções que agora também aparecem na segunda epístola aos Coríntios, com um ânimo realmente muito mais aliviado, o que faz tremendo contraste com o severo caráter dos capítulos décimo a décimo terceiro.

IV. CORRESPONDÊNCIA PAULINA COM CORINTO

1. Questão da integridade desta epístola.

A maioria dos intérpretes acredita que a primeira epístola aos Coríntios forma, essencialmente, uma unidade sólida; mas parece que a segunda epístola aos Coríntios representa uma série de missivas, que finalmente, foram reunidas, formando uma unidade, como se todas elas representassem uma única missiva escrita pelo apóstolo Paulo. —E embora que seções exatas representam missivas separadas seja uma questão em torno da qual os intérpretes não chegaram ainda a um acordo, a idéia de uma coleção de epístolas e não de uma única epístola, conta com razões que nos impelem a aceitá-la como certa. Isso não significa, contudo, que qualquer de suas porções seja posta em dúvida como paulina. Isso quer dizer meramente que o apóstolo Paulo enviou mais do que somente duas epístolas aos crentes de Corinto. A maior parte dos eruditos acredita que houve pelo menos quatro dessas missivas. (Quanto a detalhes maiores sobre esse problema, o leitor pode consultar o artigo sobre à primeira epístola aos Coríntios, sob o título «A Correspondência de Paulo com Corinto», seção IV). A essas notas são adicionadas as seguintes observações sobre as possíveis cartas separadas que podem ser distinguidas em nossa segunda epístola aos Coríntios:

Parece não haver qualquer sombra de dúvida sobre o fato de que houve uma «epístola severa», enviada pelo apóstolo Paulo aos crentes de Corinto, e que precedeu à escrita do trecho de II Cor. 1-9. Isso transparece de modo claro na passagem de II Cor. 7:5-9, que menciona tal correspondência anterior. Paulo expressa sua tristeza por ter enviado aquela carta, mas, também diz que, depois de ser sabido que a mesma se mostrara eficaz (e até mesmo os seus adversários admitiam tal fato, como se vê em II Cor. 10:10), não mais se entristecia por causa dela, já que a mesma havia contribuído para a sua reconciliação com os crentes coríntios. Essa «epístola severa», é aceita atualmente como certas porções ou mesmo a totalidade do trecho de II Cor. 10-13, onde repentinamente, a linguagem suave que Paulo vinha usando nos capítulos primeiro a nono, evidenciando o seu alívio devido à melhoria das condições entre os crentes daquela cidade, se modifica. Nesses capítulos — 10-13, aparecem repreendas e autodefesas inflexíveis, repetidas insistentemente. Pelos menos podemos supor que esses capítulos (décimo a décimo terceiro) representam uma parte daquela «epístola severa».

Todavia, aparecem outras referências àquela «epístola severa», em II Cor. 1-9. (Por exemplo, II Cor. 2:4). Paulo escreveu aquela «epístola severa» triste e lacrimejante. Também escreveu com a determinação firme de renovar a lealdade dos crentes de Corinto para com ele, e de fazê-los repelirem os adversários. (Ver II Cor. 2:9). Sua própria severidade servira tão-somente para assegurar-lhes o quão profundamente se interessava e preocupava por eles (ver II Cor. 2:3,4). Não obstante, exigiu alguma forma de punição para o líder que se opunha a ele (ver II Cor. 2:6). Foi Tito quem levou essa carta, pois Paulo lhe assegurara que os crentes de Corinto seriam novamente conquistados à amizade de Paulo, e vice-versa. (Ver II Cor. 7:14,15). E é patente que Tito também se aproveitou da oportunidade para promover a coleta que Paulo recolhia para os santos pobres da igreja de Jerusalém. (Ver II Cor. 8:6). Evidentemente Paulo haveria de ir ao encontro de Tito em Trôade, com qualquer notícia que este último pudesse trazer sobre a situação em Corinto. No entanto, Tito não compareceu ao encontro, e a angústia de Paulo se intensificou. (Ver II Cor. 2:12). Foi então que Paulo se dirigiu à Macedônia, talvez à cidade de Filipos, onde se encontrou com Tito, que lhe trazia notícias favoráveis. Foi em vista dessas notícias favoráveis que Paulo escreveu a chamada «epístola de agradecimento», a porção essencial do trecho de II Cor. 1-9.

2. *A epístola de agradecimento.* A tonalidade do trecho de II Cor. 1-9 é inteiramente diversa daquilo que aparece em II Cor. 10-13; pois aquela primeira porção da nossa segunda epístola aos Coríntios mostra a gratidão de Paulo ante o fato de que a combinação de sua *epístola severa* e da mediação de Tito havia sido suficientemente eficaz para solucionar os problemas da igreja de Corinto. (Ver II Cor. 7:5-12). Tendo sido solucionados os problemas principais, Paulo pôde dar prosseguimento aos seus

CORÍNTIOS

planos de visitar novamente a igreja de Corinto; e dessa vez o fez com alegria, e não em tristeza e lamentação, conforme sucedera na vez anterior. Era mister que Paulo fosse ali, a fim de recolher a coleta que desejava levar para os santos pobres de Jerusalém. Paulo já havia dito aos crentes da Macedônia que os crentes de Corinto estavam preparados para cumprirem a sua parte na coleta. (Ver II Cor. 9:2). Porém, para garantir que essa coleta se completaria, já que a mesma talvez tenha sido interrompida pelo conflito entre Paulo e alguns dos membros da igreja de Corinto, esse apóstolo mandou uma mensagem à sua frente para emularem os crentes à ação, no tocante à coleta. Paulo exortou os crentes de Corinto a contribuírem com generosidade, prometendo-lhes a recompensa divina em face da mesma. Por essa razão é que o apóstolo permaneceu ainda na Macedônia, completando a coleta ali feita e dando prosseguimento ao seu ministério geral do evangelho, esperando que os crentes coríntios se preparassem para fazer a sua contribuição. (Ver II Cor. 8:1-5 e 9:2). O trecho de Rom. 15:24-27 indica-nos o total sucesso desse apelo feito por Paulo.

3. Existem outras possíveis missivas, representadas nesta segunda epístola aos Coríntios. Alguns intérpretes destacam o trecho de II Cor. 6:14-7:1 como uma possível missiva curta sobre o problema do *jugo desigual*, ou mesmo como parte de uma outra missiva. Ora, isso parece fazer de nossa segunda epístola aos Coríntios uma conjunção de três cartas. Mas outras divisões ainda têm sido propostas pelos eruditos, conforme se pode verificar no artigo sobre à primeira epístola aos Coríntios, em sua seção IV. Todavia, essas três epístolas formadoras da segunda epístola aos Coríntios são as mais freqüentemente propostas.

V. TEMAS CENTRAIS

Dez são os principais temas abordados nesta segunda epístola aos Coríntios, a saber.

1. *Deus Pai*: Embora esta segunda epístola aos Coríntios não tenha tido por intuito ser um tratado doutrinário, tal como a primeira dessas epístolas, ela contém uma porção surpreendente de material doutrinário. Sobre esse tema de «Deus Pai», pode-se observar os seguintes particulares: Ele é Pai, motivo pelo qual usa de misericórdia e consola aos seus filhos (ver II Cor. 1:3). Deus é uma personalidade viva. (Ver II Cor. 3:3 e 6:16). Ele é alguém que se revela a si mesmo, o que confirma a posição central do «teísmo», o qual afirma que Deus é, não só o Criador, mas também é aquele que controla a sua criação, punindo e recompensando suas criaturas mortais. Deus se tornou conhecido principalmente através da pessoa de seu Filho, o Senhor Jesus Cristo. Desse modo, ele se faz presente entre os débeis agentes humanos postos a seu serviço. (Ver II Cor. 4:7; 6:7 e 13:4). Deus foi quem estabeleceu a ordem moral, razão pela qual deve ser respeitado e temido; mas o futuro eterno está garantido para aqueles que nele confiam. (Ver. II Cor. 1:18; 7:1 e 5:5).

2. *Realidade de Satanás* e dos poderes diabólicos: Satanás é o «deus» deste mundo (ver II Cor. 4:4), embora se disfarce como mensageiro luminoso, como mensageiro do reino da luz (ver II Cor. 11:14). Os homens, através de Satanás e da perversidade natural de suas próprias naturezas, precisam de reconciliação e da concretização da «nova criação» em Cristo. (Ver II Cor. 5:17-19). A redenção é que quebra o poder do reino das trevas. (Ver II Cor. 1:2).

3. *O Senhor Jesus Cristo*: Cristo aparece com destaque em trechos como II Cor. 1:3; 4:5 e 13:14. Ele é a imagem ou semelhança de Deus (ver II Cor. 4:4).

Ele é o Filho de Deus (ver II Cor. 1:19). Também é impecável (ver II Cor. 5:21). É Cristo quem assegura a realização das promessas de Deus aos homens, isto é, é quem garante o cumprimento das mesmas. (Ver II Cor. 1:19,20). Ele é o Redentor que traz os homens de volta a Deus, anulando a alienação que há entre os homens e o seu Criador. (Ver II Cor. 5:17-19). Jesus é o Messias de Israel, para quem os judeus deveriam olhar com expectação. (Ver II Cor. 3:12-15). Jesus é o Cristo preexistente, que não quis preservar sua anterior posição gloriosa e nem quis ignorar os homens, mas antes, empobreceu por nossa causa, dessa maneira conferindo-nos as riquezas dos céus. (Ver II Cor. 8:9). Cristo foi ressuscitado dentre os mortos, conforme se lê em II Cor. 4:14. E ele é o Senhor de todos e o Juiz de todos os homens. (Ver II Cor. 5:10).

4. *O Espírito Santo*: Ver especialmente II Cor. 13:14. O Espírito de Deus é quem produz a nova ordem, determinada por Deus e trazida à luz por Jesus Cristo, o Filho de Deus, proporcionando vida aos homens, o que o código legal de Moisés jamais poderia ter feito. (II Cor. 3:17-19). A esfera da ação do Espírito Santo é o «coração», a «alma» ou «homem interior». (Ver II Cor. 3:3). O Espírito de Cristo é o poder que transforma os crentes. (Ver II Cor. 3:6). O dom do Espírito Santo é a garantia de tudo quanto Deus promete aos homens para o futuro. (Ver II Cor. 1:22 e 5:5).

5. *Autoridade do Antigo Testamento*. As promessas de Deus (contidas nas Escrituras do A.T.) se referem aos crentes, que são o verdadeiro Israel. (Ver II Cor. 1:19,20). Porém, o código escrito, a lei de Moisés, é inferior à revelação divina que nos trouxe Cristo. (II Cor. 3:3,6). Não obstante, o A.T. se reveste de importância, não devendo ser desprezado por nós. (Ver II Cor. 3:14,15). O erro fatal dos judeus incrédulos foi não terem eles percebido o cumprimento do Antigo Testamento na nova dispensação, em Cristo Jesus.

6. *A imortalidade*. A mais completa descrição bíblica que existe sobre a «imortalidade» aparece no quinto capítulo da segunda epístola aos Coríntios. A imortalidade, todavia, não consiste em mera existência interminável; antes, consiste em uma vida de propósito e tipo específicos. No começo do estado eterno, cada crente será julgado de acordo com sua conduta nesta vida terrena. Esse julgamento determinará o nível de glória da transformação em Cristo, da capacidade de servir ao Senhor naquele novo estado. Não obstante, não devemos esperar que haja qualquer estagnação no estado eterno. Em outras palavras, é lógico supormos que o crente, tendo ficado aquém daquilo que poderia ter sido e feito, apesar disso será capaz de progredir no estado eterno, mais e mais, até que a imagem de Cristo seja aperfeiçoada nele, quando então compartilhará da própria divindade (ver II Ped. 1:4; II Cor. 3:18), que é o próprio alvo de toda a existência humana. Esse estudo paulino sobre a «imortalidade» também inclui a esperança do arrebatamento e a transformação que isso produzirá, sem que certos crentes passem pela morte física.

7. *A função e os propósitos do sofrimento do crente*. Debilidade e sofrimento são combinados com os conceitos de poder e triunfo, tal como o próprio Cristo, que era rico, se tornou pobre, tendo sofrido muito, até que triunfou em sua missão. (Ver II Cor. 13:4). Os homens são apenas vasos de barro, e devem experimentar sofrimentos e provas; porém, «o poder se aperfeiçoa com o sofrimento» (ver II Cor. 12:9). O sofrimento, pois, é um instrumento que Deus usa a

fim de levar a existência humana à perfeição, tanto como agente purificador quanto como agente desenvolvedor das graças espirituais.

8. *A esperança cristã*. A despeito das frustrações, dos sofrimentos e das provas, além do desespero ocasional, tudo isso redundará para o crente em um peso eterno de glória. (Ver II Cor. 4:10-18). Essa esperança inclui a certeza da imortalidade absoluta. (Ver II Cor. 5:1-10). Nos trechos de I Cor. 15:52 e I Tes. 4:17, percebe-se que Paulo esperava estar vivo ainda quando da «parousia» ou segundo advento de Cristo, sendo essa uma de suas grandes esperanças. A passagem de II Cor. 5:1-19 mostra-nos que Paulo continuava retendo essa esperança; porém, mesmo que isso não se concretizasse, ainda assim podemos ter a certeza de uma casa eterna, nos céus, não feita por mãos humanas. Sem importar o que venha a acontecer, haveremos de permanecer firmes em nossa fé em Cristo, esforçando-nos, quer presentes, quer ausentes, por agradá-lo. (Ver II Cor. 5:9). Toda a esperança cristã se alicerça sobre o dom inefável de Deus (ver II Cor. 9:15), o que provavelmente indica a pessoa do próprio Cristo, ou então a salvação que ele nos propicia. A esperança cristã inclui a expectação da fuga para os lugares celestiais, as dimensões da luz, conforme lemos no décimo segundo capítulo da segunda epístola aos Coríntios.

9. *O uso do dinheiro*. Está aqui em foco o espírito cristão dadivoso. Damos porque Deus nos deu em proporção infinita, bem como por causa do exemplo inspirador do próprio Cristo. (Ver II Cor. 5:18; 8:9 e 9:15). O mais importante dom de Deus que podemos dar é a nossa própria pessoa (ver II Cor. 8:5). A vida humana inteira pode ser uma forma de doação, que produz frutos dignos e aprovados pelo Senhor; e o serviço aqui focalizado é prestado tanto aos homens como a Deus, como manifestação do amor cristão. (II Cor. 8:1 e 9:14). O verdadeiro espírito de doação cristã, que agora se volta para as questões materiais, deve ser voluntário. (Ver II Cor. 9:5,7). Isso deve ser feito com boa atitude e com intensidade. (Ver II Cor. 8:2 e 9:7). O crente deve dar de modo generoso e alegre, (II Cor. 8:2 e 9:6,7,11). Também devemos dar de conformidade com a capacidade própria. (Ver II Cor. 8:11,12). O exemplo de um crente, em suas doações, encoraja a outros a seguirem o seu bom exemplo (ver II Cor. 9:2). O espírito dadivoso dos crentes edifica a fraternidade, a compreensão e o espírito de adoração mútua. (Ver II Cor. 9:12-14).

10. *Defesa do apostolado de Paulo*. Por detrás das cenas, esse tema domina grande parte da primeira e da segunda epístola aos Coríntios. Os capítulos décimo a décimo terceiro da segunda epístola são os principais trechos que abordam essa questão, onde também Paulo, ao fazer oposição aos seus adversários, revela-nos o seu íntimo, os seus conflitos e anelos, as suas esperanças, os seus desapontamentos, mas a sua esperança é permanente e imorredoura. Esta seção também ataca os adversários de Paulo, a quem ele reputava como «falsos apóstolos».

«A segunda epístola aos Coríntios fornece-nos alguns vislumbres íntimos de Paulo, mostrando-nos como ele realmente era, em momentos de maior pressão emotiva, indignado ou desanimado, ou então aliviado e grato. Tem sido dito com razão, sobre a primeira epístola aos Coríntios, que ela retira o telhado da igreja cristã primitiva, permitindo-nos espiar o seu interior. Porém, a segunda epístola aos Coríntios nos fornece um quadro ainda de maior intimidade, porquanto permite-nos olhar para o interior do coração de Paulo». (Goodspeed, Introdução à segunda epístola aos Coríntios, em sua tradução, impressa pela University of Chicago Press).

VI. Conteúdo

I. *Introdução* (1:1-11)
 1. Saudações cristãs (1:1,2)
 2. Ação de graças por seu livramento do perigo e da morte (1:3-11)
II. Paulo em Relação à Igreja de Corinto (1:12-2:4)
 1. Mudança de seus planos de visita, não por falta de sinceridade ou por volubilidade, mas para evitar outra visita dolorosa (1:12-2:4)
 2. Paulo perdoara o ofensor, contra quem escrevera em I Cor. 5, e exorta aos crentes de Corinto a fazerem o mesmo (2:5-11)
 3. Ansiedade de Paulo por ver a Tito, para saber qual o seu conceito entre os crentes de Corinto (2:12-13)
III. O Ministério Apostólico de Paulo (2:14-6:10)
 1. Paulo agradece a Deus por seu ministério (2:14-17)
 2. Os próprios crentes de Corinto autenticavam o seu ministério apostólico (3:1-3)
IV. A Superioridade do Novo Pacto (3:4-4:6)
 1. Conta com ministros qualificados por Deus (3:4-6)
 2. Ultrapassa o esplendor do antigo pacto (3:7-11)
 3. Seus ministros podem ser mais ousados (3:12-18)
 4. Consiste da *Luz* contra as trevas (4:1-6)
V. Poder Sustentador de Deus em Favor de seus Ministros (4:7-18)
 1. A vida de Jesus se manifesta em seus corpos (4:7-12)
 2. A fé na ressurreição e na glória final os sustenta (4:13-18)
VI. A Imortalidade é o Alvo de Toda a Existência (5:1-10)
 1. Poderá ocorrer através do arrebatamento (5:1-5)
 2. Poderá significar ir para o Senhor (5:6-8)
 3. Significará o juízo dos crentes (5:9,10)
VII. O Ministério da Reconciliação (5:11-6:10)
 1. Paulo desejava agradar a Deus em seu serviço concernente à reconciliação (5:11-13)
 2. Os homens são reconciliados por meio de Cristo (5:14-19)
 3. O ministério da reconciliação é urgente (5:20-6:2)
 4. Paulo era diligente nesse ministério (6:3-10)
VIII. Laços entre Paulo e a Igreja de Corinto (6:11-7:16)
 1. Apelo pelo afeto cristão mútuo (6:11-13)
 2. Evite-se a comunhão com os incrédulos de modo comprometedor (6:14-7:1)
 3. Apelo em favor do amor mútuo (7:2-4)
 4. A certeza da reconciliação produz alegria (7:5-16)
IX. As Doações Cristãs — Coleta para os Santos Pobres de Jerusalém (8:1-9:15)
 1. Que seguissem o exemplo dos macedônios (8:1-6)
 2. Que seguissem o exemplo da generosidade de Cristo (8:7-15)

3. Tito os encorajaria quanto a isso (8:16-24)
4. Que contribuíssem bem, e Deus os recompensaria liberalmente (9:1-11)
5. Dar é uma obra espiritual que leva o crente a louvar a Deus (9:12-15)

X. A Epístola Severa (10:1-13:10)
   1. Defesa contra a calúnia e os falsos líderes (10:1-11:15)
   2. Paulo mostra a grandiosidade de seus labores, demonstrando seu autêntico apostolado (11:16-12:10)
   3. Seus labores, revelações e visões mereciam a apreciação e a confiança por parte dos crentes de Corinto (12:1-10)
   4. Desejava Paulo a mudança de sentimentos para com sua pessoa antes que fosse forçado a fazer uma visita pessoal para cuidar das questões (12:11-13:10)

Conclusão: Exortações, Saudações e Bênção Finais (13:11-14)

VII. **Bibliografia:** AM EN I IB MOF NTI RO TIN VIN Z

CORÍNTIOS, TERCEIRA EPÍSTOLA AOS

Essa é uma carta atribuída a Paulo, mas escrita por um autor desconhecido. Data do século III D.C. A carta apresenta-se como uma comunicação feita por Paulo acerca do aparecimento de falsos mestres em Corinto, — onde Paulo os condena em termos claríssimos. Obteve posição canônica temporária na Igreja Siríaca, durante o século IV D.C. Mas, finalmente, foi retirada do cânon do Novo Testamento, daquele grupo cristão, quando esse cânon ficou melhor estabelecido, já no século V D.C.

CORINTO

Era outra das **importantes** cidades gregas, a qual, nos dias de Paulo, havia superado Atenas quanto à importância política e comercial. Agia como ponte terrestre entre o fluxo do comércio marítimo do Oriente com o Ocidente. Já no século VII A.C., adquirira grande poder e prosperidade, e já implantara, então, certo número de colônias. Em 146 A.C. resistiu à intrusão romana, mas foi destruída nesse processo. Durante cerca de um século ficou em ruínas. *Júlio César* fez de Corinto uma colônia romana e a reconstruiu (46 A.C.). Essa cidade se tornou conhecida por seus cultos pagãos, que consistiam em centenas de lupanares, — que promoviam a concupiscência. Este último pecado, tão generalizado em Corinto, deu origem a expressões como «corintianizar», que tem o sentido de iniciar-se em práticas imorais; também a «donzela coríntia», que simbolizava essa iniciação; e ainda «enfermidade coríntia», que indicava os resultados venéreos desses pecados de imoralidade.

Muitos edifícios e monumentos antigos têm sido escavados em Corinto, incluindo o «agorá», o centro da vida da cidade, além de muitas lojas e edifícios das proximidades, e também o templo de Apolo (datado do século VI A.C.).

A população coríntia era extremamente *cosmopolita*. Realmente, era a menos grega de todas as cidades da Grécia. Sua vida religiosa refletia a grande mistura de povos e costumes, exibindo aspectos altamente sincretistas. Contava com diversos cultos misteriosos, dentre os quais se destacava o do santuário vizinho, em Eleusis, além da adoração imoral a Afrodite. Este último culto se caracterizava sobretudo pela imoralidade e pela prostituição religiosa. Estrabão revela que havia em Corinto, dedicadas a esse culto, cerca de mil prostitutas religiosas. Ora, isso atraía um avantajado número de peregrinos, vindos do exterior, com o propósito declarado de se dedicarem à adoração religiosa. E assim, *viver como um coríntio* passou a significar uma vida entregue ao deboche.

É em razão do exposto acima que os trechos de I Tes. 4:3-7 e Rom. 1:18-25, ambos escritos de Corinto, acima de todas as demais escritas pelo apóstolo Paulo excetuando as suas duas epístolas aos Coríntios, atacam a imoralidade pagã, especialmente suas paixões infames. Embora a cidade de Corinto não fosse um centro intelectual como Atenas, Alexandria ou mesmo Tarso, mesmo assim contava com seus filósofos andarilhos em grande abundância, e a própria cidade se ufanava de sua herança intelectual.

«Na estrada que conduzia ao porto de Cencréia, aos turistas se mostrava, com veneração, o túmulo de Diógenes, o famoso cínico, contíguo ao sepulcro da famosa cortesã, Laís, talvez mostrando o gênio daquela cidade!» (G.H.C. Macgregor, Atos 18:1).

Eram os dois portos que serviam a Corinto que lhe emprestavam a sua importância comercial e o seu caráter cosmopolita. Cencréia, um desses portos, ficava cerca de pouco menos de catorze quilômetros de distância, no golfo de Sarona. Laqueum distava apenas dois quilômetros e meio a oeste do golfo de Corinto.

A principal indústria de Corinto era a cerâmica, embora houvesse vários outros produtos importantes que ali eram produzidos. O *comércio* e os negócios proliferavam, como já dissemos.

A característica topográfica dominante de Corinto era o Acrocorinto, uma rocha íngreme e de cume chato, com os seus 566 m de altura. No alto havia a Acrópole, a qual, nos tempos antigos, havia contido a *inter alia*, um templo de Afrodite, a deusa do amor, cujas atividades deram origem à imoralidade tradicional de Corinto.

Nos tempos passados, antes do século VII A.C., Corinto já era um centro importante de população. Contava com as suas próprias colônias; e à semelhança de outras localidades da Grécia, era uma cidade-estado. Do século IV A.C., até 196 A.C., Corinto foi dominada principalmente pelos macedônios; porém, foi nesse ano que a cidade foi libertada, juntamente com o resto da Grécia, por T. Quinctius Flaminius, tendo-se reunido à Liga Acaense. Corinto resistiu aos assédios romanos; mas, em 146 A.C. foi destruída pelas tropas do cônsul L. Mummius, e boa parte de seus habitantes foi vendida como escravos. Foi em 46 A.C. que Júlio César reedificou a cidade e muito se esforçou por restituir-lhe a sua primitiva glória. Augusto tornou Corinto a capital da recém-formada província da Acaia, que fora separada da Macedônia, passando a ser governada por um governador proconsular em separado.

Além das descobertas arqueológicas acima descritas, que dizem respeito a Corinto, foi encontrada uma inscrição próxima ao teatro, —que menciona o nome de Erasto, que, mui provavelmente, foi o tesoureiro de Corinto, mencionado como um dos convertidos sob os labores de Paulo, em Rom. 16:23. (Ver no NTI as notas expositivas sobre «Erasto», nesse versículo). Essa inscrição diz: «Erasto preparou este pavimento de seu próprio bolso, em apreciação por sua nomeação como sedile». (Um sedile era um oficial que cuidava das estradas, das condições sanitárias, dos jogos públicos e de outros interesses de uma cidade antiga).

CORNÉLIO

CORNÉLIO
A **importância** de sua conversão.

Ver detalhes sobre a conversão de Cornélio em Atos 10:1-11:18.

A **Grande Comissão**, conforme nos é dado no trecho de Atos 1:8, no sentido de que os discípulos deveriam evangelizar Jerusalém, Judéia, Samaria e então até os confins da terra, apresenta-nos o esboço geral da exposição do material histórico deste livro de Atos. Nos capítulos anteriores vimos como a igreja começou, cresceu, prosperou e foi então perseguida em Jerusalém, e como todas as cidades da região da Judéia ouviram o evangelho. O termo «Judéia», neste caso, evidentemente, tem por intuito incluir a totalidade da Palestina, pelo menos até onde está envolvido o alcance do ministério do evangelho. Poderíamos pensar quanto a essa designação, nas terras judaicas. Em seguida o evangelho foi a Samaria, onde habitava um povo de raça mista, mas cuja religião ainda era essencialmente judaica.

No décimo capítulo do livro de Atos é que encontramos, pela primeira vez—uma missão *oficial* entre os gentios, embora seja possível, e até mesmo provável, que alguns puros gentios já se tivessem convertido a Cristo antes dessa ocasião. Parece perfeitamente claro, entretanto, que o autor sagrado considerava este episódio como representante do começo do avanço do evangelho em territórios puramente gentílicos.

Paulo, de fato, foi o pioneiro das missões gentílicas. Ver 15:7.

Pode-se perceber, por semelhante modo, que a visão que teve o centurião, segundo se lê em Atos 10:1 e *ss*, é descrita novamente, pelo próprio Cornélio, ao chegar Pedro em Cesaréia, em Atos 10:30 e *ss*. Tudo isso foi feito pelo autor sagrado não a fim de enfatizar não somente como o evangelho penetrou entre os gentios, mas também a fim de vindicar esse avanço, visto que em seu tempo, embora não possamos entender bem tal sentimento, havia muito ressentimento, entre os crentes judeus, contra a evangelização de pagãos gentílicos puros, quando os mesmos eram admitidos com plenos direitos, na igreja cristã, através do rito inicial do batismo. Esse, de fato, foi um dos principais problemas com que a igreja primitiva se viu a braços, porquanto o núcleo original da igreja era judaica, e os seus membros, como é natural, trouxeram para a nova comunidade os seus preconceitos judaicos. Até mesmo o apóstolo Pedro teve de receber uma visão celestial, a fim de ficar plenamente convencido de que era próprio que se recebessem gentios convertidos, nas igrejas cristãs, com iguais privilégios oferecidos aos convertidos dentre o judaísmo.

Cornélio. Era um centurião romano destacado para a Palestina, que se fixara em Cesaréia, com a «coorte» ou bando chamado *Italiana*, comandante de cem homens daquela divisão do exército romano. Era conhecido como homem *temente a Deus*, talvez por causa de suas vinculações com o judaísmo, do qual, provavelmente, se tornara prosélito. Também se tornou bem conhecido por suas esmolas e por suas orações, duas qualidades altamente recomendáveis na religião judaica. «Cornélio» era um nome comum no mundo romano, desde os tempos de Cornelius Sulla, no ano de 82 A.C., o qual deu liberdade a dez mil escravos e alistou-os oficialmente como cidadãos romanos, sob o nome familiar de *gens Cornelia*. Neste caso, o vocábulo «gens» diz respeito a um «clã» uma espécie de grupo distinto dentro da sociedade. Pessoas famosas desse *clã* incluíam Cipião Africano Maior, o conquistador de Hanibal, como também Cornélio Cipião, filho desse último, que destruiu Cartago, grande rival de Roma.

Atos 10:2: *piedoso e temente a Deus com toda a sua casa, e que fazia muitas esmolas ao povo e de contínuo orava a Deus.*

O Caráter Espiritual de Cornélio.

1. Ele «temia» a Deus, uma expressão **veterotestamentária** para indicar que ele observava sua fé religiosa através de meios judaicos, como ritos, cerimônias e a lei. Portanto, ele era uma espécie de prosélito de judaísmo.

2. Parece que não fora circuncidado, pelo que não estava inteiramente identificado com a maneira judaica de viver, embora estivesse muito mais do que apenas «atraído» por aquela fé. Pedro foi criticado por haver se associado a um grupo de gentios incircuncisos. (Ver Atos 11:3).

3. Os legalistas não eram capazes de aprovar a Cornélio, conforme ele estava, mesmo que fosse um autêntico convertido ao cristianismo. Seu ingresso na comunidade cristã provocou inúmeros problemas. Os decretos que figuram em Atos 15; baixados pelo Concílio de Jerusalém, tiveram por intuito solucionar tais problemas, mas o problema do legalismo na verdade nunca foi inteiramente solucionado no seio da igreja. Meramente assumiu *formas diferentes*, em várias espécies de sacramentalismo.

Cornélio era homem com quem os judeus muito simpatizavam, pois não somente «temia» a Deus, mas também praticava a dádiva de esmolas, algo que os judeus religiosos reputavam como sinal de profunda piedade, conforme também se pensava entre os cristãos primitivos, de tal modo que nós, que damos pouca ênfase a essa parte prática, dificilmente podemos compreender. Além disso, Cornélio fazia essas esmolas «...ao povo...», frase que sem dúvida alguma indica a população judaica de Cesaréia. (No grego, «ó laos», os judeus, em contraste com *ta ethne*», as nações gentílicas). Quanto a notas expositivas sobre a importância das «esmolas», como ato piedoso enfatizado tanto no judaísmo como no cristianismo primitivo, ver Atos 3:2 no NTI.

Cornélio *orava*, isto é, conservava o hábito ou costume da oração, o que provavelmente indica a observância das horas regulares de oração, designadas pelos líderes eclesiásticos do templo de Jerusalém e das sinagogas em geral. Quanto a notas expositivas sobre essa forma cerimonial de «oração», que também fazia parte preponderante na adoração judaica, ver a exposição em Atos 3:1 no NTI. Outrossim, Cornélio era homem pessoalmente piedoso, não sendo religioso apenas formal e publicamente. Por todos esses motivos era muito respeitado entre os judeus, mas o fato de que continuava incircunciso levava-o a ser classificado por eles como mero pagão. Ora, nenhum indivíduo dessa categoria poderia ser admitido na igreja cristã (segundo a opinião dos legalistas), sob a mera condição do batismo cristão, sem primeiramente submeter-se às leis judaicas que governavam a admissão de prosélitos gentios, cuja principal provisão era a circuncisão.

A doação de esmolas e a oração eram dois dos pontos cardeais salientados pelos judeus, ao que o Senhor Jesus adicionou o jejum, no quadro que traçou diante dos fariseus, no trecho de Mat. 6:1-18.

Nesse centurião vemos a semelhança de um outro que amou ao povo de Israel, e que construiu para eles uma sinagoga, pagando as despesas do próprio bolso (ver Luc. 7:5). Podemos supor com segurança, pois, que Cornélio era homem insatisfeito com os conceitos espirituais encontrados nas religiões pagãs, tendo buscado outra maneira de encontrar a verdade, havendo aceito temporariamente o judaísmo. Deus guiava-o o tempo todo, até que pôde conduzi-lo aos pés de Cristo, que é o alvo de todo o homem.

Seriedade da busca espiritual de Cornélio

Podemos ver que esse centurião era autêntico em sua busca por Deus no fato de que trouxe sua família para ouvir a Palavra de Deus, dos lábios de Simão Pedro. Em certo sentido, nenhum homem é uma ilha, porquanto sua vida afeta às vidas de todos quantos entram em contacto com ele. De fato, se a vida de alguém não afeta àqueles que entram em contacto com ele, podemos julgar que a energia de sua busca e expressão espirituais é extremamente débil. Noutro sentido, todavia, todo indivíduo é uma ilha, porquanto a busca por Deus, por parte de cada um, é atribuição exclusiva de cada um, e ninguém pode fazer essa busca no lugar de outrem.

Cornélio, ao encontrar alguma expressão religiosa melhor do que a sua, desejou que os seus familiares também a conhecessem. O fato de que ele tinha sua família em Cesaréia mostra-nos que, provavelmente, era residente permanente ali, por ser um soldado profissional, e que planejava permanecer nessa cidade por tempo considerável. E visto que já se demorara na cidade por algum tempo, viera a conhecer e a ser conhecido pelo povo da região, tendo ficado conhecido como homem sincero e piedoso, embora não estivesse oficialmente vinculado a qualquer sinagoga.

Foi justamente um homem assim que o Espírito Santo resolveu usar como representante da introdução da igreja cristã em terreno puramente gentílico. Cornélio e sua família foram os primeiros gentios puros a serem aceitos como membros da igreja cristã, sob a condição única do batismo, sem ter havido a necessidade do rito essencialmente judaico da circuncisão. Assim sendo, ele não precisou de qualquer orientação judaica, sobre as questões religiosas, para participar dos benefícios e privilégios da igreja cristã. Foi assim que a igreja deu mais um passo, em sua expansão e desenvolvimento, até que, finalmente, veio a tornar-se uma entidade totalmente separada do judaísmo.

«Ele, *Cornélio*, criava a sua família em um ambiente religioso, como todo o homem de bem deve fazer». (John Gill em Atos 10:2).

Podemos supor com segurança que Cornélio, além das orações ritualistas ordinárias, pedisse ao Senhor, em oração, para ser guiado a uma verdade maior, mais profunda, o que, na realidade, é tanto dever como privilégio de todos os homens.

Ouvido apenas pelos santos anjos,
O bom Cornélio se ajoelhou sozinho,
Sem sonhar que sua oração e lágrimas,
Ajudariam um mundo necessitado.

Entrementes, em seu terraço,
O amado apóstolo orava a seu Senhor,
Pois em pensamento silente, distante,
Ele subiu em visão celestial.
    (Keble)

Talvez seja significativo, segundo nos sugere Matthew Henry (*in loc*), que quando a missão do evangelho chegou aos gentios, e se tornou necessário um *caso representativo* de conversão, para ensinar uma lição, à igreja, sobre como seria a nova ordem de adoração, não foi convocado um filósofo grego para ser esse indivíduo, como também não foi chamado um sacerdote pagão, o qual estaria cego pelos seus preconceitos contra quaisquer reivindicações novas de verdade, e, sim, um soldado gentio, o qual seria pessoa mais ou menos livre de quaisquer preconceitos tolhedores.

CORO

Um grupo treinado de cantores, originalmente um grupo de cantores dançarinos. O termo também se refere a um lugar, nos templos cristãos, onde o coro da Igreja posta-se e canta. Além disso, cada uma das nove *ordens* de anjos tem sido chamada por esse nome. Ver o artigo sobre *Música e Instrumentos Musicais*, no que diz respeito ao contexto bíblico para coro.

COROA Ver também **Coroas**.

Esboço:
  I. Termos Envolvidos
  II. No Antigo Testamento
  III. Em Outras Culturas
  IV. A Coroa como um Símbolo Espiritual

I. Termos Envolvidos

Há três palavras hebraicas e duas palavras gregas que precisamos considerar, a saber:

1. *Kether*, «coroa», «diadema». — Termo que figura por três vezes, sempre no livro de Ester (1:11; 2:17 e 6:8).

2. *Nezer*, «grinalda», «coroa». Palavra que ocorre por onze vezes, com esse sentido: Êxo. 29:6; 39:30; Lev. 8:9; 21:12; II Sam. 1:10; II Reis 11:12; II Crô. 23:11; Sal. 89:39; 132:18; Pro. 27:24 e Zac. 9:16.

3. *Atarah*, «coroa». Vocábulo usado por vinte e três vezes: II Sam. 12:30; I Crô. 20:2; Est. 8:15; Jó 19:9; 31:36; Sal. 21:3; Pro. 4:9; 12:4; 14:24; 16:31; 17:6; Can. 3:11; Isa. 28:1,3,5; 62:3; Jer. 13:18; Lam. 5:16; Eze. 16:12; 21:26; 23:42; Zac. 6:11,14.

4. *Diádema*, «diadema». Palavra grega que figura por três vezes, sempre no Apocalipse (12:3; 13:1 e 19:12).

5. *Stéphanos*, «coroa». Palavra grega empregada por dezoito vezes, a maior parte das vezes no Apocalipse: Mat. 27:29; Mar. 15:17; João 19:2,5; I Cor. 9:25; Fil. 4:1; I Tes. 2:19; II Tim. 4:8; Tia. 1:12; I Ped. 5:4; Apo. 2:10; 3:11; 4:4,10; 6:2; 8:7; 12:1; 14:14. Essa também é a palavra grega que era o nome do primeiro mártir cristão, Estêvão (ver Atos 6:5 ss).

II. No Antigo Testamento

A coroa era uma peça usada na cabeça, geralmente muito ornada, usada por monarcas e outras pessoas importantes. No Antigo Testamento, temos a coroa do sumo sacerdote, feita de uma placa de ouro com as palavras inscritas: «Santo ao Senhor». Essa placa era presa à sua mitra ou turbante por um cordão azul, que simbolizava a sua consagração (Êxo. 19:6; 39:30). Após o exílio babilônico, em 520 A.C., coroas de ouro e de prata foram feitas para o sumo sacerdote (Zac. 6:11-14). Após terem sido usadas, foram guardadas no templo, como emblemas do favor divino.

As coroas reais eram outorgadas como indicação de que o ofício monárquico era ocupado por decreto divino (Sal. 21:3). A coroa também simbolizava a glória (Jó 19:9; Isa. 28:5); a realeza (Pro. 27:24); o orgulho (Jó 31:36; Isa. 28:1,3). Essas coroas eram fabricadas de vários metais e, com freqüência, eram muito decoradas, algumas vezes até com pedras preciosas. Foi uma coroa assim que Davi tomou do rei dos amorreus (II Sam. 12:30), e então pô-la sobre sua própria cabeça, tal como fizeram os seus sucessores. Pelo menos em alguns casos, os reis de Israel foram formalmente coroados (II Reis 11:12).

III. Outras Culturas

A arqueologia tem descoberto evidências acerca de muitos tipos de coroas entre os egípcios, tanto através de coroas literais como mediante gravuras em murais e inscrições. Algumas vezes, essas coroas eram elaboradas e ricamente adornadas, como aquela usada por Tutancâmom. Emblemas reais também decoravam essas coroas. Elas incluíam certa variedade de caudas, mas outras consistiam em meros aros de ouro, ou um tipo de chapéu chato, com uma espiral na parte da frente, e uma elevada projeção na parte de trás. Algumas coroas eram cônicas, e outras arredondadas.

A coroa usada pelos reis assírios consistia em uma elevada mitra, freqüentemente adornada com flores ou outros objetos. Tiras de linho ou de seda eram arrumadas formando uma espiral ascendente, formando uma espécie de cone. Com freqüência, esse tipo de coroa era adornado com pedras preciosas. Os reis da Babilônia usavam uma mitra recurva, terminando em ponta. As escavações arqueológicas têm descoberto muitos aros e diademas, feitos de vários materiais, incluindo o ouro e a prata.

Os turbantes usados na Pérsia, na Pártia e na Armênia, nos tempos clássicos, eram uma espécie de quepe ou capacete, devido à sua rigidez. Os turbantes usados pelas pessoas comuns eram similares, mas feitos de tecido. Ambos os tipos são ilustrados no vaso de Dario, existente no Museo Nazionale de Nápolis, na Itália. Ao redor da testa do quepe real havia uma faixa larga, feita de material das cores branco, azul (ou púrpura), e que podia ser usada sozinha, sem o capacete, servindo de emblema de soberania. A palavra grega *diádema*, que em português deu «diadema», significa algo «enrolado em volta», embora essa palavra tenha vindo a significar uma coroa de qualquer formato.

Essa faixa simbolizava o poder despótico, e os romanos evitavam tal símbolo. Mas os romanos usavam grinaldas de folhas de carvalho ou de louro, além de aros de metal, que denotavam feitos militares ou atléticos. Júlio César usava uma coroa de louros, como general vitorioso que era; mas, quando Marco Antônio lhe ofereceu um diadema com louros, quando da festividade da Lupercália, ele não consentiu em usar tal emblema, porquanto simbolizava a realeza. E mesmo depois que Roma se tornou um império, o uso de coroas, que indicavam a realeza, continuou a ser evitado. Os primeiros imperadores preferiam a coroa de louros, celebrando as suas conquistas militares. Também havia a coroa de ponta longa, para o alto, que denotava o favor dos deuses e era símbolo dos descendentes do Sol. Essa coroa foi usada pelos imperadores romanos. Foi somente na época de Constantino que o diadema foi introduzido entre os objetos de uso real. Então os romanos começaram a imitar outros povos, e as coroas tornaram-se muito ornadas, decoradas com pedras preciosas.

IV. A Coroa como um Símbolo Espiritual

Ver o artigo separado sobre **Coroas**.

COROA DE ESPINHOS

No grego, *stéphanon eks akanthôn*. Os soldados romanos prepararam uma coroa de espinhos, para ser posta sobre a cabeça de Jesus. Foi um ato de zombaria. É possível que a planta usada para isso tenha sido a *Zizyphus spina-christi*. Esse arbusto cresce até cerca de quatro metros de altura, com dois grandes e agudos espinhos no pé de cada folha. É espécie comum na Palestina, podendo ser conseguida com muita facilidade. Mas outros estudiosos opinam que a planta usada foi a *Paliurus spina-christi*, que cresce somente de 1,20 m a 2,40 m de altura, o que teria facilitado muito a confecção da coroa, por parte dos soldados. Os espinhos dessa planta são eriçados, agudos, e aparecem em pares de comprimentos desiguais. As referências bíblicas aparecem em Mat. 27:29 e João 19:2. Essa coroa representa o escárnio da parte de homens contra outros que lhes são superiores, em uma oposição irracional e ignorante contra o plano de Deus. O Sudário de Turim (que vide), exibe as marcas do sangue derramado por causa dessa coroa de espinhos.

COROAS

Ver também, **Galardões e Julgamento do Crente**.

1. O Simbolismo: A «corona triumphalis» era feita de folhas de louro e servia para coroar os generais triunfantes. A «corona obsidionalis» era conferida aos generais que tivessem salvo o seu exército do cerco ou da rendição vergonhosa. Era tecida com grama ou outro material que pudesse ser encontrado no local da vitória. Essa coroa também era chamada de «corona graminea». A «corona myrtea» ou «corona ovalis» era feita de louro, de folhas lustrosas e espessas, que era outorgada a generais que celebrassem triunfos militares de maior ou menor envergadura. A dourada «corona muralis», fixada como ornamento, era conferida aos líderes militares que atacassem alguma muralha. A «corona castrensis» ou «valaris», feita de ouro, e ornada em imitação a paliçadas (fortificações) era dada ao primeiro soldado que escalasse o terrapleno do acampamento inimigo. Nas competições atléticas, a coroa de louro era usada como prêmio. Aquelas coroas feitas com ramos de oliveira, hera e salsa, ou então as coroas de flores, eram comumente utilizadas para os que obtinham vitórias nas competições atléticas. Nas metáforas do N.T., tais «coroas de vitória» são aludidas, e não as coroas de reis e príncipes, formadas de ouro e pedras preciosas. Exceções a isso são a coroa de espinhos, do Senhor Jesus, feita para motejar de sua «autoridade real», e a «coroa do anticristo», em Apo. 6:2, que expressa falsa realeza. Não obstante, alguns intérpretes, estranhamente, pensam que essa coroa é também de Cristo. Também pertencem a esse caráter excepcional as «coroas» de ouro que os seres celestiais depositarão aos pés de Cristo, em honra a ele, como o Grande Rei; as coroas do anticristo, que representam uma realeza temporária (ver Apo. 19:12), e as coroas de Cristo, que representam sua autoridade majestática, quando de seu segundo advento.

2. Tipos de coroas, referidas nas páginas do N.T., que simbolizam «recompensas», de várias maneiras:

a. A coroa *incorruptível* (ver I Cor. 9:25). Essa aponta para a «vida eterna» e tudo quanto nela está envolvida, incluindo suas vantagens e perfeições, dadas em recompensa pelo serviço fiel dos crentes. Ver os artigos separados sobre a *Vida Eterna* e *Salvação*. Ver também João 3:15 e Heb. 2:3 no *NTI*.

b. A *coroa da justiça* (ver II Tim. 4:8). Isso indica aquela «coroa conquistada pela retidão», mas também indica a obtenção da retidão perfeita e eterna, em que o crente passa a participar das perfeições de Cristo e da natureza moral de Deus Pai (ver Mat. 5:48). E isso envolve ser santo como Deus Pai é santo. Esse é o grande alvo de todos os remidos; mas alguns deles, ao entrarem nos lugares celestiais, por causa de seu serviço fiel e de sua piedade, terão mais elevada justiça do que outros. Isso não significa, entretanto, que alguns deles tenham algum *pecado*. Antes, alguns participaram, em mais alto grau, da santidade e da justiça positivas de Deus. A perfeição absoluta é o nosso alvo; e a eternidade inteira é a esfera na qual podemos participar da mesma. Seremos seres de notável pureza e santidade, de bondade e retidão perfeitas, como o próprio Deus Pai. (Ver Rom. 3:21 no NTI acerca de notas expositivas sobre a «retidão»). Nenhum indivíduo penetrará nos lugares celestiais sem possuir a própria retidão de Deus. Contudo, alguns entrarão ali como possuidores de mais íntimas perfeições de Deus do que outros, embora nos céus não possa haver nenhuma estagnação, e todos os seres que ali habitarem tornar-se-ão mais e mais semelhantes a Deus Pai. Será uma inquirição *eterna*.

c. *A coroa da vida* (ver Tia. 1:12). A «vida eterna» está em foco aqui, com todo o avanço na direção da natureza de Cristo. Pois a «vida eterna» não consiste apenas de existência interminável. Antes, trata-se de uma modalidade de vida . Haverá a participação na *própria espécie* de vida divina. (Ver as notas expositivas em João 5:25,26, e 6:57 no NTI quanto a esse tipo de vida, que é a vida «necessária» e «independente»). Há muitas *modalidades* de vida, a começar pelos animais unicelulares. Há os animais mais completos, há o homem, que combina a vida física com a vida espiritual. Há os anjos, que são puros espíritos. E há Deus que é a forma mais elevada de vida, a origem de toda e qualquer outra forma de vida. Ora, os remidos em Cristo estão destinados a compartilhar de sua vida e natureza, pois o próprio Cristo compartilha da vida de Deus Pai. Por conseguinte, na redenção, o homem passa a possuir uma modalidade de vida superior à dos anjos. (Ver II Ped. 1:4 e Efé. 3:19). Alguns crentes, devido ao seu serviço leal na esfera terrena, ao entrarem nos lugares celestiais, receberão uma forma de vida superior àquela conferida a outros. Contudo, conforme já dissemos, nos céus não haverá estagnação.

Em conexão com isso, alguns dos pais da igreja primitiva supunham que o «corpo ressuscitado» (ver I Cor. 15:20,35,40) será diferente para os diversos casos, ou seja, mais ou menos espiritualizado, mais ou menos semelhante à essência de Cristo, dependendo da fidelidade de cada um. Aqueles que forem dotados de uma forma superior de vida, de um tipo de vida mais espiritualizado, o que se refletirá no seu corpo ressurrecto, habitarão em dimensões espirituais mais próximas da habitação de Deus, servindo de instrumentos de serviço superior. É verdade que isso é uma «especulação», embora provavelmente seja uma verdadeira especulação teológica. Cada forma de vida tem o seu «habitat» apropriado, como os peixes vivem na água, os pássaros cruzam os ares e os anjos habitam em «lugares celestiais». E para que habitem nesta ou naquela região, cada qual receberá seu veículo apropriado. E os galardões envolverão o recebimento de veículos apropriados. Mas, como não haverá estagnação nos céus, à proporção em que alguém se for tornando mais espiritualizado, irá se desvencilhando de suas antigas algemas, de sua forma de vida mais limitada, e assim ir-se-á tornando um ser mais glorioso, similar a Cristo. Pois ser igual a Cristo, no sentido mais literal da palavra, é a significação mesma da existência, sendo esse o motivo de eterna inquirição. Não, não poderá haver estagnação nos céus, porquanto isso é contrário a tudo quanto sabemos acerca da natureza e dos desígnios divinos.

(Ver Apo. 2:10 quanto a outra referência à «coroa da vida»).

d. *A coroa da glória* (ver I Ped. 5:4). A vida nos lugares celestiais consistirá da participação na glorificação de Cristo (ver Rom. 8:29,30), e os crentes, dependendo de sua lealdade e desenvolvimento espiritual, receberão graus variegados de «glória», compartilhando da glória, da majestade, do poder, dos atributos e da natureza de Cristo em maior ou menor glória. Alguns receberão um serviço espiritual mais exaltado, por serem seres mais exaltados. Mas, uma vez mais, não haverá nenhuma estagnação nos lugares celestiais.

3. Podem ser perdidas

— Não podemos depender da fidelidade anterior como «garantia» do recebimento dos galardões. Teremos de perseverar até o fim na atitude de dedicação a Cristo. (Ver Apo. 3:11). Toda a coroa, mesmo depois de conquistada, pode ser perdida, enquanto estivermos neste mundo. A passagem de III João 8 concorda com esse princípio. O trecho de I Cor. 9:27 acrescenta a severa idéia de que até mesmo um verdadeiro discípulo pode vir a fracassar nessa carreira, perdendo assim a coroa (da vida eterna). Isso expressa uma grande verdade. Sabemos, entretanto, que finalmente, em algum lugar, neste mundo ou no outro, Cristo o trará de volta, a fim de cumprir a sua promessa de que ele não deixará perder-se qualquer de suas ovelhas, porquanto nada poderá separar-nos do seu amor (ver Rom. 8:35 e *ss*; João 10:28,29 e 17:12).

4. Elementos importantes em II Tim. 4:8.

O Senhor. Ele é o «Senhor da vida», o «Senhor da justiça» e o «Senhor de todos». É ele quem julgará que recompensa deverá ser dada; e é ele quem garante essa doação. (Ver o trecho de Rom. 1:7 no NTI e as notas expositivas ali existentes acerca do título de Jesus, «Senhor», e acerca de seu «senhorio»). Ninguém tem a Jesus como Salvador, se também não o tem como seu Senhor. Pois invocamos ao nome do «Senhor» a fim de sermos salvos (ver Rom. 10:9,10).

Reto Juiz. (Ver Atos 17:3). Ele é «justo» de tal modo que não comete equívocos nesse particular do julgamento, cumprindo perfeitamente todas as exigências da justiça, em pleno conhecimento e sabedoria. Cristo Jesus é igualmente chamado de «Juiz» em Atos 10:42 e Tia. 5:9. Deus Pai é também chamado assim em Heb. 12:23 e Tia. 4:12. Cristo Jesus, o Filho, julga por nomeação de Deus Pai, conforme aprendemos na passagem de Atos 17:31. Antes de tudo, Cristo é o Justo Juiz; mas também é o Generoso Doador, embora nunca se mostre infiel e desleal.

Naquele dia. O uso da palavra «dia», para indicar o «julgamento» ou o «segundo advento de Cristo», que resultará no julgamento, é comum nas páginas do N.T.

Também a todos quantos amam a sua vinda. Não somente o grande apóstolo dos gentios poderia obter as coroas. Todos os crentes e todos os ministros fiéis podem esforçar-se para a obtenção do mesmo alvo; e todos podem conseguir o mesmo êxito. Isso serve de encorajamento à fidelidade, porquanto não estamos em busca de alguma mera coroa corruptível.

*Quão inutilmente os homens se admiram
Para conquistar a palma, o carvalho e o louro;
E seus labores incessantes são
Coroados com alguma simples erva, ou ramo,
Cuja sombra breve e estreita
Repreende prudentemente seus labores.*

(Andrew Marvell)

O esforço terreno em prol do aprimoramento só pode conduzir o indivíduo a algo tão desapontador como isso; mas é prometido um grandioso galardão, um profundo e eterno bem-estar, para aqueles que conhecem a Cristo e o servem verdadeiramente.

5. Em Apocalipse 3:11.
Para que ninguém tome a tua coroa. É erro gigantesco interpretar essas «coroas» de modo materialista, como se dessem a entender alguma espécie de «possessão», que devamos herdar, como terrenos, mansões e várias outras formas de riquezas materiais. As «coroas» falam, figuradamente, do «avanço espiritual», — obtido, à medida que chegaremos a participar de «toda a plenitude de Deus» (Ver Efé. 3:19). A coroa da justiça, por exemplo, sem dúvida alude a como alguns crentes, acima de outros, participam da elevada justiça e santidade de Deus, das suas qualidades morais. Já que essas virtudes são infinitas, não haverá limite em que poderemos participar delas, e a eternidade inteira verá o crescimento dessa «participação», com base em nosso recebimento da própria «natureza divina» (ver II Ped. 1:4). Cristo está sendo duplicado em nós; recebemos a sua natureza moral, — e sua própria forma de ser e essência. As coroas, portanto, apontam para como participaremos de tudo isso, em graus e níveis variados. A «coroa da vida» é a participação na «vida eterna», mas em proporções abundantíssimas, além daquilo que será conferido aos que não receberem tal coroa. Em certo sentido, naturalmente, todos os crentes autênticos receberão a «coroa da vida»; mas alguns deles serão mais profundamente espiritualizados do que outros, tornando-se seres mais elevados que os restantes, — de acordo com o nosso grande modelo, Cristo. E isso, para eles, servirá de «coroa», porquanto assinalará sua dignidade e participação no prêmio, conquistadas mediante uma carreira apropriada.

Não haverá estagnação. — Todos os crentes estão destinados e finalmente participarem de toda a plenitude de Deus. Esse é o destino do homem, em Cristo. Não obteremos a mesma meramente por causa do ato da morte biológica. A árvore fica onde caiu. Em outras palavras, o grau de desenvolvimento que tivermos obtido, até o dia da morte física, será o grau que assinalará nossas pessoas, ao entrarmos nos mundos celestiais. Dali por diante, entretanto, poderemos progredir ilimitadamente. A perfeição absoluta de Deus é nosso grande alvo, e nunca haverá fim da inquirição pela perfeição. Já que haverá uma infinitude com que seremos cheios, também deverá haver um preenchimento infinito. (Ver as notas expositivas no NTI em Col. 2:10, acerca de explicações desse conceito, com documentação extraída da herança da literatura cristã, que ensina a mesma verdade).

Simbolismo judaico por detrás dessa declaração. O rabino Simon, em *Tract. Shabb. bab.* 88a (Talmude), afirma que quando ocorreu o que diz Êxo. 24:7, os israelitas foram coroados cada um com duas coroas, por seiscentos mil anjos. A primeira dessas coroas foi dada quando disseram: «Faremos». E a outra quando disseram «Seremos obedientes». Porém, por ocasião do acontecimento retratado em Êxo. 33:6, essas coroas lhes foram arrebatadas das cabeças, por um milhão e duzentos mil demônios. Finalmente, porém, Deus lhes restaurou as coroas, conforme se vê no trecho de Isa. 35:10. De conformidade com as doutrinas judaicas, não há que duvidar que a perda das coroas significava a perda da salvação pessoal, que fora ganha mediante a justificação diante de Deus; e é perfeitamente possível que o vidente João compartilhasse desse ponto de vista. Observamos que, em Fil. 3:10-14, o «prêmio» a ser conquistado na carreira é a própria «vida eterna». Certamente que a «coroa da vida», em Apo. 2:10, é a própria «vida eterna». É bem provável, por conseguinte, que João tenha feito aqui uma advertência contra a *apostasia*, ou seja, contra a perda da salvação, e não meramente contra a perda de galardões, ou mesmo da perfeita glória celestial. (Isso pode ser comparado com o que se lê em II João vs. 6: «Acautelai-vos, para não perderes aquilo que temos realizado com esforço, mas para receberdes completo galardão»).

A *metáfora* aqui tencionada poderia ser a de uma «carreira», incluindo a «coroa de louros» ou de «flores» conquistadas pelos vencedores. Ou então a coroa poderia ser a da realeza, que alguém recebe por ser rei, o que assinala a participação em seu reino e governo, por delegação. Os vencedores herdarão juntamente com Cristo (ver Apo. 2:26 e 20:5).

A diligência é requerida para que se conquiste a coroa. Essa diligência pode ser exibida pelos mártires em potencial, em tempos difíceis.

CORPO

Embora existam cerca de catorze vocábulos hebraicos de alguma maneira ligados ao corpo físico, alguns dos quais indicando porções do corpo como «costas», «barriga», etc., não há nenhum vocábulo que indique o corpo inteiro. A mais comum dessas palavras hebraicas é *basar*, que significa «carne». Porém, no Novo Testamento encontramos o termo grego *soma*, «corpo» (usado por cerca de cento e trinta vezes) e o termo grego *ptoma*, «cadáver» (usado por sete vezes: Mat. 14:12, 24:28; Mar. 6:29, 15:45; Apo. 11:8,9). A palavra *soma* aparece desde Mat. 5:29 até Apo. 18:13. É usada para indicar o corpo humano, bem como os corpos dos animais (Tia. 3:3; Heb. 13:11), os corpos vegetais, e até mesmo os corpos celestiais (I Cor. 15:35-44). E, no plural, os corpos de escravos (Apo. 18:13).

Em algumas passagens da Bíblia, o termo «corpo» é contrastado com a «alma» (Miq. 6:7; Mat. 10:28). O corpo físico é o instrumento ou veículo da vida da alma neste mundo (Deu. 12:23; Isa. 53:12; II Cor. 5:10). Pode indicar a personalidade inteira (Fil. 1:20; Rom. 12:1). Posteriormente, a teologia dos hebreus concebeu o sopro de Deus sobre o corpo, conferindo-lhe a alma residente. A teologia anterior dos hebreus compreendia isso como a mera animação da estátua de barro que Deus havia formado, sem qualquer idéia de uma alma eterna. Seja como for, o corpo físico é a manifestação inferior do ser humano, ao passo que a alma é representante do mundo dos espíritos, do qual o homem também participa. Jesus ensinou a importância secundária do corpo (Mat. 6:25-34). E Paulo reconheceu o estado de humilhação do corpo (Fil. 3:21), exortando-nos a disciplina-lo, para que obtenha uma boa expressão espiritual (I Cor. 9:27; Rom. 8:13). Além disso, o corpo físico deve ser usado para o Senhor, por ser expressão ou instrumento do espírito (I Cor. 6:13; Rom. 12:1; I Tes. 5:23).

Qualquer coisa que façamos que seja prejudicial ao corpo físico, constitui uma ofensa contra o Espírito, que usa nosso corpo como um lugar de sua habitação e expressão (I Cor. 6:13 ss). Isso contraria o ponto de vista gnóstico que fazia a matéria ser má, e que afirmava que visto que o corpo físico é material, seria a sede da maldade humana, ao passo que a alma humana não seria corrompida. Pode-se mergulhar um vaso de ouro na lama, sem alterar suas qualidades e virtudes. Assim também, para o gnosticismo, pode-se abusar do corpo das maneiras mais devassas, sem que isso prejudique a alma. De fato, de conformidade com esse ponto de vista, é vantajoso abusar do corpo, a fim de levá-lo ao fim mais prematuro possível. Todavia, o evangelho cristão rejeita a idéia da pecaminosidade exclusivamente do corpo, embora seja instrumento facilmente posto a serviço do pecado (Rom. 6:12,13). Outrossim, na qualidade de templo do Espírito, reveste-se de grande dignidade. Podemos agradecer a Deus pela saúde física, que nos permite realizar as coisas que a nossa missão requer.

O Novo Testamento ensina a real encarnação do Logos em um corpo humano (João 1:14). Isso indica que não se pode pensar que o corpo físico do homem seja a sede mesma do pecado. Platão, por outro lado, chamava o corpo de prisão e sepulcro da alma, ensinando um caminho de reformas morais e de progresso, com o intuito de liberar a alma do corpo, a fim de que a alma pudesse atingir as dimensões dos espíritos puros. O evangelho cristão não é tão severo contra o corpo, mas promete aos remidos um novo corpo, de natureza espiritual, que venha a tornar-se o veículo da alma, para expressão nos mundos celestiais (I Cor. 15:44 ss; Fil. 3:21). Quanto a um comentário pleno sobre isso, ver Fil. 3:21 no NTI.

O corpo físico foi criado por Deus, sendo bom em si mesmo, embora represente, indubitavelmente, um rebaixamento da potencialidade humana, e mesmo uma punição por causa do pecado, envolvendo-o em coisas terrenas e animais. Apesar disso, o homem tem um destino físico, inteiramente distinto de seu destino espiritual. Mesmo neste mundo, a humanidade avança para propósitos terrenos mais nobres, e cada indivíduo participa desse esforço, positiva ou negativamente. Mas, embora distinto do elevadíssimo destino espiritual, esse destino terreno está relacionado àquele. Assim sendo, para exemplificar, um cientista que faça bem o seu papel, e assim ajude a aprimorar a qualidade de vida de seus semelhantes, está agindo na qualidade de servo de Deus, ainda que não tenha consciência disso. Mas, todas as almas, — finalmente, haverão de seguir pela vereda da expressão espiritual, nos mundos não-materiais, a despeito de seguirem, então, por caminhos opostos. Este mundo físico reveste-se de um destino; e os mundos espirituais envolvem destinos mais elevados. Em nossa experiência total, participamos de ambos os destinos, como uma escola com graus inferiores e superiores de aprendizado.

Usos Metafóricos. a. O corpo humano simboliza a Igreja, com seus muitos membros e suas muitas funções (I Cor. 12:13; Rom. 12:13 ss; Efé. 1:23). b. Na Igreja, concebida como um corpo, há o Cabeça, que é Cristo, e há o corpo, que são os remidos, que cumprem as ordens do Cabeça, agora e por toda a eternidade (Efé. 1:23; Col. 1:18,24; 2:18; 3:15). c. O corpo é o novo templo que serve de habitação do Espírito Santo (I Cor. 6:13; 12:13). d. O corpo físico é o veículo da alma, fazendo-nos lembrar nosso futuro *corpo espiritual*, — que aguarda por nós nas dimensões celestiais (Fil. 3:21). e. O corpo torna-se instrumento fácil do pecado, pelo que é chamado de «corpo do pecado» e de «corpo desta morte» (Rom. 6:6; 7:24). f. As leis e ordenanças do Antigo Testamento eram meras sombras de realidades que se cumpriram em Cristo. A *totalidade* dessas coisas a serem concretizadas forma um *corpo*, que pertence a Cristo (Col. 2:17). g. O «corpo de Cristo», referido em Romanos 7:4, alude à nossa identificação com a morte de Cristo (seu corpo foi morto) o que nos torna mortos para a lei e vivos para o Espírito, a fim de podermos produzir fruto para a glória e louvor de Deus. (B UN NTI)

CORPO DE CRISTO

Expressão metafórica que aponta para a Igreja como parte integrante de Cristo, assim como um corpo e a cabeça compõem uma única entidade. Há quatro particularidades que precisamos considerar:

1. Essa expressão é aplicada exclusivamente à Igreja (I Cor. 12:13; Rom. 12:3 ss; Efé. 1:23). Ver o uso metafórico do corpo físico, no artigo sobre o *Corpo*.

2. A totalidade dessas coisas haverá de ser concretizada em Cristo, coisas essas que são apenas apresentadas simbolicamente no Antigo Testamento (Col. 2:17).

3. A expressão «corpo de Cristo» também aponta para a nossa identificação na morte de Cristo, mediante a qual passamos a viver uma vida impulsionada e inspirada pelo Espírito, como mortos para a lei e vivos para o Espírito (Rom. 7:4).

4. Quanto à controvérsia envolvida no «corpo de Cristo», como algo associado à Eucaristia, ver o artigo sobre a *Transubstanciação*.

5. *Princípios e Observações*

Rom. 12:5: *assim nós, embora muitos, somos um só corpo em Cristo, e individualmente membros uns dos outros*.

Estão ilustrados aqui os seguintes princípios básicos:

1. Existem muitos membros, o que importa em multiplicidade. Cada um deles exerce a sua respectiva função; e cada uma dessas funções é importante para a vida coletiva da igreja, onde nenhum membro individual funciona com exclusividade. Por conseguinte, há uma importância decisiva em cada um, embora tal importância não deva ser exagerada; pois o exagero da importância individual é uma falsidade, inclinando os indivíduos ao orgulho pessoal. Nenhum membro de igreja tem o direito de mostrar-se orgulhoso, porquanto depende de todos os outros para a sua própria existência.

2. Considerados juntamente, todos os membros de uma igreja constituem uma *unidade*, unidade essa em torno da pessoa de Cristo. Aqueles que estão verdadeiramente vinculados em tal unidade, dificilmente podem mostrar-se espiritualmente altivos, porquanto o orgulho da unidade consiste na combinação de todos, tendo como centro o Senhor Jesus Cristo, que é o «cabeça» do corpo, ou, conforme outras considerações, que é a «alma» da igreja. Conforme qualquer desses pontos de vista, a igreja é o seu corpo ou veículo de ação; mas o próprio Cristo é a vida e a glória reais do organismo espiritual.

3. Cada crente individual é *membro dos outros*. Cada qual está vinculado aos demais na condição de membro. Isso porque possuem uma «vida comum», um propósito comum e todos eles juntamente, embora representem muitas funções, têm uma função em comum. Cada membro precisa de todos os outros membros. Cada qual é indispensável para os demais; e os outros, por sua vez, são indispensáveis para cada qual. A expressão usada para indicar isso, neste texto, é uma expressão idiomática, segundo o grego posterior. (Com isso se pode comparar Mar. 13:19; João 8:9; III Macabeus 5:34; Luciano, *Coloecists* 9, Eusébio, História *Eclesiástica* X, iv.

CORPO DE CRISTO — CORPO, ISTO É MEU

4. Existe uma unidade essencial, mas não da espécie em que a individualidade, a importância do crente individual, se perde. Essa individualidade é perfeitamente preservada, mas não às expensas dos outros crentes individuais, e certamente não às expensas da unidade do corpo. Aquele que enfatiza a sua importância de maneira exagerada, destrói tanto a «unidade» como a «importância» do organismo inteiro. Nesse caso, não está agindo como autêntico líder espiritual no corpo, mas ter-se-á tornado uma força destruidora, que enferma e debilita o corpo.

5. O vocábulo aqui traduzido por «corpo» expressa uma «vida», isto é, a vida em Cristo. Por conseguinte, não existem membros autênticos que não tenham sido regenerados pelo Espírito Santo. Portanto, «corpo» não é equivalente aqui à *igreja visível*, e, sim, ao corpo místico de Cristo, composto daqueles que são conhecidos por Cristo, que têm experimentado algum contacto com o Espírito de Deus, naquilo que, afinal de contas, consiste em um processo místico. É por essa razão que podemos falar sobre o *corpo místico* de Cristo, composto daquele agrupamento de pessoas e indivíduos que formam uma unidade orgânica, por possuírem a vida eterna, no Espírito Santo e através dele. A principal característica desse «corpo místico» é que cada um dos seus membros tem amor pelos demais, agindo de acordo com esse amor. Porém, onde esse afeto se faz ausente, pode-se duvidar com toda razão se os indivíduos culpados realmente fazem parte do corpo místico de Cristo. (Ver Efé. 4:25 e 5:25-33).

6. O valor de cada membro é retido, mas somente até onde ele está relacionado aos outros membros, porque todos são valiosos, em vista de formarem o corpo místico de Cristo. Nenhum membro, isoladamente considerado, pode representar o corpo de Cristo, motivo também pelo qual nenhum deles tem o direito de tentar destacar-se acima dos demais, preocupando-se com sua própria promoção e importância. Porque, se assim fizer, menos se preocupará com Cristo e com a exaltação de sua pessoa, no corpo místico e através do mesmo.

«A cabeça é o centro vital orgânico do todo, em que cada coisa é considerada como relativa ao domínio e à glória da mesma, segundo vemos em Efé. 1:22». (Lange, em Rom. 12:5).

A expressão «...*em Cristo*...» é uma expressão mística tipicamente paulina, que indica a comunhão do crente individual com Cristo, através do Espírito de Deus. Essa comunhão é um fator *unificador* e *edificante*, bem como um fator transmissor de vida. O corpo inteiro tem sua vida e importância «em Cristo». (HANS NTI Z)

CORPO ESPIRITUAL

Ver completos detalhes sobre esse corpo no artigo sobre a *Ressurreição*, no seu sétimo item.

CORPO, ISTO É MEU

Esta é uma declaração importante de Cristo. Ver o artigo sobre *Jesus como o Pão da Vida*.

Mat. 26:26: *Enquanto comiam, Jesus tomou pão e, abençoando-o, o partiu e o deu aos discípulos, dizendo: Tomai, comei; isto é o meu corpo.*

Tomou Jesus um pão...isto é o meu corpo. Quanto a notas no NTí que abordam a importância e a natureza geral desse rito da ceia do Senhor, ver I Cor. 11:23. Os paralelos desta secção são Mar. 14:22-25; Luc. 22:17-20; I Cor. 11:23-25. A base é o «protomarcos». Esses versículos em Mateus seguem bem de perto a narrativa de Marcos, onde se vê que primeiramente foi partido o pão e depois foi distribuído o cálice. Essa é também a ordem que se lê em I Cor. 11:23-25, como também a de Justino, em sua *Apologia* LXVI.3. Porém, no evangelho de Lucas, no **Codex Bezae (designado D)**, além de alguns mss latinos antigos, há uma omissão de Luc. 22:19b-20, de modo que há apenas uma menção do cálice, e este precede o partir do pão, conforme se faz nas modernas orações judaicas do *Kiddush*. Por conseguinte, pode haver certa confusão na ordem desses dois acontecimentos; embora saibamos, pela narrativa do evangelho de Marcos, que é antiquíssimo, que esta pode ser reconciliada com os costumes da páscoa e com os costumes da «habburah», segundo sabemos que eram observados.

Abençoando-o. Era próprio do pai ou hospedeiro essa ação, em qualquer refeição judaica, incluindo as refeições das festividades importantes, como a da páscoa. A fórmula usual era: «Bendito és tu, ó Senhor, nosso Deus, rei do mundo, que produzes pão da terra». A adição foi feita pelo Senhor Jesus, com as palavras: «Este é meu corpo», palavras essas que têm provocado intenso debate e especulação doutrinária. Em geral, pode-se falar sobre três teorias:

1. Simbolismo. 2. Transubstanciação. 3. Consubstanciação.

Segundo a primeira interpretação (que é a posição da maioria das igrejas protestantes), quando Jesus proferiu essas palavras, *Este é o meu corpo*, quis que elas fossem aceitas figuradamente. Foram palavras simbólicas. Poderiam ser parafraseadas como: «Este cálice representa o novo pacto que será selado pelo meu sangue, o qual será derramado por vós». Uma paráfrase similar poderia ser feita com relação ao pão. Assim como comemos o pão e somos nutridos por ele, assim também a morte de Cristo não foi uma perda trágica, mas, realmente, visou o nosso benefício. Cristo é o *pão espiritual*. A idéia de que até mesmo a morte de um mártir tem valor para a salvação de Israel não era uma idéia nova; e Jesus aprofundou a significação disso com uma alusão à «expiação» operada pela sua morte, juntamente com os benefícios universais que dali procederam. Este texto é a melhor prova de que Jesus concebia a sua morte como um ato de expiação, sendo diretamente contrário à teologia moderna, a qual nega que Jesus tenha compreendido a sua morte sob esse prisma, —e que essa explicação dos evangelhos foi fornecida pela igreja, sem base alguma nas palavras mesmas de Jesus. Àqueles que argúem uma interpretação literal, — ainda que tal coisa fosse exigida, poder-se-ia mostrar que os símbolos são apresentados em linguagem não menos literária do que qualquer outra apresentação lingüística sobre qualquer outra coisa. Deve-se acrescentar aqui que a própria linguagem não pode ser forçada para que requeira um sentido simbólico ou um sentido literal. O que cremos sobre esse ponto será como dogma, preferência emotiva ou razão pessoal. Isso fica provado como verídico pelo simples fato de que no seio da própria igreja têm surgido tantos pontos de vista diferentes sobre esse texto; e no entanto, todos lêem e interpretam o mesmo texto.

Conforme a interpretação da *transubstanciação* (que vide) acreditam alguns que está em foco a «essência» ou *substância* do pão e do vinho, que seria alterada sem que os «acidentes» do pão e do vinho se modificassem. Por *acidentes* os seus defensores dizem tratar-se das características como peso, cor, gosto, extensão, ou mesmo a estrutura dos átomos

CORPO, ISTO É MEU

envolvidos. Em suma, não haveria necessidade de modificação material de qualquer espécie; e se houvesse um exame científico do pão e do vinho, antes e depois, não haveria qualquer mudança nas propriedades físicas dos mesmos. Todavia, dizem seus defensores, que isso não significa que a «substância» metafísica dos elementos não se tenha alterado. Outrossim, é mister que se compreenda o que Aristóteles quis ensinar pela palavra «substância», a fim de entender essa doutrina, posto que, de forma geral, as idéias de Aristóteles sobre a «substância» têm sido usadas para explicar a doutrina. A palavra «substância» vem dos termos latinos «sub» e «stare», «estar por baixo». A substância do pão e do vinho pode alterar-se, sem que sejam modificados os seus «acidentes». Aquele elemento místico ou metafísico que não está sujeito à percepção dos sentidos humanos, pode alterar-se e não ser descoberto por qualquer teste científico. Assim sendo, a substância do corpo e do sangue de Cristo entraria no pão e no vinho, substância essa que não está passível de qualquer verificação científica; porém, mediante um processo místico, transforma-se num elemento real, o elemento básico, do pão e do vinho. Posto não haver maneira de verificar tal «substância», tanto a sua existência como a sua descrição ficam reduzidas ao dogma. Sua aceitação fica dependendo do treinamento religioso e do doutrinamento. No que diz respeito à doutrina, visto ter sido um desenvolvimento posterior, definido em termos das idéias aristotélicas sobre «substância», idéias essas inteiramente estranhas ao pensamento da teologia do V.T., concluímos que tal doutrina não passa de uma invenção, muito engenhosa (com base no engenho especulativo de Aristóteles), mas sem qualquer fundamento nas simples palavras de Deus.

A terceira idéia, chamada de **consubstanciação** (que vide), foi inventada por Lutero, — que desejava preservar a idéia da «presença» de Cristo nos elementos da ceia, ainda que não quisesse identificar esses elementos com o corpo e o sangue de Cristo. De acordo com essa opinião, os elementos permanecem inalteráveis, a substância não se altera, mas, mediante um processo místico, a *presença* do corpo e do sangue de Cristo faz-se presente, ainda que não identificada com os elementos do pão e do vinho. Poderíamos dizer que assim é criado um «dualismo»: duas substâncias, a do pão e a do vinho, mas também do corpo e do sangue de Cristo. A substância de Cristo estaria «em, ao redor e sob» a outra substância. Essa explicação leva-nos a crer que há uma espécie de «mistura de ambas as substâncias em uma só massa». (Ver Hooker's *Eccl. Polity*). Alguns têm rejeitado essa noção à base de que ela parece criar uma onipresença do corpo e do sangue de Cristo, o que, sem dúvida, é uma doutrina monstruosa. Entretanto, em conceitos teológicos, ou filosóficos mais refinados, especialmente por novamente seguir algumas idéias de Aristóteles sobre «substância», seríamos obrigados a pensar no corpo e no sangue de Cristo como se tivessem alguma propriedade de onipresença. A maioria dos luteranos tem abandonado esse conceito, ou porque o mesmo é ambíguo ou porque simplesmente não possuímos, qualquer informação sólida sobre aqueles tipos de «substâncias» que não estão sujeitos à percepção de nossos sentidos. Simplesmente não temos meios para definir tais «substâncias», e nem podemos afirmar a sua existência salvo por dogma, revelação ou raciocínio. Assim, a mesma crítica levantada contra a transubstanciação pode ser levantada contra a consubstanciação. Não é provável que Jesus tivesse esses pensamentos na mente quando declarou: «Este é o meu corpo».

Apesar de não falarmos de qualquer transferência de substância, e nem de qualquer permanência literal do corpo e do sangue de Cristo, nos elementos da ceia, contudo, à base de outras verdades, certamente podemos pregar a *presença* de Cristo, em sentido literal, como parte integral da cena da ceia do Senhor. Jesus prometeu que onde dois ou três se reunissem em seu nome, ali estaria ele no meio deles. Isso aceitamos—literalmente, pelo que dizemos que o desfrutamento dos benefícios da presença de Cristo é uma realidade. Quando da «ceia», ele vem estar presente conosco, embora isso não signifique, de forma alguma, que ele tenha entrado nos elementos do pão e do vinho, ou que seja ingerido nesses elementos, como muitos afirmam. Pelo contrário, ele interpenetra em nossas personalidades mediante a radiação de sua energia. Bruce (*in loc.*) refere-se ao simbolismo dessa passagem como «um belo, simples, patético e poético símbolo de sua morte», rejeitando aquilo que ele apoda de *adoração fetichista*.

Devemos notar outras idéias importantes que circundam este texto:

1. Jesus tencionou instituir uma *refeição memorial*, um rito para sua futura igreja. Paulo indica isso no paralelo a esta passagem, em I Cor. 11. Jesus vai além de qualquer simbolismo geralmente compreendido na páscoa. Ele mesmo tornou-se a páscoa cristã, com todas as suas implicações da expiação. (Ver o artigo sobre a *Expiação*).

2. A compreensão dos benefícios dessa *páscoa* pode ser indicada na multiplicação dos pães para os cinco mil. Jesus é o pão espiritual, que sustenta toda a vida espiritual. Eventualmente, todos os crentes legítimos compartilharão, de modo perfeito, de sua essência e de sua natureza, através da transformação gradual na pessoa dele. Essa é a mensagem mais elevada do evangelho. Ver notas completas sobre este tema, João 6:48 no NTI.

3. Os pormenores secundários do acontecimento, tais como quando a ceia foi instituída em relação ao processo inteiro da festa pascal, são impossíveis de serem determinados com precisão. Lucas menciona a ceia antes do anúncio da traição de Judas, ao passo que Mateus e Marcos fazem-no depois. Alguns acreditam que Jesus distribuiu dois cálices (assim pensava Alford), mas outros aceitam um único cálice. Um cálice pode ter sido passado antes da ceia, e outro depois. O meter a mão no prato e a distribuição do bocado molhado, também podem ter correspondido a certas partes do cerimonial judaico. Por conseguinte, nossa moderna observação desse rito é certamente uma observância muito simplificada. Não obstante, o sentido é o mesmo, e os símbolos permanecem constantes.

4. Pelo menos temos aqui uma *alusão* ao fato de que o Cristo é o criador e o sustentador de toda a vida espiritual, e que a humanidade inteira depende dele para ter vida. Isso, naturalmente, é ensinado com clareza na passagem de Col. 1:16. Para o crente, entretanto, ele é ainda mais do que o doador e o sustentador da vida, pois a sua vida, no crente, finalmente, será compartilhada no sentido mais pleno possível. O que temos aqui, por conseguinte, é o ensinamento do sentido central do próprio cristianismo, que proclama a vida através da personalidade, da obra e da agência de Cristo. Ele é o primogênito, e nós os muitos filhos que estão sendo conduzidos à glória. Ele é tudo; nós somos a sua plenitude, de acordo com o que ensina Ef. 1:23. Essa doutrina da ceia do Senhor é mística e elevada; e no entanto, deve ser

aceita em seu sentido mais literal. De que maneira ele infunde nossos próprios seres e nos vai transformando à sua imagem, não sabemos; mas nossa ignorância acerca desse processo não diminui a realidade.

MUITOS debates têm surgido em torno da palavra «é» (no grego, *estin*), que aparece neste texto. Alguns acreditam (como os católicos romanos e Lutero, ainda que um tanto diferentemente) que o termo requer a aceitação da presença real da «essência» ou «substância». Zwínglio: que o vocábulo deve ser entendido em sentido *exclusivamente espiritual*. Calvino declarou tratar-se de uma maneira «concreta real-espiritual». Com isso ele queria dizer que se trata de uma presença espiritual nos termos que temos explicado no parágrafo anterior, mas não em quaisquer termos de troca ou infusão de «substâncias». Seria perda de tempo entrar nas longas discussões que têm anuviado muitas páginas de literatura, com tão ínfimos resultados, discussões em torno da simples palavra «é», e que vários intérpretes têm acompanhado através das páginas do N.T., a fim de ilustrar suas idéias. Basta dizer que se pode fazer com que essa palavra diga qualquer coisa que se tenha querido dizer predeterminadamente. A palavra «é» pode ser uma simples cópula, sem qualquer intenção de indicar qualquer comunicação ou transferência de «substância» ou «essência», de um sujeito para um predicado ou pronome. Contudo, pode implicar em mais do que uma mera relação gramatical; razão pela qual permanece de pé a ambigüidade. O exame da linguagem usada aqui jamais produzirá um resultado positivo, e é surpreendente ver um número tão grande de bons intérpretes entrarem nessa controvérsia. A explicação lógica sobre as crenças de alguém acerca deste texto não pode depender da linguagem do mesmo, quanto menos da simples palavra «é». Pelo contrário, convém que interpretemos mediante a consideração do que Jesus mui provavelmente quis dizer, conservando em mente o seu conceito judaico básico em segundo plano. Portanto, parece mais acertado rejeitar aquelas interpretações que dependem do engenho *filosófico de Aristóteles* sobre a teoria da «substância», pois essa filosofia não serviu de base para as palavras de Jesus, embora ela sirva de alicerce das teorias da *transubstanciação* e da *consubstanciação*. Não é provável que Jesus tivesse cultivado tais idéias, e o sexto capítulo do evangelho de João (cujo texto tem idéias paralelas às que aparecem aqui) pode ser facilmente interpretado como uma referência simbólica à vida espiritual e como essa vida nos vem inteiramente por meio de Cristo: mediante a participação nos benefícios de sua expiação e de sua própria vida e ser, mediante a graça que ele providenciou em sua ressurreição, ascensão e glorificação.

CORPORAL

Esse é o pano sobre o qual repousam os vasos usados na eucaristia; e, segundo o cerimonial da Igreja Católica Romana, a própria hóstia (que vide), até imediatamente antes da comunhão. Originalmente, essa peça de pano cobria o altar inteiro; mas, atualmente, tem apenas cerca de trinta centímetros em quadrado. O vocábulo vem do latim, *corpus*, *corpo*, porque, por meio da doutrina da transubstanciação, o corpo de Cristo viria repousar sôbre esse pedaço de pano.

CORPOS TERRESTRES E CELESTES

No grego, **sómata egigeia**. A expressão ocorre somente em I Coríntios 15:40, onde o apóstolo Paulo faz o contraste entre corpos terrestres e corpos celestes. Os estudiosos hesitam entre as opiniões se com a expressão «corpos celestes» Paulo aludia aos astros, como o sol, a lua e as estrelas, ou se ele dava a entender seres angelicais. Por outra parte, não há que duvidar que, ao empregar a expressão «corpos terrestres», o apóstolo indicava os corpos vivos que existem à face de nosso planeta. Paulo estava arquitetando um argumento a fim de lembrar que, assim como existem vários tipos de corpos, tanto na terra como nas dimensões celestiais, assim também não nos devemos admirar que, nossos futuros corpos ressurrectos terão seu caráter todo próprio.

Os corpos terrestres correspondem ao «corpo natural», o qual é contrastado ao «corpo espiritual» (I Cor. 15:44). O corpo terrestre ou natural segue o seu protótipo ou modelo, Adão; e o corpo celestial será moldado segundo o seu protótipo ou modelo, Cristo (I Cor. 15:48). Paulo chega ao clímax de seu argumento quando diz que, no caso dos remidos, a certeza da ressurreição do corpo é garantida pelo precedente que já trazemos «a imagem do que é terreno», o que significa que também traremos «a imagem do celestial» (I Cor. 15:49).

CORPUS CHRISTI

Expressão latina que significa «corpo de Cristo». É o nome de uma festividade religiosa da Igreja ocidental, celebrada na quinta feira após o domingo da Trindade, em honra à eucaristia, e em comemoração à instituição da Ceia. Essa celebração teve suas origens nas visões de Juliana de Liege, na primeira metade do século XIII. Foi oficialmente estabelecida pelo papa Urbano IV, em 1264. Sua observância tornou-se universal na Igreja ocidental. O ofício e a missa dessa festividade foram compostos por Tomás de Aquino, embora alguns historiadores duvidem dessa autoria. Ali estão contidos alguns hinos notáveis. A característica mais espetacular dessa festividade é a solene procissão da Hóstia Consagrada. Algumas igrejas ortodoxas e anglicanas também observam essa festividade. (AM C E)

CORPUS HERMETICUM

Uma coletânea de escritos neoplatônicos, de natureza astrológica e alquímica, atribuída à divindade egípcia equivalente ao deus grego, Hermes, o que explica o título dessa coletânea. Através dessas obras, o hermetismo foi promovido nos períodos de dominação grega e romana. Ver o artigo sobre *Escrituras Herméticas*.

CORREÇÃO

No hebraico temos duas palavras, e, no grego, duas, a saber:

1. *Yakach*, «raciocinar com», «reprovar», usada por cinqüenta e seis vezes com esse sentido. Por exemplo: Jó 5:17; Sal. 94:10; Pro. 3:12.

2. *Yasar*, «instruir», «castigar». Palavra usada por quarenta e duas vezes (por exemplo: Sal. 39:11; Pro. 29:17; Jer. 2:19; 10:24; 30:11; 46:28).

3. *Epanórthosis*, «retificar». Palavra grega usada apenas em II Tim. 3:16.

4. *Paideúo*, «corrigir a criança». Palavra grega usada por treze vezes: Luc. 23:16,22; Atos 7:22; 22:3; I Cor. 11:32; II Cor. 6:9; I Tim. 1:20; II Tim. 2:25; Tito 2:12; Heb. 12:6 (citando Pro. 3:11); Heb. 12:7,10; Apo. 3:19.

Corrigir é disciplinar tendo em vista a melhoria da

conduta, não sendo apenas retribuição por algum erro praticado. A palavra grega *paideúo*, que significa «correção de crianças», mostra o caráter da correção que Deus confere aos seus filhos. O trecho de I Pedro 4:6 mostra que até mesmo o julgamento no hades tem por finalidade uma função disciplinar e corretiva, não sendo apenas retributivo. Esse versículo é muito ousado, porquanto afirma que a vida espiritual pode passar por tal experiência, um conceito essencialmente perdido pela Igreja ocidental, embora preservado na Igreja oriental. A passagem de Hebreus 12:7,8 mostra-nos que Deus castiga os seus filhos para o bem deles, tal como o faz qualquer pai decente. A Igreja inteira aprova esse princípio, mas certos segmentos da mesma recusam-se a ver esse aspecto na *própria natureza* do julgamento divino, visto que esse é um ato do amor de Deus, mudando condições que, de outra maneira, não poderiam ser mudadas. É muito difícil os homens aprenderem essa grande verdade: o oposto da injustiça não é a justiça, mas o amor.

As autoridades que executam criminosos, e que sabem o que estão fazendo, acreditam que os criminosos executados de algum modo são beneficiados pela morte que sofrem, porquanto isso é uma maneira de compensar por seus erros. Não é incomum, entre os prisioneiros que esperam pela execução, suporem que a morte que sofrerão, quando merecida, pode ser benéfica para suas almas, não apenas uma dívida que têm de pagar diante da sociedade humana. Isso mostra um grande discernimento quanto à natureza até mesmo das mais severas formas de punição. Orígenes afirmava que ver no julgamento apenas o aspecto retributivo é defender uma teologia inferior. De fato, o Senhor *corrige* àqueles a quem *ama*. Todas as formas de castigo divino alicerçam-se sobre o amor de Deus. O juízo é um dedo da mão amorosa de Deus.

No Antigo Testamento, correção e juízo são meios de treinamento do caráter. Mostram que um Pai amoroso está cuidando de seus filhos (Deu. 11:2; Sal. 50:17; Jer. 17:23, 32:33). A sabedoria divina está por detrás dessa questão (Pro. 1:2; 3:7; 15:33; 23:23). As Escrituras nos ajudam como um meio de correção, de repreensão e de instrução, a fim de que sejamos ricos em boas obras (II Tim. 3:16,17). Um versículo significativo é o de Romanos 11:32, embora com raridade ouçamo-lo ser citado. «Porque Deus a todos encerrou na desobediência, a fim de usar de misericórdia para com todos». Deus tem feito os homens terminarem em miséria íntima, por causa de seus atos de desobediência, como medida disciplinadora, tendo em vista o alvo final do Senhor, que é usar de sua *misericórdia*, em última análise. Essa é a única maneira pela qual o homem pode chegar a qualquer lugar, dentro da criação de Deus. Notemos, no texto que acabamos de citar, que foi exatamente esse princípio que fez o apóstolo Paulo maravilhar-se da *sabedoria* de Deus. Quando, finalmente, entendemos o grande princípio de que todas as coisas procedem de Deus, a fim de que tudo venha a retornar a ele, então estamos preparados a entender essas questões que envolvem a correção aplicada por Deus a todos os homens. Diz Romanos 11:36: «Porque dele e por meio dele e para ele são todas as cousas. A ele, pois, a glória eternamente. Amém». Isso exprime o princípio do ato restaurador de Deus, conforme vemos em Efésios 1:10, e que envolverá, finalmente, a criação inteira. Ver o artigo sobre a *Restauração*.

Fica bem claro, portanto, o princípio da correção. Todos os atos instrutivos e corretivos de Deus, têm em mira o bem-estar do homem. Isso aplica-se tanto ao crente quanto ao incrédulo. E nenhum ato de Deus ficará sem efeito, finalmente. É precisamente isso que poderíamos esperar da parte do amor de Deus, porquanto Deus é amor. Ver I João 4:16. Contudo, isso não faz os atos de julgamento e de disciplina, impostos por Deus, tornarem-se menos sérios. É coisa muito séria alguém ter de servir um longo tempo de prisão, mesmo que, em alguma data futura, o condenado venha a ser libertado, considerando-se que, então, a dívida do criminoso, diante da sociedade, terá sido saldada. É coisa muito séria uma pessoa perder anos preciosos de vida, encarcerado, por causa de seus erros, ao passo que ele poderia ter usado aqueles anos para beneficiar a si mesmo e aos seus semelhantes, como filhos, parentes, amigos, e muitos outros. É coisa muito séria um homem desperdiçar sua vida desse modo, chegando à sepultura como um fracassado. — Também é coisa muito séria uma alma ultrapassar a morte biológica em estado de perdição, mesmo que, em algum ponto distante, o amor de Deus venha a corrigir tal situação. Podemos estar certos de que Deus nunca se apressa, embora alguns sistemas teológicos nos dêem essa impressão. Portanto, que o julgamento divino realize a sua obra. Que a instrução divina tenha os seus efeitos. Porém, se nos olvidarmos dos princípios da misericórdia e do amor divinos, dentro desse imenso quadro, quem poderia ser salvo? O que estou procurando dizer aqui, meus amigos, é que os princípios do juízo divino, de sua disciplina e do seu amor ocupam o *primeiro* lugar, no caso de todos os homens, crentes ou incrédulos. E, em *segundo* lugar, esses princípios são combinados em um único ato, com uma única motivação. Não podemos dividir Deus em pedaços, para então dizer: «Agora Deus está amando»; ou então: «Agora Deus está irado». Mesmo quando Deus manifesta mais intensamente a sua ira, ele continua amando. E isso é assim porque a sua ira é uma forma de amar, por causa daquilo que Deus tenciona fazer através de sua ira.

CORREIAS

No grego, **imás**, «correia». O termo grego aparece por quatro vezes: Mar. 1:7; Luc. 3:16; João 1:27; Atos 22:25.

As correias eram estreitas tiras de couro, usadas para segurar, amarrar, etc., alguma coisa, como, por exemplo, as sandálias. Esse é o caso de Mar. 1:7; Luc. 3:16 e João 1:27, onde João Batista refere-se às sandálias usadas pelo Senhor Jesus. Na referência do livro de Atos, a alusão é às correias com que o apóstolo Paulo estava sendo amarrado, para ser submetido à inquirição por meio de açoites, um ato ilegal porque Paulo era cidadão romano, descobrindo isso, o comandante mandou desatá-lo imediatamente.

No Antigo Testamento, precisamos considerar duas passagens correlatas, a saber: Jeremias 27:2, onde aparece o termo hebraico *moser*, que nossa versão portuguesa traduz por «brochas». Esse mesmo vocábulo aparece também em Jer. 5:5; 30:8; Sal. 11:16 e Naum 1:13, com variegadas traduções. No hebraico, devemos pensar em qualquer tipo de ligadura, de correias. Isaías 58:6, onde figura a palavra hebraica *aguddah*, «pacote», e onde o termo é usado figuradamente para indicar a carga dos impostos com que os pobres estavam sendo oprimidos em Israel. Nossa versão portuguesa traduz ali essa palavra por «ataduras», dentro da expressão «ataduras da servidão». O termo hebraico também aparece em Êxo. 12:22, onde se lê: «Tomai um molho de hissopo...», e onde «molho» é a palavra portuguesa correspondente.

CORRENTE DE CONSCIÊNCIA
Ver **Riacho da Consciência**.

CORRESPONDÊNCIA, DOUTRINA DA
Emanuel Swedenborg (que vide) aceitava, como chave para a interpretação da Bíblia e de outro material espiritual escrito, a doutrina de que todos os termos usados têm um triplo sentido: natural, espiritual e divino. Esse ponto de vista pode ser comparado ao modo *alegórico* de interpretação. Ver o artigo sobre a *Interpretação Alegórica*.

CORRESPONDÊNCIA, TEORIA DA VERDADE DA
Nesta enciclopédia, oferecemos um artigo sobre o assunto o *Conhecimento e a Fé Religiosa*. A segunda parte daquele artigo apresenta um estudo pormenorizado sobre as *Teorias da Verdade*, dentre as quais a teoria da correspondência figura. Em termos bem latos, essa teoria propõe que a verdade corresponde à realidade, e que as declarações a respeito devem exibir essa correspondência, para que sejam verazes. A linguagem é um veículo para expressão da verdade, quando suas afirmativas correspondem à verdade, e isso pode ser determinado por via da investigação. Portanto, o *empirismo* (que vide), de modo geral pode ser identificado com a correspondência, tal como a coerência, como uma teoria da verdade, é identificada com o racionalismo. A validade da correspondência sugerida precisa ser estabelecida pela experimentação, a qual repousa essencialmente, embora não de forma absoluta, sobre a percepção dos cinco sentidos físicos. Isso posto, a correspondência envolve a seguinte fórmula: declarações verazes sobre verdades verificáveis através da experimentação. A falsidade consiste na não-correspondência. Todas as teorias da verdade são parciais, pelo que essa teoria da correspondência também é falha, porquanto ignora as potencialidades representadas pela razão, pela intuição e pelo misticismo, capazes de ajudar-nos a tomar conhecimento dessas coisas, além e acima das correspondências que estabelecemos tão nitidamente. As próprias ciências físicas dificilmente poderiam suster-se de pé, ante a aplicação dessa teoria. (EP MM P)

CORRIDA
Ver **Jogos**.

CORRUPÇÃO
A apresentação bíblica desse assunto é ampla, incluindo as seguintes categorias: 1. A decadência do corpo, que é a corrupção física (Sal. 16:10). 2. Os defeitos em algum animal, que o tornavam impróprio para ser sacrificado, que é a corrupção cerimonial (Lev. 22:25). 3. A ruína moral causada pelo pecado, que é a corrupção moral (Deu. 9:12). 4. A ruína eterna, que é a corrupção escatológica (Gál. 6:18). Existe a «cova da corrupção», que talvez envolva a mesma idéia (Isa. 38:17; Sal. 30:9).

Todas as formas de corrupção estão envolvidas na nossa natureza moral, segundo Paulo ensina em I Coríntios 15:53. O próprio homem, no seu estado atual, é ali chamado de «este corpo corruptível», sendo precisamente esse o homem que terá de revestir-se da «incorruptibilidade», como cura total para a sua corrupção (vs. 54). E então tornar-se-á verdadeira a declaração que prediz: «Tragada foi a morte pela vitória. Onde está, ó morte, a tua vitória? Onde está, ó morte, o teu aguilhão? O aguilhão da morte é o pecado, e a força do pecado é a lei. Graças a Deus que nos dá a vitória por intermédio de nosso Senhor Jesus Cristo» (I Cor. 15:54-57). É por essa razão que podemos ser firmes na fé, sempre abundantes nas boas obras, sabendo que nossos esforços não são vãos. Em outras palavras, todo labor honesto e espiritual tem uma dimensão eterna.

No Novo Testamento, encontramos as palavras gregas *phthora* e *diaphthora*, ambas traduzidas por «corrupção». — A primeira delas aparece por nove vezes: denotando a decadência do corpo físico (I Cor. 15:42,50); denotando a decadência do universo físico (Rom. 8:21; Col. 2:22; II Ped. 2:2); denotando a decadência moral e religiosa (II Ped. 1:4; 2:9); denotando as destruições escatológicas (Gál. 6:8); e, estabelecendo contraste com a vida eterna (II Ped. 2:12).

CORRUPÇÃO, MONTE DA
Um outro nome desse monte é Monte da Abominação. A forma latina é *mons scandali*. A alusão é ao cume mais ao sul da terra que é conhecida como monte das Oliveiras, onde Salomão erigiu um altar para as observâncias religiosas de suas esposas pagãs (I Reis 11:7; II Reis 23:13). Esta última referência informa-nos que o rei Josias destruiu todas as construções ali existentes, por ocasião de suas reformas.

CORTANDO O NÓ GORDIANO
Górdio foi um antigo rei da Frígia que fez um nó, que, segundo um oráculo, podia ser desfeito somente pelo homem que governaria a Ásia. Ninguém foi capaz de desfazer o nó. Alexandre, o Grande, tentou mas falhou. Em consternação, ele cortou o nó com sua espada. A expressão, «cortar o nó gordiano» passou a significar, «resolver um problema por métodos falsos ou insatisfatórios». Na interpretação, seja teológica, filosófica, etc., a expressão significa o ato de dar um explicação que resolve *aparentemente* um problema, mas que, de fato, é deficiente.

CORTAR, GOLPEAR
Várias palavras hebraicas e gregas estão envolvidas no ato de *cortar*, verbos usados em sentido literal ou figurado nas Escrituras, a saber:

1. *Natach*, «cortar em pedaços». Palavra usada por dez vezes (por exemplo: Êxo. 29:17; Lev. 1:6,12; 8:20; Juí. 20:6; I Reis 18:22,23).

2. *Qara*, «cortar». Palavra usada por sessenta e quatro vezes (por exemplo: Jer. 36:26; I Sam. 15:28; I Reis 11:11,12,13,30,31). Mas, na grande maioria das vezes, esse verbo significa «rasgar».

3. *Karath*, «cortar», «derrubar». Palavra usada por cerca de cento e vinte vezes. Por exemplo: Êxo. 4:25; Lev. 17:10; 20:3,5,6; I Sam. 17:51; 24:4,5; Isa. 9:14; Eze. 14:8,13,17,19; Mal. 2:2. Esses são os verbos hebraicos principais, mais usados; mas há uma multidão de outros.

4. *Katakópto*, «retalhar-se», «cortar-se todo». Palavra grega usada por somente uma vez, em Mar. 5:5.

5. *Dichotoméo*, «cortar em dois». Palavra grega usada por duas vezes: Mat. 24:51; Luc. 12:46.

6. *Aphairéo*, «arrancar», «cortar». Palavra grega empregada por dez vezes: Mat. 26:51; Mar. 14:47; Luc. 1:25; 10:42; 16:3; 22:50; Rom. 11:27 (citando

CORTES — CORTINA DO TEMPLO

Isa. 27:9); Heb. 10:4; Apo. 22:19.

7. *Ekkópto*, «cortar». Palavra grega usada por dez vezes: Mat. 3:10; 5:30; 7:19; 18:8; Luc. 3:9; 13:7,9; Rom. 11:22,24; II Cor. 11:12.

I. Literal

O povo de Israel foi estritamente proibido de mutilar-se, em imitação a povos pagãos circunvizinhos (Lev. 19:28; 21:5; Deu. 14:1). O paganismo primitivo sempre promoveu vários tipos de mutilação, que supostamente aplacava deuses sedentos de sangue, mas que, na realidade, eram apenas um reflexo da brutalidade humana, para com o próximo e para com o próprio indivíduo. Os ritos de mutilação até hoje existem ao redor do mundo. O temor ao desprazer dos deuses leva os homens a fazerem contra si mesmos aquilo que pensam que seus deuses fariam contra eles. Foi uma concepção distorcida da divindade que levava os profetas de Baal (I Reis 18:28) a se cortarem. E eles misturavam seu próprio sangue ao sangue dos seus holocaustos.

Os Sacrifícios e Outros Objetos. Os animais sacrificados eram cortados em pedaços (Lev. 1:6); as imagens dos cananeus eram derrubadas e cortadas em pedaços (Êxo. 34:13; Deu. 7:5); árvores eram cortadas por diversos motivos (II Reis 6:4); decepar parte do corpo de um inimigo era um dos maltratos geralmente infligidos aos adversários vencidos (Juí. 1:6), ou mesmo uma ação punitiva recomendada (Mar. 9:43).

Atos de Tristeza. Virgílio descreve a irmã de Dido a rasgar-se no rosto com as unhas e a bater nos seios com os punhos, quando em profunda tristeza. Esse tipo de ação era especificamente proibido em Israel (Lev. 19:28). Todavia, muitos israelitas acabaram fazendo coisas dessa natureza, quando sofriam grandes golpes (Jer. 48:37). De fato, de outra maneira, não teriam sido proibidos de fazê-lo.

II. Golpes Figurados

Uma tribo de Israel, desobediente ou apóstata, podia ser «cortada», ou seja, destruída ou punida de algum modo (Núm. 4:18). Quando Josué derrotou povos espalhados das margens do Jordão até o mar Mediterrâneo, é dito que ele os *cortou*. Israel foi advertido de que seria cortado de sua terra se persistisse na desobediência (I Reis 9:7). Povos idólatras foram cortados ou destruídos (Isa. 14:22; Miq. 5:10-13; Zac. 9:6). Certos atos de desobediência contra a lei mosaica atraíam severo julgamento divino, como no caso daqueles que ingeriam sangue (Lev. 17:10), ou participassem em sacrifícios de crianças (Lev. 20:3,5), ou se envolvessem em atos de bruxaria (Lev. 20:6). Todos os culpados desses pecados seriam *cortados* do meio do povo.

CORTES ECLESIÁSTICAS

As igrejas Católica Romana, Oriental Ortodoxa e Anglicana mantêm em funcionamento as cortes ou tribunais eclesiásticos. Nos tempos medievais, esses tribunais tinham considerável poder civil e religioso. Enquanto à Igreja coube tratar de casos de heresia, matrimônio e testamentos, outros envolvimentos criavam alguns problemas com os governos civis. Os clérigos que se envolvessem em crimes ou outras ações prejudiciais, eram julgados pelos tribunais eclesiásticos, que não se limitavam a questões religiosas. A história registra muitos choques violentos entre a Igreja e o Estado, por motivo da jurisdição dos tribunais. Alguns governos civis utilizaram-se desses conflitos para promover a causa do Estado, ou mesmo causas pessoais dos monarcas. Houve tremendos conflitos entre Henrique II e Thomas Becket, e também entre o imperador Henrique IV e o papa Gregório VII (que vide). Terminada a Reforma protestante, as cortes eclesiásticas inglesas tiveram uma importante atuação na política da família Tudor e na política dos primeiros reis da família Stuart. Isso dizia respeito à preservação da união entre a Igreja e o Estado, sob a supremacia do rei. Essa era, precisamente, uma das principais objeções dos puritanos. Mas, quando eles atingiram o poder, fizeram a mesma coisa. Embora o poder desses tribunais estivesse se desvanecendo, continuavam mantendo jurisdição sobre certas questões matrimoniais e testamentárias, além daquelas questões estritamente eclesiásticas. — Em alguns países católicos romanos, os tribunais eclesiásticos continuam tendo funções que, em outros países, são entregues aos tribunais civis, sobretudo nos campos das heranças, dos problemas domésticos e do matrimônio. Porém, em países como os Estados Unidos da América e o Brasil, os tribunais eclesiásticos ocupam-se exclusivamente das questões de natureza religiosa.

Como Funciona uma Corte Eclesiástica? O bispo exerce suas funções através de oficiais devidamente treinados. Diante de uma decisão de um tribunal eclesiástico, pode-se apelar ao tribunal do arcebispo, se aquela decisão não for considerada justa. O tribunal supremo da Igreja Católica Romana é o *Sacra Romana Rota* da Santa Sé. Porém, em casos extremos, até mesmo as decisões desse supremo tribunal podem ser anuladas, pela chamada *Signatura Apostólica*, através da autoridade do papa. A Rota consiste em dez ou doze juízes, que devem ser padres bem versados na lei canônica. Suas decisões são publicadas sob o título de *Sanctae Romanae Rotas Decisiones*. (AM E)

CORTESIA

Essa palavra portuguesa deriva-se de *corte*, dando a entender as boas maneiras e os atos de consideração que seriam de esperar no trato entre as pessoas que vivem ali. Mais especificamente, a cortesia, conforme a conhecemos na civilização ocidental, deriva-se de padrões de gentileza iniciados na corte provençal, no século XI D.C., por algumas poucas damas dali, que assim mostraram a etiqueta e a propriedade de um comportamento decente, para servir de exemplo aos cortesãos que as cercavam.

Os costumes antigos exigiam respeito pelos estrangeiros, e ajuda, quando disso necessitassem. Os costumes orientais não-cristãos contavam com modos de cortesia altamente ritualizados. Porém, foi na sociedade feudal, nas cortes européias, que se desenvolveram esses atos de cortesia. Isso incluía o sentimento de proteção dos cavaleiros (que vide), em favor das damas. Foi aí que se desenvolveu certo tipo de etiqueta polida, para fins sociais. Em nossos dias, todos os pequenos atos de cortesia que uma pessoa mostra em relação a outras, nas visitas, como trocas de presentes ou pequenos favores, são um reflexo desses costumes medievais.

Sentido Geral. A cortesia consiste em um comportamento polido, caracterizado pelas boas maneiras e por atos de gentileza. Se for genuína, é uma pequena demonstração da lei do amor (que vide).

CORTINA DO TEMPLO

Ver sobre o **Véu do Templo**.

CORTINAS

Três palavras hebraicas têm sido assim traduzidas, a saber:

1. *Doq*, «véu fino», palavra que figura somente em Isa. 40:22. Refere-se aos céus estrelados que Deus estende como se fosse uma cortina. Provavelmente, há uma alusão à tela fina que muitos orientais estendiam sob os tetos de suas residências de verão.

2. *Yeriah*, *cortina*, «véu». Essa palavra ocorre por cinqüenta e três vezes, como em Êxo. 26:1-13; 36:8-17; Núm. 4:25; II Sam. 7:2; I Crô. 17:1; Sal. 104:2; Isa. 54:2; Jer. 4:20; 49:29; Heb. 3:7. Essa palavra está ligada ao adjetivo «trêmulo». Aponta para as dez cortinas que cobriam o tabernáculo de Moisés (Êxo. 26:1-13; 36:8-17). Essa palavra veio a tornar-se sinônimo do próprio tabernáculo, por causa de suas muitas cortinas (II Sam. 7:2). Tal vocábulo também pode indicar as paredes laterais do tabernáculo.

3. *Masak*, «véu», usada por vinte e cinco vezes, como em Êxo. 26:36,37; 35:15; Núm. 3:26. Essa palavra também servia para denotar o portão do átrio, que conduzia ao tabernáculo (Êxo. 27:16).

As cortinas do tabernáculo eram feitas de linho fino e de pêlos de cabra. Eram penduradas em sessenta colunas de madeira de acácia, sobre bases de cobre, cada coluna tinha cerca de 2,5 *m* de distância uma da outra. As cortinas dos lados norte e sul tinham 2,5 *m* de largura por 50 m de comprimento, feitas de linho fino. No lado ocidental, as cortinas tinham 2,5 m de largura por 25 m de comprimento. No lado oriental, que era o da entrada, havia duas cortinas curtas, de 2,5 m de largura por 7,5 m de comprimento, penduradas em três colunas.

As cortinas eram um item importante na vida nômade dos povos orientais, substituindo paredes e portas. Porém, mesmo nas residências de alvenaria ou de pedra, as cortinas eram um item importante.

CORUJA

Seis palavras hebraicas têm sido assim traduzidas, nas traduções em vários idiomas. Porém, a confusão é tremenda quanto a essa espécie de ave. O antigo vocabulário dos hebreus, quanto a itens da flora e da fauna não tinha um caráter científico, conforme se faz hoje em dia. Portanto, consideremos estes pontos:

1. *Yanshuph*. Ver Lev. 11:17; Deu. 14:16; Isa. 34:11. Nossa versão portuguesa diz «íbis», nas duas primeiras referências, mas «bufo», na última delas. A Septuaginta diz «íbis». A Vulgata Latina diz «coruja». Poderia estar em foco a chamada coruja águia (*Bubo ascalaphus*). Essa ave é nativa da Palestina, e poderia ser a espécie aludida nessas três referências.

2. *Kos*. Ver Lev. 11:17; Deu. 14:16; Sal. 102:6. Nossa versão portuguesa diz «mocho» nas duas primeiras referências, mas «pelicano» na última. É provável que a espécie em foco seja, realmente, o «mocho», uma espécie um tanto menor que a coruja, cujo nome científico é *Athene glaux*. Os israelitas não podiam consumir o mocho. Era uma ave comum na Palestina, conforme continua a sê-lo até os nossos dias. Visto que as aves da família da coruja são caçadoras, seu consumo era vedado na dieta dos israelitas. Ver o artigo geral sobre as *Aves da Bíblia*.

3. *Bath yaanah*. Ver Lev. 11:16; Deu. 14:15; Jó 30:29; Isa. 13:21; 34:13; 43:20; Jer. 50:39 e Miq. 1:8. Nossa versão portuguesa diz «avestruz» em todas essas oito referências. Com isso concorda a maioria dos estudiosos.

4. *Lilith*. Ver Isa. 34:14. Nossa versão portuguesa diz ali «fantasmas». Realmente, a palavra indica um demônio ou fantasma noturno; nada tem a ver com a coruja.

5. *Qippoz*. Ver Isa. 34:15. Nossa versão portuguesa diz «coruja». Porém, o verdadeiro significado da palavra é uma serpente.

6. *Tinshemeth*. Ver Lev. 11:18; Deu. 14:16; Lev. 11:30. Nossa versão portuguesa diz «gralha» nas duas primeiras dessas referências, mas diz «camaleão» na última delas. As opiniões dos especialistas estão muito divididas. Alguns pensam em uma espécie de cisne, mas outros opinam que se trata de galinhola.

Na atualidade, há várias espécies de coruja na Palestina, como a coruja águia, um pássaro grande, com 70 cm da cabeça à cauda; a coruja de orelhas curtas, que é ave migratória, de hábitos tanto noturnos quanto diurnos; a coruja de orelhas grandes, que habita nas florestas e caça rodentes, e o mocho, com a sua cor pálida, que gosta de rondar as edificações das fazendas, fazendo a sua presença notada pelos guinchos agudos que dá, enquanto voa. Essa espécie é muito comum, excetuando nos desertos. Durante o verão, a Palestina também é visitada pela coruja cuja voz é um assobio monótono, talvez semelhante à murucututu que também pode ser encontrada no norte do Brasil.

A coruja como um símbolo. Os atenienses pensavam que a coruja era uma ave sábia, conotação essa que se tornou comum até os tempos modernos. A coruja pode simbolizar uma alma que partiu deste mundo, o que é sugerido pelo canto noturno e melancólico desse pássaro. Em um sonho, a coruja pode representar a sabedoria. Pouco antes do falecimento de minha mãe, ela teve um sonho incomum, de uma coruja de asas abertas, diante de um lindo pôr-do-sol. A sabedoria maior ocorre quando a alma encontra descanso, no pôr-do-sol desta vida física.

CORVO

No hebraico, **oreb**, derivado de uma palavra que significa «negro». É vocábulo usado por dez vezes: Gên. 8:7; Lev. 11:15; Deu. 14:14; I Reis 17:4,6; Jó 38:41; Sal. 147:9; Pro. 30:17; Can. 5:11 e Isa. 34:11.

Essa ave pertence à família *Corvus corax*. O primeiro mensageiro enviado por Noé, que ficou indo e voltando, repousando sobre a arca, mas sem entrar na mesma, foi um corvo. Simbolicamente, representa a alma de tendências carnais, que nunca encontra descanso (Isa. 57:20,21). Corvos alimentaram Elias, no ribeiro de Querite (I Reis 17:4,6), quando ele temeu associar-se com pessoas que poderiam traí-lo, entregando-o ao rei Acabe. Essas aves vorazes, apesar de seu grande apetite, acharam tempo para cuidar do profeta do Senhor. Nisso encontramos uma lição sobre o infalível e ilimitado suprimento de Deus. O corvo foi destacado para mostrar como Deus cuida de toda a sua criação (Luc. 12:24). As necessidades das aves são grandes, e não semeiam e nem colhem, nem possuem armazéns, mas Deus as alimenta. Não valemos nós mais do que os corvos? Com sua voz roufenha, eles crocitam, clamando a Deus, por assim dizer; e ele os ouve. Os corvos fazem seus ninhos em lugares solitários, e assim simbolizam a desolação. O fato de que os corvos se ajuntam em torno da carniça, faz com que eles representem maus agouros, más notícias vindouras (Isa. 34:11). Por outro lado, sua cor negra azulada faz-nos lembrar os cachos de uma noiva (Can. 5:11).

••• ••• •••

CORVO MARINHO

No hebraico, **shalak**, palavra que aparece somente em Lev. 11:17 e Deu. 14:17.

Trata-se de uma ave, mencionada no Antigo Testamento, — sobre a qual pouco se sabe. As traduções falam em «pelicano», em «gavião» ou em «corvo» (esta última possibilidade refletida na nossa versão portuguesa da Bíblia, «corvo marinho»). Algumas traduções também traduzem por «pelicano» a palavra hebraica *qaath*, que aparece em Isa. 34:11 e e Sof. 2:14. Há quem pensa, que, nesse caso, deve-se pensar na «coruja». As questões da fauna e flora, na Bíblia, são extremamente confusas e difíceis de deslindar, pois os escritores sagrados não usaram uma linguagem científica (conforme fazemos atualmente), para indicar as espécies. O corvo marinho é uma voraz ave aquática do gênero *Phalacrocorax*, muito distribuído e de hábitos gregários. Tem um forte bico recurvo e um papo proeminente. Duas espécies de corvos marinhos visitam regularmente a Palestina. Alimentam-se ambas, principalmente, de peixes. Porém, não há certeza se essa é a ave que os hebreus antigos chamavam de *shalak*. O que se sabe é que a injestão de sua carne era vedada aos israelitas, pois era uma das aves imundas.

CÓS

Ver Atos 21:1. Trata-se de uma maciça ilha montanhosa do grupo das Esporades, na costa sudoeste da Ásia Menor, perto de Halicarnasso. Foi um dos portos de parada do navio que Paulo tomara, em sua viagem de Éfeso para Rodes. Evidentemente, esse lugar foi colonizado a princípio por gente vinda do Epidauro. Quando Atenas e Esparta estavam em guerra uma com a outra, o lugar sofreu as perdas maiores, às mãos dos militares de ambas aquelas cidades. A destruição chegou ao fim já no final do século V D.C. Ficou sob o controle dos atenienses até o século IV D.C. Desfrutou de um período de liberdade, por ter-se revoltado contra o jugo ateniense; mas, em seguida, caiu sob o poder da Macedônia. Era o lugar onde residia o famoso médico Hipócrates, fundador da ciência médica, no século V A.C. Nos tempos helenistas, a ilha caiu sob o controle dos reis Ptolomeus, do Egito. Filetas e Teócrito foram escritores bem conhecidos, nativos da ilha. No século II A.C., mostrou-se leal ao poder romano, tendo recebido a posição de estado livre, dentro da província da Ásia. Herodes, o Grande, foi um dos benfeitores do lugar, quando estava no poder.

A ilha é célebre por seus bons vinhos, por sua seda, algodão e manufaturas de tecidos. Tem cerca de trinta e dois quilômetros de comprimento, com quase dez quilômetros de largura. Um lugar tão pequeno, com uma história tão ilustre!

COSÃ

Nome de um homem mencionado na genealogia de Jesus, em Luc. 3:28. O termo hebraico aparentemente significa «adivinho». Era filho de Elmodã, e aparece no quinto lugar antes de Zorobabel, dentro da genealogia de José, isto é, no evangelho de Mateus. Nada se sabe sobre ele, excetuando esses fatos simples. Ver o artigo sobre a *Genealogia de Jesus*.

COSAMEU

Uma palavra encontrada em I Esdras 9:32, após o nome Simão. Porém, um nome como Simão Cosameu provavelmente é uma corrupção textual. No paralelo de Esdras 10, tal palavra é omitida. Seja como for, tal homem é nomeado entre aqueles que se desfizeram de suas esposas estrangeiras, após o retorno do cativeiro babilônico.

COSMÉTICOS

Vários tipos de cosméticos são mencionados na Bíblia. A própria palavra portuguesa vem do grego, *kósmos*, «ordem», «ornamento». Desse termo grego também se deriva a palavra portuguesa «cosmos», que significa mundo, universo, criação e a ordem divina das coisas, isto é, o universo como um sistema harmônico. A associação entre *cosmético* e *mundano* é uma aplicação falsa das palavras envolvidas, e não uma derivação verdadeira.

1. *Utensílios Associados aos Cosméticos*. Os arqueólogos têm encontrado taças de pedra calcária, vasos feitos de vários metais, pequenos potes, frascos de vidro, caixas de perfume, receptáculos de alabastro (que vide), espelhos de metal polido, espátulas de metal, colheres para ungüentos, pinças, etc., tudo associado ao uso dos cosméticos. Alguns desses objetos são altamente coloridos e decorativos, exibindo considerável habilidade na manufatura. As damas egípcias da alta sociedade favoreciam itens elaborados, feitos de marfim, com certa variedade de ilustrações da fauna e da flora. Para pintar os olhos, elas tinham pequenas caixas e tubos, e a pintura era aplicada mediante pequenas espátulas ou palitos, feitas de madeira ou de bronze.

2. *Cosméticos*. Havia certa variedade de minerais pulverizados, de óleos vegetais, de extratos, de gorduras animais, empregados como cosméticos. Azeite de oliveira era usado para ungir o corpo, nos países do Oriente Próximo e Médio, o que era considerado uma prática quase tão essencial quanto os atos de comer e beber. O azeite de oliveira também era usado nos costumes de sepultamento e lamentação pelos mortos. Havia grande variedade de perfumes, bem como pinturas em muitas cores diferentes.

3. *Pintura para os Olhos*. A maioria das pessoas, quando se olha ao espelho, gostaria de poder fazer algo sobre o seu aspecto geral. As mulheres nunca cessam de tentar. É realmente admirável como um pouco de pintura e um vestido novo podem transformar a maioria das mulheres. Qualquer porta de estábulo parece melhor quando é pintada; mas há casos difíceis. Quando eu era um jovem, era uma terrível heresia e desvio se uma moça evangélica passasse ao menos um pouco de batom nos lábios. Tal prática era considerada extremamente mundana; e um rapaz crente sério não escolheria uma esposa dentre as jovens mundanas que usavam batom. Mas, quando Billy Graham foi à Europa, dirigir campanhas de evangelização, sua esposa usava batom em público! Alguns pensaram que isso era muito mundano. Outros aprovaram. Seja como for, não demorou muito para que as mulheres crentes da Europa inteira começassem a usar batom. Na verdade, o *ascetismo* pode ser pior que um pouco de cosméticos. Posso imaginar Raquel com as suas jóias, e, naturalmente, com um pouco de pintura. Se me fosse possível encontrar-me com ela, não penso que lhe pediria para remover esses enfeites. Se eu fosse mais jovem, eu lhe pediria para doar suas jóias aos pobres e retirar a pintura. Porém, Raquel sem dúvida era uma mulher bonita, e seria errado estragar-lhe a beleza. Ademais, ela foi uma das matriarcas da nação hebréia, e isso basta para dizer algo em favor dela. Agora, que já sou homem maduro, simplesmente não consigo ficar indignado por causa de um *pouco* de

pintura e de enfeites que as mulheres queiram usar. Penso que o impulso feminino para usar cosméticos deriva-se de uma herança genética, quase impossível de vencer. A mente espiritual entende que, numa autêntica escala de valores, o que importa para a mulher crente (como para o homem crente, também) é que ela não seja idólatra, nem mentirosa, nem imoral, nem desonesta, nem invejosa, nem preguiçosa, nem viciada, etc., coisas essas que as Escrituras condenam. Para muitos crentes esclarecidos, questões como enfeites e cosméticos são questões neutras, que a Bíblia nunca condena por si mesmas, a menos que sejam usadas com intuitos pecaminosos. A moderação é um grande lema nos escritos dos antigos filósofos morais gregos, e Paulo tomou por empréstimo a idéia. Penso que essa é a resposta para essa questão, como para tantas outras. Brincando um pouco, posso até apreciar uma mulher iluminada como uma árvore de Natal, contanto que não seja a minha esposa e nem alguma parenta chegada minha! Algumas mulheres usam batom por causa de lábios ressecados e partidos; pelo que a prática deve ter algum valor medicinal. O próprio Paulo permitiu que Timóteo usasse um pouco de vinho, por causa de seu estômago adoentado (I Tim. 5:23). Porém, não permitia que qualquer ancião fosse nomeado nas igrejas cristãs, se bebesse em excesso (I Tim. 3:8). Isso não estabelece um útil e orientador precedente?

Os povos antigos faziam pinturas para os olhos de várias substâncias minerais e vegetais. Eles misturavam pós coloridos com água ou certos tipos de goma. Jó talvez seja o mais antigo livro da Bíblia, e é naquele livro que encontramos as palavras: Quéren-Hapuque, «chifre de rímel», nome de uma das filhas dele, após sua restauração à saúde e à prosperidade material. Os profetas atacaram o uso excessivo dos cosméticos (II Reis 9:30; Jer. 4:30; Eze. 23:40). Alguns intérpretes supõem que a pintura para os olhos poderia ter algum valor medicinal, protegendo os olhos das moscas; porém, penso que essa é uma interpretação por demais generosa. As mulheres usavam tais pinturas para se fazerem mais atrativas.

4. *Perfumes e Ungüentos*. Os perfumes eram muito populares na antiguidade, sendo usados igualmente por homens e mulheres. Os expositores do Antigo Testamento encontram pelo menos dezoito tipos, mencionados naquele documento. Eram usados como adorno (Can. 1:13), sendo presenteados em grande quantidade (Sabedoria de Salomão 2:7). O próprio Jesus recebeu presentes dessa natureza (Mat. 26:7 *ss*). Ungüentos e perfumes eram usados nos banhos, nos rituais mais variados e nos preparativos para o sepultamento. Eram compostos com azeite de oliveira e substâncias vegetais e animais. Eram aplicados à cabeça (Sal. 133:2; Mat. 6:17) ou ao corpo inteiro (Rute 3:3; Est. 2:2). Tintura vermelha era aplicada às palmas das mãos, às solas dos pés, às unhas e aos cabelos. Essa prática continua bastante comum entre os povos árabes. O trecho de I Samuel 8:13 fala de um típico rei que, tal como todos os monarcas dos povos ao redor, requereu os serviços de perfumistas, de cozinheiros e de padeiros, o que mostra que a manipulação e aplicação de perfumes veio a ser feita por profissionais. Ver o artigo sobre *Artes e Ofícios*.

Sabemos que o grande palácio de Mari, às margens do rio Eufrates (século XVIII A.C.), contava com sua perfumaria, onde era produzida uma vasta quantidade de cosméticos para o rei, para os seus dignitários, para os militares graduados, etc. (J. Bottero, *Archives Royales de Mari*, VII, 1957). Extratos feitos de flores que contêm agentes naturais eram usados para o fabrico de perfumes, como também os óleos extraídos da mirra e de outras gomas. A arqueologia tem desenterrado gravuras, em túmulos egípcios, que mostram a preparação de tais produtos, e, naturalmente, têm sido descobertas muitas gravuras com mulheres aplicando cosméticos em si mesmas. A rainha de Sabá, entre os muitos presentes que trouxe a Salomão, não se esqueceu de especiarias e perfumes (ver I Reis 10:2,10), e essas coisas também faziam parte do tesouro de Ezequias (II Reis 20:13).

Perfumaria Sagrada. Havia as unções realizadas nos móveis do Tabernáculo e nos sacerdotes aarônicos, em sua iniciação (Êxo. 30:22,23). A mirra, uma resina gomosa aromática, a canela aromática, a cássia e o azeite de oliveira eram misturadas nesse perfume (Êxo. 30:23-25). Ver o contexto ali, quanto ao uso desses ungüentos e perfumes.

5. *Talcos e Ruge*. Antigos talcos e ruges eram fabricados a partir do ocre. As colorações mais populares eram o vermelho e o amarelo. O ruge branco era feito de carbonato de chumbo. Tais produtos têm sido encontrados nas escavações arqueológicas. Sabemos que havia aplicadores de talco, não muito diferentes dos modernos, usados no Egito antigo. A única referência ao talco, usado como cosmético, encontra-se na Bíblia em Can. 3:6 (em português, «pós aromáticos»), embora seja provável que ali a alusão seja aos ingredientes usados na fabricação de pinturas.

6. *Os Cosméticos e os Cabelos*. Para uma mulher, ter cabelos longos é um adorno natural de considerável qualidade, conforme qualquer homem (não mulher) pode dizer-nos. Mas as mulheres pensam que são capazes de melhorar a natureza, e elas nunca cessam de fazer novas tentativas. A coisa mais desastrosa que uma mulher pode fazer contra os seus cabelos consiste em cortá-los rente. Paulo chegou a estabelecer uma norma quanto a isso, embora os crentes pareçam não dar a mínima atenção a essa recomendação apostólica (I Cor. 11:6,15). Os cabelos longos de uma mulher constituem a sua «glória», no dizer do apóstolo. As mulheres antigas tinham inúmeras maneiras de adornar aquilo que já era o seu adorno, incluindo muitos tipos de penteados. As mulheres egípcias dispunham de perucas e de inúmeros objetos para serem postos nos cabelos, como jóias, alfinetes, tiaras, etc. Um profeta fez cortante observação sobre como Jezabel penteava seus cabelos (II Reis 9:30). Pentes muito ornados tornaram-se populares, tanto para fazerem penteados como para serem usados nos cabelos. Os cabelos eram perfumados, e eram usadas tinturas para mudar-lhes a cor. Assim como os antigos homens orgulhavam-se de suas barbas, assim também as mulheres orgulhavam-se de suas cabeleiras, e tudo faziam com os cabelos para se fazerem mais bonitas. O avanço dos anos estraga bastante os cabelos e a pele das pessoas. As pessoas sempre preocuparam-se em tentar reverter essa situação. Receitas com esse propósito têm sido encontradas em papiros egípcios antiqüíssimos, de natureza médica. Uma dessas receitas trazia o encorajador título: «Livro da Transformação dos Velhos em Jovens». Essa é uma das tarefas que fazem parte das tentativas da cosmetologia, embora os cosmetólogos também tenham como um de seus alvos fazer os jovens parecerem ainda melhor. (ND SIN Z)

COSMOGONIA

Essa palavra vem dos termos gregos *kosmos*, «mundo», e *gignesthai*, «nascer». Isso posto, o termo é usado para indicar as *origens* do mundo ou do

COSMOGONIA

universo. Qualquer teoria que se proponha a dizer-nos como as coisas começaram, entra no campo da cosmogonia. A narrativa bíblica da criação, segundo a qual Deus pôs ordem ao caos, separando a luz das trevas, fazendo aparecer o sol, a luz e as estrelas, determinando o aparecimento da flora e da fauna, etc., constitui uma antiqüíssima cosmogonia. Há muitas cosmogonias antigas. Ofereço abaixo alguns exemplos disso:

Esboço:
 I. Cosmogonias Antigas
  1. Grega e Romana
  2. Egípcia
  3. Fenícia
  4. Babilônica
  5. Hebréia
 II. Indicações do Novo Testamento
 III. Lições Morais e Espirituais

I. Cosmogonias Antigas

1. *Grega e Romana*. Hesíodo (em sua *Teogonia*) propôs uma certa cosmogonia. Segundo ele, no começo o mundo não tinha forma e achava-se em estado caótico. Desse caos surgiu o primeiro espírito do amor, a saber, Eros. Do caos também teria saído a terra, de peito largo, chamado Gaea. Em seguida apareceram Érebos, as trevas, e Nix, a noite. A união destes dois últimos produziu o céu claro, o Éter, e também Hemera, o dia. Por sua vez, a terra produziu o firmamento, Urano, e o mar, Ponto. Eros foi quem uniu os casais, primeiramente Urano e Gaea, que povoaram a terra com os titãs, os gigantes e os ciclopes. Desses é que vieram os deuses do Olimpo, os heróis, e, finalmente, a raça humana. Os romanos, pouco inventivos que eram, adotaram as idéias gregas em sua forma essencial, com pouquíssimas modificações.

Os *Filósofos Pré-Socráticos*. Em suas tentativas para descobrir o elemento básico do qual todas as demais coisas se derivariam, como a água, a terra, o ar ou o fogo, ou mesmo um elemento indeterminado, esses filósofos abordaram certos aspectos da cosmogonia. O elemento mais primitivo sempre foi considerado eterno. E isso constitui um mistério. Mas o mistério sempre fez parte das origens. Quanto a alguns detalhes sobre essa questão, ver os artigos sobre *Tales, Anaximandro, Anaxímenes, Xenófanes* e *Heráclito*, cujos sistemas estão todos envolvidos nessa questão.

Platão. Esse filósofo tinha uma visão mais espiritualizada da questão, com paralelos em certos conceitos neotestamentários. Ele não acreditava que o mundo físico se tenha originado em alguma coisa física. Quanto à questão das origens, ele expunha a sua doutrina das *idéias* e das *formas*, ou dos *universais* (que vide), equivalente essencial ao mundo *noumenal* de Emanuel Kant. Contrastando com os universais, Platão falava sobre os *Particulares*, ou seja, o mundo físico, com tudo quanto no mesmo está contido. Em sua opinião, os particulares foram criados pelo *Demiurgo* (uma força mais ou menos equivalente à idéia do *Logos*, que vide, sob o título de *Verbo*) que teria usado os universais como arquétipos. Isso posto, o mundo físico seria uma imitação do mundo ideal, ou universal. Tudo quanto existiria neste mundo teria um paralelo ou arquétipo na dimensão espiritual. Os objetos físicos também poderiam combinar as idéias de vários ou mesmo de muitos arquétipos. Esse conceito é similar ao da criação por parte do Logos, a Razão Universal, de acordo com padrões, idéias e requisitos espirituais. Quanto a detalhes, ver o artigo sobre *Platão* e sobre os outros filósofos mencionados, onde é apresentado material abundante.

As idéias dos romanos, naturalmente, seguiam de perto os conceitos gregos, pois os romanos nunca foram pensadores originais no campo da metafísica.

2. *Egípcia*. De acordo com os egípcios, o universo é uma divindade que está se desenvolvendo gradualmente. Teria quatro membros essenciais: O *Kneph*, ou espírito; o *Neith*, ou matéria; o *Sevech*, ou tempo; e o *Pascht*, ou espaço. Esses membros seriam independentes e sem derivação. Os dois primeiros combinaram-se a fim de produzir o mundo visível. O *Neith* era visto como uma espécie de ovo cósmico, em torno do qual o *Kneph* pairaria como uma espécie de substância sutil, preparando o *Neith* para suas inúmeras transformações. Em primeiro lugar, viria o *Ptah*, ou seja, o fogo e a luminosidade. Em seguida, surgiram o *Pe*, firmamento, e o *Anuke*, a terra. Por cima de tudo encontra-se a abóbada celeste, que contém sutis fluidos escuros, em estado primitivo. Ali encontramos as águas acima do firmamento, conforme se vê, igualmente, na narrativa bíblica. As massas abaixo dessa abóbada tornaram-se fontes luminosas, como o sol, a lua e as estrelas. Quando o sol passou a existir, o tempo do *Ptah*, uma luminosidade generalizada, deixou de existir. Notemos que, primeiramente, houve a luz; e só mais tarde surgiram corpos luminosos específicos, como o sol, a lua e as estrelas, tal como se vê no relato bíblico.

3. *Fenícia*. Os fenícios, à semelhança dos gregos, partiam do conceito do *caos*, uma força primitiva, ou um ser, o Espírito primitivo, derivado do caos. Desse proveio o Desejo, que uniu o Espírito e a lama, nascendo assim a terra e a água. A lama ou *Mot*, tornou-se um ovo do qual se originaram as inúmeras formas de vida biológica que existem.

4. *Babilônica*. Os babilônios imaginavam um estado primitivo, que não seria nem céu e nem terra, conforme os conhecemos atualmente, algo semelhante ao caos concebido pelos gregos. O abismo seria a *mãe Tiamot*, a origem de todas as coisas. Primeiramente apareceram divindades como Lachmu, An Sar e Ki Sar, como seres criados. O começo de todas as coisas esteve envolvido em uma espécie de conflito cósmico entre o Caos e a Ordem. No *Épico da Criação*, escrito em acádico, ou Enuma Elish, o conflito teria ocorrido entre o deus da tempestade e do céu e o dragão Illuhankas. Este último triunfou a princípio; mas, quando apareceu o homem mortal, com o nome de Yupasiyas, a maré virou, e o céu obteve a vitória. Dentro da tradição dos sumérios, como o *Mito Paradisíaco de Enki* e o *Ninhursag*, lemos sobre a procriação de deuses e deusas. Através do sêmen do deus Enki, surgiu a vida vegetal. O *Mito da Criação*, da cultura babilônica, envolve algumas similaridades com a narrativa de Gênesis, o que tem sido tema de muitos comentários entre os estudiosos do Antigo Testamento. Essa história é conhecida pelo título de *Enuma Elish*, que significa «Quando do Alto», tendo sido encontrada entre os restos da biblioteca de Assurbanipal, em Nínive. Alguns fragmentos dessa obra têm sido também encontrados em Assur, Uruque e Quis. Alguns dos mais notáveis paralelos, entre outros, é o conflito entre o deus da tempestade e o dragão *Illuhankas*. O relato assemelha-se à história da serpente tentadora, que trouxe muita confusão ao jardim do Éden; o homem feito de argila; a existência de um jardim, ou paraíso; o deus Enki, que ali comeu coisas que não eram lícitas, ao que se seguiu uma maldição, mas com uma restauração posterior. Outro notável paralelo é a criação da deusa

COSMOGONIA

chamada *Ninti* (provavelmente um paralelo de Eva), cujo nome significa «senhora da costela» e «senhora que vivifica». Foi ela quem suspendeu a maldição que caíra sobre o jardim. Esses paralelos são parecidos demais para podermos dizer que não houve alguma fonte informativa comum, de alguma espécie, embora as narrativas babilônicas apareçam dentro de um contexto politeísta, e também há dois *deuses* envolvidos em ocorrências que, dentro do livro de Gênesis, envolvem Adão e Eva, que são meros seres humanos. O leitor está convidado a consultar o artigo sobre a *Babilônia*, em seu quinto ponto, *Religião e Moral*. Ali, o leitor poderá notar que esses paralelos não se limitam à história da criação e à doutrina sobre os começos. Aqueles que lêem somente a Bíblia supõem, naturalmente, que suas informações não têm paralelos; e isso faz com que se surpreendam ao descobrirem que as religiões, da mesma cultura geral, compartilham de grande número de detalhes, embora, como seja óbvio, também haja grandes diferenças.

Os hebreus legaram-nos o *monoteísmo*, e essa foi uma grande contribuição. No entanto, outros paralelos entre a Bíblia e as cosmogonias das culturas vizinhas à cultura dos hebreus, são os seguintes: o caos (uma espécie de luz primeva); luzes (sol, luz e estrelas) que vieram substituir a luz; a separação entre a porção seca e o mar; o firmamento (imaginado como uma espécie de taça invertida, feita de substância sólida, que separa as águas acima e abaixo dela). Alguns antigos supunham que as estrelas seriam perfurações nessa substância sólida, que permite que a luz celeste chegue até nós. Outros supunham que o sol, a lua e as estrelas, etc., seriam luzes penduradas na parte de baixo do firmamento. Naturalmente, ninguém desconfiava das dimensões gigantescas desses corpos luminosos.

As Diferenças. Em Gênesis temos o monoteísmo, não há ali o nascimento de deuses, e nem divindades nascidas de outras, e Adão e Eva ocupam funções que, nos mitos babilônicos, são atribuídas aos deuses. Alguns estudiosos pensam que Deus é mais transcendental na narrativa de Gênesis, e, até certo ponto, isso expressa uma verdade. Porém, na narrativa sobre o homem primitivo, no livro de Gênesis, vê-se uma grande comunhão entre Deus e o homem, como os atos de andarem e falarem um com outro, o que se aproxima da exagerada intimidade entre os deuses e os seres humanos, das narrativas pagãs. Desígnio e propósito são mais evidentes em Gênesis do que nas narrativas pagãs.

5. *Hebréia*. Em meu artigo sobre a *Astronomia*, apresento a idéia geral da cosmogonia dos hebreus, juntamente com uma ilustração. Aqui ofereço apenas um breve sumário; e o leitor poderá consultar aquele artigo. Alguns pontos principais a considerar: 1. Há o firmamento abobadado, uma sólida expansão de matéria que separa o céu da terra. 2. O céu encontra-se na luz primeva. 3. As luzes secundárias, para benefício da terra, a saber, o sol, a luz e as estrelas, estão penduradas pelo lado de dentro do firmamento. 4. Há águas acima e abaixo do firmamento, depois que as mesmas foram separadas. 5. A terra é plana. 6. Nas extremidades encontram-se montanhas que se elevam e formam os alicerces do firmamento, em seus pontos extremos. 7. O Sheol ficaria no interior da terra, mais ou menos a meio caminho entre as extremidades. Por baixo da terra estariam as colunas que a sustentam no lugar, como alicerces. A terra repousaria sobre o abismo das águas. Mas eles não explicaram sobre o que se apoiava o abismo das águas.

Orígenes impressionou o mundo dos intérpretes com suas interpretações moral, simbólica e mística. Se interpretarmos desse modo o livro de Gênesis, poderemos obter muitas lições morais e instruções espirituais importantes para a nossa fé. Mas, se insistirmos em encontrar indícios de confirmação da ciência moderna, ou teremos de ficar desapontados, ou teremos de manipular a narrativa sagrada para adaptá-la às nossas idéias, ignorando completamente o que os israelitas realmente acreditavam sobre a origem das coisas. Essa distorção é uma atividade desonesta, embora os intérpretes ultraconservadores anseiem por promovê-la de todas as maneiras. No outro extremo, há os céticos que só querem qualquer pretexto para lançarem uma sombra de dúvidas sobre os ensinos bíblicos. E uma das coisas que eles podem usar, como é óbvio, é a natureza primitiva da narrativa bíblica da criação. Devemos entender, porém, que uma ciência primitiva não significa, necessariamente, que os que a defendiam eram destituídos de iluminação espiritual. Consideremos o seguinte: sem dúvida é verdade que, apesar de todo o avanço da ciência, nossa cosmologia continua primitiva em comparação com o que ela será, digamos, dentro de cem anos. Os cientistas norte-americanos admitem que as viagens do homem à lua bem como as rochas que eles trouxeram dali, têm levantado mais dúvidas sobre à lua, do que têm resolvido. Se a lua continua misteriosa, e o homem tem podido caminhar à sua superfície, quão grandes são ainda os mistérios que circundam a infinita expansão do espaço exterior. No entanto, não é por causa de nossa ignorância sobre esse espaço exterior que não temos conhecimento científico, moral e espiritual. Simplesmente admitimos que, em todos os campos de conhecimento, científico ou espiritual, ainda estamos no começo, nos primeiros estágios de desenvolvimento. Não obstante, já somos donos de algumas grandes verdades, que dignificam nossa vida; e isso é tudo quanto a fé religiosa requer.

Interpretações que tentam reconciliar a ciência com Gênesis.

1. *O grande hiato*. Entre Gên. 1:1 e 1:2 existiu um grande hiato de tempo no qual todas as eras geológicas aconteceram. Isto explica a grande idade da terra, aliviando o problema de uma criação que aconteceu aparentemente há 6.000 anos (cálculo das genealogias).

2. *Dia=era teoria*. Os dias de Gên. não foram de 24 horas, mas sim, eras vastas. Às vezes, esta teoria é combinada com a no. 1. Imensas eras existiram entre vss. 1 e 2. Os *dias* também eram tais.

3. *Dias + intervalos*. Os dias da criação eram de 24 horas literais, mas entre eles vastas eras existiram, alternativamente.

4. *Éden somente*. A criação de Gênesis tenta nos informar somente sobre a criação de Éden, em seis dias literais. O resto da criação não está descrito na Bíblia, além da referência vaga e geral de Gên. 1:1.

5. *Eras concorrentes e sobre-impostas*. Deus, sendo um ser, além e fora do tempo, criou em tempos curtos e longos, concorrentes e sobre-impostos. Não podemos delinear dias ou eras distintas e separadas, e qualquer discussão de tempo em relação à criação é artificial.

6. *O dia revelador*. Os dias na narrativa de Gên. foram dias *de revelação*, e foram de 24 horas literais. Deus *revelou* a Moisés, *em 6 dias*, o esboço da criação, mas como ele realmente criou, e quanto tempo ele levou, são fatos não revelados.

7. *A semana dividida ou simetria dupla*. A descrição de Gênesis incorpora um método literário

COSMOGONIA

Hesíodo

O poeta grego Hesíodo em um mosaico de Monnus do século 3

Hesíodo, considerado o pai da poesia didática grega, viveu no século 8 A.C., em Ascra, na Beócia, como pastor de ovelhas. Das obras comprovadamente de sua autoria, sobreviveram dois longos poemas: a *Teogonia*, que narra a história de deuses, e *Os Trabalhos e os Dias*, que exalta o trabalho e a justiça e tece ensinamentos sobre agricultura e a vida prática.

> Pelas Musas e pelo golpeante Apolo
> há cantores e citaristas sobre a terra,
> e por Zeus, reis. Feliz é quem as Musas
> amam, doce de sua boca flui a voz.
> Se com angústia no ânimo recém-ferido
> alguém aflito mirra o coração e se o cantor
> servo das Musas hineia a glória dos antigos
> e os venturosos Deuses que têm o Olimpo,
> logo esquece os pesares e de nenhuma aflição
> se lembra, já os desviaram os dons das Deusas.
>
> Alegrai, filhas de Zeus, dai ardente canto,
> gloriai o sagrado ser dos imortais sempre vivos,
> os que nasceram da Terra e do Céu constelado,
> os da Noite trevosa, os que o salgado Mar criou.
> Dizei como no começo Deuses e Terra nasceram,
> os Rios, o Mar infinito impetuoso de ondas,
> os Astros brilhantes e o Céu amplo em cima.
> Os deles nascidos Deuses doadores de bens
> como dividiram a opulência e repartiram as honras
> e como no começo tiveram o rugoso Olimpo.
> Dizei-me isto, Musas que tendes o palácio olímpio,
> dês o começo e quem dentre eles primeiro nasceu.
>
> Hesíodo

Extraído de "Teogonia"

pelo qual o 1º dia é paralelo ao 4º, o 2º ao 5º e o 3º ao 6º, e estes pares são complementares. O fator tempo, segundo esta teoria é artificial.

Avaliação destas teorias. A simples leitura do registro de Gênesis mostra que o escritor pensava em dias literais, e bem provavelmente, de um tempo relativamente recente. Estas diversas teorias são tentativas de incorporar a história de Gênesis dentro dos conhecimentos da ciência moderna. Elas são truques teológicos e filosóficos, embora tenham elementos obviamente verdadeiros.

Uma Interpretação mais Provável: A criação como um novo início. Existem evidências em favor da criação adâmica ser uma renovação, e não uma criação absoluta. Parece que a terra já passou mudanças dos pólos mais do que 400 vezes. Isto quer dizer, que por muitas vezes vastas destruições tem arrumado, de modo diferente, os continentes, trazendo destruições quase completas da terra. Aparentemente, as últimas duas correspondem bem, em termos de tempo, às histórias bíblicas de Adão e Noé. Neste caso, a história de Adão seria uma *novo começo*, não o começo absoluto da raça humana. Existiram, portanto, muitas raças humanas anteriores à adâmica. A história bíblica, então, nos informa sobre uma renovação da raça, e esta raça é aquela que iniciou a história do homem como nós o conhecemos.

Gên. 1:1 todavia é uma declaração geral sobre Deus como o criador absoluto, de tudo, em qualquer empo.

A teoria da grande explosão da astronomia moderna pode ser combinada com a teoria das mudanças dos pólos. Existem também grandes ciclos cósmicos, não somente grandes ciclos terrestres. Há mais de 16.000.000 de anos, houve uma grande explosão de matéria condensada que deu início a criação que nós conhecemos na astronomia. Mas antes disto, houve inumeráveis explosões que iniciaram inumeráveis ciclos de bilhões de anos cada. Uma vez que o poder da explosão se dissipa, a matéria, pela força da gravidade, volta na outra direção. Uma vez que se condensa novamente, outra grande explosão ocorre. Este processo continua e é um fator sem data e totalmente além da nossa imaginação.

Conclusão. Existem grandes ciclos cósmicos e terrestres. As grandes explosões criam os cósmicos, e as mudanças dos pólos criam os terrestres. Temos ciclos terrestres dentro dos ciclos cósmicos, e todos eles são de imensa duração. Portanto, a criação cósmica que conhecemos agora é realmente uma história recente. Também, o ciclo terrestre que envolve a *raça adâmica* é recente. Além destas histórias recentes, praticamente nada sabemos sobre as obras de Deus na criação. Temos um *mysterium tremendum* que as teorias dos homens, e suas cosmogonias são infantis demais para explicar. Portanto, as diversas tentativas de reconciliar a história de Gênesis com a ciência moderna são fúteis. Também, a explicação da própria ciência sobre tudo isto é essencialmente fútil, embora perfeitamente legítima. Todas as explicações são simplesmente gritos na noite misteriosa das obras de Deus. Mas é legítimo gritar e procurar cada vez mais, por entendimentos mais aperfeiçoados.

II. Indicações do Novo Testamento

Os cristãos primitivos, sem dúvida alguma, acreditaram na veracidade essencial da narrativa de Gênesis como explicação das origens. Porém, em consonância com certas idéias filosóficas e helênicas, certos detalhes importantes foram acrescentados. O mais importante desses detalhes é o conceito do *Logos*. Essa doutrina vinha sendo desenvolvida desde cerca de 600 A.C. O leitor poderá obter uma completa descrição a respeito no artigo sobre o *Verbo*. O conceito que começou como uma força cósmica da Razão, nos escritos de Filo já recebe, algumas vezes, uma identificação pessoal, como o Anjo do Senhor. No Novo Testamento, o Logos é equiparado ao princípio do Filho do Deus triúno, o qual se encarnou como um homem. Portanto, o *Logos-Filho* é o agente por meio de quem Deus criou os mundos (Heb. 1:3; Col. 1:16). Destarte, o Filho aparece como o Pai, isto é, o Ser em quem, por meio de quem e para quem todas as coisas foram feitas. Os leitores das obras filosóficas antigas reconhecem que assim como é possível estabelecer o paralelo entre a narrativa de Gênesis e os mitos mesopotâmicos, quanto a alguns detalhes importantes, assim também podemos estabelecer o paralelo entre a doutrina neotestamentária do Logos e idéias bem parecidas do estoicismo e do platonismo, por meio do neoplatonismo (que vide). Tal como no livro de Gênesis há elementos distintivos, assim também no caso do Novo Testamento. No Novo Testamento o Logos não é apenas o criador, mas também se tornou homem, o que representa um definitivo avanço neotestamentário. Além disso, o Logos é também o Salvador, um outro grande avanço, pois isso significa que o Criador também é o Salvador. Por conseguinte, a criação assume um aspecto soteriológico. A criação dá a entender uma nova criação, dentro do processo da salvação. Os homens, portanto, são transformados segundo a imagem do Logos, passando a participar da própria natureza divina (Rom. 8:29; II Cor. 3:18; II Ped. 1:4). Isso encontra paralelo na idéia platônica da redenção, segundo a qual o homem seria reabsorvido no mundo dos universais (que vide). Desse modo, o homem deixaria de ser apenas eterno, passando a ser *imortal*. A imortalidade, por sua vez, precisa ser concebida não somente como vida sem-fim. Antes, é uma *espécie de vida*, a própria vida de Deus, segundo ela se manifesta no Cristo glorificado. Idéia tão ampla e profunda como essa, portanto, está envolvida na soteriologia do Novo Testamento.

O **autor da epístola aos Hebreus** tomou por empréstimo a visão do mundo **em duas dimensões**, mediante a qual as coisas que existem neste mundo são cópias das realidades celestes. Isso é platonismo puro, vinculado à doutrina de Platão sobre como a doutrina dos particulares da terra (todos os objetos materiais) foram criados segundo o modelo e segundo o poder das idéias, formas ou universais. Ver Heb. 8:5; 9:23,24. Quanto a um completo estudo sobre esse assunto, ver o artigo sobre a epístola aos Hebreus, em sua sexta parte, *Idéias Religiosas e Filosóficas*, quarto ponto. O trecho de Hebreus 1:3, quase certamente, é um reflexo do conceito de emanações dos estóicos neoplatônicos (que vide), sendo essa uma outra idéia que foi usada, pelo autor sagrado dessa epístola canônica do Novo Testamento, para participar de sua cosmologia. Alguns desses empréstimos são muito aptos, não havendo como negar que o Logos, ao implantar algumas de suas sementes nas filosofias e nas religiões, não concedeu aos pagãos alguns importantes conceitos. Esses conceitos, pois, foram utilizados nas revelações bíblicas, sem que a verdade sofresse qualquer violência. As coisas não precisam ser absolutamente novas, inéditas, para que sejam verdadeiras.

III. Lições Morais e Espirituais

No que diz respeito a esse assunto, podemos extrair as seguintes importantes lições morais e espirituais:

COSMOLOGIA — COSMÓPOLIS

1. Deus é a origem de todas as coisas. A matéria originou-se na Mente divina imaterial. Portanto, o mundo material sempre estaria sujeito às realidades espirituais. O mundo material não teria existência independente.

2. Na qualidade de criador do homem, Deus é o seu Senhor. O homem é responsável diante de Deus, sendo governado por imperativos morais.

3. A criação material foi criada a fim de que, da mesma, brotasse e se desenvolvesse a nova criação, espiritual.

4. Na criação material encontramos reflexos e cópias das realidades da esfera celestial. Com base na observação e no raciocínio, podemos aprender como o divino reside na matéria, e, desse modo, podemos aprender algumas coisas sobre as realidades divinas. A natureza moral do homem, como um exemplo, é um reflexo da natureza de Deus, porquanto o homem foi feito à imagem de Deus.

5. A lição da dependência. Somente Deus é independente. A vida espiritual não é algo estranho ao homem. Antes, é a própria substância de sua vida.

6. A lição do poder e da provisão. O Deus que fez todas as coisas e mostrou tanto interesse pelo homem, pode suprir todas as nossas necessidades, tanto para o tempo como para a eternidade.

7. A lição do desígnio. Foi a Mente divina que criou os mundos. Por toda a parte a criação demonstra a existência de uma Inteligência projetadora, controladora. O desígnio leva-nos a Deus, e também garante o sucesso da criação divina, em última análise, de conformidade com os planos originais de Deus.

8. A restauração. Assim como todas as coisas originaram-se em Deus, e vieram a existir pelo seu poder, assim também todas as coisas, finalmente, deverão retornar a Deus (Rom. 11:36), por meio do Filho-Logos (Col. 1:16).

Ver os seguintes artigos separados, que adicionam alguns detalhes a este verbete: *Astronomia*, *Adão*, *Cosmologia* e *Criação*. (E JAME NTI PRIT RAMM Z)

COSMOLOGIA

A palavra vem do grego **kósmos**, «mundo», e **logía**, «estudo». Portanto, o vocábulo designa a ciência geral do universo, com várias aplicações disciplinares, como segue:

1. *Um Ramo da Filosofia*. Nesse caso, ela é uma divisão da metafísica (que vide), que trata do universo como a totalidade dos fenômenos, procurando combinar especulações metafísicas com evidências científicas, dentro de um arcabouço coerente. Pode incluir a *cosmogonia* (que vide), que é a especulação acerca do começo ou nascimento da criação ou das entidades, divinas e humanas. Seus problemas são os seguintes: considerações sobre a natureza do espaço, do tempo, dos primórdios, da eternidade, da necessidade, das mudanças e da contingência. Seu método de inquirição racional e científica distinguem-na das narrativas puramente míticas sobre a origem e a natureza do universo, com freqüência ligadas à palavra «cosmogonia». A cosmogonia é tão antiga quanto a fé religiosa, conforme o artigo sobre a mesma o demonstra; mas a cosmologia filosófica teve início com os filósofos pré-socráticos, que procuravam descobrir o elemento básico de todas as coisas, e como esse elemento seria responsável pelo resto da criação. Tanto Platão, com sua doutrina dos universais (que vide) quanto Aristóteles, com os seus ensinos sobre o Impulsionador inabalável e sobre a Substância (que vide) traçaram cosmologias elaboradas. Os filósofos cristãos mesclaram conceitos bíblicos e filosóficos, em suas descrições. A renascença, a partir do século XIV D.C., começou a provocar uma radical revisão das idéias. Kant declarou que os problemas cosmológicos ultrapassam as proposições da percepção dos sentidos (conhecimento), estando sujeitos somente aos postulados da razão, da intuição e do misticismo, tornando-se uma espécie de conhecimento prático.

2. *A Cosmologia Científica*. Os cientistas podem ser deístas ou teístas (ver sobre o *deísmo* e o *teísmo*). Porém, quando abordam assuntos científicos, no tocante ao *método*, eles aderem ao ateísmo. Em outras palavras, eles aplicam o *ateísmo metódico* (que vide), o que significa que eles não tentam explicar as coisas apelando para explicações teológicas. Dentro do campo da ciência, a cosmologia é o estudo da origem e da estrutura do universo, com base em coisas como a investigação espectral da distribuição de elementos, através do universo, bem como o estudo da mudança das cores do espectro para o vermelho, associada essa mudança à recessão das galáxias, partindo de um ponto central e afastando-se mais e mais, em todas as direções, como uma explosão. A astronomia inteira, bem como certos aspectos da maioria das ciências, estão envolvidos na cosmologia científica. O método científico não se envolve em respostas finais, definitivas, como aquelas que dizem respeito à natureza do começo absoluto, ou aos propósitos a longo prazo da criação. Se um cientista vier a envolver-se em tais inquirições, já se terá tornado um filósofo. No que concerne aos grandes mistérios da natureza, a ciência põe um ponto de interrogação em tudo. Portanto, a ciência começa com o universo, conforme ele existe, procurando explicar fenômenos dentro desse contexto, jamais especulando sobre as origens, que não podem ser reproduzidas para estarem sujeitas à investigação científica.

Atualmente, os cientistas estão discutindo sobre a teoria do universo estável, ou sobre a teoria do «big bang», uma tremenda explosão que resultou na expansão do universo, que teria ocorrido pelo menos na dezesseis bilhões de anos. A teoria do «big-bang» (alguma explosão primeva) envolve implicações teológicas importantíssimas, com a possibilidade de que o universo passa, periodicamente, por longos ciclos. Nesse caso, a criação atual, para exemplificar, é apenas um dentre inúmeros ciclos, e não o único ciclo da existência que tem dominado todas as eras. A filosofia dos filósofos estóicos e neoplatônicos, mais de dois milênios atrás, propunha a teoria dos muitos ciclos, mediante a operação do Logos, que faria a criação emanar e voltar a ele, interminavelmente.

3. *A Cosmologia Teológica*. Meu artigo sobre a *Cosmogonia* explica, de modo bastante amplo, as idéias teológicas relativas à criação, seus primórdios e seus estados. Portanto, recomendamos que o leitor examine aquele artigo. Ver também o artigo sobre a *Astronomia*. Esse artigo contém especulações sobre problemas teológicos do princípio ao fim, mas especialmente sob o sétimo ponto, onde é abordada a teologia no tocante à astronomia, de modo específico. (AM C F)

COSMÓPOLIS

Os estóicos (ver sobre o estoicismo), chamavam-se *cidadãos do mundo*, e não de alguma área ou país em particular. Não criam que os padrões morais e as leis de qualquer comunidade pudessem ser corretamente preparadas pelos membros daquela comunidade.

Antes, supunham que há uma lei universal, que a razão pode perceber, governando todos os povos. Para eles, a humanidade inteira vive em uma *cosmópolis*, isto é, a grande cidade do mundo inteiro, e não em um lugar particular. Nisso, eles anteciparam a tentativa de estabelecer a lei internacional. A doutrina da cosmópolis está relacionada ao governo racional do Logos, em todos os lugares ao mesmo tempo. Razão, direito e lei derivam-se dessa força, e não de homens individuais ou das comunidades isoladas que eles formam. Há um conceito similar na Igreja cristã, visto que a *cidade celestial* é universal, para todos os povos, para todos os tempos,.e também é governada pelo Logos (chamado Cristo, por ocasião de sua encarnação). Uma verdadeira cosmópolis, porém, só será instaurada quando Deus restaurar todas as coisas (ver Efé. 1:10).

COSMOS

Essa é a transliteração da palavra grega que significa *«mundo»*, mas cujo sentido básico é «ordem» ou «adorno». Todos os conceitos em que possamos usar a palavra «mundo», envolvem-nos nesses usos, a saber: 1. Adorno pessoal, jóias, etc. (I Ped. 3:3). 2. O mundo como a súmula de tudo, o universo em ordem, no dizer de Plutarco, *Mor.* 886b (Heb. 4:3; 9:26; Fil. 2:15). Hermes, *Visão* 2.4.1, onde se lê que o mundo foi criado para benefício da Igreja. 3. O mundo como o conjunto total de todas as coisas, acima dos animais, como os homens e os anjos. Epicteto 1.9,4 (I Cor. 4:9). 4. O mundo como a terra física, o planeta terrestre (II Macabeus 3:12; Josefo, *Anti.* 9.241). 5. O mundo como lugar habitado (*Orác. Sibilinos* i.160; I Tim. 6:7). 6. O mundo como área civilizada, ou seja, em redor do mar Mediterrâneo (Col. 1:6). Foi a esse *mundo* que o evangelho atingiu, nos dias dos próprios apóstolos. 7. A terra em contraste com o céu (*Dil Chrs.* 19.59; João 3:16,17; I Tim. 1:15). 8. O mundo considerado como a humanidade (*Orác. Sibilinos* 1.189; Mat. 18:7; João 3:16,17; 6:33,51). 9. O mundo como a cena de certas vantagens terrestres, do amor, das possessões, dos cuidados com o próximo, etc. (IV Macabeus 8:23, Mar. 8:26), mas que não tem o valor nem mesmo de uma única alma. 10. O mundo dos homens, considerado como um sistema que está em estado de inimizade contra Deus (*Herm. Wr.* 6:4; Efé. 2:2; I João 5:19; João 7:4; 15:18; I Cor. 2:12). 11. O mundo como o conjunto dos *desejos mundanos*, como as ambições, o que equivale ao mundanismo (I João 2:15). Seus elementos principais e genéricos são a concupiscência da carne, a concupiscência dos olhos e o orgulho da vida. 12. A palavra «mundo» também é usada para exprimir a idéia da totalidade de algo, como dentro da frase: «Ora, a língua é fogo; é mundo de iniqüidade...» (Tia. 3:6). 13. Na filosofia, os pitagoreanos usavam essa palavra para indicar um *todo ordeiro e racional*. O vocábulo grego dá a entender aptidão e beleza, dentro do contexto da boa ordem, dentro de limites finitos. Platão usava o vocábulo em sua teoria da bondade, para indicar qualquer coisa que é dependente da organização apropriada de suas partes constituintes. Partes constituintes postas em forma compõem um *mundo*.

Na Teologia. No que diz respeito a este mundo, os mais significativos elementos são estes: Deus amou o mundo inteiro (João 3:16); o mundo inteiro é o objeto da missão evangelizadora cristã (Mat. 28:19); Cristo fez propiciação pelos homens do mundo inteiro (I João 2:2); o cosmos inteiro será restaurado (Efé. 1:10). (A F)

••• ••• •••

COSTA MARÍTIMA

No hebraico, *choph*, «porto» (em Deu. 1:7 e Eze. 22:16). E *chebel*, «corda» (em Sof. 2:5-7). No grego, *parálios*, «país costeiro» (em Luc. 6:17).

A referência é às costas marítimas do extremo leste do mar Mediterrâneo, habitadas, nos dias do Antigo Testamento, primeiramente pelos cananeus (Deu. 1:7), subseqüentemente pelos filisteus (Eze. 25:16), e, finalmente, pelos fenícios (Luc. 6:17). Era uma faixa de terra bastante fértil, estreita e dotada de poucos portos, por ausência de reentrâncias como golfos e baías, e também porque as terras ali eram baixas e as águas relativamente rasas.

COSTAS

Essa palavra vem do latim **costa**, que significa lado ou costela. Em algumas traduções, é usada no Antigo Testamento para indicar fronteiras. Atualmente, usamos esse vocábulo para indicar as costas marítimas, onde termina alguma área de terreno e começa o mar. As costas marítimas da Palestina são mencionadas, por exemplo, em Gên. 10:5; Sa. 97:1 e Jer. 47:4. As costas marítimas da Palestina eram muito regulares, sem reentrâncias como baías, pelo que não havia ali bons portos, a não ser já nas proximidades do monte Carmelo, no extremo norte da Palestina. Talvez esse seja o motivo pelo qual os israelitas apenas em raras ocasiões aventuraram-se como navegadores, como, por exemplo, na época de Salomão. Todas as tentativas posteriores, fracassaram.

COSTAS

Quatro palavras hebraicas são usadas para indicar as costas de uma pessoa, em um total de vinte e uma referências: a. *Gab*, em Sal. 129:3; Eze. 10:12 e Dan. 7:6; b. *gav*, I Reis 14:9; Nee. 9:26; Pro. 10:13; 19:29; 26:3; Isa. 38:17; 50:6 e Eze. 23:35; c. *oref* (pescoço), em Êxo. 23:27; Jos. 7:8,12; II Crô. 29:6; Jer. 2:27; 18:17; 32:33; 48:39; e d. *shekem* (ombro), em I Sam. 10:9 e Sal. 21:12. Não há qualquer importância maior em uma palavra dessa natureza senão em um trecho como o de Êxodo 33:23, onde ainda uma outra palavra hebraica, usada por quarenta vezes, com vários sentidos, como «parte posterior», «parte de trás», etc., é empregada. Ali lê-se que Moisés viu Deus pelas costas, porque a glória de seu rosto era por demais resplendente para ser contemplada. Os intérpretes chamam isso de uso metafórico ou antropomórfico, usando de vários truques para aliviar o que é uma óbvia má teologia. O texto nos dá a idéia de que Deus tem rosto e costas, como se fosse um homem, e que, de alguma maneira, as suas costas poderiam ser vistas, mas não o seu rosto, pois seu rosto resplandeceria com intensíssimo brilho. Isso só faria sentido se Deus se assemelhasse, realmente, a um homem, dotado de alguma espécie de corpo. Naturalmente, há pessoas que supõem que assim, efetivamente, sucede; mas é absurdo concebermos o Ser Supremo segundo tais termos. Só devemos apelar para a interpretação metafórica porque Deus pode revelar-se em vários graus de glória, alguns dos quais toleráveis pelo homem, mas outros não. A esses graus que podem ser tolerados, chamamos de *costas de Deus*; e àqueles graus que nos são insuportáveis, chamamos de *face de Deus*.

Uma outra palavra usada como advérbio, «por trás», mas literalmente em Pro. 10:13; 19:29 e 26:3, referindo-se às costas de um insensato, próprias para serem fustigadas, também indica as costas do prometido Messias, entregues aos que queriam feri-lo, em Isa. 50:6. Nos trechos de I Reis 14:9; Eze. 6:5; Nee. 9:26 e Isa. 38:17, essa palavra é usada como uma expressão idiomática, indicando «lançar para as costas», com o sentido de negligenciar ou ignorar.

COSTELA Ver **Mulher Feita de Costela**.

COSTUME

Do latim, **con**, «totalmente», e **suescere**, «acostumar-se com», ou seja, algo com o que alguém fica acostumado. O termo grego correspondente é *éthos*, de onde derivamos a nossa palavra *ética*, ou seja, a conduta costumeira de um povo.

I. Na Filosofia

1. De acordo com as teorias humanista e relativista, os costumes formariam a base da ética.

2. Dentro da teoria do *consensus gentium* (que vide), os costumes dos povos formar-se-iam mediante consenso coletivo, porquanto refletiriam as leis naturais e a verdade.

3. Mostesquieu (que vide) opinava que há um desenvolvimento da observação de como as sociedades tendem por considerar os *seus* costumes como se fossem normas *universais*.

4. Hume (que vide) tentou demonstrar que mesclamos os conceitos de costume e de causa, visto que o uso ou os acontecimentos habituais fazem-nos supor que há causas em operação. Hume negava o pressuposto que podemos provar que há um princípio de causa.

5. Os padrões espontâneos dos atos de uma sociedade cristalizam-se sob a forma de *mores* ou costumes, que se tornam os princípios de certo e errado, naquela sociedade. Os mores são os costumes dos povos, e não verdadeiros padrões de certo e errado.

6. Quando os costumes cristalizam-se, transformam-se em crenças éticas, e em seguida, em leis supostamente universais, de conformidade com o que diz o relativismo (que vide).

7. A ética absolutista e teísta nega que os costumes sejam a base da verdadeira ação ética. Antes, essa base vem de alguma fonte externa ao homem, como Deus, as forças naturais, forças cósmicas, etc., de tal modo que os homens receberiam as regras do certo e do errado da parte de algum poder mais alto que eles, e não dos costumes fixados através das experiências do dia-a-dia.

II. Na Religião

1. O costume é uma questão meramente humana, embora possa estar escudado nas leis naturais e nos impulsos da consciência, estando assim em harmonia com a vontade de Deus.

2. Por outro lado, os costumes podem ser totalmente perversos, acompanhando a natureza pecaminosa do homem. Os esquimós, que têm o costume de entregar a própria esposa a algum visitante que passe, para que a tenha como mulher, durante a noite, dificilmente poderão afirmar que isso é um costume correto e universal. As sociedades que seguem costumeiramente a idolatria, de forma alguma poderão afirmar que isso reflete a vontade divina. Um dito popular, que peca pela raiz, por conseguinte, é aquele que diz: «A voz do povo é a voz de Deus». Na verdade, em face da natureza pecaminosa e rebelde do homem, dificilmente a voz do povo corresponde à vontade de Deus; antes, geralmente contraria a vontade revelada de Deus. É precisamente por isso que o evangelho é pregado ao mundo inteiro, conclamando os homens ao arrependimento, ou seja, à mudança de atitude mental.

3. A *ética* alicerça-se sobre as leis naturais e sobre a revelação divina, mas jamais sobre os costumes sociais, partam eles de onde partirem.

4. Na Bíblia, encontramos uma *tradição estabelecida*, orientada por Deus, que então se torna o costume do povo (no caso específico, do povo de Israel; e nos tempos neotestamentário, dos cristãos que seguem a Bíblia) ou seja, um modo fixo de ação (I Sam. 2:13), uma norma habitual (I Sam. 27:11), ou uma forma tradicional (Gên. 40:13; Êxo. 21:9; Juí. 18:7). No Novo Testamento, o vocábulo grego *éthos* significa costume no sentido de hábito (Luc. 22:19; Atos 25:16). No evangelho de João, um termo cognato daquele vocábulo denota os costumes sociais. Essa palavra também é aplicada às tradições religiosas dos antepassados, sem importar se mosaicas ou rabínicas (Luc. 1:9; 2:42; Atos 6:14; 15:1; 16:21; 21:21; 26:3; 28:17).

COSTUMES FUNERÁRIOS

Ver o artigo geral sobre **Sepultamento**.

COSTURAR

No hebraico, **taphar**, palavra que ocorre por quatro vezes: Gên. 3:7; Jó. 16:15; Ecl. 3:7 e Eze. 13:18. No grego, *epirápto*, «costurar sobre», que aparece somente em Marcos 2:21.

A origem da técnica da costura está perdida nas brumas da antiguidade da raça humana. O livro de Gênesis relata que o primeiro casal, Adão e Eva, costurou folhas de figueira. Eles queriam fazer uma espécie de aventais, a fim de encobrir a nudez recém-percebida, segundo se lê em Gênesis 3:7. No mundo mediterrâneo antigo, tanto os homens quanto as mulheres sabiam costurar. O Senhor Jesus referiu-se a essa habilidade quando disse: «ninguém costura remendo de pano novo em veste velha...» (Mar. 1:21). Parece evidente que Paulo fazia muito trabalho de costura, quando fabricava tendas, por ser esse o seu ofício. Ver *Artes e Ofícios*.

COTA DE MALHAS

Ver o artigo geral sobre **Armadura, Armas**. Ver I Sa. 17:5,38 e I Reis 22:34. No hebraico, a palavra é *shiryon*. As cotas de malha eram de diferentes tipos. Havia desde cotas de malha de couro, fortificado com pedaços de metal, em escamas, até vestimentas inteiramente de metal. As referências bíblicas, mais provavelmente, apontam para as jaquetas de couro com metal entrelaçado, onde ficavam presas as escamas. Esse tipo de proteção tem sido encontrada pelos arqueólogos, principalmente nos relevos assírios. Fragmentos dessas peças de vestuário também têm sido encontrados em várias escavações feitas no Oriente Próximo.

COULANGES, FUSTEL DE

Suas datas foram 1830-1889. Foi um dos mais proeminentes historiadores franceses sobre o mundo antigo e sobre a história medieval. Ele tentou demonstrar que as *idéias*, e, mais particularmente, as *idéias religiosas*, são as causas das mudanças sociais, bem como o fator primário dos fenômenos sociais. Ele procurou demonstrar que o aparecimento de novas religiões e de movimentos religiosos provoca mudanças radicais na sociedade. Grande parte de sua

COURAÇA — CÔVADO

filosofia está contida no livro de sua autoria, *The Ancient City*.

COURAÇA Ver **Armadura, Arma**.

COURNOT, ANTOINE
Suas datas foram 1801-1877. Filósofo e matemático francês. Nasceu em Gray. Foi professor em Paris, Lyons e Grenoble. Foi reitor da Academia de Grenoble, e então da Academia de Dijon.
Idéias: 1. O acaso e a descontinuidade são tão reais quanto a boa ordem e a continuidade. No entanto, podemos chegar ao conhecimento da verdadeira natureza das coisas, ao que os filósofos chamam de «coisa em si mesma». 2. O método de abordagem é a vida intelectual, de acordo com o que, através de princípios mais profundos e abrangentes, as conexões de fenômenos aparentemente desvinculados podem vir a ser estabelecidas. 3. O alvo da filosofia é elaborar categorias de forma, unidade, simplicidade e simetria. 4. Nessa análise, o filósofo descobre as coisas que se caracterizam pelas qualidades de finalidade e vitalidade, e que não podem ser reduzidas a questões físicas ou químicas. Em um nível ainda mais alto, através de nossas categorias intelectuais, descobrimos Deus. A superioridade de Deus não depende do conhecimento que ele tem do futuro (o que é uma questão contingente), mas depende do fato de que, diferente do homem, ele tem seguro conhecimento do que é contingente e do que não o é.
Obras. Researches into Mathematical Principles of the Theory of Wealth; Exposition of the Theory of Chance and of Probability; An Essay on the Foundations of Our Knowledge; Treatise on the Linkage of Fundamental Ideas in the Sciences and in History. (EP P)

COURO Ver **Peles de Animais (Trabalho em Couro)**.

COUSIN, VICTOR
Suas datas foram 1692-1867. Filósofo francês nascido em Paris e ali educado. Foi professor na Escola Normal de Paris e na Sorbonne. Foi ministro da instrução pública e membro do Institut de France. Foi porta-voz do *Juste Milieu*, uma classe elitista filosófica. Foi influenciado por Locke, Condillac e pela filosofia escocesa do bom senso de Thomas Reid. Maine de Biran, Schelling e Hegel também influíram sobre o pensamento de Cousin. Ele procurou criar certa fusão de idéias, fazendo esse filósofo voltar-se para o espiritualismo (que vide).
Idéias:
1. A filosofia teria a tarefa de classificar e a necessidade de interpretar as experiências humanas, de maneira a extrair sentido das mesmas. Deveria ser um instrumento de observação, indução e análise.
2. A *espontaneidade* seria sua própria causa, servindo de importante princípio filosófico. A espontaneidade é a origem da liberdade. O homem é dotado de uma percepção espontânea, e, através disso, pode obter discernimento quanto às leis da razão, da substância e da causalidade. Partindo dessas leis, o indivíduo pode passar da psicologia para os discernimentos da ontologia (que vide).
3. Esse processo leva-nos até Deus como a causa absoluta. Deus também é a substância e a espontaneidade absolutas, a divina atividade que tem lugar sem qualquer deliberação prévia.
4. A filosofia giraria em torno de quatro pontos de vista principais: o empirismo, o idealismo, o ceticismo e o misticismo. Todos os sistemas seriam verdadeiros, mas incompletos. A função da filosofia consistiria em unir esses sistemas, provendo assim um pensamento filosófico que se ajuste à *totalidade* da consciência humana.
Obras: *Philosophical Fragments; Course in the History of Philosophy; Course in the History of Modern Philosophy; The Good and the Beautiful*. Ele também publicou muitos volumes sobre os filósofos Proclo, Descartes e Platão.

COVA DOS LEÕES
A palavra «cova» é tradução de várias palavras hebraicas e de uma palavra grega. No caso da «cova dos leões» onde Daniel foi lançado, a palavra aramaica é *gob*, usada por dez vezes (Dan. 6:7,12,16,17,19,20,23,24). O termo grego é *spélaion*, usado por seis vezes: Mat. 21:13 (citando Jer. 7:11); Mar. 11:7; Luc. 19:46; João 11:38; Heb. 11:38; Apo. 6:15. Outras palavras hebraicas podem indicar o esconderijo de algum animal feroz (Jó 37:8; Sal. 10:9; 104:22; Isa. 32:14). Também pode estar em foco uma cavidade nas rochas ou no chão, onde se oculta alguma serpente (Isa. 11:8). Pode estar em foco uma caverna ou fissura, onde os animais podem se ocultar (Juí. 6:2; Heb. 11:38; Apo. 6:15), o que, algumas vezes, é usada por pessoas que estão sendo procuradas, ou por ladrões que se ocultam da lei (Mat. 21:13; Mar. 11:17).
A cova dos leões é mencionada por dez vezes no livro de Daniel (ver acima). A história informa-nos que os babilônios e assírios guardavam leões que haviam capturado nos alagadiços, como animais para caçar ou como animais de estimação. A arqueologia tem confirmado isso nos magníficos relevos descobertos, como aqueles do governante neo-assírio, Assurnasipal II (883-859 A.C.), em Ninrode, ou de Assurbanipal, em Nínive (668-627). Os medos-persas deram prosseguimento ao costume. Na lei mesopotâmica iraniana haviam provisões para castigar por meio de provas, como enfrentar um leão e ser esmigalhado pelo mesmo. Daniel e seus companheiros foram sujeitados a esse tipo de castigo. O trecho de Jó 38:39-41 refere-se a uma cova de leões como lugar temível.

CÔVADO
Ver o artigo sobre **Pesos e Medidas**. No hebraico é *ammah*, palavra de ocorrência freqüente, pois figura por pouco mais de duzentas vezes no Antigo Testamento.
O côvado era uma medida derivada do corpo humano (Deu. 3:11). Essa medida variava de um país para outro, não havendo certeza sobre a maneira como era determinada. Parece ter sido o comprimento desde o cotovelo até o fim do dedo médio da mão, o dedo mais longo. O côvado egípcio consistia em seis larguras da mão, conforme se tem descoberto nas ruínas encontradas em Mênfis. Esse foi o côvado adotado pelos israelitas. Nos escritos rabínicos (*Mischn. Chelim*, 17.9), encontramos o côvado dividido em larguras de mão, e Josefo (*Anti.*) indica a mesma coisa, porquanto dois palmos equivalem a seis larguras de mão. Isso faz o côvado ter, aproximadamente, 44,5 cm. Em I Reis 7:26, encontramos a largura da mão usada como medida; e o palmo aparece em Êxo. 28:16. Os egípcios também dispunham de um côvado maior, o que parece estar indicado, igualmente, nos trechos de Eze. 40:5 e 43:13, o que significa que Israel tinha mais de um côvado. Esse côvado maior tem sido chamado de côvado real, que era mais longo que o côvado normal uma largura de mão, dando-lhe, aproximadamente, o

comprimento de 52 cm.

COVENANTERS

Esse foi o título dado aos que, na Escócia, contenderam resolutamente pela liberdade religiosa, entre 1637 e 1688, contra o absolutismo dos Stuarts, na Igreja e no Estado. Esse nome proveio da fé reformada, e aqueles homens estiveram envolvidos na questão. Em inglês, *covenant* significa «pacto». Os «covenanters» eram os que haviam entrado em algum pacto. O mais importante desses pactos foi chamado Pacto Nacional, assinado em 1638, na igreja de Greyfriars, em Edimburgo, na Escócia, pela maioria dos nobres e por grande número de cidadãos comuns.

O estado virtualmente agrilhoara a Igreja reformada na Escócia. Houve um ponto crítico quando o rei Carlos I introduziu um novo Livro de Cânones, que incluía uma liturgia que era contrária às convicções dos reformadores. As reclamações levaram-no a recuar por algum tempo. Ele permitiu uma Assembléia Geral, em 1637. Essa assembléia aboliu a prelazia (que vide), isto é, o tipo de governo eclesiástico segundo o qual quem exerce o poder são os bispos, os arcebispos, os metropolitanos e os patriarcas. Na Igreja Anglicana, esse poder reduz-se à autoridade dos bispos e arcebispos. Por causa dessa alteração, seguiu-se a luta armada, durante a qual os escoceses levaram a melhor. Então o rei garantiu a liberdade religiosa, embora não tivesse cumprido a sua palavra. Em 1643; os escoceses entraram na Liga Solene, com o parlamento inglês. Rebentou a guerra civil, o exército parlamentar triunfou, e Carlos I foi executado. Porém, a luta estava longe do fim. Carlos II prometeu defender os covenanters; e, no entanto, começou grande opressão contra eles. Foram executados importantes líderes dos covenanters, como Argyle, Sir Archibald Johnston, e vários outros. Muitos ministros do evangelho foram banidos, milhares de pessoas foram encarceradas, e todos sofreram perseguição. Porém, o processo histórico estava do lado dos covenanters. Em 1688, a revolução, sob a direção de Guilherme de Orange, garantiu a liberdade religiosa na Escócia. (B C)

COVERDALE, MYLES

Suas datas foram 1488-1568. Foi o tradutor da primeira Bíblia completa impressa no idioma inglês (1535), e editor da Grande Bíblia (1539), a primeira das versões *autorizadas* em inglês. Coverdale sentiu que teria de sair das ilhas britânicas para as terras continentais européias, a fim de escapar da perseguição, acusado de heresia como fora. O bispo de Exeter, em 1551, privou-o de sua sé por ocasião da subida ao trono da rainha Maria. Os chamados hereges, em muitos casos, fizeram grande contribuição para a fé religiosa. Obviamente, houve e há hereges autênticos, que foram e continuam sendo forças negativas. Mas estamos falando dos que são tachados *hereges* sem o serem. A morte de Henrique VIII, em 1547, permitiu que os reformadores se tornassem mais fortes, e, no tempo do reinado de Eduardo VI, Coverdale foi feito bispo de Exeter, em 1551. Porém, poucos anos mais tarde, quando Maria I, a Católica, subiu ao trono, Coverdale precisou fugir novamente para terras continentais. Em Genebra, na Suíça, Coverdale participou na produção da Bíblia de Genebra, lançada pelos calvinistas, —que veio a ser a versão inglesa favorita dos puritanos e de muitos outros grupos evangélicos. Finalmente, foi ultrapassada pela versão autorizada de 1611, intitulada em inglês King James Version. Quando Isabel I subiu ao trono, Coverdale regressou à Inglaterra. Nunca mais recebeu posições eclesiásticas importantes, mas foi-lhe dada uma pensão vitalícia, em Londres. Faleceu nessa cidade, a 20 de janeiro de 1569. Foi um homem da Bíblia do começo ao fim, pelo que a sua vida foi muito útil à causa do cristianismo evangélico. (AM E)

COXA

Há duas palavras hebraicas e uma palavra grega a considerar, neste verbete, a saber:

1. *Yarek*, «coxa», palavra que ocorre por trinta e quatro vezes, das quais vinte e uma vezes com esse sentido. Por exemplo: Gên. 24:2,9; 32:25,31,32; Núm. 5:21,22,27; Juí. 3:16,21; Can. 3:8; Eze. 21:12; 24:4.

2. *Yarekah*, «coxa». Palavra aramaica que aparece somente em Dan. 2:32.

3. *Merós*, «coxa». Palavra grega que ocorre somente em Apo. 19:16.

A coxa é a parte superior da perna de uma pessoa, entre os quadris e o joelho. A coxa é suportada pelo maior, mais longo e mais forte osso do corpo humano, o fêmur. Tem a forma de um cone invertido e truncado. Na parte superior, a coxa é limitada pela virilha, pelo períneo, na parte interna, pela dobra das nádegas, na parte detrás, e pelos quadris, lateralmente. Na parte inferior, a coxa é limitada pela proeminência do joelho, na parte da frente, e pelo chamado espaço poplíteo ou dobra da perna. Além do fêmur, a coxa consiste em fortes músculos, além dos vasos sangüíneos, vasos linfáticos e nervos, estruturas todas essas rodeadas por uma faixa fibrosa forte, como se fora a casca de uma árvore.

O deslocamento da junta da coxa com os quadris ocorre na porção superior do fêmur, mais comumente em um movimento para a frente, embora também se reconheça um movimento para trás. Quando o Anjo do Senhor tocou no nervo da coxa de Jacó (Gên. 32:25), sem dúvida fê-lo na dobra de uma das nádegas. Alguns estudiosos pensam que isso produziu o deslocamento da própria junta. Se isso realmente ocorreu, então Jacó deve ter ficado com o movimento afetado da perna correspondente, precisando apoiar-se sobre o dedão do pé. Deve-se notar que a cabeça do fêmur, nesses casos, eleva-se dentro de seu soquete, de tal modo que os músculos da área ficam mais curtos. Esses músculos encurtados talvez correspondam à descrição de Gênesis 32:32, «...o nervo do quadril, na articulação da coxa...»

Uma outra interpretação sobre a injúria sofrida por Jacó é aquela que pensa no «moderno diagnóstico, muito em moda, do rompimento do disco intervertebral, o que produz uma dor ciática muito severa e intratável, por motivo de pressão das extremidades nervosas». Com base nesse outro ponto de vista, o «nervo do quadril» seria o nervo ciático. Todavia, essa interpretação envolve a dificuldade de se explicar como o toque na coxa poderia ter produzido a injúria do disco da vértebra.

É digno de nota que os patriarcas de Israel tinham por costume pôr uma mão debaixo da coxa, em conexão com juramentos solenemente feitos (ver Gên. 24:2; 47:29). Também era costume cingir a espada de encontro à coxa (Sal. 45:3). Assim sucedia porque a mão chega àquela altura com naturalidade, e o cabo da espada, pois, tornava-se facilmente acessível, em algum inesperado encontro com o inimigo (Can. 3:8). Em contraste com isso, bater uma mão de encontro à coxa servia de manifestação externa de vergonha e surpresa (Jer. 31:19; Eze. 21:12). O gesto era feito como se alguém apalpasse em busca de uma espada que não estava ali, e o indivíduo percebesse, subitamente, que estava desarmado.

Em último lugar, mas não menos importante, é a observação que, por ocasião do aparecimento triunfal de Jesus, ele trará sobre a coxa a inscrição «Rei dos reis e Senhor dos senhores» (Apo. 19:16).

COZBI

O nome provém do acádico **kuzbu**, «volúpia». Mas outros pensam que o nome significa «enganadora». Esse era o nome de uma mulher midianita, filha de Zur, que Finéia executou juntamente com seu amante israelita, Zinri, em cerca de 1452 A.C. Essa tribo de nômades montados em camelos invadiu a Palestina na época dos juízes de Israel. Introduziram maus costumes, como a idolatria e a imoralidade, além de outros danos de ordem material. O nome de Cozbi aparece somente em Núm. 25:15,18. Os príncipes de Midiã foram feridos em número de cinco, porquanto os israelitas haviam sido corrompidos no deserto, pelos midianitas (Jos. 13:21). Após a morte de Cozbi, houve outra guerra de Israel contra os midianitas.

COZEBA

No hebraico, «falsidade». Nome de uma pequena aldeia, localizada nas terras altas da Judéia (I Crô. 4:22), que alguns estudiosos têm identificado com a moderna Khirbet ed-Dilb. A arqueologia tem descoberto ali peças de cerâmica do início da era do Ferro. Mas outros eruditos identificam-na com Quezibe, uma aldeia na fronteira da Sefelá, no centro do território de Judá (Gên. 38:5). Também há quem conjecture tratar-se do moderno Tell el-Beida, cerca de cinco quilômetros a oeste de Adulão.

COZINHADO

No hebraico, **nazid**, vocábulo que ocorre por seis vezes: Gên. 25:29,34; II Reis 4:38-40; Ageu 2:12. Essa palavra significa algo «cozinhado», segundo se vê em Gên. 25:29,34. Nessa referência, temos o preço que Esaú pagou a Jacó, para perder o seu direito de primogenitura. O vs. 34 informa-nos que o cozinhado era preparado com lentilhas. Poderia ter sido preparado com vários legumes, porquanto só precisava ser algo cozido, — sem necessidade de ser algo específico. Em Ageu 2:12, um «cozinhado» é mencionado lado a lado com vários outros mantimentos. O trecho de II Reis 4:39 informa-nos que os discípulos de Eliseu prepararam uma panela com cozinhado para comerem.

Usos figurados. Com base na narrativa sobre Jacó e Esaú, um «cozinhado» veio a significar qualquer coisa de grande valor, pelo que se pagou um preço ridículo. Ou, por extensão, a insensatez de sacrificar alguma coisa importante ou valiosa, em troca de algo sem valor.

COZINHAR, COZINHEIRO

A palavra hebraica **tabbach**, usada com o sentido de «cozinheiro» apenas por duas vezes — I Sam. 9:23,24 — também tinha os sentidos de açougueiro, executor e guarda. A conexão é que um cozinheiro geralmente era quem abatia os animais para consumo humano. Em todas as casas havia cozinheiros e cozinheiras não profissionais; mas também os havia profissionais (Gên. 40:1; I Sam. 9:23,24). As escravas e servas com freqüência também eram cozinheiras (I Sam. 8:13), mas as donas de casa também sabiam cozinhar (Gên. 18:6; 27:9). Também havia cozinheiros (Gên. 18:7; 25:29; 27:31). Gideão sabia como cozinhar e cozer bolos (Juí. 6:19). Um cozinheiro é sugerido no trecho de Lucas 17:8. É possível que, nas atividades do templo de Jerusalém, os sacerdotes se ocupassem no cozimento das carcaças dos animais abatidos, o que também podia ser feito por auxiliares.

Utensílios de Cozinha. A arqueologia tem iluminado amplamente essa questão. Esses utensílios eram os mais variados, de vários metais, tamanhos e formatos. Alguns deles eram largos e fundos, outros estreitos e rasos. Quanto à configuração geométrica eram quase esféricos. Alguns tinham duas asas, e outros, uma só. Alguns desses utensílios tinham perfurações por onde se passava um cordão, para facilitar-lhes o transporte. Havia grelhas, panelas, jarras, taças, copos, frigideiras, etc., feitas de barro ou de vários metais. Também havia facas e colheres. Referências bíblicas a potes, panelas, caldeirões, cestas, pratos, frigideiras, etc., aparecem em Êxodo 16:3; I Samuel 2:14; II Reis 2:20; 4:38; 21:13; 25:15 e II Crônicas 35:13.

Sentidos Simbólicos e Psicológicos. A preparação de uma refeição simboliza **suprimentos**. Quanto mais elaborada for essa preparação, mais abundante será o suprimento. Além disso, o ato de cozinhar pode simbolizar a preparação do crente para alguma coisa, ou a realização de alguma tarefa específica. O ato de cozinhar, igualmente, pode retratar a transformação de matérias primas em algo útil, ou seja, a realização de alguma tarefa ou projeto. Pode indicar progresso na apreensão da verdade. Virar alguma coisa em uma panela pode indicar o ato de pensar, de raciocinar sobre alguma coisa, ou o ato de procurar alguma resposta. A dificuldade em engolir algo pode indicar a relutância em aceitar algum ensinamento, idéia ou circunstância externa. Uma *panela redonda*, que apareça em uma visão ou sonho, pode simbolizar a ansiedade da pessoa para expandir seus horizontes e experiências.

Em sentido negativo, o ato de cozinhar pode simbolizar o planejamento ou a execução de projetos com maus desígnios. Também há o caldo das bruxas, como símbolo de mágica e adivinhação, ou então de maldições e obras malignas. De outras vezes, o ato de cozinhar pode envolver sentidos psicossomáticos, como advertência contra certos alimentos ou maneiras de preparar os mesmos. Mas, talvez na maioria dos casos, sonhar com o ato de cozinhar, com alimentos ou com refeições, significa apenas que a pessoa está com fome. Portanto, nada de precipitações na interpretação dos sonhos! (CHE S UN Z)

COZINHAS

No hebraico, **bashal**, «cozinhar». Enquanto a versão portuguesa diz, em Ezequiel 46:24: «São estas as *cozinhas*, onde os ministros do templo cozerão...», o original hebraico diz algo como: «São estes os *lugares*, onde os ministros do templo cozerão...». A cena fazia parte de uma visão que Ezequiel teve sobre o templo de Jerusalém, no tocante a um dos quatro subátrios do átrio exterior, onde o povo poderia preparar seus sacrifícios, nas lareiras ali providas com esse propósito. Os sacerdotes cozinhavam suas ofertas em suas próprias cozinhas (vs. 19,20), a fim de que não entrassem em contato com coisas imundas e nem com pessoas não consagradas. (Z)

••• ••• •••

CRANMER, THOMAS

Reformador religioso inglês e arcebispo de Canterbury. Nasceu em Aslockton, em Nottinghamshire, em 1489. Faleceu em 1556. Educou-se na Universidade de Cambridge; foi membro do Colégio de Jesus. Mas casou-se, e perdeu o posto. Porém, após o falecimento de sua esposa, retornou ao ministério. Foi ordenado em 1520, notabilizando-se por seus estudos das Escrituras e da teologia; e recebeu o doutorado em 1526. As doutrinas da Reforma protestante (que vide) abalaram a Universidade de Cambridge na época de Cranmer. E ele mesmo declarou-se contrário à idéia da supremacia papal. Seus contínuos estudos da Bíblia e dos escritos patrísticos afastavam-no cada vez mais dos padrões do catolicismo romano. Envolveu-se nos problemas do divórcio de Henrique VIII, e, finalmente, já como arcebispo, declarou nulo o primeiro casamento do rei. Antes mesmo disso obtivera o favor real, tendo sido recompensado com o cargo de capelão real e de arquidiácono de Tauton. Foi enviado ao estrangeiro em missão diplomática, em 1530, ao imperador Carlos V, da Alemanha. Estando na Alemanha, casou-se secretamente com uma sobrinha do reformador luterano Andreas Osiander. Em 1532, o rei da Inglaterra chamou-o de volta, nomeando-o arcebispo de Canterbury. Foi consagrado a 30 de março de 1533.

Cranmer estava preparado para efetuar reformas ainda mais amplas na Igreja Anglicana. Influenciou a formulação dos *Dez Artigos*, de 1536, os primeiros da Igreja da Inglaterra. Também contribuiu com alguma coisa para o *Livro do Bispo*, desse mesmo ano. Promoveu, igualmente, a publicação da Bíblia em inglês, e participou da preparação do *Livro de Oração Comum*, em suas edições de 1549 e 1552. A edição de 1662, dessa obra, continua sendo usada pela denominação anglicana. Cranmer também tomou parte na formulação dos *Quarenta e Dois Artigos*, de 1553, os quais terminariam sendo reduzidos aos famosos *Trinta e Nove Artigos*.

Quando Eduardo VI tornou-se rei, Cranmer recebeu a grande responsabilidade de dirigir as reformas que alteraram em muito a Igreja Anglicana, o que incluiu a produção das obras acima citadas. Então ocorreu a calamidade. Maria I sucedeu a Eduardo VI no trono. E essa rainha, pelo menos temporariamente, fez a Igreja Anglicana reverter às suas raízes católicas, incluindo o reconhecimento da autoridade do papa. Cranmer foi acusado de traição, por causa de envolvimentos políticos que eram então desaprovados. Foi forçado a contemplar os martírios de Latimer e Ridley (ver os artigos sobre eles), e foi condenado por heresia, em 1556. Suas ordens clericais foram canceladas, e foi forçado a retratar-se, sob pressões. Porém, no dia de sua execução, em Oxford, a 21 de março de 1556, repudiou suas retratações, e experimentou a execução na fogueira, com grande coragem. Um toque dramático foi que ele manteve sua mão direita nas chamas, até ela ser consumida, porquanto com aquela mão assinara sua retratação. Através de Cranmer é que a Igreja Anglicana alicerçada suas reivindicações de sucessão apostólica, o que a Igreja Católica Romana repudia. Ver o artigo sobre a questão da *Sucessão Apostólica*. Mas, com ou sem a sucessão apostólica, Cranmer deixou sua marca indelével na história da Igreja, como força positiva em prol da verdade, sem importar os erros em que tenha caído. (AM E P)

CRANTOR

Filósofo grego que viveu entre os séculos IV e III A.C. Nasceu em Soli, na Cilícia. Provavelmente estudou com Xenócrates (que vide) e com Pólemon (que vide). Foi membro da primeira Academia (que vide) de Platão. Seu interesse básico eram as questões éticas, embora tenha composto o primeiro comentário conhecido sobre o *Timaeus* de Platão, um diálogo metafísico e científico. Além desse comentário ele fez um estudo sobre a *Dor*.

CRASHAW, RICHARD

Suas datas foram 1613-1649. Foi um poeta inglês, educado em Cambridge por algum tempo, membro da Peterhouse. Tornou-se católico romano nos seus últimos anos ali, e, por motivo das perseguições que sofreu, finalmente, mudou-se para o continente europeu. Sua principal obra foi *Steps to the Temple*, escrita quando ele ainda era nominalmente um anglicano. Assinala-se por um êxtase devocional quase sem-par na língua inglesa. Em 1646 foi a Roma e foi apresentado ao papa, após o que foi galardoado com um ofício eclesiástico no santuário de Loreto. Faleceu ali, a 21 de agosto de 1649. Foi um grande desvio para um homem que fora criado como puritano, e cujo pai fora ministro protestante.

CRATES

Esse foi o nome de nada menos de três filósofos gregos, a saber:

1. Crates de Atenas, que sucedeu Pólemon, como líder da Academia de Platão (270-268 A.C.). Ele interessava-se, acima de tudo, pela ética.

2. Crates de Malo, do século II A.C. Foi filósofo estóico, líder da biblioteca de Pérgamo. Opunha-se a Aristarco. Foi líder da escola alexandrina.

3. Crates de Tebas. Foi um filósofo cínico da porção final do século IV A.C. Foi famoso estudante de Diógenes, e também o último grande representante do cinismo (que vide). Ajudou a desenvolver o chamado ensaio satírico, que se tornou o padrão do modo de expressão daquela escola.

CRÁTILO

Viveu em torno de 410 A.C. Foi filósofo sofista grego (que vide). Desenvolveu uma forma radical da doutrina de Heráclito, ao afirmar que tudo está em estado de fluxo, ao ponto em que não se pode pisar por duas vezes no mesmo rio. Essa foi a doutrina que ajudou Platão a afirmar que o *conhecimento* não pode alicerçar-se sobre a percepção dos sentidos, e nem sobre o mundo material em constante fluxo. Isso posto, o conhecimento deve estar fundamentado sobre a razão, a intuição e o misticismo. O conhecimento verdadeiro dependeria do mundo das *idéias* ou *universais* (que vide). Platão escreveu um diálogo intitulado *Crátilo*. Nesse diálogo, Platão atribui a Crátilo a noção de que os nomes das coisas naturalmente são vinculadas às coisas, as quais, de alguma maneira, apegam-se corretamente. Porém, a doutrina do fluxo de todas as coisas labora contra tal noção, porquanto qualquer coisa que vive em constante modificação na natureza dificilmente pode ter um nome que reflita verazmente qualidades específicas fixas e naturais.

CRÉDITO, CREDOR (Ver também sobre **Juros**).

No hebraico, **nashah**, palavra que ocorre por onze vezes no Antigo Testamento, por duas vezes com o claro sentido de credor, a saber, II Reis 4:1 e Isaías

CREDO — CREDO CONSTANTINOPOLITANO

50:1. No Novo Testamento temos a palavra grega *daneistés*, «emprestador», que aparece somente em Lucas 7:41.

A Bíblia, no Antigo e no Novo Testamentos, fala sobre os credores, pessoas que emprestam dinheiro ou bens a alguém, que passa a ser o devedor. A lei mosaica (ver Deu. 23:19) não permitiu que um judeu cobrasse juros de outro judeu. Mas podiam ser cobrados juros dos estrangeiros que se encontrassem em Israel. Usualmente, nos casos de empréstimo, algo de valor servia de penhor, por parte do devedor, o que era confiscado caso o pagamento da dívida não fosse feita. As leis, tanto na cultura hebréia como em outras culturas antigas, eram bastante brutais quanto a esse aspecto. Basta dizer que a família inteira de um homem podia ser vendida à escravidão se ele não pagasse as suas dívidas. Ver II Reis 4:1. Juros eram cobrados (Lev. 25:37; Deu. 23:20), e isso dava margem a tremendos abusos. Jesus acusou os fariseus de devorarem as casas das viúvas. Isso mostra como pessoas religiosas, impelidas pela ganância, são capazes de atos de desumanidade. Tais explorações são contrárias à lei do amor, que é o cumprimento dos requisitos morais da lei inteira (Rom. 13:9,10). No trecho de Lucas 7:41, temos a menção ao credor (no grego, *daneistés*) que perdoou generosamente ao devedor, que lhe devia imensa quantia. Em seguida, Jesus fez a pergunta: «Qual deles, portanto, o amará mais?», após ter-se referido a um devedor muito menor, cuja dívida não fora perdoada. A resposta óbvia à pergunta de Jesus é que quem mais foi perdoado, mais ama. Esse texto espiritualiza a questão, fazendo-a ilustrar o perdão dos pecados e o plano da redenção, traçado pelo Senhor Deus. Esses benefícios espirituais deveriam inspirar-nos ao amor a Deus, que é o Grande Credor, ao passo que todos os homens são os devedores.

CREDO Ver também sobre **Credos**.

Essa palavra vem do latim, com o sentido de «creio». Essa é a palavra por detrás do vocábulo português «credo». Ver o artigo abaixo sobre os *Credos*. Em relação ao termo latino *credo*, há vários «slogans» usados por teólogos e filósofos, que têm provocado considerável discussão. Consideremos os seguintes:

1. *Credo quia absurdum est*, «Creio porque é absurdo». E também: *Credo quia impossibile est*, «Creio porque é impossível». Essas são famosas declarações de Tertuliano (que vide), o qual enfatizava com elas a doutrina da fé, que não corresponde à compreensão e à investigação humanas. A verdade com freqüência reveste-se de uma aura fantástica. Quanto mais a ciência descobre, mais isso torna-se óbvio. Muito mais ainda, certas grandes verdades espirituais não se adaptam à lógica humana. Aquilo que os homens pensam ser absurdo ou impossível, bem pode corresponder à verdade dos fatos. Por outro lado, essa atitude pode tornar-se uma desculpa para a *credulidade* (que vide), que é a crença fácil e tola.

2. *Credo ut intelligam*, «Creio para poder compreender». Essa declaração foi feita por Agostinho, e também foi utilizada por Anselmo (ver os artigos a respeito deles). Essa declaração ensina-nos que a crença pode ser necessária para a boa compreensão das coisas, ao passo que a atitude do ceticismo deixa a pessoa nas trevas.

3. *Credo*, «Creio». Essa palavra introduz vários credos importantes da Igreja cristã.

4. Na missa da Igreja Católica Romana, o *credo* é a terceira parte, uma repetição do Credo Niceno (que vide).

CREDO ATANASIANO

Com freqüência denominado **Quicunque Vult**, por causa das palavras iniciais, sendo um dos três credos chamados ecumênicos. Os outros dois são o apostólico e o niceno (ver os artigos). Originou-se no Ocidente, mas os seus conceitos tiveram vasta influência por toda a Igreja. Foi incluído como um apêndice nos Ofícios Horários da Igreja Ortodoxa Oriental. O *Athanasium* originalmente era uma espécie de comentário sobre o *fides Athanasii* ou sobre o credo niceno. A maioria dos eruditos vêem-no como pós-agostiniano, mas outros argumentam em favor de uma origem nos dias de Apolinário, ou seja, pré-nestoriano (ver o artigo a respeito). Seja como for, não foi escrito por Atanásio (ver o artigo), embora seu nome tivesse sido incluído como um campeão da ortodoxia, que o credo pretendia promover. Nos primeiros séculos foi altamente considerado entre os monges como próprio para a meditação e a memorização. Com a reavivamento da música sacra sob Carlos Magno (ver o artigo), passou a ser usado como um cântico, e foi posto no ofício de Prime (ver o artigo). No primeiro Livro de Oração de Eduardo VI (1549), foi decidido que deveria ser cantado ou recitado após o Benedictus, nas festividades maiores. No quinto Livro de Oração da Inglaterra (1662), que continua sendo o único livro oficial da Oração Comum na Igreja Anglicana, ficou decidido que a confissão fosse entoada ou recitada na Oração Matinal em vez do Credo dos Apóstolos, nas treze festividades, incluindo todas as principais festividades.

O Credo:

«A fé católica é esta: adoramos um Deus em trindade, e a trindade em unidade: nem confundindo as pessoas e nem dividindo a substância. Pois há uma pessoa do Pai, outra do Filho e outra do Espírito Santo. Mas a deidade do Pai, do Filho e do Espírito Santo, é apenas uma; a glória é igual, a majestade é co-eterna. Tal como é o Pai, assim é o Filho e assim é o Espírito Santo; a saber, não criado, incompreensível, eterno. O Pai não foi feito de ninguém, nem criado e nem gerado. O Filho é apenas do Pai; nem feito e nem criado, mas gerado. O Espírito Santo é do Pai e do Filho; nem feito, nem criado, nem gerado, mas procedente».

Esse credo foi originalmente composto para opor-se a vários presumíveis erros acerca da cristologia e da divindade. Várias controvérsias produziram suas declarações distintivas, tendo sido originalmente escrito com um zelo fanático, para censurar os hereges. Assim, foi prefaciado como segue:

«Quem tiver de ser salvo, antes de tudo é mister que se apegue à fé católica, fé essa que, se alguém não a guardar sã e sem mácula, sem dúvida perecerá eternamente. E a fé católica é esta».

Por causa disso, muitos têm sentido que à sua atitude falta a característica do amor, pelo que não deveria ser incluído nos cultos. (AM B S)

CREDO CONSTANTINOPOLITANO

Um outro nome para esse credo é Credo Niceno-Constantinopolitano. O concílio de Calcedônia, de 451 D.C. (que vide), atribuiu esse credo ao concílio de Constantinopla, de 381 D.C. Esse credo difere do Credo Niceno, de 325 D.C., por haver adicionado a declaração, a respeito do Espírito Santo, como procedente do Pai. A declaração completa diz: «O Espírito Santo, o Senhor e Doador da Vida, procede do Pai, e, juntamente com o Pai e o Filho, é adorado e glorificado, e o qual falou através dos profetas». Esse credo também acrescentou algumas declarações sobre a Igreja, o batismo e a ressurreição, assemelhando-se muito à fórmula de Epifânio (que vide), de 374 D.C. Ver o artigo sobre os *Credos da Cristandade*. (E)

CREDO DOS APÓSTOLOS

Esse credo é usado no culto da Igreja Católica e também por muitos grupos protestantes, como uma afirmação tradicional de crenças fundamentais. Lemos no Livro da Oração Comum, da Igreja Anglicana:

«Creio em Deus, o Pai Todo-Poderoso, criador do céu e da terra. E em Jesus Cristo, Seu Filho unigênito e nosso Senhor, o qual foi concebido pelo Espírito Santo, nasceu da Virgem Maria, sofreu sob Pôncio Pilatos, foi crucificado, morto e sepultado. Desceu ao inferno. Ao terceiro dia ressuscitou dentre os mortos. Subiu ao céu e assenta-se à mão direita de Deus Pai, Todo-Poderoso. Dali virá para julgar a vivos e mortos. Creio no Espírito Santo, na Santa Igreja Universal, na comunhão dos santos, no perdão dos pecados, na ressurreição do corpo e na vida eterna. Amém».

Essa forma do credo é uma elaboração local de uma forma romana mais antiga, usada no sudoeste da França no século VII. Tirânio Rufino, que escreveu um comentário sobre o credo, no começo do século XV, declarou que o mesmo foi escrito pelos apóstolos, sob a inspiração do Espírito de Deus, pouco depois da ressurreição de Cristo. Segundo uma tradição, foi entregue à Igreja de Roma sem alteração, porque nenhuma heresia jamais se teria originado em Roma, e porque era publicamente usado por ocasião do batismo e da confissão. Nenhum erudito aceita tal afirmativa como veraz hoje em dia, exceto no sentido secundário, que o credo preserva em seus pontos essenciais, a crença dos apóstolos, e que certamente é muito antigo.

Dentro da obra *Tradição Apostólica* de Hipólito há um credo romano constante de perguntas e respostas, datado do começo do século III D.C., que pode ter sido a fonte principal do Credo dos Apóstolos. Diz como segue:

«Crês em Deus, o Pai Todo-Poderoso? Crês em Jesus Cristo, o Filho de Deus que nasceu pelo Espírito Santo da Virgem Maria, morreu e foi sepultado, ressuscitou dentre os mortos ao terceiro dia, subiu ao céu e está sentado à mão direita do Pai, e virá para julgar vivos e mortos? Crês no Espírito Santo e na Santa Igreja e na ressurreição dos mortos?»

Parece termos aqui uma confissão batismal. Adições feitas à mesma aparentemente produziram o credo, conforme o conhecemos atualmente. Naturalmente, as doutrinas ali contidas são ensinos neotestamentários, encontrados em trechos como I Cor. 8:6; I Tess. 1:9,10; I Cor. 15:1-11, e nos vários evangelhos. A expressão «santa Igreja» pode ser encontrada em uso desde os meados do século II D.C., e o item do perdão de pecados, dentro da confissão batismal, tornou-se corrente pelos fins desse mesmo século. Ou esses itens já eram usados e foram adicionados ao credo em data anterior, ou um ou dois desses itens talvez já fizessem parte da formulação original.

Entretanto, os últimos itens a serem adicionados foram: 1. A descida de Cristo ao hades, conceito baseado em I Ped. 3:18 - 4:6 e Efé. 4:9. Esse figura no credo de Sirmium, em 359 D.C. 2. A noção de «vida eterna», baseada em vários credos orientais, e que, naturalmente, é uma doutrina do Novo Testamento. 3. A noção de «comunhão dos santos», que com essas palavras aparece pela primeira vez em Nicetas de Remesiana, no fim do século IV D.C. A idéia de «comunhão» sugere a outra adição, «Santa Igreja Universal», onde se manifesta essa comunhão.

O próprio credo exprime doutrinas neotestamentárias diretas, mas várias lendas cresceram ao redor do mesmo. As primeiras lendas foram aquelas já aludidas, refletidas nas declarações de Rufino. Lendas mais elaboradas apareceram como a afirmação de que todos os doze apóstolos contribuíram com algum artigo especial. Assim, presumivelmente Pedro entrou com «Creio em Deus, o Pai Todo-Poderoso»; André (ou João) adicionou: «e em Jesus Cristo, Seu Filho, nosso Senhor», etc.

Supostos estágios de desenvolvimento: 1. A antiga fórmula romana, pelos meados do segundo século cristão. 2. A fórmula expressa por Rufino (390 D.C.), que continha algumas adições. 3. Uma fórmula grega, conhecida por Marcelo de Ancira, do século quarto. 4. Uma fórmula breve, usada na Inglaterra, até o tempo da conquista normanda. 5. A forma atualmente conhecida, contida no Livro de Ação Comum dos anglicanos, fixada pelo século VII. Portanto, o credo foi um desenvolvimento, e nenhum concílio eclesiástico jamais fixou o texto do credo oficialmente. Pelo século XII, sua forma presente era usada por toda a parte no Ocidente e a prática de recitar o credo no culto diário e por ocasião dos atos de batismo, tornara-se comum; dois costumes que prevalecem até hoje.

Criação de credos. Até mesmo nas páginas do Novo Testamento encontramos exemplos de credos antigos. Quase certamente o trecho de Mat. 28:19 é um deles, tal como se dá em I Cor. 12:3. Paulo escreveu sobre um «padrão de ensino», segundo o qual eram «treinados» os novos convertidos (Rom. 6:17). Timóteo fez uma boa «confissão» perante muitas testemunhas (I Tim. 6:12), sendo bem provável que isso tivesse envolvido alguma afirmação credal padronizada. Ver também II Tim. 2:8 e 4:1. Pelos meados do segundo século, existiam credos em forma primitiva, sobretudo para o rito do batismo, que incluíam elementos existentes no Novo Testamento.

Importância atual dos credos. Muitas igrejas, denominações e organizações missionárias têm credos que se tornam padrões mediante os quais membros são aceitos ou rejeitados. Nenhum desses credos representa a gama inteira do ensino neotestamentário, pois cada um deles amolda-se às interpretações das várias denominações. Por exemplo, o relato da descida de Cristo ao hades, a fim de realizar ali uma missão misericordiosa (I Ped. 4:6), contida em I Ped. 3:18 - 4:6, e que faz parte do Credo dos Apóstolos, é geralmente ignorado por muitas denominações evangélicas da atualidade, embora se revista de imensas implicações quanto à extensão e abrangência da missão de Cristo. Ver o artigo sobre a *Descida de Cristo ao hades*. (AM B E S Z)

CREDO NICENO Ver **Nicéia, Credo de**.

CREDO QUIA ABSURDUM EST

Ver o artigo sobre **Credo**.

CREDO QUIA IMPOSSIBILE EST

Ver o artigo sobre **Credo**.

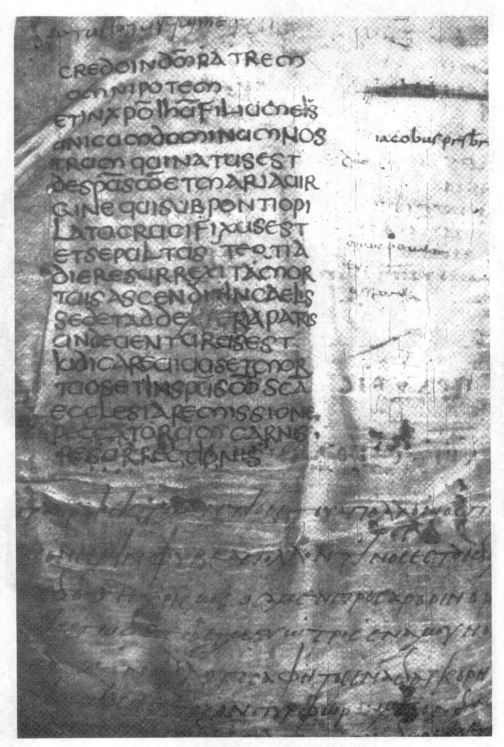

Cópia antiga do Credo Apostólico — Cortesia, Bodleian Library

JESUS E OS PESCADORES CONCERTANDO AS REDES

CREDO — CREDULIDADE

CREDO UT INTELLIGAM
Ver o artigo sobre **Credo**.

CREDOS

Os principais credos cristãos são discutidos em artigos separados. Ver acerca dos seguintes: Credo dos Apóstolos, Credo Atanasiano, Credo Niceno, Confissão de Augsburgo, Confissão de Westminster. Sob o título *Confissões da Igreja Histórica*, esses e outros credos são descritos, onde também são dadas informações gerais sobre as atividades credais da Igreja cristã ao longo dos séculos. Ver também o artigo sobre *Cristologia e Cristianismo*. O budismo (que vide) alude a uma vereda em oito passos. Maimônides (que vide) preparou um credo para o judaísmo (ver sob esse título, ponto onze, *Aspectos Históricos*).

1. Classificação Geral dos Credos Cristãos. Esses credos foram divididos apenas por questão de classificação, nos seguintes tipos: ecumênicos, católicos ocidentais, ortodoxos orientais, eclesiásticos provinciais, protestantes, declarações democráticas e seitas e cultos. Os credos ecumênicos são o Credo dos Apóstolos, o Credo Niceno e o Credo Atanasiano. Esses e outros são ventilados nesta enciclopédia de acordo com suas divisões distintas, no artigo sobre *Confissões da Igreja Histórica*. O Credo dos Apóstolos, que esteve em processo formativo durante muito tempo, resultou parcialmente da oposição ao gnosticismo e às idéias de Márcion, por parte da antiga Igreja cristã. Modelos dos primeiros credos encontram-se nas confissões simples do próprio Novo Testamento, como o sumário paulino do evangelho, no décimo quinto capítulo de I Coríntios, os elementos da Grande Comissão (que vide), em Mateus 28:19,20, e as fórmulas de I João, feitas contra antigas expressões do gnosticismo (II João 1:1-4; 2:22; 4:1-3,14 ss. Ver também II Cor. 1:21 ss; I Ped. 1:2; I Tim. 2:5 ss; 6:13 ss; II Tim. 4:1; Rom. 1:3; 8:34; Fil. 2:5-11; I Ped. 3:18 ss). Algumas dessas declarações, como aquelas dos credos formais que mencionamos abaixo, surgiram em face da oposição a crenças falsas. O Credo Niceno foi, essencialmente, uma definição de cristologia, uma tentativa para solucionar as controvérsias em torno da pessoa de Cristo. Adições feitas a isso, como o *filioque* de séculos posteriores, foram definições subseqüentes. O Credo Atanasiano girou em torno de uma controvérsia, tendo exibido uma atitude dura, o que impediu seu uso maior pela Igreja cristã. Não obstante, ali estão contidas algumas importantes definições.

2. A Autoridade dos Credos. Tanto a Igreja Ocidental quanto a Igreja Oriental têm imenso respeito pelos credos, que formam uma das bases de sua autoridade. A Bíblia e a tradição, conforme são vistos nos escritos dos chamados pais da Igreja e nos credos, são fundamentais. Ver o artigo sobre a *Autoridade*, no tocante a uma declaração geral sobre atitudes, no que concerne a essa questão. Para os grupos protestantes e evangélicos, a Bíblia é a única autoridade reconhecida; mas seus credos certamente têm sido usados como meios de separar os fiéis dos não fiéis e dos hereges. Muitas igrejas e escolas contam com credos muito rígidos, os quais, se não forem seguidos à risca, são usados como instrumentos para provocar o isolamento e a exclusão. Assim sendo, se o protestantismo não se declara favorável à autoridade dos credos, na prática diária ali se dá grande valor aos mesmos.

3. Considerações Históricas. Os credos são meios convenientes, usados pela Igreja cristã histórica, para definir as suas crenças, como também para refinar as mesmas no decorrer dos séculos, conforme as circunstâncias históricas assim exigiram. Esses credos tornaram-se declarações de fé, além de serem testes comprobatórios da ortodoxia. Não raramente, têm servido como instrumentos de perseguição e hostilidade contra aqueles que não têm concordado com as estipulações desses credos.

4. Inadequações. Você já leu algum credo onde seja mencionada a lei do amor, que é o maior de todos os princípios espirituais, a prova mesma da espiritualidade? O pano de fundo polêmico dos credos tem servido para eliminar automaticamente esse princípio, ou os formuladores dos credos simplesmente esqueceram-se desse princípio básico? Além disso, esses credos não fazem justiça à fé e à experiência cristãs. Não dão resposta a perguntas críticas como aquelas que envolvem os preconceitos raciais, o pacifismo, o desarmamento, e outros grandes problemas com que se debate a sociedade. Os credos tendem mais por apresentar declarações formais e intelectualizadas da fé cristã, enfatizando a letra, que pode matar, e não o Espírito, que vivifica. Um credo tende por furtar um homem de sua liberdade intelectual, que é um atributo e um direito básico do homem, porquanto requer conformidade com suas estipulações, geralmente inflexíveis e incompletas. (AM E P ROU)

CREDULIDADE

Essa palavra alude à *crença fácil*. De fato, algumas pessoas têm a *vontade de crer*, geralmente ligada ao desejo de ter conforto mental, em busca de perguntas fáceis e finais para problemas complexos. As pessoas religiosas como uma classe, inclinam-se mais para a credulidade do que a maioria das pessoas, visto que estão condicionadas a crer. Por isso mesmo, há tantas doutrinas e sistemas diferentes que dependem da crença fácil. Por outro lado, também existe a *vontade de não crer*, porquanto há pessoas que repeliram definitivamente a fé religiosa, assumindo uma disposição contrária e cética diante das realidades religiosas e espirituais. Para estas últimas, não é aceitável nem mesmo a crença baseada em evidências convincentes, e explicações alternativas são buscadas para justificar eventos místicos e espirituais incomuns. Essas explicações alternativas são muitas, se alguém dedicar tempo suficiente às investigações. Convido o leitor a examinar o artigo sobre *Satya Sai Baba*, quanto a uma moderna demonstração de fatos admiráveis que ele está realizando em nossos próprios dias. O relato inteiro da vida de Jesus é uma poderosíssima confirmação da legitimidade da crença. Mas, visto que vivemos afastados dele por cerca de dois mil anos, as pessoas inclinam-se a pensar que esses relatos bíblicos sobre Jesus são apenas mitos criados pela Igreja cristã. Personagens como esse homem indiano demonstram que os evangelhos são muito cautelosos em seu relato sobre o que Jesus foi e realizou, e não exagerados. Todavia, isso não justifica a grande proliferação de seitas e credos, que são aceitos, sem qualquer tipo de prova e exame, por imensas multidões. Isso mostra a quanto chega a credulidade. Agostinho afirmou: «Creio para que possa compreender». Ele partia do pressuposto que a mente aberta à fé é a que melhor pode compreender as coisas, ao passo que as mentes céticas habitam em uma espécie de trevas auto-impostas. A crença, como qualquer outra coisa na vida, deveria ser submetida a teste. Há algumas linhas mestras, a saber: *O teste moral*. As crenças devem promover a moralidade e a espiritualidade. *O teste das Escrituras*. As crenças religiosas precisam concordar em espírito com a revelação que nos foi dada na Bíblia, ainda que não necessariamente em cada detalhe. *O teste da autoridade*. Na Igreja cristã há uma longa história da interpretação, a qual, apesar de não ser uma autoridade final, é algo comprovado pela antiguidade. *O teste do amor*. As crenças que fomentam os sentimentos de hostilidade, de exclusivismo e de formas disfarçadas de ódio, como de uma pessoa contra outra, ou como de um grupo contra outro, envolvem algo de muito errado. *O teste da ciência* e de outras disciplinas do conhecimento. Algumas crenças que os homens defendem alicerçam-se sobre uma falsa idéia do mundo e dos acontecimentos antigos. A ciência moderna tem esclarecido certo número dessas coisas no campo da geologia, da física e da astronomia. Para exemplificar, a grande antiguidade do universo é comprovada pela astronomia, de maneira tal que falar em termos de uma criação com apenas seis mil anos de idade é exprimir a mais crassa ignorância dos fatos. Ver o artigo sobre a *Autoridade*, quanto a outras sugestões quanto ao teste a que nossas crenças devem ser submetidas.

CREMAÇÃO

Ver o artigo geral sobre *Sepultamento, Costumes de*, sob o terceiro ponto, *Cremação*.

CREMER, HERMANN

Suas datas foram 1834-1903. Foi professor em Greifswald. Um influente pioneiro luterano na teologia bíblica, que interpretava as doutrinas paulinas do pecado, da justificação e do julgamento, com base na consciência, de maneira forense e energética. Enfatizava a teologia bíblica e diminuía a importância da teologia especulativa.

CRENÇA (CRER)

Este artigo procura responder à pergunta: No que consiste o ato de crer? As idéias a respeito são variadas:

1. *Na Filosofia*. Seria considerar veraz uma proposição, por dispor de certo respaldo em evidências, ainda que essas evidências não fossem conclusivas. A crença é mais forte que a opinião, e mais fraca que o conhecimento. Pode ser um estágio no caminho para o conhecimento, se não puderem ser recolhidas evidências mais conclusivas. Tradicionalmente, na filosofia a crença também tem sido identificada com certo estado mental, conforme se vê nos escritos de Descartes, onde se confirma ou nega alguma proposição. Nos escritos de Hume, a crença aparece como um estado passivo, que ocorre ou está prestes a ocorrer, no tocante a alguma proposição. No behaviorismo (ver o artigo) nega-se que a crença seja um estado mental introspectivo, porquanto depende de reiterada percepção dos sentidos quanto a objetos físicos. Em Ortega Y Gasset (ver o artigo), trata-se do assentimento pré-racional, que é o poder por detrás das idéias.

2. *Na Teologia*. A crença equivale à fé. Isso é uma realidade, mesmo que não seja aceita pela teologia popular. (Ver o artigo sobre a *fé*). Na teologia popular, a crença é muito mais o assentimento diante de uma proposição ou credo. A Bíblia ensina que a fé é «dom de Deus» (Efé. 2:8), pelo que Paulo foi capaz de dizer: «...a fé não é de todos» (II Tes. 3:2), referindo-se àqueles que não receberam do alto o dom da fé. Portanto, a fé é uma operação do Espírito Santo, mediante a qual o indivíduo não somente crê em certas realidades, mas também é transformado por elas. Essas realidades giram todas em torno da pessoa e da obra de Jesus Cristo. Quem crê, crê em Jesus Cristo, em tudo quanto ele é e representa. E quem não crê, descrê de Jesus Cristo. Paralelamente, é fé na palavra de Cristo. Aquele que crê, depende do que Cristo disse. Confiança em Cristo e fé em sua palavra, são aspectos que podem ser vistos em trechos como: a. Nas palavras de Jesus ao ex-cego que fora expulso da sinagoga: «Crês tu no Filho do homem? Ele respondeu, e disse: Quem é, Senhor para que eu nele creia? E Jesus lhe disse: Já o tens visto, e é o que fala contigo. Então afirmou ele: Creio, Senhor; e o adorou» (João 9:35-38). b. Na definição teológica oferecida por Paulo: «E assim, a fé vem pela pregação, e a pregação pela palavra de Cristo» (Rom. 10:17). Portanto, na Bíblia, crer não é apenas assentir diante de certas proposições de um credo. Antes, é a confiança em Jesus Cristo, com a conseqüente outorga da alma eterna aos seus cuidados. Isso, por sua vez, conduz à transformação do homem interior segundo a imagem de Cristo, através do poder do Espírito (Rom. 8:29; II Cor. 3:18).

3. *Crença Fácil*. Essa é uma das pragas do evangelicalismo. Trata-se da suposição de que quando alguém aceita como verdadeiras certas crenças a respeito de Cristo, Deus fica na obrigação de salvar aquela pessoa. A crença fácil não envolve quaisquer requisitos morais, e nem é fonte da transformação espiritual. É mera crença em um credo qualquer. Não há salvação sem santificação (Heb. 12:14).

CRENÇA RELIGIOSA e O Problema de Verificação
Ver **Verificação de Crenças Religiosas**.

CRENÇA VERDADEIRA JUSTIFICADA
Ver **Gettier, Problema de**.

CRESCAS, HASDAI BEN ABRAHAM
Filósofo judeu espanhol. Nasceu em Barcelona, em aproximadamente 1340. Faleceu em 1412. Opunha-se ao racionalismo e aristotelianismo de Maimônides e Gersonides (que vide, no artigo sobre o *Judaísmo*, primeiro ponto, *Aspectos Históricos*, 13-15). Sua filosofia asseverava a centralidade da lei do amor e a necessidade de revelação (que vide). Spinoza foi influenciado por suas idéias referentes à distinção dos atributos e propriedade da criação e do livre-arbítrio. Ver sobre *Spinoza*, pontos 6, 7 e 9.

Escritos: *The Light of the Lord; Treatise*.

CRESCENTE FÉRTIL
A expressão refere-se àquela região, começando pelo golfo Pérsico e ampliando-se na direção noroeste até os vales dos rios Tigre e Eufrates, e daí continuando para oeste, até à costa nordeste do mar Mediterrâneo, incluindo o vale do rio Nilo. Embora a área adjacente ao crescente fértil seja estéril, a própria região é muito fértil, o que explica o seu nome. Tem-se tornado comum afirmar que as primeiras evidências da civilização procedem dessa região; mas, atualmente, a arqueologia está descobrindo evidências ainda mais antigas de civilização na África. Seja como for, a história dessa área é antiqüíssima, tendo sido sempre o centro das maiores potências do mundo, até à época dos gregos e romanos, quando a civilização gravitou um tanto mais para o ocidente. Essa região era uma espécie de encruzilhada de

civilizações, sobretudo daquelas mencionadas na Bíblia.

CRESCER, CRESCIMENTO

Crescer é aumentar em peso e tamanho, mediante a assimilação de nutrientes e a multiplicação das células. Esse verbo também indica qualquer tipo de progresso, prosperidade, incremento, cultivo ou realização. Há notáveis conotações metafóricas e espirituais. Em Atos 12:24, temos o crescimento e a multiplicação da Palavra de Deus (o evangelho), com o aumento do número de cristãos. Ver também Atos 19:20 quanto a esse tipo de conexão. Lemos que o corpo místico inteiro de Cristo cresce (Efé. 2:21). Aos recém-convertidos ao cristianismo é recomendado que se alimentem com o leite sincero da Palavra, a fim de que cresçam, ou se desenvolvam espiritualmente (I Ped. 2:2). A mesma idéia é aplicada a todos os crentes, em II Ped. 3:18. Paulo agradecia a Deus, quando via outros crentes crescendo na fé (II Tes. 1:3).

Meios Espirituais de Crescimento. Da mesma maneira que nossos corpos físicos precisam de certa variedade de nutrientes para que se desenvolva apropriadamente, outro tanto sucede à alma. Há meios de crescimento espiritual. Esses meios são os seguintes: 1. O treinamento intelectual no estudo dos documentos espirituais, como a Bíblia, ou outros livros que nos confiram conhecimento útil. 2. A oração e a meditação, quando o crente solicita e recebe, ou aguarda por instruções recebidas intuitivamente. 3. A santificação. 4. A prática da lei do amor, incluindo toda a forma de boas obras. O amor cristão é a prova mesma da espiritualidade (I João 4:8 ss). 5. O toque místico, que consiste na iluminação por meio da meditação ou por meio do uso dos dons espirituais. Aquele que prática todos esses meios de forma diligente, será um gigante espiritual.

CRETA

Creta é uma ilha montanhosa que fica no mar Mediterrâneo, ao sul do mar Egeu. Tem cerca de duzentos e cinqüenta quilômetros de comprimento, variando em largura de onze a cinqüenta e seis quilômetros. É provável que os *quereteus*, que faziam parte da guarda pessoal de Davi, fossem provenientes da ilha de Creta, embora a própria ilha nunca seja chamada por nome nas páginas do A.T. As referências a essa ilha, no N.T., ficam em Atos 27:7,12,13,21 e em Tito 1:5. É dito, em Atos 2:11, que havia crentes presentes no dia de Pentecoste, quando houve o derramamento inicial do Espírito Santo. Paulo fez uma parada em Creta, durante a sua viagem a Roma, antes do seu primeiro período de encarceramento. (Ver Atos 27:7-13,21). Paulo também aconselhou aos marinheiros que passassem ali o inverno; mas, preferindo eles ignorar seus conselhos, mais tarde tiveram de sofrer naufrágio, segundo se vê no vigésimo sétimo capítulo do livro de Atos.

O que sabemos acerca da história dessa ilha se deriva principalmente das descobertas arqueológicas. Desde a era neolítica já havia ali a ocupação humana (quarto milênio A.C.), e na idade do bronze já se tinha erguido uma poderosa civilização. O centro dessa civilização era Cnossos, um local escavado por Sir Arthur Evans. No período de 2600-2000 A.C. houve significativa expansão comercial. A escrita, em tabletes de argila e de cobre tem sobrevivido daquele período, onde uma primitiva escrita pictográfica era usada (2000-1650 A.C.). Posteriormente foi uma escrita chamada linear A, uma forma simplificada daquela (1750-1450 A.C.).

O clímax da civilização cretense foi atingido na primeira metade da idade do bronze (minoano posterior, 1600-1400 A.C.). O linear B, uma forma arcaica do grego, era o idioma desse tempo, o qual foi decifrado em 1953 por M. Ventris. Mui provavelmente invasores gregos tinham modificado a linguagem para isso, ao passo que a escrita anterior provavelmente era de origem semita. Perto do fim da idade do bronze (minoano posterior III, 1400-1125 A.C.), gregos dórios chegaram à ilha, que, então, se tornou, essencialmente, uma colônia grega.

Já desde o início de sua história registrada havia muitas cidades na ilha, levando-se em conta seu tamanho minúsculo. Se pudermos crer na Odisséia de Homero (*lib.* xix.v. 172-179), contava com noventa cidades naqueles tempos tão remotos, embora outras fontes informativas falem até em cem cidades. Nos dias do apóstolo Paulo, o número de judeus ali habitando era grande, provavelmente devido à sua importância comercial. As localidades mencionadas nas páginas do N.T., pertencentes àquela ilha, são *Bons Portos* (um porto marítimo) e a cidade de Laséia, nas proximidades (ver Atos 27:8). A população atual dessa ilha é de cerca de quinhentos mil habitantes. Creta também tem o nome de Candia.

Pelo que se lê na passagem de Tito 1:5, conclui-se que já havia um bom número de igrejas ali, quando Paulo enviou Tito para aquele lugar, porquanto o apóstolo dos gentios e outros já haviam evangelizado bastante aquela ilha. É provável que após ter sido solto de seu primeiro aprisionamento em Roma o apóstolo tenha visitado a ilha e feito algum trabalho ali. Porém, tendo a necessidade de dirigir-se a outros lugares, exortou a Tito que desse prosseguimento a seu trabalho, consagrando anciãos ou pastores qualificados nas igrejas. Esta carta a Tito nos dá a impressão que reflete esse período de liberdade de Paulo, antes de seu segundo encarceramento em Roma e seu martírio final; e isso significa que essa epístola foi escrita antes da segunda epístola a Timóteo.

Não dispomos da narrativa da quarta viagem missionária de Paulo ao Ocidente, mas especificamente, à Espanha, excetuando várias alusões à mesma nos escritos dos primeiros pais da igreja (ver as notas expositivas adicionadas ao trecho de Atos 28:31 no NTI), pelo que é impossível fazermos qualquer declaração dogmática sobre o tempo em que Paulo evangelizou a ilha de Creta. Todavia, a resposta comumente feita a essa indagação é que isso foi feito entre o primeiro e o segundo período de aprisionamento. Na verdade, a narrativa do livro de Atos fornece-nos apenas um esboço, — sendo possível que tal trabalho tenha sido efetuado rapidamente, antes de seu primeiro período de aprisionamento, mas acerca do que simplesmente não dispomos de qualquer registro histórico na Bíblia.

CRETENSES

Os cretenses eram os habitantes da ilha de Creta, localizada ao largo das costas gregas e da Ásia Menor, na parte centro-oriental do mar Mediterrâneo. Nessa ilha havia cerca de cem cidades. As mais importantes eram Cnossos, Cortina, Lictoso, Licastos, Polixos, Paesto, Cidon, Manetusa e Dietina. Creta é uma ilha recoberta de montanhas, com cerca de duzentos e cinqüenta e um quilômetros de comprimento, e uma largura que varia entre onze e cinqüenta e seis quilômetros. Não é mencionada no A.T., embora provavelmente os cretenses sejam os mesmos *quereteus*, que formavam parte da guarda pessoal de Davi, eram originários da ilha de nome Caftor, o que provavelmente indicava a ilha e as terras costeiras adjacentes que caíram dentro de seu domínio, durante o segundo milênio A.C.

O apóstolo Paulo visitou a ilha de Creta pelo menos por duas vezes, em suas viagens missionárias (ver Atos 27:6-13,21), bem como houve uma terceira visita após o seu aprisionamento, quando ali deixou Tito, para dar continuidade ao trabalho de evangelização que fora por ele iniciado. A descrição nada lisonjeira dos cretenses, na passagem de Tito 1:12, é uma citação do poeta Epimênides, de Creta. Esse autor é igualmente citado no trecho de Atos 17:28a. Sabe-se, pelas descobertas arqueológicas, que se falava uma forma de grego arcaico ali, pelo menos desde 1000 a 1500 A.C., sem dúvida devido aos invasores gregos da ilha. Antes desse período, a história da ilha continua sob discussão, entre os estudiosos. Mas pelo menos se sabe que o idioma grego ali se tornou dominante desde cedo.

CRIAÇÃO

Esboço:
I. Discussão Preliminar
II. Origens da Criação
III. Pontos de Vista Bíblicos da Criação
IV. Significados da Criação
V. Alguns Poucos Problemas Especiais
VI. A Criação Cristocêntrica
VII. Interpretações que Tentam Reconciliar a Ciência com Gênesis

I. Discussão Preliminar

A palavra portuguesa «criar» vem do latim, **creare**, «produzir», «gerar». A palavra tem seus sentidos filosófico e teológico em relação à origem do mundo, do homem e de outros seres, tanto físicos quanto espirituais. A maioria das religiões supõe que o mundo, conforme o conhecemos, foi produzido por alguma força cósmica ou divina, com base em um estado anterior. Esse estado anterior poderia ser o caos, embora com os elementos já existentes, inteiramente desorganizados, ou poderia ser o vácuo, de onde foram extraídos os mundos, mediante o poder divino. As religiões mais primitivas parecem preferir a idéia do *caos*; e, ocasionalmente, esse vocábulo chega a ser utilizado para falar de uma divindade ou força cósmica, uma espécie de entidade por seus próprios direitos. Os gregos, em sua maior parte, falavam em termos de matéria já existente, que foi então posta em ordem. Esse é o ponto de vista dos mórmons; portanto, nesse grupo, temos um representante do ponto de vista do caos. O segundo ponto deste artigo apresenta dez opiniões diferentes sobre as origens.

Historicamente falando, a criação refere-se àquele primeiro ato mediante o qual o Deus *auto-existente* trouxe à existência o que não tinha forma de existência independente. Em certo sentido, pois, a criação torna-se uma subdoutrina da doutrina do próprio Deus; pois, uma vez que algo existe, além de Deus, já precisamos definir a natureza dessa existência em relação à sua origem, tanto do ponto de vista da responsabilidade quanto do ângulo do destino. É razoável pensar que se a criação teve começo em Deus, então também deverá continuar e encontrar cumprimento em Deus. O Novo Testamento define essa questão ao dizer que tudo foi criado *da parte de* Deus, *por* Deus e *para* Deus, de tal maneira que, em todos os estágios, enfatiza-se a dependência da criação a Deus. Ver Romanos 11:36. Esse versículo enfatiza o mistério das operações de Deus. E não há mistério maior do que o da criação divina. Por conseguinte, não podemos esperar que nossas idéias sejam mais do que meras sugestões.

O Credo dos Apóstolos (que vide) começa confessando fé em Deus, Todo-poderoso, Pai, criador dos céus e da terra. Portanto, essa doutrina é cêntrica para a fé cristã. Mas, no que concerne ao seu *modus operandi*, há muitas opiniões. A Bíblia testifica sobre a centralidade dessa doutrina, dando início aos seus ensinamentos com o relato da criação. O gnosticismo afirmava que uma criação imperfeita requer que se postule que ela foi criada por uma divindade imperfeita. Os mestres gnósticos partiam daí para a idéia de que essa divindade imperfeita é o Deus do Antigo Testamento, ao passo que um Deus superior, se não mesmo o maior de todos, estaria envolvido na revelação neotestamentária. Todavia, a maior parte dos luminares da Igreja repudia esse ponto de vista. De acordo com a teologia do A e NT, o verdadeiro Deus, como Criador de todas as coisas, é o alicerce indispensável da teologia. No cristianismo, essa doutrina, quando aplicada ao homem, indica sua total dependência em Deus, e não apenas quanto à sua origem, mas também quanto à sua continuação e ao seu destino. Lutero, em seu *Pequeno Catecismo*, asseverou: «...Deus criou a mim e a tudo quanto existe; ele deu-me o corpo e a alma, e continua a sustentá-los, os meus membros e os meus sentidos, a minha razão e todas as demais faculdades de minha mente...»

Em séculos recentes, com o surgimento da ciência avançada e com a diversificação das posições teológicas, têm vindo à tona muitos debates relativos à criação. O ponto de vista cosmológico dos hebreus (ver a ilustração acerca disso no artigo sobre a Astronomia) na verdade não concorda com aquilo que sabemos ser a verdade acerca da terra e do espaço, embora muitos teólogos conservadores adaptem *continuamente* essas idéias, a fim de fazê-las concordar com a ciência moderna. Entretanto, esses teólogos não se esforçam por descobrir no que os hebreus realmente acreditavam, preferindo ocupar-se em uma atividade apologética, e não na busca pela verdade. Porém, se a cosmologia dos hebreus não concorda com os fatos científicos conhecidos, então o debate não somente é legítimo, mas também absolutamente necessário, se tivermos de compreender qualquer coisa sobre o mundo, sobre suas origens e sobre seus propósitos. Ver o artigo sobre a *Cosmogonia*, quanto à idéias dos povos antigos sobre a origem das coisas.

A fé, a razão e a revelação concordam entre si que Deus é a causa da criação. Porém, quando começamos a abordar os detalhes, descobrimos inúmeros mistérios, para os quais não encontramos solução. Isso posto, a teologia explica melhor o porquê da criação, e não o *como*. E a ciência, por sua vez, não faz idéia certa sobre esse *como* da criação. E isso significa que temos de confessar a nossa ignorância sobre o ponto. Ainda que a ciência venha a desenvolver, algum dia, uma física perfeita, podendo responder a todas as perguntas atinentes a essa disciplina, teremos de lembrar-nos que nem todas as perguntas são questões de física e que precisamos de todas as variedades de disciplinas ou ciências para chegarmos a qualquer porção apreciável da verdade. Isso posto, não devemos esperar solucionar o dilema da criação somente através da ciência. Gilbert Ryle apresentou uma ilustração do problema que estamos abordando. Digamos, por exemplo, que a ciência,

CRIAÇÃO

mediante a física e outras disciplinas, possa explicar exatamente o que sucede em um jogo de bilhar. Não há ali movimentos físicos que não possam ser explicados. Porém, — uma vez chegado a essa explicação, ainda teríamos de levar em conta as *regras* do jogo, com as estratégias e os propósitos dos *jogadores*. Mas, para esses tipos de problemas, a física não conta com qualquer explicação. Ora, se podemos dizer isso acerca de um simples jogo, quanto mais acerca do imenso e misterioso universo no qual vivemos!

É sob essa luz que a história bíblica da criação deveria ser compreendida. Estamos procurando descobrir as regras do jogo, bem como o papel que o Jogador e os jogadores desempenham. No livro de Gênesis não devemos buscar um comentário sobre o aspecto físico da criação. Se o fizermos, encontramos uma cosmologia que não se presta para tal exame. É verdade que podemos ser desonestos, distorcendo o que o autor sagrado escreveu ali, fazendo suas palavras ajustarem-se àquilo que sabemos, em nossos dias, ser verdade; mas isso é desonesto. A nossa teologia começa pelo alicerce do conceito que criou e trouxe à existência os universos e os seres materiais e imateriais; e, que, por causa desse fato, todas as coisas criadas têm que buscar continuamente em Deus a razão de sua existência e o seu destino. A teoria da criação chamada *ex nihilo*, apesar de supor erroneamente que Deus criou tudo «do nada» (visto que do nada, nada é feito; *ex nihilo, nihil fit*), ela está com a razão, ao fazer tudo dependente e contingente, excetuando Deus. A criação espiritual é que torna necessária a criação material, e é precisamente isso que está envolvido na redenção. Pois, na nova criação, os remidos haverão de participar da natureza divina, tornando-se assim seres necessários, ou seja, seres que *não podem* deixar de existir. Ver o artigo separado sobre a *Criação Ex Nihilo*.

II. Origens da Criação

1. O elemento ou **substância original**, do que tudo veio a ser, é indefinido e desconhecido. Desse elemento desconhecido é que surgiram os quatro elementos básicos, a terra, o ar, o fogo e a água. Toda a vida ter-se-ia originado de um ou outro desses elementos, ou de todos eles, coletivamente. E todas as demais coisas teriam sido criadas por um processo de condensação ou rarefação. O filósofo grego, Anaximandro, ao empregar essa teoria geral, tornou-se o pai da teoria evolucionária. Ele escolheu a água como elemento básico, tendo postulado que a vida se originou no mar, através de um processo de desenvolvimento que se teria originado na água. Somente há pouco é que os cientistas que aceitam a teoria evolucionária, decidiram que a água não pode oferecer o meio ambiente necessário para tal desenvolvimento. Anaximandro viveu em cerca de 550 A.C.

2. *A eternidade da matéria*. Aqueles que explicam a origem da vida, conforme é esboçado no parágrafo acima, tiveram a necessidade de postular a eternidade da matéria. A maioria dos filósofos que empregavam a teoria do «hilozoísmo», ou seja, que a vida faz parte inerente da matéria, —que emerge por meio de algum processo natural e que é o nome aplicado ao conceito que acabamos de apresentar, criam que a própria matéria é eterna. Alguns postulavam um elemento «indefinido», desconhecido, que existiria por detrás e anterior a tudo quanto se conhece atualmente. Porém, até mesmo nesse caso, tal elemento era considerado material. Ainda outros acreditavam que a vida inteira se originou de elementos conhecidos por nós, como o fogo, a água, a terra e o ar. Podemos observar muitas «causas». Em outras palavras, uma coisa seria causada por outra, essa ainda por outra, «ad infinitum». Imaginar uma retrogressão infinita de «causas dependentes», não é mais difícil, filosoficamente falando, do que supor que há uma única causa *primária* e «independente», ou seja, única causa que não foi ela mesma causada.

3. Alguns filósofos antigos, como Platão, não aceitavam a matéria como a substância primária, mas antes, postulavam uma *substância espiritual*, do que a própria matéria ter-se-ia desenvolvido. Platão chamava isso de «o universal». Uma força cósmica, o «demiurgo», teria criado o mundo material, utilizando-se dos universais como padrões. Os próprios universais seriam eternos. Basicamente, embora pluralístico, o conceito não é diferente do conceito cristão. Dá ao «espírito» a posição primária, ao passo que a matéria seria mera «imitação» da espiritualidade, ou seja, tanto temporária como secundária.

4. *A criação como um ato eterno de Deus*. É difícil contemplar qualquer tempo em que a criação não existia, pois então poderíamos indagar: «O que fazia Deus, quando somente ele existia?» Poderíamos imaginar um Deus inativo? Por essa razão é que Orígenes, pai da igreja de cerca de 225 D.C., supunha que a criação, bem como a vida toda, fazem parte de um eterno e contínuo ato criador de Deus, o qual seria a fonte originária de toda a vida. Apesar de que as formas de vida podem modificar-se, a vida criada seria coexistente com Deus, ou, pelo menos, os elementos básicos dos quais se soergueu a vida. Deus, portanto, reveste-se de posição primária, quanto à importância e grandeza, embora não de posição primária, quanto ao tempo. Formas e tipos de criação vieram à existência, isto é, têm um começo; mas a própria criação, de alguma maneira, é um eterno ato de Deus.

5. *A criação como um pensamento eterno de Deus*. Clemente, pai da igreja que viveu no começo do terceiro século de nossa era, acreditava que nem sempre a criação existiu como uma realidade, mas sempre fez parte do pensamento de Deus. Já dentro do tempo, Deus concretizou o seu pensamento. E assim as coisas vieram à existência.

6. *A criação ex nihilo*. Deus teria criado a tudo, «do nada», mediante o poder de sua palavra. Houve tempo em que somente Deus existia. A vida humana foi criada por um ato especial, da matéria já existente, para em seguida receber a infusão do princípio espiritual. Usualmente, na teologia moderna, essa teoria é descrita como Deus a transformar sua própria energia em matéria e outras formas de vida; pelo que essa teoria não é realmente uma idéia que fala da criação «derivada do nada». O trecho de Heb. 11:3, segundo pensam alguns estudiosos, dá apoio a essa teoria.

7. *O panteísmo*. De acordo com essa teoria, Deus não «cria» e, sim, «emana». Ele emana a si mesmo, pelo que tudo faz parte de Deus, sendo alguma forma de sua essência. Deus é o Cabeça do universo, e o universo é o corpo de Deus. Deus seria como o grande Sol central; e o mundo e toda a vida humana que nele existe, seriam os seus «raios». Deus pode ser pessoal ou impessoal em tais sistemas. O panteísmo moderno com freqüência é evolucionário em seu caráter. As «emanações» teriam um «modus operandi», evolucionário.

8. *A eternidade da matéria*, tendo Deus como *organizador*. O mormonismo aceita a idéia da matéria eterna, mas crê que ela existia na forma de caos.

955

CRIAÇÃO

Assim sendo, Deus a teria organizado; nesse caso, o ato de Deus não teria sido criador, e sim, organizador.

9. *O ponto de vista do ceticismo.* A ciência moderna acredita que é impossível solucionar o problema da origem. A única coisa que podemos saber é aquilo que podemos investigar com os nossos sentidos de percepção (empirismo). E é óbvio que questões como «causa primária», «causa independente», «origem», «destino», «Deus», «alma», etc., são temas fora da investigação científica.

10. *Fulguração.* Ver *Leibniz, Idéias*, ponto 3.

11. *O ponto de vista neotestamentário.* Deus cria por meio do seu Filho, um agente pessoal; e, nessa energia, traz tudo à existência, material ou espiritual. Ele criou a tudo «em Cristo» e «para Cristo».

III. Pontos de Vista Bíblicos da Criação

A Bíblia não ensina uma criação **ex nihilo**. A narrativa de Gênesis pode dar a entender que, antes de Deus, nada existia, mas isso não é a mesma coisa que uma criação *ex nihilo*. O trecho de Hebreus 11:3 afirma que Deus fez o mundo de coisas «que não aparecem», o que é uma expressão bastante vaga. Essas palavras poderiam indicar coisas *imateriais*; mas nunca «do nada». A epístola aos Hebreus tem um marcante tom neoplatônico, no estilo de Filo; e isso poderia indicar que esse versículo da epístola teria uma perspectiva platônica. Platão supunha que os mundos físicos vieram à existência por via do trabalho do Demiurgo, que os constituiu usando os arquétipos dos universais (que vide). Os universais são eternos, existindo em uma espécie de céu platônico. Os teólogos cristãos têm-se utilizado dessa idéia, afirmando que os universais são as idéias da mente divina. Nesse caso, então somente a mente divina existia, antes do universo físico. E há um precedente para isso, até mesmo no diálogo *Leis*, de Platão, onde Deus parece substituir a complexa doutrina das idéias ou universais. Seja como for, mesmo nesse caso, não temos a idéia do «nada», de onde tudo teria procedido. Os teólogos cristãos modernos, aproveitando idéias extraídas da teoria atômica, supõem que Deus transformou sua própria energia em matéria, e isso pelo poder da sua vontade, exemplificada na sua Palavra proferida. Sem dúvida esse é um conceito superior, que substitui corretamente a idéia da criação *ex nihilo*. Portanto, talvez possamos afirmar com segurança que o primeiro conceito bíblico da criação é que houve tempo em que somente Deus existia. Orígenes teve dificuldades com esse conceito. Os teólogos da antiguidade perguntavam: «O que fazia Deus, quando somente ele existia?» Essa pergunta nos deixa indagando curiosamente. Assim sendo, alguns teólogos, como Orígenes, falavam em termos da criação como um ato eterno de Deus, ou como eternamente existente na mente divina, que se tornou concreta mediante um ato criativo. Contudo, apenas nos divertimos, ao falar sobre essas idéias, porque, na realidade, não temos respostas para quebra-cabeças dessa natureza.

Pontos de vista Cosmológicos. Os capítulos primeiro e segundo do livro de Gênesis fornecem-nos a narrativa da criação, primeiramente do mundo físico, e, em seguida, do homem. Os eruditos do idioma hebraico asseguram-nos de que a primeira parte desse relato, sobre a criação do mundo físico, foi escrita em hebraico bem antigo; e que a segunda parte do relato, acerca do homem, em hebraico mais recente, embora ainda no estilo clássico. Portanto, é difícil pensar como um mesmo autor original pode ter sido o autor de ambas as porções. Isso significaria que o segundo capítulo de Gênesis é uma espécie de doutrina repensada da criação, especialmente no que tange à criação do homem. Em meu artigo sobre a *Cosmogonia*, demonstrei que certo número das idéias envolvidas forma um paralelo bem definido das narrativas da criação originadas na área da Mesopotâmia, sobretudo no caso das histórias da criação dos babilônios. A maioria dos eruditos concorda que havia um fundo comum de idéias, provenientes de várias culturas da época e daquela área, que foi usado para prestar subsídios para os registros bíblicos. Os eruditos bíblicos afirmam que, apesar de tais empréstimos serem óbvios, a inspiração divina elevou a qualidade dos relatos, mormente ao injetar nos mesmos o conceito monoteísta.

Esse ponto de vista pode ser defindido. Mas seria uma desonestidade ocultar do leitor que, apesar desse refinamento, que é teologicamente instrutivo, continuamos com uma antiga cosmologia que é bastante defeituosa. Quando os hebreus aludiam ao firmamento, para exemplificar, não se referiam ao céu estrelado. Antes, eles imaginavam alguma espécie de substância sólida, abobadada sobre a terra, separando as águas que haveria por cima de águas que haveria por baixo dessa abóbada. Eles supunham que essa substância sólida assemelhava-se a uma taça invertida, cujas bordas pousavam sobre regiões montanhosas, nas extremidades de uma terra plana. Eles pensavam que essa abóbada tivesse janelas, por onde passava a chuva e a luminosidade celeste. Também pensavam que as luzes do sol, da lua e das estrelas eram corpos relativamente pequenos, pendurados na parte inferior da abóbada, para servirem de luminares da terra.

Os antigos também pensavam que o *hades* seria uma região literal, abaixo da superfície da terra. E a terra era retratada como uma terra plana que repousava sobre águas do abismo, e que havia colunas por baixo de tudo, apoiando a estrutura inteira. Não havia resposta para a pergunta sobre onde repousavam as águas do abismo. Todos esses conceitos são refletidos em referências bíblicas, o que ilustro nos artigos sobre *Astronomia* e *Cosmogonia*, nesta enciclopédia. É melhor sermos honestos a qualquer dia da semana, reconhecendo as coisas conforme elas são, não nos envolvendo em adaptações desonestas sobre idéias antigas, para que se ajustem à ciência moderna. No século XXI haverá uma nova ciência astronômica, e os evangélicos conservadores da época estarão fazendo novas adaptações da narrativa de Gênesis, para que se ajustem às novas descobertas científicas. Isso não é buscar pela verdade com seriedade. É apenas uma tentativa para preservar o conforto mental, mediante a suposição de que todas as coisas ditas no relato bíblico expressam verdades científicas. E os que assim pensam, não admitem qualquer evidência em contrário. Ver o ponto I.4 no artigo sobre a *Cosmogonia*, quanto a paralelos entre o livro de Gênesis e as histórias da criação provenientes da Babilônia.

Elementos Teológicos. Convido o leitor a examinar meu artigo sobre a *Cosmogonia*, terceiro ponto, *Lições Morais e Espirituais*, onde alisto oito itens.

Indicações do Novo Testamento. O segundo ponto do artigo sobre **Cosmogonia** aborda alguns detalhes sobre como o Novo Testamento faz adições às idéias do Antigo Testamento, no tocante à criação. A doutrina do *Logos* é a mais importante dessas adições. O Novo Testamento apresenta-nos a doutrina da nova criação ou criação espiritual, que se deriva da antiga

CRIAÇÃO

criação. Acerca disso apresento um artigo separado, intitulado *Criação Espiritual*.

IV. Significados da Criação

1. **Exibe a magnificência de Deus e o seu poder infinito**, mostrando que essas qualidades também residem no Filho. Fica implícito que a bondade infinita de Deus está em foco; pois confiamos que o mais elevado poder do universo é também o poder mais beneficente e altruísta. Um Deus dotado de tal poder não pode usá-lo arbitrariamente. O mesmo poder que criou, se volta para a redenção, pelo que deverá haver um vasto recolhimento dos perdidos.

2. **A criação exige a existência de Deus** (argumentos cosmológico e etiológico). Deve haver alguma *causa* da criação. Um retrocesso infinito de causas dependentes é uma idéia contrária à razão e repugnante à esperança. Aquele que é a causa da criação física também é a *causa* e a *origem* de todo o bem-estar humano; e assim como Deus é eficaz em uma dessas dimensões, assim também o é na outra.

3. **Assim como existe uma *vida física*, também deve haver uma «vida espiritual».** A criação original (física) foi feita de maneira que dela emergisse a criação «espiritual». (Ver as notas expositivas sobre esse conceito, em João 1:4 no NTI). O propósito de Deus, ao criar o homem, foi o de exaltá-lo infinitamente. A queda não alterou esse plano. A exaltação completa se acha em Cristo (ver Rom. 8:29,30).

4. **A vida espiritual é extraída da criação física**, mediante a «iluminação». (Ver Efé. 1:18,19 sobre esse conceito). A transição que há em João 1:4, da «vida» para a «luz», subentende a mesma coisa.

5. **Deus é a única fonte originária de todo o bem-estar**, e Cristo é o seu mediador (ver Col. 1:16).

6. **A vida inteira, portanto, deve ser dirigida na direção de Deus** (ver I Cor. 8:6).

7. **A doutrina da criação não foi revelada para satisfazer à nossa curiosidade**, e, sim, visa nossa instrução espiritual. Fala-nos do mundo eterno e do Deus eterno do qual se originou essa criação (ver Heb. 11:1). Nossa fé deve ser dirigida na direção desse mundo, que é o nosso verdadeiro lar.

V. Alguns Poucos Problemas Especiais

1. *A filosofia da narrativa da criação*. Alguns intérpretes insistem em encarar o relato de Gênesis como perfeito, científico e sem erros. Isso obriga-os a todas as formas de contorsão na exposição desse relato bíblico. Já expus as razões pelas quais devemos rejeitar esse ponto de vista, no terceiro ponto, acima. Há referências a outros artigos, onde maiores detalhes são apresentados. O valor da narrativa bíblica da criação encontra-se em seu aspecto teológico. A porção que envolve questões da física não devem ser salientadas por nós. Quando assim fazemos, atolamo-nos em grandes dificuldades, que só servem para criar debates acirrados.

2. *Paralelos com cosmogonias antigas*. É difícil para as pessoas que conhecem somente a Bíblia, entenderem que havia um fundo comum de conhecimento, sobre o qual se estribaram as diversas narrativas da criação, incluindo o relato bíblico. Para essas pessoas, dizer que o relato de Gênesis é superior devido à sua *teologia* (embora não quanto ao aspecto físico), — não serve de consolo —. Lamento não poder consolá-las quanto à questão. — Afirmar que a inspiração divina pode utilizar tal fundo, fazer acréscimos ao mesmo, elevar a sua qualidade, e infundir ao mesmo um valor espiritual e teológico, também não parece muito confortador para os estudiosos ultraconservadores, cujo dogma lhes afiança que isso não pode ter acontecido. Também gostaria de consolar os ultraconservadores; mas, se a verdade entra em conflito com isso, então prefiro a verdade.

3. *Como havia luz*, antes do sol ter sido criado? Vemos nisso o antigo conceito da luz primeva. O sol, a lua e as estrelas aparecem como luzes secundárias, preparadas especificamente para iluminarem a terra. Os hebreus não faziam idéia da vastidão do espaço exterior, e nem das dimensões dos corpos celestes. Antes, imaginavam que todos eles estavam pendurados por baixo da abóbada do firmamento (a taça invertida), feita de substância sólida, que separaria os céus da terra.

4. *A antiguidade da criação e da terra*. A maioria dos estudiosos tem abandonado a tentativa de descobrir a idade da terra, através das genealogias bíblicas. A astronomia mostra-nos que está chegando até nós luz que foi emitida pelas galáxias há, pelo menos, dezesseis milhões de anos. As evidências mostram que o sistema solar tem entre quatro a cinco milhões de anos de antiguidade. Alguns eruditos bíblicos pensam que uma grande expansão de tempo deve ser postulada entre Gênesis 1:1 e Gênesis 1:2. Isso significaria que há uma criação inicial, no passado indeterminado; e, muito depois, uma renovação. Isso abriria espaço para todas as eras geológicas. Além disso, isso nos permitiria reconhecer que a terra física é antiqüíssima, sem nenhum conflito como o relato de Gênesis. Alguns estudiosos chegam a pensar que criaturas semelhantes a homens poderiam ter vivido durante a criação original e a criação renovada, e que a narrativa bíblica de Gênesis nos oferece somente uma nova criação da raça adâmica.

Em minha opinião, essa espécie de interpretação, apesar de fornecer-nos um meio de reconciliar as descobertas científicas com o relato bíblico, na verdade é apenas uma adaptação ao avanço do conhecimento, e não um reflexo do que o autor sagrado estava procurando transmitir. Os registros geológicos mostram que os pólos têm mudado de posição ao menos por quatrocentos vezes, com deslizamentos correspondentes da crosta terrestre. Isso tem produzido vastas destruições, rearranjo de continentes, fins de antigos ciclos e inícios de novos ciclos. Ao que parece, as duas últimas dessas vastíssimas destruições correspondem, cronologicamente falando, às datas de Adão e do dilúvio de Noé. Isso poderia significar que tanto Adão quanto Noé representam novos começos, e não começos absolutos. Adão teria sido o primeiro homem da raça, conforme o conhecemos agora, e não o primeiro homem, em sentido absoluto. Quanto a detalhes sobre a questão da imensa antiguidade da criação, ver os artigos sobre *Antediluvianos*, *Adão* e *Astronomia*. O terceiro ponto deste último artigo tem o título: *A Imensa Antiguidade da Criação*, onde são expostos vários argumentos a respeito.

5. *Os dias do livro de Gênesis*. Teriam sido dias literais de vinte e quatro horas? Grande controvérsia ruge entre os eruditos, até mesmo sobre essa particularidade. Alguns deles afirmam que devemos pensar em dias literais de vinte e quatro horas, salientando a expressão «Houve tarde e manhã...» que assinala cada novo dia. Outros, esperando encaixar todas as vastas eras geológicas dentro do esquema da narrativa, expandem esses dias para que se tornem grandes períodos de tempo. Alguns deles declaram que cada dia teria durado mil anos, usando o trecho de Sal. 90:4 como justificação, onde se lê que, para o

CRIAÇÃO

Senhor um dia é como mil anos. Argumentos como esse são fúteis. Em primeiro lugar, é óbvio que o autor sagrado pensava que estavam envolvidos dias literais de vinte e quatro horas, embora o sol não tenha sido criado senão já no quarto dia. Outros dizem que os luminares celestes só *se tornaram visíveis* no quarto dia, embora existentes antes disso. Essa opinião envolve uma interpretação desonesta, a fim de dar solução a um problema trivial. O autor sagrado simplesmente não se preocupava com tais pormenores, ainda que os mesmos viessem a produzir alguma incongruência. Dias com duração de mil anos não representam nem uma gota, no balde das eras geológicas. E a teoria dos dias prolongados em nada contribui para solucionar os enigmas da criação. Tenho para mim que os dias de vinte e quatro horas são apenas uma conveniência literária da narrativa, sem qualquer significação do ponto de vista da física e da geologia. Uma outra interessante mas ridícula idéia acerca dos *dias* da criação é aquela que diz que o modo da criação foi revelado no processo de seis dias literais, ao autor sagrado, nada tendo a ver com a criação propriamente dita. Os evolucionistas, por sua vez, tentam explicar o *modus operandi* do desenvolvimento gradual das espécies. Porém, isso é uma outra tentativa que fracassa.

Acredito no seguinte: nenhuma das interpretações que diz respeito ao problema dos dias da criação contribui em qualquer coisa para o nosso conhecimento do aspecto físico da criação, pelo que as controvérsias sobre esses detalhes são fúteis. A Bíblia simplesmente não foi escrita para ensinar *como* Deus criou todas as coisas. Seu propósito é teológico, e não científico.

VI. A Criação Cristocêntrica

Talvez fosse melhor dizermos *a criação Logos cêntrica*. Temos nisso um importante dado teológico. Ofereço ao leitor um artigo separado a respeito, intitulado: *Criação Realizada No, Por Meio De, e Para o Filho*.

VII. Interpretações que tentam reconciliar a ciência com Gênesis

1. *O grande hiato*. Entre Gên. 1:1 e 1:2 existiu um grande hiato de tempo no qual todas as eras geológicas aconteceram. Isto explica a grande idade da terra, aliviando o problema de uma criação que aconteceu aparentemente há 6.000 anos (cálculo das genealogias).

2. *Dia = era teoria*. Os dias de Gên. não foram de 24 horas, mas sim, eras vastas. Às vezes, esta teoria é combinada com a de no. 1. Imensas eras existiram tanto entre vss. 1 e 2, como também os *dias*.

3. *Dias + intervalos*. Os dias da criação eram de 24 horas literais, mas entre eles vastas eras existiram, alternativamente.

4. *Éden somente*. A criação de Gênesis tenta nos informar somente sobre a criação do Éden, em seis dias literais. O resto da criação não está descrita na Bíblia, além da referência vaga e geral de Gên. 1:1.

5. *Eras concorrentes e sobreimpostas*. Deus, sendo um ser, além e fora do tempo, criou em tempos curtos e longos, concorrentes e sobreimpostos. Não podemos delinear dias ou eras distintas e separadas, e qualquer discussão de tempo em relação à criação é artificial.

6. *O dia-revelador*. Os dias na narrativa de Gên. foram dias *de revelação*, e foram de 24 horas literais. Deus *revelou* a Moisés, *em 6 dias*, o esboço da criação, mas como ele realmente criou, e quanto tempo ele levou, são fatos não revelados.

7. *A semana-dividida ou simetria dupla*. A descrição de Gênesis incorpora um método literário pelo qual o 1º dia é paralelo ao 4º, o 2º ao 5º e o 3º ao 6º, e estes pares são complementares. O fator tempo, segundo esta teoria é artificial.

Avaliação destas teorias. A simples leitura do registro de Gênesis mostra que o escritor pensava em dias literais, e bem provavelmente, de um tempo relativamente recente. Estas diversas teorias são tentativas de incorporar a história de Gênesis dentro dos conhecimentos da ciência moderna. Elas são truques teológicos e filosóficos, embora tenham elementos obviamente verdadeiros.

Uma interpretação mais provável: a criação como um novo início. Existem evidências em favor da criação adâmica ser uma renovação, e não uma criação absoluta. Parece que a terra já passou mudanças dos pólos mais do que 400 vezes. Isto quer dizer, que por muitas vezes, vastas destruições tem arrumado, de modo diferente, os continentes, trazendo destruições quase completas da terra. Aparentemente, as últimas duas correspondem bem, em termos de tempo, às histórias bíblicas de Adão e Noé. Neste caso, a história de Adão seria um *novo começo*, não o começo absoluto da raça humana. Existiram, portanto, muitas raças humanas anteriores à adâmica. A história bíblica, então, nos informa sobre uma renovação da raça, e esta raça é aquela que iniciou a história do homem como nós o conhecemos. Gên. 1:1, todavia, é uma declaração geral sobre Deus como o criador absoluto, de tudo, em qualquer tempo.

8. *A teoria da grande explosão* da astronomia moderna pode ser combinada com a teoria das mudanças dos pólos. Existem também grandes ciclos cósmicos, não somente grandes ciclos terrestres. Há mais de 16.000.000 de anos, houve uma grande explosão de matéria condensada que deu início à criação que nós conhecemos na astronomia. Mas antes disto, houve inumeráveis explosões que iniciaram inumeráveis ciclos de bilhões de anos cada. Uma vez que o poder da explosão se dissipa, a matéria, pela força da gravidade, volta na outra direção. Uma vez que se condensa novamente, outra grande explosão ocorre. Este processo continua e é um fator sem data e totalmente além da nossa imaginação.

Conclusão. Existem grandes ciclos cósmicos e terrestres. As grandes explosões criam os cósmicos, e as mudanças dos pólos criam os terrestres. Temos ciclos terrestres dentro dos ciclos cósmicos, e todos eles são de imensa duração. Portanto, a criação cósmica que conhecemos agora é realmente uma história recente. Também, o ciclo terrestre que envolve a *raça adâmica* é recente. Além destas histórias recentes, sabemos praticamente nada sobre as obras de Deus na criação. Temos um *misterium tremendum* que as teorias dos homens, e suas cosmogonias são infantis demais para explicar. Portanto, as diversas tentativas de reconciliar a história de Gênesis com a ciência moderna são fúteis. Também, a explicação da própria ciência sobre tudo isto é essencialmente fútil, embora perfeitamente legítima. Todas as explicações são simplesmente gritos na noite misteriosa das obras de Deus. Mas é legítimo gritar e procurar cada vez mais, por entendimentos mais aperfeiçoados. (AM B C E Z)

CRIAÇÃO, realizado no, por meio de, e para o Filho.

O Ensino de Col. 1:16 sobre o *Logos*, chamado Cristo na sua encarnação.

1. *Porque nele foram criadas todas as coisas*. A criação *em Cristo* refere-se ao seu caráter como *Alfa*.

CRIAÇÃO POR MEIO DE CRISTO

O termo *nele* implica que todos os universos, todos os seres, existem como um desdobramento da mente de Deus, acerca de como deveria ser a natureza de tudo, segundo a natureza e exigências do *Logos*. O Logos é o padrão ou plano utilizado na criação. No caso do homem, ele é o padrão da natureza que o homem, na salvação, deve compartilhar, Rom. 8:29, dando a ele, a natureza divina, II Ped. 1:4. O Logos (Cristo) é, então o arquétipo da criação. Tudo foi criado por consideração a seu ser. A expressão *nele* também implica que foi *seu poder* que realizou a criação, em conjunto com o poder do Pai. O Logos, na qualidade de *arquétipo* da criação, equivale à idéia platônica das *Idéias* ou *Formas* que agem como o padrão para a criação das coisas terrenas. Note como *para ele* (ver explicações a seguir) fala sobre o Logos como o *Ômega*. Assim, o Logos é ao mesmo tempo o Alfa e o Ômega da criação. A criação também é *por ele*. Ele é o agente efetivo dela.

2. *Tudo foi criado por meio dele*. Isso se refere ao fato de que a criação veio à existência através do poder e da agência de Cristo. O vocábulo grego *dia* é usado do mesmo modo como em João 1:3. (Ali são dadas notas expositivas completas sobre esse aspecto de sua criação). Observemos que a idéia de «através dele» não denota qualquer inferioridade, como se Deus tão-somente tivesse se utilizado de Cristo para criar as coisas, como se ele mesmo não fosse o criador real. Pode-se verificar que, em Heb. 2:10, a mesma coisa é dita a respeito de Deus Pai; é «através dele» que tudo existe.

Notemos que a expressão **ta panta** é reiterada. Até os elevados poderes angelicais, juntamente com todas as outras coisas e seres, fazem parte da criação realizada por Cristo. E isso, mostra que sob hipótese alguma Cristo pode ser considerado parte da criação. Ele pertence a uma espécie distinta da criação. Os gnósticos afirmavam que a criação procedera de Deus como emanação, descendo de um poder angelical para outro, como emanações de vários graus da glória de Deus, a força criadora; —as emanações, pois— continuaram até se manifestarem na forma de espíritos, incluindo as almas humanas; e daí passaram à matéria, cuja forma mais inferior de emanações estaria tão afastada da luz de Deus que habitaria em trevas totais. Antes, Cristo é a causa primária e original; a causa mediadora também. Tudo veio à existência por meio dele, por seu ato de criação. Cristo, pois, não foi apenas mais um estágio de interminável sucessão de emanações, ao que os gnósticos o tinham reduzido; antes, ele foi a causa de todos os estágios da criação, que não é visto como uma emanação da parte de Deus, pois Deus é distinto de sua criação não compartilhando com ela de sua natureza, como o termo «emanação» geralmente indica. Assim é que evitamos a noção «panteísta», que sempre se faz inerente em qualquer teoria de «emanação».

Criado. Notemos aqui o tempo perfeito, em vez do aoristo. Este último apontaria para o ato de criação, mas o perfeito salienta o «estado resultante». Tudo quanto existe, conforme o conhecemos hoje em dia, «existe» devido à energia criadora de Cristo. Isso dá a entender, naturalmente, um ato criador original. Eles «foram criados» (aoristo) «nele», conforme nos mostra a primeira porção deste versículo; o ato criador original residia em Cristo, dependendo dele; e então todas as coisas «permanecem criadas», no estado em que as encontramos, através do seu poder criador. Isso pode ser comparado ao trecho de Heb. 1:10, que diz: «No princípio, Senhor, lançastes os fundamentos da terra, e os céus são obras das tuas mãos». Essas palavras se referem ao ato criador realizado por Cristo.

Para ele. No grego temos as palavras «eis auton». Assim como a palavra «nele» refere-se a Cristo em seu caráter como o «Alfa», assim também «para ele» refere-se a Cristo como o *Ômega* (ver Apo. 1:8). Isso significa que a criação visava ao seu benefício, à sua glória, aumentando a estatura de seu governo; pois ele é o «alvo» de toda a criação. Essa é a idéia do primeiro capítulo da epístola aos Efésios, onde o vemos como o ponto central em redor de quem tudo se reunirá harmoniosamente. Dentro da teoria gnóstica das «emanações», tudo retornaria a Deus e seria absorvido por ele, por seu Deus e sua fonte originária. Deus é visto como o poder que sustenta a tudo, enquanto tudo existiria como emanações de seu ser. Isso expressa uma verdade, embora mal formulada. «Todas as coisas», por assim dizer, são emanações de Cristo, mas distintas dele. Contudo, todas essas coisas retornam a Cristo, sendo absorvidas por ele, e os remidos chegarão a participar de sua própria natureza, sem jamais perderem sua individualidade. Tudo foi criado a fim de que — finalmente — encontrasse nele a razão da existência. Interveio a queda, mas a redenção que há em Cristo restaurou o desígnio original, chegando mesmo a aumentá-lo. Por isso é que Cristo é aquele que *preenche a tudo em todos* (conforme se aprende em Efé. 1:23).

De Que Modo Cristo É O Alvo?

1. Não podemos compreender esse fato plenamente, a menos que observemos cuidadosamente que ele é o *alvo* de «todas as coisas», tal como foi a causa de tudo. Se reduzirmos esse conceito em qualquer grau, perderemos de vista o conhecimento apropriado do que significa ser Cristo o alvo de toda a criação. Se fizermos dele o Alfa, mas não o Ômega, não o estaremos honrando com a nossa doutrina.

2. Col. 1:16 ensina-nos a mesma coisa que se aprende em Efé. 1:10: a «restauração geral» de tudo, em Cristo, o «reajuntamento de toda a criação», e isso «em redor» de Cristo, para que ele se torne o cabeça de todos. Essa restauração é intitulada, na epístola aos Efésios, de «o mistério da vontade de Deus», ou seja, aquilo que Deus está fazendo em suas muitas realizações, e através de muitas eras.

3. No que diz respeito aos eleitos, isso redunda para eles em «redenção», isto é, na participação na própria imagem e natureza de Cristo (ver Rom. 8:29), na sua plenitude (ver Col. 2:10), em ser a sua plenitude (ver Efé. 1:23), na participação na natureza e nos atributos divinos (Efé. 3:19), e, por conseqüência, em ser o principal agente da glória de Cristo, nos mundos eternos (ver Efé. 1:23). Isso tudo significa que a igreja estará ocupada na eternidade com a tarefa de tornar Cristo «tudo para todos» (ou seja, a restauração), conforme alguns intérpretes parafraseiam aquele versículo. Essa «natureza» e «atividade» da igreja, conferirão a Cristo a sua glória mais exaltada, porquanto somos o seu corpo, os membros através dos quais ele atua; e a glorificação do corpo será necessariamente a glorificação do Cabeça.

4. No que concerne aos perdidos, antecipamos que haverá uma «restauração», em contraste com a redenção dos eleitos. Aquela será uma glória secundária, uma existência digna de ser vivida, que redundará em glória positiva para Cristo, embora não queira dizer, que os não-eleitos venham a compartilhar da natureza divina. Tais seres serão uma ou mais espécies distintas, de natureza inferior. Não obstante, Cristo será tudo para eles, a motivação, a alegria e o propósito da sua existência. O próprio julgamento

CRIAÇÃO — CRIAÇÃO ESPIRITUAL

será um dos meios da realização da *restauração*, I Ped. 4:6. Ver o artigo sobre *Restauração*.

5. E que dizer sobre os demais seres espirituais? Cristo também será o cabeça deles, e o propósito de sua existência. Presumimos que os anjos caídos poderão ser restaurados, embora pouquíssima seja a nossa informação bíblica a esse respeito. Nada sabemos, especificamente, do tipo de destino que foi determinado para os seres angelicais. Mas, sem importar exatamente qual seja, estará centralizado em torno de Cristo.

6. A criação física: a ordem será restaurada, a maldição divina será suspensa. — Finalmente, surgirá uma nova criação, e isso fará parte da restauração geral.

7. Cristo criou todas as coisas; e tudo retornará a ele novamente. O mesmo conceito é declarado no tocante a Deus Pai. (Ver I Cor. 8:6 e Rom. 11:36).

Cristo Jesus é o Senhor dos senhores,
Ele é o Rei dos reis;
Ele é também o Sol da justiça,
E a cura ele traz em suas asas.
(John Mason).

«Ele é a finalidade da criação, contendo a razão, em si mesmo, de por que a criação existe, e por que é como é». (Alford, em Col. 1:16).

«Ele mesmo é o fim. Assim, enquanto entre os homens se debatia acerca do fim, se seria o prazer, a especulação, a virtude, a indiferença ou o que as escolas filosóficas pudessem dizer, para nós basta dizer que a finalidade é Cristo». (Cramer, «Catenae in N.T.», sobre I Ped. 4:7). Isso empresta a Col. 1:16 um excelente tom *moral*. Agora mesmo, em tudo, em toda a inquirição espiritual, Cristo é o alvo e o padrão, tal como, — finalmente —, em todas as coisas e de todos os modos, ele será o centro.

Cristo é o fim, pois Cristo foi o começo,
Cristo é o começo, pois o fim é Cristo.
(F.W.H. Meyers, St. Paul, pág. 53).

Em tudo isso vemos claramente como devemos confiar plenamente em Deus, através da fé, e da lealdade a Cristo. Assim se define a vida eterna.

«Estou começando a perceber que posso e devo crer em Deus, e estou simplesmente assustado. Tenho ficado acostumado a viver sem ele, até certo ponto. Se admitir a mim mesmo que Deus é real, sei que terei de fazer algo a respeito, e sinto que minha vida inteira será transtornada. E procuro evitar essas modificações desconhecidas mas possíveis». (*Finding God* - Ray Long & Richard R. Smith).

Se usarmos a terminologia aristotélica, então Cristo será:

1. A causa *material*. Pois ele é a substância na qual tudo tem seu potencial, do que tudo o mais se desenvolve. (Isso é semelhante à idéia do «nele», que figura em Col. 1:16).

2. A causa *formal*. Em outras palavras, nele se acha o plano de desenvolvimento e seu potencial. Essa idéia também faz parte inerente da palavra «nele», que há em Col. 1:16.

3. A causa *eficiente*. Pois ele é o agente da criação, a força criadora. (Essa idéia é expressa pelas palavras «por ele», em Col. 1:16).

4. A causa *final*. Porquanto nele se cumprem todos os desenvolvimentos ou fruições da vida; ele é o alvo na direção do qual se move a criação. (Isso é expresso dentro do conceito sugerido pelas palavras «para ele», em Col. 1:16).

Cristo, por conseguinte, é o *Alfa*, o *Mu* e o *Ômega* da vida: o começo, o meio e o fim. Ele é o padrão, a razão, o agente, o sustentador e o alvo da vida.

CRIAÇÃO ESPIRITUAL

A Nova Criação, (Efé. 2:10).

1. Isso, quanto ao aspecto físico (ver Rom. 1:20). Devemos a Deus nossa própria existência. Ele é o Alfa.

2. Porém, também somos sua criação espiritual. Ele é o Ômega. Movemo-nos na direção dele. (Ver I Cor. 8:6 e II Cor. 5:17). Isso é conseguido através de nossa comunhão mística com Cristo (ver as notas a respeito em I Cor. 1:4 no NTI), pois, «nele», temo-nos tornado novas criaturas.

3. Mui provavelmente, ambas as idéias acima expressas, estão em foco aqui, conforme as vemos ligadas entre si em João 1:4. Da «vida» original é que emergiu a «luz», isto é, a «nova vida iluminada». A criação física foi feita a fim de que, dela, pudesse emergir a criação espiritual.

4. Essa declaração é parcialmente polêmica. Visto que somos «criação» dele, dificilmente podemos ser nossos próprios criadores. Isso é óbvio, no que concerne à criação física. Para certas pessoas, entretanto, isso não é tão óbvio no tocante à criação espiritual, porquanto elas se esforçam por refazer-se através das obras, dos sacramentos e das cerimônias religiosas. Na verdade, porém, isso nos vem pela graça divina: Deus nos tornou naquilo que somos; nossos destinos dependem dele. Ele forma em nós a imagem de Cristo (ver Rom. 8:29). Ele nos proporciona sua própria natureza e seus atributos (ver Efé. 3:19). Toda essa realização está muito acima das possibilidades humanas. Tudo nos vem pela graça.

Dele. Esse vocábulo é enfático. Pois a feitura é «dele», isto é, de Deus, e não nossa. Embora tenham sido empregadas palavras gregas diferentes, há uma certa antítese entre «obras» e «feitura». Assim sendo, a salvação não vem de «obras», mas de «feitura». Também não vem de «obra humana», e, sim, de *feitura divina*. É interessante saber que o nosso vocábulo português «poema» se deriva do termo grego aqui traduzido por «feitura». Portanto, somos «um poema» ou «uma composição de Deus», porquanto nossa graça e beleza estética pertencem à sua arte, e não ao nosso próprio engenho. Naturalmente que podemos fazer essa aplicação como uma ilustração, pois não há que duvidar que o apóstolo dos gentios não tinha em mente a idéia de «poema», —quando escrevera Efé. 2:10. Não obstante, essa mesma palavra grega significa uma composição poética, tendo sido assim utilizada por diversos autores antigos. A única outra ocasião, em todo o N.T., onde essa palavra é novamente usada, é em Rom. 1:20, e onde a alusão é à criação física.

Criados, Efé. 2:10. Comenta Vincent (*in loc.*), como segue: «Ver sobre João 1:3. Originalmente esse verbo significava 'tornar habitável', 'popular', e, portanto 'fundar'. Deus é chamado de *ktistes*, em I Ped. 4:19 e de 'o ktistes' 'aquele que criou', em Rom. 1:25. (Comparar com Apo. 4:11). *Ktisis* é termo usado para indicar a súmula total das coisas criadas, segundo se vê em Mar. 10:6 e Rom. 8:22».

Como Opera essa Nova Criação

1. Ela nos orienta na direção de um destino planejado por Deus. Ela esboça o curso de nossas vidas, neste mundo e para sempre.

2. Ela torna cada um de nós uma pessoa singular, singular em sua missão (ver as notas sobre isso em Apo. 2:17 no NTI).

CRIAÇÃO EX NIHILO — CRIACIONISMO

CRIAÇÃO EX NIHILO

O latim, «ex nihilo» significa «do nada». A criação «do nada» é o ponto de vista tradicional cristão, em contraste com a idéia grega da reforma da matéria previamente existente. Na primitiva teologia cristã, quando a doutrina do Logos ou Verbo estava sendo utilizada para explicar o *modus operandi* da criação, estabeleceu-se a idéia de que ninguém pode falar sobre o Logos eterno e sobre a eternidade da matéria, ao mesmo tempo. O gnóstico Basílides (que vide), antecipou a doutrina e Hiérocles de Alexandria (que vide) apegou-se a uma versão da mesma. Tomás de Aquino supunha que Deus sustenta a sua criação por meio de alguma lei geral. Descartes (que vide) referiu-se ao poder sustentador de Deus de maneira tal que, à sua maneira de apresentar a idéia, Deus estaria criando novamente o mundo, a cada instante. Os teólogos modernos falam em termos do poder criador e sustentador de Deus como uma energia divina. Isso significa que temos uma criação mediante a energia de Deus, e não «do nada». Mas, com essa qualificação, o antigo nome ainda assim é retido. Como é óbvio, o que vem do nada é o nada, ou seja, *ex nihilo nihil fit* (do nada, nada é feito). Ver o artigo geral sobre a *Criação*, quanto às várias idéias concernentes à origem da criação, além de outras questões envolvidas no assunto.

CRIAÇÃO NOVA Ver **Nova Criação**.

CRIACIONISMO

Consideremos dois pontos principais a respeito:

1. *No Tocante à Alma*. No que diz respeito à alma, o *criacionismo* é uma dentre várias teorias referentes à sua origem. Quanto a um completo estudo sobre a questão, ver o artigo geral sobre a *Alma*, sob as teorias de sua origem. Essa teoria afirma que, no momento da concepção ou do nascimento, Deus cria *de novo* a alma humana, para utilizar-se do corpo físico como um veículo. Trechos bíblicos usados em apoio a essa teoria são: Zac. 12:1; Isa. 42:5 e Heb. 12:9. Entretanto essas passagens dificilmente provam o ponto; e a própria idéia envolve uma teologia deficiente. Simplesmente não há passagens bíblicas claras acerca da origem da alma, embora sua existência e seu destino sejam pontos claramente ensinados na Bíblia.

Dificuldades Dessa Opinião. Em primeiro lugar, essa teoria força Deus a depender do ato procriativo do homem. Deus também não cessaria em criar almas, a cada nova concepção ou nascimento humano, o que reflete uma situação ridícula e nada econômica quanto ao tempo de Deus. O *traducionismo* (que vide) procura isentar Deus dessa contínua atividade criativa, afirmando que os poderes de criação dos pais, que são seres não apenas físicos, mas também espirituais, naturalmente produzem tanto o corpo quanto a alma. Isso teria sido estabelecido como uma lei natural, inerente ao esquema natural das coisas. Segundo penso, essa teoria é superior à primeira, embora ainda não corresponda à realidade total dos fatos. Em segundo lugar, o criacionismo envolve certas dificuldades teológicas. É impossível imaginarmos que Deus haveria de criar uma alma decaída. Na verdade, a doutrina cristã afirma que as almas humanas caíram em Adão, por ocasião do pecado original. Portanto, as almas já chegam como entidades pecaminosas na esfera terrestre. Por outra parte, o criacionismo requer a negação dessa doutrina, dando a entender que *é o corpo*, por estar poluído, que contamina a alma, assim que a alma entra em contato com o corpo. Qualquer pessoa que estuda a teologia sabe que tal doutrina é um reflexo do gnosticismo. Os mestres gnósticos supunham que a própria matéria é má, e que o espírito é puro. Assim sendo, o corpo físico seria mal e contaminado, mas não o espírito. No entanto, a doutrina cristã nunca encarou o próprio corpo como pecaminoso, embora aceite que o mesmo é instrumento fácil do pecado. Antes, a *entidade espiritual* é que é pecaminosa, o homem real, a alma. Portanto, a alma é que já chega neste mundo como um ser caído, e então apossasse-se do corpo físico como seu veículo de expressão. O corpo não é mau por si mesmo. E como poderia sê-lo? É apenas um montículo de matéria, embora uma máquina admirável. A concepção da matéria como má é uma noção gnóstica clara. No entanto, muitos teólogos cristãos precisam recorrer ao gnosticismo a fim de defender a teoria do criacionismo.

Criados do Nada? Boaventura e Tomás de Aquino (ver os artigos a respeito deles) aplicaram a idéia do *ex nihilo* ao criacionismo. Presumivelmente, Deus criaria as almas do nada, da mesma maneira que, presumivelmente, teria criado o mundo do nada. Porém, do nada, nada se origina (*ex nihilo, nihil fit*). Nem todos os teólogos, entretanto, que advogam o criacionismo, apegam-se à idéia do *ex nihilo*. A idéia do criacionismo tem-se mostrado dominante na Igreja ocidental e na Igreja oriental, como também em muitas denominações protestantes. Tertuliano, seguindo os estóicos, ensinava o *traducionismo*. Lutero não sabia qual decisão tomar entre essas duas teorias, mas a maioria dos luteranos tem preferido o traducionismo. Outras idéias alternativas são a da eternidade da alma (Platão), como participante dos universais (que vide); ou a idéia da *preexistência* (que vide) da alma, posição assumida pela maioria dos pais gregos da Igreja. Essa é a teoria que parece mais lógica, em face das razões que enumero no artigo com esse título.

2. *Criacionismo Cosmológico*. Esse é o conceito que diz que o começo de todas as coisas ocorreu mediante um ato criativo de Deus, e não em virtude de alguma emanação de seu próprio ser (panteísmo). Essa idéia nega que a matéria tenha existido desde a eternidade, tendo sido apenas reformada ou posta em boa ordem. Esse ensino dá a entender que houve um tempo em que somente Deus existia. Tudo constitui um grande mistério, que não nos foi revelado!

3. *Criacionismo Antropológico* (origem do homem). Esse é o ensino que diz que o homem foi criado por Deus por um ato especial e imediato, de tal maneira que o homem não é produto de evolução. A idéia inclui a noção que, tanto o corpo quanto a alma, foram criados como uma unidade. Todavia, a idéia mais antiga dos hebreus foi que o ato criador de Deus envolveu somente o corpo, e que *isso* inclui o homem interior chamado alma nas traduções, porquanto, na antiga teologia hebraica não haveria qualquer noção sobre um ser *imaterial*. Essa idéia aparece mais tarde nos Salmos e nos livros dos profetas, estando ausente do Pentateuco. A teoria da evolução apareceu, com algumas poucas exceções, como um conceito de como o homem *biológico* veio à existência, e nada pretende falar sobre o espírito humano. Isso posto, essa teoria também nada tem a ver com o homem essencial, real, o espírito humano. Estritamente falando, portanto, nem o livro de Gênesis e nem a teoria da evolução informam-nos como o homem real veio à existência. Mas, de acordo com a *interpretação cristã*, o registro de Gênesis fornece-nos a narrativa sobre a origem do homem, em corpo e alma. Ver o artigo sobre a *Evolução*. (B C P)

••• ••• •••

CRIANÇA

CRIANÇA

Esboço:
1. O Termo
2. As Escrituras e as Crianças
3. Usos Bíblicos Figurados
4. As Crianças e a Ética
5. A Idade da Responsabilidade e da Salvação

1. O Termo

O heb. **yeled** aparece 87 vezes no A.T. (Exemplos: Gên. 21:8,14,16; Êxo. 2:3,6-10; Rute 4:16; I Sam. 12:15,18,19,21,22; I Reis 3:25; II Reis 4:18,26,34; Ecl. 4:13,15; Isa. 9:6; Jer. 31:20). No grego, *paidíon*, palavra que ocorre por cinqüenta e três vezes, de Mat. 2:8 a I João 3:7. E também *país*, que aparece por vinte e quatro vezes, de Mat. 2:16 a Atos 20:12, com o sentido de «servo», «criado», «filho», etc.

No Antigo Testamento, a palavra acima algumas vezes é usada no plural a fim de designar somente um descendente masculino (I Crô. 2:31; II Crô. 24:25), em cujos casos a palavra «filhos» dá a entender, genericamente, descendência, da qual todos morreram, exceto o último nome mencionado. Tanto no Antigo quanto no Novo Testamento, os termos envolvidos são usados com considerável latitude, conforme é demonstrado pelas várias definições. Um uso comum consiste em designar a descendência, sem importar quão remota. Assim, os «filhos» de uma personagem qualquer podem ser seus descendentes remotos.

2. As Escrituras e as Crianças

a. **Uma criança era considerada, entre os israelitas, uma bênção de Deus**; e muitos filhos eram um sinal do favor divino, ao passo que as pessoas estéreis eram olhadas com menosprezo (Gên. 11:30; 30:1; I Sam. 2:5; II Sam. 6:23 e Sal. 127:3).

b. *Posição da Criança*. O fato de que as crianças eram, por muitas vezes, vendidas como escravas ou entregues a algum credor, a fim de ser paga uma dívida, mostra o pouco respeito que se tinha pelas crianças, em Israel (ver II Reis 4:1; Isa. 50:1; Nee. 5:5). Um pai hebreu exercia poder ilimitado sobre seus filhos, meninos ou meninas. Os pais é que escolhiam os cônjuges para seus filhos (Gên. 21:21; Êxo. 21:9-11; Juí. 14:2,5). Um pai podia anular um voto sagrado feito por uma filha, embora não por um filho. Dos pais esperava-se que entregassem seus filhos para serem mortos, se se tornassem culpados de abusar de um dos genitores (Êxo. 21:15,17; Lev. 20:9). Jesus referiu-se a essa lei em Mat. 15:4 e Mar. 7:9. Antes da legislação mosaica, um pai podia designar quem era o seu filho primogênito, usualmente filho de uma esposa favorita, sem importar se esse filho era, ou não, o mais velho. Ver Gên. 49:3. Os privilégios dos primogênitos eram consideráveis. Ver sobre o *Direito de Primogenitura*.

c. *Os Infantes*. Bebês recém-nascidos eram cuidados por parteiras ou servas (Gên. 35:17; 38:28; Êxo. 1:15). A criança recém-nascida era banhada em água, esfregada com sal, envolta em panos e cuidada pela mãe (Gên. 21:7; I Sam. 1:23), com a ajuda de outras pessoas, conforme indicado acima, dependendo das posses da família. Os meninos eram circuncidados ao oitavo dia de nascidos. Ver o artigo sobre a *Circuncisão*. Os nomes dados às crianças dependiam de algumas circunstâncias que envolviam o nascimento (Gên. 25:25 *ss*; 35:18; 38:29), ou de algum desejo ou esperança por parte da mãe (Gên. 4:25; 29:32), ou em honra a algum parente (Luc. 1:61). Quarenta dias após o nascimento de um menino, ou oitenta dias após o nascimento de uma menina, a mãe precisava oferecer um sacrifício de purificação no templo (Lev. 12:1-8), apresentando a criança a Deus, e remindo-a com certa importância em dinheiro (Núm. 18:15 *ss*; 4:47). —O desmame usualmente só ocorria aos dois, ou mesmo aos três anos de idade (II Macabeus 7:27). Isso era celebrado (Gên. 21:8), e eram feitos os sacrifícios apropriados (I Sam. 1:23,24).

d. *Treinamento*. A mãe da criança era sua principal treinadora (Pro. 31:1; II Tim. 1:5 e 3:15). As filhas eram estritamente supervisionadas até no casamento. Quando uma criança atingia os cinco anos de idade, os pais tomavam um papel mais ativo na sua educação; e, no caso de famílias mais abastadas, eram contratados professores (Núm. 11:12; Isa. 49:23; II Reis 10:1; Gál. 3:24). Havia grande empenho na educação religiosa das crianças, bem como na arte da leitura e da escrita (Êxo. 12:26; 13:8,14; Deu. 4:10; 6:7). As escolas são uma invenção comparativamente recente. Os meninos eram treinados em uma profissão qualquer, usualmente a do seu pai. Gamaliel, nos dias de Jesus, conforme somos informados, foi o primeiro judeu a estabelecer escolas para meninos, nas cidades.

e. *As Crianças Diante da Lei*. A reverência aos pais era uma exigência absoluta (Êxo. 20:12; Lev. 19:3), sem o que uma criança não podia prosperar espiritualmente, segundo se cria. Se uma criança amaldiçoasse a seus pais, imediatamente ficava debaixo de uma maldição divina (Deu. 27:16). Se um filho fizesse alguma violência contra seus pais, era executado (Êxo. 21:15,17; Lev. 20:9). Se um filho se tornasse um alcoólatra, um glutão, um malfeitor, ignorando as advertências de seu pai, seria morto por apedrejamento, pelos anciãos da cidade (Deu. 21:18-21). O primeiro filho a ser declarado primogênito, não podia, posteriormente, perder esse direito, porque seu pai, depois dele, gerara um filho através de alguma esposa mais favorecida, e queria mudar seu parecer sobre a questão (Deu. 21:15-17). A lei permitia que um pai anulasse um voto de uma filha sua (Núm. 30:4,5). Ele tinha autoridade para contratar casamento para seus filhos, e podia vender uma filha como concubina; mas não podia vendê-la a um povo estrangeiro (Êxo. 21:7 *ss*). Os filhos podiam ser vendidos a fim de ser paga alguma dívida, podendo até mesmo ser vendidos à servidão (II Reis 4:1; Isa. 50:1; Nee. 5:5). Os filhos nascidos como escravos, filhos de escravos, permaneciam como escravos (Gên. 14:14; 15:3 e 17:23).

f. *Filhos Ilegítimos*. Esses não tinham direito à herança (Gên. 21:10; Gál. 4:30). Não recebiam qualquer treinamento formal, eram excluídos da congregação e eram desprezados (Deu. 23:2; Juí. 11:2).

g. *Adoção de Filhos*. Na antiga Mesopotâmia, conforme somos informados dos documentos de Nuzi, havia o costume de adotar filhos. Abraão adotou um herdeiro (Gên. 15:3), embora não houvesse qualquer legislação formal para isso, até onde sabemos. Os casos bíblicos de adoção usualmente ocorrem em um meio ambiente estrangeiro, como a adoção de Moisés por parte da filha de Faraó (Êxo. 2:10), ou a adoção de Ester por Mordecai (Est. 2:7,15). Em alguns casos, os adotados já eram descendentes da mesma linhagem (Gên. 48:5,12; Rute 4:16,17). As referências neotestamentárias, conforme se vê em Rom. 8:15 e Gál. 4:5, têm um pano de fundo romano. Naquela sociedade, a prática era regulamentada por lei, conferindo a posição de plena filiação. Ver o artigo sobre a *Adoção*.

3. Usos Bíblicos Figurados

JESUS ABENÇOANDO AS CRIANÇAS

Aquele que habita no esconderijo do Altíssimo, à sombra do Onipotente descansará. Direi do Senhor: Ele é meu refúgio, a minha Fortaleza, e Nele confiarei. Porque ele te livrará do laço do passarinheiro e da peste perniciosa. ELE te cobrirá com suas penas, e debaixo de suas asas estarás seguro: a sua Verdade é escudo e broquel. Não temerás espanto noturno, nem seta que voe de DIA, nem peste que ande na escuridão, nem mortandade que assole ao meio dia. Mil cairão ao teu lado, e dez mil à tua direita, mas tu não serás atingido. Somente com teus olhos olharás e verás a recompensa dos ímpios.

Porque tu, ó Senhor, és o meu refúgio! O Altíssimo é tua habitação. Nenhum mal te sucederá, nem praga ALGUMA chegará à tua tenda. Porque aos seus anjos dará ordem a teu respeito, para te guardarem em todos os teus CAMINHOS.

Salmos 91 1-11

Caligrafia de Darrell Steven Champlin

CRIANÇA

a. As crianças simbolizam um estado de ignorância e de trevas intelectuais (Mat. 11:16; I Cor. 13:11; 14:20; Efé. 4:14 e Heb. 5:13).

b. Israel, em sua agonia na escravidão egípcia, é comparado a uma criança abandonada, ou a um infante que jaz em seu próprio sangue (retratando a crueldade dos egípcios) (Eze. 16:1-14).

c. A expressão «filho de» ou «filhos de» indica alguma característica especial, como «filhos da luz», aqueles que possuem iluminação espiritual (Luc. 16:8), ou «filhos da obediência», aqueles que obedecem às leis espirituais (I Ped. 1:14). Pelo lado negativo, encontramos expressões como «filhos do inferno» (Mat. 23:15); «filhos do maligno» (Mat. 13:38), «filhos deste mundo» (Luc. 16:8).

d. Os «filhos da ressurreição» serão aqueles que participarão da vida eterna, já com seus corpos ressuscitados (Luc. 20:36).

e. Os «filhos de Deus» são os remidos, uma expressão extremamente freqüente, sobretudo no Novo Testamento (João 1:12).

f. Os «filhos de Abraão» são aqueles que seguem em sua tradição espiritual, sem importar se judeus ou gentios, os quais, por isso mesmo, são herdeiros de sua herança espiritual (Luc. 3:8; João 8:39 e Gál. 3:7).

g. Todos aqueles que chegam ao reino de Deus devem ter a mesma atitude humilde dos filhos (Mat. 18:3).

4. As Crianças e a Ética

a. A primeira responsabilidade da educação das crianças cabe aos pais; e só secundariamente à Igreja e às instituições de ensino. Por isso encontramos aquele mandamento que diz: «Ensina a criança no caminho em que deve andar, e ainda quando for velho não se desviará dele» (Pro. 22:6). É com base nessa idéia que a Igreja Católica Romana diz que se lhe for confiada o treinamento de uma criança, até que ela chegue aos sete anos de idade, provavelmente ela não se afastará dos ensinamentos católicos depois disso. Os evangélicos, naturalmente, também crêem nesse princípio, pelo que têm estabelecido muitas escolas religiosas, em face da corrupção crescente do sistema escolar público, e devido à ausência de treinamento apropriado no lar. Apesar desse sistema contar com alguns pontos positivos, também tem seu aspecto negativo. Os cristãos por procuração não são, necessariamente, os melhores; pois, passada a supervisão de seus superiores, coisas desastrosas podem acontecer. Um soldado precisa enfrentar a batalha, a fim de aprender a lutar. Um boxeador precisa treinar suas habilidades *lutando*. Assim sendo, a saturação das escolas cristãs com freqüência cria mais indiferença do que espiritualidade. Não há que duvidar que muitos missionários têm caído no erro sério de confiar o treinamento de *seus* filhos a terceiros, usualmente nas escolas, ao passo que eles ensinam a filhos *alheios*, em algum campo missionário estrangeiro, em vez de ensinarem a seus próprios filhos.

b. *Fracassos*. Apesar de todos os esforços de seus pais, as crianças freqüentemente deixam de corresponder ao desafio, mesmo dos pais mais piedosos, os quais apóiam seu ensino com o próprio exemplo. Como poderíamos explicar esses casos? Meus amigos, preciso dizer-lhes o que acredito. A alma é preexistente, trazendo consigo toda a bagagem espiritual acumulada em uma longa existência. Isso pode ser aprimorado ou prejudicado pelas circunstâncias da vida. Os pais piedosos com freqüência recebem as almas de boas entidades, e, nesses casos, o treinamento *parece* operar esplendidamente. Mas, a verdade é que essas crianças já trazem consigo um bom caráter espiritual, que haverá de manifestar-se com ou sem treinamento. Todavia, o treinamento de uma criança pode transmitir-lhe essa boa qualidade ainda mais positivamente, pois a espiritualidade é uma qualidade que sempre é passível de crescimento. Porém, se uma alma má nasce de bons pais, seus *melhores esforços* poderão fracassar miseravelmente. Um dos mais violentos assassinos da história criminal dos Estados Unidos da América era filho de um piedoso líder evangélico. Esse, é claro, é um exemplo radical; mas os exemplos dessa ordem são tão abundantes que precisamos mudar de idéia quanto ao conceito inteiro do treinamento de crianças. No caso de João Batista, somos informados pelas Escrituras que ele foi cheio do Espírito Santo desde o ventre materno (Luc. 1:15). Paulo era um vaso especial, escolhido desde antes do seu nascimento (Gál. 1:15). Podemos dizer que esses eram casos especiais, dependendo da decisão do Senhor. Porém, observando o que está ocorrendo com as crianças de nossos dias, vemos como, com a mesma família, com o mesmo treinamento, com os mesmos pais, nas mesmas escolas, nas mesmas igrejas, as crianças acabam mostrando ser inteiramente diferentes, tanto no sentido espiritual quanto no tocante a outras questões. Em face disso, tenho chegado à conclusão que está em jogo muito mais do que o treinamento e o meio ambiente. As pessoas gostam de afirmar que João Batista e Paulo representam *exceções* divinas, mas penso que eles representam ilustrações da *regra*. Os pais alexandrinos da Igreja acreditavam na preexistência da alma, sem a reencarnação. Mas, com ou sem a reencarnação (que vide), precisamos considerar a possibilidade de que o começo de uma alma pode dar-se por impulso divino, em uma remota eternidade passada, nada tendo a ver com a geração do corpo. Assim, a alma teria uma história inteiramente separada do corpo físico. Ver o artigo sobre a *Alma, Sua Origem*. Ali exponho as diversas teorias sobre a origem da alma.

Era comum à teologia judaica posterior que seus profetas cumpriram mais de uma missão terrena. Isso se reflete em Mat. 16:14. Alguns judeus pensavam que Jesus era Jeremias, ou algum dos outros profetas do Antigo Testamento, que havia retornado. O mesmo princípio teria aplicação a entidades negativas, como o anticristo, que seria a volta à vida de um imperador romano, saído do próprio abismo (que vide), ou do hades (que vide) (ver Apo. 17:8,11). Aquilo que a doutrina supostamente ortodoxa tem chamado de exceções, bem podem ser exemplos de uma verdade geral. Precisamos aprender através da experiência, e o conhecimento é algo que sempre está sujeito a desenvolvimento. Quando vejo o que sucede às crianças, filhos de pais piedosos, percebo que a palavra «treinamento», apesar de contar muito, não conta a história inteira. Estudos recentes demonstram que cerca de metade dos criminosos, nos Estados Unidos da América, não foram criados sob condições domésticas e sociais que, normalmente, fomentariam um mau caráter. Ademais, muitos criminosos procedem de lares perfeitamente normais, e, desde seus primeiros anos, são diferentes, mentindo, furtando e tratando outras pessoas de maneira errada. Nessas crianças há algo que já veio com eles, desde que nasceram. Alguns estudiosos têm pensado em defeitos cerebrais, nesses casos; porém, nenhuma prova foi colhida quanto a isso, até agora. Portanto, precisamos considerar a possibilidade da *herança espiritual*, e não apenas a

CRIANÇA

herança genética e o meio ambiente, a fim de compreender alguns dos nossos mais críticos problemas.

Por outra parte, há os casos daquelas crianças que, sem nenhum treinamento especial, — até mesmo em um meio ambiente doméstico e social negativo, elevam-se acima da média, chegando a grandes realizações seculares e espirituais. Também não penso que isso ocorre por mero acidente. É que tais crianças já trouxeram consigo um caráter espiritual básico e bem formado, que haverá de manifestar-se, sem importar as circunstâncias contrárias, como um lar negativo, uma péssima vizinhança, ou qualquer outro fator adverso. Se alguém mergulhar um objeto de ouro na lama, esse objeto continuará sendo de ouro, e a lama não conseguirá penetrar no metal. Mas, se alguém mergulhar um objeto de chumbo em água pura e cristalina, esse objeto continuará sendo de chumbo. Tempo e esforço são capazes de modificar qualquer coisa; e é disso que o evangelho trata. Contudo, essa modificação se processa lenta e laboriosamente. E a conversão, apesar de elevar as pessoas, não as eleva todas ao mesmo nível. De fato, a vida de muitas pessoas supostamente convertidas continua extremamente deficiente em qualidade espiritual. É que em cada vida há um caráter espiritual básico já em operação, não estando envolvido apenas aquilo que acontece neste mundo. O que já aconteceu à alma, no passado remoto, é extremamente importante, e não apenas na vida terrena.

c. *Influências Cristãs*. A influência do judaísmo no mundo, e, em seguida, do cristianismo, muito contribuiu para eliminar alguns terríveis abusos. O judaísmo fazia finca-pé contra o sacrifício de crianças (Lev. 18:21). A Igreja cristã condena o aborto provocado. Orfanatos cristãos tornaram-se uma instituição comum a começar em cerca de 361 ou 363 D.C. A Igreja cristã promove o funcionamento de instituições educacionais e hospitalares para as crianças. Robert Raikes deu início à Escola Dominical, e F.D. Maurice promoveu a legislação a respeito do labor infantil, com base na ética cristã. Talvez o fator mais significativo que ocorre atualmente nos Estados Unidos da América, no que concerne às crianças que nascem de pais evangélicos, seja o fenomenal desenvolvimento das escolas evangélicas. É possível que isso tenha por modelo o empreendimento da Igreja Católica Romana e de grupos ortodoxos orientais.

5. A Idade da Responsabilidade e da Salvação

Um problema teológico de grandes proporções está envolvido no caso da salvação das crianças. Que sucede aos infantes que morrem? Com que idade uma criança torna-se responsável pelos seus atos? Há diversas respostas para essas perguntas:

a. *Os Céticos*. Esses dizem que a questão envolve um mistério para o qual não há nenhuma boa resposta.

b. *A Igreja Católica Romana*. Os infantes não-batizados não são considerados responsáveis por seus atos, mas também não estão na Igreja. Portanto, se vierem a morrer, irão para o *limbo* (que vide), que não seria nem o céu e nem o inferno. Não há descrições sobre o tipo de vida que as crianças levam ali. Mas alguns teólogos dão ouvidos a filósofos gregos, que tinham boas idéias quanto à questão, e que viveram antes da era cristã. Portanto, no romanismo há muita discussão filosófica a esse respeito! Os teólogos chamam o limbo de lugar de felicidade, embora ali ninguém recebesse a *Visão Beatífica* (que vide). Os indivíduos mentalmente incompetentes também seriam enviados para o limbo. Por conseguinte, felizes os que nascem retardados, pois outros, que têm algum bom senso, são enviados para o inferno! Segundo o catolicismo, os infantes *batizados* iriam para o céu. Os protestantes e evangélicos consideram o limbo uma pura invenção, porquanto sabem que o ato do batismo não altera o destino de uma pessoa, por ser apenas o símbolo externo de uma operação do Espírito. Portanto, eles preferem pensar que os retardados mentais e os infantes que morrem vão para o céu.

c. *O Ponto de Vista Calvinista Radical*. Visto que as crianças são criaturas caídas, se morrerem, elas irão diretamente para o inferno, embora para uma região de menor punição; mas para o inferno, não obstante. E elas ficam eternamente condenadas. Isso pode parecer uma posição lógica, se nos apegarmos somente às passagens bíblicas que dizem respeito ao julgamento geral; mas tal posição é repugnante e ridícula.

d. *A Idade da Responsabilidade*. A maioria dos estudiosos protestantes fala em termos de uma certa idade que, quando a criança atinge, torna-se responsável por seus atos. Os teólogos da Idade Média presumiam que, com a idade de cerca de doze anos, as crianças atingem essa fase da responsabilidade. Os mórmons preferem pensar que isso se dá quando a criança chega aos oito anos de idade. De acordo com essa doutrina, antes dessa idade, uma criança, embora tenha cometido pecados, não é responsabilizada pelos mesmos. Outro tanto pode ser dito acerca dos mentalmente deficientes. Essas pessoas, mediante a graça divina geral, iriam para o céu quando morressem. Naturalmente, isso é uma *idéia racional*, e não uma doutrina das Escrituras. Alguns apontam para o trecho de II Samuel 12:13 como texto de prova. Davi declara ali que não poderia trazer sua criança de volta, mas que ele poderia ir até ela. Porém, isso não fala necessariamente sobre o céu; poderia indicar a morte e o envolvimento no Sheol, etc. Além disso, não se trata de um versículo dogmático, em uma passagem dogmática. Para mim, seja como for, toda essa idéia não faz sentido. Mediante qual bafejo da sorte algumas pessoas morrem quando ainda infantes e outras nascem idiotas?' Deve haver alguma idéia melhor, que se aproxime mas da verdade!

e. *A Preexistência da Alma e a Morte dos Infantes*. Quando, mais acima neste artigo, discutíamos sobre o *treinamento* das crianças, especulamos dizendo que faz sentido supor que a alma humana é preexistente. Se isso é verdade, então isso nos dá certa margem de segurança para falarmos sobre a salvação dos infantes que morrem nessa fase inicial da vida. A alma, que já tem uma longa história espiritual, já possui suas qualidades espirituais específicas. Ao associar-se ao corpo físico, ela poderá melhorar ou piorar, sem importar se essa associação tem de ocorrer apenas por uma vez ou por diversas vezes. Se a alma assumiu um corpo físico, mas morreu ainda na infância, então nada de especial sucedeu à qualidade espiritual dessa alma. Nada de significativo foi ganho, e nada de significativo foi perdido. Talvez os pais é que possam aprender alguma lição significativa, em meio ao sofrimento que tiverem de experimentar com a morte de sua criança infante e isso pode revestir-se de algum valor. A própria alma, porém, não retorna ao inferno, embora *algumas* almas más talvez retornem à região do hades, se é dali que elas vieram (ver Apo. 17:8). Tal alma, por não ter sido uma missionária que veio cumprir alguma missão terrena, como João Batista, não retorna aos lugares celestiais, porquanto nem veio dali. Há muitos lugares espirituais que não podemos

964

CRIANÇAS — CRIATURAS VIVAS

classificar como céu ou inferno. É para lugares assim que essas almas retornam, pois dali elas vieram. A morte do corpo físico, no qual habitaram por um breve período, é apenas uma curiosidade, e não um evento determinador do destino da alma. Na verdade, o trecho de I Pedro 4:6 mostra que a própria morte biológica não determina o destino final de alguém, porquanto Cristo ampliou a sua missão para que envolvesse até mesmo o hades (ver I Ped. 3:18 ss), e assim o evangelho foi anunciado aos mortos, até mesmo naquele lugar de juízo. Isso significa que Cristo pode atingir os homens em qualquer lugar, tanto nesta vida como depois da morte biológica. O trecho de Efésios 4:9,10 mostra-nos que a descida de Cristo ao hades (que vide) bem como a sua ascensão ao céu, tiveram o mesmo propósito, isto é, *preencher todas as coisas*, fazendo o Logos tornar-se tudo para todos. O *mundo intermediário*, que não deixou de existir, continua sendo um lugar sujeito ao poder de Cristo. As almas que dali emanam continuam sujeitas à redenção, e a morte de corpos infantis, nos quais habitaram por algum tempo, não exerce qualquer efeito na determinação de seu destino.

Essa interpretação por certo não agrada aos católicos romanos, pois acreditam na existência do limbo. Muitos protestantes e evangélicos, que ignoram certos trechos bíblicos que nos fornecem um quadro mais otimista, preferirão continuar com seu ponto de vista racionalista sobre a idade da responsabilidade das crianças. Porém, alguns da Igreja Ortodoxa Oriental e da Igreja Anglicana, que seguem aspectos da teologia dos pais gregos da Igreja, verão nessa explicação um profundo sentido. Na verdade, nessa idéia não há novidade alguma, quanto às suas bases teológico filosóficas. Os pais gregos da Igreja não limitavam o fim da oportunidade de salvação por ocasião da morte física, conforme a Igreja ocidental prefere fazer. A alma é maior do que isso e não pode ser limitada dessa maneira. Ver mais detalhes no artigo **Infantes, Morte e Salvação dos**. (H ID UN NTI Z)

CRIANÇAS, A IDADE DA RESPONSABILIDADE E DA SALVAÇÃO

Ver sobre *Criança*, ponto 5, mas especialmente o artigo intitulado, *Infantes, Morte e Salvação dos*.

CRIANÇAS, AS TRÊS, CANÇÃO DAS
Ver **Três Crianças, Canção das**.

CRIANÇAS MORIBUNDAS E FENÔMENOS PSÍQUICOS Ver **Parapsicologia**, seção X.

CRIATIVIDADE

Esse é o processo humano mediante o qual algo de inédito e diferente é produzido pelo homem. De algumas vezes, isso é concebido como produto da utilização de alguma *faculdade especial* que jaz dormente na maioria dos homens. De algumas vezes, os sonhos, a hipnose ou certos estados alterados da consciência podem atingir essa faculdade, fazendo-a exprimir-se.

1. Nos escritos de Freud (que vide), a criatividade pessoal é a sublimação e a emergência do sublimado como alguma nova forma de expressão.
2. Whitehead (que vide) afirmava que a criatividade é a categoria do final, e que o universo está envolvido, momento após momento, em um avanço criativo.
3. Lossky (que vide) considerava a criatividade como a característica essencial tanto de Deus quanto do homem.

4. Berdyaev (que vide, pontos primeiro a quarto) asseverava que a autocriação caracteriza tanto o homem quanto Deus. Em ambos os casos, teríamos uma espécie de criação *ex nihilo*, ou seja, criação com base no nada.
5. Wieman (que vide) falou sobre o *evento criativo* (que vide), que consistiria na pessoa de Deus e em suas obras. Haveria quatro subeventos, igualmente envolvidos na criação, e que produzem o *bem criativo*.

Cientistas, inventores, músicos, poetas, filósofos, teólogos, etc., têm todos falado em *eriatividade*. Isso depende de inspiração de alguma sorte, quando um homem ultrapassa as suas capacidades normais e produz algo inspirado e nobre. Alguns eventos criativos, mui provavelmente, são inspirados por entidades superiores ao homem, os quais contribuem para formar os pensamentos do homem, capacitando-o a produzir coisas extraordinárias, como escrever livros notáveis em prosa ou poesia, ou fazer importantes descobertas científicas. Esse processo pode ser psíquico ou metafísico, pessoal ou extrapessoal, particular ou coletivo.

CRIATURAS VIVAS

Essa é uma espécie de referência geral e vaga a todos os animais que foram criados (Gên. 1:21,24; 2:19). Ezequiel usou a expressão para aludir a seres angelicais, como os querubins (Eze. 1:5; 13:15,19,20, 22). As *quatro* criaturas vivas tinham, cada uma, quatro rostos, de um homem, de um leão, de um boi e de uma águia. Esses animais, com ou sem razão, tornaram-se símbolos dos quatro evangelhos, na concepção de alguns cristãos antigos. Mateus seria o homem; Marcos, o boi; Lucas, o leão; e João, a águia. Aqueles que costumam ler diretamente os manuscritos antigos, ou então através de microfilmes, ocasionalmente encontrarem representações pictográficas, ou alusões mencionadas, nas introduções aos manuscritos.

A figura dos querubins, as quatro criaturas vivas, passou para o Novo Testamento, em Apocalipse 4:6-9, onde eles são descritos como seres que estão sempre diante do trono de Deus. Cada um deles tinha seis asas (quatro, segundo a descrição de Ezequiel). As quatro representações animais são retidas, mas, no livro de Ezequiel, cada um desses animais caracteriza um dos seres angelicais. Isso significa que, em Ezequiel, cada ser tem as características dos outros três.

Em tudo isso está envolvida uma elaborada angelologia judaica, que se deriva, pelo menos em parte, das obras pseudepígrafes, e, em parte, deriva-se da angelologia de outros povos semitas. Ver as notas expositivas no NTI, no trecho de Apo 4:6, quanto a outros detalhes. Há muitas interpretações metafóricas a respeito da questão, sobre o que comentamos nas notas referidas. Ireneu (170 D.C.) pensava que esses quatro querubins representavam aspectos da obra de Jesus Cristo, como também os evangelhos específicos, conforme se disse acima. Cada animal falaria de um aspecto do ministério de Cristo. O leão representaria o seu poder; o boi, o seu caráter sacerdotal, porquanto o boi era usado nos holocaustos; o homem representaria a sua encarnação; e a águia representaria o seu Espírito. Agostinho, porém, preferia uma outra interpretação, a saber: Mateus, o leão; Lucas, o boi; Marcos, o homem; e João, a águia. Tudo isso, naturalmente, não passa de especulação e fantasia, com base no método alegórico de interpretação. Ver sobre a *Interpretação Alegórica*. Esse método de interpretação tem algum valor. De fato, há ocasiões em que se torna até necessário. Porém, também é capaz de produzir muitas fantasias, criadas pela imaginação dos intérpretes.

CRIME

Ver o artigo seguinte, **Crimes e Castigos**, onde há considerações bíblicas a respeito. A palavra não ocorre no Antigo Testamento, embora a idéia seja freqüente. Mas, quando chegamos ao Novo Testamento, há duas palavras gregas que devem ser consideradas:

1. *Aitía*, «causa». Esse termo figura por vinte vezes: Mat. 19:3,10; 27:37; Mar. 15:26; Luc. 8:47; João 18:38; 19:4,6; Atos 10:21; 13:28; 22:24; 23:28; 25:18,27; 28:18,20; II Tim. 1:6,12; Tito 1:13; Heb. 2:11.

2. *Égklema*, «acusação». Essa palavra aparece só por duas vezes, em Atos 23:29 e 25:16.

Um ato criminoso ocorre quando alguma lei, pública, moral ou espiritual, é quebrada. Todavia, a rigor, só se deve considerar a transgressão contra alguma lei expressa em código vigente. Esse é o ponto de vista dos criminalistas, naturalmente. Há sérios crimes morais que não são alistados nesses códigos. As leis variam muito de país para país, seguindo situações e crenças culturais, políticas e religiosas. Algumas leis são baixadas com o intuito de beneficiar os legisladores, e não a sociedade em geral. O castigo contra os criminosos é profundamente influenciado pelo poder, pelo dinheiro, pelo prestígio pessoal e pelas opiniões dos juízes ou dos jurados. Na maioria dos casos, há grande latitude de aplicação e interpretação das leis, sobre o que se fazer exatamente, no que concerne a certos crimes. As detenções, por sua vez, têm fracassado em larga escala nas tentativas de *reforma* dos criminosos. Essa reforma seria o ideal do sistema penal de qualquer país. Mas, bem pelo contrário, muitos criminosos saem das penitenciárias ainda mais habilidosos quanto ao crime. A sociologia e a psicologia não podem conferir uma autêntica conversão religiosa (que vide), e os esforços das igrejas cristãs, evangélicas ou não, apesar de sinceros, são inadequados para a tarefa. As detenções são, entretanto, centros de recolhimento dos elementos mais daninhos à sociedade, o que resulta na proteção dos cidadãos ordeiros e pacíficos. Na verdade, as organizações policiais confessam que seu papel se assemelha ao dos «lixeiros», que recolhem aqueles que se tornaram perigosos ao convívio normal na sociedade. Isso significa que o sistema carcerário, com todo o sistema judicial que o envolve, confessa-se impotente para solucionar o aspecto da reabilitação dos criminosos. O papel principal das forças policiais é preventivo; mas até mesmo isso é grandemente diminuído pelo fato de que a polícia só pode agir quando o crime já se consumou ou há fortes indícios de configuração. Nos Estados Unidos da América, cujas estatísticas são de fácil acesso aos pesquisadores, o retorno dos criminosos às prisões chega a orçar em sessenta por cento. Mas, sabendo-se que apenas uma pequena porcentagem dos criminosos é apanhada, e, menos porcentagem ainda é encarcerada, poderíamos indagar qual a real porcentagem dos criminosos que volta à senda do crime, depois de soltos. Sem dúvida, essa porcentagem é altíssima.

A perversidade da alma humana. A mente criminosa. Muito se ouve falar sobre como as condições adversas, sociais e econômicas, são causas da vida criminosa. Não se pode negar que isso é uma das causas. Porém, estudos sérios sobre a *mente criminosa* têm revelado fatos perturbadores. Para exemplificar, nos Estados Unidos da América, somente metade dos criminosos tem razões sociais e econômicas para se voltarem para o crime, como meio de sobrevivência. A outra metade consiste, comprovadamente, em pessoas *diferentes*, desde seus primeiros anos de vida. Quando ainda crianças já furtavam, brigavam e demonstravam sinais de descontentamento, embora, em muitos casos, pertencentes a famílias sem quaisquer problemas financeiros especiais, cujos irmãos e irmãs são totalmente normais. Além disso, a falta de dinheiro não explica o fato de que a maioria dos criminosos ofende em todas as três áreas principais do crime: desonestidade, destruição da propriedade alheia e assaltos sexuais.

O elo entre o *crime infantil* e o *crime adulto* é extremamente comum. Assim, nos Estados Unidos da América, oitenta por cento dos criminosos adultos condenados, também tiveram uma vida de crimes quando crianças e jovens. Estudos feitos na Suécia tentaram provar que a mente criminosa está ligada a defeitos cerebrais, e que o meio ambiente social tem pouco efeito sobre a porcentagem das pessoas que se entregam ao crime. Porém, à teoria ainda faltam evidências mais sólidas, antes que possa ser aceita de modo definitivo.

Por outra parte, aqueles que acreditam na preexistência da alma, com ou sem a reencarnação, insistem na idéia de que a alma já chega a este mundo pervertida, impelida por tendências criminosas, porquanto ao longo de sua história, anterior a esta vida terrena, teria acumulado uma bagagem má. Seja como for, parece que o problema da criminalidade é, essencialmente, uma questão espiritual, ao passo que as causas psicológicas e ambientais são secundárias. Muitos criminosos apreciam a vida de crimes, tal como um atleta aprecia a competição esportiva, ou um boxeador gosta de castigar o adversário e ser castigado por ele. Lembro-me de meus dias de colégio, quando eu praticava o futebol americano, uma modalidade esportiva brutal e potencialmente perigosa. Lembro-me de ter conversado com um colega, que acabara de participar de uma peleja especialmente violenta, como representante de nosso colégio. Durante a partida, ele sofrera algumas contusões pequenas. Com um sorriso, ele comentou: «Puxa, como foi divertido!» Aqueles que tratam com os criminosos sabem que eles apreciam a excitação proveniente de seus atos ousados; gostam muito dos tiroteios com a polícia. Há quem goste de matar outros seres humanos, relatando entre bravatas as suas aventuras, como se tudo fosse uma festa. Isso nada tem a ver com a falta de dinheiro. Tem a ver com a perversão do ser humano.

A Bíblia fornece-nos algumas orientações sobre a questão. O Antigo Testamento ensina a lei de Talião, «olho por olho, dente por dente». Ver Êxodo 21:24. A lei levítica é muito rígida e pormenorizada. Caim (Gên. 4:11-16) recebeu a primeira sentença perpétua, embora tivesse cometido um homicídio. Houve certa razão para esse abrandamento da pena; mas a legislação posterior, mosaica, teria requerido a pena de morte para Caim. Paralelamente ao conceito da retaliação, a Bíblia também ensina insistentemente a necessidade da ministração de ensinos espirituais, o que pode resultar em genuína transformação moral das pessoas. Além disso, o trecho de I Pedro 4:6 mostra-nos que o julgamento, incluindo o julgamento divino contra os pecadores, tem um efeito restaurador. E a passagem de Efésios 1:10 ensina que o plano de Deus a longo prazo é vir a restaurar todas as coisas.

CRIMES E CASTIGOS

Os castigos e juízos impostos por Deus participam desse plano restaurador. Nas operações de Deus, não existe tal coisa como justiça bruta, que só procura a retaliação. A ira de Deus sempre é temperada pelo amor de Deus, sendo, na verdade, um dedo da amorosa mão do Senhor. Um julgamento severo é apenas uma disciplina severa, e não uma questão de vingança, embora também inclua esse fator. Há coisas que Deus pode fazer, mediante o julgamento, que não poderia fazer de qualquer outra maneira.

Retribuição Apropriada. Alguns crimes exigem uma severa retribuição. A lassidão humana em nada ajuda para reformar uma alma criminosa. Alguns criminosos, empedernidos na senda do crime, alegram-se quando se vêem diante da morte. Destarte, eles sentem que sua dívida diante da sociedade foi saldada, e que as suas *almas* foram beneficiadas. Parece haver nisso um discernimento autêntico. Sem dúvida, a morte biológica não é o fim da oportunidade da alma, conforme o trecho de I Pedro 4:6 demonstra. Isso posto, quando um criminoso paga pelos seus crimes, encontra-se em melhor situação para buscar e receber a redenção espiritual. Isso permite que ele se desfaça da má bagagem, pelo menos parcialmente, que pesava sobre a sua alma, tornando-se assim mais receptivo da mensagem espiritual que, finalmente, pode chegar até ele. (BEC H)

CRIMES E CASTIGOS

Este artigo aborda as considerações bíblicas a respeito, e não tanto um apanhado de opiniões sociológicas e criminalísticas.

Esboço:
I. Elementos do Ensino Bíblico
II. Classificação dos Crimes
III. Sumário dos Castigos

I. Elementos do Ensino Bíblico

1. *Palavras Empregadas.* Necessariamente, há uma grande afinidade entre os conceitos de crime, culpa, pecado e castigo, nas páginas da Bíblia. As palavras empregadas nas Escrituras ilustram esse fato. No Antigo Testamento há palavras hebraicas como *avon*, que significa «iniqüidade», «punição», etc., usada por mais de duzentas e trinta vezes; *resha*, «maldade», geralmente palavra aplicada a desvios religiosos, empregada por trinta vezes; *chet*, «falta», uma palavra que mostra o elo religioso com o conceito de crime, usada por cerca de trinta e três vezes. Essa palavra é usada para indicar pecados contra Deus ou contra seres humanos (Gên. 41:9; Deu. 19:15). No Novo Testamento, as palavras gregas mais importantes, envolvidas no conceito, são: *Hamartia, asebeia, adikia, parakoe, anomia, paranomia* e *paráptoma*. *Hamartia* e seu cognato, *hamártema*, significam «errar o alvo», sendo usualmente empregadas para traduzir o termo hebraico *chet*, quando trechos do Antigo Testamento são referidos no Novo Testamento. *Asebeia* significa «impiedade», sendo o equivalente geral do termo hebraico *resha*. Essa palavra indica os pecados de fundo religioso, principalmente. *Adikia*, «injustiça», pode ter esse sentido, mas também é aplicada a qualquer ato injusto. *Parakoe* tem o sentido básico de desobediência ativa. *Paranomia* é uma transgressão da lei ou de normas estabelecidas. *Parábasis* também é a transgressão da lei (Rom. 4:15). *Paráptoma* é um passo em falso, indicando uma falta de menor gravidade. Essa grande variedade de vocábulos fala sobre as diversas maneiras como os homens transgridem, pecam e tornam-se culpados por desobedecerem às leis divinas ou às leis humanas.

2. *A Conexão Religiosa.* No Oriente Próximo e Médio, a jurisprudência sempre esteve vinculada à idéia do divino, à idéia dos deveres diante de Deus ou das divindades. Quase sempre a crença era de que a mente divina estava por detrás das legislações humanas, pelo que também a primeira responsabilidade era diante desse poder divino. No prólogo das leis de Ur-Namu, Nana, o deus-lua dos sumérios aparece no quadro. O código de Hamurabi contava com o respaldo da autoridade do deus Shamash. Isso tem sido descoberto pela arqueologia, mediante uma estrela que mostra esse deus apresentando leis a Hamurabi. Naturalmente, a maior ilustração possível da conexão religiosa com as legislações é o relato do livro de Êxodo, onde as tábuas da lei aparecem como compostas pelo próprio Yahweh. Isso nos transmite a idéia de que não há como prejudicar ao próximo sem ofender, ao mesmo tempo, a Deus. Não é por acidente que os dois grandes mandamentos, o de amar a Deus de todo o ser, e ao próximo como a si mesmo, aparecem no Novo Testamento (Mat. 22:37-40) como o cumprimento de toda a lei e dos profetas.

3. *Uma Ética Absoluta.* Ver o artigo sobre a *Ética*, onde aparecem três tipos principais de sistemas éticos: a ética relativa, a ética absoluta e a ética de valores, esta última meio termo entre as outras duas. A ética ensinada na Bíblia é *absoluta*. Isso significa que as leis que devem governar a conduta devem ser tidas como finais e decisivas, e não sujeitas ao capricho e às modificações humanas. Isso é assim porque a ética, na Bíblia, depende da revelação divina, e não da experiência humana.

4. *Um Código Exigente.* No Antigo Testamento encontramos a lei do «olho por olho e dente por dente». Ver Êxodo 21:24. Isso aponta para uma retribuição ao pé da letra. E grande parte da legislação levítica está envolvida no delineamento preciso dos crimes, com seus castigos específicos. A pena de morte é aplicada a questões que, segundo a concepção moderna, nos deixam chocados. Para exemplificar, um filho desobediente a seus pais deveria ser apedrejado até à morte, pela congregação, dando ênfase ao ensino que a delinqüência juvenil simplesmente não podia constituir um problema permanente na sociedade judaica. A legislação levítica era bastante ampla. Um assassino deveria ser executado, mas outro tanto se dava no caso dos blasfemos. O relato sobre Jesus e a mulher apanhada em flagrante adultério, no oitavo capítulo do evangelho de João, mostra que o Senhor Jesus aplicava maior dose de misericórdia, injetando assim, na lei mosaica, a lei do amor, para contrabalançar o princípio da retribuição. Isso assinala um avanço tipicamente cristão, porquanto o oposto da injustiça não é apenas a justiça, mas também o amor.

II. Classificação dos Crimes

1. **Crimes Contra Deus**

a. *Idolatria* (Êxo. 20:3-6). Para esse pecado, a pena de morte era imposta (Êxo. 22:20), o que mostra a seriedade da questão, impressa sobre as mentes do povo de Israel. Naturalmente, nem sempre a pena era cumprida. Se alguma comunidade se tornasse culpada desse pecado, a mesma era totalmente destruída, incluindo as propriedades e os animais (Deu. 13:12-16). Como é óbvio, todos os objetos usados no culto idólatra eram completamente destruídos. Mas, que dizer sobre certos santuários idólatras tão concorridos do catolicismo, onde a venda de imagens e outros objetos religiosos é a principal

CRIMES E CASTIGOS

atividade e a principal fonte de renda? E onde o ganho de rios de dinheiro explica por qual razão esse comércio nefando não cessa?

b. *Sacrifício de Infantes*. Israel deixou-se envolver nesse tipo de pecado, imitando os povos vizinhos. Os ídolos cananeus pareciam vorazes por sangue.

c. *Bruxaria, Adivinhação e Espiritismo*. Essas práticas eram estritamente proibidas. Os líderes desses cultos demoníacos deveriam ser mortos (Deu. 18:10,11; Lev. 20:27). Naturalmente, Israel tinha suas próprias formas de adivinhação, no que estava envolvido o próprio sumo sacerdote. Ver o meu artigo sobre a *Adivinhação*. Portanto, em certo sentido, a adivinhação só é proibida quando não é «aprovada» pelos costumes judaicos, dentro da sociedade judaica!

d. *Blasfêmia*. O terceiro mandamento proibia o uso superficial do nome do Senhor. E, naturalmente, qualquer linguagem abusiva contra Deus ou contra as coisas sagradas, era proibida. As calúnias e críticas acerbas contra as autoridades humanas, supostamente estabelecidas por direito divino, estavam inclusas nessa proibição. A pena de morte estava decretada contra os blasfemos (Êxo. 22:28; Lev. 24:11-23; Êxo. 22:28).

e. *Profecia Falsa*. Esta assumia duas formas diversas: profecia falsa em nome de Yahweh; e profecia em nome de algum deus pagão. Em qualquer das modalidades, a pena de morte era imposta (Deu. 18:20-22; Jer. 26:8,9).

f. *Quebra do Sábado*. O sábado comemorava o término da obra criativa do Senhor, devendo ser considerado um dia santo. Leis complexas controlavam a questão, sendo elas rigidamente observadas (Êxo. 16:23; 20:9,10; Lev. 23:3; Êxo. 31:13). Nem mesmo os animais podiam ser postos a trabalhar em dia de sábado, por ser um dia reservado exclusivamente à adoração religiosa. A pena de morte era imposta aos ofensores (Núm. 15:32-36; Êxo. 31:14-17).

g. *Desafio à Autoridade da Lei de Deus*. Esse crime envolvia Deus e a sua lei, ou então podia ser cometido contra os representantes de Deus (Núm. 15:27,30,31; Deu. 17:8-12), contra o qual também estava decretada a pena de morte.

2. Crimes Contra o Homem

a. *Homicídio*. Desde Gên. 9:6 vemos que a pena de morte era requerida. O sexto mandamento do decálogo (que vide) seguia essa regra (Êxo. 21:12). O homicídio acidental contava com a provisão das cidades de refúgio (que vide). O homicida involuntário precisava permanecer em uma das cidades de refúgio, sob pena de ser morto pelo vingador do sangue. Isso significa que sua punição era uma forma de prisão perpétua. Ver Êxo. 21:13; Núm. 35:22-25. Posteriormente, o rei parece ter tido autoridade para intervir em tais casos, assim modificando a legislação caso a caso (II Sam. 13:19; 14:7; I Reis 2:34). Homens poderosos, protegidos pelas autoridades, podiam matar, mesmo que não acidentalmente, sem serem punidos. Várias leis secundárias circundavam a questão. Se dois homens estivessem brigando, e a esposa grávida de um deles tentasse intervir e fosse morta no esforço, o assassino teria de ser morto (Êxo. 21:22-25). Um touro que matasse a um homem, teria de ser morto. Um ladrão invasor, que atacasse à noite, podia ser morto, e nenhuma pena seria imposta ao seu executor. Mas, se atacasse durante o dia, o executor poderia sofrer alguma retribuição (Êxo. 22:3).

b. *Assaltos*. As perdas e injúrias resultantes de assaltos estavam sujeitas à lei de Talião (no latim, *talis*, «tal»), ou seja, a lei que exigia retribuição tal e qual, sempre que possível. Os ferimentos eram retribuídos com ferimentos; as propriedades furtadas eram recompensadas por propriedades equivalentes. No caso de danos corporais contra algum escravo, disso poderia resultar a sua emancipação (Êxo. 21:24,26,27).

c. *Furtos e Apropriação Indébita*. A legislação mosaica requeria a devolução do que fosse furtado, além de vinte por cento em compensação (Lev. 6:2-7). O trecho de Lev. 19:13 classifica os ladrões entre os opressores. Igualmente entre estes estavam os que não cumpriam seus acordos ou deixavam de pagar os seus trabalhadores. Quanto a esse particular, o código de Hamurabi era muito mais severo, requerendo a pena de morte (lei 22). Mas, se um ladrão entrasse na casa de alguém, em qualquer hora do dia ou da noite, podia ser morto em autodefesa, e nenhuma pena incidiria sobre seu executor (Êxo. 22:1,3,4). Um crime praticado durante o dia não era considerado sério, segundo essa legislação babilônica, e a lei procurava evitar que o executor de um ladrão fosse penalizado em qualquer sentido. No caso de roubo de animais, a devolução de dois animais era a pena, incluindo o animal que fora furtado; mas, se o animal originalmente furtado tivesse sido morto ou negociado, então a devolução consistia em quatro animais. Se o ladrão não pudesse saldar a sua dívida, então era vendido como escravo, até que a restauração fosse feita.

d. *Crimes Sexuais*. Em contraste com o costume greco-romano, as religiões do Oriente Próximo não contavam com a prostituição religiosa, e as experiências sexuais pré-maritais e extramaritais eram consideradas infrações sérias. A atitude dos gregos e romanos diante do sexo era mais relaxada, em todas as categorias. Os códigos sumério, babilônico, assírio e hitita, e não apenas o código hebreu, impunham castigos em questões de desvios sexuais. A preservação da família era considerada questão importantíssima, pelo que as leis da herança e da adoração religiosa pura, avultavam em importância. Isso explica as seguintes leis, dentro da cultura dos hebreus: 1. O *homossexualismo*, punido com a morte de ambos os envolvidos (Lev. 18:22,29; 20:13). 2. *Adultério*, que consiste na atividade sexual fora do casamento, mas por parte de pessoas casadas, era um pecado proibido pelo sétimo mandamento (Êxo. 20:14), cuja punição era o apedrejamento de ambos os envolvidos (Lev. 20:10; Deu. 22:24). O noivado era considerado um casamento preliminar, pelo que a mesma lei do adultério pesava sobre os noivos (Deu. 22:23,24). 3. *Fornicação*, ou seja, as atividades sexuais, de pessoas solteiras, era algo proibido, e os pais tinham a responsabilidade de proteger as suas filhas, para que não se tornassem prostitutas (Lev. 19:29). Quanto à sociedade em geral, não incidiam penas, mas a filha de um sacerdote, que se prostituísse, deveria ser executada (Lev. 21:7), sendo queimada na fogueira (Lev. 21:9). De modo surpreendente, como paralelo de tal severidade, um israelita (que não fosse sacerdote) podia casar-se com uma prostituta arrependida. 4. *Sedução e Violação*. A sedução é uma espécie de violação, embora reconhecida como menos séria que a violação forçada, ou estupro. Contudo, a sedução também envolve violência, embora do tipo mental e psicológico. Algumas vezes, envolve o poder do dinheiro, ou alguma vantagem qualquer, capaz de convencer a mulher a ceder. Porém, também se reconhece que uma mulher pode querer ser seduzida, embora nunca o declare. Outrossim, as mulheres convidam à

CRIMES E CASTIGOS

sedução mediante a maneira como se vestem e agem. Ademais, algumas vezes a mulher é que seduz o homem. Por causa dessa variedade de fatores, a sedução é considerada menos séria que a violação. Porém, a sedução contra uma mulher casada era considerada adultério, pelo que ambos os envolvidos estavam sujeitos à pena de morte. A violação era punida com a morte do homem culpado (Deu. 22:25-27). Se um homem seduzisse uma virgem (que não estivesse noiva) que consentisse com o ato, então ele poderia corrigir o erro casando-se com ela legalmente, além de pagar uma multa a seu pai. Se o pai não permitisse o casamento, a jovem não se casava, e o culpado tinha de pagar uma importância adicional. Se um sedutor se casasse com a jovem a quem seduzira, nunca poderia divorciar-se dela (Deu. 22:29). 5. *Incesto.* Todas as variedades de incesto requeriam a pena de morte (Lev. 20:11). Relações sexuais com a própria sogra ou com a mãe de uma concubina eram punidas com a execução na fogueira. Irmão e irmã, sobrinho e tia, cunhado e cunhada são outros casos especificamente mencionados. Ver as referências abaixo, onde são mencionados os vários casos: Lev. 20:11,12,17; 19:21 e Deut. 27:33. Entretanto, um homem podia casar-se com a viúva de um seu irmão, e até mesmo estava nessa obrigação, se seu irmão e aquela mulher não tivessem tido filhos. 6. *Atividades sexuais durante o período menstrual* eram proibidas, provavelmente por duas razões: primeira, as mulheres estão mais sujeitas à promiscuidade durante esse período por ser um tempo de esterilidade. Em segundo lugar, havia o sentimento que o sangue da menstruação era contaminador (Lev. 18:19; 20:18). O próprio marido era aconselhado a abster-se de relações com sua esposa menstruada, ou seria considerado ritualmente imundo pelo espaço de uma semana (Lev. 15:24).

e. *Desonra aos Pais.* Até mesmo os ataques verbais, como uma maldição, ou um ataque físico contra os pais, eram punidos com a morte do culpado (Êxo. 21:15,17). Além disso, um filho podia ser morto meramente por ser desobediente contumaz e preguiçoso, ou viciado em bebidas alcoólicas. Nesses casos, era responsabilidade dos pais apresentarem queixa diante do tribunal local (Deu. 21:18-21). Essa medida visava a impedir a propagação do mau exemplo, para que não se propagasse a atitude de desobediência entre os filhos.

f. *Seqüestro.* Usualmente, os casos de seqüestro envolviam o plano para vender a pessoa seqüestrada como escrava. Sem importar qual o plano envolvido, o culpado era punido com a execução capital (Êxo. 21:16; Deu. 24:7).

g. *Perjúrio e Processo Malicioso.* Se alguém mentisse em tribunal, a fim de prejudicar a outrem, e isso fosse descoberto, então o culpado sofria a mesma pena que fora imposta ao caluniado. Essa era a primeira lei do código de Hamurabi; mas ali era imposta automaticamente a pena de morte. A razão dessa severidade era impedir que os tribunais fossem manipulados para qualquer tipo de vantagem pessoal ou vingança (Deu. 19:19,20).

h. *Dano à Propriedade.* A substituição em espécie ou em dinheiro era exigida nesses casos (Êxo. 22:5; Lev. 24:18,21). Animais que escapassem de seus proprietários deveriam ser protegidos. Os buracos onde eles pudessem cair, teriam de ser tapados (Êxo. 21:33,34). Mesmo no caso de propagação acidental de fogo, se passasse de uma propriedade para outra, com destruição das plantações, os prejuízos sofridos tinham de ser compensados. Isso ensinava as pessoas a serem cuidadosas (Êxo. 22:6).

i. *Fianças Desonestas.* Se alguém entregasse algo como garantia, por algo que fora tomado por empréstimo, e a outra pessoa guardasse para si mesma o objeto penhorado, tinha de devolver em dobro (Êxo. 22:9). E se o caso envolvesse furto, digamos, de um animal que tivesse sido deixado como penhor, então a pessoa culpada tinha de devolver o objeto ou animal furtado, e outro tanto, de acordo com o valor calculado (Êxo. 22:10,11).

j. *Opressão Social.* Viúvas, órfãos e estrangeiros eram vítimas de tratamento abusivo. Contra tais opressores era proferida uma maldição divina, como se o próprio Deus estivesse defendendo tais casos, a fim de que a justiça fosse servida (Êxo. 22:21-24). O povo de Israel precisava lembrar-se de que já sofrera a opressão no Egito, devendo respeitar aos menos privilegiados, que poderiam ser vítimas de exploração e opressão.

III. Sumário das Punições

1. *A Pena de Morte*

a. *Por apedrejamento.* As ofensas assim punidas eram o infanticídio como parte da adoração idólatra (Lev. 20:2-5); a adivinhação (Lev. 20:27); a blasfêmia (Lev. 24:15,16); a violação do sábado (Núm. 15:32-36); a idolatria e a adoração falsa (Deu. 17:2-7); a profecia falsa (Deu. 13:1-5); desobediência contumaz dos filhos (Deu. 21:18-21); e o adultério (Deu. 22:22,23).

b. *À espada.* Essa era a punição imposta aos assassinos (Núm. 35:19,21), aos idólatras (Deu. 13:15); e aos apóstatas (Êxo. 32:27).

c. *Na fogueira.* Era a punição imposta aos casos de incesto com uma mulher e sua mãe (Lev. 20:14), bem como a fornicação da parte da filha de um sacerdote (Lev. 21:9).

2. *A Mutilação*

Se em uma briga, a mulher de um deles injuriasse o órgão sexual masculino do outro homem, a mão dela seria decepada (Deu. 25:12). A mutilação também era imposta aos que ferissem maliciosamente a outras pessoas (Êxo. 21:24,25). Em tais casos, os membros da família do ofensor não eram atingidos, o que também ocorria nas leis dos babilônios e assírios. O trecho de Deu. 24:16 anuncia o princípio de não retaliação contra os membros das famílias dos ofensores desses casos.

3. *Açoites*

Parece que não havia crimes especificamente associados à punição com açoites, exceto quando um marido acusasse falsamente sua esposa de ter tido experiências sexuais antes do casamento. Também presume-se que muitas ofensas secundárias podiam ser castigadas desse modo, por ordem de oficiais (Deu. 22:18; 25:1-3). A disciplina doméstica geralmente era efetuada desse modo.

4. *Aprisionamento*

No Egito, José foi sentenciado à prisão, mas, no começo da história de Israel, essa medida parece ter sido empregada somente para a detenção de pessoas que estavam aguardando julgamento. Posteriormente, temos o caso de Jeremias, —que foi lançado em uma masmorra, sob a acusação de traição (Jer. 37:15,16). Se o aprisionamento era uma punição ocasional, faltam-nos informações a respeito; mas o fato é que a legislação levítica nada diz a esse respeito.

5. *Multas*

A compensação pelo furto de algum objeto ou por alguma propriedade danificada, fazia-se por meios monetários ou pela substituição em espécie (Êxo. 22:1-4; Deu. 22:18,19). A lei sempre requeria a restauração de cem por cento, e, às vezes, de até quatrocentos por cento, dependendo do caso. Se um homem deflorasse uma virgem (não um caso de violação, que era punido com a pena capital), então o homem culpado tinha de pagar ao pai da jovem a quantia que geralmente correspondia ao dote pago (Deu. 22:29), a menos que o casal acabasse se casando (Êxo. 22:16).

6. *Escravização*

Um ladrão que não pudesse fazer devolução, era escravizado pelo espaço de seis anos, ou até que pudesse devolver aquilo que havia furtado (Êxo. 21:2). Era mister que ele juntasse a isso vinte por cento, se tivesse furtado um animal. A devolução do animal furtado e de um outro animal, como compensação, fazia parte da lei levítica. No caso de não poder devolver o animal furtado, então tinha de restaurar quatro animais (Êxo. 22:3). As pessoas que não pudessem saldar as suas dívidas, também deveriam ser vendidas à servidão (II Reis 4:1; Nee. 5:5; Amós 2:6). Também havia a escravização voluntária, quando uma pessoa queria evitar a pressão econômica, mas sem qualquer vinculação a crime (Lev. 25:39 *ss*). (CLAR ND PRIT VA Z)

CRIPTA

Vem do latim, **crypta**. Indica uma abóbada subterrânea, oculta. Em relação ao cristianismo, temos de considerar os lugares subterrâneos de sepulcro, ou catacumbas (que vide). O termo veio a ser usado para indicar alguma escavação feita por baixo de uma igreja, com propósito de sepultamento.

CRIPTOCALVINISMO

Vem do grego **krypto**, «oculto», em combinação com o termo que alude à doutrina de João Calvino (que vide). A expressão criptocalvinismo foi usada como termo para expressar opróbrio, durante a época das controvérsias doutrinárias da última metade do século XVI, pelos aderentes estritos da teologia de Lutero, a fim de apelidarem os seus adversários, igualmente luteranos. Esses últimos haviam sido «contaminados» pelos pontos de vista de Calvino, a respeito de certos itens da cristologia (que vide), ou acerca da Ceia do Senhor, da predestinação, etc. Alguns suspeitos dessa contaminação eram os teólogos de Wittenberg, como Major, Eber, Crell e o médico Caspar Peucer, que era genro de Melanchton. O crítico mais acerbo deles era Matthia Falacius (que vide).

CRISE, TEOLOGIA DA

Essa é uma expressão usada para referir-se a uma modalidade de teologia iniciada pouco depois da Segunda Guerra Mundial por Karl Barth, seus discípulos e simpatizadores.

Interpretação da Expressão. 1. Dentro da teologia otimista dos séculos XIX e XX, alguns teólogos supõem haver encontrado elementos enfermiços e inadequados, pelo que pensaram que uma nova teologia deveria substituir aquela, saudável, própria para tempos de crise e de tomada de decisões. 2. A teologia passara por uma crise quando os teólogos liberais alemães deram aprovação à nefanda política do governo nazista, que produziu tanto morticínio e destruição. Uma nova teologia era necessária, para reverter esse tipo de atividade. 3. Dentro da teologia de Karl Barth, a expressão *crise* é usada para aludir ao juízo (no grego, *krisis*) de Deus, que foi concebido como um julgamento que sobrevém apenas sobre os empreendimentos humanos, incluindo seus aspectos moral e religioso. Barth reenfatizou certos ensinos paulinos e da Reforma protestante, que punham em destaque o elemento divino da teologia, em oposição às especulações humanas.

A teologia de crise também se chama teologia *dialética*. Afasta-se das tendências liberais e aproxima-se mais do cristianismo original, com repúdio às inclinações germânicas, que sintetizavam a doutrina cristã com a ideologia política dos socialistas nacionais alemães, uma ideologia racista. Sua influência tomou vulto na Europa e nos Estados Unidos da América, nas décadas de 1920 e 1930. Sua influência pode ser vista nos ensinos da Declaração de Barmen (que vide), de maio de 1934, que, em oposição à doutrina dos cristãos alemães, nega explicitamente a validade das revelações *subordinadas* na história, na natureza e na raça humana, reconhecendo *exclusivamente* a revelação de Deus em Jesus Cristo, da qual testificam a Igreja e o Espírito Santo. A controvérsia entre Barth e Emil Brunner, em 1934, foi uma outra ilustração da natureza da teologia da crise. Brunner defendia o lugar legítimo da teologia natural no cristianismo, mas Barth reiterava sua teoria de revelação exclusiva, assim negando a validade da teologia natural. Apesar de que a influência da teologia da crise vem declinando desde 1945, está bem viva nos escritos de vários teólogos, incluindo Dietrich Bronhoeffer, que tomou por empréstimo idéias e sentimentos da teologia da crise. Também há indícios nos escritos de Eduard Thurneysen, Friedrich Gogarten e Paul Tillich. (C MAC)

Ver o artigo sobre *Dialética, Teologia da*. Este artigo acrescenta informação valiosa sobre o assunto da *Teologia da Crise*.

CRISIPO

Filósofo grego, nascido na Cilícia, estudou em Atenas, sob Cleantes e Zeno. Ele foi o terceiro principal líder estóico, tendo chefiado essa escola de 232 a 208 A.C. Ele sistematizou a doutrina de Zeno e de Cleantes. Muito fez para defender o estoicismo (que vide), contra o ceticismo da academia. Ele argumentava de forma soberba. Diógenes Laércio disse a respeito dele: «Se os deuses usam da dialética, então não usam outra senão a de Crisipo». Ele escreveu muito, especificamente porque foi o apologista do estoicismo.

Idéias:

1. As idéias gerais do estoicismo não são reiteradas aqui. O leitor poderá examinar o artigo sobre esse assunto.

2. Crisipo ultrapassou a lógica aristotélica quanto a alguns particulares, tendo criado princípios que até hoje fazem parte do cálculo. Quanto a isso, ele antecipou o moderno assunto do cálculo proposicional.

3. Ele contribuiu para a definição da modalidade (que vide). Cícero disse que Crisipo seguia a definição do *possível*, de Filo de Megara, no sentido de que certas coisas serão verdadeiras quando as circunstâncias externas não as impedem de ser o que são, bem como a definição do *necessário*, como aquilo que é autêntico e não pode tornar-se falso, nem em si mesmo, e nem através das circunstâncias externas.

4. No tocante às teorias da verdade, Crisipo expunha o critério que inclui tanto *apresentações* como *noções comuns*, que fariam parte da consciência

do ser humano.

5. *Idéias éticas importantes*, fora do estoicismo normal. O bem e o mal são fatores contrários essenciais, relacionados, respectivamente, à racionalidade e à irracionalidade. A maldade cósmica é uma irracionalidade que se opõe à razão universal do Logos. (Ver o artigo sobre o *Logos*, com o título de Verbo). A conduta ideal pode ser atingida mediante a vida caracterizada pela razão, tanto pessoal quanto cósmica.

6. *Deus*. Segundo Crisipo, há certas coisas específicas que podemos dizer a respeito de Deus, incluindo declarações como aquelas que dizem que Ele é uma entidade material, não pessoal, mas imanente por todo o universo, sendo esse o princípio do Logos, ou Razão Cósmica. Crisipo identificava Deus com o elemento essencial, o *fogo*. Ele acreditava que todas as coisas existem em ciclos, e que, finalmente, todas as coisas serão absorvidas pelo fogo primitivo. Mas, o fim de um ciclo seria, ao mesmo tempo, o início de um novo ciclo. É curioso observarmos que essa idéia estóica não está distante da moderna teoria astronômica do «big bang», que supõe que um ciclo termina quando começam a ser atraídos de volta os elementos projetados para fora, mediante uma grande explosão anterior, somente para que, uma vez reunidos esses elementos, ocorra uma nova grande explosão. Ver o artigo sobre a *Astronomia*, sob o sétimo ponto, quanto a uma discussão sobre essa questão. O artigo envolve importantes implicações teológicas.

Escritos. Foi dito que Crisipo escreveu setecentos e cinqüenta tratados, dos quais sobreviveram até nós alguns fragmentos, conforme se vê na obra de J. von Arnim, *Stocorum veterum fragmenta*, em três volumes, 1903-1924. (E P EP)

CRISMA

Vem do grego **chrio**, «ungir». É palavra usada para indicar a aplicação do azeite bento, empregado nos três sacramentos que, de acordo com a Igreja Católica Romana, conferem caráter (que vide), a saber, o batismo, a crisma ou confirmação e a ordenação. Esse ponto de vista é compartilhado pela Igreja Ortodoxa Oriental. A crisma também é usada em outras cerimônias solenes, como na dedicação de altares, igrejas, etc. A Igreja Anglicana usa a unção por ocasião da coroação dos monarcas ingleses, os quais, após o ato, são chamados «ungidos do Senhor». A maioria dos protestantes tem descontinuado a prática, no tocante a objetos e coisas, devido ao fato de que o mesmo não tem precedentes no Novo Testamento, e por causa da obscuridade de seu simbolismo. Mas, alguns grupos evangélicos têm dado prosseguimento à «unção», como a chamam, dos ministros, por ocasião de sua consagração, ou dos enfermos, quando solicitam a unção com azeite, em atendimento ao que diz o trecho de Tiago 5:14,15.

CRISOL

No hebraico a palavra é **matsreph**, «vaso de refinar», «crisol». Aparece somente por duas vezes, em Pro. 17:3 e 27:21.

O crisol era um vaso feito de cerâmica, capaz de resistir a temperaturas muito elevadas, usado para refino de metais como a prata e o ouro. O processo de refino simboliza os exames e juízos de Deus, que testam o coração humano, reconhecendo a verdadeira natureza de um indivíduo qualquer. O processo também se assemelha ao tipo de louvor que um homem recebe, e que serve de juiz de seu caráter. Ver *Acrisolar*.

CRISÓLITO

Trata-se de uma pedra preciosa transparente, amarela ou esverdeada. A palavra aparece somente em Apo. 21:20. No grego, o termo significa «pedra dourada». Mas o vocábulo grego tem sido variegadamente aplicado, também podendo significar o topázio (que vide). Ver Êxodo 28:17. A palavra também pode indicar o crisoberilo, o zircônio, a turmalina e a apatita, todas as quais têm um tom amarelado. Porém, a referência mais comum é mesmo ao topázio. A crisólita moderna consiste em silicato de magnésio, com alguns traços de ferro. Essa gema verde amarelada também é chamada olivina ou peridoto, embora esta não seja descrita como «dourada». No trecho de Apocalipse 21:20, essa pedra é mencionada como uma das gemas que adornarão os alicerces da Nova Jerusalém.

CRISOLORAS, MANUEL

Suas datas aproximadas foram 1355-1415 D.C. Foi homem de nobre nascimento, enviado à Itália pelo imperador grego, a fim de solicitar ajuda militar para reforçá-lo em sua resistência aos turcos. Estabeleceu-se em Florença, a convite das autoridades da cidade, e tornou-se o primeiro mestre importante do grego, na Itália. Faleceu a caminho para o concílio de Constança.

CRISÓPRASO

Uma pedra preciosa mencionada somente em Apocalipse 21:20 como uma das gemas que adornarão os alicerces da Nova Jerusalém. O termo representa o antigo nome de certa variedade de berilo verde amarelado (que vide), embora outras pedras dessa coloração também tenham sido chamadas por esse nome. Na Idade Média, muitas pessoas atribuíam a essa pedra, como a outras também, a capacidade de brilhar no escuro. O que estava realmente envolvido? Minhas fontes informativas nada adiantam a esse respeito. Porém, de acordo com a moderna mineralogia, o termo é empregado para indicar certa variedade maçã esverdeada de calcedônia (que vide). Sua cor deve-se à presença de óxido de níquel, de mistura com sílica de grão muito fino.

CRISÓSTOMO, JOÃO

Suas datas foram 347-407 D.C. Seu nome era João de Antioquia, apelidado *Crisóstomo*, «boca de ouro», por causa de sua eloqüência quando falava em público ou escrevia. Se alguém pensa que ele não merecia o apodo, basta ler algo que ele escreveu. De fato, de acordo com o que diz uma de minhas fontes informativas, ele era «dotado de inigualável eloqüência no púlpito». Ele nasceu em Antioquia da Síria. Sua educação inicial foi excelente, essencialmente obra de sua mãe, Antusa. Em seus dias, desde então, poucos têm podido pregar como ele fazia. Seus escritos têm o mesmo poder e graça, tendo-o tornado um dos mais distinguidos representantes da escola antioqueana de teologia. Seus sermões não somente eram eloqüentes, mas também eram teologicamente importantes. Esses sermões também fornecem-nos importantes informações sobre os costumes de sua época, do ponto de vista da história e das idéias.

CRISÓSTOMO — CRISTANDADE

Após o período em que sua mãe esteve significativamente envolvida, a sua educação foi guiada por Andragácio, com ênfase na filosofia grega, e por Libânio, um famoso sofista pagão, que lhe ensinou a retórica. Ele tornou-se advogado em Antioquia, sendo provável que nunca tenha perdido uma causa que defendeu. Posteriormente, após três anos de instrução com o bispo Melécio, de Antioquia, ele foi batizado como cristão. Ele evitou ser eleito como bispo, em 370 D.C., porquanto queria internar-se em um mosteiro, seguindo a vida monástica. Sua mãe opunha-se a tal idéia; mas, quando ela faleceu, ele cumpriu a sua vontade. Passou a viver como um eremita, nas colinas da cidade, tendo mesmo usado uma caverna como residência, durante algum tempo. Tão grandes foram os rigores a que se sujeitou, durante esse período de sua vida, que sua saúde ficou permanentemente prejudicada, pois João Crisóstomo submetia-se a muitas e severas penitências. Isso requereu seu retorno a Antioquia, o que ele fez em 380 D.C. Naquele mesmo ano, foi nomeado diácono. Em 386 D.C., tornou-se ancião ou presbítero. Em 387 D.C. foi feito patriarca de Constantinopla.

Envolveu-se nas controvérsias em torno de Orígenes, por causa do que foi banido. Isso ocorreu porque alguns daqueles que estavam sendo perseguidos, por se terem posto ao lado de Orígenes, quanto a várias idéias, apelaram para a proteção de João Crisóstomo. Aquele que protege a um herege deve sofrer como herege. As tentativas de João, para ajudar no caso, foram zombeteiramente rejeitadas. Muitas inverdades foram divulgadas, e a imperatriz Eudóxia decretou o banimento de João Crisóstomo. Entrementes, pessoas eram maltratadas, injuriadas e mortas, até mesmo através de ações militares. Mas, conforme os perseguidores costumam dizer, essa era a justiça santa. Seu principal adversário foi Teófilo, patriarca de Alexandria. A mente desse homem era dominada por pensamentos de sangue, ódio e homicídio. Ele organizou o ilegal sínodo do Carvalho, que decretou o banimento de João Crisóstomo, em 403 D.C. A verdade, porém, foi que, de forma pouco diplomática, João chamara todos eles de «um bando de hipócritas». Além disso, os seus sermões continham muitas revelações embaraçosas sobre a vida pessoal da imperatriz Eudóxia. Por essa razão, ela deu apoio àquele sínodo, e João foi denunciado de forma escaldante, tendo sido acusado de toda uma série de erros, incluindo imoralidade, ofensas contra a Igreja e alta traição. O povo quase fez um levante, no dia em que João Crisóstomo deixaria a cidade; mas ele foi capaz de pacificá-los com a sua grande eloqüência, podendo deixar a cidade em paz. Porém, havia uma grande surpresa à espera de todos. Na noite que se seguiu à partida de João Crisóstomo, ocorreu um violento abalo sísmico que sacudiu a cidade. Teófilo, que gostava de abalar a outros, mas que não gostava de ser sacudido por Deus, deixou apressadamente Antioquia e retornou a Alexandria, onde continuou a presidir pomposamente como patriarca. Assim, após apenas três breves dias, João Crisóstomo reentrou na cidade, de forma realmente triunfal. No entanto, continuou pregando e atacando a vida pessoal e orgulhosa da imperatriz. Desnecessário é dizer que ela ficou muito irada, e que Teófilo voltou à cidade para dar início a outro julgamento contra João Crisóstomo. Os adeptos de Teófilo, durante as vigílias da páscoa, no ano de 404 D.C., armados e inclinados à violência, invadiram o templo de João, arrebataram-no e levaram-no para o exílio em Cúcuso, na Armênia. Dessa vez, nenhum terremoto fez reverter a ordem dos acontecimentos.

Antes disso, tanto Teófilo quanto João Crisóstomo haviam procurado obter o apoio da Igreja ocidental. João Crisóstomo foi o vencedor nesse conflito, e Inocente Honório tentou obter o retorno de João do exílio. Porém, as autoridades eclesiásticas, no Oriente, ignoraram tudo isso, e João foi sujeitado a um banimento ainda mais severo, tendo sido levado para Pítius, às margens do mar Negro. Porém, enquanto estava a caminho, não podendo resistir ao rigor das intempéries, morreu durante a viagem. Suas últimas palavras, em grego, foram: *Doksa to Theo panton eneken*, que significam: «Graças a Deus por tudo». Por sua vez, o povo recusou-se a reconhecer o novo patriarca e seu sucessor, até que o imperador Teodósio II, em 438 D.C., fez que os ossos de João Crisóstomo serem trazidos de volta, depositando-os na abóbada imperial. Depois que os venezianos assolaram Antioquia, no ano de 1204, seus ossos foram enviados para a catedral de São Pedro, em Roma. A festa em sua comemoração é celebrada a 27 de janeiro no Ocidente, e a 13 de novembro, na Igreja Grega. Aqueles que perseguiram a João Crisóstomo são melhor relembrados devido exatamente a isso, por haverem perseguido a um homem bom, superior a eles, de acordo com qualquer padrão espiritual.

Escritos: Há um certo número de tratados, como aquele intitulado *Sobre o Sacerdócio*; 386 cartas, 236 das quais foram escritas durante o seu exílio; muitos sermões pregados em Antioquia; muitos valiosos comentários sobre trechos da Bíblia, que se caracterizam pela interpretação da escola antioqueana. Ver o artigo sobre a *Escola Antioqueana*. (AM E)

CRISPO

No grego, *Krispos*, derivado do latim, *crispus*, *encaracolado*. Ele foi o presidente de uma sinagoga judaica em Corinto (Atos 18:8). Converteu-se sob a pregação de Paulo (I Cor. 1:4). Foi uma das poucas pessoas a quem Paulo batizou pessoalmente. O livro *Atos de Pilatos* (2:4), provavelmente tece comentários sobre ele. Alguns manuscritos antigos, por equívoco, põem o seu nome no lugar do de Crescente, em II Timóteo 4:10. A tradição (*Const. Apostól.* 7:46) faz dele bispo de Egina, em tempos posteriores; mas, não temos meios de averiguar se essa tradição coincide com a realidade dos fatos.

CRISTANDADE

A palavra indica o **mundo cristão**. Tem uma aplicação geral a qualquer época, quando se refere a todos os aspectos da fé e das instituições cristãs, coletivamente consideradas. Também pode apontar para os cristãos, coletivamente falando. A palavra também tem um significado específico, quando se refere à Idade Média, àquela época em que a Igreja Católica Romana tinha autoridade para fazer impor a sua vontade sobre as crenças e práticas do mundo europeu daqueles mil anos. O zênite dessa autoridade ocorreu quando o papa Gregório VII (1021-1085), escreveu às nações para lembrar-lhes que, desde a época de São Pedro, a sé de Roma havia sido a suserana delas. A desintegração da cristandade, nesse sentido, começou quando chegava ao fim da Idade Média, com o surgimento da renascença, do nacionalismo e do secularismo. A renascença (que vide), e então a Reforma protestante, emprestaram maior impulso à quebra do monopólio da Igreja Católica Romana, quanto ao seu poder secular e religioso. A princípio, os reformadores protestantes trataram da questão das relações entre o estado e a Igreja; mas o golpe de morte fora desfechado. A

CRISTÃO — CRISTIANISMO

revolução francesa anunciou o estado secular. Em vários países, até os nossos dias, a Igreja Católica Romana exerce grande autoridade quanto a questões políticas; mas isso é apenas uma mera sombra do que já houve. A cristandade foi um grandioso ideal, promovido pela *Cidade de Deus*, obra de Agostinho. Mas esse ideal deu ocasião para muitos abusos, e para muitos dogmas sem fundamento. Acresça-se a isso que não é provável que Jesus tivesse se preocupado com esse tipo de poder secular. Não obstante, deve-se reconhecer que a Igreja Católica Romana, ao agir como o fez, não somente preservou a civilização, mas também foi a campeã da civilização, em meio a um mundo em turbulência, que se estava desintegrando quanto aos seus valores culturais. De fato, a Igreja Católica Romana preservou a civilização pelo espaço de mil anos, tal como Israel o fará, durante o futuro milênio. A despeito dos abusos, isso estava dentro do plano divino. (C)

CRISTÃO

1. *Origem e Referências Bíblicas*. Essa palavra veio à existência como uma espécie de apelido, análogo a «metodista», «quacre», etc. Foi nome aplicado pelos não-cristãos da era apostólica aos primeiros seguidores de Cristo. A palavra é empregada pela primeira vez no livro de Atos, onde se lê que os discípulos de Jesus foram pela primeira vez designados «cristãos» em Antioquia da Síria. Não sabemos dizer se o nome foi cunhado pelos próprios crentes, ou se foram pessoas não-cristãs que o inventaram; mas, o mais provável é que se trata dessa última possibilidade. No Novo Testamento há três referências onde esse apelido é empregado: Atos 11:26; 26:28 e I Pedro 4:16. Isso dá a entender que, desde bem cedo, esse título veio a designar os seguidores da nova fé cristã.

2. *O Termo*. A palavra parece ser uma manipulação latina, onde nomes plurais, terminados em *iani*, podiam designar os soldados de algum general, para exemplificar. Assim, temos *galiani*, indicando os homens de Galba (Tácito, *Hist.* i.51), ou os *augustiniani*, os que pertenciam a Augusto; e os *caesariani*, para indicar os escravos e súditos de César. Assim, é possível que *christian*(o)i, o que já envolve uma adaptação da forma plural do grego, indicasse os soldados de Cristo, aqueles que lutaram pela sua causa. Mas o sentido dessa palavra também pode ter sido «da casa de Cristo» ou «partidários de Cristo». Seja como for, essa palavra é a forma adjetivada do termo grego *Christós*, «ungido», pelo menos quanto ao seu uso, ainda que não, talvez, quanto à sua origem.

3. *Usos*. a. Esse título era usado tanto pelos próprios cristãos como pelos não-cristãos, para *distinguir* os seguidores da nova fé dos pagãos e dos judeus, tal como até hoje tem alguma função, distinguindo os cristãos dos judeus, islamitas, hindus, etc. b. Trata-se de uma *designação genérica* de todas as denominações e seitas cristãs. c. Também é uma espécie de designação para pessoas dotadas de sensibilidade religiosa e moral, inteiramente à parte de sua associação com qualquer grupo religioso. É por isso que dizemos: «Ele agiu como um cristão». Com essa maneira frouxa de falar, falamos usando noções cristãs. d. Um adjetivo, derivado da doutrina de Cristo. e. Um sinônimo para indicar a descendência humana. f. Um ser humano, em distinção a um animal irracional. g. Um *nome denominacional*, para indicar uma igreja cristã, ou seja, os campbelitas, h. Teologicamente, o termo é usado para indicar um verdadeiro crente em Jesus Cristo, similar ao seu uso original. i. Mas, também há um uso pejorativo, indicando aqueles que pertencem a grupos cristãos, considerados inferiores aos grupos cristãos a que pertence quem assim fala, ou considerados inteiramente falsos. Para exemplificar, um crente (evangélico), pode considerar um cristão católico inferior a si mesmo, reservando o termo «cristão» para o tal, ao mesmo tempo em que reserva o termo «crente», para indicar a si mesmo. Alguns cristãos unitários têm rejeitado a designação «cristão» como termo por demais restritivo para indicar sua doutrina. No passado, alguns mórmons aplicavam a palavra a outros grupos, embora não a si mesmos, porém esse costume parece haver desaparecido entre eles.

4. *Cristo e Cresto*. O Codex Vaticanus traz a forma *chrestianos* em todas as passagens do Novo Testamento. Essa forma também é comum nas primeiras inscrições. O termo grego *chrestós*, porém, significa «bom», «gentil», e as evidências demonstram que essa era uma derivação alternativa para «cristãos». Portanto, é duvidoso se a base original dessa palavra era *christós* ou *chrestós*. Porém, isso é muito provável que os não-cristãos estivessem acostumados a chamar os seguidores de Cristo de «bons» ou «gentis»; e isso significa que *christós* é a base da palavra, embora a variante, sem dúvida, existisse. Sem importar qual a derivação exata, o fato é que o adjetivo espalhou-se rapidamente. Tácito, o historiador romano, informa-nos que, nos tempos de Nero, a população geral de Roma empregava a palavra para designar os membros da nova fé em Cristo. (A B C ND W WA)

CRISTIANISMO

Esboço:
1. O Termo.
2. Suas Origens.
3. Principais Períodos Históricos.
4. Principais Divisões Históricas.
5. Idéias Principais.
6. Cristianismo, A Fé Universal.

1. O Termo. Quanto às origens da palavra «cristianismo», ver o artigo sobre os *Cristãos*. O termo «cristão» aparece por três vezes nas páginas do Novo Testamento, embora o termo «cristianismo» nunca figure ali. Entretanto, essa palavra veio à existência no século II D.C., como designação da religião que se desenvolvera em torno da pessoa do Senhor Jesus Cristo. Esse vocábulo encontra-se, pela primeira vez, nos escritos de Inácio (Rom. iii), quando ele falava sobre aquele sistema e sua prática religiosa, o qual é odiado pelo mundo. Em Magn. x e em Phila vi, Inácio usou a palavra para fazer contraste com o judaísmo. Em Magn. x ele a empregou para denotar aquele sistema de fé que incorpora a Verdade e requer uma vida que corresponda a essa verdade. Atualmente, a palavra «cristianismo» geralmente é empregada como sinônimo da religião cristã, em distinção às outras fés, como o judaísmo, o islamismo, etc., ou então, em oposição a vários *ismos*, como o humanismo, o marxismo, etc. O termo refere-se, igualmente, aos crentes, considerados coletivamente, ou ao estado próprio de um cristão, conforme se vê em uma frase como: «O cristianismo dele ainda não estava bem desenvolvido».

2. Suas Origens. A fé cristã teve começo com a pessoa e com os ensinamentos de Jesus, o Cristo. Ele pertencia à raça judaica, de acordo com sua natureza humana. Mas ele era a encarnação do Logos de Deus. O décimo sexto capítulo de Mateus mostra-nos que o movimento cristão não foi um ramo acidental do

CRISTIANISMO

judaísmo. A cultura romana antiga concebia o cristianismo como uma mera divisão herética da fé judaica. Porém, a narrativa de Lucas e Atos foi escrita para demonstrar que o cristianismo era uma entidade por si mesma, um avanço espiritual em relação ao judaísmo, e não um mero fragmento do judaísmo, criado por motivo de disputas teológicas. Vários pensadores liberais têm pensado que o real originador do cristianismo foi o apóstolo Paulo, porquanto é em seus escritos que obtemos a autoridade para o Jesus teológico, em contraste com o Jesus histórico. Antes da missão paulina, segundo eles acreditam, o movimento cristão era apenas uma espécie de judaísmo concorrente. Porém, essa suposição só pode ser mantida se rejeitarmos muitas das declarações do próprio Jesus no tocante ao seu poder, autoridade e caráter distintivo, como se fossem meras invenções da Igreja cristã de épocas posteriores. O trecho de Mateus 16:16 ss, é uma passagem que diz respeito a esse problema. O trecho de Mateus 22:41 ss, que encerra a exaltada doutrina de Jesus sobre o Messias, é outra passagem dessa ordem. Em todos os quatro evangelhos, ficamos impressionados com o caráter *distintivo* de Jesus Cristo. Ele era por demais importante e poderoso para ser apenas um outro profeta judaico. As formulações paulinas são reflexos dessa doutrina, com um pouco mais de definição. É um erro fatal diminuir a importância do que os evangelhos dizem sobre Cristo. Os evangelhos mostram-se modestos, e não exagerados, em suas declarações sobre Jesus. Ver João 20:30,31. O advento do Pentecoste, com seu derramamento do Espírito Santo (ver Atos 2), assinalou o tempo em que a Igreja recebeu poder, embora isso já tivesse começado em forma preliminar. A maioria dos cristãos afirma que o Pentecoste (que vide) foi o começo real da Igreja. Essa declaração, naturalmente, não ignora o fato de que houve um começo *preliminar*.

3. Principais Períodos Históricos.

a. *O Período Apostólico*, até 100 D.C. Os apóstolos de Cristo propagaram a sua mensagem, e dentro desse breve período, os principais centros do mundo romano tinham alguma forma da nova fé, ali representada (Col. 1:6).

b. *Período Pós-Apostólico, Antes de Constantino*, 100-313 D.C. O cristianismo propagou-se por toda parte, embora sofrendo oposição e perseguição, até mesmo oficial, por parte de uma longa linha de imperadores romanos. A Igreja esforçou-se para combater as primeiras divisões e heresias, como o gnosticismo (que vide). Clemente de Roma, Irineu, Tertuliano, Clemente de Alexandria e Orígenes foram importantes teólogos cristãos desse período.

c. *De Constantino a Gregório*, 313-590 D.C. Com a conversão nominal do imperador romano Constantino, o cristianismo tornou-se uma espécie de Igreja oficial. Esta obteve poder político e formalizou o seu credo. Os *concílios* formalizaram a sua fé: o de Nicéia, de 325 D.C., que produziu o credo niceno (que vide); o de Constantinopla I, de 381 D.C.; o de Éfeso, de 431 D.C.; o de Calcedônia, 451 D.C.; o de Constantinopla II, 553 D.C. O monasticismo desenvolveu-se, pelo menos em parte, como uma solução racional para os excessos ascéticos dos devotos. Surgiram várias heresias, como o arianismo, o nestorianismo, o monofisitismo e o pelagianismo (ver os artigos).

d. *Período de Gregório I a Carlos Magno*, 590-800 D.C. Esse período viu a cristianização dos povos germânicos. Também foi o período durante o qual o Egito, a África e a Espanha (que então incluía Portugal), perderam terreno para os islamitas. Dois importantes concílios ocorreram durante essa fase: o de Constantinopla III, 680 D.C., e o de Nicéia II, 787 D.C.

e. *De Carlos Magno ao Papa Gregório VII*, 800-1073 D.C. Esse foi um tempo durante o qual a autoridade papal desenvolveu-se extraordinariamente, quase cumprindo a doutrina de Agostinho de que a Igreja deve ser superior ao estado e deve ser também sua mestra. Essa autoridade só atingiu seu ponto culminante quando do pontificado de Gregório VII, o qual fez as coroas da Europa entenderem que a sé de Roma as dominava à sua vontade. Nesse período, houve o Concílio de Constantinopla IV, de 869 D.C. E, no ano de 1054 D.C., a Igreja Oriental separou-se da Igreja Ocidental, em torno da questão do *filioque* do credo niceno (que vide). Ver também sobre a *Igreja Ortodoxa Oriental*. Naturalmente, houve também outras causas (talvez mais decisivas), dessa separação. cujos elementos se vinham formando há séculos.
— Foi no século XI D.C., que a Igreja Católica Romana adicionou o notório *filioque* ao terceiro artigo do credo niceno. Isso fazia o Espírito Santo proceder tanto do Pai *quanto do Filho*. A Igreja Ortodoxa Oriental, porém, objetava a essa adição. Ver o artigo geral sobre os *Credos*.

f. *Período de Bonifácio VII às Teses de Lutero*, 1295-1517 D.C. Os principais acontecimentos desse período foram o concílio de Viena, 1311; a carreira de João Wycliff, cerca de 1365; o concílio de Constança (João Huss), 1414-1418; o concílio de Basiléia, 1431; a queda de Constantinopla, 1453; e o quinto concílio de Latrão, 1512-1517.

g. *Das Teses de Lutero à Paz de Westphalia*, 1517-1648. Nesse período houve a Reforma protestante, bem como as carreiras de Lutero, Calvino e Zwínglio. Também houve o concílio de Trento (1543-1563).

h. *De 1648 aos Nossos Dias*. Nesse período temos o desenvolvimento da Igreja Católica Romana e das igrejas protestantes; o Ato da Tolerância, da Inglaterra, de 1689; o concílio do Vaticano, 1869; o movimento ecumênico, que aumentou de intensidade a partir do início do século XX. Houve também o surgimento e o desenvolvimento do liberalismo e a fragmentação das denominações protestantes; surgiu o movimento pentecostal; houve a politização de grandes áreas do catolicismo romano, e, em menor intensidade, das igrejas protestantes, através de ideologias políticas, especialmente através da *teologia de libertação* (que vide).

4. Principais Divisões Históricas.

a. A Igreja Apostólica, até 100 D.C.

b. A Igreja Primitiva, de 100 a 325 D.C.

c. A Igreja Católica antiga, de 325 até 1054 D.C.

d. A Igreja Católica Romana e a Igreja Ortodoxa Oriental, de 1054 aos nossos dias.

e. O ramo Protestante da Igreja, a começar em cerca de 1529, quando o apelido «protestante» foi aplicado aos príncipes alemães que, por ocasião da dieta de Speyer, em 1529, protestaram contra a decisão de anular seu direito de controlar as questões religiosas em seus respectivos territórios.

As igrejas protestantes fazem toda a autoridade espiritual e religiosa repousar sobre as Escrituras Sagradas, não reconhecendo o papa como uma figura religiosa singular. Se combinarmos todos os grupos, os cristãos representam cerca de duas sétimas partes da população do mundo. Apesar da longa separação e de uma grande variedade, a qual tende sempre por aumentar, as três divisões principais compartilham de

CRISTIANISMO

certas características identificadoras, pelo que merecem o epíteto de grupos «cristãos» (que vide). Essas características incluem o reconhecimento especial dos ensinamentos de Jesus Cristo; o reconhecimento que Ele é o Mensageiro especial de Deus, o Messias, a pessoa divino-humana. Usualmente, reconhece-se alguma forma de doutrina da Trindade; o uso de certos sacramentos ou ordenanças, que incorporam ou simbolizam importantes itens da fé cristã; o reconhecimento do Antigo e do Novo Testamento como autoritários, e, portanto, de um grande corpo de ensinos, mantido em comum, apesar das disputas sobre muitas questões. Os códigos morais desses vários grupos cristãos são bastante similares. Todos defendem as idéias da imortalidade da alma, da necessidade da redenção e do julgamento divino, que se seguirá após a morte física ou por ocasião da segunda vinda de Cristo.

5. Idéias Principais.

a. *Crenças Sobre Cristo.* O caráter distintivo do cristianismo gira em torno do caráter distintivo de Jesus Cristo. Mesmo para os estudiosos liberais, Jesus Cristo é distintivo pelo menos quanto ao poder de sua missão e quanto à representação vital de como Deus interveio decisivamente na história humana. Para os estudiosos conservadores de todas as variedades, é importante defender alguma forma do ensino de sua divindade. Jesus é concebido como o instrumento do principal revelação de Deus, o que explica o grande desenvolvimento do Novo Testamento, em contraste com o Antigo Testamento. A vida de Cristo incorpora uma *missão divina salvadora.* Jesus é intitulado tanto o Salvador quanto o Messias. Os ensinamentos sobre Jesus constituem a porção central do cristianismo, em contraste com todas as demais fés. Ver o artigo sobre a *Cristologia,* o qual inclui uma declaração detalhada sobre essa questão.

b. *Crenças Sobre Deus.* O cristianismo é uma fé *teísta.* O teísmo (que vide) ensina que Deus não somente criou, mas também ele mantém um contínuo interesse pela sua criação. Ele intervém, ele recompensa pelo bem praticado; ele pune pelo mal. Ele dirige o curso da história humana e tem um propósito final para os homens, e também para toda a criação; e ele revela a sua vontade a profetas e a santos. Em contraste com isso, o deísmo (que vide) diz que apesar disso ter sido originado por alguma grande força originadora, pessoal ou impessoal, a criação foi abandonada por essa força, tendo sido deixada aos caprichos das leis naturais. Em outras palavras, Deus não guiaria, nem interviria, nem recompensaria e nem puniria. Deus seria totalmente transcendental e indiferente.

Entretanto, as doutrinas básicas sobre Deus originaram-se no berço do cristianismo da fé judaica (que vide). Ali há uma noção teísta sobre Deus. Ali há também a atuação da esperança messiânica e das sementes do cristianismo. Ali Deus é exposto como um ser poderoso, santo, justo, amoroso e bom, em grau infinito. O cristianismo herdou todas essas idéias. Entretanto, temos uma elevação do conceito de Deus no cristianismo, em vista da qual ele se tornou menos o Capitão de um exército e mais o Pai universal. A missão gentílica da Igreja primitiva estava alicerçada no conceito da universalidade de Deus e de seu interesse por todos os homens.

c. *Crenças Sobre o Espírito Santo.* No Antigo Testamento, o Espírito divino é mencionado. No Novo Testamento, ele já aparece em união e comunhão com o Pai e com o Filho (ver sobre a *Trindade*). A missão atual do Espírito consiste em promover e desenvolver a obra do Filho. O Espírito Santo também vem residir em todos os crentes individuais, a fim de promover a transformação de cada um deles segundo a imagem do Filho (Rom. 8:29). É dessa forma que os remidos chegarão a compartilhar da espiritualidade divina, de uma maneira que o judaísmo nunca imaginou.

d. *Crenças Sobre o Homem.* O homem é uma criatura caída, embora originalmente criada por Deus. A redenção (que vide) consiste no retorno do homem ao estado primitivo, impecável, embora também envolva um avanço para além desse estado. Mas, o que significa esse «para além» é variegadamente interpretado, na Igreja Católica Romana, na Igreja Ortodoxa Oriental ou nas diversas igrejas protestantes. Uma declaração geral a respeito afirma que o homem, nesse retorno, recebe o perdão dos pecados, a total libertação do princípio do pecado, a imortalidade da alma, e também uma forma de vida espiritual, quando entra nos mundos celestiais. Ali não mais haverá morte, enfermidades ou tristezas. Muitos, entretanto, ficam estagnados quando chegam a esse ponto, supondo que o estado que será alcançado, com sua glória correspondente, depende daquilo que cada indivíduo terá feito em uma única vida na face da terra. Ver os artigos sobre os *Galardões* e sobre as *Coroas.* Entretanto, os pais alexandrinos da Igreja, seguidos por muitos na Igreja Ortodoxa Oriental e na Igreja Anglicana, supõem que o estado eterno não se caracterizará pela estagnação. Até que ponto uma alma humana poderá progredir? O alvo da salvação (que vide) é a participação na natureza divina, de modo real e finito. Isso significa que a Trindade continuará à parte e sem igual, e que a natureza de Deus será duplicada nos remidos, em graus extraordinários, mas finitos. Os trechos de II Pedro 1:4 e Colossenses 2:10 declaram essa doutrina; e o trecho de II Coríntios 3:18 ensina que só poderemos chegar a esse elevado estado se formos atravessando muitos estágios de glória. Ver o artigo sobre a *Salvação.* O evangelho que inclui noções como o perdão dos pecados, a transferência para o céu e a estagnação nesse ponto deriva-se, essencialmente, de textos extraídos dos evangelhos sinópticos e do livro de Atos. Mas o evangelho que inclui noções como a participação na própria natureza de Cristo e a glorificação eterna (que vide) deriva-se, principalmente, de textos paulinos e petrinos. Como é óbvio, essa mensagem mais profunda resultou de uma revelação mais ampla que foi dada aos apóstolos durante o período de transição, quando o cristianismo estava se separando do judaísmo.

e. *Crenças Sobre Princípios Éticos.* O cristianismo está pesadamente endividado com o judaísmo, quanto a esse particular. O espírito dos Dez Mandamentos é retido de muitas maneiras, no Novo Testamento. Ensinamentos bíblicos, como a queda do homem, a sua necessidade de redenção como criatura decaída, a promessa da recompensa futura, com base na conduta de cada um (ver a idéia inteira das recompensas e o segundo capítulo de Romanos), a ameaça de julgamento contra os impenitentes (ver o artigo sobre o *Julgamento*), etc., são idéias compartilhadas pelo judaísmo e pelo cristianismo. Naturalmente, Jesus não foi apenas um rabino judeu. Ele espiritualizou a lei, fazendo o mal esconder-se até mesmo nos motivos dos homens, e não se externalizar apenas em atos cometidos. Isso posto, o adultério agora não consiste apenas no ato, mas até no pensamento, segundo se aprende em Mateus 5:28. O homicídio agora não é apenas o ato, mas é também o ódio que lhe dá a força, como se aprende em Mateus 5:21,22. A fórmula reiterada de Jesus: «Ouvistes que

CRISTIANISMO

foi dito aos antigos... Eu, porém, vos digo...», sem dúvida foi uma maneira pela qual ele alertou os seus ouvintes ao fato de que ele não somente era algum intérprete autorizado da lei, mas era a própria Autoridade, que podia manifestar-se independentemente e acima da lei. Jesus foi o *Novo Moisés*, — que trouxe à luz um novo código moral.

A lei do amor. Para o judaísmo, o amor consistia em um hebreu cuidar de outro hebreu. O judaísmo, porém, não dava grande importância ao amor pelos gentios, pois, de fato, em parte alguma do Antigo Testamento encontra-se algum mandamento para os hebreus amarem a seus vizinhos gentios. Já no Novo Testamento, o próximo é qualquer pessoa, sem importar sua raça, que esteja em necessidade. Não foi por acidente que Jesus escolheu um *samaritano* (que vide), em sua parábola do bom samaritano (Luc. 10:33 ss). Os samaritanos eram considerados pessoas desprezíveis pelos judeus; e, no entanto, naquela parábola, foi um samaritano que mostrou misericórdia por um total estranho. Nisso, o amor de Deus é exibido como universal. Deus amou o mundo (João 3:16). O ato salvatício visa a todos. No Novo Testamento, pois, o amor torna-se a princesa de todas as virtudes, o solo onde todas as demais virtudes são cultivadas (I Cor. 13 e Gál. 5:22,23). O trabalho do Espírito consiste em cultivar essa virtude (bem como todas as demais), em cada remido. Isso posto, no Novo Testamento o amor aparece como uma operação divina, e não apenas como uma emoção humana. Isso significa que os princípios éticos começam a fazer parte das verdades místicas, onde o espírito de um homem entra em comunhão com Deus, e mediante o que um homem vai sendo transformado segundo a imagem de Cristo. Isso equivale a dizer que a ética torna-se ali uma subdivisão da teologia.

f. *Crenças sobre as Sagradas Escrituras*. Faz parte da fé cristã, teísta como ela é, que Deus revelou-se através do Antigo e do Novo Testamentos. Ver o artigo sobre a *Revelação*. Os livros que resultaram dessa revelação são considerados sagrados, autoritários, e são reputados como autoridade básica sobre a qual está firmada a fé cristã. Ver o artigo sobre as *Sagradas Escrituras*.

g. *Crenças Sobre os Sacramentos ou Ordenanças*. Quanto a notas expositivas completas sobre a questão, ver os artigos sobre ambos esses assuntos. Um sacramento supostamente transmite poderes espirituais especiais, uma marca ou caráter que realiza uma operação espiritual. Uma ordenança, porém, é apenas um ato simbólico, com o propósito de lembrar-nos as realidades espirituais, e que, por si mesma, não transmite qualquer poder espiritual. Certos segmentos do cristianismo ensinam os sacramentos; outros, as ordenanças; mas ambos os segmentos concordam sobre os princípios espirituais envolvidos, ainda que não quanto ao *modus operandi* do poder espiritual.

6. Cristianismo, a Fé Universal. Qualquer fé religiosa que afirme ter importância e aplicação para todos os homens pode ser chamada *universal*. O judaísmo não começou com tal ponto de vista, mas terminou sendo uma fé universal. O dubismo, o hinduísmo e o islamismo são fés universais. Muitos grupos menores e seitas também, poderiam ser considerados universais. Muitos cristãos negam a validade das reivindicações de outras fés, de que são fés universais, tachando-as de falsas e espúrias. Quanto a esse particular, penso que os pais gregos da Igreja, como quanto a diversas outras questões, exibiram uma sabedoria maior do que isso. Eles partiam da idéia de que o princípio universal, o *Logos*

(ver o artigo sobre o *Verbo de Deus*) implanta suas sementes entre todos os homens. Em face disso, eles supunham que a melhor porção da filosofia grega, especialmente aquela exposta por Platão, serviu de aio para conduzir os gentios a Cristo, da mesma maneira que a lei exerceu essa função, no tocante aos judeus. Se aplicarmos esse ponto de vista, então poderemos afirmar que o Logos, encarnado sob a forma de Jesus Cristo, tem um ministério muito mais amplo do que geralmente se supõe. Isso significaria que outras fés religiosas, que não são chamadas cristãs, ainda contam com as sementes do Logos, operante nelas. Sabemos que a *restauração* geral (que vide), ensinada em Efésios 1:10, dá a entender que a restauração só poderá ocorrer através da operação feita por muitos séculos, incluindo até mesmo uma parte da eternidade futura. A segunda vinda de Cristo (ver sobre a *Parousia*) assinalará uma grande *transição* no trato de Deus com os homens, e *não* um ponto final. Após esse evento, ou melhor, uma série de eventos que faz parte da segunda vinda de Cristo, haverá muitas longas eras, e os processos remidor e restaurador continuarão em seus efeitos. O alvo disso será o de fazer Cristo tornar-se tudo para todos (Efé. 1:23). Estou supondo que, até mesmo em nossos dias, estão sendo feitas contribuições para os propósitos de Deus que não dizem respeito somente à fé cristã, contribuições essas que envolvem não somente outras religiões, mas também a filosofia, os movimentos históricos, as ciências, e todas as atividades por causa das quais o conhecimento e a espiritualidade estão avançando. A promessa divina é que, finalmente, *tudo* será unificado e centralizado em torno de Cristo. Quando examinamos os conceitos de outras fés religiosas, podemos notar, quanto a vários pontos básicos, uma certa similaridade de idéias, embora tais idéias sejam expressas mediante uma terminologia diferente. Uma das primeiras coisas que um filósofo aprende é reconhecer que uma idéia qualquer pode ser expressa de diferentes maneiras, através de certa variedade de termos. Os estudos no campo das religiões comparadas demonstram que há muitas idéias que estão sendo expressas de diversas maneiras, e que, quanto à sua base, são as mesmas.

O Caráter Distintivo do Cristianismo. O que dissemos acima não tem o propósito de afirmar que todas as fés religiosas expressam igualmente a verdade de Deus, ou que sejam idênticas quanto ao seu valor intrínseco. O caráter distintivo do cristianismo repousa sobre o caráter distintivo da pessoa de Jesus Cristo e de sua missão. O cristianismo reivindica especialmente que seu fundador é uma encarnação direta do Logos (João 1:1), ou seja, era uma pessoa de natureza divino-humana. Essa é uma reivindicação distintiva; e, visto que ela é verdadeira, situa o cristianismo em uma posição distintiva e ímpar. O cristianismo envolve uma revelação distintiva sobre Deus e sua vontade, bem como uma revelação ética superior. Não somente isso, mas também se a idéia dos pais gregos da Igreja, sobre a doutrina do Logos, corresponde à verdade, então essa é a *mesma Pessoa* que, em *outros* sistemas religiosos, lhes transmitiu seus mais importantes valores, posto que mesclados com noções humanas distorcidas. Isso significaria que esses outros sistemas receberam vislumbres, ao passo que, no cristianismo, temos a efulgência mesma da revelação divina. Mas também significa que toda a glória pertence a Cristo, e que seu modo de operar está muito acima de nossos dogmas e de nossas crenças denominacionais!

Há um outro fator que deveria ser observado nesta discussão. É que quando lemos sobre outras fés religiosas, para nossa surpresa, encontramos pontos que manifestam uma grande sabedoria, com idéias que aprimoram nossa maneira de pensar sobre as coisas. Na realidade, encontramos alguns dos mais preciosos tesouros nos lugares mais inesperados. Isso reveste-se de grande valor para nós, ensinando-nos que a ignorância nunca teve qualquer vantagem. Além disso, em conexão com isso, deveríamos observar a mesma coisa quando lemos a respeito das crenças e tradições válidas de outras denominações, dentro do contexto cristão. Todas as denominações cristãs encerram verdades e erros, pontos de fortaleza e de debilidade. Quanto mais aprendemos sobre elas todas, tanto melhor torna-se a nossa visão da verdade. Desse modo, quanto a alguns pontos, abandonamos sem senso de perda certos aspectos das crenças de nossas respectivas denominações, porque encontramos alguns aspectos melhores da verdade, preservados em algum outro segmento do cristianismo evangélico. Isso pode constituir uma surpresa para aqueles que, desde a infância, têm sido ensinados a supor que uma certa denominação é *a* representante da verdade cristã. Tal idéia, portanto, é apenas uma parte da mitologia denominacional. (AM BR E HU HUS P R WW)

CRISTIANISMO SECULAR
Ver **Secularização do Cristianismo**.

CRISTO
O artigo que segue é o tratado principal sobre aquele assunto. Outros artigos relacionados também são importantes e esclarecem ainda mais o assunto. *Ver:* Cristo, Como a Verdade; Cristo, Como a Vida; Cristo Como o Caminho; Fundamento da Igreja, Cristo como; Cristo, Conhecer Segundo a Carne; Cristo-Consciência; Divindade de Cristo; Humanidade de Cristo; Missão Universal do Logos (Cristo); Cristo-Misticismo; Cristo, O Corpo De; Cristo, Tentação de; Cristo Vivo; Crucificação de Cristo; Ressurreição de Cristo; Ascensão de Cristo; Descida de Cristo ao Hades; Cristologia; Messias; Jesus Teológico e Histórico; Ensinos de Jesus; Ética de Jesus; *Jesus* (artigo geral); Mediador, Cristo, o único.

1. O Termo. A palavra portuguesa **Cristo** é transliteração do adjetivo verbal grego, *Christós*, que significa «ungido». Essa palavra hebraica, por sua vez, traduz o termo hebraico *mashiach*, que tem o mesmo sentido. Essa palavra hebraica foi absorvida pelo grego sob a forma modificada de *messias*, conforme se vê em João 14:1 e 4:25. É daí que vem a nossa palavra portuguesa Messias. Em Israel, desde os tempos mais remotos, os sumos sacerdotes (Êxo. 29:7) e os reis eram ungidos. Essa unção servia de confirmação externa da escolha divina, que conferia a eles os seus respectivos ofícios. É dito acerca de Saul e Davi que, por ocasião de sua unção, o Espírito de Yahweh desceu sobre eles poderosamente (I Sam. 10:6 *ss,* 16:13). Aí há um texto de prova bíblico em favor da idéia da transmissão de caráter (que vide), ou seja, a noção de que os sacramentos deixam certa *marca* sobre a pessoa que os recebe, conferindo-lhe a graça divina que a transforma em seu caráter. Ver também trechos bíblicos como I Sam. 24:6,10; Sal. 2:2; 18:50; 20:6; 132:10,17; 89:38,51. No trecho de Salmos 105:16 lemos que os patriarcas foram consagrados ao serviço de Deus, o que dá a entender unção. O rei da Pérsia, Ciro (Isa. 45:1), foi ungido por Deus para realizar certa tarefa divina, o que no serve de informação bastante instrutiva. Algumas referências do livro dos Salmos cabem dentro do contexto messiânico, dando a entender o aparecimento do *Ungido*. Os escritos do período intertestamentário também têm algumas indicações messiânicas. A obra Salmos de Salomão, de 50 A.C., é fortemente messiânica, referindo-se à vinda do Rei que seria impulsionado pelo Espírito, que seria forte no temor de Deus, e subjugaria a muitos povos, não pelo poder militar, mas pela energia espiritual. Ele reuniria um povo que seria os filhos de Deus. Mas somente o povo de Israel seria beneficiado diretamente. Essa predição não emprega o termo «Messias», mas o conceito está presente. Não há que duvidar que, antes mesmo dos tempos do Novo Testamento, havia expectações messiânicas entre os judeus. Portanto, não nos devemos admirar que, mesmo naquele período, aquela idéia fosse exposta de maneira formalizada, com textos de prova apropriados. Esperava-se que Deus visitasse o seu povo de maneira toda especial (Luc. 1:68). Na porção inicial dos evangelhos sinópticos, temos, em operação, o *segredo messiânico*. Jesus não se declarava o Messias. Os estudiosos liberais afirmam que ele ainda nem tinha certeza disso. Os eruditos conservadores asseveram que ele tinha certeza do fato, mas que apenas evitava declará-lo em público. O trecho de Mateus 16:13-20 oferece-nos a afirmação clássica dos evangelhos sinópticos, onde se lê que Pedro percebeu, por revelação divina, o caráter messiânico de Jesus. Por ocasião de seu julgamento, Jesus declarou francamente que era o Messias (Mar. 14:61 *ss*), embora tenha-se recusado a dar uma resposta direta à pergunta feita pelo sumo sacerdote (Mat. 26:63 *ss*; Luc. 22:66 *ss*). Não obstante, a resposta dada por Jesus foi tomada como uma afirmação, sendo essa uma das razões pelas quais Jesus foi condenado à crucificação, porquanto, segundo eles pensavam, Jesus teria blasfemado.

No evangelho de João, o caráter messiânico de Jesus é declarado desde o começo (João 1:41,49). Isso coaduna-se com a intenção desse livro, onde a missão divina é vista em operação na pessoa divina, a fim de trazer a salvação ao povo escolhido. Nesse quarto evangelho não temos conflitos, nem dúvidas e nem qualquer segredo messiânico, porque ali o Espírito revela seu propósito tão obviamente que não há espaço algum para especulações. O termo «Messias», através de sua tradução grega, e, daí, para o português, tornou-se parte integrante do nome de Jesus, pois ele é Jesus, o Cristo, ou então, o Senhor Jesus Cristo, ou o Filho, Jesus Cristo, que é nosso Senhor (Rom. 1:3,7; 5:11; I Cor. 1:2; 5:4; II Cor. 1:2; Efé. 1:3; Fil. 1:2; Col. 2:6; I Tes. 1:1; II Tes. 1:1; I Tim. 1:1; II Tim. 1:2; Tito 1:4; File. 3). O trecho de Tiago 1:1 reflete o uso.

2. O Cristo Vivo. Alguns intérpretes supõem que uma vez que o termo «Cristo» tornou-se parte do nome próprio de Jesus, tal termo teria perdido o seu significado original. Porém, tal idéia é absurda, quando consideramos os pontos abaixo: a. Com freqüência, mesmo nas igrejas gentílicas, o núcleo da comunidade compunha-se de judeus convertidos; b. mesmo quando isso não era assim, a mensagem cristã era apresentada como cumprimento das Escrituras judaicas, e o ensino a respeito do Messias, embora não fosse uma idéia pagã, deve ter sido um assunto comumente ventilado na Igreja. Basta-nos lembrar que as «Escrituras» da Igreja primitiva eram os livros do Antigo Testamento, e que só gradualmente o cânon do Novo Testamento desenvolveu-se e assumiu proporções importantes. Assim, onde fosse iniciada uma igreja cristã, ali estava sendo ensinado o Antigo Testamento como base de sua autoridade.

a. *Jesus e o Messias*. A fé humana é verdadeiramente fraca. Pareceria que Jesus nada mais tinha para provar, após a vida que ele viveu, após o poder que ele demonstrou possuir. Mas os homens, distantes dos eventos, especulam que os cristãos primitivos inventaram o relato inteiro, e alguns chegam ao extremo de declarar que Jesus nunca existiu, tendo sido apenas uma figura fictícia, para preencher uma esperança messiânica frustrada. Acresça-se a isso a atividade *demitizadora* (que vide) do evangelho. Os homens declaram que houve dois Jesus, um histórico e o outro teológico. O Jesus histórico estaria irremediavelmente perdido em meio a tradições e mitos. O Jesus teológico seria apenas criação da Igreja. Isso significa que nada se sabe mesmo, sobre Jesus. Tal idéia é simplesmente absurda. Em primeiro lugar, porque não havia interesse algum pela criação de um Jesus teológico, a menos que houvesse *notáveis fatos históricos* que tivessem inspirado tal teologia. Em segundo lugar, se encontramos notáveis fatos históricos, que fazem parte da história de Jesus, então só nisso já temos base para um Jesus teológico autêntico. Temos necessidade de explicar a vida que Jesus viveu. Como é óbvio, nenhum homem comum poderia ter vivido como ele viveu. Como Jesus poderia ser tão incomum. Os primeiros cristãos, bem como os primeiros grupos hereges, envolveram-se na atividade da *cristologia* (que vide), procurando apresentar explicações. Todo gênio criador que vem a este mundo, sem importar se negativo ou se positivo, provoca uma reação significante entre os homens. Depois, em redor de cada um desenvolve-se uma abundante literatura. Quando surgem tais condições, sabemos que algo de incomum sucedeu. Pelos fins do século II D.C., havia cerca de vinte grupos que haviam aparecido, cada qual afirmando saber expor melhor a pessoa e os pontos de vista de Jesus, o Cristo. A própria existência desses grupos demonstra o impacto que Jesus exerceu sobre os homens. Acompanhando esses movimentos, houve a produção de abundante literatura, incluindo o nosso Novo Testamento. Essa *atividade literária* serve de uma outra prova do poder da vida de Jesus.

b. *Considerações Modernas*. Atualmente vive o homem santo hindu, Satya Sai Baba (que vide), o qual está realizando os milagres de Jesus, em plena luz do dia, defronte mesmo dos céticos e dos cientistas. Muitos deles se têm tornado seus discípulos, e *instantaneamente*, como se viu no caso de Jesus. Eles admitem que toda a estrutura de suas idéias, geralmente alicerçada sobre o ceticismo (que vide), ruiu diante do que esse homem é capaz de fazer. Não estou entrando aqui no mérito das reivindicações de Baba, que têm significação teológica, e nem estou fazendo confronto entre ele e Jesus. Somente menciono esse fenômeno moderno para mostrar que há homens de gigantesco poder espiritual, e que nossas explicações naturais e céticas são incapazes de explicar tais homens. As dúvidas que têm sido levantadas acerca de Jesus, resultam da debilidade do caráter espiritual dos homens. Jesus realizou aquilo que os evangelhos dizem que ele fez. De fato, os evangelhos mostram-se muito cautelosos em suas afirmações sobre Jesus, procurando não exagerar, conforme se vê em João 20:30,31.

c. *Afirmações com Base na Ignorância*. Se um político radical qualquer, um general do exército, um déspota destruidor que propaga o terror, etc., tomar sobre si a tarefa de emitir opiniões sobre valores religiosos, nenhuma pessoa sensata haverá de tomar a sério o que tal indivíduo diz. Se um faxineiro qualquer começar a falar comigo sobre astronomia, proferindo toda a espécie de absurdos, não haverei de considerá-lo uma autoridade sobre questões astronômicas. Se um mecânico de automóveis apresentar-se para submeter-me a uma intervenção cirúrgica, dizendo que ele sabe consertar bem automóveis, e que, por isso mesmo, me deixará curado, não me sentirei inclinado a aceitar o seu oferecimento. E se um indivíduo que se mostra cético, que nunca viu um milagre suceder, que sempre foi ensinado a duvidar, em todas as escolas que freqüentou, sem importar quão intelectual ele pareça ser, o que significa que lhe falta profundeza espiritual, vier a declarar que Jesus não pode ter feito aquilo que os evangelhos lhe atribuem, não me deixarei impressionar pelo que ele disser. A verdade é que Jesus foi um homem dotado de capacidades espirituais e de realizações muito acima das experiências dos céticos. É impossível nos pronunciarmos sobre as coisas, de modo inteligente, se não tivermos experiência sobre as coisas acerca das quais falamos. Os apóstolos tinham grande experiência no campo no qual Jesus operava. Eles chegaram à conclusão de que Jesus era o Cristo (Messias), o Filho de Deus de modo todo especial. A teologia continua procurando defini-lo, e as declarações feitas a respeito dele mostram que isso não é uma atividade apenas legítima, mas também *necessária*. O ceticismo, porém, não nos leva a parte alguma. Preciso admitir, neste ponto, que nossos termos teológicos, por si mesmos, têm inúmeras aplicações que ultrapassam em muito às nossas experiências, sem importar quão grandes estas sejam; e, por essa precisa razão, devemos continuar a estudar e a investigar, a fim de percebermos melhor a *natureza* daquilo em que cremos.

3. A Operação Presente. O Cristo que agora está vivo e operante no mundo, é muito mais do que a influência da vida de Jesus, que prossegue entre os homens. Grandes homens inspiram-nos para fazer o melhor, é verdade. Seus ensinos instruem-nos e ajudam-nos. Porém, o *Cristo vivo* transcende a tudo isso. Isso é comprovado na experiência de muitas pessoas do mundo atual. As vidas dos discípulos originais foram profundamente afetadas por Jesus. Nossas vidas também são afetadas por seu Espírito, que é o seu *alter ego*. Há criatividade e inspiração no ministério do Espírito Santo, o qual cuida para que o significado do Cristo vivo continue vital no mundo. A teologia é uma coisa linda. Porém, mais lindo ainda é o poder espiritual que nos foi posto à disposição. Isso é exibido diariamente na vida dos crentes. Há uma transformação moral; há obras de ensino, caridade e filantropia. Ademais, há o lado místico da fé, onde os poderes espirituais continuam operando milagres e iluminando os homens. O Cristo vivo, no mundo atual, continua a levar avante o plano traçado em favor dos homens pela graça divina. Há uma criatividade espiritual, do Espírito Santo atuante. O Cristo vivo é a cristividade de Deus solta entre os homens. Limites e obstáculos estão sendo derrubados em todos os lugares. Em minha própria vida tenho visto isso acontecer, e ouso afirmar que o leitor também tem sido testemunha disso. (E NTI W)

CRISTO, COMO A VERDADE

João 14:6. **E a verdade**. Quanto a este particular, poderíamos destacar os pontos seguintes:

1. Jesus é a verdade de *Deus* porque, na qualidade de «Logos» eterno (ver João 1:1), ele é a perfeita revelação de Deus e de sua verdade, e isso não meramente para os homens, mas também para todos os seres criados.

2. Jesus é, especialmente, a *revelação de Deus* aos

CRISTO — CRISTO, COMO A VIDA

homens, no que concerne à salvação deles. Sua própria pessoa representa realmente essa verdade, porque nele, segundo os eternos conselhos divinos (ver Efé. 1:3-5), ele sempre esteve unido a Deus Pai, e o plano da redenção dessa maneira se originou dele. Assim sendo, em sua encarnação, ele trouxe essa verdade da redenção aos homens. Em sua ascensão, ressurreição e glorificação, ele assegura aos remidos a mais plena participação em toda a sua glória e em sua natureza divina. Portanto, por esses motivos ele é a verdade metafísica do homem.

3. Jesus é a *verdade do caminho* pelo qual os homens devem retornar a Deus, porquanto ele é o exemplo supremo e o ilustrador desse caminho. Essa é a verdade envolvida em sua encarnação. Tudo quanto o homem precisa saber está contido em sua pessoa. Jesus é a verdade ética do homem.

4. Dessa maneira, em sua própria pessoa, Cristo Jesus combina *tudo* quanto os homens precisam saber, crer e ser, tanto no que diz respeito à natureza de Deus como no tocante à natureza e à posse da redenção e da glória eterna.

5. Jesus é a verdade, *em oposição* à religião falsa, como o judaísmo desviado e obstinado. Ele é aquela verdade para a qual apontava a lei mosaica, e da qual o pacto do A.T. era apenas uma sombra pálida. Ele é a materialização da verdade espiritual, e não meramente um profeta de Deus ou uma representação parcial polêmica cristã contra os judeus incrédulos, que rejeitaram ao seu próprio Messias. O autor sagrado queria que tais pessoas soubessem que tudo aquilo em que confiavam, como uma revelação da parte de Deus, nada significava à parte da pessoa de Jesus Cristo, posto ser ele a concretização de toda a verdade de Deus, ao passo que Moisés, a lei e os profetas meramente apontavam para Cristo.

6. Em sua *própria essência*, Cristo também é a verdade de Deus, porquanto ele mesmo é divino, e assim nos tem mostrado qual é a natureza de Deus ou a verdadeira forma de vida que ele possui, a qual ele está transmitindo aos homens através de Cristo. Essa é justamente a mensagem de um trecho como Col. 2:9, onde se lê: «...porquanto nele habita corporalmente toda a plenitude da divindade...» Ou então do trecho de Col. 1:15: «Ele é a imagem do Deus invisível...». Ver João 18:38.

7. O *Logos* (Cristo) planta suas sementes em filosofias e religiões não-cristãs como atos preparatórios à Restauração (que vide). Portanto, sua exclusividade é ao mesmo tempo uma universalidade, porque opera através de uma multiplicidade de meios. As verdades nas religiões, nas filosofias, e nas ciências, são *todas elas*, as verdades universais do Logos. Seu campo de atividade é universal.

CRISTO, COMO A VIDA

João 14:6: E a vida. O evangelho, em sua totalidade, leva-nos a compreender a veracidade dos pontos abaixo discriminados.

1. Jesus é a *vida* devido ao fato de que, na qualidade de *Logos* divino e eterno, ele *compartilha* da mais elevada forma de toda espécie de vida, a vida do próprio Deus. Por conseguinte, ele é verdadeiramente divino.

2. Essa vida divina, porém, Jesus *transmite aos homens* regenerados, tal como a mesma lhe foi transmitida, quando de sua encarnação humana. Os trechos de João 5:26 e 6:57 ensinam-nos justamente esse tema, que os teólogos e filósofos denominam de *vida necessária* ou *vida independente*. Trata-se de uma vida «necessária» por ser o tipo de vida que não pode cessar de existir. E é «independente» porque não depende de qualquer outro ser, para sua continuação e renovação. Ela é a sua própria continuação e renovação. Somente Deus tem essa forma de vida, a qual é chamada de «vida eterna» não somente porque não tem princípio e nem fim, mas porque se trata de uma espécie de vida: a vida que ele conferiu ao Senhor Jesus, quando de sua encarnação, e que o Senhor Jesus, por sua vez, pela autoridade que recebeu da parte do Pai, conferiu a todos os homens que dele se valem, a fim de recebê-la. Dessa forma, os remidos tornar-se-ão verdadeiramente «eternos», tal como o próprio Deus é eterno. Ora, Jesus dá-nos essa vida, e ela se encontra na sua própria pessoa.

3. Em sua encarnação, o Senhor Jesus veio ensinar aos homens como *devem compartilhar* dessa sua vida, porque ele demonstrou aos homens como a recebeu, mediante uma transformação moral e metafísica. Quando ele ressurgiu triunfalmente do sepulcro, trouxe essa forma de vida aos homens por haver saído da sepultura como o primeiro homem realmente imortal. Quando de sua ascensão e glorificação, Jesus veio participar ainda mais intensamente da vida de Deus, na qualidade de primeiro homem imortal, tornando-se assim as primícias de muitos outros homens igualmente imortais. Dessa maneira, Cristo está conduzindo muitos filhos à glória, os quais participam dessa mesma vida. É esse aspecto mais completo que denominamos «vida eterna».

4. Jesus transmite a vida real, não como símbolo, e, sim, como *um fato*, em contraste com o judaísmo, que não passava de um símbolo, segundo os ensinamentos dos profetas, na lei de Moisés e nos ritos cerimoniais. Nisso encontramos, novamente, certo elemento da polêmica cristã primitiva, dirigida contra os judeus incrédulos e outros incrédulos, os quais confiavam em meras exterioridades ou sombras, ao mesmo tempo em que rejeitavam a substância mesma da vida, concretizada na pessoa de Jesus Cristo.

5. Jesus Cristo é a vida, tanto a *vida futura* como o *princípio e a fonte* originária de toda a vida, pelo que também aquele que não se achega a Deus, por intermédio dele, está sujeito à condenação, à morte espiritual. (Ver João 3:15).

Ninguém vem ao Pai senão por mim. O destino legítimo do homem é chegar até às regiões onde habita Deus Pai, retornando assim a ele; mas isso não meramente em sentido especial, e, sim, com todo o seu ser, participando finalmente da *perfeita natureza moral* de Deus, compartilhando de sua natureza *divina* tal como Cristo Jesus dela participa. Portanto, os homens que não atingem esse alvo, —ficam aquém do destino preparado por Deus para o homem, na criação original, porque o homem foi feito à imagem de Deus, sendo afetado especificamente em sua pessoa pelo modelo que é Cristo, em tudo quanto Cristo foi e fez, bem como em tudo quanto Cristo é e está fazendo. Assim, pois, não participar dessa glória é o mesmo que a morte espiritual. Isso significa que o alvo é Deus Pai. E é exclusivamente por intermédio de Cristo que esse alvo pode ser atingido.

A exclusividade e universalidade de Cristo:

1. Na eternidade passada, o Logos revelou Deus a todos os seres inteligentes. (Ver João 1:18).

2. Em sua missão terrena, o Logos, encarnado em Jesus, se fez visivelmente o único caminho de retorno ao Pai. (Ver João 1:14; Gál. 1:8,9). Atos 4:12 tem uma declaração similar.

3. A idéia toda de filhos serem desenvolvidos segundo a imagem do Filho, II Cor. 3:18, através da

CRISTO — CRISTO-CONSCIÊNCIA

energia do Espírito, prova a exclusividade do Filho, porquanto existiria algum outro Filho unigênito? Essa transformação segundo a imagem de Cristo é a salvação. (Ver Heb. 2:3).

4. O filho, agora glorificado, continua sendo o único mediador entre Deus e os homens, I Tim. 2:5; (ver também Heb. 8:6; 9:15 e 12:24).

5. Na posição de Logos, tendo retornado à glória, ele continua sendo o Salvador. Muitos pais da igreja opinavam que o Logos prosseguia em sua missão remidora entre as almas humanas que ultrapassaram a barreira da morte física. (Ver I Ped. 4:6). A descida de Cristo ao hades tornou isso possível, I Ped. 3:18. Outros crêem que essa missão pós-morte melhorou o estado dos perdidos, não lhes oferecendo a salvação dos eleitos contudo.

6. Portanto, aprendemos que o Logos é o único Salvador, e que sua missão não se limita à sua encarnação terrena, embora todos os benefícios que ele confira aos homens dependam da mesma. João 14:10.

7. O *Logos* (Cristo) planta suas sementes em filosofias e religiões não-cristãs como atos preparatórios à Restauração (que vide). Portanto, sua exclusividade é ao mesmo tempo uma universalidade, porque opera através de uma multiplicidade de meios. As verdades nas religiões, nas filosofias, e nas ciências, são *todas elas*, as verdades universais do Logos. Seu campo de atividade é universal.

CRISTO COMO O CAMINHO

O *Logos* (Cristo) é o *caminho* para Deus, para os lugares celestiais e para a transformação espiritual. É também o *pioneiro* no caminho da espiritualidade (que vide), Heb. 2:10. Ele é o caminho *atual* e será o caminho para a salvação *além do sepulcro*. Ver I Ped. 4:6. Será sempre o caminho para uma *glorificação* crescente e eterna. Ver o artigo separado sobre *Caminho, Cristo como*, que oferece mais detalhes.

CRISTO COMO O FUNDAMENTO DA IGREJA

Ver **Fundamento da Igreja, Cristo como**.

CRISTO, CONHECER segundo a carne

Antes conhecemos a Cristo segundo a carne, II Cor. 5:16. Uma frase um tanto obscura, que tem admitido diversas interpretações, a saber:

1. Paulo não se referia a qualquer conhecimento de Cristo no tocante à sua vida e ministério terrenos.

2. Nem pretende dar a entender que antes conhecera pessoalmente a Jesus, ainda que, indiretamente, talvez estivesse repreendendo alguns elementos do partido «de Cristo», que se ufanavam disso.

3. Por igual modo, também não falava de Cristo como o Messias judaico, conforme a sua anterior estimativa e maneira de pensar.

4. Ainda mais fora do alvo é aquela explanação que pensa que Paulo alude a algum tempo «após» a sua conversão, quando seu conceito de Cristo ainda era um tanto inferior, ficando muito aquém do que alguém deveria pensar a seu respeito, por ser mera «estimativa humana». É possível que haja alguma verdade nessa opinião, porquanto Paulo poderia tê-la usado como crítica contra os seus oponentes judaizantes. Por conseguinte, Paulo poderia ter dito: «Antes eu tinha uma estimativa de Cristo semelhante à vossa agora, situando-o abaixo de Moisés, para todos os efeitos práticos. Mas esse é um mero ponto de vista humano, errôneo, que desde então já abandonei». Tudo isso pode exprimir uma verdade, mas não parece ser aquilo que Paulo desejou frisar em II Cor. 5:16. Não existe qualquer registro histórico que Paulo tenha algum dia pregado um evangelho legalista, o que precisaríamos admitir se tivéssemos de aceitar essa interpretação.

5. Antes, Paulo se refere nesse ponto a um período anterior à sua conversão, quando tinha a Jesus Cristo em péssimo conceito, quando blasfemava o seu nome, pensando ser ele um mestre herético e turbulento, inimigo de Moisés. Paulo tivera uma opinião de Cristo conforme a opinião dos fariseus e saduceus até ali. Mas essa opinião ele abandonou.

Infelizmente, para muitos, o conhecimento «acerca de Cristo», e as afirmações em um credo, têm tomado o lugar do «conhecimento de Cristo», corretamente e através do Espírito Santo. De viagem para o estado da Georgia, nos Estados Unidos da América do Norte, um morávio se encontrou com João Wesley e lhe perguntou: «Você já conhece a Jesus?» Wesley retrucou: «Sei que ele é o Salvador do mundo». «Sim, mas, você já o conhece»? veio a resposta: eis aí um bom ponto. Podemos saber muitas coisas sobre Cristo, sem conhecê-lo. (Com isso se pode comparar o trecho de Fil. 3:10 e *ss*).

CRISTO-CONSCIÊNCIA

Esse é apenas um outro nome para a *elevada iluminação* dada através das operações do Espírito, de tal modo que o crente venha a compartilhar da mente de Cristo em grau significativo. Trata-se de uma espécie de versão cristianizada daquilo que se chama *consciência cósmica* (que vide). O trecho de I Cor. 2:16 mostra-nos que todos os crentes, até certo ponto, possuem a mente de Cristo; mas há muitos níveis dessa participação. Na Igreja Ortodoxa Oriental, muitas pessoas envolvem-se na busca intensa pela *iluminação* (que vide). Quanto maior a iluminação obtida, maior a consciência de Cristo que o crente obtém. Há muitos meios de desenvolvimento espiritual. Esses meios incluem o estudo das Escrituras e dos livros espirituais, o desenvolvimento do intelecto com vista à melhoria espiritual, a oração, a meditação, a santificação, a prática da lei do amor ou das boas obras. Também há os toques místicos. Não basta estudar e orar. Precisamos da intervenção direta do Espírito em nossas vidas, se tivermos de atingir qualquer grau apreciável de espiritualidade. O Espírito Santo pode intervir em nossas vidas por meio da iluminação. A iluminação espiritualiza as nossas mentes, e as nossas almas são profundamente transformadas. A meditação (que vide) é um método testado e honrado para ajudar-nos na experiência da iluminação. De algumas vezes, a iluminação é dada como dom de Deus, repentinamente. Porém, quando examinamos esses casos, verificamos que isso ocorre como recompensa pela vida cristã de alta qualidade. Isso ocorreu com Tomás de Aquino, — que, durante toda a vida, esteve ocupado na busca intelectual pela verdade, anotando as suas descobertas. Tomás de Aquino combinava isso com uma vida de santidade pessoal. Pouco tempo antes de sua morte, ele recebeu, subitamente, uma significativa iluminação, quando estava entrando na capela. Tão grande foi a iluminação recebida que ele declarou que todos os seus escritos anteriores pareciam palha, comparativamente falando. Vejo nessa experiência de Tomás de Aquino uma *recompensa* pela vida que ele viveu, do começo ao fim de sua intensa inquirição espiritual.

Por ocasião da *visão beatífica* (que vide), o crente recebe altíssima iluminação espiritual, mediante a qual chega a participar plenamente da mente de

CRISTO, DIVINDADE DE — CRISTO, MISSÃO UNIVERSAL DE

Cristo. Essa iluminação também nos transforma a alma. A participação na natureza divina torna-se uma realidade, embora em escala finita. Não obstante, a *mesma natureza* que Deus possui é compartilhada com os seus filhos (II Cor. 3:18; II Ped. 1:4). Possuir alguém a natureza divina, necessariamente o torna participante da natureza divina. Desse modo, a consciência torna-se *coletiva*, e não individual. Várias religiões orientais têm tido um discernimento, quanto a isso, que muitas religiões ocidentais têm perdido. Ali fala-se sobre a absorção do ser na pessoa de Deus, com a perda da individualidade. Isso exprime uma verdade, em certo sentido. A alma individual, assim absorvida, deixa de ser uma entidade isolada, passa a fazer parte da mente divina e a inteligência e o conhecimento tornam-se coletivos. Nesse sentido é que o indivíduo deixa de existir e não no sentido que a pessoa deixa de existir. Antes, a vida e a expressão individuais são preservadas, conforme já foi explicado. Visto que essa grandiosa participação na mente divina torna-se uma realidade, até certo ponto, mesmo na vida terrena, e, em grau mais pleno, na *imortalidade*, por meio do *Logos*, ao qual chamamos de *Cristo*, quando de sua encarnação, isso se denomina *Cristo-consciência*.

Paulo refere-se à iluminação espiritual em Efésios 1:17 ss. Não pode haver qualquer crescimento cristão considerável sem isso, e o Espírito de Deus está envolvido na questão, do começo ao fim. Atraímos a intervenção direta do Espírito de Deus, em nossas vidas, pela qualidade e sinceridade de nossa inquirição espiritual. Cumpre-nos usar todos os meios do desenvolvimento espiritual. O crente em desenvolvimento vai recebendo uma iluminação crescente. Quando esta atinge um grau suficientemente elevado, então o crente começa a participar da mente de Cristo de modo significativo. Desse modo, obtemos a Cristo-consciência, porquanto a consciência dele torna-se a nossa consciência; e isso nos envolve em uma vida comunal, e não apenas individual. Isso é um aspecto da própria salvação da alma. Em conexão com esse assunto, seria útil se o leitor examinasse o artigo sobre o *Misticismo*. Esse termo alude ao contacto direto da alma com poderes espirituais superiores, sendo esse o principal meio de crescimento e de conhecimento espirituais. As *revelações* são uma subcategoria do misticismo. Ver sobre *Revelações*.

CRISTO, DIVINDADE DE

Ver o artigo sobre a **Divindade de Cristo**.

CRISTO, ENVIADO DO PAI

O tema de que o Senhor Jesus foi enviado por parte de Deus Pai é reiterado por mais de quarenta vezes no evangelho de João, o que subentende os seguintes pontos:

1. A Preexistência de Cristo.
2. A sua missão divina messiânica, que visava a redenção dos homens.
3. A sua união com Deus Pai.
4. A sua autoridade, recebida da parte do pai.
5. O fato de que ele é o representante das regiões celestes.

«Quando a sua missão terrena houvesse de terminar, na sua morte, isso não significaria derrota, mas antes, o retorno a Deus Pai, até onde os seus inimigos não poderiam segui-lo. Essa declaração foi esclarecida ante os seus discípulos, tendo servido como mensagem de consolo. (Ver João 13:33; 14:19 e 16:16-19). Mas, para os seus opositores, serviu de mensagem de condenação». (Wilbert Howard, comentando acerca de João 7:33).

Referências: João 3:17; 4:34; 5:23,34, 36-38; 6:29, 38-40,44,57; 7:16,18,28,29,33; 8:16,18,26,29,42; 9:4; 10:36; 12:44,45,49; 13:16,20; 14:24; 15:21; 16:5; 17:3,18,21,23,25; 20:21.

CRISTO, FEITO PECADO

Ele o fez pecado por nós (II Cor. 5:2). Nem por isso o Senhor Jesus se tornou um «pecador», porquanto isso seria contra tudo o que é possível imaginar com respeito a Cristo, contrário também à declaração sobre sua impecabilidade. Essa frase fala antes de sua *total identificação* com os pecadores a fim de que possa ser reputado como um deles, já que se tornou o portador do pecado de todos eles. (Com essa declaração se pode comparar o trecho de Rom. 8:3, que declara que Deus enviou Cristo «...em semelhança de carne pecaminosa...»). Em Rom. 8:3, uma vez mais, não há nenhuma idéia de que Cristo tinha pecado; antes, ele se identificou totalmente com os pecadores, tendo tomado a natureza deles, mas não a natureza de Adão antes da queda, ou alguma natureza angelical. É verdade que Jesus tinha um corpo enfraquecido por causa da queda, a natureza pecaminosa do homem, mas sem qualquer pecado. (Comparar também com Gál. 3:13, onde aprendemos que Cristo se fez «maldição» por nós). Consideremos ainda os pontos seguintes:

1. A linguagem dessas vigorosas assertivas provavelmente se originou da tradição das ofertas judaicas, como a das ofertas pelo pecado e pela culpa, que aparecem no quarto capítulo do livro de Levítico, bem como a oferta do bode expiatório, no décimo sexto capítulo desse mesmo livro. De acordo com vários comentadores, pois, na realidade o «pecado» indica aqui a «oferta pelo pecado» (conforme afirmou Agostinho, com freqüência, em sua controvérsia contra os pelágios). Isso estaria em perfeito acordo com os tipos simbólicos judaicos que Paulo tão bem conhecia. Isso equivale a dizer que Cristo foi quem levou sobre si os nossos pecados. E não há que duvidar que sem importar o exato sentido dessa frase, o fato é que não podemos admitir qualquer forma de corrupção na pessoa de Cristo e em sua experiência expiatória.

2. Outros eruditos explicam aqui a palavra *pecado* como se isso indicasse a *natureza humana* sujeita ao sofrimento e à morte, resultados do pecado. Assim fala Rom. 8:3.

3. *Um mistério*. A expressão fala da nossa identificação mística com Cristo na sua morte, e nos efeitos da mesma. Nesta mesma identificação, temos uma fusão com ele na sua justiça e vida. Ele se identificou na nossa morte. Nós nos identificamos na sua vida. Na morte, ele tomou nossos pecados. Na vida, nós tomamos sua justiça.

CRISTO, HUMANIDADE DE

Ver o artigo sobre a **Humanidade de Cristo**.

CRISTO, LUZ DO MUNDO

Ver o artigo sobre a **Humanidade de Cristo**.

CRISTO, MEDIADOR, o ÚNICO

Ver **Mediador, Cristo, o Único**.

CRISTO, MISSÃO UNIVERSAL DE

Ver o artigo sobre a **Missão Universal de Cristo**.

CRISTO — CRISTO, O CORPO DE

CRISTO (LOGOS), MISSÃO UNIVERSAL DE
Ver o artigo sobre **Missão Universal do Logos (Cristo)**.

CRISTO-MISTICISMO

1. A expressão **em Cristo**, se encontra por 164 vezes nas epístolas de Paulo. Conforme a maioria dos intérpretes, ela indica comunhão mística. Os crentes, por meio do Espírito, desfrutam de um genuíno contacto com Cristo, por causa do que estão sendo transformados segundo a sua imagem, e, portanto, estão adquirindo suas qualidades morais e também metafísicas (ver as notas em Col. 2:10 no NTI).

2. Por conseguinte, a expressão subentende a participação no tipo de vida eterna que ele prometeu. (Ver o artigo sobre a *Vida Eterna*).

3. Estar *em Cristo* significa que o Espírito está conduzindo o crente de um estágio de glória para outro, *ad infinitum*. (Quanto a notas completas sobre esse conceito, ver II Cor. 3:18 no NTI). Fica obviamente implícita a presença habitadora do Espírito (no crente, como seu templo—ver as notas em Efé. 2:20 no NTI).

4. *Em Cristo*, os homens têm salvação, ou seja, a participação na própria forma de vida que Deus tem, a sua vida necessária e independente (ver no NTI as notas em João 5:25,26, e sobre a *salvação*, em Heb. 2:3). A salvação é mediada através da filiação (ver Rom. 8:14-17), e nenhum indivíduo fora de Cristo (e, portanto, que não esteja «nele»), poderá aspirar a ser salvo.

5. Portanto, estar *em Cristo* significa participar da inteira plenitude de Deus (ver Efé. 3:19), isto é, possuir os seus atributos divinos, com base na participação em sua natureza.

6. Em segundo lugar, a expressão quer dizer «estar identificado com a comunidade cristã». Isso confere ao crente um novo endereço. Portanto, todo o crente tem dois endereços, um deles puramente humano, a localidade onde ele vive; o outro é de ordem espiritual, a identificação com Cristo e a sua comunidade remida.

7. Essa expressão também fala de nossa união com Cristo, em seus aspectos presente e eterno. Esse é o tema mais freqüente dos escritos de Paulo.

No trecho de Rom. 6:3, aprendemos que fomos todos «batizados em Cristo». Uma vez mais, a comunhão ou participação em uma nova vida é o tema central. Em Rom. 8:10 lemos que Cristo está em nós. Podemos notar, em I Cor. 1:2, que esse estar em Cristo atua como elemento santificador. O trecho de I Cor. 1:30, por sua vez, mostra-nos que isso significa a obtenção da sabedoria, da retidão, da santificação e da redenção que há em Cristo. E a passagem de II Cor. 5:17 ensina-nos que aqueles que estão em Cristo devem ser, necessariamente, novas criaturas, seres que perenemente estão sendo transformados, até que Cristo seja perfeitamente formado neles. (Ver II Cor. 3:18 e as notas expositivas a respeito, no NTI, quanto a esse tema). Ora, o alvo final de tudo isso é a perfeição absoluta. (Ver Rom. 8:28). E Efé. 2:13 é a passagem que mostra que o estado de alienação de Deus é eliminado por essa nova participação na vida de Cristo. Essa, pois, é a comunhão mística do corpo com a cabeça, da Noiva com o Noivo celeste.

Estar em Cristo, outrossim, significa estar em uma nova *posição escatológica*, isto é, sob o favor divino, no tocante ao segundo advento de Cristo e ao julgamento final, bem como no que concerne às realizações potenciais da eternidade. Mas está envolvido ainda mais do que isso, conforme as notas expositivas acima demonstram. Ver as referências seguintes, que usam essa expressão: Rom. 3:24; 6:3; 8:1,10; 12:5; 13:14; 16:7; I Cor. 1:2,4,30; 3:11; 15:22; 16:24; II Cor. 5:17; 13:5; Gál. 2:20,21; 3:27,28; 5:6; Efé. 1:1,3; 2:13; 3:17; Fil. 1:21; 3:3; Col. 1:27; 3:3,11 e II Tim. 2:1,10.

CRISTO, MITO DE Ver **Mito de Cristo**.

CRISTO, O CORPO DE

No Novo Testamento, essa expressão é empregada de três modos diversos:

1. *O Corpo Humano e Literal de Jesus Cristo*. O trecho de Hebreus 10:5 ensina que foi preparado um corpo humano para o Filho de Deus. Mateus e Lucas narram o nascimento virginal de Jesus. Lucas 2:21 é trecho que menciona a sua circuncisão. I João 4:2,3 negam o valor do ensino docético dos gnósticos, os quais se tornaram incômodos nos tempos da Igreja primitiva. Eles negavam que Jesus tivesse um verdadeiro corpo humano (o qual, para eles, seria apenas uma ilusão), ou então afirmavam que o Espírito de Cristo viera tomar posse do homem Jesus, embora fosse uma entidade diferente dele. Ver o artigo sobre o *Docetismo*. Contrastando com isso, o Novo Testamento ensina tanto a realidade do corpo físico de Jesus quanto a identidade de Jesus-Cristo, como uma única pessoa. Seu corpo padecia dos limites ordinários que os homens enfrentam, com seus problemas e necessidades (Heb. 5:7,8). Foi um corpo humano real que foi cravado na cruz (João 19:34,35; Heb. 10:20). Quando da ressurreição, o soerguimento físico, corporal de Jesus é enfatizado nos evangelhos (Mat. 28:9; Luc. 24:37-40). A ressurreição e a glorificação do corpo físico de Jesus garantem a ressurreição e a glorificação dos crentes (I Cor. 15:20-23).

2. *O Corpo de Cristo Simbolizado na Ceia do Senhor*. Os católicos romanos e os luteranos supõem que há uma genuína presença do corpo de Cristo nos elementos da Ceia do Senhor ou Eucaristia. Isso é explicado com base na substância do corpo, que não é igual aos seus meros acidentes. Ver o artigo sobre a *Transubstanciação*. A maioria dos protestantes supõe que passagens como Mat. 26:26; Mar. 14:22; Luc. 22:19 e I Cor. 11:24 indicam como o pão *simboliza* o corpo de Cristo. Quando Jesus fez a declaração ali constante, ele só pôde ter falado metaforicamente, porque o pão continuou sendo pão, e ele continuou dono do seu próprio corpo físico. O que ele quis dizer é que se dava gratuitamente em favor de todos, espiritualmente falando, tal como partira o pão e o distribuíra gratuitamente entre os seus discípulos. E agora, o seu dom espiritual é recebido mediante a fé no coração. Os méritos de cada lado da questão são discutidos no artigo aludido. Ver também sobre *Jesus como o Pão da Vida*.

3. *A Igreja*. Cristo é a Cabeça, e a Igreja é o seu corpo (Efé. 1:22,23 e 4:15,16). O corpo de Cristo, a Igreja, tem muitos membros cada qual dotado de uma função específica, tal como sucede a um corpo físico humano (Rom. 12:4-8; I Cor. 12:4-31). A Igreja universal é o corpo místico de Cristo. É um corpo místico por não ser palpável, por ser uma união espiritual, um *organismo espiritual*, e não alguma organização. Cada membro desse organismo espiritual está diretamente relacionado a Cristo como a Cabeça, que é quem dá poder, controla e inspira. O

trecho de Efésios 2:11 ss. enfatiza a união entre judeus e gentios, dentro desse corpo. Na epístola aos Colossenses, a unidade do *cosmos* inteiro, sob a liderança de Cristo, está em pauta (Col. 1:16-19 e 2:10).

Implicações Possíveis da Metáfora. 1. A participação da comunidade na mesa do Senhor sugere que os muitos membros da comunidade participam de tudo em união, tal como acontece a um corpo humano, com seus diversos membros (I Cor. 10:16,17). 2. Os filósofos estóicos também falavam em uma eclesia ou reunião pública, chamando-a de corpo unificado, composto de muitos indivíduos, que são os membros daquela comunidade. Paulo tinha conhecimento das idéias estóicas, e tomou por empréstimo certas dessas metáforas, em seus ensinamentos éticos, sendo possível que a sua metáfora do corpo humano tenha sido influenciada por essa filosofia. 3. Israel, no Antigo Testamento, algumas vezes é retratado como uma *personalidade corporal*, como na figura simbólica da vinha, em Salmos 80:8. Isso sugere um corpo e seus respectivos membros. 4. O crente é intimamente identificado com Cristo em seus sofrimentos, da mesma forma que um membro qualquer do corpo compartilha dos sofrimentos de outros membros, porquanto formam uma única unidade (ver Atos 9:4,5 e Col. 1:24).

Implicações Teológicas. 1. A redenção é comunal, e não uma questão meramente pessoal. O corpo inteiro terá de ser remido, ou a obra ficará incompleta. 2. A participação em um destino comum faz parte óbvia da metáfora. Esse destino é muito elevado e glorioso. 3. A participação na mesma natureza, no caso da Cabeça e de todos os membros do corpo, sem dúvida faz parte do quadro. Isso transparece em passagens onde a metáfora não é incorporada, como II Pedro 1:4; Colossenses 2:10. Ver os artigos sobre a *Transformação Segundo a Imagem de Cristo* e sobre a *Salvação*. 4. A Igreja, em sua função e propósito, é uma extensão da *encarnação* de Cristo (que vide), realizando a sua obra, vivendo a sua vida e manifestando o seu poder e a sua glória. 5. O trecho de Efésios 1:23 mostra-nos que isso prosseguirá no estado eterno. A Igreja continuará sendo composta por membros do corpo de Cristo, e funcionará como uma força remidora e restauradora entre todos os seres inteligentes, contribuindo para que Cristo *preencha todas as coisas*. Isso fornece-nos alguma indicação da obra da Igreja, no estado para além da vida física. Trata-se da mesma obra, mas elevada a um nível superior, operando em esferas espirituais, e não em esferas físicas. (HANS NTI Z)

CRISTO, TENTAÇÃO DE

No grego, «tentar» é **peiradzo**, que significa «submeter a teste». Essa palavra é usada por trinta e seis vezes no Novo Testamento, desde Mat. 4:1 até Apo. 3:10. a. Esse teste pode ser concebido em um bom sentido, como quando Deus prova a alguém, a fim de determinar o seu caráter e potencial espiritual, segundo se vê em Gênesis 22:1 ou no livro de Jó. Essa sondagem pode ter aspectos positivos, no desenvolvimento do caráter espiritual da pessoa. b. Tentar ao erro e ao pecado, em sentido negativo, como na epístola de Tiago. Ali é dito que Deus não tenta a ninguém, mas que o homem é tentado por causa das suas próprias concupiscências, a fazer o que é errado (Tia. 1:13,14).

1. *As Escrituras*. Trechos bíblicos como Mat. 4:1-11; Mar. 1:12,13; Luc. 4:1-13; Heb. 2:18; 4:15,16; Heb. 2:18 e 4:15 mostram que Jesus foi tentado quanto a todos os pontos possíveis, ao longo de sua vida, e não meramente no incidente relatado no começo dos evangelhos sinópticos.

2. *Presumível Lugar da Tentação de Cristo*. O local tradicional da tentação é o monte Quarantina, localizado não muito distante da presumível localidade onde Jesus teria sido batizado por João Batista. Marcos 1:12 diz que, imediatamente após o seu batismo, Jesus dirigiu-se ao lugar onde foi tentado pelo diabo; daí a conexão entre os dois lugares. Essa colina é a mais elevada que há nas imediações, de onde se divisa uma visão espetacular do vale do rio Jordão. É um lugar de desolação, o que concorda com as descrições bíblicas a respeito.

3. *Circunstâncias*. A carreira inicial de Jesus foi um período de reconhecimento do Messias, pelo que houve a voz proveniente do céu: «Tu és o meu Filho amado, em ti me comprazo» (Luc. 3:22). O ministério público de Jesus estava a ponto de começar, e um grande Mestre precisava ser submetido à prova, para que ficasse certo de que ele era poderoso, pois, do contrário, não podia ensinar ao povo.

4. *Natureza da Tentação de Jesus*. Essa tentação envolveu as várias áreas enumeradas no trecho de I João 2:16, a saber: a. *A concupiscência da carne*. Jesus havia jejuado e, presumivelmente, seria tentado a transformar pedras em pães, a fim de satisfazer sua fome física. Essa tentação foi por ele repelida com base em Deuteronômio 8:3. O homem não vive só de pão; pois jamais pode olvidar-se do pão espiritual, ou não poderá ser um mestre. b. *A concupiscência dos olhos*. Jesus poderia ser tentado a fazer algo que prontamente conquistasse a admiração pública. Seria um espetáculo, se ele se tivesse lançado do pináculo do templo, e tivesse sobrevivido. Talvez esse pináculo fosse o pórtico de Salomão, que se elevava a mais de noventa metros de altura, acima do vale do Cedrom. Jesus poderia desafiar a providência divina, fazendo reivindicações desnecessárias da parte da mesma. Mas ele recusou-se a fazer tal coisa. Saul cedeu diante de uma tentação similar, quando ofereceu um sacrifício que cabia exclusivamente ao sacerdote Samuel. c. *O orgulho da vida*. A Jesus foi oferecido um imenso poder, facilitado pelo «deus» deste mundo, que era capaz de cumprir a sua oferta. Mas isso teria envolvido a abjeta adoração a esse falso «deus», e isso, naturalmente, seria contrário ao mandamento de Deus de que se deve adorar exclusivamente a Deus (Deu. 6:10 e 10:20).

5. *Teologia da Tentação de Cristo*. O Messias precisava ser tentado a fim de comprovar o seu caráter espiritual. Ninguém haverá de seguir um mestre que não foi devidamente testado. Ver Heb. 2:18 e 4:15. Em sua humanidade, Jesus precisava desenvolver-se à semelhança de todos os filhos de Deus. Ele foi *aperfeiçoado* mediante as coisas que sofreu (Heb. 2:10). Isso serve de indicação de sua autêntica humanidade, bem como de sua identificação com os homens, em sua encarnação. Ver o artigo sobre a *Humanidade de Cristo*.

Jesus Poderia ter Caído em Pecado? As Escrituras declaram que Jesus foi tentado em todos os pontos, à nossa semelhança, embora nunca tivesse caído em pecado (Heb. 4:15). Lemos em II Coríntios 5:21: «Àquele que não conheceu pecado, o fez pecado por nós...» Impõe-se, pois, a indagação: Jesus poderia ter caído em transgressão? Bons intérpretes dão-nos respostas contraditórias. Se a nossa explicação partir do ângulo de sua divindade, então teremos de responder com um «não», pois, como é patente, Deus não pode ser pecador. Mas, se nossa resposta partir do ponto de vista de sua humanidade, então teremos de responder afirmativamente, porquanto a natureza humana sempre estará sujeita ao pecado. E, se tomarmos essa última posição, poderemos argumentar que, a menos que Jesus tivesse podido pecar, a vida pura que ele viveu revestir-se-ia de menor significação para nós. Se Jesus tivesse enfrentado tentações, mas não tivesse podido ceder diante das mesmas, com base em sua superior natureza (divina ou humana), então o fato de que ele não cedeu teria pouca significação para nós. Alguns intérpretes supõem que afirmar que Jesus não poderia ter pecado, é retroceder ao *docetismo* (que vide), que não reconhece a humanidade autêntica de Cristo. Não há que duvidar que as modernas Igrejas evangélicas têm caído nesse erro, embora professem verbalmente que acreditam na verdadeira humanidade de Jesus Cristo. Ver o artigo sobre a *Humanidade de Cristo*. Ver também sobre a *Divindade de Cristo*.

Um outro Argumento. Embora fosse um **ser humano**, ainda assim Jesus não teria podido pecar. Pode-se arquitetar um argumento em prol de um Jesus impecável, inteiramente à parte de considerações sobre a sua divindade. Se Jesus tivesse sido um grande mestre espiritual, que tivesse encontrado solução para o problema do pecado, mesmo no *nível humano*, inteiramente à parte de sua natureza divina, então ele poderia ter sido o tipo de ser que simplesmente não sentia tentação para cair em pecado. Essa impecabilidade poderia basear-se em seu desenvolvimento espiritual superior, como simples homem. Alguns eruditos supõem que até mesmo pessoas comuns podem chegar ao ponto da inteira santificação, embora também suponham que, uma vez atingido esse elevado estágio de desenvolvimento espiritual, o indivíduo pode cair novamente em pecado. Suponhamos, entretanto, que Jesus tivesse alcançado esse elevado estágio espiritual, mas de modo tão magnificente que *não houvesse chance* dele retroceder ao pecado. É apenas lógico supor que a natureza humana pode chegar a esse ponto. Um grande poder espiritual poderia chegar a esse nível de desenvolvimento, mesmo sem ser um ente divino.

A Doutrina da Polaridade. Talvez fosse útil aplicar, neste ponto, a doutrina da **polaridade** (que vide). Certas verdades não podem ser devidamente entendidas, a menos que consideremos os seus dois pólos. Por conseguinte, ninguém pode, realmente, compreender as doutrinas do livre-arbítrio ou do determinismo, sem levar ambos esses lados em consideração. Na verdade, esses são os dois pólos de uma verdade maior. Outro tanto ocorre no caso das doutrinas da divindade e da humanidade de Cristo. Isso envolve um grande mistério. Em uma única pessoa, Jesus Cristo, encontramos os dois elementos: o divino e o humano. Ninguém pode compreender o Jesus-Logos-Cristo sem examinar os pólos opostos desse conceito. Isso posto, considerando o problema que indaga se Jesus podia ter pecado, precisamos considerar seriamente tanto as respostas afirmativas quanto as respostas negativas, visto que ambas nos dão indicações sobre a verdade maior envolvida. Não obstante, terminamos com um mistério essencial. Meus amigos, nossa teologia não resolve e nem mesmo pode solucionar todos os problemas. E o problema que ora ventilamos pode ser um daqueles problemas insolúveis.

Conclusão. Quanto a mim mesmo, considerando todas as facetas do problema, penso que a melhor explicação é aquela que diz que Jesus, embora um ser humano, desenvolveu um tipo de *humanidade ideal* de acordo com a qual o problema do pecado simplesmente inexistia. Ele, simplesmente, estava acima da possibilidade de cair em pecado. Devemos nos lembrar que o pecado não faz parte necessária do ser humano; foi-lhe imposto por ocasião da queda. O pecado é uma perversão da verdadeira humanidade. Em conseqüência, é perfeitamente possível que Jesus, possuidor de uma *humanidade verdadeira*, estivesse totalmente acima do problema do pecado. Portanto, inteiramente à parte da questão de sua divindade, Cristo não somente era impecável, mas também nem podia ser tentado a pecar. Essa é a estatura moral que buscamos, e onde haveremos de chegar. Antes mesmo de chegarmos a esse ponto, também estamos sendo transformados de modo a compartilhar moralmente das virtudes positivas de Deus, como o amor, a gentileza, a bondade, etc., que constituem o lado positivo de nossa transformação moral. Essa transformação moral provoca a transformação metafísica, visto que a santificação (que vide) é imprescindível à transformação metafísica e à glorificação final. Essa glorificação inclui a participação na própria natureza divina (II Ped. 1:4), um importantíssimo princípio moral, ao qual dou uma posição secundária nesta discussão. Muitos problemas precisam ser examinados desse ponto de vista. *Não acredito* que possamos solucionar a questão da impecabilidade de Jesus, nem a questão de sua incapacidade de pecar, meramente apelando para a sua divindade. Isso deixa sem solução muitos problemas relacionados à sua humanidade, e esta é uma doutrina por demais negligenciada em nossas igrejas evangélicas modernas. Os pais alexandrinos da Igreja, entretanto, pensavam que Jesus, como ser humano, também era preexistente, e que a sua elevada espiritualidade, como ser humano, derivava-se dessa preexistência como um *espírito humano*. As duas naturezas de Jesus, a divina e a humana, existem por causa de uma fusão que ocorreu em face de sua encarnação. Eram preexistentes tanto o princípio divino quanto o princípio humano, e ambos esses princípios estavam presentes na encarnação. Isso envolve um grande mistério, e coisa alguma que possamos dizer aqui satisfará a todas as perguntas que sejam levantadas. De fato, não há maneira inteiramente satisfatória de alguém manifestar-se sobre esse assunto. As teologias usualmente exageram um ou outro lado da questão, ou enfatizam um aspecto para ignorar totalmente o outro.

Quanto ao que um Jesus impecável, que não poderia pecar, deveria significar para nós, digo que ele tornou-se o *modelo* de uma *humanidade ideal* que não somente podemos, mas que, finalmente, *devemos* emular. Isso é verdade porque não pode haver glorificação sem a santificação absoluta (Heb. 12:14). Portanto, apesar de seu exemplo estar, agora, fora de nosso alcance, não será para sempre. Ele é o *Pioneiro* no caminho (Heb. 2:10); seremos transformados à sua imagem e participaremos na sua natureza divina (II Ped. 1:4, Rom. 8:29, II Cor. 3:18, Efé. 3:19).

CRISTO, ÚNICO MEDIADOR
Ver **Mediador, Cristo, o Único**.

CRISTO VIVO
Esse título enfatiza um importante aspecto da doutrina de Cristo (que vide). Ver sobre *Cristologia*. Faz parte das tendências dos evangélicos conservadores, em primeiro lugar, ignorarem a humanidade de Jesus, perdendo-se em meio a complexos argumentos sobre a sua deidade. Esquecem-se de que há uma

importante mensagem para nós na humanidade de Cristo, e não apenas em sua divindade. Ver sobre a *Humanidade de Cristo*. Esses estudiosos têm exibido a tendência, mediante o destaque exagerado sobre os credos, de se esquecerem que a doutrina cristã fala sobre um Cristo que continua vivo e pode e quer fazer parte de nossa vida diária, mediante a influência do seu Espírito. Em outras palavras, é possível alguém salientar a letra do Novo Testamento, olvidando-se do Espírito. Mas sempre será uma verdade que a letra mata, mas o Espírito vivifica.

Por sua parte, os cristãos liberais, no seu afã de redescobrirem o Jesus histórico e de demitizarem as narrativas evangélicas, chegam a ignorar e a mostrar-se céticos diante da doutrina de um Cristo vivo que, através do contacto místico, pode entrar em contacto conosco, influenciando-nos poderosamente a vida diária. Mas, apesar de que houve um Jesus histórico, que foi o Cristo (o Messias dos judeus), e apesar de que haverá um Cristo escatológico, que intervirá futuramente na história humana, também há um Cristo vivo, que nos convida a aprender que há um poder espiritual posto à nossa disposição, para o dia de hoje, e não somente para ontem ou para amanhã.

A operação de Deus, por meio do Cristo vivo, faz violento contraste com a lei mosaica, que sempre exige, mas não é um poder impulsionador e produtivo. A mensagem cristã inclui o anúncio que Jesus, em sua missão terrena, trouxe toda uma nova expressão espiritual para nós. Também faz parte dessa mensagem que o Espírito Santo, em sua atual operação, faz a missão de Cristo tornar-se uma realidade viva para nós. A lei já foi o mestre do mundo religioso. Mas agora esse Mestre é Cristo, e a lei é apenas uma de suas servas. A lei era uma excelente legislação moral. Mas a lei do Espírito é um meio de transformação presente, de tal modo que a imagem de Cristo vai sendo formada nos crentes. Finalmente, eles passarão a compartilhar da própria natureza divina (II Ped. 1:4). Hesíodo, o poeta grego, especulou acerca da possibilidade da *psyche* (alma humana) tornar-se um *daemon* (divindade, de acordo com o uso clássico dessa palavra grega). A resposta cristã é um avanço monoteísta e patrístico para além dessa especulação. É um avanço monoteísta porque o Deus eterno, em três Pessoas, sempre é ímpar e infinito. Mas a alma humana só pode tornar-se divina em sentido finito, embora de modo crescente, crescendo sempre na participação na própria natureza de Deus e em seus atributos. Naturalmente, devemos conceber um processo eterno, visto que a finitude deverá ir sendo absorvida pela infinitude de Deus. Visto que há uma infinitude que nos haverá de encher, também deverá haver um preenchimento infinito (Efé. 1:23). Isso requer o avanço de um estágio de glória para o próximo, mediante o poder transformador do Espírito (II Cor. 3:18). É precisamente nesse ponto que a doutrina do Cristo vivo torna-se tão importante, por ser a garantia da concretização desse elevado desígnio divino. De acordo com a transformação metafísica, há também — a transformação moral —, sem a qual se torna impossível qualquer avanço espiritual (Heb. 12:14). O Cristo vivo é a criatividade de Deus liberada na história humana. E a resposta cristã à especulação de Hesíodo (ver acima) é uma resposta patrística porque Deus Pai é o grande alvo de toda a existência, na direção do qual iremos caminhando passo a passo. Isso ocorrerá por ocasião da restauração de tudo (que vide) quando Deus será tudo em todos (ver I Cor. 15:25-28).

Como é liberada a criatividade de Deus? Foram preparados para nós diversos meios que permitem que o Cristo vivo opere em nós. Poderíamos intitulá-los «meios de crescimento espiritual». Eis a lista: 1. O estudo das Escrituras Sagradas e outros livros que tendem a edificar-nos a espiritualidade, aumentando o nosso *conhecimento* útil. O intelecto, por si só, é capaz de uma maravilhosa obra de transformação. 2. O uso da oração e de sua irmã gêmea, a meditação. A oração busca a Deus, falando com ele, pedindo e recebendo. A meditação espera que Deus fale, de tal modo que o crente possa ser informado intuitiva e misticamente. Porém, a meditação também pode envolver a comunhão com o Ser divino, não sendo apenas um meio para recebermos conhecimento. 3. O caminho da santificação. A nossa transformação espiritual é impedida pelo pecado e pela ausência das virtudes espirituais. A santificação liberta-nos do pecado e leva-nos a participar das virtudes de Deus, em Cristo. 4. O caminho das boas obras, ou seja, o uso da *lei do amor*. A maior de todas as verdades morais é a lei do amor, que requer que sirvamos ao próximo. 5. O toque místico, que nos vem através da iluminação, mediante a meditação, com o uso dos dons espirituais e outras experiências místicas, que põem a nossa alma em contacto com o Ser divino. Ver o artigo sobre o *Misticismo*. É grandioso sermos capazes de ler a Bíblia e orar. Porém, há outros meios de desenvolvimento espiritual que precisam ser empregados, se o Cristo vivo tiver de mostrar-se atuante em nós, hoje em dia.

CRISTOLOGIA

Esboço:
1. Várias Definições
2. A Base Bíblica
3. A Cristologia nos Concílios e nas Controvérsias
4. Declarações Cristológicas dos Pais da Igreja
5. Outros Desenvolvimentos e Opiniões
6. O Mistério

1. Várias Definições

Schleiermacher definiu o cristianismo como um «monoteísmo — em que tudo está vinculado a Cristo, o Redentor». É impossível alguém conceber uma versão da religião cristã à parte da posição central ocupada por Cristo. De fato, não podemos entender o cristianismo sem o Cristocentrismo. A cristologia, pois, é o nome da interpretação teológica do sentido da pessoa e da obra de Cristo, e, como tal, é uma definição da natureza essencial do próprio cristianismo. Ver o artigo sobre o *Cristianismo*. A preocupação central da cristologia é a doutrina da pessoa e da obra de Jesus Cristo. Diz respeito à sua natureza divino-humana, à sua encarnação, à sua revelação de Deus, aos seus milagres, aos seus ensinamentos, à sua morte expiatória, à sua ressurreição e ascensão, à sua intercessão em nosso favor, à sua parousia, ao seu ofício de Juiz, à sua posição de Cabeça de todas as coisas, à sua centralidade dentro do mistério da vontade de Deus, dentro da restauração (que vide). Ver o artigo separado sobre *Cristo*. Na introdução àquele artigo, vários outros artigos são mencionados, relativos ao assunto, suplementando o que é dito aqui.

2. A Base Bíblica

a. *No Antigo Testamento*. A cristologia começa no Antigo Testamento, onde encontramos muitos textos de prova, usados pelos cristãos, para mostrar que Jesus Cristo era uma figura predita, tendo cumprido a expectativa messiânica do povo judeu. O trecho de

CRISTOLOGIA

Gênesis 3:15 dá início à lista desses textos de prova. Nas notas expositivas no NTI, em Atos 3:22, ofereço uma lista das profecias messiânicas que se cumpriram em Jesus; e essa lista consiste de cerca de quarenta referências extraídas do Antigo Testamento, com suas contrapartes neotestamentárias. O leitor pode encontrar essa mesma lista, nesta enciclopédia, no artigo *Profecias do Antigo Testamento Cumpridas em Jesus*.

b. *No Novo Testamento*:

i. *Humanidade*. A humanidade de Cristo é subentendida em todas as páginas do Novo Testamento. Ele nasceu como um bebê, de uma mãe humana, cresceu, aprendeu, experimentou fome, ansiedade, dúvida, desapontamento, surpresa e foi aperfeiçoado, pelo que sofreu, foi humilhado, padeceu e morreu. Ver as seguintes referências: Luc. 2:40; 7:9; Mar. 2:15; 14:33; 15:34; Gál. 4:4; João 1:14; Heb. 2:9,10; 5:7,8; Mat. 27:1 ss. Quanto ao desenvolvimento desse assunto, ver o artigo sobre a *Humanidade de Cristo*.

ii. *Impecabilidade*. Embora fosse um ser humano, é declarado que ele não cometeu pecado. (Ver Heb. 4:15; II Cor. 5:21; I Ped. 2:22). Porém, poderia ele ter caído em pecado? Quanto a essa pergunta, ver o artigo sobre *Cristo, Tentação de*, sob o quinto item, *A Teologia da Tentação de Cristo*; e ver também sobre a *Impecabilidade de Jesus*.

iii. *Filho do Homem*. Em Mateus 8:20, onde a humanidade de Cristo está em pauta, ele aparece como um homem típico ou representativo, ou seja, a humanidade é ilustrada em Cristo. Porém, o trecho de Marcos 14:62 tem o título «Filho do homem» com o trecho de Daniel 7:13 em mente, aquela figura celestial e elevada autoridade espiritual, um ideal que representa o povo de Deus. Esse título também pode salientar a sua humildade e aparente insignificância (Mar. 2:10; 2:28; Luc. 12:19). O evangelho de João usa o título em contextos que enfatizam sua preexistência (João 2:13 ss; 6:62 ss e 8:6 ss). Nos escritos de Paulo, ele é o homem descido do céu, o segundo Adão (Rom. 5 e I Cor. 15).

iv. *Servo*. Jesus é Aquele que cumpre supremamente a vontade de Deus, e, dessa maneira, serve melhor aos homens. Ele é o Servo Sofredor retratado no livro de Isaías. Ver Mat. 12:18; Mar. 10:45; Luc. 24:26. Foi na qualidade de Servo que Cristo ofereceu a si mesmo pelos pecados do seu povo (João 1:29; Isa. 53).

v. *Humilhação*. Por ocasião da encarnação (que vide), ele deixou de lado a sua glória celestial, a fim de poder obter glória para os homens (Fil. 2:5 ss, João 1:14).

vi. *Encarnação*. O Logos encarnou-se na forma de Jesus (João 1:14). Da mesma maneira que ele assumiu a natureza humana, assim também o homem, por intermédio dele, haverá de assumir a sua natureza divina (Rom. 8:29; II Cor. 3:18; Col. 2:10; II Ped. 1:4). Ver o artigo sobre a *Encarnação*.

vii. *Cristo, o Messias*. Em sua encarnação, Cristo tomou sobre si mesmo a incumbência de cumprir a missão do Messias, que é chamado Cristo, em grego. (Ver Atos 10:38; João 1:41; Rom. 9:5). Ver o artigo sobre o Messias, e o artigo sobre o *Cristo*.

viii. *Divindade*. A encarnação consistiu no fato de que o Logos de Deus tornou-se o homem Jesus. Ora, o Logos é Deus (João 1:1). O Filho do homem é, por igual modo, o Filho de Deus (Mat. 11:27; Mar. 13:32; João 20:17). O Filho e o Pai são um só (João 5:19,30; 16:32). Ele vive cheio de toda a plenitude de Deus (Gál. 2:9). Quanto a completos detalhes sobre essa questão, ver o artigo sobre a *Divindade de Cristo*.

ix. *O Logos*. Ver João 1:1. Neste particular, a filosofia é empregada, porque a doutrina do Logos tem uma longa história na filosofia e foi tomada por empréstimo pela cristologia. Foi um apto subsídio para ajudar a expressar a divindade de Cristo, e isso mediante a idéia da encarnação. Ver o artigo sobre o *Verbo*, quanto a detalhes completos sobre a questão.

x. *O Redentor*. A realização expiatória de Cristo, vinculada a outros aspectos de sua missão, produz a redenção. Ver Rom. 3:24; 8:23; I Cor. 1:30; Col. 1:14; Heb. 9:12,15. Ver o artigo sobre a *Redenção*, e também sobre a *Expiação*.

xi. *O Restaurador de Tudo*. Ver o trecho de Efésios 1:10 quanto ao mistério da vontade de Deus, que é a restauração universal em torno de Cristo. Ver o artigo sobre a *Restauração*.

xii. *O Senhor de Tudo*. Cristo não é apenas o Salvador. Ele também é o Senhor. E, no devido tempo, haverá de impor o seu senhorio sobre todas as coisas, de modo palpável e evidente. Doutra sorte, seu caráter de Salvador seria anulado. Ver Rom. 10:9,10; Fil. 2:11. Ver o artigo sobre o *Senhorio de Cristo*.

xiii. *Mediador*. Ver o trecho de Heb. 7:24 ss, quanto ao ofício de Cristo de Mediador e Sumo Sacerdote (que vide).

3. A Cristologia nos Concílios e nas Controvérsias

a. *Antes do Concílio de Nicéia* (que vide), as seguintes doutrinas eram correntes, várias das quais influenciadas pelo neoplatonismo (que vide): o *ebionismo* (que vide). Era de origem judaica. Negava a encarnação. Jesus seria apenas humano. O *docetismo* (que vide). Era de origem gnóstica. Cristo seria um elevado poder espiritual, pois seria um anjo, sendo divino apenas em sentido secundário; e a sua natureza humana seria apenas uma representação teatral. O *basilidianismo* (que vide), ensinava que Cristo tornou-se divino por ocasião de seu batismo em água. Os *alogoi* (que vide) e os *artemonitas* (que vide), ensinavam que Jesus era humano, embora impulsionado por uma energia divina. O *patripassianismo* (que vide), ensinava que só há um Deus, chamado, alternativamente, Pai ou Filho, pelo que o próprio Pai foi crucificado. O *sabelianismo* (que vide), dizia que o Filho é apenas um dos três modos pelos quais a Substância Divina costuma manifestar-se.

b. *O Arianismo* (que vide). Esse sistema opunha-se diretamente à cristologia defendida pelo credo Niceno. Esse credo afirmava que Cristo foi eternamente gerado, não fazendo parte da criação de Deus. Além disso, esse credo declarava Cristo da mesma substância que o Pai. Ário (que vide), em contraste, afirmava que Cristo possuía tanto a natureza divina quanto a natureza humana, embora tivesse sido criado em um tempo definido, por um ato da vontade de Deus. Seria subordinado a Deus e teria uma substância *diferente*. Portanto, só o Pai seria o verdadeiro Deus.

c. *Cristologias que Provocaram Declarações de Concílios*. O *apolinarianismo* (que vide) foi um dos assuntos tratados pelo concílio de Calcedônia, de 451 D.C. Esse sistema ensina que Cristo era possuidor de corpo humano, mas que o *Logos* (ver sobre o *Verbo*) veio a ser a alma humana de Jesus. Portanto, foi criado um ser divino que não tinha alma humana. Nesse concílio também foi denunciado o *Nestorianismo* (que vide), sistema que asseverava que Cristo tinha tanto a natureza divina quanto a natureza humana, mas sem haver comunicação entre as duas. O *eutiquianismo* (que vide) ensinava que Cristo possuía as duas naturezas, embora a natureza humana tivesse sido inteiramente absorvida pela natureza divina, pelo que tudo quanto Cristo fazia era

CRISTOLOGIA

divino. Todas essas doutrinas foram condenadas pelo concílio de Calcedônia, e as doutrinas do credo niceno foram confirmadas.

d. *Cristologias que Levaram ao Concílio de Constantinopla III, em 689 D.C.* O *monofisitismo* (que vide), ensinava que Cristo tinha apenas uma natureza, a humana, que era uma espécie de qualidade contingente da natureza divina. O *monotelitismo* (que vide), ensinava que, visto ser Cristo apenas uma pessoa, ele também só tem uma vontade. O concílio de Constantinopla III opôs-se a essas idéias e reafirmou a posição assumida no concílio de Calcedônia.

e. O *protestantismo* (que vide), exibe muitas formas em sua cristologia. Os protestantes conservadores têm cristologias bastante similares, se não mesmo idênticas às do catolicismo ortodoxo, mas vários ramos do protestantismo têm adotado idéias dos *ismos* acima mencionados. O protestantismo, de modo geral, usa de cuidados para resguardar sua cristologia de uma indevida invasão da exagerada exaltação a Maria, mãe de Jesus, a fim de que Cristo receba toda a glória. Isso resulta também no fato de seu ofício como *mediador* é preservado de infrações.

4. Declarações Cristológicas de Vários Pais da Igreja

a. *Os Pais Apostólicos,* 90-140 D.C., como Clemente de Roma, referiram-se a Cristo em termos exaltados, refletindo os ensinamentos do Novo Testamento. Em II Clemente encontramos: «Irmãos, devemos pensar sobre Jesus Cristo como Deus, como o Juiz dos vivos e dos mortos». Esses pais combateram os ebionitas e os docéticos.

b. *Os Apologistas. Justino* (cerca de 100-165 D.C.) e *Teófilo* de Antioquia defenderam o evangelho ante os ataques dos pagãos. A doutrina do Logos era o principal instrumento de defesa cristã, com a incorporação de fortes argumentos e tendências filosóficas. De acordo com o pensamento platônico, o Logos teria assumido posição inferior à do Pai, mas essa também é uma idéia paulina do Filho, quando este é visto na humilhação de sua encarnação (I Cor. 15:58). *Melito* de Sardes aludia a Cristo como Deus e como homem. Suas datas foram 140-200 D.C. Ele atacou o gnosticismo e expôs um ponto de vista bíblico de Cristo. *Tertuliano* (cerca de 160-220 D.C.) combateu o gnosticismo e o monarquianismo ou sabelianismo. Ele foi o primeiro dos pais da Igreja a afirmar que o Pai e o Filho são de *uma mesma substância,* e falou sobre as três pessoas da deidade. *Irineu* (140-200 D.C.) combateu o gnosticismo usando a cristologia do Novo Testamento. Não somente ensinava a divindade de Cristo, mas também declarou enfaticamente que: «Ele tornou-se naquilo que somos, a fim de tornar-nos aquilo que ele é». Isso equivale à idéia da participação na natureza divina, em um sentido perfeitamente real, da mesma forma que Cristo, de maneira perfeitamente real, participou da natureza humana (II Ped. 1:4 e Col. 2:9,10).

c. *Orígenes.* Suas datas foram 185-254 D.C. Ele teve grande influência sobre o desenvolvimento da cristologia no Oriente. Usou a expressão *geração eterna* ao referir-se à filiação de Cristo, a fim de evitar qualquer idéia de um começo em sua pessoa, ou de que ele tivesse sido criado pelo Pai. Empregou o termo *homoousios,* ao afirmar que o Filho é dotado da mesma substância que o Pai. Não obstante, sua cristologia envolvia a idéia errônea de subordinação do Filho ao Pai (ver I Cor. 15:28), expressa segundo termos platônicos. Em sua missão, Cristo teria sido um ser intermediário, preenchendo o espaço entre o ser totalmente transcendental de Deus e este mundo criado. Como poderia ser de outro modo? Deus precisa do seu Mediador (que vide). Orígenes ensinava a doutrina da alma humana preexistente de Jesus, visto que ele acreditava na alma preexistente, e não excetuava à regra nem mesmo a natureza humana de Cristo. Todavia, o Logos não seria apenas preexistente, mas também eterno. Por ocasião da encarnação, pois, houve a fusão dessas duas naturezas. Ver os artigos sobre *Orígenes* e sobre o *Origenismo.* Foi Orígenes, mais do que qualquer outra figura cristã, quem finalmente, destruiu a influência do gnosticismo na Igreja. No entanto, na posterior controvérsia ariana, sua teologia complexa era usada por ambos os lados dessa controvérsia.

d. *Ário.* Suas datas foram cerca de 265-336 D.C. Ele negava a possibilidade de qualquer emanação divina, ou de qualquer distinção dentro da deidade. Ele ensinava que o Logos foi criado do nada, por Deus, antes do início do tempo, conforme o conhecemos agora. Embora o Logos tenha apenas uma forma de divindade, ele poderia ser chamado divino, posto não ser o verdadeiro Deus, e nem ter a mesma substância do Pai. O concílio de Nicéia opôs-se a esses pontos de vista, em cerca de 325 D.C. Atanásio (ver abaixo), foi o grande opositor de Ário, nessas suas idéias distorcidas.

e. *Atanásio* (298-373 D.C.). Defendia a doutrina de uma só substância, possuída pelo Pai e pelo Filho. Alicerçava seus argumentos não em seus raciocínios acerca do Logos, mas na natureza da redenção. Na redenção (que vide), faz parte do plano de Deus levar os remidos a compartilharem de sua natureza. Para realizar isso, Deus precisou assumir a natureza humana. Portanto, Deus encarnou-se. E foi em seu estado encarnado que ele resolveu o problema do pecado, tendo igualmente aberto o caminho para o homem progredir até Deus. E isso deve incluir uma transformação tão radical da alma humana que, finalmente, através da transformação metafísica, aquilo que antes era apenas humano, tornar-se-á divino, compartilhando da real natureza de Deus. Concordo plenamente com essa idéia, e provi, nesta enciclopédia, um artigo sobre esse assunto. Ver *Divindade, Participação do Homem na.* A salvação consiste na filiação a Deus. Os filhos realmente participarão da natureza do Pai, embora em sentido infinito. Não obstante, sempre haverá um maior desenvolvimento nessa participação, pois, visto que há uma infinitude com que seremos cheios, também deverá haver um preenchimento infinito (ver Col. 2:10; II Cor. 3:18). A glorificação (que vide) será um processo eterno, e não um acontecimento dentro do tempo.

f. *Apolinário* (310-390 D.C.). Afirmava que não podia entender o mistério do Deus homem (e quem pode?), pelo que raciocinava que o Logos era apenas um homem. Ao explicar o homem, ele apelava para a idéia platônica da tríada, referindo-se ao homem como composto por: 1. corpo; 2. alma irracional ou animal; 3. alma racional ou intelecto (no grego, *nous*), que é a porção mais elevada do homem, aquela que sobrevive à morte física. Essa *nous* (a alma), de acordo com essa doutrina, foi substituída pelo Logos, na pessoa de Jesus Cristo. Portanto, em Cristo não devemos pensar em uma humanidade verdadeira, mas em uma espécie de nova criação. Essa doutrina, pois, nega a verdade da encarnação.

g. *Gregório Nazianzeno* (329-390 D.C.). Ele condenou o ponto de vista acima definido e defendeu tanto a divindade verdadeira quanto a humanidade verdadeira de Cristo. As idéias de Apolinário foram condenadas pelo concílio de Constantinopla (381 D.C.).

h. *Nestor*, falecido em 451 D.C. Foi bispo de Constantinopla. Recusava-se a usar a expressão «mãe de Deus», a qual, a princípio, fora criada para enfatizar è divindade de Cristo. Cristo era divino, e Maria fora sua mãe. Originalmente, a expressão não tinha por intuito dizer que Deus tem mãe, em qualquer sentido. Nestor, entretanto, negava a verdadeira divindade de Cristo, asseverando que ele apenas foi um homem que serviu de instrumento da deidade. As declarações de Nestor são confusas, pois, ao mesmo tempo em que falava sobre o Deus homem, também parecia pensar que havia duas naturezas, atuando lado a lado, em uma única manifestação, embora não chegasse a pensar na fusão dessas duas naturezas. Nestor argumentava que Deus não pode sofrer, pelo que foi o lado humano de Cristo que morreu. É verdade que foi o lado humano de Cristo que morreu, visto que Deus não pode morrer; porém, a maneira de Nestor tentar resolver o mistério da pessoa de Cristo não satisfez aos teólogos da Igreja. Essa separação de pessoas, em Jesus Cristo, foi condenada pelo concílio de Calcedônia de 451 D.C., e também pelo concílio de Éfeso, de 431 D.C.

i. *Cirilo* (que vide), o inteligente mas violento patriarca de Alexandria, em cerca de 412 D.C., opôs-se aos nestorianos, tendo servido de instrumento da condenação dos mesmos. Ele também combateu a doutrina de Apolinário (que vide), asseverando que a humanidade de Cristo era completa e inteira, mas sem subsistência independente (no grego, *anupóstasis*).

j. *Êutico*, um discípulo de Cirilo, continuou pensando sobre o problema e terminou ensinando que as duas naturezas de Cristo estavam fundidas em uma só, ficando assim eliminadas as claras distinções entre a natureza divina e a natureza humana em Jesus Cristo. Isso se assemelhava ao docetismo (que vide), pelo que sua posição foi condenada pelo concílio de Calcedônia de 451 D.C. Esse concílio pronunciou-se em favor das duas naturezas de Cristo, coexistindo uma com a outra, sem nenhuma fusão ou conversão, mas também sem divisão e separação alguma.

l. *Leôncio de Bizâncio*, antes de 553 D.C., continuou meditando sobre esse problema, desejando apresentar uma declaração que fosse aceita por todos. Escreveu tratados contra os nestorianos, os monofisistas e os apolinarianos, o que mostra que ele era habilidoso polemista. Apresentou uma fórmula que a miioria dos teólogos aceitou. Ele ensinava que a natureza de Cristo não era uma hipóstase independente. No lugar disto, era *en-hipostática*, isto é subsistia no *Logos* e através do *Logos*. Essa teoria foi aprovada pelo segundo concílio de Constantinopla, em 553 D.C.

m. *Sérgio de Constantinopla* continuou meditando sobre o problema, e decidiu que o mesmo ainda não havia sido resolvido. Por essa razão, criou a doutrina chamada *monotelitismo*, o que indica «uma só operação divino-humana», ou uma só vontade atuante na pessoa de Cristo. Aqueles que defendiam essa posição supunham que, embora houvesse duas naturezas em Cristo, haveria apenas uma energia divino humana, o que significaria que em Cristo não haveria duas vontades, as quais poderiam entrar em choque uma a outra, mas apenas uma vontade.

n. *Honório I*, bispo (papa) de Roma, 625-741 D.C, também defendia a teoria da vontade única em Cristo. Mas a Igreja Ocidental, em 649 D.C., declarou-se favorável à idéia das duas vontades de Cristo, e o sexto concílio ecumênico de Constantinopla, em 680 D.C., declarou que a posição do papa Honório era uma heresia! O termo usado pela formulação desse concílio foi *dioteletismo*, que significa que Cristo tinha duas naturezas em operação, mas que a natureza humana sempre se mostrou sujeita à natureza divina.

5. Outros Desenvolvimentos e Opiniões

a. *A Igreja da Idade Média*. A Igreja Católica Romana aderiu de perto às declarações dos concílios em favor de uma cristologia ortodoxa. Seus pontos de vista foram enriquecidos pela teologia de Agostinho (354-430 D.C.) (que vide), o qual frisava a real humanidade de Cristo, a sua obra expiatória e as experiências místicas. A humanidade de Cristo tornou-se um importante elemento na devoção mística de Bernardo de Clairvaux (1091-1153). Ele enfatizava a possível união da alma com Cristo, sob a figura da noiva e do Noivo. Punha-se ênfase sobre a divindade de Cristo, por alguns teólogos de seu tempo, conforme atualmente se faz nas igrejas evangélicas, as quais, para todos os propósitos práticos, embora não quanto à teoria, eliminaram a humanidade de Cristo de suas teologias.

b. *Os Reformadores Protestantes*. Lutero ensinava a verdadeira humanidade e a verdadeira divindade de Cristo, referindo-se à *maravilhosa troca* de influências entre uma e outra dessas naturezas, como também à comunicação dos atributos envolvidos. Desse modo, temos uma doutrina da interpenetração mútua das naturezas divina e humana de Cristo, algo similar à mescla de naturezas (conforme pensava Êutico), o que a cristologia do concílio de Calcedônia procurava evitar. No luteranismo posterior, a posição de Lutero provocou uma controvérsia a respeito do ponto em que a humanidade do Filho de Deus compartilha com os atributos divinos e atua, juntamente com os mesmos. Se levarmos isso longe demais, perderemos de vista a real humanidade de Cristo. Além disso, nesse exagero, poremos em perigo a idéia inteira da *kenosis* (que vide), isto é, o esvaziamento do Logos quanto às suas prerrogativas divinas, por ocasião da encarnação.

Calvino aprovava os pronunciamentos ortodoxos dos concílios, mas rejeitava a tendência de Lutero para o erro de Êutico, preferindo defender a idéia de duas naturezas distintas, embora nunca separadas. Para ele, a salvação depende das propriedades de ambas as naturezas. A natureza divina opera através da natureza humana; mas, ao mesmo tempo, a salvação também envolveria a obra de Jesus, em sua perfeita obediência e santificação, em lugar de todos os homens, em sua própria pessoa, pois a humanidade de Jesus não foi apenas o instrumento, mas também a causa material da salvação. A salvação só pode tornar-se realidade mediante o cumprimento dos três ofícios de Cristo como Profeta, Sacerdote e Rei. Essa é uma boa teologia, concordando com a mensagem da epístola aos Hebreus, em trechos como 2:10 e 5:8. Jesus tanto foi *aperfeiçoado* quanto *aprendeu a obediência* pelas coisas que sofreu e experimentou. Infelizmente, em muitas igrejas calvinistas de nossos dias, a teologia popular ressalta tanto a divindade de Cristo que se perdem de vista aqueles importantes pontos teológicos que estão envolvidos na humanidade Cristo. Ver sobre a *Humanidade de Cristo*.

c. *Fragmentação dos Protestantes*. Visto que os grupos protestantes não se sentem obrigados diante dos pronunciamentos dos concílios, eles têm representado entre si todos os desvios cristológicos que temos visto neste artigo. A partir do século XIX, a tendência

CRISTOLOGIA — CRITÉRIOS

dos grupos protestantes tem sido desviar-se da doutrina calcedônica das duas naturezas de Cristo. Schleiermacher constituiu uma cristologia que vê em Cristo uma consciência única e arquétipa de total dependência filial ao Pai; e assim ele enfatizava o lado humano, às expensas do lado divino de Cristo. Alguns teólogos luteranos têm salientado fortemente a idéia de *kenosis* (que vide), supondo que a encarnação requeria um verdadeiro esvaziamento de atributos como onipotência, onipresença e onisciência, embora retendo os atributos morais essenciais da divindade. Assim, se Cristo continuou sendo divino em sua natureza, ele não reteve a forma de Deus, durante o período da encarnação (que vide). Naturalmente, há indícios neotestamentários em favor dessa posição, conforme aqueles trechos da epístola aos Hebreus e as declarações do próprio Senhor Jesus de que ele não sabia tudo, como se vê em Mar. 13:32. É óbvio que a humanidade de Cristo limitava os seus atributos divinos, pois, do contrário, não poderia haver doutrina da encarnação. Essa doutrina, entretanto, tem provocado muita discussão.

d. *Abordagem de Estudiosos Liberais*. Muitos liberais vêem pouco sentido em todas as controvérsias e suas minúsculas distinções. Eles dispõem-se a chamar Jesus de *divino*, mas somente no sentido de que Deus *irrompeu* por meio de Jesus, manifestando assim a sua vontade e os seus atributos. Eles não partem da idéia de que, em Jesus, havia a mesma substância do Pai, ou da idéia de que ele era divino, por ser a encarnação literal do Logos de Deus. Nesse caso, o termo divindade envolve muito mais o que ele foi e realizou, dotado de poder da parte de Deus, embora isso não refletisse uma natureza divina essencial. Em outras palavras, eles negam a doutrina que expõe Jesus como o próprio Deus.

6. Mistério
Debates surgem na cristologia porque estamos tratando de um *mistério*. Um mistério é um segredo divino, atualmente já revelado, que ainda retém elementos difíceis que dificultam a compreensão e a explicação. Para nós é impossível criar qualquer formulação que explique como tanto a natureza divina quanto a natureza humana podem, realmente, habitar em uma única pessoa, ao mesmo tempo. Nossas explicações tendem por diminuir o fator humano para acomodar-se ao fator divino, ou então vice-versa. Ou então, podemos desistir da questão inteira e chamá-la de um *paradoxo*; ou mesmo podemos rejeitar o assunto inteiro, intitulando-o de um mito.

Porém, a última resposta que nos interessa aqui é a mitológica. Quem era Jesus e o que ele fez, permanece um dos grandes mistérios da vida. Na verdade, alguns teólogos têm dito que o mistério de Cristo ainda é maior que o mistério do Pai. Jesus mesmo declarou: «...ninguém conhece o Filho senão o Pai...» (Mat. 11:27). Não obstante, há coisas que podemos dizer, pelo que o debate sobre as naturezas divina e humana, existentes em Cristo, é um debate legítimo. Porém, uma de nossas grandes dificuldades consiste em não sabermos no que consiste a *divindade*. Nossa ciência e nossa filosofia ainda não conseguiram mostrar-nos no que consiste a divindade, embora contemos com muitas descrições parciais. Na verdade, a nossa teoria atômica não passa disso, uma *teoria*, que está sendo submetida a uma constante modificação, à medida que nossos fatores atinentes vão sendo descobertos. Assim, como podemos falar de maneira muito inteligente sobre o que significa ser *divino*? Isso ainda está completamente fora de nosso alcance. Podemos falar sobre os atributos e as obras divinas com algum sucesso; mas, quando podemos descrever a *natureza* de Deus, nosso sucesso é praticamente nulo. Esse é o *mysterium tremendum*. Esse *mysterium tremendum* entrou na existência humana, na pessoa de Jesus Cristo. Enquanto estivermos deste lado da existência, não seremos capazes de explicar *Cristo*. Não obstante, quando tentamos fazê-lo, podemos dizer algumas coisas úteis. (AM B C HAV KN NE P)

CRITÉRIO

A palavra vem do grego, **kritérion**, do verbo *krineĩn*, «decidir», «ajuizar». Um cognato grego, *krités*, significa «juiz». Um critério é um padrão com a ajuda do qual se pode chegar a um juízo certo; ou então é um teste, uma regra ou medida para se distinguir entre o falso e o verdadeiro, ou então o imperfeito e o perfeito. Há muitos critérios usados na determinação da verdade. No artigo sobre a *Fé Religiosa e o Problema da Verificação*, apresento aqueles critérios que se aplicam ao campo da teologia e da religião. No artigo intitulado o *Conhecimento e a Fé Religiosa*, sob o segundo ponto, exponho as teorias da verdade ou os critérios da verdade.

CRITÉRIOS DE UMA GUERRA JUSTA

Seria correto um país enviar tropas com o propósito específico de matar os homens (e a população em geral) de outro país? Os pacifistas respondem com um sonoro «não»! Porém, os outros retrucam dizendo que os pacifistas alegram-se em participar da liberdade e dos benefícios de uma guerra da qual eles não quiseram participar. Ver os artigos sobre *Pacifismo* e *Objetores Conscientes*. Talvez devêssemos formular a pergunta nos seguintes termos: «Sob quais circunstâncias podemos preferir fazer um erro menor, a fim de evitar um erro maior?» As respostas a essa indagação são muitas:

1. *Os Pais da Igreja*. Eles lamentaram as tragédias da guerra, exortando os crentes a buscarem a paz e a amarem a seus inimigos. Alguns deles recusaram-se a prestar serviço militar; mas a Igreja cristã, como um todo, nunca foi expoente do pacifismo. Ambrósio repreendeu o imperador Teodósio por causa das atrocidades cometidas a seu mando em Tessalônica. Mas, em nossos dias, os homens estão arquitetando justificativas para a guerra.

2. *Cícero*. Foi ele o escritor da primeira proposta de uma guerra supostamente justa. Ele alistou seis pontos: a. Uma guerra deve visar à defesa e à segurança nacional, e não ser apenas alguma aventura. b. Só deve ser deflagrada quando todas as negociações tiverem fracassado. c. Deve ser formalmente declarada, com a devida antecedência, sem golpes de traição. d. Deve ter por finalidade a obtenção da paz, e não a mera destruição do inimigo. e. Devem ser poupados os prisioneiros e os que se renderem. f. Somente soldados legítimos deveriam participar das guerras justas.

3. *Agostinho* (em *Cidade de Deus* xix) criticou as regras de Cícero como destituídas de realismo. A sociedade humana, não-remida, jamais haverá de observar regras assim, por melhores que os homens pareçam ser. Nenhuma guerra é inteiramente justa. Entretanto, a *paz* pode ser justa, e a guerra pode ser necessária a fim de garantir a paz. As guerras só deveriam ser iniciadas por ordem das autoridades devidamente constituídas, que dirigem as nações. Os soldados deveriam combater com arrependimento no coração, e não impelidos pelo sentimento do ódio. A

CRÍTIAS — CRÍTICA DA BÍBLIA

justiça precisa levar Deus em consideração, pois todas as nossas ações serão julgadas, se agradaram a ele ou não.

4. *Tomás de Aquino* (em *Summa Theologica* ii.2.a,40) escreveu sobre a necessidade de guerras justas e de intenções corretas. A moralidade de uma guerra depende desses fatores, e não das conseqüências finais. Deveríamos lutar a fim de garantir a paz, e não a fim de matar. A justiça precisa concordar com a lei, e a lei deve visar ao *bem comum*.

5. Os *reformadores* do século XVI renovaram os conceitos de Agostinho, adicionando a idéia bíblica de que o Estado é um agente da justiça retributiva de Deus, pelo que as guerras deveriam ser iniciadas em autodefesa, para pôr fim às injustiças, em cujo caso seriam permissíveis. Ver Rom. 13:1-5; I Ped. 2:13,14.

6. *John Lock* resolveu contribuir para a idéia, dando a entender que, algumas vezes, as guerras são necessárias, quando não há qualquer autoridade internacional para encontrar solução para os casos de flagrante injustiça. O lado vencedor não deveria ter jurisdição sobre os não-combatentes da nação derrotada, e nem a nação vencida deveria ser obrigada a aceitar qualquer forma de governo escolhida pelo vencedor. Essas sugestões, porém, não parecem ajustar-se às modernas nações industrializadas. Nessas nações, a força civil industrial é que possibilita as guerras, e a mudança de governo pode ser necessária para garantir uma paz duradoura.

Gigantes problemas não têm respostas fáceis e simples. Assim, — quando a matança *en masse* está envolvida, é indiscutível que ninguém jamais será capaz de definir, de forma adequada, no que consistiria uma guerra justa. Porém, piores ainda que as chamadas guerras justas são as «guerras santas», quando os homens enganam a si mesmos, ao pensarem que a guerra deve ser feita em nome de Deus e em defesa da fé religiosa. Geralmente, os fanáticos é que iniciam as «guerras santas», pelo que de santas elas só têm o nome. (H)

CRÍTIAS DE ATENAS

Filósofo grego do século V A.C. Nasceu em Atenas e tornou-se um dos filósofos sofistas (que vide). Estudou com Górgias e Sócrates. Tornou-se um líder político. Foi banido de Atenas; mas depois retornou para governar novamente. Foi um dos mais inescrupulosos dentre os trinta tiranos. Em sua teoria política, ele afirmava que tanto a lei quanto a religião são invenções das pessoas investidas de autoridade, e que o principal instrumento que elas usam, a fim de controlar as multidões, é o *medo*. O medo é o receio da punição, e qualquer modificação efetuada precisa ser realizada por esse intermédio. (P)

CRÍTICA ALTA

Este termo significa a *crítica bíblica* em todos os assuntos que vão além da *crítica textual*. Pode ser positiva ou negativa, o termo em si é *neutro*. Algumas pessoas usam a palavra *introdução* como um sinônimo. Questões como autoria, proveniência, integridade, data, problemas especiais de livros bíblicos fazem parte da *crítica alta*. A *crítica baixa* (que vide) é a crítica textual. Ver o artigo geral sobre *Crítica da Bíblia*.

CRÍTICA BAIXA

Esse é um outro nome dado à **Crítica Textual**. Ela é chamada «baixa» a fim de ser contrastada com a «alta», e não por ser inferior. A crítica textual examina os textos do ponto de vista dos manuscritos, com o propósito de restaurar o original mediante a comparação com os manuscritos existentes. A «alta crítica», por sua vez, estuda tudo quanto está fora da questão do texto, incluindo problemas como autoria, data, proveniência, destino, integridade, problemas especiais, etc. O artigo sobre *Manuscritos do Novo Testamento*, juntamente com informações sobre os mesmos, também expõe os princípios da crítica textual, sob os pontos quinto a oitavo.

CRÍTICA DA BÍBLIA

Esboço do Artigo

1. Definições e Funções
2. Esboço Histórico da Crítica da Bíblia
3. Evidência Positiva de Satya Sai Baba e dos Gigantes Espirituais
4. Crítica da Forma
5. Atividade Crítica
6. Crítica Textual
7. Conclusão e Avaliação.
8. Bibliografia

1. Definições e Funções

A expressão **baixa crítica** é usada para designar a crítica textual. — A expressão **alta crítica** é usada para indicar o estudo crítico da Bíblia que envolve qualquer coisa fora do próprio texto, como as questões de autoria, propósito, problemas lingüísticos, pano de fundo histórico, unidade, proveniência, datas, problemas especiais, etc. Essa expressão tem assumido um certo sentido negativo por causa dos abusos que têm estado associados a esse tipo de atividade. Porém, os estudiosos mais conservadores, que defendem a autoria mosaica do Pentateuco, praticam a alta crítica tanto quanto aquele que faz julgamentos negativos. Talvez um título melhor para a alta crítica seja «crítica literária», ao passo que a expressão «introdução» não é tão boa, porque o termo já é usado para indicar outro tipo de estudo.

A Função. Os princípios usados para aquilatação e exame de qualquer outra literatura são aplicados à Bíblia. Isso inclui a investigação histórica, a aplicação do que se conhece no tocante às características da transmissão de textos, estilos de caligrafia, escolas históricas de escribas, tipos de materiais usados em vários séculos, problemas lingüísticos, panos de fundo históricos que indicam datas, idéias que caracterizam períodos que influenciaram os autores, etc. Naturalmente, a crítica é absolutamente necessária, porquanto não pode haver verdadeira exegese de um texto bíblico sem a crítica. Entretanto, deveríamos resguardar-nos contra o ceticismo, que não é apenas o resultado, mas, algumas vezes, até mesmo a motivação por detrás das atividades de alguns críticos.

2. Esboço Histórico da Crítica da Bíblia

a. *Pano de Fundo*. Quando os saduceus rejeitaram todos os escritos do Antigo Testamento, excetuando o Pentateuco, estavam agindo como críticos da Bíblia. *Idem*, quando os fariseus aceitaram todos os trinta e nove livros da Bíblia. Quando a congregação judaica da dispersão julgou que deveria adicionar catorze outros livros (chamados apócrifos), estavam aplicando pelo menos alguns princípios comuns à crítica da Bíblia, a fim de justificar um cânon expandido. Quando os gnósticos, na época da Igreja primitiva, rejeitaram totalmente o Antigo Testamento, supondo que seu «deus» era uma divindade secundária e imperfeita, criador de nosso mundo imperfeito,

CRÍTICA DA BÍBLIA

também estavam aplicando princípios próprios da crítica da Bíblia. Porfírio (300 D.C.), discípulo de Plotino, em sua polêmica contra o cristianismo, usou a crítica textual da Bíblia como um de seus instrumentos. Ele via o livro de Daniel como composição muito mais recente do que realmente era, como se ele tivesse escrito história, e não profecia. (Ver o artigo sobre Porfírio).

A escola de Antioquia (não uma instituição, mas uma postura teológica), de 400 D.C., opunha-se à interpretação alegórica, que era comumente usada pelos pais alexandrinos da Igreja. Ambas essas escolas estavam aplicando princípios de crítica da Bíblia, embora produzindo resultados diferentes. A escola de Antioquia também aplicava considerações gramático-históricas em seus estudos, método esse que figura entre os métodos usados na crítica da Bíblia (ver os artigos sobre essas duas escolas). Ver sobre o *método alegórico* de interpretação. Portanto, nessas antigas atividades, encontramos os primórdios da crítica da Bíblia. Porém, tal tipo de atividade, de forma organizada como uma metodologia, pertence à história relativamente recente.

b. *A Reforma*. Quando da compilação do *Textus Receptus* por Erasmo, contemporâneo de Lutero, no começo do século XVI, encontramos os verdadeiros primórdios da crítica textual ou baixa crítica. Não tardou para que se patenteasse que os manuscritos por ele usados eram de qualidade inferior, embora muito tempo se passasse até que o texto do Novo Testamento chegasse ao estado purificado em que se encontra hoje. Ver o artigo sobre os *Manuscritos, Novo Testamento*, que inclui os princípios da crítica textual. Vários dos reformadores rejeitaram um ou mais dos livros do Novo Testamento, como indignos de ocuparem lugar no cânon. Assim, Lutero rejeitava a epístola de Tiago, por causa de sua posição contrária à justificação pela fé. E ele também considerava Judas e Apocalipse como livros de valor secundário, em relação ao resto do Novo Testamento. Calvino rejeitava o Apocalipse, não tendo comentado sobre o mesmo em todo o seu longo comentário do Novo Testamento. E também rejeitava a segunda epístola de Pedro. Ver o artigo sobre o *Cânon*, que fornece informações detalhadas sobre a questão. Em tudo isso vemos atividades próprias da crítica da Bíblia, não aplicadas de forma negativa, mas honestamente, por homens dotados de fé, que queriam um Novo Testamento o mais puro possível, embora suas conclusões reduzissem um tanto o cânon universalmente aceito em nossos dias.

c. *Período Moderno*. A crítica da Bíblia começou a florescer no século XVIII, contra um pano de fundo racionalista (ver o artigo sobre o *Racionalismo*). Havia então o desejo de dar maior relevância ao cristianismo, diante das tendências do pensamento contemporâneo. O racionalismo alemão tomou a posição que considerava suspeita toda e qualquer evidência, até que fosse provada válida. Essa abordagem não podia deixar de redundar em ceticismo.

O Antigo Testamento passou a ser rigorosamente examinado, algumas vezes sofrendo ataques da parte dos críticos. Houve o surgimento da hipótese de múltiplas fontes formativas do Pentateuco. Alguns supunham que Moisés utilizou-se de várias fontes, que ele reuniu (conforme dizia Jean Astruc, que postulava duas fontes), ao passo que outros afirmavam que Moisés nada tivera a ver com a autoria da coletânea do Pentateuco. A. Geddes e J.S. Vater (fins do século XVIII e começo do século XIX), viam várias fontes, e não apenas duas, o que acabou evoluindo para a famosa teoria JEDP (quatro fontes), de Hermann Hupfeld (1853), Karl Graf e Abraham Kuenen (1869), em vários estágios. Essa teoria supõe que havia uma fonte jeovista (J), uma fonte eleoimista (E), uma fonte deuteronômica (D) e uma fonte sacerdotal (P). Esses símbolos estariam baseados na incidência preferida do nome divino, por algum autor particular, ou então nos tipos específicos de materiais registrados (presumivelmente por diferentes autores). Essa questão é ventilada mais detalhadamente no artigo sobre Gênesis — que comenta individualmente sobre cada uma dessas fontes. O mesmo tipo de atividade foi aplicado ao livro de Isaías, aos Salmos, a Daniel e a outros livros do Antigo Testamento. Os artigos sobre esses livros oferecem-nos exemplos desses esforços da crítica da Bíblia. Ver sobre *J.E.D.P.(S.)*.

Novo Testamento. Um dos primeiros problemas a serem abordados foi a questão das fontes informativas dos evangelhos sinópticos. Lachmann (1835) demonstrou que Marcos era o evangelho original, e que em seguida foi usado como uma das primeiras fontes de Mateus e Lucas. Isso desenvolveu-se na teoria dos quatro documentos, de B.B. Streeter (1874-1937), a saber: Marcos, Q, L e M. Ver o artigo sobre o *Problema Sinóptico*, quanto a detalhes sobre a questão.

Os Milagres. Thomas Woolson (falecido em 1731) supunha, sobre bases céticas, que os milagres de Jesus eram criações de pessoas supersticiosas, muito tempo depois da morte de Jesus. H.S. Reimarus (falecido em 1768), asseverou que as fabulosas narrativas sobre Jesus eram falsificações deliberadas, dos discípulos de Jesus, sobre aquilo que realmente se sucedeu. Fr. Schleiermacher (falecido em 1834), tentou preservar a posição cêntrica de Cristo, embora supondo que os evangelhos haviam sido artificialmente construídos, a partir de uma miscelânea de retalhos separados da tradição oral. A chamada *crítica da forma*, do século XX, emprega o conceito básico dessa teoria. D.F. Straus, em seu Lebem Jesu (1835) apresentou Jesus como um sábio judeu ideal, cujas memórias foram preservadas em meio a inúmeros adornos. Frederick Christian Baur (1792-1860) foi o fundador da Escola de Tubingen, tendo proposto uma primitiva *tese* judaica no tocante à vida de Jesus, encabeçada por Pedro, mas com uma subseqüente *antítese*, que procurou embelezar a biografia de Jesus, conferindo-lhe estatura divina, encabeçada por Paulo. E a *síntese* (segundo os moldes hegelianos) teria sido provida pelo evangelho de João, que para ele pertencia a uma data fantasticamente posterior, cerca de 170 D.C. Mas, um pequeno fragmento de papiro, P(52), do evangelho de João e pertencente ao começo do século II D.C., destruiu a teoria. No entanto, Baur sentia que a história cristã primitiva precisava ser reescrita, a fim de desnudá-la de suas emendas apócrifas, bem como dos relatos exagerados de entusiastas, a fim de sabermos o que realmente aconteceu. Dessa forma, Baur distinguiu entre o Jesus histórico e o Jesus teológico. Interessante é observar que apesar da estrutura central de sua teoria (dialética hegeliana) ter sido abandonada pela maioria dos especialistas, sua oposição entre Pedro e Paulo tem persistido como noção de muitos estudiosos. W. Boosset (1892) e Adolf von Harnack (1899) opinavam que era mister eliminar quaisquer emendas supersticiosas e religiosas, a fim de se ficar apenas com o Jesus *histórico*. Segundo eles, Jesus seria um meio liberal eloqüente, que proclamava o evangelho da paternidade universal de Deus e a fraternidade universal dos homens. Porém, Johanne Weiss (1892) reagiu contra tão

CRÍTICA DA BÍBLIA

simplista modernização de Jesus, tendo sido secundado por Albert Schweitzer (nasceu em 1875), o qual insistiu em seu livro *Quest for the Historical Jesus* (1906), que Jesus era um crente apaixonado no iminente fim do mundo e no imediato estabelecimento do reino de Deus sobre a terra. Nisso, Jesus estaria equivocado, segundo Schweitzer supunha; porém, acreditaria em tais coisas.

É possível que a principal tendência da erudição liberal, a partir do ano de 1906, tenha sido aquela promovida por Rudolf Bultmann (nasceu em 1884). De acordo com essa tendência, precisamos demitizar os registros bíblicos a fim de chegarmos ao Jesus real. Mas a tentativa terminou em *ceticismo* quanto ao método, considerado fútil, visto que até os evangelhos sinópticos encerram declarações que promovem a deidade de Cristo. Não obstante, alguns estudiosos continuam fiéis ao método. Ver os artigos sobre *Bultmann* e a *Demitização*, quanto a detalhes sobre a questão. —A neoortodoxia de Karl Barth não foi outra coisa senão uma reação contra o extremo liberalismo alemão. O sistema de Karl Barth também faz parte da crítica da Bíblia. Ver o artigo separado sobre ele, quanto a detalhes.

3. Evidência Positiva de Satya Sai Baba e dos Gigantes Espirituais

Satya Sai Baba é um dos «homens santos» do hinduísmo, que, em nossos dias, está operando milagres feitos por Jesus, diante de testemunhas próximas e dignas de confiança. Ele tem criado matéria, tem ressuscitado os mortos e tem curado toda a variedade de enfermidades. Ele afirma ser uma reencarnação de Jesus, deixando os céticos admirados e consternados. Muitos se têm tornado discípulos seus instantâneos e fiéis, porquanto aquilo que ele faz é espantoso e inacreditável. Não quero entrar no mérito de suas reivindicações, mas apenas mencionar suas atividades. O artigo a seu respeito entra em maiores detalhes. Seja como for, suas obras demonstram claramente que negar aquilo que Jesus realizou equivale a não reconhecer o que realmente sucede nas vidas humanas, através do poder de gigantes espirituais. Ver o artigo sobre *Sathya Sai Baba*.

Há grandes maravilhas neste mundo; há milagres; há ocorrências admiráveis, realizadas por pessoas incrivelmente poderosas. Portanto, os evangelhos em nada exageram, mas chegam mesmo a subestimar modestamente o que Jesus realizou e quem ele, na verdade, foi neste mundo. Seremos apenas uns insensatos se permitirmos que nossos preconceitos a priori, como o ceticismo, governem a nossa maneira de pensar acerca da espiritualidade e suas potencialidades. Satya Sai Baba é apenas um homem santo, um poderoso homem espiritual. E há muitos outros, maiores e menores. As experiências religiosas fecham as portas diante do ceticismo e abrem-nas para a fé. Não obstante, a alta crítica tem trazido à tona muitos problemas que precisam ser examinados, tendo destacado muitas verdades que antes eram ignoradas. Porém, o que quero salientar neste parágrafo é que o *descobrimento* de várias fontes informativas, incorporadas em um livro, ou informes que modificam nossas idéias sobre autoria, influências históricas sobre as idéias (pois nada se desenvolve no vácuo), etc., pouco ou nada têm a ver com a mensagem espiritual em geral. Essa mensagem caracteriza-se pelo poder, pela redenção, pela restauração, estando envolvida em um imenso otimismo. — Não devemos permitir que o ceticismo venha sombrear essa mensagem. — O arcabouço literário, através do qual a mensagem espiritual é transmitida, pode envolver e realmente envolve muitos problemas, mas isso não é suficiente para obscurecer a *Luz* que nos foi enviada, a despeito dos defeitos dos homens e de seus livros!

4. Crítica da Forma

Crítica da Forma é um método de pesquisa que surgiu na Alemanha, a partir de 1919, quando Martin Dibelius (ver o artigo) publicou sua obra *From Tradition to Gospel*. O método havia sido antecipado por outros, como Johannes Weiss (ver o artigo) e Hermann Gunkel (ver o artigo). A crítica da forma é uma tentativa para recuperar as *unidades* da tradição oral que circulavam antes dos evangelhos serem escritos. Segundo são concebidas, essas unidades incluiriam antigas *narrativas*, como o relato da paixão, parábolas, declarações ou ensinos, *relatos de milagres* e *lendas*. Tudo estaria baseado em graus variegados de verdade, de mistura com a ficção. Alguns intérpretes também lançaram-se à tarefa de distinguir níveis dentro dessas supostas unidades, como o material judaico primitivo e o material helenista posterior. Supõe-se que os evangelhos resultaram de um tipo de recolhimento de fragmentos, em que as peças foram sendo ajustadas umas às outras, algumas vezes habilidosamente, e outras vezes, de forma crua. Alguns supõem que essas tradições foram essencialmente *preservadas* pela Igreja; mas outros pensam que os cristãos inventaram a maioria dessas tradições. Seja como for, a tradição concentrada nos evangelhos seria uma espécie de esforço comunitário, e não de iniciativa particular. Isso significa que haveria uma certa canonização de material, desde o começo.

Essa teoria, apesar de conter elementos de verdade, também tem seus exageros. Marcos, o evangelho original, certamente parece haver sido escrito apressadamente, para narrar uma história que todos já conheciam; e não por alguém que agisse como redator, alinhavando pedaços provenientes de muitas fontes. Nota-se ali um senso de urgência, com base em narrativas de testemunhas oculares, o que é embotado por uma exagerada crítica da forma. Ver o artigo separado sobre o assunto, onde há mais detalhes.

5. Atividade dos Críticos

Qualquer estudo introdutório a algum livro da Bíblia naturalmente incluirá várias formas de crítica. Essa é uma atividade necessária, tornando-se prejudicial somente quando guiada pelo ceticismo, que busca encontrar erros e embotar a verdade, em vez de lançar luz sobre ela. As introduções aos livros da Bíblia, nesta Enciclopédia, geralmente incluem uma discussão sobre aspectos como autoria, proveniência, unidade e integridade, variantes no texto grego, problemas difíceis e especiais, data, destinatários, propósitos, etc. O leitor, no tocante à introdução a qualquer livro das Escrituras, poderá perceber a mão da crítica plenamente ilustrada, nessas introduções.

6. Crítica Textual

Crítica Textual, é também chamada «baixa crítica». Quanto a esse assunto, ver o artigo separado sobre os *Manuscritos, Antigo e Novo Testamentos*, onde, juntamente com informações gerais, são discutidos os princípios básicos da crítica textual. Quanto ao Novo Testamento, ver especificamente o ponto sexto, *Princípios da Restauração do Texto*, que inclui os tipos de texto e os testemunhos que lhes dizem respeito; o ponto sétimo, *Ilustrações* de como as formas corretas são escolhidas, quando há variantes no texto; e o ponto oitavo, *Esboço Histórico da Crítica Textual do Novo Testamento*. A crítica textual do

CRÍTICA DA BÍBLIA

Antigo Testamento está incluída no artigo sobre os Manuscritos, no tocante àquele documento.

7. Conclusão e Avaliação

a. A crítica, por si mesma, é uma atividade absolutamente necessária para o nosso conhecimento da Bíblia, e muitos resultados positivos têm resultado de todas as diversas modalidades de crítica que temos ventilado.

b. Já passou a época em que se podia usar a Bíblia como uma espécie de entidade mágica. Não nos devemos tornar culpados nem de *bibliomancia* (ver o artigo) — e nem de *bibliolatria* (que vide). — Nada teríamos a ganhar se encorajássemos o erro piedoso, só para satisfazer a pessoas que gostam de respostas simples. Se há algo que caracteriza a verdade das coisas é que a verdade não é simples. Nela está envolvida a tremendamente complexa mente divina, com o resultado que pareceremos um bando de símios pendurados nas árvores, quando nos pomos a examinar a Mente de Deus, tão acima está ela de nós. Portanto, quando Deus permitiu que algo de sua mente transparecesse em um livro, não deveríamos pensar que é fácil compreender tudo quanto ele diz ali.

c. Além disso, é ridículo ignorar o *lado humano* da Bíblia. Para exemplificar, há muitos erros gramaticais no grego do Novo Testamento. Nesse documento a linguagem foi expressa em diversos níveis de qualidade, desde o grego quase clássico da epístola aos Hebreus, até o grego de rua, com todos os seus vícios, do evangelho de Marcos. Além disso, há o grego como segundo idioma, no Apocalipse, cujo autor pensava em aramaico e imitava a gramática aramaica no grego por ele produzida, com os resultantes erros gramaticais. Haveríamos de explicar isso, dizendo que o Espírito Santo é um mau gramático?

d. Além disso, existem diversos *níveis de revelação*. Encontramos trechos místicos, de autêntico êxtase, nos escritos de Paulo, como porções do oitavo capítulo de Romanos, do décimo terceiro capítulo de I Coríntios, do segundo capítulo de Filipenses e do primeiro capítulo de Efésios. Pode-se contrastar isso com o tratado didático da epístola de Tiago, com seu judaísmo quase puro, em que a luz cristã só rebrilha aqui e acolá. Em Tiago encontramos o tipo de ensino que se poderia ouvir nas sinagogas, em qualquer sábado. Há ali grandes verdades, mas não empapadas na típica revelação cristã. É ridículo tentar harmonizar o que Tiago diz com os avançados conceitos de Paulo. Tiago continuava promovendo conceitos judaicos, que estavam começando a mesclar-se com os conceitos cristãos. A crítica destaca coisas assim, forçando-nos a relacionar as atitudes expressas por Tiago à divisão da Igreja primitiva em torno do legalismo, conforme se vê no décimo quinto capítulo de Atos, levando-nos a concluir que esse livro surgiu em meio àquela controvérsia, como representante do espírito antipaulino, de certos segmentos da Igreja primitiva, que ainda eram mais judaicos do que cristãos. Mas, os harmonizadores, buscando conforto mental, insistem em reconciliar Tiago e Paulo. Mas isso é anti-histórico e antidoutrinário. Não precisamos de tal esquema para fortalecer-nos a fé.

e. Outrossim, sem dúvida há *vários tipos* de fontes informativas dos evangelhos. Torna-se óbvio que as declarações ali constantes nem sempre foram ditas dentro das associações em que são postas. Com isso quero dizer que, nos evangelhos, há declarações postas dentro de certos acontecimentos históricos com os quais não estavam originalmente vinculados. Assim, no evangelho de Mateus, há vários grandes blocos de declarações de Jesus, como as bem-aventuranças, o sermão da montanha e as parábolas do reino que são óbvios *sumários*, provavelmente de muitas declarações de Jesus, que não foram proferidos em uma *única* ocasião, conforme aquele evangelho dá a entender. Isso é facilmente provado mediante a simples comparação do material de Mateus e Lucas, por exemplo, que aparece dentro de diferentes engastes históricos. Acresça-se a isso que a ordem dos acontecimentos nem sempre é a mesma em um e em outro evangelho. Tenho ilustrado isso abundantemente em meus artigos, apresentados nesta Enciclopédia, sobre o *Problema Sinóptico* e a *Historicidade dos Evangelhos*. Ver o item específico décimo segundo: *O que não significa a historicidade*, dentro do artigo sobre esse assunto.

f. Há problemas reais que envolvem pontos como *unidade* e *integridade* da Bíblia. As epístolas de I e II Coríntios representam uma correspondência entre Paulo e os crentes de Corinto, e não apenas duas epístolas, pois poderiam envolver nada menos que quatro epístolas diversas. É bem possível que a epístola aos Romanos, segundo a conhecemos, inclua material que, originalmente, não fazia parte da mesma. Falamos especificamente sobre o décimo sexto capítulo, que parece ser uma curta epístola aos crentes de Éfeso, e que terminou sendo agregada à epístola aos Romanos, onde se tornou seu capítulo dezesseis. Com freqüência, quando tratamos de tais problemas, não podemos fornecer informações mais precisas, o que se dá sobretudo com certos livros do Antigo Testamento, que quase certamente incorporam blocos de material reunidos por compiladores, uma atividade perfeitamente normal em todas as produções literárias.

g. E, continuando somente a fornecer exemplos de alguns tipos de problemas textuais, finalmente podemos discernir *níveis e diferenças de doutrina*, dentro do próprio Novo Testamento, e não meramente quando são contrastados o Antigo e o Novo Testamentos. Todos admitem que o Novo Testamento é doutrinariamente mais avançado do que o *A*. Nesse caso, por qual motivo certas porções do Novo Testamento não seriam doutrinariamente mais evoluídas do que outras porções do mesmo Novo Testamento? Os evangelhos refletem a doutrina cristã segundo o nível a que ela chegara até o fim do ministério de Jesus. Mas ele afirmou: «Tenho ainda muito que vos dizer, mas vós não o podeis suportar agora; quando vier, porém, o Espírito da verdade, ele vos guiará a toda a verdade...» (João 16:12,13). Já falei sobre o exemplo de Tiago, cujos conceitos foram ultrapassados pela revelação paulina. Além disso, consideremos os *mistérios* referidos por Paulo. Um mistério é uma verdade recém-revelada, que não fora revelada antes. Se já fosse conhecida, não seria um mistério. Portanto, de cada vez em que Paulo diz: «Eis que vos digo um mistério», era como se ele estivesse dizendo: «Eis uma nova verdade, que só agora está sendo revelada». E então Paulo nos leva a verdades acima de verdades ensinadas em outras porções do Novo Testamento, que outros autores sagrados desconheciam até então. Assim, no primeiro capítulo de Efésios, quando Paulo fala sobre «o mistério da vontade de Deus», ele nos dá um vislumbre do que Deus finalmente tenciona fazer em prol da humanidade, que ultrapassa a antiga doutrina de juízo, refletida em várias porções do Novo Testamento.Ora, essa intenção divina final é muito mais otimista, no tocante ao destino humano, do que transparece em outras porções do Novo Testamento. Ver o artigo

CRÍTICA DA BÍBLIA — CRITICISMO

sobre a *Restauração*, que demonstra isso.

Por outra parte, se mantivermos a atitude que o Novo Testamento é perfeitamente homogêneo em sua exposição de doutrinas, então essa verdade ficará oculta, para nosso próprio detrimento. Por igual modo, quando Pedro afiança que o evangelho foi pregado a mortos (I Ped. 4:6), quando Cristo desceu ao hades, entre sua morte e ressurreição (I Ped. 3:18 ss), ele aumenta e amplia a nossa esperança, demonstrando que Cristo *pode atingir os homens em todos os lugares*, incluindo no lugar mesmo do juízo. Mas, se eu vier a supor que Pedro não podia ter conhecimento de algo sobre o que os demais autores sagrados nada comentaram, então perderei uma preciosa verdade ensinada na Bíblia. No entanto, Paulo revela-nos que a descida de Cristo ao hades teve o mesmo propósito que sua subida dali, ou seja, tornar-se tudo para todos (Efé. 4:8 ss). O Senhor chegará a «preencher a tudo», tornando-se assim tudo para todos, a própria *essência de toda a existência*, bem como sua origem, propósito e alvo. Mas, se eu aferrar-me exclusivamente a Hebreus 9:27, que proclama que a oportunidade de salvação termina por ocasião da morte biológica, terei deixado de entender que algumas porções do Novo Testamento ultrapassam a outras em profundidade, oferecendo-nos novas verdades, e das mais preciosas.

Sabendo que esses informes bíblicos mais profundos são complementares, e não contraditórios com o que o resto da Bíblia nos ensina, isso não enfraquece a nossa fé nos ensinamentos bíblicos, antes, enriquece o nosso entendimento sobre o plano de Deus. Paulo não cessava de orar por seus convertidos, no sentido de que recebessem «...espírito de sabedoria e de revelação no pleno conhecimento dele, iluminados os olhos do vosso coração, para saberdes qual é a esperança do seu chamamento, qual a riqueza da glória da sua herança nos santos» (Efé. 1:17,18). Mesmo que não saibamos colocar todos os ensinos em sua exata seqüência ou ordem de importância, isso é melhor do que eliminar de nosso sistema de doutrinas alguns dos ensinamentos mais profundos da Bíblia, somente porque não se encaixam dentro de nossa limitada compreensão.

Aspectos positivos e bons da crítica. Devo dizer que a crítica da Bíblia pode ser positiva e boa. Com a sua ajuda, posso ter uma atitude mais otimista e uma maior confiança na missão de Cristo. Todavia, sou contrário ao uso negativo da crítica que só tenciona destruir e negar. A verdade é que alguns críticos partem da intenção de destruir a fé, por causa de alguma distorção psicológica que os leva a destruir em vez de edificar. Alguns deles parecem indignados diante da Igreja cristã e seus ensinos. Outros sentem-se insatisfeitos com o próprio cristianismo. Certo crítico alemão chegou ao extremo de negar a *existência* de Jesus, dizendo que a Igreja foi que O inventou!

Todas essas atividades baseadas no negativismo devem ser ignoradas por nós, porquanto não produzirão coisa alguma de proveitoso. Porém, os esforços honestos para melhorar o nosso conhecimento das realidades divinas, mesmo quando nos parecem bizarras, com freqüência produzem *alguns* resultados positivos, capazes de fomentar nosso conhecimento da Bíblia. Também sinto-me na obrigação de dizer que alguns evangélicos muito conservadores fazem parecer importantes para a fé aquilo que, realmente, não tem importância. Conversei com certo homem que nada sabia sobre o idioma grego, em que foi escrito o Novo Testamento, mas que dizia ter a *certeza* de que não podia haver erros gramaticais no texto, porquanto ele tinha a *certeza* de que a Bíblia não pode conter erros de qualquer espécie! Essa *certeza*, baseada na ignorância, de modo algum é louvável. É triste quando a fé de uma pessoa repousa sobre questões triviais como boa ou má gramática. E ainda é mais lamentável quando o conforto mental de alguém é preservado pela ignorância proposital.

A verdade de Deus nunca fica estagnada, e nem nos é perfeitamente revelada neste lado da existência. Ela chega até nós gradualmente, e de várias maneiras. Descobrir a verdade é uma aventura excitante, pois precisamos investigá-la sob muitos ângulos diversos. Também tenho observado que quanto mais sábios nos tornamos, mais otimistas ficamos, e mais respeitamos e confiamos na missão do Logos, Jesus Cristo. Não precisamos de um arcabouço literário perfeito para dispormos de uma boa apreciação da grandeza do plano divino em favor dos homens. Há uma profunda verdade naquela declaração que diz: «Precisamos de mais fé, e de menos crença». É mediante essa fé mais profunda que nosso espírito avança para mais perto de Deus. E, à medida que avançamos, mais percebemos e desejamos a sua luz.

8. *Bibliografia*. AM BUL E GRAN GT GU HAH ID NTI ME MO PF TEN YA YO Z

A Ti, Alma Eterna, seja louvor!
Quem, de dias antigos, até nossos,
Através das almas de santos e profetas, Senhor,
Tem mandado tua Luz, teu Amor,
 — Tua Palavra —

CRÍTICA DE FORMA

Ver o artigo sobre **Crítica da Bíblia**, quarto ponto.

CRÍTICA DE TEXTO

Ver sobre os **Manuscritos Bíblicos**.

CRÍTICA HISTÓRICA

Ver o artigo geral sobre **Crítica da Bíblia**.

CRÍTICA LITERÁRIA

Ver **Crítica da Bíblia**.

CRITICISMO

Essa palavra deriva-se do verbo grego **krínein**, «julgar», «ajuizar», «discernir». O termo é usado nos campos da filosofia, da teologia e da ética.

1. *Na Filosofia*. Esse vocábulo é aplicado à filosofia de Emanuel Kant (que vide), conforme se vê em suas obras *Critique of Pure Reason, Critique of Practical Reason* e *Critique of Judgment*. O seu objetivo era investigar a natureza e os limites do entendimento humano. De modo geral, o termo aplica-se ao uso de um juízo discriminador, de uma avaliação das atividades filosóficas.

2. *Na Teologia e na Religião*. Ali o termo é usado para referir-se à *alta crítica*, isto é, o exame cuidadoso de idéias e documentos, na busca por informações sobre questões como autoria, data, proveniência, problemas especiais, etc., ou seja, qualquer coisa que esteja fora do próprio texto, os manuscritos que estão por detrás das traduções. Esse tipo de estudo também é chamado, embora impropriamente, de *introdução*. O título «alta crítica», por si mesmo é neutro. Pode indicar resultados positivos ou negativos. Visto que a

alta crítica alemã afirmava muitas coisas contrárias à posição dos teólogos conservadores, bem como algumas coisas contrárias ao bom senso e à verdade, a expressão «alta crítica» absorveu uma conotação negativa, para muitas pessoas. A «baixa crítica», por sua vez, é o estudo dos manuscritos antigos, a fim de ser estabelecido o original mais próximo possível, o qual é traduzido para outros idiomas que não sejam o hebraico e o grego. Ver o artigo separado sobre a *Crítica Bíblica*.

3. *Na Ética*. O termo «criticismo» tem sido usado com freqüência para indicar as atitudes censuradoras e as declarações que degradam, desmoralizam e, com freqüência, críticas injustas a outras pessoas. — A isso pode dar-se simplesmente o título de julgamento. Essa prática é condenada em Mat. 7:1 ss e Rom. 2:1 ss. Porém, nenhuma outra atitude errada é mais comum na Igreja cristã do que isso, sem importar se estamos pensando nas denominações evangélicas ou nos membros individuais das igrejas evangélicas.

CRÍTICOS DE JESUS

João 8:46: *Quem dentre vós me convence de pecado? Se digo a verdade, por que não me credes?*

1. Para aqueles que defendem a total abstinência de bebidas alcoólicas, parece suspeito o ato de Jesus, que criou vinho da água. Outros vêem nele apenas um revolucionário, quando se utilizou de açoites contra os cambistas que infestavam o templo. Ainda outros pensam que os evangelhos simplesmente exageraram o quadro de santidade que pintam sobre Jesus.

2. Se Jesus reivindicou divindade para si mesmo, então, conforme asseveram alguns, ele foi um homem blasfemo, no dizer de certos teólogos modernos.

3. Mais basicamente ainda, alguns têm pensado que o ideal de Jesus quanto ao homem — não-violento, humilde, submisso — apenas degrada o ser humano. Muitos outros têm pensado que seu código ético é impraticável.

Alguns incrédulos têm ido tão longe que asseguram que Jesus nos guia erradamente. Assim é que Nietzsche declarou: «...ter vinculado o N.T. juntamente com o A.T., formando um único volume, é talvez a *maior audácia e pecado* contra o Espírito que a Europa, literariamente, tem contra a sua própria consciência». (*Beyond Good and Evil*, Edinburg: T.N. Foulis, 1909, pág. 71). E Freud asseverou: «O que o mundo chama de seu código de moral requer mais sacrifício do que vale a pena, e a sua conduta não é ditada nem pela honestidade e nem é estabelecida pela sabedoria». (*Introductory Lectures on Psycho-Analysis*, Londres: George Allen and Unwin, 1923, pág. 362).

As virtudes de Cristo são desprezadas por alguns, como Nietzsche, o qual afirmou que as suas *virtudes* nem virtudes são, mas antes, são fraquezas, enfermidades, estúpidas repressões, uma espécie de *moralidade escrava*. Acreditava esse filósofo que Cristo equivocou-se ao defender os fracos e os idosos, ao procurar reprimir as paixões humanas. Pois dessa maneira, segundo ele, a fraqueza se transmuta em mérito; a covardia dos caracteres fracos se transforma em «paciência», e a vingança justa é destruída pelo espírito de *perdão*. E o resultado de tudo isso, ainda segundo o mesmo pensador, é que «...o cristão europeu é um anão, uma espécie quase cômica...de tal modo que parece que alguma vontade isolada tem governado a Europa durante dezoito séculos, a fim de fazer um sublime aborto do homem...» (*Beyond Good and Evil*, pág. 84).

Observemos, no entanto, o que sucede aos homens, quando se afastam de Deus. Todavia, é possível que Nietzsche preferisse uma Europa sob o tacão de Hitler do que uma Europa sob o jugo suave de Cristo. «As bestialidades e as inacreditáveis enormidades que têm surgido (entre os homens que rejeitam a Cristo) têm chocado e envergonhado a todos nós, mostrando-nos o quanto devemos a ele (Cristo)». (Arthur John Gossip em João 8:46).

O desafio lançado pelo Senhor Jesus foi muito ousado; mas, através dos séculos, tem permanecido de pé e tem satisfeito a muitos.

Jesus era incomparável

1. Se nos referirmos ao poder de sua vida, aqui vivida então, e à sua influência permanente, quem pode comparar-se com Jesus?

2. Porém, sua excelência moral era mais notável que seus milagres, pois ele mesmo era um milagre espiritual e moral. Sócrates foi um exemplar de excelência moral, em confronto com seus contemporâneos, mas ficamos chocados diante de certas permissividades éticas que ele manifestou. Maomé exibia um espírito fervoroso de espiritualidade, que chega a impressionar; porém, em seus anos finais de vida — degenerou perigosamente.

3. Jesus afirmou que quando fosse levantado, atrairia a si mesmo *todos* os homens (João 12:32). Nada se tem podido dizer, nem nada tem sido registrado na história, quer de natureza político social quer de natureza religioso moral, que tenha diminuído a importância de suas reivindicações. Ele era a encarnação do Logos divino, e, em sua humanidade, destituída de pecado, embora tivesse tido a necessidade de aprender como homem, mediante a obediência ao Pai (ver Heb. 5:7 ss; ver Fil. 2:7 quanto à *humanidade* de Cristo).

CROÇA

Esse é o nome do cajado pastoral de um bispo católico romano. Simboliza sua jurisdição episcopal e seu ofício pastoral. Tem a forma típica de um cajado de pastor, com uma das extremidades recurva.

CROCE, BENEDETTO

Suas datas foram 1866-1952. Filósofo italiano, nascido em Pescasseroli. Fixou residência em Nápolis. Foi historiador e crítico de arte. Não ocupou postos acadêmicos, mas fundou um jornal, *La Critica*. Serviu como senador, membro do gabinete italiano e ministro da educação. Mas, durante o período do fascismo, de Benito Mussolini, separou-se da vida pública.

Idéias:

1. A filosofia e a história não podem ser divorciadas uma da outra, pois ambas estudam o desenvolvimento do espírito. A filosofia do espírito está envolvida nas disciplinas da estética, da lógica, da economia e da ética.

2. Na estética, o âmago é formado pela individualidade e pela liberdade. Os artistas possuem uma função intuitiva que os capacita a perceber a essência da realidade, e suas obras de arte provocam nos contempladores a mesma reação. A individualidade de cada um é retratada e cultivada nas formas de arte. A própria linguagem é uma expressão estética.

3. A lógica é a esfera da verdade universal. Mas Croce estava interessado, não nos universais abstratos, e, sim, nos universais concretos, e como estes conferem-nos discernimento quanto à natureza das

coisas reais.

4. A economia é a esfera da experiência prática, controlada pelo critério da utilidade. A lei é uma utilidade social, ajustando-se às categorias do instrumental e do econômico.

5. A ética é a esfera da experiência prática, que diz respeito ao universal. Abarca a consciência do espírito, como um todo. Com base nisso, podemos derivar certo senso de dever, que ultrapassa as inclinações individuais.

Essas disciplinas, em seu conjunto, expressam o espírito. As descrições dessas disciplinas constituem a filosofia. O espírito é universal e individualizado de pessoa para pessoa.

Obras: *Philosophy of Spirit; Philosophy of the Practical; History, its Theory and Practice; The Essence of Aesthetic; Politics and Morals; Poetry; History as the Story of Liberty; My Philosophy.* (AM P)

CROCODILO

Essa palavra não é usada em muitas traduções, embora muitos pensem que a palavra esteja em foco em Jó 41:1, onde o original hebraico diz *leviatã* (embora nossa versão portuguesa diga ali «crocodilo», talvez seguindo a *Revised Standard Version*, em inglês). É provável que esteja em foco o crocodilo do rio Nilo. Que esse animal está em foco é deduzido com base nos hábitos mencionados, como o fato de que é difícil de ser morto, que seu couro é duro e quase impenetrável, que suas costas contam com escamas, que ele faz o fundo do rio borbulhar como uma panela que ferve, etc., coisas essas que aparecem em Jó 41:7,13,15,26 e 31. Na antiguidade, esse animal era encontrado em toda a extensão do rio Nilo. Mas a caça ao mesmo reduziu em muito a área de seu habitat. Outras regiões, conhecidas pelo povo de Israel, também dispunham de crocodilos. Por essa razão, antes e depois do êxodo, os israelitas tinham consciência da existência deles. Alguns supõem que o «crocodilo» também esteja em foco no trecho de Eze. 29:3 ss. (o que é refletido em nossa versão portuguesa). Mas outros estudiosos preferem pensar no «dragão», uma figura simbólica de Faraó. Em Levítico 11:39 algumas traduções dizem «crocodilo da terra» (o que também se dá com a nossa versão portuguesa). De acordo com as leis levíticas, os répteis eram imundos, impróprios para o consumo humano. O crocodilo pode ser chamado de «grande lagarto», não sendo franqueado à alimentação humana. As dimensões médias do crocodilo, no Oriente Próximo, em nossos dias, são menores que na antiguidade; porém, mesmo na atualidade podem atingir cinco metros, pesando uma tonelada. Esse réptil é carnívoro, alimentando-se de insetos e de toda a espécie de presas. Algumas vezes, tornam-se comedores de seres humanos.

CROMWELL, OLIVER

Suas datas foram 1599-1658. Nasceu em Untingdon, na Inglaterra. Estudou na escola de gramática dirigida pelo puritano Thomas Beard, bem como no Sidney Essex College, de Cambridge. Foi membro do parlamento inglês, de 1640 a 1649. Simpatizava com os puritanos, e era hostil aos bispos e ao clero anglicanos. Foi um hábil líder militar, cujo exército derrotou as tropas de Carlos I. Tornou-se protetor do reino, entre 1653 e 1658, e, através de sua influência, foi decretada a tolerância religiosa na Inglaterra para todos, excetuando os católicos romanos, os anglicanos e as seitas extremistas. Cromwell tentou estabelecer uma igreja nacional inglesa. Era calvinista em seus dogmas, e mostrou-se muito influente no estabelecimento do *congregacionalismo* (que vide).

CRÔNICAS DOS VIDENTES

Algumas traduções, como a nossa versão portuguesa, dizem em II Crônicas 33:19, em vez dessa expressão, «história escrita por Hozai». Está em pauta algum livro ou registro, onde ficaram registrados por escrito a oração de Manassés, a sua pecaminosidade e os seus atos de impiedade. Contudo, a palavra «Hozai», poderia ser um nome próprio, referindo-se ao autor do livro antigo que continha essas crônicas, da mesma forma que Isaías registrou os atos e as obras de Ezequias (II Crô. 32:32). Outros estudiosos preferem entender «Hozai» como «videntes». Nesse caso, estariam em foco os profetas que estiveram envolvidos no reinado de Manassés, em várias ocupações.

CRÔNICAS, LIVROS DE

Esboço:
1. Declaração Geral
2. O Título
3. Autoria
4. Data
5. Autenticidade Histórica
6. Fontes Literárias
7. Motivo e Propósito
8. Filosofia e Teologia
9. Canonicidade
10. Alguns Problemas
11. Conteúdo
12. Bibliografia

1. Declaração Geral

I e II Crônicas são livros históricos do Antigo Testamento, contidos na terceira e última divisão do cânon hebraico (que vide), *os Escritos e os Hagiógrafos* (que vide). Originalmente, esses livros formavam um único volume. Esses livros narram desde Adão até Ciro (538 A.C.), dando atenção especial a Davi (que vide) e aos reis subsequentes de Judá. Essas obras têm sinais de ser uma revisão de livros anteriores e canônicos do Antigo Testamento, sobretudo com base em I e II Samuel e I e II Reis (que vide), de acordo com os interesses e idéias do autor. O autor exibe um interesse especial pelo templo de Jerusalém (que vide), com sua adoração e ritos. Ele também demonstrou um interesse especial pela doutrina da retribuição divina. A tradição judaica atribui a obra desses dois livros a Esdras (que vide); mas muitos eruditos modernos supõem que os mesmos pertencem a um período posterior, isto é, à primeira metade do século III A.C., de autoria do mesmo autor que escreveu os livros de Esdras e Neemias (que vide). Se Esdras viveu na primeira metade do século IV A.C., entretanto, não é impossível que ele tivesse sido, realmente, o autor sagrado. Além de usar os livros canônicos históricos como fontes informativas (Gênesis a II Reis), parece que outras fontes também foram usadas. O valor especial dos livros de Crônicas reside nas explicações e avaliações feitas pelo autor sagrado acerca das idéias e instituições do judaísmo de sua época. Alguns estudiosos supõem que esses livros são suplementares, escritos no espírito dos escritos sacerdotais, P.(S.), embora representem um estágio posterior dos mesmos. Ver o artigo sobre as fontes informativas do

CRÔNICAS

Pentateuco.

2. O Título. O título «Crônicas» foi usado pela primeira vez já nos fins do século IV D.C., em seu equivalente latino, por Jerônimo (que vide). A LXX, a versão grega do Antigo Testamento, compilada no século II A.C., emprega o nome *Paralipomena*, que significa «coisas omitidas», a saber, omitidas de outros livros do Antigo Testamento, e que o autor sagrado desejava suprir. O nome hebraico desses livros é *Dibre Hayamim*, que significa «anais» ou «história». Nas Bíblias grega e latina e na maioria dos idiomas hebraicos, os livros de Crônicas aparecem entre os livros de Reis e de Esdras, ou entre os livros de Esdras e Neemias. Porém, na Bíblia hebraica, aparecem num fim dessa coletânea. Originalmente, eles eram um único volume. A divisão retrocede até à LXX, o que não foi adotado na Bíblia hebraica senão já na Idade Média. Entretanto, não há qualquer evidência de que, originalmente, os livros de Crônicas e Esdras-Neemias formavam um único volume.

3. Autoria. A tradição judaica atribui os livros de Crônicas a Esdras, ao escriba que é personagem nos livros de Esdras e Neemias (Esd. 7:6). A tradição talmúdica (Baba Bathra 15a) confirma essa opinião. O trecho de II Macabeus 2:13-15 indica que Neemias reuniu uma extensa biblioteca (que vide), a qual, provavelmente, esteve à disposição de Esdras, para usá-la como fonte informativa. O relato de Esdras-Neemias cobre aproximadamente o primeiro século do estado judeu restaurado, após o retorno do exílio babilônico em 539 A.C., aludindo, principalmente, às atividades de Esdras e Neemias, após uma breve narrativa sobre o retorno dos judeus e a reconstrução do templo de Jerusalém. É bem provável que Esdras tenha sido o autor de ambos esses livros. Também é possível que ele tenha sentido que um relato atualizado da história de Israel seria útil para conscientizar a sua geração sobre a importância do templo e da tradição judaica em geral. Os livros de Crônicas, segundo parece, resultam desse desejo. O elo entre o final dos livros de Crônicas e o começo do livro de Esdras, bem como a similaridade de ponto de vista desses livros, sugere que eles formam uma unidade; e isso, por sua vez, sugere uma autoria única. Adições de natureza histórica, muito tardias para Esdras, podem ser explicadas como obra de escribas posteriores, os quais atualizaram os livros. Assim, nas genealogias, em I Crô. 3:19-25, os nomes dos descendentes de Zorobabel, até à sexta geração (na LXX, até à décima primeira geração), e a lista dos sumos sacerdotes, em Nee. 12:22, continuam até Jadua que, conforme Josefo explica, viveu na época de Alexandre, o Grande, tendo falecido em 333 A.C., o que ultrapassa à época de Esdras, pelo que deve representar essas adições às quais acabamos de nos referir. Em favor da autoria de Esdras temos igualmente o fato de que nenhum dentre os demais nomes sugeridos adapta-se tão bem aos fatos, como um todo, como o nome de Esdras.

4. Data. Esdras retornou a Jerusalém em 457 A.C. O templo de Jerusalém foi reconstruído em 520-515 A.C., mas a lassidão geral prevalecia no tocante à observância apropriada das instituições judaicas. Portanto, Esdras anelava por melhorar a situação. Neemias retornou à Palestina em 444 A.C., e, novamente, em 432 A.C., como governador do novel estado judaico, provendo à liderança necessária no tocante à reconstrução das muralhas da cidade. Provavelmente, foi durante esse período de ajustamento e reorientação que Esdras escreveu os dois livros de Crônicas. O arqueólogo W.F. Albright defendeu a autoria de Esdras, datando a escrita desses livros entre 400 e 350 A.C. Porém, alguns estudiosos pensam em uma data tão tardia quanto 250 A.C., supondo que escribas posteriores fizeram uma compilação, incluindo algum material que, obviamente, dizia respeito a um período posterior ao de Esdras. Porém, esse material pode ser justificado como adições feitas por escribas posteriores, com o intuito de atualizar a obra.

5. Autenticidade Histórica. O autor sagrado aventura-se a incluir material ainda não contido nos livros canônicos anteriores do Antigo Testamento. Os críticos têm posto em dúvida a historicidade desse material adicional. Todavia, W.F. Albright dá-nos a seguinte garantia: «Os livros de Crônicas contêm grande quantidade de material que aborda a história de Judá, e que não se encontra nos livros dos Reis e... o valor histórico desse material original está sendo confirmado pelas descobertas arqueológicas» (*Bulletin Am. School of Oriental Research* 100, 1945, pág. 18). É verdade que o autor sagrado usou muitas fontes informativas (ver o ponto sexto, abaixo), mas parece que ele se mostrou cuidadoso na seleção que fez. Acresça-se a isso que é bom lembrar que os hebreus eram muito sensíveis à história, e que pelo menos desde 1000 A.C. em diante, os relatos apresentados por ele têm sido achados bastante exatos.

6. Fontes Informativas Literárias. O próprio autor sagrado refere-se a vários escritos que contêm novas informações sobre a história de Israel; e, apesar de não afirmar especificamente que se utilizou deles, isso é o que se pode deduzir. Os livros de Crônicas distinguem-se por serem as obras do Antigo Testamento que mais alusões fazem a fontes externas aos livros sagrados.

Muitas dessas fontes informativas estão agora perdidas.

As Fontes Informativas:

1. *Registros oficiais*, talvez existentes na biblioteca de Neemias, incluindo outros livros do Antigo Testamento:

   a. A história do Rei Davi (I Crô. 27:24).
   b. Os livros canônicos dos Reis (II Crô. 16:11; 25:26; 27:7; 28:26; 32:27; 35:27 e 36:8).
   c. O livro da história dos reis (II Crô. 24:27).
   d. A prescrição de Davi, rei de Israel, e a de Salomão, seu filho (II Crô. 35:4).

2. *Escritos e registros proféticos*:

   a. Samuel (I Crô. 29:29).
   b. Natã (I Crô. 29:29 e II Crô. 9:29).
   c. Gade (I Crô. 21:9).
   d. Ido (II Crô. 9:29; 12:15 e 13:22).
   e. Aías (II Crô. 9:29).
   f. Semaías (II Crô. 20:34).
   g. Jeú, filho de Hanani (II Crô. 12:15).
   h. Isaías (II Crô. 26:22; 32:32).
   i. Hozai (II Crô. 33:19).

3. *Diversas outras fontes*. Listas genealógicas e documentos oficiais (II Crô. 32:10-15); as cartas de Senaqueribe (II Crô. 32:10-15); as palavras de Asafe e Davi (II Crô. 29:30); o documento com planos para a construção do templo de Jerusalém (I Crô. 28:19). Essas fontes informativas não são, necessariamente, todas elas, documentos separados. Além dos escritos canônicos do Antigo Testamento, que contêm a essência da mensagem dos profetas, também há um número regular de escritos que lhes são semelhantes, mas que nunca fizeram parte do cânon do Antigo Testamento.

7. Motivos e Propósitos. Esdras já vinha atuando

CRÔNICAS

ativamente em Jerusalém, como mestre da lei, por mais de uma década, antes que Neemias chegasse como governador, em 444 A.C. A obra de Neemias renovou os interesses espirituais do povo judeu, o que pode ter sido aproveitado por Esdras como a ocasião apropriada para reforçar esse avanço, pondo em dia os escritos históricos de Israel. Se o povo judeu adquirisse maior orgulho a respeito de sua história e de suas tradições religiosas, sentir-se-ia mais fortalecido em uma época de renovação. Alianças foram renovadas, as festas religiosas foram celebradas (Nee. 8-10). O livro não declara especificamente o seu propósito; mas, com base em seu conteúdo, podemos obter uma boa idéia sobre esse propósito. O autor sagrado não queria meramente repetir a história. Ele não apresentou fatos, deixando muitos deles sem serem mencionados. Porém, por detrás dessa sua nova narração da história, ele tinha um certo propósito teológico e filosófico. Por exemplo, ao descrever o reinado de Davi, ele demonstrou a supremacia militar e os interesses religiosos desse grande rei de Israel. Ele relatou, com abundância de detalhes, as coisas que Davi realizou, como se estivesse dizendo obviamente ao povo: «É chegado o tempo de restaurar as coisas, em consonância com o estilo davídico». Ele retratou Salomão sob luzes favoráveis, visto que foi Salomão quem construiu o templo de Jerusalém. Sem dúvida é significativo que a apostasia de Salomão, tão cuidadosamente delineada no décimo primeiro capítulo de I Reis, seja inteiramente omitida nas Crônicas. É que o autor sagrado queria projetar um exemplo positivo, que pudesse ser seguido; e ele não queria obscurecer esse ponto, narrando os aspectos negativos do relato. E o autor sagrado usou do mesmo esquema ao relatar os atos de outros reis. As virtudes deles foram enfatizadas, para que pudessem servir de bons exemplos.

8. Filosofia e Teologia. A fim de transmitir a sua mensagem, o autor sagrado teve a inspiração de apresentar pontos de vista e propósitos específicos. Ele tinha uma certa filosofia a comunicar.

a. *A lei da colheita segundo a semeadura*. Deus ocupa-se da retribuição, de uma maneira ativa. A história não é algo que meramente acontece. Há uma reconhecida relação entre causas e efeitos, e essas causas e efeitos estão baseados em condições morais. O vigésimo primeiro capítulo de II Reis, que é a base de II Crônicas 33, diz muita coisa má a respeito de Manassés. Porém, nas mãos do autor sagrado dos livros de Crônicas, esses atos errados não foram relatados, porquanto isso seria incompatível com o longo e pacífico reinado de Manassés. E ele também teve o cuidado de narrar o exílio e o arrependimento de Manassés, mostrando como ele retornou a Israel a fim de levar uma vida caracterizada pela piedade (II Crô. 33:11-13).

b. *A questão da autoridade*. A fim de que a vontade de Deus seja cumprida entre o povo, é mister que haja uma autoridade apropriada, estabelecida entre os homens, com líderes legítimos. Os primeiros 405 versículos dos livros de Crônicas enfatizam esse tema.

c. *O Davidismo*. Davi é o grande herói que o autor sagrado pinta com cores brilhantes, a fim de que ele pudesse ser o grande exemplo heróico para o povo judeu seguir. As questões éticas sempre foram importantes. O autor sagrado diz que Davi traçou planos cuidadosos para a construção do templo, algo que não é revelado em outras fontes informativas. No entanto, isso era importante para o propósito do autor sagrado. Ele precisava de exemplos claros sobre o uso apropriado do templo e de seus rituais. Davi e Salomão servem de exemplo sobre a preocupação apropriada a respeito dessas coisas. Precisamos estar interessados em cumprir a vontade de Deus.

d. *Uma ênfase exclusiva*. Os lances mais antigos do Antigo Testamento, como a história dos patriarcas, o êxodo, a conquista da Palestina, etc., quase não são mencionados. Isso se harmoniza com o propósito do autor sagrado de salientar o templo de Jerusalém. Por essa razão, a sua narrativa não é proporcional, e, quanto a esse aspecto, deixou de ser história, para tornar-se muito mais uma crônica. Poderíamos chamar essa narrativa de história *selecionada*, compilada para servir a um propósito religioso e prático. Alguns eruditos fazem objeção a essa distorção, acusando o autor sagrado de ter querido reescrever a história. Porém, parece melhor supormos que essa porção do livro não tinha o propósito específico de ser história, no seu sentido comum. Há porções dos livros de Crônicas que são mais tratados religiosos, historicamente baseados.

9. Canonicidade. Desde que se completou o cânon do Antigo Testamento ou Bíblia hebraica (que vide), os livros de Crônicas foram incluídos. Esses livros foram incluídos por Josefo dentro dos vinte e dois livros de que consistia o cânon hebreu. Mas então a arrumação dos livros era outra, e esse número correspondia aos nossos mesmos trinta e nove livros. Segundo se pode depreender de seus escritos, parece que Josefo acreditava que o cânon do Antigo Testamento completou-se por volta de 400 A.C. Os livros de Crônicas ficavam dentro da classe dos *Escritos*, a terceira divisão do cânon hebraico. Aparecem em último lugar dentro da coletânea da Bíblia hebraica original; mas isso parece estar de acordo com um arranjo histórico, não servindo de indicação de prioridade canônica. Quanto a maiores detalhes sobre a questão ver o artigo sobre o *Cânon do Antigo Testamento*.

10. Alguns Problemas:

a. A questão da data e da autoria é criada pelo problema que cerca o trecho de I Crô. 3:19-24, bem como a lista dos sumos sacerdotes, em Neemias 12:22. Ambas as passagens ultrapassam da época de Esdras. Podemos encarar isso como indicação de que os livros foram escritos após a época de Esdras ou então como indicação de que a obra original foi expandida por escribas posteriores. Ver a discussão sob *Data* e sobre *Autoria*.

b. Alguns críticos não se satisfazem com a implicação dos livros de Crônicas de que Davi fez todos os planos relativos ao templo de Jerusalém e estabeleceu as guildas de cantores. Esses supõem que isso promove uma espécie de davidismo, segundo o qual Davi seria manipulado como uma espécie de herói, a fim de inspirar o povo a interessar-se pelo templo e seu ritual. Porém, o arqueólogo W.F. Albright descobriu evidências em prol da assertiva de que essas guildas musicais não somente remontam aos dias de Davi, mas até mesmo aos tempos dos cananeus, muito antes da época de Davi (*The Old Testament and Archeology*, conforme citado por Alleman e Flack, em *Old Testament Commentary*, pág. 63). E há fontes informativas egípcias que se referem a músicos cananeus durante o segundo milênio A.C.; e os fundadores das guildas musicais, nos registros do Antigo Testamento, têm nomes cananeus.

c. *Novos informes históricos*. Nos pontos onde os livros de Crônicas vão além da história canônica do Antigo Testamento, têm sido levantadas algumas dúvidas. Sobre tais questões, entretanto, Albright afirma que as descobertas arqueológicas têm confirmado coerentemente a historicidade do livro de Crônicas. Ver o quinto ponto, sobre *Autenticidade Histórica*.

11. Conteúdo:
I. *Genealogias de Adão a Saul* - I Crô. 1:1-9:44.
  1. De Adão a Noé, 1:1-4.
  2. Dos filhos de Noé a Jacó e Esaú, 1:5-54.
  3. Os filhos de Jacó, 2:1-9:44.
     a. Judá, a linhagem real, 2:1-4:23.
     b. Outras tribos, 4:24-8:40.
     c. Levi, 6:1-81.
     d. Oficiais do templo, 9:1-34.
     e. Saul, 9:35-44.
II. *Davi, o Grande Exemplo* — I Crô. 10:1-29:30.
  1. Morte de Saul, 10:1-14.
  2. A captura de Sião e os guerreiros de Davi, 11:1-12:40.
  3. Davi como rei, 13:1-22:1.
  4. Contribuição de Davi para o templo, 22:1-29:30.
III. *História de Salomão* — II Crô. 1:1-9:31.
  1. Sua prosperidade, 1:1-17.
  2. Construção do templo, 2:1-7:22.
  3. Sua obra e sua morte, 8:1-9:31.
IV. *Os Reis de Judá* — 10:1-36:23.
  1. De Reoboão a Zedequias, 10:1-36:21.
  2. O decreto de Ciro, o exílio e o retorno, 36:22,23.
  12. *Bibliografia*.ALBR AM BRI IB KEI ND ROW Z

CRONISTA

No hebraico significa **alguém que faz lembrar**. Ocupava importante função oficial em Israel, como arauto. O cronista era um dos diversos importantes oficiais da corte real de Israel. (Quanto aos nomes dos outros, ver em II Sam. 8:16-18 e I Crô. 18:14-17; II Sam. 20:23-26; I Reis 4:1-6). Embora os termos hebraicos ocorram por nove vezes, os deveres exigidos do cronista nunca são mencionados na Bíblia. Se o termo «cronista» descreve o ofício, então ele deve ter estado ligado ao registro dos eventos oficiais da nação. Contudo, essa tarefa parece ter sido função do escriba real. Uma outra possibilidade é que ele era um oficial vocal, uma espécie de relações públicas do governo. Esse parece ter sido o caso de Joá, filho de Asafe, um cronista durante o reinado de Ezequias. Juntamente com dois outros oficiais, ele representou o rei Ezequias nas negociações com o Rabsaqué que representava Senaqueribe, rei da Assíria (II Reis 18:18,37; Isa. 36:3,22). Um outro Joá, filho de Joacaz, foi cronista durante o reinado de Josias (II Crô. 34:8). Juntamente com Safã e Maaséias, ele foi delegado para pagar os trabalhadores que repararam o templo, durante a reforma do mesmo. Finalmente, Josafá foi o cronista durante os reinados de Davi e Salomão, embora a natureza de seu ofício não seja indicada (II Sam. 8:16; 20:24; I Reis 4:3; I Crô. 18:15). A menção dos cronistas, desde Davi a Josias, indica que o ofício prosseguiu até o fim da monarquia.

CRONOLOGIA DO ANTIGO TESTAMENTO
Esboço:
  I. Definição e Declaração Geral
  II. Alguns Métodos Usados nas Datas
  III. Problemas Comuns da Cronologia
  IV. Metodologia
  V. Períodos Bíblicos Específicos
  VI. Cronologia Literária
  VII. Gráficos Históricos e Literários

I. Definição e Declaração Geral

A cronologia é a ciência que nos permite fixar datas, arranjando o tempo passado em períodos ou divisões, além de situar os locais dos eventos nos lugares certos, dentro desse arranjo. Os cronologistas dão a entender que há dois tipos principais de fixação de datas: a. *Fixação relativa*: Os períodos e os eventos são postos em *relação* a uma seqüência estabelecida, mostrando que alguns eventos são anteriores ou posteriores a outros, embora sem qualquer tentativa específica de determinar datas exatas. Os eventos ou períodos que ocorrem ao mesmo tempo são chamados *sincrônicos*. Mas os eventos ou períodos que ocorrem em tempos diferentes são chamados *discrônicos*. b. *Fixação cronométrica*: Essa forma de fixação de datas apresenta datas exatas ou aproximadas, ou então apresenta um período dentro do qual certos eventos tiveram lugar, como de 12.000 até 10.000 A.C. Esse segundo método é o grande alvo dos historiadores; mas, com freqüência, é impraticável.

II. Alguns Métodos Usados nas Datas

a. *Paralelos históricos e literários*. Algumas vezes, uma data exata ou aproximada pode ser estabelecida relacionando-se a mesma a um outro evento histórico mencionado na literatura, que ocorreu na mesma época. Ver exemplos acerca desses paralelos em Lucas 2:1 e 3:1.

b. *Referências astronômicas*. Os astrônomos são capazes de datar qualquer acontecimento astronômico do passado; e, se houver referências literárias a esse acontecimento, então pode-se determinar uma data exata. O trecho de Mateus 2:2, onde é aludida a estrela de Belém, talvez uma alusão a uma rara conjunção de planetas, nos fornece uma data aproximada para o nascimento de Cristo.

c. *Registros históricos paralelos*. Os povos antigos conservavam registros históricos. E, apesar de que usualmente eram repletos de inexatidões, eles nos provêem muito material para a fixação de datas.

d. *Fixação do tempo pelo método do carbono* 14. Esse método mede o carbono 14 restante em qualquer matéria que fora viva. É que o carbono 14 vai decrescendo em quantidade em qualquer organismo animal ou vegetal, após a morte do mesmo, de uma maneira uniforme. O nível de carbono 14 restante, em qualquer objeto animal ou vegetal, encontrado pela arqueologia, pode ser comparado com o nível do mesmo animal ou vegetal vivo, o que nos fornece uma data aproximada de sua morte. Esse método pode estabelecer datas com bastante acurácia até cerca de sessenta mil anos. Após isso a mostragem do tempo torna-se *mais curta* do que realmente se passou. Ver o artigo separado sobre essa fixação de datas pelo método do *Carbono* 14, quanto a uma declaração mais detalhada e informativa.

e. *Fixação do tempo pelo método do potássio argônio*. Esse sistema pode fixar a antiguidade das coisas que ultrapassam o alcance do método do carbono 14. Tal método alicerça-se sobre a perda de radioatividade do potácio 40 em cálcio 40, e daí, para o argônio 40, utilizando proporções conhecidas em termos de taxas conhecidas de transformação. Esse método pode retroceder um milhão de anos de forma bastante exata. E as datas ainda mais antigas, estabelecidas de acordo com esse método, provavelmente não erram muito da realidade. A perda de

CRONOLOGIA DO ANTIGO TESTAMENTO

radioatividade nos meteoritos sugere que o nosso sistema solar foi formado há cerca de 4.700.000.000 de anos atrás.

f. *Termoluminiscência*. Esse método tem sido usado para se datar objetos de cerâmica. Quando um objeto de argila é aquecido ao rubro em um forno, cada eléctron volta a uma posição estável e emite uma luz que pode ser fotografada. Se um fragmento antigo de cerâmica for reaquecido em laboratório, pequenas quantidades de luz serão emitidas pelo fragmento. Essa quantidade de termoluminiscência indicará quanta perda de radiação foi sofrida por cada eléctron. Portanto, a quantidade de termoluminiscência serve de medida do tempo que se passou desde que a peça de cerâmica foi fabricada. O Museu da Universidade da Pennsylvania, nos Estados Unidos da América, muito tem trabalhado para refinar esse método. O método aprimorado consiste em bombardear a peça de cerâmica para ela ser analisada mediante raios X.

g. *Fixação de datas mediante a obsidiana*. De acordo com esse método é medida a camada de hidrogênio deixada sobre a obsidiana (uma rocha vulcânica vítrea), mediante a absorção de água.

h. *Magnetismo termorremanescente*. O magnetismo remanescente, causado pelo aquecimento (usualmente em um forno), é comparado com a direção e intensidade sempre mutáveis do campo magnético do globo terrestre.

i. *Teste pela fluorina*. Segundo esse método, datas relativas podem ser estabelecidas comparando-se o conteúdo da fluorina restante, em ossos antigos e ossos recentes.

j. *Análise do Pólen*. A identificação e enumeração dos tipos de pólen presentes em um objeto antigo qualquer podem ser comparados com uma escala de tempo, comparando-se esse objeto com outros espécimes de data conhecida.

l. *Camadas de sedimentação*. De conformidade com esse método, as camadas de sedimentos, deixadas pelas geleiras, são contadas e correlacionadas a informes similares, colhidos em outros lugares.

m. *Dendrocronologia*. As árvores contam com anéis de crescimento sobrepostos, resultantes da passagem de épocas específicas. Esse método pode datar árvores com até três mil anos de antiguidade.

III. Problemas Comuns da Cronologia

a. *A vasta antiguidade da terra*. Na verdade, a história real da terra é desconhecida. A narrativa sobre Adão fornece-nos um começo recente. Muitos eruditos da Bíblia estão convencidos, através das investigações científicas, de que houve eras pré-adâmicas, completas até com raças pré-adâmicas, que nada têm a ver com a Bíblia, excetuando o ponto que o começo de todas as coisas foi determinado divinamente, nossos métodos de fixação de datas são alistados sob o segundo ponto, acima, fazendo-nos retroceder até quase cinco bilhões de anos, no tocante à antiguidade do nosso sistema solar, e até, pelo menos, dezesseis bilhões de anos, no que concerne ao início do universo. Ver o artigo sobre *Astronomia*. Por conseguinte, podemos dizer com toda a verdade e certeza que a história de Adão é história relativamente *recente*. Sentimo-nos inteiramente perdidos na incerteza, quando temos de tratar com os primórdios verdadeiramente antigos.

b. *A inexatidão dos registros antigos*. Essa inexatidão deve-se mais à ausência de pontos de referência. Os registros antigos com freqüência estavam mais interessados na simetria do que na exatidão dos registros dos reinados e acontecimentos importantes. Os eventos são algumas vezes mencionados somente em relação a certas dinastias.

c. *Alterações nas inscrições antigas*. Várias inscrições recentemente achadas, provenientes do Egito, segundo se tem descoberto, foram alteradas em algum tempo no passado. Além disso, sabe-se que certos monarcas, por um orgulho estúpido, deixaram alistadas batalhas que eles supostamente venceram, mas nas quais nunca se envolveram. Além disso, certas ocorrências, que realmente tiveram lugar, são exageradas e distorcidas, para satisfazer a soberba de governantes.

d. *O uso de números redondos*. Lemos que Saul, Davi e Salomão reinaram, cada um, durante quarenta anos. Ora, isso seria uma incrível coincidência. Portanto, podemos pensar em números propositalmente arredondados. Ou, segundo alguns estudiosos pensam, seria uma maneira oriental de expressar longos reinados.

e. *Ausência de calendários exatos e formalizados* (ver sobre *Calendário*). Essa ausência não permitia que os acontecimentos fossem exatamente registrados, no tocante ao tempo. Vários povos contavam suas datas a partir de vários começos históricos, reais ou imaginários. Além disso, a duração dos anos variava de sistema para sistema.

f. *Conflitos de autoridade*. O trecho de II Crônicas 21:20 revela-nos que o rei Jeorão tinha trinta e dois anos de idade quando começou a reinar, tendo morrido após um reinado de oito anos, com a idade de quarenta anos, portanto. Mas o capítulo seguinte (vs. 22), diz-nos que seu filho mais jovem, Acazias, o sucedeu, tendo quarenta e dois anos de idade quando subiu ao trono. Isso significaria que Acazias nasceu dois anos antes de seu pai, e que os seus irmãos mais velhos nasceram antes mesmo disso. O trecho paralelo de II Reis (8:26) fala em vinte e dois anos, e não em quarenta e dois anos. E isso significa que, no original hebraico, a letra *mem* foi escrita, por engano, em lugar da letra *cafe*. No entanto, a Septuaginta fala em vinte anos, não correspondendo nem a quarenta e dois e nem a vinte e dois. Portanto, em algum ponto, houve erros de transcrição, pelo menos. Naturalmente, os harmonizadores só faltam perder a cabeça na tentativa para explicar essas discrepâncias, porquanto não gostam de erros no texto bíblico que perturbem suas teorias de inspiração. Acresça-se a isso que esses erros podem ter sido introduzidos no processo de cópia, através dos séculos. Por essa razão, John Gill, em seu comentário sobre o Antigo Testamento, alista I Crônicas 22:2 como trecho que merecia certa explicação, mas terminou dizendo: «Parece melhor reconhecermos que houve aqui um erro de cópia, que facilmente poderia ter ocorrido, devido à similaridade entre os números quarenta e dois e vinte e dois». Questões cronológicas não envolvem pontos de fé, embora algumas pessoas pensem assim.

g. *Os historiadores antigos*, em contraste com os historiadores modernos, com freqüência não estavam interessados pela exatidão dos registros, esforçando-se apenas por uma narrativa bem organizada, mas permitindo a existência de grandes hiatos de tempo. Mas a falha oposta também era comum. Os reinados de alguns monarcas eram aumentados, quanto ao número de anos, para que fosse obtida uma certa data. Ver o item abaixo.

h. *Os monarcas hebreus*. É bem provável que nenhuma outra cronologia tenha recebido maior atenção, por parte dos eruditos, do que a dos hebreus. Nas narrativas sobre os reinados dos monarcas de Judá e de Israel, a duração de cada reinado foi

CRONOLOGIA DO A. TESTAMENTO

registrada com referências cruzadas, dizendo-nos em qual ano do reinado de algum rei de Judá, algum rei de Israel subiu ao trono. Apesar de um esquema assim, a cronologia envolvida está maculada por problemas insolúveis. Para começar, os anos registrados totais dos reis de Judá, até à queda de Samaria, envolvem trinta e um anos a mais que dos reis de Israel, durante o mesmo período, e nenhuma referência cruzada, após os dois primeiros reinados, está rigidamente correta. Os anos que se passaram entre o primeiro e o segundo templos de Jerusalém foram exatamente quatrocentos e oitenta anos. Os anos dos reis de Israel foram de duzentos e quarenta. O período desde a partida de Abraão, de Ur, ao êxodo, foi de quatrocentos e oitenta anos, e do êxodo até o primeiro templo, também foi de quatrocentos e oitenta anos. Notemos como os duzentos e quarenta anos são exatamente a metade de quatrocentos e oitenta. É evidente que os cronistas hebreus estavam procurando atingir a simetria, e não a exatidão, em seus registros históricos. Os estudiosos modernos acreditam que os reinados do período da monarquia foram propositalmente alongados nas narrativas, para que se amoldassem ao período de quatrocentos e oitenta anos, e também que o período do exílio dos hebreus, no Egito, foi alongado, para fazê-lo coincidir com as invasões dos hicsos. Além disso, os tradutores da Septuaginta, quando tomaram conhecimento, através da obra recentemente publicada de Maneto, intitulada *Aegyptiaca* (em cerca de 280 A.C.), de que o rei egípcio, Menes, havia reinado em data ainda mais antiga do que se pensava, — alongaram as vidas dos patriarcas hebreus, para que a história do povo hebreu fosse mais antiga que a dos egípcios. Talvez tivessem feito isso com base na idéia de que a antiguidade envolve uma certa glória. Parece que precisamos reconhecer que os números eram manipulados para obtenção de resultados como simetria, glorificação ou conveniência. Mas não eram considerados importantes para efeito de exatidão. Ora, isso não se adapta à moderna maneira de pensar sobre as coisas. Os critérios mudam com a passagem do tempo, e os critérios antigos não eram os mesmos que usamos. No entanto, declarações como essas não agradam aos harmonizadores, os quais têm a idéia fixa de que a inspiração envolve certos detalhes, como números exatos. Porém, a verdade dos fatos é mais importante do que a harmonia a qualquer preço.

i. *Genealogias*. Os registros genealógicos existentes na Bíblia deixam grandes hiatos de tempo, para efeito de simetria. Basta-nos examinar o trecho de Mateus 1:17, com catorze gerações simétricas em cada grupo: de Abraão a Davi; de Davi ao cativeiro babilônico; e do cativeiro babilônico até o Cristo. Essa simetria forçada provavelmente tinha finalidades mnemônicas, para ajudar à memória dos leitores quanto ao tempo envolvido. Há alguma evidência, nas genealogias do Antigo Testamento, que, às vezes, um homem qualquer, em vez de envolver um só indivíduo, envolvia toda a história de um clã ou de uma tribo, devendo-se pensar em várias gerações, e não em uma somente. Atualmente, os estudiosos admitem que as genealogias representam muito mais tempo do que o resultado obtido pela soma das idades das pessoas envolvidas. Por isso, a erudição bíblica abandonou o método de calcular a passagem do tempo com a ajuda das genealogias. Isso não foi levado em conta pelo bispo Ussher, um dos primeiros estudiosos modernos a lançar mão do método da contagem do tempo através das genealogias bíblicas. Os escritores sagrados não visavam tanto a uma cronologia exata, mas antes, visavam à simetria, para efeito de facilitar a memorização. Ver as notas no NTI, sobre Mateus 1:1, quanto a evidências que confirmam o que acabamos de dizer.

IV. Metodologia

O antigo método de fixação de datas mediante os números dados nas genealogias bíblicas é extremamente inexato. Isso é assim porque existem hiatos feitos propositalmente com finalidades de simetria; porque certos eventos alistados ocorreram paralelamente, e não consecutivamente; porque um único nome pode representar toda uma linhagem, ou uma tribo, e não uma única pessoa; porque quase certamente houve raças pré-adâmicas que não foram levadas em conta na narrativa de Gênesis, que só se interessa por uma história relativamente recente, isto é, a partir de Adão em diante. Há evidências geológicas de cerca de quatrocentas mudanças dos pólos do globo terrestre. Quando isso sucede, a crosta da terra desliza, os continentes são rearranjados e os oceanos ocupam novas localizações. Isso envolve destruições cataclísmicas, em que tudo quanto há à face do planeta, por assim dizer, tem um novo começo. As duas últimas mudanças de pólos correspondem, a grosso modo, aos relatos atinentes a Adão e a Noé. E isso permite-nos presumir que eles representam *novos começos* na história humana, e não começos absolutos. A maior parte das descobertas arqueológicas, em face das vastas destruições envolvidas nesses eventos cataclísmicos, abarcam somente a história recente, ou seja, o período relatado na Bíblia. Entretanto, há muitos outros períodos, anteriores a esse, que antecedem à nossa era não somente por milhares, mas até mesmo por milhões de anos, e sobre os quais a Bíblia nada nos informa, a não ser, talvez, em termos extremamente vagos, nos nos seus primeiros dois versículos. Isso é assim porque a Bíblia não foi escrita para ensinar-nos a história geológica do mundo, mas para explicar o plano de Deus acerca da humanidade. Pode ter havido, portanto, muitas civilizações irrecuperáveis para os registros históricos, excetuando alguma descoberta ocasional, que não se ajusta ao resto dos fatos conhecidos. Alguns estudiosos chegam a pensar que há alguma evidência material e literária que nos permite imaginar o uso da energia atômica, por civilizações passadas, com a conseqüente destruição das mesmas. Por esses e outros motivos, solicito ao leitor que examine o artigo intitulado os *Antediluvianos*. Esse artigo, além de exibir as evidências que há em prol dessa idéia, aborda o problema da harmonização, da reconciliação e da cronologia, o que não repito neste artigo.

Métodos Atuais. Muitos eruditos modernos, além de se escudarem nos dados cronológicos oferecidos na Bíblia, procuram estabelecer ou confirmar datas por meio da arqueologia. Isso nos permite examinar os acontecimentos de muitas civilizações que não são mencionadas na Bíblia—não necessariamente anteriores a Adão—mas que nos ajudam a estabelecer melhor as datas. Assim, têm sido encontradas muitas inscrições antigas onde são mencionados nomes e lugares referidos na Bíblia. A partir de 620 A.C., há um arcabouço cronológico que nos é provido pelo cânon de Ptolomeu, além de outras fontes informativas clássicas, como os escritos de Meneto. Acrescente-se a isso os tabletes e inscrições da Babilônia. Antes mesmo desses, temos os registros assírios. Certo eclipse do sol, mencionado em antigas fontes literárias, e que agora sabemos ter ocorrido a 15 de junho de 763 A.C., fornece-nos um meio de fixar datas para eventos de antes e de depois desse eclipse. Assim, há as listas de reis da Assíria que nos fazem

CRONOLOGIA DO A. TESTAMENTO

recuar até cerca de 2000 A.C., sem falar em listas de reis babilônicos, similares. Não há que duvidar que essas listas envolvem inexatidões e manipulações, tal como se dá no caso das listas dos reis hebreus, mas, pelo menos, através dessas fontes, podemos obter uma idéia geral da cronologia de períodos até dois milênios A.C. As fontes informativas egípcias ajudam-nos a estabelecer datas desde 1200 até 2100 A.C. Essas fontes incluem listas de reis, registros sobre alguns fenômenos astronômicos, mediante os quais alguns reinados podem ser datados com precisão. Destarte, as dinastias XI e XII do Egito podem ser agora datadas entre 2134 a 1786 A.C., enquanto que as dinastias de XVIII a XX ficam entre 1570 a 1085 A.C., com um erro máximo de, talvez, dez anos. As datas relativas à Mesopotâmia, entre 2000 e 1500 A.C., dependem em grande parte da data que atribuimos a Hamurabi, da Babilônia; e, nesse caso, provavelmente há uma margem de erro de cem anos ou mesmo mais.

Quanto mais retrocedemos para além do ano 2000 A.C., maiores incertezas fazem-se presentes. Para datas anteriores a 3000 A.C.; precisamos depender, quase exclusivamente, de métodos de fixação de datas como o do carbono 14, ou de outros métodos, enumerados no segundo ponto, acima. É possível determinar datas, com notável exatidão; os vários níveis de ocupação humana que as escavações arqueológicas vão descobrindo; e assim vamos retrocedendo de uma civilização a outra. A partir da época de Salomão em diante, até Cristo, podem ser estabelecidas datas com maior exatidão. Mas, quanto mais recuamos, de Salomão para trás, maiores dificuldades encontram os cronologistas, em suas pesquisas.

V. Períodos Bíblicos Específicos

a. Período pré-adâmico. Evidências extrabíblicas certamente indicam não apenas a existência do mundo físico antes de Adão, mas até mesmo de raças pré-adâmicas de seres inteligentes. Ver o artigo sobre os *Antediluvianos*, quanto a evidências a esse respeito. Esse artigo também menciona meios através dos quais os estudiosos da Bíblia procuram reconciliar essa questão com as declarações e considerações bíblicas. A arqueologia tem descoberto objetos pré-adâmicos; e vários métodos de fixação de datas, conforme se vê no segundo ponto deste artigo, confirmam a grande antiguidade do nosso sistema solar e do universo. Atualmente, estamos recebendo luz de estrelas e galáxias que precisaram de dezesseis bilhões de anos para chegar até nós. A luz precisa de cerca de sessenta mil anos ao menos para atravessar, de um extremo a outro, a nossa própria galáxia, ou Via Láctea, que é o nosso próprio pequeno universo, sendo ela apenas uma dentre muitos bilhões de galáxias. E agora, devemos falar em «nosso próprio pequeno universo» porque o nosso sol é apenas um dentre muitos bilhões de sóis que se encontram na Via Láctea. Além da Via Láctea, há outras dezesseis galáxias que nos estão mais próximas, além de incontáveis bilhões de outras galáxias, mais distantes, espalhadas pelo universo. A Via Láctea é aquilo que vemos a cada noite, com exceção de algumas pequenas manchas de luz, visíveis a olho nu, que vêm de fora da nossa própria galáxia. Portanto, a Via Láctea, a despeito de suas descomunais dimensões, é apenas o nosso portão de entrada. No entanto, para que a luz atravesse de uma ponta à outra na nossa Via Láctea, é preciso de cerca de sessenta mil anos.

O método de fixação de datas através do potássio argônio nos dá quase cinco bilhões de anos como a idade de nosso próprio sistema solar.

Portanto, quando a Bíblia diz, no seu primeiro versículo, «No princípio criou Deus...», está em pauta um começo muito remoto e misterioso. E quando lemos que Deus criou Adão, podemos pensar em um outro começo, bem mais recente. Imaginemos a verdadeira história do globo terrestre como uma enciclopédia de muitos volumes de mil páginas cada um. Nesse caso, podemos imaginar a história de Adão como um verbete que aparece na última página do último volume dessa enciclopédia. As demais páginas desse último volume estão quase inteiramente perdidas para nós, excetuando um ou outro indício muito raro. E todos os demais volumes anteriores estão irremediavelmente perdidos para nós. É que grandes **cataclismos sepultaram** para sempre a história verdadeiramente antiga da terra, e apenas ocasionalmente vem à tona alguma coisa que está narrada nas páginas anteriores desse último volume da imaginária enciclopédia. Nossa cronologia, excetuando alguns raros itens, não consegue examinar coisa alguma das primeiras novecentas e noventa e nove páginas do último volume. O que sabemos é que Deus já estava nesse último volume, e em todos os volumes anteriores; que a terra surgiu em algum desses volumes; que houve outras criaturas inteligentes na terra, antes do aparecimento do *Homo sapiens*, a raça adâmica. Não há como encaixar, dentro dos supostos seis mil anos que se passaram, desde a criação da terra, até os nossos dias, todas as ocorrências geológicas que a ciência já tem podido descobrir.

Isso posto, ninguém pode dizer: «Seis mil anos é a idade da criação de Deus».

b. De Adão a Noé. O método genealógico vale-se dos trechos de Gênesis 5:1-32 e de Gênesis 7:6 como base de seus cálculos. Os estudiosos das tabelas patriarcais, após terem verificado como os hebreus manipulavam suas genealogias, nas quais há tão frequentes omissões, onde um nome pode representar toda uma linhagem, com muitas gerações, etc.—problemas esses sobre os quais já nos manifestamos, acima—são forçados a ignorar o método cronológico usado pelo bispo Ussher (que vide), o qual estabeleceu que a data da criação teria ocorrido em cerca de 4000 A.C. A tentativa de manutenção desse método de fixação de datas só consegue levar-nos aos mais crassos absurdos. Parece justo dizermos, mesmo quando defendemos a historicidade de Adão, do que não abrimos mão, que as genealogias envolvidas contêm somente alguns dos nomes mais importantes, saltando, em muitos casos, por cima de muitas gerações. É que o propósito desses registros bíblicos não era o de fornecer-nos uma história cronológica, mas apenas mostrar-nos a linhagem ou descendência de Jesus Cristo. Para tanto, bastou um relato histórico *geral* da raça humana, e não foi preciso fornecer-nos uma história *detalhada* da mesma.

Se a história de Adão representa apenas um novo começo, e não um começo absoluto, então não temos necessidade de apelar para razões apologéticas (que governam quase todas as discussões sobre questões cronológicas, por parte dos eruditos conservadores mais rígidos), e nem precisaremos distorcer nossas idéias, procurando encontrar lugar para as tremendas expansões de tempo que se ajustem às descobertas arqueológicas e da ciência em geral. Alguns estudiosos têm conseguido fazer a cronologia bíblica retroceder para até 10.000 A.C., mas isso não representa ao menos uma gota no balde cheio da história descoberta pela arqueologia, e não representa nem ao menos alguns átomos de água, no grande

CRONOLOGIA DO A. TESTAMENTO

oceano da história da geologia. Por conseguinte, é com muita dose de verdade que o Dicionário Bíblico de Unger afirma que o trecho de Gênesis 1:1 situa a origem do universo no «passado sem data, dando margem a todas as eras esboçadas pela ciência da geologia». Quanto ao aparecimento do homem à face da terra, esse mesmo autor considera os supostos 4000 anos de Ussher como algo «insustentável, à luz dos fatos arqueológicos confirmados». Unger, grande estudioso presbiteriano, estava entre aqueles que fazem a cronologia da Bíblia retroceder até cerca de dez mil anos antes de Cristo. Mas a arqueologia fala em datas muito mais antigas do que isso, a menos que suponhamos que tal período seja o período *adâmico*, mas não como representante do *homem* como uma entidade. Conforme já dissemos acima, é interessante o fato de que a história bíblica sobre Adão corresponde, a grosso modo, **ao grande cataclismo** anterior ao próximo passado, quando então houve uma mudança de pólos, tal como a história sobre Noé **corresponde ao último desses cataclismos passados**. Se encararmos as questões envolvidas por esse prisma, então a narrativa bíblica concordará com justeza àquilo que se conhece, cientificamente falando, acerca da atual raça humana, acerca da qual se manifesta a maioria de nossas descobertas arqueológicas. No que concerne à teoria da *Evolução*, que, naturalmente, diz respeito à cronologia mais antiga do homem, ver o artigo sobre esse assunto.

Ilustração sobre Datas Bíblicas:
Os informes dados no gráfico abaixo foram extraídos do texto hebraico do Antigo Testamento, do Pentateuco samaritano e da Septuaginta. O Pentateuco samaritano pertence cerca de 430 A.C., e a Septuaginta pertence cerca de 283 A.C.
Observações. 1. A base é Gênesis 5:1-32 e 7:6. 2. Os números indicam a idade de cada indivíduo nomeado, quando algum filho (não necessariamente o mais velho dos filhos) nasceu, ou então, algum evento específico ocorrido, que ajuda a cronologia. 3. As três fontes informativas mencionadas acima são especificadas, mediante as abreviações Heb., Sam. e LXX.

Anos Desde A Criação Até o Dilúvio

Nome	Heb.	Sam.	LXX
Adão	130	130	230
Sete	105	105	205
Enos	90	90	190
Quenã	70	70	170
Maalalel	65	65	165
Jarede	162	62	162
Enoque	65	65	165
Matusalém	187	67	167
Lameque	182	53	188
Noé	600	600	600
Total de Anos	1.656	1.307	2.242

c. Do Dilúvio até Abraão
1. **A grande era dos patriarcas.** — A cronologia pré-abraâmica está alicerçada sobre as genealogias de Gênesis 5 e de Gênesis 11:10-26, separadas, uma da outra, pelo dilúvio da época de Noé. A declarada imensa idade dos primeiros patriarcas, vários dos quais viveram mais de novecentos anos, tem deixado perplexos a alguns intérpretes. O fato de que as antigas lendas pagãs da Suméria dizem-nos que somente *8 reis* conseguiram viver por um período de 241 mil anos tem feito alguns estudiosos suporem que estamos tratando, na Bíblia, com mitos antigos

idênticos. Há mesmo intérpretes que supõem que, tanto nas narrativas pagãs quanto nas narrativas bíblicas, um único nome pode representar toda uma tribo, o que explicaria a imensa duração da vida dos primeiros homens nomeados na Bíblia. Por outro lado, apesar de poder ter havido exageros, o fato de que tanto as narrativas bíblicas quanto as narrativas pagãs falam nessas vidas muito longas pode servir de indicações de que isso, realmente, sucedia. Em nossos dias, alguns cientistas estão dizendo que a nossa é a última geração de homens mortais. Claro que nisso há um exagerado otimismo. Mas é que a ciência está às vésperas de conseguir avanços tão fantásticos que as enfermidades poderão ser derrotadas, e as células do corpo humano poderão recuperar a vitalidade perdida. Se isso chegar a suceder, o que tem sido prometido a um milênio, bem poderá tornar-se uma realidade. A Bíblia prevê que, durante o milênio futuro, se alguém então morrer com cem anos de idade, será considerada uma criança (ver Isaías 66:20). Os místicos contemporâneos também afirmam que estamos nos aproximando da época em que será normal os homens viverem durante séculos. No que me diz respeito, aceito o que o Antigo Testamento diz sobre a longevidade dos primeiros homens, como algo perfeitamente razoável. Contudo, sabendo o que sabemos sobre as genealogias bíblicas, também precisamos afirmar que elas podem consistir apenas em esboços, e não em registros completos. Portanto, conforme diversos intérpretes têm dito, é bem possível que não sejamos capazes de determinar o tempo que se escoou entre o dilúvio e Abraão, com qualquer grau de certeza.

2. *Os períodos arqueológicos e os patriarcas*. Essa informação foi oferecida no artigo sobre a Arqueologia, parte I, pelo que não a repetimos aqui. A leitura daquele material suprirá o leitor com muitas informações atinentes ao período entre Noé e Abraão. A época de Abraão pode ser identificada como a Idade do Bronze Média (2000-1500 A.C.), sendo dito que ele chegou à terra de Canaã em cerca de 2086 A.C. O período dos patriarcas ocuparia as datas de 2086 a 1871 A.C. A era patriarcal e a era de Davi seriam, respectivamente, 2000 e 1000 A.C.

3. *Ilustração Sobre Datas*:
Os informes do gráfico abaixo foram extraídos do texto hebraico, do Pentateuco samaritano e da Septuaginta.
Observações: 1. **A base do gráfico é Gênesis 11:10-26.** 2. Os números indicam a idade de cada indivíduo nomeado, quando um filho (não necessariamente o mais velho) nasceu, ou então algum evento específico ocorrido, que nos ajuda na cronologia. 3. As três fontes informativas mencionadas acima são especificadas mediante as abreviações *Heb., Sam. e LXX.*

Nome	Heb.	Sam.	LXX
Sem	100	100	100
Arfaxade	35	135	135
Cainã			130
Selá	30	130	130
Éber	34	134	134
Peleque	30	130	130
Reú	32	132	132
Serugue	30	130	130
Naor	29	79	179
Terá	70	70	70
Nasce Abraão			
Anos de Sem,	100	100	100

CRONOLOGIA DO A. TESTAMENTO

	Heb.	Sam.	LXX
antes do dilúvio			
Anos do dilúvio até Abraão	290	940	1.170

Essas datas, naturalmente, não levam em conta possíveis hiatos; pois, quando muito, elas são apenas sugestivas. Os eruditos modernos, baseados em informes bíblicos, com algumas adaptações, supõem que o dilúvio teve lugar pelo menos 3.284 anos antes de Abraão. O método de interpretação cronológica de Ussher abria espaço para apenas 353 anos, entre o dilúvio e o nascimento de Abraão. Porém, tal cálculo não concorda com os períodos conhecidos da história do Egito e da Mesopotâmia, com abundantes evidências arqueológicas.

4. *Comentários sobre o Dilúvio.*

Naturalmente, esse foi um dos grandes eventos da história recente da humanidade, do ponto de vista geológico. As evidências em favor da realidade do dilúvio são abundantes, não somente na geologia, mas também em fontes literárias e nas lendas antigas dos povos. Não há razão alguma para supormos que as muitas lendas que se referem ao dilúvio derivam-se todas dos registros bíblicos. Essas lendas são, por si mesmas, fontes informativas independentes. Fica implícito que houve áreas em que algumas poucas pessoas sobreviveram. A narrativa bíblica conta acerca de uma família sobrevivente. Mas, há evidências que alguns eruditos aceitam, para provar que o dilúvio não foi universal. Os chineses, por exemplo, conseguiram fazer história, *embaixo da água*. Não há qualquer registro histórico, entre eles, que fale de interrupção mediante alguma grande catástrofe. É quase certo de que o dilúvio de Noé representa a última grande catástrofe causada por uma mudança dos pólos magnéticos da terra. Quando há uma mudança de pólos, a crosta da terra desliza para novas posições, os continentes assumem novas formas, os leitos dos oceanos mudam de lugar, e, naturalmente, há tempestades incríveis, com ventos incrivelmente violentos e inundações destrutivas.

Os místicos contemporâneos asseguram que estamos bem perto de um **cataclismo universal** dessa magnitude. Pode ser que algo assim ponha fim à nossa era, dando origem a uma nova era áurea, o milênio. Quanto a notas expositivas completas sobre a questão, bem como sobre o dilúvio de Noé, ver o artigo sobre o *Dilúvio*. As evidências geológicas sugerem que o globo terrestre já experimentou cerca de quatrocentas dessas catástrofes, pois, nas rochas, há evidências de muitas alterações dos pólos magnéticos. Na verdade, toda a história que conhecemos, com algum detalhe, é de tempos recentes. Quanto à data do dilúvio, o bispo Ussher pensava em 2500 A.C., mas a data real deve ter sido consideravelmente mais antiga do que isso. Todavia, não há como estabelecer a data exata desse **cataclismo**.

d. De Abraão ao Êxodo:

1. *Conjecturas sobre as datas de patriarcas específicos:*
   Abraão, 2000-1850 A.C.
   Isaque, 1900-1750 A.C.
   Jacó, 1800-1700 A.C.
   José, 1750-1650 A.C.

A entrada de Jacó e de sua família no Egito, é datada em cerca de 1700 A.C. Se essa conjectura está correta, então o poder de José no Egito corresponde ao período dos hicsos na história do Egito, quando governantes de origem semítica tornaram-se Faraós do Egito. Isso talvez explique a mistura de elementos egípcios e semitas, em Gênesis 37:1. Desnecessário é dizer que os intérpretes variam de opinião quanto a essa questão. Abaixo damos um gráfico baseado em informações dadas na Enciclopédia Pictórica da Bíblia, de Zondervan. Deve-se observar que as datas oferecidas variam daquelas dadas acima, em cerca de cem anos. Mas, quando tratamos de questões de tão grande antiguidade, levando em conta as incertezas que circundam as genealogias, esse tempo não é por demais significativo.

2. *Gráfico Ilustrativo*

Evento	Datas Heb.	LXX	Gênesis
Nasce Terá	2291	2263	11:32, 12:4
Abraão entra em Canaã	2091	2058	12:4
Nasce Ismael	2080	2047	16:16
Nasce Isaque	2066	2033	25:26
Morre Sara	2029	1996	23:1
Isaque casa-se	2026	1993	25:20
Nascem Jacó e Esaú	2006	1973	47:9
Morre Abraão	1991	1958	25:7
Jacó foge para Harã	1929	1896	30:24-26
José vendido ao Egito	1898	1865	37:2
Isaque morre	1886	1853	35:28
José obtém o poder	1885	1852	41:54
Jacó desce ao Egito	1876	1843	Êxo. 12:40

3. *Estadia no Egito.* O texto hebraico diz que essa estadia perdurou por 430 anos; mas a Septuaginta fala em 215 anos. Ver Êxo. 12:40. A LXX diz como segue: «O tempo em que os filhos de Israel habitaram na terra do Egito *e na terra de Canaã* (foi de) quatrocentos e trinta anos». Essa declaração tem o apoio do Pentateuco samaritano. Se isso reflete a declaração original, então o tempo em que os filhos de Israel estiveram no Egito foi muito mais curto. O trecho de Atos 7:6 (parte do discurso de Estêvão) dá um número arredondado, «quatrocentos anos». No entanto, Gálatas 3:17 diz que o tempo entre a aliança estabelecida com Abraão e a outorga da lei foi de quatrocentos e trinta anos, o que concorda bem de perto com a declaração da Septuaginta. É óbvio, pois, que as diversas declarações bíblicas não se harmonizam entre si, por terem sido influenciadas por mais de uma tradição cronológica. No NTI, em Gálatas 3:17, provi uma nota sobre o problema da cronologia, no tocante a essa questão. Tal problema não é passível de qualquer boa solução. É que, nessa questão de datas, estamos abordando diferentes tradições antigas. A experiência de todos os estudiosos é que, usualmente, quanto mais longa a data, mais correta. Todavia, esse critério talvez não se aplique ao problema atual.

e. Do Êxodo à Construção do Templo

1. *Duração.* Esse período durou quatrocentos e oitenta anos, de acordo com o texto hebraico (I Reis 6:1), mas 440, de acordo com a Septuaginta. Questões difíceis iniciais são: Em qual ponto da história o Egito começou a oprimir sistematicamente ao povo de Israel? Quem foi o Faraó da opressão, que não conhecia a José (Êxo. 1:8)? Os estudiosos têm oferecido várias sugestões. Os candidatos favoritos são Ramisés II (1237-1225 A.C.), Aames I, fundador da XVIIIª Dinastia, chamada de Novo Império (1570 A.C.), e Tutmés III (1504-1450 A.C.). Alguns pensam que Ramisés seria tanto o faraó da opressão quanto o faraó do êxodo, a despeito do fato de que Êxodo 4:19 refere-se à morte do opressor pouco antes do êxodo. Os argumentos em favor deste ou daquele

CRONOLOGIA DO A. TESTAMENTO

nome alicerçam-se sobre as descobertas arqueológicas; porém, cada opinião está sujeita a alguma forma de objeção, o que nos deixa na dúvida. Contra Tutmés III temos o argumento que mais tempo seria necessário do que as suas datas permitem, para que a história de Israel tivesse ocorrido durante o seu reinado, a julgar pelo que sabemos mediante a história, através da arqueologia. Mediante cálculos bíblicos, chegamos a uma data de cerca de 1445-1446 A.C. Isso corresponderia a Tutmés III como o opressor de Israel; e seu filho, Amenhotepe II, como o Faraó do êxodo.

2. *A Data do Êxodo*. Se o informe de I Reis 6:1 está correto, então podemos fixar uma data quase precisa, pois sabemos quando, mais ou menos, o templo de Jerusalém foi construído. Essa construção teve início no quarto ano do reinado de Salomão, em cerca de 967 A.C. Se retrocedermos no tempo por quatrocentos e oitenta anos, isso nos dará uma data entre 1446 e 1448 A.C. Todavia, isso depende da exatidão histórica da genealogia em questão. A experiência dos estudiosos com as questões genealógicas demonstra que, com freqüência, elas atendem mais às demandas da simetria do que às exigências da verdadeira cronologia. Visto que os próprios informes bíblicos não concordam entre si, defrontamo-nos com um problema que não é passível de solução fácil e boa.

3. *As Vagueações pelo Deserto*. Os trechos de Deuteronômio 8:2 e Êxodo 16:35 dizem especificamente que esse período durou quarenta anos. Porém, alguns eruditos aceitam a cifra como figurada, porque quarenta é o número simbólico de julgamento. Outras referências ao número quarenta, com esse sentido, são Gênesis 7:4; Juí. 13:1 e Mateus 4:2. Ainda outros estudiosos pensam que se trata de um número redondo, que permite considerável variação.

4. *De Josué até o Reinado de Davi*. Como delinear esse período, cronologicamente falando, é algo que tem deixado os intérpretes perplexos. De fato, há quem diga que, quanto a esse período, não se pode obter grande sucesso enquanto a arqueologia não nos fornecer maiores informações, ou não as obtivermos mediante a literatura. Se levarmos em conta todos os informes bíblicos disponíveis, obteremos cerca de quinhentos e oitenta anos, o que, como é claro, é demais para adaptar-se à referência em I Reis 6:1. O problema consiste em como combinar os informes que falam sobre as opressões por parte de potências estrangeiras, em comparação com o tempo alocado aos vários juízes. A única maneira de conseguirmos harmonia com o trecho de I Reis 6:1 consiste em supor que os períodos mencionados acerca das opressões e dos juízes se justapõem. Desse modo, se esses períodos não forem calculados de modo consecutivo, poderemos reduzir consideravelmente o total. A arqueologia nos tem dado evidências suficientes para concluirmos que, no Oriente Próximo, a cronologia não alista os eventos de modo necessariamente sincrônico. Os antigos meramente alistavam cada série de governantes e reinados separadamente, como se sempre estivessem em sucessão; e isso alonga o tempo realmente envolvido. Um exemplo disso é o Papiro Torino, com sua lista de reis egípcios. Ali há listas de todas as cinco dinastias, da XIIIª à XVIIª, em grupos sucessivos. Ali aparecem cento e cinqüenta governantes, e seus reinados ocupariam, pelo menos, quatrocentos e cinqüenta anos. No entanto, com base em fontes arqueológicas, sabe-se que todos os Faraós precisam ajustar-se em um período de cerca de duzentos e dezesseis anos. Conclui-se daí que certos Faraós reinaram contemporaneamente, e não sucessivamente. Condições similares ocorrem na história das cidades-estados da Suméria e do antigo reino babilônico. Uma de minhas fontes informativas, no tocante ao período em questão, alista vinte e cinco listas, sobre algumas das quais a Bíblia nos dá algumas informações quanto à duração do tempo. Se incluirmos nas vagueações pelo deserto, quarenta anos, e mais o período da conquista, duzentos e trinta anos, chegaremos a um total de seiscentos e vinte e três anos. Mas a opressão sob Jabim, a opressão sob Midiã e a opressão sob Amom, etc., terão então de ser concebidas como inclusas nesses informes, que dizem por quanto tempo governou cada um dos juízes. Dessa forma, os seiscentos e vinte e três anos poderão ser consideravelmente reduzidos. Porém, como conseguir o feito, de maneira exata, já é questão que envolve os eruditos em considerável trabalho de harmonização.

5. *Lista Ilustrativa*

	Anos
Vagueações pelo deserto	40
Período da conquista	230
Israel serve a Cusã-Risataim (Juí. 3:8)	8
Livramento por Otniel (Juí. 3:11), com um período de descanso	40
Israel serve a Eglom (Juí. 3:14)	18
Livramento por Eúde (Juí. 3:30), com um período de descanso	80
Opressão por Jabim (Juí. 4:3)	20
Livramento por Débora (Juí. 5:31), com um período de descanso	40
Opressão pelos midianitas (Juí. 6:1)	7
Livramento por Gideão (Juí. 8:28), com um período de descanso	40
Abimeleque reina em Israel (Juí. 9:22)	3
Tola julga Israel (Juí. 10:2)	23
Jair julga Israel (Juí. 10:2)	22
Opressão pelos amonitas (Juí. 10:8)	18
Jefté julga Israel (Juí. 12:7)	6
Ibsã julga Israel (Juí. 12:9)	7
Elom julga Israel (Juí. 12:11)	10
Abdom julga Israel (Juí. 12:14)	8
Opressão pelos filisteus (Juí. 13:1)	40
Sansão julga Israel (Juí. 15:20; 18:31)	20
Período de Eli (I Sam. 4:18)	40
Samuel julga Israel (I Sam. 8:2)	20
Reinado de Saul (Atos 13:21)	40
Reinado de Davi (I Reis 2:11)	40
Reinado de Salomão antes da construção do templo	3
Total	623

f. **Da Fundação do Templo de Salomão até a sua Destruição**

A era dos reis hebreus vai de cerca de 1000 a 587 A.C.

1. *Monarquia Unida*: Davi, 1000-971 A.C. Salomão, 971-926 A.C.

O templo foi fundado em cerca de 967 A.C. As datas são aproximadas, envolvendo conjecturas.

2. *A Dupla Monarquia*: 926-587 A.C.

Judá		Israel	
Reoboão	926-918 A.C.	Jeroboão I	926-907
Abias	910-908	Nadabe	907-906
Asa	908-872	Baasa	906-883
Josafá	872-852	Elá	883-882
Jeorão	852-845	Zinri	882

CRONOLOGIA DO A. TESTAMENTO

Judá	Ano			
Acazias	845-844	Onri	882-871	Josias 639-609 Samaria
Atália	845-839	Acabe	871-852	Jeoacaz 609
Jeoás	839-800	Acazias	852-851	Jeoaquim 608-598
		Jeorão	851-845	Jeoachim 598
		Jeú	845-818	Zedequias 598-587
Amazias	800-785	Jeoacaz	818-802	Queda de 587
Uzias	785-747	Joás	802-787	Jerusalém
		Jeroboão II	787-747	
Jotão (rei e regente)	758-743	Zacarias	747-746	
		Salum	747-746	
		Menaém	746-737	
Acaz	742-725	Pecaías	736-735	
Ezequias	725-697	Peca	734-733	
Manassés	696-642	Oséias	732-724	
Amom	641-640	Queda de Samaria	721	

a. *Tabela de Sincronismos*. Dados encontrados no Antigo Testamento provêm informações sobre como os reinados dos monarcas de Judá corresponderam aos de Israel. Essa informação mostra-nos em qual reinado um certo rei de Israel começou a reinar, em comparação com um ano específico do reinado de algum rei de Judá, conforme se vê abaixo:

••• ••• •••

Judá	Ano	Israel	Ano	Referência Bíblica
Reoboão	1	Jeroboão	1	
Abias	1	Jeroboão	18	I Reis 15:1
Asa	1	Jeroboão	21	
Asa	2	Nadabe	1	I Reis 15:25
Asa	26	Baasa	1	I Reis 15:28,33
		Nadabe	2	
Asa	26	Elá	1	I Reis 17:8
		Baasa	24	
Asa	27	Zinri	7	I Reis 15:10
Asa	27	Onri	1	I Reis 16:16
Asa	38	Acabe	1	I Reis 16:29
		Onri	12	
Josafá	1	Acabe	4	
Asa	41			
Josafá	1	Acabe	5	
Josafá	17	Acazias	1	I Reis 12:51
		Acabe	21	
Josafá	18	Jorão/Acabe	1/22/2	
		Acazias		
Josafá/Jeorão	22/1	Jorão	5	II Reis 8:25
Jeorão/Acazias	1	Jorão	12	

b. *Dificuldades do Sincronismo*. Embora os hebreus tenham-nos deixado as mais detalhadas informações sobre seus reis, em relação a outros povos, incluindo a lista acima de sincronismos, até nisso os eruditos têm encontrado várias manipulações com o propósito de obter simetria, ou com outras finalidades. No tocante a uma declaração sobre a questão, ver 3.h, *Problemas Comuns da Cronologia — Reis Hebreus*. Os eruditos encontram muitos erros e incoerências nessas informações. Certo investigador, levando em consideração o problema inteiro da cronologia, entre os povos orientais, declarou: «Os orientais sempre dão números definidos, mas nunca computam». Parece ter havido a tentativa de fazer o período entre a construção do templo, por Salomão, e a reconstrução do mesmo, por Zorobabel, ser exatamente de quatrocentos e oitenta anos. Já pudemos encontrar esse mesmo número, designando o período desde o êxodo até à construção do templo. Além disso, convenientemente, a duração do reino do norte, Israel, teria sido exatamente a metade disso, ou seja, duzentos e quarenta anos. É óbvio que questões de simetria, e não de cronologia estrita, estavam ali em foco.

c. *Cronologia Pós-Exílica*
Fontes Informativas. Quanto a esse período histórico, temos os livros do Antigo Testamento como Esdras, Neemias e Daniel. Este último oferece-nos apenas algumas informações. Mas o livro canônico de Ester, e os livros apócrifos de Tobias e Judite, embora pertencentes a esse período, não nos oferecem qualquer ajuda sobre questões cronológicas. No entanto, I e II Macabeus também fornecem-nos informações a respeito. As descobertas arqueológicas atinentes a esse período são inúmeras. A questão inteira é ilustrada mediante referências literárias de fontes seculares, produzidas por outros povos envolvidos. Os gráficos abaixo do sétimo ponto, *Gráficos Históricos e Literários*, fornecem-nos as informações desejadas. Muitos outros detalhes podem ser encontrados no artigo separado, intitulado *Período Intertestamental*.

VI. Cronologia Literária. Esse assunto é inteiramente coberto pelos dois gráficos sob o ponto sétimo, abaixo. O primeiro gráfico trata da cronologia literária do Antigo Testamento, e o segundo trata dos livros apócrifos e pseudepígrafes.

Bibliografia. AM FIN IB KI THI UN Z

CRONOLOGIA DO A. TESTAMENTO
VII. GRÁFICOS HISTÓRICOS E LITERÁRIOS
TABELA I. Os Livros do Antigo Testamento

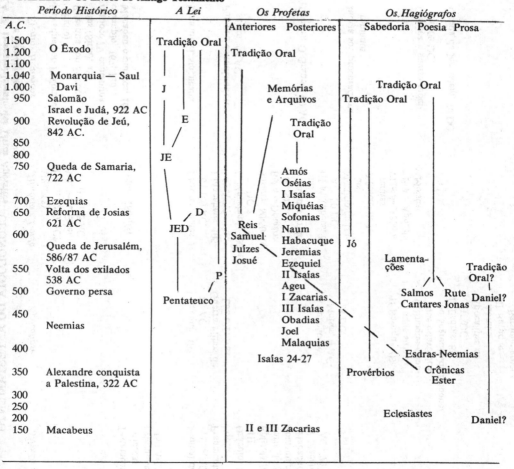

TABELA II. Desenvolvimento dos Livros Apócrifos e Hagiógrafos — CRONOLOGIA DO A. TESTAMENTO

AC	Eventos Históricos	História e Lenda	Apocalipse	Sermão e Ensaio	Sabedoria	Salmos
250	Palestina sob Ptolomeus (Egito)	Ahikar (?) Tobias, 220 AC? Adições a Ester, c. 181-145 AC				
200	Palestina sob Selêucidas (Síria), 198 Antíoco IV contamina o templo, 167; Judas Macabeu o purifica, 164 AC.					
150	Dinastia Hasmoneana	Judite, 180-100	I Enoque, 183-80 AC. Guerra Filhos da Luz e Trevas	Testamento 12 Patriarcas I Baruque, 150 AC.	Sabedoria de Jesus Ben Siraque (Eclesiástico), 180 AC.	
63	Pompeu conquista Jerusalém, 63 AC.	I Esdras, antes de 100 AC. I Macabeus, 105-65 AC.? II Macabeus, 100 AC Susana, 80-50 AC Bel e o Dragão, 80-50 AC Vidas dos Profetas III Macabeus, 50 AC-50 DC. Martírio de Isaías Crônicas de Jeremias Vida de Adão e Eva / Apo. de Moisés/		Manual de Disciplina, 100 AC? Fragmentos Sadoquitas Oráculos Sibilinos III Epístola Jeremias Carta de Aristéias Comentário sobre Habacuque 1,2 IV Macabeus, 50 AC - 70 DC.	Sabedoria de Salomão 50 AC-10 DC	Cântico dos Três Jovens Salmos da Seita de Qumran Salmos de Salomão
50	Herodes, O Grande, 40 AC		Assunção de Moisés, 4 AC-28 DC.			
DC 1	Judéia sob procuradores romanos					
66	Começa a guerra judaica, 66 DC.		II Baruque /Baruque siríaco/ II Enoque /Enoque eslavônico ou Segredos de Enoque/ II Esdras, 88-117 DC. Apocalipse de Abraão III Baruque /Baruque grego/		Ditos dos Pais /Pirke Aboth, 10-100 DC?/	Oração de Manassés
100	Queda de Jerusalém, 70 DC					

CRONOLOGIA DO ANTIGO TESTAMENTO

TABELA III — História de Israel e seus vizinhos: os Selêucidas; os Hasmoneanos

PERÍODO INTERTESTAMENTAL

a. ISRAEL PÉRSIA EGITO SÍRIA

ISRAEL

Data:	
538	Zorobabel Sheshbazaar; alguns voltaram a Jerusalém.
537	O começo da reconstrução do templo
	Interrupção da construção do templo
520	A construção recomeçada
516	O templo é completado (3 de Adar, 10 de março)
458	Ezra vai a Jerusalém
445-433	O Templo de Neemias em Jerusalém

IMPÉRIO PERSA:

539-540	Ciro
530-522	Cambises
522-486	Dario I
486-465	Xerxes I (Assuero)
464-423	Artaxerxes I
423-404	Dario II Nothus
404-359	Artaxerxes II Mnemon
359-337	Artaxerxes III Ochus
338-335	Arses
336-331	Dario III Codomanus
331-323	Alexandre de Macedônia

ISRAEL

324	Israel sob o domínio da Síria
282	Ptolomeu I Soter
320	A Judéia torna-se parte do império de Ptolomeu, anexada por Ptolomeu I
198	A Palestina torna-se parte do império sírio, permanecendo até os Macabeus
167-40	Os Macabeus (hasmoneanos) A libertação de Israel Matatias, o pai, inspirou a revolta
166-161	Judas Macabeu
160-143	Jonatan Macabeu
143-135	Simão Macabeu
135-104	João Hircano I
104-103	Aristóbolo I
103-76	Alexandre Jannaeus
76-67	Rainha Salomé Alexandra e Hircano II
67-40	Hircano II e Aristóbolo II
63	Pompeu estabelece o protetorado romano; Israel é dominado
40	Herodes o Grande apontado como *rei dos judeus*
37-4	Governo de Herodes

EGITO

323	Ptolomeu I Soter
285-246	Ptolomeu II, Philadelphus
246-222	Ptolomeu III, Euergetes
222-205	Ptolomeu IV, Philopater
204-180	Ptolomeu V, Epiphanes

SÍRIA

312-281	Seleuco, I Nicator
281-261	Antíoco, I Soter
261-246	Antíoco, II Theos
246-225	Seleuco II
225-223	Seleuco III Soter
223-187	Antíoco III, O Grande
187-175	Seleuco IV
175-163	Antíoco IV Epiphanes
163-162	Antíoco V
162-150	Demétrio I
139-129	Antíoco VII Sidetes

CRONOLOGIA DO ANTIGO TESTAMENTO

PERÍODO INTERTESTAMENTAL

b. *OS REIS SELÊUCIDAS*

Os Números Indicam A Ordem Do Reinado De Cada Um

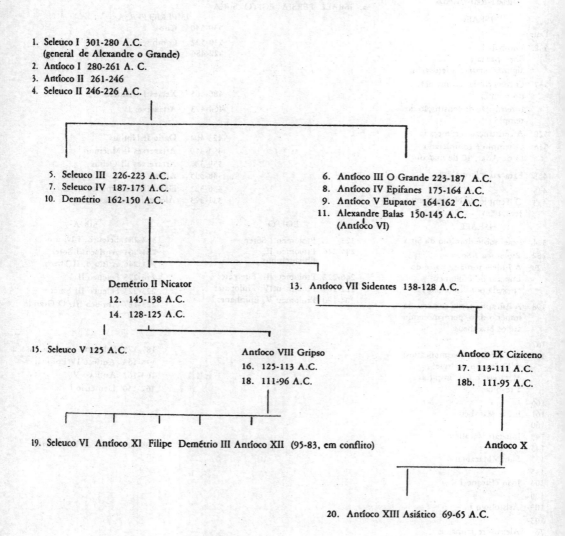

A palavra *Seleucidae* (plural) vem do nome de Seleuco Nicator, general de Alexandre, o Grande (312 A.C.). Esse general, depois da morte de Alexandre, começou a dinastia que governou a maior parte da Ásia Menor, Síria, Pérsia e Báctria (312-64 A.C.).

CRONOLOGIA DO ANTIGO TESTAMENTO

PERÍODO INTERTESTAMENTAL
c. *OS HASMONEANOS*

Os números indicam a ordem do reinado de cada um.

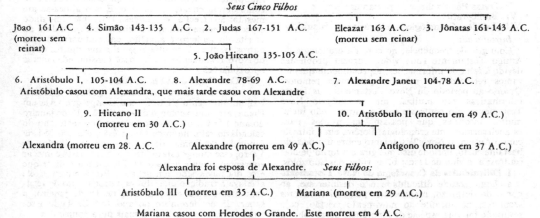

Mariana casou com Herodes o Grande. Este morreu em 4 A.C.

d. *OS HERODIANOS*
Foram Incluídas Todas As Referências Bíblicas

Antípater, procurador da Judéia 47-43 A.C.
|
Herodes o Grande 37 A.C. (Mat. 2:1 e Luc. 1:5)

Mariana (neta de Hircano) hasmoneana	Mariana (filha do sumo sacerdote Simão)	Maltace (samaritana)		Cleópatra
Aristóbulo (esposo de Berenice, filha de Salomé, irmã de Herodes o Grande)	Herodes Filipe I (esposo de Herodias, filha de Agripal e mãe de Salomé (Mat. 14)	Herodes Antipas (tetrarca, Mat. 14:1; Luc.3:1, 19; 9:7; Mar.6: 14. 4 A.C.-39 D.C.)	Arquelau (Mat. 2:22) 4 A.C. - 6 D.C.	Filipe o Tetrarca (Luc. 3:1) (Herodes Filipe II) 4 A.C. - 34 D.C
Herodes de Cálquis (esposo de Berenice filha de Agripa I)	Agripa I 41-44 D.C. (Atos 12)			
Agripa II (Atos 25:13)	Berenice (Atos 25:13) Segundo casamento com Herodes de Cálquis	Drusila (Atos 24:24) Segundo casamento com Félix		

HISTÓRIA JUDAICA DE 63 A. C. A 70 D. C.

1. Início do domínio romano: 63 A.C.-4 A.C. Poder *indireto*, luta entre Roma e os hasmoneanos.
2. Poder *indireto*, governo de Herodes (sujeito a Roma): 40 A.C.-44 D.C.
3. Judéia, Samaria, Iduméia (que constituíam a província romana da Judéia) governada por *procuradores romanos*: 6 D.C.-41 D.C.
4. Palestina inteira governada por Agripa: 41 D.C.-44 D.C.
5. Palestina inteira governada diretamente *por Roma*, até à destruição de Jerusalém: 44 D.C.-70 D.C.

CRONOLOGIA DO N. TESTAMENTO

CRONOLOGIA DO NOVO TESTAMENTO
Esboço
Introdução
I. Dificuldades da Cronologia do Novo Testamento
II. Cronologia da Vida de Jesus
III. Cronologia da Era Apostólica
IV. Cronologia das Epístolas Paulinas
V. Datas Pós-Paulinas Importantes
VI. Bibliografia
VII. Tabelas Cronológicas Literárias e Históricas

Introdução:
Com grande freqüência, no caso da cronologia do Antigo Testamento (que vide), surgem problemas devido à falta de informações, especialmente quando vamos retrocedendo para tempos mais remotos. Quanto ao período do Novo Testamento, as fontes informativas são muitas; mas o próprio Novo Testamento, em contraste com o Antigo, não inclui muitos informes que possam ser usados para estabelecermos uma cronologia. Porém, em contraste com o Antigo, o Novo Testamento cobre um período bastante curto, período esse que gira em torno de dois centros: a. a vida de Jesus; b. as vidas dos apóstolos.

I. Dificuldades da Cronologia do Novo Testamento
a. Uma grande dificuldade é o desinteresse, ao ponto do desprezo, manifestado pelos historiadores seculares, no tocante ao movimento cristão, cujo resultado foi uma espécie de ignorância geral sobre a questão; ou então, quando esses historiadores disseram algo, fizeram-no de maneira muito breve e desinformada. Para exemplificar, Tácito falou sobre Jesus, explicando que o nome «cristão» provinha de *Cristo*, que teria sido título dado a certo judeu que fora executado.

b. Durante o século I D.C., várias maneiras de computar a passagem do tempo estavam em uso, sendo difícil agora interpretarmos os itens em termos do calendário que usamos em nossos dias. Além disso, os numerais romanos eram difíceis de manusear.

c. As datas geralmente eram dadas em relação à distância em que estava a subida ao trono de algum imperador, ou então em relação ao ano em que algum cônsul romano assumira seu ofício. Tais informes não correspondiam a qualquer calendário então em uso.

d. Os romanos usavam um calendário solar, ao passo que os judeus usavam um calendário lunar. E, para complicar ainda mais o quadro, o calendário judaico tinha um começo para o ano civil e outro começo para o ano religioso. Ver os vários artigos sobre os *Calendários*. O ano lunar de doze meses sofria uma defasagem de dez ou onze dias em relação ao ano solar, diferença essa que se ia acumulando a cada ano. Os judeus tentavam solucionar esse problema adicionando um décimo terceiro mês ao tempo do equinócio de inverno, sete vezes a cada dezenove anos, ou seja, uma vez a cada três anos, mais ou menos. Mas isso somente resultava em confusão geral, quando se tentavam comparar datas.

e. As pessoas dos tempos bíblicos não davam muita importância à questão de datar com exatidão os eventos, além de usarem expressões inexatas. Além disso, o cômputo de datas era feito de forma inclusiva, de tal modo que o primeiro e o último dias (ou qualquer designação de tempo mencionado) eram incluídos nessa contagem. Assim, «três dias e três noites» (Mat. 12:40) poderia significar qualquer porção dos mesmos, incluindo o primeiro dia mencionado. Jesus morreu na cruz às 15:00 horas da sexta-feira e ressuscitou no fim da madrugada do domingo, o que significa que esteve morto por, no máximo, quarenta horas. No entanto, de acordo com a maneira de contar dos judeus, ele esteve, realmente, no coração da terra, por «três dias e três noites». E, em Atos 20:31, os «três anos» envolvem apenas vinte e sete meses, o que dá em pouco mais de dois anos.

f. Apesar de haver informes cronológicos específicos no Novo Testamento, com freqüência os intérpretes sentem dificuldade em saber exatamente como devem encarar a questão. E isso aplica-se até mesmo ao trecho de Lucas 1:3, que foi dado especificamente para ajudar-nos a localizar a data da escrita do terceiro evangelho, em comparação com outros eventos. O resultado geral é que muitas datas do Novo Testamento precisam ser consideradas meras aproximações.

II. Cronologia da Vida de Jesus
O Nascimento de Jesus. Quando Dionísio Exíguo, do século VI D.C., um monge que vivia em Roma, atribuiu o começo da era cristã a 1° de janeiro do ano I D.C., que foi o quadragésimo sexto ano do calendário reformado de Júlio César, e o ano 754 da fundação de Roma, de acordo com os cálculos de Varro, esse monge estava fazendo a era cristã começar convenientemente nessa data. Ele chegou a dizer que esse dia havia sido um sábado. Provavelmente, ele aceitava a tradição que situava o nascimento de Jesus exatamente uma semana antes de 1° de janeiro, a saber, 25 de dezembro do ano 1 A.C. Tudo isso, entretanto, não passava da mais pura conjectura.

Maneiras de Determinar a Data do Nascimento de Jesus:
Há três pontos de referência que nos podem guiar na determinação da data do nascimento de Jesus, a saber:

1. *O recenseamento romano*, mencionado em Lucas 2:1,2. Lucas informa-nos que o nascimento de Jesus teve lugar em Belém, especificamente porque José e Maria tinham ido até ali para se alistarem, para efeito de pagamento de impostos, quando do recenseamento. Eles tinham ido até ali, porque aquela era a sua cidade nativa. Também somos informados de que Quirínio era, na ocasião, governador da Síria. As dificuldades a esse respeito surgem de imediato, porque as fontes informativas fora do Novo Testamento não indicam que Quirínio teria sido um dos governadores da Síria, e nem que ele determinou que se fizesse um recenseamento. Os acontecimentos durante o reinado de Augusto foram documentados de forma deficiente, pelo que é possível que, se Quirínio governou a Síria apenas por um breve período, seu nome simplesmente tivesse sido omitido nos poucos registros históricos provenientes da época. Uma inscrição danificada, que existe no Museu de Latrão, menciona um governador, cujo nome não é dado, e que teria governado a Síria por duas vezes; e é possível que esse homem tenha sido Quirínio. Acresça-se a isso que o título de *Legatus Caesaris* podia ser privilégio de dois homens ao mesmo tempo. Nesse caso, um deles cuidava das questões políticas, e o outro cuidava das questões militares. Quirínio pode ter sido um co-regente da Síria.

Parece-nos, entretanto, que Lucas tinha razão em suas assertivas. Temos algum conhecimento do padrão seguido nos recenseamentos romanos. Esses recenseamentos eram feitos a cada catorze anos, começando em 90 até 258 D.C. Sabe-se que um outro recenseamento foi efetuado em 62 D.C. Se esse padrão foi uniformemente seguido, então um outro recenseamento deve ter sido efetuado em 8 A.C., outro em 6 D.C., outro em 20 D.C. e outro em 34 D.C., e ainda outro em 48 D.C. Entretanto, sabemos

1012

CRONOLOGIA DO N. TESTAMENTO

que alguns recenseamentos eram locais ou regionais. As palavras usadas por Lucas, «toda a população do império, para recensear-se», parecem indicar um dos recenseamentos universais; porém, isso nos daria a data de 8 A.C. como a data do nascimento de Cristo. Porém, a tarefa de organizar o recenseamento nas províncias mais distantes precisou de considerável tempo para concretizar-se, sendo perfeitamente possível que, naqueles lugares, só tenha ocorrido considerável tempo após 8 A.C. Um ano ou dois não seria exagerado. Com base nas indicações dadas pelos recenseamentos, pois, só podemos dizer que Jesus deve ter nascido em 6 ou 7 A.C., ou mesmo antes. Isso significa uma diferença de mais de meia década, em relação à opinião de Dionísio Exíguo.

2. *A Estrela de Belém*, segundo se lê em Mateus 2:2. O cometa de Halley foi avistado em 12 A.C. Sendo um espetáculo brilhante, pode ter sido considerado como arauto Daquele que é a Luz do Mundo. Nesse caso, Jesus teria nascido em um domingo, 25 de dezembro de 12 A.C. Mas essa data é muito atrasada. Além disso, os antigos geralmente pensavam que os cometas eram portentos malignos.

Muitos astrônomos e intérpretes da Bíblia de nossos dias têm suposto que a *estrela* foi, na realidade, uma rara conjunção de planetas, envolvendo, principalmente, Saturno, Júpiter e Marte, o que teria ocorrido no signo de Peixes. Em prol dessa idéia pode ser dito que Peixes simbolizava Israel, e também que um apropriado símbolo do cristianismo seria um *peixe*. De fato, posteriormente, assim sucedeu, quando i/ch/th/us (palavra grega para peixe) tornou-se uma abreviatura de «Jesus/Cristo/de Deus/Filho». Porém, é possível que em tudo isso haja apenas muita fantasia. Talvez seja significativo quando certos místicos modernos afirmam que, em fevereiro de 1962, houve uma similar rara conjunção de planetas. E eles supõem que, juntamente com outros indícios, teria sido então que o anticristo nasceu. Se isso é verdade, então a idéia de conjunção de planetas assume uma outra significação. Acresça-se em favor dessa idéia que os magos (que vide), eram astrólogos do Oriente, os quais podem ter suposto que uma rara conjunção de planetas em Peixes (que simbolizava Israel), naturalmente indicaria o nascimento de um rei de Israel. Naturalmente, outras interpretações têm sido oferecidas acerca dessa estrela, como aquelas que dizem que seria uma personalidade divina, ou algum fenômeno celeste divinamente provocado. Quanto a comentários completos sobre a questão inteira, ver as notas sobre o trecho de Mateus 2:2, no NTI.

Se a estrela de Belém foi, realmente, essa conjunção de planetas, então o nascimento de Jesus poderia ser datado em cerca de 6 ou 7 A.C., quando esse fenômeno teve lugar.

3. *A Morte de Herodes*. O Herodes (pois houve diversos deles) referido na narrativa do nascimento de Jesus morreu em 4 A.C., e continuava vivo e ativo quando chegaram os magos, talvez dois anos mais tarde. Portanto, sabemos que Jesus deve ter nascido antes dessa data. Isso fortalece a conjectura do ponto dois, acima. Josefo informa-nos que houve um eclipse de luz imediatamente antes do falecimento de Herodes (*Anti*. xvii.6,4). Os astrônomos têm calculado que houve um eclipse de luz visível na Palestina a 23 de março de 5 A.C. Outros eclipses da lua foram visíveis ali a 15 de setembro de 5 A.C., a 12 de março de 4 A.C., e a 1º de janeiro de 1 A.C. Josefo também registra que Arquelau, que sucedeu a Herodes (ver Mat. 2:22), foi deposto em 6 D.C., no décimo ano de seu reinado (*Anti*. xvii.13.2; *Guerras* ii.7,3). Esses detalhes apontam todos para 4 A.C. como a data da morte de Herodes. Sabemos que a sua morte ocorreu na primavera, visto que ele morreu pouco antes da páscoa (*Anti*. xvii.6,6-9,3). Poderíamos supor que o infante Jesus continuou na Palestina por algum tempo, algo menos do que dois anos, antes da fuga da família para o Egito. Portanto, adicionando quatro e mais dois, chegamos cerca de 6 D.C., o que corresponde à rara conjunção dos planetas, mencionada no segundo ponto, acima.

a. *O Dia e o Mês do Nascimento de Jesus*. Solicito que o leitor examine o meu artigo sobre o *Natal*, onde se aprende por que a data de 25 de dezembro foi escolhida como o dia em que se comemora o nascimento de Jesus. Essa data não era observada como a data do nascimento de Jesus, senão depois da ascensão de Constantino ao trono imperial. Fora até então um feriado pagão, que foi substituído por um feriado cristão. Antes de Constantino, muitos cristãos preferiam a data de 6 de janeiro. No entanto, não havia evidências históricas em favor de qualquer dia particular. O fato de que os pastores estavam cuidando de seus rebanhos nas colinas da Judéia (ver Luc. 2:8), mostra-nos que o tempo não podia ser durante os meses de dezembro e janeiro, pois então era inverno. No hemisfério norte do globo terrestre, o inverno ocorre nos meses de dezembro, janeiro e fevereiro.

b. *O Batismo de Jesus*. Lucas presta-nos uma informação que tem a ver com a cronologia referente a esse evento, ao dizer que o ministério de João Batista começou no décimo quinto ano do reinado de Tibério César (Luc. 3:1). Josefo afirma que Tibério sucedeu a Augusto, por ocasião da morte deste (*Anti*. xviii. 2:2). Augusto faleceu a 19 de agosto de 14 D.C. Isso faria o começo do ministério de João Batista corresponder ao ano 29 D.C. Porém, a maioria dos cronologistas pensa que essa data é tardia demais. Eles preferem supor que Lucas referia-se ao tempo em que Tibério tornou-se co-imperador com Augusto, o que sucedeu em cerca de 11 D.C. Eusébio assevera que Jesus foi batizado no quarto ano da governança de Pilatos, e que Pilatos foi nomeado mais ou menos no décimo segundo ano do reinado de Tibério (*Hist*. 1:10). Todavia, desconhecemos com qual autoridade Eusébio declarou tal coisa, além do que a sua informação nos daria um ministério um tanto posterior para João Batista. Lucas diz-nos que Jesus foi batizado quando tinha cerca de trinta anos de idade (Luc. 3:23). Se essa informação é exata, então Jesus deve ter sido batizado em cerca de 26 D.C., e quanto a isso, não precisamos de quaisquer outras evidências. De fato, todas as evidências que demos até agora são acompanhadas por dificuldades, de tal modo que não podemos fixar datas com qualquer grau de certeza. Os orientais não eram muito exatos nessa questão de números, e as palavras usadas por Lucas, «cerca de trinta anos» (Luc. 3:23), poderiam indicar um pouco menos ou um pouco mais do que trinta anos. Sabe-se, porém, que, na sociedade judaica, os homens não ocupavam posições de liderança enquanto não chegavam aos trinta anos de idade, o que significa que Jesus, na realidade, tinha um pouco mais de trinta anos ao dar início ao seu ministério.

c. *Duração do Ministério de Jesus*. Os intérpretes procuram calcular a duração do ministério do Senhor observando quais e quantos feriados religiosos judaicos são mencionados nos evangelhos. Mas, logo surge o primeiro problema quando se considera que o evangelho de João menciona várias dessas festas religiosas que não figuram nos evangelhos sinópticos. Já em João 6:4 encontramos uma páscoa que não figura nas narrativas sinópticas. Alguns eruditos textuais supõem que isso representa uma adição escribal no evangelho de João, embora não haja qualquer evidência em favor disso, nos manuscritos. Outros eruditos opinam que os informes de João sobre festividades não indicam qualquer cronologia, visto que o quarto evangelho não é ordenado em forma cronológica. Isso significaria que os feriados específicos mencionados estão cronologicamente fora de ordem, ou então que tais feriados são totalmente artificiais, sendo meros artifícios literários, para ornar os ensinamentos de Jesus. Seja como for, se seguirmos somente os feriados mencionados nos evangelhos sinópticos (Mateus, Marcos e Lucas), obteremos um ministério de cerca de apenas um ano para Jesus. Hort chega a um ministério de Jesus de apenas um ano, ignorando o trecho de João 6:4, supondo que se trata de uma adição primitiva ao texto original. Historiadores bíblicos, em anos recentes, têm suposto que os evangelhos sinópticos estão mais perto da verdade, do ponto de vista da cronologia. Os conservadores, porém, mostram-se relutantes em sacrificar os informes joaninos; mas essa relutância em nada ajuda a explicar as escassas informações dadas pelos evangelhos sinópticos. O problema que um intérprete bíblico precisa explicar consiste no seguinte: 1. rejeitar a cronologia dos evangelhos sinópticos; 2. rejeitar a cronologia do evangelho de João; ou 3. fazer ainda o que é mais duvidoso, tentando reunir tais informes, como se, cronologicamente, eles fossem suplementares, e não estivessem, realmente, em conflito. A maioria dos eruditos modernos prefere ficar com os evangelhos sinópticos quanto a esse ponto, embora não haja como termos certeza quanto a isso. Eusébio referia-se a um ministério de Jesus de três ou quatro anos (*Hist.* i.10.39,40). Mas a sua autoridade provavelmente era o evangelho de João, pelo que nada de novo é acrescentado como evidência. Alguns pais da Igreja, como Clemente de Alexandria (Stromata, i.21), supõem que Isaías 61:2 e Lucas 4:18, ao falarem no «ano aceitável» do Senhor, queriam indicar que, na realidade, o ministério de Jesus perdurou apenas por um ano. Porém, mesmo que isso correspondesse à cronologia dos evangelhos sinópticos, não é provável que as próprias Escrituras quisessem indicar um ano literal, quando usaram essa expressão.

d. *A Crucificação*. A simples aritmética nos poderia fornecer o ano da crucificação de Jesus; mas as conclusões diferem, em consonância com a cronologia a ser seguida, se a dos evangelhos sinópticos ou a do evangelho de João, conforme foi discutido no parágrafo acima. Se Jesus nasceu em A.C., viveu por trinta anos, iniciou o seu ministério, que teria durado apenas um ano, então deve ter sido crucificado em 26 D.C. Mas, se o seu ministério prolongou-se por três anos, então ele deve ter sido crucificado em cerca de 29 D.C. Os pais da Igreja em nada nos ajudam nesse particular. Eles limitam-se aos informes bíblicos. Assim, Clemente de Alexandria fala em 28 D.C.; mas Eusébio fala em 33 D.C. (*Hist.* i.10). Tudo depende também do que atribuirmos ao nascimento de Jesus, e isso varia em alguns anos, dependendo de como manipularmos as informações. O *dia* é mesmo mais fácil de ser fixado do que o ano, porquanto sabemos que foi em uma *sexta-feira*, na época da páscoa, e, portanto, a 14 ou 15 do mês de Nisã (correspondente ao nosso abril). O dia de sexta-feira tem sido posto em dúvida, mas penso que o leitor verá, com base nas evidências oferecidas no artigo sobre o *Dia da Crucificação*, que a sexta-feira é o dia certo. O trecho de João 19:31 afirma especificamente que o corpo de Jesus foi tirado da cruz a fim de que ali não permanecesse no sábado, o qual, segundo a maneira de contar os dias, entre os judeus, começaria às 18:00 horas. Além disso, o quarto evangelho informa-nos que o dia da crucificação era a parasceve, ou preparação, que era a antiga expressão hebraica, que terminou entrando no idioma grego, para indicar a véspera do sábado, ou seja, a sexta-feira. E o trecho de Lucas 23:54 diz que o dia da crucificação foi no dia da preparação, e que o sábado logo teria início. A cronologia de Lucas permite apenas três dias (ver Luc. 23:52 - 24:1), a saber: 1. a preparação; 2. o sábado; e 3. o primeiro dia da semana. O artigo acima mencionado explica como isso pode ser reconciliado com a expressão três dias e três noites, como o tempo da permanência do corpo de Jesus no sepulcro. Há um artigo separado sobre esse ponto, com o título de *Três Dias e Três Noites*. Que o dia foi uma sexta-feira, é claro; mas o *ano*, continua em dúvida.

As horas de trevas. Se o período de trevas, que ocorreu enquanto Jesus esteve sobre a cruz (ver Mat. 27:45), ocorreu devido a algum eclipse do sol, então isso nos forneceria uma indicação astronômica. Entretanto, sabemos que um eclipse, naquela ocasião, era algo impossível, porque era tempo da lua cheia, uma das características da páscoa. Além disso, nenhum eclipse do sol continuaria pelo espaço de três horas. A explicação das três horas de trevas, se é que foi um fenômeno natural, deve ter sido uma *nuvem de poeira cósmica*, pelas quais, algumas vezes, passa o nosso globo, e em face do que as trevas podem sobrevir à terra, por várias horas, mesmo durante o horário diurno. Ver as notas em Mateus 27:45, no NTI, quanto a completas explicações sobre essa questão, além de outras especulações acerca das trevas.

A refeição da páscoa, a crucificação e problemas de harmonização. A crucificação teve lugar a 14 ou 15 do mês de Nisã? Os evangelhos sinópticos parecem concordar com o evangelho de João, quanto a esse ponto. Quanto a completas explicações ver as notas no NTI, em Mateus 26:17.

III. A Cronologia da Era Apostólica

a. *A Conversão de Paulo*. Diversos fatores dificultam a determinação de datas, quanto a esse período do Novo Testamento. Tudo parte da data da crucificação de Jesus. A partir dessa data, teremos de acrescentar algum tempo para cobrir o período durante o qual Paulo perseguiu a Igreja cristã, durante esse tempo ele esteve ativo em muitos lugares, viajando por várias cidades, atrás de judeus cristãos (Atos 26:11).

Paulo informa-nos que Aretas era governante de Damasco quando ele mesmo teve de fugir daquela cidade, tendo sido descido dentro de uma cesta, pela muralha da cidade abaixo (II Cor. 11:32), o que sucedeu depois que ele havia permanecido por três anos na Arábia (Gál. 1:17,18). Dispomos de várias informações a respeito de Aretas, sogro de Herodes Ãntipas, mas coisa nenhuma tão específica que nos possa ajudar, com bases extrabíblicas, a determinarmos quaisquer datas exatas relativas ao apóstolo dos gentios. Aretas I era chamado «rei dos árabes»; mas Roma obteve domínio sobre aquela área, pelo que parece que o Aretas aludido por Paulo era uma espécie de rei vassalo em Damasco, dotado de alguma independência, mas sob o controle dos romanos. Aretas teve uma disputa com Ãntipas (que vide), e o imperador Tibério enviou Vitelo, procônsul da Síria, a fim de ajudar Ãntipas. Porém, antes que o seu exército pudesse atacar, Tibério faleceu, e o exército

CRONOLOGIA DO N. TESTAMENTO

foi chamado de volta. Ora, a morte de Tibério ocorreu a 6 de março de 37 D.C. Portanto, o tempo referido em II Coríntios 11:32 provavelmente ocorreu antes da morte de Tibério, porquanto vemos que Aretas acabou responsável pela cidade de Damasco. Todo esse raciocínio, entretanto, fornece-nos apenas um período aproximado: três anos (a permanência de Paulo na Arábia) antes da morte de Tibério, embora tal período possa ter sido consideravelmente mais longo. Isso posto, os eruditos citam datas a começar de 33 D.C. em diante. Podemos começar no tempo da crucificação de Jesus, adicionar um ano para as perseguições movidas por Paulo, e chegar entre os anos 27 e 30 D.C. para a sua conversão, e talvez 33 D.C. para o incidente ocorrido em Damasco. Porém, isso estaria baseado na cronologia dos evangelhos sinópticos acerca da crucificação, e na suposição de que Paulo perseguiu a Igreja somente pelo espaço de um ano, antes de sua conversão.

b. *A Morte de Tiago*. Supõe-se que a morte desse apóstolo ocorreu logo no início do reinado de Agripa I. A Agripa fora dada a tetrarquia de Filipe, e então a de Antipas o que ocorreu em 39 D.C., calculando-se em bases extrabíblicas. Ele tornou-se o rei de Judá, Samaria e Abilene em 41 D.C., e reinou pelo total de sete anos, somente três dos quais sobre a Judéia. O trecho de Atos 12:23 parece dar a entender que ele morreu por ocasião da festa, quando foi ferido por um anjo; e Josefo diz que ele só sobreviveu mais cinco dias. A sua morte ocorreu em 44 D.C. Se supormos que o aprisionamento de Pedro e a morte de Tiago ocorreram durante o começo da autoridade de Antipas sobre a Judéia, então o ano de 41 D.C. poderia ter sido a data desses acontecimentos.

c. *A Fome na Época de Cláudio*, referida em Atos 11:29. O problema com relação a alusão que Lucas faz a esse período de fome é que vários deles tiveram lugar no império romano, durante o reinado de Cláudio, de 41 a 54 D.C. Os historiadores romanos Tácito e Suetônio, bem como Josefo, informam-nos sobre diversos períodos de fome, pelo que é difícil determinar a qual desses períodos Josefo se referia. A declaração lucana de que essa fome ocorreu «por todo o mundo» indica uma fome muito severa, na época do reinado de Cláudio. É possível que a linguagem usada por Lucas tenha sido um tanto exagerada. No entanto, Josefo informa-nos acerca do grande número de judeus que morreram de fome na época de C. Cuspius Fadus e de Tibério Alexandre, em 44-46 e 46-48 D.C., respectivamente. É possível que Lucas se tenha referido a um desses períodos. Mas alguns intérpretes supõem que é preferível pensar entre 41 e 45 D.C., e que esta última data é a mais preferida. O começo das viagens missionárias de Paulo não ocorreu muito após essa fome, conforme o livro de Atos nos mostra.

d. *A Vida de Paulo*. Não muito depois da fome mencionada acima, sob o ponto «C», teve início a carreira missionária de Paulo, talvez no ano 46 D.C. A cronologia sobre a vida de Paulo é dificultada pelos próprios informes bíblicos. Há considerável dificulda- de para a harmonização do que nos diz Lucas, no livro de Atos, com referência às cartas de Paulo. Sempre que aparecem diferenças, a maior parte dos eruditos modernos prefere as próprias palavras de Paulo, supondo que Lucas não estava procurando dar-nos qualquer descrição detalhada, e nem qualquer cronologia exata. Isso pode ser prontamente demons- trado pelo fato de que os três longos anos de permanência de Paulo, na Arábia, imediatamente após a sua conversão, são inteiramente omitidos por Lucas. Devemos situar esse período, como se fosse uma cunha, entre os versículos 21 e 22 do nono capítulo do livro de Atos. Com base na narrativa de Atos, poderíamos supor que a visita de Paulo a Jerusalém (Atos 9:26 ss), quando então se encontrou com os outros apóstolos, ocorreu pouco tempo após a sua conversão. E, no entanto, o trecho de Gálatas 1:18 nos fornece um período intermediário de três anos.

1. *Problemas de Harmonia*

A questão das viagens missionárias de Paulo serem precisamente três, é posta em dúvida por alguns. Pode ter havido outras viagens missionárias, mais curtas ou mais longas. A narrativa de Lucas parece ser uma espécie de sumário de eventos principais. Os informes que o próprio Paulo nos dá não cabem com justeza dentro dos eventos das três viagens. Antes mesmo disso, a visita a Jerusalém, em conjunção com o episódio da fome (Atos 11:27 ss), é omitida nas epístolas paulinas, a não ser que Gálatas 2:1-10 seja uma referência a essa visita. Quanto a esse problema de cronologia, bem como a outros pontos difíceis de harmonia, envolvendo Lucas e Paulo, nas notas expositivas no NTI, em Atos 11:27, tecemos comentários que são apropriados. É possível que tanto Lucas quanto Paulo nos tenham fornecido dados parciais, e que, juntando as mesmas, possamos obter um quadro mais completo, embora não possam ser perfeitamente manipulados, no tocante à harmo- nia e à cronologia. Parece que, seja como for, no que concerne a visita vinculada à fome, é mais acertado identificá-la com Gálatas 2:1-10, e não com a visita relacionada ao concílio, relatada em Atos 15:1-32.

2. *A Primeira Viagem Missionária* (Atos 13:3 ss). Se tirarmos proveito do esboço lucano, para efeito de conveniência, poderíamos datar a primeira viagem missionária em cerca de 46 D.C., pouco após o período da fome de Atos 11:28. O concílio apostólico, nesse caso, deve ter ocorrido no ano 48 D.C. O trecho de Atos 2:1-10, por conseguinte, não deve ser identificado com esse concílio, o qual, na realidade, é historiado no décimo quinto capítulo de Atos, conforme já foi dito acima.

3. *A Segunda Viagem Missionária* (Atos 15:36 ss). Essa viagem teria coberto a data de 49 - 52 D.C., aproximadamente.

4. *A Terceira Viagem Missionária* (Atos 18:23 ss). Essa viagem, que teve início assim que a outra terminou, poderia ser datada entre 53 e 57 D.C.

5. *Uma Quarta Viagem Missionária?* O livro de Atos nada diz sobre uma suposta quarta viagem missionária. Mas muitos eruditos, com base em informes existentes nas epístolas pastorais, bem como nos escritos dos primeiros pais da Igreja, supõem que Paulo fez uma viagem missionária na qual chegou até a Espanha, entre seu primeiro e seu segundo períodos de aprisionamento, ou seja em 64 ou 65 D.C.

Detalhes dessas viagens. O leitor deveria consultar o artigo intitulado *Paulo, Sua Importância*, I, Vida, pontos terceiro a oitavo.

6. *Primeiro Período de Detenção*. Narrado em Atos 28, o primeiro período de aprisionamento ocupou os anos de cerca de 61 a 63 D.C. Ver os detalhes sobre esse episódio no artigo sobre Paulo, I, 7.

7. *Intervalo Entre o Primeiro e o Segundo Períodos de Detenção*. Esse intervalo é deduzido das epístolas de Paulo, mais precisamente de suas epístolas pastorais, e não do livro de Atos. Esse intervalo ocupou os anos de 63 a 65 D.C., tendo incluído uma quarta viagem missionária. Ver o artigo sobre Paulo, I,8. Ver também as notas expositivas sobre Rom. 15:24, no NTI, onde Paulo expressa o desejo de ir até

CRONOLOGIA DO N. TESTAMENTO

a Espanha, e que, aparentemente, ele finalmente cumpriu.

8. Segundo Período de Detenção. Esse episódio não é mencionado no livro de Atos, cuja narrativa só vai até o primeiro período de detenção; mas é subentendido pelas atividades narradas nas epístolas pastorais do próprio Paulo, onde transparece um ministério após aquele que foi registrado no livro de Atos, mas que, segundo o apóstolo já previa, terminaria com a sua morte (II Tim. 4:6,7). Esse período deve ter ocupado os anos de 66 e 67 D.C. Ver o artigo sobre Paulo I,9.

9. Morte de Paulo. As tradições asseveram que Paulo foi executado por decapitação na via Óstia, imediatamente fora de Roma, por ordem de Nero. Visto que Nero morreu em 68 D.C., é bem provável que a morte de Paulo tenha ocorrido em 67 D.C.

10. Tabela da Vida de Paulo:

Eventos	Datas
Nascimento	c. de 1 DC.
Conversão	34
Visita de fome, a Jerusalém	45
Primeira viagem missionária	46-48
Concílio de Jerusalém	49
Segunda viagem missionária	49-52
Terceira viagem missionária	53-57
Aprisionamento em Jerusalém	57
Aprisionamento em Cesaréia	57-60
Primeiro aprisionamento em Roma	61-63
Quarta viagem missionária	64-65
Segundo aprisionamento em Roma	66-67
Morte	67

IV. Cronologia das Epístolas Paulinas. No artigo intitulado, *Paulo, a Importância de*, no décimo ponto, damos a seqüência em que foram escritas as epístolas desse apóstolo, com os eventos históricos paralelos. A principal diferença entre esta apresentação e aquela oferecida ali é que, neste ponto, à epístola de Gálatas damos o primeiro lugar, dentro da seqüência cronológica. As razões para termos dado essa primeira posição à epístola aos Gálatas são amplamente ventiladas naquele artigo, sob o segundo ponto, *Data e Proveniência*. Se aceitarmos a autoria paulina das epístolas pastorais, então poremos as mesmas no fim da coletânea de escritos paulinos, relacionando-as ao período de liberdade de Paulo, após seu primeiro aprisionamento em Roma, e durante seu segundo período de aprisionamento naquela cidade. Mas, se elas são deuteropaulinas, então temos de atribuir-lhes uma data ainda posterior. Seja como for, os artigos sobre cada uma das epístolas paulinas nos fornece detalhes abundantes sobre suas datas e sobre as circunstâncias históricas que as acompanharam. Torna-se claro, através de algumas referências nas epístolas paulinas, como em Colossenses 4:16, que Paulo escreveu epístolas que não foram preservadas para nós. Entretanto, a coletânea de que dispomos é suficientemente extensa para representar devidamente a teologia paulina. Naturalmente, é possível que alguns itens doutrinários, bem interessantes, como também dados históricos, poderiam estar contidos nas epístolas de Paulo que não chegaram até nós, e que, por isso mesmo, terão de permanecer como um mistério, a menos que, algum dia, a arqueologia as traga à luz.

Tabela Cronológica das Epístolas de Paulo

Epístola	Local de Escrita	Data
Gálatas	Antioquia da Síria	49 DC.
I Tessalonicenses	Corinto	51
II Tessalonicenses	Corinto	51-52
I Coríntios	Éfeso	55
II Coríntios	Macedônia	56
Romanos	Corinto	57
Efésios	Roma	61-62
Colossenses	Roma	61-62
Filemom	Roma	61-62
Filipenses	Roma	61-62
I Timóteo	Macedônia? Espanha?	64
Tito	Macedônia? Espanha?	64
II Timóteo	Roma	67

Observações. 1. As epístolas aos Colossenses, aos Efésios e a Filemom formam um grupo, pelo que provavelmente foram escritas estando Paulo aprisionado em Éfeso, em uma data anterior àquela que aparece na tabela acima. Ver a introdução à epístola aos Colossenses, em II, Data e Proveniência, quanto a informações sobre essa especulação. Se a data anterior for aceita, então deveremos pensar no ano 54 D.C. 2. Vários lugares têm sido sugeridos como o local onde foram escritas as epístolas pastorais, uma questão discutida no artigo sobre I Timóteo, sob a parte III, Data e Proveniência. 3. A epístola aos Hebreus não é de autoria paulina, conforme se vê nas razões alistadas no artigo sobre aquela epístola, sob a parte I, Autoria.

V. Datas Pós-Paulinas Importantes

a. Fuga dos cristãos de Jerusalém para Pela, antes da destruição de Jerusalém, entre 66 e 70 D.C.

b. A destruição de Jerusalém, no ano 70 D.C.

c. Perseguição contra os cristãos, durante o reinado de Domiciano, entre 81 e 96 D.C.

d. Literatura *neotestamentária* pós-paulina, como as epístolas de Pedro, a epístola de Judas, as epístolas joaninas e o Apocalipse. O gráfico que aparece sob o sexto ponto relaciona todos os livros do Novo Testamento a eventos históricos, onde também as datas podem ser averiguadas. Além disso, na introdução a cada livro, é discutido o problema das datas.

e. Literatura secular, relacionada ao movimento cristão. Um artigo separado é apresentado sobre *Livros Apócrifos*, parte III; *Novo Testamento: Livros Apócrifos e Outra Literatura Cristã Antiga*. As datas desses escritos, paralelamente a certos eventos históricos, são expostas no gráfico que há sob o ponto sexto deste artigo.

f. Morte do apóstolo João, cerca do ano 100 D.C., que pôs fim à era apostólica. A questão do martírio de João, se ele foi martirizado ou não, e quando, talvez requeira que ele tenha morrido muito antes do que se pensa. A maioria dos estudiosos, entretanto, rejeita uma data anterior àquela tradicionalmente aceita. Esse problema é amplamente discutido no artigo sobre a primeira epístola de João, sob a parte III, Data, Proveniência e Destino.

VI. Bibliografia. BOY FIN IB ID ISBE OG UN Z

CRONOLOGIA DO NOVO TESTAMENTO

VII. Tabelas Cronológicas Literárias e Históricas:
a. Cronologia da Literatura do Novo Testamento e Literatura relacionada ao Novo Testamento.

Desenvolvimento da Literatura do Novo Testamento e de outra Literatura Cristã Primitiva
Datado e Comparado com a História Geral e com a História Narrada no Novo Testamento

DATAS	HISTÓRIA GERAL	HISTÓRIA DO NOVO TESTAMENTO	LITERATURA
Até 47 A.C.	Antípatre, procurador da Judéia (pai de Herodes, o Grande)		
50 A.C.	Herodes, o Grande (40-4 A.C.)	Nacimento de Jesus (8-4 A.C.)	
1 D.C.	César Augusto (27 A.C.-14 D.C.)		
14 D.C.	Tibério (14-37 D.C.)		
26 D.C.	Pôncio Pilatos, procurador (26-36 D.C.)	Pregação de João Batista (28 D.C.)	
30 D.C.		Crucificação de Jesus (30 D.C.)	
		Desenvolvimento da igreja	
32 D.C.		Conversão de Paulo (32-39 D.C.)	
		Paulo em Jerusalém (37-38 D.C.)	
38 D.C.	Gaio e Calígula (37-41 D.C.)		
46 D.C.	Cláudio (41-54 D.C.)	Evangelização do sul da Galácia (45-46 D.C. Atos 13-14)	
	Fome na Palestina (46 D.C.)	Concílio de Jerusalém (46-47 D.C. Atos 11:30; 15:2; Gál. 2:11)	
50 D.C.	Expulsão dos judeus de Roma, sob Cláudio (49 D.C.)	Primeira viagem missionária de Paulo (46-47 D.C. Atos 13-14)	
51 D.C.	Gálio, procônsul da Acaia (51-52 D.C.)	Segunda viagem missionária de Paulo (48-51 D.C. Atos 16-17)	
		Paulo em Corinto (50 D.C. Atos 18)	I Tes. (50 D.C.)
53 D.C.	Félix, procurador (52-58 D.C.)	Terceira viagem missionária (53 D.C. Éfeso, 54-57; Atos 19)	I Cor. (54-55 D.C.) Marc. (50-54 D.C.)
58 D.C.	Nero (54-68 D.C.)	Paulo em Macedônea e na Grécia (55-58 D.C. Atos 20:1-6; 21:17)	Gál. (54-55 D.C.)
	Festo, procurador (58-62 D.C.)	Paulo em Jerusalém (56 D.C. Atos 21)	II Cor. (55 D.C.)
59 D.C.		Paulo em Roma (59 D.C. Atos 28)	Rom. (56 D.C.) Col. (59 D.C.)
61 D.C.		Fim da história de Atos (61 D.C.)	File. (59-61 D.C.) Fil. (59-61 D.C.)
62 D.C.		Martírio de Tiago, irmão do Senhor (62 D.C.)	Efé. (59-61 D.C.) I e II Tim. (61-62 D.C.) Tito (61 D.C.)
64 D.C.	Perseguição de Nero (64 D.C.)	Martírio de Paulo (61-64 D.C.)	I Ped. (60-64 D.C.?)
66 D.C.		Começa a revolta dos judeus. Cristãos fogem para Pela (66 D.C.)	
70 D.C.	Galva, Oto, Vitélio (68-69 D.C.) Vespasiano (69-79 D.C.)	Queda de Jerusalém (70 D.C.) Perseguições de Domiciano (81-96 D.C.)	Heb. (70-80 D.C.) Tiago (75-80) Luc.-Atos (75-80 D.C.) Mat. (75-80 D.C.)
81 D.C.	Pompeu (79 D.C.) Tito (79-81 D.C.)		
100 D.C.		Morte de João (100 D.C.)	Apo. (100 D.C.) João (100 D.C.) I, II, III João (100 D.C.) Judas (100 D.C.) I Clem. (100 D.C.) Inácio (100 D.C.)
	Plínio persegue os cristãos (112 D.C.)		
	Inácio martirizado em Roma (115 D.C.)		

CRONOLOLGIA DO NOVO TESTAMENTO

Cronologia Literária, cont.

segundo século

Didache (140 D.C.)
II Ped. (150 D.C.)
II Clem. (150 D.C.)
Pastor de Hermas (130-150 D.C.)
Ev. de Tomé (100-150 D.C.)
Ev. dos Egípcios (150 D.C.)
Ev. de Pedro (160 D. C.)
Ev. de Nicodemos (Séc. II-V?)
Ev. da Infância (séc. II-V)
Atos de João (150-160 D.C.)
Atos de Pedro (160 D.C.)
Atos de Tomé (180-200 D.C.)
III Cor. (200 D.C.)
Ep. Laodicenses (180 D.C.?)
Paulo e Sêneca (190 D.C.?)
Apo. de Pedro (180 D C.)
Apo. de João (180 D.C.)
Apo. de Tiago (125-180 D.C.?)
Apo. de Paulo (225- D.C.)

CRONOLOGIA DO NOVO TESTAMENTO

b. História Secular Relacionada a Eventos Registrados no Novo Testamento.

ACONTECIMENTOS DURANTE OS TEMPOS DO NOVO TESTAMENTO

ROMA	PALESTINA	NOVO TESTAMENTO
Primeiro Triunvirato: Júlio César, Pompeu, Crássio 60 A.C.	Conquista de Jerusalém por Pompeu, 63 A.C. João Hyrcanus II, 63-40 A.C.	
Segundo Triunvirato: Otávio, Lepidus, Antonio, 43 A.C.		
Augusto (Otávio), 31 A.C. - 14 D.C.	Herodes o Grande recebeu o poder e reinou (37-4 A.C.)	Jesus nasceu, primavera de 4 D.C. João Batista, quase ao mesmo tempo.

	ITUREA, Trachonitis, Palestina do Norte	GALILÉIA	JUDÉIA	
	Filipe, 4 A.C. 34 D.C.	Herodes Antipas 4 A.C. - 39 D.C.	Arquelau, 4 A.C. - 6 D.C.	Censo sob Quirino ou Cirênio. Fuga de Jesus para o Egito, morte de Herodes 4 A.C. Volta de Jesus à Palestina
				Nascimento de João, o apóstolo (2? D.C.)
Nascimento de Sêneca (3? D.C.)			Vários procuradores 6-41 D.C. (Pilatos 26-36)	Nascimento de Paulo, o apóstolo (5 D.C.)
		Insurreição de Judas da Galiléia (7 D.C.)	Morte de Hillel, queda de Arquelau, Judéia feita província romana (6 D.C.)	A primeira visita de Jesus ao templo, 9 D.C. (Luc. 2:41)
Morte de Augusto, Reinado de Tibério, 14-37 D.C.		Edificação de Tiberíades por Antipas (18 D.C.)		Morte de José (20? D.C.)
Morte de Livy e Ovídio, 18 D.C.				Batismo de Jesus, começo de seu ministério (28 D.C.)
				Ministério de Jesus (28 D.C.)
Calígula, 37-41 D.C. Cláudio, 41-51 D.C. Nero, 54-58 D.C. Galva, OTO, Vitélio, 68 D.C. Vespasiano 69-79 D.C.	Agripa I 37-44 D.C. Agripa II 53-93 D.C.	Agripa I 39-44 D.C. Agripa II 54-93 D.C.	Agripa I 41-44 D.C. Procuradores 44-66. (Félix 52-60; Festus 61-62) Primeira revolta dos judeus 66 D.C. Queda de Jerusalém 70 DC.	Crucificação 31 D.C. Conversão de Paulo 32 D.C. Paulo perante Festus 61 D.C. Paulo em Roma, 62 D.C.

CRUCIFICAÇÃO

CRUCIFICAÇÃO
Mat. 27:35: *Então, depois de o crucificarem, repartiram as vestes dele, lançando sortes, para que se cumprisse o que foi dito pelo profeta: Repartiram entre si as minhas vestes, e sobre a minha túnica lançaram sortes.*

Depois de o crucificarem. (Ver o artigo sobre a *Expiação*). A crucificação é modo muito antigo de execução. O *stauros* (vocábulo grego) para «poste», «cruz» originalmente era um poste de ponta afiada, em cima do qual as vítimas eram lançadas, para ficarem ali suspensas e torturadas. Era usado na Pérsia e em Roma dos tempos antigos. Os judeus suspendiam um criminoso, após a sua morte, com o propósito de servir de exemplo (ver Deut. 21:22,23). Ao tempo de Cristo, três tipos de cruzes eram usadas — uma que se assemelhava à nossa letra X (chamada cruz de Santo André), outra parecida com nossa letra T (chamada cruz de Santo Antônio), e a cruz latina, de desenho bem conhecido †. Não há absoluta certeza sobre a modalidade de cruz que foi empregada quando da execução de Jesus, mas a maioria dos estudiosos acredita que tenha sido a de último tipo. A crucificação sempre tinha lugar fora dos muros da cidade e a vítima carregava a sua cruz até o local da execução. As mãos (provavelmente no pulso ou no metacarpo) eram cravadas, primeiramente a direita, e então a esquerda, enquanto o condenado jazia sobre a terra. As autoridades diferem sobre o ponto dos pés serem cravados em separado ou se ambos eram cravados juntos. Não havia apoio para os pés, propriamente dito, mas alguma espécie de apoio em torno dos pés era usado. O mais provável é que na cruz os pés da vítima ficassem a apenas cerca de um palmo da terra. — A morte usualmente demorava muito, raramente exigindo menos de trinta e seis horas, e ocasionalmente se prolongava por nada menos de nove dias. As dores eram intensas, e as artérias da cabeça e do estômago ficavam grossas de sangue. Às vezes declarava-se febre traumática e tétano. Quando era desejável apressar a morte da vítima, as pernas eram despedaçadas com golpes aplicados com um pesado cacete ou martelo. O próprio nome da cruz era motivo de opróbrio, culpa e ignomínia. *Cícero* declarou: «O próprio nome (da cruz) deveria ser excluído não só do corpo, mas também dos pensamentos, dos olhos e dos ouvidos dos cidadãos romanos». Era uma execução reservada aos criminosos mais vis. Constantino (imperador romano em cerca de 300 D.C.), após a sua conversão ao cristianismo, embora nominalmente apenas, aboliu essa prática.

Uma Morte em Jerusalém
Artigo extraído por permissão da Revista Time, secção «Ciência», edição de 18 de janeiro de 1971.

Foi um período de grande intranqüilidade e agitação na antiga Judéia. Desassossegados sob o governo pagão de Roma, os judeus da Palestina, no primeiro século da era cristã, por repetidas vezes desafiaram os seus conquistadores com gestos ousados de oposição e atos francos de rebelião. A resposta dos romanos usualmente era imediata e cruel. Talvez porque tenha participado em um desses levantes ou tenha cometido alguma outra ofensa grave, aos olhos dos severos governantes de Jerusalém, um jovem judeu, chamado *Yehohanan* (forma hebraica para *João*), foi sentenciado à morte. A semelhança de milhares de outros judeus — incluindo Jesus de Nazaré — que também fora condenado pelos procuradores romanos durante aqueles anos de turbulência, Yehohanan morreu lenta e dolorosamente na cruz.

Primeira Evidência
A morte de **Yehohanan** foi esquecida prontamente. Nenhum documento foi jamais encontrado que registrasse o seu crime ou relembrasse a sua execução. No entanto, depois de quase dois mil anos, foi ele agora súbita e sensacionalmente desenterrado das brumas da história. Na semana passada arqueólogos israelenses anunciaram que haviam identificado os restos mortais do desafortunado jovem, por haverem encontrado claras evidências sobre sua terrível execução.

Os eruditos israelenses, que estudaram seu achado por mais de dois anos, antes de fazerem o seu anúncio, mostraram-se compreensivelmente cautelosos. O que descobriram e autenticaram foi a primeira firme evidência física de uma crucificação real, no antigo mundo mediterrâneo. Embora a história registre que essa forma de punição tenha continuado a ser usada pelos romanos, até o século IV D.C. (até que foi finalmente banida por lei, pelo imperador Constantino I, que legalizou o cristianismo no império), a única evidência física anterior sobre a crucificação era extremamente tênue. Consistia de alguns poucos ossos, escavados na Itália e na **Romênia**, que continham perfurações nos braços e nos calcanhares, e que poderiam ter sido feitos durante crucificações. Mas nunca se descobrira qualquer traço dos cravos que teriam sido utilizados para penetrar no corpo das vítimas, fixando-as à cruz.

A nova evidência arqueológica, que é um subproduto de intensas escavações e dos projetos de construção efetuados pelos israelenses, nos territórios conquistados durante a Guerra de Seis Dias, é muito mais substancial. Em junho de 1968, um ano depois que as tropas israelenses ocuparam a cidade inteira de Jerusalém, os trabalhadores começaram a aplainar um trecho rochoso de terreno, com tratores, em um local que distava quase dois quilômetros da antiga Porta de Damasco daquela cidade, na direção norte, como preparativos para o soerguimento de um moderno complexo de edifícios de apartamentos. E quase imediatamente descobriram que aquele local, denominado Giv'at ha-Mivtar (que significa Colina da Fronteira) estava coalhado de sepulcros que datavam dos tempos bíblicos.

Convocado pelo *Departamento de Antigüidades e Museus de Israel*, o arqueólogo Vasilius Tzaferis não demorou em abrir quinze ossuários, ou seja, sarcófagos de pedra, que continham os esqueletos de trinta e cinco pessoas, onze homens, doze mulheres e doze crianças. Pelo menos cinco daqueles judeus tinham tido morte violenta. Mas Tzaferis ficou especialmente intrigado pelo que encontrou em um dos ossuários, que continha os ossos de uma criança de três ou quatro anos de idade, e os ossos de um adulto cujo nome — Yehohanan — estava escrito em letras aramaicas quase ilegíveis, do lado de fora. Os ossos do calcanhar desse homem estavam atravessados pelos restos enferrujados de um cravo com dezoito centímetros de comprimento.

Com base nesses frágeis ossos, um anatomista e antropólogo romeno, da Universidade Hebraica de Jerusalém, *Nicu Haas*, foi capaz de compor um quadro surpreendentemente detalhado do jovem: teria entre vinte e trinta anos de idade, e era de estatura média para aquele período (1,65 m), sendo dotado de feições delicadas e agradáveis, que pareciam aproximar-se do ideal helênico; talvez tivesse usado barba, e aparentemente jamais realizara qualquer trabalho realmente árduo — o que indicava

CRISTO NO CALVÁRIO

LEVANTANDO A CRUZ

CRUCIFICAÇÃO

sua possível origem nas classes abastadas. Excetuando os ferimentos que lhe foram infligidos durante sua crucificação, parece que gozava de saúde realmente excepcional. Suas únicas deformações físicas eram um palato levemente aberto e uma certa assimetria quase imperceptível em seu crânio, que talvez fosse sinal de um nascimento difícil.

Cravo Torto

O único cravo tão revelador foi preservado por uma estranha ocorrência. Por causa de um nó muito duro na madeira de oliveira da cruz, o cravo se entortou de leve para um lado, quando estava sendo fincado a marteladas em seu lugar. Mais tarde, quando aplicaram o tradicional golpe de misericórdia (pancada forte que fraturava ambas as pernas e que apressava a morte da vítima, causando hemorragia e choque), aparentemente o cravo torto mostrou estar firmemente fixado na cruz, tendo impedido todos os esforços de tirar o cadáver da cruz. A única maneira prática pela qual isso pôde ser feito, segundo escreve Haas no *Israel Exploration Journal*, foi «decepar os pés e então remover o complexo inteiro — cravo, placa de madeira que ajudava a manter os pés em posição, e os pés — da cruz». Em seguida, essas porções cortadas foram segundo todas as aparências, sepultadas imediatamente, juntamente com o resto do corpo, em uma sepultura temporária; pois os costumes judaicos proíbem que um corpo fique exposto por muito tempo depois da ocorrência da morte. Subseqüentemente, os restos mortais de Yehohanan foram desenterrados por seus amigos ou parentes, tendo sido removidos para seu lugar de descanso permamente, do lado de fora da cidade, onde permaneceram intocados até o ano de 1968.

A data exata da execução já não transparece com tanta clareza. Porém, se levarmos em conta os vasos e outros artefatos existentes na caverna, conforme verificaram os eruditos israelenses, poderemos fazer um cálculo aproximado: tudo poderia ter tido lugar desde 7 D.C., quando os judeus se levantaram contra os romanos, protestando por motivo de um recenseamento oficial, ou já no final da década antes da destruição do Segundo Templo e da dispersão dos judeus, em 70 D.C.

A Agonia de Jesus

O período e o lugar da execução desse jovem animou comparações com a própria paixão de Jesus Cristo na cruz—o que, segundo crêem os eruditos, teve lugar em cerca de 30 D.C., quando Jesus já havia passado dos trinta anos de idade.

Ao fixar a data para o início da era cristã, o monge cita do século VI D.C., Dionísio Exíguo, introduziu um equívoco de pelo menos quatro anos no cálculo do ano do nascimento de Jesus. Além disso, os evangelhos não fornecem uma data precisa nem para o nascimento e nem para a morte de Cristo.

Porém, o diretor de antiguidades de Israel, Abraham Biran, bem como certo número de eruditos bíblicos cristãos, prontamente advertiram contra a tentativa de identificar o esqueleto como se fosse o de Jesus. Conforme salientou o Dr. Bruce Metzger, do Princeton Theological Seminary: «Não temos, em absoluto, qualquer conhecimento acerca da estatura física de Jesus». Outrossim, o executado era mais jovem que Jesus, e os evangelhos historiam que os soldados romanos, em contraste à sua prática regular, não quebraram as pernas de Jesus antes de sua morte; mas feriram-lhe o lado do cadáver com uma lança. Tanto os arqueólogos como os eruditos bíblicos se mostraram compreensivelmente preocupados. Qualquer sugestão, ainda que remota, de que o corpo era o de Jesus, poderia desafiar duas das crenças cristãs mais centrais; a ressurreição, ou seja, a doutrina de que Cristo ressuscitou dentre os mortos, três dias após a sua crucificação; e a ascensão, que assegura que Jesus subiu corporalmente aos céus, quarenta dias mais tarde.

Embora o descobrimento feito em *Giv'at ha-Mivtar* não acrescente qualquer nova informação sobre a vida de Jesus, pode dar uma nova dimensão ao seu sofrimento final. Segundo a arte religiosa clássica, Jesus crucificado geralmente aparece em uma posição ereta, preso à cruz por cravos atravessados em suas mãos estendidas e através de seus pés. Na opinião de alguns estudiosos, entretanto, essa interpretação acerca da crucificação desde há muito tem parecido altamente improvável. Pois se o peso principal do corpo ficasse dependurado pelas mãos, o corpo da vítima ficaria arqueado para fora; tornar-se-ia extremamente difícil o funcionamento. De conformidade com a reconstituição da crucificação de Yehohanan, feita por Haas—o que talvez mostre a maneira típica usada nas crucificações da Palestina antiga—os cravos bem poderiam ter sido fixados através dos antebraços, a fim de que houvesse maior apoio, ao mesmo tempo que as pernas da vítima eram torcidas para um lado e dobradas. Haas chama isso de *posição compulsória e desnatural*. Porém, explica ele que isso teria servido aos propósitos dos executores perfeitamente bem: teria prolongado tanto a vida como a agonia da vítima.

De conformidade com os costumes romanos, os crucificados não eram tirados da cruz; eram ali abandonados, a fim de morrerem lentamente. Suas carnes eram dadas às aves ou aos animais ferozes. Havia ocasiões em que o sofrimento dos condenados era abreviado, acendendo-se uma fogueira ao pé da cruz, ou permitindo que leões ou ursos os despedaçassem. Mas os judeus não permitiam tais coisas; e também insistiam em que se desse sepultamento aos mortos na cruz. O ato de quebrar as pernas dos crucificados, **na realidade era** uma espécie de *golpe de misericórdia*, a fim de apressar a morte; e o transpassar com a lança também era outra forma de «golpe de misericórdia». Alguns comentaristas acreditam que foi quando estava sendo cravado na cruz que Jesus proferiu aquelas palavras: «Pai, perdoa-lhes, porque não sabem o que fazem» (Luc. 23:34). A tortura da cruz era a forma de punição mais horrenda, desumana e sem misericórdia que jamais foi inventada pelo homem, e a palavra *excruciante*, termo moderno para indicar tortura ou dor intensas, se deriva desse vocábulo—*cruz*.

Temos um hino favorito que diz:

Sob a cruz de Jesus,
Quero tomar meu lugar...

Por instinto, preferíamos tomar lugar em toda parte, menos ali, porquanto em parte alguma achamos uma acusação tão patente contra a iniqüidade humana. Ali vemos claramente demonstrada a iniqüidade do homem. A própria história do mundo, com todos os seus conflitos e guerras, e até mesmo com as divisões e as contendas no seio da própria igreja cristã, serve de mais um testemunho acerca da maldade do homem. É na cruz que encontramos *nossa natureza vil*, nossas propensões ao pecado, nossas expressões de maldade. Na cruz, entretanto, sofreu e morreu, o homem da alma mais pura que a terra já conheceu. Buttrick diz em Mat. 27:35: «Como poderíamos exibir ainda a natureza humana, exceto quando essa natureza humana é lançada na misericórdia e poder de Deus?»

CRUCIFICAÇÃO

Na Via Dolorosa, Jesus lutara sob o peso de sua cruz. Fora açoitado com um açoite cuja ponta era munida de um pedacinho de metal. Foi espancado até quase não poder ser reconhecido, e a caminho do Calvário foi com ferimentos abertos, a derramar sangue. Nessas condições é que foi cravado na cruz. Foi vítima de exposição ao sol e ao calor, a enxames de moscas, e aos insultos de homens dotados de mentes sádicas. Quando a altivez humana—tal como a de Caifás, que cobiçava ouro e posição, ou como a de Pilatos, que desejava governar, se desenvolve plenamente, crucifica Cristo de novo. Aprendemos, então, que é à sombra da cruz, que devemos tomar nosso lugar, pois dali flui o sangue que dá vida. Jesus identificou-se conosco, sofrendo em favor de toda a humanidade, a ira que pertence ao pecado e o precede. Por conseguinte, a sua morte é a nova páscoa. Por conseguinte, o seu poder permanece até hoje, para salvar-nos do pecado que o enviou à cruz. O desespero do expositor é o fato de não existirem paralelos para a obra de Cristo. Mas o crânio daquela colina atualmente está partido mediante a coragem e a compaixão de Deus, em Cristo, pelo que agora há nele o nascimento de uma vida nova para todos quantos vivem neste mundo.

As Chagas

Divinas mãos e pés, peito rasgado.
Chagas em brandas carnes imprimidas,
Meu Deus, que, por salvar almas perdidas,
Por elas quereis ser crucificado.

Outra fé, outro amor, outro cuidado,
Outras dores às Vossas são devidas,
Outros corações limpos, outras vidas,
Outro querer no vosso transformado.

Em vós se encerrou toda a piedade,
Ficou no mundo só toda a crueza,
Por isso cada um deu o que tinha.

Claros sinais de amor, ah! saudade!
Minha consolação, minha firmeza,
Chagas do meu Senhor, redenção minha.

(Frei Agostinho da Cruz, Portugal: 1540-1619).

CRUCIFICAÇÃO, Dia da. Ver **Dia da Crucificação, Sexta-Feira.**

CRUCIFICAÇÃO, Narrativa do Calvário

João 19:17-42 comparado com os *Sinópticos*.
Ver os paralelos nos trechos de Mat. 27:45-61; Mar. 15:33-47 e Luc. 23:44-56. Novamente encontramos o fato de que diferentes fontes informativas foram utilizadas pelo autor do quarto evangelho em comparação com as fontes usadas pelos autores dos evangelhos sinópticos, pois apesar de grande parte do material ser idêntico, existem algumas notáveis diferenças que tornam óbvia a sugestão que, neste ponto, houve uma variedade de fontes. Sabemos que o evangelho de João encerra menos de dez por cento do material dos evangelhos sinópticos, e isso é prova suficiente de que o seu autor não contava com qualquer desses evangelhos à sua frente, quando compilou o seu próprio evangelho. Porque se tivesse contado com os mesmos evangelhos, não resta dúvida de que teria usado muito mais do que os dez por cento. É óbvio também que até quando o quarto evangelho contém material semelhante, em alguns pontos particulares, esse material é bastante diferente.

As diferenças básicas entre os evangelhos sinópticos e o evangelho de João no que diz respeito a João 19:17-42.

1. O evangelho de João *omite* a história de Simão o cireneu, que foi forçado a ajudar a carregar a pesada cruz de Jesus, porquanto Cristo estava por demais debilitado fisicamente para tão grande esforço, e ainda lhe era necessário fazer a caminhada da área do templo até fora dos muros de Jerusalém, onde ficava o lugar da sua crucificação. Todos os evangelhos sinópticos, entretanto, incluem essa narrativa. Provavelmente as fontes informativas usadas pelo quarto evangelho não continham essa história, pelo que também o seu autor não a incluiu em suas descrições históricas. Alguns estudiosos têm sugerido, entretanto, que mui provavelmente ele sabia da ocorrência, tendo-a omitido propositalmente, porquanto gnósticos heréticos, até mesmo em seus dias, como Basílides fez uma geração mais tarde, diziam que Simão e Jesus trocaram de lugar, de tal modo que Jesus realmente não morreu na cruz. (Encontramos essa idéia mencionada por Irineu, um dos primeiros pais da Igreja, em 150 D.C., em seu livro *Contra as Heresias*, I.24.4). Sabemos que há um forte elemento antignóstico e antidocético no evangelho e nas epístolas de João, sendo possível que foi justamente por esse motivo que o autor sagrado do quarto evangelho omitiu a história, a fim de evitar qualquer sugestão de que Jesus não morreu na cruz. Todavia, não há meios de provarmos a questão, nem para um lado e nem para outro.

2. A narrativa das mulheres que se lamentavam, enquanto seguiam o Senhor Jesus ao local da crucificação, também é apresentada exclusivamente pelo *terceiro* evangelho (ver Luc. 23:27-31).

3. O título, posto por Pilatos no alto da cruz de Jesus, apresenta *variações diversas* em todos os quatro evangelhos. O evangelho de João é o único que nos dá a informação que foram escritas as palavras «Jesus, o Nazareno», como também é o único que ajunta que o título da acusação fora escrito em hebraico, em latim e em grego. Pelos informes históricos ficamos sabendo que mui provavelmente isso era uma medida usual, porquanto em outros casos, títulos em diversos idiomas foram escritos e expostos em público, como nos sepulcros dos grandes personagens, etc.

4. A objeção feita pelos principais sacerdotes dos judeus, ante o título posto na cruz, *Rei dos Judeus*, ocasião em que desejavam que fosse dito «Ele disse...», isto é, que Jesus é quem fizera tal reivindicação, e não que ele fosse realmente o rei dos judeus, são informes que aparecem somente no quarto evangelho. (Ver João 19:21,22).

5. O oferecimento que fizeram a Jesus, de uma bebida amortecedora dos sentidos, evidentemente para aliviar as dores próprias da crucificação, é informação que aparece somente nos trechos de Mat. 27:34 e Mar. 15:23.

6. A divisão das vestes de Jesus Cristo, entre os soldados, é narrada nos evangelhos de Mateus, Marcos e João; mas somente este último diz-nos que suas vestes foram divididas em *quatro partes*, ou seja, uma parte para cada soldado. E somente o evangelho de João, por igual modo, informa-nos que quanto à túnica sem costura de Jesus, os soldados lançaram sortes, para ver com qual deles ficaria a mesma, cumprindo assim a profecia de Sal. 22:18. (Ver João 19:23,24).

7. Somente o evangelho de João fala-nos sobre a presença de Maria, mãe de Jesus, de outras mulheres e do apóstolo João, ao pé da cruz. (Ver João 19:25-27).

8. Os evangelhos sinópticos são os únicos que registram como diversos indivíduos ou grupos se prostraram diante da cruz, incluindo os principais

CRUCIFICAÇÃO — CRUELDADE

sacerdotes, com o fito de insultarem a Jesus, estando ele encravado na mesma. (Ver Mar. 15:29-32; Mat. 27:39-44 e Luc. 23:35-43).

9. Somente o evangelho de Lucas registra como *um* dos ladrões, que também havia participado ativamente das zombarias contra Jesus, finalmente se arrependeu, e como o Senhor Jesus lhe prometeu que ainda naquele dia estaria com ele no paraíso. (Ver Luc. 23:39-43). O evangelho de Lucas, entretanto, não indica que esse ladrão penitente houvesse zombado de Jesus, mas os evangelhos de Mateus e Marcos deixam isso claro, ainda que em termos gerais.

10. As declarações feitas por Jesus, estando na cruz, são diferentes em cada evangelho. (Quanto a uma completa descrição sobre essa questão, ver as notas no NTI em João 19:26).

11. O fato de que sobrevieram trevas, que sombrearam a terra inteira pelo espaço de três horas é registrado exclusivamente pelos evangelhos sinópticos. (Ver Mat. 27:45-50; Mar. 15:33-37 e Luc. 23:44-46).

12. *Os diversos fenômenos* que acompanharam a crucificação de Jesus são omitidos no relato do evangelho de João, como por exemplo, o véu do templo, que se rasgou de cima a baixo (Ver Mar. 15:38; Mat. 27:41 e Luc. 23:45). O testemunho do centurião, acerca da grandeza moral de Jesus também é omitido pelo quarto evangelho. (Ver Mar. 15:39; Mat. 27:54 e Luc. 23:47). A grande consternação e lamentação das mulheres é outro pequeno detalhe histórico omitido pelo autor do quarto evangelho. (Ver Mar. 15:40; Mat. 27:55,56 e Luc. 23:28-49).

13. O fato de que as pernas do Senhor Jesus não tiveram de ser quebradas, a exemplo do que os soldados fizeram com os dois ladrões, e também o de um soldado ferir o corpo já morto de Jesus com uma lança, entre as costelas, e como saiu sangue e água pelo ferimento, aparece apenas no quarto evangelho. (Ver João 19:31-37).

14. O fato de que *Pilatos* se maravilhou com a morte súbita de Jesus, aparece exclusivamente na passagem de Mar. 15:44,45.

15. O fato de que *Nicodemos* acompanhou José de Arimatéia quando do sepultamento do Senhor Jesus, é exposto apenas pelo evangelho de João. (Ver o versículo trinta e nove, que também descreve a quantidade de perfumes e especiarias trazidos para o embalsamamento do corpo de Jesus, segundo o costume judaico, que também só aparece no evangelho de João).

16. O fato de que o sepulcro de Jesus ficava em um jardim, é detalhe oferecido a nós somente no evangelho de João. (Ver João 19:41).

17. Que foi posta uma guarda de soldados para vigiar o túmulo de Jesus, é informe histórico dado somente no trecho de Mat. 27:62-66.

No que diz respeito à ordem dos acontecimentos, por ocasião da crucificação.

1. No caminho para o Gólgota, as mulheres se lamentam. Foi a Via Dolorosa. (Luc. 23:27-31).
2. Chegada ao Gólgota. (Mat. 27:33; Mar. 15:22; Luc. 23:33 e João 19:17).
3. Ofereceram uma mistura amortecedora dos sentidos, que Jesus rejeitou. (Mat. 27:34 e Mar. 15:33).
4. A crucificação. (Mat. 27:35-38; Mar. 15:24-28; Luc. 23:33-38 e João 19:18-24).
5. Declaração de Cristo, na cruz: «Pai, perdoa-lhes» (Luc. 23:34).
6. Vestes de Jesus são divididas, e sua túnica inconsútil é dada por sorte a um dos soldados. (Mat. 27:35; Mar. 15:34; Luc. 23:34 e João 19:23,24).
7. O povo, os principais sacerdotes, os soldados e os passantes, todos zombam de Jesus. (Mat. 27:39-44; Mar. 15:29-32 e Luc. 23:35-38).
8. O incidente dos ladrões que escarneciam de Jesus, até que um deles, finalmente, se arrepende. (Mat. 27:44; Mar. 15:32 e Luc. 23:29-43).
9. Segunda declaração de Cristo, na cruz: «Em verdade te digo que hoje estarás comigo no paraíso» (Luc. 23:43).
10. Terceira declaração de Cristo, na cruz, à sua mãe e ao apóstolo João, respectivamente: «Mulher, eis aí o teu filho...Eis aí a tua mãe» (João 19:26,27).
11. As trevas de três horas sobre a terra. (Mat. 27:45; Mar. 15:33 e Luc. 23:24).
12. Quarta declaração de Cristo, na cruz: «Deus meu, Deus meu, por que me abandonaste?» (Mat. 27:46 e Mar. 15:34-36).
13. Quinta declaração de Cristo, na cruz: «Tenho sede» (João 19:28).
14. Sexta declaração de Cristo, na cruz: «Está consumado!» (João 19:30).
15. Sétima declaração de Cristo, na cruz: «Pai, nas tuas mãos entrego o meu espírito» (Luc. 23:46).
16. O Senhor entrega o espírito. (Mat. 27:50; Mar. 15:37; Luc. 23:37; Lu. 23:46 e João 19:30).

CRUCIFIXO

Essa palavra vem do latim, *crucifixus*, que se deriva de *crux*, «cruz», e *figere*, «fixar». Em outras palavras, uma cruz que é fixada. O item representa Cristo na cruz, usado como símbolo cristão. Desde o começo do cristianismo, a cruz tem sido um emblema cristão. O crucifixo começou a ser usado de modo geral em cerca do século VI D.C. A princípio, os crucifixos traziam uma imagem vestida, representando Cristo, por razões de modéstia. Porém, os artistas orientais começaram a retratar a cena de forma mais realista, provavelmente em resultado da controvérsia monofisista (que, vide). De acordo com esta posição a verdadeira humanidade de Cristo era negada, para todos os propósitos práticos. A representação mais realista de Cristo, no Ocidente, só ocorreu no século IX D.C. em diante. O crucifixo era uma extensão do uso privado e litúrgico da cruz. As cruzes celtas com freqüência serviam a um propósito didático, porquanto eram inscritas de forma a representar vários mistérios da fé cristã. Alguns crucifixos eram tão elaboradamente preparados, representando os sofrimentos e os ferimentos de Cristo, que eram mais símbolos da desolação e dos padecimentos humanos do que da vitória de Jesus Cristo sobre a morte.

CRUELDADE

Em certo sentido, a história da humanidade é a história da crueldade humana. Os próprios relatos bíblicos, por serem realistas, deixam-nos chocados com seus vívidos relatos de intermináveis guerras, matanças e destruições de vidas e bens. As histórias infantis não escapam dessa praga, visto que a sensação de suspense, assim obtida, quase sempre depende da ameaça à vida e ao bem-estar. Muitas das histórias infantis são francas narrativas de matanças e malefícios. Os modernos entretenimentos, na literatura, no cinema, no teatro e na televisão dependem muito da idéia dos morticínios. O extremo oposto de tudo isso é a lei do amor, cuja voz dificilmente pode ser ouvida entre os brados de crueldade. Há muitas formas de crueldade. Os dicionários definem a palavra «cruel» como «a disposição para infligir sofrimento em outras pessoas». Esse sofrimento pode ser físico, mental ou moral. A crueldade, pois, é a indiferença diante do sofrimento alheio, com ausência de misericórdia, de parceria com algum ato positivo de maldade. Muitos casamentos terminam sob a alegação de «crueldade mental». E também devemos pensar na crueldade que os homens praticam contra o mundo animal. Os olhos dos coelhos têm sido usados como campo de teste para novos produtos químicos, que depois às mulheres usam, a fim de se verificar se eles têm algum efeito cáustico sobre tecidos humanos sensíveis. O gado é apertado em pequenos cubículos, onde não podem se movimentar, sendo forçados a ingerir grandes quantidades de alimentos, para estarem prontos para o abate, a curto prazo. As crianças arrancam as pernas e as asas dos insetos, somente para vê-los tremendo de agonia. Homens que possuem dois automóveis na sua garagem, e residências luxuosas, saem para caçar e matar animais selvagens por puro esporte, porquanto nunca conheceram a fome. Verdadeiramente, o homem é um ser decaído; e uma das maneiras pela qual ele demonstra isso mais claramente são as suas múltiplas formas de crueldade, do que todos nós somos culpados de algum modo, fisicamente, ou mediante a imposição de sofrimento mental. Quão distante de tudo isso é a atitude que transparece nas palavras de Jesus: «Vinde a mim, todos vós que estais cansados e oprimidos, e eu vos aliviarei. Tomai sobre vós o meu jugo, e aprendei de mim, que sou manso e humilde de coração; e achareis descanso para as vossas almas» (Mat. 11:28,29).

CRUSIUS, CHRISTIAN AUGUST

Suas datas foram 1612-1775. Foi um filósofo e teólogo alemão. Nasceu em Leuna. Foi educado em Leipzig, onde se tornou professor e onde, finalmente, se tornou reitor da universidade. Opunha-se à tradição de Leibniz e Wolff e foi um dos líderes do movimento pietista. Exerceu notável influência sobre Emanuel Kant (que vide).

Idéias:

1. O princípio da *cogitabilitas*, ou cogitabilidade, indica que aquilo que não pode ser concebido como falso é verdadeiro, e que aquilo que nem pode ser cogitado é falso.

2. Entre a falsidade e a verdade, ficam situadas quase todas as proposições, sobre as quais só podemos ter uma certeza moral, que repousa sobre a indução, a hipótese ou a força do testemunho.

3. Tudo quanto sabemos sobre a causalidade deriva-se de nossa própria experiência sobre a constante conjunção dos eventos.

4. Crusius declarava-se favorável à idéia do livre-arbítrio, principalmente com base no fato de que o determinismo (que vide) não é capaz de explicar o mal moral, e nem pode manusear sozinho essa questão.

5. Ele rejeitava o argumento ontológico (que vide), acreditando que as provas da existência de Deus podem ser estabelecidas sobre bases morais. Ver sobre o *Argumento Moral* em prol da existência de Deus.

6. A ontologia não pode estar fundamentada sobre a lógica; mas a lógica de qualquer indivíduo pressupõe a ontologia, de alguma maneira.

7. A revelação bíblica é a fonte final da verdade, no que concerne às questões de suprema importância.

Obras: Instructions for a Reasonable Life; Sketch of Necessary Rational Truths; The Way to Certainty and Reliability of Human Knowledge.

CRUZ

Esboço:
I. Costumes Antigos Seculares e Bíblicos
II. Simbolismos Neotestamentários
III. Um Símbolo Antigo
IV. Usos Modernos

I. Costumes Antigos Seculares e Bíblicos

Ver o artigo sobre a **Crucificação**, que inclui detalhes sobre as cruzes antigas e o uso que se fazia delas. Dentro da cultura hebréia, os cadáveres eram deixados pendurados em árvores como medida de opróbrio, além de servir de advertência a possíveis ofensores (Deu. 21:22,23; Jos. 10:26). Mas a crucificação, como forma de punição capital, não era usada. Ver o artigo sobre *Crimes e Castigos*. O símbolo dessa maldição é atrelado à cruz de Cristo, no Novo Testamento (Atos 5:20; 13:29; I Ped. 2:24; Gál. 3:13), onde o elemento de opróbrio e vergonha é destacado.

A crucificação também era praticada entre os fenícios e os cartagineses, e, posteriormente, pelos romanos. Contudo, um cidadão romano não podia ser crucificado. A cruz era a punição capital reservada à classe criminosa mais abjeta, bem como aos escravos. Nas páginas do Novo Testamento, a cruz é um dos símbolos da morte de Jesus, pelo que se reveste de profundo sentido teológico. Contudo, não devemos pensar que na Bíblia aparece a idéia de «crucifixos» e da veneração aos mesmos. Ver o artigo sobre *Cruz de Cristo, Efeitos*; que nos apresenta a teologia envolvida. Paulo referia-se ao evangelho como «evangelho da cruz», visto que sua mensagem girava em torno do ato expiatório de Cristo, e os efeitos do mesmo.

II. Simbolismos Neotestamentários

Os sofrimentos de Jesus tornaram-se o grande lema que indica a extensão da agonia e da resolução que se fazem necessários para o solucionamento do problema do pecado. Há vários simbolismos em torno dos detalhes da crucificação de Jesus, como «fora da cidade», etc. Portanto, devemo-nos separar do mundo e sua maneira de viver, levando sempre o opróbrio de Cristo (Heb. 13:13).

Jesus foi *levantado* na cruz, e assim ficou capacitado a atrair todos os homens a si mesmo (João 12:32).

A tabuleta escrita, posta sobre a cruz, simboliza a maldição proferida pela lei contra a humanidade; por causa do pecado. Agora, essa maldição foi removida, devido ao sangue expiatório de Cristo (Col. 2:14).

A cruz era o cúmulo da humilhação, vinculada à doutrina da humanidade e da missão terrena de Cristo (Fil. 2:8,9).

Levar a própria cruz é um símbolo de discipulado cristão sério (Mat. 16:25; João 12:26; Mar. 8:34-36). Jesus levou a sua própria cruz, e os seus discípulos terão de fazer outro tanto.

A cruz tornou-se símbolo de nossa união mística com Cristo, mediante a qual novos desejos e novos poderes são liberados, em uma nova vida espiritual (Gál. 2:19,20; Rom. 6:6).

Podemos compartilhar da missão de Cristo, o que inclui sofrimentos e dificuldades, que teremos de enfrentar (Col. 1:24).

CRUZ — CRUZ DE CRISTO, EFEITOS

A cruz serve de símbolo do propósito ímpar de Deus, na missão realizada por Jesus (Atos 2:23; Mat. 16:21; Mar. 14:36; Fil. 2:8).

A cruz é símbolo da nossa reconciliação com Deus, por meio de Jesus Cristo (II Cor. 5:19).

A cruz é o grande sinal do ato remidor de Deus, na história da humanidade (I Cor. 1:18).

III. Um Símbolo Antigo

A cruz é um dos mais antigos e universais símbolos conhecidos pelo homem. Os egípcios usavam uma cruz em forma de «T», com um círculo no alto. Isso formava uma combinação que simbolizava a vida vindoura, após a morte biológica. Essa cruz se chama *crux ansata*, parecendo-se com isto: ⚲ — Esse mesmo símbolo transmitia a idéia de sabedoria secreta, para os fenícios e os índios astecas, da América Central. Quando o círculo era posto abaixo da cruz, significava a *bondade*. Também havia vários tipos de cruzes, usadas como símbolos astronômicos. A cruz com os quatro braços do mesmo comprimento +, representava os supostos quatro elementos básicos da natureza: terra, ar, água e fogo, dos quais se derivariam todos os demais elementos existentes. Alimentos e outros itens eram assinalados com essa cruz, quando usados com propósitos religiosos nas religiões da Índia, da China, da Pérsia, da Assíria e da Babilônia, embora não saibamos dizer qual o significado desse símbolo. A cruz suástica 卐 era usada no budismo para indicar a completa resignação espiritual; e os índios da América do Norte consideravam-na um símbolo das leis que governam os ventos e as águas. Há evidências de que essa cruz já era usada desde a Idade do Bronze, tendo existido como um símbolo religioso em culturas tão diversas quanto a dos indianos, a dos persas, a dos chineses, a dos japoneses e a dos ameríndios. É possível que originalmente fosse um símbolo pictográfico do sol em revolução. Não é claro o motivo pelo qual esse símbolo foi adotado pelos nazistas. Mas, nesse caso, é justo chamá-la pelo outro nome que a torna conhecida, cruz torta, porque o nazismo perverteu tudo quanto é sagrado para o cristianismo bíblico.

Os judeus não tinham nenhuma palavra especial para «cruz», pelo que se referiam a ela como uma «árvore». A exposição de cadáveres, sobre estacas ou árvores era governada pela lei mosaica (Deu. 2:22,23). Foi apenas natural que a *árvore* dos judeus viesse a ser associada à cruz de Cristo, levando a *vergonha* da raça, passando a ser desprezada pelos próprios judeus (Col. 2:14; Atos 5:30; I Ped. 2:24).

IV. Usos Modernos

Ver o artigo sobre o **Crucifixo**, quanto ao uso por certos cristãos de uma pequena cruz, feita de vários materiais, para uso devocional e litúrgico, particular ou público. Cruzes têm servido para decorar templos, altares, etc., em todas as civilizações cristãs. Até mesmo cemitérios são assinalados por cruzes, cada uma delas indicando um sepulcro. Crucifixos de mão são usados pelos bispos católicos romanos em suas bênçãos e atos litúrgicos. João Crisóstomo (407 D.C.) usou crucifixos nas procissões, quando procurou chamar de volta certos cristãos à posição ortodoxa e a um sério discipulado cristão. Imensas cruzes, erigidas nos mercados, serviam de estruturas que protegiam as pessoas das intempéries. Também serviam para, ao pé das mesmas, serem publicados decretos e mensagens as mais diversas. As áreas dos asilos eram marcadas por quatro cruzes, na Inglaterra, e imensas cruzes, postas à beira das estradas, na França, tinham a mesma função. Algumas cruzes, como aquelas usadas pelos povos celtas, serviam para propósitos didáticos, com vários mistérios cristãos inscritos nas mesmas. Os arautos, tanto civis quanto religiosos, têm usado o emblema da cruz como um sinal distintivo de seu ofício. A cruz papal foi planejada para representar essa idéia. Cerca de vinte e duas nações européias usam cruzes em suas decorações de honra, incluindo até mesmo alguns países comunistas.

O artigo sobre o *Crucifixo* é suplementar a este artigo, devendo ser examinado juntamente com este, para maiores informações. Ver também o artigo sobre a Teologia da Cruz, sob o título *Cruz de Cristo, Efeitos*. (AM DU E NTI)

CRUZ DE CRISTO, EFEITOS

Os efeitos da cruz de Cristo; o significado da cruz:

1. Substituição pelos pecadores (ver Isa. 53:4-6; Mat. 20:28; II Cor. 5:21; I Tim. 2:5,6; Heb. 2:9 e I Ped. 3:18).

2. Sofrimento vicário (ver Heb. 2:9; I Ped. 3:18; I João 2:2; 4:10; Heb. 2:17 e Rom. 3:25).

3. Mediação entre Deus e o homem (ver Col. 1:20). Ele estabeleceu a paz pelo sangue de sua cruz (ver I Cor. 15:25-28; João 7:38; 16:7; 14:16; Atos 2:33 e Gál. 3:13,14).

4. Base de intercessão em prol dos pecadores (ver I Tim. 2:5,6; I João 2:1,2; Apo. 5:6 e Fil. 2:8-10).

5. Cristo pôs fim ao princípio da lei, tanto como uma base suposta de justificação como também como meio de santificação ou guia na vida cristã diária (ver João 1:17; Rom. 4:4,14; 10:4; 11:6; Gál. 3:3,10-13; 4:19-31; 5:1 e Atos 15:10).

6. Redenção da servidão ao pecado, seu julgamento e seu domínio sobre a vida do crente. (Ver o sexto capítulo da epístola aos Romanos, Col. 1:1-3 e Gál. 2:20).

7. Reconciliação com Deus (ver Rom. 5:1,10,11; II Cor. 5:19,20; Efé. 2:16 e II Cor. 5:18).

8. *Propiciação* para com Deus e pelo pecado (ver Rom. 3:25; I João 2:2; 4:10 e Heb. 9:5).

9. Julgamento contra o pecado, com a destruição do princípio do pecado e de seus frutos (ver Rom. 5:15,17,18; 8:3,6:14). A natureza pecaminosa, pois, é assim judicialmente destruída—agora é debilitada e então será eliminada (ver Rom. 6:10; Col. 2:14,15; João 16:11; Rom. 6:1—8:13 e Gál. 5:22,23, que mostram que é o poder do Espírito Santo que vence).

10. A cruz é a base do *perdão*: o perdão consiste na purificação do pecado. É o saldar ou apagar das antigas dívidas. (Ver Rom. 3:25; 4:7; Atos 2:38; 3:19 e I João 1:1-2:2).

11. A cruz é a base pela qual é deferido o justo juízo divino (ver Rom. 9:22; I Ped. 3:20 e II Ped. 3:9,15).

12. Ela fez expiação pelos pecados cometidos antes da missão do Messias e desde então, «cobrindo o passado»; e eis que os sacrifícios de animais apenas tipificavam essa verdade, não sendo a sua realidade. (Ver Heb. 10:4; Rom. 3:25 e Heb. 9:15).

13. Finalmente, significará a salvação nacional de Israel. (Ver Rom. 11:25-27). Isso envolverá a possessão final das terras que lhes foram prometidas, as bênçãos terrenas e a restauração nacional. (Ver Isa. 66:22; Jer. 31:36; II Sam. 7:16; Jer. 33:5,17,21). Mas também está em foco a salvação pessoal, conforme é indicado pela passagem do décimo primeiro capítulo da epístola aos Romanos.

14. Serve ela de base para as bênçãos milenares e eternas que sobrevirão a todas as nações (ver Apo. 21:23; Mat. 25:31-46; Isa. 60:3,12; 61:9; 62:2; Atos

15:17 e Rom. 11:15).

15. Significou igualmente a derrota dos poderes angelicais pervertidos, o despojamento dos principados e poderes. (Ver Col. 2:15; Apo. 12:7; 20:10; Mat. 25:41 e João 12:31).

16. A cruz é a base da pacificação entre judeus e gentios, no seio da igreja cristã, entre Deus e o homem, e por todo o universo, no que atinge a todos os seres. (Ver Rom. 5:1; Col. 1:20; Efé. 2:11,12; 2:14-18; Col. 2:14,15; I Cor. 15:26-28).

17. Purificação das coisas nos céus e uma restauração universal. Isso é parcialmente envolvido pelo ponto anterior. (Ver Heb. 9:11,12,21-23). Essa «purificação» pode ser, pelo menos em parte, a «remoção da ira de Deus», por causa do pecado, que «vem do céu». Portanto, uma espécie de purificação tem tido lugar. Porém, as Escrituras indicam que a queda no pecado abalou até mesmo os céus. Anjos malignos agora habitam nos «lugares celestiais» (ver Efé. 6:12), e o abalo dessa rebelião levou os próprios céus a sofrerem poluição. De alguma maneira, a cruz e a missão de Jesus Cristo cuidam de todos esses aspectos. Ver o artigo sobre a *Restauração*.

Alguns intérpretes supõem que a redenção dos anjos está aqui envolvida, porquanto isso faz parte da restauração de tudo a Cristo, conforme o primeiro capítulo das epístolas aos Efésios e aos Colossenses indicam ser necessário. A restauração dos homens, nas esferas celestes ou espirituais, que não servem de habitação dos remidos, também pode estar em foco, de acordo com os trechos de I Ped. 3:18-20 e 4:6. O primeiro capítulo da epístola aos Efésios, entretanto, indica uma grande restauração universal, em Cristo, confirmado em espírito pelo segundo capítulo da epístola aos Filipenses. Cristo é o Salvador de todos os mundos, em todos os mundos. Isso não significa que todas as criaturas humanas virão à salvação conhecida pelos eleitos, porquanto as Escrituras ensinam que isso nunca acontecerá; mas haverá *uma espécie* de restauração em escala universal, não obstante. Deus corrige o erro do pecado, de tal maneira que o mesmo perde o seu aspecto de «inimizade», desespero e «perda total». Qualquer que seja a redenção que exista, de qualquer modalidade, — tudo ainda procederá de Cristo, de seus méritos, de sua cruz, de sua ressurreição, como produto de sua missão. Nem por isso estaremos degradando a sua cruz e a sua missão. Pelo contrário, elevamos infinitamente sua importância e escopo. Ver as notas sobre Efé. 1:10 e Col. 1:16 no NTI.

18. A cruz trouxe luz e esperança até mesmo para o submundo dos espíritos em perdição. Para alguns intérpretes, isso significa a possibilidade de completa salvação além-túmulo, mas outros pensam que haverá, pelo menos, a melhoria das condições existentes nas dimensões dos perdidos, de tal modo que propósito e existência possam honrar a Deus, beneficiando os espíritos humanos em alguma coisa. Os trechos de I Ped. 3:18-20 e 4:6 assim parecem ensinar. Mas esse efeito da cruz precisa, ainda assim, ser aceito livremente, mediante a volição humana, podendo ser rejeitado, tal como sucede neste lado da existência.

CRUZ, TEOLOGIA DA

Ver o artigo sobre *Cruz de Cristo, Efeitos*. Ver também os artigos gerais sobre *Crucificação* e *Cruz* que fornecem informações suplementares.

•••

CRUZ VERMELHA

Uma organização internacional, formada originalmente para cuidar dos feridos no campo de batalha. Quando as forças militares das nações desenvolveram melhor suas próprias unidades para fazer este serviço, além de continuar com o mesmo, a Cruz Vermelha estendeu suas atividades para incluir assistência às famílias das vítimas da guerra, e aos prisioneiros. Esta organização também se mostra ativa em tempos de desastres naturais, como terremotos, dilúvios, etc. Nos países árabes uma organização semelhante, mas separada, O Crescente Vermelho substitue a Cruz Vermelha. Muitos países têm suas organizações aliadas à Cruz Vermelha. Na Pérsia, ela funciona sob o nome de Leão Vermelho. Florence Nightingale (1820-1919), na Guerra Crimeana (1854) e Clara Barton (1821-1912) na Guerra Civil dos E.U.A., forneceram uma inspiração para este tipo de serviço. Mas o próprio movimento começou pelo trabalho filantrópico do suíço, Jean Henri Dunant. Observações, de primeira mão, dos sofrimentos que resultam da guerra o impressionaram (1859), e conseqüentemente, ele começou o trabalho que finalmente resultou na Cruz Vermelha, organizada em 1865. O movimento assim tinha — origem suíça — e continua centralizada na Suíça, embora seja agora verdadeiramente internacional. Cada sociedade nacional é autônoma, mas, através de uma comissão, mantém ligações internacionais. Em relação aos seus membros não há discriminação quanto ao sexo, religião e raça.

Serviços da Cruz Vermelha moderna incluem, além dos serviços tradicionais, relacionados à guerra, assistência aos acidentados, instrução em cuidados médicos, pronto socorro, enfermagem, nutrição, etc.

Em meio ao ódio e matança, as coisas que os homens, na sua loucura, praticam uns contra os outros, é bom ver alguma manifestação do amor de Deus, operando neles.

Ver o artigo geral sobre *Movimentos Sociais Cristãos*. (AM E H)

••• ••• •••

CRUZADAS

Vem do latim bárbaro, **cruciata**, «assinalado com a cruz». Passou pelo termo francês *croisade* e pelo termo espanhol *cruzada*. Originalmente, o termo aludia a uma série de guerras efetuadas com o propósito de recuperar lugares santos do cristianismo, então sob o poder dos islamitas. Essas campanhas perduraram do século XI ao século XIII. Em sentido secundário, uma cruzada passou a ser qualquer expedição enviada para criar uma sensação, luta contra os pagãos ou hereges; ou então está em foco qualquer campanha militar que, supostamente, defende uma boa causa. Finalmente, passou a indicar qualquer ação vigorosa, movimento ou trabalho que visa a uma causa específica.

Causas das Cruzadas Originais. Com o declínio do poder do califado de Bagdá, dos monarcas abácidas, os turcos seldjuques conquistaram a Armênia, subjugaram a Asia Menor, e estabeleceram sua capital em Nicéia. E então marcharam sobre Jerusalém, capturando-a no ano de 1076. Muitos atos de atrocidade foram cometidos contra os peregrinos cristãos. Os povos do ocidente europeu sentiram-se impelidos à ação. Pedro, o Eremita (que vide), além de outros, passaram a pregar abertamente a guerra contra os islamitas. Quando do concílio de Clermont

CUBE — CUIDADO (ANSIEDADE)

(1095), foi tomada a decisão de enviar um exército a fim de eliminar os islamitas que controlavam a Terra Santa. A guerra foi proclamada pelo papa Urbano II (que vide). Naturalmente, os barões feudais irrequietos viram nessa circunstância uma maneira de se enriquecerem ainda mais, além de se divertirem um pouco. As guerras santas só são «santas» no nome. As principais cruzadas foram seis, a saber:

Primeira cruzada. Foram capturadas as cidades de Antioquia da Síria, em 1098, e de Jerusalém, em 1099. Foi então estabelecido o chamado reino latino (1099-1143).

Segunda cruzada. Ocorreu entre 1147 e 1149. Houve a queda de Edessa, em 1144, diante dos islamitas. Então, mediante os esforços do papa Eugênio III e de Bernardo, o imperador Conrado III e Luís VII, da França, foram convencidos a iniciar uma segunda cruzada. Essa cruzada fracassou.

Terceira cruzada. Durou de 1189 a 1192. O papa Gregório VIII ordenou essa cruzada, porquanto Jerusalém havia sido capturada por Saladino, o líder das forças islâmicas aliadas. Uniram suas forças o imperador Frederico Barbarroxa, Filipe Augusto, da França, Ricardo I, da Inglaterra, e Guilherme, da Sicília. Frederico morreu afogado, em 1190. A cidade de Acre caiu diante dos cruzados após grande morticínio; os líderes cristãos puseram-se a discutir. Jerusalém não foi conquistada pelos cruzados, mas Saladino prometeu retornar à verdadeira Cruz (houve muitas dessas cruzes através da história), pagando indenização. Foram estabelecidas condições de paz; aos peregrinos foi garantido o direito de trânsito e foi estabelecido o intercâmbio comercial. O sucesso foi apenas parcial, e o fracasso foi considerável.

Quarta cruzada. De 1202 a 1204. O império latino ampliou suas fronteiras às custas da cidade cristã de Constantinopla, que foi capturada pelos cruzados em julho de 1205. O império latino dominou ali de 1205 a 1261. O poder bizantino foi quebrado, e os turcos otomanos obtiveram a hegemonia. Constantinopla tornou-se um ponto de resistência contra o islamismo, embora as dificuldades estivessem longe de ser resolvidas.

Quinta cruzada. Essa também tem sido chamada de Cruzada das Crianças. Ocorreu em 1212. Esse foi o nome dado a um movimento popular pietista, que teve pequena duração na Europa. Foi assim chamada porque um número razoavelmente grande de crianças participou dessa cruzada. Seu objetivo era libertar o local do Santo Sepulcro dos islâmicos. Somente algumas poucas crianças atingiram as margens do mar Mediterrâneo, mas não conseguiram obter transporte. Algumas crianças atingiram a cidade de Marselha, na França, onde caíram nas mãos de negociantes inescrupulosos, que as venderam como escravas no Norte da África. Essa cruzada, pois, foi a que terminou de maneira mais trágica.

A cruzada de Frederico II. Durou de 1228 a 1229. Essa cruzada não foi oficialmente reconhecida, visto que esse monarca estava sob a pena de exclusão. Ele concluiu um tratado com El Kamil, do Egito, em 1229, e coroou-se rei de Jerusalém. Porém, o seu sucesso não foi reconhecido pelo clero católico.

Outras cruzadas, de menor porte, foram efetuadas, como aquela de Teobaldo, rei de Navarra, entre 1239 e 1240; bem como as de Ricardo da Cornuália e de Simão de Montfort, em 1240.

Sexta cruzada. Durou de 1248 a 1254. Foi encabeçada por Luís IX, da França. Sofreu uma série de derrotas e foi aprisionado em Damieta, em 1249, por Turan Shah. Este último foi assassinado no ano seguinte. Foi conseguido um armistício de quinze anos, com seu sucessor, Musa do Egito. Em 1270, Luís IX dirigiu outra cruzada, mas morreu de uma praga, em Cartago, naquele mesmo ano. Eduardo I, da Inglaterra, que o havia acompanhado na aventura, deixou a Palestina em 1271. Isso assinalou o fim das cruzadas genuínas. Mas também houve a cruzada de Pio II, o autor da bula *Execrabilis*, de 1464, que assinalou o fim desse movimento.

Resultados. O aparecimento de novas cidades. O fomento da importância da cavalaria (que vide). A decadência do sistema feudal. O desenvolvimento de monarquias nacionais. A separação definitiva entre a cristandade e o islamismo, com poderes hostis constantes. O aumento do poder papal. A tomada de consciência de que as raízes do cristianismo estão na Palestina. Um pesado envolvimento militar por parte da Igreja Católica, o que teve tremendas conseqüências posteriores. (AM E)

CUBE

Esse vocábulo encontra-se somente em Ezequiel 30:5, referindo-se a um lugar ou a um povo que entrara em aliança com o Egito, na época de Nabucodonosor (c. de 610 A.C.). Algumas traduções dizem ali Lude, o que seria a Líbia. A Septuaginta diz Lube. O trecho de Naum 3:9 alista os nomes líbios, cuxitas, egípcios e Pute, tal como em Ezequiel.

CUDWORTH, RALPH

Suas datas foram 1617-1688. Foi um filósofo platonista inglês, líder de Cambridge (que vide). Nasceu em Aller, em Somersetshire. Foi estudante e então professor em Cambridge, e mestre do Colégio de Cristo; foi um dos consultores do governo de Oliver Cromwell (que vide).

Idéias:

1. As principais idéias metafísicas são a existência de Deus, a naturalidade das distinções morais (a natureza as contém e ensina) e a realidade da liberdade humana.

2. Ele combatia o ateísmo e o atomismo mecânico refletidos em filósofos como Hobbes (que vide). O atomismo, por si mesmo, não precisa ser ateu, conforme é demonstrado pelo sistema dos estóicos. Porém, alguns distorcem o atomismo, a fim de dar apoio ao ateísmo. Os princípios mecânicos não são suficientes como explicação da natureza. É mister postular os princípios espirituais, não-materiais, para que se tenha uma explicação mais satisfatória.

3. O conhecimento consiste em mais do que uma coleção de impressões dos nossos sentidos. Antes, é um fato eterno e auto-subsistente, na mente de Deus. Portanto, regras e distinções morais têm uma natureza perene, embora, na sociedade humana, fiquemos confusos quando tratamos sobre essas coisas.

Obras: The True Intellectual System of the Universe; A Treatise Concerning Eternal and Immutable Morality; A treatise of Free Will. (P)

CUIDADO (ANSIEDADE)

No hebraico há uma palavra principal a ser considerada, e, no grego, duas a saber:

1. *Deagah,* «cuidado ansioso», palavra que ocorre por seis vezes, e que tem sido variegadamente traduzida por «temor», «cuidado» ou «ansiedade» (por

exemplo, Eze. 4:16).

2. *Phronéo*, «preocupar-se», palavra grega que aparece por vinte e cinco vezes no Novo Testamento: Mat. 16:23; Mar. 8:33; Atos 28:22; Rom. 8:5; 11:20; 12:3,16; 14:6; 15:5; I Cor. 13:11; II Cor. 13:11; Gál. 5:10; Fil. 1:7; 2:2,5; 3:15,19; 4:2,10; Col. 3:2; I Tim. 6:17.

3. *Merimnáo*, «cuidar», «ansiar»; e seu substantivo mérimna, «cuidado», «ansiedade». O verbo figura por dezoito vezes: Mat. 6:25,27,28,31,34; 10:19; Luc. 10:41; 12:11,22,25,26; I Cor. 7:32-34; 12:25; Fil. 2:20; 4:6. O substantivo por seis vezes: Mat. 13:22; Mar. 4:19; Luc. 8:14; 21:34; II Cor. 11:28; I Ped. 5:7.

O ser humano é um criatura fraca e dependente. Sente-se perdido, a boiar no tempestuoso mar da vida, tendo pouca certeza acerca de onde veio, quem ele é, e, menos ainda, para onde está indo. As filosofias, as religiões, e, estranha e estupidamente, até a política, procuram fornecer-lhe alguma orientação, algum propósito. Quanto a essa ansiedade, o trecho de I Pedro 5:7 oferece ao crente a solução certa: «...lançando sobre ele toda a vossa ansiedade, porque ele tem cuidado de vós». Poderíamos traduzir com mais efeito essa frase de Pedro, sem em nada distorcer o original grego: «para que tanto cuidado, se ele cuida de vós?» Na verdade, não há necessidade alguma de ansiedade, no caso do crente, pois o Senhor anseia por nós. Ver o artigo sobre *Cuidar*, *Cuidado*. Em Mateus 13:22, há menção aos cuidados deste mundo, que levam os perdidos a ansiarem e preocuparem-se com as necessidades básicas da vida e com questões econômicas, sentindo-se oprimidos por elas, sabendo que é mister preservar, proteger e usar devidamente o dinheiro. De tais cuidados, os pobres estão isentos. Há também aquele cuidado piedoso (II Cor. 7:11), que produz o arrependimento. E outros exibem um cuidado espiritual por outros crentes e pelas igrejas locais, o que é uma virtude espiritual positiva (II Cor. 11:28). Jesus proibiu a ansiedade frívola com coisas meramente materiais e oculares (Mat. 6:25-34), mas o evangelho por toda a parte elogia o nosso interesse e preocupação pelos nossos semelhantes, o que é apenas outra maneira de ver a lei do amor em operação. Ver o artigo sobre o *Amor*.

CUIDADO, CUIDADOS

Há dois vocábulos gregos que fazemos bem em examinar, nessa conexão:

1. *Spoudé*, «pressa», palavra que aparece por doze vezes: Mar. 6:25; Luc. 1:30; Rom. 12:8,11; II Cor. 7:11,12; 8:7,8,16; Heb. 6:11; II Ped. 1:5; Jud. 3.

2. *Mello*, «importar-se», «cuidar de», palavra que aparece por cerca de cento e dez vezes, desde Mat. 2:13 até Apo. 10:17.

Ansiedade e cuidado são idéias correlatas; mas se a primeira enfoca a noção de «preocupação sem motivo», a segunda dá a entender a noção de «interesse» pelo bem-estar de outrem, pelo bom estado de algo. Ver *Ansiedade*.

O substantivo *spoudé*, «pressa», é usado nas páginas sagradas para indicar não somente a idéia de urgência, mas também de solicitude ou diligência. Para exemplificar, lemos que Paulo recomendou: «No zelo não sejais remissos» (Rom. 12:11), onde o termo «zelo» é esse substantivo grego. Paulo queria dizer que não devemos ser preguiçosos em nossa solicitude por servir ao próximo. Outro tanto se vê em II Cor. 8:16: «Mas, graças a Deus, que pôs no coração de Tito a mesma solicitude por amor de vós».

O verbo *mello*, que, na maioria das vezes dá a idéia de algo que está prestes a ocorrer, também transmite a idéia de cuidado com outrem, segundo se vê, por exemplo, em II Cor. 7:11: «Porque, quanto cuidado não produziu isto mesmo em vós, que, segundo Deus, fostes contristados!» Impelidos pelo senso de urgência e de interesse por Paulo, os crentes de Corinto mudaram de atitude em relação ao apóstolo, conforme ele esclarece no versículo seguinte: «...para que a vossa solicitude a nosso favor fosse manifesta entre vós, diante de Deus».

CULLMAN, OSCAR

Nasceu em 1902, em Strasbourg, na Alemanha. Foi professor do Novo Testamento e da Igreja Eclesiástica em Basiléia, na Suíça, e professor do cristianismo primitivo na Sorbonne, em Paris.

Idéias:

1. Ele era um expositor da **Heilsgeschichte** (história da salvação), que alude ao *Já* (a primeira vinda de Cristo) e ao *Ainda Não* (a segunda vinda de Cristo, ou *parousia*). Atualmente, nos encontraríamos em um intervalo na tensão, entre eventos decisivos. Esse intervalo caracteriza-se pela *temporalidade*, sendo essa a base de todas as ações éticas, importante em todas as considerações acerca da salvação que está em processo.

2. A *possibilidade* de vivermos em consonância com a ética cristã deriva-se da vitória de Cristo no passado. A *urgência* da ética cristã deriva-se do próximo grande evento, a *parousia*, que é a futura vitória de Cristo.

3. O «dever moral» do cristianismo repousa sobre a *ontologia*, o ser real do Espírito. Porém, há uma certa tensão entre esse dever moral e aquilo que fazemos, entre o *Já* e o *Ainda Não*. A fé seria a reação ética aquilo que é retratado pelo batismo na água, o novo nascimento que nos identifica com Cristo.

4. O Espírito é o *É* da nossa fé, a primeira parcela da salvação. A obra do Espírito é um *dokimazein*, um «teste», através do qual ele nos está desenvolvendo no campo da ética cristã.

5. Visto que a realização do Espírito é dinâmica e feliz, não se caracteriza por qualquer renúncia negativa do mundo, mediante a atitude ascética. Antes, é uma experiência jubilosa; e onde se instala o negativismo, desaparece a alegria cristã.

Obras: Christ and Time; Salvation in History; Church and State; The State in the New Testament. (H)

CULPA

No hebraico temos duas palavras, e no grego, três, a saber:

1. *Asham, ashem*, «culpado». Palavras hebraicas usadas por dezessete vezes com esse sentido. Por exemplo: Gên. 42:21; Lev. 4:13,27; 5:2-5, 17; 6:4; Núm. 5:6; Juí. 21:22; Esd. 10:19.

2. *Rasha*, «iníquo». Palavra hebraica usada por dez vezes com o sentido de culpado. Por exemplo: Núm. 33:31; II Crô. 19:2; Jó 34:18; Sal. 1:1,4-7; 73:12.

3. *Upódikos*, «sob justiça». Palavra grega que ocorre por apenas uma vez, em Rom. 3:19.

4. *Opheílo*, «endividado». Termo grego que aparece por trinta e cinco vezes: Mat. 18:28,30,34; 23:16,18; Luc. 7:41; 11:4; 16:5,7; 17:10; João 13:14; 19:7; Atos 17:29; Rom. 13:8; 15:1,27; I Cor. 5:10; 7:36; 9:10; 11:7,10; II Cor. 12:11,14; Efé. 5:28; II Tes. 1:3; 2:13; File. 18; Heb. 2:17; 5:3,12; I João 2:6; 3:16; 4:11; III

João 8.

5. *Ênochos*, «sujeito a». Palavra grega usada por dez vezes: Mat. 5:21,22; 26:66; Mar. 3:29; 14:64; I Cor. 11:27; Heb. 2:15; Tia. 2:10.

Ver o artigo geral sobre o *Pecado*. A culpa é uma condição moral ou legal que resulta da violação de uma lei, escrita, moral, intuitiva ou espiritual. Há muitas formas de culpa que não estão contidas nos códigos legais municipais ou nacionais. O Antigo Testamento não estabelece uma clara distinção entre o pecado e a culpa, porquanto todo pecado envolve culpa. Porém, dentro do jargão legal, para que haja culpa, alguma lei expressa deve ter sido violada. As traduções variam quanto ao uso da palavra. Assim, em inglês, a King James Version só usa o termo por duas vezes no Antigo Testamento (Deu. 19:13; 21:9), ao passo que a Revised Standard Version se utiliza do termo por cento e nove vezes. Outro tanto se dá no caso do adjetivo cognato, «culpado».

Ser culpado equivale a merecer castigo. Na filosofia moral, como nos escritos de Kant, e isso com base bíblica, todo pecado envolve culpa. Mas as leis civis estabelecem uma seleção daquelas coisas que mais prejudicam a sociedade como um todo. Os pecados particulares e o senso pessoal de culpa não são levados em conta nessas leis civis. No entanto, ensina-nos a Bíblia que «o salário do pecado é a morte» (Rom. 3:23), pelo que todo o pecado tem sua devida penalidade, por isso podemos dizer que todo pecado envolve culpa. — Lev. 4:13; 5:2 indica que a quebra de qualquer dos mandamentos de Deus, cerimoniais ou morais, incorre em culpa. O trecho de Tiago 2:10 afirma que quebrar um ponto da lei, apesar dos demais mandamentos não estarem sendo desobedecidos, resulta em culpa.

O senso de culpa é um dos mais importantes capítulos da psicologia, porque muitos dos males do homem resultam do senso de culpa que ele abriga. Para os psicólogos freudianos, a culpa está ligada à formação do *superego*, que age como uma espécie de policial interno, que controla os impulsos básicos, disfarçando-os sob a forma de sonhos. Em uma criança, o senso de culpa é uma espécie de identificação com um de seus pais que a desaprova. Na vida adulta, a criança transfere seu conceito de culpa a várias formas de autoridade, nem sempre envolvendo questões de certo ou errado. Portanto, o senso de culpa pode ser falso e patológico. Apesar disso, mesmo admitindo-se que tais coisas sucedem, quem pode compreender como funcionam a mente e os sentimentos humanos? Também é verdade que há erros genuínos diante dos quais a consciência humana reage mediante o senso de culpa ou de falta de dignidade. A culpa é um fato da condição humana mesmo quando um indivíduo não quer admitir o fato (Rom. 3:19). A cura da culpa, sobre bases bíblicas, depende, em primeiro lugar, do *reconhecimento do pecado*; em segundo lugar, do *arrependimento*; em terceiro lugar, da *restituição*, na medida do possível, devido a danos feitos contra outras pessoas. Do arrependimento e da fé resulta a conversão. A santificação é uma obra do Espírito de Deus, sem cuja atuação jamais ocorre. Esses são os meios bíblicos para tratarmos com o senso de culpa. A mudança nas atitudes e nas ações é algo absolutamente necessário para quem quer livrar-se do senso de culpa.

CULPA DE SANGUE

A expressão aparece em trechos como Salmos 51:14; Êxodo 22:2; I Samuel 25:26,33, II Samuel 21:1 e Oséias 12:14. Quando um ser humano tira a vida de outro, torna-se culpado de sangue. Porém, no trecho de Ezequiel 18:13, certa variedade de pecados, como furto, homicídio, adultério, opressão dos pobres, desonestidade, idolatria, etc., faz com que os culpados sejam dignos de morte; e isso também importa em culpa de sangue. (Ver também Salmos 39:8). Em Israel, a culpa de sangue era fator poluidor da terra (Núm. 35:33 ss), e o derramamento de sangue inocente *contaminava* (Deu. 19:10; I Reis 2:5). Tal culpa de sangue precisava ser vingada (I Reis 2:31 ss). Estavam excluídos da tal classificação casos como os de execução judicial, homicídio em autodefesa e homicídio não-intencional (Êxo. 22:2 e Lev. 20:9). Era provido asilo aos homicidas involuntários, para que não fossem mortos pelo vingador da família (Núm. 35:9 ss). Também não era classificado como tal o ato de tirar a vida de um ladrão, durante a noite, porquanto tal ladrão era perigoso e podia tirar a vida de suas vítimas. Mas, se houvesse a morte de um ladrão durante o dia, podia haver um caso de culpa de sangue (Êxo. 22:2 ss). A culpa de sangue era levada muito a sério em Israel, de tal modo que se a sociedade não tomasse a devida vingança, ou não pudesse fazê-lo, Deus intervinha em favor da parte envolvida e prejudicada (Gên. 4:10-12; Isa. 26:21; Eze. 24:6-9). Seja como for, a culpa precisava ser expiada (II Sam. 4:11) podendo até mesmo afetar a descendência de alguém que se tornasse culpado de sangue (II Sam. 3:28 ss; 21:1-9; I Reis 21:29; Mat. 27:25). (Z)

CULTIVADOR DE SICÔMOROS

Essa expressão encontra-se somente em Amós 7:14, em todo o Antigo Testamento, onde o profeta Amós mostra que trabalhava nessa ocupação, e não reivindicava associação alguma à linhagem dos profetas. Era claro, pois, que Deus havia feito intervenção em sua vida, e que ele tinha uma importante mensagem a entregar. Um cultivador de sicômoros podava as árvores e fazia uma pequena operação nos frutos verdes, a fim de promover o amadurecimento e uma colheita mais abundante.

CULTOS DE FERTILIDADE
Ver **Fertilidade, Cultos de**.

CULTURA
Esboço:

I. Definições
II. Cultura Segundo a Filosofia
III. Pontos de Vista Cristãos da Cultura

I. Definições

Há muitas definições da cultura, como:

1. Um empreendimento coletivo, segundo o qual os homens conseguem estabelecer um estilo de vida distinto, com base em valores comuns.

2. «Aquele todo complexo que inclui conhecimentos, crenças, artes, princípios morais, leis, costumes e quaisquer outras capacidades e hábitos adquiridos pelos homens, como membros da sociedade». (E.B. Tylor).

3. A totalidade da invenção e da realização humana, incluindo todos os princípios, agências e técnicas de controle que os homens têm adquirido sobre a natureza física e o comportamento humano, bem como todas as experiências pessoais e sociais que

eles têm acumulado, intercambiado e transmitido, por meio de instrumentos e símbolos.

4. Todas as expressões criativas dos homens, em todos os campos do empreendimento humano.

5. Em sentido limitado, a expressão que os homens têm conseguido nas artes liberais.

6. Essa palavra vem do latim *colere*, «cultivar». Portanto, a cultura é um cultivo, sem importar os meios empregados para tanto.

O vocábulo não entrou na linguagem senão já no século XVIII, embora o uso possa ser percebido ao longo da história, mas expresso de muitas formas diferentes.

II. Cultura Segundo a Filosofia

1. *Platão e Aristóteles*. Na academia, eles estabeleceram os meios da produção e propagação da cultura, mediante o aprendizado formal.

2. A *escola do cinismo* (que vide) considerava a cultura humana como algo degenerado, procurando voltar as mentes dos homens para a simplicidade da natureza.

3. No *estoicismo* (que vide) o ideal de um mundo culto consistia na idéia de que o indivíduo é cidadão do universo, e não apenas de alguma cidade-estado.

4. A *cultura grega* disseminou-se pelo mundo inteiro, na época de Alexandre, o Grande. Continuou muito influente no mundo romano, incluindo aspectos como a filosofia, as artes e várias ciências. Os primeiros teólogos-filósofos cristãos, como Justino, Agostino e Boethius (ver os artigos) promoveram os ideais gregos dentro da cultura cristã em desenvolvimento.

5. *Emanuel Kant*, em sua obra *Crítica do Julgamento*, promoveu certa idéia da cultura que girava em torno do gênio e do refinamento das sensibilidades estéticas.

6. *Saint Simon* falava sobre *épocas críticas* e *épocas orgânicas*, como meios transformadores da cultura. Ver o artigo a respeito dele, nos pontos segundo e terceiro, onde fornecemos explicações.

7. *Fichte* considerava que a principal realização possível da cultura seria um mundo dominado pela ética, devidamente organizado e constituído.

8. *Hegel*, ao falar sobre o Espírito Absoluto, que seria o poder criativo e orientador de todas as coisas e acontecimentos, fazia da cultura um cultivo desse Espírito.

9. *Schlegel* (que vide, no segundo ponto) supunha que a cultura definitiva poderá ser alcançada mediante a fusão da ciência e da vida diária.

10. *Splengler* distinguia entre cultura e civilização. A primeira indicaria as possibilidades vitais de uma sociedade e as realizações ou concretizações dessas possibilidades. A segunda aludiria às formas e pretensões externas da sociedade.

11. *Matthew Arnold* pensava que a cultura conduz à *perfeição*. A cultura conquistaria a barbárie e o espírito combativo dos homens.

12. Os sociólogos e os filósofos não concordam se há ou não alguma diferença entre cultura e civilização. Ver o artigo sobre a *Civilização*, onde essas noções são ilustradas.

13. A *dialética materialista* supõe que a cultura é determinada por considerações materiais, especialmente pelas condições econômicas em torno das quais as classes da sociedade se entrechocam.

14. *Huizinga* pensava que a cultura perfeita é resultado da devida harmonia entre os valores materiais e os valores espirituais, e que o homem se acha no vórtice de um drama, no qual são cultivados os valores humanos. Ele se referia ao homem como o *homo ludens*, «o homem que joga». Alguns pensadores metafísicos hindus opinam nesses termos, considerando que a inquirição do homem pela espiritualidade é uma espécie de gigantesco drama cósmico, com muita diversão de intermeio, de tal modo que a comédia é o resultado final.

15. *Pontos de vista cristãos*. Ver secção III onde se sumariam esses pontos.

III. Pontos de Vista Cristãos da Cultura

1. O cristianismo concebe um *mundo em dois andares* — o mais elevado, de cunho espiritual; e o mais baixo, de cunho material. Embora o nível mais elevado seja o alvo, e também o nível mais importante, a ênfase sobre os deveres cristãos para com o próximo, demonstra que o ponto de vista cristão precisa incluir a idéia que a cultura humana é importante *em si mesma*. Os homens estão encarregados de missões mais elevadas ou mais modestas. Eles buscam o bem da alma (nível mais elevado), mas também o desenvolvimento das instituições terrenas (nível mais modesto). Com freqüência, esses alvos são mutuamente dependentes, como é o caso de muitos homens que servem ao próximo e participam das realizações humanas, das instituições, etc., embora como *parte* do ideal espiritual. Algumas pessoas, no presente, têm apenas uma missão mais modesta, como os cientistas. Eles adiam para outra ocasião os interesses da alma. Porém, se servirem bem em seu papel, também estarão servindo a Deus, embora indiretamente. Finalmente, porém, poderão enveredar pela inquirição da alma. A humanidade como um todo, e até mesmo as nações, individualmente falando, têm missões a cumprir neste mundo. Não obstante, finalmente, todos os seres humanos haverão de envolver-se nos interesses do outro mundo, embora alguns só o façam após a morte física. Para alguns, isso significa que o farão tarde demais; para outros, parece haver uma segunda chance, pois o destino da alma não parece ser fixado somente nesta vida. Em todas as atividades humanas dignas, há uma certa cultura envolvida, um cultivo que está em progressão.

2. Em *sentido bem amplo*, a própria criação é cultivo de Deus, cujo principal propósito é a salvação dos cidadãos do mundo (João 3:16), mediante a realização do Filho de Deus (Col. 1:16). Por conseguinte, a terra torna-se o campo de provas desse elevadíssimo propósito divino.

3. Em *sentido mais estrito*, a Igreja cristã tem-se saído bem na promoção da civilização e da cultura humanas. Durante a Idade Média, a Igreja Católica foi a encarnação mesma da cultura, servindo de meio através do qual a instrução nas letras e o desenvolvimento das artes se processavam. Idealmente, a Igreja cristã deveria injetar na cultura humana os princípios cristãos que promovem as virtudes da honestidade, da harmonia e do amor. A Igreja cristã também deveria alertar os homens acerca de um caminho mais elevado e civilizado, a caminhada da alma como elemento orientador de qualquer cultura humana.

4. Existe aquele país celestial do qual este mundo é apenas uma sombra e uma pobre imitação, um conceito antecipado por Platão e utilizado pelo escritor da epístola aos Hebreus (11:16).

5. Os *dualistas cristãos* supõem que o homem está vivendo em duas dimensões ao mesmo tempo: a física e a espiritual. Porém, os mais radicais não vêem qualquer utilidade na dimensão física, e convidam os

cristãos a se desligarem de qualquer participação significativa nessa dimensão. Outros cristãos, entretanto, permitem tal participação, mas supõem que isso serve somente para promover melhor os interesses da alma, nada vendo de significativo naquilo que acontece no mundo físico, à parte dos interesses espirituais.

6. Os *conversionistas cristãos*, quando radicais, supõem que o único uso que os crentes podem fazer deste mundo é serem missionários que buscam a conversão da sociedade. Porém, eles não vêem qualquer bem na própria sociedade, e não recomendam a ninguém a participação ativa na sociedade, exceto como um meio de promover a causa da evangelização.

7. Os *anticulturistas cristãos*, como Tertuliano, vêem apenas o mal na cultura humana, denunciando qualquer participação dos crentes na política, nas artes e na filosofia, como atividades pagãs e produtos indesejáveis dos esforços de homens perdidos.

8. Os *incorporacionistas cristãos* têm por intuito misturar-se em todas as atividades seculares e culturais, o que diminui seu caráter distintivo como cristãos.

9. Os *sintetistas cristãos*, como Tomás de Aquino, supõem que a Igreja cristã deveria mostrar-se ativa na promoção de todas as variedades de cultura, como parte de suas funções, levando assim a Igreja a ocupar-se em maior número de coisas das quais ela tem tempo e energia para desincumbir-se a contento.

10. Os *nacionalistas cristãos* mostram-se orgulhosos das realizações culturais de suas nações particulares, supondo que parte do trabalho missionário cristão consiste em impor a outros povos os próprios padrões culturais dos missionários, e não apenas os valores religiosos. Nisso revela-se uma espécie de identificação inconsciente entre o cristianismo e a cultura ocidental, em suas realizações.

11. Os *absorvedores cristãos* dizem-se incapazes de distinguir entre a cidade de Babel e a cidade de Sião, absorvendo-se assim nos empreendimentos seculares e humanos que são próprios dos filhos de Babel, e não dos filhos de Sião. Esses olvidam-se que há uma cidade eterna, que tem alicerces perenes (Heb. 11:10).

12. Os *isolacionistas cristãos* reconhecem a necessidade de atividades culturais, mas separam-se formando comunidades exclusivistas, afastando-se assim de todas as comunidades pagãs o mais possível. Eles possuem suas próprias comunidades e escolas, e só se mesclam com o mundo exterior nas questões comerciais, embora somente até onde não ponham em risco a própria sobrevivência.

Três atitudes gerais, concernentes à cultura, do ponto de vista cristão, podem ser salientadas, a saber: a. Cristo *contra* a cultura; b. Cristo *da* cultura; e c. Cristo *acima* da cultura. De conformidade com o livro de Richard Neibuhr, *Christ and Culture*, isso sumaria a questão. Essas atitudes têm sido ilustradas de forma mais elaborada nos pontos acima. Quanto a «a», ver os números 5, 6 e 12. Quanto a «b», ver os números 1, 3, 9 e 11, que podem ilustrar aspectos positivos e negativos. Quanto a «c», ver os números 1, 5 e 6 como aplicações possíveis. (C E NIE P)

CULTURA E FÉ RELIGIOSA

Ver o artigo sobre a **Cultura**, terceiro ponto.

CULTURA ÉTICA

Essa expressão designa uma cultura que salienta os princípios éticos como o centro da religião. A idéia foi introduzida por Félix Adler (1851-1933), na cidade de Nova Iorque, nos Estados Unidos da América. Terminou se transformando em um movimento internacional, com centros em várias cidades do mundo. O culto dominical consiste em música, leitura, discursos éticos e um período de meditação. Apesar do fato de que a religião cristã não pode ser reduzida a princípios éticos, o evangelho do *fácil creísmo* (que vide) alerta-nos para o fato de que, em muitos lugares da igreja evangélica de nossos dias, não se dá a devida ênfase à ética.

CULVERWEL, NATHANAEL

Suas datas aproximadas são 1618 e 1651. Foi um filósofo inglês, nascido em Londres e educado em Cambridge, onde também ensinou. Esteve sob a influência do platonismo de Cambridge, mas combinava as idéias de Aristóteles com as idéias de Platão, e ambas essas idéias com o neoplatonismo, o escolasticismo e o calvinismo. Ele frisava a autoridade absoluta de Deus, não apenas no campo da eleição divina, mas também na ética e nas leis naturais. (P)

CUM

Cidade aramaica mencionada somente em I Crônicas 18:8. Ficava localizada ao norte de Arã-Zobá, no lado oriental das montanhas do Líbano. Em II Samuel 8:8, que é o texto paralelo, figura o nome «Berotai»; embora alguns estudiosos pensem que, evidentemente, não se trata da mesma localidade. Davi levou daquela área alguns itens de bronze, como despojos de guerra.

CUMBERLAND, RICHARD

Suas datas foram 1631-1718. Foi filósofo e teólogo inglês. Nasceu em Londres e educou-se em Cambridge. Foi eclesiástico, tendo sido nomeado como um dos pregadores oficiais de Cambridge. Foi bispo de Peterborough. Professor de filosofia, refutou idéias de Thomas Hobbes (que vide).

Idéias:

1. A moralidade repousa sobre leis naturais imutáveis, válidas e obrigatórias, inteiramente à parte das leis dos estados e governos. Os seres racionais têm consciência dessas leis. As leis decretadas pelos homens refletem as leis naturais, mas a consciência de cada indivíduo serve ainda de guia mais seguro.

2. O homem exibe uma tendência natural para o altruísmo, o que se verifica até entre certos animais. Nisso está envolvida uma certa lei natural. O *bem coletivo* contribui para o bem de cada indivíduo, mediante o que há uma felicidade geral. O comportamento contrário traz somente a miséria. O princípio defendido por Cumberland, de *bem coletivo*, como uma lei natural básica, antecipou a ênfase do utilitarismo (que vide).

3. O princípio da *benevolência universal*. Nenhum ato seria moralmente bom a menos que contribua para a felicidade dos homens em geral. As ações morais sempre envolveriam a comunidade, e não apenas indivíduos isolados.

4. As ações virtuosas são guiadas por princípios determinadores como o da felicidade, o da miséria e o da retribuição futura.

Obras: De Legibus Naturae.

••• ••• •••

CUMI
Ver sobre **Talitha Cumi**.

CUMPRIMENTO
Ver sobre **Realizar, Realização**.

CUNEIFORME
Essa palavra significa «em forma de cunha», referindo-se ao tipo de escrita usado pelos sumérios, após o período de escrita pictográfica, para representar os fonemas de seu idioma. Essa forma de escrever foi tomada por empréstimo pelos babilônios, assírios, hititas, elamitas e persas, para escreverem seus respectivos idiomas. A escrita cuneiforme é uma espécie de escrita semipictográfica, cujos caracteres eram impressos sobre a argila mole, com o uso de um estilete. Os tabletes de argila que recebiam a escrita eram usados quando ainda moles, e então eram endurecidos ao sol ou em fornos, o que os tornava duros e de longa duração. Mais ou menos em meados do segundo milênio A.C., os cananeus de Ugarite usavam esse método de escrita. Mas ultrapassaram os símbolos cuneiformes semipictográficos, desenvolvendo um verdadeiro alfabeto, embora limitado somente aos fonemas consonantais. A escrita cuneiforme babilônica desenvolveu-se até tornar-se um modo internacional de comunicação escrita, de tal modo que muita correspondência diplomática era efetuada entre as nações para as quais o idioma babilônico era uma língua estrangeira. Para exemplificar, temos as cartas de Tell el-Amarna (que vide), entre os reis cananeus e a corte egípcia. E então no século VII A.C., os persas desenvolveram um sistema cuneiforme todo próprio, com quarenta e dois sinais, trinta e seis dos quais eram fonéticos, todos consistindo em sílabas abertas, ou seja, sílabas que terminam com alguma vogal. Essa forma de escrita é bastante diferente de outras escritas cuneiformes de outras culturas, e pode ter representado um desenvolvimento independente. Ver os artigos sobre *Escrita* e *Alfabeto* (Z).

CURA
De acordo com o vocabulário da Igreja Católica Romana, um padre responsável pela *cura das almas*. Na França, esse é o título dado a um padre paroquiano assistente. Na Inglaterra, é o título de alguém que assiste a um reitor ou vigário.

CURA
Ver também o artigo sobre **Curas pela Fé**.

A universalidade da cura. A antropologia tem comprovado a universalidade de duas atividades «sobre-humanas». — Essas são a profecia e a cura. Normalmente, essas funções têm sido vinculadas a rituais religiosos, geralmente administrados mediante cerimônias estranhas e exóticas. Porém, as duas funções não são de cunho necessariamente religioso ou espiritual (conforme nós os crentes, entendemos essas palavras), porquanto podem ocorrer inteiramente à parte do sentimento religioso. Por exemplo, os estudos dos sonhos têm demonstrado que todos os seres humanos possuem certa habilidade de «ver o futuro». Os sonhos mesclam, em forma simbólica, o passado, o presente e o futuro, de tal modo que todas as pessoas têm consciência, pelo menos no nível subconsciente, de eventos futuros em suas vidas. Naturalmente, isso ainda não é o dom de profecia, que visa principalmente, a instrução moral, ainda que ocasionalmente, inclua um vislumbre de eventos vindouros. Além disso, através de toda a história dos homens e em todas as culturas, tem havido aqueles que possuem poderes de cura. Apesar de poder-se admitir que existem poderes demoníacos envolvidos em muitas curas, no caso de certas pessoas, contudo, a cura pode ser algo perfeitamente natural e humano, através do uso de qualidades inatas ao espírito humano.

A fotografia Kirliana. Trata-se de uma forma de fotografia que se utiliza do processo radiológico. É capaz de detectar a radiação de energia que emana dos seres vivos, mas que são invisíveis para o olho humano. Com esse processo (que agora vem sendo experimentado em várias partes do mundo), a «aura» humana pode ser fotografada e vista. Trata-se de um campo de luz que circunda o ser humano, estendendo-se até cerca de quatro metros além do corpo. Todas as coisas vivas, além disso, possuem esse campo de luz. Existe antes da formação da porção física, e mesmo depois do desaparecimento dessa porção. Os ovos de rãs, por exemplo, têm um campo de luz entre dez e quinze centímetros. Mediante a mesma luz pode-se determinar onde se desenvolverão as várias partes da rã, e evidentemente, essa é a força que controla o desenvolvimento. No caso da amputação dos dedos, dos braços ou das pernas de um homem, a fotografia Kirliana continua exibindo a luz dos dedos, braços ou pernas amputados. Em outras palavras, a porção psíquica continua presente, antes e depois, pois é independente da porção material. Estudos como esses, naturalmente, ajudam na aproximação científica da alma, pois demonstram que aquilo que atualmente chamamos de parte «física», não é a totalidade da personalidade humana.

No tocante às curas, tem sido demonstrado, através da fotografia Kirliana, que quando há uma cura, a luz da pessoa que cura a outrem decresce, mas a aura da pessoa curada aumenta. Outrossim, aquele que cura perde peso. Evidentemente, essa energia desconhecida tem certo peso. Portanto, nas curas, pode haver certa transferência de energias vitais. Isso mostra que falar alguém de meras curas psicológicas, crendo que não existem curas reais de condições físicas adversas, é um absurdo.

Fontes da cura. O que dissemos acima mostra que a cura pode ter origem totalmente humana, por ser uma qualidade inerente do espírito humano, sem qualquer interferência do Espírito de Deus, de outros espíritos, etc. Até mesmo quando a cura ocorre por alguma influência direta de um ser espiritual ou do Espírito Santo, parece haver o mesmo «mecanismo». Em outras palavras é transferida alguma energia vital daquele que cura para aquele que recebe a cura. Talvez por isso é que até no caso do poderoso Senhor Jesus, é dito que «dele saiu virtude» (ver Luc. 6:19 e 8:46). É fato bem conhecido que, nas curas, o terapeuta chega a um ponto em que suas energias se esgotam, e ele não pode mais curar. O descanso normalmente restaura essa energia, embora, em alguns casos, tal poder se perca inteiramente, após diversos meses ou anos de uso. Nada disso visa indicar que as curas não podem transcender ao que é humano; pois evidentemente esse é o caso, ainda que possa utilizar-se de energias vitais humanas como seu «modus operandi». Naturalmente, também pode ultrapassar inteiramente a tudo quanto é meramente humano, normalmente, porém, não é assim que as coisas são. No caso de transcender aos poderes

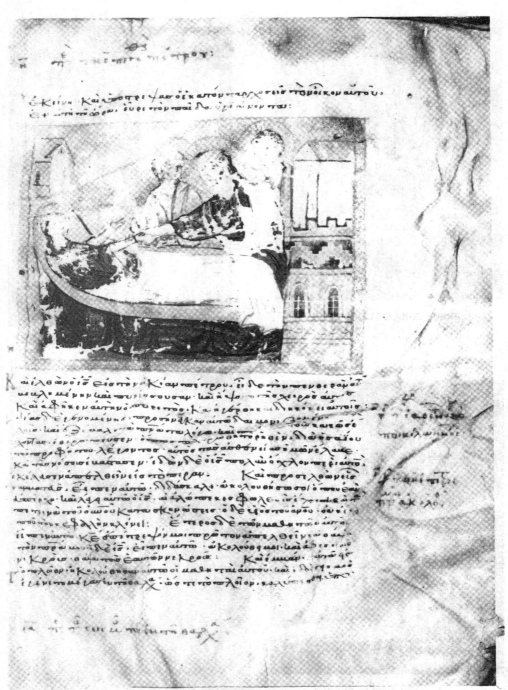

Rockefeller-McCormick Ms 965, Mat. 8:14 ss.
Jesus Cura a Sogra de Pedro
Cortesia, University of Chicago

JESUS CURA OS DOENTES

O HOMEM CEGO DE NASCENÇA

JESUS CURA OS LEPROSOS

CURANDO A LEPRA

CURA

humanos, só podem essas curas ser de origem demoníaca, ou então inspiradas pelo Espírito Santo, e, quem sabe, por poderes angelicais.

O dom das curas. (Ver as notas expositivas sobre isso, na introdução ao décimo segundo capítulo da primeira epístola aos Coríntios no NTI). O dom de curas pode envolver qualquer dos níveis de origem acima mencionados. Em outras palavras, Deus pode dar a certas pessoas a habilidade de usarem suas energias curadoras latentes, que todos os seres humanos possuem, mas que não podem e não sabem usar. Tal pessoa pode demonstrar poderes de cura desde a meninice; e sua missão pode ser a de curar, contanto que use tal capacidade como um elemento de instrução espiritual. A cura raramente, se é que alguma vez, serve apenas para curar alguma enfermidade física; antes, deve servir de demonstração da dimensão espiritual da existência. Quando assim acontece, sem importar seu nível, é algo belíssimo e um gracioso dom de Deus. As curas provavelmente podem ser efetuadas mediante o ministério dos anjos, que operam através de instrumentos humanos. Nesse caso, o poder pode ser repentinamente dado à pessoa, e ser notável. Além disso, pode agradar a Deus curar diretamente, através do seu Santo Espírito. Mas, uma coisa é certa: as curas são um fato, uma belíssima realidade. No entanto, pode ser um instrumento perigoso e mesmo prejudicial, usado nas mãos de ímpios, em cujo caso pode ser igualmente real, mas não dedicado à glória de Cristo.

A oração confiante pode curar. Todos os homens são terapeutas em potencial, «ocasionalmente»; e a oração de muitos crentes certamente tem tal efeito. Normalmente, entretanto, as curas espirituais são efetuadas por aqueles que são dotados para tanto, tal como alguns são dotados para ensinar, outros para profetizar, outros para falar em línguas, e ainda outros para interpretá-las. Cada crente individual tem sua missão específica, e deveria ocupar-se de seu desenvolvimento. Cumpre-nos orar pedindo os dons espirituais, desejando-os ardentemente (ver I Cor. 14:31), mas o amor deve ser desenvolvido, a fim de controlar o uso dos dons espirituais. Naturalmente, no processo de nossa transformação segundo a imagem de Cristo, teoricamente poderíamos possuir todos os dons espirituais; e, de fato, eventualmente haveremos de possuir aqueles que forem úteis nas esferas espirituais, além do sepulcro. No entanto, para efeito de uso na igreja cristã, que ninguém se assenhoreie de outro, mas antes, tudo deve ser feito com base no amor (ver I Cor. 12:30), embora uma pessoa possa exercer mais de um dom, segundo a experiência o demonstra.

Considerando as declarações acima, vemos que a passagem de Tiago 5:14-18, sobre as curas espirituais, está longe de envolver questões ultrapassadas, obsoletas. As curas são uma realidade viva hoje em dia. Tiago nos fornece algumas regras sobre a questão, tal como a oração unida dos anciãos da igreja e a unção com óleo. Essas medidas têm mostrado ser valiosas, embora outros métodos se tenham mostrado igualmente eficazes. Podemos supor que, juntamente com a unção com óleo, a imposição de mãos deve ser efetuada; e a maioria dos terapeutas pratica esse método. Os filmes de raios-X capturam a energia que emana das mãos dos terapeutas e essa energia cura tanto plantas e animais como os seres humanos.

Tiago 5:14: *Está doente algum de vós? Chame os anciões da igreja, que estes orem sobre ele, ungindo-o com óleo em nome do Senhor.*

Certamente estão em foco os doentes no *corpo físico*, e não aqueles que sofrem de distúrbios emocionais ou psicológicos, embora esses distúrbios sejam enfermidades reais. E certamente o texto não fala de «enfermidades espirituais», conforme alguns têm crido erroneamente, como se as curas fossem algo do passado, e não do presente.

Presbíteros. Estão aqui em foco os líderes principais da igreja, sem designação específica quanto às funções que exercem, como mestres, pastores, etc. (Ver I Tim. 5:1,17 quanto ao uso desse vocábulo, bem como quanto ao desenvolvimento dos anciãos liderantes na igreja cristã. Ver acerca do «presbitério» em I Tim. 4:14). A igreja cristã primitiva copiou a sinagoga em questões de governo eclesiástico, e a primeira coisa feita foi reconhecer certos homens, de grande espiritualidade, como líderes das igrejas, os quais ocupavam, individualmente, funções diversas, para benefício da comunidade cristã.

Os anciãos ou presbíteros, quando de sua consagração, recebiam dons espirituais, normalmente através da imposição de mãos. (Ver I Tim. 4:14). Portanto, esperava-se que fossem capazes de curar, pelo menos alguns deles; e sua oração unida era reputada mais do que o exercício da eloqüência verbal. Antes, tinham o poder de Deus. Por conseguinte, que os enfermos lhes fossem levados. Deus haveria de levantar aos enfermos, porquanto o próprio Senhor resolvera cuidar dos casos de enfermidade por esse método.

Façam oração sobre ele. Podemos supor que a imposição de mãos também era aplicada aos enfermos, sendo medida eficaz nas curas. Outrossim, a oração é uma força criadora, que pode alterar as condições físicas, pois nos vincula ao poder de Deus. (Ver Efé. 6:18 no NTI quanto à nota expositiva geral sobre a «*oração*»). No tocante a esse costume entre os judeus (pois Tiago não nos apresentava nenhuma novidade), ver *Sanhedrin* 101,1; *Shabbath* 127b e *Sota* 14a. *Amachoth Zutarti* têm uma extensa passagem sobre esse costume, e seu fraseado se assemelha extraordinariamente ao rito da «extrema-unção» da Igreja Católica Romana, em nossos dias. Portanto, essa prática, em algumas de suas formas, é mais antiga que a era cristã, ainda que tenha sofrido algumas modificações entre os cristãos. É normal, pois, para aqueles que crêem na extrema-unção como um *sacramento*, verem em Tiago 5:14 um texto de prova. Mas a «extrema-unção» não se tornou prática formalizada da Igreja Católica Romana, bem como um dos sete sacramentos, até o século XII D.C., ainda que tivesse existido sob forma informal desde muito antes disso. Recebeu definição autoritária em um decreto, no concílio de Trento, ao tempo de Lutero (1545 ---) O texto da epístola de Tiago 5:14 foi usado como apoio neotestamentário. (Ver secção xiv, *Doctrina de sacr. extr. unct.* cap.). A Igreja Ortodoxa Grega, entretanto, retém a prática original. Ela unge os *corpos enfermos*, visando sua *recuperação* à saúde, e *não* em benefício da *alma*, antes da morte, visando o perdão dos pecados. A idéia entre as igrejas protestantes segue o pensamento esposado pela Igreja Ortodoxa Grega.

A idéia que a unção com óleo envolve alguma graça espiritual, tendente ao perdão de pecados, certamente se deriva de tradições dogmáticas, e não do próprio N.T., pois na Bíblia certamente tal idéia nunca é ensinada. (Ver também *Baba Bathra* 116 e Talmude Babilônico *Shabbath* 13b, quanto à prática da «oração pelos enfermos»).

CURA — CURAS PELA FÉ

Óleo. Os antigos consideram o azeite de oliveira dotado de propriedades medicinais (ver Luc. 10:34). Contudo, nunca se pensou que o azeite fosse capaz de curar toda e qualquer enfermidade. Portanto, sabemos que era usado meramente como sinal visível e tangível do poder de Deus; e os primitivos cristãos criam que o Senhor curaria o enfermo, quando assim fizessem, porque, com tal ação, confirmavam sua fé em Deus. É possível que alguns primitivos cristãos criam que o azeite tivesse algum poder «sacramental» verdadeiro. Em outras palavras que comunicasse a graça da cura. Mas é provável que a maioria deles visse no azeite um mero meio de confirmação da fé. Era algo que faziam a fim de mostrar sua fé. Alguns crentes da atualidade continuam usando o óleo desse modo e com essa atitude, e não como se o mesmo tivesse propriedades sacramentais.

A palavra *sacramento*, usada na cristandade, não significa apenas alguma coisa «sagrada», conforme se poderia pensar, com base no próprio termo. Seu sentido teológico é «um meio físico que transmite graça espiritual», como se, sem tal meio físico, não se pudesse esperar a transmissão da graça espiritual. Assim é que alguns pensam que sem a água do batismo, não pode haver regeneração. Entretanto, isso é fazer da fé religiosa algo «mágico». Na verdade, em todas as suas manifestações graciosas, o Espírito opera com ou sem qualquer sinal visível. Pois o contacto dos homens com o Espírito de Deus é «místico», e não «sacramental».

Também não deveríamos reduzir Tiago 5:14, fazendo-o ensinar que a oração e a unção com óleo meramente prepara psicologicamente o enfermo, de tal modo que, com fé e confiança, seu corpo natural tenha aumentado a sua resistência às enfermidades. É claro que nisso há certa verdade; mas a cura é efetuada através de uma energia real, e essa energia pode fazer qualquer coisa. Algumas vezes opera até mesmo à parte da fé, e a despeito do ridículo lançado pela própria pessoa que recebe a cura. Não sabemos muito sobre o que governa as curas, embora saibamos que estão envolvidos fatores espirituais e normais, além da fé. Normalmente a fé é algo necessário; mas nem sempre. Jesus ressuscitou a mortos, e não foi a fé deles que operou. Assim também muitas crianças são curadas, — quando não se pode pedir qualquer fé da parte delas. Contudo, usualmente a fé é necessária.

O óleo usado na cura. Era fato tanto na cultura judaica como na pagã, e não meramente da cristã, que se usava o azeite na unção dos enfermos. (Ver Isa. 2:6; Luc. 10:34; *Galeno, Med. temp.* ii, *Tal Jerus.* em *Berakoth*, 3:1). Algumas vezes era misturado vinho com azeite, conforme se vê nessa última referência. (Ver também o Talmude *Jerusa.*, em *Maasar Sheni* 53:3; Bab. em Joma 77:2; Jerusal. em *Shab.* 14:3. Quanto aos primitivos escritores cristãos, ver Tertuliano, *Ad Scapulam* 4; Orígenes, *Hom.* ii. sobre Levítico 4, Cirilo de Alex., *de adorat. in spir. et ver.* vi. par. 211). Em alguns lugares, tais práticas eram recomendadas em substituição à magia pagã. Após o século IV D.C. idéias sacramentais começaram a entrincheirar-se firmemente na igreja, no tocante a essas coisas. Antes do fim do século VIII de nossa era, o «perdão dos pecados» já estava vinculado a esse costume; e o óleo já vinha sendo usado não para efeitos curadores, mas para a transmissão da graça perdoadora. Essa idéia, naturalmente, provinha de grande antiguidade, *Irineu* (i.21:5) menciona que Márcion, o gnóstico, ungia os moribundos com azeite e água, o que supostamente lhes protegia as almas contra poderes espirituais hostis, ao passarem para a dimensão dos espíritos. Portanto, os gnósticos tinham idéias sacramentais. (Quanto a notas expositivas sobre o desenvolvimento da prática da *extrema-unção* na igreja cristã ocidental, ver o parágrafo que comenta sobre as palavras «façam oração sobre ele». Em alguns setores da igreja antiga, o azeite veio a ser usado para unção, antes do batismo, e com intenções sacramentais).

Em nome do Senhor. Provavelmente está em foco o Senhor Jesus Cristo, o Grande Médico. Cristo também é o Senhor de todas as enfermidades e doenças da alma. O uso de seu nome faz da unção com óleo um ato espiritual, e não um mero tratamento médico. Os primitivos cristãos criam que continua presente o poder de Cristo para curar, tal como nos dias de sua carne, embora ele não se faça visivelmente presente.

CURA DAS ALMAS

Uma expressão usada pelas igrejas Católica Romana e Anglicana para descrever o trabalho pastoral dos padres. Por ocasião da ordenação de um padre, torna-se seu dever cuidar do bem-estar espiritual de seus paroquianos, o que envolveria a cura das almas. Fica entendido, dentro desse contexto, que ele precisa administrar os sacramentos, visitar os seus paroquianos e supervisionar questões que dizem respeito à sua área de serviço.

CURA, INCLUÍDA NA EXPIAÇÃO?

Ver o artigo sobre **Doenças**, seção IV, **A Teologia da Doença**.

CURAS, DOM DE

Ver os artigos sobre **Cura** e **Curas pela Fé**.

CURAS PELA FÉ

Ver o artigo geral sobre a **Cura**. A expressão denota as curas que ocorrem contra ou acima das expectativas e possibilidades da ciência médica, dependendo da fé da pessoa curada, do curador, ou de ambos. Os milagres de cura, realizados por Jesus, foram desse tipo (Mat. 9:22,29; 9:2; Mar. 9:24; Mat. 10:1), como também os milagres de cura efetuados pelos apóstolos (Atos 3:16; 5:14,15; 19:9).

Modos Empregados:

1. *Imposição de mãos.* Os estudos modernos no campo da parapsicologia (que vide) mostram-nos que uma energia real pode ser transferida desse modo, do curador para a pessoa curada. Algumas vezes, as mãos não tocam no paciente, mas apenas pairam sobre ele, e, no caso de algumas pessoas, isso parece produzir melhores resultados. Outras vezes, os curadores obtêm melhores efeitos usando ambas as mãos, uma diante da outra, com a área afetada do paciente entre elas. É possível que isso estabeleça um certo fluxo de energias, de uma mão para a outra, atravessando a região enferma.

2. *Unção com Azeite.* Isso é recomendado em Tiago 5:14. Trata-se de um ato simbólico, representando a fé expressa na oração, sabendo-se que é o Espírito de Deus quem, realmente, efetua a cura.

3. *Oração simples*, novamente na expectativa da intervenção divina.

4. A *visualização* tem sido usada por algumas

CURAS PELA FÉ — CURRAIS

pessoas com sucesso. Trata-se da visualização da enfermidade, como se já estivesse curada, mediante a imaginação. Também pode estar envolvida alguma coisa que possa ajudar na cura. O Dr. Carl Simonton tem obtido muitas curas totais ou parciais de câncer, dessa maneira, com a cooperação dos pacientes. Certo paciente imaginou que suas células brancas do sangue eram como gigantescos ursos polares, marchando pela corrente sangüínea e consumindo as células cancerosas. Outros pacientes simplesmente visualizam o desaparecimento do tumor, vendo a área afetada inteiramente curada.

5. A *hipnose*, em outras oportunidades, tem demonstrado notáveis poderes de cura. É possível que a hipnose seja outro mecanismo de visualização, apenas.

6. A *sugestão mental* de que a doença foi sanada, em momentos de oração ou de meditação, ou sob hipnose, também tem sido empregada.

7. *Poderes Externos*. Não há que duvidar que os seres angelicais podem curar. Outro tanto pode ser dito sobre a própria alma, o nosso *eu* mais alto. A cura pela fé é possível, mesmo sem qualquer intervenção divina. Os espíritos (ver sobre o espiritismo) supõem que espíritos humanos desencarnados podem curar, dizendo mesmo que alguns desses espíritos têm uma missão de cura, em benefício da humanidade. Isso parece ter ocorrido, em alguns casos. Em outros casos, talvez haja outras entidades espirituais envolvidas, sobre as quais nada sabemos. O poder dos demônios, algumas vezes, pode estar envolvido nas curas, com ou sem o espiritismo. Precisamos exercer cautela quanto às maneiras de cura empregadas, a fim de não nos expormos à ação de poderes negativos, que só podem nos prejudicar.

8. *Autocura*. Nossa própria alma, ou «eu» superior, pode efetuar a cura do corpo físico. Estudos recentes sobre múltiplas personalidades demonstram que quando uma das personalidades está exercendo o controle, o corpo físico reage à mesma. Para exemplificar, quando certa personalidade está no controle, a pessoa pode tornar-se míope; mas, quando a outra personalidade exerce o controle, a pessoa recupera sua boa visão. Outro tanto sucede no caso de diversas enfermidades, incluindo coisas sérias como a epilepsia. Diferem também a pressão sangüínea o número de pulsações e os eletroencefalogramas. Apesar de que tais efeitos possam ser explicados, em alguns casos, pela influência de entidades que se apossam das pessoas, causando as diversas manifestações de personalidade, o mais provável é que, na maioria dos casos, estejamos tratando apenas com questões mentais. Fragmentos da psique tornam-se pessoas diferentes, por assim dizer, e cada um desses fragmentos é capaz de influenciar o organismo físico de maneira significativa. Se fôssemos capazes de manipular o nosso poder mental, poderíamos curar qualquer tipo de enfermidade.

9. *Intervenções Divinas*. Há casos de curas de enfermidades físicas que se processam independentemente de quaisquer mecanismos humanos. Cremos que alguns dos milagres efetuados por Jesus pertenciam a essa categoria, ao passo que outras curas podem envolver algum outro nível de entidade e poder. Ver o artigo sobre *Satya Sai Baba*, como exemplo de um poderoso curador moderno.

10. *Curas Psicossomáticas*. Há doenças de origem mental. Com a alteração das atitudes mentais, é removido o efeito físico correspondente.

Conforme demonstrei, há todo um complexo *modus operandi* envolvido nas curas. Quando Deus está por detrás de qualquer dessas maneiras, a cura é boa. Nessa classe podemos incluir as curas efetuadas pela medicina tradicional. Devemos dar a Deus o crédito pelas curas assim obtidas, bem como ser gratos pela saúde de que desfrutamos, a fim de podermos cumprir as nossas respectivas missões na terra. Este artigo foi escrito para ser lido juntamente com aquele outro, intitulado *Cura*, onde prestamos outras informações a respeito.

Cumpre-nos acrescentar o seguinte: Algumas vezes, as curas psíquicas ou as curas pela fé precisam de algum tempo para se processarem, tal como nos casos de curas por meios puramente físicos. Podem ser necessárias várias aplicações da energia curativa, como também mais de uma maneira de curar. As curas pela fé, na maioria dos casos, envolvem um processo. Somente os grandes curadores, como Jesus Cristo, os apóstolos e alguns profetas são capazes de realizar curas instantâneas, a cada vez em que o tentam. A maioria dos curadores prefere tratar os pacientes conforme fazem os médicos, exigindo um certo prazo e diversas sessões de tratamento. Mas isso em nada detrata o poder ou a viabilidade das curas por meio da fé.

Um outro fato. Muitas enfermidades físicas têm causas mentais. Poderíamos frisar emoções negativas como o ódio, a hostilidade e a ansiedade. Todos esses estados de alma podem ter efeitos físicos adversos. A ciência vem reconhecendo cada vez mais essa realidade. Às vezes, quando as pessoas corrigem o estado de suas almas, ocorre a cura do corpo. A vereda certa para todo o tipo de cura é a vereda espiritual. Aquele que odeia pode terminar canceroso. Aquele que ama pode remover um câncer, tanto do corpo quanto do espírito.

CÚRIA ROMANA

O corpo das congregações sagradas, ao qual o papa delega parte de sua jurisdição, que eles usam no governo da Igreja Católica Romana. No momento, a Cúria Romana consiste em doze congregações, três tribunais e cinco ofícios. Desde o século XI, a Cúria tem sido o mais elevado órgão eclesiástico, administrativo e judicial. A crescente complexidade do ofício papal e da administração da Igreja Católica Romana tem exigido a existência desse corpo especial. Cada congregação que faz parte desse órgão é presidida por um cardeal-prefeito, com a assistência de um secretário e de um segundo secretário. As principais questões de cada congregação são discutidas em uma *congregatio plenaria*, da qual participam todos os oficiais eclesiásticos principais envolvidos. (AM E)

CURRAIS

Esse verbete envolve quatro palavras hebraicas e duas palavras gregas, a saber:

1. *Gedereth tson*, «cerca para o rebanho», expressão que aparece em Núm. 32:16,24,36 e Sof. 2:6.

2. *Miklah*, «restrições». Palavra hebraica que figura em Sal. 50:9; 78:70 e Hab. 3:17.

3. *Mishpethayim*, «currais duplos». Palavra que aparece somente em Juí. 5:16, com esse sentido.

4. *Naveh*, «habitação». Palavra que ocorre por quatro vezes com esse sentido: Isa. 65:10; Jer. 23:3; Eze. 34:14.

5. *Aulè tōn probáton*, «átrio das ovelhas». Expressão grega que aparece somente em João 10:1.

6. *Probatikós*, «pertencente às ovelhas». Palavra

CURSIVOS — CURTIDOR

grega que ocorre somente em João 5:2.

O curral ou aprisco era um lugar fechado que servia para proteger as ovelhas dos azares das intempéries, dos ladrões e das feras. Localizado perto da residência de um dos proprietários, ou armado nas colinas onde as ovelhas pastavam, o curral não tinha telhado, suas paredes eram feitas de pedra, e contava apenas com uma porta, que servia de entrada e de saída. Usualmente abrigava diversos rebanhos, cada um dos quais retinha a sua identidade, visto que cada pastor conhecia suas ovelhas e era bem conhecido por elas, havendo entre pastor e ovelhas uma grande relação de dependência. (Ver João 10:3-5).

CURSIVOS

Essa palavra indica os manuscritos da Bíblia, além de outros documentos, escritos com letras minúsculas, ligadas umas às outras, e não com letras separadas, como nos manuscritos *unciais*, que também eram escritos com letras maiúsculas. A escrita cursiva foi um passo na direção da escrita chamada «manuscrita», em contraste com a escrita impressa. A partir do século X D.C., esse estilo de escrita tornou-se comum, usado nos manuscritos do Novo Testamento, o que significa que isso nos confere uma maneira aproximada de datar os diversos manuscritos. Ver o artigo geral sobre os *Manuscritos da Bíblia*. Uma palavra alternativa para indicar esse tipo de manuscrito é *minúsculo*, porquanto as letras empregadas eram menores que aquelas usadas nos manuscritos unciais. Dessas letras menores, ou de caixa baixa, foi que se desenvolveram as letras latinas e gregas da atualidade. Os primeiros livros impressos tinham tipos que imitavam essas letras minúsculas.

CURSO

Essa palavra portuguesa vem do latim, **cursus**, «correr». Há certa variedade de palavras hebraicas e gregas assim traduzidas, a saber:

1. *Merutsah*, «corrida». Palavra hebraica usada por quatro vezes: Jer. 8:6; 23:10; II Sam. 18:27.

2. *Mesillah*, «estrada». Palavra hebraica que ocorre por vinte e cinco vezes, como em Juí. 5:20; Núm. 20:19; I Sam. 6:12; II Sam. 20:12,13; Isa. 7:3; 11:16; 19:23; 33:8; Jer. 31:21.

3. *Drómos*, «estrada», «corrida». Palavra que figura por três vezes: Atos 13:25; 20:24; II Tim. 4:7.

4. *Trochós*, «roda». Palavra grega usada somente em Tia. 3:6, onde é empregada metaforicamente, para indicar o curso da vida.

5. *Aion*, «era». Palavra grega usada cerca de cento e cinco vezes, desde Mat. 6:13 até Apo. 22:5. Essa palavra é usada para indicar várias idéias, como o curso natural das coisas, o curso da conduta humana (Efé. 2:2), etc. O mundo e a humanidade correm em ciclos, cada qual com suas características próprias. O crente deve evitar o curso deste mundo, ditado pelo espírito das trevas (Efé. 2:2).

6. *Euthudroméo*, «correr em linha reta». Palavra grega que é usada somente em Atos 16:11 e 21:1.

Essa palavra também pode referir-se a uma sucessão em ordem, como no caso das turmas de trabalhadores de Salomão, que se revezavam a cada mês, dez mil deles de cada vez (I Reis 5:14). Nesse caso, nossa versão portuguesa prefere a palavra «leva». É o mesmo caso dos «turnos» dos sacerdotes e levitas, que serviam no templo de Jerusalém. Esses turnos foram organizados por Davi, e vinte e quatro dessas divisões foram estabelecidas por ele em Israel (I Crô. 24:1-19; II Crô. 8:14; 35:4,5). (A Z)

CURTIDOR

No Antigo Testamento, o resultado do trabalho dos curtidores de couros e peles aparece com relativa freqüência, mas não é mencionado nunca o próprio «curtidor». Entretanto, essa profissão aparece no Novo Testamento. No grego, «curtidor» é *burseús*, uma palavra que aparece por três vezes: Atos 9:43; 10:6,32.

A ausência de menção a essa profissão, no Antigo Testamento, talvez se deva ao fato de que os judeus consideravam a ocupação muito indesejável, porquanto, além de envolver odores muito fétidos e repulsivos, há também cenas nada atrativas, se não mesmo a contaminação cerimonial, tão cara aos judeus, cuja religião muito se baseava em princípios cerimoniais. Por essa razão, bem podemos imaginar que Simão, o curtidor (Atos 9:43), encontrou entre os discípulos de Jesus um companheirismo que antes lhe vinha sendo negado entre os seus compatriotas judeus. Quando Pedro escolheu a casa de Simão, o curtidor, para ser sua residência e base de operações, enquanto ele esteve em Jope, esse apóstolo mostrou que o cristianismo eliminara dele muitos preconceitos. É interessante observar que a casa de Simão, o curtidor, ficava à beira-mar, o que continua sucedendo às residências dos curtidores da costa da Síria, até os nossos próprios dias. A proximidade do mar facilitava tanto o acesso à água salgada, tão necessária à arte dos curtumes, como também o ar livre da praia facilitava a dispersão dos maus odores próprios de tais lugares. Os curtumes antigos eram muito simples, pois geralmente consistiam de apenas um ou dois aposentos, e de um pátio. As cubas onde os couros e as peles ficavam mergulhados eram feitas de pedra sólida escavada, ou então de várias pedras, rebocadas por dentro e por fora.

As peles ou couros eram besuntadas pelo lado interno com uma pasta de visgo. Em seguida eram enroladas, ficando assim até que todos os pêlos se soltassem. Então, os pêlos em uma das superfícies, e qualquer carne e gordura, pelo lado de dentro, eram removidos. Então as peles eram novamente mergulhadas em uma solução de visgo, fezes de cães e fermento, mais ou menos conforme se faz, até hoje, nos curtumes que ainda não usam os recursos da química moderna. As peles assim tratadas eram mergulhadas em sumagre (*Rhus coriaria*), até hoje usada, com esse propósito, na Síria e na Palestina.

Após secar, o couro é enegrecido em uma das superfícies esfregando-se na mesma uma solução de vinagre fervido com pedaços de cobre. E, finalmente, o couro é amaciado com azeite de oliveira. Naturalmente, conforme já demos a entender, esses processos mais primitivos foram substituídos por processos químicos muito mais eficientes. Mas, antigamente, para o fabrico das peles vermelhas de carneiros (ver Êxo. 25 *ss*), esfregava-se o couro com uma solução de *kermes* (similar ao *murex*, um tipo de gastrópode, de onde os antigos extraíam uma espécie de tintura púrpura) e azeite de oliveira. Então o couro era polido com uma pedra lisa.

No Líbano, algumas vezes os curtidores usavam a casca do pinho. Os árabes usam o suco de uma certa planta do deserto, para tirar os pêlos e curtir as peles. No caso dos odres (receptáculos feitos de couros de animais pequenos, como cabras, ovelhas, etc.), os pêlos não eram removidos. A curtição, nesse caso, fazia-se enchendo-se o receptáculo, após a remoção de toda carne e gordura, com gravetos de madeira de carvalho e água. Esses «receptáculos» ficavam repousando, de pernas para cima, durante semanas, ao ar livre. Esses odres são referidos em trechos tanto do Antigo quanto do Novo Testamentos: Jos. 9:4-13; Osé. 7:5; Mat. 9:17; Mar. 2:22 e Luc. 5:37.

É provável que, nos tempos bíblicos, o couro fosse usado mais extensamente do que os registros bíblicos nos dão a entender. Sabemos que os egípcios usavam o couro em trabalhos ornamentais. Eles conheciam a arte de estampar sobre o couro. As esculturas antigas mostram-nos que havia métodos para uso do couro no fabrico de sandálias, de arreios para os cavalos e os carros de combate, coberturas de cadeiras e assentos, decorações para harpas, sarcófagos, etc. Há duas referências na Bíblia (Mat. 3:4 e II Reis 1:8) que mostram que também havia cinturões feitos de couro. Também eram fabricadas vestes de couro (Lev. 13:48 e Núm. 31:20). Tendas, igualmente, eram fabricadas com couro, e não apenas com tecidos (Êxo. 25:5; Núm. 4:6). O couro também era muito usado na vida militar. Muitos artigos militares eram feitos desse material, como capacetes, aljavas, arreios de carruagens, fundas e escudos. Estes últimos eram feitos de madeira, forrada de couro bem azeitado, para impedir que o couro rachasse e também para impedir a penetração de dardos (II Sam. 1:21; Isa. 21:5). Sandálias feitas com couro de animais marinhos eram um sinal de luxo (Êxo. 16:10), embora seja provável que, tal como no Egito e na Assíria, o couro mais fino fosse usado para forrar leitos, coberturas de cadeiras e de outros móveis.

As peles, quando usadas para bolsas de alta qualidade, eram curtidas com sal mineral, usualmente o alúmen, importado das margens do mar Morto ou do Egito; ou então essas peles eram tratadas como se fossem o pergaminho.

CUSÃ

Trata-se de um outro nome para Cuxe (que vide), ou então alude a uma região da Arábia ocupada pelos cuxitas (Hab. 3:7). A Septuaginta diz, nessa referência, «Etiópia». Alguns eruditos pensam que essa palavra designa um antigo nome dado à região contínua a Midiã. Isso significaria que a mulher cuxita de Moisés talvez fosse apenas uma mulher midianita. Ver sobre *Cuxita* (*Mulher Etíope*).

CUSA, NICOLAU DE
Ver **Nicolau de Cusa**.

CUSÃ-RISATAIM

Esse era o nome de um rei e conquistador militar hitita. Primeiramente, ele anexou a Mesopotâmia (Mitani), e então assolou a Palestina, na época dos juízes hebreus (Juí. 3:7-10). Os historiadores fixam seu reinado em cerca de 1361-1352 A.C. Vestígios de suas conquistas continuam evidentes em Bete-Seã, uma poderosa fortaleza em Esdrelom, e em outras localidades. Israel passou oito anos em subserviência a esse homem. Otniel, genro de Calebe, tornou-se o libertador de Israel. Os historiadores não concordam entre si quanto à identidade desse monarca e seu território. Ele pertencia à área dos dois rios (Tigre e Eufrates), conforme é indicado pelo termo aramaico «Arã-naharaim», ou seja, «Arã dos dois rios». Esse era o seu nome hebraico. Arã é nome conhecido nas cartas de Tell el-Amarna e nos manuscritos egípcios. Nesse caso, Cusã-Risataim pode ter sido um hitita (ou heteu, segundo a palavra preferida nas Escrituras). Outros estudiosos supõem que a palavra «Arã», na realidade significa Edom, e que o nome original era «Edom das Duas Iniqüidades», o que, realmente, poderia ser o sentido do nome hebraico, pois *rishathaim* significa «iniqüidades». Nesse caso, algum tipo de corruptela entrou na palavra, talvez deliberadamente. Mas isso não passa de especulação, pelo que a maioria dos eruditos prefere a outra interpretação.

CUSAÍAS

No hebraico, «arco de Yahweh». Ele era um levita merarita, cujo filho, Etã, foi nomeado para ser o principal assistente de Hemã, para cuidar da música do templo. Ele serviu nessa ocupação durante o tempo de Davi (I Crô. 15:17). É chamado pelo nome de Quisi, em I Crô. 6:44. Cerca de 975 A.C.

CUSI

No hebraico, «negro». Nome de duas pessoas diferentes, nas páginas do Antigo Testamento:

1. O pai de Selemias, bisavô de Jeudi. Jeudi fora enviado pelos magnatas judeus para convidar Baruque a ler diante deles o rolo de Jeremias (Jer. 36:14), em cerca de 604 A.C.

2. Um filho de Gedalias, pai do profeta Sofonias (Sof. 1:1), em cerca de 620 A.C.

CUSI

Um lugar mencionado no livro apócrifo de Judite (7:17), perto de Ácraba, às margens do ribeiro Mocmur. Provavelmente ficava na Palestina central, ao sul da moderna Nablus.

CUSPIR Ver **Saliva**.

CUSTÓDIA ROMANA

Atos 23:17: *Chamando Paulo um dos centuriões, disse: Leve este moço ao comandante, porque tem alguma coisa que lhe comunicar.*

Podemos ver como o sobrinho do apóstolo Paulo tivera acesso fácil onde ele estava detido. É que havia vários tipos de aprisionamento e custódia, reconhecidos pelas leis romanas, conforme a descrição dada abaixo:

1. Havia a *custódia pública* («detenção pública»), era o encarceramento em uma prisão pública, que era o pior tipo de cárcere dos tempos antigos, onde imperavam as piores condições imagináveis. Paulo sofreu esse tipo de encarceramento por diversas vezes, em Filipos, e também, provavelmente, em Éfeso. (Quanto a notas expositivas sobre as «prisões antigas», ver Atos 16:24 no NTI).

2. *Custódia libera* («detenção livre»), que se limitava a indivíduos de alta estirpe, quando esperavam ser julgados por qualquer ofensa que porventura tivessem cometido. Nesses casos, o acusado era entregue aos cuidados de um magistrado ou senador, que assumia a responsabilidade de garantir o comparecimento do réu, no dia do julgamento.

3. *Custódia militaris* («detenção militar»), em que o acusado era entregue à vigilância de um soldado. Tal soldado se tornava o responsável pelo acusado, sob pena de perder a própria vida, se este escapasse. Ordinariamente, nesses casos, a mão esquerda do

CUTA — CUXE

soldado era acorrentada à mão direita do prisioneiro. Este geralmente era conservado nas acomodações militares, embora, noutras ocasiões, lhe fosse permitido permanecer em uma casa particular, sob a vigilância do soldado. O aprisionamento de Paulo, em Jerusalém, pertenceu à categoria da «custódia militaris». (Quanto a notas expositivas sobre o ofício militar dos «centuriões», ver Atos 21:32 no NTI).

Paulo não se demorou a agir e «...traçou os seus planos tão energicamente como se Jesus não lhe tivesse prometido que veria Roma (ver Atos 23:11)». (Robertson em Atos 23:17). O homem tem a responsabilidade de agir como se tudo dependesse dele, embora deva pensar como se tudo dependesse de Deus; e Paulo seguia esse preceito. Essa é uma norma que pode ajudar-nos a obter pleno sucesso em nossa missão na vida.

Paulo não esperou por algum milagre celeste para livrá-lo da prisão, mas antes, fez uso dos meios ao seu alcance, sem duvidar de coisa alguma, mas crendo que tudo fora determinado por Deus. «Aquele que não se mexe para ajudar a si mesmo, de conformidade com os meios e os poderes ao seu dispor, não recebeu nem razão e nem revelação capaz de assegurar-lhe que receberá qualquer assistência da parte de Deus». (Adam Clarke em Atos 23:17). «Ele não desconfiou da veracidade das palavras de Cristo, mas creu mui firmemente nelas; não obstante, julgou fazer parte de seu dever utilizar-se dos meios que a providência divina tinha posto em seu caminho, a fim de preservá-lo e conservá-lo em segurança». (John Gill em Atos 23:17).

CUTA

Precisamos considerar uma cidade e um indivíduo, que aparece em um livro apócrifo da Bíblia, a saber:

1. Uma das mais importantes cidades da antiga Babilônia, que alguns estudiosos pensam ter sido a mais antiga capital do império sumério (II Reis 17:24,30). O Tell Ibrahim assinala o local, em nossos dias. Ficava cerca de trinta e dois quilômetros a nordeste da cidade da Babilônia. Têm sido efetuadas escavações no local, a partir de 1881. Houve grandes descobertas, incluindo um santuário, erguido em memória de Ibrahim (Abraão), e também um templo dedicado a Nergal, rei do submundo. Essa cidade tinha certa importância comercial. Senaqueribe a destruiu, mas Nabucodonosor a reconstruiu e adornou. Esse foi um dos lugares de onde Sargão II deportou colonos para repovoarem o norte de Israel, depois da queda de Samaria, em 721 A.C. Os habitantes de Cuta tornaram-se o elemento dominante ali, de tal modo que os habitantes de Samaria vieram a ser chamados cuteanos. Em resultado disso, muitas palavras de origem não semita entraram na língua dos samaritanos. Desnecessário é dizer que não existe tal coisa como pura, em qualquer povo.

2. Cuta (na Septuaginta, Coutha), aparece no livro apócrifo de I Esdras 5:32. Ali a palavra aparece como nome de um indivíduo, um exilado, cabeça de uma família de servos do templo, que retornaram juntamente com Zorobabel a Jerusalém, após o cativeiro babilônico. Nas listas paralelas de Esd. 2:52 e Nee. 7:54, não figura o nome desse homem.

CUXE

Há duas pessoas e um lugar com esse nome, nas páginas da Bíblia:

1. Um filho (provavelmente o mais velho) de Cão, cujo nome aparece na genealogia dos descendentes de Noé. Lemos ali: «Cuxe gerou a Ninrode...» (Gên. 10:8; I Crô. 1:10). Certo número de descendentes aparece nessas listas.

2. Um benjamita mencionado no título do sétimo Salmo. Lemos que esse salmo foi composto acerca das palavras desse benjamita. Coisa nenhuma se conhece a seu respeito, mas o contexto indica que ele era inimigo de Davi, que procurou oportunidade para fazer-lhe algum mal, mas falhou (Sal. 7:15).

3. *A terra e o povo de Cuxe*. Essa palavra pode referir-se à terra (Isa. 11:11; 18:1; Sof. 1:1; Est. 1:1), ou ao povo que habitava a terra de Cuxe (Isa. 20:5; Jer. 46:9; Eze. 38:5). Geralmente essa palavra é traduzida por «Etiópia», conforme se vê na Septuaginta, seguida por muitas traduções modernas. Em outras traduções, porém, temos as traduções «Cuxe», e «cuxita». Não se conhecem as dimensões exatas da região designada por esse nome, embora devamos pensar na área geográfica conhecida desde a antiguidade como Etiópia, aquela seção da África contígua ao Egito e ao mar Vermelho, atualmente chamada também Abissínia (II Reis 11:9; Est. 1:1; Eze. 29:10). Porém, a referência ao lugar, em Gên. 2:13 e 10:8, é a uma Cuxe asiática (mesopotâmica) anterior, provavelmente pertencente aos cassitas. O termo veio referir-se a uma área mais ampla, correspondente ao que comumente se chama Núbia. A referência talvez seja simplesmente a Arábia, visto que, em II Crônicas 21:16, lemos que os árabes residiam perto dos etíopes, o que talvez seja explicado pelo fato de que entre eles havia somente a estreita língua do mar Vermelho. Alguns estudiosos afirmam que, na época, a Etiópia não consistia em uma população negra; mas essa contenção esbarra com o significado da própria palavra hebraica, *cush*, que significa «tez queimada». A questão ainda não foi resolvida definitivamente.

a. *História de Cuxe*. A região é mencionada inicialmente como parte do Egito, nos dias do monarca egípcio Sesóstris I, 1971-1930 A.C. Em cerca de 1000 A.C., Cuxe rompeu com o Egito e tornou-se um estado independente, cuja capital era Nápata. Alguns séculos mais tarde, Cuxe conseguiu predomínio sobre o Egito inteiro. Houve então a XXVª dinastia, ou dinastia etíope, de 715 a 663 A.C. Nessa época, o rei Tiraca veio fazer guerra contra Ezequias (Isa. 37:9). Finalmente, foi obrigado a recuar, por intervenção dos assírios, em cerca de 689-676 A.C.

b. *Elementos*. O termo Etiópia foi usado metaforicamente para indicar um lugar lo mais distante possível (Eze. 29:10). O trecho de Isaías 45:14 pode sugerir que o povo daquele lugar consistia em mercadores. Aparentemente, estavam em foco árabes cuxitas (II Crô. 21:16). Os etíopes, conforme Judá os conhecia, eram uma raça de aparência notável (Isa. 18:2).

c. *Confusão com os Cuxitas Mesopotâmicos*. O trecho de Gênesis 2:13 deve ter sido um lugar diferente, mas com o mesmo nome. Moisés teve uma esposa cuxita (Núm. 12:1). Seria ela da Mesopotâmia ou da Etiópia?

d. *Os Etíopes na Bíblia*. Os principais reis de Cuxe, mencionados na Bíblia, foram Zerá e Tiraca. Houve um corredor que trouxe a notícia da morte de Absalão a Davi, que pertencia a essa raça (II Sam. 18:21-23). Um outro cuxita era um adido à corte real de Judá, nos dias do cerco de Jerusalém pelos babilônios, em 587 A.C. Houve um cuxita que teve dó de Jeremias, quando este estava atolado em um poço com lama, e que providenciou para tirar o profeta daquele lugar (Jer. 38:7 ss). E também houve o eunuco etíope, no relato de Atos 8:27, —que era tesoureiro da rainha Candace, da Etiópia.

CUXITA (MULHER ETÍOPE)

O trecho de Números 12:1 informa-nos que Moisés casou-se com uma mulher etíope. Cuxe ou Etiópia era a região ao sul da primeira catarata do rio Nilo. A Septuaginta e a Vulgata Latina apresentam essa mulher como natural da Etiópia. Mas as tradições judaicas identificam-na com Zípora, pensando que ela era natural de Cusã, que aparece em Habacuque 3:7. Cusã também tem sido região identificada com a Etiópia; mas outros preferem pensar em Midiã, ou algum aliado desse território. As lendas judaicas sugerem que antes de Moisés fugir para o deserto de Midiã, ele foi comandante em chefe de uma campanha egípcia contra a Etiópia. Tarbis, a filha do rei etíope, ter-se-ia apaixonado por ele, do que resultou o casamento dos dois. Porém, quase todas as lendas desse tipo não passam de invenções românticas, pelo que a questão da identidade exata da esposa cuxita de Moisés continua sujeita a debates.

CUZA

A palavra vem do aramaico. Seu significado é *jarrinha*. Ele era procurador de Herodes Antipas. Sua esposa, Joana, era uma das mulheres que empregavam seus meios financeiros para atender às necessidades de Jesus e seus apóstolos (Luc. 8:3 e 24:10). Joana esteve entre as mulheres que foram ao túmulo de Jesus para ungir-lhe o corpo com especiarias, na manhã da ressurreição (Luc. 24:10). No tocante a Cuza, o termo «procurador» parece indicar que ele gerenciava as propriedades de Herodes. Como tal, provavelmente ele fora escolhido segundo considerações políticas. A ausência de qualquer menção a ele, nas narrativas dos evangelhos, excetuando essa única informação que temos, pode significar que ele era indiferente para com a mensagem cristã, ou então que ele já havia falecido quando Lucas nos prestou a informação. Mas, o fato de que sua esposa tornara-se discípula de Jesus mostra-nos que, mesmo nessa fase inicial, o evangelho penetrara em todos os níveis da sociedade.

••• ••• •••

Sua opinião é importante para nós. Por gentileza, envie seus comentários pelo e-mail **editorial@hagnos.com.br**

Visite nosso site:
www.hagnos.com.br

Esta obra foi impressa na Imprensa da Fé.
São Paulo, Brasil.
Outono de 2021.